Who's Who in America®

Who's Who in America®

2006

60th Edition
Volume 1 ✦ A-L

562 Central Avenue
New Providence, NJ 07974 U.S.A.
www.marquiswhoswho.com

Who'sWho in America®

Marquis Who's Who®

Published by Marquis Who's Who LLC.

For information, contact:
Marquis Who's Who
562 Central Avenue
New Providence, New Jersey 07974
1-908-673-1001
www.marquiswhoswho.com

WHO'S WHO IN AMERICA is a registered trademark of Marquis Who's Who LLC.

International Standard Book Number 0-8379-6990-5 (Set, Classic Edition)
0-8379-6991-3 (Volume 1, Classic Edition)
0-8379-6994-8 (Set, Deluxe Edition)
0-8379-6995-6 (Volume 1, Deluxe Edition)
International Standard Serial Number 0083-9396

Manufactured in the United States of America.

Table of Contents

Preface

"WHO'S WHO IN AMERICA *shall endeavor to list those individuals who are of current national reference interest and inquiry either because of meritorious achievement or because of the position they hold."*

Albert Nelson Marquis
Founder, 1899

Marquis Who's Who is proud to present the 2006 Anniversary Edition of *Who's Who in America.* The 60th edition features over 100,000 profiles of prominent individuals representing virtually every major field of endeavor. This special commemorative edition also features **The Who's Who 60**, our editors' choices of 60 extraordinary individuals covering every decade from the 1890s to the present.

In 1899, our first year of publication, Marquis biographees numbered 8,602. While the number of individuals profiled in *Who's Who in America* has grown substantially, our selection standards remain stringent. Fewer than one in 2,900 Americans are included in the 2006 edition of *Who's Who in America.*

While the vast majority of the individuals profiled on the following pages are American, *Who's Who in America* also includes the biographies of select individuals from around the world whose lives have had considerable impact and influence in America.

On the pages that follow, you will find Olympic champions, Nobel and Pulitzer Prize winners, university presidents, accomplished artists, renowned entertainers, entrepreneurs, and leaders representing hundreds of industries. Our 2006 Edition includes some long-established biographees like Rosa Parks, Lee Iacocca, and Jack Nicklaus, as well as many intriguing first-time listees. *Who's Who in America* also includes the profiles of thousands of remarkable achievers who, despite extraordinary accomplishments in everything from breakthrough medical research to cutting-edge technological innovations, have not as yet become household names. The 2006 Edition also includes the Who's Who 60, our selections of the most influential Americans who have appeared on the pages of *Who's Who in America* since our very first edition.

Our profiles provide you with critical biographical information, including educational background, family history, work history, civic activity, memberships, honors, and awards. In many cases, hobbies and special interests are also listed.

One Principle Governs Selection

As in all Marquis Who's Who biographical volumes, the individuals profiled in *Who's Who in America* are selected on the basis of current reference value. Factors such as position, noteworthy accomplishments, visibility, and prominence in a field are all taken into account. An individual's desire to be listed is not sufficient reason for inclusion. Similarly, wealth and social position are not relevant criteria. Of course, Marquis Who's Who has never charged a fee for publishing a biography, nor is purchase of the book ever a factor in the selection of biographees. Final decisions concerning inclusion or exclusion are made following extensive discussion, evaluation, and deliberation.

Biographical information is gathered in a variety of manners. In most cases, we invite our biographees to submit their biographical details. In many cases, though, the information is collected independently by our research and editorial staffs, which use a wide assortment of tools to gather the most complete, accurate, and up-to-date information available. Sketches researched by Marquis Who's Who are followed by an asterisk (*).

Responding to Your Reference Needs

As a complement to the biographical profiles, the Geographic and Professional Indexes featured in Volume 2 make *Who's Who in America* an even more productive research tool. Through these indexes, users can identify and locate individuals in any of thirty-eight professional categories, as well as by country, state, or city. Each entry contains name and occupation description.

The Geographic Index lists names in the United States under state and city designations, as well as biographees in American territories. Canadian listings include provinces and cities. Names in Mexico and other countries appear by city. Biographees whose addresses are not published in their sketches are found under Address Unpublished.

The Professional Index includes categories ranging alphabetically from Agriculture to Social Science. Within each area, the names appear under geographic subheadings. Names without published addresses appear at the end of each professional area listing under Address Unpublished. If the occupation does not fall within one of the specified areas, the name is listed under Unclassified.

Some biographees have professions encompassing more than one area; each of these appears under the field best suited to the biographee's occupation. Thus, while most bankers are listed under Finance: Banking Services, investment bankers are found in Finance: Investment Services. A biographee with two or more diverse occupations is found under the area that best fits his or her professional profile.

Our Challenge

While the Marquis Who's Who editors exercise the utmost care in preparing each biographical sketch for publication, it is inevitable in a publication involving so many profiles that occasional errors will appear. Users of this publication are urged to notify the publisher of any issues so that adjustments can be made, which will not only be reflected in all subsequent editions of the book but which can now be immediately displayed via Marquis Who's Who on the Web.

We sincerely hope that this volume will be an indispensable reference tool for you. We are always looking for ways to better serve you and welcome your ideas for improvements. In addition, we continue to welcome your Marquis Who's Who nominations. Feel free to submit these via our Web site (www.marquiswhoswho.com) or by e-mail and postal mail.

Our Utmost Thanks

Without the cooperation and assistance of those profiled on the pages that follow, *Who's Who in America* would not be possible. We would like to specifically thank our biographees for reviewing and editing their profiles. As a consequence, *Who's Who in America* remains the unchallenged leader in the field of biographical reference works. For this we are truly grateful.

Key to Information

[1] GIBSON, OSCAR JULIUS, [2] physician, medical educator; **[3]** b. Syracuse, N.Y., Aug. 31, 1937; **[4]** s. Paul Oliver and Elizabeth H. (Thrun) G.; **[5]** m. Judith S. Gonzalez, Apr. 28, 1968; **[6]** children: Richard Gary, Matthew Cary, Samuel Perry. **[7]** BA magna cum laude, U. Pa., 1960; MD, Harvard U., 1964. **[8]** Diplomate Am. Bd. Internal Medicine, Am. Bd. Preventive Medicine. **[9]** Intern Barnes Hosp., St. Louis, 1964-65, resident, 1965-66; clin. assoc. Nat. Heart Inst., NIH, Bethesda, Md., 1966-68; chief resident medicine U. Okla. Hosps., 1968-69; asst. prof. cmty. health Okla. Med. Ctr., 1969-70, assoc. prof., 1970-74, prof., chmn. dept., 1974-80; dean Coll. Medicine U. Okla. , 1978-82; v.p. med. staff affairs Bapt. Med. Ctr., Oklahoma City, 1982-86, exec. v.p., 1986-88, chmn., 1988-95, chmn, CEO, 1995—; **[10]** mem. governing bd. Ambulatory Health Care Consortium, Inc., 1979-80; mem. Okla. Bd. Medicolegal Examiners, 1985—; mem. Okla. Bd. of Med. Ethics, 1994—. **[11]** Contrb. articles to profl. jours. **[12]** Bd. dirs., v.p. Okla. Arthritis Found., 1982—; trustee N. Ctrl. Mental Health Ctr., 1985—. **[13]** Served U.S. Army, 1955-56. **[14]** Recipient R.T. Chadwick award Overlook Hosp., 1968; Am. Heart Assn. grantee, 1985-86, 88, 1995-96. **[15]** Fellow Assn. Tchrs. Preventive Medicine; mem. AAAS, AMA, Am. Fedn. Clin. Rsch., Assn. Med. Colls., Masons, Shriners, Sigma Xi. **[16]** Republican. **[17]** Roman Catholic. **[18]** Avocations: swimming, weight lifting, travelling. **[19]** Home: 6060 N Ridge Ave Oklahoma City OK 73126 **[20]** Office: Bapt Med Ctr 1986 Cuba Hwy Oklahoma City OK 73120*

KEY

[1] Name
[2] Occupation
[3] Vital statistics
[4] Parents
[5] Marriage
[6] Children
[7] Education
[8] Professional certifications
[9] Career
[10] Career-related
[11] Writings and creative works
[12] Civic and political activities
[13] Military
[14] Awards and fellowships
[15] Professional and association memberships, clubs and lodges
[16] Political affiliation
[17] Religion
[18] Avocations
[19] Home address
[20] Office address
[*] Researched by Marquis Who's Who

Table of Abbreviations

The following abbreviations and symbols are frequently used in this book.

**An asterisk following a sketch indicates that it was researched by the Marquis Who's Who editorial staff and has not been verified by the biographee.*

A

A Associate (used with academic degrees only)
AA, A.A. Associate in Arts, Associate of Arts
AAAL American Academy of Arts and Letters
AAAS American Association for the Advancement of Science
AACD American Association for Counseling and Development
AACN American Association of Critical Care Nurses
AAHA American Academy of Health Administrators
AAHP American Association of Hospital Planners
AAHPERD American Alliance for Health, Physical Education, Recreation, and Dance
AAS Associate of Applied Science
AASL American Association of School Librarians
AASPA American Association of School Personnel Administrators
AAU Amateur Athletic Union
AAUP American Association of University Professors
AAUW American Association of University Women
AB, A.B. Arts, Bachelor of
AB Alberta
ABA American Bar Association
ABC American Broadcasting Company
AC Air Corps
acad. academy, academic
acct. accountant
acctg. accounting
ACDA Arms Control and Disarmament Agency
ACHA American College of Hospital Administrators
ACLS Advanced Cardiac Life Support
ACLU American Civil Liberties Union
ACOG American College of Ob-Gyn
ACP American College of Physicians
ACS American College of Surgeons
ADA American Dental Association
a.d.c. aide-de-camp
adj. adjunct, adjutant
adj. gen. adjutant general
adm. admiral
adminstr. administrator
adminstrn. administration
adminstrv. administrative
ADN Associate's Degree in Nursing
ADP Automatic Data Processing
adv. advocate, advisory
advt. advertising
AE, A.E. Agricultural Engineer
A.E. and P. Ambassador Extraordinary and Plenipotentiary
AEC Atomic Energy Commission
aero. aeronautical, aeronautic
aerodyn. aerodynamic
AFB Air Force Base
AFL-CIO American Federation of Labor and Congress of Industrial Organizations
AFTRA American Federation of TV and Radio Artists
AFSCME American Federation of State, County and Municipal Employees
agr. agriculture
agrl. agricultural
agt. agent
AGVA American Guild of Variety Artists
agy. agency
A&I Agricultural and Industrial
AIA American Institute of Architects
AIAA American Institute of Aeronautics and Astronautics
AIChE American Institute of Chemical Engineers
AICPA American Institute of Certified Public Accountants
AID Agency for International Development
AIDS Acquired Immune Deficiency Syndrome
AIEE American Institute of Electrical Engineers
AIM American Institute of Management
AIME American Institute of Mining, Metallurgy, and Petroleum Engineers
AK Alaska
AL Alabama
Ala. Alabama
ALA American Library Association
alt. alternate
Alta. Alberta
A&M Agricultural and Mechanical
AM, A.M. Arts, Master of
Am. American, America
AMA American Medical Association
amb. ambassador
A.M.E. African Methodist Episcopal
Amtrak National Railroad Passenger Corporation
AMVETS American Veterans of World War II, Korea, Vietnam
ANA American Nurses Association
anat. anatomical
ANCC American Nurses Credentialing Center
ann. annual
ANTA American National Theatre and Academy
anthrop. anthropological
AP Associated Press
APA American Psychological Association
APGA American Personnel Guidance Association
APHA American Public Health Association
APO Army Post Office
apptd. appointed
Apr. April
apt. apartment
AR Arkansas
ARC American Red Cross
arch. architect
archeol. archeological
archtl. architectural
Ariz. Arizona
Ark. Arkansas
ArtsD, ArtsD. Arts, Doctor of
arty. artillery
AS American Samoa
AS Associate in Science
ASCAP American Society of Composers, Authors and Publishers
ASCD Association for Supervision and Curriculum Development
ASCE American Society of Civil Engineers
ASHRAE American Society of Heating, Refrigeration, and Air Conditioning Engineers
ASME American Society of Mechanical Engineers
ASNSA American Society for Nursing Service Administrators
ASPA American Society for Public Administration
ASPCA American Society for the Prevention of Cruelty to Animals
assn. association
assoc. associate
asst. assistant
ASTD American Society for Training and Development
ASTM American Society for Testing and Materials
astron. astronomical
astrophys. astrophysical
ATLA Association of Trial Lawyers of America
ATSC Air Technical Service Command
AT&T American Telephone & Telegraph Company
atty. attorney
Aug. August
AUS Army of the United States
aux. auxiliary
Ave. Avenue
AVMA American Veterinary Medical Association
AZ Arizona
AWHONN Association of Women's Health Obstetric and Neonatal Nurses

B

B. Bachelor
b. born
BA, B.A. Bachelor of Arts
BAgr, B.Agr. Bachelor of Agriculture
Balt. Baltimore
Bapt. Baptist
BArch, B.Arch. Bachelor of Architecture

BAS, B.A.S. Bachelor of Agricultural Science
BBA, B.B.A. Bachelor of Business Administration
BBB Better Business Bureau
BBC British Broadcasting Corporation
BC, B.C. British Columbia
BCE, B.C.E. Bachelor of Civil Engineering
BChir, B.Chir. Bachelor of Surgery
BCL, B.C.L. Bachelor of Civil Law
BCLS Basic Cardiac Life Support
BCS, B.C.S. Bachelor of Commercial Science
BD, B.D. Bachelor of Divinity
bd. board
BE, B.E. Bachelor of Education
BEE, B.E.E. Bachelor of Electrical Engineering
BFA, B.F.A. Bachelor of Fine Arts
bibl. biblical
bibliog. bibliographical
biog. biographical
biol. biological
BJ, B.J. Bachelor of Journalism
Bklyn. Brooklyn
BL, B.L. Bachelor of Letters
bldg. building
BLS, B.L.S. Bachelor of Library Science
BLS Basic Life Support
Blvd. Boulevard
BMI Broadcast Music, Inc.
BMW Bavarian Motor Works (Bayerische Motoren Werke)
bn. battalion
B.&O.R.R. Baltimore & Ohio Railroad
bot. botanical
BPE, B.P.E. Bachelor of Physical Education
BPhil, B.Phil. Bachelor of Philosophy
br. branch
BRE, B.R.E. Bachelor of Religious Education
brig. gen. brigadier general
Brit. British, Brittanica
Bros. Brothers
BS, B.S. Bachelor of Science
BSA, B.S.A. Bachelor of Agricultural Science
BSBA Bachelor of Science in Business Administration
BSChemE Bachelor of Science in Chemical Engineering
BSD, B.S.D. Bachelor of Didactic Science
BSEE Bachelor of Science in Electrical Engineering
BSN Bachelor of Science in Nursing
BST, B.S.T. Bachelor of Sacred Theology
BTh, B.Th. Bachelor of Theology
bull. bulletin
bur. bureau
bus. business
B.W.I. British West Indies

C

CA California
CAA Civil Aeronautics Administration
CAB Civil Aeronautics Board
CAD-CAM Computer Aided Design–Computer Aided Model
Calif. California
C.Am. Central America
Can. Canada, Canadian
CAP Civil Air Patrol
capt. captain
cardiol. cardiological
cardiovasc. cardiovascular
CARE Cooperative American Relief Everywhere
Cath. Catholic
cav. cavalry
CBC Canadian Broadcasting Company
CBI China, Burma, India Theatre of Operations
CBS Columbia Broadcasting Company
C.C. Community College
CCC Commodity Credit Corporation
CCNY City College of New York
CCRN Critical Care Registered Nurse
CCU Cardiac Care Unit
CD Civil Defense
CE, C.E. Corps of Engineers, Civil Engineer
CEN Certified Emergency Nurse
CENTO Central Treaty Organization
CEO chief executive officer
CERN European Organization of Nuclear Research
cert. certificate, certification, certified
CETA Comprehensive Employment Training Act
CFA Chartered Financial Analyst
CFL Canadian Football League
CFO chief financial officer
CFP Certified Financial Planner
ch. church
ChD, Ch.D. Doctor of Chemistry
chem. chemical
ChemE, Chem.E. Chemical Engineer
ChFC Chartered Financial Consultant
Chgo. Chicago
chirurg. chirurgical
chmn. chairman
chpt. chapter
CIA Central Intelligence Agency
Cin. Cincinnati
cir. circle, circuit
CLE Continuing Legal Education
Cleve. Cleveland
climatol. climatological
clin. clinical
clk. clerk
C.L.U. Chartered Life Underwriter
CM, C.M. Master in Surgery
CM Northern Mariana Islands
CMA Certified Medical Assistant
cmty. community
CNA Certified Nurse's Aide
CNOR Certified Nurse (Operating Room)
C.&N.W.Ry. Chicago & North Western Railway
CO Colorado
Co. Company
COF Catholic Order of Foresters
C. of C. Chamber of Commerce
col. colonel
coll. college
Colo. Colorado
com. committee
comd. commanded
comdg. commanding
comdr. commander
comdt. commandant
comm. communications
commd. commissioned
comml. commercial
commn. commission
commr. commissioner
compt. comptroller
condr. conductor
Conf. Conference
Congl. Congregational, Congressional
Conglist. Congregationalist
Conn. Connecticut
cons. consultant, consulting
consol. consolidated
constl. constitutional
constn. constitution
constrn. construction
contbd. contributed
contbg. contributing
contbn. contribution
contbr. contributor
contr. controller
Conv. Convention
COO chief operating officer
coop. cooperative
coord. coordinator
CORDS Civil Operations and Revolutionary Development Support
CORE Congress of Racial Equality
corp. corporation, corporate
corr. correspondent, corresponding, correspondence
C.&O.Ry. Chesapeake & Ohio Railway
coun. council
CPA Certified Public Accountant
CPCU Chartered Property and Casualty Underwriter
CPH, C.P.H. Certificate of Public Health
cpl. corporal
CPR Cardio-Pulmonary Resuscitation
C.P.Ry. Canadian Pacific Railway
CRT Cathode Ray Terminal
C.S. Christian Science
CSB, C.S.B. Bachelor of Christian Science
C.S.C. Civil Service Commission
CT Connecticut
ct. court
ctr. center
ctrl. central
CWS Chemical Warfare Service
C.Z. Canal Zone

D

D. Doctor
d. daughter
DAgr, D.Agr. Doctor of Agriculture
DAR Daughters of the American Revolution
dau. daughter
DAV Disabled American Veterans
DC, D.C. District of Columbia
DCL, D.C.L. Doctor of Civil Law
DCS, D.C.S. Doctor of Commercial Science
DD, D.D. Doctor of Divinity
DDS, D.D.S. Doctor of Dental Surgery
DE Delaware

Dec. December
dec. deceased
def. defense
Del. Delaware
del. delegate, delegation
Dem. Democrat, Democratic
DEng, D.Eng. Doctor of Engineering
denom. denomination, denominational
dep. deputy
dept. department
dermatol. dermatological
desc. descendant
devel. development, developmental
DFA, D.F.A. Doctor of Fine Arts
D.F.C. Distinguished Flying Cross
DHL, D.H.L. Doctor of Hebrew Literature
dir. director
dist. district
distbg. distributing
distbn. distribution
distbr. distributor
disting. distinguished
div. division, divinity, divorce
divsn. division
DLitt, D.Litt. Doctor of Literature
DMD, D.M.D. Doctor of Dental Medicine
DMS, D.M.S. Doctor of Medical Science
DO, D.O. Doctor of Osteopathy
docs. documents
DON Director of Nursing
DPH, D.P.H. Diploma in Public Health
DPhil, D.Phil. Doctor of Philosophy
D.R. Daughters of the Revolution
Dr. Drive, Doctor
DRE, D.R.E. Doctor of Religious Education
DrPH, Dr.P.H. Doctor of Public Health, Doctor of Public Hygiene
D.S.C. Distinguished Service Cross
DSc, D.Sc. Doctor of Science
DSChemE Doctor of Science in Chemical Engineering
D.S.M. Distinguished Service Medal
DST, D.S.T. Doctor of Sacred Theology
DTM, D.T.M. Doctor of Tropical Medicine
DVM, D.V.M. Doctor of Veterinary Medicine
DVS, D.V.S. Doctor of Veterinary Surgery

E

E, E. East
ea. eastern
E. and P. Extraordinary and Plenipotentiary
Eccles. Ecclesiastical
ecol. ecological
econ. economic
ECOSOC Economic and Social Council (of the UN)
ED, E.D. Doctor of Engineering
ed. educated
EdB, Ed.B. Bachelor of Education
EdD, Ed.D. Doctor of Education
edit. edition
editl. editorial
EdM, Ed.M. Master of Education
edn. education
ednl. educational
EDP Electronic Data Processing
EdS, Ed.S. Specialist in Education
EE, E.E. Electrical Engineer
E.E. and M.P. Envoy Extraordinary and Minister Plenipotentiary
EEC European Economic Community
EEG Electroencephalogram
EEO Equal Employment Opportunity
EEOC Equal Employment Opportunity Commission
E.Ger. German Democratic Republic
EKG Electrocardiogram
elec. electrical
electrochem. electrochemical
electrophys. electrophysical
elem. elementary
EM, E.M. Engineer of Mines
EMT Emergency Medical Technician
ency. encyclopedia
Eng. England
engr. engineer
engring. engineering
entomol. entomological
environ. environmental
EPA Environmental Protection Agency
epidemiol. epidemiological
Episc. Episcopalian
ERA Equal Rights Amendment
ERDA Energy Research and Development Administration
ESEA Elementary and Secondary Education Act
ESL English as Second Language
ESPN Entertainment and Sports Programming Network
ESSA Environmental Science Services Administration
ethnol. ethnological
ETO European Theatre of Operations
Evang. Evangelical
exam. examination, examining
Exch. Exchange
exec. executive
exhbn. exhibition
expdn. expedition
expn. exposition
expt. experiment
exptl. experimental
Expy. Expressway
Ext. Extension

F

F.A. Field Artillery
FAA Federal Aviation Administration
FAO Food and Agriculture Organization (of the UN)
FBA Federal Bar Association
FBI Federal Bureau of Investigation
FCA Farm Credit Administration
FCC Federal Communications Commission
FCDA Federal Civil Defense Administration
FDA Food and Drug Administration
FDIA Federal Deposit Insurance Administration
FDIC Federal Deposit Insurance Corporation
FE, F.E. Forest Engineer
FEA Federal Energy Administration
Feb. February
fed. federal
fedn. federation
FERC Federal Energy Regulatory Commission
fgn. foreign
FHA Federal Housing Administration
fin. financial, finance
FL Florida
Fl. Floor
Fla. Florida
FMC Federal Maritime Commission
FNP Family Nurse Practitioner
FOA Foreign Operations Administration
found. foundation
FPC Federal Power Commission
FPO Fleet Post Office
frat. fraternity
FRS Federal Reserve System
FSA Federal Security Agency
Ft. Fort
FTC Federal Trade Commission
Fwy. Freeway

G

G-1 (or other number) Division of General Staff
GA, Ga. Georgia
GAO General Accounting Office
gastroent. gastroenterological
GATE Gifted and Talented Educators
GATT General Agreement on Tariffs and Trade
GE General Electric Company
gen. general
geneal. genealogical
geod. geodetic
geog. geographic, geographical
geol. geological
geophys. geophysical
geriat. geriatrics
gerontol. gerontological
G.H.Q. General Headquarters
GM General Motors Corporation
GMAC General Motors Acceptance Corporation
G.N.Ry. Great Northern Railway
gov. governor
govt. government
govtl. governmental
GPO Government Printing Office
grad. graduate, graduated
GSA General Services Administration
Gt. Great
GTE General Telephone and Electric Company
GU Guam
gynecol. gynecological

H

HBO Home Box Office
hdqs. headquarters
HEW Department of Health, Education and Welfare
HHD, H.H.D. Doctor of Humanities
HHFA Housing and Home Finance Agency
HHS Department of Health and Human Services
HI Hawaii
hist. historical, historic

HM, H.M. Master of Humanities
HMO Health Maintenance Organization
homeo. homeopathic
hon. honorary, honorable
Ho. of Dels. House of Delegates
Ho. of Reps. House of Representatives
hort. horticultural
hosp. hospital
HS, H.S. High School
HUD Department of Housing and Urban Development
Hwy. Highway
hydrog. hydrographic

I

IA Iowa
IAEA International Atomic Energy Agency
IATSE International Alliance of Theatrical and Stage Employees and Moving Picture Operators of the United States and Canada
IBM International Business Machines Corporation
IBRD International Bank for Reconstruction and Development
ICA International Cooperation Administration
ICC Interstate Commerce Commission
ICCE International Council for Computers in Education
ICU Intensive Care Unit
ID Idaho
IEEE Institute of Electrical and Electronics Engineers
IFC International Finance Corporation
IGY International Geophysical Year
IL Illinois
Ill. Illinois
illus. illustrated
ILO International Labor Organization
IMF International Monetary Fund
IN Indiana
Inc. Incorporated
Ind. Indiana
ind. independent
Indpls. Indianapolis
indsl. industrial
inf. infantry
info. information
ins. insurance
insp. inspector
insp. gen. inspector general
inst. institute
instl. institutional
instn. institution
instr. instructor
instrn. instruction
instrnl. instructional
internat. international
intro. introduction
IRE Institute of Radio Engineers
IRS Internal Revenue Service
ITT International Telephone & Telegraph Corporation

J

JAG Judge Advocate General
JAGC Judge Advocate General Corps
Jan. January
Jaycees Junior Chamber of Commerce
JB, J.B. Jurum Baccalaureus
JCB, J.C.B. Juris Canoni Baccalaureus
JCD, J.C.D. Juris Canonici Doctor, Juris Civilis Doctor
JCL, J.C.L. Juris Canonici Licentiatus
JD, J.D. Juris Doctor
jg. junior grade
jour. journal
jr. junior
JSD, J.S.D. Juris Scientiae Doctor
JUD, J.U.D. Juris Utriusque Doctor
jud. judicial

K

Kans. Kansas
K.C. Knights of Columbus
K.P. Knights of Pythias
KS Kansas
K.T. Knight Templar
KY, Ky. Kentucky

L

LA, La. Louisiana
L.A. Los Angeles
lab. laboratory
L.Am. Latin America
lang. language
laryngol. laryngological
LB Labrador
LDS Latter Day Saints
LDS Church Church of Jesus Christ of Latter Day Saints
lectr. lecturer
legis. legislation, legislative
LHD, L.H.D. Doctor of Humane Letters
LI, L.I. Long Island
libr. librarian, library
lic. licensed, license
L.I.R.R. Long Island Railroad
lit. literature
litig. litigation
LittB, Litt.B. Bachelor of Letters
LittD, Litt.D. Doctor of Letters
LLB, LL.B. Bachelor of Laws
LLD, L.L.D. Doctor of Laws
LLM, L.L.M. Master of Laws
Ln. Lane
L.&N.R.R. Louisville & Nashville Railroad
LPGA Ladies Professional Golf Association
LPN Licensed Practical Nurse
LS, L.S. Library Science (in degree)
lt. lieutenant
Ltd. Limited
Luth. Lutheran
LWV League of Women Voters

M

M. Master
m. married
MA, M.A. Master of Arts
MA Massachusetts
MADD Mothers Against Drunk Driving
mag. magazine
MAgr, M.Agr. Master of Agriculture
maj. major
Man. Manitoba
Mar. March
MArch, M.Arch. Master in Architecture
Mass. Massachusetts
math. mathematics, mathematical
MATS Military Air Transport Service
MB, M.B. Bachelor of Medicine
MB Manitoba
MBA, M.B.A. Master of Business Administration
MBS Mutual Broadcasting System
M.C. Medical Corps
MCE, M.C.E. Master of Civil Engineering
mcht. merchant
mcpl. municipal
MCS, M.C.S. Master of Commercial Science
MD, M.D. Doctor of Medicine
MD, Md. Maryland
MDiv Master of Divinity
MDip, M.Dip. Master in Diplomacy
mdse. merchandise
MDV, M.D.V. Doctor of Veterinary Medicine
ME, M.E. Mechanical Engineer
ME Maine
M.E.Ch. Methodist Episcopal Church
mech. mechanical
MEd., M.Ed. Master of Education
med. medical
MEE, M.E.E. Master of Electrical Engineering
mem. member
meml. memorial
merc. mercantile
met. metropolitan
metall. metallurgical
MetE, Met.E. Metallurgical Engineer
meteorol. meteorological
Meth. Methodist
Mex. Mexico
MF, M.F. Master of Forestry
MFA, M.F.A. Master of Fine Arts
mfg. manufacturing
mfr. manufacturer
mgmt. management
mgr. manager
MHA, M.H.A. Master of Hospital Administration
M.I. Military Intelligence
MI Michigan
Mich. Michigan
micros. microscopic, microscopical
mid. middle
mil. military
Milw. Milwaukee
Min. Minister
mineral. mineralogical
Minn. Minnesota
MIS Management Information Systems
Miss. Mississippi
MIT Massachusetts Institute of Technology
mktg. marketing
ML, M.L. Master of Laws
MLA Modern Language Association
M.L.D. Magister Legnum Diplomatic
MLitt, M.Litt. Master of Literature, Master of Letters
MLS, M.L.S. Master of Library Science
MME, M.M.E. Master of Mechanical Engineering

MN Minnesota
mng. managing
MO, Mo. Missouri
moblzn. mobilization
Mont. Montana
MP Northern Mariana Islands
M.P. Member of Parliament
MPA Master of Public Administration
MPE, M.P.E. Master of Physical Education
MPH, M.P.H. Master of Public Health
MPhil, M.Phil. Master of Philosophy
MPL, M.P.L. Master of Patent Law
Mpls. Minneapolis
MRE, M.R.E. Master of Religious Education
MRI Magnetic Resonance Imaging
MS, M.S. Master of Science
MS, Ms. Mississippi
MSc, M.Sc. Master of Science
MSChemE Master of Science in Chemical Engineering
MSEE Master of Science in Electrical Engineering
MSF, M.S.F. Master of Science of Forestry
MSN Master of Science in Nursing
MST, M.S.T. Master of Sacred Theology
MSW, M.S.W. Master of Social Work
MT Montana
Mt. Mount
MTO Mediterranean Theatre of Operation
MTV Music Television
mus. museum, musical
MusB, Mus.B. Bachelor of Music
MusD, Mus.D. Doctor of Music
MusM, Mus.M. Master of Music
mut. mutual
MVP Most Valuable Player
mycol. mycological

N

N, N. North
NAACOG Nurses Association of the American College of Obstetricians and Gynecologists
NAACP National Association for the Advancement of Colored People
NACA National Advisory Committee for Aeronautics
NACDL National Association of Criminal Defense Lawyers
NACU National Association of Colleges and Universities
NAD National Academy of Design
NAE National Academy of Engineering, National Association of Educators
NAESP National Association of Elementary School Principals
NAFE National Association of Female Executives
N.Am. North America
NAM National Association of Manufacturers
NAMH National Association for Mental Health
NAPA National Association of Performing Artists
NARAS National Academy of Recording Arts and Sciences
NAREB National Association of Real Estate Boards
NARS National Archives and Record Service
NAS National Academy of Sciences
NASA National Aeronautics and Space Administration
NASP National Association of School Psychologists
NASW National Association of Social Workers
nat. national
NATAS National Academy of Television Arts and Sciences
NATO North Atlantic Treaty Organization
NATOUSA North African Theatre of Operations, United States Army
nav. navigation
NB New Brunswick
NBA National Basketball Association
NBC National Broadcasting Company
NC, N.C. North Carolina
NCAA National College Athletic Association
NCCJ National Conference of Christians and Jews
ND, N.D. North Dakota
NDEA National Defense Education Act
NE Nebraska
NE, N.E. Northeast
NEA National Education Association
Nebr. Nebraska
NEH National Endowment for Humanities
neurol. neurological
Nev. Nevada
NF Newfoundland
NFL National Football League
Nfld. Newfoundland
NG National Guard
NH, N.H. New Hampshire
NHL National Hockey League
NIH National Institutes of Health
NIMH National Institute of Mental Health
NJ, N.J. New Jersey
NLRB National Labor Relations Board
NM New Mexico
N.Mex. New Mexico
No. Northern
NOAA National Oceanographic and Atmospheric Administration
NORAD North America Air Defense
Nov. November
NOW National Organization for Women
N.P.Ry. Northern Pacific Railway
nr. near
NRA National Rifle Association
NRC National Research Council
NS, N.S. Nova Scotia
NSC National Security Council
NSF National Science Foundation
NSTA National Science Teachers Association
NSW New South Wales
N.T. New Testament
NT Northwest Territories
nuc. nuclear
numis. numismatic
NV Nevada
NW, N.W. Northwest
N.W.T. Northwest Territories
NY, N.Y. New York
N.Y.C. New York City
NYU New York University
N.Z. New Zealand

O

OAS Organization of American States
ob-gyn obstetrics-gynecology
obs. observatory
obstet. obstetrical
occupl. occupational
oceanog. oceanographic
Oct. October
OD, O.D. Doctor of Optometry
OECD Organization for Economic Cooperation and Development
OEEC Organization of European Economic Cooperation
OEO Office of Economic Opportunity
ofcl. official
OH Ohio
OK Oklahoma
Okla. Oklahoma
ON Ontario
Ont. Ontario
oper. operating
ophthal. ophthalmological
ops. operations
OR Oregon
orch. orchestra
Oreg. Oregon
orgn. organization
orgnl. organizational
ornithol. ornithological
orthop. orthopedic
OSHA Occupational Safety and Health Administration
OSRD Office of Scientific Research and Development
OSS Office of Strategic Services
osteo. osteopathic
otol. otological
otolaryn. otolaryngological

P

PA, Pa. Pennsylvania
P.A. Professional Association
paleontol. paleontological
path. pathological
PBS Public Broadcasting System
P.C. Professional Corporation
PE Prince Edward Island
pediat. pediatrics
P.E.I. Prince Edward Island
PEN Poets, Playwrights, Editors, Essayists and Novelists (international association)
penol. penological
P.E.O. women's organization (full name not disclosed)
pers. personnel
pfc. private first class
PGA Professional Golfers' Association of America
PHA Public Housing Administration
pharm. pharmaceutical
PharmD, Pharm.D. Doctor of Pharmacy
PharmM, Pharm.M. Master of Pharmacy
PhB, Ph.B. Bachelor of Philosophy

PhD, Ph.D. Doctor of Philosophy
PhDChemE Doctor of Science in Chemical Engineering
PhM, Ph.M. Master of Philosophy
Phila. Philadelphia
philharm. philharmonic
philol. philological
philos. philosophical
photog. photographic
phys. physical
physiol. physiological
Pitts. Pittsburgh
Pk. Park
Pky. Parkway
Pl. Place
P.&L.E.R.R. Pittsburgh & Lake Erie Railroad
Plz. Plaza
PNP Pediatric Nurse Practitioner
P.O. Post Office
PO Box Post Office Box
polit. political
poly. polytechnic, polytechnical
PQ Province of Quebec
PR, P.R. Puerto Rico
prep. preparatory
pres. president
Presbyn. Presbyterian
presdl. presidential
prin. principal
procs. proceedings
prod. produced (play production)
prodn. production
prodr. producer
prof. professor
profl. professional
prog. progressive
propr. proprietor
pros. atty. prosecuting attorney
pro tem. pro tempore
PSRO Professional Services Review Organization
psychiat. psychiatric
psychol. psychological
PTA Parent-Teachers Association
ptnr. partner
PTO Pacific Theatre of Operations, Parent Teacher Organization
pub. publisher, publishing, published
pub. public
publ. publication
pvt. private

Q

quar. quarterly
qm. quartermaster
Q.M.C. Quartermaster Corps
Que. Quebec

R

radiol. radiological
RAF Royal Air Force
RCA Radio Corporation of America
RCAF Royal Canadian Air Force
RD Rural Delivery
Rd. Road
R&D Research & Development
REA Rural Electrification Administration
rec. recording
ref. reformed
regt. regiment
regtl. regimental
rehab. rehabilitation
rels. relations
Rep. Republican
rep. representative
Res. Reserve
ret. retired
Rev. Reverend
rev. review, revised
RFC Reconstruction Finance Corporation
RFD Rural Free Delivery
rhinol. rhinological
RI, R.I. Rhode Island
RISD Rhode Island School of Design
Rlwy. Railway
Rm. Room
RN, R.N. Registered Nurse
roentgenol. roentgenological
ROTC Reserve Officers Training Corps
RR Rural Route
R.R. Railroad
rsch. research
rschr. researcher
Rt. Route

S

S, S. South
s. son
SAC Strategic Air Command
SAG Screen Actors Guild
SALT Strategic Arms Limitation Talks
S.Am. South America
san. sanitary
SAR Sons of the American Revolution
Sask. Saskatchewan
savs. savings
SB, S.B. Bachelor of Science
SBA Small Business Administration
SC, S.C. South Carolina
SCAP Supreme Command Allies Pacific
ScB, Sc.B. Bachelor of Science
SCD, S.C.D. Doctor of Commercial Science
ScD, Sc.D. Doctor of Science
sch. school
sci. science, scientific
SCLC Southern Christian Leadership Conference
SCV Sons of Confederate Veterans
SD, S.D. South Dakota
SE, S.E. Southeast
SEATO Southeast Asia Treaty Organization
SEC Securities and Exchange Commission
sec. secretary
sect. section
seismol. seismological
sem. seminary
Sept. September
s.g. senior grade
sgt. sergeant
SHAEF Supreme Headquarters Allied Expeditionary Forces
SHAPE Supreme Headquarters Allied Powers in Europe
S.I. Staten Island
S.J. Society of Jesus (Jesuit)
SJD Scientiae Juridicae Doctor
SK Saskatchewan
SM, S.M. Master of Science
SNP Society of Nursing Professionals
So. Southern
soc. society
sociol. sociological
S.P.Co. Southern Pacific Company
spkr. speaker
spl. special
splty. specialty
Sq. Square
S.R. Sons of the Revolution
sr. senior
S S Steamship
S S S Selective Service System
St. Saint, Street
sta. station
stats. statistics
statis. statistical
STB, S.T.B. Bachelor of Sacred Theology
stblzn. stabilization
STD, S.T.D. Doctor of Sacred Theology
std. standard
Ste. Suite
subs. subsidiary
SUNY State University of New York
supr. supervisor
supt. superintendent
surg. surgical
svc. service
SW, S.W. Southwest
sys. system

T

TAPPI Technical Association of the Pulp and Paper Industry
tb. tuberculosis
tchg. teaching
tchr. teacher
tech. technical, technology
technol. technological
tel. telephone
Tel. & Tel. Telephone & Telegraph
telecom. telecommunications
temp. temporary
Tenn. Tennessee
Ter. Territory
Ter. Terrace
TESOL Teachers of English to Speakers of Other Languages
Tex. Texas
ThD, Th.D. Doctor of Theology
theol. theological
ThM, Th.M. Master of Theology
TN Tennessee
tng. training
topog. topographical
trans. transaction, transferred
transl. translation, translated
transp. transportation
treas. treasurer
TT Trust Territory
TV television
TVA Tennessee Valley Authority
TWA Trans World Airlines
twp. township

TX Texas
typog. typographical

U

U., univ. University
UAW United Auto Workers
UCLA University of California at Los Angeles
UDC United Daughters of the Confederacy
U.K. United Kingdom
UN United Nations
UNESCO United Nations Educational, Scientific and Cultural Organization
UNICEF United Nations International Children's Emergency Fund
UNRRA United Nations Relief and Rehabilitation Administration
UPI United Press International
U.P.R.R. United Pacific Railroad
urol. urological
U.S. United States
U.S.A. United States of America
USAAF United States Army Air Force
USAF United States Air Force
USAFR United States Air Force Reserve
USAR United States Army Reserve
USCG United States Coast Guard
USCGR United States Coast Guard Reserve
USES United States Employment Service
USIA United States Information Agency
USMC United States Marine Corps
USMCR United States Marine Corps Reserve
USN United States Navy
USNG United States National Guard
USNR United States Naval Reserve
USO United Service Organizations
USPHS United States Public Health Service
USS United States Ship
USSR Union of the Soviet Socialist Republics
USTA United States Tennis Association
USV United States Volunteers
UT Utah

V

VA Veterans Administration
VA, Va. Virginia
vet. veteran, veterinary
VFW Veterans of Foreign Wars
VI, V.I. Virgin Islands
vice pres. vice president
vis. visiting
VISTA Volunteers in Service to America
VITA Volunteers in Technical Assistance
vocat. vocational
vol. volunteer, volume
v.p. vice president
vs. versus
VT, Vt. Vermont

W

W, W. West
WA Washington (state)
WAC Women's Army Corps
Wash. Washington (state)
WATS Wide Area Telecommunications Service
WAVES Women's Reserve, US Naval Reserve
WCTU Women's Christian Temperance Union
we. western
W. Ger. Germany, Federal Republic of
WHO World Health Organization
WI Wisconsin
W.I. West Indies
Wis. Wisconsin
WSB Wage Stabilization Board
WV West Virginia
W.Va. West Virginia
WWI World War I
WWII World War II
WY Wyoming
Wyo. Wyoming

X Y

YMCA Young Men's Christian Association
YMHA Young Men's Hebrew Association
YM & YWHA Young Men's and Young Women's Hebrew Association
yr. year
YT Yukon Territory
YWCA Young Women's Christian Association

Z

zool. zoological

Alphabetical Practices

Names are arranged alphabetically according to the surnames, and under identical surnames according to the first given name. If both surname and first given name are identical, names are arranged alphabetically according to the second given name.

Surnames beginning with De, Des, Du, however capitalized or spaced, are recorded with the prefix preceding the surname and arranged alphabetically under the letter D.

Surnames beginning with Mac and Mc are arranged alphabetically under M.

Surnames beginning with Saint or St. appear after names that begin Sains, and are arranged according to the second part of the name, e.g., St. Clair before Saint Dennis.

Surnames beginning with Van, Von, or von are arranged alphabetically under the letter V.

Compound surnames are arranged according to the first member of the compound.

Many hyphenated Arabic names begin Al-, El-, or al-. These names are alphabetized according to each biographee's designation of last name. Thus Al-Bahar, Neta may be listed either under Al- or under Bahar, depending on the preference of the listee.

Also, Arabic names have a variety of possible spellings when transposed to English. Spelling of these names is always based on the practice of the biographee. Some biographees use a Western form of word order, while others prefer the Arabic word sequence.

Similarly, Asian names may have no comma between family and given names, but some biographees have chosen to add the comma. In each case, punctuation follows the preference of the biographee.

Parentheses used in connection with a name indicate which part of the full name is usually omitted in common usage. Hence, Chambers, E(lizabeth) Anne indicates that the first name, Elizabeth, is generally recorded as an initial. In such a case, the parentheses are ignored in alphabetizing and the name would be arranged as Chambers, Elizabeth Anne.

However, if the entire first name appears in parentheses, for example, Chambers, (Elizabeth) Anne, the first name is not commonly used, and the alphabetizing is therefore arranged as though the name were Chambers, Anne.

If the entire middle name is in parentheses, it is still used in alphabetical sorting. Hence, Belamy, Katherine (Lucille) would sort as Belamy, Katherine Lucille. The same occurs if the entire last name is in parentheses, e.g., (Brandenberg), Howard Keith would sort as Brandenberg, Howard Keith.

For visual clarification:

Smith, H(enry) George: Sorts as Smith, Henry George
Smith, (Henry) George: Sorts as Smith, George
Smith, Henry (George): Sorts as Smith, Henry George
(Smith), Henry George: Sorts as Smith, Henry George

In commemoration of the 60th Edition of **Who's Who in America**®

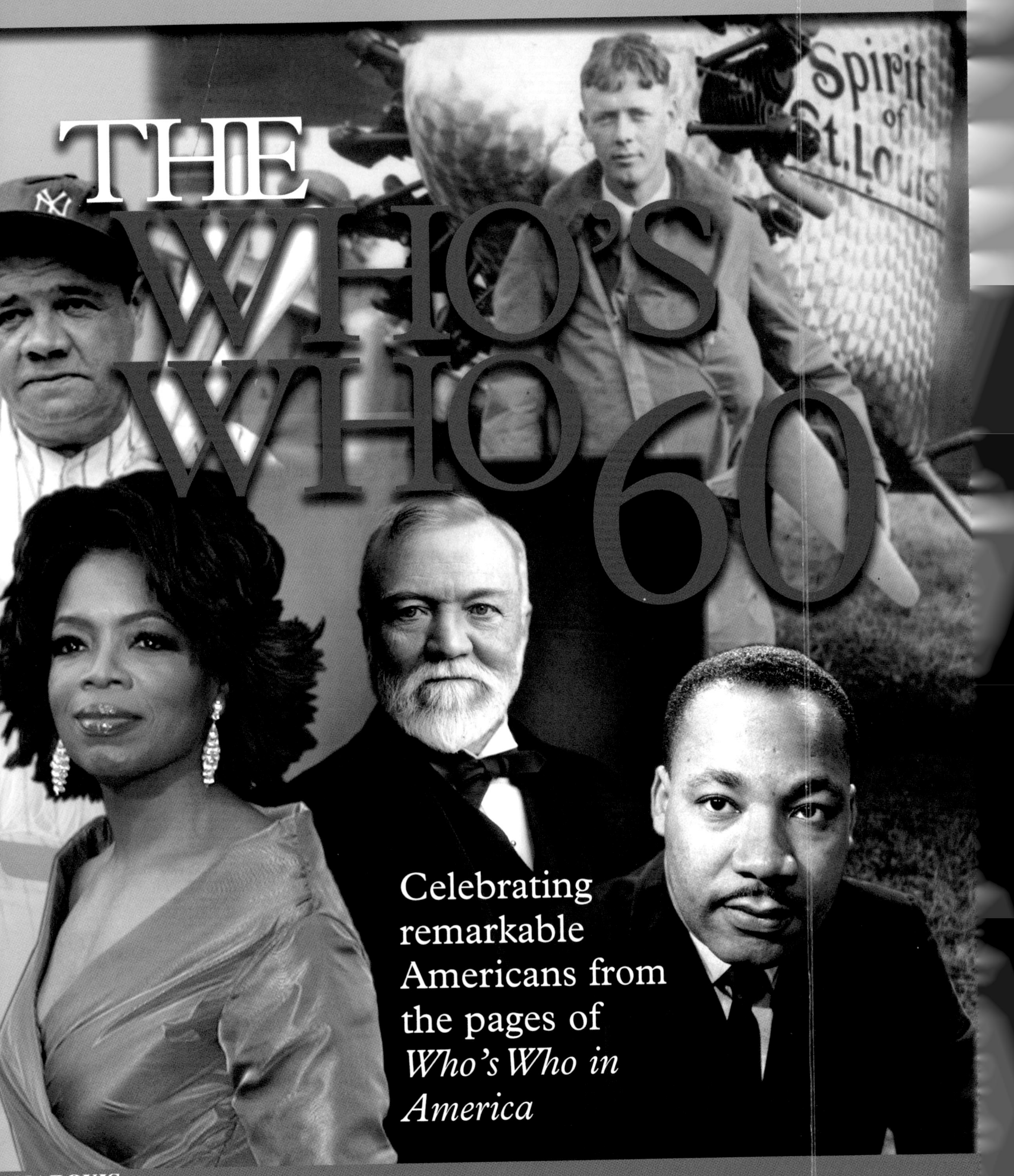

Introduction

The *Who's Who 60* was created to commemorate the 60th Edition of **Who's Who in America**. Our formula for selecting honorees was a simple one: select five individuals from each of the twelve decades we've been publishing **Who's Who in America**. From each decade, beginning with the 1890s, we have chosen one individual to represent each of the following five areas:

- Science and Technology
- Newsmakers
- Business and Industry
- Sports
- Entertainment, Arts and Letters

The *Who's Who 60* presents Americans doing what Americans do best. The individuals profiled on the following pages are innovators, dreamers, achievers. Many of them opened doors for future generations, while others have been called upon to lead the country through difficult, tumultuous times. Some have entertained us. Others have awed us with their athletic achievements.

From Thomas Edison to Bill Gates, from Edith Wharton to Stephen King, from John D. Rockefeller to Meg Whitman, the editorial staff of Marquis Who's Who has selected individuals who have helped to define their eras.

To compile the list, our editorial and research staffs were called upon to nominate individuals for consideration.

- Individuals who had enormous impact in their fields of endeavor
- Individuals who helped to define their eras
- Individuals whose achievements have stood the test of time.

While other publications and media outlets have chosen their own lists, they have done so only as a sideline to their regular businesses. At Marquis Who's Who, we have been evaluating the influence and power of individuals since 1899, and we do it every single day of the week.

In a few cases, multiple individuals were chosen in the same decade in the same category. That is why you will find both Wright Brothers (Orville and Wilbur), the Robber Barons (John D. Rockefeller and Andrew Carnegie), the Google team of Sergey Brin and Larry Page, the baseball kings of the 1950s (Mantle, Mays and Snider), and the intense NBA rivals Larry Bird and Magic Johnson.

Each decade is represented in a two-page spread complete with archival photographs, a newspaper front page illustrating a key historical event of the decade, and a timeline representing events, discoveries and achievements of the decade.

Obviously, all of the members of the *Who's Who 60* have appeared on the pages of **Who's Who in America**. All of the individuals featured in the decade of the 1890s were included in the very first edition of **Who's Who in America**. And all of the living members of the *Who's Who 60* can be found in this, the 60th Edition.

EDISON, Thomas Alva, inventor; *b.* Milan, Ohio, Feb. 11, 1847; *s.* Samuel Ogden Jr.
and Nancy (Elliott) Edison; married Mary G. Stilwell, Dec. 25, 1871 (dec. Aug. 9,
1884); children: Marion Estelle, Thomas Alva, William Leslie; married Mina Miller,
Feb. 24, 1886; children: Madeleine, Charles, Theodore. Spent 3 months at sch., Port
Huron, Mich., then received instruction from his mother; hon. Ph.D., Union Coll., 1878.
Began selling newspaper and candy on the Grand Trunk Railroad to Detroit, 1859; wrote
and printed Grand Trunk Herald, 1862; telegraph operator in towns throughout
Midwest, 1863-67, with Western Union Telegraph Co., Boston, 1868-69; gen. mgr.
Samuel Laws' Gold Indicator Co., NYC, 1869; co-founder Pope, Edison & Co., 1869,
bought by Gold & Stock Telegraph Co. along with stock-ticker inventions, 1870, with
money established workshop at Newark, NJ, 1870-76, removing to Menlo Park, NJ,
1876-82, and later to West Orange, NJ, 1887-31; co-organized Edison Electric
Illuminating Co. of NY, 1880, Edison Electric Light Co., 1878, other electric companies,
eventually consolidated into General Electric Co., 1892; consolidated later companies
into Thomas A. Edison, Inc., 1911, pres. 1911-26; tested 17,000 plants for domestic
source of rubber, 1927-31, as Edison Botanic Research Co. Head of US Naval
Consulting Bd., 1915-21. Recipient Albert Medal, British Soc. Arts, 1892, John Fritz
Medal, Am. Engineering Societies, 1908, Rumford Medal, Am. Acad. Arts & Sciences,
1908, Congressional Gold Medal for development and application of inventions that
have revolutionized civilization in the last century, 1928; named Chevalier French
Legion of Honor, 1878, promoted to Comdr., 1889; elected to Nat. Acad. Sciences,
1927. First patent for electric vote recorder, June 1, 1869; made numerous telegraphic
improvements: automatic repeater, transmitters, receivers, the duplex, quadruplex, &
sextuplex systems, carbon rheostat, automatic printers & tape; worked to improve typing
machine, 1871; invented electric pen, 1875, phonograph, 1877, the microphone, the
microtasimeter for detection of small changes in temperature, the megaphone, first
practical incandescent lamp, 1879, a method to make plate glass, magnetic ore separator,
compressing dies, composition brick, a cement process, an all-concrete house, an
electric locomotive, patent, 1893, fluoroscope, nickel-iron battery, universal motor,
1907, electric safety lantern, 1914, many others; developments in motion pictures,
kinetograph & kinetoscope, Edison Co. produced over 1700 movies, synchronized
movies with phonograph, 1904; opened first central power station, London, 1882, Pearl
Street, NYC, 1882; first observed phenomenon to be known as Edison Effect, 1880;
since commencement of European War, 1914, designed, built and operated successfully
several benzol plants, also 2 carbolic acid plants and other chemical plants for making
myrbane aniline oil, aniline salt, and para-phenylenediamine; acquired 1093 patents
throughout his life. Died West Orange, NJ, Oct. 18, 1931.

The timeline concludes with the actual Marquis Who's Who profiles of the honorees as they currently appear in the Marquis Who's Who database and as part of **Marquis Who's Who on the Web**, our online database featuring over 1.2 million profiles.

As in any project involving subjectivity, there was serious debate over virtually every individual presented in the *Who's Who 60*. We are certain that you will agree with some of our decisions and disagree with others. We, of course, would love to hear your opinions and suggestions.

The 1890s

Thomas Edison

Science and Technology

Of all of the brilliant scientists produced in the United States, none can rival Edison for the sheer scope and impact of his work. Edison earned 1,093 patents, the first coming at the age of 21, and the last after his death in 1931.

Edison received a patent for his most far-reaching invention, the electric light bulb, in 1879, but continued to produce revolutionary inventions over the following 50 years.

The 1890s was a prolific period for Edison. The Edison General Electric Company merged with Thomson-Houston to form the General Electric Company in 1892, allowing him to turn his attention from the electrical business to two other areas in which he made a significant impact: the phonograph and motion pictures. While he received numerous patents in each of these fields, he received none for his work with x-rays, which culminated in his invention of the fluoroscope in 1896. He refused to patent the machine, allowing doctors to utilize the technology without incurring licensing fees.

Despite the notion of many that Edison was a "genius" he consistently attributed his success to "hard work," as evidenced in his famous line, "Genius is 1 percent inspiration and 99 percent perspiration."

Susan B. Anthony

Newsmaker

Long after the end of the Civil War and the end of slavery, America still treated women as second-class citizens. While there were many key figures in the women's rights movement of the late 19th century, few had the impact of Susan B. Anthony.

Anthony's advocacy for multiple social, political and economic causes spanned the entire second half of the 19th century. As early as 1868, Anthony's newspaper, *The Revolution*, had published an editorial demanding an eight-hour work day and equal pay for equal work.

Anthony was the co-founder (along with Elizabeth Stanton) of the American Equal Rights Association, an organization devoted to equal voting rights and equal economic rights.

In 1892, at the age of 72, Anthony became president of the National American Woman Suffrage Association. Despite her advanced age, she traveled the country and spent much of the decade campaigning in the West to ensure that the territories where women had the right to vote were not blocked from inclusion in the Union.

Anthony would not live to see the fruits of her labor. When the 19th Amendment, granting women the vote, was finally ratified in 1920, it was called the Susan B. Anthony Amendment.

John Philip Sousa

Entertainment, Arts and Letters

The music of John Philip Sousa is as much a part of the American landscape as a game of baseball or a wedge of apple pie. Sousa's upbeat music was a reflection of the exuberance of a young nation just beginning to feel its oats.

Sousa "The March King," composed all kinds of music, from operas to ragtime, but his legacy is his 135 marches. His father was a trombonist in the US Marine Band and he enlisted his son in the Marines at the tender age of 13. By 1880, Sousa was elevated to be the conductor of the Marine Band, called "The President's Own."

Over the following years, Sousa faithfully served under a series of presidents including Rutherford B. Hayes, James Garfield, Grover Cleveland and William Henry Harrison.

It was in 1892, though, that Sousa left the Marine Band and went out on his own, forming his first civilian band. The band toured all over the world, but Sousa still had time to compose many of his most memorable works including *The Liberty Bell, The Manhattan Beach March*, and *King Cotton.*

On Christmas day, 1896, Sousa would compose his most enduring work- *Stars and Stripes Forever.* One hundred years later, President Ronald Reagan honored Sousa in declaring *Stars and Stripes Forever* as the official march of the United States of America.

1890 — Alice Sanger becomes first female White House staffer

1891 — James Naismith invents Basketball

1892 — Francis Bellamy writes "Pledge of Allegiance"

1893 — Coca-Cola trademarked

1894 — Hershey Bar introduced

Andrew Carnegie & John D. Rockefeller

Business and Industry

America's emergence as a political and military power on the world stage was a direct result of the country's development into a major economic force. More than any other individuals at the turn of the century, Andrew Carnegie (top) and John D. Rockefeller (bottom) helped to transform America into a world power.

Both men rose from humble beginnings, amassed unfathomable fortunes and then disbursed much of their gains through prolific philanthropic undertakings.

Carnegie, who came to America at the age of 13, began his working life earning $1.20 a week as a mill worker. As he worked his way out of poverty, Carnegie invested virtually every penny he earned. By the time he was 21, his investments were paying him more than three times his salary. Investing in everything from railway cars to oil, Carnegie became wealthy by the age of 40.

He would not begin to amass his huge fortune, though, until he went into the steel business in 1875. The business grew quickly and Carnegie would soon merge several steel companies under the umbrella of Carnegie Steel. When Carnegie sold his interests to J.P. Morgan for $480 million, he instantly became the richest man in the world. Much of the rest of his life would be devoted to contributions to education and world peace.

Like Carnegie, Rockefeller built his fortune from the bottom up, starting his career as a bookkeeping clerk. Only four years later, however, Rockefeller was able to form his own business, the earliest predecessor to what would eventually become the Standard Oil conglomerate. By 1863 he realized that the future was in oil, and by 1868, his company, then called Rockefeller, Andrews & Flagler, was the largest refiner in the world. Two years later The Standard Oil Company was formed, and Rockefeller remained at its helm through its various reorganizations until it was dissolved in 1911.

Although Rockefeller retained his title of president at Standard Oil until 1911, he was largely retired from active business by 1897, and began devoting his time, and a fortune estimated to have peaked at $900 million, to philanthropic activities.

Cy Young

Sports

There is a reason why, to this day, the best pitchers in baseball are rewarded with the Cy Young award.

Denton True "Cy" Young was the single most dominant pitcher in baseball at the turn of the century. Pitching for teams like the Cleveland Spiders and St. Louis Perfectos (the predecessors to the Cardinals), Young put up numbers that are unimaginable by today's standards.

In the 1890s, he topped the 20-win mark nine years in a row and turned in three seasons with over 30 wins. Between 1891 and 1896, Young averaged 31 victories a year. His career total of 511 wins may be the single most untouchable record in baseball, rivaled only by his 749 complete games.

In the 1890s, Young averaged nearly 400 innings per year, topping out at an unfathomable 453 innings in 1892. Today, a pitcher who throws 200 innings in a season is considered to be a workhorse.

For his efforts, by the year 1899, Young was earning the National League maximum wage of $2400. Towards the end of his life, in the early 1950s, Young couldn't believe how much salaries had gone up.

"Gosh, all a kid has to do these days is spit straight and he gets forty-thousand dollars to sign," he said wistfully.

1895 — Stephen Crane writes "The Red Badge of Courage"

1896

1897 — Thomas Edison patents movie projector

1898 — Teddy Roosevelt and the Rough Riders take San Juan Hill

1899 — First Edition of *Who's Who in America* Published

The 1900s

The Wright Brothers

Science and Technology

The historic first flight of the legendary Wright Brothers, the flight that guided the world into the aviation age, was little more than a hop-skip-and-jump. With Orville at the controls, the famed flight lasted a mere 12 seconds, covering an uninspiring distance of 120 feet.

Despite the brevity of the flight, one fact was unmistakable. Theirs was the first controlled and sustained flight in a power-driven, heavier-than-air machine. It was a flight that would be an early step in our path to the cosmos.

The flight took place on Thursday, December 17, 1903 in the small town of Kitty Hawk, North Carolina. They attempted three more flights that day, with the final flight–with Wilbur at the helm–carrying 852 feet and lasting a full 59 seconds.

The Wright Brothers were bicycle makers by trade. Though neither Wilbur nor Orville had a high school diploma, they approached their obsession with scientific precision, creating their own laboratory, wind-tunnel and workshop to create what was to become the first successful airplane.

Their achievements are best summed up in the words below, taken from the plaque in their honor at the Smithsonian Institution...

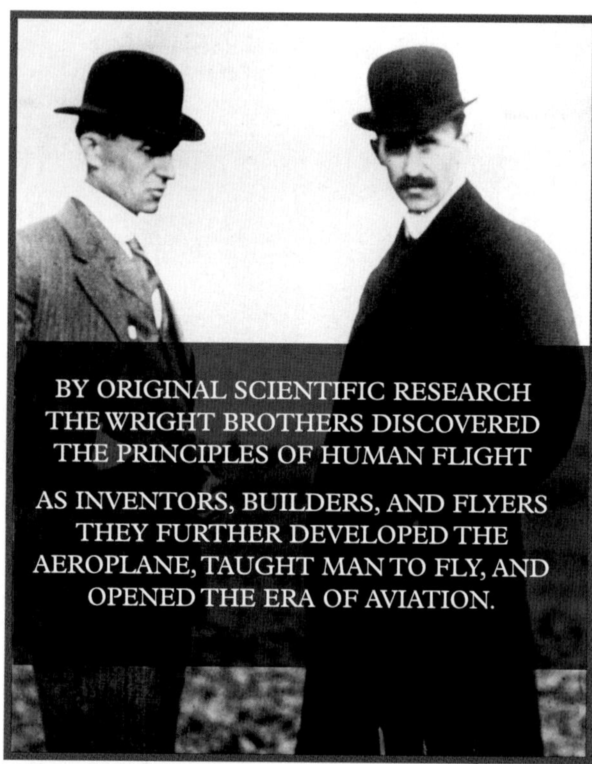

BY ORIGINAL SCIENTIFIC RESEARCH
THE WRIGHT BROTHERS DISCOVERED
THE PRINCIPLES OF HUMAN FLIGHT
AS INVENTORS, BUILDERS, AND FLYERS
THEY FURTHER DEVELOPED THE
AEROPLANE, TAUGHT MAN TO FLY, AND
OPENED THE ERA OF AVIATION.

Teddy Roosevelt

Newsmaker

The path from war hero to president is a well-worn one in American history. From George Washington to John F. Kennedy, there is a long and proud history of great military figures becoming great political leaders.

Such was the case with Teddy Roosevelt, whose heroics in the Spanish American War propelled him into one of t country's most memorable and successful presidencies.

A lieutenant colonel in the legendary Rough Riders, Roosevelt led t charge at the battle of San Juan. Upon his return to civilian life, Roosev ran for governor of New York on an anti-corruption platform. He won th election in 1898 and just two years later was elected as vice-president unc William McKinley. Still a relative political neophyte, Roosevelt ascended the presidency when McKinley was assassinated in 1901.

Upon taking office, Roosevelt immediately embarked upon a course major initiatives. On the economic front, Roosevelt took on big business a became known as the "trust-buster." In race relations, he took the unprec dented step of inviting Booker T. Washington to the White House to discu both scientific issues and race relations. Internationally, Roosevelt comm sioned the building of the Panama Canal and won the Nobel Peace Prize f his efforts in ending the Russo-Japanese conflict.

Roosevelt, like Thomas Jefferson before him, was a true renaissance ma Among other talents, he was an accomplished writer, hunter, orat zoologist and conservationist.

It took an assassination attempt, leaving him with a bullet wound to th chest, to slow him down. Though he survived the wound, Roosevelt wou see out the rest of his days in relative quiet.

George M. Cohan

Entertainment, Arts and Letters

What can you say about a man brought America such incredible hits *You're A Grand Old Flag, Yankee Doodle* *Give My Regards to Broadway* and (*There*? How about, thank you.

Indeed, America owes a huge thank you the contributions of George M. Cohan, greatest writer, producer, composer, a and dancer Broadway has ever known the musical theater is one of Ameri greatest gifts to world culture, then Co is the greatest gift to musical theater.

1900 — "Wonderful Wizard of Oz" published

1901 — J.P. Morgan buys Carnegie Steel

1902 — Helen Keller writes "The Story of my Life"

1903 — Wright Brothers first flight

1904 — U.S. hosts its fir Olympics in St. Lo

Henry Ford

Business and Industry

Henry Ford didn't invent the automobile; he simply figured out a way to mass produce them. Utilizing advanced assembly line efficiencies and streamlining the entire production process, Ford was able to make a huge volume of quality, affordable automobiles.

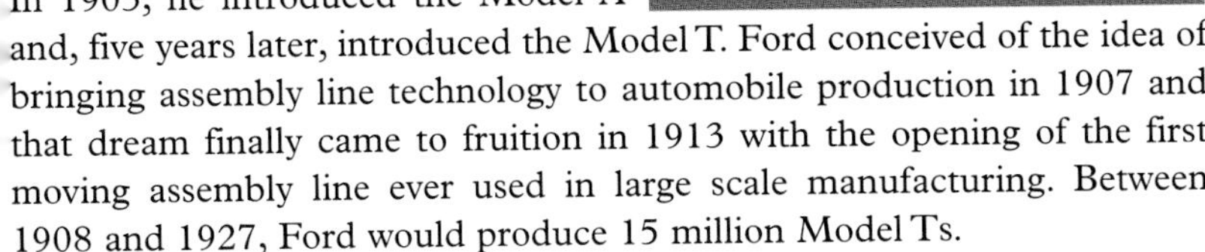

Ford's automotive career began while he was still in the employ of Thomas Edison. Ford joined the Edison Illuminating Company in Detroit in 1891, working his way up to the position of Chief Engineer. When Ford told Edison of his vision of building affordable automobiles, Edison gave him enormous encouragement.

While still in Edison's employ, Ford built his first automobile, the Quadricycle. Three years later, Ford quit working for Edison to devote himself full time to the manufacturing of automobiles.

In 1903, he introduced the Model A and, five years later, introduced the Model T. Ford conceived of the idea of bringing assembly line technology to automobile production in 1907 and that dream finally came to fruition in 1913 with the opening of the first moving assembly line ever used in large scale manufacturing. Between 1908 and 1927, Ford would produce 15 million Model Ts.

"There is one rule for the industrialist and that is: Make the best quality of goods possible at the lowest cost possible, paying the highest wages possible," he said.

Cohan never knew a life outside the theater. Virtually from the day he was born, Cohan sang, danced and acted with his family in the Vaudeville act "The Four Cohans." By his teens, Cohan was the driving force behind the act, handling the bulk of the writing, comedy and dancing responsibilities.

Cohan began writing songs at the age of 13 and had written his first musical at the age of 23. By the time he was done, Cohan had written more than 40 plays, written over 500 songs and had made over 1,000 stage appearances.

Cohan's defining musical, *Little Johnny Jones*, premiered in 1904 and featured *Yankee Doodle Boy* and *Give My Regards to Broadway*. His music reflected the unprecedented level of optimism in America. There were fortunes to be made, seemingly by anyone with a dream and willingness to work, and Cohan's music captured that feeling perfectly.

Cohan's life was immortalized forever in the movie *Yankee Doodle Dandy*, where the role of Cohan was played brilliantly by James Cagney. Cohan saw the film just weeks before his death in 1942.

Honus Wagner

Sports

Honus Wagner, the man they called "The Flying Dutchman," may have played a century ago, but remains at the heart of any contemporary discussion of the greatest baseball player ever.

Based on Wagner's statistics alone, it's hard to argue against him.

Between 1900 and 1909, while playing for the Pittsburgh Pirates, Wagner led the National League in hitting seven times and stolen bases five times. By the time his career ended, Wagner was the all-time National League leader in hits, runs, RBI, doubles, triples, stolen bases and games. He batted over .300 for 17 years in a row, a remarkable testament to his consistency.

Not only is he universally recognized as the best shortstop of his era, he was equally dominant at every other position he played— and he played every position except for catcher.

Legendary manager John McGraw, who saw everyone from Ty Cobb to Babe Ruth play, called Wagner the best baseball player ever. Even Sam Crawford, himself a Hall of Famer and a teammate of the legendary Ty Cobb for 12 seasons, called Wagner the best ever.

Wagner's 1909 American Tobacco Company trading card sold in 2000 on eBay for the record price of $1.265 million.

The Times

HEART IS TORN FROM GREAT CITY.

San Francisco Nearly Destroyed By Earthquakes and Fire—Hundreds of Killed and Injured—Destruction of Other Coast Cities—California's Greatest Horror.

1905 — B&O railroad introduces electric locomotives

1906

1907 — First Ziegfeld Follies opens

1908 — Henry Ford builds Model T

1909 — Peary reaches North Pole

The 1910s

George Washington Carver

Science and Technology

It is almost impossible to measure the full extent of George Washington Carver's contributions. With the creation of more than 500 new agricultural products, Carver almost single-handedly saved the economy of the rural American south.

The son of slaves, Carver made strides thought impossible for black men of his generation. Carver was forced to move away from his family just to find a high school that would accept black students. Having completed high school at the top of his class, Carver became the first African American to enroll at what is now Iowa State University.

At the invitation of Booker T. Washington, Carver joined the faculty of Tuskegee Institute. It was there that Carver did most of his breakthrough agricultural research. Carver created well over 300 products from peanuts and another 100 from sweet potatoes. He developed new hybrids of cotton.

Carver's research revolutionized agriculture in the southern states, by introducing the science of crop rotation. By alternating such nutrient-depleting crops as cotton with soy and peanuts (crops that replenished the soil), farms could not only remain active and productive, but it helped to diversify and enrich the economy of the south.

Carver refused to reap what would have been substantial financial rewards from his patents, giving away his discoveries for free. Carver's contributions and life are best summed up by the words that grace his gravestone...

"He could have added fortune to fame, but caring for neither, he found happiness and honor in being helpful to the world."

Woodrow Wilson

Newsmaker

Long before he became one of the most influential presidents in American history, Woodrow Wilson made his mark as a scholar.

Wilson had impressive academic credentials: an undergraduate degree from Princeton, a law degree from the University of Virginia and a Ph.D. from Johns Hopkins. He returned to Princeton where he quickly ascended to the school's presidency.

Wilson's political career advanced just as quickly. In 1910, he successfully ran for governor of New Jersey and just two years later he was nominated as the Democratic Party candidate fo president. With Republican William Howard Taft and Progressive Party candidate Theodore Roosevelt splitting the vote, Wilson easily defeated both men.

Wilson helped to create the Federal Trade Commission and was behind the passage of the Federal Reserve Act. Wilson was also the driving force behind key child labor laws and laws limiting the hours demanded o railroad workers.

Wilson was re-elected in 1916 on a platform of keeping America out o the European conflict, but it was a promise he could not keep. In Apri of 1917, the United States declared war on Germany and it was the contributions of American troops that turned the tide of World War I. The biggest regret of Wilson's political career was his failure to get the Congress to ratify the Versailles Treaty, which would have assured America's presence in the League of Nations.

Wilson won the Nobel Peace Prize for his efforts in bringing the world together after the war.

Edith Wharton

Entertainment, Arts and Letters

In a time when women were supposed to be seen and not heard, Edith Wharton emerged as one of the defining literary voices of her age.

Born to wealth and privilege, Wharton had a front row seat to the life of the burgeoning upper class in early 20th century America. She possessed an almost unique ability to look upon her contemporaries with the distanced and jaundiced eye of a social anthropologist.

In her books and articles, Wharton chronicled the clashes between the "old money" and the "nouveau riche" and had a keen eye for the social and sexual politics of the day.

One of her most famous and enduring works was *The House of Mirth*, a book that eviscerated the world of the newly rich and ostentatious.

NAACP founded

Break-up of Standard Oil

The New York Times.

TITANIC SINKS FOUR HOURS AFTER HITTING ICEBERG; 866 RESCUED BY CARPATHIA, PROBABLY 1250 PERISH; ISMAY SAFE, MRS. ASTOR MAYBE, NOTED NAMES MISSING

Titanic sinks

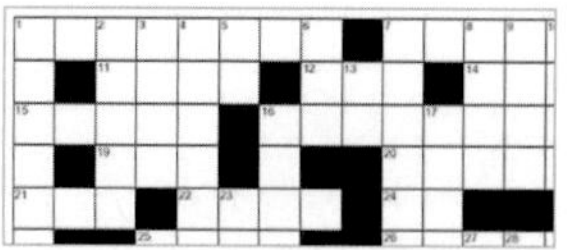

First crossword puzzle introduced in New York World

Panama Canal ope

1910 1911 1912 1913 1914

Louis B. Mayer

Business and Industry

Louis B. Mayer was a movie mogul before the term even existed.

In 1907, when Mayer was just 22, he purchased a dilapidated movie theater in the town of Haverhill, Massachusetts. Mayer refurbished the theater and turned it into a success. Within a few years, Mayer owned the largest theater chain in New England.

Mayer's experience as a theater owner taught him that the real money in the movie theater business was in distribution, so he formed his first distribution company—the Louis B. Mayer Company. One of the first deals by the company (in 1915) was the New England rights to distribute D.W. Griffith's *Birth of a Nation*, which turned out to be the biggest movie of its time.

The rest, as they say in Hollywood, is history.

The $450,000 earned by Mayer off of *Birth of a Nation* gave him the bankroll he needed to expand his interests into movie production. In 1917, and still barely into his 30s, Mayer moved out west to the creative heart of the movie business. That year he would form the company that would soon evolve into Metro Goldwyn Mayer Studios (MGM).

In a career that would span five decades, Mayer would be the business mind behind such enormous blockbusters as *Ben Hur, Wizard of Oz, Gone With the Wind, Mutiny on the Bounty* and even the Marx Brothers' *Night at the Opera.*

Her characters were thinly veiled versions of many of America's wealthiest individuals.

The decade covering 1910 to 1920 was a particularly fruitful one for Wharton. In short succession, she wrote *Ethan Frome* (1911), *The Reef* (1912), and *The Custom of the Country* (1913). Later in the decade, she wrote dispatches during World War I for various newspapers. At the end of the decade, she wrote her most acclaimed work, *The Age of Innocence*, which was published in 1920, and became the first woman to win the Pulitzer Prize in fiction.

Jim Thorpe

Sports

Jim Thorpe wasn't simply the greatest athlete between 1910 and 1920. He may well have been the greatest athlete ever.

Both of Thorpe's parents were part Native American, with his father having Sac and Fox heritage and his mother, Potowatomi and Kickapoo blood. Thorpe went to school at the Carlisle (Pa.) Indian Industrial School. While there, he led the school's football team to the National Collegiate Championship, defeating such traditional powerhouses as Harvard and Army along the way. That feat would be the modern equivalent of an MIT beating the likes of Nebraska and Oklahoma.

As a track star, Thorpe won gold medals in both the pentathlon and decathlon (the two most demanding and multi-disciplined events) at the 1912 Olympic games. Thorpe would end up having a Hall of Fame career in professional football and was named the National Football League's first president.

If those achievements weren't enough, Thorpe also played major league baseball for six seasons, playing for the Giants, Reds and Braves between 1913 and 1919.

"He was the greatest athlete of his time, maybe the greatest of any time in any land and he needed no gilded geegaws to prove it," wrote Red Smith, one of the greatest sportswriters in history. "The proof is in the records and the memories of the men who knew him and watched him and played with him."

1915 — Film, "Birth of a Nation," opens

1916 — Lincoln Logs introduced

1917 — First Pulitzer Prizes awarded

1918 — Armistice Day: World War I ends

1919 — Prohibition signed into law

The 1920s

Philo Farnsworth

Science and Technology

If you are asking yourself, "Who is Philo Farnsworth and what is his name doing among these luminaries?" don't feel too badly. Of all of the great inventors of the 20th century, Farnsworth is among the most obscure. Yet his invention, the television, is among the most ubiquitous.

Farnsworth was a most unlikely genius. The son of Iowa farmers, Farnsworth had to travel by horse to get to high school. At the age of 14, though, Farnsworth not only came up with the idea for television, he had worked out most of the technical details.

In 1928, while still just 22, Farnsworth would receive his first patent for his television. It would be many years before he would be able to fully enjoy the fruits of his invention. He became embroiled in a lengthy legal dispute with RCA, which claimed that their employee, Vladimir Zworykin, had invented television first. It wasn't until 1934, after years of litigation, that the US Patent Office sided with Farnsworth.

Ironically, as television became an almost universal appliance, Farnsworth objected to his own children watching.

"There's nothing on it worthwhile, and we're not going to watch it in this household," he told them. "And I don't want it in your intellectual diet."

Farnsworth's genius wasn't limited to television. He earned over 300 patents in his life, including the first simple electron microscope and the first cold cathode-ray tube.

Charles Lindbergh

Newsmaker

The 1920s was the decade of the celebrity. America was in love with the like of Charlie Chaplin, George Gershwin, Al Jolson, Rudolph Valentino… to nam but a few. But no one captured the imagination of the country quite lik Charles Lindbergh.

Lindbergh's historic non-stop crossing of the Atlantic aboard the Spirit of St. Louis instantaneously transformed him into a national hero. The flight, which began at 7:52 AM on May 20, 1927 at Long Island's Roosevelt Field, ended 33 1/2 hours and 3,610 miles later at LeBourget Field, in Paris. The crowd of 40,000 Parisians that greeted Lindbergh's arrival was dwarfed by the crowd that honored him in New York City at the ticker-tape parade down 5th Avenue in his honor.

Lindbergh would spend the following years writing about the flight and traveling across America speaking to enormous crowds about the glorious future of flight.

Lindbergh's later years were marked by controversy and tragedy. In 1932, Lindbergh's infant son was kidnapped and murdered. The alleged kidnapper, Bruno Hauptman, was convicted and executed for the crime.

Lindbergh's popularity took a severe hit in the years leading up to World War II. He was vocal in his opposition to America's entry into World War II and was seen by many to be both a Nazi sympathizer and an anti-Semite.

F. Scott Fitzgerald

Entertainment, Arts and Letters

If ever an author became the embodiment of an era, it was F. Scott Fitzgerald, who both lived and chronicled American life in the Roaring 20s.

Fitzgerald's three major works of the 1920s captured the essence of the American scene and spirit in a way no other author of the time could. *The Great Gatsby* is far more than a great book from the 1920s… it is widely recognized as one of the finest American novels of any era.

In his personal life, Fitzgerald lived as fast and hard as the tragic heroes of his books. He drank and par-

1920 — 19th Amendment gives women the right to vote

1921 — William H. Taft named Chief Justice of the United States

1922 — First Issue of "Reader's Digest" published

1923 — Time Magazine debuts

1924 — George Gershwin composes "Rhapsody in Blue"

David Sarnoff

Business and Industry

In many ways, Sarnoff is the father both of radio and television. Though not an inventor or a technologist himself, Sarnoff had the gift of seeing profitable ways to capitalize on new technologies.

As an employee of American Marconi, Sarnoff was exposed to the technology of radio. At the time, radio technology was used almost exclusively in the shipping industry. In a memo written to his supervisor in 1915, Sarnoff outlined his plan to turn radio into an entertainment medium, making "radio a household utility in the same sense as the piano or phonograph."

While the memo was ignored, Sarnoff did not abandon his idea. In what would become a defining moment in the history of radio, Sarnoff got the rights to broadcast the 1921 fight between Jack Dempsey and Georges Carpentier. As thousands gathered around the few existing radios to listen, a new medium had been launched. Going under the trade name Radiola, sales in 1924 skyrocketed to over $80 million.

Sarnoff's next step of genius was to bring single broadcasts to a national audience through networking radio stations across the country. To do so, he created a subsidiary called the National Broadcasting Company, a company known to this day simply as NBC.

Sarnoff's vision did not stop with the radio. After seeing a prototype for a television in 1923, he would set up a special subsidiary of NBC to experiment with this even more fascinating medium. By 1941, NBC had begun the first commercial broadcasts in this medium.

Babe Ruth

Sports

Babe Ruth was a superstar long before the term was coined. Ruth wasn't merely the best player in baseball during his era... there was nobody else even in the ballpark. Bigger than life, Ruth turned the New York Yankees into the most dominant team the game has ever known.

Ruth began his career as a dominating pitcher, but his hitting prowess resulted in his conversion to a full-time outfielder. After Ruth shattered the home-run record in 1919 (with 29), he was traded to the Yankees for the price of $100,000 together with a $350,000 loan. The loan would finance the enormously successful play, *No No Nannette*, but the success of the show proved to be a small return on the enormous price of trading Ruth away.

The Red Sox, which had won the World Series in 1918 with Ruth on the mound, would not win another world series until 2004. With Ruth in their lineup, the Yankees would become the most dominant team in the history of the game.

In his first season as a Yankee, Ruth hit 54 home runs, shattering his own record in the process. As the 1920s would progress, Ruth would break that record twice, hitting 59 homers in 1921 and 60 in 1927. That record would stand until 1961. By the end of the decade, Ruth had amassed 516 home runs (339 more than anyone in history.) Ruth would retire after the 1935 season with 714 home runs, a mark that wouldn't be broken for 39 years.

Off the field, Ruth was bigger than life. He loved New York City and he was a regular at bars and clubs and was a notorious womanizer. When he was earning $80,000 back in 1930, a reporter noted that the president, Herbert Hoover, only made $75,000.

"Heck," Ruth was reported to have replied. "I had a better year than he did."

tied with the newly wealthy on Long Island and battled fiercely with his equally volatile wife, Zelda.

Fame and success came early for Fitzgerald. *This Side of Paradise* was published when he was only 24. Two years later, he wrote *The Beautiful and the Damned*. He was not yet 30 when he wrote *The Great Gatsby* and it would be another decade before his final novel, *Tender is the Night*, would arrive.

For most of his life, Fitzgerald's fame had more to do with his personal excesses than his literary successes. His tumultuous marriage to Zelda was fodder for the newspapers. The two were known for their lavish lifestyle, wild parties, alcoholism and subsequent breakdowns.

He was in the middle of writing *The Last Tycoon* when he died—at the age of 44—of a massive heart attack.

Scopes Monkey Trial challenges teaching of evolution

1925

Gertrude Ederle swims the English Channel

1926

The New York Times.

LINDBERGH DOES IT! TO PARIS IN 33½ HOURS; FLIES 1,000 MILES THROUGH SNOW AND SLEET; CHEERING FRENCH CARRY HIM OFF FIELD

1927

Mickey Mouse debuts

1928

Stock Market crash ends the great bull market of the 1920's

1929

The 1930s

Robert Goddard

Science and Technology

Like many other visionaries, Robert Goddard was vilified, denounced and dismissed for his revolutionary theories.

Before Goddard, the prevailing wisdom was that it was impossible to establish propulsion outside of the Earth's atmosphere, thus precluding any kind of outer space travel. Goddard theorized that liquid fuels were the key to space flight and he spent a lifetime proving his theory.

He had his first successful launch of a rocket in 1926, sending the 11-foot missile 41 feet in the air at a speed of 60 miles per hour.

It wasn't until 1930, though, when Goddard received a $100,000 grant to continue his research that he was able to make substantial breakthroughs. Over the course of the decade, Goddard's rockets reached heights of 9,000 feet and speeds that exceeded the speed of sound. Ironically, it was Goddard's design that was first utilized by German scientists who turned Goddard's work into the V-2 rockets that were used to devastating effect in London.

Goddard would die from throat cancer in 1945, but it was his design that was used to create the Redstone missile, which was the rocket used to send the first American astronauts into space.

Franklin Delano Roosevelt

Newsmaker

America entered the 1930s mired in a miserable economic depression and reeling from the inept presidency of Herbert Hoover. At a time when the country was desperate for new and effective leadership, Franklin D. Roosevelt came forward and turned the country's fortunes around.

Roosevelt, whose promising political career was nearly ended by a serious case of polio, won the first of his four presidential elections in a landslide, beating Hoover by seven million votes. When he took office, there were 13 million unemployed and only a handful of banks still open. In his inaugural speech, Roosevelt said the immortal words "the only thing we have to fear is fear itself."

With such key "New Deal" programs as the Public Works Administration, the Tennessee Valley Administration, and the National Recovery Act, Roosevelt helped to reduce the rampant unemployment and begin to ease the country's economic woes.

Roosevelt tried his hardest to remain neutral as war raged in Europe, but as England and France came under siege, the United States provided substantial economic and munitions support to the Allied cause. With the bombing of Pearl Harbor followed closely by the declaration of war against America by Germany and Italy, Roosevelt mobilized the American war effort.

Roosevelt would live to see the United States turn the tide of the war, but would die shortly before the conflicts would come to an end.

To this day, Roosevelt remains one of the most beloved presidents in history.

John Steinbeck

Entertainment, Arts and Letters

No discussion of great American writers is complete without a serious look at the life and works of John Steinbeck. Steinbeck, more than any other writer, became the voice of the depression years, giving a name and a face to the countless ordinary men and women who summoned extraordinary will just to survive.

Steinbeck's genius was his ability to show the heroic character in the most "common" of men. His heroes were migrant workers, laborers, ordinary men and women who faced almost unimaginable adversity and yet managed to keep hope alive and continue to dream.

Artist Grant Wood paints "American Gothic"

1930

Star-Spangled Banner becomes National Anthem

1931

Amelia Earhart becomes first woman to fly solo across the Atlantic

1932

End of Prohibition

1933

Securities and Exchange Commission formed

1934

Walt Disney

Business and Industry

From the first crude drawings he sold as a seven-year-old to the magical worlds he created in California and Florida, Walt Disney spent a lifetime devoted to the entertainment and enchantment of the masses.

Disney, who began his professional career as a commercial artist, discovered the art of animation and was hooked. At the age of 21, with his first crude films in hand, Disney moved to Hollywood, where he set up shop with his brother, Roy.

After a few modest successes, Disney created his most enduring character, Mickey Mouse, in 1928. With the advent of sound technology in movies, Disney was the first to use sound with animation and created the famous short "Steamboat Willie," which introduced the world to Mickey Mouse.

It was in the 1930s, though, that Disney would show the full extent of his talents and vision. He introduced Technicolor into animated films in 1932 and earned his first Oscar that same year.

In 1937, Disney would take on his most ambitious project, a full-length animated film. Disney invested $1.5 million (in the heart of the depression) in *Snow White and the Seven Dwarfs*. The film was such a resounding success that it bankrolled such subsequent classics as *Bambi, Pinocchio, Fantasia* and *Dumbo*.

Having revolutionized the film industry, Disney's vision and drive led him to create first Disneyland and then Disneyworld. He also embraced the medium of television. His *Wonderful World of Color, The Mickey Mouse Club* and *Zorro* were some of the most successful shows in the early years of television.

Disney never thought of himself as a "genius" or as the producer of significant art. His goal was simply to entertain.

"Somehow I can't believe there are any heights that can't be scaled by a man who knows the secret of making dreams come true," he said.

Steinbeck's first three novels garnered little in the way of attention. It was only after he moved to California that he began producing his best work. In 1935 he wrote *Tortilla Flat* and followed that effort up with *In Dubious Battle* in 1936, *Of Mice and Men* in 1937, *The Long Valley* in 1938 and his masterpiece, *Grapes of Wrath* in 1939. Steinbeck would not be nearly as prolific in later years, but still produced such classics as *The Pearl, Cannery Row* and *East of Eden*.

It wasn't until 1962, long after his finest works were written, that Steinbeck was honored with the Nobel Prize in Literature. Steinbeck's legacy was captured wonderfully in his New York Times obituary, where Charles Poore wrote:

"His place in [U. S.] literature is secure. And it lives on in the works of innumerable writers who learned from him how to present the forgotten man unforgettably."

Jesse Owens

Sports

The 1936 Berlin Olympic Games were–in the mind of Adolph Hitler–going to be a showcase not just for the dominance of Germany, but for the superiority of the Aryan race.

It was Jesse Owens, a black track star from America, who almost single-handedly made a mockery of Hitler's vision. Owens dominated the 1936 Olympic games, capturing the 100-meter dash, the 200-meter dash, the broad jump, and anchoring the gold-medal-winning 400-meter relay team.

A year earlier, Owens may have enjoyed the greatest single day ever turned in by a track athlete. Competing for Ohio State University (which wouldn't allow him to live on campus because he was black) in the Big Ten Championships, Owens set three world records and tied a fourth, all within a 70-minute span.

While Owens was able to help dispel the myth of Aryan superiority, he was not able to break down racial barriers at home. Upon his return from Berlin, Owens could not get a job, was not given any endorsements and was generally treated as a second-class citizen.

"After I came home from the 1936 Olympics with my four medals, it became increasingly apparent that everyone was going to slap me on the back, want to shake my hand or have me up to their suite," Owens said. "But no one was going to offer me a job."

The New York Times

HINDENBURG BURNS IN LAKEHURST CRASH; 21 KNOWN DEAD, 12 MISSING; 64 ESCAPE

Social Security Act passed

1935

Hoover Dam completed

1936

1937

Action Comics introduces Superman

1938

"Gone with the Wind" premieres

1939

The 1940s

J. Robert Oppenheimer

and the makers of the atom bomb

Science and Technology

Led by J. Robert Oppenheimer, the members of the infamous "Manhattan Project" forever changed the face of warfare with the development and deployment of the first atomic bombs.

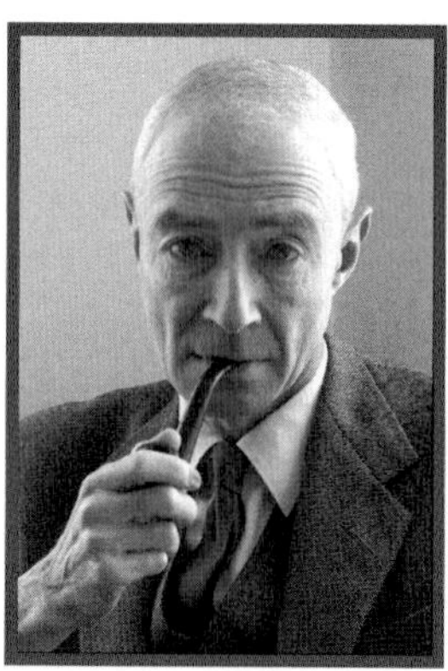

As World War II progressed, rumors were circulating that Germany was close to completion on a devastating weapon that would utilize the destructive powers of nuclear fission. Such a bomb, it was believed, could decide the fate of the war and the future of the world.

It was at this point that the government gave the green light to develop such a bomb before the Germans could. Oppenheimer, appointed the head of the project by General Leslie Groves, brought together many of the finest physicists working in America at the time, a group that included Edward Teller, Leó Szilárd, Enrico Fermi, Richard Feynman and Hans Bethe. Each man contributed a piece of the puzzle that would eventually produce the first successful atomic bombs.

After the first successful test of the bomb on July 16, 1945, President Harry Truman wasted no time in putting the weapon to use. Just three weeks later, on August 6, 1945, the uranium bomb was dropped on Hiroshima. Three days later, a plutonium bomb was dropped on Nagasaki. While hundreds of thousands of civilians were killed by the blast and the radiation that lingered, the bomb was credited with the quick end to the war in the Pacific.

"We knew the world could not be the same," Oppenheimer said. "I remember the line from the Hindu scripture, the Bhagavad Gita: 'I am became Death, the destroyers of worlds.' I suppose we all thought that, one way or another."

George Marshall

Newsmaker

George Marshall, more than any other individual of the time, deserves credit for both his execution of the allied strategy in World War II and for his remarkable post-war plan that helped bring stability and ultimately prosperity to the ravaged European continent.

Marshall not only directed the Allied operations in Europe and the Pacific; he is credited with creating the strategy behind the Normandy Invasion. No less than Winston Churchill called Marshall "the true organizer of victory."

In 1947, in his capacity as Secretary of State, Marshall outlined his plan for the post-war recovery in Europe. Known forever as "The Marshall Plan," it called for a massive infusion of support (ultimately over $13 billion) to promote economic and technological growth in Western Europe.

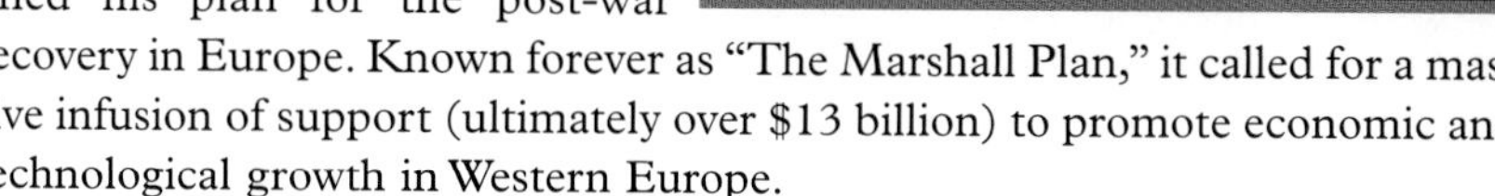

For his efforts, Marshall earned the 1953 Nobel Prize. He was also named Time Magazine's Man of the Year twice in the 1940s, first for his war efforts and then for his peacetime efforts.

Despite his personal efforts at achieving peace, Marshall was wisely skeptical about man's ability to maintain the peace.

"If man does find the solution for world peace it will be the most revolutionary reversal of his record we have ever known," he said.

Humphrey Bogart

Entertainment, Arts and Letters

There was no shortage of star power during the 1940s. From Ernest Hemingway to William Faulkner, from Jimmy Stewart to Katharine Hepburn, from Frank Sinatra to Judy Garland, the 1940s were a golden age in all of the arts.

Somehow, Humphrey Bogart was able to stand out from this stellar group. While his career spanned many decades, the 1940s saw many of Bogart's definitive works. In a remarkably prolific decade, Bogart starred in *Maltese Falcon, Casablanca,*

EXTRA!

Los Angeles Times

INVASION

1940 — Igor Sikorsky's helicopter makes its first free flight

1941 — Joe DiMaggio hits successfully in 56 straight games

1942 — Artist Edward Hopper paints "Nighthawks"

1943 — "Oklahoma!" opens on Broadway

1944

William Levitt

Business and Industry

William Levitt built much more than just homes. He built the foundation for an entire way of life. As the father of modern American suburbia, Levitt brought affordable home ownership to countless thousands in the years following World War II.

Levitt's genius was in taking the American dream of home ownership and making it a reality by creating small, cookie-cutter homes that were accessible to even the most modest of incomes. The first Levitt homes cost just under $7000 and homes could be secured with no down-payment and a refundable deposit of only $100.

Using assembly line methods borrowed from the great Henry Ford, Levitt created his first planned community, Levittown, in 1947. Homes were broken down into component parts, manufactured in separate locations, and then assembled on-site. With vast open acreage and the proximity to New York City, Long Island offered a great location for those who would work in Manhattan, but didn't want to raise their families in the city. Built on the site of a former potato farm, Levittown fit 17,000 homes neatly onto the property.

Among the first residents of Levittown were hundreds of GIs, who had just returned from service overseas. Levittown would prove to be the prototype for many other communities across American and the world. By the time he sold his company, in 1968, Levitt had built more than 140,000 homes.

To Have and Have Not, The Big Sleep, Key Largo, High Sierra and *The Treasure of the Sierra Madre.*

He played heroes and anti-heroes, good guys and bad guys. Though hardly a screen idol, he managed to produce remarkable screen chemistry with the likes of Lauren Bacall, Ingrid Bergman and Mary Astor.

By 1947, Bogart was the highest paid actor in the world and had started his own production company. As remarkable as his career was in the 1940s, the 1950s would see Bogart win his only Oscar in 1951 for *The African Queen,* and earn another nomination, three years later, for *The Caine Mutiny*. Bogart's only other nomination came for his classic role as Rick Blaine in *Casablanca*.

In 1999, the American Film Institute would name Bogart as the Greatest Male Star of All Time.

Jackie Robinson

Sports

Before Martin Luther King, before Malcolm X, and long, long before the likes of Jesse Jackson, Barbara Jordan and Colin Powell, there was Jackie Robinson.

It was Robinson, the man who broke Major League Baseball's color line, who opened the door for so many to follow. The integration of baseball helped put America on a path that would lead to the integration of the military, of schools, and of neighborhoods. Robinson is cited as a hero not just to the ballplayers who followed in his footsteps, but to African Americans who were given opportunities in all fields where barriers had existed before.

While there were a number of African American ballplayers with talent equal to or greater than his, Robinson was chosen to be the first to make the majors because of his education (UCLA), his military service and his demeanor. Branch Rickey, the Brooklyn Dodgers' executive who signed Robinson, knew that the success or failure of his experiment would fall squarely on Robinson's shoulders. If Robinson failed, in any way, the integration of baseball could have been set back by many years.

Robinson did not disappoint. Despite being faced with the worst kinds of racism, Robinson thrived from the very start. He won Rookie of the Year honors in 1947 and MVP honors two years later. He was one of the key players during the glory years of the Brooklyn Dodgers.

"A life is not important except in the impact it has on other lives," Robinson said.

That would make Robinson, without question, one of the most important Americans of the 20th century.

1945 — Victory in Europe Day

1946 — Dr. Spock's "Baby and Child Care" published

1947 — Chuck Yeager breaks sound barrier

1948 — Bic Ballpoint pen

1949 — William Faulkner wins Nobel Prize for literature

The 1950s

Jonas Salk

Science and Technology

It is hard to imagine, today, just how terrifying an illness polio was. It struck quickly and with devastating results, including death and paralysis. By the 1950s, there was an average of 40,000 cases a year. In 1952, that number peaked at 57,879 cases.

Jonas Salk, who had first worked in epidemiology battling the flu virus, turned his attention to polio in the late 1940s. Working out of the University of Pittsburgh Medical School, Salk worked eight years before developing the first polio vaccine. The result was an immediate and dramatic reduction in the number of polio cases in America.

Though he could have made a fortune from his discovery, Salk refused to patent the vaccine, so that it could be utilized worldwide at minimal cost.

Salk was not alone in the pursuit of a polio vaccine. Researchers across the country had made key discoveries along the way. It was Salk, though, who beat the others to the punch, using killed polio virus and delivering it via injection. Several years after the Salk Vaccine, Albert B. Sabin developed a "live" vaccine that could be taken orally. Between the two vaccines, polio has been virtually eliminated in Western nations and greatly reduced worldwide.

While Salk will forever be remembered for his polio vaccine, he spent his entire life in an effort to eradicate disease, spending the final years of his life attempting to develop an AIDS vaccine.

Rosa Parks

Newsmaker

Rosa Parks, whose name is forever linked with the civil rights movement, neve intended to be a hero, a leader or a symbol. She was simply a black woman wh had suffered one indignity too many. Years of living as a second-class citizer caught up with her on that historic day.

On December 1, 1955, after a long day at work, Parks took a seat in the fift row of a Montgomery bus. That was the first row where blacks were allowed t sit so long as no white person was standing. Three stops later, the bus was nearing capacity and there were no seats open in the front of the bus for whites.

The black riders in the middle of the bus were told to go to the back. All di except for Parks.

The enraged driver put the emergency brake on and demanded that she go to the back, but Parks quietly refused. The driver got off of the bus, returned with a policeman, and the rest, as they say, is history.

Parks received a fine of $14, a fine she appealed. It would take a huge effort and a year's time, but in the end, the Supreme Court ruled Montgomery's segregation laws to be unconstitutional.

While the case was pending, a boycott of the Montgomery busses was called for and led by Martin Luther King, Jr. Because black riders represented 75% of the ridership, this would cost the bus company enormous financial losses.

Many years after the incident, Parks was asked why she had done it.

"Have you ever been hurt and the place tries to heal a bit, and you just pull the scar off of it over and over again?" she explained.

Marilyn Monroe

Entertainment, Arts and Letters

Though it has been over 40 years since the tragic death of Marilyn Monroe, she remains—to this day—a cultural icon. While remembered by many for her beauty and sexuality, Monroe was a truly remarkable actress, one who could handle the toughest dramatic roles and the broadest comedic roles with equal aplomb.

While her acting career began in the 1940s, Monroe became an enormous star in the 1950s, appearing in 23 films during the decade. She had leading roles in some of the decade's biggest hits, including *All About Eve, the Asphalt Jungle, Gentlemen Prefer Blondes, Bus Stop, How to Marry a Millionaire* and *Some Like it Hot.*

1950 — Diner's Club becomes the first credit card

1951 — *I Love Lucy* debuts

1952 — Hemingway's "The Old Man and the Sea" published

1953 — Scrabble introduced to mass market

PART I Los Angeles Times

Order May Cut Off McCarthy Inquiry

NATIONALISTS SINK RED GUNBOAT OFF FORMOSA

Supreme Court Outlaws Segregation in Schools

REDS STAND FIRM AT PEACE SESSION

1954

Ruth Handler

Business and Industry

At a time when there were precious few women in business and even fewer entrepreneurs, Ruth Handler helped build the Mattel toy empire from scratch. Working with her husband (a furniture maker by trade) Handler took advantage of the baby boom to create a wide variety of toys for an ever growing market.

Mattel's early success came from the sales of plastic ukuleles, toy pianos and other instruments for children. An early Mattel music box sold over 20 million units.

Mattel grew enormously after Handler decided to invest heavily in advertising, becoming one of the first companies to truly exploit television as an advertising medium.

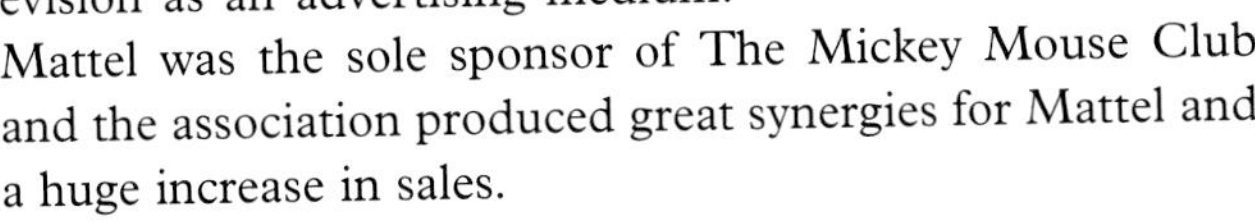

Mattel was the sole sponsor of The Mickey Mouse Club and the association produced great synergies for Mattel and a huge increase in sales.

Mattel's real breakthrough would come in 1959, with the introduction of the Barbie Doll. More than 350,000 Barbies were sold in the first year and over one billion (including Barbie's sidekicks, Ken, Skipper, etc.) have been sold to date. To put things into perspective, an average of two Barbie Dolls are sold every second of every day.

Among the innovations created by Handler was the idea of selling clothes and accessories for her dolls, which was a multi-million dollar industry in itself. So many Barbie outfits are made that Mattel is actually the fourth largest maker of women's clothes.

The Barbie Doll is such an American icon that it was buried in the official "America's Time Capsule" in 1976.

Mickey Mantle, Willie Mays & Duke Snider

Sports

In the 1950s, baseball was king and New York City was the center of the baseball universe. The New York Yankees, New York Giants and Brooklyn Dodgers dominated the baseball world in those years, combining for 15 World Series appearances and nine championships.

At the heart of each of these teams was a Hall-of-Fame centerfielder. For the Yankees, it was Mickey Mantle, while the Giants had Willie Mays and the Dodgers, Duke Snider. Who was the best? This was the question that launched a thousand debates.

The debate has made virtually every major list of top sports debates, including ESPN's definitive list of the top 10 sports arguments ever.

The three men combined for 21 all-star game appearances in the 1950s. Mantle won two MVP awards in the 1950s, Mays one and Snider none. But Snider hit more home runs in that decade than either Mays or Mantle. Mantle clearly had the best season of the decade, winning the American League triple crown in 1956, batting .353, with 52 home runs and 130 RBI.

All three men would be immortalized in the Hall of Fame and all three remain etched in the memories of any fortunate enough to have seen them play.

"Snider, Mantle and Mays," said Red Smith, the legendary sportswriter. "You could get a fat lip in any saloon by starting an argument as to which was best."

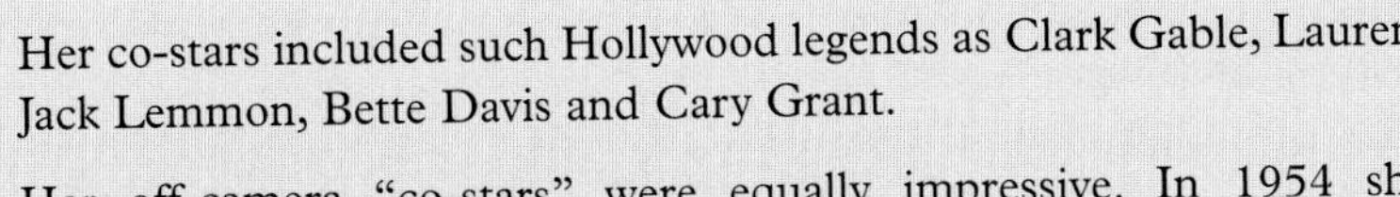

Her co-stars included such Hollywood legends as Clark Gable, Laurence Olivier, Jack Lemmon, Bette Davis and Cary Grant.

Her off-camera "co-stars" were equally impressive. In 1954 she married Joe DiMaggio. Doomed by DiMaggio's jealousy, the marriage lasted a mere nine months. Two years later, she wed playwright Arthur Miller, in what was called one of the more improbable marriages in history. This marriage, too, was brief.

She was also rumored to have had affairs with both Robert and John F. Kennedy and her "Happy Birthday" to the president remains the most memorable rendition of the song— ever.

Bill Haley and the Comets record "Rock around the Clock"
1955

Elvis Presley's breakout year
1956

Little Rock schools integrated
1957

Hula Hoop introduced
1958

Alaska and Hawaii join the union
1959

The 1960s

Neil Armstrong

Science and Technology

On May 25, 1961, just three weeks after Alan Shepherd had become the first American launched into space, President John F. Kennedy made the following stunning announcement: "I believe this Nation should commit itself to achieving the goal, before this decade is out, of landing a man on the moon and returning him safely to earth. No single space project in this period will be more impressive to mankind, or more important for the long-range exploration of space."

Even for a generation who had grown up on Flash Gordon and other space adventures, Kennedy's mandate seemed to be impossibly over-optimistic.

What would ensue over the next eight years was nothing short of remarkable: the first man in orbit, the first space walk, the Gemini missions, the first moon orbit (and breathtaking view of the Earth), and, ultimately, the historic flight of Apollo 11.

It was on July 20, 1969 that Armstrong stepped out of the lunar module and uttered the words "One small step for man… one giant leap for mankind." When Apollo 11 splashed down to Earth on July 24, Kennedy's vision was complete.

While Armstrong was just one man out of thousands who deserve credit for the incredible march to the moon, he has become the symbol for America's greatest single moment in technology.

Martin Luther King Jr.

Newsmaker

While there were many key figures in the Civil Rights Movement, no individual is more closely tied with this movement than Martin Luther King.

King first came to national attention during the 1950s with his involvement in the 1955 Montgomery bus strike, but it was not until the 1960s that he became the living embodiment of the Civil Rights Movement.

The King-led demonstrations in Birmingham, Alabama in 1963 were the catalyst for the passage of the Civil Rights Act of 1964. It was also in 1963 that King delivered the unforgettable "I have a dream" speech on the steps of the Lincoln Memorial. That same year, King was named as *Time Magazine*'s Man of the Year. The following year he would be honored with the Nobel Peace Prize.

As the decade of the 1960s progressed, King not only continued to speak out on racial issues, but was also a key figure in the anti-war movement.

In 1968, just one day after delivering his "I've been to the Mountaintop" speech, King was gunned down by an assassin.

"I've been to the mountaintop," King said in that speech. "I've seen the promised land. I may not get there with you. But I want you to know tonight, that we, as a people, will get to the promised land."

Bob Dylan

Entertainment, Arts and Letters

Bob Dylan's fingers on the throat of his guitar might as well have been his fingers taking the pulse of America during the tumultuous decade of the 1960s. With songs like *Blowin' in the Wind, Maggie's Farm, Masters of War* and *The Times They Are A Changin'* Dylan provided the signature voice for his generation.

When Dylan arrived on the scene in the early 1960s, most music was about cruising in cars, surfing and teenage love gone wrong. It was Dylan who used a gruff voice, a cynic's eye and a poet's heart to change the course of music forever. Dylan sang poignantly about war, poverty, racism and the battle of the

1960 — John F. Kennedy elected as youngest president ever

1961 — Yankee Outfielder Roger Maris hits 61st home run

1962 — Rachel Carson writes Silent Spring

1963 — Martin Luther King Jr. delivers "I have a dream" speech

1964 — The Beatles play to millions on Ed Sulliva

Ray Kroc

Business and Industry

You don't know the McDonald brothers, Dick and Maurice. But you certainly know Ray Kroc. It is Kroc—and obviously not the McDonald brothers—who will forever be known as the genius behind the McDonald's hamburger empire.

When Kroc first encountered the McDonalds, he was a blender salesman, and the McDonald brothers were one of his best clients. The McDonald brothers succeeded by applying assembly line efficiencies to their kitchens, allowing them to produce meals both quickly and inexpensively. While the McDonald brothers seemed content to enjoy success on a relatively small scale, Kroc had other ideas.

Kroc convinced the brothers to allow him to be the exclusive seller of McDonald's franchises. Kroc was so successful in this endeavor that he was able to purchase the entire business from the McDonald brothers in 1961 for the bargain price of $2.7 million.

By 1963, there were already 500 restaurants and the franchise sold its billionth hamburger. By the time the 1960s had come to an end, McDonald's was selling 3.5 million hamburgers a day and had topped the 5 billion burger mark.

Today, there are over 30,000 McDonald's in well over 100 countries. Kroc summed up his success in this way:

"The two most important requirements for major success are: first, being in the right place at the right time, and second, doing something about it."

---

generations. His songs became the backdrop to history, played at anti-war rallies, at the 1968 Democratic Convention riots and on virtually every college campus in America.

Obviously, Dylan's wasn't the only voice of protest. He had been preceded by the likes of Woody Guthrie and Pete Seeger, and was a contemporary of the likes of Peter, Paul and Mary, Phil Ochs, Joan Baez and Tom Paxton. But it is still Dylan who stands out as the leading voice of the era.

Even today, perhaps especially today, his words and music still resonate.

"Come mothers and fathers throughout the land and don't criticize what you can't understand. Your sons and your daughters are beyond your command. Your old road is rapidly aging, please get out of the new one if you can't lend your hand, for the times they are a changin'."

Muhammad Ali

Sports

What more can you say about someone simply known as "The Greatest?"

A legendary boxer, a controversial figure in the anti-war and civil rights movements and a major figure in the American Muslim community... Ali's impact both domestically and worldwide is undeniable.

As a boxer, Ali was grace and power personified. After winning the Gold Medal in the 1960 Olympics, Ali turned pro and immediately set his sights on the heavyweight title. After 19 impressive victories, Ali got his shot against the heavily favored Sonny Liston. On February 25, 1964, the 22-year-old Ali stunned the boxing world with his six-round knockout— a result Ali (then known as Cassius Clay) had boldly predicted.

The following day, Ali again stunned the boxing world with his announcement that he had become a member of the Nation of Islam.

As the Vietnam war escalated, Ali was called upon to serve in the Army. Based on his religious beliefs, Ali applied for conscientious objector status from the Army, but his request was denied. When he refused to serve, he was sentenced to five years in prison. The conviction would subsequently be overturned by the Supreme Court, but Ali would lose three critical years from the peak of his career.

Ali returned to the ring in the 1970s and enjoyed a remarkable comeback, including classic fights with Joe Frazier and George Foreman.

Ali's legacy was far greater than anything he ever did in the ring. He was a black man who refused to cow-tow to "proper" behavior. He was a Muslim, who was willing to go to jail for his beliefs. He remains a hero and role model to millions around the world.

he Sound of Music shatters ox office ecords

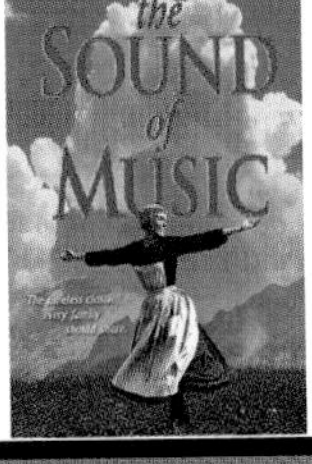

1965

Michael DeBakey implants first artificial heart

1966

Thurgood Marshall becomes first black Supreme Court justice

1967

First public demonstration of computer mouse

1968

The New York Times

MEN WALK ON MOON

ASTRONAUTS LAND ON PLAIN; COLLECT ROCKS, PLANT FLAG

1969

The 1970s

Herbert Boyer & Stanley Cohen

Science and Technology

A conversation that began with a couple of deli sandwiches ended with one of the most profound advances in the history of science.

Stanley Cohen (right), a Stanford University professor, and Herbert Boyer (left), a University of California professor, met at a conference in Hawaii, where they were both presenting papers on their research. Cohen had been working on ways to splice genes together, but couldn't find a way to merge the splices together, while Boyer had just recently discovered an enzyme that had the capacity to do just that.

The two immediately began the process of creating the framework for recombinant DNA (gene splicing), the basis of the entire biotechnology revolution. Together, they figured out how to take a piece of foreign DNA, introduce it into a simple cell called a "plasmid," and turn that plasmid into a factory recreating the original DNA over and over again.

To put it simply, they were able to splice together genes from two different organisms to create an entirely new variation. Their work produced myriad innovations, including synthetic insulin, interferon, and human growth hormone. It also set the stage for future generations of scientists to use and advance the technology to make advancements in science, medicine and agriculture.

For their efforts, they were awarded numerous scientific honors, including the Lemelson-MIT Prize, the National Medal of Science and the National Medal of Technology.

Cohen and Boyer's collaboration, not only resulted in great recognition in the scientific community, it made them both fabulously wealthy. Licenses from their patents have earned them over $250 million.

Richard Nixon

Newsmaker

Thirty years after Richard Nixon resigned in disgrace, his legacy remains a jumbled collection of contradictions and paradoxes. History looks at Nixon in almost Shakespearian terms: a great and powerful leader whose foibles and weaknesses led to a tragic and pathetic downfall.

On the one hand, Nixon was a visionary, opening long closed doors to China and Russia. On the other, it was his hunger for power and control that led Nixon down a path that would end with the Watergate crisis and, ultimately, with his decision to resign the presidency in the face of a near certain impeachment.

After serving as vice president under Dwight Eisenhower for two terms, Nixon took on John F. Kennedy in the 1960 presidential election. While Nixon would lose that race, he would return in 1968 with a convincing victory over Hubert Humphrey.

Though Nixon had failed to deliver on his promise of getting America out of Vietnam, he was still able to get re-elected in a landslide victory over George McGovern. It was a series of illegal activities committed during the re-election campaign (most notably the break-in at the Watergate Hotel and the attempted cover-up) that led to Nixon's 1974 resignation.

Woody Allen

Entertainment, Arts and Letters

While America was struggling with the Vietnam War, Watergate, and multiple cultural revolutions, Woody Allen provided us with some much needed comic relief.

The decade began with the release of *Bananas*, a hilarious send up of South American revolution. He continued with *Play It Again Sam, Everything You Wanted to Know About Sex…, Sleeper* and *Love and Death*, a brilliant parody of the great works of Russian fiction.

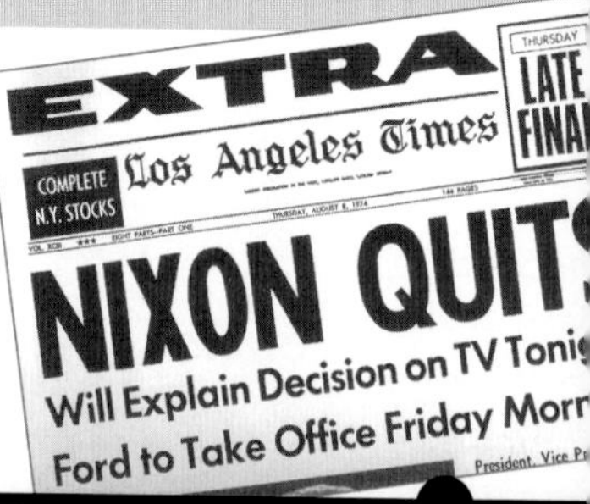

1970 — Amtrak formed

1971 — "All in the Family" debuts

1972 — Nixon is the first US President to visit China

1973 — Sears Tower Completed

1974

Sam Walton

Business and Industry

If Sam Walton's life were a novel, you would dismiss it as corny and unbelievable. But his story is a real one and as classic an American tale as you will ever read.

He grew up on a farm, worked to help support his family, had a stellar academic record and then went off to serve his country, rising to the rank of Captain in the US Army intelligence corps.

Upon his return from service, Walton took $5,000 of his own savings and borrowed $20,000 to buy his first department store. Walton sold out five years later (doubling his initial investment) and then opened the first Walton's 5 and 10 in 1950.

In quick order, Walton added one store and then another and another. The Wal-Mart chain began in 1962 and grew steadily through the decades. It was in the 1970s, though, that Wal-Mart enjoyed its most explosive growth. The company went public in 1970 and by 1979 had grown to 276 stores and had passed the $1 billion mark in sales.

His success was based on the principles of selling as many different products as possible and selling them as cheaply as he could. Through efficiencies in purchasing, staffing and even the structure of his stores, Walton was able to offer his goods at prices well below the competition. He kept his employees happy and motivated with profit-sharing plans (an innovation at the time).

"The secret of successful retailing is to give your customers what they want," Walton said. "And really, if you think about it from your point of view as a customer, you want everything."

With *Annie Hall*, Allen's vision took a very different direction. *Annie Hall* was a sophisticated romantic comedy which effortlessly blended humor with pathos. *Annie Hall* would beat out *Star Wars* for Best Picture of the Year and also earn Oscars for Allen (writing and directing) and Diane Keaton (Best Actress).

Allen stunned his fans with his next work, *Interiors*, his first drama. While jarring to those expecting another comedy, *Interiors* was given near universal raves and earned five Oscar nominations.

As the years have gone on, Allen has continued to be a prolific and successful writer/actor/director, moving seamlessly between his comedic and dramatic efforts.

"I don't want to achieve immortality through my work," he said. "I want to achieve it through not dying."

Billie Jean King

Sports

It is a discredit to Billie Jean King to have her listed on these pages merely as the sports figure of the 1970s. A huge figure in the women's rights movement, she just as easily could have been considered a newsmaker. A brilliant labor organizer and business woman, she could have been listed in that category as well. Finally, as a consummate performer, King would fit in easily as an entertainer.

King's tennis prowess ranks her among a handful of players at the top of her sport. She holds the record of 20 Wimbledon titles (singles and doubles); four US Open titles and had a victory in both the French Open and Australian Open.

While she dominated women's tennis, King will always be most remembered for her 1973 match against Bobby Riggs. In what was called "The Battle of the Sexes," King crushed Riggs 6-4, 6-3, 6-3, beating the 55-year-old former Wimbledon champion in all aspects of the game.

Life Magazine named King as one of the 100 most important Americans of the 20th Century. In 1971 King became the first woman athlete, in any sport, to earn over $100,000. In 1975, Seventeen Magazine reader's poll voted King the most admired woman in the world, beating out Israeli Prime Minister Golda Meir.

The following year was an extremely busy one for King. She founded *WomenSports* magazine, started the Women's Sports Foundation, and formed World Team Tennis.

"In the '70s we had to make it acceptable for people to accept girls and women as athletes," she said in an interview with ESPN. "We had to make it OK for them to be active. Those were much scarier times for females in sports."

1975 VCR introduced

1976 America celebrates its bicentennial

1977 Star Wars debuts

1978 Camp David Accords

1979 Sony Walkman introduced

The 1980s

Bill Gates

Science and Technology

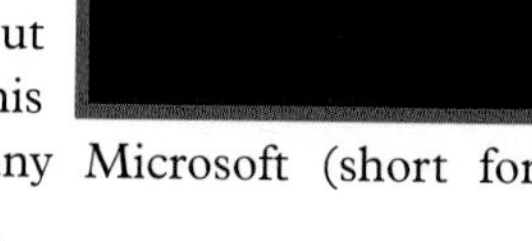

No single name is more synonymous with the computer revolution than Bill Gates. Gates was the driving force behind Microsoft, the world's most powerful and influential technology company. It is the rare individual, business, or school in this county that doesn't rely on some form of technology developed by Microsoft.

Born in 1955, Gates was already programming computers at the age of 13 and had sold his first program at the age of 17. Gates attended Harvard University, but dropped out to devote his time to his new company Microsoft (short for microcomputer software).

It would be another six years, with the development of MS-DOS and the adoption of MS-DOS in the very first IBM personal computers, that Microsoft began to emerge as a major player in the technology world.

The 1980s saw Gates introduce Microsoft Word (1983), Windows (1985) and the entire Microsoft Office Suite by the end of the decade. By 1990, this tiny company had reached $1 billion in annual sales and had revolutionized the way America did business.

Gates' contributions go far wider than just the technology world. He is the single most prolific philanthropist in history, with the Bill and Melinda Gates Foundation having already granted over $7 billion to causes ranging from education to global health.

Ronald Reagan

Newsmaker

Only in America can a B-movie actor transform himself into one of the most influential and revered presidents in history.

There was more than a little skepticism when Reagan announced his candidacy for the presidency in 1980. Though he had previously served as governor of California, he was still considered to be something of a political lightweight.

Reagan presented himself as the alternative to Jimmy Carter's America, a country humbled by a weak economy and the Iran hostage crisis. It was a message that resonated with the American people. Reagan overwhelmed Carter in the 1980 election and would ride a wave of immense popularity to an even more decisive victory over Walter Mondale in 1984.

Reagan's domestic tenure was marked by his "trickle down economics" policy of cutting taxes and bringing economic incentives to big business. While he amassed an enormous deficit, the 1980s proved to be one of the country's most prosperous decades.

On the international front, Reagan oversaw a massive increase in defense spending and was credited, in part, with the downfall of the Soviet Union. It was during his 1987 speech in Berlin that Reagan uttered his most famous line: "General Secretary Gorbachev, if you seek peace, if you seek prosperity for the Soviet Union and Eastern Europe, if you seek liberalization: Come here to this gate! Mr. Gorbachev, open this gate! Mr. Gorbachev, tear down this wall!"

Stephen King

Entertainment, Arts and Letters

Stephen King's legacy may well be measured more in nightmares than Pulitzers, but his contributions to the American literary landscape cannot be denied or dismissed. It is almost impossible to find a person who hasn't had the pleasure of being terrified by one or more of Stephen King's many books or movies.

King who once called himself "the literary equivalent of a Big Mac and fries," has sold nearly as many books as McDonalds has sold burgers. In the 1980s, he penned no less than seven of the top-25 best-selling novels of the decade.

Miracle on Ice —US defeats Russia in Olympic ice hockey en route to gold medal

The New York Times

REAGAN TAKES OATH AS 40TH PRESIDENT; PROMISES AN 'ERA OF NATIONAL RENEWAL'

MINUTES LATER, 52 U.S. HOSTAGES IN IRAN FLY TO FREEDOM AFTER 444-DAY ORDEAL

Michael Jackson's "Thriller"

Camcorders introduced

Macintosh computer debu

1980 1981 1982 1983 1984

Lee Iacocca

Business and Industry

Lee Iacocca guaranteed his place among America's greatest businessmen with his orchestration of the remarkable turnaround of Chrysler Corporation in the 1980s.

Iacocca arrived at Chrysler after a distinguished career at Ford. At Ford, Iacocca was credited with the design of the Mustang, an accomplishment that helped propel him to the company's presidency. After a falling out with Henry Ford II, Iacocca moved on to Chrysler, a company on the verge of bankruptcy.

One of Iacocca's first moves at Chrysler was to go directly to the U.S. Congress, asking for (and receiving) an unprecedented loan guarantee of $1.2 billion. The loan allowed Chrysler to stay in business long enough for Iacocca to work his magic.

Using ideas that had been rejected by Ford, Iacocca first introduced the K-car in 1980. The K-car was not only inexpensive, but had excellent gas mileage. The enormous success of the K-car was followed up by the introduction of the mini-van, which was the vehicle that inspired the SUV. In the late 1980s, Chrysler acquired the American Motors Corporation, which gave Chrysler a key new brand, Jeep.

In the 1980s, he also served as chairman of the Statue of Liberty–Ellis Island Foundation and distinguished himself as an author. His 1984 autobiography was the best selling non-fiction book of both 1984 and 1985.

Among the unforgettable works penned by King during the 1980s, were *Cujo*, *Firestarter*, *Pet Semetary*, *The Mist*, *The Talisman*, and *It*. In the same decade he produced two far more subtle works, *Misery* and *Rita Hayworth* and the *Shawshank Redemption*. Those two went on to become two of his most successful movie projects.

The undisputed king of the horror genre, King has a remarkable knack for identifying our deepest psychological fears and then gleefully exploiting them. He can take our best friends, our cats and dogs, and turn them into evil incarnate. He can take the family car and turn it into a weapon of vengeance. He can even turn a senior prom into a bloodbath of biblical proportions.

"People want to know why I do this, why I write such gross stuff," King once explained. "I like to tell them I have the heart of a small boy... and I keep it in a jar on my desk."

Magic Johnson & Larry Bird

Sports

There are few rivalries in the history of sport that had the intensity, the drama and the mutual respect shared by Larry Bird (left) and Magic Johnson (right). Muhammad Ali had Joe Frazier, Jack Nicklaus had Arnold Palmer, but the career-long rivalry between Bird and Johnson produced some of the most epic games in the history of college and professional basketball.

During the 1970s, the National Basketball Association was in deep trouble. Attendance was down, interest was waning and the league revenues were at dangerously low levels.

It was with the arrival of two remarkable rookies, Johnson (with the Los Angeles Lakers) and Bird (with the Boston Celtics) that the entire league's fortunes turned around. The rivalry between Johnson and Bird had begun with the 1979 NCAA Championship game and continued fiercely through the ensuing decade.

During the 1980s, the two would garner more than their share of individual and team accolades. Bird would win Rookie of the Year honors, three MVPS and three NBA championships, and would be named to the All-NBA first team nine times. In the decade, Johnson would help lead the Lakers to five NBA championships while earning two MVP honors and seven All-NBA first team nominations.

Both men saw their careers cut short by illness and injury. For Johnson, it was the stunning revelation that he had contracted the HIV virus. For Bird, it was a series of severe back injuries.

Both men ended up on the NBA's 1996 list of the 50 greatest players ever and both are members of the NBA Hall of Fame.

Pete Rose breaks career hits record — 1985

Fox Network debuts — 1986

"Black Monday" stock market crash — 1987

Human Genome Project begins — 1988

B-2 Stealth Bomber introduced — 1989

The 1990s

Francis Collins

Science and Technology

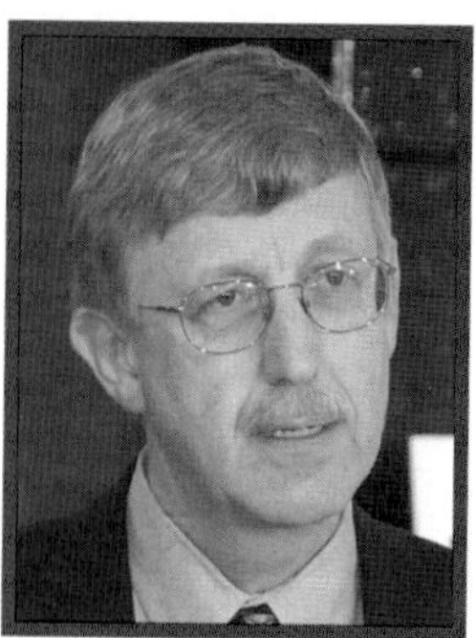

As the Director of the Human Genome Project, Francis Collins may well go down as one of the most important figures in the history of medicine and health.

Though his name is not widely known outside of the scientific community, Collins' work (and the work of his team) laid the groundwork for enormous advances in understanding the cause and nature of disease and, with that knowledge, the tools to eradicate disease.

Simply put, the Human Genome Project provided the world with an "instruction manual" to human genetics. Armed with a fully mapped guide to the human genome, scientists have already begun the process of looking into the nature of health and disease. The work of the Human Genome Project has already given science profound insights into the nature of such diseases as cystic fibrosis, neurofibromatosis, Huntington's disease, adult acute leukemia and diabetes.

The implications for the future are boundless. Beyond merely giving us better tools to recognize and diagnose disease, the Human Genome may provide ways to see what diseases are "programmed" into individuals and allow doctors to ambush the disease, eliminating it long before the first symptoms would materialize.

Collins, while taking great pride in his work, is quick to point out that he is only one individual in a team consisting of approximately 1000 researchers worldwide. No one man could have begun to tackle the huge job of the Human Genome Project. But only one man was there to lead it all— Francis Collins.

"But this is, I think, one of the most exciting moments in all of science, Collins said. "We have only the faintest glimmer of what a lot of this information is really telling us."

Bill Clinton

Newsmaker

Love him or hate him, and there are plenty on both sides of the ledger, Bill Clinton was the defining American personality of the 1990s. When the decade began, Clinton's name was barely known outside the confines of Arkansas politics. By the time the 1990s had come to a close, Clinton was one of the most recognized and powerful figures in the world.

After leaving Arkansas for Georgetown, Oxford and Yale Law School, Clinton returned to his roots and immediately began to pursue his career in politics. Just five years out of law school, Clinton was elected Governor.

Clinton stunned the world in 1992, beating out George H.W. Bush and Ross Perot for the presidency. In 1996, he became the first Democratic President since Franklin D. Roosevelt to win a second term. His tumultuous presidency was marked by both achievements and shortcomings.

During his presidency, the largest deficit in history turned into a budget surplus. By the time Clinton left office, over 20 million new jobs had been created, resulting in the lowest unemployment levels in 30 years. Internationally, he brokered the Oslo Accords, bringing the best hopes for peace in the Middle East in decades, and also was instrumental in ending the oppressive regime of Slobodan Milosevic.

What could have been remembered as a great presidency was tarnished by his affair with Monica Lewinsky. The affair led to Clinton's impeachment and subsequent acquittal in the Senate.

Stephen Spielberg

Entertainment, Arts and Letters

It is hard to imagine a person who hasn't been touched in some way by one of the many epic films of Steven Spielberg. A masterful director, Spielberg has the rare ability to create films that can both blow you away in their sheer scope and move you with their profound, human stories.

Early in his career, Steven Spielberg demonstrated a remarkable capacity to create entertaining movies on a grand

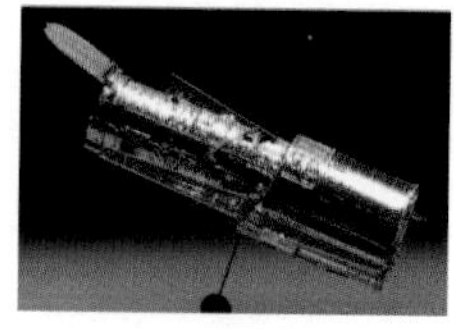

Launch of the Hubble space telescope

1990

Clarence Thomas appointed to Supreme Court

1991

Johnny Carson hosts his final *Tonight Show*

1992

Toni Morrison wins Nobel Prize for Literature

1993

Yahoo launched

1994

Jeff Bezos

Business and Industry

n 1990, the Internet was still a highly technical tool being used almost exclusively by the academic and military communities. By the end of the decade, thanks in great part to Jeff Bezos, the Internet would be utilized as the greatest innovation in commerce since Henry Ford's creation of the assembly line.

Educated as an electrical engineer and computer scientist at Princeton, Bezos began his professional career in the world of finance, but quickly turned his attention to the Internet when he learned that between 1993 and 1994, Internet usage had increased by 2,300 percent.

Armed with this piece of information, Bezos made the determination that the one field where the Internet could make the biggest impact was the world of books. At that point in time, there was no single print catalogue that covered the entire universe of publishing.

It didn't take long for this dream to become a reality. Launching Amazon.com in July of 1995, Bezos had sold books in 50 states within 30 days. Within two months, sales were up to $20,000 a week. From there, sales simply skyrocketed.

In 1997, Bezos took the company public,. In 1999, Amazon.com's sales exceeded $1.6 billion. By the end of the decade, Amazon.com had serviced 17 million customers in 150 countries. For his efforts, Bezos was recognized by *Time Magazine* as "Man of the Year."

scale. With movies like *Close Encounters of the Third Kind, Jaws, E.T.* and the *Indiana Jones* saga, Spielberg was able to amaze us, terrify us and leave us spellbound.

It was in the 1990s, though, that Spielberg tackled many of his most serious and memorable subjects. Between 1993 and 1998 Spielberg directed *Schindler's List, Amistad* and *Saving Private Ryan*, taking on issues of genocide, slavery and war. He won the Oscar for Best Director for both *Schindler's List* and *Saving Private Ryan*. Both films were also nominated for Best Film, with *Schindler's List* taking the Oscar.

It's not that Spielberg forgot his action/adventure/fantasy roots during the 1990s. The decade also saw him direct *Jurassic Park* and *Jurassic Park II*, two wildly successful blockbusters.

Michael Jordan

Sports

Of all the decisions made in compiling this elite list of 60, there were few easier choices than this one. While there were many sports legends during the 1990s (do the names Mark McGwire and Sammy Sosa ring a bell?), Michael Jordan's achievements in the 1990s, both on the court and off, were nothing short of legendary.

In the 1990s, Jordan led the Chicago Bulls to six NBA championships, earning four Most Valuable Player awards along the way. The 1990s also saw Jordan's leadership of the 1992 Olympic "Dream Team" that dominated the rest of the world en route to a Gold Medal. He most likely would have achieved even more during the decade if he hadn't quit basketball for nearly two full seasons as he pursued his ill-fated dream of becoming a Major League Baseball player.

In the business world, Jordan's impact nearly equaled his impact on the court. His endorsements of Nike, Coke, Hanes, McDonald's, Rayovac, Wheaties and Gatorade make him one of the highest paid endorsers in history. Jordan's association with Nike may have been the greatest single marriage in the history of sports marketing.

Jordan even brought his Midas touch to the film industry. His movie, *Space Jam*, which combined live actors with such animated characters as Bugs Bunny and Daffy Duck, grossed over $230 million worldwide.

Mark McGwire breaks Roger Maris home run record

Los Angeles Times

Clinton Acquitted

Votes Fall Far Short of Conviction

Hyde Regrets the Strategy, Not the Fight

Perjury charge rejected, 55-45. Obstruction charge tally is 50-50. President offers apology and calls for reconciliation.

Glad It's Over, but Not Glad It Happened

Amazon.com debuts

1995

Palm Pilot introduced

1996

Mars Pathfinder lands on Mars

1997

1998

1999

The 2000s

Sergey Brin and Larry Page

Science and Technology

I Google. You Google. Everybody Googles.

The very name Google has become more than just part of the Internet landscape, it has become part of the vernacular. Every day millions of visitors come to Google.com to get information on every topic under the sun. From high school students doing homework assignments to employers checking out the background of potential employees, Google has become a primary research tool.

While there are hundreds of search engines, none has proven to be as useful and pervasive as the one created by Sergey Brin (right) and Larry Page (left). Page and Brin met as graduate students at Stanford University, with each taking an immediate dislike for the other.

Fortunately, their shared passion for data mining helped them to overcome their initial personality issues. In 1998, the two introduced Google in a paper entitled: The Anatomy of a Large-Scale Hypertextual Web Search Engine. At the time, Google was searching 24 million Web pages and, according to the paper, the immediate goal was to scale up to 100 million pages.

As of late 2004, Google was searching over 8 billion pages. In 2004, Google had nearly $3.5 billion in revenues (99% from advertising) and that number was expected to be substantially higher in 2005. Google is in the process of expanding its horizons well beyond the world of a mere search engine. They have already launched a mail service, a networking community and a sophisticated mapping program. While they have delved into other areas, don't expect them to neglect their bread-and-butter.

"The ultimate search engine would basically understand everything in the world, and it would always give you the right thing," Page said in an interview with *Business Week*. "And we're a long, long ways from that."

George W. Bush

Newsmaker

The beginning of our 43rd President's first term focused primarily on domestic issues such as social security privatization, tax relief, and education reform.

All of that changed on September 11, 2001.

With the multiple hijackings and the attacks on the World Trade Center and Pentagon, America was thrust into a new world. The global war on terror would become the defining issue of Bush's presidency. Bush has executed that war on many fronts, first in Afghanistan, then in Iraq and has been working with governments around the world in an effort to contain what has become a global problem.

Bush faced yet another major crisis early in his second term. Hurricane Katrina created devastation in Louisiana, Mississippi and Alabama. While there was an inadequate response from local and state governments, Bush conceded that the response by the Federal Government–most notably the Department of Homeland Security–could have been far swifter and more decisive.

Bush's legacy will ultimately depend largely on his ability to deal with the continuing global war on terror and how he handles the aftermath of the single greatest natural disaster in American history.

Oprah Winfrey

Entertainment, Arts and Letters

Looking at Oprah Winfrey's resume, it is almost impossible to fathom the scope and range of her enormous success.

- As a journalist, Winfrey debuted on-air at the age of 19.
- As a television personality, Winfrey has had the No. 1 talk show in America for nearly 20 years, watched by over 30 million viewers each week.
- As an actress, Winfrey has been nominated for an Academy Award and a Golden Globe.

2000 — Millennium Edition (54th) of *Who's Who in America* inducted into the White House Millennium Time Capsule

2001

The New York Times

U.S. ATTACKED

HIJACKED JETS DESTROY TWIN TOWERS AND HIT PENTAGON IN DAY OF TERROR

President Vows to Exact Punishment for 'Evil'

A CREEPING HORROR

2002 — Halle Berry is first African American woman to win Best Actress Oscar

2003 — *The DaVinci Code* published

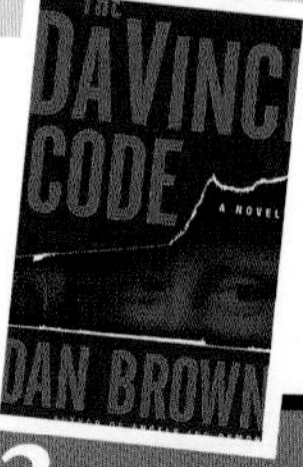

2004 — Red Sox win first World Series since 1918

Meg Whitman

Business and Industry

Thanks to CEO Meg Whitman, eBay has grown from a tiny auction site into one of the most successful businesses in the world. eBay, a site that was built with the idea of trading Pez dispensers, now handles over $30 billion in transactions annually, with no slowdown in sight.

Whitman came to eBay armed with a Harvard MBA and a long track record of success during stints at Walt Disney, FTD and Hasbro. When she arrived at eBay in 1998, the company was in its relative infancy, with revenues under $6 million annually. Under Whitman's stewardship, eBay has grown from a grass-roots curiosity into a multi-billion dollar conglomerate. By the end of 2004, revenue figures had topped the $3 billion mark and, based on first-half results, revenues for 2005 are expected to exceed $4 billion.

How big is eBay today? Based on a July 2005 survey, 724,000 Americans reported that eBay was their primary or secondary source of income. Another 1.5 million Americans supplement their income by selling on eBay. In the second quarter of 2005, there were 440 million new listings on eBay and 64.6 million active users.

There have been many accolades for Whitman. She was on *Time* Magazine's list of the 100 most influential people in the world in both 2004 and 2005. She was ranked #1 in *Worth*'s 2002 list of best CEOs.

- As a producer, Winfrey has her own production company, one that not only produces her show, but created the immensely popular Dr. Phil as well.
- As a publisher, Oprah magazine is one of the most successful and fastest-growing ventures in history.
- With her Oprah Book Club, Winfrey has become one of the most influential people in the book publishing industry. An endorsement from Winfrey is a virtual guarantee of a best-seller.
- Winfrey is also co-founder of Oxygen Media (a 24-hour women's cable network) and Oprah.com.
- As a philanthropist, Winfrey is deeply involved in multiple charities, working primarily in the areas of education and children's health and safety.

Her successes, in so many fields, have made her a billionaire and Forbes ranked her as the 9th most powerful woman in the world.

"I don't think of myself as a poor, deprived ghetto girl who made good," she said. "I think of myself as somebody who from an early age knew I was responsible for myself, and I had to make good."

Tiger Woods

Sports

Tiger Woods has emerged as the single most influential figure on the American sports scene. A golfing prodigy from the time he was a toddler, Woods is well on his way to becoming the greatest golfer in the history of the sport as well as the greatest corporate spokesman ever.

Though just under 30 years old, Woods has seemingly been around forever. At the age of two, he was on television in a putting contest with Bob Hope. By the age of five, he had been featured in *Golf Digest* Magazine. In junior competitions, he dominated amateur golf in a way no other player had in history.

Turning pro in 1996, Woods continued his unprecedented success. He won two tournaments as a rookie and, by 1997, had already established himself as the No. 1 player in the world.

His 2000 season was one of the greatest enjoyed by any golfer in history. He won 11 tournaments that year, shattering his own record for earnings. More importantly, he came up with consecutive victories in the US Open, British Open and PGA. Woods has continued his mastery of the golf world, earning Player of the Year honors in 2000, 2001, 2002, and 2003.

After a relatively disappointing 2004 season, Woods roared back in 2005 to enjoy yet another remarkable season, He won his fourth Masters, finished second at the US Open, won his second British Open at St. Andrews and finished fourth at the PGA.

Woods is so venerated as golfer and as a person that he has earned far more money from endorsements than any other active athlete. He was recognized by *Forbes* magazine as the No. 1 athlete and No. 2 celebrity overall in terms of earnings.

Lance Armstrong wins 7th Tour de France

2005

1890's

Science and Technology

Thomas Edison

Edison, Thomas Alva, inventor; b. Milan, Ohio, Feb. 11, 1847; s. Samuel Ogden Jr. and Nancy (Elliott) Edison; married Mary G. Stilwell, Dec. 25, 1871 (dec. Aug. 9, 1884); children: Marion Estelle, Thomas Alva, William Leslie; married Mina Miller, Feb. 24, 1886; children: Madeleine, Charles, Theodore. Spent 3 months at sch., Port Huron, Mich., then received instruction from his mother; hon. Ph.D., Union Coll., 1878. Began selling newspaper and candy on the Grand Trunk Railroad to Detroit, 1859; wrote and printed Grand Trunk Herald, 1862; telegraph operator in towns throughout Midwest, 1863-67, with Western Union Telegraph Co., Boston, 1868-69; gen. mgr. Samuel Laws' Gold Indicator Co., NYC, 1869; co-founder Pope, Edison & Co., 1869, bought by Gold & Stock Telegraph Co. along with stock-ticker inventions, 1870, with money established workshop at Newark, NJ, 1870-76, removing to Menlo Park, NJ, 1876-82, and later to West Orange, NJ, 1887-31; co-organized Edison Electric Illuminating Co. of NY, 1880, Edison Electric Light Co., 1878, other electric companies, eventually consolidated into General Electric Co., 1892; consolidated later companies into Thomas A. Edison, Inc., 1911, pres. 1911-26; tested 17,000 plants for domestic source of rubber, 1927-31, as Edison Botanic Research Co. Head of US Naval Consulting Bd., 1915-21. Recipient Albert Medal, British Soc. Arts, 1892, John Fritz Medal, Am. Engineering Societies, 1908, Rumford Medal, Am. Acad. Arts & Sciences, 1908, Congressional Gold Medal for development and application of inventions that have revolutionized civilization in the last century, 1928; named Chevalier French Legion of Honor, 1878, promoted to Comdr., 1889; elected to Nat. Acad. Sciences, 1927. First patent for electric vote recorder, June 1, 1869; made numerous telegraphic improvements: automatic repeater, transmitters, receivers, the duplex, quadruplex, & sextuplex systems, carbon rheostat, automatic printers & tape; worked to improve typing machine, 1871; invented electric pen, 1875, phonograph, 1877, the microphone, the microtasimeter for detection of small changes in temperature, the megaphone, first practical incandescent lamp, 1879, a method to make plate glass, magnetic ore separator, compressing dies, composition brick, a cement process, an all-concrete house, an electric locomotive, patent, 1893, fluoroscope, nickel-iron battery, universal motor, 1907, electric safety lantern, 1914, many others; developments in motion pictures, kinetograph & kinetoscope, Edison Co. produced over 1700 movies, synchronized movies with phonograph, 1904; opened first central power station, London, 1882, Pearl Street, NYC, 1882; first observed phenomenon to be known as Edison Effect, 1880; since commencement of European War, 1914, designed, built and operated successfully several benzol plants, also 2 carbolic acid plants and other chemical plants for making myrbane aniline oil, aniline salt, and para-phenylenediamine; acquired 1093 patents throughout his life. Died West Orange, NJ, Oct. 18, 1931.

Newsmaker

Susan B. Anthony

Anthony, Susan Brownell, reformer; b. Adams, Mass., Feb. 15, 1820; d. Daniel and Lucy (Read) A. Ed. in school maintained by father for his own and neighboring children, Battenville, N.Y.; ed., Friends' Boarding School, West Phila., 1837–38. Taught school from age 15 to 30; aided in organizing the first State women's temperance soc., 1852; organizer and sec. Women's Nat. Loyal League during Civil War. After the war, entirely devoted to the women's suffrage movement; founded "The Revolution," exclusively woman's rights paper, 1868; managed it several yrs.; co-founder, with Elizabeth Cady Stanton, Am. Equal Rights Assn., 1866, Nat. Woman Suffrage Assn., 1869, pres., 1892-1900 (then Nat. Am. Woman Suffrage Assn.); arrested and tried for voting under the Fourteenth Amendment in 1872; engaged in 78 different State campaigns for a constl. amendment enfranchising woman; granted a hearing before committees of every Congress since 1869. Joint author with Mrs. Elizabeth Cady Stanton and Mrs. Matilda Joslyn Gage of The History of Woman Suffrage (3 vols.), and of Vol. IV with Ida Husted Harper; contributed to leading mags. and lectured in England and throughout the U.S. Died 1906.

Business and Industry

Andrew Carnegie

Carnegie, Andrew, philanthropist; b. Dunfermline, Fifeshire, Scotland, Nov. 25, 1835; m. Louise Whitfield, 1887; 1 daughter: Margaret. Came with family to U.S., 1848, settling in Pittsburgh. Lord rector, St. Andrew's University, 1903-07, LL.D., 1905; lord rector, Aberdeen University, 1912-14, and LL.D.; also LL.D., universities of Glasgow, Edinburgh, Birmingham, Manchester, McGill University (Montreal), Queen's College (Toronto), Erskine College, Allegheny College, University of Pa., Brown University, Cornell University, Hamilton College; Dr. Political Science, University of Groningen. First work was as weaver's assistant in cotton factory, Allegheny, Pa.; telegraph messenger boy in Pittsburgh office of Ohio Telegraph Company, 1851; learned telegraphy, entered employ Pa. R.R. and became telegraph operator, advancing by promotions until he became superintendent Pittsburgh division Pa. system; joined Mr. Woodruff, inventor of the sleeping car, in organizing Woodruff Sleeping Car Company, gaining through it nucleus of his fortune; careful investments in oil lands increased his means; during Civil War served as superintendent military railways and government telegraph lines in the East. After war developed iron works of various kinds and established, at Pittsburgh, Keystone Bridge Works and Union Iron Works. Introduced into this country Bessemer process of making steel, 1868; was prime owner a few years later of Homestead and Edgar Thomson Steel Works, and other large plants as head of firms of Carnegie, Phipps & Company and Carnegie Bros. & Company; interests were consolidated, 1899, in the Carnegie Steel Company, which in 1901 was merged in the United States Steel Corporation, when he retired from business. Author: An American Four-in-Hand in Britain, 1883; Round the World, 1884; Triumphant Democracy, 1886; The Gospel of Wealth, 1900; The Empire of Business, 1902 (translated into 8 languages); The Life of James Watt, 1906; Problems of Today, 1909. Commander Legion of Honor, France, 1907; Grand Cross, Order of Orange Nassau; Grand Cross, Order of Danebrog. Hon. member American Institute Architects, American Society Mining Engineers, American Institute Mining Engineers. Life trustee Carnegie Corporation of New York ($125,000,000 foundation to carry on various works in which he has been engaged); trustee Cornell University, from 1890. Has received freedom of 54 cities of Great Britain and Ireland. Has given libraries to many towns and cities in the U.S. and Great Britain, and large sums in other benefactions, including $24,000,000 to Carnegie Institute, Pittsburgh; $5,200,000 to New York for the establishment of branch libraries; $22,000,000 to Carnegie Institution of Washington; $10,000,000 to Scotch universities; $5,000,000 to fund for benefit of employees of Carnegie Steel Company; $1,000,000 to St. Louis Public Library; $5,000,000 to the Carnegie Hero Fund Commission, Pittsburgh; $1,150,000 to the Carnegie Hero Fund Trust, Dunfermline, Scotland (for Great Britain); $1,000,000 to the Hero Fund for France; $1,500,000 to the Hero Fund for Germany; $230,000 to the Hero Fund for Belgium; $125,000 to the Hero Fund for Denmark; $200,000 for the Hero Fund for Holland: $230,000 to the Hero Fund for Sweden; $130,000 to the Hero Fund for Switzerland; $750,000 to the Hero Fund for Italy; $125,000 to the Hero Fund for Norway; $3,500,000 to the Carnegie Dunfermline Trust; $1,500,000 for the Peace Temple at The Hague; $1,500,000 to United Engineering Society. Total benefactions exceed $300,000,000, including over $60,000,000 for over 3,000 municipal library buildings: also building and grounds for Pan-American Union, Washington. 1906; $16,250,000 for Foundation for Advancement of Teaching in U.S., Can., and Newfoundland. Died Aug. 11, 1919.

John Davison Rockefeller

Rockefeller, John Davison, capitalist, philanthropist; b. in Richford, New York, July 8, 1839; s. William Avery and Eliza (Davison) R.; m. Laura C. Spelman, Sept. 8, 1864 (died 1915); children—Bessie (Mrs. Charles A. Strong, dec.), Alta (Mrs. E. Parmalee Prentice), Edith (Mrs. Harold Fowler McCormick, dec.), John Davison. Moved to Cleveland, Ohio, 1853; public school education. Was clerk in forwarding and commission house; at 19 partner in firm of Clark & Rockefeller, commission merchants; firm became Andrews, Clark & Co., and engaged in oil business; in 1867 the firm, then Rockefeller, Andrews & Flagler, operated a large oil refinery at Cleveland, and in 1870, the business was consolidated with others in the Standard Oil Co.; other interests were later acquired and the Standard Oil Trust was formed, 1882, but dissolved, 1892, after which the Standard Oil Co. operated as a New Jersey corporation until it dissolved in 1911, with Mr. Rockefeller, president until Dec. 4, 1911, when he retired. It is estimated that the total amount given by Mr. Rockefeller for philanthropic and charitable purposes up to 1921 exceeded $500,000,000. Nearly four-fifths of this sum went to the four great charitable corporations which he created: the Rockefeller Foundation, General Education Board, The Laura Spelman Rockefeller Memorial, and The Rockefeller Institute for Medical Research. Republican. Baptist. Died May 23, 1937.

Sports

Cy Young

Young, Cy (Denton True Young), professional baseball player; b. Gilmore, Ohio, Mar. 28, 1867; s. McKenzie Young. Player with profl. baseball team, Canton, Ohio, 1890; pitcher Cleve. Spiders, 1890–98, St. Louis Perfectos and Cardinals, 1899-1900, Boston Americans, Somersets, Pilgrims and Red Sox, 1901-08, Cleve. Naps and Indians, 1909–11, Boston Braves, 1911; mgr. Boston Red Sox, 1907. Achieved lifetime record of 511 victories against 313 losses; pitched 3 no-hitters, 1897, 1904, 1908; pitched first perfect game in Am. League history, May 5, 1904; won 35 games, lost 10, for .778 season, 1895; maintained win-loss record of over .700 for 5 seasons, over .600 for 11 seasons; holds major league record for complete games with 751; elected to Baseball Hall of Fame, 1937; Cy Young Award created to honor the best pitchers in baseball, 1956. Died Nov. 4, 1955.

Entertainment, Arts, and Letters

John Philip Sousa

Sousa, John Philip, composer, conductor, bandmaster; b. Washington, D.C., Nov. 6, 1854; s. John Antonio Sousa and Maria Elisabeth Trinkhaus; m. Jane van Middlesworth Bellis, Dec. 30, 1879. Studied music theory and composition with George Felix Benkert, a noted Washington orch. leader and tchr. Dir. US Marine Band, 1880–92; Europe tour The Sousa Band, 1900, Second European tour, 1901, Third European tour, 1905, World Tour: NY, Great Britain, Canary Islands, South-Africa, Australia, New Zealand, Fiji Islands, Hawaii, Can., 1910. Composer: (marches) Moonlight on the Potomac Waltzes, 1872, The Gladiator, 1886, Semper Fidelis (traditionally known as the "official" march of the Marine Corps), 1888, The Washington Post, 1889, The Thunderer, 1889, The Stars and Stripes Forever, 1896, The Liberty Bell March, 1893, Manhattan Beach March, 1893, King Cotton, 1895, Hands Across the Sea, 1899, Fairest of the Fair, 1908, US Field Artillery, 1917, The Gallant Seventh, 1922, The Black Horse Troop, 1924, Daughters of Texas, 1929, (operettas) The Queen of Hearts, 1885, The Smugglers, 1882, Desiree, 1883, El Capitan, 1895, The Bride Elect (libretto), 1897, The Charlatan (lyrics), 1898, Chris and the Wonderful Lamp, 1899, The Free Lance, 1905, The American Maid, 1909; conductor : The President's Own, serving under presidents Hayes, Garfield, Cleveland, Arthur and Harrison, 1880–92; (Broadway plays) Gilbert & Sullivan's H.M.S. Pinafore, 1875; and many others. With USMC, 1967–75, joined US Naval Reserve, 1917. Achievements include invention of the sousaphone; testified before Congress in 1927 and 1928 for composers' rights; the first Sousa Band concert was performed September 26, 1892 at Stillman Music Hall in Plainfield, NJ; enshrined in the Hall of Fame for Great Americans in a ceremony at the John F. Kennedy Ctr. for the Performing Arts, 1976; The Stars and Stripes Forever was declared the Nat. March of the US by an Act of Congress on Dec. 10, 1987. Died Mar. 6, 1932; buried Congressional Cemetery, Washington, DC.

1900's

Science and Technology

The Wright Brothers

Wright, Wilbur, æronaut; b. nr. Millville, Indiana, Apr. 16, 1867; Son of Milton and Susan Catharine (Koerner) W.; brother of Orville W.; ed. high schs., 4 yrs., Richmond, Ind., and Dayton, O.; (hon. B.S., Earlham College, Ind., 1909; LL.D., Oberlin College, Ohio, 1910); unmarried. Owned shop for sale and repair of bicycles; from 1903, with his brother, Orville, devoted time to heavier-than-air flying machine, patented by Wright Bros. in leading countries of world. With brother first to fly with a heavier-than-air machine, Dec. 17, 1903. Has made numerous flights in U.S. and abroad; sold a machine to U.S. Govt. for $30,000. Awarded gold medal by French Academy Sciences, 1909, Aero Club of France, 1908; Aero Club of United Kingdom, 1908; Acad. of Sports of France, 1908; Aeronautical Soc. Gt. Britain, 1908; Congress of U.S., 1909; State of Ohio, 1909; City of Dayton, 1909; Aero Club America, 1909; Cross of Chevalier of Legion of Honor, French, 1909; also many others. Mem. Aero Club of America. Home: Dayton, Ohio. Died May 30, 1912.

Wright, Orville, inventor; b. Dayton, Ohio, Aug. 19, 1871; s. Milton and Susan Catharine (Koerner) W.; ed. pub. and high schs. to 1890; hon. B.S., Earlham Coll., Ind., 1909, LL.D., 1931; Dr. Tech. Sci., Royal Tech. Coll., Munich, 1909; LL.D., Oberlin, 1910, Harvard Univ., 1930, Huntington (Ind.) Coll., 1935; Sc.D., Trinity, 1915, Cincinnati, 1917, Ohio State U., 1930; M.A., Yale, 1919; Dr. Engring., Univ. of Michigan, 1924; D.Sc., Otterbein Coll., Westville, Ohio, 1947; Doctor of Engineering, University of Dayton, 1943; unmarried. Owned shop for sale and repair of bicycles; with his brother, Wilbur, was the first to fly with a heavier-than-air machine, Dec. 17, 1903, and with him the inventor of the system of control used in flying machines of today; dir. Wright Aeronautical Laboratory, Dayton, O. Awarded the Collier trophy, 1913, for development of the automatic stabilizer; gold medals: Aero Club of France, 1908; Aero Club of United Kingdom, 1908; Acad. of Sports of France, 1908; Aeronautical Soc. Gt. Britain, 1908; Congress of U.S., 1909; State of Ohio, 1909; City of Dayton, 1909; Aero Club America, 1909; French Acad. Sciences, 1909; Cross of Chevalier of Legion of Honor, French, 1909; Cross of Officer of Legion of Honor, 1924; Langley medal, Smithsonian Inst., 1910; Elliott Cresson medal, Franklin Inst., 1914; Albert medal, Royal Soc. Arts, 1917; The John Fritz medal, 1920; bronze medal, International Peace Society; The John Scott medal, 1925; Washington award, 1927; Distinguished Flying Cross awarded, Feb., 1929; Daniel Guggenheim medal, 1930; Franklin medal, 1933; Medal for Merit, 1947; hon. mem. Aero Club of Sarthe, France, Aeronautical Society, Great Britain, Aero Club of United Kingdom, Osterreichischen Flugtechnischen Vereines, Vienna, Verein Deutscher Flugtechniker, Berlin, American Society Mech. Engrs., Aeronautical Soc. America, Nat. Aeronautic Assn. (gov. at large, 1929-39), Nat. Exchange Club, Ohio Society of New York, Inst. of Aeronautical Science, 1932, Franklin Inst., Nat. Fedn. Post Office Clerks, Inst. of Mech. Engrs., London, Air Line Pilots Assn., Inc.; hon. fellow Royal Aeronautical Soc.; mem. Nat. Inventors Council, Nat. Acad. Sciences, Nat. Museum Engring. and Industry (v.p., 1924), Nat. Adv. Com. for Aeronautics, A.A.A.S., Franklin Inst., S.A.E., Engineers' Club of Dayton (hon. life); hon. scout Boy Scouts America. Mem. Daniel Guggenheim Fund for Promotion of Aeronautics; chmn. advisory com., Daniel Guggenheim Sch. of Aeronautics, New York Univ.; hon. Aircraft Pilot Certificate No. 1, issued by Civil Aeronautics Authority, 1940. Home: Park and Harmon Avs. Office: 15 N. Broadway, Dayton. O. Died Jan. 30, 1948; buried Woodlawn Cemetery, Dayton.

Newsmaker

Theodore Roosevelt

Roosevelt, Theodore, 26th President of the United States; b. NYC, Oct. 27, 1858; s. Theodore and Martha (Bulloch) R.; m. Alice Hathaway Lee, Oct. 27, 1880 (dec. 1884); 1 child, Alice; m. Edith Kermit Carow, Dec. 2, 1886; children: 4 sons and a daughter. Fifth cousin of Franklin Delano Roosevelt, 32nd pres. AB, Harvard U., 1880; LLD, 1902, Columbia U., 1899, Hope Coll., 1901, Yale U., 1901, Northwestern U., 1893, U. Chgo., 1903, U. Calif., 1903, U. Pa., 1905, Clark U., 1905, George Washington U., 1909, Cambridge U., 1910; D.C.L., Oxford U., 1910; PhD, U. Berlin, 1910. Mem. NY Legis., 1882-84; commr. U.S. Civil Svc. Commission, 1889-95; police commr. City of NY, 1895-97; asst. sec. U.S. Navy, 1897-98; resigned from military; gov. New York State, 1899-1900; elected v.p. U.S., 1901; succeeded to presidency on death of William McKinley, 1901-05; elected Pres. of U.S., 1905-09; contbg. editor The Outlook, 1909-14. Spl. ambassador of U.S. at funeral of King Edward VII, 1910; addresses before univs. and learned socs.; lectr. Royal Geog. Soc., London, 1914; rancher; hunter, Africa, 1909-10; explorer in Brazil, 1914, a tributary of the Madeira River named in his honor by govt. Author: The Winning of the West, 1889-96, History of the Naval War of 1812, 1882, Hunting Trips of a Ranchman, 1885, Life of Thomas Hart Benson, 1886, Life of Gouverneur Morris, 1887, Ranch Life and Hunting Trail, 1888, History of New York, 1890, The Wilderness Hunter, 1893, American Ideals and Other Essays, 1897, The Rough Riders, 1899, Life Of Oliver Cromwell, 1900, The Strenuous Life, 1900, Works (8 vols.), 1902, The Deer Family, 1902, Good Hunting, 1907, True Americanism, African and European Addresses, 1910, African Game Trails, 1910, The New Nationalism, 1910, Realizable Ideals (the Earl lectures), 1912, Conservation of Womanhood and Childhood, 1912, History as Literature and Other Essays, 1913, Theodore Roosevelt, An Autobiography, 1913, Life Histories of African Game Animals (2 vols.), 1914, Through the Brazilian Wilderness, 1914, America and the World War, 1915, A Booklover's Holidays in the Open, 1916, Fear God, and Take Your Own Part, 1916, Foes of Our Own Household, 1917, National Strength and International Duty, 1917; contbr. to leading mags. and reviews. Del. Rep. Nat. Conv., 1884; candidate for mayor NYC, 1886. Organized with Surgeon (later Maj.-Gen.) Leonard Wood, 1st U.S. Cav., lt. col. of regt., which disting. itself in Cuba; promoted to col. for gallantry at battle of Las Guasimas, mustered out Sept. 1898; candidate for Pres. for Progressive Party, 1912 (shot during campaign speech); adv. of civil svc. and other reforms, nat. and mcpl.; nominated for Pres., Progressive Party, 1916, declined; offered to raise an army divsn., after declaration of war, to go to France, offer declined by Pres. Wilson, 1917. Recipient Nobel Peace Prize, 1906 (first Am. winner). Presented with first "Teddy Bear" named in his honor, 1903. Republican. Died Jan. 6, 1919 at Sagamore Hill, NY.

Business and Industry

Henry Ford

Ford, Henry, automobile manufacturer; b. Dearborn Township, Mich., July 30, 1863; s. William and Mary (Litogot) Ford; m. Clara J. Bryant, Apr. 11, 1888; 1 child, Edsel Bryant. D Engring., U. Mich., 1926; LLD, Colgate U., 1935. Apprentice machinist Detroit, 1879–81; engr. Edison Illuminating Co., Detroit, 1891–93, chief engr., 1893–99; chief engr., ptnr. Detroit Automobile Co., 1899–1901; organized, engr. Henry Ford Co., 1901–02; v.p., chief engr. Ford Motor Co., 1903–06, pres., 1906–19, 1943–45, opened factory, Highland Park, Mich., 1910, all prodn. being done at Rouge Plant, Dearborn, Mich., 1927. Model A introduced, 1903; began manufacturing of the Model T, 1908; introduced first moving automobile assembly line, 1913; announced plan of profit-sharing with employees paying $5 for an 8 hour day, 1914; chartered ship and conducted party to Europe with object of organizing a conf. of peace advocates to influence belligerent govts. to end WWI, 1915; built Henry Ford Hosp. at cost of $7,500,000; apptd. by Pres. Wilson mem. Wage Umpire Bd., 1918; developed Tri-Motor airplane, 1926; first V-8 Ford car built, 1932. Author: My Life and Work, 1923, Today and Tomorrow, 1926, Edison As I Knew Him, 1930, Moving Forward, 1931. Dem. candidate for US Senate against Truman H. Newberry, 1918; dedicated The Edison Inst. (now Henry Ford Mus. and Greenfield Village), 1929, open to pub., 1933. Mem. Soc. Automotive Engrs., Detroit Bd. Commerce, various clubs. Died Apr. 7, 1947.

Sports

Honus Wagner

Wagner, Honus (John Peter Wagner), professional baseball player; b. Mansfield, Pa., Feb. 24, 1874; Player with Louisville Colonels, 1897–99, Pitts. Pirates, 1900–17, mgr., 1917. Named to Baseball Hall of Fame, 1936. Achievements include Nat. League pennants 1901-1903, 1909; World Series champion, 1909; batted over .300 for 17 consecutive seasons with career average of .329; 8 time Nat. League batting champion; led league in stolen bases five times; most valuable baseball card in history. Died Dec. 6, 1955.

Entertainment, Arts, and Letters

George M. Cohan

Cohan, George M(ichael), comedian, actor; b. Providence, R.I., June 3, 1878; S. Jerry John and Helen Frances (Costigan) C.; m. Ethel Levy, actress; d. Georgette; m. Agnes Nolan, Jul. 4, 1908; children: Mary Helen, Helen Frances, George M. First appearance, Haverstraw, N.Y., at 9 yrs. of age, in Daniel Boone; appeared in Peck's Bad Boy, 1890; later in vaudeville, in The Four Cohans; starred in Little Johnny Jones, 1904-06, in George Washington Jr., 1906-07, in I'd Rather Be Right, 1937-38. Author: (plays) The Wise Guy; The Govenor's Son (three-act comedy); Running for Office; Little Johnny Jones (prod. 1904); Forty-five Minutes from Broadway (prod. 1905); George Washington Jr., (prod. 1906); Popularity (prod. 1906); The Talk of New York; Fifty Miles from Boston (prod. 1907); The Man Who Owns Broadway (prod. 1908); The Yankee Prince (prod. 1909); Get-Rich-Quick Wallingford (prod. 1910); The Little Millionaire (prod. 1911); Seven Keys to Baldpate (prod. 1913); Hit-the-Trail Holiday, 1915; The Tavern, 1920; The Song and Dance Man, 1923; American Born, 1925; The Baby Cyclone (farce), 1927; Billie (musical play), 1928; Gambling Drama, 1929; also many popular songs; best known for the songs: You're A Grand Old Flag, Yankee Doodle Boy, Give My Regards to Broadway, and Over There. Wrote more than 40 plays and 500 songs, and made over 1000 stage appearances in lifetime. Died Nov. 5, 1942.

1910's

Science and Technology

George Washington Carver

Carver, George Washington, educator; b. Diamond Grove, Mo., 1864; was born of slave parents on a farm; in infancy, lost father; was stolen and carried into Ark. with mother, who was never heard of again; was bought from captors for a race horse valued at $300. BS in Agr., Iowa State Coll. Agrl. and, Mechanic Arts, 1894, MS Agr., 1896; DSc, Simpson Coll., 1928. Elected mem. faculty, in charge of greenhouse Iowa State Coll. Agrl. and Mechanic Arts; tchr. Tuskegee Inst., from 1896; dir. Dept. of Agrl. Rsch.; apptd. collaborator Bur. of Plant Industry USDA (divsn. mycology and disease survey), from 1935. Recipient Spingarn medal 1923, Roosevelt medal, 1939. Mem. Royal Soc. of Arts/London. Achievements include creating over 300 products from peanuts and over 100 from sweet potatoes. Died Jan. 5, 1943.

Newsmaker

Woodrow Wilson

Wilson, Woodrow, 28th President of the United States; b. Staunton, Va., Dec. 28, 1856; s. Rev. Joseph R. and Jessie (Woodrow) W.; m. Ellen Louise Axson, June 24, 1885 (dec. 1914); 3 daughters; m. Edith Bolling Galt, Dec. 18, 1915. Student, Davidson Coll., 1874–75; AB, Coll of N.J. (now Princeton U.), 1879, AM, 1882; grad. in law, U. Va., 1881; post-grad., John Hopkins U., 1883–85, PhD, 1886; LLD, Wake Forest U., 1887, Tulane U., 1898, Johns Hopkins U., 1902, Rutgers U., 1902, U. of Pa., 1903, Brown U., 1903, Harvard, 1907, Williams, 1908, Dartmouth, 1909; LittD, Yale, 1901. Bar: 1882. Assoc. prof. history and polit. economy Bryn Mawr Coll., 1885-88; prof. history and polit. economy Wesleyan U., 1888-90; prof. Princeton U., N.J., 1890-1910; prof. jurisprudence and polit. economy, 1890-95; prof. jurisprudence, 1895-97; prof. jurisprudence and politics, 1897-1910; pres. Princeton U., N.J., 1902-10; gov. State of N.J., 1911-13; receiving 435 electoral votes elected Pres. U.S., 1912, pres., 1913–17; re-elected, 1917–21. Left for France on the troopship George Washington Dec. 4, 1918, at the head of Am. Commn. to Negotiate Peace; arrived at Brest, Dec. 13, at Paris, Dec. 14; visited Eng., Dec. 26-30, 1918, Italy, Jan. 2-6, 1919, Belgium, June 18-19, 1919; delivered many addresses and given hon. degrees by various univs. of allied countries; returned to U.S., arriving in Boston, Feb. 24, 1919; left New York on 2d trip to Europe, Mar. 5, after speaking at closing session Peace Treaty, June 28, 1919; returned to U.S., arriving in New York, July 8, 1919. Author: Congressional Government, a Study in American Politics, 1885, The State: Elements of Historical and Practical Politics, 1889, Division and Reunion, 1829-1889, 1893, An Old Master and Other Political Essays, 1893, Mere Literature, and Other Essays, 1893, George Washington, 1896, A History of the American People, 1902, Constitutional Government in the United States, 1908, The State: Elements of Historical and Practical Politics, new edit., 1911, Free Life, 1913, The New Freedom, 1913, When a Man Comes to Himself, 1915, On Being Human, 1916. Recipient Nobel Peace Prize, 1919. Democrat. Died Feb. 3, 1924 in Washington, D.C.

Business and Industry

Louis Burt Mayer

Mayer, Louis Burt, producer; b. Minsk, Russia, July 4, 1885; arrived in US, 1904, naturalized, 1912; s. Jacob and Sarah (Meltzer) M.; m. Margaret Shenberg, June 14, 1904 (div.); children: Edith, Irene; m. Lorena L. Danker, Dec. 4, 1948. Ship and indsl. plant salvaging bus., 1906; operator of theater Orpheum (formerly the Gem), Haverhill, Mass., 1907; acquired movie houses throughout New Eng.; formed own distribution co. Louis B. Mayer Co.; controlled New Eng. rights D.W. Griffith's Birth of a Nation; joined Alco Co. (later Metro Pictures), NYC; moved to LA and started own prodn. co., 1917; merged co. with Metro Pictures and The Goldwyn Co. to form Metro-Goldwyn-Mayer, 1924, West coast head; del. Rep. Nat. Conv., 1928; vice chmn. Calif. Rep. State Ctrl. Com. Trustee, L.A. Jewish Orphans. Involved in prodn. of movies including Ben Hur, The Wizard of Oz, Gone With the Wind, Mutiny on the Bounty, and Night at the Opera. Decorated Officer Legion Hon., 1937, Cross of White Lion, Czechoslovakia, 1938. Mem. C. of C., LA C. of C., Cmty. Welfare Fedn., LA Nat. Housing Com. for Congested Areas, Comml. Bd. LA; Mason (Shriner). Jewish. Clubs: Hillcrest Country, All Year Club of Southern Calif. Died Oct. 29, 1957.

Sports

Jim Thorpe

Thorpe, James Francis (Jim Thorpe), athlete; b. near Prague, Okla., May 28, 1888; s. Hiram and Charlotte (View) T.; m. Iva Miller, 1913; m. Frieda Kirkpatrick, 1926; m. Patricia Askew, 1945. Student, Carlisle (Pa.) Indian Indsl. Sch., 1907-12. Profl. baseball player NY Giants, 1913-19, Boston Braves, 1919; profl. football player Canton Bulldogs, 1915-17, 1919-20, 1926, Cleve. Indians, 1921, Oorang Indians, 1922-23, Rock Island Independents, 1924, NY Giants, 1925, Chgo. Cardinals, 1928; first pres. NFL, 1920. Author: (with T.F. Collison) Jim Thorpe's History of the Olympics, 1932. Named to Pro Football Hall of Fame, 1963. Achievements include leading Carlisle Indian Indsl. Sch.'s football team to Nat. Collegiate Championship, defeating Harvard, Army, U. Pa., U. Minn., 1912; being voted All Am. player, 1908, 11, 12; winning Olympic Gold Medals in decathlon and pentathlon, Stockholm, 1912; winning championships with Canton Bulldogs, 1916, 17, 19. Died Mar. 28, 1953.

Entertainment, Arts, and Letters

Edith Wharton

Wharton, Edith (Newbold Jones), novelist; b. N.Y., 1862; d. George Frederic and Lucretia Stevens (Rhinelander) Jones; m. Edward Wharton, 1885. LittD (hon.), Yale U., 1923. Author: The Greater Inclination, 1899, The Touchstone, 1900, Crucial Instances, 1901, The Valley of Decision, 1902, Sanctuary, 1903, The Descent of Man, and Other Stories, 1904, Italian Villas and Their Gardens, 1904, Italian Backgrounds, 1905, The House of Mirth, 1905, Madame de Treymes, 1907, The Fruit of the Tree, 1907, The Hermit and the Wild Woman, 1908, Motor-flight Through France, 1908, Artemis to Actaeon, 1909, Tales of Men and Ghosts, 1910, Ethan Frome, 1911, The Reef, 1912, The Custom of the Country, 1913, Xingu, 1916, Fighting France, 1915, Summer, 1917, The Marne, 1918, French Ways and Their Meaning, 1919, In Morocco, 1920, The Age of Innocence, 1920 (Pulitzer Prize for fiction, 1921), Glimpses of the Moon, 1922, A Son at the Front, 1923, False Dawn, 1924, New Year's Day, 1924, Old Maid, 1924, The Spark, 1924, The Mother's Recompense, 1925, The Writing of Fiction, 1925, Here and Beyond, 1926, Twilight Sleep, 1927, The Children, 1928, Hudson River Bracketed, 1929, Certain People, 1930, A Backward Glance (autobiography), 1934. Decorated Legion of Honor of France, Chevalier Order of Leopold of Belgium; recipient gold medal Nat. Inst. Arts and Scis. Mem. AAAL. Died Aug. 11, 1937.

1920's

Science and Technology

Philo Farnsworth

Farnsworth, Philo Taylor, research engineer; b. Beaver, Utah, Aug. 19, 1906; s. Louis Edwin and Serena (Bastian) F.; m. Elma Gardner, May 27, 1926; children: Philo Taylor, Kenneth Gardner (dec.), Russell S., Kent. Student, BYU, 1923-25; ScD (hon.), Ind. Inst. Tech., 1951; DSc (hon.), BYU, 1968. With Farnsworth Television and Radio Corp. and predecessor firms, Ft. Wayne, Ind., 1926-58; former pres., dir. Farnsworth Rsch. Corp. divsn. ITT; former v.p., tech. dir. Farnsworth Electronics Co.; lab cons. ITT. Founder, pres., dir. Philo T. Farnsworth Assocs. Inc. Holder of more than 300 U.S. and fgn. patents in television, radar and electronics. Recipient BYU Alumnus award, 1937, hon. mention Eta Kappa Nu, 1937, Morris Leibnan Meml. Prize Inst. Radio Engrs., 1941, 1st medal Television Broadcasters Assn., 1944, Disting. Alumnus award BYU, 1953; named one of 10 outstanding young Am. Pioneers, 1940. Fellow AAAS, IEEE; mem. Franklin Inst., Am. Phys. Soc., Sigma Xi, Eta Kappa Nu. Lds Ch. Achievements include invention of TV. Came up with idea at age 14. Applied for first patent in 1927, which was granted in 1930. Died Mar. 11, 1971; buried Provo UT.

Newsmaker

Charles Lindbergh

Lindbergh, Charles Augustus, aviator; b. Detroit, Feb. 4, 1902; s. Charles Augustus (mem. Congress from 6th Minn. Dist., 1907-17) and Evangeline Lodge (Land) L.; married Anne Spencer Morrow, May 27, 1929; children—Charles A. (dec.), Jon Morrow, Anne, Scott, Land Morrow, Reeve; Grad. high sch., Little Falls, Minn., 1918; matriculated in mech. engring., U. Wis., 1920; left univ. to enroll in Flying Sch., Lincoln, Neb., Feb. 1922; M. Aero., N.Y. U., 1928; LL.D., Northwestern U. and U. Wis., 1928; hon. M.S., Princeton, 1931. Made his first airplane flight April 9, 1922; first double parachute jump while on exhibition trip in Nebraska with another aviator, June 1922; bought first airplane - a Govt. "jenny" for $500, April, 1923 and took first flight alone the next day. Enrolled as flying cadet U.S. Air Service Res. at Brooks Field, San Antonio, Tex., Mar. 19, 1924, later advanced to col. 1st lt. Mo. N.G., 1925, later col. Made first flight as airmail pilot from Chgo. to St. Louis, April 15, 1926; went to San Diego, Calif. to order airship to be made, to be entitled The Spirit of St. Louis, Feb. 28, 1927; took off from San Diego in The Spirit of St. Louis May 10, 1927 and landed at Curtiss Field, Long Island., May 12, (stopping at St. Louis), flying time 21 hours, 20 minutes - a record achievement from coast to coast; took off alone May 20, 1927, on non-stop transatlantic flight, from Roosevelt Field N.Y. via New Foundland, Ireland and England and landed at Paris, France next day, covering an estimated distance of 3,600 miles in 33_ hours; given reception by French govt., and later at Brussels, London, Washington, N.Y.C.; officially welcomed by President Coolidge on return to Washington; subsequently given enthusiastic reception in New York and other American cities; made air tour to 75 cities in U.S. under auspices of Daniel Guggenheim Foundation for Promotion of Aeronautics, and upon invitation of President Calles of Mexico made non-stop flight from Washington, D.C. to Mexico City, a distance of 2,100 miles, in 27 hrs. 10 minutes; later visited Central America and West Indies, including Havana, Cuba. Made survey of U.S. airplane prodn. for U.S. Army, 1939; toured U.S. making radio speeches urging U.S. to keep out of war, 1941; with Ford Motor Co. at Willow Run bombing plant March, 1942. Helps found Transcontinental & Western Air (T&WA), later Trans World Airlines, 1929; dir. Pan Am. World Airways. Author: Of Flight and Life, 1948; The Spirit of St. Louis, 1953. Trustee Panamin Found., Inc., Carnegie Instn., 1934; World Wildlife Bd. Trustees, 1966-72; civilian advisor Pacific Theatre, developed fuel efficient methods to increase range of fighter planes, flew 50 combat missions, 1944; recommissioned to Air Force by Pres. Eisenhower and promoted to brigadier general, 1954. Recipient Congl. Medal of Honor (U.S.), Distinguished Flying Cross, Distinguished Service Cross; Woodrow Wilson medal and 25,000 for good will flight to Mexico, Central Am. and West Indies, Langley medal (Smithsonian Instn.); Hubbard Medal (Nat. Geog. Soc.); Cross of Honor (U.S. Flag Assn.); Medal of Valor (N.Y. State); German Eagle, 1938 and many others; decorated Chevalier Legion of Honor (French); Royal Air Cross (Brit.); Order of Leopold (Belgian) and others; Winner Orteig 25,000 prize for 1st N.Y. to Paris nonstop flight, also various other tokens of recognition; recipient Wright Bros. Meml. Trophy, 1949, Guggenheim Medal, 1954; Pulitzer award, Distinguished Am. biography, 1954. Died Aug. 26, 1974.

Business and Industry

David Sarnoff

Sarnoff, David, communications executive; b. Uzlian, Minsk, Russia, Feb. 27, 1891; came to U.S., 1900; s. Abraham and Lena (Privin) S.; m. Lizette Hermant, July 4, 1917; children: Robert William, Edward, Thomas Warren. Student, Pratt Inst.; DSc, St. Lawrence U., 1927, Marietta Coll., 1935, Suffolk U., 1939, Pa. Mil. Coll., 1952; DLitt, Norwich U., 1935; DCS, Oglethorpe U., 1938, Boston U., 1948; LLD, Jewish Theol. Sem. Am., 1946, Bethany Coll., 1946, John Carroll U., 1950, U. Pa., 1952, Fairleigh Dickinson Coll., 1953, U. So. Calif. Pratt Inst., 1954; LHD, U. Louisville, 1950; D in Engring., Drexel Inst. Tech., 1953; DSc, U. Notre Dame, 1955, Temple U., 1958; LLD, Fordham U., 1955, Dropsie Coll., 1957, U. R.I., 1957. Messenger boy Comml. Cable Co., N.Y.C., 1906; office boy Marconi Wireless Telegraph Co., N.Y.C., 1906-09; mgr. Marconi Sta., Sea Gate, N.Y., 1909-11; wireless operator SS. Harvard, 1910, John Wanamaker's, N.Y.C., 1911-12; from radio inspector to comml. mgr. Marconi Co., N.Y.C., 1912-19; from comml. mgr. to pres. RCA Comm. Inc. (formerly Marconi Co.), N.Y.C., 1919-30, chmn. bd., 1947-69, hon. chmn., 1970-71; founder subsid. Nat. Broadcasting Co. (NBC), 1926. Wireless operator S.S. Beothic, Newfoundland, equipped vessel and made trip as operator to Arctic ice fields on sealfishing expds., 1911; instr. Marconi Inst., 1912; bd. dirs. Chatham Sq. Music Sch. Author: Looking Ahead, 1968. Trustee Am. Heritage Found., Ednl. Alliance, Thomas A. edison Found., Nat. Found. Infantile Paralysis, United Seamen/s Svc., Inc., U.S. Coun. Internat. C. of C., Pratt Inst., N.Y.U., councillor; bd. dirs. Armed Forces Comms. Assn.; nat. chmn. Am. Red Cross Fund Campaign, 1954; chmn. Nat. Security Tng. Commn., 1955. Commd. lt. col., S.C. Res., U.S. Army, 1924, col., 1931, brig. gen., 1944; brig. gen. Army of U.S. Hon. Res. Decorated Officer Polonia Restituta (Poland), Chevalier Legion of Honor, Officer Legion of Honor, Comdr. Legion of Honor (France), Officer Order Oaken Crown (Luxembourg), Legion of Merit, Medal for Merit, U.S. Treasury's Silver Medal, Richard J.H. Gettheil Medal; recipient Horation Alger award, 1951, Gold Citizenship Medal and Citation of VFW, 1950, Pub. Svc. award of merit Civl Svc. Leader, 1951, Ann. award Radio-TV Mfrs. Assn., 1952, Founder award Inst. Radio Engrs., 1953, First ann. Keynoter award Nat. Assn. Radio and TV Broadcasters, 1953, Engring. and Sci. award Drexel Inst. Tech., 1953, numerous others; hon. fellow Weizmann Inst. Sci. Fellow IEEE, Royal Soc. Arts (London); mem. Brit. Instn. Radio Engrs. (hon.), Acad. Polit. Sci., Armed Forces Adv. Com., N.Y. State C. of C., Coun. Fgn. Rels., Mil. Govt. Assn., Mil. Order World Wars, Nat. Aero. Assn., Nat. Inst. Social Scis., N.Y. Soc. Mil. and Naval Officers World Wars, Grant Monument Assn. (trustee), Naval Order U.S. (life), U.S. Naval Inst., Am. Shakespeare Festival Found., Crusade for Freedom (chmn. greater N.Y. com. 1951), Newcomen Soc. Eng., Res. Officers Assn., Radio Pioneers, Vet. Wireless Operators Assn., Radio Club Am., India House Club, Century Country Club, Lotos Club, Rockefeller Ctr. Luncheon Club (N.Y.C.), Army-Navy Club, Met. Club, Fed. City Club (Washington), Beta Gamma Sigma, Tau Delta Phi. Achievements include coming up with idea for "radio music box" that would make the radio a "household utility". Died Dec. 12, 1971; buried Valhalla Cemetery Valhalla NY.

Sports

Babe Ruth

Ruth, Babe (George Herman Ruth), professional baseball player; b. Balt., Feb. 6, 1894; m. Helen Woodford, 1914 (dec.); d., Dorothy; m. Claire Hodgson, Apr. 1929; 1 adopted step daughter, Julia. Signed as pitcher-outfielder Balt. Orioles (Balt.-Providence Club of Internat. League), 1913; pitcher Boston Red Sox, 1914-20; outfielder N.Y. Yankees, N.Y.C., 1920-34; v.p., asst. mgr., part-time player Boston Braves (Nat. League), 1935; coach Bklyn. Dodgers (Nat. League), 1938. Voted most valuable player Am. League, 1923; mem. Am. League All Star Team, 1933; played in 10 World Series, 1915, 16, 18, 21, 22, 23, 26, 27, 28, 32, total of 41 games; in total series games made most runs (37), most home runs (15), most strikeouts (30); pitched most innings in Series game, Boston against Bklyn., Oct. 9, 1916; as pitcher had most consecutive scoreless innings in total Series, 29 2/3 (13 1/3, Oct. 9, 1916; 9, Sept. 5, 1918; 7 1/3, Sept. 9, 1918); held lowest earned run average in season for left-handed pitcher, Boston (Am. League), 1.75, 1916; highest batting average in Am. League, .692 for 21 yrs.; held numerous other records, including: most runs in season, Am. League, 177 in 152 games, 1921; most home runs in major leagues, 714 (708 Am. League, 6 Nat. League), 1914-35; most home runs in season, 60 in 151 games, 1927; most yrs. leading Am. League in home runs, 12 (1918-25 and 1926-31); most runs batted in, Am. League, 2197 (1914-34); most yrs. leading Am. League in runs batted in, 6 (1919-23, 1926, 1928); world record for strikeouts, 1330 in 22 yrs. Broadcast radio program, 1943-44; appeared in films, including Pride of the Yankees, 1942; cons. to William Bendix in his role as Babe Ruth, in The Babe Ruth Story. Died Aug. 16, 1948.

Entertainment, Arts, and Letters

F. Scott Fitzgerald

Fitzgerald, Francis Scott Key (F. Scott Fitzgerald), writer; b. St. Paul, Sept. 24, 1896; s. Edward and Mary (McQuillan) F.; m. Zelda Sayre, Apr. 3, 1920; d. Frances Scott. Student, Newman Sch., Lakewood, N.J., 1911–13, Princeton U., 1913-17. Screenwriter Metro Goldwyn Mayer, 1937–38. Author (novels): This Side of Paradise, 1920, The Beautiful and Damned, 1922, The Great Gatsby, 1925, Tender Is the Night, 1934, The Last Tycoon (an unfinished novel), 1941; (short story collections) Flappers and Philosophers, 1920, Tales of the Jazz Age, 1922, All the Sad Young Men, 1926, Taps at Reveille, 1935; (plays) The Vegetable, 1923. Served to 1st lt., U.S. Army Inf., 1917-19, adc Brig. Gen. J.A. Ryan, 1918-19. Died Dec. 21, 1940.

1930's

Science and Technology

Robert Goddard

Goddard, Robert Hutchings, physicist; b. Worcester, Mass., Oct. 5, 1882; s. Nahum Danford and Fannie Louise (Hoyt) G.; m. Esther Christine Kisk, June 21, 1924. BS, Worcester Poly. Inst., 1908; AM, Clark U., 1910, PhD, 1911, ScD, 1945. Instr. Worcester Poly. Inst., 1909-11, Princeton U., 1912-13; instr. and fellow, physics Clark U., 1914-15, asst. prof., 1915-19, prof., 1919-43; dir. of rsch. Bur. of Aeronautics, Navy Dept., 1942-45. Engaged in rocket rsch. under Daniel and Florence Guggenheim Found. grants; cons. engr. Curtiss-Wright Corp., 1943-45; dir. rsch. U.S. Signal Corps, Worcester Poly. Inst. and Mt. Wilson Observatory, Calif., World War, 1918. Fellow AAAS; mem. Am. Phys. Soc., Am. Meteorol. Soc., Inst. Aeronautical Scis., Nat. Aeronautic Assn., Geophys. Union, Sigma Xi, Sigma Alpha Epsilon. Achievements include pioneering research on rockets; world's first flight of a liquid-fuel rocket, 1926. Died Aug. 10, 1945.

Newsmaker

Franklin Delano Roosevelt

Roosevelt, Franklin Delano, 32nd President of the United States; b. Hyde Park, N.Y., Jan. 30, 1882; s. James and Sara (Delano) R.; m. Anna Eleanor Roosevelt, Mar. 17, 1905; children: Anna Eleanor Boettiger, James, Elliott, Franklin D., John A. BA, Harvard U., 1904; postgrad., Columbia U. Law Sch., 1904-07; LLD, Rutgers U., 1933, William and Mary Coll., 1934, U. Notre Dame, 1935; LittD, Rollins Coll., 1936; D in Civil Law, Oxford (Eng.) U., 1941. Bar: N.Y. 1907. Lawyer Carter, Ledyard & Milburn, N.Y.C., 1907-10; ptnr. Roosevelt & O'Connor, N.Y.C., 1924-33; mem. N.Y. State Senate, 1910-13; resigned, 1913; asst. sec. U.S. Navy, 1913-20; gov. State of N.Y., 1929-33; pres. U.S., 1933-45; established programs including Pub. Works Adminstrn., TVA, Nat. Recovery Act. In charge of inspection U.S. Naval forces in European waters, 1918, and of demobilization in Europe, 1919. Author: Whither

Bound, 1926, The Happy Warrior–Alfred E. Smith, 1928, Government–Not Politics, 1932, Looking Forward, 1933, On Our Way, 1934. Dem. nominee for v.p. of U.S., 1920; mem. Hudson-Fulton Celebration Commn., 1909, Plattsburgh Centennial, 1913; mem. Nat. Commn. Panama P.I. Expedition, 1915; overseer Harvard U., 1918-24; pres. Am. Nat. Red Cross, Ga. Warm Spring Found.; sr. warden St. James Episc. Ch., Hyde Park. Mem. Naval History Soc., N.Y. Hist. Soc., Holland Soc., Alpha Delta Phi, Phi Beta Kappa, Masons. Democrat. Episcopalian. Died Apr. 12, 1945; interred at Hyde Park, N.Y.

Business and Industry

Walt Disney

Disney, Walter E., producer, animator; b. Chgo., Dec. 5, 1901; s. Elias and Flora (Call) D.; m. Lillian Marie Bounds, July 13, 1925; children: Diane (Mrs. Ron Miller), Sharon (Mrs. Robert Brown). MS (hon.), U. So. Calif., 1938; MA (hon.), Yale U., 1938, Harvard U., 1940; AFD (hon.), UCLA, 1963. Comml. artist, 1919; cartoonist Kansas City Film Ad, 1920-22; prodr. Alice Comedies, N.Y.C., 1923-26, Oswald, the Rabbit for Universal, 1926-28; bd. dirs., exec. prodr. Walt Disney Prodns., from 1928. Founder Disneyland, 1954; prodr. Disneyland TV and Mickeymouse Club TV programs over ABC-TV, 1954–. Prodr.: Mickey Mouse, Silly Symphony Cartoons, from 1928, Three Little Pigs, 1933 (cert. from Acad. Motion Picture Arts), Snow White and the Seven Dwarfs (Acad. Motion Picture Arts and Scis. award), 1938, Ferdinand the Bull, 1939, Fantasia (plaque Dowling Found., scroll N.Y. Critics of N.Y.C., medal N.Y. Schs. Music), Pinocchio, 1940, The Reluctant Dragon, Dumbo, 1941, Bambi, 1942, Saludos Amigos, 1942, Victory Through Air Power, 1943, The Three Caballeros, 1944, Make Mine Music, 1946, Song of the South, 1946, Fun and Fancy Free, 1947, Melody Time, 1948, So Dear to My Heart, 1949, Ichabod and Mr. Toad, 1949, Cinderella, 1950, Treasure Island, 1950, Alice in Wonderland, 1951, The Story of Robin Hood, 1952, Peter Pan, 1953, Sword and Rose, 1953, Rob Roy, 1954, 20,000 Leagues Under the Sea, 1954, Siam, 1954, Lady and the Tramp, 1955, other true life adventure nature films; elaborated true-life adventures to full features including: The Living Desert, 1953, The Vanishing Prairie, 1954, The African Lion, 1955, Secrets of Life, 1956; prodr. live action features: Littlest Outlaw, 1955, Johnny Tremain, Old Yeller, Westward Ho, The Wagons, 1957, Lapland, Blue Men of Morocco, of the People and Places series, released to 1957; prodr. TV shows Zorro, 1957, Walt Disney Presents, 1958-61, Walt Disney's Wonderful World of Color, NBC-TV, 1961-66; pictures include: Sleeping Beauty, The Shaggy Dog, Darby O'Gill and the Little People, Third Man on the Mountain, 1959, Toby Tyler, Kidnapped, The Sign of Zorro, Pollyanna, Jungle Cat, Ten Who Dared, Swiss Family Robinson, 1960, One Hundred and One Dalmations, The Absent Minded Professor, Nikki, Wild Dog of the North, Greyfriars Bobby, The Parent Trap, Babes in Toyland, 1961, Moon Pilot, Bon Voyage, Big Red, Almost Angels, The Legend of Lobo, in Search of the Castaways, 1962, Son of Flubber, Miracle of the White Stallions, Savage Sam, Summer Magic, The Incredible Journey, The Sword in the Stone, 1963, The Misadventures of Merlin Jones, A Tiger Walks, The Three Lives of Thomasina, The Moon Spinners, Mary Poppins, Emil and the Detectives, 1964. Served as R.C. ambulance driver, AEF, France, 1918-19. Recipient 39 awards Acad. Motion Picture Arts and Scis., 4 Emmy awards Acad. TV Arts and Scis., more than 800 awards and decorations for work. Mem. Order DeMolay, Am. Soc. French Legion of Honor, Art Workers' Guild of London (hon.). Died Dec. 15, 1966.

Sports

Jesse Owens

Owens, Jesse (James Cleveland Owens), former Olympic athlete, public relations executive; b. Danville, Ala., Sept. 12, 1913; s. Henry and Emma (Alexander) O.; m. Ruth Solomon, 1931; children: Gloria, Beverly, Marlene. AB, Ohio State U., 1937. Mem. U.S. Olympic Track Team, Berlin, Germany, 1936; with Office Civilian Def., Phila., 1940-42; dir. Negro personnel Ford Motor Co., 1942-46; sec. Ill. Athletic Commn., Chgo., 1952-55; former sports specialist Ill. Youth Commn.; pres. Jesse Owens & Assocs., Chgo. Briefly led orch. and acted in films; ambassador of sports U.S. Dept. of State, 1955. With mil. WWII. Mem. Alpha Phi Alpha, Elks. Achievements include setting three world records and tying a 4th at Big 10 Championships, 1935; winning four Olympic Gold Medals for 100-meter dash, 200-meter dash, broad jump, and as part of 400-meter relay team, Berlin, 1936. Baptist. Died Mar. 31, 1980.

Entertainment, Arts, and Letters

John Steinbeck

Steinbeck, John Ernst, writer; b. Salinas, Calif., Feb. 27, 1902; s. John Ernst and Olive (Hamilton) S.; m. Carol Henning, 1930 (div. 1943); m. Gwyn Conger, Mar. 29, 1943; children: Tom, John; m. Elaine Scott, Dec. 28, 1950. Student, Stanford U., 1919. War columnist overseas. Author: (novels) Cup of Gold, 1929, The Pastures of Heaven, 1932, To a God Unknown, 1933, Tortilla Flat, 1935, In Dubious Battle, 1936, Of Mice and Men, 1937, The Red Pony, 1937, The Grapes of Wrath, 1939, The Forgotten Village, 1941, The Moon is Down, 1942, Cannery Row, 1945, The Wayward Bus, 1947, The Pearl, 1947, Burning Bright, 1950, East of Eden, 1952, Sweet Thursday, 1954, The Short Reign of Pippin IV, 1957, The Winter of Our Discontent, 1961; (short stories) Saint Katy the Virgin, 1936, Nothing So Monstrous, 1936, How Edith McGillicuddy Met R.L.S., 1943, The Crapshooter, 1957; (short story collection) The Long Valley, 1938; (non-fiction) Their Blood is Strong, 1938, Sea of Cortez, 1941, Bombs Away, 1942, A Russian Journal, 1948, Once There Was a War, 1958, Travels with Charley, 1962, America and Americans, 1966. Recipient Pulitzer Prize, 1940, Nobel Prize for lit., 1962, Presdl. Medal of Freedom, 1964. Died Dec. 20, 1968.

1940's

Science and Technology

J. Robert Oppenheimer

Oppenheimer, J. Robert (Robert Oppenheimer), physicist; b. N.Y.C., Apr. 22, 1904; s. Julius S. and Ella (Freedman) O.; m. Katherine Puening Harrison, Nov., 1940; children: Peter, Katherine. AB, Harvard U., 1925; postgrad., Cambridge (Eng.) U., 1925-26; PhD, Göttingen U., 1927. Nat. rsch. fellow, 1927-28; Internat. Edn. Bd. fellow U. Leyden, U. Zurich, 1928-29; asst. prof. physics U. Calif., Calif. Inst. Tech., 1929-31, assoc. prof., 1931–36, prof., 1936–47; dir., prof. physics Inst. for Advanced Study, Princeton U., 1947-67. Dir. Los Alamos (N.Mex.) Sci. Lab., 1943-45, chmn., gen. advisory com., Atomic Energy Commn., 1946-53 Recipient Enrico Fermi award, 1964. Achievements include directing the Manhattan Project which successfully developed and tested the first atom bomb on July 16, 1945 in Alamogordo, N. Mex. Died Feb. 18, 1967.

Newsmaker

George C. Marshall

Marshall, George Catlett, military officer; b. Uniontown, Pa., Dec. 31, 1880; s. George Catlett and Laura (Bradford) M.; m. Elizabeth Carter Coles, Feb. 11, 1902 (dec. 1927); m. Katherine Boyce Tupper Brown, Oct. 15, 1930); stepchildren: Molly B. Winn., Clifton Stevenson (dec.), Lt. Allen Tupper. Student, Va. Mil. Inst., 1897–1901; hon. grad., U.S. Inf.-Cav. Sch., 1907; grad., Army Staff Coll., 1908; DSc, Washington and Jefferson Coll., 1939; PhD Mil. Sci, Pa. Mil. Coll., 1940, Norwich U., 1942; LLD, William and Mary Coll., 1941, Trinity Coll., 1941, Columbia U., 1947, Princeton, 1947. Commd. 2nd lt. inf., 1901; promoted through grade to maj. gen., 1939; instr. Army Staff Coll., 1908-10; with A.E.F., 1917-19; gen. staff qst divsn., chief ops. 1st Army chief staff 8th Army Corps.; instr. Army War Coll., 1927; asst. comdt. Inf. Sch., 1927-32; comdr. 8th Inf., 1933; sr. instr. Ill. Nat. Guard, 1933-36; comdg. gen. 5th Brig. U.S. Army, 1936-38; chief war plans div. gen. staff, 1938; deputy chief staff U.S. Army, 1938-39; chief staff, 1939; chief staff rank of gen., 1939-45; gen. Army, 1944. Apptd. spl. rep. of Pres. to China with personal rank of Ambassador, 1945; coun. of fgn. min., Moscow, London, U.N. Gen. Assembly, N.Y., 1947; appt. sec. state 1947; sec. def. 1950-51; pres. ARC, 1949-50; chmn. U.S. del. Coronation Queen Elizabeth, 1953. Recipient Gold Medal, D.S.M. with oak leaf cluster Silver Star, Victory Medal with 5 bars U.S., Croix de Guerre with Palm, Silver Medal of Valor (Montenegro), Grand Croix Legion of Honor (France), Officer Order of Saints Maurice and Lazarus, Officer Order of the Crown, Italy, Order of La Soledaridad, Panama, Grand Comdr. Order of Merit, Brazil, Star of Aldon Calderon, Ecuador, Gran Oficial del Sol del Peru, Grand Cross of Ouissam Alaouite, Morocco, Military Order of Merit, 1st Class, Cuba, Order del Merito, Chile, Knight Grand Cross, Order of the Bath, Britain, Order of Suvarov, 1st Degree, USSR, Theodore Roosevelt Disting. Svc. Medal of Honor, 1945, Varieties Clubs Humanitarian award, 1947, Freedom House award, 1947, Nat. Planning Assn. Gold Medal, 1949, Nat. Civic Svc. award, Order Eagles, 1949, N.Y. Bd. Trade award for Disting. svc. and contbrn. to Am. Way, 1949, U.S. Conf. of Mayors award for Disting. Pub. Svc., 1949, Disabled Am. Vets. N.Y. Chpt. Citizenship award, 1950, Disting. Svc. Medal, Am. Legion, 1951, Four Freedoms Found. award, 1952, Nobel Peace Prize, 1953. Mem. Soc. Cin., Kappa Alpha; Clubs: Army and Navy, Alibi Washington, Army and Navy Country, Army and Navy San Francisco, Metropolitan N.Y. Achievements include authoring Marshall Plan for post-war recovery in Europe, 1947. Episcopalian. Died Oct. 16, 1959; buried Arlington Nat. Cemetery.

Business and Industry

William Levitt

Levitt, William Jaird, builder; b. Bklyn., Feb. 11, 1907; s. Abraham and Pauline (Biederman) L.; m. Rhoda Kirshner, Nov. 16, 1929; children: William Jaird, James R.; m. Alice Kenny, Jan., 1959; m. Simone Korchin, Nov. 1969. DCS, St. John's U.; LHD, Yeshiva U.; PhD, Bar Ilan U. Founder-chmn. Levitt & Sons, Inc., until 1969; chmn. bd. William J. Levitt, Inc., Levitt Industries, Inc., Internat. Community Corp. Bd. overseers Albert Einstein Coll. Medicine; bd. dirs. Am. Health Found.; trustee North Shore U. Hosp.; pres. Levitt Found. Served as lt. USNR, 1942-45, PTO. Recipient Frank P. Brown medal Franklin Inst. Pa., 1965. Achievements include creating Levittown, 1st mass produced home devel. Home: Greenvale, NY. Died Jan. 28, 1994.

Sports

Jackie Robinson

Robinson, Jack Roosevelt (Jackie Robinson), former professional baseball player, entrepreneur; b. Cairo, Ga., Jan. 31, 1919; s. Jerry and Mallie (McGriff) Robinson; m. Rachel A. Isum, Feb. 10, 1946; children: Jack Roosevelt Jr. (dec. 1971), Sharon A., David R. Student, Pasadena Jr. Coll., UCLA, 1939-41; LLD (hon.), Bethune Cookman Coll., 1951, Howard U., 1957. Profl. football player LA Bulldogs (Pacific Coast Football League), 1941, Honolulu Bears, 1941; profl. basketball player LA Red Devils, 1946–47; baseball player Kansas City Monarchs, Am. Negro League, 1945; profl. baseball player signed contract with Bklyn. Dodgers, 1945, played with Montreal Royals farm team, 1946, Bklyn. Dodgers, 1947–56; traded to NY Giants, 1956; ret., 1957; v.p. Chock Full O'Nuts Co., NYC, 1957–64; co-founder Freedom Nat. Bank of Harlem, 1964, chmn. bd., 1964–72; staff mem. Gov. Nelson Rockefeller, 1964–68, spl. asst. for cmty. affairs; worked on campaign of presdl. candidate Hubert H. Humphrey, 1968; founder Jackie Robinson Constrn. Co., 1970. Author: (with Alfred Duckett) I Never Had it Made: An Autobiography of Jackie Robinson, 1972. Mem. bd. parole Conn. State Prison; bd. dirs., cons. ATI; dir. YMCA Greater NYC, bd. mgrs. Harlem branch Served to 2nd lt. U.S. Army, 1942–44. Named Rookie of Yr., Major League Baseball, 1947, MVP, 1949; named to All-Star Team, 1949–56, UCLA Hall of Fame, 1984; recipient Alumni of Yr. Award, UCLA, 1962, Presdl. Medal Freedom, 1984. Mem. NAACP (chmn. Fight for Freedom Fund 1957, Spingarn Medal 1956), Nat. Conf. Christians and Jews. Achievements include First black baseball player in the US major leagues in the 20th century. Played his first major league game on April 15, 1947; Member of the Bklyn. Dodgers World Series Championship Team, 1955; Inducted into the Baseball Hall of Fame, July 23, 1962; Major League Baseball's Rookie of Yr. Award renamed Jackie Robinson Award, 1987; Major League Baseball dedicated the 1997 season to him. Died Oct. 24, 1972.

Entertainment, Arts, and Letters

Humphrey Bogart

Bogart, Humphrey DeForest, actor, producer; b. NYC, Dec. 25, 1899; s. Belmont DeForest and Maude (Humphrey) Bogart; m. Helen Menken, May 20, 1926 (div. 1927); m. Mary Philips, Apr. 3, 1928 (div. 1937); m. Mayo Methot, Aug. 21, 1938 (div. 1945); m. Lauren Bacall, May 21, 1945; children: Stephen Humphrey, Leslie Howard. Grad., Trinity Sch., NYC, 1916; student, Phillips Acad., Andover, Mass. Founder prodn. co. Santana Pictures, 1947. Actor: (films) Life, 1920, Up the River, 1930, A Devil with Women, 1930, Body and Soul, 1931, The Bad Sister, 1931, A Holy Terror, 1931, Love Affair, 1932, Big City Blues, 1932, Three on a Match, 1932, Midnight, 1934, The Petrified Forest, 1936, Bullets or Ballots, 1936, Two Against the World, 1936, China Clipper, 1936, Isle of Fury, 1936, Black Legion, 1937, The Great O'Malley, 1937, Marked Woman, 1937, Kid Galahad, 1937, San Quentin, 1937, Dead End, 1937, Stand-In, 1937, Swing Your Lady, 1938, Crime School, 1938, Racket Busters, 1938, Men Are Such Fools, 1938, The Amazing Dr. Clitterhouse, 1938, Angels with Dirty Faces, 1938, King of the Underworld, 1939, The Oklahoma Kid, 1939, Dark Victory, 1939, You Can't Get Away with Murder, 1939, The Roaring Twenties, 1939, The Return of Doctor X, 1939, Invisible Stripes, 1939, Virginia City, 1940, It All Came True, 1940, Brother Orchid, 1940, They Drive by Night, 1940, High Sierra, 1941, The Wagons Roll at Night, 1941, The Maltese Falcon, 1941, All Through the Night, 1942, The B[illegible] Shot, 1942, Across the Pacific, 1942, Casablanca, 1942 (Acad. Awar[illegible] nomination for best actor, 1944), Action in the North Atlantic, 194[illegible] Sahara, 1943, Passage to Marseille, 1944, To Have and Have Not, 194[illegible] Conflict, 1945, The Big Sleep, 1946, Dead Reckoning, 1947, The Tw[illegible] Mrs. Carrolls, 1947, Dark Passage, 1947, The Treasure of the Sierr[illegible] Madre, 1948, Key Largo, 1948, Knock on Any Door, 1949, Tokyo Jo[illegible] 1949, Chain Lightning, 1950, In a Lonely Place, 1950, The Enforce[illegible] 1951, Sirocco, 1951, The African Queen, 1951 (Acad. Award for be[illegible] actor, 1952), Deadline - U.S.A., 1952, Battle Circus, 1953, Beat th[illegible] Devil, 1953, The Caine Mutiny, 1954 (Acad. Award nomination for be[illegible] actor, 1955), Sabrina, 1954, The Barefoot Contessa, 1954, We're N[illegible] Angels, 1955, The Left Hand of God, 1955, The Desperate Hours, 1955 The Harder They Fall, 1956. Served USN. Named Greatest Male Star [illegible] All Time, Am. Film Inst., 1999. Died Jan. 14, 1957; buried Forest Law[illegible] Meml. Park.

1950's

Science and Technology

Jonas Salk

Salk, Jonas Edward, physician, scientist; b. NYC, Oct. 28, 1914; s[illegible] Daniel B. and Dora (Press) Salk; m. Donna Lindsay Salk, June 8, 1939 children: Peter Lindsay, Darrell John, Jonathan Daniel; m. Francoise Gilot, June 29, 1970. BS, CCNY, 1934, LLD (hon.), 1955; MD, NYU 1939, ScD (hon.), 1955; LLD (hon.), U. Pitts., 1955; PhD (hon.) Hebrew U., 1959; LLD (hon.), Roosevelt U., 1955; ScD (hon.), Turin U. 1957, U. Leeds, 1959; ScD (hon.), Hahnemann Med. Coll., 1959; ScD (hon.), Franklin and Marshall U., 1960; DHL (hon.), Yeshiva U., 1959 LLD (hon.) , Tuskegee Inst., 1964. Fellow in chemistry NYU, 1935–37 fellow in exptl. surgery, 1937–38, fellow in bacteriology, 1939–40; Intern Mt. Sinai Hosp., NYC, 1940–42; NRC fellow Sch. Pub. Health, U Mich., 1942–43, research fellow epidemiology, 1943–44, research assoc., 1944–46, asst. prof. epidemiology, 1946–47; assoc. research prof. bacteriology Sch. Medicine, U. Pitts., 1947–49, dir. virus research lab., 1947–63, research prof. bacteriology, 1949–55, Commonwealth prof. preventive medicine, 1955–57, Commonwealth prof. exptl. medicine, 1957–63; founder and dir. Salk Inst. Biol. Studies, 1963–75, resident fellow, 1963–84, founding dir., from 1976, disting. prof. internat. health scis., from 1984. Cons. epidemic diseases sec. war, 1944–47; sec. army, 1947–54; mem. commn. on influenza Army Epidemiol. Bd., 1944–54, acting dir. commn. on influenza, 1944; mem. expert adv. panel on virus diseases WHO; adj. prof. health scis., depts. psychiatry, cmty. medicine and medicine U. Calif., San Diego, 1970. Author: Man Unfolding, 1972, The Survival of the Wisest, 1973, Anatomy of Reality, 1983; (with Jonathan Salk) World Population and Human Values: A New Reality, 1981; contbr. articles to sci. jours. Decorated chevalier Legion of Honor France, officer; recipient Criss award, 1955, Lasker award, 1956, Gold medal of Congress and presdl. citation, 1955, Howard Ricketts award, 1957, Robert Koch medal, 1963, Mellon Inst. award, 1969, Presdl. medal of Freedom, 1977, Jawaharlal Nehru award for internat. understanding, 1979, Jehan Sadat Peace award (posthumous), Women's Internat. Ctr., 2004. Fellow: APHA, AAAS, Am. Acad. Pediat. (hon.; assoc.); mem.: Soc. Exptl. Biology and Medicine, Assn. Am. Physicians, Inst. Medicine (sr.), Am. Acad. Neurology, Am. Coll. Preventive Medicine, Delta Omega, Alpha Omega Alpha, Phi Beta Kappa. Achievements include development of vaccine, preventive of poliomyelitis, 1955 (refused to patent vaccine, thereby receiving no personal profits from the discovery). Died June 23, 1995.

Newsmaker

Rosa Parks

Parks, Rosa Louise, civil rights activist; b. Tuskegee, Ala., Feb. 4, 1913; d. James and Leona McCauley; m. Raymond Parks, Dec. 18, 1932 (dec. 1977). Student, Ala. State Teachers Coll.; hon. degree, Shaw Coll. Former seamstress and housekeeper, Montgomery, Ala., Detroit, from 1957; office mgr. for Congressman John Conyers, Jr., from 1965; co-founder Rosa and Raymond Parks Inst. for Self-Development, Detroit, 1987–. Author: Quiet Strength, 1994; guest appearance: (TV series) Touched by an Angel, 1999 (31st NAACP Image award for outstanding supporting actress in a drama series for Touched by an Angel, 2000). Formerly active Montgomery Voters League; mem. youth coun. NAACP, sec. Montgomery br., 1943; active SCLC. Recipient Spingarn medal NAACP, 1970, Martin Luther King Jr. award, 1980, Congl. Gold Medal of Honor, 1999. Achievements include triggering the Montgomery bus boycott after her arrest on Dec. 1, 1955 for refusing to give up her seat to a white passenger; the 382-day bus boycott (organized by Martin Luther King Jr. and other civil rights leaders) led to the 1956 U.S. Supreme Court ruling that the Alabama bus segregation laws were unconstitutional. Office: Rosa & Raymond Park Inst Ste 2200 65 Cadillac Sq Detroit MI 48226

Business and Industry

Ruth Handler

Handler, Ruth, inventor, manufacturing executive; b. Denver, Colo., Nov. 4, 1916; d. Jacob and Ida Mosko; m. Elliot Handler, June 26, 1938; children: Barbara, Ken. Studied, Art Center College of Design, Pasadena, Calif. Co-founder (with Elliot Handler) Mattel Creations (later Mattel, Inc.), Hawthorne, Calif., 1945, exec. v.p., 1948–67, named pres., 1967, co-chmn., 1973–75; founder, pres. line of prosthetic breasts, Nearly Me, for cancer survivors Ruthton Corp., 1975–91. Autobiography Dream Doll: The Ruth Handler Story, 1994. Achievements include spokesperson and advocate for early breast cancer detection after surviving the disease; inventing the Barbie Doll in 1959, the first mass-marketed adult-looking doll for girls; The Barbie Doll set sales records for Mattel - in its first year, 350,000 were sold; by 2002 over 1 billion Barbies had been sold in over 150 countries. Died Apr. 27, 2002.

Sports

Willie Mays

Mays, Willie Howard, Jr., (Say Hey Kid), retired professional baseball player; b. Westfield, Ala., May 6, 1931; s. William Howard and Ann M.; m. Margherite Wendell Chapman, 1956 (div. 1961), 1 adopted son, Michael; m. Mae Louise Allen, Nov. 27, 1971. LHD (hon.), Yale Univ., 2004. Baseball player Birmingham Black Barons, 1948-50, Trenton Inter-State League, 1950-51, Mpls. Millers, Am. Assn., 1951, N.Y. Giants, 1951-57, San Francisco Giants, 1958-72, N.Y. Mets, 1972-73; with Bally's Park Place, Atlantic City, 1980–; pub. rels. exec. San Francisco Giants, 1986-98, retired, 1998. Author: Willie Mays: My Life In and Out of Baseball, 1966, Say Hey: The Autobiography of Willie Mays, 1988. Served with AUS, 1952-54. Named Most Valuable Player Nat. League, 1954, 65; named Player of Yr. Sporting News, 1954, Baseball Player of Decade Sporting News, 1970, Male Athlete of Yr. AP, 1954, NL Rookie of Yr., 1951, Sporting News Player of the Year award, 1954, All-Star Game, 1954-73; recipient Hickok belt, 1954, Golden Bat ward to commemorate 600 home runs, Gold Glove award (12 times), st Commissioner's award, 1970, Golden Plate awarded to America's Captains of Achievement by Am. Acad. Achievement, 1976, Spirit of Life ward City of Hope, 1988, Sportsman of Decade, Cong. Racial Equality, 991, Legendary Star award HBO Video; inducted into Ala. Sports Hall f Fame, Baseball Hall of Fame, 1979, Black Hall of Fame, 1973, Calif. Sports Hall of Fame. Achievements include being the holder of 4th place n major league homeruns (660); lifetime batting average of .302; signed fetime pub. rels. contract with San Francisco Giants, 1993. Office: Baseball Hall of Fame PO Box 590 Cooperstown NY 13326-0590

Duke Snider

Snider, Edwin D. (Duke Snider), retired baseball player; b. L.A., Sept. 9, 1926; Baseball player Bklyn. Dodgers, 1947-57, N.Y. Mets, 1963, San Francisco Giants, 1964; scout L.A. Dodgers, 1965, 67-68; minor league mgr., 1965-68; batting instr., broadcaster San Diego Padres, 1969-71; broadcaster Montreal Expos, 1973. Named to Baseball Hall of Fame, 980; selected to All-Star Team, 1950, 52-56, 63; mem. World Series Champions, 1954. Office: c/o Nat Baseball Hall Fame PO Box 590 Cooperstown NY 13326-0590

Mickey Mantle

Mantle, Mickey Charles, former professional baseball player, marketing consultant; b. Spavinaw, Okla., Oct. 20, 1931; s. Elvin Clark and Lovell (Richardson) M.; m. Merlyn Louise Johnson, Dec. 23, 1951; children: Mickey Elvin, David Harold, Billy Giles (dec.), Danny Merle. Grad. high sch. Signed with N.Y. Yankees, 1949, played with Independence (Mo.) farm team, 1949, played with Joplin (Mo.) farm team, 1950, 1st baseman, outfielder, 1951-68, appeared in World Series games, 1951-53, 1955-58, 1960-64. Inducted into Baseball Hall of Fame Cooperstown, N.Y., 1974 Home: Dallas, Tex. Died August 13, 1995.

Entertainment, Arts, and Letters

Marilyn Monroe

Monroe, Marilyn (Norma Jean Mortenson), actress; b. Los Angeles, June 1, 1926; d. Gladys Pearl (Monroe) Baker; m. James Dougherty, June 19, 1942 (div. 1946); m. Joe DiMaggio, Jan. 14, 1954 (div. Oct. 27, 1954); m. Arthur Miller, June 29, 1956 (div. Jan. 20, 1961). Student, pub. schools, Calif.; studied with Lee Strasburg, Actors' Studio, NYC, 1955. Worked as model appearing on many popular magazine covers; first Playboy centerfold, 1953; co-founder Marilyn Monroe Productions, 1956. Actor: (films) *The Shocking Miss Pilgrim*, 1947, *Dangerous Years*, 1947, *Scudda Hoo! Scudda Hay!*, 1948, *Ladies of the Chorus*, 1948, *Love Happy*, 1949, *A Ticket to Tomahawk*, 1950, *The Asphalt Jungle*, 1950, *All About Eve*, 1950, *The Fireball*, 1950, *Right Cross*, 1950, *Home Town Story*, 1951, *As Young as You Feel*, 1951, *Love Nest*, 1951, *Let's Make It Legal*, 1951, *Clash by Night*, 1952, *We're Not Married!*, 1952, *Don't Bother to Knock*, 1952, *Monkey Business*, 1952, *O. Henry's Full House*, 1952, *Niagara*, 1953, *Gentlemen Prefer Blondes*, 1953, *How to Marry a Millionaire*, 1953, *River of No Return*, 1954, *There's No Business Like Show Business*, 1954, *The Seven Year Itch*, 1955, *Bus Stop*, 1956, *The Prince and the Showgirl*, 1957, *Some Like It Hot*, 1959 (Golden Globe for best motion picture actress - musical/comedy, 1960), *Let's Make Love*, 1960, *The Misfits*, 1961, *Something's Got to Give* (final film, never completed), 1962. Recipient Golden Globe for female world film favorite, 1954, 1962. Died Aug. 5, 1962; buried Westwood Village Meml. Pk. Cemetery, Los Angeles.

1960's

Science and Technology

Neil Armstrong

Armstrong, Neil A., former astronaut; b. Wapakoneta, Ohio, Aug. 5, 1930; s. Stephen A.; children: Eric, Mark. BS In Aero. Engring., Purdue U., 1955; MS in Aero. Engring., U. So. Calif. With Lewis Flight Propulsion Lab., NACA, 1955; then aero. research pilot for NACA (later NASA, High Speed Flight Sta.), Edwards, Calif.; astronaut Manned Spacecraft Center, NASA, Houston, 1962-70; command pilot Gemini 8; comdr. Apollo 11; dep. assoc. adminstr. for aeros. Office Advanced Research and Tech., Hdqrs. NASA, Washington, 1970-71; prof. aerospace engring. U. Cin., 1971-79; chmn. AIL Sys., Inc., 1989-2000, EDO Corp., 2000-02. Mem. Pres.'s Commn. on Space Shuttle, 1986, Nat. Commn. on Space, 1985-86. Served as naval aviator USN, 1949-52, Korea. Recipient numerous awards, including Octave Chanute award Inst. Aero. Scis., 1962, Presdl. Medal for Freedom, 1969, Exceptional Service medal NASA, Hubbard Gold medal Nat. Geog. Soc., 1970, Kitty Hawk Meml. award, 1969, Pere Marquette medal, 1969, Arthur S. Fleming award, 1970, Congl. Space Medal of Honor, Explorers Club medal. Fellow AIAA (hon., Astronautics award 1966), Internat. Astronautical Fedn. (hon.), Soc. Exptl. Test Pilots; mem. Nat. Acad. Engring. Achievements include being the first man to walk on the Moon, July 20, 1969. Office: EDO Corp 60 E 42nd St Ste 5010 New York NY 10165

Newsmaker

Martin Luther King, Jr.

King, Martin Luther, Jr., civil rights leader, clergyman; b. Atlanta, Jan. 15, 1929; s. Martin Luther and Alberta (Williams) K.; m. Coretta Scott, June 18, 1953; children: Yolanda Denise, Dexter Scott, Bernise Albertina, Martin Luther III. AB, Morehouse Coll., 1948, LHD, 1957; BD, Crozer Theol. Sem., 1951; PhD (J. Louis Crozer fellow), Boston U., 1955; DD (hon.), Chgo. Theol. Sem., 1957, Boston U., 1959, Wesleyan Coll., 1964, Springfield Coll., 1964, St. Peter's Coll., 1965; LLD (hon.), Howard U., 1957, Morgan State Coll., 1958, Lincoln U., 1961, U. Bridgeport, 1961, Jewish Theol. Sem., 1964, Yale U., 1964, Hofstra U., 1965, Grinnell Coll., 1967; LHD (hon.), Ctrl. State Coll., 1958, Oberlin Coll., 1965; DCL (hon.), Bard Coll., 1962, U. New Castle Upon Tyne, 1967; LittD (hon.), Keuka Coll., 1963; D. of Social Sci. (hon.), Amsterdam Free U., 1965; spl. student, U. Pa., Harvard U. dept. philosophy. Ordained Bapt. min., 1948; pastor Dexter Ave. Bapt. Ch., Montgomery, Ala., 1954; co-pastor (with his father) Ebenezer Bapt. Ch., 1960-68; pres. SCLC, 1957-68; v.p. Nat. Sunday Sch. and Bapt. Tng. Union Congress Nat. Bapt. Conv., Inc. Crusader for civil rights, peace, and non-violence. Author: Stride Toward Freedom, 1958, The Measure of a Man, 1959, The Strength of Love, 1963, Why We Can't Wait, 1964, Where do we go From Here? Chaos or Community, 1967; Letter From a Birmingham Jail, Apr. 16, 1963; contbr. articles to popular and religious publs. Pres. Montgomery Improvement Assn., 1955. Selected one of 10 outstanding personalities of 1956, Time mag., 1957; named Man of the Year, Time mag., 1963, American of the Decade, Laundry, Dry Cleaning, and Die Workers Internat. Union, 1963; recipient Spingarn Medal, NAACP, 1957, Nobel Peace prize, 1964, John Dewey award, U.S. Fedn. of Teachers, 1964, John F. Kennedy award, Catholic Coun. Chgo., 1964; also numerous awards for leadership in the Civil Rights movement. Mem. NAACP, Elks, Alpha Phi Alpha, Sigma Pi Phi. Achievements include mobilizing and leading the 382-day Montgomery bus boycott that led to the 1956 U.S. Supreme Court ruling that Alabama's segregated bus laws were unconstitutional; arrested over 25 times and assaulted at least four times for participating and leading numerous peaceful Civil Rights demonstrations; delivering the "I Have a Dream" speech on the steps of the Lincoln Meml. to a crowd estimated at 250,000 on Aug. 28, 1963; youngest recipient of the Nobel Peace Prize. Assassinated Memphis, Tenn. Apr. 4, 1968; a martyr. Buried Atlanta, Georgia.

Business and Industry

Ray Kroc

Kroc, Raymond A., food service executive, professional sports team executive; b. Chgo., Oct. 5, 1902; m. Ethel Fleming (div.); 1 child, Marilyn; m. Jane Dobbins Green (div.); m. Joan Smith, Mar. 8, 1969. Student, Oak Park (Ill.) pub. schs. Salesman Lily Tulip Cup Co., 1922–25, 1926–41; musical dir. Sta. WGES, Chgo.; worked in real estate, Ft. Lauderdale, Fla., 1925–26; founded own co. to distribute Multimixers, 1941; founder, chmn. McDonald's Corp., Chgo., 1955–77, became sole owner, 1961, sr. chmn., 1977-84; owner San Diego Padres, 1974-84. Author: (book) Grinding It Out: The Making of McDonalds, 1977. Served in Ambulance Corps, WWI. Died Jan. 14, 1984.

Sports

Muhammad Ali

Ali, Muhammad (Cassius Marcellus Clay), retired professional boxer; b. Louisville, Jan. 17, 1942; s. Marcellus and Odessa (Grady) Clay; m. Sonji Roi, August 14, 1964 (div. Jan. 10, 1966); m. Kalilah Tolona (Belinda Boyd), Apr. 17, 1967 (div. 1977) children: Rasheeda, Jamilla, Maryum, Muhammed Jr.; m. Veronica Porshe, June 19, 1977 (div. 1986), children: Hana, Laila; m. Yolanda Williams, Nov. 19, 1986, 1 child, Asaad; two other children Miya, Khalilah. Ed. pub. schs., Louisville. Profl. boxer, 1960–79, 1980–81; ret., 1981. Film appearances: The Greatest, 1976, Freedom Road (TV), 1978; author: The Greatest: My Own Story, 1975, (with Thomas Hauser) Healing, 1996, (with Hana Ali) More Than a Hero, 2000, (with Hana Ali and Hana Yasmeen Ali) The Soul of a Butterfly: Reflections on Life's Journey, 2004. Named the greatest heavyweight champion of all time, Ring Mag., 1987, Muhammad Ali Mus., Louisville Galleria opened, 1995; named to U.S. Olympic Hall of Fame, 1983, World Boxing Hall of Fame, 1986, Internat. Boxing Hall of Fame, 1990, Sport in Soc. Hall of Fame, 1994; recipient 6 Kentucky Golden Gloves titles, Olympic gold medal in boxing, 1960, Nat. Golden Gloves titles, 1959–60, Jim Thorpe Pro Sports award, lifetime achievement, 1992, Essence award, 1997. Mem. World Community Islam. Achievements include being a light heavyweight champion AAU, 1959, 60; light heavyweight champion Golden Gloves, 1959, heavyweight champion, 1960; light heavy weight champion Olympic Games, 1960, world heavyweight champion, 1964-67, 74-78, 78-79.

Entertainment, Arts, and Letters

Bob Dylan

Dylan, Bob (Robert Allen Zimmerman), singer, composer; b. Duluth, Minn., May 24, 1941; s. Abe Zimmerman and Beatrice Rutman; m. Sara Rowndes, Nov. 22, 1965 (div. June 19, 1977); children: Jakob, Jesse, Samuel, Anna, Maria; m. Carolyn Y. Dennis, June 4, 1986 (div. Oct. 1992); d. Desiree Gabrielle. Self-taught on guitar, piano, autoharp, harmonica; student, U. Minn., 1960; Mus D (hon.), Princeton U., 1970. Performer numerous tours and concerts, 1960–. Musician: (albums) Bob Dylan, 1962, The Freewheelin' Bob Dylan, 1963, The Times They Are A-Changin', 1964, Another Side of Bob Dylan, 1964, Bringing It All Back Home, 1965, Highway 61 Revisited, 1965, Blonde on Blonde, 1966, John Wesley Harding, 1967, Bob Dylan's Greatest Hits, 1967, Nashville Skyline, 1969, Self Portrait, 1970, New Morning, 1970, Bob Dylan's Greatest Hits, Vol. 2, 1971, Dylan, 1973, (soundtrack) Pat Garrett and Billy the Kid, 1973, Planet Waves, 1974, Blood on Tracks, 1975, Desire, 1976, Hard Rain, 1976, Street Legal, 1978, Masterpieces, 1978, Slow Train Coming, 1979, At Budokan, 1979, Saved, 1980, Shot of Love, 1981, Infidels, 1983, Real Live, 1984, Empire Burlesque, 1985, Biograph, 1985, Knocked Out Loaded, 1986, Down In The Groove, 1988, Oh Mercy, 1989, Under the Red Sky, 1990, The Bootleg Series, Vols. 1-3, 1991, Good as I Been to You, 1992, World Gone Wrong, 1993 (Grammy Award for Best Traditional Folk Album, 1994), Greatest Hits, Vol. 3, 1994, Unplugged, 1995, Time Out of Mind, 1997 (Grammy Award for Album of Yr., 1998, Grammy Award for Best Contemporary Folk Album, 1998), The Best of Bob Dylan, 1997, The Bootleg Series, Vol. 4: The Royal Albert Hall Concert, 1998, Essential Bob Dylan, 2000, The Best of Bob Dylan, Vol. 2, 2000, The Very Best of Bob Dylan, 2000, Love and Theft, 2001 (Grammy Award for Best Contemporary Folk Album, 2002), The Bootleg Series, Vol. 5, Live 1975, 2002, (soundtrack) Masked and Anonymous, 2003, Bootleg Series, Vol. 6 Live 1964, 2004; musician: (with various artists) The Concert for Bangladesh, 1971 (Grammy Award for Album of Yr., 1973), (soundtrack) The Last Waltz, 1976, Bob Dylan 30th Anniversary Concert Celebration, 1993; musician: (with The Band) Before the Flood, 1974, The Basement Tapes, 1976; musician: (with Traveling Wilburys) Traveling Wilburys Vol. 1, 1988 (Grammy Award for Best Rock Performance by a Duo or Group with Vocal, 1990), Traveling Wilburys Vol. 3, 1990; musician: (with Grateful Dead) Dylan and the Dead, 1988; composer: (songs) Blowin' in the Wind, Like a Rolling Stone (Named Greatest Rock 'n' Roll song of All Time Rolling Stone mag., 2004), Lay, Lady, Lay, Subterranean Homesick Blues, Forever Young, Gotta Serve Somebody, Don't Think Twice, It's Alright, A Hard Rain's A-Gonna Fall, The Times They are A-Changin', Just Like a Woman, I'll Be Your Baby Tonight, I Shall Be Released, Mr. Tambourine Man, Tangled Up In Blue, others; dir., editor (films) Eat the Document, 1972; appeared in: (documentaries) Don't Look Back, 1967; actor: (TV films) The Madhouse on Castle Street, 1963; (films) Pat Garret and Billy the Kid, 1973, Hearts of Fire, 1987; actor, composer, dir., editor, writer (films) Renaldo and Clara, 1978, actor, composer, writer Masked and Anonymous, 2003, Songs appear in films including Easy Rider, 1969, In the Name of the Father, 1993, Jerry Maguire, 1996, The Big Lebowski, 1997, American Beauty, 1999, The Hurricane, 1999, Girl Interrupted, 1999, Wonder Boys, 2000 (Acad. Award for best original song for Things Have Changed, 2001), High Fidelity, 2000, Blow, 2001, Monster's Ball, 2001, Vanilla Sky, 2001, Gods and Generals, 2003, The Hunted, 2003, and many others; author: Tarantula, 1971, Writings and Drawings, 1973, Tarantula: Poems, 1994, (book of sketches) Drawn Blank, 1994, (memoirs) Chronicles, Vol. 1, 2004. Named to Rock and Roll Hall of Fame, 1988; recipient Grammy Award for Best Male Rock Vocal Performance, (for Gotta Serve Somebody), 1980, Lifetime Achievement Award, Grammy Awards, 1991, Grammy nomination for Best Rock Performance by a Duo or Group, (with Roger McGuinn, Tom Petty, Neil Young, Eric Clapton, and George Harrison for My Back Pages), 1997, Grammy Award for Best Male Rock Vocal Performance, (for Cold Irons Bound), 1998. Achievements include devising and popularizing folk-rock. Office: Columbia Records 550 Madison Ave New York NY 10022-3211

1970's

Science and Technology

Herbert W. Boyer

Boyer, Herbert Wayne, retired biochemist; b. Pitts., July 10, 1936; m. Grace Boyer, 1959. BA, St. Vincent Coll., Latrobe, Pa., 1958, DSc (hon.) (hon.), 1981; MS, U. Pitts., 1960, PhD, 1963. Mem. faculty U. Calif., San Francisco, 1966–, prof. biochemistry, 1976–91, prof. emeritus, 1991–. Co-founder, dir. Genentech, Inc., South San Francisco, Calif. Recipient V.D. Mattai award, Roche Inst., 1977, Albert and Mary Lasker award for basic med. research, 1980, Golden Plate award, Am. Acad. Achievement, 1981, Moet Hennessy-Louis Vuitton prize, 1988, Jerome H. Lemelson-MIT prize for excellence in invention and innovation, 1996, Nat. Tech. medal, 1989, Nat. Sci. medal, NSF, 1990. Fellow: AAAS; mem.: NAS, Am. Soc. Biol. Chemists, Am. Acad. Arts and Scis. Achievements include obtaining, with Stanley N. Cohen, first patent in the field of recombinant deoxyribonucleic acid (DNA), 1980.

Stanley Cohen

Cohen, Stanley Norman, geneticist, educator; b. Perth Amboy, N.J., Feb. 17, 1935; s. Bernard and Ida (Stolz) Cohen; m. Joanna Lucy Wolter, June 27, 1961; children: Anne, Geoffrey. BA, Rutgers U., 1956; MD, U. Pa., 1960, ScD (hon.), 1995, Rutgers U., 1994. Intern Mt. Sinai Hosp., N.Y.C., 1960-61; resident Univ. Hosp., Ann Arbor, Mich., 1961-62; clin. assoc. arthritis and rheumatism branch Nat. Inst. Arthritis and Metabolic Diseases, Bethesda, Md., 1962-64; sr. resident in medicine Duke U. Hosp., Durham, N.C., 1964-65; Am. Cancer Soc. postdoctoral rsch. fellow Albert Einstein Coll. Medicine, Bronx, 1965-67, asst. prof. devel. biology and cancer, 1967-68; mem. faculty Stanford (Calif.) U., 1968–, prof. medicine, 1975–, prof. genetics, 1977–, chmn. dept. genetics, 1978-86, K.-T Li Prof., 1993–. Mem. com. recombinant DNA molecules NAS-NRC, 1974; mem. com. on genetic experimentation Internat. Coun. Sci. Unions, 1977–96. Trustee U. Pa., 1997–2002. With USPHS, 1962–64. Named to Nat. Inventors Hall of Fame, 2001; recipient Burroughs Wellcome Scholar award, 1970, Mattia award, Roche Inst. Molecular Biology, 1977, Albert Lasker basic med. rsch. award, 1980, Wolf prize, 1981, Marvin J. Johnson award, 1981, Disting. Grad. award, U. Pa. Sch. Medicine, 1986, Disting. Svc. award, Miami Winter Symposium, 1986, Nat. Biotech award, 1989, de la Vie prize, LVMH Inst., 1988, Nat. Medal Sci., 1988, City of Medicine award, 1988, Nat. Medal of Tech., 1989, Spl. award, Am. Chem. Soc., 1999, Lemelson MIT Prize, MIT, 1996, Albany Med. Ctr. prize in medicine and biomedical rsch., 2004, The Shaw prize in Life Sci. and Medicine, 2004; Guggenheim fellow, 1973, faculty scholar, Josiah Macy, Jr., 1975–76. Fellow: AAAS, Am. Acad. Microbiology; mem.: NAS (chmn. genetics sect. 1988–91), Inst. Medicine, Assn. Am. Physicians, Am. Soc. Clin. Investigation, Am. Soc. Pharmacology and Exptl. Therapeutics, Am. Soc. Microbiology (Cetus award 1988), Genetics Soc. Am., Am. Soc. Biol. Chemists, Phi Beta Kappa, Sigma Xi, Alpha Omega Alpha. Achievements include obtaining, with Herbert Boyer, first patent in the field of recombinant deoxyribonucleic acid (DNA), 1980. Office: Stanford U Sch Med Dept Genetics Rm M-322 Stanford CA 94305

Newsmaker

Richard Nixon

Nixon, Richard Milhous, 37th President of the United States; b. Yorba Linda, Calif., Jan. 9, 1913; s. Francis A. and Hannah (Milhous) N.; m. Thelma Catherine Patricia Ryan, June 21, 1940 (dec.); children: Patricia (Mrs. Edward Finch Cox), Julie (Mrs. Dwight David Eisenhower II). AB, Whittier Coll., 1934; LL.B. with honors, Duke U., 1937. Bar: Calif. 1937, U.S. Supreme Ct. 1947, N.Y. State 1963-69. Practiced law in, Whittier, Calif., 1937-42; atty. Office Price Adminstrn., Washington, Jan.-Aug. 1942; mem. 80th-81st U.S. Congresses from 12th Calif. Dist.; senator from Calif. U.S. Senate, 1950-53; v.p. served under Pres. Dwight D. Eisenhower U.S., 1953-61; Republican candidate for Pres. of U.S., 1960; Republican nominee for gov. Calif., 1962; counsel firm Adams Duque & Hazeltine, L.A., 1961-63; mem. firm Mudge Stern Baldwin & Todd, N.Y.C., 1963-64; ptnr. firm Nixon Mudge Rose Guthrie & Alexander, N.Y.C., 1964-68; elected 37th Pres. of U.S., 1968, 72; inaugurated, 1969, 73; resigned, 1974. Hon. chmn. Fund for Democracy and Devel., 1992. Author: Six Crises, 1962, RN, 1978, The Real War, 1980, Leaders, 1982, Real Peace, 1984, No More Vietnams, 1985, 1999: Victory Without War, 1988, In the Arena: A Memoir of Victory, Defeat and Renewal, 1990, Seize the Moment: America's Challenge in a One-Superpower World, 1992, Beyond Peace: The Spiritual Deficit in America, 1994. Hon. chmn. Boy Clubs Am.; trustee Whittier Coll., 1939-68. Served to lt. comdr. USNR, 1942-46, PTO. Mem. Order of Coif. Republican. Soc. Of Friends. Home: New York, NY. Died Apr. 22, 1994.

Business and Industry

Sam Walton

Walton, Sam Moore, retail executive; b. Kingfisher, Okla., 1920; m. Helen Walton; children: Samuel Robson, John, Jim, Alice. BA, U. Mo., 1940. With J. C. Penney Co., Des Moines, 1938-42; franchise owner, operator Ben Franklin Stores, 1945-62; co-founder Wal-Mart Stores, Bentonville, Ark., 1962, chmn., chief exec. officer, 1974-88, chmn., until 1992, also bd. dirs. Served with U.S. Army, 1942-45. Recipient Presdl. Medal of Freedom, 1992. Avocations: tennis, quail hunting. Home: Bentonville, Ark. Died Apr. 5, 1992.

Sports

Billie Jean King

King, Billie Jean Moffitt, retired professional tennis player; b. Long Beach, Calif., Nov. 22, 1943; d. Willard J. and Betty Moffitt; m. Larry King, Sept. 17, 1965, (div. 1987). Student, Calif. State U. at Los Angeles, 1961-64; PhD (hon.), Calif. State U., 1997; hon. degree, Trinity Coll., 1998; PhD (hon.), U. Pa, 1999, U. Mass., 2000. Amateur tennis player, 1958-67; profl., 1968–84; mem. Tennis Challenge Series, 1977, 78; dir., ofcl. spokesperson World Team Tennis, Chgo., 1985–; commentator, analyst Wimbledon and other tennis events HBO, N.Y.C. Winner, Singles champion tournaments include: Wimbledon, 1966-68, 1972-73,75, U.S. Open, 1967, 1971-72, 74, Australian Open, 1968, French Open, 1972; Doubles champion Wimbledon, 1961-62, 65, 67-68, 70-73, 79 U.S. Open, 1965, 67, 74, 80, French Open, 1972; mixed doubles champion Wimbledon, 1967, 71, 73, 74, U.S. Open, 1967, 71, 73, French, 1967, 70, Australian, 1968; winner 29 Virginia Slims singles titles, 1970-77, four Colgate titles, 1977, Fedn. Cup, 1963-67, 76-79, Wightman Cup, 1961-67, 70, 77-78; World Tennis Team All-Star, three times; host Colgate women's sports TV spl. The Lady is a Champ, 1975; sports commentator ABC-TV, 1975-78; founder Women's Tennis Assn., 1973, pres., 1973-75, 1980-81; founder, Women's Sports Found, 1974, Profl. World TeamTennis, 1974, World TeamTennis Profl. League, 1981, World TeamTennis Recreational League, 1985, World TeamTennis Charities, 1987; co-founder, pub. WomenSports mag., 1974, Kingdom, Inc., San

Mateo, Calif.; founding mem., Women's Sports Legends; first woman commr. (Team Tennis League) profl. sports history, 1984; TV commentator HBO-Sports Wimbledon coverage; capt. Fed. Cup for USA, 1995; cons. Virginia Slims World Championship Series; mem., Planned Parenthood, US Profl. Tennis Assn., US Profl. Tennis Registry, Chgo. Area Women's Sports Assn., advisory bd., Areta Sports award nomination com., Jim Thorpe Pro sports nomination com. award, sports advisory bd. for the Vic Braden Neurology Rsch. Inst., USTA Player Devel. Com.; bd. dirs. Challenger Ctr., Elton John AIDS Found., S.A.F.E., Nat. AIDS Fund, Altria Group, Inc., Women's Sports Found.; amb. Adventures in Movement Charity; coach Fed. Cup Women's Tennis Team, 1995-96, 1998-03, USA Olympic Women's Tennis Team, 1996, 2000; nat. spokesperson Literary Vols. Am.; tennis tchr. to profls. Author: *Tennis to Win*, 1970, (with Kim Chapin) Billie Jean, 1974, (with Greg Hoffman) *Tennis Love: A Parent's Guide to the Sport*, 1978, (with Frank Deford) *The Autobiography of Billie Jean King*, 1982 (with Cynthia Starr) *We Have Come a Long Way, The Story of Women's Tennis*, 1988. Named Sportsperson of Yr., 1972, Top 40 Athletes, 1994, Sports Illustrated; Woman Athlete of Yr., A.P., 1967, 73, Top Woman Athlete of Yr., 1972; Woman of Yr., *Time* mag., 1976, One of 10 Most Powerful Women in Am., *Harper's Bazaar*, 1977, One of 25 Most Influential Women in Am., *World Almanac*, 1977, One of 100 Most Important Ams. of 20th Century, *Life* mag., 1990, woman of the Year, *Women in Sports & Events, 2002*; named to Internat. Tennis Hall of Fame, 1987, Nat. Women's Hall of Fame, 1990, Chgo. Gay and Lesbian Hall of Fame, 1999, Court of Champions, USTA Nat. Tennis Ctr., 2003; WTA Hon. Membership award, 1986, Female Teaching Pro of the Decade, 1994, Lifetime Achievement award, March of Dimes, 1994, Flo Hymnal award, Women's Sports Found, 1997, Player Who Makes a Difference award, 1997, US Olympic Com. Nat. Tennis Coach of the Year award, 1997, Nat. Women's Law Ctr. honoree, 1997, Elizabeth Blackwill award for Courage, William & Hobart Smith Colleges, 1998, Arthur Ashe award for Courage, ESPN, 1999, Community Role Model award, LA Gay & Lesbian Ctr., 1999, NFL Players Assn. Lifetime Achievement award, 1999, *Sports Illustrated* Athletes Who Changed the Game award, 1999, Capitol award, GLAAD, 2000, Radcliffe medal, Radcliffe Coll., 2002, Internat. Olympic Com. Women & Sport World Trophy, 2002, Nat. Assn. Collegiate Women Athletic Administrators award of Honor, 2002, Philippe Chatrier award, Internat. Tennis Fedn., 2003. Won 71 singles titles, including 12 Grand Slam singles titles; won 20 Wimbledon titles; first woman to win more than $100,000 in a single season in any sport; highest singles ranking 1(five times between 1966-72); defeated Bobby Riggs in The Battle of the Sexes tennis match, Sept. 20, 1973, Houston, Tex. Office: Billie Jean King Ste 983 960 Harlem Ave Glenview IL 60025

Entertainment, Arts, and Letters

Woody Allen

Allen, Woody (Allen Stewart Konigsberg), director, actor, writer; b. N.Y.C., Dec. 1, 1935; s. Martin and Nettie (Cherry) Konigsberg; m. Harlene Rosen, 1954 (div. 1960); m. Louise Lasser, 1964 (div. 1969); ptnr. Mia Farrow; 1 child , Satchel; adopted children: Moses, Dylan; m. Soon-Yi Previn, 1997; adopted children: Bechet, Manzie Tio Student, NYU, 1953, CCNY, 1953. Writer TV comedy for Sid Caesar, 1957, Art Carney, 1958-59, Herb Shriner, 1953; appeared in numerous nightclubs, TV shows, from 1961; author screenplay, also appeared in motion picture What's New Pussycat?, 1964-65; screenplay, dir., actor Take the Money and Run, 1969, Bananas, 1971, What's Up Tiger Lily?, 1966, Everything You Always Wanted to Know About Sex But Were Afraid to Ask, 1972, Sleeper, 1973, Love and Death, 1975, The Front, 1976, Manhattan (Brit. Acad. award 1979, N.Y. Film Critics award), Stardust Memories, 1980; writer, dir., prodr., actor films Annie Hall, 1977 (N.Y. Film Critics Circle award for Best Dir. and Best Screenplay 1977, Acad. awards for best film, best direction, Nat. Soc. Film Critics Screenwriting award), Zelig, 1983, Broadway Danny Rose, 1984, Hannah and Her Sisters, 1986 (Acad. award for best screenplay, D.W. Griffith award for best dir. Nat. Bd. Rev. of Motion Pictures), New York Stories (Oedipus Wrecks segment), 1989, Mighty Aphrodite, 1995 (Acad. award nominee for best screenplay 1996), Everyone Says I Love You, 1996, Deconstructing Harry, 1997, Count Mercury Goes to the Suburbs, 1997, Celebrity, 1998, Sweet and Lowdown, 1999, Small Town Crooks, 2000, The Curse of the Jade Scorpion, 2001, Hollywood Ending, 2002, Anything Else, 2003; writer, dir., narrator film Radio Days, 1987; screenplay, dir. films Interiors, 1978, Purple Rose of Cairo, 1985, A Midsummer Night's Sex Comedy, 1982, September, 1987, Another Woman, 1988, Crimes and Misdemeanors, 1989, Alice, 1990, Shadows and Fog, 1992, Husbands and Wives, 1992, Manhattan Murder Mystery, 1993, Bullets Over Broadway, 1994, Mighty Aphrodite, 1995; dir. Melinda and Melinda, 2004; author play: Don't Drink the Water, 1966 (actor, dir. of TV movie, 1994), The Floating Lightbulb, 1981, (one act) Death Defying Acts, 1995, Sounds from a Town I Love (TV movie), 2001; play, screenplay Play It Again, Sam, 1969, film, 1972; actor, film King Lear, 1988, Scenes From a Mall, 1990, Cannes...les 400 coups, 1997, Waiting for Woody, 1998, Impostors, 1998, AFI's 100 Years...100 Movies, 1998, Antz, 1998, Wild Man Blues, 1998, Stuck on You, 1998, Company Man, 1999 Picking Up the Pieces, 1999; author: Getting Even, 1971, Without Feathers, 1975, Side Effects, 1980; guest appearances (TV) Just Shoot Me, The Tonight Show; writer, director (off Broadway play) A Second Hand Memory, 2004; contbr. numerous pieces to Playboy, New Yorker, other mags. Recipient Sylvania award, 1957; Spl. award Berlin Film Festival, 1975; nominated for Emmy award as TV writer, 1957. Democrat.

1980's

Science and Technology

Bill Gates

Gates, Bill (William Henry Gates III), computer software company executive; b. Seattle, Wash., Oct. 28, 1955; s. William H. and Mary M. (Maxwell) G.; m. Melinda French, January 1, 1994; children–Jennifer Katherine, Rory John, Phoebe Adele. Grad. high sch., Seattle, 1973; student, Harvard U., 1973-75. Co-founder Traf-O-Data Co., Seattle, 1972–73, Microsoft Corp. (formerly Micro Soft), Albuquerque, 1975; gen. ptnr. Microsoft Corp., 1975–77, pres., 1977–82, chmn. bd., 1981–, exec. v.p. development activities, 1982–83, chief software architect Redmond, Wash., 1999–; founder Corbis, 1989. Bd. dirs. ICOS Corp., 1990–, Berkshire Hathaway Inc., 2004–. Author: The Future, 1994, The Road Ahead, 1995, Business at the Speed of Thought, 1999. Founder William H. Gates Found., 1994–2000; co-founder Gates Learning Found. (formerly Gates Library Found.), 1997–2000, Bill and Melinda Gates Found., 2000–. Recipient Howard Vollum award, Reed Coll., Portland, Oreg., 1984, Nat. medal Tech. U.S. Dept. Commerce Tech. Adminstrn., 1992, Hon. Knighthood, UK, 2005; named CEO of Yr., Chief Executive mag., 1994; named one of Top 200 Collectors, ARTnews Mag., 2004, one of 100 Most Influential People, Time Mag., 2005. Avocation: Collector 19th Century Am. Art. Office: Microsoft Corp 1 Microsoft Way Redmond WA 98052-8300

Newsmaker

Ronald Reagan

Reagan, Ronald Wilson, 40th President of the United States; b. Tampico, Ill., Feb. 6, 1911; s. John Edward and Nelle Clyde Wilson Reagan; m. Jane Wyman, Jan. 25, 1940 (div. June 28, 1948); children: Maureen E. (dec. 2001), Michael E. (adopted); m. Nancy Davis, Mar. 4, 1952; children: Patricia Ann, Ronald Prescott. AB, Eureka Coll., 1932, MA (hon.), 1957. Actor GE Theatre, 1954-62; gov. State of Calif., 1967-74; businessman, rancher, commentator on public policy, 1975-80; Pres. of U.S., 1981-89. Sports announcer, motion picture and TV actor, 1932–66; Actor: (films) *Love is on the Air*, 1937, *Sergeant Murphy*, 1937, *Swing Your Lady*, 1938, *Accidents Will Happen*, 1938, *Cowboy from Brooklyn*, 1938, *Boy Meets Girl*, 1938, *Girls on Probation*, 1938, *Brother Rat*, 1938, *Going Places*, 1938, *Secret Service of the Air*, 1939, *Dark Victory*, 1939, *Naughty But Nice*, 1939, *Hell's Kitchen*, 1939, *The Angels Wash Their Faces*, 1939, *Smashing the Money Ring*, 1939, *Code of the Secret Service*, 1939, *Brother Rat and a Baby*, 1940, *An Angel from Texas*, 1940, *Knute Rockne All American*, 1940, *Tugboat Annie Sails Again*, 1940, *Santa Fe Trail*, 1940, *The Bad Man*, 1941, *Million Dollar Baby*, 1941, *International Squadron*, 1941, *Nine Lives Are Not Enough*, 1941, *Kings Row*, 1942, *Juke Girl*, 1942, *This is the Army*, 1943, *For God and Country*, 1943, *Cadet Classification*, 1943, *Stallion Road*, 1947, *The Hagen Girl*, 1947, *The Voice of the Turtle*, 1947, *John Loves Mary*, 1949, *Murder in the Air*, 1949, *Night Unto Night*, 1949, *The Girl from Jones Beach*, 1949, The *Hasty Heart*, 1949, *Louisa*, 1950, *Storm Warning*, 1951, *The Last Outpost*, 1951, *Bedtime for Bonzo*, 1951, *The Big Truth*, 1951, *Hong Kong*, 1952, *The Winning Team*, 1952, *She's Working Her Way Through College*, 1952, *Law and Order*, 1953, *Tropic Zone*, 1953, *Prisoner of War*, 1954, *The Jungle Trap*, 1954, *Cattle Queen of Montana*, 1955, *Tennessee's Partner*, 1955, *Hellcats of the Navy*, 1957, *The Killers*, 1964, (voice): *The Young Doctors*, 1961, (Host): (TV series) *The Orchid Award*, 1953–54, *Death Valley Days*, 1965–66; Author: (autobiography) *Where's the Rest of Me?*, 1965, *Speaking My Mind: Selected Speeches*, 1989, *An American Life: The Autobiography*, 1990. Mem. Calif. State Rep. Ctrl. Com., 1964-66; del. Rep. Nat. Conv., 1968, 72; chmn. Rep. Gov. Assn., 1968-73; mem. presdl. Commn. CIA Activities Within U.S., 1975; bd. dirs. Com. Present Danger, Washington, 1977; cand. for Rep. nomination for Pres., 1976. Served as capt. USAAF, 1942-45. Recipient Great Am. Decade award, Va. Young Am. Freedom, Man Yr. Free Enterprise award, San Fernando Valley Bus. & Profl. award, 1964, Am. Legion award, 1965, Horatio Alger award, 1969, George Washington Honor medal, Freedoms Found. Valley Forge award, 1971, Disting. Am. award; inducted into Nat. Football Found. Hall Fame, Am. Patriots Hall Fame. Mem. SAG (pres. 1947-52, 59), Am. Fedn. Radio & TV Artists, Lions, Friars, Tau Kappa Epsilon. Republican. Died June 5, 2004.

Business and Industry

Lee Iacocca

Iacocca, Lee (Lido Anthony Iacocca), former automotive manufacturing executive, venture capitalist; b. Allentown, Pa., Oct. 15, 1924; s. Nicola and Antoinette (Perrotto) I.; m. Mary McCleary, Sept. 29, 1956 (dec.); m. Darrien Earle, March 30, 1991; children- Kathryn Lisa Hentz, Lia Antoinette Nagy. BS, Lehigh U., 1945; ME, Princeton U., 1946. With Ford Motor Co., Dearborn, Mich., 1946-78, successively mem. field sales staff, various merchandising and tng. activities, asst. dirs. sales mgr. Phila., dist. sales mgr. Washington, 1946-56, truck mktg. mgr. div. office, 1956-57, car mktg. mgr., 1957-60, vehicle market mgr., 1960, v.p.; gen. mgr. Ford Motor Co. (Ford div.), 1960-65, v.p. car and truck group, 1965-69, exec. v.p. of co., 1967-69, pres., 1970-78, Ford N. Am. automobile ops.; pres., chief operating officer Chrysler Corp., Highland Park, Mich., 1978-79, chmn. bd., chief exec. officer, 1979-93; prin. Iacocca Ptnrs., 1994–; pres. Iacocca Assocs., L.A.; founder EV Global Motors. Bd. dirs. Chrysler Fin. Corp. Author: Iacocca: An Autobiography, 1984, Talking Straight, 1988. Past chmn. Statue of Liberty-Ellis Island Centennial Commn. Wallace Meml. fellow Princeton U. Mem. NAE, Tau Beta Pi. Clubs: Detroit Athletic. Office: 16201 Stagg St Van Nuys CA 91406-1716

Sports

Larry Bird

Bird, Larry Joe, professional athletics manager, former professional basketball coach; b. West Baden, Ind., Dec. 7, 1956; s. Joe and Georgia B; m. Dinah Mattingly, Oct. 1, 1989. Student, Ind. U., 1974, Northwood Inst., West Baden, Ind., 1974; BS, Ind. State U., 1979. Player Boston Celtics, 1979-92, spl. asst. to exec. v.p., 1992-97; head coach Ind. Pacers, Indianapolis, Ind., 1997–2000; pres., basketball ops. Ind. Pacers., 2003–. Author: (with Bob Ryan) Drive, 1989; Actor (film) Blue Chips, 1994. Mem. US Gold Medal team World Univ. Games, Sophia, Bulgaria, 1977; NBA championship team, 1981, 84, 86; NBA All-Star Team, 1980-88, 1990-92; gold medal Olympic basketball team (Dream Team), Barcelona, 1992; named Collegiate Player of Yr. AP, UPI and Nat. Assn. Coaches, 1978-79; Rookie of Yr. NBA, 1980; MVP NBA All-Star Game, 1982, NBA, 1984-86, NBA Playoffs, 1984, 86; named to All-NBA first-team, 1980-88; named one of 50 Greatest Players in NBA history, 1996; inducted into Basketball Hall of Fame, 1998.

Magic Johnson

Johnson, Magic (Earvin Johnson Jr.), former professional basketball coach and player, professional sports team executive, development company executive; b. Lansing, Mich., Aug. 14, 1959; s. Earvin and Christine Johnson; m. Earleatha "Cookie" Kelly, Sept. 1991; children: Earvin III, Elisa, Andre. Student, Mich. State U., 1976-79. Basketball player LA Lakers, 1979–91, 1996, head coach, 1994, v.p., co-owner, 1994–; sportscaster NBC-TV, 1993-94; chmn., CEO Johnson Devel. Corp., 1993–; chmn. Magic Johnson Entertainment, Magic Johnson Productions & Magic Johnson Enterprises, 1997–; co-chmn. exec. steering com. for diversity NASCAR, 2004–. Author: (autobiography) Magic, 1983; (with Roy S. Johnson) Magic's Touch, 1989; What You Can Do to Avoid AIDS, 1992; My Life, 1992. Established the Magic Johnson Found., 1991. Named Most Outstanding Player, NCAA Divsn. I Tournament, 1979, NBA Finals MVP, 1980, 1982, 1987, NBA MVP, 1987, 1989, 1990, NBA All-Star Game MVP, 1990, 1992, Player of Yr., Sporting News, 1987; named one of 50 Greatest Players in NBA History, 1996; named to All-NBA first team, 1983–91, All-NBA Second Team, 1982, NBA All-Rookie Team, 1980, NBA All-Star Team, 1980, 1982–92, Mich. State U. Athletics Hall of Fame, 1992, Naismith Meml. Basketball Hall of Fame, 2002; recipient All-Around Contributions to Team Success Award, IBM, 1984, Schick Pivotal Player Award, 1984, J. Walter Kennedy Citizenship Award, NBA, 1992. Achievements include being mem. of NCAA Championship Team, 1979, NBA Championship Team, 1980, 82, 85, 87, 88, US Olympic Basketball gold medal winning team, 1992; chosen first overall in 1979 NBA Draft; holder of career record for highest assists-per-game avg. (11.2), career playoff record for most assists (2346), NBA Finals single-series record for highest assists-per-game avg. (14.0), 1985, NBA Finals single-series highest assists-per-game avg. by a rookie (8.7 1980, NBA Finals single-game record for most points by rookie (42 1980. Office: Johnson Devel Corp & Magic Johnson Found 910 Wilshire Blvd Beverly Hills CA 90212-3415

Entertainment, Arts, and Letters

Stephen King

King, Stephen Edwin, novelist, scriptwriter; b. Portland, Maine, Sep 21, 1947; s. Donald and Nellie Ruth (Pillsbury) K.; m. Tabitha Jan Spruce, Jan. 2, 1971; children: Naomi Rachel, Joseph Hillstrom, Owe Phillip. BS, U. Maine, 1970. Tchr. English, Hampden (Maine) Acad 1971-73; writer in residence U. Maine at Orono, 1978-79. Novels includ *Carrie*, 1974, *Salem's Lot*, 1975, *The Shining*, 1976, *The Stand*, 1978, *Th Dead Zone*, 1979, *Firestarter*, 1980, *Cujo*, 1981, *Different Seasons*, 198 *The Dark Tower I: The Gunslinger*, 1982, *Christine*, 1983, *Pet Sematar* 1983, (with Peter Straub) *The Talisman*, 1984, *Cycle of the Werewolf*, 198 *Skeleton Crew*, 1986, *It*, 1986, *The Eyes of the Dragon*, 1987, *Misery*, 198 *The Dark Tower II: The Drawing of the Three*, 1987, *The Tommyknocker* 1987, *The Dark Half*, 1989, *The Stand, the Complete and Uncut Edition* 1990, *The Dark Tower III: The Waste Lands*, 1991, *Needful Things*, 199 *Gerald's Game*, 1992, *Dolores Claiborne*, 1992, *Insomnia*, 1994, *Ros Madder*, 1995, *Desperation*, 1996, *The Green Mile*, 1996, *The Dark Towe IV: Wizard & Glass*, 1997, *Bag of Bones*, 1998, *The Girl Who Loved Tor Gordon*, 1999, *Storm of the Century*, 1999, *Dreamcatcher*, 2001, (wit Peter Straub) *Black House*, 2001, *From A Buick 8*, 2002, *Dark Tower V Wolves of the Calla*, 2003, *Dark Tower VI: Song of Susannah*, 2004, *Th Dark Tower VII: The Dark Tower*, 2004; (collections) *Night Shift*, 197 *Different Seasons*, 1982, *Skeleton Crew*, 1985, *Four Past Midnight*, 199 *Nightmares and Dreamscapes*, 1993, *Hearts in Atlantis*, 1999, *Everything Eventual: 14 Dark Tales*, 2002; (as Richard Bachman) *Rage*, 1977, *Th Long Walk*, 1979, *Roadwork*, 1981, *The Running Man*, 1982, *Thinner* 1984, *The Bachman Books: Four Early Novels*, 1986, *The Regulators*, 1996 (non-fiction) *Danse Macabre*, 1981, *On Writing: A Memoir of the Craft* 2000, (with Stewart O'Nan) *Faithful: Two Diehard Boston Red Sox Fan Chronicle the Historic 2004 Season*, 2004; (original screenplays *Creepshow*, 1982, *Cat's Eye*, 1984, *Silver Bullet*, 1985, *Maximum Overdrive*, 1986, *Golden Years*, 1991, *Sleepwalkers*, 1992; creator, write (TV mini-series) *The Stand*, 1994, *The Shining*, 1997, *Storm of the Century*, 1999, *Kingdom Hospital*, 2004; actor (films): *Knightriders*, 1981 *Creepshow*, 1982, *Maximum Overdrive*, 1986, *Creepshow II*, 1988; dir (films) *Maximum Overdrive*, 1986. Recipient Medal for Disting. Contbn to Am. Letters, The Nat. Book Found., 2003. Mem. Author's Guild Am. Screen Artists Guild, Screen Writers of Am., Writer's Guild. Democrat Office: 49 Florida Ave Bangor ME 04401-3005

1990's

Science and Technology

Francis Collins

Collins, Francis S., federal agency administrator, geneticist, physician b. Apr. 14, 1950; BS in Chemistry, U. Va., 1970; PhD in Physical Chemistry, Yale U., 1974; MD, U. N.C., Chapel Hill, 1977. Residency and chief residency in internal medicine N.C. Memorial Hospital, Chapel Hill, 1978–81; fellow in human genetics Yale U., 1981–84; prof. internal med. and human genetics, chief med. genetics U. Michigan, Howard Hughes Med. Inst, 1984–93; dir. Human Genome Project, 1992–2003; chief, genetic and molecular biology NIH, 1993; dir. Nat Ctr. for Human Genome Rsch. (became Nat. Human Genome Rsch Inst. in 1997), NIH, Bethesda, Md., 1993–; sr. investigator, Genome Technology Br. Nat. Human Genome Rsch. Inst., NIH, Bethesda, Md. Overseer Internat. Human Genome Sequencing Consortium; lectr. in field. Contbr. articles to profl. jours.; contbd. foreward Coming to Peace with Science: Bridging the Worlds Between Faith and Science, 2004. Vol. physician rural missionary hosp., Nigeria. Co-recipient Gairdner Found. Internat. award for work on cystic fibrosis, 1990; recipient Mendel medal, Biotechnology Heritage award, Chemical Heritage Found. and Biotechnology Industry Orgn., 2001, Gairdner Found. Internat. award for merit, 2002; named Va. Outstanding Scientist of Yr., Sci. Mus. of Va., 2001 Mem.: IOM, NAS, AMA (Scientific Achievement award 2001). Achievements include working on methods of crossing large stretches of DNA to identify disease genes, which was named "positional cloning"; identifying the gene for cystic fibrosis with Lap-Chee Tsui and Jack Riordan in 1989; identifying the neurofibromatosis gene with colleagues in 1990; identifying the defective gene that causes Huntington's Disease with colleagues in 1993; identifying the gene for multiple endocrine neoplasia type 1 and the M4 type of adult acute leukemia with colleagues; overseeing a complex multidisciplinary project, Human Genome Project, aimed at mapping and sequencing the entire human DNA, and determining aspects of its function. A working draft of the human genome sequence was announced in June, 2000, an initial analysis was published in February, 2001, and the completed sequence was announced in April, 2003; founding of the National Human Genome Research Institute Division of Intramural Research (DIR) in 1994, which has developed into one of the nation's premier research centers in human genetics; serving as strong advocate for protecting privacy of genetic information and as a national leader in efforts to prohibit gene-based insurance discrimination. Office: Nat Human Genome Rsch Inst NIH Bldg 31/4B09 31 Center Dr 9000 Rockville Pike Bethesda MD 20892 Office Phone: 301-496-0844. Fax: 301-402-2218.

Newsmaker

Bill Clinton

Clinton, Bill (William Jefferson Clinton), 42nd President of the United States; b. Hope, Ark., Aug. 19, 1946; s. Virginia Dell Cassidy and William Jefferson Blythe IV; m. Hillary Rodham, Oct. 11, 1975; 1 child, Chelsea Victoria. BS in Internat. Affairs, Georgetown U., 1968; postgrad., Oxford U., 1968-70; JD, Yale U., 1973. Prof. U. Ark. Sch. Law, Fayetteville, 1973-76; pvt. practice law, 1973-76; atty. gen. State of Ark., Little Rock, 1977-79, gov., 1979-81, 83-92; of counsel Wright, Lindsey & Jennings, Little Rock, 1981-82; pres. US, Washington, 1993-01; spl. envoy for tsunami reconstruction UN, 2005–. Chmn. So. Growth Policies Bd., 1985-86. Author: (memoir) *My Life*, 2004 (Grammy Award for Spoken Word Album, 2005, *Publishers Weekly* Bestseller, *NY Times* Bestseller, Biography of Yr., Brit. Book Awards, 2005, Audiobook of Yr., Audio Publ. Assn., 2005). Chmn. Edn. Commn. of the States, 1986-87, mem. steering com.; mem. Task Force on Adolescent Edn., Carnegie Found.; chmn. Dem. Leadership Coun., 1990-91. Rhodes scholar Univ. Coll., Oxford U., 1968-70; named one of most influential people, TIME mag., 2005. Mem. ABA, Ark. Bar Assn., Nat. Govs. Assn. (vice chmn. 1986, chmn. 1986-87, exec. com., fin. com., com. on human resources, com. on internat. trade and fgn. rels., task force on rural devel., co-chmn. task force for edn. 1990-92). Democrat. Address: 55 W 125th St New York NY 10027

usiness and Industry

effrey Bezos

ezos, Jeffrey Preston, multimedia executive; b. Albuquerque, N. 1ex., Jan. 12, 1964; s. Miguel and Jacklyn Bezos; m. Mackenzie Tuttle, 993. Degree in Elec. Engring. and Computer Sci., summa cum laude, rinceton U., 1986. With FITEL, NY, 1986–88, Bankers Trust Co., NY, 988-90, v.p., 1990, D.E. Shaw & Co., NY, 1990-94, sr. v.p., 1992-94; under Amazon.com Inc., Seattle, 1994–, chmn., 1994–, pres., 1994–99, 000, CEO, 1996–, treas., sec., 1996–97; founder Blue Origin, Seattle, 000–. Mem. staff FITEL, NY, 1986-88; bd. dirs., Drugstore.com, 1998–'amed Person of the Year, TIME mag., 1999; named one of 40 Under) Richest, Fortune, 2003. Mem. Phi Beta Kappa. Live on the Internet ıly 16, 1995, first book sold: Fluid Concepts & Creative Analogies: omputer Models of the Fundamental Mechanisms of Thought; 'unding Blue Origin, builders of low cost vehicles that would send pas-engers into space on short flights. Office: Amazon com Inc 1200 12th ve S Ste 1200 Seattle WA 98144

ports

Aichael Jordan

ordan, Michael Jeffrey, retired professional basketball player, former rofessional sports team executive, retired baseball player; b. Bklyn., Feb. 7, 1963; s. James and Deloris Jordan; m. Juanita Vanoy, Sept. 1989; chil-ren: Jeffrey Michael, Marcus James, Jasmine. Student, U. N.C., 981–84. Basketball player Chgo. Bulls, 1984–93; baseball player Chicago White Sox AA Team, 1994-95; basketball player Chgo. Bulls, 995–98; pres. basketball ops. Washington Wizards, 1999–2000, player, 001–03. Owner Michael Jordan's: The Restaurant, 1993–; founder ordan Brand Clothing, 1997–. Author: RareAir: Michael on Michael, 993; actor: (films) Space Jam, 1996, He Got Game, 1998. Named Rookie of Yr., NBA, 1985, Seagram's NBA Player of Yr., 1987, Slam-Dunk Championship winner, 1987-88, NBA All-Star Game Most Valuable Player, 1988, 1996, 1998, NBA Def. Player of Yr., 1988, NBA Most Valuable Player, 1988, 1991, 1992, 1996, 1998, Male Athlete of Yr., AP, 1991-93, NBA Finals MVP, 1991–93, 1996–98; named to Sporting News All-Am. first team, 1983–84, NBA All-Star team, 1985–93, 996–98, 2002–03, All NBA First Team, 1987–93, 1996–98, NBA All-Def. Team, 1988–93, 1996–98; recipient Naismith award, 1984, Wooden award, 1984, IBM award, 1985, 1989, Schick Pivotal Player award, 1985, 989. Achievements include holding record for most points in an NBA playoff game with 63; mem. NCAA divsn. 1 championship team, 1982, NBA champion Chgo. Bulls, 1991-93, 96-98, US Olympic basketball gold medal team, 1984, 92.

Entertainment, Arts, and Letters

Steven Spielberg

Spielberg, Steven, film director; b. Cin., Dec. 18, 1946; m. Amy Irving, Nov. 27, 1985 (div. 1989); children: Max Samuel; m. Kate Capshaw Oct. 12, 1991; children: Theo (adopted), Sasha, Sawyer, Mikaela (adopted), Destry, Jessica (stepchild). BA, Calif. State U., Long Beach; D of creative arts (hon.) , Brandeis U., 1986; DHL (hon.) , Yale U., 2002. Founder Amblin Entertainment (Universal Studios), Dreamworks SKG (with Jeffrey Katzenberg and David Geffen). Dir.: (films) *The Last Gun*, 1959, *Jaws*, 1975, 1941, 1979, *Raiders of the Lost Ark*, 1981 (Acad. Award nomination for best dir., 1982), *Indiana Jones and the Temple of Doom*, 1984, *Indiana Jones and the Last Crusade*, 1989, Hook, 1991, *Jurassic Park*, 1993, *The Lost World: Jurassic Park*, 1997, *Minority Report*, 2002, *War of the Worlds*, 2005; (TV films) *Columbo: Murder by the Book*, 1971, *Duel*, 1971, *Something Evil*, 1972, *Savage*, 1973, (episodes for TV series) *The Name of the Game*, 1968, *Marcus Welby, M.D.*, 1969, *Night Gallery*, 1970, *The Psychiatrist*, 1971, *Owen Marshall: Counselor at Law*, 1971; exec. prodr.: (films) *I Wanna Hold Your Hand*, 1978, *Used Cars*, 1980, *Continental Divide*, 1981, *Gremlins*, 1984, *Fandango*, 1985, *Back to the Future*, 1985, *Young Sherlock Holmes*, 1985, *The Money Pit*, 1986, *An American Tail*, 1986, *Harry and the Hendersons*, 1987, *Innerspace*, 1987, *Three O'Clock High*, 1987, **batteries not included*, 1987, *Who Framed Roger Rabbit*, 1988, *The Land Before Time*, 1988, *Tummy Trouble*, 1989, *Dad*, 1989, *Back to the Future Part II*, 1989, *Joe Versus the Volcano*, 1990, *Yume*, 1990, *Back to the Future Part III*, 1990, *Roller Coaster Rabbit*, 1990, *Gremlins 2: The New Batch*, 1990, *Arachnophobia*, 1990, *Cape Fear*, 1991, *Trail Mix-Up*, 1993, *We're Back! A Dinosaur's Story*, 1993, *I'm Mad*, 1994, *The Flintstones*, 1994, *Casper*, 1995, *Balto*, 1995, *Twister*, 1996, *The Lost Children of Berlin*, 1997, *Men in Black*, 1997, *Deep Impact*, 1998, *The Mask of Zorro*, 1998, *The Last Days*, 1998, *The Haunting*, 1999, *Eyes of the Holocaust*, 2000, *Shrek*, 2001, *Evolution*, 2001, *Jurassic Park III*, 2001, *Price for Peace*, 2002, *Men in Black II*, 2002; (TV films) *Class of '61*, 1993, *Survivors of the Holocaust*, 1996, *Shooting War*, 2000, *Semper Fi*, 2001, *We Stand Alone Together*, 2001, *Burma Bridge Busters*, 2003; (TV miniseries) *Band of Brothers*, 2001 (Emmy for outstanding miniseries, 2002), *Broken Silence*, 2002, *Taken*, 2002 (Emmy for outstanding miniseries, 2003), Into the West, 2005; (TV series) *The Plucky Duck Show*, 1992, *Family Dog*, 1992, *SeaQuest DSV*, 1993–96, *ER*, 1994, *Pinky and the Brain*, 1995–98, *Freakazoid!*, 1995–97, *Toonsylvania*, 1998–2000, *Pinky, Elmyra & the Brain*, 1998; prodr.: (films) *An American Tail: Fievel Goes West*, 1991; writer (films) *Ace Eli and Rodger of the Skies*, 1973, dir., prodr. *E.T. the Extra-Terrestrial*, 1982 (Acad. Award nomination for best dir., 1983, Acad. Award nomination for best picture, 1983), *Twilight Zone: The Movie*, 1983, *The Color Purple*, 1985 (Acad. Award nomination for best picture, 1986), *Empire of the Sun*, 1987, *Always*, 1989, *Schindler's List*, 1993 (Acad. Award for best dir., 1994, Acad. Award for best picture, 1994, Golden Globe for best dir., 1994), *Amistad*, 1997, *Saving Private Ryan*, 1998 (Acad. Award for best dir., 1999, Acad. Award nomination for best picture, 1999, Golden Globe for best dir., 1999, Disting. Pub. Svc. Award USN, 1999), *Catch Me If You Can*, 2002, *The Terminal*, 2002, dir., writer *Fighter Squad*, 1961, *Escape to Nowhere*, 1961, *Firelight*, 1964, *Slipstream*, 1967, *Amblin'*, 1968, *The Sugarland Express*, 1974, *Close Encounters of the Third Kind*, 1977 (Acad. Award nomination for best dir., 1978), prodr., writer *Poltergeist*, 1982, exec. prodr., writer *The Goonies*, 1985, (TV series) *Amazing Stories*, 1985–87, *Tiny Toon Adventures*, 1990–92, *Animaniacs*, 1993–98, dir., prodr., writer *Artificial Intelligence: AI*, 2001, asst. dir. action scenes (films) *Star Wars III: Revenge of the Sith*, 2005. Mem. adv. bd. Sci. Fiction Mus. and Hall of Fame. Recipient Man of Yr. award Hasty Pudding Theater, Harvard U., 1983, Outstanding Directorial Achievement award for feature films, Dirs. Guild Am., 1985, Film award, Brit. Acad. Film and TV Arts, 1986, Irving Thalberg Mem. award, Acad. Motion Picture Arts and Scis., 1987, Golden Lion award for career achievement, Venice Film Festival, 1993, Life Achievement award Am. Film Inst., 1995, John Huston award, Artists Rights Found., 1995; named Entertainment Weekly's Most Powerful Person in Entertainment, 1997, Lifetime Achievement award, Dir. Guild Am., 2000; named one of 50 Most Powerful People in Hollywood Premiere mag., 2004, 2005; knighted Order of British Empire, 2001. Fellow Brit. Acad. Film and TV Arts. Achievements include winning film contest with 40-minute war movie, Escape to Nowhere, at age 13; made film Firelight at age 16, and made five films while in coll.; became TV dir. at Universal Pictures at age 20. Office: Creative Artists Agy 9830 Wilshire Blvd Beverly Hills CA 90212-1804

2000's

Science and Technology

Sergey Brin

Brin, Sergey, information technology executive; b. Moscow, Aug. 21, 1973; BS in Math. and Computer Sci. with honors, U. Md., College Park, 1993; MS, Stanford U., 1995; MBA, Instituto de Empresa. Co-founder, pres. tech., asst. sec. Google, Inc., Mountain View, Calif., 1998–; also bd. dirs. Spkr. World Econ. Forum, Technol., Entertainment and Design Conf.; spkr. in the field. Author: (Articles) Extracting Patterns and Relations from the World Wide Web; Scalable Techniques for Mining Casual Structures; Beyond Market Baskets: Generalizing Association Rules to Correlations; co-author (with Larry Page): Dynamic Data Mining: A New Architecture for Data with High Dimensionality; guest appearence on Charlie Rose Show, CNBC, CNNfn. Named one of World's 100 Most Influential People, Time Mag., 2005; fellow NSF. Office: Google Inc 1600 Amphitheatre Pkwy Mountain View CA 94043 Office Fax: 650-618-1499.

Larry Page

Page, Larry, information technology executive; BS in Engring., U. Mich.; postgrad., Stanford U.; MBA (hon.), Instituto de Empresa. Co-founder, founding CEO Google, Inc., Mountain View, Calif., 1998–2001, pres. products, 2001–, also bd. dirs. Spkr. in field; spkr. World Econ. Forum. Mem. nat. adv. com. U. Mich. Coll. Engring., Ann Arbor, Mich. Named Global Leader for Tomorrow, World Econ. Forum, 2002, Young Innovator Who Will Create the Future, MIT Tech. Review Mag., Innovator of Yr., Research and Development Mag.; named one of World's 100 Most Influential People, Time Mag., 2005; recipient Engring. Graduate award, U. Mich. Alumni Soc. Mem.: Nat. Acad. Engring., Eta Kappa Nu. Office: 1600 Amphitheatre Pkwy #41 Mountain View CA 94043-1351 Office Phone: 650-623-4000. Office Fax: 650-618-1499.

Newsmaker

George W. Bush

Bush, George Walker, 43rd President of the United States; b. New Haven, Conn., July 6, 1946; s. George Herbert Walker and Barbara (Pierce) Bush; m. Laura Lane Welsh, Nov. 5, 1977; children: Barbara, Jenna. BA in History, Yale U., 1968; MBA, Harvard U., 1975. CEO Bush Exploration, Midland, Tex., 1975–83; chmn., CEO Spectrum 7 Energy Corp., Midland, Tex., 1983–87; dir. Harken Energy Corp. (formerly Spectrum 7 Energy Corp.), Midland, Tex., 1986; sr. advisor George Herbert Walker Bush Presidential campaign, 1988; mng. gen. ptnr. Tex. Rangers (baseball franchise), 1989–94; gov. State of Tex., Austin, 1994–2000; pres. US, Washington, 2001–. Co-author (with Karen Hughes): A Charge to Keep, 1999. Pilot Texas Air Nat. Guard, 1968–70. Named Person of the Year, *Time* mag., 2004; named one of most influential people, 2005; recipient Big D award, Dallas All Sports Assn., 1989. Mem.: Delta Kappa Epsilon (pres. 1965–68). Republican. Achievements include first Governor in Texas history to be elected to two consecutive four-year terms; won re-election as Pres. in 2004. Office: The White House 1600 Pennsylvania Ave NW Washington DC 20500

Business and Industry

Meg Whitman

Whitman, Meg (Margaret C. Whitman), internet company executive; b. LI, N.Y., Aug. 4, 1956; m. Griffith R. Harsh IV; children: Griff, Will. BA in Econs., Princeton U., 1977; MBA, Harvard U., 1979. Brand asst. Procter & Gamble, 1979–81; v.p. Bain & Co., 1982–89; sr. v.p. mktg. & consumer products divsn. Walt Disney Co, Burbank, Calif., 1989–92; corp. v.p. strategic planning Stride Rite Corp., 1992–93, exec. v.p. Keds divsn., 1993–94, pres. Stride Rite divsn., 1994–95; pres., CEO Florists' Transworld Delivery (FTD), 1995–97; gen. mgr. preschool divsn. Hasbro Inc., 1997–98; pres., CEO eBay, Inc., San Jose, Calif., 1998–. Bd. dirs. eBay, Inc., 1998–, Staples Inc., 1999, The Goldman Sachs Group Inc., 2001–02, Procter & Gamble Co., 2003–, The Gap Inc., 2003–, DreamWorks Animation SKG, Inc. Bd. trustees Princeton U. Named Number One on List of Best CEO's, Worth, 2002; named one of 25 Most Powerful Business Mgrs. (annually since 2000), Business Week, 25 Most Powerful People in Business, Fortune, 2004, Most Powerful Women in American Business, World's 100 Most Influential People, Time Mag., 2004, 2005, Most Powerful Women, Forbes mag., 2005. Avocation: fly fishing. Office: eBay Inc 2145 Hamilton Ave San Jose CA 95125

Sports

Tiger Woods

Woods, Tiger (Eldrick Woods), professional golfer; b. Cypress, Calif., Dec. 30, 1975; s. Earl and Kultida W., m. Elin Nordegren, Oct. 5, 2004. Student, Stanford U. Winner Optimist Internat. Jr. World Championship, 1984, 1985, 1988, 1989, 1990, 1991, Ins. Youth Golf Classic (youngest ever to win), 1990, 1992, second pl., PGA Nat. Jr. Championship, 1990, semi-finalist, U.S. Jr. Amateur Championship, 1990, CIF-So. Calif. H.S. Invitational Championship, 1991, So. Calif. Jr. Championship, 1991, PING/Phoenix Jr. Championship, 1991, 1992, Edgewood Tahoe Jr. Classic, 1991, L.A. City Jr. Championship, 1991, Orange Bowl Jr. Internat. Championship, 1991, U.S. Jr. Amateur Championship (youngest ever to win), 1991, U.S. Jr. Amateur Championship (only golfer to win twice), 1992, U.S. Jr. Amateur Championship, 1993, Nabisco Mission Hills Desert Jr. Championship, 1992, Pro Gear San Antonio Shootout, 1992, So. Calif. Jr. Best Ball Championship, 1993, U.S. Amateur Championship (youngest ever to win, also largest come-back ever), 1994, U.S. Amateur Championship, 1995, 1996, Western Amateur Championship, 1994, So. Calif. Golf Assn. Amateur Championship, 1994, Pacific Northwest Amateur Championship, 1994, William Tucker Invitational, 1994, Jerry Pate Invitational, 1994, Stanford Invitational, 1995, Walt Disney World/Oldsmobile Classic, 1996, Las Vegas Invitational, 1996, NCAA Championship, 1996, John A. Burns Invitational, 1996, Cleve. Golf Championship, 1996, Tri-Match Championship (Stanford U., Ariz. State U., U. Ariz.), 1996, Cougar Classic, 1996, Pac-10 Championship (shot course record 61), 1996, NCAA West Regional, 1996, Masters Tournament, 1997, 2001, 2002, 2005, Mercedes Championships, 1997, 2000, Asian Honda Classic, 1997, GTE Byron Nelson Classic, 1997, Motorola Western Open, 1997, 1999, Johnnie Walker Classic, 1998, 2000, BellSouth Classic, 1998, PGA Grand Slam, 1998, 1999, 2000, 2001, 2002, Meml. Tournament, 1999, 2000, 2001, PGA Championship (fifth youngest ever to win), 1999, Buick Invitational, 1999, 2003, Deutsche Bank-SAP Open, 1999, 2001, 2002, WGC NEC Invitational, 1999, 2000, 2001, Nat. Car Rental Classic, 1999, Tour Championship, 1999, WGC Am. Express Championship, 1999, 2002, 2003, World Cup individual and team titles (with Mark O'Meara), 1999, AT&T Pebble Beach Pro-Am, 2000, Bay Hill Invitational, 2000, 2001, 2002, 2003, U.S. Open Championship, 2000, 2002, Brit. Open Championship, 2000, 2005, PGA Championship, 2000, Bell Can. Open, 2000, World Cup (with David Duval), 2000, The Players Championship, 2001, Williams World Challenge, 2001, Buick Open, 2002, WGC Accenture Match Play, 2003, Western Open, 2003. Mem. U.S. Team World Amateur Team Championships, Versailles, France, 1994, Walker Cup Match, Porthcawl, Wales, 1995; qualified for U.S. Ryder Cup Team, 97, 99; qualified for U.S. Presidents Cup Team, 98; qualified for U.S. Ryder Cup Team, 2002; qualified for U.S. Presidents Cup Team, 2000; qualified for U.S. Ryder Cup Team, 04. Named Player of Yr., Am. Jr. Golf Assn., 1991, Golf Digest, 1991, 1992, Golf World, 1993, 1994, L.A. Times, 1994, Orange County, 1994, So. Calif. Player of Yr., 1991, 1992, 1993, Nat. Amateur of Yr., Titleist-Golfweek, 1991, 1992, Orange County League MVP, 1994, Pac-10 Player of Yr., 1995, 1996, First Team All-Am., 1995, 1996, Sportsman of Yr., Sports Illustrated, 1996, 2000, Reuters, 2000, PGA Tour Rookie of Yr., 1996, Fred Haskins Coll. Player of Yr. award, 1996, Jack Nicklaus Coll. Player of Yr., 1996, Male Athlete of Yr., AP, 1997, 1999, 2000, Male Athlete of Yr. (with Ken Griffey, Jr.), ESPN, 1997, Male Athlete of Yr., 1999–01, World Sportsman of Yr., World Sports Acad., 1999, Most Powerful Person in Sports, Sporting News, 2000, World Champion of Champions, L'Equipe, France, 2000; named to First Team Rolex Jr. All Am., 1991, 1992; recipient Dial award, 1993, Jack Nicklaus award, PGA Am., Golf Writers Assn. Am., 1997, 1999–03, Byron Nelson award, PGA Tour, 1999–03, Vardon Trophy, PGA of Am., 1999–03, Mark H. McCormack award as No. 1 player on world ranking, 1999–03. Achievements include being the youngest player, first African Am., first Asian Am., and having largest margin of victory (12 strokes) to win Masters Tournament, 1997; being first player ever to win U.S. Open, Brit. Open and PGA Championship in same yr. (2000); first player ever to hold all 4 maj. golf championships at the same time, 2001; ranked No. 1 player in world for a record 264 consecutive weeks, 1999-04. Office: PGA PO Box 109601 100 Avenue Of Champions Palm Beach Gardens FL 33418-3665

Entertainment, Arts, and Letters

Oprah Winfrey

Winfrey, Oprah, television talk show host, actress, television producer; b. Kosciusko, Miss., Jan. 29, 1954; d. Vernon Winfrey and Vernita Lee. BA in Speech Comm. and Performing Arts, Tenn. State U. News reporter Sta. WVOL Radio, Nashville, 1971-72; reporter, news anchorperson Sta. WTVF-TV, Nashville, 1973-76; news anchorperson Sta. WJZ-TV, Balt., 1976–78, host morning talk show People Are Talking, 1978–83; host talk show A.M. Chgo. Sta. WLS-TV, 1984; host The Oprah Winfrey Show, Chgo., 1985–, Oprah After the Show, Chgo., 2002–; nationally syndicated, 1986–; host series of celebrity interview spls. Oprah: Behind the Scenes; owner, prodr., chmn., CEO Harpo Prodns., 1986–. Ptnr., co-founder Oxygen Media, an Internet and cable TV co., 2000–; founder, editl. dir. O, The Oprah Magazine in conjunction with Hearst Mags., 2000; launched (mag.) first internat. edit., O, The Oprah Magazine in South Africa, 2002-, O at Home, 2004-; online leader, Oprah.com, launched Live Your Best Life, 2003-; started Oprah Book Club. Appeared in films The Color Purple, 1985 (nominated Acad. award and Golden Globe award), Native Son, 1986, There Are No Children Here, 1993, Beloved, 1998 (prodr.), About Us: The Dignity of Children, 1997 (TV), Before Women Had Wings, 1997 (TV; also prodr. ABC series Oprah Winfrey presents); prodr. Dr. Phil (TV series), 2002–; Listen Up: The Lives of Quincy Jones (TV spl.), 1990; prodr., actress ABC-TV miniseries The Women of Brewster Place, 1989, also series Brewster Place, 1990; exec. prodr. (ABC Movie of the Week) Overexposed, 1992; host, supervising prodr. celebrity interview series Oprah: Behind the Scenes, 1992, ABC Aftersch. Spls., 1991-93; host, exec. prodr. Michael Jackson Talks...to Oprah-90 Prime-Time Minutes with the King of Pop, 1993; exec. prodr. (TV) Nine, 1992, Oprah Winfrey Presents: Their Eyes Were Watching God, 2005; exec. prodr. TV miniseries: Oprah Winfrey Presents: The Wedding, 1998, David and Lisa, 1998, Tuesdays with Morrie, 1999, Amy and Isabelle, 2001, Their Eyes Were Watching God, 2005; voice (video) Our Friend, Martin, 1999; guest appearances: The Fresh Prince of Bel-Air, 1992, Ellen, 1997, Home Improvement, 1999, The Hughleys, 1999, Mad TV, 2002, Desperate Housewives, 2005, and several others. Established Oprah Winfrey Found., 1987–, Oprah's Angel Network, 1997–, ChristmasKindness South Africa, 2002–, Oprah Winfrey Scholars Program. Recipient Woman of Achievement award NOW, 1986, Emmy award for Best Daytime Talk Show Host, 1987, 91, 92, 94, 95, 97, Hon. Nat. Book Award for influential contbn. to reading and books, 1999, Nat. Book Found's 50th Anniversary gold medal, 1999, America's Hope award, 1990, Industry Achievement award Broadcast Promotion Mktg. Execs./Broadcast Design Assn., 1991, Image awards NAACP, 1989, 91, 92, 94, Entertainer of Yr. award NAACP, 1989, CEBA awards, 1989, 90, 91, George Foster Peabody's 1995 Individual Achievement award, 1996, Gold Medal award IRTS, 1996, Lifetime Achievement award NATAS, 1998, People's Choice award, 1997, 98, Horatio Alger award, 1993, Bob Hope Humanitarian award, 2002, Marian Anderson Award, Phila., 2003, AAP Honors award, Assn. Am. Publishers, 2003, Disting. Svc. award, Nat. Assn. Broadcasters, 2004; ranked #1 Most Powerful In Industry, Entertainment Weekly, 1998, 200 Greatest Pop Culture Icons, VH1, 2003; named Broadcaster of Yr. Internat. Radio and TV Soc., 1988, TV Performer of Yr., TV Guide, 1997, Most Important Person in Books and Media, Newsweek, 1997; named one of 50 Most Beautiful in the World, People, 1997, America's 25 Most Influential People of the 20th Century, Time, 1998, 100 Most Powerful Women in Entertainment, Hollywood Reporter, 2004, 100 Most Influential People, Time Mag., 2005, Most Powerful Women, Forbes mag., 2005, Nat. Freedom Award, Nat. Civil Rights Mus., 2005; named to List American Billionaires, Fortune, 2003; inducted to Television Hall of Fame, 1994, Broadcasting and Cable Hall of Fame, 2002; elected to Nat. Women's Hall of Fame, Seneca Falls, NY. Initiated a campaign to establish a national database of convicted child abusers, and testified before U.S. Senate Judiciary Committee on behalf of National Child Protection Act in 1991, as a result, President Clinton signed the "Oprah Bill" into Law on December 20, 1993, establishing the national database used by law enforcement agencies around the world; third woman in American entertainment industry to own her own studio; first African-American woman to reach billionaire status; after receiving Lifetime Achievement award in 1998, permanently withdrew name from Daytime Emmy Award consideration; Oprah and Oprah Winfrey Show received a total of 39 Daytime Emmy awards: seven for Outstanding Host; nine for Outstanding Talk Show; 21 in the Creative Arts categories; and one for supervising producer of the ABC School Special, Shades of Single Protein. Office: Oprah Winfrey Show Harpo Studios 1058 W Washington Blvd Chicago IL 60607 Address: Harpo Prodn PO Box 909715 Chicago IL 60607 Office Phone: 312-633-0808.

Who'sWho in America®

Biographees A - L

AABERG, THOMAS MARSHALL, SR., academic administrator; b. St. Paul, Sept. 5, 1936; m. Judith S. Young, June 17, 1961; children: Thomas M. Jr., Leigh, Sarah. BA, Dartmouth Coll., 1958, MS, 1959; MD, Harvard U., 1961; MSPH in Preventive Medicine, U. Okla., 1967. Diplomate Am. Bd. Ophthalmology. Asst. prof. ophthalmology Med. Coll. Wis., Milw., 1969-71, assoc. prof. ophthalmology, 1971-76, prof. ophthalmology, 1976-88; chmn. dept. ophthalmology Sch. Medicine Emory U., Atlanta, 1988—. Surgeon USPHS, 1966-68. Office: Emory Eye Ctr Ste B 4405 1365-B Clifton Rd NE Atlanta GA 30322-1013 E-mail: ophttma@emory.edu.

AADAHL, JORG, engineering executive; b. Trondheim, Norway, June 16, 1937; came to U.S., 1966; s. Ottar P. and Gurli (Lockra) A.; m. Inger R. Holst, July 13, 1973; children: Erik, Nina. MS in Mech. Engring., Tech. U. Norway, 1961; MBA, U. San Francisco, 1973. Rsch. fellow Tech. U. Norway, Trondheim, 1961-62; mgr. arc welding devel. NAG, Oslo, 1964-66; mfg. engr. Varian Assocs., Palo Alto, Calif., 1966-67; sr. tech. writer Lynch Comm. sys., 1967-69; indsl. engr., project mgr. United Airlines, San Francisco, 1969-74, bus. mgr., 1974-75, sr. systems analyst, 1976-81; strategic planning specialist Magnex Corp., San Jose, Calif., 1981-82; cons. in mgmt., 1982-84; founder, pres. Safeware, Inc., San Mateo, Calif., 1984—; founder, prin. CampuSafe Sys., 1996—. Developer Safechem Hazardous Chem. Mgmt. Sys. Author: Strength Analysis, Welded Structures, 1967; editor Nordic Highlights, 1972; contbr. articles to profl. jours. Recipient Cert. of Honor, San Francisco Bd. Suprs., 1973. Mem. Leif Erikson League (pres. 1973), Norwegian Soc. Profl. Engrs., Environment and Safety Data Exch. (founding mem., dir.). Office: Safeware Inc PO Box 6745 San Mateo CA 94403-2366 E-mail: safechem@aol.com.

AADALEN, DAVID KEVIN, lawyer; b. Hamilton, Calif., Dec. 23, 1953; s. Arlie Vernon and Irma Jean (Willig) A.; m. Rhonda Kay Kramer, May 29, 1976; children: Luke David, Amy Johanna, Adam Ross. Student, U. Kans., 1971; BA, Washburn U., 1975, JD, 1979. Bar: Kans. 1980, U.S. Dist. Ct. Kans. 1980. Pvt. practice, Topeka, 1980-93; sr. v.p. trust dept. mgr. Mercantile Bank of Topeka, 1993-95; ptnr. Clutter & Aadalen, LLP, 1997—. Judge pro tempore Shawnee County Dist. Ct., 1988—. Deacon Topeka Bible Ch., 1981-91; bd. dirs. Cair Paravel Latin Sch., Inc., 1995-2000. Named Outstanding Young Man in Am., U.S. Jaycees, 1982. Mem. Kans. Bar Assn., Topeka Bar Assn. (probate com.), Christian Legal Soc. Republican. Home: 3517 SW Oak Pky Topeka KS 66614-3220 Office: Clutter & Aadalen LLP 2201 SW 29th St Topeka KS 66611-1908

AADLAND, THOMAS VERNON, minister; b. Mpls., Dec. 24, 1950; s. Otto Sidney and Dorothy Jean (Holmquist) A.; m. Mary Joanne Pratt, June 27, 1981; children: Evangeline Faith, Brigitta Hope, Andrew Paul, Marian Joy. AB in Philosophy, Wheaton Coll., 1973; MDiv, Luther Theol. Sem., 1980. Ordained to ministry Am. Luth. Ch., 1980. Assoc. pastor Christ Luth. Ch., Duluth, Minn., 1980-91, sr. pastor, 1991—99; sec. Am. Assn. Luth. Chs., Mpls., 1987-93; min. Christ. Luth. Ch., 1980—99. Presiding pastor, Amer. Assn. of Lutheran Chs., 1999—, bd. dirs. Lake Superior Life Care Ctr., Duluth, Minn., 1987-90, pres. Lake Superior chpt. Luths. for Life, 1996—99, nat. bd. dirs., 2003—, sec., 2004—. Lutheran. Home: 13986 Dallas Ave Rosemount MN 55068-7108 Office Phone: 952-884-7784. E-mail: aadland@aol.com. *I believe Americans cannot escape the religous question. The enjoyment of our freedoms—in some vitally important sense—depends upon a humble and grateful recognition that the source of our fundamental rights to life, liberty and property is transcendent: they derive not from the generosity of the State but from the magnanimity of God, in Whose image we are created.*

AADNESEN, CHRISTOPHER, rail transportation executive, consultant; b. Salt Lake City, Nov. 2, 1948; s. Grant C. and Helen Jane (Ray) Aadnesen; m. Helen Elizabeth Twelves, Aug. 14, 1973 (div. 1988); children: Aric Paul, Brian James, Nicholas Twelves; m. Betty Jean DeLeon, Aug. 19, 1988; stepchildren: Brooke Binham, Brad Binham. BA in English, U. Utah, 1971, MBA, 1973; PMD, Harvard U., 1990. Gen. mgr., founder Thaddeus Duncan Co., Salt Lake City, 1968-72; divsn. supt. Western Pacific R.R., Sacramento, 1978-82; gen. supt. of transp. Mo. Pacific R.R., Spring, Tex., 1983-84; asst. gen. mgr. So. Region Union Pacific R.R., Spring, Tex., 1984-88, gen. dir. pers. svcs. Omaha, 1988-89, asst. v.p. ops. adminstrn., 1989-90, asst. v.p. employee devel. and involvement, 1990-91, sr. asst. v.p. field ops., 1992-93, sr. asst. v.p. transp., 1993-95, pres. capitol city group, pres. capitol city mgmt. assocs., 1996—; COO Transp. Ferroviara Mexicana, S.A. de C.V., 1996-99, exec. v.p., 1999-2000; exec. v.p., COO Tex. Mexican Rlwy. Co., 1999-2000; chmn. Port Terminal R.R. Assn., 2000-01. Bd. dirs. Georgetown Rail Equipment Co. Campaign mgr. County Commr., Quincy, Calif., 1978; commr. planning and zoning Georgetown, 2001—; bd. dirs. Palace Theatre, Georgetown, Tex., 2001—. With USN, 1967—69. Mem.: Am. Assn. R.R. Supts., Georgetown C. of C., Cimarron Hills Country Club, Berry Creek Country Club, Field Club Omaha, Happy Hollow Country Club, Rotary, Beta Theta Pi. Republican. Episcopalian. Avocations: guitar, golf, fishing. Home: 30205 Oak Tree Dr Georgetown TX 78628-1143 Office: Capitol City Group 4500 Williams Dr Ste 212 PO Box 255 Georgetown TX 78628

AAGAARD, JAMES KJERSGAARD, music educator; b. Portland, Oreg., June 24, 1947; s. George Merritt and Miriam Augusta Aagaard; m. Norlene Rene Emerson; 1 child, Emerson Jens. AA, Waldorf Coll., 1967; BA, St. Olaf Coll., 1970; MA, U. No. Iowa, 1976. Music dir. East Chain Schs., Fairmont, Minn., 1970—74; band dir. Waldorf Coll., Forest City, Iowa, 1974—75; music dir. U. Wis., Richland Ctr., Wis., 1976—. Dir. Ocooch Chorale, Richland Ctr., 1979—; artistic dir. Coppertop Summer Theater, Richland Ctr., 1985—95; dir. Richland Music Projects, Richland Ctr., 1990—. Mem.: Wis. Choral Dirs. Assn. (dir. allstate coll. choir 2003—), Am. Choral Dirs. Assn., Soc. American Music. Office: Univ Wisconsin Richland 1200 Hwy 14 W Richland Center WI 53581

AALBERS-SELLE, LAURIE LYNN, music educator; b. DesMoines, Iowa, Apr. 21, 1962; d. Duane Lee and Darlene Faye Aalbers; m. Dennis Lee Selle, Apr. 29, 1989; children: Colton, Cody, Cassie. BA, Ctrl. Coll., 1984; MA, Pacific Luth. U., 1992. Acct. City of Auburn, Wash., 1987—89; music specialist Sumner Sch. Dist., Sumner, Wash., 1989—. Treas. exec. bd. Evergreen Orff Chpt., Wash., 1999—; artist-in-residence Wash. State Arts and Pierce Co. Arts, 1999, 2001, 02. Com. chair Boy Scouts Am., 2004—05, den leader, 2002—04. Mem.: Music Educators Nat. Conf., Am. Orff-Schulwerk Assn., Phi Delta Kappa. Avocations: camping, hiking, painting, antiques, music. Office: Sumner Sch Dist #320 1202 Wood Ave Sumner WA 98390

AALBERTS, NOLA JEAN, social worker, administrator; b. Orange City, Iowa, Feb. 19, 1941; d. Gradus C. Aallberts and Auriel Mae Aalberts. BASW, Gustavus Adolphus Coll., 1963; MS in Mgmt., U. South Fla., 1977. Peace Corps vol., Guatemala, 1963—65; tchr. Am. Sch. Guatemala, Guatemala City, 1969—73; dir. Mitchell County Homemaker-Home Health Aide Svc., Osage, Iowa, 1969—73; dir., head start North Iowa Cmty. Action Orgn., Mason City, Iowa, 1973—74; program dir., homemaker-home health aide svc. Family Services Ctr., Clearwater, Fla., 1974—78; program assoc. Nat. HomeCaring Coun., N.Y.C., NY, 1978—80, program dir., 1980—83; dir., homemaker-home health aide sect. Iowa State Dept. of Health, Des Moines, 1983—85; dir., homemaker-home health aide divsn. Nat. Assn. for Home Care, Washington, 1985—89, adminstrv. dir., 1986—87; dir. of accreditation and edn. Found. for Hospice and Homecare, Washington, 1987—89; coord. for mission stewardship and supr. for native am. ministries, Ctrl. Am. and Ecuador Ref. Ch. in Am., Corona, Calif., 1989—2001, Orange City, Iowa, 1999—2001; coord. Healthy Families NW Iowa, 2001, NW Iowa Cmty. Empowerment, and Child Welfare Decategorization, Orange City, Iowa, 2001—. Adj. prof. Spanish Northwestern Coll., Orange City, Iowa, 2001—02; past advisor, state and nat. programs Health Care Financing Adminstrn.; past advisor Depts. Elderly and Adult Svcs., Social Svcs. and Health, N.H., Mo., Nebr., Iowa, N.Y., N.J.; past tchr. seminars on supervision in home care, N.H., Mo., Nebr., Iowa, N.Y., N.J. Contbr. articles to mags.; co-author: home care curricula for supervision and home care aides. State adv. com. Healthy Families Iowa program (HOPES), 2001—; mem. Iowa Early Childhood Devel. Stakeholders, 2003—, Mayor's Task Force on Child Care, Orange City, Iowa, 2002. Recipient Disting. Alumni award, Gustavus Adolphus Coll., 1986, Excellence in Edn. asward, Nat. Assn. Home Care, Spl. Contbns. award, Mental Health Ctr. North Iowa. Mem.: Iowa Empowerment Coordinators. Avocations: walking, hiking, travel.

AALL, CHRISTIAN BERGENGREN, software company executive; b. St. Louis, Dec. 7, 1955; s. Christian Hiorth Aall and Ruth (Bergengren) Perkins; m. Esther Drugowitsch, Aug. 5, 1983; children: Christian Daniel, Nathalie Caroline. MME, Swiss Fed. Inst. Tech., Zürich, 1980; MBA, Internat. Mgmt. Devel. Inst., Lausanne, Switzerland, 1987. Project mgr. Cementos Apasco S.A., Apasco, Mexico, 1981-82; cons. Holderbank (Switzerland) Mgmt. & Cons. Ltd., 1982-86; mgr. systems and strategic planning GM Europe Parts and Accessories, Zürich, 1988-91; comptr. GM Europe Parts & Accessories, Ruesselsheim, Germany, 1991-92; comptr. sales Adam Opel AG, Ruesselsheim, 1992-95; mng. dir. Opel Master Lease GmbH, Ruesselsheim, 1996-98; pres. Daidalos Cons., Wellesley, Mass., 1998-2001; dir. internat. ops. Daidalos Unternehmensberatung GmbH, Wolfratshausen, Germany, 1998—2001; CEO C2 Remktg., Inc., Los Altos, Calif., 2001—02; pres. Aall Devel., Inc., Wellesley, 2003—. Bd. trustees Frankfurt Internat. Sch., 1995-97, chmn. bldgs. and grounds com., treas., chmn. fin. com. 1997-98; treas. IMD Alumni Deutschland e.V., 1995-99. E-mail: caall@comcast.net.

AAMODT, ROGER LOUIS, federal agency administrator; b. San Francisco, Dec. 9, 1941; s. Rodney Lee and Barbara Helen (Quinn) A.; m. Janet Roberta Hall, Sept. 15, 1962 (div. 1995); children: Sandra Marie, Aaron Lee; m. Diane Sue Dwyer, Apr. 27, 1997. Student, Antioch Coll., 1959-60; BS cum laude, U. Utah, 1966; PhD, U. Rochester, 1972. Rsch. asst. dept. radiol. health U. Utah, Salt Lake City, 1965-66; sect. chief dept. nuclear medicine Clin. Ctr., NIH, Bethesda, Md., 1971-83; grants assoc. NIH, Bethesda, 1983-84; program dir. cancer diagnosis br. Nat. Cancer Inst., NIH, Rockville, Md., 1984-96, chief resources devel. br. cancer diagnosis program, 1997—2005; cons. Aamodt Enterprises, 2005—. Pres. Internat. Soc. for Biol. and Environ. Repositories, 2002—03. Author (with others): Textbook of Nuclear Medicine, 1978; contbr. refence tables to Human Health and Disease, 1977, more than 50 articles to profl. jours. Pres. Calvin Park Civic Assn., Rockville, 1974-94.—. Spl. Health Physics fellow U.S. Atomic Energy Commn., 1966-69, NDEA fellow, 1969-71. Mem. AAAS, Am. Soc. Investigative Pathology, Internat. Soc. Analytical Cytology, NIH Microcomputer Club (sec.-treas. 1983-84). Democrat. Methodist. Achievements include research on zinc absorption and metabolism in humans; organization of the NCI Cooperative Human Tissue Network, Cooperative Breast Cancer Tissue Resource, and Cooperative Prostate Cancer Tissue Network.

AAMOTH, GORDON M., medical association administrator; b. Apr. 12, 1940; MD, Northwestern U., 1966. Intern U. Calif., San Francisco, 1966—67, fellow, 1968—69, residency, 1969—73; clinical prof. of orthopaedic surgery U. Minn., dir. Abbott NW private rotation for orthopaedic surgery; pres. Am. Bd. of Orthopaedic Surgery. Office: Am Bd Orthopaedic Surgery 400 Silver Ceder Ctr Chapel Hill NC 27514 also: U Minn Depart of Orthopaedic Surgery 2512 S 7th St R200 Minneapolis MN 55454

AANSTOOS, CHRISTOPHER MICHAEL, psychology professor; b. Saipan Island, U.S. Trust, Apr. 4, 1952; s. Anthony Matthew and Frances Henrietta (Jambrick) A.; children: Megan, Elizabeth, Lucas Matthew. BA, Mich. State U., 1974; MA, Duquesne U., 1976, PhD, 1982. Instr. Pa. State U., McKeesport, 1979—82; asst. prof. psychology U. West Ga., Carrollton, 1982-87, assoc. prof., 1987-92, prof., 1992—, chmn., 1995-96. Contracted rschr. Pitts. Sch. Dist., 1979, Opaion, 2001; manuscript reviewer Harcourt, Brace, Jovanovich, NYC, 1983, New Ideas in Psychology, 1984—85, Saybrook Inst., 1986, Metaphor and Symbolic Activity, 1985—88, Sage, 1989, Guilford, 1990; nat. adv. panel Existential-Humanistic Inst.; adv. coun. Ctr. Study Psychology Psychiatry; program chmn. Symposium for Qualitative Rsch., Perugia, Italy, 1987, Perugia, 99; lectr. in field. Editor: Exploring the Lived World, 1984, The World of the Infant, 1987, The Humanistic Psychologist, 1985—2002, Human Growth and Development, 1990, Studies in Humanistic Psychology, 1991; editor: (assoc.) Jour. Theoretical Philos. Psychology, 1986—89; editor: (cons.) Jour. Phenomenological Psychology, 1982—, Jour. Humanistic Psychology, 1989, Jour. Psychology of Religion, 1991—94, Psychotherapy Patient, 1996—, Ethical Human Scis. and Svcs., 1999—; contbr. articles to profl. pubs. Vol. West Ga. Coll. Spkrs. Bur., 1983—; coord. fund drive Am. Heart Assn., U. West Ga., 1985. Faculty Rsch. grantee U. West Ga., 1983-85, 89-90, 92-93. Fellow APA (exec. bd. divs. 24, 32, program chmn. divsn. 24 1991, pres. divsn. 32 1997-98); mem. AAUP, Human Sci. Rsch. Assn. (program chmn. 1984), Southeastern Psychol. Assn., Assn. Qualitative Rsch. Psychology (chmn. program com. 1987-97), Chess Fedn. West Ga., Phi Beta Kappa. Home: 2175 Hog Liver Rd Carrollton GA 30117-9308 Office: U West Ga Psychology Dept Carrollton GA 30118-0001

AARHUS, CRAIG H., music educator, director; b. Sylacauga, Ala., Mar. 14, 1974; s. Betty Aarhus; m. Amy Folsom, June 10, 1976. B in Music Ed., Auburn U., 1997; MA, U. Iowa, 2002. Asst. band dir. Miss. State U., Mississippi State, 2003—. Founder, dir. Starkville/Miss. Stat4e U. Cmty. Band, Mississippi State. Fellow, U. Iowa, 2005—. Presbyterian. Avocation: tennis. Office: Mississippi State U Band PO Box 6162 Mississippi State MS 39762 Office Phone: 662-325-2323. Personal E-mail: craigaarhus@hotmail.com.

AARIM-HERIOT, NAJIA, history professor, researcher; b. Meknes, Morocco, Dec. 19, 1959; d. Jelloul Aarim and Rabha El Khalssi; m. Kirk Heriot, Dec. 14, 2001; children: Adam H. Heriot, Neil S. Heriot. MA Doctorat 3EME cycle, Universite De Grenoble, France, 1984; PhD, Temple U., 1996. Prof. Brit. and Am. studies Universite Moulay Ismail, Meknes, Morocco, 1984—98; assoc. prof. history SUNY- Fredonia, 1998—. Author: (articles, book) Chinese Immigrants, African Americans, and Racial Anxiety in the United States, 1848-1882 (hon. mention Gustavus Myers Ctr. for the Study of Bigotry and Human Rights book award, 2004). Mem.: Orgn. Am. Historians, Am. Hist. Assn. Avocations: reading, travel, arts, cooking. Office: SUNY-Fredonia Dept Of History Fredonia NY 14063 Office Fax: 716-673-3332. E-mail: aarim@fredonia.edu.

AARON, BENJAMIN, law educator, arbitrator; b. Chgo., Sept. 2, 1915; s. Henry Jacob and Rose (Weinstein) A.; m. Eleanor Opsahl, May 24, 1941; children: Judith, Louise. AB, U. Mich., 1937; LL.B., Harvard U., 1940; postgrad., U. Chgo., 1940-41. With Nat. War Labor Bd., 1942-45; mem. labor adv. com. to Supreme Comdr. Allied Powers, Tokyo, 1946; research assoc. Inst. Indsl. Relations; lectr. labor law, dept. econs. UCLA, 1946-51, assoc. dir., 1957-60, dir., 1960-75, prof. law, 1960-86, prof. emeritus, 1986—. Faculty mem. Salzburg (Austria) Seminar in Am. Studies, 1958, 67; arbitrator labor-mgmt. disputes, 1946—; pub. mem. WSB, Washington, 1951-52; mem. Statutory Arbitration Bd. in R.R. Dispute, 1963-64; chmn. Calif. Farm Labor Panel, 1965-66; mem. Nat. Commn. on Tech., Automation and Economic Progress, 1965-66; pub. mem. Adv. Council on Employee Welfare and Pension Benefit Plans, 1966-68; vis. prof. Harvard U., 1972, U. Mich., 1979; mem. pub. rev. bd. U.A.W., 1975—; mem. arbitration services adv. com. Fed. Mediation and Conciliation Service, 1974-82; mem. ILO Com. of Experts on Application of Convs. and Recommendations, 1986-94; charter emeritus fellow Coll. of Labor and Employment Lawyers, 1996—. Author: Legal Status of Employee Benefit Rights Under Private Pension Plans, 1961; Editor: The Employment Relation and The Law, 1957, Labor Courts and Grievance Settlement in Western Europe, 1970, Comparative Labor Law jour, 1979-85; co-editor: Industrial Conflict: A Comparative Legal Survey, 1972; Public-Sector Bargaining, 1979; mem. editl. bd. Internat. Labor Law Reps., 1974—2005. Fellow Ctr. for Advanced Study in Behavioral Scis., 1966-67; vis. fellow Clare Hall, Cambridge (Eng.) U., 1973, Australian Nat. U., 1982; named First Southwestern Legal Found. Rsch. Fellows Disting. Scholar in Residence, 1971; first Howard W. Wissner Meml. Lectr. Tulane U., 1971; Phi Beta Kappa vis. scholar, 1978-79 Mem. ABA (sec. sect. labor rels. law 1975-76), AAUP, Internat. Soc. Labor Law and Social Security (chmn. U.S. nat. com., internat. exec. com. 1967-83, v.p. N.Am. region 1982-85, pres. 1985-88, hon. pres. 1988—), Nat. Acad. Arbitrators (pres. 1962, bd. govs.), Indsl. Rels. Rsch. Assn. (exec. bd. 1965-68, pres. 1972, mem. CCH labor law reports panel of experts 1987-92), Am. Arbitration Assn. (mem. adv. coun. L.A. 1975-76, Disting. Svc. award 1981). Home: 316 18th St Santa Monica CA 90402-2406 Office: UCLA 405 Hilgard Ave Los Angeles CA 90095-1476 Office Phone: 310-825-1296.

AARON, CHESTER, retired medical educator, writer; b. Butler, Pa., May 7, 1923; s. Albert Aaron and Celia Charleson; BA, U. Calif., Berkeley, 1955; MA, San Francisco State U., 1960. Chief technologist x-ray dept. Alta Bates Hosp., Berkeley, 1957—72; prof. St. Mary's Coll., Moraga, Calif., 1973—98; ret., 1998—. Tchr., cons. in field, Calif., 1997—. Author: About Us, 1967, An American Ghost, 1973, Gideon, 1982, Garlic is Life, 1996, Garlic Kisses, 2001, Home To The Sea, 2004, Whispers, 2004, Willa's Poppy, 2005, 4 audio books, 2005. With U.S. Army, 1943—45, Germany. Recipient award, Hartford Found., 1950, Chapelbrook Found., 1953, Nat. Endowment Arts, 1960. Mem.: Authors' Guild, Screenwriters' Guild. Home: PO Box 388 Occidental CA 95465 Personal E-mail: chgarlic@comcast.net.

AARON, DAVID L., diplomat, author; b. Chgo., Aug. 21, 1938; m. Chloe W. Aaron; 1 child. BA, PhD (hon.), Occidental Coll.; MA, Princeton U. With Fgn. Svc., 1962—, polit. and econ. officer Guayaquil, Ecuador; internat. rels. officer Dept. of State, 1964-66; polit. officer NATO, Paris, 1966; with Arms Control and Disarmament Agy.; sr. staff mem. Nat. Security Coun., 1972-74; legis. asst. Senator Walter F. Mondale, Minn., 1974-75; task force leader select com. intelligence U.S. Senate, 1975-76; dep. asst. to pres. for nat. security, 1977-81; v.p. Oppenheimer and Co., Inc., 1981-85; writer, lectr. Lantz-Harris Agy., 1985-93. Sr. advisor Mondale Presdl. Campaign, 1984; cons. 20th Century Fund, 1990-92, sr. fellow, 1992-93; bd. dirs. quest value dual purpose fund Oppenheimer Capital Corp.; amb., U.S. rep. Orgn. Econ. Cooperation and Devel., Paris, 1996.; presdl. spl. envoy for cryptography, 1996; undersec. internat. trade dept. Commerce, 1997-00; sr. internat. adv. Dorsey & Whitney, 2000-2003; sr. fellow RAND, 2003—. Author: State Scarlet, Agent of Influence, Crossing By Night; contbr. articles to profl. jours. Staff mem. Carter-Mondale Presdl. Campaign; bd. dirs. Atlantic Coun. Decorated Nat. Def. medal. Mem. Nat. Dem. Inst. Internat. Affairs (bd. dirs.), Coun. Fgn. Rels., Internat. League Human Rights (bd. dirs.), Authors Guild, Pacific Coun. on Internat. Policy. Office: RAND 1700 Main St Santa Monica CA 90407-2138 Office Phone: 310-393-0411. E-mail: daaron@rand.org.

AARON, HANK (HENRY L. AARON), professional baseball team executive; b. Mobile, Ala., Feb. 5, 1934; s. Herbert and Estella A. Aaron; m. Billye Suber Aaron, Nov. 1973; 1 child, Ceci; children: Gail, Hank, Lary, Gary-(dec.). Ed. pub. schs. Former semi-pro baseball player; baseball player Milw. Braves (became Atlanta Braves 1966), 1954—76; v.p. player devel. Atlanta Braves, 1976—89, sr. v.p., asst. to pres., 1989—, also bd. dirs.; owner Hank Aaron Automotive Group, 1999—. Mem. Nat. League All-Star Team, 1955—74, Am. League All-Star Team, 1975, World Series Championship Team, 1957; broke Babe Ruth's career home run record with 715th home run, April 8, 1974; holder major league record for most home runs (755), most runs batted in (2297). Author: (autobiography) I Had A Hammer: The Hank Aaron Story, 1991. Pres. No Greater Love, 1974; nat. chmn. Friends of Fisk for Athletics; organizer Hank Aaron Scholarship Fund; sponsor Hank Aaron Celebrity Bowling Tournament for Sickle Cell Anemia, 1972; mem. exec. bd. PUSH; mem. nat. bd. Big Bros./Big Sisters Am., NAACP; state chmn. Wis. Easter Seal Soc., 1975; nat. sports chmn. Nat. Easter Seal Soc., 1974; mem. Atlanta bd. Am. Cancer Soc. Named Most Valuable Player, Nat. League, 1957, Player of Yr., Sporting News, 1956, 1963, MLB All-Century Team, 1999; named to Baseball Hall of Fame, 1982; recipient Nat. League Gold Glove Award, 1958—60. Office: Atlanta Braves PO Box 4064 Atlanta GA 30302-4064

AARON, HENRY J., economist; BA, UCLA, 1958; MA, Harvard U., 1960, PhD, 1963. Sr. fellow econ. studies The Brookings Inst., Washington. Former asst. sec. for planning and evaluation Dept. Health, Edn., and Welfare; bd. dirs. Ctr. on Budget and Policy Priorities, Abt Assocs., Am. Tax Policy Inst.; rsch. and adv. bd. Stanford Inst. Econ. Policy Rsch., 1991—; mem. Inst. Medicine, 1986—. Author: (book) Serious and Unstable Condition: Financing America's Health Care, 1991, The Problem that Won't Go Away: Reforming U.S. Health Care Financing, 1996; co-author: The Painful Prescription: Rationing Hospital Care, 1984, The Comparable Worth Controversy, 1986, Can America Afford to Grow Old? Paying for Social Security, 1989, Countdown to Reform: The Great Social Security Debate, 1998; editor: Setting National Priorities: Policy for the Nineties, 1990, Behavioral Dimensions of Retirement Policy, 1999; co-editor: Uneasy Compromise: Problems of a Hybrid Income-Consumption Tax, 1988, Setting Domestic Priorities: What Can Government Do?, 1992, Economic Effects of Fundamental Tax Reform, 1996, Setting National Priorities: The 2000 Election and Beyond, 1999, Coping with Methuselah: The Impact of Molecular Medicine on Biology and Society, 2004, Health in Restoring Fiscal Sanity, 2005, Meeting the Long Term Fiscal Challenge, 2005, Can We Say No? The Challenges of Health Care Rationing, 2005; contbr. articles to profl. jours. Guggenheim fellow, 1996—97. Mem.: NAS (mem. Inst. Medicine), AAAS, Adv. Coun. on Social Security (former chmn.), Nat. Acad. Social Ins. (chmn. bd. dirs.), Am. Econ. Assn. (former v.p.). Office: 1775 Massachusetts Ave NW Washington DC 20036 Office Phone: 202-797-6128. Business E-Mail: haaron@brookings.edu.

AARON, HENRY JACOB, economics professor; b. Chgo., June 16, 1936; s. David and Betty (Cooper) A.; m. Ruth Kotell, May 5, 1963; children: Jeffrey, Melissa. AB, UCLA, 1958; MA, Harvard U., 1960, PhD, 1963. Assoc. prof. econs. U. Md., 1967-75, prof., 1975-77, 79-89; sr. fellow Brookings Instn., 1968-78, 96—, 1996—, dir. econ. studies, 1990-96; asst. sec. planning and evaluation HEW, Washington, 1977-78. Sr. staff economist Pres.'s Coun. Econ. Advisers, 1966-67; mem. Gov. Md. Coun. Econ. Advisers, 1968-75;

vis. prof. econs. Harvard U., 1974; mem. bd. dirs. Abt Assocs., 1979—, Ctr. on Budget and Policy Priorities, 1994—; chmn. Adv. Coun. on Social Security, 1978-79; trustee Tchrs. Ins. and Annuity Assn., 1984-87; trustee Georgetown U., 1995-97, bd. dirs.; mem. vis. com. dept. econs. Harvard U., 1985-89; mem. Inst. Medicine, 1986—, mem. com. on econ. future of baseball, 1990-92; rsch. adv. coun. Joint Ctr. Polit. Studies, 1984-89; v.p. Nat. Acad. Social Ins., 1986-96, chmn. bd. dirs., 1998—; rsch. adv. bd. Com. Econ. Devel., 1988-92; mem. adv. com. Stanford Inst. for Econ. Policy Rsch. Stanford U., 1991—. Author: Who Pays the Property Tax?, 1974, Politics and the Professors, 1978, Serious and Unstable Condition: Financing America's Health Care; co-author: The Peculiar Problem of Taxing Life Insurance Companies, 1983, The Economic Effects of Social Security, 1984, The Painful Prescription: Rationing Hospital Care, 1984, Assessing Tax Reform, 1985, Can America Afford To Grow Old?, 1988, (with Robert Reischauer) Countdown to Reform: The Great Social Security Debate; editor: Setting National Priorities: Policies for the Nineties, 1990, Serious and Unstable Condition: Financing America's Health Care, 1991; co-editor: Setting Domestic Priorities: What Can Government Do?, 1992, Values and Public Policy, 1994. Economic Effects of Fundamental Tax Reform (edited with William Gale), 1996, (with Robert D. Reischaver) Countdown to Reform: The Great Social Security Debate, 1998, Jour. Econ. Perspectives, Jour. Pub. Econs., Jour. Health Econs.; contbr. articles to profl. jours. Mem. adv. com. Ctr. for Econ. Policy Rsch., Stanford U. Ctr. for Advanced Study in the Behavioral Scis. fellow, 1996-97, Guggenheim fellow, 1996-97. Mem. Am. Econ. Assn. (exec. com. 1978-81, v.p. 1991), Am. Acad. Arts and Scis., Assn. Pub. Policy and Mgmt. (pres. 1998-99). Home: Apt #41 2101 Connecticut Ave NW Washington DC 20008 Office: 1775 Massachusetts Ave NW Washington DC 20036-2103 Business E-Mail: haaron@brookings.edu.

AARON, HUGH, writer; b. Worcester, Mass., Nov. 30, 1924; s. Barnet and Gertrude Rose Aaron; m. Joyce Charlotte Gomberg, June 19, 1955 (div. June 1988); children: Suzanne Ruth, Andrew Mark, Elizabeth Ann; m. Ann Marie Stein, Apr. 29, 1989. AB, U. Chgo., 1951. Supr. Apex Tire & Rubber Co., Pawtucket, R.I., 1955-57, Elfskin Corp., Worcester, 1958-60; mgr. Plastic Materials Inc., Slatersville, R.I., 1960-65; pres. Customcolor Inc., Cumberland, R.I., 1966-85; writer Belfast, Maine, 1985—. Author: Business Not as Usual, 1993, When Wars Were Won, 1995, It's All Chaos, 1996, Letters from the Good War, 1997, Driven, Notes of a Neurotic Entrepreneur, 1995, Go West Old Man, 1996, Quintet, 2005; (children's stories) Suzy, Fair Suzy, 1998, Andy in the Morning, 2000; author of essays, short stories, plays, novels. With USN, 1943-45. Mem. Maine Writers and Pubs. Alliance. Avocations: reading, sailing, gardening, hiking. Home: 6 Henderson Lane Cushing ME 04563 E-mail: haaron@adelphia.net.

AARON, KATHLEEN F., librarian; BS, Calif. State Poly. U., 1972; MLS, Calif. State U., 1975. Libr. Riverside (Calif.) City and County Pub. Libr., 1976-79; reference libr. Inland Libr. Sys., Riverside, 1979-83, reference coord., 1983-92, exec. dir., 1992—. Pres. Tierra del Sol Regional Libr. Network, 2000—. Mem. ALA, Calif. Libr. Assn. Office: Inland Libr Sys PO Box 468 Riverside CA 92502-0468

AARON, KENNETH ELLYOT, lawyer; b. Phila., Nov. 3, 1948; s. Neal L. and Dorothea G. Aaron; m. Phyllis A. Carroll, May 29, 1969; children: Seth Joel, Joshua Scott. BS in Econs., U. Pa., 1970, JD, 1973. Bar: Pa. 1973, U.S. Dist. Ct. (ea. dist.) Pa. 1973, U.S. Ct. Appeals (3d cir.) 1974, U.S. Supreme Ct. 1977, U.S. Dist. Ct. (we. and ea. dist.) Pa. 1993, Del. 2001, Fla. 2001, U.S. Dist. Ct. Del. 2001, U.S. Dist. Ct. (so. and no. dists.) Fla. 2001; cert. bus.bankruptcy law specialist Am. Bankruptcy Bd, Cert. Assoc. Astor & Weiss, Phila., 1973-76; ptnr. Casper & Davidson, P.C., Phila., 1976-80; pvt. practice Phila., 1980-83; ptnr. Garfinkel & Volpicelli, Phila., 1983-86, Mesirov, Gelman, Jaffe, Cramer & Jamieson, Phila., 1986-91, Buchanan Ingersoll P.C., Phila., 1991-2001, Weir & Ptnrs., Phila., 2001—. Mem. Ea. Dist. Pa. Bankruptcy Conf., vice chmn. edn. com. 1991, co-chmn. 1992, co-chmn. legis com., 1993; trustee Phila. Bar Found., 1997-2000. Author: Foreclosure and Repossession, 1989; contbr. chpts. to books Commr. Haverford (Pa.) Twp. Planning Bd., 1978—80; chmn. Lower Merion Zoning Bd., 1993—; planning commr. Lower Merion Twp. Planning Bd., Ardmore, Pa., 1992. Recipient Tax Writing award Nat. Assn. Accts., 1970, Am. Jr. award in Creditors' Rights, 1973. Mem.: Phila. Bar Found. (trustee 1997—2000), Phila. Bar Assn. (chmn. commn. on insolvency issues in real estate 1989—), Hias & Coun. (v.p. 1999—2002), Rotary (pres. Haverford Twp. 1982—83). Avocations: sports, camping, golf. Office: Weir & Ptnrs 1339 Chestnut St Ste 500 Philadelphia PA 19107 Office Phone: 215-665-8181. Business E-Mail: kaaron@wgirpartners.com.

AARON, LARRY GENE, secondary school educator, writer, minister; b. Danville, Va., Oct. 10, 1945; s. Conley Lee and Virginia Evelyn Aaron; m. Bonita Louise Becker (div.); m. Nancy Cody Ikenberry, June 3, 1989; children: Lori Cramton, Christie Wright, John. B in Biology, Va. Tech., 1968; B in Religious Edn., Midwestern Bapt. Coll., 1974; MDiv, Liberty Bapt. Theol. Sem., 1986; D in Ministry, Luther Rice Sem., 1999. Assoc. pastor, interim Christian Heritage Ch., Danville, 1993—94; tchr., chair dept. sci. Chatham H.S., Va., 1997—2004. Instr., adj. faculty Nat. Coll. Bus. Tech., Danville, 1996—; instr. Piedmont Regional Govs. Sch., 2003-05 Author: Barefoot Boy: An Anthology of Blue Ridge Poems. Recipient Va. medal Va. Soc. SAR, 1997-98, Meritorious Svc. medal, 2000, Liberty medal Nat. Soc. SAR, First Place Feature Writing Series award Va. Press Assn., 2000, 02, named State of Yr. Aerospace Edn. Found. Va., 2004, Tchr. of Yr. Chatham HS, 2004-05, HS Educator of Yr. Pittsylvania County Schs., 2005 Mem. Soc. Protozoologists, Va. Assn. of Sci. Tchrs. Avocations: backpacking, biking. Home: 185 Martindale Dr Danville VA 24541 Personal E-mail: lgaar@juno.com.

AARON, M. ROBERT, electrical engineer; b. Phila., Aug. 21, 1922; s. Edward A. and Beatrice A.; m. Wilma Spiegelman, Nov. 18, 1944; children: Richard, James. BSE.E., U. Pa., 1949, MSE.E., 1951. Research engr. Franklin Inst. Research Labs., Phila., 1949-51; with Bell Telephone Labs. Inc., Murray Hill, N.J., 1951-89, supr., 1954-68, dept. head, 1968-89; ret., 1989; cons., 1989—. Lectr., tchr. in field. Mem. adv. com. Whippany (N.J.) Sch. Bd., 1950's. Guest editor for tech. jours., 1971-99; contbr. articles to profl. jours., poems to various jours.; patentee in field. Tutor NAACP Program, Red Bank, N.J., 1966-68. Served to lt. (j.g.) USCG, 1942-45. Co-recipient computers and communications prize Found. for Computers and Communications Promotion, 1988. Fellow IEEE (mem. fin. bd. 1976-77, awards bd. 1987-89, 93, co-recipient Alexander Graham Bell medal 1978, Centennial medal 1984, Millenium medal 2000), Internat. Engring. Consortium; mem. Nat. Acad. Engring., IEEE Circuits and Systems Soc. (assoc. editor 1969-71, pres. 1973), IEEE Comm. Soc. (chmn. awards bd. 1975-79, 80-84, bd. govs. 1986-89, Meritorious Svc. award 1985, fellow evaluation 1992-96, disting. lectr. 1995, lifetime svc. award 1997, Christopher Columbus internat. telecomms. award 1999), Student Soc. for Stem Cell Rsch. (mem. adv. bd. 2004—), Internat. Myeloma Found. Home and Office: 2427 Presidential Way Apt 901 West Palm Beach FL 33401-1359 Office Phone: 561-687-2345. E-mail: b.aaron@ieee.org.

AARON, MARCUS, II, lawyer; b. Pitts., Oct. 24, 1929; s. Marcus Lester and Maxine (Goldmark) A.; m. Barbara Goldman, Feb. 6, 1955; children: Susan, Judith, Barbara. AB, Princeton U., 1950; JD, Harvard U., 1953. Bar: Pa. 1953, D.C. 1953, U.S. Dist. Ct. (we. dist.) Pa. 1956, U.S. Supreme Ct. 1969, U.S. Ct. Appeals (3d cir.) 1971. Assoc. Glick, Berkman & Engel, Pitts., 1956-64; ptnr. Klett, Rooney, Lieber & Schorling, P.C., Pitts., 1965-99, sr. counsel, 2000—. Asst. solicitor City of Pitts., 1957—67; bd. dirs. Homer Laughlin China Co., Newell, W.Va., 1967—, sec., 1972—88, v.p., 1980—88, pres., treas., 1989—2001. Trustee Western Pa. Sch. for Blind Children, Pitts., 1969—2001, pres., 1982—90; bd. dirs. Blue Cross of Western Pa., Pitts., 1972—86, sec., 1984—86; bd. dirs. Ctr. Engring., Inc., State College, Pa., 1984—92; trustee Rodef Shalom Congregation, Pitts., 1991—2001, hon. trustee, 2002—, treas., 1996—98, v.p., 1998—2001. Mem.: ABA, Allegheny County Bar Assn., Pa. Bar Assn. Democrat. Jewish. Home: 2298 Pacific Ave #6 San Francisco CA 94115-1435 Office: Klett Rooney Lieber & Schorling 1 Oxford Ct Fl 40 Pittsburgh PA 15219-6498 E-mail: maaron@KlettRooney.com.

AARON, MERIK ROY, financial executive, educator, lawyer; b. N.Y.C., May 22, 1947; s. Harry and Gertrude S. (Scherl) A.; m. Karen M. Snyder, 1984; children: Stacey Lynn, Lauren Jill. BA, L.I. U., 1969, MA, 1971; profl. diploma, Hofstra U., 1975; EdD, Nova Southeastern U., 1982; JD, Touro Coll., 1991. Bar: N.J. 1992, U.S. Dist. Ct. N.J. 1992, Conn. 1992, U.S. Dist. Ct. (so. and ea. dists.) N.Y. 1992, D.C. 1993, Minn. 1993, N.Y. 1994, U.S. Ct. Appeals (fed. cir.) 1995, U.S. Ct. Appeals Armed Forces 1995, U.S. Ct. Fed. Claims 1995, U.S. Supreme Ct. 1995. Dist. sci. supr. Carle Place (N.Y.) Pub. Schs., 1969-80; dist. dir. sci. Lawrence (N.Y.) Pub. Schs., 1980-84; dir. curriculum Bellmore-Merrick Cen. H.S. dist., Merrick, NY, 1984—91; law clk. Liotti & Skelos, Garden City, NY, 1991—92; gen. counsel Cliff Data Sys., Lyndhurst, NJ, 1992-94; prin. dep. town atty. Town of Hempstead, NY, 1994—. Pres. Mervic Enterprises, Smithtown, N.Y., 1980—; adj. prof. Nassau C.C., 1975—, Syracuse U., 1974-80. Trustee Carle Place Bd. Edn., 1981-86; rep. candidate of N.Y. State Assembly, 20th assembly dist., 1996, Nassau County Legislature, 2001; exec. bd. five Towns Cmty. Coun., Woodmere, N.Y., 1998-99; exec. leader North Woodmere Rep. Com., 1999—; commr. Storm Water Drainage Com., Inc., Village of Hewlett Harbor, N.Y., 2003-04, Village Attorney, Inc., Village of Hewlett Harbor, 2004—. Recipient Outstanding Contbrns. to Edn. award, Nassau County, 1981, Outstanding Sci. Supr. award, State of N.Y., 1986, Nation's Outstanding Sci. Supr. award, 1991, Profl. Excellence award Nassau C.C., 2000. Mem. ABA, Nat. Sci. Tchrs. Assn. (exec. bd. 1986), Nat. Sci. Suprs. Assn. (exec. bd. 1983-88, pres. 1986-87), N.Y. State Sci. Suprs. Assn. (pres. 1982-83), N.Y. Acad. Scis. (life), Nassau County Sci. Suprs. Assn. (pres. 1979), Am. Assn. Sex Educators, Counselors and Therapists (cert.), Bar Assn. Nassau County (chmn. fee conciliation com. 2000-02, mem. grievance com. 2002—), N.Y. State Bar Assn., Nassau Lawyers Assn. L.I. (pres. 2004-05), L.I. U./C.W. Post Campus Alumni Assn. (bd. dirs. 1997-99), Phi Delta Kappa (exec. bd. 1988), Phi Alpha Delta, Civic Club, Kiwanis (life, pres. Westbury, N.Y. club 1982-83, pres. Five Towns N.Y.Club 1998-99), North Woodmere Rep. Club (pres. 1992-99), Woodmere Mchts. Assn. (v.p. 2000—), Masons, Shriners. Republican. Office: Town Atty's Office 1 Washington St Hempstead NY 11550-4921 Personal E-mail: eddjd@aol.com.

AARON, ROGER S., lawyer; b. Cleve., 1942; AB magna cum laude, Dartmouth Coll., 1964; MBA with high distinction, Dartmouth Coll., Amos Tuck School of Business Adminstrn., 1965; LLB, JD, Yale U., 1968. Bar: NY 1969. Sr. ptnr. for corporate Skadden, Arps, Slate, Meagher & Flom, NYC, serves on Policy Com. Lectr. in field. Mem. ABA. Office: Skadden Arps Slate Meagher Flom 4 Times Sq New York NY 10036-6522 Office Phone: 212-735-3300. Fax: 212-735-2000; Office Fax: 917-777-3300. Business E-Mail: raaron@skadden.com.

AARON, SHIRLEY MAE, tax consultant; b. Covington, La., Feb. 28, 1935; d. Morgan and Pearl (Jenkins) King; m. Richard L. King, Feb. 16, 1952 (div. Feb. 1965); children: Deborah, Richard, Roberta, Keely; m. Michael A. Aaron, Nov. 27, 1976 (dec. July 1987). Adminstrv. asst. South Central Bell, Covington, La., 1954-62; acct. Brown & Root, Inc., Houston, 1962-75; timekeeper Alyeska Pipeline Co., Fairbanks, Alaska, 1975-77; adminstrv. asst. Boeing Co., Seattle, 1979-93; pres. Aaron Enterprises, Seattle, 1977—; owner Gabriel's Dinner Club, La., 1993—. Contbr.: Who's Cooking What in America by Phyllis Hanes, 1993. Bd. dirs. Burien 146 Homeowners Assn., Seattle, 1979—, pres., 1980-83, 92. Mem. NAFE. Avocation: singing, art. Home: 131 Gerard St Mandeville LA 70448-5808

AARON, STEWART D., lawyer; b. 1958; BS, Cornell Univ., 1980; JD summa cum laude, Syracuse Univ., 1983. Bar: NY 1984, US Supreme Ct. 1988. Ptnr., securities enforcement, litig. Arnold & Porter LLP, NYC, 2005—. Notes and comments editor Syracuse Law Rev., 1982—83. Fellow: NY Bar Found.; mem.: NY County Lawyers Assn., NY State Bar Assn., Order of Coif. Office: Arnold & Porter LLP 399 Park Ave New York NY 10022-4690 Office Phone: 212-715-1114. Office Fax: 212-715-1399. Business E-Mail: Stewart.Aaron@aporter.com.

AARONSON, DAVID ERNEST, lawyer, educator; b. Washington, Sept. 19, 1940; s. Edward Allan and May (Rosett) A.; m. Laura Dine, 1991; stepchildren: Dara Prushansky, Jared Prushansky. BA in Econs, George Washington U., 1961, MA, 1964, PhD, 1970; LL.B., Harvard U., 1964; LL.M. (E. Barrett Prettyman fellow), Georgetown U., 1965. Bar: D.C. bar 1965, Md. bar 1975, U.S. Supreme Ct. bar 1969. Research asst. Office of Commr., Bur. Labor Stats., U.S. Dept. Labor, Washington, 1961; staff atty. legal intern program Georgetown Grad. Law Ctr., Washington, 1964-65; rsch. assoc. patent rsch. project dept. econ. George Washington U., Washington, 1966; assoc. firm Aaronson and Aaronson, Washington, 1965-67, ptnr., 1967-70; prof., B.J. Tennery Scholar Am. U. Law Sch., Washington, 1970—; prof. Sch. Justice, Coll. Pub. and Internat. Affairs, 1981-92; dep. dir. Law and Policy Inst., Jerusalem, summer, 1978. Interim dir. clin. programs Md. Criminal Justice Clinic, 1971-73, founder prosecutor criminal litigation clinic, 1972, co-dir. trial practice program, 1982—2004, dir. trial practice program, 2004—; vis. prof. Law Sch. of Hebrew U., Jerusalem, 1978; trustee Montgomery-Prince George's Continuing Legal Edn. Inst., 1983-1997. Author: Maryland Criminal Jury Instructions and Commentary, 1975, (with N.N. Kittrie and D. Saari) Alternatives to Conventional Criminal Adjudication: Guidebook for Planners and Practitioners, 1977, (with B. Hoff, P. Jaszi, N.N. Kittrie and D. Saari) The New Justice: Alternatives to Conventional Criminal Adjudication, 1977, (with C.T. Dienes and M.C. Musheno) Decriminalization of Public Drunkenness: Tracing the Implementation of a Public Policy, 1981, Public Policy and Police Discretion: Processes of Decriminalization, 1984, (with R. Simon) The Insanity Defense: A Critical Assessment of Law and Policy in the Post-Hinckley Era, 1988, Maryland Criminal Jury Instructions and Commentary, 2d rev. edit., 1988; contbr. articles to profl. jours. Mem. Friendship Heights Village Coun., 1979. Recipient Outstanding Cmty. Svc. award, 1980; Outstanding Tchr. award Am. U. Law Sch., 1978, 81, Scholar/Tchr. of Yr. award Am. U., 1989; Pauline Ruyle Moore scholar in Pub. Law, 1983; B.J. Tennery scholar, 1990—. Mem. ABA (criminal justice sect. rules of ct. prof. and evid. com. 1991—), D.C. Bar Assn. (chmn. criminal code rev. com. 1971-73), Md. State Bar Assn. (criminal law sect. coun. 1984—, chmn. 1989-90, Robert C. Heeney award 1999), Assn. Am. Law Schs. (elected to sect. coun., criminal justice sect. 1999—), Montgomery County (Md.) Bar Assn., Am. Law Inst., Phi Beta Kappa. Office: Am U Law Sch 4801 Massachusetts Ave NW Washington DC 20016-8196 Office Phone: 202-274-4201. E-mail: daarons@wcl.american.edu.

AARONSON, ROBERT JAY, air transportation executive; b. Temple, Tex., June 8, 1942; s. Leonard and Ruth (Lader) A.; m. Louise Elaine Loia, June 6, 1967; children: Steven Bradford, Suzanne Denise. AB, Brown U., 1964; M in Govtl. Adminstrn., Wharton Sch., U. Pa., 1965. Spl. asst. Southeastern Pa. Transp. Authority, Phila., 1965-67; transp. rep. Urban Mass Transp. Adminstrn., Washington, 1967-69; transp. adviser HUD, 1969-71; aviation adminstr. Md. Dept. Transp., Balt., 1972-78; asso. adminstr. for airports FAA, Washington, 1978-81; dir. aviation Port Authority of N.Y. and N.J., N.Y.C., 1981-89; pres. Air Transport Assn. Am., Washington, 1989-92; exec. v.p. Lockheed Air Terminal, Inc., Burbank, Calif., 1993-94, Airport Group Internat., Inc., Glendale, Calif., 1995-97; pres. Strategies For Airports, Inc., Encino, Calif., 1997-98; exec. v.p. Lufthansa Cons. GmbH, Encino, Calif., 1999—2002; dir. gen. Airports Coun. Internat., Geneva, 2002—. Lectr. Royal Aero. Transport Course, Oxford U. Samuel S. Fels fellow, 1964-65 Mem. Nat. Assn. State Aviation Ofcls. (pres. 1978), Airport Operators Coun. Internat. (chmn. 1987-88), Am. Assn. Airport Execs., Wings Club (pres. 1992). Address: Geneva Airport PO Box 4 1215 Geneva 15 Switzerland Office Phone: 422-717-8585. E-mail: raaronson@compuserve.com.

AARSLEFF, HANS, linguistics educator; b. Rungsted Kyst, Denmark, July 19, 1925; came to U.S., 1948, naturalized, 1964; s. Einar Faber and Inger (Lotz) A. BA, U. Copenhagen, 1945; PhD, U. Minn., 1960. Instr. English U. Minn., 1952-56; instr. Princeton U., 1956-60, asst. prof., 1960-65, assoc. prof., 1965-72, prof., 1972-97. Author: The Study of Language in England 1780-1860, 1967, From Locke to Saussure: Essays on the Study of Language and Intellectual History, 1982, Introduction to Wilhelm von Humboldt, On Language, 1988; editor, translator: Condillac, Essay on the Origin of Human Knowledge, 2001; assoc. editor: The Historiography of Linguistics, bd. editors: Jour. History Ideas, 1979—; contbr. articles to jours. and books. Jr. fellow Council of Humanities Princeton U., fall 1962; fellow Am. Council Learned Socs., 1964-65, 72-73, NEH, 1975-76 Fellow Am. Acad. Arts and Scis.; mem. Am. Philos. Soc., Royal Danish Acad. Scis. and Letters (fgn.). Office: Princeton U Dept English Princeton NJ 08544-0001

AASEN, LAWRENCE OBERT, public relations executive; b. Gardner, N.D., Dec. 5, 1922; s. Theodore and Clara Olina (Brenden) A.; m. Martha Ann McMullan, Nov. 25, 1954; children: David Lawrence, Susan Clare. PhB, U. N.D., 1947; MS, Boston U., 1949. With McGraw Hill Pub. Co., N.Y.C., 1952-54, N.Y. Life Ins. Co., 1954-67, asst. v.p., 1965-67; exec. sec. Better Vision Inst., N.Y.C., 1967-87; pres. Publicity, Inc., Westport, Conn., 1988—. Author: North Dakota Postcards 1900-1930, 1999, North Dakota Images 1900-1940, 2000. Dem. commiteeman Westport; elected mem. Rep. Town Meeting, 1970. With AUS, 1943-45. Mem. Pub. Rels. Soc. Am., Am. Soc. Assn. Execs. Congregationalist. Home: 31 Ellery Ln Westport CT 06880-5203 Office Phone: 203-227-6126. E-mail: aasenm@aol.com.

AATRAPI, MARJANE, writer, illustrator; b. Rasht, Iran, 1969; arrived in Vienna, 1984, Strasbourg, arrived in Iran, 1989, arrived in Paris, 1994; married. Student, Lycee Francais, Tehran, Iran. Contbr. NY Times, The New Yorker, others. Author: Persepolis: The Story of an Iranian Childhood, 2003, Persepolis 2: The Story of a Return, 2004, Embroideries, 2005. Office: c/o Pantheon Books 201 E 50th St New York NY 10022*

ABAKANOWICZ, MAGDALENA, artist, sculptor; b. Falenty, Poland, June 20, 1930; d. Konstanty and Helena (Domaszowska) A.; m. Jan Kosmowski, Sept. 22, 1956 Grad., Warsaw Acad. Fine Arts, 1954; D (hon.), Royal Coll. Art, London, 1974, RI Sch. Design, 1992, Acad. of Fine Arts, Lódz, Poland, 1998, Pratt Inst., NYC, NY, 2000, Mass. Coll. Art, 2001; DHC (hon.), Sch. of the Art Inst. Chgo., Chgo., Ill., 2002; Dr. (hon.), Acad. of Fine Arts, Poznan, Poland, 2002, Sch. Art Inst. Chgo., 2002. Prof. Acad. Fine Art, Poznan, Poland, 1965, 1979. Prin. works include monumental space forms of woven fibres, circles of figurative sculptures of burlap, wood, metals, stone and clay drawings, paintings, exhibited in group shows at Internat. Biennale de Tapisserie, Lausanne, 1962—79, Biennale of Art, São Paulo, 1965, Venice Biennale, 1968, Biennale of Art, São Paulo, 1979, Venice Biennale, 1980, ROSC, Dublin, 1980, Nat. Gallery, Berlin, 1983, ARS '83, Helsinki, 1983, Mus. Moderner Kunst Vienne, 1984, Nürnberg Triennale of Drawing, 1985, Sydney Biennale of Art, 1986, Mus. Modern Art, NYC, 1987, County Mus., 1987, Hirshorn Mus., Washington, 1988, Olympic Pk., Seoul, 1988, Mus. Nacional Belas Artes, Rio de Janeiro, 1992, Fuji San Kei Biennial, Japan, 1993, Europa-Europa, Bonn, Germany, 1994, Muzeum Narodove, Warsaw, 1994, Centro Galego de Arte Conteporanea Santiago de Compostela, 1994, Royal Festival Hall, London, 1995, Mus. Ludwig, Cologne, Germany, 1995, Les Champs Elysees, Paris, 1996, The Nasher Collection, Guggenheim Mus., NYC, 1997, Guggenheim Mus., Bilbao, Spain, 1997—98, Mus. D'Art Moderne Ville de Paris, 1997, Arco, Madrid, 1998, Mus. Würth Künzelsau, Germany, 2000, Nat. Gallery Jeu de Paume, Paris, 2000, Mus. Würth, Germany, 2000, Open 2002, Venice, 2002, one-woman shows include Museo Reina Sofia, Madrid, 2004, Three Rivers Art Festival, 2001, exhibited in group shows at Les Jardins Du Palais Royal, Paris, 2000, Europalia, 201, Musee D'Art Moderne, France, 2001, Den Haag Sculpture, Haque, Holland, 2001, Maque, Holland, 2001, La Parade des Animaux, Monte Carlo, Monaco, 2002, Open 2002, Lido, Italy, Museo Nacional Centro de Arte Reina Sofia, Madrid, 2004, one-woman shows include Kunsthaus Zurich, 1968, Nationalmuseum Stockholm, 1970, Pasadena Art Mus., Calif., 1971, Art Mus., 1971, Dusseldorf Kunsthalle, 1972, Whitechapel Art Gallery, London, 1975, Nat. Gallery of Victoria, Melbourne, 1976, Muzeum Sztuki, Lodz, Poland, 1978, Mus. d'Art Moderne de la Ville de Paris, 1982, Mus. Contemporary Art, Chgo., 1982, Mus. d'Art Contemporain, Montreal, 1983, Portland Art Mus., Oreg., 1984, Dallas Mus. Fine Arts, 1984, Xavier Fourcade Gallery, NYC, 1985, Turske & Turske Gallery, Zürich, Mücsarnok Palace, Budapest, Hungary, 1988, Städel Kunstinstitut, Frankfurt, 1989, Marlborough Gallery, NYC, 1989, Sezon Mus., Tokyo, 1991, Mus.Modern Art, Shiga, 1991, Art Tower, Mito, 1991, Hiroshima Art Mus., 1991, Walker Art Ctr., Mpls., 1992, Inst. Contemporary Art P.S. 1 Mus., NY, 1993, BWH Kraków, 1993, Hiroshima City Mus. Contemporary Art, 1993, Kordegarda, Warsaw, 1994, Marlborough Gallery, Madrid, 1994, Fundacio Miro a Mallorca, 1994, Ctr. Polish Sculpture, Oronsko, 1995, Yorkshire Sculpture Park, 1995, Manchester City Art Galleries, 1995, Ujazdowski Castle, Warsaw, 1995, Galerie Marwan Hoss, Paris, 1996, Charlottenborg Exhbn. Hall, Copenhagen, 1996, Oriel Mostyn, Wales, 1996, Marlborough Gallery, NYC, 1997, Doris Freedman Plz., NY, Galerie Marvan Moss, Paris, 1997, Gallery Starmach, Krakow, 1998, Muzeum Sztuki, Lodz, Poland, 1994, Met. Mus. Art, NYC, 1999, Jardins du Palais Royal, Paris, 1999, Marlborough Gallery, NY, 2000, NYC, 2000, Pillsbury and Peters Fine Art, Dallas, 2001, Grant Selwyn Fine Arts, LA, 2001, Gerald Peters Gallery, Santa Fe, N.Mex., 2001, Muzeum Narodowe (Nat. Mus.), Poznan, Poland, 2002, Mart, Museo di Arte Moderna e Contemporaranem, Trento, Rovereto, Italy, 2003, Beck & Eggeling, Inst. Fine Art, Dusseldorf, Germany, 2003, Mus. Beelden Aan Zee, Germany, Holland, 2003, Marlborough Fine Art, London, Eng., 2003, Marlborough Gallery, NY, 2003, Mus. of Art, Lucerne, Switzerland, 2003, Savannah Mus. of Art and Designe, Georgia, 2004, Schleswig Holstein Mus., Schloss-Gottorf, Germany, 2004, Represented in permanent collections Galerie Saint Severin, Paris, Muzeum Sztuki, Lodz, Mus. Modern Art, N.Y.C., Kyoto, Japan, Stedelijk Mus., Amsterdam, Australian Nat. Collection, Canberra, Ctr. Georges Pompidou, Paris, Mus. Contemprary Art, Chgo., Nat. Mus., Stockholm, Met. Mus., NYC, LA County Mus., Israel Mus., Jerusalem, Mus. Moderner Kunst, Vienna, Spazzi d'Arte, Italy, Va. Mus. Fine Art, Richmond, W. Lehmbruck Mus., Duisburg, Storm King Art Ctr., N.Y., Mus. Ludwig, Cologne, Hess Collection, Napa, Calif., Nasher Collection, Tex., Mus. Nacional Centro Arte Reina Sofia, Madrid, Mus. D'Art Moderne Ville Paris, Paris, Nelson-Atkins Mus. Art, Mo., Nat. Gallery Art, Washington, exhibitions include Open, exhi. of Sculptures and Installation, Venice and Lido, Italy, 2002. Mem. Presdl. Coun. for Culture, 1992—. Decorated officier de l'Ordre des Arts et Lettres (France), 1999, Comdr. Cross with Star, Order of Polonia Restituta, 1998; recipient prize 1st class Min. of Culture, Poland, 1965, Gold medal VIII Biennale of Art, Sao Paulo, 1965, Polish State prize Stiftung F.V.S. Hamburg, Vienna, 1979, Alfred Jurzykowski prize, 1982, award for distinction in sculpture, NY, 1993, Leonardo da Vinci World award of Arts, 1997, Cavaliere Nell Ordine Al Merito Della Republic Italiana, 2000, Orden Pour le Merite fur Wissenschaften und Kunste Berlin, 2000, Comdr. Del'Ordre Arts et des Lettres, Paris, 2004. Mem. Am. Acad. Arts and Letters (hon.), Polish Assn. Authors., Akademie der Kunste (hon.), Sachsische Akademie der Kunste, Dresden, Germany (hon.), Orden Pour le merite fur Wissenschaften und Kunste, Berlin. Address: Bzowa 1 02-708 Warsaw Poland E-mail: magdalena@abakanowicz.art.pl.

ABATE, CATHERINE M., retired state legislator; b. Margate, NJ, Dec. 8, 1947; d. Joseph and Carolyn (Fiore) A.; m. Ronald E. Kliegerman, Oct. 28, 1978; 1 child, Kyle. BA, Vassar Coll., 1969; JD, Boston U., 1972. Bar: N.Y. 1973, U.S. Dist. Ct. (so. dist.) N.Y. 1976. Staff atty. Legal Aid Soc., NYC, 1972-74, 75-78, supervising atty., 1979-81, dir. tng., 1981-85, acting chairperson Gov.'s Taskforce Criminal Justice, 1983; chairperson NY State Platform Criminal Justice, 1984, NY Crime Victims Bd., 1988-90; exec. dep. commr. NY State Div. Human Rights, 1986-88; commr. NYC Dept. Probation, 1990-92, NYC Dept. Correction, 1992-94; mem. NY State Senate, Albany, 1995-98; pres., CEO Cmty. Healthcare Network, 1999—. Dist. leader Dem. Party, 1981-86; 1st vice chmn. county com. Dem. Party, N.Y. County; bd. dirs. Village Nursing Home, 1987-99; bd. mem. Naral, 1999—, Correctional Assn., 1999—, Eleanor Roosevelt Legacy Com., 2003, Citizen Action, 2001—; chair 2001—; pres. bd. Family Planning Advs., 2004—. Mem. Bar Assn. City N.Y. (criminal cts. com. 1982-86), Nat. Assn. Crime Victims Compensation Bd. (bd. dirs. 1989-90), Nat. Orgn. Italian-Am. Women (bd. dirs. 1986-2003, chief judge's CPL com., 1999—, prisoner legal svcs. com., 1999—). Roman Catholic. Avocation: tennis. Home: 303 Mercer St New York NY 10003-6706 Office Phone: 212-366-4500 ext. 262. Business E-Mail: cabate@chnnyc.org.

ABATE, JOHN E., electrical engineer, consultant; b. Paterson, N.J., July 25, 1931; s. Joseph and Lucy Abate; m. Mary Ann Parrillo, July 9, 1955; children: John F., Robert J., Mark J., Holly A. BSEE, NCE, 1954; MSEE, Stevens Inst. Tech., 1960; ScD in Elec. Engring., N.J. Inst. Tech., 1967. Registered profl. engr., N.J. Astronautic engr. Kearfott Inc., Little Falls, NJ, 1956—63; tech. mgr., mem. tech. staff Bell Labs., Holmdel, NJ, 1963—98; comm. cons. AT&T Labs., Holmdel, 1998—2001. Chmn. synchronization stds. group Am. Nat. Stds. Inst. T1X1.3, 1983-86; mem. U.S. Nat. Bur. Stds. Panel for Basic Stds., 1986-89; expert in field of comm. network synchronization. Contbr. over 20 articles to profl. jours., conf. procs. and mags. Cubmaster Cub Scouts, Holmdel, 1968-70; chmn. ch. coms., Holmdel, 1968-70. 1st lt. USAF, 1954-56. Bell Labs. fellow, 1991, AT&T fellow, 1996; named to Alumni Honor Roll, N.J. Inst. Tech. Alumni Assn., Newark, 1992, Disting. Alumni, NCE, Newark, 1964; recipient commendation Nat. Security Agy., Washington, 1956. Mem. IEEE (sr., life). Roman Catholic. Achievements include invention of adaptive delta modulator used in NASA space shuttle communications system, Bell Labs fellow in 1991 for fundamental contributions national and international in area digital synchonization planning for public and private communication networks and AT&T fellow in 1996. Home: 20 Pearce Ct Manasquan NJ 08736 Office: PO Box 664 Manasquan NJ 08736

ABATEMARCO, TRACY J., lawyer; BA summa cum laude, SUNY, Albany, 1988; JD, Georgetown U., 1991. Bar: NY 1991, Conn. 1992, US Dist. Ct. So. Dist. NY, US Dist. Ct. Ea. Dist. NY. Ptnr. Wilson, Elser, Moskowitz, Edelman & Dicker LLP, NYC. Mem.: NY State Bar Assn., Phi Beta Kappa. Office: Wilson Elser Moskowitz Edelman & Dicker LLP 23rd Fl 150 E 42nd St New York NY 10017-5639 Office Phone: 212-490-3000 ext. 2613. Office Fax: 212-490-3038. Business E-Mail: abatemarcot@wemed.com.

ABAUNZA, DONALD RICHARD, lawyer; b. New Orleans, Oct. 25, 1945; s. Alfred E. and Virginia (White) A.; m. Carolyn Thompson; 1 child, Richard. BA, Vanderbilt U., 1966; JD, Tulane U., 1969. Bar: La. 1969, U.S. Dist. Ct. (ea. dist.) La. 1969, U.S. Dist. Ct. (we. dist.) La. 1980, U.S. Supreme Ct. 1986. Ptnr. Liskow & Lewis, New Orleans, 1977—, mng. ptnr., 1996—2003. Adj. faculty Tulane Sch. Law, 1981-89. Fellow Am. Coll. Trial Lawyers; mem. La. Bar Assn. (Pres.'s award 1988). Office: Liskow & Lewis 1 Shell Sq 50th Fl 701 Poydras St New Orleans LA 70139-5099 Office Phone: 504-556-4110. Business E-Mail: drabaunza@liskow.com.

ABBAS, AMR EL-SAYED, cardiologist; b. Cairo, July 21, 1970; s. El-Sayed Abbas Saleh and Raifa Aly Salama. MD, Ain Shams U., Cairo, 1993. Diplomate Am. Bd. Internal Medicine, Am. Bd. Echocardiography, Am. Bd. Cardiology. Intern Ain Shans Univ. Hops., Cairo, 1993—94, ob-gyn. resident, 1994—97; internal medicine resident Maricopa Med. Ctr., Phoenix, 1997—2000; cardiology fellow Mayo Clinic, Scottsdale, Ariz., 2000—03; interventional cardiology fellow/cardiologist William Beaumont Hosp., Royal Oak, Mich., 2003—. Mem., pub. rev. com. Mayo Clinic, Scottsdale, Ariz., 2003; reviewer Am. Jour. Cardiology; presenter in field. Contbr. articles to profl. jours., including Am. Jour. Cardiology, Jour. Am. Coll. Cardiology, Internat. Jour. Cardiology (Morton Fuch's Ednl. award, 2000). Med. reporter African Olympic Games, Cairo, 1991, Internat. Conf. Population and Devel., Cairo, 1994; bd. mem. Internat. Fedn. Med. Students Assn., Cairo. Grantee, Am. Heart Assn. Mem.: AMA, Egyptian Med. Syndicate, Am. Coll. of Cardiology (assoc.), Mayo Clinic Alumni. Office: William Beaumont Hosp 3601 W 13 Mile Rd Royal Oak MI 48073 Office Phone: 248-551-4176. E-mail: aabbas@beaumont.edu.

ABBAS, MIKE ALLAN, science educator; b. Redmond, Oreg., Apr. 5, 1967; s. Roger Allan and Linda Allan Abbas; 1 child, Zack. BS in Edn., Western Oreg. U., Monmouth, 1994; M in Ednl. Leadership, Northern Ariz. U., Flagstaff, 2004. Cert. prin. Ariz. Tchr. science Cibola H.S., Yuma, Ariz., 1994—2001, campus mentor tchr., 2001—. Head wrestling coach Cibola H.S., 1999—2001. Named Outstanding Tchr., Tandy Corp., 1997. Mem.: ASCD, Yuma County Profl. Educators. Avocations: camping, scuba diving, woodworking. Home: 4577 W 19th St Yuma AZ 85364-4880 Office: Cibola HS 4100 W 20th St Yuma AZ 85364

ABBAS BORHAN, RICHAT, medical association administrator; s. Abbas Borhan and Maria Abliz; m. Hamra Borhan Turahmat, Nov. 14, 1969; children: Zerina R. Borhan, Tilman Borhan, Davron Borhan. PhD, Ohio State U., 1994. Rsch. asst. Coll. Pharmacy, Ohio State U., Columbus, 1990—94; pharmacokineticist Toxicology Divsn., Armstrong Lab., Wright-Patterson AFB, Dayton, Ohio, 1994—96; mgr., sr. pharmacokineticist Otsuka Am. Pharm., Inc., Rockville, Md., 1996—2000; dir., staff scientist Emisphere Techs., Inc., Tarrytown, NY, 2000—02; assoc. clin. dir., clin. pharmacologist Hoffmann-La Roche, Inc., Nutley, 2002—04; dir. clin. pharmacology Wyeth Rsch., Collegeville, 2004—. Contbr. over 80 articles to profl. jours. and sci. confs. Recipient Sci. and Tech. Achievement award, U.S. Air Force Material Command, 1996, Sci. Achievement award, Dept. Air Force, 1996; Rsch. Assistantship scholar, Ohio State U., 1990 - 1994. Mem.: Am. Soc. Clin. Pharmacology and Therapeutics, Am. Assn. Pharm. Scientists (assoc.). Achievements include development of new drug; patents for oral insulin; oral cromolyn; research in pharmacokinetics; design clinical trials for new drug development. Office Phone: 484-865-8577.

ABBASI, TARIQ AFZAL, psychiatrist, educator; b. Hyderabad, India, Aug. 13, 1946; came to U.S., 1976, naturalized, 1983; s. Shujaat Ali and Salma Khatoon (Siddiqui) A.; m. Kashifa Khatoon, Nov. 10, 1972; children—Sameena, Omar, Osman. B.S., Madrasa-I-Aliya, Hyderabad, 1964; M.B.B.S., Osmania Med. Coll., Hyderabad, 1970; Diploma in Psychol. Medicine, St. John's Hosp., U. Sheffield (Eng.), 1976. Diplomate Am. Bd. Psychiatry and Neurology; diplomate in psychiatry Royal Coll. Physicians of Eng. Sr. house officer St. John's Hosp., Lincoln, Eng., 1972-73, registrar, 1973-76; resident in psychiatry Rutgers Med. Sch., Piscataway, N.J., 1976-79, chief resident, 1979, dir. adult in-patient services Community Mental Health Ctr., Rutgers Med. Sch., also asst. prof. psychiatry, 1979-82; staff psychiatrist Northville Regional Psychiat. Hosp. (Mich.), 1982-83, div. dir., 1983-2002; cons. psychiatrist Rahway State Prison (N.J.), 1979-82; clin. instr. psychiatry Wayne State U. Med. Sch., Detroit. Mem. Am. Psychiat. Assn., Mich. Psychiat. Soc. E-mail: taabbasi@aol.com. also: 33200 Dequindre Rd Ste 200 Sterling Heights MI 48310-5916 also: 30700 Telegraph Rd Ste 2560 Bingham Farms MI 48025-4526 Office Phone: 248-213-0501. E-mail: tabbasi@comcast.net.

ABBASSIAN-KASHI, MANDANA, industrial engineer, systems engineer; b. Tehran, Iran, Sept. 4, 1973; arrived in U.S., 1995; d. Reza Abbassian and Zahra Navabi; m. Ali R. Nowroozi, Aug. 18, 1994; 1 child, Naseem Emma Nowroozi. BS, Shahid Beheshti U., Tehran, 1995; MS, U. So. Calif., 1997. Inventory control analyst Mark Fabrics Inc., L.A., 1997—99; master production scheduler Boeing Satellite Sys., L.A., 2001—. Avocations: travel, skiing, water-skiing, windsurfing, movies. Home: 321 S Lilac Ct Anaheim CA 92808 Office: Boeing Satellite Sys Inc 2006 E El Segundo El Segundo CA 90245-0902 E-mail: mabbassian@hotmail.com.

ABBATE, ANTONIO, cardiologist; b. Formia, Latina, Italy, Nov. 5, 1976; s. Gerardo Abbate and Amalia Ferraro; m. Vera Di Trocchio, May 15, 2004. MD, U. Campus Bio-Medico, 2000. Lic. Italy, 2001. Cardiology fellow Cath. U. of Sacred Heart, Rome, 2000—04; resident in internal medicine Va. Commonwealth Univ. Med. Coll., Richmond, 2004—. Contbr. articles to profl. jours. Home: 10025 Bellona Ct Richmond VA 23238 Office: Va Commonwealth Univ Med Coll Virginia Campus Richmond VA Personal E-mail: abbatea@yahoo.com.

ABBE, CHARLES J., manufacturing executive; b. 1941; Sr. ptnr. McKinsey & Co., Inc., San Francisco; various sr. mgmt. positions Raychem Corp., 1989-96; v.p., gen. mgr. Santa Rosa divsn. Optical Coating Lab., Inc., 1996-98, dir., pres., CEO, 1998-2000, sr. v.p., sr. oper. officer, 2000; pres., COO JDS Uniphase Corp., San Jose, 2000—. Office: 163 Baypointe Pkwy San Jose CA 95134 Office Fax: 408-954-0760.

ABBE, COLMAN, investment banker; b. NYC, Sept. 24, 1932; s. Leo Theodore and Beatrice (Shiff) A.; m. Nancy Adele Hyams, June 23, 1963; children: Elizabeth, Leo, Richard. BS in Acctg., Bucknell U., 1953; MBA, NYU, 1962. CPA NY. Ptnr. Belsky & Abbe CPAs, N.Y.C., 1960-70; stockbroker Loeb Rhoades, N.Y.C., 1971-72; pres. Sagittarius Fund, N.Y.C., 1973, OCG Tech. Inc., N.Y.C., 1973, Profl. Mediquip Inc., Scarsdale, N.Y., 1974-80, Abbe & Co., Inc., 1984—; mng. dir. corp. fin. Evans & Co. Inc., N.Y.C., 1985-87, Reich & Co., Inc., N.Y.C., 1988-90; vice chmn., sr. mgr., dir. investment banking Laidlaw Internat. Inc., N.Y.C., 1991-93; chmn. AB Capital Markets, N.Y.C., 1993-94. Trustee Heart Rsch. Found., N.Y.C., 1982-92, pres., 1986; pres. Am. Friends of HAIFA Med. Ctr., 1989-93. Mem. AICPA, N.Y. State Soc. CPAs. Democrat. Jewish. Office: Abbe & Co Inc 26 Lawrence Rd Scarsdale NY 10583-7209 Office Phone: 914-723-3736. Personal E-mail: colman26@verizon.net.

ABBE, ELFRIEDE MARTHA, sculptor, graphics designer; b. Washington; d. Cleveland Jr. and Frieda (Dauer) A. Student, Art Inst. Chgo., 1937; B.F.A., Cornell U., 1940; postgrad., Syracuse U., 1947. Author and illustrator: books including The Plants of Virgil's Georgics, 1965; One-woman exhbns. include Carnegie-Mellon U., 1962, 69, Cornell U., 1963, Trinity Coll., Hartford, 1964, Arts Club of Washington, 1972, Cornell Club of N.Y., 1977, Copley Soc. Boston, 1978, Woods-Gerry Gallery, R.I. Sch. Design, 1983; represented in permanent collections Met. Mus. Art., Watson Library, Boston Mus. Fine Arts, Cin. Art Mus., Dumbarton Oaks, Washington, Houghton Library, Harvard U., Hunt Library, Carnegie-Mellon U., N.Y. Pub. Library, Rosenwald Collection Nat. Gallery, Kew Gardens Library, Royal Bot. Garden, Edinburgh, Nat. Library, Canberra, Australia; sculpture placed in Mann Library, Kroch Library and Morrison Hall, Cornell U., McGill U., N.Y. Bot. Gardens, Hunt Library, Pitts., Pres.'s Office, Keene (N.H.) State Coll., Herzog August Bibliothek, Wolfenbüttel, Fed. Republic Germany (bronze bust of founder), Abbe Mus., Bar Harbor, Maine (bronze bust of founder Dr. Robert Abbe). Recipient Gold medals Pen and Brush, N.Y.C., 1964, Margaret Sussman Meml. award 1987, Gold medals Nat. Arts Club, 1970, Gold medals Acad. Artists Assn., Springfield, Mass., 1976, Founders' Prize Pen and Brush, 1977; Bd. Dirs. award Salmagundi Club N.Y., 1978; Elliot Liskin award, 1979, Catherine Lorillard Wolfe Club award, 1993. Fellow Nat. Sculpture Soc. (Barrett-Colea prize 1984); mem. Nat. Soc. Mural Painters, Phi Kappa Phi.

ABBETT, ROBERT KENNEDY, artist, writer; b. Hammond, Ind., Jan. 5, 1926; s. Clarence Corodon and Vere Kennedy Abbett; m. Marilyn Kay Smith; children: Robert Smith, Linda J. BS, Prudue Univ., W. Lafayette, Ind., 1946; BA, Univ. Mo., Cloumbia, Mo., 1947. Illustrator Stevens-Gross Studio, Chgo., 1947—49, Bielefeld Studios, Chgo., 1952—53, Chaite Studios, N.Y., 1953—54; freelance illustrator Darien, Conn., 1954—70; gallery painting, 1970—. Career cons., country wide, 1998—; writing freelance, 1983—; tchg. Scotdale Artists Sch., 1986—96. Represented in permanent collections Mus. of Nat History, Norman, Okla., Nat. Cowboy and Western Heritage Mus., Okla. City, Genesco County Mus. of Wildlife Art, Mumford, N.Y., Dog Mus. of Am., St. Louis, Mo., Soc. of Illustrators, N.Y.C., Nat. Bird Dog Mus., Grand Junction, Tenn., over 120 ltd. edit. prints, exhibitions include Nat. Cowboy and Western Heritage Mus., Oklahoma City, 1974—2004, Artists of Am., Denever Rotary, 1982—85, 1990—93, Soc. of Am. Impressionists, 1984, Nat. Western & Wildlife Art Collectors Annual, 1984 (Wildlife Artist of the Yr., 1984), Birds in Art, Leigh Yawkey Woodson Mus., 1984—87, The Era of the Pet, Univ. Pa., 1984, Thomas Gilcrease Mus., Tulsa, 1984—88, 1995—96, Cheyenne Frontier Days, Old West Mus., 1985, 1990, The Dog in Art, Acad. of the Arts, Md., 1999, exhibitions include 20th annv. Sports Edge King Gallery, N.Y., 1992, sculpter bronze edit., Grey Water, sculpter brone edit., Whoa!, Dare, T.V. special, Robert K. Abbett, Conn. Profile, WVIT TV Hartford, 1987, The Fall Colors of Robert Abbett, Pub. TV, Okla. City; author: The Outdoor Paintings of Robert K. Abbett, 1976, ABBETT, Masters of the Wild Series, by Michael McIntosh, 1989, Wings from Cover, The Upland Images of Robert K. Abbett and Ed Gray, 1996, A Season for Painting, 2001; contbr. articles numerous pub. to profl. jour. Air cadet USN, 1943—45. Recipient First prize, Salmagundi Summer Exhibit, NYC, 1972, Top Ten Wildlife Artists, 100th Annversary issue of Sport's Afield Mag., 2004, Wildlife Artists Award of Excellence, Sporting Classics Mag., 2004. Mem.: Soc. Animal Artist. Republican. Achievements include protraitures of Jimmy Stewart, Sam Walton, Margaret Meade. Avocations: photography, maintaining 56 rural acres.

ABBEY, G(EORGE) MARSHALL, lawyer, retired health facility administrator; b. Dunkirk, N.Y., July 24, 1933; s. Ralph Ambrose and Grace A. (Fisher) A.; m. Sue Carroll, July 13, 1974; children: Mark, Steven, Michael, Lincoln BA with high distinction, U. Rochester, 1954; JD with distinction, Cornell U., 1957. Bar: N.H. 1957, Ill. 1965. Atty. McLane, Carleton, Graf, Greene & Brown, Manchester, N.H., 1957-65, Baxter Internat. Inc., Deerfield, Ill., 1965-69, gen. counsel, 1969-72, sec., gen. counsel, 1972-75, v.p., sec., gen. counsel, 1975-82, sr. v.p., gen. counsel, 1985-90, sr. v.p., sec., gen. counsel, 1990-93; of counsel Bell Boyd & Lloyd, Chgo., 1997—2000; pvt. practice Law Office of G. Marshall Abbey, 1993-97, 2000—. Editor Cornell Law Rev., 1956-57. Mem. vis. com. Law Sch., U. Chgo., 1978-81; dir. Coun. Puerto Rico-U.S. Affairs, 1988-92; mem. indsl. adv. coun. U. P.R.; dir. P.R.-USA Found., 1975-93, B.U.I.L.D., Chgo., 1980-84, bus. adv. com. B.U.I.L.D. Inc.; bd. dirs. Hundred Club of Lake County, Ill., 1976-86; dir. Food and Drug Law Inst., 1975-93; bd. dirs. Evanston Inventure, 1986-88; former trustee Winnetka Congl. Ch.; dir. Nat. Com. for Quality Health Care, 1988-93; mem. Northwestern U. Corp. Coun. adv. bd., 1976-93; dir. P.R. Cmty. Found., 1986-94; bd. dirs. Better Bus. Bur. Chgo. and No. Ill., 1991-93; mem. Conf. Bd's. Coun. Chief Legal Officers and Legal Quality Coun., 1991-93. Mem. ABA, Ill. Bar Assn., Lake County Bar Assn., Chgo. Bar Assn., Health Industry Mfrs. Assn. (chmn. legal/regulatory affairs 1976-78, bd. dirs. 1978-80, chmn. govt. affairs com. 1980-81), Univ. Club, Exmoor Country Club, Bankers Club (P.R.), Order of the Coif, Phi Beta Kappa. Office: 836 Skokie Blvd Northbrook IL 60062-4001

ABBEY, LINDA ROWE, artist, educator; d. Robert Bradford and Elizabeth Spencer Rowe; m. Bruce James Abbey, Aug. 23, 1969; 1 child, Jason James. AA, Piedmont Coll., Charlottesville, Va., 1986; BA, Hanover Coll., Hanover, Ind., 1966. Cert. tchg. N.J., 1969, Va., 1975. Tchg. english as a fgn. lang. Peace Corps, Bizerte, Tunisia, 1966—68; tchg. english to italian navy officers Shenker Inst., Rome, Italy, Taranto, Italy, 1969—69; fourth grade tchr. Princeton Regional Sch., Princeton, NJ, 1969—72; title I tchr. Charlottesville City Sch., Charlottesville, Va., 1974—89; fifth grade tchr. St. Anne's Belfield Sch., Charlottesville, Va., 1989—90; artist self-employed, Syracuse, NY, 1990—. Watercolor tchr. to adults and children, Syracuse, NY, 1993—; watercolor tchr. Everson Mus. of Art, Syracuse, NY, 1997—2001; vol. artist McKinley Brighton Elem. Sch., Syracuse, NY, 1995—; judge of artwork for on my own time show Syracuse U., Syracuse, NY; founding mem. Pleiades, A Group Of Six To Eight Artists Who Exhibit Together, Syracuse, NY, 1998—. One-woman shows include Watermark Gallery, Balt., Md., Fox & Fowle, Architects, N.Y.C., Straun Art Gallery, Jacksonville, Ill., prin. works include painting of Syracuse U.'s chancellor's house (The Brochure received a bronze medal from the Coun. for Advancement and Support of Edn., 2001), prin. works include 12 paintings in a Plexi frame to raise money for Onandaga Park trees damaged in the 1998 Labor Day Storm, 1998—2000, exhibitions include AAUW Invitational Show, Skaneateles, N.Y., Rene Foteuil Gallery, N.Y.C., Edith Barrett Fine Arts Gallery, Utica Coll., Utica, N.Y., Goodsight Gallery with Pleiades, Cazenovia, N.Y., Veerhoff Gallery, Washington, SUNY Ints. of Tech., Utica/Rome, N.Y., Lagerquist Gallery, Atlanta, Ga., Artifice Gallery, Syracuse, N.Y., Gallery 210 Juried Exhbn., Fine Details Gallery, Skaneateles, N.Y., Kirkland Art Ctr., Ctrl. N.Y. Juried Show, Clinton, N.Y., Adirondacks Nat. Exhbn. of Am. Watercolors, Old Forge, N.Y., Represented in permanent collections, TV program. Organizer of art show for over 50 artists in neighborhood Art on the Porches, Syracuse, 2001—04. Recipient Golden Rule Award, JC Penny and McKinley Brighton Sch., Syracuse, NY, 1997, Best Watercolor, Delavan Award, Hon. Mention, Cazenova Caral Mus. Show, 1992, 1994, 1996, Second Pl. Watercolor, SUNY Inst. Tech., Regional Art Show, 2000; grantee John DeFrancisco N.Y. Arts and Cultural Grant Fund and Cultural Resources Coun., 2003, 2004. Mem.: Onondaga Art Guild (assoc.; sec. 1998—99, pres. 1999—2000).

ABBINANTE, CHRISTOPHER, finance company executive; married; 2 children. BA in History, Loyola U., 1972; MBA, U. Chgo., 1985; JD, LLM. From atty. trainee to sr. v.p. Chgo. (Ill.) Title Ins. Co., 1976—2000; sr. v.p. Fidelity Nat. Fin. (acquired Chgo. Title Corp.), Santa Barbara, Calif., 2000—02; exec. v.p. Fidelity Nat. Fin., 2002—, co-COO, 2002—. Office: Fidelity National Financial 4050 Calle Real Santa Barbara CA 93110

ABBOT, EDWARD PIERCE, lawyer; b. Glen Ridge, N.J., Mar. 19, 1958; s. Alden Peek and Harriet Gere (Francisco) A.; m. Jill Victoria Comer, June 13, 1982; children: Edward Pierce Jr., Kelly Elizabeth. BA, George Washington U., 1980; JD, Fordham U., 1985. Bar: N.Y. 1986, N.J. 1986, Pa. 1994, U.S. Dist. Ct. N.J. 1986, U.S. Supreme Ct. 1992. Assoc. McCarter & English, Newark, 1985-88; ptnr. Anderson Kill Olick & Oshinsky, P.C., N.Y.C., 1988-96, Smith Abbot, L.L.P., N.Y.C., 1996—. Mem. ABA, N.J. State Bar Assn., N.Y. State Bar Assn. Office: Smith Abbot LLP 377 Broadway New York NY 10013 E-mail: edabbot@aol.com.

ABBOT, WILLIAM WRIGHT, history professor; b. Louisville, Ga., May 20, 1922; s. William Wright and Lillian (Carswell) A.; m. Eleanor Pearre, Mar. 31, 1958; children— William Wright, John Pearre. Student, Davidson (N.C.) Coll., 1939-41; AB, U. Ga., 1943; MA, Duke U., 1949, PhD, 1953; LHD, Coll. William and Mary, 1998. Tchr. Louisville Acad., 1946-47, McCallie Sch., 1951-52; from asst. prof. to prof. history Coll. William and Mary, 1953—61, 1963—66; assoc. prof. Northwestern U., 1958-59, Rice U., 1961-63; James Madison prof. history U. Va., 1966-92, emeritus, 1992—, chmn. history dept., 1972—74. Author: The Royal Governors of Georgia, 1754-1775, 1957, The Colonial Origins of the United States, 1607-1763, 1975; editor in chief: The Papers of George Washington, 1977-92, Colonial Series, Vols. I-X, Revolutionary War Series, Vols. I-VI, Confederation, Vols. I-VI, 1992-97, Presidential, Vols. I-V, Retirement Series, Vols. I-IV, 1998; editor Jour. So. History, 1961-63; book rev. editor William and Mary Quar., 1955-61, editor, 1963-66; bd. editors Va. Quarterly Rev., 1971-90. Served to lt. USNR, 1943-46. Mem. Inst. Early Am. History and Culture (coun. 1976-79), So. Hist. Assn. (exec. coun. 1978-81), Mass. Hist. Soc., Am. Antiquarian Soc., Va. Hist. Soc. (hon.), Gridiron Club (U. Ga.), Raven Soc. (U. Va.), Phi Beta Kappa (pres. Alpha chpt. 1984-87). Home: 804 Rugby Rd Charlottesville VA 22903-1629

ABBOTT, A. DWIGHT, retired astronautical engineer; BS in Aero. Engring., Purdue U., 1958, MS in Indsl. Mgmt., 1964. Gen. mgr. bus. mgmt. for space tech. applications, prin. dir. design engring., prin. dir. space transp. devel. for space launch ops. Aerospace Corp., L.A., 1960—2000; gen. mgr. systems engring. Aeronautics and Space Engring. Bd., Nat. Academies, Washington, 1960—2000. Mem. dean's vis. com. sch. engring. Purdue U., West Lafayette, Ind. Mayor Palos Verdes Estates (Calif.) City Coun.; bd. dirs. So. Calif. Coun. Govts. Fellow: AIAA (mem. pub. policy com.); mem.: AAAS, Planetary Soc. Avocation: flying. Home: 1825 Via Estudillo Palos Verdes Estates CA 90274

ABBOTT, ALDEN FRANCIS, lawyer, federal official; b. Bethesda, Md., Nov. 10, 1951; s. Roger Sloane and Suzanne Jeanne (Dupuy) Abbott; m. Ljubica Visich, May 3, 1980; 1 child, Roger Visich. Cert., U. Madrid, 1972; BA, U. Va., 1974; JD, Harvard U., 1977; MA in Econs., Georgetown U., 1984. Bar: D.C. 1977, U.S. Supreme Ct. 1992. Atty. Office of Legal Policy FTC, Washington, 1977-80; atty. Fried, Frank, Harris, Shriver & Kampelman, Washington, 1980-82; spl. counsel Office of Legal Policy U.S. Dept. Justice, Washington, 1982-84, spl. asst. to asst. atty. gen. antitrust divsn., 1984-86, sr. counsel Office of Legal Counsel, 1987-89; counselor to gen. counsel U.S. Dept. Commerce, Washington, 1989-92, chief counsel Nat. Telecom. and Info. Adminstrn., 1992-94, asst. gen. counsel fin. and litig., 1994-2001, acting gen. counsel, 2001; asst. dir. for policy evaluation, Bur. of Competition FTC, Washington, 2001—, assoc. dir. for policy and coordination, 2004—. Adj. prof. Sch. Law George Mason U., Arlington, Va., 1991—; vis. fellow All Souls Coll., Oxford, England, 2005 Comment and note editor Harvard Internat. Law Jour.; contbr. numerous articles to profl. jours. Mem. Fed. Comm. Bar Assn. (internat. sect.), U.S. Supreme Ct. Bar, Henry Simons Soc., Phi Eta Sigma, Phi Beta Kappa. Avocations: foreign languages and travel, swimming, reading, skiing. Home: 1611 Westmoreland St Mc Lean VA 22101-5166 Office: US Fed Trade Commn 6th & Penn Ave NW Washington DC 20580 Business E-Mail: aabbott@ftc.gov.

ABBOTT, ALORIS JEAN, retired medical/surgical nurse, retired nursing administrator; b. Maynard, Minn., July 22, 1931; d. Bernt O. and Melvina (Gerde) Docken; m. Roy L. Abbott, Jan. 2, 1987; children: Dianne Weber, Susan Milewski. Diploma, Broadlawns Sch. Nursing, Des Moines, 1952. Cert. oper. rm. nurse, nursing adminstr. Head nurse Iowa Meth. Med. Ctr., Des Moines; pvt. scrub nurse Des Moines; head nurse oper. rm., recovery rm., nursing coord. oper. rm. VA Med. Ctr., Des Moines, oper. rm.-recovery rm. coord., ret., 1991. Mem. adv. bd. Des Moines Area CC; bd. dirs. Coun. Nursing Adminstrn. Mem.: ANA, Nurses Orgn. VA, Assn. Oper. Rm. Nurses (v.p. ctrl. Hawkeye chpt.). Home: 3519 Crestmoor Pl Des Moines IA 50310-4322

ABBOTT, BARRY ALEXANDER, lawyer; b. New Haven, Aug. 20, 1950; s. Harold and Norma (Kaufman) A.; 1 child, Anne Stewart. AB, Dartmouth Coll., 1972; JD, U. Fla., 1975; MBA, Stanford U., 1977. Bar: Fla. 1975, Calif. 1976, U.S. Dist. Ct. (so. dist.) Fla. 1976, U.S. Dist. Ct. (no. dist.) Calif. 1976, U.S. Ct. Appeals (9th cir.) 1976, U.S. Supreme Ct. 1979, D.C. 1985, N.Y. 1986. Assoc. Morrison & Foerster, San Francisco, 1977-83, ptnr., 1983-94; dir. Howard Rice Nemerovski Canady Falk & Rabkin, San Francisco, 1994—. Adj. faculty mem. Boalt Hall Sch. Law, U. Calif., Berkeley, 1998; lectr. corp., comml. and fin. inst. law various orgns.; mem. Fed. Res. Bd. Consumer Adv. Coun., 1992-94, chmn. consumer credit com., 1993-94, mem. governing com. Conf. on Consumer Fin. Law; mem. Am. Coll. Consumer Fin. Svcs. Attys., 1995—, bd. regents, 1995-98, sec., 2002-05, treas., 2005—. Co-author: Truth in Lending: A Comprehensive Guide; contbr. articles to profl. jours. Named one of Outstanding Young Men of Am., U.S. Jaycees, 1980. Fellow Royal Soc. Arts (Silver medal 1972); mem. ABA (chmn. young lawyers divsn. bus. law com. 1987-88, chmn. ins. products subcom. 1987-92, vice chmn. consumer fin. svcs. commn. 1995-96, active various coms.), Calif. Bar Assn. (vice chair fin. instns. com. 1991-92, chair 1992-93, mem. ins. law com. 1994-96, mem. bus. law sect. exec. com. 1996-99, treas. 1997-98, vice chair 1998-99), Fla. Bar Assn., D.C. Bar Assn., N.Y. State Bar Assn., San Francisco Bar Assn. (chmn. membership com. 1984-86, bd. dirs. 1982, 87-88, Merit award 1985, 2004), Barristers Club (bd. dirs. 1981-83, treas., pres. 1982), Order of Coif, Phi Beta Kappa, Phi Kappa Phi. Clubs: World Trade (San Francisco), Commonwealth (Calif.). Republican. Office: Howard Rice 3 Embarcadero Ctr Ste 700 San Francisco CA 94111-4024 Office Phone: 415-434-1600. Business E-Mail: babbott@howardrice.com.

ABBOTT, BEVERLY STUBBLEFIELD, artist; b. Greensboro, NC, Dec. 12, 1940; d. Robert L. and Helen W. Stubblefield; m. Ira H. A. Abbott, May 7, 1960; children: Ira Robert, Leslie Ann. Represented by Seaside Art Gallery, Nags Head, NC. Exhibitions include Leigh Yawkey Woodson Art Mus., 1996—97, Seaside Art Gallery, 1996—2005, Village Gallery, 1997—99,

Germantown Gallery, 1999—2004, Fla. Wildlife Art Expo, 1999—2005, Southeastern Wildlife Expo, 2002, Miniature Art Soc. Fla., 2003—05, Pawprints on My Heart, 2000, Paw Prints through the Years, 2004, prin. works include Va. Living Mus. Wildlife Arts Festival, 2003, World Federation of Miniaturists, Smithsonian Inst., 2004, Paper Mill Internat. Miniature art exhbn., 2004, Paper Mill Internat. Miniature Art Exhbn., 2005, 71st Miniature Painters, Sculptors and Gravers Soc. of Washington, 2004, 71st Minature Paitners, Sculptors and Gravers Soc., Washington, DC, 2004. Grantee, Susan K. Black Found., 2002. Mem.: Hampton Arts League (Merit award 1997), Atlantic Wildfowl Heritage Mus., James River Camera Club (pres. 1994), Langley Kennel Club (life; show chmn. 1977, 1984). Avocations: travel, photography. Home: 13 Delta Cir Newport News VA 23601-3117

ABBOTT, CHARLES FAVOUR, lawyer; b. Sedro-Wolley, Wash., Oct. 12, 1937; s. Charles Favour and Violette Doris Abbott; m. Oranee Harward, Sept. 19, 1958; children: Patricia, Stephen, Nelson, Cynthia, Lisa, Alyson. BA in Econs., U. Wash., 1959, JD, 1962. Bar: Calif. 1962, Utah 1981, Wash. 2005. Law clk. Judge M. Oliver Koelsch, U.S. Ct. Appeals (9th cir.), San Francisco, 1963; assoc. Jones, Hatfield & Abbott, Escondido, 1964; pvt. practice Escondido, 1964-77, Provo, Utah, 1983-93; of counsel Mueller & Abbott, Escondido, 1997—; ptnr. Abbott, Thorn & Hill, Provo, 1981-83, Abbott & Abbott, 1993—98; pres. Charles F. Abbott PC, 1998—; of counsel Abbott & Walker, PC, 1998—. Presenter in field. Author: How to Do Your Own Legal Work, 1976, 2d edit., 1981, How to Win in Small Claims Court, 1981, How to Be Free of Debt in 24 Hours, 1981, How to Hire the Best Lawyer at the Lowest Fee, 1981, The Lawyers's Inside Method of Making Money, 1979, The Millionaire Mindset, 1987, How to Make Big Money in the Next 30 Days, 1989, Business Legal Manual and Forms, 1990, How to Make Millions in Marketing, 1990, Telemarketing Training Course, 1990, How to Form A Corporation in Any State, 1990, The Complete Asset Protection Plan, 1990, Personal Injury and the Law, 1997, Fen-Phen Fallout--The Medical and Legal Crisis, 1998; mem. editl. bd. Wash. Law Rev. and State Bar Assn. Jour., 1961-62; bd. editors Phen-fen Litigation Strategist, 1998-2000; contbr. articles to profl. jours. Mem. ATLA, Utah Bar Assn., Calif. Bar Assn., U.S. Supreme Ct. Bar Assn., Wash. State Bar Assn. Home: 4411 N Sheffield Dr Provo UT 84058 Office: Charles F Abbott PC 3651 N 100 E Ste 300 Provo UT 84604-4521 Office Phone: 800-366-2040. Business E-Mail: charles@abbott-abbott.com.

ABBOTT, CHARLES WARREN, lawyer; b. Miami, Jan. 16, 1930; s. Voyle E. and Katherine (Paschall) A.; m. Betty Jo Eckholdt, Jan. 9, 1959; children: Brenda Jean, Katherine Louise, Abigail Jill. BS in Bus. Adminstrn., U. Fla., 1951, JD, 1953. Bar: Fla. 1955, U.S. Dist. Ct. (so. dist.) Fla. 1955, U.S. Dist. Ct. (ctrl. dist.) Fla., U.S. Supreme Ct. 1960, U.S. Ct. Appeals (11th cir.) 1981, U.S. Dist. Ct. (no. dist.) Fla. 1981; cert. mediator Supreme Ct. Fla. Assoc. Maguire, Voorhis & Wells, P.A., Orlando, Fla., 1955-59, ptnr., 1959-68, dir., 1968—95, of counsel, 1995—98; ptnr. Holland & Knight LLP, Orlando, Fla., 1998—. Mem. judicial nominating commn. Fifth Appellate Dist., 1984-88, chmn. 1987-88. Chmn. Goldenrod Fire Control Dist., 1966-79; mem. Orange County Emergency Med. Svcs. Coun., 1984, 91-94; dir. Fla. Found. for Spl. Children; trustee U. Fla. Law Ctr. Assn, 2002—. Served with JAGC, USAF, 1953-55; served to capt. USAFR, 1951-62. Fellow Am. Coll. Trial Lawyers; mem. ABA, Fla. Bar Assn., Orange County Bar Assn., Fla. Def. Lawyers Assn. (sec.-treas. 1983, v.p. 1984, pres. 1985), Def. Rsch. Inst. (state chmn. 1981-85, so. regional v.p. 1986-88, nat. dir. 1988-91), Fedn. Ins. Corp. Counsel, Am. Bd. Trial Advs. (charter, treas. 1991-92, sec. 1992-93), First Ctrl. Fla. Am. Inns of Ct. (charter mem., treas., pres. 1992-93), Phi Delta Phi. Democrat. Methodist. Home: 2035 Summerland Ave Winter Park FL 32789-1453 Office: Holland & Knight LLP PO Box 1526 200 S Orange Ave Ste 2600 Orlando FL 32801 Office Phone: 407-244-1124. Business E-Mail: charles.abbott@hklaw.com.

ABBOTT, DAN-SAN, parachute designer; b. Canton, Kwantong, China, Aug. 10, 1923; came to U.S., 1925; s. Harry Wayne and Mary Alice (Carr) A.; m. Noami Irene Abbott, Mar. 15, 1946 (div. 1953); children: Sandra, Daniel, Danielle; m. Patricia Lee Brown, June 15, 1958. Parachute rigger Security Parachute Co., Oakland, Calif., 1946-49; parachute supr. Calif. Air N.G., Hayward, 1949-53; design engr. Security Parachute Co., San Leandro, Calif., 1953-64, mgr. engring., 1964-68, v.p., 1968-77; dir. ops. Guardian Parachute, Santa Ana, Calif., 1977-88; dir. mktg. FXC Corp., Santa Ana, 1986-88; cons. World War I Aviation Documentation Svc., Ceres, Calif., 1988—. Artist Oakland Nat. Engraving, 1946. Contbr. articles to profl. jours. Recipient Achievement award Don Beck Meml. award, 1990, Award for Editl. Excellence, Over the Front, 1988, 90. Mem. Soc. of the First World Aviation Historians, League of WWI Aviation Historians, WWI Aeroplances Inc, NRA. Republican. Presbyterian. Avocations: painting, watercolor painting, drawing, writing. Home and Office: 1800 Stone Cress Ct Ceres CA 95307 E-mail: dansanabbott@charter.net.

ABBOTT, DAVID HENRY, manufacturing executive; b. Milton, Ky., July 6, 1936; s. Carl and Rachael (Miles) A.; m. Joan Shefchik, Aug. 14, 1976; children— Kristine, Gina, Beth, Linsey BS, U. Ky., 1960, MBA, 1961. With Ford Motor Co., Louisville, Mpls. and Dearborn, Mich., 1961-69; div. controller J I Case Co., Racine, Wis., 1970-73, gen. mgr. service parts supply div., 1973-75, v.p., 1975, v.p. and gen. mgr. constrn. equipment div., 1975-77, v.p., gen. mgr. Drott div. Wausau, Wis., 1977-79, exec. v.p. worldwide constrn. equipment, 1979-81; pres., chief operating officer Portec, Inc., Oak Brook, Ill., 1981-87, also dir.; pres., chief exec. officer, dir. E.D. Etnyre & Co., Oregon, Ill., 1988—2002, ret., 2002. Dir. Oak Brook Bank, 1982-88. Served with U.S. Army, 1958 Mem. Constrn. Industry Mfrs. Assn. (bd. dirs. 1979-81, 82-2002, chmn. 1992), Am. Rd. and Transpn. Builders Assn. (dir. 1988—2002). Republican. Home: 2461 Saddlewood Ct Lanark IL 61046

ABBOTT, DAVID L., agricultural products executive; BS, Univ. Vt. CEO Purina Mills, St. Louis; pres., CEO E-markets Inc., Ames, Iowa. Mem.: Nat. FFA Found. (bd. mem.), Am. Feed Ind. Assn. (past pres.). Office: E-markets Inc Ste 108 1606 Golden Aspen Dr Ames IA 50010-8011*

ABBOTT, DOUGLAS EUGENE, engineering educator; b. Glendale, Calif., Apr. 20, 1934; s. Richard Edward and Eva (Pogue) A.; m. Doris Bernice Newmark, Dec. 16, 1956; children: Sandra Lee, Jodi Frances, Shari Evalinis, Traci Bernice. B.M.E., Stanford U., 1956, M.M.E., 1957, PhD, 1961. Asst. head fluid mechanics sect. Vidya div. Itek Corp., Palo Alto, Calif., 1960-64; lectr. Stanford U., 1963-64; asso. prof. Purdue U., 1964-69, prof., 1969-77, dir. thermal scis. and propulsion center, 1972-77; prof., chmn. dept. mech. engring. and mechanics, dir. computer-aided design/computer-aided mfg. ednl. program Lehigh U., Bethlehem, Pa., 1977-83, vice provost for computing and info. services, 1983-85; assoc. vice chancellor for info. technologies U. Mass.-Amherst, 1985-96; cons. in comms. technologies Amherst, 1996—. Staff cons. Midwest Applied Sci. Corp., Lafayette, Ind., 1964-72; energy controls div. Bendix Corp., South Bend, Ind., 1967-75, Westinghouse Research and Devel. Center, Pitts., 1970-75, ERDA, 1975-77; chmn. air breathing propulsion adv. com. Air Force Office of Sci. Research, 1973-83, Tech. Concepts, Inc., Sudbury, Mass., 1985-88; bd. dirs. Univ. Programs in Computer Aided Engring., Design and Mfg., 1984-91. Mem. governing bd. Five Coll. Libr., 1991-96. Hon. research fellow Sci. Research Council, U.K., 1971-72 Fellow AAAS, Am. Phys. Soc.; mem. ASME, AIAA, N.Y. Acad. Scis., Nat. Computer Graphics Assn. (bd. dirs. 1985-87, treas. 1987-89), Nat. Computer Graphics Assn. Ednl. Found. (bd. dirs. 1989-92, stewardship coun. 2004—), Trout Unltd. (bd. dirs. Pioneer Valley chpt. 1995—), Pi Tau Sigma. Home: 150 Wendell Rd Shutesbury MA 01072-9754 Office Phone: 413-253-9422. E-mail: abbott@oit.umass.edu.

ABBOTT, EDWARD LEROY, finance executive; b. Dayton, Ohio, Dec. 18, 1930; s. Roy Edward and Mildred Eileen (Filler) A.; m. Elizabeth Joan Grahame, June 8, 1957; children: Jay Edward, Julie Beth Abbott Holland. AB, Wittenberg U., 1952; postgrad., Ohio State U., 1952-53. With Northwestern Mut. Life Ins. Co., 1956-73, regional mgr. Washington, 1970-73; with Acacia Mut. Life Ins. Co., Washington, 1973-83, exec. v.p., treas., 1978-83; vice chmn., exec. v.p. CenTrust Savs. Bank, Miami, Fla., 1983-87; chmn., pres., CEO Capital-Union Savs., Baton Rouge, 1987-90; pres. CEO, dir. Firststate Fin., Orlando, Fla., 1992-97, Heritage Hill Farm, 1998—. Served with U.S. Army, 1954-55. Mem. Alpha Tau Omega. Republican.

ABBOTT, GEOFFREY WINSTON, physiologist, researcher; b. Bradford-On-Avon, Wiltshire, England, June 14, 1970; s. Ronald and Helen Mary (Black) Abbott. B.Sc. in Zoology with honors, Durham U., Eng., 1991; M.Sc. in Molecular Pathology and Toxicology with distinction, U. Leicester, Eng., 1993; Ph.D. in Biochemistry, U. London, 1997. Wellcome trust prize travelling postdoctoral rsch. fellow Yale U. Sch. of Medicine, New Haven, 1997—99, postdoctoral assoc., 1999—2001; asst. prof., dept. of medicine Cornell U., Weill Med. Coll., New York, 2001—, asst. prof., dept. of pharmacology, 2001—. Editl. adv. bd. mem. Jour. of Pharmacology & Exptl. Therapeutics, Bethesda, Md., 2004—. Contbr. chapters to books, articles to profl. jours. Recipient Cornell U. Weill Med. Coll. 11th Ann. Dept. of Medicine Investigator award, Michael Wolk Found., 2002; grantee, NIH, 2004—, Am. Heart Assn., 2002—. Mem.: Am. Heart Assn., Biophysical Soc., Soc. for Neuroscience. Achievements include patents for MinK-related genes, formation of potassium channels and association with cardiac arrhythmia; patents pending for vovel small molecule modulators of ion channels; co-discoverer of the KCNE gene family of potassium channel beta subunits; co-discoverer of the first example of a molecular genetic basis for acquired cardiac arrhythmia; co-discoverer of novel roles for potassium channel ancillary subunits in mammalian brain; co-discoverer of the molecular basis for bradycardia in patients under propofol general anesthesia; research in first usage of RNA interference technique in Xenopus oocytes. Home: 1161 York Avenue Apt 8K New York NY 10021 Office: Cornell University Weill Med College Starr 463 520 East 70th Street New York NY 10021 Office Phone: 212-774-7026. Home Fax: 212-774-7390; Office Fax: 212-774-7390. Personal E-mail: gwa2001@med.cornell.edu.

ABBOTT, GEORGE LINDELL, librarian; b. Rutland, Vt., July 11, 1941; s. F. George and Eva Marie (Fields) A.; m. Sandra Jean Baker, Aug. 6, 1966; 1 child, Brian George. BA in Math., St. Michael's Coll., 1963; MLS, Syracuse U., 1966. Cataloguer St. Michael's Coll., Winooski, Vt., 1963-64; cataloguer libr. Syracuse (N.Y.) U., 1966-70, media librarian, 1970-80, head dept. media svcs., 1980—. Cons. in field. Contbr. articles to various publs.; editor Videodisc/VideoTex jour., 1980-82. Recipient Watson Davis award, Am. Soc. for Info. Sci. and Tech., 1987. Mem. ALA, Am. Soc. Info. Sci. (bd. dirs. 1981-85), Internat. Fedn. of Libr. Assns. and Instns. (standing com. audiovisual and multimedia sect., 2003—), Libr. and Info. Tech. Assn. (bd. dirs. 1985-88), Soc. Motion Picture and TV Engrs., Beta Phi Mu. Avocations: microcomputing, cinema. Office: Syracuse Univ Libr 222 Waverly Ave Syracuse NY 13210-2412 Office Phone: 315-443-2438.

ABBOTT, GREG WAYNE, state attorney general, former state supreme court justice; b. Wichita Falls, Tex., Nov. 13, 1957; s. Calvin Roger and Doris Lacristia (Jacks) Rowley A.; m. Cecilia Therese Phalen, Aug. 15, 1981; 1 child, Audrey. BBA, U. Tex., 1981; JD, Vanderbilt U., 1984. Bar: Tex. 1985, U.S. Dist. Ct. (so. dist.) Tex. 1985. Atty. Butler & Binion, Houston, 1984-92; judge 12th State Dist. Ct., Houston, 1992-96; justice Texas Supreme Ct., 1996—2000; partner Bracewell & Patterson, LLP; atty. gen. State of Tex., 2003—. Prof. U. Tex.; mem. com. on Pub. Trust and Confidence in Tex. Cts., Jury Task Force Implementation Project; mem. cert. bd. Tex. Ct. Reporters; exec. com. Family Law 2000 Task Force. Dir. Houston Ctr. for Barrier Free Living, 1986-87; capt. March of Dimes Team Walk, Houston, 1986-87; mem. Gov.'s Com. to Promote Adoption; bd. dirs. Tex. Inst. Rehab. and Rsch., Maywood Children and Family Svcs.; bd. trustees Goodwill Industries; adv. bd. Career and Recovery Resources Inc. Named Disabled Person of Yr. Harris County Com. on Employment of Disabled Persons, 1985, Outstanding Young Texan Tex. Jaycees, 1995; recipient Am. Jurisprudence award Am. Jur, 1983, Named Outstanding Trial Judge, Texas Assn. of Civil Trial and Appellate Specialists, 1995. Mem. State Bar Tex. (com. on legal advt. 1988, Supreme Ct. liason for com. on jud. ethics, jud. conduct commn., code of jud. conduct), Houston Bar Assn. (Houston's Outstanding Young Lawyer 1994), Houston Young Lawyers Assn., Tex. Assn. State Judges (exec. com.). Republican. Roman Catholic. Avocations: snow-skiing, travel, swimming. Office: Capitol Station PO Box 12548 Austin TX 78711-2548

ABBOTT, HERSCHEL LEE, JR., lawyer; b. Little Rock, Ark., Sept. 4, 1941; s. Herschel Lee and Wanda Catherine (Jones) Abbott; m. Anne Elizabeth Hamilton, Dec. 21, 1963; children: Cathryn Boyd, Herschel Lee. BA, Tulane U., 1963; LLB, 1966. Cert.: Birmingham Eng. U./Birmingham Eng. 1962, bar: La. 1966, US Dist. Ct. (ea.,cid., we. dist.)/La. 1966, US Ct. Apls. (5th cir.) 1971, US Sup. Ct. 1973. Assoc. Jones, Walker, Waechter, Poitevent, Carrere & Denegre, ptnr., sr. ptnr.; gen. counsel BellSouth Corp, La., 1991—95; assoc. gen. counsel BellSouth Telecommunications, Atlanta, 1995—96; Pres., Louisiana Operations BellSouth Corp., 1996—2001, v.p. governmental affairs, 2001—. Trustee St. Martin's Episcopal Sch.; pres. New Orleans Area Bayou River Health Sys. Agy., 1976—77. Capt. JAGC USAF, 1970, maj. Res. USAF, 1970—78. Decorated Bronze Star. Mem.: New Orleans Bar Assn., Fed. Bar Assn., La. Bar Assn., Am. Judicature Soc., ABA, Am. Law Inst. Republican. Office: c/o BellSouth Corp 1155 Peachtree St NE Atlanta GA 30309

ABBOTT, HIRSCHEL THERON, JR., lawyer; b. Clarksdale, Miss., Jan. 11, 1942; s. Hirschel Theron Sr. and Ona Belle (Williamson) A.; m. Mimi Eugenia DuPre, June 14, 1969; children: Barkley, Chip. BBA in Acct., U. Miss., Oxford, 1964; JD, U. Va., Charlottesville, 1971. Bar: La. 1971, Miss. 1971, U.S. Dist. Ct. (ea. dist.) La. 1971, U.S. Ct. Appeals (5th cir.) 1981, U.S. Tax Ct. 1988; bd. cert. tax law specialist. Lawyer Stone Pigman Walther Wittmann LLP, New Orleans, 1971—75, ptnr., 1975—. Bd. dirs. Episcopal Housing for Srs., Inc., Lambeth House, Inc.; past trustee, sec. Preservation Resource Ctr., New Orleans; past bd. mem., chmn. Trinity Episcopal Sch. Bd. Trustees; past trustee, treas. La. Civil Svc. League; past bd. mem. Uptown Neighborhood Improvement Assn.; past mem., chmn. La. Jefferson Scholarship Selection Com. U. Va.; past regional chmn. La. U. Va. Law Sch. Annual Giving Fund; past mem. of vestry Trinity Episcopal Ch.; past mem. Adv. Bd. Jr. League New Orleans. Recipient Monte M. Lemann award, La. Civil Svc. League, 1989. Fellow Am. Coll. Trust and Estate Counsel (past mem. charitable planning and exempt orgns. com.), La. Bar Found.; mem. ABA (tax sect., bus. law sect., real property trusts probate sect.), La. Bar Assn. (past chmn. tax law specialization commn., tax sect., corp. sect., successions, donations and trusts sect.), Miss. State Bar Assn., New Orleans Estate Planning Coun., Assn. Employee Benefit Planners. Epicopalian. Office: Stone Pigman Walther et al 546 Carondelet St New Orleans LA 70130-3588 Office Phone: 504-593-0809. E-mail: habbott@stonepigman.com.

ABBOTT, HORACE PORTER, English literature educator; b. Balt., Nov. 21, 1940; s. Horace P. and Barbara Ann (Trueblood) A.; m. Anita Vaivods, June 25, 1966; children: Jason, Byram. BA, Reed Coll., Portland, Oreg., 1962; MA, U. Toronto, Ont., Can., 1964, PhD, 1968. From asst. prof. to assoc. prof. U. Calif., Santa Barbara, 1966-82, prof., 1982—, chair of English, 1983-87, 90, acting dean humanities and fine arts, 1992-94, acting dir. Interdisciplinary Humanities Ctr., 1999—2001. Lectr., instr. Yeats Summer Sch., Sligo, Ireland, 1989. Author: The Fiction of Samuel Beckett, 1973, Diary Fiction, 1984, Beckett Writing Beckett, 1996, The Cambridge Introduction to Narrative, 2002; (poetry) Cold Certainties and Changes Beyond Measure, 1988; editor On the Origin of Fictions, 2001. Pres. Foothill Preservation League, Santa Barbara, 1996-2004. Recipient William Stafford award Poetry Assn. Wash., 1977. Mem. MLA, Samuel Beckett Soc. (pres. 1962-64). Office: U of Calif Dept English Santa Barbara CA 93106

ABBOTT, JAMES SAMUEL, III, marketing executive; b. Cleve., Nov. 19, 1918; s. James Samuel and Dorothy (Wilbor) A.; m. Mary Margaret Torrance, Oct. 13, 1957; 1 child, James Samuel. Student, Cornell U., 1941. Sales engr. Nat. Acme Co., Cleve., Chgo., 1945-63, chief sales engr. Cleve., 1963-67, sales mgr., 1967-69; mktg. mgr. Cleveland Twist Drill Co., Cleve., 1969-83; pres. James S. Abbott Consulting, Inc., Gates Mills, Ohio, 1983—. Contbr. articles to profl. jours. Mem. pk. bd. Village of Gates Mills, Ohio, 1979-86. Capt. USAF, 1941-45. Mem. Soc. Founders-Patriots (gov. 1968-69), Soc. Colonial Wars, Western Res. Hist. Soc., Clev. Mus. Natural History, U.S. Horse Cavalry Assn., Mayfield Country Club. Avocations: history, antiques, fly fishing, golf, tennis. Home: 7059 Hillcreek Ln Gates Mills OH 44040-9629

ABBOTT, KENNETH WAYNE, law educator; b. Albany, NY, July 25, 1944; s. Walter Miles and Ruth Bessie (Lasher) Abbott; m. Ann Wadsworth, June 8, 1968; children: Thomas A., Carolyn R.; m. Deborah deSchweitz, May 17, 1980. BA, Cornell U., 1966; JD magna cum laude, Harvard U., 1969. Bar: Mass 1969, NY 1970. Assoc. Harris, Beach, Wilcox, Robin & Levey, Rochester, NY, 1970—77; vol. VISTA, 1969—70; rsch. fellow Harvard U. Law Sch., 1977—78; assoc. prof. Northwestern U. Sch. Law, Chgo., 1978—82, prof., 1982—93, Elizabeth Froehling Horner prof. of law and commerce, 1993—; interim dir. Ctr. for Internat. and Comparative Studies, Chgo., 1999—2000, dir., 2000—; vis. prof. Cornell U., 1983—84. Contbr. articles to profl. jours. Mem.: Am. Assn. for Comparative Study of Law, Am. Soc. Internat. Law, ABA. Office: Northwestern U Sch Law 357 E Chicago Ave Chicago IL 60611-3059 E-mail: k-abbott@law.northwestern.edu.*

ABBOTT, KEVIN CHARLES, lawyer; b. Pitts., May 7, 1956; BA in Polit. Sci. magna cum laude, Ind. U. of Pa., 1978; JD magna cum laude, U. Pitts., 1981. Bar: Pa. 1981, W.Va. 1997, Commonwealth Ct. Pa. 1981, US Ct. Appeals 3rd Cir. 1982, US Ct. Appeals 6th Cir. 1982, US Dist. Ct. No. Dist. Ohio 1982, US Dist. Ct. We. Dist. Pa. 1983, US Dist. Ct. Mid. Dist. Pa. 1991, US Dist. Ct. No. Dist. W.Va. 1997, US Dist. Ct. So. Dist. W.Va. 1999, US Dist. Ct. Ea. Dist. Pa. 1999. Law clk. to Honorable Leroy Contie, Jr US Dist. Ct. No. Dist. Ohio, 1981-82, US Ct. Appeals 6th Cir., 1982-83; assoc. Thorp, Reed & Armstrong, Pitts., 1983-90, ptnr., 1990—2000, Reed Smith LLP Pitts., 2000—, Pitts. practice group leader litig. group, head energy & natural resources group. Case note editor U. Pitts. Law Rev., 1981. Bd. trustees Energy and Mineral Law Found. Recipient Fed. Bar Assn. prize, 1981; Provost's scholar U. Pitts., 1981; Owens fellow U. Pitts., 1978. Mem. ABA, Pa. Bar Assn., Allegheny County Bar Assn., Am. Arbitration Assn., Order of Coif. Office: Reed Smith LLP 435 Sixth Ave Pittsburgh PA 15219 Office Phone: 412-288-3804. Office Fax: 412-288-3063. Business E-Mail: kabbott@reedsmith.com.

ABBOTT, LAURENCE FREDERICK, physics educator; b. Toronto, Ont., Can., May 15, 1950; came to U.S., 1957; s. Norman John and Ursula (Herbst) A.; m. Catherine Mitchell Davis, Apr. 6, 1974; children: Paul Davis, Karen Chapin. Student, Oberlin Coll., 1968-71; PhD in Physics, Brandeis U., 1977. Rsch. assoc. Stanford (Calif.) Linear Accelerator, 1977-79; asst. prof. Brandeis U., Waltham, Mass., 1979-80, assoc. prof., 1982-88, prof. physics, 1988—. Sci. assoc. European Orgn. for Nuclear Rsch. (CERN), Geneva, 1980-81; mem. adv. bd. Theoretical Advanced Summer Inst., Dept. Energy, Washington, 1988—. Editor: Inflationary Cosmology, 1986, (with Terrence J. Sejnowski) Neural Codes and Distributed Representations: Foundations of Neural Computation (Computational Neuroscience), 1999; mem. editl. bd. Phys. Rev., 1987—; editorial adv. bd. Network, England, 1989—; contbr. numerous articles to profl. jours.; patentee in field. Sloan Found. fellow, 1983-85; rsch. grantee Dept. Energy, 1979—; recipient Pioneer award, NIH, 2004. Achievements include research in analytic techniques and computer simulation to study the electrical characteristics of single neurons. Office: Brandeis U 415 South St Waltham MA 02454 Business E-Mail: abbott@brandeis.edu.

ABBOTT, LAWRENCE E., lawyer; b. Miami, Fla., May 18, 1944; BA, St. Edward's U., 1967; JD, Tulane U. La., 1972. Bar: La. 1972, U.S. Dist. Ct. (ea. dist.) La. 1972, U.S. Dist. Ct. (we. dist.) La. 1974, U.S. Dist. Ct. (mid. dist.) La. 1975, U.S. Supreme Ct. 1979, U.S. Ct. Appeals (5th cir.) 1981, U.S. Ct. Appeals (11th cir.) 1984, Tex. 1996. D.C. 1996. Mem. Abbott, Simses & Kuchler, Houston, New Orleans and Covington, La. Mem. ABA (products, gen. liability and consumer law com., rail and motor carrier law com., toxic and hazardous substances and environ. law com. 1995—), Maritime Law Assn. U.S. (mem. internat. law sea com. 1984—, mem. subcom. offshore exploration and devel. 1984—, mem. com. river and ocean towing 1985—), Average Adjusters Assn. U.S. (assoc.), La. State Bar Assn. (asst. examiner com. on bar admissions 1994—), La. Assn. Def. Counsel, New Orleans Bar Assn., New Orleans Def. Counsel Assn., Southeastern Admiralty Law Inst., Def. Rsch. Inst., Inc., La. Bar Found., La. Assn. R.R. Trial Counsel, Am. Arbitration Assn., La. Assn. Bus. and Industry, Phi Delta Phi. Office: Abbott Simses Knister & Kuchler 400 Lafayette St Ste 200 New Orleans LA 70130-3229 E-mail: Larry-Abbott@abbott-simses.com.

ABBOTT, LORRAINE A., musician, educator; b. Buffalo, N.Y., Dec. 4, 1962; d. Murray Abbott and Rita Abbott-Klos; m. Edwin K. Bradley, Jr., Dec. 24, 2001; children: Matthew Edwin, Hannah Lorraine. BFA in Piano Performance, SUNY, Buffalo, N.Y., 1985, MusM in Piano Performance, 1988, MusM in Chamber Music, 1996; MusD in Chamber Music, U. Miami, 2002. Freelance pianist, pvt. tchr., Miami, 1996—2003, Buffalo, 2003—. Grad. tchg. asst. U. Miami, 1996—99; pianist South Beach Chamber Ensemble, Miami, 1997—2003, Arabesque Chamber Ensemble, Miami, 1998—; pianist, organist, dir. choir Deerhurst Presbyn. Ch., Buffalo. Recipient Arts and Letters Achievement award, SUNY, 1985; Garahee Music scholar, 1982—85. Mem.: Nat. Guild Piano Tchrs., Am. Guild Organists, Pi Kappa Lambda. Home: 75 W Maplemere Rd Williamsville NY 14221 Office Phone: 716-432-8647. Personal E-mail: keenly50@msn.com.

ABBOTT, NELSON THOMAS, lawyer; b. Escondido, Calif., Jan. 30, 1966; s. Charles FaVour and Oranee (Harward) A.; m. Kirstin Nielson, Aug. 6, 1987; children: Michael, Katie, Caroline, David. BA, Brigham Young U., 1989, MBA, JD, 1993. Bar: Utah 1994, U.S. Dist. Ct. Utah, 1994. With Abbott, Abbott & Walker, Orem, Utah, 1994—98, Nelson T. Abbott, LLC, Orem, Utah, 1998, Abbott, Spencer & Smith, LLC, Orem, Utah, 1998—2002, Abbott & Assocs., Provo, Utah, 2002—03, Abbott & Walker, P.C., Provo, 2003—. Author: How to Create Barriers to Protect Your Assets, 1990; co-author: How to Form a Corporation in Any State, 1990; contbr. articles to profl. jours. Bd. dirs. Utah Valley Mgmt. Soc., Tri-Connections, Inc. Mem. ATLA, Utah Trial Lawyers Assn., Beta Gamma Sigma. Republican. Mem. Lds Ch. Office: Abbott & Walker PC 43 W 300 North Provo UT 84601

ABBOTT, REBECCA PHILLIPS, museum director, consultant, photographer; b. Giessen, Germany, Jan. 10, 1950; d. Charles Leonard and Janet Alice (Praeger) Phillips. BA, Emory and Henry Coll., 1973; postgrad., Georgetown U., 1975, Am. U., 1982-88. Assoc. univ. registrar Am. U., Washington, 1977-81, assoc. dir. adminstrv. computing, 1981-84, dir. adminstrv. computing, 1984-88; dir. membership Nat. Mus. of Women in the Arts, Washington, 1988-89, dir., 1989-98; cons. in fine arts, 1998—. Fine arts photographer. Selected solo exhbns., Includes Anton Gallery, Public Places Private Views, 1992, The Wind, 1994, Canal Views, 1996, Burton Marinkovich Fine Art, Shadows at 18th and K, 1998; Selected group exhbns. includes The Annex Gallery, Metaphysical Landscapes,1989, Embassy of Japan: East Meets West, 1995, Nippon Gallery, Assimilations, 1997. Mem. Am. Assn. Mus., Mus. Art Table.

ABBOTT, REGINA A., neurodiagnostic technologist, consultant, business owner; b. Haverhill, Mass., Mar. 5, 1950; d. Frank A. and Ann (Drelick) A. Student, Pierce Bus. Sch., Boston, 1967-70, Seizure Unit Children's Hosp. Med. Ctr. Sch. EEG Tech., 1970-71. Registered electroneurodiagnostic technologist Advanced Fuller Sch. Massage Therapy, 2001, nat. cert. massage therapist Nat. Cert. Bd. Therapeutic Massage and Bodywork. Tech. dir. electrodiagnostic labs. Salem Hosp., 1972-76; lab. dir. clin. neurophysiology Tufts U. New Eng. Med. Ctr., Boston, 1976-78; clin. instr. EEG program Laboure Coll., Boston, 1977-81; adminstrv. dir. dept. Neurology Mt. Auburn Hosp., Cambridge, Mass., 1978-81; tech. dir. clin. neurophysiology Drs. Diagnostic Service, Virginia Beach, Va.; tech. dir. neurodiagnostic ctr. Portsmouth Psychiatric Ctr., 1981-87; founder, pres., owner Commonwealth Neurodiagnostic Services, Inc., 1986—, Hands on HealthCare, 2001—,

Hands On-Site, LLC, 2004—. Co-dir. continuing edn. program EEG Tech., Boston, 1977-78; mem. adv. com. sch. neurodiagnostic tech. Laboure Coll., 1977-81, Sch. EEG Tech. Children's Hosp. Med. Ctr., Boston, 1980-81; assoc. examiner Am. Bd. Registration of Electroencephalographic Technologists, 1977-83; mem. guest faculty Oxford Medilog Co.; cons. Nihon Kohden Am., 1981-83; cons., educator Teca Corp., Pleasantville, N.Y., 1981-87; clin. evaluator Calif. Coll. for Health Scis., 1995—. Contbr. articles to profl. jours. EIL scholar, Poland/USSR, 1970; recipient Internat. Woman of Yr. award in bus. and sci. Internat. Biographical Ctr., London, 1993-94. Mem.: NAFE, Am. Soc. Electroneurodiagnostic Technologists, Am. Massage Therapy Assn. Avocations: running, art collecting, photography, reading, investing.

ABBOTT, ROBERT DEAN, psychology professor; b. Twin Falls, Idaho, Dec. 19, 1946; s. Charles Dean and Billie June (Moore) A.; m. Sylvia Patricia Keim, Dec. 16, 1967; children: Danielle, Matthew. BA, Calif. Western U., San Diego, 1967; MS, U. Wash., 1968, PhD, 1970. Asst. prof., assoc. prof. Calif. State U.-Fullerton, 1970-75; asst. prof., prof. ednl. psychology U. Wash., Seattle, 1975—; dir. Ctr. Inst. Devel. and Research, Seattle, 1983-92. Author: Elementary Multivariate Statistics, 1983; contbr. over 150 articles to profl. jours. Calif. State scholar, 1964-67 Fellow Am. Psychol. Assn.; mem. Am. Ednl. Research Assn., Am. Stats. Assn., Psychometric Soc. Office: Ednl Psych 312 Miller PO Box 353600 Seattle WA 98195-3600

ABBOTT, WILLIAM SAUNDERS, lawyer; b. Medford, Mass., June 2, 1938; s. Charles Theodoric and Evelyn (Saunders) A.; m. Susan Shaw, June 24, 1961; children: Cathryn, Stephen, David. AB, Harvard U., 1960, LLB, 1966. Bar: Mass. 1967, U.S. Dist. Ct. Mass., U.S. Ct. Appeals (D.C. cir.). White House fellow, 1966-67; regional coord. U.S. Agrl. Programs Asia USDA, 1967-68; gen. counsel Cabot, Cabot & Forbes Co., Boston, 1968-77; prin. Simonds, Winslow, Willis & Abbott, Boston, 1977—. Mem. Harvard Law Review. Pres. The Wildlands Trust Southeastern Mass., 1984—90, 1996—97, Nat. Found. to Improve TV, 1970—; mem. Arlington Bd. Selectmen, 1970—73. Lt. USN, 1960—63. Mem.: Boston Bar Assn., Mass. Bar Assn., Phi Beta Kappa. Home: 33 Herring Way Plymouth MA 02360-3225 Office: Simonds Winslow Willis & Abbott 50 Congress St Ste 925 Boston MA 02109-4075 Office Phone: 617-523-5520. E-mail: wabbott1@aol.com.

ABBOTT, WILLIAM THOMAS, private investigator; b. Guthrie, Okla., Jan. 6, 1938; s. Benjamin Franklin and Eva Mae (Lattin) A.; m. Jerri Evelyn Stacy, Apr. 20, 1974. BS, Cen. State U., Okla., 1960; Casualty Claim Law Assoc., Am. Ednl. Inst., 1975. Cert. Fraud Examiner, Assn. Cert. Fraud Examiners, 1996. Claim adjuster Crawford and Co., Lubbock, Tex., 1964-67, Tulsa, 1967-70; sr. claim specialist State Farm Ins. Co., Tulsa, 1970-2000; pvt. investigator Abbott Investigations, Inc., Tulsa, 2000—. Bd. dirs. Okla. Arson Adv. Coun., chmn., 1996—. Mem. Young Reps., 1967, Tulsa Met. Ministries, 1971-75, Tulsa Mental Health Hotline, 1971-73, Okla. Hist. Soc.; pres., bd. dirs. Vis. Nurse Assn. Tulsa, 2003-05. With USMC, 1960-64. Mem. Am. Legion, Internat. Assn. Arson Investigators (bd. dirs. Okla. chpt. 1985-93, pres. 1991), Assn. Cert. Fraud Examiners (Tulsa chpt.), Tulsa Claims Assn. (pres. 1981, Claimsman of Yr. 1979), pres. Mt Carmel Cemetery Assn., Noble Co., Okla., Internat. Assn. Spl. Investigation Units (bd. dirs. Okla. chpt. 1998-2000), Santa Fe Trail Assn., League Am. Bicyclists (life), Adventure Cyclists, Tulsa Bicycle Club, Nat. Off-Road Bicycle Assn. Republican. Methodist. Avocations: bicycling, state and regional history, writing. E-mail: tulsatracker@aol.com.

ABBOUD, ALFRED ROBERT, banker, consultant, investor; b. Boston, May 29, 1929; s. Alfred and Victoria (Karam) A.; m. Joan Grover, June 11, 1955; children: Robert G., Jeanne Frances, Katherine Jane. BS cum laude, Harvard U., 1951, LL.B., 1956, MBA, 1958. Bar: Mass. 1957, Ill. 1959. Asst. cashier First Nat. Bank of Chgo., 1960-62, asst. v.p., 1962-64, v.p., 1964-69, sr. v.p., 1969-72, exec. v.p., 1972-73, vice chmn. bd., 1973-74, dep. chmn. bd., 1974-75, chmn. bd., CEO, 1975-80; pres., COO Occidental Petroleum Corp., L.A., 1980-84; pres. A. Robert Abboud & Co., Fox River Grove, Ill., 1984—; chmn., CEO First City Bancorp. of Tex. Inc., Houston, 1988-91. Author: Money in the Bank: How Safe Is It?, 1988. Capt. USMC, 1951-53. Decorated Purple Heart, Bronze Star; Baker scholar, 1958. Mem. Econ. Comml. Club, The Chgo. Club, Harvard Club Chgo., Harvard Club N.Y.C., Barrington Hills Country Club. Home: 209 Braeburn Rd Barrington IL 60010-9637 Office: PO Box 33 212 Stone Hill Ctr Fox River Grove IL 60021-0033 Office Phone: 847-639-0101.

ABBOUD, FRANCOIS MITRY, physician, educator; b. Cairo, Jan. 5, 1931; arrived in U.S., 1955, naturalized, 1963; s. Mitry Y. and Asma (Habac) Abboud; m. Doris Evelyn Khal, June 5, 1955; children: Mary Agnese, Susan Marie, Nancy Louise, Anthony Lawrence. Student, U. Cairo, 1948—52; MBBCh, Ein Chams U., 1955; D (hon.), U. Lyon, France, 1991; DSc (hon.), Med. Coll. Wis., 1994. Diplomate Am. Bd. Internal Medicine, Am. Bd. Cardiovasc. Disease (bd. govs. 1987-93). Intern Demerdash Govt. Hosp., Cairo, 1955; resident Milw. County Hosp., 1955—58; Am. Heart Assn. rsch. fellow cardiovasc. labs. Marquette U., 1958—60; Am. Heart Assn. advanced rsch. fellow U. Iowa, 1960—62, asst. prof., 1961—65, assoc. prof. medicine, 1965—68, prof. medicine, 1968—, prof. physiology and biophysics, 1975—, Edith King Pearson chair of cardiovascular rsch., 1988—, dir. cardiovasc. divsn., 1970—76, chmn. dept. internal medicine, 1976—2002, dir. cardiovasc. rsch. ctr., 1974—, assoc. v.p. for rsch., 2003—. Attending physician U. Iowa Hosps., 1961—, VA Hosp., Iowa City, 1963—; chmn. rsch. rev. com. Nat. Heart, Lung and Blood Inst., 1978—80, adv. coun., 1995—99. Editor Circulation Rsch., 1981—86, Procs. Assn. Am. Physicians, 1995—2000, assoc. editor Advances in Internal Medicine, 1991—96, Physiology in Medicine, 2002—, editl. bd. Medicine, 1992—. Recipient European Traveling fellowship, French govt., 1948, NIH Career Devel. award, 1962—71. Master: ACP (award for outstanding work in sci. related to medicine 2000); mem.: AMA, Am. Coll. Cardiology (Disting. Scientist award 2004), Assn. Patient Oriented Rsch. (founding mem.), Am. Acad. Arts and Scis., Internat. Soc. Hypertension (Merck Sharp & Dohme Internat. award for rsch. in hypertension 1994), Am. Soc. Pharmacology and Exptl. Therapeutics (award exptl. therapeutics 1972), Am. Clin. and Climatol. Assn. (councillor 1992), Am. Physiol. Soc. (chmn. circulation group 1979—80, chmn. clin. physiology sect. 1979—83, publ. com. 1987—90, Wiggers award 1988, Carl Ludwig lecture award 2000), Assn. Am. Physicians (treas. 1979—84, councillor 1984—89, pres.-elect 1989—90, pres. 1990—91), Assn. Profs. Medicine (bd. dirs. 1993—97, Robert H. Williams Disting. Chmn. of Medicine award 1993), Assn. Univ. Cardiologists, Am. Fedn. Clin. Rsch. (pres. 1971—72), Am. Heart Assn. (bd. dirs. 1977—80, pres.-elect 1989—90, pres. 1990—91, past chmn. rsch. coms., award of merit 1982, Disting. Achievement award 1988, CIBA award for hypertension rsch. 1990, Gold Heart award 1995, Rsch. Achievement award 1999), Soc. Exptl. Biology and Medicine, Ctrl. Soc. for Clin. Rsch. (pres. elect 1984—85, pres. 1985—86), Am. Soc. Clin. Investigation, Inst. Medicine NAS, Alpha Omega Alpha (bd. dirs. 1989—), Sigma Xi. Achievements include research and publications in cardiovascular physiology on neurohumoral control of circulation and molecular mechanisms and gene regulation of baroreceptor activation. Home: 24 Kennedy Pky Iowa City IA 52246-2780 Office: Carver Coll Medicine Univ Iowa 318 CMAB VPR Iowa City IA 52242-1101

ABBOUD, JOSEPH M., fashion designer; b. Boston, May 5, 1950; s. Joseph and Lila (Sallah) A.; m. Lynn Weinstein, June 6, 1976. BA cum laude, U. Mass, 1972. Buyer, merchandiser Louis of Boston, 1972-80; salesman, designer Polo-Ralph Lauren, N.Y.C., 1980-84; designer, cons. Chanel, Paris, 1984-86; designer, prin. Joseph Abboud Co., N.Y.C., 1986—. Recipient men's knitwear design award Woolknit Assocs., 1986, Cutty Sark award as most promising menswear designer, 1987, Woolmark award as best designer of menswear, 1988, Spl. Achievement award Neckwear Assn. Am., Inc., 1994; named Menswear Designer of Yr., Coun. Fashion Designers Am., 1989, 90. Avocations: tennis, squash, running, fiction. Office: 650 5th Ave Fl 27 New York NY 10019-6108

ABBRUZZESE, JOHN ANTHONY, JR., psychologist, retired administrator, educator; b. Pitts., Dec. 19, 1928; s. John A. and Frances (Curcio) A.; m. Jean Dezzutti, Sept. 27, 1952; children: John A. III, Mark R., Eugenia F. BS, U. Pitts., 1949, MEd, 1954; PhD, Western U., San Diego, 1957. Cert. tchr., sch. adminstr., psychologist, Pa. Chemistry and physics tchr., various locations, Pa., 1950-51, 53-55; tchr. spl. edn., psychyol. examiner Allegheny County schs., 1955-56; psychologist Monroe County schs., Pa., 1956-66, asst. supt., 1966-69, supt., 1969-71; pvt. practice psychology, 1962—; mem. staff Pocono Med. Ctr., Pa., 1968—. Asst. exec. dir. Colonial Northampton Intermediate Unit, Pa., 1971-73, dir. spl. edn., 1973-82, exec. dir., 1982-93, exec. dir. emeritus, 1993—. Contbr. articles to profl. jours. Bd. dirs. Easter Seal Soc., Monroe County, Pa., 1957-85. Sgt. U.S. Army, 1951-53. Recipient numerous awards for profl. and civic contbns., including Brace for an Ace award Easter Seals Soc., 1970, Silver Beaver award Boy Scouts Am. Minsi Trails Coun., 1992. Mem. APA, Am. Coll. of Forensic Examiners, Am. Assn. Sch. Adminstrs., Am. Vocat. Assn., Nat. Assn. Sch. Psychologists, Nat. Rehab. Assn., Coun. Exceptional Children, Coun. Adminstrs. and Suprs. Spl. Edn., Pa. Assn. Chief Sch. Adminstrs., Lehigh Valley Psychol. Assn., Pa. Psychol. Assn., Mideast Pa. Sch. Psychologists Assn., Pa. Vocat. Assn., Pa. Assn. Sch. Adminstrs., Eastern Pa. Assn. Ret. Sch. Supts (pres. 1997-98), Rotary, Pa. Schoolmen, Phi Delta Kappa Democrat. Roman Catholic. Home: 1033 Locust Ln Stroudsburg PA 18360-9708 Office: 1320 N 5th St Stroudsburg PA 18360-2648 Business E-Mail: jaajr@ptd.net.

ABCARIAN, HERAND, surgeon, educator; b. Ahvaz, Iran, Jan. 23, 1941; arrived in U.S., 1966; s. Joseph and Stella (Banki) A.; m. Karen Jane Berger, May 10, 1969; children: Gregory, Ariane, Margot. MD, Teheran U., 1965. Intern Cook County Hosp., Chgo., 1966—67, resident in gen. surgery, 1967—71, resident in colon and rectal surgery, 1971—72, chmn. colon and rectal surgery, 1972—93; head dept. surgery, Turi Josefson prof. U. Ill. Coll. Med., Chgo., 1989—; exec. dir. Am. Bd. Colon & Rectal Surgery, Taylor, Mich. Assoc. editor: Diseases of Colon and Rectum, 1981—95. Fellow ACS (various coms. and offices), Am. Soc. Colon and Rectal Surgeons (sec. 1985-87, pres. 1988-89), Can. Soc. Colon and Rectal Surgeons (hon.); mem. Am. Surg. Assn., Soc. Am. Gastroendoscopic Surgeons (founder), Sydney Soc. Colon and Rectal Surgeons (hon.), Assn. Coloprotology of Gt. Britain (hon. fellow). Republican. Roman Catholic. Avocations: visual arts, music, philately. Office: U Ill 840 S Wood St # 518 Chicago IL 60612-7317 Also: Am Bd Colon & Rectal Surgery 20600 Eureka Rd Ste 713 Taylor MI 48180-5376 Office Phone: 312-996-2061. Business E-Mail: abcarian@uic.edu.

ABDEL DAYEM, HUSSEIN MAHMOUD, nuclear medicine physician, radiology educator; b. Cairo, Apr. 5, 1934; s. Mahamaud and Shafika (El Sayed) A.D.; m. Sept. 19, 1968; children: Amani, Essmaeel. MB, BChir, Cairo U., 1959, MD in Radiology, 1967. Diplomate Am. Bd. Nuclear Medicine, Am. Bd. Radio Therapy. Instr. radiology Faculty of Medicine Cairo U., Egypt, 1967-70; resident, fellow Roswell Park Cancer Inst., Buffalo, 1970-72; dir. nuc. medicine Erie County Med. Ctr., Buffalo, 1972-81; assoc. prof. radiology SUNY, Buffalo, 1972-81; prof., chmn. dept. nuc. medicine Kuwait U., 1981-90; adj. mem. Meml. Sloan Kettering Cancer Ctr., N.Y.C., 1990-92; dir. nuc. medicine St. Vincent's Hosp., N.Y.C., 1992—; prof. radiology N.Y. Med. Coll., N.Y.C., 1992—. Sr. registrar Cancer Ctr. Kuwait, 1969-70; vis. prof. Med. Coll. Wis., 1990. Contbr. numerous articles to profl. jours. and chpts. to 7 text books on nuc. medicine; mem. editl. bd. Jour. Nuc. Medicine, European Jour. Nuc. Medicine. Mem. Soc. Nuc. Medicine (pres. Asia and Oceana fedn. 1988-92, vice chmn. sci. program 1994, 1st prize nuc. medicine rsch. 1984, 3rd prize, 1986), Am. Coll. Nuc. Physicians, Am. Coll. Nuc. Medicine, Radiol. Soc. N.Am. Moslem. Home: 71 Hoover Dr Cresskill NJ 07626-1705 Office: St Vincent's Hosp 153 W 11th St New York NY 10011-8305

ABDELGHANI, ASSAF A., medical educator; b. Arrabeh, Jordan, Dec. 30, 1937; s.1971; s. Assaf and Rukayya Arabi; m. Laila Abdelghani, Jan. 1, 1981; children: Ramsy, Samy. BS, Am. U., Beirut, Lebanon, 1967; MS, Tulane U., 1972, DS, 1978. Prof. Tulane U., New Orleans, 1975—, lab. dir., 1993—, chmn. dept. environ. health, 1999—. Office: Tulane U 1430 Tulane New Orleans LA 70112

ABDEL-GHANY, MOHAMED, family economics educator; b. Cairo, Mar. 24, 1940; came to U.S., 1965; s. Ibrahim Abdel-Ghany and Aischa Hassanen; children from a previous marraige: Tamara, Sonya, Mary Katherine. BS, Cairo U., 1962; diploma, Inst. Nat. Planning, Cairo, 1963; MS, Iowa State U., 1972; PhD, U. Mo., 1974. Asst prof. consumer sci. U. N.C., Greensboro, 1974-78; assoc. prof., head dept. consumer sci. U. Ala., Tuscaloosa, 1978-82, prof., chmn. consumer sci. dept., 1982-90, prof. consumer sci., dir. internat. affairs, Coll. Human Environ. Scis., 1990—. Vis. prof. Chiba U., Japan, 1990; mem. econ. rsch. group USDA, 1991, U. Qatar, Doha, 1991, U. B.C., Can., 1992, 93, 95, 97, 98, 2001, U. Pertanian, Malaysia, 1993; cons. Agy. Internat. Devel., Cairo, 1980, U. Ga., 1996. Contbr. articles to profl. jours. Mem. Am. Assn. Family and Consumer Scis. (chair rsch. sect. 1984-86, assoc. editor 1996—, Family Econs. Rsch. award 1998), Assn. Consumer Rsch. (policy bd. Jour. Consumer Rsch. 1983-85), Am. Coun. Consumer Interest (bd. dirs. 1977-79, treas. 1997-2000, v.p. 2000, pres. 2001-02, Disting. Fellow award 1999), Internat. Soc. Quality of Life Studies (v.p. 1999, Fellow award 2000), Asian Consumer and Family Econs. Assn. (pres. 1999-2001). Avocations: chess, Karate, ballroom dancing. Office: U Ala Dept Consumer Scis Box 870158 Tuscaloosa AL 35487-0154 E-mail: mabdel-g@ches.ua.edu.

ABDEL-KADER, REHAB FAROUK, education educator, researcher; b. Al-Mansourh, Egypt, July 26, 1974; U.S., 1997; d. Farouk Mahmood Abdel-Kader and Ehsan Mohammed El-Demerdash; m. Medhal Awad El-Hadek, Aug. 26, 1996; 1 child, Roem; 1 child, Ranah. BS in computer engrng., Suez Canal U., 1986; MSc, Tukagee U., 1998; PhD, Auburn U., 2003. Grad. tchg. asst. Tuskegee U., Ala., 1997—2000, instr., 2000—01; grad. rsch. asst. Auburn U., 2001—03; asst. prof. Ga. So. U., 2003—. Mem.: IEEE, Soc. of Women Engineers. Avocations: reading, travel. Home: 1309 Sunset Circle Statesboro GA 30458 Office: Ga Southern U Sch Tech Statesboro GA 30460

ABDEL-KHALIK, SAID IBRAHIM, nuclear and mechanical engineering educator; b. Alexandria, Egypt, Aug. 9, 1948; came to U.S., 1969; s. Ibrahim Saad and Esha Farag (Ahmad) A.-K.; m. Sharon Lora Duncan; 1 child, Faith Austen Khalik. BS summa cum laude, Alexandria U., 1967; MS in Mech. Engrng., U. Wis.-Madison, 1971, PhD in Mech. Engring., 1973. Postdoctoral fellow in chem. engrng. U. Wis., Madison, 1973-74, asst. prof. nuclear engrng., 1976-78, assoc. prof., 1978-82, prof., 1982-87; Ga. Power disting. prof. nuclear engrng. Ga. Inst. Tech., Atlanta, 1987-89, assoc. dir. sch. mech. engrng., 1990-92, so. nuclear disting. prof., 1993—; instr. Alexandria U., 1967-69; sr. engr. Babcock & Wilcox, Lynchburg, Va., 1975. Guest rsch. scientist Nuclear Rsch. Ctr., Karlsruhe, Fed. Republic Germany, 1979; vis. prof. EPFL, Inst. de Genie Atomique, Lausanne, Switzerland, 1982; cons. Kewaunee Nuclear Plant, Green Bay, Wis., 1983—93, So. Nuclear Vogtle, Hatch, and Farley Nuclear Plants, 1999-, numerous rsch. orgns. and govtl. agys. Contbr. articles to profl. jours. Fellow Am. Nuclear Soc., ASME; chair Fusion Energy Divsn. Am. Nuclear Soc. 2005; mem. Am. Soc. Engrng. Edn. (Glenn Murphy award 1999), Profl. Reactor Operators Soc., Am. Inst. Physics, Assn. Egyptian-Am. Scholars, Sigma Xi, Phi Kappa Phi. Achievements include patents in field. Avocations: sailing, chess. Home: 3579 Midvale Cove Tucker GA 30084-3210 Office: Sch Mech Engring Ga Inst Tech Atlanta GA 30332-0405 Office Phone: 404-894-3719. E-mail: said.abdelkhalik@me.gatech.edu.

ABDELLAH, FAYE GLENN, retired public health service executive; d. H. B. and Margaret (Glenn) Abdellah. BS in Tchg., Columbia U., 1945, MA in Tchg., 1947, EdD, 1955; LLD (hon.), Case Western Res. U., 1967, Rutgers U., 1973; DSc (hon.), U. Akron, 1978, Cath. U. Am., 1981, Monmouth Coll., 1982, Ea. Mich U., 1987, U. Bridgeport, 1987, Georgetown U., 1989; D in Pub. Svc. (hon.), Am. U., 1987; LHD, D in Pub. Svc., U. S.C., 1991; D in Mil. Nursing (hon.), USUHS, 2002. RN N.Y., D.C. Commd. officer USPHS, Rockville, Md., 1949, advanced through grades to rear adm., 1970, dep. surgeon gen., chief nurse officer, 1970—87, dep. surgeon gen., 1981—89, chief nursing edn. br., divsn. nursing, 1949—59, surgeon gen., 1989; chief rsch. grants br. Bur. Health Manpower Edn., NIH, HEW, Rockville, 1959—69; dir. Office Rsch. Tng. Nat. Ctr. for Health Svcs. R & D, Health Svcs. Mental Health Adminstrn., Rockville, 1969; acting dep. dir. Nat. Ctr. for Health Svcs. R & D, Rockville, 1971, Bur. Health Svcs. Rsch. and Evaluation, Health Resources Adminstrn., Rockville, 1973; dir. Office Long-Term Care, Office Asst. Sec. for Health, HEW, Rockville, 1973—80; exec. dir. Grad. Sch. Nursing Uniformed Svcs. U. Health Scis., Bethesda, Md., 1993—, founding dean, prof. emeritus, 2001—. Prof. nursing, Emily Smith chair U. S.C., Columbia, 1990—91; dean, prof. Grad. Sch. Nursing, Uniformed Svcs. U. Health Scis., 1993—2002, founding dean, prof. emerita, 1993—2002. Author: Effect of Nurse Staffing on Satisfactions with Nursing Care, 1959, Patient Centered Approaches to Nursing, 1960, Better Patient Care Through Nursing Research, 1965, 2d edit., 1979, 3d edit., 1986, Intensive Care, Concepts and Practices for Clinical Nurse Specialists, 1969, New Directions in Patient Centered Nursing, 1972, Preparing Nursing Research for the 21st Century, 1994; contbr. articles to profl. jours. Named to TC Nursing Hall of Fame, Columbia U., 1999, Nat. Women's Hall of Fame, 2000; recipient Mary Adelaide Nutting award, 1983, Oustanding Leadership award, U. Pa., 1987, 1999, Disting. Svc. award, 1973—89, Surgeon Gen.'s medal and medallion, 1989, Achievement award in aging, Allied-Signal, 1989, Gustav O. Lienhard award, Inst. Medicine NAS, 1992, Breaking Ground in Women's Health award, 2001, G.W. "Sonny" Montgomery award, Dept. Vets. Affairs, 2002. Fellow: Am. Acad. Nursing (charter, past v.p., pres.); mem.: AAAS, ANA (hon.), APA, Assn. Mil. Surgeons U.S., Douglas Soc., Phi Lambda Theta, Sigma Theta Tau (Disting. Rsch. Fellow award 1989). Home: 3713 Chanel Rd Annandale VA 22003-2024

ABDEL-RAHMAN, EIHAB M., mechanical engineer, researcher; b. Mansoura, Egypt, July 23, 1966; s. Muhamad Abdel-Rahman. PhD, U. Toledo, 1997. Faculty rsch. assoc. Va. Tech, Blacksburg, Va., 1997—. Mem.: ASME. Office: Virginia Tech Dept of Engineering Science & Mechanics Blacksburg VA 24061 Office Phone: 540-231-3246. Office Fax: 540-231-2290.

ABDELRAHMAN, TALAAT AHMAD MOHAMMAD, financial executive; b. Kafr Saqr, Sharkia, Egypt, Sept. 13, 1940; came to U.S., 1970; s. Ahmad Mohammad and Zeen Elmahdi (Hassan) A.; m. Soher T. Ali (Dec. Feb. 1979); children: Manar, Neven, Nancy, Amon; m. Ekram T. Kandil (div. May 1994); m. Moushira El Shafei, Jan. 1996 (div. Jan. 2005). BS in Mgmt., Cairo U., 1965, BA in Law, 1969, PhD in Fin., 1987; MBA in Acctg., NYU, 1974. Fin. analyst Nat. Bank Egypt, Cairo, 1965—70; Euro-dollar specialist Bankers Trust Co., N.Y.C., 1970—74; sr. cost acct. Phelps Dodge Cable & Wire, Yonkers, NY, 1974—75; fin. cons. East Orange, NJ, 1975—76; asst. treas. ITT Fed. Electric, Paramus, NJ, 1976—82, mgr. fin. Jed, Saudi Arabia, 1982—86, mgr. corp. fin. Paramus, 1987—91; owner 7-Eleven, Woodridge, NJ, 1991—97; gen. dir., chmn., pres., co-owner Franconia Pediat. & Family Med. Ctrs., Alexandria, Va., 1997—2003; real estate investor, 2003—. Bd. dirs. ITT Howard/Egypt, Cairo, Talkan USA, Inc., Morganville, N.J.; owner 7-Eleven Franchise, Wood Ridge, N.J., 1991-96, Hackensack, N.J., 1992-96, Family Food Store Inc., T/A Broadway Stop & Shop, Fair Lawn, N.J., 1993-95. Contbr. articles to profl. jours. Pres. Bergen County Islamic Ctr., 1995-96. Avocations: windsurfing, swimming. Mailing: 1108 Samy Dr Tampa FL 33613 Office Phone: 813-961-0846.

ABDELRAZIG, YASSIR A., engineering educator; b. Khartoum, Khartoum, Sudan, 1968; arrived in U.S., 1994; PhD, Purdue U., 1999. Rsch. assoc. Purdue U., West Lafayette, Ind., 1999; asst. prof. Fla. State U., Tallahassee, 1999—. Mem.: ASCE. Achievements include research in FSU Cornerstone Research Award - $100, 000. Office: Fla A & M U Fla State U Coll Civil Engring 2525 Pottsdamer St Tallahassee FL 32310

ABDELSAMAD, MOUSTAFA HASSAN, dean; b. Mar. 12, 1941; B in Commerce with honors, Cairo U., 1961; MBA, George Washington U., 1965, DBA, 1970. Assoc. dean Va. Commonwealth U., Richmond, Va., 1977-88; dean, finance prof. U. Mass., N. Dartmouth, Mass., 1988-91; prof. fin. Tex. A&M U., Corpus Christi, Tex., 1991—, dean Coll. Bus., 1991—. Cons. in field Editor-in-chief SAM Advanced Mgmt. jour., 1985—. Mem. Fin. Mgmt. Assoc., Soc. Advancement Mgmt. (mgmt. excellence award, 1991, 1998, pres. excellence award, 1996, Phil Carroll Advancement Mgmt. finance award, 1989, internat. pres. 1983-86, 96—), Tex. Coun. Coll. Bus. Edn., So. Bus. Adminstrn. Assoc. Office: Dean Coll Business Tex A&M U Corpus Christi Corpus Christi TX 78412 E-mail: moustafa@cob.tamucc.edu.

ABDELSAYED, WAFEEK HAKIM, accounting educator; b. Fayoum, Egypt, Aug. 16, 1958; came to U.S., 1970; s. Fr. Gabriel H. and Tahani (Mikhael) A. BBA, Hofstra U., 1979; MBA, Adelphi U., 1983, MS, 1984; PhD, U. Conn., 1996. CPA Fla., N.Y.; cert. fraud examiner Assn. of Cert Fraud Examiners; cert. fin. mgr; cert. control assesment, Inst. Internal Auditors, 2002, cert. gov. auditing profl., 2003. Staff acct. KPMG Peat Marwick, L.I., N.Y., 1981-82, Deloitte & Touche, L.I., 1983-84; prof. acctg. dept. So. Conn. State U., New Haven, 1984—. Contbr. rsch. papers to profl. publs. (Competitive Paper award 1991, Becker's Outstanding Rsch. award 1991). Mem. bd. deacons Virgin Mary Coptic Orthodox Ch., treas. Scholar N.Y. State Soc. CPA's, 1983. Mem. AICPA, N.E. Bus. and Econs. Assn. (bd. dirs.), Am. Acctg. Assn., Inst. Mgmt. Accts. (cert. mgmt. acct., cert. fin. mgmt.), Inst. Internal Auditors (cert. internal auditor), Cert. Govt. Financial Mgr., Assn. of Govt. Accts, Conn. Soc. CPAs, Beta Gamma Sigma, Beta Alpha Psi. Egyptian/Christian Orthodox. Avocations: coin and stamp collecting, photography. Home: PO Box 170 North Haven CT 06473-0170 Office: So Conn State U Sch Bus 501 Crescent St New Haven CT 06515-1330 Office Phone: 203-392-5690. E-mail: abdelsayedw1@southernct.edu.

ABDENUR, ROBERTO MAMERI PINTO, ambassador; b. Rio de Janeiro, May 5, 1942; married; 3 children. B in Econ., London Sch. of Econ.; law student, Pontifical Cath. U. of Rio de Janeiro. Div. of comm. and archives Brazilian Min. of External Rels., 1964—65, trade policy div., 1966—67, acting head, Tech. Section of Analysis and Planning to under sec. for Policy Planning, 1968, cabinet staff mem., 1969, asst. to sec.-gen, 1975—78, dep. min., 1993—95; Brazilian dep. consulate gen. to consulate gen. London, 1969—73; first sec. Washington, 1973—75; amb. to Equador, Quito, 1985—88, to China, Beijing, 1989—93, to Germany, Berlin, 1995—2002, to Austria, Vienna, 2002—04, to US, Washington, 2004—. Fluent in Portuguese, Spanish, English, French, German. Office: Embassy of Brazil 3006 Mass Ave NW Washington DC 20008

ABDESSALAM, SHAHAB, pediatrician, surgeon, oncologist; b. Phila., Feb. 11, 1968; s. Adel Abdessalam and Sylvia Saylor; m. Cindy Frazier, May 21, 1997; children: Malik, Safiyah, Nayera. BS, Ohio State U., 1991, MD, 1995. Cert. Am. Bd. Surgery (cert. in gen. surgery and surg. critical care). Gen. surgery resident U. Nebr. Med. Ctr., Omaha, 1995—2000; sugical oncology fellow Ohio State U. Hosps., Columbus, 2000—03, Columbus Children's Hosp., 2003—04, pediatric surg. fellow, 2004—. Mem.: AMA, Zollinger Surg. Soc., Soc. Critical Care Medicine, Soc. Surg. Oncology, Am. Assn. Cancer Rsch., Phi Beta Kappa. Avocations: skiing, golf, tennis, running, biking. Office: Columbus Children's Hosp ED 379 700 Children's Dr Columbus OH 43205 Office Phone: 614-722-3923. Personal E-mail: sabdessalam@hotmail.com.

ABDO, VIRGINIA RICHIE, secondary school educator; b. Dallas, Mar. 11, 1929; d. James Logan and Sara Virginia (Ogletree) Richie; m. Milton Kalil Abdo, June 2, 1956; children: Anthony Logan, David Kalil, Ernest Alan. BA, So. Meth. U., 1954, MA, 1979. Cert. tchr. Tchr. El Centro Jr. Coll., Dallas, 1968-70, Berkner High Sch., Richardson, Tex., 1970—98; ret., 1998. Musician Mesquite Symphony Orch., New Philharm. Symphony, Irving. Contbr. reviews to music mags. Bd. dirs. Dallas Opera, Dallas Chamber Music Soc., Greater Dallas Youth Orchestras; active Dallas Symphony, So. Meth. U. Conservatory, Met. Opera, Santa Fe Opera, Seattle Opera, Lyric Opera of Chgo., San Francisco Opera, Gesellschaft Der Freunde von Bayreuth,

Germany, Houston Grand Opera, Wagner Soc. N.Y., Wagner Soc. Am., Dallas Mus. of Art, Kimbell Art Mus., Art Inst. Chgo., Met. Mus. Art., MEadows Mus. Art, Women's Mus. Art, Washington, Friends of So. Meth. U. Librs., Friends of Sta. WRR. Mem. Am. Assn. Tchrs. of German, Tex. Fgn. Lang. Assn., Dallas Goethe Ctr., Alliance Francaise, So. Meth. U. Alumni Assn., Highland Park High Sch. Alumni Assn., Wagner Soc. of Dallas (founder, pres. 1990, bd. dirs.), Phi Beta Kappa (sec., treas. North Tex. chpt. 1988-90), Mu Phi Epsilon, Alpha Lambda Delta, Delta Phi Alpha. Avocations: music, playing viola and violin in amateur groups and chamber music groups. Home: 3234 Amherst Ave Dallas TX 75225-7620

ABDOO, ELIZABETH A., lawyer; b. Apr. 1958; BA, JD, Georgetown U. Bar: 1987. Sr. v.p., asst. gen. counsel Orbital Sciences Corp., 1996—2001; sr. v.p., gen. counsel Host Marriott Corp., Bethesda, Md., 2001—03, corp. sec., 2001—, exec. v.p., gen. counsel, 2003—. Office: Host Marriott Corp 6903 Rockledge Dr Ste 1500 Bethesda MD 20817

ABDRISAEV, BAKTYBEK, ambassador; b. Kyrgyz Republic, Apr. 17, 1958; married; 2 children. Degree in automatics and telemechs., Bishkek Poly. Inst., 1980, postgrad., 1987; PhD in Physics, Belorussian Acad. Sci. Jr. sci. fellow Bishkek Poly. Inst. (now Kyrgyz Tech. U.), 1980—84, sr. sci. fellow, 1988—91; sci. fellow Inst. Physics, Acad. Scis., Kyrgyzstan, 1991—92; expert Internat. Rels. Dept. Office of Pres., Kyrgyzstan, 1993, head, 1996; mem. parliament Kyrgyz Republic, 1995, ambassador to U. S. and Can., 1996—. Office: Embassy of Kyrgyz Republic to US and Can 1732 Wisconsin Ave NW Washington DC 20007

ABDUL, PAULA (PAULA JULIE ABDUL), singer, dancer, choreographer; b. San Fernando, Cailf., June 19, 1963; d. Harry and Lorraine A.; m. Emilio Estevez, Apr. 29, 1992 (div. 1994); m. Brad Beckerman, Oct. 14, 1996 (div. 1998). Student, Calif. State Univ., Northridge; studied tap, jazz with Joe Tramine, the Bella Lewitzky Co. Laker Girls head cheerleader, head choreographer L.A. Lakers basketball team; choreography for Jacksons singing group, Janet Jackson, ZZ Top, Arnold Schwarzenegger, Tom Hanks, The Tracey Ullman Show, others. Albums: Forever Your Girl, 1988, Shut Up and Dance, 1990, Spellbound, 1991, Head Over Heels, 1995; Actress (TV films) Junior High School, 1978, Touched By Evil, 1997, Amy Fuentes, The Waiting Game, 1998, Denise Walton, Mr. Rock 'n' Roll: The Alan Freed Story, 1999; (voice) Robots, 2005; choreographer (films) Private School, 1983, A Smoky Mountain Christmas, 1986, Dragnet, 1987, Can't Buy Me Love, 1987, The Running Man, 1987, Coming to America, 1988, Bull Durham, 1988, Action Jackson, 1988, Dance to Win, 1989, The Karate Kid Part III, 1989, She's Out of Control, 1989, The Doors, 1991, Jerry Maguire, 1996, American Beauty, 1999, Black Knight, 2001, The Master of Disguise, 2002, (TV series) The Tracy Ullman Show, 1987, (TV) The 17th Annual Am. Music Awards, 1990, 62nd Annual Academy Awards, 1990, (video) ZZ Top: Greatest Hits (Velcro Fly), 1992; singer, Side Out, 1990; exec. prodr. (video) Paula Abdul: Cardio Dance, 1998; judge American Idol, 2002-; guest appearahcess include: Top of the Pops, 1989, 1990, 1995, Spin City, 1998, The Wayans Bros., 1999, Sabrina, the Teenage Witch, 1999, Mad TV, 2002, The Bernie Mac Show, 2004, Fashion In Focus, 2005, Less Than Perfect, 2005, The Contender, 2005, "So You Think You Can Dance", 2005 and several others. Recipient Soul Train award for best video, 1989, best choreography, 1989, Am. Video Arts award choreographer of yr. 1990, Nat. Acad. Video Arts and Scis., 1987, Emmy awards: best choreography for the Tracy Ullman Show, 1988-89, Outstanding Achievement in Choreography for Am. Music Awards, 1990; MTV awards: best choreography, Janet Jackson's Nasty video, 1986, best female video, best dance video, best choreography in a video, best editing in a video for hit Straight Up, 1989, Am. Music awards: for choreography on ZZ Top's Velcro Fly video, 1987, Favorite Pop-Rock Female, 1990, 1992, Favorite Dance artist, 1990; People's Choice awards: Favorite Female Musical Performer, 1990, 1991; named to Nickelodeon's Kids Choice Hall of Fame; represented by star on Hollywood Blvd. Mailing: American Idol Fox Broadcasting PO Box 900 Beverly Hills CA 90213-0900*

ABDUL-JABBAR, KAREEM (LEW ALCINDOR, LEWIS FERDINAND ALCINDOR), professional basketball coach; b. N.Y.C., Apr. 16, 1947; s. Ferdinand Lewis and Cora Alcindor; m. Habiba (Janice Brown), 1971 (div. 1973); children: Habiba, Kareem, Sutana, Amir. BA, UCLA, 1969. Basketball player with Milw. Bucks, 1969—75, L.A. Lakers, 1975—89; owner Kareem Productions; asst. coach L.A. Clippers, 2000—01; cons. Ind. Pacers, 2001—02; head coach, Okla. Storm U.S. Basketball League, 2002; cons., scout NY Knicks, 2004—. Commentator ESPN, Bristol, Conn. Actor: (films) Game of Death, 1978, The Fish that Saved Pittsburgh, 1979, Airplane, 1980, Fletch, 1985; (TV series) Mannix, 1971, Emergency!, 1974, The Man from Atlantis, 1977, Dinah!, 1977, The Way It Was, 1977, Diff'rent Strokes, 1982, Pryor's Place, 1984, Tales from the Darkside, 1985, Stingray, 1987, 21 Jump Street, 1990, Good Sports, 1991, Uncle Buck, 1991, Amen, 1991, Matrix, 1993, The Critic, 1994, The Fresh Prince of Bel-Air, 1994, Full House, 1995, Martin, 1996, Everybody Loves Raymond, 1996, Living Single, 1997, Boston Common, 1997; (TV miniseries) The Stand, 1994; author (with Peter Knobler): Giant Steps: An Autobiography of Kareem Abdul-Jabbar, 1983; author: (with Mignon McCarthy) Kareem, 1990; author: (with Stephen Singular) A Season on the Reservation: My Soujourn with the White Mountain Apaches, 2000; author: (with Alan Steinburg) Black Profiles in Courage: A Legacy of African-American Achievement, 2000; author: (with Anthony Walton) Brothers in Arms, 2004. Named Rookie of the Yr., NBA, 1970, Most Valuable Player, 1971, 1972, 1974, 1976, 1977, 1980, NBA Playoff Most Valuable Player, 1971, 1985, NCAA Tournament Most Outstanding Player, 1967, 1968, 1969; named to All-Star Game, NBA, 1970—87, 35th Anniversary All-Time Team, 1980, Basketball Hall of Fame, 1995; recipient Maurice Podoloff Cup. Moslem. Achievements include becoming NBA all-time leading scorer, 1984; being a mem. of NBA Championship Team, 1971, 80, 82, 85, 87, 88; being mem. of NCAA Championship Team, 1967, 68, 69. Avocation: jazz.*

ABDUL-JABBAR, KARIM, retired professional football player; b. L.A., June 28, 1974; m. Sabria; 1 child, Ibarhim Abdullah. BS in Econs., UCLA, 1997. Running back Miami Dolphins, 1996-98, Cleve. Browns, 1998-99, Indianapolis Colts, 2000—. Holder club rookie rushing record; voted to all-rookie teams Football News Pro Football Writers Am. and Coll. and Pro Football Newsweekly; named AFC Offensive Player of the Week. Office: Indianapolis Colts RCA Dome PO Box 535000 Indianapolis IN 46253-5000

ABDULLAEV, YALCHIN, neuroscientist, educator; b. Baku, Azerbaijan, Aug. 19, 1960; s. Gulhuseyn and Almas Abdullaev; m. Naida Velieva, Nov. 24, 1987 (div. June 20, 2003); 1 child, Mikail. MS, Azerbaijan State U., Baku, 1982; PhD, Inst. Exptl. Medicine, St. Petersburg, Russia, 1987; MD, St. Petersburg Med. Acad., 1994. Rsch. asst. Inst. Physiology, Azerbaijan Acad. Scis., Baku, 1982-84; grad. stud. Inst. Exptl. Medicine, St. Petersburg, 1984-87, jr. rsch. scientist, 1987-89, sr. rsch. scientist, 1989-90, Brain Ctr., St. Petersburg, 1990-94; asst. prof. U. Oreg., Eugene, 1994-96, U. Louisville, 1996—2005; rsch. scientist U. Oreg., 2005—. Mem. grad. faculty U. Louisville, 1996—; rsch. dir. Cognitive Neurosci. Lab., 1996—. Mem. editl. bd.: Internat. Jour. Psychophysiology, 1992—96; mem. editl. bd. The Sci. World, 2002—, Med. Sci. Monitor, 2003—; contbr. more than 60 rsch. articles to profl. jours. Mem.: Internat. Orgn. Psychophysiology, Internat. Orgn. Human Brain Mapping, Soc. Neurosci., Am. Psychol. Soc. Avocations: swimming, running, Judo, reading. E-mail: yabdullaev@yahoo.com.

ABDULLAH, BASHAR Y., pharmacist, researcher; s. Yousif A. and Rasmia S. Almanaseer; m. Muna M. Habib, July 9, 1986; children: Yasamin B., Yasser B., Taha B., Weseem B. BS in Pharmacy, U. Baghdad, 1986. Lic. pharmacist Iraqi Bd. Pharmacist, 1986. Pharmacist, formulation devel. Abbott labs, North Chicago, Ill., 1996—2001; research assoc. III Baxter Healthcare, Round Lake, 2001—. Mem.: Am. Assn. Pharm. Scientists, The Sci. Adv. Bd. (assoc.; online cmty. 2001). Achievements include patents for United States patent no. 6, 008, 192 (Hydrophilic Binary Systems for the Adminstration of Lipophilic Compounds); Patent no. 98910361.9-2112 from the European Patent office, (Hydrophilic Binary Systems for the Adminstration of Cyclosporine); Hydrophilic Binary Systems for the Administration of Lipophilic Compounds; Hydrophilic Binary Systems for the Adminstration of Cyclosporine; development of Norvir Capsules; Gengraf capsules; research in 1998 Chairman Award from Abbott labs pharmaceutical and Analytical Research and Development; first to Awarded year 2000 Abbott Achievment Award; development of Generic Veterinary products of 1% Iodine solution and Neomycin Suspention. Home: 2272 N Sarazen Dr Vernon Hills IL 60061 Office: Baxter Healthcare WG3-3S Route 120 and Wilson Rd Round Lake IL 60073

ABDUR-RAHIM, SHAREEF (JULIUS SHAREEF ABDUL-RAHIM), professional basketball player; b. Marietta, Ga., Dec. 11, 1976; s. William and Aminah Abdur-Rahim; m. Delicia (DeeDee) Abdur-Rahim; 1 child, Jabri. Forward, guard Vancouver Grizzlies NBA, 1996—2001, Altanta Hawks NBA, 2001—03, Portland Trail Blazers, 2003—05; forward Sacramento Kings NBA, 2005—. Guest Jamie Foxx Show. Founder The Future Found., Rebound America (to raise funds for 9/11 victims), 2001. Named one of Good Guys in Sports, The Sporting News; named to NBA All-Rookie First Team, 1996—97, Third Team All-Am., AP. Achievements include third overall draft pick, NBA Draft, 1996. Avocations: pool, collecting basketball jerseys, movies. Mailing: c/o Sacramento Kings Arco Arena One Sports Plz Sacramento CA 95834*

ABE, GREGG KOYEI, music educator; b. Honolulu, June 22, 1958; s. Charles Sadaichi and Diane Aiko Abe; m. Julie Yukiko Fujii, Apr. 30, 1988; children: Kayla, Gregg. BE, U. Hawaii, 1983. Cert. tchr. Hawaii. Asst. dir. bands Castle HS, Kaneohe, Hawaii, 1984—85; dir. bands Roosevelt HS, Honolulu, 1985—. Named Music Educator of the Yr., Hawaii Music Awards, 1996, Outstanding Educator, Oceanic TV, 2001. Mem.: Am. Sch. Band Dirs. Assn. (Tchr. of the Yr. S.W. Region 1998), Am. Fedn. Musicians, Phi Beta Mu. Office: Roosevelt High School 1120 Nehoa St Honolulu HI 96822-2566 E-mail: rhsband58@hotmail.com.

ABE, NOBUYASU, international organization administrator; b. Akita, Japan, Sept. 9, 1945; m. Akiko Sugawara; 2 children. Studied, U. Tokyo, Japan; studied Polit. Sci., Amherst Coll. Joined Japanese Fgn. Svc., 1967; served in the Japanese missions Internat. Orgn., Geneva, 1977—79, UN, NYC, 1987—90, 1996—97, Internat. Orgn., Vienna, Switzerland, 1999—2001; private sec. to Foreign Min. Kiichi Miyazawa Tokyo, 1974—76; dir., policy planning, 1984—86; sous-Sherpa for the G7 Summits, 1992—94; dir.-gen. for Arms Control and Sci. Affairs, 1997—99; amb. of Japan to the Kingdom of Saudi Arabia, 2001—03; under-sec.-gen., disarmament affairs, 2003—. Internat. fellow, Weatherhead Ctr. for Internat. Affairs Harvard U., 1986—87, consul-gen., Japan, 1994—96. Achievements include helping organize the Tokyo Forum for Nuclear Nonproliferation and Disarmament and particpated in mnay internat. activities for disarmament and nonproliferation; instrumental in bringing about the Japanese ratification of the Ottawa Conv. to Ban Anti-personnel Landmines; in Vienna, leading the efforts to promote the entry into force of the Comprehensive Test Ban Treaty and to conclude the negotiation on the FIrearms Protocol of the Anti-Organized Crime Conv. Office: UN Hdqr First Avenue at 46th St New York NY 10017 Office Phone: 212-963-1234. Office Fax: 212-963-4879.

ABEBE, HENOK, engineer, researcher; s. Abebe Mulat; m. Abebaye Hailu. BSc, Addis Ababa U., 1987; MSc in Physics, Calif. State U., L.A., 1996; MSc in Math., Claremont Grad. U., 1998; PhD, Claremont U., 2002. Faculty Calif. State U., L.A., 1996—2000; device modeling, very large scale integration engr. U. So. Calif., Info. Sci. Inst. Mosis, Marina del Rey, 2000—. Faculty Calif. State U., L.A., 2002—. Office: USC Info Sci Inst MOSIS 4676 Admiralty Way Marina Del Rey CA 90292 E-mail: abebeh@isi.edu.

ABEDI, SHAROKH, mathematician, educator; s. Mashallah Abedi and Sakineh Rezaie. MS in Math., U. Ark., 1988. Grad. tchg. asst. U. Ark., Fayetteville, 1984—88, instr. math. Pine Bluff, 1988—. Mem. Iranian-Am. Assn. Ark., Little Rock, 1992—2005. Mem.: Am. Math. Soc., Math. Assn. Am. Avocations: reading, volleyball, basketball. Office: U Ark 1200 N Univ Dr Pine Bluff AR 71601 Office Phone: 870-575-8760. Office Fax: 870-575-4659. E-mail: abedi_s@uapb.edu.

ABEGG, MARTIN GERALD, retired academic administrator; b. Alliance, Nebr., Oct. 3, 1925; s. Frank and Mary Anna (Newberry) A.; m. Barbara Louise Chamberlain, June 29, 1946; children: Martin Gerald, Robert Miles. BS in Gen. Engring, Bradley U., 1947; MS in Civil Engring, U. Colo., 1951; PhD in Civil Engring, Rensselaer Poly. Inst., 1960; LL.D. (hon.), Ill. Coll., 1982; L.H.D. (hon.), Bradley U., 1993. Registered profl. engr., Ill. registered land surveyor, Ill. Instr. engring. Bradley U., 1947-50, asst. prof., 1950-55, asso. prof., 1955-60, prof., 1960—, head dept. civil engring., 1960-63, dean Coll. Engring. and Tech., 1963-70, pres., 1971-92, pres. emeritus, 1992—. Engring. aide Ill. Div. Hwys., Dixon, 1946, civil engr., Peoria, Ill., 1948; park dist. engr., Peoria, 1953-55; cons. engr. Norman Porter & Assos., N.Y.C., 1956-57, 59. Served to lt. (j.g.) USNR, 1943-46. Recipient Putnam award Bradley U., 1961, Disting. Engring Alumnus award U. Colo., 1986, Disting. Alumnus award Bradley U., 1992. Mem. Am. Soc. C.E., Sigma Xi, Sigma Tau, Phi Kappa Phi, Omicron Delta Kappa, Tau Beta Pi, Chi Epsilon. Home: 116 Warbler Way Georgetown TX 78628-4804 E-mail: mgabegg@dcwis.com.

ABEL, CARLOS ALBERTO, immunologist; b. Buenos Aires, May 7, 1930; came to U.S., 1959, naturalized, 1969; s. Carlos Alberto and Rosa Blanca (Molinero) A.; m. Amalia Carmen Minieri, June 15, 1959. BS, M. Belgrano Coll., 1948; MD, U. Buenos Aires, 1957. Intern St. Joseph's Hosp., Providence, 1959-60; fellow in pediatrics U. Md., Balt., 1960-64, resident in pediatrics, 1964-66; advanced rsch. fellow Scripps Clinic, La Jolla, Calif., 1966-69; vis. scientist U. Oxford, Eng., 1969-70; mem. div. basic immunology Nat. Jewish Hosp., Denver, 1970-84; sr. scientist Med. Rsch. Inst., San Francisco, 1984-92; dir. immunochemistry ICR/Med. Rsch. Inst., 1986-89; chmn. sci. coun. Med. Rsch. Inst., 1993—. Biotech. cons.; vis. scholar U. Calif.-Berkeley, 1982. Contbr. articles to profl. jours. Mem. Am. Assn. Immunologists, Am. Assn. Pathologists, Biochem. Soc. (Eng.), British Soc. for Immunology, Sociedad Argentina de Immunologia, Assn. Latino Americana Immunologia, Soc. Clin. Immunology. Democrat. Roman Catholic. Achievements include research in structure and function of glycoproteins from the surfaces of lymphocytes; study of their role in cell-cell interactions, structure of antibodies, glycobiology. Home: 523 Cragmont Ave Berkeley CA 94708-1205 E-mail: carlosabel@comcast.net.

ABEL, ELIZABETH A., dermatologist; b. Hartford, Conn., Mar. 16, 1940; d. Frederick A. and Rose (Borovicka) Abel; m. Barton Lane; children: Barton F. Lane, Geoffrey Lane, Suzanne Lane Franklin. Student, Colby-Sawyer Coll., 1957-60; BS, Wash. Hosp. Ctr. Sch. Med. Tech., 1961, U. Md., 1965, MD cum laude, 1967. Diplomate Am. Bd. Dermatology. Intern San Francisco Gen. Hosp., 1967-68; resident in medicine, fellow in oncology U. Calif. Med. Ctr., San Francisco, 1968-69; resident in dermatology NYU Med. Ctr., 1969-72, chief resident, 1971-72, USPHS research trainee in immunology, 1972-73; dep. chief dept. dermatology USPHS Hosp., S.I., N.Y., 1973-74; instr. clin. dermatology Columbia U. Coll. Physicians and Surgeons, N.Y.C., 1974-75, Stanford (Calif.) U. Sch. Medicine, 1975-77, clin. asst. prof. dermatology, 1977-82, asst. prof. dermatology, 1982-90, clin. assoc. prof., 1990-96, clin. prof., 1996—. Asst. editor Jour. Am. Acad. Dermatology, 1993-98; mem. med. adv. bd. The Nat. Psoriasis Found., 1993-95. Contbr. articles to profl. sci. jours. Mellon Found. fellow, 1983, 87. Fellow Am. Acad. Dermatology; mem. N.Am. Clin. Dermatologic Soc., San Francisco Dermatologic Soc., Internat. Soc. Dermatology, Pacific Dermatologic Assn., Women's Dermatologic Soc., Noah Worcester Dermatologic Soc., Alpha Omega Alpha. Avocations: piano, golf, travel, reading. Office: 2660 Grant Rd Ste D Mountain View CA 94040-4315 Office Phone: 650-938-6244.

ABEL, GREGORY E., utility company executive; B of Commerce with honors, U. Alberta, Can. Chartered acct., Can. With Price Waterhouse, San Francisco, Calif. Energy Co., Inc., 1992, sr. v.p.; pres., COO MidAm. Energy Holdings Co., Des Moines, 1997—. CEO CE Electric UK, England, MidAmerican Funding, LLC., Kern River Gas Transmission Co., Northern Natural Gas Co.; dir. MidAmerican Energy Holdings Co., HomeServices Am., Inc., Mpls.; bd. dir. Edison Electric Inst. Bd. and exec. com. Greater Des Moines Partnership; Iowa Bus. Coun.; bd. dir. Wells Fargo, Iowa; exec. bd. Mid-Iowa Coun. Boy Scouts Am. Mem.: Alberta Inst. Chartered Accts., Canadian Inst. Chartered Accts. Office: Mid Am Energy Holdings Co 666 Grand Ave Des Moines IA 50309

ABEL, MARY ELLEN KATHRYN, quality control executive, chemist; b. Cleve., Nov. 3, 1949; d. Arthur L. and Dorothy Virginia (DeLura) Jaklic; m. Burton E. Abel, June 22, 1990; stepchildren: Stephanie, Russell E., Christopher A., Darrell A.; 1 child, Matthew Anthony. AA with honors, Lakeland C.C., 1985; BS in Chemistry magna cum laude, Lake Erie Coll., Painesville, Ohio, 1991. Lab technician W.S. Tyler Inc., Cleve., 1969-71, C-E Tyler, Cleve., 1974-76; quality control mgr., environ. coord. Morton Salt, Painesville, 1977—. Treas. com. mem. Boy Scouts Am., 1988-90, sr. mem. explorer scouts marksmanship post, 1987-90, sec. local com., 1987-90; mem. Lake County Indsl. Cmty. Awareness Emergency Response Adv. Panel, 1987-90, 2000—; mem. citizens' rep. Lake County Solid Waste Policy Bd., 2000—. Mem. NAFE, AAUW, Am. Chem. Soc., Gold Wing Road Riders Assn. Republican. Roman Catholic. Avocations: travel, photography, tutoring math. Home: 391 Manhattan Pkwy Painesville OH 44077-5024 Office: Morton Salt A Rohm and Haas Co PO Box 428 Grand River OH 44045-0428 E-mail: mabel@mortonsalt.com.

ABEL, ROBERT BERGER, science administrator; b. Providence, July 21, 1926; s. Abraham Lincoln and Betty Ruth (Berger) A.; m. Nancy Marilyn Klein, Oct. 4, 1953; children: Alan Stewart, Deborah Jane. BS in Chemistry, Brown U., 1947; MEA, George Washington U., 1961; PhD, Am. U., 1972. Chemist Woods Hole (Mass.) Oceanographic Inst., 1947-50; oceanographer U.S. Navy Hydrographic Office, Suitland, Md., 1950-55; asst. to dir. U.S. Navy Hydrog. Office, 1955-60; asst. research coordinator Office Naval Research, Washington, 1961-64; exec. sec. Interagy. Com. Oceanography, 1960-67; asst. exec. sec. Nat. Council Marine Resources and Engring. Devel., 1967-68; dir. Nat. Sea Grant Program, Dept. Commerce, 1966-77; asst. v.p. Tex. A&M U., 1977—80; v.p. N.J. Marine Scis. Consortium, Fort. Hancock, 1979-81, pres., 1981-93; sr. sci. Stevens Inst. Tech., Hoboken, N.J., 1993—. Instr. oceanography USNR Officers Sch., 1960-65, Fairleigh Dickinson U., 1966-83, U. Va., 1976-77; instr. ocean mgmt. Rutgers U., 1980-84; dir. Israel Oceanographic and Limnol. Rsch. Ltd., Inc.; mem. panel Nat. Acad. Scis.; mgr. Cooperative Marine Tech. Program for Middle East, 1980—; mem. N.J. Marine Fisheries Coun., 1993—; mem. N.J. Aquaculture Adv. Coun.; chmn. adv. com. Jersey Shore Partnership; cruise lectr. Cunard, Crystal, Holland Am., Celebrity, Lindblad and Seabourne Lines. Pres. Cris-Mar Manor Civic Assn., 1957-61; bd. dirs. Tantallon Civic Assn., 1973-74, Ctr. Ocean Law and Policy; v.p. Jewish Congregation; chmn. Zoning Bd., Shrewsbury, N.J., 1990-2001. With USNR, 1944-46. Recipient Spl. award Prince of Monaco, 1952, Superior Civilian Svc. award Navy Dept., 1963, Disting. Svc. award, 1967, Disting. Alumnus award George Washington U., 1983, Compass Disting. Svc. award, 1987, Disting. Svc. award Egyptian Nat. Inst. Oceanography and Fisheries; Gold medal Dept. Commerce, 1973; named Man of Yr. Nat. Sea Grant Program, 1977; decorated Order Jules Richard, Monaco, 1951. Mem. Am. Chem. Soc., Rsch. Soc. Am. (past pres. chpt.), Marine Tech. Soc. (pres. 1974-75), Am. Geophys. Union, Am. Soc. Oceanography (pres. 1971-72), Cosmos Club (Washington), Brown Club (N.J.). Jewish. Home: 55 Queen Ann Dr Shrewsbury NJ 07702-4127 Office: Stevens Inst Tech Davidson Labs 711 Hudson St Hoboken NJ 07030 Office Phone: 201-216-5314. E-mail: rbanka@aol.com.

ABEL, SEAN JOSEPH, music educator; b. Columbia, Mo., July 19, 1965; s. Sara M and David E Abel. MusB in Edn., U. Kans., 1988; MEd, Lindenwood U., 2005. Teacher Certification Mo. Dept. of Edn., 1988. Dir. of bands and choirs Maysville R-I Jr./Sr. H.S., Mo., 1988—92; dir. of bands Nishna Valley CSD, Emerson, Iowa, 1992—95, Woodbury Ctrl. CSD, Moville, Iowa, 1995—96; substitute tchr. Sioux City Iowa Pub. and Parochial Schools, 1996—97; asst. dir. of bands/dir. of jazz studies Jefferson City Pub. Schools, Mo., 1997. Home: 221 Boonville Rd Jefferson City MO 65109 Office: Jefferson City HS 609 Union St Jefferson City MO 65101 Office Phone: 573-659-3072. Office Fax: 573-632-3483. Personal E-mail: sabel@mchsi.com. Business E-Mail: sean.abel@jcps.k12.mo.us.

ABELE, JOHN E., medical products executive; m. Mary Abele; 3 children. BS in Physics and Philosophy, Amherst Coll., 1959. With Advanced Instruments, Inc.; co-founder, chmn., dir. Boston Sci., Natick, Mass., 1979—. Founder Kingbridge Centre, Canada. Trustee Mus. of Sci., Boston; chmn. First Orgn.; founder Argosy Found., 1995. Achievements include first to develop medical technology and products that reduce risk, trauma, cost and recovery time; invention of steerable catheter in 1969; patents in field. Office: Boston Sci One Boston Scientific Pl Natick MA 01760-1537

ABELES, CHARLES CALVERT, retired lawyer; b. Norfolk, Va., Nov. 3, 1929; s. Charles T. and Sally (Taylor) A.; m. Mehitable Mackay-Smith, Sept. 30, 1961; children— Nathaniel C., Damaris S., Jessica A.K. AB, Harvard U., 1952; JD, U. Va., 1958. Bar: Va. 1958, D.C. 1958, U.S. Dist. Ct. (D.C. dist.) 1958, U.S. Ct. Appeals 1958. Assoc. Hogan & Hartson, Washington, 1958-62; assoc. Kieffer & Moroney, Washington, 1962-64, ptnr., 1964-69, Lichtman, Abeles, Anker & Nagle, Washington, 1969-77, Wald, Harkrader & Ross, Washington, 1977-85, Piper & Marbury, Washington, 1986-95. Trustee Corina Higginson Trust. Author articles in field Served to lt. (j.g.) USN, 1952-55 Mem. D.C. Bar, Transplant Recipients Internat. Orgn. (past sec., nat. bd. dirs., past pres. local chpt.). Clubs: Metropolitan (Washington). Democrat. Home: 4339 Westover Pl NW Washington DC 20016

ABELES, KIM VICTORIA, artist; b. Richmond Heights, Mo., Aug. 28, 1952; d. Burton Noel Wright and Frances Elizabeth (Sander) Hoffman. BFA in Painting, Ohio U., 1974; MFA in Studio Art, U. Calif., Irvine, 1980. Free-lance artist, L.A., 1975—. Lectr. varius schs. and art ctrs., 1980—; vis. disting. artist Calif. State U., Fullerton, 1985-87; assoc. prof. Calif. State U., Northridge, 1998—; artist-in-residence Art Mill, Czech Republic, 2005. Author, illustrator Crafts, Cookery and 'Country Living, 1976, Kim Abeles, 1988, Kim Abeles: Encyclopedia Persona, 1993, author, photographer: Impressions, 1979; co-author: Surface tension Problematics of Site, 2003; work featured in Artery, 1979, Pacific Poetry and Fiction Review, 1980, Fiction Internat., 1985; one-woman shows include U. Calif., Irvine, 1979—80, Mcpl. Art Gallery, LA, 1981, L.A. City Hall, 1982, Phyllis Kind Gallery, Chgo., 1983, Karl Bornstein Gallery, Santa Monica, Calif., 1983, 1985, 1987, Pepperdine U., Malibu, Calif., 1985, A.I.R. Gallery, N.Y.C., 1986, Chapman Coll., Orange, Calif., 1986, Mount St. Mary's Coll., L.A., 1987, Atlanta Pavilion, 1990, Calif. Mus. of Sci. and Industry, L.A., 1991, Laguna Art Mus. Satellite Gallery, Costa Mesa, Calif., 1991, Turner-Krull Gallery, L.A., 1992, Lawrence Miller Gallery, N.Y.C., 1992, Santa Monica Mus. Art, L.A., 1993, Nat. Mus. Fine Arts, Santiago, Chile, 1996, Mus. Modern Art, Rio de Janeiro, 1996, Cmplejo Cultural Recoleta, Buenos Aires, 1986, Centro Cutural Consolidado, Caracas, 1997, Cepa Gallery, Buffalo, 1998, A.R.T., Inc., N.Y.C., 1989, Contemporary Arts Ctr., Cin., 2000, Art Resources Transfer, N.Y.C., 2001, Intersection, San Francisco, 2001, Calif. Sci. Ctr., L.A., 2000—01, Coll. Environ. Design, Calif. Poly. U., Pomona, 2002, El Camino Coll., L.A., 2003, exhibited in group shows at Silpakorn U., Bangkok, 2002, exhibitions include Mus. of Contemporary Art, L.A., L.A. County Mus. Art, Calif. African-Am. Mus., Allen Meml. Art Mus., Ohio, Represented in permanent collections Marriott Hotels, City of Pasadena, San Fernando Valley Constituent Svc. Ctr., Marvin Braude San Fernando Valley Constituent Svc. Ctr., Dept. Transp., L.A., one-woman shows include El Camino Coll., LA, 2003, exhibited in group shows at Mus. Kampa, Czech Republic, Nat. History Mus., LA, 2005, Hanoi U. Fine Arts, Vietnam, 2005. Honored for Outstanding Student Rsch. & Creative Achievement U. Calif.,

1979; recipient U.S. Steel award Exhbn. of the Associated Artists of pitts., 1977, Clean Air award Air Quality Mgmt. Dist., Calif., 1992; hand Hollow Found. fellow, 1984, Design Team fellow Panorama City Libr., Calif., 1992-93, J. Paul Getty Trust Fund for the Visual Arts fellow, 1994; Pollock-Krasner Found. grantee, 1990, Calif. Arts Coun. grantee, 1990, L.A. Cultural Affairs grantee, 1991, 95, 96, U.S. Info. Agy. grantee, 1995-97; commissioned by Panorama City Pub. Libr., L.A., 1993, Met. Transp. Authority, L.A., 1995, Dept. Transp., L.A., 2000; recipient Richard Neutra award for Profl. Excellence, 2001. Office Phone: 213-626-4623. Personal E-mail: kimabeles@earthlink.net.

ABELES, NORMAN, psychologist, educator; came to U.S., 1939, naturalized, 1944; s. Felix and Bertha (Gronich) A.; m. Jeanette Bueller, Apr. 14, 1957; children: Linda, Mark. BA, NYU, 1949; MA, U. Tex., 1952, PhD, 1958. Diplomate: Am. Bd. Profl. Psychology (Midwest regional bd. 1972-78, chmn. regional bd. 1975-77; nat. trustee 1975-77). Fellow in counseling U. Tex., Austin, 1956-57; instr. Mich. State U., East Lansing, 1957-59, asst. prof., 1959-64, asso. prof., 1964-67, prof. psychology, 1968—, dir. psychol. clinic, 1978—, co-dir. clin. tng., 1981-96, asst. dir. counseling center, 1965-71. U.S. State Dept. ednl. exch. prof. U. Utrecht, Netherlands, 1969, vis. prof., 1975; cons. Peace Corps, 1965-69; vocat. cons. Social Security Office of Hearings and Appeals, 1962—; med. advisor Social Security Office of Hearings and Appeals, 1986—; mem. Mich. Commn. Cert. of Psychologists, 1962-77, chmn., 1966-68; mem. coun. Nat. Register Health Svc. Providers in Psychology, 1974—, vice chmn., 1975-80; del. White House Conf. on Aging, 1995, 2002, 2005; mem. geriatric and gerontology adv. com. to Sec. of VA. Editor: Acad. Psychology bull., 1978-82; cons. editor Am. Jour. Alzheimers Disease and other Dementias, Jour. Personality Assessment, 1988—, Clin. Psychology: Sci. and Practice, 1994—, Clin. Psychology Rev., 1995-98, Profl. Psychology: Rsch. and Practice, 1979-81, 89—, editor, 1983-88; contbr. articles to profl. jours. Served with U.S. Army, 1954-56. Fulbright-Hays grantee, 1969; recipient Disting. Psychologist award Mich. Soc. Clin. Psychologists, 1984; Disting. Practitioner, Nat. Acad. Practice, 1982; Arthur Furst Ethics Lectureship medal Pacific Grad. Sch. Psychology, 1996; Dept. Vets. Affairs Spl. Contbns. award, Battle Creek Mich., 1997. Fellow APA (coun. reps. 1972-75, 77-79, 89-91, 93-95, 99—, policy and planning bd. 1975-79, chmn. 1976, rec. sec. 1980-86, chmn. edn. and tng. bd. 1988, bd. ednl. affairs 1999-2001, com. on internat. rels. in psychology 2002-04, pres. divsn. psychotherapy and divsn. clin. psychology 1990, publs. and comm. bd. 1990-96, chmn. 1995, pres.-elect 1996, pres. 1997, bd. dirs. divsn. psychotherapy 2000—, pres. divsn. internat. psychology 2005, pres. sect. IX assessment divsn. clin. psychology 2004, ethics com. 2005—), Am. Psychol. Found. (sec. 2002—), Coun. Sci. Socs. Pres.; mem. Midwestern Psychol. Assn., Mich. Psychol. Assn. (legis. chmn. 1964-72, pres. 1971-72, Disting. Psychologist 1974), Internat. Union Psychol. Scis. (U.S. com. 1999—), Sigma Xi. Home: 953 Rosewood Ave East Lansing MI 48823-3126 Office: Mich State U Dept Psychology 110C Psychology Bldg East Lansing MI 48824-1117 Office Phone: 517-353-7274. Business E-Mail: abeles@msu.edu.

ABELES, RICHARD ALAN, lawyer; b. Chgo., June 28, 1937; s. Jerome Guthmann Sr. and Jeanne Katherine (Rosenbacher) Abeles; m. Kathleen Sue Koretz, Jan. 28, 1968; 1 child, Elizabeth Amy. BA, Amherst Coll., 1959; JD, Harvard U., 1963. Bar: Ill. 1963, N.Mex. 1976. Atty. Altheimer & Gray, Chgo., 1963-69; hon. consul of Costa Rica State of N.Mex., 1976-84; pvt. practice Chgo., 1971-75, Santa Fe, 1976—. Founding pres. Santa Fe Children's Mus., 1987-95; trustee Santa Fe Prep. Sch., 1993-99; elected ofcl. Santa Fe Met. Water Bd., 1988-90. Mem.: N.Mex. Assn. Grantmakers (treas. 2003—). Avocations: sailing, basketball, travel. Home and Office: 3730 Old Santa Fe Trl Santa Fe NM 87505-4573 Fax: 505-984-2040. E-mail: rick@abeles.net.

ABELES, SIGMUND M., painter, sculptor, printmaker; b. N.Y.C., Nov. 6, 1934; s. Samuel and Henrietta (Banner) A.; m. Anne Merck (div. 1998); children: David Paul, Shoshanna Lynn, Maxwell Merck Abeles. Student, Pratt Inst., 1952-53, Art Students' League, 1954, Skowhegan Sch. (scholar), 1955-56, Bklyn. Mus. Sch. (Graphics scholar), 1956-57; AB in Art, U. S.C., 1955; MFA, Columbia U., 1957; DA (hon.), Coastal Carolina U., 2000. Faculty Swain Sch. Design, New Bedford, Mass., 1961-64; resident artist Wellesley (Mass.) Coll., 1964-69; asst. prof. art Boston U., 1969-70; prof. U. N.H., 1970-87, prof. emeritus, 1987—; artist-in-residence U. So. Maine, Gorham, 1990. Instr. workshop Acad. Realist Art, Seattle, 1995, Art Students League, N.Y.C., 1997-2000; instr. advanced drawing workshop Nat. Acad. Sch. Fine Arts, N.Y.C., 1997-98; bd. dirs. Artist Fellowship, N.Y.C. One man shows include Bates Coll. Mus., Lewiston, Maine, 1999, Thomas Williams Fine Arts, London, 2000, Art 2003, London, Thomas Williams Fine Arts and Drawing Studio, Tucson, Burroughs/Chapin Art Mus., Portland Mus. Art, others; group shows include Pinkard Gallery, Bunting Ctr., Md., Coll. Art, Balt., 2001, Randall Bryan Art Gallery, 2001, S.C. State Mus., Columbia, 1999, Denise Bibro Gallery, N.Y.C., 1999, Atrium Gallery U. Conn., 1992, John Szoke Gallery, N.Y.C., 1989, Am. Artists Galleries, 1986, others; represented in permanent collections including Albert & Victoria Mus., London, The Brit. Mus., London, Libr. Congress, Washington, Mus. Modern Art, N.Y.C., Met. Mus. Art, N.Y.C., Museo de Arte, Ponce, P.R., Phila. Mus. Art, Mus. Find Art, Boston, Fitz William Mus., Cambridge, England, Munson-Proctor-Williams Inst., Ithaca, N.Y., Whitney Mus. Am. Art, N.Y.C., The Old Print Shop, Whilliam P. Carl Fine Prints, Northampton, Mass., Portfolio Art Gallery, Columbia, SC, Yale U. Art Gallery, New Haven, Conn., others; vis. sculptor Johnson Atelier, Tech. Inst. for Sculpture, 1977; traveling retrospective exhbn. New Eng. Coll., Henniker, N.H., McKissick Mus., U. S.C., Columbia, Checkwood Mus. Art, Nashville, Fitchburg (Mass.) Mus. Art, 1992-93; (subject of) The Observant Hand, Forty Years of the Drawing of Sigmund Abeles, So. Meth. U. Gallery, Dallas, 1998; archive for his papers set up at South Carolinian Libr., U. S.C., 1998—, study archive for prints at Bates Coll. Mus. Art, 1998—, grant to paint Chateau Rochefort-en-tene-France, 2000. Nat. Inst. Arts and Letters grantee, 1965, Nat. Coun. Arts and Humanities sabbatical grantee, 1966, Louis Comfort Tiffany Found. grantee, 1967, U. N.H. Grad. Sch. Sculpture grantee, 1973, Am. Jewish Com. grantee for acad. seminar in Israel, 1981, Florsheim Found. grantee, 1992, residency grantee Chateau Rochefort en Terre, Brittany, France, 2000; recipient Am. Master/Printmaking award Am. Artist mag., 1996; subject of "Sigmund Abeles, A Monograph" essays by Charles Simic and Robert Doty, 1992. Mem. NAD (Leo Meisner prize 1983, academician 1990, mem. coun., corr. sec. 1991—), Soc. Am. Graphic Artists, Pastel Soc. Am. (Hall of Fame honoree 2004). E-mail: sabelesart@aol.com. *I strive to observe life with a penetrating eye that I hope can go beyond surface reality to reveal psychological and visual truth, even some magic.**

ABELITE, JAHNIS JOHN, lawyer; b. McMinnville, Tenn., Oct. 10, 1950; s. Augusts and Alexandrine Rita Olga (Tilga) A.; m. Nora Lynn Whitley Baar, May 19, 1990. BA, U. Wash., 1972; JD, U. Puget Sound, 1975. Bar: Wash. 1981, U.S. Dist. Ct. (we. dist.) Wash. 1983. Assoc. Dolack, Hansler et al, Tacoma, 1975-77; legal liaision State of Wash., Olympia, 1977-78, contract specialist Tacoma, 1978-80; contract adminstr. Data I/O Corp., Redmond, Wash., 1980-88; pvt. practice Bothell, Wash., 1981-88, Seattle, 1989—. Counsel West Coast Latvian Edn. Ctr., Mountlake Terr., Wash., 1982—; bd. dirs. Latvian Credit Union, Seattle. Mem. ABA, Fed. Bar Assn., Wash. State Trial Lawyers Assn., Seattle-King County Bar Assn. Lutheran. Office: Ste #302 16710 Smokey Pt Blvd Arlington WA 98223-8435 E-mail: abelaw@nocharge.com.

ABELL, ANNA ELLEN, primary school educator; b. Phila., Nov. 24, 1945; d. Elwood George Daeche and Anna Pauline Pflaumer; m. DeLeon Abell, Aug. 24, 1974; children: Sara Abigail, Beth Ann, Rebecca Nöel. B in Music Edn., Westminster Choir Coll., 1967; postgrad., Assn. Christian Sch. Internat., Piscataway Unified Sch. Dist. Educator Piscataway (N.J.) Sch. Dist., 1967—74; pvt. music tchr. Orange Coast Christian Sch., San Clemente, Calif., 1982—89, 6th grade tchr., 1989—90; jr. high tchr. Dana Point (Calif.) Christian Sch., Calif., 1991—94; 5th grade tchr. Capo Beach Calvary Sch., Dana Point, 1994—98, kindergarten tchr., 1998—. Distbr. JuicePlus/NSA, Dana Point, 2001—. Choral mem. Sanctuary Choir, San Clemente, Calif., 1990—; bell choir mem. Sounds of Bronze, San Clemente, Calif., 1992—. Mem.: Assn. Christian Schs. Internat. Republican. Presbyterian. Avocations: cooking, reading, health and nutrition.

ABELL, DAWN GABBITAS, elementary school, high school educator, administrator; b. Detroit, Sept. 23, 1947; B of Art Edn., Ea. Mich. U., 1969; MEd in Sch. Adminstrn., Winthrop U., 1982. Tchr. 1st grade Learning Improvement Ctr. Melvindale (Mich.) Northern-Allen Park, 1969-79; interior designer, owner La Maison Magnifique, Dearborn, Mich., 1975-79; tchr. art, remedial reading and writing Clover (S.C.) Sch. Dist. 2, 1979-85; tchr. gifted Cherokee County Sch. Dist. I, Gaffney, S.C., 1985-87; dist. vocat. coord. for spl. populations Aiken (S.C.) County Pub. Schs., 1987-89; asst. dir. S.C. Coun. Vocat./Tech. Edn., Columbia, 1989-90; vocat. coord. Richland County Sch. Dist. 1, Columbia, 1990-92; curriculum supr. Beaufort-Jasper Career Edn. Ctr., Ridgeland, S.C., 1992-93; tech. prep. dir., tchr. art Gaston County Schs., Gastonia, N.C., 1993-96; asst. prin. Union County Schs., Monroe, N.C., 1996-97; elem. prin., spl. advisor vocat. edn. Wilson County Schs., Lebanon, Tenn., 1997-98; asst. prin. Midwood H.S. (alt. sch. and TAPS Teen Pregnancy Program), 1998-2000, Starmount Elem. Sch., Charlotte-Mecklenberg Sch. Sys., Charlotte, NC, 2000—01, Sedgefield Mid. Sch., 2001—02; tchr. Lake Wylie Elem. Sch., 2002—. Owner The Learner's Edge Inc., Gastonia, 1987-88; tchr. Gaston Coll. Interior Design, 2004; facilitator nat. career devel. teleconf./workshop, Dallas, N.C., 1994. Organizer/creator Focus: Special Populations 2000 Conf., 1990; contbr. articles to profl. jours. Mem. ASCD, Nat. Assn. Sec. Sch. Prins., Am. Vocat. Assn., S.C. Vocat. Dirs. Assn., N.C. Educators Assn., Internat. Tech. Edn. Prevention Network, Nat. Bus. Edn. Assn., Mktg. Edn. Assn., S.C. Network for Women in Adminstrn. Avocations: horseback riding, antiques, american history, painting, fishing. E-mail: dga901@aol.com.

ABELL, GREGORY ALAN, physicist; b. Cin., Ohio, Sept. 23, 1954; s. Raphael and Mary Lou Abell; m. Annabelle Signada Sayson, July 17, 1998; children: Nicole, Gregory A. Jr. BS, Univ. Cin., Cin., Ohio, 1995, BS, 1996, MS, 1997. Diplomate Am. Bd. Radiology, cert. theraputic radiologic physics Am. Bd. Radiology. Radiation biophysicist Loma Linda Univ., Lama Linda, Calif., 1997—98, med. physicist, 1999—2002, St. Francis Hosp., Honolulu, 2002—03; chief physicist Cancer Inst. of Maui, Wailuku, Hawaii, 2003—04; tech. dir. Ctrs. for Radiation Oncology, Brandon, Fla., 2004—. Contbr. articles pub. to profl. jour. Mem.: Am. Assn. of Physicist & Medicine, Golden Key Nat. Honor Soc., Sigma Pi Sigma. Avocations: photography, fishing, canoeing, hiking, travel. Office Phone: 813-661-6339.

ABELL, NANCY L., lawyer; b. L.A., July 19, 1950; BA with honors, Pitzer Coll., 1972; JD, UCLA, 1979. Bar: Calif. 1979. Extern clk. to Hon. Shirley Hufstedler U.S. Ct. Appeals (9th cir.), 1978; ptnr. Paul, Hastings, Janofsky & Walker LLP, LA, 1986—, chairperson employment law dept. Bd. govs. Inst. Corp. Counsel, 1989— (chairperson, 1994-95). Author: (with P.W. Cane) AM Employer's Guide to the Americans with Disabilities Act, 1991, An Employer's Guide for Preparing Affirmative Action Programs. Fellow Coll. Labor and Employment Lawyers, Inc.; mem. ABA (mgmt. co-chair trial advocacy subcom., employee rights and responsibilities com., labor and employment law sect. 1991-94); Order of Barristers, Order of Coif. Office: Paul Hastings Janofsky & Walker LLP 515 S Flower St Fl 23 Los Angeles CA 90071-2300 Office Phone: 213-683-6162. Office Fax: 213-996-3162. Business E-Mail: nancyabell@paulhastings.com.

ABELL, RICHARD BENDER, federal official, lawyer; b. Phila., Dec. 2, 1943; s. Lon Edward Welch, Jr. and Charlotte Amelia (Bender) A., stepfather Ernest George Abell; m. Lucia del Carmen Lombana-Cadavid, Dec. 2, 1968; children: David, Christian, Rachel. BA in Internat. Affairs, George Washington U., 1966, JD, 1974. Bar: Pa. 1974. Vol. Peace Corps, Colombia, 1967-69; assoc. Reilly & Fogwell, West Chester, Pa., 1974-80; asst. dist. atty. Chester County, Pa., 1974-79; staff mem. to US Senator Richard Schweiker US Senate, Washington, 1979-80; dir. Office of Program Devel. Peace Corp., Washington, 1981-83; dep. asst. atty. gen. US Dept. Justice, Washington, 1983-86, asst. atty. gen., 1986-90; spl. master US Ct. Fed. Claims, Washington, 1991—. Mem. adj. faculty Del. Law Sch., Wilmington, 1975-77, West Chester State U., 1976; bd. dirs. Fed. Prison Industries, Inc., 1985-91; chmn. Nat. Crime Prevention Coalition, 1986-90; mem. adv. bd. Nat. Inst. Corrections, 1986-90; co-chmn. adv. com. Nat. Ctr. for State and Local Law Enforcement Tng., 1987-90; vice chmn. rsch. and devel. rev. bd. Dept. Justice, 1987-89; mem. nat. drug policy bd. Enforcement Coordinating Group and Coordinating Group for Drug Abuse Prevention and Health, The White House, Washington, 1988-89. Author: Peter Smith of Westmoreland County, Va. (Died 1741) and Some Descendents, 1996, Sojourns of a Patriot: Field and Prison Papers of An Unreconstructed Confederate, 1998. Chmn. Young Rep. Nat. Fedn., Washington, 1979-81; mem. exec. com. Rep. Nat. Com., 1979-81; mem. fed. coordinating coun. on Juvenile Justice and Delinquency Prevention, 1986-90; mem. Pres.'s Task Force on Adoption, 1987-88; mem. Pres.'s Commn. on Agrl. Workers, 1988-93. With U.S. Army, 1969-71. Decorated Purple Heart, Army Commendation medal for heroism, Air medal; recipient Jefferson Davis Hist. gold medal, 2000. Mem.: Order Indian Wars US, Sons of Revolution, Soc. Colonial Wars, Soc. Cin., Aztec Club of 1847. Anglican-Catholic. Mailing: US Ct Fed Claims Office Spl Masters 717 Madison Pl NW Washington DC 20005

ABELL, SARA NIGHTINGALE, music educator, musician; b. Toledo, Ohio, Apr. 28, 1952; d. Homer Scott and Alice (Walbolt) Nightingale; m. Ralph "Casey" Abell, May 10, 1986; children: Alison Margaret, Nathan Samuel. MusB, Bowling Green State U., 1974; MusM, Coll. Conservatory Music U. Cin., 1978, D in Music Edn., 1993. Elem. music tchr. Toledo Pub. Schs., 1974—76; music edn. tchg. asst. Coll.-Conservatory Music, U. Cin., 1976—78; elem. music tchr. Mt. Healthy Pub. Schs., Cin, 1979—84; tchr. pre-sch. music classes Musical Arts Ctr., Cin, 1980—82; music edn. tchg. asst. Coll.-Conservatory of Music U. Cin, 1983—86; pre-sch. music tchr. Little Lambs Children's Ctr., Columbus, Ohio, 1994—97; pre-sch. and elem. music tchr. Acad. Fine Arts, Highland Village, Tex., 1999—2002; dir. music Trinity Presbyterian Ch., Flower Mound, Tex., 2002—. Mem.: Tex. Music Educators Assn., Music Educators Nat. Conf., Sigma Alpha Iota (Denton Alumni chpt.), Ariel Club in Tex. Fedn. Women's Clubs.

ABELOV, STEPHEN LAWRENCE, marketing executive, consultant; b. NYC, Apr. 1, 1923; s. Saul S. and Ethel (Esterman) Abelov; m. Phyllis S. Lichtenson, Nov. 18, 1945; children: Patricia C., Gary M. BS, NYU, 1945, MBA, 1950. Asst. divsn. mgr. Nat. Silver Co., NY, 1945; sales rep. Angelica Uniform Co., NY, 1945—50, asst. sales mgr., 1950—56, western regional mgr. L.A., 1956—66; v.p. Angelica Uniform Co. of Calif., 1958—66, nat. v.p. sales, 1966—72; v.p. Angelica Corp., 1958—88, cons., 1988—92, group v.p. mktg., 1972—80; exec. v.p., chief mktg. officer Angelica Uniform Group, 1980—88. Vis. lectr. mktg. NYU Grad. Sch. Bus. Adminstrn. Contbr. articles to profl. jours. Vice comdr. Am. Legion; mem. vocational adv. bd. VA; adv. bd. Woodcraft Rangers; bd. dirs. Univ. Temple. Served with USAF, 1942—44. Mem.: various trade assns., Inst. Environ. Scis., Health Industries Assn. Am. (dir.), Am. Mktg. Assn., Am. Soc. for Advancement Mgmt. (chpt. pres.), Am. Assn. Contamination Control (dir.), U.S. Power Squadron, Coast Guard Aux. (Flotilla comdr., dist. officer), B'nai B'rith (past pres.), St. Louis Coun. on World Affairs, NYU Alumni Assn., Lake of the Ozarks Yachting Assn., Moorings Yacht Club (v.p.), Sales Execs. Club (bd. dirs.), Aqua Sierra Sportsmen Club, NYU Club, Men's Club (exec. v.p.), Town Hall Club, Phi Epsilon Pi (treas.). Home: 9821 Log Cabin Ct Saint Louis MO 63124-1133

ABELS, GUSTA J., artist, art and art history educator; b. N.Y.C., May 20, 1932; d. Max Emanuel and Selma G. Zuckerman; m. Robert Samuel Abels, Mar. 9, 1958; children: Julienne Claire Chevan, Margot Ellen. AB, Barnard Coll., 1954; MFA, Columbia U., 1956. Tchr. upper sch. art and art history Vail Deane Sch., New Providence, N.J., 1981-90; tchr. h.s. art history Wardlaw-Hartridge Sch., Edison, N.J., 1993-98; adj. prof. drawing and painting Seton Hall U., South Orange, N.J., 1992-98; instr. art history and painting Guilford Handcraft Ctr., Conn., 1999—. Solo and group exhbns. of painting in galleries in N.J., N.Y.; works in pvt. collections. Chair Livingston (N.J.) Arts Coun., 1996-98; county committeeperson Dem. Party, Livingston, 1987-98. Fulbright scholar, Antwerp, Belgium, 1954-55. Mem. Art Students League N.Y. (life). Jewish. Home: 28A Harbour Vlg Branford CT 06405-4472

ABELSON, ALAN, columnist; b. N.Y.C., Oct. 12, 1925; s. Harry Carl and Vivian (Finkelstein) A.; m. Virginia Eloise Peterson, Sept. 1, 1951; children—Justin Adams, Reed Vivian. BS in Chemistry and English, CCNY, 1946; MA in Creative Writing, U. Iowa, 1947. Reporter N.Y. Jour. Am., N.Y.C., 1949-56, stock market columnist, 1952-56; with Barron's, The Dow Jones Bus. and Fin. Weekly, N.Y.C., 1956—, mng. editor, 1965-81, editor, 1981-93; columnist Up & Down Wall St., 1966—. Bus. corres. NBC-TV News at Sunrise, 1982-90. Office: Barron's 200 Liberty St New York NY 10281-1003

ABELSON, HAROLD, electrical engineer, educator; Chief scientist, internet tech. group Hewlett-Packard; prof. computer sci. and engring. MIT, Cambridge, Mass., 1990—. Vis. scholar Phi Beta Kappa, 2003—04; co-dir., Project iCampus MIT/Microsoft Alliance for Rsch. in Edu. Tech.; mem., steering com. MIT/Hewett-Packard Alliance; serving on the MIT Project on Math. and Computation; co-dir. MIT Edu. Tech. Coun.; founding dir. Creative Commons; dir. Public Knowledge; advisor Cambridge U., Ctr. for Applied Rsch. in Edu. Tech.; serving on MIT Com. on Outside Profl. Activities; mem. MIT Press Mgmt. Bd.; mem. adv. bd. MIT Academic Media Prodn., MIT OpenCourseWare. Recipient MIT Convocation Program award, 1992. Office: MIT Dept Elec Engring and Computer Sci 200 Technology Sq NE43-429 Cambridge MA 02139 Office Phone: 617-253-5856. Office Fax: 617-258-8682. E-mail: Hal@mit.edu.

ABELSON, HERBERT TRAUB, pediatrician, educator; b. St. Louis, Feb. 19, 1941; s. Benjamin J. and Ann (Traub) Abelson; m. Constance Faye Caldwell, May 17, 1968; children: Matthew, Rebecca, Jonathan, Daniel. AB with high honors, U. Ill., 1962; MD, Washington U., St. Louis, 1966. Diplomate Am. Bd. Pediat., Am. Bd. Pediatric Hematology-Oncology. Intern pediat. U Colo. Med. Ctr., Denver, 1966—67; resident Boston Children's Hosp., 1969—71; staff assoc. Nat. Cancer Inst. NIH, Bethesda, Md., 1967—69; Jane Childs Meml. Fund for Med. Rsch. fellow NIH, 1971, spl. postdoctoral fellow, 1972; teaching fellow Med. Sch. Harvard Coll., Boston, 1970—71, instr. pediat., 1973—74, asst. prof., 1974—79; tutor in med. scis., 1977—79; assoc. prof. Harvard Coll., Boston, 1979—83; vis. prof., Ctr. for Cancer Rsch. MIT, Cambridge, 1982—83; prof., chmn. dept. pediat. Med. Sch. U. Wash., Seattle, 1983—95; prof., chmn., physician-in-chief dept. pediat. U. Chgo., 1995—2004, assoc. dean. admissions Pritzker Sch. Medicine, 2005—. Rsch. fellow in hematology Children's Hosp. Med. Ctr., Boston, 1971—73; rsch. assoc. in biology MIT, 1971—73; mem. exec. com. Am. Med. Sch. Pediatric Dept. Chairmen, 1989—91; lectr. U. Wash., 1990; mem. pediatric residency rev. com. Accreditation Coun. for Grad. Med. Edn., 1992—97; examiner Am. Bd. Pediatrics, 1988—, bd. dirs., 1992—97, sec.-treas., 1995, chmn. elect., 1995—96, chmn., 1996—97; endowed chair U. Chgo., 2004. Contbr. articles to profl. jours. Lt. comdr. USPHS, 1967—69. Recipient Rsch. Career Devel. award, NIH, 1975—80, Alumni achievement award, Washington U., 2001. Fellow: Am. Acad. Pediat.; mem.: Am. Soc. Pediat. Hematology (fin. com.), Am. Bd. Med. Spltys. (fin. com.), Am. Pediatric Soc., Soc. Pediatric Rsch., Am. Soc. Clin. Oncology, Am. Assn. Cancer Rsch., Am. Soc. Hematology (mem. sci. subcom. on pediatric hematology 1987—91). Avocations: aviation, squash, cooking. Office: Univ Chgo Office Medical Edn 924 E 57th St BSLC104 MC1000 Chicago IL 60637-1455 Office Phone: 773-702-3650. Business E-Mail: habelson@bsd.uchicago.edu.

ABELSON, JOHN NORMAN, biology professor; b. Grand Coulee Dam, Wash., Oct. 19, 1938; BS, Wash. State U., 1960; PhD, Johns Hopkins U., 1965; postgrad., Lb. Molecular Biology, Cambridge, Eng., 1965—68. Asst. prof. dept. chemistry U. Calif.-San Diego, 1968—73, assoc. prof., 1973—77, prof., 1977—82; prof. biology Calif. Inst. Tech., Pasadena, 1982—. Founding bd. dirs. Agouron Inst., La Jolla, Calif., 1979—; co-founder Agouron Pharmaceuticals, Inc. Asst. editor Analytical Biochemistry, 1980—87, mem. editl. bd. (Journal) Jour. Biol. Chemistry, 1981—85, mem. editl. com. Ann. Rev. Inc., 1982—; editor: Methods in Enzymology, —; contbr. articles to profl. jours.; Mem. editl. com Ann. Rev. Biochemistry. Mem.: Am. Acad. Arts and Scis., NAS, Am. Chem. Soc., Am. Soc. Biol. Chemists. Home: 1097 Blanche St Apt 316 Pasadena CA 91106-3062 Office: Calif Inst Tech 147-75 1200 E Calif Blvd Pasadena CA 91125-0001

ABELT, RALPH WILLIAM, bank executive; b. Elmhurst, Ill., Feb. 16, 1929; s. P. Alfred and Clara S. (Springhorn) A.; m. Patricia Mitchell, Feb. 2, 1952; children: Susan E., Christopher M., Leslie A. BS, U. Colo., 1952; MBA, Ind. U., 1953. Acct. Marion Hutchinson, C.P.A., Denver, 1952; v.p. comml. banking Continental Ill., Chgo., 1953-77; pres., chief exec. officer, dir. Bank One of Northeastern Ohio, NA, Painesville, 1977-83; chmn., chief exec. officer Bank One Cleve., NA, 1983-86; pres., chief exec. officer Work in N.E. Ohio Council, 1988-91. Dir. KnowledgeWorks Found., Cin. Past pres., mem. exec. bd., area v.p. N.E. Ohio coun. Boy Scouts Am., Painesville, 1981; dir. Holden Arboretum, Kirtland, Ohio, 1986-2005; hon. corp. dir. Ohio Motorists Assn. Served with USMC, 1946-48. Mem. Kirtland Country Club. Home: 4711 Figgie Dr Willoughby OH 44094-7947 E-mail: custcraft@aol.com.

ABER, JOHN WILLIAM, finance educator, consultant; b. Canonsburg, Pa., Sept. 9, 1937; s. John William and Rose (Lauda) A.; m. Cynthia Louise Sousa, Nov. 24, 1962; children: John, Valerie, Alexander. BS, Pa. State U., 1959; MBA, Columbia U., 1965; DBA, Harvard U., 1972. Cons. Univ. Affiliates, Inc., Boston, 1969-71; asst. prof. fin. Ga. State U., Atlanta, 1971-72, Boston U., 1972-78, assoc. prof., 1978-97, prof., 1997—. Bd. dirs. Managers Funds, Appleton Growth Fund, Third Ave. Funds. McKinsey scholar Columbia U.; fellow Harvard U. Home: 51 Columbia St Brookline MA 02446-2407 Office: Boston U 595 Commonwealth Ave Boston MA 02215-1704 Office Phone: 617-353-4404. Business E-Mail: jackaber@bu.edu.

ABERBACH, JOEL DAVID, political science educator, author; b. New York City, June 19, 1940; s. Isidore and Miriam (Meltzer) A.; m. Joan F. Gross, June 17, 1962; Children: Ian Mark, Amy Aberbach Arbreton, Matthew Daniel, Rachel Aberbach Metz. AB, Cornell U., 1961; MA, Ohio State U., 1963, Yale U., 1965, PhD, 1967. Asst. prof. U. Mich., Ann Arbor, 1967-72, research scientist, 1967-88, assoc. prof., 1972-78, prof., 1978-88; sr. fellow Brookings Inst., Washington, 1977-80; dir. Ctr. for Am. Politics and Pub. Policy, UCLA, 1986—2004; disting. prof. UCLA, 2004—. Cons. Commn. on the Op. of the Senate, Washington, 1976, U.S. Office of Pers. Mgmt., Washington, 1983, Nat. Pub. Radio, Washington, 1983-84, U.S. Govt. Accountability Office, 2004—. Author: Keeping a Watchful Eye, 1990; co-author: Race in the City, 1973, Bureaucrats and Politicians in Western Democracies, 1981, In the Web of Politics, 2000; co-editor: The Role of the State in Taiwan's Development, 1994, Institutions of Democracy: The Executive Branch, 2005. Del. Mich. Dem. Conv., Detroit, 1972; editorial bd. Congress and the Presidency, Washington, 1981—, Governance, Oxford, Eng., 1987-98, Italian Rev. of Pub. Policy, 2001--, Pub. Orgn. Rev., 2000--. Research grantee Nat. Sci. Found., Washington, 1969-73, 1978-81, 1986-89, 1993-98. Fellow Brookings Inst., Ctr. for Advanced Study in Behavioral Scis., Swedish Collegium for Advanced Study in the Social Scis.; mem. Am. Polit. Sci. Assn., Rsch. Com. on Structure and Orgn. Govt. of Internat. Polit. Sci. Assn. (exec. bd. 1985-89, co-chmn. 1989—, co-chair exec. branch comm. Annenberg Found. Insts. of Democracy Project, 2003-), Phi Beta Kappa. Jewish. Home: 10453 Colina Way Los Angeles CA 90077-2041 Office: UCLA 4250 Public Policy Bldg Los Angeles CA 90095-1484 Office Phone: 310-206-5720. E-mail: aberbach@polisci.ucla.edu.

ABERCROMBIE, NEIL, congressman; b. Buffalo, June 26, 1938; s. G. Don and Vera June (Giersdorf) Abercrombie; m. Nancie Ellen Caraway, July 18, 1981. BA, Union Coll., 1959; MA, U. Hawaii, 1964, PhD in Am. studies, 1974. Mem. Hawaii Ho. Reps., 1974—86, Hawaii Senate, 1978—86, U.S. Congress 1st Hawaiian dist., 1986—87, 1991—, mem. resources com., armed svcs. com., nat. security com. Mem. Honolulu City Coun., 1988—90. Co-author: Blood of Patriots. Democrat. Office: US Ho Reps 1502 Longworth House Office Building Washington DC 20515-0001

ABERE, ANDREW EVAN, economist, educator; b. N.Y.C., June 16, 1961; s. Frank Joseph and Ruth (Mofenson) A.; m. Lisa Joy Watine, Nov. 5, 1989; children: Spencer David, Amanda Emily. BA, Columbia U., 1983, MA in Econs., 1986, PhD in Econs., 1991. Economist Skadden, Arps, N.Y.C., 1987-91, Ernst & Young, N.Y.C., 1991-95, Princeton (N.J.) Econ. Group, Inc., 1995—. Instr. dept. econs. Columbia U., N.Y.C., 1987-89, lectr., 1989-90, adj. asst. prof. econs., 1991-96; adj. asst. prof. dept. econs. NYU, 1991; part-time lectr. dept. econs. Rutgers U., 1997-2003. Columbia U. fellow, 1985-87, 89-91. Mem. Am. Econ. Assn., Am. Law and Econs. Assn. Office Phone: 609-279-0600. E-mail: a.abere@econgroup.com.

ABERLIN, BETTY KAY, actress; b. N.Y.C., Dec. 30, 1942; d. Harry Ageloff and Daisy Kinstein. BA in Creative Writing, Bennington Coll. Actor: (musical theater) Sandhog, I'm Getting My Act Together; (TV series) Mr. Rogers' Neighborhood, 1969—2001, The Smothers Brothers; (films) Dogma, Jersey Girl; co-founder, on-air talent Sta. WYEP-FM, Pitts.; author: Stop Me Before I Love Again, Girl Steps Out of Car - Gets Blown Up, The Blonding of America, Nightclub, Potter's Field, The White Pages; contbr. to PoetsAgainstTheWar.com, FreshYarn.com. Vol. chaplain's office Rikers Island, N.Y.C.; vol. Children's Hosp., L.A. Jewish Christian. Avocations: writing, art. Personal E-mail: bettykayday@earthlink.net.

ABERMAN, HAROLD MARK, veterinarian; b. Chgo., Aug. 5, 1956; s. Howard Oscar and Goldie Esther Aberman. BS, Purdue U., 1979, MSE, 1987, BSE, 1986, DVM, 1983. NIH postdoctoral fellow Purdue U., West Lafayette, 1983-87; dir. sci. and biol. affairs Howmedica div. Pfizer, Rutherford, 1987-99; pres. Applied Biol. Concepts, Los Alamitos, Calif., 1996—; dir. devel. Orthop. Rsch. Inst., Long Beach, Calif., 1999-2001, med. device cons., 2001—; dir. sci. affairs, chief sci. officer Synthes Spine, West Chester, Pa., 2003—. Adj. prof. N.C. State U., Raleigh, 1988—, Miss. State U., Starkville, Miss., 1990—, Purdue U., 1991—. Contbr. articles to profl. jours. Mem. ASME, AVMA, Am. Animal Hosp. Assn., Ortho. Rsch. Soc., Soc. Biomechanics, Acad. Surg. Rsch. Jewish. Office: Applied Biol Concepts 12581 Silver Fox Rd Los Alamitos CA 90720-5234 also: Synthes Spine 1302 Wrights Ln E West Chester PA 19380 Office Phone: 610-719-5682. Personal E-mail: haroldabc@aol.com.

ABERNATHY, DIANE ELLEN, elementary school educator; b. Bethesda, Md., Sept. 1, 1949; d. Gene Dixon and Jean Ellen (Ryan) Robertson; m. Paul Abernathy, Oct. 30, 1976 (div. 1987); 1 child, Emily Marie. BA, Ball State U., 1971, MA, 1972; endorsement gifted/talented edn., Purdue U., 1990. Cert. tchr., Ind. Tchr. Jennings County Schs., North Vernon, Ind., 1972—. Problem-solving coach Future Problem Solvers, North Vernon, 1984-92; curriculum chair Performance Based Accredidation, 1999-01; chair gifted/talented curriculum com. Jennings County Schs., North Vernon, 1987-91, gifted/talented counsel, 1991-96, curriculum senate, 1989-91; judge, workshop leader Odyssey of the Mind, Dept. Edn., Indpls., 1988—; state problem capt. Odyssey of the Mind, 1999-01, judge world finals, 1999. Pastor, parish com. 1st United Meth. Ch., North Vernon, 1993-96; mem. Fist Bapt. Ch. North Vernon; Pub. Law 21 com. 2002—. Mem. Internat. Assn. for Childhood Edn., Delta Kappa Gamma, Delta Theta Tau (com. chair 1983-85, sec. 1986-88, pledge trainer 1997-99). Avocations: reading, atvs, travel. Home: 404 S Elm St North Vernon IN 47265-2102 Office: Jennings County Schs 810 W Walnut St North Vernon IN 47265-1461 E-mail: dabernat@seidata.com.

ABERNATHY, FREDERICK HENRY, mechanical engineering educator; b. Denver, Colo., June 19, 1930; s. Henry James and Irene Sarah (Lehman) A.; m. AnnaMaria Herbert, June 18, 1961; children: Sarah, Marian, Pauline. BSME, Newark Coll. Engring., 1951; postgrad., Oak Ridge Sch. Reactor Tech., 1952; SM, Harvard U., 1954, PhD, 1959. Gordon McKay prof. engring. Harvard U., Cambridge, Mass., 1963—, Abbott and James Lawrence prof. mech. engring., 1995—; dir. engring. divsn. NSF, Washington, 1972-73, dir. energy-realted rsch., 1973-74; prof. engring. Harvard U. Dir. Textile/Clothing Tech. Corp., Cambridge, 1985-87, Harvard Ctr. for Textile and Apparel Rsch., 1991—. Fellow Am. Phys. Soc., Am. Acad. Arts and Scis.; mem. ASME, Am. Soc. Engring. Edn., Sigma Xi. Office: Harvard Univ Divsn Engring/Applied Scis Pierce Hall Cambridge MA 02138 E-mail: fha@deas.harvard.edu.

ABERNATHY, JAMES LOGAN, public relations executive; b. Kansas City, Mo., Jan. 23, 1941; s. James Logan and Caryl (Nicolson) A.; m. Kevin Kearns, Sept. 12, 1981; 1 child, Nell Logan. Student, Brown U., 1959-64. Assoc. dir. investor relations CBS Inc., N.Y.C., 1967-72; v.p. investor relations Warner Communications Inc., N.Y.C., 1972-74, ABC Inc., N.Y.C., 1974-79, v.p. corp. affairs, 1979-84; chmn. Abernathy/MacGregor Group Inc., N.Y.C., 1984—. Trustee, chmn., dir. Caron Found., Wernersville, Pa., 19836; trustee Hackley Sch., Tarrytown, N.Y., 1982-89; overseer Brown U. Sch. Medicine, 1996—; dir. Nat. Coun. on Alcoholism and Drug Addiction, 2000. Mem. Investor Relations Assn. (pres. 1979-80), Nat. Investor Relations Inst., Knickerbocker Club (N.Y.C.), Doubles Club (N.Y.C.), Devon Yacht Club (L.I.). Home: 130 E End Ave New York NY 10028-7553 Office: Abernathy MacGregor Group Inc 501 Madison Ave New York NY 10022-5602

ABERNATHY, RONALD FITTZ, pharmacist; b. Richmond, Va. s. Richard Fittz and Neta (Tarkington) A. BS in Pharmacy, Med. Coll. Va., 1970. Registered pharmacist, Va., Md. Pharmacist in charge Drug Fair, Falls Ch., Va., 1970-86, pharmacist, mgr. Arlington, Va., 1986-88, Rite Aid, Arlington, 1988-98, Safeway, Reston, Va., 1998—. Mem. Am. Pharmacist Assn., Va. Pharmacist Assn., Potomac Pharmacist Assn., Phillips Collection (assoc.), Phi Delta Chi (social chmn. 1969-70). Episcopalian. Avocation: computers.

ABERNATHY, SHIELDS B., allergist, immunologist, internist; b. Bronxville, N.Y., Mar. 14, 1951; m. Leslie Abernathy; children: Amelia, Camille, Lant. BA, Ohio Wesleyan U., 1973; MS, Harvard U., 1975; MD, Med. Coll. Pa., 1979. Diplomate Am. Bd. Internal Medicine, Am. Bd. Allergy and Immunology, eligible Am. Preventive Medicine, Nat. Bd. Med. Examiners; Qualified Med. Examiner Calif.; Fed. Aviation Med. Examiner; ACLS Am. Heart Assn. Intern in internal medicine L.A. County/U. So. Calif. Med. Ctr., L.A., 1979-80; resident in internal medicine Hosp. of Good Samaritan, L.A., 1980-81; resident UCLA Wadsworth VA Med. Ctr., 1981-82, fellow allergy and immunology, 1982-84. Instr. pub. edn. programs; med. philanthropic facilitator, Philippines, 2000, India, 2001, Indochina, 2001, Amazon, 2002, Africa, 2004; rschr. in field. Fellow Am. Coll. Allergy and Immunology, Am. Acad. Allergy and Immunology; mem. Am. Med. Health Assn., Am. Pub. Health Assn. (internat. health sect.). Office: 1050 Las Tablas Rd Ste 3 Templeton CA 93465-9792 Office Phone: 805-434-1000. E-mail: sabernats@sbcglobal.net.

ABERNATHY, THOMAS EDWARDS, IV, lawyer; b. Chattanooga, Feb. 18, 1941; BA, Vanderbilt U., 1963, JD, 1967, U. Va., 1967. Bar: Tenn. 1967, US Dist. Ct. (ea. dist.)/Tenn. 1967, US Ct. Fed. Claims 1970, US Supreme Ct. 1970, US Dist. Ct. (no. dist.)/Ga. 1972, Ga. Ptnr. Smith, Currie & Hancock, Atlanta, 1971—. Contbr. articles profl. jour. Chmn. Metro-Atlanta adv. bd. Salvation Army, 1997—2000, past chmn. Metro-Atlanta Social Svcs. adv. coun. Capt. JAGC U.S. Army, 1967—71. Fellow: Am. Coll. Constrn. Lawyers (founder, bd. govs. 2003—05); mem.: ABA (chair pub. contract law sect. 1983—84, mem. constrn. com. litigation sect., forum com. on the constrn. industry, mem. fidelity and surety com. tort ins. practice sect.), Am. Arbitration Assn. Office: Smith Currie & Hancock 233 Peachtree St NE Ste 2600 Atlanta GA 30303-1530 Office Phone: 404-582-8013. E-mail: teabernathy@smithcurrie.com.

ABERNETHY, DAVID F., lawyer; b. Harrisburg, Pa., May 29, 1958; s. Gerald Lester and Carol Marie (Thompson) A.; m. Phyllis Karen Simon, Sept. 3, 1983; children: Maxwell Simon, Andrew Simon. AB, Syracuse U., 1980, JD, 1982. Bar: Pa. 1982, U.S. Ct. Appeals (3rd cir.) 1986, U.S. Supreme Ct. 1986, U.S. Dist. Ct. (ea. dist.) Pa. 1987, N.J. 1994, U.S. Dist. Ct. N.J. 1994, U.S. Dist. Ct. (mid. dist.) Pa. 1996. Assoc. Pepper, Hamilton & Scheetz, Phila., 1982, Drinker, Biddle & Reath LLP, Phila., 1986-92, ptnr., comml. litig., 1992—, and chair, pro bono com. Capt. U. S. Army JAGC, 1983-87. Recipient Spiegelberg award Am. Coll. Trial Lawyers, 1982. Mem. ABA, Pa. Bar Assn., Phila. Bar Assn., Order of Coif, Phi Beta Kappa. Office: Drinker Biddle & Reath LLP One Logan Sq 18th & Cherry Sts Philadelphia PA 19103-6996 Office Phone: 215-988-2503. E-mail: david.abernethy@dbr.com.

ABERNETHY, ROBERT JOHN, real estate developer; b. Indpls., Feb. 28, 1940; s. George Lawrence and Helen Sarah (McLandress) A. BA, Johns Hopkins U., 1962; MBA, Harvard U., 1968; cert. in real estate fin. and constrn., UCLA, 1974. Asst. to chief scientist Phoenix missile program Hughes Aircraft Co., L.A., 1968-69, asst. program mgr. Iroquois night fighter and night tracker program, 1969-71, asst. to contr. space and comm. group, 1971-72, contr. tech. divsn., 1972-74; pres. Am. Std. Devel. Co., L.A., 1974—, Transit Cmty. Devel. Corp., 1997-2001. Bd. dirs., chmn. audit com. Pub. Storage, Inc., Glendale, Calif., Marathon Nat. Bank, L.A., 1984-2003, Tech Net, L.A. Bancorp, Met. Water Dist., So. Calif., Met. Transp. Authority, L.A. County; pres. Self Svc. Storage Assn., San Francisco, 1978-83. Active Albert Schweitzer Found.; asst. to dep. campaign mgr. Humphrey for Pres., Washington, 1968; commr. L.A. Planning Commn., 1984—88, L.A. Telecom. Commn., 1992—93, Calif. Transp. Commn., 1998—2001, Calif. State Bd. Edn., 2000—; vice chmn. L.A. Econ. Devel. Coun., 1988—93; chmn. Calif. Tech. Adv. Com. on Aeronautics, Ctr. for Study Dem. Inst., Santa Barbara, Calif., 1986—; bd. dirs. Met. Transp. Authority Los Angeles County, South Bay Civic Light Opera, L.A. Children's Mus., World Children's Transplant Fund, French Found. for Alzheimers Rsch., Pacific Coun. on Internat. Policy; adv. bd. mem. Peabody Conservatory, 1992—, Ctr. Talented Youth, 1992—, Nitze Sch. Advanced Internat. Studies, 1993—, Harvard Ptnrs., 1996—, Inst. Acad. Achievement of Youth, 1999—; bd. vis. Davidson Coll.; bd. dirs. L.A. Theatre Ctr., 1986—92, YMCA; mem. Coun. on Fgn. Rels., L.A. Com. on Fgn. Rels., Calif Arts Coun., 2001—; trustee Johns Hopkins U., 1991—. Lt. USNR, 1962—66. Mem. So. Calif. Planning Congress (bd. dirs.), Parker Found. (bd. dirs.), California Club, St. Francis Yacht Club, Jonathan Club, Calif. Yacht Club, Alpha Lambda. Address: PO Box 834 Redondo Beach CA 90277 E-mail: rabernethy@techcenter.net.

ABERSON, LESLIE DONALD, lawyer; b. St. Louis, May 30, 1936; s. Hillard and Adele (Wenneker) A.; m. Regene Jo Lowenstein, Oct. 16, 1960; children: Karen, Angie, Leslie. BS, U. Ky., 1957, JD, 1960. Bar: Ky. 1960, U.S. Dist. Ct. (we. dist.) Ky. 1964, U.S. Tax Ct. 1968, U.S. Supreme Ct. 1975. Dir. Bank of Louisville. Bd. dirs. Ky. Athletic Hall of Fame, 1965—2003, NCCJ; past bd. dirs. Jewish Hosp. Louisville, Louisville Med. Rsch. Found.; past pres. B'rith Sholom Temple; bd. dirs., past v.p. Jewish Cmty. Fedn. Louisville; bd. dirs. Louisville Free Pub. Libr. Found. Recipient Louis Cole Young Leadership award. Mem.: Louisville Bar Assn., Ky. Bar Assn., U. Ky. Law Sch. Alumni Assn. (bd. dirs.). Home: 5431 Harbortown Cir Prospect KY 40059-9257 Office: Rothschild Aberson & Miller Suite 102 5940 Timber Ridge Dr Prospect KY 40059

ABETTI, PIER ANTONIO, electrical engineer, consultant, finance educator; b. Florence, Italy, Feb. 7, 1921; came to U.S., 1946; s. Giorgio and Anna (Garino) A.; m. Elizabeth Burr Nelson, June 11, 1948; children: George E., Frank A. Student, Poly. Inst., Turin, Italy, 1940-44; D of Indsl. Engring., U. Pisa, Italy, 1945; MSEE, Ill. Inst. Tech., Chgo., 1948; PhD in Elec. Engring., Ill. Inst. Tech., 1953. Registered profl. engr., Mass. Advanced devel. engr. Gen. Electric Co., Pittsfield, Mass., 1948-56, mgr. project EHV, 1957-62, mgr. pvt. telephone sys. Lynchburg, Va., 1971-73, mgr. Europe strategic planning Brussels, 1974-79, cons. R & D Schenectady, N.Y., 1980-81; dep. gen. mgr. UNIVAC-Europe, Lausanne, Switzerland, 1963-64; prof. mgmt. of tech. and entrepreneurship Rensselaer Poly. Inst., Troy, N.Y., 1982—, dir. Ctr. for Entrepreneurship New Tech. Ventures, 1988-92. Adj. prof. MIT, Troy, NY, 1951-52, Berkshire CC, Pittsfield, Mass., 1958-60; vis. prof. U. Calgary, Can., 1986-87, U. Tech., Compiègne, France, 1988-92, Internat. U., Japan, 1991, 93, Elec. Rsch. Inst., Cuernavaca, Mex., 1992, Helsinki Sch. Econs. and Bus. Adminstrn., 1994-2005, U. Oulu, Finland, 1997, Korean Advanced Inst. Sci. and Tech., 1995-97, U. Stellenbosch, South Africa, 1994, Gordon Inst. Tufts U., 1987-2005, Duxx Sch. Bus. Leadership, Monterrey, Mex., 1997-2000, Queensland U. Technol., Brisbane, Australia, 1998, 2000-03, Nat. Coll. Ireland, Dublin, 1998-2004, Danish U. Tech., 1999-2001, Technol. Inst. of Costa Rica, 1999-2000, U. Udine, Italy, 2001, Help Inst., Malaysia, 2002-03, Nat. U. Singapore, 2003, Bus. Sch. 10 November U., Tunisia, 2004-05; cons. in field. Author: Linking Technology and Business Strategy, 1990, (with J. Maldifassi) The Defense Industries of Argentina, Brazil, Chile, 1994; assoc. editor Internat. Jour. Entrepreneurship and Innovation Mgmt., 2001—; contbr. articles to profl. jours Pres. Berkshire Mycol. Soc., Pittsfield, 1954-59; pres. Berkshire Film Soc., 1955-58. Recipient Coffin award GE, 1952, Internat. prize Montefiore Inst., 1953, Recognition award Italian Hist. Soc. Am., 1953, Kaufmann Found. award Entrepreurship Educator of Yr. Finalist, 1993. Fellow IEEE (chmn. Volta scholarship 1961-66, mem. awards bd. 1984-86, chmn. scholarship awards 1984-86); mem. Am. Mgmt. Assn. (R&D coun. 1985-92), Italian Soc. for Sci. Progress (hon.), Eta Kappa Nu (Recognition award 1953), Tau Beta Pi. Office Phone: 518-276-6834. Business E-Mail: abetti@rpi.edu. *In my life I have always tried to learn from my predecessors in science and technology and innovate based on their teaching and my original thinking.*

ABHYANKAR, SHREERAM S., mathematics professor; b. Ujjain, India, July 22, 1930; came to U.S., 1951, naturalized, 1989; s. Shankar Keshav and Uma (Tamhankar) A.; m. Yvonne Margit Kraft, June 5, 1958; children: Hari Shreeram, Kashi Shreeram. BSc, Bombay U., 1951; AM, Harvard U., 1952, PhD, 1955; DHD (hon.), U. Angers, 1998. Rsch. instr. Columbia U., N.Y.C., 1955-56, vis. asst. prof., 1956-57; asst. prof. Cornell U., Ithaca, N.Y., 1957-58; vis. asst. prof. Princeton (N.J.) U., 1958-59; assoc. prof. Johns Hopkins U., Balt., 1959-63; pres. math. Purdue U., West Lafayette, Ind., 1963-67, Marshall disting. prof. math., 1967—, prof. indsl. engring., 1987—, prof. computer scis., 1988—. Vis. lectr. Harvard U., 1960-61; vis. prof. Munster U., Erlangen U., summer 1963, Matsci., Madras, India, fall 1963, Tata Inst., Bombay, 1969-70, 75-76, spring 1974, Kyoto U., fall 1976, U. Ky., fall 1978, U. Paris, spring 1980, ENS St. Cloud, France, spring 1982, U. Nice, spring 1983, U. Sydney, spring 1986, U. Strasbourg, spring 1991, Ohio State U., spring 1995; vis. assoc. prof. Yale U., spring 1963; spkr. numerous profl. meetings, univ., insts., symposia, confs., and congresses, 1960—. Author: Ramification Theoretic Methods in Algebraic Geometry, 1959, Local Analytic Geometry, 1964, Resolution of Singularities of Embedded Algebraic Surfaces, 1966, 2d enlarged edit. 1998, A Glimpse of Algebraic Geometry, 1971, Algebraic Space Curves, 1971, Lectures on Expansion Techniques in Algebraic Geometry, 1977, Weighted Expansions for Canonical Desingularization, 1982, Enumerative Combinatorics of Young Tableaux, 1988, Algebraic Geometry for Scientists and Engineers, 1990; also over 150 articles. Recipient Herbert Newby McCoy award Purdue U., 1973, Medal of Honor, U. Valliadolid, Spain, 1990; grantee NSF, 1960-87, 89-91, 89-2002, Office Naval Rsch., 1986-90, Army Rsch. Office, 1988-90, Nat. Security Agy., 1992-99; rsch. fellow Alfred P. Sloan Found., 1958-60. Fellow Indian Nat. Sci. Acad., Indian Acad. Scis.; mem. Am. Math. Soc., Math. Assn. Am. (Lester R. Ford prize 1977, Chauvenet award 1978), Phi Beta Kappa. Achievements include research in algebraic geometry, commutative and local algebra, theory of functions of several complex variables, quantum electrodynamics, circuit and invariant theory, combinatorics, computer aided design, and robotics. Home: 111 Waldron St West Lafayette IN 47906-2836 Office: Purdue U Div Math Sci West Lafayette IN 47907 Business E-Mail: ram@cs.purdue.edu.

ABID, ANN B., art librarian; b. St. Louis, Mar. 17, 1942; d. Clarence Frederick and Luella (Niehaus) Bartelsmeyer; m. Amor Abid (div. 1969); children: Rod, Kady; m. Cleon R. Yohe, Aug. 10, 1974 (div.); m. Roldo S. Bartimole, Feb. 1, 1991. Cert. in Librarianship, Washington U., St. Louis, 1976. Asst. to libr. St. Louis Art Mus., 1963-68, libr., 1968-85; head libr. Cleve. Mus. Art, 1985—. Vis. com. univ. librs. Case We. Res.U., 1987-90, co-chairperson, 1990. Co-author: Documents of Surrealism, 1918-1942, 1981, Planning for Automation of the Slide and Photograph Collections at the Cleveland Museum of Art: A Draft Marc Visual Materials Record, 1998; contbr. articles to profl. jours. Grantee Mo. Coun. Arts, 1978, Mo. Com. Humanities, 1980, Nat. Hist. Pubs. and Records Commn., 1981, Reinberger Found., 1987, Japan Found., 1996. Mem. ALA, Art Librs. Soc. N.Am. (chmn. mus.-type-of-libr. group nat. chpt. 1979-81, chmn. New Orleans 1980, nominating com. 1980, 84, Wittenborn awards com. 1981, 90, v.p., pres.-elect 1987-88, pres. 1988-89, past pres. 1989-90, chmn. N.Am. art libr. resources com. 1991-93, search com. new exec. dir. 1993-94. chmn. fin. com. 1996-98, presenter numerous papers, chmn. nominating com. 1999-2000, co-chair conf. program com. 1999-2000), Soc. Am. Archivists, Midwest Mus. Conf. (co-chmn. program com. ann. meeting 1982), Spl. Librs. Assn., Rsch. Librs. Group (shares exec. group 1996-98, shares participation com. 1997-99). Office: Cleve Mus of Art 11150 East Blvd Cleveland OH 44106-1711 E-mail: aabid@clevelandart.org.

ABIDI, S. MANZOOR, neurologist; b. Lucknow, India, Jan. 9, 1940; arrived in U.S., 1965; s. S. Maqbool and Afsar Begum (Zaki) Abidi; children: Nicholas, Zeena. MD, King George's Med. Coll., Lucknow, 1962. Rotating intern King George's Med. Coll., Lucknow, 1962-63, med. resident, 1963-65; internal medicine resident Huron Rd. Hosp., Cleve., 1965-66; psychiatry resident Phila. Gen. Hosp., 1966-68; neurology resident Temple U. Hosp., Phila., 1968-71; pvt. practice Regional Neurol. Group, NJ, 1973-78, Neurol. Regional Assocs., Maple Shade, NJ, 1978—, N.J. Med. Inst., Maple Shade, 1997—. Asst. neurologist Cooper Med. Ctr., Camden, NJ, 1972—73, assoc. neurologist, 1974, attending neurologist, 1974—75; asst. neurologist Pa. Hosp., Phila., 1972—74; neurologist Garden State Cmty. Hosp., 1973—77, chief neurology, 1977—88, attending neurologist, 1989—92, mem. exec. com. bd. trustees; chief attending neurologist Underwood Meml. Hosp., Woodbury, NJ, 1975—79, attending neurologist, 1979—82; assoc. neurologist Burlington County Meml. Hosp., Mt. Holly, NJ, 1975—84, chief divsn. neurology, 1984—94; cons. neurologist South Ocean County Hosp., Manahawkin, NJ, 1975—2002, Hampton Hosp., Rancocas, NJ, 1986—94; neurologist John F. Kennedy Meml. Hosp.-Univ. Med. Ctr., 1980—85, attending neurologist, 1984—85, Zurbrugg Meml. Hosp., Riverside, NJ, 1984—85; chief neurology Marlton divsn. W. Jersey Hosp., 1993—95; chief neurology sect. W. Jersey Health Sys., Berlin, Camden, Marlton, Vorhees, NJ, 1995—2003, trustee, 1992—2000. Fellow: Royal Soc. Gt. Britian; mem.: AMA (alt. del. N.J. 1995—2000, del. N.J. 2000—), Coun. Indian Orgns. Greater Phila. (Profl. Excellence award 2005), Phila. Neurol. Soc., Acad. Medicine N.J. (trustee 1999—2000, treas. 2000—01, 2d v.p. 2002—), Burlington County Med. Soc. (pres. 1990—91), N.J. Med. Soc. (trustee 1992—2001, 2d v.p. 2001—02, 1st v.p. 2002—03, pres.-elect 2003—04, pres. 2004—05), Am. Electroencephalography Soc., Am. Acad. Neurology. Home: 4 Silverwood Rd Moorestown NJ 08057-2118 Office: 504 Route 38 E Maple Shade NJ 08052-2039 Office Phone: 856-866-0466. E-mail: abidi@yahoo.com.

ABI-GHANEM, GEORGES VICTOR, civil engineer, environmental engineer; b. Dakar, Senegal, Feb. 16, 1954; Came to U.S. 1976. s. Victor and Souad (Syriani) Abi-G. Maitrise Es-Science with honors, Universite Claude-Bernard, Academie de Lyon, France, 1975; Diplome d'Ingénieur Civil, ESIB, Lebanon, 1976; MS in Water Resources Engring., Stanford U., 1977; MS in Structures and Mechanics, Princeton U., 1980, PhD in Continuum Physics, 1982. Rsch. engr. U. Delft, The Netherlands, 1975; rsch. assoc. U. Ariz., 1977-78; rsch. and teaching asst. Sch. of Engring. and Applied Sci. Princeton U., 1978-82; chief engr., gen. mgr. EWA, Inc., Mpls., 1983-87, prin. scientist, 1987-90, ARDI Corp., Mpls., 1983—. Cons. to fed. and state agys. and various corps. in U.S. and abroad, 1977—; tech. reviewer Water Resources Rsch., Soc. Petroleum Engrs. Jour. and SIAM, 1982-92; observer Audits of U.S. DOE Contracts on High-Level Nuclear Waste Disposal Projects, 1987; tech. reviewer R&D grant applications Nat. Scis. and Engring. Rsch. Coun. of Canada, 1987—, Oversight of US DOE Environ. Restoration and Waste Mgmt. Activites, 1988-90; peer reviewer Hanford Environ. Dose Reconstruction Project, Hanford, Wash., 1990-94. Co-author: (with V. V. Nguyen and H. O. Pfannkuch) Practical Solutions to Chemical Spillages and Groundwater Contamination; contbr. articles to Water Resources Research, Physical Review, Jour. of Physics, Jour. of Mathematical Physics, others; author numerous publs. in conf. proceedings and tech. reports. Recipient grad. studies scholarship, 1976-77. Mem. Am. Math. Soc., Am. Phys. Soc., Am. Geophys. Union. Achievements include development of models for simulation of flow and transport of chemicals and radionuclides in air, water and geological media, of stochastic based criteria for the evaluation of environmental/health monitoring network designs, of remedial action strategies for hazardous/nuclear wastes site clean-up; characterization of scale dependent rock properties for analysis and survivability of deep underground structures subject to shock wave impulses; structural stability criteria for the construction and performance of new and improved materials; modelling of surface physics processes and thin film growth; Neuromorphic Systems design & stability criteria; research in hazardous/nuclear waste technology and monitoring design for environmental systems, in atmospheric chemistry and physics of air pollution, in physics of state transition in solids, and in image formation, compression of complex information, and associative memory in neural webworks. Address: PO Box 50058 Minneapolis MN 55405-0058

ABISH, CECILE, artist; b. N.Y.C. m. Walter Abish. B.F.A., Bklyn. Coll., 1953. Instr. art Queens Coll. Vis. artist U. Mass, Amherst, Cooper Union, Harvard U. Solo exhbns. include Newark Coll. Engring., 1968, Inst. Contemporary Art, Boston, 1974, U. Md., 1975, Alessandra Gallery, N.Y.C., 1977, Wright State U., Dayton, Ohio, 1978, Carpenter Ctr., Cambridge, Mass., 1979, Anderson Gallery, Va. Commonwealth U., Richmond, 1981, SUNY-Stony Brook, 1982, Ctr. for Creative Photography, Tucson, 1984, Books & Co., N.Y.C., 1996; group exhbns.: Detroit Inst. Art, 1969, Aldrich Mus. Art, 1971, 10 Bleecker St., N.Y.C., 1972, Lakeview Ctr. Arts, Peoria, Ill., 1972, Bykert Gallery, N.Y.C., 1971-74, Michael Walls Gallery, N.Y.C., 1975, Fine Arts Bldg. Gallery, N.Y.C., 1976, Mus. Modern Art, N.Y.C., 1976, Hudson River Mus., 1979, Atlanta Arts Festival, 1980, New Mus., N.Y.C., 1980, 81, Kuntsgebaude, Stuttgart, Fed. Republic Germany, 1981, Long Beach (Calif.) Mus., 1983, Edith C. Blum Art Inst., Bard Coll., Annandale-on-Hudson, N.Y., 1984, Mus. Modern Kunst, Vienna, Austria, 1985, U. R.I., Kingston, 1985, Art Defense Galleries, Paris, 1993, Architektur Zentrum, Vienna, 1993, Artists Space, N.Y.C., 1994, Islip Art Mus., N.Y., 1995, P.S. 1 Contemporary Art Ctr., N.Y., 1999; numerous commns.; represented in permanent collections; published photo works: Firsthand, 1978, Chinese Crossing, 1986, 99: The New Meaning, 1990. Nat. Endowment Arts fellow, 1975, 77, 80; CAPS fellow, 1975. Mem. Coll. Art Assn. Office: Cooper Station PO Box 485 New York NY 10276-0485

ABIZAID, JOHN PHILIP, military officer; b. Redwood City, Calif., Apr. 1, 1951; m. Kathleen Denton; children: Sharon, Chritine, David. Grad., US Mil. Acad., 1973; Infantry Officer Basic & Advanced Training, Armed Forces Staff Coll.; MA in Area Studies, Harvard U.; Olmsted scholar, U. Jordan, Amman. Commd. 2nd lt. U.S. Army, 1973, advanced through grades to gen., 2003; comdt. cadets U.S. Mil. Acad., West Point, NY, 1997-99; comdr. First Infantry Div., Wurzburg, Germany, 1999—2000; dir. of strategic plans and policy Joint Staff, Washington, 2000—01, dir., 2001—03; dep. comdr., Combined Forces Command U.S. Ctl. Command, MacDill AFB, Fla., 2003, comdr., 2003—. US Army War Coll. sr. fellowship Hoover Institution, Stanford U. Decorated Bronze Star US Dept. of Defense; recipient Disting. Svc. medal, Superior Svc. medal, Legion of Merit, Combat Infantryman's Badge, Master Parachutist Badge with Gold Star, Expert Infantryman's Badge. Office: US Ctrl Command 7115 S Boundary Blvd MacDill AFB Tampa FL 33621-5101*

ABLARD, CHARLES DAVID, lawyer; b. Enid, Okla. s. Charles Ross and Mary M. (Pattie) A.; m. Doris Maria Perl, Nov. 14, 1959; children— Jennifer, Jonathan, Catherine BA, U. Okla., 1952, JD, 1954; LLM, George Washington U., 1959. Bar: D.C. Jud. officer U.S. Post Office Dept., Washington, 1958-60; ptnr. Ablard and Harrison, Washington, 1960-63; v.p., counsel Mag. Pubs.

Assn., Washington, 1963-69; gen. counsel USIA, Washington, 1969-72; assoc. dep. atty. gen. Dept. Justice, Washington, 1972-74; assoc. dean Vt. Law Sch., South Royalton, 1974; gen. counsel Dept. Army, Washington, 1975-77; ptnr. Gage and Tucker, Washington, 1979-92, Faegre and Benson, Washington and Mpls., 1992-97, Perkins, Smith, Cohen & Crowe, Washington and Boston, 1997—. Adj. prof. Cath. U., Washington, 1984; mem. Fgn. Srv. Grievance Bd., 1998—. Contbr. articles to profl. jours. Bd. dirs. Hist. Alexandria Found., Pub. Diplomacy Found.; commr. Alexandria Hist. Restoration and Preservation Commn.; mem. coun. Adminstrv. Conf. U.S., Washington, 1970-73; mem. Bd. Internat. Broadcasting, Washington, 1980-84; bd. dirs. Radio Free Europe/Radio Liberty, Washington, 1983-84. With USAF, 1954-56. Fellow Ctr. for Internat. Studies, Cambridge U., Eng., 1974; recipient Profl. Achievement award George Washington U., 1976, Disting. Civilian Service award Dept. Army, 1975, 76 Fellow Am. Bar Found. (life); mem. ABA (chmn. adminstrv. law sect. 1984-85), English Speaking Union U.S. (bd. dirs.). Clubs: Cosmos (Washington); Army-Navy Country (Arlington, Va.); Small Point (Maine). Republican. Episcopalian. Home: 803 Hall Pl Alexandria VA 22302-3405 Office: 1001 Pennsylvania Ave NW Washington DC 20004-2505

ABLE, EDWARD H., association executive; BA in Chemistry, Emory U., 1967; MBA, George Washington U., 1973. Cert. assn. exec. Staff aide to U.S. Senator Richard B. Russell, 1967-68; staff aide to U.S. Senator Mike Mansfield, 1968; acct. exec. Exec. Cons., Inc., Washington, 1971-73; asst. dir. resident assoc. program Smithsonian Instn., Washington, 1973-77; exec. v.p. Am. Soc. Landscape Architects, Washington, 1977-86; pres., CEO Am. Assn. Mus., Washington, 1986—. Lectr. in field. Author: (with others) Principles of Association Management, 1988. Bd. dirs. Nat. Humanities Alliance, 1986—, officer, 1990—, Nat. Cultural Alliance, 1991—; mem. founding bd. dirs. Nat. Ctr. Non-profit Bds., 1987—, vice chair, 1993-99; coun. mem. U.S. Com. World Heritage, 1988—; bd. mem. Nat. Ctr. for Non-Profit Enterprise. Capt. U.S. Army, 1968-71. Decorated Bronze Star. Fellow Am. Soc. Assn. Execs. (bd. dirs. 1987-90, chmn. mgmt. conf. 1988, instr. 1985—, frequent speaker meetings and convs. 1981—, chmn. grad. studies commn. 1986-87, mem. nat. edn. com. 1984-86, vice-chmn. 1985, chmn. 1986, bd. dirs. membership dirs. sect. 1982-83, Key award 1990, vice-chmn. fellows 1987-88, chmn. 1988-89), bd. dirs., 1994—; Greater Washington Soc. Assn. Execs. (chief exec. officer conf. com. 1982-83), Univ. Club (Washington). Office: Am Assn Museums 1575 I St NW Ste 400 Washington DC 20005-1113

ABLE, KENNETH PAUL, biology professor; b. Louisville, Feb. 5, 1944; s. William Morris and Viola (Bridwell) A.; m. Mary Allen, Jan. 28, 1967; 1 child, Joshua. BS, U. Louisville, 1966, MS, 1968; PhD, U. Ga., 1971. Asst. prof. SUNY, Albany, 1971-77, assoc. prof., 1977-84, prof., 1984—2003, prof. emeritus, 2003—. NSF grantee, 1974-2000. Fellow Animal Behavior Soc., Am. Ornithologists' Union (treas. 1981-85, elective councilor 1999-2002, William Brewster medal 1996); mem. Internat. Soc. Behavioral Ecology, Am. Soc. Naturalists, Am. Birding Assn. (dir. 1986-95, 99—2003). Business E-Mail: KenAble@direcway.com.

ABLE, WARREN WALTER, natural resource company executive, physician; b. Seymour, Ind., Mar. 3, 1932; s. Walter Cudwith and Edith (Harmon) A.; m. Joan Graham, May 6, 1956; children: Susan, Nancy, Cynthia, Wally. AB, Ind. U., 1953, MD, 1956, JD, 1968. Bar: Ind. 1968. Intern Indpls. Gen. Hosp., 1956-57; surgeon USPHS, 1957-59; pres. Able Ventures, Inc., Columbus, Ind., 1968—. Bd. dirs. Salin Bank & Trust. Editor: Lawyer's Medical Cyclopedia, 1967-68. Bd. dirs. Bartholomew Consol. Sch. Corp., Columbus, 1970-74; trustee Christian Theol. Sem., 1991—2003. Mem. AMA, Ind. Med. Soc., ABA, Ind. Bar Soc., Nat. Benevolent Assn. (bd. dirs. 1983-90). Democrat. Mem. Christian Ch. (Disciples Of Christ). Avocations: aviation, farming. Home and Office: 4253 E Windsor Ln Columbus IN 47201-9681

ABLER, RONALD FRANCIS, geography educator; b. Milw., May 30, 1939; s. Ambrose Francis and Lucille Bernice A.; m. Barbara Ruth Bailey, Apr. 23, 1983; children: Frederick F., Kenneth J. BA, U. Minn., Mpls., 1963, MA, 1966, PhD, 1968. Prof. Pa. State U., University Park, 1967-95; exec. dir. Assn. Am. Geographers, Washington, 1990—2002. Dir. geography program NSF, Washington, 1984-88; vis. prof. Stockholm Sch. Econs., 1982-83, U. Minn., Mpls., 1972-74, U. B.C., Vancouver, 1971. Editor: A Comparative Atlas of America's Great Cities, 1976; co-editor: Atlas of Pennsylvania, 1989, Geography's Inner Worlds, 1992. Councilman State College (Pa.) Borough, 1978-82. Recipient Publ. award Geog. Soc. Chgo., 1976, Centenary medal Royal Scottish Geog. Soc., 1990, Spl. Recognition award NSF, Washington, 1988, Victoria medal Royal Geog. Soc./Inst. Brit. Geographers, 1996, Samuel Finley Breese Morse medal Am. Geog. Soc., 2004. Fellow AAAS, Assn. Am. Geographers (pres. 1985-86, exec. dir. 1990—2002, Honors 1995), Cosmos Club, Internat. Geog. Union (sec. gen. and treas. 2000—). Avocation: beekeeping. Home: 2246 N Pollard St Arlington VA 22207-3805 Office: Internat Geog Union 2246 N Pollard St Arlington VA 22207-3805 Office Phone: 202-431-6271. E-mail: rabler@aag.org.

ABLER, WILLIAM LEWIS, paleopsychologist; b. Chgo., Dec. 6, 1943; s. Julius and Elizabeth (Engelman) A. B.A., U. Pa., 1966, M.A., 1968, Ph.D., 1971. Postdoctoral fellow Stanford U., Calif., 1971-74; asst. prof. Ill. Inst. Tech., Chgo., 1974-81; paleopsychology researcher, Chgo., 1981— . Author: Shop Tactics, 1973. Contbg. author: Scientfic Illustration: A Guide for the Beginning Artist. Contbr. articles to sci. jours. Patentee in field. Mem. Linguistic Soc. Am., Acoustical Soc. Am., Entomol. Soc. Am. Home: 3350 S Michigan Ave Chicago IL 60616-3818

ABLESON, DONALD WILLIAM, automobile industry executive; b. Ypsilanti, Mich., May 24, 1937; s. Guy Franklin and Katherine Ann (Pratt) A.; m. Muriel Ruth Studt, Aug. 22, 1959; children: Michael, Bruce, Christopher, Kimberly. B of Ind. Engring., Kettering U., Flint, Mich., 1960; MBA, Mich. State U., 1978. Registered profl. engr., Mich. Engr. in charge GMC-Fisher Body, Warren, Mich., 1972-78, gen. supt. Livonia, Mich., 1978-80, GMC-Pontiac, Mich., 1980-84; plant mgr. GM-Chevrolet-Pontiac-Canada, Pontiac, 1984-87, Tarrytown, N.Y., 1987-90, program mgr. Warren, Mich., 1990-96; dir. splty. vehicles GM-Mid/Luxury Car Group, Warren, 1997-98; exec. dir. splty. vehicle activity NA Car Group, Warren, 1999—. Chmn., dir. Westchester C.C. Found., Mt. Pleasant, N.Y., 1988-94; dir. GMI Alumni Bd., Flint, 1980; chmn. Birmingham (Mich.) Mid. Sch. Com., 1983, West Bloomfield (Mich.) Cable TV Com., 1985. Recipient citation Birmingham Sch. Bd., 1983, proclamation Westchester County, 1990. Mem. Soc. Automotive Engring. (bd. dirs. 1987-90, chmn. 1965-68, chmn. Detroit sect. 1982-83, chmn. sects. bd. 1987-88, chmn. strategic planning com. 1990-91, chmn. bd. trustees SAE Found. 1992-98, chmn. fin. com. 1994-97, pres. 1999-2000, pres. SAE Found. Can. 1999—). Avocations: skiing, sailing, photography, wildlife, hiking. Office: GM Corp 480-210-251 30001 Van Dyke Ave Warren MI 48093-2350

ABLIN, RICHARD JOEL, immunologist, educator; b. Chgo., May 15, 1940; s. Robert Benjamin and Minnie Edith (Gordon) A.; m. Linda Lee Lutwack; 1 son, Michael David. AB, Lake Forest Coll., 1962; PhD in Microbiology, SUNY, Buffalo, 1967; DSc (hon.), Lake Forest Coll., 2005. Diplomate Am. Bd. Clin. Immunology and Allergy; cert. specialist in pub. health and med. lab. microbiology Nat. Registry Microbiologists of Am. Acad. Microbiology. Grad. asst. dept. biology SUNY-Buffalo, 1963-65, research asst., summer 1963, research fellow, 1965-66; USPHS postdoctoral fellow dept. microbiology Sch. Medicine, lectr., lab instr., 1966-68; instr., research asst. Rosary Hill Coll., 1965-66; research cons. program med. edn. AID, Paraguay, 1968; dir. div. immunology Millard Fillmore Hosp. Rsch. Inst., Buffalo, 1968-70; head sect. immunology, renal unit Meml. Hosp. of Springfield, 1970-73; dir. sect. immunobiology div. urology dept. surgery Cook County Hosp. and Hektoen Inst. for Med. Research, Chgo., 1973-75, sr. sci. officer div. immunology, 1976-83; sr. mem. sci. staff, clin. immunologist Cook County Hosp., 1973-75; asst. prof. medicine So. Ill. U., 1971-73; assoc. prof. microbiology Univ. Health Sci. (Chgo. Med. Sch.), 1973-74; rsch. assoc. prof. urology, dir. immunology unit dept. urology SUNY, Stony Brook, 1983—89; pres., dir. Robert Benjamin Ablin Found. for Cancer Rsch., Evergreen Park, Ill., 1979—; dir. sci. investigation Tetragenex Pharms., Inc., Park Ridge, NJ, 1991—2003, consulting scientist, 2003—. Mem. Univ. Senate, 1986-89, 89-92, Univ. Governing Coms., 1984-92; acad. del. United Univ. Professions, 1986-88, 88-90; vis. rsch. prof. Coll. Medicine U. Ariz., Tucson, Ariz., 2001-04; rsch. prof. dept. microbiology and immunology Ariz. Coll. Medicine and the Ariz. Cancer Ctr., Tucson, 2005—; organizer, presenter, instr., participant numerous nat. and internat. profl. meetings, symposia, seminars. Editor: Allergologia et Immunopathologia, 1980—84; co-editor: Cancer Metastasis-Biology and Treatment, 2000—; contbg. editor: Current Perspectives in Allergologia and Immunopathologia, 1974—84, Ill. Med. Jour., 1975—88, Cancer Watch, 2001—; adv. editor: Jour. Cancer, 1976—89, assoc. editor: Low Temperature Medicine, 1975—, Jour. Investigational Allergology and Clin. Immunology (formerly Allergologia et Immunopathologia), 1985—95, Jour. Exptl. Therapeutics and Oncology, 2003—; mem. editl. bd. Immunology and Allergy Practice, 1979—95, Medikon, 1974—80, TumorDiagnostik and Therapie, 1980—98, Am. Jour. Reproductive Immunology and Microbiology, 1980—91; mem. editl. adv. bd.: Med. Sci. Rsch., 1984—2000; mem. editl. bd. Cellular and Molecular Biology, 1985—87, Chemistry Today, 1991—97, Early Pregnancy: Biology and Medicine, 1995—; mem. editl. bd.: Internat. Jour. Oncology, 1996—; mem. editl. bd. Current Oncology, 1998—, Advances in Therapy, 1999—, Prostate Jour., 1999—2001, Bratislava Med. Jour., 1999—, Exptl. Biology and Medicine, 2000—, UroOncology, 2000—, Annals Clin. and Lab.Sci., 2000—, Clin. and Applied Immunology Revs., 2001—, Clin. and Diagnostic Lab. Immunology, 2002—, Cancer Therapy, 2003—; contbr. chapters to books, articles to profl. jours.; mem. editl. bd.: Current Opinion in Oncology, 2005. Chief Sangamo Nation Y-Indian Guides, Springfield, 1972-73; mgr. Skokie Indians' Boys' Baseball, Ill., 1973-74, 77, 80, 81, bd. dirs., 1979-83, exec. v.p., 1981-82; mgr. Little League Three Villages, Setauket, N.Y., 1986; cubmaster N.W. Suburban coun. Boy Scouts Am., 1974-78, asst. scoutmaster, 1975-77; mem. exploring divsn. Suffolk County coun. Boy Scouts Am., 1985-88; pres., dir. Spirit of Chgo. Hockey Club Found., Evergreen Park, Ill., 1982—. Recipient Nat. Pres. Leader's Dist. Boy Scouts Am., 1975; named Cubmaster of Yr. Boy Scouts Am., 1977 Fellow: Assn. Clin. Scientists, Am. Coll. Cryosurgery (adv. bd. 1977—78, v.p. 1977—79, parliamentarian 1977—79, adv. bd. 1980—81, 1984—99), Am. Coll. Allergy and Immunology, Indian Cryogenics Coun. (hon.); mem.: AAAS, Metastasis Rsch. Soc., Am. Assn. Cancer Rsch., Am. Assn. Immunologists, Am. Soc. Microbiology, Assn. Med. Lab Immunologists, Brit. Assn. Surg. Oncology, Buffalo Collegium Immunology, Internat. Soc. Andrology, Internat. Soc. Chronobiology, Internat. Soc. Immunology Reprodn., N.Y. Acad. Scis., Soc. Cryobiology, Soc. Exptl. Biology and Medicine, Soc. Leukocyte Biology, Soc. Protozoologists, Soc. Study Reprodn., Transplantation Soc., Japan Soc. Low Temperature Medicine (hon.), Internat. Soc. Cryosurgery (hon.; pres. 1977—80, bd. dirs. 1980—, hon. life pres.), Cryoimmunotherapeutic Study Group (chmn.), Witebsky Ctr. Microbial Pathogenesis and Immunology, Sigma Xi, Phi Beta Kappa (Theta of Ill. at Lake Forest Coll.). Achievements include identification of prostate specific antigen (PSA), used as tumor marker in prostate cancer, and of human thymic specific antigen providing means for differentiation of thymic lymphocytes from other lymphoid cells and the development of antithymocyte globulin (selectively immunosuppressive for thymocytes) used in renal allograft (transplant) recipients; development of concept of cryoimmunotherapy for treatment of cancer. Office: Univ Ariz Coll Medicine Health Scis Ctr Dept Micro and Immunology 1501 N Campbell Ave PO Box 245049 Tucson AZ 85724-5049 Office Phone: 520-662-8319. Business E-Mail: ablinrj@email.arizona.edu. *One of the saddest things in life is to have the opportunity to do something and not to take advantage of it.*

ABLOW, JOSEPH, artist, educator; b. Salem, Mass., Aug. 16, 1928; s. Benjamin and Eva (Smith) A.; m. Roselyn Karol, June 23, 1956; 1 child, Rachel. BA, Bennington Coll., 1954; MA, Harvard U., 1955. Instr. Middlebury (Vt.) Coll., 1955-58; asst. prof. Bard Coll., Annandale, NY, 1959-61, Wellesley (Mass.) Coll., 1962-63; assoc. prof. Boston U., 1972-95, chmn. div. of art, 1964-67, prof. of art, 1972-95, prof. emeritus, 1996—2003. Vis. assoc. prof. MIT, Cambridge, 1969-70; vis. prof. Amherst (Mass.) Coll., 1975-76, vis. artist, 2003; vis. scholar Cambridge (Mass.) Humanities Seminar, MIT, 1973-82; mem. adv. com. Bunting Inst., Radcliffe Coll., Cambridge, 1984-87; lectr. Amherst Coll., 1975, 78, 82, Univ. N.H., 1980, 82, 2005, Inst. of Contemporary Art, Boston, 1980, Nieman Found., Harvard Univ., 1982, 83, MIT, 1984, St. John's Univ., Collegeville, Minn., 1986, Fitchburg Art Mus., 1987, Salve Regina Coll., Newport, R.I., 1990, and others. One-man shows include Boris Mirski Gallery, Boston, 1961, 65, 69, Pucker Gallery, Boston, 1979, 81, 83, 87, 91, 94, 2001, The Trustman Art Gallery, Simmons Coll., Boston, 1983, Fitchburg Art Mus., Miami U., Oxford, Ohio, 1987; retrospective exhbn. Amherst Coll., 2003, Boston U., 2004; represented in permanent collections Bard Coll., Middlebury Coll., DeCordova and Dana Mus., Univ. Mass. Harbor Campus, Mead Art Gallery, Amherst Coll., Rose Art Mus., Brandeis U., others; contbg. editor Bostonia Mag., Boston, 1986-89; contbr. articles to profl. jours. Mem. bd. dirs. Jewish Cultural Endowment, Boston Univ., 1988-95. Recipient Paige traveling fellowship Mus. Fine Arts, Boston, 1951, Fulbright grant in painting, Paris, 1958-59, Silver medal award for best article of the yr. Coun. for Advancement and Support of Edn., 1987, Boston U. Sch. for the Arts disting. faculty award, 1996. Avocation: music. Home: 16 Monmouth Ct Brookline MA 02446-5634 Office: Boston U Sch Visual Art 855 Commonwealth Ave Boston MA 02215-1303

ABLOW, KEITH RUSSELL, writer; b. Boston, Nov. 23, 1961; s. Allan Murray and Jeanette Norma (Mezansky) A. ScB, Brown U., l983; MD, Johns Hopkins U., l987. Reporter Newsweek, N.Y.C., 1984; columnist Balt. Evening Sun, Boston Herald, 1985-89, Washington Post, 1990—; intern in psychiatry Tufts U.-New Eng. Med. Ctr. Hosps., Boston, 1987-88, resident, 1988-91; chief resident 1991—, 1991-92; columnist Washington Post, 1990—; cons. psychiatrist WCVB TV, Boston, 1992—; med. dir. Tri-City Mental Health Ctr., 1992-94; assoc. med. dir. Heritage Health Systems, 1993-94; corr. Med. News Network, 1993—; med. dir. FHC New Eng., 1994-96; outpatient psychiatrist Boston Regional Med. Ctr., 1996—. Med. editor Lifetime Med. TV, L.A. and Astoria, N.Y., l986-89; founder, CEO, memorymountain.com. Author: (novels) Denial, 1997, Projection, 1999, Compulsion, 2002, Psychopath, 2003, Murder Suicide, 2004, The Architect, 2005, (non-fiction) Medical School: Getting In, Staying In, Staying Human, 1987, How to Cope With Depression, 1989, To Wrestle With Demons, 1992, Anatomy of a Psychiatric Illness, 1993, The Strange Case of Dr. Kappler, 1994, Without Mercy: The Shocking True Story of a Doctor Who Murdered, 1996, Inside the Mind of Scott Peterson, 2005; columnist Mental Health Infosource Website, 1996—. Trustee White Pines Coll., Chester, N.H., 1989-91. Recipient Optimate award Am. Soc. Profl. Italians, 1990. Mem. AAAS, AMA (sr. editor, creative cons. Pulse 1986-87, Jerry L. Pettis award 1987), Am. Psychiat. Assn., Am. Med. Writers Assn. (Will Solimene award 1991, 92, Best Trade Book, 1993). Democrat. Avocation: writing fiction.*

ABLOW, ROZ KAROL (ROSELYN KAROL ABLOW), painter, curator; b. Allentown, Pa. BA, Bennington Coll., 1954; student, Boston U. Fellow Bunting Inst., 1988; instr. Newton Arts Ctr., Mass., 1989-92, New Arts Ctr., Newton, Mass., 1993-95. Curator New Arts Ctr., Newton, Mass., 1994. One-person shows at Amherst (Mass.) Coll., 1976, Impressions Gallery, Mass., 1979, Clark Gallery, Lincoln, Mass., 1984, Pine Manor Coll., Brookline, Mass., 1991, Miami U., Oxford, Ohio, 1995, Art Guild of Old Forge, NY, 2002; group shows include Smithsonian Traveling Exhbn., 1978-80, Fitchburg Art Mus., 1988, Bunting Inst., Radcliffe Coll., 1988, David Brown Gallery, Provincetown, Mass., 1988, Pratt Graphic Ctr. Internat. Monotype Show, 1989, Gallery 30, Burlingame, Calif., 1993, New Art Ctr., Newton, Mass., 1994, Pucker Gallery, 2004, others; represented in permanent collections Mobil Corp., Chemical Bank, NY, New Eng. Mutual Life Ins. Co., Boston, Conn. Gen. Life, Hartford, Sears, Roebuck & Co., Chgo., Broadway Crown Plaza Hotel, NY, Pucker Gallery, Boston. Bunting Inst. fellow Radcliffe Coll., 1988; grantee Mass. Arts Lottery Coun., 1990-91. Address: Pucker Gallery Boston MA 02116 Office Phone: 617-734-3652.

ABNEY, MARTHA MCEACHERN, music educator; b. Bremen, Ga., Dec. 6, 1957; d. James Sterling and Nancy Hughes McEachern; m. Jeffrey Robert Abney, June 8, 2002; children: Laura, Steve, Ginger, Sam, Ellen, Peter. B of Music Edn., West Ga. Coll., 1987, M of Music Edn., 1992. Tchr. music Bremen City Schs., Ga., 1987—98, Carroll County Schs., Villa Rica, 1998—, State U. West Ga., Carrollton, 1999—. Music dir. Bremen 1st United Meth. Ch., 1992—95. Mem.: Ga. Music Educators Assn., Am. Choral Dirs. Assn., Spirit Atlanta Alumni Assn. (assoc.). Republican. Methodist. Home: 34 Woodstream Ln Tallapoosa GA 30176 Office: Villa Rica High Sch 600 Rocky Branch Rd Villa Rica GA 30180 Office Phone: 770-459-5185. Business E-Mail: martie.abney@carrollcountyschools.com.

ABNEY, SHERRIE R., lawyer, mediator, arbitrator; d. Clyde A. and Helen R. Hughey; children: Donald J. Raley, Teresa Gay Quarm, Darrell W. Raley. BA in Edn., Ctrl. State U., 1971; MFA, U. Okla., 1972; MEd, U. Tex., El Paso, Tex., 1979; JD, Okla. City (Okla.) Sch. Law, 1988. CLU The Am. Coll., 1984. Mgr. N.Y. Life Ins., Dallas, 1983—90; prin. Law Offices Sherrie R. Abney, Dallas and Carrollton, Tex., 1991—. Co-founder, bd. dirs. Tex. Collaborative Law Coun., Dallas, 2004—; chmn. ADR Sect., Dallas, 2001—02. Co-author: (practice forms and materials) Protocols of Practice, Participation Agreement and Practice Forms for Civil Collaborative Lawyers. Mem.: Coll. State Bar Tex., Dallas (Tex.) Bar Assn. (chmn. collaborative law study group 2004—), Assn. Atty. Mediators (bd. dirs. 2003—). Office: Law Offices of Sherrie R Abney 2840 Keller Springs Road Ste 204 Carrollton TX 75006 Office Phone: 972-417-7198. Office Fax: 972-417-9655. E-mail: sra169@comcast.net.

ABO, RONALD KENT, freelance/self-employed architect; b. Rupert, Idaho, July 10, 1946; s. Isamu and Ameria (Hachiya) A.; m. Lisa A. Wiesley; children: Tamiko N., Reiko D., Ryan A., Emily A. BArch, U. Colo., 1969. Lic. architect, Colo. Designer SLP & Ptnrs., Denver, 1968-71; dir. Community Design Ctr., Denver, 1971-72; assoc. Barker, Rinker, Seacat, Denver, 1972-76; pvt. practice Denver, 1976-80; pres. Abo Gude Architects, Denver, 1980-84, Ron Abo Architects, Denver, 1984-91, Abo Architects PC, Denver, 1991-94, Abo Copeland Architecture, 1995—2002, ACLP Architecture, Inc., 2002—. Design instr., thesis advisor U. Colo., Denver. Prin. works include Morrison Horticultre Ctr., 1983 (W.O.O.D. Inc. citation 1983), Highland Square, 1982 (AIA citation 1983), Roxborough Elem. Sch., 1990, Tropical Discovery Ctr. Denver Zoo, 1992, New Denver Internat. Airport Concourse Bldgs., 1993, Nederland Middle/H.S., 1996, Julesburg Welcome Ctr., 1997, Rocky Mountain Mfg. Acad., 1998. Active Denver Comty. Leadership Forum, 1986, Colfax-on-the-Hill, 1988—, U. Colo. Alumni Bd., Workforce Devel. Bd., 1990—, Savid House. Recipient Design Excellence award W.O.O.D. Inc., Denver, 1982, Martin Luther King Bus. Social Responsibility award, 1998. Mem. AIA (bd. dirs., pres.-elect Denver chpt. 1990, pres. 1991, pres.-elect Colo. chpt. 1997, pres. 1998), Asian C. of C. (pres. 1998), Colo. Aikido Assn. (head instr. Denver Buddhist Temple Aikido), Lions Club (bd. dirs.). Democrat. Avocation: aikido (4th degree black belt). Office: ACLP Architecture INC 1660 Wynkoop St Ste 900 Denver CO 80202 E-mail: rka@aclparchitecture.com.

ABOLINS, MARIS ARVIDS, physicist, educator; b. Liepaja, Latvia, Feb. 5, 1938; came to U.S., 1949, naturalized, 1956; s. Arvids Gustavs and Olga Elizabete (Grintals) A.; m. Frances Delano, Dec. 19, 1959 BS magna cum laude, U. Wash., 1960; MS, U. Calif.-San Diego, 1962, PhD, 1965. Research asst. U. Calif.-San Diego, 1960-65; physicist Lawrence Berkeley Lab., 1965-68; assoc. prof. physics Mich. State U., East Lansing, 1968-73, prof. physics, 1973—. Cons. U.S. Dept. Energy; sci. assoc. CERN, Geneva, 1976-77; vis. research scientist, Saclay, France, 1977, Fermi Nat. Accelerator Lab., 1990-92, Saclay, France, 1997; mem. tech. adv. com. Argonne Nat. Lab., 1971-72; mem. prep. com. Fermilab, 1978-79; chmn. Fermilab Users' Exec. Com., 1982-83; mem. SSC Users Exec. Com., 1988-91; chmn. bd. dirs. ATLAS Trigger/DAQ Instnl., 1997-99. NSF research grantee, 1971—; Disting. Faculty award 1998. Fellow Am. Phys. Soc. (exec. com. div. particles and fields 1984-86); mem. AAAS, Patria, Phi Beta Kappa, Sigma Xi. Home: 1430 Fairoaks Ct East Lansing MI 48823-1812 Office: Mich State U Dept Physics And Astro East Lansing MI 48824 Office Phone: 517-355-9200 x2121. Business E-Mail: abolins@pa.msu.edu.

ABORN, FOSTER LITCHFIELD, insurance company executive; b. Providence, July 8, 1934; s. John Russell and Helene Cecile (Hesse) A.; m. Sara Holbrook; children: Justin, Hilary. BA, Dartmouth Coll., 1956, MBA, 1957; exec. prog., 1978. Asst. v.p. Mellon Bank N.A., Pitts., 1957-68; asst. investment officer John Hancock Ins. Co., 1968—72, second v.p., 1972—78, v.p., 1978—84, sr. v.p., Treas. & Fin. Services, 1984—87, sr. v.p., Corp. Mktg. Rsch., 1984, sector head, Investment & Pension Group, 1987—92; vice chmn. & chief investment officer John Hancock Fin. Svcs., Inc., 1992—2000; bd. dir. John Hancock Life Ins., 2000—. Dir.,mem. of com. of fin., John Hancock Life Insurance Co.; mem. adv. com. One Liberty Ventures; mem. investment com., Kairos Fund, L.P.; adv. dir., Debt Exchange, LLC; dir., Seniorlink Incorp., cMarket, Inc. Trustee, dir., & chmn. fin. com. Beth Israel Deaconess Med. Ctr.; chmn. investment com. Controlled Risk Ins. Co.; chmn. exec. adv. bd. & capital campaign steering com. Bay Cove Human Services; dir. SquashBusters; overseer Huntington Theatre Co. Mem. Univ. Club Boston. Office: John Hancock Finl Svcs PO Box 111 C-02-01 Boston MA 02117-0111

ABOTT, MICHAEL LARRY, physician; b. Bklyn., Mar. 22, 1952; s. Jerome and Lynn (Gross) A.; m. Beth Ellen Friedberg, Aug. 10, 1975; children: Stephen, Richard. BS, Bklyn. Coll., 1974; MD, Autonomous U. de Guadalajara, Mex., 1978. Diplomate Am. Bd. Internal Medicine, Am. Bd. Pulmonary Diseases, Am. Bd. Critical Care, Am. Bd. Geriatrics. Pvt. practice, Bklyn., 1984—; assoc. attending physician N.Y. Meth. Hosp., Bklyn., 1984—, Victory Meml. Hosp., Bklyn., 1984—, Maimonides Med. Ctr., Bklyn., 1995—; CEO, United Med. Assocs., 1998—. Med. dir. Lily Pond Nursing Home, S.I., 1984—, Garden of Eden Home, Bklyn., 1984-2001; dir. pulmonary Medspect Imaging, Bklyn., 1990—; mem. steering utility com. Bklyn. Physicians, Ind. Physicians Assn., 1995, mem. exec. com. Meth. Hosp., 1995; chmn. quality assurance N.Y. Meth. Hosp., 2001—. Fellow ACP, Am. Coll. Chest Physicians; mem. AMA, Am. Acad. Geriatrics, Soc. Critical Care Medicine, N.Y. State Soc. Internal Medicine, Thoracic Soc., Kings County Med. Soc. Office: 7124 18th Ave Brooklyn NY 11204 also: 263 7th Ave Brooklyn NY 11215 Office Phone: 718-234-3333.

ABOU-SAYED, HATEM, plastic surgeon; s. Ahmed S. and Kadreya E. Abou-Sayed. BS, U. Calif., Berkeley, 1992; MD, U. Calif. San Francisco, 1996. Diplomate Am. Bd. of Surgery, 2002, Am. Bd. of Plastic Surgery, 2004. Intern dept. surgery Mass. Gen. Hosp., Boston, 1996—97, resident dept. surgery, 1997—2001; resident divsn. plastic surgery U. Calif., 2001—03; plastic surgeon Plastic Surgery of Palm Beach, Palm Springs, Fla., 2003—. Musician: (popular music) Hookah Smoke. Recipient Academic Excellence award, UCSF Alumni Faculty Assn., 1996; scholar Regents scholar, U. Calif.-Berkeley, 1988—92; Nat. Merit Scholar Edward Frank Kraft, 1988. Mem.: Palm Beach County Med. Soc., AMA, ACS (assoc.), Alpha Omega Alpha, Phi Beta Kappa, Eta Kappa Nu, Tau Beta Pi. Office: Plastic Surgery of Palm Beach PA 1620 South Congress Ave Ste 100 Palm Springs FL 33461 Office Fax: 561-968-1800. Personal E-mail: temsayed@hotmail.com.

ABOUSSIE, MARILYN, retired judge; b. Wichita Falls, Tex., June 9, 1948; m. John A. Hay, Jr., Dec. 9, 1973; 1 child, John A. III. BA, Midwestern U., 1969; JD, U. Tex., 1974. Bar: Tex. 1974. Assoc. Foreman, Dyess, Prewett, Rosenberg & Henderson, Houston, 1974-76; pvt. practice San Angelo, Tex., 1976-78; ptnr. Smith, Davis, Rose, Finley & Hofmann, San Angelo, Tex., 1978-83; judge 340th Dist. Ct., San Angelo, 1983-86; justice Tex. Ct. Appeals, Austin, 1986-98, chief justice, 1998—2003; ret., 2003. Mem. ABA, State Bar Assn. of Tex. Episcopalian. Office Phone: 325-658-9758.

ABRAHAM, ANDREW, lawyer; b. Phoenix, Jan. 14, 1958; s. Willard B. and Dale W. (Wiener) A.; m. Ann N. Boland, May 29, 1983. BA, Claremont McKenna, 1979; JD, Ariz. State U., 1982. Bar: Ariz. 1982, U.S. Dist. Ct. Ariz. 1982, U.S. Ct. Appeals (9th cir.) 1982. Law clk. Ariz. Supreme Ct., Phoenix, 1982-83; with Burch and Cracchiolo, Phoenix, 1983—. Judge pro tem Maricopa County Ariz. Superior Ct. Mng. editor Ariz. State U. Law Jour., 1981-82. Mem. Ariz. State U. Coll. Law Alumni Assn. (pres. 1991). Office: Burch and Cracchiolo 702 E Osborn PO Box 16882 Phoenix AZ 85011-6882 Office Phone: 602-274-7611. Business E-Mail: AAbraham@bcattorneys.com.

ABRAHAM, EDWARD, medical educator; b. Chgo., Apr. 17, 1952; s. Willard and Shirley Dale (Wiener) A.; m. Norma-May Isakow, Nov. 22, 1989 BA, Stanford U., 1974, MD, 1978. Diplomate Am. Bd. Internal Medicine, Critical Care. Asst. prof. UCLA Sch. Medicine, L.A., 1981—87, assoc. prof., 1987—93, U. Colo. Health Sciences Ctr., Denver, 1993—95, prof. medicine, 1995—2000, Roger Sherman Mitchell prof. pulmonary and critical care medicine, 2000—, head divsn. pulmonary scis. and critical care medicine, 2000—, vice chair dept. medicine, 2002—. Contbr. articles to profl. jours.; chpts. to books. Area program com. Am. Friends Svc. Com., Denver, 2004. Recipient Pres.'s citation, Soc. Critical Care Medicine, 1999, 2002, 2004. Fellow Am. Coll. Chest Physicians; mem. Soc. Critical Care Medicine (Young Investigator award 1985), ACP, Western Soc. Clin. Investigators, Shock Soc., Am. Fedn. Clin. Research. Avocation: jogging. Office: U Colo Health Sci Ctr Box C272 4200 E Ninth Ave Denver CO 80262 Office Phone: 303-315-3397. Office Fax: 303-315-5632. E-mail: edward.abraham@uchsc.edu.

ABRAHAM, HENRY JULIAN, political science professor; b. Offenbach am Main, Germany, Aug. 25, 1921; s. Fredrick and Louise (Kullmann) A.; m. Mildred Kosches, Apr. 13, 1954; children: Philip F., Peter D. AB summa cum laude, Kenyon Coll., 1948, LHD (hon.), 1972; MA, Columbia U., 1949; PhD, U. Pa., 1952; LLD (hon.), U. Hartford, 1982, Knox Coll., 1982; LittD (hon.), St. Joseph's U., 1987; LLD (hon.), Old Dominion U., 1996. Faculty U. Pa., 1949-72, prof. polit. sci., 1962-72; Doherty prof. govt. and fgn. affairs U. Va., 1971-78, James Hart prof., 1978-97, James Hart prof. emeritus, 1997—. Vis. prof. Swarthmore Coll., CCNY, Colo. U., Columbia U., Richmond Law Sch., Copenhagen U., U. Stockholm, Aarhus U., Lund U., Goteborg U., U. Oslo, U. Helsinki, U. Uppsala, U. Amsterdam, U. London, univs. in India and Iran, 1978, univs. in Peru, Bolivia, Brazil, Paraguay, Argentina, 1979, univs. in Japan, China, Taiwan, The Philippines, New Zealand, and Australia, 1982, univs. in Republic of Korea, 1982, 84. Author: Compulsory Voting, 1955, Government as Entrepreneur, 1956, Courts and Judges, 1959, Elements of Democratic Government, 1964, Essentials of National Government, 1971, Justices & Presidents, 1992, American Democracy, 1990, Justices, Presidents and Senators, 1999, The Judiciary, 1997, The Judicial Process, 1998, Freedom and the Court, 2003. Mem. com. on non-discrimintion Phila. Bd. Edn., 1962; mem. vis. com. on govt. Lehigh U., 1967-71; trustee fedn. Jewish Agys. Greater Phila., 1970-72, Kenyon Coll., 1987-93; mem. Va. Commn. on Bicentennial of Constn. of U.S., 1985-92, Va. Coun. on Human Rights, 1999-2002. Recipient award excellence undergrad. teaching U. Pa., 1959, 67, Kite and Key Teaching award, 1967, award excellence undergrad. teaching U. Va., 1978, Thomas Jefferson award U. Va., 1983, U. Va. Alumni Teaching award, 1986, Disting. Svc. award Va. Social Sci. Assn., 1982, Disting. Prof. award U. Va. Alumni Assn., 1986, First Lifetime Achievement award, org. sec. on law & courts, Am. polit., sci. Assn., 1993, others; NEH, 1975, 76, 78, 80, 81, NSF fellow, 1965, fellow Am. Philos. Soc., 1961-67, 79, Rockefeller Found. fellow, 1978, Earhart fellow, 1984, Bradley Found., 1989-97. Mem. Fellows in Am. Studies (pres. 1966), Am. Polit. Sci. Assn. (v.p. 1980-82), Raven Soc., Am. Soc. for Legal History, So. Polit. Sci. Ass. (rec. sec. 1980-81), Soc. of Fellows, English-Speaking Union, Met. Opera Guild, Nat. Trust, Golden Key, Greencroft Club (v.p. 1985-87, Charlottesville, Va.), Z Club, Imp Club, Yale Club (N.Y.C.), Capitol Hill Club, Oliver Turner Soc., Phi Beta Kappa (vis. scholar 1970-71), Pi Sigma Alpha, Pi Gamma Mu, Omicron Delta Kappa. Home: 250 Pantops Mountain Rd Apt 5311 Charlottesville VA 22911 Office: Univ Va 232 Cabell Hall Charlottesville VA 22904 Office Phone: 434-924-3192. *Basically—a commitment to hard work; to discipline; to a maintenance of a sense of humour; to a rejection of pompousness and egomania; to a resolute embrace of merit. Above all, an abiding faith in drawing a viable line between the rights and obligations of individuals and those of society without which the democratic process can neither work nor survive.*

ABRAHAM, JACOB A., computer engineering educator, consultant; b. Kerala, India, Dec. 8, 1948; came to U.S., 1970; s. Jacob and Annamma (Chacko) A.; m. Ruth Anne Dick, July 19, 1975; children— Nathan Thomas, Sarah Anne BS, U. Kerala, 1970; MS, Stanford U., 1971, PhD, 1974. Acting asst. prof. Stanford U., Calif., 1974-75; asst. prof. computer engring. U. Ill., Urbana, 1975-80, assoc. prof., 1980-83, prof., 1983-88; prof. and Cockrell Family Regents Chair in Engring. #8 U. Tex., Austin, 1988—, dir. Computer Engring. Rsch. Ctr., 1989—. Cons. Aerospace Corp., Digital Equipment Corp., GE, GTE, Hewlett-Packard Co., IBM Corp., Intel, Sperry, 1979—; dir. rsch. program in reliable very large scale integration architectures U. Ill., 1984-88. Assoc. editor JETTA, 1992—; adv. editor Asken Assocs. Pub., 1987-89; contbr. over 200 articles to profl. confs., jours. and books. Recipient Best Paper award IEEE-Assn., IEEE Emanuel R. Piore award, 2005, Computing Machinery Design Automation Conf., 1993. Fellow IEEE (assoc. editor transactions on computer-aided design of integrated circuits and systems 1984-86, assoc. editor transactions on very large scale integration systems 1992-93, chair Computer Sci. Tech. Com. on Fault-Tolerant Computing, 1991-92); fellow Assn. Computing Machinery, Sigma Xi. Mem. Ch. of S. India Achievements include 1 patent. Office: U Tex Computer Engring Rsch Ctr 1 University Sta C8800 Austin TX 78712-0323

ABRAHAM, JAME, medical researcher; b. Kannur, Kerala, India, May 31, 1966; came to U.S., 1993; s. Abraham and Lucy Abraham; m. Shyla Jovitha Abraham, Nov. 30, 1994; 1 child, Abel Sebastian. MB, BChir, Calicut Med. Coll., Kerala, 1991. Diplomate Am. Bd. Internal Medicine. Intern Calicut Med. Coll., Kerala, 1990-91; jr. resident All India Inst., Delhi, 1992-93; resident U. Conn. Sch. Medicine, 1994-97; fellow NIH, Bethesda, Md., 1997—. Editor: Manual of Oncology, 1999; contbr. articles to profl. jours. Recipient Howard Levine award, 1997, Dept. Int. med., U. Conn., Pfizer/Roerig prize, 1998. Mem. ACP, Am. Soc. Clin. Oncology. Avocations: writing, reading. Office: Nat Cancer Inst 12N 226 Bldg 10 Bethesda MD 20892-0001

ABRAHAM, JUNIOR EASSA, secondary school educator; b. Detroit, Oct. 16, 1947; s. Eassa Joseph and Selma Matilda (Zarick) A. BS, Wayne State U., 1969, MEd, 1975. Cert. tchr., Mich. Grades 9-12 math. tchr., lab. facilitator Detroit Bd. Edn., 1990—94. Math. tutor Grosse Pointe Learning Ctr., Grosse Pointe Farms, Mich., 1984-; Homework Hotline operator Great Cities program NEA/Mich. Edn. Assn., Detroit, 1994-2000 Deacon Revelation Knowledge Ch., Detroit, 1994-2004. Office: Henry Ford HS 20000 Evergreen Rd Detroit MI 48219-2075 E-mail: jabraham@sbcglobal.net.

ABRAHAM, KATHARINE GAIL, economics professor; b. Dayton, Ohio, Aug. 28, 1954; d. William Hamilton and Roberta Taylor (Grannis) A.; m. Graham Neil Horkley, May 25, 1985; children: Ian Robert Horkley, Benjamin William Horkley. Student, Carleton Coll., 1972-74; BS, Iowa State U., 1976; PhD, Harvard U., 1982. Asst. prof. Sloan Sch. Mgmt. MIT, Cambridge, Mass., 1980-85; rsch. assoc. Brookings Inst., Washington, 1985-87; assoc. prof. econs. U. Md., College Park, 1987-91, prof. econs., 1991-97. Commnr. labor stats. U.S. Bur. Labor Stats., 1993—; rsch. assoc. Nat. Bur. Econ. Rsch., 1987-95. Author 2 books; assoc. editor Quar. Jour. Econs., 1985-92; bd. reviewers Indsl. Rels., 1984-93; contbr. articles to profl. jours. Named Outstanding Young Alumnus Iowa State U., 1988; recipient Disting. Achievement Citation award Iowa State U. Alumni Assn., 1999; grad. fellow NSF, 1977-80. Mem. Am. Econ. Assn., Indsl. Rels. Rsch. Assn., Com. on the Status Women in the Econs. Profession.

ABRAHAM, KENNETH SAMUEL, law educator; b. Kearny, NJ, June 19, 1946; s. Saul Jerome and Helen Beverly (Godin) A.; m. Susan R. Stein, Apr. 5, 1981. AB, Ind. U., 1967; JD, Yale U., 1971. Bar: Md. 1977, Va. 1988. Assoc. Mazer & Lesemann, Hackensack, NJ, 1971-73; asst. prof. law U. Md., Balt., 1974-77, assoc. prof., 1977-80, prof., 1980-84; prof. law U. Va., Charlottesville, 1984—, Class 1962 prof., 1988—2002, Robert E. Scott Disting. prof & Class 1966 Rsch. prof., 2002—. Assoc. reporter ALI, Phila., 1986—91; vis. asst. prof. Case Western Res. U., Cleve., 1974, Johns Hopkins U., 1976; vis. prof. U. Va., 1983—84, Harvard U., 2003. Author: Distributing Risk: Insurance, Legal Theory, and Pub. Policy, 1986, Insurance Law and Regulation, 3d edit., 2000, Environmental Liability Insurance Law, 1991, The Forms and Functions of Tort Law, 2d edit., 2002; also articles. Mem. Am. Law Inst. (coun.), Phi Beta Kappa. Home: 770 Covey Hill Rd Charlottesville VA 22901-3268 Office: U Va Sch Law 580 Massie Rd Charlottesville VA 22903-1738*

ABRAHAM, NICHOLAS ALBERT, lawyer, real estate developer; b. Boston, Sept. 17, 1941; s. Nicholas and Ida (Ghiz) A.; m. Evie Stathopoulos, June 30, 1968; children: Annise, Nicholas. BS, Boston U., 1963, JD, 1966. Bar: Mass. 1966, U.S. Dist. Ct. Mass. 1968, U.S. Ct. Appeals (1st cir.) 1971. Sr. ptnr. Abraham-Hanna, P.C., Boston, 1968-88; CEO Boston Investors Fund, Inc., 1988-93; pres., CEO Abraham Properties Inc., Boston, 1993—. CEO., chmn., founder STOR/GARD, Inc., 1996—. Author: Doing Business in Egypt, 1979, Doing Business in Saudi Arabia, 1980, Doing Business in Kuwait, 1982. Bd. of trustees Boston U. Coll. of Bus. Adminstrn., 1968; chmn. fund raising com. Boy Scouts Am., 1968; coach Weston Little League; founder of Weston Youth Hockey League, 1985. Served with U.S. Army, 1966-67; to lt. comdr. USN, 1967-74. Republican. Eastern Orthodox. Office: Abraham Properties Inc 581 Boylston St Fl 3 Boston MA 02116-3608

ABRAHAM, SPENCER (EDWARD SPENCER ABRAHAM), former secretary of energy; b. East Lansing, Mich., June 12, 1952; s. Eddie and Julie Abraham; m. Jane Hershey, 1990; children: Julie, Betsy, Spencer. BA in Social Sci.and Polit. Sci., Mich. State U., 1974; JD, Harvard U., 1979. Asst. prof. law Thomas M. Cooley Law Sch., 1981-83; chmn. Mich. Republican Party, 1983-90; dep. chief of staff to Vice President Dan Quayle The White House, Washington, 1990-91; co-chmn. Nat. Republican Congressional Com., 1991-93; of counsel Miller, Canfield, Paddock & Stone, 1993-94; U.S. senator from Mich., 1995-2001; mem. budget, commerce, sci., transp., judiciary, and small bus. committees; sec. U.S. Dept. Energy, Washington, 2001—05. Disting. vis. fellow Hoover Inst., 2005—; bd. dirs. Occidental Petroleum Corp., LA, 2005—. Mem.: Electricity Advisory Bd. (also secretary), 2001. Republican. Office: Hoover Inst Stanford U Stanford CA 94305

ABRAHAM, TEENA, pharmacist, educator; b. New Delhi, Apr. 1, 1972; d. M.E. and Kunjamma Eappen; m. Titus Abraham, Mar. 27, 1972; 1 child, Alana Elyse. BS in Pharmacy, L.I. U., 1995, PharmD, 1998, MS in Pharmacy, 2002—02. Registered pharmacist NY, Pa., Tex., cert. Bd. Pharm. Specialties, 2001. Pharmacist Randall's, Pasadena, Tex., 1995—96; resident in critical care pharmacotherapy U. of Scis./Hahnemann U. Hosp., Phila., 1998—99; asst. prof. of pharmacy practice Arnold And Marie Schwartz Coll. Of Pharmacy, L.I. U., Bklyn., 1999—; dir. of clin. pharmacy svcs. NY Meth. Hosp., Bklyn., 1999—; adj. asst. prof. of nursing Hunter Coll., CUNY, N.Y.C., 2002—. Mem.: AAUP, Am. Coll. Clin. Pharmacy, Soc. Critical Care Medicine, Am. Soc. Health-system Pharmacists. Avocations: working out, travel. Office: NY Meth Hosp 506 Sixth Street Brooklyn NY 11215

ABRAHAM, TONSON, chemist, researcher; b. Bombay, Dec. 21, 1948; arrived in U.S., 1970; s. Thykadavil Jorge and Annie (Joseph) Abraham; m. Iona Marianne Joseph, June 17, 1978; children: Akash, Kavi. B in Tech., Indian Inst. Tech., Kanpur, India, 1970; PhD in Organic Chemistry, Cath. U. Am., 1976. Fellow NRC, Washington, 1976-78; postdoctoral fellow No. Ill. U., DeKalb, 1978-79; vis. asst. prof. Ill. State U., Normal, 1979-80; polymer scientist Wright-Patterson Air Force Base, Fairborn, Ohio, 1980-86; sr. scientist Owens-Corning Fiberglas, Granville, Ohio, 1986; R & D assoc. B.F. Goodrich Co., Brecksville, Ohio, 1987-94; polymer chemist Argonne (Ill.) Nat. Lab., 1994-96; rsch. prin. Advanced Elastomer Sys., Akron, Ohio, 1996—. Contbr. articles to profl. jours. Mem.: Am. Chem. Soc. Roman Catholic. Achievements include research in synthesis and applications of thermoplactic elastomers; biodegradable polymers; water swellabel and water soluble polymers; synthesis of high temperature; oil resistent elastomers; fluoroelastomers; hydrogenation of polymers; homogeneous hydrogenation catalysts; thermosetting resin precursors for aerospace composites; chemistry of indoles; patents in field. Home: 16936 Deer Path Dr Strongsville OH 44136-6260 Office: Santoprene Specialty Products 388 S Main St Akron OH 44311-1065 Office Phone: 330-849-5222. E-mail: tonson.abraham@santoprene.com.

ABRAHAM, WILLIAM JOHN, JR., lawyer; b. Jan. 17, 1948; s. William John and Constance (Dudley) A.; m. Linda Omeis, Aug. 31, 1968; children: Richard W., Heidi K. BA with honors, U. Ill., 1969; JD magna cum laude, U. Mich., Ann Arbor, 1972. Bar: Wis. 1973, U.S. Supreme Ct. 1975. Jud. clk. U.S. Ct. Appeals (D.C. cir.), Washington, 1972-73; ptnr. Foley & Lardner, Milw., 1973—. Former mem. mgmt. com., former chmn. bus. law dept; bd. dirs. The Vollrath Co., Windway Capital Corp., Phillips Plastics Corp., Quad/Graphics, Inc., Park Bank, L'eft Bank Wine Co., Ltd., TransPro, Inc.;, Hi-Liter, LLC lectr. MBA program U. Wis. Mem. adv. bd. Wis. Policy Rsch. Inst.; mem. Greater Milw. Com.; chmn. Children's Rsch. Inst.; bd. dirs. Children's Health Sys. of Milw.; past bd. dirs. United Way of Greater Milw., Family Svc. of Milw., Milw. Zool. Soc.; bd. dirs., former chmn. Children's Hosp. Found. Named All-Am. Big 10 Fencing Champion, 1968—69. Mem. ABA, State Bar of Wis. (former chmn. legis. com.), Milw. Bar Assn., Barristers, Tripoli Country Club (bd. dirs., pres.), Milw. Athletic Club, Milw. Club, Desert Mountain Country Club. Office: Foley & Lardner 777 E Wisconsin Ave Ste 3800 Milwaukee WI 53202-5367 Office Phone: 414-297-5667. E-mail: wabraham@foley.com.

ABRAHAM-HELMAN, CHERYL GOODRICH, medical education company executive; b. Denver, Dec. 10, 1946; d. Herbert Linn and Frances Louola (Turner) Goodrich; m. Ken Helman, June 21, 1999; children by previous marriage— Anthony, Matthew, Jeffrey, Kristin. B.A. in Mgmt./Journalism, St. Mary's Coll., 1978. Cert. meeting planner; Clk., Social Security Adminstrn., Kansas City, Kans., 1965-66; sec. Calif. Credit Union, Hayward, Calif., 1966-68; tchr. San Ramon Schs., Danville, Calif., 1968-76; owner, mgr. Target Tng. Assocs., Danville, 1976—; owner www.atouchofelegance.com, 1998—, Eagle Mt. Ranch, 1999—; CEO Symposia Medicus, Pleasant Hill, Calif., 1978—; columnist/freelance writer Herald News, Danville, 1976-82; cons., counselor, asst. organizer Venture Sch., Danville, 1978-79. Contbr. articles to profl. jours. Mem. Nat. League Am. Pen Women (state pres. 1979-80). Home: 2086 Pleasant Hill Rd Pleasant Hill CA 94523-3541 Office: Symposia Medicus Ste 210 399 Taylor Blvd Pleasant Hill CA 94523 Office Phone: 925-969-1789. Business E-Mail: cabraham@symposiamedicine.org.

ABRAHAMS, ROBERT M., lawyer; b. NYC, Nov. 21, 1948; s. Ralph M. and Mathilda (Moses) Abrahams; m. Carol J. Popkin, Aug. 8, 1970; children: Kathryn, Emily, Daniel. BA, Hobart Coll., 1969; JD, Hofstra U., 1976. Bar: NY 1977, registered: US Dist. Ct. (So. Dist.) NY 1977, US Dist. Ct. (Ea. Dist.) NY 1977, US Ct. Appeals (2nd Cir.) 1980, US Supreme Ct. 1980, US Ct. Appeals (3rd Cir.) 1984, US Tax Ct. Assoc. Paul, Weiss, Rifkind, Wharton & Garrison, NYC, 1976-80; assoc. then to ptnr. Schulte Roth & Zabel LLP, NYC. Instr. trial advocacy program Hofstra U., 1984—88. Editor-in-chief Hofstra U. Law Rev., 1975. Bd zoning appeals Village of Thaston, NY, 1982—97; mem. Mediation Panel US Dist. Ct. (So. Dist.) NY, 1998—. Fellow: NY Bar Found.; mem.: NY Bar Assn. (Task Force on Foreclosure Reform, Real Property Sect., Litig. Sect.), ABA (Litig. Sect., trial practice com., RICO subcom 1984—). Office: Schulte Roth & Zabel 919 Third Ave New York NY 10022-4774 Office Phone: 212-756-2355. Office Fax: 212-593-5955. Business E-Mail: robert.abrahams@srz.com.

ABRAHAMS, SIDNEY CYRIL, physicist, crystallographer; b. London, May 28, 1924; arrived in U.S., 1948; s. Aaron Harry and Freda (Cohen) A.; m. Rhoda Banks, May 1, 1950; children: David Mark, Peter Brian, Jennifer Anne. BSc, U. Glasgow, Scotland, 1946, PhD, 1949, DSc, 1957; PhD with honors, U. Uppsala, Sweden, 1981; PhD (hon.), U. Bordeaux, 1997. Rsch. fellow U. Minn., Mpls., 1949-50; mem. staff MIT, Cambridge, 1950-54; rsch. fellow U. Glasgow, 1954-57; mem. tech. staff Bell Labs., Murray Hill, NJ, 1957-82; disting. mem. tech. staff AT&T Bell Labs., Murray Hill, 1982-88; Humboldt sr. scientist Inst. Crystallography, U. Tübingen, Germany, 1989-90. Guest scientist Brookhaven Nat. Lab., Upton, N.Y., 1957-90; vis. prof. U. Bordeaux, France, 1979, 90; Humboldt sr. scientist U. Tübingen, 1995; adj. prof. physics So. Oreg. U., 1990—. Mem. editl. bd. Rev. Sci. Instruments, 1963-65; co-editor Anomalous Scattering, 1975; editor World Directory of Crystallographers, 1977; editor-in-chief Acta Crystallographica, 1978-87; book rev. editor Ferroelectrics, 1975—. Recipient Sr. U.S. Scientist award, Alexander von Humboldt Found., 1989-90. Fellow AAAS, Am. Phys. Soc.; mem. Am. Crystallographic Assn. (pres. 1968, mng. editor 1965-90), Royal Soc. Chemistry, Am. Inst. Physics (chmn. pub. policy com. 1981-91), Internat. Union Crystallography (chmn. commn. on crystallographic apparatus 1972-75, commn. on jours. 1978-87, commn. on crystallographic nomenclature 1978-2002), Internat. Union Pure and Applied Chemistry (rep. interdivsnl. com. on nomenclature and symbols 1984-2001, interdivsnl. com. terminology, nomenclature and symbols 2001-04), Sigma Xi (founding pres. So. Oreg. State Coll. 1993-95). Avocations: photography, hiking. Home: 89 Mallard St Ashland OR 97520-7316 Office: So Oreg U Physics Dept Ashland OR 97520 Business E-Mail: sca@sou.edu.

ABRAHAMSEN, ABEL, wholesale and retail import company executive; b. Trondheim, Norway, Sept. 7, 1923; came to U.S., 1944; s. Salamon Abrahamsen and Mirjam Fischer; m. Anne Katrine Gaaso, Nov. 22, 1954; children: Anne C.L., Synnove J. Student, Cathedral Sch., Trondheim, 1941; B Engring., Stockholm Tech. Inst., 1943; postgrad., U. So. Calif., 1946-47. Prodr. documentary movies Abrahamsen Family, Trondheim, 1938-41, Stockholm, 1941-44, RNAF Camp Little Norway, Toronto, Ont., Can., 1944-45; freelance cameraman N.Y.C., 1947-50; cameraman CBS-TV, N.Y.C., 1950-58; pres. Norwegian Silver Corp., N.Y.C., 1958-95, Norsk, Inc., N.Y.C., 1963-95, Ege Area Rugs, N.Y.C., 1975—. Co-chmn. Norwegian Immigration Sesquicentennial Commn., 1975; initiater cooperation between Rusk Inst. Rehab. Medicine NYU Med. Ctr. and Norwegian Sunnaas Rehab. Hosp., Oslo, 1998. Contbr. articles to Reader's Digest, 1949-53. Trustee Norwegian Seamen's Ch., N.Y.C., 1976—, Thanks to Scandinavia, N.Y.C., 1968-74; pres. Norwegian-Am. C. of C., 1973-76, Norwegian Club, N.Y.C., 1995-97. Nav. Sgt. Royal Norwegian AF, 1945-46. Hon. fellow Am. Scandinavian Found., 1946-47; recipient Knight's Cross 1st Class, Royal Norwegian Order of St. Olav, 1976, award for outstanding contbns. to development of trade rels. with Norway, Export Coun. Norway, 1984, award City of N.Y. and U.S. World Trade Fair, 1960, Gift and Art Buyer award, 1963. Mem. Norwegian Immigration Assn. (founder and chmn. 1996-98, chmn. emeritus 2000). Avocations: making movies, music, WWII and holocaust studies. Home and Office: 165 E 66th St New York NY 10021

ABRAHAMSON, HARMON BRUCE, chemist, educator; b. Cokato, Minn., Aug. 26, 1952; s. Harvey Benhart and Ruth Anne (Werner) A.; m. Cathy Lee VandenHeuvel, May 24, 1974 (div. 1979); m. Julie Kristine Conrad, May 22, 1982; children: Joel Theodore, Krista Rachel, Peter Craig. BChem, U. Minn., 1974; PhD, MIT, 1978. Asst. prof. U. Okla., Norman, 1978-84, U. N.D., Grand Forks, 1984-88, assoc. prof., 1988-95, prof. chemistry, 1995—, chmn. dept. chemistry, 1996—2003. Vis. assoc. prof. Ohio State U., Columbus, 1991-92; ad hoc reviewer NSF, Petroleum Rsch. Fund. Contbr. numerous articles to profl. jours.; ad hoc reviewer Jour. Am. Chem. Soc., Inorganic Chemistry, Organometallics, Jour. Organometallic Chemistry, Jour. Chem. Edn., Synthesis and Reactivity in Inorganic and Metal-Organic Chemistry. Vol. presenter, instr., exhibits and grants com. Dakota Sci. Ctr., 1994-02. Recipient Alpha Chi Sigma Freshman Chemistry award U. Minn., 1971, M. Cannon Sneed award in inorganic chemistry, 1974; NSF predoctoral fellow MIT, 1975-78, U. Okla. Coll. Arts and Scis. Summer fellow, 1979, Jr. Faculty Summer Rsch. fellow, 1982; grantee Assoc. Western Univs., 1993, ESPSCoR/ASEND, 1993, NSF (EPSCoR and ASEND), 1987-91, 86-90, dept. Energy, 1986-89, Am. Chem. Soc.-Petroleum Rsch. Fund, 1982-87, 79-82, Rsch. Corp., 1982-84, Dept. Def., Office of Naval Rsch., 1979-80, Dept. Health and Human Svcs./Pub. Health Svc., 1995-03, Dept. of Edn., 200- Mem. Am. Chem. Soc. (chmn. Red River Valley sect. 1988-89, Nat. Coun., 2000-), Inter-Am. Photochem. Soc., Sigma Xi (U. Okla. chpt. sec. 1980-81, U. N.D. chpt. pres. 1994-95), Tau Beta Pi (Minn. Alpha v.p. 1973-74). Lutheran. Avocations: reading, woodworking, computers. Office: Univ of North Dakota PO Box 9024 Grand Forks ND 58202-9024

ABRAHAMSON, SHIRLEY SCHLANGER, state supreme court justice; b. NYC, Dec. 17, 1933; d. Leo and Ceil (Sauerteig) Schlanger; m. Seymour Abrahamson, Aug. 26, 1953; 1 son, Daniel Nathan. AB, NYU, 1953; JD, Ind. U., 1956; SJD, U. Wis., 1962. Bar: Ind. 1956, N.Y. 1961, Wis. 1962. Asst. dir. Legis. Drafting Research Fund, Columbia U. Law Sch., 1957-60; since practiced in Madison, Wis., 1962-76; mem. firm LaFollette, Sinykin, Anderson & Abrahamson, 1962-76; justice Wis. Supreme Ct., Madison, 1976-96, chief justice, 1996—. Bd. visitors Ind. U. Sch. Law, 1972-02, U. Miami Sch. Law, 1982-97, U. Chgo. Law Sch., 1988-92, Brigham Young U., Sch. Law, 1986-88, Northwestern U. Law Sch., 1989-94; chmn. Wis. Rhodes Scholarship Com., 1992-95; chmn. nat. adv. com. on ct.-adjudicated and ct.-ordered health care George Washington U. Ctr. Health Policy, Washington, 1993-95; mem. DNA adv. bd. FBI, U.S. Dept. Justice, 1995-2001; bd. dirs. Inst. Jud. Adminstrn., Inc., NYU Sch. Law; chair Nat. Inst. Justice's Commn. Future DNA Evidence, 1997-2001; prof. U. Wis. Sch. Law, 1966-92; v.p. Conference of Chief Justices, 2002-. Editor: Constitutions of the United States (National and State) 2 vols, 1962. Mem. study group program of rsch., mental health and the law John D. and Catherine T. MacArthur Found., 1988-96; mem. coun. fund for rsch. on dispute resolution Ford Found., 1987-91; bd. dirs. Wis. Civil Liberties Union, 1968-72; mem. ct. reform adv. panel Internat. Human Rights Law Group Cambodia Project, 1995-97. Mem. ABA (coun., sect. legal edn. and admissions to bar 1976-86, mem. commn. on undergrad. edn. in law and the humanities 1978-79, standing com. on pub. edn. 1991-95, mem. commn. on access to justice/2000 1993-02, mem. adv. bd. Ctrl. and East European law initiative 1994-99, mem. consortium on legal svcs. and the public 1995-2001, vice-chair ABA Coalition for Justice 1997-2000), Wis. Bar Assn., Dane County Bar Assn., 7th Cir. Bar Assn., Nat. Assn. Women Judges, Am. Law Inst. (mem. coun. 1985-), Am. Philos. Soc., Am. Acad. Arts and Scis. Office: Wis Supreme Ct PO Box 1688 Madison WI 53702-1688

ABRAHM, JANET LEE, hematologist, oncologist, educator, palliative care specialist; b. San Francisco, Mar. 14, 1949; d. Paul Milton and Helen Lesser Abrahm; m. David Rytman Slavitt, Apr. 16, 1978. Student U. Calif., Berkeley, 1969; BA, U. Calif., San Francisco, 1970, MD, 1973. Diplomate in internal medicine, hematology and oncology Am. Bd. Internal Medicine; ciplomate Am. Bd. Hospice and Palliative Medicine. Intern and resident medicine Mass. Gen. Hosp., Boston, 1973-75, hematology fellow, 1975-76; chief resident medicine Moffitt Hosp. U. Calif., San Francisco, 1976-77; hematology/oncology fellow Hosp. U. Pa., Phila., 1977-80; postdoctoral fellow medicine U. Pa., Phila., 1977-78, postdoctoral trainee medicine, 1977-80, asst. prof. medicine, 1980-86, Hosp. U. Pa. and VA Med. Ctr., Phila., 1986-89, assoc. prof. medicine, 1989-2000; attending physician Hosp. U. Pa., Phila., 1980-93; from staff physician to faculty scholar Phila. VA Med. Ctr., 1982—97, faculty scholar Project Death in Am., 1997—2000; med. dir. Wissahickon Hospice UPHS, 1998-2000; assoc. prof. medicine and anesthesia Harvard Med. Sch., 2001—; attending physician Dana-Farber Cancer Inst., Brigham and Women's Hosp., Boston, 2001—. Prin. investigator Palliative Care Fellowship Grant, 1996-2001, 03—; mem. concensus panel on End-of-Life Care, ACP, 1997—; chmn. adv. com. Cancer Care VA Dist. 4, 1987-90; sec. subspecialty bd. hematology Am. Bd. Internal Medicine, 1987-92, sec. SEP subcom. hematology, 1993-95; mem. tech. adv. group Cancer Care Region 1, 1990-95; med. oncology cons. cancer pain consultation panel Ctr. for Continuing Edn. U. Pa. Sch. Nursing, 1990-2000; mem.

quality of life and cancer edn. com. Pa. Cancer Adv. Bd., 1994-97; mem. human resources coun. of VHA VISN, 1996-97, councillor Region 1, AVOCOM, 1996-97, TAPC mem., 2000-02, Am. Acad. Hospice and Palliative Medicine, 1999-, ACP, 2000-, others; attending physician Brigham and Women's Hosp., Boston, 2001—; dir. pain and palliative care program Dana-Farber Career Inst., Boston, 2001—. Author: Pain Management and Antiemitu Therapy in Hematolgic disorders in Hematology: Basic Principles and Practice, 1994, 2005, Anemia, Pain Management in Geriatric Secrets, 1996, 2000, 2004, A Physician's Guide to Pain and Symptom Management in Cancer Patients, 2000, 2d edit., 2005, Caring For Patients at the End of Lipppin Clinical Oncology, 2004, Specialized Care of the Terminally Ill, An Cancer, Principles & Practices of Oncology, 2005; reviewer New Eng. Jour. Medicine, JAMA, Cancer, Archives Internal Medicine, Annals Internal Medicine, mem. editl. bd. Jour. Palliative Medicine, 2004—; contbr. numerous articles to profl. jours. Recipient Manual award Merck, 1973; Fife Medicine scholar, 1973. Fellow: ACP, Am. Acad. Hospice and Palliative Medicine (bd. dirs. 2002—); mem.: Am. Pain Soc., Am. Assn. Cancer Edn. (program com. 1993), Am. Soc. Clin. Oncology, Am. Soc. Clin. Hypnosis, Am. Soc. Hematology, Alpha Omega Alpha, Phi Beta Kappa. Home: 35 West St #5 Cambridge MA 02139 Office: Dana Farber Cancer Inst 44 Binney St Boston MA 02115 E-mail: jabrahm@partners.org.

ABRAM, BLANCHE SCHWARTZ, music educator, pianist; b. NYC, June 28, 1925; d. Irving Al and Celia (Smith) Schwartz; m. Joseph Kushner (div. 1957); m. Irving Abram, May 19, 1957; children: Rachel, Michael, Anne Marie, David. BA, Bklyn. Coll., 1945; postgrad., NYU, 1945-46. Music faculty 92d St Y Sch. Music, N.Y.C., 1945—97; music lectr. NYU Sch. Continuing Edn., N.Y.C.; sr. prof. music Hofstra U., Hempstead, N.Y., 1965—; pianist, co-dir. Am. Chamber Ensemble, N.Y.C., 1965—; pianist Drucker Trio, N.Y.C., 1980—. Judge in competitions Contbr. articles to profl. jours. Founder, chmn. South Shore Cmty. Arts Coun., L.I., N.Y., 1951-56; founder creative arts program Roosevelt (N.Y.) Cmty. Rels. Coun., 1962. Recipient Pathfinder award in arts Twp. of Hempstead, 1998, citation for outstanding contgn. in artistry 92d St Y, 1966; N.Y. State Coun. on Arts grantee, 1989—. Mem. N.Y. State Music Tchrs. Assn., Music Tchrs. Nat. Assn. (cert. master tchr.). Avocations: hiking, dancing, reading. Home: 2320 Surrey Ln Baldwin NY 11510-3024 E-mail: babram20@optonline.net.

ABRAM, DONALD EUGENE, retired federal judge; b. Des Moines, Feb. 8, 1935; s. Irwin and Freda Phyllis (Gibson) A.; m. Frances Jennette Cooley, Apr. 22, 1962; children: Karen Lynn, Susan Ann, Scott Alan, Diane Jennette. BS in Bus., U. Col., 1957, JD, 1963. Ptnr. Phelps, Fonda, Hays, Abram and Shaw (now Peterson & Fonda, PC), Pueblo, Colo., 1963-75; dist. judge Colo. 10th Jud. Dist., Pueblo, 1975-81; chief U.S. magistrate judge U.S. Dist. Ct. State of Colo., 1981-00; ret., 2000. Lectr. law in criminal procedure U. Denver Sch. of Law, 1983-90; adj. prof. sociology, instr. bus. law U. So. Colo., Pueblo, 1977-81. Mng. editor, bd. dir. Colo. Law Review, 1961-63. Vice chmn. Pueblo County Rep. Party, 1973-75; city councilman Pueblo, 1970-73; pres. Pueblo city coun., 1972-73, Pueblo Goodwill Industries, 1965, Pueblo United Fund, 1968; chmn. consolidation planning com. Pueblo County Sch. Dists. 60, 70, 1968-70; mem. gov.'s. milit. affairs adv. com., 1975-78; mem. gov.'s. commn. children and families, 1978-80. Lt. (j.g.) USN, 1957-60, capt. Res. ret. Recipient Disting. Svc. award Colo. Jaycee, 1970, Disting. Citizen Svc. award, Pueblo Rotary, 1975. Mem. Fed. Magistrate Judges Assn. (pres. 1990-91), Pueblo C. of C.(bd. dirs. 1972, chmn. edn. com. 1970-71), Colo. Bar Assn. (1st v.p. 1975-76), Nat. Coun. U. S. Magistrates (dir., officer 1984-89), Juvenile Judges Assn. Colo. (chmn. 1979-80), Colo. Navy League (state pres. 1976-78). Lutheran. Office: US Dist Ct US Courthouse C-566 1929 Stout St Denver CO 80294-1929

ABRAMO, GUY P., information technology executive; BSCE, N.J. Inst. Tech.; MBA, Georgetown U. Various positions including mgr. planning and bus. analysis, regional mgr. adminstrn. and controls, asst. gasoline bus. mgr. Mobile Oil Co.; sr. v.p. mktg. worldwide, co-chair eSolutions group Ingram Micro, Inc., 1998—2000, chief info. officer, 2000, exec v.p., chair strategy and info. officer Santa Ana, Calif., 2000—. Office: Ingram Micro Inc 1600 E St Andrew Pl PO Box 25125 Santa Ana CA 92799

ABRAMOVIC, MARINA, artist; b. Belgrade, Yugoslavia, 1946; PhD (hon.), Art Inst. Chgo., 2004. Instr. Acad. Fine Arts, Novi Sad, 1973—75; visiting prof. Académie des Beaux-Arts, Paris, 1983, Hochschule der Kunst, Berlin, 1990—91, Hochschule für Bildende Kunst, Hamburg, 1992—96, prof. Braunschweig, 1997; artist in residence Atelier Calder, Saché, 2001. One-woman shows include Art must be Beautiful Artist must be Beautiful, Art Festival, Copenhagen, Denmark, 1975, Breathing out/Breathing in (with Ulay), Studenski Kulturni Center, Belgrade, 1977, Charged Space (with Ulay), Brooklyn Mus., European Performance Series, NY, 1978, Rest Energy (with Ulay), ROSC 80, Dublin, 1990, Nightsea Crossing (with Ulay), Mus. Contemporary Art, Chgo., 1982, Die Mond der Sonne (with Ulay), The House, Santa Monica, 1987, The Lovers: The Great Wall Walk (with Ulay), The Great Wall China, 1988, Dragon Heads, Kunstmuseum, Bonn, Germany, 1992, Delusional (with Charles Atlas), Theater am Turin, Frankfurt, Germany, 1994, Cleaning the House, Sean Kelly Gallery, NY, 1995, The Biography, Schouwburg, Groningen, 1996, Balkan Baroque, Biennale di Venezia, Venice, Italy, 1997, Luminosity, Sean Kelly Gallery, NY, 1997, Artist Body-Pub. Body, Mus. Contemporary Art, Valencia, Spain, 1998, The House with the Ocean View, 2003 (NY Dance & Performance Award, 2003), Directions, Hirschhorn Mus. & Sculpture Garden, 2001, Moving Pictures, Soloman R. Guggenheim Mus., NY, 2002, exhibited in group shows at Whitney Biennial Exhbn., Whitney Mus. Am. Art, 2004. Recipient Niedersächsicher Kunstpreis, 2003. Mailing: c/o Solomon R Guggenheim Mus 1071 5th Ave New York NY 10128*

ABRAMOWICZ, HELEN KAUFMAN, psychiatrist; b. New Haven, May 24, 1943; d. Samuel and Ann (Hankin) K.; m. Mark Abramowicz, June 1, 1969; children: Sarah, Michael, David. BA, Smith Coll., 1964; MD, Albert Einstein Coll. Medicine, 1968. Diplomate Am. Bd. Pediatrics, Am. Bd. Psychiatry and Neurology, subspecialty in Child Psychiatry. Intern, resident Bronx (N.Y.) Mcpl. Hosp., 1968-70; fellow devel. disabilities Rose F. Kennedy Ctr., Bronx, 1970-72; attending physician pediatrics Bronx (N.Y.) Mcpl. Hosp, 1972-75; psychiatry resident Montefiore Hosp., Bronx, 1975-77; child psychiatry fellow N.Y. Hosp., White Plains, 1978-79; psychiatry instr. N.Y. Hosp./Cornell U., White Plains, 1979-90, psychiatry asst. prof., 1990—, pres. faculty coun., 1991-92; pvt. practice adult and child psychiatry Larchmont, N.Y., 1979—. Workshop presenter in field. Fellow Am. Psychiat. Assn., Am. Acad. Child and Adolescent Psychiatry, Westchester Psychiat. Soc. (treas. 1985-87, sec. 1987-88, pres. 1989-92). Avocations: gardening, opera, travel, reading, math. puzzles. Home and Office: 19 Locust Ave Larchmont NY 10538-3820 Office: 25 Central Park W Apt 1L New York NY 10023-7205 Office Phone: 914-834-0872.

ABRAMOWITZ, ELKAN, lawyer; b. N.Y.C., Mar. 10, 1940; S. Harry and Claire L. (Liebreich) A.; m. Susan Isaacs, Dec. 7, 1943; children: Andrew, Elizabeth. AB, Brown U., 1961; LLB, N.Y. U., 1964. Bar: N.Y. 1964. Law clk. U.S. Dist. Ct. (so. dist.) N.Y., 1964-66; asst. U.S. atty. So. Dist. N.Y., 1966-70, chief criminal divsn., 1976-77; pvt. practice N.Y.C., 1970-76, 77-79; with Morvillo Abramowitz Grand Iason & Silberberg, N.Y.C., 1979—. Mem. faculty Nat. Inst. Trial Advocacy, 1977—. Mem. ABA, N.Y. State Bar Assn., Assn. Bar City of N.Y., Fed. Bar Coun. Office: 565 5th Ave New York NY 10017 Office Phone: 212-880-9500. Business E-Mail: eabramowitz@magislaw.com.

ABRAMOWITZ, MORTON I., former ambassador; b. Lakewood, N.J., Jan. 20, 1933; s. Mendel and Dora (Smith) Abramowitz; m. Sheppie Glass, Sept. 13, 1959; children: Michael, Rachel. BA, Stanford U.; MA, Harvard U., 1955. Joined U.S. Fgn. Service, 1960; 3d sec., vice consul Taipei, Formosa, 1960-62; with Fgn. Area and Lang. Trng. Ctr., Taichung, Taiwan, 1962-63; consul, polit. officer Hong Kong, 1963-66; assigned Bur. Econ. Affairs, 1966-68; Sr. Inter dept. Group, 1968-69; spl. asst. under-sec. state, 1969-71; research assoc. Inst. for Strategic Studies, 1971; asst. to sec. of def., 1972-73; polit. adviser to Comdr.-in-Chief Pacific, 1973-78; also dep. asst. sec. def. for Inter-Am., E. Asia and Pacific, 1974-78; amb. to Thailand, Bangkok, 1978-83; U.S. rep. to Mutual and Balanced Force Reduction Negotiations Vienna, 1983-85; dir., asst. sec. Bur. of Intelligence and Rsch., 1985-89; amb. to Turkey, 1989-91. Author (with Richard Moorsteen): Remaking China Policy, 1972; author: Moving the Glacier, the Two Koreas and the Powers, 1972, East Asian Actors and Issues, China, Can We Have a Policy, 1997, Turkey's Transformation and American Policy, 2000, Turkey and the United States - Allies in Need, 2003; contbr. articles to jours. and newspapers. Pres. Carnegie Endowment for Internat. Peace, Washington, 1991—97; bd. dirs. Internat. Crisis Group, 1997—, Internat. Rescue Com., Nat. Endowment for Democracy, Open Soc. Inst., Freedom House. With AUS, 1957. Recipient Disting. Pub. Svc. award, Dept. Def., 1976, Sec. Def. Disting. Svc. award, 1978, Joseph C. Wilson award, 1980, Pres.'s award for Disting. Fed. Svc., 1981, 1985, 1988, Nat. Intelligence Disting. medal, 1989. Mem.: Am. Acad. Arts and Scis., Phi Beta Kappa.

ABRAMOWITZ, ROBERT LESLIE, lawyer; b. Phila., May 1, 1950; s. Nathan P. and Lucille H. (Rader) A.; m. Susan Margaret Stewart, Dec. 1, 1974; children: David, Catherine. BA, Yale U., 1971; JD, Harvard U., 1974. Bar: Pa. 1974, N.J. 1975. Assoc. Ballard, Spahr, Andrews & Ingersoll, Phila., 1974-81, ptnr., 1981-90; ptrn. Morgan Lewis & Bockius, LLP, Phila., 1990—. Adj. prof. law Villanova U., 1986—2001. Trustee Moorestown (N.J.) Friends Sch., 1981-90, Rock Sch. of Pa. Ballet, 1990—; pres. Harvard Law Sch. Assn. Greater Phila., 1999-2001. Mem. ABA, Am. Coll. Employee Benefits Counsel, Phila. Bar Assn. (exec. com. probate sect. 1982-85, pension com. 1985-94, chair 1987-89), Am. Coll. Tax Counsel, Athenaeum Phila., Yale Club, Merion Cricket Club. Home: 623 Pembroke Rd Bryn Mawr PA 19010-3613 Office: Morgan Lewis & Bockius LLP 1701 Market St Philadelphia PA 19103-2903 Office Phone: 215-963-4811.

ABRAMS, ARTHUR JAY, physician; b. Camden, N.J., Apr. 9, 1938; s. Morris and Sophia Sarah (Kates) A.; m. Marianne Ritto Abrams, June 8, 1963; children: Suzanne Beth, Cheryl Lyn, Robert Dwight. BA, Rutgers U., Camden, N.J., 1959; MD, Hahnemann U., 1963. Diplomate Am. Bd. Dermatology. Intern Madigan Army Med. Ctr., Tacoma, Wash., 1963-64; resident, chief resident Letterman Army Med. Ctr., San Francisco, 1964-67; dermatologist, Far East cons. 249th Gen. Hosp. U.S. Army, Tokyo, 1967-69; asst. chief dermatologist Tripler Army Med. Ctr., Honolulu, 1969-70; staff dermatologist El Camino Hosp., Mountain View, Calif., 1970—; clin. assoc. prof. dermatology Stanford U. Med. Ctr., 1979—; dermatology cons. San Jose (Calif.) State U., 1994—; maj. U.S. Army, 1963-70. Mem. AMA, Calif. Med. Assn., Pacific Dermatol. Assn., San Francisco Dermatol. Soc. Avocations: volleyball, walking. Office: 763 Altos Oaks Dr Ste 4 Los Altos CA 94024-5400

ABRAMS, DAN, news correspondent, lawyer; b. NYC, May 20, 1966; BA cum laude, Duke U., 1988; JD, Columbia U., 1992. Anchor, reporter Court TV, New York, NY, 1992—97, Teen Court TV; gen. assignment correspondent NBC News, 1997—, chief legal correspondent; anchor MSNBC, host, The Abrams Report; contbr. Jewish World Review. Jewish. Office: NBC News 30 Rockefeller Plaza New York NY 10112 E-mail: abramsreport@msnbc.com.*

ABRAMS, DOUGLAS CARL, social studies educator; b. Tarboro, NC, Jan. 7, 1950; s. Era Glenn and Edna Louise Abrams; m. Linda Marie Perry, Aug. 2, 1980; children: Jessica Louise, Benjamin Perry. BA, Bob Jones U., 1972; cert., Sorbonne U. Paris, 1974; MA, N.C. State U., 1974; PhD, U. Md., 1981. Prof. Bob Jones U., Greenville, SC, 1974—, dir. Africa team, 1991—, chair dept. social studies edn., 1992—; tchg. asst. U. Md., College Park, 1977—81; instr. U. Coll., U. Md., College Park, 1981—81. Outside reader Harcourt Press, N.Y.C., 1994—94; program participant Citadel, Conf. on the Civil Rights Movement in S.C., Charleston, 2003—; presenter and spkr. in field. Author: (historical monograph) Selling the Old-Time Religion: American Fundamentalists and Mass Culture, 1920-1940, Conservative Constraints: North Carolina and the New Deal; book rev. contbr. to various jours.:; contbr. chapters to books, articles to profl. jours. Named alt. Fulbright lectr. for Kenya, Fulbright Scholar Program, 1995—96; grantee, NEH, 1983, 1986, Am. Coun. Learned Socs., 1988, So. Bapt. Hist. Commn., 1989, Inst. for the Study Am. Evangelicals, 1992; Hearst fellow, U. Md., 1980. Mem.: So. Hist. Assn. (assoc.), Orgn. Am. Historians (assoc.). Republican. Avocations: reading, gardening, walking, music, travel. Home: One Oriole Greenville SC 29609 Office: Bob Jones Univ Box 34627 Greenville SC 29614 Personal E-mail: clabrams@charter.net. Business E-Mail: cabrams@bju.edu.

ABRAMS, ELLIOTT, federal official; b. NYC, Jan. 24, 1948; s. Joseph and Mildred (Kauder) Abrams; m. Rachel Decter, Mar. 9, 1980; children: Jacob, Sarah, Joseph BA, Harvard U., 1969, JD, 1973; MS in Internat. Rels., London Sch. Economics, 1970. Atty. Breed, Abbott & Morgan, Boston, 1973—75; asst. counsel US Senate Permanent Subcom. on Investigations, Washington, 1975; spl. counsel Sen. Henry M. Jackson, 1975-76, Sen. Daniel P. Moynihan, 1977-78, chief of staff, 1978-79; atty. Verner, Liipfert, Bernhard & McPherson, Washington, 1979—81; asst. sec. for internat. orgn. affairs US Dept. State, Washington, 1981, asst. sec. for human rights and humanitarian affairs, 1981-85, asst. sec. for Inter-Am. affairs, 1985-89; sr. fellow Hudson Inst., Washington, 1990-96; pres. Ethics and Pub. Policy Ctr., Washington, 1996-2001; spl. asst. to Pres., sr. dir. for democracy, human rights, and internat ops. NSC, Washington, 2001—02, spl. asst. to Pres., sr. dir. for Near East and North African Affairs, 2002—05; dep. asst. to pres. The White House, Washington, 2005—; dep. nat. security advisor for global democracy strategy NSC, Washington, 2005—. Bd. dirs. Inter-Am. Found., 1985—90; commr. US Commn. on Internat. Religious Freedom, 1999—2001, chmn., 2000—01; columnist Beliefnet. Author: Undue Process, 1992, Security and Sacrifice, 1995, Faith or Fear: How Jews Can Survive in a Christian America, 1997. Mem.: Am. Com. for Peace in Chechnya, Coun. Fgn. Rels. Republican. Office: Nat Security Coun 347 Old Exec Office Bldg Washington DC 20504

ABRAMS, GERALD DAVID, pathologist, educator; b. Detroit, Apr. 27, 1932; s. Arthur and Esther (Kushner) A.; m. Gloria Sandra Turner, June 6, 1954; children— Kathryn, Nancy AB, Wayne U., 1951; MD, U. Mich., 1955. Diplomate Am. Bd. Pathology. House officer pathology U. Mich., Ann Arbor, 1955-59, instr. pathology, 1959-60, asst. prof. pathology, 1963-66, assoc. prof. Ann Arbor, Mich., 1966-69, prof., 1969—2002, prof. emeritus, 2002—, dir. anatomic pathology, 1985-89; asst. chief dept. exptl. pathology Walter Reed Army Inst. Rsch., 1961-62. Dep. med. examiner Washtenaw County, Mich., 1963—; cons. physician Ann Arbor VA Hosp., 1970—2002. Served to capt. M.C., US Army, 1961-62 Markle scholar John and Mary Markle Found., 1963-68; recipient Elizabeth Crosby Teaching award U. Mich., 1969, 87, 96, Kaiser-Permanente Teaching award U. Mich., 1978; Lifetime achievement Award in Med. Edn., 2002. Mem. AAAS, US-Can. Acad. Pathology, Mich. Soc. Pathologists Office: U Mich Dept Pathology Ann Arbor MI 48109 Business E-Mail: gabrams@umich.edu.

ABRAMS, HAROLD EUGENE, lawyer; b. Pensacola, Fla., Jan. 18, 1933; s. Samuel Ralph and Sadie (Gerhardt) A.; m. Nancy Gray, June 22, 1958; children: Shari Abrams Marx, Eric Gray. BA, U. Mich., 1954; JD, Harvard U., 1957. Bar: Ga. 1958, D.C. 1976, U.S. Supreme Ct. 1970. Law clk. to presiding judge U.S. Ct. Appeals (5th cir.), Atlanta, 1957-58; assoc. Kilpatrick & Cody, Atlanta, 1958-63; ptnr. Kilpatrick Stockton, Atlanta, 1963—. Pres. Atlanta Tax Forum, 1990-91, Atlanta Estate Planning Coun., 1991-92; bd. dirs. Randall Bros., Inc., Atlanta, Selig Enterprises, Inc., Atlanta. Contbr. articles on tax and estate planning to profl. publs. Pres. Buckhead Little League, Atlanta, 1972-73; bd. dirs. Atlanta chpt. Am. Jewish Com., 1987-2001, Atlanta Jewish Fedn., 1996—; sec. Ronald McDonald's Children's Charities, Atlanta, 1988—. With U.S. Army, 1957-58. Fellow Am. Coll. Tax Counsel; mem. State Bar of Ga. (chmn. tax sect. 1964-65), So. Fed. Tax Inst. (trustee 1964-2001, pres. 1970-71, treas. 1986-95), Atlanta Lawyers Club. Avocations: tennis, travel. Office: Kilpatrick Stockton LLP 1100 Peachtree St NE Ste 2800 Atlanta GA 30309-4530 Office Phone: 404-815-6600. Business E-Mail: habrams@kilpatrickstockton.com.

ABRAMS, HERBERT KERMAN, physician, educator; b. Chgo., 1913; BS, Northwestern U.; MD, MS, U. Ill., 1940; MPH, Johns Hopkins U., 1947. Intern Cook County Hosp., Chgo., 1940-41; chief Bur. of Adult Health, Calif. Health Dept., 1947-52; dir. Chgo. Union Health Service, 1952-66; prof., chair dept. community medicine Chgo. Med. Sch.-Mt. Sinai Hosp., Chgo., 1966-68; prof., head dept. family community medicine U. Ariz., Tucson, 1968-78, prof. emeritus, 1990—; dir. Ariz. Ctr. for Occupl. Safety and Health, 1978-83. Surgeon USPHS, 1942-46. Mem.: APHA, AMA, Physicians for a Nat. Health Program, Internat. Physicians Prevention Nuclear War, Physicians for Social Responsibility, Am. Coll. Occupl. Environ. Medicine, Assn. Tchrs. Preventive Medicine, Ariz. Med. Assn. Office: U Ariz Dept Family and Cmty Medicine PO Box 245143 Tucson AZ 85724-5143 E-mail: hka@u.arizona.edu.

ABRAMS, HERBERT LEROY, radiologist, educator; b. N.Y.C., Aug. 16, 1920; s. Morris and Freda (Sugarman) Abrams; m. Marilyn Spitz, Mar. 23, 1943; children: Nancy, John. BA, Cornell U., 1941; MD, Downstate Med. Ctr., N.Y., 1946. Diplomate Am. Bd. Radiology. Intern L.I. Coll. Hosp., 1946—47; resident in internal medicine Montefiore Hosp., Bronx, NY, 1947—48; resident in radiology Stanford (Calif.) U. Hosp., 1948—51; practice medicine specializing in radiology Stanford U., Calif., 1951—67, mem. faculty Sch. Medicine, 1951—67, dir. divsn. diagnostic roentgenology Sch. Medicine, 1961—67, prof. radiology Sch. Medicine, 1962—67; Philip H. Cook prof. radiology Harvard U., 1967—85, now prof. emeritus, chmn. dept. radiology, 1967—80; prof. radiology Stanford U. Sch. Medicine, 1985—90, prof. emeritus, 1990—; clin. prof. U. Calif. Sch. Medicine, San Francisco, 1986—. Radiologist-in-chief Peter Bent Brigham Hosp., Boston, 1967—80; chmn. dept. radiology Brigham and Women's Hosp., Boston, 1981—85; radiologist-in-chief Sidney Farber Cancer Inst., Boston, 1974—85; R.H. Nimmo vis. prof. U. Adelaide, Australia; mem.-in-residence Ctr. for Internat. Security and Cooperation, Stanford U., 1985—; mem. radiation study sect. NIH, 1962—66; cons. to hosps., profl. socs. Author (with others): Angiocardiography in Congenital Heart Disease, 1956, Congenital Heart Disease, 1965, Coronary Arteriography: A Practical Approach, 1983, Brigham Guide to Diagnostic Imaging, 1986, Assessment of Diagnostic Technology in Health Care; editor: Abrams' Angiography, 3d edit., 1983; author: The President Has Been Shot: Confusion, Disability and the 25th Amendment, 1992, 1994, The History of Cardiac Radiology, 1996; mem. editl. bd.: Investigative Radiology, editor-in-chief, founder: Cardiovasc. and Interventional Radiology, 1978—88, Postgrad. Radiology, 1983—99. Named David M. Gould Meml. lectr., Johns Hopkins, 1964, William R. Whitman Meml. lectr., 1968, Leo G. Rigler lectr., Tel Aviv U., 1969, Holmes lectr., New Eng. Roentgen Ray Soc., Boston, 1970, Ross Golden lectr., N.Y. Roentgen Ray Soc., N.Y.C., 1971, Stauffer Meml. lectr., Phila. Roentgen Ray Soc., 1971, J.M.T. Finney Fund lectr., Md. Radiol. Soc., Ocean City, 1972, Aubrey Hampton lectr., Mass. Gen. Hosp., Boston, 1974, Kirklin-Weber lectr., Mayo Clinic, 1974, Crookshank lectr., Royal Coll. Radiology, 1980, Alpha Omega Alpha lectr., vis. prof., U. Calif. Med. Sch., San Francisco, 1961—65, W.H. Herbert lectr., U. Calif., Caldwell lectr., Am. Roentgen Ray Soc., 1982, Percy lectr., McMaster Med. Sch., 1983, Charles Dotter lectr., Soc. Cardiovasc. and Interventional Radiology, 1988, Philip Hodes lectr., Jefferson Med. Coll., 1988, David Gould Meml. lectr., Johns Hopkins U., 1991, Hymer Friedell lectr., Western Res. Sch. Medicine, 1993, Felix Fheischner Meml. lectr., Harvard Med. Sch., 1997, Charles Dotter Meml. lectr., Am. Heart Assn., 1998; fellow, Nat. Cancer Inst., 1950, Spl. Rsch. fellow, Nat. Heart Inst., 1960, 1973—74, Henry J. Kaiser sr. fellow, Ctr. for Advanced Study in Behavioral Sci., 1980—81. Fellow: Am. Coll. Cardiology, Am. Coll. Radiology, Royal Coll. Radiology (Gt. Britain) (hon.), Royal Coll. Surgery (Ireland) (hon.); mem.: NIH (chmn. consensus panel on MRI, internat. blue ribbon panel radiation effects rsch. found. Hiroshima 1996, working group on disability of U.S. pres. 1995—98), NAS (com. biol. effects of low-level ionizing radiation BEIR VII 1999—), Inst. of Medicine NAS (com. on biol. effects of low level ionizing radium 1999—), Nat. Coun. Health Tech. Assessment, Soc. Chmn. Acad. Radiology Depts. (pres. 1970—71), Soc. Cardiovasc. Radiology (Gold medal 2000), Internat. Physicians for Prevention of Nuc. War (founding v.p., participant Nobel Peace prize 1985), N.Am. Soc. Cardiac Radiology (pres. 1979—80), Radiol. Soc. N.Am. (Gold medal 1995), Am. Soc. Nephrology, Am. Heart Assn., Inst. Medicine, Assn. Univ. Radiologists (Gold medal 1984), Alpha Omega Alpha, Phi Beta Kappa. Achievements include Naming of Abrams Conf. Rm. in radiolog and Women's Hosp., 1984; establishment of Herbert L. Abrams ann. lecturesh of Harvard Med. Sch., 1985; dedication of endowed Herbert L. Abrams Directorship of Vascular and Interventional Radiology at Brigham and Women's, 2002. Home: 714 Alvarado Stanford CA 94305 Office: Stanford U Sch Medicine 300 Pasteur Dr Stanford CA 94305-5105 E-mail: hlabrams@stanford.edu.

ABRAMS, J.J. (JEFFREY J. ABRAMS), television producer, writer; b. NYC, June 27, 1966; s. Gerald W. Abrams; m. Katie McGrath; children: Henry, Gracie. Attended, Sarah Lawrence Coll. Actor: (films) Six Degrees of Separation, 1993, Diabolique, 1996; prodr., writer, actor: Regarding Henry, 1991; exec. prodr., dir., writer: (TV series) Felicity, 1998—2002; Alias, 2001—; Lost, 2004—; exec. prodr., writer: (films) Forever Young, 1992; prodr.: The Pallbearer, 1996; actor, prodr.: (films) The Suburbans, 1999; writer, prodr.: Joy Ride, 2001; writer Gone Fishin', 1997; (screenplay) Armageddon, 1998. Office: William Morris Agency 1 William Morris Place Beverly Hills CA 90212*

ABRAMS, JONATHAN, Internet company executive; BS in Computer Science, McMaster U. Software engr. Bell-Northern Rsch. (now Nortel R&D); lead java scientist Nortel Computing Tech. Lab; software engr. Netscape Comm., 1996, CrossWorlds Software; founder, CTO HotLinks Network Inc., 1999—2001, CEO, 1999—2000, acting v.p. of engring., 1999; lead, engring. group Bitfone Corp., 2001; founder, CEO Friendster Inc., Sunnyvale, Calif., 2002—. Adv. bd. mem. Silicon Valley Assn. of Startup Entrepreneurs. Office: Friendster Inc 415 N Mary Ave Ste 112-280 Sunnyvale CA 94085

ABRAMS, LAURA SUE, social worker, educator; b. Ithaca, N.Y., June 6, 1967; d. Richard Lee and Jane Shack Abrams; m. Owen B. Fighter; 1 child, Eli Abrams Fighter. BA in History of Ideas, Brandeis U., 1989; MSW, U. Calif. Berkeley, 1993; PhD of Social Welfare, U. Calif. Berkeley, Berkeley, 2000. Cert. Study of Women, Gender, and Sexuality U. Calif., Berkeley, 2000. Sch. social worker Oakland Unified Sch. Dist., Calif., 1993—95; rsch. assoc. Stanford U., Palo Alto, Calif., 1995—96; instr. social work U. Minn., St. Paul, 1996—. Contbr. articles to profl. jours. Bd. mem. Youthlink Minn., Mpls., 2003. Recipient Lois and Samuel Silberman award, 2002; grantee rsch., Minn. Agrl. Expt. Sta., 2001. Mem.: Soc. for the Study of Social Problems, Inst. for the Advancement of Social Work Rsch. (assoc.), Coun. on Social Work Edn. (assoc.). Office: U Minn 105 Peters Hall 1401 Gortner Ave Saint Paul MN 55108

ABRAMS, LEE NORMAN, lawyer; b. Chgo., Feb. 28, 1935; s. Saul E. and Evelyn (Cohen) A.; m. Myrna Parker, Dec. 26, 1965; 1 dau., Elana Shira. AB, U. Mich., 1955, JD, 1957. Bar: Ill. 1957, U.S. Supreme Ct. 1961, U.S. Tax Ct. 1972. Assoc. firm Mayer, Brown, Rowe & Maw and predecessors, Chgo., 1957-66, ptnr., 1966—. Mem. visitors com. U. Mich. Law Sch., 1970—; bd. assocs. Nat. Coll. Edn., Chgo., 1973-80. Recipient Gold medal AICPA, 1958. Mem. ABA (coun. antitrust sect. 1975-77, fin. officer 1977-81, program chair antitrust sect. 1988-91, vice chair antitrust sect. 1991-92, chmn. forum on franchising 1982-85, chmn. antitrust com. sect. bus. law 1995-99), Chgo. Bar Assn. (antitrust law com. 1970-85), Ill. State Bar Assn. (antitrust section coun. 1994-2001), U.S. C. of C. (antitrust and trade regulation com. 1974-80), Briarwood Country Club, Royal and Ancient Golf Club of St. Andrews (Scotland). Office: Mayer Brown Rowe & Maw & predecessors 71 S Wacker Dr Chicago IL 60606 Office Phone: 312-701-7083. Business E-Mail: labrams@mayerbrownrowe.com.

ABRAMS, LEIGH JEFFREY, manufacturing executive; b. N.Y.C., July 28, 1942; BBA, Baruch Coll., 1964; CPA, N.Y. Sr. auditor Ernest & Whinney, N.Y.C., 1964—68; exec. v.p. Drew Industries Inc., White Plains, NY,

1969—78, pres., CEO, dir., of specialty bldg. products mfg., 1979—. Bd. dirs. Impac Mortgage Holdings, Inc. Chmn., bd. dirs. YMCA; bd. dirs. Impac Mortgage Holdup Inc.; cons. Jr. Achievement Westchester, Inc., bd. dirs., 1992—, chmn. bd. Westchester chpt.; former soccer coach Dad's Club, White Plains; baseball mgr. Elmsford (N.Y.) Little League. Mem. AICPA, N.Y. Soc. CPAs. Home: 91 Ridge Rd Hartsdale NY 10530-2212 Office: Drew Industries Inc 200 Mamaroneck Ave White Plains NY 10601 Office Phone: 914-428-9098. E-mail: leigh@drewindustries.com.

ABRAMS, MARC, lawyer, political organization worker; b. NYC, Mar. 23, 1957; s. Stephen Robert and Virginia Ornstein Abrams; 1 child, Lawrence Christopher. BA magna cum laude, Wesleyan U., Middletown, Conn., 1978; MA, JD, U. Mich., 1981. Bar: Conn. 1982, N.Y. 1986, D.C. 1987, Pa. 1987, Oreg. 1989, U.S. Dist Ct. (so. dist.) N.Y. 1986, U.S. Dist. Co. (ea. dist.) Pa. 1988, U.S. Dist. Ct. Mont. 1989, U.S. Cir. Ct. (3d, 4th and 9th cirs.), U.S. Dist. Ct. Oreg. 1989, U.S. Supreme Ct. Asst. prof. U. Oreg., 1981-83; exec. dir. Student Press Law Ctr., 1983-85; pvt. practice, 1985—2002; sr. asst. atty. gen. State of Oreg., 2002—. Talk show host KXL-AM, 2002—; commentator KATU-TV, 2005—. Co-author: Law of the Student Press, 1983, Confronting Wrongful Discharge Under Oregon and Washington Law, 1989. Vice chair Lane County (Oreg.) Dem. Ctrl. Com., 1981-82, Multnomah County (Oreg.) Dem. Ctrl. Com., 1991-92; mem. Oreg. Dem. State Ctrl. Com., 1981-82, 91—, Multnomah Edn. Svc. Dist. Bd., 1993-97, chmn., 1996-97; fin. chair Oreg. State Dem. Party, 1993-95, vice chair, 1994-97, chmn., 1997-99; mem. Portland Sch. Bd., 1995-2003, vice chair, 1998-2002; treas. Assn. State Dem. Chairs, 1998-99. Recipient Johnnie Phelps medal Vets. for Human Rights, 1995. Jewish. Office: 1162 Court St NE Salem OR 97301 Business E-Mail: marc.abrams@state.or.us.

ABRAMS, MEYER HOWARD, language educator; b. Long Branch, NJ, July 23, 1912; s. Joseph and Sarah (Shanes) A.; m. Ruth Gaynes, Sept. 1, 1937; children: Jane, Judith. AB, Harvard U., 1934, MA, 1937, PhD, 1940; postgrad. (Henry fellow), Cambridge (Eng.) U., 1934-35; D.H.L. (hon.), U. Rochester, 1978, Northwestern U., 1981, U. Chgo., 1982, Western Md. Coll., 1985, Le Moyne Coll., 1993; D.H.L. (hon.) (hon.), Carleton Coll., 2003. Instr. Harvard, 1938-42; research asso. psycho-acoustic lab. Harvard U., 1942-45; asst. prof. English, Cornell U., Ithaca, N.Y., 1945-47, asso. prof., 1947-53, prof., 1953-60, Frederic J. Whiton prof. English, 1960-73, Class of 1916 prof. English, 1973-83, prof. emeritus, 1983—. Adv. editor W.W. Norton & Co., Inc., 1961—; bd. editors various Cornell publs. Hon. sr. fellow Sch. Criticism and Theory, Cornell U., Fulbright lectr. Royal U. Malta, Cambridge U., 1953; Roache lectr. U. Ind., 1963; Alexander lectr. U. Toronto, 1964; Ewing lectures UCLA, 1975; Cecil Green lectr. U B.C., 1980; Lamont lectures Union Coll., 1995; Mem. founders group Nat. Humanities Ctr.; mem. coun. of scholars Libr. of Congress, 1980-94, chmn. coun. of scholars, 1984-94. Author: The Milk of Paradise, 1934, 2d edit., 1970, The Mirror and the Lamp: Romantic Theory and the Critical Tradition, 1953, A Glossary of Literary Terms, 1957, 8th edit., 2005, Natural Supernaturalism: Tradition and Revolution in Romantic Literature, 1971, The Correspondent Breeze: Essays on English Romanticism, 1984, Doing Things with Texts: Essays in Criticism and Critical Theory, 1989, also publs. on mil. communications; editor: The Poetry of Pope, 1954; Editor: Literature and Belief, 1958, The Romantic Poets: Modern Essays in Criticism, 1960, rev. edit., 1975, The Norton Anthology of English Literature, 1962, 7th edit., 1999, Wordsworth: A Collection of Critical Essays, 1972, (with others) Wordsworth's Prelude: Norton Critical Edition, 1979. Recipient Christian Gauss prize Phi Beta Kappa, 1954, James Russell Lowell prize, 1971, Am. Acad. award humanistic studies, 1984, Disting. Scholar award Keats-Shelley Assn., 1987, Am. Acad. and Inst. Arts and Letters award for lit., 1990; Rockefeller fellow, 1946; Ford fellow, 1952; Guggenheim fellow, 1958, 60-61; fellow Center for Advanced Study in the Behavioral Scis., Palo Alto, Calif., 1967-68; vis. fellow All Soul's Coll., Oxford, 1977. Mem. AAUP, MLA (exec. council 1961-64), Am. Acad. Arts and Scis., Am. Acad. Arts and Letters, Am. Philos. Soc., Brit. Acad. (corr. fellow), Phi Beta Kappa, Sigma Xi. Home: 378 Savage Farm Dr Ithaca NY 14850-6505 Office Phone: 607-255-3428. Business E-Mail: mha5@cornell.edu.

ABRAMS, NORMAN, law educator, academic administrator; b. Chgo., July 7, 1933; s. Harry A. and Gertrude (Dick) A.; m. Toshka Alster, 1977; children: Marshall David, Julie, Hanna, Naomi. AB, U. Chgo., 1952, JD, 1955. Bar: Ill. 1956, US Supreme Ct. 1967. Assoc. in law Columbia U., 1955-57; rsch. assoc. Harvard U., 1957-59; sec. Harvard-Brandeis Coop. Rsch. for Israel's Legal Devel., 1957-58, dir., 1959; mem. faculty law sch. UCLA, 1959—, prof. law, 1964—, co-dir. Ctr. for internat. and strategic studies, 1982-83, chmn. steering com., 1985-87, 88-89, assoc. dean law, 1989-91, vice chancellor acad. pers., 1991-2001, interim exec. v. chancellor, 1998, interim dean law, 2003—04. Reporter for So. Calif. indigent accused persons study Am. Bar Found., 1963; cons. Gov. Calif. Commn. L.A. Riots, 1965, Pres.'s Commn. Law Enforcement and Adminstrn. Justice, 1966-67, Nat. Commn. on Reform of Fed. Criminal Laws, 1967-69, Rand Corp., 1968-74, Ctr. for Adminstrv. Justice, ABA, 1973-77, Nat. Adv. Commn. on Criminal Justice Stds., Organized Crime Task Force, 1976; spl. hearing officer conscientious objector cases Dept. Justice, 1967-68; vis. scholar Inst. for Advanced Studies, Hebrew U., summer, 1994; vis. prof. Hebrew U., 1969-70, 86, Bar Ilan U., 1970-71, 78, U. So. Calif., 1972, Stanford U., 1977, U. Calif., Berkeley, Calif., 1977; spl. asst. to U.S. atty. gen. Dept. Justice, 1966-67, prof.-in-residence Criminal Divsn., 1966-67 Author: (with others) Evidence, Cases and Materials, 7th edit., 1983, 8th edit., 1988, 9th edit., 1997, Federal Criminal Law and Its Enforcement, 1986, 2d and 3d edits. (with S. Beale), 1993, 2000, Anti-terrorism and Criminal Enforcement, 2003, 2d edit., 2005; mem. editl. bd. Criminal Law Forum, 1990—, Jour. Nat. Security Law and Policy, 2004—. Chmn. Jewish Conciliation Bd., LA, 1975-81; bd. dir. Bet Tzedek, 1975-85, LA Hillel Coun., 1979-82, Shalhevet HS, 1998—; chmn. So. Calif. region Am. Prof. for Peace in Middle East, 1981-83; bd. dir. met. region Jewish Fedn., 1982-88, v.p. 1982-83; pres. Westwood Kehillah Congregation, 1985. Mem. Internat. Soc. for Reform of Criminal Law (mem. exec. com. 1994—), Phi Beta Kappa. Office: UCLA Law School 405 Hilgard Ave Los Angeles CA 90095-9000 Office Phone: 310-794-4056. Business E-Mail: abrams@law.ucla.edu.

ABRAMS, RICHARD LEE, physicist; b. Cleve., Apr. 20, 1941; s. Morris S. and Corinne (Tobias) A.; m. Jane Shack, Aug. 12, 1962; children: Elizabeth, Laura. B. Engring. Physics, Cornell U., Ithaca, N.Y., 1964, PhD, 1968. Mem. tech. staff Bell Telephone Labs., Whippany, N.J., 1968-71; sect. head Hughes Rsch. Labs., Malibu, Calif., 1971-75, dept. mgr., 1975-83; chief scientist Space and Comm. Group Hughes Aircraft Co., El Segundo, Calif., 1983-89; chief scientist Hughes Rsch. Labs., Malibu, Calif., 1989-96, cons., 1997—. Program co-chmn. Conf. on Laser Engring. and Applications, Washington, 1979; chmn. Conf. on Lasers and Electro-Optics, Phoenix, 1982 Assoc. editor: Optics Letters, 1979-82; patentee in field. Fellow IEEE (assoc. editor Jour. Quantum Electronics 1980-83, bd. editors Proc. 1987-89, Centennial medal 1989), Optical Soc. Am. (bd. dirs. 1982-85, v.p. 1988, pres. 1990); mem. IEEE Quantum Electronics and Applications Soc. (adminstrve. com. 1980-83, v.p. 1982, pres. 1983), Tau Beta Pi, Phi Kappa Phi. Clubs: Riviera Country (Pacific Palisades, Calif.). Home: 922 Enchanted Way Pacific Palisades CA 90272-2823 E-mail: rla11@cornell.edu.

ABRAMS, ROBERT, lawyer, state attorney general; b. Bronx, N.Y., July 4, 1938; s. Benjamin and Dorothy (Kaplan) A.; m. Diane B. Schulder, Sept. 15, 1974; children: Rachel Schulder, Becky Schulder. BA, Columbia U., 1960; JD, NYU, 1963; LLD (hon.), Hofstra U., 1979, Yeshiva U., 1984, L.I. U., 1989, Pace U., 1991. Mem. N.Y. State Assembly, 1965-69; pres. Borough of Bronx, 1970-78; atty. gen. State of N.Y., 1979-93; ptnr. Stroock & Stroock & Lavan, N.Y.C., 1994—. Panel mem. of disting. neutrals CPR Inst.; dir. Sterling Nat. Bank, Sterling Bancorp.; commr. NYC Charter Revision Commn. Contbr. articles to profl. publs.; writer column Nat. Law Jour., N.Y. Law Jour., N.Y. Times, N.Y. Newsday, N.Y. Post, N.Y. Daily News, Buffalo News, Albany Times Union, Ganette Suburban Newspapers, The Harvard Environ. Law Rev., NYU Law Rev., Columbia Jour. Environ. Law, Pace Environ. Law Rev., Washburn Law Rev., Albany Law Rev., Pace Law Rev., The Jour. of State Gov. Pres. Citizens Union Found., Help Am. Vote Act - Impace and Potential for NY, Century Found.; del. Dem. Nat. Conv., 1972, 76, 80, 84, mem. platform com., 1988; elector Electoral Coll., 1988; co-chair Nat. Jewish Dem. Coun., N.Y. State; apptd. mem. Charter Revision Commn., 2004. Recipient Adam Clayton Powell Pub. Svc. award, Interfaith award Coun. Chs., N.Y.C., Bronx Community Coll. medallion for Svc., Scroll of Honor plaque United Jewish Appeal, Benjamin Cardozo award for legal excellence Jewish Lawyers Guild, Brotherhood award B'nai B'rith, Man of Yr. award NAACP, Alumni Achievement award NYU Sch. Law, Environmentalist of Yr. award Environ. Planning Lobby N.Y., Disting. Pub. Svc. Citation Bus. Coun. N.Y. State, N.Y. State Sheriff's Assn. award, Nat. Crime Victims award, Torch of Liberty award Anti-Defamation League, Anatoly Scharansky Freedom award N.Y. Conf. Soviet Jewry, Environmentalist of Yr. award L.I. Pine Barrens Soc., Il Leone de San Marco Hon. Italian Am. award, Cavaliere medal Pres. Italy, Pres. award Marist Coll., Hubert Humphrey Humanitarian award United Fedn. Tchrs., Law Day award N.Y. State Trial Lawyers Assn., Contbns. to Urban Law award Fordham Law Jour., Deans medal Law Sch. NYU, Margaret Sanger award N.Y. State Family Planning Advocates, Lehman/LaGuardia Civic Achievement award Anti-Defamation League B'nai B'rith and Commn. on Social Justice of the Order of Sons of Italy, Father of the Yr. award Nat. Father's Day Com., B'nai Zion Bill of Rights award, Avodah award Jewish Tchr's. Assn., Man of the Yr. award N.Y. State Consumer Assembly, Rodef Tzedek Pursuer of Justice award Restructionist Rabbinical Coll., Humanitarian award Rochester Labor and Religious Coalition, Special Recognition award Profl. Women in Construction and Allied Industries, Humanitarian award Long Island Assn. for Children with Learning Disabilities, Man of the Yr. award Mental llness Found., N.Y. State Ct's. Man of the Yr. award Shamrai Tzedek Soc., Grand Marshall award Schenectady Labor Coun. Labor Day Parade, Louis Brandeis award Zionist Orgn. Am., Lubavich Tzivos Hashem award, Chassidius in Am. Exemplary Leadership award Bostoner Chassidum, Recognition for Pub. Svc. award Greater Buffalo AFL-CIO Coun., Effort on Behalf of the Elderly award Workmen's Circle Home & Infirmary For the Aged, Dedication Concerning Reproductive Rights award N.Y. Coun. of Jewish Women, Citation of Appreciation N.Y. State Assn. of Architects, Pesach-Tikvah Hope Developer award, Pub. Svc. award N.Y. Soc. Clin. Psychologists, Cmty. Achievement award Am. Orthodox Fedn., State Svc. award Nat. Columbus Day Com., Environmentalist of the Yr. award Sierra Club, Svc. award N.Y. State Jewish War Veterans, Cadet award N.Y.C. Mission Soc., Disting. Achievement award AMIT Women, Man of the Yr. award Nassau County Police Res. Assn., Ann. award Lubavitch Youth Orgn., Appreciation award Japanese C. of C. of N.Y., Friend of the Cmty. award Empire State Pride Agenda, Roland Smith award Capital Region chpt. N.Y. Civil Liberties Union, Scharansky Freedom award L.I. Com. on Soviet Jewry, Cert. of Honor award N.Y. League of Histadrut, Scouting For the Handicapped Outstanding Svc. award Greater N.Y. Coun. of Boy Scouts of Am., Citizen of the Yr. award We. N.Y. Labor Coalition, Svc. award Citizen's Coun. for the Cmty. of Mentally Retarded, Rockland Hosp. Guild, Man of the Yr. award The Shield Inst. for Retarded Children, Maccabean Svc. award N.Y. Bd. of Rabbis, Thurgood Marshall award Bridge Builders Albany, Pro Choice award Naral N.Y., Dist. Humanitarian award Insts. Applied Human Dynamics, Life-Long Dedication award Holocaust Meml. Com., Disting. Cmty. Svc. award Am. Friends of Bnei Akiva; named Man of Yr. St. Patrick's Home Aged and Infirm, Man of Yr. State Israel Bonds; named Outstanding New Yorker, N.Y.C. Coun. Mem. N.Y. State Bar Assn. (Environ. Acheivement award), Assn. Bar City of N.Y., Nat. Assn. of Attys. Gen. (pres. 1988-89, chmn. environ. protection com. 1982-85, chmn. antitrust com. 1985-88, chmn. civil rights com. 1990-92, chmn. ea. regional conf. of attys. gen. 1983-84, Wyman award for Outstanding Atty. Gen. in the Nation 1991, Assn. Bar City of NY commn. campaign fin. reform, Bellotti award). Democrat. Office: Stroock & Stroock & Lavan 180 Maiden Ln Ste 3989 New York NY 10038-4937 Office Phone: 212-806-5546. Office Fax: 212-806-6006. Business E-Mail: rabrams@stroock.com.

ABRAMS, ROGER IAN, lawyer, educator; b. Newark, July 30, 1945; s. Avel S. and Myrna (Posner) A.; m. Frances Elise Kovitz, June 1, 1969; children: Jason, Seth. BA, Cornell U., 1967; JD, Harvard U., 1970. Bar: Mass. 1970, U.S. Dist. Ct. Mass. 1971, U.S. Ct. Appeals (1st cir.) 1971. Law clk. to Judge Frank M. Coffin U.S. Ct. Appeals (1st cir.), Boston, 1970-71; assoc. Foley, Hoag & Eliot, Boston, 1971-74; prof. law Law. Sch. Case Western Res. U., Cleve., 1974-86; dean Law Ctr. Nova U., Ft. Lauderdale, Fla., 1986-93; dean Law Sch. Rutgers U., Newark, 1993-1998; prof. law sch. Rutger U., Newark, 1993-99; Herbert J. Hannuch scholar Rutgers U., Newark, 1998-99; dean Northeastern U., Boston, 1999—2002, Richardson prof. law, 1999—. Labor arbitrator Fed. Mediation Svc., 1975—; vis. prof. law Harvard Law Sch., 2005-. Author: Legal Bases: Baseball and the Law, 1998, The Money Pitch: Baseball Free Agency and Salary Arbitration, 2000, The First World Scenes and the Baseball Fanatics of 1903, 2003; contbr. articles to law jours. Recipient Gen. Counsel's Advocacy award NAACP, Boston, 1974; inductee Union N.J. Hall of Fame, 1995. Fellow Mass. Hist. Soc.; mem. Am. Law Inst., Am. Bar Found., Am. Arbitration Assn. (labor arbitrator). Democrat. Jewish. Avocations: swimming, distance walking, reading. Office: Northeastern Univ Sch Law 400 Huntington Ave Boston MA 02115-5005 Office Phone: 617-373-2068. Business E-Mail: rabrams@neu.edu.

ABRAMS, ROSALIE SILBER, retired state agency official; b. Balt., June 2, 1916; d. Isaac and Dora (Rodbell) Silber; 1 child, Elizabeth Joan. RN, Sinai Hosp.; postgrad., Columbia U.; BS, Johns Hopkins U., 1963, MA in Polit. Sci. Pub. health nurse USNR, 1945-46; bus. mgr. Sequoia Med. Group, Calif., 1946-47; asst. bus. mgr. Silber's Bakery, Balt., 1947-53; mem. Md. Ho. of Dels., 1967-70, Md. Senate, 1970-83, majority leader, 1978-82; chmn. Dem. Party of Md., 1978-83, chmn. fin. com., 1982-83; dir. Office on Aging, State of Md., 1983-95, ret., 1995. Chair World War II Meml. Commn., 1996-2000; mem. Balt. City Commn. on Aging, 1997—2000; host Outlook TV show, 1983-90; guest lectr., witness before congl. coms. Platform com. on nat. healthcare Dem. Nat., Com., 1979—; chmn. Md. Humane Practices Commn., 1978-83, mem., 1971-74; mem. New Coalition, 1979-83, State-Fed. Assembly Com. on Human Resources, 1977-83, Md. Comprehensive Health Planning Agy., 1972-75, Md. Commn. on Status of Women, 1968—, Am. Jewish Com. Chair Med. Supplies Com. for Needy and Elderly in Odessa, Ukraine; chair dept. human resources, dept. health and mental hygiene, transp., housing and cmty. devel., econ. and employment devel., Interagy. Com., 1984-95; bd. dirs. Sinai Hosp., Balt., 1973-2000, Balt. Jewish Coun., Cross Country Improvement Assn., 1969—2000, Fifth Dist. Reform Dems., 1967—2000; chmn. legis. com. Balt. Area Coun. on Alcoholism, 1973-75; mem. adv. bd. long term care project U. Md., Balt., 1986; mem. Md. Adv. Com. for Adult and Cmty. Svcs., 1984; mem. nat. adv. bd. Pre-Retirement Edn. Planning, 1986—93; mem. State Adv. Coun. on Nutrition, 1988—; spl. trustee Sheppard-Pratt Hosp., 1992-2000. With Nurse Corps USN, 1944-46. Recipient Louise Waterman Wise Cmty. Svc. award, 1969, award Am. Acad. Comprehensive Health Planning, 1971, Balt. News Am. award, Women of Distinction in Medicine, 1971, traffic safety award, Safety First Club of Md., 1971, ann London Scott Meml. award for legis. excellence, Md. chpt. NOW, 1975, Md. Nurses Assn., 1975, svc. award Balt. Area Coun. on Alcoholism, 1975, First Citizens award Md. Senate Pres., 1999, named to Md. Women's Hall of Fame, Md. Commn. for Women and Women Legislators of Md. Gen. Assembly, 1994, numerous others; 1st ann. Rosalie S. Abrams Firsts award awarded by Women Legislators of Md., 2004, Nursing Spectrum award, 2005. Mem. AAUW, AARP, Md. Order Women Legislators (pres. 1973-75), Nat. Conf. State Legislatures (human resources and urban affairs steering com. 1977-83), Nat. Legis. Conf. (human resources task force, intergovtl. rels. com. 1975-83), Md. Gerontol. Assn. (bd. dirs. 1984—), Nat. Fedn. Dem. Women, Am. Jewish Congress, Am. Soc. on Aging, Md. Gerontol. Assn., Sigma Theta Tau Nursing Soc. Home: North Oaks 725 Mt Wilson Ln Apt 729 Baltimore MD 21208

ABRAMS, ROZ, newscaster; married; 2 children. BS in Sociology, Western Mich. U.; MA in Speech, U. Mich. Anchor KRON-TV, San Francisco, CNN; anchor/reporter WXIA-TV, Atlanta; with WABC-TV, NYC, 1986—2003, weekend anchor, gen. assignment reporter, anchor Eyewitness News at 5 PM, host program Making It; co-anchor 5pm and 11pm news WCBS-TV, NYC, 2004—. Editl. adv. bd. Making Waves Am. Women in Radio and TV, 2003—. Co-chair NY Reads Together. Recipient numerous awards including Centennial award for svc. and achievement in media Greater Harlem C. of C.

ABRAMS, WILLIAM F., lawyer; b. Indpls., Sept. 21, 1954; AB with honors, Stanford U., 1976; JD, U. Santa Clara, 1979. Bar: Calif. 1979, U.S. Dist. Ct. (all Calif. dist., Md., Del.), U.S. Tax Ct., U.S. Ct. Appeals (8th, 9th cir.), U.S. Supreme Ct. 1983. Past mem. Orrick, Herrington & Sutcliffe, San Francisco; ptnr. Intellectual Property practice, head IP Litigation team Pillsbury Winthrop Shaw Pittman, Palo Alto, Calif. Instr. Stanford Univ. Mng. editor Santa Clara Law Rev., 1978; contbr. articles to profl. jours.; frequent legal commentator in print & broadcast media. Bd. dir. Youth Law Ctr., San Francisco, Silicon Valley Campaign for Legal Svcs., Hear My Voice, Ann Arbor, Palo Alto Babe Ruth League. Named a No. Calif. Super lawyer, San Francisco Mag., 2004; named one of Silicon Valley's Top 300 Lawyers, San Jose Mag., 2001—04; recipient Human Biology Excellence in Advising award, 2004. Mem. ABA, Am. Intellectual Property Law Assn., State Bar Calif., Santa Clara County Bar Assn. (trustee), Fed. Cir. Bar Assn., Intellectual Property Owners Assn., INTA, Bar Assn. San Francisco, Assn. Bus. Trial Lawyers, William A. Ingram Inn of Ct. Office: Pillsbury Winthrop Shaw Pittman 2475 Hanover St Palo Alto CA 94304-1114 Office Phone: 650-233-4668. Office Fax: 650-233-4545. Business E-Mail: william.abrams@pillsburylaw.com.

ABRAMS FINGER, IRIS DALE, retired elementary school educator; b. Ironton, Ohio, Jan. 22, 1939; d. Frank Abrams and Pearl (Moore) Schwab; m. Robert James Roderick Sr., July 20, 1957 (div. Nov. 1971); children: Robert James Roderick Jr., Elizabeth Ann Roderick Travis; m. Henry Waterman Bromley Jr., May 14, 1972 (div. June 1987); one child: Henry Waterman Bromley III; m. Grover Cleveland Finger III, Apr. 1, 1989; stepchildren: Lynn Hall, Adam Finger, Sara Mason. Degree in Early Childhood and Elem. Edn., U. South Fla.; degree in Design, Jackson Coll., Honolulu. Cert. mid. sch. math. tchr., TESLA, and gifted edn. Children's libr. Ft. Myers Pub. Libr., Fla., 1955—57; workmen's compensation payroll adminstr. San Diego, 1964—66; permanent substitute tchr. Sigsbee Elem. Sch., Key West, Fla., 1968—70; part time libr. Danielson Libr., Conn., 1970—71; residential design Bateman Homes, Leigh Acres, Fla., 1971—72; structural steel designer So. Machine and Steel, Ft. Myers, Fla., 1972—73; dir. Ft. Myers Bus. Coll., Fla., 1973—77; structural prestress concrete designer Southland Prestress, Dean Steel and Kirby MaCumber Steel, 1977—83; tchr. Lee County Sch. Bd., Ft. Myers, Fla., 1983—2004, team leader, math. coach, 1983, 1994—95; with Bonita Spring Mid. Sch., 1994—96, equity coord., 1995—96; ret., 2004. Pres. PTA, Key West, 1966-68; Fla. Art League, Ft. Myers, 1984-86; hosp. nurse ARC, 1964-66, med. evacuation for Vietnam wounded Philippine Islands Subic Hosp.; mem. Treasury of Island Coast Uni-Serve; rep. to Lee County Safety Com. Recipient Pres. Regan Achievement Award, 1976, Pres. Johnson People to People Award and Plank Award for sch. constrn. at San Meguel, Philippines, 1960; named to Wall of Tolerance, 2004, Wall at Justice Ctr., Montgomery, Ala., 2004. Mem.: NEA, Navy Wives and Navy Relief Soc., Lee County Math. Coun., Fla. Math. Coun., Rep. Assembly, Tchrs. Assn. Lee County, Fla. Tchrs. Profession, Am. Legion, VFW Aux., Pioneer Club Ft. Myers, Phi Beta Kappa (program chmn., treas.), Alpha Delta Kappa. Republican. Methodist. Avocations: art, crafts, reading, travel, family socials, swimming. Home: 186 Price St Naples FL 34113 Personal E-mail: gfinger3@comcast.net.

ABRAMSKY, ROGER, education educator; s. Morris and Mildred Abramsky; m. Jacquelyn Stone, Sept. 29, 1987; children: Jack, Melissa. AA, Middlesex C.C., Middletown, Conn., 1984; BA, Ea. Conn. State U., Willimantic, Conn., 1986. Cert. pub. speaking Am. Soc. For Positive Thinking, 2004. Fin. analyst Computer Sci. Corp., Wethersfield, Conn., 2000—; founder, motivational spkr. Am. Soc. For Positive Thinking, South Windsor, Conn., 2003—. Motivational speaker and educator (public speaking seminars) Improve Yourself Through Positive Thinking, Positive Thinking and Confidence Building, Confidence, Confidence, Confidence, Speak Easy, The Art of Public Speaking, motivational speaker, educator (conf.) Overcoming Obstacles, Positive Thinking At Any Age, Maximize Your Confidence, Mastering the Art of Public Speaking. Rnc team leader Rep. Nat. Com., Washington, 2004. Conservative. Achievements include Founder of the Am. Soc. For Positive Thinking. Avocations: finance and investing, motivational public speaking, Alaskan Malamute dogs, writing. Office Phone: 860-644-9608. Business E-Mail: positivethinkinggetsresults@yahoo.com.

ABRAMSON, ARTHUR SEYMOUR, linguistics educator, researcher; b. Jersey City, Jan. 26, 1925; s. Seymour Vallie (Olshan) A.; m. Ruby Melamed, June 27, 1952 (div. May 1985); children: Joseph B., David N. Student, Rutgers U., 1942-43; BA, Yeshiva U., 1949; MA, Columbia U., 1950, PhD, 1960. Tchr. English and French Pub. High Schs., Jersey City, 1950-53; research staff Haskins Labs., N.Y.C., 1959-63, 64-65, research assoc., 1963-64, 65—; assoc. prof. speech CUNY, 1963-64, prof. communication arts and scis., 1965-67; prof. linguistics U. Conn., Storrs, 1967-92, prof. emeritus, 1992—, head dept. linguistics, 1967-74. Fulbright tchr. Bangkok and Songkhla, Thailand, 1953-55; vis. prof. Lady Davis Fellowship Trust, Jerusalem, 1981. Author: The Vowels and Tones of Standard Thai: Acoustical Measurements and Experiments; editor Language and Speech, 1975-87; contbr. numerous articles to profl. jours. With U.S. Army, 1943-46, ETO. Am. Coun. Learned Socs. fellow, 1973-74, Ford Found. fellow, Thailand, 1973-74. Fellow Acoustical Soc. Am., Internat. Soc. Phonetic Scis. (v.p. 1985-91); mem. MLA, Permanent Coun. for Orgn. Internat. Congresses of Phonetic Scis., Linguistic Soc. Am. (sec.-treas. 1974-78, v.p. 1982, pres. 1983), Internat. Phonetic Assn. (coun. 1986-90), Am. Soc. Phonetic Scis., S.E. Asian Linguistics Soc., Siam Soc., Conn. Acad. Arts. and Scis., Phi Kappa Phi. Democrat. Jewish. Home: 1559 Stafford Rd Apt 2 Storrs Mansfield CT 06268-1210 Office: Haskins Labs 300 George St New Haven CT 06511-6624 also: U Conn Dept Linguistics 337 Mansfield Rd Unit 1145 Storrs Mansfield CT 06269-1145 Office Phone: 203-865-6163. E-mail: arthur.abramson@uconn.edu.

ABRAMSON, EDWARD J., magazine publisher; Publisher Car and Driver, Ann Arbor, Mich., Home Mag., N.Y.C., 1999—2000; v.p. Hachette Filipacchi Mags., 2000—, group pub., 2000—. Office: Hachette Filipacchi Magazines Inc 1633 Broadway New York NY 10019-6708 also: Car & Driver 2002 Hogback Rd Ann Arbor MI 48105 Office Phone: 212-767-6098, 734-971-3600. Office Fax: 734-971-9188. E-mail: eabramson@hfmmag.com.*

ABRAMSON, HANLEY NORMAN, pharmacy educator; b. Detroit, June 10, 1940; s. Frederick Jacob and Lillian (Kampner) A.; m. Young Hee Kim, Aug. 4, 1967; children: Nathaniel, Deborah, Stephen. BS in Pharmacy, Wayne State U., 1962; MS in Pharm. Chemistry, U. Mich., 1963, PhD in Pharm. Chemistry, 1966. Registered pharmacist. Rsch. assoc. The Hebrew U., Jerusalem, 1966-67; asst. prof. Wayne State U., Detroit, 1967-73, assoc. prof., 1973-78, prof., 1978—, chmn. dept. pharm. sci., 1986-95, interim dean Eugene Applebaum Coll. of Pharmacy and Health Scis., 1987—88, assoc. provost, 1991-95, assoc. dean, 1996-99, dep. dean pharmacy, 2000—02. Author numerous published articles in field of medicinal chemistry. Bd. trustees 1st Bapt. Ch. of Oak Park, Mich., 1974-78; deacon Bloomfield Hills (Mich.) Bapt. Ch., 1986-89; dir. Met. Detroit Alliance for Minority Participation, 1994-2000. Recipient rsch. grants Mich. Heart Assn., Detroit, 1967-76, Nat. Cancer Inst., Bethesda, Md., 1982-91. Mem. AAAS, Am. Chem. Soc., Am. Pharm. Assn., Am. Assn. Colls. Pharmacy. Baptist. Avocations: astronomy, coin collecting/numismatics, baseball history, classical music. Home: 5530 Hammersmith Dr West Bloomfield MI 48322-1452 Office: Wayne State U 3607 Applebaum Bldg Detroit MI 48201 Office Phone: 313-577-1711. Business E-Mail: ac2531@wayne.edu.

ABRAMSON, HYMAN NORMAN, engineering and science research executive; b. San Antonio, Mar. 4, 1926; s. Nathan and Pearl (Westerman) A.; m. Idelle Rebecca Ringel, Apr. 20, 1947; children: Phillip David, Mark Donald. BSME, Stanford U., 1950, MS in Engring. Mechanics, 1951; PhD in Engring. Mechanics (So. Fellowship Fund fellow), U. Tex., Austin, 1956.

Engr. U.S. Naval Air Missile Test Center, Point Mugu, Calif., 1947—48; project engr. Chance Vought Aircraft Co., Dallas, 1951-52; assoc. prof. aero. engrng. Tex. A&M U., 1952-55; sect. mgr., dept. dir. S.W. Research Inst., San Antonio, 1956-72, v.p. div. engrng. scis., 1972-85, exec. v.p., 1985-91, also bd. dirs. Mem. many research adv. coms. U.S. Govt.; bd. dirs. Broadway Nat. Bank. Author: An Intro to the Dynamics of Airplanes, 1958, reprinted, 1971; contbr. numerous articles to profl. publs.; editor: (with others) Applied Mechanics Surveys, 1966, The Dynamic Behavior of Liquids in Moving Containers, 1966; assoc. editor: (with others) Applied Mechanics Revs, 1954-85; editorial adv. bd.: (with others) Jour. Computers and Structures, 1970—, Aeros. and Astronautics, 1975-80. Mem. Greater San Antonio C. of C., and City of San Antonio Market Sq. Adv. Com., 1973-77; mem. U.S. Bicentennial Com. of San Antonio, 1975-76; mem. adv. bd. dirs. U.S. Alamo, Inc., 1985-90; mem. adv. bd. Karta Techs., 1991—. Served with USN, 1943-45. Fellow AIAA (Disting. Service award 1973, dir., Structures, Structural Dynamics and Materials medal 1991), ASME (v.p., gov., hon. mem. 1979, Gold medal 1999); mem. Nat. Acad. Engring., Soc. Naval Architects and Marine Engrs., Nat. Acad. Engring. Mexico, AAAS, Sigma Xi. Republican. Jewish. Home: 1511 Spanish Oaks San Antonio TX 78213-1635 Office: SW Research Inst PO Box 28510 San Antonio TX 78228-0510 Office Phone: 210-522-2207.

ABRAMSON, MARC A., dentist; Degree, Mich. State U.; DDS, U. Mich. Sch. Dentistry, Ann Arbor, 1977. Gen. practice residency St. Vincent's Med. Ctr., Toledo; solo dental practice Garden City, Mich.; dentist Exceptional Dental, Cambridge Dental Group, Dearborn Heights, Mich., 2002—. Office: Exceptional Dental Cambridge Dental Group 27281 W Warren Dearborn Heights MI 48127 Office Phone: 313-274-4040, 313-278-8800. Office Fax: 313-274-8080.*

ABRAMSON, NORMAN, retired engineering educator, electronics executive; b. Boston, Apr. 1, 1932; s. Edward and Esther (Vaslavsky) A.; m. Joan Freulich, July 4, 1954; children: Mark David, Carin Lynn. AB, Harvard U., 1953; MA, UCLA, 1955; PhD, Stanford U., 1958. Asst. prof. Stanford (Calif.) U., from 1958, assoc. prof., to 1965; vis. prof. U. Calif., Berkeley, 1965, Harvard U., Cambridge, Mass., 1965-66; prof. U. Hawaii, Honolulu, 1966-94; v.p. Aloha Networks, Inc., San Francisco, 1994-2001, Hokupâa Technologies, Honolulu, 2002—. Vis. prof. MIT, 1981-82; cons. Internat. Telecom. Union, Geneva, UNESCO, Paris, UN Devel. Program, N.Y.C. Author: Information Theory and Coding, 1963; co-editor: Computer Communication Networks, 1973; editor: Multiple Access Communications, Foundations for Emerging Technologies, 1993. Recipient Koji Kobayshi Computers and Communications award Inst. of Elec. and Electronics Engrs., 1995, Tech. award Rhein Found., 2000. Fellow: IEEE Info. Theory Soc. (Golden Jubilee award for Tech. Innovation 1998), IEEE, Internat. Engring. Consortium. Achievements include patents in field. Home: 521 Lake St San Francisco CA 94118-1216 E-mail: norm@post.harvard.edu.

ABRAMSON, PAUL ROBERT, political scientist, educator; b. St. Louis, Nov. 28, 1937; s. Harry Benjamin and Hattie Abramson; m. Janet Carolyn Schwartz, Sept. 11, 1966; children— Lee Jacob, Heather Lyn BA, Washington U., St. Louis, 1959; MA, U. Calif.-Berkeley, 1961, PhD, 1967. Asst. prof. polit. sci. Mich. State U., East Lansing, 1967-71, assoc. prof. polit. sci., 1971-77, prof. polit. sci., 1977—. Lady Davis vis. prof. Hebrew U. Jerusalem, 1994. Author: Generational Change in American Politics, 1975, The Political Socialization of Black Americans, 1977, Political Attitudes in America, 1983; co-author: Change and Continuity in the 1980 Elections, 1982, rev. edit., 1983, Change and Continuity in the 1984 Elections, 1986, rev. edit., 1987, Change and Continuity in the 1988 Elections, 1990, rev. edit., 1991, Change and Continuity in the 1992 Elections, 1994, rev. edit., 1995, Value Change in Global Perspective, 1995, Change and Continuity in the 1996 Elections, 1998, Change and Continuity in the 1996 and 1998 Elections, 1999, Change and Continuity in the 2000 Elections, 2002, Change and Continuity in the 2000 and 2002 Elections, 2003; contbr. articles to profl. jours. Served to lt. U.S. Army, 1960—62. Woodrow Wilson fellow, 1959-60; Ford Found. faculty research fellow, 1972-73; Fulbright grantee sr. lectr. Hebrew U. of Jerusalem, 1987-88. Mem. Am. Polit. Sci. Assn., Midwest Polit. Sci. Assn., So. Polit. Sci. Assn., Am. Sociol. Assn., Internat. Polit. Sci. Assn., Phi Beta Kappa Home: 2830 Turtlecreek Dr East Lansing MI 48823-6333 Office: Mich State U Dept Polit Sci East Lansing MI 48824-1032 Office Phone: 517-353-3285. Business E-Mail: abramson@msu.edu.

ABRAMSON, SARA JANE, radiologist, educator; b. New Orleans, La., May 12, 1945; m. Walter Squire; children: Harrison, Russell, Zachary, Andrew. BA, Sarah Lawrence Coll., 1967; postgrad., Tulane U., 1967-69; MD, Mt. Sinai Sch. Medicine, 1971. Diplomate Am. Bd. Radiology, cert. added qualifications pediat. radiology. Intern in pediatrics Mt. Sinai Hosp., N.Y.C., 1971-72, resident in pediatrics, 1972-73; resident in radiology St. Luke's Children's Mercy Hosp., Kansas City, Mo., 1973-76; asst. prof. radiology U. Mo., 1976-79, Harvard U. Med. Sch., Cambridge, Mass., 1979-81; fellow in pediatric radiology Children's Hosp., Boston, 1979-81; asst. prof. radiology Columbia Coll. Physicians & Surgeons, N.Y.C., 1981-88, assoc. prof. radiology, 1988-93; assoc. attending radiologist Babies Hosp. Columbia Presbyn. Med. Ctr., N.Y.C., 1981-93, dep. dir. divsn. pediatric radiology, 1992-93; assoc. prof. radiology Cornell U. Med. Coll., N.Y.C., 1993-99, prof., 1999—; assoc. attending radiologist, assoc. mem. Sloan-Kettering Cancer Ctr., Meml. Hosp., N.Y.C., 1993-98, attending radiologist, mem., 1999—. Mem. radiology elective program Columbia U. Med. Sch., N.Y.C., 1981-93, radiology residency program reevaluation, 1984-93, program coord. affiliated hosps. teaching program, 1991-93, med. student advisor, 1991-93; mem. faculty coun. Columbia U., 1987-93; cons. in pediatric radiology Blythedale Children's Hosp., 1982—, Bet Israel Hosp., N.Y.C., 1983—, Harlem Hosp., N.Y.C., 1983—, N.Y. Foundling Hosp., 1988—, Lenox Hill Hosp., 1990—, Morristown Meml. Hosp., 1990—; lectr., presenter in field. Contbr. over 40 articles to profl. jours., chpts. to books. Named Radiology Tchr. of Yr., Columbia Coll. Physicians and Surgeons, 1992, 93, 94, 2004. Fellow Am. Coll. Radiology (del. N.Y. chpt. 1991—, alt. del. 1984-91, alt. del. from Soc. for Pediat. Radiology 1992-2005, 2005—, co-chair nominating com. 2000-2002); mem. AMA, Soc. for Pediat. Radiology (bd. dirs. 2000-2003), Radiology Soc. N.Am., European Soc. for Pediat. Radiology, Soc. Thoracic Radiology, Am. Assn. Ultrasound in Medicine, Am. Assn. Women in Radiology, N.Y. Roentgen Soc. (exec. com. 1999—, sec.-treas. 1991-94, v.p. 1996-97, pres.-elect 1997-98, pres. 1998-99, moderator, pediat. program chair spring conf. 1991), N.Y. State Radiological Soc. (chmn. residents sect. 1998—, sec.-treas. 2002-2004, pres.-elect 2004-2005, pres. 2005-2006, guest lectr. spring conf. 1990-98), Children's Oncology Study Group, Caffey Soc., Neuhauser Soc., Kirkpatrick Soc. Office: Sloan-Kettering Cancer Ctr 1175 York Ave New York NY 10021-7169 Office Phone: 212-639-2184.

ABRAMSON, STEPHANIE W., former advertising executive, lawyer; b. Dec. 24, 1944; BA, Radcliffe Coll., 1966; JD, NYU, 1969. Bar: N.Y. 1969. Mem. Morgan, Lewis & Bockius, N.Y.C.; exec. v.p. and gen. counsel Young & Rubicam Inc, N.Y.C. 1996—2001; legal officer, chief corp. devel. officer Heidrick & Struggles Internat. Inc., N.Y.C, 2001—03.

ABRAVANEL, ALLAN RAY, lawyer; b. N.Y.C., Mar. 11, 1947; s. Leon and Sydelle (Berenson) A.; m. Susan Ava Paikin, Dec. 28, 1971; children: Karen, David. BA magna cum laude, Yale U., 1968; JD cum laude, Harvard U., 1971. Bar: N.Y. 1972, Oreg. 1976. Assoc. Paul, Weiss, Rifkind, Wharton & Garrison, N.Y.C., 1971-72, 74-76; fellow Internat. Legal Ctr., Lima, Peru, 1972-74; from assoc. to ptnr. Stoel, Rives, Boley, Fraser & Wyse, Portland, Oreg., 1976-83; ptnr. Perkins Coie, Portland, 1983—. Editor, pub. Abravanel Family Newsletter. Chair Oreg. Internat. Trade Com., Oreg. Dist. Export Coun. Mem.: ABA. Office: Perkins Coie LLP 1120 NW Couch St Portland OR 97209-4125 Office Phone: 503-727-2000. E-mail: aabravanel@perkinscoie.com.

ABREU, BOBBY, professional baseball player; b. Aragua, Venezuela, Mar. 11, 1974; 1 child, Emily Paola. With Astros, 1990-97, right fielder, 1997-98; outfielder Phila. Phillies Maj. Baseball League, 1998—. Named Home Run Derby Champion, MLB All-Star Game, 2005; named to Nat. League All-Star Team, 2005. Office: Phila Phillies PO Box 7575 Philadelphia PA 19101-7575 also: Philadelphia Phillies Veterans Stadium 3501 South Broad Street Philadelphia PA 19148*

ABREU, LUIS ALBERTO, lawyer; b. Pinar Del Rio, Cuba, Apr. 20, 1956; came to U.S., 1961; s. Arnaldo Jesus and Justa (Villar) A.; m. Sallie Brown Shadrick, Aug. 23, 1980; children: Sarah, Maria. BA, Davidson Coll., 1978; JD, U. Fla., 1981. Bar: Va. 1981, U.S. Bankruptcy Ct. 1981, U.S. Ct. Appeals (4th cir.) 1981. From assoc. to ptnr. Clement & Wheatley, Danville, Va., 1981—2003; prin. Carter Craig, Attys. at Law, Danville, Va., 2003—. Chmn. Local Human Rights Com., Danville, Va., 1986—89; commr. Commn. Archtl. Rev.; bd. dirs., pres. YMCA, 1992; mem. planning and budget com. United Way; bd. dirs. Danville Sci. Ctr. Alex Hemby scholar Davidson Coll., 1974-78; recipient Bob Griese award Miami Touchdown Club, 1976. Mem.: ABA, Mental Health Assn. (bd. dirs.), Va. Bar Assn., Danville Mus. Fine Arts, Hist. Soc., Lions (pres. 1984—85). Republican. Roman Catholic. Avocations: racquetball, house restoration. Home: 250 Shoreham Dr Danville VA 24541-5149 Office: Carter Craig 126 S Union St Danville VA 24541 Office Phone: 434-792-9311. Business E-Mail: labreu@ccbbk.com.

ABRIKOSOV, ALEXEI ALEXEYEVICH, physicist; b. Moscow, June 25, 1928; s. Aleksey Ivanovich and Fanny Davidovna (Vulf) Abrikosov; m. Svetlana Yuriyevna Bun-kova, 1977; 3 children. Degree, Moscow U., 1948; DS in Physics and Math., Inst. Phys. Problems, Moscow, 1955; DS (hon.), Lausanne U., 1975, Bordeaux U., 2003, Laughborough U., 2004. Rsch. assoc., sr. scientist Inst. Phys. Problems USSR Acad. Scis., Moscow, 1948-65, head dept. L.D. Landau Inst. Theoretical Physics, 1965-88; dir. Inst. High Pressure Physics, Moscow, 1988-91; disting. sci. Argonne Nat. Lab., Ill., 1991—. Prof. Moscow Univ, 1951—68, Gorky Univ, 1971—72, Moscow Physical Eng Inst, 1974—75; head chair theoretical physics Moscow Inst Steel and Alloys, 1976—92. Author: Quantum Field Theory Methods in Statistical Physics, 1962, Introduction to the Theory of Normal Metals, 1972, Fundamentals of the Theory of Metals, 1987; contbr. articles to profl jours. Recipient Lenin Prize, 1966, Fritz London Award, 1972, State Prize, 1982, Landau Prize, Acad Sci USSR, 1989, Int John Bardeen Award, 1991, Nobel prize in physics, 2003. Fellow: Am. Acad. Arts and Scis., Am. Physics Soc.; mem.: NAS, Royal Soc. London (fgn.), Russian Acad. Scis. Office: Argonne Nat Lab 9700 Cass Ave Argonne IL 60439-4803 Office Phone: 630-252-5482. E-mail: abrikosov@anl.gov.

ABRIL, MARCIA (ELA I. CARDINAS), writer; b. Jesus Maria, Santander, Colombia, Mar. 21, 1928; came to U.S., 1985; d. Jorge Benjamin and Ana Isabel (Valenzuela) Tellez; m. Rafael A. Cardenas, Mar. 12, 1959; children: Willyam, Harold, Alix, Ela, Rafael, Katiana. BA in Edn. and Psychology, Normal Superior A. Narino, Malaga, Santander, 1950. Prodr. Continental Network Channel 14 TV, Miami, Fla., 1989. Participant/writer Mcpl. Matanzas en el Exilio, Miami, Fla., 1986. Author: Para ti Cartagena, 1982, Aguilas e Ilusiones, 1986, Insolito, 1990, 2d edit., 1995, Girasol y Yo, 1994, Viento y Sol, 1995; author/composer: Colombia Aqui Esta tu Gente, Miami, 1986. Vol. Empresa Promotora de Turismo, Cartagena, 1982-83; benefactor Biblioteca Nacional, Bogota, Colombia, 1982, U. Nacional de Colombia, Bogota, 1982; guest/participant Primer Encuentro de la Cultura Hispanoamericana, Bogota, 1983. Recipient Honorary award Municipio de Matanzas en el Exilio, Miami, 1986, Meritory award Eva Am. Prodns., 1995, Cert. of Recognition, U.S. Libr. of Congress, 1995. Roman Catholic. Avocations: writing, dance, swimming, reading. Office: 815 SW 8th St Miami FL 33130-3703

ABRIOLA, LINDA M., civil engineer, environmental engineer; BS in Civil Engring., Drexel U., 1976; MS in Civil Engring., Princeton U., 1979, MA in Civil Engring., 1980, PhD in Civil Engring., 1983. Project engr. Procter and Gamble Mfg. Co., S.I., NY, 1976—78; rsch. asst. dept. civil engring. Princeton U., NJ, 1979—83, postdoctoral rschr. dept. civil engring., 1983—84; vis. assoc. prof. dept. petroleum engring. U. Tex., Austin, 1991; vis. scientist dept. geotech. engring. Universitat Politecnica de Cataluna, Barcelona, 1992; asst. prof. dept. civil and environ. engring. U. Mich., Ann Arbor, 1984—90, assoc. prof. dept. civil and environ. engring., 1990—96, prof., dir. Environ. and Water Resources Engring. Program, 1996—2003; dean engring., prof. civil and environ. engring. Tufts U., 2003—. Mem. environ. engring. com. USEPA Sci. Adv. Bd., 1990—96; mem. com. on groundwater clean-up alternatives NRC, 1991—94, mem. water sci and tech. bd., 1994—97; mem. sci. adv. com. Western Region Hazardous Substance Rsch. Ctr., 1995—. Contbr. articles to profl. jours. Recipient Presdl. Young Investigator award, NSF, 1985, Faculty award for Women Scientists and Engrs., 1991, Outstanding Educator award, Assn. for Women Geoscientists, 1996; Vis. Scientist's grant, Spanish Ministry of Edn. and Sci., 1992, Disting. Darcy lectr., Nat. Groundwater Assn., 1996. Mem.: Nat. Acad. Engring., Am. Geophys. Union (hydrology divsn. 1992—94), Assn. Environ. Engring. Profs. (bd. dirs. 1990—92). Office: Dean Engring Tufts U Medford MA 02155

ABRON, LILIA A., chemical engineer; b. Memphis, Mar. 8, 1945; d. Ernest and Bernice (Wise) A.; children: Fredeick, Ernest, David. BS in Chemistry, Lemoyne Coll., 1966; MS in Sanitary Engring., Washington U., 1968; PhD in Chem. Engring., U. Iowa, 1971. Profl. engr. Free lance cons., Washington, 1971-74; asst. prof. Howard U., Washington, 1974-81; chief environ. div. Delon Hampton & Assocs., Washington, 1975-78; pres., CEO Peer Cons., Rockville, Md., 1978—. Com. mem. Nat. Coun. Examiners, Clemson, S.C. Pres. Jack & Jill Am., Inc., D.C. Chpt., 1990-92; bd. dirs. Bapt. Home for Children, Washington. Recipient Women Owned Bus. Enterprise award DOT, 1988, Balti. Outstanding Minority Bus. award Fed. Exec. Bd., 1987; named Alumnus of Yr. Lemoyne Owen Coll., 1988. Fellow Am. Acad. Arts & Scis.; mem. AAAS, Water Environ. Fedn., Am. Soc. Civil Engrs., Am. Water Works Assn., Sigma Xi Office: PEER Cons 12300 Twinbrook Pkwy Ste 410 Rockville MD 20852-1650

ABSHIRE, GEORGE EDWIN, mathematician, educator; b. Cushing, Okla., June 8, 1952; s. Lewis and Willa Mae Abshire; m. Judy Sullivan, Aug. 14, 1956. BS in Edn., East Ctrl. U., 1978; MEd, Okla. U., 2004. Nat. bd. cert. tchr. 1999. Tchr. math. Jenks (Okla.) Mid. Sch., 1982—. Author: Developing Mathematical Fluency. Recipient Tchr. Yr. award, Okla. State Dept. Edn., 2002. Mem.: Okla. Coun. Tchrs. Math. (treas. 2001—05). Home: PO Box 1092 Jenks OK 74037-1092 Office: Jenks Middle School 205 East B Street Jenks OK 74037 Office Phone: 918-299-4411. Office Fax: 918-298-0652. E-mail: george.abshire@jenksps.org.

ABSHIRE, MARY YOUNG, dietitian, small business owner; b. El Campo, Tex., Jan. 10, 1952; d. Robert Joshua and Virginia (Braden) Young; m. Russell John Abshire, June 22, 1978; children: Russell Braden, Marissa Michelle, Ryan Ross. BS in Foods and Nutrition, U. Tex., 1973. Registered dietitian; lic. dietitian, Tex. Dietetic trainee U. Tex. Sys. Cancer Ctr.-M.D. Anderson Hosp., Houston, 1974-75; regional dietary cons. Nat. Living Ctrs. Inc., Victoria, Tex., 1975-77, quality assurance dietitian Houston, 1977-78, corp. dietitian, dietary coord., 1978-81; restaurant owner, operator Virginia Young, Inc., El Campo, Tex., 1980-86; ind. cons. El Campo, 1981-88; v.p. nutrition and dietary svcs. The Arboretum Group, Inc., Victoria, 1988-94; owner, pres. Abshire & Assocs., Inc., El Campo, 1994-98; co-owner Allied Dietary Cons., Inc., 1998—. Author: (how to books) Dietary Forms for Long Term Care, 1994, Dietary Inservices for Long Term Care, 1994, Documentation for Long Term Care, 2000, Dietary Cost Control, 2001. Mem.: Tex Health Care Assn. (certs. and stds. com., peer rev. com. 1978—81), Tex. Cons. Dietitians in Health-Care Facilities (chair elect/chair 1990—91), Dietitians in Health-Care Facilities, Nutrition Entrepreneurs Practice Group, Gerontol. Nutritionists Practice Group, Tex. Cons. Gerontol. Dietitians Practice Group (chair-elect/chair 1996—97), Am. Dietetic Assn. (registered dietitian), Omicron Nu, Beta Sigma Phi. Avocations: crafts, reading, travel. Home and Office: Allied Dietary Cons Inc 2409 Hutchins Ln El Campo TX 77437-2113 E-mail: abshire@wcnet.net.

ABSTON, DUNBAR, JR., management executive; b. Memphis, Jan. 26, 1931; s. Dunbar and Esther (Cook) A.; m. Constance Condon, Apr. 29, 1978; children— Lauri Abston Arnold, Dunbar III, Linda Abston Larsen, Frank Norfleet; stepchildren— Selden Early Popwell, Martha McKellar Early, William Cole Early III, Elizabeth Early Gore. AB, Princeton U., 1953; MBA, Harvard U., 1955; M.Phil., Oxford U., 1989. Joined Parts Inc., Memphis, 1959, chmn., 1979; pres. parent co. Parts Industries Corp., Memphis, 1981-83, pres., chief exec. officer, 1983-87; pres., proprieter Abston Mgmt. Co., Memphis, 1987—. Pres. Tract-O-Land Plantation; ptnr. Abston Farms, Lake Comorant, Miss., Abston-Norfleet Realty Co., Memphis, Abston Sod Farm LLC, Lake Comorant, Miss., 2000—. Past chmn. Memphis Symphony Orch., Memphis Plough Community Found.; trustee Rhodes Coll., Lawrenceville Sch. Baker scholar Harvard U., 1954. Mem. Automotive Warehouse Distbrs. Assn. (past chmn.), Memphis Econ. Club (past chmn.), Phi Beta Kappa. Republican. Presbyterian. Home: 4010 Dumaine Way Memphis TN 38117 Office: Abston Mgmt Co 4727 Spottswood Ave Memphis TN 38117-4818 Office Phone: 901-763-4727. Personal E-mail: dabstonjr@aol.com.

ABT, JEFFREY, art educator, art historian, artist, writer; b. Kansas City, Mo., Feb. 27, 1949; s. Arthur and Lottie (Weinman) A.; m. Mary Kathleen Paquette, July 16, 1972; children: Uriel, Danya. BFA, Drake U., 1971, MFA, 1977. Curator collections Wichita (Kans.) Art Mus., 1977-78; gen. mgr. Billy Hork Galleries, Ltd., Chgo., 1978-80; exhbns. coordinator U. Chgo. Libr., 1980-86; asst. dir. Smart Mus. of Art, U. Chgo., 1986—87, acting dir., 1987—89; assoc. prof. dept. art and art history Wayne State U., Detroit, 1989—, dept. chair, 1989-94, mem. adv. bd. Humanities Ctr., 1993-95. Author: A Museum on the Verge: A Socioeconomic History of the Detroit Institute of Arts, 1882-2000, 001; exhbn. catalogues The Printer's Craft, 1982, The Book Made Art, 1986; one-man shows include Cliff Dwellers, 1997, Cary Gallery, 1998, Wayne State U., 1999, 2003, Worthington Arts Coun. Gallery, 2000; editor ann. Book and Paper Group Am. Inst. for Conservation, 1985-86; editor exhbn. catalogue Up From the Streets: Detroit Art from the Duffy Warehouse Collection, 2001; mem. editl. bd. Wayne State U. Press, 1990-96, 2002—, chmn. editl. bd., 1996—2001; illustrator: Water: Sheba's Story, 1997; contbr. articles and book revs. to profl. jours., chpts. to books and encys. Bd. dirs. Hyde Pk. Jewish Cmty. Ctr., Chgo., 1988-89, Detroit Artists Market, 1994—, sec., 1996-99, pres., chmn. bd. dirs., 1999-2001, hon. dir., 2004—; trustee Ragdale Found., Lake Forest, Ill., 1985-96, nat. adv. coun., 1996—; intercultural programs com., 1990-92, libr. adv. com., 1990-96, edn. adv. com., 1992-95, Detroit Inst. Arts; visual arts com. Detroit Festival of the Arts, 1989-92; juror art exhbns., 1986—; dir. Reva and David Logan Found., Chgo., 2003—. Recipient numerous purchase prizes, awards and commns. for artistic work, 1974—, award of merit Mich. Hist. Soc., 2002, Bd. Govs. award Wayne State U., 2003; Hebrew Union Coll.-Jewish Inst. Religion fellow, Jerusalem, 1971-72; grantee IMS, NEA, NEH, Rockefeller Archive Ctr., Rockefeller U., Logan Found., Wayne State U. Humanities Ctr., Kaufman Meml. Trust, Woodrow Wilson Nat. Fellowship Found. Mem. Am. Assn. Mus., Coll. Art Assn., Assn. Mus. History (co-founder). Office: Wayne State U Dept Art and Art History 150 Art Bldg Detroit MI 48202 Office Phone: 313-993-6785. Business E-Mail: j_abt@wayne.edu.

ABT, STEVEN R., civil engineer, educator, dean; b. Cheyenne Wells, Colo; BCE, Colo. State U., 1973, MSCE, 1976, PhDCE, 1980. Hydraulics staff engr. Leonard Rice Engring., Denver, 1974-76; instr. Colo. State U., Ft. Collins, 1976-80, from asst. prof. to assoc. prof., 1980-88, prof., 1988—, exec. asst. dean, 1997—2004, interiim dean, 2004—05. Cons., Ft. Collins, 1976—. Editor, co-editor Proceedings; contbr. more than 78 articles to profl. jour. 2d lt. C.E., US Army, 1973, brig. gen. USAR, 1973—. Fellow ASCE; mem. Transp. Rsch. Bd., Internat. Erosion Control Assn. Office: Colo State U Engring and Rsch Ctr Fort Collins CO 80523-1372 E-mail: sabt@engr.colostate.edu.

ABTS, CYNTHIA MARIE, music educator; b. Ft. Ord, Calif., Jan. 21, 1977; d. Gerald Francis and Martha Abts. MusB, Humboldt State U., 1998; MusM, Ohio State U., 1999. Adj. instr. music Ind. Wesleyan U., Marion, Ind., 2000—02; instr. music Dickinson (N.D.) State U., 2002—. Prin. percussionist, timpanist Bismarck-Mandan Symphony Orch., ND, 2003—. Office: Dickinson State Univ 291 Campus Dr Dickinson ND 58601 Office Phone: 701-483-2557. E-mail: cindy.abts@dickinsonstate.edu.

ABTS, HENRY WILLIAM, retired banker; b. Columbus, Nebr., July 3, 1918; s. Matthew C. and Irene (Xanders) A.; m. Virginia Lung, Nov. 7, 1942; children: Bruce M., Susan A. (Mrs. J. Farnham). BS, Butler U., 1941. Asst. mgr. indsl. relations Union Carbide Co., Kokomo, Ind., 1945-54, personnel mgr. N.Y.C., 1954-56, dir. indsl. relations South Charleston, W.Va., 1956-60; v.p. personnel Cummins Engine Co., Inc., Columbus, Ind., 1960-68, v.p. adminstrn., sec., 1968-82, ret., 1982; v.p. Columbus Bank and Trust, 1982-87, pres., chief exec. officer, 1987-88; ret., 1988. Mem. regional adv. bd. Liberty Mut. Ins. Co. Served to capt. USAAF, 1941-45. Recipient Disting. Alumnus award Butler U., 1981, Cmty. Svc. award Columbus C. of C., 1985; named Outstanding Young Man Kokomo Jr. C. of C., 1951, Boss of Year Columbus Jr. C. of C., 1963, Athletic Hall of Fame, Butler U., 1996. Mem. Ind. C. of C., Ind. Golf Assn. (past pres., dir.), Phi Delta Theta. Mem. Christian Ch. Clubs: Otter Creek Golf (past pres.), Harrison Lakes Country (past pres.); Columbus Rotary (past pres.). Home: 9544 Raintree Dr S Columbus IN 47201-4817

ABUBAKR, SAID MOHAMMED, chemical engineering educator; b. Irbid, Jordan, Sept. 23, 1948; came to U.S., 1977; s. Abdellatif and Khaireh (Hrais) A.; m. Doha M. Serieh, Jan. 24, 1984; children: Haniene, Tamer, Maher, Majdy. BS in Petroleum Engring., Moscow Inst. Petrochems., 1974; MSChemE, Mich. State U., 1981, PhD in Chem. Engring., 1982. Prodn. engr. Jordan Petroleum Refinery, Zarga, 1974-77; instr. Mich. State U., East Lansing, 1977-82; asst. prof. Yarmouk U., Irbid, 1982-84, U. Wis., Stevens Point, 1984-87, from assoc. prof. to prof., 1987-93; project leader USDA Forest Products Lab., Madison, Wis., 1993—2002; prof. chair paper and printing sci. and engring. Western Mich. U., Kalamazoo, 2002—. Mem. adv. bd. U. Wis.-Stevens Point Gesell Inst., 1988-93, U. Wis.-Stevens Point, 1993—. Editor: Anthology of Paper Recycling, 1996; contbr. more than 100 sci. papers to profl. publs., author/co-author four books. Recipient Tchg. Excellence award U. Wis., 1987, Sec.'s Honor award USDA, 1995-97, Tech. Transfer award Forest Svc. Chief, 1997. Fellow TAPPI (mem. divsn. coun. forestry bd. 1997—, vice chair fiber recycling 1997—); mem. AIChE. Achievements include research in area of paper recycling and removal of contaminants from recycled paper using enzymatic deinking, fiber loading and fractionation; inventions in field. Office: Western Mich U A217 Parkview 4601 Campus Dr Kalamazoo MI 49008-5462 E-mail: sabubakr@wmich.edu.

ABUGHALI, NAZHA, pediatrician, consultant; b. Beirut, Aug. 27, 1960; d. Fawzi and Suliema Abughali; m. Mohamed A. Ali, June 13, 1989; children: Marwan M. Ali, Dana M. Ali, Nadeen Ali, Ahmad Ali. MD, Am. U. Of Beirut, Beirut, Lebanon, 1981—85. Diplomate in the Am.Bd. of Pediatrics 1989, Diplomate in Pediatric Inf. Dis. 1994. Pediatric infectious dis. Metro Health Med. Ctr., Cleveland, Ohio, 2001—; pediatric infectiuos dis. cons. Cleve. Clinic Found., Ohio, 2001—; pediatrician Children's Physicians, West Palm Beach, Fla., 1999—2001; pediatric infectiuos dis. staff Metrohealth Med. Ctr., Cleveland, Ohio, 1993—98. Head of pediatric tb services Cuyahoga Co. Tb Clin., Cleveland, Ohio, 2001—; med. dir. of pediatric in patient Metro Health Med. Ctr., Cleveland, Ohio, 2002—; asst. prof. of pediat. Case Western Res. U., Cleveland, Ohio, 1994—. Fellow: Am. Acad. Of Pediat. (corr.; us 1990); mem.: Pediatric Infectiuos Dis. of Pediat. (corr.; us 1993). Achievements include research in pediatric Tuberculosis. Office: Metrohealth Med Ctr 2500 Metrohealth Dr Cleveland OH 44109 Business E-Mail: nabughali@metrohealth.org.

ABUHOFF, DANIEL MARK, lawyer; b. Westbury, NY, Jan. 7, 1954; s. Ralph Leo and Fleur (Karastoff) A.; m. Tamsen Carol Granger, Oct. 16, 1982; children: Granger, Sadie, Ezekiel. AB, Princeton U., 1975; JD, Columbia U., 1978. Bar: NY 1979. Assoc. Debevoise & Plimpton LLP, NYC, 1978-88, ptnr., mem. litig. dept., 1988—. Mem. non-profit coord. com. NY Real

Property Task Force. Mem. ABA (litigation sect., antitrust sect.), Assn. Bar City NY Office: Debevoise & Plimpton LLP 919 Third Ave New York NY 10022 Office Phone: 212-909-6381. Office Fax: 212-909-6836. E-mail: dmabuhoff@debevoise.com.

ABUL-HAJ, SULEIMAN KAHIL, pathologist; b. Palestine, Apr. 20, 1925; came to U.S., 1946, naturalized, 1955; s. Sheik Khalil and S. Buteina (Oda) Abul-H.; m. Elizabeth Abood, Feb. 11, 1948; children: Charles, Alan, Cary. *The roots of the Abul-Haj family date back to the 7th century, A.D. Arab armies invaded North Africa and intermarried with local inhabitants, the Berbers. The Berbers were Barbarian Germanic hords who invaded Rome and then moved into and settled in North Africa. Tarique Bin Ziyad, born to Berber mother and an Arab father, was the founding ancestor. Tarique commanded the Arab armies that conquered Spain in 711 A.D. Jabal Tarique, anglicized to Gibraltar, was named after him, which means the Mount of Tarique. The name Abul-Haj, father of the pilgrims, was dubbed in the 12th century following the treaty between Saladdin and the Crusaders.* BS, U. Calif., Berkeley, 1949; MS, U. Calif., San Francisco, 1951, MD, 1955. Intern Cook County Hosp., Chgo., 1955-56; resident U. Calif. Hosp., San Francisco, 1949, Brooke Gen Hosp., 1957-59; chief clin. and anatomic pathology Walter Reed Army Hosp., Washington, 1959-62; assoc. prof. U. So. Calif. Sch. Medicine, L.A., 1963-96; sr. surg. pathologist Los Angeles County Gen. Hosp., 1963; dir. dept. pathology Cmty. Meml. Hosp., Ventura, Calif., 1964-80, Gen. Hosp. Ventura County, 1966-74; dir. Pathology Svc. Med. Group, 1970—. Cons. Calif. Tumor Tissue Registry, 1962-96, Camarillo State Hosp., 1964-70, Tripler Gen. Hosp., Hawaii, 1963-67, Armed Forces Inst. Pathology, 1960-69. Contbr. articles to profl. jours. Bd. dirs. Tri-Counties Blood Bank, Am. Cancer Soc. Maj., M.C., U.S. Army, 1956-65. Recipient Calif. Honor Soc. award, 1949, Borden award, 1955, Achievement cert. Surgeon Gen. Army, 1962, Internat. medal of Honor, Internat. Living Legends. Fellow Coll. Am. Pathologists; mem. AAAS, AMA, Inte rnat. Coll. Surgeons, World Affairs Coun., World Peace and Diplomacy Forum. Achievements include research in cardiovascular disease, endocrine, renal, skin diseases, also cancer. Home and Office: 105 Encinal Way Ventura CA 93001-3317 Office Phone: 805-648-1232. Personal E-mail: eabulhaj@earthlink.net.

ABU-MOSTAFA, AYMAN SAID, application developer, consultant; b. Giza, Egypt, June 1, 1953; came to U.S., 1978; s. Said S. Abu-Mostafa and Faiza A. Ibrahim. BME, Cairo U., 1976; MS in Mech. and Aerospace Engring., Okla. State U., 1980, PhD, 1984. Tchg. asst. Cairo U., Giza, Egypt, 1978, Okla. State U., Stillwater, 1978-79, rsch. assoc., 1979-81; software engr. SEAM Internat. Corp., Palos Verdes, Calif., 1984-87; computing and networking cons. Calif. State U., Los Alamitos, 1987-92; sr. sys. analyst Allied Signal Aerospace, Torrance, Calif., 1992-93; pres., CEO NeuroDollars, Inc., Huntington Beach, Calif., 1993-97; sr. programmer analyst Softnet Systems, Irvine, Calif., 1997-99; software solutions cons. Borland Software Corp. (formerly known as StarBase Corp.), Santa Ana, Calif., 1999—2003; software devel. engr. Capita Techs., Inc., 2003—04. Author papers, articles in field. Undergrad. fellow Ministry of Higher Edn., Cairo, 1971, 72, 76; NASA/Ames grantee, 1979-81. Mem. AIAA, IEEE, Assn. for Computing Machinery. Avocations: reading, computers, languages, music. E-mail: ayman1@aol.com.

ABU-MOUSTAFA, ADEL H., medical educator, dean; b. Cairo, Nov. 18, 1939; came to U.S., 1962; s. Abdulhamid and Zanab (Ayad) Abu-moustafa; m. Magda Ismail Kabbany, Oct. 10, 1962; children: Heidi, Sally, Sherief. BSc, Cairo U., 1960; MA, Harvard U., 1964; PhD, Boston U., 1969. Instr. Boston Coll., Chestnut Hill, Mass., 1964-67; from asst. prof. to assoc. prof. Salem (Mass.) State Coll., 1967-70, prof., 19770-72, dean undergrad studies, 1972-74, acting acad. dean, 1974-76, dean acad. svcs., 1976-79, exec. v.p., 1979-83; adminstrv. counselor King Faisal U., Saudi Arabia, 1983-86; dir. svcs. to higher edn. Acad. for Ednl. Devel., Washington, 1983-87; dir. assoc. dean internat. health affairs Tufts U. Sch. Medicine, Boston, 1987—, dean internat. health affairs, 1997—. Team leader consortium of U.S. Univs. and U.S. Dept. Treasury, U.S. Saudi Commn. on Econ. Cooperation to assist King Faisal U., Saudi Arabia, 1983-87. Contbr. articles to profl. jours. Mem. exec. com. Fletcher Sch. Law and Diplomacy, 1987—. Mem. Arab Am. Physicians. Moslem. Avocation: politics. Office: Tufts U Sch Medicine 136 Harrison Ave Boston MA 02111-1817 Office Phone: 617-636-0355. Business E-Mail: adel.abu-moustafa@tufts.edu.

ABUT, CHARLES C., lawyer; b. Jan. 11, 1944; BA, Columbia U., 1969; JD, Cornell U., 1972. Bar: NJ 1972, DC 1979, NY 1980, U.S. Supreme Ct. 1976, cert.: (matrimonial atty.), accredited family law mediator:. Assoc. Hannoch & Weisman, Newark, 1972-74; arbitrator Am. Arbitration Assn., 1978—. Lectr. Inst. CLE, 1989-2000. Author: Celebrity Goodwill, 1989. With Mil. Police, U.S. Army, 1964-67. Fellow Am. Acad. Matrimonial Attys.; mem. ABA, ATLA, N.J. Trial Lawyers Assn., Masons, Psi Upsilon. Office: 1 Executive Dr Fort Lee NJ 07024-3309 E-mail: ccaesq@att.net.

ACAMPORA, RALPH JOSEPH, brokerage firm executive; b. NYC, Oct. 2, 1941; s. Ralph J. and Teresa (Fusco) Acampora; m. Rosemary Sherlock; stepchildren: Mathew, Ross J. BA, St. Joseph's Sem., Yonkers, N.Y., Iona Coll. With Harris, Upham & Co. (merged with Smith Barney), N.Y.C., 1969-80; sr. v.p., tech. analyst Kidder Peabody & Co., N.Y.C., 1980-90, Prudential Equity Group, N.Y.C., 1990—, mng. dir. tech. rsch. Tchr. N.Y. Inst. Fin., 1970—. Author: The Fourth Mega Market, 2000. Bd. dirs. Hudson River Performing Arts Ctr. Mem.: Security Industry Assn. (bd. dirs.), Security Traders Assn. (bd. dirs.), NY Soc. Security Analysts (bd. dirs.), Internat. Fedn. Technician Analysts (founder, 1st chmn. 1986—92), Market Technicians Assn. (founder assn. libr. 1975, pres. 1979—80, 2001—03, chartered, founder 1970s, Hon. award 1987). Republican. Roman Catholic. Avocation: study of World War II. Home: 350 Albany St Ph 1 New York NY 10280-1415 Office: Prudential Equity Group 1 New York Plz New York NY 10004-1901

ACCARDI, JAMES (JIMMI) LEONARD, musician; b. Bklyn., Jan. 20, 1950; s. James Vincent and Angelina (Mastrogiulio) Accardi; m. Kathleen Monahan (div.); children: James John, Kimberly Flower; m. Margaret Iredell Foard; 1 child, Christobal Moriah Moscoso Fitzpatrick. Grad., Patchogue (L.I.) H.S., 1968. Guitarist on tour Chubby Checker, 1972, Davey Jones and Mickey Dolenz, 1977; musician, songwriter with original bands NY, 1973—76; guitarist recording with Rupert Holmes, NY, 1975; guitarist, vocalist. songwriter with The Laughing Dogs, 1976—79; rec. artist with The Laughing Dogs Columbia Records, NY, 1978—79; guitarist, bass player Eddy Dixon, Wilson Cloud Chamber, NY, 1980—90; guitarist Harry Nillson, Calif., 1993; performing artist, composer, songwriter Calif., 1990—. Studio keyboard player, drummer, rec. engr., arranger, prodr., 1970—. Musician: (albums) The Laughing Dogs, 1979, The Laughing Dogs Meet their Makers, 1979, The Long Lost Night, 1992, Great Italian Love Songs of the '50s, Hidden Bones, Roots I and II, (Jimmi Accardi and the Gold Rush Boys) Songs of the Gold Rush, Keep on Rockin'!, Rock & Roll Party; composer: (films and TV including soundtrack) The Complete Beatles, Loveless; musician: (albums) Workstation, The Bardos, Song for Inanna, 1985—90, The Skandhas, 1986, Punky But Chic: The American New Wave Scene. DJ Jimmi Accardi's Rock & Roll Party KVMR-FM Radio, Nevada City, Calif., 1999—. Recipient Billboard Top Picks. Mem.: BMI. Avocation: painting. Home: PO Box 1181 Penn Valley CA 95946 Personal E-mail: jimmi_accardi@oro.net.

ACCARDI, LARRY J., food service executive; m. Kathy Accardi; 3 children. BBA, U. Memphis. Joined Sysco Corp., Houston, 1976, dir. program accounts Memphis, 1976—82, dir. mktg., 1982—84, v.p. mktg., 1984—85, sr. v.p. mktg./merchandising, 1985—89, pres., COO Jackson, Miss., 1989—92, CEO, 1992—95, pres., CEO Atlanta, 1995—98, sr. v.p. ops. N.E. region Houston, 1998—2000, exec. v.p. merchandising svcs. and multi-unit sales, 2000—, pres. splty. distbn., 2000—. Office: Sysco Corp 1390 Enclave Pkwy Houston TX 77077-2099

ACCATINO, STEVEN C., instrumental music educator, orchestra conductor; s. Charles B and Ruth E Accatino; m. Carolyn S Vanderbilt, Sept. 1, 2002; children: Megan E, Adrienne A, Kimberly E Vanderbilt, Peter C, Emily N. AA, Diablo Valley Coll., 1968—70; BA, Calif. State U., 1970—72; MS, So. Oreg. U., 1993—95. California State Teaching Credential Calif. Dept. of Edn., 1973. Dir., instrumental music Ygnacio Valley H.S., Concord, Calif., 1980—; music dir., condr. Young Artists Symphony Orch., Walnut Creek, Calif., 1997—. Treas. Contra Costa County Band Directors Assn., Concord, Calif., 2003—. Musician: Western Internat. Band Clinic (Order of the Phoenix, 1995). Scout leader Boy Scouts of Am., Concord, Calif., 1996—99. Recipient Eagle Scout award, Boy Scouts of Am., 1967. Mem.: Music Educators Nat. Conf. (assoc. Nationally Registered Music Educator 1997), Assn. of Calif. Symphony Orch. (assoc.), Calif. Band Directors Assn. (assoc.). Avocations: travel, music, model railroading. Office: Ygnacio Valley HS 755 Oak Grove Rd Concord CA 94518 Office Phone: 925-685-8414. Office Fax: 925-685-1435. Personal E-mail: saccatino@earthlink.net.

ACCOMANDO, ANNETTE LE FEBVRE, language educator; b. New Orleans, Mar. 15, 1958; d. Elvin Stanley Jr. and Mary Eleanor (Trosclair) Le Febvre; m. Gerard Joseph Accomando, July 25, 1981; children: Maria Ann, Mary Madeline, Joseph Gerard. Student, U. New Orleans, 1981, 1990—, MEd, 1985. Tchr. St. Maurice Parochial Sch., New Orleans, St. Bernard Parish Sch. Bd., Chalmette, La.; instr. St. Bernard Parish Community Coll., Chalmette, La.; instr. English as 2d langauge St. Bernard Parish Sch. Bd., Chalmette, La.; asst. prof. Nunez Community Coll., Chalmette. Mem. Internat. Reading Assn., La. Reading Assn., St. Bernard Coun. Reading Assn. (chair, pres.), S.W. Regional Coun. English in Two Yr. Colls., La. Tchrs. English to Speakers of Other Languages, NTE, Am. Ednl. Rsch. Assn., SERA, Greater New Orleans Tchrs. English, Alpha Theta Epsilon, Delta Kappa Gamma.

ACCORDINO, FRANK JOSEPH, architect; b. Bklyn., July 14, 1946; s. Carmine Anthony and Elvira Helen (Saccone) A.; m. Sheila May Lloyd, Sept. 6, 1969. BS, SUNY, N.Y. Inst. Tech., 1969; MArch, U. N.Mex., 1971. Registered architect, N.Y., Ill.; cert. Nat. Council Archtl. Registration Bds. Project architect Gencorelli & Salo Architects, Mineola, N.Y., 1971-74, Grove Haack & Assocs., P.C., Architects, Engrs., Planners, Ft. Lauderdale, Fla., 1974-76; v.p., dir. Cashin Assocs., P.C., Architects, Engrs., Planners, Mineola, N.Y., 1976-79; prin. architect Frank Accordino, AIA, Merrick, N.Y., 1979-80; sr. architect, facilities devel. Eastern Airlines, Inc., Miami, Fla., 1980-83; sr. architect Dean Witter Reynolds, Inc., N.Y.C., 1983-84; regional dir. constrn. and engring. Avis Rent A Car System, Inc., Garden City, NY, 1984-87, v.p. corp. facilities, 1987—2002; prin. architect Frank Accordino, AIA, Glen Cove, NY, 2002—, Palm City, Fla., 2002—. Mem. AIA. Republican. Roman Catholic. Office Phone: 772-418-7105.

ACCORSI, ERNEST WILLIAM, JR., professional football team executive; b. Hershey, Pa., Oct. 29, 1941; s. Ernest William Sr. and Mary Doris (Nardi) A.; m. Judy Ann Nangle, Sept. 9, 1967 (div. Aug. 1985); children: Michael Ryan, Sherlyn Paige, Patrick Vincent. BA, Wake Forest U., 1963; postgrad., Temple U., 1967. News dir. St. Joseph's U., Phila.; sportswriter Phila. Inquirer, 1966-69; with sports info. dept. Pa. State U., University Park, 1969-70; pub. relations dir. Balt. Colts, Owings Mill, Md., 1970-75, asst. gen. mgr., 1977-82, gen. mgr., 1982-84; asst. to pres. NFL, N.Y.C., 1975-77, Cleve. Browns, 1984-85, exec. v.p. football ops., 1985—92; exec. mgr. bus. affairs Baltimore Orioles, 1992—94; asst. gen. mgr. New York Giants, 1994—98, gen. mgr., 1998—. Bd. dirs. Nat. Football Found., N.Y.C., 1983. Served with U.S. Army N.G., 1964. Recipient Columbia award Italian-Am. Orgns. Md., Balt., 1982; named Grand Marshall Conv. Council Colts' Corrals, 1983. Mem. Advt. Club Balt. (bd. dirs.) Democrat. Roman Catholic. Office: Gaints Stadium East Rutherford NJ 07073

ACERRA, MICHELE (MIKE ACERRA), engineering and construction company executive; b. Messina, Italy, Apr. 15, 1937; came to U.S., 1978; s. Luigi and Matilde Mazzullo A.; m. Elena Fino, May 31, 1975; children— Marco Eugenio, Matilde Enrica Jennifer. Dr. Chem. Engring., Politecnico, Milan, Italy, 1962. Vessels designer Foster Wheeler Italiana, Milan, 1962, asst. mgr. drawing office, 1963, project engr., 1963-70, project mgr., 1970-74; pres. Glitsch Italiana, Rome, 1974-78; pres., chief oper. officer, dir. 8 subs. cos. Glitsch, Inc., Dallas, 1978-86; pres., chief exec. officer Foster Wheeler USA Corp., Perryville, N.J., 1986-89; corp. v.p. indsl. and environ. group Foster Wheeler Corp., Perryville, N.J., 1989-94; v.p. Foster Wheeler Energy Internat. Inc., 1994-97; dir. 4 subs.; v.p., mgr. BOC JV Foster Wheeler Power Sys., 1997-99; pres. Tray, Inc., Clinton, N.J., 2000—. N.Am. mktg. and sales mgr. Baretti S.P.A.; cons. in engring. and contrn., expert mfg. and arbitrations. Roman Catholic. Avocations: reading, gardening, travel. Office Phone: 908-832-9290. E-mail: meacerra@earthlink.net.

ACETO, VINCENT JOHN, librarian, educator; b. Schenectady, N.Y., Feb. 5, 1932; s. Henry and Gilda (Maietta) Aceto; m. Jean Louise Rasey, Aug. 27, 1955 (div. 1974); children: David, Paul Andrew; m. Kveta Urbanova, June 16, 1993. AB, MA, SUNY, 1953, MLS, 1959; postgrad., Case Western Res. U., 1959, 62, 65-66. Tchr. Scotia (N.Y.)-Glenville Ctrl. Schs., 1956-57; high sch. libr. Burnt Hills (N.Y.)-Ballston Lake Ctrl. Schs., 1957-59; libr. dir. Town of Ballston Pub. Libr., Burnt Hills, 1958-60; Fulbright lectr. U. Dacca, East Pakistan, 1964-65; asst. prof. Sch. Libr. Sci., SUNY, Albany, 1959-62, assoc. prof. libr. sci., 1963-69, prof., 1969—, assoc. dean, 1987-93, interim dean, 1993-95, co-dir. film and TV documentation ctr., 1983—, Disting. Svc. prof., 2000—. Libr. cons. various pub. schs., N.Y. State Edn. Dept., U.S. Dept. Edn., USA Govt. of Bangladesh, 1965, Govt. of Cyprus, 1992, 94; dir. U.S. Office Edn. insts. and traineeships. Joint Editor: Film Lit. Index; contbr. articles to profl. jours. Prs., Filmdex Par II, Inc., 1973-90; bd. dirs. Freedom Forum, Schenectady, 1970-78, chmn., 1976-78; trustee Shenendehowa Pub. Libr., 1995—, v.p., 1996-97, 2000, pres., 1997-99, pres., 2002-; mem. Shenendehowa Ctrl. Pub. Schs. Bd. of Edn., 2002—, v.p., 2004—. Served with AUS, 1954-56. Collins fellow U. Albany, 1997. Mem.: NEA, ALA, Soc. Cinema Studies, Am. Soc. Info. Scis., Am. Soc. Indexers, Hudson-Mohawk Libr. Assn. (v.p. 1964—66), N.Y. Libr. Assn., East Pakistan Libr. Assn., Pakistan Libr. Assn., Idaka Forum, Shenendehowa Rotary Club, Rotary, Phi Delta Kappa, Kappa Phi Kappa. Democrat. Unitarian Universalist. Office: SUNY Albany Sch Info Sci and Policy 1400 Washington Ave Albany NY 12222-0100 Home: 27 Wheeler Dr Clifton Park NY 12065 Personal E-mail: vaceto1@nycap.rr.com. Business E-Mail: aceto@albany.edu.

ACEVEDO-VILA, ANIBAL, governor, former congressional representative; b. Río Piedras, P.R., Feb. 13, 1962; s. Salvador Acevedo-Colón and Elba Vilá; m. Luisa Gándara, June 29, 1987; children: Gabriela, Juan-Carlos. BA, U. P.R., 1982, JD, 1985; LLM, Harvard U., 1987. Law clk. to Hon. Federico Hernández-Denton Supreme Ct. of P.R., San Juan, 1985-86; law clk. to Hon. Levin H. Campbell U.S. Ct. Appeals (1st cir.), Boston, 1987-88; legis. affairs aide to Gov. Rafael Hernandez Colon San Juan, 1989-92; mem. at-large P.R. Ho. of Reps., San Juan, 1991—2001, ho. minority leader, 1997-2001; pres. Popular Dem. Party, 1997-99, v.p., 1999—; resident commr. U.S. Ho. Reps from P. R., 2001—05; gov. Commonwealth of PR, San Juan, 2005—. Editor-in chief U. P.R. Law Jour., 1984—85, columnist El Nuevo Dia, 1993—96; author: En Honor a la Verdad. Mem. governing bd. Popular Dem. Party, San Juan, 1995-. Mem. P.R. Bar Assn. Democrat. Avocation: reading. Office: La Fortaleza PO Box 9020082 San Juan PR 00902

ACHARYA, JAYANT NARAHARI, neurologist, educator; b. Pune, Maharashtra, India, Apr. 6, 1961; s. Holenarsipur Gururaja and Vasumathi Narahari; m. Vinita Jayant Thakur, June 12, 1994; children: Neil Jayant, Nathan Jayant. MB BS, B.J. Med. Coll., Pune U., India, 1983; MD, Pune U., India, 1986; DM in Neurology, NIMHANS, Bangalore U., India, 1991. Diplomate Am. Bd. Psychiatry and Neurology, Am. Bd. Clin. Neurophysiology. Resident in medicine Sassoon Gen. Hosps., Pune, 1984—86; lectr. medicine B. J. Med. Coll., Pune, 1987; resident in neurology NIMHANS, Bangalore, 1987—92; asst. prof. neurology M. S. Ramaiah Med. Coll., Bangalore U., Bangalore, 1993—94; clin. fellow in epilepsy and clin. neurophysiology Cleve. Clinic Found., 1994—97; resident in neurology Wake Forest U. Bapt. Med. Ctr., Winston-Salem, NC, 1997—2001; asst. prof. neurology U. Pitts. Med. Ctr., 2001—03; assoc. prof. neurology St. Louis Univ. Hosp., 2003—. Mem. residency task force com. U. Pitts. Med. Ctr., 2002—03; tchr. Wake Forest U. Sch. Medicine, Winston-Salem, 1998—2001; evaluator Wake Forest U. Sch. of Medicine, Winston-Salem, 1999—2000; tchr. U. Pitts. Sch. Medicine, 2001—. B. J. Med. Coll., Pune, 1985—87, NIMHANS, Bangalore, 1991—92, Cleve. Clinic Found., 1996—97; spkr. in field. Contbr. 14 articles to profl. jours., 4 chpts. to med. textbooks. Recipient Hindustan Ciba-Geigy Gold medal, Neurol. Soc. India, 1991, Internat. Young Investigator award, Internat. League Against Epilepsy, 1993. Mem.: AMA, Am. Soc. Neuroimaging, Am. Acad. Neurology, Am. Epilepsy Soc., Neurol. Soc. India (life), Indian Acad. Neurology (life), Indian Epilepsy Assn. (life). Avocations: music, painting, literature, philosophy, sports. Office: St Louis Univ Hosp Dept Neurology Greater Midwest Epilepsy Treatment Ctr 3635 Vista Ave at Grand Blvd Saint Louis MO 63110 Office Phone: 314-577-8026.

ACHARYA, VINITA J, neurologist, researcher, educator; d. Dattatraya Balaji and Shubhada Dattatraya Thakur; m. Jayant Narahari Acharya, June 12, 1994; children: Neil Jayant, Nathan Jayant. MB, Topiwala Nat. Med. Coll., Bombay, 1984; MD, U. Bombay, 1989. Lectr. in medicine T.n. Med. Coll., Bombay, 1989—91, lectr. in neurology, 1991—94; fellow in epilepsy The Cleve. Clinic Found., Cleve., 1995—97; fellow in epilepsy and neurosonology Wake Forest U. Sch. Medicine, Winston Salem, NC, 1997—2000, stroke fellow, 2001; asst. prof. neurology St. Louis U. Rschr. & spkr. in field. Contbr. articles to med. jours. Recipient Doris Flynn International Fellowship award. Mem.: Am. Epilepsy Soc. (assoc. Young Investigator award), Am. Acad. Neurology (assoc.). Office: Saint Louis U 3635 Vista Ave @ Grand Blvd Saint Louis MO 63110 Office Phone: 314-768-3000. Office Fax: 314-268-5101. Business E-Mail: acharyav@slu.edu.

ACHAUER, BRUCE MICHAEL, plastic surgeon; MD, Baylor U., 1967. Intern San Francisco Gen. Hosp., 1967-68; resident in gen. surgery U. Calif., Irvine, 1970-74, rsch. in plastic surgery, 1974-76, adj. prof. surgery, 1994—; fellow in plastic surgery Queen Victoria Hosp., East Grinstead, U.K., 1976; pvt. practice U. Calif. Irvine Med. Ctr., Orange, 1977—; mem. staff St. Joseph Hosp., 1977—; mem. active staff Children's Hosp. of Orange County, 1977—; pvt. practice plastic surgery Orange. Mem. courtesy staff Med. Ctr. of GGG, 1985—; dir. Am. Bd. Plastic Surgery, 1995—. Fellow Am. Acad. Pediatrics; mem. AMA, Am. Assn. Plastic Surgeons, Am. Cleft Palate Assn., Am. Soc. for Surgery of Hand, Am. Soc. Plastic and Reconstructive Surgeons (sec. ednl. found.).

ACHEBE, CHINUA, writer, humanities educator; b. Ogidi, Nigeria, Nov. 16, 1930; s. Isaiah Okafo and Janet N. (Iloegbunam) A.; m. Christie Chinwe Okoli, Sept. 10, 1961; children: Chinelo, Ikechukwu, Chidi, Nwando. Student, Univ. Coll., Ibadan, Nigeria, 1948—52; BA, U. London, 1953; DLitt (hon.), Dartmouth Coll., 1972; DUniv, Stirling U., Scotland, 1975; DLitt (hon.), U. Southampton, Eng., 1975; LLD (hon.), U. Prince Edward Isl., Can., 1976; LHD (hon.), U. Mass., 1977; DLitt (hon.), U. Ife, Nigeria, 1978, U. Nigeria, Nsukka, 1981, U. Kent, Canterbury, Eng., 1982, Mt. Allison U., Sackville, Can., 1984, U. Guelph, Can., 1984, Franklin Pierce Coll., 1985, Ibadan U., 1989; DUniv, Open U., Eng., 1989; LLD (hon.), Georgetown U., 1990, Port Harcourt (Nigeria) U., 1991; DLitt (hon.), Skidmore Coll., 1991, CCNY, 1992, Fitchburg State Coll., 1994; DLitt, Harvard U., 1996, Binghamton U., 1996, Bates Coll., 1996, Fairleigh Dickinson U., 2002; LHD (hon.), Westfield Coll., 1989, New Sch. for Social Rsch., 1991, Hobart and William Smith Coll., 1991; LHD, Marymount Manhattan Coll., 1991; LHD (hon.), Colgate U., 1993; DLitt, Syracuse U., 1997, Trinity Coll., 1999, Ohio Wesleyan U., 1999, U. Witwatersrand, South Africa, 2000; LHD, Cape Town U., South Africa, 2002; DLitt, Haverford Coll., 2001. Prodr., contr., dir. Nigerian Broadcasting Co., Lagos, 1954-66; sr. rsch. fellow in African studies U. Nigeria, 1967-72, prof. dept. English, 1976-81, emeritus prof., 1985—. Vis. prof. English U. Mass., Amherst, 1972-75, U. Conn, Storrs, 1975-76, Afro-Am. studies U. Mass., Amherst, 1987-88; pro-chancellor Anambra State U. Tech., Enugu, Nigeria, 1986-88; Regent's lectr. UCLA, 1984; dir. Heinemann Ednl. Books (Nigeria) Ltd.; vis. fellow and Ashby lectr. Clare Hall, Cambridge (Eng.) U., 1993. Author: (novels) Things Fall Apart, 1958, No Longer at Ease, 1960, Arrow of God, 1964, A Man of the People, 1966, Anthills of the Savannah, 1988; (poetry) Christmas in Biafra, 1975, Collected Poems, 2004; (short stories) Girls at War, 1972; (essays) Morning Yet on Creation Day, 1975; The Trouble with Nigeria, 1983, Hopes and Impediments-Selected Essays, 1965-87, 1988; (essay and poems) Another Africa, 1998; (non-fiction) Home and Exile, 2000, (children's stories) The Flute, 1978, The Drum 1978. Mem. coun. Lagos (Nigeria) U., 1966; mem. East Ctrl. State Libr. Bd., 1971-72, Anambra State Arts Coun., 1977-79; Goodwill amb. UN Population Fund, 1998—. Recipient Lit. award New Statesman, 1965, Commonwealth Poetry prize, 1973, Nat. Creativity award Nigeria, 1999, St. Louis Lit. award 1999; Rockefeller fellow, 1960-61; UNESCO fellow, 1963. Friedenspreis (Peace Prize) Germany, 2002. Fellow: MLA (hon.), Nigerian Acad. Letters, Royal Soc. Lit. (hon.); mem.: Royal African Soc. (v.p. London 1998), Nonino Risit D'Aur, Am. Acad. Arts and Scis. Office: Bard Coll Dept Lang and Lit Annandale On Hudson NY 12504

ACHEE, ROLAND JOSEPH, lawyer; b. New Orleans, Dec. 12, 1922; s. Benjamin Elphege and Marie Josephine (Cazenave) A.; m. Jean Winifred Lant, Feb. 19, 1955; 1 child, Marie Alaine Achee Mayo. BA, Centenary Coll., 1944; JD, La. State U., 1949. Bar: La. 1949, U.S. Dist. Ct. (we. dist.) La. 1950, U.S. Ct. Appeals (5th cir.) 1960. Ptnr. Rountree, Cox, Guin & Achee, Shreveport, La. Editor-in-chief La. Law Review, 1948-49. Chmn. Selective Svc. Bd. No. 10, Shreveport, 1965. Lt. (j.g.) USNR, 1944-46, PTO. Named Outstanding Asst. City Atty. U.S., Nat. Inst. Mcpl. Officers, 1988. Fellow Am. Coll. Trial Lawyers; mem. ABA, La. State Bar Assn. (past. chmn. profl. responsibility, legal ethics adv. com. 1991—), Shreveport Bar Assn. (chmn. ethics com. 1975-77, pres. 1984), Am. Legion (comdr. 1961), Elks (life, Exalted Ruler 1958), Order of Coif. Home: 182 Bruce Ave Shreveport LA 71105-3711 Office: Rountree Cox Guin & Achee PO Box 1807 400 Travis St Ste 1200 Shreveport LA 71101-5565

ACHELPOHL, STEVEN EDWARD, lawyer, political organization worker; b. Wichita, Kans., July 15, 1950; s. Ray Edward and Juanita J. (Barnes) A.; m. Shelley R. Kiel (div. Sept. 1987); m. Sara K. Nabity, Nov. 24, 1989; children: Joseph E., Samuel B., Raechel A., Ryan Sullivan, Peter Sullivan. BA, U. Nebr., 1972, JD with distinction, 1975. Bar: Nebr. 1975, U.S. Dist. Ct. Nebr. 1975, U.S. Ct. Appeals (8th cir.) 1981. Law clk. hon. Donald R. Ross U.S. Ct. Appeals, Omaha, 1975-77; atty. McGrath, North, O'Mally, Kratz, Omaha, 1977-80, Dwyer, O'Leary & Martin, Omaha, 1980-83; ptnr. Schumacher & Achelpohl, Omaha, 1983-92; assoc. Smith Peterson, Omaha, 1992-93; pvt. practice Omaha, 1994—. Active Dem. Nat. Com., 2001—; chair Neb. Dem. Party, 2001—. Fellow: Neb. State Bar Found., Am. Coll. Trial Lawyers. Democrat. Avocations: golf, baseball. Home: 6420 Underwood Ave Omaha NE 68132-1812 Office: 1823 Harney St Ste 1010 Omaha NE 68102-1900 Office Phone: 402-346-1900. E-mail: achelpohl@usa.net.

ACHENBAUM, ALVIN ALLEN, marketing and management consultant; b. N.Y.C., Dec. 11, 1925; s. Benjamin and Dora (Dworin) A.; m. Barbara Ann Greenwald, June 24, 1951 (dec. Apr. 1992); children: Jonathan Peter, Lisa Jane, Martha Beth; m. Leila Lebendig, June 6, 1993. BS, UCLA, 1950; MS, Columbia U., 1951. Mgr. market rsch. McCann-Erickson, N.Y.C., 1951-57; exec. v.p., sec., dir. Grey Advt., Inc., N.Y.C., 1957-71; exec. v.p. J. Walter Thompson Co., 1971-74; chmn. bd. dirs. Canter, Achenbaum, Assocs., Inc., N.Y.C., 1974-89; vice chmn. bd. dirs. Backer, Spielvogel, Bates Worldwide, N.Y.C., 1989-93; pres. Achenbaum Assocs. Inc., N.Y.C., 1992-95; chmn. Achenbaum Bogda Assocs. Inc., N.Y.C., 1996—. Bd. dirs. MARC, Inc. Mem. edit. bd. Jour. Advt. Rsch. Mem. Citizens Adv. Com. of Irvington, 1970—; mem. Middle Eastern affairs com. Anti-Defamation League; adv. com. Assn. Consumer Research.; Trustee Mktg. Sci. Inst.; Am. Mktg. Assn. Found.; editl. bd. Mktg. Mgmt. Mag. Named to Market Research Hall of Fame. Mem. Market Rsch. Coun. N.Y., Copy Rsch. Coun. N.Y., Am. Mktg. Assn. (v.p. global mktg. div., bd. dirs., found. trustee), Am. Econ. Assn., Assn. Pub. Opinion Rsch., Beta Gamma Sigma. Home: 225 Central Park W New York

NY 10024-6026 Office: Achenbaum Bogda Assocs Inc 225 Central Park W Apt 723 New York NY 10024-6033 Office Phone: 212-579-3333. Business E-Mail: al@abaconsulting.com. E-mail: alvinache@aol.com.

ACHESON, ALLEN MORROW, retired engineering executive; b. Tanta, Egypt, June 12, 1926; s. Samuel Irvine and Hazel Lenore (Welker) A.; m. Mary Jean Baird, Aug. 5, 1950 (div. May 1978); children: Rebecca R., Jennifer E., Scott A., Jon M. BS in Mech. Engring., Iowa State U., 1950; LLD, Tarkio Coll., 1985. Registered profl. engr., Mo. Sta. supt. Iowa Pub. Svc. Co., Carroll, 1950—54; engr. Proctor & Gamble Co., 1954—55, Iowa-Ill. Gas & Electric Co., 1955—56; mgr. City Power & Light Co., Independence, Mo., 1956—60; mgmt. adviser Yanhee Electricity Authority, Bangkok, 1960—63; exec. v.p. Black & Veatch Internat., Kansas City, Mo., 1964—73, pres., 1973—88, chmn., 1989—91; gen. ptnr. Black & Veatch, Kansas City, 1974—75, exec. ptnr., 1975—91; ret., 1991. Trustee Tarkio (Mo.) Coll., 1964-77, chmn., 1975-77; elder Trinity and Rolling Hills Presbyn. Ch. With USNR, 1944-46. Recipient Profl. Achievement citation Coll. Engring., Iowa State U., 1976, Marston medal, 1992. Mem. Am. Cons. Engrs. Coun. (chmn. internat. engring. divsn., past pres. award 1992); mem. ASME (life). Home: 723 W 100th St Kansas City MO 64114 Personal E-mail: aacheson@hotmail.com.

ACHESON, AMY J., lawyer; b. Pitts., July 16, 1963; d. Willard Phillips and Patricia Louise (Marshall) A. BA, Haverford Coll., 1984; JD cum laude, U. S.C., 1987. Bar: Pa. 1987, U.S. Dist. Ct. (we. dist.) Pa. 1987, U.S. Ct. Appeals (10th cir.) 1989, U.S. Ct. Appeals (3d cir.) 1988, U.S. Ct. Appeals (4th cir.) 1993. Atty. Reed, Smith, Shaw & McClay, Pitts., 1987—95; shareholder Berger Law Firm, Pitts., 1995—99; of counsel Ogg, Jones, Cordes & Ignelzi, Pitts., 1999—. Mem. S.C. Law Rev., 1985-87. Fin. officer Ret. Sr. Vol. Program Allegheny County, Pitts., 1990-91; treas. Parents League for Emotional Adjustments, Pitts., 1990-91; mem. adv. bd. Pa. Dept. Correction, Community Svc. Ctr. No. 1, Pitts., 1990-97; bd. mgrs. The Woodwell, Pitts., 1992-97, v.p., 1998-2000; bd. dirs. Presbyn. Seniorcare Network, Inc., 2000—; bd. trustees Shadyside Presbyn. Ch. Nursery Sch., 2001—. Mem. ABA (jud. adminstrn. div. com., chmn. subcom. on discipline of fed. judges, 1990-91), ATLA (life mem.), Allegheny County Bar Assn. (young lawyers sect. coun. 1990-91), Order of the Coif, Order of the Wig and Robe. Office: Riverview Pl 245 Fort Pitt Blvd Pittsburgh PA 15222-1511 E-mail: amyacheson@aol.com.

ACHESON, DAVID CAMPION, retired lawyer, policy analyst, writer; b. Washington, Nov. 4, 1921; s. Dean G. and Alice (Stanley) Acheson; m. Patricia Castles, May 1, 1943 (dec. 2000); children: Eleanor Dean, David Campion, Peter Wesley. BA, Yale U., 1942; LLB, Harvard U., 1948. Bar: DC, Pa., U.S. Supreme Ct. With Office Gen. Counsel AEC, 1948—49; with firm Covington & Burling, Washington, 1950—61, mem. firm, 1958—61; U.S. atty. for DC, 1961—65; spl. asst. to sec. treasury, 1965—67; v.p., sr. v.p., gen. counsel Communications Satellite Corp., 1967—74; ptnr. Jones, Day, Reavis & Pogue, Washington, 1974—78, Drinker Biddle & Reath, Phila. and Washington, 1978—87. Author (with others): Effective Washington Representation, 1983, Acheson Country: A Memoir, 1993; co-author (CSIS report): A More Effective Civil Space Program, 1988; editor: This Vast External Realm, 1973; editor: (with David McLellan) Among Friends, 1980. Mem. presdl. commn. on Challenger accident, 1986; pres. Atlantic Coun. U.S., 1993—99. Mem.: Met. Club. Episcopalian. Home: 2700 Calvert St NW Washington DC 20008-2621 Personal E-mail: dcampach@aol.com.

ACHESON, LOUISE SEYMOUR, physician, educator; b. Assiut, Egypt, Jan. 12, 1953; d. Willard Phillips and Patricia Louise A.; children: Elizabeth, Emily. BA in Chemistry, Oberlin Coll., 1972; MD, Harvard Med. Sch., 1976; MS in Family Medicine, Case Western Res. U., 1987. Diplomate Am. Bd. Family Practice. Resident in family practice U. Wash. Affiliated Hosps., Seattle, 1976-79; pvt. practice Seattle, 1980-84; prof. family medicine, onocology, reproductive biology Case Western Res. U., Cleve., 1984—. Assoc. editor Archives of Family Medicine, 1993-2000; contbr. articles to profl. jours. Mem. adv. bd. Middlefield (Ohio) Amish Birth Ctr., 1989-. Mem. Am. Soc. Human Genetics (assoc.), Am. Coll. Med. Genetics, Am. Soc. Preventive Oncology, Am. Acad. Family Physicians, Soc. Tchrs. Family Medicine, N.Am. Primary Care Interest Group. Avocations: reading, outdoor activities. Office: Case Western Res U Sch Medicine 11100 Euclid Ave Cleveland OH 44106-5036

ACHILLE, JOHN GARLAND, lawyer; b. Cannonsburg, Pa., May 19, 1953; s. John J. and Anne (Chapell) A.; m. Diana Moore, July 29, 1978. BS, Pa. State U., 1975; postgrad., Western New Eng. Coll., 1975-76; JD, Del. Law Sch., 1978. Bar: Pa. 1978, U.S. Dist. Ct. (we. and ea. dists.) Pa. 1978, N.J. 1979, U.S. Dist. Ct. (so. dist.) N.J. 1979. Investigator, rschr. Atty. Gen. Mass., 1976, Cmty. Legal Svcs., Brookville, Pa., 1977; office mgr. Laurel Legal Svcs., Brookville, Pa., 1977; rsch. asst. to justice Thomas A. Pitt Chester County, Pa., 1978; atty. pvt. practice, Phila. and Brookville, 1978—. Mem. ABA, Pa. Bar Assn., Assn. Trial Lawyers Am., Pa. Trial Lawyers Assn., Jefferson-Phila. County Bar Assn., Kiwanis. Methodist. Avocations: flying, sailing, scuba diving, skiing. Home: 1 Caldwell Ct Brookville PA 15825-1015 Office: 379 Main St Brookville PA 15825-1221

ACHIN, MILOS KOSTA, historian, writer; b. Knjazevac, Yugoslavia, Feb. 28, 1915; came to U.S., 1950; s. Kosta Sava and Vuka (Vujic) A.; divorced; children: Vuka, Kosta. Student, Mil. Acad., Belgrade, 1934, Air Force Sch., Pancevo, 1938. Capt., editor Yugoslav Guerrila, Free Mountains, 1941-44; dir. UN IRO Ctr., Trieste, Gorica, 1948-50; writer Free Serbian Press, 1950—. Author: Srbija Gori, 1960, Prolog Buducnosti, 1963, Branioci Kosova, 1973, Kosovski Kristali, 1976, Povratak Suncu, 1982, Koreni & Iskorenjeni, 1982, Vremeplov, 1984, Od Kosmaja do Kosmosa, 1989, 95, 100 Strele do Stratospere, 1994, General Mihailovic and Ravna Gora, 19 Vols., 1996, Tales of Socialist Yugoslavia, Yugoslavia in Our Time, 1991, Yugoslavia Dismembered, 1992, Draža Mihailović: A Biography, 3 Vols., 1997, numerous other books, essays, short stories and articles. Capt. Royal Yugoslav Air Force, 1938-41. Rankovich Charitable and Ednl. Fund grantee, 1988, 89. Mem. Soc. Serbian Writers and Artists Abroad, N.Am. Soc. Serbian Studies. Home and Office: 6221 Walhonding Rd Bethesda MD 20816-2138

ACHINSTEIN, PETER JACOB, philosopher, educator; b. N.Y.C., June 30, 1935; s. Asher and Betty (Comras) A.; children: Jonathan, Sharon, Betty, married L. Suzanne Brown, June 16, 2005. AB, Harvard, 1956, AM, 1958, PhD, 1961; postgrad. (Knox Traveling fellow), Oxford U., Eng., 1959-60. Asst. prof. U. Iowa, Iowa City, 1961-62; asst. prof. philosophy Johns Hopkins Balt., 1962-64; asso. prof., 1964-68; prof., 1968—; chmn. dept. philosophy, 1968-77; vis. prof. M.I.T., Cambridge, 1965-66, Stanford (Calif.) U., 1967, City U. N.Y., 1973; mem. adv. panel NSF, 1968-70, 79-81; Lady Davis vis. prof. Hebrew U., Jerusalem, spring 1976. Author: Concepts of Science, 1968, Law and Explanation, 1971, The Nature of Explanation, 1983, Particles and Waves: Historical Essays in the Philosophy of Science, 1991 (Lakatos award 1993); The Book of Evidence, 2001; editor: (with Stephen Barker) The Legacy of Logical Positivism, 1969, The Concept of Evidence, 1983, (with Laura J. Snyder) Scientific Methods, 1994; Science Rules, 2004, Scientific Evidence, 2005; mem. editl. bd. Philosophy of Sci., 1973-2000. Guggenheim fellow, 1966-67 Fellow AAAS (chair history and philosophy of sci. sect. L 1995); mem. Philosophy of Sci. Assn. (bd. govs.), Internat. Union History and Philosophy (del. U.S. 1967-73, 79-86), Phi Beta Kappa. Office: Johns Hopkins U Dept Philosophy Baltimore MD 21218 E-mail: peter.achinstein@jhu.edu.

ACHOLONU, WILFRED W., JR., clinical pharmacy specialist, educator; b. Owerri, Imo, Nigeria, July 18, 1953; arrived in U.S., 1974; s. Wilfred W. and Esther Rose Acholonu; m. Ezioma G. Onwuchekwa, May 25, 1991; children: Ikenna Colin, Ezioge Celest. BS in Pharmacy, Oreg. State U., 1980, MS in Pharmacology and Toxicology, 1984; PharmD, U. Fla., 1994. Cert. Bd. Pharm. Spltys. Resident hosp. pharm. VA Med. Ctr., Portland, Oreg., 1983—84; staff pharmacist Olin E. Teague VA Med. Ctr., Temple, Tex., 1984—89, VA Med. Ctr., Gainesville, Fla., 1989—94; assoc. clin. prof. pharmacy practice U. Fla., Gainesville, 1996—; clin. pharmacy specialist VA Med. Ctr., Gainesville, 1994—. Mem. PET com. VA Med. Ctr., Gainesville. Contbr. articles to profl. jours. Mem.: Am. Soc. Health Sys. Pharmacists, Am. Coll. Clin. Pharmacy, Coll. Psychiatric and Neurologic Pharmacists. Avocations: tennis, racquetball, basketball. Office: North Fla/South Ga VHS 1601 SW Archer Rd Gainesville FL 32608 Office Phone: 352-376-1611 ext. 6459. E-mail: wilfred.acholonu@med.va.gov.

ACHON, RAQUEL ANDREA, music educator, consultant; b. Ctrl. Preston, Cuba, May 5, 1927; arrived in U.S., 1947; d. Crescencio Gutierrez and Basilisa Semorile; m. David Achon, Dec. 25, 1957; 1 child, David. BA, Instituto Santiago, 1947; diploma, Martin Coll., 1949; BS in Arts, Peabody Coll., 1951. Pvt. music tchr., Downey, Calif., 1968—. Cons. in field. Editor: Celebrenos II, 1983, El Himnario, 1998, 1999. Pianist Crusader's Class, 2004; vice-chair, editor United Meth. Hymnal, 1989; pianist Downey (Calif.) United Meth. Ch., 1995. Named to Hall of Fame, Am. Coll. Musicians, 1990. Mem.: Am. Coll. Musicians. Republican. Methodist. Avocations: collecting angels, collecting boxes. Home: 12029 Gurley Ave Downey CA 90242

ACHORD, JAMES LEE, retired gastroenterologist; b. Dayton, Ohio, Sept. 24, 1931; s. Lonnie M. and Ethel E. (Collins) A.; m. Patsy Jane Moore, Dec. 18, 1954; children: J. Michael, Ann Elizabeth, Andrew P. Student, Emory U., 1949-52, MD, 1956. Intern Emory Hosp., 1956-57; resident Emory U., Atlanta, 1959-62, instr., assoc. prof., 1962-71; med. dir. Med. Ctr. Cen. Ga., Macon, 1971-75; assoc. dean, prof. East Tenn. State Sch. Medicine, Johnson City, 1975-76; prof., dir. div. digestive diseases U. Miss. Med. Ctr., Jackson, 1976-98, prof. emeritus, 1998. Editor book revs. Am. Jour. Gastroenterology, 1985-91, Dig. Dis. Sci., 1994-96; mem. editl. bd. Am. Jour. Clin. Gastroenterology, 1999—; contbr. numerous articles and editls. to profl. jours. and chpts. to books. Capt. U.S. Army, 1957-59. Master ACP (gov. Miss. chpt. 1993-97), Am. Coll. Gastroenterology (pres. 1983-84); mem. Am. Assn. Study Liver Disease, Am. Gastroent. Assn., Am. Soc. Gastroenterologic Endoscopy. E-mail: jamesachord@cs.com.

ACHORN, ROBERT COMEY, retired newspaper publisher; b. Westboro, Mass., Mar. 31, 1922; s. Edward Welt and Mabel (Comey) A.; m. Jean Mary Berlo, Sept. 23, 1950 (dec. 1980); children: Nancy Louise (Mrs. Eric Engberg), Susan Jean, Edward Christopher, Judith Joyce (Mrs. Albert Berry), Carole Lee (Mrs. Ralph Abislaiman); m. Ann Bouvier, Aug. 20, 1982. AB, Brown U., 1943. Reporter Worcester (Mass.) Telegram, 1946-53; editorial writer Evening Gazette, Worcester, 1953-60, mng. editor, 1964-67; editor editorial pages Worcester Telegram & Gazette, 1964-67, assoc. editor, 1967-70, editor, 1970-73, v.p., editor, 1973-81, assoc. pub., exec. v.p., 1981-82, pub., 1982-87, dir., 1982-88, pres., 1986-87, Beacon Communications Corp., 1984-85, vice chmn., 1985-87; pres. Worcester Telegram & Gazette, Inc., 1985-87. Bd. dirs. Blackstone Valley Regional Devel. Corp., 1991-95; mem. newspaper adv. bd. UPI, 1974-78. Pres. United Way of Ctrl. Mass., Worcester, 1973—75; v.p. The Meml. Hosp., 1976; vice chmn. Ctrl. Mass. chpt. ARC, 1976—84, chmn., 1984—86; media chmn. Mass. Bar-Press Com., 1976—77; chmn. trustees Worcester Found. Exptl. Biology, 1984—87; trustee Old. Sturbridge Village, 1986—2001, hon. trustee, 2001—; trustee U. Mass. Med. Ctr. Found., 1991—2002, Sutton Coun. on Aging, 1993—99, U. Mass. Meml. Found., 1998—2002. Fellow Acad. New Eng. Journalists; mem. UPI New Eng. Newspaper Editors (pres. 1969), Am. Soc. Newspaper Editors, New Eng. Newspaper Assn. (pres. 1986-87), New Eng. Soc. Newspaper Editors (pres. 1968), New Eng. AP News Execs. Assn. (pres. 1971), Am. Antiquarian Soc., Soc. Profl. Journalists, Worcester Club, Worcester Econ. Club (pres. 1975), Bohemian Club, Nat. Press Club, St. Wulstan Soc., Worcester Torch Club, Phi Beta Kappa.

ACHTENHAGEN, FRANK, economics professor; b. Berlin, May 28, 1939; s. Wilhelm and Kaethe (Ulrich) A.; m. Roswitha Manski, Sept. 30, 1965 (dec. Feb. 1990); children: Claudia, Leona; m. Susanne Weber, Nov. 11, 1994. Diploma, Free U. Berlin, 1963, D in Econs., 1969; D in Econs. (hon.), U. St. Gallen, Switzerland, 1991; D in Philosophy (hon.), U. Helsinki, Finland, 2000. Referendar Senate of Berlin, 1963-65; asst. prof. econs. Free U. Berlin, 1966-69; assoc. prof. U. Münster, Germany, 1969-71; prof. econs., dir. U. Göttingen, Germany, 1971—. Author 20 books, 1969—. Mem. German Soc. for Edn. Rsch. (treas. 1980-88), Am. Ednl. Rsch. Assn., European Assn. for Rsch. on Learning and Instrn. Evangelical. Avocations: tennis, skiing. Home: Am Goldgraben II D-37073 Göttingen Germany Office: Georg August U Platz Goettinger Sieben 5 D-37073 Göttingen Germany

ACHTERMAN, GAIL LOUISE, lawyer; b. Portland, Oreg., Aug. 1, 1949; AB in Econs. with distinction, Stanford U., 1971; MS in Natural Resource Policy and Mgmt., U. Mich., 1975, JD cum laude, 1974. Bar: Oreg. 1974, U.S. Dist. Ct. Oreg. 1978, U.S. Supreme Ct. 1978, U.S. Ct. Appeals (fed. and 10th cirs.). Atty.-advisor U.S. Dept. Interior, 1975-78; asst. for natural resources Gov. Neil Goldschmidt, 1987-91; mem. Stoel Rives LLP, Portland, 1978-2000; dir. Inst. for Natural Resources, Oreg. State U., Corvallis, 2003—. Exec. dir. Deschutes Resources Conservancy, 2000—03; adj. prof. forest policy, Coll. Forestry Oreg. State U., 1991—. Mem. Oreg. Water Resources Commn., 1981-85, Gov.'s Growth Task Force, 1998; mem. pres.'s bd. advisors Oreg. State U., 2000—03, Oreg. Transp. Commn., 2000—. Mem. N.W. Environment Watch (bd. dirs.), Oregon Garden (bd. dirs.), Am. Leadership Forum, Oreg. Women's Forum, Portland C. of C. (bd. dirs. 1996-99). Office: Oreg State U INR Dirs Office 210 Strand Ag Hall Corvallis OR 97331-5712

ACIMAN, CAROLE V., lawyer; b. Cotonou, Rep. of Benin, 1964; Diploma, Maitrise, Université de Paris-Panthéon-Sorbonne, 1986; D.E.S.S., Université de Nanterre-Paris, 1988; LLM, NYU Sch. Law, 1990. Bar: N.Y. 1991, Second Cir., U.S. Dist. Ct., So. and Ea. Dists. N.Y. 1992, U.S. Supreme Ct. 1999. Counsel Hughes Hubbard & Reed LLP, New York. Trade adv. Govt. France; adj. asst. prof F-law Sch. Continuing and Profl. Studies, NYU; dir. Global Nomads Group, Inc.; Dir. Women's eNews; mem. adv. bd. Inst. Law, Sci. and Tech, Seton Hall Sch. Law. Mem. Internat. Adv. Bd. Taking it Global Youth Assn.; dir. Global Youth Action Network, Inc. Recipient Rising Star award, N.Y. County Lawyers' Assn., 1999, Women of the Future award, N.Y. Women's Agenda, 2000. Mem.: ABA (Sci & Tech. Sec. 1988—), Law Alumni Assn, NYU Sch. Law (dir.), Nat. Conf. Women's Bar Assn (dir., pres. 2005). Office: Hughes Hubbard & Reed LLP One Battery Park Plaza New York NY 10004-1482 Office Phone: 212-837-6000. E-mail: aciman@hugheshubbard.com.

ACKER, ANDREW FRENCH, III, mathematics professor, researcher; b. New London, Conn., May 9, 1943; s. Andrew French Jr. and Miriam Luce (Woodhull) A.; children: Denise, Marcella, Joseph, Laurel; m. Melissa Ann Stanton, Aug. 10, 1991; children: Michael, Christian. BS, Union Coll., Schenectady, 1965; PhD, Boston U., 1972; Prof Dr, Karlsruhe U., Germany, 1982. Lectr. Boston U., 1969-72; asst. prof. La. State U., New Orleans, 1972-73; asst. U. Karlsruhe, 1973-83; assoc. prof. math. Iowa State U., Ames, 1983-87, Wichita (Kans.) State U., 1987-91, prof., 1991—. Guest rschr. U. Heidelberg, Germany, summer 1987. Contbr. articles to math. jours. Mem. Am. Math. Soc., Sigma Xi, Pi Mu Epsilon. Achievements include contributions to the analytical treatment of free boundary problems in elliptic partial differential equations, especially flow-surface and flow-interface problems in fluid dynamics, with emphasis on the existence, uniqueness, convexity and geometry of solutions; development of operator methods for successive approximation of free boundaries. Home: 1213 Farmstead St Wichita KS 67208-2628 Office: Wichita State U Dept Math Wichita KS 67260-0033 E-mail: acker@math.twsu.edu.

ACKER, ANN E., lawyer; b. Chgo., July 21, 1948; BA magna cum laude, St. Mary's Coll., 1970; JD cum laude, Loyola U., 1973. Bar: Ill. 1973. Asst. corp. counsel City of Chgo.; partner Chapman and Cutler, Chgo. Mem.: Nat. Assoc. of Bond Lawyers, Chicago Bar Assoc., Amer. Bar Assoc. Office: Chapman and Cutler 111 W Monroe St Ste 1700 Chicago IL 60603-4006 Office Phone: 312-845-3710. Office Fax: 312-701-2361. E-mail: acker@chapman.com.

ACKER, FREDERICK GEORGE, lawyer; b. Defiance, Ohio, May 7, 1934; s. Julius William and Orah Louise (Dowler) A.; m. Cynthia Ann Wayne, Dec. 1, 1962; children: Frederick Wayne, Mary Katherine, Richard Hoghton, Jennifer Ruth. Student, Ind. U., 1952-54; BA, Valparaiso U., 1956; MA, Harvard U., 1957, JD, 1961; postgrad., U. Manchester (Eng.), 1957-58. Bar: Ill. 1961, Ind. 1961. Ptnr. Winston & Strawn, Chgo., 1961-88, McDermott, Will & Emery, Chgo., 1988—2003, counsel, 2003—. Co-chmn. Joint Prin. and Income Act. com., Chgo., 1976-81. Co-author: (portfolio) Generation-Skipping Tax, 1991; contbr. articles to profl. jours. Bd. dirs. Max McGraw Wildlife Found., Dundee, Ill., 1984-03, chmn., pres. 1997-01; trustee L.S. Wood Ednl. Trust, Chgo., 1975—, Ill. chpt. The Nature Conservancy, Chgo., 1981-90, chmn., 1986-90. Danforth Found. fellow, 1956; Fulbright scholar, 1957. Mem. Trout Unlimited, Fulbright Assn. (bd. dirs. 1994-2000, pres. 2000), Met. Chgo. Club, Anglers Club, Coleman Lake Club. Lutheran. Avocations: hunting, fishing. Home: 543 N Madison St Hinsdale IL 60521-3213 Office: McDermott Will & Emery 227 W Monroe St Ste 3100 Chicago IL 60606-5096

ACKER, FREDERICK WAYNE, lawyer; b. Chgo., Feb. 28, 1966; s. Frederick George and Cynthia Ann (Wayne) A.; m. Anette Kjeldaas, June 3, 1988; children: Chelsea Kirsten, Ingrid Noelle, Stein Frederick, Ryan Alexander. BA, St. Olaf Coll., 1988; JD, U. Notre Dame, 1992; Splty. Degree, U. Oslo, Norway, 1993. Bar: Mich. 1993, Ill. 1994, U.S. Dist. Ct. (no. dist.) Ill. 1995, U.S. Ct. Appeals (7th cir.) 1997, U.S. Ct. Appeals (fed. cir.) 1997, Calif. 2000, U.S. Dist. Ct. (no., ctrl., so. and ea. dists.) Calif. 2000. Vis. scholar Notre Dame Law Sch., South Bend, Ind., 1993; atty. Stamos & Trucco, Chgo., 1994-98, Hahn, Loeser & Parks, Columbus, Ohio, 1998—99, Bingham McCutchen, San Francisco, 2000—. Author: The Lost Treasure of Ferando Montoya, 2003, The Case of the Autumn Rose, 2003, Dead Man's Rule, 2005; columnist Minn. Spectator, 1988-90; mem. Notre Dame Law Rev Campaign mgr. Gilbertson for Congress, Mpls., 1988, Fintzen for Rep., Geneva, Ill., 1997; pres. Notre Dame Federalist Soc., 1991-92. Thomas J. White scholar, 1989. Mem. ABA. Republican. Evangelical Christian. Avocations: fiction and editorial writing, Scandinavian lang. and hist., fishing, theology. Office: Bingham McCutchen Three Embarcadero Ctr San Francisco CA 94111 Office Phone: 415-393-2380. E-mail: rickacker@yahoo.com.

ACKER, KATHLEEN ALICE RUSIN (KATHLEEN ALICE RUSIN ACKER), writer, editor, poet; b. Port Jefferson, N.Y., Sept. 4, 1945; d. Edward and Alice Catherine (Gniazdowski) Rusin.; m. David Henry Acker, Aug. 24, 1968 (div. 1979); children: Sherry Lynn Acker, Wendy Kay Acker. AAS, Suffolk County C.C., Selden, 1965. Dental asst., receptionist Rosner & Marson, DDS, Port Jefferson, 1963-65; legal sec. Block, Namm & Baranello, Port Jefferson, 1965-67; exec. sec. Hoffman Majesty, Inc., Port Jefferson, 1967; sr. steno Physics Dept. SUNY, Stony Brook, 1968-74, sr. steno Ecology & Evolution Dept., 1976-78; legal sec. Howard Bergson & Roy Dragotta, Port Jefferson, 1978-80; talent agt. Gary Reynolds Talent Assocs., Hicksville, N.Y., 1982; legal sec. Neil Abelson, Port Jefferson, 1983-85; exec. asst. J.B. Kimberly & Assoc., Woodbury, N.Y., 1985-86; office svcs. mgr., personnel cons. Arrow Employment Agy., Melville, N.Y., 1986-90; author, editor, poet. Emcee, judge, singer talent shows and Karaoke contest, Long Island, 1990-93. Author: Love Takes Time, 1996; editor, contbg. writer: The Colors of God's Love, 1994, editor, contbg. writer, photographer: Rainbow Spirit, 2001; editor, contbg. writer Knowledge From The Source, 2004; contbr. poetry anthology Dance on the Horizon, 1994; editor, contbg. writer, poet: newsletter Family Self Sufficiency Program, 1993—95. Sec., organizer "Blockettes" Group, Campaign to Elect Frederic Block, Esq. to State Assmbly, Port Jefferson, 1966; co-chmn. Post Office Customer Adv. Coun., Commack, N.Y., 1992-95. Mem. NAFE, Nat. Mus. Women in the Arts, Internat. Soc. Poets (Named Internat. Poet of Merit 1994, 96, 97), Babylon Citizens Coun. on the Arts, Internat. Platform Assn., Filmmakers Connection, LI Film/TV Found. Democrat. Roman Catholic. Avocations: photography, the arts, travel, alternative healing, the paranormal, painting. Home: 123 N Country Rd Port Jefferson NY 11777-2121

ACKER, LOREN CALVIN, medical products executive; b. Lamar, Colo., Mar. 3, 1934; s. John C. and Ada M. (Ecton) Acker; m. Judy N. Willms, Sept. 17, 1955 (dec. Oct. 1968); children: Cheryl Acker Hoge, Keith B., Karen Acker Kime; m. Darla S. Copeland, July 24, 1976. BSME, Fresno State Coll., 1956; cert. in bus. and mgmt., U. Calif., Berkeley, 1961; MBA, U. Santa Clara, 1966. Flight test NASA, Edwards, Calif., 1954-56; engring. mgr. Westinghouse, Sunnyvale, Calif., 1956—68; engring. mgr. and assoc. dir. Kitt Peak Nat. Obs., Assn. of U. for Rsch. in Astronomy, Sebra, 1968—73; founder, chmn., CSO Engr. & Rsch. Assocs., Inc., Tucson, 1973—. Founder, gen. ptnr. Winged Foot Assocs., Tucson, 1974—; founder NYPA Inc., Tucson, 1986; founder, mgr bd. Electrophysiology LLC, Tucson, 2000—03; founder WoofSpa and Resort, N.Y.C., 2003. Chmn. pk. and recreation City of Cupertino, Calif., 1968; founder, mem. So. Ariz. Leadership Coun., 1997—; bd. dirs. Sonoran Sea Aquarium, 1999—; chmn. bioindustry Greater Tucson Econ. Coun., 1994—99; master engring. Ariz. Indsl. Partnership, 2000—; mem. agrl. and biosystem coun. U. Ariz., 1999—. Entrepreneurial fellow, U. Ariz., 1999. Mem.: Internat. Soc. Cellular Therapy, Am. Soc. Apherises, Am. Assn. Blood Banks, Audubon Soc., Nature Conservancy, Sierra Club. Republican. Achievements include patents in field. Avocations: skiing, tennis. Home: 4831 E Winged Foot Pl Tucson AZ 85718-1727 Office: 100 N Tucson Blvd Tucson AZ 85716-4740

ACKER, MARTIN HERBERT, psychotherapist, educator; b. N.Y.C., Dec. 15, 1921; s. Irving and Rose Martha (Katz) A.; m. Joan Elise Robinson, Apr. 29, 1948; children— Michael Christopher, David, Jonathon, Steven Anthony; m. Julia Ann Payne, Feb. 14, 1976 PhD, NYU, 1963. Lic. psychologist, Oreg. Prof. counseling and psychology U. Oreg., Eugene, 1961-86, prof. emeritus, 1986—, chmn. counseling, 1963-68. Vis. prof. Fed. City Coll., Washington, 1968-69, U. Victoria, B.C., Can., 1974, Fredrich Karls U., Tübingen, Germany, 1987; psychotherapist, Eugene, 1974—; dir. BeBusk Meml. Clinic, 1983-85. Mem. adv. com. Lane County Adult Corrections; bd. dirs. Lane Mental Health Assn., Pearl Buck Ctr.; mem. budget com. Sch. Dist. 4J, Eugene, 1994—. Mem. Am. Pers. and Guidance Assn. (bd. dirs. 1967-68), Soc. Sci. Study Sex, Oreg. Psychol. Assn., Am. Rehab. Counselors Assn. (pres. 1968-69), Men's Studies Assn. (co-chair 1986-90), Lane County Psychologists Assn. (pres. 1985-86), Friars Club. Home: 2733 Kismet Way Eugene OR 97405-1284 E-mail: macker@oregon.uoregon.edu.

ACKER, ROBERT FLINT, microbiologist; b. Chgo., Aug. 24, 1920; s. Robert Booth and Mary (Flint) A.; m. Phyllis Catharine Fry, Jan. 2, 1948; children: Catharine Elizabeth, Barbara Fenner, Robert Macdonald, James Christopher. BA, Ind. U., 1942, MA, 1948; PhD, Rutgers U., 1953. Asst. prof. Iowa State U., Ames, 1954-59; asst. chief cancer chemotherapy dept., chief quality control dept. Microbiol. Assocs., Inc., Bethesda, Md., 1959-61, chief dept. cell and media prodn., 1961-62; dir. microbiology program Office of Naval Research, Dept. Navy, Washington, 1962-69; dir. office of rsch. coord., asst. dean faculties for research, prof. biol. scis. Northwestern U., Evanston, Ill., 1969-74; exec. dir. Am. Soc. Microbiology, Washington, 1974-81, Nat. Found. Infectious Diseases, Bethesda, Md., 1981-86; pres. Bionox Corp., Tucson, 1985-92. Mem. bacteriology and mycology study sect. NIH, 1964. Author: (with R.R. Jennings) The Protistan Kingdom, 1970; editor: Proc. 24th Internat. Congress on Marine Corrosion and Fouling, 1972; editorial bd.: Applied Microbiology, 1962-73. V.p., bd. dirs. Iona House Sr. Svc. Ctr., Washington, 1978-79, pres., 1979-81; trustee Massanetta Conf. Ctr., 1983-86; bd. dirs. Am. Type Culture Collection, 1983-89; pres. Sunrise Mountain Ridge Homeowners Assn., 1994-95; bd. elders Potomac United Presbyn. Ch., Md., 1967-69, Winnetka (Ill.) Presbyn. Ch., 1972-74, Nat. Presbyn. Ch., Washington, 1983-86, St. Andrew's Presbyn. Ch., Tucson, 1989-91, 1998-2000. Eli Lilly & Co. postdoctoral fellow, 1953—54. Fellow Am. Acad. Microbiology, Soc. for Indsl. Microbiology (pres. 1986-87, Charles Porter award 2001); mem. Am. Soc. for Microbiology, Am. Inst. Biol. Sci. (coun. 1983-91), Cosmos Club. Home and Office: Apt 4102 5950 N Fountains Ave Tucson AZ 85704-7859 Personal E-mail: rfacker@flash.net.

ACKER, RODNEY, lawyer; b. Jacksonville, Tex., Sept. 29, 1949; s. Mike and Dorothy (Kennedy) Acker; m. Judy Bruyere, Sept. 2, 1972; children: Amy, Shelley, Rachel, Sam. BBA, U. Tex., Arlington, 1971; JD with honors, Tex. Tech, 1974. Bar: Tex. 1974, US Dist. Ct. No., So., Ea., We. Districts Tex., US Ct. Appeals 5th & 11th Circuits, US Supreme Ct.; cert. in civil trial law. Law clk. to Hon. Eldon Mahon, US Dist. Ct., Ft. Worth, 1974-76; assoc. Kendrick, Kendrick & Bradley, Dallas, 1976, Jenkens & Gilchrist, P.C., Dallas, 1976-79, ptnr., then shareholder, 1979—, mng. shareholder Dallas office. Fellow Am. Bar Found., Tex. Bar Found., Dallas Bar Found., Am. Coll. Trial Lawyers; mem. ABA, State Bar Tex., Dallas Bar Assn., Am. Bd. Trial Advocates, State Bar Coll., Patrick E. Higginbotham Am. Inns of Ct., Securities Industry Assn., Tex. Assn. Bank Counsel, Tex. Assn. Defense Counsel, Tex. Judicature Soc., Phi Delta Phi. Baptist. Office: Jenkens & Gilchrist Ste 3700 1445 Ross Ave Dallas TX 75202-2799 Office Phone: 214-855-4336. Office Fax: 214-855-4300. Business E-Mail: racker@jenkens.com.

ACKER, ROSE L., elementary school educator; b. Washington, May 10, 1945; d. Samuel L. and Bessie L. Acker. BA, Howard U., 1970; MA, U. D.C., 1979; EdD, George Washington U., 1994. Coord., instr. U. D.C., Washington; dictaphone transcriber editor NEA of Sch. Adminstrs., Washington; with U.S. Office Personnel Mgmt., Washington; sec.-adminstrv. aide H. Vogel Law Firm; educator D.C. Pub. Schs., Washington; counselor Fairfax County Pub. Sch., Ft. Belvoir Elem. Sch., Va. Recipient Regional Supts. Cert. of Merit, Outstanding Tchr. of Yr. award. Mem. LWV, Internat. Reading Assn., Am. Assn. Counseling and Devel., D.C. Alliance Sch. Educators, Nat. Coun. Negro Women (life), George Washington Alumni Assn., Delta Sigma Theta (life), Pi Lambda Theta, Chi Sigma Iota, Phi Delta Kappa (past pres., del., Bessie Gabbard Disting. award Leadership 2002-2003). Home: 1301 Delaware Ave SW Washington DC 20024-3911

ACKER, VIRGINIA MARGARET, nursing consultant; b. Madison, Wis., Aug. 11, 1946; d. Paul Peter and Lucille (Klein) A. Diploma in nursing, St. Mary's Med. Ctr., Madison, 1972; BSN, Incarnate Word Coll., San Antohio, 1976; MS in Health Professions, S.W. Tex. State U., 1980; postgrad., U. Tex., 1992-93. RN, Tex. Staff nurse St. Mary's Hosp., Milw., 1972-73, Kenosha (Wis.) Meml. Hosp., 1973-74, S.W. Tex. Meth. Hosp., San Antonio, 1974-75, Met. Gen. Hosp., San Antonio, 1975-76; instr. Bapt. Meml. Hosp. Sys. Sch. Nursing, San Antonio, 1976-83; DON, Meml. Hosp., Gonzales, Tex., 1983-84; instr., DON, Victoria Coll., Cuero, Tex., 1984-86; DON, Rocky Knoll Health Care Facility, Plymouth, Wis., 1986-87, Unicare Health Facilities, Milw., 1987-88; coord. nursing edn. St. Nicholas Hosp., Sheboygan, Wis., 1989-90; instr. U. Wis., Oshkosh, 1990-92, St. David's Hosp., Austin, Tex., 1992-95; coord. quality improvement Bailey Square Surgery Ctr., Austin, 1995-98; coord. regulation compliance South Austin Hosp., 1998—2003; program dir. Prevent Inc., 2003—. Roman Catholic. Avocations: cross-stitching, reading, camping, fishing. Home: 129 Copano Cove Rd Rockport TX 78382 Personal E-mail: virginia_acker@yahoo.com.

ACKERLY, WENDY SAUNDERS, construction company executive; b. Chgo., July 23, 1960; d. Robert S. Jr. and Linda Ackerly. BS in Atmospheric Sci., U. Calif., Davis, 1982; postgrad., U. Nev., Reno, 1985. Programmer U. Calif, Davis, 1982-83; cons. software Tesco, Sacramento, 1983; software engr. Bently Nev. Corp., Minden, Nev., 1984-85; mgr. computer scis. Jensen Electric Co., Reno, 1985-86, software engr. Cameron Park, Calif., 1986-89; sr. engr. Aerojet, Sacramento, 1989-96, test ops. specialist, 1996-98; dir. design and devel. Kerry King Constrn., Inc., 1998—, sec.-treas., 1991—. Mem. Nat. Space Soc., Planetary Soc., U.S. Tennis Assn., Calif. Aggie Alumni Assn. Republican. Avocations: tennis, hiking, travel, piano. Office: PO Box 269 Rescue CA 95672-0269

ACKERMAN, ARLENE, school system administrator; BA in Elem. Edn., Harris Stowe Tchrs. Coll.; MA in Ednl. Adminstrn. an dpolicy, Washington U.; MA in Edn., EdD in Adminstrn., Planning and Social Policy, Harvard U. Supt. Washington (D.C.) Pub. Schs., 1997—99, San Francisco United Sch. Dist., 1999—. Bd. mem. WestEd Regional Edn. Lab., 2003—; mem. Bay Area Sch. Reform Collaboration; program advisor BROAD-Urban Supts. Acad. Trustee San Francisco Fine Arts; bd. govs. San Francisco Symphony; active San Francisco Workforce Investment Bd. Recipient Apple for the Tchr. award, Iota Lambda Sorority, Disting. Alumni award, Harris Stowe Tchrs. Coll.; McDonnell Douglas fellow. Mem.: ASCD, Presdl. Commn. on Hist. Black Colls. and Univs., Nat. Assn. Black Sch. Educators, Coun. of the Great City Schs. (chair), Am. Assn. Sch. Adminstrs., Phi Delta Kappa. Office: 555 Franklin St San Francisco CA 94102*

ACKERMAN, ARLENE ALICE, accountant, business consultant, artist, writer; b. Omaha, Mar. 24, 1936; d. Walter Nelson and Mildred Eleanor (Krimlofski) A. BA in Social Sci. and Econs., San Francisco State U., 1962; MA in Polit. Sci., Purdue U., 1967; grad., U.S. Dept. Def. Info. Sch., 1973, U.S. Army Command-Gen. Staff Coll., 1977. CPA, Ind. Acct., adminstr. Peeples & MacDonald, CPAs, Sacramento, 1961-66; acct. chief acct.'s office Purdue U., West Lafayette, Ind., 1966-67; adj. gen. and info. officer, editor newspaper 123d Army Res. Command, Ind., 1972-75; mng. ptnr. Piano Showcase, Indpls., 1975-83; adminstr. Bennett Thrasher & Co. CPAs, Atlanta, 1983-86, Melvin Belli Law Offices, San Francisco, 1990; bus. cons. Ackerman & Assocs., Indpls., 1986-90; acctg. mgr., acting CFO Lera Dynalectric, San Francisco, 1991-94; CFO Nat. Home Bus. Assn., St. Helena, Calif., 1994-96; prin. Ackerman & Assocs., Fairfax, Calif., 1996-2000; fin. analyst Exodus Comm., Inc., Santa Clara, Calif., 2000—. Editor Mus. Indian Heritage Newsletter, Indpls., 1971-77; exhibited in group shows at Marin Agrl. Land Trust, San Rafael, Calif., 1993, Marin County Fair & Exposition, San Rafael, 1993, 96, Marin Soc. Artists, Ross, Calif., 1993, 94, Monterey Peninsula Mus. Art Christmas Miniature Show, 1993, Artisans Gallery, Mill Valley, Calif., 1993-95, Sonoma-Marin Fair, Petaluma, Calif., 1993-94, San Mateo (Calif.) County Fair, 1992-94, Sonoma County Fair, Santa Rosa, Calif., 1993-95; contbr. articles to Army profl. jours. Mem. Atlanta Feminist Women's Chorus. Officer U.S. Army, 1956-61, 67-71; col. USAR, ret., 1988. Mem. Soc. Children's Book Writers and Illustrators (assoc.), Marin Soc. Artist, San Francisco Early Music Soc., Nat. Assn. Miniature Enthusiasts. Avocations: classical piano, painting, drawing, writing children's stories, miniature artist. Home: 977 Citadel Dr Atlanta GA 30324 E-mail: ladycolonel@comcast.net.

ACKERMAN, BRUCE ARNOLD, law educator; b. NYC, Aug. 19, 1943; s. Nathan and Jean (Rosenberg) A.; m. Susan Gould Rose, May 29, 1967; children: Sybil Rose, John Mill. BA summa cum laude, Harvard U., 1964; LLB with honors, Yale U., 1967. Bar: Pa. 1970. Law clk. US Ct. Appeals (2d cir.), New York, 1967-68; law clk. to assoc. justice John M. Harlan US Supreme Ct., Washington, 1968-69; prof. law and public policy analysis U. Pa., Phila., 1969-74; prof. law Yale U., New Haven, 1974-82, Sterling prof. law and polit. sci., 1987—; Beekman prof. law and philosophy Columbia U., NYC, 1982-87. Author: Private Property and the Constitution, 1977, Social Justice in the Liberal State, 1980 (Gavel award ABA), (with Hassler) Clean Coal/Dirty Air, 1981, Reconstructing American Law, 1984, We the People: Foundations, 1991, The Future of Liberal Revolution, 1992, (with Golove) Is NAFTA Constitutional?, 1995, We the People: Transformations, 1998, The Failure of the Founding Fathers: Jefferson, Marshall, and the Rise of Presidential Democracy, 2005, (with others) The Uncertain Search for Environmental Quality, 1974 (Henderson prize Harvard Law Sch.). Cmdr. French Order Merit Henry Phillips prize in Juris Prudence, Am. Philol. Soc.; Guggenheim fellow, 1985. Fellow Am. Acad. Arts and Scis.; mem. Am. Law Inst. Office: Yale U Law Sch PO Box 208215 New Haven CT 06520-8215*

ACKERMAN, DAVID P., lawyer; b. Wilmington, Del., Feb. 22, 1957; BA with honors, Bucknell Univ., 1979; JD, George Washington Univ., 1982. Bar: Fla. 1983, US Dist. Ct. (so., no., middle dist. Fla.), US Ct. Appeals (11th cir.). Law clk. Judge James C. Paine, US Dist. Ct.; ptnr. Gunster Yoakley & Stewart, 1983—96; founding ptnr., bus. litigation Ackerman Link & Sartory, West Palm Beach, Fla., 1996—. Past chmn. Judicial Nominating Commn. for 15th Judicial Cir., Palm Beach County, Fla.; trustee, past pres. Legal Aid Soc., Palm Beach County, Fla. Contbr. articles to CLE publ. Named one of Fla. Legal Elite, Fla. Trend mag., 2004; recipient Pro Bono Svc award, Legal Aid Soc. Palm Beach County. Fellow: Am. Coll. Trial Lawyers; mem.: ABA, Fla. Bar (mem. exec. council Bus. Law sect.), Palm Beach County Bar Assn. Office: Ackerman Link & Sartory LLP Suite 1250 Esperante 220 Lakeview Ave West Palm Beach FL 33401 Office Phone: 561-838-4100. Office Fax: 561-838-5305. Business E-Mail: dackerman@alslaw.com.

ACKERMAN, DEBORAH, lawyer; b. Santa Monica, CA, 1950; BA, So. Meth. U., 1972; JD, St. Mary's U., 1979. Ptnr. Oppenheimer, Rosenberg, Kelleher & Wheatley, 1979—87, Cauthorn & Tobin, 1987—88; asst. gen. counsel S.W. Airlines Co., Dallas, 1988—2001, v.p., gen. counsel, asst. sec., 2001—. Mem.: ABA. Office: Southwest Airlines Customer Rels PO Box 36647 1CR Dallas TX 75235-1647 also: Southwest Airlines 2702 Love Field Dr Dallas TX 75346 Office Phone: 214-792-4000. Office Fax: 214-792-5015.

ACKERMAN, EUGENE, biophysics professor; b. Bklyn., July 8, 1920; s. Saul Benton and Dorothy (Salwen) A.; m. Dorothy Hopkirk, June 5, 1943; children— Francis H., Emmanuel T., Amy R. Ackerman de Canésie. BA, Swarthmore Coll., 1941; Sc.M., Brown U., 1943; PhD, U. Wis., 1949; postgrad., U. Pa., 1949-51, fellow, 1957-58. Instr. Brown U., 1943; from asst. prof. to prof. biophysics Pa. State U., 1951-60; mem. faculty U. Minn. Mayo Grad. Sch. Medicine, 1960-67, prof. biophysics, 1965-91, Hill Family Found. prof. biomed. computing, prof. biometry also computer scis., 1967-79, prof. dept. lab. medicine and pathology, 1969-91, prof. emeritus, 1991—, dir. div. health computer sci., 1969-79; staff cons. biophysics Mayo Found. and Mayo Clinic, 1960-67; dir. computer facility Mayo Found., 1964-65. Cons. bioacoustics USAF, 1957-62; mem. epidemiology and biometry tng. com. NIH, 1963-67, spl. study sect. ultrasonic applications, 1965-67, spl. study sect. lab. med. scis., 1967-69, computer and biomath. sci. study sect., 1969-73; dir. nat. resource for simulation of stochastic micropopulation models, 1983-90 Author: Biophysical Science, 1962, (with L. Ellis and L. Williams), 2d edit., 1979; (with L. Gatewood) Math Models in the Health Sciences, 1979, (with L. Elveback and J. Fox) Infectious Disease: Simulation of Epidemics and Vaccination Strategies, 1984; editor Biophys. Jour., 1983-87; also articles, tech. reports, chpts. in books. Rsch. grantee Am. Cancer Soc., 1953-56, NSF, 1958-64, NIH, 1954-90 Mem. Biophys. Soc., Am. Physiol. Soc., Assn. Computing Machinery, IEEE, Phi Beta Kappa, Sigma Xi, Gamma Alpha. Mem. Soc. Of Friends. Home: 11301 Park Ridge Dr W Minnetonka MN 55305-2551 Office: U Minn Health Ctr Box 511 MMC 420 Delaware St SE Minneapolis MN 55455-0374 Business E-Mail: acker004@umn.edu.

ACKERMAN, F. DUANE (DUANE ACKERMAN), telecommunication industry executive; b. Plant City, Fla., 1942; m. Kappy Ackerman; 4 children. BS, MS, Rollins Coll., MIT. With Bell South Corp., Orlando, Fla., 1964—, vice-chmn., group pres., 1991-95, vice-chmn., COO, 1995-97, pres., 1997—2005, CEO, 1997—, chmn. Atlanta, 1998—. Bd. dirs. Wachovia Corp.; Chmn. Nat. Security Telecom. Advisory Com. Bd. dirs. Ctrl. Atlanta Progress, The Commerce Club; trustee Rollins Coll. Mem.: bd. dirs. Allstate Corp., Homeland Security Advisory Coun., Atlanta C. of C. Office: BellSouth Corp 1155 Peachtree St NE Atlanta GA 30309-3610

ACKERMAN, FELICIA NIMUE, philosophy educator, writer; b. Bklyn., June 23, 1947; d. Arthur and Zelda (Sondack) A. AB summa cum laude, Cornell U., 1968; PhD, U. Mich., 1976. Asst. prof. philosophy Brown U., Providence, 1974-79, assoc. prof., 1979-91, prof., 1991—. Vis. asst. prof. philosophy UCLA, 1976; vis. hon. lectr. logic and metaphysics U. St. Andrews, Scotland, 1983; sr. Fulbright lectr. Hebrew U., 1985. Contbr. articles and short stories to various mags. Recipient O. Henry award for short story pub. in Prize Stories, 1990; fellow Ctr. for Advanced Study in Behavioral Scis., NEH, 1988-89. Mem. ACLU, NAACP (asst. sec. Providence br.), Am. Philos. Assn., Amnesty Internat. Office: Brown U Dept Philosophy PO Box 1918 Providence RI 02912-1918 Office Phone: 401-863-3240. Business E-Mail: felicia_ackerman@brown.edu.

ACKERMAN, GARY LEONARD, congressman; b. Brooklyn, N.Y., Nov. 19, 1942; s. Max and Eva (Barnett) A.; m. Rita Tewel, May 27, 1967; children: Lauren Meredith, Corey Brian, Ari David. BA, Queens Coll., 1965. Tchr. N.Y.C. Pub. Schs., 1966-70; founder Queens (N.Y.) Tribune, 1970—89; owner Multi Media, Queens, 1972—; mem. N.Y. Senate, 1979-83, 98th-108th Congresses from 5th N.Y. dist., Washington, 1983—; mem. internat. rels. com.; mem. banking and fin. svcs. com. Mem. Queens Coll. Alumni Assn. Democrat. Office: US States Capitol Office 2243 Rayburn Ho Office Bldg Washington DC 20515-3205 E-mail: gary_ackerman@mail.house.gov.*

ACKERMAN, GERALD MARTIN, art historian, consultant; b. Alameda, Calif., Aug. 21, 1928; s. Alois M. and Eva L. Ackerman. BA, U. Calif.-Berkeley, 1952; postgrad., U. Munich, Germany, 1955-58; PhD, Princeton U., 1964. Instr. Bryn Mawr Coll., Pa., 1960-64; asst. prof. Stanford U., Calif., 1964-70; assoc. prof. dept. art Pomona Coll., Claremont, Calif., 1970-75, prof., 1975-89, chmn. dept. art, 1972-82; prof. emeritus, 1989—. Fulbright prof. U. Leningrad, 1980; prof. Florence (Italy) Acad. Art, 1996—. Author: The Life and Work of J.L. Gerome, 1986, American Orientalists, 1994, Gerome, 2000, Les Orientalistes de l'Ecole britannique, 1991, The Barque-Gerome Drawing Course, 2003. Named Appleton eminent scholar, Fla. State U., 1994. Democrat. Home: 360 S Mills Ave Claremont CA 91711-5331 Office Phone: 909-626-6594. Personal E-mail: gackerman@pomona.edu.

ACKERMAN, JACK ROSSIN, investment banker; b. N.Y.C., Feb. 8, 1931; s. Robert M. and Florence (Rossin) Ackerman; m. Dana Lowenthal, Nov. 29, 1974; children: Ellen, Jay, Robin, Bradley. BA, Harvard U., 1953, MBA, 1955. With Bache Halsey Stuart Shields, Inc., N.Y.C., 1955-80; mng. dir. Drexel Burnham Lambert, Inc., N.Y.C., 1980-88; pres. Bond Review Inc., N.Y.C., 1988-91; mng. dir. Ladenburg Thalmann & Co. Inc., N.Y.C., 1991-93, Brill Securities, 1993-94, Burnham Securities, Inc., 1994-96. Bd. dirs. Jewish Found. Edn. Women, 1980; trustee, v.p. Jewish Bd. Family and Children's Svcs. Mem.: Harvard Club N.Y.C., Century Country Club (Purchase, N.Y.).

ACKERMAN, JACOB LEWIS, ophthalmologist; b. Berlin, July 22, 1947; s. Joseph and Pearl (Ziment) A.; m. Elaine Marsha Horowitz, Aug. 10, 1969 (dec. Mar. 2002); children: Rita, Karen, Steven, Julie; m. Judith Fay Rosenfeld, Oct. 6, 2002. MD, Albert Einstein Coll. Medicine, 1971. Assoc. dir. Brook Plaza Ophthalmology, Bklyn., 1975—, Brook Plaza Ambulatory Surgery Ctr., Bklyn., 1989—; asst. prof. of ophthalmology SUNY Health Sci. Ctr., Down State Med. Ctr., 1981—. Exec. bd. dirs. Met. Ophthalmic Ambulatory Surg. Ctr. Assn., Bronx. Contbr. articles to profl. jours. Sec. Young Israel of Lawrence-Cedarhurst, 1993. Avocations: tennis, writing, talmud, art, torah. Office: Brook Plaza Ophthalmology Assocs 1901 Utica Ave Brooklyn NY 11234-3213 Home: 138-15 Union Turnpike Flushing NY 11367-3250 Office Phone: 718-968-8700. E-mail: jfjamd2000@yahoo.com.

ACKERMAN, JAMES, fine arts educator; b. San Francisco, Nov. 8, 1919; s. Lloyd S. and Louise (Sloss) A.; m. Mildred Rosenbaum, Apr. 11, 1947 (dec. Jan. 10, 1986); children: Anne, Anthony, Sarah; m. Jill Slosburg, Aug. 1987; 1 child, Jesse August. AB, Yale U., 1941; MA, NYU, 1947, PhD, 1952; LHD, Kenyon Coll., 1961; DFA, Md. Inst., 1972, Mass. Coll. Art, 1984; LHD, U. Md., 1976; DArch, U. Venice, 1985. Part-time instr. Yale U., 1946-48; rsch. fellow Am. Acad. in Rome, 1949-52; from asst. prof. to prof. U. Calif., 1952-60; editor in chief Art Bull., 1956-60; prof. fine arts Harvard U., 1960—, chmn. dept. fine arts, 1963-68, 82-84, Arthur Kingsley Porter prof. fine arts, 1984-90, prof. emeritus, 1990. Slade prof. fine art, fellow King's Coll., Cambridge U., 1969-70; vis. fellow Coun. Humanities, Princeton, 1960-61; fellow Am. Coun. Learned Socs., 1964-65, N.Y. Humanities Inst., spring 1992; Mellon sr. scholar Can. Ctr. for Architecture, 2001; vis. prof. fine arts NYU, 1992; sr. fellow NEH, 1974-75; Mellon lectr. Nat. Gallery Art, 1985; Schapiro prof. art history Columbia U., 1989-90, 91; vis. prof. architecture MIT, 1996, Harvard, 1996-97. Author: The Cortile del Belvedere, 1954, The Architecture of Michelangelo, 1961 (winner Alice D. Hitchcock award Soc. Archtl. Historians 1961, Charles R. Morey award 1963), (with Rhys Carpenter) Art and Archaeology, 1963, Palladio, 1967, Palladio's Villas, 1967, The Villa: Form and Ideology of Country Houses, 1990, Distance Points, 1991, Origins, Imitation, Conventions, 2002; co-editor: Annali d'Architettura, 1992-95, Conventions of Architectural Drawing, 2000; films Looking for Renaissance Rome (with Kathleen Weil-Garris), 1975, Palladio the Architect and His Influence in America. Trustee The Artists Found., pres., 1977-79; mem. council of scholars Library of Congress, 1980-82. Recipient medal for svc. in art edn. Nat. Gallery Art, 1966, Centennial citation U. Calif., 1968, Honors AIA 1987, Gold medal Inst. per la Storia dell'Arte Lombarda, 1987, Archtl. History award AIA, 1991, Paul Oskar Kristeller Lifetime Achievement award Renaissance Soc. Am., 1998, Internat. Balzan prize, 2001; decorated grand officer Order of Merit, Republic of Italy, 1985, Premio Daria Borghese, 1995; Guggenheim fellow, 1992-93. Fellow Am. Acad. Arts and Scis., Am. Philos. Soc., Brit. Acad., Accademia Olimpica (corr.), Royal Acad. Arts and Scis., Accademia of St. Luca (Rome, hon.), Ateneo Veneto, Royal Acad. Uppsala (corr.), Bavarian Acad. Scis. (corr.). Home: 12 Coolidge Hill Rd Cambridge MA 02138-5510 Office: Harvard U Sackler Mus Cambridge MA 02138 E-mail: jsackerm@fas.harvard.edu.

ACKERMAN, JEROME LEONARD, biomedical researcher; BS in Chemistry cum laude, SUNY, Stony Brook, 1971; PhD in Physical Chemistry, MIT, Cambridge, 1976. Postdoctoral fellow U. Calif., Berkeley, 1976-77; asst. prof. chemistry U. Cin., 1977-82, assoc. prof. chemistry, 1982-85; asst. prof. radiology Harvard Med. Sch., Boston, 1985-95, assoc. prof. radiology, 1995—; dir. NMR spectroscopy Mass. Gen. Hosp., Charlestown, 1985—. Co-founder SkelScan, Inc.; cons. in field. Editor: (book) Advanced Tomographic Imaging Methods for the Analysis of Materials, 1991; contbr. numerous articles to profl. jours. Mem. Internat. Soc. for Magnetic Resonance in Medicine, Exptl. Nuclear Magnetic Resonance Conf. (mem. exec. com. 1991—, conf. chair 1999). Achievements include research in magnetic resonance studies of bone and synthetic biomaterials. Office: Biomaterials Lab Matinos Ctr Mass Gen Hosp Rm 2320 149 13th St Charlestown MA 02129-2000 E-mail: jerry@nmr.mgh.harvard.edu.

ACKERMAN, LENNIS CAMPBELL, retired management consultant; b. L.A., July 28, 1917; s. Lennis Howard and Ethel (Campbell) A.; m. Barbara Bohlken, July 27, 1941; children: Nancy (Mrs. Michael H. Burnaugh), Janet (Mrs. Robert W. Lesser), John, Barbara (Mrs. H.D. Arnold), George. AB, UCLA, 1940. With Texaco Co., L.A., 1940-43, Schenley Distillers, San Francisco, 1945-48; merchandiser Richfield Oil Corp., San Francisco, 1949-52; sales rep. Walker Mfg. Co., 1952-56, mktg. adminstr., 1956-58; v.p., gen. mgr. Can. subs. Galt Metal Industries, 1958-63, v.p. internat. ops. parent co., 1963-65, v.p. mktg., 1965, pres., 1966-68; pres., chief exec. officer Newport News Shipbldg. and Dry Dock Co., 1969-73; exec. v.p. Tenneco, Inc., 1972-73; group v.p. Questor Corp., 1973-78; assoc. dean Sch. Bus. Adminstrn. Coll. William and Mary, Williamsburg, Va., 1978-83. Sec. Va. Port Authority, 1971-73; mem. Sch. Bus. Adminstrn. Sponsors, Inc., Coll. William and Mary, 1970-79, chmn., 1970-72. Served with USAAF, 1943-45. Mem. Soc. Automotive Engrs., Pine Valley Golf Club, Beta Gamma Sigma (hon.), Alpha Sigma Phi. Episcopalian. Home and Office: Apt 129 5700 Williamsburg Landing Dr Williamsburg VA 23185-8077 Personal E-mail: budackman1@cox.net.

ACKERMAN, LISA MARILYN, foundation administrator, consultant; b. Danville, Pa., May 19, 1960; d. Bruce David and Jean Mamie (Pedevill) A. BA, Middlebury Coll., 1982; MBA, NYU, 1986. Intern Internat. Found. for Art Rsch., N.Y.C., 1982; adminstrv. asst. Samuel H. Kress Found., N.Y.C., 1982-84, program adminstr., 1984-87, chief adminstrv. officer, 1987-93, v.p., 1993—2003, exec. v.p., 2003—03; bd. mem. Hist. House Trust, N.Y.C., 2003. Cons. Internat. Found. for Art Rsch., 1985-86; rsch. cons. survey on art-deco comm. architecture, 1987-93; bd. dirs. U.S. chpt. Internat. Coun. of Monuments and Sites; mem. adv. coun. The Gallery of the Am. Bible Soc., 2003—. Contbr. articles to profl. jours. Vol. Planned Parenthood, NYC, 1982-83, Middlebury Coll. Alumni Assn., 1982-86, edn. dept. Mus. Modern Art, NYC, 1989-94; bd. dirs. St. Ann Ctr. for Restoration and the Arts, 1992-97, Jewish Heritage Coun., 1993-95, Historic House Trust of NYC, 2003—; active Middlebury Coll. Arts Coun., 1998—; bd. advisors Neighborhood Preservation Ctr., 1999—; pres. Friends of Roberto Longhi Found., 2000—, NY Preservation Archive Project, 2000—, Ptnrs. for Sacred Places, 1997-2003. Avocation: dance. Office: Samuel H Kress Found 174 E 80th St New York NY 10021-0439 Office Phone: 212-861-4993. E-mail: lisa@shkf.org.

ACKERMAN, LORETTA ANN, retired secondary school educator; b. Ellwood City, Pa., Nov. 8, 1937; d. Joseph Michael and Margaret (Petro) Fancsalszki; m. John McKay Ackerman, June 25, 1960 (dec.); children: Michael, Melisa, Melana. BS in Edn., Indiana U. Pa., 1959; MEd, Ashland (Ohio) U., 1990. Cert. tchr., Ohio. Tchr. Lorain (Ohio) Schs., 1959-60, Olean (N.Y.) City Schs., 1961-63; tchr. social studies Fredericktown (Ohio) Schs., 1972—2000; ret., 2000. Mem. Libr. Bd., Fredericktown, 1988—; mem. Fredericktown Bd. Edn.; mem. Fredericktown Cmty. Found. bd. Named Fredericktown Tchr. of Yr., 1993; scholar Martha Holden Jennings Found., 1992-93. Avocations: travel, reading. Home: 81 W Sandusky St Fredericktown OH 43019-1251

ACKERMAN, MARSHALL, publishing company executive; b. N.Y.C., Jan. 22, 1925; s. Albert and Beatrice (Munstuk) A.; m. Carol Lipman, June 8, 1948; children: Stark, Scott, A. Marc. AB, Harvard U., 1949; MS in Journalism, Northwestern U., 1950. Dir. employee relations Gimbel Bros., N.Y.C., 1950-51; account exec. Leonard Wolf & Assoc. (advt. agy.), N.Y.C., 1951-54; with Rodale Press, Inc., 1954-91, exec. v.p., 1967-91, vice chmn. bd., 1978-91; pub. Prevention mag., 1977-86, Theatre Crafts mag., 1967-78, vice chmn., Western divsn., 1986-91; ind. cons. health food industry, health media, 1992—2002. Pres. bd. assocs. Cedar Crest Coll., Allentown, Pa., 1976—78, trustee, 1983—87; pres. Pa. Stage Co., Allentown, 1978—80; chmn. Santa Barbara chpt. Am. Inst. Wine and Food, 1998—2003. Charge de Presse, Confrerie de la Chaine des Rotisseurs, Bailliage de Santa Barbara, 1998-2003; Decorated Bronze Star, Purple Heart. Home and Office: 894 Toro Canyon Rd Santa Barbara CA 93108-1642 E-mail: mackermanm@aol.com.

ACKERMAN, MELVIN, investment company executive; b. Bronx, N.Y., Feb. 6, 1937; s. Norman Ackerman and Lilly (Ostreicher) Warshaw; m. Jennie Wang, Sept. 19, 1964; children: Lori, Julie, Melissa. Student, Bklyn. Coll., 1956, 59. Trader Myron A. Lomasney & Co., N.Y.C., 1960-62; sr. v.p. E.F. Hutton & Co., N.Y.C., 1963-88. Exch. arbitrator Am. Stock Exch., N.Y.C., 1984-88; mem. options adv. com. Phila. Stock Exch., 1980-88, Am. Stock Exch., 1975-88; ind. cons., 1988—; dir. BBFD Investment Co.; ptnr. Breckenridge Holding Co. With USMC, 1956-58. Mem. Securities Traders Assn. N.Y., Securities Industry Assn. (credit div., options and derivative products com., 1983-88). Jewish.

ACKERMAN, PAGE, retired librarian, educator; b. Evanston, Ill., June 30, 1912; d. John Bernard and Florence Page. BA, Agnes Scott Coll., Decatur, Ga., 1933; B.L.S., U. N.C., 1940. Cataloger Columbia Theol. Sem., 1942-43; post librarian U.S. Army, Aberdeen Proving Ground, Md., 1943-45; asst. librarian Union Theol. Sem., Richmond, Va., 1945-49; reference librarian UCLA, 1949-54, asst. univ. librarian, 1954-65, asso. univ. librarian, 1965-73, univ. librarian, 1973-77, prof. Sch. Info. and Library Sci., 1973-77, 82, 83; vis. prof. Sch. Librarianship, U. Calif., Berkeley, 1978, 80. Recipient award of distinction in libr. sci. UCLA Alumnae Assn., 1977, Disting. Career Citation, Assn. Coll. and Rsch. Librs., 1989. Mem. ALA, AAUW (Status of Women award 1973), Calif. Libr. Assn., Coun. on Libr. Resources (bd. dirs. 1975-90). Home: c/o Rebecca Holt Esq 520 S Sepulveda Blvd Ste 400 Los Angeles CA 90049-3547 E-mail: page@ucla.edu.

ACKERMAN, PHILIP CHARLES, utilities executive, lawyer; b. Kenmore, N.Y., Feb. 14, 1944; s. Harold Lewis and Marion (Ehrhardt) Ackerman; m. Nancy Margaret Weig, Sept. 11, 1967; children: David Philip, Kathryn Elizabeth. BS in Acctg., SUNY, Buffalo, 1965; LLB, Harvard U., 1968. Bar: N.Y. 1968. Atty. Iroquois Gas Corp., Buffalo, 1968-72, asst. sec., 1972-74; sec. Nat. Fuel Gas Distbn. Corp., Buffalo, 1975—84, gen. counsel, 1978—84, sr. v.p., 1983—84, exec. v.p., 1989—95, pres., 1995—99, bd. dirs.; sr. v.p. Nat. Fuel Gas Supply Corp., 1984—88, exec. v.p., 1988—90, 1994—2002; v.p. Nat. Fuel Gas. Co., Buffalo, 1980—89, sr. v.p., 1989—99, dir., 1994—, pres., 1999—, CEO, 2001—, chmn. bd., 2002—. V.p. Seneca Resource Corp., 1978—89, pres., 1989—96, also bd. dirs.; mem. regional adv. bd. J. P. Morgan Chase. Mem.: Gas Tech. Inst. (bd. dirs. 2002—), Bus. Coun. N.Y. State (bd. dirs. 2002—), Buffalo Soc. Natural Sci. (bd. mgrs. 1982—, vice chmn. 1990—99, chmn. 1999—), Am. Gas Assn. (bd. dirs. 1999—, chmn. security, integrity and reliability com. 2001—04). Office: Nat Fuel Gas Co 6363 Main St Williamsville NY 14221

ACKERMAN, RAYMOND BASIL, advertising agency executive; b. Pitts., Aug. 7, 1922; s. Charles Raymond and Teresa Jane (Grasinger) A.; m. Lucille Frances Flanagan, June 14, 1948; children: Patricia Ann Mehring, Ann Carol Adams, Ray K., Susan Marie Fuller, Mark, Amy Lou Shaver. BS, Oklahoma City U., 1951, PhD (hon.) in Comml. Sci., 1996. Mem. display advt. staff Okla. Pub. Co., Oklahoma City, 1947-52; account exec. Knox-Ackerman Advt., Oklahoma City, 1952-53; pres. Ackerman Assos., Oklahoma City, 1954-74; chmn. bd. Ackerman McQueen, Inc., advt. agy., Oklahoma City, Tulsa, Dallas, Washington, 1975-92; chmn. emeritus Ackerman McQueen, Inc., 1992—. Bd. dirs. LSB Industries; past internat. pres. Worldwide Ptnrs. affil. Author: Tomorrow Belongs to Oklahoma, 1964; subject of biography Old Man River by Bob Burke with Joan Gilmore, 2002. Pres., gen. chmn. Oklahoma City United Appeal, 1964-66, trustee, 1967—; chmn. Oklahoma City Salvation Army, 1968; pres. Oklahoma City Better Bus. Bur., 1966; gen. chmn. Nat. Finals Rodeo Oklahoma City, 1965-84; past bd. dirs. Jr. Achievement, Oklahoma City, Okla. Water Devel. Found., Redlands Coun. of Girl Scouts, Urban League, Mercy Hosp.; past pres., bd. dirs. St. Anthony Hosp. Found.; past pres. Omniplex Sci. Mus., Oklahoma City; past trustee Oklahoma City Youth Park; campaign chmn., pres. Allied Arts Found., Oklahoma City, 1986-88, mem. exec. com., 1989—, Oklahoma City Cmty. Coun., 1989-2003; bd. dirs. Kirkpatrick Ctr. Mus. Complex, Oklahoma City, 1973-2004, pres. 1990-92; trustee, mem. exec. com., Oklahoma City U., 1988—; bd. dirs. Red Earth Indian Ctr., 1987-2004, Oklahoma City Pub. Sch. Found., 1990—; adv. bd. Enterprise Sq., 1994—; mem. last frontier coun. Boy Scouts Am. Rear Adm. USNR, ret. Recipient Silver medal Am. Adv. Fedn., 1982, Lifetime Svc. award Oklahoma City United Appeal, 1992, Pathfinder award Oklahoma County Hist. Soc., 1992, Outstanding Grad. award, Oklahoma City U., 1964, Disting. Alumnus award, 1991, Leadership Okla. award, 2001, Dean A. McGee award Downtown Now, Oklahoma City, 2000, Archbishop Beltran Cmty. Svc. award, 2000, Gov. Okla.'s Arts award, 2000, Lifetime Achievement award Nat. Assn. Fund Raising Execs., 2000, Sales and Mktg. Execs. Internat. Acad. Achievement award, 2000, Leadership Okla., 2001, Father of Yr. award Am. Diabetes Assn., 2003; named Humanitarian of Yr. Oklahoma County Arthritis Found., 1992, Okla. Living Treasures for Tomorrow Okla. Health Ctr. Found., 2004; named to Okla. Hall of Fame, 1993, Okla. Commerce and Industry Hall of Honor, 1998; named Ray Ackerman Leadership award in his honor United Way of Ctr. Okla., 2004. Mem. Naval Res. Assn. (nat. pres. 1969-71), Navy League (nat. bd. dirs. 1972-76, pres. Okla. chpt. 1974-76), Okla. Heritage Assn. (bd. dirs.), Oklahoma City C. of C. (bd. dirs., chmn. 1991, creation of Ray Ackerman award 1993), Oklahoma City Advt. Club (pres. 1954, Disting. Svc. award 1964), Am. Assn. of Advt. Agys. (past chmn. southwest coun.), Quail Creek Golf and Country Club, Rotary, Fortune Club, others. Home: 12905 Laurel Valley Ct Oklahoma City OK 73142-5167 Office: 1100 Valliance Bank 1601 NW Expressway St Oklahoma City OK 73118-1467

ACKERMAN, RICHARD CHARLES, lawyer, state legislator; b. Long Beach, Calif., Dec. 5, 1942; s. Jay Fuller and Marge Mae (Lyon) A.; m. Linda Irene Vranesic, May 4, 1968; children: Lauren, Marc, Brett. AB in Math., U. Calif., Berkeley, 1964; JD, Hastings Sch. Law, 1967. Ptnr. Ackerman, Mordock & Bowen, Fullerton, Calif., 1982—. Mem. city coun. City of Fullerton, 1980-92; pres. Orange County Waste Mgmt., Santa Ana, Calif., 1982-95; v.p. So. Calif. Hazardous Waste Mgmt., L.A., 1982-95; mem. Calif. State Assembly, 1994-2000, mem. Calif. State Sen., 2000-. Named Ofcl. of Yr., O.C. Com. Persons with Disabilities, 1996. Mem. Orange County Bar Assn., Fullerton C. of C. (pres., Man of Yr. 1983, Educator of Yr. 1996), Fullerton Rotary Club (pres.), Elks, Fullerton Yacht Club (commodore 1976—). Republican. Presbyterian. Avocations: sailing, racquetball, reading. Office: Ackerman Mordock & Bowen 305 N Harbor Blvd Ste 303 Fullerton CA 92832-1901 also: 17821 East 17th St Tustin CA 92780

ACKERMAN, ROBERT WALLACE, metal products executive; b. N.Y.C., Sept. 14, 1938; s. Emory Graham and Margaret Wallace A.; m. Margaret Tracy Dealy, Dec. 30, 1964; children: Ashley, Graham, Todd. BS, Yale U., 1960; MBA, Harvard U., 1962, DBA, 1968. CPA, N.Y. Cons. Arthur Young & Co., N.Y.C., NY, 1962-66; asst. prof. Harvard Bus. Sch., Boston, 1968-72, lectr., 1972-74; v.p. fin. and adminstrn. Preco, Inc., West Springfield, Mass., 1974-78; pres., bd. dirs. Premoid Corp., West Springfield, 1979-86, Whitman Products Ltd., West Warwick, RI, 1977-86; sr. research fellow Harvard Bus. Sch., 1986-88; pres., CEO Lincoln Pulp & Paper, Inc., 1988-92, Sheffield Steel Corp., 1992-99, chmn., CEO Sand Springs, Okla., 1999-2000; ptnr. Watermill Ventures, Waltham, Mass., 2000—. Author: The Social Challenge to Business, 1975, (with Hugo Uyterhoeven and John Rosenblum) Strategy and Organization, Text and Cases, General Management, 1973, 2d. edit., 1977, (with Raymond Bauer) Corporate Social Responsiveness, 1976. Deacon 1st Ch. in Cambridge Congl., 1970—; bd. dirs. Wildlife Conservation Trust, 1977—; chair adv. bd. Nature Conservancy, Mass., 1994—. Served with AUS, 1963 Mem.: AICPA, Steel Mfrs. Assn. (chmn. 1998—2000), N.Y. State Soc. CPA's, Am. Acad. Mgmt. (gov. 1972—73), Timber Owners of New Eng. (pres. 1977—, bd. dirs.), Harvard Club (Boston), The Kittansett Club (Maron, Mass.), Yale Club (N.Y.C.). Home: 274 Beacon St Boston MA 02116- Office: Watermill Ctr 800 South St Waltham MA 02453-1435

ACKERMAN, ROGER G., ceramics engineer; m. Maureen Ackerman; 4 children. Grad., D, Rutgers U.; PMD program, Harvard U. Engr., sales, mgmt. positions Corning (N.Y.) Inc., 1962—72, pres. Corhart Refractories Co., 1972—75, gen. mgr., v.p. Ceramic Products Divsn., 1975—80, sr. v.p., 1980—81, dir. Mfg. and Engring. Divsn., 1981—83, pres. MetPath Inc., 1983—85, pres. Specialty Materials, 1985—90, pres., COO, 1990—96, chmn., CEO, 1996—2001; ret., 2001. Bd. dirs. Pittston Co., Mass. Mutual Life Ins. Co., Dow Corning Corp.; trustee Corning Inc. Found., Corning Mus. Glass; mem. bd. overseers Rutgers U. Found. Office: Corning Inc PO Box 45 Phoenix NY 13135 E-mail: ackermanrg@corning.com.

ACKERMAN, RUDY SCHLEGEL, artist, educator; b. Allentown, Pa., Mar. 30, 1933; s. Harvey J. and Alma (Schlegel) A.; m. Rosemarie Ercolani, 1953; children: Sally Ann, Ann Marie. BS in Art Edn., Kutztown U., 1958; MS in Edn., Temple U., 1961; EdD in Art Edn., Pa. State U., 1967. Art specialist So. Lehigh State U., Coopersburg, Pa., 1958-63; prof., chmn. dept. art Moravian Coll., Bethlehem, Pa., 1963-2000, prof. arts and humanities, 1990—; exec. dir. Baum Sch. of Art, Allentown, Pa., 1965—. Commd. works include sculpture installations at Lehigh U., Pa. State U., Bethlehem Sculpture Garden, Moravian Coll., various pvt. collections; lectr. in field. Pres. Allentown Arts Commn., 1992—. With U.S. Army, 1953-55. Mem. Coll. Art Assn., Nat. Guild of Schs. of the Arts. Home: 2708 W Washington St Allentown PA 18104-3839 Office: Art Dept Moravian Coll Bethlehem PA 18018 E-mail: BaumSchool@aol.com.

ACKERMAN, SIGURD HOWARD, psychiatrist; b. Millville, NJ, Feb. 25, 1940; s. William H. and Ethel (Kessler) A.; m. Cecelia M. McCarton, Apr. 25, 1983; children: Elizabeth, Rebecca, McCarton. BA, Harvard U., 1962; MD, Tufts U., 1966. Intern Kings County Hosp., Bklyn., 1966-67, resident in medicine, 1967-68; resident in psychiatry Montefiore Med. Ctr., Bronx, NY, 1970-73; dir. psychiatry St. Luke's Roosevelt Hosp. Ctr., N.Y.C., 1989—98, med. dir., exec. v.p., 1991-93; prof. clin. psychiatry Columbia U. Coll. Physicians and Surgeons, N.Y.C., 1989—, assoc. dean, 1991-93; pres., CEO St. Luke's-Roosevelt Med. Ctr., N.Y.C., 1998—2001; pres., med. dir. Silver Hill Hosp., Inc., New Canaan, Conn., 2003—. Rsch. Scientist Devel. award level I and II, NIMH, 1976-84. Home: 97 Sagamore Rd Stamford CT 06902-8007 Office: Silver Hill Hosp 208 Valley Rd New Canaan CT 06840 Office Phone: 203-801-2215. Business E-Mail: sackerman@silverhillhospital.org.

ACKERMAN, VALERIE B., former sports association executive; b. Nov. 7, 1959; m. Charlie Rappaport; children: Emily, Sally. Grad., U. Va., 1981, UCLA Sch. Law, 1985. Assoc. Simpson, Thacher & Bartlett, N.Y.C.; staff atty. NBA, 1988, spl. asst. to commr., 1990-92, dir. bus. affairs, 1992—94, v.p. bus. affairs, 1994—96; pres. WNBA, 1996—2005. Bd. dirs. USA Basketball; exec. com. Naismith Meml. Basketball Hall of Fame. Trustee March of Dimes. Named to, GTE Acad. All-Am. Hall of Fame, 1999, Scholar Athlete Hall Fame, Inst. for Internat. Sport, 2003; recipient Disting. Alumna award, U. Va. Women's Ctr., 1997.

ACKERS, GARY KEITH, biophysical chemistry educator, researcher; b. Dodge City, Kans., Oct. 25, 1939; s. Leo Finley and Mabel Ida (Hostetler) A.; children: Lisa, Sandra, Keith. BS in Chemistry and Math., Harding Coll., Searcy, Ark., 1961; PhD in Physiol. Chemistry, Johns Hopkins U., 1964. Instr. physiol. chemistry Johns Hopkins U. Sch. Medicine, Balt., 1965-66, prof. biology and biophysics, 1977-89, dir. Inst. Biophys. Rsch., 1987-89; asst. prof. biochemistry U. Va. Sch. Medicine, Charlottesville, 1966-67, assoc. prof., 1967-72, prof. biochemistry and biophysics, 1972-77; prof. biochemistry and molecular biophysics Washington U., St. Louis, 1989—, head dept. biochemistry and molecular biophysics, 1989-96. Instr. physiology Marine Biol. Labs., Woods Hole, Mass., 1974-76; chmn. Gordon Conf. on Proteins, 1985; disting. lectr. Red Cell Club, 1997—. Mem. editorial bd. Analytical Biochemistry, 1970-79, Biophys. Chemistry, 1973-78, Proteins, Structures, Functional Genetics, 1991—; contbr. over 150 articles to sci. jours. Guggenheim fellow, 1972-73; recipient NIH Merit award, 1987. Fellow Biophys. Soc. (coun. 1972-74, 80-83, pres. 1984-85, Cole rsch. award 1994); mem. Am. Chem. Soc. (program chair biol. chem. divsn. 1994), Am. Soc. Biochem. Molecular Biology. Office: Washington U Med Sch Dept Biochem and Molecular Biophysics 660 S Euclid Ave Saint Louis MO 63110-1010

ACKERSON, CHARLES STANLEY, minister, social worker; b. St. Louis, June 19, 1935; s. Charles Albert and Glenda Mae (Brown) A.; m. Carol Jean Stehlick, Aug. 18, 1957; children: Debra Lynn, Charles Mark, Heather Sue. AB, William Jewell Coll., 1957; MDiv, Colgate Rochester Div. Sch., 1961. Ordained to ministry Am. Bapt. Ch., 1961; LCSW. Pastor Glens Falls (NY) Friends Meeting, 1961-65; assoc. pastor Delmar Bapt. Ch., St. Louis, 1965-68; resource dir. Block Partnership, 1968-71; group home dir. Northside YMCA, 1971—72; group home supr. St. Louis Juvenile Ct., 1973-74; program dir. Youth Opportunities Unltd., casework supr. St. Louis County Juvenile Ct., 1974-83; pastor St. Jordan's and St. John's United Chs. of Christ, 1976—; youth svcs. specialist St. Louis County Dept. Human Svcs., 1985-94; assoc. dir. Gen. Protestant Children's Home, 1994-99; residential dir. Mo. Bapt. Children's Home, 1999-2000; instr. sociology, adminstrn. of justice and human svcs. Mo. Bapt. U., 1980—. Exhibit coord. Dog Mus., 1989—91; cons. Am. Youth Found., 1990—2001; mem. ordination coun. area V Great Rivers region Am. Bapt. Chs. U.S.A., 1982—84; chmn. youth focus group Interfaith Partnership Met. St. Louis, 1985—88; chmn. St. Louis Area Youth Svcs. Network, 1987—89. Chmn. group home com. Mo. Coun. on Criminal Justice, 1973-75; chmn. cts. and instns. subcom. Juvenile Delinquency Task Force for Gov. Mo. Action Plan for Pub. Safety, 1976. Mem.: Nat. Juvenile Ct. Svcs. Assn., Soc. for the Sci. Study Religion, Am. Correctional Assn., Mo. Juvenile Justice Assn., Nat. Coun. Juvenile and Family Ct. Judges (mem. faith law and morality com.), Mo. Conservation Fedn., Nat. Audubon Soc., Smithsonian Instn. Assn., Three Rivers Kennel Club of Mo. (past pres.), Cairn Terrier Club Am., Lambda Chi Alpha. Democrat. Baptist. Home: 1221 Havenhurst Rd Ballwin MO 63011-4402 Personal E-mail: cackersn@swbell.net.

ACKERSON, PATRICIA KATHLEEN FREIS, art educator, artist; b. Plainfield, N.J., Sept. 22, 1970; d. Peter Charles and Kathleen Claire Freis; m. Richard Stephen Ackerson, June 15, 1996. BFA in Illustration and Design, Marywood Coll., Scranton, Pa., 1993. Woodshop asst. K & S Marine Woodcraftsmen, Long Branch, NJ, 1988—90; designer / woodcrafter Long Br. Mfg. & Design, Long Branch, NJ, 1992—94; full-time asst. tchr. Metuchen-Edison YMCA, Metuchen, NJ, 1995—98, part-time asst. tchr., 1999—; art tchr. St. Francis Cathedral Sch., Metuchen, 1999—. Calligrapher, Edison, NJ, 1984—; custom-made craft designer, Edison, 1990—; freelance illustrator, Edison, 1990—; calligrapher NJ Polic Benevolent Assn. Contbr. program design St. Francis of Assisi Cathedral bull.; carbothello drawings/paintings, Barron Arts Ctr. Exhbn.; illustrator (calendar cover) St. Francis of Assisi Sch. calendar, calligrapher St. Francis of Assisi. Mem.: Nat. Mus. of Women in the Arts (hon.; mem. 2003—), Nat. Cath. Ednl. Assn. (assoc.; mem. 2003—). Roman Catholic. Avocations: reading, drawing, music, travel. Home: 61 Sixth St Edison NJ 08837 Office: St Francis Cathedral Sch 528 Main St Metuchen NJ 08840 Personal E-mail: pattifa@aol.com.

ACKLEY, ROBERT O., lawyer; b. Chgo., July 24, 1952; s. William O. and Jeannette E. (Mitchell) A.; m. Patricia Ann Cerney, May 24, 1980; children: Matthew, Allison, Elizabeth, Anne, Kathryn, Kimberly. BA, No. Ill. U., 1974; MA., No. Mich. U., 1977; JD, John Marshall Law Sch., Chgo., 1988. Bar: Ill. 1988, U.S. Dist. Ct. (no. dist.) Ill. 1988, U.S. Ct. Appeals (7th cir.), 2003. Adminstrv. intern, asst. to city mgr. City of Marquette, Mich., 1976—77; adminstrv. asst. to town mgr. Town of Glastonbury, Conn., 1978; supr. Continental Bank, Chgo., 1979; chief methods analyst dept. fin. City of Chgo., 1980—81, chief supr. ops. dept. revenue, 1981—84; pres. Ackley & Assocs., Chgo., 1984—88; law clk., adminstrv. asst. to chief justice Thomas J. Moran Supreme Ct. of Ill., Lake Forest, 1988—90; atty. Cassiday, Schade & Gloor, Chgo., 1990—91; pvt. practice Chgo., 1991—2002; ptnr. Sarles & Ouimet, Chgo., 2003—, Woodstock & Dallas. Bd. dirs. Ill. Pro Bono Ctr., 1997-2002; adj. prof. Roosevelt U., Chgo., 1989-90; mem. panel arbitrators Cir. Ctr. of 19th Jud. Cir., 1991-97, Cir. Ct. Cook County, 1993-97; detention screening atty. pretrial svcs. Cir. Ct. of Cook County, 1991—; drugs panel atty. Office of State Appellate Defender, 1992—. Bd. dirs. Bryn Mawr-Broadway Ridge Mchts. Assn., Chgo., 1984-87; panel mem. Capital Resource Ctr., 1991, Community Econ. Devel. Law Project. Fellow Ill. Bar Found.; mem. Nat. Assn. Counsel Children, Ill. Bar Assn., Chgo. Bar Assn., Lake County Bar Assn. (pro bono svc. award 2000), Ill. Appellate Lawyers Assn., Acad. Polit. Sci. (life), Nat. Coun. Juvenile and Family Ct. Judges, McHenry County Bar Assn. (Pro Bono Svc. award, 2004). Home: 606 Buckingham Pl Libertyville IL 60048-3326 Office: 131 E Calhoun St Woodstock IL 60098 Office Phone: 815-334-9500. Business E-Mail: ackley@calcon.net.

ACKLIN, HAILEY ERIN, music educator; b. Springfield, Mo., Jan. 18, 1977; d. Ronald Gene and Marsha Lynn Acklin. AA, State Fair CC, Sedalia, Mo., 1997; MusB, S.W. Bapt. U., Boliver, Mo., 2000; EdM, Ctrl. Mo. State U., 2005. Tchr. Smithton (Mo.) R-6 Schs., 2002—. Mem.: Mo. State Tchrs. Assn., Mo. Music Educators Assn., Nat. Assn. Music Edn. Baptist. Avocations: music, reading. Office: Smithton R6 Sch Dist 505 S Myrtle Smithton MO 65350

ACKOFF, RUSSELL LINCOLN, systems analyst, educator; b. Phila., Feb. 12, 1919; s. Jack and Fannie (Weitz) A.; m. Alexandra Makar, July 17, 1949 (dec. Feb. 1987); children: Alan W., Karen B., Karla S.; m. Helen Wald, Dec. 20, 1987. BArch, U. Pa., 1941, PhD in Philosophy, 1947; DSc, U. Lancaster, 1967; DSc (hon.), Washington U., St. Louis, 1993, U. Lincolnshire and Humberside, U.K., 1999, Fla. Internat. U., 2001; DL (hon.), U. New Haven, 1997; Dr. (hon.), Pontificia U. Cath. del Peru, Lima, 1999. Asst. instr. philosophy U. Pa., Phila., 1941-42, 46-47; asst. prof. philosophy and math. Wayne U., Detroit, 1947-51; assoc. prof., prof. ops. rsch. Case Inst. Tech., Cleve., 1951-64; Silberberg prof. systems scis. U. Pa., 1964-86, chmn. dept. stats. and ops. rsch., 1964-66, chmn. grad. faculty ops. rsch., 1964-69, dir. Mgmt. Sci. Ctr., 1964-67, 69-70, chmn. Busch Ctr., 1970-74, 76-79, chmn. social systems sci. unit, 1974-78, 86—, Anheuser-Busch prof. emeritus of mgmt. scis., 1986—. Chmn. INTERACT: The Inst. Interactive Mgmt., 1986—; methodological cons. U.S. Bur. Census, 1950-51; cons. Eastern Airlines, Emerson Electric Co., Gen. Foods Co., Mobil Oil Co., Nat. Acad. Scis., Nat. U. Mex., Sci. and Tech. Rsch. Coun., Turkey, Western Electric Co.; bd. dirs. Mantua Indsl. Devel. Corp.; August A. Busch Jr. vis. prof. mktg. Washington U., St. Louis, 1989-95; mem. core faculty Union Inst., Cin., 1989-91, Ackoff Ctr. Advanced Sys. Approaches Univ. Penn., 2000—; vis. prof. U. Hull, U.K., 2005—. Author: (with C.W. Churchman) Psychologistics, 1946, Methods of Inquiry, 1950, (with C.W. Churchman and M. Wax) Measurement of Consumer Interest, 1947, The Design of Social Research, 1953, (with C.W. Churchman and E.L. Arnoff) Introduction to Operations Research, 1957, Progress in Operations Research, I, 1961, Scientific Method, 1962, (with P. Rivett) A Manager's Guide to Operations Research, 1963, (with M. Sasieni) Fundamentals of Operations Research, 1968, A Concept of Corporate Planning, 1970, (with F.E. Emery) On Purposeful Systems, 1972, Redesigning The Future, 1974, (with T.A. Cowan et al) Designing a National Scientific and Technological Communication System, 1976, The Art of Problem Solving, 1978, Creating the Corporate Future, 1981, (with E. V. Finnel, J. Gharajedaghi) A Guide to Controlling Your Corporation's Future, 1984, (with P. Broholm and R. Snow) Revitalizing Western Economics, 1984, Management in Small Doses, 1986, Ackoff's Fables, 1991, The Democratic Corporation, 1994, Exploring Personality: An Intellectual Odyssey, 1998, Ackoff's Best, 1999, Re-Creating the Corporation, 1999, (with Sheldon Rovin) Redesigning Society, 2003, Beating the System, 2004; editor: Management Science, 1965-70, Systems and Mgmt. Ann, 1974; assoc. editor Ops. Rsch., 1953-65, Conflict Resolution, 1964-70; book rev. editor Philosophy of Science, 1947-53; mem. abstracting staff: Biological Abstracts, 1950-51; adv. editor mgmt. sci. John Wiley & Sons, 1964-86; mem. adv. bd. Math. Spectrum, 1968-86; mem. editl. bd. Management Decision, 1968-86, Reflections, 2001-03; editl. assoc. European Jour. Operational Research; contbr. articles to profl. jours. Bd. dirs. Tallberg Found., Sweden, 1997—2000, Ctr. for Quality Mgmt., Cambridge, Mass., 1996—2004; mem. UN Devel. Adv. Coun., 1996—. Recipient award ASTD, 1993, award for outstanding achievement in sys. thinking and practice U.K. Sys. Soc., 1999. Fellow Am. Statis. Assn., Ops. Rsch. Soc. Am. (v.p., pres. 1956-57), Internat. Acad. Mgmt., Inst. Mgmt. Cons.; mem. Internat. Acad. Mgmt., Russian Acad. Natural Scis. (fgn. mem.), Inst. Mgmt. Scis. (v.p. 1965), Operational Rsch. Soc. (U.K.) (Silver medal 1971), Soc. Gen. Systems Rsch. (pres. 1987-88), Oprational Rsch. Soc. India, Peace Rsch. Soc., Sigma Xi, Tau Sigma Delta. Achievements include Ackoff Ctr. for Advancement of Sys. Approaches (2000) and the Russell L. Ackoff Endowment (2001) established at U. Pa. Home: Benson House 101 930 Montgomery Ave Bryn Mawr PA 19010-3044 Office: # 201 1021 W Lancaster Ave Ste 201 Bryn Mawr PA 19010-2635 Office Phone: 610-526-9374. Personal E-mail: rlackoff@aol.com.

ACKOUREY, PAUL PHILIP, lawyer; b. Scranton, Pa., Dec. 27, 1958; s. Paul Peter and Jean Helene (Dorris) A.; m. Bernadette Ackourey. BA, MA, U. Scranton, 1980; JD, Dickinson Sch. Law, 1983. Bar: Pa., U.S. Dist. Ct (mid. dist.) Pa., U.S. Ct. Appeals (3rd cir.), U.S. Supreme Ct. Assoc. Levy & Preate, Scranton, 1983-85; ptnr. Spizer & Ackourey, Scranton, 1985—93, Paul Philip Ackourey, Scranton, 1994—. Lectr. U. Scranton, 1987, Am. Inst. Paralegal Studies, Scranton, 1986—. Named one of Outstanding Men of Am., 1986. Mem. ACLU, Lackawanna County Bar Assn., Pa. Bar Assn., Assn., Am. Bankrupty Inst., PA Assn. of Criminal Def. Lawyers, Nat. Assn. of Criminal Def. Lawyers, Wyo. Cty. Bar Assn., NEPA Trial Lawyers Assn. Office: 116 N Washington Ave 1st Fl Scranton PA 18503 Office Phone: 570-342-4242.

ACKOUREY, PETER PAUL, lawyer; b. Scranton, Pa., Dec. 18, 1954; s. Paul Peter and Regina Helene (Dorris) A.; m. Christine Marie Van Wert, Aug. 6, 1977; children: Abigail Regina, Kenneth Jamal, Jemeille Irene, Mary Rose. BA in History, U. Scranton, 1974; JD, Harvard U., 1977. Bar: Pa. 1977, N.J. 1989. Assoc. Drinker Biddle & Reath, Phila., 1977-83; assoc. counsel Mellon Bank Corp., Phila., 1983-88; ptnr. Drinker Biddle & Reath LLP, Princeton, NJ, Florham Park, NJ, 1988—2005; shareholder Buchanan Ingersoll P.C., Princeton, 2005—, Phila., 2005—. Co-ptnr. in charge of Princeton office Drinker Biddle & Reath LLP, 1995—2000, bd. mem. mng. ptnrs., 1996—2000. Mem. ABA, Pa. Bar Assn., N.J. Bar Assn., Phila. Bar Assn. Avocations: U.S. history, baseball. Office: Buchanan Ingersoll PC 700 Alexander Pk Princeton NJ 08540-6347 Office Phone: 609-987-6807. Business E-Mail: ackoureypp@bipc.com.

ACOBA, SIMEON RIVERA, JR., state supreme court justice, educator; b. Honolulu, Mar. 11, 1944; s. Simeon R. and Martina (Domingo) A. BA, U. Hawaii, 1966; JD, Northwestern U., Chgo., 1969. Bar: Hawaii 1969, U.S. Dist. Ct. Hawaii, U.S. Ct. Appeals (9th cir.). Law clk. Hawaii Supreme Ct., Honolulu, 1969-70; housing officer U. Hawaii, Honolulu, 1970-71; dep. atty. gen. State of Hawaii, Honolulu, 1971-73; pvt. practice, Honolulu, 1973-80; judge 1st Circuit Ct. Hawaii, Honolulu, 1980-94, Intermediate Ct. Appeals Hawaii, Honolulu, 1994-2000; assoc. justice Hawaii Supreme Ct., 2000—. Atty. on spl. contract divsn. OSHA, Dept. Labor, Honolulu, 1975—77, Pub. Utilities divsn., State of Hawaii, 1976—77; campaign spending com. State of Hawaii, 1976; staff atty. Hawaii State Legislature, 1975; instr. criminal law Hawaii Pacific U., 1992—. Bd. dirs. Hawaii Mental Health Assn., 1975—77, Nuuanu YMCA, 1975—78, Hawaii Youth at Risk, 1990—91; mem. Gov.'s Conf. on Yr. 2000, Honolulu, 1970, Citizens Com. on Adminstrn. of Justice, 1972, State Drug Abuse Commn., 1975—76, Com. to Consider the Adoption of ABA Model Rules of Profl. Conduct, 1989—91; mem. Judicial Edn. Com., 1992—93, Hawaii State Bar Assn. Jud. Adminstrn. Com., 1992—94, Permanent Com. Rules Penal Procedure and Cir. Ct. Rules, 1992—96; subcom. chmn. Supreme Ct. Com. Pattern Jury Instrns., 1990—91; mem. Hawaii Supreme Ct. Ad Hoc Com. Jury Master List, 1991—92. Recipient Liberty Bell award, 1964. Mem.: Hawaii Bar Assn. (dir. young lawyers sect. 1973). Office: Hawaii Supreme Ct 417 S King St Honolulu HI 96813-2912

ACOMB, ROBERT BAILEY, JR., lawyer, educator; b. New Orleans, July 28, 1930; s. Robert Bailey and Catherine (Ryan) A.; m. Greta LeBlanc, Apr. 25, 1953; children: Robert III, Dwight J., Greta, William Ryan, John. BBA, Tulane U., 1951, JD, 1953. Bar: La. 1953, U.S. Dist. Ct. (ea. and mid. dist.) La. 1953, U.S. Ct. Appeals (5th cir.) 1955, U.S. Supreme Ct. 1967, U.S. Ct. Appeals (7th cir.) 1976, U.S. Ct. Appeals (11th cir.) 1981, U.S. Dist. Ct. (we. dist.) La. 1989. Assoc. Jones, Walker, Waechter, Poitevent, Carrere & Denegre, New Orleans, 1953-56, ptnr., 1956, sr. ptnr., 1968—. Adj. prof. law Tulane U., New Orleans, 1969—; bd. dirs. Attys. Liability Assurance Soc. Ltd., Hamilton, Bermuda, 1979-2001; pres. bd. dirs. Christian Bros. Found., Inc., New Orleans, 1976-78; trustee Christian Bros. Retirement Fund, New Orleans, 1989—. Author: Maritime Personal Injury & Death, 4th edit., 1993; editor: Damages Recovered, 1984; contbr. articles to profl. jours.; chmn. adv. editors: Tulane Maritime Law Jour., 1976-93. Chmn. Archbishop's Community Appeal, New Orleans, 1993; pres. Tulane U. Assocs., New Orleans, 1990-92. Decorated knight grand cross Equestrian Order of Holy Sepulchre of Jerusalem, knight of St. Gregory, Pope John Paul II. Fellow Am. Coll. Trial Lawyers (state chair 1972—), Am. Bar Found.; mem. ABA (mem. standing com. on admiralty, chmn. 1979-83), New Orleans Bar Assn. (Disting. Maritime Lawyer 1996), Tulane Maritime Law Ctr. (chmn. 1982—), Maritime Law Assn. U.S. (proctor, mem. exec. com. 1981-84), Tulane Maritime Law Inst. (chmn. 1991—), Tulane U. Alumni Assn. (pres. 1989-90, Vol. of Yr. 1992), Navy League U.S. (pres. New Orleans chpt. 1987-88, state pres. 1990-94), Assn. Average Adjusters U.S. (chmn. 1992-93), Mil. Order Fgn. Wars (comdr. La. Commandery), New Orleans Country Club, Boston Club, Pickwick Club, Stratford Club, Order of St. Louis. Roman Catholic. Avocations: photography, travel, sports, teaching. Office: Jones Walker Waechter Poitevent Carrere & Denegre 201 Saint Charles Ave Fl 48 New Orleans LA 70170-1000 Office Phone: 504-582-8112. Office Fax: 504-582-8010. Business E-Mail: bacomb@joneswalker.com. E-mail: bacomb@jwlaw.com.

ACOSTA, ALEX (RENE ALEXANDER ACOSTA), prosecutor, former federal agency administrator; b. Miami; BA, JD, Harvard U. Law clk. U.S. Ct. Appeals (3rd cir.); assoc. Kirkland & Ellis, 1995—97; sr. fellow Ethics & Pub. Policy Ctr., 1997—2000; prin. dep. asst. atty. gen. civil rights divsn. US Dept. Justice, Washington, 2001—02, asst. atty. gen. civil rights divsn., 2003—05, interim US atty. (so. dist.) Fla. Miami, 2005—. Mem. NLRB, 2002—03. Recipient Disting. Leadership award, Arab Am. Anti-Discrimination Com. Mich., 2004, Excellence in Govt. Svc. award, Mex.-Am. Legal Def. and Edn. Fund, 2003, Hugh A. Johnson, Jr. Meml. award, DC Hispanic Bar Assn., 2003, Friend in Govt. award, Am.-Arab Anti-Discrimination Com., 2005. Office: US Atty Office 99 N E 4th St Miami FL 33132

ACOSTA, RAYMOND LUIS, federal judge; b. N.Y.C., May 31, 1925; s. Ramon J. and Carmen J. (Acha-Jimenez) Acosta-Colon; m. Marie Hatcher, Nov. 2, 1957; children: Regina, Gregory, Ann Marie. Student, Princeton U., 1948; JD, Rutgers U., 1951. Bar: N.J. 1953, U.S. Supreme Ct. 1956, P.R. 1959. Sole practice, Hackensack, N.J., 1953-54; spl. agt. FBI, San Diego, Washington, Miami, Fla., 1954-58; asst. U.S. atty. San Juan, P.R., 1958-61; sole practice, 1961-67; trust officer Banco Credito y Ahorro Ponceno, San Juan, 1967-80; U.S. atty. Dist. P.R., Hato Rey, 1980-82; judge U.S. Dist. Ct. P.R., San Juan, 1982—. Alt. del. U.S.-P.R. Commn. on Status, 1962-63; mem. Gov.'s Spl. Com. to Study Structure and Orgn. Police Dept., P.R., 1969 Contbr. articles to profl. jours. Pres. United Fund, P.R., 1979. Served with USN, 1943-46, Normandy. Recipient Merit cert. Mayor of San Juan, 1973. Mem. Fed. Bar Assn. (pres., P.R. 1967), P.R. Bankers Assn. (chmn. trust div. 1971, 75, 77), P.R. Bar Assn., Soc. Former Spl. Agts. FBI. Office: US Courthouse & PO Bldg Ste 348 300 Recinto Sur St San Juan PR 00901

ACQUAH, SARAH NIPAH, agricultural educator; b. Kumasi, Ghana, Mar. 10, 1945; d. Johan Nipah and Kate Bempah; m. Emmanuel Turkson Acquah, May 13, 1978; children: Isaac H., Catherine H. Diploma in home sci., U. Ghana, Accra, 1971; BSc, MSc, Ohio State U., 1975, PhD in Ext. Edn., 1977. Agrl. instr. Ministry Agr., Kumasi, 1966-69; asst. to v.p. acad. affairs U. Md. Ea. Shore, Princess Anne, Md., 1985-86, faculty rsch. assoc., 1987-96, dir. internat. student advisor, 1996—, project assoc. African Lang., 1992—, instr. agrl. and ext. edn., 1997—. Internat. student advisor U. Md. Ea. Shore, Princess Anne, 1996—, new student orientation com., 1997—, retention com., 1998-99, faculty rsch. com., 1998-99. Bd. mem., ch. mem. Asbury United Meth., Salisbury, 1986—. Scholar Ghana Govt., 1969, U. Md. Ea. Shore, Princess Anne, Ohio State U., Columbus, 1973-74, Altrusa Internat.; grantee USDA, 1986-89, 93-96, 96-99, USAID, 1986-91, UMES, 1990-91, 98-99. Mem. Am. Vocat. Edn. Rsch. Assn., Md. Assn. for Higher Edn., U. Md. Internat. Faculty and Adminstrs. Assn., Soroptimist Internat. (bd. mem. 1992-93). Avocations: basketball, tennis, reading, travel. Home: 614 Frene Ave Salisbury MD 21801 Office: Univ Md Eastern Shore Backbone Rd Princess Anne MD 21853 E-mail: sqacquah@mail.umes.edu.

ACREE, ANGELA DENISE, lawyer; b. Portales, N.Mex., Oct. 29, 1959; d. Elick Henry and Velma Joan Acree; m. Robert Franklin Torp, May 23, 1998. BS, U. Houston, 1986; MBA, S.W. Mo. State U., 1991; JD, U. Mo., 1997. Bar: Mo. 1997, Ill. 1998. Sole practice, Murphysboro, Ill., 1998—2000; asst. prosecutor Greene County, Mo., 2000—02; with Burkart & Hunt PC, 2002—03; mcpl. judge Springfield, Mo., 2003—; with Bankruptcy Clinic, LLC, Springfield, 2003—. Contbr. articles to profl. jours. With USAF, 1979-83. Mem.: Mo. Mcpl. and Assoc. Cir. Judges Assn., Springfield Met. Bar Assn., Mo. Bar Assn. Avocations: golf, canoeing, paragliding. Home: 3431 S Valley View Ave Springfield MO 65804-4677 Office: Bankruptcy Clinic LLC 1736 E Sunshine Ste 702 Springfield MO 65804 Office Phone: 417-886-5940.

ACREE, G. HARDY, airport executive; Previous positions with Anchorage Internat. Airport, Alaska, Phila., Indpls., and Riverside/San Bernardino area airports; mgr., dep. dir. aviation Bush Intercontinental Airport, Houston, 1995—99; dir. Sacramento County Airport Sys., Sacramento Internat. Airport, Calif., 1999—. Office: Sacramento County Airport Sys Sacramento Internat Airport 6900 Airport Blvd Sacramento CA 95837 Office Phone: 916-874-0719. E-mail: Acreeh@saccounty.net.*

ACRIVOS, ANDREAS, chemical engineering professor; b. Athens, Greece, June 13, 1928; m. Juana Vivo, Sept. 1, 1956. BSChemE, Syracuse U., 1950; MS, U. Minn., 1951, PhD, 1954. Instr. U. Calif., Berkeley, 1954-55, asst. prof., 1955-59, assoc. prof., 1959-62; prof. Stanford (Calif.) U., 1962-88; Einstein prof. CCNY, 1988-2001. Prof. emeritus, CCNY, 2001—. Contbr. articles to profl. jours. Guggenheim Found. fellow, 1959, 76; recipient Bingham Medal, 1994, Soc. Rheology, Nat. medal of Science, 2001. Fellow AIChE (awards 1963, 68, 84), Am. Phys. Soc. (Fluid Dynamics prize 1991); mem. NAS, NAE, Am. Acad. Arts and Scis., Am. Chem. Soc., Soc. Rheology. Office: CCNY Levich Inst 138th St at Convent Ave New York NY 10031 Business E-Mail: acrivos@sci.ccny.cuny.edu.

ACTON, DAVID, lawyer; b. Phila., Feb. 13, 1933; s. Kenneth Davis and Mary (Musselman) A.; m. Barbara Ann Sullivan, June 18, 1955; children—Lauren Doane, Paul Bodine; m. Jane Thomas Young, June 24, 1978. AB, Yale, 1955; JD, U. Pa., 1960. Assoc. Krusen, Evans & Byrne, Phila., 1960-63; asst. sec., asst. gen. counsel Leeds & Northrup Co., Phila., 1963-65, sec., gen. counsel North Wales, Pa., 1965-71; v.p., gen. counsel K.S. Sweet Assos., King of Prussia, Pa., 1971-75; practice in Bryn Mawr, Pa., 1975-77; v.p. Crockett Mortgage Co., Valley Forge, Pa.; gen. mgr. Hershey's Mill, 1977-82; exec. v.p. Ultec, Inc., Exton, Pa., 1982-85; arbitrator and mediator, 1986—. Bd. dirs. Nat. Ctr. for the Am. Revolution. Mem. Phila. Bar Assn., Colonial Soc. Pa., Mensa, Union League Club, Merion Cricket Club, Yale Club (Phila.), Chevaliers du Tastevin. Home and Office: 233 Righters Mill Rd Gladwyne PA 19035-1532 Office Phone: 610-649-4972. E-mail: d.acton1326@comcast.net.

ACTON, DAVID L(AWRENCE), automobile company executive; b. Detroit, Apr. 12, 1949; s. Lawrence E. and Johannah (Cassimatis) A.; m. Dianne Patience McNeill, Sept. 5, 1981; children: Andrew, Stephen, Amy. BME, Gen. Motors Inst., Flint, Mich., 1973; MBA, U. Mich., 1978. Assoc. engr. Hydra-matic div. GM, Ypsilanti, Mich., 1973-74, project engr., 1974-77, supr. indsl. engring., 1977-78, asst. supt. indsl. engring., 1978-81, asst. supt. progress tracking, quality and reliability Detroit, 1981-83, sr. adminstr., 1983-85, mgr. program planning B-O-C- car group, 1985, program mgr. Allanté elec. test system, 1985-87; mgr. elec. design and processing Cadillac Motor Car Co., Detroit, 1987-91, mgr. electrical product systems, 1991-93; chief engr. elec./electronics Cadillac luxury car divsn. GM, Flint, Mich., 1993-96, dir. elec. engring. mid-luxury car group, 1996-97, dir. elec. engring. N.Am. ops. Warren, Mich., 1997-98, chief vehicle engr. OnStar divsn. Troy, Mich., 1998-2000, exec. dir. global telematics, 2000—02, dir. global telematics portfolio planning, 2002—04; pres., CEO Charter Mobile Info. Inc., Owosso, 2004—05; v.p. YGOMI LLC, Owosso, 2005—. Bd. dirs. Its Am. Mem.: SAE, Convergence Transp. Electronics Assn. (bd. dirs.). Office: 120 Exchange St Ste 200C Owosso MI 48867

ACZÉL, JANOS DEZSÖ, mathematician; b. Budapest, Hungary, Dec. 26, 1924; s. Dezsö and Irén (Adler) A.; m. Susan Kende, Dec. 14, 1946; children: Catherine, Julie. MA, PhD, U. Budapest, 1947; DSc, Hungarian Acad. Sci., 1957; Dr. honoris causa, U. Karlsruhe, 1990, U. Graz, 1995, Silesian U. Katowice, 1996, U. Miskolc, 1999, U. Debrecen, 2003. Faculty U. Szeged, Hungary, 1948-50; prof. math. Tech. U., Miskolc, 1950-52, Kossuth U., Debrecen, Hungary, 1952-65, U. Waterloo, Ont., Can., 1965-93, disting. prof., 1969-93, disting. prof. emeritus, 1993—; vis. prof. U. Fla., Gainesville, 1963-64, 81, Stanford U., 1964, U. Köln, Germany, 1965, U. Giessen, 1966, 70, Ruhr U., Bochum, 1968, Fla. Atlantic U., 1968, U. Pavia, 1968, 69, Ist. Naz. Alta Matematica, Rome, 1971, Monash U., Clayton, Victoria, Australia, 1972, Ahmadu Bello U., Zaria, Nigeria, 1975-76, U. Lecce, Italy, 1976, Calif. Inst. Tech., 1978, Karl-Franzens U., Graz, Austria, 1979, 1986, 1991, 1993, 1999, 2003, Okayama U. (Japan), 1984, U. Milan, 1985, 91, U. Hamburg, 1985, U. Politécnica Catalunya, Barcelona, 1986, 92, U. Bern, Switzerland, 1986, U. Karlsruhe, Germany, 1992, 98, U. Calif., Irvine, 1994, 1996—2002, 2004—05. Cons. Naval Ocean Systems Ctr., San Diego, 1979-81; chmn. Internat. Symposium of Functional Equations, 1962-96, hon. chmn., 1997—; Jeffrey lectr. Acadia U., 1984, Marshak lectr. UCLA, 1998. Author (with S. Gołąb): Funktionalgleichungen der Theorie der geometrischen Objekte, 1960; author: Vorlesungen über Funktionalgleichungen und ihre Anwendungen, 1961, Ein Blick auf Funktionalgleichungen und ihre Anwendungen, 1962, Dover reedition, 2005, Lectures on Functional Equations and Their Applications, 1966, On Applications and Theory of Functional Equations, 1969; author: (with Z. Daróczy) On Measures of Information and Their Characterizations, 1975; author: A Short Course on Functional Equations Based Upon Recent Applications to Social and Behavioral Sciences, 1987; author: (with J. Dhombres) Functional Equations in Several Variables with Applications to Mathematics, Information Theory and to the Natural and Social Sciences, 1989, Russian trans., 2003; editor: Functional Equations: History, Applications and Theory, 1984, Aggregating Clones, Colors, Equations, Iterates, Numbers and Tiles, 1995, (jours.) Rendiconti di Matematica e delle sue Applicazioni, Inequalities and their Applications, Scientiae Mathematicae Japonicae, Results of Mathematics, Mathware and Soft Computing, Publicationes Mathematicae, Comptes Rendus Mathématiques de l'Académie des Sciences Canada, (book series) Theory and Decision Libr.-Math. and Methods Series; translator (hon. editor-in-chief): Aequationes Mathematicae. Recipient M. Beke award J. Bolyai Math. Soc., 1961, Hungarian Acad. Scis. award, 1958, 62, Cajal medal Spanish Nat. Coun. Sci. Rsch., 1988, J. Kampé de Feriet award Internat. Conf. on Info. Processing and Mgmt. of Uncertainty in Knowledge-based Sys., 2004. Fellow Royal Soc. Can., Hungarian Acad. Scis. (fgn.); mem. Can. Math. Soc., Am. Math. Soc., N.Y. Acad. Scis. Achievements include initiation of modern theory of functional equations; gave gen. theorems and applications to geometry, algebra, analysis, econs., mathematical psychology, utility, decision, probability and info. theory; theories of mean values, measurement, and webs. Office: U Waterloo Pure Math Dept Waterloo ON Canada N2L 3G1 E-mail: jdaczel@math.uwaterloo.ca.

ADA, ALMA FLOR, education educator, writer; b. Camagüey, Cuba, Jan. 3, 1938; came to U.S., 1970; d. Modesto Arturo Ada and Alma Lafuente; children: Rosalma, Alfonso, Miguel, Gabriel Zubizarreta. Diploma in Spanish studies, U. Complutence, Madrid, 1960; B of Humanities, U. Cath., Lima, Peru, 1963, PhD, 1965. Assoc. prof. Emory U., Atlanta, 1970-72; prof. Mercy Coll. Detroit, 1972-75; prof. Sch. Edn. U. San Francisco, 1976—2004, prof. emeritus, 2004—. Author: The Gold Coin (Christopher award 1991), My Name is María Isabel, 1993, The Unicorn of the West, 1994, Dear Peter Rabbit, 1994, Where the Flametrees Bloom, 1995, Gathering the Sun, 1997, Under the Royal Palms, 1998 (Pura Belpré award 2000), The Lizard and the Sun, 1997, The Malachite Palace, 1998, Yours Truly, Goldilocks, 2002, Three Golden Oranges, 1999, Friend Frog, 2000, With Love, Little Red Hen, 2003, I Love Saturdays...y domingos, 2003, A pesar del amor, 2003, A Magical Encounter: Latino Children's Literature in the Classroom, 2003, Gateways to the Sun, 2001-03, Pio Peep: Spanish Nursery Rhymes, 2004, Mamá Goose: A Treasury of Nursery Rhymes in Spanish and English, 2005; co-author: Authors in the Classroom. A Transformative Education Experience, 2003. Recipient Ann. award L.A. Bilingual Dirs. Assn., 1993, Calif. State PTA Assn., Simon Weisenthal Mus. of Tolerance award, 1998, Gold medal Parenting Mag., 1998, Purá Belpré, 2000; scholar Radcliffe Inst. Harvard U., 1965-67; Fulbright scholar, 1966-68. Mem. Internat. Bd. Books for Young People, Nat. Assn. for Bilingual Edn., Calif. Assn. for Bilingual Edn. Office: U San Francisco Ignatian Heights San Francisco CA 94117 Office Phone: 415-383-8047. Personal E-mail: almaflorada@yahoo.com.

ADACHI, ATHAN KEN, civil engineer; b. Honolulu, July 18, 1951; s. Kenneth Korji and Dorothy Takako (Fujioka) Adachi; m. Marleen Takako Kuboyama, Feb. 13, 1993. BSCE, U. Hawaii, 1974; cert., Ind. U., 1989. Registered prof. engr., Hawaii. Project engr. Avanti Constrn. Co., Honolulu, 1974—77; engr. cons. Unemori Engring. Co., Wailuku, Hawaii, 1977—79; civil engr. IV County of Maui, Wailuku, 1979—85, asst. dist. engr., 1986—2004, civil engr. VIII, 2004—. Bd. dirs. Maui Assn. for Retarded Citizens, 1983—94; coord. Blood Bank of Hawaii, Maui United Way, 1985—2003; asst. leader Grace Bible Ch. Recipient Silver award, United Way, Cert. of Recognition, Cert. of Merit for Disting. svc. to Cmty., others. Mem.: Water Environment Fedn., Christian Leadership Min., Christian Coalition, U. Hawaii Alumni Assn., Toastmasters (Disting. Competent award), U.S. Tennis Assn., Coll. Engring. Club. Home: 98-660 Moanalua Loop #279 Aiea HI 96701-5199 Office: City & County Honolulu Dept Environ Svcs Divsn of Environ Quality 1000 Uluohia St Ste 303 Kapolei HI 96707 Office Phone: 808-692-5096. Business E-Mail: aadachi@honolulu.gov.

ADADE, ANTHONY KWASI, import export company executive; b. Kumasi, Ashanti, Ghana, Sept. 16, 1957; came to U.S., 1976; s. Opanin Kofi and Abena (Nyantah) Fofie; m. Florence Yaa Dapaah, Dec. 16, 1990; 1 child, Chrystal Ama. AS, Northeastern U., 1984, BS, 1986; MEd, Cambridge (Mass.) Coll., 1988. Cert. computer programmer. Dir. human resources Newton (Mass.) Plastics Corp., 1980-87; pres., chief exec. officer N.H. Corp., Somerville, Mass., 1988—. Cons. African Studies Ctr., Boston U., 1985-86; dir. edn. outreach UN Assn. Greater Boston, 1985-87; advising Mem. Ashanteman Coun., Ghana, 1987. Founding exec. mem. Ashanteman Assn. of New Eng., Springfield, Mass., 1990—. Mem. Boston Computer Soc., United Nations Assn. of Greater Boston, World Affairs Coun., The White Brotherhood Lodge of Ghana (full minister). Roman Catholic. Avocations: ping pong/table tennis, soccer, photography, walking. Office: NH Corp 19 Beacon Pl Fl 3 Somerville MA 02143-4305 also: PO Box 3120 Kumai Ghana Western Sahara also: PO Box 9183 955 Massachusetts Ave #254 Cambridge MA 02139

ADAIR, ELEANOR REED, environmental biologist; b. Arlington, Mass., Nov. 28, 1926; d. Kenneth Clarke and Margaret Reed; m. Robert Kemp Adair, June 21, 1952; children: Douglas, Margaret, James (dec.). BA, Mt. Holyoke Coll., 1948; MA, U. Wis., 1951, PhD, 1955. From rsch. asst. to lectr., sr. scientist Yale U., New Haven, 1960—. From asst. fellow to fellow John B. Pierce Lab., New Haven, 1966—96; sr. scientist Electromagnetic Radiation Effects, Air Force Rsch. Lab., Brooks AFB, Tex., 1996—2001, sr. scientist emeritus, 2001—; cons. sci. adv. bd. EPA, 1983—89. Editor: Microwaves & Thermoregulation, 1983; contbr. articles to jours. Bd. dirs. Am. Himalayan Found., 1990—. Fellow AAAS, APA, IEEE, Am. Inst. Med. and Biol. Engring., N.Y. Acad. Scis.; mem. Bioelectromagnetics Soc. Avocations: birdwatching, gardening, Buddhism. Home: 50 Deepwood Dr Hamden CT 06517

ADAIR, ROBERT KEMP, physicist, educator; b. Ft. Wayne, Ind., Aug. 14, 1924; s. Robert Cleland and Margaret (Wiegman) Adair; m. Eleanor Reed, June 21, 1952; children: Douglas McVeigh, Margaret Guthrie, James Cleland. Ph.B., U. Wis., 1947, PhD, 1951, DSc (hon.), 1994. Instr. physics U. Wis., Madison, 1950-53; physicist Brookhaven Nat. Lab., Upton, NY, 1953-58, assoc. dir. high energy and nuc. physics, 1987-88; mem. faculty Yale U., New Haven, 1958—, prof. physics, 1961-72, Eugene Higgins prof. physics, 1972-88, Sterling prof. physics, 1988—94, Sterling prof. emeritus, 1994—, chmn. dept. physics, 1967-70, dir. divsn. phys. scis., 1977-80, sr. rsch. scientist, 1994—. Physicist Nat. Baseball League, 1987—89. Author (with Earle C. Fowler): (book) Strange Particles, 1963; author: Concepts in Physics, 1969, The Great Design, 1987, The Physics of Baseball, 1990; assoc. editor: Phys. Rev., 1963—66, Phys. Rev. Letters, 1974—76; editor, 1978—84. With inf. U.S. Army, 1943—46. Guggenheim fellow, 1954, Ford Found. fellow, 1962—63, Sloan Found. fellow, 1962—63. Fellow: Am. Acad. Arts and Scis., Am. Phys. Soc. (chmn. divsn. particles and fields 1972—73); mem.: NAS (chmn. physics sect. 1986—89, sec. class phys. scis. 1989—92, chmn. class phys. scis. 1992—94). Home: 50 Deepwood Dr Hamden CT 06517-3415 Office: Yale U Dept Physics Sloane Physics Lab PO Box 208121 New Haven CT 06520-8121 Business E-Mail: adair@hepmail.physics.yale.edu.

ADAIR, WENDELL HINTON, JR., lawyer; b. Ft. Benning, Ga., Mar. 17, 1944; s. Wendell H. Sr. and Jacqueline (Moore) A.; children: Elizabeth Carroll, John Michael, Benjamin David. BA, Emory U., 1966, postgrad., 1966-67; JD, U. Chgo., 1969. Bar: Ill. 1969, N.Y. 2000. Assoc. Ross, Hardies, O'Keefe, Babcock & Parsons, Chgo., 1969-72; ptnr. Mayer, Brown & Platt, Chgo., 1972-89, McDermott, Will & Emery, Chgo., 1989—99, Stroock & Stroock & Lavan LLP, N.Y.C., 1999—. Editor: K & A Restructuring Register, (legal bulletin) The Jour. of Corp. Renewal. Bd. dirs. ARC Mid-Am. chpt. 1991-99, Chgo. Opera Theatre, 1993-99; mem. Evanston Zoning Amendment Com., 1980-83. Mem. ABA (bus. sect., bcy. sect., natural resources sect., pub. utilities sect.), Ill. Bar Assn., Fed. Energy Bar Assn. (bd. dirs. 1985-87, program chmn. 1990-91), NY Bar Assn., Am. Gas Assn. (bd. dirs. legal sect. 1986-89), Turnaround Mgmt. Assn. (program and publs. coms.). Clubs: Econ. (Chgo.), Chicago. Republican. Office: Stroock & Stroock & Lavan 180 Maden Ln New York NY 10038 Office Phone: 212-806-5870. E-mail: wadair@stroock.com.

ADAIR, WENDY HILTY, university official; b. Gary, Ind., Aug. 10, 1949; d. Robert Merle Hilty and Marjorie Ellen (Akers) Gurasich; m. James Bynum Adair, June 3, 1972 (div. Oct. 1988). BA, U. Okla., 1971; MBA, U. Houston, 1990. Grad. asst. U. Okla., Norman, 1971—72; pub. rels. assoc. Okla. Regional Med. Program, Oklahoma City, 1972—73; asst. dir. vols. VA Hosp., Oklahoma City, 1973—75; writer U. Tex. Health Scis. Ctr., Houston, 1975—78; asst. dir. media U. Houston, 1978—80, dir. media rels., 1980—83, dir. univ. rels., 1983—87, assoc. v.p. for pub. rels., 1987—95, assoc. vice chancellor pub. affairs, 1995—97, assoc. vice chancellor, v.p., 1997—. Freelance writer gen. mags., Houston, 1975-88; pub. rels. cons. Houston Dist. Dental Soc., 1978-86. Pub. rels. com. mem. United Way Gulf Coast, Houston, 1994-98, allocations com. mem., 1990-98; bd. dirs. Children at Risk, 1993-2000; active Boy Scouts Am., Houston, 1987; pub. rels. coun. mem. Tex. Med. Ctr.; chair bd. Ctr. AIDS, 1998-2003; bd. dirs. Initiatives for Children. Recipient Field Dir.'s award and commendation VA, 1975, Matrix award Women in Communications, Houston, 1988, 2 silver and bronze awards Nat. Admissions Mktg., 1988, Best of Tex. award Tex. Pub. Rels. Soc., 1988, bronze, silver and gold award Houston Advt. Club, 1988), named Houston Marketer of Yr. Am. Mktg. Assn., 2002 Mem. Internat. Assn. Bus. Communicators (pres. Houston 1989-90, Regional Merit award 1989, Houston Communicator of Yr. 1991), Nat. Assn. State Univs. (nat. exec. com. 1989-91, 95—), Pub. Rels. Soc. Am. (chair-elect), Coun. for Advancement and Support of Edn. (nat. adv. com., nat. pub. rels. program award 1987, silver pub. rels. grand award 1988, nat. bronze award 1989, dist. gold award 1995, dist. awards 1996, 97, 98, 99, 2000), Houston Press Club (bd. dirs. 1990-92). Unitarian Universalist. Avocations: walking, writing, dogs, music, pottery. Office: U Houston Office Pub Affairs Houston TX 77204-2021

ADAKU, CHIOMA, non-profit organization administrator; b. Oak Ridge, Tenn., Feb. 19, 1968; d. Orin Walter and Ethel Louise Sykes; m. Jarvis T. Griffin, Nov. 30, 2002; children: Daisha S. Ortiz, Willie Williams. BS, Knoxville Coll., 1990; BA, Bristol U., 1990, MBA, 1992. Contract adminstr. Dept. Energy, Oak Ridge, 1990—99; grantwriter Child & Family Tenn., Knoxville, 1999—2001; devel. dir. Tenn. Indsl. Renewal Network, Knoxville, 2002—. Cons. in organizational devel., marketing, and grassroots. Ind. filmmaker: (documentaries) Apartheid in Appalachia, 2003; (film) From the Backyard to Brazil, 2003; From the Mountains to Mexico, 2003; author: (book) Emmaus in Appalachia, 2002. Pres. Cmty. Edn. Fund, 2002—; candidate for state rep. Rep. Party, Knoxville, 1999; v.p. Women Polit. Caucus, Knoxville, 2001—02; chair bd. dirs. Tribe One, Knoxville, 2003; bd. dirs. Appalachian Cmty. Fund, Knoxville, 2002. Recipient Knoxville Leadership award, Cmty. Action Ctr., 1996, Knoxville's First and Next Leadership award, Sincere Seven, 2003, Leadership Award, Cmty. Action Com., YWCA Tribute to Women award, 2003. Mem.: NAACP (v.pres. Knoxville chpt. 2000—), Assn. Profl. Fundraiser (assoc.), Ea. Stars, Zeta Phi Beta (charter 1986—90). Republican. Achievements include communitiy based research Apartheid in Appalachia on African-American history and health. Office: Tenn Indsl Renewal Network 1515 E Magnolia Ave Knoxville TN 37917

ADAM, JENNIFER JEAN, music educator, choral conductor; d. David Harold Adam; m. Matthew James Herman, May 24, 2003. MusB in Music Edn. and Violin Performance, Wilkes U., Wilkes-Barre, Pa., 1998; postgrad., West Chester U., West Chester, Pa/, 2021; MusM in Vocal Performance and Choral Conducting, Temple U., Phila., 2001. Elem. music tchr. West Chester Area Sch. Dist., West Chester, Pa., 2001—02; instr. West Chester U., West Chester, 2003—04; h.s. / mid. sch. music tchr. Conestoga Valley Sch. Dist., Lancaster, Pa., 2001—. Singer The Lyric Consort, Scranton, Pa., 1996—; faculty mem. The Performing Arts Inst. of Wyo. Sem., Kingston, Pa., 1999—; dir. of chorale Berks Classical Children's Chorus, Shillington, Pa., 2003—. Grantee Meet the Musician I grantee, Conestoga Valley Edn. Found., 2002, Composition for Women's Chorus, Mid. Sch. Chorus and Orch. grantee, 2003, Masterclass and Performance by U. of Pretoria, South Africa, Choir, 2004. Mem.: Am. Choral Dirs. Assn. (assoc.), Music Educator's Nat. Conf. (assoc.), Sigma Alpha Iota (life). Independent. Lutheran. Avocation: cooking. Office: Conestoga Valley School District 2110 Horseshoe Rd Lancaster PA 17601 Office Phone: 717-397-5231 3165. E-mail: jennifer_adam@cvsd.k12.pa.us.

ADAM, JOHN, JR., insurance company executive emeritus; b. Braintree, Mass., Dec. 14, 1914; s. John and Harriet E. (Hubley) A.; m. Ruth E. Maddock, Dec. 27, 1945. AB, Oberlin Coll., 1937; LL.D. (hon.), Clark U., 1974. Underwriter Glens Falls Ins. Co., 1938-39, mgr. inland marine dept., 1939-40; with Central Mut. Ins. Co., 1940-60, v.p., 1957-60, Worcester Mut. Ins. Co., 1960, pres., 1960-79; also dir. pres., dir. Hanover Ins. Cos., 1969-79, dir., 1979, pres. emeritus, 1979—; pres. Heald, Inc., 1979-87. Chmn. adv. com. Mich. Investment Fund, M.B.W. Venture Ptnrs. Author: More Sales for You, 1949, also articles. Chmn. Mass. Bd. Higher Edn., 1972-77; past pres. Greater Worcester Community Found. Mem. Worcester C. of C. (past pres., dir.), Worcester County Music Assn. (past pres.), C.P.C.U. Soc. (nat. pres. 1967, dir.), Worcester Econ. Club (past pres.), Boston Sales Execs. Club (past pres.)

ADAM, JOSEPH J., musician; b. Washington, Iowa, Feb. 12, 1961; s. Leo A. and Eveline M. Adam. MFA, U. Iowa, 1986. Cathedral organist St. James Cathedral, Seattle, 1993—; affiliate artist U. Puget Sound, Tacoma, 1997—. Musician: (competition) St Albans Internat. Organ Competition (1st prize, 1991). Office: St James Cathedral 804 Ninth Ave Seattle WA 98104 Office Phone: 206-382-4597. Business E-Mail: jadam@stjames-cathedral.org.

ADAMANY, DAVID WALTER, law and political science educator; b. Janesville, Wis., Sept. 23, 1936; s. Walter Joseph and Dora Marie (Mutter) Adamany. AB, Harvard U., 1958, JD, 1961; MS, U. Wis., 1963, PhD in Polit. Sci., 1967; LLD (hon.), Adrian Coll., 1984; AAS (hon.), Schoolcraft Coll., 1986; D. Engring. (hon.), Mich. Tech. U., 1987; D in Pub. Svc. (hon.), Eastern Mich. U., 1997. Bar: Wis. 1961. Spl. asst. to atty. gen. State of Wis., Madison, 1961—63, exec. pardon counsel, 1963; commr. Wis. Pub. Svc. Commn., 1963—65; instr. polit. sci. Wis. State U., Whitewater, 1965—67; asst. prof., then assoc. prof. Wesleyan U., Middletown, Conn., 1967—72, dean coll., 1969—71; assoc. prof., then prof. polit. sci. U. Wis., Madison, 1972—77; v.p. acad. affairs, prof. Calif. State U., Long Beach, 1977—80, U. Md., College Park, 1980—82; disting. prof. law and polit. sci. Wayne State U., Detroit, 1982—2000, pres., 1982—97, pres. emeritus, 1997; CEO Detroit Pub. Schs., 1999—2000; pres. Temple U., Phila., 2000—, Laura Carnell prof. law and polit. sci. Chmn. Wis. Coun. Criminal Justice, 1973—75, Wis. Elections Bd., 1976—77; sec. Wis. Dept. Revenue, 1973—75. Author: Financing Politics, 1969, Campaign Finance in America, 1972; co-author: Borzoi Reader in American Politics, 1972, American Government: Democracy and Liberty in Balance, 1975, Political Money, 1975; editl. bd.: Social Sci. Quarterly, 1973—, State and Local Govt. Rev., 1974—80; contbr. articles to profl. jours. Mem. exec. com. Detroit Med. Ctr., 1982—97; chmn. Mich. Bicentennial of U.S. Constrn. Commn., 1986—88; mem. Mich. Civil Svc. Commn., 1996—99; bd. dirs. Greater Phila. First, 2001—, African Am. Mus. Phila., 2001—; mem. Wis. Gov.'s Commn. on Campaign Fin. Reform, 1996—97;

bd. dirs. Detroit Inst. Arts Founders Soc., 1983—92, Detroit Symphony Orch., 1983—89, Detroit Econ. Growth Corp., 1984—92, Karmanos Cancer Inst., 1982—97, New Detroit, 1982—95, Blue Cross Blue Shield Found. Mich., 1995—2000, Gilmour Fund, 1996—, HOPE Fund of Cmty. Found. of S.E. Mich., 1995—2000, Temple U. Health Sys., 2000—. Mem.: ABA (commn. on coll. and univ. legal studies 1992—95), ACLU, Pres.'s Coun. State Univs. (chmn. 1982—97), Am. Polit. Sci. Assn., Wis. Bar Assn., Greater Phila. C of C (exec. com. 2000—), Nat. Adv. Com. on Instl. Quality and Integrity (U.S. dept. edn. 1994—2000), Can.-U.S. Fulbright Commn. (bd. dirs. 1993—97). Democrat. Office: Temple U Rm 200 Sullivan Hall 1330 W Berks Street Philadelphia PA 19122-6087

ADAMCIK, JOE ALFRED, retired chemistry professor, lawyer; b. Taylor, Tex., June 28, 1930; s. Joseph John Adamcik and Pearle Mae Offield. BS, U. Tex., Austin, 1951, MA, 1954; PhD, U. Ill., 1958; JD, Tex. Tech. U., 1991. Bar: Tex. 1991. Asst. prof. chemistry Tex. Tech. U., Lubbock, 1957-61, assoc. prof. chemistry, 1961-88; ret., 1988; practiced in Lubbock, 1991-95; ret., 1995. Mediator Dispute Resolution Ctr., Lubbock, 1991—2004. Contbr. articles to profl. chemistry jours. Fellow AAAS, Tex. Acad. Sci. (v.p.); mem. Am. Chem. Soc. (dir. 1981-88), Am. Geophys. Union, Royal Soc. Chemistry. Avocation: computers. Home: 5223 42d St Lubbock TX 79414 Personal E-mail: jadamcik@aol.com.

ADAMEK, CHARLES ANDREW, lawyer; b. Chgo., Dec. 24, 1944; s. Stanley Charles and Virginia Marie (Budzban) A.; m. Lori Merriel Klein; children: Donald Steven, Elizabeth Jean. BA with honors, U. Mich., 1966, JD, 1969. Bar: Ill. 1969, Calif. 1978. Clk. U.S. Dist. Judge U.S. Fed. Cts., Chgo., 1969-71; assoc. atty. Lord Bissell & Brook, Chgo., 1971-77, ptnr., 1977-78, L.A., 1978—. Mem. ABA, Ill. State Bar Assn., State Bar Calif., Nat. Assn. Railroad Trial Counsel(emeritus mem.). Roman Catholic. Avocations: banjo, hockey. Office: Lord Bissell & Brook 300 S Grand Ave Ste 800 Los Angeles CA 90071-3119 Office Phone: 213-687-6721. Business E-Mail: cadamek@lordbissell.com.

ADAMIAN, GREGORY HARRY, academic administrator; b. Somerville, Mass., Sept. 17, 1926; s. Adam K. and Sandy (Martin) Adamian; m. June Mouradian, July 6, 1958 (dec. Jan. 1967); children: Douglas, Daniel; m. Deborah Murdza, Jan. 1, 1978. AB, Harvard, 1947; MPA, JD, Boston U., 1951, LLD (hon.), 1991; DCS (hon.), Bentley Coll., 1991. Bar: Mass. 1951. Since practiced in, Cambridge; lectr. law and econs. Suffolk U., 1953-54; prof. law Bentley Coll., Waltham, Mass., 1955-67, chmn. dept. law, 1968-70, pres. coll., 1970-91, chancellor, 1991—. Lectr. real estate law Am. Savs. and Loan Inst. Pres. and trustee emeritus Bentley Coll. Lt. USN, 1944—47. Recipient Boyan Humanity award, Armenian Students Assn., 1973, Silver Shingle Disting. Svc. award, Boston U. Law Sch., 1986, Humanities award, 1990, Significant SIG medal, 1997, St. Sahag & St. Mesrob medal, Armenian Ch., 1998. Mem.: ABA, Am. Bus. Law Assn., Boston Bar Assn., Mass. Bar Assn., Nat. Assn. Armenian Studies and Rsch., Oakley Country Club, Shriners, Masons. Mem. Armenian Apostolic Ch. Office: Bentley Coll Office of Chancellor Waltham MA 02452

ADAMO, KENNETH R., lawyer; b. Staten Island, NY, Sept. 27, 1950; BS, ChE, Rensselaer Polytech. Inst., 1972; JD, Union U., Albany, 1975; LLM, John Marshall Law Sch., 1989. Bar: Ill. 1975, N.Y. 1976, Ohio 1984, Tex. 1988, U.S. Patent and Trademark Office. Ptnr. Jones, Day, Reavis & Pogue, Cleve. Mem.: Internat. Bar Assn. Office: Jones Day Reavis & Pogue N Point 901 Lakeside Ave Cleveland OH 44114 Address: 2727 N Harwood Dallas TX 75201 Office Phone: 241-969-4856. Business E-Mail: kradamo@jonesday.com.

ADAMS, A. JOHN BERTRAND, public information officer, consultant; b. Liverpool, Eng., Nov. 22, 1931; came to U.S., 1962, naturalized, 1971; s. Wilfrid and Francine Sophia (Bertrand) A.; m. Vibeke Dinsen, June 3, 1963 (div. 1975); m. Judith Ann Duff, Oct. 15, 1978; 1 dau., Caroline Louise. Corr. London Daily Telegraph, 1952-56; editor, bur. chief, asst. dir. news Radio Free Europe, Bonn and Munich, W.Ger., 1956-62; Africa corr. ABC News, 1963; writer, exec. CBS News, N.Y.C., 1964-70; assoc. dir. advt. and pub. rels. Investment Co. Inst., 1971-72; dir. pub. affairs U.S. Price Commn., Washington, 1972-73; pres. John Adams Assocs., Inc., Washington, 1973—; founding chmn. The WORLDCOM Group, N.Y.C., London, Tokyo, 1987. Bd. dirs. King Comm. Group, Washington. Author: (with J.M. Burke) Civil Rights: A Current Guide to the People, Organizations and Events, 1970; editor: Energy Policy: Industry Perspectives, 1975. Bd. dirs. Psychiat. Inst. Found., Washington, 1974-79, Nat. Coun. Fireworks Safety, 1986-96, Radio Free Europe Radio Liberty Fund, 1987—, Am. Com. for Aid to Poland, 1989-97, Am. Friends of Queen Mary Coll., U. London, 1990—, Friends of Benjamin Franklin House, London, 1990—; exec. dir. Eviron. Industry Coun., 1975-80; mem adv. bd. Gallaudet Coll. for Deaf, Washington, 1977-79. Lt. King's Shropshire Light Inf., Brit. Army, 1951-52, Korea. Recipient Knight's Cross, Order of Merit, Govt. of Poland, 1998, Disting. Svc. award U.S. Price Commn., 1973. Mem. Pub. Rels. Soc. Am. (Silver Anvil award 1978, 84, Hall of Fame, 1999), Nat. Press Club, Fed. City Club, Univ. Club (Washington), Severn River Yacht Club (Annapolis, Md.). Office: John Adams Assocs 807 National Press Building Washington DC 20045 Home: Oakleigh Farm 38065 Kite Ln Lovettsville VA 20180 Office Phone: 202-737-8400. Business E-Mail: jadams@johnadams.com.

ADAMS, ALBERT T., lawyer; b. Cleve., Ohio, Dec. 20, 1950; BA, Harvard Coll., 1973; MBA, Harvard Bus. Sch., 1977; JD, Harvard Law Sch., 1977. Bar: Ohio 1977, US Tax Ct., 1977. Ptnr. Baker & Hostetler, Cleve., chmn. Cleve. office, 1996—, mem. policy com. Mem.: ABA (mem. bus. law section, mem. com. on developments in bus. financing), Cleve. Bar Assn., Ohio Bar Assn. Office: Baker & Hostetler 3200 Nat City Ctr 1900 E 9th St Ste 3200 Cleveland OH 44114-3475 Office Phone: 261-861-7499. Office Fax: 216-696-0740. Business E-Mail: aadams@bakerlaw.com.*

ADAMS, ALFRED GRAY, lawyer; b. Winston-Salem, NC, Feb. 28, 1946; s. Carlton Noble and Elizabeth (Walker) A.; m. Elizabeth Lark; children: Alfred Gray Jr., Amanda Laing. BA, Wake Forest U., 1968, JD, 1973. Bar: NC 1973; cert. specialist bus., comml., indsl. real estate property transactions. Ptnr. Van Winkle, Buck, Wall, Starnes & Davis, P.A., Asheville, NC, 1973-94, Kilpatrick Stockton L.L.P., Winston-Salem, 1994-2000, Womble, Carlyle, Sandridge & Rice, PLLC, Winston-Salem, 2001—. Adj. prof. law Wake Forest U., 1996-2005. Assoc. editor: Wake Forest Law Rev., 1972. Chmn. Buncombe County Tax. Adv. Com., Asheville, 1983; Leadership Cir. chair United Way, 2000; pres. Wake Forest U. Alumni Coun., 2003—04; bd. dirs. Downtown Winston-Salem Partnership, 2002—, Downtown Winston-Salem Found., 2003—. Named Top Real Estate Atty. NC Legal Elite in NC Bus. Mag.; James Mason scholar Wake Forest U., 1972. Mem. NC Bar Assn. (bd. govs. 1987-90, real property sec. vice chmn. 1982-83, chmn. 1983-84, writer, lectr. real property and future interests bar rev. course 1981-83, real property curriculum adv. com. 1984-91, chmn. 1988-91, seminar planner and lectr. real property 1987-2003, chmn. cont. legal edn. com. 1991-93), Am. Coll. Real Estate Lawyers, Am. Coll. Mortgage Attys. (state chair 1995-2002, bd. regents 1996-98, sec. 1998, pres. 2000-01), Biltmore Forest Country Club (bd. govs. 1993-94), Forsyth Country Club (bd. dirs. 2003—, pres. 2005), Old North State Club, Rhododendron Royal Brigade of Guards (capt. Ensign Class 1986). Republican. Methodist. Home: 115 Sullivan Way Winston Salem NC 27104-4911 Office: One W Fourth St Winston Salem NC 27101 Office Phone: 336-721-3642. Business E-Mail: aadams@wcsr.com.

ADAMS, ALFRED HUGH, retired academic administrator; b. Punta Gorda, Fla., Mar. 8, 1928; s. Alfred and Irene (Gatewood) A.; m. Joyce Morgan, Nov. 10, 1954; children: Joy, Al, Paul; m. Lynda K. Long, Apr. 20, 1999. AA, U. Fla., 1948; BS, Fla. State U., 1950, MS, 1956, Ed.D., 1962; L.H.D., Fla. Atlantic U., 1972. Asst. coach varsity football Fla. State U., 1955-58, asst. dir. housing, instr. edn., 1958-62, asst. dean men, asst. prof. edn., 1962-64; supt. pub. instrn. Charlotte County, Fla., 1965-68; pres. Broward Community Coll., Ft. Lauderdale, Fla., 1968-87; exec. dir. Performing Arts Ctr. Authority, Ft. Lauderdale, 1987-88; pres. Broward Performing Arts Found., Ft. Lauderdale, 1990-91. Bd. dirs. Am. Council on Edn.; vis. lectr. in higher edn. Inst. Higher Edn., U. Fla., com. on internat. edn. relations, com. on mil-higher edn. relations; adv. com. Inst. Internat. Edn.; dir. Sun Bank/South Fla., N.A.; Vice chmn. Gov. Fla. Commn. Quality Edn., 1968-70; mem. Gov.'s Adv. Com. Edn., 1966-70; mem. regional council Southeastern Edn. Corp., 1966-69; mem. commn. adminstrv. affairs Am. Council on Edn., 1973; pres. Pub. Instns. Higher Learning in So. States, 1975; adv. com. Joint Coun. on Econ. Edn.; chmn. AACJC Internat./Intercultural Consortium, S.E. Fla. Ednl. Consortium; chmn. coun. pres. Fla. Cmty. Colls.; trustee South Fla. Edn. Center, Pub. Service TV Mem. editorial bd., Soc. for Coll. and Univ. Planning. Pres. United Way, 1973; bd. dirs. local chpt. ARC, 1971; bd. dirs. Opera Guild, Ft. Lauderdale, pres., 1983-85; bd. dirs. Coll. Consortium Internat. Studies; exec. dir. Performing Arts Ctr. Authority, Ft. Lauderdale; pres. Broward Performing Arts Found., Ft. Lauderdale. Comdr. USNR. Decorated knight Internat. Constantinian Order; recipient Liberty Bell award, 1975, Patriot award Freedoms Found., Disting. Alumnus award Fla. State U., A. Hugh Adams Coll. Gold Key. cert. of recognition Fla. Ho. of Reps., Disting Omicron Delta Kappa Alumnus of Yr., 1987; named Patriot Fla. Bicentennial Commn., Fla. State U. Sports Hall of Fame. Mem. Fla. Tchr. Edn. Adv. Council, Fla. Edn. Council Ethics Com. Sch. Adminstrs., Am. Assn. Sch. Adminstrs., Ft. Lauderdale C. of C. (v.p.), Profl. Practices Commn., Fla. Assn. Colls. and Univs. (pres. 1975), Naval Res. Assn., Res. Officers Assn., U.S. Naval Inst. (life), Broward Minutemen (pres.), Fla. Inter-agy. Law Enforcement Planning Council, Omicron Delta Kappa, Phi Theta Kappa. Clubs: Gulfstream Sailing, Fort Lauderdale; Tower (gov. 1985-86). Lodges: Kiwanis. Baptist. Home: 1633 Sand Castle Rd Sanibel FL 33957

ADAMS, ALICE, sculptor; b. N.Y.C., Nov. 16, 1930; d. Charles P. and Loretto G. (Tobin) A.; m. William D. Gordy, Feb. 7, 1969; 1 dau., Katherine Adams Gordy. Student, Adelphi Coll., 1948-50; BFA, Columbia U., 1953; postgrad. (French Govt. fellow), 1953-54; postgrad. Fulbright Travel grantee, L'Ecole Nat d'Art Decoratif, Aubusson, France, 1953-54. Lectr. Manhattanville Coll., Purchase, N.Y., 1960-79; instr. sculpture Sch. Visual Arts, 1980-87. One-woman shows include N.Y.C., 1972, 74, 75, Hal Bromm Gallery, N.Y.C., 1979, 80; exhibited in group shows at Whitney Mus. Am. Art, N.Y.C., 1971, 73, Indpls. Mus. Art, 1974, Nassau County Mus. Fine Arts, Roslyn, N.Y., 1977, Wave Hill, Riverdale, N.Y., 1979, Mus. Modern Art, N.Y.C., 1984, Lehman Coll. Art Gallery, N.Y.C., 2000-01; represented in permanent collections Weatherspoon Gallery U. N.C., Greensboro, U. Nebr., Everson Mus., Syracuse, N.Y., Haags Gemetemuseum, The Hague, Netherlands, Am. Craft Mus., N.Y.C., Edwin I. Ulrich Mus., Wichita, Kans.; pub. commissions include Bot. Garden, Toledo, Ohio, Port Authority of N.Y. and N.J., Thomas Jefferson U., Phila., N.Y.C. Bd. Edn., State of Conn., Denver Internat. Airport, N.Y.C. Metro. Transp. Authority, U. Tex. San Antonio, Broward County, Fla., U. Del., Newark, Montclair State U., Station N.J. Transit; design team Seattle Transit Project, St. Louis Metro-Link Project, Midland Metro, Birmingham, Eng., Charlotte (N.C.) Area Transit Sys., 2003-05. Creative Artists Pub. Svc. grantee, 1973-74, 76-77, Nat. Endowment for Arts Artists grant, 1978-79, Richard Florsheim grant, 1999, Am. Acad. of Arts and Letters grant, 1984; Guggenheim fellow, 1981-82; Rockefeller Found. resident, Bellagio, Italy, 2002. Home: 3370 Fort Independence St Bronx NY 10463-4502

ADAMS, ANNETTE MARIE, finance educator; d. Warren H. Hafner and June L. Leenhouts; m. Leon J. Adams, July 20, 1985; children: Leon-Ryan, Tristan Nicole. AAS, Monroe C.C., Rochester, N.Y., 1995; B in Bus. Edn. cum laude, Nazareth Coll. Rochester, 1997; M in Mgmt. Sci., Roberts Wesleyan Coll., 2003. Cert. bus. and distributive edn. N.Y., 2005, qualification N.Y., 1998, profl. sec. Kans., 2000. Dept. adminstrv. aide Mobil Chem. Corp., Victor, NY, 1986—88; adminstrv. asst. engring. dept. Xerox Corp., Rochester, NY, 1991—93; adj. prof. secretarial programs Monroe C.C., Rochester, 1998—2001; substitute bus. tchr. Webster (N.Y.) H.S., 1999—2000; bus. tchr. Nazareth Acad. H.S., Rochester, 2000—02; bus. dept. chairperson Bishop Kearney H.S., Rochester, 2002—; adj. prof. careers and skills NTID at Rochester Inst. Tech., 2005—. Adj. prof. adminstrv. secretarial Bryant and Stratton Coll., Rochester, 2000—; adj. prof. bus. Finger Lakes C.C., Canandaigua, NY, 2003—, Rochester Inst. Tech. Named N.Y. State Ethnic Baking Champion, 2003, 2004; scholar, Monroe C.C., 1993, 1994, 1995; Writer's scholar, Nazareth Coll., 1995, 1996, 1997. Mem.: Internat. Assn. Adminstrv. Profls. (assoc.), N.Y. State Bus. Edn. Assn. (assoc.), Nat. Bus. Edn. Assn. (assoc.), Monroe County Bus. Educators Assn. (assoc.). Independent. Roman Catholic. Avocations: travel, acting, baking/cooking, writing, dance. Home: 1163 Belmont Dr Farmington NY 14425 Office Phone: 585-342-4000 216.

ADAMS, ANTHONY WALTER, composer; b. Fort Dodge, Iowa, Nov. 12, 1948; s. Donald K. Adams and Geneva Lavonne Schluter; m. Wanda Simpson (div.); m. Deborah Young (div.); children: Carley Elizabeth, Samantha Suzanne. Pvt. studies with, Elmer Bernstein, Alfred Sendry, Nelson Riddle, Jerry Goldsmith, Dr. Russell L. Baldwin, George Tremblay, Dr. Frederick Finnell, Joe Reisman, Dave Pell, Hugo Friedhofer, Eddy L. Manson; Pvt. Studies, Earle Hagen; AA, San Bernardino Valley Coll., 1969; PhD (hon.), Internat. U., 1988; DHL (hon.), Loyola U., L.A., 1994. Composer/arranger in residence Saddleback Concert Chorale, Mission Viejo, Calif., 1978—82; composer, condr. Am. Soc. Music Arrangers and Composers; Calif. Inst. for the Arts; UCLA, 1979—84; composer, arranger L.A. Pops Orch., 1982—85; music dir., arranger, condr. Hollywood (Calif.) Pops Orch., 1984—92; composer, arranger, prodr. The Music Scultors, London, 1998—2000; rec. engr., prodr. various artists L.A., 2000—04; music pub. Orphium Music Enterprises, Dublin; clinician/workshop instr. Saddleback Coll., UCLA, U. So. Calif., CalArts, Grand Canyon U.; music pub. Kumara Music Pub., Adams and Daughters Music Pub., Pinon Music, L.A., Kumara Music Prodns., LTD, London. Dir./officer Soc. of Singers, Hollywood Media Assn., Am. Soc. Music Arrangers and Composers;, L.A., 1978—88. Composer: (film score) King Of The Streets, The Prey, The Legend Of Jedediah Carver, Little Pioneers, Mourning, Shiney Mountain, The Beast Within, (television score) Oh, Little Town, Mariposa Storyteller, The Real Samuel Clemons, Remmington Steele, Hotel, Knot's Landing, Highway To Heaven, Little House On The Prarie, Falcon Crest, The Devlin Connection, Trauma Center, Newhart, National Geographic; music orchestrator (film score) Under The Volcano, Good Morning, Vietnam, Airplane, Time After Time, Victor/Victoria, The Glass Managerie, That's Life, Sunset, Nightwing, Ice Castles; composer: (television score) From The Manor; music orchestrator (film score) The Spy Who Loved Me, Sophie's Choice, The Outlaw Josey Wales, The Black Bird, composer/arranger/producer (television, record, and concert arr.) Various Artists; composer: (television score) Aventuras Vascas (BAFTA, 2000); music arranger (recordings and concerts) Artists: Lesley Garrett, John Williams (guitar), Barry White, John Denver, Jenifer McClaren, Benny Carter, Melissa Manchester, Johnny Mathis, Doc Severinsen, Lola Falana, Earle Klugh, The Lettermen, others; composer: (television score) Mersey Me; music arranger (instrumental recordings and concerts) BBC Concert Orch., London Symphony Orch., Royal Philharmonic Orch., Boston Pops Orch., 101 Strings, Virgina Pops Orch., Dallas Symphony Orch., Pitt. Symphony Orch0, Cin. Pops Orch., Las Vegas Phil. Orch., others; prodr.: (recordings (albums/cds) For RCA Records, Capital Records, Concorde Records, Alshire Records, ABC-Dunhill Records, London Records; composer: (concert works) Fanfare for Americans, Nocturne De La Mer, The Crossing, American Overture, A Christmas Chorale, Concerto for Violin, Prima Volta, Reveries, Waltz ala King, Major Williams March, Symphony for Orchestra, Cameo for Chamber Orchestra; music arranger (live television) Grammy Awards, Emmy Awards, The Oscars, others; author: (screenplays) Atlantis, Best Town By A Dam Site, Strangers Among Us; composer: (opera) Nosferatu, Marie Lavois, Saint Joan; actor: (television series) Amazing Stories (They Only Come Out At Night); musician: (conductor) Concerts with Hollywood Pops Orchestra, London Symphony Orchestra, English Chamber Orchestra, Royal Philharmonic Orchestra, Los Angeles Pops Orchestra; arranger/conductor (concert and worldwide bbc broadcast) Mellenium New Year's Eve at the London Millenium Dome. Nominee Emmy award, Acad. TV Arts and Scis., 1982, Grammy award, NARAS, 1982, 1996; recipient 6 Gold and 3 Platinum Albums, Rec. Industry Assn. Am., Grammy award, NARAS, 1989. Mem.: NATAS, NARAS, ASCAP, Motion Picture Acad. Am., Am. Fedn. Musicians. Home: 15737 Hesby St Encino CA 91436 Personal E-mail: muzik4you@sbcglobal.net.

ADAMS, ARLIN MARVIN, lawyer, retired judge, arbitrator, mediator; b. Phila., Apr. 16, 1921; s. Aaron M. and Mathilda (Landau) A.; m. Neysa Cristol, Nov. 10, 1942; children: Carol (Mrs. Howard Kirshner), Judith A., Jane C. BS in Econs. with highest honors, Temple U., 1941; LLB with honors, U. Pa., 1947, MA in Econs., 1950; DHL (hon.), Temple U., 1964; DSc (hon.), Phila. Coll. Optometry, 1965; LLD (hon.), Phila. Coll., 1966, Susquehanna U., 1985, Muhlenberg Coll., 1986, Villanova U., 1987, U. Pa., 1998. Bar: Pa. 1947; U.S. Ct. Appeals (3rd cir.), 1947. Law clk., Chief Justice Horace Stern Pennsylvania Supreme Ct., 1947; assoc. firm Schnader, Harrison, Segal & Lewis, Phila., 1947-50, sr. partner, 1950-63, 66-69; sec. pub. welfare Commonwealth of Pa., Phila., 1963-66; judge U.S. Ct. Appeals (3d cir.), Phila., 1969-87; counsel Schnader, Harrison, Segal & Lewis, Phila., 1987—. Apptd. ind. counsel to investigate Dept. HUD, 1990-95; apptd. spl. counsel Pa. Commn. of Police, 1994-95; instr. Am. Inst. Banking, Phila., 1949-52; lectr. fed. practice Law Sch., U. Pa., Phila., 1952-56, lectr. constl. law, 1972-97; endowed chair, Arlin M. Adams Professorship Constl. Law, U. Penn. Law Sch., 2004. Author: Law and Religion, 2 vols., 1991, A Nation Dedicated to Religious Liberty, 1990; Editor-in-chief Law Review U. Penn., 1947; contbr. articles to profl. jours. Pres. Annenberg Inst., 1988—91; chmn. bd. dirs. Moss Rehab. Hosp., Phila., 1962—63; trustee U. Pa., 1985—; chmn. U.S. Supreme Ct. Jud. Fellows Commn., 1987—93, Fels Inst. Govt., Phila., 1967—77, Sch. of Social Work, Bryn Mawr (Pa.) Coll., 1967—78, Diagnostic and Rehab. Ctr., Phila., 1971—72; chmn. overseers U. Pa. Law Sch., 1985—92; trustee Med. Coll. of Pa., 1974—80, hon. trustee, 1981—98; trustee German Marshall Meml. Fund, 1972—84, Lewis H. Stevens Trust, Bryn Mawr Coll., 1972—78, Columbia U. Ctr. for Law and Econ. Studies, U. Pa. Inst. for Law and Econs., William Penn Found.; hon. trustee Phila. Mus. Art, 1998—; mem. Cardinal's Commn. re Abuse of Children, 2002. With USNR, 1942—45, North Pacific. Recipient Disting. Service award U. Pa. Law Sch., 1981, Justice award Am. Jud. Soc., 1982, John Courtney Murray award DePaul U., 1987, Cresset award Rosemont Coll., 1988, Gold Medallion award Chapel of Four Chaplains, Founders award Temple U., 1997, Phila. award, 1997. Mem. ABA (del. ho. of dels. 1966-67, 75-77, chmn. trade assn. com.), Am. Law Inst., Am. Bar Found., Pa. Bar Assn. (pres. jr. bar 1950, del. ho. of dels. 1967-71), Phila. Bar Assn. (chancellor 1967, Gold Medal award 1999), Am. Judicature Soc. (pres. 1975-77, Justice award), Am. Philos. Soc. (sec. 1980-83, v.p. 1987-92, pres. 1993-99), Am. Acad. Arts and Scis., Arlin Adams Law and Soc. Inst., Phila. Club, Union League, Sun. Breakfast Club, Legal Club (pres. 1986-91), Jr. Legal Club, Order of Coif, Beta Gamma Sigma.

ADAMS, AUSTIN A., bank executive; b. N.C., 1943; Grad., Appalachian State Univ., 1965. Head of operations and automation First Union Corp., 1985—2001; exec. v.p., head of technology and operation Bank One Corp., 2001, exec. v.p., chief info. officer, 2001—04, JPMorgan Chase (acquired Bank One), 2004—. Named a Premier 100 IT Leader, Computerworld mag., 2004; recipient Disting. Alumni award, Appalachian State Univ., 1996. Office: JPMorgan Chase 1 Bank One Plz Chicago IL 60670

ADAMS, BARBARA, English language educator, poet, writer; b. NYC, Mar. 23, 1932; d. David S. Block and Helen (Taxter) Block Tyler; m. Elwood Adams, June 6, 1952; (dec. 1993); children: Steven, Amy, Anne, Samuel. BS, SUNY, New Paltz, 1962, MA, 1970; PhD, NYU, 1981. Prof. English Pace U., N.Y.C., 1984—2000, dir. bus. comm., 1984—2001. Poet in residence Cape Cod Writers' Conf., 1988. Author: Double Solitaire, 1982, The Enemy Self: The Poetry & Criticism of Laura Riding, 1990, Hapax Legomena, 1990, Negative Capability, 1999 (1st Prize for Fiction); (poetry) The Ordinary Living, 2004; (play) God's Lioness and the Crow: Sylvia Plath and Ted Hughes, 2000; author numerous poems; contbr. articles to profl. jours. Recipient 1st prize for poetry NYU and Acad. Am. Poets, 1975, 1st prize for fiction Negative Capability contest, 1999; Penfield fellow NYU, 1977. Mem. PEN, Poetry Soc. Am., Poets and Writers. Home: 59 Coach Ln Newburgh NY 12550-3818

ADAMS, BARBARA, lawyer; b. Hutchinson, Kans., Nov. 17, 1951; d. Robert Thomas and MaryJane (Lewis) Adams; m. John B. Rosenthal, Apr. 22, 1983 (div. 1986); children: Anna Adams-Sarthou, Kari Torp, Sian Torp. BA, Smith Coll., 1973; JD, Temple U., 1978. Bar: Pa. 1978, US Dist. Ct. Ea. Dist. Pa. 1978, US Ct. Appeals 3rd Cir. 1978. Rsch. ofcl. Schuylkill County Office Tech. Assistance, Pottsville, Pa., 1974-75; mgr. First Valley Bank, Bethlehem, Pa., 1975-77; clk. Duane Morris LLP, Phila., 1977—78, assoc., 1978—85, ptnr., 1986—, chair firm fin. practice group. Co-author booklet: Business Political Action in Pennsylvania, 1977; editor PABL Update newsletter, 1991-92. Coord. housing task force Rendell Transition Team, Phila., 1991-92; policy com. co-chair of housing Gov.-elect Rendell Transition Team, 2002; commr. Ind. Charter Commn. of City of Phila., 1992—94, Phila. Gas Commn., 1995-98; bd. mem. & sec. Phila. Neighborhood Enterprise, 1989-93; treas. Reading Terminal Market Corp., 1994-2001, bd. mem., 1997-2001; co-founder Pa. Energy Buyers Forum, 1997-, mem. mgmt. com., sec./treas.; bd. mem. Phila. Assn. Cmty. Devel. Corporations, 1998-, People's Emergency Ctr., 2003-. Mem. ABA (sect. pub. utility; charter mem. forum on affordable housing and cmty. devel. law), Pa. Bar Assn., Phila. Bar Assn. (bus. law sect.), Nat. Assn. Bond Lawyers, Pa. Assn. Bond Lawyers (bd. dirs. 1991-97). Avocations: interior decorating, travel. Office: Duane Morris LLP One Liberty Pl Philadelphia PA 19103-7396 Office Phone: 215-979-1225. Office Fax: 215-979-1020. Business E-Mail: badams@duanemorris.com.

ADAMS, BARBARA RUTH, minister; b. Chgo., May 12, 1941; d. Walter H. and Stephanie (Polgar) Froehlich; m. J. Rodger Adams, July 28, 1962; children: Catherine, Robert. BS, Marquette U., 1962; MSW, U. Ill., 1978. Chaplain St. John's Regional Med. Ctr., Oxnard, Calif. Bd. dirs. Cath. Social Svcs., Ventura County, Calif. Home: 2239 S Hill Rd Ventura CA 93003-6723

ADAMS, BERNARD SCHRODER, retired college president; b. Lancaster, Pa., July 20, 1928; s. Martin Ray and Charlotte (Schroder) A.; m. Natalie Virginia Stout, June 2, 1951; children: Deborah Rowland, David Schroder. BA, Princeton, 1950; MA, Yale, 1951; PhD, U. Pitts., 1964; LL.D. (hon.), Lawrence U., 1967; cert., Inst. for Ednl. Mgmt., Harvard U., 1975. Asst. dir. admissions, instr. English Princeton, 1953-57; dir. admissions and student aid U. Pitts., 1957-60, spl. asst. to chancellor, 1960-64; dean students, lectr. English Oberlin (Ohio) Coll., 1964-66; pres. Ripon (Wis.) Coll., 1966-85, Ft. Lewis Coll., Colo., 1985-87; ednl. cons. pvt. practice, Colo. Springs, 1987-88; v.p. resources Goodwill Industries, Colorado Springs, Colo., 1988-96. Dir. Wis. Power & Light Co., Newton Funds, 1970-85; cons., examiner Commn. on Instns. Higher Edn., North Cen. Assn. Colls. and Secondary Schs., 1972-87, exec. commr., 1981-86; bd. dirs. Four Corners Opera Assn., 1985-87, pres., 1986-87. Contbr. articles to profl. jours. Bd. dirs. Keep Colorado Springs Beautiful, 1990—99; bd. dirs. Colo. chpt. Nat. Assn. Fundraising Execs., 1990—94; bd. dirs. Colorado Springs Music Vols., 1992—98, 2000—, Ctr. Prevention Domestic Violence, 1995—2001. 1st lt. USAF, 1951—53. Woodrow Wilson fellow, 1951 Mem. Assoc. Colls. Midwest (bd. dirs. 1966-85, pres. 1973-75), Wis. Assn. Ind. Colls. and Univs. (bd. dirs. 1966-85, pres. 1969-71, 83-85). Home: 90 Ellsworth St Colorado Springs CO 80906-7954

ADAMS, BRYAN, vocalist, composer, photographer; b. Kingston, Ont., Can., Nov. 5, 1959; Vocalist, 1976—; composer various bands including Prism, Bachman-Turner Overdrive, Bob Welch, Kiss, 1977—. Albums include Bryan Adams, 1980, You Want It, You Got It, 1982, Cuts Like a Knife, 1983, Reckless, 1985, Into the Fire, 1987, Live! Live! Live!, 1988, Waking Up the Neighbors, 1991, So Far, So Good, 1993, 18 Til I Die, 1996, Bryan Adams Unplugged, 1997, On A Day Like Today, 1998, The Best of Me, 1999, (soundtrack) Spirit: Stallion of the Cimarron, 2002, Room Service, 2004; singles include Straight from the Heart, Cuts Like a Knife, 1983,

Heaven, One Night Love Affair, It's Only Love, 1985, Heat of the Night, Victim of Love, Only the Strong Survive, Hearts On Fire, 1987, Thought I Died and Gone to Heaven, 1991, (Everything I Do) I Do It for You (Acad. award nominee for best original song 1992), Can't Stop This Thing We Started, There Will Never Be Another Tonight, (with Michael Kamen and Robert John Lange, from Don Juan DeMarco) Have You Ever Loved a Woman, 1995 (Acad. award nominee for best original song 1996); contbr. to soundtracks: Robin Hood: Prince of Thieves, The Three Musketeers (with Rod Stewart & Sting), Don Juan DeMarco; photographer (books) Made in Canada, 1999, Haven, 1999, American Women, 2005. Decorated with Order of B.C., Order of Canada; recipient multi-platinum record, #1 single in Am., Can., U.K., Sweden, Finland, Denmark, Norway; named Artist of Decade, Canadian Recording Industry; nominated for 6 Grammys and 7 Juno awards, 1992, many other awards in music. Office: ICM 40 W 57th St New York NY 10019*

ADAMS, CAROL H., dean; d. Wilfred L. and Sadie Dean Hoskins; m. John W. Adams, Apr. 10, 1966; children: Craig J., Dina R. BA in Edn., Mich. State U., 1965; MS in Edn., CUNY, Queens, 1975. Tchr. K-6 N.Y.C. Bd. Edn., 1965—72; tech. cons. Green Leigh Assocs., N.Y.C., 1972—74; instr. tchr. edn. York Coll. CUNY, Jamaica, 1974—75; instr. SUNY Brockport, Rochester, 1975—77; prof. devel. edn. Monroe C.C., Rochester, 1977—91, acad. dean, 1991—. Cons. Greenleigh Assn., N.Y.C., 1972—74; cons. tchr. edn. Corning C.C., NY, 2003. Bd. dirs. YWCA, Rochester, 1989—; mem. steering com. AALDP United Way, Rochester, 1992—93; mem. adv. bd. youth/family project U. Rochester, 2000. Recipient Women's History award, Rochester City Sch. Dist., 1997, Chancellor's award for excellence, SUNY, 2000. Mem.: AAUW, Nat. Inst. Leadership Devel., Am. Assn. Women in Cmty. and Jr. Colls., Nat. Assn. Devel. Edn., The Links (v.p. 2002), Leaders League for Innovation, Phi Delta Kappa. Home: 106 Elmore Rd Rochester NY 14618 Office: Monroe Community Coll 1000 E Henrietta Rd Rochester NY 14623

ADAMS, CHARLES FRANCIS, advertising executive, real estate company executive; b. Detroit, Sept. 26, 1927; s. James R. and Bertha C. (DeChant) A.; m. Helen R. Harrell, Nov. 12, 1949; children: Charles Francis, Amy Ann, James Randolph, Patricia Duncan. BA, U. Mich., 1948; postgrad., U. Calif., Berkeley, 1949; student additional study, Oxford U., 1996. With D'Arcy-MacManus & Masius, Inc., 1947-80, exec. v.p., dir., 1970-76, pres., chief operating officer, 1976-80; pres. Adams Enterprises, 1971—; exec. v.p., dir. Washington Office, Am. Assn. Advt. Agys., 1980-84. Chmn., chief exec. officer Wajim Corp., Detroit; past mem. steering com. Nat. Advt. Rev. Bd.; mem. mktg. com. U.S. Info. Agy.; pres. Internat. Visitors Ctr. of the Bay Area, 1988-89. Author: Common Sense in Advertising, 1965, Heroes of the Golden Gate, 1987, California of the Year 2000, 1992, The Magnificent Rogues, 1999, Murder By The Bay, 2005 Past chmn. exec. com. Oakland U. Mem. Am. Assn. Advt. Agys. (dir., mem. govt. rels. com.), Advt. Fedn. Am. (past dir.), Nat. Outdoor Advt. Bur. (past chmn.), Nat. Golf Links Am. Club (Southampton, LI), Olympic Club, The Family Club, Theta Chi, hon. mem. Alpha Delta Sigma, (hon.). Republican. Roman Catholic. Home: 2240 Hyde St # 5 San Francisco CA 94109-1509 Office: 10 W Long Lake Rd Bloomfield Hills MI 48304-2707

ADAMS, CHARLES GEOFFREY, minister, educator; b. Arkansas City, Kans., Aug. 23, 1948; s. Robert Nelson and Helen Louise A.; m. Cheryl Lynn Triplitt, Aug. 14, 1970; children: Sarah Wagner, Rebekah Herzog. B in Ministry, Luther Rice Sem., 1982; M in Sacred Lit., Trinity Theol. Sem., 1993, PhD, 2002; DD, Md. Bible Coll. and Sem., 1995. Youth pastor First Bible Bapt. Ch., Wichita, Kans., 1969-71; youth pastor and assoc. pastor Kansas City (Mo.) Bapt. Temple, 1971-74; sr. pastor Kansas City Bapt. Temple, 1984—; interim pastor Iglesia Bautista Emanuel, San Jose, Costa Rica, 1975; missionary Bapt. Internat. Missions, Inc., Managua, Nicaragua, 1976; pastor Iglesia Bautista Miramonte, San Salvador, El Salvador, 1976-84. Prof. Inst. Biblico Emanuel, San Jose, 1975, Inst. Biblico Por Ext. Que Dice la Biblia, Kansas City, 1990—; prof., pres. Inst. Biblico Miramonte, San Salvador, 1976-84; del. Internat. Congress on Itinerant Evangelism, Billy Graham Assn., Amsterdam, The Netherlands, 1983; pres. Shepherd Sch. Min., Kansas City, 1985—; pres. bd. dirs. Reality Living Pub., Kansas City, vice-chmn. Heart America Billy Graham Crusade, mem. bd. trustees Christar, 2004-. Author: Reality Living, 1990, Psalm 119: A Journey Into the Heart of God, 1993, Job: Adventures in the Land of Uz, 1994, Filemon, 2002. Mem. Mayor's Task Force on Drugs, City of Kansas City, 1984. Mem.: Evangelical Holiletics Soc. Baptist. Avocations: black belt, shotokan karate, travel, alpine skiing. Home: 4607 Norwood Ct Kansas City MO 64133 Office: Kansas City Bapt Temple 5460 Blue Ridge Cutoff Kansas City MO 64133 E-mail: jadams@kcbt.org.

ADAMS, CHARLES JAIRUS, lawyer; b. Randolph, Vt., Feb. 17, 1917; s. Charles B. and Jeanette E. (Metzger) A.; m. Mary E. Tobey, July 5, 1942; children: Mary Jean, Carol Ann. BS in Elec. Engring, Norwich U., 1939; LL.B., Boston U., 1951. Bar: Vt. 1951. Student engr. Gen. Electric Co., also New Eng. Power Co., 1939-41; plant supt. Demeritt Co., Waterbury, Vt., 1946-48; practiced in Montpelier and Waterbury, 1951-98; partner firm Adams, Darby & Laundon, 1980-86; of counsel Darby, Laundon, Stearns, Thorndike & Kolter, 1987-98. Treas. Vt. Bar Assn., 1951-55; atty. gen. State of Vt., 1962-63; chmn. State of Vt. Legis. Apportionment Bd., 1972-80; mem. adv. com. on civil rules Vt. Supreme Ct., 1971-82 Trustee Village of Waterbury, 1956-57, 88-90, pres., 1958; moderator Town of Waterbury, 1961; mem. Waterbury Pub. Libr. Assn., 1961-93. Mem. Am. Legion, Norwich U. Gen. Alumni Assn. (pres. 1960-61), Partridge Soc. (bd. fellows), Masons. Congregationalist. Home: Apt D-326 6955 Carlisle Ct Naples FL 34109

ADAMS, CHARLES LYNFORD, English language educator; b. Joliet, Ill., May 11, 1929; s. Charles Lynford and Eloise A. (Henault) A.; m. Joan Marie Johnson, June 6, 1953; children— Rebecca Lynn, Stephen Thomas. BA, Mich. State U., 1951; MA, U. Ill., 1952; PhD, U. Oreg., 1959. Instr. English U. Ore., 1959-60; asst. prof. U. Nev., Las Vegas, 1960-65, assoc. prof., 1965-67, prof. English, 1967-96, prof. emeritus English, 1996—. Las Vegas rep. U. Nev. System Grad. Sch., 1964-66, coordinator grad. studies, 1966-68, dean grad. studies, 1968-71 Editor: Studies in Frank Waters. Mem. adv. com. Univ. Mus. Soc. Served with AUS, 1954-56. Mem. MLA, Nat. Coun. Tchrs. English, Nev. Coun. Tchrs. English, So. Nev. Coun. Tchrs. English, Rocky Mountain MLA, Conf. Coll. Composition and Comm., AAUP, Nat. Soc. Profs., Frank Waters Soc., Phi Kappa Phi. Home: 1921 E Saint Louis Ave Las Vegas NV 89104-3805 Office: 4505 S Maryland Pkwy Las Vegas NV 89154-5011 E-mail: adamsc@unev.edu.

ADAMS, CHARLES P., JR., lawyer; b. Jackson, Miss., Feb. 28, 1949; BSBA cum laude, Georgetown U., 1971; JD, Georgetown U. Law Ctr., 1974. Bar: Miss. 1975. Mng. ptnr., transactions and corp. advisory svcs. Adams and Reese, LLP (merged with Stokes Bartholomew Evans & Petree, P.A. July, 2005), Jackson, Miss. Editor: Law & Policy in Internat. Bus., 1973—74. Mem.: Miss. Bar, Hinds County Bar Assn., Barristers (chmn. coun. 1973—74), Phi Delta Phi. Office: Adams and Reese LLP Capitol Bldg 111 E Capitol St Ste 350 Jackson MS 39201 Office Phone: 601-292-0720. Office Fax: 601-355-9708. Business E-Mail: charles.adams@arlaw.com.*

ADAMS, CHERYL, newscaster; Grad., Marquette U. Coll. Journalism. Creator weekly news setment The Parent Place Sta. WXIN-TV, Indpls., anchor, 1994—. Nominee Emmy awards (5); recipient Outstanding Journalist award, Luth. Child and Family Svcs.; fellow, Casey Journalism Ctr. Children and Families, U. Md., 1997. Mem.: Indpls. Assn. Black Journalists.

ADAMS, CHRISTINE HANSON, advertising executive; b. Hackensack, N.J., May 24, 1950; d. Kenwood Alwin and Doris (Rogers) Hanson; m. L. Ashby Adams III, June 1, 1974 (div. Aug. 1993); 1 child, Nathaniel Kaufman. BA, Lafayette Coll., 1972; MBA, Duke U., 1979. Med. sales rep. Hoffman-LaRoche, Nutley, N.J., 1972-75; sr. market rsch. analyst Burroughs Wellcome Co., Research Triangle Park, N.C., 1976-77, product planner, 1978; dir. market research Sterling Drug Inc., N.Y.C., 1979-81; group product mgr. Pfizer Inc., N.Y.C., 1981-83; account supr. Kallir Philips Ross Inc., N.Y.C., 1983, v.p., account group supr., 1984-86; v.p., account supr. Baxter Gurian and Mazzei Inc., Beverly Hills, Calif., 1987-89, account group v.p., 1990-91, sr. v.p. account group, supr., 1991-93, sr. v.p. mgmt. supr., 1994; sr. v.p. group acct. dir. Kallir Philips Ross Inc, N.Y., 1994-96; sr. v.p. mgmt. supr. Torre Lazur Comm., Parsippany, N.J., 1996-98; v.p., mgmt. supr. Integrated Comm. Corp., Lawrenceville, N.J., 1998-2000; sr. v.p. mgmt. supr. Nelson Comms., Inc., Princeton, N.J., 2001—. Cons. advt. Wellness Cmty., Santa Monica, Calif., 1988-92. Active membership com. St. Michael's Episcopal Ch., Studio City, Calif., 1987-93, altar guild, 1988-93, tchr. Sunday sch., 1990-91. Named Young Career Woman Bus. Profl. Women's Assn., Chapel Hill, N.C., 1978. Mem. Healthcare Mktg. and Comms. Coun., Healthcare Businesswomen's Assn. Republican. Avocations: fashion design, sewing, music, 19th-century English Literature. Home: 8 Villa Dr Princeton Junction NJ 08550-1241 Office: Integrated Comm Corp 989 Lenox Dr Ste 300 Lawrenceville NJ 08648-2315 E-mail: adamskaufman@home.com.

ADAMS, CHRISTOPHER STEVE, JR., retired electronics executive, military officer; b. Shreveport, La., July 8, 1930; s. Christopher Steve and Armenda Lee (Tanner) A.; m. Mary Alene Mitchell, Aug. 22, 1953; children: Cynthia, Charlotte, Cheri, Christopher III. A.S., Tarleton State U., 1950; BS, Tex. A&M U., 1952. Commd. U.S. Air Force, 1952, advanced through grades to maj. gen., 1979, B-36, B-52 pilot Ramey AFB, P.R.; dir. plans and policy J-5, Def. Nuclear Agy., Washington, 1970-73; comdr. 90th Strategic Missile Wing, 1973-75; comdr. 12th Air Div., 1975-78; chief of staff SAC, 1982-83; ret., 1983; assoc. dir. Los Alamos Nat. Lab., 1983—86; v.p. bus. devel. Andrew Corp., Dallas, 1987-94, ret., 1994. Author: The Cold War Series, 6 books, 1999—2004. Decorated D.S.M., Def. Superior Service medal, Legion of Merit (2), Air Force Commendation medal, Air medal (2); recipient Disting. Alumnus award Tarleton State U., 1990, Disting. Alumnus award Tex. A&M U., 1991. Presbyterian. Home: 9408 Gimmee Ct Granbury TX 76049 Personal E-mail: cadams@itexas.net. *America the beautiful. I have dedicated my life through service to preserve our freedom. There is no better place on earth— I know, I've been there.*

ADAMS, CONSTANCE ST. ONGE, artist; b. Burlington, Vt., Apr. 15, 1937; d. Joseph Alcide and Beryl Anna (Thibault) St. Onge; m. Edward L. Adams III, Aug. 10, 1963; children: Matthew Stuart, Suzanne St. Onge Adams. Pre-med student, U. Vt., 1955-57; student, No. Seattle Community Coll., 1979-89; studied sculpture with, Rosa Estebanez/Louise McDowall, 1977-78. Cert. computer ops. Analyst/programmer RCA Conn. Gen., San Francisco/Hartford, Conn., 1958-60, 60-63; sculptor Seattle and Edmonds, Wash., 1979—. Principal works include: (stone sculptures) Wind God, 1985, Sky Seeker, 1987, The Bath, 1988, Greek Man and Woman, 1984, cash prizes, Edmonds Art Festival. Exhibitor at Stonington Gallery, Seattle, 1985-89, Lynn McCallister Gallery, Seattle, 1985, Legends Gallery, Seattle, 1986, Gallerie Marie one-person show, Edmonds, 1985. Donated work Polar Bear On Ice to Edmonds Pub. Libr., 1989. Democrat. Avocation: duplicate bridge. Home: 7286 E Raintree Ln Port Orchard WA 98366-8426

ADAMS, CURT MATTHEW, director, researcher, social studies educator; b. Tulsa, Okla., May 7, 1973; s. George Xavier and Barbara Lee Adams; m. Victoria Kay Adams, Nov. 25, 2000; 1 child, Brody. BA, U. Tulsa, Okla., 1997, MA, 1999; EdD, Okla. State U., Stillwater, 2003; at David L. Clark grad. student seminar, UCEA, Columbia, Mo., 2003. Tchr. social studies Thomas Edison H.S., Tulsa, 1998—2000; counselor Bishop Kelley H.S., 2000—02; dir. trust rsch. project Okla. State U., 2002—; dir. San Miguel Sch. Tulsa, 2002—. Accreditation coord. Cath. Schs. Tulsa, Okla., 2003—04. Mem.: Am. Edn. Rsch. Assn. Roman Catholic. Office: San Miguel Sch Tulsa 2434 E Admiral Blvd Tulsa OK 74110-5323 Home: 1524 E 36 Pl Tulsa OK 74105

ADAMS, CYNTHIA ANN, librarian, media specialist, writing instructor; b. Thomaston, Ga., Nov. 27, 1942; d. Emory Ellis and Marian (Moseley) A. AB, Mercer U., 1964; MEd, U. Ga., 1972; EdS, Ga. State U., 1994. Cert. English tchr., career libr. media specialist, Ga. Libr. media specialist Walton County Bd. Edn., Monroe, Ga., 1972-74, Madison County Bd. Edn., Danielsville, Ga., 1974-80; tchr. English, libr. media specialist Westwood Bd. Trustees, Thomaston, 1981-82; libr. media specialist Harris County Bd. Edn., Hamilton, Ga., 1983—97; instr. writing, asst. computer lab. Gordon Coll., Barnesville, Ga., 1997—. Book reviewer Sch. Libr. Jour., 1973-74; author numerous poems; exhibited at Nat. Mus. Women in the Arts, Washington Mem. visual arts com. Thomaston Upson Arts Coun.; vol. Am. Heart Assn. Grad. study scholar. Mem. Kappa Delta Pi. Achievements include research in preservation of paper collections in archives. Home: 630 S Center St Thomaston GA 30286-4133 Office: Gordon Coll 419 Coll Dr Barnesville GA 30204 Business E-Mail: c_adams@gdn.edu.

ADAMS, DANIEL FENTON, law educator; b. Reading, Pa., July 29, 1922; s. Daniel Snyder and Carrie Betsy (Vought) A.; m. Eloise Williams, Sept. 6, 1968. AB, Dickinson Coll., 1947; LL.B., Dickinson Sch. Law, 1949. Bar: Pa. 1951, Ark. 1984. Prof. law Dickinson Sch. Law, Carlisle, Pa., 1949-65, asst. to dean, 1952-54, 56-60, acting dean, 1954-56, asst. dean, 1960-65; prof. Sch. Law U. Ark., Little Rock, 1965-70, 77-93, prof. emeritus, 1993—; asst. dean U. Ark. Sch. Law, Little Rock, 1966-70, acting dean, 1981-82, interim dean, 1989-91; prof. U. Miss. Sch. Law, Oxford, 1970-77. Vis. prof. Stetson U. Sch. Law, St. Petersburg, Fla., 1976-77, 99-00, U. Tenn. Coll. Law, 1993. Contbr. articles to profl. jours. Served with U.S. Army, 1943-44 Mem. ABA, Pa. Bar Assn., Ark. Bar Assn.

ADAMS, DANIEL NELSON, lawyer; AB, Yale U., 1932; LLB, Harvard U., 1935. Bar: N.Y. 1937. Sr. counsel Davis Polk & Wardwell, N.Y.C. Mem. ABA, N.Y. State Bar Assn., Assn. of Bar of City of N.Y., N.Y. County Lawyers Assn., Am. Law Inst. Office: Davis Polk & Wardwell 450 Lexington Ave Fl 31 New York NY 10017-3982

ADAMS, DAVID FRANKLYN, music educator; b. Albuquerque, May 17, 1939; s. John Marian and Mary Louise Adams, Kenneth Jewell and Peggy Crowther (Stepmother); m. Vickie Sharon Mobley, June 8, 1998; m. Gail Lenore Ingraham, June 10, 1966 (div. Oct. 28, 1983); children: Christina Ann Cox, Tamara Gail Olarte, Wendy Michelle Swoope. Diploma, Mesa Coll., 1974. Musician Denver Affair, Las Vegas, 1969—73; band dir. Burlington H.S., Colo., 1967—68; pianist USAF Bicentennial Band, Fort Meade, Md., 1974—76, US Army Field Band, 1977—79; stage band dir. 1st Army Band, Fort Carson, Colo., 1979—80; rhythm vocal br. head Armed Forces Sch. of Music, Norfolk, Va., 1980—86; acting band comdr. US Army Band, Fort Hamilton, NY, 1986—87; counselor Army Cmty. Services, 1988—90; pvt. tchr., musician Albuquerque, 1990—95; band dir., tchr. Bosque Prep. Sch., 1996—98; dir. jazz studies Acad. Music, Norfolk, Va., 1999—2000; band dir. An Achievable Dream Acad., Newport News, 2001—. Resident jazz musician Va. Beach Pub. Schs., Virginia Beach, 2001—01, all-city jazz band dir., 2002—02; founder, dir., prodr. Young Razzcals Jazz Project, 1992—. Composer: (music) The Magic of Christmas; author: (poetry book) The Reason for the Rhyme. Squadron comdr. CAP, Fort Meade, 1977—79, mission pilot Norfolk, Va., 1980—90, dir. aerospace edn. Albuquerque, 1990—95. With U.S. Army, 1974—90. Recipient Grover Loening Aerospace award, CAP, 1991, Frank G. Brewer Aerospace award, Regional CAP, 1995, Nat. CAP, 1995, Cmty. Svc. award, Arts Coun. Coop., 1997, Outstanding Leadership and Performance, Young Razzcals Jazz Project, 2001, 2002. Mem.: Internat. Assn. Jazz Educators, Nat. Assn. Music Edn. Achievements include development of Jazz for the very young, see website www.young-razzcalsjazzproject.com. Avocations: flying, running, writing, scuba diving, hang-gliding. Home: 5228 Dundee Ln Virginia Beach VA 23464 Office Phone: 757-373-6622. Home Fax: 757-479-1454; Office Fax: 757-247-1720. Personal E-mail: darazzcaljazz@cs.com.

ADAMS, DAVID G., lawyer; b. Monroe, La., Jan. 30, 1952; BA, U. Southwestern La., 1973; JD, NYU, 1977. Bar: Ga. 1977, US Dist. Ct. (no. dist.) Ga. 1977, US Dist. Ct., DC 1995, US Ct. Appeals (4th and 10th cirs.) 1999, US Dist. Ct., Dist. Md. 1999. Dir. Policy Develop. and Coordination Staff, assoc. chief counsel for drugs/litig. atty. FDA, 1978—94; ptnr., chmn. Food & Drug Group Venable LLP, Washington, DC. Tchr. food & drug law George Washington U. Law Sch. Contbr. articles to profl. jours. Root-Tilden Scholar. Mem.: ABA (chmn Food & Drug Law Comt., Bus. Law Sect.), DC Bar. Office: Venable LLP 575 7th St NW Washington DC 20004 Office Phone: 202-344-8014. Office Fax: 202-344-8300. E-mail: dgadams@venable.com.

ADAMS, DAVID HUNTINGTON, judge; b. Cleve., May 30, 1942; s. Donald Croxton and Nancy Adams; m. Mary Watson, Dec. 4, 1982; children from previous marriage: Ann Arendell, David Huntington, Susanna Camp. AB, Washington and Lee U., 1965, JD, 1968. Bar: Va. 1968, U.S. Dist. Ct. (ea. dist.) Va. 1968, U.S. Ct. Appeals (4th cir.) 1968, U.S. Supreme Ct. 1973. Law clk. U.S. Dist. Ct., Norfolk, Va., 1968-69; assoc. law firm Willcox, Savage, Norfolk, 1969-72; ptnr. law firm Agelasto, Bernard & Adams, Norfolk, 1972-74, Taylor, Walker, Bernard & Adams, Norfolk, 1974-78, Taylor, Walker & Adams, Norfolk, 1974-87, Clark & Stant, P.C., 1987-93; judge U.S. Bankruptcy Ct. (ea. dist. Va.), 1993—. Master of the bench James Kent Am. Inn of Ct., 1994-99, pres., 1995; lectr. bankruptcy practice joint com. on cont. legal edn. Va. Bar Found., 1981, 89, 93—; adminstrv. hearing officer Commonwealth of Va., 1974-89; mem. 4th Cir. Jud. Coun., 2003—, Adminstrv. Office Bankruptcy Judges Adv. Coun., 2001—04, Bankruptcy Judges Adv. Group, 2001—04, Adminstrv. Office Joint Adv. Com., 2003-2005. Author: Virginia Landlord/Tenant Law, 1980. Bd. dir. Heritage Mus., Norfolk, 1991-94, Virginia Beach Neptune Fest., 1997—, King Neptune XXVI; chmn. Neptune Found., 2002; pres. Bay Colony Civic League, Virginia Beach, 1978, Princess Anne Hills Civic League, Virginia Beach, 1988; mem. 4th Cir. Jud. Conf., 1974—;, 4th Cir. Jud. Coun., 2002—; mem. 2d dist. ethics com. Va. State Bar, 1983-84. Recipient Superior Pub. Svc. award, Sec. of Navy, 2004. Mem.: ABA, Va. Bar Assn. (bd. dir. bankruptcy sect. 1990—93, mem. coun. jud. sect. 1995—, chmn. 1997), Virginia Beach Bar Assn., Norfolk-Portsmouth Bar Assn., Nat. Conf. Bankruptcy Judges (bd. govs. 1996—2000, sec. 2000, pres. 2004—05), Am. Bankruptcy Inst., Hampton Roads Naval Historical Found. (bd. dir. 2005—), Hampton Roads Coun. Navy League U.S. (life; pres. 2000—04, nat. dir. 2002—04), N.Y. Yacht Club, Cavalier Golf and Yacht Club (bd. dir. 1993—98, commodore 1994). Episcopalian. Avocations: yachting, swimming, bicycling. Office: United States Bankruptcy Ct Walter E Hoffman US Courthouse 600 Granby St Norfolk VA 23510-1915 Business E-Mail: david_adams@vaeb.uscourts.gov.

ADAMS, DAVID PARRISH, historian, epidemiologist, educator; b. Jacksonville, Fla., Aug. 2, 1958; s. David Parrish and Gloria Ann (Nesmith) A.; m. Teri Ann Becker, Aug. 31, 1985; 1 child, Morgan Becker. BA, Emory U., 1980; AM, Washington U., St. Louis, 1982; PhD, U. Fla., 1987; MPH, Ohio State U., 1994. Resource faculty dept. family medicine U. Fla., Gainesville, 1983-87; assoc. prof. dept. humanities Columbus (Ohio) State C.C., 1987-95; rsch. dir. Cabarrus Family Medicine Residence Program, Concord, N.C., 1995—; cons. assoc. dept. cmty. and family medicine Duke Med. Ctr., Durham, N.C., 1996—; assoc. prof. dept. health sci. Armstrong Atlantic State U., 2001—. Adj. faculty dept. history Ohio Dominican Coll., Columbus, 1987-95; adj. asst. prof. dept. family medicine Ohio State U., Columbus, 1990-95, post-doctoral rschr. AHEC program, 1995, lectr. dept. history, 1995; adj. asst. prof. dept. family medicine Ponce (P.R.) Sch. Medicine, 1993; rsch. dir. Cabarrus Family Practice Residence program Cabarrus Meml. Hosp., Concord, N.C.; cons. assoc. dept. cmty. and family medicine Duke U., 1995—; vis. asst. prof. med. humanities program Davidson Coll., 1996—; adj. asst. prof. Coll. Nursing, U. Tenn.-Knoxville; adj. asst. prof. dept. family medicine Quillen Coll. Medicine, Ea. Tenn. State U., 1998—; cons. in field; assoc. prof. Atlantic State U; clin. asst. prof. Med. Coll. Ga Dept. Family Medicine. Author: The Greatest Good to the Greatest Number: Penicillin Rationing on the American Home Front, 1940-45, 1991, American Board of Family Practice: A History, 1999; contbr. articles to profl. jours. Med. Humanities fellow U. Ill., Chgo., 1992; grant-in-aid U. Wis., 1985; grantee NIH, 1989, Ohio Acad. Family Physicians, 1991. Mem. APHA, Am. Assn. History of Medicine, Am. Hist. Assn., Orgn. Am. Historians, Soc. Tchrs. Family Medicine, Am. Soc. Tropical Medicine and Hygiene. Democrat. Mem. United Ch. of Christ. Achievements include research in general and family practice; evolution of family practice; penicillin, dentistry and SBE; wartime penicillin policy; community oriented primary care.

ADAMS, DAVID PORTERFIELD, III, business appraiser; b. Nashville, Oct. 10, 1961; s. David Porterfield Adams and Elizabeth (Morgan) Spiegel; m. Pamela Beverforden, Oct. 12, 1991; children: Porter, Trevor. BS in Mech. Engring., Ga. Inst. Tech., 1986, MBA, 1988. CPA. From cons. to mgr. KPMG Peat Marwick, Atlanta, 1988-94; mgr. Coopers & Lybrand, Atlanta, 1994-96; pres. Adams Capital Inc., Atlanta, 1996—. Bd. advisors The George West Mental Health Found., Applied Systems Intelligence, Inc., Nat. Assn. Corp. Dirs., Atlanta. Co-author: Closely Held Business Valuation, 1995, Minority Interests & Discounts, 1995; author: ESOP Valuation, 2000. Fellow Ga. Soc. CPAs (bd. dirs., mgmt. com.); mem. AICPAs, Am. Soc. Appraisers, The Georgian Club. Avocations: skiing, hiking, reading, building. Office: Adams Capital Inc 600 Galleria Pkwy SE #1850 Atlanta GA 30339-5990

ADAMS, DAVID R., dermatologist; b. Sunbury, Pa., Jan. 4, 1956; s. William R. and Pearl I. Adams; m. Stephanie A. Wetzel, May 21, 1977; children: Jennifer E., Karen E., Michael D. BS in Pharmacy, Phila. Coll. Pharmacy and Sci., 1978; PharmD, U. Ill., Chgo., 1992; MD, Pa. State Coll. Medicine, 1997. Registered pharmacist Pa., 1978, diplomate Am. Bd. Dermatology. Intern Pa. State Hershey Med. Ctr., 1997—98, resident, 1998—2001, asst. prof. dermatology, 2001—; chief dermatologist VA Med. Ctr., Lebanon, Pa., 2001—. Contbr. articles to profl. jours. Vol. Skin Cancer Screening, 2001—. Fellow: Am. Acad. Dermatology. Republican. Evang. Free Ch. Avocations: running, fishing, hunting, photography. Home: 99 Brownstone Dr Hershey PA 17033 Office: Pa State Hershey Med Ctr Dept Dermatology UPC II Ste 4300 Hershey PA 17033 Office Phone: 717-531-8307. Business E-Mail: dadame@psu.edu.

ADAMS, DEAN (LEWIS ADAMS), theater director; b. Seattle, July 22, 1957; s. Brockman and Mary Elizabeth (Scott) A.; m. Kristin Cook Gilbert, June 20, 1981. BA in Drama and English, Tufts U., 1980; MA in TV-Film, U. Md., 1986; MFA in Directing, Fla. State U., 2002. Mgr. stage prodn. Shakespeare and Co., Washington, 1975—79; asst. stage mgr. Arena Stage, Washington, 1976; tech. dir. St. Albans Sch., Washington, 1980—82; dir. theater Loomis Chaffee Sch., Windsor, Conn., 1982—88, Westminster Sch., Simsbury, Conn., 1989—99; freelance theater dir. Artistic dir. Centennial Theater Festival, Simsbury, 1989—; asst. prof. theater, Kennesaw State U., Kennesaw, Ga., 2002—; artistic dir., Kennesaw State Univ. Dir. (U.K. tour) Dining Room, 1985; dir., producer (1st Chinese tour of Am. mus.) Once Upon a Mattress, 1987. Bd. dirs. Farmington Valley Music Found. Grantee Ford Found., 1984; scholar Tufts U., 1978-80. Mem. Internat. Brotherhood Magicians, Soc. Am. Magicians, Soc. of Stage Dirs. and Choreographers, Actors Equity Assn., Assn. of Performing Arts Presenters. Democrat. Episcopalian. Home and Office: 1512 Tennessee Walker Dr Roswell GA 30075 Office: Kennesaw State Univ 1000 Chastain Rd Kennesaw GA 30144 Office Phone: 770-420-4408. Personal E-mail: deanadams@msn.com. Business E-Mail: dadams@kennesaw.edu.

ADAMS, DEANNA RUTH, writer, educator; b. Cleve., Feb. 17, 1954; d. Virginia and Joseph Fedorko; m. Jeffrey Alan Adams, July 16, 1983; children: Danielle, Tiffany. AA, Lakeland C.C., 1986. Instr. Poets & Writers League of Greater Cleve., Cleve.; conf. coord., motivational spkr. Lakeland C.C., Kirtland, 2001—, pop culture historian, instr.; writing instr. Wildwood Cultural Ctr., Mentor. Author: (book) Rock 'n' Roll and the Cleveland Connection, Kent State U. Press, 2002 (Ohioana award Finalist/Assoc. Recorded Sound Collections award Finalist, 2003). Mem.: Internat. Women's Writing Guild, Poets & Writers' League Greater Cleve. (assoc.), Rock and Roll Hall Fame and Mus. Personal E-mail: DEENCR@aol.com.

ADAMS, DEBORAH ROWLAND, lawyer; b. Princeton, NJ, July 28, 1952; d. Bernard S. and Natalie S. Adams; m. Charles L. Campbell, June 16, 1990. BA, Colo. Coll., Colorado Springs, 1974; JD, U. Colo., 1978. Bar: Ind. 1978, Colo. 1978, U.S. Dist. Ct. Colo. 1978. Atty. Legal Svcs. Orgn. Ind., Indpls., 1978-79, Pikes Peak Legal Svcs., Colorado Springs, 1979-80, Pub. Defender's Office, Colorado Springs, 1980-81; assoc. Ranson, Thomas, Cook and Livingston, Colorado Springs, 1982-84; pvt. practice Colorado Springs, 1985—. Mem. state Jud. Nominating Commn. for 4th Jud. Dist., 1994-99; Colo. State Grievance Com., 1997-98, Atty. Regulation Com., 1999. Bd. dirs. Domestic Violence Prevention Ctr., 1980-86, pres., 1982-84; bd. dirs. Pikes Peak Legal Svcs., 1983-88, pres., 1986-87, Colo. Coll. Bus. and Cmty. Alliance Bd., 1998-2002, Citizens Project Bd., 1999-2002, CASA, 1999-2004, Emily Griffith Ctr., 2002—, v.p., 2003-05, Colo. Bar Found., 1993-2005, pres 2003-04; bd. dirs. Chins Up, 1991-97, state bd. dirs. Legal Aid Found., 1994-2000, v.p., 1997-99; mem. Colorado Springs Leadership Inst., 1997, mem. adv. bd., 1998-2003. Recipient Pro Bono award Pikes Peak Legal Svcs., 1988; named Atty of Yr. El Paso County Legal Secs. Assn., 1990, Wagon Wheel Girl Scouts Cmty. Svc. Award. Mem. Colo. Bar Assn. (family law sect. 1991-2005, bd. govs. 1994-97, exec. counsel 1995-97, nominating com. 1996), El Paso County Bar Assn. (pres. 1995-96), El Paso County Bar Found. (founding mem.), Colo. Bar Assn., Colo. Women's Bar Assn., Women Lawyers Assn. of the 4th Jud. Dist., Zonta Club Colorado Springs (pres. 1989-90, co-chair dist. 12 regional conf. 1991-92, Zontian of Yr. 1990-91). Democrat. Avocations: tennis, mountain biking, travel, snowboarding. Office: 2 N Cascade Ave Ste 1010 Colorado Springs CO 80903-1629 Office Phone: 719-471-7727. Personal E-mail: dradams@pcisys.net.

ADAMS, DELPHINE SZYNDROWSKI, lawyer; b. East Chicago, Ind., May 24, 1953; d. Joseph C. and Rachael L. Szyndrowski; m. Dave Adams. BA, Ind. U., 1974; JD, Golden Gate U., 1985. Bar: Calif. 1986, U.S. dist. Ct. (all dists.) Calif. 1986, U.S. Ct. Appeals (9th cir.) 1986. Assoc. Goldberg, Stinnett & Macdonald, San Francisco, 1986-87, Bronson, Bronson & McKinnon, San Francisco, 1987-91, Santa Rosa, Calif., 1991-93, ptnr., 1993-95, San Francisco, 1995-96; atty. pvt. practice, Santa Rosa, 1996—. Co-author: (chpt.) Real Estate Litigation, 1994. Mem. adv. coun. Red Empire Ballet Assn., Santa Rosa, 1992-94. Mem. Engrng. Contractors Assn. (adv. coun. 1996—), North Coast Builders Exch., Assoc. Gen. Contractors. Avocations: gardening, motorcycling, reading, music. Office: PO Box 1902 Santa Rosa CA 95402-1902 Fax: (707) 577-8010. E-mail: lawofcdsa@yahoo.com.

ADAMS, DENNIS PAUL, artist; b. Des Moines, Nov. 15, 1948; s. Paul Thomas Adams and Stella Vernita (Kirkland) MacGregor; children: Jack Walker, Todd Dennis. BFA, Drake U., 1969; MFA, Tyler Sch. Art, Phila., 1971. Assoc. prof. MIT, Cambridge, 1996-99, prof., dir. visual arts program, 1999—2001; prof. Cooper Union, 2002—, dean, 2004—05. Vis. prof. Parsons Sch., N.Y.C., 1990-99, Cooper Union, N.Y.C., 1988-90, Ecole Des Beaux-Arts, Paris, 1992, Rijksakademie, Amsterdam, 1992-, Akademie Der Bildenden Künste, Munich, 1993-94, MIT, Cambridge, 1994—; asst. prof. Tyler Sch. Art, 1976, Ohio Sch. Art, Athens, 1972-75. One-man shows include de Appel Found., Amsterdam, The Netherlands, 1988, The Clocktower, N.Y.C., 1988, Galerie Meert-Rihoux, Brussels, 1989, John Weber Gallery, N.Y.C., 1989, Galerie Gabrielle Maubrie, Paris, 1990, Kent Fine Art, N.Y.C., 1990, Hirschhorn Mus., Washington, 1990, Mus. Modern Art, N.Y.C., 1991, Fundacio la Caixa, Barcelona, Spain, 1992, Portikus, Frankfurt, Germany, 1993, Muhka, Antwerpen, 1994, Contemporary Arts Mus., Houston, 1994, Queens Mus., N.Y.C., 1996, Kent Fine Art, 1997, Galerie, Gabrieele Maubrie, Paris, Mus. Contemporary Art, Zagreb, 1999, Galerie Lumen Travo, Amsterdam, 2000, 13 Quai Voltaire, Paris, 2000, Mus. Contemporary Art, Balt., 2001, Kent Gallery, N.Y.C., 2002, Pabellon Villanueva Royal Botanical Garden, Madrid, 2004, Mies Van Der Rome Pavillion, Barcelona, 2004, Galerie Gabrielle Maubrie, Paris, 2004; contbr. articles to profl. jours. Bd. govs. N.Y. Found. for Arts, N.Y.C., 1989-92. NEA fellowship grantee, 1984, 88, 95; recipient Visual Artists Project award N.Y. State Coun. on Arts, 1984, NY Found. Arts fellowship, 2004. Home: 42 Walker St New York NY 10013-3514 E-mail: dadams@mit.edu.

ADAMS, DIANE LORETTA, physician; b. St. Louis, Nov. 3, 1948; m. William McKinley Adams; children: Kareem McKinley, Dawn Caron, Akeem Michael. BS, Howard U., 1969; MD, N.J. Med. Sch., 1976; MPH, Johns Hopkins U., 1980, resident in gen. preventive medicine, 1980. Resident in family practice Howard U. Hosp., Washington, 1976-79; chief med. officer USCG Shipyard, Curtis Bay, Md., 1980-83, Bur. Engraving and Printing, Washington, 1983-85; med. officer St. Elizabeth Hosp., Washington, 1985-86; rsch. analyst Office Asst. Sec. Health, Rockville, Md., 1987-90; chief minority health svcs. rsch. program Agy. Health Care Policy and Rsch., Rockville, 1990-93; congl. fellow office of Congressman Louis Stokes U.S. Ho. of Reps., Washington, 1990; sr. med. adv. Agy. Health Care Policy and Rsch., Rockville, 1993-99, Agy. Healthcare Rsch. and Quality, Dept. Health/Human Svcs., 1999-2000, cons., 2000—; clin. assoc. prof. dept. phys. therapy U. Md., 1993—2000; dir. health policy, rsch. and profl. med. affairs Nat. Med. Assn., 2001—02. Cons. rep. AIDS Task Force, 1987-93; lectr. intensive bioethics Georgetown U. Kennedy Inst. Ethics, 1991; sr. health policy fellow, Ga. Ctr. Advanced Telecommns. Tech. Editor: Health Issues for Women of Color: A Cultural Diversity Perspective, 1995. Named to, Md. Women's Hall of Fame, 1997, Black Coll. Alumni Hall of Fame in Medicine, 2001, Women of Achievement in Md. History, 2002; recipient Adminstrs. Outstanding Cmty. Svc. award, Agy. Health Care Policy and Rsch., 1996. Mem.: APHA, Am. Coll. Preventive Medicine, Alpha Kappa Alpha (mem. internat. program com. 1998—2002, Outstanding Comt. Svc. award 1981—85). Avocation: equitation. Home: 17032 Barn Ridge Dr Silver Spring MD 20906-1106

ADAMS, EARL WILLIAM, JR., economics professor; b. Lansing, Mich., Nov. 13, 1937; s. Earl William and V. Crystal (Woodruff) A.; m. Barbara Joan Charlton, Aug. 4, 1964; children: Earl William, III, Nicholas Charlton. BA, U. Mich., 1959; PhD, Mass. Inst. Tech., 1971. Asst. prof. econs. Amherst Coll., 1963-66, U. Pitts., 1966-72; Andrew Wells Robertson prof. econs. Allegheny Coll., Meadville, Pa., 1972—. Vis. asst. prof. U. Mass., 1966; rsch. dir. bus. taxation Pa. Tax Commn., 1979-81; mem. adv. coun. Pa. Blue Shield, 1980-82, mem. corp., 1982. Contbr. to profl. publs. Woodrow Wilson fellow, 1959 Mem. Am. Econs. Assn., Pa. Econs. Assn., Phi Beta Kappa, Phi Kappa Phi. Home: 187 Grandview Ave Meadville PA 16335-1415 Office: Allegheny Coll Dept Econs Meadville PA 16335 Business E-Mail: eadams@allegheny.edu.

ADAMS, EDMUND JOHN, lawyer; b. Lansing, Mich., June 6, 1938; s. John Edmund and Helen Kathryn (Pavlick) A.; m. Mary Louise Riegler, Aug. 11, 1962 (dec. May 2004). BA, Xavier U., 1960; LLB, U. Notre Dame, 1963. Bar: Ohio 1963. Assoc. Paxton & Seasongood, Cin., 1965-70, Frost & Jacobs (now Frost Brown Todd), 1970-71, ptnr., 1971-2000, mem. exec. com., 1985-88, 90-96, mng. ptnr., 1994-96, chmn., 1996-2000, of counsel, 2000—; tournament counsel Western & Southern Fin. Group Tennis Masters Tournament, 2003—05. Author: Catholic Trails West, The Founding Catholic Families of Pennsylvania, Vol. 1, 1988, Vol. 2, 1989. Mem. Ohio Bd. Regents, 1999—, sec., 2002—03, vice-chmn., 2003-04, chmn, 2005—; mem., com. co-chair Ohio Gov.'s Commn. on Higher Edn. and the Economy, 2003-04; trustee Jewish Hosp., 1995-2001, Cin. Internat. Vis. Ctr., 1989-91, Japan Am. Soc. Greater Cin., 1988-96, Ursuline Acad., 1992-94; trustee S.W. Ohio Regional Transit Authority, 1980-91, pres., 1983, 88; trustee Sister Cities Assn. Greater Cin., 1984-91, chmn., 1984-90; trustee Econ. Ctr. for Edn. and Rsch., 1996—, exec. com., 1999-, vice-chmn., 2002-04, chmn., 2005—; chmn. USTA Nat. Father and Son Clay Ct. Tennis Championships, 1990-92; exec. com. Hamilton County Rep., 1982—, fin. com., 1990—, chmn., 1992-94, ctrl. com., 2000—, adv. bd. Elder HS, 2002—, Ohio Coll. Access Network, 2005-, adv. bd. Ohio Coll. Access Network, 2005-. 1st lt. U.S. Army, 1963-65. Fellow Am. Coll. Bankruptcy; mem. ABA, Ohio Bar Assn., Cin. Bar Assn., Cin. Tennis Club (trustee 1990-98, treas. 1992-93, sec. 1994-95, pres. 1996-98, historian 2001—), Met. Club. (bd. dirs. 1996-2001). Roman Catholic. Home: 3210 Columbia Pky Cincinnati OH 45226-1042 Office: Frost Brown Todd 2500 PNC Ctr 201 E 5th St Cincinnati OH 45202-4182 Personal E-mail: adamschoice@cinci.rr.com. Business E-Mail: eadams@fbtlaw.com.

ADAMS, EDWIN MELVILLE, retired diplomat, actor, writer; b. Gridley, Ill., Sept. 28, 1914; s. Edwin Melville and Crystal (Montgomery) A. AB, U. Ill., 1936, LL.B., 1939; postgrad., The Hague Acad. Internat. Law, summer 1951. Bar: Ill. 1939. Atty. State Farm Ins. Cos., Bloomington, Ill., 1939-42; officer charge Brazil area World Trade intelligence div., State Dept., Washington, 1942-43, negotiator German external assets agreements with neutral countries, 1946-48; successively assigned by State Dept. to, London, Paris, Bern and Frankfort; as U.S. negotiator at internat. econ. confs., 1948-50; econ. attache Am. embassy, The Hague, 1950-52; charge Italian econ. affairs State Dept., 1952-55; dep. chief mut. def. affairs, 2d sec. Am. embassy, Rome, Italy, 1955-58, chief mut. def. affairs, 1st sec., 1958-61; officer in charge econ. affairs for N. Africa Dept. State, 1961-64, career mgmt. officer, 1964-65; spl. asst. to dep. under sec. state, 1965-67; asso. dean Fgn. Service Inst., 1967-68; cons. Dept. State, 1968-72. Host: radio show Passport, WAMU, 1972—; author, narrator radio show, NBC-TV show, Venice, My Love, 1972; pub. broadcasting The Social Responsibility of Business; radio shows My Beloved Italy; star radio shows, CBS-TV show, The Empty Frame, 1973; appeared in films The Last Detail, 1974, Airport, 1975, Three Days of the Condor, 1975, Franklin and Eleanor, The Other Side of Midnight, Company, The Seduction of Joe Tynan, Justice for All, First Monday in October, BBC's Double Image; author: Petty Destiny, 2004. U.S. del. Conf. of African States on Devel. of Edn. in Africa, 1961. Served to lt. (j.g.) USNR, 1943-46, PTO. Decorated cavaliere ufficiale Order of Merit of Italian Republic. Mem. Screen Actors Guild, AFTRA, Actors Equity, Phi Delta Phi, Phi Kappa Sigma. Espicopalian. Lodge: Masons (Washington).

ADAMS, ELIZABETH HERRINGTON, banker; b. Tulsa, May 25, 1947; d. James Dillon and Helen (Allderdice) Herrington; m. Phillip Hollis Hackney, Mar. 5, 1977 (dec. Jan. 1990); m. Keith R. Adams, Sept. 4, 1993. Student, No. Ariz. U., 1965-67, 68-69. With Coldwater (Kans.) Nat. Bank, summers 1964-67, The Ariz. Bank, Phoenix, 1969, Flagstaff, 1970-71; asst. cashier The Wilmore (Kans.) State Bank, 1972—2001, The Coldwater Nat. Bank, 1974-83, cashier, ops. officer, 1984—; v.p. The Coldwater (Kans.) Nat. Bank, 1998—2002, sr. v.p., 2002—. Bd. dirs. The Coldwater Nat. Bank. Bd. dirs. Pioneer Lodge Nursing Home, Coldwater, 1984-89; mem. sch. site coun., 1993-94; life mem. Girl Scouts, chmn. Neighborhood Cookie Drive, 1991-95; bd. dirs., mem. strategic planning com. Wheatbelt Area Girl Scout Coun., 1994-96—; elder 1st Presbyn. Ch., Coldwater; Kans. Lung Assn. Vol. Spkrs. Bur., 1998—; mem. Ch. Session Bd., Coldwater, 1994-2000. Mem. Fin. Women Internat., Cmty. Bankers Assn. Kans. (membership com. 1991-94, INPAC com. 1992-93), Kans. Ind. Bankers (gen. svcs. com. 1986-87), PEO, Alpha Omicron Pi, Lake Coldwater Archtl. Rev. Bd. Republican. Avocation: music (pianist). Office: Coldwater Nat Bank PO Box 726 Coldwater KS 67029-0726

ADAMS, EULA L., data storage executive; BS in Acctg., Morris Brown U.; MBA, Harvard Bus. Sch. bd. dirs. MasterCard Internat. Former ptnr. Deloitte and Touche; CEO Western Union, exec. v.p. and gen. mgr. Telesvcs. First Data Corp., Atlanta, 1991-98, pres. First Data Resources and Teleservices, 2000—03, exec. v.p., pres. First Data Merchant Svcs. subs., 1998—2003; v.p. global services Storage Technology Corp., Louisville, Colo., 2004—. Bd. dirs. Solidus Networks, Inc, NetBank, Inc. Named one of 50 Most Powerful Black Executives, Fortune mag., 2002. Office: 1 StorageTek Dr Louisville CO 80028 Office Phone: 303-673-5151.

ADAMS, F. GERARD, economist, educator; b. Apr. 28, 1929; s. Walter and Margot Adams; m. Heidi Vernon; children: Leslie, Colin, Loren, Mark. BA, U. Mich., 1949, MA, 1951, PhD, 1956. Instr. dept. econs. U. Mich., Ann Arbor, 1952—56; economist Calif. Tex. Oil Corp., N.Y.C., 1956—59; cons. economist, mgr. gen. econs. dept. Compagnie Française des Pétroles, N.Y.C. and Paris, 1959—61; mem. faculty U. Pa., Phila., 1961—98, prof. econs. and fin.; McDonald prof. Northeastern U., Boston, 1998—; Freeman prof. Johns Hopkins U., Balt., 2002. Dir. Econs. Research Unit, 1961-98, chmn. Faculty Senate, 1987-88; chmn. profl. bd. WEFA Group, Phila., 1969-91. Author: (with others) An Econometric Analysis of International Trade, 1969, (with J.R. Behrman) Econometric Models of World Agricultural Commodity Markets, 1976, Commodity Exports and Economic Development, 1982, (with L.R. Klein) Industrial Policies for Growth and Competitiveness, 1983, The Business Forecasting Revolution, 1986; editor: (with S.A. Klein) Stabilizing World Commodity Markets - Analysis, Practice and Policy, 1978, The Macroeconomic Dimensions of Arm Reduction, 1992, Economic Activity, Trade and Industry in the U.S.-Japan-World Economy, 1993, East Asian Development: Will the Miracle Survive?, 1998; Public Policies in East Asian Development: Facing New Challenges, 1999, Macroeconomics for Business and Society, 2002, The E-Business Revolution and the New Economy,2003. Home: 39 Stafford Rd Newton Center MA 02459-1818 E-mail: adams@ssc.upenn.edu, f.adams@neu.edu.

ADAMS, GEORGE BELL, lawyer; b. NYC, Sept. 16, 1930; s. George Bell and Mary Josephine (Smith) Adams; m. Lucy Elizabeth Ahearn, Sept. 10, 1952; children: Lucy S., Marea F., George B. Adams Jr., Alison E. BA, Yale U., 1952; LLB cum laude, Harvard U., 1957. Bar: N.Y. 1957, U.S. Dist. Ct. (so. and ea. dists.) N.Y. 1965, U.S. Ct. Appeals (2d cir.) 1973. Assoc. Debevoise, Plimpton, Lyons & Gates, NYC, 1957-65; ptnr. Debevoise & Plimpton, NYC, 1966-97, chmn. corp. dept., 1988-93, mng. ptnr. London, 1993-96, of counsel NYC, 1998—. Trustee Sarah Lawrence Coll., Bronxville, NY, 1977—, chmn. bd. trustees, 1987—91, vice chmn., chmn. exec. com., 1981—87; bd. dirs., exec. com. United Way of NYC, 1982—95, chmn. nominating com., 1985—93; fellow Pierpont Morgan Libr., NYC, 1977—, coun. of fellows, 1983—87, Yale U. Coun., 1983—90, chmn. alumni publs., 1979—83; trustee, mem. exec. com. Am. Trust for Brit. Libr., 1998—; bd. visitors CUNY Law Sch., 2003—; bd. dirs. New Amsterdam Singers, 1997—, Lawyers Alliance for World Security, 1989—98, Am. Assn. Internat. Com. of Jurists, 1998—, Greater NY Fund, NYC, 1977—84, pres., 1981—84. 1st lt. U.S. Army, 1952—54. Fellow, Davenport Coll., Yale U., 1983—90. Fellow: Am. Bar Found., Royal Soc. for Arts; mem.: ABA, Assn. Bar City NY, Century Assn., Pilgrim Soc., Racquet and Tennis Club, Cosmos Club. Office: Debevoise & Plimpton 919 3rd Ave Fl 44 New York NY 10022-3904 Business E-Mail: gbadams@debevoise.com.

ADAMS, HAROLD LYNN, architect; b. Palmer, Tex., May 15, 1939; s. Charles Roy and Lola (Beck) A.; m. Janice Lindhurst, Aug. 29, 1963; children: Harold Lynn, Abigail, Ashley, Sam. BS in Architecture, Tex. A&M U., 1962. Registered architect 44 states and U.K.; 1st class registered architect Japan. Draftsman Pratt Box Henderson, Dallas, 1960; intern William B. Tabler & Assocs., N.Y.C., 1961-62; architect John Carl Warnecke & Assocs., Washington, 1962-66; pres. RTKL Assocs., Inc., Balt., 1967-87, chmn. bd., 1987—2003, chmn. emeritus, 2003—. Regent Am. Archtl. Found., 1989—, chmn., 2000—; cons. Nat. Caital Planning Commn., 1992; dir. Lincoln Elec. Corp., 2001—, Legg Mason, 1987—, Renaissance Weekend, 1996—, Comml. Metals Corp., 2003-. Contbg. author: Current Techniques in Architectural Practice, Representative Am. Speeches, 1987-88, Technology: Trap or Triumph. Chmn. archtl. divsn. United Fund Drive, 1972; mem. task force on econ. devl. Balt. C. of C., 1975; pres. Econ. Devel. Coun. of Balt.; exec. com. Mt. Washington Country Sch. for Boys, 1976-77; bd. mgrs. Black Rock YMCA, 1971; vice chmn. GBC Found.; mem. Greater Balt. Com. on Edn., 1977-80, Com. on Planning, 1980-82; bd. dirs. Greater Balt. Com., 1983-90; mem. devel. coun. Tex. A&M U., 1982-90; mem. vis. com. Dept. Architecture U. Md., 1985-87; trustee Md. Inst. Coll. Art, Balt., 1984—, Maryvale Prep. Sch., Brooklandville, Md., 1985-89, Peale Mus., Balt., 1985-92, Balt. City Life Mus., 1985-92; regent Morgan State U., Balt., 1985-87; regent Am. Architecture Found., 1989-98, chmn., 2000—; trustee Balt. Fgn. Rels. Coun., 1987-93, Walter Gallery Art, 1987—; Balt. Metro. YMCA, 1987-90; chmn. World Trade Ctr. Inst., Md., 1990-99; mem. svcs. policy adv. com. U.S. Trade Rep., 1990—; bd. dirs. Internat. Visitors Ctr., 1990-92; mem. U.S.-China Bus. Coun., U.S.-Korea Bus. Coun.; adv. bd. Korea Econ. Inst. of Am.; chmn. Downtown Partnership Balt.; commr. Md. Econ. Devel. Comm.; chair Nat. Bldg. Mus., 1998—. Recipient Featherlite Design award Tex. A&M U., 1962; recipient Davidson Design award Tex. A&M U., 1962, Alpha Rho Chi medal, 1962, Tau Sigma Delta Gold medal Assn. Collegiate Schs. Architecture, 1993, Gov.'s award World Trade Ctr. Md., 1996, Outstanding Alumni award Tex. A&M U., 1998. Fellow AIA (pres. Balt. chpt. 1973-74, chmn. large firm roundtable 1984—, chancellor Coll. of Fellows 1997-98, nat. dir. 1999—, Kemper medal 1997); mem. Urban Land Inst., Am. Inst. Architects (chmn. large firm roundtable 1984—), Soc. Am. Mil. Engrs. (Urban medal 1997), Bursar Coll. of Fellows (vice chancellor), Royal Inst. Brit. Architects, Japan Inst. Architects, Center Club (Balt.), Met. Club (Washington), Cosmos Club, The Athenaeum (London). Democrat. Baptist. Home: 1601 The Terraces Baltimore MD 21209-3636

ADAMS, HAZARD SIMEON, language educator, writer; b. Cleve., Feb. 15, 1926; s. Robert Simeon and Mary (Thurness) A.; m. Diana White, Sept. 17, 1949; children: Charles Simeon, Perry White. AB, Princeton, 1948; MA, U. Wash., 1949, PhD, 1953. Instr. English Cornell U., 1952-56; asst. prof. U. Tex., 1956-59; vis. assoc. prof. Washington U., St. Louis, 1959; from assoc. prof. to prof. Mich. State U., 1959-64; Fulbright lectr. U. Dublin, 1962-63; prof. U. Calif.-Irvine, 1964-77, founding chmn. English dept., 1964-69; dean Sch. Humanities, 1970-72, vice chancellor acad. affairs, 1972-74; co-dir. Sch. Criticism and Theory, 1975-77; sr. fellow, 1975-88; hon. sr. fellow, 1988—; prof. English and comparative lit. U. Wash., Seattle, 1977-97, Byron W. and Alice L. Lockwood prof. humanities, 1988-97, prof. emeritus, 1997—. Prof. English U. Calif., Irvine, 1990-94. Author: Poems by Robert Simeon Adams, 1952, Blake and Yeats: The Contrary Vision, 1955, 2d edit., 1969, The Contexts of Poetry, 1963, William Blake: A Reading of the Shorter Poems, 1963, Poetry: An Introductory Anthology, 1968, The Horses of Instruction, 1968, Fiction as Process, 1968, The Interests of Criticism, 1969, William Blake: Jerusalem, Selected Poems and Prose, 1970, The Truth About Dragons, 1971, Critical Theory Since Plato, 1971, 3d edit., 2004, Lady Gregory, 1973, The Academic Tribes, 1976, 2d edit., 1988, Philosophy of the Literary Symbolic, 1983, Joyce Cary's Trilogies, 1983, Critical Theory Since 1965, 1986, The Book of Yeats's Poems, 1991, Antithetical Essays, 1991, Critical Essays on William Blake, 1991, The Book of Yeats's Vision, 1995,The Farm at Richwood and Other Poems, 1997, Many Pretty Toys, 1999, Home, 2001; mem. editl. bd. Epoch, 1954-56, Tex. Studies Lit. and Lang., 1957-68, Studies in Romanticism, 1966—, Blake Studies, 1969-80, Modern Lang. Quar., 1977-84. Served to 1st lt. USMC, 1943-45, 51. Guggenheim fellow, 1974-75 Mem. Internat. Assn. Univ. Profs. English, Am. Conf. for Irish Studies, Phi Beta Kappa. Home: 3930 NE 157th Pl Lake Forest Park WA 98155-6730 Personal E-mail: HAdams3048@aol.com.

ADAMS, HENRY, museum director, writer; b. Boston, May 12, 1949; s. Thomas Boylston and Ramelle (Cochrane) A.; m. Marianne Berardi, Apr. 12, 1989. BA, Harvard U., 1971; MA, Yale U., 1977, PhD, 1980. Asst. prof. U. Ill., Champaign, 1981-82; curator fine arts Carnegie Mus., Pitts., 1982-84; Samuel Sosland curator Am. Art Nelson-Atkins Mus. Art, Kansas City, Mo., 1984-93; dir. Cummer Mus. Art, Jacksonville, Fla., 1994—95; interim dir. Kemper Mus. Art, Kansas City, Mo., 1996; curator, Am. Art Cleve. Mus. Art, 1996; prof., Am. Art Case Western Reserve Univ., Cleve., 1997—. Adj. prof. U. Kans., U. Mo., Kans. Author: Thomas Hart Benton: An American Original, 1989, Thomas Hart Benton: Drawing from Life, 1990, Albert Bloch: The American Blue Rider, 1997, Eakins Revealed: The Secret Life of an American Artist, 2005, (with others) John La Farge, 1989; contbr. articles to jours. in field. Recipient Arthur Kingsley Porter prize Coll. Art Assn., 1985, William F. Yates Disting. Svc. medal William Jewell Coll., 1989, Frances Blanshard prize Yale U., Inst. of Mus. Svcs. Nat. Mus. Svc. award for Cummer Mus., 1994. Office: Mather House Case Western Reserve Univ 11201 Euclid Ave Cleveland OH 44106-7110 E-mail: henry.adams@case.edu.

ADAMS, HERBERT RYAN, management consultant, retired minister, mediator; b. Phila., Apr. 19, 1932; s. Leander Hampton and Helen Marguerite (Richards) Adams; m. Carol Anne Levine, Aug. 27, 1956 (div.); children: Ashley Pozefsky, Joshua, Lee, Rachel; m. Mary Ryan, Aug. 20, 1977. AB, Colby Coll., 1954; student, Harvard Div. Sch., 1955-56, Kent State U., 1957, Boston U., 1963; EdD, Harvard U., 1972. Ordained to ministry Congregationalist Ch., 1952, Unitarian Universalist, 1968. Minister Fairfield and Pine Point, Maine, 1950-56, Chelsea, Mass., 1962-66, Lexington, Mass., 1967-75, Winnetka, Ill., 1978-87, South Paris, Maine, 1988-94, West Paris, Maine, 1991-94; iterim Ithaca, NY, 1997-98, Santa Fe, 1998-99, Port Charlotte, Fla., 2001-02; editor Allyn and Bacon, Boston, 1959-62; sr. editor Ginn & Co., Boston, 1962-68; v.p. mktg. Visual Learning Corp., Cambridge, Mass., 1968-71; dir. Sci. Rsch. Assocs. divsn. IBM, Chgo., 1975-83; v.p. Laidlaw Bros., River Forest, Ill., 1983-84, pres., CEO, 1984-87; pres. Ryan-Adams Cons. Svcs., Center Lovell, Maine, 1994—. Author: Poetry on Film, 1970, Listening Your Way to Management Success, 1983; contbr. articles to profl. jours. Tchr. Greenville (Pa.) HS, 1956—58, Euclid (Ohio) HS, 1958—59, Lexington (Mass.) HS, 1968—69, Harvard Gradh. Sch. Edn., 1971—72, Oxford Hills (Maine) HS, 1987—88; prin. Oxford Hills Jr. HS, 1989—91. Recipient Coe Found. award, DePauw U., 1958, cert. of Merit, VFW, 1989, Disting. Pres. award, Norway-Paris Kiwanis, 1996. Mem.: Lovell Hist. Soc., Mediators Maine, Lovell Land Trust, Oxford Hills Ret. Tchrs. Assn., Girard Coll. Alumni Assn. (life), Unitarian Universalist Ret. Mins. Assn., Lake Kezar Country Club. Home: 252 Brentwood Dr Lake Placid FL 33852 E-mail: herbadams@webtv.net.

ADAMS, HILARY SHIELS, theater director; b. Washington, Nov. 3, 1972; d. Lawrence Curtis and Barbara (Johnston) Adams. BA, Evergreen State Coll., 1995. Asst. to David Harry Hwang, 2001—02. Dir.: (Broadway plays) Flower Drum Song, 2001, Reckless, (N.Y.C. theatrical prodns.) It's Called the Sugar Plum, 1997, What Neighbors Are For, 1997, Stills, 1997, 70 Scenes of Halloween, 1998, 100 Variations of a Family Theme, 1998, Whiskey Talking, 1998, Women of Manhattan, 1999, Kaleidoscope and the Flying Machine, 1999, A Boy Who was a Bird, 2001, Moby Dick, 2002, 2004 (Nominee for Outstanding Dir., Nominee for Outstanding Play, Nominee for Outstanding Actor), The Ice Factory Festival, 2002, Obie Award Winning Season, 2002, The Worthy Matron of the Eastern Star, 2003, Traindog, 2003, Still Asking for Trouble, 2003, Once Upon a Mattress, 2004; assoc. dir.: Peter Pan, 2004; A Real Cowboy, 2004; Romantic, 2005; Hamlet, 2005; Mickey Mouse is Dead, 2005; Beauty and the Beast, 2005; 2nd asst. dir. Titanic, 1996—97; asst. dir.: And Out of the Light, 1996; The Price of Love, 1996; Hansel and Gretel, 1996; Reincarnation, 1996; Bedfellows, 1997; Griller, 1998; The Fastest Clock in the Universe, 1998; (Broadway plays) Aida, 2000—01; A Little Night Music, 2002; (regional prodns.) Moonlight and Magnolias, 2005; 31 staged readings: including NY premiers by David Henry Hwang, OyamO, Jenny Lyn Bader. Manhattan Theatre Club Directing fellowship, 2004, 2005, Directing fellowship, Drama League, 2005. Mem.: Works Prodns. (co-founder, artistic dir.), First Light Theatre Co., N.Y. Coalition of Profl. Women in the Arts and Media (bd. mem.), Lincoln Ctr. Theatre Dirs.' Lab, Soc. of Stage Dirs. and Choreographers (observerships 1995—96, 2002). Office Phone: 212-462-9453. E-mail: HilaryAdams@mac.com.

ADAMS, HUNTER (PATCH ADAMS), internist, health facility administrator; b. Washington, May 28, 1945; Student, Sewanee U.; BA, George Washington U., 1967; MD, Med. Coll. Va., 1971. Resident pediat. Georgetown U. Hosp., Washington, 1971; founder, dir. Gesundheit Inst., Arlington, Va., 1971—92. Author: House Calls: How We Can All Heal the World One Visit at a Time, 1998; co-author: Gesundheit!: Bringing Good Health to You, the Medical System, and Society through Physician Service, Complementary Therapies, Humor, and Joy, 1998. Recipient Inst. of Noetic Sci. award for Creative Altruism, 1994. Office: Gesundheit Institute PO Box 50125 Arlington VA 22205 Address: Gesundheit Inst Hosp Found PO Box 98072 Washington DC 20090-8072*

ADAMS, INGRID G., federal government intelligence specialist; b. Washington, Oct. 11, 1959; d. Norbert Green and Marion Zeno Joseph; m. Keith Michael Adams, Mar. 1994 (div. Apr. 21, 1998); 1 child, Oliver; children:

Ashaunta, Diondra, Dana Tumblin. BA magna cum laude in Psychology, So. U., 1983. Case worker Office Family Security State of La., Hahnville, La., 1984—87, supr. eligibility worker Thibodaux, La., 1987—88; import specialist U.S. Customs Svc., New Orleans, 1989—98; intelligence specialist Dept. Homeland Security, New Orleans, 1998—. Ind. assoc. Pre Paid Legal Svcs., Ada, Okla., 2003—; spkr. Green's Consulting Co., St. Rose, La., 2003. Mem. com. Curtis Johnson Campaign, St. Rose, 1999, Dems. for Mary Landreu, St. Rose, 1999; bd. dir. Dem. Women Orgn., 1998—2001. Mem.: Positive Women/Men of New Orleans, St. Charles Hist. Found., So. U. Alumni Assn. (2d v.p. 2001—03). Democrat. Baptist. Avocations: writing, singing, dance, stamp collecting/philately, reading. Home: 309 Turtle Creek Lane Saint Rose LA 70087 Office: Dept Homeland Security 423 Canal St Rm 242 New Orleans LA 70130

ADAMS, J. PHILLIP, oil industry executive; BA in Fin. and Acctg., Utah State U., 1978. With Brown and Davis, CPAs, 1978—80, Flying J. Inc., Brigham City, Utah, 1980—, CEO, 1992—. Office: Flying J Inc PO Box 150310 Ogden UT 84415-0310

ADAMS, JAMES CHARLES, lawyer; b. Cleve., June 20, 1949; s. Charles Otterbein and Loraine Ida (Bagnoli) Adams; m. Donna Elaine Roe, Aug. 7, 1971 (dec. 1983); 1 child, Heather Anne; m. Naz D. Edwards, Aug. 29, 1998. BA, Mich. State U., 1971; JD, U. Mich., 1974. Bar: Mich. 1974, U.S. Dist. Ct. (ea. dist.) Mich. 1974. Assoc. Honigman Miller Schwartz, Detroit, 1974—75, Dykema Gossett, PLLC, Detroit, 1975—82, ptnr., 1982—86, Simpson & Moran, Birmingham, Mich., 1986—87; prin. James C. Adams, Traverse City, Mich., 1987—93, Adams & Assocs., Traverse City, 1993—95; ptnr. Running, Wise, Ford & Phillips, Traverse City, 1995—98; mem. Dykema Gossett PLLC, Detroit, 1998—. Mem.: ABA, Detroit Bar Assn., Phi Kappa Phi, Order of the Coif. Home: 3 Northwick Ct Ann Arbor MI 48105 Office: Dykema Gossett PLLC 400 Renaissance Ctr Ste 35 Detroit MI 48243-1501 Office Phone: 313-568-6527.

ADAMS, JAMES FREDERICK, psychologist, educator, academic administrator; b. Andong, Korea, Dec. 27, 1927; s. Benjamin Nyce and Phyllis Irene (Taylor) A.; m. Carol Ann Wagner, Jan. 17, 1980; children— James Edward, Dorothy Lee Adams Vanderhorst, Robert Benjamin BA In Psychology, U. Calif.-Berkeley, 1950; Ed.M. in Counseling and Psychology, Temple U., 1951; PhD in Exptl. Psychology, Wash. State U., 1959. Cert. psychologist, Wash., Pa.; lic. psychologist, Pa. Psychometrician Measurement and Research Ctr., Temple U., Phila., 1951-52; asst. prof. psychology Whitworth Coll., Spokane, Wash., 1952-55; teaching and research asst. State U. Wash., 1955-57; research assoc. Miami U., Oxford, Ohio, 1957-59; asst. prof. psychology Coll. Liberal Arts, Temple U., 1959-62, assoc. prof., 1962-66, prof., 1966-80, chmn. dept. counseling psychology, 1969-72; vis. prof. psychology Coll. Soc. Scis., U. P.R., Rio Piedras, 1963-64, Coll. Scis., Cath. U., Ponce, P.R., 1971-72; chmn. dept. counseling psychology Coll. Edn., Temple U., 1973-77, coordinator div. ednl. psychology, 1974-76; grad. dean, prof. psychology Grad. Coll., U. Nev., Las Vegas, 1980-85; acad. (sr.) v.p. Longwood Coll., Farmville, Va., 1985-86. Author: Problems in Counseling: A Case Study Approach, 1962, Instructors Manual for Understanding Adolescence, 1969; (exhbn. catalogue with J. D. Selig) Colonial Spanish Art of the Americas, 1976; (comml. pamphlet with C. L. Davis) The Use of the Vu-graph as an Instructional Aid, 1960; editor: Counseling and Guidance: A Summary View, 1965, Understanding Adolescence: Current Developments in Adolescent Psychology, 1968, 4th edit., 1980, Human Behavior in a Changing Society, 1973, Songs that had to be Sung (by B. N. Adams), 1979; contbr. chpts., articles, tests and book revs. to profl. publs. Served to cpl. USMC, 1945-46 Recipient Alexander Meiklejohn award AAUP, 1984; James McKean Cattell research fund grantee Miami U., Oxford, Ohio, 1958, Bolton fund research grantee Temple U., 1960, 62, faculty research grantee Temple U., 1961, 63, Commonwealth of Pa. research grantee Temple U., 1969, 70, 71, 72, summer research fellow Temple U., 1979; recipient scholarship U. Munich, 1955; James F. Adams endowment for psychology established at Wash. State U., Pullman, 2003. Fellow Am. Psychol. Assn. (divs. 26, 17); mem. Eastern Psychol. Assn., Western Psychol. Assn., Interam. Soc. Psychology, Sigma Xi, Psi Chi Scholarship established in his name at U. Nev., Las Vegas. Home: 130 Palacio Rd Corrales NM 87048-9648

ADAMS, JAMES MICHAEL, nuclear physicist; b. Brookline, Mass., Dec. 5, 1957; s. Michael James and Elizabeth (Corchary) A.; m. Linda Gail Sheehan Adams, Dec. 26, 1990; children: Kelley Marie, Megan Marie. AB, Coll. of the Holy Cross, Worcester, Mass., 1979; MS, Pa. State U., 1990, PhD, 1995. Lt. sr. grade USN, Washington, 1979-84; sr. engr. Westinghouse Electric Corp., Pitts., 1984-88; rsch. asst. Pa. State U., University Park, 1988-94; rsch. fellow U. Mich., Ann Arbor, Mich., 1995-96; guest rschr., physics lab. Nat. Inst. Stds. and Tech., Gaithersburg, Md., 1995-96; rsch. physicist Neutron Interactions & Dosimetry Group Physics Lab. Nat. Inst. Stds. and Tech., Gaithersburg, 1996—. Contbr. articles to profl. jours. including Phys. Rev., Applied Physics Letters, Surface Sci., Hyperfine Interactions, Ferroelectrics, Materials Sci. and Engring., Nuclear Tech. Vol. Alpha Cmty. Ambulance Svc., State College, Pa., 1994; asst. scoutmaster Boy Scouts Am., Framingham, Mass., 1975. Lt. USN, 1979-84. Recipient Grad. scholarships Am. Nuclear Soc., 1990-93, Inaugural Nuc. Energy Rsch. Initiative grant; named Inst. of Nuclear Power Op. scholar, 1988-89, Pa. State U. Grad. fellow The Pa. State U., 1991-92, Deans fellow, 1988-90. Mem. ASTM (sec., mem. com.), Am. Phys. Soc., Am. Nuc. Soc., Sigma Xi, Sigma Pi Sigma, Tau Beta Pi, Alpha Nu Sigma. Achievements include research in hyperfine interactions, surface physics, fundamental neutron physics, neutron spectroscopy and dosimetry, neutron source calibrations, and nuclear reactor analysis. Home: 21503 Fox Field Cir Germantown MD 20876-5944 Office: Nat Inst Stds and Tech 100 Bureau Dr Mail Stop 8461 Gaithersburg MD 20899

ADAMS, JAMES THOMAS, surgeon; b. Rochester, N.Y., Mar. 28, 1930; s. Thomas and Sarah A.; m. Jacqueline K. Stemmler, July 7, 1952; children— Pamela, Mark, Sari Lynn. AB, Washington U., St. Louis, 1951, MD, 1955. Intern, then resident in surgery Barnes Hosp., St. Louis, 1955-60; mem. faculty U. Rochester Med. Sch., 1962—, prof. surgery, 1977—. Author papers in field, chpts. in books. Served as officer M.C. USAR, 1960-62. Mem. Am. Surg. Assn., Soc. Internat. de Chirurgie, Soc. U. Surgeons, Central Surg. Assn., Soc. Vascular Surgery, Am. Gastroenterol. Assn., Soc. Surgery Alimentary Tract, Am. Assn. Surgery Trauma, Phi Beta Kappa, Sigma Xi, Alpha Omega Alpha. Clubs: Oak Hill Country (Rochester). Achievements include co-designing inferior vena cava clip. Office Phone: 716-275-2726. Personal E-mail: jadams06@rochester.rr.com. E-mail: james-adams@urmc.rochester.edu.

ADAMS, JO-ANN MARIE, lawyer; b. L.A., May 27, 1949; d. Joseph John and Georgia S. (Wein) A. AA, Pasadena C.C., 1968; BA, Pomona Coll., 1970; MA, Calif. State U., L.A., 1971; MBA, Pacific Luth. U., 1983; JD, Santa Clara U., 1996. Cert. in telecom. and info. resource mgmt. Secondary tchr. South Pasadena (Calif.) Unified Schs., 1970-71; appraiser Riverside County (Calif.) Assessor's Office, 1972-74; systems and procedures analyst Riverside County Data Processing Dept., 1974-76, supr. systems analyst, 1976-79; systems analyst computer Boeing Computer Svcs. Co., Seattle, 1979-81; sr. systems analyst Thurston County Ctrl. Svcs., Olympia, Wash., 1981-83, data processing systems mgr., 1983-84; data processing systems engr. IBM Corp., 1984-87; realtor assoc. Dower Realty, 1987-92; corp. sales rep. UniGlobe Met. Travel, 1988-89; project mgr. Servco Pacific, 1989-90, Scott Software Systems, 1990-91; systems analyst Dept. Atty. Gen., 1991-93; pvt. practice Honolulu, 1996—; with Bervar & Jones, 2002—03. Cons. in field, 1993—; corp. counsel RightWorks Corp., 2000-01, Law Offices Thomas R. Hogan, 1999; instr. Riverside City Coll., 1977-79; adj. prof. Santa Clara U., 1997-2000. Actor: films and TV shows. Chair legis. task force Riverside/San Bernardino chpt. NOW, 1975-76, chpt. co-chair, 1978; mem. ethics com. Calif. NOW, Inc., 1978; alt. del. Calif. Dem. Caucus, 1978; del. Hawaii Dem. Caucus, 2002; mem. Gay, Lesbian, Bisexual and Transgender Caucus of Hawaii Dem. Party, Hawaii Dem. State Ctrl. Com.; bd. dirs. Honolulu Gay and Lesbian Cultural Found. Mem. ABA, NAFE, Santa Clara Calif. Bar Assn. (mem. rainbow com. 1994-2000, chair 1998, minority access com. 1 999-2000, nominating com. 2000), Pomona Coll. Alumni Assn., Santa Clara U. Alumni Assn. Home: 411 Hobron Ln # 801 Honolulu HI 96815-1210 Office: Seven Waterfront Plz 500 Ala Moana Blvd Ste 400 Honolulu HI 96813-4920 Office Phone: 808-528-2100. Personal E-mail: jadamsesq@aol.com.

ADAMS, JODY, chef, restaurant owner; m. Ken Rivard; children: Oliver Rivard, Roxanne Rivard. Student, Brown U. Apprentice, class asst. Nancy Verde Barr; chef Seasons restaurant, Boston, 1983—86; sous chef Hamersley's Bistro, Boston, 1986—90; exec. chef Michela's, Boston, 1990—94; ptnr., chef Rialto, Cambridge, 1994—; ptnr. Sapphire Restaurant Group, Cambridge, 1994—, blu, Boston, 2001, Noik, Cambridge, Mass., 2002. Named Best Chef, Boston Mag., 1997; named one of Five Rising Stars, Restaurant Hospitality, 1992, Am.'s Best Young Chef's to Keep Your Eye On, Esquire mag., 1992, Am.'s Ten Best new Chefs, Food and Wine mag., 1993; named to Fine Dining Hall of Fame, Nation's Restaurant News, 2000; recipient Perrier-Jouet Best Chef award N.E., James Beard Found., 1997. Office: Sapphire Restaurant Grp 20 Univ Rd Cambridge MA 02138

ADAMS, JOEY LAUREN, actress; b. Little Rock, Jan. 6, 1971; Appeared in films Dazed and Confused, 1993, Coneheads, 1993, The Program, 1993, Sleep With Me, 1994, The Pros & Cons of Breathing, 1994, S.F.W., 1994, Mallrats, 1995, Drawing Flies, 1996, Bio-Dome, 1996, Michael, 1996, Chasing Amy, 1997 (Golden Globe award nominee 1998, Chgo. Film Critics Assn. award 1998), A Cool, Dry Place, 1998, Big Daddy, 1999, Bruno, 2000, Beautiful, 2000, Harvard Man, 2001, (voice) Dr. Dolittle 2, 2001, In the Shadows, 2001, Jay and Silent Bob Strike Back, 2001, Grand Champion, 2002, Beeper, 2002, The Big Empty, 2003, A Promise Kept, 2003; appeared in TV movies One the Edge, 2001, Remembering Charlie, 2003; appeared in tv series Top of the Heap, 1991, Vinnie & Bobby, 1992, Second Noah, 1996; guest tv appearances include Married with Children, 1987, Double Rush, 1995, Hercules, 1998, Dinner for Five, 2001, Stripperella, 2003. Office: ICM 8942 Wilshire Blvd Beverly Hills CA 90211-1934

ADAMS, JOHN A., lawyer; b. Fargo, N.D., Dec. 31, 1954; BA, Brigham Young U., 1978, JD, 1981. Bar: Utah 1981, U.S. Dist. Ct. Utah 1984, Utah Ct. Appeals (D.C. cir.) 1981, U.S. Ct. Appeals (fed. cir.) 1984, U.S. Supreme Ct. 1984. Atty. Ray, Quinney & Nebeker, PC, Salt Lake City. Mem.: Utah State Bar (pres. 2002—). Office: Ray Quinney and Nebeker PO Box 45385 36 S State St Ste 1400 Salt Lake City UT 84145-0385

ADAMS, JOHN CARTER, JR., insurance executive; b. Williston, Fla., June 13, 1936; s. John Carter and Katharine Anna (Beall) A.; m. Leila Nora Johnson, Nov. 28, 1958; children: Julia Katharine, Ruth Anne. BSBA, U. Fla., 1958. Agt. Pan Am Ins. Co., 1958-59; acct. exec. Guy B. Odum & Co., Inc., 1959-63, v.p., 1963-66, exec. v.p., 1966-71, pres., 1971-76, Jay Adams & Assocs., Inc., Daytona Beach, Fla., 1976-85, Hilb Rogal & Hamilton Co., Daytona Beach, Fla., 1986-89, CEO, 1986-92, chmn., 1986-98, mem. oper. com. Richmond, Va., 1988-95, chmn. oper. com., 1987-93, sr. v.p. ops., 1989-90, exec. v.p. sales and mktg., 1991-93, exec. v.p., COO, 1993-94, exec. v.p. ops., 1994-99; exec. v.p. Brown & Brown Inc., Daytona Beach, 1999—2004, mem. leadership coun., 2004—. Bd. dirs. Consol. Tomoka Land Co., chmn. compensation com., 1990-, mem. audit com., 2004—, mem. exec. com.; chmn. adv. bd. Daytona Beach region Am. Pioneer Savs. Bank, Orlando, Fla., 1986-90. Mem. bd. visitors Embry-Riddle Aero. U., Daytona Beach, 1967-69, trustee, 1969—, mem. exec. com., 1972—, vice chmn. bd. 1981—, chmn. exec. com, 1983—, devel. coun. chmn. fund drive Hunt Meml. Libr. Embry-Riddle Aero U., 1985; chmn. Commitment 2000 Fund Drive Embry-Riddle Aero U.; campaign chmn. Easter Seal Soc., 1969, trustee, 1970-73, pres., 1972-73; bd. dirs. YMCA, Daytona Beach, 1968-76, 78—, treas., 1970, v.p., 1971-82, pres., 1983; mem. Metro Bd. Daytona Beach YMCA, 1992-2001, trustee, 2002—; dir. Futures, Inc., 1985-93, pres., 1987; dir. Nat. Intercollegiate Sports Festival, 1985-87; gen. campaign chmn. United Way of Volusia County, Fla., 1977, pres., 1979, dir., 1976-82, trustee, 1985—; chmn. Civic League of Halifax Area, 1983-84, exec. com., 1977-92; chmn. Fla. Internat. Festivals, Inc., 1990-91, bd. dirs. 1987—, exec. com., 1991—, chmn. Lively Arts Ctr. Inc., 1997-2002, chmn. emeritus, 2003-; mem. Tourist Devel. Coun. Volusia County 1983-85, Halifax Advt. Authority, 1985; bd. dirs. Volusia County Bus. Devel. Coun., 1984-92, Daytona Beach Cmty. Found., 1984-87, Fla. State C. of C., 1985-86. Served with USNR, 1953-61. Recipient Disting. Svc. award Bd. visitors Embry-Riddle Aero. U., 1975, Champion Higher Ind. Edn. in Fla. award Ind. Colls. and Univs. of Fla., 1973, 1st Ann. Herbert M. Davidson Cmty. Svc. award United Way of Volusia County, 1992, J. Saxton Lloyd Outstanding Cmty. Svc. award Civic League of the Halifax Area, 2003; named Citizen of Yr., Boys and Girls Club of Volusia-Flagler Counties, 2000, Ctrl. Fla. Coun. Boy Scouts Am., 2001; established John C. Adams Cmty. Svc. award Embry-Riddle Aero U., 1990. Mem. Daytona Beach C. of C. (bd. govs. 1968-70, v.p. bus. and govt. 1970, pres. 1975, gen. campaign chmn. devel. fund drive 1984, Louis Fuchs Man of Yr. award 1985), Volusia County Insurors Assn. (pres. 1971-72), Fla. Assn. Ins. Agts. (bd. dirs. 1978-81), Coun. Ins. Agts. and Brokers (bd. dirs. 1989—, co-chmn. exec. liasion com., mem. fin. and audit com. 1993-94, sec. 1994-95, treas. 1995-96, vice chmn. 1996-97, chmn. 1997-98, co-chmn. nominating com. 1998-99), Rotary (bd. dirs. 1989-91). Republican. Episcopalian. Office: Brown & Brown Inc PO Box 2412 220 S Ridgewood Ave Daytona Beach FL 32115 Personal E-mail: jadamsindaytona@aol.com. Business E-Mail: jadams@bbdaytona.com.

ADAMS, JOHN COOLIDGE, composer, conductor; b. Worcester, Mass., Feb. 15, 1947; s. Carl John and Elinore Mary (Coolidge) A. Studied with Leon Kirchner, Earl Kim, Roger Sessions, Harvard U., AB magna cum laude, 1969, MA, 1971. Former composer-in-residence, condr. San Francisco Symphony Orch., 1979—85. Artistic advisor, San Francisco Symphony Orch., from 1978, former composer-in-residence, San Francisco Symphony Orch.; dir., New Music Ensemble, from 1972-81; faculty mem., San Francisco Conservatory, 1972-83; composer-in-residence, Marlboro Festival, 1970; musical compositions include Electric Wake, 1968, Heavy Metal, 1971, American Standard, 1973, Kataadn, 1973, Onyx, 1976, Phrygian Gates, 1977, Shaker Loops, 1978; Onyx, Grounding, Sermon, Common Tones, 1979, Harmonium, 1980, Grand Pianola Music, 1982, Harmonielehre, 1985, Nixon in China, 1987 (Grammy for best contemporary composition, 1989), The Death of Klinghoffer, 1991, Chamber Symphony, 1993 (Royal Philharmonic Soc. Music award, 1994), Violin Concerto (Grawemeyer award for music, 1995), Naive and Sentimental Music, 1999, On The Transmigration of Souls, 2002 (Pulitzer prize for music, 2003). Named to rank of Chevalier dans l'Ordre des Artes et des Lettres, French Ministry of Culture; recipient Cyril Magnin Awd. for Outstanding Achievement in the Arts, Calif. Gov's. Awd. for Lifetime Achievement in the Arts. Office: Boosey & Hawkes 24 E 21st St New York NY 10010 also: California Artists Mgt 41 Sutter St # 420 San Francisco CA 94104-4903

ADAMS, JOHN HAMILTON, lawyer; b. NYC, Feb. 15, 1936; s. John and Barbara (Johnston) A.; m. Patricia Brandon Smith, Sept. 30, 1963; children: Katherine L., John H., Ramsay W. BA, Mich. State U., 1959; LL.B., Duke U., 1962. Bar: NY 1963. Assoc. Cadwalader, Wickersham & Taft, NYC, 1962-65; asst. US atty. So. Dist. NY, NYC, 1965-69; co-founder and exec. dir. Nat. Resources Def. Coun., Inc., NYC, 1970-98, pres., 1998—. Chmn. Open Space Inst., N.Y.C., 1979—. Bd. dirs. Catskill Ctr. for Conservation, Arkville, N.Y., 1974—, Hudson River Found. Sci. and Environ. Rsch., Inc., 1981—, Winston Found. World Peace, 1984—, World Resources Inst., 1987—. Recipient As They Grow award Parents mag., 1989, Frances K. Hutchinson award Garden Club Am., 1990, Disting. Alumni award Duke U., 1991. Mem. Am. Conservation Assn. (bd. dirs. 1985—), Century Assn. Office: Natural Resources Def Coun Inc 40 W 20th St New York NY 10011-4211 Office Phone: 212-727-4535. E-mail: jcoifman@nrdc.org.

ADAMS, JOHN HURST, bishop; b. Columbia, S.C., Nov. 27, 1929; s. Eugene Avery and Charity A. (Nash) A.; m. Dolly Desselle, Aug. 25, 1956; children: Gaye Desselle, Jann Hurst; 1 child, Madelyn Rose. AB, Johnson C. Smith Coll., 1948; STB, Boston U., 1951, STM, 1953; DD, Wilberforce U., 1956, Paul Quinn Coll., 1972. Ordained deacon A.M.E. Ch., 1948, elder A.M.E. Ch., 1952, bishop A.M.E. Ch., 1972. Pastor Bethel A.M.E. Ch., Lynn, Mass., 1950—52; prof. Wilberforce (Ohio) U., 1952—56; pres. Paul Quinn Coll., Waco, Tex., 1956—62, chmn. bd., 1972—; pastor 1st A.M.E. Ch., Seattle, 1962—68, Grant A.M.E. ch., L.A., 1968—72; 87th A.M.E. bishop 10th Dist. Tex. councils chs., 1972—; bishop 2d Dist., 1986—89; sr. bishop Atlanta, 1989—92, 7th Episcopal Dist., Columbia, SC, 1992—. Author: Ethnic Education in Black Church, 1970. Bd. dirs. Nat. Coun. Chs., Nat. Conf. Black Churchmen, Nat. Bd. Black United Funds, People United to Save Humanity (PUSH), Tex. Coun. Chs. Named Man of Yr., B'nai B'rith, 1964, Urban League, Seattle, 1965. Mem.: Boulé, Alpha Phi Alpha. Office: 110 Pisgah Church Rd Columbia SC 29203-9351*

ADAMS, JOHN JILLSON, lawyer; b. Toledo, Nov. 12, 1934; s. Theodore Floyd and Esther (Jillson) A.; m. Barbara Barr, June 6, 1959; children: Leigh Ann Adams Miller, Leslie, Julie. BA, Denison U., 1956; LLB, U. Va., 1959. Bar: Va. 1959, D.C. 1967, U.S. Ct. Appeals (4th, 6th and D.C. cirs.), U.S. Supreme Ct. Assoc. Hunton & Williams, Richmond, Va., 1960-65, ptnr. Washington, 1967—; assoc. dir. Am. United for Separation of Ch. and State, Washington, 1965-66; spl. asst. U.S. State Dept., Washington, 1966-67. Served with USAR, 1959-65. Mem. ABA, Va. Bar Assn., D.C. Bar Assn. Baptist. Home: 8546 Georgetown Pike Mc Lean VA 22102-1206 Office: Hunton & Williams 1900 K St NW Washington DC 20006-1110

ADAMS, JOHN LEWIS, bank executive; BBA in Fin, U. Tex., 1966, JD, 1969. With Tex. Commerce Bancshares, Inc., Houston, 1973, exec. v.p; pres. Tex. Commerce Bank-Houston, N.A. (subs.), 1983; dir., now chmn. Tex. Commerce Bank-Dallas; chmn., CEO Group 1 Automotives. Office: Tex Commerce Bank NA 712 Main St Houston TX 77002-3223*

ADAMS, JOHN M., library director; b. Chgo., June 10, 1950; s. Merlin J. and Esther (Bohn) A.; m. Nancy Ileen Coultas, June 12, 1970; 1 child, Arwen Lee BA in English, U. Ill., 1972, M.L.S., 1973. Grad. asst. U. Ill. Libr., Urbana, 1972-73; libr.-reference Sherman Oaks Libr., L.A., 1973-75; libr. philosophy dept. L.A. Pub. Libr., 1975-77, head gen. reading svc., 1977-78; dir. Moline Pub. Libr., Ill., 1978-83, Tampa (Fla.)-Hillsborough County Pub. Libr. System, 1983-91; dir., county librarian Orange County (Calif.) Public Library System, 1991—. Dir. Tampa Bay Libr. Consortium, Fla., 1983-91, Santiago Libr. System, 1991—, chmn., 1999; mem. adv. com. on pub. librs. OCLC, 1992-95; bd. govs. Am. Rsch. Ctr. in Egypt, 2003—. Contbr. articles to profl. jours. Pres. Orange County chpt. Am. Rsch. Ctr. in Egypt, 2002—; bd. dirs. Planned Parenthood of Tampa, 1984. Recipient Frontier award ALA Mag., 1981; named Outstanding Young Man, Moline Jaycees, 1983. Mem. ALA (J.C. Dana award 1982, 93, 2004), Calif. Libr. Assn., Calif. County Librs. Assn., Orange County C. of C. Avocations: music, tennis. Office: Orange County Pub Libr 1501 E Saint Andrew Pl Santa Ana CA 92705-4930 Office Phone: 714-566-3040. Business E-Mail: jadams@ocpl.org.

ADAMS, JOHN MARSHALL, lawyer; b. Columbus, Ohio, Dec. 6, 1930; s. H.F. and Ada Margaret (Gregg) A.; m. Janet Hawk, June 28, 1952; children: John Marshall, Susan Lynn, William Alfred. BA, Ohio State U., 1952; JD summa cum laude, 1954. Bar: Ohio 1954. Mem. Cowan & Adams, Columbus, 1954—55; asst. city atty. City of Columbus, 1955—56; mem. Knepper, White, Richards & Miller, 1956-63; practiced in Columbus, 1963—74; ptnr. Porter, Wright, Morris & Arthur, Columbus, 1975—91, of counsel, 1992—. Vice chmn. Ohio Bar Liability Ins. Co., 1990-93, chmn., 1994-2002, chair emeritus, 2002—; trustee Ohio Legal Ctr. Inst., 1976-81, Ohio Lawpac, 1980-89. Fellow Am. Coll. Trial Lawyers, Am. Bar Found., Ohio Bar Found. (trustee 1975-84); mem. ABA, Ohio State Bar Assn. (exec. com. 1975-80, pres. 1978-79, Ohio Bar medal 1994), Columbus Bar Assn. (bd. govs. 1970-76, pres. 1974-75), Lawyers Club (pres. 1968-69), 6th Cir. Jud. Conf. (life), Am. Contract Bridge League (life master), Order of Coif, Grey Oaks Country Club (Naples, Fla.), Scioto Country Club, Delta Upsilon, Phi Delta Phi. Republican. Home: 2535 Canterbury Rd Columbus OH 43221-3081 Office: 41 S High St Columbus OH 43215-6101

ADAMS, JOHN QUINCY, adult education educator, consultant; b. Gary, Ind., Sept. 6, 1950; s. John Quincy and Fannie (Simpson) A.; m. Becky Jo Yonan (div. 1978); m. Pearlie Mae Strother, June 26, 1980; children: Leia, Jabari. PhB, Grand Valley State Coll., 1975; MA, Ind. U., 1977; PhD, U. Ill., 1989. Tchr. Ctr. for World Studies, Grand Rapids, Mich., 1975-77, Catalyst H.S., Peoria, Ill., 1977-78; asst. prof. Ill. State U., Normal, 1978-83; tchg. asst. U. Ill., Urbana, 1983-84; dir. Minority and Intercultural Affairs, Joliet (Ill.) Jr. Coll., 1985-88; asst. prof. Western Ill. U., Macomb, 1988-93, dir. ednl. opportunity, 1993-97, prof., 1997—. Prof. PBS teleclass Dealing with Diversity, 1992, 99. Co-author (CD Rom) Multicultural Prism, 1999; co-editor (anthology) Multicultural Education: Strategies for Implementation in Colleges and Universities, vol. 1-5, 1991-96, (anthology and video) Multicultural Prism: Voices from the Field, 1994. Mem. adv. bd. Golden Apple Orgn., Chgo. Cpl. USMC, 1970-74. Recipient Pacesetter award for multicultural edn. Ill. State Bd. Edn., 1981, Leadership award Ill. Com. on Black Concerns in Higher Edn., 1989, Connections 2000 award Ill. State Bd. Edn., 1993. Mem. ASCD, Ill. Staff and Curriculum Developers Assn. (pres. 1992-94, adv. bd. 1995—, Leadership award 1994), Phi Kappa Phi. Avocations: frisbee golf, poetry, music. Home: 1 Bacon Woods Macomb IL 61455 Office: Western Ill Univ 1 University Cir Macomb IL 61455-1390 Fax: 309-298-2222. E-mail: jabari@macomb.com.

ADAMS, JOHN S., insurance company executive; V.p., corp. fin. and svcs. Old Republic Internat. Corp., Chgo., sr. v.p., chief fin. officer, 2001—04, v.p., fin., 2004—. Office: Old Rep Internat Corp 307 N Michigan Ave Chicago IL 60601 Office Phone: 312-346-8100 ext. 205. Office Fax: 312-726-0309.

ADAMS, JOHN STEPHEN, geography educator; b. Mpls., Sept. 7, 1938; s. Edward Francis and Ellen Cecilia (Cullen) A.; m. Judith Estelle Nielsen, Sept. 1, 1962; children: John D., Ellen Anastasia, Martin Francis, David Joseph Cullen. BA, U. St. Thomas, 1960; MA, U. Minn., 1962, PhD, 1966. Rsch. asst., rsch. fellow Upper Midwest Econ. Study, Mpls., 1960-64; teaching asst. dept. geography U. Minn., Mpls., 1964-66, assoc. prof., then prof. geography, 1970—, now prof. geography, planning and pub. affairs, dir. Sch. Pub. Affairs and H.H. Humphrey Inst. Pub. Affairs, 1976-79, chmn. dept. geography Mpls., 1981-84 92-93, 1999—2005, Fesler-Lampert prof. Urban and Regional Affairs Mpls.; asst. prof. geography Pa. State U., State College, 1966-70. Rsch. asst. N. Star Rsch. and Devel., Inc., Mpls., 1964; Fulbright prof. geog. Econ. U. Vienna, Austria, 1975-76; vis. prof. geography U. Wash., Seattle, 1979; vis. prof. geography and environ. engring. U.S. Mil. Acad., West Point, N.Y., 1990-91; vis. prof. geography and earth scis. Marie Curie-Sklodowska U., Lublin, Poland, 1997; mem. nat. adv. com. H.H. Humphrey N.-S. Fellowship Program, Inst. Internat. Edn., N.Y.C., 1979-81, coord. at U. Minn., 1981-87, 89-90; econ. geographer in residence Bank of Am., San Francisco, 1980-81; mem. exec. com. Nat. Com. Rsch. on 1980 census Social Sci. Rsch. Coun., N.Y.C., 1981-88; bd. dirs. Consortium of Social Sci. Assns., Washington, 1983-85, FVB Energy Inc.; mem. geography panel Coun. for Internat. Exchange of Scholars, Washington, 1983-85, chair, 1986, mem. Soviet-Eastern European panel, 1990-93; mem. geography div. adv. com. U.S. Bur. Census, Washington, 1985; Bush sabbatical fellow, 1987-88, Fulbright prof. geography Moscow State U., 1988. Author: (with R. Abler and P. Gould) Spatial Organization, 1971, (with Abler and K. Lee) A Comparative Atlas of America's Great Cities, 1976 (Geog. Soc. Chgo. award 1977), Housing America in the 1980s, 1987); editor: Contemporary Metropolitan America, 4 vols., 1976, Urban Policy Making and Metropolitan Dynamics, 1976, (with B. Van Drasek) Minneapolis-St. Paul People, Place and Public Life, 1993; mem. editl. bd. Geographia Polonica, Govt. and Policy, Urban Geography, Eurasian Geography and Economics. Bd. dirs. Newman Ctr., Mpls., 1983—88, 1994—2002. Sr. Scientist Rsch. fellow NSF, Berkeley, Calif., 1980-81. Mem. Assn. Am. Geographers (nat. sec. 1975-78, v.p. 1981-82, pres. 1982-83, honors award 1988), Nat. Coun. Geog. Edn., Mpls. Com. Fgn. Rels. Democrat. Roman Catholic. Avocations: photography, coin collecting/numismatics, gardening. Home: 2611 W 49th St Minneapolis MN 55410-1902 Office: U Minn Dept Geography 267 19th Ave S Minneapolis MN 55455-0499 Office Phone: 612-625-0571. Business E-Mail: adams004@umn.edu.

ADAMS, JOSEPH ANDREW, internist, health facility administrator, educator; b. Tarrytown, NY, Jan. 21, 1956; s. Elijah Adams and Blanche Macoff; m. Linda Freda Barr, Aug. 11, 1984; children: Zachary Elijah, Jackson Barney. BA, U. Pa., 1978; MD, U. Md., 1984. Diplomate Am. Bd. Internal Medicine (added qualification in geriatric medicine). Pvt. practice internal medicine, Towson, Md., 1988—; med. dir. Blakehurst Life Care Cmty., Towson, 1995—. Clin. asst. prof. U. Md. Sch. Medicine, Balt., 1999—. Contbr. articles to profl. jours. Pres. Smoke Free Md. Coalition, Balt., 1997—97, Md. Childrens Initiative Edn. Fund, Inc., Balt., 1998—99; sec. Smoke Free Balt. County Coalition, Towson, 1999—2002; bd. dirs. Balt. County Med. Assn., Towson, 1998—2002; bd. dirs. Md. & DC chpts. Asthma and Allergy Found. of Am., Balt., 2000—02. Recipient Physician Recognition award for Continuing Med. Edn., AMA, 1991, Best Article of 1995 award, Md. Med. Jour., 1995, Disting. Svc. award, Am. Lung Assn. Md., 1996, 2001, Physician's Disting. Svc. award, Balt. County Med. Assn., 1997; grantee, Md. Dept. Health and Mental Hygiene, 2000. Fellow: ACP, Am. Soc. Internal Medicine (life); mem.: APHA, Am. Soc. Addiction Medicine. Liberal. Jewish. Avocations: jogging, cooking. Home: 1405 Berwick Rd Towson MD 21204 Office: 6701 N Charles St Ste 4104 Towson MD 21204

ADAMS, JOSEPH KEITH, lawyer; b. Provo, Utah, Apr. 3, 1949; s. Joseph S. and Marian (Bellows) A.; m. Myrle June Overly, Sept. 2, 1971; children: Derek J., Bret K., Stephanie, Julie K., Scott J., Laura. BA summa cum laude, Brigham Young U., 1973; JD, Harvard U., 1976. Bar: Utah 1976, U.S. Dist. Ct. Utah 1976, U.S. Tax Ct. 1983. Assoc. Van Cott, Bagley, Cornwall & McCarthy, Salt Lake City, 1976-82, shareholder, 1982-98; also bd. dirs. Van Cott, Bagley, et al, Salt Lake City, 1993-97, chmn. tax and estate planning sect., 1995-98; ptnr. Stoel, Rives, LLP, Salt Lake City, 1998—. Adj. faculty Brigham Young U. Law Sch., Provo, 1993. Co-author: Practical Estate Planning Techniques, 1990. Planned giving com. Restoration Cathedral Madeleine, Salt Lake City, 1991-93; pres. Utah Planned Giving Roundtable, Salt Lake City, 1994, Salt Lake City Estate Planning Coun.; planned giving com. U. Utah Hosp. Found., 1994; bd. dirs. Salt Lake C.C. Found., 1982-98; chair Salt Lake profl. adv. group LDS Found.; stake pres. LDS Ch. David O. Mackay scholar Brigham Young U., 1967-73. Fellow Am. Coll. Trust and Estate Counsel; mem. ABA (real property, probate and trust sect.), Utah State Bar (exec. com., past chmn. estate planning probate sect.), Harvard Alumni Assn. Utah (chair bd. dirs. 1980-90), Harvard Law Sch. Assn. Utah (vice chair). Republican. Mem. Lds Ch. Avocations: skiing, reading, golf. Office: Stoel Rives LLP 201 S Main St Ste 1100 Salt Lake City UT 84111-4904 Office Phone: 801-328-3131. E-mail: jkadams@stoel.com.

ADAMS, JOYCE M., retired academic administrator; b. Dickinson, Tex., Dec. 21; d. Clarence L. and Effie R. Adams. BS, Prairie View A&M U., 1965; MS, Tex. Woman's U., 1978, PhD, 1996. RN Tex. Staff nurse M.D. Anderson Hosp., Houston, 1967—73; instr., prof. San Jacinto Coll., Houston, 1973—94, dept. chmn., 1994—98, assoc. dean, 1998—2003, dean program devel. instl. effectiveness and health careers, 2003—04; ret., 2004. V.p. Bd. of Vocat. Nurse Examiners for State of Tex. Bd. dirs. Eastwood Health Clinic, Houston, 1999—2003, Benevolent Mission Internat., Houston, 1994—2003; chair health com. Shalom Zone Mobile Health Ministries, Houston, 1998—2003. Mem.: ANA, Tex. Nurses Assn., Sigma Theta Tau. Home: 5434 Botany Lane Houston TX 77048 Personal E-mail: jadams0513@aol.com.

ADAMS, JULIAN TIMOTHY, psychologist; s. Julian and Bertha Ozella Adams; m. Sharlene Frances Bunge, Nov. 15, 1992; m. Martha Jo House, Mar. 22, 1975 (div. July 0, 1990); children: Julian Mclane, Thomas Daniel, Timothy James. BS, Columbus Coll., Ga., 1974—76; MA, U. W. Fla., Pensacola, 1983—84; PhD, Forest Inst. Profl. Psychology, Springfield, Mo., 1987—91. Lic. clin. psychologist Va., 1995, Ariz., 1991. Clin. psychologist U.S. Army, 1989—94; CEO Psychol. Assessments, Interventions and Resources, Inc., Annandale, Va., 1994—2002; clin. psychologist Ednl. and Devel. Intervention Services, U. S. Army Hosp., Heidelberg, Germany, 2002—; rehab. psychologist Veterans Adminstrn., Washington, 2002. Adv. bd. mem. Am. Bd. Psychol. Specialties, 1996—99. Auxillary police officer Fairfax County Police Dept., Va., 1996—99; rape crisis counselor Lakeview Ctr. Inc., Pensacola, Fla., 1983—86, helpline counselor, 1983—86. Fellow, Wash., D.C. Area Geriatric Edn. Consortium, 1996. Home: CMR 442 Box 214 Ae Apo 09042 Germany

ADAMS, JULIE KAREN, clinical psychologist; b. Portland, Oreg., Dec. 12, 1955; d. Allen Hays and Susanna Angelina (Meyers) A. B, Willamette U., 1977; M, Ctrl. Wash. U., 1982; cert. in bus. adminstrn., U. Wash., 1986; D, Pacific U., 1992; MS, Columbia U., 2000. Lic. clin. psychologist; cert. counselor, sch. psychologist, Wash. Sch. psychologist Highline Sch. Dist., Seattle, 1987-90; psychology intern Elmcrest Psychiat. Hosp., Portland, Conn., 1990, clinician, 1991; rsch. asst. Yale U., New Haven, Conn., 1991; clinician Advanced Clin. Svcs., Seattle, 1991-93; postdoctoral fellow U. Wash., Seattle, 1991-93; acad. counselor Johns Hopkins U., Balt., 1993; behavior intervention specialist Edmonds (Wash.) Sch. Dist., 1993-94, Marysville Sch. Dist., Marysville, Wash., 1994-99; instr. Seattle U., 1995-99. Guest spkr. in field to profl. assns., also Pacific U., U. Wash., U. Oreg., 1989—. Freelance writer: Psychology Today Mag., reporter: Wash. Psychologist Newsletter; contbr. (book chpt.) Women in Communication; contbr. articles to profl. jours. Mem. tng. com., kids week com., nursing home com., pub. policy com. Jr. League of Seattle, 1988—; health care researcher Wash. State Legis., Olympia, 1993; campaigner Bush for Pres., Seattle, 1988, 92; rsch. asst. to state senator Oreg. State Legis., Salem, 1985; press page nat. conv. Rep. Nat. Com., Detroit, 1980; student grad. v.p., faculty rep. com. Pacific U. Sch. of Profl. Psychology, 1989-90; bd. dirs. Jr. League, Seattle. Mem. APA (health psychology com. student rep. 1992-93), Wash. Psychol. Assn. (coun. reps.), Wash. State Psychol. Assn. Coun., Soc. Profl. Journalists, Willamette U. Alumni Assn. (bd. dirs. 1983-88), Vols. for Outdoor Wash. (bd. dirs. 1986-87), City Club of Seattle (membership com. 1986-88), Jr. League Seattle (bd. dirs. 2004-2005), Psi Chi, Beta Alpha Gamma. Avocations: writing, skiing, american history, reading, travel. Home: 9226 46th Dr NE Marysville WA 98270 Business E-Mail: ja365@columbia.edu.

ADAMS, KAREN HOEVE, university administrator; b. Holland, Mich., Jan. 3, 1961; d. Erville Wayne and Nella Ruth (Heemstra) Hoeve; m. James Franklin Adams Jr., July 1, 1989; children: Lucas James, Matthew Wayne (twins). BA, Calvin Coll., 1983; MS in Edn., Ind. U., 1985, EdD, 1995. Asst. dir. student fin. assistance Bloomington Office Student Fin. Assistance, Ind. U., 1985-89; computing edn. trainer Ind. U. Computing Svcs., Bloomington, 1989-91, planning and comms. adminstr., 1991—97; chief staff Office V.P. for Info. Tech. and Rsch. Ind. U., 1997—. Bd. dirs. Bloomington Pops, 1993—. Home: 2301 E Arden Dr Bloomington IN 47401-6890 Office: Office of VP for Info Tech 601 East Kirkwood Ave Bloomington IN 47405

ADAMS, KENNETH FRANCIS, automotive executive; b. Danbury, Conn., Feb. 4, 1946; s. Donald and Evelyn Trocola (Mulvihill) Adams; m. Annette Talarico, Sept. 28, 1968; children: Amy, Ella Louise, Elizabeth. Student, Mt. St. Mary's Coll., 1964—68. C.P.A., Conn. Mgr. Price Waterhouse & Co., Bridgeport, Conn., 1968—74; v.p. fin. and adminstrn., dir. Saab Cars USA, Inc., Norcross, Ga., 1974—. Served with USAR, 1968—74. Mem.: AICPA, Inst. Mgmt. Accts., Fin. Exec. Inst., Conn. Soc. CPAs. Roman Cath. Office: Saab Cars USA Inc 9565 Red Bird Ln Alpharetta GA 30022

ADAMS, KENNETH ROBERT, gaming analyst, writer, consultant, historian; b. Carson City, Nev., Sept. 8, 1942; s. Maurice Adams and Gertrude Aloha (Wilson) Burke; children: John Anthony, James Joseph. Prin. Ken Adams and Assoc., Sparks, Nev., 1990—. Coord. gaming history series of the oral history program U. Nev., continuing edns. gaming mgmt. program adv. com., 1988-97, chmn., 1988. Co-author: Playing the Cards That Are Dealt, 1992, Always Bet on the Butcher, 1994, War Stories, 1995, Dwayne Kling: Luck in the Residue of Design, 2001; publ., assoc. editor: Nev. Gaming Almanac, 1991—, Nev. Gaming Directory, 1997—, The Adams Report. Chmn. mktg. com. Downtown Improvement Assn., 1994—, pres., 2001—; steering com., chmn. gaming com. Festival Reno, 1984-86; mem. adv. bd. Leadership Reno Alumni Assn., 1995-97. Mem. Internat. Platform Assn. Office: Ken Adams & Assocs 210 Marsh Ave Ste 103 Reno NV 89509-1698 Office Phone: 775-322-7722. Office Fax: 775-322-7806.

ADAMS, LAVONNE MARILYN BECK, critical care nurse, nursing educator; b. Bridgeport, Conn., Feb. 22, 1965; d. Adolf and Hazel B. (Henderson) Beck. ASN, Kettering Coll. Med. Arts, 1985; BSN, Wright State U., 1988; MSN, Andrews U., 1992, PhD, 2003. CCRN. Staff nurse Kettering (Ohio) Med. Ctr., 1985-89, resource staff nurse, 1989-95, instr. in nursing, 1989-92; asst. prof. nursing Kettering (Ohio) Coll. Med. Arts, 1992—99, Southwestern Adventist U., Keene, Tex., 1999—2003, assoc. prof., 2003—04; asst. prof. nursing Tex. Christian U., Harris Sch. Nursing, Ft. Worth, 2004—; PRN staff nurse Huguley Mem. Hosp., 2002—. Asst. leader kindergarten divsn. Seventh-day Adventist Ch., Kettering, 1987—93, Arlington Seventh Day Adventist Ch., 2001—03; mem. Southwestern Sem. Oratorio Chorus, 1999—. Mem.: Am. Assn. Critical Care Nurses, Pi Lambda Theta, Sigma Theta Tau, Phi Kappa Phi. Avocations: music, travel. Home: 7000 Welch Ct Fort Worth TX 76133-6726 Office: TCU Harris Sch Nursing TCU Box 298620 Fort Worth TX 76129

ADAMS, LEE STEPHEN, lawyer, banker; b. St. Louis, June 3, 1949; s. Albert L. and Margaret C. (Donoghue) A. AB, Rutgers Coll., 1971; JD, Georgetown U., 1974. Bar: D.C. 1975, Mo. 1975, Ohio 1982, Calif. 1995. Asst. dean Georgetown U. Law Ctr., Washington, 1974-76, adj. prof. law, 1973-76; sr. counsel to bd. govs. FRS, Washington, 1976-81; v.p., gen. counsel Fed. Res. Bank, Cleve., 1981-82, sr. v.p., gen. counsel, 1982-86; dep. gen. counsel Bank One Corp., Columbus, Ohio, 1986-95, v.p., gen. counsel, 1986-91; of counsel Morrison & Foerster, San Francisco, 1995-98, ptnr. Washington, 1999—, group chair fin. svcs. Lectr. law Cath. U. Law Sch., Washington, 1977-81 Mem. Columbus Country Club. Office: Morrison & Foerster 2000 Pennsylvania Ave NW Washington DC 20006-1812 Home: 539 Virginia Ave Saint Louis MO 63119-4229

ADAMS, LEE TOWNE, lawyer; b. Chatham, Ont., Can., July 12, 1922; arrived in U.S., 1923; s. Lee Eugene and Josephine Towne A.; m. Muriel Kathryn Stang, June 29, 1946; children: Nancy Louise, Carol Josephine, Jane Bertha. BA, U. Rochester, 1943; JD, Yale U., 1949. Atty. pvt. practice, Forestville, N.Y., 1949-72; mcpl. atty. various towns and villages, 1955-72; judge State of N.Y., Chautauqua County, 1972-93; retired, 1993—. Trustee Presbytery of Western N.Y., 1970-76; dir., vice chmn. Presbyn. Homes Western N.Y., 1984-90. Lt. USN, 1943-46. Mem. VFW, Am. legion, Submarine Vets. WWII, Masons, Jamestown Consistory, Ismaila Temple, Phi Beta Kappa. Republican. Avocations: gardening, reading. Home: 21 Pearl St PO Box 306 Forestville NY 14062-0306

ADAMS, LELAND RICHARD, retired accountant; b. Spickard, Mo., May 17, 1928; s. Thomas Lavern and Hattie Bell (Long) A. AA, Trenton Jr. Coll., 1949; BS, N.W. Mo. U., 1951. Acct. U.S. Govt., ret., 1982. Vol. Mo. Dept. Corrections, Probation and Parole; mem. Johnson County, Kans. Bicentennial Com., chmn. subcom. rec. cemetery inscriptions, 1974-76, Kans. Mus. Bd., 1978-87, pres., 1986; treas. Shawnee Mission Indian Hist. Soc., 1987-88; v.p. Atchison County, Kans. Hist. Soc., 1988-89. Mem. SAR (Kans. state sec. Delaware Crossing chpt. 1977), Johnson County Geneal. Soc. (organizer, 1st pres. 1973-75), Kans. Coun. Geneal. Socs. (pres. 1975-77), Am. Family Records Assn. (v.p. 1981-82), Fedn. Geneal. Socs. (dir., treas., dir. nat. conv. Kansas City 1985), Atchison County Kans. Geneal. Soc. (pres. 1991-93)Vols. Nat. Archives (organizer, 1st pres. Kansas City chpt. 1986-88), VFW (comdr. Post 846 1965-66, adminstrv. surgeon 1969-74), Toastmasters (pres. 1972).

ADAMS, LEOCADIA, secondary school educator, writer; b. Clinton, Mass., Oct. 9, 1947; d. Leokadia Marianna Donat; children: Erik Paul, Keith David. BS in edn., vocational home econ., Ctrl. Mo. State U., 1972, MA in edn., spl. edn., learning disabilities, emotionally disturbed, 1987. Pre-sch. dir. La Petite Acad., Overland Park, Kans., 1973—74; vocat. home econ. instr. Martin Luther King Jr. H.S., Kansas City, Mo., 1974—75, Longfellow Elem., Kansas City, Mo., 1975—76; instr. needle arts, head dept. St. Teresa's Acad., Kansas City, Mo., 1976—83; owner The Light Ho., Kansas City, 1983—84; learning disabilities specialist. itinernant tchr. Kans. City Sch. Dist., 1985—86; learning disabilities specialist Westport Mid. Sch., Kansas City, 1986—89, SW H.S., Kansas City, 1989—90, Satchel Paige Elem. Sch., Kansas City, 1990—96, Chester R. Anderson Alternative Mid. Sch., Kansas City, 1997—98, 1997—99, Ctrl. Mid. Sch., 1999—2000, Van Horn H.S., Independence, Mo., 2000—. Author: (text book) Beginning to Advanced Sewing, (cookbook) Drink's On Me, 1994; prodr.: (seminars and workshops on sewing) Variety of Titles Depending on Workshop, 1980—84, (director) (fashion shows) Varied, 1977—83,: Poland's History and Culture, 1988—95; guest columnist: Post Eagle; contbr. columns in newspapers; editor: website. Zone coord., block capt. 49/63 Neighborhood Coalition, Kansas City, 1974—79, co-chmn. edn. com., 1974—75, chmn. govt. com., 1977; campaign mgr. Jim Dolan for State Rep., Kansas City, 1977—78; vol. Elect Ed Growney, Kansas City, 1978—88. Named to Wall of Freedom, Birmingham, Ala. Mem.: Coun. Exceptional Children, Assn. Supervision and Curriculum Devel., Phi Delta Kappa. Roman Catholic. Avocations: reading, classical music, gourmet cooking, Polish studies, sewing. Personal E-mail: lodgia@sbcglobal.net.

ADAMS, LILIANA OSSES, music performer, harpist; b. Poznan, Poland, May 16, 1939; came to U.S., 1978, naturalized, 1990; d. Sylwester and Helena (Koswenda) O.; m. Edmund Pietryk, Sept. 4, 1965 (div. Aug. 1970); m. Bruce Meredith Adams, Feb. 3, 1978. MA, Music Acad. Poznan, Poland, 1971. Prin. harpist Philharm. Orch. of Szczecin, Poland, 1964-72, Imperial Opera and Ballet Orch., Tehran, Iran, 1972-78; pvt. music tchr. Riyadh, Saudi Arabia, 1979-81; soloist Austrian Radio, 1981-86; solo harpist, pvt. tchr. harp and piano Antioch, Calif., 1986—. Music cons. Schs. and Librs., Calif., 1991—. Contbr. articles to profl. jours. Mem. Am. Fedn. of Musicians, Am. Harp Soc., Music Tchrs. Assn. Calif., Internat. Soc. of Harpers, U.K. Harp Assn., Internat. Harp Ctr. (Switzerland). Home: PO Box 233 Antioch CA 94509-0023 E-mail: harpliliana@comcast.net.

ADAMS, LISA KAY, artist; b. Bristol, Pa., Aug. 3, 1955; d. Charles Joseph Jr. and Liese-Lotte (Leiss) Adams. Student, U. Heidelberg, Germany, 1976; BA, Scripps Coll., Claremont, Calif., 1977; MFA, Claremont Grad. U., 1980. Artist in residence Nordic Inst. Contemporary Art, 1999. Exhibited in one-person shows at Newspace, L.A., 1989, 90, 92, 93, Daniel Maher Gallery, L.A., 1991, Century Gallery, Sylmar, Calif., 1992, William Turner Gallery, Venice, Calif., 1994, Coll. So. Nev., North Las Vegas, 1995, Miller Fine Art, L.A., 1997, Gallery Paradiso, Costa Mesa, Calif., 1998, New Image Art, L.A., 1999, Crazy Space, Santa Monica, Calif., 2000, The Living Room, Santa Monica, 2001, Patricia Correa Gallery, Santa Monica, 2002, The Sandbox, Venice, Calif., 2003, The Office, Huntington Beach, Calif., 2004, White Box Gallery, Marina del Rey, Calif., 2005; group shows include U. Calif., Irvine, Soho Ctr. for Visual Arts, N.Y.C., East Hawaii Cultural Ctr., Hilo, Santa Monica (Calif.) Art Complex, L.A. Mcpl. Art Gallery, Lanning Gallery, Houston, Dorothy Goldeen Gallery, Santa Monica, Calif., William Turner Gallery, Venice, Calif., Sandberg Inst., Hoorn, The Netherlands, Raid Projects, L.A., Triple Candie, N.Y.C., Healing Arts Gallery, Bklyn.; represented in permanent collections at Aratex, Burbank, Calif., Laguna Mus. of Art, Laguna Beach, Calif., Nippon Steel USA Inc., L.A., Sun Am., L.A.; also pvt. collections. Bd. dirs. Side St. Projects, 1994-95. Brody Arts Fund fellow, 1992; recipient Fulbright Sr. award, 1996; Durfee Arc grantee, 2001. Mem. L.A. Contemporary Exhbns. Home and Office: PO Box 2456 Venice CA 90294-2456

ADAMS, LORETTA, marketing executive; b. Panama; BS in Internat. Mktg., Am. U., 1962; postgrad. in Econs., U. Panama, Panama City, 1963-64. Mgmt. trainee Sears Roebuck & Co., Panama City, Panama, 1962-63, mgmt. pers., 1963-65; supr. internat. advertising projects Kenyon & Eckhardt Advertising, Inc., N.Y.C., 1965-68; asst. rsch. dir. divsn. L.Am. and Far E. Richardson-Vicks Internat., Mexico City and Wilton, Conn., 1968-69, rsch. dir. divsn. Mex. and L.Am., 1969-75, mem. top mgmt. strategic planning team, 1975-78; founder, pres. Mkt. Devel., Inc., San Diego, 1978—. Contbr. articles to profl. jours. Mem. Am. Mktg. Assn., European Soc. for Opinion & Market Rsch., Advt. Rsch. Found., Coun. Am. Survey Rsch. Orgns., Market Rsch. Assn. Office: Market Devel Inc 600 B St Ste 1600 San Diego CA 92101-4584

ADAMS, LUDWIG HOWARD, lawyer; b. Pitts., Dec. 11, 1954; s. Ludwig and Alberta Anne (Howard) A.; m. Lynn Ann Krapcho, Sept. 12, 1981; children: Kimberly Lynn, Justin Andrew. BA, MA, U. Pa., 1976; JD, Columbia U., 1979; LLM in Taxation, NYU, 1988. Bar: D.C. 1979, N.Y. 1986, U.S. Tax Ct. 1991. Trial atty. tax divsn. U.S. Dept. Justice, Washington, 1979-84; assoc. Cahill Gordon & Reindel, N.Y.C., 1984-90, sr. atty., 1990-96, counsel, 1996—98, ptnr., 1999—. Editor, author Columbia Jour. Transnational Law, 1978-79. Mem. ABA (tax sect.), N.Y. State Bar Assn. (tax sect.). Presbyterian. Office: Cahill Gordon & Reindel 80 Pine St Fl 19 New York NY 10005-1702

ADAMS, MARGARET BERNICE, retired museum official; b. Toronto, Ont., Can., Apr. 29, 1936; arrived in U.S., 1948, naturalized, 1952; d. Robert Russell and Kathleen Olive (Buffin) A.; m. Alberto Enrique Sánchez-Quiñonez, Nov. 30, 1956 (div. 1960). AA, Monterey Peninsula Coll., 1969; BA, San Jose State U., 1971; MA, U. Utah, 1972. Curator ethnic arts Civic Art Gallery, San Jose, Calif., 1971; staff asst. Utah Mus. Fine Arts, Salt Lake City, 1972; lectr., curator Coll. Seven, U. Calif., Santa Cruz, 1972-74; part-time educator Cabrillo Coll., Aptos, Calif., 1973, Monterey Peninsula Coll., 1973-84; dir. U.S. Army Mus., Presidio of Monterey, 1974-83; chief. mus. br. Ft. Ord Mil. Complex, 1983-88. Guest curator Am. Indian arts Monterey Peninsula Mus. Art, 1975-88. Author: Indian Tribes of North America and Chronology of World Events in Prehistoric Pueblo Times, 1975, Historic Old Monterey, 1976; contbg. editor Indian Am., Writing on the Wall, WWII Patriotic Posters, 1987; contbr. articles to jours. Mem. Native Am. adv. panel AAAS, Washington, 1972-78; mem. rev. and adv. com. Project Media, Nat. Indian Edn. Assn., Mpls., 1973-78; working mem. Program for Tng. Am. Indian Counsellors in Alcoholism Counselling and Rehab. Programs, 1972-74; mem. hist. adv. com. Monterey County Bd. Suprs., 1987-89. Grad. fellow, dean's scholar U. Utah, 1972; dean's scholar Monterey Peninsula Coll., 1969, San Jose State U., 1971. Mem. Am. Anthrop. Assn., Am. Assn. Museums, Soc. Am. Archeology, Nat., Calif., Indian Edn. Assns. Home: 2281 W 155 S Hurricane UT 84737-4425

ADAMS, MARK KILDEE, lawyer; b. Des Moines, Oct. 8, 1938; s. Walter Bunting and Regina (Kildee) A.; m. Helen von Bachmayr Larsen, May 22, 1982; 1 child, Kirsten. AB, Harvard U., 1960, JD, 1966. Bar: N.Mex. 1966, U.S. Dist. Ct. N.Mex. 1966, U.S. Ct. Appeals (10th cir.) 1970, U.S. Claims Ct., Zuni Pueblo Tribal Ct. Assoc. Rodey, Dickason, Sloan, Akin & Robb, Santa Fe, 1966-70, ptnr., 1970—, dir. Santa Fe office. Co-author: N. Mex. Environ. Law Handbook; author: Unitization of Solid Mineral Properties, 1982, Minimum Work Clauses in Mining Leases, 1976. Capt. U.S. Army, 1960-62. Mem. ABA, Albuquerque Bar Assn. (bd. dirs. 1976-78), Lawyers Club (officer 1980-84). Republican. Office: Rodey Dickason Sloan Akin & Robb PA 315 Paseo de Peralta Santa Fe NM 87501 Office Phone: 505-954-3903. Office Fax: 505-954-3942. Business E-Mail: mkadams@rodey.com.

ADAMS, MARTHA JEAN MORRIS, art educator, artist; d. Frank Elliott and Theodosia Ellen (Dever) Morris; m. John Hines Adams, Sr., Aug. 3, 1962; children: John Hines Jr., Jean Karole Adams Meares. BS in Edn., Elizabeth City State U., 1985. Art tchr. Hertford County Schs., Winton, NC, 1986—99, 2002—, Franklin County Schs., Louisburg, NC, 1999—2000, Vance County Schs., Henderson, NC, 2000—02. Mem. county-wide sch. improvement com. Hertford County Schs., Winton, 1993—94; program enhancement chmn. Riverview Elem., Murfreesboro, NC, 1994—96; mem. exec. bd. Profl. Educators N.C., Raleigh, 1993—2003. Vol. Spl. Olympics Riverview Elem., Ahoskie, NC, 1992—96; participant N.C. Ctr. for Advancement Tchg., Cullowhee, 1996, 1999; Sunday sch. tchr. Grantee, N.C. Arts Coun., 1993—94, U.S. Govt., 1995—97. Mem.: Nat. Art Edn. Assn. Baptist. Avocations: reading, cooking. Home: 103 Springlake Dr Murfreesboro NC 27855 Office: Ahoskie Elem Sch 200 N Talmage Ave Ahoskie NC 27910

ADAMS, MARY A., retired assistant principal; b. Trimble, Tenn., June 20, 1933; d. Ira Sr. and Diora (Pierce) Bingham; children: Cheryl R. Gray, Gregory S. Adams. BS, Tenn. State U., 1954; MS, Hofstra U., 1975. Cert. math. tchr. N.Y., ednl. adminstrn. N.Y. Cartographic engr. aide TVA, Chattanooga, 1954—55; asst. to placement dir. Tenn. State U., Nashville, 1955-56; statistical programmer IBM, Poughkeepsie, N.Y., 1956-59; tchr. math. Bellmore-Merrick Sch. Dist., Merrick, N.Y., 1961-80, asst. prin., 1980-94; ret., 1994. Trustee Roosevelt (N.Y.) Pub. Lib., 1993—, Nassau C.C., Garden City, N.Y., 1995—; bd. dirs. Literacy Vols. Am., Nassau County chpt.; mem. adv. bd. Nassau County, Hempstead, N.Y., 1992—; committeewoman Roosevelt (N.Y.) Dem. Com., 1991-2001; covenor Citizens in Support of African-Am. Mus., Hempstead, N.Y., 1991—. Recipient Edn. award Women on the Job, Inc., 1993, Cmty. Svc. award March of Dimes, 1993, Chi Eta Phi sorority, 1994, Martin Luther King award Nassau County, 1994, Sojourner Truth Cmty. Svc. award Profl. & Bus. Women Am. Ctrl. Nassau chpt., Hon. Resolution Recognition award N.Y. Com. Col. Trustees, 2001, Gov.'s award for Excellence, State of N.Y., 2001, Harriett Turman Humanaterian Achievement award, 2005; named Outstanding Citizen Assembly of State of N.Y., 2000. Mem. NAACP, Am. Ethnic Coalition, Tenn. State U. Nat. Alumni Assn. (pres. 1994-98, archivist 1998—), Roosevelt Dem. Club. (treas. 1991-2001), Nat. Coun. Negro Women. Democrat. Presbyterian. Avocation: music. Home: 200 E Pennywood Ave Roosevelt NY 11575-1209

ADAMS, MENDLE EUGENE, minister; b. Bath County, Va., July 1, 1938; s. Earl and Margaret M. (Godsey) A.; m. N. Ruth Williams, Feb. 2, 1957; children: David Mendle, Brian Richard, Josef Wayne, Vicki Ruth. AB, Ind. Wesleyan U., 1967; MA in Religion, Christian Theol. Sem., 1969; postgrad., Aquinas Coll., 1977, Harvard U., 1978. Ordained to ministry Meth. Ch. as deacon, 1968, as min., United Ch. of Christ, 1981; orders accepted The Old Cath. Order, 1993; received into Order of St. Francis of The Orthodox Cath. Ch., 2002. Pastor Windfall (Ind.) Pilgrim Ch., 1960-63, Mt. Olive Meth. Ch., Marion, Ind., 1963-67, Mt. Comfort United Meth. Ch., Indpls., 1967-69, United Meth. Ctr., Donnybrook, Maxbass, Lansford, N.D., 1979, Hope Congl. United Ch. of Christ, Granville, N.D., 1980-82, 1st Congl. United Ch. of Christ, McPherson, Kans., 1982-87; chaplain ecumenical campus Okla. State U., Stillwater, 1987-91; interim pastor Peace United Ch. of Christ, Loyal, Okla., 1988, 1st Christian Ch. (Disciples of Christ), Stillwater, 1990, Bethel Congl. Ch., Edmond, Okla., 1991; organizing min. High Point United Ch. of Christ, Boone County, Ky., 1991-99; pastor St. Peter's United Ch. of Christ, Cin., 1997—. Ednl. trips to Israel-Palestine, 1980, Nicaragua, 1983, The Philippines, 1985, Ukraine, 2000. Co-author: Touching Center Adventures in Christ Consciousness, 1990, Medical-educational Trip to Ukraine, 2000. Mem. Ind. Solid Waste Com., 1976, Ind. and Okla. group for Equal Rights Amendment to the U.S. Constn., 1977, 1981; bd. dirs. McPherson Family Life Ctr., 1983—84, Interfaith Chapel, Cin./No. Ky. Internat. Airport, 1992—; chmn. com. McPherson Cmty. Nursing Home, 1984; mem. Gov.'s Task Force on AIDS, Okla., 1987—88, Gov.'s Cabinet on Children's Issues, 1988—91, Ecumenical Coun. on Maternal and Infant Health, So. Gov.'s Leadership Coun., 1989—91; cert. mediator Okla. Dispute Resolution, Supreme Ct. Okla., 1991; mem. Ind. Ho. of Reps., 1975—76, Chs. Uniting in Global Mission, 1992—; co-chmn. United Ch. Assembly of Greater Cin.; mem. Earth Spirit Rising Com., 1999; bd. dirs. IMAGO, Inc., 1999—2001. Recipient Honored Legislator citation Ind. Coun. Chs., 1976. Mem.: Masons (32d degree York Rite). Democrat. Home: 6113 Webbland Pl Cincinnati OH

45213-1405 *Upon being ordained Deacon, Bishop Richard Raines counseled, "The Divine call is where your abilities intersect human needs." I have sought to discern that call and respond in Christ's name; trusting in Providence for a spiritual legacy.*

ADAMS, MICHAEL FRED, academic administrator, political scientist, educator; b. Montgomery, Ala., Mar. 25, 1948; s. Hubert W. and Jean (Taylor) A.; m. Mary Lynn Ethridge, June 7, 1969; children: David Winston, Stephen Taylor. BA, Lipscomb U., 1970; MA, Ohio State U., 1971, PhD, 1973. Asst. prof. Ohio State U., 1973-74; chief of staff for Sen. Howard Baker, Washington, 1975-79; advisor to gov. State of Tenn., Nashville, 1981-82; v.p. Pepperdine U., Malibu, Calif., 1982-88; pres. Centre Coll., Danville, Ky., 1988-97, U. Ga., Athens, 1997—. Chmn. Nat. Assn. Ind. Colls. and Univs., 1995-96, Assoc. Colls. of South; mem. coun. for advancement and support of edn. NCAA Pres. Commn., 1992-94; chmn. Commn. on Colls. of So. Assn. Colls. and Schs.; vice chmn. task force that founded Coun. for Higher Edn. Accreditation; chair Am. Coun. on Edn., 2000. Author: Rhetorical Strategies of Howard Baker, 1973; contbr. articles to various publs. Pres. Circle K Internat., Chgo., 1970; nominee for U.S. Congress, Nashville, 1980; mem. site host com. 1984 Olympiad, L.A.; elder Christian Ch. Recipient Bronze Quill award Internat. Assn. Bus. Communicators, 1986, Excellence award Nat. Sch. Pub. Relations Soc., 1985; Ohio State U. grad. fellow, 1970-73 Mem. Young Pres. Orgn., Speech Comm. Assn., Ctr. for Study of Presidency, Univ. Club (N.Y.C.), Coun. Fgn. Relations. Republican. Avocations: golf, reading, travel. Office: U Ga Adminstrn Bldg Athens GA 30602 Office Phone: 706-542-1214.

ADAMS, MIGNON STRICKLAND, library director; b. Chickasha, Okla. d. Augustus and Donna Vea (Forehand) S.; m. David Geliebter, Nov. 20, 1992; children: Melinda Bartscherer, Benjamin Adams. BS, Eastern Ill. U., 1962; MSLS, U. Ill., 1966, postgrad., 1968-70. Coord. media svcs. Sch. Dist. #7, Tolono, Ill., 1962-66; campus sch. libr. Eastern Ill. U., Charleston, 1966-67; libr. dir. Lake Land Coll., Mattoon, Ill., 1967-69; coord. libr. instruction SUNY, Oswego, 1971-82, assoc. dir. info. svcs., 1981-85; dir. libr. svcs. Phila. Coll. Pharmacy and Sci., 1985—. Bd. dirs. Health Scis. Librs. Consortium, Phila., Tri-State Coll. Libr. Coop., Phila. Author: Teaching Library Skills for Academic Credit, 1985; contbr. articles to profl. jours. Overseer Phila. Monthly Meeting of Friends, Phila., 1989—. Mem. ALA, Assn. of Coll. and Rsch. Librs. (chair coll. libr. sect. 1992-93), Am. Assn. Colls. and Pharmacy (chair librs. and ednl. resources sect. 1989-91), Del. Valley Assn. of Coll. and Rsch. Librs. (bd. dirs., chair 1989-91). Mem. Soc. Of Friends.

ADAMS, NANCY R., nurse, retired military officer; b. Rochester, N.Y., Apr. 20, 1945; BSN, Cornell U., 1968; MSN, Cath. U. Am., 1974; grad., U.S. Army War Coll. Advanced through grades to maj. gen. U.S. Army, 1991; comdr. William Beaumont Army Med. Ctr., S.W. Regional Med. Command; chief Army Nurse Corps; asst. surgeon gen. for pers. and comdr. U.S. Army Ctr. for Health Promotion and Preventive Medicine; lead agt. TRICARE Region VII U.S. Army; chief nurse Frankfurt Army Regional Med. Ctr., 1987—89; staff asst. profl. affairs and quality assurance Office of Asst. Sec. of Def., asst. inspector gen., dir. intensive care nursing course; nursing cons. Army Surgeon Gen., 1989—91; commd. Nurse Corps U.S. Army, 1991—95; commdg. gen. Tripler Army Med. Ctr., Hawaii, 1998—2002; sr. advisor to the dir. TRICARE Mgmt. Activity, 2002—. Decorated Legion of Merit, Meritorious Svc. medal; recipient Disting. Svc. medal, Defense Superior Svc. medal. Fellow: Am. Acad. Nursing; mem.: ANA, Am. Orgn. of Nurse Execs., Assn. of Mil. Surgeons of the U.S., Sigma Theta Tau. Home: 5575 Seminary Rd Apt 207 Falls Church VA 22041-3555

ADAMS, PATRICK O., career officer; b. Cape Gireadeau, Mo. m. Jean Marie Means; children: Patrick Jr., Christine. BS in Pub. Adminstrn., U. Mo., 1968; MS in Internat. Rels., Auburn U., 1983. Commd. 2d lt. USAF, 1968; advanced through grades to brig. gen., 1995; personnel officer Air U., Maxwell AFB, Ala., 1969-71; aide-de-camp mil. assistance and adv. group Hdqs. Command, Tehran, Iran, 1971-72; personnel officer De Nang Air Base, Republic South Vietnam, 1972-73, Udorn Royal Thai Air Base, Thailand, 1973; chief field activities Air Force Mil. Personnel Ctr., Randolph AFB, Tex., 1991, mem. air staff tng. program, 1973-75; personnel officer office asst. for col. assignments Hdqs. USAF, Washington, 1975-78, dir. svc., 1995—97; personnel officer office asst. for col. assignments Air Force Manpower and Personnel Ctr., Randolph AFB, Tex., 1978-80, asst. exec., exec. officer to comdr., 1980-82; chief mil. personnel Tinker AFB, Okla., 1983-84; exec. officer to comdr. in chief Mil. Airlift Command, Scott AFB, Ill., 1985-87, dir. personnel programs, asst. sr. officer matters, 1988-90; comdr. 3440th Tech. Tng. Group Lowry Tech. Tng. Ctr., Colo., 1987-88; dir. personnel Air Mobility Command, Scott AFB, Ill., 1993-94, spl. asst. to comdr., 1994-95; chief Mil. Liaison Team Bulgaria European Command, Sofia, 1994; dir. manpower and personnel Joint Staff/J1, Washington, 1995—2000; ret. Former pres. Air Force Meml. Found. Decorated Legion of Merit with oak leaf cluster, Airman's medal, Bronze Star medal.

ADAMS, PAULINE DEHAART, artist, consultant; b. Heerlen, Limburg, The Netherlands, July 20, 1926; d. Pieter and Adriana Cornelia (Zijp) DeHaart; children: Peter D., Diane L., Laurie J., Steven M. BA, U. Rochester, 1964, MA, 1966. Artist, tchr. The Harley Sch., Rochester, N.Y., 1958-64; registrar Mus. of Arts and Scis., Rochester, 1965-66, Seattle Art Mus., Seattle, 1966-76; workshop chmn. Northwest Watercolor Soc., Seattle, 1989—; freelance portrait artist. Home hopitality hostess World Affairs Coun., Seattle, 1986-90. Mem. Netherlands Bus. Assn. (bd. dirs. 1986—), Mountaineers. Republican. Avocations: hiking, artist. Home and Office: 15810 143rd Ave SE Yelm WA 98597-9169

ADAMS, PETER FREDERICK, academic administrator, civil engineer; b. Halifax, N.S., Can. m. Barbara Adams, Oct. 11, 1957; 3 sons. B.Eng., N.S. Tech. Coll., 1958, M.Engr., 1961; PhD, Lehigh U., 1966. With Internat. Nickel Co. Can., 1958-59, Dominion Bridge Co., 1974-75; mem. faculty U. Alta., Edmonton, 1960-89, prof. civil engring., 1971-89; dean Faculty of Engring., 1976-84; pres. Ctr. for Frontier Engring. Research, 1984-89, Tech. U. N.S., Halifax, 1989-92, Can. Inst. Petroleum Industry Devel. (now Can. Petroleum Inst.), Edmonton, Alta., Can., 1992—; chmn. Churchill Corp., 1993—. Lectr. in field. Author: (Krentz & Kulak) Canadian Structural Steel Design, 1973, (Krentz & Kulak) Limit States Design in Structural Steel, 1977. Past pres. Aspen Gardens Community League;past chmn. Salvation Army Red Shield Appeal. Fellow Can. Soc. Civil Engring. (Sanderson award 1986), Can. Acad. Engring., Engring. Inst. Can.; mem. ASCE (A.B. Anderson award 1986), Internat. Assn. Bridge & Structural Engring. (hon.), Can. Stds. Assn., Toastmasters (past pres.). Office: Canadian Inst Petroleum 4220 98th St Edmonton AB Canada T6E 6AI

ADAMS, PHYLLIS CURL, nursing educator; b. Houston, Sept. 15, 1947; d. Kenneth H. and Helen (Phillips) Curl; m. Todd E. Adams, Aug. 28, 1982. BSN, Dillard U., 1969; MSN, Ohio State U., 1972; EdD, Tex. So. U., 1989; postmasters FNP, Tex. Woman's U., 1995. RN; cert family nurse practitioner. Charge nurse The Meth. Hosp., Houston, 1969-71, practitioner, asst. mgr., 1981—90, staff nurse, 1990—95; faculty coord. Columbus (Ohio) Tech. Inst., 1973-81; coord., asst. prof. Sch. Nursing U. Tex. Health Sci. Ctr., Houston, 1990-95, spl. asst. to pres. for Office of Campus Diversity, 1993—95; asst. prof. U. Tex. Sch. Nursing, Arlington, 1995—2001, asst. clin. prof., 2001—. FNP, Ft. Worth, 1997—2001, Cmty. Partnership of Tarrant County, Ft. Worth, 2001—; dir. FNP program U. Tex. Sch. Nursing, Arlington, 2000—. Contbr. articles to profl. jours. Mem. ANA, Am. Assn. Nurse Practitioners, Tex. Nurses Assn. (bd. dirs. 1994-95, mem. dist. 4), Minority Faculty Assn., Sickle Cell Assn. Ft. Worth (bd. dirs.), Nat. Black Orgn. Nurses, Sigma Theta Tau, Phi Delta Kappa. Avocations: frog collecting, aerobics, reading, skeet. Home: 1225 Chinkapin Pl Flower Mound TX 75028-3229 Office: U Tex-Arlington Sch Nursing PO Box 19407 411 S Nedderman Dr Arlington TX 76019 Office Phone: 817-272-2776. E-mail: pcadams@uta.edu.

ADAMS, QUENTIN MARK, neurologist; b. San Antonio, Jan. 23, 1956; s. Ronald Dean and Marjorie Loree Adams; m. Carol Louise Adams, Mar. 12, 1982; children: Melanie, Quentin, Dylan. BS in Chem. Engring., U. Tex., Austin, 1978; MD, U. Tex., San Antonio, 1985; MBA, Tex. Christian U., 2000. Diplomate Am. Bd. Neurology. Process design and computer engr. Dow Chem. Co., Freeport, Tex., 1978—81; intern in internal medicine Tex. Tech. U., Lubbock, 1985—86; resident in neurology U. Tex. Southwestern Med. Ctr., Dallas, 1986—89, clin. assoc. prof., 1989—; neurologist Arlington, Tex., 1989—. Med. dir. Rehab. Care Therapy Ctr., Arlington, 1992—96; healthcare analyst EIF at Tex. Christian U., 1999—2000; clinic attending, neurology U. Tex., Southwestern, 1989—; guest spkr. Peripheral Neuropathy Assn., Ft. Worth, 1999—2001. Contbr. articles to profl. jours. Asst. coach Colleyville (Tex.) Baseball, 1996—, Colleyville Basketball. Recipient 1st place rsch. award, Tex. Neurol. Soc., 1987. Mem.: Am. Acad. Clin. Neurophysiology, Nat. Headache Found., Am. Acad. Neurology. Avocations: reading, coaching, sculpture museums, security analysis. Office: 3150 Matlock Rd # 405 Arlington TX 76015

ADAMS, RANALD TREVOR, JR., retired air force officer; b. Ft. Sill, Okla., Mar. 7, 1925; s. Ranald Trevor and Mary (King) A.; m. Jeannette Malloy Chichester, May 3, 1947; children: Ranald T. III, Mary M., Jeannette M. Student, Va. Poly. Inst., 1941-43; BS, U.S. Mil. Acad., 1946; MS, George Washington U., 1966. Commd. 2d lt. USAF, 1946, advanced through grades to lt. gen., 1978; served in Korean conflict, 1950-51; served in Vietnam, 1968-69; comdr. 408 Fighter Group, 1969-71; asst. dep. chief staff ops. N.Am. Air Def. Command, 1971-73; comdr. 26 N.Am. Air Def. Command Region/Air Div. Luke AFB, Ariz., 1973-74; dep. insp. gen. inspection and safety Norton AFB, Calif., 1974-77; dir. InterAm. Def. Coll., Ft. McNair, D.C., 1977-78; chmn. Interam. Def. Bd., Washington, 1978-81, ret., 1981; cons., 1981-91. Decorated Legion of Merit, Meritorious Service medal, D.S.M., D.F.C., Air medal. Mem. Air Force Assn., Order Daedalians (flight capt. 1973) Home and Office: 1002 Emerald Dr Alexandria VA 22308-2626

ADAMS, REID C., JR., lawyer; b. Kinston, NC, June 26, 1956; married; 2 children. BA cum laude, Wake Forest U., 1978; JD cum laude, Wake Forest Sch. Law, 1981. Bar: NC 1981, admitted to practice: US Dist. Ct. (Middle and Western Districts, NC), Dist. Ct. Appeals (4th & 11th Circuits). Clerk Morris, Rochelle, and Duke, Kinston, NC, 1979, Divsn. Youth Svcs., NC Dept. Human Resources, Raleigh, NC, 1980; assoc. Nichols Caffrey Hill Evans & Murrelle, Greenboro, NC, 1981—85; practice group leader, insurance, govt. & tort litig. sect. Womble Carlyle Sandridge & Rice, PLLC, Winston-Salem, NC, mem. pro bono com. Pres. bd. dirs. Legal Aid Soc. of NW NC, 1996—2001; bd. dir. Legal Svcs. NC, exec. com. chair, grievance com. Hankins Scholar, Wake Forest U. Mem.: ABA (mem. pro bono adv. com.), NC Bar Assn. (mem. litig. sect.), Forsyth County Bar Assn. (liasion, vol. lawyers program, chair, pro bono com.). Avocations: golf, reading. Mailing: Womble Carlyle Sandridge & Rice PLLC PO Box 84 Winston Salem NC 27102 Office: Womble Carlyle Sandridge & Rice PLLC One West 4th St Winston Salem NC 27101 Office Phone: 336-721-3674. Office Fax: 336-733-8333. Business E-Mail: radams@wcsr.com.

ADAMS, REX, dean; m. Ellen Cates; three children. BA in Polit. Sci. magna cum laude, Duke U., 1962. Govt. rels. trainee Mobil Internat., London, 1965-70; dir. employee and govt. rels. Mobil Oil, Libya, 1970-72, pers. dir. European ops. London, 1972-75; mgr. recruitment and placement Mobil Oil Corp., 1975-79, mgr. employee rels. exploration and producing divsn., 1979-84; v.p. employee rels. Mobil Corp., 1984-88; v.p. adminstrn. Mobil Oil Corp. and Mobil Corp., 1988-96; prof. bus. adminstrn., dean Fuqua Sch. Bus. Duke U., 1996-2001, dean emeritus, 2001—. Bd. dirs. PBS, AMVESCO PLC, Vintage Pet., Alleghany Corp., Vera Inst. Justice; trustee Com. for Econ. Devel. and Woods Holes Oceanog. Instn.; former trustee Duke U. and Va. Union U. Rhodes scholar Merton Coll., Oxford U., 1962. Fellow Nat. Acad. Human Resources (disting.); mem. Phi Beta Kappa. Office: 1900 Faucette Mill Rd Hillsborough NC 27278

ADAMS, RICHARD GEORGE, writer; b. Newbury, Berkshire, Eng., May 9, 1920; s. Evelyn George Beadon and Lilian Rosa (Button); m. Elizabeth Acland, Sept. 26, 1949; children: Juliet Vera Lucy, Rosamond Beatrice Elizabeth. MA, Oxford U., 1948. With Brit. Home Higher Civil Svc. Ministry Housing and Local Govt., 1948-74; asst. sec. Dept. Environ., 1968-74. Writer-in-residence U. Fla., 1975, Hollins Coll., 1976. Author: Watership Down, 1972 (Guardian award Children's Lit. 1972, Carnegie Medal 1972), Shardik, 1974, (with Max Hooper) Nature Through the Seasons, 1975, The Tyger Voyage, 1976, The Adventures and Brave Deeds of the Ship's Cat on the Spanish Main: Together with the Most Lamentable Losse of the Alcestis and Triumphant Firing of the Port of Chagres, 1977, The Plague Dogs, 1977, (with Max Hooper) Nature Day and Night, 1978, Introduction to Faithful Ruslan, 1979, The Unbroken Web: Stories and Fables, 1980, Voyage Through the Antarctic, 1982, The Girl in a Swing, 1980, Maia, 1985, The Bureaucats, 1985, A Nature Diary, 1985, The Legend of Te Tuna, 1986, Traveller, 1988, The Day Gone By, 1990, Tales from Watership Down, 1996, The Outlandish Knight, 2000; editor, contbr. Occasional Poets, 1986. Served with Brit. Army, 1940—46. Fellow: Royal Soc. Lit.; mem.: Royal Soc. for Prevention of Cruelty to Animals (former pres.). Mem. Ch. Of Eng. Home: 26 Church St Whitchurch Hampshire England

ADAMS, ROBERT BARRY, pathologist; b. Birmingham, Ala., July 24, 1928; m. Jean Glaze, Sept. 2, 1950; children: Jeanmarie, Robert Barry Jr. BS in Chemistry & Biology, Birmingham So., 1950; MD, Med. Coll. Ala., 1956. Rotating intern Lloyd Noland Hosp., Fairfield, Ala., 1956-57; pathology resident Bapt. Meml. Hosp., Memphis, 1957-59; mem. med. corps U.S. Army, San Antonio, 1959-61; instr., prof. Med. Coll. Ala., Birmingham, 1961-64; dir. pathology lab. Bapt. Med. Ctr., Montgomery, Ala., 1964-79, St. Margaret's Hosp., Montgomery, Ala., 1972—; med. dir. Ala. Reference Lab., Montgomery, 1972—, Ala. Reference Lab./LabSouth, Montgomery, 1995—. Pres. Ala. Assn. Pathologists, Birmingham, 1969-71, Med. Coll. Ala. Alumni Assn., 1993-95; edn. leader Sch. Med. Tech. Bapt. Hosp., St. Margaret's Hosp., Auburn U. Montgomery, Ala. Reference Lab., 1968—, Pres., bd. trustees Judson Coll., Marion, Ala., 1985-88; pres. Nat. Coll. Ala. Alumni, Birmingham, 1993-95; sec.-treas. Montgomery County Med. Soc., 1990-92. Recipient Algernon Sidney Sullivan award Judson Coll., 1985. Mem. AMA, Am. Soc. Clin. Pathology, Am. Assn. Blood Banks (inspector 1963-86), Am. Soc. Nuc. Medicine, Coll. Am. Pathologists, Med. Soc. Montgomery County, Cornerstone Soc., Alpha Omega Alpha. Baptist. Office: Lab Corp Am 543 S Hull St Montgomery AL 36104-4609

ADAMS, ROBERT BRERETON, lawyer; AB, Boston Coll., 1961; JD, NYU, 1965. Bar: N.Y. 1965. Dep. county atty. Nassau County, N.Y., 1965-67; assoc. Cullen & Dykman, 1968-70; v.p., asst. gen. counsel Chase Manhattan Corp., 1971-86, sr. v.p., dep. gen. counsel N.Y.C., 1986-97; ptnr. Kelley, Drye & Warren, N.Y.C., 1998—. Office: Kelley Drye & Warren 101 Park Ave Fl 29 New York NY 10178-0062 Office Phone: 212-808-7710. Business E-Mail: radams@kelleydrye.com.

ADAMS, ROBERT EDWARD, journalist; b. Geneseo, Ill., Apr. 27, 1941; s. Horace Mann and Florence (Beidelman) A. BS, U. Ill., 1963. Reporter Champaign-Urbana Courier, 1962-64; reporter, city staff St. Louis Post-Dispatch, 1966-72, Washington corr., 1972-93, asst. Washington bur. chief, 1981-83, Washington bur. chief, 1983-93. Washington commentator Sta. KMOX, St. Louis, 1984—; founding mem. St. Louis Journalism Rev., 1970 Recipient reporting award Nat. Civil Service League, 1975, polit. reporting award Lincoln U., Jefferson City, Mo., 1984, Raymond Clapper Meml. award for Washington Corr., 1987, citation for excellence Overseas Press Club, for series on Soviet Union, 1988; co-recipient Fgn. Corr. award Overseas Press Club Am., 1984, Nat. Headliner award, 1986. Mem. Nat. Press Club, Internat. Platform Assn., Com. to Protect Journalists, Washington Ind. Writers, The Gridiron Club, Sigma Delta Chi (Outstanding Young Reporter award St. Louis chpt. 1969). Roman Catholic. Home: Apt 707 2500 Wisconsin Ave NW Washington DC 20007-4504 Office: 529 14th St NW Washington DC 20045-1000 Office Phone: 202-333-1026. Personal E-mail: adams707@earthlink.net. Business E-Mail: badams@lwv.org.

ADAMS, ROBERT JONATHAN, chemistry educator, biology educator; b. El Paso, Oct. 16, 1975; s. Gerald Clarence and Sharon Koepp Adams; m. Jennifer Leigh Bannister, May 29, 1999. BS in BioChemistry, Roberts Wesleyan Coll., 1998. Cert. tchr. N.Y. Tchr. chemistry and biology Hilton (N.Y.) H.S., 1999—. Home: 570 Blossom Rd Rochester NY 14610 Office: Hilton HS 400 East Ave Hilton NY 14468

ADAMS, ROBERT MCCORMICK, anthropologist, educator; b. Chgo., July 23, 1926; s. Robert McCormick and Janet (Lawrence) Adams; m. Ruth Salzman Skinner, July 24, 1953 (dec.); 1 child, Megan. PhB, U. Chgo., 1947, MA, 1952, PhD, 1956; DSc (hon.), U. Pitts., 1985, Dartmouth Coll., 1989; LHD (hon.), Hunter Coll., CUNY, 1986, Coll. William and Mary, 1989, Brandeis U., 1992; LD (hon.), Harvard U., 1992; PhD (hon.), U. Copenhagen, 2002. Archaeol. field tng. in, Jarmo, Iraq, 1950—51, Mexico, 1953; field studies history irrigation and urban settlement, 1956—77; Homewood prof. dept. anthropology and near ea. studies, 1956—77, 1956—77; reconnaissance and excavation ancient Mayan settlement patterns Chiapas, Mexico, 1958—61; mem. faculty dept. anthropology, Oriental Inst. U. Chgo., 1955—84, assoc. prof. Oriental Inst., 1961—62, prof., 1962—84, dir. Oriental Inst., 1962—68, 1981—83, dean div. social scis., 1970—74, 1979—80, provost, 1982—84; sec. Smithsonian Instn., Washington, 1984—94; Homewood prof. dept. anthropology and near ea. studies Johns Hopkins U., 1984—94. Adj. prof. U. Calif., San Diego, 1993—; fellow Inst. for Advanced Study, Berlin, 1995—96; resident dir. Baghdad Sch., Am. Schs. Oriental Rsch., 1968—69; chmn. assembly behavioral and social scis. NRC, 1972—76, chmn. commn. on behavioral and social scis. and edn., 1987—93. Author: The Evolution of Urban Society, 1966; author: (with H.J. Nissen) The Uruk Countryside, 1972; author: Heartland of Cities, 1981, Paths of Fire: An Anthropologist's Inquiry into Western Technology, 1996; editor (with C.H. Kraeling): City Invincible: A Symposium on Urbanization and Cultural Development in the Ancient Near East, 1960; editor: (with C.S. Schelling) Corners of a Foreign Field, 1979; editor: (with N.J. Smelser and D.J. Treiman) Behavioral and Social Science Research: A National Resource, 1982; editor: Trends in American and German Higher Education, 2002. Trustee Nat. Opinion Rsch. Ctr., 1970—94, Nat. Humanities Ctr., 1976—83, Russell Sage Found., 1978—91, Santa Fe Inst., 1984—, Am. U. Beirut, 1989—94, Morehouse Coll., 1989—94, German Am. Acad. Coun., 1993—99. Recipient UCLA medal, 1989, Great Cross of Vasco Nuñez de Balboa, Panama, 1993, Gold medal, Am. Inst. Archaeology, 2002, award of merit, Field Mus., 2003. Fellow: AAAS, Mid. East Studies Assn., Am. Acad. Arts and Scis., Iraqi Acad. (assoc.), Am. Anthrop. Assn.; mem.: NAS, Coun. Fgn. Rels., Am. Philos. Soc., German Archaeol. Inst., Soc. Am. Archaeology (Disting. Svc. award 1996), Sigma Xi. Business E-Mail: rmadams@ucsd.edu.

ADAMS, ROBERT T., lawyer; b. 1954; BA in Economics, Colgate U.; MS in Economics, SUNY, Stonybrook; JD, Pace U., 1986. Bar: NY 1987, Conn. 1987, US Dist. Ct. So. Dist. NY, NY Dist. Ct. Ea. Dist. NY. Ptnr. Wilson, Elser, Moskowitz, Edelman & Dicker LLP, White Plains, NY. Mem.: ABA (entertainment & sports law sect.), NY State Bar Assn. (entertainment & sports law sect.). Office: Wilson Elser Moskowitz Edelman & Dicker LLP 3 Gannett Dr White Plains NY 10604 Office Phone: 914-323-7000 ext. 4201. Office Fax: 914-323-7001. Business E-Mail: adamsr@wemed.com.

ADAMS, ROBERT WAUGH, state agency administrator, economist, educator; b. Johnstown, Pa., Oct. 26, 1936; s. Robert Waugh and Mary Louise (Pyle) A.; m. Karen Day, June 13, 1964; children: Robert W. and Tara Anne Adams Mason. BS in Acctg., Pa. State U., 1958; MBA, U. Louisville, 1967. Acct., comptr., v.p. lending Citizens Fidelity Bank, Louisville, 1959-77; dir. fin., planning, and from dep. exec. dir. to exec. dir. Ky. Housing Corp., Frankfort, 1977-96; owner Adams Consulting Co., Louisville, 1996—2004, ret., 2004. Past pres. Bank Adminstrv. Inst., 1966, Planning Exec. Inst., 1970, Fin. Exec. Inst., 1974. Bd. dirs. Habitat for Humanity, Ctr. for Non Profit Excellence. Capt. U.S. Army Infantry, 1958-62. Mem. Louisville Boat Club (past pres.). Republican. Roman Catholic. Home and Office: 5210 Tamerlane Rd Louisville KY 40207-1160

ADAMS, ROGER C., lawyer; b. 1944; married. BA cum laude, Bowdoin Coll., 1966; JD, Boston Coll., 1969. Bar: 1969. With criminal divsn. US Dept. Justice, 1972-93, counsel to dep. atty. gen., 1993-97, acting pardon atty., 1997—98, pardon atty., 1998—. Mem. Maine Bar Assn. Office: US Dept Justice Office Pardon Atty 500 1st St NW Ste 400 Washington DC 20530-0001*

ADAMS, RONALD G., elementary school educator; b. Boston, July 7, 1948; s. Russell Lawrence and Alice Gertrude (LeCorn) A.; m. Patricia Marie Sullivan, Mar. 15, 1950; children: Ronald Patrick, Michael Joseph, Kevin Russell. BS, U. Mass., 1975; MEd, Cambridge Coll., 1992. Cert. tchr. English, reading, adult basic edn., Mass. Tchr. English Quincy (Mass.) Pub. Sch., 1975-81, tchr. grade 7, 1983—; tchr. grade 7/8 Lincoln (Mass.) Pub. Schs., 1981-83. Mem. adv. bd. Mass. Carnegie Coun.: Turning Points, Dept. Edn., Mass., 1991-93; founding mem. Internat. Space Educators Coun., Huntsville, Ala., 1992-93; on-air moderator PBS Annenberg documentary series Primary Sources in Teaching American History, 2001. Prodr. TV documentary Quincy Shipbuilding, 1989 (award Dept. Edn. 1990); co-author: (booklet) Not Me, I Can Handle It, 1985 (Gov.'s award 1986); cons. TV series A Century of Women, TBS, 1994 (A&E Cable award 1992). Founder Winnie the Welder Day, City of Quincy, 1991-93; coach Houghs Neck Women's Softball League, Quincy, 1980-85; vol. Cub Scouts, Weymouth, Mass., 1989-93; mem. edn. steering com. Amnesty Internat., Somerville, Mass., 1989-93; mem. adv. bd. U.S. Naval Shipbldg. Mus., Quincy, 1992-93. Recipient Nat. Ednl. award Cable in Classroom, 1992, George Washington medal Freedoms Found., 1992, Young Prodr.'s award Continental Cablevision, 1992, A World of Difference Tchr. award Anti-Defamation League, 1994, Giraffe award, Reebok Internat. Youth-in-Action Human Rights award, 1995, Minn. Advocates for Human Rights award, 1997, Domestic Partnership award US AID, 1998, Anti-defamation League's Global Activism award 1998, 99, Darryl Williams Human Rights Leadership award Northeastern U., 1999, Bearer of Light award Union of Am. Hebrew Congregations, 1999, Hero Among Us award Boston Celtics, 2000, Global Edn. award The Peace Corps, 2000; named Tchr. of Yr., Mass. Dept. Edn., 1992, Nat. Consumers League Trumpeter award, 1998, Citizen of the Yr. 2000, Quincy Sun Newspaper. Fellow Mass. Acad. Tchrs. (history coord. 1992-93), Boston Writing Project; mem. NEA (Human and Civil Rights award 2000Applegate/Dorros Peace and Global Edn. award 2000), Nat. State Tchrs. of Yr., Nat. Coun. Social Studies, Nat. Coun. Tchrs. English, Mass. Tchrs. Assn. (Human Rights award 1991), Quincy Edn. Assn. (exec. bd. 1980-81). Avocation: football. Home: 8 Coolidge Ave Weymouth MA 02188-3605 Office: Broad Meadows Middle Sch 50 Calvin Rd Quincy MA 02169-2516

ADAMS, SCOTT, cartoonist; b. Windham, NY; s. Paul and Virginia Adams. BA in Econs., Hartwick Coll., 1979; MBA, Univ. Calif., Berkeley. Cert. hypnotist. Bank teller, computer programmer; engr. Pacific Bell, San Ramon, Calif., 1986—95; cartoonist, Dilbert United Features Syndicate, 1989—. Cartoon, Dilbert, syndicated in 1,550 newspapers in 35 countries; author: The Dilbert Principle: Cubicle's-Eye View of Bosses, Meetings, Management Fads, and Other Workplace Afflictions, 1996, Dogbert's Top Secret Management Handbook, 1996, The Dilbert Future: Thriving on Business Stupidity in the 21st Century, 1997, Random Acts Of Management, 2000, Dilbert and the Way of the Weasel: A Guide to Outwitting Your Boss, Your Coworkers, and the Other Pants-Wearing Ferrets in Your Life, 2002, Words You Don't Want to Hear During Your Annual Review, 2003. Office: c/o United Media 200 Madison Ave New York NY 10016-3903

ADAMS, SCOTT LESLIE, accountant; b. Seattle, Nov. 23, 1955; s. Brock and Mary Elizabeth (Scott) A.; m. Crystal Hood, Aug. 7, 1978; children: Brock, Justin, Betsy, Brooke. BS in Acctg. magna cum laude, Jones Coll., 1984. CPA. Dist. dir. The Scott Co., Washington, 1972-75; pres. Slade Corp., Greenbelt, Md., 1977-80; shift supr. U.S. Ho. Reps., Washington, 1977-82; acct. Comprehensive Bus. Svcs., Jacksonville, Fla., 1984-85; prin. Contemporary Bus. Svcs., Jacksonville, 1985—, Tax Consultants, P.A., 1991—. Pres. Small Bus. Assocs., Jacksonville; v.p. Adams Mgmt. Svcs. Chmn. fin. com, chmn. deacons Westside Bapt. Ch.; treas. Jacksonville West Camp, Gideons U.S.A., 1987—. Mem. AICPA, Nat. Soc. Pub. Accts., Nat. Soc. Tax Practitioners, Fla. Inst. CPA's, Nat. Assn. Accts., Small Bus. Network, Jacksonville C. of C. Republican. Avocations: swimming, tennis. Home: 4984 Ortega Forest Dr Jacksonville FL 32210-8112 Office: Contemporary Bus Svcs 4070 Herschel St Ste 1 Jacksonville FL 32210-2249 E-mail: scott@cbsjax.com.

ADAMS, SHARON BUTLER, minister, philosopher, researcher; b. Chgo., Oct. 30, 1949; d. Lionel Augustus and Clara Bernice Butler; m. Vernon McFadden Jr., June 13, 1968 (div. Oct. 1977); children: Vernon McFadden III, Aleceia Marie McFadden. Ordained min. African-Am. Universal Ministry. Engrng. technician Servitron, Baton Rouge, 1976—78; instr. Coml. Bus. Coll, Baton Rouge, 1978—80; project mgr. Minority Engrs. La., Baton Rouge, 1980—86; cleric adminstr. Baton Rouge African-Am. Cath. Cong., 1997—98, cleric adminstr., So. Region Baton Rouge, 1998—99; interim pastor Imani Temple, Baton Rouge, 1998—99; pastor Ch. of the Living God, Baton Rouge, 1999—2002. Advisor Kwanzaa celebration A-A Universal Apostolic Ministry, Baton Rouge, 1999—; dir. Females in Ministry, Baton Rouge, 1999—; spiritual adv. Jazz and Heritage Festival, New Orleans, 2001—; cons. NAACP, New Orleans, 2001; advisor La. Dept. of Environ. Quality, 1990; owner ADHD-Alarm, 2004—. Author to newspapers and jours. Panelist New Orleans Jazz & Heritage Festival, 2002, Jazz Festival, 2003; bd. dirs. Cmty. Devel. Project, Baton Rouge, 1998, La. Dem. Project, Baton Rouge, 2000. Recipient Kwanzaa Celebration award, Mayor & Metr. Coun. of Baton Rouge, 2001. Mem.: Internat. Black Environ. & Econ. Justice, Soc. Am. Music. Avocation: reading, sewing, singing and playing musical instruments. Office Phone: 225-383-6479. E-mail: asharon@bellsouth.net.

ADAMS, THOMAS LAWRENCE, lawyer; b. Jersey City, Apr. 14, 1948; s. Lawrence Ignatius and Dorothy Tekla (Halgas) A. BS, N.J. Inst. Tech., 1969; JD, Seton Hall U., 1975. Bar: N.J. 1975, U.S. Dist. Ct. N.J. 1975, U.S. Patent Office 1975, N.Y. 1976. Sys. engr. Grumman Aerospace, Bethpage, N.Y., 1969-71; sr. engr. Weston Instruments, Newark, 1971-74; mem. patent staff RCA, Princeton, NJ, 1974-75; corp. atty. Otis Elevator, N.Y.C., 1975-77; ptnr. Goebel & Adams, Morristown, NJ, 1978-80, Behr & Adams, Morristown and Edison, NJ, 1981—2000. Mem. Seton Hall Law Rev. Mem. Livingston (N.J.) Twp. Coun., 1985-88, dep. mayor, 1987; mem. Livingston Environ. Commn., 1984-87; chmn. Livingston Rep. County Com., 1992-98. Mem. N.J. Patent Law Assn., Trial Attys. N.J., N.J. Bar Assn. (chmn. patent, trademark, copyright law and unfair competion 1991), Morris County Bar Assn., KC (grand knight 1980), Tau Beta Pi, Eta Kappa Nu. Office Phone: 973-463-0100. Business E-Mail: adams@newidea.com.

ADAMS, THOMAS LYNCH, JR., lawyer; b. Fayette County, Ky., Nov. 22, 1941; s. Thomas Lynch and Amanda (Keith) A.; m. Anne Randolph, Aug. 13, 1974 (div. 1992); children: Thomas Lynch III, Randolph T., Alexander K., Andrew D. BA in History, U. Va., 1963; JD, Vanderbilt U., 1970. Bar: Ky. 1970, DC 1970, Tenn. 1970. Appellate atty. U.S. Dept. Justice, Washington, 1970-72; minority counsel U.S. Senate Commerce Com., Washington, 1972-75; legal counsel SBA, Washington, 1975; asst. gen. counsel FTC, Washington, 1975-77; govt. rels. Rep. Steel Corp., Washington, 1977-83; dep. gen. counsel U.S. EPA, Washington, 1983-86, asst. adminstr., presdl. appointee, 1986-89; ptnr. Dechert, Price & Rhoads, 1989-93; environ. dir. Internat. Paper, 1993; counsel to pres. America's Clean Water Found., 1994-95; of counsel Perkins Coie, Washington, 1995-2000; pres. Oxygenated Fuels Assn., Washington, 2000—02, sr. advisor dept. energy, asst. sec. environ. mgmt., 2002—. Lt. (j.g.) USNR, 1963-67. Mem. ABA, Ky. Bar Assn., DC Bar Assn., Met. Club, Beta Theta Pi. Office Phone: 202-586-3179.

ADAMS, THOMAS MERRITT, lawyer; b. St. Louis, Sept. 27, 1935; s. Galen Edward and Chloe (Merritt) A.; m. Sarah McCardell Davis, June 6, 1959; children: Mark Merritt, John Harrison, William Shields, Thomas Bondurant. AB, Washington U., St. Louis, 1956, JD, 1960; postgrad., London Sch. Econs., 1957; LLM, George Washington U., 1966. Bar: Mo. 1960, Calif. 1971. Atty. SEC, Washington, 1964-66; asst. dir., asst. gen. counsel Investment Bankers Assn., Washington, 1966-68; pres. Transamerica Investment Mgmt., 1969-80; ptnr. Lanning Adams & Peterson, 1980—. Author: State and Local Pension Funds, 1968; contbr. articles to profl. jours. Chmn. Salina (Kans.) Community Ambassador program, 1961. Served to capt. USAF, 1960-63. Decorated Air Force Commendation medal. Mem. Phi Beta Kappa. Episcopalian. Office: Lanning Adams & Peterson 11777 San Vicente Blvd #750 Los Angeles CA 90049-5067

ADAMS, THOMAS TILLEY, lawyer; b. Orchard Park, N.Y., Oct. 9, 1929; s. Floyd Tilley and Clara Elizabeth (Potter) A.; m. Virginia Rives Smith, Sept. 1, 1956; children: Julia, Janet, Claire, Douglas. BA, U. Buffalo, 1951; JD, Cornell U., 1957. Bar: N.Y. 1957, U.S. Ct. Appeals (2d cir.) 1962, U.S. Supreme Ct. 1962, Conn. 1964. Tchr. Lake Shore Cen. Sch., Angola, NY, 1953-54; assoc. Davies, Hardy & Schenck, N.Y.C., 1957-63; prin. Gregory & Adams P.C., Wilton, Conn., 1963—2001, of counsel, 2002—. Lectr. Cornell U. Law Sch., Ithaca, N.Y., 1962-65, emeritus mem. adv. coun., 1990—; adj. assoc. prof. law Fordham U., N.Y.C., 1973-76; adviser Dana Fund Internat. and Comparative Legal Studies, Toledo, 1976-91; assoc. bd. dirs. Union Trust Co., Stamford, Conn., 1982-94; mem. adv. bd. Norwalk Savs. Soc., 1993-97. Town atty. Town of Wilton, 1966-71; pres. Five Town Found., Norwalk, Conn., 1983-85, trustee, 1989-91; chmn. bldg. com. Wilton High Sch., 1966; bd. dirs. Woodcock Nature Ctr., Wilton-Ridgefield, Conn., 1997-99, trustee Norwalk Hosp., 1974, Wilton Library Assn., Inc., 2000-2001, Elizabeth Raymond Ambler Charitable Trust, 2004—. Capt. USAF, 1951—53, Korea. Recipient Silver Beaver award Boy Scouts Am., 1980, Disting. Alumnus award Cornell Law Sch., 1990. Mem. ABA, Am. Judicature Soc. (dir. 1991-92), Norwalk-Wilton Bar Assn. (pres. 1990), Stamford-Norwalk Regional Bar Assn. (bd. dirs. 1991-93), Conn. Bar Assn. (ethics com. 1970-75, 92-93, mem. coun. bar pres.'s 1988-90), N.Y. Bar Assn., Assn. Bar City of N.Y., Silver Spring Country Club (gov. 1998-2004, asst. sec. 2003-04), Algonquin Roundtable of 21st Century, Cornell Club (N.Y.), Phi Delta Phi. Episcopalian. Home: 55 Deer Run Rd Wilton CT 06897-1204 also: Rogers Rock Clb Ticonderoga NY 12883 Office: Gregory & Adams PC 190 Old Ridgefield Rd Wilton CT 06897-4023 Office Phone: 203-762-9000. Office Fax: 203-834-1628.

ADAMS, THOMAS WALTON, corrections official; b. Midland, Mich., Apr. 15, 1947; s. Lawrence Walton and Elizabeth (Miller) A.; m. Karen Lynn Perry. BS with honors, Mich. State U., 1973, MS, 1987. Probation agt. 75th Dist. Ct., Midland, 1973—2003; cmty. corrections coord. Midland County, 2003—. Mem. Midland County Alcohol Svcs. Bd., 1975-78, Midland-Gladwin County Community Mental Health Bd., 1978-87, chmn. 1980-82; mem. allocation panel Midland County United Way, 2002—; mem. adv. Mt. Pleasant Regional Ctr. for Devel. Disabiities, 1988-89; active Act 511 Bd., 1990—; adv. bd. Midland County Jail, 1991-93; bd. dirs. FACE, 1995—; mem. violence/gang task force Midland County, 1998-2004; co-chair Domestic Violence Coordinating Coun., Midland County, 2000—. Named One of Outstanding Young Men Am., 1982; recipient Liberty Bell award, Midland Bar Assn., 1983. Mem.: Am. Correctional Assn., Sigma Chi, Alpha Phi Sigma. Avocations: stereo equipment, music, photography. Office: Adult Probation Courthouse Midland MI 48640 Home: 2605 Hearthstone Cir Midland MI 48642

ADAMS, TIMOTHY D., federal agency administrator; BA, MS, U. Ky. Dep. assoc. dir. office policy and devel. Exec. Office of Pres., Washington; co-founder, mgmt. dir. G-7 Group, Washington, 1993—2000; policy dir. Bush-Cheney Presdl. Campaign, Washington, 2000; chief of staff U.S. Dept. Treasury, Washington, 2001—03, under sec. internat. affairs, 2005—. Office: US Dept Treasury 1500 Pennsylvania Ave Rm 4440 Washington DC 20220 Office Phone: 202-622-0656. Office Fax: 202-622-0417.*

ADAMS, VALENCIA I., telecommunications industry executive; b. Atlanta; BBA, Ga. State U.; postgrad. in Mgmt., Columbia U., Emory U. COO consumer svcs. BellSouth Corp., Atlanta, v.p., chief diversity officer, 2002—. Former mem. adv. coun. to pres. BellSouth Telecom. Inc.; mentor BellSouth Mentor Exch. Program; trustee Ga. Coun. on Econ. Edn.; bd. dirs. BellSouth Found., Prevent Child Abuse Ga., Possible Woman Found. Chairperson Met. Atlanta United Way Campaign, 1998. Named Woman of Yr., Women Looking Ahead News Mag., 2004; recipient Jr. Achievement Vol. award, Gov. Ga., Bus. Assoc. of Yr. award, Am. Bus. Women's Assn. Mem.: Atlanta C. of C. (life). Office: BellSouth Corp 1155 Peachtree St NE Atlanta GA 30309-3610 Office Phone: 404-249-2365.

ADAMS, VELMA M., assistant principal, consultant; b. Balt., Oct. 1, 1945; d. George and Anna Jones; m. Kenneth G. Adams, Jan. 5, 1946; 1 child, Mark. MusB in Edn., Howard U., 1968; MusM, Morgan State U., 1978; Profl. Cert. for Adminstrn. and Supervision, Queens Coll. Cert. bldg. and dist. adminstrn. N.Y., 1996. Choral and gen. music tchr. Balt. City Pub. Schs., 1968—80; vocal and gen. music tchr. Uniondale (N.Y.) Pub. Schs., 1980—99, asst. prin., 2000—; discipline supr. Lawrence Rd. Jr. High, Uniondale, 1999—2000. Second step character edn. trainer. Recipient Jenkins PTA award, PTA of Turtle Hook Mid. Sch., 1998. Mem.: ASCD, The Mid. Sch. Adminstr., Curriculum Audit Mgmt. Ctrs., Inc. (assoc.), Nassau Music Educators Assn. (life; pres.). Democrat. Episcopalian. Achievements include development of peer mediation program. Avocations: avid reader, mediation consultant, curriculum auditor, rehearsal and show pianist, computer enthusiast. Home: 71-24 Sutton Place #2 Fresh Meadows NY 11365 Office: Lawrence Rd Middle School 50 Lawrence Rd Hempstead NY 11550 Office Phone: 516-918-1503. Business E-Mail: vadams@uniondaleschools.org. E-mail: velmaa1@hotmail.com.

ADAMS, WAYNE VERDUN, pediatric psychologist, educator; b. Rhinebeck, N.Y., Feb. 24, 1945; s. John Joseph and Lorena Pearl (Munroe) A.; m. Nora Lee Swindler, June 12, 1971; children: Jennifer, Elizabeth. BA, Houghton Coll., 1966; MA, Syracuse U., 1969, PhD, 1970; postgrad., U. N.C., 1975. Diplomate Am. Bd. Profl. Psychology (hon.); lic. psychologist, N.Y., Oreg. Asst. prof. Colgate U., Hamilton, NY, 1970-75; chief psychologist Alfred I. DuPont Inst., Wilmington, Del., 1976-86; dir. divsn. psychology, dept. pediat. DuPont Hosp. for Children (formerly Alfred I. DuPont Inst.), Wilmington, 1987-99; mem. Del. Bd. Licensure in Psychology, 1983-86, bd. pres., 1986; assoc. prof. pediat. Thomas Jefferson Coll. Medicine, Phila., 1995-99; prof. psychology George Fox U., Newberg, Oreg., 1999—, chair grad. dept. clin. psychology, 2001—. Grant reviewer NIH, 1999—. Cons. editor Jour. Pediatric Psychology, 1980-83, guest reviewer, 1984—; co-author 5 nationally used psychol. tests in field; contbr. over 25 articles to profl. jours. Fellow APA, Nat. Acad. Neuropsychology; mem. Soc. Pediatric Psychology, Del. Psychol. Assn. (exec. com. 1979-82, pres. 1981-82), Oreg. Psychol. Assn. Office: George Fox U Grad Dept Clin Psychology Box 6141 414 N Meridian St Newberg OR 97132-2697 Office Phone: 503-554-2761.

ADAMS, WESTON, former diplomat, military officer, lawyer; b. Columbia, S.C., Sept. 16, 1938; s. Robert and Helen Hayes (Calhoun) A.; m. Elizabeth Nicholson Nelson, Mar. 2, 1962; children— Robert VI, Weston III, Daniel Wallace, Julian Calhoun II AB in History, U. S.C., 1960, LL.B., 1962. Bar: S.C. 1962. Research dir. S.C. Republican Orgn., Columbia, 1966-67; trust officer S.C. Nat. Bank, Columbia, 1967-70; assoc. counsel Select Com. on Crime, U.S. Ho. of Reps., Washington, 1970-71; solo practice Columbia, 1971-84, 86—; ambassador to Malawi U.S. Dept. of State, Lilongwe, 1984-86. Mem. S.C. House of Reps., 1972-74; presdl. elector U.S. Electoral Coll., S.C., 1980; del. Rep. Nat. Conv., Kansas City, Mo., 1976, New Orleans, 1988, Houston, 1992, alt. del., Detroit, 1980, San Diego, 1996; mem. diplomatic adv. com. and exec. com. bus./industry adv. com. Am. Bicentennial Presdl. Inaugural, 1989; mem. U.S. presdl. del. to inauguration of Pres. of Dominican Republic, 1982; United Nations Day Chmn. for the State of S.C., honoring its 50th Anniversary, 1995; mem. UNESCO, 1982-84. Capt. USAF, 1963—66, with US Air Force Res., 1966—73, maj. Spl. Ops. Adv. Group, 2001—, SC, brig. gen. Spl. Ops. Adv. Group, SC. Recipient Order of Palmetto, Gov. S.C., 1974. Mem. S.C. Bar, Richland County Bar Assn., U. S.C. Alumni Assn., U. South Carolina Hist. Soc., S.C. Soc. of Cincinnati, Order First Families N.C., Magna Charta Barons (Somerset chpt.), St. Andrews Soc., Soc. Colonial Wars, Huguenot Soc. of S.C., Soc. Lower Richland, Jamestowne Soc., Welcome Soc. Pa., The Society of First Families of S.C. 1670-1700, Most Venerable Order Hosp. St. John Jerusalem, Coun. Am. Ambs., Knight Grand Cross, Imperial Order of Holy Trinity (Imperial Ethiopia), Knight Grand Cross, Order of St. Michael of Wing (Portugal-Braganza), Clubs: Palmetto Columbia). Episcopalian.

ADAMS, WILBURN CLIFTON, communications educator; b. Huntsville, Ala., Feb. 14, 1943; s. Wilburn Clifton and Pauline Marie (Pennington) A.; m. Sara Ruth Shook, July 25, 1970; 1 child, Ami Rhae. BA, U. Ala., 1968; MS, Fla. State U., 1970, PhD, 1973. Asst. prof. Ctrl. Mo. State U., Warrensburg, 1972-77, assoc. prof., 1977-82, prof., 1982-99, prof., dir. of forensics, 1999-2000, prof. emeritus, 2000—. Chmn. curriculum com. Ctrl. Mo. State U., 1987—88, chmn. stds. com., 1992—93, sponsor speech comm. soc., 1979—99, co-dir. 1st nat. officiated debate tournament, 1993; vis. lectr. Fgn. Affairs Coll., Beijing, 2000—01; acad. advisor Chao Yang Culture Ctr., 2000—01; prof. U. Md. Univ. Coll.-Asia, 2001—03. Contbr. articles to profl. jours., lit. mags., and newspapers; creater games Sieze, Communication Activities Clock, timshel holiday cards. Sgt. U.S. Army, 1964-66. Named Outstanding Tchr. Speech and Theatre Assn. of Mo., 1975; receipient Podium of Honor, Ctrl. Mo. Forensics Squad, 1996. Mem. Elks (trustee 1997-99, exalted ruler 1989-90). Personal E-mail: clifton_adams@yahoo.com.

ADAMS, WILLIAM D., academic administrator; b. Pontiac, Mich., Aug. 18, 1947; s. Waldemar Harmon Adams and Charlotte Elizabeth (Drea) Rising; m. Catherine Spaulding Bruce, Oct. 10, 1993; children: Sean Douglass Vallant, Carmen Milena. BA magna cum laude, The Colo. Coll., 1972; PhD, U. Calif., Santa Cruz, 1982. Vis. asst. prof. dept. polit. sci. U. N.C., Chapel Hill, 1983—84, U. Santa Clara, Calif., 1984—85; instr. great works in western culture program Stanford U., Calif., 1985—86, program coord. great works in western culture program, 1986—88; exec. asst. to pres. Wesleyan U., Middletown, Conn., 1988—93, v.p., sec., 1993—95; pres. Bucknell U., Lewisburg, Pa., 1995—2000, Colby Coll., Waterville, Maine, 2000—. Contbr. articles to profl. jours. 1st lt. U.S. Army, 1966—69. Office: Colby Coll Office of Pres 4601 Mayflower Hl Waterville ME 04901-8846 E-mail: wadams@colby.edu.

ADAMS, WILLIAM HENSLEY, ecologist, educator; b. Nashville, Aug. 14, 1929; s. William Hensley and Mary Pauline (Vaughn) A.; children: Deska Lee, Norma Dee, Anita Rice, Patricia Lynn; m. Mary Lou Adams, 1999. AB, U. Tenn., 1951; postgrad., U. Okla., 1951, Tulane U., 1953-54; MS, La. State U., 1956; PhD, Auburn U., 1959. Grad. research asst. Auburn U., 1956-59; sr. research biologist Tenn. Game and Fish Commn., 1959-60; chmn. dept. biology, prof. biology Tenn. Wesleyan Coll., 1960-64, dean Coll. Arts and Scis.; prof. biology Tenn. Technol. U., Cookeville, 1964-66; with div. pre-coll. edn. in sci. NSF, 1966-68, div. undergrad. edn. in sci., 1969-73, div. higher edn. in sci., 1973-75, div. sci. edn. devel. and research, 1975-77, div. sci. improvement, 1977-81; cons., 1981—; pres. BIADA Constrn. Devel. Co. and Empire Realty Investment Co., Vienna, Va., 1990-92; broker ERA Real Estate, Hilton Head, SC, 1992—. Mem. NSF Research Participation for Coll. Tchrs. Highlands Biol. Sta., 1961, NSF Summer Inst. Radiation Biology Oak Ridge Inst. Nuclear Studies, 1961, NSF Summer Inst. Comparative Anatomy Harvard, 1962, NSF Summer Inst. Marine Biology Duke Marine Lab., 1963, NSF-Tenn. Acad. Sci. Vis. Scientist Program, 1962-66; dir. NSF Coop. Coll.-Sch. Sci. Program, 1963-65; mem. Commn. Undergrad. Edn. in Biol. Scis. Southeastern Regional Conf., 1965, Advanced Placement Reader in Biology, 1965; Oak Ridge Inst. Nuclear Scis. Radiation Biology Conf., 1965 Mem. Savanah River Site Citizens Adv. Bd. Served to lt. col. Med. Service Corps, USAF, 1951-53, 68-69. Recipient Sigma Xi-Research Engring. Soc. Am. grant-in-aid, 1960-61, Tenn. Wesleyan Coll. Faculty award, 1962, Tenn. Technol. U. faculty research grant, 1966 Fellow Explorers Club; mem. Am. Soc. Mammalogists (honorarium 1959), Am. Ornithologists Union, Cooper Ornithol. Soc., Wilson Ornithol. Soc., Wildlife Soc. Home: 4 Field Sparrow Ct Hilton Head Island SC 29926-1881 Office: 840 Wm Hilton Pkwy Hilton Head Island SC 29928 Business E-Mail: adamshhi@hargray.com. *Increasingly, people in positions of responsibility are abdicating their concomitant role as respected leaders and thereby failing to set good examples for young people to follow, especially at a time when they need high standards for self-emulation. Therefore I challenge young people to set forceful leadership as their highest personal goal in life and remember, as I have, that attainment of this goal will require the stamina necessary to remount their white chargers each time and no matter how often they are unseated.*

ADAMS, WILLIAM ROGER, historian, consultant; b. Mpls., Nov. 4, 1935; s. Jacob Anthony and Clara Louise (Jordan) A.; m. LaVonne May Turgeon, June 24, 1961; children: James Jacob, April Louise. BA, U. Minn., 1961, MA, 1967; PhD, Fla. State U., 1974. Analyst USIS, 1964-69; asst. prof. history Fla. State U., 1972-75; exec. dir. Fla. Bicentennial Commn., 1975-77; dir. Historic St. Augustine (Fla.) Preservation Bd., 1977-85. Pres., prin. cons. Historic Property Assocs.; dir. City of St. Augustine Dept. Hist. Preservation, 1999—; bd. dirs. Fla. Trust Historic Preservation, 1979-81, Fla. Hist. Soc., 1980-88. Served with AUS, 1955-57. Office: Historic Property Assocs PO Box 1002 Saint Augustine FL 32085-1002 Personal E-mail: hpa9@aol.com.

ADAMSON, DAN KLINGLESMITH, retired science association executive; b. Vernon, Tex., Oct. 12, 1939; s. Earl Larkin and Edith (Klinglesmith) A.; m. Eva Diane Pope, Aug. 18, 1962; children: Larkin, Rebecca, Amy, Sarah Student, U. Mo., 1958-59; BA in History, Southwestern U., Georgetown, Tex., 1962. Tchr. pub. schs., Jefferson County, Colo., 1962-64; asst. dir. Soc. Petroleum Engrs., Dallas, 1964-67, editor jour., 1967-71, gen. mgr., 1972-79, exec. dir., 1979—2001. Mem. Am. Soc. Assn. Execs., Council Engrng. Sci. Soc. Execs. Republican. Methodist. E-mail: dadamson@spemail.org.

ADAMSON, GEOFFREY DAVID, endocrinologist, surgeon; b. Ottawa, Ont., Can., Sept. 16, 1946; came to U.S., 1978, naturalized, 1986; s. Geoffrey Peter Adamson and Anne Marian Allan; m. Rosemary C. Oddie, Apr. 28, 1973; children: Stephanie, Rebecca, Eric. BSc with honors, Trinity Coll., Toronto, Can., 1969; MD, U. Toronto, 1973. Diplomate Am. Bd. Ob-Gyn., Am. Bd. Laser Surgery; cert. Bd. Reproductive Endocrinology. Resident in ob-gyn. Toronto Gen. Hosp., 1973-77, fellow in ob-gyn., 1977-78; fellow reproductive endocrinology Stanford (Calif.) U. Med. Ctr., 1978-80; practice medicine specializing in infertility Los Gatos, Calif., 1980-84; instr. Stanford U. Sch. Medicine, 1980-84, clin. asst. prof., 1984-92, clin. assoc. prof., 1992-95, clin. prof., 1995—; assoc. clin. prof. Sch. Medicine U. Calif., San Francisco, 1992—; founder, chmn., CEO Advanced Reproductive Care Inc., Palo Alto, Calif., 1997—. Tech. adviser WHO, 2003—. Editor: (textbook) Endoscopic Management of Gynecologic Disease, 1996, Modern Management of Endometriosis, 2005; mem. editl. bd. Can. Doctor mag., 1977—83, Jour. Am. Assn. Gynecol. Laparoscopists, 1996—, Fertility and Sterility, 2000—03, mem. editl. adv. bd. Mid. East Fertility Soc., 2004—, mem. editl. bd. others; assoc. editor: Mid. E. Fertility Soc., 2004—. Fellow, Ont. Ministry of Health, 1977—78. Fellow ACS, Royal Coll. Surgeons Can., Am. Coll. Ob-Gyns.; mem. AAAS, AMA, Am. Assn. Gynecol. Laparoscopists (adv. bd., bd. trustees, sec., treas. 2002-03, v.p. 2003-04, exec. com. 2002—, v.p. 2003-04, pres. 2004-05), Am. Soc. Reproductive Medicine (com. mem., bd. dirs. 1997-99, 2000-03, exec. com., 2002-04), Soc. Reproductive Endocrinologists (charter), Soc. Reproductive Surgeons (charter, bd. dirs., sec., treas., v.p., pres., past pres.), Soc. Assisted Reproductive Tech. (treas., dir., v.p., pres., past pres. bd. dirs. 1991—), Nat. Coalition Oversight of Assisted Reproductive Technicians (vice-chair 2001-03, chair 2003-05), Internat. Com. Monitoring Assisted Reproductive Techs. (2000-), Internat. Fedn. Fertility Socs. (audit com. 2001—), Pacific Coast Reproductive Soc. (dir., sec., v.p., pres., past pres.), Pacific NW Ob-Gyn Soc. (hon. life), Pacific Coast Ob-Gyn. Soc., Soc. Gynecologic Surgeons, San Francisco Gynecol. Soc. (past pres.), Soc. for Gynecologic Investigation, Bay Area Reproductive Endocrinologists Soc. (founding pres., hon. life), Gynecol. Laser Soc., N.Y. Acad. Scis., Shufelt Gynecol. Soc., Peninsula Gynecol. Soc. (past pres.), Calif. Med. Assn., San Mateo County Med. Assn., Santa Clara County Med. Assn., Am. Fedn. Clin. Rsch., Nat. Resolve (bd. dirs. 1991-2001, sec., treas., Lifetime Svc. award 1999), Can. Assn. Interns and Residents (hon. life, pres. 1977-79, bd. dirs. 1974-79, rep. AMA resident physician sect. 1978-79, rep. Can. Med. Protective Assn. 1975-78, rep. Can. Med. Assn. 1975-78, Disting. Svc. award 1980), Profl. Assn. Interns and Residents Ont. (bd. dirs. 1973-76, v.p. 1974-75, pres. 1975-76), Royal Coll. Physicians and Surgeons Can. (com. exams. 1977-80), Ont. Med. Assn. (sec. interns and residents sect. 1973-74). Avocations: hiking, ice hockey, skiing. Office: 540 University Ave Ste 200 Palo Alto CA 94301-1929 E-mail: gdadamson@arcfertility.com.

ADAMSON, JAMES B., retail executive; b. 1948; Various positions The Gap, 1975-84, B. Dalton Bookseller, 1984—86, Target Stores, 1986—88; exec. v.p. mktg. Revco Inc., 1988—91; various positions, CEO Burger King Corp., 1991-95; chmn., pres., CEO Advantica Restaurant Group, Spartanburg, SC, 1995—2001; chmn, CEO Kmart Corp., 2002—03.

ADAMSON, JEROME DALE, JR., art dealer, consultant; b. Glendale, Calif., July 14, 1944; m. Gayle Harriet Guptill, June 22, 1968; children: David Scott, Laurie Anne Adamson Wippler. BA, Whittier Coll., 1967. Pvt. art dealer, collector, L.A., 1976—80; owner, dir. Adamson-Duvannes Galleries, 1980—. Co-editor (pub.): (exhbn. catalogue) With an Eye Toward Collecting California Paintings, American Art 1830-1940: A Century Observed, The California Vision: Watercolors in the California Style. Mem.: Art Dealers Assn. Calif. (pres. 2001—). Avocations: reading, antiques, travel, hiking, fishing. Office: Adamson-Duvannes Galleries 484 S San Vicente Blvd Los Angeles CA 90048 Office Phone: 323-653-1015.

ADAMSON, LYNDA G., literature educator, writer; b. Erwin, NC, Aug. 22, 1945; d. Norman E. and Irma Smith Gossett; m. Frank M. Adamson Jr., Dec. 18, 1971; children: Frank M. III, Gregory T. BA, U. NC, 1967, MA, 1968; PhD, U. Md., 1981. Prof. English Prince George's Coll., Largo, Md., 1969—2001, chair lit. dept., 1986—87, chair English dept., 1995—2001, prof. emerita, 2001—. Creator travel study program Prince George's Coll. Author: (reference work) Thematic Guide to the Modern American Novel, 2002, Recreating the Past: A Guide to American and World Historical Fiction for Children and Young Adults, 1994, A Reference Guide to Historical Fiction for Children and Young Adults, 1987, Notable Women in American History: A Guide to Biographies and Autobiographies, 1999, American Historical Fiction Novels for Adults and Young Adults, 1999, World Historical Fiction for Adults and Young Adults, 1999, Notable Women in World History: A Guide to Biographies and Autobiographies, 1999, Literature Connections to American History, K-6, 1998, Literature Connections to American History, 7-12, 1998, Literature Connections to World History, K-6, 1998, Literature Connections to World History, 7-12, 1998; contbr. articles to profl. jours. Editor dir. Woodmont Civic Assn., Arlington, Va.; vol. Arlington Ctrl. Libr.; choir Foundry United Meth. Ch., Washington, 1985—; sec., instr. Arlington Learning in Retirement Inst., 2002—04. Recipient Faculty Excellence award, Faculty Senate at Prince George's Coll., 1995; grantee, NEH, 1989, ALA, 1999—2000. Mem.: U.S. Bd. on Books for Young Adults, Internat. Rsch. in Children's Lit., Capital Choices, Choral Arts Soc. Washington. Democrat. Methodist. Avocations: travel, music, miniatures, art. E-mail: ladamson@alumni.unc.edu.

ADAMSON, TERRENCE BURDETT, lawyer; b. Floyd County, Ga., Nov. 13, 1946; s. Sollie Burdett and Lois Antoinette (Rogers) A.; m. Ede E. Holiday, June 8, 1985; children: Terrence Morgan, Kathlyn Watson Holiday, Elizabeth Rogers Holiday. BA, Emory U., 1968, JD with distinction, 1973.

Bar: Ga. 1973, U.S. Supreme Ct. 1978, D.C. 1981. Reporter Atlanta Constn., 1968-70; law clk. to Hon. Griffin B. Bell U.S. Ct. Appeals (5th cir.), 1973-74; assoc. Hansell & Post, Atlanta, 1974-77; spl. asst. U.S. Atty. Gen., 1977-79; ptnr. Hansell & Post, Atlanta and Washington, 1979-86, Dow, Lohnes & Albertson, Atlanta, 1986-91, Donovan, Leisure, Rogovin & Schiller, Washington, 1991-93, Kaye, Scholer, Fierman, Hays & Handler, LLP, Washington, 1993—98; exec. v.p. Nat. Geographic Soc., 1998—. Henry Luce scholar Ishii Law Office, Tokyo, 1975-76, scholar selector, 2002-; dir. office pub. affairs, chief spokesman U.S. Dept. Justice, Washington, 1978-79; bd. dirs. Nat. Geographic Ventures, 1996—; bd. dirs., mem. exec. com. State Justice Inst., Alexandria, Va., U.S. Presdl. appointment, 1990, 92, 94, Senate confirmed 1990, 92, 95. Contbr. articles to newspapers, mags. and law revs. Trustee Asia Found., 1984—, vice chmn. 1991-95, chmn. bd. 1995-2000; mem. steering com. Nat. Libel Def. Resource Com., 1987-91, co-chair Biennial Media Seminar, 1987-96; trustee The Nat. Faculty, 1990—; site selection com. 1988 Dem. nat. conv.; mem. U.S. Nat. Com. for Pacific Econ. Coop., 1983—, Leadership Atlanta, 1988-89, bd. trustee, exec. com., bd. councillors, gen. counsel, Carter Presdl. Ctr., Atlanta, 1983—; mem. Coun. for Excellence in Govt., 1991-94; mem. Clinton-Gore transition, 1992-93. Kennedy fellow Inst. Politics, Harvard U., 1979 Fellow Soc. Values in Edn.; mem. ABA (law and media project, conf. com. on lawyers and media 1987-90, cable defamation and media law com. 1992-93), U.S. Supreme Ct. Hist. Soc., Ga. Bar Assn., D.C. Bar Assn., Order of Coif, Order of Barristers, Omicron Delta Kappa. Democrat. Office: National Geographic Soc 1145 17th St NW Washington DC 20036-4688 Office Phone: 202-857-7449. Business E-Mail: tadamson@ngs.org.

ADAMSON, THOMAS CHARLES, JR., aerospace engineer, consultant; b. Cicero, Ill., Mar. 24, 1924; s. Thomas Charles and Helen Emily (Koubek) Adamson; m. Susan Elizabeth Huncilman, Sept. 16, 1949; children: Thomas Charles III, William Andros, Laura Elizabeth. BS, Purdue U., 1949; MS, Calif. Inst. Tech., 1950, PhD, 1954. Rsch. engr. Jet Propulsion Lab., Pasadena, Calif., 1952-54; assoc. rsch. engr. U. Mich., Ann Arbor, 1954-56, asst. prof., 1956-57, assoc. prof., 1957-61, prof., 1961-93, prof. emeritus, 1993—, chmn. dept. aerospace engring., 1983-92; ret., 1993. Mem. François-Xavier Bagnoud Aerospace Prize Bd., 1992—2003, chmn., 1992—2000. Editor (with M. F. Platzer): Transonic Flow Problems in Turbo Machinery, 1977; contbr. articles to profl. jours. Trustee Mich. Aviation Hall of Fame, 1987—. With U.S. Army, 1943—46, ETO. Named to Hall of Fame, Lyons Twp. HS, 2000; recipient Disting. Faculty Achievement award, U. Mich., 1980; Guggenheim fellow, 1950—52. Fellow: AIAA; mem.: Am. Phys. Soc., Sigma Xi. Episcopalian. Home: 667 Worthington Pl Ann Arbor MI 48103-6138 Office: U Mich Dept Aerospace Engring 1320 Beal Ave Ann Arbor MI 48109-2140 Business E-Mail: tcajr@umich.edu.

ADAMS-PASSEY, SUELLEN S., retired elementary school educator; b. Cin. d. Raymond J. and Thelma P. (Munk)Sweany; m. Douglas Passey; children; Amy, Jacqueline, James, Sarah, Kristina, Zoya. BS in Edn., Kent State U. Cert. elem. tchr., Wash. Tchr. 4th and 5th grades Chgo. Jr. Sch., Elgin, Ill.; gen. dir., program developer Courtyard Theatre, Edmonds, Wash.; tchr. 4th grade Edmonds (Wash.) Dist. 15; tchr. 4th, 5th and 6th grades combination class Martha Lake Elem. Sch., Lynnwood, Wash.; founder Suellen Adams Sch. of Hope for Orphans, Armenia, 2003. Bd. dirs. Pub. Edn. Fund for Dist. 15, 1985-87; pres. Seattle Storytellers Guild, 1985-88; bd. dirs. Seattle Folklore Soc. 1998-2004, founder and chair, concert com. 1988-2002, dir. Crackerbarrel Mornings, 1982-87, co-chair, student subsidy program, 1989-2000, Seattle Opera Guild.

ADAR, EYTAN, computer engineer, researcher; arrived in U.S., 1985; s. Aharon and Tsvia R. Adar. BS, MIT, 1997, MEE, 1998. From undergrad. to grad rschr. lab. computer sci. MIT, Cambridge, 1993—98; rsch. scientist Xerox PARC, Palo Alto, Calif., 1998—2001, HP Labs, Palo Alto, 2001—. Co-founder Outride, Redwood Shores, Calif., 2002. Recipient Anna Pogosyants UROP award, MIT, 1996. Mem.: ACM, IEEE. Achievements include discovery of free-riding on peer to peer sys; patents in field; patents pending in field; research in privacy; info. retrieval; social networks on the internet. Personal E-mail: eytan@alum.mit.edu.

ADARKAR, ADITYA, humanities educator; PhD, U. Chgo., 2001. Asst. prof., classics and gen. humanities Montclair State U., Upper Montclair, NJ, 2001—. Office: Montclair State Univ Classics and General Humanities Montclair NJ 07043

ADATTO, IRVING JACK, physician; b. Chgo., Oct. 23, 1930; BS, U. Ill., Chgo., 1952, MD, 1954. Diplomate Am. Bd. Internal Medicine, Am. Bd. Cardiovascular Diseases. Intern Cook County Hosp., Chgo., 1954-55; resident in gen. internal medicine U. Ill. Hosps., Chgo., 1955-57, fellow in clin. cardiology, 1957-59; chmn. cardiac bd. Luth. Gen. Hosp., Park Ridge, Ill., 1963-66, chmn. dept. medicine, 1968-69, chief CCU, 1965-72; pvt. practice, Des Plaines, Ill., 1972—. Author: (booklets) Living with Heart Disease, 1973, Hypertension, 1975. Fellow Am. Coll. Chest Physicians (emeritus), Am. Coll. Cardiology. Office: Maine Ridge Med Assocs ltd 9301 Golf Rd Des Plaines IL 60016-1667 Office Phone: 847-296-8151.

ADAWI, IBRAHIM HASAN, physics professor; b. Palestine, Apr. 18, 1930; came to U.S., 1951, naturalized, 1961; s. Hasan and Dabella (Miari) A.; children: Omar, Nadia, Yasmin, Rhonda, Tariq. BS in Engring. Physics, Washington U., St. Louis, 1953; PhD in Engring. Physics, Cornell U., 1957. Mem. tech. staff RCA Labs., Princeton, N.J., 1956-60; research cons. Battelle Meml. Inst., Columbus, Ohio, 1960-68; adj. prof. elec. engring. Ohio State U., 1965-68; prof. physics U. Mo., Rolla, 1968-97, emeritus prof. physics, 1997—. Vis. prof. U. Hamburg, W.Ger., winter 1977, Sch. Math. and Physics, U. East Anglia, Norwich, Eng., fall 1982; Fulbright lectr. Rabat, Morocco, 1982; sr. scientist Motorola, Phoenix, summer 1979; rsch. leader Internat. Ctr. Theoretical Physics, Trieste, Italy, summers 1982, 83, 85. Jr. fellow Cornell U., 1953-54; J. McMullen scholar, 1954-55; Sigma Xi fellow, 1955-56 Mem. Am. Phys. Soc Home: 10540 County Road 3010 Rolla MO 65401-7754 Office: U Mo-Rolla Dept Physics Rolla MO 65401 Business E-Mail: adawi@umr.edu. *Goals in science, and perhaps in life, are seldom reached; they are only approached asymptotically. The higher we soar the more dazzling is the panorama, but the wider is the horizon, and the frontiers of knowledge keep expanding.*

ADAWI, NADIA SHARON, energy executive; b. Princeton, NJ, Aug. 29, 1958; d. Ibrahim Hasan and Gerda (Obert) Adawi; m. Patrick John Loll, June 18, 1983. BSEE, U. Mo., 1980; MBA, Yale U., 1997. Electronics engr. FCC, Washington, 1980-81; cons. engr. Washington, 1981-89; asst. dir. advanced cellular tech. Ameritech Mobile Communications, Schaumburg, Ill., 1989-93; regional ops. mgr. Ericsson, Inc., Schaumburg, 1993-95; bus. ethics cons. Arthur Andersen, N.Y.C., 1997-99; dir. ops. The Energy Cooperative, Phila.; pres. Phila. Fry-o-Diesel LLC. Mem. Sustainable Bus. Network of Greater Phila.; treas. Greater Phila. Clean Cities. Named one of Phila. Bus. Jour. Women of Distinction, 2001. Mem.: Am. Solar Energy Soc. Avocations: music, literature, travel. Home: 329 S 46th St Philadelphia PA 19143-1801 E-mail: nsadawi@aol.com.

ADCOCK, ALBERT EUGENE (GENE), manufacturing executive; b. Christopher, Ill., Mar. 11, 1937; s. Omer Leon and Erva Doris Advock; m. Sylvia H. Adcock, Nov. 25, 1992; children: Mark, Chris. AA in Air Traffic Control Mgmt., Johnson County C.C., Olathe, Kans., 1972; BA in Econs. and Bus. Adminstrn., Park Coll., 1975; MBA, Webster U., 1977. Enlisted USAF, 1955, advanced through grades to master sgt.; assigned to Hdqrs. USAF Mil. Airlift Command, Scott AFB, Ill., 1975-76; ret., 1977; logistics engr. McDonnel Aircraft Co., St. Louis, 1977-79; high frequency radio networks comm. officer Hdqs. Air Force Comm. Command, Scott AFB, 1979-80; mktg. mgr. air traffic control navigational aids E-Sys. Montek Divsn., Salt Lake City, 1980-81; mktg. mgr. ground and aircraft radar transponders Govt. Electronics divsn. Motorola, Tempe, Ariz., 1981-87; regional mktg. mgr. Harris RF Comm., Sacramento, 1987-88; U.S. govt. mktg. mgr. night vision equipment Litton Electro-Optics Divsn., Tempe, 1988-91; v.p. bus. devel. Night Vision Equipment Co., Inc., Emmaus, Pa., 1991—. Author: Night Vision Reference Ency.—Optical Surveillance, 1999. Decorated Bronze Star medal with oak leaf cluster, Air medal with six oak leaf clusters. Mem. Air Commando Assn. (life), Combat Control Assn (life), Airlift-Tanker Assn. (life), Nat. Def. Indsl. Assn., Armed Forces Comm. and Electronics Assn. Office: Night Vision Equipment Co Inc PO Box 266 Emmaus PA 18049 E-mail: gene@nvec-night-vision.com.

ADCOCK, BETTY-LEE, real estate company executive, real estate broker; b. Waldo, Kans., Nov. 19, 1921; d. Ralph Preston and Hazel (Pangburn) Beatty; m. Charles Warren Adcock, Feb. 17, 1945; 1 dau., Roberta Lee. B.S. in Journalism, Kans. State Coll., 1946; grad. Realtors Inst. Lic. real estate broker, Hawaii; cert. residential specialist, residential broker. Mem. pub. relations staff Boeing Airplane Co., Wichita, Kans., 1942-45; biographical staff AP, N.Y.C., 1945-46; real estate salesman and broker, Honolulu, 1972—; prin. broker, pres., owner Adcock, Ltd., real estate mktg., Honolulu, 1983—2005; retired. Recipient Girl Scout Award of Merit, Kitzingen, Germany, 1960, spl. award Am. Cancer Soc., Middlebury, Vt., 1956. Mem. Nat. Assn. Realtors. Hawaii Assn. Realtors, Honolulu Bd. Realtors, Honolulu Zool. Soc., Friends of Waikiki Aquarium, Nat. Trust for Historic Preservation, Honolulu Art Acad., Friends of Iolani Palace, Bishop Mus., Hawaii Hist. Soc., Hawaii Humane Soc., Hist. Hawaii Found., Chi Omega. Republican. Episcopalian. Home and Office: Adcock Ltd 2415 Aha Aina Pl Honolulu HI 96821-1001

ADCOCK, MURIEL W., special education educator; b. Chgo. BA, U. Calif. Sonoma State, Rohnert Park, 1979. Cert. spl. edn. tchr., Calif., Montessori spl. edn. tchr. Tchr. The Concordia Sch., Concord, Calif., 1980-85; tchr., cons. Tenderloin Community Children's Ctr., San Francisco, 1985-86; adminstr. Assn. Montessori Internat.-USA, San Francisco, 1988, tchr., advisor, 1989—. Course asst. Montessori Spl. Edn. Inst., San Francisco, 1985-87, tchr. spl. edn., 1990, tchr. cons., 1991—, rschr. 1992—. U.S. mng. editor World Futures: The Jour. of Gen. Evolution, 2000—; contbr. articles to profl. jour. Sec. Internat. Forum World Affairs Coun., San Francisco, 1990-95, program chair, 1993-95, pres./founder Club of Budapest, U.S., 2000—. Mem. ASCD, Am. Orthopsychiat. Assn., Internat. Soc. Sys. Scientists, Internat. Sys. Inst., Assn. Montessori Internat., N.Am. Montessori Tchrs. Assn., Assn. Childhood Edn. Internat., Smithsonian Assocs., N.Y. Acad. Scis., Internat. Sys. Inst. Avocations: general evolutionary systems theory, sustainable development, human capacity building. Office: 4040 Civic Center Dr Ste 200 San Rafael CA 94903

ADCOCK, PETER ANTHONY, chemistry professor, researcher; b. Brisbane, Queensland, Australia, Aug. 16, 1959; s. Allan John and Elizabeth Mary (Cockburn) Adcock; m. Lydia Panares Collingwood Adcock, Sept. 8, 1990. BS with honors, James Cook U., Townsville, Queensland, 1980; PhD, U. Western Sydney, NSW, Australia, 1999. Grad. rsch. scientist Electrolytic Zinc Co., Hobart, Australia, 1981—90; sr. electrochemist Pasminco Rsch. Ctr., Newcastle, 1990—96; post doctoral rsch. fellow A.J. Parker Coop. Rsch. Ctr., Murdoch U., Perth, 1999; ANUTech rsch. assoc. Ctr. for Sustainable Energy Sys., Australian Nat. U., Canberra, 2000—01; post doctoral rsch. assoc. Los Alamos (N.Mex.) Nat. Lab., 2001—04; sr. rsch. assoc. Northeastern U., Boston, 2004; asst. prof. chemistry Campbellsville (Ky.) U., 2004—. Contbr. articles to profl. jours. Grantee, Australian Dept. Industry, Tech. and Regional Devel., 1993—96, U. Western Sydney, 2000; A.J. Parker CRC Rsch. fellow, Murdoch U., 1999. Mem.: Am. Chem. Soc., Electrochem. Soc., Royal Australian Chem. Inst. (sec. electrochemistry divsn. 1994—97, North Queensland sect. Student prize 1979). Roman Catholic. Achievements include discovery of alkylideneamido complexes of ruthenium and synthetic methodology for same; development of CO-mitigation to make Pt fuel anodes competitive with Pt alloys in presence of CO; method to map conditions to generate electrodeposits of a given morphology, e.g. ultrafine, unoriented crystallites; spouted bed electrowinning processes for zinc; invention of micro-fluidized bed electrodeposition; patents pending for non-invasive acoustic technique for mixing and segregation of fluid suspensions in microfluidic applications; patents for controlling processes for the electrolytic recovery of metals, measuring light reflectance. Avocations: karaoke, standardbred bloodlines. Office: Campbellsville Univ UPO 1361 1 University Dr Campbellsville KY 42718 Office Phone: 270-789-5054. Office Fax: 270-789-5170. E-mail: palcadcock@hotmail.com.

ADCOCK, RICHARD PAUL, lawyer; b. Chgo., May 14, 1955; s. Horace John and Louise Kathreen (Gallagher) A. AB with distinction in Econs., U. Ill., 1977; JD, Columbia U., 1980. Bar: Calif., 1980. Assoc. Lawler, Felix & Hall, L.A., 1980-82; corp. counsel Technicolor, Inc., L.A., 1982-83; assoc. counsel Nat. Med. Enterprises, L.A., 1983-85, sr. assoc. counsel, 1985-86, asst. gen. counsel, 1986-87; v.p., sec., gen. counsel The Hillhaven Corp., Tacoma, Wash., 1987-90, sr. v.p., sec., gen. counsel, 1990-95. Chmn. legal subcom. Am. Health Care Assn., Washington, 1993-95. Mem. ABA, Am. Corp. Counsel Assn., Nat. Health Lawyers Assn.

ADCROFT, PATRICE GABRIELLA, former editor; b. Scranton, Pa., Apr. 15, 1954; d. Joseph Raymond and Patricia Ann (Ryan) Adcroft. BA In Mag. Journalism and Creative Writing, Syracuse U., 1976. Editor-in-chief Carbondale (Pa.) Miner Mid Valley Gazette, 1976—77; staff writer Good Housekeeping Mag., N.Y.C., 1978—80; mng. editor Family Media/Alive and Well, N.Y.C., 1980—81; freelance writer, editor N.Y.C., 1981—82; sr. editor CBS Mags. Family Weekly, N.Y.C., 1982—84, Omni Mag., N.Y.C., 1984—85, exec. editor, 1985—86, editor-in-chief, 1986—90; Editor-in-Chief Seventeen Magazine, 1998—2001; exec. editor Marie Claire, 2004—. Vis. prof. Syracuse U., 1992—93. Editor-in-chief Omni Future Medical Almanac, 1987, NetGuide Mag., 1994—95, deputy editor InStyle Mag., 1995—98; author: (novels) Every Day Doughnuts; contbr. writer Arthur C. Clarke's 2019, 1986, Omni Book of Continuum, 1982. Bd. advisors SCI Ctr. for Advanced Studies in Mgmt. Wharton Sch., U. Pa. Roman Catholic. Office: Marie Claire 250 W 55th St New York NY 10019

ADDABBO, DOMINIC LUCIAN, lawyer; b. N.Y.C., Dec. 13, 1951; s. Joseph P. and Grace (Salamone) A.; m. Marianna G. Riverso, Jan. 12, 1980; children: Grace, Lisa, Joseph. BA, St. John's U., 1973, JD, 1976. Bar: N.Y. 1977, Fla. 1978, U.S. Dist. Ct. (ea. and so. dists.) N.Y. 1978. Asst. dist. atty. Queens Dist. Attys. Office, KEw Gardens, N.Y., 1977-81; coun. to pres. Queens Borough Pres., KEw Gardens, N.Y., 1981-83; ptnr. Addabbo & Greenberg, Forest Hills, N.Y., 1983—. Pres. United Exec. Dem. Club, Ozone Park, N.Y., 1981-86, state commiteeman N.Y. State Dem. Party, Queens, 1982-86. Mem. Fla. Bar Assn., N.Y. State Bar Assn., Queens County Bar Assn., Asst. Dist. Attys. Assn. Roman Catholic. Avocations: music, songwriting, Karate. Office: Addabbo & Greenberg 11821 Queens Blvd Forest Hills NY 11375-7201 Office Phone: 718-268-0400. Business E-Mail: mail@queenslaw.com.

ADDERLEY, TERENCE E., personnel director; b. 1933; BBA, U. Mich., 1951, BMA, 1956. Fin. analyst Standard Oil Co. NJ, 1956-57; with Kelly Svcs., Inc., Troy, Mich., 1957-61, v.p., 1961-65, exec. v.p., 1965-67, pres., COO, 1967—, chmn., CEO, 1998—, also bd. dirs. Office: Kelly Svcs Inc 999 W Big Beaver Rd Troy MI 48084-4716

ADDIE, HARVEY WOODWARD, retired secondary education educator, music director; b. Birmingham, Ala., June 14, 1930; s. LeRoy and Frances (Driscoll) A.; m. Gwendolyn Marie Mendes, June 5, 1955; children: Cynthia Marie Corra, Julie Ann Lorch, Mary Elizabeth Dunaway. MusB, Coll. Pacific, 1959; MusM, U. Pacific, 1970. Cert. life music tchr., Calif. Mgr. dept. S.H. Kress and Co., Santa Monica and Stockton, Calif., 1953-55; head produce, mgr. area Safeway Stores Inc., Lodi, Stockton, Calif., 1955-61; tchr. music Manteca (Calif.) Elem. Sch. Dist., 1959-61, San Joaquin County Sch. Music Office, Stockton, 1961-71; mgr. store Bill's Music Sales, Stockton, 1971-73; dir. music El Dorado High Sch., Placerville, Calif., 1973, Stockton Unified Sch. Dist., 1973-89. Pres. San. Joaquin County Band Dirs. Assn., Stockton, 1984-86, Stagg High Sch. Faculty Assn., 1984-85. 1st. v.p. San Joaquin Concert Ballet Assn., Stockton, 1966; bd. dirs. Stockton opera Assn., 1968, Stockton Concert Band Assn., 1986-88. Served to cpl. U.S. Army, 1951-53, Korea. Mem. Assn. Jazz Edn., Calif. Music Educators Assn. (bd. dirs. 1983-87), Stockton Tchrs. Assn. (treas. 1986-89), Am. Fedn. Musicians (life mem., bd. dirs., sec.-treas. 1992—, pres. 1995—), Calif. Tchrs. Assn. (state coun. 1986-89), Noble Grand Fraternal Order of Odd Fellows (dist. dep. Grand Master Calif., trustee Saratoga Home 1994-97). Democrat. Methodist. Avocations: fishing, golf, computers. Home: 1426 W Euclid Ave Stockton CA 95204-2903 Office: Stockton Musicians' Assn 33 W Alpine Ave Stockton CA 95204-3607

ADDIEGO, RUSSELL FRANCIS, middle school educator; b. San Francisco, Apr. 22, 1955; s. Phillip Francis and Emma Marie Addiego. Assoc. in Sci., City Coll. of San Francisco, 1975; BA, San Francisco State U., 1977, MA, 1985. Tchr. 8th grade Aptos Mid. Sch., San Francisco Unified Sch. Dist., 1977—, gifted and talented edn. program coord., 1996—. Mem. supt.'s gifted and talented edn. task force San Francisco Unified Sch. Dist., 2001—02. Mem. Nat. Trust for Hist. Preservation, 2000, Neighborhood Emergency Response Team, San Francisco, 1998, ACLU, 1996, People for the Am. Way, 1999. Mem.: ASCD, Nat. Mid. Sch. Assn., Nat. Assn. for the Gifted, Calif. Assn. for the Gifted, Phi Delta Kappa. Democrat. Roman Catholic. Avocations: San Francisco history, architecture, theatre, classical and popular music. Office: Aptos Middle School 105 Aptos Avenue San Francisco CA 94127 Office Phone: 415-469-4520. Office Fax: 415-333-9038. E-mail: raddieg@sfusd.edu.

ADDIS, KAY TUCKER, newspaper editor; AB in English, Coll. of William and Mary, 1970. Editor The Virginian-Pilot, Norfolk, 1996—. Office: The Virginian-Pilot 150 W Brambleton Ave Norfolk VA 23510-2075 also: Virginian Pilot P O Box 449 Norfolk VA 23501-0449

ADDIS, LAIRD CLARK, JR., philosopher, educator, musician; b. Bath, N.Y., Mar. 25, 1937; s. Laird Clark and Dora Ersel (Webber) A.; m. Patricia Karen Peterson, Dec. 20, 1962; children— Kristin, Karin. BA, U. Iowa, 1959, PhD, 1964; MA (Woodrow Wilson fellow), Brown U., 1960. Instr. U. Iowa, Iowa City, 1963-64, asst. prof., 1964-68, asso. prof., 1968-74, prof. philosophy, 1974—2004, chmn. dept. philosophy., 1977-85, emeritus, 2004—. Sr. Fulbright lectr. State U. Groningen, Netherlands, 1970-71 Author: (with Douglas Lewis) Moore and Ryle: Two Ontologists, 1965, The Logic of Society, 1975, Natural Signs, 1989, Of Mind and Music, 1999; contbr. articles to profl. jours. Mem. Am. Philos. Assn., Philosophy of Sci. Assn., Am. Soc. for Aesthetics, Am. Fedn. Musicians, Quad City Symphony Orch. (ret.), Soc. Humanist Philosophers. Home: 20 W Park Rd Iowa City IA 52246-2304 Office: U Iowa Dept Philosophy Iowa City IA 52242 Office Phone: 319-335-0021. Business E-Mail: laird-addis@uiowa.edu.

ADDISON, BRIAN MICHAEL, lawyer; b. Norwalk, Ohio, Mar. 2, 1954; s. William Edward and Betty Mae (Urban) A.; m. Jeanne Lorraine Brown, Jan. 17, 1981; children: Stephen Christian, Andrew Michael, Jeremy Thomas. BA with distinction, Pa. State U., 1976, MBA, 1990; JD cum laude, Dickinson Sch. Law, 1979. Bar: Pa. 1979, U.S. Dist. Ct. (ea. dist.) Pa. 1979, U.S. Dist. Ct. (mid. dist.) Pa. 1982, U.S. Supreme Ct. 1981. Law clk. IRS, Washington, summer 1978; assoc. German, Gallagher & Murtagh, Phila., 1979-82; sr. counsel Hershey (Pa.) Foods Corp., 1982-94; ptnr. McNees, Wallace & Nurick, Harrisburg, Pa., 1994; corp. counsel DENTSPLY Internat. Inc., York, Pa., 1994-97, v.p., sec., gen. counsel, 1998—. Mediator U.S. Dist. Ct. (mid. dist.) Pa. mediation panel. Vice chmn. Conewago Zoning Hearing Bd., 1995, Dauphin County. Mem. ABA (antitrust law sect., vice chair corp. counseling com. 1993-95, editor an titrust compliance handbook, co-editor corp. counseling newsletter, bus. law sect. mem., labor and employment law sect. mem.), Pa. Bar Assn. (chair alt. dispute resolution com. 1990-93, corp., banking and bus. law sect. mem., antitrust com., corp. counsel com., labor rels. law sect. mem.), Dauphin County Bar Assn. (bd. dirs. 1991-93, chair alt. dispute resolution com. 1987-90), York County Bar Assn., York County Bar Found. (bd. dirs. 1998—, treas. 2001—), Am. Corp. Counsel Assn., Pi Sigma Alpha. Avocation: golf. Office: DENTSPLY Internat Inc Susquehanna Commerce Ctr 221 W Philadelphia St York PA 17405-0872 Office Phone: 717-845-7511. Office Fax: 717-849-4753. E-mail: baddison@dentsply.com, bmaesq@aol.com.

ADDISON, FERGUSON LOFTON LIGHTBOURNE, retired bank executive; b. Punta Gorda, Fla., Sept. 10, 1922; s. Locke and Maysoura Lofton (Hall) Addison. BA, Harvard U., 1950. Safety patrol sponsor Coconut Grove Elem. Sch., Miami, Fla., 1952—53. Svc. cons. Dun & Bradstreet, Miami, 1954—57. Feature writer: Dun's Bull. The Gold Coast Story, 1956. Pres. Shaughnessy Club, First Nat. Bank, Palm Beach, 1962. With USNR, 1942—46. Mem.: English Speaking Union, Martin County Hist. Soc., Harvard Club of Palm Beach (organizer 1962, pres. 1964—65). Achievements include receiving approval from the Fla. Dept. of State of the nomination of W.S. Lightbourn as a Great Floridian, 2000 and Frances Langford into Fla. Women's Hall of Fame, 2002. Avocations: genealogy, antiques. Home: 300 Forest Hill Blvd West Palm Beach FL 33405-4614

ADDISON, HERBERT JOHN, consulting editor, writer; b. Berkeley, Calif., Nov. 21, 1932; s. Herbert and Clara Virginia (Mason) A.; m. Geraldyne Elaine Harvey, Aug. 17, 1957; children: Bradley Thomas, Gregory James. BA, U. Calif.-Berkeley, 1958; MA, NYU, 1959. Office-personnel mgr. Thomas Y. Crowell Co., N.Y.C., 1958-65; editor-in-chief coll. dept. Holt, Rinehart & Winston, Inc., N.Y.C., 1965-70; v.p., gen. mgr. coll. dept. Thomas Y. Crowell Co., N.Y.C., 1970-74; exec. editor coll. dept. John Wiley & Sons, Inc., N.Y.C., 1974-78; gen. mgr. coll. dept. Oxford U. Press, Inc., N.Y.C., 1978-82, v.p., exec. editor bus., 1982-2000, cons. editor, 2000—. Adj. lectr. NYU, 1977-83 Author: Books and Bucks: The Business of College Textbook Publishing, 1980. Trustee Adult Sch. Montclair, N.J., 1976-80; mem. Civic Conf. Com., Glen Ridge, N.J., 1974-77, 2004—; mem. Glen Ridge Hist. Preservation Commn., 2005—. Served with U.S. Army, 1953-55. Mem. Acad. Mgmt. Home: 46 Sherman Ave Glen Ridge NJ 07028-1441 Personal E-mail: herb.addison@verizon.net.

ADDISON, JAMES W., lawyer; b. Langdale, Ala., Aug. 18, 1946; BA, Clemson U., 1968; JD, U. Va., 1971. Bar: Ga. 1971. Assoc. Hansell, Post, Brandon & Dorsey, 1971—74, Troutman Sanders LLP, Atlanta, 1974—76, ptnr., 1976—, sect. chief, real estate law, mem. exec. com. Named a Super Lawyer, Law & Politics and Atlanta Mag., 2004. Mem. ABA, State Bar Ga., Internat. Bar Assn., Phi Kappa Phi. Office: Troutman Sanders LLP Ste 5200 600 Peachtree St NE Atlanta GA 30308-2216 Office Phone: 404-885-3103. Office Fax: 404-885-3900. Business E-Mail: james.addison@troutmansanders.com.

ADDISON, JOHN TOWERS, economics educator, consultant; b. Dudley, U.K., May 9, 1946; came to U.S., 1981; s. Roland William Addison and Ida Iris Halford; m. Aleta Marie Pillick, June 24, 1978 (div. Oct. 1986). BSc in Econs., London Sch. Econs., 1967, MSc in Econs., 1968, PhD, 1971. Econ. adviser Office Manpower Econs., London, 1971-72; lectr. U. Aberdeen, Scotland, 1972-80; from assoc. prof. to prof. econ. U. S.C., Columbia, 1981—2002, Hugh C. Lane prof. econ. theory, 2002—; prof. U. Hull, U.K., 1996-97; Olin vis. prof. Ctr. Study of Am. and Bus. Washington U., St. Louis, 1997-98. Author: The Market for Labor, 1979, The Economic Analysis of Unions, 1986; editor: Job Displacement, 1991, Labor Markets & Social Security, 1998, International Handbook of Trade Unions, 2003; mem. editl. bd. Jour. Labor Rsch., 1981—, Springer Verlag, 1998—, Jour. Internat. Econs. and Econ. Policy, 2003—. Anglican. Avocations: coin collecting/numismatics, tennis. Home: 117 Spring Valley Ct Columbia SC 29223-5950 Office: U SC Dept Econs Moore Sch Bus Columbia SC 29208-0001 Office Phone: 803-777-4608. Business E-Mail: ecceaddi@moore.sc.edu.

ADDISON, LINDA LEUCHTER, lawyer, writer, commentator, columnist; b. Allentown, Pa., Nov. 25, 1951; d. Marcus and Sophie Theresa (Tisch) Leuchter; m. Max M. Addison, Sept. 10, 1977; 1 child, Alexandra Leuchter Addison. BA with honors, U. Tex., 1973, JD, 1976. Bar: Tex. 1976, U.S. Dist. Ct. (so. dist.) Tex. 1977, U.S. Dist. Ct. (no. dist.) Tex. 2000, U.S. Dist. Ct. (ea. dist.) Tex. 2003, U.S. Ct. Appeals (5th cir.) 1981, U.S. Ct. Appeals (fed. cir.) 2003, U.S. Supreme Ct. 2003. Assoc. Fulbright & Jaworski LLP, Houston, 1976—83, ptnr., 1984—, exec. com., tech. ptnr., 2002—. Expert on fed. and Tex. evidence. Author: Texas Practice Guide: Evidence, 2004; mng. editor Tex. Law Rev. 1975-76; contbr. chpt. to book, articles to profl. jours. Trustee U. Tex. Law Sch. Found., 1994—; mem. fed. jud. evaluation com. of Sens. Hutchison and Cornyn, 1997-; exec. com. chancellor's coun. U. Tex. Sys., 1999-; bd. dirs. Holocaust Mus. Houston, 2001-; mem. Commn. of 125, U. Tex., Austin, 2003-04, vice chmn. task force of centennial commn., 1981-83. Named one of Am.'s Top 50 Women Litigators, Nat. Law Jour., 2001, Tex. Go To Litigators, Tex. Lawyer, 2002, Most Fascinating People in Houston, Friends of Tex. Med. Ctr. Libr., 2001, Hon. Barrister, U. Tex. Sch. Law bd. advocates, 2000, Outstanding Young Lawyer of Houston, 1984-85, Woman on the Move, Tex. Exec. Women, 2000, Woman to Watch, Jewish Women Internat., 2002; named one of Best Lawyers in Am., Woodard and White, 2003, 04, Tex. Super Lawyers, Tex. Monthly, 2003, 04; named to Chambers & Ptnrs. USA, 2004, 05. Fellow: Tex. Bar Found. (life; trustee 2003—), Houston Bar Found. (life), Am. Bar Found. (life); mem.: ABA, Am. Bd. Trial Advs., World Internat. Patent Orgn. (arbitration and mediation ctr. domain name panel 2002—), Am. Intellectual Property Law Assn., Am. Arbitration Assn. (internat. panel 1992—, panel of neutrals, large complex case panel), Houston Young Lawyers Assn. (chmn. cont. legal edn. com. 1977—78, bd. dirs. 1978—81, Outstanding Chmn. award), Tex. Young Lawyers Assn. (bd. dirs. 1981—83), Houston Bar Assn. (chmn. cont. legal edn. com. 1981—82, mem. jud. evalns. com. 1982—83, Pres.'s award for outstanding svc. 1982), State Bar Tex. (chmn. bar jour. com. 1988—90, adminstr. rules evidence com. 1988—90, chmn. bar jour. com. 1991—99), Tex. Law Rev. Ex-Editors Assn. (life), Abbot, Friar Soc., United Way, deTocqueville Soc., Anti-Defamation League (bd. dirs. S.W. Region 1992—94), Omicron Delta Kappa. Office: Fulbright & Jaworski LLP 1301 McKinney St Ste 5100 Houston TX 77010-3095

ADDO, CHARLES KWAME, municipal official; b. Techiman, B/A, Ghana, Feb. 16, 1957; s. James Kwabena Addo and Mary Abena Brefo-Inkum; 5 children. Student, SUNY Maritime Coll., Bronx, 1977—79; BS, Mercy Coll., Dobbs Ferry, N.Y., 1996; MBA, L.I. U., 1999; postgrad., Walden U., 2002—. Cert. merchant marine officer. Shipdeck officer Golotrade Shipping and Chartering, N.Y.C., 1981—90; adj. prof. Mercy Coll., Dobbs Ferry, 1999—. Author: Corporate Mergers and Acquisitions: A Case Study, 2000, Burdens of the Mirage Dream, 2001. Methodist. Avocation: writing.

ADDUCCI, JOSEPH EDWARD, obstetrician, gynecologist; b. Chgo., Dec. 1, 1934; s. Dominee Edward and Harriet Evelyn (Kneppreth) A.; m. Mary Ann Tiertje, 1958; children: Christopher, Gregory, Steven, Jessica, Tobias. BS, U. Ill., 1955; MD, Loyola U., Chgo., 1959. Diplomate Am. Bd. Ob-Gyn., Nat. Bd. Med. Examiners. Intern Cook County Hosp, Chgo., 1959-60; resident in ob-gyn Mt. Carmel Hosp., Detroit, 1960-64; practice medicine specializing in obstetrics and gynecology Williston, ND, 1996—; chmn. dept. ob-gyn. Mercy Hosp., 1994—. Chief staff, chmn. obstetrics dept. Mercy Hosp., Williston, gov. bd., 1996, chmn. dept. surgery; clin. prof. U. ND Med. Sch., 1973—; gov. bd. Mercy Hosp. Cath. Health Corp.; mem. coun. Accreditation Coun. for Gynecologic Endoscopy, 1999—. Mem. N.D. Bd. Med. Examiners, 1974—, past chmn.; project dir. Tri County Family Planning Svc.; past pres. Tri County Health Planning Coun.; mem. governing bd. Mercy Hosp., Williston, N.D. With Med. Corps, AUS, 1964-66. Fellow Am. Soc. Abdominal Surgeons, ACS (regent ND 1990—), Am. Coll. Obstetrics and Gynecologists (sect. chmn. ND), Internat. Coll. Surgeons (regent 1972-74, 88-89), Am. Fertility Soc., Am. Assn. Internat. Lazar Soc., Gynecol. Lataropists, ND Obstetricians and Gynecologists Soc. (pres. 1966, 76); mem. Am. Soc. for Colopscopy and Colpomicroscopy, Am. Soc. Cryosurgery, Am. Soc. Contemporary Medicine and Surgery, Am. Assn. Profl. Ob-Gyn., Pan Am. Med. Assn., Am. Coll. Surgeons (regent 1989— N.D.), Kotana Med. Soc. (pres. 2003—), Elks. Home: 1717 Main St Williston ND 58801-4244 Office: Med Ctr Dept Ob-Gyn Williston ND 58801 Office Phone: 701-572-0316. Personal E-mail: jadducci@prodigy.net.

ADDUCCI, STEVEN A., lawyer; b. 1965; BA summa cum laude, U. ND, 1987, JD with honors, 1990. Bar: DC, US Ct. Appeals, DC Cir. Ptnr. Venable LLP, Washington, DC. Mem. bd. dirs. Am. Red Cross, Alexandria, Va. Mem.: ABA, Energy Bar Assn., Fed. Bar Assn. (mem. Adminstrv. Law & Regulatory Practice and Health Law Forum Sects.), DC Bar Assn. (mem. Adminstrv. Law and Agency Practice, Environment, Energy and Natural Resources and Health Law Sects.), Phi Alpha Delta. Office: Venable LLP 575 7th St NW Washington DC 20004 Office Phone: 202-344-4361. Office Fax: 202-344-8300. E-mail: saadducci@venable.com.

ADDY, ALVA LEROY, mechanical engineer; b. Dallas, S.D., Mar. 29, 1936; s. Alva Isaac and Nellie Amelia (Brumbaugh) A.; m. Sandra Ruth Turney, June 8, 1958 BS, S.D. Sch. Mines and Tech., 1958; MS, U. Cin., 1960; PhD, U. Ill., 1963. Engr. Gen. Electric Co., Cin., also Lancaster, Calif., 1958-60; prof. mech. engring. U. Ill., Urbana, 1963-98, prof. emeritus, 1998—, dir. mech. engring. lab., 1965-97, assoc. head mech. engring. dept., 1980-87, head, 1987-98. Aerodynamics cons. U.S. Army Missile Command, Redstone Arsenal, Ala., summers 1965-98; cons. U.S. Army Research Office, 1964—; cons. in high-speed fluid dynamics to indsl. firms, 1963—; vis. research prof. U.S. Army, 1976; lectr. Von Karman Inst. Fluid Dynamics, Brussels, 1968, 75, 76 Fellow ASME, AIAA (assoc.), Am. Soc. for Engring. Edn. (Ralph Coates Roe award 1990); mem. Sigma Xi, Pi Tau Sigma, Sigma Tau. Home: 726 Elk Run Rd Spearfish SD 57783

ADECHI, JOEL WASSI, international organization administrator; b. Dakar, Senegal, 1949; married; 4 children. Received law degree, U. Brazzaville, 1973; received advanced law degree, U. Orléans, France, 1974; hold diploma in diplomacy, Inst. Internat. Pub. Adminstrn., Paris. Second counsellor and later Chargé d' affaires Embassy of Benin, Democratic Republic of Congo, 1978—85, min. counsellor Ottawa, Canada, 1990—94, Permanent Mission of Benin to the UN, 1994—96; dir. of Cabinet; dir. of State Protocol; dir. of Am. Sect. Foreign Ministry of Benin; dir. of the African and Arab Countries Sect.; permanent rep. of Benin UN, NY. Office: UN Hdqs First Ave at 46th St New York NY 10017

ADEDEJI, ADEBAYO, economist, retired federal official, academic administrator; b. Ijebu-Ode, Ogun, Nigeria, Dec. 21, 1930; came to Ethiopia, 1975; s. L.S. and Adeola Adedeji; m. Aderinola Ogun, Aug. 11, 1957; children: Adedoyin, Funso, Adekunle, Adeleke, Adeniyi, Adeola, Adefunke, Adeyinka, Adepoju, Adedipe, Adeoye. Diploma in Local Govt. Adminstrn., Univ. Coll., U. Ibadan, 1953-54; B.Sc. in Econs., London U., 1958; M.P.A., Harvard U., 1961; PhD in Econs., U. London, 1967; Litt.D. (hon.), Ahmadu Bello U., 1976; LL.D. (hon.), U. Dallhousie, 1984, U. Zambia, 1984, U. Calabar, 1987; DSc (hon.), Obafemi Awolowo U., 1989; DSc (hon.), U. Ibadan, 1997, Ogun State U., 1998. Sr. prin. sec. for revenue and budget Nigerian Civil Service, 1958-63; dep. dir. Inst. Adminstrn. U. Ife, 1963-67, dir. Inst. Adminstrn., prof. pub. adminstrn., 1967-75; fed. commr., minister Nigeria Ministry for Econ. Devel. in Reconstruction, 1971-75; under-sec.-gen., exec. sec. UN Econ. Commn. for Africa, Addis Ababa, Ethiopia, 1975—91; dir. African Ctr for Development and Strategic Studies, 1991—. Mem. ad hoc com. of experts fin. UN and specialized agys., 1965; mem. expert com. on restructuring econ. and spl. sectors UN, 1975; chmn. senate UN Inst. for Namibia, 1975—90; trustee dept. econs. Boston U., 1975—85; chmn. Western Nigerian Govt. Broadcasting Corp., 1966—67; mem. Nigerian Nat. Manpower Bd., 1968—71; chmn. Directorate of Nat. Youth Svc. Corps, 1973—75; founder African Ctr. for Devel. and Strategic Studies, 1991—; mem. panel of high level experts on restructuring UN, chmn. devel. program, 1994, mem. adv. bd. African Futures project, 1998—, team leader evaluation and assessment devel. assistance framework, 1998, 2000, team leader on future of staff coll., 00; spl. envoy of pres. Nigeria on Zimbabwe inter-party dialogue post pres. election, 02; contbr. UN Intellectual History Project, 2005; spl. advisor on transition of Orgn. African Unity to African Union; mem. eminent persons panel African Peer Rev. Mechanism. Author: as a factor in Africa's Development and miodernization, Africa, the Third World and the search for a New Econ. Order, 1976, Africa: The Crisis of Devel. and the Challenge of a New Econ. Order, 1977, The Political Class, the Higher Civil Svc. and the Challenge of Nation Building, 1981, The Deepening Internat. Econ. Crisis and its Implications for Africa, 1982; editor: Indigenization of African Econs., 1981, Econ. Crisis in Africa: African Perspectives on Devel. Problems and Potentials, 1985, Towards the Dawn of the Third Millenium and the Beginning of the 21st Century, 1986, Towards a Dynamic African Econ., 1989, NIgeria in the Year of its Centenary, 2014, 1989, Economics of Development in a World of Changing Ideologies and values, 1989, Preparing Africa for the Twenty-First Century: Agenda for the 1990's, 1991, The African Alternative Framework to Structural Adjustment Programmes for Socio-economic Recovery and Transformation: A Human-Centred and Holistic Development Paradigm, 1992, Africa Within the World: Beyond Disposession and Dependence, 1993, South Africa and Africa: Within or Apart?, 1996, Nigeria: Renewal From the Roots? The Struggle for Dem. Devel., 1997, Sub-Sahara Africa and a New Strategy for International Development in the 21st Century, 1997, Comprehending and Mastering African Conflicts - The Search for Sustainable Peace and Good Governance, 1999, People-Centered Democracy in Nigeria? The Search for Alternative Systems of Governance at the Grassroots, 2000, African Development and Governance Strategies in the 21st Century-Looking Back to Move Forward, 2004, Essays in Honour of Adebayo Adedeji at Seventy, 2004. Decorated grand officer Order of Mono Togo; named a comdr. Order of Merit, Islamic Republic Mauritania, comdr., Republic of Gambia, 1988; named grand comdr. Order of Disting. Svc. first class, Zambia, grand comdr. Order of Lion, Senegal, 1987, grand comdr. most excellent Order of Eagle, Namibia, 1995, grand officer Order of the Niger, 1988, comdr., Fed. Republic Nigeria, 2001; recipient Faculty prize in Econs., U. Coll. Leicester, 1956—57, Gold Mercury Internat. award, 1982; subject of numerous books. Fellow Nigerian Inst. Mgmt. (dir. 1968-75), Nigerian Econ. Soc. (pres. 1971-72), African Assn. for Pub. Adminstrn. and Mgmt. (v.p. 1971-74, pres. 1975-85), African Acad. Sci. Anglican. Avocations: photography, tennis, golf. Home: Asiwaju Ct GRA Erunwon Rd PO Box 203 Ijebu Ode Nigeria Office: African Ctr Devel Strategic Studies PO Box 203 Ijebu Ode Nigeria E-mail: acdess@hyperia.com, executivedirector@acdess.org.

ADELBERG, ARNOLD MELVIN, mathematics professor, researcher; b. Bklyn., Mar. 17, 1936; s. David and Evelyn (Brass) A.; m. Harriet Diamond, June 30, 1962; children: Danielle Hamill, Erica. BA, Columbia U., 1956; MA, Princeton U., 1959, PhD, 1996. Instr. Columbia U., N.Y.C., 1959-62; instr., asst. prof., assoc. prof., prof. Grinnell (Iowa) Coll., 1962—, Myra Steele prof. math., 1991—. Chair math. dept., sci. div. several times, chmn. faculty Grinnell Coll., 1974-76. Contbr. articles to profl. jours. Mem. Math. Assn. Am., Am. Math. Soc. Avocations: bridge, chess. Home: 1930 Manor Cir Grinnell IA 50112-1136 Office: Grinnell Coll Math Dept PO Box 805 Grinnell IA 50112-0805 Business E-Mail: adelbe@math.grinnell.edu.

ADELL, HIRSCH, lawyer; b. Novogrodek, Poland, Mar. 11, 1931; arrived in U.S., 1937; s. Nathan and Nachama (Wager) A.; m. Judith Audrey Fuss, Feb. 8, 1963; children— Jeremiah, Nikolas, Balthasar, Valentine. Student, CCNY, 1949—52; BA, UCLA, 1955, LLB, 1963. Bar: Calif. 1963. Adminstrv. asst. to State Senator Richard Richards, 1956-60; ptnr. Warren & Adell, LA, 1963-75, Reich, Adell, Crost & Cvitan, LA, 1975—. Gen. counsel Ctrl. Valley Trust, 2003—. Served with AUS, 1953-55. Mem. ABA (labor and employment law sect.) Home: 545 S Norton Ave Los Angeles CA 90020-4610 Office: Reich Adell Crost & Cvitan 3550 Wilshire Blvd Ste 2000 Los Angeles CA 90010-2421 Office Phone: 213-386-3860. Business E-Mail: hirscha@racclaw.com.

ADELMAN, GRAHAM, heavy manufacturing company executive; Grad., U. Va.; degree magna cum laude, U. Miami. Fed. law clk.; asst. counsel FINA, Inc.; sr. v.p., gen. counsel, sec., bd. dirs. Western Co. N.Am., to 1995; sr. v.p., gen. counsel, sec., chmn. ops. com. Global Indsl. Tech. Inc., Dallas, 1995—. Office: Global Indsl Tech Inc Ste 25000 LB 31 2121 San Jacinto St Dallas TX 75201

ADELMAN, HOWARD, philosophy educator; b. Toronto, Jan. 7, 1938; s. Harry Adelman and Frances (Duviner) Bromstein; m. Margaret Dorothy Smith, May 31, 1960; children: Jeremy Ian, Shonagh Eva, Rachel Esther, Eric Reuben; m. Nancy Jean Garrett, June 15, 1985; children: Daniel Jacob, Gabriel Benjamin. BA, U. Toronto, 1961, MA, 1963, PhD, 1971. From asst. prof. to assoc. prof. philosophy York U., Toronto, Ont., 1966-80, prof. North York, Ont., 1981-83, acting dean Atkinson Coll., 1973-74, dir. grad. programme in philosophy, 1980-83, 95-96, dir. Ctr. for Refugee Studies, 1986-93, chmn. senate, 1981-82. Lady Davis vis. prof. Hebrew U., 1977-78; vis. fellow, Princeton U., 2003-. Author: Beds of Academe, 1970, The Holiversity, 1973, Canada and the Indochinese Refugees, 1982; co-author: Early Warning and Conflict Management: The Genocide in Rwanda, 1996; editor: Refugee Policy: Canada and the United States, 1991, Legitimate and Illegitimate Discrimination: New Issues in Migration, 1993, Immigration Policy and Practice in Canada, 2002; co-editor: African Refugees, 1994, Immigration and Refugee Policy: Australia and Canada Compared, 1994, (with John Simpson) Multiculturalism, Jews and Canandian Identity, 1996, Immigration and Refugee Policy: Canada and Europe, 1998, The Path of a Genocide: The Rwanda Crisis from Uganda to Zaire, 1998, (with Govind Rao) War and Peace in Zaire/Congo, 2004; editor Refuge, 1982-93; contbr. articles to profl. jours. Harvard Harvey Harnick scholar, Queen Elizabeth II scholar, Can. Coun. Writing scholar; Grad. fellow Province of Ont.; grantee Ctrl. Mortgage and Housing Corp., Slater Found., 1980, SSHRC, 1983, 90-93, Aktinson Coll., 1982-86, CIDA, 1991, UNESCO, 1991, CEIC, 1982, 86-93, Ford Found., 1984, 86-89, IDRC, 1982, 92, ICMC, 1982, Ditchley Conf., 1983, OECD, 1995, Rsch. Travel grant, 1998, Rsch. grant CIC, 1999, Travel grant YUFA, 2001, Rsch. grant USIP, 2001, others; recipient Gerstein award, 1996, Marvin Gelber award, 1996, European Task Force award, 1996, John Holmes Found. award, 1997, SSHRC, 1997. Home: 64 Wells Hill Ave Toronto ON Canada M5R 3A8 Office: York U Philosophy Dept 4700 Keele St North York ON Canada M3J 1P3 E-mail: hadelman@yorku.ca, howardadelman@rogers.ca.

ADELMAN, JONATHAN REUBEN, political science professor; b. Washington, Oct. 30, 1948; s. Benjamin and Kitty (Sandler) A. BA, Columbia U., 1969, MA, 1972, M in Philosophy, 1974, PhD, 1976. Vis. asst. prof. Columbia U., N.Y.C., 1977; vis. asst. prof. U. Ala., Tuscaloosa, 1977-78; asst. prof. Grad. Sch. Internat. Studies U. Denver, 1978-85, assoc. prof., 1985-92, prof. polit. sci., 1992—; sr. rsch. analyst Sci. Applications, Inc., Denver, 1981-87, 96—; hon. prof. People's U., Beijing, 1996—; sr. fellow Found. for the Def. of Democracies, 2001—03; hon. prof. Beijing U., 1996—. Cons., 1988-89, 96—; Lady Davis vis. assoc. prof. Hebrew U., Jerusalem, 1986; vis. fellow Soviet Acad. Scis., 1989, 90, Chinese Inst. Contemporary Internat. Rels., Beijing, 1988, People's U., Beijing, 1990, 94, 96, 97, 98, 99, 2000; vis. prof. Beijing U., 1989, 98, U. Haifa, Israel, 1990, Ctrl. European U., Budapest, 2000; vis. spkr. Soviet Acad. Scis., 1990, Barcelona (Spain) U. and Complutense U., 1990, Cambridge (Eng.) U., 1991, Nat. Taiwan U., 1998, 99; vis. lectr., Japan, India, Hong Kong, Yugoslavia, Spain, 1990, 91, Germany, 1991, Bulgaria, 1991; vis. spkr. Conf. for Study of European Ideas, Aalborg U., Denmark, 1992; vis. prof. People's U., Beijing, 1990, 97, Janus Pannonius U., Pecs, Hungary, 1981. Author: The Revolutionary Armies, 1980, Revolution, Armies and War, 1986, Prelude to the Cold War: Tsarist, Soviet and U.S. Armies in Two World Wars, 1988, Torrents of Spring: Soviet and Post Soviet Politics, 1994; co-author: The Dynamics of Soviet Foreign Policy, 1988; editor: Communist Armies in Politics, 1982, Terror and Communist Politics, 1984, Superpowers and Revolution, 1986; co-editor: Contemporary Soviet Military Affairs: The Legacy World War II, 1989; contbr. numerous articles in fieod to profl. jours. Charles Phelps Taft fellow U. Cin., 1976-77; Am. Philos. Soc. grantee, 1980. Mem. Am. Polit. Sci. Assn., Am. Assn. Advancement Slavic Studies. Democrat. Jewish. Office: U Denver Grad Sch Internat Studies Denver CO 80208-0001 Office Phone: 303-871-2548. Business E-Mail: jadelman@du.edu.

ADELMAN, MICHAEL SCHWARTZ, lawyer; b. Cambridge, Mass., June 6, 1940; s. Benjamin Taft and Sally Frances (Schwartz) A.; m. Amy Kay, June 15, 1962; children: Robert, Jonathon. Student, Boston U., 1958—59; BA in English with honors, U. Mich., 1962, JD cum laude, 1967. Bar: Mich. 1968, Miss. 1974; cert. for death penalty post-conviction collateral relief cases. Assoc. Zwerdling, Miller, Klimist & Maurer, Detroit, 1968-69; ptnr. Philo, Maki, Ravitz, Glotta, Adelman, Cockrel & Robb, Detroit, 1969-70, Glotta, Adelman & Dinges, Detroit, 1970-74, Andalman, Adelman & Steiner P.A., Hattiesburg, Miss., 1974-86, Adelman & Steiner P.A., Hattiesburg, 1986—2005, Michael Adelman, P.A., 2005—. Pres., bd. dirs. Miss. Ctr. Legal Svcs., Hattiesburg. Contbr. short stories: The Deputy, The Detention Center to New Renaissance. Treas. Hattiesburg Area Equal Rights Coun.; mem. Hattiesburg Biracial Adv. Com., 1987-89, chmn., 1988-89; v.p. state bd. dirs. NAMI, 2000—. Recipient Ralph T. Abernathy award Jackson County (Miss.) So. Christian Leadership Conf., 1978. Mem.: ABA, South Ctrl. Miss. Bar Assn. (pres. 2002). Address: 33 Camellia Ct Hattiesburg MS 39402-6112 Office Phone: 601-544-8291. E-mail: adelst33@aol.com.

ADELMAN, PAMELA BERNICE KOZOLL, education educator; b. Milw., Dec. 26, 1945; d. Harry and Rebecca (Sharp) Kozoll; m. Steven H. Adelman, June 30, 1968; children: David, Robert. BS, U. Wis., Madison, 1967; MA, Northwestern U., 1972, PhD, 1982. Cert. tchr., Ill. Chair edn. dept. Barat Coll., Lake Forest, Ill., 1986-97; tchr. Peckham Jr. High Sch., Milw., 1967-68, Fairview Sch., Skokie, Ill., 1968-70; learning disabilities specialist Sch. Dist 28, Northbrook, Ill., 1971-77; instr., rsch. asst. Northwestern U., Evanston, Ill., 1977-80; lectr., asst. prof., then assoc. prof. Barat Coll., Lake Forest, Ill., 1977-90, prof. edn., 1990-99, dir. learning opportunities program, 1985-99, chmn. edn. dept., 1986-97, grad. dean, 1997-99, chmn. edn. dept., 1986-97; founding exec. dir. Hyde Park Day Sch., 1999—, Hyde Park Day Sch. North, Chgo., 2004—. Cons. Deerfield (Ill.) Pub. Schs., 1986-90; proposal reviewer State of N.J., Trenton, 1986-87; mem. Pres.'s Com. on Hiring of Disabled, 1990; higher edn. adv. coun. State of Ill.; mem. Coun. Chgo. Area Deans of Edn., 1992-99, chair, 1998-99; comprehensive sys. of pers. devel. adv. com. Ill. State Bd. Edn.; presenter in field. Co-author: Learning Disabilities, Graduate School, and Careers, 1990; co-editor: Success for College Students with Learning Disabilities, 1993; consulting editor Learning Disabilities Focus, 1989-92, Jour. Developmental Edn., 1990-98, Jour. of Postsecondary Edn. and Disabilities, 1991-95; contbr. articles to ednl. publs. Chair Sch. Dist. 107 Caucus, Highland Park, Ill., 1982; bd. dirs. Jewish Children's Bur., Chgo., 1985—, pres., 1994-96; co-author brochure for Ill. Dept. Human Rights, Chgo., 1986; bd. dirs. Jewish Fedn. Met. Chgo., 1996. Paul A. Witty fellow Northwestern U., 1978-80; grantee Lloyd A. Fry Found., 1985-86, McDonald's Corp., Chgo., 1986, Kraft Corp., Chgo., 1989, Thorn River Found., 1990—. Fellow Internat. Acad. for Rsch. in Learning Disabilities; mem. Internat. Dyslexia Assn. (bd. dirs. Ill. br. 2000—), Coun. Exceptional Children, Learning Disabilities Assn. Am., Coun. Learning Disabilities. Avocations: reading, walking, music, swimming. Office: Hyde Park Day Sch 1375 E 60th St Chicago IL 60637-2856 Office Phone: 773-834-5081.

ADELMAN, RICK, professional basketball coach; b. Lynwood, Calif., June 16, 1946; m. Mary Kay Adelman; children: Kathryn Mary, Laura, R.J., David. Master's, Loyola Marymount U. Profl. basketball player, San Diego, 1968-70, Portland (Oreg.) Trail Blazers, 1970-73, asst. coach, 1983-89, head coach, 1989-94; basketball player Chgo., New Orleans, Kansas City, and Omaha, 1973-75; head coach Chemeketa Community Coll., Salem, Oreg., 1975-83, Golden State Warriors, Oakland, Calif., 1995-97, Sacramento Kings, 1998—. Office: Sacramento Kings ARCO Arena One Sports Parkway Sacramento CA 95834

ADELMAN, ROBERT PAUL, retired construction executive, lawyer; b. N.Y.C., Dec. 7, 1930; s. Saul and Eva (Ochs) A.; m. Renee Gratum, June 7, 1953 (dec. Apr. 1998); children: Michael, Susan, John; m. Judith A. Turner, Jan. 9, 1999. BA, Columbia U., 1952, JD, 1954. Bar: N.Y. 1954, U.S. Supreme Ct. 1960. Assoc. Winthrop, Stimson, Putnam & Roberts, N.Y.C., 1956-64; with Celanese Corp., N.Y.C., 1964-71; v.p., treas., gen. counsel Calina Industries, Inc., N.Y.C., 1971-73; chief fin. officer Rockefeller Group, Inc., N.Y.C., 1975-84; chmn., chief exec. officer, pres. Rogers Group, Inc., Nashville, 1984-88, chmn., 1988-92, vice chmn., 1992—2001, cons. to the pres. and CEO, 2001—04. Mem. Fin. Execs. Inst., 1973-84, Conf. Bd. Exec. Coun., 1985-90; bd. dirs. N. European Oil Royalty Trust, 1987—, chmn. audit com., 1995—; bd. dirs. Coml. Paving & Recycling Co., 2004—. Treas. and chief fin. officer N.Y. State Urban Devel. Corp., 1973-75; trustee The Jackson Lab., 1981—. Served with U.S. Army, 1954-56, instr. Corps of Cadets U.S. Mil. Acad., West Point, N.Y. Mem. University Club (N.Y.C.), Amelia Island Club. Avocations: sailing, golf. Home: 1540 Piper Dunes Pl Amelia Island FL 32034-6610

ADELMAN, STANLEY JOSEPH, lawyer; b. Devils Lake, N.D., May 20, 1942; s. Isadore Russell Adelman and Eva Claire (Robins) Stoller; m. Mary Beth Petchaft, Jan. 30, 1972; children: Laura E., Sarah A. BS, U. Wis., 1964, JD, 1967. Bar: Ill. 1967, U.S. Dist. Ct. (no. dist.) Ill. 1967, Wis. 1968, U.S. Ct. Appeals (7th cir.), U.S. Dist. Ct. (ea. dist.) Wis. 1979, U.S. Supreme Ct. 1982, U.S. Ct. Appeals (10th cir.) 1984, U.S. Ct. Appeals (fed. cir.) 1987. Assoc. Sonnenchein, Carlin, Nath & Rosenthal, Chgo., 1967-75, ptnr., 1975-85, DLA Piper Rudnick Gray Cary US LLP, Chgo., 1985—, co-chmn. litigation dept., 1985-91, 96-97, profl. responsibility ptnr., 1992-94, mem. mgmt. policy com., 1985-97, co-chmn. complex litigation practice group, 1997-98, pro bono ptnr., 2003—05. Bd. dirs. Legal Assistance Found., Chgo., 1982—83. Fellow Nat. Inst. Trial Advocacy; mem. Chgo. Bar Assn., Chgo. Coun. Lawyers, Am. Inns of Ct. (pres. Markey/Wigmore chpt. 1998-99), Lawyers Club Chgo., Order of Coif. Jewish. Home: 115 Crescent Dr Glencoe IL 60022-1303 Office: DLA Piper Rudnick Gray Cary US LLP 203 N La Salle St Ste 1900 Chicago IL 60601-1210 Office Phone: 312-368-4095. Business E-Mail: stanley.adelman@dlapiper.com.

ADELMAN, STEVEN ALLEN, theoretical physical chemist, educator; b. Chgo., July 4, 1945; s. Hyman and Sarah Adelman; m. Barbara Stolberg, May 13, 1974 BS, Ill. Inst. Tech., 1967; PhD, Harvard U., 1972. Postdoctoral fellow MIT, Cambridge, 1972-73; postdoctoral fellow U. Chgo., 1973-74; asst. prof. chemistry Purdue U., West Lafayette, Ind., 1975-77, assoc. prof., 1977-82, prof., 1982—. Cons. Exxon Rsch. Co., Los Alamos Nat. Lab.; vis. prof. U. Paris, 1985; nominator 1994 Nobel Prize in Chemistry, Royal Swedish Acad. Scis.; Renaissance Weekend Participant, 2003. Contbr. articles to profl. jours.and chapters to books. Vol. U.S. Peace Corp., Ankara, Turkey, 1969-70. Fellow Alfred P. Sloan Found., 1976-78, Guggenheim Found., 1982-83; NSF grantee, 1976—; named Outstanding Sr. in Chemistry, Am. Inst. Chemistry, 1967. Fellow Am. Phys. Soc.; mem. AAAS, Am. Chem. Soc., Am. Statis. Assn., Math. Assn. Am., Sigma Xi. Achievements include creating the mathematical and physical foundation for studying chemical reaction dynamics on solid surfaces and in liquid solution; developing the theory of fast variable/slow bath irreversible motion; making basic contributions to the theory of friction on molecules and to the theory of liquid phase vibrational energy relaxation. Avocations: long-distance running, strength training, turkish language and literature. Home: 3037 Courthouse Dr W Apt 2C West Lafayette IN 47906-1035 Office: Purdue U Dept Chemistry 560 Oval Dr West Lafayette IN 47907-2084 Office Phone: 765-494-5277. Business E-Mail: saa@purdue.edu.

ADELMAN, STEVEN HERBERT, lawyer; b. Dec. 21, 1945; s. Irving and Sylvia (Cohen) A.; m. Pamela Bernice Kozoll, June 30, 1968; children: David, Robert. BS, U. Wis., Madison, 1967; JD, DePaul U., 1970. Bar: Ill. 1970, U.S. Dist. Ct. (no. dist.) Ill. 1970, U.S. Ct. Appeals (7th cir.) 1975. Ptnr. Keck, Mahin & Cate, Chgo., 1970-93, Lord, Bissell & Brook, Chgo., 1993—. Bd. dirs. Bur. Jewish Employment Problems, Chgo., 1983—, pres. 1991, 92;

employment relations com. Chgo. Assn. Commerce and Industry, 1982-90. Contbr. chpts. to books, articles to profl. jours. Named one of leading labor and employment lawyers in Ill., Leading Lawyers Network; recipient, Leading Atty. Network. Fellow Coll. Labor and Employment Lawyers; mem. ABA (Silver key award 1969), Chgo. Bar Assn. (chmn. labor and employment law com. 1988-89), Ill. State Bar Assn., Chgo. Coun. Lawyers, Decalogue Soc. Office: Lord Bissell & Brook 115 S La Salle St Ste 3200 Chicago IL 60603-3902 E-mail: sadelman@lordbissell.com.

ADELMAN, WILLIAM J., JR., biophysicist; b. Mt. Vernon, N.Y., Jan. 29, 1928; s. William Joseph Adelman and Helen Emma Carlock; m. Jean Alma Mayo, Sept. 3, 1951; children: Everett M., John W., Willa J. BS, Fordham U., 1950; MS, U. Vt., 1952; PhD, U. Rochester, 1955. Aviation physiologist Sch. Aviation Medicine, Randolph AFB, 1955—56; instr. U. Buffalo (N.Y.) Sch. Medicine, 1956—57, asst. prof. physiology, 1957—59; neurophysiologist Lab. Biophysics Nat. Inst. Neurol. Diseases and Blindness, NIH, Bethesda, Md., 1959—62; prof. physiology dept. physiology U. Md. Sch. Medicine., Balt., 1962—72; chief lab. biophysics Nat. Inst. Neurol., Communicative Disorders, and Stroke, NIH, Bethesda, 1972—89. Treas. Soc. Gen. Physiology; trustee Marine Biol. Lab., Woods Hole, Mass. Editor: Biophysics and Physiology Excitable Membranes, 1971; contbr. articles to profl. jours.; newspaper art critic:. Recipient Spl. Recognition award, USPHS, 1985; fellow, AAAS, 1965; grantee in field; spl. fellow, NIH, 1969. Avocation: fine art. Home: 160 Locust St Falmouth MA 02540-2674

ADELMAN, WILLIAM JOHN, retired academic administrator, industrial relations specialist; b. Chgo., July 26, 1932; s. William Sidney and Annie Teresa (Goan) A.; m. Nora Jill Walters, June 26, 1952; children: Michelle, Marguerite, Marc, Michael, Jessica. Student, Lafayette Coll., 1952; BA, Elmhurst Coll., 1956; MA, U. Chgo., 1964. Tchr. Whitecross Sch., Hereford, Eng., 1956-57, Jefferson Sch., Berwyn, Ill., 1957-60, Morton High Sch., Berwyn, 1960-66; mem. faculty dept. labor and indsl. relations U. Ill., Chgo., 1966-91, prof., 1978-91, prof. emeritus, 1991—; coordinator Chgo. Labor Edn. Program, 1981-87. Lectr. Road Scholar Program, Ill. Humanities Coun., 1997. Author: Touring Pullman, 1972, Haymarket Revisited, 1976, Pilsen and the West Side, 1981; writer: film Packingtown U.S.A., 1968; narrator: Palace Cars and Paradise: Pullman's Model Town, 1983. Bd. dirs. Chgo. Regional Blood Program, 1977-80; mem. Ill. State Employment Security Adv. Bd., 1974-75; Democratic candidate U.S. Ho. of Reps. from 14th dist. Ill., 1970; organizer Haymarket Centennial Events, 1986; chmn. adv. bd. Jane Addams' Hull House, 1991-99; mem. adv. bd. Maxwell St. Mus., 2001—; mem. Haymarket Monument Adv. Panel, 2002-04. Ill. Humanities Council grantee, 1977; German Marshall Fund U.S. grantee, 1977; recipient Tradition of Excellence award Oak Park/River Forest H.S., 1993, Eugene V. Debs award Midwest Labor Press assn., 1995. Mem. Ill. Labor History Soc. (founding mem., v.p., Union Hall of Honor 1993), Am. Fedn. Tchrs., Doris Humphrey Soc. (v.p. 1990—). Unitarian Universalist. Home and Office: 613 S Highland Ave Oak Park IL 60304-1524 Personal E-mail: www.dooper@aol.com.

ADELSBERG, HARVEY, hospital administrator; b. Bronx, N.Y., Aug. 5, 1931; s. Joseph and Becky (Rindner) Adelsberg; m. Miriam Levine, June 20, 1964; children: Jonathan, Risa, Seth. BA, NYU, 1953, MPA, 1960, postgrad., 1960—65. Adminstrv. resident Beth David Hosp., N.Y.C., 1953—54; adminstrv. asst. Met. Jewish Geriatric Center, Bklyn., 1954—58; asst. dir. Kingsbrook Jewish Med. Center, Bklyn., 1958—61, Hosp. for Joint Diseases, N.Y.C., 1961—64; exec. dir. Theresa Grotta Center for Restorative Svcs., Caldwell, NJ, 1964—70; asst. dir. Mt. Sinai Hosp., N.Y.C., 1970—72; cons. med. care and svcs. to aged Fedn. Jewish Philanthropies, N.Y.C., 1972—74; exec. dir. Daus. of Miriam Center for Aged, Clifton, NJ, 1974—76, exec. v.p., 1977—95, exec. v.p. emeritus, 1996; adj. prof. MBA health sys. mgmt. program Fairleigh Dickinson U., Coll. of Bus., 2002—. Adj. asst. prof. health care adminstrn. Bernard M. Baruch Coll., Mt. Sinai Sch. Medicine, CUNY, 1973—, U. Medicine and Dentistry, N.J., 1995; mem. adv. com. Rutgers U., 1969—; mem. adj. prof. N.J. Grad. Sch. Pub. Health, 1995; cons. Consulting Svcs. Inst., 1995; mem. N.J. Licensing Bd. for Nursing Home Adminstrs., 1969—, vice chmn., 1969—77; mem. Adv. Council on Aging, Livingston, NJ, 1977—; sr. exec. fellow long term care studies MBA Health Sys. Mgmt. Program Fairleigh Dickinson U., 2002; sr. exec. fellow long term care studies. V.p. Solomon Schechter Day Sch. of Essex and Union, 1980—; trustee Synagogue of Suburban Torah Center, Livingston, 1978—; v.p. Temple Beth Shalom, Livingston, 1970—71, 1973, trustee, 1968—70, 1975—; mem. governing com. Camp Ramah, Wingdale, NY, 1979—; exec. bd. Jewish Communal Svc. Assn., 1993—; trustee Hosp. and Council Met. N.J., 1967—70, Health and Hosp. Council So. N.Y., 1972—74, N.J. Assn. Non-Profit Homes for Aging, 1976—, Jewish Cmty. Housing Corp., Paterson, NJ, 1975—; trustee tng. Dist. 1199J, 1990; bd. govs. Greater N.Y. Hosp. Assn., 1972—74; agt. Daus. of Miriam Found., 1984. Fellow: Am. Geriatric Soc., Am. Coll. Nursing Home Adminstrs., Am. Coll. Hosp. Adminstrs.; mem.: APHA, Am., N.J. hosp. assns., B'nai B'rith (v.p. 1960—64), Hosp. Exec. Club. Home and Office: 27 Tuxedo Dr Livingston NJ 07039-2452 Office Phone: 973-992-0498. E-mail: harveyadelsberg@aol.com.

ADELSMAN, JEAN (HARRIETTE ADELSMAN), newspaper editor; b. Indpls., Oct. 21, 1944; d. Joe and Beatrice Irene (Samuel) A. BS in Journalism, Northwestern U., 1966, MS in Journalism, 1967. Copy editor Chgo. Sun-Times, 1967-75, fin. news editor, 1975-77, entertainment editor, 1977-80, asst. mng. editor features, 1980-84; now mng. editor Daily Breeze, Torrance, Calif. Office: Daily Breeze 5215 Torrance Blvd Torrance CA 90503-4077

ADELSON, EDWARD, physicist, educator, musician; b. Bklyn., Aug. 19, 1934; s. Barnet and Sarah (Strongin) A.; m. Juliane A.W. Riedel, Aug. 5, 1961 (div. June 1982). BA, NYU, 1956; postgrad. (Woodrow Wilson fellow), Eastman Sch. Music, 1956-57; MS, Ohio State U., 1965, PhD, 1974. Prin. physicist Battelle Mem. Inst., Columbus, Ohio, 1957-71; lectr. Ohio State U., Columbus, 1974-88, acad. program specialist, 1988—. Cons. in field. Author: Student Companion for Reese's University Physics, vol. 2, 2001; editor test books; contbr. articles to profl. jours. Organist, choirmaster emeritus St. Alban's Episcopal Ch., Bexley, Ohio. Mem.: AAAS, Am. Guild Organists, Am. Assn. Physics Tchrs., Am. Phys. Soc., Chrichton Club, Sigma Pi Sigma, Phi Beta Kappa. Home: 6384 Falkirk Pl Columbus OH 43229-2045 Office: Ohio State U Smith Lab Columbus OH 43210

ADELSON, LAWRENCE SETH, electronics executive, lawyer; b. San Francisco, Mar. 28, 1950; s. Joseph Bernard Adelson and Edna Sylvia (Kamener) Fraiberg; m. Pamela Joan Williams, Dec. 1, 1984; 1 child, Emily. BA, U. Mich., 1972; JD, Harvard U., 1975. Bar: Ill. 1977, U.S. Dist. Ct. (no. dist.) Ill. 1977, U.S. Ct. Appeals (7th cir.) 1980. Law clk. to judge U.S. Ct. Appeals for 9th Cir., Honolulu, 1975-76; assoc. Isham Lincoln & Beale, Chgo., 1976-85; gen. counsel CMC Real Estate Corp., Chgo., 1985-90, v.p., 1987-90, v.p., gen. counsel, 1988-90, CMC Heartland Ptnrs., Chgo., 1990—. V.p. and gen. counsel Chgo.-Milw. Corp., 1988—, Heartland Tech., Inc., 1998—; chmn., CEO Heartland Tech., Inc., 2002—; CEO Heartland Ptnrs., 2002—. Editor Harvard Law Rev., 1973-75. Pres., bd. dirs. Gus Giordano Jazz Dance; pres. West Ctrl. Assn., 1997-2000. Mem. Chgo. Bar Assn. (chmn. law week subcom. 1982, neighborhood outreach project 1983-84, membership com. 1987-88), Lawyers Club. Jewish. Office: Heartland Tech Inc 303 N Jefferson Ct, Ste 305 Chicago IL 60661

ADELSON, M(AURICE) B(ERNARD), IV, lawyer; b. Memphis, Apr. 24, 1952; s. M.B. and Clare (Walker) A.; m. Mary Ina Lindeman. BA, Va. Mil. Inst., 1973; MS, Fla. Inst. Tech., 1979, MBA, 1982; JD, Fla. State U., 1986. Bar: Fla. 1987, fed. cts. Commd. officer U.S. Army, 1973, advanced through grades to maj., 1981, ret., 1993; project mgr. Army R&D Command, Dover, NJ, 1978-82, Breed Corp., Fairfield, N.J., 1982-83; pvt. practice law Tallahassee, 1987—90; asst. gen. counsel land use litigation Fla. Dept. Community Affairs, 1990-91; sr. asst. gen. counsel and permitting atty. Fla. Dept. Environ. Protection, 1991—2001; atty. Tallahassee office Law Offices of Arthur C. Koski, P.A., Boca Raton, Fla., 2001—03; atty. Law Offices of M.B. Adelson IV, P.A., 2003—. Contbr. articles to profl. jours. Decorated Army Commendation medal, Meritorious Service medal, others. Mem. Fla. Bar. Republican. Avocations: woodworking, rugby, canoeing, cooking, photography. Office: 3387 E Lakeshore Dr Tallahassee FL 32312-1456 Office Phone: 850-523-0606. E-mail: mba4@earthlink.net.

ADELSON, ROGER DEAN, history professor, historian, editor; b. Abilene, Kans., July 11, 1942; s. Orlie Austin and Winnifred Graham (McClure) A.; m. Sally Isabelle Squires, Sept. 1966 (div. Apr. 1978). BA, George Washington U., 1964; MA, Washington U., 1967, PhD, 1972; BLitt, Oxford (Eng.) U., 1970. Danforth fellow Washington U., St. Louis, 1964-67; sr. rsch. fellow St. Antony's Coll., Oxford U., 1972-73; lectr. history Harvard U., Cambridge, Mass., summer 1974; asst. prof. Ariz. State U., Tempe, 1974-78, assoc. prof., 1978-95, prof., 1996—; editor Historian, 1990-95, cons. editor, 1995—2001, mem. editl. bd., 2002—. Vis. prof. Am. Grad. Sch. Internat. Mgmt., Glendale, Ariz., 1980s, Pepperdine U., Malibu, Calif., 1994, 95, 96; dir. Global History Project, 1995-97. Author: Mark Sykes: Portrait of an Amateur, 1975, London and the Invention of the Middle East, 1995, Speaking of History, 1996. Founding. pres. Soc. for Internat. Devel., Ariz., 1983; charter mem. Coun. Fgn. Rels., Phoenix, 1976. Mem. Conf. Hist. Jours. (pres. 1995-97), Phi Alpha Theta (historian 1990-95, editl. bd. 1997--). Avocations: bicycling, swimming, gardening, entertaining. Office: Ariz State U Dept History PO Box 874302 Tempe AZ 85287-4302 Office Phone: 480-965-4594. Business E-Mail: adelsonr@asu.edu.

ADELSON, SHELDON G., hotel executive; b. Aug. 4, 1933; m. Miriam Ochshorn, 1991; children: Adam Arthur, Matan Sarel. Paperboy; mortgage broker; investment adv.; fin. cons.; chmn., CEO Interface Group Inc., Needham, Mass., 1974; chmn., CEO, treas. Las Vegas Sands, Inc., 1989—, Las Vegas Sands Corp., 2004—; founder COMDEX Trade Shows, 1991—95, Sands Expo & Convention Ctr., 1990—, Venetian Resort-Hotel-Casino, 1991—. Mem., US Holocaust Meml. Coun. US Holocaust Meml. Mus., Washington. One of 10 richest people in Am.; 19th richest person in world, 2005. Office: Venetian Resort Hotel Casino 3355 Las Vegas Blvd S Las Vegas NV 89109 Office Phone: 702-414-1000. Office Fax: 702-414-4884.

ADELSTEIN, S(TANLEY) JAMES, pathologist, educator; b. NYC, Jan. 24, 1928; s. George and Belle (Schild) Adelstein; m. Mary Charlesworth Taylor, Sept. 20, 1957; children: Joseph Burrows, Elizabeth Dunster. BS, MS, MIT, 1949, PhD in Biophysics, 1957; MD, Harvard U., 1953. Med. house officer Peter Bent Brigham Hosp., Boston, 1953-54, sr. asst. resident physician, 1957-58, chief resident, 1959-60; fellow Howard Hughes Med. Inst., 1957-58, Henry A. and Camilus Christian fellow, 1959-60; Moseley travel fellow Harvard U. Med. Sch., Boston, 1958-59, instr. anatomy, then asst. prof., 1961-68, assoc prof. radiology, 1968-72, prof., 1972-89, Paul C. Cabot prof. med. biophysics, 1989-97, prof. pathology, Daniel S. Tosteson univ. prof., 1997—2003, Paul C. Cabot disting. prof. med. biophysics, 2003—, dean for acad. program, 1978-97. Dir. Nat. Coun. for Radiation Protection Measurements, 1980—2002, v.p., 1982—2002, hon. v.p., 2002—; cons. Med. Found. fellow, 1960—63; Walter Dandy lectr. Johns Hopkins U., 1996; John Cameron lectr. U. Wis., 1998; Lauristen Taylor lectr. Nat. Coun. for Radiatide Photection, 2000; radiation rsch. bd. NAS, 1999—2002, chair, 2002—05, nuclear and radioactive studies bd., 2005—; biol. rsch. adv. com. Dept. Energy, 2001—; John Cameron lectr. U. Wis., 1998; L. Taylor lectr. Nat. Coun. for Radiation Protection, 2000; rsch. coll. adv. bd. U. Tasmania, 2003—. Mem. editl. bd.: Investigative Radiology, 1972—80, Postgrad. Radiology, Radiology Rsch., 1990—94; editor (assoc. editor): Jour. Nuc. Medicine, 1975—81; contbr. articles to profl. jours. Trustee Am. Bd. Nuc. Medicine, 1972—78; mem. fellowship adv. com. Whitaker Found., 1991—97. Recipient Career Devel. award, NIH, 1965—68; fellow Nat. Found., MIT, 1957, Fogarty Sr. Internat., 1976. Fellow: AAAS, Am. Coll. Nuc. Physicians; mem.: Inst. Medicine, Boylston Med. Soc., Soc. Nuc. Medicine (trustee 1970—74, Blumgart award 1983, Aebersold award 1986, Dr. Hevesy award 1999), Radiation Rsch. Soc. (councillor 1975—78), Assn. Radiation Rsch., Biophys. Soc., Am. Chem. Soc., Alpha Omega Alpha, Tau Beta Pi, Sigma Xi. Office: Harvard Med Sch 25 Shattuck St Boston MA 02115-6027

ADEMA, DANIEL JOHN, real estate company executive; b. New Market, Ontario, Can., Apr. 26, 1976; s. Dwight Eugene Adema and Lorraine Elizabeth Israels; m. Angela Eron Russell, Apr. 25, 2002. BS in Mktg., Metro State Coll., Denver, 1999. Asst. dist. chair Rocky Mountain News, Ft. Collins, Colo., 1999; pres. Adema Enterprises, Englewood, 1999—2005; v.p. ops. Letts Contracting, Aurora, 2003—04; realty chair Colo. Real Estate Network, Denver, 2004—. Author: Penny Miracles, 1998. Republican. Office: Adema Enterprises PO Box 262271 Littleton CO 80163

ADERHOLDT, TRACI EAVES, music educator; b. Rutherfordton, N.C., Mar. 3, 1964; d. Julian Bobby and Alice Faye (Waldrop) Eaves; m. James Lamar Aderholdt, June 17, 2000. B in Music Edn., U. N.C., 1986; M in Music Edn., Converse Coll., 1992. Drama tchr. Montgomery County Sch., Troy, NC, 1986—87; gen. music tchr. Shelby City Sch., Shelby, NC, 1987—2001, 2002—, Gaston County Sch., Gastonia, NC, 2001—02. Music dir. Greater Shelby Cmty. Theater, Shelby, 1988—95; pianist Cleve. County Choral Soc., Shelby, 1988—99, Eastside Bapt. Ch., Shelby, 1991—97, First Bapt. Ch., Kings Mt., NC, 1997—. Mem.: Am. Choral Dir. Assn. (SSA all-state coord. 1994—95), Music Educators Nat. Conf. Baptist. Avocations: antiques, painting, coin collecting/numismatics, drawing. Home: 357 Beattie Rd Kings Mountain NC 28086

ADERHOLT, ROBERT B., congressman, lawyer; b. Haleyville, Ala., July 22, 1965; m. Caroline McDonald; children: Mary Elliot, Robert Hayes. BA, Birmingham Southern U., 1987; JD, Samford U. Cumberland School of Law, 1990. City judge, Haleyville, Ala., 1992—96; asst. legal advisor to Al. gov., 1995—96; mem. U.S. Congress from 4th Ala. dist., 1997—, mem. appropriations com., vice chmn. military quality of life subcom., mem. transp., treasury subcom., housing and urban develop. subcom. & interior and environ. subcom. Mem. Helsinki Commn. on Security and Cooperation in Europe. Republican. Office: US Ho of Reps 1433 Longworth Bldg Washington DC 20515-0104 also: Dist Off 247 Carl Elliott Bldg 1710 Ala Ave Jasper AL 35501*

ADETUNJI, BABATUNDE ABAYOMI, forensic psychiatrist; s. Babajide Aderogba and Florence Oluyemi Adetunji; m. Oluyemisi Hannah Quadri, Sept. 20, 1990; children: Oluwadamilola Temidayo, Opeposi Abimbola, Oluwanifemi Aderonke. BSc with honors in health sci., Obafemi Awolowo U., Nigeria, 1980—84; M in human ecology, Vrije U., 1990—93; MSc, U. London, 1995—97. Medical Doctor Obafemi Awolowo U., 1987, diplomate Royal coll. of Physicians and Surgeons of Ireland, 2000, Conjoint Bd. of Guys Hosp. and U. of Bahrain, 1999. Staff forensic psychiatrist Redford Lodge Hosp., London, 1998—2001; cons. psychiatrist and dir. Medikhelp Cons. Ltd., London, 2001—02; attending psychiatrist Kirby Forensic Psychiat. Ctr., Manhattan, NY, 2004—05, MHM-Correctional Services, Phila., 2005—. Dir. Medikhelp Cons. Ltd., London, 2001—; locum cons. in forensic psychiatry Broadmoor Hosp., Crowthorne, England, 2001—02, Three Bridges Medium Secure Unit, Ealing, England, 2001—02; medicolegal cons. Bajikijaye Solicitors, Toronto, Canada, 2001—04; locum cons. in geriatric psychiatry Princess Alexandra Hosp., Harlow, England, 2004, Lincolnshire Cmty. NHS Trust, Lincoln, England, 2004—04; locum cons. psychiatrist Oxleas NHS Trust, Sidcup, England. Book reviewer Royal Society of Medicine Press; contbr. articles to profl. jours. Recipient Internat. Cert. in Human Ecology, UNESCO, 1993; Belgian Govt. schorlaship (ABOS), Belgian Govt., 1990—93. Fellow: Royal Acad. of Medicine of Ireland, Am. Soc. of Addiction Medicine; mem.: Am. Coll. of Forensic Examiners Internat., Assn. of European Psychiatrists, Am. Acad. of Psychiatry and the Law, Brit. Acad. of Forensic Sciences, Internat. Acad. of Law and Mental Health, Soc. of Expert Witnesses, NY Acad. of Sciences, Brit. Assn. of Med. Managers, Acad. of Experts. Achievements include design of information package on HIV-AIDS in 3 Nigerian languages; risk monitoring inventory for mental health multidisciplinary team (RMI-MDT); research in assessment of the effectiveness of day hospitals using preadmission and 6-months intra-admission questionnaire scores; perception of mental health professionals with regards to issue of racism in psychiatry; community hypertension survey; AIDS awareness survey. Office: MHM-Correctional Services Mod Ii 8001 State Rd Philadelphia PA 19136 Office Phone: 215-685-7167. Office Fax: 215-685-7166. Personal E-mail: medikhelp@yahoo.com.

ADHIKARY, BIMAL BABU, structural engineer; b. Kathmandu, Nepal, Sept. 13, 1965; s. Madhu Bilas and Sasikala Adhikary; m. Namrata Adhikary, June 25, 1972. BS, Nat. Inst. of Tech., India, 1990; MS, Asian Inst. of Tech., Thailand, 1995; PhD, Saitama U., Japan, 2000. Project engr. Frank Lam & Assoc., Austin, Tex.; project mgr. Encotech Engring. Con., Austin, Tex., 2004—. Contbr. articles pub. to profl. jour. Recipient Best Paper Award, Japan Soc. of Civil Engrs., 2000; fellow Monbusho, Japanese Govt., 1997-2000, DAAD, German Govt., 1993-1995, Colombo Plan, Indian Govt. Mem.: ASCE, Am. Concrete Inst., Sigma Xi. Achievements include research in Reviewer, Jour. of Constrn. and Bldg. Materials. Home: 12113 Metric Blvd #435 Austin TX 78758 Office: Encotech Engring Cons Inc 8500 Bluffstone Cove Ste B-103 Austin TX 78759 Personal E-mail: bimaladhikary@gmail.com.

ADIGA, GIRIDHAR U., geriatrician, pharmacologist, researcher, internist; arrived in U.S., 1999; s. Krishna Uppoor Adiga; m. Mamatha Adiga. MB, BChir, Gulbarga U., Bellary, India, 1992; MD, All India Inst. Med. Scis., New Delhi, 1997. Diplomate Am. Bd. Internal Medicine, 2002, cert. Edn. Commn. for Fgn. Med. Grads., 1994, geratric medicine ABIM, 2003. Med. officer Dhanvanthri Nursing Home, Bellary, 1992—93; resident med. officer ophthalmology All India Inst. Med. Scis., New Delhi, 1993—93, postgrad. resident in pharmacology, 1994—97; resident med. officer cancer surgery Safdarjung Hosp., Govt. Delhi, New Delhi, 1993—93; sr. demonstrator Maulana Azad Med. Coll., New Delhi, 1998—99; resident internal medicine Our Lady Mercy Med. Ctr., N.Y. Med. Coll., Bronx, 1999—2002; fellow geriatric medicine N.Y. Med. Coll., Bronx, 2002—03; with Halifax Med. Specialists, P.A., Roanoke Rapids, NC, 2003—. Presenter in field; clin. preceptor Univ. N.C. Sch. of Medicine, Chapel Hill. Contbr. articles to profl. jours., chapters to books. Mem.: AMA, Am. Med. Dirs. Assn., Am. Geriat. Soc., Am. Coll. Clin. Pharmacology. Achievements include discovery of and characterization of Iatrogenic anemia in the elderly; research in diuretic activity of Benincasa hispida; role of life style factors on the occurance of diabetes in India; review on vitamin B12 deficiency in older adults; HIV disease and gastrointestinal manifestations in older adults; Review on Myths and Facts on Growth Hormone; Review on human helminthic infections; Review of clinical and toxicological aspects of snake bites; discovery of altered vitamin B12 metabolism in acute pneumonia; research in anti ulcer activity of B. hispida; anti inflammatory activity of pefloxacin; diuretic activity of Benincasa hispida; Characterization and role of IL2 therapy in skeletal complications of renal cell carcinoma; Reviewed and characterectized Ritchter's conversion of CLL to Hodgkin's disease; Impact of iatrogenic anemia on mortality; Toxicological studies on Benincasa hispida. Office: Halifax Med Specialists PA 270 Smith Church Rd Roanoke Rapids NC 27870 E-mail: adiga_69@yahoo.com.

ADINOLFI, MARION DARLYNE, research scientist; b. Bronx, NY, Oct. 16, 1941; d. Carlo and Frances Moscato; m. Vincent John Adinolfi Sr., June 1, 1956; children: Vincent John Jr., Richard Anthony. BA, Coll. of New Rochelle, New Rochelle, NY, 1979; Master of Metaphysical Sci., U. of Metaphysics, Studio City, CA, 2001, Dr. of Metaphysical Sci., 2002. Pres. Adino Asbestos, Bronx, NY; tech. rschr. N.Y.C.; 11c spl. edn. educator St. Raymond's H.S., Bronx; english educator St. Martin's of Tours, Bronx; tech. rsch. scientist Adino Asbestos, Bronx; ny realty owner F&S Crest Co., Bronx; pastoral counselor N.Y.C.; metaphysical practitioner; ordained min.; dr. of metaphysical. V.p. F&S Crest Co., New York, NY, 1974—2002; metaphysical cons. Pvt. Practice, New York, NY, 1984—2002. Author: of various Anti-aging, Performance Enhancement, & Entertainment Computer Programs; contbr. articles to profl. newspapers and jours. R-Consevative. Achievements include development of pheromonal cologne and perfume fragrances; completed 2 placebo studies in pheromonal research. Avocations: reading, pheromonal research, golf, swimming, gift wrapping. Home: 828 Calhoun Ave Bronx NY 10465

ADIZES, ICHAK, management consultant, writer; PhD, Columbia U. Prof. Hebrew U., Jerusalem, Tel Aviv U., Stanford (Calif.) U., Columbia U., N.Y.C., UCLA; founder, profl. dir. Adizes Inst., Santa Barbara, Calif., 1975—; acad. dean Adizes Grad. Sch. for Study of Change and Leadership, Santa Barbara, Calif. Lectr. in field. Author: Self-Management, 1975, How to Solve the Mismanagement Crisis, 1979, Corporate Lifecycles: How and Why Corporations Grow and Die and What to Do About It, 1988, Mastering Change; The power of Mutual Trust and Respect in Personal Life, Business and Society, 1992, The Pursuit of Prime, 1996, Managing Corporate Life Cycles, 1999, The Ideal Executive: Why You Cannot Be One and What to Do About It, 2004, Management/Mismanagement Styles: How to Identify A Style and What to Do About It, 2004, Leading the Leaders: How to Enrich Your Style of Management and Handle People Whose Style Is Different From Yours, 2004; contbr. articles to profl. jours., newspapers. Office: Adizes Inst 2815 E Valley Rd Santa Barbara CA 93108-1611 Fax: (805) 565-0741. Office Phone: 805-565-2901. E-mail: ichak@adizes.com.

ADJARIAN, MAUDE MADELEINE, literature educator, researcher; b. Santa Monica, Calif., Oct. 10, 1965; BA Comparative Lit., U. of Calif., Berkeley, 1987; PhD Comparative Lit., U.of Mich., Ann Arbor, 1994. Adj. instr., women's studies/program in personal devel. UC Berkeley Ext., San Francisco, 1995—97; instr., English Skyline H.S., Oakland, Calif., 1997—2000; assoc. rschr. U. of Ariz., Dept. Women's Studies, Tucson, 2000—; adj. instr., English Pima C.C., Tucson, 2000—. Reader, English lit. exam. Edn. Testing Services, Princeton, NJ, 2000—; referee Coll. Lit., West Chester, Pa.; adj. lectr. women's studies U. Ariz., 2003—; reviewer Choice, 2004—. Contbr. articles literary criticism and revs. to various jours.; editor: Michigan Feminist Studies, 1993—94; author: Allegories of Desire: Body Nation and Empire in Modern Caribbean Literature by Women, 2004. Vol.literacy tutor Berkeley Pub. Libr., Mich., 1995—97. Grantee U. of Mich. Departmental Fellowship, Program in Comparative Lit., 1988—89, Rackham Discretionary Grant, Rackham Grad. Coll., U. of Mich., 1990. Program in Comparative Lit., Departmental Block Grant, U. of Mich., 1990. Mem.: MLA, Am. Comparative Lit. Assn., African Lit. Assn., Phi Beta Kappa. Office: Univ of Ariz Dept Womens' Studies Comm 108 PO Box 210025 Tucson AZ 85721 E-mail: adjarian@u.arizona.edu.

ADJEMIAN, VART K., agricultural products executive; B in Commerce, Cairo U.; MBA, UCLA. Joined Conti, 1975, contr. Allied Mills, CEO ContiIndustries, CEO commodity mktg. group, sr. v.p. South Am. divsn., sr. v.p. fin. and adminstrn., gen. mgr. Europe; exec. v.p., COO ContiGroup Cos., N.Y.C., 2001—. Office: Conti Group Cos 277 Park Ave New York NY 10172

ADKERSON, RICHARD C., mining executive; BA with honors, Miss. State U., 1969, MBA, 1970. Prof. acctg. fellow SEC, Washington, 1976-78; ptnr., mng. dir., head worldwide oil and gas practice Arthur Anderson & Co.; various positions with Freeport-McMoRan Copper & Gold Inc., New Orleans, 1989-97, pres., COO, 1997—2000, pres., CEO, 2000—; co-chmn. McMoRan Exploration Co. Trustee Nat. D-Day Mus.; v.p., bd. dir., mem. exec. com. Miss. State Univ. Found.; mem. adv. bd. Coll. Bus. & Ind. & Agribus. Inst., Miss. State Univ.; mem. Bus. Council New Orleans & River Region; mem. develop. bd. Fellowship Christian Athletes New Orleans; mem. exec. bd. adv. Coucn Coll., La. State Univ.; mem. Pres. Council Xavier Univ.; mem. bd. vis. M.D. Anderson Cancer Ctr.; mem. adv. bd. Crosby Arboretum. Office: Freeport McMoRan Copper and Gold Inc 1615 Poydras St New Orleans LA 70112*

ADKINS, J. K., writer, professional society administrator; b. Newark, N.J., Jan. 22, 1974; d. Linda C. Britt and James Warren Adkins III. Pres. Kappa Phi Iota Lit. Sorority, Newark, 1997—; moderator PoetryFamily, Montclair, NJ,

2001—. Author: Escapades of a Type A Personality, 1999, Pink Satin Sunrise, 2000, Facets of Being, 2001, (albums) Multifaceted, 2002. Seaman USCG, Newport, R.I. Recipient Glam Slam Championship Trophy, Nuyorican Poets' Cafe, 1999, Winner's Cert., Def Poetry Jam Online, 2001. Mem.: Poetic Shades of Brown Poetry Cir. Home: 37 The Crescent Montclair NJ 07042 Office: Pink Diamond PO Box 22176 Newark NJ 07101 Business E-Mail: pink_diamond@go.com.

ADKINS, JEANNE M., state agency administrator; b. North Platte, Nebr., May 2, 1949; BA, U. Nebr. Journalist; mem. Colo. Ho. of Reps., 1988—99, chairwoman judiciary com., vice-chairwoman legal svcs. com., mem. fin. com., regional air quality control coun., state edn. accountability commn.; dir. policy and planning Colo. Dept. Edn.; dir. Colo. Student Loan Program, 2002—. Founding sec. Douglas County Econ. Devel. Coun., bd. dirs., 1988. Fellow Vanderbilt U. Govt., Gates fellow JFK Sch. Govt. State/Local Program, Toll fellow. Mem. Am. Soc. Newspaper Editors, Soc. Profl. Journalists, Suburban Newspaper Assn. Republican. Baptist. Office: CSLP 999 18th St Ste 425 Denver CO 80202

ADKINS, RODNEY, computer company executive; Joined IBM, 1981, various positions as an engr. with prod. devel., bus. operations and gen. mgmt., 1981—2001, gen. mgr. pervasive computing White Plains, NY, 2001—03, v.p., systems group devel., 2003—. Bd. govs. IBM Academy Tech.; co-chmn., multi-cultural people in tech. IBM; co-chmn. Nat. Black Family Tech. Awareness; bd. dirs. Peopleclick, Inc. Pres. advisory coun. Ga. Tech; bd. trustees Ga. Tech Rsch. Corp. Mem.: Exec. Leadership Coun., Nat. Society Black Engineers. Office: IBM 1133 Westchester Ave White Plains NY 10604

ADKINS, THOMAS SAMUEL, library director; b. Portsmouth, Ohio, Oct. 24, 1965; s. Millard Elwood and Ruth Caroline (Shultz) A. BS, Ohio U., 1988; MLS, Kent (Ohio) State U., 1993. Tchr. Cmty. Action Agy., Portsmouth, Ohio, 1988, Scioto County Schs., Portsmouth, 1988-89; ext. svcs. coord. Portsmouth Pub. Libr., 1989-95; dir. G.A. Wilson Pub. Libr., Waverly, Ohio, 1996—. Chairperson Libr. Adv. Coun., Wellston, Ohio, 1997. Author: Lucasville Cemeteries, 1988; editor: A Backward Glance, vol. 1, 1987, vol. 2, 1990. Mem. Cmty. Svcs. Coun., Waverly, Ohio, 1996—; treas. Lucasville (Ohio) Hist. Soc., 1986—; mem. Valley Alumni Scholarship Com., Lucasville, 1990—; govt. rels. com. Ohio Libr. Coun., 1998—, treas. bd. dirs., 2000-2002, pres. 2004; participant Libr. Leadership Inst., Snowbird, Utah, 1999. Recipient Diana Vescelius Meml. award, 1998. Mem. ALA (Emerging Leaders 2000), Pike County C. of C. (bd. dirs.). Avocations: book collecting, local history, movies, travel.

ADKINSON, ANN M., elementary and special education educator; b. Chgo., Nov. 22, 1957; d. Ernest G. and Thelma L. (Hill) Williams; m. Douglas P. Adkinson, July 30, 1983; children: Courtney Ann, Bryan Douglas. BS in Edn., U. Tex., 1979; MEd, Sam Houston State U., Huntsville, Tex. Cert. elem. and spl. edn. tchr., supr., Tex. Spl. edn. tchr. Roth Elem. Sch., Spring, Tex., Klein Ind. Sch. Dist. Mem. NEA, Coun. for Exceptional Children. Avocations: reading, skiing, planting, aerobics. Home: 11 Pebble Hollow Ct Spring TX 77381-4803

ADKINSON, BRIAN LEE, manufacturing executive; b. Lebanon, Ind., July 10, 1959; s. Marion Leroy and Edith Marie (Shonkwiler) A.; m. Pamela Lea Dinkins, June 12, 1982; children: Katherin Elizabeth, Anna Mary Josephine. BS in Fin., Ind. U., 1982; postgrad., Keller Sch. Mgmt., 1992—93. Asst. bank examiner FDIC, Chgo., 1980-81; acctg. assoc. battery prodn. Union Carbide Co., Bennington, Vt., 1982-83; sr. ptnr. AC Sales Assocs., Murfreesboro, Tenn., 1983-89; spl. mkts. mgr. Chgo. Cutlery Housewares, div. Gen. Housewares Corp., Terre Haute, Ind., 1989-90; nat. sales mgr. Gerber Legendary Blades, a Fiskers Co., Portland, Oreg., 1990-91, Fiskers Inc, Wausau, Wis., 1992-94; mktg. mgr. Fiskars Inc., Wausau, Wis., 1994-98, dir. mktg., 1998-99; group dir. sales/mktg. Recreation Group, 1999-2000; gen. mgr. Fiskars Outdoor Leisure Products, 2000; mng. dir. Fiskar U.K. Ltd., 2000—02; v.p. Jensen Co., Racine, Wis., 2002—03; v.p. sales and mktg. Walnut Hollow INc., Dodgeville, Wis., 2003—. Spl. examiner-in-charge Union Carbide Credit Union, Bennington, 1982-83, acctg. adv. co. store, 1982-83; mem. industry stds. com. Hobby Industries Assn. Patentee in field. Vol. Zionsville (Ind.) Christian Ch., 1975-82, Ctrl. Christian Ch., Murfreesboro, 1983-87; mem. edn. com. Trinity United Meth. Ch., Murfreesboro, 1987-89, chmn. fin. com., 1989-89, adminstrv. bd., 1988-89; bd. dirs. Wesley Found., Mid. Tenn. State U., Murfreesboro, 1989; mem. Rutherford County Humane Soc., Beasley, 1987-89. Mem. Am. Mgmt. Assn., Am. Mktg. Assn., Ind. U. Alumni Membership Assn. (Nashville chpt.), Sigma Pi (mem. alumni assn., Hobby & Craft Industry of Am., Am. Hardware Manufacturer's Assn Republican. Methodist. Avocations: investments, reading, sports, computer science. Office Phone: 608-574-1496. Personal E-mail: alegandron@yahoo.com.

ADKISON, RON, lawyer; b. Nacogdoches, Tex., Jan. 8, 1955; s. Robert Edward and Doris Ozelle (Pollard) A.; m. Tanya Regina Williamson, June 2, 1979 (div. Dec. 1984); 1 child, Veronica Alexis Adkison; m. Donna Elaine Dennis, Apr. 1, 1990 (divorced); 1 child, Alexander Aron; m. Tamra Bryan, July 4, 2001. BA, Stephen F. Austin U., 1976; JD, Baylor U., 1978. Bar: Tex. 1979, U.S. Dist. Ct. (ea., we., so. and no. dists.) Tex., U.S. Ct. Appeals (5th cir.), U.S. Supreme Ct. Atty. Wellborn & Houston, Henderson, Tex., 1979; ptnr. Wellborn, Houston, Adkison, et al., Henderson, Tex., 1980—. Regent Stephen F. Austin State U., Nacogdoches, 1993-99; chair bd. regents, 1995-96. Fellow Am. Bd. Trial Advs., Tex. Inst. for Legal Ethics and Professionalism; mem. Coll. State Bar Tex. (Disciplinary Rev. com., Adminstrn. Rules Civil Evidence com.), Tex. Trial Lawyers Assn. (dir., chair Toxic Torts com.), Henderson Country Club (pres. 1989-94). Avocations: golf, aviation. Office: Wellborn Houston Adkison et al 300 W Main St Henderson TX 75652-3109 Office Phone: 903-657-8544. Personal E-mail: t-adkison@msn.com.

ADKISSON, PERRY LEE, university system chancellor; b. Hickman, Ark., Mar. 11, 1929; s. Robert Louis and Imogene (Perry) A.; m. Frances Rozelle, Dec. 29, 1956 (dec. 1995); m. Gloria Ray, May 16, 1998; 1 dau., Jean Amanda. BS, U. Ark., 1950, MS, 1954; PhD in Entomology, Kans. State U., 1956; DS (hon.), U. Ark., 1997; DHL, Tex. A&M U., 2001. Asst. prof. entomology U. Mo., 1956-58; assoc. prof. Tex. A&M U., 1958-63, prof., 1963-67, Disting. prof. entomology, 1967—, head dept. entomology, 1967-78, v.p. for agr. and renewable resources, 1978-80, dep. chancellor for agr., 1980-83, dep. chancellor, 1983-86, chancellor, 1986-91, regent's prof., 1991-95. Cons. Internat. AEC, Vienna, 1969-74; chmn. sci. adv. panel Gov. Tex. on Agrl. Chems., 1970-72; chmn. Tex. Pesticide Adv. Com., 1972; mem. panel experts on integrated pest control UN/FAO, Rome, 1971-78, chmn., 1992-96; mem. Structural Pest Control Bd., Tex., 1972-78, NRC World Food and Nutrition Study Team, 1977; chmn. com. biology pest species NRC, 1974; mem. environ. studies bd., study group problems pest control NAS-NRC, 1973-75; mem. U.S. directorate UNESCO Man and the Biosphere Program, 1975-77; mem. bd. on agr. NRC, 1985-87, mem. Nat. Sci. Bd., 1985-96; mem. governing bd. Internat. Crops Rsch. Inst. for Semi-Arid Tropics, 1982-88; mem. rsch. adv. com. Agr. for Internat. Devel., 1986; mem. com. on life scis. NRC, 1985-85; mem. Tex. Sci. and Tech. Coun., 1986-88; mem. Standing Com. for Internat. Plant Protection Congresses, 1984—, adv. dir. Export-Import Bank U.S., 1987. Mem. editorial com. Ann. Rev. Entomology, 1973-78; contbr. articles to profl. jours. Exec. dir. G.H.W. Bush Presdl. Libr. Ctr. and Bush Libr. Found., 1991-93. With M.C., U.S. Army, 1951-53. Recipient Faculty Disting. Achievement award for rsch. Tex. A&M U., 1965, Alexander Von Humboldt award, 1980; Disting. Svc. award Am. Registry Prof. Entomology, 1979, Disting. Scientist of Yr. award Tex. Acad. Scis., 1982, Disting. Alumnus Svc. award Kans. State U., 1980, Disting. Svc. award Am. Inst. Biol. Sci., 1987, Nat. 4-H Alumni award, 1988, Outstanding Alumnus award Coll. of Agr. and Home Econs., U. Ark., 1990, Disting. Alumni award U. Ark., 1990, Disting. Svc. award Am. Agrl. Editors Assn., 1992, Wolfe Prize in Agr., 1994-95, World Food prize, 1997, medallion alumni award Kans. State U., 1999; USPHS postdoctoral fellow Harvard U., 1963-64; Tex. Heritage Hall of Honor, 1998. Fellow AAAS, Entomol. Soc. Am. (governing bd. 1971-75, pres. 1974, Bussart Meml. award 1967, Founders Meml. lectr. 1985); mem. Am. Acad. Arts and Scis., Kans. Entomol. Soc., Internat. Orgn. Biol. Control, Am. Registry Profl. Entomologists (governing council 1976-78, pres. 1977), Nat. Acad. Scis., Phi Kappa Phi, Sigma Xi. Office: Tex A&M U Dept Entomology College Station TX 77843-0001

ADLEMAN, LEONARD M., computer scientist, educator; m. Lori Bruce, 1983; 3 children. BS, U. Calif., Berkeley, 1968; PhD in Computer Sci., U. Calif., 1976. Assoc. prof. math. MIT, Cambridge, 1976-80; faculty computer sci. U. So. Calif., L.A., 1980-85, asst. prof., 1985, Henry Salvatori prof. computer sci., 1985—. Asst. prof. math. RSA Data Security, 1983—. Recipient Koji Kobayashi Computers and Comm. award, IEEE, 2000, ACM Turing award, 2002, ACM Paris Kanallakis award, 1996, Alexander von Humboldt Fellowship and Disting. Alumnus award, 1995. Mem. NAE. Office: U So Calif Dept Computer Sci Los Angeles CA 90089-0001 E-mail: adleman@pollux.usc.edu.

ADLER, AMY M., law educator; b. 1963; BA summa cum laude, Yale U., 1985, JD, 1990. Bar: NY 1993. Law clk. to Judge John M. Walker, Jr. US Ct. Appeals 2nd Cir., NYC, 1990—91; litig. assoc. Debevoise & Plimpton, NYC, 1992—94; fellow Freedom Forum Media Studies Ctr. Columbia U., 1994—95; asst. prof. law NYU Sch. Law, 1996—99, assoc. prof., 1999—2001, prof., 2001—. Office: NYU Sch Law Vanderbilt Hall Rm 314K 40 Washington Sq S New York NY 10012-1099 Office Phone: 212-998-6645. E-mail: adlera@juris.law.nyu.edu.

ADLER, BARBARA ARLENE, artist; b. Bklyn., Mar. 10, 1941; d. Abraham and Rose (Luftik) Turetsky; m. Don Adler, Feb. 21, 1961; children: Eric, Michael. Student, Bklyn. Coll., 1959-61. Exhbns. include: S.I. Mus., 1981, 82, S.I. Snug Harbor Cultural Show, 1981, Fisher Galleries, Washington, 1981, Salmagundi Club, 1981, Washington Sq. Outdoor Art Exhibit, 1981, 82 (Laurette McDonald award), 84 (Honorable Mention), 85 (Honorable mention), N.Y. Coliseum, 1983, Knickerbocker Artists (John J. Karpick Meml. award), 1981, 84, Gracie Sq. Art Show, 1985; represented in permanent collection at Roads Galleries, N.Y.C., Ariel Gallery, Soho, N.Y. Mem. S.I. Mus., S.I. Cultural Club. Home: 31 Elwood Ave Staten Island NY 10314-6020

ADLER, BARRY E., law educator, academic administrator; b. 1960; BS, Cornell U., 1982; JD, U. Chgo., 1985. Bar: NY 1987. Law clk. to Hon. Frank H. Easterbrook US Ct. Appeals 7th Cir., Chgo., 1985—86; assoc. Cleary, Gottlieb, Steen & Hamilton, NYC, 1986—88; asst. prof. George Mason U. Sch. Law, 1988—92; assoc. prof. Emory U. Sch. Law, 1992—94; vis. assoc. prof. U. Va. Sch. Law, 1993—94, prof., 1994—96, Sullivan & Cromwell rsch. prof. law, 1995—96; vis. prof. NYU Sch. Law, 1995—, prof., 1996—, Charles Seligson prof. law, assoc. dean info. systems & tech., 2002—. Cons. legal reform project Harvard Inst. Internat. Devel., 1995; vis. prof. Yale U., 1997, Columbia U., 1998. Mem.: Am. Law & Economics Assn. (bd. dirs. 2001—04). Office: NYU Sch Law Vanderbilt Hall Rm 424 40 Washington Sq S New York NY 10012-1099 Office Phone: 212-998-6660. Office Fax: 646-349-1747. E-mail: barry.adler@nyu.edu.

ADLER, CHARLES DAVID, lawyer; b. N.Y.C., June 29, 1945; s. Hans J. and Frieda (Nayer) A.; m. Judith Lampert, Mar. 26, 1969; 1 child, Kate Devon. Student, Am. U., 1963-65, Queens Coll., N.Y.C., 1965-67; JD, N.Y. Law Sch., 1970. Bar: N.Y. 1971, U.S. Dist. Ct. (so. and ea. dists.) N.Y. 1975, U.S. Supreme Ct. 1977, U.S. Ct. Appeals (2d cir. 1985), U.S. Ct. Appeals (11th cir.) 1988, Ariz. 1991. Acting dir. law adv. bur., sr. trial atty. N.Y.C. Legal Aid Soc., 1971-76; ptnr. Goltzer & Adler, N.Y.C., 1976—. Mem. faculty trial advocacy program Cardozo U. Law Sch., N.Y.C., 1981—, Hofstra U. Law Sch., N.Y.C., 1989, Legal Aid Soc., N.Y.C., 1980—. Mem. Dem. Jud. Screening Com., N.Y.C., 1985; pres. Vol. Com. of Lawyers. Mem. Nat. Assn. Criminal Def. Lawyers, N.Y. State Assn. Criminal Def. Lawyers (charter mem.), Internat. Criminal Bar Assn., N.Y. Criminal Bar Assn., Bar Assn. City of N.Y. (chair criminal law com., 1998-2001), Ctr. for Cmty. Alternatives (pres.). Avocation: pvt. pilot. Home: 35 W 9th St New York NY 10011-8901 Office: Goltzer & Adler 100 Church Street New York NY 10007

ADLER, CHARLES SPENCER, psychiatrist; b. N.Y.C., Nov. 27, 1941; s. Benjamin H. and Anne (Greenfield) A.; m. Sheila Noel Morrissey, Oct. 8, 1966 (dec.); m. Peggy Dolan Bean, Feb. 23, 1991 BA, Cornell U., 1962; MD, Duke U., 1966. Diplomate Nat. Bd. Med. Examiners, Am. Bd. Psychiatry and Neurology. Intern Tucson Hosps. Med. Edn. Program, 1966-67; psychiat. resident U. Colo. Med. Sch., Denver, 1967-70; pvt. practice medicine specializing in psychiatry and psychosomatic medicine Denver, 1970—. Chief divsn. psychiatry Rose Med. Ctr, 1982-87; co-founder Applied Biofeedback Inst., Denver, 1972-75; prof. pro tempore Cleve. Clinic, 1977; asst. clin. prof. psychiatry U. Colo. Med. Ctr., 1986—, chief psychiatry and psychophysiology Colo. Neurology and Headache Ctr., 1988-95; med. dir. Colo. Ctr. for Biobehavioral Health, Boulder, 1994—. Author: (with Gene Stanford and Sheila M. Adler) We Are But a Moment's Sunlight, 1976, (with Sheila M. Adler and Russell Packard) Psychiatric Aspects of Headache, 1987; contbr. (with S. Adler) sect. biofeedback med. and health ann. Ency. Britannica, 1986; chpts. to books, articles to profl. jours.; mem. editorial bd. Cephalalgia: an Internat. Jour. of Headache, Headache Quar. Emeritus mem. Citizen's Adv Bd. Duke U. Ctr. Aging and Human Devel. Recipient Award of Recognition, Nat. Migraine Found., 1981; N.Y. State regents scholar, 1958-62 Fellow Am. Psychiat. Assn.; mem. AAAS (rep. of AAPB to med. sect. com.), Am. Assn. Study Headache, Internat. Headache Soc. (chmn. subcom. on classifying psychiat. headaches), Am. Acad. Psychoanalysis (sci. assoc.), Biofeedback Soc. Colo. (pres. 1977-78), Assn. for Applied Psychophysiology and Biofeedback (rep. to AAAS, chmn. ethics com. 1983-87, bd. dirs. 1990-93, Sheila M. Adler cert. honor 1988). Jewish. Office: 955 Eudora St Apt 1605 Denver CO 80220-4341 Office Phone: 303-333-0505.

ADLER, CHRISTOPHER ALAN, composer, educator; b. Mountain View, Calif., Sept. 27, 1972; s. Gordon Alan and Pamela Adler; m. Supeena Insee Adler, Nov. 21, 2003. BS in Math., BS in Music, MIT, 1994; PhD in Music Composition, Duke U., Durham, N.C., 1999. Assoc. prof. of music U. of San Diego, 1999—, dir. of music program, 2002—05. Pianist and composer-in-residence NOISE, San Diego, 2003—; pianist Christopher Adler Trio, San Diego, 2000—; editor San Diego New Music newsletter, 2003—. Composer: (compact disc) Epilogue for a Dark Day, Tzadik Records TZ 8004; musician: Transcontinental, the Christopher Adler Trio (9 Winds Records), (mini-compact disc) Christopher Adler, khaen, ArtShip Recordings, (compact disc) Nathan Hubbard, Skeleton Key Orchestra (Circumvention Records). Mem.: ASCAP, Am. Music Ctr., Soc. for Ethnomusicology. Office: University of San Diego Music Program 5998 Alcala Pk San Diego CA 92110 Office Phone: 619-260-7502.

ADLER, DAVID AVRAM, psychiatrist; b. N.Y.C., Aug. 25, 1947; s. Jack and Myril (Stangen) A.; m. Jill Sonneborn, Oct. 5, 1975; children: Jonathan Michael, Eliza Kate. BA, U. Rochester, 1969; MD, Yale U., 1973. Diplomate Am. Bd. Psychiatry and Neurology. Internship, residency Mass. Mental Health Ctr., 1973-76; dir. South Boston Ct. Clinic, Bay Cove Mental Health Ctr., Boston, 1976-79; dir. partial hospitalization programs New Eng. Med. Ctr., Boston, 1979-82; dir. aftercare svcs. Bay Cove Mental Health Ctr., Boston, 1979-86; asst. chief div. adult psychiatry New Eng. Med. Ctr. Hosps., Boston, 1982-83, assoc. chief div. adult psychiatry, 1983-84, dir. ambulatory adult psychiatry svcs., 1983-86, chief divsn. adult psychiatry, 1984-93, sr. psychiatrist, 1993—. Adj. scientist The Health Inst., Inst. Clin. Rsch. and Health Policy Studies, New Eng. Med. Ctr., 1993-97, sr. scientist, 1997—, dir. mental health svcs. rsch. group, 1997—; assoc. prof. psychiatry Tufts U. Sch. Medicine, Boston, 1984-90, prof. psychiatry, 1990—, vice chair faculty senate, 1995-96, chair, 1996-97; adj. assoc. prof. Simmons Coll. Sch. Social Work, Boston, 1986-91, adj. prof., 1991-97; prof. medicine Tufts U. Sch. Medicine, 2000—; assoc. The Levinson Inst., Belmont, Mass., 1987-93; sr. cons. The Levinson Inst., Waltham, Mass., 1993—. Author 2 books; contbr. articles to profl. jours. Mem. cen. physicians planning com. Tufts Associated Health Plan, Waltham, Mass., 1983-88. Recipient Twenty-Five Yr. Disting. Svc. award Bay Cove Human Svcs., Boston, 2004, Henry Solomon Rsch. award Mass. Mental Health Ctr., Boston, 1975, ROI-Award NIH, 1997-2002, 2002—. Fellow Am. Psychiat. Assn. (disting. fellow); mem. Group for Advancement Psychiatry (chair com. on psychopathology 1981-92, publ. bd. 1994—, chmn. publs. bd. 1996—), Mass. Psychiat. Soc., Mass. Med. Soc. Avocations: reading, gardening, tai chi. Office: New Eng Med Ctr Hosps PO Box 1007 750 Washington St Boston MA 02111-1526

ADLER, DAVID NEIL, lawyer; b. Bklyn., Apr. 11, 1955; s. Leonard Howard and Elaine (Holder) A. Student, Colgate U., 1973-75; BA, NYU, 1977; JD, St. John's U., 1980. Bar: N.Y. 1981, U.S. Dist. Ct. (ea. and so. dists.) N.Y. 1986, U.S. Tax Ct. 1989. Pvt. practice, Kew Gardens, N.Y., 1982—. Contbr. articles to profl. jours. Mem. Queens County Bar Assn. (com. chmn. 1983—, co-editor Queens Bar Bull. 1987—, bd. mgrs. 1989—, officer 1993—, pres. 1998), N.Y. State Bar Assn. (exec. com. trusts and estates). Office: 12510 Queens Blvd Kew Gardens NY 11415-1519

ADLER, EDWARD I., media and entertainment company executive; b. NYC, Jan. 12, 1954; s. Walter S. and Justine (Rosenberg) P.; m. Shari Goldman; children: Alexander Justin, Jillian Haly. BA, Vassar Coll., 1976; MA in Journalism, NYU, 1979. Reporter Time Mag. subs. Time Inc, N.Y.C., 1976-79; sports programming exec. Home Box Office Inc. subs. Time Inc., N.Y.C., 1979-81; news editor TV-Cable Week Mag. subs. Time Inc., N.Y.C., 1981-83; sr. assoc. corp. pub. affairs Time Inc., N.Y.C., 1983-88; mgr. media rels. corp. comm. Time Warner Inc., N.Y.C., 1989-93, dir. media rels. corp. comm., 1993-97, v.p. corp. comm., 1997-2000, sr. v.p. corp. comm., 2000—04, exec. v.p. corp. comm., 2004—. Bd. dirs. NY Cares, Big Apple Circus. Bd. dirs. City Parks Found. Mem.: Internat. Radio and TV Soc. Office: Time Warner Inc One Time Warner Ctr New York NY 10019 Business E-Mail: edward.adler@timewarner.com.

ADLER, ERWIN ELLERY, lawyer; b. Flint, Mich., July 22, 1941; s. Ben and Helen M. (Schwartz) A.; m. Stephanie Ruskin, June 8, 1967; children: Lauren, Michael, Jonathan BA, U. Mich., 1963, LL.M., 1967; JD, Harvard U., 1966. Bar: Mich. 1966, Calif. 1967. Assoc. Pillsbury, Madison & Sutro, San Francisco, 1967-73; assoc. Lawler, Felix & Hall, L.A., 1973-76, ptnr., 1977-80, Rogers & Wells, L.A., 1981-83, Richards, Watson & Gershon, L.A., 1983—. Bd. dirs. Hollywood Civic Opera Assn., 1975-76, Children's Scholarships Inc., 1979-80 Mem. ABA (vice chmn. appellate advocacy com. 1982-87), Calif. Bar Assn., Phi Beta Kappa, Phi Kappa Phi. Jewish. Office: Adler Law Group 350 S Figueroa St Ste 557 Los Angeles CA 90071

ADLER, FRED PETER, retired electronics company executive; b. Vienna, Mar. 29, 1925; came to U.S., 1942, naturalized, 1947; s. Michael and Ellida (Bronner) A.; m. Alicia Gulkis, 1950; children; Michael Steven, Andrew David; m. Adrienne Wilcox, 1991. BSEE with honors, U. Calif., Berkeley, 1945; MSEE (Charles A. Coffin fellow), Calif. Inst. Tech., 1948, PhD magna cum laude, 1950. Elec. engr. GE Rsch. and Cons. Labs., 1945-47; project engr. Jet Propulsion Lab., 1950; with Hughes Aircraft Co., 1950-70, sr. staff physicist, dept. mgr., 1954-57, mgr. advanced planning, 1957-59, dir. advanced projects labs., 1959-61, v.p., mgr. space systems div., 1961-66, v.p., asst. group exec. Aerospace Group, 1966-70; pres. Nadgeco Ltd., 1970—73, chmn. bd., 1973-77; v.p., group exec. aerospace groups Hughes Aircraft Co., 1973-81, sr. v.p., pres. electro-optical and data sys. group, 1981-87; dir. Jefferson Ctr. for Character Edn., Monrovia, Calif., 1973-99, chmn. bd., 1988-99; ret., 1999. Co-author: text Guided Missile Engineering, 1959; also articles tech. jours. Fellow AIAA; mem. N.Y. Acad. Scis., Sigma Xi, Tau Beta Pi. Home: 10795 Woodbine St Apt 208 Los Angeles CA 90034 Personal E-mail: fredad690@cs.com.

ADLER, FREDA SCHAFFER (MRS. G. O. W. MUELLER), criminologist, educator; b. Phila., Nov. 21, 1934; d. David and Lucia G. (de Wolfson) Schaffer; children by previous marriage: Mark, Jill, Nancy. BA, U. Pa., 1956, MA, 1968, PhD (fellow), 1971. Instr. dept. psychiatry Temple U., Phila., 1971; research coordinator Addiction Scis. Center, 1971-72; research dir. sect. on drug and alcohol abuse Med. Coll. Pa., 1972-74, asst. prof. psychiatry, 1972-74; asso. prof. criminal justice Rutgers U., Newark, 1974-79, prof., 1979-82, disting. prof., 1982—, acting dean grad. sch. criminal justice, 1986-87. Bd. dirs. Internat. Sci. and Profl. Adv. Coun. UN Programs in Crime Prevention and Criminal Justice; vis. fellow Yale U., 1976; cons. to Nat. Commn. on Marijuana and Drug Abuse, 1972-73, NYU Sch. Law, 1972-74; mem. faculty Nat. Jud. Coll., U. Nev., 1973—, Nat. Coll. Criminal Def. Lawyers and Pub. Defenders U. Houston, 1975; mem. adv. com. Gen. Fedn. Women's Clubs, 1975-77; UN rep. Internat. Prisoner Aid Assn., 1973-75, Centro Nat. di Prevenzione e Difesa Sociale, 1989—, Internat. Soc. Social Def., regional sec. gen., 1991—, bd. dirs.; sec. bd. dirs. Inst. for Continuous Study of Man, 1974-77, v.p., 1977—; adv. bd. Internat. Jour. Comparative and Applied Criminal Justice, 2005— Author: Sisters in Crime, 1975, The Incidence of Female Criminality in the Contemporary World, 1981, Nations Note Obsessed with Crime, 1983; co-author: A Systems Approach to Drug Treatment, 1975, Medical Lollypop, Junkie Insuline or what?, 1974, Criminology of Deviant Women, 1978, Outlaws of the Ocean, 1985, Criminology, 1991, 2005, Criminal Justice, 1993, 2003, Criminal Justice: The Core, 1996, Kriminologia, 2000, Criminology and the Criminal Justice System in the United States of America: Criminology and the Criminal Justice System: United States and Georgia, 2003; contbr. numerous articles on criminology and psychiatry to profl. jours.; editor: Advances in Criminological Theory, 1987—; mem. editl. bd.: Criminology, 1971—73, Jour. Criminal Law and Criminology, 1982—, The American Sociologist, 1999—; co-editor: Politics, Crime and the International Scene, 1972—, Revue Internationale de Droit Penal, 1974—, European Jour. Criminology, 2003—; assoc. editor: LAE Jour., 1977—85, cons. editor: Jour. Criminal Law and Criminology, mem. adv. bd.: Internat. Jour. Comparative and Applied Criminal Justice, 2005—. Bd. dirs. U. Pa. Alumnae Assn., 1974—77, The Police Found., 1996—2002. Recipient (with G.O.W. Mueller) Beccaria medal in Gold Deutsche Kriminologische Gesellschaft, 1979; fellow Max Planck Inst. Fgn. and Internat. Law and Criminology, 1984, Am. Soc. Criminology, 1994, Northeastern Criminal Inst. Assn., 2002; named Cecil H. and Ida Green Honors Prof., Tex. Christian U., 1998, Ind. U. Disting. Scholar of Crime, Law, and Justice, 1999, Excellence award minorities and women's sect. Acad. Criminal Justice Scis., 2001. Mem. Am. Soc. Criminology (pres. 1994-95, Herbert Bloch award 1972, fellow 1995), Am. Sociol. Assn., Internat. Assn. Penal Law, U. Pa. Alumnae Assn. (bd. dirs. 1974-77), Chi Omega Home: 30 Waterside Plz Apt 37J New York NY 10010-2628 Office: Rutgers U Sch Criminal Justice 123 Washington St Newark NJ 07102-3094 Personal E-mail: freadler@nyc.rr.com, fre-adler@cox.net, f-adler@cox.net.

ADLER, FREDERICK RICHARD, lawyer, corporate financial executive; b. N.Y.C., Apr. 4, 1926; s. Samuel and Rose (Axelrod) A.; m. Catherine R. George, Apr. 25, 1986; Christopher Wells, Frederick George Richard; children by previous marriage: Barbara Ilene, James Richard, Susan Ruth Chapman, Elizabeth Anne Wertheimer. BA, Bklyn. Coll., 1948; JD magna cum laude, Harvard U., 1951; Doctorate (hon.), Technion-Israel Inst. Tech., 1998. Bar: N.Y. 1952. Assoc. Reavis & McGrath, N.Y.C., 1951-58, ptnr., 1959-89, Fulbright, Jaworski, Reavis & McGrath, N.Y.C., 1989-91; ret. sr. ptnr. Fulbright & Jaworski, N.Y.C., 1991-95, of counsel, 1996—; dir., chmn. exec. com. Data Gen. Corp., Westbo, Mass., 1968-99; mng. ptnr. VENAD Assocs., Adler & Co. Bd. dirs. Sentigen Holding Corp., Colo., SIT Investment Assocs., Minn. Trustee Tchrs. Ins. and Annuity Assn., 1977-95; bd. mgrs./overseers Meml. Sloan-Kettering Cancer Ctr.; mem. dean's adv. bd. Harvard Law Sch; trustee Horace Mann School; With U.S. Army, 1943-45. Mem. Harvard Club, Met. Club, Maroon Creek Club (Aspen, Colo.), Univ. Club (N.Y.), Atlantic Golf Club (Southampton, N.Y.), Old Oaks Country Club (Purchase, N.Y.), Palm Beach Country Club (Palm Beach, Fla.), N.Y. Athletic Club. Office: 220 Sunrise Ave Palm Beach FL 33480-3869

ADLER, HOWARD BRUCE, lawyer; b. N.Y.C., Apr. 29, 1951; s. Mandel and Dora (Rosenblatt) A.; m. Tanya Jean Potter; 1 child, Alexandra. BA, Johns Hopkins U., 1972; JD, NYU, 1975. Bar: N.Y. 1976, U.S. Dist. Ct. (ea. and so. dists.) N.Y. 1976, D.C. 1979, U.S. Dist. Ct. D.C., 1979, U.S. Ct. Appeals (D.C. cir.) 1979. Assoc. Shearman & Sterling, N.Y.C., 1975-79, Arnold & Porter, Washington, 1979-82; mng. counsel Mellon Bank N.A., Pitts., 1982-84; exec. v.p., gen. counsel The Riggs Nat. Bank of Wash. D.C., Riggs Nat. Corp., 1984-87; ptnr. Gibson, Dunn & Crutcher LLP, Washington, 1987—. Contbr. articles to profl. jours. Finalist Top Washington Lawyers Corp./Fin., Washington Bus. Jour., 2004; named one of Tier 1 Leading Lawyers for Bus. corp./comml., Checkers USA, 2005. Mem. ABA (banking law com.), Fed. Bar Assn. (exec. coun. banking law com. 1990-98), D.C. Bar (treas. 1996-97, steering com. corp., fin. and securities law sect., 1991-96, chmn. 1994-95, vice chmn. 1993-94, budget com. 1996-97, chmn. task force of lawyers for econ. redevel. of D.C. 1997-99), Archdiocesan Legal Network of Washington (adv. bd. 1995-2002), Congl. Country Club, Met. Club, Knights of Malta. Avocation: civil war history. Home: 11103 Cripplegate Rd Potomac MD 20854 Office: Gibson Dunn & Crutcher LLP 1050 Connecticut Ave NW Ste 900 Washington DC 20036-5306 Office Phone: 202-955-8589. Business E-Mail: hadler@gibsondunn.com.

ADLER, IRA JAY, lawyer; b. NYC, Jan. 1, 1942; s. Ralph and Beatrice (Rosenblum) A.; m. Laraine Sheila Garfinkel, July 4, 1965; children: Jodi, Michael. BA, NYU, 1963, JD, 1966. Bar: N.Y. 1966. Ptnr. Certilman, Balin, Adler & Hyman, LLP, East Meadow, NY, 1973—. Contbr. to profl. publs. Mem. N.Y. State Bar Assn., Nassau County Bar Assn., L.I. Builders Inst. (bd. dirs. 1985—), Real Estate Inst. C.W. Post (bd. dirs. 1986—), N.Y. State Builders Assn. (bd. dirs. 1988—) Office: Certilman Balin Adler & Hyman LLP 90 Merrick Ave East Meadow NY 11554-1571

ADLER, IRVING, mathematician; b. N.Y.C., Apr. 27, 1913; s. Marcus and Celia (Kress) A.; m. Ruth Relis, June 2, 1935 (dec. 1968); children: Stephen L., Peggy A.; m. Joyce Lifshutz, Sept. 16, 1968 (dec. 1999). BS, CCNY, 1931, DHL (hon.), 2002; MA, Columbia U., 1938, PhD, 1961; DSc (hon.), St. Michael's Coll., 1990. Tchr. pub. high schs., N.Y.C., 1932-46; chmn. dept. math. Textile High Sch., N.Y.C., 1946-52; instr. math. Columbia U., N.Y.C., 1957-60, Bennington Coll., North Bennington, Vt., 1961, So. Vt. Coll., Bennington, 1983; researcher in math. biology North Bennington, 1972—. Lectr. in field. Author 49 books; co-author 34 books; contbr. articles to profl. jours.; contbg. editor Sci. and Society, 1981—; mem. editl. bd. Sci. and Nature, 1978-89. Recipient awards for outstanding sci. books for children Children's Book Coun. and Nat. Sci. Tchrs. Assn., 1972, 75, 80, 90, Townsend Harris medal for outstanding achievement CCNY Alumni Assn., 1993. Fellow AAAS, Vt. Acad. Arts and Sci.; mem. Am. Math. Soc., Math. Assn. Am., Nat. Council Tchrs. Math., Soc. for Indsl. and Applied Math., Authors League, Townsend Harris Hall of Fame, 1996, Phi Beta Kappa, Sigma Xi. Democrat. Jewish. Avocation: vegetable gardening. Home: 297 Cold Spring Rd North Bennington VT 05257-9767 E-mail: iadler@sover.net.

ADLER, JAMES BARRON, publishing executive; b. N.Y.C., Mar. 8, 1932; s. George G. and Mollie (Barron) A.; m. Esthy Lehmann, June 26, 1956; children: Laura Frances, Eric Stephen. AB magna cum laude, Harvard U., 1953. With NBC, N.Y.C., 1956-57, R.R. Bowker Co., N.Y.C., 1957-61, Random House, Inc., N.Y.C., 1961-64, G.P. Putnam's Sons, N.Y.C., 1964-67; founder James B. Adler, Inc., 1967; founder, pres., chmn. Congressional Info. Service, Inc., Washington, 1969-81; mng. partner Adler Assos., 1981—; pres. Adler & Adler Pubs., 1983—. Chmn. Greenwood Press, Inc., 1976-79; mem. U.S. Nat. Advisory Commn. Internat. Documentation Fedn., 1972-73 Served with U.S. Army, 1954-55. Recipient Profl. award Spl. Libraries Assn., 1972; Product of Yr. award Info. Industry Assn., 1971, 76 Mem. ALA, Am. Soc. Info. Sci. Clubs: Cosmos, Nat. Press. Home: 5630 Wisconsin Ave Apt 1205 Chevy Chase MD 20815-4457 Office: 5530 Wisconsin Ave Chevy Chase MD 20815-4404

ADLER, JEFFREY D., media consultant, management consultant; b. Cleve., July 10, 1952; s. Bennett and Edythe Joy (Eisner) A.; m. Colleen Ann Bentley, May 29, 1983. BS in Journalism, Northwestern U., 1975. Porter, waiter, bartender Amtrak, Chgo., 1975-76; reporter Enterprise-Courier, Oregon City, Oreg., 1977, Las Vegas Sun, 1977-80, O.C. Daily Pilot, Costa Mesa, Calif., 1982-85; v.p. pub. affairs Englander Comm., Newport Beach, Calif., 1985-86; pres. Adler Wilson Campaign Svcs., Laguna Hills, Calif., 1990-95, Adler Pub. Affairs, Long Beach, Calif., 1987—. Chair bd. dirs. Pacific Pub. Radio (KKJZ-FM), Long Beach, 2002—. Mem. Am. Assn. Polit. Cons. Democrat. Jewish. Home: 33 Pomona Ave Long Beach CA 90803-3426 Office: Adler Pub Affairs 200 Pine Ave Ste 300 Long Beach CA 90802-3038 Office Phone: 562-435-5551. Business E-Mail: jeffadler@adlerpa.com.

ADLER, JEREMY ANDREW, physician assistant; b. Boston, Nov. 20, 1973; s. Martin E. and Eileen S. Adler; m. Danielle E. Beaty, Dec. 27, 1997; 1 child, Jacob Edward. BS in Gen. Biology, U. Calif., San Diego, 1995; BS in Physician Asst. Studies, SUNY, Stony Brook, 1999; M in Physician Asst. Studies, U. Nebr., 2001. Cert. physician asst. Nat. Commn. Certification Physician Assts., 1999. Pain mgmt. physician asst. Pacific SW Pain Ctr., La Mesa, Calif., 1999—. Fellow: Am. Acad. Physician Assts., Am. Acad. Pain Mgmt. (cert.); mem.: San Diego Soc. Physician Assts. (co-founder), Calif. Acad. Physician Assts. (group leader), Alpha Eta, Golden Key. Avocations: golf, auto restoration, travel. Office: Pacific SW Pain Ctr 8881 Fletcher Parkway #360 La Mesa CA 91942 Office Phone: 619-460-2700.

ADLER, JERRY, journalist, writer; BA, Yale U., 1970. Reporter Jour. Commerce, 1970—72, NY Daily News, 1972—79; assoc. editor Newsweek, 1979—80, gen. editor, 1980, sr. writer, 1981—93, sr. editor, 1993—. Author (with Allen Gerson): (book) The Price of Terror: The History-Making Struggle for Justice After Pan Am 103, 2001. Finalist Spl. Interest award, Nat. Mag., 1993; recipient Sidney Hillman award, 1987, First Prize award, NY Bar Assn., 1988, 2d Pl. Nat. Headliner award. Office: Newsweek 251 W 57th St New York NY 10019-1894 Office Phone: 212-445-4000.

ADLER, KENNETH R., oncologist; b. Bklyn., Sept. 22, 1947; BS, U. Pitts., 1968; MD, Albany (N.Y.) Med. Coll., 1973. Diplomate Am. Bd. Internal Medicine, Am. Bd. Hematology. Intern Albany Med. Ctr. Hosp., 1973—74, resident in internal medicine, 1974—76, resident in hematology and oncology, 1976—78; oncologist Carol G. Simon Cancer Ctr., Morristown (N.J.) Meml. Hosp. Clin. asst. prof. medicine N.J. Med. Sch. Named one of Top Drs. in N.Y. Met. Area, Castle Connolly, Top Drs. 2003, N.J. Monthly Mag. Office: Carol G Simon Cancer Ctr Morristown Meml Hosp 100 Madison Ave Morristown NJ 07960 Office Phone: 973-538-5210. Business E-Mail: kenneth.adler@ahsys.org.

ADLER, LARRY, marketing professional; b. Frankfort, Ind., Dec. 18, 1938; s. Leon Sidney and Roslyn Jane (Woolf) A.; m. Ruthlee Figlure, Oct. 9, 1960; children: Laurie Kaye, Mark Allan, Joy Ellen. BS in Mktg. and Journalism, Ind. U., 1960. Asst. circulation and promotion mgr. McCall Corp., 1960-61; circulation and promotion mgr. Bartell-Media, Inc., 1961-63; sales promotion mgr. Golden Press, Inc., 1963-64; audio-visual dir., licensing mdse. dir., periodical publs. dir., advt. sales and mktg. dir. periodical div. Western Pub. Co., N.Y.C., 1964-74; v.p., pub., dir., treas. Washingtonian mag. and books Washington Mag., Inc., 1974-79; pres. Am. Program Bur., 1980; communications cons., 1980; pres., chmn. Adler Enterprises Ltd., 1981—, Adler Media, Inc., 1981—. Pres. Bergen Cablevision, Inc., Bergen County, N.J., 1970-72; asso. profl. lectr. Publs. Specialists program George Washington U., 1977-79 Creator, host: TV show Toy Fair News, 1968-73; exec. prodr. (TV programs) Jazz at the Smithsonian, 1981, Great Shark Hunt, 1981, Ireland by Rail, Tomb of Jesus, 1981, Operation Animal Shield, 1981. Pres. Englewood (N.J.) Jaycees, 1965-66; mem. bd. edn. High Sch. Planning Com., Tenafly, N.J., 1969; program chmn. Tenafly Action Conf. on Edn., 1969; exec. bd. Tenafly, 1968-70; mem. steering com., long range planning com. Tenafly Bd. Edn., 1971-72; chmn. Tenafly Citizens Communications Com., 1971-72, Tenafly Townwide Com., 1972-73; chmn. bd. dirs. Capital Children's Mus., 1977-83; Bd. dirs. Englewood Boys Club, 1967-69. Mem. City and Regional Mag. Assn. (founder, pres., treas.), Ind. U. Alumni Assn., Alpha Delta Sigma, Zeta Beta Tau (v.p. 1960) Office: 6849 Old Dominion Dr Mc Lean VA 22101-3705 E-mail: adlermedia@aol.com.

ADLER, MARGOT SUSANNA, journalist, radio producer, radio coorespondent, writer; b. Little Rock, Apr. 16, 1946; d. Kurt Alfred and Freyda (Nacque) A. BA, U. Calif., Berkeley, 1968; MS, Columbia U., 1970. Newscaster Sta. WBAI-FM, N.Y.C., 1968-71, host talk show, 1972-90; chief Washington bur. Pacifica News Svc. Network; corr., prodr. All Things Considered, Morning Edit., Nat. Pub. Radio, N.Y.C., 1978—, host Justice Talking, 1999—. Instr. radio comms. Goddard Coll., Plainfield, Vt., 1977; instr. religion and ecology Inst. for Social Ecology, Vt., 1986-93. Author: Drawing Down the Moon, 1979, Heretic's Heart, 1997; co-prodr., dir. (radio drama) War Day, 1985; contbr. articles to prof. jours. Nieman fellow Harvard U., 1982. Mem. Phi Beta Kappa. Avocations: swimming, bird watching, science fiction. Home: 333 Central Park W New York NY 10025-7145 Office: Nat Pub Radio 801 2nd Ave Rm 701 New York NY 10017-4781 Office Phone: 212-878-1435. Business E-Mail: madler@npr.org.

ADLER, MATTHEW, law educator; BA summa cum laude, Yale U., 1984, JD; MLitt, St. Antony's Coll., Oxford U., 1986. Law clk. for Judge Harry Edwards US Ct. Appeals, DC Cir., 1991—92; for Judge Sandra Day O'Connor US Supreme Ct., 1992—93; assoc. litig. dept. Paul, Weiss, Rifkind, Warton & Garrison, NYC, 1994; asst. prof. U. Pa. Law Sch., Phila., 1995—2000, prof., 2000—. Vis. prof. U. Va. Law Sch., 2002, U. Chgo. Law Sch., 2003. Contbr. articles to law jours. Office: U Pa Law Sch 3400 Chestnut St Philadelphia PA 19104 Office Phone: 215-898-4571. Office Fax: 215-573-2025. E-mail: madler@law.upenn.edu.*

ADLER, MICHAEL I., lawyer; b. San Francisco, May 10, 1949; BA in Polit. Sci. summa cum laude, UCLA, 1971, JD, 1976; MA, Columbia U., 1973. Bar: Calif. 1977. Extern to Hon. Matthew O. Tobriner Calif. Supreme Ct., 1975; law clerk to Hon. William B. Enright U.S. Dist. Ct. (so. dist.) Calif., 1976-77; mem. mitzlell Solberbery & Knubb, L.A., 1977—97; ptnr. Lichter, Grossman, Nichols & Adler, Inc., L.A., 1997—. Mem. entertainment law symposium com. UCLA, 1979—; instr. UCLA Extension, 1980. Woodrow Wilson fellow, 1972; Columbia U. Presdl. fellow, 1973. Mem. ABA, State Bar Calif., L.A. County Bar Assn., Beverly Hills Bar Assn., Phi Beta Kappa, Phi Eta Sigma. Office: Lichter Grossman Nichols & Adler Inc 9200 W Sunset Blvd Ph 1200 Los Angeles CA 90069-3607 E-mail: madler@lgna.com.

ADLER, NANCY ELINOR, psychologist, educator; BA, Wellesley Coll., 1968; MA, Harvard U., 1971, PhD, 1973. Asst. prof. psychology U. Calif., Santa Cruz, 1972-76, assoc. prof. psychology, 1976-77, assoc. prof. med. psychology dept. psychiatry and pediat. San Francisco, 1977-84, prof. med. psychology depts. psychiatry and pediat., 1984—, dir. health psychology program, 1988—, program dir. NIMH tng. program, 1991—, vice chair dept. psychiatry, 1994—; dir. Ctr. for Health and Cmty., 1998—. Vis. asst. rsch. psychologist Inst. Personality Assessment and Rsch., U. Calif., Berkeley, 1975; mem. peer rev. panel Ad Hoc Sci. Study Sects., Nat. Inst. Child Health and Human Devel., 1977—, Nat. Heart, Lung and Blood Inst., 1993; adv. com. for five-yr. plan Demographic and Social Scis. Br., Ctr. for Population RSch., Nat. Inst. Child Health and Human Devel., 1986-87, adv. com., 1991-2000; sr. rsch. scientist in psychology Yale U., New Haven. 1994-95; review com. Intramural Rsch. NIMH, 1997, sci. adv. bd. Ctr. Advancement Health, Washington, 1995-96, bd. trustees, 1996—; grant reviewer NSF, Social Scis. and Humanities Rsch. Coun. Can., Soc. Behavioral Medicine, March of Dimes, Ctrs. for Disease Control, Econ. and Social Rsch. Coun.; presenter in field. Author: (with others) Health Psychology-A Handbook: Theories, Applications, and Challenges of a Psychological Approach to the Health Car System, 1979, Preventing Preterm Birth: A Parent's Guide, 1988, SES & Health in Industrialized Nations, 1999; adv. bd. Ency. Mental Health, 1995—; assoc. editor Health Psychology, 1984-90, Women's Health: Research in Gender, Behavior and Policy, 1994-98; mem. editl. bd. Jour. Population and Environment, 1982-88, Health Psychology, 1994—; manuscript reviewer Jour. Personality and Social Psychology, Jour. Nervous and Mental Disease, Personality and Social Psychology Bull., Jour. Health and Social Behavior, Jour. Applied Social Psychology, Basic and Applied Social Psychology, Psychology Women Quarterly, The Western Jour. Medicine, Jour. Am. Med. Assn., Am. Jour. Pub. Health, many others; contbr. articles in field. Recipient Best Rsch. Paper award Soc. for Adolescent Medicine, 1984; NSF fellow, 1968-72, U. Calif. Regents Summer fellow, 1974; grantee in field. Fellow: Am. Psychol. Soc., APA (sec.-treas. divsn. 34 1975—78, pres. divsn. 34 1979—80, planning com. for nat. conf. on tng. in health psychology 1982—83, chairperson fellow com. divsn. 34 1982—86, participant Arden House conf. on edn. and tng. in health psychology 1983, chairperson nominations com. 1989—90, task force on promotion of population psychology 1992—97); mem.: Inst. of Medicine, Soc. for Rsch. on Adolescence, Assn. Med. Sch. Profs. Psychology, Soc. Advancement Social Psychology, Internat. Assn. Applied Psychology, Soc. Exptl. Social Psychology, Phi Beta Kappa, Sigma Xi.

ADLER, NORMAN TENNER, dean, psychologist, educator; b. Chgo., June 7, 1941; BA, Harvard U., 1962; MA in Endocronology, U. Calif., 1967. Rsch. prof. dept. elec. engring. Drexel U., 1985-93; prof. psychology in psychiatry sch. medicine U. Pa., 1988-93, assoc. dean coll. Sch. Arts and Scis., 1989-93; vice provost rsch. Northeastern U., 1993-95; prof. psychology Yeshiva U., N.Y.C., 1995—, dean, 1995—. Organizer, Roundtable on Liberal Learning in Rsch. Univs. Am. Assn. Colls., 1994—. Recipient Charles A. Dana Found. Prize, 1988; grantee John Simon Guggenheim Fellow, 1985—86, Harry Frank Guggenheim Fellow, 1985—86. Mem.: AAAS, Endocrine Soc., Am. Soc. of Zoologists, Society for Neuroscience, Soc. for Neuroethology, Internat. Soc. for Devel. Psychobiology, Animal Behavior Soc., Am. Psychol. Assn. (chair, Sci. Awards Com. 1993—95). Office: Benjamin N Cardozo Schf Law Brookdale Ctr 55 Fifth Ave New York NY 10003-4391 Office Phone: 212-960-5214. Office Fax: 212-960-5245. E-mail: adler@ymail.yu.edu.

ADLER, PATRICIA ANN, sociologist, educator; b. N.Y.C., Sept. 7, 1951; d. Benjamin Theodore and Judith Ann (Goldhill) Heller; m. Peter Adler, Aug. 20, 1972; children: Jori Ann, Brye Jacob. AB in Sociology summa cum laude, Washington U., St. Louis, 1973; MA in Sociology, U. Chgo., 1974, U. Calif., San Diego, 1975, PhD in Sociology, 1984. Instr. Tulsa Jr. Coll., 1981-83; rsch. assoc. U. Tulsa, 1983-84, asst. prof., 1984-85; asst. prof. sociology Okla. State U., Stillwater, 1985-86; asst. prof. U. Colo., Boulder, 1987-93, assoc. prof., 1993-99, prof., 1999—. Vis. asst. prof. sociology Washington U., St. Louis, 1986-87 Author: Wheeling and Dealing, 1985, 2d edit., 1993; author: (with others) The Social Dynamics of Financial Markets, 1984, The Sociologies of Everyday Life, 1980, Membership Roses in Field Research, 1987, Blackboards and Blackboards, 1991, Peer Power, 1998, Sociological Odyssey, 2001, Paradise Laborers, 2004 (Outstanding Book award North Ctrl. Sociol. Assn., 2005); editor: Jour. Contemporary Ethnography, 1986—94, (ann. series) Sociol. Studies of Child Devel., 1984—92; assoc. editor: Social Problems Jour., 1984—87, Jour. Urban Life, 1982—86, Administrative Science Quarterly, 1989—; contbr. articles to profl. jours.; author (with others): Constructions of Deviance, 1994, 1997, 2000, 2003—. Mem. Am. Sociol. Assn. (com. regulation rsch. 1992-95, chair alcohol and drug sect. 1993-94, chair sociology of emotions sect., 2005—), Soc. for Study Social Problems, Am. Soc. Criminology, Sociologists for Women in Soc., Soc. for Study of Symbolic Interaction (publ. com. 1985-88, program chmn. 1984, 86), Midwest Sociol. Soc. (bd. dirs. 1993-95), Pacific Sociol. Assn. (pub. com. 1991-94, com. on coms. 1992-95), Phi Beta Kappa. Avocations: aerobics, travel, photography, body building. Office: Dept Sociology 327 UCB U Colo Boulder CO 80309-0327 Business E-Mail: adler@colorado.edu.

ADLER, POSY (ROSLYN ADLER), artist, educator; b. Chgo., Feb. 6, 1916; d. Leon and Julia (Sonnenschein) Woolf; m. Leon Adler, Nov. 1, 1937 (dec.); children: Larry, Janet. BE, Nat. Coll. Edn., Evanston, Ill., 1975; MFA in Sculpture, Goddard Coll., Plainfield, Vt., 1975; studied with Roger Armstrong, Eliot O'Hara, Barbara Neijna, Robert Stoetzer. Art tchr. Miami (Fla.)-Dade Coll., Miami, Fla., 1964-84; sculpture tchr. Saddleback Coll., Mission Viejo, Calif., 1984—. Art tchr. Newport Harbor Mus., Irvine Fine Arts Ctr., Met. Art Ctr., Dade County C.C., New Sch. Fine Arts. Exhibited at Art Angles, Calif., Artist's Unlimited, Fla., Bacardi Art Gallery, Fla., Blunt Gallery, Ctr. for the Arts, Boca Raton, Fla., Design Ctr. South, Calif., Grove House Gallery, Fla., Jockey Club Art Gallery, Fla., U. Fla. Lowe Art Gallery, Fla., Met. Art Ctr., Fla., Mus. Science, Miami, Neiman Marcus Art Gallery, Rauchbach Galleries, Tolley Gallery, Turnberry Gallery; commissions include: Sherman Gardens, Calif., Sports Clinic, Laguna Hills, Calif., Temple Or Olom, Miami; represented in permenant collections Clubhouse 3 Leisure World, Laguna Woods, Calif. Ind. state v.p. Mental Health Soc., Frankfort, 1954-55, bd. dirs., Miami, Fla., 1957-62; hospice vol., Laguna Hills, Calif., 1990-99; vol. Adult Day Care Ctr., Laguna Hills, 1999. Mem. Am. Crafts Coun., Orange Co. Fine Arts, Ceramic League Miami, Creative Arts Guild, Dana Point Coastal Arts Coun., Florida Craftsman, Laguna Arts Assn., Miami Cultural Arts Alliance, Nat. League Am. Penwomen (pres. Laguna Beach br.), Nat. Mus. Women in the Arts, Niguel Art Assn., Sculptors of Fla., Women's Caucus for Art. Democrat. Jewish. Avocations: travel, sculpting, painting, craft work. E-mail: posyadler@1world.net.

ADLER, RAPHAEL, retired humanities educator, speech pathology/audiology services professional; b. N.Y.C., Feb. 21, 1922; s. Marcus and Celia (Kress) A.; m. Minna Adler, Sept. 23, 1948; children: Ava Dee, Roxanne, Margo Celeste. BA, Wayne State U., 1953, M in Edn., 1962; PhD, Walden U., 1981. Cert. tchr. secondary schs., Mich.; cert. speech pathologist Am. Speech and Hearing Assn. Tchr. dept. English/speech Berkley (Mich.) Sch. Dist., 1954-68; prof. Oakland C.C., Union Lake, Mich., 1968-92, prof. emeritus, 1992—2002; pres. P.W. Mulligan Enterprises, LLC. Dir. speech and hearing St. Joseph Mercy Hosp., Pontiac, Mich.,1965-84; owner, dir., pres. Speech Pathology Svcs., Southfield, Mich., 1972-86; cons. hosps., nursing homes, VNA, S. Oakland County Health Dept.; bd. dirs. Motion Picture Inst. Mich. Author: The Magical Adventures of Pee Wee Mulligan, 2001. Com. mem. Am. Heart Assn. of Mich., past chmn.; chmn., bd. trustees State of Mich . Stroke Com. Recipient many speaking citations and awards, 1953-62, Toastmasters Internat. 1971, Mrs. Horace Elgin Dodge award Am. Heart Assn. Mich., 1989, 92, 95. Avocations: reading, gardening, writing, poetry.

ADLER, RICHARD, composer, lyricist; b. N.Y.C., Aug. 3, 1921; s. Clarence and Elsa (Richard) A.; children by previous marriage: Andrew H., Christopher E. (dec.); children: Katherine J.S.; 1 stepson, Charles A. Shipman. AB, U. NC, 1943; D in Music and Theatre, Wagner Coll., 2003. Mem. advt. dept. Celanese Corp. Am., 1946-50; White House cons. on the arts, 1965-69. Cons. on arts gov. N.C. Adv. bd. Inst. Outdoor Drama, 1968-83, N.C. School arts, 1963—; commd. by Harvard U. to write a march for 50th Anniversary of Neiman Found. Journalist Soc., 1989. Collaborator (with Jerry Ross); on music and lyrics for musicals John Murray Anderson's Almanac, 1953, Pajama Game, 1954, Damn Yankees, 1955; composer, lyricist Kwamina, 1961, TV prodns. Little Women, 1959, Gift of the Magi, 1959; produced and staged White House Press Corrs. and Photographers show for Pres. Kennedy and Prime Minister MacMillan, 1962, N.Y.'s Birthday Salute for Pres. Kennedy, 1962, Inaugural Anniversity Salute to Pres. Kennedy, 1963, Salutes to Pres. Johnson, 1964, Inaugural Gala for Pres. Lyndon Johnson, 1965; producer, composer, lyricist: ABC-TV Stage 67 Musical Olympus 7-0000, fall 1966; composer, lyricist: A Mother's Kisses, 1968; producer: revival Pajama Game, 1973; producer: Rex, 1976; co-producer-composer: Music Is, 1976, Yellowstone Overture (Pulitizer prize nomination); commd. by Dept. of Interior to write Wilderness Suite (Pulitzer prize nomination), 1983, recorded by Utah Symphony; commd. by Statue of Liberty/Ellis Island Found. to write The Lady Remembers (Pulitzer prize nomination), recorded by Detroit Symphony, Retrospectrum (Pulitizer prize nomination); commd. by Chgo. City Ballet to write Eight by Adler, 1984 (Emmy award for TV version 1985); commd. by City of Chgo. to write (ballet) Chicago for sesquicentennial, 1987; commd. by Olympic Com. to write fanfare and overture for U.S. Olympic Festival, 1987, commd. by U. N.C. to write suite to commemorate bicentennial, 1993, recorded by London Symphony Orch.; author: (autobiography) You Gotta Have Heart, 1990; collaborator lyrics, composer: Off Key, 1995; composer The House of Bernarda Alba, 1998, Wilderness Suite Ballet, 2001, Notes on My Life, 2002. Trustee John F. Kennedy Ctr. for Performing Arts, 1964-77, exec. com., 1975-77; bd. dirs. Southampton Cultural Com. Lt. (j.g.) USNR, 1943-46. Recipient Antoinette Perry award, Donaldson award, Variety Critics Poll for Pajama Game 1954, Damn Yankees 1955, Antoinette Perry nomination Kwamina 1962, Pulitzer Prize nomination Retrospectrum 1980, Yellowstone Overture 1981, Playmaker Life Time Achievement award dept. dramatic art U. N.C., 1999, Richard Rodgers award ASCAP Found., 2002; Pulitzer prize nominee for rec. The Statue of Liberty Suite; named to Songwriters Hall of Fame, 1984; Hon. Park Ranger award Nat. Park Service, 1984. Mem. Dramatists Guild (exec. coun. 1958-68), Songwriters Guild Am. (bd. dirs., exec. com., exec. v.p. 1985—), New Dramatists (bd. dirs. 1974-2001), Nat. Hypertension Assn. (bd. dirs. 1978—). Address: 8 E 83d St New York NY 10028-0418 E-mail: reldar2@aol.com.

ADLER, RICHARD MELVIN, architect, planner; b. N.Y.C., Mar. 25, 1928; s. Jacob William and Betty (Uffer) A.; children: Robin Sheryl, Joy Lois; m. Marie Fusco, 1986. Registered architect, N.Y., others. Airport architect Port Auth. N.Y., 1952-58; ptnr. Brodsky Hoff & Adler, N.Y.C., 1959-71; pres. BHA Architects & Engrs., N.Y.C., 1971-75, Brodsky & Adler, N.Y.C., 1975-80, R.M. Adler & Assocs., Peterborough, N.H., 1993—. Pres. Adler, Goodman A Kolab For Architects & Engrs., Great Neck, 1993—; chmn. bd. Geller Termotto & Adler, Teaneck, N.J., 1982—, Clendening Adler, Arlington, Tex., 1983—. Elected to budget com., Peterborough, 1998—; chmn. capital improvement com. Town of Peterborough, 1996—. Served to 1st lt., N.Y. Nat. Guard, 1948-63. Recipient disting. svc. award Engrs. News Record, 1974, creative design award ASCE, 1973. Mem. AIA (emeritus; merit award 1977, bd. dirs. L.I. chpt. 1988, chair profl. practice L.I. chpt.), N.Y. Soc. Architects, Wings Club, Constrn. Specifications Inst., Queens C. of C. Republican. Jewish.

ADLER, ROBERT, electronics engineer; b. Vienna, Dec. 4, 1913; came to U.S., 1940, naturalized, 1945; s. Max and Jenny (Herzmark) A.; m. Mary F. Buehl, 1946 (dec. Jan. 1993); m. Ingrid C. Koch, 1998. PhD in Physics, U. Vienna, 1937. Asst. to patent atty., Vienna, 1937-38; lab. Sci. Acoustics, Ltd., London, Assoc. Rsch., Inc., Chgo., 1940-41; research group Zenith Radio Corp., Chgo., 1941-52, assoc. dir. research, 1952-63, v.p., 1959-77, dir. research, 1963-77, EXTEL Corp., Northbrook, Ill., 1978-79, v.p. research, 1979-82; tech. cons. Zenith Electronics Corp., 1982-97, Motorola, 1997—2001, Elo Touch Sys., 1997—. Contbr. articles to profl. jours. Fellow IEEE (Edison medal 1980); mem. Nat. Acad. Engring. Achievements include 200 patents: invention of ultrasonic remote control for TV sets, electromechanical I.F. filter, electron beam parametric amplifier, ultrasonic touch system; research on improved touch system using Love waves. Home: 1380 Ridge Rd Northbrook IL 60062-4626 Office Phone: 847-562-0126. Personal E-mail: rbtadler@aol.com.

ADLER, ROBERT MARTIN, lawyer; b. Toledo, Ohio, Oct. 2, 1943; s. Charles J. and Barbara (Sechback) A.; m. Andrea Rosenberg, June 12, 1966; children: Rebecca J., David C. BA, Oberlin Coll., 1965; JD, U. Mich., 1968. Bar: D.C. 1969. Trial atty. tax divsn. U.S. Dept. Justice, Washington, 1968-74; ptnr. Stiller, Adler & Schwartz, Washington, 1974-81; pvt. practice Law Offices Robert M. Adler, Washington, 1981-91; sr. ptnr. Drinker Biddle & Reath, Washington, 1991-96; ptnr. O'Connor & Hannon, L.L.P., Washington, 1996—. Chmn. Stiller Meml. Found., Washington, 1979-91. Avocation: sailing. Office: O'Connor & Hannan LLP 1666 K St NW Ste 500 Washington DC 20006-1217

ADLER, SAMUEL HANS, retired conductor, composer; b. Mannheim, Germany, Mar. 4, 1928; came to U.S., 1939, naturalized, 1945; s. Hugo Chaim and Selma (Rothschild) A.; m. Carol Ellen Stalker, Feb. 14, 1960 (div. 1989); children: Deborah Ruth, Naomi Leah; m. Emily Freeman Brown, June 8, 1991. MusB, Boston U., 1948; MA, Harvard U., 1950; MusD (hon.), So.

Methodist U., 1969; DFA (hon.), Wake Forest U.; D.F.A. (hon.), St. Mary's Coll., Ind., 1986; DMus (hon.), St. Louis Conservatory, 1986. Music dir. Temple Emanu-El, Dallas, 1953-66; prof. composition North Tex. State U., Denton, 1957-66; Eastern regional dir. contemporary music project Ford Found., 1966-70; prof. composition Eastman Sch. Music, U. Rochester, N.Y., 1966-94; hon. prof. U. Wales, Cardiff, 1984-89; ret., 1994; tchr. Julliard Sch. Music, N.Y.C. Lectr., condr. throughout world Condr. Dallas Chorale, 1954—57, Dallas Lyric Theatre, 1955—59; composer: 6 symphonies, 4 operas, 8 string quartets, sonatas for piano, violin (4), cello, flute, viola, guitar, oboe, clarinet, organ, saxophone, concertos for piano (3), violin, horn, cello, flute, saxophone quartet, organ, woodwind quintet, guitar, viola, also for orch. and band, chamber and choral works, songs; author: Choral Conducting, 1971, 2d revised edit., 1985, Sight Singing, 1979, 2d revised edit., 1996, The Study of Orchestration, 1982, 3d edit., 2002. Served with AUS, 1950-52. Grantee Nat. Endowment Arts, Ford Found., Rockefeller Found.; recipient 6 1st prizes Tex. Composers Contest, Charles Ives award, 1965, Lillian Fairchild award, 1968, Deems Taylor award, 1983, Am. Acad. and Inst. Arts and Letters award, 1990; Guggenheim fellow, 1984-85; named Composer of the Yr. Music Teachers' Nat. Assn. 1986, 87, Composer of the Yr. Am. Guild of Organists, 1989, 91. Mem.: ASCAP (awards 1960—), Music Tchrs. Nat. Assn., Music Educators Nat. Conf., Phi Beta Kappa, Phi Mu Alpha Sinfonia, Am. Acad. Arts and Letters. Jewish. E-mail: sadlercomp@yahoo.com.

ADLER, SARA, arbitrator, mediator; b. Chgo., Jan. 26, 1942; d. Matthew Michael and Mildred Paula (Eckhaus) Lewison; m. James N. Adler, Aug. 19, 1967; children: Michael, Philip, Matthew. AB, U. Chgo., 1961; JD, UCLA, 1969. Bar: Calif. Cons. Inst. Criminal Justice Adminstrn. U. Calif., Davis, 1969-71; assoc. Law Office of Sara Radin, L.A., 1971-72; assoc. dir. Paralegal Tng. Inst. U. So. Calif., L.A., 1972-74; assoc. Wyman, Bautzer, et al, L.A., 1974-78; arbitrator, mediator Dispute Resolution Svcs., L.A., 1978—. Fellow: Coll. Labor and Employment Lawyers; mem.: ABA (neutral co-chair ADR in Labor/employment Law 1995—98, neutral mem. coun. Labor & Employment sect.), Labor and Employment Rsch. Assn. (nat. bd. dirs. 2005—), L.A. County Bar Assn. (chmn. labor and employment sect. 1997—98), Indsl. Rels. Rsch. Assn. (pres. so. Calif. 1991—92, v.p. 2005—, nat. exec. bd. mem. 2005—, exec. bd. mem. 2005), Nat. Acad. Arbitrators (regional chair 1994—96, bd. govs. 2000—03, v.p. 2005—), Am. Arbitration Assn. (bd. dirs., exec. com., labor mgmt. law task force, employment ADR steering com.). Avocations: travel, theater, bridge. Office: Dispute Resolution Svcs 1034 Selby Ave Los Angeles CA 90024-3106 Office Phone: 310-474-5170. Personal E-mail: sadlerarb@earthlink.net.

ADLER, SEYMOUR JACK, social services administrator; b. Chgo., Oct. 22, 1930; s. Michael L. and Sarah (Pasnick) A.; m. Barbara Fingold, Mar. 24, 1958; children: Susan Lynn Adler, Karen Sandra Adler-Marder, Michelle Lauren Adler-Morrison. BS, Northwestern U., 1952; MA, U. Chgo., 1958. Caseworker Cook County Dept. Pub. Aid, Chgo., 1955; juvenile officer Cook County Sheriff's Office, 1955—56; U.S. probation-parole officer U.S. Dist. Ct., Chgo., 1958—68; exec. dir. Youth Guidance, Chgo., 1968—73; dir. court svcs. Juvenile Ct. Cook County, Chgo., 1973—75; exec. dir. Meth. Youth Svcs., Chgo., 1975—85; program mgr. Dept. Social Svcs., Kenosha, Wis., 1985—91, dir., 1992—95, Dept. Human Svcs., Kenosha, 1996—99, coord. Kenosha Yes, Juvenile Justice Project, 1999—2002; cmty. liaison Wis. Coun. on Children and Families, 2002—. Mem. Ill. Law Enforcement Commn., 1969—72; instr. corrections program Chgo. State U., 1972—75; instr. Harper Coll., 1977, St. Joseph's Coll., 1978; case developer Nat. Ctr. on Instns. and Alternatives, 1985—86; mem. soc. sci. adv. com. Carthage Coll., 1997—. Chair adminstrn. com. Joint Youth Devel. Program, 1973—75; bd. dirs. Kenosha Area Family and Aging Svcs., Inc., Child Care Assn. Ill., 1979—84; exec. bd. Kenosha br. NAACP, 1998—, W-2 steering com., 1998—99, v.p., 2004—; chair ethics bd. Village Twin Lakes, 2003—. 1st lt. USMCR, 1952—55. Recipient Meritorious Svc. award Chgo. City Colls., 1968, Appreciation award NAACP, 1999, Svc. award, 2003, award Kenosha County Foster Parents Assn., 2000. Mem. NASW (del. Assembly 1977, 1979, 1981, 1984, 1987, chmn. Chgo. dist. 1978-80, com. inquiry Wis. chpt. 1990—, leadershipID com. 2002-05), Ill. Acad. Criminology (pres. 1972, Morris J. Wexler award 1975, Pres.'s award 1997, Svc. award 2004), Kenosha Coalition on Homeless, Holiday House, Concerned Citizens' Coalition and Healthy Communities/Healthy Youth, Alpha Kappa Delta, Tau Delta Phi. Home: 232 Grandview Ln Twin Lakes WI 53181-9572 Office: Kenosha Dept Human Svcs 8600 Sheridan Rd Kenosha WI 53143 Office Phone: 262-605-6521. Business E-Mail: sadler@co.kenosha.wi.us.

ADLER, SHELLEY, b. Detroit, Sept. 28, 1945; d. Calvin Jerome and Florence Jeanne (Cohen) Goodman; m. Norman T. Adler, 1968 (div. 1986); children: Shira Tamar, Tanya Aviv, Ari Chaim, Kiva Tal, Tahg Khorin; co-parent of Keshet Tari Weinstein, Mical Ruach Weinstein. BA in English, UCLA, 1966, MA in English, 1968; MS in Edn., U. Pa., 1972; MS in Counseling, Villanova U., 1983. Cert. tchr., Calif. Barber. Poet: 4 Lyric Poets, 1968, Voices of Two Women, 1974, Poems of a Pervert, 1975, Seasons, 1980, Little Rages, 1985, Alice's Hat, 1997. Committeeman Narberth (Pa.) City, 1973-75; mem. task force Phila., 1984, 85. Sgt. U.S. Women's Army Res., 1973-75. Democrat. Jewish. Home: 19220 Prairie St Northridge CA 91324-2725

ADLER, STEPHEN J., editor-in-chief; b. NYC; m. Lisa Grunwald; children: Elizabeth, Jonathan. BA, Harvard Coll., 1977; JD, Harvard Law Sch., 1983. Reporter Tampa Times, Tallahassee Democrat; editor The American Lawyer, 1983—88; legal editor The Wall Street Journal, 1988—94, spl. projects editor Page One, 1994—97, dep. Page One editor, 1997—99, dep. mng. editor, 1999—2005; editor-in-chief BusinessWeek Mag., NYC, 2005—. Author: The Jury: Trial and Error in the American Courtroom (ABA Silver Gavel Award, 1995); editor: Letters of the Century, 1999. Office: BusinessWeek 43rd Fl McGraw-Hill Bldg 1221 Ave of Americas New York NY 10020-1093 Office Phone: 212-512-2511.

ADLER, STEPHEN LOUIS, physicist; b. N.Y.C., Nov. 30, 1939; s. Irving and Ruth Adler; children: Jessica Wendy, Victoria Stephanie, Anthony Curtis; m. Sarah C. Brett-Smith, 1995. AB summa cum laude, Harvard U., 1961; PhD, Princeton U., 1964. Jr. fellow Soc. Fellows Harvard U., 1964—66; rsch. assoc. Calif. Inst. Tech., 1966; mem. Inst. for Advanced Study, Princeton, NJ, 1966—69, prof. Sch. Natural Scis., 1969—, N.J. Albert Einstein prof. Sch. Natural Scis., 1979—2003. Vis. lectr. dept. physics Princeton U., 1969—. Author: (with R.F. Dashen) Current Algebras, 1968, Quaternionic Quantum Mechanics and Quantum Fields, 1995, Quantum Theory as an Emergent Phenomenon, 2004; contbr. articles to profl. jours. Recipient J.J. Sakurai prize Am. Phys. Soc., 1988, Dirac medal Internat. Ctr. Theoretical Physics, Trieste, Italy, 1998. Fellow Am. Acad. Arts and Scis., AAAS, Am. Phys. Soc.; mem. Nat. Acad. Scis., Phi Beta Kappa, Sigma Xi. Home: 287A Nassau St Princeton NJ 08540-4618 Office: Sch Natural Scis Inst Advanced Study Einstein Dr Princeton NJ 08540 Office Phone: 609-734-8051.

ADLERSBERG, JAY BEN, internist; b. Pitts., Nov. 25, 1944; s. Herman and Mathilda (Marshall) A.; 1 child, Zoe. BS magna cum laude, U. Pitts., 1965; MD, U. Pa., 1969. Diplomate Am. Bd. Internal Medicine, Nat. Bd. Med. Examiners. Intern in internal medicine NYU Med. Ctr., N.Y.C., 1969-70, jr. asst. resident, asst. resident medicine Bellevue Hosp., 1970-72, NIH fellow in rheumatology/immunology, 1972-74; asst. prof. medicine divsn. rheumatic diseases/immunology Albert Einsteon Coll. Medicine, Bronx, 1974-80; assoc. attending physician Bronx (N.Y.) Mcpl. Hosp. Ctr., 1976-80; attending physician Beth Israel Med. Ctr., N.Y.C., 1980—, Lenox Hill Hosp., N.Y.C., 1986—; asst. prof. medicine Mt. Sinai Sch. Medicine, N.Y.C., 1980—. Assoc. attending physician Hosp. for Joint Diseases/Orthopaedic Inst., N.Y.C., 1980—; attending physician Hosp. Albert Einstein Coll. Medicine, 1974-80, Montefiore Hosp. Med. Ctr., Bronx, 1974-76; teaching asst. in medicine NYU Med. Ctr., 1972-74; teaching fellow in rheumatology Bellevue Hosp., 1972-74; keynote speaker Jonas Salk Scholarship Awards CUNY, 1993. Contbg. corr. ABC News Now, 1992—; weekly med. corr. The Health Show, ABC News, 1987-90; med. reporter Eyewitness News, WABC-TV, N.Y., 1983—; co-host Arthritis Telethon, WOR-TV, N.Y.C., 1982-86; guest host Healthline, WNYU-AM Radio, N.Y.C., 1980; contbr. weekly health column Bridgehampton (N.Y.) Sun, 1980-81. Master of ceremonies gala Cystic Fibrosis Found., 1990, S.I. Hospice Assn., 1990; mem. med. and sci. com. N.Y. chpt. Arthritis Found., 1985-88, dir. bd. dirs., 2005—. Named one of Best Drs. in N.Y., N.Y. Mag., 1998; included in How to Find the Best Doctors, New York, 1998, 99, 2000, 01, 02, 03, 04, George Foster Peabody award Excellence Journalism, 2001; Am. Cancer Soc. grantee, 1977-79. Fellow Am. Coll. Rheumatology; mem. AMA, N.Y. Acad. Scis., Am. Rheumatism Assn., N.Y. Rheumatism Assn., Med. Soc. County of N.Y., Med. Soc. State of N.Y., Phi Beta Kappa. Avocations: road bicycling, skiing, tennis, reading. Office: 220 E 69th St New York NY 10021-5737 Office Phone: 212-570-1800. Personal E-mail: drjay@medasso.com.

ADNET, JACQUES JIM PIERRE, astronautical and electrical engineer, consultant; b. Sermaize-les-Bains, Marne, France, Dec. 12, 1929; arrived in U.S., 1947; s. Julien Charles and Aline Georgette (Klein) A.; m. Mildred Ann Pruet, June 8, 1952 (div. Apr. 1982); children: Denise E., Lisa A., Paul A.; m. Helen Ilene Milam, Nov. 3, 1990. BA with honors, U. Fla., 1951, BEE with honors, 1960; MS in Astronautics, AF Inst. Tech., 1965; grad., Indsl. Coll. Armed Forces, 1972. Interpreter (civilian) U.S. Army, France, 1945—46; enlisted USAF, 1951, commd. 2d lt., 1952, advanced through grades to lt. col., 1968, elec. warfare officer Wiesbaden, Germany, 1954—57; with Radar Evaluation Flight Air Def. Command, Griffiss AFB, NY, 1957—58; flight test engr. USAF Sys. Command, Hanscom Field, Mass., 1960—61, subsys. devel. engr., 1961—63, site implementation engr. France, Belgium, Italy, 1968; chief space sys. divsn. USAF Fgn. Tech. Divsn., Dayton, Ohio, 1968—71; R&D dir. aero. sys. divsn. USAF Sys. Command, Dayton, 1971—73, ret., 1973; instr., course dir. Air Force Acad., Colorado Springs, Colo., 1974—81; tech. cons. and tech. translator Adnetech, Colorado Springs, 1973—. Dir. Dept. Def. Protocol Office Paris Internat. Air and Space Show, 1969, 71, 73, 75, 77; translator for U.S. Army in France, 1945—46; recognized as expert translator fed. and city cts. Author: When I See a "Forty and Eight"..., 2001; contbr. articles to profl. jours. Dir. of protocol 1986 World Cycling Championships, Colorado Springs, 1985-86; active Tri-Lakes (Colo.) Comprehensive Plan Com., Tri-Lakes Land Use Com.; co-founder Am. Air Mus. Britain; active Air Force Acad. Environ. Coun., 1999—. Decorated Air Force Meritorious Svc. medal; recipient Ordre Nat. Du Mérite French Govt., Paris, 1982, French Legion of Honor, 2004; named hon. citizen of Sermaize les Bains, France; Groupe Scolaire Jacques Adnet named in his honor, 2001. Mem. AIAA (sr.), VFW, Nat. Space Soc., Planetary Soc., Am. Legion, Air Force Assn., The Ret. Officers' Assn., USAF Acad. Ecole de l'Air Exch. Assn. (hon., exec. sec.), USAF Acad. Environ. Coun., U. Fla. Alumni Assn., Air and Airways Comm. Svc. Alumni Assn., Nat. Air Intelligence Ctr. Alumni Assn. Roman Catholic. Achievements include design modifications and conceptual design of electronic warfare equipment; direction of analysis of foreign space systems and equipment; design of unique passively heated solar homes. Home and Office: Adnetech 4360 Diamondback Dr Colorado Springs CO 80921-2364 Fax: 719-481-0082. Office Phone: 719-481-2887. Personal E-mail: adnet@direcway.com.

ADOLPH, KATHRYN ANN, passenger service employee; b. Hartington, Nebr., Dec. 20, 1945; d. Edmund Leonard and Elizabeth Claire Arens; m. Lester Leroy Adolph, Jan. 2, 1965 (div. July 1998); children: Leslie Marie, Edmund Glenn. BS in Adult and Occupation Edn., Kans. State U., 1981. Passenger svc. employee TWA, Kansas City, Mo., 1978—2001, Am. Airlines, Kansas City, 2001—. Industry expert (TV appearance) CNN. Avocations: writing, photography.

ADOLPHSON, VANESSA, counseling administrator, educator, chemist; b. Bakersfield, Calif., Oct. 13, 1973; d. Juan A. and Elena L. Garza; m. David J. Adolphson, Apr. 28, 2001; children: Marissa E., Blake J. BS in Chemistry, Calif. State U. Bakersfield, 1996; MS in Sch. counseling, U. La Verne, 2000, MEd in Ednl. Mgmt., 2003. Sch. counselor Winterstein Adult Ctr., Sacramento, 2000—; counselor Stanford Home For Children, Sacramento, 1998—2000. Evening sch. adminstr. Winterstein Adult Ctr., Sacramento, 2001—. Activist Foster Youth Forum, Sacramento, 1998—2000. Mem.: Phi Sigma Sigma (life; jud. bd. 1994—95). D-Conservative. Roman Catholic. Avocations: travel, tennis, painting. Office: Winterstein Adult Center 900 Morse Ave Sacramento CA 95864 Office Phone: 916-971-7414. Personal E-mail: vangarza@hotmail.com. E-mail: vadolphson@sanjuan.edu.

ADOMAVICIUS, JONAS, gastroenterologist, writer; b. Pernarava, Lithuania, Dec. 15, 1911; arrived in U.S., 1949; s. Anupras Adomavcius and Marija (Rimkute) Adomavicius. MD, Vytautes the Great U., Kaunes, Lithuania, 1938. Radio health show host (in Lithuanian); med. columnist in Lithuanian Lang. Weekly Newspaper. Author: 10 books; contbr. columns in newspapers Dienovydis (Lithuanian Lang. Newspaper), Draugas Lithuanian lang. daily Chgo., Lietuvill (bi-weekly), Ameikos Lietuviy Balsas (Lithuanian lang. weekly); author: Die Medizinische Fakultat der Eberhard-Karls-Universitat zu Tübingen der Grad enes Doctors der Medizin, Kvieslys Sveikaton. Mem.: Am. Gastroenterology Soc. Home and Office: 6515 S California Ave Chicago IL 60629

ADOQUEI, SAM, art educator, artist; b. Accra, Ghana, Jan. 20, 1962; came to U.S., 1981; s. Tetteh Adoquei and Adjeley Adjei. Diploma, Ghanatta Coll. Arts, 1978; grad., Opportunities Indsl. Ctr., Ghana, 1986; student, Art Student League N.Y., 1986. Artist, N.Y.C., 1986—; art instr. Ghanatta Coll. Fine Arts; mem. faculty Nat. Acad. Design, N.Y.C., Ednl. Alliance, N.Y.C.; represented by Portrait Inc. Instr. Ednl. Allience, N.Y.C., 1995—, Nat. Acad. Design, N.Y.C., 1993—, N.Y. Acad. Art, 1997—. Exhibited in shows including Salmagundi Art Club, Allied Artists Am., Knickerbocker Artists, Hudson Valley Art Assn., Nat. Acad. Design BiAnn. Exch.; designer textbook covers; contbr. articles to profl. jours. Recipient Honorable Mention award Nat. Portrait Competition Artists Mag., 1989, 3rd place award in portrait competition Artists Mag., Grumbacher Gold medal award Knickerbocker Artists 41st Ann. Award of Best Traditional Oil Painting Nat. Open Exhibition, 1991. Mem. Salmagundi Art Club, Knickerbocker Club. Home: 46-36 Oceania St Bayside NY 11361 Studio: 32 Union Sq E New York NY 10003-3209

ADOUR, COLLEEN MCNULTY, artist, educator; BFA in Studio Arts, cum laude, Syracuse U., 1980, postgrad. in MFA program in Studio Arts, 1980—84; grad. level ceramics, Alfred U., 1994; MFA in Art History, magna cum laude, SUNY, Binghamton, 2002. Daytime supr., art and music libr. Bartle Libr., SUNY, Binghamton, 2000—02; art tchr., lectr. Broome CC, SUNY, Binghamton, 2003—. Pub. info. mgr. Everson Mus. Art, Syracuse, NY, 1982—84. Notary pub. Dept. State, Divsn. Licensing Svcs., Albany, NY, 1998—; insp. of elections Broome County Bd. Elections, Binghamton, 1998—2003. Mem.: Binghamton U. Medieval and Renaissance Group (assoc.; v.p., treas. 2000—). Office: Adour Art & Pottery PO Box 1196 Vestal NY 13850-1196

ADREAN, LEE, communications executive; B Acctg. summa cum laude, Bucknell U.; MBA, Harvard U. With Providian Corp.; exec. v.p., CFO First Data Corp.; CFO, exec. v.p. fin. and adminstrn. EarthLink. Trustee, chmn. investment com. Bucknell U. Mem. Fin. Execs. Inst., Ga. State CFO Roundtable. Office: 1430 W Peachtree St Ste 400 Atlanta GA 30309

ADREON, BEATRICE MARIE RICE, pharmacist; b. Huntington, W.Va., July 23, 1929; d. Lloyd Emerson and Beatrice (Odell) Rice; student Mary Washington Coll., 1947-49; B.S. in Pharmacy, Med. Coll. Va., 1952; M.A. in Spl. Studies and Women's Studies, George Washington U., 1976; m. Harry Barnes Adreon, Jr., Dec. 27, 1952. Summer vol. worker pharmacies De Paul Hosp., Norfolk, Va., 1949, U.S. Marine Hosp., Norfolk, 1950; pharmacist Washington Clinic, 1954-71; counselor George Washington U., 1976-77, cons. gerontology health scis. dept., 1977—; cons. medicine control traffic patterns nursing homes Cross & Adreon, Washington, 1962-87; founder, pres. Pharmacy Counseling Services, Inc., 1978—. Instr. advanced first aid ARC, 1952—, civil def. instr., 1952—; vol. Spanish Edn. Devel. Center, Washington, 1972; mem. Arlington (Va.) Community Services Bd., 1980-83; chmn. com. substance abuse. Recipient Arnold and Marie Schwartz award in pharmacy, 1980. Mem. Acad. Pharmacy Practice and Mgmt., Am. Pharm. Assn., Va. Pharm. Assn., Potomac Pharmacists Assn., Am. Inst. History of Pharmacy, Nat. Council Patient Info. and Edn. (task force pub. info.), Panhellenic Assn., Kappa Epsilon. Episcopalian (mem. bishop's com. neighborhood services 1967-69, chmn. services for aged div. 1967-69). Contbr. articles in field to profl. jours. Home: 4524 19th Rd N Arlington VA 22207-2352

ADREON, HARRY BARNES, architect; b. Norfolk, Va., July 18, 1929; s. Harry Barnes and Helen Rae (Medairy) A.; m. Beatrice Marie Rice, Dec. 27, 1952. MS in Architecture, Va. Poly. Inst. and State U., 1952; postgrad., George Mason U. Law Sch., 1977-78; grad., USMC Pack and Equitation Sch., U.S. Army Engr. Sch., Ft. Belvoir, Va. Registered architect, Va., Md., D.C. Pvt. practice architect in Va., Md. and Washington; ptnr. Cross & Adreon, Architects, Washington, Va., 1961-87; prin. Harry B. Adreon, Architect, Arlington, Va., 1987—. Pres. Arlington Kiwanis Club, 1984; mem. com. on mgmt. Arlington YMCA, 1982-84; mem. Arlington Commn. on Physically Disabled Persons, 1987-93, Arlington County Fire Prevention Code Appeals Bd., 1990; chmn. Arlington County chpt. ARC, 1990-92, damage assessment technician Disaster Svcs. Human Resources Sys. Capt. USMCR, 1952. Recipient Dorothy Brunsman Outstanding Svc. award ARC, 1997; named Arlington Cmty. Hero, 1999. Mem. AIA (commr., dir. D.C. Met. chpt. 1978-79, Nat. Design Honor award 1968), Constrn. Specifications Inst. (pres. D.C. Met. chpt. 1972-74, Nat. Pres.'s plaque 1974, Carl Ebert award D.C. Met. chpt. 1990, cert. constrn. specifier), Kiwanis (Hixon award). Episcopalian (Vestryman 1961, 67, 71). Home and Office: 4524 19th Rd N Arlington VA 22207-2352

ADRI, (ADRI STECKLING COEN), fashion designer; b. St. Joseph, Mo. Ed., Sch. Fine Arts, Washington U., St. Louis, Parson Sch. Design. With B.H. Wragge; owner, pres. Adri Studio, Ltd., NYC, 1983—. Critic Parsons Sch. Design, 1982—; with Claire McCardell in 2-person showing, Innovative Contemporary Fashion, Smithsonian Instn., Washington, 1971. Two-woman show (with Claire McCardell) Smithsonian Instn., Washington, 1972. Recipient Coty award, 1982, Internat. Best Five award, Tokyo, 1986. Office: 143 W 20th St 11th Fl New York NY 10011-3630

ADRIAN, BARBARA (MRS. FRANKLIN C. TRAMUTOLA), artist; b. N.Y.C., July 25, 1931; d. Allen Isaac and Mildred (Brown) A.; m. Franklin C. Tramutola, July 26, 1972. Student, Art Students League, 1947-54, Hunter Coll., 1951, Columbia Sch. Gen. Study, 1952-54. Art cons. Doyle-Dane-Bernbach, advt. agy., 1960, A.H. Macy, N.Y.C., 1960-61, Saks Fifth Avenue, 1960, Black, Starr & Gorham, 1960; instr. art workshop Jamaica, N.Y., 1958-59; pvt. tchr. art, 1960—; instr. Art Students League, N.Y.; represented by Harman-Meek Gallery, Naples, Fla. One man shows, G. Gallery, 1957, San Juan, P.R., 1951, Grippi Gallery, N.Y.C., 1963, Banfer Gallery, N.Y.C., 1966, Eileen Kuhlik Gallery, 1973, Century Assn., N.Y.C., 1998; exhibited in group shows, G. Gallery, 1955-59, City Center Gallery, N.Y.C., 1954, N.Y.C. Festival, 1957, Portland (Maine) Mus., 1958, Workshop Gallery, N.Y.C., 1959, Grippi Gallery, 1960-63, Lane Gallery, Calif., 1962-63, Mus. Gallery, Lubbock, Tex., 1962-63, The Gallery, Norwalk, Ohio, 1962, Gallery 777, Plainview, L.I., N.Y., 1963, NAD, 1963, 81, Butler Art Inst., Youngstown, Ohio, 1963, Gallery Modern Art, N.Y.C., 1969, Child Hassam Fund Purchase Exhbn., N.Y.C., 1968, Orr's Gallery, San Diego, 1968, Pa. Acad. Fine Arts, Phila., 1980, Art Students League, N.Y.C., 1982, Norman A. Eppink Art Gallery, Emporia State U. (Kans.), 1983, Assn. of Bar of City of N.Y., 1986, Loyola Law Sch., Los Angeles, 1986, Blanden Meml. Art Mus., Ft. Dodge, Iowa, 1986-87, Minn. Mus. Art, St. Paul, 1987, Sunrise Art Mus., Charleston, W.Va., 1987, Capricorn Gallery, Washington, Kenmore Gallery, Phila., Whitney Mus. Am. Art, Albrecht Art Mus., Minn. Mus. Art, St. Paul, Nat. Acad. Design, N.Y.C., 2003-04, Century Assn., N.Y.C., 2003-04; represented in permanent collections, Grippi Gallery, Summer Found., Butler Inst., McMay Mus., U. So. Ill., San Antonio, Corcoran Gallery, Washington, Assn. of Bar of City of N.Y., Loyola U. Law Sch., Los Angeles, Blanden Meml. Art Mus., Ft. Dodge, Iowa, Minn. Mus. of Art, St. Paul, Sunrise Art Mus., Charleston, W. Va., Ark. Arts Ctr., Little Rock; also pvt. collections in, U.S., P.R., Mex.; Recipient (Benjamin Altman prize 1968), Nat. Acad. Design Invitational Exhbn., 1991. Recipient Dorothy Lapham Ferriss award, 1983, Walker award, 1985, Spring Oil Exhbn. Forbes Inc. award, 1990, Elizabeth Morse Genius award, 1992. Mem. NAD (academician), Century Assn. Address: 420 E 64th St New York NY 10021-7853 Gallery: Harmon-Meek Gallery 601 5th Ave S Naples FL 34102-6601 Office Phone: 212-371-3598.
I want to paint the magic of man, and that magic, both real and phantasmagorical, by which he lives and feels. Art to me is more than a profession, it is the expression of all life.

ADRIANOPOLI, BARBARA CATHERINE, librarian; b. Fort Dodge, Iowa, Jan. 27, 1943; d. Daniel Joseph and Mary Dolores (Coleman) Hogan; m. Carl David Adrianopoli, June 28, 1969; children: Carlin, Laurie. BS, Mundeline Coll., 1966; MLS, Rosary Coll., 1975; postgrad., Ozark Rsch. Inst., 1999—2000. Cert. in Pranic Healing and Dowsing Ozark Rsch. Inst. Dir. br. and extension svcs. Schaumburg Twp. (Ill.) Dist. Libr., 1979—. Mem. diversity com. North Suburban/Suburban Libr. Sys., Wheeling, Ill., 1995—; mem. commn. Hoffman Estates History Mus., 2004; co-chair Dorothy Brown Clk. of Cook County Cts. Adv. Com. on Women's Issues, 20026. Columnist local newspaper, 1995—, Sr. Connection, 2000—; contbr. articles to profl. jours. Mem. com. Schaumburg Twp. Disabled, 1981-95; historian Village of Hoffman Estates, 1986-99; adv. com. Hoffman Estates Sister Cities, 1996-98, Hoffman Estates History Commn., 2004—; asst. coach St. Viator H.S., 1999-2003; mem. adv. bd. Cmty. Nutrition Network, 1994—; organizer, mem. Northwest Corridor-St. Patrick's Day Parade com., 1986-2003; trainer A World of Difference Anti-Defamation League, 1994; mem. Com. For Choices For Success-Seminars For Young Women, 1996-2002; mem. Hoffman Estates Sr. and Disabled Commn., 2001; apptd. 8th Dist. State Dem. Com. Women, 2002; treas. Hoffman Estates History Mus., 2005—. Recipient Hoffman Estates Citizen of Yr. award, VFW, 1995. Mem.: ALA, Ill. Libr. Assn. Home: 1105 Kingsdale Rd Hoffman Estates IL 60194-2378 Office: Schaumburg Twp Pub Libr 130 S Rosedale Rd Schaumburg IL 60193 Personal E-mail: cadriano@sbcglobal.net.

ADRION, WILLIAM RICHARDS, academic administrator, computer and information sciences educator, writer; b. Nov. 2, 1943; s. Vernon Richards and Mary Leone (Carlock) A.; m. Jacqueline Cotner, July 3, 1971; children: Carrie Buchanan, Emily Richards. BS, Cornell U., 1966, ME, 1967; PhD, U. Tex., 1971. Computer engr. Honeywell EDP, Waltham, Mass., 1969—70; asst. prof. U. Tex., Austin, 1971—72; area chmn., asst. prof. Oreg. State U., Corvallis, 1972—78; dir. program NSF, Washington, 1976—78, 1980—85, dep. divsn. dir., 1968—86, chief scientist computer rsch., 1986; group mgr. Nat. Bur. Stds., 1978—80; prof. U. Mass., Amherst, 1986—, chmn. computer scis., 1986—94, dir. Ctr. Realtime Intelligent Complex Computing Sys., 1988—. Chmn. bd. dirs., pres. Applied Computing Sys. Inst. of Mass., Inc., 1989-99, Applied Computing Sys. Inst. of Mass., Inc. Labs., 1990-99; cons. Applied Theory Assocs., Corvallis, 1973-78, Tektronix, Portland, Oreg., 1974-76, Lawrence Livermore (Calif.) Labs., 1985-88, Radio Free Europe/Radio Liberty, Munich, 1981-82; prof., lectr. Am. U., Washington, 1978; vis. prof. U. Calif., Berkeley, 1984-85, U. Paris-Sud, 1992—; adj. rsch. prof. Georgetown U., 1985-86; gen. chair internat. conf. on Software Engring, 1994, 97; dir. divsn. EIA/CISE, 2000-02; sr. scientist CISE, 2002-03; dir. Commonwealth Info. Tech. Initiative U.Mass., 2004— Contbr. articles to profl. jours. Named Outstanding Young Faculty, Am. Soc. Engring. Edn., 1973; recipient Disting. Svc. award ACM/Spl. Interst Group on Software Engring., 1996. Fellow AAAS, Assn. Computing Machinery (editor-in-chief Trans. on Software Engring. and Methodology 1989-95); mem. IEEE, Soc. Indsl. and Applied Math., N.Y. Acad. Scis., Computer Rsch. Assn. (bd. dirs. 1988-96, chmn. govt. ops. 1990-94), CSNET (exec. com. 1986-89), Sigma Xi, Phi Kappa Phi. Home: 104 Wildflower Dr Amherst MA 01002-3447 Office: U Mass Dept Computer Sci CS Bldg 140 Governors Dr #316 Amherst MA 01003-4610

ADROUNIE, V. HARRY, retired public health service officer, science educator, environmentalist; b. Battle Creek, Mich., Apr. 29, 1915; s. Haroutune Asadour and Dorthy (Kalaidjian) A.; m. Emalea Riley, June, 1943 (div. Jan. 1980); children: Harry Michael, Vee Patrick; m. Agnes M. Slone, June 26, 1981. BS, St. Ambrose U., 1940, BA, 1959; MS in Environ. Health, PhD in Environ. Health, PhD in Pub. Health, We. States U. Profl. Studies, 1984. Diplomate Am. Bd. Indsl. Hygiene, Am. Acad. Sanitarians; registered sanitarian Calif., Mich., Pa. Enlisted U.S. Army, 1941, commd. 2d. lt., 1943; advanced through grades to lt. col. USAF, ret., 1968; founder, tech. dir. ARA Environ. Svcs., 1968—72; dir. environ. health div. Chester County Health Dept., Pa., 1972—75, Berrien County Health Dept., Berrien County, Mich., 1975—78; prof. environ. health Sch. Pub. Health U. Hawaii, Manoa, 1978—80; dean, prof. Sch. Pub. Health, We. States U. Profl. Studies, Mo., 1980—83; vis. prof. environ. and pub. health Am. U., Armenia, 1995. USAF rep. U.S. Interdepartmental Com. on Nutrition for Nat. Def., 1959—61; cons. Health Mobilization Program USPHS Surgeon Gen., 1957—61; mem. USAF Surgeon Gen.'s med. goodwill tour all S.A.m. countries, 1960; chmn., vis. assoc. prof. dept. environ. health, faculty med. scis. Am. U. Beirut, 1963—66, chmn. dept. environ. health, 1964—66; charter mem. Mid. East RSH-UN Welfare Relief Agy. Pub. Health Examining Bd. for Mid. East, 1963—66; cons. Mid. East UN Welfare Relief Agy., 1964—66; founder, coord. 1st and 2nd Environ. Health Symposium of Mid. East, 1965—66; mem. Mich. Hazardous Waste Policy Com., 1990—91, Mich. Underground Storage Fin. Policy Bd., 1994—2001; adj. instr., adv. com. environ. health Ferris State Coll., Big Rapids, Mich., 1974—75, Big Rapids, 1977—78. Contbr. numerous articles to profl. jours.; author many manuals and tng. booklets for USAF and other orgns., several books. Chmn. Barry County Solid Waste Planning and Oversight com., 1981—; mem. Barry County Dept. Human Svcs., 1996—, vice chmn., 1998—, chmn., 2003—; vice chmn. Hastings City Planning Commn., 1984—; mem., vice chmn., co-founder sci. adv. and policy bd. Mich. Ground Water Survey, Inc., 1983—90, chmn., 1988—91; chmn. adv. coun. South Ctrl. Mich. Commn. on Aging, 1981—91; charter mem. UL Underwriters adv. coun. environ. and pub. health, 1996—2005, emeritus mem., 2005—; appointed mem. Vision 2020 Com. St. Ambrose U., 2000—01; past adult leader Boy Scouts Am.; chmn. com. negative aspects environ. health on children, tchrs., and tng. manual, 2003—05; co-founder, co-chair Environ. Med. Coordinating Coun., 2004—. Decorated Legion of Merit, USAF, 1966; named Alumnus of Yr., Hastings H.S., 1961; recipient Walter S. Mangold award Nat. Environ. Health Assn., 1963, spl. recognition Mich. Environ. Health Assn., 1992, Safety Person of World Safety Orgn., 1991, State of Mich. White Pine award, 1998; congl. act named after him, Mich., 2004. Mem.: APHA (pres. 1995—97, emeritus conf., task force on aging 2002—), NRA (life; cert. rifle marksmanship instr.), VFW (life), Indonesian Environ. Health Assn. (co-founder 1979), World Safety Orgn. (bd. dirs. 1986—95, cert. bd. 1987—2000, editl. bd. 1988—2000), Global Health Assn., Internat. Pub. Health Soc. (charter-emeritus), Mich. Assn. Local Environ. Health Adminstrs. (pres., founder 1976, V. Harry Adrounie award named in his honor 2001), Mich. Environ. Health Assn. (life; pres. 1991—92), Assn. Mil. Surgeons (life), Nat. Environ. Health Assn. (life; pres. 1961—62), Am. Legion (comdr. post 45 1989—90), Air Force Assn., Mil. Officers Assn. Am. (life), Disabled Vets. Assn. (life), Kiwanis (pres. Hastings, Mich. chpt. 1985—86), Moose, Elks (life). Home: 1905 N Broadway Hastings MI 49058-1086 Personal E-mail: vee1@voyager.net.

ADSIT, RUSSELL ALLAN, landscape architect; b. Syracuse, N.Y., June 11, 1952; B of Landscape Arch., U. Ga., 1975; M of Agribus. Mgmt., Miss. State U., 1997. Registered landscape arch., Ala., Ark., Ga., Ky., Miss., Tenn. Landscape designer Landscape Svcs., Birmingham, Ala., 1975-76; pres., owner, gen. mgr. Adsit Landscape and Design Firm, Inc., Memphis, 1976-94; owner Natural Design Solutions, Memphis, 1995-98; prin. Fisher & Arnold, Inc., Memphis, 1998—. Instr. Toro U., 1990-91, Tenn. Fedn. Garden Clubs, 1990-92, Miss. State U., 1995-98; spkr. Hinds C.C., Jackson, Miss. Mem. Intern Program at Cobelskill Program, 1991-92, Co-op Program at Miss. State U., 1980-92, Econs. Amenities Task Force, 1982; mem. finance com. Asbury Meth. Ch., 1991-92. Named Outstanding Small Bus. of Yr., Memphis Bus. Jour., 1981, Outstanding Bus. Vol., Memphis Bot. Garden Found., 1988. Fellow Am. Soc. Landscape Archs. (chmn. membership application rev. com. 1978-80, water mgmt. ednl. seminar 1979, pres. Tenn. chpt. 1980-81, 84-85, chmn. nat. coun. chpt. pres. 1981, judges panel Miss. ann. awards 1981, spkr. nat. conv. Cin. 1985, Tenn. trustee 1987-93, judges facilitator Okla. ann. awards 1987, mem. ann. conf. organizing com. Tenn. chpt. 1989, chpt. membership com. 1989-91, publs. bd. 1991-92, fin. and adminstrn. com. 1991-92, v.p. 1999-2000, merit award 1979, 80, honor award 1981); mem. Assn. Turf and Ornamental Mgrs. (charter, pres. 1986), Assoc. Landscape Contractors Am. (distinction award 1990, 92, 93, merit award 1991), So. Nurserymen's Assn., Memphis Bot. Garden Found. (bd. dirs. 1984-92, chmn. master plan selection com. 1987, 2d v.p. 1989-90), West Tenn. Nursery and Landscape Assn., Tenn. Nursery Assn., Memphis Hort. Soc., Memphis Assn. Bldg. Owners and Mgrs., Memphis C. of C. (small bus. coun., chmn. small bus. connection 1992). Office: 9180 Crestwyn Hills Dr Memphis TN 38125-8538

ADU, FREDDY, professional soccer player; b. Tema, Ghana, June 2, 1989; Professional soccer player D.C. United, Washington, 2004—. Mem. U.S. under 17 Nat. Soccer Team, 2002—03. Named Chevy Young Male Athlete of the Year, U.S. Soccer, 2003; named to MLS All-Star Team, 2004. Achievements include one of the youngest atheletes to ever compete in a major professional sport; graduated High School in an accelerated program; mem. MLS Cup Champion D.C. United, 2004. Office: c/o DC United 2400 East Capitol St SE Washington DC 20003*

ADU, HELEN FOLASADE See SADE

ADUBATO, RICHARD ADAM (RICHIE ADUBATO), professional basketball coach; b. Irvington, NJ, Nov. 23, 1937; m. Carol Begerow, July 25, 1989; children: Beth, Scott, Adam. grad., postgrad. degree, William Paterson Coll., Wayne, NJ. Head coach Our Lady of the Valley High Sch., Orange, NJ; asst. coach Upsala Coll., East Orange, NJ, 1969-72, head coach, 1972-78; asst. coach Detroit Pistons, Detroit, 1978-79, head coach, 1979-80; scout Atlanta Hawks, Atlanta, 1980-82; asst. coach New York Knicks, N.Y.C., NY, 1982-86, Dallas Mavericks, Dallas, 1986-89, head coach, 1989-93; asst. coach Cleveland Cavaliers, 1993-96; head coach Orlando Magic, 1996-97, New York Liberty (WNBA), 1998—. Named to William Paterson Hall of Fame. Office: New York Liberty 2 Penn Plz New York NY 10121-0101

ADUJA, MELODIE WILLIAMS, state senator; b. Honolulu, Jan. 25, 1960; m. Lee Williams; children: William, Amber. BA, Hawaii Loa Coll., Kaneohe, 1981; ML, Golden Gate U. Sch. of Law, 1991, JD, 1987. Legis. aide State Rep. Alfred Lardizabal, 1982—83; dep. processing atty. Prosecutor's Office, Honolulu, 1987—91; atty. Law Office of Melodie R. Williams Aduja, 1992—; commr. Transport. Commn. City and County of Hawaii, 1999—2000; senator Hawaii State Senate, 2002—. Dir. Nat. Kidney Found. of Hawaii, 1997—98; bd. mem. Hina Mauka Recovery Ctr., 1998—2001; dir. No Hope in Dope, Inc., 1998—2001; mem. Kahaluu Neighborhood Bd., 1999—2001; dir. Hawaii Filipino Lawyers Assn., 1993—94; mem. San Francisco Area Women Tax Lawyers, 1992—93. Mem.: Calif. State Bar. Democrat. Roman Catholic. Office: State Capital Rm 231 415 S Beretania St Honolulu HI 96813 E-mail: senaduja@Capitol.hawaii.gov, melodie@aduja.com.

ADYA, SAURABH N., research engineer; b. Nangal, Punjab, India, Mar. 1, 1978; s. Naresh G. and Madhu N. Adya; m. Nidhi G. Adroja, Jan. 20, 2003. BE, Mangalore U., 1999; MS, U. Mich., 2002, PhD, 2004. Rschr. IBM Austin Rsch. Labs, Austin, Tex., 2002—03; sr. r&d engr. Synplicity Inc., Sunnyvale, Calif., 2004—; integrated circuit design engr. Tex. Instruments, Bangalore, India, 1999—2000; grad. student rsch. asst. U. of Mich., Ann Arbor, Mich., 2000—04; summer intern Siemens Comm. Software, Bangalore, India, 1998—98. Contbr. articles to profl. jours. Interact club pres. Rotary Internat., Mithapur, India, 1994—95. Recipient Rsch. Mentor award, U. of Mich. Coll. of Engring., 2004, Design Automation Conf. scholar for grad. students, IEEE, ACM, 2001, Team award for Design Planning, Synplicity, 2004. Mem.: IEEE. Hindu. Achievements include research in Unification of Partitioning, Floorplanning and Placement. Personal E-mail: adyasaurabhn@gmail.com.

ADZICK, NICK SCOTT, surgeon, pediatric surgery educator; b. Omaha, May 14, 1953; MD, Harvard Coll., 1975; postgrad., 1979. Resident gen. surgery Mass. Gen. Hosp., 1979-83, 85-86; resident surg. rsch. U. Calif., San Francisco, 1983-85; resident pediat. surgery Boston Children's Hosp., 1986-88; faculty U. Calif., San Francisco, 1988—; surgeon-in-chief The Children's Hosp., Phila.; C. Everett Koop prof. pediat. surgery U. Pa. Sch. Medicine, 1995—; pediat. surgery tng. program dir., dir. Ctr. for Fetal Diagnosis and Treatment. Fellow ACS; mem. AMA, Am. Acad. Pediat. (surg. sect.), Am. Coll. Physician Execs., Am. Pediat. Surg. Assn., Am. Surg. Assn., Assn. for Acad. Surgery, Soc. Univ. Surgeons, Nat. Inst. Medicine, Internat. Fetal Medicine and Surgery Soc., Brit. Assn. Pediat. Surgery, Pacific Assn. Pediat. Surgeons, Wound Healing Soc., Coll. Physicians Phila., John Morgan Soc., Ravdin-Rhoads Surg. Soc. E-mail: adzick@email.chop.edu.

AEHLERT, BARBARA JUNE, health facility administrator; b. San Antonio, June 17, 1956; d. Bobby Ray and Ronella Su (Light) Mahoney; m. Dean A. Aehlert, Sept. 6, 1980; children: Andrea, Sherri. AA in Nursing, Glendale (Ariz.) C.C., 1976; BS in Profl. Arts, St. Joseph's Coll., Windham, Maine, 1997. Cert. ACLS instr., BLS instr., emergency med. tng./paramedic instr. Gen. mgr. Hosp. Ambulance Svc., Phoenix, 1982-83; critical care nurse Samaritan Health Svcs., Phoenix, 1978-80, coord. patient transp., 1980-82, mgr. clin. programs, 1983-92; dir. emergency med. svcs. edn. EMS Edn. and Rsch., 1992-97; pres. S.W. EMS Edn. Inc., Glendale, Ariz., 1997—. EMS coord., City of Mesa Fire Dept., 2001-04. Author: ACLS Quick Review Study Guide, 2d edit., 2001, ACLS Quick Review Slide Set, 1994, ACLS Quick Review Study Cards, 2003, PALS Study Guide, 2d edit., 2004, ECGs Made Easy, 2d edit., 2001, ECGs Made Easy Lesson Plans, 1996, Mosby's Computerized Paramedic Test Generator, 1996, Aehlert's EMT Basic Study Guide, 1997, ECGs Made Easy Study Cards, 2003, Mosby's Comprehensive Pediatric Emergency Care, 2005. Republican.

AELION, C. MARJORIE, science educator; BS summa cum laude, U. Mass., 1980; MSCE, MIT, 1983; PhD, U. N.C., 1988. Park ranger Nat. Park Svc., Cape Cod Nat. Seashore, South Wellfleet, Mass., 1976-78; biologist, resource assessment divsn. Nat. Marine Fisheries, Woods Hole, Mass., 1978-84; rsch. asst. MIT, Cambridge, Mass., 1981-83, U. Mass.-Amherst, Amherst, Peru, 1983-84, U. N.C., Chapel Hill, 1986-88, tchg. asst., 1987; hydrologist U.S. Geol. Survey, Water Resources Divsn., Columbia, S.C., 1988-91, faculty mem., 1991-97; asst. prof. dept. environ. health scis. U. S.C., Columbia, 1991-97, assoc. prof., 1997-2001, prof., 2001—. Presenter in field. Contbr. articles to profl. jours. Fulbright-Hayes scholar, 1980-81; Bd. Govs.' fellow U. N.C., 1984-86, Dissertation fellow, 1988, NSF fellow in engring., 1993; grantee U.S. EPA, 1991-93, Hazardous Waste Mgmt. Rsch. Fund, 1991-94, 99-2002, Nat. Geographic Soc., 1992, S.C. Dept. Health and Environ. Control and Hazardous Waste Mgmt. Rsch. Fund, 1991-94, U. S.C., 1993-94, NSF, 1993-00, 99—, Fulbright Scholar, 2002; grad. student travel grantee award U. N.C., 1988; Rsch. Fellowship, Internat. Agrl. Ctr., The Netherlands, 2002. Mem. Am. Chem. Soc., Am. Soc. Microbiology, Assn. for Women in Sci. (sec. S.C. chpt. 1996-97, pres. S.C. chpt. 1997-98), Soc. Women Engrs., Soc. Environ. Toxicology and Chemistry, Phi Kappa Phi, Delta Omega. Office: U SC Environ Health Scis Dept Columbia SC 29208-0001

AELONY, YOSSEF, physician; b. Dayton, Ohio, Nov. 5, 1937; s. David and Janet Aelony; m. Ginette C. Aelony, July 22, 1966; children: Auram, Shana. MD, Minn. U., 1965; BA, U. Mann, 1961. Diplomate Am. Bd. Pulmonary Disease. Physician Kaiser Permanente, Harbor City, Calif., 1973—. Author: Practice Thoracoscopy, 1990. Maj. U.S. Army, 1967—70. Named Exceptional Physician, Permanente Harbory City, 1992. Fellow: ACP, Am. Coll. Chest Physicians.

AFAR, DANIEL E. H., pharmacologist, researcher; b. Frankfurt/Main, Germany, Dec. 18, 1961; s. Joseph E. Afar and Arlette Balaila; m. Melody S.W. Pong, Dec. 28, 2004. BSc in Biology, McGill U., Montreal, Que., Can., 1984, MSc in Pharmacology, 1987; PhD in Biochemistry, U. Ottawa, Ont., Canada, 1992. Post-doctoral fellow UCLA, L.A., 1992—97; rsch. scientist Agensys, Inc, Santa Monica, Calif., 1997—2000; sr. scientist Eos Biotech. Inc., South San Francisco, Calif., 2000—03; dir. oncology Protein Design Labs, Inc., Fremont, Calif., 2003—. Contbr. articles to profl. jours. Spl. fellow, Leukemia Soc. Am., 1995—97, Postdoctoral fellow, Med. Rsch. Coun. of Can., 1992—95. Mem.: Shotokan Karate of Am. (Yodan (4th level black belt) 2000). Achievements include patents for serpentine transmembrane antigens expressed in human cancers and uses thereof; G protein-coupled receptor up-regulated in prostate cancer and uses thereof; a secreted brain specific protein expressed and secreted by prostate and bladder cancer cells; gene expressed in prostate cancer; secreted protein called 36P6D5 characteristic of tumors; C-type lectin transmembrane antigen expressed in human prostate cancer and uses thereof; PTANS: testis specific proteins expressed in prostate cancer; G protein-coupled receptor up-regulated in prostate cancer and uses thereof; serpentine transmembrane antigens expressed in human cancers and uses thereof; diagnosis and therapy of cancer using SGP28-related molecules.

AFDAHL, LEE J., musician, director, composer; b. Baldwin, Wis., Aug. 22, 1949; s. Marcus S. and Jeanne A. (Snyder) Afdahl. BA, Luther Coll., 1971. Dir. music, organist First Luth. Ch., Muskegon, Mich., 1971—73, Trinity United Meth. Ch., Grand Rapids, Mich., 1973—85, Arlington Hills Luth. Ch., St. Paul, 1985—91, First Presbyn. Ch., Rochester, 1991—. Conductor Internat. Handbell Symposium, Adelaide, Australia, 1994; mem. Handbell Conf., Bristol, England, 1996. Contbr. articles to profl. jours.; composer: numerous handbell compositions. Conductor Rochester Boychoir, 1995—2004. Mem.: ASCAP, Churisters Guild, Am. Choral Dirs. Assn., Am. Guild Organists, Am. Guild English Handbell Ringers. Office Phone: 507-282-1618. Business E-Mail: afdahl.lee@fpcrochester.org.

AFERZON, MARK, otolaryngologist; b. Kmelnitsky, Ukraine, July 7, 1971; U.S., arrived in U.S., 1979; s. Semyon and Bella Aferzon; m. Ruslana Aferzon, Aug. 5, 2000; 1 child, Matthew. BA in Computer Sci., Brown U., 1993, MD, 1997. Diplomate Am. Bd. Otolaryngology. Resident otolaryngolgy Geisinger Health Sys., Danville, 1999—2002; active staff Griffin Hosp., Derby, Conn., 2002. Courtesy staff Milford Hosp., Conn., 2004. Contbr. articles to profl. jours., chapter to book. Clin. Rsch. grant, Geisinger Med. Ctr., 2000—02. Fellow: ACS; mem.: AMA, Am. Acad. Otolaryngology, New Haven County Med. Assn. Avocations: soccer, swimming, volleyball, tennis. Office: 101 Elizabeth St Derby CT 06418

AFFELDT, JOHN ELLSWORTH, retired physician; b. Lansing, Mich., May 26, 1918; s. John Ferdin and Pearl Heald (Gardner) Affeldt; m. Nancy Faye Spomer, Sept. 2, 1942; children: John C., Elizabeth Affeldt Westberg, Cindy L. BS, Andrews U., Berrian Springs, Mich., 1939; MD, Loma Linda (Calif.) U., 1944. Intern Detroit Gen. Hosp., 1943—44; resident in internal medicine White Meml. Hosp., Los Angeles, 1946—49; fellow in pulmonary physiology Harvard Sch. Pub. Health, 1949—51; med. dir. Rancho Los Amigos Hosp., Downey, Calif., 1956—64, Los Angeles County Dept. Hosps., 1964—72, Los Angeles County Dept. Health Services, 1972—77; pres. Joint Commn. Accreditation Hosps., Chgo., 1977—86; med. advisor Beverly Enterprises, Fort Smith, Ark., 1986—97. Served with U.S. Army, 1944—47. Mem.: ACP, AMA, Calif. Assn. Med. Dirs. (pres. 1993—94), Los Angeles County Med. Assn., We. Soc. Clin. Rsch., Ins. Medicine NAS, Am. Congress Rehab. Medicine. Home: 5140 Bareback Sq PO Box 8432 Rancho Santa Fe CA 92067-8432

AFFELDT, THOMAS MICHAEL, lawyer; b. Cedar Rapids, Iowa, Sept. 22, 1946; s. Chester Nicklaus and Helen Mae (Pleshek) A.; m. Susan Lee Shaffer, June 20, 1970; children: Diane Maurine, Nancy Lee. BBA, U. Iowa, 1968; JD, U. Tulsa, 1972. Bar: Okla. 1972, U.S. Dist. Ct. (no. dist.) Okla. 1972, U.S. Dist. Ct. Appeals (10th cir.) 1972, U.S. Tax Ct. 1972. Assoc. Blackstock, Joyce & Pollard, Tulsa, 1972-73; atty./advisor SEC, Washington, 1973-75; ptnr. Savage, O'Donnell, Scott, McNulty & Affeldt, Tulsa, 1975-96, Savage, O'Donnell, McNulty & Affeldt, Tulsa, 1996—. With USAR, 1968-74. Mem. ABA, Okla. Bar Assn., Tulsa County Bar Assn., Oil Capital C. of C. (pres. 1978-80), KC, St. Pius X Men's Club. Democrat. Roman Catholic. Office: Savage O'Donnell McNulty & Affeldt Ste 600 601 S Boulder Ave Tulsa OK 74119-1306 Office Phone: 918-599-8400.

AFFLECK, BEN, actor; b. Berkeley, Calif., Aug. 15, 1972; m. Jennifer Garner, June 29, 2005. Actor: (films) School Ties, 1992, Dazed and Confused, 1993, Mallrats, 1995, Going All the Way, 1997, Chasing Amy, 1997, Armageddon, 1998 (Favorite Supporting Actor in Sci. Fiction Blockbuster Entertainment award, 1999), Phantoms, 1998, Reindeer Games, 1999, Forces of Nature, 1999 (Favorite Actor in Comedy/Romance Blockbuster Entertainment award, 2000), Dogma, 1999, 200 Cigarettes, 1999, Daddy and Them, 1999, Boiler Room, 1999, Bounce, 2000 (Favorite Actor in Drama/Romance Blockbuster Entertainment award, 2001), Jay and Silent Bob Strike Back, 2001, Pearl Harbor, 2001, The Sum of All Fears, 2002, Changing Lanes, 2002, The Third Wheel, 2002, Daredevil, 2003, Gigli, 2003; (films) Paycheck, 2003, Jersey Girl, 2004, Surviving Christmas, 2004; actor, writer Good Will Hunting, 1997 (Oscar award Best Writing Screenplay Written Directly for Screen, 3d pl. Boston Soc. Film Critics award Best Screenplay, Broadcast Film Critics Assn. award Best Screenplay-Motion Picture, Golden Satellite award Best Motion Picture Screenplay-Original, London Critics Cir. award Screenwriter of Yr., others); prodr.: Stolen Summer, 2002; exec. prodr.: (TV series) Project Greenlight, 2001, Push, Nevada, 2002, Project Greenlight 2; (films) Crossing Cords, 2001, Speakeasy, 2002, The Battle of Shaker Heights, 2003. Office: c/o Endeavor Talent Agency LLC 9701 Wilshire Blvd 10th Fl Beverly Hills CA 90210

AFFLECK, MARILYN, retired sociology educator; b. Logan, Utah, July 1, 1932; d. Clark B. and Velda (Bryson) A.; children: Michelle Alisa, Kimberly Kay, Lacey Dawn. BA, U. Okla., 1954; MA, Brigham Young U., 1957; PhD, UCLA, 1966. Instr., Central State Coll., Edmond, Okla., 1958-60; asst. prof. Fla. State U., Tallahassee, 1966-68; asst. prof. sociology U. Okla., Norman, 1968-70, asso. prof., 1971-90, interim dean Grad. Coll., 1978-79, asst. dean, 1976-82. Editor Free Inquiry in Creative Sociology Jour., 1984-90. Recipient AMOCO Good Teaching award U. Okla., 1974 Mem. Okla. Sociol. Assn. (pres. 1974-75), South Ctrl. Women's Studies Assn. (treas. 1979-83), Phi Beta Kappa. Democrat. Mem. Lds Ch. Home: 6395 Corky Dr NE Norman OK 73026-3135

AFFLICK, GILBERT LESLIE, editor, journalist; b. Lucea, Jamaica, Apr. 18, 1931; arrived in US, 1979; s. Jack Gilbert and Hattie Laura (Kennedy) Afflick; m. Pearly Brown Dickens, Dec. 26, 1991 (dec. Nov. 1997); m. Shirley Veronica Goldsmith (div.); 1 child, Gregory Julian. *Fierce ambition fueled the launching platform for the first generation of Jamaica-born Afflicks, a farming family, to acquire higher education and work in the professions. Father, Jack, left his parents' small farm to become a railway clerk in 1918. Brother, Clive, BSC in Theology, Philadelphia Biblical College, 1959, MA in History, Temple University, 1965, Doctor of Arts, Miami University, 1989, is a teacher. Brother, Martin, BSc, University of West Indies, Jamaica, 1966, MA, New School University, 1982, is an economist. Brother, Paul is a businessman in Palm Coast. Brother, Peter, is an engineer for Amtrak. Brother, David, is a retired TV cameraman. Sister, Hope, is a retired accounting clerk.* Cert. in journalism, U. West Indies, 1960. Acctg. clk. Jamaica Pub. Works Dept., Kingston, 1949—53; sports reporter Daily Gleaner, Kingston, 1953—58; copy editor Daily Gleaner and Star, Kingston, 1959—68; sports editor, features editor, night editor Jamaica Daily News, Kingston, 1973—79; editor Merrill Lynch IBK, NYC, 1982—2001. Author: The Farmer and the Thief, 2004; contbr. articles to profl. jours. Active Orphans Internat., NY, 2000; assoc. mem. Nat. Trust Historic Preservation, 1999. Fellow, Commonwealth Press Union, 1962. Independent. Avocations: reading, theater, photography, travel, cycling. Home and Office: 13 Flanders Ln Palm Coast FL 32137 Personal E-mail: gilbertaffleck@msn.com.

AFFONSO, DYANNE D., dean; BSN, U. Hawaii, 1966; MN in Nursing, U. Wash., 1967; MA in Clin. Psychology, U. Ariz., 1980, PhD in Clin. Psychology, 1982. Asst. prof. sch. nursing U. Miss., 1967-68; OB staff nurse, night charge nurse Kinchloe AFB Hosp., Mich., 1968-70; instr. sch. nursing U. Hawaii, 1970-73; asst. prof. coll. nursing U. Ariz., 1974-77, assoc. prof. coll. nursing, 1978, coord. psychiatric mental health nursing coll. nursing, 1982-84, joint appointment in psychology dept. psychology, 1983; assoc. prof. sch. nursing U. Calif., San Francisco, 1984-87, prof. sch. nursing, 1988; prof., dean sch. nursing Emory U., Atlanta, 1993-98, assoc. prof. women's & children's divsn. sch. pub. health, 1993—. Prof. sch. nursing Emory U., Atlanta, 1998—. Contbr. articles to profl. jours.; presenter in field. Mem. NAS (mem. inst. medicine 1994), NIH (mem. adv. coun. nat. inst. child health & human devel. 1979-83, mem. agenda com. nat. inst. child health & human devel. 1982, mem. scientific rev. com. nat. ctr. nursing rsch. 1986, mem. adv. coun. nat. ctr. nursing rsch. 1986-88, mem. steering com. rsch. patient outcomes nat. ctr. nursing rsch. 1991, sec.'s conf. 1993, charter mem. adcv. coun. office rsch. on women's health 1995). Office: Emory U Sch Nursing 531 Asbury Cir Atlanta GA 30322-0001

AFFRONTI, LEWIS FRANCIS, SR., b. Rochester, N.Y., Aug. 12, 1928; s. John and Mary (Least) A.; m. Aileen Ledford, June 2, 1956; children: John, Lewis, Mary Louise, Eileen. BA, U. Buffalo, 1950, MA, 1951; PhD, Duke U., 1958. Rsch. assoc. Buffalo VA Hosp., 1951-52, Roswell Meml. Cancer Inst., 1954, TB Henry Phipps Inst. U. Pa., 1957-58; asst. prof. Sch. Medicine, George Washington U., Washington, 1962-65, assoc. prof., 1965-72, prof. microbiology, 1972-93, prof. emeritus, 1994—, chmn. dept. microbiology, 1973-93. Cons. AVCO Rsch. Corp., VA Hosp., Martinsburg, W.Va., VA Hosp. Ctr., Wilmington, Del.; U.S. rep. WHO Conf. on Skin Test Antigens and Vaccines, Geneva, 1966; mem. med. adv. bd. VA, Wilmington. Mem. editl. bd. Infection and Immunity, 1972-78. Bd. dirs. Lynchburg (Va.) unit Am. Cancer Soc., 1996. Commd. officer USPHS (CDC), 1958-62; with USAF, 1952-54. NIH Spl. fellow, 1969; Nat. Tb fellow for Internat. Conf. on Tb Moscow, 1971; Nat. Tb fellow for Internat. Conf. on Tb Tokyo, 1973; Washington Acad. Sci. fellow; Recipient WHO Exch. Rsch. Workers award, 1970, Scientist Emeritus award Soc. Expl. Biology and Medicine, Washington, 1994; interacad. exch. program award NAS, 1980. Fellow Am. Acad. Microbiology, Assn. Med. Sch. Microbiology Chmn. (sec.-treas. 1976-86, bd. dirs. 1976-86), Washington Acad. Sci.; mem. AAAS (life), Am. Soc. Microbiology, Am. Assn. Immunologists, Reticuloendothelial Soc., Am. Thoracic Soc., Assembly on Microbiologists and Immunologists (sec. 1971-72), The Protein Soc., Toastmasters Internat. (Atlanta), Mil. Order World Wars, KC, Sigma Xi (local pres. 1986-87). Office: George Washington U Med Ctr Dept Microbiology 2300 I St NW Washington DC 20037-2336

AFGHANI, AFROOZ, medical educator; MPH, UCLA, 1994; PhD, U. So. Calif., L.A., 2001. Postdoctoral fellow, rsch. assoc. U. So. Calif., L.A., 2001—02; assoc. prof. Touro U. Internat., Cypress, Calif., 2002—. Rschr. U. So. Calif., 2001—; lectr. UCLA, 2002—. Author: (book chpt.) Trends in Smoking and Health Research, Trends in Exercise and Health Research; contbr. articles and reports to med. jours. Office: Touro Univ Internat 3d Fl 5665 Plaza Dr Cypress CA 90630

AFIELD, WALTER EDWARD, psychiatrist, educator, health facility administrator; b. N.Y.C., Dec. 28, 1935; s. Walter Edward and Mollie Evelyn (MCGovern) A.; m. Nancy Browning, Dec. 27, 1973; children: Walter Edward, Neva Browning. AB, U. Pa., 1956; MD, Johns Hopkins U., 1960. Intern Grady Meml. Hosp., Atlanta, 1960-61; fellow in psychiatry Harvard U., Cambridge, Mass., 1961-64, 66-67; asst. prof. psychiatry Johns Hopkins U., Balt., 1967-70, dir. dept. child psychiatry, 1967-70; prof. U. South Fla. Coll. Medicine, 1970-74, chmn. dept. psychiatry, 1970-74; exec. dir. Tampa Bay Neuropsychiat. Inst., Tampa, Fla., 1970—; chmn., chief exec. officer The Mental Health Programs Corp., Tampa, 1985-92. Author: The Children of

Resurrection City, 1970; contbr. articles to profl. jours. Pres. Fla. Lyric Opera, 1976—. Capt. USAF, 1964-66. Fellow Am. Coll. Psychiatrists; mem. AMA, Am. Acad. Neurology, University Club, Tampa Yacht Club. Republican. Roman Catholic. Home: 4619 W Bay To Bay Blvd Tampa FL 33629-7610 Office: 5820 W Cypress St Ste B Tampa FL 33607-1785 Office Phone: 813-636-8811. E-mail: hogheavn@tampabay.rr.com.

AFIFI, ADEL KASSIM, physician; b. Akka, Palestine, Oct. 19, 1930; came to U.S., 1984; naturalized, 1988; s. Kassim and Zeinnab (Akki) A.; m. Larryanna Patten, June 17, 1960; children: Rema, Walid. MD, Am. U., Beirut, 1957; MS, U. Iowa, 1965. Intern Am. U. of Beirut, 1956-57, resident in internal medicine, 1959-61; resident in neurology U. Iowa, 1962-64, fellow in neuroanatomy, 1961-62; fellow in neurology N.Y. Neurol. Inst., 1964-65; fellow in electron microscopy Johns Hopkins U., Balt., 1967-68; asst. prof. Am. U., Beirut, 1965-69, assoc. prof., 1969-74, prof., 1974-84, asst. dean Coll. Medicine, 1969-78, chmn. Dept. Human Morphology, 1969-84; prof. U. Iowa, Iowa City, 1984—. Author: Atlas of Microscopic Anatomy, 1974, 89, Basic Neuroscience, 1980, 86, Compendium of Anatomical Variation, 1988, Atlas of Human Anatomy, 1991; contbr. articles to jours. in field. Trustee Diana Tamari Sabbagh Found., Beirut, 1979—, Med. Welfare Fund, Switzerland, 1991—; mem. King Faisal Internat. Prize in Medicine, Riyadh, Saudi Arabia, 1981-85. Fulbright scholar U. Iowa, 1980-81. Mem. Am. Neurol. Assn., Am. Acad. Neurology, Child Neurology Soc., Soc. for Neurosci., Alpha Omega Alpha. Home: 1147 Penkridge Dr Iowa City IA 52246-4933 Office: U Iowa Coll Medicine Dept Anatomy Iowa City IA 52242

AFIFI, ALAA YOUSSEF, cardiothoracic surgeon; b. Cairo, Jan. 19, 1965; arrived in U.S., 1972; s. Youssef S. Afifi and Samia A. Salem. BS in Biology magna cum laude, Siena Coll., 1985; MD magna cum laude, Albany Med. Coll., 1989. Diplomate Nat. Bd. Med. Examiners, Am. Bd. Surgery, Am. Bd. Thoracic Surgery. Intern Wilford Hall USAF Med. Ctr., Lackland AFB, 1989-90, resident, 1990-91, Keesler USAF Med. Ctr., Keesler AFB, Miss., 1991-93, chief resident, instr. surgery, 1993-94, chief cardiothoracic surgery, dir. surg. ICU, 1999-2000; jr. fellow, instr. cardiothoracic surgery U. Rochester (N.Y.) Med. Ctr., 1994-95, chief fellow, instr., 1995-96; asst. prof. surgery Uniformed Svcs. U. Health Scis., Bethesda, Md., 1999—; attending cardiothoracic surgeon Biloxi (Miss.) VA Med. Ctr., 1996-2000, Meml. Hosp. Gulfport, Miss., 1998-2000, Ellis Hosp., Albany Med. Ctr., St. Peter's Hosp., Albany, NY, 2000—. Presenter in field. Contbr. articles to profl. jours. Recipient Ralph D. Alley award Cardiothoracic Surgery, 1989, award, Soc. Laparoendoscopic Surgeons, 1994; Presdl. scholar, 1981—85. Fellow: ACS, So. Thoracic Surgeons Assn., Soc. Thoracic Surgeons, Am. Coll. Cardiology, Am. Coll. Chest Physicians; mem.: AMA, Soc. Air Force Clin. Surgeons, Monroe County Med. Soc., Med. Soc. State N.Y., Am. Heart Assn., Sigma Xi, Alpha Omega Alpha, Delta Epsilon Sigma, Alpha Kappa Alpha. Avocations: travel, sports, landscaping, photography. Home: 10 Sable Sands Newport Coast CA 92657 Office Phone: 714-973-9903. Personal E-mail: alaaafifi@msn.com.

AFRICA, COLBY TAIT, information technology executive, poet; b. Santa Fe, Sept. 23, 1974; s. Deirdre Africa. Sr. software engr. Critical Path Tech. Svcs., Inc., Redmond, Wash., 1995—97; product mgr. Microsoft Corp., Redmond, 1997—99; software devel. mgr. Pacific Edge Software, Inc., Kirkland, Wash., 1999—2000, chief software arch., 2000—01; pres. PM Blvd., LLC, Alexandria, Va., 2001—; chief tech. officer Robbins-Gioia, LLC, Alexandria, 2004—. Chairperson Project Mgmt. XML Working Group, Kirkland, 1999—2001. Author: (poetry) Strands of Sanity (Editors Choice award Poetry.com, 2003). Mem.: IEEE (assoc.). E-mail: colbyafrica@hotmail.com.

AFSARY, CYRUS, artist; b. Oct. 18, 1940; s. Mehraban Afsary and Mehrbanoo Jamasbi; children: Bonnie, Jacqui-Mitra. BA in Art, U. Mid. East, 1962, BA in Interior Design, 1971. Resident artist Grand Gallery, Las Vegas, Nev., 1975-80; freelance artist Las Vegas, 1980-88, Scottsdale, Ariz., 1988—. Art tchr., Mid. East, 1967-68; participant Artists of Am., 1988, 92. Works featured in Southwest Art, 1987, Midwest Art, 1988, Arts of the West, 1988 Recipient Exceptional award Pastel Soc. Am., 1986; named Best of Show, C.M. Russell Show, 1985, Best Oil, Amarillo Rotary Club Art Show, 1991, chosen Ofcl. Poster Artist, 1991. Mem. Nat. Acad. Western Art (gold medal 1987, Robert Lougheed gold medal 1988, silver medal 1989), N.W. Rendezvous Art (merit award 1987). Avocations: photography, reading, music (new age). Studio: PO Box 3217 Scottsdale AZ 85271-3217 E-mail: ca@cyrusafsary.com.

AFSHINNIA, FARSAD, endocrinologist, researcher; b. Tehran, Iran, Mar. 16, 1970; s. Manouchehr Afshinnia and Shahin Salehpour; m. Parisa Jahanbani, Mar. 21, 1969. MD, Isfahan U. of Med. Sci., Isfahan, Iran, 1995. Cert. ECFMG Pa., 2001, ACLS Am. Heart Assn., 2002. Rschr. Endocrine/Metabolism Rsch. Ctr., Isfahan, Iran, 1995—98; instr. of methodology and biostats. Isfahan U. of Med. Sci., Isfahan, Iran, 1995—2000; physician VA Hosp. of Janbazan Found., Isfahan, Iran, 1995—97; pvt. practice Isfahan, Iran, 1997—99; couns. methodologist Ednl. Devel. Ctr. of Isfahan U. of Med. Sci., Isfahan, Iran, 1998—2000; physician Baharestan Razi Med. Ctr., Baharestan., Iran, 1999—2000, Brookdale U. Hosp. and Med. Ctr., Bklyn., 2002—. Cons. Ednl. Devel. Ctr. of Isfahan U. of Med. Scie., Isfahan, Isfahan, Iran, 1998—2000. Editor: Applied Data Analysis, 1999—; contbr. articles to profl. jours. Founder Baharestan Razi Med. Ctr., Baharestan, Iran, 1998—99. Sr. lt. Physician of Land Force of Army, 1995—97, Isfahan. Recipient Prize of the best rschr. of Isfahan U. of Med. Sci., Isfahan U. of Med. Sciences., 1994, Cert. of Rsch. in Medicine, Isfahan U. of Med. Sci., 1996. Mem.: Iranian Med. Coun. (corr.), N.Y. Acad. Sci. (corr.), Am. Diabetes Assin. (corr.), AMA (corr.), ACP (assoc. Cert. of Merit 2003). Office: Brookdale University Hosp 1 Brookdale Plaza Brooklyn NY 11212 Personal E-mail: afshinnia@hotmail.com.

AFTERMAN, ALLAN B., accountant, educator, financial consultant, researcher; b. Chgo., Jan. 25, 1944; s. Joseph and Ruth Gertrude (Jacobson) Afterman; m. Joan Elaine Hoffman, Apr. 30, 1974; children: Debra, Lori, Julie, Robin. BBA, Roosevelt U., 1964; PhD, U. Birmingham, Eng., 1989. CPA Calif. Asst. dir. securities exchange com. practices Alexander Grant & Co., Chgo., 1967—70; nat. staff mgr. Touche Ross & Co., Chgo., 1970—73; nat. tech. dir. Practice Devel. Inst., Chgo., 1977—82; acctg. prof. U. Ill., Chgo., 1983—88, dir. exec. edn.; mem. faculty grad. sch. bus. U. Chgo., 1992—99. Cons. to govts. Author: Accounting and Auditing Disclosure Manual, 1982, Compilation and Review, 1983, Accounting and Auditing Update, 1984, SEC Accounting and Auditing Update, 1985, GAAP Practice Manual, 1985 (Best Loosleaf Bus. Reference award Profl. and Scholastic Divsn. Assn. Am. Pubs., 1985), Accounting and Tax Highlights, 1986, Handbook of SEC Accounting and Disclosure, 1987, Credit Analyst's Report, 1988, Financial Reporting and Disclosure Manual in the United Kingdom, 1989, Public Accounting Practice Manual, 1990, Governmental Accounting & Auditing Disclosure Manual, 1991, Nonprofit Accounting and Auditing Disclosure Manual, 1992, Auditing Standards and Practices in Poland, 1993, SEC Regulation of Public Companies, 1994, International Financial Accounting, Reporting & Analysis, 1994, U.S. Securities Regulation of Foreign Issuers, 1995, Charities Accounting and Auditing Disclosure Manual in the United Kingdom, 1996, Audit Committee Governance Report, 2000, Corporate Financial Management, 2001, Guide to Preparing Mathamemtics Discussion, 2005, Guide to Preparing Pretax and Information Statements, 2005. Mem.: AICPA, N.Y. Soc. CPAs, Practicing Law Inst., Am. Acctg. Assn. Jewish. Home: 3900 Mission Hills Rd Apt 302 Northbrook IL 60062-5721 Office: 600 Central Ave STE 322 Highland Park IL 60035-3257 Office Phone: 847-433-6222. Business E-Mail: allan@allanafterman.com.

AFTERMAN, JEAN, professional sports team executive; BA in History of Art, U. Calif., Berkeley, 1979; JD, U. San Francisco, 1991. Aide Don Nomura, 1994—99; pvt. practice, 1999—2001; asst. gen. mgr. N.Y. Yankees, Bronx, 2001—, v.p., 2003—. Office: NY Yankees Yankee Stadium E 161 St & River Ave Bronx NY 10451

AGADJANYAN, MICHAEL GRANT, education educator; b. Yerevan, Armenia, Sept. 6, 1950; s. Grant Michael Agadjanyan and Shushan Khachatrian; m. Irina Y Petrushina; 1 child, Anna Marie. PhD, Inst. Epidemiology and Microbiology, USSR Acad. Medicine, 1974—78; DSc, Inst. Epidemiology and Microbiology, USSR Acad. Medicine, Miscow, Russia, 1980—90. Vis. prof. The Wistar Inst., Phila., 1991—93, U. Pa,The Inst. Viral Preparations, Russia, 1993—2000; prof. Inst. Molecular Medicine, Huntington Beach, Calif., 2000. Contbr. articles to over 80 profl. jours. Recipient Sci. awards, NIH, CRDF, 1997—2001. Mem.: Armenian Acad. Sciences (hon.), Am. Assn. Microbiology, Immunology (assoc.). Achievements include patents in field. Office: The Inst for Molecular Medicine 15162 Triton Lane Huntington Beach CA 92649 E-mail: magadjanyan@immed.org.

AGAJANIAN, GILDA, pianist; d. Oganes and Azatuhi A. BA, U. So. Calif., 1973, Grad. Study, 1974-76; Diploma, Am. Coll. of Musicians, Austin, Tex., 1981, Artist Diploma, 1984. Russian educator, Calif., 1976-81; music educator Gilda Agajanian Piano Studio, La Habra Heights, Calif., 1987—; profl. classical pianist Calif., 1985—; entrepreneur, ptnr. Aggie's Restaurants, Calif., 1981-89. Mem. Westshore Musicians Club (pres. 1992-95), Music Tchrs. Nat. Assn., Calif. Assn. Profl. Music Tchrs. (chmn. recitals 1992—), Dominant Club (sec. 1994-96), Nat. Guild of Piano Tchrs. Avocations: Slavic language and literature, exotic birds, horticulture, cats, dogs. Office: Gilda Agajanian Piano Studio 2039 N Cypress St La Habra Heights CA 90631

AGALLIANOS, DENNIS DIONYSIOS, psychiatrist; b. Galati, Romania, Jan. 1, 1923; arrived in U.S., 1957; s. Dionysios Nicholas and Eleni (Craciun) Agallianos; m. Georgia-Lee Virginia Foden, June 20, 1964 (dec. 2004); 1 child, Helen Penelope. BA, Classical Gymnasium, Galati, Romania, 1941; MD, Victor Babes Med. Sch., Cluj, Romania, 1948. Diplomate Am. Bd. Psychiatry and Neurology. Pvt. practice, Romania, 1948-49; preparator urol. dept. Victor Babes Med. Sch., 1949-51; intern. urol. dept. U. Athens Med. Sch., Greece, 1951-54; asst. prof. urology Med. Sch. U. Athens, Greece, 1956-57; staff physician Polikliniki Athinon, Athens, 1954-56; intern, resident French Hosp., N.Y.C., 1957-58; resident in psychiatry Brattleboro Retreat, 1958-60; resident, staff psychiatrist Spring Grove State Hosp., Balt., 1960-64, chief of divsn., 1965-68; staff psychiatrist Brattleboro (Vt.) Retreat, 1969-76, chief of profl. svc., 1976-80, dir. older adult program, 1980-92; asst. prof. psychiatry Dartmouth Med. Sch., Hanover, 1978—95; pvt. practice, 1992—2000; locum tenens staff psychiatrist, 2000—. Adj. asst. prof. clin. psychiatry Dartmouth Med. Sch., Hanover, 1995—2000. Contbr. articles to profl. jours. Pres. Parish Coun. St. George Greek Orthodox Ch., Keene, NH, 1985—86; sustaining mem. Greek Orthodox Archdiocese N. and S.Am., 1966—; founding father United Greek Orthodox Charities, 1967. Recipient Exemplary Psychiatrist award, Nat. Alliance Mentally Ill, 1994; grantee, NIMH. Fellow: Am. Psychiat. Assn. (life Disting. life fellow); mem.: AMA, Vt. State Med. Soc., Vt. Psychiat. Assn. Home: PO Box 759 Brattleboro VT 05302-0759 E-mail: dagallia@sover.net.

AGANI, FATON HILMI, anatomist, educator; b. Gjakova, Kosovo, Oct. 4, 1956; arrived in U.S., 1992; s. Hilmi and Mukades Agani. MD, U. Prishtina, Kosovo, 1980; MS, U. Zagreb, Croatia, 1987; PhD, U. Prishtina, 1990. Cert. MD Yugoslavia. Rsch. fellow Brookhaven Nat. Lab., Upton, L.I., NY, 1985; postdoctoral rschr. Case Western Res. U., Cleve., 1992—95, Johns Hopkins U., Balt., 1995—98; instr. Case Western Res. U., 1998—99, asst. prof. anatomy, 2000—. Achievements include discovery of basic mechanisms of cell response to hypoxia; effects of insulin-like growth factor (IGF-1), nitric oxide (NO), role of mitochondria on regulation of transcription factor hypoxia-inducible factor 1 (HIF-1). Avocations: painting, running, reading. Office: Case Western Res U Euclid Ave 10900 Cleveland OH 44106 E-mail: fxa5@po.cwru.edu.

AGAPITO, J. F. T., mining engineer, mineralogist; ACSM in Mining Engring., Camborne Sch. Mines, Eng.; MS in Mine Ventilation/Mining Engring., U. Mo., Rolla; PhD in Rock Mechanics/Mining Engring., Colo. Sch. Mines. Profl. engr., Colo., Wash. Miner, technician Beralt Wolfram & Tin, Ltd., Portugal, 1958-60, South Crofty, Ltd., Eng., 1958-60; ventilation engr. White Pine (Mich.) Copper Co., 1964-66, mine rsch. engr., 1966-68; instr. Colo. Sch. Mines, Golden, 1968-72; sr. rock mechanics engr. Atlantic Richfield Co., Grand Valley, Colo., 1972-74; assoc. Golder Assocs., Inc., Grand Junction, Colo., 1974-76; ind. cons. mining engr., 1976-78; pres. J. F. T. Agapito & Assocs., Inc., Grand Junction, 1978—. Contbr. articles to profl. jours. Recipient Rock Mechanics award Soc. Mining, Metallurgy and Exploration, 1992. Fellow Inst. Mining and Metallurgy (Eng.); mem. AIME, Internat. Soc. Rock Mechanics. Office: J F T Agapito & Assoc Inc 715 Horizon Dr Ste 340 Grand Junction CO 81506-8727

AGARWAL, BANKE, gastroenterologist, educator; b. New Delhi, Aug. 3, 1965; s. Nathmal and Vijaya Agarwal. MBBS, Jawaharlal Inst. for Postgraduate Med. Edn. and Rsch., India, 1989; MD, Jawaharlal Inst. Med. Edn. and Rsch., India, 1992. Abim Am. Bd. of Internal Medicine, 1996, ABIM Gastroenterology Am. Bd. of Internal Medicine, 2000. Instr. in medicine Harvard Med. Sch., Boston, 1999—2000; asst. prof. of medicine MD Anderson Cancer Ctr., Houston, 2000—02, St. Louis U. Sch. Medicine, St. Louis, 2002—. Dir., advanced gastrointestinal endoscopy Divsn. of Gastroenterology and Hepatology, St. Louis U. Sch. of Medicine, St. Louis, 2002—; course dir. Ann. Symposia on Gastrointestinal Cancers, 2002—. Recipient Charles Flood Rsch. Prize, Coll. of Physicians and Surgeons of Columbia U., 1999. Mem.: Am. Soc. of Gastrointestinal Endoscopy, Am. Gastroenterology Assn. (Young Clinician Award 1998). Achievements include Conceived and developed the annual symposium on Gastrointestinal Cancers to promote their multidisciplinary management; development of one of nation's largest referral clinical practice specializing in diagnosis and staging of gastrointestinal cancers. Office: Saint Louis Univ Sch Medicin 3635 Vista Ave Saint Louis MO 63105 Office Phone: 314-577-8764. Office Fax: 314-577-8757. Personal E-mail: agarwalb@slu.edu.

AGARWAL, JAMES, education educator; b. Calcutta, West Bengal, India; s. Joel and Sorola Agarwal; m. Pritam Patricia Agarwal, May 17, 1995; children: Johanan, Joseph, Joel, Joshua. BCom, St. Xavier's Coll. U. Calcutta, 1983; PGD in PM&IR, Xavier Inst., 1985; MBA, Atlanta U., 1989; PhD, Ga. Inst. Tech., 1993. Asst./assoc. prof. U. Regina, Canada, 1993—2001; assoc. prof. U. Calgary Haskayne Sch. Bus., Canada, 2002—. Chair mktg. dept. U. Calgary Haskayne Sch. Bus., 2002—04. Author: (Jour. Bus. Ethics) Ethical Climate Dimensions in a Not-for-Profit Organization: An Empirical Study (Manitoba Internat. Mktg. Competition award, 1997), (Non-Profit Mgmt. and Leadership) Factors Influencing Ethical Climate in a Not-for-Profit Organization: Research Propositions (Listed in Canadian Who's Who and Who's Who in Canadian Bus., 2004), (Mgmt. Internat. Rev.) Does NAFTA Influence Mexico's Product Image? A Theoretical Framework and an Empirical Investigation in Two Countries (Saskatchewan Wheat Pool Professorship award, 1998), (Jour. Internat. Mktg.) Internationalization and Entry Modes: A Multitheoretical Framework and Research Propositions (William Darden Best Paper award, Acad. Mktg. Sci. Conf., 2000), (Internat. Mktg. Rev.) Heterogeneity of Regional Trading Blocs and Global Marketing Strategies: A Multicultural Perspective (ANBAR Citation of Excellence, MCB Press, U.K., 1997). Recipient Saskatchewan Wheat Pool Rsch. award, Saskatchewan Wheat Pool, 1997—98, 1999—2000; grantee Health Rsch. grant, Saskatchewan Health, Can., 1994, rsch. on non-profit orgns., Kahanoff Found. Queen's U., Ontario, 2000, Rsch. grant, Haskayne Sch. Bus. U. Calgary, 2002, Social Scis. and Humanities Rsch. Coun., Can., 2002. Mem.: Am. Mktg. Assn., Am. Acad. Mktg. Sci. Avocation: travel. Office: Univ Calgary 2500 Univ Dr NW T2N 1N4 Calgary Canada Office Fax: 403-282-0095. Business E-Mail: james.agarwal@haskayne.ucalgary.ca.

AGARWAL, PAVAN K., lawyer; BSEE summa cum laude, U. Md., 1993; JD with highest honors, George Washington U. Law Ctr., 1996. Bar: Va. 1996, D.C., U.S. Patent & Trademark Office. Law clk. to Hon. Alvin A. Schall U.S. Ct. Appeals, Fed. Cir.; ptnr. Foley & Lardner LLP, Washington, chmn. electronics & software practice group. Adj. prof. George Washington U. Law Ctr., Washington; patent editor Fed. Cir. Bar Jour. Co-author: Patenting In-Line With Fed. Cir., 2003. Mem.: Guiles S. Rich Am. Inns Ct., ABA, Am. Intellectual Property Law Assn. Office: Foley & Larnder LLP 3000 K St NW Ste 500 Washington DC 20007-5101 Office Phone: 202-945-6162. Office Fax: 202-672-5399. Business E-Mail: pagarwal@foley.com.

AGARWAL, RAMESH KUMAR, aeronautical scientist, researcher, educator; b. Mainpuri, India, Jan. 4, 1947; came to U.S., 1968; s. Radhakishan and Parkashvati (Goel) A.; m. Sugita Goel, Oct. 26, 1976; children: Vivek, Gautam. BS, U. Allahabad, 1965; BTech, Indian Inst. Tech., 1968; MS, U. Minn., 1969; PhD, Stanford U., 1975. Rsch. assoc. NASA Ames Rsch. Ctr., Moffett Field, Calif., 1976-78; McDonnell Douglas fellow, program dir. McDonnell Douglas Aerospace, St. Louis, 1978-94; Bloomfield disting. prof., chair aerospace engring. Wichita (Kans.) State U., 1994-96, Bloomfield disting prof., exec. dir. Nat. Inst. Aviatn Rsch., 1997—2001; William Palm prof. engring., dir. Aerospace Rsch. and Edn. Ctr. Washington U., St. Louis, 2001—. Affiliate prof. Washington U., St. Louis, 1986-95. Contbr. more than 200 articles to profl. jours. Fellow AIAA, AAAS, ASME, SME, Soc. Automotive Engring., Royal Aero. Soc., IEEE, Am. Phys. Soc.; mem. Am. Helicopter Soc., Tau Beta Pi, Sigma Gamma Tau, Pi Tau Sigma. Office: Washington U Dept Mech Engring Saint Louis MO 63130 Office Phone: 314-935-6091. Business E-Mail: rka@me.wustl.edu.

AGARWAL, RAVI PRAKASH, mathematician, educator; arrived in U.S., 2002; MSc, Indian Inst. Tech., Madras, 1969, PhD, 1973. Prof. math. Fla. Inst. Tech., Melbourne, 1992—. Office: Florida Inst Tech Dept Math Melbourne FL 32901 Personal E-mail: agarwal@fit.edu.

AGARWAL, SHASHI KANT, cardiologist; b. Jullundur, Punjab, India, June 15, 1952; arrived in U.S., 1975; s. Vadhika Ram and Raj Aggarwal; children: Neil, Ayna. Cert. bd. cert. internal medicine and cardiovascular diseases, bd. cert. managed care medicine and disability analysts. Attending cardiologist Orange (N.J.) Meml. Hosp.; pvt. practice Orange. Tchr. U. N.Mex., Albuquerque, St. Michael's Med. Ctr., Newark, 1979-81, asst. to chief of cardiology, 1980-81; dir. divsn. cardiology South Amboy Meml. Hosp., 1991; ofcl. physician India Festival Com.; lectr. in field. Author, editor: (monthly newsletter) Good Health Long Life; reviewer: Catheterization and Cardiovasc. Diagnosis; appeared on weekly TV show To Your Health, 1995-96; contbr. numerous articles to profl. publs. Del. citizen amb. program People to People Internat., Med. Writers Del. to Russia and Estonia, 1997; gen. sec. Overseas Indian Congress, 1993-95; v.p. Asian Am. Heritage Coun., 1994-97; mem. nat. fin. com. Nat. Rep. Party, 1995-96; mem. Rep. Senatorial Trust, Nat. Rep. Congl. Com., Rep. Presdl. Legion of Merit; life mem. Rep. Presdl. Task Force; mem. steering com. Vedic Cultural Ctr. Project N.Y.; pres. Asian Music Acad., 1997-98, Asian Am. Heritage Coun., 1997-99, Pragya Mission USA Inc. Recipient Physician's Recognition award AMA, 1992-95, 95-98, 98-01, Rep. Presdl. award, 1994, Rep. Senatorial Medal of Freedom, 1994, News India Times Contbr.'s award, 1994, Rep. Presdl. Legion of Merit medal 1995, Key to West Orange, N.J., 1996, 98, Internat. Cultural Diploma of Honor, 1997, Med. Medal of Honor for Treatment of the Indigent, 1997, Chmn.'s Spl. award Asian Am. Heritage Coun., 1997 Fellow Am. Coll. Cardiology (cert.), Am. Coll. Chest Physicians, Am. Coll. Internat. Physicians, Interam. Coll. Physicians, Acad. Medicine of N.J.; mem. ACP, Internat. Coll. Physicians (founder N.J. chpt.), Am. Soc. Spiritual Medicine (founder), Am. Assn. Cardiologists of Indian Origin (life), Am. Assn. Physicians from India (patron), Am. Coll. Nuclear Physicians, Am. Sleep Disorders Assn., Am. Inst. Ultrasound Medicine, Am. Coll. Physician Execs., Soc. Critical Care Medicine, Heart Friends Around the World, Am. Acad. Family Physicians (supporting), Am. Philatelic Soc., Asian Am. Polit. Coalition (life), Mensa. Republican. Hindu. Avocations: flying, boating, singing, music. Office: 290 Central Ave Orange NJ 07050-3414 Fax: (973) 676-5858. Office Phone: 973-676-1234. E-mail: skagarwal@pol.net.

AGASSI, ANDRE KIRK, professional tennis player; b. Las Vegas, Nev., Apr. 29, 1970; s. Mike and Elizabeth Agassi; m. Brooke Shields, Apr. 19, 1997 (div. 1999); m. Steffi Graf, Oct. 22, 2001; children: Jaden Gil, Jaz Elle. Profl. Tennis player ATP Tour, 1986—. Mem. U.S. Davis Cup Team, 1988—, U.S. Olympic Tennis Team, Atlanta, 1996. Founder, Andre Agassi Charitable Foundation, 1994, Andre Agassi Boys & Girls Club, 1997, Andre Agassi College Prep Academy, 2001 Named Most Improved Player of the Year, ATP, 1988, Player of the Year, 1999, Most Caring Athlete, USA Today, 1996, 2001, Champion of Champions, L'Equipe, 1999; recipient Arthur Ashe Humanitarian Award, ATP, 1995, 2001, Outstanding Men's Tennis Performer, ESPY Awards, 2000. Achievements include oldest player to be ranked no. 1 in the ATP entry system, 2003; winner Wimbledon, 1992, U.S. Open, 1994, 1999, Australian Open, 1995, 2000, 2001, 2003, Roland Garros, 1999; Gold medal, U.S. Men's Singles, Atlanta Olympic Games, 1996; mem. U.S. Davis Cup Championship Teams, 1990, 1992, 1995; winner 60 career singles titles, 1 doubles title, ATP Tour. Address: International Mgmt Group 1 Erieview Plz Ste 1300 Cleveland OH 44114-1715 Office: ATP Tour Internat 201 ATP Tour Blvd Ponte Vedra Beach FL 32082

AGASSI, SHAI, application developer, director; BS in Computer Sci., Israel Inst. Tech. Founder TopTier Software, 1992—2001, Quicksoft Ltd., Quicksoft Media; CEO SAP portals SAP AG, Walldorf, Germany, 2001, dir. tech. and strategy, 2002—, mem. exec. bd., 2002—. With Israeli Army. Achievements include patents in field. Office: SAP AG Neurottstrasse 16 69190 Walldorf Germany

AGATA, BURTON C., lawyer, educator; b. NYC, Feb. 7, 1928; s. Max and Augusta (Steger) A.; m. Dale S. Granirer, Dec. 24, 1955; children: Seth Hugh, Abby Fran. AB, U. Mich., 1947, JD, 1950; LLM in Trade Regulation, NYU, 1951. Bar: NY 1951. Counsel divsn. NY State Banking Dept., 1955-59; ptnr. firm Burstein & Agata, Mineola and NYC, 1959-61; prof. Mont. U., 1961-62, N.Mex. U., 1962-63, Houston U., 1963-69; counsel Nat. Commn. on Reform Fed. Criminal Laws, 1968-70; prof. law Hofstra U., 1970-2001, Max Schmertz disting. prof. law, 1982-2001, disting. prof. emeritus, 2001—, interim dean, 1989; mem. faculty Nat. Inst. Trial Advocacy, 1977-81; dir. N.E. Regional Program, 1981-84. Spl. counsel NYC Charter Revision Commn., 1987-89, NY State Senate Minority, 1982-87; cons. Fed. Jud. Ctr., 1972, Inst. Jud. Adminstrn., 1973, HEW, 1971, White House Spl. Action Office Drug Abuse Prevention, 1973, NY State Temp. Com. on Constl. Revision, 1993-95; chmn. NY State Task Force, Stds. and Go als for Prosecution and Def., 1977-79; cons. Adv. Com. on Qualifications of Counsel, 2d Ct., 1977; bd. dirs. Nassau Economic Opportunity Commn., 1972-73; reporter-cons. action unit on criminal justice system NY State Bar Assn., 1986-90. Contbr. articles to law jours. With JAGC U.S. Army, 1951-54. Food Law fellow NYU, 1951, fellow U. Wis., 1963. Fellow Am. Bar Found. (life); mem. Am. Law Inst. (life), ABA (state antitrust law commn. 1980-2001, vice chair com. on professionalism sr. lawyers divsn. 1996-2000), NY State Bar Assn. (exec. com. criminal justice sect., chmn. com. rev. of criminal law 1987-2003, spl. com. on pre-sentence reports 1989-2001, Donnelly Act com. 1990-2001), Assn. Bar City of NY (criminal cts. com. 1970-73, penology com. 1973-76, criminal justice coun. 1983-85, antitrust com. 1986-89), Fed. Jud. Coun., Assn. Am. Law Schs. (chmn. criminal law sect. 1973). Office: 209 Mt Merino Rd Hudson NY 12534 Personal E-mail: vze2vnja@verizon.net.

AGATSTON, ARTHUR STEPHEN, cardiologist; b. N.Y.C., Jan. 22, 1947; s. Howard James and Adell (Paymer) A.; m. Sari Agatston, Mar. 7, 1983; children: Evan, Adam. BA, U. Wis., 1969; MD, NYU, 1973. Diplomate Am. Bd. Internal Medicine, Am. Bd. Cardiovascular Disease. Intern Montefiore Hosp. Med. Ctr., N.Y.C., 1973-74, resident in medicine, 1974-76; fellow in cardiology NYU Med. Ctr., N.Y.C., 1977-79; dir. noninvasive cardiology Mt Sinai Med. Ctr., Miami Beach, Fla., 1980—. Assoc. prof. medicine, U. Miami, Fla. Contbr. articles to profl. jours., chpts. to books in field; author, The South Beach Diet, 2003, The South Beach Diet Cookbook: More than 200 Delicious Recipes That Fit the Nation's Top Diet, 2004, The South Beach Diet Good Fats/Good Carbs Guide: The Complete and Easy Reference for All Your Favorite Foods, 2004 (Publishers Weekly Bestseller). Fellow Am. Coll. Cardiology (del. Fla. chpt. 1992-96); mem. Am. Heart Assn. (pres. Greater Miami chpt. 1992). Address: 4300 Alton Rd Miami Beach FL 33140-2800*

AGAZZI, SIVIERO, neurosurgeon; s. Evandro and Lucia Agazzi. MD, U. of Geneva Sch. of Medicine, 1991—96. Swiss Neurosurgery Board Certification FMH, Swiss Med. Fedn., Switzerland, 2003. Resident Dept. Neurosurgery Ul. Lousanne, Switzerland, 1996—2002; faculty U. of Lausanne Dept. of Neurosurgery, Lausanne, Switzerland, 2002—03; skull base and cerebrovascular surgery fellow U. of South Fla. Dept. of Neurosurgery, Tampa, Fla., 2003—05, faculty, 2005—. Sci. reviewer for grant applications Nat. Med. Rsch. Coun., Singapore. Contbr. articles to profl. jours. Mem.: AMA, Am. Assn. of Neurol. Surgeons, Swiss soc. of Neruosurgery, Swiss Med. Fedn. Office: Univ of South Fla Dept Neurosurgery 4 Columbia Dri Ste 730 Tampa FL 33606 Office Phone: 813-259-0901. E-mail: sagazzi@hsc.usf.edu.

AGBEH, ANTHONY ODEY, education educator, consultant; arrived in US, 1979; s. Jonas Offum and Rosemary Agbede Agbeh; m. Elizabeth Adeshi Agbeh, Dec. 9, 1991; children: Antonia, Rosemary, Samuel, Patricia. BS, Fla. Internat. U., 1982, MS, 1983. Dir. Wiley Coll., Marshall, Tex.; dept. chmn. Morris Brown Coll., Atlanta; prof. Ferris State U., Big Rapids, Mich.; assoc. prof. Northampton Coll., Bethlehem, Pa. Mgr. Victoria Sta., Miami, Fla. Sec. Conv. and Vis. Bur., Big Rapids, 1994—2002, bd. dirs., 2002—04. Fellow: Am. Hotel and Lodging Assn. (bd. trustees 1996—2002, hospitality educators com. 2002); mem.: KC, Lehigh Valley Realtors. Home: 116 Independence Ct Bethlehem PA 18020 Office: Northampton Coll Bethlehem PA 18020 Office Phone: 610-861-4114. Personal E-mail: aagbeh@yahoo.com.

AGBETSIAFA, DOUGLAS KOFI, financial consultant, management consultant; b. Anloga, Volta, Ghana; arrived in U.S., 1976; s. Benjamin K. Agbetsiafa and Rebecca Afafa Agbakpe; m. Patricia Ann Williams. BS, U. Ghana, 1971, MS, 1975; MA, Western Ontario, 1976; PhD, U. Notre Dame, 1980. Secondary sch. tchr. Mininstry Edn., Accra, Ghana, 1966-68; instr. U. Western Ontario, London, 1973-75, U. Notre Dame, 1976-80; prof. econs., acad. senate pres., spl. asst. to chancellor Ind. U., South Bend. Contbr. articles to profl. jours. Sec.-treas. United Way St. Joseph's County, bd. dirs., 1987—; trustee Urban League, South Bend, 1988; bd. dirs., trustee Urban Leauge South Bend and St. Joseph's County, 1996—. Mem.: Assn. Global Bus. (program dir. 1993—94, v.p. program dir. 1995—), Bus. Assn. Latin Am. Studies, Ind. Acad. Soc. Sci., Midsouth Acad. Econs. and Fin. (bd. dirs.), Midwest Econ. Assn., Western Econ. Internat., Internat. Bus. Assn., Am. Statis. Assn., Am. Econ. Assn. Am., Am. Math. Soc., Math. Assn. Am., U. Notre Dame Alumni Assn., South Bend-Mishawaka C. of C. (bd. dirs., mem. minority bus. devel. task force). Avocations: raquetball, reading poetry, gardening, travel. Home: 224 N Sunnyside Ave South Bend IN 46617-3332 Office: Ind U 1700 Mishawaka Ave South Bend IN 46615-1400 Office Phone: 574-520-4208. Business E-Mail: dagbetsi@iusb.edu.

AGBO, EDDY C., research scientist, veterinarian; m. Ebby Ezinne Agbo, Sept. 27, 1998; children: Chidera Crystal, Ezinwa Lydia. MS, Wageningen U., Netherlands; DVM, U. Ibadan, Nigeria; PhD, Utrecht U., Netherlands. Cert. rsch. scientist Vet. Coun. Nigeria, 1991. Scientist Inst. Animal Sci. and Health (Id-Lelystad), Netherlands, 1998—99, rsch. scientist, 1999—2003, Ctrl. Inst. Disease Control, Lelystad, 2003, Johns Hopkins U., Balt., 2003—. Mem. Netherlands Soc. Parasitology, 2002—04. Grantee, Netherlands Sci. Orgn. Rsch. Tropical Diseases, 1999—2003; Netherlands Grad. fellow, 1994—95, Wageningen U. Grad. Rsch. fellow, 1996—98. Mem.: AAAS. Office: Johns Hopkins Sch Medicine 725 N Wolfe St Baltimore MD 21205 Business E-Mail: eagbo@jhmi.edu.

AGEE, BOB R., academic administrator, educator, minister; b. Brownsville, Tenn., Sept. 30, 1938; s. Edwin L. and Katie L. (Stewart) A.; m. Nelle Rose; children— Nancy Denise, Robyn Janelle BA, Union U., Tenn., 1960; M.Div., So. Bapt. Theol. Sem., 1964, D.Min., 1974; PhD, Vanderbilt U., 1986. Ordained to ministry Baptist Ch. Pastor Shively Heights Bapt. Ch., Louisville, 1964-70; pastor Ardmore Bapt. Ch., Memphis, 1970-75; dean, v.p. religious affairs Union U., Jackson, Tenn., 1975-82; pres. Okla. Bapt. U., Shawnee, 1982-98, pres. emeritus, 1998—. Mem. edn. commn. So. Bapt. Conv., 1985-93, chmn., 1987-90; bd. dirs. Co-op Svcs. Internat. Edn. Consortium, chmn., 1988-90; cons. evaluator North Ctrl. Assn. Colls. and Univs., 1987—; bd. dirs. Nat. Assn. Ind. Colls. and Univs., 1986-90, 93—. Author Bibl. study materials and articles Mem. human relations com. Memphis Bd. Edn., 1972-74; mem. Memphis Mayor's Crime Commn., 1973-75; mem. Okla. Ind. Coll. Found., 1982-98, chmn., 1985-87. Inducted into Okla. Higher Edn. Hall of Fame, 1999. Mem. Soc. Coll. and Univ. Planning, Shawnee C. of C. (bd. dirs. 1983-98), So. Bapt. Theol. Sem. Alumni Assn. (nat. pres. 1985-86), AAUP, Am. Assn. Univ. Adminstrs., Nat. Assn. Ind. Colls. and Univs. (bd. dirs. 1988-97), Coun. for Christian Colls. and Univs. (bd. dirs. 1997-2003), Assn. So. Bapt. Colls. and Schs. (exec. dir. 1998—, exec. dir. consortium global edn. 1998-2002). Republican. Avocations: racquetball, golf, fishing, writing. Office: PO Box 11655 Jackson TN 38308-0127

AGEE, CLAUDIA, clerk, receptionist, tax consultant; b. Selma, Ala., Nov. 11, 1939; d. Claude and M. Marie (McConico) Thomas; m. Cleveland Agee Jr. (dec.); children: Debbie K., Danita McCary, Cleveland III (dec.), La Shondria, Ed'Keia, Mondena, Tocara, Lil Freddie, Mondeno Agee; m. William Stokes, Feb. 5, 2005. Student, Booker T. Washington, 1973, Birmingham Bapt. Bible Coll., 1989, Bessemer Tech., 1992; AA in Office Adminstrn., Bessemer State Tech. Coll., 1997. Bookkeeper, gen. mgr. Thomas Deli, Birmingham, AmSouth Corp. Revolving Credit Rsch., Birmingham; garment mgr. NLS, Birmingham; svc. clk., bookkeeper Minority Literacy Expo; office mgr., personal sec. Ross Gardner, ENT Specialist. Mem. The Bidders Orgn. (sec.), Order Ea. Star (sec. Lodge 385), Zeta Phi Lambda (Beta Psi chpt. honoree 1976). Home: 1346 45th St W Birmingham AL 35208-1919

AGEE, G. STEVEN, state supreme court justice; b. Roanoke, Va., Nov. 12, 1952; BA, Bridgewater Coll.; JD, U. Va.; LLM in Taxation, NYU. Mem. 7th dist. Va. Ho. of Dels., 1982—94; judge Va. Ct. Appeals, Richmond, 2001—03; justice Va. Supreme Ct., Richmond, 2003—. Former mem. Va. Criminal Sentencing Commn. Trustee Bridgewater Coll. Served in Judge Advocate General Corps USAR, 1985—97. Mem.: Roanoke County-Salem Bar Assn. (former pres.), Va. Bar Assn., DC Bar Assn. Office: Supreme Ct Va 100 N 9th St 5th Fl Richmond VA 23219

AGEE, NELLE HULME, retired art history educator; b. Memphis, May 22, 1940; d. John Eulice and Nelle (Ray) Hulme; m. Bob R. Agee, June 7, 1958; children: Denise, Robyn. Student, Memphis State U., 1971—72; BA, Union U., Jackson, Tenn., 1978; postgrad., Seminole Okla. Col., 1982, Okla Bapt. U., 1984; MEd, Ctrl. State U., Edmond, Okla., 1989. Cert. tchr. art, history Ky., Tenn., Okla. Offices svcs. supr. So. Bapt. Theol. Sem., Louisville, 1961—64; kindergarten tchr. Shively Heights Bapt. Ch., Louisville, 1965—70; editl. asst. Little Publs., Memphis, 1973—75; tchr. art Humboldt HS, Tenn., 1978—82. Vis. artist-in schs. Tenn. Arts. Commn., Nashville, 1978, 81, 82; adj. prof. art history Seminole Col., Okla., 1985—86, 1989; asst. prof. art and edn. Okla. Bapt. U., 1989—98; spkr. art orgns, ch. groups; tchr. art workshops Humboldt City Sch. Sys.; tchr. Cultural Arts Day Camp, Jackson, Tenn., 1982. Exhibited in various shows. Nat. pres. ministers' wives conf. So. Bapt. Conv., 1988; vol. Mabee-Gerrer Mus., Shawnee; bd. dirs. Robert Dotson Foun., Mabee-Gerrer Mus., Family Resource Ctr., 1993—98; active vol. Salvation Army Aux., Shawnee. Recipient Disting. Classroom Tchr. award, Tenn. Edn. Assn., 1982. Mem.: Goals 2000, Alpha Delta Kappa, Delta Kappa Gamma. Republican. Baptist. Avocations: stained glass, pottery, travel. Home: 14 Woodmanor Pl Jackson TN 38305-1718

AGEE, WARREN KENDALL, journalism educator; b. Sherman, Tex., Oct. 23, 1916; s. Frederic M. and Minnie E. (Logsdon) A.; m. Edda Robbins, June 1, 1941; children: Kim Kendall, Robyn Kendall Ansley. BA cum laude, Tex. Christian U., 1937; MA, U. Minn., 1949, PhD, 1955. Mem. editorial staff Ft. Worth Star-Telegram, 1937-48; instr. journalism Tex. Christian U., 1948-50, asst. prof., 1950-55, asso. prof., 1955-57, prof., 1957-58, chmn. dept., 1950-58, faculty adviser student publs., 1949-58; prof. journalism, dean sch. journalism W.Va U., 1958-60; mem. ednl. adv. com. WJPB-TV, Fairmont and Weston, W.Va., 1959-60; nat. exec. officer Soc. Profl. Journalists, Sigma Delta Chi, 1960-62; prof. journalism, dean Evening Coll., Tex. Christian U., Ft. Worth, 1962-65; dean William Allen White Sch. Journalism, U. Kans., Lawrence, 1965-69, Henry W. Grady Coll. Journalism and Mass Communication U. Ga., 1969-75, prof. journalism, 1975-87, dean and prof. emeritus, 1987—; vis. scholar U. Tex., fall 1975; copy editor Atlanta Constn., summer 1977. Combat corr. USCG Res., 1941-44; pub. info. specialist USCG Res. Hdqrs., 1944-45; mem. adv. screening com. journalism, com. internat. exchange of persons Conf. Bd. Assn. Rsch. Couns., Washington, 1958-62; mem. Am. Coun. Edn. for Journalism and Mass Communication, 1958-60, 65-67, mem. accrediting com., 1969-76, vice chmn., 1973-74, chmn., 1974-76, chmn. appeals bd., 1977, 79, 81, 83; mng. dir. William Allen White Found., 1965-69, trustee, 1970—; mng. dir. George Foster Peabody Radio and TV awards, 1969-75, Sigma Delta Chi Nat. Journalism Awards, 1960-62; assoc. James M. Cox Jr. Ctr. Internat. Mass Comm. Tng. and Research, U. Ga., 1985—. Author: (with Edwin Emery and Phillip H. Ault) Introduction to Mass Communications, 1960, 12th rev. edit., 1997, Reporting and Writing the News, 1983, (with Dennis L. Wilcox, Ault) Public Relations: Strategies and Tactics, 1986, 8th edit., 2003, (with Nelson Traquina) O Quarto Poder Frustrado: Os Meios de Comunicacão Social No Portugal Pós-Revolucionário, 1988; also articles.; editor: The Press and the Public Interest, 1968, Mass Media In A Free Society, 1969, (with Emery and Ault) Perspectives on Mass Communications, 1982, Maincurrents in Mass Communications, 1986, rev. edit., 1989; assoc. editor, bus. mgr.: The Quill, 1960-62; press rev. columnist, contbg. editor, 1977-82; adv. editl. bd. Journalism Quar, 1955-60. Mem. Athens (Ga.) Internat. Rels. Cmty. Coun., pres., 1980-82; pres. Friends of Mus. Art U. Ga., 1974-75; mem. Howard Blakeslee Media Awards judging com. Am. Heart Assn., 1976-94, chmn. judging com., 1980-94. Recipient Journalism award Fort Worth Press, 1936, Outstanding News Writing award Ft. Worth Profl. chpt. Sigma Delta Chi, 1946, Carl Towley award Journalism Edn. Assn., 1969, Outstanding Achievement award U. Minn., 1973, Wells Meml. key Sigma Delta Chi, 1978, Disting. Teaching award Soc. Profl. Journalists, 1987, Alumni Hall of Excellence award Tex. Christian Univ. Dept. Journalism; Fulbright grantee to Portugal, 1982, 85. Mem.: Soc. Profl. Journalists, Southwestern Journalism Congress (sec. 1957—58), Am. Studies Assn., Am. Soc. Journalism Sch. Adminstrs. (pres. 1956), Assn. Edn. in Journalism and Mass Comm. (pres. 1958, Disting. Leadership award 2001), Gridiron Club (Ft. Worth), Rotary, Phi Beta Delta, Alpha Sigma Lambda, Phi Kappa Sigma, Alpha Chi, Kappa Tau Alpha (50 yr. journalism edn. svc. award 1987), Sigma Delta Chi (pres. Fort Worth profl. chpt. 1954—55, sec. Tex. 1957—58, nat. v.p. campus chpt. affairs 1966—69, leader coun. 1982—, v.p. N.E. Ga. profl. chpt. 1978—79, pres. 1979—80). Presbyterian. Home and Office: 130 Highland Dr Athens GA 30606-3212 *One abiding goal has been to spread and deepen public understanding of the fundamentals of our democratic society as embodied in the Bill of Rights in general and the First Amendment in particular. That public understanding has been seriously eroded in recent decades. Only through a renewed, vastly broadened national effort to teach these principles in our schools and other social institutions, and through the media of mass communication, will this erosion be halted and our nation, as we have known it, survive.*

AGERSBORG, HELMER PARELI K., pharmaceutical company executive, researcher; b. Decatur, Ill., Dec. 2, 1928; s. Helmer Pareli and Jennie E. (Dunbar) A.; m. Marcella Felchlia; children— Eric, Kristin, Karen BA, Harvard U., Cambridge, 1949; BS, So. Ill. U., Carbondale, 1953; PhD, U. Tenn., Memphis, 1957. Asst. physiology U. Tenn., Memphis, 1954-57, instr. physiology, 1957-58; clin. physiologist Wyeth Labs., Phila., 1958-61, mgr. toxicology, 1961-69, assoc. dir. research, 1969-76, v.p. research and devel., 1976-85, sr. v.p. research and devel., 1985-87; pres. Wyeth Ayerst Research, 1987-91; CEO, pres. Fieldcastle, Inc., Wayne, Pa., 1991—2005, Afferon Corp., 1991—2005, Maret Corp., 1994-98. Mem. Am. Soc. Pharmacology and Exptl. Therapy, Am. Physiol. Soc., Am. Soc. Zoology, Soc. Toxicology Home: 336 Saint Andrews Pl Blue Bell PA 19422-1290 E-mail: afferonha@aol.com.

AGGARWAL, KUL, internist, cardiologist, educator; b. Nairobi, Kenya, Jan. 2, 1952; s. Labhu Ram and Kaushalya Devi (Gupta) A.; m. Archana Goel, July 26, 1979; children: Ruchi, Neha. MB, BS, Panjab U., 1975, MD, 1978. Diplomate in internal medicine, cardiovasc. disease, interventional cardiology and echocardiograhy Am. Bd. Internal Medicine. Intern Med. Coll. and Hosp., Amritsar, 1974—75; resident in internal medicine Willingdon Hosp., New Delhi, 1981—84, Nat. Health Svc., London, 1986—89, N.Y. Med. Coll.-Lincoln Hosp., 1990—92; fellow in cardiology U. Mo. Sch. Medicine, Columbia, 1992—95, mem. staff, 1995—, asst. prof. internal medicine, 1995—. Staff cardiologist Harry S. Truman Meml. VA Hosp., Columbia. Fellow ACP; mem. Am. Coll. Cardiology, Royal Coll. Physicians (London), Royal Coll. Physicians (Dublin, Ireland). Office: U Mo Health Scis Ctr 1E-66 Divsn Cardiology One Hospital Dr Columbia MO 65212 Office Phone: 573-884-6092. Business E-Mail: aggarwalk@health.missouri.edu.

AGGARWAL, VINOD K., political science professor; b. Seattle, Wash. BA in Polit. Sci., U. Mich., 1975; MA in Polit. Sci., Stanford U., 1977, PhD in Polit. Sci., 1981. Special adviser on trade Nnegotiations United Conference on Trade and Develop., Geneva, 1989; prof. polic. sci. U. Calif., Berkeley, Calif., 1980—, prof. Haas Sch. of Bus., 1992—, dir. APEC Study Ctr., 1996—. Bd. mem. Calif. Council for Internat. Trade; mem. Council on Foreign Relations, 1987—92; charter mem. Pacific Council on Internat. Economic Policy; editor in chief Bus. and Politics; chair Polit. Economy of Industrial Societies, 1991—94; rsch. fellow and guest scholar Brookings Inst.; fellow Woodrow Wilson Internat. Ctr. for Scholars; consultant Mexican Govt., US Dept. of Commerce, WTO, OECD, Group of Thirty, IFAD, World Bank. Author: Liberal Protectionism: The International Politics of Organized Textile Trade, 1985, International Debt Threat: Bargaining Among Creditors and Debtors in the 1980s, 1987, Debt Games: Strategic Interaction in International Debt Rescheduling, 1996. Grantee Rockefeller Internat. Relations Fellowship, 1984—85, Council on Foreign Relations Internat. Affairs Fellowship, 1987. Mem.: Am. Polit. Sci. Assn. (chair internat. polit. economy div. 1994), Am. Economic Assn. Office: U Calif BASC 802 Barrows Hall 1970 Berkeley CA 94720-1970*

AGGREY, ORISON RUDOLPH, former ambassador, consultant, academic administrator; b. Salisbury, N.C., July 24, 1926; s. J.E. Kwegyir and Rose Rudolph (Douglass) A.; m. Francoise Fratacci, Nov. 5, 1966; 1 dau., Roxane Rose. BS, Hampton Inst., 1946; MS, Syracuse U., 1948; fellow Ctr. for Internat. Affairs, Harvard U., 1964-65; LLD, Livingstone Coll., 1977. Publicity asst. United Negro Coll. Fund, 1947, 50; reporter Cleve. Call and Post, 1948-49; corr. Chgo. Defender, 1949; publicity dir. Bennett Coll., 1950; info. officer, vice consul Am. Consulate Gen., Lagos, Nigeria, 1951-53; asst. dir. USIS, Lille, France, 1953-54; asst. cultural affairs officer Am. embassy, Paris, 1954-57; dir. USIS Cultural Ctr., Paris, 1957-60; dep. pub. affairs adviser for Africa Dept. State, 1961-64; acting chief French br. Voice of Am., 1965; 1st sec., dep. pub. affairs officer Am. embassy, Kinshasa, Democratic Republic of Congo, 1966-68; program mgr. Motion Picture and TV Service, USIA, 1968-70; dir. West African affairs Dept. State, 1970-73; ambassador to The Gambia and Senegal, 1973-77; ambassador to Romania, 1977-81; career min. info., 1979; career min., 1981; Dept. State fgn. affairs sr. fellow, rsch. prof. diplomacy Georgetown U., Washington, 1981-83; spl. asst. Office Analysis Soviet Union and Eastern Europe Dept. State, Washington, 1983-84; internat. rels. cons., 1984-87, 94—; dir. Patricia Roberts Harris pub. affairs program Howard U., 1987-90; acting dir. Howard U. Press, 1988-90, dir., 1990-94. Mem. adv. coun. Joint Ctr. for Polit. and Econ. Studies. Decorated grand officer Senegalese Nat. Order of Lion, 1977; recipient Meritorious Svc. award USIA, 1955, Superior Svc. award, 1960; Hampton Inst. Alumni award, 1961, Meritorious Svc. award Pres. of U.S., 1984, Chancellor's medal Syracuse U., 1984, Meritorious Achievement award Fla. A&M U., 1985, Disting. Achievement award Dillard U., 1987. Mem. Soc. Prodigal Sons State of N.C., Acad. Jazz Paris (hon.), Assn. Black Am. Ambassadors, Assn. Diplomatic Study and Tng. (bd. dirs.), Am. Acad. Diplomacy (former trustee Phelps Stokes Fund, exec. com. Atlantic Coun.), Fed. City Club, Alpha Phi Alpha, Sigma Delta Chi, Alpha Kappa Mu, Sigma Pi Phi. Home: Apt 1406 320 Twenty-Third St S Arlington VA 22202

AGHABEGIAN, DIANA E. BORTNOWSKY, English language educator, publisher; b. Santa Monica, Calif., Apr. 25, 1963; d. Michael and Lillian Kristine (Panka) Bortnowsky; m. Armond Aghabegian, Mar. 7, 1986; children: Alex Michael, Nicole Eugenia. BA in English Lit., UCLA, 1984; MA in English Lit., Calif. State U., Carson, 1988. Cert. lifetime tchg. credential, Calif. Instr. English, West Los Angeles Coll., Culver City, Calif., 1989-93, El Camino Coll., Torrance, 1990-91, Santa Monica Coll., 1990—. Pub. Blue Rabbit Press, West Hills, Calif., 1997—. Editor Full Moon lit. mag., 1997-2000; contbr. poetry to lit. mags. Mem. Santa Monica Coll. Concert Chorale. Mem. MLA, L.A. Libr. Assn., UCLA Alumni Assn. Democrat. Roman Catholic. Avocations: choral singing, poetry, bicycling. Office: Santa Monica Coll 1900 Pico Blvd Santa Monica CA 90405-1628 E-mail: aghabegian_diana@smc.edu.

AGHAJANIAN, GEORGE KEVORK, medical educator; b. Beirut, Apr. 14, 1932; (parents Am. citizens); s. Ghevont M. and Araxi (Movsessian) A.; m. Anne E. Hammond, Jan. 10, 1959; children: Michael, Andrew, Carol, Laura. AB, Cornell U., 1954; MD, Yale U., 1958. Asst. prof. psychiatry Sch. of Medicine Yale U., New Haven, 1965-68, assoc. prof. psychiatry Sch. of Medicine, 1968-70, assoc. prof. psychiatry and pharmacology Sch. of Medicine, 1970-74, prof. psychiatry and pharmacology Sch. of Medicine, 1974—, founds. fund prof. Sch. of Medicine, 1985. Contbr. more than 300 articles to profl. jours. Capt. U.S. Army, 1963—65. Recipient Hoffheimer prize Am. Psychiat. Assn., 1981, Scheele medal Swedish Acad. Pharmacy, 1981, Merit award NIH, 1990-2000, Hillarp award Internat. Amine Group, 1996, Lieber prize NARSAD, 1998. Fellow Am. Coll. Neuropsychopharmacology (Efron award 1975); mem. Soc. for Pharmacology and Exptl. Therapeutics, Soc. for Neurosci., Internat. Brain Rsch. Orgn., Inst. of Medicine, Inst. of Medicine of NAS. Achievements include research in electrophysiological and pharmacological properties of brain serotonergic, noradrenergic, and dopaminergic neurons. Office: 34 Park St New Haven CT 06519-1109 E-mail: george.aghajanian@yale.edu.

AGHAYERE, ABIEYUWA (ABI AGHAYERE), civil engineer, educator, structural engineer; b. Nigeria; m. Josie Aghayere, Dec. 28, 1985; children: Osa, I.T., O.D., Eghosa. BS, U. Lagos, 1981; MS, MIT, 1983; PhD, U. Alberta, 1988. Lic. profl. engr., Ont., 1992. Project engr. Halsall Associates Ltd, Toronto, Canada, 1988—96; asst. prof. Rochester Inst. Tech., NY, 1996—2002, assoc. prof., 2002—, prof., 2005—. Recipient Eisenhart Outstanding Tchg. award, Rochester Inst. Tech., 2004-2005. Mem.: Profl. Engineers Ont., Am. Inst. Steel Constrn., Am. Concrete Inst. Office: Rochester Inst Tech 78 Lomb Memorial Dr Rochester NY 14623 Office Phone: 585-475-2183.

AGHDASHLOO, SHOHREH, actress; b. Tehran, Iran, May 11, 1952; m. Houshang Touzie, 1985; 1 child, Tara; m. Aydin Aghdashloo, 1972 (div. 1980). BA in Internat. Rels., 1984. Actor: (films) Shatranje bad, 1976, Gozaresh (The Report), 1977, Sootah Delaan, 1978, Guests of Hotel Astoria, 1989, Twenty Bucks, 1993, Maryam, 2000, Surviving Paradise, 2000, America So Beautiful, 2001, House of Sand and Fog, 2003 (best supporting actress award L.A. Film Critics Assn., 2003, best supporting actress award N.Y. Film Critics Cir., 2003, Ind. Spirit award for best supporting female, 2004, Acad. award nomination for best supporting actress, 2004), The Exorcism of Emily Rose, 2005, (guest appearances): (TV series) Martin, 1993, "24", 2005.*

AGIN, HERBERT, real estate company executive; Student, Hunter Coll., Bklyn. Law Sch. Indsl. specialist Sutton & Towne, 1972, dir. indsl. properties, v.p., mgr. regional office; resident mgr., v.p. Coldwell Banker, 1979; prin., mng. ptnr. Sutton & Edwards, 1982, pres., CEO, 1990; chmn. TCN Worldwide. Office: Sutton & Edwards 981 Marcus Ave New Hyde Park NY 11042-3200

AGISIM, PHILIP, advertising and marketing company executive; b. Newark, Jan. 12, 1919; s. Isidore and Jennie (Socket) A.; m. Blanche Tedlow, June 14, 1942; children: Leslie Wayne, Elliot Steven. BS, Rutgers U., 1941; MBA, N.Y. U., 1949. Asst. market research dir. Crowell-Collier Pub. Co., N.Y.C., 1945-49; asso. market research dir. Cowles Pub. Co., N.Y.C., 1949-54; research and planning dir. J.B. Williams Co., N.Y.C., 1954-59, v.p., advt. dir., 1970-71; research dir. Parkson Advt. Agy., N.Y.C., 1959-63, v.p., 1963-69, exec. v.p., 1971-72, vice chmn., 1972-77, pres., 1978—, chief exec. officer, 1980-84, also bd. dirs. Vice chmn. Ohlmeyer Advt., 1984; pres. Product Opportunities Unltd., Inc., 1985-92; ptnr. Ron Meyer and Assocs.; bd. dirs. Trevor, Cole, Reid & Monroe Inc., TCRM Commercial Corp., The Harlem Times Corp., REsidential Fin. Svcs. Inc. Contbr. articles in field to profl. jours. Mem. Nat. Acad. TV Arts and Scis., Am. Mktg. Assn., Friars Club. Jewish. Home: 650 Park Ave New York NY 10021-6115 Office: Trevor Cole Reid & Monroe 515 Madison Ave New York NY 10022-5403 Office Phone: 212-371-3933.

AGLER, RICHARD DEAN, rabbi; b. NYC, May 11, 1952; s. Eugene and Sylvia (Spieler) A.; m. Mindy Steinberg, June 19, 1976; children: Jesse Allen, Talia Faith, Sarah Suzan. BA in Polit. Sci., NYU, 1973; MA in Hebrew Lit., Hebrew Union Coll.-Jewish Inst. Religion, 1976; DDiv honoris causa, Hebrew U., 2003. Ordained rabbi, 1978. Rabbi Stephen Wise Free Synagogue, N.Y.C., 1978-80, Temple Beth Shalom, Vero Beach, Fla., 1980-82, Temple Beth El, Boca Raton, Fla., 1982-84; founding rabbi Congregation Bnai Israel, Boca Raton, 1984—. Bd. dirs. Anti Defamation League, Palm Beach County. V.p. Handgun Control of Palm Beach County, Fla., 1983-93; co-founder Boca Raton Black-Jewish Fellowship, 1984—; founder Ctr. for Justice, Boca Raton, 1989—; co-founder Black-Jewish Coalition Quality Pub. Edn. Named Outstanding Young Man Am., 1989. Mem. Ctr. Conf. Am. Rabbis, South Palm Beach County Rabbinical Assn. (pres. 1991-93), S.E. Assn. Ctrl. Conf. Am. Rabbis (spirituality chair 1984-2002), Assn. Reform Zionists of Am. (life, bd. dirs.), Palm Beach County Bd. Rabbis. Jewish. Avocations: literature, athletics, sailing. Office: Congregation Bnai Israel 2200 Yamato Rd Boca Raton FL 33431-4325

AGNE, PHYLLIS G., artist, educator; b. N.Y.C., May 20, 1932; d. John J. and Anna (Rosen) Gross; 1 child, Wendy Agne Reed. Student, Art Students League, 1950-51; BA, Hunter Coll., CUNY, 1970; MFA, Columbia U., 1972. Lectr. Wagner Coll., Staten Island, N.Y., 1971-72, Fairleigh Dickinson U., Madison, N.J., 1972; assoc. prof. U. Conn., Waterbury, 1973-92. Vis. faculty fellow Yale U./Carnegie Mellon Inst. Solo exhbns. include Fulton Gallery, NYC, 1960, 1963, 1965, 1973, Mattatuck Mus., Waterbury, Conn., 1979, The Waterbury Club, 1986, Eierweiss Gallery, New Haven, Conn., 1992, Promenade Gallery, The Bushnell, Hartford, Conn., 1998, William Benton Mus., Storrs, 1996, others; group exhbns. include Conn. Women Artists Juried Exhbns., New Haven, Norwich and Hartford, 1976-86, Discovery Mus., Bridgeport, Conn., 1987, 89, 93, Mattatuck Mus., 1993, Slater Meml. Mus., Norwich, 1986, 88, 89, New Haven Paint & Clay Club, Inc., 1980—, CUNY Grad. Ctr., N.Y.C., 1978, L'Atelier Gallery, Essex, Conn., 1985, Nat. Drawing Assn., N.Y.C., 1987, 1988, 1989, 1993, 1994, Galerie Triangle, Washington, 1988, Erector Sq. Gallery, New Haven, 1990, Aetna Gallery, Hartford, 1991, Inter Art Galerie Reich, Cologne, Germany, 1999-03, many others; represented in permanent collections William Benton Mus. Art Storrs, Conn., Slater Meml. Mus., Norwich, Conn., Mattatuck Mus., Waterbury, Conn., The Amity Art Found., Am. Brands, Anco Wood Specialties, Inc., The Delong Corp., The New Haven Paint and Clay Club, Tarlow, Levy, Harding and Droney, A.M. Sachs, Fulton Gallery, Mimi Kazon, Irena Urdang De Tour, and numerous pvt. collections. William Graf scholar Women's Trade Union League; U. Conn. Rsch. Found. grantee. Mem. Am. Artists Profl. League, Nat. Drawing Assn., Conn. Women Artists, New Haven Paint and Clay Club (v.p., archivist). Avocations: music, gardening.

AGNEW, ALFONSO FERNANDEZ, mathematics professor; b. Arcadia, Calif., Jan. 24, 1969; s. Richard Francis and Lia Paula Agnew; m. Victoria Elizabeth Nichols, July 26, 2004; 1 child, Alfonso Fernandez Jr. BA in Math., BS in Physics, Calif. State U., Fullerton, 1994; MS in Math., PhD in Math., Oreg. State U. Vis. asst. prof. So. Meth. U., Dallas, 1999—2001; asst. prof. math. Calif. State U., Fullerton, 2001—. Office: Ca State Univ Fullerton 880 N State College Blvd Fullerton CA 92834 Office Phone: 714-278-5568.

AGNEW, CHRISTOPHER MACK, minister, historian; b. Santa Barbara, Calif., Aug. 7, 1944; s. Jack and Agnes Emma (Mack) A.; m. Suzanne Marie Souder, June 1, 1974 (div.); m. Elizabeth Lewis Lyddane, Apr. 25, 1998. AB, Bucknell U., Lewisburg, Pa., 1967; MA, U. Del., Newark, 1975, PhD, 1980; STM, Gen. Theol. Sem., N.Y.C., 1991. Ordained to ministry as deacon Episcopal Ch., 1991, as priest Episcopal Ch., 1992. Reference libr. Dover (Del.) Pub. Libr., 1969—72; tchg. asst. dept. history U. Del., Newark, 1972—76; manuscript libr. Hist. Soc. Del., 1979—81; asst. prof. history and Can. studies SUNY, Plattsburgh, 1981—84; registrar Diocese of Del., Wilmington, 1985—89; assoc. ecumenical officer Episcopal Ch., N.Y.C., 1989—94; deacon St. Thomas' Ch., Newark, 1991—92; priest-in-charge St. Marks, Teaneck, NJ, 1992; priest assoc. All Angels Ch., N.Y.C., 1992—95; interim rector St. Martin's, Maywood, NJ, 1994—95, All Hallows, Wyncote, Pa., 1995, St. Michael's, Litchfield, Conn., 1995—97, Ch. of the Ascension, Norfolk, Va., 1997, St. Peter's in Great Valley, Paoli, Pa., 1997—99; priest in charge St. Paul's, Owens, Va., 2000—02; interim rector Vauter's Ch., Loretto, Va., 2002—, St. Paul's, Nomini Grove, Va., 2002—. Exec. bd. Episcopal Diocesan Ecumenical Officers, 1989—94; mem. Episcopal-Reformed Episcopal Dialogue, 1989—94, NCC Christian-Muslim Rels. Commn., 1989—91, NCC Christian-Jewish Rels. Commn., 1989—99, NCC Interfaith Working Group, 1990—95; mem. planning com. Nat. Workshop on Christian Unity, 1990—94; mem. Faith and Order Commn., 1991—95; chmn. NCC Christian-Jewish Rels. Commn., 1991—99; mem. Parliament of the Worlds Religions, 1993, Interfaith Rels. Commn., 1996—99, Episcopal-Reformed Episcopal-Anglican Province of Am. Dialogue, 2003—, Episc. Russian Orthodox Joint Coordinating Com., 1990—91. Editor: The Ecumenical Bull., 1989-94, Anglican Statements on the Church: Selected Documentary Sources for a Study of Anglican Ecclesiology, 1994; author: God With Us, 1986; contbr. articles to profl. jours. Mem. Ecumenical Interfaith Commn. Diocese of Va., 2000—, co-chmn., 2004—; mem. faith and order workgroup Va. Coun. Chs., 2002—, chmn. workgroup, 2004—, chair, 2004—, mem. coord. cabinet, 2003—. Mem. Nat. Episc. Historians Assn. (mem. exec. bd. 1995-99), Hist. Soc. Episc. Ch. (bd. dirs. 2005—), Order Crown Charlemagne U.S. (asst. chaplain 1997-2005, chaplain 2005—), Assn. for Preservation Va. Antiquities (trustee No. Neck br. 2004-), Orgn. Am. Historians, Am. Hist. Assn., N.Am. Acad. Ecumenists (mem. exec. bd. 2004—), Can. Hist. Assn., Assn. Can. Studies in U.S., Interim Ministry Network, Mil. Order of Loyal Legion of U.S. (chaplain-in-chief 1995—), Mil. Order of Stars and Bars, Soc. Colonial Wars, N.Am. Guild of Change Ringers. Home: 12433 Richards Ride King George VA 22485

AGNEW, HAROLD MELVIN, physicist; b. Denver, Mar. 28, 1921; s. Sam E. and Augusta Agnew; m. Beverly Jackson, May 2, 1942; children: Nancy E. Agnew Owens, John S. AB, U. Denver, 1942; MS, U. Chgo., 1948, PhD, 1949; PhD (hon.), Coll. Santa Fe, 1980, U. Denver, 1992. With Los Alamos Sci. Lab., 1943-46, alt. div. leader, 1949-61, leader weapons div., 1964-70, dir., 1970-79; pres. Gen. Atomics, San Diego, 1979-85, also bd. dirs., 1985—. Sci. adviser Supreme Allied Comdr. in Europe, Paris, 1961-64; chmn. Army Sci. Adv. Panel, 1965-70, San Diego County adv. bd.; mem. aircraft panel President's Sci. Adv. Com., 1965-73; mem. USAF Sci. Adv. Bd., 1957-69, Def. Sci. Bd., 1965-70, Gov. of N.Mex.'s Radiation Adv. Coun., 1959-61; sec. N.Mex. Health and Social Svcs., 1971-73; chmn. gen. adv. com. ACDA, 1974-77, mem., 1977-81; mem. aerospace safety adv. panel NASA, 1964-70; mem. U.S. Army Sci. Bd., 1978-80, White House Sci. Coun., 1982-89; adj. prof. U. Calif., San Diego, 1988—. Mem. council engring. NRC, 1978-82; mem. Los Alamos Bd. Ednl. Trustees, 1950-55, pres., 1955; trustee San Diego Mus. Art, 1983-87; mem. Woodrow Wilson Nat. Fellowship Found., 1973-80; N.Mex. State senator, 1955-61; sec. N.Mex. Legis. Council, 1957-61; chmn. N.Mex. Senate Corp. Commn., 1957-61; mem. Fed. Emergency Agy., 1982-88; bd. dirs. Fedn. Rocky Mountain States, Inc., 1975-77, Charles Lee Powell Found., 1993—; chmn. U. Calif. San Diego Chancellors Assocs., 1998-2000. Recipient Ernest Orlando Lawrence award AEC, 1966; Enrico Fermi award Dept. Energy, 1978; Pres's. medal, U. of Calif., 2003. Fellow Am. Phys. Soc., AAAS; mem. Nat. Acad. Scis., Nat. Acad. Engring., Council on Fgn. Relations, Phi Beta Kappa, Sigma Xi, Omicron Delta Kappa. Home: 322 Punta Baja Dr Solana Beach CA 92075-1720

AGNEW, JOHN A., education educator; b. Millom, Cumbria, England, Aug. 29, 1949; arrived in U.S., 1971; s. Herbert and Anne (MacPherson) A.; children: Katherine, Christine. BA, Exeter U., Eng., 1970; Cert. Edn., Liverpool U., Eng., 1971; MA, Ohio State U., 1973, PhD, 1976. From asst. prof. to prof. Syracuse (NY) U., 1975—96; prof. UCLA, 1996—, chair dept. geography, 1998—2002. Dir. social sci. program Syracuse U., 1981—88; vis. prof. U. Chgo., 1992, U. Cambridge, England, 1992, U. Iowa, 1995, Univ. Coll., London, 1996, U. Durham, 2003, Queen's U., Belfast, 2003, Emmanuel Coll., Cambridge, 2004; Hettner lectr. U. Heidelberg, 2000; Guggenheim fellow UCLA, 2003—04. Author: Place and Politics, 1987, The U.S. in World Economy, 1987, Rome, 1995, Geopolitics: Re-Visioning World Politics, 1998, 2d edit., 2003, Place and Politics in Modern Italy, 2002, Making Political Geography, 2002, Hegemony, The New Shape of Colonial Power2005; co-author: Mastering Space, 1995, The Geography of World Economy, 1989, 4th edit., 2003; editor: The City in Cultural Context, 1984, The Power of Place, 1989, American Space/American Place, 2002, Companion to Political Geography, 2002, The Marshall Plan Today: Model and Metaphor, 2004; co-editor Geopolitics, 1999—; mem. editl. bd. Polit. Geography, Nat. Identities, Global Networks, Scottish Geog. Jour., European Jour. Internat. Rels., Progress in Human Geography. Fellow: AAAS, Royal Geog. Soc.; mem.: N.Y Acad. Sci., Am. Polit. Sci. Assn., Coun. European Studies, Am. Assn. Geographers. Office: UCLA 1255 Bunche Hl Los Angeles CA 90095-1524 Office Phone: 310-825-1713. Business E-Mail: jagnew@geog.ucla.edu.

AGNEW, KATHLEEN DIANNE CROSBIE, language educator; b. Tulsa, Okla., June 16, 1946; d. James Conn and Madeline Madge (Baldwin) Crosbie; m. James Alford Tulley, Jan. 28, 1968 (div. 1991); children: Jennifer R., Scott A.; m. David Dutilh Agnew, June 21, 1997. BA, Butler U., 1968. Lic. secondary tchr. Tchr. East Ladue Jr. HS, 1968—74, Sweet Grass County HS, Big Timber, Mont., 1975—2005. Mem. Sweet Grass County Task Force At Risk Children, 1985-90; organist, vestry St. Mark's Episcopal Ch., Big Timber, 1991-98; mem. Mont. task force on tchr. edn. std., 1999; cabinet mem. Carnegie Libr. Capital Campaign, 2003-2005. Recipient Milken Educator award Milken Family Found., 1997; Excellence in Tchg. English and Am. Studies award Am. Coun. Tchr. Russian and Am. Coun. Collaboration in Edn. and Lang. Study, 1998. Mem. NEA, Nat. Coun. Tchr. English, Mont. Assn. Tchr. English and Lang. Arts, Mont. Edn. Assn. (pres., sec), Sponsors Sch. Publ. (v.p., pres.); participant in NEH seminar "Shakespeare: Enacting the Text", 2003. Avocations: piano, writing, photography, painting. Office: Sweet Grass County HS PO Box 886 Big Timber MT 59011-0886 Personal E-mail: kagnew5514@hotmail.com.

AGNEW, PETER TOMLIN, employee benefit consultant; b. Orange, NJ, Nov. 20, 1948; s. William Harold and Janet Elisabeth (Gittinger) A.; m. Linda W. Seyffarth; children: Jonathan, Stephen, Douglas, Karen; 1 step child, Kristin Seyffarth. BA in English cum laude, Amherst Coll., 1971; MBA in Fin., NYU, 1976. CLU. Asst. investment officer Mutual Benefit Life, Newark, 1971—78; exec. v.p., bd. dir., prin. Post & Kurtz, Inc., N.Y.C., 1978—85, exec. v.p., prin., 1993—, also bd. dirs., pres., treas., 1998—; sr. regional dir. Minet, N.Y.C., 1985—92. Pres. P. Tomlin Agnew Assocs., Glen Ridge, N.J., 1982—. Contbr. articles to profl. jours. Capt. United Way, Newark, 1978; assoc. class agt. Amherst Coll. Alumni Fund, 1980—, class agt., 1993—; exec. bd. Rep. Congl. Leadership Coun., 1988-92; vice chair Civic Conf. Com. of Glen Ridge, 1998-99, Glen Ridge Rep. Club; asst. treas. Glen Ridge Congl. Ch.; parents coun. Hamilton Coll., 1997-2001, Skidmore Coll., 2002-03; mem. Glen Ridge Bd. Edn., 2005—. Fellow Life Mgmt. Inst.; mem. Soc. CLU (con. chmn. N.Y. chpt. 1984), Assn. Advanced Life Underwriters, Nat. Assn. Securities Dealers, Yale Ins. Group (chmn. 1988-90), Glen Ridge Country Club, Downtown Assn. Avocations: swimming, bridge, skiing, music, golf. Home: 75 Glen Ridge Pky Glen Ridge NJ 07028-1821 Office Phone: 212-766-8800. Personal E-mail: pagnew236@aol.com.

AGNEW, ROBERT, retired psychologist, poet; b. Flat River, Mo., Mar. 12, 1944; s. Thomas Henry Agnew and Iva Matilda Johnson-Agnew, Carrol Wayne and Nadine Evelyn Agnew Taylor; m. Deloris Kay Pruett, Aug. 29, 1973. BGS, SE Mo. State U., 1972, MA in Psychology, 1973; PhD of Psychology, U. of So. Miss., 1977. Cert. Psychologist Bd. of Healing Arts/Mo., 1984. Dir. children svcs. NE Nebr. Comprehensive Mental Health Ctr., Norfolk, 1978—83; clin. dir. SE Ozark Mental Health Ctr., Poplar Bluff, Mo., 1983—86; chief of psychology John J. Pershing V.A. Hosp., Poplar Bluff, Mo., 1986—95. Adj. prof. Three Rivers C.C., Poplar Bluff, Mo., 1984—85; cons. Mingo Job Corp, Puxico, Mo., 1985—90, Oakdale Residential Care, Poplar Bluff, 1990—95, Poplar Bluff Police Dept., Poplar Bluff, 1992—94. Author (poet): (poetry) Dance of the Sun, You and I, The Road that Never Ends, The Best Poems and Poets of 2003, The Best Poems and Poets of 2004. E-5 USN, 1966—70.

AGNEW, SAMUEL GERARD, orthopaedic traumatologist; b. New Orleans, Oct. 22, 1958; s. Thomas A. and Elizabeth (De la Houssaye) A.; m. Denise Kachler, May 3, 1986; children: Taylor Frances, Caroline Elizabeth. BS, U. S.C., 1980; MD, Tulane U., 1984. Diplomate Am. Bd. Orthopaedic Surgeons. Chief trauma orthopedic dept. orthopedics, asst. prof. U. Miss. Med. Ctr., Jackson, 1990-91; chief orthopedic trauma, asst. prof. U. Ark. for Med. Scis., Little Rock, 1991-95; chief orthopedic trauma, assoc. prof. U. Fla., Jacksonville, 1995—. Vis. lectr. Hennepin County Med., 1994, Pa. Orthopaedic, 1994. Author: Orthopedic Clinics of North America, 1992. Fellow Am. Acad. Orthopaedics; mem. ACS, Orthopedic Trauma Assn., Am. Assn. for Surgery of Trauma, Assn. for Advancement of Automotive Medicine. Office: PEE DEE Orthopaedic Assn PO Drawer 1771 Florence SC 29503

AGNO, JOHN G., management consultant; b. Gloversville, NY, Dec. 8, 1940; s. John G. and Margretta (Luff) Anagnostopulos; m. Karen Clark Mikus, June 29, 1985 (div. Nov. 2002). BBA, U. Fla., 1962. Mktg. specialist Eastman Kodak Co., Rochester, N.Y., 1965-73; gen. mgr. sanitation appliance divsn. Thetford Corp., Ann Arbor, Mich., 1973-80; v.p. mktg. and adminstrn. Stirling Power Systems Corp. divsn. McDonnell Douglas Corp., Ann Arbor, 1980-87; pres. Signature, Inc., Ann Arbor, 1983—. Deacon First Presbyn. Ch., Ann Arbor; bd. dirs. Washtenaw United Way, 1991-95; bd. dirs. YMCA, 1995-2000. 1st lt. U.S. Army, 1963-65. Mem. Recreational Vehicle Industry Assn. (chmn. mktg. commn. 1978-82, bd. dirs. 1981-83), Turnaround Mgmt. Assn., Ann Arbor Country Club, Rotary. Republican. Home: 4701 Midway Dr Ann Arbor MI 48103-9427 Office: Signature Inc PO Box 2086 Ann Arbor MI 48106-2086 Office Phone: 734-426-2000. Business E-Mail: johnagno@signatureseries.com, info@coachthee.com.

AGNONE, ANTHONY, lawyer; BS, Mt. St. Mary's Coll., 1975; JD, U. Balt., 1978. Asst. to dean U. Balt. Law Sch., 1978—83; lead negotiator Ea. Athletic Svcs., Hunt Valley, Md. Adj. prof. sports law U. Balt. Sch. Law; bd. dirs. Susquehanna Bank. Mem.: Sports Lawyers Assn. (bd. dirs.), Fed. Bar, W.Va. State Bar. Office: Eastern Athletic Svcs 11350 McCormick Rd Ste 800 Plazal Hunt Valley MD 21031 Office Phone: 410-229-0080. Business E-Mail: tagnone@easfootball.com.

AGONAFER, MULUGETA GABRIEL, political science professor; b. Shoa/Addis Abeba, Ethiopia; arrived in U.S., 1973; s. Agonafer Gashi and Wudnesh Kebede; m. Addis Alem Bekele, May 18, 1991; 1 child, Kokeb Mulugeta BSc in Electronics Engring. Tech., Purdue U., 1978; BA in Polit. Sci., Ind. U., 1979; MA in Polit. Sci., Western Wash. U., 1981, PhD (hon.) in Internat. Rels., Comparative Politics and African-Polit. Economy, 1990. Tchr. April 27th H.S., Jimma, Ethiopia, 1971-73; instr. Pa. State U., McKeesport, 1987-91, Strayer Coll., Woodbridge, Va., 1991-92; prof. Sprinfield (Mass.) Coll., 1992—. Reader Ednl. Testing Svcs., Princeton, N.J., 1995—. Mem. editl. bd.: Jour. Pub. Policy, 1999—; contbr. articles to profl. jours. Bd. dirs. Ethiopian Rsch. Coun., Washington, 1992-97; dir. Africa project YMCA, Springfield, 1998-2000 Mem. Am. Polit. Sci. Assn., African-Am. Devel. Edn., Rsch. and Tng. Inst. (founder, pres. 1994—). Democrat. Ethiopian Orthodox. Avocation: soccer. Home: 194 North St Belchertown MA 01007 Office: Springfield Coll 263 Alden St Springfield MA 01109 Office Fax: 413-748-3236. Personal E-mail: aadert@hotmail.com. Business E-Mail: mulugeta_agonafer@spfldcol.edu.

AGOSTA, VITO, mechanical and aerospace engineering educator; b. N.Y.C., July 26, 1923; s. John and Elizabeth (Alvares) A.; m. Mary Frago, Aug. 9, 1952; children: John, Diana, Charles. MS in Engring., U. Mich., 1949; PhD, Columbia, 1959. Registered profl. engr., N.Y. Thermodynamicist DeLaval Steam Turbine Co., 1946—47; mem. faculty Poly. Inst. N.Y., Bklyn., 1950—, prof. mech. and aerospace engring., 1962—, prof. emeritus, 1986—; prof. Queen Mary Coll., London U., NY, 1966—67, London U., 1966—67; pres. Propulsion Scis., Inc., Huntington, NY, 1966—75, Fuels Systems Design Corp., Huntington, NY, 1975—94, Propulsion Scis. Co., Huntington, 1989—. Cons. in field in fluid dynamics in transportation sys., energy sys., boilers, engines & alternate fuels. Served with AUS, 1943—45. Recipient Alexander Hamilton award, Grand Army Rep., 1943; grantee, Fulbright Found., 1966—67. Mem. ASME, Sigma Xi, Tau Beta Pi. Democrat. Roman Catholic. Achievements include invention of non-miscible liquid emulsifier; modulating oil burner; design of and mfr. of modulating fuel emulsifier systems for engines and boilers; research in combustion instability in rocket motors; supersonic combustion of two phase systems; air and thermal pollution; heat transfer analysis in reacting fuels; ventilation in Boston and New York City automobile tunnels; air movement studies in train stations; use of ammonia as a hydrogen carrier and an alternative fuel additive in engines and burners; patents for the process of hydrodynamic emulsification; hydrodynamic proportionate mixing of liquids; chemical mixing and metering apparatus. Avocation: photography. Home: 42 Cherry Ln Huntington NY 11743-2945 Office: Propulsion Scis Co 300 Broadway Huntington Station NY 11746-1405 Office Phone: 631-219-0708. Personal E-mail: vagosta@optonline.net.

AGOSTA, WILLIAM CARLETON, chemist, educator; b. Dallas, Jan. 1, 1933; s. Angelo N. and Helen Carleton (Jones) A.; m. Karin Solveig Engstrom, July 2, 1958; children— Jennifer Ellen, Christopher William. BA, Rice Inst., 1954; AM, Harvard U., 1955, PhD, 1957. NRC postdoctoral fellow Oxford (Eng.) U., 1957-58; Pfizer postdoctoral fellow U. Ill., Urbana, 1958-59; asst. prof. U. Calif., Berkeley, 1959-61; liaison scientist U.S. Navy, Frankfurt, Germany, 1961-63; asst. prof. chemistry Rockefeller U., N.Y.C., 1963-67, assoc. prof., 1967-74, prof., 1974-98, prof. emeritus, 1998—. Vis. prof. U. Innsbruck, 1995, Princeton U., 1996; cons. in field; officer Chiron Press, Inc., 1977-85; mem. NRC Associateship Programs Chem. Scis. Panel, 1997—2005; mem. Noxious Weed Control Bd., San Juan County, Wash., 2002—. Author: Chemical Communication, 1992, Bombardier Beetles and Fever Trees, 1996, Thieves, Deceivers, and Killers, 2001; mem. editl. adv. bd. Jour. Organic Chemistry, 1984-88; contbr. articles to profl. jours. Bd. dirs. San Juan Cmty. Home Trust, 2003—, pres., 2004—. John Angus Erskine fellow U. Canterbury (N.Z.), 1981 Fellow AAAS; mem. Chem. Soc. London, Am. Chem. Soc., Interam. Photochem. Soc., European Photochemistry Assn., Am. Soc. Photobiology, Internat. Soc. for Chem. Ecology, Phi Beta Kappa, Sigma Xi. Home: PO Box 1547 Friday Harbor WA 98250-1547 Office: U Wash Friday Harbor Labs Friday Harbor WA 98250 Office Phone: 360-378-0816. E-mail: agosta@u.washington.edu.

AGOSTI, DEBORAH ANN, retired senior justice; BA cum laude, U. Toledo, 1973, JD, 1976. Bar: Nev., U.S. Supreme Ct. Dep. pub. defender Montgomery County, Ohio, 1977; sr. staff atty. Sr. Citizens Legal Assistance Program, Washoe County, 1977—79; dep. dist. atty., 1979—82; justice of the peace Reno Twp., Nev., 1982—85; dist. judge 2d Jud. Dist., Reno, 1985—99; justice Nev. Supreme Court, Carson City, 1999—2004, sr. justice, 2005—. Trustee Nat. Jud. Coll., 2001—, Pretrial Svcs. Resource Ctr., 1999—; co-chmn. jury improvement commn. Supreme Ct. of Nev., 2001—; mem., dean's adv. bd. U. Toledo Coll. Law. Chmn. Task Force to Revitalize Interest in Attendance at Washoe County Bar Meetings, 2001—. Named Outstanding Young Woman for State of Nev., 1983, One of Am.'s 100 Young Women of Promise, Good Housekeeping mag., 1985, Reno's Outstanding Woman for 1986, One of Three Outstanding Young Nevadans, Reno Jaycees, 1986, Outstanding Women Lawyer, No. Nev. Women Lawyer's Assn., 1993, Judge of Yr., Nev. Dist. Judge's Assn., 1989, Woman of Achievement, Nev. Women's Fund, 1998, Woman of Distinction, Nat. Assn. Women Bus. Owners-So. Nev. Chpt., 2004, One of Nev.'s First One Hundred Women Attys., Woman of Distinction, Soroptimists of Reno, 2005. Master: Bruce Thompson Inn of Ct.; mem.: No. Nev. Women Lawyers Assn., Nat. Assn. Women Judges, Soroptimists Internat. of Truckee Meadows (life mem., Woman of Distinction 2001). Office: Supreme Ct Nev 201 S Carson St Carson City NV 89701-4702 Office Phone: 775-684-1600. E-mail: dagosti@nvcourts.state.nv.us.

AGOSTINELLI, ROBERT FRANCESCO, investment banker; b. Rochester, NY, May 21, 1953; BA, St. John Fisher Coll., 1976; MBA, Columbia U., 1981. Assoc. Jacob Rothschild, London, 1981-82; v.p. investment banking Goldman, Sachs & Co., NYC and London, 1982-87; sr. mng. dir. investment banking Lazard Frères & Co. LLC, NYC, 1987-96; bd. dirs. Rhone Group/Rhone Capital, NYC, 1996—. Supervisory bd. mem. Lazard GmbH; non-exec. mem. adv. com. Frontera S.A.; mem. Coun. on Fgn. Rels.; Vorstand Clariden Bank; dir. Lazard Spa; dir., former vice-chmn. Coun. US and Italy; European Inst., Am.-Italian Cancer Found.; dir., mem. exec. com. Almatis B.V.; non-resident fellow The Pierpont Morgan Libr.; dir. in field; advisor in field. Bd. dirs. Soc. des Amis du Museè d'Art Moderne; supporting fellow The Frick Collection; mem. NY-Rome Sister City Adv. Com. Office: Rhone Group 630 5th Ave Ste 2710 New York NY 10111-0100

AGRANOFF, BERNARD WILLIAM, biochemist, educator; b. Detroit, June 26, 1926; s. William and Phyllis (Pelavin) A.; m. Raquel Betty Schwartz, Sept. 1, 1957; children: William, Adam. MD, Wayne State U., 1950; BS, U. Mich., 1954. Intern Robert Packer Hosp., Sayre, Pa., 1950-51; commd. surgeon USPHS, 1954-60; biochemist Nat. Inst. Neurol. Diseases and Blindness, NIH, Bethesda, Md., 1954-60; mem. faculty U. Mich., Ann Arbor, 1960—, prof. biochemistry, 1965—; R.W. Gerard prof. of neurosci. in psychiatry, 1991. Rsch. biochemist Mental Health Rsch. Inst., 1960—, assoc. dir., 1977-83, dir. 1983-95, dir. neurosci. lab., 1983-2000; vis. scientist Max Planck Inst. Zellchemie, Munich, 1957-58, Nat. Inst. Med. Rsch., Mill Hill, Eng., 1974-75; Henry Russel lectr. U. Mich., 1987; cons. pharm. industry, govt. Contbr. articles to profl. jours. Fogarty scholar-in-residence NIH, Bethesda, Md., 1989-95; named Mich. Scientist of Yr. Mus. of Sci., Lansing, 1992. Fellow AAAS, Am. Acad. Arts and Scis., N.Y. Acad. Sci., Am. Coll. Neuropsychopharmacology; mem. Am. Soc. Biochemistry and Molecular Biology, Am. Chem. Soc., Inst. Medicine of NAS, Internat. Soc. Neurochemistry (treas. 1985-89, chmn. 1989-91), Am. Soc. Neurochemistry (pres. 1973-75). Achievements include research in brain lipids, biochem. basis of learning, memory and regeneration in the nervous system, human brain imaging. Office: U Mich C 560 MSRB II 1150 W Medical Center Dr Ann Arbor MI 48109-0669 E-mail: agranoff@umich.edu.

AGRAST, MARK DAVID, lawyer; b. Cleve., Mar. 31, 1956; s. Harold and Charlotte Agrast; life ptnr. David Michael Hollis. BA summa cum laude, Case Western Res. U., 1978; postgraduate Rhodes Scholar, Oxford Univ., 1978—81; JD, Yale U., 1985. Bar: Ohio 1986, D.C. 1988, U.S. Supreme Ct. Atty. Jones Day Reavis & Pogue, Washington, 1985—91; sr. legis. asst. Hon. Gerry E. Studds, U.S. Ho. of Reps., Washington, 1992—97; counsel and legis. dir. Hon. William D. Delahunt, U.S. Ho. of Reps., Washington, 1997—2003; sr. v.p. for domestic policy Ctr. for Am. Progress, Washington, 2003—. Rhodes scholar, Oxford U., 1978—81. Fellow: Am. Bar Found.; mem.: ABA (chair sect. individual rights and responsibilities 2002—03, bd. of governors, 2004-, exec. bd. ctr. for human rights, 2003-). Office: Ctr Am Progress 805 15th St NW Ste 400 Washington DC 20005 also: Center American Progress 10th Fl 1333 H St NW Washington DC 20005

AGRAWAL, DHARMA PRAKASH, engineering educator; b. Balod, India, Apr. 12, 1945; came to U.S., 1976; s. Saryoo Prasad and Chandra K. Agrawal; m. Purnima Agrawal, June 7, 1971; children: Sonali, Braj. BE, Ravishankar U., Raipur, India, 1966; ME with honors, Roorkee (India) U., 1968; DSc in Tech., Fed. Inst. Tech., Lausanne, Switzerland, 1975. Lectr. M.N.R. Engring. Coll., Allahabad, India, 1968-72, Roorkee U., 1972-73; asst. Fed. Inst. Tech., Lausanne, 1973-75; instr., postdoctoral work So. Meth. U., Dallas, 1976-77; asst. prof., then assoc. prof. Wayne State U., Detroit, 1977-82; assoc. prof. N.C. State U., Raleigh, 1982-84, prof., 1984-98; OBR Disting. prof. U. Cin., 1998—. Gen. co-chair Advanced Computing Conf., 1997—2000; Fulbright sr. specialist, 2002; keynote spkr. Internat. Conf. on Parallel and Distributed Sys., 1997; presenter in field. Co-author: Introduction to Wireless and Mobile Systems, 2003; editor: Advanced Computer Architecture, 1986, Advances in Distributed System Reliability, 1990, Distributed Computing Network Reliability, 1990; editor: Jour. Parallel and Distg. Computing, 1984, Computer mag., 1986-91. Fellow IEEE (chair tech. com. on computer architecture, IEEE Computer Soc. 1991-94, chair McDowell Award and Harry Grode Award coms. 1991-99, chair Eckerdt Mauchley award in computer architecture, program chair internat. conf. on parallel processing 1994, chair disting. visitor program, workshop chair internat. conf. on parallel processing 1995, gen. chair fourth internat. workshop on modeling analysis and simulation of computer and telecom. sys. 1996, 2001, editor jour. 1992-96), AAAS, AIM, Internat. Conf. on Mobile Adhoc Sensor Sys. (gen. chair), Assn. Computing Machinery, World Innovation Found.; mem. Sigma Xi. Office: U Cin ECE&CS PO Box 210030 Cincinnati OH 45221-0030 Office Phone: 513-556-4756. E-mail: dpa@ececs.uc.edu.

AGRAWAL, HARISH CHANDRA, neuroscientist, educator; b. Allahabad, Uttar Pradesh, India; came to U.S., 1964, naturalized, 1982; s. Shambhu and Rajmani Devi A.; m. Daya Kumari Bhushan, Feb. 6, 1960; children— Sanjay, Sanjeev B.Sc., Allahabad U., 1957, M.Sc., 1959, PhD, 1964. Med. research assoc. Thudichum Psychiat. Lab., Galesburg, Ill., 1964-68; lectr. dept. biochemistry Charing Cross Hosp., London, 1968-70; prof. neurology Washington U. Sch. Medicine, St. Louis, 1970—. Mem. neurology study sect. NIH, 1979-82 Author: Handbook of Neurochemistry, 1969, Developmental Neurobiology, 1970, Biochemistry of Developing Brain, 1971, Membranes and Receptors, 1974, Proteins of the Nervous System, 1980, Biochemistry of Brain, 1980, Handbook of Neurochemistry, 1984; contbr. numerous papers on various aspects of myelin proteins and their role in demyelinating disrders. Jr. research fellow Council Sci. and Indsl. Research, New Delhi, 1960-62, sr. research fellow, 1963-64; Research Career Devel. award Nat. Inst. Neurol. and Communicative Disorders, 1974-79 Mem. Internat. Soc. Neurochemistry, Internat. Brain Rsch. Orgn., Am. Soc. Neurochemistry, Am. Soc. Biol. Chemists and Molecular Biologists, Am. Soc. Physiology. Home: 3500 Mystic Pointe Dr #3207 Aventura FL 33180 Office: Washington U Dept Neurology 660 S Euclid Ave Dept Saint Louis MO 63110-1093

AGRAWAL, KRISHNA CHANDRA, pharmacology educator; b. Calcutta, India, Mar. 15, 1937; naturalized; s. Prasadi Lal and Asarfi Devi (Agrawal) A.; m. Mani Agrawal, Dec. 2, 1960; children— Sunil, Lina, Nira BS in Pharmacy, Andhra U., Waltair, India, 1959, MS, 1960; PhD, U. Fla., 1965. Cert. in pharm. chemistry. Research assoc. dept. pharmacology Yale U. Sch. Medicine, New Haven, 1966-69, instr., 1969-70, asst. prof., 1970-76, assoc. prof., 1976; assoc. prof. dept. pharmacology Tulane U. Sch. Medicine, New Orleans, 1976-81, prof., 1981—, interim chmn., 1996-99, regents prof., chmn., 1999—. Cons. mem. Southeastern Cancer Study Group, 1980—85; mem. adv. com. on instnl. grants Am. Cancer Soc., 1980—85; mem. AIDS and Related Rsch. Rev. Group NIH, 1989—94, 1999—2002; mem. oncology merit rev. com. Vets. Adminstrn., 2002—04; exptl. therapeutics NIH,

2002—05. Conbr. articles to profl. jours.; patentee radiosensitizers for hypoxic tumor cells and compositions; novel AZT analogs. Grantee Nat. Cancer Inst., 1976-89, WHO, 1979-82, La. Bd. Regents, 1981-82, Nat. Inst. Allergy and Infectious Diseases, 1987—, Dept. Def., 1994-96, Nat. Heart Lung and Blood Inst., 1997—. Fellow Am. Inst. Chemists; mem. Am. Chem. Soc., Am. Assn. Cancer Rsch., Internat. Soc. Antiviral Rsch., Radiation Rsch. Soc., Am. Soc. Pharmacology and Exptl. Therapeutics, Am. Soc. Hematology, Sigma Xi. Home: 26 Olympic Ct New Orleans LA 70131-8614 Office: Tulane U Sch Medicine Dept Pharmacology New Orleans LA 70112 Office Phone: 504-988-2628. Business E-Mail: agrawal@tulane.edu.

AGRAWAL, PIYUSH C., school system administrator; b. Khairagarh, Agra, India, June 26, 1936; arrived in U.S., 1976; s. Ram C. and Chameli (Kiran) Agrawal; m. Sudha Sita Bansal, May 18, 1963; children: Seema, Sukrit, Akhil. BSc, Agra (India) U., 1955, MSc, 1963; BEd, Delhi U., 1958; MS, SUNY, Albany, 1972, EdS, 1978, EdD, 1979. Tchr., dept. head Delhi Adminstrn., 1958-68; expert UNESCO, Liberia, 1971—76, 1968—70; dir. metric edn. Regional Planning Ctr., Albany, 1977-79; supr. math. Dade County Pub. Sch., Miami, Fla., 1979-94; assoc. supt. Piscataway Bd. Edn., 1992-94, dep. supt., 1994-97, acting supt., 1997-98; chmn. & CEO APS Tech., Inc., 2000. Cons. in field; Fla. state coord. nat. math. competition Am. Jr. HS Math. Exam., 1989—92; rev. panelist Am. 2000 proposals New Am. Schs. Devel. Corp., 1992; tchr. enhancement program NSF, 1992; mem. nat. adv. panel Md. Pub. TV, 1993—95; mem. nat. adv. coun. South Asian affairs, 1994—, vice chair, 1998—. Author: numerous books and booklets. Mem. U.S. Census 2000 Adv. Com. on Asian and Pacific Islander Populations, 1994—, chair, 1995, 1997, 1999, 2000, 2001; mem. Fla. House Spkr.'s Task Force on Math., Sci., and Computer Edn., 1982—83; nat. selection com. mem. Presdl. Awards for Excellence in Sci. and Math. Tchg., 1990, state selection com. mem., 1987, 1990, 1991; chmn. Secondary math. Fla. State Textbook Adoption Coun., 1984. Mem.: Asian-Am. Fed. of Fla. (pres. 2003—), Asian Am. Cmty. Forum (founding Chair 2002), Asian Am. Found. (chair 2001—), Asian Am. Alliance (founding mem. 2001—, chair 2002—), Mid. States Assn. Colls. and Schs. (task force 1993—95), Fla. Leadership Alliance for Improving Math. Edn. (founder 1991), Dade County Sch. Adminstrs. Assn. (v.p. 1985—86), Fla. Assn. Instrnl. Supr. and Adminstrs. (bd. dirs. 1985—86), UNESCO Staff Assn. (pres. 1971—76), Fla. Assn. Math. Supr. (pres. 1986—87), Fla. Coun. Tchrs. Math. (pres. 1990—92), U.S. Metric Assn. (ann. conf. chmn. 1982), Assn. Indians in Am. (nat. v.p. 1984—88, 1992—94, trustee 1997—, nat. pres. 2000—04). Home: 1625 Eagle Bnd Weston FL 33327-1615 Office: APS Techs Inc 630 W 84th St Hialeah FL 33014-3617 E-mail: sudhapca@aol.com.

AGRAWAL, RAKESH, industrial engineer, researcher; b. Ara, Bihar, India, Nov. 3, 1953; came to U.S., 1975; s. Girdhar Lal and Bimla; m. Manju Agrawal, June 18, 1980; children: Udit, Numit. BTech, Indian Inst. Tech., Kanpur, 1975; MChE, U. Del., 1977; ScD, MIT, 1980. From process engr. to process mgr. Air Products and Chems., Allentown, Pa., 1980-90, sr. engring. assoc., 1990-92, prin. engring. assoc., 1992-96, chief engr. process synthesis, 1996—2003, fellow, 2003—. Trustee Cache Corp., Austin, 1997—. Contbr. over 60 articles to profl. jours.; holder over 400 patents in field. Fellow Indian Inst. Chem. Engrs. (hon.); mem. AIChE (mem. chem. engring. operating tech. coun. 1999—, cons. editor Separations, AIChEJ 1999—, Inst. award for Excellence in Indsl. Gases Tech. 1998, Gerhold award in separations 2001), NAE. Avocations: exercise, photography, reading. Office: Air Products and Chems 7201 Hamilton Blvd Allentown PA 18195-1526 E-mail: agrawar@apci.com.

AGRE, JAMES COURTLAND, physiatrist; b. Northfield, Minn., May 2, 1950; s. Courtland Leverne and Ellen Violet (Swedberg) A.; m. Patti Dee Soderberg, Aug. 6, 1982. MD, U. Minn., 1976, PhD, 1985. Cert. diplomate Nat. Bd. Med. Examiners, bd. cert. Am. Bd. Phys. Medicine and Rehab. Rsch. fellow dept. phys. medicine and rehab. U. Minn., Mpls., 1979-80, instr. dept. phys. medicine and rehab., 1980-84; asst. prof. dept. phys. medicine and rehab. U. Wis., Madison, 1984-90, assoc. prof. dept. rehab. medicine, 1990-93, chmn. dept. rehab. medicine, 1991-97, prof. dept. rehab. medicine, 1993-97; practitioner in svc. Ministry Health Care, Rhinelander and Eagle River, Wis., 1997—. Mem. editorial bd. and contbr. articles to Archives of Phys. Medicine and Rehab., 1988-2000. Ski coord. Wis. Ski for Light, Madison, 1985-95. Fellow Am. Acad. Phys. Medicine and Rehab. (Elizabeth and Sidney Licht award 1989, Excellence in Sci. Writing award 1990), Am. Coll. Sports Medicine (New Investigator award 1991). Office: Ministry Health Care 930 E Wall St Eagle River WI 54521 Office Phone: 715-477-3000. Business E-Mail: jagre@shsmh.org.

AGRE, PETER COURTLAND, medical educator; b. Northfield, Minn., Jan. 30, 1949; BA in Chemistry with honors, Augsburg Coll., 1970. Postdoctoral fellow dept. pharmacology Johns Hopkins, 1974—75; from intern to resident Case Western Res. U., 1975—78; postdoctoral fellow dept. medicine, hematology/oncology divsn. U. NC, Chapel Hill, 1978—80, clin. asst. prof. medicine, 1980—81; sr. clinical rsch. scientist Wellcome Labs., Research Triangle Park, NC, 1980—81; from rsch. assoc. to instr. dept. cell biology/anatomy and medicine Johns Hopkins Sch. Medicine, 1981—83, asst. prof. dept. medicine and cell biology/anatomy, 1984—88, assoc. prof., 1988—93; sabbatical dept. embryology Carnegie Inst., Washington, 1988—89; co-dir. office of rsch. planning dept. medicine, 1990—94; dir. grad. program in cellular and molecular medicine Johns Hopkins, 1996—99, chmn. adv. bd. grad. program in cellular and molecular medicine, 1999—2005; vice chancellor, sci., tech. and prof. cell biology Duke Univ. Med. Ctr., Durham, NC, 2005—. Recipient Clin. Investigator award, Nat. Heart, Lung and Blood Inst., 1981—85, Basil O'Connor award, March of Dimes Birth Defects Found., 1986—88, Established Investigator award, Am. Heart Assn., 1987—92, Young Investigator award, Am. Federation Clinical Rsch., 1991, Disting. Alumnus award, Augsburg Coll., 1995, Nobel prize for chemistry, 2003. Mem.: NAS, Am. Soc. Nephrology (Homer Smith award 1999), Am. Soc. for Biochemistry and Molecular Biology, Am. Physiol. Soc., Am. Soc. for Clinical Investigation, Am. Soc. for Cell Biology, Interurban Clinical Club (hon.). Office: Vice Chancellor Sci Tech Duke Univ Med Ctr Trent Dr Durham NC 27710

AGREN, TINA SMITH, librarian, archivist; b. Springfield, Mass., Mar. 1, 1947; d. Stephen Owen Smith and Phyllis M. Grant; life ptnr. Dwight John Wilcoxson; children: Sarah Jean(dec.) children: Eric Douglas, Jason Christopher. BS, U. N.H., 1969. LCSW Maine, 1992, Tex., 1992. Bus. ptnr. Agren Appliance, Auburn, Maine, 1978—92; social worker, dir. admissions Life Care Ctr. Plano - Homestead of McKinney, Tex., 1992—94; tour guide Sabbathday Lake Shaker Village, New Gloucester, Maine, 1999—2001; libr., archivist Shaker Libr. - Sabbathday Lake Shaker Village, 2001—. Hospice vol. Androscoggin Home Health, Lewiston, Maine, 1992—2001. Mem.: Maine Archives and Mus., So. Maine Libr. Dist., New Eng. Archivists. Unitarian-Universalist. Avocations: antiques, cooking, gardening, reading, walking. Office: Sabbathday Lake Shaker Village 707 Shaker Rd New Gloucester ME 04260 Office Phone: 207-926-4597. Office Fax: N/A. E-mail: brooks1@shaker.lib.me.us.

AGRESS, HARRY, JR., radiologist, nuclear medicine physician; s. Harry and June W. Agress. BA in Math., Tufts U., 1968, MD, 1972. Diplomate Am. Bd. Radiology, Am. Bd. Nuclear Medicine, Nat. Bd. Med. Examiners. Intern Mt. Sinai Med. Ctr., NYC, 1972—73; fellow NIH, Bethesda, Md., 1973—75; resident in diagnostic radiology Columbia-Presbyn. Med. Ctr., NYC, 1975—78; from asst. to attending physician Hackensack (NJ) U. Med. Ctr., 1980—96, sr. attending radiologist, 1996—, chmn. dept. radiology, 2005—; asst. clin. prof. Columbia U. Coll. Physicians and Surgeons, NYC, 1980—88, assoc. clin. prof. radiology, 1988—2001, clin. prof., 2002—, chmn. dept. radiology, 2005—. Dir. divsn. nuclear medicine Positron Emission Tomagraphy Ctr., Hackensack, 1978—; bd. dirs. GE Med. Sys., Milw.; oral exam examiner Am. Bd. Radiology, Tucson, 1999—; faculty Positron Emission Tomagraphy Learning Ctr., Reston, Va., 2002—; lectr., spkr., presenter in field. Contbr. chapters to books, articles to profl. jours. Bd. vis. Mary Inst. St. Louis Country Day Sch., 2003—. Lt. comdr. USPHS, 1973—75. Mem.: AMA, Radiol. Soc. NJ, NJ Med. Soc., Acad. Molecular Imaging, Radiol. Soc. N.Am., Soc. Nuclear Medicine, Am. Coll. Radiology. Achievements include research in positron emission tomography detection of unexpected asymptomatic cancers. Avocations: piano, photography, golf. Office: Hackensack Univ Med Ctr Dept Radiology 30 Prospect Ave Hackensack NJ 07601 Office Phone: 201-996-2196.

AGREST, EMMANUIL M., mathematician, physicist, educator; b. Moscow, Jan. 30, 1945; s. Matest M and Riva S Agrest; m. Larisa S Shaldjian, Aug. 6, 1968; children: Igor, Yan. PhD Math. and Physics, N.N. Andreyev Acoustics Inst., Moscow, 1975; M.S. Math. and Mechanics, Moscow State U., 1968. Docent of department of Algebra and Geometry Supreme Certifying Bd. of the Coun. of Ministers of USSR, 1986. Rsch. fellow Acoustics Inst., Sukhumi, Georgia, 1969—80; asst. prof. Abkhazian State U., Sukhumi, Georgia, 1980—86, head of algebra and numerical methods dept., 1986—92; asst. prof. Johnson & Wales U., Charleston, SC, 1993—96, assoc. prof., 1996—2000, prof., 2000—; adj. faculty Coll. of Charleston, Charleston, SC, 1993—2002. Mem.: Am. Math. Soc., The Math. Assn. of Am. Achievements include invention of A device for automatic tractor navigation, inventors certificate # 1099865 USSR, 1984; research in Mathematical modelling of nonlinear effects in acoustical cavitation. Office: Johnson & Wales University 801 W Trade St Charlotte NC 28202 Office Phone: 980-598-1479. E-mail: emmanuil.agrest@jwu.edu.

AGRESTA, ANTHONY JOHN, academic administrator, educational consultant, language educator; b. Jersey City, Apr. 8, 1933; s. Charles Vincent and Pauline Grace (Truncellito) Agresta; m. Carla Perls, Aug. 9, 1997; m. Elizabeth Ann Smelser, Nov. 13, 1955 (div. Sept. 23, 1965); m. Nancy Mae Laraway, Oct. 29, 1966 (div. Mar. 13, 1974); children: Anthony II, Lisane, Suzanne. BS, Fairleigh Dickinson U, Teaneck, NJ, 1955; MS, William Paterson U, Wayne, NJ, 1961; PhD, US U of Am., Wash. DC, 1974; dip. in Orthotics, New York Sch. of Med., New York, NY, 1982; rev. ordained, Universal Life Ch., Modesto, CA, 1997; DD, Am. Inst. of Holistic Theology, Youngstown, OH, 2001. Income tax prep., H & R Block, 1988; cert. tchr.: K-8 NJ, 1958, counselor: K-12 NJ, 1967, prin.: K-12 NJ, 1968, sch.administrator NJ, 1969, metaphysical psychology N.Y.C., hypnosis holistic practitioner, child psychol. Am. Assoc. of Christian Coun., 2003. Elem. guidance Rochelle Pk. Pub. Sch., Rochelle Pk., NJ, 1955—60, asst. prin., 1960—62; dir. of guidance Wallington (NJ) Elem. Schs., 1963—64; prin. Wallington Bd. of Ed., 1964—70; HS prin. Wallington HS, 1971—81; CEO B&H Shoe Shoppes, Inc., Hackensack, NJ, 1982—86, Red Bank, NJ, 1982—86; dir. of guidance Paramus Catholic HS, Paramus, NJ, 1986—89; dir. of fin. aid Gibbs Coll., Montclair, NJ, 1989—90; adj. prof. English William Paterson U., Wayne, NJ, 1991—, grad. office coord., 1992—93, ESL tchr., curriculum developer continuing edn. program, 1995—2002, writing ctr. tutor, 1996—2000; acad. coord. Hispanic Inst., Paramus, NJ, 1998—. Income tax preparer H & R Block, 1988—92, Budget Tax, Saddle Brook, NJ, 1991—; metaphysics lectr., 1996—98; co-chair Healthy Families Bergen County, Englewood, NJ, 1998—2002; pres. Master Learning Inst., Saddle Brook, NJ, 2000—, cons. owner, 2000—. Inventor (shoes) automatic shoe measure, 1980; editor: (ESL textbooks) Let's Get Down to Bus. (idioms), 2000. Councilman, chair, pub. works Mcpl. Town Coun., Emerson, NJ, 1979—81; chair, substance abuse coun. Paramus Cath. HS, Paramus, NJ, 1987—89. SFC USAR, 1953—61, vessel examiner US Coast Guard Auxilary, 1988—96. Nominee disting. prin., Wallington, NJ, 1979—80; recipient Cert. of Honor, Wallington PTA, 1971, Cert. of Merit, Mid. States Assoc. of Secondary Sch./Coll., 1971, Achievement award, IRS/ Newark, NJ, 1989, Cert. of Merit, Hispanic Inst. /Paramus, NJ, 1990. Mem.: Am. Fed. of Tchr., Healthy Families Bergen Coun. (co-chair 2001—02), Tchr. of Eng. Second language. Achievements include writing of by-laws/constn. for Healthy Families Bergen County; dir. elementary sch. guidance prog; wrote grants and coord. remedial svc; development of curriculum staff evaluation, adult edn. and tech. studies curriculum writing of all final exams, course outlines, all levels, Hispanic Institute; federal title programs Wallington Schools, Rochelle Park Schools. Home: 531 Saddle River Rd Saddle Brook NJ 17663-4638 Office: Hispanic Inst for Rsch and Devel 17 Arcadian Ave Paramus NJ 17652

AGRESTI, MIRIAM MONELL, psychologist; b. N.Y.C., Mar. 23, 1926; d. James McCloud and Marion Henrietta (Zippel) Monell; children: Robert, Carol. BS, Queens Coll., 1947; MA in Sci. Edn., Columbia U., 1949; PhD in Clin. Psychology, Yeshiva U., 1976; postgrad., Ackerman Inst. Family Therapy, 1977-81, L.I. Jewish Hosp. Human Sexualality Ctr. Lic. psychologist, N.Y. Diplomate Am. Bd. Family Psychology (fellow, pres. 1984-85). Psychology intern Creedmoor Psychiat. Ctr., Queens, N.Y., 1963-64, family therapist, 1964-69; psychologist Northeast Nassau Psychiat. Ctr., Kings Park, N.Y., 1969-72; adminstrv. dir. Friendship House Day Hosp., Glen Cove, N.Y., 1972-74; psychologist and team leader Ctrl. Islip (N.Y.) Psychiatr. Ctr., 1974-75; tchr., coord. family therapy program Pilgrim Psychiat. Ctr., West Brentwood, N.Y., 1976-80; pvt. practice psychotherapy, 1977—. Pres. Nassau County Med. Ctr., 1990-95; co-dir. L.I. Family Inst., 1976-79; cons. family therapy Cath. Charities, 1979, St. Vincent's Hall, 1979, Nassau County Mental Health Assn., 1980; adj. faculty Sch. Edn., C.W. Post Coll., L.I. U., 1972, CUNY, 1978-80, St. John's U., 1983, Hofstra U., 1985-88. Exec. dir. movie/videotape Beware the Gaps in Medical Care for Older People (1st prize Am. Film Festival). Fellow Am. Orthopsychiat. Assn.; mem. APA, N.Y. State Psychol. Assn., Nassau County Psychol. Assn., Am. Assn. for Marriage and Family Therapy (pres. L.I. chpt. 1981-83, sec. N.Y. state divsn. 1996-98), Pi Lambda Theta. Unitarian Universalist. Address: 1110 Dee Ln Woodbury NY 11797 Office Phone: 516-921-3924.

AGRESTO, JOHN THOMAS, former college president, education consultant; b. Brooklyn, NY, Jan. 7, 1946; m. Catherine Agresto; children: Mollie, Meghan. AB magna cum laude in polit. sci./history, Bost. Coll., 1967; PhD in polit. sci., Cornell U., 1974; LHD (hon.), Kenyon Coll., 1989. Vis. lectr. U. Toronto, 1971-72; asst. prof. Kenyon Coll., Gambier, Ohio, 1972-78; projects dir. Nat. Humanities Ctr., Triangle Park, N.C., 1979-82; asst. chmn. NEH, Washington, 1982-85, acting chmn., 1985-86, dep. chmn., 1985-89; pres. St. John's Coll., Santa Fe, 1989-2000, John Agresto & Assocs., Santa Fe, 2000; sr. advisor for edn. Coalition Provisional Authority, Iraq, 2003—04. Vis. assoc. prof. Duke U., Durham NC; mem. faculty New Sch. for Social Rsch., NYC, 1988-89; pres. Madison Ctr., Washington, 1989. Author: The Supreme Court and Constitutional Democracy, 1984; editor, contbr. Liberty and Equality Under the Constitution, 1983; co-editor (with Peter Riesenberg) The Humanist as Citizen: Essays on the Uses of the Humanities, 1982; contbr. numerous articles to profl. jours.; speaker, panelist in field. Trustee Pontifical Coll. Josephinum; former mem. Ind. Commn. Arts; former mem. Columian Quincentenary Commn. Nat. Humanities Ctr. fellow, 1978-79. Mem. Am. Polit. Sci. Assn., Nat. Assn. Scholars, Sons of Italy in Am., Am. Acad. Liberal Edn. (founding chmn.).

AGRUSA, JEROME, tourism studies educator; b. N.Y.C. s. Jerry Agrusa and Joyce Tenney. BS, U. Houston, 1987, M in Hospitality Mgmt., 1990; PhD, Tex. A&M U., 1996. Cert. food mgmt. profl. Nat. Restaurant Assn., hospitality educator Am. Hotel/Motel Assn. Prof. Houston C.C., 1990—91; lectr. Tex. A&M U., College Station, 1991—94; mng. ptnr. Mirage United Hotels, Bolzano, Italy, 1993—96; assoc. prof. U. So. Miss., Hattiesburg, 1994—97; endowed rsch. prof. U. La., Lafayette, 1997—2002; prof. Hawaii Pacific U., Honolulu, 2002—. Pres. JFA, Inc., Internat. Consulting, Honolulu, 1987—; main resource spkr. Asian Productivity Orgn., Nadi, Fiji, 2003—. Editor Jour. Tchg. in Travel & Tourism, assoc. editor Asia Pacific Jour. Tourism Scis., mem. editl. rev. bd. Internat. Jour. Tourism Scis. Named Assoc. Mem. of Yr., La. Restaurant Assn., 2001; recipient Vis. Scholar award, Nat. Tourism Found., 1998; grantee, La. Tourism Commn., 1998, Dept. Natural Resources and U.S. Dept. Energy, 2000. Mem.: Travel & Tourism Rsch. Assn. (bd. dirs. 2002—05), Asia Pacific Tourism Assn. (bd. dirs. 1997—2004), Sigma Xi, Phi Beta Delta (pres. 2001—02). Avocations: golf, swimming, movies. Office: Hawaii Pacific U 1164 Bishop St Ste 912 Honolulu HI 96813 Fax: 808-544-9396. Office Phone: 808-544-9341. E-mail: jfagrusa@aol.com.

AGUAYO, ALBERTO JUAN, neuroscientist; b. Argentina, July 16, 1934; MD, U. Cordoba, Argentina, 1959; Dr. Honoris Causa, U. Lund, Sweden. Cert. specialist in neurology, Que., cert. EEG specialist, Que. Intern Port Arthur Gen. Hosp., 1960-61; resident in neurology Toronto Gen. Hosp., 1961-62, resident in medicine, 1962-63; resident in neurology Montreal Gen. Hosp., 1964-65; prof. neurology and physiology McGill U., 1977—; prof. medicine McGill U. and Montreal Gen. Hosp. Rsch. Inst., 1976—, asst. dept. physiology, 1981—, dir. Ctr. for Rsch. in Neurosci., 1985—; sec.-gen. Internat. Brain Rsch. Org., 2001. Mem. sci. adv. bds. and coms. including Med. Rsch. Can., Howard Hughes Med. Inst., Am. Paraplegic Assn., Ipsen Found., Max Planck Inst., Munich, Germany, Friedrich Miescher-Inst., Basle, Switzerland. Co-editor Current Opinion in Neurobiology; mem. editorial bd. European Jour. Neurosci., Experimental Brain Rsch., Brain Rsch., Synapse, Jour. of Neural Transplantation, Jour. Neurobiology; mem. adv. bd. Neuroscis. Rsch.; mem. internat. adv. bd. NeuroReport. Decorated Order of Can.; recipient Gairdner Found. Internat. award, Ipsen award on Neural Plasticity, WH Helmerich III award for Outstanding Achievement in retina rsch., Leo Parizeau Prize in Biology Assn. Canadienne-Française pour l'Avancement des Sciences, 1993, Killam prize for health scis. Can. Coun. for Arts, 1999, recognition award for outstanding contbns. in field of visual rsch. Alcon Labs., 1998, Prix du Que.-Wilder Penfield award, 1994, prize Ameritec Found., 1993, Christopher Reeve Rsch. medal, 1999; rsch. fellow Banting Inst., U. Toronto, 1963-64, Montreal Gen. Hosp., 1965-66, traveling fellow McLaughlin Found., 1966-67, Reeve medal, 2000. Fellow Royal Soc. Can., AAAS; mem. Inst. Medicine of the NAS (U.S), N-Am. Soc. for Neurosci. (pres.), Can. Neurol. Soc. (pres.), Can. Assn. of Neuroscientists (pres.), Third World Congress of the Internat. Brain Rsch. Orgn. (pres.), Can. Neurosci. Found. (v.p., bd. dirs.), Soc. Neurosci. (pres. 1987-88), Internat. Brain Rsch. Orgn. (sec.-gen. 2001). Office: McGill U Gen Hosp Rsch Inst 1650 Cedar Ave Montreal PQ Canada H3G 1A4 E-mail: mcio@musica.m.gill.ca.*

AGUERO, JOSEPH EDWARD, psychology professor, psychologist, educator; b. Havana, Cuba, July 14, 1946; s. Enrique and Maria Teresa (Carillo) Aguero; m. Sonia Dionisia Socorro, Dec. 4, 1964 (div. Mar. 6, 1970); children: Diane Carol(dec.), Joseph Edward Jr., Thomas Arthur, Wendy Marie. BA, Ind. U. NW, Gary, 1974; MS, Purdue U., 1977, PhD, 1982. Vis. instr. St. Mary's Coll. Md., St. Mary's City, Md., 1980—81; asst. prof. psychology MUCIA/Institut Teknologic MARA, Shah Allam, Malaysia, 1986—88, U. Wis. Ctr., Menasha; prof. psychology U. PR at Mayaguez, 1988—. Author: (text book (in Spanish) The Psychology of Human Sexuality: A Social-Psychological and Humanist Perspective; contbr. chapters to books. External evaluator Hogar Portal de Amor, San German, PR, 2002—05. Mem.: APA (assoc.). Roman Catholic. Avocations: computer games, music, gardening. Home: PO Box 5733 Mayaguez PR 00681 Office: U PR at Mayaguez Dept Social Scis PO Box 9266 Mayaguez PR 00681 Office Phone: 787-265-3839. Personal E-mail: jaguero@lycos.com.

AGUERREBERE, JOSEPH A., academic administrator; b. E Los Angeles; BA in polit. sci, U. So. Calif.; M in edn. admin., U. So. Calif; Doctorate in ednl. admin., U. So. Calif. Pres. Nat. Bd. for Profl. Tchg. Standards, Arlington, Va., 2003—; dep. dir. edn., sexuality and religion unit Ford Found., NYC; assoc. prof. to prof. Calif. State U., Grad Edn. Dept. Office: Nat Bd Profl Tchg Standards 1525 Wilson Blvd Ste 500 Arlington VA 22209

AGUIAR, ADAM MARTIN, chemist, educator; b. Newark, Aug. 11, 1929; s. Joaquim Ramahlo and Emilea Andrada (Nunes) A.; m. Laura E. Brand, Sept. 2, 1980; children: Justine Diane, David Laurence, Adam Albert, Erick Arthur, Aaron Benjamin, Evan Joaquim. BS, Fairleigh Dickinson U., 1955; MA, Columbia U., 1957, PhD, 1960. Chemist Otto B. May, Newark, 1948-55; asst. prof. Fairleigh Dickinson U., Rutherford, NJ, 1959-63; asst. prof. chemistry Tulane U., New Orleans, 1963-65, assoc. prof., 1965-67, prof., 1967-72, head dept. chemistry Newcomb Coll. divsn., 1970; dean grad. and research programs William Paterson Coll., Wayne, NJ, 1972-73; rsch. prof. Rutgers U., Newark, 1973-75; prof. chemistry Fairleigh Dickinson U., Madison, NJ, 1975-93, chmn. dept. chemistry/geol. scis., 1984-89; pres. Seltox Corp., NJ, 1980—. Adj. prof. chemistry Monmouth U., West Long Branch, N.J., 1993—; adj. prof. humanities Ocean County Coll. ext. Fairleigh Dickinson U., 2004; cons. chem. firms in La. and N.J. Contbr. articles to profl. jours. Union Carbide fellow, 1957; NIH fellow, 1959; recipient other grants. Mem. AAUP, Am. Chem. Soc., AAAS, N.Y. Acad. Sci., Ctr. for Profl. Advancement, Sigma Xi, Phi Lambda Epsilon, Phi Omega Epsilon. Home: 37 Wyncrest Ln Neptune NJ 07753-7421 Personal E-mail: adamatt@att.net.

AGUIAR, ELIZABETH JOAN, publishing executive, educator; b. Union City, Tenn., Nov. 16, 1954; d. John Roland and Doris Olson Beck; m. Albert Anthony Aguiar, Nov. 30, 1991; 1 stepchild, Cassandra Nicole. BA, Bowling Green State U., 1977; MA, George Washington U., 1979. Dean Coll. Undergraduate Bus. and Mgmt. U. Phoenix, 1993—99; assoc. v.p. acad. pub. Apollo Group, Inc., Phoenix, 1999—2001, v.p. acad. pub., 2001—. Mem. resource project team, chmn. bd. initiative, 2000—02. Author: (fiction) Big Book, 2002, Managing Service for Success, 1987, 1989; mem. editl. bd. Future mag., U. Phoenix Alumni Network, 2003—. Avocations: reading, art. Home: 1224 E Grandview Rd Phoenix AZ 85022 Office: Apollo Group Inc 4615 E Elwood St Phoenix AZ 85040 Office Phone: 480-557-1736. Office Fax: 480-921-4271. Business E-Mail: ejaguiar@apollogrp.edu.

AGUIGUI, IGNACIO CRUZ, lawyer; b. Agana Heights, Guam, Dec. 3, 1970; s. Joaquin Tyquiengco and Teresita Cruz Aguigui. BA magna cum laude, Yale U., 1991; JD with honors, Columbia Law Sch., 1997. Bar: Calif. 1997, U.S. Ct. Appeals (9th cir.) 1997, U.S. Dist. Ct. (no. dist.) Calif. 1997, Guam 1999, U.S. Dist. Ct. Guam 1999, U.S. Dist. Ct. (ctrl. dist.) Calif. 2001. Spl. asst. to the gov. Office of Gov. of Guam, Hagatna, 1993—94; extern law clk. U.S. Dist Ct. (so. dist.) N.Y. Hon. Barrington D. Parker, Jr., N.Y.C., 1995; atty. Morrison & Foerster LLP, San Francisco, 1997—98; atty. Superior Ct. Guam Chambers of Hon. Katherine A. Maraman, Hagatna, 1998—99; atty. Calvo and Clark, LLP, Tamuning, 1999—2002; legal counsel Camacho/Moylan Gubernatorial Transition Com., Hagatna, 2002; ptnr. Lujan, Unpingco, Aguigui & Perez LLP, Hagatna, 2003—; counsel to gov. Office Gov. Guam, Hagatna, 2003. V.p., bd. dirs. Guam Legal Svcs. Corp., Hagatna, 2000—03. Mem. Rep. Party of Guam, Hagatna, Guam Election Commn., Hagatna, 2002—04, Guam Pub. Libr., Hagatna, 1991—92. Recipient Centennial Scholar award, NIH, 1987, U.S. Congl. award, Office of Guam's Del. to the U.S. Ho. of Reps., 1987, Prin.'s award, Inarajan H.S., Inarajan, Guam, 1987, Robin Berlin Meml. prize, Yale U., 1989, Valedictorian award, Inarajan H.S., Inarajan, Guam, 1987; fellow Pub. Svc. fellow, Columbia Law Sch., 1994; Profl./Tech. scholar, Govt. of Guam, 1994-1997, Harlan Fiske Stone scholar, Columbia Law Sch., 1996, Merit scholar, Govt. of Guam, 1987-1991, Summer Rsch. fellow, U. Calif., Berkeley, 1989, U. Calif., San Francisco, 1990. Mem.: ABA (assoc.). R-Liberal. Roman Catholic. Avocations: travel, music, french language and culture. Home: Oka Towers 303 162 Western Blvd Tamuning GU 96913 Office Phone: 671-727-2881. E-mail: iaguigui@aya.yale.edu.

AGUILAR, JULIA SHELL, publishing executive; BS in Sociology and Psychology, MS in Social Work Adminstrn., Va. Commonwealth U. Dir. human resources Times-Advocate, Escondido, Calif., 1982—84; v.p. human resources L.A. Daily News, 1984—87; dir. human resources John P. Scripps Newspapers, 1987—90; pres., then pub. San Luis Obispo (Calif.) County Telegram-Tribune, 1990—98; dir. mgmt. devel. E.W. Scripps Co., Cin., 1998—2000; gen. mgr. Knoxville (Tenn.) News-Sentinel, 2000—. Office: Knoxville News-Sentinel 2332 News Sentinel Dr PO Box 59038 Knoxville TN 37950-9038

AGUILAR, MIRIAM REBECCA, technology project manager; b. Torrance, Calif., Feb. 6, 1963; d. Samuel Conklin and Victoria Lizarraga Aguilar; children: Samantha Victoria Reed, Olivia Linda Reed. AA in Liberal Arts, L.A. Harbor Coll., 1984; BA in Anthropology Minor Art History, Colo. State U., 1998; M of Internat. Pub. Mgmt., Monterey Inst. of Internat. Studies, 2001. Cert. travel counselor Travel and Trade Career Inst. IT market analyst Kagan World Media, Carmel, Calif., 2000; tech. project mgr. CTB McGraw-

Hill, Monterey, Calif., 2001—. Proposed design and devel. for creation of Internat. Lang. and Culture Meml. Mus. and Rsch. Ctr. World Trade Ctr. Author: (pub. project) Developing and Designing An Administrative Model for an International Language and Culture Museum and Research Center. Bd. dirs. internat. programs Internat. Lang. and Culture Found., Monterey, 1999. Mem.: Internat. Lang. and Culture Found. (life; bd. dirs. internat. programs 1999, treas. 2002). Avocations: reading, travel, gardening, research, yoga. Home: 930 Casanova Ave #7 Monterey CA 93940 Personal E-mail: miriama0246@yahoo.com.

AGUILAR-BRYAN, LYDIA, medical educator, researcher; b. Mexico City, Feb. 25, 1951; m. Joseph Bryan; 1 child. MD, U. Nacional Autonoma de Mex., 1975; PhD in Population Studies, U. Tex., 1985. Rsch. assoc. Inst. Biomed. Rsch., U. Nacional Autonoma de Mex., Mexico City, 1985—86, Baylor Coll. of Medicine, Dept. of Medicine, Divsn. of Endocrinology, Houston, 1987—88, postdoctoral fellow, 1988—90, instr., 1990—91, asst. prof., 1991—; prof. M.D. Anderson Cancer Ctr. U. Tex. Contbr. articles to profl. jours. Recipient postdoctoral fellowship, Juvenile Diabetes Found., 1988—90. Mem.: AAAS, Endocrine Soc., Biophys. Soc., Am. Diabetes Assn. (Rsch. grantee 1995—).

AGUILERA, CHRISTINA, vocalist; b. Dec. 18, 1980; Vocalist New Mickey Mouse Club, 1994-96; vocalist theme song for Disney animated film Mulan, 1998 (Golden Globe nominee for best original song in a motion picture); debut album Christina Aguilera (RCA), 1999 (Grammy award, Best New Artist, 2000), My Kind of Christmas, 2000, Mi Reflejo, 2000, Complete, 2002, Stripped, 2002 (Grammy award, Best Female Pop Vocal Performance for song "Beautiful", 2003); singles: What A Girl Wants, 1999, The Christmas Song, 1999, Genie in a Bottle, 1999; video: The Genie Gets Her Wish, 1999. Recipient ALMA award, best new artist, 1999.

AGUIRRE, BENIGNO EMILIO, sociology educator; b. Trinidad, Las Villas, Cuba, Oct. 25, 1947; came to U.S., 1961, naturalized, 1970; m. Lauriece Chitwood; children— Carlos, Benigno E., Jr. B.A., Fla. State U., 1970; M.A. in Latin Am. Studies, Tulane U., 1972; Ph.D. in Sociology, Ohio State U., 1977. Mem. faculty Tex. A&M U., College Station, 1979, assoc. prof. sociology, 1985—; mem. faculty council Sterling C. Evans Library; research assoc. Disaster Research Ctr., Ohio State U., 1975-77. HEW fellow; Tex. A&M grantee, 1977-83, 81. Contbr. articles to profl. jours. Mem. team Com. Natural Disasters Nat. Research Council, 1982; cons. Family Violence Br., Tex. Dept. Human Resources, Austin, 1983. Mem. Sociol. Assn., Latin Am. Studies Assn., Nat. Council Family Relations, Soc. Study Social Problems, So. Sociol. Assn. Office: Dept Sociol Tex A&m Univ College Station TX 77843-0001 Home: 35 Winslow Rd Newark DE 19711-5209

AGUIRRE, DIEGO, retired radiologist; MD, Universidad El Bosque, Bogota, 1997, diagnostic radiologist degree, 2003. Cert. med. dr. Ministry of Edn., Colombia, 1998. Assoc. rsch. U. Calif., San Diego, 2003—. Contbr. articles to profl. jours. E-mail: daguirre@ucsd.edu.

AGUIRRE, EDUARDO, JR., ambassador, former federal agency administrator; b. Cuba; m. Tere Aguirre; 2 children. Grad., La. State U.; degree (hon.), U. Tacnologica Santiago, Dominican Rep. With Texas Commerce Bank, 1969, Bank of Am., 1978—2000, pres., 1999—2000; vice chmn., 1st v.p. Export-Import Bank of U.S., Washington, 2001—02; Dir. Bureau of Citizenship & Immigration Services US Dept. Homeland Security, Washington, 2003—05; US amb. to Spain & Andorra US Dept. State, Madrid, 2005—. Hon. prof. Beijing Polytech U., Ctrl. U. Nationalities, Beijing; former chmn. bd. trustees Tex. Bar Found.; Founding chmn. bd. dirs. Houston Livestock Show and Rodeo; former chmn. bd. dirs. Tex. Children's Hosp.; regent U. Houston System Bd. of Regents, 1995—2001, chmn., 1996—98. Office: US Dept State 8500 Madrid Pl Washington DC 20521*

AGUIRRE, FERNANDO, food products executive; b. Mex. BSBA, So. Ill. U. With Procter & Gamble, 1980—2004, pres., gen. mgr. P&G Brazil, 1992—96, pres. P&G Mex., 1996—99, v.p. global and U.S. snacks and food products, 1999—2000, pres. global feminine care, 2000—04; pres., CEO Chiquita Brands Internat., Inc., Cin., 2004—, also. chmn. bd. dirs. Bd. dirs. Univision Comm., Inc.; chmn. emeritus corp. adv. bd. Marshall Sch. Bus. U. So. Calif. Office: Chiquita Brands Internat 250 E 5th St Cincinnati OH 45202

AGUIRRE, PABLO EDUARDO, management consultant; b. Montevideo, Uruguay, Apr. 11, 1965; came to U.S. 1966; s. Carlos Alberto and Lydia (Guaragna) A. BS, U. Md., 1987; M of Mgmt., Kellogg Grad. Sch., 1993. Cons. Andersen Consulting, Washington; sr. cons. Deloitte Consulting, Washington, SRI Consulting, Arlington, Va.; bd. dirs. Atomic Tangerine, Arlington. Avocations: golf, reading, travel, motorcycle riding. Home: 6583 Sand Wedge Ct Alexandria VA 22312 E-mail: pea94@aol.com.

AGUIRRE, PASCAL GEORGE ARTHUR, management consultant; b. Ales, Gard, France, Apr. 5, 1968; s. Juan Fernando Arturo and Andree Louise Aguirre; m. Irina Lutskaya, July 20, 1998; 1 child, Ariel Andre, Arthur. BA in Econs., Boston (Mass.) U., 1994, MS, 1993, MBA, 1994. Sr. v.p. and practice leader Adventis, Corp., Boston, 1994—. Contbr. columns in newspapers. Dir. Bird St. Cmty. Ctr., Boston, 2004—05. Mem.: Porsche Club Am., Aircraft Owners and Pilots Assn., Rotary Internat., Beta Gamma Sigma. Republican. Roman Catholic. Avocations: flying, windsurfing, driving, oenology. Office: Adventis Corp 10 St James Ave Boston MA 02116 Office Phone: 617-421-9990. Office Fax: 617-421-9994. E-mail: paguirre@adventis.com.

AGUIRRE, ROBERT DAVID, literature educator; b. Redwood City, Calif., Oct. 3, 1961; PhD, Harvard U., 1990. Asst. prof. UCLA, 1989—97; assoc. prof. Wayne State U., Detroit, 1997—. Author: (book) Informed Empire Mexico and Central America in Victorian Culture, 2005. Andrew W. Mellon Post-Doctoral fellowship, John Carter Brown Libr., 1999-2000. Office: Wayne State Univ English Dept Detroit MI 48202 Office Phone: 313-577-2450. Business E-Mail: r.aguirre@wayne.edu.

AGUIRRE-BACA, FRANCISCO, publisher, consultant; b. León, Nicaragua, Jan. 7, 1920; came to U.S., 1947; s. Horacio and Pilar (Baca) Aguirre-Muñoz; m. Gladys Sacasa Aguirre, Dec. 27, 1941; children: Gladys, Francisco Xavier, Mariangeles, Rafael Eugenio, Guiomar, Alejandra. JD, U. Granada, Nicaragua, 1947. Various sr. positions Nicaraguan Armed Forces, 1940-47; rep., coord. numerous L.Am. newspapers and mags. Washington, 1947-53; co-founder, co-pub. Diario Las Americas, Miami, Fla., 1953—; founder Francisco Aguirre & Assocs. Latin Am. Newspapers and mag., Washington, 1960; dir. Pan Am. Divsn. Am. Road Builders Assn., Washington, 1948-53; co-founder, co-pub. Diario Las Americas, Miami, Fla., 1953; founder Francisco Aguirre & Assoc., Washington, 1960; amb. to III Summit Iberoamerican Chiefs of State Del. Dominican Republic, Salvador, Bahia, Brazil, 1993, amb. to IV Summit Iberoamerican Chiefs of State, 1994, Del. Republic Panama, Cartajena, Colombia, 1994; amb. to IV Summit Iberoamerican Pres. and Heads of States Nicaraguan Del., Santiago, Chile, 1996, amb. to official visit to His Holiness John Paul II Vatican City, Italy, 1996, amb. to Summit of the Ams. Santa Cruz, Bolivia, 1997; amb. to inauguration new Pres. Nicaragua Arnoldo Aleman Lacayo U.S. Del., Managua, Nicaragua, 1997; amb. to official visit to Republic China Nicaraguan Del., Taiwan, 1998, amb. II Summit of the Ams. Santiago, Chile, 1998, amb. XXVIII Gen. Assembly OAS Caracas, Venezuela, 1998. Internam. cons. Ambassador Extraordinary and Plenipotentiary of Nicaragua in Spl. Missions, Panama in Spl. Missions, 2002. Bd. dirs. Panamerican Divsn., Am. Rd. Builders Assn., 1948. Knight Order of St. Gregory, Sovereign Order of Malta; decorated by govts. of Argentina, Ecuador, Panama, Dominican Republic, Spain, Nicaragua, Republic of China (Taiwan). Mem. Hist. Georgetown Club, City Club, Nat. Press Club, Univ. Club, Congl. C.C. Republican. Roman Catholic. Home: 4951 Rockwood Pkwy NW Washington DC 20016-3247

AGUIRRE-BATTY, MERCEDES, Spanish and English language educator, literature educator, educator; b. Cd Juarez, Mex., Dec. 20, 1952; came to U.S., 1957. d. Alejandro M. and Mercedes (Péon) Aguirre; m. Hugh K. Batty, Mar. 17, 1979; 1 child, Henry B. BA, U. Tex., El Paso, 1974, MA, 1977; PhD in Edn., Capella U., 2005. Cert. online tchr., Calif. Instr. ESL Paso del Norte-Prep Sch., Cd Juarez, 1973-74; tchg. asst. ESL and English U. Tex., El Paso, 1974-77; instr. ESL English Lang. Svcs., Bridgeport, Conn., 1977-80; instr. Spanish and English, coord. modern lang. Sheridan (Wyo.) Coll., 1980—, pres. faculty senate, 1989-90; pres. faculty senate, chair dist. coun. No. Wyo. C.C. Dist., 1995-96. Planning com. No. Wyo. C.C. Dist., 1996-97; mem. advanced placement faculty Spanish cons. Coll. Bd. Ednl. Testing Svc., 1996-99; adj. prof. Spanish, U. Autonoma Cd Juarez, 1975; adj. prof. Spanish and English, Sacred Heart U., Fairfield, Conn., 1977-80; spkr. in field. Bd. dirs. Wyo. Coun. for the Humanities, 1988-92; translator county and dist. cts., Sheridan; vol. Wmen's Ctr.; translator Sheridan County Meml. Hosp.; del. Citizen Ambassador Program, People to People-India, 1996. NEH fellow, 1991-92; Wyo. State Dept. Edn. grant, 1991. Mem. MLA (del. assembly 1998-2000, 2004-), Wyo. Fgn. Lang. Tchrs. Assn. (pres. 1990-92), Am. Assn. Tchrs. Spanish and Portuguese (founder, 1st pres. Wyo. chpt. 1987-90), TESOL, Sigma Delta Mu (v.p. 1992-99, pres. 2000—), Sigma Delta Pi (Alpha Iota chpt. pres. 1974-75). Avocations: travel, reading, archeology, languages, geography. Office: Sheridan Coll NWCCD 3059 Coffeen Ave Sheridan WY 82801-9133

AGUIRRE-SACASA, FRANCISCO XAVIER, international banker, diplomat; b. Managua, Nicaragua, Sept. 4, 1944; s. Francisco and Gladys (Sacasa) A.; m. Maria de los Angeles, Oct. 6, 1968; children: Rafael Ignacio, Roberto Francisco, Georgiana Eugenia. BS in Fgn. Svc., Georgetown U., 1966; JD, Harvard U., 1969. Contributing writer Christian Sci. Monitor, Boston Herald Traveler, Boston Globe, Wall Street Jour., Fin. Times, Wash. Post, Wash. Times, La Prensa (Nicaragua), Diario Las Americas, 1968—; young profl. and loan officer The World Bank, Washington, 1969-76, div. chief, 1977-86, asst. dir., 1986-87, sr. ops. advisor, 1987-88, dir., external affairs, 1988-90, dir. Africa region, 1990-95, dir. ops. evalutation dept., 1995-97; ambassador to U.S., Canada govt. Nicaragua, Washington, 1997—. Named one of Nicaragua's Citizen of the Century, 2000; OAS scholar Harvard U., 1966-68. Mem. Nat. Press Club, Nicaraguan Acad. Geography and History, Am.-Nicaraguan Found. (treas.), U. Mobile Latin Am. Campus (adv. bd.), Zamorano Agrl. Sch. (internat. adv. bd.), Congl. Country Club (Bethesda, Md.), Harvard Club of Washington, Univ. Club (Wash.), Hist. Georgetown Club (Wash.). Roman Catholic. Avocations: carpentry, golf, farming. also: Valhalla Farm 11302 Obannons Mill Rd Boston VA 22713-4132 Office: Embassy of Nicaragua 1627 New Hampshire Ave NW Washington DC 20009-2573 Home: 4823 Yuma St NW Washington DC 20016-2061

AGVANIAN, YOURI, mathematician, educator, physicist; b. Yerevan, Armenia, Sept. 22, 1950; s. Martiros and Eranuhe Agvanian; m. Anahit Hovhanesyan; children: Zara, Elina. BS, Yerevan State U., Armenia, 1972; MS, Moscow U., 1980, PhD, 1990. Prof. physics, dean Yerevan Poly. U., 1973—92; prof. math. Pasadena City Coll., Calif., 1998—2000, L.A. Mission Coll., Sylmar, Calif., 1998—, Moor Park Coll., Calif., 1998—; prof. physics, astronomy Calif. State U., L.A., 1999—2001; prof. math. Calif. State Poly. U., Pomona, 2000—. Author: Transforamtion of Drops in NonHomogenious Temperature and Concentration Binary Vescous Environments, 1978, The Theory of Diffusive Magnetism of "Flying" High Heat Transferring Spherical Drops, 1978, The Theory of Thermal Magnetism of Spherical Drops in a Binary Liquid, 1979; contbr. articles to profl. jours. Mem.: Math. Assn. Am., N.Y. Acad. Sci., Am. Math. Soc., Am. Phys. Soc. Office: Calif State Polytechnic U 3801 West Temple Ave Pomona CA 91768

AGWU, IDIKA UME, chemist, educator, reading specialist; m. Ugo Idika Agwu, July 25, 2001; children: Adanna Brittany, Bessy Anele, Ume Brian. BS in Chemistry Edn., U. Lagos, 1990; MEd in Curriculum & Instrn., Loyola Coll., 2001; MEd in Reading, Bowie State U., 2002; post masters cert. in adminstrn. and supervision, Coppin State U., Balt., 2005. Advanced Profl. Cert. in Chemistry Md. State Dept. of Edn., 2001, Advanced Profl. Cert. in Reading Md. State Dept. of Edn., 2002, cert. Adminstrn. & Supervision Coppin State U., Md., 2005. Chemistry educator Abia State Sch. Mgmt. Bd., Aba, Nigeria, 1992—98; sci. tchr. Parkdale HS, Riverdale, Md., 1999—2000, Suitland HS, Forestville, Md., 2000—02; reading specialist Dodge Pk. Elem. Sch., Landover, 2002—04, Adelphi Elem. Sch., Md., 2004—, sch. test coord., 2004—; math. tchr. Adult Basic Edn., Suitland HS, Forestville, 2003—05; tchr. writing enrichment Crossland Saturday Sch., Temple Hills, 2004—05. Ind. contractor Porter Edn. & Comm., Landover, Md., 2003—; site supr. Am. Reads, Adelphi Elem. Sch., 2004—; coord. Ptnrs. in Print, Adelphi Elem. Sch., 2004—; sch. test coord. Adelphi Elem. Sch., 2004—. Chair sch. planning & mgmt. team Adelphi Elem. Sch., 2004; mem. sch. planning & mgmt. team Dodge Pk. Elem. Sch., Landover, 2002—04, coord. spelling bee, 2002—04, chair book fair, 2002—04; mem. Adelphi Elem. Sch. PTA, 2004; mem. sch. improvement team, multidisciplinary team & curriculum and assessment com. Adelphi Elem. Sch., 2004; chair reading com. Dodge Pk. Elem. Sch., 2002—04; mem. Dodge Pk. Elem. Sch. PTA, 2002—04. Recipient cert. of Appreciation, Suitland H.S., 2001—02, Dodge Pk. Elem. Sch., 2003—04. Mem.: NEA, Sci. Tchrs. Assn. Nigeria, Geol. Assn. Am., Prince George's County Educators Assn., Md. State Tchrs. Assn., Internat. Reading Assn. Member Lds Ch. Achievements include presenting workshops to teachers on four square writing, balanced literacy workshop, reciprocal teaching, reading centers, cooperative learning, writing objectives, and running records; presenting workshops to teachers on directed reading assessment and test security and administration. Avocations: soccer, reading, writing, music, movies, ping pong/table tennis. Home: 2414 Kirtland Ave Forestville MD 20747 Office: Adelphi Elem Sch 8820 Riggs Rd Adelphi MD 20783 Office Phone: 301-906-9133. Personal E-mail: iagwu@yahoo.com.

AGWU, NKECHI MADONNA, mathematics professor; b. Enugu, Enugu, Nigeria, Oct. 8, 1962; arrived in U.S., 1987; d. Jacob Ukejeh Agwu and Europa Lauretta Durosimi Wilson; m. Nicholas C. B. Ogbonna; 1 child, Ngozichukwuka Jacob A. D. BS with honors, U. of Nigeria, Nsukka, 1984; MS, U. of Conn., 1991; PhD, Syracuse U., 1995. Statistician Fed. Office of Stats., Enugu, 1984—85; lectr. Kaduna (Enugu) Poly., Kaduna, 1985—87; prof./dir. of the tchg. learning ctr. Borough of Manhattan C.C., CUNY, N.Y.C., 1995—. Ednl. cons. New Visions for Pub. Schs., N.Y.C., 2000—01, Algebra Project, N.Y.C., 1998—2000. Author: (curriculum development) Using a Threaded Discussion Web-based Software to Teach Statistics (Am. Math. Assn. 2-Year Colls. INPUT award, 2000); editor: (jour.) Mathematics in College, American Journal of Undergraduate Research. Named to Project Kaleidoscope Faculty for the Twenty-First Century Class of 1997, 1997—2002; recipient Performance Excellence award, Profl. Staff Congress, CUNY, 2000, Nigerian Fed. Govt. Merit award, 1981—84, tchg. assistantship, Syracuse U., 1991—95, tchg. assistantship, U. of Conn., 1987—91, Internat. Conf. on Tech. in Collegiate Math. Travel award, Addison-Wesley, 2002, Nat. Grad. Student Dissertation Travel award, Am. Ednl. Rsch. Assn. Divsn K, 1994, N.Y.C. Literacy Assistance Ctr. mini-grant, N.Y.C. Literacy Assistance Ctr. and Profl. Devel. Consortium, 1998, N.Y.C. Literary Assistance Ctr. and Profl. Devel. Consortium, 1999; Vis. Fellow, Edn. Testing Svc., 2003, Fulbright U.S. Fellow, 2004. Mem.: Internat. Biographical Assoc. (life), Math. Assn. of Am. (life Math. Assn. of Am. Inst. in the History of Math. and Its Uses in Tchg. Profl. Devel. award 1997—2001), Am. Math. Assn. 2-Year Colls. (life Travel award 1997). Office: Borough of Manhattan C C 199 Chambers St New York NY 10007 Office Phone: 212-220-1337. Business E-Mail: nagwu@bmcc.cuny.edu.

AGYENKWAH, KENNEDY SETH, communications executive; b. Accra, Ghana, May 20, 1953; came to U.S., 1989; s. Seth Kwabena Apeasah and Mercy Afua Addae; m. Sylvia Afari, June 23, 1984 (div. June 1994); m. Sandra Dee, Nov. 23, 1995; children: Osiris, Kwasi. BA in Mgmt., Met. State U., 2000. Instr. bus. edn. Ghana Edn. Svc., Somanya, 1974-76; prin. course tutor, writer Inst. Adult Edn., U. Ghana, Legon, 1978-79; founder, vice prin., dir. African Meth. Episcopal Zion U., Monrovia, Liberia, 1980-86; instr., bus. mgr., asst. dir. Don Bosco Poly., Monrovia, 1981-89; CEO Pan African Internat. Marketplace, Mpls., 1993-97, African Comm. Network, Mpls., 1997—. Project cons., writer Don Bosco Poly., Monrovia, 1988-89. Author: (poems and essays) African Personality, 1993, (book) African Ethoes, 1998, Organize the Village-Core Values Game and Rites of Passage Game, 2001. Gen. sec. Ananda Marga Yoga Soc., Monrovia, 1984-89; mem. steering com. North Washington Indsl. Park, Mpls., 1995; cons. Coun. Black Minnesotans African Resource Ctr., St. Paul, 2000-01; mem. adv. bd. race, poverty initiative, U. Minn. Law Sch., Mpls.; elder, chief organizer, facilitator Global African Village, 1998—; bd. dirs. Network Devel. Children African Descent, 2005 Fellow British Soc. Commerce. Home and Office: African Comm Network 2923 Dupont Ave N Minneapolis MN 55411-1343

AHALT, MARY JANE, management consultant; b. Elizabethville, Pa., Oct. 11, 1914; d. George Lewis and Grace Eva (Cooper) Zeigler; m. Arthur Montraville Ahalt, Mar. 29, 1935 (dec. Sept. 1958); children: Mary Jane Ahalt Barker, Arthur Montraville Monty. Student, U. Md., 1949-51, 63-65. Relief tchr., dir. Calvert Nursery Sch., Riverdale, Md., 1943-45; off-campus housemother U. Md., College Park, 1939-93, typist, 1951-58; prin. stenographer U. Md. Coll. Agr., College Park, 1958-59; sec. I, III, and IV U. Md. Coll. Edn., College Park, 1959-78; sec. to dean U. Md., College Park, 1960-76; sec., bookkeeper Entomology Soc. Am., College Park & Washington, 1951-53; cons. office practice and mgmt. College Park, 1978—. Panel mem. College Park Bus. and Profl. Women, St. Louis, 1994, College Park, 1995; cons. Project Return, Prince George's County Mental Health Assn., 1970-72. Historian archivist History of Maryland Business and Professional Women, 1983-86; co-prodr. cable TV program Women's Changing Roles: Finding a Balance, 1991. Sec. coun. Hope Luth. Ch., College Park, 1956-61, 69-74, pres. Luth. Ch. Women, 1952, 74, 87, mem. adv. bd. dist. bd., 1975-87; mem. Prince George's County Internat. Women's Task Force, 1974-76; mem. aux. Nat. Luth. Home for Aged, 1960-98; asst. leader Jr. H.S. Girl Scout troop, 1951-54; co-chair publicity com. Prince George's County Internat. Women's Yr. Task Force, 1974-76, mem. recognition of woman of month com., 1974-76; mem. by-laws com. Women's Action Coalition of Prince George's County, 1976-77; chair parish-staff rels. com. Hope Luth. Ch., 1988; judge Most Beautiful Youth, Prince George's County; coord./pres. archives com. Charlestown Cmty. Inc., 1998—. Named Prince Georgian of Yr., Prince George County Citizens, 1989, Womanof Hist. Note Prince George County Bus. and Profl. Women, 1988, Woman of Achievement in Prince George's County History, 1994; named to Women's Hall of Fame, Prince George's County, Commn. for Women, 1990; recipient Beautification award Com. for a Better Environ., College Park, 1990. Mem. College Park Bus. and Profl. Women (charter, historian, archivist 1964-93, mem. Cable TV 1983-89, 89—, pres. 1966-68, Woman of Yr. award 1976), Md. Fedn. Bus. and Profl. Women's Clubs (bd. mem. 1967—, pres. 1973-74, Md. BPW Woman of Yr. award 1976), Nat. Fedn. Bus. and Profl. Women's Clubs (nat. bd. 1973-74, founder career advancement scholar com. 1975-76) Avocations: landscaping, sewing, reading, card games, volunteering. Home: 2527 Lyons Dr Annapolis MD 21403-4212

AHANONU, CHUKWUMA SMART, education educator; s. Samuel Owowo Ahanonu Onyemaobi and Mgbakwa Adline Ahanonu, Onyenaemeribe; m. Ijeoma Ahanonu, Sept. 18, 1970; children: Chidinmma Valerie children: Okechikanma, Cecilia Nkechinyere Isabel, Nwanyidirim Ahanonu-Acord, Nwachi. BS in Spl. Edn., Psychology, Utah State U., 1979, MS in Spl. Edn., 1983, Philosophy of Spl. Edn. degree, 1986. Profl. Adminstrv. and Supr. (K-12) UT State Office of Edn., 1990. Spl. educator Granite Sch. Dist., Salt Lake City, 1979—81; asst. pastor First Presbyn. Ch., Logan, Utah, 1983—91, Preston Presbyn. Cmty. Ch., Idaho, 1983—91; spl. educator, dept. chair, soccer coach Logan City Sch. Dist., Utah, 1984—91; spl. educator, soccer coach Davis County Sch. Dist., Farmington, Utah, 1991—93; assoc. prof. Weber State U., Ogden, Utah, 1993—2000; assoc. prof., acting dept. chair Miss. Valley State U., Itta Bena, 2000—. Edn. cons. Project Success Inc., Ogden, Utah, 1993—2000, adv. bd. mem., 1994—97, exec. bd. mem., edn. rep., 1997—2000. Author: (jour. article) UT Acad. of Scis. (Best Paper Presentation, 1999), (poems) The time is now; Early Morning; Onye Oma; Ochi Gi; Legacy; story teller (African folklore) Nwa aka-adighi ukporo. Pres. Phi Delta Kappa Weber State U. Chpt., Ogden, Utah, 1998—99; edn. divsn. chair UT Acad. of Scis., Arts and Letters, Salt Lake City, 1999—2000; miss. valley state univ. student chpt. advisor Coun. for Exceptional Children, Itta Bena, Utah, 2001—03. Recipient Best Poster Session award, Assn. for Behavior Analysis, 1985, Exemplary Collaboration Cert. and Cash Award, Weber State U., 1995; grantee Faculty Vitality Grant, Hemingway, 1998—99, Evaluative Rsch. and Capacity Bldg. Grant, NSF and Miss. Dept. of Edn., 2003—. Mem.: Kappa Delta Pi (student chpt. co-advisor 2002—03), Phi Delta Kappa Internat. Fratanity (weber state chpt. sec., v.p., del. i, pres. 1994—2000, Presdl. Plaque 1999), The Coun. for Exceptional Children (student chpt. advisor 1994—2003). Methodist. Avocations: photography, reading, sewing, computers, teaching. Office: Miss Valley State U 14000 Hwy 82 W Box 7243 Itta Bena MS 38941 E-mail: cahan@mvsu.edu.

AHCHING, PETER LEIATAUA, translator; s. Leiataua Peter Ah Ching; m. Tina Renee AhChing; 1 child, Rocco Leiataua. BS, Calif. State U., Fresno, 1995; postgrad., U. Hawaii, 2003—. Sci. rsch. cert. U. Calif., San Diego, Scripps, 1994. Founder and exec. officer Samoan Med. Interpreters and Legal Translators Hawaii, Honolulu, 2002—. Author, editor, translator: Polynesian Interconnections: Samoa to Tahiti to Hawaii. Active St. Patricks Cath. Ch., Honolulu, 1998—. Scholar, Hawaii Cmty. Scholarships, 1998—. Fellow: Theta Chi (assoc.; scholarship chmn., v.p. 1992—95, Outstanding Svc. award 1995); mem.: Hawaii Fed. and State Ct. Officers (assoc.; ct. officer 2003—). Roman Catholic. Avocations: basketball, weightlifting, football, golf, surfing. Office: John A Burns School of Medicine HI East-West Rd Dole St Honolulu HI 96822 Office Phone: 808-225-1728. Personal E-mail: ahchingp@hawaii.edu.

AHDOUT, SHAHLA MARVIZI, mathematics professor; b. Tehran, Iran, Apr. 30, 1954; came to the U.S., 1977; d. Yagob and Pari (Eshraghian) Marvizi; m. Benjamin Khosrow Ahdout, July 1, 1982; 1 child, Isaac. BS, Arya Mehr U., Tehran, 1977; PhD, MIT, 1981. Postdoctoral fellow Inst. for Advanced Study, Princeton, N.J., 1981, Math. Rsch. Inst., Berkeley, Calif., 1982; asst. prof. U. Calif., Berkeley, 1983-85; assoc. prof. L.I. U., Greenvale, N.Y., 1985—. Grad. advisor math. L.I. U., 1989—. Office: Long Island U C W Post Greenvale NY 11548

AHEARN, DYLAN SHEPHARD, environmental scientist, researcher; b. NY, 1974; m. Jennifer McDowell; children: Kai Wood, Malia Wood. PhD, U. of Calif., 1999—2004. Rsch. asst. Hawaiian Volcano Obs., Kilauea, 1996—97; staff rschr. Hawaii Sci. Drilling Project, Hilo, 1999; grad. rschr. U. of Calif., 1999—2004, post doctoral rschr., 2004—; environ. cons. West Yost and Assoc., Davis, Calif., 2004—. Recipient Best Presentation, State of the Rivers Conf., 2001, Outstanding Student Presentation award, Am. Geophys. Union, 2000, CALFED, 2000. Mem.: Am. Soc. Limnology and Oceanography, N.Am. Benthological Soc., Am. Geophys. Union (assoc.). Office: Univ of Calif Davis 3119 Plant and Environ Sci Building Davis CA 95616 Office Phone: 530-752-3073. Personal E-mail: dsahearn@ucdavis.edu.

AHEARN, GERALDINE, medical/surgical nurse, writer, poet; b. Bklyn., Aug. 14, 1950; d. Louis Principessa and Patricia Donato; m. James J. Ahearn, Aug. 13, 1972 (div. June 4, 2001); children: Alicia Danielle, Katherine Ann. AA, Suffolk County CC, Selden, N.Y., 1971; diploma in nursing, Ctrl. Islip State Hosp. Sch. Nursing, 1974. LPN, N.Y., Ariz., RN N.Y., Ariz., cert. CCRN, Am. Heart Assn., EKG technician, Am. Heart Assn. RN Bayshore (N.Y.) Hosp., 1970—83, Farmingville (N.Y.) Clinic, 1986—87, Sachem Schs., Farmingville, 1988—93; hosp. CCRN cardiac care NY, 1978—83; hosp. CCRN severely disabled children, 1989—90; freelance writer Mesa, Ariz., 1993—. Instr. CPR ARC, Coram, NY, 1986—90, instr. first aid, 1986—90, instr. CPR, Bohemia, NY, 1986—90. Author: (book) Inspirations, 2001, Words to Live By, 2001, Life's Poetic Journey, 2002, (series) The Nurse in the Purse, Vol. 1, 2001, (book) From America's Most Wanted, 2005; contbr. poetry to anthologies. Leader Girl Scouts U.S., Farmingville, 1988—91;

cmty. leader Am. Online, 2001—04; catechist Farmingville Ch., 1985—87. Republican. Roman Catholic. Avocation: gardening. Home and Office: 3506 E Caballero St Mesa AZ 85213 E-mail: HrT4Angel@aol.com.

AHEARN, JAMES, columnist; b. S. Bend, Ind., Dec. 26, 1931; s. Francis T. and Loretto (Lorden) A.; m. Mary Ann Boesch, June 7, 1954; children—Michael James, Mary Elizabeth, Sarah Katharine, Margaret Ann. BA, Amherst Coll., 1953; Nieman fellow, Harvard U., 1970-71. Reporter UPI, Boston, Newark and Trenton, N.J., 1957-61; state house corr. The Record, Hackensack, N.J., 1961-65, editorial writer, then editor editorial page, 1965-77, mng. editor, 1977-87, assoc. editor, 1987-91, contbg. editor, 1993—. Served with USNR, 1953-57. Office: 150 River St Hackensack NJ 07601-7110

AHEARN, JAYNE NEWTON, liturgist, editor, writer; b. Sheboygan, Wis., Dec. 30, 1942; d. Norman Edward and Grace Daniels Newton. BS, U. of Wis., 1966; PhD, Ariz. State U., 1973; MA, U. of Notre Dame, 1991. Dir. of liturgy and ritual St. Raphael the Archangel Cath. Ch., Oshkosh, Wis., 2003—; dir. of liturgy Blessed Sacrament Cath. Ch., Midland, Mich., 1996—2003; dir. of liturgy and campus ministry St. Francis of Assisi Parish, Muncie, Ind., 1994; dir., office of worship Diocese of Townsville, Australia, 1992—94; liturgist, editor Holy Trinity Cath. Ch., Honolulu, 1985—89; asst. rsch. prof. U. of Hawaii, Honolulu, 1976—84. Internat. peer rev. com. mem. Pastoral Liturgy, Freemantle, Western Australia, Australia, 2003—, assoc. editor, 1991—2003. Contbr. book. Fellow Genetics Rsch. Tng. grant, NIH, 1967-1970; Hawaiian Drosophila Project Post-doctoral fellow, NSF, 1972-1976. Mem.: Nat. Pastoral Life Ctr., Nat. Assn. of Pastoral Musicians, Liturgy Network of the Notre Dame Ctr. for Liturgy, Liturgical Conf., Fedn. of Diocesan Liturgical Commns., Australian Acad. of Liturgy, NY Acad. of Scis. (life), Phi Beta Kappa. Avocations: photography, gardening. Office: St Raphael Catholic Ch 830 South Westhaven Dr Oshkosh WI 54904 Office Phone: 920-233-8044.

AHEARN, JOSEPH AUGUST, military officer, civil engineer; b. Galesburg, Ill., Sept. 5, 1936; s. Joseph Aloysius and Mary Ethel (Rinella) A.; m. Nona Maria Fallon, Nov. 9, 1963; children: Stacia C., Gianna R., Trienel K., Joseph F. BSCE, Notre Dame U., 1958; MS in Engring., Syracuse U., 1967; postgrad., Harvard U., 1988. Registered profl. engr., Mass. Commd. 2d lt. USAF, 1958, advanced through grades to maj. gen., 1988; dep. comdr., then comdr. 554th Red Horse Squadron, Cam Rhan Bay Air Base, Vietnam, 1970-71; squadron comdr., base civil engr. Craig AFB, Ala., 1971-74; insp. gen., civil engring. staff officer Hdqrs. Air Tng. Command, Randolph AFB, Tex., 1974-76; chief housing div. Directorate Engring. and Svcs., DCS/Logistics and Engring., Hdqrs. USAF, Washington, 1976-78; student Indsl. Coll. Armed Forces, Ft. Leslie J. McNair, D.C., 1978-79; chief programs div. Directorate Engring. and Svcs., DCS/Logistics and Engring., Hdqrs. USAF, 1979-83; dep. chief of staff for engring. and svcs. Hdqrs. USAF Europe, Ramstein Air Base, Fed. Republic Germany, 1983-86; dep. dir. engring. and svcs. DCS/Logistics and Engring., Hdqrs. USAF, Washington, 1986-89; civil engr. Hdqrs. USAF, Washington, 1989—92; sr. v.p., regional mgr. Mid-Atlantic region CH2M Hill Inc., 1994, pres. transp. bus. group; vice chmn. CH2M Hill Cos. Chmn. bd. dirs. Air Force Commissary Svc., 1988-91; bd. dirs. Air Force Exch. Svc., 1985-91; mem. Air Force Bd., Air Force Coun., 1988-91, bd. advisors Def. Commissary Agy., 1991, environ. protection com. Hdqrs. USAF, 1990-91. Author numerous publs., brochures and policy documents on mil. civil engring. Centurion Mil. Archdiocese Cath. Ch. Decorated D.S.M., Legion of Merit, Bronze Star, Def. Meritorious Svc. medal, Meritorious Svc. medal with 3 oak leaf clusters; Cross of Honor in Gold (Fed. Republic Germany); Honor medal (Republic of Vietnam); recipient Engring. Honor award U. Notre Dame, 1990. Mem. NAE (bldg. futures coun.), NSPE, ASCE (Pres. award 1999), AIA (hon.), Soc. Am. Mil. Engrs. (nat. pres. 1991, bd. dirs. 1991—), Civil Engring. Rsch. Found. (vice chmn. bd. dirs. 1990-91), Profl. Housing Mgmt. Assn., Am. Pub. Works Assn., Army Navy Country Club, Air Force Order of Sword, Tau Beta Pi. Avocations: sports, theater, museums, family activities. Home: 5620 S Beech Cir Littleton CO 80121-3913 Office: CH2M Hill Cos 9191 S Jamaica St Englewood CO 80112 *When we set out to contribute to mankind's quest for a better world, the enormity of people's needs and the enormity of opportunity become at once overwhelming and compelling. I know of nothing more professionally rewarding that to act to improve the lot of mankind, one small step at a time.*

AHEARN, WILLIAM BARRY, English language educator; b. Montague, Mass., Jan. 29, 1950; s. William Gorey and Frances Barbara (Keller) A.; m. Pamela Lander Gray, Dec. 17, 1983; 1 child, Thomas Gray. BA, Trinity Coll., Hartford, Conn., 1973; MA, Johns Hopkins U., 1975, PhD, 1978. Asst. prof. English Tulane U., New Orleans, 1982-86, assoc. prof., 1986-98, prof., 1998—. Author: Zukofsky's A, 1983, William Carlos Williams and Alterity, 1994; editor: Pound/Zukofsky Letters, 1987, Pound/Cummings Letters, 1996, The correspondence of William Carlos Williams and Louis Zukofsky, 2003. Am. Coun. Learned Socs. grantee, 1985. Mem. MLA, William Carlos Williams Soc. Home: 2021 Pine St New Orleans LA 70118-5456 Office: Tulane U Dept English 6823 Saint Charles Ave New Orleans LA 70118-5665

AHEARNE, JOHN FRANCIS, science foundation director, researcher; b. New Britain, Conn., June 14, 1934; s. Daniel Paul and Balbena Marian (Baloski) A.; m. Barbara Helen Drezek, June 19, 1956; children: Thomas, Paul, Mary Ann, Robert, Patricia. B of Engring. Physics, Cornell U., 1957, MS in Physics, 1958; MA, Princeton U., 1963, PhD, 1966. Nuc. weapons analyst USAF, 1959-61; assoc. prof. physics USAF Acad., 1964-69; from analyst to dir. tactical air Office Asst. Sec. Def. for Systems Analysis, 1969-72; dep. asst. sec. def. for gen. purpose programs, 1972-74; prin. dep. sec. def. manpower and res. affairs, 1974-76; staff White House Energy Office, 1977; dep. asst. sec. Dept. Energy, 1978; commr. U.S. Nuc. Regulatory Commn., 1978-83, chmn., 1980-81; mgmt. cons. Comptr. Gen of U.S., 1983-84; v.p., sr. fellow Resources for the Future, 1984-89; exec. dir. Sigma Xi, The Sci. Rsch. Soc., Research Triangle Park, NC, 1989-96; dir. Sigma Xi Ctr., Research Triangle Park, 1995-99; dir. ethics program Sigma Xi, Research Triangle Park, 1999—; lectr. pub. policy Duke U., Durham, NC, 1995—. Adj. fellow Resources for Future, 1992—; adj. prof. civil and environ. engring. Duke U., 1996-2002; adj. prof. U. Colo., 1966-69; adj. fellow Resources for the Future, 1992—; vice-chmn. Nat. Rsch. Coun. Bd. on Radioactive Waste Mgmt., 1997-99, chmn., 2000—04; chmn. adv. com. on nuc. facility safety U.S. Dept. Energy, 1988-91, environ. mgmt. adv. bd., 1994-2002, co-chmn. adv. com. on external regulation, 1995-96, nuc. energy rsch. adv. com., 1998—, vice chmn., 2002—; chmn. risk perception and comm. com. NAS, 1987-89, chmn. future nuc. power com., 1990-93, com. on tech. bases for Yucca Mountain Stds., 1993-96, com. on risk characterization, 1994-97, dual use techs. and export controls com., electrometallurg. tech. com., co-chmn. burning plasma experiment assessment com., 2002-04, co-chmn. forum on the environment, 1995-97, vice-chmn. com. risk assessment and mgmt. marine sys., 1996-98, com. on battlefield radiation exposure, 1996-99, chmn. com. to rev. rsch. under EPACT, 1997-99, co-chmn. com. on end points of U.S. and Russian nuc. waste, 2001—03, com. on indigenization of programs to prevent leakage, jt. acad. com. on counterterrorism challenges for Russia and the US, 2002—, chmn. com. on earth penetrator nuc. weapons, 2004-; chair com. Opportunities US-Russian Coop. Combating Radiological Terrorism, 2004-; mem. pres.'s coun. for nat. labs. U. Calif., 1992—; vice-chmn. U.S. Commn. for IIASA, 1992-93, chmn., 1994-98; adv. com. Princeton Plasma Physics Nat. Lab., 1993-98; co-chmn. panel on opportunities in plasma sci. tech. NAS, 1992-96, reactor panel for disposition of weapons plutonium, 1992-96; bd. dirs. Wis. Energy Corp.; lectr. Colo. Coll., 1966-69; pres. com. adv. S&T Energy R&D panel, 1997-98; USGAO exec. coun. Info. Mgmt. and Tech., 1997-2004; mem. adv. coun. Jet Propulsion Lab., 2004—. Bd. dirs. Woodstock Theol. Ctr., chmn., 1980-85. Gen. Electric Coffin fellow, 1957-58; recipient Dept. Def. Disting. Civilian Svc. medal and bronze palm, Sec. Def. Meritorious Svc. medal; named Boss of Year D.C. chpt. Nat. Secs. Assn., 1976. Fellow AAAS, Am. Phys. Soc. (chmn. forum on physics and soc. 1996-97, chair panel on pub. affairs 2003—04), Am. Acad. Arts and Scis., Soc. Risk Analysis; mem. NAE, Nat. Acads. (nat. assoc.), Nat. Coun. for Radiation Protection and Measurement, Am. Nuc. Soc., Soc. for Risk Analysis (past pres.), Sigma Xi. Democrat. Roman Catholic. Office Phone: 919-547-5213. Business E-Mail: ahearne@sigmaxi.org.

AHERIN, DARREL WILLIAM, lawyer; b. Colfax, Wash., July 11, 1946; s. Don Lewis and Leona Margaret (Edwards) A.; m. Freda Jean Kieffer, June 27, 1968 (dec.); children: Daniel Winston, Dustin Wynne; m. Michelle Rae Messley, June 26, 1982; children: Alex William. BA, Lewis Clark State Coll., 1969; JD, U. Idaho, 1973. Pvt. practice, Lewiston, Idaho, 1973—; ptnr. Aherin, Rice & Anegon (formerly Aherin, Rice & Brown), Lewiston, 1973—. Active Planning & Zoning Com., Genesee, Idaho, 1996—. Mem. ATLA (gov. 1996—), Idaho Trial Lawyers Assn. (sec., treas., pres.), Western Trial Lawyers (gov. 1995—), Lewis Clark State Coll. Alumni (pres.). Home: PO Box 337 Genesee ID 83832-0337 Office: Aherin Rice & Anegon 1212 Idaho St Lewiston ID 83501-1941

AHERN, JOHN JAMES, software company executive; b. Bklyn., June 12, 1940; s. John and Bertha Elizabeth (Lehman) A.; m. Margaret Patrician Swift, July 15, 1961; children: Elizabeth, Deirdre. Asst. mgr. quality control Ramcor Inc., Huntington, N.Y., 1965-67; pvt. cons. Huntington, N.Y., 1967-69; field engr. Harris Corp., Syosset, N.Y., 1969-75, Litton Data Systems, Van Nuys, Calif., 1975-76; product support mgr. Millenium Info. Systems, Sunnyvale, Calif., 1976-77; mgr. engr. Argosystems, Inc., Sunnyvale, Calif., 1977-79; dir. quality assurance Support Sys. Assocs., Inc., Hauppauge, N.Y., 1979-92; pres., CEO Jadal Techs., Ltd., Bohemia, N.Y., 1992—. Author (copywright) Carat, 1988, Info-Trak, 1990, One-to-One, 1992. With USAF, 1957-65. Mem. Am. Soc. Quality Control. Avocations: golf, bowling, gardening, cooking. Home: 10 Wilson Commons Yaphank NY 11980-2041

AHERN, JOHN W., pharmacist; s. John T. and Ruth A. Ahern; m. Nancy I. Diehl, Nov. 6, 1999; children: Megan E. children: Caleb D. BS in Pharmacy, U. R.I., 1994; PharmD, SUNY, Buffalo, 1996. Cert. pharmacotherapy with added qualifications in infectious diseases Bd. Pharm. Specialties, 1997. Pharmacy intern Cath. Med. Ctr., Manchester, 1989—94; tchg. asst. SUNY at Buffalo, Amherst, NY, 1994—95; pharmacy resident Millard Fillmore Hosp., Buffalo, 1996—97; clin. coord. Kent Gen. Hosp., Dover, Del., 1997—98; pharmacist clinician infectious disease Fletcher Allen Health Care, Burlington, Vt., 1998—. Contbr. chapters to books, articles to profl. jours. Mem.: Am. Coll. Clin. Pharmacy, Soc. Infectious Diseases Pharmacists (assoc.). Achievements include research in dosing of cefazolin in hemodialysis patients. Office: Fletcher Allen Health Care 111 Colchester Ave Burlington VT 05401 E-mail: john.ahern@vtmednet.org.

AHERN, JOSEPH JAMES, JR., television station executive; b. Phila., June 9, 1945; s. Joseph James Ahern Sr. and Frances E. Murray; m. Lynn Barbara Pettit, Apr. 5, 1969; 1 child, Meredith Lynn. Student, St. Joseph's U., Phila., 1964-68. Salesman Phila. Evening Bull., 1968-70, Sta. WDVR-FM, Phila., 1970-73, Sta. WPVI-TV, Phila., 1973-75; sales mgr. Sta. WLS-TV, Chgo., 1975-77, sta. mgr., 1981-85, v.p., gen. mgr., 1985-86, pres., gen. mgr., 1986—97; nat. sales mgr. spot sales ABC-TV, Detroit, 1977-78; gen. sales mgr. Sta. WABC-TV, N.Y.C., 1978-81; pres., gen. mgr. KGO-TV, San Francisco, 1998—2002, WBBM-TV, Chgo., 2002—. Bd. dirs., gen. chmn. United Cerebral Palsy, Chgo., 1981-86; bd. dirs., sec. Spl. Children's Charities, Chgo., 1983-86; bd. dirs., exec. bd. State St. Council, Chgo., 1985-86; bd. dirs., v.p. Starlight Found., Chgo., 1985-86; bd. dirs. library bd. Northwestern U., Evanston, Ill., 1985-86; bd. dirs. Childrens Meml. Found., 1987. Named Man of Yr., WE-TIP, Inc., 1984, Gen. Mgr. of Yr., Pub. Affairs Dirs. Chgo., 1985, Media Man of yr., 1986; recipient One Ch. One Child award Dept. Children and Family Services, Chgo., 1986, Spirit of Life award City of Hope, Distng. Vol. award Chgo. Pub Schs., citation U.S. Dept. Health and Human Services Regional, 1987. Mem. Acad. TV Arts and Scis. (bd. dirs. Chgo. chpt. 1982-86), Ill. Film Inst., Chgo. Urban League (bus. adv. council 1986). Clubs: Broadcast Ad, East Bank (Chgo.). Republican. Presbyterian. Avocations: running, weightlifting, wine. Office: CBS 2 Chicago 630 N McClurg Court Chicago IL 60611

AHERN, MICHAEL JAMES, lawyer; b. Red Wing, Minn., Aug. 20, 1951; s. Andrew Alyosious and Cecelia Mame (Ackerman) A.; m. Sharon Marie Kaufman, June 21, 1975; children: Ryan Michael, Emily Treise. BA, U. Minn., 1973; JD, William Mitchell Coll. Law, 1977. Bar: Minn. 1977, U.S. Dist. Ct. Minn. 1977, U.S. Ct. Appeals (8th cir.) 1992. Law clk. Van Valkenburg, Comaford, Moss, Fassett, Flaherty & Clarkson, Mpls., 1976-77; atty. Moss & Barnett, P.A., Mpls., 1977-80, shareholder, atty., 1980-98, also bd. dirs.; ptnr., co-chmn., legis. practice group Dorsey & Whitney LLP, Mpls., 1999—. Contbr. chpt. to book Minnesota Administrative Procedure. Bd. dirs., chmn. Group Health Plan, Inc., St. Paul, 1978-88; vice chmn. Midwest Assurance Co., Inc., St. Paul, 1990-93; bd. dirs. Group Health Inc. Adminstrs. and Medcenters Managed Care Inc., 1993-95. Mem. ABA, Minn. State Bar Assn. (exec. com. 1980-93, chair adminstrv. law sect. 1991-92), Hennepin County Bar Assn. (chair environ. law sect. 1986-87), Minn. Govtl. Rels. Coun. (pres. 1989). Office: Dorsey & Whitney LLP 50 S Sixth St Minneapolis MN 55402-1498 Office Phone: 612-340-2881. Office Fax: 612-340-2868. Business E-Mail: ahern.michael@dorsey.com.

AHLBERG, JAMES GEORGE, lawyer; b. Brockton, Mass., Jan. 14, 1951; s. G. Harold and Ruth C. (Apland) A.; m. I. Elaine Bloom, June 24, 1972; children: Matthew, Erik. BA, North Park Coll., 1974; JD, U. Ill., 1978. Bar: Ill. 1978, U.S. Dist. Ct. (no. dist.) Ill. 1979, (central dist.) Ill. 1988. Ptnr. Fearer, Nye, Ahlberg & Chadwick, Rochelle and Oregon, Ill., 1978—. Bd. dirs. Prairie State Legal Svcs., 1979-82, sec. bd., 1981-82 Mem. Ill. Bar Assn. Evangelical. Home: PO Box 82 Rochelle IL 61068-0082 Office: Fearer Nye Ahlberg & Chadwick 420 4th Ave Rochelle IL 61068-1640

AHLEM, LLOYD HAROLD, psychologist; b. Moose Lake, Minn., Nov. 7, 1929; s. Harold Edward and Agnes (Carlson) A.; m. Anne T. Jensen, Dec. 29, 1952; children: Ted, Dan, Mary Jo, Carol, Aileen. AA, North Park Coll., 1948; AB, San Jose State Coll., 1952, MA, 1955; Ed.D., U. So. Calif., 1962. Tchr. retarded children Fresno County (Calif.) Pub. Schs., 1953-54; psychologist Baldwin Park (Calif.) Sch. Dist., 1955-62; prof. psychology Calif. State U., Stanislaus (formerly Stanislaus State Coll.), Turlock, Calif., 1962-70; pres. North Park U., Chgo., 1970-79, dir., 1966-70; exec. dir. Covenant Village Retirement Center, Turlock, 1979-89; dir. spl. projects Covenant Retirement Communities, Chgo., 1989-93; dir. Emanuel Med. Ctr., Turlock, Calif., 1984-99, Merced Mut. Ins. Co., Atwater, Calif., 1993—2005; chmn. Capital Corp. of West, Merced, Calif., 1995—2002; ret. Author: Do I Have To Be Me, 1974, How to Cope: Managing Change, Crisis and Conflict, 1978, Help for the Families of the Mentally Ill, 1983, Living and Growing in Later Years, 1992; columnist Covenant Companion, 1972-90. Decorated comdr. Order of Polar Star Sweden. Mem. Assn. Colls. Ill. (vice chmn. 1975-79) Mem. Covenant Ch. Club: Rotary (Paul Harris fellow 1987). Home: 2125 N Olive C-11 Turlock CA 95382

AHLERS, GLEN-PETER, SR., law library director, educator, consultant; b. N.Y.C., Mar. 15, 1955; s. LeGrande Jacob and Joan (Stoltz) A.; m. Sondra Sue Wadley, May 17, 1987; children: Glen-Peter II, Sandia Marie, Gavin Patrick, Sierra Le Ann Rose, Stacia Camille, Sienna Catherine. BS, U. N.Mex., Albuquerque, 1979; MA, U. of South Fla., 1983; JD, Washburn U., 1987. Bar: Kans. 1987, U.S. Dist. Ct. Kans. 1987, U.S. Ct. Mil. Appeals 1988, D.C. 1990. Reference asst. U. N.Mex. Sch. Law, Albuquerque, 1979-83; asst. dir. Washburn Sch. Law Libr., Topeka, 1983-87; assoc. libr. dir. Wake Forest U., Winston-Salem, N.C., 1987-90; libr. dir., assoc. prof. D.C. Sch. Law, Washington, 1990-92, U. Ark., Fayetteville, 1992-2000, prof., 2001—02; assoc. dean info. services Barry U. Dwayne O. Andreas Sch. of Law, Orlando, Fla. Computer and libr. cons. Ctr. for R&D in Law-Related Edn., Winston-Salem, 1987-90; adj. prof. Sch. of Law Wake Forest U., Winston-Salem, N.C., 1987-90; Mid-Am. Law Sch. Libr. Consortium, 1992-2002, bd. dirs. Consortium of Southeastern Law Librs., 1988-90, pres. 2000-02. Author: History of Law School Libraries in the United States, 2002, Election Laws of the United States, 1995; co-author: Notary Law and Practice, 1997; editor The Maall Newsletter, 1984-87, The Scrivener, 1992—2004; tech. editor Washburn Law Jour., 1985-86; contbr. articles to profl. jours. Mediator N.C. Neighborhood Justice Ctr., Winston-Salem, 1989-90. Mem. ABA, ALA, Fla. Bar Assn., Am. Assn. Law Librs., Southwestern Assn. Law Librs. (pres. 1995-97), Southeastern Assn. of Law Librs., Mid Am. Assn. Law Librs. (pres. 1999-2000), Scribes (exec. dir. 1997—), Phi Kappa Phi, Kappa Delta Pi, Beta Phi Mu. Avocation: writing. Home: 1069 Winding Waters Cir Winter Springs FL 32708-6326 Office: Barry U Dwayne O Andreas Sch of Law 6441 E Colonial Dr Orlando FL 32807-3650 Office Phone: 321-206-5701. Business E-Mail: gahlers@mail.barry.edu.

AHLERS, GUENTER, physicist, researcher; b. Bremen, Germany, Mar. 28, 1934; came to U.S., 1951; s. William Carl and Ida Pauline (Cornelson) A.; m. June Bly, Aug. 24, 1964 BS in Chemistry, U. Calif., Riverside, 1959; PhD in Physical Chemistry, U. Calif., Berkeley, 1963. Mem. tech. staff Bell Labs., Murray Hill, NJ, 1963—78; prof. physics U. Calif., Santa Barbara, 1979—. Chair fundamental physics discipline working group NASA, 1998—99. Contbr. numerous articles to profl. jours. Recipient Tenth Fritz London Memorial award, 1978, Alexander von Humboldt Senior U.S. Scientist award, 1989—90. Fellow AAAS, Am. Phys. Soc., Am. Acad. Arts & Sci.; mem. NAS. Home: 523 Carriage Hill Ct Santa Barbara CA 93110-2022 Office: U Calif Dept Physics Santa Barbara CA 93106 Personal E-mail: guenter@stc.ucsb.edu.

AHLERS, LINDA L., retail executive; BA, U. Wisc. Buyer, Target Stores Dayton Hudson Corp., 1977-83, divsn. mdse. mgr., Target Stores, 1983-85, dir. mdse. planning and control, 1985-88, v.p. mdse. planning and control, 1988, sr. v.p. Target Stores, 1988-95, exec. v.p. merchandising, dept. store divsn., 1995-96; pres., dept. store divsn. Dayton Hudson Corp. (now Marshall Field's), 1996—; bd. dirs. Dayton Hudson Corp., 1997—. Dir. Guthrie Theatre; mem. Com. of 200, Detroit Renaissance Bd., Minn. Women's Econ. Roundtable. Office: Target Corp 1000 Nicollet Mall Minneapolis MN 55403-2467

AHLERS, ROLF WILLI, philosopher, theologian; b. Hamburg, Germany, June 22, 1936; arrived in US, 1966; s. Arthur W. and Ilse F. (Freund) A.; m. Luise Kuse, July 1965; children: Christoph Matthias, Marcus Andreas. BA, Drew U., 1958; MDiv, Princeton Theol. Sem., 1961; Dr. Theol., U. Hamburg, 1966. Wissenschaftlicher Assoc. Seminar Für Systematische Theologie und Sozialethik, U. Hamburg, Germany, 1962-66; asst. prof. religion Ill. Coll., Jacksonville, 1966-72; Reynolds prof. philosophy and religion Russell Sage Coll., Troy, 1973—. Author: The Barmen Declaration of 1934: Archeology of a Confessional Text, 1986, The Community of Freedom: Karl Barth and Presuppositionless Theology, 1989; author, editor: System and Context/System und Kontext: Early Romantic and Early Idealistic Constellations, New Athenaeum/Neues Athenaeum, vol. VII, 2004. NEH grantee, 1972-73; Soc. for Health and Human Values grantee, 1975. Mem.: Hegel Soc. Am., Am. Acad. Religion, Am. Philos. Soc, Internationale Hegel Vereinigung, Internationale Fichte Gesellschaft, Fichte Soc. N.Am. Presbyterian. Home: 3 Academy Rd Albany NY 12208-3102 Office: Russell Sage Coll Philosophy Dept Troy NY 12180 Office Phone: 518-244-2322. *The cunning of history, pure grace and keen sense of self made me the person who I am.*

AHLSTROM, RONALD GUSTIN, artist; b. Chgo., Jan. 17, 1922; s. Frederick Karl and Gertrude (Gustin) A.; m. Nancy Costa; 1 son, Arn Gustin. Ed., U. Chgo., Art Inst. Chgo.; B.F.A., 1955. Asst. dir. McCormick Pl. Gallery, 1960-63; dir. Tacoma Art Mus., 1963—. One-man shows include Barat Coll., Lake Forest, Ill., 1958, Blackhawk Restaurant, Chgo., 1961, collages at Main St. Galleries, Chgo., 1969, J. Faulkner Galleries, Chgo., 1970, 71, Spiesberger Gallery, Skokie, Ill., 1975, Zriny-Hayes Gallery, Chgo., 1978; group shows include Chgo. and vicinity ann., Art Inst. Chgo., 1955, 56, 59, 61, 62, 64, other shows at Art Inst., 1957, 58, Inst. Jewish Studies, 1956, 1020 Art Ctr., 1957, Navy Pier, 1957, 58, Old Town Art Center, 1959, B.C. Holland Gallery, 1961, McCormick Pl. Art Gallery, 1961, 62, 63, Hyde Park Art Ctr., 1963, Studio 22, 1970, all Chgo., C. McNider Mus., Mason City, Iowa, 1971, Touchstone Gallery, N.Y.C., 1973; exhibited in Chgo. Artists European Tour Exhibit, USIA, 1957-59, Festival of Fine Arts, Lake Forest, 1958, Soc. of Four Arts Exhibit, West Palm Beach, Fla., 1959, E. Mich. Coll. at Ypsilanti, 1960, Corcoran Gallery Art, Washington, 1961, Tacoma Art Mus., 1963, 5 Abstractionists, Main St. Galleries, 1968; represented in permanent collections Tacoma Art Mus., Barat Coll. Gallery, Gutenberg Mus., Mainz, Germany, Art Inst. Chgo., Blue Cross, Chgo., Atlantic-Richfield, Chgo., Ill. Bell Telephone, Container Corp. Am., Chgo., also in numerous pvt. collections; work represented in book Collage and Foundation Art (Meilach and Ten Hoor), 1964, Collage and Assemblage, Trend and Techniques (Meilach and Ten Hoor), 1973. Served with U.S. Army, 1942-46. Recipient Clyde M. Carr prize for painting, 1955, Alumni of Sch. Art Inst. prize, 1959, Jane Broadus Clark prize, 1958; Singer & Sons prize, Navy Pier; Abel Fagan prize Festival Fine Arts, Lake Forest, 1958; Ford Found. purchase prize Seattle Art Mus., 1964 Achievements include being represented in The Art of Collage (Gerald F. Brommer Davis) 1978, Collage and Found Art, MEilach & Tenhoor, Collage and Assemblage, Meilach & Tenhoor. Home: 121 W Park Dr Lombard IL 60148-3320 E-mail: nahlstrom@msn.com.

AHMAD, AHMAD ATIF, historian, educator; b. Cairo, Aug. 24, 1971; s. Atif Ahmad Abul-Himal and Asmaa al-Shafi'i Abul-Aynayn; m. Elizabeth Lee-Hood. BA, Cairo U., 1992, MA, 1997; PhD, Harvard U., 2005. Editor, Islamic legal history Ency. of Islamic Scis., Safeer Publs., Cairo, 1991—97; lectr. Cairo U., Tufts U., Medford, Mass., 2004—05; instr. Harvard U., Cambridge, MA, Mass., 1999—2005; asst. prof. Islamics Macalester Coll., St. Paul, 2005—. Author: (book) Appellate System in Islamic Law, Arabic, Cairo, 1997; contbr. articles to profl. jours. Mem.: Am. Hist. Assn. Home: 1600 Grand Ave Saint Paul MN 55105 Office: Harvard Univ 1430 Mass Ave Cambridge MA 02138

AHMAD, IBRAHIM A., statistics educator; BS in Econometrics, U. Cairo, 1965; MS, Fla. State U., 1970, PhD, 1973. Instr. dept. statistics U. Cairo, 1965-68; grad. asst. dept. statistics Fla. State U., 1968-72; statistical cons. auditor gen. office State of Fla., 1972-75; from asst. to assoc. prof. dept. math. and statistics McMaster U., 1975-80; assoc. prof. dept. math. scis. U. Memphis, 1978-80; assoc. prof. dept. maths. U. Md., 1980-83; coord. statistics program, 1980-83; prof. dept. maths. U. S. Fla., 1983-87; coord. statistics program, 1983-87; prof. dept. statistics No. Ill. U., 1987—, dir. divsn. statistics, 1987-94. Asst. prof. Meml. U. Newfoundland, 1975-76; assoc. prof. U. Petroleum and Minerals, Dhahran, Saudi Arabia, 1980-81; prof. King Saud U., Saudi Arabi, spring, 1985; vis. scientist Armamatn Lab. Eglin AFB, summer, 1988; vis. disting. prof. U. Brasilia (Brazil), spring, 1996; rsch. Fulbright prof. Damascus (Syria) U., 1994-95; organizer 8th Annual Midwest Conf. on Statistical Scis., 1996; referee grante agys.; invited spkr. in field; supr. PhD student; cons. in field. Founding editor: Jour. Non Parametric Statistics; internat. corr. editor: Saudi Arabia's Jour. Mathematical Scis.; reviewer mathematical revs., methods abstracts; mem. editl. bd. Arab Jour. Scientific Rsch.; referee econometric jours. Disting. vis. scholar dept. econs. U. We. Ont., 1987, 89; vis. scholar dept. econ. London Sch. Econs. and Polit. Scis., 1989, dept. maths. and statistics U. Brasilia, 1996, 97; rsch. grantee Meml. U., 1975, McMaster U., 1976, 77, 78, Memphis State U., 1979, U. Md., 1983, USF, 1984, 86, King Saud U., 1985, Natural Sci. and Engring. Coun., 1975-80, Army, 1979-81, AFOSR, 1988, 89, Fulbright, 1994-95, NSF Travel Grant, 1991, indsl. grantee Caterpillar Internat., 1989, G.D. Searle Pharms., 1990-92, Hauser-Ross Eye Inst., 1992. Fellow Royal Statistical Soc.; mem. Am. Statistical Assn., Internat. Statistical Inst., Inst. Mathematical Statistics, Arabian Mathematical Soc. (bd. dirs.), Malaysian Acad. Scis. (hon., adv. editor Jour. Maths. and Computer Scis.), Statistical Soc. Can., Mathematical Assn. Am. Achievements include research in nonparametric statistics, density estimation and robust procedures, reliability and lifetesting in probabilistic models, inference, applied probability, renewal theory and operation research. Office: No Ill U Divsn Statistics Dekalb IL 60115 Home: 4345 Steed Ter Winter Park FL 32792-7630

AHMAD, IRSHAD, physicist, nuclear scientist; b. Azamgarh, India, Nov. 1, 1939; came to U.S., 1962; s. Aquil and Tahira (Khatoon) A.; m. Fauzia Mazhar, Jan. 23, 1969; children: Fahim, Mateen, Sabina. MS, U. Pacific, 1965; PhD, U. Calif., Berkeley, 1966. Postdoctoral fellow Lawrence Berkeley (Calif.) Lab., 1966, Argonne (Ill.) Nat. Lab., 1966-68, asst. chemist, 1968-71, chemist, 1971-85, physicist, 1985—. Mem. Am. Phys. Soc., Am. Chem. Soc., Sigma Xi. Office: Argonne Nat Lab D 203 9700 Cass Ave Argonne IL 60439-4803

AHMAD, JAMEEL, civil engineer, researcher, educator; b. Lahore, Punjab, Pakistan, May 22, 1941; came to U.S. 1962; s. Naseer and Iftikhar (Dean) Bakhsh; m. Rosalba Quiroz, March 31, 1983; 1 child, Monica. BSc, Punjab U., Lahore, 1962; MS, U. Hawaii, 1964; PhD, U. Pa., 1967. East-west ctr. fellow U. Hawaii, Honolulu, 1962-65; rsch. fellow U. Pa., Phila., 1965-67; asst. prof. Widener U., Chester, Pa., 1967-68, Cooper Union, N.Y.C., 1968-71, assoc. prof., 1971-80, prof. civil engring., 1979—, chmn. civil engring., 1980—; dir. rsch. Cooper Union Rsch. Found., N.Y.C., 1983—; sr. advisor Verdant Power LLC, Arlington, Va., 2003—. Dir. High Techs., Inc., N.Y.C., 1986—; bd. dirs. Consortium of N.Y.C. Engring. Colls. and Univs., Mayor's Office of Constrn., 1994—, fellow Rsch. Inst. for the Study of Man, 2002. V.p. Vilmanor Cmty. Assn., N.Y.C., 1992, West Side Cmty. Assn., N.Y.C., 1976. Mem. ASCE (Outstanding Svc. award 1985), ASME, Am. Soc. Engring. Edn., Am. Inst. Steel Constrn., Structural Engring. Inst., Pakistan League Am. (bd. dirs., Abdus Salam medal disting. rsch. engring. scis. 1993), Chi Epsilon, Phi Happa Phi. Achievements include patents for fleximech reinforcement system, asphalt reinforcement system. Office: Cooper Union Coll 51 Astor Pl New York NY 10003-7132 Office Phone: 212-353-4294. E-mail: ahmad@cooper.edu. *My philosophy of life is best exemplified by the great 19th century industrialist/philanthropist Peter Cooper - concentrate on giving something back to society. As the founder of the only tuition-free private college in America, his legacyhas benefited generations of young people since 1849.*

AHMAD, JOSEPH YOUSUF, lawyer; b. Bloomington, Ind., Sept. 13, 1962; BA with honors, Lawrence U., 1984; JD, U. Mich., 1987. Bar: Tex.; bd. cert. Tex. Bd. Legal Splization, 1996. Law clerk, U.S. Dist. Ct. (we. dist.) Mich. Hon. Benjamin F. Gibson, Mich., 1987-89; assoc. Miller, Bristow & Brown, Houston, 1989-90, Crain, Caton & James, Houston, 1990-93; shareholder Ahmad Zavitsanos & Anaipakos, PC, Houston, 1993—. Mem. ATLA, ABA (litig., labor and employment secs.), Houston Bar Assn., Tex. Bar Assn. (labor, litig. secs.), Nat. Employment Lawyers Assn. Office: Ahmad Zavitsanos & Anaipakos PC 1221 Mckinney St Ste 3460 Houston TX 77010-2009 Office Phone: 713-655-1101.

AHMAD, MIRZA MUZAFFAR, economic advisor; b. Qadian, India, Feb. 28, 1913; came to U.S., 1972; d. Mirza and Sarwar (Sultana) Bashir; m. Amatul Q. Ahmad, May 8, 1939; 1 child, Zahir Ahmad. BA, Gov. Coll., Lahore, India, 1933; BA wtih honors, London U., 1935; postgrad. law, Middle Temple, London, 1935; postgrad., Corpus Christie Coll., Oxford, London, 1938. Several govt. positions, India, 1939-47; additional chief sec. West Pakistan Province, 1959-62; sec. commerce Govt. of Pakistan, 1962, sec. fin., 1963-66, fed. minister, fin. minister planning commn., 1966—70, econ. adviser, fin. adviser to the pres., 1970-71, adviser for fgn. loans and consortium, 1971-72; exec. dir. bd. World Bank, 1972-74; dep. exec. sec., staff mem., con. Joint Ministerial Com. of Bd. Govs. World Bank and IMF, 1974-93. Mem. Pakistan del. to Commonwealth Prime Ministers' Conf., 1962, 64; negotiator with World Bank for Indus Basin Devel. Fund, 1964; leader Pakistan del. to 8th consortium meeting, Washington, 1966, Pakistan del. to meetings of Econ. Coun. of Indonesia-Pakistan Econ. and Cultural Cooperation, 1966-69, Pakistan del to ministerial meetings Colombo Plan Conf., Geneva, 1987, Pakistan del. to People's Republic of China, 1967; chmn. ministerial meetings 17th Colombo Plan Conf., 1966. Amir/pres. Ahmadiya Movement in Islam, Inc. Recipient Hilal Quaid Azam award, Sitari Pakistan award Pres. of Pakistan. Moslem. Home: 9920 New London Dr Potomac MD 20854-4845 Office: Ahmadiya Movement in Islam Baitur Rahman 15000 Good Hope Rd Silver Spring MD 20905-4120 Office Phone: 703-287-0095. E-mail: zmahmad@aol.com.

AHMAD, MOGHISUDDIN, chemist, researcher; b. Dhanbad, India, July 1, 1950; arrived in U.S., 1979; s. Moinuddin Ahmad and Zaibun Nesa; m. Athar Bano Hussain, Mar. 23, 1985; children: Waseem, Raees. BS with honors, Aligarh (India) Muslim U., 1971, MS, 1973, MPhil., 1975, PhD, 1978. Postdoctoral fellow Aligarh Muslim U., 1978-79; rsch. assoc. dept. biochemistry and biophysics Tex. A&M U., College Station, 1979-81; rsch. assoc. dept. food sci. Oregon State U., Corvallis, 1981-88; chemist Lipids dept. Sigma Chem. Co., St. Louis, 1988—95, chemist II bio-organics dept., 1995—2001; assoc. dir. lipid chemistry NeoPharm, Inc. R&D, Waukegan, Ill., 2001—02, dir. lipid chemistry, 2002—03; v.p. Lipid Chemistry, 2003—. Contbr. articles to profl. jours. Mem.: Am. Chem. Soc., Am. Oil Chemists Soc. (bd. dirs. phospholipid divsn. 2005—). Avocations: reading, writing. Office Phone: 847-887-0800. Business E-Mail: moghis@neopharm.com.

AHMAD, SALAHUDDIN, nuclear scientist, physicist; b. Sylhet, Bangladesh, Nov. 25, 1954; arrived in Can., 1978; came to U.S., 1990; s. Jalal and Momtaz (Begum) A.; m. Munawar Sultana, June 1, 1978; 1 child, Nahid Rubaba. MSc, Dhaka U., Bangladesh, 1975; PhD, U. Victoria, B.C., Can., 1981. Diplomate Am. Bd. Radiology. Lectr. Dhaka U., 1978; postdoctoral rsch. assoc. U. Victoria, 1981; rsch. scientist U. Paris South, Orsay, France, 1982-83; profl. rsch. assoc. U. Sask., Saskatoon, Can., 1983-84; rsch. assoc. Triumf Nat. Lab., Vancouver, 1984-86, U. B.C., Vancouver, 1987-89; faculty fellow, rsch. asst. prof. Rice U., Houston, 1990-96; rsch. assoc. MD Anderson Cancer Ctr., U. Tex., Houston, 1996-98; asst. prof. radiology Baylor Coll. Medicine, Houston, 1999—2004; chief physicist radiotherapy VA Med. Ctr., Houston, 1999—2004; assoc. prof. radiation oncology U. Okla. Health Sci. Ctr., Okla. City, 2004—. Contbr. more than 130 articles to sci. jours. and conf. procs., including Physics Letters, Phys. Rev., Phys. Rev. Letters, Nucl. Phys., Nucl. Instr. & Methods Bangladeshi rep. World Muslim Youth Conf., Abha, Saudi Arabia, 1977; founder, pres. Bangladesh-Can. Cultural Assn., Vancouver, 1988-89, Bangladesh-Am. Lit., Art and Cultural Assn., Houston, 1992-95, 98-99, 2004—. Raja Kalinarayan scholar U. Dhaka, 1974-75; fellow Can. Commonwealth Fellowship Com., 1978-81. Mem. Am. Assn. Physicist in Medicine, Am. Coll. Med. Physics. Business E-Mail: salahuddin-ahmad@ouhsc.edu. E-mail: kintukeno@hotmail.com.

AHMAD, SHAH MAHMOOD, chemical engineer, consultant; b. Lahore, Punjab, Pakistan, Mar. 25, 1967; came to U.S., 1992; s. Syeo Muhammad and Mahmooda Begum Ahmad; m. Muzaffara Bushra Dahri, Dec. 29, 1996. BSChemE, U. Engring. Lahore, 1990; MSChemE, Western Mich. U., 1995. Profl. engr. Shift engr. Rupali (Toray) Polyester, Lahore, 1991; process engr. Glaxo Ltd. U.K., Lahore, 1991-92; rsch. asst. Western Mich. U., Kalamazoo, 1992-95; project mgr. EDM Consulting Inc., Vicksburg, Mich., 1995-96; cons. compliance Pharmacia & Upjohn, Kalamazoo, 1996—. Cons. BASF, Holland, Mich., 1995-96, Remote Control Inc., Allegan, Mich., 1997—. Asst. to editor Jour. Asia Pacific Bus., 1994-95. Vol. Western U. Mich. Librs., Kalamazoo, 1993; sec. publ. Ahmadiyya Movement Islam, Detroit, 1997—. Mem. Am. Inst. Chem. Engrs. Achievements include developer Software Program "Emergency Relief System Design Basis". Office: Pharmacia & Upjohn OU1305-87-1 Kalamazoo MI 49001

AHMAD, SHAMOON, hematologist, oncologist, consultant; b. Pakistan; arrived in U.S., 1988; MB, BChir, Dow Med. Coll., Karachi, Pakistan, 1987; law student, U. Nev., 2004—. Diplomate Am. Bd. Hosp. Physicians, Am. Bd. Hematology, Am. Bd. Oncology, Am. Bd. Internal Medicine, lic. physician Pa., Ala., N.Y., Nev. Resident in internal medicine Seton Hall U., NJ, 1989—92; fellow in hematology Mt. Sinai Sch. Medicine, N.Y.C., 1992—93, 1995—96, fellow in neoplastic diseases, 1996—97, fellow in bone marrow transplant, 1997—98; dir. blood and marrow transplant program Comprehensive Cancer Ctrs. of Nev., Las Vegas, 1998—. Asst. med. dir. Jackson County (Ala.) Rural Health Project, Scottsboro, 1993—95; chair cancer com., sect. chief hematology/oncology Sunrise Hosp. and Med. Ctr., Las Vegas, 2001—02; part-time med. dir. therapeutic apheresis program United Blood Svcs., Las Vegas, 2002—; chair pain com. Sunrise Hosp. and Med. Ctr., 2002—, vice chmn. instnl. rev. bd., 2002—03; mem. gov.'s task force on prostate cancer State of Nev., 2004—; pres. Physician & Legal Consultants, Inc., 2004; lectr., presenter in field. Contbr. articles to profl. jours. Named to Who's Who in So. Nev., In Bus. Las Vegas mag., 2003; recipient Physician's Recognition award, AMA, 1992—2000, Curtsey Las Vegas award, C. of C., Las Vegas, 2002. Fellow: ACP, Am. Bd. Hosp. Physicians; mem.: Am. Coll. Legal Medicine, Am. Coll. Physician Execs., Am. Soc. Blood and Marrow Transplantation, Clark County Med. Soc. (bylaws, policies and procedures com., profl. stds. coun. 2002—), Nev. State Med. Assn. (coun. on pub. health 2002—), Assn. Cmty. Cancer Ctrs. (ho. dels. 2003—), Am. Soc. Clin. Oncology (clin. practice com. 2003—), Nev. Oncology Soc. (pres. 2003—). Office: PO Box 60327 Las Vegas NV 89160 Office Phone: 702-952-3400. Fax: 702-458-2436. E-mail: shamoonahmad@yahoo.com.

AHMAD, SYED HASAN, ambassador; b. Feni, Feb. 1, 1936; married; 3 children. MS in Physics, U. Dhaka, 1956; diploma in Geophysics, Imperial Coll. Sci. and Tech., London, 1958; M Applied Geophys., U. London, 1959; diploma in Devel. Adminstrn., London Sch. Econs., 1969. Exec. Burmah Oil Co., Chittagong; sr. exec. Pakistan Shell Oil Co.; with Civil Svc. Pakistan, 1960—; sec. East Pakistan Indsl. Devel. Corp.; exec. dir. Ea. Refinery, Titas Gas Transmission and Distbn. Co.; dep. commr. Mymensing; econ./comml. counselor Bangladesh Embassy, Bonn, Germany, Kuwait; chmn. Bangladesh Petroleum Corp., Bangladesh, Bangladesh Oil and Gas Corp. (Petrobangla), Bangladesh; sec. Ministry of Commerce, Bangladesh; sec. rwy. divsn. Ministry of Comms.; dir. gen. Bangladesh Rwy.; sec. Ministry of Health; chmn. Tarrif Commn.; sec. Ministry of Textiles; prin. sec. Prime Min., Bangladesh; ambassador to Belgium Bangladesh Fgn. Svc., 1992—96, ambassador to U.S. Washington, 2002—. Ind. cons.Asian Devel. Bank; chmn. coun. advisors BNP. Office: Bangladesh Embassy 3510 International Dr NW Washington DC 20008

AHMANN, JOHN STANLEY, retired psychologist; b. Struble, Iowa, Oct. 17, 1921; s. Henry Francis and Philomine (Wictor) Ahmann; children: Sandi Ann, Sheri Kay, Gregory Steven, Shelly Joan. *A descendant of Johann Adolph Ahmann of Marl, Germany, John Stanley Ahmann was born and raised in midwestern United States. His four children are: daughter Sandi (Ahmann) Ashley, BS Colorado State U., EdS U. of Kansas, a licensed professional counselor in Montana; daughter Sheri (Ahmann) Carmon, BA U. of Northern Colorado, is a real estate broker associate in Colorado; son Steve Ahmann, BS Montana State U., a teacher in Montana; and daughter Shelly Ahmann, BA and MD U of Colorado, a surgeon in Georgia. Each has an abiding love of the Rocky Mountain west and its environment.* BA, Trinity Coll., 1943; BS, Iowa State U., 1947, MS, 1949, PhD, 1951. Instr. profl. studies Iowa State U., 1949-51, prof. edn. and psychology Ames, 1975—, disting. prof. edn., 1981—, chmn. dept. profl. studies, 1975-84; asst. prof. div. ednl. psychology and psychol. measurement Cornell U., 1951-54, asso. prof., 1954-58, prof., 1958-60; prof. psychology Colo. State U., 1960-75; assoc. dir. Human Factors Rsch. Lab., 1969-71, asst. to pres., 1961-64, head dept. psychology, 1962-64, acad. v.p., 1964-69; retired. Adj. prof. psychology and edn. U. Denver, 1971—76; vis. prof. Colo. State U., 1951, Wash. State U., 1960, Western Wash. U., 1970; cons. rsch. programs U.S. Dept. Edn.; cons. evaluation ednl. programs, Colo., NY, La., Tex., Ark., Hawaii, Ga., Ariz., Ohio, Minn., Iowa; project dir. Nat. Assessment Ednl. Progress, 1971—75; dir. various fed. and state sponsored rsch. projects; hon. lectr. Mid-Am. State U. Assn., 1976—77. Author: (book) Statistical Methods in Educational and Psychological Research, 1954, Evaluating Student Progress, 6th edit., 1981, Evaluating Elementary School Pupils, 1960, Testing Student Achievement and Aptitudes, 1962, Measuring and Evaluating Educational Achievement, 2d edit., 1975, How Much Are Our Young People Learning?, 1976, Needs Assessment for Program Planning in Vocational Education, 1979, Academic Achievements of Young Americans, 1983; assoc. editor: Ednl. Studies, 1975—79. With USNR, 1943—46, PTO. Recipient Laureate award, Iowa State U., 1975. Fellow: APA, AAAS; mem.: Nat. Coun. Measurement Edn., Am. Ednl. Rsch. Assn., Psi Chi, Alpha Chi Sigma, Phi Lambda Upsilon, Phi Delta Kappa, Phi Kappa Phi, Sigma Xi. Home: 3738 Franklin Ave Loveland CO 80538-2204

AHMED, ATIF ALI, pathologist; b. Khartoum, Sudan, Mar. 7, 1965; s. Ali Ahmed Hussein and Habiba F Aljarrari; m. Susan J Veit, Apr. 5, 2004. MBBS, U. Khartoum, Sudan, 1988. Cert. Anatomic Pathology and Clinical Pathology Am. Bd. of Pathology, 2003. Tchg. asst., resident in pathology and microbiology U. Khartoum, 1991—94; med. intern Mt. Vernon Hosp., NY, 1995—96; resident in pathology Columbia U., NY, 1996—98, U. Okla., 1998—2000; post-residency fellowship in pediat. pathology NYU, 2000; clin. fellow Nat. Cancer Inst., NIH, Bethesda, Md., 2003—04; attending pathologist Children's Nat. Med. Ctr., Washington, 2004—. Enhanced profl. info. pathologist Nat. Cancer Inst., NIH, Bethesda, Md., 2003—04. *Place of employment, the Children's National Medical Center, is one of the best 10 pediatric hospitals in America, according to U.S. News and World Report. It has academic and research affiliations with the George Washington University, Georgetown University, and the National Institutes of Health.* Contbr. articles various profl. jours. Tchg. Albert-Einstein Coll. of Medicine, Bronx, NY, 2002—03. Fellow Advanced subspecialty in Pediatric Pathology, U. South Fla., 2002. Fellow: Assn. of Clin. Scientists, Coll. of Am. Pathologist. Achievements include research in expression of C-kit in Ewing family of tumors: A comparison of different immunohistochemical protocols; Fryns syndrome-like phenotype with mosaic chromosomal translocation; placenta membranacea: A developmental anomaly with diverse clinical presentation; antimicrobial agent resistance in bacterial isolates from patients with diarrhea and urinary tract infection in the Sudan; interstitial cells of Cajal in children. Office: Childrens Nat Med Ctr 111 Mich Ave NW Washington DC 20009 Office Fax: 202-884-4030. Personal E-mail: atifaahmed@yahoo.com.

AHMED, ELIAS, microbiologist; b. Hyderabad, India; arrived in U.S., 1972; s. Ariff Mohammed and Bashirunissa Begum; m. Elizabeth Louise Snyder, Dec. 16, 1972. BS, Sind Muslim Coll., Pakistan, 1968; MS in Microbiology, U. Karachi, 1970. Med. technologist Variety Children's Hosp., Miami, Fla., 1973—77; supr. microbiology Easton (Pa.) Hosp., 1978; med. technologist Northside Hosp., Atlanta, 1978—79; med. technologist II Quest Diagnostics, Horsham, Pa., 1979—. Editor: On Track diversity newsletter (Quest Diagnostics); contbr. poetry to numerous books. Mem.: Am. Soc. Microbiology, Am. Soc. Clin. Pathologists, Acad. Am. Poets. Republican. Moslem. Avocations: writing poetry, tennis, photography, travel. Home: 281 Riverview Rd King Of Prussia PA 19406-2020 Office: Quest Diagnostics 900 Business Ctr Horsham PA 19044 E-mail: eliahm@msn.com.

AHMED, IQBAL, psychiatrist, consultant; b. Tumkur, Karnataka, India, Aug. 23, 1951; arrived in US, 1976, naturalized, 1982; s. Rahimuddin Ahmed and Arifa (Banu) Rahimuddin; m. Lisa Suzanne Rose, Oct. 9, 1983; children: Yasmin, Jihan. BS, MB, St. John's Med. Coll., 1975. Diplomate in gen. psychiatry, geriatric psychiatry and psychosomatic medicine Am. Bd. Psychiatry and Neurology. Intern St. Martha's Hosp., Bangalore, India, 1974-75; resident in psychiatry U. Nebr. Med. Ctr., Omaha, 1976-79; fellowship in consultation Boston U. Sch. Medicine, 1979-81; staff psychiatrist in consultation liaison psychiatry Boston City Hosp., 1981-87, staff psychiatrist, geriatric psychiatry, 1983-85, dir. geriatric neuropsychiatry unit, 1985-87, dir. geriatric psychiatry, 1988-92; assoc. dir. consultation liaison psychiatry New England Med. Ctr., Boston, 1989-92. Asst. prof. psychiatry Boston U. Sch. Medicine, 1981—87, Tufts U. Sch. Medicine, Boston, 1987—92; dir. med. student edn. in psychiatry Boston City Hosp., 1981—87; chief spl. svcs. Hawaii State Hosp., 1991—94, pres. med. staff, 1994—95, chief geriatric psychiatry, 1994—; assoc. prof. dept. psychiatry U. Hawaii John A. Burns Sch. Medicine, 1992—97, prof. dept. psychiatry, 1997—; vice chmn. dept. psychiatry U. Hawaii, 1999—2001; cons. Triple Army Med. Ctr., 1997—; program dir. gen. and geriatric psychiatry residency programs U. Hawaii, 1998—2004; dir. pyschopharm. Adult Dept. Mental Health State of Hawaii, Honolulu, 2003—; dir. geriatric psychiatry Queens Med. Ctr., Honolulu, 2003—, vice chmn. edn., dept. psychiatry, 1999—2004. Contbr. articles to profl. jours., chapters to books. Mem. Mass. State Dem. Party Minority Caucus, Boston, 1983. Finalist Parker Palmer Courage to Teach award, Accreditation Council Grad. Med. Edn., 2004; recipient Irma Bland award, APA, 2005. Fellow: Am. Psychiat. Assn., Acad. Psychosomatic Medicine, Am. Psychiat. Assn. (disting.), Royal Coll. Psychiatrists; mem.: Am. Coll. Psychiatrists, Internat. Coll. Geriatric Psychoneuropharmacology (founding mem.), Am. Assn. Geriatric Psychiatry, Am. Neuropsychiat. Assn. Democrat. Avocations: web surfing, snorkeling. Office: 1356 Lusitana St Fl 4 Honolulu HI 96813-2421 Business E-Mail: ahmedi@dop.hawaii.edu.

AHMED, JAMIL, rehabilitation service physician; Grad., Karachin U.; MD, Sindh Med. Coll. Resident Maimonides Med. Ctr./Boston U. Med. Ctr.; attending physician, rehabilitation medicine Erie Country Med. Ctr., Buffalo, clin. instructor, rehabilitation medicine. Office: Erie Country Med Ctr Ste G-200H 462 Grider St Buffalo NY 14215 Address: Erie County Med Ctr Rehabilitation Medicine G-217 462 Grider St Buffalo NY 14215 Office Phone: 716-898-5059, 716-898-6126. Business E-Mail: jahmed@ecmc.edu, ahmed7@buffalo.edu.*

AHMED, NASIM, surgeon; b. Chittagong, Bangladesh, Bangladesh, July 4, 1962; s. Zaibun Nisa and Wasiul Hasan; m. Syeda Shahnaz Akhtar, May 17, 1994; children: Zain Nasim, Zuha Nasim. MBBS, Dow Med. Coll. Karachi Pakistan, 1987. Diplomate Am. Bd. of Surgery, 1999, Am. Bd. Surg. Critical Care, 2000. Asst. dir. of trauma & surg. critical care Jersey Shore U. Hosp., Neptune, NJ, 2001—. Dir. critical care UniMed Med. Ctr., Minot, ND, 2000—01; clin. asst. prof. surgery Robert Wood Johnson Med. Sch., New Brunswick, NJ, 2002—. Contbr. articles to profl. jours. Scholar Pres. of Pakistan Scholarship, Govt. of Pakistan. Fellow: Am. Coll. Surgeons; mem.: AAAS, N.Y. Acad. of Sci., Am. Physiology Soc., Soc. Critical Care, Am. Coll. Chest Physician. Home: 1919 Fiddlers Run Toms River NJ 08755 Office: Jersey Shore University Hospital 1945 State Rt 33 Neptune NJ 07754 Office Phone: 732-776-4749. Business E-Mail: nahmed@meridianhealth.com.

AHMED, S. BASHEER, research and development company executive, educator; b. Kurnool, Andhra, India, Jan. 1, 1934; s. S. M. and K.A. (Bee) Hussain; m. Alice Cordelia Pearce; 1 child, Ivy Amina. BA, Osmania Coll., Kurnool, 1955; MA, Osmania U., Hyderabad, India, 1957; MS, Tex. A&M U., 1963, PhD, 1966. Asst. prof. Tenn. Tech. U., Cookeville, 1966-68, Ohio U., Athens, 1968-70; vis. fellow Princeton U., N.J., 1977-78; prof. Western Ky. U., Bowling Green, 1970-80; prof. Mgmt. Scis. Lubin Grad. Sch. Bus., dir. doctoral program Pace U., NYC, 1982-92, prof. emeritus, 1993—2003; pres. Princeton Econ. Rsch., Inc., 1980-99, Pearce Cons. Svcs., 2000—. Cons. Oak Ridge (Tenn.) Nat. Lab., 1969-77, Inst. for Energy Analysis, Oak Ridge, 1975, Honeywell Corp., Mpls., 1985. Author: Quantitative Methods for Business, 1974, Nuclear Fuel and Energy Policy, 1979; author, editor: Technology, International Stability, and Growth, 1984. Mem. cirs. bd. The Kennedy Ctr., 1997-2000. Recipient Achievement award Oak Ridge Nat. Lab., 1977, IEEE Centennial Medal, 1983, Millennium medal, 2000. Fellow AAAS, Systems, Man, and Cybernetics Soc. (pres. 1980-82). Home: 817 Albemarle Dr Bowling Green KY 42103 Office Phone: 202-862-1164. E-mail: sbahmed@aol.com.

AHMED, SYED Z., anthropologist; b. Meerut, India, Aug. 19, 1923; s. Syed Riazuddin and Shah Jehan Begum; m. Susan Ahmed, Feb. 20, 1944; 1 child, Suraiya. PhD, Eng. Leader Sahara Recon Expdn., North Africa; prodr. 40 scientific documentary films for TV, Europe; pres., exec. prodr. Xploration Internat. Rschr., traveler numerous expdns. worldwide. Author: Twilight of an Empire in India, Twilight of an Empire in China, Twilight on the Silk Road, Ruwenzori: A Land Journey Through Europe to Central Africa, Twilight on Caucausus, Incredible Journeys Around the World, Tales of Imperial China and Asia, 1997, Travel in Shangri-La, 1998, East of Tien Shan, 1998, An Imperial Affair, 1999, I Was a Geisha, 1999, Zenith of an Empire, 2001, A Daring Escape, 2002, Bambuti, 2004, Manchukou, 2004, Chaghatai, 2004. Islamic.

AHMED, WALID KHAIRY MOHAMED, electrical engineer; b. Cairo, Dec. 5, 1968; arrived in Canada, 1992, arrived in US, 1997; s. Khairy Mohamed Sulaiman and Rafia Zaki Ahmed; m. Nevin El-Sayed Ali Sultan, 1995; children: Maryam, Marwa, Omar. BSc with honors in electrical engring., commn. and electronics engring., Ain Shams U., Egypt, 1991; PhD in electrical and computer engring., Queen's U. at Kingston, Canada, 1997. Registered electrical engr. Syndicate of Engrs. of Egypt, 1991, cert. green belt six sigma 2005. Rsch. asst. Wireless Commn. Lab., Dept. Electrical and computer engring., Queen's U. at Kingston, Ontario, Canada, 1992—97; DSP engr. Radio DSP Dept., Nortel Tech., Ottawa, Canada, 1997; tech. staff, design supr. Bell Labs., Wireless Organ. Consumer Products Organ., Lucent Tech., Holmdel, NJ, 1997—98; tech. staff Bell Labs., Performance Analysis Dept. Bell Labs Advanced Commn. Tech. Ctr., Lucent Tech., Holmdel, NJ, 1998—2001; tech. lead, prin. engr. Tyco Electronics, Sys. Engring, M/A-COM, NJ, 2001—03, sr. prin. engr., tech. lead mgr., 2003—; tchr., lab. asst. Benha Higher Inst. of Tech., Dept. Electrical Engring., Egypt, 1991; tchr., lab asst. Sin Shams U., Ept. of Electronics and Commn. Engring., Faculty of Engring., Egypt, 1992—97; adj. prof. Wesley J. Howe Sch. Tech. Mgmt., Stevens Inst. of Tech., NJ, 2002—. Reviewer various profl. jours. and papers. Pres. student assn. Queen's U. at Kingston, Ontario, Canada, 1994—95. Named Sr. Prin. Engr., Tyco Electronics; recipient Sr. mem. of IEEE award, IEEE, 2000, Commn. Soc. Cert. of Appreciation, 2001; scholarship, Canadian Internat. Devel. Agency, 1992—94, Grad. scholarship, Gov. of Ontario, 1995—96. Mem.: IEEE (sr. mem. 2000—). Achievements include many patents and original research publications on wireless communications networks and systems, signal processing, and wireless transeiver design. Avocations: Karate, reading, music. Office: MA COM Tyco Electronics 250 Indl Way Eatontown NJ 07724 E-mail: walidmail@yahoo.com.

AHMOSE, NEFERTARI A., journalism educator; b. Kingston, Jamaica, Oct. 3, 1951; arrived in U.S., 75; d. Cecil Alexander Rose and Florence Rhodian Daley. Student, L.A. Valley Coll., 1975. Journalist Jamaica Daily News, 1974—80; pub. African Expression, Bronx, NY, 1982—91; founder Afrikan People Stock Exchange, 1982—; politician Kemet-Kush, Ensley, Ala., 1985—2001; founder Afrikan U. in West, Bklyn., 1996—, Wafrakan Ins. Co., 2003—, Merkhutu Currency Kiafrafan Lang. Kiafrakan Corp. Leader Wafrakan Empress Afrikan Diasporan Nation. Author: Black Sovereign-The Black Alternative, 1992, Harmonization, Unification and Standardization in Afrikan Tribal Vernaculars into Afrikan Language-Dictionary and Grammar, 1996, Ki-Afrakan-English Exercise, 1997, Ki-Afrakan Grammar, 1996, Ki-Afrakan Dictionary, 1996, Incorp. Afrakan Standard Language, 1994, Sex Education for Youngsters, 1994, Kemet Calendar, 2000. Founder Afrikan Bank and Investment Trust, Merkhutu Currency, Kemet-Kush (now Wafrakan Polit. Party), NY, 2000—. Mailing: PO Box 971 Bronx NY 10472 Office Phone: 718-601-9419.

AHN, CHOONG YONG, economics professor; b. Taegu, Republic of Korea, Jan. 3, 1941; s. Wha Sun (Whang) A.; m. Sun Hye Kim, Dec. 20, 1972; 1 child, Jae Churl. BA, Kyungpook Nat. U., Taegu, 1963; MA, U. Hawaii, 1968; PhD, Ohio State U., 1972. Postdoctoral fellow Ohio State U., Columbus, 1972-74; prof. econs. Chung-Ang U., Seoul, 1974—2002. Chmn. bd. dirs. Chohung Bank, 1999-2002; cons. Bank of Korea, Seoul, 1990-92, World Bank, Washington, 1978-88; chief tech. advisor UN Indsl. Devel. Orgn., Vienna, 1985, 91; pres. Korea Inst. for Internat. Econ. Policy, 2002—; dean grad. sch. internat. studies Chung-Ang U., 1997-2000. Editor: Jour. Econ. Devel., 1985-96; contbr. articles to profl. jours. Pres. Korean Assn. East-West Ctr. Alumni, Seoul, 1986-87; pres. Korean Asn. Ohio State U. ALumni Assn., 1999-2000. 2d lt. Korean Army, 1963-65. Named Economist of Yr. Maeil Economic Daily Paper, Korea, 1984; recipient Okita Policy Rsch. award NIRA, Japan, 2000. Mem. Korean Econometric Soc. (pres. 1991-92), Fedn. Korean Industries (mem. adv. bd. 1980—), Presdl. Commn. Sci. and Tech. (mem. adv. bd. 1989-90), Korean Econ. Assn., Korean Internat. Econ. Assn. (pres. 1994), Korean Futurist Soc., Presdl. Econ. Adv. Coun. Avocations: golf, mountain climbing, reading. Office: 300-04 Yomgok-dong Seocho-gu Seoul 137-747 Republic of Korea

AHN, DONG H, insurance company executive; Grad. in econ. and polit. sci., Yale U. Various mgmt. positions The Travelers Ins. Co., 1982—95; sr. v.p., dir. of the employer market segment, group benefits divsn. Hartford Life Ins. Co., 1995—2002; exec. dir. group ins. Aetna Inc., 2002, sr. v.p., group ins., 2002—. Office: Aetna Inc 151 Farmington Ave Hartford CT 06156

AHN, HONGSHIK, statistician, educator; b. Seoul, Korea (South), Aug. 19, 1961; s. Yong Jin Ahn; m. Hyesun Chung, May 21, 1988; children: Rachel Suejin, Andrew Jeehyun. PhD, U. Wis., Madison, 1987—92. Staff fellow Nat. Ctr. Toxicological Rsch., Jefferson, Ark., 1992—93, math. statistician, 1994—96; asst. prof. Stony Brook U., NY, 1996—99, assoc. prof., 1999—. Vis. scientist Nat. Ctr. Toxicological Rsch., 1997—; assoc. editor Comm. Stats., 2000—. Grantee SPIR Project, Veeco UPA, 1997, First Ind. Rsch. Support and Transition award, NIH, 1998-2003. Mem.: Am. Statis. Assn. (v.p., program com. chair ctrl. Ark. Chpt. 1994—96), Internat. Biometric Soc., Ea. North Am. Region (regional adv. bd. 2004—). Home: 109 Erin La Setauket NY 11733 Office: Stony Brook U Dept Appl Math and Stats Stony Brook NY 11794-3600 Office Phone: 631-632-8372. Business E-Mail: hahn@ams.stonybrook.edu.

AHN, JOONHONG, engineering educator, nuclear engineer; s. Chul Joong Ahn and Boon Nam Park; m. Junghae Park, Nov. 10, 1961; children: Taewoo, Jise. PhD, U. Calif., 1988; DEng, U. Tokyo, 1989. Lectr. U. Tokyo, 1991—93; assoc. prof. Tokai U., Hiratsuka, Japan, 1993—95; asst. prof. U. Calif., Berkeley, 1995—99, assoc. prof., 1999—. Steering com. Atomic Energy Soc. of Japan, Tokyo, 1993—95. Jr. Scientist fellow, Japan Soc. Promotion of Sci., 1988—90. Mem.: Am. Nuc. Soc. Office: Univ Calif Berkeley Dept Nuclear Engr Berkeley CA 94720-1730 Office Phone: 510-642-5107.

AHN, SHI HYUN, professional golfer; b. Inchon, Korea, Sept. 15, 1984; Winner three events Apache Dream Tour, 2002; winner CJ Nine Bridges Classic, 2003. Mem. Korean Nat. Team, 2000—01. Recipient Louise Suggs Rolex Rookie of Yr., 2004. Achievements include being the youngest internat. winner in LPGA history and sixth youngest winner in LPGA history. Avocation: quilting. Office: c/o LPGA 100 International Dr Daytona Beach FL 32124-1092

AHN, SUHNNE, music educator; b. New York, NY, Dec. 9, 1963; d. Choong-sik and Inkyong Ahn. BA, Yale U., 1982—86; AM, Harvard U., 1986—90, PhD, 1986—97. Dean Harnwell Coll. Ho.; UPenn, Phila., 2002—; musicology faculty Peabody Conservatory of The Johns Hopkins U., Balt., 1997—; dir. of student affairs Peabody Prep. of The Johns Hopkins U., Balt., 1997—2002; musicology faculty Sch. of Music, U. of Md., Coll. Pk., 1995—96. Mem. bd. of spl. advisors Renovation in Music Edn., Wash., DC, 2004—. Recipient Deutscher Akademischer Austauschdient, DAAD, 1989; fellow Oscar Straus Schafer Tchg. fellowship, Music Dept. of Harvard U., 1993; Peabody Faculty Devel. grant, Peabody Inst., 1999. Mem.: AAUW, Am. Musicological Soc. Office: Harnwell Coll House UPenn 3820 Locust Walk Philadelphia PA 19104-6134 Office Phone: 215-573-3497.

AHO, BRIEN, photojournalist; Grad., Syracuse Military Photojournalism, 2002. Photojournalist USN, Fleet Combat Camera, Atlantic. Recipient Four Time First pl. Winner in Mil. Photography of Yr. Competition. Mem.: Eddie Adams Workshop (staff mem. 1999—). Home: 603 Trout Run Odenton MD 21113-3617

AHO, HOLLY KATHLEEN, artist; b. Robinsdale, Minn., Feb. 15, 1975; d. Thomas and Janice Moen; m. Chad Marcus Aho, Oct. 10, 1998; children: Noel Lockhart, Lukas, Thomas, Timothy. Adminstr., artist Art Epiphany, Glencoe, Minn., 2004—; artist Studio 14 Art Gallery, 2001—. Cons., art McLeod County, Glencoe, 2004—. Painting, Horizons (Hon. Mention, 2004). Home: 1327 Ford Ave Glencoe MN 55336 Personal E-mail: oasis@studio14artgallery.com.

AHO, PAUL RICHARD, artist, art educator; b. Milw., Sept. 3, 1954; s. John Toivo Aho and Doris Niemczyk; m. Anne Fredrika Wall (div.); 1 child, Eliza Allen; m. Barbara Jolly (div.). BFA magna cum laude, Fla. State U., 1977; MFA, U. So. Fla., 1979. Dir. visual arts svc. Palm Beach County Cultural Coun., Fla., 1990—94; exhib. coord., N.Am. sales rep. Internat. Fine Art Expositions, Stuart, Fla., 1994—95; dean Sch. Art, Armory Art Ctr., West Palm Beach, Fla., 1996—2003; chief program dir. Palm Beach Photographic Ctr., Delray Beach, Fla., 2003—04; adj. faculty Fla. Atlanta U., Boca Raton, 2004—. A Passion for Paint-Selected Works by Wayne Thiebaud, 1998, Selected Works by Philip Pearlstein, 1999, Thought Through My Eyes-Graham Nickson, Armory Art Ctr., 2001, Nelson Shanks-Portraits and Paintings From the Figure, Armory Art Ctr., 2002, Janet Fish- A Sea of Color, Armory Art Ctr., 2003, one-man shows include Kinzelman Art Cons., Houston, 2004, Studio E, Abacoa, Fla., 2004, exhibitions include Seoul Arts Ctr., 1997, Gallery Camino Real, 1998, Jon Oulman Gallery, Mpls., 1998, Atrium Gallery, U. Conn., 1998, Ritter Gallery, Fla. Atlantic U., Boca Raton, 1998, N.Y. Studio Sch., 2000, Gallery Camino Real, Boca Raton, 2001, Boca Raton Mus. Art, 2002, ArtServe, Ft. Lauderdale, 2003, Fla. Atlantic U., Boca Raton, 2004, Jones Ctr. Contemporary Art, Austin, Tex., 2004, Arcaute Arte Contemporaneo, San Pedro Garza Garcia Mex., 2004, Somerhill Gallery, Chapel Hill, N.C., 2004, Schmidt Ctr. Gallery, 2004. Founding chmn., mem. profl. artists com. Palm Beach County Cultural Coun., 1988—90, bd. dirs., 1988—90; co-chair Arts Against Aids, West Palm Beach, 1994; ex officio Palm Beach County Cultural Coun., 1988—90; mem. steering com. Palm Beach County Sch. of Arts, 1994; mem. Palm Beach County Art Adv. Com., 2000—04. Recipient Ubertalli Meml. award for Artistic Achievement, Palm Beach County Cultural Coun., 1987; fellow, So. Fla. Cultural Consortium, 1995. Mem.: Coll. Art Assn. Avocation: surfing. Home: 1385 NE Meyer's Ter Jensen Beach FL 34957 Office Phone: 561-832-5222. Personal E-mail: kobalt@earthlink.net.

AHRARI, EHSAN M., political science professor, dean; b. Hyderabad, India, Nov. 24, 1945; came to U.S. 1968; s. Mohammed Hashmatullah and Sayyeda Ahrari; m. Sharon Leyland Ahrari. BA, Ea. Ill. U., 1971, MA, 1972; PhD, So. Ill. U., 1976. Grants specialist Jackson County Housing, Murphreesboro, Ill., 1977; vis. asst. prof. Ea. Ill. U., Charleston, 1977-79, Kean Coll. N.J., Union, 1980; asst. prof. polit. sci. Eastern Carolina U., Greenville, 1980-86; assoc. prof. polit. sci. Miss. State U., 1986-90; prof. Middle East and Southwestn Asian Studies Air War Coll., Maxwell AFB, Ala., 1990-94; prof. internat. security & strategy joint & combined warfighting sch. Joint Forces Staff Coll., Nat. Def. U., Norfolk, Va., 1994—, assoc. dean of joint and combined warfighting sch., 1995—96. Sr. rsch. fellow Ctr. for Internat. Security and Strategic Studies, Miss. State U. Author: The Dynamics of Oil Diplomacy, 1980, OPEC-The Failing Giant, 1986, Ethnic Groups and U.S. Foreign Policy, 1987, The Gulf and International Security: The 1980's and Beyond, 1989, the Persian Gulf After the Cold War, 1993, The Middle East in Transition, 1994, Change in the Continuity in the Middle East, 1996, The New Great Game in Central Asia, 1996; contbr. book revs. and articles to profl. jours. NEH fellow, 1979, 84-85. Mem. Am. Polit. Sci. Assn., Am. Soc. Pub. Adminstrn. (bd. dirs. Ea. N.C. chpt. 1985-86, pres. Ea. N.C. chpt. 1985-86, editl. bd. Internat. Jour. Pub. Adminstrn.), Pi Sigma Alpha, Pi Alpha Alpha. Democrat. Muslim. Avocations: photography, tennis, racquetball, travel. Home: 5904 Mount Eagle Dr #1010 Alexandria VA 22303-2539 Personal E-mail: eahrari@cox.net.

AHRENDTS, ANGELA, apparel executive; 3 children. Grad., Ball State U., 1981. Pres. Pringle of Scotland; with Warnaco, Inc., v.p. Valentino intimate apparel and Ungaro intimate apparel; v.p. sales Carmelo Pomodoro, pres.; v.p. merchandising Donna Karen Co., 1992, pres. Donna Karen Collection, 1992; v.p. gen. mdse. mgr. Henri Bendel; v.p. corp. merchandising and design Liz Claiborne, Inc., N.Y.C., 1998—2000, sr. v.p. corp. merchandising, group pres., 2000—02, exec. v.p., 2002—. Recipient Alumni Achievement award, Ball State U., 2003. Achievements include featured in Time Magazine Style and Design Women in Fashion Power List, 2004. Office: Liz Claiborne Inc 1441 Broadway New York NY 10018

AHRENS, FRANKLIN ALFRED, veterinary pharmacology educator; b. Leigh, Nebr., Apr. 27, 1936; s. Alfred Henry and Agnes Elizabeth (Higgins) A.; m. Katherine Aldene Henning, May 8, 1960; children— Jeffrey, Gregory, Matthew, Kristin D.V.M., Kans. State U., 1959; MS, Cornell U., 1965, PhD, 1968. Instr. U. Minn.-St. Paul, 1959-60; asst. prof. pharmacology Coll. Vet. Medicine, Iowa State U., Ames, 1968-70, assoc. prof. pharmacology, 1970-75, prof. pharmacology, 1975—2001, chmn. dept. vet. physiology and pharmacology, 1982-90; prof. emeritus Coll. Vet. Medicine Iowa State U., 2001—. Served as capt. USAF, 1960-63, lt. col. Air N.G., 1971-91. Recipient Norden Disting. Tchr. award Iowa State U., 1981; NIH spl. research fellow Cornell U., 1967-68 Mem. AVMA, N.Y. Acad. Scis., Assn. Mil. Surgeons U.S., Sigma Xi Democrat. Lutheran.

AHRENS, HENRY WILLIAM, art educator, consultant, puppeteer; b. Bklyn., Apr. 11, 1918; s. Otto Conrad and Caroline Johanna (Schoneck) A.; m. Marjorie June Brooks, Dec. 18, 1965. BFA, Pratt Inst., Bklyn., 1941; MA, Columbia U., 1943; EdD, NYU, 1964. Art tchr. Lincoln Sch., Tchrs. Coll. Columbia U., N.Y.C., 1941-42; art supr. Bd. Edn., South River, N.J., 1946-47, art tchr. Elizabeth, N.J., 1947-52; assoc. prof. SUNY, Buffalo, 1952-57; prof. art The Coll. of N.J., 1957-83, chmn. art dept., 1965-70, 72-75, ret., 1983, prof. emeritus, 1987—. Cons. Thomas A. Edison State Coll., Trenton, 1975-93; exch. prof. U. Frankfurt, Frankfurt Am Main, W. Ger., 1970-71; lectr. in field; mem. original puppet prodns. in Can., Europe and U.S., 1947—. Served alt. mil. duty Civilian Pub. Svc., 1943-46. Recipient Frank A. Rexford medal for Cooperation in Govt., 1937. Mem. Art Educators N.J. (hon. life, 1st v.p., pres.), Puppeteers of Am. (religious cons. 1969-76), Mercer County Ret. Tchrs. Assn. (life mem.), N.J. Edn. Assn. (life mem.), NEA (life mem.), Union Internat. Del La Marionettes, The Greater Phila. Area Puppetry Guild (hon. life), Puppeteers of Am., Phi Delta Kappa (life). Mem. Religious Soc. Friends (Quakers). Home and Office: Chandler Hall Phelps 102 90 Barclay Ct Newtown PA 18940

AHRENS, KENT, museum director, art historian; b. Martinsburg, W.Va. s. Fred E. and Mary C. (Routzahn) A. AB, Dartmouth Coll., 1961; MA, U. Md., 1966; PhD, U. Del., 1972. Mem. faculty Fla. State U., Tallahassee, 1971-74, Randolph-Macon Woman's Coll., Lynchburg, Va., 1974-77; mem. curatorial staff Wadsworth Atheneum, Hartford, Conn., 1977-78; mem. faculty Georgetown U., Washington, 1979-82; dir. Everhart Mus., Scranton, Pa., 1982-90, Rockwell Mus., Corning, N.Y., 1990-95, Civic Fine Arts Ctr., Sioux Falls, S.D., 1996-97, Kennedy Mus. of Art, Ohio U., Athens, 1997—2000; mus. cons., 2000—; dir. devel. Cmty. Action, Athens, 2002—. Mem. task force on art activities Lynchburg Bicentennial Commn., 1975-76; project evaluator Md. Com. Humanities, 1980-82; adv. panel Lucan Ctr., Scranton, Pa., 1983-84; mus. adv. com. Pa. Hist. and Mus. Commn., 1984-86; trustee Williamstown (Mass.) Regional Art Conservation Lab., Inc., 1984-92; art mus. adv. panel Pa. Coun. on Arts, 1984-87; adv. panel Pa. Fedn. Mus. and Hist. Orgns., 1989-90; adv. com. on exhbns. at Pa. Gov.'s residence, 1987-90; juror Regional Art '89, Marywood Coll. Art Galleries, Scranton, 1989, Regional 1991, Arnot Art Mus., Elmira, 1991, Cmty. Cultural Ctr., Brookings, SD, 1996; juror Fiber and Textile Exhibn. Civic Fine Arts Ctr., Sioux Falls, SD, 1996, Wilbur Stilwell Student Awards Exhibn., U. SD, Vermillion, 1997, Zanesville (Ohio) Art Ctr., 2000; adj. prof. Sch. Art, Ohio U., Athens, 1997-2000, percent for art com., 1997-99. Author: (with others) Rembrandt in the National Gallery of Art, 1969; author: The Drawings and Watercolors by Truman Seymour (1824-1891), Everhart Mus. 1986; co-author: Frederic C. Knight (1898-1979), Everhart Mus., 1987; author: The Oils and Watercolors by Edward D. Boit (1840-1915), Everhart Mus., 1990, Cyrus E. Dallin: His Small Bronzes and Plasters, Rockwell Mus., 1995, others; contbg. author: American Paintings and Sculpture: Illustrated Catalogue, Nat. Gallery of Art, 1970, Wadsworth Atheneum Paintings: The Netherlands and German-speaking Countries, 1978, Dictionary of Women Artists, 1997, Allgemeines Künsterlexikon, 1999—; author: Currier & Ives: Selection from the Nation-wide Collection, Kennedy Mus. Art, 2000; Small Bronzes by Harriet W. Frishmuth, Kennedy Mus. of Art, 2001. Vol. Bosnia-Herzegovina Heritage Rescue, London, 1995-2001; trustee, bd. dirs. Bosnia-Herzegovina Heritage Rescue, Inc., USA, 2001-03; trustee Cmty. Shares of Mid Ohio, 2004—, v.p., 2005—. 1st lt. U.S. Army, 1962—64. Recipient grant-in-aid Am. Philos. Soc., 1975; Samuel H. Kress fellow Nat. Gallery of Art, 1968-69; Chester Dale fellow Nat. Gallery Art, 1970-71; NEH fellow, 1973-74, Mus. Mgmt. Inst., J. Paul Getty Trust, 1991, award for superior vol. svc. Am. Assn. Mus., 1999, award The Fund Raising Sch., Ctr. on Philanthropy, Ind. U., Indpls., 2004. Mem. Coll. Art Assn., Am. Assn. Mus. (on-site surveyor mus. assessment program 1984-89, 92—, accreditation com. 1986, 90—), Mus. Assn. Pa. (chmn. 1984-90), Mid-Atlantic Assn. Mus., Ohio Assn. Non-profit Orgns.(peer rev., standards on excellence, 2005-), Rotary, Elks. Office: Hocking-Athens-Perry Cmty Action PO Box 340 Athens OH 45701 Office Phone: 740-592-6601.

AHRENS, LYNN, lyricist; b. NY, Oct. 1, 1948; m. Neil Costa. BA in Comms., Syracuse U., 1970. Author book, lyricist: Once On This Island, 1995 (Olivier award best musical, Tony nominations for best book and score, NAACP award for best playwright), Lucky Stiff, 1988 (Helen Hayes award for best musical), lyricist: My Favorite Year (Lincoln Ctr. Theatre), 1993, Ragtime, 1998 (Grammy nomination, Tony award, Drama Desk award, Outer Critics Cir. award), Anastasia, 1997 (2 Acad. award nominations, 2 Golden Globe nominations), Bartok the Magnificent, 1999, With Voices Raised (Boston Pops), 1999, Seussical, 2000 (Grammy nomination), A Man of No Importance, 2002 (Outer Crix Cir. award for best musical, 2003), co-author, lyricist: A Christmas Carol (Madison Sq. Garden), 1994—2004, Schoolhouse Rock, 1973—85 (Emmy award, 4 Emmy nominations), 1992—98. Mem.: NARAS, ASCAP, Dramatists Guild Coun., Acad. Motion Picture Arts and Scis. Office: c/o William Morris Attn Peter Franklin 1325 Avenue Of The Americas New York NY 10019-6026

AHRENS, THOMAS H., communications executive; b. N.Y.C., Oct. 25, 1919; BA magna cum laude, U. Buffalo, 1938; JD, Harvard U., 1941; certificate in Culinary Arts, N.Y.C. Tech. Coll., 1953. Bar: N.Y. 1944. Dir. Edward F. Gallaher Prodns., 1946—; lectr. wines and beverages N.Y.C. Tech. Coll., 1953-55, prof. hotel and restaurant mgmt., 1971—; dir. rsch., security analyst Templeton, Dobbrow and Vance, 1962-64; pres. Chef Phillip, Inc., 1956-69. Author radio and TV scripts on wines, gastronomy and music, 1946— . Mem. chmn.'s coun. Lincoln Ctr. for Performing Arts. 2d lt. AUS, 1942-45. Decorated officer Chaine des Rotisseurs; Confrerie Saint Etienne d'Alsace; Chevaliers du Tastevin; Commanderie des Cordons Bleus de France; Medaille de la Ville de Paris, 1976 Mem. ABA, N.Y. Soc. Security Analysts, Phi Beta Kappa. Clubs: Harvard, Paris-American, Met., Met. Opera (all N.Y.C.); Travellers, Cercle de l'Union Interalliée (Paris). Home: 333 E 69th St New York NY 10021-5549

AHRENS, WILLIAM HENRY, architect; b. NYC, May 12, 1925; s. John Karl and Sophie (Hashage) A.; m. Joyce Nolan, Mar. 27, 1951. Student, R.I. Sch. Design, 1946; AB in Architecture, Princeton U., 1950, M.F.A. in Arch. and Urban Planning, 1953; postgrad., Tehran U., 1960. Chief architect Litchfield, Whiting, Bowne, Iran, 1958-61, Rome, 1961-64; dir. internat. ops. Whiting Assos., Rome, 1964-67; architect William H. Ahrens, AIA, Rome, Italy, 1967-95. Chmn. John's Island Archtl. Review com., 1997—. Prin. archtl. works include ITT Sheraton Hotels, Tunisia and Iraq, Marriott Hotels, Egypt and Iran, Esso Hotels, Bologna, Italy and Bordeaux, France, Holiday Inn at Salalah Oman, Univ. of Dallas Rome Campus, various projects for NATO, Pontifical N.Am. Coll., Vatican City State. Trustee John Cabot U.; adv. bd. U. Dallas, U. Rome; bd. regents Marymount Internat. Sch., Rome; councilman Indian River Shores, Fla., 2003—. With USAAF, WWII, PTO. Recipient Pub. Svc. award Tehran Lions Club, 1961, Rector's award Pontifical N.Am. Coll., Rome, 1994. Mem. AIA (award 1953), Princeton Club (NYC), John's Island Club, Circolo del Golf Club (Rome), Knight of Malta, Knight of St. Gregory, Met. Club (NYC). Home: John's Island 371 Silver Moss Dr Indian River Shores FL 32963-3430

AHRENSFELD, THOMAS FREDERICK, retired lawyer; b. Bklyn., June 30, 1923; s. Frederick Herman and Madeline Florence (Moffett) A.; m. Joan Ann McGowan, Mar. 17, 1944; 1 child, Thomas Frederick. AB, Bklyn. Coll., 1948; LL.B., Columbia U., 1948. Bar: N.Y. 1948. Assoc., then ptnr. Conboy, Hewitt, O'Brien & Boardman, N.Y.C., 1948-58; sec., assoc. gen. counsel Philip Morris Inc., N.Y.C., 1959-70, v.p., gen. counsel, 1970-76, sr. v.p., gen. counsel, 1976-85, Philip Morris Cos., Inc., N.Y.C., 1985-88. Trustee Trinity-Pawling Sch. Corp., 1976-98; elder Presbyn. Ch. 1st lt. USAAF, 1942-45. Decorated D.F.C., Air medal with oak leaf clusters. Mem. ABA, N.Y.C. Bar Assn., N.Y. Athletic Club, Mt. Kisco (N.Y.) Country Club, Johns Island (Fla.) Club. Home: 450 Beach Rd Vero Beach FL 32963

AHSANULLAH, MOHAMMAD, statistics educator; b. Tangra, Bengal, India, Aug. 31, 1936; s. Sam Ali and Nazmun Nesa; m. Masuda Gowas; children: Omar, Tabassum, Nisar. BS with honors, Presidency Coll., Calcutta, India, 1957; MS, Calcutta U., 1959; PhD, N.C. State U., 1969. Asst. prof. N.D. State U., Fargo, 1968-69; rsch. scientist Nat. Health and Welfare Can., Ottawa, 1969-74; prof. U. Brasilia (Brazil), 1974-76; rsch. scientist Nat. Health and Welfare, Ottawa, 1976-79; prof. U. Brasilia, 1979-81; vis. prof. Nat. U. of Mex., Mexico City, 1981-82; assoc. prof. Temple U., Phila., 1982-84; prof. stats. Rider Coll., Lawrenceville, N.J., 1984—. Author: Introduction to Record Values, 1988; editor. Jour. Applied Statis. Sci.; contbr. more than 125 articles to profl. jours. Fellow Royal Statis. Soc.; mem. Inst. Math. Stats., Am. Statis. Assn., Internat. Statis. Inst. Home: 91 Stallion Cir Fstrvl Trvose PA 19053-1509 Office: Rider Univ 2083 Lawrenceville Rd Lawrenceville NJ 08648-3099

AHSANUZZAMAN, ABU NOMAN, environmental engineer, hydrogeologist; m. Rizwana Haque, Jan. 6, 1998; 1 child, Raeed R. Zaman. PhD, U. Okla., 2004. EIT Tex. Rsch. asst. U. Okla., Norman, 1997—2001; sr. scientist Shaw E & I, US EPA, Ada, Okla., 2002—04. Lectr. Bangladesh U. Engring. and Tech., Dhaka, 1994—96. Contbr. articles to profl. jours. Pres. Student Assn. Bangladesh, Norman, 1997—98. Named Hon. Citizen of Okla., 1997; Cleo Cross scholar, U. Okla., 1999. Mem.: Am. Geophys. Union, Nat. Ground Water Assn., Sigma Xi. Achievements include patents pending for tool for assessing health risk involved in applying animal waste for fertilization; development of model for pollutant transport through groundwater. Office: Shaw E & I 919 Kerr Rsch Dr Ada OK 74820 Office Phone: 580-436-8587. E-mail: ahsanuzzaman.abu@epa.gov.

AHUJA, JAGDISH CHAND, mathematics professor; b. Rawalpindi, West Pakistan, Dec. 24, 1927; came to U.S., 1966, naturalized 1972; s. Nihal Chand and Ishwardai (Chhabra) A.; m. Sudarshan Sachdeva, May 18, 1955; children— Naina, Anita BA, Banaras U., 1953, MA, 1955; PhD, U. B.C., 1963. Sr. math. tchr. D.A.V. High Sch., Nairobi, Kenya, 1955-56; tchr. math. Tanzania, 1956-58; teaching asst. U. B.C., 1958-61, teaching fellow, 1961-63, stats. lab. instr., 1959-61, lectr. stats., 1961-63; asst. prof. math. U. Calgary, Can., 1963-66; assoc. prof. math. Portland State U., Oreg., 1966-69, prof. math., 1969—. Contbr. articles to profl. jours.; referee profl. jours., reviewer profl. jours. Mem. Inst. Math. Stats. Home: 4016 Orchard Dr Lake Oswego OR 97035-2406 Office: Portland State U Dept Math PO Box 751 Portland OR 97207-0751 Office Phone: 503-725-3627. Business E-Mail: ahujaj@pax.edu.

AIBEL, HOWARD J., arbitrator, mediator; b. NYC, Mar. 24, 1929; m. Katherine Webster, June 6, 1952; children: David Webster, Daniel Walter, Jonathan Brown. AB magna cum laude, 1950; JD cum laude, Harvard U., 1951. Bar: N.Y. 1952. Assoc. White & Case, NYC, 1952-57; trade regulation counsel GE, 1957-60, spl. litigation counsel elec. equipment antitrust cases, 1960-64; antitrust counsel ITT Corp., NYC, 1964-66, v.p., assoc. gen. counsel, 1966-68, sr. v.p., gen. counsel, 1968-87, exec. v.p., gen. counsel, 1987-92, exec. v.p., chief legal officer, 1992-94; ptnr. LeBoeuf Lamb Greene & MacRae, NYC, 1994-99, of counsel, 1999-2001. Vice chmn. Fund for Modern Cts., 1985-95; mem. AAA/ABA/AMA Com. Health Care Dispute Resolution, 1997-2000, trustee, Sacred Heart U. Fairfield, CT, 2003—; dir. Farrel Corp., 1994—. Mem. vis. com. Northwestern U. Law Sch., 1984—90; mem. adv. com. Corp. Counsel Ctr., chmn., 1986—87; trustee Lawyers Com. for Civil Rights, 1991—95, U. Bridgeport, 1989—91, chmn. adv. com. Sch. Law, 1987—92; cons. trustee Westport Nature Ctr. for Environ. Activities; mem. dean's adv. com. Harvard Law Sch., 2004—; commr. Conservation Commn., Weston, Conn., 2004—; dir. Westport Country Playhouse, 2005—; bd. dirs. Alliance of Resident Theatres, NY, 1986—, chmn., 1989—2002, chmn. emeritus, 2002—; bd. dirs., 1st v.p. Westport Arts Ctr., 1993—96. Ret. lt. comdr. USNR, 1946—66. Fellow Am. Bar Found. (life); mem. ABA (bus. law sect. corp. governance 1994-98), Am. Law Inst. (elected mem.), Am. Arbitration Assn. (chmn. exec. com. 1992-95, chmn. bd. dirs. 1995-98), Assn. Gen. Counsel, pres. Harvard Law Sch. Assn. NY, 1992-94, v.p. Harvard Law Sch. Assn., 1994-2002, Am. Judicature Soc. (bd. dirs. 1994-2001, exec. com. 1996-2001), Harvard Clubs NYC. Democrat. Unitarian Universalist. Home and Office: 183 Steep Hill Rd Weston CT 06883-1924 Personal E-mail: howardaibel@sbcglobal.net. Business E-Mail: hjaibel@post.harvard.edu.

AIDINOFF, M(ERTON) BERNARD, retired lawyer; b. Newport, RI, Feb. 2, 1929; s. Simon and Esther (Miller) A.; m. Celia Spiro, May 30, 1956 (dec. June 28, 1984); children: Seth G., Gail M.; m. Elsie V. Newburg, Nov. 29, 1996. BA, U. Mich., 1950; LLB magna cum laude, Harvard U., 1953. Bar: D.C. 1953, N.Y. 1954. Law clk. to Judge Learned Hand, U.S. Ct. of Appeals, N.Y.C., 1955-56; with Sullivan & Cromwell, N.Y.C., 1956-63, ptnr., 1963-96, sr. counsel, 1997—. Bd. dirs. Am. Internat. Group Inc., Goldman Sachs Philanthropy Fund; mem. adv. com. to IRS commr., 1979-80, 85-86. Editor in chief The Tax Lawyer, 1974-77. Trustee Spence Sch., 1971-79; mem. adv. com. Gibbs Bros. Found., 1965-94; mem. vis. com. Harvard U. Law Sch., 1976-82, 99—; adv. dir. Met. Opera Assn., 1989-2002; chmn. bd. dirs. St. Luke's Chamber Ensemble, 1988-2001, chmn. emeritus, 2001—; nat. campaign chair Campaign to Save Touro Synagogue; pres. Soc. Friends of Touro Synagogue, 2002-03; chair Touro Synagogue Found., 2003—. 1st lt. JAGC, AUS, 1953-55. Recipient Judge Learned Hand award Am. Jewish Com., 1997. Mem.: ABA (vice chmn. sect. taxation 1974—77, chmn.-elect 1981—82, chmn. 1982—83, chmn. commn. taxpayer compliance 1983—88, Ho. of Dels. 1988—91, sect. taxation Disting. Svc. award 2003), Am. Law Inst. (chmn. tax program com. 1988—, John Minor Wisdom award 1995), Assn. Bar City of N.Y. (exec. com. 1974—78, chmn. exec. com. 1977—78, v.p. 1978—79, chmn. taxation com. 1979—81, chmn. govt. ethics com. 1988—90), NY State Bar Assn., The Parks Coun. (bd. dirs. 1995—97), Human Rights First (bd. dirs. 1986—, treas. 1997—2002), Coun. Fgn. Rels., East Hampton Hist. Soc. (trustee 1983—89, 1990—95), Found. for a Civil Soc. (bd. dirs. 1994—, vice chmn. 1997—98, chmn. 1999—), Guild Hall (trustee 1989—94, treas. 1993—94, 1995—2002, trustee 1995—2003), Met. Club, Century Assn., India Ho., Phi Beta Kappa. Home: 980 5th Ave New York NY 10021-0126 Office: Sullivan & Cromwell 125 Broad St New York NY 10004-2498 Office Phone: 212-558-3708. E-mail: aidinoffmb@sullcrom.com.

AIELLO, ELIZABETH BLACKWELL, secondary school educator; b. Chgo., Nov. 24, 1946; d. William Thomas and Betty Louise (Landis) Blackwell; m. John William Aiello, Mar. 7, 1970; 1 child, Sarah Elizabeth. EdB, Ind. U., 1968; MS in Reading, Western Ill. U., 1992. Cert. tchr. 6-12 reading endorsement, Ill. Tchr. S.E. H.S., Springfield, Ill., 1968-69, St. Aloysius Sch., Springfield, 1971-72, St. Patrick Sch., Springfield, 1974-75, St. Agnes Sch., Springfield, 1977—. Mem. DAR, Internat. Reading Assn., Nat. Coun. English Tchrs., Ctrl. Ill. Reading Coun., Nat. Cath. Educators Assn., Alpha Upsilon Alpha. Home: 156 Maple Grove Springfield IL 62707-9567 Office: St Agnes Sch 251 N Amos Ave Springfield IL 62702-4792 Office Phone: 217-793-1370.

AIELLO, ERIN JANELLE, research scientist; b. San Jose, Calif., Feb. 9, 1978; BS magna cum laude, U. Calif. Irvine, 2000; MPH, U. Wash., 2002. Data coord., rsch. asst. Fred Hutchinson Cancer Rsch. Ctr., Seattle, 2000—02; rsch. assoc. Group Health Coop., Seattle, 2002—. Mammogram density cons. Fred Hutchinson Cancer Rsch. Ctr., Seattle, 2002—. Mem.: Am. Soc. Preventive Oncology, Am. Assn. Cancer Rsch. (assoc.). Avocations: singing, dance, running, travel. Office: Group Health Coop 1730 Minor Ave Ste 1600 Seattle WA 98101 E-mail: aiello.e@ghc.org.

AIELLO, JUDITH A., music educator; b. Newton, Iowa, Aug. 17, 1939; d. Delmar Harry Grosvenor and Helen Edrie Jacobs; m. Frank John Aiello, Aug. 13, 1966; children: Rose Helen, Dominic. BA, Vennard Coll., 1961; B in Music Edn., Drake U., 1963, M in Music Edn., 1966. Cert. educator, Iowa, N.Y., S.D. Piano tchr. St. John's Sch., Des Moines, 1962-63; ch. organist Luth. Ch., Des Moines, 1962-63; tchr. music K-8 Davis County Schs., Bloomfield, Iowa, 1963-65; tchr. music 3-6 Westchester County Schs., Port Chester, N.Y., 1966-67; staff accompanist U. S.D., Vermillion, 1968-69; tchr. music K-8 Vermillion Pub. Schs., 1975-94; pvt. piano tchr. Vermillion, 1995—. Organist St. Agnes Ch., Vermillion, 1980-2000. Mem. Nat. Guild Am. Musicians, Music Tchrs. Nat. Assn., Federated Music Club (pres. 1990-99), Delta Kappa Gamma. Roman Catholic. Avocations: organizing bible study groups, gardening. Home: 30174 448th Ave Volin SD 57072-7021

AIELLO, STEPHEN, public relations executive; BA in History, NYU; MA in History, Columbia U.; PhD in Urban Studies, Union Grad. Sch. Former adminstr. N.Y.C. Bd. Edn., pres., 1974-80; former prof. Fordham U., N.Y.C.; spl. asst. ethnic affairs White House, Washington, 1980-81; exec. dir. N.Y.C. Ednl. Constrn. Fund; v.p., dir., civic affairs Burson-Marsteller, 1983-86, exec. v.p., pub. affairs, 1987-89, dir. pub. affairs, 1991-92; exec. v.p., gen. mgr. Cohn & Wolfe, N.Y.C., 1989-90, exec. v.p., gen. mgr. N.Y., 1992-93, pres., CEO, 1993—2003; sr. counselor pub. affairs Hill & Knowlton, N.Y.C., 2003—. Chair ethnic/urban coun. Nat. Dem. Com.; former chmn. N.Y. Urban Coalition, N.Y.C. Youth Bd., NYU Creative Arts Team; former mem. Nat. Ctr. for Urban Ethnic Affairs, Nat. Dropout Prevention Fund; former trustee N.Y. State Dem. Com.; former chmn. Cmty. Svcs. Soc. N.Y.; dir. Nat. Italian Am. Found., Kappa Delta Pi; pres. N.Y.C. Bd. Edn., 1976-79. Office: Hill & Knowlton Third Floor 466 Lexington Avenue New York NY 10017

AIGEN, BETSY PAULA, psychotherapist; b. N.Y.C., Sept. 13, 1938; d. Abraham H. and Gertrude (Rosenblum) Wasserman; m. Ronald Aigen, Dec. 7, 1957 (div. Jan. 1979); m. Isadore Schumukler, June 20, 1982; children: Jennifer Loren, Samantha Devin. BA, New Sch. Social Research, 1971; MA, Columbia U., 1972; D of Psychology, Rutgers U., 1980. Group co-leader, asst. psychotherapist Inst. Rational Psychotherapy, N.Y.C., 1967-72; asst. course instr. Columbia U., N.Y.C., 1971-72; psychotherapist Mt. Carmel Guild, Englewood, N.J., 1980-82, SELF Edn. Learning and Feeling, N.Y.C., 1982—; founder, dir. Surrogate Mother Program, N.Y.C., 1985—. Cons. Police Chief Tng. Community Workshops Assn., N.Y.C., 1973-74, Richmond Fellowship Mental Health Halfway Houses, Eng. and U.S., 1970-75. Contbr. articles to profl. jours. Chmn. Tenants Com., N.Y.C., 1975-85; active Profl. Theatre, 1956-67. Mem. Nat. Orgn. Women, RESOLVE, Adoptive Parents Com., Am. Psychol. Assn., N.Y. St. Psychol. Assn., N.J. St. Psychol. Assn., N.Y. Assn. Feminist Therapists. (co-founder, charter), Am. Orgn. Surrogate Parenting Practitioners (founder, charter). Democrat. Jewish. Home: 220 W 93rd St Apt 1A New York NY 10025-7412 Office: Surrogate Mother Program Childbirth Cons Svcs 220 W 93rd St Apt 1A New York NY 10025-7412

AIGNER, DENNIS JOHN, economics professor, consultant; b. L.A., Sept. 27, 1937; s. Herbert Lewis and Della Geraldine (Balasek) A.; m. Vernita Lynne White, Dec. 21, 1957 (div. May 1977); children: Mitchell A., Annette N., Anita L., Angela D.; m. Gretchen Camille Bertolet, Dec. 22, 1992. BS, U. Calif.-Berkeley, 1959, MA, 1962, PhD, 1963. Asst. prof. econs. U. Ill., Urbana, 1962-67; from assoc. prof. to prof. U. Wis., Madison, 1967-76; prof., chmn. dept. econs. U. So. Calif., L.A., 1976-88; dean grad. sch. mgmt. U. Calif., Irvine, 1988-97, prof. grad. sch. mgmt., 1988—, assoc. dean sch. environ. sci. and mgmt. Santa Barbara, 1998-2000, acting dean, 2000-01, dean, 2001—05, adj. prof., 2005—. Pres. Dennis Aigner Inc., L.A., 1978—; dir. Analysis Group Econs. Author: Introduction to Statistical Decision Making, 1968, Basic Econometrics, 1971; editor: Latent Variables in Socio-Economic Models, 1977; co-editor: Jour. Econometrics, 1972-91. Fulbright fellow Belgium, 1970, Israel, 1983, Bren fellow U. Calif. Santa Barbara, 1998—2004; NSF grantee, 1968-70, 70-72, 73-76, 79-81, 84-86. Fellow Econometric Soc.; mem. Am. Statis. Assn., Am. Econ. Assn. Office: Sch Environ Sci Mgmt U Calif Santa Barbara CA 93106 Office Phone: 805-893-8579, 949-824-6229. E-mail: djaigner@bren.ucsb.edu.

AIKAWA, JERRY KAZUO, internist, educator; b. Stockton, Calif., Aug. 24, 1921; s. Genmatsu and Shizuko (Yamamoto) A.; m. Chitose Aihara, Sept. 20, 1944; 1 son, Ronald K. AB, U. Calif., 1942; MD, Wake Forest Coll., 1945. Intern, asst. resident N.C. Baptist Hosp., 1945-47; NRC fellow in med. scis. U. Calif. Med. Sch., 1947-48; NRC, AEC postdoctoral fellow in med. scis. Bowman Gray Sch. Medicine, 1948-50, instr. internal medicine, 1950-53, asst. prof., 1953; established investigator Am. Heart Assn., 1952-58; exec. officer lab. service Univ. Hosps., 1958-61, dir. lab. services, 1961-83, dir. allied health program, 1969—, assoc. dean allied health program, 1983—, pres. med. bd.; assoc. dean clin. affairs asst. prof. U. Colo. Sch. Medicine, 1953- 60, assoc. prof. medicine, 1960-67, prof., 1967—, prof. biometrics, 1974—, assoc. dean clin. affairs, 1974—. Pres. Med. bd. Univ. Hosps. Fellow ACP, Am. Coll. Nutrition; mem. Western Soc. Clin. Research, So. Soc. Clin. Research, Soc. Exptl. Biology and Medicine, Am. Fedn. Clin. Research, AAAS, Central Soc. Clin. Research, AMA, Assn. Am. Med. Colls., Phi Beta Kappa, Sigma Xi, Alpha Omega Alpha Office: U Colo Sch Medicine 4200 E 9th Ave Denver CO 80220-3706 Home: 501 E Ironwood DR Phoenix AZ 85020-1044

AIKEN, CHARLES SHELTON, geographer, educator; b. Thyatira, Miss., Aug. 20, 1938; s. Claude Lavelle and Frances Jewell (Smith) Aiken; m. Mary Ann Ford, Aug. 22, 1970; children: Charles Ford, John William. BS, U. Memphis, 1960; MA, U. Ga., 1962, PhD, 1969. Instr. U. Memphis, 1962—65; from asst. prof. to assoc. prof. U. Tenn., Knoxville, 1969—78, prof., 1978—. Cons. Nat. Atlas of U.S., Washington, 1970—73; guest prof. U. Bonn, Germany, 1994. Author: The Cotton Plantation South Since the Civil War, 1998. Fellow: Am. Geog. Soc.; mem.: Assn. Am. Geographers (pres. S.E. divsn. 1985—87, J. B. Jackson prize 1999, Rsch. Honors award S.E. divsn. 1987). Democrat. Ch. Of Christ. Avocations: golf, reading, writing. Office: U Tenn Burchfiel Geography Bldg Dept Geography Knoxville TN 37996

AIKEN, CLAYTON HOLMES, singer; b. Raleigh, NC, Nov. 30, 1978; s. Vernon Grissom and Faye (Parker) Aiken. Student, U. NC at Charlotte. Founder Bubel/Aiken Found. for children. Singer: (single) This is the Night, 2003, (albums) Measure of a Man, 2003 (triple platinum), Merry Christmas with Love, 2004; singer: (with various artists) American Idol Season 2: All Time, 2003; singer, runner up (TV series) American Idol: The Search for a Superstar, 2003; performer: Miss America Pageant, 2003, An American Idol Christmas, 2003, The Nick at Nite Holiday Special, 2003, Fromage, 2003; co-author (with Allison Glock): (books) Learning to Sing: Hearing the Music in Your Life, 2004. Address: Clay Aiken Official Fan Club PO Box 90217 Raleigh NC 27675 Office: Bubel/Aiken Found PO Box 90307 Raleigh NC 27675 Address: c/o The Firm Mgmt Agy Jacobson & Colfin PC 19 W 21st St New York NY 10010

AIKEN, MICHAEL THOMAS, former academic administrator; b. El Dorado, Ark., Aug. 20, 1932; s. William Floyd and Mary (Gibbs) Aiken; m. Catherine Comet, Mar. 28, 1969; 1 child, Caroline R. BA, U. Miss., 1954; MA, U. Mich., 1955, PhD, 1964. Asst. prof. U. Wis., Madison, 1963—67, assoc. prof., 1967—70, prof., 1970—84, assoc. dean coll. arts and scis., 1980—82; prof. U. Pa., Phila., 1984—93, dean sch. arts and scis., 1985—87, provost, 1987—93; chancellor U. Ill., Urbana, 1993—2001, Champaign/Urbana, 1993—2001. Co-author: The Dynamics of Idealism, 1971, Economic Failure, Alienation, and Extremism, 1968; co-editor: Complex Organizations: Critical Perspectives, 1981, The Structures of Community Power, 1970. Mem.: Am. Sociol. Assn. (sec. 1986—89). E-mail: aiken@uiuc.edu.

AIKEN, PETER HAYNES, systems engineer, educator, architect, consultant; b. Washington, Jan. 17, 1959; s. Benjamin Hayes and Susan (Benck) Aiken. BS, Va. Commonwealth U., 1981, MS, 1984; PhD, George Mason U., 1989. Sr. engr. Va. Commonwealth U., Richmond, 1980-85, asst. prof. info. systems Sch. Bus., 1992-98, assoc. prof. infosys., dir. Inst. for Data Rsch., 1998—; rsch. asst. George Mason U., Fairfax, Va., 1985-89, vis. asst. prof., 1989-93, dir. Hypermedia Tech. Lab., 1989-92; computer scientist Ctr. for Info. Mgmt. U.S. Dept. Def., Vienna, Va., 1992—. Cons. many leading internat. orgns. including: Carnegie-Mellon U., Deutsche Bank, Eli Lilly & Co., Hoffman La Roche Inc., Mattel, Time Life, Inc. Office Sec. Defense and many more. Author: (book) Data Reverse Engineering, 1995; author: (with W. C. Fikelstein) Building Corporate Portals Using XML. Recipient Internat. Achievement award, Data Mgmt. Assn. Internat., 2001, Cmty. award, 2005; scholar George Mason Inst., 1985—88. Mem.: IEEE (sr.), Assn. Computing Machinery. Avocations: playing electric bass, photography. Office: School of Bus Dept of ISY 1015 Floyd Ave Richmond VA 23284-4000 Home: 13155 Country Garden Ln Montpelier VA 23192-3028 Fax: (804) 828-8884. Office Phone: 804-828-0174. E-mail: paiken@acm.org.

AIKEN, VERNOY FRED, government agency administrator; b. Atlanta, Jan. 30, 1938; s. Vernoy Grady and Anne Whitehead Aiken; m. Sue Carol Camp, Aug. 1, 1959; 1 child, Susan Leigh Aiken Grier. *Mother and father were recognized in 1985 as "Citizens of the Year" for their community work by the Paulding County Chamber of Commerce in Georgia. Mother, father, and all three of their children, Fred, Jody, and Eugenia were named Family of the Year by the Kennesaw Mountain Chapter of the March of Dimes in Marietta, Georgia for their fundraising efforts in 1976. Vernoy Aiken Road bears the name of his father and namesake. Daughter, Susan Leigh Grier, graduated from the University of Georgia in 1989, is a corporate trainer for the Automatic Data Processing Corporation, married David Grier, and has one child, Caroline Aiken Grier, age 2.* Student, U. Ga., 1960; LLB, Atlanta Law Sch., 1965; banking cert., La. State U., 1969. V.p. Cobb Bank and Trust, Smyrna, Ga., 1973—79; owner Alfredo's Restaurant, Dallas, Ga., 1975—89; state rep. Ga. State Ho. Reps., Atlanta, 1980—92; dist. rep. U.S. Congressman Newt Gingrich, 1992—97; dist. dir., sr. dist. rep. U.S. Congressman Bob Barr, Marietta, Ga., 1997—2003; econ. devel. and devel. gov. rels. specialist Ga. Dept. Labor, Atlanta, 2003—. Bd. mem. SafePath Child Advocacy Ctr.; active No. Ga. Svcs. for Blind and lOW Vision, Cancer Crusade, March of Dimes; past pres. Smyrna Rotary, Marietta-Metro Rotary. Sgt. Ga. Air Nat. Guard. Named Outstanding Legislator, Ga. Mcpl. Assn., 1980. Mem. Cobb City C. of C. (past pres.), Jaycees. Republican. Avocations: reading, golf, watching College football, Nascar auto racing. Home: 4020 Pineview Dr Smyrna GA 30080 Office: Ga Dept Labor Ste 650 148 International Blvd Atlanta GA 30303-1751 Office Phone: 404-232-3789.

AIKENS, MARTHA BRUNETTE, national park service administrator; b. Jayess, Miss., Aug. 23, 1949; d. Walter and Elnora La Doris (Bridges) A. BS in Social Sci., Alcorn State U., 1971; postgrad., George Williams Coll., 1974, Fla. Internat. U., 1977, George Washington U., 1979, Pa. State U., 1979, U. So. Calif., D.C. Ext., 1980. Social worker Pearl River County Devel. Corp., Picayune, Miss., 1971—72; environ. ednl. specialist Nat. Park Svc., Homestead, Fla., 1973—75, environ. ednl. coord., 1973—75, comm. specialist, 1976—78; park mgr. Bklyn., 1978—79, Dept. Interior's Mgmt. Program, 1979—80, St. Augustine, Fla., 1979—83, Washington, 1983—88; dir. training and employee devel. Nat. Park Svc., 2002—. Instr., cons. Coll. African Wildlife Mgmt., Tanzania, 1980, Fed. Law Enforcement Tng. Ctr., Glynco, Ga., 1983—, Stephen T. Mather Employee Devel. Ctr., Harper's Ferry, W.Va., 1988—91; supt. Independence Nat. Hist. Pk., Phila., 1991—2002; chair Nat. Pk. Svc. Women's Conf., New Orleans, 1991. Author: tchrs. guides on Everglades Nat. Park, 1973—76, park brochure, 1977; contbr. chapters to books chpts. to books. Active Dept. Interior's Partnership in Edn. Commn., Washington, 1983—, Fed. Interagy Commn. on Edn., Washington, 1983—, Nat. Park Svc. Employee Rels. Task Force, Washington, 1983—, 21st Century Task Force, 1988—, Salt River Bay Nat. Hist. Pk. and Ecol. Preserve Adv. Commn., 1993—, Strategic Planning Task Force, Atlanta, 1981—83, S.E. Regional Equal Opportunity Commn., Atlanta, 1982—83; bd. trustees Walnut St. Theatre, Phila., 1993—; bd. dirs. Peopling of Phila., 1993—; mem. Leading by Example, 1992—. Recipient Star 104.5 Woman of Yr. award, 1993, Image award, YWCA. Office: Dept Training & Employee Devel Nat Park Svc 1849 C St NW Washington DC 20240*

AIKMAN, ALBERT EDWARD, lawyer; b. Norman, Okla., Mar. 11, 1922; s. Albert Edwin and Thelma Annette (Brooke) A.; m. Shirley Barnes, June 24, 1944; children: Anita Gayle, Priscilla June, Rebecca Brooke. BS, Tex. A&M U., 1947; JD cum laude, So. Meth. U., 1948, LLM, 1954. Bar: Tex. (no. dist.) 1948, U.S. Supreme Ct. 1956, U.S. Ct. Appeals (5th dist.), U.S. Tax Ct. Tax ct. staff atty. Phillips Petroleum Co., Amarillo, Tex., 1948-49; sole practice pvt. practice, Amarillo, Tex., 1949-53; tax counsel Magnolia Petroleum Co. (Mobil), Dallas, 1953-56; ptnr. Locke, Purnell, Boren, Laney & Neely, Dallas, 1973-81; of counsel Pickens Energy Corp., Dallas, 1981-96, Ptnrs. in Exploration, Dallas, 1997—; couns. Ptnrs. in Exploration, LLC, Dallas, 1997—. Contbr. articles to profl. jours. Served in inf. U.S. Army, 1943-45. Mem. ABA, Tex. Bar Assn., Dallas Bar Assn. Methodist. E-mail: aikmanae@aol.com.

AIKMAN, TROY, former professional football player; b. West Covina, Calif., Nov. 21, 1966; Student, Okla. U., UCLA. Quarterback Dallas Cowboys NFL, 1989—2000; ret. from football, April 9, 2000. Mem. Super Bowl Championship Team, 1992, 93, 95. Co-host (with Brad Sham) weekly radio show, 1989—2000, co-host (with Pat Summerall) TV program, co-host (with Bruce Murray) Troy Aikman Football Show, Sporting News Radio, 2003. Founder The Troy Aikman Found., 1992—. Named Super Bowl Most Valuable Player, 1992, TV's Top Newcomer, Sports Illustrated, 2001; named to Sporting News Coll. All-Am. team, 1988, Pro Bowl team, 1991, 1992, 1993, 1994, 1996, Sporting News NFL All-Pro team, 1993. Mailing: The Troy Aikman Found PO Box 3427 Coppell TX 75019 also: SPRINGboard Agency PO Box 581 Grapevine TX 76099*

AILES, ROGER EUGENE, television producer, consultant; b. Warren, Ohio, May 15, 1940; s. Robert Eugene and Donna Marie (Cunningham) Ailes; m. Elizabeth Tilson, Feb. 14, 1998; 1 child. B.F.A., Ohio U., 1962, D in Communications (hon.), 1989. Assoc. dir. Sta. KYW-TV, Cleve., 1962-63, prodr., dir., 1963-65; prodr. Mike Douglas Show Westinghouse Broadcasting Corp., Phila., 1965-67, exec. prodr., 1967-68; exec. prodr. TV for Richard M. Nixon, 1968; chmn. Ailes Comm., Inc., NYC, 1969—92; exec. v.p. TV News Inc., NYC, 1975-76; pres. CNBC, NYC, 1993-96, America's Talking, NYC, 1993; chmn., CEO, Fox News, NYC, 1996—; exec. editor FOXNews.com, 2000—; chmn. Fox Television Stations, 2005—. Former cons. WCBS-TV; communications cons. to polit. and bus. leaders; v.p. Conf. Personal Mgrs. Author: You Are the Message: Secrets of the Master Communicators, 1987; producer: Broadway mus. Mother Earth, 1972, (play) Hot-L Baltimore, 1973-76 (4 Obie awards, 1973); exec. producer, dir.: (TV spl.) The Last Frontier, 1974, Television and the Presidency, 1984 (Emmy award); producer, dir.: (TV spl.) Fellini: Wizards, Clowns and Honest Liars (Emmy nominee 1977); exec. producer: Tomorrow: Coast to Coast, 1981, The Rush Limbaugh Show, 1992-96, A Current Affair, The Maury Povich Show, The Leeza Show; co-exec. prodr.: An All-Star Salute to Our Troops, 1991. Polit. cons. Reagan '84, Bush '88. Recipient 2 Emmy awards for The Mike Douglas Show, 1967, 68, award for Shakespeare prodn., Fine Arts Mag., 1964, Liberty Bell award, Advt. Alliance Phila., 1971, Commendation award for contbn. comm., Ohio U., 1972, Silver Cir. award, Nat. Acad. TV Arts and Scis., 1999. Mem. AFTRA, Dirs. Guild Am., Radio and TV News Dirs. Assn. Office: Fox News 1211 Ave of Americas New York NY 10036*

AILEY, D. BRIAN, music educator; b. Chattanooga, May 23, 1962; s. Michael L. Ailey and Gladys E. Eldridge, Donald S. Eldridge (Stepfather). MusB, Carson-Newman Coll., Jefferson City, Tenn., 1985. Cert. music tchr. Tenn., 1993. Vocal music tchr. North Whitfield Mid. Sch., Dalton, Ga., 1988—90; vocal music/video prodn. tchr. Tyner Mid. Sch., Chattanooga, 1990—99; vocal music tchr. Chattanooga Mid. Sch., 1999—2000, Hixson Mid. Sch., Hixson, Tenn., 2000—; pianist, tenor sect. leader Brainerd United Meth. Ch., Chattanooga, 1990—. Tenor soloist Chattanooga Symphony and Opera Chorus, 1987—97; first tenor soloist Chattanooga Bach Choir, 1989—2000; tenor soloist Chattanooga Choral Arts, 1991—98. Mem.: Music Educators Nat. Conf., East Tenn. Vocal Assn. (jr. high/mid. sch. v.p. 2004—). Christian. Avocations: antique electronics collecting, walking, amateur composer, classic car restoration. Home: 3837-B North Terr Chattanooga TN 37411-5122 Office: Hixson Middle School 5401 School Dr Hixson TN 37343 Office Phone: 423-870-0600. Personal E-mail: brinchatt@aol.com. E-mail: ailey_brian@hcde.org.

AILLONI-CHARAS, DAN, marketing executive; b. Ploiesti, Romania, May 22, 1930; came to U.S., 1950, naturalized, 1960; s. Max and Felicia (Lupescu) Charas; m. Miriam C. Taytelbaum, Oct. 8, 1957; children: Ethan Benjamin, Orrin, Adam. AB with honors, U. Calif., Berkeley, 1952, MA, 1953; PhD, NYU, 1968. Mem. editl. staff San Francisco Call Bull., 1953-54; exec. sec. TAHAL, 1955-56; project dir. Marplan divsn. Interpub., N.Y.C., 1958-60; supr. advt. studies NBC, N.Y.C., 1960-62; dir. consumer and comm. rsch. Forbes Rsch., Inc., N.Y.C., 1962-63; mgr. market rsch. Chesebrough-Pond's, Inc., N.Y.C., 1963-64, new products mgr., 1964-68, mgr. internat. mktg. services dept., 1968-69; pres. Stratmar Sys., Inc., Port Chester, NY, 1969-91, CEO, 1991—2001, chmn., 2001—; asst., then prof. mktg. Pace U., 1963-85. Mem. adv. bd. Premium Incentive Show, 1986-92, Nat. Premium Incentive Show, 1987-92; lectr. Israel Inst. Tech., 1956-58, dir. extension divsn. no. region, 1956-58. Author: Promotion: A Guide to Effective Promotional Planning, Strategies and Execution, 1984; editor: Mktg. Rev., 1960-63, Proc. 1st Ann. Conf. on Rsch. Design, 1964, New Directions in Research Design, 2d Conf., 1965, Planning, 1968-71; bd. editors Jour. Consumer Mktg., 1982—, Jour. of Brand and Product Mgmt., 1991—, Jour. Svc. Mktg., 1992—; contbr. to Brandweek, Mktg. News, Chain Drug Rev., MMR, New Product News. Trustee Inst. Advanced Mktg. Studies, 1965-66, Philharmonic Symphony of Westchester, 1977-80; bd. dirs. Young Men's Bd. Trade, 1960-63, state dir., N.Y. StatJr. C. of C., 1962-63; bd. advisers Ad Expo, 1978; 1st v.p. Student World Affairs Coun. Northern Calif., 1953-54, chmn. Asilomar World Affairs conf., 1954; founder Israel Assn. Grads. Social Scis. & Humanities, 1955; pres. Haifa Jr. C. of C., 1956-57. Coro Found. fellow, 1953; Univ. honors scholar NYU, 1968. Mem. Am. Mktg. Assn. (pres. N.Y. chpt. 1965-66, nat. v.p. 1970-71), Promotion Mktg. Assn. Am. (bd. dirs. 1978-98, chmn. edn. com. 1979-81, 82-91, chmn. premium show com. 1982-91, exec. com. 1986-87, 89-93, 94-95, 96-97, 99-2000, chmn. nat. conf. 1988, 96, v.p. 1989-93, 94-95, chmn. retailers and mfrs. conf. 1992, 93, chmn. in-store mktg. coun. 1993-94), N.Am. Soc. Corp. Planning (bd. dirs. 1970-72), Nat. Assn. Chain Drug Stores (nat. industry adv. bd. 1992—2003), Am. Friends of the Coll. Mgmt. (chmn. 1999-2004), Soc. Profl. Journalists, Nat. Press Club, Coro Alumni Assn. (nat. bd. dirs. 1989-95), Sigma Delta Chi, Phi Sigma Alpha. Office: Stratmar Bldg 109 Willett Ave Port Chester NY 10573-4287 E-mail: dailloni@stratmar.com.

AIMAN, ROBERT WILLIAM, elementary school educator, vocational school educator; b. Warrin, Mich., Mar. 11, 1973; s. William Russell Aiman; m. Kimberly P. Purcell, Dec. 7, 2002; children: Cheyenne Melody, Shawnee Morgan, Cherokee Rose, Dakota Dawn. BS, Utah State U., 1997; MSc, Brigaham Young U., 2004. Tchr. tech. and engring. Am. Fork (Utah) Jr. H.S., 1997—. Mem.: Assn. Career and Tech. Eduation (Program Excellence award 2000, Outstanding Tech. Edn. Program award 2000). Avocations: woodworking, fishing, hunting, camping. Office Phone: 801 756 8543 110.

AINBINDER, BRUCE, lawyer; b. Bklyn., Nov. 17, 1961; BS, U. Fla., 1984; MBA, Adelphi U., 1990; JD cum laude, St. John's U., 1993. Bar: NY 1994, US Dist. Ct. Ea., So., No. & We. Districts NY 1994. Ptnr. Wilson, Elser, Moskowitz, Edelman & Dicker LLP, NYC. Mem.: ABA, NY Bar Assn. Office: Wilson Elser Moskowitz Edelman & Sicker LLP 23rd Fl 150 E 42nd St New York NY 10017-5639 Office Phone: 212-490-3000 ext. 2136. Office Fax: 212-490-3038. Business E-Mail: ainbinderb@wemed.com.

AINLAY, STEPHEN CHARLES, academic administrator, educator; b. South Bend, Ind., July 30, 1951; s. Charles William and Dorothy Marie (Breunlin) A.; m. Judy Renee Gardner, Aug. 16, 1975; children: Jesse Gardner, Jonathan Charles. BA in Sociology, Goshen (Ind.) Coll., 1973; MA in Sociology, Rutgers U., 1977, PhD in Sociology, 1981. Asst. prof. Coll. of the Holy Cross, Worcester, Mass., 1982-87, assoc. prof., 1987-93, prof. sociology and anthropology, 1993—, dir. Ctr. for Interdisciplinary and Spl. Studies, 1993—, v.p. for acad. affairs, dean of the Coll., 1996—. Cons. Am. Found. for the Blind, N.Y.C., 1980-81; vis. scholar St. Edmunds Coll., Cambridge U., Eng., 1987. Author: Day Brought Back My Night, 1989; co-author: Mennonite Entrepreneur, 1995; editor: The Dilemma of Difference, 1986, Making Sense of Modern Times, 1986. Mem. adv. bd. Mass. Assn. for Blind, Worcester, Audio Jour., Worcester, 1992-94; mem. Coun. on Aging, Holden, Mass., 1992-94; mem. exec. com. Colls. of Worcester Consortium, 2002-04. Princeton U. postdoctoral fellow, 1981-82. Mem. Soc. for Sci. Study of Religion, Am. Conf. Acad. Deans (bd. dirs., vice chair). Office: College of the Holy Cross 1 College St Worcester MA 01610-2322 Office Phone: 508-793-2541. Business E-Mail: sainlay@holycross.edu.

AINLEY, DAVID JAMES, systems engineer, electrical engineer; b. San Diego, May 4, 1956; s. James Edward and Vivian Marie (Magnuson) A.; m. Mary Claire Howell, Oct. 22, 1988; children: Elena Estelle, Chloe Abigayle, Parker Vance. AS, SUNY, Albany, 1981; AA, U. Ctrl. Fla., 1985, BSE in Elec. Engring., 1988. Sr. assoc. sys. engr. Lockheed Space Ops., Kennedy Space Ctr., Fla., 1988-91; sr. design engr. McDonnell Douglas Space and Def. Sys., Kennedy Space Ctr., 1991—96. With USN, 1977-83, USNR, 1983-2001. Mem. Internat. Coun. on Sys. Engring. Avocations: reading, scuba diving, model building, hiking, water and snow skiing. Home: 10 Saint Mary Dr Hudson NH 03051-5077

AINSLEY, WILLIAM FRANKLIN, geographer, educator; b. Elizabeth City, NC, Aug. 5, 1944; s. William Franklin Ainsley, Sr. and Doris Gregory Ainsley; m. Mary Magdolene Fennell, June 23, 1968; children: Susan Elizabeth, Mark Benjamin. BA in Biblical Studies, U. NC, 1966, MA in Geography, PhD in Geography, U. NC, 1977; MDiv, Southeastern Bapt. Theological Seminary, 1969. Instr. U. NC, Chapel Hill, NC, 1972—73, Wilmington, NC, 1973—77, asst. prof. to assoc. to prof., 1977—. Bd. trustees Cape Fear Mus., Wilmington, NC, 1979—82; mem. Historic Dist. Comm., Wilmington, 1982—84; bd. dir. Pioneer Am. Soc., Wilmington, 1987—. Author: North Carolina: Its Land and People, 1988, World Geography, 1991, Front Porches and Parlors: Historical Architecture of Faison, NC, 1994. Internat. programs chair Wilmington-Cape Fear Rotary Club, Wilmington, NC, 1998—. Recipient Tchg. Excellence award, U. NC Bd. of Gov., 2004, H.H. Douglas Dist. Svc. award, Pioneer Am. Soc., 2003, Edn. of Yr. award, NC Geographical Soc., 2003. Mem.: NC Geographical Soc. (pres. 1988—89), Assn. of Am. Geographers, Pioneer Am. Soc. (sec., treas. 1989—). Democrat. Home: 1705 Princess St Wilmington NC 28405 Office: Univ NC Earth Sci Dept 601 S Coll Rd Wilmington NC 28403 Office Phone: 910-962-3493. Office Fax: 910-962-7077. E-mail: ainsleyf@uncw.edu.

AINSLIE, GEORGE WILLIAM, psychiatrist; b. Ithaca, N.Y., Sept. 19, 1944; s. George William and Elizabeth Lee Ainslie; m. Elizabeth Boyd Keeney, June 25, 1966; children: Matthew Forrest, Roger Scott, Eleanor Ruth. BA, Yale Coll., 1965; MD, Harvard Med. Sch., 1969. Diplomate Am. Bd. Psychiatry and Neurology; cert. adult psychiatry. Intern Mary Imogene Bassett Hosp., Cooperstown, N.Y., 1969-70; resident in psychiatry Mass. Mental Health Ctr., Boston, 1970-71, 73-75; fellow Harvard U. Health Svcs., Cambridge, Mass., 1975-76; asst. clin. dir. Mass. Mental Health Ctr., Boston, 1976-79; psychiatrist VA Med. Ctr., Coatesville, Pa., 1979-90, chief psychiatrist, 1990—. Asst. prof. Jefferson Med. Coll., Phila., 1979-85, assoc. prof., 1985-92; clin. prof. Temple U. Med. Coll., Phila., 1992—; rsch. assoc. Harvard Lab. Exptl. Psychology, Cambridge, Mass., 1967-78. Author: Picoeconomics: The Strategic Interaction of Successive Motivational States Within The Person, 1992, Breakdown of Will, 2001; contbr. articles on motivational conflict to profl. jours. Surgeon, USPHS, 1971-73. Mem. Players Club Swarthmore (stage dir.), Phi Beta Kappa. Avocations: dramatics, antiquarian book dealer. Office: Dept Psychiatry VA Med Ctr 116A Coatesville PA 19320 Office Phone: 610-383-0260. Business E-Mail: Ainslie@Coatesville.va.gov, George.Ainslie@va.gov.

AINSWORTH, KENT P., engineering company executive; BS, San Jose U., 1970. With URS Corp., San Francisco, 1987—, former v.p., contr., v.p., CFO, 1991—, sec., 1994—, exec. v.p., 1996—. Office: URS Corp 600 Montgomery St 25th Fl San Francisco CA 94111 Office Phone: 415-774-2700.*

AINSWORTH, LOUIS LYNDE, lawyer, manufacturing executive; b. Moline, Ill., Aug. 31, 1947; s. Calvin and Elizabeth (Carney) A.; m. Susan H. Hopper, Mar. 22, 1969; children: Katherine E., Lucy A. BA summa cum laude, Seattle U., 1972; JD cum laude, William Mitchell Coll., St. Paul, 1977. Bar: Minn. 1977, U.S. Dist. Ct. Minn. 1977, U.S. Ct. Appeals (8th cir.) 1981. Assoc., ptnr. Wiese & Cox Ltd., Mpls., 1977-84; ptnr. Henson & Efron, P.A., Mpls., 1984-97; sr. v.p. and gen. counsel Pentair, Inc., St. Paul, 1997—, sec., 2002—. Office: Pentair Inc 5500 Wayzata Blvd Golden Valley MN 55416-1259

AINSWORTH, PENNE, accountant, educator; b. Manhattan, Kans., Apr. 21, 1958; d. Eugene and Shirley Wendt; m. Scott Ainsworth, June 25, 1977; children: Heather Grable, Dusty. BS, Kans. State U., 1983, MS in Acctg., 1984; PhD, U. of Nebr., 1988. CPA Kans., 1985, cert. Mgmt. Acct., Inst. of Cert. Mgmt. Accountants, 1992, CIA, Inst. of Internal Auditors, 1995. Asst. prof. Kans. State U., Manhattan, 1987—93, assoc. prof., 1993—97, U. of Wyo., Laramie, 1997—2001, prof., dept. of acctg., 2001—, chair, dept. of acctg., 2004—. Author: (textbook) Introduction to Accounting: An Integrated Approach. Recipient Coll. of Bus. Outstanding Sr. Tchg. award, U. of Wyo., 1999, 2001, 2004, John P. Ellbogen Meritorious Tchg. award, 2002. Mem.: Am. Assn. for Higher Edn., Inst. of Mgmt. Accts., Am. Acctg. Assn. Office: University of Wyoming Dept 3275 1000 E University Ave Laramie WY 82071 Business E-Mail: penne@uwyo.edu.

AIONA, JAMES R., JR., lieutenant governor; b. Honolulu, June 8, 1955; m. Vivian Welsh; children: Makana, Ohulani, Kulia, Kaimilani. BA in Polit. Sci., U. of the Pacific; JD, U. Hawaii. Law clk. hon. Wendell K. Huddy Cir. Ct. Judge First Cir. Hawaii, 1981—82; dep. pros. atty. City and County Honolulu, 1982—85, dep. corp. counsel City Attys. Office, 1985—87, chief litigator, 1987—90; family ct. judge 1st Cir. State Hawaii, 1990—93, cir. ct. judge 14th divsn., 1993—96; adminstrv. judge Drug Ct. Program, 1996—98; ret., 1998; pvt. practice, 1997—2002; part-time family dist. ct. judge, 1999—2002; lt. gov. State of Hawaii, Honolulu, 2002—. Asst. basketball coach varsity boys St. Lous H.S.; vol. soccer coach AYSO; vol. youth baseball coach Makakilo-Kapolei; vol. judge H.S. mock trials competition State of Hawaii; bd. mem. The Salvation Army, Reid J.K. Richards Found., Youth At Risk Adv. Coun., Maryknoll Schs., 1995—98. Republican. Office: Exec Chambers Hawaii State Capitol Honolulu HI 96813

AISENBERG, IRWIN MORTON, lawyer; b. Worcester, Mass., Aug. 8, 1925; s. William and Esther (Lewis) A.; m. Lois P., Sept. 4, 1955 (div. Apr. 1986); children: Karen Sue Portner, Sondra Lee, David Craig, Steven Bennett; m. Hana Jane Barton, June 19, 1999. BS in Chem Engring., Carnegie Mellon U., 1946; JD, Georgetown U., 1957. Bar: DC 1958, US Ct. of Customs and Patent Appeals 1958, US Ct. Appeals (DC cir.) 1958, US Supreme Ct. 1964, NJ 1965, Va. 1969, US Ct. Appeals (fed. cir.) 1982; registered profl. engr., Mass. Patent examiner US Patent Trademark Office, Washington, 1954-57; assoc. atty. Wenderoth, Lind & Ponack, Washington, 1957-63; chief patent counsel Sandoz, Inc., Hanover, NJ, 1963-67; pvt. practice Washington, 1967-75; ptnr. Berman, Aisenberg & Platt, Washington, 1975-91, mng. ptnr., 1980-85; ptnr. Jacobson Holman PLLC, Washington, 1991—. Lectr. Franklin Pierce Law Sch., Concord, NH, 1980-88; mem. appeal bd. Nat. Register Health Svc. Providers Psychology, 1987-89. Mem. editl. adv. bd. IDEA, Jour. of Law and Tech., 1981-95; bd. editors: Patent Strategy and Management; author: Attorney's Dictionary of Patent Claims, 1985, with yearly supplements, Patent Law Precedent, 1991, 2d edit., 1992, Modern Patent Law Precedent, 3d edit., 1997, 5th edit., 2003; contbr. articles to profl. jours.; patentee in field. Served to cpl. US Army, 1950-52. Mem. ABA, Internat. Assn. Protection Indsl. Property, Am. Intellectual Property Law Assn., Am. Arbitration Assn. (mem. panel arbitrators). Clubs: Kenwood Golf Country, Am. Contract Bridge League (life master). Jewish. Home: 8508 Meadowlark Ln Bethesda MD 20817-2921 Office: Jacobson Holman PLLC Jenifer Bldg 400 7th St NW Washington DC 20004 Office Phone: 202-638-6666. Business E-Mail: iaisenberg@jhip.com.

AITCHISON, SUANN, elementary school educator; b. Paterson, N.J., Oct. 1, 1941; d. Archie Wilson and Isabell (Farrow) A. BA, William Paterson Coll., 1963, MEd, 1976; student, Fairleigh Dickinson U., 1991, St. Peter's Coll., 1996. Cert. elem. edn., reading tchr., elem. reading specialist. Tchr. 3d grade Fair Lawn (N.J.) Pub. Schs., 1963-64, 70-71, tchr. 2d grade, 1964-70, 71-87, tchr. reading, 1987-95, reading specialist, 1997—; tchr. reading and math. Fair Lawn (N.J.) Bd. Edn., 1996—; literacy specialist grades 6-8 Meml. and Thomas Jefferson Mid. Schs., Fair Lawn, 2003—. Adj. prof. William Paterson Coll., 1977; developer curriculum guides for remedial reading, 1989, lang. arts and reading for ESL children, 1989, lang. arts and reading for gifted children, 1989, libr. skills and lit. for neurologically impaired children, 1991; mem. Coun. Basic Edn., 1997; com. mem. Bergen County Celebrates Excellence and Pride in our Pub. Schs., 1997. Active Observation and Evaluation Revision Com., 1995, Cerebral Palsy Ctr.; choir Ch. in Radburn, 1993—95; mem. Garretson Forge Found., 1993—95; assoc. Cerebral Palsy Ctr., 1993—95; mem. com. Bergen County Celebrates Excellence and Pride in Edn., 1997; mem. Coun. for Basic Edn., 1997, Borough Fair Lawn Family Aquatic Study Com., 1997—; dist. reading tchr. family literacy reading take home program grades 1-2 elem. schs., 1999—; mem. 1st class Fair Lawn Police Dept.'s Citizen's Police Acad. Course, 2002; reapptd. mem. adv. com. Ams. with Disability Act, 2002—; com. mem. Fair Lawn Rep. County Com., 1986—98, rec. sec., 1994; vol. Gov. Whitman primary and gen. election campaigns, 1992; mem. Fair Lawn mayor and coun. adv. com. Ams. With Disabilities Act, 1996. Mem. AAHPERD, ASCD (premium mem. 1995—), AAUW, N.J. Reading Assn. (North Jersey coun. 1987-95), Coun. Exceptional Children, N.J. ASCD, Math. Assn. Am., Nat. Coun. Tchrs. of English, Coun. Ednl. Diagnostic Svcs., Fair Lawn Rep. Club (trustee 1997), Fair Lawn Pride Com. Assn., Nat. Assn. Secondary Prins. Baptist. Avocations: singing, reading, restaurant dining, theater, concerts. Home: 38-56 Van Duren Ave Fair Lawn NJ 07410-5018 Office: Fair Lawn Bd Edn 37-01 Fair Lawn Ave Fair Lawn NJ 07410-4919

AITKEN, ANDREW C., lawyer; b. Washington, DC, May 24, 1961; BS, Loyola Coll., Md., 1983; JD, Cath. U. of Am., 1988. Bar: Md. 1988, US Dist. Ct., Dist. of Md. 1989, US Ct. Appeals, Fed. Cir. 1991, US Patent and Trademark Office 2000. Law clk. to Hon. L. Leonard Ruben Cir. Ct. of Montgomery County, Md., 1988—89; ptnr. Intellectual Property Litig. and Patent Prosecution Depts. Venable LLP, Washington, DC. Bd. mem. CYO. Mem.: ABA, Patent Lawyers' Club of Washington, DC, Am. Intellectual Property Law Assn., Md. State Bar Assn. Office: Venable LLP 575 7th St NW Washington DC 20004 Office Phone: 202-344-8165. Office Fax: 202-344-8300. E-mail: acaitken@venable.com.

AITKEN, DOUG, artist; Student, Marymount Coll., Palos Verdes, Calif., 1986—87; BFA, Art Ctr. Coll. Design, Pasadena, Calif., 1991. One-man shows include ACl Project Room, N.Y.C., 1993, 303 Gallery, 1994, 1997, 1998, Pasco Art Ctr., Holiday, Fla., 1994, Taka Ishil Gallery, Tokyo, 1996, 1998, Gallery Side Two, 1998, Jiri Svestka Gallery, Prague, 1998, Doug Lawing Gallery, Houston, 1999, Victoria Miro Gallery, London, 1999, Dallas Mus. Art, 1999, Pitti Discovery Series, Florence, Italy, 1999, Galerie Eva Presenhuber, Zurich, 2005, exhibited in group shows at AC Project Room, N.Y.C., 1991, 1993, 1998, Stux Gallery, 1992, New Mus. Contemporary Art, 1992, Christopher Middendorf Gallery, Washington, 1992, Rushmore Estate, 1993, 303 Gallery, 1993, Santa Monica Mus. Art, 1994, Ma'nes Space, Prague, 1994, Espace Montjoie, Paris, 1994, Flash Art Mus., Trevi, Italy, 1994, Lisson Gallery, London, 1994, Mus. Lab. Art Contemporanea, Rome, 1995, Musee Art Ville Paris, 1995, Elga Wimmer Gallery, N.Y.C., 1996, Lauren Wittles Gallery, 1996, Basilico Fine Arts, 1996, Bard Ctr. Curatorial Studies, Annandale-on-Hudson, 1996, Kunsthalle N.Y., 1996, Kunstraum Vienna, 1996, Galleria Civica Art Modern Contemporanes Turin, Italy, 1996, Bonnefanten Mus., Maastricht, The Netherlands, 1996, Modern Gallery, Ljublijana, 1997, Tivoli Gallery, 1997, San Casciano Dei Bagni, Italy, 1997, Taka Ishii Gallery, Tokyo, 1997, Galleri Index, Stockholm, 1997, Cubitt Gallery, 1997, Whitney Mus. Am. Art, N.Y.C., 1997, Photographer's Gallery, 1998, Mus. Ludwig, Cologne, Germany, 1998, Walker Art Ctr., 1998, Long Beach (Calif.) Mus. Art, 1998, Galerie Peter Kilchmann, Zurich, 1998. Office: c/o 303 Gallery 525 W 22nd St New York NY 10011-1100

AITKEN, IAM, health facility administrator; Grad., Northern Ill. U. With Ill. Dept. Mental Health and Disabilities; v.p., CEO Four Winds-Chgo. Hosp., Lemont, Ill.; v.p. health sys. devel. Rock Creek Ctr., Lemont; with Menninger Clinic, Tex., 1996—, pres., chief exec. officer. Office: The Menninger Clinic 2801 Gessner PO Box 809045 Houston TX 77280-9045

AITKEN, PAUL ARTHUR, composer, conductor; b. Listowel, Ontario, Canada, Nov. 10, 1970; s. Donald Arthur and Elke Aitken; m. Stephanie Michelle Sharp, July 15, 2000; children: Michael Charles, Wilson Arthur. MusB in Edn, U. Western Ont., London, Canada, 1989—93; MusM, So. Ill. U., 1996. Lectr. So. Ill. U., Carbondale, Ill., 1996—97; dir. of music ministries Cathedral of Rockies, Boise, Idaho, 2002. Composer: (choral composition) Flanders Fields (Raymond W. Brock Meml. Student Composition Competition, 1999), (songs) Huron Carol. Mem.: Am. Guild Organists, Am. Choral Dirs. Assn. (regional chair, nwacda 2004). Office: Cathedral of Rockies 717 N 11th St Boise ID 83702 Office Phone: 208-343-7511. Business E-Mail: paitken@boisefumc.org.

AITKEN, ROBERT CAMPBELL, engineer; b. Vancouver, B.C., Can., Apr. 21, 1963; came to U.S., 1990; s. Robert and Mary Elizabeth A.; m. Denise Kathleen Maloney, Aug. 2, 1986; children: Robert James, Colin Campbell. BS with hons., U. Victoria, B.C., Can., 1985, MS, 1986; PhD, McGill U., Montreal, Que., Can., 1990. Rsch. assoc. Alberta Rsch. Coun., Calgary, Alberta, Can., 1986-87; mem. tech. staff Agilent Technologies, Santa Clara, Calif., 1990—. Tech. program com. mem. Internat. Conf. on Computer-Aided Design, Santa Clara, 1993-94, local arrangements chmn., 1995, tutorials chmn., 1996-97, panels chmn., 1998; tech. program com. Custom Integrated Cirs. Conf., Santa Clara, 1995-97; panel and poster chmn. Test Synthesis Workshop, Santa Barbara, Calif., 1995, fin. chmn., 1996-97, vice-chair, 1998, gen. chair, 1999; mem. program com. Internat. Test Conf., 1996-2000, vice chair program com., 2001. Assoc. editor: IEEE Transactions on Comp.-Aided Design, 1997—. Recipient award for Best paper, Internat. Test Conf., Balt., 1992, Atlantic City, 2000, hon. mention, Balt., 1991; named Indsl. Mentor in Yr. Semiconductor Rsch. Corp., 1998. Mem. IEEE. E-mail: rob.aitken@agilent.com.

AITKEN, WYLIE A., lawyer; b. Detroit, Jan. 4, 1942; AA, Santa Ana Coll., Calif. State Coll.Fullerton; LLB, Marquette U., 1965. Bar: Calif. 1966, U.S. Dist. Ct. (Ctrl. dist. Calif.). Founding ptnr. Aitken, Aitken & Cohn, Santa Ana, Calif. Assoc. editor: Marquette Law Review, 1963—65; contbr. articles to profl. jours. Named So. Calif. Super Lawyer, OC Bus. Jour., 2004; named one of Top 100 Influential Lawyers, Calif., 1998—2003; recipient Jurisprudence award, Anti Defamation League, 2003. Mem.: Robert A. Banyard Am. Inns of Ct., Am. Bd. Trial Advocates (Plaintiff Trial Lawyer of Yr. 1998), Nat. Bd. Trial Advocacy, Assn. Trial Lawyers Am. (mem. bd. govs. 1977—), Calif. Trial Lawyers Assn. (mem. state bd. 1970—73, chmn. consumer protection com. 1972, v.p. 1973—75, pres. 1977), Orange County Trial Lawyers Assn. (Bus. Trial Lawyer of Yr.), State Bar Calif., Celtic Bar Assn. Orange County (founding mem.), Orange County Bar Assn. Office: Aitken Aitken & Cohn 3 Imperial Promenade Ste 800 Santa Ana CA 92707 Office Phone: 866-434-1424. E-mail: wylie@aitkenlaw.com.

AIT-SAHALIA, YACINE, finance educator; PhD, MIT, 1993. Prof. fin. U. Chgo., 1993—98; Otto A. Hack prof. Princeton U., NJ, 1998—. Dir. Bendheim Ctr. Fin. Princeton U., 1998; rschr. in field. Dir. Western Fin. Assn. Office: Princeton Univ Bendheim Ctr Fin 26 Prospect Ave Princeton NJ 08540 Office Phone: 609-258-4015.

AIUTO, RUSSELL, science education consultant; b. Monroe, Mich., July 13, 1934; s. Crispino and Maria (d'Aiuto) A.; m. Nancy Jane Obenauf, Dec. 17, 1955 (dec. 1980); children: Mary T. Carroll, Susan M. Summa; m. Beverly Bradley, Jan. 3, 1981 BA, Ea. Mich. U., 1958, U. Mich., 1995; MA, U. N.C., 1963, PhD, 1971. Tchr. speech, drama Monroe High Sch., Mich., 1958-61; prof. biology Albion Coll., Mich., 1966-82, provost, 1982-85; pres. Hiram Coll., Ohio, 1985-88; div. dir. tchr. preparation and enhancement NSF, Washington, 1988-90; program mgr. Nat. Sci. Tchrs. Assn., Washington, 1990-93, Coun. Ind. Colls., 1993-95. Cons. Gygi Found., Dundee, Mich., 1984— Author: Mencken and Sara, 1980, Ring Lardner's America, 1984, Dorothy Parker, 1986; co-author: Science Interactions, 3 vols., 1993; contbr. articles to profl. jours. Vice chmn. Albion Improvement Com., 1983-85 NSF grantee, 1968 Mem. Sigma Xi, Omicron Delta. Episcopalian. Avocation: collecting books. Home: 9631 Duffer Way Gaithersburg MD 20886-1309

AIYER, JAY KUMAR, lawyer; b. London; m. Nirja Sharma; 2 children. BA in Govt. and Economics, MPA, U. Tex., Austin; JD, S. Tex. Coll. of Law. Bar: Tex. 1995. Former sr. mgmt. consultant Deloitte and Touche; former staff mem. Sen. Rodney Ellis; former chief of staff Mayor Lee P. Brown; of counsel Chamberlain, Hrdlicka, Williams, White & Martin; now atty. immigration and public law priv. practice. Mem. Gulfton Youth Develop. Commn.; bd. dirs. Alief YMCA; mem. Southwest Houston Rotary, Leadership Houston, Ctr. for Houston's Future; mem. bd. trustees Houston Community Coll. System. Office: 6524 San Felipe PMB 412 Houston TX 77057*

AIZEN, ICEK, psychology professor, consultant; s. Mendel and Pesa Ajzen; m. Rachel K. Klotz, June 5, 1966; children: Ron Michael, Jonathan Oren. BA, Hebrew U. Jerusalem, Israel, 1962—66; MA, U. Ill., 1966—67, PhD, 1967—69. Asst. prof. U. Ill., Champaign, 1969—71, U. Mass., Amherst, 1971—74, assoc. prof., 1974—78, prof., 1978—. Assoc. chair, dept. psychology U. Mass., 1987—93, head personality and social psychology program, 1997—. Author: (book) Attitudes, Personality, and Behavior. Recipient Fulbright Travel award to Bulgaria, Coun. Internat. Exch. of Scholars, 1995, Christiansen Meml. award in Psychology, U. Bergen, Norway, 2002. Fellow: Am. Psychol. Soc.; mem.: Soc. Exptl. Social Psychology, Soc. Personality and Social Psychology. Avocations: travel, reading, music. Office: U Mass Tobin Hall 135 Hicks Way Amherst MA 01003-9271 Office Phone: 413-545-0509. Business E-Mail: aizen@psych.umass.edu.

AIZEN, RACHEL K., clinical psychologist; b. Tel-Aviv, Israel; MA, U. Ill., 1968, PhD, 1970; postgrad. in clin. psychology, U. Mass., 1980-83. Lic. psychologist, Mass.; nat. cert. sch. psychologist. Asst. prof. Tel-Aviv U., 1972-73; psychologist Northampton (Mass.) State Hosp., 1971-72; clin. psychologist Amherst (Mass.) Sch. System, 1974—; pvt. practice Amherst, Mass, 1974—; intern VA Med. Ctr., Northampton, 1982-83; clin. psychologist Shieba Med. Ctr., Israel, 1985-86; fellow in neuropsychology Mass. Mental Health Hosp., Boston, 1987-88. Cons. psychologist Mass. Rehab., 1974—, various local agys. and cts. Cons. editor The Am. Psychologist, 1974; co-author: Psychological Counseling: Principles, Strategies and Intervention, 1990; contbr. articles to profl. jours. Mem. APA (divsn. clin. and psychoanalysis), NEA, Nat. Assn. Sch. Psychologists. Avocations: travel, art. Office: 48 N Pleasant St Ste 204 Amherst MA 01002-1758 Office Phone: 413-256-3456.

AIZEN, VLADIMIR B., geographer, educator; s. Berthold M. and Valerie V. Eisen; m. Vera V. Teterina, Oct. 8, 1969 (div. June 8, 1981); m. Valentina P. Smirnova, Nov. 4, 1982 (div. Feb. 3, 1991); m. Elena M. Karapetyance, Feb. 29, 1992; children: Valeria V., Alexei V., Sergey V., Alexander V. BC, Inst. Engring. Hydrology and Melioration, Tashkent, Uzbekistan, 1975; MSc, Kyrgyz State U., Bishkek, 1981; PhD, Inst. Geography, Russian Acad. Scis., Moscow, 1988. Cert. hydrologist, Am. Inst. Hydrology. Engr. Dept. Hydrometeorology, Bishkek, Kyrgyzstan, 1975—82; sr. scientist Inst. of Geography, Russian Acad. of Scis., Moscow, 1982—92; assoc. prof. Coll. Environ. Sci. and Mgmt. U. Calif., Santa Brabara, 1994—2001; vis. rschr. Scott Polar Rsch. Inst. U. Cambridge, England, 1992—93; prof. dept. geography U. Idaho, Moscow, 2001—. Cons. Asian Devel. Bank, Tokyo, 1997—98; vis. prof. Niigata (Japan) U., Japan, 1996—97. Author: (book) Glaciers and Environment in the Qinghai-Xizang (Tibet) Plateau. The Gongga Mountain.; contbr. more than 200 articles to profl. publs. Grantee, Russian Acad. Scis., 1988—91, NASA, 1994—97, Japanese Soc. Promotion Sci., 1996, NSF, 1997, 2003—, U.S. Dept. Energy, 1998—2004, 2003, Nato Collaborative Linkage Grant, 1999, U.S. Nat. Geog., 2002. Mem.: Internat. Glaciological Soc., Nat. Geog. Soc. (assoc.), Am. Geophys. Union. (assoc.), Internat. Assn. Hydrological Sciences (assoc.), Am. Permafrost Soc. (assoc.). Office: U Idaho Mines Bld PO Box 443025 Moscow ID 83844-3025 Office Fax: 208-885-5724. Business E-Mail: aizen@uidaho.edu.

AIZENMAN, MICHAEL, mathematics professor, physics professor, researcher; b. Aug. 28, 1945; m. Marta Beatriz Gershanik; children: Nurith Celina, Ya'ir Gideon. BS, Hebrew U., Jerusalem, Israel, 1969; PhD, Yeshiva U., 1975. Postdoctoral vis. mem. Courant Inst. Math. Scis. Courant Inst. Math. Scis. NYU, 1974-75, prof., 1987-90; postdoctoral position to asst. prof. physics Princeton (N.J.) U., 1975-82, prof. math. and physics, 1990—; from assoc. prof. to prof. math. and physics Rutgers U., New Brunswick, N.J., 1982-87. Vis. prof. Institut des Hautes Etudes Scientifiques, Bures-sur-Yvette, U. Paris, 1984-85, Inst. Advanced Study, 1991. Mem. Nat. Acad. Scis., 1997. Sloan fellow, 1981-84, Guggenheim fellow, 1984-85; Fairchild scholar, 1992; recipient Giudo Stampacchia prize Scuola Normale Superior di Pisa, 1982, Excellence in Rsch. award Rutger U. Bd. Trustees, 1987, Norbert Wiener award Am. Math. Soc. and Soc. Indsl. and Applied Math., 1990. Achievements include rsch. in physics and math. with focus on math. analysis of issues arrising in statis. mechanics, theory of Schrödinger operators and disorder effects, random fields and stochastic geometry. Office: Princeton U 347 Jadwin Hall Washington Rd Princeton NJ 08544-0708

AIZIN, GREGORY, physicist, educator, researcher; b. Brest, Belarus, Oct. 13, 1958; came to U.S., 1994; s. Ruvim and Dora (Bershadskaya) A.; m. Natalie Dykhne, Nov. 1, 1990; children: Sophia, Rebecca. MS in Physics, Belarus State U., Minsk, 1981; PhD in Physics, Inst. Gen. Physics, Moscow, 1986. Jr. rsch. scientist Inst. Radio Engring. and Electronics of Russian Acad. Scis., Moscow, 1985-87, rsch. scientist, 1987-94; rsch. assoc. dept. physics and astronomy Hunter Coll., CUNY, N.Y.C., 1994-97; asst. prof. phys. scis. Kingsborough C.C., CUNY, Bklyn., 1997-2000, assoc. prof. phys. scis., 2000—04, prof. phys. scis., 2004—. Contbr. articles to profl. jours. Rsch. awardee cuny, 1998—, U.S. Army Rsch. Office, 2005—. Mem. Am. Phys. Soc. Achievements include contribution to the theory of low-dimensional electron systems at semiconductor interfaces. Office: Kingsborough Coll/CUNY Dept Phys Scis 2001 Oriental Blvd Brooklyn NY 11235-2333 Office Phone: 718-368-5765. E-mail: gaizin@kbcc.cuny.edu.

AIZPURUA, JAVIER, physicist, researcher; b. Donostia-San Sebastián, Spain, Jan. 29, 1971; s. Aizpurua Jose Agustin and Iriazabal Juncal. MSc in Physics, U. Zaragoza, 1994; PhD, U. Basque Country, 1998. Postdoctoral rschr. Chalmers U. Tech., Gothenburg, Sweden, 1998—2000; assoc. prof. U. Basque Country, Bilbao, Spain, 2000—01; guest rschr. Nat. Inst. Standards and Tech., Gaithersburg, Md., 2001—04; rsch. fellow Donostia (Spaine) Internat. Physics Ctr., 2004—. Contbr. articles to profl. jours. Mem.: Am. Phys. Soc. Office: Donostia International Physics Center Paseo Manuel Lardizabal 4 Donostia-San Sebastián 20018 Spain Office Phone: +34-943-015624. Office Fax: +34-943-015600. E-mail: aizpurua@sc.ehu.es.

AJA-HERRERA, MARIE, fashion designer, educator; b. Bedford, Eng., Mar. 19, 1955; d. Henry and Ariadne Swiejkowski; m. Manny Anjel Aja-Herrera, Oct. 24, 1981. BA in Fashion, U. Ctrl. England, 1977; MA in Fashion/Textiles, Lodz U./Krakow U., Poland, 1980; MA in Design Studies, Ctrl. St. Martins, England, 1995; postgrad. cert. in Edn., U. London, 1981. Head fashion dept. Southend Coll. Essex U., 1981—84; head womenswear design (Byblos) Ghirombelli/Pacanina Modas/Santini S.A., Barcelona, Milan, London, 1984—88; head womenswear design Jefferson Internat. PLC, Hong Kong, 1988—89; sales exec., design & edn. coord. Lectra Sys., 1989; chair fashion design, chair fashion merchandising Am. Coll. in London, 1989—92; design dir. CAD, knitwear, textiles Jacques Vert PLC, 1992—95; dean faculty of art and design Am. U. Dubai, United Arab Emirates, 1995—96; head of design Twins/NIKE Enterprise PLC, 1996—97; chair fashion design Savannah (Ga.) Coll. Art & Design, 1997—. Cons. Herrera UK Ltd., 1982-95. Fellow: Soc. Artists & Designers (lic.); mem.: Textile Inst., Polish Union Artists, The Fashion Group Internat., Clothing & Footwear Inst. Avocations: horse riding, skiing, collecting antiques, travel. Office: Savannah Coll Art & Design HR-Clinard Hall Drayton St Savannah GA 31401-5644 Office Phone: 912-525-6661. Business E-Mail: mcajaher@scad.edu.

AJELLO, EDITH H., state legislator; b. Apr. 26, 1944; d. Kenneth Aaron and Rozella Christine (Ewoldt) Hanover; children: Linell, Aaron. BA, Bucknell U., 1966. Store mgr. V. George Rustigian Rugs, Inc., 1981-93, 94—; interim exec. dir. Vols. in Providence Schs., 1993; mem. R.I. Ho. of Reps., 1993—. Democrat. Home and Office: 29 Benefit St Providence RI 02904-2743 Business E-Mail: rep-ajello@rilin.state.ri.us.

AJZENBERG-SELOVE, FAY, physicist, researcher; b. Berlin, Feb. 13, 1926; came to U.S., 1940, naturalized, 1946; d. Mojzesz A. and Olga (Naiditch) A.; m. Walter Selove, Dec. 18, 1955. BS in Engring., U. Mich., 1946; MS, U. Wis., 1949, PhD, 1952; DSc (hon.), Smith Coll., 1995, Mich. State U., 1997, Haverford Coll., 1999—. Rsch. fellow Calif. Inst. Tech., 1952, 54; lectr. Smith Coll., 1952-53; cons., fellow MIT, Cambridge, 1952-53; from asst. prof. to rsch. assoc. prof. Boston U., 1953-57; mem. faculty Haverford Coll., 1957-70, prof. physics, 1962-70, acting chmn. dept. physics, 1967-69; rsch. prof. U. Pa., Phila., 1970-73, prof. physics, 1973—, assoc. chmn., 1989-93. Vis. asst. prof. Columbia, summer 1955, Nat. U. Mexico, summer 1955; lectr. U. Pa., 1957; cons. in field, 1962-63; vis. assoc. Calif. Inst. Tech., 1973-74; Exec. sec. com. physics faculties in colls. Am. Inst. Physics, 1962-65, mem. adv. com. manpower, 1963-68, adv. com. vis. scientists program, 1963-67; commr. Commn. on Coll. Physics, 1968-71; exec. sec. ad hoc panel on nuclear data compilations NAS-NRC, 1971-75; mem. Commn. on Nuclear Physics, Internat. Union Pure and Applied Physics, 1972-78, chairperson. 1978-81; mem. U.S. del. low energy nuclear physics to USSR, AEC, 1966; mem. Distinguished Faculty Awards Commn. Commonwealth of Pa., 1976; mem. nuclear sci. adv. com. Dept Energy-NSF, 1977-80; mem. numerical data adv. bd., assembly math. and phys. scis. NRC, 1977-79; lectr. U. Minn., 1994 Author: A Matter of Choice, Memoirs of a Female Physicist, 1994; editor: Nuclear Spectroscopy, vol. A and B, 1960; bd. editors Phys. Rev. C., 1981-83. Mem. Bower awards com. Franklin Nat. Meml., 1993. Recipient Christian R. and Mary F. Lindback award for disting. teaching, 1991, Nicholson medal for humanitarian svc. Am. Phys. Soc., 1999, 1st Disting. Alumni fellow in Physics, U. Wis., 2001; Smith-Mundt fellow, 1955; Guggenheim fellow, 1965-66. Fellow AAAS (mem. governing coun. 1974-80, mem. com. on coun. affairs 1977, 78), Am. Phys. Soc. (chairperson divsn. nuclear physics 1973-74); mem. AAUP, NRC (mem. phys. scis. panel, associateship program 1988-91), Am. Inst. Physics (mem. com. on pub. edn. and info. 1980-83), Phi Beta Kappa, Sigma Xi (nat. lectr. 1973-74). Home: 118 Cherry Ln Wynnewood PA 19096-1209 Office: U Pa Philadelphia PA 19104-6396

AKAIKE, HIROKO, music educator, conductor; arrived in U.S., 1997; d. Hiroshi and Etsuko Akaike. B in Music Edn., Kunitachi Coll. Music, Tokyo, 1995; M in Music Performance, Shenandoah U., 1999, MS in Music, 2003. Lic. tchg. Va. Tutor, accompanist Shenandoah U., Winchester, Va., 1998—2003; substitute tchr. Winchester Pub. Sch., 2002—03; band, choir dir. Highland County Pub. Sch., Monterey, Va., 2003—. Pvt. piano, vocal instr., 1997—; pianist Wesleyan Fellowship Ch., Winchester, 1998—2003; asst. music dir., conductor Mary Washington Coll., Fredericksburg, Va., 1999; music dir. Highland County Arts Coun., Monterey, 2004—. Contbr. articles to newspaper. Musician West Minster Canterbury Nursing Home, Winchester, 1999—2003. Named Employee of Month, Highland County Pub. Schs., 2003; fellow, Shenandoah U., 1999—2003; scholar, Ikueikai, 1991—95, Kunitachi Coll. Music, 1991—95. Mem.: Conductors Guild, Va. Edn. Assn., Nat. Assn. Music Educators. Avocations: dance, reading. Office: Highland County High Sch PO Box 430 Monterey VA 24465 Office Phone: 540-468-2181. Personal E-mail: hakaike@yahoo.com.

AKAKA, DANIEL KAHIKINA, senator; b. Honolulu, Sept. 11, 1924; s. Kahikina and Annie (Kahoa) A.; m. Mary Mildred Chong, May 22, 1948; children: Millannie, Daniel, Gerard, Alan, Nicholas. BEdn, U. Hawaii, 1952, MEdn, 1966. Tchr., Hawaii, 1953-60; vice prin., then prin. Ewa Beach Elem. Sch., Honolulu, 1960-64; prin. Pohakea Elem. Sch., 1964-65, Kaneohe Elem. Sch., 1965-68; program specialist Hawaii Compensatory Edn., 1978-79, from 1985; dir. Hawaii OEO, 1971-74; spl. asst. human resources Office Gov. Hawaii, 1975-76; mem. 95th-101st Congresses from 2d Dist., Hawaii, 1977-90; U.S. senator from Hawaii, 1990—; mem. Indian affairs com., vets. affairs com., armed svcs. com., energy & natural resources com., govt. affairs com., Indian affairs com., ethics com. U.S. Senate, mem. Senate dem. policy com. Chmn. Hawaii Principals' Conf. Bd. dirs. Hanahauoli Sch.; mem. Act 4 Ednl. Adv. Council, Library Adv. Council.; Trustee Kawaiahao Congl. Ch. Served with U.S. Army, 1945-47. Named Friend of Nat. Parks, Nat. Parks Conservation Assn., 2005; recipient Adam Smith award for excellence in econ. edu., Nat. Council on Econ. Edu., 2005. Mem. NEA, Musicians Assn. Hawaii. Democrat. Office: US Senate 141 Hart Senate Office Bldg Washington DC 20510-0001*

AKELLA, UMASUNDARI SRIVENKATA, research scientist; arrived in U.S., 1997; d. Sriramchandramurty Venkata and Kamala Akella; m. Mukul Anand Krishna, Aug. 9, 2000. BA in Sociology, U. of Delhi, 1994, MA in Sociology, 1996; MS in Sociology, Okla. State U., 1999; postgrad., SUNY, Stony Brook, 1999. Rsch. and tchg. asst. Okla. State U., Stillwater, 1997—99, SUNY, Stony Brook, NY, 1999—; instr. Ctr. For Survey Rsch., SUNY, Stony Brook, NY, 2002—, SUNY, Stony Brook, NY, 2002—. Contbr. book rev. Women's Studies International Forum. Mem. Nat. Svc. Scheme, Delhi, 1991—94; vol. worker Cheshire Home for Mentally Challanged Children, Delhi, 1989—93; mem. SPIC MACAY, Delhi, 1991—94. Recipient Grad. Merit Tuition scholarship, SUNY, 1999, Summer Travelling fellowship, Ctr. for Devel. Econs., Delhi Sch. of Econs., 1995, Nat. Merit scholarship. Mem.: Ea. Sociol. Soc., Am. Sociol. Assn., Alpha Kappa Delta (life). Achievements include research in impact of corporate organizational structure and work policies on women executives in the United States; coalition formation between environmental organizations and labor unions in Oregon. Office: SUNY Dept Sociology Stony Brook NY 11794-43 E-mail: uakella@ic.sunysb.edu.

AKEMANN, DAVID R., lawyer; b. Elgin, Ill., Oct. 31, 1951; s. Theodore H. and Lois (Marr) A.; m. Vickie C. Skala, Aug. 5, 1978; children— Carrie, Julie, Collin. B.S., Brigham Young U., 1972; J.D., Lewis U., 1978. Bar: Ill. 1978, U.S. Dist. Ct. (no. dist.) Ill. 1978, U.S. Ct. Appeals (7th cir.) 1979, U.S. Supreme Ct. 1981. Clk. States Atty. Office, Kane County, Geneva, Ill., 1977-78; asst. states atty., 1978-79, chief civil divsn., 1979—87; sole practice, Elgin, 1978—92; elected states atty., 1992-2000; asst. atty. gen., 2000-03; Apptd. commnr. Ill. Industrial Commn., 2003. Recipient Am. Jurisprudence Constn. Law award Lawyers Coop. Pub. Co., 1978. Mem. ABA, Ill. Bar Assn., Kane County Bar Assn., Ill. Pub. Employers Labor Relations Assn. (prin.). Methodist. Home: 420 Hoxie Ct Elgin IL 60123-3220 E-mail: dakemann@mail.state.il.us.

AKENSON, DONALD HARMAN, historian, educator; b. Mpls., May 22, 1941; s. Donald Nels and Fern L. (Harman) A. BA, Yale U., 1962; PhD, Harvard U., 1967; LittD (hon.), McMaster U., 1995; HHD (hon.), U. Lethbridge, 1996; LittD (hon.), Guelph U., 2000; DLaws (hon.), Regina U., 2002. Allston Burr sr. tutor Dunster House, Harvard U., 1966-67; asst. prof. history, asst. dean Yale Coll., 1967-70; assoc. prof. history Queens U., Kingston, Ont., Canada, 1970-74, prof., 1974—2003, Douglas chair Canadian and colonial hist., 2003—; hon. prof. U. Aberdeen, 2002—; Beamish rsch. prof. migration studies U. Liverpool, England, 1997—2002; sr. editor McGill-Queens Univ. Press, 1982—. Hon. rsch. fellow Queens U., Belfast, 1976-77, sr. rsch. fellow, 1995-96; hon. prof. edn. Trinity Coll., Dublin, 1976-77; hon. lectr. Australian Nat. U., 1985; Cecil H. Green disting. vis. prof. Green Coll., U. B.C., 1995; guest artist Yaddo Colony, 1985; writer-in-residence Bellagio Ctr., Lake Como, Italy, 1993; hon. rsch. prof. Irish and Scottish studies U. Aberdeen, Scotland, 2002—; Freilich Found. lectr. Australian Nat. U., 2003. Author: The Irish Education Experiment: The National System of Education in the Nineteenth Century, 1970, The Church of Ireland: Ecclesiastical Reform and Revolution 1800-1885, 1971, Education and Enmity: The Control of Schooling in Northern Ireland 1920-50, 1973, The United States and Ireland, 1973, A Mirror to Kathleen's Face: Education in Independent Ireland 1922-60, 1975, Local Poets and Social History: James Orr, Bard of Ballycarry, 1977, Between Two Revolutions: Islandmagee, County Antrim, 1798-1920, 1979, The Lazar House Notebooks, 1981, A Protestant in Purgatory: Richard Whately, Archbishop of Dublin, 1981, The Irish in Ontario, 1984, Brotherhood Week in Belfast, 1984, Being Had: Historians, Evidence, and the Irish in North America, 1985, The Orangeman: The Life and Times of Ogle Gowan, 1986, The Edgerston Audit, 1987, Small Differences: Irish Catholics and Irish Protestants, 1815-1922, 1988, Half the World from Home; Perspectives on the Trial in New Zealand, 1990, At Face Value: The Life and Times of Eliza McCormack/John White, 1990 Occasional Papers on the Irish in South Africa, 1991, God's Peoples: Covenant and Land in South Africa, Israel and Ulster, 1992, The Irish Diaspora A Primer, 1993, Conor: A Biography of Conor Cruise O'Brien, 1994, If the Irish Ruled thr World: Montserrat 1630-1730, 1997, Surpassing Wonder. The Invention of the Bible and the Talmuds, 1998, Saint Saul: A Skeleton Key to the Historical Jesus, 2000, Intolerance. The E. Coli of the Human Mind, 2004, An Irish History of Civilization, 2 vols., 2005; editor: Canadian Papers in Rural History, 1978-96; sr. editor McGill-Queen's U. Press, 1982—. Recipient rsch. award Can. Coun., 1974-83, 91-94, Am. Coun. Learned Socs., 1976-77, Chalmers prize, 1985, Landon prize, 1987, Grawemeyer award for improving world order, 1993, Biography medal U. B.C., 1994, Trillium prize, 1995, Molson Laureate, 1996; Guggenheim fellow, 1981-85, John David Stout rsch. fellow Victoria U., 1988-89, Univ. fellow Rhodes U., 1990. Fellow Royal Soc. Can., Royal Hist. Soc. (U.K.); mem. Am. Conf. Irish Studies, Phi Beta Kappa. Office: Queens U Dept History Kingston ON Canada K7L 3N6

AKER, SUSAN K., elementary school educator; b. Bklyn., Aug. 4, 1951; d. Mike and Rose Kriegsman; m. David Aker, Sept. 1, 1974; children: Michael, Jessica. BA, CUNY, 1973, MS, 1975, Long Island U., 1976, MS, 1991, Coll. New Rochelle, 1998. Cert. early childhood edn., elem. edn., spl. edn., libr. sci., sch. adminstrn. and supervision. Tchr. 4th grade Yeshiva Crown Heights, Bklyn., 1974-75; tchr. 6th grade Hebrew Acad. Nassau County, Bethpage, NY, 1975-76; libr. Jericho (NY) Jewish Ctr., 1978-81, Half-Hollow Hills Pub. Libr., Dix Hills, NY, 1978-81; libr. media specialist Uniondale (NY) Free Sch. Dist., 1989-90, Hempstead (NY) Union Free Sch. Dist., 1990-92; tchr. P.S. 105 NYC Bd. Edn., Bronx, 1993—; adj. prof. Mercy Coll., Yorktown; mentor NYC Dept. Edn., Region 2, Bronx, 2004—. Internal geography cons. NYC Bd. Edn., 1996—, staff devel. workshop presenter, 1996—. Contbr. articles to TeacherLink. Grantee United Fedn. Tchrs., 1997, NY Geographic Alliance, 1998, 99, McDonald's Corp., 2001. Mem.: ASCD, N.Y. Reading Assn., Assn. Early Childhood Internat., N.Y. Geog. Alliance, Phi Delta Kappa. Home: 23 Southern Rd Hartsdale NY 10530-2128

AKER, SUZANNE DEVERSE, physical movement educator; b. Kansas City, Mo., Sept. 19, 1926; d. Earnest Hillborn and Clara Maude Scruggs; m. Meredith Eugene Aker, Jan. 28, 1960 (div. Feb. 1977); children: alan Morrow, Jan Ameen, John Bettis, Elizabeth Aker, Laura Greer. Student, Ballet Theater Sch., 1953; BA, Tulsa U., 1962. Cert. profl. dance tchr. Profl. dancer Burchmann Dancers, Hollywood, N.Y., 1944-45; tchr. Tulsa U., 1959-62; chmn. dept. dance Tex. Tech. U., Lubbock, 1962-69; founding artistic dir., choreographer, tchr. Ballett Lubbock, 1969-2000; phys. movement tchr. Covenant Health Sys., Lubbock, 2000—. Choreographer Tex. Tech. U., 1963-85, Lubbock Theater Ctr., 1965-76, Lubbock Christian U., 1981-90; choreographer, tchr. Wayland Bapt. U., Plainview, Tex., 1979-83. Assoc. Cmty. of Holy Spirit Episcopal Convent, 1985—. Nat. Endowment for Arts grantee, 1980; recipient Pathfinder's award Lubbock C. of C., 1987. Mem. Chi Omega (v.p. 1946), Alpha Psi Omega (hon.), Delta Psi Kappa (hon.). Avocations: icon painting, dance related artwork. Home: 5016 27th St Lubbock TX 79407 Office Phone: 806-725-6579.

AKERELE, EVARISTO OLANREWAJU, psychiatrist, educator; b. Ibadan, Nigeria, July 14, 1960; arrived in U.S., 1993; s. Abiodun and Elizabeth Folashade Akerele; m. Corina Elena Dutcus, Aug. 17, 1989; children: Andreea F., Christa A. BS in Biochemistry with honors, U. London, 1983; postgrad., U. Craiova, Romania, 1983—84; MD, Inst. Medicine & Pharmacy, Cluj-Napoca, Romania, 1990. Diplomate Am. Bd. Psychiatry and Neurology. Intern Harlem Hosp. Ctr., Columbia U., N.Y.C., 1994—95, resident, 1995—98; asst. clin. psychiatry Columbia U., N.Y.C., 1998—2000, fellow, 1998—2000, asst. prof., 2000—. Staff physician Abyssinian House, 1997—99; attending Harlem Hosp. Ctr., 1998—2000; attending physician Columbia-Presbyn. Hosp., 1998—; assoc. med. dir. Substance Treatment and Rsch. Svc., 2000—; co-dir. addiction psychiatry fellowship Columbia U.; presenter in field. Contbr. articles to profl. jours. Mem. Nat. Alliance for Mentally Ill. Recipient Rsch. related to women, gender and drug abuse award, Nat. Inst. Drug Abuse, 1999, Dir.'s award, 2000, K-12 Rsch. Career Devel. award, 2000—; grantee, Eli Lilly, 2000—02; Alcohol Med. scholar, 2001—03. Mem.: Am. Acad. Addiction Psychiatry, Am. Psychiat. Assn. (vice chair residents com. N.Y. county dist. br. 1996—97, chair residents com. N.Y. chpt. 1997—98, bd. trustees 1999—2000, chair early career psychiatrists 2003—, chair minority fellowships selection com., Nat. Substance Abuse fellow 1998—2000). Roman Catholic. Office: 1051 Riverside Dr Unit 66 New York NY 10032

AKERLIND, CHRISTOPHER, lighting designer, set designer; Lighting designer (Broadway plays) The Piano Lesson, 1990, Philadelphia, Here I Come!, 1994, Seven Guitars, 1996, The Tale of the Allergist's Wife, 2000, Reckless, 2004, The Light in the Piazza, 2005 (Tony award, best lighting design of a musical, 2005, Drama Desk award, outstanding lighting design, 2005, Outer Critics Circle award, outstanding lighting design, 2005), (plays) Carnage, A Comedy, Love and Anger, Mad Forest, Traps, Owners, Blown Sideways Through Life, The Lights, The Rez Sisters, Day Standing on Its Head, The Day the Bronx Died, Fallen Angel, Slavs!, Iphigenia and Other Daughters, Silence, Cunning, Exile, Troilus and Cressida, The Skriker, Therese Raquin, The Dying Gaul, Freedomland, Sueno, Waste, The Butterfly Collection, First Love, Everything That Rises Must Converge, Room, This Thing of Darkness, Well, 2004, Between Us, Belle Epoque, 2005, Score, Olly's Prison, Oedipus, La Dispute, Uncle Vanya, Enrico IV, Misalliance, Nicholas and Alexandra, A Midsummer Night's Dream, Pericles, King Lear, lighting and set designer Cymbeline, Don Juan. Recipient Obie award, sustained excellence in lighting design, Village Voice, Michael Merritt award, design & collaboration.*

AKERLOF, CARL WILLIAM, physics professor; b. New Haven, Mar. 5, 1938; s. Gosta Carl and Rosalie Clara (Hirschfelder) A.; m. Carol Irene Ruska, Sept. 4, 1965; children— Karen Louise, William Gustav BA, Yale U., 1960; PhD, Cornell U., 1967. Research assoc. U. Mich., Ann Arbor, 1966-68, asst. prof., 1968-72, assoc. prof., 1972-78, prof. physics, 1978—. Contbr. articles to profl. jours. Incorporator Ann Arbor Hands-On Mus. Fellow Am. Phys. Soc.; mem. Am. Astron. Soc. Office: U Mich Randall Lab Physics Dept Physics Ann Arbor MI 48109

AKERLOF, GEORGE ARTHUR, economics professor; b. New Haven, June 17, 1940; s. Gosta Carl and Rosalie C. Akerlof; m. Janet Louise Yellen, July 7, 1978; 1 child, Robert. BA, Yale U., 1962; PhD, MIT, 1966; D Econs. (hon.), U. Zurich, Switzerland, 2000. Cassell prof. of money and banking London Sch. Econs., 1978-80; assist. prof. U. Calif., Berkeley, 1966—70, assoc. prof., 1970—77, prof., 1977—78, 1980—; sr. fellow Brookings Instn., Washington, 1994—. Bd. dirs. Nat. Bur. Econ. Rsch., 1997—; mem. bd. editors Quar. Jour. Econs., 1983—, Am. Econ. Rev., 1983-90. Author: An Economic Theorist's Book of Tales, 1984; co-author: Efficiency Wage Theories of Unemployment, 1988; co-editor Jour. Econs. and Politics, 1990—; contbr. articles to profl. jours. Recipient Woodrow Wilson fellow, 1962—63, Cooperative fellow NSF, 1963—66, Fulbright fellow, 1967—68, Nobel Prize in Economics, 2001. Fellow Am. Acad. Arts and Scis.; mem. Am. Econ. Assn. (mem. exec. com. 1988-91, v.p. 1995), Can. Inst. Advanced Rsch. (assoc.), Russell Sage Round Table on Behavioral Econs. Office: U Calif Dept Econs 549 Evans Hall # 3880 Berkeley CA 94720-3880*

AKERS, BROCK CORDT, lawyer; b. Milw., Oct. 30, 1956; s. John Norman Akers and Lucille Henrietta (Cordt) Galassini; m. Colleen Elizabeth Cullen, Nov. 24, 1984; children: Cordt Cullen, Allison Kathleen, Bradley Christopher. BA, Tex. Christian U., 1978; JD, U. Tex., 1981. Bar: Tex. 1981, U.S. Dist. Ct. (so., ea., no. and wes. dists.) Tex. 1981, U.S. Ct. Appeals (5th cir.) 1981, U.S. Supreme Ct. 1988; cert. in civil trial law Nat. Bd. Trial Advocacy; cert. in personal injury and civil trial law Tex. Bd. Legal Specialization. Assoc. Vinson & Elkins, Houston, 1981-89; ptnr. Phillips & Akers, Houston, 1989—. Mem. ABA, Houston Bar Assn., Am. Bd. Trial Advocates, Tex. Assn. Def. Counsel (v.p., bd. dirs.), Def. Rsch. Inst. Republican. Roman Catholic. Avocation: golf. Home: 3704 Garnet St Houston TX 77005-3716 Office: Phillips & Akers Phoenix Tower 3200 Southwest Fwy Houston TX 77027-7528 Office Phone: 713-552-9595. E-mail: brock.akers@phillipsakers.com.

AKERS, FRANK H., JR., engineer, director; BS in Engring., U.S. Naval Acad., 1966; MMAS in Operational Art, U.S. Army Command & Gen. Staff Coll.; AM in History, PhD in History, Duke U., 1975; graduate in Strategy & Policy, U.S. Army War Coll., 1985; graduate in Nat. Security, Indsl. Coll. of Armed Forces, 1970; graduate Sr. Exec. Program, U. Mich., 1986, Harvard U., 1995; graduate, Lockheed Martin Sr. Leadership Inst., 1998. Commd. lt. U.S. Army, 1966, advanced through grades to brig. gen., ret., 1996; dir. nat. security ops. Lockheed Martin Energy Sys., Oakridge, Tenn., 1996—97, dir. advanced tech., 1997—99, v.p. advanced tech., 1999—. Decorated Legion of Merit U.S. Army, Bronze Star, Purple Heart; recipient Disting. Svc. Medal, Defense Superior Svc. Medal. Office: Oak Ridge National Lab PO Box 2008 MS6242 Oak Ridge TN 37831-6242

AKERS, JENNIFER ANN, aeronautical engineer; d. James and Hazel Akers. MSME, So. Ill. U., 2005. Tchg. asst. So. Ill. U., Carbondale, 2003—05; aero. engr. Lockheed Martin, Ft. Worth, 2005—. Mem.: ASME (finalist Best STudent Paper award for dynamic systems and controls), Soc. Women Engrs., Phi Theta Kappa. Office: Lockheed Martin Fort Worth TX

AKERS, SAUNDRA RUTH, retired disability rights advocate; b. Urbana, Ohio, July 21, 1943; d. Henry Albert and Clara Velma (Stultz) Crum; m. Larry Roger Akers, Mar. 1, 1964 (div. Feb. 1986); children: Crystal Annette Castle, H. Roger, Noel Justin, Pride A. Cert. paralegal, Am. Inst. Paralegal Practice. Mgr. Marathon Sta., Columbus, Ohio, 1972—73; nursing assoc., mental health tech., mental health tech. supr. Columbus Devel. Ctr., residential area program planner, vocat. habilitation specialist; disability rights advocate Ohio Legal Rights, Columbus; ret., 2005. Liaison Gov.'s Coun. People with Disabilities, 1997—, Ohio Devel. Disability Coun., 1994—97. Author: Curious Concepts, 2005. Sec. Citizen's Com., Hilliard, Ohio, 1973. Mem.: Toastmasters Internat. Avocations: public speaking, creative writing, genealogy. Home: 3260 Colony Hill Ln Columbus OH 43204

AKERS, SHARRON LOELLA, language educator; b. Rexburg, Idaho, Aug. 21, 1935; d. Ferry Henry Larter and Mabelle Irene Luthy-Larter; children: Shanna, Drienne, Gustin. *Going by pen name S. L. Larter, was born to Ferry Henry Larter and Mabelle Irene Lüthy Larter on a cattle ranch in Idaho. Mother's ancestry comes from England, Switzerland and France. Both maternal grandparents migrated through Ellis Island. Father's ancestry follows the early colonies, which include John Howland, who signed the Mayflower contract and John Brown (Brown University) from England, and include Chad Brown and Obadiah Holmes, famous English preachers. The name Larter dates through Scottish history, the Vikings, and the Germanic Tribes who settled East Anglia (the home of the Larters).* AA, Columbia Basin Coll., 1992; BA, Coll. Global Deployment, Vancouver, Wash., 2001; MA magna cum laude, Coll. Global Deployment, 2002. Missionary Columbia Foursquare, Richland, Wash., 1987—90; sec. Columbia Basin Coll., Pasco, Wash., 1990—92; salesperson K-Mart, Kennewick, Wash., 1990—92; libr. Wash. State U., Richland, 1992—93, receptionist, 1993—94; missionary Yuma, Ariz., 1987—96; mem. staff Leviton Mfg., San Diego, 1994—96; substitute tchr. Joint Sch. Dist. # 111, Arco, Idaho, 1999—2002; reporter Magic Valley Times News, Twin Falls, Idaho, 2002—03; tchr. English as 2d lang. Coll. So. Idaho, Twin Falls, 2002—04. Author: The Truth Sayers, 2004; sculptor The Protector. Prodr., dir. Mackay (Idaho) Cultural and Art Assn., 2000—01, v.p., 2000—01; bd. dirs., vol. Vets. of Custer County and the High Country Resource Conservation and Devel. Inc., 1999—; leader 4-H Club, Idaho, 1965—71; youth leader M-H Club, 1965—; mem. election bd. Mackay Precinct, 2002; tchr., sec., ordain min., missionary Vida Theol. Inst. Internat. Ch. of Foursquare Gospel, Tijuana, Mexico, 1987—90; tchr., sec., missionary The Redeemed Evang. Mission, Lagos, Nigeria, 1998—99. Mem.: Am. Legion Aux., Gamma Phi Delta. Republican. Mem. Internat. Ch. Of The Foursquare Gospel. Avocations: hiking, travel, painting, gardening, white-water rafting. Home: 304 E 300 N Jerome ID 83338 Office Phone: 208-644-9437. Personal E-mail: sharronakers@ltlink.com.

AKHAVAN, FARHAD, electrical engineer; b. Tehran, Iran, Dec. 30, 1967; came to U.S., 1989; s. Akbar Akhavan and Shahpar Karimi. MS in Physics, MSEE, U. Mo., Rolla, 1992, PhD in Elec. Engring., 1998. Postdoctoral rsch. assoc. Optical Scis. Ctr. U. Ariz., Tucson, 1998-2000, asst. rsch. scientist Optical Scis. Ctr., 2000; sr. optical engr. Nortel Networks Inc., Wilmington, Mass., 2000—. Advisor Nat. Security Agy., Md., 1998-2000. Contbr. articles to profl. jours. Grantee NASA, 2000. Mem. IEEE, Optical Soc. Am., Soc. Optical Engrs. Avocation: classical readings of ancient civilizations. E-mail: farhad@nortelnetworks.com.

AKHONDI, HOSSEIN, internist, researcher; b. Tehran, Iran, Nov. 16, 1968; s. Mahmood Akhondi and Parvaneh Espahbodi. MD, Iran U., Tehran, 1995. Diplomate Am. Bd. Internal Medicine. Instr. anatomy and neuroanatomy Iran U. Med. Scis., Tehran, 1990—95; hospitalist physician Police Hosp., Tehran, 1995—97; emergency room physician Day Gen. Hosp., Tehran, 1997—99; rsch. asst. Mercer U., Savannah, Ga., 1999—2001, internal medicine resident, 2001—. Mem. rsch. com. Mercer U. Meml. Hosp., Savannah, 2000—, mem. quality mgmt. resident liaison com., 2000—; presenter in field. Contbr. articles to profl. jours. Mem. nat. screening team for rheumatic heart diseases Ministry Health, Tehran, 1993—94. Recipient Continued Med. Edn. course prize, MAYO Clinic, 2000. Fellow: Iranian Med. Coun. (licentiate; young physicians 1995—97); mem.: AMA, Ga. Chpt. Physicians, ACP - Am. Soc. Internal Medicine (assoc. Second place for best original rsch. presentation 2002, Second place for an oral presentation award 2001), So. Med. Assn. (mem. resident adv. com. 2002—, First place for oral presentation 2002). Achievements include research in description of association of tongue piercing with infective endocarditis; presented first case of subclavian vein thrombosis after weigh lifting; role of positive pressure ventilation in treating patients with diastolic heart failure; role of illicit drug use in spinal cord infarct; development of antibody coated bacteria in UTI differentiation; research in ESR in Alzheimer and non-Alzheimer dementia; are physicians using evidence based medicine in atrial fibrilation; discovery of the correlation of SPECT brain scan, Tau and Beta-42 protein with Alzheimer disease. Avocations: movies, reading, chess, tennis. Office: Southern Md Hosp 7503 Surratts Rd Clinton MD 20735 Personal E-mail: h68akhond@hotmail.com.

AKHOURY, RAVI, insurance company executive; BS in engring., Indian Inst. Tech.; MS in quantitative methods, SUNY. V.p. Equitable Life, 1973; v.p., mem. investment policy com. Fischer, Francis, Trees and Watts; dir. MacKay Shields, 1984—, pres., 1989—92, chmn., CEO, 1992—; exec. mgmt. com. New York Life Ins. Co., N.Y.C., 1997—, exec. v.p., 1997—. Mem.: Fin. Affairs Com. NY Acad. Scis., Innerdoorway.com (dir.), Bharti Tele-Ventures (dir.).

AKHTAR, MUHAMMAD I., neurologist, researcher; arrived in U.S., 1994; s. Akhtar Hussain and Mushtary Begum; m. Huda Mohsin Qureshi; children: Hadiya children: Sumaiyaa. MD, Sindh Med. Coll., Karachi, 1991; postgrad., Ohio State U., 2002. Chief resident Ohio State U. Med. Ctr., Columbus, 2001, cons. neurologist, 1999—2002, So. Ohio Med. Ctr., Portsmouth, 2003—. Scholar, Am. Neurol. Assn., 2002. Mem.: AMA, W.Va. Med. Assn., Columbus Med. Assn., Am. Acad. Neurology (resident scholarship 2002), Pakistan Internat. Neurosci. Soc., So. Med. Assn. (hon.), Am. Headache Soc. (hon.), Pakistan Med. Coun. (hon.). Home: 3351 Seneca Dr Portsmouth OH 45662 Office: So Ohio Med Ctr 1735 27th St C Ste 102 Portsmouth OH 45662 Personal E-mail: drakhtar@hotmail.com. Business E-Mail: AkhtarM@somc.org.

AKIBA, LORRAINE HIROKO, lawyer; b. Honolulu, Dec. 28, 1956; d. Lawrence H. and Florence K. (Iwasa) Katsuyama. BS with honors, U. Calif., Berkeley, 1977; JD, U. Calif., San Francisco, 1981. Bar: Hawaii 1981, U.S. Dist. Ct. Hawaii 1981, U.S. Ct. Appeals (9th cir.) 1981, U.S. Supreme Ct. 1986. Dir. State of Hawaii Dept. Labor and Indsl. Rels., 1995—2000; ptnr. Cades, Schutte, Fleming & Wright, Honolulu, 1981—94, McCorriston Miller Mukai and MacKinnon, Honolulu, 2000—. Lawyer rep. 9th Cir. Jud. Conf., 1991-94; mem., past treas. Hawaii Inst. for Continuing Legal Edn., Honolulu, 1987—. Chairperson attys. divsn. Aloha United Way, Honolulu, 1991, 2004, statewide chairperson, 1995; mem. State of Hawaii Environ. Coun., Honolulu, 1990-94, chair, 1992. Named one of Outstanding Young Women Am., 1985. Mem. ABA, Hawaii Bar Assn., Hawaii Women Lawyers Assn., Hawaii Women Lawyers Found. (pres. 1988-92), Honolulu Club, Phi Beta Kappa. Office: McCorriston Miller Mukai MacKinnon LLP PO Box 2800 Honolulu HI 96803-2800 Office Phone: 808-529-7300. E-mail: akiba@m4law.com.

AKIL, HUDA, neuroscientist, educator, researcher; b. Damascus, Syria, May 19, 1945; came to U.S., 1968; d. Fakher and Widad (Al-Imam) A.; m. Stanley Jack Watson Jr., Dec. 21, 1972; children: Brendon Omar, Kathleen Tamara. BA, Am. U., Beirut, Lebanon, 1966, MA, 1968; PhD, UCLA, 1972. Postdoctoral fellow Stanford U., Palo Alto, Calif., 1974-78; from asst. prof. to prof. psychiatry and neuroscience U. Mich., Ann Arbor, 1979—, co-dir., sr. rsch. scientist Mental Health Rsch. Inst. Mem. adv. bd. Neurex Corp., Menlo Park, Calif., 1986—, Neurobiol. Techs., Inc., 1994-97; sec. Internat. Narcotics Rsch. Conf., 1990-94. Editor: (jour.) Pain and Headache: Neurochemistry of Pain, 1990; contbr. articles over 300 articles to profl. jours., 1971—2001. Recipient Pacesetter award Nat. Inst. Drug Abuse, 1993, Pasarow award Pasarow Found., 1994, Bristol-Myers Squibb award, 1998, Edward Sachar award Columbia U., 1998; Rockefeller scholar, Beirut, 1963-66; Alfred P. Sloan fellow, Stanford, Calif., 1974-78; grantee Nat. Inst. Drug Abuse, Washington, 1978—, NIMH, Washington, 1980—, Markey Found., U. Mich., 1988-97. Fellow Am. Acad. Arts & Scis., Am. Coll. Neuropsychopharmacology (pres. 1997-98), U. Mich. Soc. Fellows; mem. Inst. Medicine/NAS,

Soc.for Neuroscience (pres. 2002-03). Achievements include first to produce physiological evidence for existence of naturally occurring opiate-like substances (endorphins) in brain; described phenomenon of stress-induced analgesia; described functions and regulation of endorphins in brain and pituitary gland; contributed to understanding of biological mechanisms of morphine tolerance and physical dependence; (with colleagues) cloned two main types of opiate receptors, described critical brain circuits relevant to stress and depression. Office: Mental Health Rsch Inst 205 Zina Pitcher Ann Arbor MI 48109-2214*

AKIMOTO, MARTIN WAYNE, mental health services professional; b. Chgo., July 24, 1949; s. Ned E. and Emmy (Tsujimoto) A.; m. Barbara Wendley, June 11, 1983; children: Emily, Ellen. BS in Psychology, U. Utah, 1972, MSW, 1974. Cert. suicide intervention trainer, Calif.; lic. social worker. Social worker Protective Svc. Davis County, Div. Family Svc., Utah, 1974; pvt. practice Simi Psychotherapy Group, Simi Valley, Calif., 1979-87; field work supr. U. So. Calif., 1983-85; sr. psychiat. social worker Simi Valley Mental Health, Ventura County Mental Health Dept, 1975-76, Conejo Valley Mental Health, 1976-87; coord. outpatient children's svc. Ventura County Mental Health, Thousand Oaks, 1987-88; regional supr. children's svcs. Ventura County Mental Health Dept., 1988-92, program supr. options program, 1992-2000; sr. program mgr. Butte County Dept. Behavioral Health, Chico, 2000—. Vol. lectr., rap session leader Planned Parenthood of Utah, 1972-73. Office: Butte County Dept Behavioral Health Youth Svc Adminstrn 500 Cohasset Ste 28 Chico CA 95926 Office Phone: 530-879-3875. E-mail: makimoto@buttecounty.net.

AKIN, ANN FOSTER, special education educator; b. Danbury, Conn., Apr. 11, 1953; d. Thomas Joseph and Sarah Foster; m. Kent Brown Akin, Aug. 22, 1981; children: Hannah Kathleen, Nicholas Kent. BA in Psychology, Elem. Edn. and Edn. for Blind, Dominican Coll., 1976; EdM Edn. of Blind and Visually Impaired, Boston Coll., 1981. Cert. tchr. for blind and partially seeing, elem. edn. N.Y., 1977. Itinerant tchr. for blind and visually impaired Bd. Coop. Ednl. Svcs., Ashville, NY, 1977—. Coord. religious edn. St. Mary's Ch., Mayville, NY. Mem.: AAUW, Coun. for Exceptional Children, Assn. for the Edn. and Rehab. Blind and Visually Impaired, Mayville-Chautauqua Lions Club (pres. 2003—), Eta Nu (pres. 1989—90).

AKIN, CHARLES S., academic administrator; b. Dallas, Tex., Jan. 19, 1940; s. Charles Wesley and Faye Fern Akin; m. Cynthia Gaye Miller, Dec. 28, 1974; children: Kanda, Chad, Charles Jr., Wesley. BS in edn., U. N. Tex., 1962, MS in edn., 1965. Cert. pub. sch. administr. State of Tex. Tchr. Pine Tree HS, Longview, Tex., 1962—66, Henderson County Jr. Coll., Athens, Tex., 1966—74; dir. Trinity Valley C.C., Terrell, Tex., 1974—82; dean Trinity Valley C.C., Evening Coll., Athens, Tex., 1982—88, Trinity Valley C.C.,Palestine Campus, Palestine, Tex., 1988—; v.p. C. of C., Palestine, 1989—91. Bd. dirs. Mus. East Tex. Culture, 1989—95. Recipient Office of Yr. award, Athens Police Dept., 1970; Paul Harris fellow, Palestine Rotary Club, 1995. Mem.: Tex. Assn. Coll. Tech. Educators, Tex. C.C. Tchrs. Assn., Palestine Rotary Club (pres. 1995), Terrell Noon Lions Club (pres. 1980). Meth. Office: Trinity Valley CC PO Box 2530 Palestine TX 75802 Office Phone: 903-729-0256. Office Fax: 903-729-2325. E-mail: cakin@tvcc.edu.

AKIN, STEVEN PAUL, finance company executive; b. Hackensack, N.J., Apr. 6, 1945; s. Richard Ernest and Lucille F. (Mosher) A.; m. Jane Goddard, Nov. 24, 1973; children: Kyla, Sus. BA in Econs., Ohio Wesleyan U., 1969; postgrad., Columbia U., Harriman, N.Y., 1986. Lic. series 7 and 24, NASD, NYSE. Mgmt. trainee customer svc. mgmt. N.Y. Telephone, 1969-78; asst. v.p. customer svc. United Tel. Co. Ohio, Mansfield, 1978-85; v.p. ops. United Tel. Co. Ind., Warsaw, 1985-86, United Tel. Co. Midwest, Overland Park, Kans., 1986-87; sr. v.p., then pres. US Sprint, Kansas City, Mo., 1987-92; pres. Fidelity Retail Investor Svcs., Boston, 1992-95, Fidelity Brokerage Svcs., Inc., Boston, 1995-97, Fidelity Retail Customer Svcs., Boston, 1995-96; pres., chief info. officer Fidelity Investments Sys. Co., Boston, 1997-99; pres. Fidelity Capital, 1999—2002; pres., CEO Colt Telecomms., London, 2002—04; pres., CEO EVP Corp. Svcs. Fidelity, 2004—. Pres. Mansfield Symphony, 1985—86, Lyric Opera, Kansas City, Kans., 1991—92; trustee Kents Hill Sch., Kents Hill, Maine, 2002—, Boston Lyric Opera, 2002—03, 2005—. Home: 55 Hillcrest Rd Weston MA 02493-2020 Office: Fidelity 82 Devonshire St F5E Boston MA 02109

AKIN, W. TODD, congressman, former state legislator; b. N.Y.C., July 5, 1947; m. Lulli Boe, 1971; six children. BS, Worcester Poly. Inst.; MDiv, Covenant Theol. Sem. Mo. State rep. Dist. 86, 1988-2000; corp. mgmt. Laclede Steel Co.; bus. mgr., educator; former mktg. profl. IBM Computer Systems; mem. U.S. Congress from 2d Mo. dist., 2001—, mem. armed svcs. com., small bus. com., sci. com., chmn. workforce, empowerment and govt. programs subcom. Officer Army Engrs. Republican. Office: 117 Cannon Ho Office Bldg Washington DC 20515-2502*

AKINAKA, ASA MASAYOSHI, lawyer; b. Honolulu, Jan. 19, 1938; s. Arthur Yoshinori and Misako (Miyoshi) A.; m. Betsy Yoshie Kurata, Oct. 7, 1967; children— David Asa Yoshio, Sarah Elizabeth Sachie. BA magna cum laude, Yale U., 1959; postgrad. (Rotary Found. fellow), Trinity Coll., Oxford U., 1959-60, Yale Law Sch., 1960-61; LL.B., Stanford Law Sch., 1964. Bar: Hawaii bar 1964. Research asst. U.S. Senator Oren Long, Washington, 1961-62; pvt. practice law Honolulu, 1964—. Bd. visitors Stanford Law Sch., 1971-74. Mem. Am. Bar Assn., Hawaii State Bar Assn. (pres. 1977), Nat. Conf. Bar Presidents, Pacific Club, YMCA (bd. dirs., v.p. 1970-81). Democrat. Episcopalian. Office: PO Box 1035 Honolulu HI 96808-1035

AKINCI, FEVZI, health science association administrator, educator; BS in Health Admin., Hacettepe U., 1991; MHA, St. Louis U., 1995, PhD in Health Svc. Rsch., 1998. Asst. prof. King's Coll., Wilkes-Barre, Pa., 1998—2004; asst. prof. health policy, adminstrn. Wash. State U., Spokane, Wash., 2004—. Bd. mem. Bus. Health Adminstrn. Assn., Chicago, Ill., 2001, Behavioral Health Rsch. Inst., Scranton, Pa., 2000—04, Health Care Mgmt. Forum Northeastern Pa., Scranton, Pa., 2001—04, Ethics Inst. Northeastern Pa., Dallas, Pa., 2002—04, Ctr. Health Promotion, King's Coll., Wilkes-Barre, Pa., 2002—04, Mercy Health Partners NE Region, Scranton, Pa., 2002—04; mem. NE Regional Cancer Inst., Scranton, Pa., 2001—02. Recipient Mary Grumble Levy award, St. Louis U., 1998, Disting. Rsch. award, Allied Acad. Fall Internat. Conf., Las Vegas, 2001, Mark R. Leffler Scholar of the Year award, King's College, Wilkes Barre, PA, 2003. Fellow: Commn. Accreditation Healthcare Mgmt. Edn. (CAHME); mem.: APHA, Commission Accreditation Healthcare Mgmt. Edn. (CAHME) Criteria Rev. Com., AUPHA Fin. Economics Faculty Forum, Am. Coll. Health Care Executives, Acad. Health. Office: Washington State Univ PO Box 1495 Spokane WA 99210-1495 Office Phone: 509-358-7985. Office Fax: 509-358-7984. E-mail: akinci@wsu.edu.

AKINS, CARY WILLARD, surgeon, educator; b. July 13, 1944; AB, Harvard Coll., 1966; MD, Harvard U., 1970. Diplomate Am. Bd. Thoracic Surgery. Resident in gen. surgery Mass. Gen. Hosp., Boston, 1970—74, fellow in cardiac surgery, 1975, clin. prof. surgery, dir. clin. cardiac rsch./end results cardiac surgery; fellow in cardiac surgery Southampton Western Hosp., Eng., 1974. Office: Mass Gen Hosp White 503 55 Fruit St Boston MA 02114-2696 Office Phone: 617-726-8218.

AKINS, GEORGE CHARLES, accountant; b. Feb. 22, 1917; s. Guy Brookins and Eugenie (Swan) A.; m. Jane Babcock, Mar. 27, 1945 (dec. May 3, 2003). AA, Sacramento City Coll., 1941. Acct., auditor Calif. Bd. Equalization, Dept. Fin., Sacramento, 1940—44; contr.-treas. DeVons Jewelers, Sacramento, 1944—73, v.p., contr., 1973—80, v.p., CFO, dir., 1980—84; individual acctg. and tax practice Sacramento, 1944—. Contbg. author: Portfolio of Accounting Systems for Small and Medium-Sized Business, 1968, Portfolio of Accounting Systems for Small and Medium-Sized Business, rev. edit., 1977. Acct., cons. Mercy Children's Hosp. Guild, Sacramento, 1957—77. With USAF, 1942. Mem.: Northwestern Pacific Railroad Hist. Soc., Internat. Platform Assn., Calif. Hist. Soc., Nat. Soc. Accts., Soc. Calif. Pioneers, Mendocino County Hist. Soc. (life), USN League (life), Drake Navigators Guild, Sacramento County Hist. Soc. (life), Crocker Art Mus. (life), Comstock, Commonwealth Club of Calif. Republican. Roman Catholic. Home and Office: 96 S Humboldt St Willits CA 95490-3539

AKINS, VAUGHN EDWARD, retired engineering company executive; b. Gowanda, NY, Sept. 28, 1934; s. Elsworth D. and Alice (Carlton) A.; m. Muriel M. Hoglund, May 15, 1960 (dec. 1992); children: Sonja L., Coleen R., Joseph E. Student, U.S. Naval Schs., 1956-57, IBM Engring. Sch., 1961-65. Lab. specialist IBM, Poughkeepsie, N.Y., Boulder, Colo., East Fishkill, NY, 1959—69; test mgr. Semi, Phoenix, 1969-74; mgr. computer-aided mfg. and test engring. semicondr. R&D Motorola Corp., Mesa, Ariz., 1974-84; applications mgr. (SIM) Motorola Corp. New Enterprises Group, Mesa, 1984-86; mgr. computer integrated mfg. semicondr. products sector Motorola Corp., Phoenix, 1986-87; with start-up team SEMATECH, Inc., Austin, Tex., 1988-93, dir. internat. standards programs, 1989-93, mgr. incubator programs, 1992; mgr. strategic integration Motorola Ctr. Advanced Computer Products, Austin, 1993-96; ret. Motorola Wireless Sys. Ctr., Austin, 1996-98; cons. in field, 2000—. Personal and bus. coach. Precinct committeeman N.Y. State Conservative Party, 1963; instr. first aid ARC, 1971-78; chair U.S. exec. com. S.E.M.I., Inc., mem. exec. com. internat. standard program, 1987-1993. With USNR, 1953-59. Mem. IEEE (sr.), NRA, Electrochem. Soc. (cons. to exec. bd., co-chmn. founding com. Automation in Mfg. chpt., exec. com. electronics divsn. 1985-92), World Future Soc Republican. Fundamentalist. Home: 560 Waterleaf Blvd Kyle TX 78640 Office Phone: 512-217-9312. Personal E-mail: vakins@ieee.org.

AKINS, ZANE VERNON, agricultural products executive; b. Bethel, Kans., Apr. 13, 1940; s. Gerald Vernon and Vesta Jean (Rutherford) A.; m. Kay Ellen Cowan, Aug. 17, 1963; children: Michael Scott, Deborah Lynn, Christine Sue. BS in Agr., U. Mo., 1962. Farmer, 1962-64; svc. technician No. Ohio Breeders Assn., Tiffin, 1964-66; program dir. Holstein Assn. Am., Brattleboro, Vt., 1966-73, mgr. sire devel. svc., 1973-77, adminstrv. asst., 1977-78, CEO, 1978-90; exec. v.p. Holstein-Friesian Svcs., Inc., Brattleboro, 1978-90; pres. Zane Akins and Assocs., West Brattleboro, 1991—. Pres., chmn. bd. dirs. Nat. Integrated Techs. Inc., 1996—; bd. dirs. Earthwide Assocs., Inc., pres. 1994—; pres. A&S Assocs., Ltd., 1995—; bd. dirs. Vt. Nat. Bank, 1987-2000, Earthwide Sys. Inc., v.p., 1995—; v.p. Earthwide Products Corp., 1996—; bd. dirs. Vt. Fin. Svcs., 1987-2000, chmn. exec. com., 1995-96, chmn. audit com., 1996-97, chmn. loan com., 1997-98; regional leader Primerica Fin. Svcs., 1991—; chmn. bd. dirs. Anitech Internat. Inc., Boulder, Colo., 1991-92; trustee N.E. Delta/Vt. Dental Soc., Inc., 1990-99, chmn., 1995-99; chmn. bd. NEDA, 1999--; pres. Vt. Natural Food Products Inc., 2001--. Bd. dirs. Windham County United Way, 1980-84; corporator Brattleboro Meml. Hosp., 1980—, chmn. pub. rels. com., 1982-83, bd. dirs., 1983-86; pres. Windham County Humane Soc., 1992-93; bd. dirs. Brattleboro Area Boys & Girls Club, 1998-2002, treas., 1999-2002. Sears & Roebuck scholar, Freshman Curators scholar, Borden's scholar, U. Mo., 1958-59, Sophomore Curators scholar, Campus Chest scholar, 1958-60; recognized as Man of the Yr. Tri-State Breeders Coop., 1984; recipient Citation of Merit U. Mo., 1986. Mem. Purebred Dairy Cattle Assn. (bd. dirs. 1978-90, Recognition award 1991), Nat. Soc. Livestock Records Assn. (v.p. 1982-84), Nat. Pedigree Livestock Coun. (pres. 1984-86, sec., treas. 1989—, Disting. Svc. award 1993), Nat. Coop. Dairy Herd Improvement Programs (policy bd. 1980-90), Geonomics Inst., Boston Dist. Export Coun., Brattleboro C. of C. (bd. dirs. 1979-81), Alpha Zeta (Centennial Honor Roll 1997), Alpha Gamma Rho (regional v.p. 1980-84, bd. dirs. 1984-90, grand pres. 1986-89, Man of Yr. award Chgo. Alumni chpt. 1991, Bro. of the Century 2004). Congregationalist. Home and Office: 177 Palermo Pl Lady Lake FL 32159-0094

AKISKAL, HAGOP SOUREN, psychiatric researcher, educator; b. Beirut, Jan. 16, 1944; U.S., 1969; s. Stephen Jacques and Vehanoushe Dickran (Bedrossian) A. MD, Am. U., Beirut, 1969; Dr. honoris causa, U. Lisbon, 2003. Instr. U. Tenn., Memphis, 1972-73, asst. prof., 1973-77, assoc. prof., 1977-80, prof. psychiatry, dir. sect. affective disorders program, 1975—, dir. med. student edn., 1974-78. Co-dir. Sleep Disorders Ctr., Bapt. Meml. Hosp., Memphis, 1983—; Eli Robins lectr. Washington U., 1980; sr. sci. advisor Nat. Inst. Mental Health, 1990-94; prof. psychiatry, dir. Internat. Mood Ctr., U. Calif. San Diego, 1995—. Editor (editor-in-chief): Jour. of Affective Disorders, 1986—. Recipient Anna Monika prize, 1999, Affective Disorders prize, NARSAD, 2001, Jean Delay prize, World Psychiat. Assn., 2002, Ellis Island medal of honor, 2003. Fellow Am. Psychiat. Assn., Soc. Biol. Psychiatry (Gold medal 1995), Am. Coll. Psychiatrists, Am. Coll. of Neuropsychopharmacology, Royal Coll. of Psychiatrists (hon.), French Nat. Academy Medicine (fgn. mem., Paris), Armenian Nat. Acad. Scis. (hon.). Office: U Calif Psychiatary 0603 9500 Gilman Dr La Jolla CA 92093-5004 Office Phone: 858-552-8585 2226. Business E-Mail: hakiskal@ucsd.edu.

AKIYAMA, TOSHIO, cardiologist, educator, researcher; b. Shimizu, Japan, Mar. 10, 1941; came to U.S., 1968; m. Akiko Okamura Akyama; children: Naoko, Sachiko. MD, Kyoto Prefectural U. Med., 1966. Cert. in internal medicine, specialty in cardiovasc. disease. Rotating intern U.S. Naval Hosp., Yokosuka, Japan, 1966—67; med. resident, 3d internal medicine dept. Kyoto Prefectural U. Medicine, 1967; staff physician Atomic Bomb Casualty Commn., Hiroshima, Japan, 1967—68; intern Rochester Gen. Hosp., 1968-69, resident in medicine, 1969-70, Strong Meml. Hosp.-U. Rochester, 1970-71, resident in cardiology, 1972-73; fellow in cardiology Emory U., Atlanta, 1971-72, U. Chgo., 1973-75; dir. heart sta. Strong Meml. Hosp., Rochester; prof. medicine with unltd. tenure U. Rochester Sch. Medicine, 1993—. Reviewer NIH study sect. Biomed. Tech. Spl. Emphasis Panel; cons. Exec. com. for Japanese Med. Specialist Joint commn. Mem. editl. bd. Jour. Electrocardiology, Jour. Arrhythmia, Japanese Circulation Jour., Jour. Arrhythmia, Acta Medica Mem. Biologica; contbr. over 160 articles to profl. jours Chmn. Rochester Hamamatsu Sister City Com., chmn., 1998-2000. Fellow Am. Coll. Cardiology; mem. Am. Heart Assn., N.Am. Soc. of Pacing and Electrophysiology, Japanese Med. Soc. (exec. com. joint commn. med. specialist sys.), Japanese Clin. Cardiology Soc. Office: U Rochester Med Ctr Dept Cardiology 601 Elmwood Ave Box 679 Rochester NY 14642-8679 Office Phone: 585-275-1667. E-mail: toshio_akiyama@urmc.rochester.edu.

AKKARA, JOSEPH AUGUSTINE, chemist, educator; arrived in US, 1964, naturalized, 1980; s. Augustine Aippu Akkara and Theresa Anthony Kolapran; m. Mary Ann Malaickel, Aug. 18, 1969; children: Augustine Viju, Jeena Theresa. PhD in Biochemistry, U. Mo., 1969. Med. rschr. Med. Coll. Trivandrum, Kerala, India, 1959-61; tech. asst. Ctrl. Food Technol. Rsch. Inst., Mysore, India, 1961-64; grad. asst., rsch. assoc. Sch. Medicine U. Mo., Columbia, 1964-69; rsch. assoc. Rockefeller U., N.Y.C., 1969-71, Brookdale Hosp. Med. Ctr., Bklyn., 1971-73, chief radioassay, 1973-80; sr. scientist Med. Rsch. Inst., Worcester, Mass., 1980-81; biochemist stat. Toxicology Svc. Boston, 1981-84; rsch. chemist U.S. Army Natick Rsch. and Engring. Ctr., 1984-99; program dir. NSF, 1999—. Adj. faculty Framingham State Coll., 1996-99; mem. biotechnology adv. bd. Mass. Bay Coll.; advisor NRC; bd. dirs. Invention Evaluation. Recipient R&D award U.S. Army, 1992, 96, Inventor of Yr. award U.S. Army Soldier Sys. commd., 1998. Mem. Materials Rsch. Soc., Am. Chem. Soc., N.Y. Acad. Scis., Kerala Assn. New Eng. (pres. 1986-87), Indian Assn. Greater Boston (sec. 1986-88, 1st v.p. 1988-89), Lions Club, Rotary, Sigma Xi (pres. Natick chpt. 1998-99). Roman Catholic. Achievements include patents and publications in synthesis, modification, characterization, and applications of polymers and materials for electro-optic and high performance multifunctional applications; enzymology, nutrition, endocrinology, analytical chemistry, and research program management. Home: 7520 Walnut Hill Ln Falls Church VA 22042-3539 E-mail: jakkara@nsf.gov, jaakkara@aol.com.

AKOS, FRANCIS, retired violinist, conductor; b. Budapest, Hungary, Mar. 30, 1922; came to U.S., 1954; s. Karoly and Rose (Reti) Weinberg; m. Phyllis Malvin Sommers, June 7, 1981; children from previous marriage: Katherine Elizabeth, Judith Margaret. Baccalaureate, Budapest, 1941; MA, Franz Liszt Acad. Music, Budapest, 1940, PhD, 1941. Concertmaster, Budapest Symphony Orch., 1945-46, Royal Opera and Philharmonic Soc., Budapest, 1947-48, Gothenburg (Sweden) Symphony Orch., 1948-50, Municipal Opera (now Deutsche Oper), West Berlin, Ger., 1950-54, Mpls. Symphony Orch., 1954, asst. concertmaster, Chgo. Symphony Orch., 1955—, ret., 2003, concertmaster emeritus, 1997-, also performed as soloist; performed at Salzburg Festival, 1948, Scandinavian Festival, Helsinki, Finland, 1950, Berlin Festival, 1951, Prades Festival, 1953, Bergen Festival, 1962, Vienna Festival, 1962, founder, condr., Chgo. Strings, chamber orch., 1961, condr., Fox River Valley Symphony, Aurora, Ill., 1965-73, Chicago Heights (Ill.) Symphony, 1975-79, Highland Park Strings, 1979—. Prizewinner Hubay competition, Budapest, 1939, Remenyi competition, Budapest, 1939 Home: 1310 Maple Ave Evanston IL 60201-4325 Personal E-mail: violak1310@yahoo.com.

AKOURIS, DIANNE FRANCES, school system administrator; b. Nenno, Wis., Aug. 19, 1940; d. Sylvester X. and Marcella H. Hefter; m. John G. Akouris, June 19, 1976. BS in Edn., Alverno Coll., 1969; MA in Reading, Northeastern Ill. U., 1988. Cert. advanced study of supr. Nat. Louis U., 1992, elem. and secondary tchg. Ill. Tchr. Parochial Archdioceses of Chgo., 1959—64, St. Mary's Sch., Holly Springs, Miss., 1964—66, Parochial Archdioceses of Chgo., 1966—85, Cook County, Chgo., 1985; tchrs. aide Westnorthfield Elem. Sch. #31, Glenview, Ill., 1985—86; comm. tchr. Waukeban Pub. Sch. #60, Waukegan, Ill., 1986—87; tchr. Fremont Sch. Dist., Fremont, Ill., 1987—88, Waukegan Pub. Sch., Waukegan, Ill., 1988—2000, summer bridges coord., 2000; facilitator Waukegan Tchrs. Acad., Waukegan, Ill., 2000—. Coop. tchr. Barat Coll., Lake Forest, Ill., 1995, Lake Forest, 97, Nat. Louis U., Evanston, Ill., 1999. Co-author: (article) The California Reader, 1990. Presenter Ill. State Kindergarten Conf., Rosemont, Ill., 1992; moderator League of Women Voters, Libertyville, Ill., 1993, WKRS Radio Station, Waukegan, Ill., 1993; presenter Ill. Reading Coun., Columbus, Ohio, 2001. Nominee Golden Apple award, Golden Apple Found., 2000; recipient First Grant award, First Bank of Am., 1995, Excellence in Tchg., Classic Cheverlot of Waukegan, 2000. Mem.: Lake County Curriculum Resource Coun., Internat. Reading Assn., Assn. for Supervision and Curriculum Devel., Ill. Principals Assn. Achievements include development of Kindergarten Extend Education Through Parents (K.E.E.P.), 1991-1994. Avocations: gardening, reading, choir. Home: 2004 Sunset Ct Zion IL 60099 Office: Waukegan Tchrs Acad Lincoln Ctr 1201 N Sheridan Rd Waukegan IL 60085 Office Phone: 847-599-2787. Office Fax: 847-360-5654. E-mail: dakouris@waukeganschools.org.

AKSEN, GERALD, arbitrator, lawyer, educator; b. N.Y.C., Feb. 16, 1930; s. David and Bess (Stein) A.; m. Phyllis Schwadron, June 3, 1957 (dec.); 1 child, Lisa Susan. AB, CCNY, 1951; MA, Columbia U., 1952; LLB, NYU, 1958. Bar: N.Y. 1959, U.S. Dist. Ct. (so. and ea. dist.) N.Y. 1961, U.S. Supreme Ct. 1964. Assoc. Flood & Purvin, N.Y.C., 1958-61; assoc. gen. counsel Am. Arbitration Assn., N.Y.C., 1962-63, gen. counsel, 1964-80; ptnr. Reid & Priest L.L.P., N.Y.C., 1981-98, Thelen Reid & Priest L.L.P., N.Y.C., 1998—2002. Adj. prof. NYU, N.Y.C., 1968-2001; mem. First Dept. Jud. Screening Com., 1983-93; bd. dirs. U.S. Coun. Internat. Bus., 1982—; ICC Inst. World Bus. Law, 1992—; vice chmn. ICC Internat. Ct. Arbitration, 2000-02; pres. Coll. Coml. Arbitratiors, 2002-03. Bd. dirs. Nat. Inst. Consumer Justice, 1971-72, World Arbitration Inst. 1984-2000; mem. adv. bd. Inst. for Internat. and Comparative Law, 1988—; pvt. adjudications com. Ctr. for Pub. Resources, 1988-2002. 1st lt. U.S. Army, 1952-55. Fellow Am. Bar Found; mem. ABA (ho. of dels. 1985-87, chmn. sect. internat. law and practice 1982-83), N.Y. State Bar Assn., Assn. Bar City of N.Y. (chmn. adv. com. on ADR 1992-93), London Ct. Internat. Arbitration, Am. Arbitration Assn. (bd. dirs. 1982-95), Citizens Union (bd. dirs. 1983-86), Am. Soc. Internat. Law. Office Phone: 212-603-2174. E-mail: gaksen@thelenreid.com.

AKUTSU, YOSHIHIRO, communications educator; b. Utsunomiya, Tochigi, Japan, Apr. 13, 1932; s. Miyoshi and Fumi (Owada) A.; m. Masako Ota, May 3, 1963. BA, Internat. Christian U., Mitaka, Tokyo, 1958, MA in Edn., 1960; PhD in Communication, Mich. State U., 1969. Instr. Internat. Christian U., 1969-71, asst. prof., 1971-74, assoc. prof., 1974-77, prof., 1977—2003, prof. emeritus, 2003—. Chmn. divsn. edn. Internat. Christian U., 1980-82, dir. pub. info. office, 1985-87, dean of students, 1988-90, dean Coll. of Liberal Arts, 1991-93. Co-author: Explorations in Mass Communication, 1970, Public Communication, 1975; editor Jour. Communication, 1976. Advisor social edn. Mitaka-City, 1983-91. Mem. Japan Soc. for Study of Audio-Visual Edn. (bd. dirs. 1972-94), Japan Soc. for Study of Radio-TV Edn. (bd. dirs. 1977-94), Japan Soc. Ednl. Sociology (bd. councillors 1987-97), Japan Assn. for Ednl. Media Study (bd. dirs. 1994—), Japan Soc. for Child Study (bd. dirs. 1994—). Avocations: noh song, Go. Home: 4-12-11 Josuiminami Kodaira Tokyo 187-0021 Japan Office: Internat Christian U 3-10-2 Osawa Mitaka Tokyo 181-8585 Japan

ALADJEM, HENRIETTA H., writer; b. Romania, Jan. 21, 1917; arrived in U.S., 1941, naturalized, 1947; d. Alfred and Mina Hirs; m. Albert T. Aladjem, Apr. 1941 (dec.); children: Albert T. Jr., Ingrid Winifred Nercesian, Martha Louise Climo. Student, Harvard U., 1941—45, Simmons Coll., 1943—44, U. Sofia. Founder, mem. acquisition dept. Harvard Weidner's Libr., Cambridge, Mass., 1941—45; writer, 1972—. Guest lectr. med. schs., Boston; cons. in field. Editor: Lupus News, 1973—96, Lupus World, 1996—; author: The Sun Is My Enemy, 1972, Understanding Lupus: What It Is, How to Treat It, How to Cope with It, 1982, In Search of the Sun, 1988, A Decade of Lupus, 1991, A Patient's Story, 1986, The Challenges of Lupus, 1998; contbr. articles to profl. publs. Recipient Pres.'s Vol. Action award, Pres. Ronald Reagan, The White Ho., 1985, Disting. Health Comm. award, New Eng. chpt. Am. Med. Writers Assn., 1992, Harold Swanberg Disting. Svc. award, Nat. Am. Med. Writers Assn., 1994, prize for nonfiction article, New Eng. Writer's Conf. Mem.: Lupus Found. Am. (co-founder 1972, adv. bd., Achievement award various chpts., Disting. Svc. award 1986).

ALAFOUZO, ANTONIA, marketing and business strategy professional; b. Cairo, Oct. 13, 1952; came to U.S., 1982; d. Pano Antony and Agni-Maria (Ranos) A.; m. Thomas D'Ambola Jr., May 29, 1988; 1 child, Tatiana Maryana. BSc in Econ., Brunel U., London, 1975; Diploma in Econ. and Politics, Oxford (Eng.) U., 1977, M of Philosophy, PhD, 1980; MBA, Henley U., 2003. Staff reporter The Economist, London, 1973-75, contbg. writer, 1975-82; mktg. exec. Rubenstein, Wolfson Co., N.Y.C., 1982-87; founder, pres. Markcom Ltd. (now Zoelics-Markcom), N.Y.C., 1987—97; sr. prin. Zoetics-Markcom, 1997—. Contbg. writer Fin. Report, London, 1975-82; cons. writer Fin. Times, London, 1980-82; cons. communications and econs. World Gold Council, N.Y.C., 1982—. Contbr. reports to fin. publs. Mem. Inst. Journalism Internat., Oxford Union Soc. Avocations: travel, languages, tennis, marksmanship, horse riding. Office: Zoetics-Markcom 270 Lafayette St New York NY 10012-3327

ALAM, AKM A., ceramics engineer; b. Dhaka, Bangladesh, Apr. 8, 1948; arrived in U.S., 1993; s. Emad Uddin Ahmed and Meherun Nessa Khatun; m. Mahmuda Alam, Nov. 12, 1970; children: Mahmudul, Mahbubul. BSc, U. Dhaka, 1969; diploma in ceramic tech., Tajimi Tech. Inst., 1975. Instr. Inst. Glass and Ceramics, Dhaka, 1978—84; ceramic engr. UN Devel. Program, Georgetown, Guyana, 1984—93, Terra Designs Inc., Dover, NJ, 1996—2000, Sherle Wagner Internat., Fall River, Mass., 2000—. Mem.: Am. Ceramic Soc. Avocations: travel, music, reading. Home: 808 Caton Ave Brooklyn NY 11218 Office: Sherle Wagner Internat 1 Lewiston St Fall River MA 02721 Office Phone: 508-678-5800. Office Fax: 508-678-5884. E-mail: advtec04@comcast.net.

ALAM, A.N.M. MAHBUB UL, engineer, educator; b. Dhaka, Bangladesh, Aug. 26, 1940; naturalized, U.S., 1993; s. Abdul Mannan Mirdha and Ambia Khatun; m. Saleha Khatun, June 11, 1967; children: M. Nayeem Ul, Shuvo Mayeen Ul. BS in Agrl. Engring., Am. U. of Beirut, 1961, MS in Irrigation Engring., 1978; PhD, Colo. State U., 1985. Chief ext. officer Epwapda, Bwdb, Kushtia, Dhaka, Bangladesh; prin. sci. officer Bangladesh Agrl. Rsch. Coun., Dhaka, 1978—80; rsch. assoc. Colo. State U. and USDA-ARS, Fort Collins, 1985—88; ext. irrigation specialist Colo. State U., Fort Collins, 1988—95;

asst. prof. Kans. State U., Garden City, 1996—2000, assoc. prof., ext. specialist irrigation, 2000—. Reviewer: Applied Engring. in Agr.; contbr. articles to profl. jours. Organizer of youth program on water and natural resources Childrens Water Festival, River Festival, and Earth Awareness Rschrs. for Tomorrows Habitat (EARTH), Delta (CO), Garden City and Wichita(KS), Kans., 1990; pres. Kushtia Shahitya Parishad (Kushtia Lit. Coun.), Bangladesh; founder Tarun Krishak (orgn. for rural farm youth), Kushtia, Bangladesh, 1965—70. Sr. Fulbright scholar, J. William Fulbright Fgn. Scholarship Bd., 2003-2004, Rsch. grant, Kans. Corn Commn., 1997-2004, Rsch. grants, Kans. Dept. of Health and Environ., 1998 to present, Rsch. and demonstration grant, Kans. Water Office, 1999 - 2004. Mem.: Am. Water Resources Assn., Am. Soc. of Agrl. Engrs. (Kans. sect. chair 2002—04, Blue Ribbon 1998), Irrigation Assn. (life), Epsilon Sigma Phi. Avocations: travel, international programs. Office: Kans State Univ SWREC 4500 E Mary St Garden City KS 67846 Office Phone: 620-275-9164. Business E-Mail: malam@ksu.edu.

ALAOUA, MOHAMMAD D., cardiologist; s. Safouh and Suaad Alaoua; m. Najlaa Alwan, Mar. 7, 1995; children: Hadi, Waseem. MD, Damascus U., 1993. Cert. Am. Bd. Internal Medicine, 1998, bd. cert. cardiovascular disease Am. Bd. Internal Medicine, 2001, bd. cert. nuclear cardiology Md., 2004. Cardiologist Metro Physicians and Specialists, Chgo., 2001—02, The Heart Specialists Ltd., 2002—04, Eau Claire Heart Inst., Wis., 2004—. Named chief fellow, Adv. Ill. Masonic Med. Ctr., 2001. Fellow: Am. Coll. Cardiology; mem.: Am. Soc. Nuc. Cardiology.

ALAPONT, JOSÉ MARIA, automotive executive; b. Spain; Degree in indsl. engring., Tech. Sch. Valencia, Spain; degree in philology, Univ. Valencia, Spain. With Ford Motor Corp., 1974—90; ops. dir. through group v.p. Valeo Group, 1990—97; exec. dir., through pres. internat. ops. Delphi Automotive Sys., 1997—2003; CEO, dir. IVECO S.p.A., Torino, Italy, 2003—05; chmn., pres., CEO Federal Mogul Corp., Southfield, Mich., 2005—. Office: Federal Mogul Corp 26555 Northwestern Hwy Southfield MI 48034*

ALARCON, ARTHUR LAWRENCE, federal judge; b. LA, Aug. 14, 1925; s. Lorenzo Marques and Margaret (Sais) A.; m. Sandra D. Paterson, Sept. 1, 1979; children— Jan Marie, Gregory, Lance BA in Polit. Sci., U. So. Calif., 1949, LLB, 1951. Bar: Calif. 1952. Dep. dist. atty. L.A. County, 1952—61; legal adv. to gov. State of Calif., Sacramento, 1961—62, exec. asst. to Gov. Pat Brown, 1962—64; chmn. Calif. parole bd., 1964; judge L.A. Superior Ct., 1964—78; assoc. justice Calif. Ct. Appeals, L.A., 1978—79; judge U.S. Ct. Appeals for 9th Circuit, L.A., 1979—92; sr. judge, 1992—. Adj. prof. Southwestern U. sch. of law, L.A., 1985—, Loyola Marymount sch. of law, 1993—94. With U.S. Army, 1943—46, ETO. Decorated Bronze Star, Purple Heart; recipient Infantry badge, Expert Rifleman medal, Four Battle Stars, ETO Ribbon. Mem.: ABA, LA Bar Assn. Office: US Ct Appeals 9th Cir 1607 US Courthouse 312 N Spring St Los Angeles CA 90012-4701 also: US Ct Appeals 95 Seventh St San Francisco CA 94103

ALARCON, RENATO DANIEL, psychiatry educator, researcher, medical facility executive; b. Arequipa, Peru, Apr. 11, 1942; came to U.S., 1967; s. Jose Romulo and Rosa Aurea (Guzman) A.; m. Graciela E. Solis, June 8, 1967; children: Patricia, Sylvia, Daniel. MD, Cayetano Heredia U. Med. Sch., Lima, Peru, 1966; MPH, Johns Hopkins U., 1972. Diplomate Am. Bd. Psychiatry and Neurology. Fellow in psychosomatic medicine Johns Hopkins U. Sch. Medicine, Balt., 1967-68, resident in psychiatry, 1968-72; asst. prof. psychiatry U. Peru-Cayetano Heredia, Lima, 1972-76, assoc. prof. psychiatry, 1976-80; prof. psychiatry U. Ala. Sch. Medicine, Birmingham, 1981-83; chief of adult svcs. Univ. Hosp.-U. Ala. Med. Ctr., Birmingham, 1981-92; chief affective disorders program U. Ala. Sch. Medicine, Birmingham, 1991-93; chief psychiatry svc. VA Med. Ctr., Atlanta, 1993—; prof., vice chmn. dept. psychiatry Emory U. Sch. Medicine, Atlanta, 1993—. Cons. Pan Am. Health Orgn., Washington, 1974-87; examiner Am. Bd. Psychiatry and Neurology, 1989—. Author: Psicoterapia, 1979, Psiquiatria, 1986, Identidad de la Psiquiatria Latinoamericana, 1990; co-editor: Enciclopedia Iberoam, Psiquiatria, Buenos Aires, 1990-94; assoc. editor Acta Psiq. Am. Latin, 1989-94; book rev. editor Depression and Anxiety; editor Cull Div. and Mental Health; contbr. numerous articles to psychiat. jours. Active Physicians for Social Responsibility, 1982, Amnesty Internat., 1986. Rockefeller Found. scholar, 1988; named Exemplary Psychiatrist, Nat. Alliance for the Mentally Ill, 1992. Fellow APA, Am. Soc. Hispanic Psychiatrists (pres. 1994-96); mem. Am. Coll. Psychiatrists, Am. Psychopathology Assn. (group adv. psych.). Roman Catholic. Avocations: reading, classical music, writing, soccer, biking. Office: Atlanta VA Med Ctr 1670 Clairmont Rd Decatur GA 30033-4004

ALARCON, ROGELIO ALFONSO, internist, researcher; b. Yungay, Nuble, Chile, Feb. 14, 1926; arrived in U.S., 1954; s. Alfredo and Carmen Rosa (Carrasco) A. BS, U. Chile, Concepcion, 1943; MD, U. Chile, Santiago, 1950. Staff physician internal medicine U. Chile Hosp. Salvador, Santiago, 1951-52, Hosp. Gonzalez Cortez, Santiago, 1952-54; resident medicine Meml. Ctr. for Cancer and Allied Diseases, N.Y.C., 1955-56; fellow internal medicine George Washington U. Hops., George Washington Sch. Medicine, Washington, 1956-57; resident internal medicine Lemuel Shattuck Hosp., Boston, 1957-58; rsch. fellow pathology Children's Cancer Rsch. Found., Children's Hosp. Med. Ctr., Boston, 1958-60; rsch. assoc. Children's Cancer Rsch. Found., Boston, 1960-74, Harvard Med. Sch., Boston, 1962-76, Cancer Rsch. Inst., New Eng. Deaconess Hosp., Boston, 1974-76; staff physician Boston Children's Hosp. Med. Ctr., Wrentham, Mass., 1977-79, VA Med. Ctr., Phila., 1979-80, Bedford, Mass., 1980—2002. Contbr. articles to profl. jours. Mem. Am. Chem. Soc., N.Y. Acad. Scis. Roman Catholic. Achievements include discovery of the enzymatic generation of acrolein, a highly cytotoxic aldehyde, from biogenic polyamines; development of a fluorometric method to measure minimal amounts of acrolein; research in the growth inhibitory effects of oxidized spermine on mammalian cells, research involving acrolein in cell growth regulation, and identification of acrolein as a metabolite of cyclophosphamide and related chemotherapeutic agents. Home: 33 Pond Ave Apt B-915 Brookline MA 02445-7163

ALATIS, JAMES EFSTATHIOS, university dean emeritus; b. Weirton, W.Va., July 13, 1926; s. Efstathios and Vasiliki (Galanoudis) A.; m. Penelope Mastorides, Dec. 30, 1951; children: William, Stephen, Anthony. BA, W.Va. U., 1948; MA, Ohio State U., 1953; PhD, 1966. Fulbright lectr. English U., Athens, 1955-57; English testing and teaching specialist Dept. State, 1959-61; specialist for lang. research U.S. Office Edn., 1961-65, chief lang. sect., 1965-66; asso. dean Sch. Langs. and Linguistics, Georgetown U., Washington, 1966-73, dean, 1973-94; dean emeritus Georgetown U., Washington, 1994—, sr. advisor to exec. v.p. internat. lang. programs and rsch., 1994-96, sr. advisor to Dean of Georgetown Coll. for internat. langs. programs and rsch., 1996—; assoc. prof. linguistics Sch. Langs. and Linguistics, Georgetown U., Washington, 1966-75; disting. prof. linguistics and modern Greek Georgetown U., Washington, 1994—. Exec. sec. TESOL, 1966-87, exec. dir. emeritus, 1987—; pres. Joint Nat. Com. for Langs., 1980-88, bd. dirs. 1998—, TESOL Internat. Rsch. Found., 1999—; mem. Greek Orthodox Archbishop's commn., 1999; bd. advisors U.S. Dept. Agriculture Grad. Sch. Author: (with Peter Lowenberg) The Three Circles of English: A Conference in honor of Braj B. Kachru, 2002; editor: Studies in Honor of Albert H. Marckwardt, 1972, (with Kristie Twaddell) English as a Second Language in Bilingual Education, 1976, (with Ruth Crymes) Human Factors in ESL, 1977, (with Gerli and Brod) Language in American Life, 1978, Internat. Dimensions of Bilingual Education, 1978, (with G. R. Tucker) Language in Public Life, 1979, Current Issues in Bilingual Education, 1980, (with others) The Second Language Classroom: Directions for the 1980s, 1981, Applied Linguistics and the Preparation of Second Language Teachers: Toward a Rationale, 1983, (with John J. Staczek) Perspectives on Bilingualism and Bilingual Education, 1985, (with Deborah Tannen) Language and Linguistics: The Interdependence of Theory, Data, and Application, 1986, Language Teaching, Testing, and Technology: Lessons from the Past with a View Toward the Future, 1989, Linguistics, Language Teaching and Language Acquisition: The Interdependence of Theory, Practice, and Research, 1990, Quest for Quality: The First 21 Years of TESOL, 1991, Linguistics and Language Pedagogy: The State of the Art, 1991, Language, Communication and Social Meaning, 1993, Strategic Interaction and Language Acquisition: Theory, Practice and Research, 1993, Educational Linguistics, Cross-Cultural Communication, and Global Interdependence, 1994, (with others) Linguistics and the Education of Language Teachers: Ethnolinguistic, Psycholinguistic, and Sociolinguistic Aspects, 1995, (with others) Linguistics, Language Acquisition and Language Variation: Current Trends and Future Prospects, 1996, (with others) Aspects of Sociolinguistics in Greece, 1997, (with others) Language in Our Time: Bilingual Education and Official English, Ebonics and Standard English, Immigration and the Unz Initiative, 1999, (with others) Linguistics, Language, and the Professions: Education, Journalism, Law, Medicine and Technology, Georgetown Univ. Round table on Languages and Linguistics, 2000, Linguistics, Language, and the Real World: Discourse and Beyond, Georgetown Univ. Round Table on Languages and Linguistics, 2001 (with Deborah Tannen) Georgetown University Round Table on Language and Linguistics, 2001; mem. editl. bd. World Englishes, English Today. Served with USNR, 1944-46. Recipient N.E. Conf. award, 1985, Pres.'s award Nat. Assn. for Bilingual Edn., 1987. Mem. MLA, Am. Coun. on Teaching Fgn. Langs., Linguistic Soc. Am (del. 1966-69), Nat. Assn. Fgn. Student Affairs (dir. 1965-66), Def. Lang. Inst. (bd. visitors), Phi Beta Kappa. Home: 5108 Sutton Pl Alexandria VA 22304-2704 Office: Georgetown U Int'l Langs Prog & Rsch 37th & 0 St Washington DC 20057-0001 Office Phone: 202-687-5659. Business E-Mail: alatisj@georgetown.edu.

ALATSIS, DESPINA KATHERINE, music educator, director; m. Leonidas Alatsis, 1975; 2 children. MusB, Pacific Lutheran U., 1975; MS in Edn. Adminstrn., City U., 1987. Choir dir. Tacoma Pub. Schs., Tacoma, 1976—2005; vocal coach pvt. practice, Tacoma, 1976—87; Greek folk dance coach St. Nicholas Greek Orthodox Ch., Tacoma, 1990—94. Recipient Class Act Tchr. award, KSTW 11 TV, 1993. Mem.: Music Educators Nat. Assn. Office: Stadium HS 6229 S Tyler Tacoma WA 98409 Business E-Mail: dolatsi@tacoma.k12.wa.us.

ALATZAS, GEORGE, delivery service company executive; b. Salonika, Greece, Sept. 30, 1940; came to U.S., 1954; s. Gus Alatzas and Georgia Karayanidou; m. Ida Elizabeth Feldman, Sept. 26, 1965; children: Dennis, Ari. AA in Liberal Arts, Middlesex Community Coll., 1979; student, Rutgers U. Dept. mgr. Bamberger's N.J. div. Macy's Dept. Store, Newark, 1959-61, 63-65; buyer Koos Bros., Rahway, N.J., 1965-67; sales rep. Bassett (Va.) Furniture, 1967-69; store mgr. W&J Sloane, Union, N.J., 1969-72, Steinbach & Co., Freehold, N.J., 1972-78; owner, pres. Lawyers & Corp. Messenger Svc., Bridgewater, NJ, 1978-84; pres., chief exec. officer Pegasus Delivery Systems, Inc., Somerville, N.J., 1984—; pres. It's All About the Flag, Inc. Pres. Just In Time Inc. fin. mgmt. and support svcs., It's All About the Flag Inc.; bd. dirs. Alternarives Inc. Instr. swimming Am. Legion Children's Camp, Newburgh, N.Y., 1957-58; instr. marksmanship reservation Boy Scouts Am., Yards Creek, and Blairstown, N.J., 1980-83; pres. Office Condominium Assn. Ctr. at Raritan. With U.S. Army, 1961—63, Command Sgt. Major USAR, 1973—75. Recipient Somerset County Businessman of Yr. award, 1999; Paul Harris fellow. Mem. Assn. U.S. Army, Nat. Alliance Businessmen, 78th Divsn. NCO Assn., 78th Divsn. Vets. Assn., N.J. Bus. and Industry Coun., Rotary (Somerville/Bridgewater chpt. pres. 2003-04), Somerset County C. of C. (bd. dirs.) Greek Orthodox. Avocations: tennis, golf, walking. Office: Pegasus Delivery Systems Inc 1124 Us Highway 202 Ste B14 Raritan NJ 08869-1475 Personal E-mail: gapegasus@aol.com.

ALAUPOVIC, ALEXANDRA VRBANIC, artist, educator; b. Slatina, Yugoslavia, Dec. 21, 1921; d. Joseph and Elizabeta (Papp) Vrbanic; m. Peter Alaupovic, Mar. 22, 1947; 1 child, Betsy. Student Bus. Sch., Zagreb, Yugoslavia, 1940-41, Acad. Visual Arts, Zagreb, Yugoslavia, 1944-48; postgrad. Acad. Visual Arts, Prague, Czechoslovakia, 1949, Art Sch., U. Ill., 1959-60; MFA, U. Okla., 1966; came to U.S., 1958. Sec., Arko Liquer & Yeast Factory and Distillery, Zagreb, 1941-44; instr. U. Okla., Norman, 1964-66; instr. three dimensional design sculpture Oklahoma City U., 1969-77, Okla. Sci. Found., Oklahoma City, 1969-75; one-woman shows at Okla. Art Ctr., Oklahoma City, U. Okla. Mus. Art, Norman, La Mandragore Internat. Galerie d'Art, Paris, 1984; exhibited art in group shows retrospective 50 yrs. Struggle, Growth and Whimsy, 1987-88, Okla. Art Ctr., Springfield (Mo.) Art Mus., Okla. U. Mus., Norman, 7th Ann. Temple Emanuel Brotherhood Arts Festival, Dallas, Salon des Nation, Paris, 1983; since statehood twevle Okla. artists Art. Mus., Okla. 1996; represented in permanent collections Okla. U. Art Mus., Okla. State Art Collection, Okla. Art Ctr., Mercy Health Ctr. Recipient Jacobson award U. Okla., 1964; hon. mention in sculpture Philbrook Art Ctr., Tulsa, 1967; 1st sculpture award Philbrook Art Ctr., Tulsa, 1970; biography included in Virginia Watson Jones' Contemporary American Women Sculptors, 1986, Jules and Nancy Heller's North American Women Artists of 20th Century, 1995; State of Okla. Art commemdation, 1996. Mem. Internat. Sculpture Center, Lausanne, Suisse, Prestige de la Peinture et de la Sculpture d'Aujourd'hui dans le Monde, 1992, Paris, 1995. Home and Office: 11908 N Bryant Ave Oklahoma City OK 73131-4823

ALAUPOVIC, PETAR, biochemist, educator; b. Prague, Czechoslovakia, Aug. 3, 1923; came to U.S., 1957; married, 1947; 1 child. ChemE, U. Zagreb, 1948, PhD in Chemistry, 1956; DHC (hon.), U. Lille, France, 1987, U. Buenos Aires, 1994, U. Goteborg, 1999. Rschr. pharms. rsch. lab. Chem Corp, Prague, 1948-49; rschr. organic lab. Inst. Indsl. Rsch., Yugoslavia, 1949-50; asst. agrl. faculty U. Zagreb, 1951-54, asst. chem. inst. med. faculty, 1954-56; rsch. biochemist U. Ill., 1957-60; with cardiovascular sect. Okla. Med. Rsch. Found., Oklahoma City, 1960—, head lipoprotein lab., 1972-92, also head Lipid and Lipoprotein Lab. Prof. rsch. biochemistry, sch. med. U. Okla., 1960—. Assoc. editor Lipids, 1974-78. Named Disting. Career Scientist Okla. Med. Rsch. Fund, 1990; NIH grantee, 1961-95. Mem. AAAS, Am. Soc. Biol. Chemists, Am. Chem. Soc., Am. Heart Assn. (Spl. Recognition award 1994), Am. Oil Chemistry Soc. Achievements include research on chemistry of naturally occuring macromolecular lipid compounds such as serum and tissue lipoproteins and bacterial endotoxins, on biochemistry of red cell membranes; isolation and characterization of tissue lipases. Office: Okla Med Rsch Found Lipid and Lipoprotein Lab 825 NE 13th St Oklahoma City OK 73104-5005 Office Phone: 405-271-7703. Business E-Mail: alaupovicp@omrf.ouhsc.edu.

ALAV, FARAMARZ, cardiologist, internist; b. Akstafa, Azerbaijan, Jan. 26, 1958; s. Ahmed Alav and Ashraf Abulmulla; m. Kristina Jalilova, Nov. 7, 2000; children: Emil, Ceila children: Emin. MD, Azerbaijan State Med. Inst., Baku, Azerbaijan, 1974—80. Intern Rsch. Inst. Cardiology, Baku, Azerbaijan, 1980—81; emergency unit physician Ctrl. Hosp. Emergency Unit, Baku, Azerbaijan, 1981—86; fellow Inst. Advanced Med. Studies, Baku, Azerbaijan, 1986—88; cardiologist Diagnostic Ctr., Baku, Azerbaijan, 1988—93; internist Bonab Ctrl. Hosp., Bonab, Iran, 1993—94; telemetry technician St. Joseph Hosp., Orange, 1995—98; resident in internal medicine Wayne State U. Sinai-Grace Hosp., Detroit, 1988—2001; physician in internal medicine United Family Care, Fontana, Calif., 2001—. Contbr. articles to profl. jours. Recipient award for Outstanding Performance and Svc. to the Cmty., State Bd., 1995. Mem.: Am. Soc. Internal Medicine, Am. Coll. Physicians. Office: PO Box 610 Rialto CA 92377-0610 Office Phone: 909-874-2371. Personal E-mail: falav@hotmail.com.

ALBA, JESSICA, actress; b. Pomona, Calif., Apr. 28, 1981; Actor: (films) Camp Nowhere, 1994, Venus Rising, 1995, P.U.N.K.S., 1999, Never Been Kissed, 1999, Idle Hands, 1999, Paranoid, 2000, The Sleeping Dictionary, 2003, Honey, 2003, Sin City, 2005, Fantastic Four, 2005; (TV films) Too Soon for Jeff, 1996; (TV series) Flipper, 1995—96, Dark Angel, 2000—02, (guest appearance) The Secret World of Alex Mack, 1994, Chicago Hope, 1996, Beverly Hills 90210, 1998, The Love Boat: The Next Wave, 1998, Entourage, 2004. Office: Endeavor Talent Agency 9701 Wilshire Blvd 10th Fl Beverly Hills CA 90212*

ALBACH, HORST, economist; b. Essen, Germany, July 6, 1931; s. Karl Albach; m. Renate Gutenberg; children: Rolf, Karin, Dirk. Student, U. Cologne, 1952-56, D of Econs., 1958; PhD (hon.), Helsinki U., Stockholm U., Graz U., Kiel U., Bielefeld U., Alcala de Henares U., Cottbus U., Bowdoin Coll. Lectr., Cologne, 1960; prof., 1961; sci. adv. com. Fed. Econs. Ministry, 1967—2004; vice-chmn. German Sci. Coun. Wissenschaftsrat, 1974-77, bd. econ. advisors, 1978-83; pres. Berlin Acad. Scis., 1987-90; prof. corp. policy Humboldt U., Berlin, 1994-99; dean exec. MBA program, Herbert Quandt prof. internat. mgmt. Koblenz (Germany) U., 1987—2001. Dir. Sci. Ctr. Berlin, 1990-99. Author: Wirtschaftlichkeitsrechn. bei unsich. Erwartungen, 1959, Investition u. Liquidität, 1962 (also in Japanese), Beitr. z. Unternehm. plan., 1969, 2d edit., 1978, Culture and Technical Innovation, 1994, 2d edit., 2000, Allgemeine Betriebswirfschaftslehre, 2000, 3d edit., 2001; co-author: numerous publs.; contbr. articles to profl. jours. Mem. Rhineland-Westphalian Acad. Sci., Royal Swedish Acad. Sci., Acad. Scis. Morals and Politics, Order Pour le Mérit for Arts and Scis. Office: 49 Wald St D-53177 Bonn Germany Personal E-mail: profalbach@aol.com.

ALBACH, RICHARD ALLEN, microbiology educator; b. Chgo., Mar. 31, 1930; s. Maurice and Martha (Silverman) A.; m. Janice Elaine Boewe, Jan. 23, 1962; children: Michael, Karren, Kimala, David, Brian, Julie, Barry. BS, U. Ill., 1956, MS, 1958; PhD, Northwestern U., 1963. Asst. prof. U. Health Scis., Chgo. Med. Sch., North Chicago, Ill., 1968-69, assoc. prof., 1969-73, prof., 1973—2003, vice-chmn., 1975-82, acting chmn., 1982-83, prof. emeritus, 2003—. Editl. cons. Yearbook Med. Pubs., Chgo., 1975-81; vis. prof. St. George's U. Sch. Medicine, Grenada, 1992—. Contbr. articles to profl. jours. With U.S. Army, 1953-55. Recipient Trustees Rsch. award Chgo. Med. Sch., 1968, Tchg. Prof. of Yr. award, 1976, 78, 82; fellow Abbott Found., 1961; grantee NIH, 1965-78. Fellow Am. Acad. Microbiology (emeritus); mem. Am. Soc. Microbiology, Soc. Protozoologists (exec. com. 1984-89, chmn. awards com. 1995-1999), Ill. Soc. Microbiology (membership chmn. 1969-70). Achievements include research in biology of parasitic protozoa. Office: Rosalind Franklin Sch Medicine Sci 3333 Green Bay Rd North Chicago IL 60064-3037 Office Phone: 847-578-3230. E-mail: richard.albach@rosalindfranklin.edu.

ALBAIN, KATHY S., oncologist; b. Monroe, Mich., June 4, 1952; d. James Jay and Elizabeth G. (Jakscy) A. BS in Chemistry summa cum laude, Wheaton Coll., 1974; MD, U. Mich., 1978. Diplomate Am. Bd. Internal Medicine, Am. Bd. Oncology. Instr. physical diagnosis U. Mich. Med. Sch., 1978; intern U. Ill. Med. Ctr., Chgo., 1978-79, resident in internal medicine, 1979-81, clin. instr. medicine, 1980-81; instr. in medicine U. Ill. Hosps. and Clinics, 1980-81; fellow dept. medicine sect. hematology/oncology U. Chgo. Med. Ctr./U. Chgo. Hosps. and Clinics, 1981-84; asst. prof. medicine Loyola U. Chgo. Strich Sch. Medicine, 1984-91, assoc. prof. medicine divsn. hematology/oncology, 1991—; attending physician Hines (Ill.) VA Hosp., 1984—, Loyola U. Chgo. Foster G. McGaw Hosp., 1984—. Co-investigator multidisciplinary lung cancer staging and rsch. group U. Chgo. and Michael Reese Hosp. Med. Ctrs., 1982-84; coord. ann. breast cancer screening program Sr. Ctr. LaGrange, Ill., 1985-91; mem. med. adv. bd. Y-Me Nat. Breast Cancer Orgn., 1987—; co-dir. Multidisciplinary Breast Care Ctr. Loyola U. Med. Ctr., 1991—, dir. Multidisciplinary Lung Cancer Evaluation Ctr., 1994—; mem. oncology med. adv. bd. Eli Lilly and Co., 1993—; co-investigator nat. surg. adjuvant breast and bowel project U. Chgo., 1982-84; mem. breast cancer com., breast cancer working group, lung cancer com., lung cancer working group S.W. Oncology Group, 1986—, mem. gynecol. cancer com. and working group, 1989—, sarcoma and brain coms., 1990—, chair com. on women's health, 1992—; mem. intergroup lung cancer working cadre Nat. Cancer Inst., 1993—, mem. breast cancer intergroup com. on correlative scis. Nat. Cancer Inst., 1995, mem. breast cancer intergroup chairs com., 1994—; clin. trials co-chair Sec. of HHS Nat. Breast Cancer Action Plan, 1993-94; mem. adv. panel State of Ill. Breast and Cervical Cancer Rsch. Fund, 1994—; charter mem. adv. com. on rsch. in women's health NIH, 1995—; mem. Early Breast Cancer Trialists' Collaborative Group, 1995—; mem. clin. trials working group Sec. of Health Nat. Breast Cancer Action Plan, 1995—; rschr., lectr., presenter in field. Reviewer jours. Cytometry, Breast Cancer Rsch. and Treatment, Cancer Rsch., Jour. Clin. Oncology, Cancer, Chest; contbr. articles to profl. publs. Mem. sr. choir Grace Luth. Ch., River Forest, Ill. Nat. Cancer Inst. fellowship tng. grantee, 1981-84, grantee Bristol-Myers, 1988-93, Squibb Mark Co., 1989, UpJohn Co., 1990, 92, Office Rsch. on Women's Health/Nat. Cancer Inst., 1992, 93-95, Nat. Cancer Inst., 1993—. Mem. ACP, Am. Assn. Cancer Rsch., Am. Fedn. Clin. Rsch., Am. Soc. Clin. Oncology, Internat. Assn. for Study of Lung Cancer, Christian Med. and Dental Soc. Home: 220 S Maple Ave Oak Park IL 60302-3031 Office: Loyola U Med Ctr Divsn Hematology/Oncology 2160 S 1st Ave Maywood IL 60153-3304

ALBALA, DAVID MOIS, urologist, educator; b. Chgo., Dec. 25, 1955; m. Francene Ann Salerno, Oct. 23, 1999; 1 child, Jack. BA, Lafayette Coll., Easton, Pa., 1978; MD, Mich. State U., 1983. Prof. urology Loyola U. Med. Ctr., Maywood, Ill., 1990—2000, Duke U. Med. Ctr., Durham, NC, 2000—. Fellow, White House, 1995—96. Mem.: Am. Urol. Assn. Office: Duke Univ Medical Center Rm 1112 DUMC #3457 Durham NC 27710 Office Phone: 919-684-5416. Office Fax: 919-681-7423. Personal E-mail: albal002@mc.duke.edu.

ALBAN, ROGER CHARLES, small business consultant; b. Columbus, Ohio, Aug. 3, 1948; s. Charles Ellis and Alice Jacqueline (Hosfeld) A.; children: Allison Ann, Roger Charles II, Charles Michael (dec. June 1998); m. Linda Bayer Lusk, Aug. 30, 1997 (div. Nov. 2001). Student pub. schs. With Alban Equipment Co., Columbus, 1963—, sales mgr., 1972-75, gen. mgr., 1975-85, treas., 1978-85, v.p., 1980-85, pres., 1985-99, ret., 1999-00; exec. mgr. Infiniti of Dublin, Ohio, 2000—01. Mem. Grandview Heights Bd. Edn., Columbus, 1978-85, pres., 1979, v.p., 1982, legis. liaison, 1978-79, 83-84, re-elected mem., 1992-93; elected Grandview Heights City Coun., 1986; mem. Met. Ednl. Coun., Columbus Area Leadership PRogram, 1982-83; trustee Builders Exch. Benefit Trust, 1987-98, chmn., 1996. Mem. Assoc. Equipment Distbrs. (lt. dir. region 6 1980, 85, 86, 88, dir. 1989-91, chmn. light equipment dist. com. 1985, chmn. sales and mktg. com. 1988, elected dir. region 6 1989-92, chmn. lt. equipment steering com. 1998), Ohio Sch. Bds. Assn. (all-ctrl. region bd. 1984), Bldg. Industry Assn. Ctrl. Ohio, Am. Rental Assn., Builders Exch. Ctrl. Ohio (dir. 1990-99, elected treas. 1996, 2nd v.p. 1996, v.p. 1997, pres. 1998), Am. Mgmt. Assn., Nat. Right to Work Com., Nat. Fedn. Ind. Bus., Ohio Equipment Distbrs. Assn. (dir. 1982, 84-91, pres. 1983), Roundtable, Mensa (chpt. exec. com. 1979-80), Rotary (elected Columbus dir. 1994-97), Downtown Columbus Club. Home and Office: 4572 Carriage Hill Ln Columbus OH 43220-3802 E-mail: bigalban@mindspring.com.

ALBANDAR, JASIM MOSA, dental researcher, scientist; b. Baghdad, Iraq, May 21, 1954; arrived in Norway, 1980; s. M. Mosa Albandar and Bedria Jebbar; m. Mona Albandar, Jan. 1, 1988; children: Heidar, Hazim, Joseph. DDS, Coll. Dentistry, Baghdad, 1976; diploma periodontology, Dental Faculty, Oslo, 1984, DDS, 1987, PhD, 1989. Dental diplomate and periodontal cert. Clin. instr. U. Baghdad, Iraq, 1976-79, asst. prof., 1984; clin. instr. U. Oslo, Norway, 1980-83, statis. computing cons., 1985; postgrad. fellow Dental Faculty, Oslo, 1987-90, assoc. prof., 1992-93; dentist, dental surgery Pub. Dental Health, Akershus, Norway, 1991; vis. scientist NIH, Bethesda, Md., 1994—. Referee Cmty. Dentistry and Oral Epidemiology, Aarhus, Denmark, 1989-94, Jour. Dentistry, Eng., 1992-94. Contbr. articles to profl. jours. Recipient Waerhaug's prize Scandinavian Soc. Periodontology, 1984. Mem. Scandinavian Soc. Dental Rsch., Internat. Assn. Dental Rsch., Norwegian Dental Assn. Office: NIDR 45 Center Dr Bethesda MD 20892-0001

ALBANESE, JAY SAMUEL, criminologist, educator; b. Mineola, N.Y., Feb. 10, 1953; s. Samuel S. and Doris (Mather) A.; m. Leslie Elizabeth King, July 12, 1980; children: Thomas, Kelsey. BA, Niagara U., 1974; MA, Rutgers U., 1976, PhD, 1981. Chief Internat. Ctr. Nat. Inst. Justice, 2002—; prof. Niagara U., Niagara Falls, NY, 1981-96; prof. govt. and pub. policy Va. Commonwealth U., Richmond, 1996—. Vis. prof. Simon Fraser U., Vancouver, B.C., Can., 1988. Author: Dealing with Delinquency, 2d edit., 1993, Crime in America, 1993 White Collar Crime in America, 1995, Criminal Justice, 1999, 3d edit., 2005, Organized Crime in Our Times, 2004; editor:

Contemporary Issues in Organized Crime, 1995, Organized Crime: World Perspectives, 2003; contbr. articles to profl. jours. Recipient Sears Found. Tchg. Excellence award, 1989-90, Founder's award, Acad. Criminal Justice Scis., 2000, Elske Smith Disting. Lectr. award Va. Commonwealth U. Coll. Humanities and Scis., 2001 Fellow Acad. Criminal Justice Scis., 2002/ mem. Am. Soc. Criminology, Internat. Assn. Study Organized Crime (exec. dir. 2002—), Northeastern Assn. Criminal Justice Scis. (pres. 1988-89), Acad. Criminal Justice Scis.(pres. 1995-96), White Collar Crime Res. Consortium (pres. 2000-02), Phi Kappa Phi. Office: PO Box 50484 Washington DC 20091-0484

ALBANESE, THOMAS, entrepreneur; b. Passaic, NJ, June 27, 1930; s. Charles and Viola (Gueritey) A.; m. Theresa Mary Perez, Aug. 8, 1953; children: Thomas II, John, Theresa Lynn, Richard Charles, Michael Quintin. Grad. Garfield (NJ) H.S. Pres. Thomas Albanese Inc., Clifton, NJ, 1958-60; founder, pres. Albanese Products Inc., Las Vegas, Nev., 1960—; exec. cons. The Norlen Co., Las Vegas, 1971—; exec. dir. The Las Vegas Chili Co., 1982—; owner The Chef Tomal Co., Las Vegas, 1995—. Creator Gourmet Chili Meals and Desserts-La Chilafesta, 1982, Mr. B's Hang All Kit, 1971; patentee plumbing sys. Founder Double TT Rancho, dir., 1986—. With USAF, 1951-55. Mem. United Assn. Plumbers and Pipefitters, Plumbers and Pipefitters Local 525. Avocations: designing, inventing.

ALBANI, THOMAS J., investor; b. Hartford, Conn., May 3, 1942; s. Charles A. and Marie F. Albani; m. Suzanne Beardsley, Sept. 3, 1966; children: Karin, Steven. BA, Amherst Coll., 1964; MBA, Wharton Sch. U. Pa., 1967. Asst. product mgr. Gen. Mills Inc., Mpls., 1967-69; dir. mktg. Am. Can Co., Greenwich, Conn., 1969-73; mgmt. cons. McKinsey and Co., Inc., N.Y.C., 1973-78; gen. mgr. GE, Bridgeport, Conn., 1978-84; group v.p. Black & Decker, Inc., Bridgeport, 1984; pres. Sunbeam No. Am. Appliance Div. Allegheny Internat., Oak Brook, Ill., 1984-86; pres. appliance bus. Allegheny Internat. Inc., Pitts., 1986, exec. v.p., COO, 1986-89; prin. New Eng. Cons. Group, Westport, Conn., 1990-91; pres., CEO Electrolux Corp., Atlanta, 1991-98; pres. Canopache Cons., Siasconset, Mass., 1999—. Bd. dirs. Select Comfort Corp., Igloo Products Corp. Office: Canopache Cons PO Box 855 Siasconset MA 02564-0855 Home: 31 Island Pl Orchid FL 32963-9505 Personal E-mail: tjalbani@aol.com.

ALBANO, ANDRES, JR., real estate developer, real estate broker; b. Honolulu, Apr. 16, 1941; s. Andres Pacis and Florence (Paglinawan) A.; m. Sandra Kam Mee Ymas, Nov. 29, 1961; children: Cheryl Ann, Denise Lynn. BEE, U. Hawaii, 1965, MBA, 1972. Engr. nuclear power USN, 1965—67; elec. engr. FAA, Honolulu, 1967—69, Honolulu Bd. Water Supply, 1969—79; exec. v.p. MidPac Devel. Ltd., Honolulu, 1979—84; pres. Albano & Assocs., Honolulu, 1984—; prin. broker Gen. Growth Mgmt. of Hawaii, Inc., 1993—96; ptnr., v.p., dir. devel., cons. CB Richard Ellis Hawaii, Inc., Honolulu, 1998—. Bd. regents U. Yasall; bd. dirs. The U. Vakon Rsch. Corp. Mem. NSPE, Hawaii Soc. Profl. Engrs. (pres. 1979-80), Devel. Assn. Hawaii (pres. 1992-93), Hawaii Developers Coun. (pres. 1995-96, 99-00), Rotary, Beta Gamma Sigma. Roman Catholic. Avocations: tennis, karate, weightlifting. Home: 748 Kokomo Pl Honolulu HI 96825-1603 Office: CB Richard Ellis Hawaii Inc Am Savs Bank Tower 1001 Bishop St Ste 2000 Honolulu HI 96813 Office Phone: 808-521-1200. Business E-Mail: andres.albano@cbre.com.

ALBANO, DAVID WARREN, financial executive, business analyst; b. Orange, N.J., Mar. 16, 1959; s. Nicholas Henry Jr. and Anne (Warren) A. BA, U. Pa., 1982; MBA, NYU, 1990. Gen. sales mgr. Sta. WZIP, South Daytona, Fla., 1985-88; fin. analyst Motion Picture Assn. Am., N.Y.C., 1990-93; sr. fin. analyst Children's TV Workshop, N.Y.C., 1994-96, fin. dir., 1996-2000; asst. v.p. internat. fin. Sesame Workshop, N.Y.C., 2000—03; v.p. fin. and acctg. Global Consumer Licensing, N.Y.C., 2003—. Home: 32 West 40th St Apt 11A New York NY 10018

ALBANO, MICHAEL J., former mayor; m. Michele Garreffi; children: Jonathan, Michael, Christopher. BS, Springfield Coll., 1974; MS, Am. Internat. Coll., 1976; MPA, U. Hartford, 1981. Probation officer Westfield Dist. Ct., 1974-82; mem. staff Office of the State Auditor, 1994-95; spl. parole bd. mem., 1993-94; mem. Mass. parole bd., 1982—94; mayor City of Springfield, Mass., 1996—2004. Adj. faculty mem. Asnutuck C.C., Enfield, Conn., 1979-81, 92-94, Springfield Tech. C.C., 1977-81, U. Mass., 1992; vis. lectr. criminal justice Westfield State Coll./Suffolk U., Boston. Springfield Youth commr., 1980-81; mem. Springfield Sch. com., 1985-90; commr. Springfield Conservation, 1990-92; mem. Springfield City Coun., 1991—, pres., 1994-95.

ALBANO, MICHAEL SANTO JOHN, lawyer; b. Bklyn., Jan. 13, 1944; s. Alexander Joseph and Josephine (Giannetto) A.; m. Grace Alma Hoelzel, Mar. 14, 1944; children: Christine Grace, Sarah Michelle. BA, U. Mo., Kansas City, 1965, JD, 1968. Bar: Mo. 1968, U.S. Dist. Ct. (we. dist.) Mo. 1968. From assoc. to shareholder Welch, Martin & Albano LLC, Independence, Mo., 1968—. Contbr. articles to profl. jours. Recipient Practitioner of Yr. award U. Mo. Kansas City Law Alumni, 2001, Presdl. Citation for Alumni Svc. U. Mo.-Kansas City, 2003; named one of the Best of the Best Lawyers in Greater Kansas City Area, Kansas City Bus. Jour., 2002, 04; Tchrs. Assn. scholar, 1963-64, U. Mo. scholar, Kansas City, 1963-66. Mem. ABA (chmn. family law sect. 1984-85), Am. Acad. Matrimonial Lawyers (pres. 1993-94), Mo. Bar Assn.(Practitioner of the Year, 2004), Kansas City Bar Assn., Am. Coll. Family Trial Lawyers (diplomate, mem. exec. com. 1994-2005, U. Mo. Kansas City All Alumni Assn. (pres. 2001-03), Phi Delta Phi. Democrat. Lutheran. Office: 311 W Kansas Ave Independence MO 64050-3715 E-mail: mjalbano@wmamlaw.com.

ALBANO, PASQUALE CHARLES, management educator, management and organization development consultant; b. Bayonne, N.J., Dec. 3, 1941; s. Armando and Marie (Fasulo) A.; m. Norma Agnes Eichholz, July 16, 1960; children: Donna, Nancy, Susan, Carol. BS in Edn.-Social Sci. cum laude, Monmouth U., 1967; postgrad., Rutgers U., 1969—2001; MA in Mgmt. magna cum laude, Pepperdine U., 1976; cert. in orgnl. cons., U.S. Army Tng. Ctr., 1979; EdD in Leadership and Policy summa cum laude, Temple U., 1987. Cert. tchr. social scis., N.J.; orgn. devel. cons. Personnel-employee devel. specialist Hdqs. Army Comm.-Electronics Command, Ft. Monmouth, N.J., 1967-69; chmn. mgmt. devel. dept. army edn. ctr. Hdqs. Army Comm. Command, Ft. Monmouth, N.J., 1969-75, dir. northeastern U.S. regional tng. ctr., 1975-78, orgnl. effectiveness officer R & D ctr., 1978-81, chief orgnl. effectiveness office, 1981—85, chief leadership rsch. office, 1985-87, chief orgnl. consulting office, 1987—94; pvt. practice cons., 1993—. Tchr. U.S. Army Pers. Mgmt. Program, Ga., Wash., Pa., NJ, Ala., Ariz., Va., NY, Okla., SC, Panama, 1976—78, Internat. Assn. Quality Cirs., Internat. Pers. Mgmt. Assn., Info. Resource Mgmt. Assn., USAR, 1981—91, Am. Mgmt. Assn., 1995—, Ctr. for Bus. and Inds., Monmouth and Ocean Counties, 1995; adj. prof. mgmt. and social psychology small bus. mgmt. Kean Coll., Union, NJ, 1981—96, Brookdale C.C., NJ, 1975—93, Pepperdine U., L.A., 1977—81, Temple U., Phila., 1987—88, grad. sch. bus. Fairleigh Dickinson U., 1990—; adj. prof. tchr. mgmt. and orgnl. psychology in MBA and spl. corp. onsite edn. programs Rutgers U., 1997—, adj. prof. M of Adminstrv. Sci. program, Jewish and Israeli fgn. student program, 2002; adj. prof. orgnl. behavior St. Peter's Coll., Jersey City, 2003—; tchr. interpersonal rels. Ocean County Coll., 1971—73; creative thinking Brookdale C.C., 1972—73; mem. small bus. adv. coun., 1996; cons. Mut. UFO Network, 1998; global CEO Inst. Chartered Fin. Analysts, India, 2002—; adj. prof. global mgmt., internat. bus., strategic planning N.J. City Univ., Jersey City, 2003—; adj. prof. human behavior, orgnl. behavior, introductory mgmt. St. Peter's Coll., Jersey City, 2003—, adj. prof. managerial decision making bus. policy, mgtm. of innovation, 2004—; reviewer coll. textbooks Prentice-Hall Pubs., 2003—; presenter Bayonne Hist. Soc., 2003; program instr. Brookdale Coll. Communiversity, Camp Evans, Belmar, NJ, 2003; presenter NRC Nuclear Regulatory Comm. Hearing, NJ, 2004; adj. prof. by invitation U. Canada-West, 2005; submitted testimony to N.J. Legis. Hearing on Nuc. Security/Pub. Safety, 2005. Author: Transactional Analysis on the Job, 1974, Retention of Engineers and Scientists, 1983, The Effects of an Experimental Training Program on the Creative Thinking Abilities of Adults, 1987, Value-Adding Leadership, 1988, Tapping the Potential to Contribute, 1998, One Summer, A Thousand Days, 2001, The Cloud Shaman, 2001, Fires Burning Deep Inside, 2001, Turn the Sandglass Over, 2001, Skyline Drive: A Poetic Journey Through Business Life, 2001; contbr. poetry anthologies Anagram: Art and Literature of Asian Americans, 1998, Snow and Barn, The Golden Wings, Bytes of Poetry, 2001—02, Taj Mahal Rev., India, 2002, developer mgmt. tng. curriculum for Monmouth and Ocean County Adult Edn. Commn., 1996, also instnl. materials for tng. tel. crisis hotline ctr. workers Contact USA, ednl. programs for lab. software engrs. and orgnl. surveys of U.S. Army, 1995, merger, mgmt. and original design tng. programs, 1996—, internet-based orgnl. learning assessment; contbg. editor: workingmanaging.com (U.K.), 2004; contbr. world wide web articles to numerous publs., materials for use in tng. sr. officers, fgn. mil. officers U.S. Army and Command Gen. Staff Coll.; contbr.: strategic planning, thinking, adaptive leadership and self-mastery arts Russia Jour. Bus., Globiz internat. bus. jour., 2004—, author ednl. materials. Tchr. human rels. ednl. assns. Monmouth and Ocean Counties, 1970-74, Fed. Women's Program, 1980, ESL Cmty. and Family Svcs., Monmouth, 1990-93; pvt. tutor English Citizenship; vol. Habitat for Humanity Internat., 1995-96, Contact USA, 1995-96, Presbyn. Youth Program, 1965; mem. NAACP, 1963-64; mem. Small Bus. Adv. Coun., Ocean County Coll., 1996; vol. Sierra Club, Wilderness Soc., Save the Planet, Nat. Resources Def. Coun., Nat. Wildlife Fedn., True Majority, Oceans Conservancy, League of Conservation Voters, Consumers Union, Am. Fed. of Tchrs., Move On.org, Common Cause, 2002—, NJ Pub. Int. Rsch. Group, 2004—. With U.S. Army, 1958-60. Recipient Bernard Watson award William Penn Found., 1987, Quality Circle Devel. commendation U.S. Army, 1981, Devel. Sci. Pers. commendation, 1983, Creative Edn. Techniques commendation, 1988, ESL Textbooks commendation U.S. Army Materiel Command, 1992, Mgmt. Devel. Curriculum commendation, 1992, numerous World Wide Net awards for creative writing, 1998. Mem. ASTD, ACLU, Creative Edn. Found., Internat. Transactional Analysis Assn., Adult Edn. Assn., Nat. Assn. Retired Fed. Employees, Nat. Speleol. Soc., Archaeol. Inst. of Am., Soc. Advancement of Mgmt., Acad. Mgmt., World Future Soc., Assn. of U.S. Army, Internat. Platform Assn. (elected), Union Concerned Scientists,Jersey Shore Quality Coun., Nat. Space Soc., Inst. Noetic Sciences, Acad. of Am. Poets, Planetary Soc. (cons. mutual UFO network 1998), Search for Extraterrestrial Intelligence Inst., Mensa, Phi Alpha Theta, Phi Delta Kappa. Avocations: investigating mysteries, exploring caves and ancient ruins, digging fossils, inventing, poetry. Personal E-mail: charlesalbano@webtv.net. *There is a continuity in life that comes of one's core identity, the whispered voice of youth. When heeded, it unfailingly provides motivation, persistence, satisfaction and direction. Life's purpose is not given; it is self-determined. Compounded of breaks, burdens, chance, successes, failures, myths and realities, we are nevertheless, self-made. Living well means respecting life, living to one's potential, adding value, and reducing pain and suffering of others. Success must be measured against how well one has met his/her own standards and purposes in living.*

ALBANO, PATRICK MARINO, historian, educator, archivist; b. Teaneck, N.J., Apr. 25, 1949; s. Patrick Marino Albano and Ann Elizabeth Sharp; 1 child, Patricia June. D, Drew U., 2001. Asst. prof. history Shippensburg (Pa.) U., 2000—02, Lock Haven (Pa.) U., 2002—04; asst. prof. Fairmont State U., W.Va., 2004. Author: Helots and Hiwis (Robert L. Chapman prize, 2001). Staff sgt. USMC, 1968—77. Vis. scholar, U. So. Calif., 2002; Mil. History Seminar fellow, U.S. Mil. Acad., West Point, 2001, NEH grantee, U. So. Calif., 2002. Mem.: Soc. US Mil. Hist., U.S. Mil. (assoc.). Home: 1108 Allegheny Dr Blakeslee PA 18610 Personal E-mail: moscow2015@hotmail.com.

ALBARRACIN, DOLORES, psychologist, educator; d. Carlos and Marta R. Albarracín; m. Martin P. Repetto, June 1, 1962; children: Maria de los Angeles Repetto, Martin J. Repetto. PhD, U Ill., Champaign-Urbana, 1997. Asst. prof. Psychology Dept., U. Fla., Gainesville, Fla., 1997—; grad. asst. and fellow Psychology Dept., U. Ill., Champaign-Urbana, Ill., 1992—97. Author: (jour. article) Jour. of Personality and Social Psychology, Health Psychology, 2000, Jour. of Personality and Social Psychology, 2001, Psychol. Bull., 2001; Personality and Social Psychology Bull., 2001, Advances in Exptl. Social Psychology, 2002, Health Psychology, 2003; editor: (book) Handbook of attitudes and attitude change, 2004. Recipient Scientist Devel. Award, NIMH, 1999-2003; grantee R 03 Rsch. Grant, 1997-1999, R 01 Rsch. Grant, NIH, 2001-2006. Mem.: Soc. of Intermerican Psychology (us rep. 2000—02), Am. Psychol. Soc., Soc. of Personality and Social Psychology, APA, Soc. of Exptl. Social Psychology. Home: 3629 SW 97th Way Gainesville FL 32608 Office: University Fla Psychology Dept Gainesville FL 32611 Office Phone: 352-392-0601 252. E-mail: dalbarra@ufl.edu.

ALBAUGH, JAMES F., aerospace transportation executive; b. May 31, 1950; BA in Math. and Physics, Willamette U.; MCE, Columbia U. Joined Boeing co., Hanford, Wash., 1975, mgr. process engring., plant mgr. El Paso, Tex., v.p. ops. autonetics electronic sys. divsn.; pres. Rocketdyne Propulsion & Power; sr. v.p., pres. space and comm. Boeing Space Transp., 1998—2002, pres., CEO integrated defense systems, 2002—. Mem. Nat. Security Telecom. Adv. Com., 2003—. Mem. corp. adv. com. Harvey Mudd Coll.; bd. dirs. St. Joseph Ballet. Mem. AIAA (sr.), Nat. Mgmt. Assn. (gold knight, silver knight), Interant. Cad. Astronautics, Nat. Def. Industrial Assoc. (Bob Hope Dist. Citizen award, 2001), Air Force Assoc., Am. Astronautical Soc. Office: Boeing Integrated Def Sys PO Box 516 Saint Louis MO 63166 Office Phone: 314-232-0232.

ALBEE, ARDEN LEROY, geologist, educator; b. Port Huron, Mich., May 28, 1928; s. Emery A. and Mildred (Tool) A.; m. Charleen H. Ettenheim, 1978; children: Janet, Margaret, Carol, Kathy, James, Ginger, Mary, George. BA, Harvard U., 1950, MA, 1951, PhD, 1957. Geologist U.S. Geol. Survey, 1950-59; prof. geology Calif. Inst. Tech., 1959—2002, prof. emeritus, 2002—; chief scientist Jet Propulsion Lab., 1978-84, dean grad. studies, 1984—2001, project scientist Mars Observer and Global Surveyor Missions, 1984—. Cons. in field, 1950; chmn. lunar sci. rev. panel NASA, 1972-77, mem. space sci. adv. com., 1976-84; mem. exam. bd. T.O.E.F.L. (Test of English as a Foreign Lang.), 1995-97; mem. Grad. Record Exam. Bd., 1995-98; mem. exec. com. Assn. Grad. Schs., 1995-97. Assoc. editor Jour. Geophys. Rsch., 1976-82, Ann. Rev. Earth Space Scis., 1978—; contbr. numerous articles to profl. jours. Bd. regents L.A. Chiropractic Coll., 1990-98. Recipient Exceptional Sci. Achievement medal NASA, 1976 Fellow Mineral Soc. Am. (assoc. editor Am. Mineralogist 1972-76), Geol. Soc. Am. (assoc. editor bull. 1972-89, councilor 1989-92), Am. Geophys. Union. Office: Calif Inst Tech Mail Code 150-21 Pasadena CA 91125-0001 E-mail: aalbee@gps.caltech.edu.

ALBEE, EDWARD FRANKLIN, playwright, writer; b. Mar. 12, 1928; s. Reed A. and Frances (Cotter) Albee. Student, Trinity Coll., 1946-47. Disting. prof. U. Houston, 1988—. Author: (plays) The Zoo Story, 1958, The Death of Bessie Smith, The Sandbox, 1959, The American Dream, 1960, Who's Afraid of Virginia Woolf?, 1962 (Tony award best play, 1963), The Ballad of the Sad Cafe (adaption of Carson McCullers' novella), 1963 (Tony nom. best play, 1964), Tiny Alice, 1964 (Tony nom. best play, 1965), Malcolm, 1966, A Delicate Balance, 1966 (Pulitzer Prize for drama, 1967, Tony nom. best play, 1967), Everything in the Garden, 1968, Box and Quotations from Chairman Mao, 1970, All Over, 1971, Seascape, 1975 (Pulitzer prize for drama, 1975, Tony nom. best play, 1975), Counting the Ways, 1976, Listening, 1977, The Man Who Had Three Arms, 1981, The Lady from Dubuque, 1979, adaptation of Lolita (Nabokov), 1980, Finding the Sun, 1982, Marriage Play, 1987, Three Tall Women, 1991 (Pulitzer Prize for drama, 1994), Fragments, 1993, About the Baby, 1996, Occupant, 2001, The Goat, Or Who is Sylvia?, 2002 (Tony award best play, 2002), Petal and Jerry, 2004; dir.: (plays) Happy Days, 1993, Alley Theatre, 1991. Pres. Edward F. Albee Found. Named to Theater Hall of Fame, 1985; recipient gold medal in drama Am. Acad. and Inst. Arts and Letters, 1980, Nat. Medal of Arts, 1996, Kennedy Ctr. honoree, 1996, Spl. Tony award for Lifetime Achievement in Theatre, 2005. Mem.: Nat. Inst. Arts and Letters, Dramatists Guild Coun. Address: 14 Harrison St New York NY 10013-2842

ALBEE, GEORGE WILSON, psychology professor; b. St. Marys, Pa., Dec. 20, 1921; s. George W. and Maude (Allen) A.; m. Constance Impallaria, Aug. 6, 1955 (dec.); children: Alexander, Luke, Maud, Sarah; m. Margaret Moon-Mui Tong, Dec. 20, 1985. AB, Bethany Coll., 1943, ScD (hon.), 1969; MS, U. Pitts., 1947, PhD, 1949; PhD (hon.), Stirling U., Scotland, 1998. Rsch. psychologist Western Psychiat. Inst., Pitts., 1949-51; asst. exec. sec. Am. Psychol. Assn., Washington, 1951-53; Fulbright prof. Helsinki (Finland) U., 1953-54; assoc. prof. psychology Western Res. U., Cleve., 1954-56, prof., 1957-71, chmn. dept. psychology, 1957-60, 63-66, Ladd disting. prof. psychology, 1959-71; prof. psychology U. Vt., Burlington, 1971-92, prof. emeritus, 1992—; courtesy prof. Fla. Mental Health Inst. U. South Fla., Tampa, 1994—. Cons. VA, Surgeon Gen. of Army, Pres.'s Com. on Mental Retardation, Peace Corps, 1962-65; vis. fellow Brit. Psychol. Soc., 2003. Author: Mental Health Manpower, 1959, Emerging Concepts of Mental Disorder, 1969, The Uncertain Future of Clinical Psychology, 1970, The Future of Psychology, 1974, The Protestant Ethic, Sex, and Psychotherapy, 1978; editor: Primary Prevention of Psychopathology, 1977; gen. editor: (with Justin M. Joffe) series of books on primary prevention of psychopathology; humor columnist The Longboat Observer. Mem. Vt. Psychology Licensing Bd., 1972-75; dir. task force on manpower Joint Commn. Mental Illness and Health, Cambridge, Mass., 1957-59; program com. Nat. Assn. for Mental Health, 1968-70; dir. task group in prevention Pres.'s Commn. Mental Health, 1977-78; com. on prevention Nat. Mental Health Assn., 1985-86; bd. dirs. Internat. Coun. Psychologists, 1985-88, 98-00; prevention com. World Fedn. Mental Health, 1992—, Biennial Albee lectr. on prevention. Recipient Alumni Achievement award in sci. Bethany Coll., 2000. Fellow APA (bd. profl. affairs, coun. reps., bd. dirs. 1965-70, 77-80, pres. div. clin. psychology 1967, nat. pres. 1969-70, policy and planning bd. 1972-75, chairperson com. on human resources 1973-76, mem. com. on sci. and profl. ethics 1990-92, bd. for advancement of psychology in pub. interest 1999-2002, task force on governance 2003, Disting. Profl. Contbn. award 1975, Gold medal for lifetime contbns. in the pub. interest 1993, Presdl. citation 2001. pres. divsn. gen. psychology, 2004-), Am. Psychol. Soc. (founding fellow); mem. AAAS, AAUP, Am. Bd. Profl. Psychology (bd. dirs. 1975-78, treas. 1976-80), Ea. Psychol. Assn., Midwestern Psychol. Assn., Ohio Psychol. Assn. (pres. 1963-64), Vt. Psychol. Assn., New Eng. Psychol. Assn. (pres. 1978-79, Disting. Contbn. award 1997), Am. Assn. Applied and Preventive Psychology (1st pres. 1990-92, Lifetime Achievement award in prevention psychology 1997), Psychologists for Social Responsibility (pres. 1999, steering com. 2001—), Soc. for Gen. Psychology (pres. divsn. 1 2005), Phi Beta Kappa, Sigma Xi, Psi Chi. Home: 7157 Longboat Dr N Longboat Key FL 34228-1047 Office Phone: 941-387-8096. Personal E-mail: gwallee@webtv.net.

ALBEE, GLORIA, playwright; b. Brockton, Mass., Apr. 26, 1931; d. Earl Fredric and Rita Marie (Walls) Albee; m. Leonard Goodman, Jan. 13, 1961 (div.); 1 child, Anna Albee Goodman. Student, Boston U., 1948-49, U. Wash., 1972-74, Sarah Lawrence Coll., 1975-76, Hunter Coll., 1986-92. Playwright: Medea, 1975, Helen of Sparta, 1991; plays produced include Medea, Nothing Personal, The Yellow Wallpaper. Recipient John Golden Theatre award Hunter Coll., 1986, Mary M. Fay award in poetry Hunter Coll., 1990, Honorable Mention award Jane Chambers Playwriting Award, 1994; Rockefeller Bros. Found. grantee; Nat. Arts Club Lit. scholar, 1990. Mem. Dramatists Guild. Home: The Lillian Booth Actors Home 155-175 W Hudson Ave #14 Englewood NJ 07631-1609

ALBER, JOHN I., lawyer; AB, Ind. U., 1974; JD, So. Ill. U., 1979. Bar: Ill. 1979, Mo. 1979, US Dist. Ct., Ea. Dist. Mo. 1981. Ptnr., mem. exec. com. Bryan Cave LLP, St. Louis. Office: Bryan Cave LLP One Metropolitan Square 211 North Broadway, Ste 3600 Saint Louis MO 63102 Office Phone: 314-259-2144. E-mail: jialber@bryancave.com.

ALBERG, JAMES L., lawyer; b. NYC, July 11, 1952; BA cum laude, Union Coll., 1974; JD, Boston Univ., 1977. Bar: NY 1978, DC 1979, Mass. 1986, Ga. 1994, US Dist. Ct. (DC, ea. dist. Mass.), UK (registered fgn. lawyer). Atty. Gen. Electric Corp., Citibank; sr. v.p. & gen. counsel Dun & Bradstreet Software, 1989—96; ptnr., chmn. global sourcing group Pillsbury Winthrop Shaw Pittman, Washington, 1996—. Contbr. articles to profl. jours. Mem.: ABA, DC Bar Assn., Computer Law Assn. Office: Pillsbury Winthrop Shaw Pittman 2300 N St NW Washington DC 20037-1128 Office Phone: 202-663-9123. Office Fax: 202-663-9120. Business E-Mail: james.alberg@pillsburylaw.com.

ALBERG, TOM AUSTIN, investment company executive, lawyer; b. San Francisco, Feb. 12, 1940; s. Thomas A. and Miriam A. (Twitchell) A.; m. Mary Ann Johnke, June 8, 1963 (div. July 1989); children: Robert, Katherine, John; m. Judith Beck, Aug. 8, 1989; children: Carson, Jessica. AB, Harvard Coll., 1962; JD, Columbia U., 1965. Bar: N.Y. 1965, Wash. 1967. Assoc. Cravath, Swaine & Moore, N.Y.C., 1965-67, Perkins, Cole, Stone, Olsen & Williams, Seattle, 1967-71, ptnr., 1971-90, chmn. exec. com., 1986-90; exec. v.p. legal and corp. affairs McCaw Cellular Comm. Inc., Kirkland, Wash., 1990-95; pres., CEO, dir. Personal Connect Comm. Corp., Kirkland, 1995—; prin. Madrona Investment Group, 1996—. Pres., COO, dir. Lin Broadcasting Inc., Kirkland, 1991-95; bd. dirs. Active Voice Corp., VISIO Corp., Emeritus Corp., Amazon Com., Inc.; pres. Seattle Legal Svcs., 1973-74; lectr. on securities and fin. law. Editor Law Rev., Columbia U. Contbr. articles to profl. jours. Pres. Intiman Theatre, Seattle, 1981-83, Pacific Sci. Ctr. Found., Seattle, 1982-84; chmn. Discovery Inst., 1991—, Seattle Commons, 1991-94; trustee Children's Hosp. Found., 1992-95, Pacific Sci. Ctr., 1994—, U. Puget Sound, 1994—, Sta. KING-FM, 1994—. Stone scholar Columbia U., 1963-65. Mem. ABA, Wash. State Bar Assn. (chmn. corp. sect. 1975-76, securities com. 1974-75), Univ. Club, Seattle Yacht Club. Office: Madrona Investment Group LLC 1000 2nd Ave Ste 3700 Seattle WA 98104-1053

ALBERGER, WILLIAM RELPH, lawyer, legislative staff member; b. Portland, Oreg., Oct. 11, 1945; s. Relph Griffin and Ferne (Ahlstrom) A.; children: Eric Griffin, Blake Eugene. BA, Willamette U., 1967; MBA, U. Iowa, 1971; JD, Georgetown U., 1973. Bar: D.C. 1974. Spl. asst. to U.S. Senator Bob Packwood, 1969-71; legis. asst. U.S. Rep. Al Ullman, Washington, 1972-75, adminstrv. asst., 1975-77, House Com. on Ways and Means, 1977; vice-chmn. U.S. Internat. Trade Commn., Washington, 1978-80, chmn., 1980-82; pvt. practice Washington, 1982—. Mem. ABA (chmn. standing com. customs law 1983-85), D.C. Bar Assn., Internat. Bar Assn. Democrat. Avocations: softball, tennis, fantasy sports. Office Phone: 703-461-3791. E-mail: bill.alberger@comcast.net.

ALBERS, CHARLES EDGAR, retired investment company executive; b. Flushing, NY, Nov. 30, 1940; s. Edwin M. and Olive F. (Van Dyke) A.; m. Judy Mae Hite, Dec. 18, 1961 (dec. June 1998); children: Robert, Karin, Laura. AB, Kenyon Coll., 1962; MBA, Columbia U., 1967. CFA. Portfolio mgr. Guardian Park Ave. Fund, Inc., N.Y.C., 1972—98; pres. Guardian Stock Fund, N.Y.C., 1983—98; sr. v.p. Oppenheimer Funds, N.Y.C., 1998—2003; portfolio mgr. Oppenheimer Main St. Fund, N.Y.C., 1998—2003; ret., 2003. Trustee, dir. Interweave, Inc., 2004-. Named to honor roll Forbes Mut. Fund 9 times, Variable Annuity Mgr. of Yr. Morningstar, 1996; Woodrow Wilson fellow, 1962-63. Mem. Short Hills Club, Beacon Hill Club, Columbia Club, Cato Inst., Appalachian Mountain Club. Avocations: platform tennis, reading, mountain hiking. Personal E-mail: chuckalbers@aol.com.

ALBERS, DOLORES M., secondary school educator; b. Lander, Wyo., June 2, 1949; AA, Casper Coll., 1969; BS, U. No. Colo., 1972; postgrad., U. N.C., U. Wyo., Chadron State. Physical edn. instr. for grades K-12, 6th and 8th grade sci. tchr. Bent County Sch. Dist. 2, McClave, Colo., 1972-75; physical edn./health instr. Sweetwater County Sch. Dist. # 2, Green River, Wyo.,

1972—. Mem. phys. edn. coun. Mid. and Secondary Schs., 1999—2003, chmn. phys. edn. coun., 2002—03. Mem., chmn. Green River Parks and Recreation Bd.; coord. Hoops for Heart; co-chmn. United Way Sweetwater County, 1999-2001. Named Tchr. of Yr., Ctrl. Dist., 1994—95, Nat. Assn. Sport and Phys. Edn., 1995. Mem. AAHPERD, AALR, ASCD/NFOIA, NEA, Wyo. Edn. Assn., Wyo. Assn. Health, Phys. Edn., Recreation and Dance (Tchr. of Yr. award 1994-95), Green River Edn. Assn., Nat. Assn. for Sport and Phys. Edn., Mid. and Secondary Sch. Phys. Edn. Coun. (chmn. 2002-03). Roman Catholic. Avocations: snowboarding, backpacking, woodworking, crewel, cross country skiing. Home: 1745 Massachusetts Ct Green River WY 82935-6229 Office: Green River HS 1615 Hitching Post Dr Green River WY 82935-5771

ALBERS, GREGORY W., neurologist; MD, U. Calif., San Diego, 1980. Prof. neurology Stanford (Calif.) U., 1989—, dir. Stanford Stroke Ctr., 1992—. Office: Stanford Stroke Ctr 701 Welch Rd # 325 Palo Alto CA 94304 Office Phone: 650-723-4448. Office Fax: 650-723-4451.

ALBERS, JAMES WILSON, neurologist; b. Detroit, Oct. 28, 1943; s. James Milton and Willa Jean (Wilson) A.; m. Janet Mary Rakocy, May 10, 1968; children— Jeffrey, Matthew, Katherine, Elizabeth BS in E.E., U. Mich., 1965, MS, 1966, MS, 1968, PhD, 1970, MD, 1972. Diplomate Am. Bd. Neurology. Instr. neurology Mayo Clinic, Rochester, Minn., 1976; asst. prof. neurology Med. Coll. Wis., Milw., 1976-79; assoc. prof. neurology U. Mich., Ann Arbor, 1979-83, prof., 1983—, dir. neuromuscular program, 1979—. Contbr. articles to profl. jours. Recipient Henry W. Woltman award Neurology Dept. Mayo Clinic, 1978 Fellow Am. Acad. Neurology; mem. Am. Assn. Electromyography and Electrodiagnosis (bd. dirs. 1984—), Mich. Neurologic Assn. (sec. treas. 1985—), Sigma Xi, Eta Kappa Nu, Tau Beta Pi Home: 3889 Waldenwood Dr Ann Arbor MI 48105-3006 Office: Univ Mich Med Ctr Dept Neurology B4952 CFOB Ann Arbor MI 48109

ALBERS, JANE E., social worker, psychotherapist; b. Medford, Mass., July 18, 1940; d. Allan S. and Margaret E. Henry; m. Richard R. Albers Sr., June 11, 1961; children: Judy, Rick, Daniel. BA, Edison State Coll., 1997; MSW, E. Carolina U., 2000. LCSW N.C., cert. clin. addiction specialist N.C., clin. supr. N.C. Counselor Carrier Found., Glen Mead, NJ, 1983—87, Wilmington (NC) Treatment Ctr., 1988, Southeastern Ctr. Mental Health, Wilmington, 1988—98, outpatient clin. supr., 1998—. Avocations: water-skiing, reading, gardening, jogging. Office: Southeastern Ctr Mental Health MH/DD/SAS 2023 S 17th St Wilmington NC 28401 E-mail: albers@secmh.org.

ALBERS, SHERYL KAY, state legislator; b. Sauk County, Wis., Sept. 9, 1954; d. Marcus J. and Norma Anderson Gumz; 1 child, Joel Albert. BA, Ripon Coll., 1976; JD, U. Wis., 2004. Mem. Wis. State Assembly, 1991—, mem. judiciary com., children and families com., chmn. property rights/land mgmt. com. Assembly Rep. Caucus Wis., 1987-91; mem. Local Emergency Planning Com. Juneau County; mem. Joint Com. on Fin., 1996-2000; mem. Sauey Foun. Scholarship Com. Recipient Campbell award Sauk County Rep. Com., 1981, 90, Top 10 County award Wis. State Rep. Party, 1982, Pacesetter award Wis. Forage Coun., 1983, Bovay award Rep. Party Wis., 1990; named one of Outstanding Farmers Sauk County Farm Bur., 1982. Mem. Sauk County Farm Bur. (dir., treas. 1977-82), Sauk County Hist. Soc., Agrl. Bus. Coun. Wis., Kiwanis. Republican. Office: Hazelbaker and Assoc SC 3240 University Ave Ste 3 Madison WI 53704 Office Phone: 608-266-8531. Business E-Mail: Rep.Albers@legis.state.wi.us.

ALBERSON, BARBARA, health science association administrator; b. L.A., July 22, 1950; d. Solomon Nathan and Rae Spar Gimpel; m. Jack Alberson, Feb. 17, 1979. Pub. health educator San Diego Pub. Health Dept., 1974-78, Sacramento County Health Dept., 1979-81; health edn. cons. II Calif. Dept. of Aging, 1981-89, chief state and local injury control sect., 1989—. Mem. spl. panel for prevention of pediatric injuries Ctr. for Disease Control and Prevention, 1997-99; tng. cons. safe communities Nat. Hwy. Traffic Safety Adminstrn., 1998-2000. Bd. dirs. Calif. Coalition for Children's Safety and Health, 1994—, Calif. Coalition Against Driving Under the Influence, 1996—, alliance for Edn. Solutions, 1996—; Women's Am. Orgn. for Rehab. and Tng., 1974—. Fellowship Pub. Health Edn. Leadership Inst. Assn. of State and Territorial Dirs. of Health Promotion and Pub. Health Edn., 2000—; recipient Outstanding Achievement Calif. Office of Traffic Safety, 2000, Outstanding Partnership award Calif. Healthy Cities, 1998. Mem. APHA; mem. State and Territorial Dirs. of Injury Prevention. Avocations: gardening, cats.

ALBERT, ALAN DALE, lawyer; b. Christiansburg, Va., Feb. 6, 1956; s. Horace Wendell and Alma Juanita (Morris) A.; m. Charlotte Lynne Anders, Sept., 27, 2003; children: Amber Lynne Reed, Alexander, Caroline. AB magna cum laude, Harvard Coll., 1979; MPhil, Oxford U., 1981; JD cum laude, Harvard U., 1985. Bar: Va. 1985, U.S. Dist. Ct. (ea. dist.) Va. 1989, U.S. Ct. Appeals (4th cir.) 1989, U.S. Bankruptcy Ct. (ea. dist.) Va. 1991, U.S. Ct. Appeals (fed. cir.) 2003 U.S. Supreme Ct. 2005. Instr. in legal methods, teaching fellow in fed. litigation Harvard Law Sch., 1983-85; teaching fellow faculty arts and scis. Harvard U., 1984-85; law clk. Office of the Legal Adviser U.S. Dept. State, 1984; rsch. dir., speech writer Baliles for Gov., Richmond, Va., 1985; dir. policy devel. Gov.'s Transition Office Commonwealth of Va., Richmond, 1985-86, spl. asst. to Gov. of Va., 1986-89; assoc. Mays & Valentine, Norfolk and Richmond, 1989-93, ptnr., 1994—2000, Troutman Sanders LLP, Norfolk and Richmond, Va., 2001—04; shareholder, v.p. LeClair Ryan PC, 2004—. Author books on environ. law, real estate and land use law, freedom of info. and pub. records access; editor Harvard Law Rev., 1983-85; contbr. articles to profl. jours. Vol. Dem. nat., state and local polit. campaigns and com. activities, 1976—; exec. dir. Va. Dems., 1988; bd. dirs. Va. Opera, 1990—; bd. trustees Va. Symphony, 2004—; co-founder, gen. coun. Commonwealth Theatre Co.; mem. Leadership Metro Richmond, 1987-88. Harvard Nat. scholar, 1974-79, George C. Marshall scholar, 1979-82, European Consortium Polit. Rsch. scholar, 1982, Pres.'s Disting. Svc. award Treas. Assn. of Va., 1995, 2003. Mem. ABA, Fed. Bar Assn., Am. Intellectual Property Law Assn., Va. Bar Assn. (sect. bd. govs. 1991-94), Va. State Bar, Tidewater Legal Aid Soc. (bd. dirs. 1990-93), Norfolk-Portsmouth Bar, Virginia Beach Bar, Town Point Club, Owl Club, Phi Beta Kappa. Office: 999 Waterside Dr Ste 2525 Norfolk VA 23510 Address: 951 E Byrd St Richmond VA 23219 Office Phone: 757-441-8914. E-mail: aalbert@leclairryan.com.

ALBERT, ARNOLD, medical association administrator; BS in Med. Tech., Fairleigh Dickenson U., Teaneck, N.J., 1972; MBA in Acctg. and Fin., Iona Coll., New Rochelle, N.Y., 1976. Cert. trainer/ targeted selections Dedicated Dimensions Inc., 2004, med. practice exec. Intern med. tech. Bergen Pines Hosp., Paramus, NJ, 1971—72; med. tech. Mary Immaculate Hosp., Queens, NY, 1972—76; exec. dir. Somerset County Med. & Dental Group, Princess Anne, Md., 1976—79; v.p. fin. and adminstrn. Ctr. Addictive Illnesses, Morristown, NJ, 1979—82; founder and COO Prime Health Sys./Modern Healthcare Concepts, 1981—95; COO Image Enhancing Dermatology, Inc., San Jose, Calif., 1996—97; sr. v.p. and COO Dental Health Mgmt., Inc., Nashville, 1997—98; v.p. ops. InterDent, Inc., El Segundo, Calif., 1998—2001; cons. Premier Dental Group, Beverly Hills, 2001—02; dir. Vanderbilt Med. Group, Nashville, 2002—. Adj. prof. bus., healthcare and entrepreneurship U. Calif., Berkeley, U. Md., Mercy Coll., Dobbs Ferry, NY, Morris County (N.J.) C.C. Mem.: Dental Group Mgmt. Assn., Am. Coll. Med. Practice Execs., Med. Group Mgmt. Assn. Address: 8108 Poplar Wood Ln Nashville TN 37221

ALBERT, DANIEL MYRON, ophthalmologist, educator; b. Newark, Dec. 19, 1936; s. Maurice I. and Flora Albert; m. Eleanor Kagle, June 26, 1960; children: B. Steven, Michael. BS, Franklin and Marshall Coll., 1958; MD, U. Pa., 1962; MA (hon.), Harvard U., 1976; D honoris causa, Louis Pasteur U., Strasbourg, 1992; MS, U. Wis., Madison, 1997. Diplomate Am. Bd. Ophthalmology. Intern Hosp. U. Pa., 1962-63, resident, 1963-66; surgeon USPHS, 1966-68; NIH spl. fellow in ophthalmic pathology Armed Forces Inst. Pathology, 1968-69; asst. prof. ophthalmology Yale U. Sch. Medicine, 1969-70, assoc. prof., 1970-75, prof., 1975-76; practice medicine specializing in ophthalmology; assoc. surgeon Mass. Eye and Ear Infirmary, 1976-86, surgeon, 1986-92, dir. David G. Cogan eye pathology lab., 1979-92; prof. ophthalmic pathology Harvard U. Med. Sch., 1976-84, David G. Cogan prof. ophthalmology, 1984-92; Frederick Allison Davis prof., dept. ophthalmology U. Wis., Madison, 1992—, chmn. dept. ophthalmology, 1992—2002, emeritus chmn., 2002—. Author: (with Scheie) A History of Ophthalmology at the University of Pennsylvania, 1965, Textbook of Ophthalmology, 8th edit. 1969, 9th edit. 1977; co-author: Jaeger's Atlas of Ophthalmology, 1972, (with Puliafito) Foundations of Ophthalmology, 1979, Men of Vision, 1993, (with Jakobiec) Atlas of Clinical Ophthalmology, 1996; editor: (with Edwards) The History of Ophthalmology, 1996, John Jeffries' Lectures on the Diseases of the Eye, 1998, Ophthalmic Surgery: Principles and Techniques, 1998, A Physician's Guide to Health Care Management, 2002, (with Polans) Ocular Oncology, 2003, (with Lucarelli) Clinical Atlas of Procedures in Ophthalic Surgery, 2003; co-editor (with Jakobiec) Principles and Practice of Ophthalmology, 1994, 2d edit., 1999, A Physician's Guide to Healthcare Management, 2002, Dates in Ophthalmology, 2002, (with Lucarelli) Clinical Atlas of Procedures in Ophthalmic Surgery, 2003, (with Polans) Ocular Oncology, 2003; editor Archives of Ophthalmology, 1994—; contbr. articles to profl. jours. Recipient Oliver Meml. medal, U. Pa., 1962, Friedenwald award, 1981, Von Sallmann award in vision and ophthalmology, Internat. Conf. for Eye Rsch., 1988, award, Humboldt Found., 1991, MacKenzie medal, Scottish Ophthal. Soc., 1992, Lighthouse Pisart Vision award, The Lighthouse Inc., 1997, Lorenz E. Zimmerman (WARF) professorship, 1999, Disting. Alumni award, U. Pa. Sch. Medicine, 2001, Weisenfeld award, Fight for Sight, 2003; William and Mary Greve scholar, 1978—79, Alcon Rsch. Inst. scholar, 1984—85. Fellow ACS; mem. Am. Assn. Ophthalmic Pathology (Zimmerman medal 1993), Am. Acad. Ophthalmology (Jackson Meml. lectr. 1996), Am. Bd. Ophthalmology (dir. 1997—), Macula Soc. (W. Richard Green award 2003), Fight for Sight (Mildred Weisenfeld award 2003), New Eng. Ophthal. Soc. (Taylor Smith Gold medal 2004). Jewish. Home: 1106 Wellesley Rd Madison WI 53705-2230 Office: U Wis Hosp and Clinics Dept Ophthalmology F4/334 600 Highland Ave Madison WI 53792-3284 Office Phone: 608-263-9798.

ALBERT, ELIZABETH FRANZ (MRS. HENRY B. ALBERT), investor, artist, conservationist; b. Chgo., Nov. 9, 1923; d. Herbert George and Louise Anders Franz; m. Henry Burton Albert, Oct. 24, 1964 (dec. July 1980). Student, Chevy Chase Jr. Coll., 1942. Investor stock market, real estate. Breeder several champion Miniature Poodles. Exhibitions include portraits, still life (various painting awards); contbr. biology textbook; editor: biology textbook. Former mem. Landmarks Preservation Coun. Chgo. Mem.: Am. Farmland Trust, Nat. Trust Hist. Preservation, Cousteau Soc. (founding mem.), Natural Resources Def. Coun., Environ. Def. Fund (Osprey Soc.), Nat. Mus. Women in the Arts (charter mem.), Chgo. Symphony Orch. Soc., Art Inst. Chgo. (life). Republican. Episcopalian. Achievements include design of a house in college within the architectural field; conservationist who campaigned against the herbicide Dacthal which causes lymphoma and Parkinson's Disease and is used by lawn care companies, home owners, farmers, and golf course greens keepers. Avocations: music, renovating houses, antiques, gardening, reading. Home: 316 Courtland Ave Park Ridge IL 60068

ALBERT, GARETT J., lawyer; b. Sept. 7, 1943; m. Eleanor Lanier Culbertson, Oct. 2, 1971. BA cum laude, Columbia U., 1965; postgrad., Harvard U. Bus. Sch., 1967-68; JD, Harvard U., 1968. Bar: D.C. 1969, N.Y. 1970. Atty. U.S. Atomic Energy Commn., 1968; assoc. Hughes Hubbard & Reed, N.Y.C., 1969-77; ptnr. Hughes Hubbard & Reed, LLP, N.Y.C., 1977—. Contbr. articles to various publs. including James Joyce Quar. Bd. dirs., pres. Perlman Music Program; bd. dirs. Mannes Coll. Music, Nat. Acad. Design, Nat. Corp. Fund for Dance, Paul Taylor Dance Found. Winner U.S. Nat. Powerlifting Championship, Nat. Physique com., Tournament of Champions, 1996, Mr. USA, 1996, Kevin Levrone Bodybuilding Classic, 1995, and other masters powerlifting and bodybuilding championships. Mem. Union Club, Quogue (N.Y.) Field Club. Office: Hughes Hubbard & Reed LLP 1 Battery Park Plz Fl 12 New York NY 10004-1482

ALBERT, GERALD, clinical psychologist; b. NYC, Nov. 13, 1917; s. Andrew I. and Eleanor (Walder) A.; divorced; m. Norma Holm Haskell, 1983 (dec. 2004); children: Jay Harvey, Laurie Ellen Albert Moxham BA. CCNY, 1938; MA, New Sch. for Social Research, 1958; EdD, Columbia U., 1964; Cert. psychoanalytic tng. program, L.I. Inst. Mental Health, Queens, N.Y., 1964. Editor Vulcan and Creston Pubs., N.Y.C., 1939-45; nat. dir. advt., pub. relations Universal Pictures, div. ednl. films, N.Y.C., 1945-50; exec. dir. Advt. Enterprises and Continental Research Inst., Queens, N.Y., 1951-64; asst. to full prof. LIU, 1964-85, prof. Emeritus, 1985—; dir. L.I.U. C.W. Post Counseling Ctr., 1964-70. Psychologist, supervising psychologist, clin. dir. L.I. Consultation Ctr., 1966-86, clin. cons., 1986-95; pvt. practice marriage and individual therapy, 1958—. Author: (cassette) How To Choose and Keep a Marriage Partner, 1980, The Wonderful Magic of No-Fault Living, 1990, Japanese edit., 1996, (feature series for website) Making Your Marriage Work Better, 2001-02; editor-in-chief Jour. Contemporary Psychotherapy, 1985-87; contbr. articles to profl. jours. Recipient 1st prize Most Effective Comms./Newsletters Cmty. Agys. Pub. Rels. Assn., 1983. Fellow Am. Assn. for Marriage and Family Therapy (L.I. Family Therapist of Yr. 1993, founder L.I. recorded telephone series "Helpful Hints for Happier Marriage" 1995, contbr. to webpage, 2001); mem. APA, Am. Soc. for Psychical Rsch., Nat. Coun. Family Rels., Soc. Clin. and Exptl. Hypnosis, Soc. Sci. Exploration, Internat. Soc. for Study of Subtle Energy and Energy Medicine, Inst. Noetic Scis. Office: 1900 Hempstead Tpke East Meadow NY 11554-1724 Office Phone: 516-794-6848.

ALBERT, JANYCE LOUISE, human resources specialist, retired business educator, banker, consultant; b. Toledo, July 27, 1932; d. Howard C. And Glenola Mae (Masters) Blessing; m. John R. Albert, Aug. 7, 1954; children: John R., James H. Student, Ohio Wesleyan U., 1949-51; BA, Mich. State U., 1953; MS, Iowa State U., 1980. Asst. pers. mgr./tng. sup. Sears, Roebuck & Co., Toledo, 1953-56; tchr. adult edn. Tenafly Pub. Schs. (N.J.), 1966-70; pers. officer, tng. officer, tng. and edn. mgr. Iowa Dept. Transp., Ames, 1974-77; coll. recruiting coord. Rockwell Internat., Cedar Rapids, Iowa, 1977-79, engring. adminstrn. mgr., 1979-80; employee rels. and job evaluation analyst, recruiter Phillips Petroleum Co., Bartlesville, Okla., 1980-81; v.p., dir. pers. Rep. Bancorp, Tulsa, 1981-83; sr. v.p. and dir. human resources First Nat. Bank, Rockford, Ill., 1983-94; dir. bus. divsn. Rock Valley Coll., Rockford, Ill., 1994-99, ret., 1999; human resources cons. Furst Group, Rockford, 2000—04. Advisor to Nat. Profl. Secs. Assn.; mem. adv. com. Zion Devel. Corp., 1999-2002. Bd. dirs. Rocvale Children's Home, 1986-97, 99-2001, pres. 1991-94; bd. dirs. United Way of Ames, 1976-77; mem. employee svc. comm., Rockford Pub. Schs., 1988-92; acct. exec. United Way Rockford, 1993-98, acct. sec. head, 1996, allocations com., 2000-01; bd. dirs. Rockford Human Resources Cmty. Action Program; chair legis. com. Rockford Human Svcs. Dept., 1989-92; chair Rockford State of Ill. Job Svcs. Employers Coun., 1990-97; publicity chmn. Tenafly 300th Ann. Celebration, 1969; task force Rockford Bd. Edn., 1993-94; gala com. Janet Wattles Mental Health Ctr., 1990; deacon Collegiate Presbyn. Ch., Ames, 1972-75; adv. coun. Rockford YWCA, 1986, fund drive task force, 1998-99, co-chair YWCA Leader Luncheon, 1986-87; advisor Rockford chpt. ARC, 1991-2004; mem. Mayor's Task Force for Rockford Project Self-Sufficiency, 1986-89, chmn. adv. coun., 1991; chair info. and referral com., bd. dirs. Contact, 1994-2003; bd. dirs. Rockford Symphony Orch., 1992-95, sec. 1994-95; bd. dirs. Rockford Leadership Found., 1994-96; chair pers. com. Rockford Ctrl. Area Commn., 1997-99, v.p., bd. dirs.; fund drive taskforce Blackhawk Day Nursery, 1998-99; bd. dirs. Rock Valley Coll. Found., 2000-03, co-chmn. governance com., 2001-03; mem. session 1st Presbyn. Ch., Rockford, 2000-01, chair mktg. task force, 2003, mem. space allocation task force, 2004; ctrl. steering com. Ctr. for Learning in Retirement, 2000-01. Pres.'s scholar Mich. State U., 1951-53; recipient YWCA Kate O'Connor award for Women in Labor Force, 1984; named Bd. Mem. of Yr. Rockford Human Resources Community Action Program, 1992. Mem.: Ill. Consortium Internat. Travel (mentor The Netherlands 1997), Employee Benefits Assn. No. Ill. (membership chmn.), Am. Soc. Pers. Adminstrn., Crusader Clin. Found. (bd. dirs. 1997—2003, v.p. bd. dirs. 2000, pres. bd. 2001—02, chmn. 2001—), Rockford Pers. Assn. (adv. coun. 1983—91, co-chmn. programs 1985—86), Rockford C. of C. (leadership program 1989, Athena event com. 1990—, chmn. Rockford Athena chpt. 1991, pres. coun. 1991—94, internat. bus. coun. 1993—99, transp. com., human resources com., Nat. Athena Found. award 1991, Woman of Yr.), Rockford Network (past chair 1985—86, awards com. 1995—97), World Trade Coun. (bd. dirs. 1994—97), Womenspace (bd. dirs. 1993—95, mktg. com. 1993—99, awards com. 1995—98, adv. bd. 1996—2005), Rockford Panhellenic Coun. (sec. 1992—93, treas. 1993—94, v.p. 1994—95, pres. 1995—96, Woman of Yr. award 1994, Rockford Lifescape Sr. of Yr. award 1999), P.E.O., Rockford Rotary Internat. (membership com. 1999—2003, chair steering com. 2000—01, co-chair membership com. 2001—03, Svc. Above Self com. 2004—05, bd. dirs. 2004—, 2005—, co-chair Rockford Acad. Event), Phi Kappa Phi, Alpha Gamma Delta, Sigma Epsilon. Home and Office: 5587 Thunderidge Dr Rockford IL 61107-1756 Fax: 815-282-8248. Office Phone: 815-282-8248. E-mail: janycealbert@hotmail.com.

ALBERT, KRISTEN ANN, music educator; b. Harrisburg, Pa., July 29, 1962; d. Charles Orth and Kathryn Johnson Froehlich; m. Douglas Lee Albert, Aug. 31, 2001. BS in Edn., Millersville U., 1983; EdM, Shippensburg U., 1989. Cert. instrnl. II Pa. Dept. Edn., 1983, specialist II Pa. Dept. Edn., 1989. Music specialist Warwick Sch. Dist., Lititz, Pa., 1984—84, Manheim Twp. Sch. Dist., Lancaster, Pa., 1984—89, guidance counselor, 1990—92, Hempfield Sch. Dist., Landisville, Pa., 1989—90; music specialist Lampeter (Pa.)-Strasburg Sch. Dist., 1992—2000; instr. music edn. West Chester (Pa.) U., 2001; asst. prof. music edn. West Chester U. Pa., 2001—, chmn. Dept. Music Edn., 2005—. Co-dir. Children's Choir Lancaster, 2000—. Musician: Allegro: The Chamber Orch. Lancaster, 2001—; contbr. articles to profl. jours. ETeaching/eLearning grant, West Chester U., 2002, 2003. Mem.: OAKE, Orgn. Am. Kodaly Educators, Am. Choral Dirs. Assn., Tech. Inst.: Music Edn. (instr.), Music Educators Nat. Conf. Lutheran. Avocations: golf, reading, computers. Office: West Chester Univ Pa Swope Hall West Chester PA 19383 Office Phone: 610-738-0495.

ALBERT, MARTIN LAWRENCE, behavioral neurologist, writer, educator, biomedical researcher; b. Lawrence, Mass., Jan. 7, 1939; s. Benjamin and Alice (Kaminsky) A.; m. Phyllis Gloria Cohen, Dec. 25, 1960; children: David, Michael, Rachel. MD, Tufts U., 1963; PhD, U. Paris, France, 1971. Diplomate Am. Bd. Psychiatry and Neurology. Intern Maimonides Med. Ctr., Bklyn., 1963-64; resident in neurology Boston U. Med. Sch./Boston VA Hosp., 1966-69; fellow in behavioral neurology Boston U. Med. Sch., 1969-71, Laboratoire de Neuropsychologie, Hopital Ste-Anne, Paris, 1969-71; chief, clin. neurology Boston VA Med. Ctr., 1978-83; clin. dir., co-prin. investigator Aphasia Rsch. Ctr. Boston U., 1979-96, prof. neurology Sch. Medicine, 1980—, dir. behavioral neuroscis., dept. neurology, 1983-92, dir. Aphasia Rsch. Ctr., 1996—; dir. med. rsch. svc. Dept. of Veterans Affairs, Washington, 1992-95. Cons. in behavioral neurosci. WHO, Geneva, Switzerland, 1981—; cons. to Pres.' Office of Sci. and Tech. Policy, Washington, 1993-95; Sackler scholar Inst. Advanced Studies Tel Aviv U., 1996; vis. prof. neurology Hebrew U. Med. Sch., Jerusalem, 1993, Hosp. de la Salpetriere, Paris, France, 2001-02; nat. adv. coun. Program in Bioethics Dept. VA, Washington, 1995—; nat. adv. coun. Nat. Inst. Gen. Med. Scis. NIH, 1992-93. Author: Human Neuropsychology, 1978, The Bilingual Brain, 1978, Clinical Aspects of Aphasia, 1981, Language in the Aging Brain, 1981, Manual of Aphasia Therapy, 1991, Clinical Neurology of Aging, 1984, 2d edit., 1994, Manual of Aphasia and Aphasia Therapy, 2004; contbr. over 200 articles to profl. jours. Mem. adv. bd. program in med. ethics Hebrew Coll., Boston, 1987; mem. adv. bd. U.S. Israel Mental Health Fedn., Worcester, Mass., 1991. Capt. U.S. Army, 1965-66. Grantee NIH, 1970—. Fellow Am. Acad. Neurology (co-founder, chmn. sect. geriatric neurology 1989-91); mem. Acad. Aphasia (bd. govs. 1986-88), Am. Neurol. Assn., Nat. Aphasia Assn. (v.p. 1988—). Jewish. Achievements include introduction of the concept subcortical dementia; development new treatment approaches for aphasia, including melodic intonation therapy and pharmacotherapy for aphasia; development of the field of language in aging and dementia, created popular diagnostic tests in behavioral neuroscience. Office: VA Boston Healthcare Sys 12A 150 S Huntington Ave Boston MA 02130-4817 Office Phone: 617-232-9500. Business E-Mail: malbert@bu.edu.

ALBERT, MICHAEL SALVATORE, pathologist, medical laboratory executive; b. Buffalo, Oct. 3, 1960; s. Salvatore Michael and Francine Joan (Anzalone) A.; m. Melissa Renee Albert, Sept. 20, 1996; children: Nathan, Jared, Hadley, Emma. BS in Biology, U. Dallas, 1982; MD, Albany (N.Y.) Med. Coll., 1986. Diplomate Nat. Bd. Med. Examiners, Am. Bd. Pathology. Intern dept. surgery St. Lukes-Roosevelt Hosp., N.Y.C., 1986-87; trauma clin. rsch. fellow Albany Med. Ctr., 1987-88; resident in pathology Strong Meml. Hosp., Rochester, N.Y., 1988-93; assoc. pathologist Mercy Hosp. of Buffalo, 1993-97, chmn. dept. pathology, 2001—; chief of pathology United Meml. Med. Ctr., Batavia, 1997—2001; pres., chmn. bd. dirs. X-Cell Lab., Amherst, NY, 2000—02, 2005; treas., bd. dirs. Ea. Great Lakes Pathology, PC, 2002—. Medico-legal cons. Paul Beltz Attys., PC, Buffalo, 1996-2001; founding mem., shareholder Eastern Gt. Lakes Pathology, PC, Amherst, 1996—. Fellow Coll. Am. Pathologists; mem. NY State Soc. Pathologists (past v.p.), Sigma Xi. Republican. Mem. Assembly of God Ch. Avocations: hunting, fishing, camping, photography, shooting sports. Home: 180 Independence Dr Orchard Park NY 14127 Office: Mercy Hosp of Buffalo 565 Abbott Rd Buffalo NY 14220 Business E-Mail: malbert3258@adelphia.net.

ALBERT, RONALD PETER, lawyer; b. Utica, N.Y., Sept. 10, 1956; AB in Econs. magna cum laude, U. Calif., Davis, 1979; JD, U. Calif., Berkeley, 1983; postgrad., Golden Gate U., 1989-91. Bar: Calif. 1983, N.Y. 1985; lic. real estate broker, Calif. Adj. prof. bus. law Syracuse U. Utica Coll., 1988-89; assoc. Griffinger, Levinson, Freed & Heinemann, San Francisco, 1989-93; pvt. practice, Sausalito, Calif., 1994—. Lectr. real estate law U. Calif. Haas Sch. Bus., Berkeley, 1992-98; pres. Sausalito Exch. Co., 1995—. Supreme Ct. editor U. Calif. Law Rev., 1982-83. Mem. Planning Commn., City of Sausalito, 1997-2002, chmn., 1999-2002; active Tax-Aid, San Francisco; mem. Sausalito City Coun., 2002—. Mem. Calif. State Bar, Bar Assn. San Francisco (vol. lawyers svc. program). Office: 66 George Ln Ste 101 Sausalito CA 94965-1890 Fax: 415-332-9216.

ALBERT, ROSS ALAN, lawyer; b. Boston, Nov. 22, 1958; s. Richmond G. and Mary (Day) A.; m. Nancy Ada Christian, July 16, 1983. AB, Harvard U., 1982, postgrad., 1985—86; JD, U. Calif., Berkeley, 1986. Bar: Mass. 1986, DC 1988, Ga. 2002, U.S. Dist. Ct. Md. 1987, U.S. Dist. Ct. (no. dist.) Ga. 2005, U.S. Ct. Appeals (4th cir.) 1987, U.S. Ct. Appeals (5th cir.) 1993, U.S. Ct. Appeals (DC cir.) 1994, U.S. Ct. Appeals (2d cir.) 1994, U.S. Ct. Appeals (6th cir.) 1994, U.S. Ct. Appeals (9th cir.) 1994, U.S. Ct. Appeals (11th cir.) 1994, U.S. Supreme Ct. 1994, U.S. Ct. Appeal (8th cir.) 1995. Jud. law clk. U.S. Dist. Ct. Md., Balt., 1986-88; assoc. Wilmer, Cutler & Pickering, Washington, 1988-93; spl. counsel Office of Gen. Counsel-appellate group U.S. SEC, Washington, 1993-97, counsel to commr. Norman S. Johnson, 1997-2000, sr. spl. counsel Divsn. of Enforcement, 2000-01; of counsel Morris, Manning & Martin LLP, Atlanta, 2001—. Assoc. editor Calif. Law Rev., 1985-86. Democrat. Office: Morris Manning & Martin LLP 1600 Atlanta Fin Ctr 3343 Peachtree Rd Atlanta GA 30326 Office Phone: 404-504-7768. Personal E-mail: ra81@post.harvard.edu. E-mail: raa@mmmlaw.com. *Notable cases include: U.S. vs. Lincoln, U.S. Dist. Ct. N.D. Ga. & U.S. Ct. App. 11th Cir., assisted at trial and served as lead appellate counsel for largest securities fraud prosecution in Georgia history; Vail vs. SEC, U.S. Ct. App. 5th Cir., successfully argued novel disciplinary case arising from broker's theft of funds from a political group; SEC vs. Midwest Investments, Inc., U.S. Ct. App. 6th Cir., drafted brief and successfully argued case of first impression, a jurisdictional challenge to the SEC's* *ability to regulate interstate securities fraud; SEC vs. Grossman, U.S. Ct. App. 2d Cir., drafted brief and successfully argued case involving challenge to misappropriation theory of insider-trading.*

ALBERT, SUSAN WITTIG, writer; b. Maywood, Ill., Jan. 2, 1940; d. John H. and A. Lucille (Franklin) Webber; m. William Albert, 1986; children by previous marriage: Robert, Robin, Michael. BA, U. Ill., 1967; PhD, U. Calif.-Berkeley, 1972. Instr. U. San Francisco, 1969-71; asst. prof. to assoc. prof. U. Tex., Austin, 1971-79; assoc. dean Grad. Sch., U. Tex., Austin, 1977-79; dean Sophie Newcomb Coll., New Orleans, 1979-81; dean of faculty. grad. dean S.W. Tex. State U., San Marcos, 1981-82, v.p. acad. affairs, 1982-86, prof. English, 1981-87. Founder Story Circle Network, Inc., 1997. Author: Work of Her Own, 1992, Writing From Life, 1996; author: (China Bayles novels) Thyme of Death, 1992, Witch's Bane, 1993, Hangman's Root, 1994, Rosemary Remembered, 1995, Rueful Death, 1996, Love Lies Bleeding, 1997, Chile Death, 1998, Lavender Lies, 1999, Mistletoe Man, 2000, Bloodroot, 2001, Indigo Dying, 2003, An Unthymely Death, 2003, A Dilly of a Death, 2004; author: Dead Man's Bones, 2005; author: (Robin Paige novels) Death at Bishop's Keep, 1994, Death at Gallows Green, 1995, Death at Daisy's Folly, 1997, Death at Devil's Bridge, 1998, Death at Rottingdean, 1999, Death at Whitechapel, 2000, Death at Epsom Downs, 2001, Death at Dartmoor, 2002, Death at Glamis Castle, 2003, Death in Hyde Park, 2004, Death at Blenheim Palace, 2005; author: (Cottage Tales of Beatrix Potter novels) The Tale of Hill Top Farm, 2004, Cottage Tales of Beatrix Potter novels: The Tale of Holly How, 2005; editor: With Courage and Common Sense: Memoirs from the Older Women's Legacy Circles, 2003; contbr. articles to profl. jours. Danforth grad. fellow, 1967—72. Home and Office: PO Box 1616 Bertram TX 78605 E-mail: china@tstar.net.

ALBERTHAL, LESTER M., JR., retired information processing services executive; b. Corpus Christi, Tex., Feb. 27, 1944; married. BBA, U. Tex., 1967. With EDS, Plano, Tex., 1968—; v.p. ins. group Electronic Data Systems Corp., Plano, 1979-84, v.p. bus. ops. Dallas, from 1984, pres., 1986-96, CEO, 1987-99, also dir., chmn., 1989—. Office: Electronic Data Systems H2-7W-40 5400 Legacy Dr # 40 Plano TX 75024-3199

ALBERTINI, WILLIAM OLIVER, retired telecommunications industry executive; b. Mt. Carmel, Pa., June 29, 1943; s. William F. and Phyllis (Newman) A.; m. Katherine M. Keliher, Aug. 27, 1966; children: Elizabeth M., William O. Jr. BS, U. Notre Dame, 1965; MBA, Lehigh U., 1967; MS, MIT, 1982. With Bell of Pa., Harrisburg, 1967-83, dist. sales mgr. Allentown, 1973-74, dist. plant mgr., 1974-77, div. mgr. customer services Harrisburg, 1979-81, gen. pub. relations supr. community relations Phila., 1982-83; acctg. mgr. AT&T Co., Basking Ridge, N.J., 1977-79; dir. investor relations Bell Atlantic Corp., Phila., 1983-85, asst. v.p. bus. planning and fin. mgmt. network services div. Arlington, Va., 1985, v.p., sec., treas. Phila., 1985—. Exec. v.p., CFO Bell Atlantic Global Wireless, Phila., 1989-99; bd. mem. Triump Group, Black Rock, Inc., Airgas, Inc., Charming Shoppes, Am. Water Works Co. Bd. dirs. United Cerebal Palsy Campaign, Harrisburg, 1979-81, pres., 1980-81. Served as staff sgt. USAF, 1967-68. Fellow Soc. Sloan Fellows (bd. govs. 1982-86); mem. Stockholder Relations Soc. N.Y. (adv. bd. 1985—), Fin. Execs. inst. (adv. bd. 1985—, com. investment employee benefit assets). Clubs: Eagles Mere (Pa.) Country (bd. dirs. 1976—, pres. 1986—); Merion Golf (Ardmore, Pa.). Republican. Roman Catholic. Avocations: golf, tennis, platform tennis. Office: Bell Atlantic Corp 1717 Arch St Philadelphia PA 19103-2713

ALBERTS, BARRY S., lawyer; b. Chgo., Feb. 2, 1946; s. Irving and Evelyn Alberts; m. Susan Weinstein, Apr. 28, 1974; 1 child, Jaime Eliana. BA cum laude, Miami U., 1968; JD, U. Chgo., 1971. Bar: Ill. 1971, U.S. Dist. Ct. (no. dist.) Ill. 1971, U.S. Ct. Appeals (7th cir.) 1989, U.S. Ct. Appeals (6th cir.) 1996, U.S. Ct. Appeals (2d cir.) 1997. Ptnr. Schiff Hardin LLP, Chgo. Adj. prof. law Northwestern U. Law Sch., Chgo., 1991—98, Chgo., 2003; lectr. law U. Chgo. Law Sch., 1995—2005. Contbr. articles to profl. jours. Mem. bd. dirs. Chgo. Children's Choir, 2002—05. Mem. Am. Law Inst. (hon.), ABA (co-chair ethics and professionalism sect. litig. 1998-2002, trial evidence com., 1995-98, task force ethical guidelines settlement negotiations 2001-2002), Acad. Laureates Ill. Lawyers (hon., bd. regents), Ill. State Bar Assn. (hon.), Chgo. Bar Assn., Chgo. Coun. Lawyers, Lincoln-Am. Inn of Ct., Phi Beta Kappa. Office: Schiff Hardin LLP 6600 Sears Tower Chicago IL 60606-6473 Home: 200 Dempster St Evanston IL 60202-1406 Office Phone: 312-258-5611. Business E-Mail: balberts@schiffhardin.com.

ALBERTS, BRUCE MICHAEL, cell biologist, former foundation administrator; b. Chicago, Ill., Apr. 14, 1938; s. Harry C. and Lillian (Surasky) A.; m. Betty Neary, June 14, 1960; children: Beth L., Jonathan B., Michael B. AB in Biochemical Scis. summa cum laude, Harvard Coll., 1960; PhD in Biophysics, Harvard U., 1965. Postdoctoral fellow NSF Institut de Biologie Moleculaire, Geneva, 1965-66; asst. prof. dept. chemistry Princeton U., NJ, 1966-73, assoc. prof. dept. biochemical scis., 1971-73, Damon Pfeiffer prof. life scis., 1973-76; prof., vice chmn. dept. biochemistry and biophysics U. Calif., San Francisco, 1976-81, Am. Cancer Soc. Rsch. prof., 1981-85, prof., chmn., 1985-90, Am. Cancer Soc. Rsch. prof. of biochemistry, 1990-93; pres. NAS, Washington, 1993—2005; chmn. NRC, Washington, 1993—. Trustee Cold Spring Harbor Lab., 1972-75; adv. panel human cell biology NSF, 1974-76; adv. coun. dept. biochemical scis. and molecular biology Princeton U., 1979-85; chmn. vis. com. dept. biochemistry and molecular biology Harvard Coll., 1983-86; chmn. mapping and sequencing the human genome Nat. Rsch. Coun. Com., 1986-88; bd. sci. couns. divsn. arthritis and metabolic diseases NIH, 1974-78, molecular cytology study sect. 1982-86, chmn. 1984-86; program adv. com. NIH Human Genome Project, 1988-91; sci. adv. bd. Jane Coffin Childs Meml. Fund for Med. Rsch., 1978-85, Markey Found., 1984—, Fred Hutchinson Cancer Rsch. Ctr., Seattle, 1988—; com. mem. corp. vis. dept. biology MIT, 1978—, dept. embryology Carnegie Inst., Washington, 1983—; faculty rsch. lectr. U. Calif., San Francisco, 1985; sci. adv. com. Marine Biological Lab., Woods Hole, Mass., 1988—; bd. dirs. Genentech Rsch. Found., Fed. Am. Socs. for Experimental Biology; adv. bd. Bethesda Rsch. Labs. Life Tech. Inc., Nat. Sci. Resources Ctr., Smithsonian Inst., 1990—; com. mem. adolescence and young adulthood/sci. standards, Nat. Bd. Profl. Teaching Standards, 1991—. Co-author: The Molecular Biology of the Cell, 1989; editor: Mechanistic Studies of DNA Replication and Genetic Recombination, 1980; editorial bd. Jour. Biological Chemistry, 1976-82, Jour. Cell Biology, 1984-87; assoc. editor Annual Reviews Cell Biology, 1984—; essay editor Molecular Biology of the Cell, 1991—; contbr. numerous articles to profl. jours. including Saunders Sci. Publ., Current Sci., Ltd. Fellow NSF, 1960-65; recipient Eli Lilly award in biological chemistry Am. Chemical Soc., 1972, Baxter award for Disting. Rsch. in Biomedical Scis. Assn. Am. Med. Colls., 1992; named Lifetime Rsch. Prof. Am. Cancer Soc., 1980, Outstanding Vol. Coord. Calif. Sch. Vol. Partnership, 1993. Gairdner Found. Internat. award, 1995. Fellow AAAS; mem. NAS (commn. life scis. Nat. Rsch. Coun. 1988—, chmn. 1988-93, adv. bd. Nat. Sci. Resources Ctr. 1990—, Nat. Com. Sci. Edn. Standards and Assessment 1992—, com. mem. Nat. Edn. Support System for Tchrs. and Schs. 1992—, U.S. Steel Found. award 1975), Am. Chemical Soc., Am. Soc. for Cell Biology, Am. Soc. for Microbiology, Genetics Soc. Am., Am. Soc. Biochemistry and Molecular Biology (councilor 1984—), Am. Philos. Soc., European Molecular Biology Orgn. (assoc.), Phi Beta Kappa.*

ALBERTS, MARION EDWARD, retired physician; b. Hastings, Nebr., Mar. 14, 1923; s. Eddie and Mary Margaret (Hilbers) A.; m. Jeannette McDaniel, Dec. 25, 1944; children: Kathryn (dec.), Brian, Deborah, Timothy BA, U. Nebr., 1944, MD, 1948. Lic. Am. Bd. Pediatrics. Intern Iowa Meth. Hosp., Des Moines, 1948-49; resident in pediatrics Raymond Blank Hosp. Children, Des Moines, 1949-50, 52-53; practice medicine specializing in pediatrics Des Moines, 1953-88; ret., 1988. Chief pediatrics Mercy Hosp., 1953-69, 74-78, chief med. staff, 1966; mem. med. staff Iowa Luth. Hosp., 1953-88, Iowa Meth. Hosp., 1953-88, Broadlawns Polk County Hosp., 1983-88; instr. clin. pediatrics Coll. Osteo. Medicine and Surgery, 1970-82 Author: History of the Polk County Medical Society 1951-2001, 2003; sci. editor Iowa Medicine, 1971—97; contbr. articles to profl. jours. Pres. Polk County Tb and Respiratory Diseases Assn., 1965, 66, 70. Comdr. USNR, 1943-45, 50-52 (ret.) 1983. Recipient Whitaker Interstate Teaching award Interstate Postgrad. Med. Assn., 1980; Service award Sisters of Mercy, 1978 Fellow Am. Acad. Pediatrics, AMA (recognition awards 1969—), Iowa Med. Soc.; mem. Masons, Kiwanis. Presbyterian (elder). Home: 5991 Pommel Cir West Des Moines IA 50266-6324

ALBERTS, RENÉE MILLER, counselor, alcohol/drug abuse services professional; b. N.Y.C., Oct. 17, 1930; d. Julius and Bertha (Brookner) Miller; m. Henry Celler Alberts, Jan 13, 1950; children: Jo Alberts Lord, Nina Alberts Charnley, Hope Alberts Megonical, Jody Alberts Naleppa. BA, Queens Coll., 1950; MA, U. Va., 1979; postgrad., Va. Poly. U.; cert. in cmty. alcohol edn., Howard U., 1973. Cert. substance abuse counselor, Va.; lic. profl. counselor, Va. Substance abuse counselor, asst. dir., then acting dir. Fairfax Alcohol Safety Action Program, Va., 1972—89; substance abuse coord. Mt. Vernon Ctr. Cmty. Mental Health, Alexandria, Va., 1989—2001; overseer mental health, mental retardation and alcohol and drug svcs. Fairfax, Falls Church Cmty. Svcs. Bd., 2001—, chair mental health com., 2003—, vice chair, 2005—. V.p. Va. Coalition on Women, Alcohol and Drugs, Fairfax, 1985-96; mem. dual diagnosis subcom. Met. Washington Coun. Govts., 1990-2001; bd. apptd. Woman's Collaborative on HIV/AIDS, 1995-2001.

ALBERTSEN, PETER C., surgeon, educator; b. N.Y.C., Jan. 8, 1953; s. Torkild and Else Albertsen; m. Pamela S. Stanton, Mar. 10, 1979; children: Kristen, Karl. AB, Princeton U., 1974; MD, Columbia U., 1978; MS, U. Wis., 1990. Diplomate Am. Bd. Urology. Resident New Eng. Deaconess Hosp., Boston, 1978—80, Brady Urol. Inst., Johns Hopkins Hosp., Balt., 1980—84, instr., 1985—86; asst. prof. U. Conn. Health Ctr., Farmington, 1987—94, assoc. prof., 1994—2000, divsn. chief, residency program dir., 1995—, prof., 2000—. Mem. tech. assessment panel Nat. Blue Cross/Blue Shield, 1997—; mem. epidemiology and disease control study sect. NIH, 1986—89; mem. cause of death com. Nat. Cancer Inst., 1999—; chmn. ambulatory ops. com. Univ. Physicians, 1991—93, chmn. managed healthcare com., 1992—93, interim med. dir., 1993—96; bd. mem. Drug Utilization Rev. State of Conn. Dept. Income Maintenance, 1991—95; reviewer jours. in field; rschr. in field; trustee Am. Bd. Urology, 2000—. Mem. editl. bd. Urology, 1993—, Urology Times, 1993—, PDQ Screening and Prevention, 1997—, The Prostate Jour., 1997—; contbr. numerous articles to profl. jours., chapters to books. Grantee, Berlex Labs., 1991—94, USPHS, 1991—93, Covance/Merck Rsch. Labs., 1991—99, Pfizer, Inc., 1991—95, NIH, 1994—2001, Dept. Pub. Health and Addiction Svcs., 1995—96, Conn. Dept. Pub. Health, 1996—2001, Agy. Health Care Policy and Rsch., 1998—. Fellow AMA, Am. Coll. Genitourinary Surgeons, Am. Urol. Assn. (Conn. rep. to New Eng. sect. 1997-98, pres. New Eng. sect. 2004—), Am. Assn. Clin. Urologists (pres. 2005—), Hartford Med. Soc. (bd. dirs. 1994-2000, sec.-treas. 1996-97, v.p. 1997-98, pres. 1998-99, mem. com. on third party payors 1989-95). Office: U Conn Dept Surgery 263 Farmington Ave Farmington CT 06030-0002 E-mail: albertson@nso.ucnc.edu.

ALBERTSON, CHRISTIERN GUNNAR (CHRIS ALBERTSON), commentator, music critic, writer; b. Reykjavik, Iceland, Oct. 18, 1931; came to U.S., 1957, naturalized, 1963; s. Thordur and Yvonne (Broberg) A.; m. Hanne Elisabeth Christensen, 1954 (div. 1958). Student, Kent Coll., Canterbury, England, 1947-49; grad., Acad. Merc. Art, Copenhagen, 1952. Gen. mgr. Storyville Club, Copenhagen, 1952-54; prodr., writer U.S. Armed Forces Radio and TV, Iceland, 1954-57, WCAU Radio, Phila., 1957-58; disc jockey WHAT-RM Radio, Phila., 1958-60; prodr. Riverside Records, N.Y.C., 1960-62; continuity dir. WNEW Radio, N.Y.C., 1963-64; gen. mgr. WBAI-FM Radio, N.Y.C., 1964-66; dir. BBC programs Hartwest Prodns., N.Y.C., 1966-67; co-prodr., host weekly TV series The Jazz Set, PBS Network, 1972-73; pres. Video One, Inc., 1976-79; prodr., co-host weekly cable TV series Doin' It, 1976-77; entertainment editor Beauty Trade Mag., 1978-79; prodr. Bessie Smith blues series Columbia Records, 1970; U.S. jazz reporter Danish Radio, 1972-75; U.S. music corr. Berlingske Tidende, Copenhagen, 1960-64. Talent cons. Dupont Show of Week, 1961. Author: Bessie-Biography of Bessie Smith, 1972, rev. edit., 2003, Empress of the Blues, 1974; contbg. author: Bluesland, 1992, Jazz: A Listener's Companion, 2000; contbg. editor: Oxford Biographical Encyclopedia of Jazz, 1998; writer story and script The Alberta Hunter Story, TV mini-series, 1980, (film) Really The Blues, 1997, (TV documentary, DVD) My Castle's Rockin', 1988, The Story of Jazz, 1994; contbg. editor Stereo Review, 1973-99, A Plus Mag., 1983-96, Sound & Vision, 1999-2000; editl. cons. Routes Mag., 1978-80, 91-95; contbr. articles to Down Beat, Saturday Rev., Rolling Stone, N.Y. Times, Jazz Forum, Sound & Image, MacWeek, N.Y. Amsterdam News, Timeline, others; assoc. producer, cons. (film) Bessie, 1974; music cons. (film) Buddy Can You Spare A Dime, 1974. Mem. adv. bd. N.Y. Jazz Mus., 1972-75. Recipient Grand Prix du Disque, Montreux Jazz Festival, 1971, Trendsetter of Yr. award Billboard, 1971, CEBA award for distinction, 1964, Critics Poll Best Liner Notes award Living Blues Mag., 1993. Mem. Nat. Acad. Rec. Arts & Scis. (Grammy award 1971, Trustees award 1971, Grammy nominations 1977, 97). Address: 444 Central Park W New York NY 10025-4378 E-mail: calbertson@nyc.rr.com.

ALBERTSON, CHRISTOPHER ADAM, librarian; b. Oak Park, Ill., Dec. 10, 1951; Student, U. New Orleans, 1969—70; BA magna cum laude, U. Tex.-Arlington, 1972; MLS, N. Tex. State U., 1973. Cataloger Orange (Tex.) Pub. Libr., 1974-75, asst. libr., 1975-79, city libr., 1979-81, Tyler (Tex.) Libr., 1981—. Contbr. articles to profl. jours. Mem. ALA, ASPA, Am. Mgmt. Assn., Am. Soc. Info. Sci., Tex. Libr. Assn., Rotary. Presbyterian. Home: 3100 Pounds Ave Tyler TX 75701-8034 Office: Tyler Pub Library 201 S College Ave Tyler TX 75702-7381 Office Phone: 903-593-7323. Business E-Mail: citylibn@tylertexas.com.

ALBERTSON, JOSEPH LESTER, JR., lawyer; b. Mar. 13, 1933; s. Joseph Lester and Ethel Sanford (Martin) A.; m. Jennie Holmes Snider, Jan. 31, 1958; children: Joseph Lester III, Margaret C., Jennie H.S. AB, Williams Coll., 1954; LLB; JD, N. Law Sch., 1958. Bar: N.Y. 1958, U.S. Dist. Ct. (so. dist.) N.Y. 1962, U.S. Tax Ct. 1965. Ptnr. Albertson, Simmons & Albertson, New Rochelle, 1990—. Dir. Chase Manhattan, N.B.W., N.Y. Bd. govs. New Rochelle Hosp. Med. Ctr., 1968+, New Rochelle Day Nursery, 1965-90, Home for Aged of New Rochelle, 1962-70; chmn. Larchmont Village Traffic Commn., 1973; trustee Boys Club New Rochelle, 1969 +1 . Mem. ABA, N.Y. State Bar Assn., Westchester County Bar Assn., New Rochelle Bar Assn., Phi Delta Phi, Williams Club, Boca Grande Club. Home: PO Box 1997 Boca Grande FL 33921-1997 Office: 271 North Ave New Rochelle NY 10801-5104

ALBERTSON, TERRY L., lawyer; b. Montebello, Calif., Nov. 15, 1946; s. Vern G. and June L. (Wodei) A.; m. Kathleen A. Blackburn, June 3, 1968; children: Sarah, Andrew. AB magna cum laude, Georgetown U., 1968; AM, Yale U., 1969; JD, Harvard U., 1974. Ptnr. Crowell & Moring, Washington, 1974—. Contbr. articles to profl. jours. Sgt. U.S. Army, 1969-71, Vietnam. Named one of leading govt. contract lawyers in Washington, Legal Times. Office: Crowell & Moring 1001 Pennsylvania Ave NW Fl 10 Washington DC 20004-2595

ALBERTY, ROBERT ARNOLD, chemistry professor; b. Winfield, Kans., June 21, 1921; s. Luman Harvey and Mattie (Arnold) Alberty; m. Lillian Jane Wind, May 22, 1944; children: Nancy Lou, Steven Charles, Catherine Ann. BS, U. Nebr., 1943, MS, 1944; PhD, U. Wis., 1947; DSc (hon.), U. Nebr., 1967, Lawrence U., 1967. Engaged in rsch. blood plasma fractionation for U.S. Govt., 1944—46; mem. faculty U. Wis., 1946—67, prof. chemistry, 1955—67, assoc. dean letters and sci., 1961—63, dean Grad. Sch., 1963—67; prof. chemistry MIT, 1967—91, dean Sch. Sci., 1967—82, prof. emeritus, 1991—. Cons. NSF, 1958—83, NIH, 1962—72; chmn. commn. on human resources NRC, 1974—77; dir. Colt Industries, 1978—88, Inst. for Def. Analysis, 1980—86; pres. phys. chemistry divsn. Internat. Union Pure and Applied Chemistry, 1991—93. Co-author: Experimental Physical Chemistry, 1970, Thermodynamics of Biochemical Reactions, 2003, Physical Chemistry, 2005. Recipient Eli Lilly award biol. chemistry, 1955; fellow Guggenheim, Calif. Inst. Tech., 1950—51. Fellow: AAAS; mem.: NAS, Am. Acad. Arts and Scis. (coun. 1991—94, 2003—), Am. Chem. Soc. (chmn. com. on chemistry and pub. affairs 1978—80), Inst. Medicine, Sigma Xi, Phi Beta Kappa. Home: 931 Massachusetts Ave Cambridge MA 02139-3171 Office: MIT 77 Massachusetts Ave Rm 6-215 Cambridge MA 02139-4307

ALBIN, BARRY G., lawyer, rabbi; b. Wichita, Kans., Sept. 6, 1948; s. Frederick Eugene Albin and Eloise Nelda Riley; m. Marianne Kay Olish, Aug. 8, 1970 (div. Feb. 1997); children: Thomas C., Michael A., Benjamin J., Joshua S. BA, U. Kans., 1970, JD, 1973; cert. in data processing, Kansas City C.C., 1981. Bar; Kans. 1973, U.S. Dist. Ct. Kans. 1973. Staff counsel Wyandotte Legal Aid Soc., Kansas City, Kans., 1974-76; pvt. practice Kansas City, 1976-83, 85—; gen. mgr. Chameleon Dental Products, Kansas City, 1983-85; grand hierophant, CEO Modern Rite of Memphis, Inc., 2002. Lectr. bus. law Maple Woods C.C., Kansas City, Mo., 1978; staff counsel Kans. State Dept. Social and Rehab. Svcs., Kansas City, 1986-91; legal counsel Mid. Am. Gay Ecumenical Found., Kansas City, Mo., 1975-80, Phylaxis Soc., 1999-2005, N.E. Kans. Valley, AASR, 1995—, Chi Rho Fraternity, Grand Tribune, 2001-05; bd. Strawberry Hill Neighborhood Assn., Inc.; steering com. Kans. City Downtown Shareholders; pres. Bus. of Strawberry Hill, Inc.; energetic healer and exorcist. Author: Climbing Jacob's Ladder, 1981, Believers Commentary on Mark, 1985, Believers Commentary on Barnabas, 1986, Catechism of Nasorean Church, 1995. Mebbaker rabbi Nasorean Orthodox Qahal, Kansas City, 1985—; rabbi Congregation B'nai Or; state treas. Green Party, 2000—02; bd. dirs. Wyandotte Interfaith Sponsoring Coun., 2004—. Mem. Internat. Soc. Study of Subtle Energies and Energy Medicine, Common Cause (state sec. 1978, state v.p. 1978-79), Inst. Noetic Sci., Masons (various offices 1989—), Dist. Dep. Grand Master of 4th Dist. Kans., Scottish Rite (33d degree), York Rite (Knight York Cross of Honor), Masonic Brotherhood of Blue Forget-Me-Not, Blue Lodge. Democrat. Avocations: computers, reading, hiking, teaching, scripture. Office Phone: 913-342-1986. E-mail: balbin@kc.rr.com.

ALBIN, BARRY TODD, state supreme court justice; b. Bklyn., July 7, 1952; m. Inna Albin; 2 children. BA with high honors, Rutgers U., 1973; JD, Cornell U., 1976. Bar: N.H. 1976, U.S. Supreme Ct. 1984, U.S. Ct. Appeals (3d cir.) 1985. Dep. atty. gen. N.J. Div. Criminal Justice, Trenton, 1976-78; asst. prosecutor Passaic County, Paterson, NJ, 1978-79, Middlesex County, New Brunswick, NJ, 1979-82; assoc. Wilentz, Goldman & Spitzer, Woodbridge, NJ, 1982—86, partner, 1986—99; judge NJ Supreme Ct., 2002—. Pres. NJ Assn. of Criminal Defense Lawyers, 1999—2000; mem. NJ Supreme Ct. Criminal Practice Com., 1987—92. Trustee Nat. Conf. of Christians and Jews, Edison, N.J., 1986. Mem. N.J. Bar Assn., Middlesex County Bar Assn. Office: Richard J Hughes Complex PO Box 970 25 W Market St Trenton NJ 08625-0970

ALBIN, KELLI JEAN, art educator, artist; b. West Plains, Mo., Nov. 14, 1965; d. Forest Porter and Mary Maxine Albin. BA in Comml. Art, Oral Roberts U., 1987; M in Elem. Edn., SW Mo. State U., 1997. Cert. art and spl. reading K-12 tchr. Color separator Rainbow Colorworks, West Plains, 1987—90; art tchr. West Plains Elem., 1990—92; mem. libr. staff West Plains Pub. Libr., 1992—97; art tchr. Howell Valley Sch., West Plains, 1993—97, Dora (Mo.) R-3 Schs., 1997—. Photographs, paintings, drawings, (1st pl. ribbon, 1987, 2004). Mem.: Nat. Art Edn. Assn. Avocations: photography, painting, drawing. Office: Dora R-3 PO Box 17 Dora MO 65637

ALBIN, LESLIE OWENS, biology professor; b. Spur, Tex., Jan. 8, 1940; s. John Leslie and Ottie Maude (Lassetter) A.; m. Monta Kay Gragg, Sept. 3, 1961 (div. 1982); children: Leslie Susan Albin Gann, Kimberly Ann Albin. BA, McMurry Coll., Abilene, 1962; MA, N. Tex. State U., 1969. Instr. biology E. Cen. State U., Ada, Okla., 1969-71; rsch. assoc. M.D. Andrson Hosp. & Tumor Inst., Houston, 1971; asst. prof. biology Western Tex. Coll., Snyder, 1971-74, assoc. prof. biology, 1974-77; prof. Austin (Tex.) C.C., 1977—, chmn. divsn. natural scis., 1978-95, head dept. biology, 1977-97. NDEA fellow, 1968. Mem. Am. Inst. Biol. Scis., Faculty Assn. Western Tex. Coll. (pres. 1973-74), Faculty Assn. Austin C.C. (pres. 1987-88), Faculty Senate Austin C.C., Tex. C.C. Tchrs. Assn., Tex. Acad. Sci., Am. Soc. for Microbiology, Alpha Chi. Office: Austin Community Coll Cypress Creek Campus 1555 Cypress Creek Rd Cedar Park TX 78613-3607 Business E-Mail: lesalbin@austincc.edu.

ALBINO, JOSEPH XAVIER, writer, educator, photographer; b. Syracuse, N.Y., Mar. 19, 1937; s. Samuel and Frances Carmella Albino; m. Mary Louise Albino, July 30, 1960; children: Mary Susan, Anne Louise, Christine Francesca, Julie Marie, Melody Jo. BA English, Le Moyne Coll., Syracuse, N.Y., 1959; MS in English Edn./Composition, Syracuse U., 1983. English educator and writer/photographer various colls., Cortland, Morrisville, and Herkimer, NY, 1982—; photographer/writer Fortune 500 firms, 1960—80. Vol. Mental Health Assn. of Onondaga County, Syracuse, NY, 1995—2001; amateur radio operator K2GWO; consecrated mem. OPUS Santorum Angelorum, 1988—. Roman Catholic. Avocations: hiking, canoeing, swimming, amateur radio operator. Home: 221 Hillbrook Road Syracuse NY 13217 Mailing: PO Box 21 Camillus NY 13031 Office Phone: 315-487-5710. E-mail: saintjoe@dreamscape.com.

ALBINO, JUDITH ELAINE NEWSOM, university president; b. Jackson, Tenn. m. Salvatore Albino; children: Austin, Adrian. BJ, U. Tex., 1967, PhD, 1973. Mem. faculty sch. dental medicine SUNY, Buffalo, 1972-90, assoc. provost, 1984-87, dean sch. arch. and planning, 1987-89, dean grad. sch., 1989-90; v.p. acad. affairs and rsch, dean system grad. sch. U. Colo., Boulder, 1990-91, pres., 1991-95, pres. emerita, prof. psychiatry, 1995-97; pres. Calif. Sch. Profl. Psychology Alliant Internat. U., San Francisco, 1997—. Contbr. articles to profl. jours. Acad. Adminstrn. fellow Am. Coun. on Edn., 1983; grantee NIH. Fellow APA (treas., bd. dirs.); mem. Behavioral Scientists in Dental Rsch. (past pres.), Am. Assn. Dental Rsch. (bd. dirs.). Fax: 415-771-5908. E-mail: jalbino@alliant.edu.

ALBOM, MITCH DAVID, sports columnist; b. Passaic, N.J., May 23, 1958; s. Ira and Rhoda Albom. BA in Sociology, Brandeis U., 1979; M in Journalism, Columbia U., 1981, M in Bus. Adminstrn., 1982. Sportswriter, Ft. Lauderdale News and Sun-Sentinel, Florida, Panelist, ESPN's Sports Reporters, feature reporter, ESPN-TV, contributing commentator, ESPN radio, WLLZ-FM, Detroit, sports director, 1985-, sports columnist, Detroit Free Press, 1985-, Sunday Sports Albom, co-host, 1988-, WDIV-TV, Detroit, broadcaster and commentator, 1987. Author: (book) The Live Album, 1988, The Live Albom II, 1990, The Live Albom III, 1992, Tuesdays With Morrie, 1997, The Five People You Meet In Heaven, 2003; co-author Bo: The Bo Schembecher Story, 1989; playwright: And The Winner Is, (Purple Rose Theatre, Chelsea, Mich.), 2005. Chmn. Hospice Mich. Fundraising, 1987—; speaker, vol. Heart Assn. Mich., 1985—, Am. Cancer Soc. Mich. Pub. Broadcasting, 1985—. Named #1 Sports Columnist in U.S.A. AP Sports Editors, 1987, 88, 89, #1 Sports Columnist in Mich. AP and UPI, 1985, 86, 87, 88, #1 Sports News Story in U.S.A., 1985, #1 Sports Columnist in Mich. United Press Internat., 1986, 87, 88, #1 Sports Columnist in Mich. Nat. Assn. Sportswriters and Broadcasters, 1988, 89, #2 Outstanding Writer Nat. Headliners award, 1989. Mem. Baseball Writers Am., Football Writers Am., Tennis Writers Am. Avocation: former musician. Office: Detroit Free Press Inc 600 W 4th St Detroit MI 48226*

ALBRACHT, JUDITH MARIE, elementary school educator; b. Carlinville, Ill., Jan. 20, 1951; s. Adolph Selvo and Winifred Louise Otwell; m. Robert D Albracht, July 3, 1969; children: Renee Marie Stein, Kelley Ann Maintz. BS in cum laude, Southern Ill. U., 1974, MS, 1990. Chpt. math instr. Hillsboro Unit Schools, Ill., 1975—80, tchr., 1980—. Pres. La Seitoma, 1980. Mem.: Ill. Fedn. Teachers (bd. mem. 1980—2005). Democrat. Cath. Avocations: travel, antiques, reading, gardening. Home: 532 Lakeside Knolls Dr Hillsboro IL 62049

ALBRECHT, CHRIS, broadcast executive; b. Queens, NY, July 24, 1952; BA in Dramatic Lit., Hofstra U., 1973. Talent mgmt. consultant ABC, N.Y.C., 1975; talent agent Internat. Creative Mgmt., Los Angeles, Calif., 1980—85; sr. v.p. original programming, West Coast HBO Pictures, Los Angeles, Calif., 1985—90; pres. HBO Independent Productions, Los Angeles, Calif., 1990—95; pres. original programming HBO Pictures, N.Y.C., 1995—2002, chmn., CEO, 2002—. Bd. dirs. Museum of TV & Radio, 2003—. Mem.: Am. Film Inst. (bd. trustees). Office: HBO Pictures 1100 Ave of Americas New York NY 10036

ALBRECHT, KATHE HICKS, art historian, visual resources manager; b. Ann Arbor, Mich., Aug. 21, 1952; d. Richard Brian and Mafalda (Brasile) Hicks; m. Mark Jennings Albrecht, July 20, 1973; children: Nicole, Alexander, Olivia. BA in Art History, UCLA, 1975; MA in Art History, Am. U., 1989. Slide libr. asst. Am. U., Washington, 1986—88, visual resources curator, 1991—; pres.-elect Visual Resources Assn., 2003, pres., 2004—. Co-coord. Mus. Ednl. Site Licensing Project (Nat. Initiative Getty), 1994; presenter Southeastern Coll. Art Conf., Georgetown U., 1995, Richmond, Va., 1997, Norfolk, Va., 1999; mem. Conf. on Fair Use (Dept. of Commerce) VRA rep. to Digital Future Coalition, 1996—; mem. Nat. Initiative for a Networked Cultural Heritage, 1996-2003. Vol. Fairfax County Pub. Sch. Sys., 1980-2000; re-election com. Rep. Nat. Com., Washington, 1984; Rep. precinct worker Mason dist., 1980s. Grantee Getty Art History Info. Program, 1994-97; Am. U. (image processing, database devel.), 1995, 2003. Mem.: Visual Resources Assn. (pres. Mid-Atlantic region 1995—96, 2000—02, chair nat. membership com. 1995—97, chair intellectual property rights com. 1996—2000, pres.-elect 2003—04, pres. 2004—), Southeastern Coll. Art Conf., Am. Assn. Mus., Coll. Art Assn., Art Librs. Soc. N. Am. Presbyterian. Avocation: antique and prints collecting. Office: Am Univ 4400 Massachusetts Ave NW Washington DC 20016-8001 Office Phone: 202-885-1675. E-mail: kalbrec@american.edu.

ALBRECHT, RALPH P., lawyer; b. Watertown, NY; BS, Va. Polytechnic Inst. and State Univ., 1989; JD, George Mason U., 1997. Bar: DC 1997, Ct. Appeals for Fed. Cir. 1999, US Patent and Trademark Office. Mem. Sterne, Kessler, Goldstein & Fox; rschr. IBM Corp., 1985—97; ptnr., co-chair Patent Prosecution Practice Group, mem. Intellectual Property Litig. Dept. Venable LLP, Washington, DC. Contbr. articles tp profl. jours. Mem.: ABA, Capital Telecom. Profls., Am. Intellectual Property Law Assn., Patent, Trademark and Copyright Sect., Bar Assn. of DC (chair 2003—04, exec. coun. mem., newsletter editor, Outstanding Svcs. Award 1999, 2000, 2002). Office: Venable LLP 575 7th St NW Washington DC 20004 Office Phone: 202-344-8166. Office Fax: 202-344-8300. E-mail: rpalbrecht@venable.com.

ALBRECHT, RICHARD RAYMOND, retired manufacturing executive, lawyer; b. Storm Lake, Iowa, Aug. 29, 1932; s. Arnold Louis and Catherine Dorothea (Boettcher) A.; m. Constance Marie Berg, June 16, 1957; children: John Justin, Carl Arnold, Richard Louis, Henry Berg. BA, U. Iowa, 1958, JD with highest honors, 1961. Bar: Wash. 1961. Assoc. Perkins, Coie, Stone, Olsen & Williams, Seattle, 1961-67, ptnr., 1968-74; gen. counsel U.S. Dept. Treasury, Washington, 1974-76; v.p., gen. counsel, sec. Boeing Co., Seattle, 1976-81, v.p. fin., contracts and internat. bus., 1981-83, v.p., gen. mgr. Everett div., 1983-84; exec. v.p. Boeing Comml. Airplane Group, Seattle, 1984-97, sr. advisor, 1997-2000. Bd. dirs. Esterline Technologies Corp., Wash. Dental Svc. Mem. bd. regents Wash. State U., 1987-2000. With AUS, 1955-58. Recipient Outstanding Citizen of Yr. award Seattle-King County Municipal League, 1968-69, Disting. Alumni award U. Iowa, 2002. Mem. ABA, Wash. State Bar Assn., Am. Judicature Soc., Order of St. John (officer 1992-99, comdr. 1999-04, knight 2004-), Order of Coif, Rainier Club, Broadmoor Golf Club, Wing Point Golf Club, Seattle Tennis Club, Sigma Nu, Omicron Delta Kappa, Phi Delta Phi. Home: PO Box 10669 Bainbridge Island WA 98110 Office: Perkins Coie LLP 1201 3rd Ave Ste 4800 Seattle WA 98101-3099 Office Phone: 206-855-8896. Business E-Mail: dick@albrecht.net.

ALBRECHT, RONALD FRANK, anesthesiologist; b. Chgo., Apr. 17, 1937; s. Frank William and Mabel Dorothy (Cassens) A.; children: Ronald Frank II, Mark Burchfield, Meredith Ann. AB, U. Ill., 1958, BS, 1959, MD, 1961. Diplomate Am. Bd. Anesthesiology. Intern U. Cin. Hosp., 1961-62; resident in anesthesiology U. Ill. Hosp., Chgo., 1962-64, attending physician, 1966-73, 89—; clin. assoc. NIH, Bethesda, Md., 1964-66; practice medicine specializing in anesthesiology Chgo., 1966—; asst. prof. anesthesiology U. Ill., Chgo., 1966-70, clin. assoc. prof., 1970-73, prof. anesthesiology, head dept. Coll. Medicine, 1989—; chief dept. anesthesiology U. Ill. Hosp., Chgo., 1989—, pres. med. staff, 1999-2001. Chmn. dept. anesthesiology Michael Reese Med. Ctr., Chgo., 1971—; prof. anesthesiology U. Chgo., 1973-89. Contbr. articles to profl. jours. Served to lt. comdr. USPHS, 1964-66. Fellow Am. Coll. Anesthesiologists; mem. AMA, Internat. Anesthesia Rsch. Soc., Am. Soc. Anesthesiologists, Assn. Anesthesists Gt. Britain and Ireland, Am. Physiol. Soc., Soc. Acad. Anesthesiology Chairs, Assn. Anesthesiology Program Dirs. (pres. 1991-93), Ill. Soc. Anesthesiologists (pres. 1980-81), Ill. State Med. Soc., Chgo. Med. Soc., Chgo. Soc. Anesthesiologists (pres. 1986-90), Assn. Univ. Anesthesiologists. Presbyterian. Home: 1020 Chestnut Ave Wilmette IL 60091-1732 Office: U Ill Chgo Coll Medicine Dept Anesthesiology MC/515 1740 W Taylor St Ste 3200 Chicago IL 60612-7239 Office Phone: 312-996-4020. Business E-Mail: ralbrech@uic.edu.

ALBRECHT, RONALD LEWIS, financial services executive; b. Derby, Conn., Dec. 30, 1935; s. Lewis Davis and Gladys Imogene (Spear) A.; m. Mikyong Kim, Dec. 28, 1968; children: Rondi Kim, Kathryn Lynn, Karen Ann. BS in Agr., U. Vt., 1957; BBA in Bus. Mgmt., Baylor U., 1966; MA in Bus. Mgmt., Cen. Mich. U., 1975. Commd. 2d lt. USAF, 1957, advanced through grades to lt. col., 1973, comdr. detachment Sioux City AB, Iowa, 1957—60, air traffic control officer Cheveston, England, 1960—62, dir. air traffic control HQ12 Waco, Tex., 1962—66, comdr. detachment Kimpo AB, Republic of Korea, 1967—68, comdr. squadron Sewart AFB Tenn., 1969—70, comdr. squadron Holloman AFB, 1970—73, staff officer, air traffic control HQ air force systems command Andrews AFB, 1973—75, dep. comdr. group Pentagon, 1975—77, staff officer electronics HQ joint staff Yongson, Republic of Korea, 1977—79, staff officer air traffic control communications area Rome, NY, 1979—80, retired, 1980; real estate broker Bangor, Maine, 1980—; retirement, investment and fin. planning exec. Bangor (Maine) Savs. Bank, 1981—87; pres. Maine Fin. Mgmt. Svcs.,Inc. and Albrecht Fin. Svcs., P.A., Bangor, 1987—. Instr. Los Angeles Community Coll., Seoul, Korea, 1977-79, Husson Coll. Bangor, 1981-84. Mem. loaned exec. bd. div. planning com. United Way of Penobscot Valley, Bangor, 1981—, Rep. Party, Bangor, 1981—. Hood Dairy scholar U. Vt., 1955. Mem. Fin. Planning Assn. (v.p. programs, co-founder 1985, pres. Maine chpt. 1988-89), Inst. Cert. Fin. Planners, Internat. Cert. Fin. Planners (bd. standards and practices), Ret. Officers Assn., Am. Assn. Ret. Persons, Air TrafficControl Assn., Armed Forces Communications Electronics Assn., Kiwanis (2d and 1st v.p. Bangor Club, pres. 1987-88), Masons, Anah Temple, Valley of Tokyo, Orientof Japan and Korea. Avocations: reading, hiking, gardening, travel. Office Phone: 207-945-5533. E-mail: rla@midmaine.com.

ALBRECHT, STAN LEROY, academic administrator, sociologist, educator; b. Fremont, Utah, July 13, 1942; s. Rex LeRoy and Alta (Taylor) A.; m. Joyce Van Wagoner; children: Sheri, Michael, Bryant, Rachelle, Stacia. BS, Brigham Young U., 1966; MA, Wash. State U., 1968, PhD, 1970. Asst. prof. Utah State U., Logan, 1970-74, exec. v.p., provost, 2000—05, pres., 2005—; assoc. prof. Brigham Young U., Provo, Utah, 1974-78, prof., 1978—, dean, 1988-89, acad. v.p., 1989. Vis. asst. prof. SUNY, Albany, 1973. Author: Social Psychology, 1981, 87, Divorce and Remarriage, 1980, Research Methods, 1984. Mem. Am. Sociol. Assn., Rural Sociol. Soc. (v.p. 1986). Democrat. Mem. Lds Ch. Avocations: hiking, fishing. Office: Utah State U 1420 Old Main Hill Logan UT 84322-1420 Home: 818 E Summit Dr Smithfield UT 84335

ALBRECHT, THOMAS W., lawyer; b. Coral Gables, Fla., July 6, 1954; BA summa cum laude, U. Dayton, 1975; JD cum laude, U. Chgo., 1979. Bar: Ill. 1979. Ptnr. Sidley Austin Brown & Wood, Chgo., co-head, global securitization and structured fin. practice group, mng. ptnr. Chgo. office, and mem. mgmt. and exec. committees. Contbr. articles to profl. journals. Recipient Hinton Moot Ct. Cup. Mem. ABA, Chgo. Bar Assn., Am. Coll. of Comml. Fin. Lawyers, Order Coif. Office: Sidley Austin Brown & Wood LLP Bank One Plz 10 S Dearborn St Chicago IL 60603 Office Phone: 312-853-7213. Office Fax: 312-853-7036. Business E-Mail: talbrecht@sidley.com.

ALBRECHT, WILLIAM PRICE, economist, educator, government official; b. Pitts., Jan. 7, 1935; s. William Price and Jane Lanier (Moses) A.; m. Alice Annette Cooper, June 14, 1956 (div. Nov. 1975); children— William, Alison, Jonathan, Jeffrey; m. Fran Jaecques, July 4, 1976 AB, Princeton U., 1956; MA, U. S.C., 1962, Yale U., 1963, PhD, 1965. Asst. prof. U. Iowa, Iowa City, 1965-70, assoc. prof., 1970-82, prof. econs., 1982-88, assoc. dean Coll. Bus. Adminstrn., 1984-88; self-employed antitrust cons., 1978-88; commr. Commodity Futures Trading Commn., Washington, 1988-93; prof. econs. U. Iowa, Iowa City, 1993—, dir. Inst. for Internat. Bus., 1998—2003, Justice prof. Internat. Bus., 2000—. TV fin. advisor. Author: Economics, 1974, 4th edit., 1986, Black Employment, 1970, Microeconomic Principles, 1979, Macroeconomic Principles, 1979 Candidate U.S. Ho. of Reps., 1970; legis. asst. U.S. Senator Dick Clark, 1974. Served to lt. USN, 1956-61 Mem. Am. Econ. Assn., Midwest Econ. Assn. (v.p. 1981-82). Avocations: tennis, farming. Home: 5770 NE Morse Rd Solon IA 52333-8806 Office: U Iowa Dept Econs Iowa City IA 52242 Office Phone: 319-335-3125. Business E-Mail: william-albrecht@uiowa.edu.

ALBRETHSEN, ADRIAN EDYSEL, metallurgist, consultant; b. Carey, Idaho, June 20, 1929; s. Norman Carl and Dollie Gustina (Brown) A.; m. Joan Alice Phelan, July 8, 1961; children: Thomas, Eric, Carl. BS in Mining Engring., U. Idaho, 1952, MSMetE, 1958; PhD in Mineral Engring., MIT, 1963. Analytical chemist Bunker Hill Co., Kellogg, Idaho, 1954-55; mining engr. Anaconda Co., Butte, Mont., 1955-57; rsch. asst. MIT, Cambridge, 1958-63; sr. engr. GE, Richland, Wash., 1963-65; sr. rsch. engr. Battelle Meml. Inst., Richland, Wash., 1965-66, ASARCO, Inc., South Plainfield, N.J., 1966-86; plant metallurgist Nord Ilmenite Corp., Jackson, N.J., 1989-92; cons. pvt. practice, Bridgewater, N.J., 1986—. 1st lt. USAF, 1952-54, Korea. Mem. ASM Internat., Soc. Mining Engrs., Sigma Xi. Avocation: gardening. Home: 485 Vicki Dr Bridgewater NJ 08807-1941

ALBRIGHT, GIFFORD HARRY, retired architectural engineering educator, consultant; b. Pottsville, Pa., Feb. 14, 1931; s. Harry Clayton and Grace Reinhart Albright. BArch in Engring., Pa. State U., 1953; MS, MIT, 1955. Rsch. projects dir. U.S. Naval Civil Engrs. Corps, Washington, 1956—58; prof. archtl. engring. Pa. State U., University Park, 1958—91, dept. head archtl. engring., 1962—83; program dir. NSF, Washington, 1983—88; prof. ermeritus archtl. engring. Pa. State U., 1991—. Bldg. rsch. cons. G. H. Albright Assocs., State College, 1958—. Author: (technical publication) Planning Atomic Shelters- A Handbook. Chair, bldg. code appeals bd. Borough of State Colege, State College, Pa., 1965—68; councilman Triangle Nat. Frat., Plainfield, Ind., 1982—86; pres. PS Alumni Chpt., Triangle Frat., 1965—69. Lt. j.g. USNR. Mem.: Am. Concrete Inst., Earthquake Engring. Rsch. Inst., Am. Soc. Heating, Ventilation and Refrigeration Engrs., Constrn. Specification Inst. (advisor 2004—), Pa. State Ret. Faculty Staff Club (pres. 2004—), Pa. State Faculty Staff Club (pres. 1998—99). Home: P O Box 196 State College PA 16804-0196 Personal E-mail: gha1@psu.edu.

ALBRIGHT, JACK LAWRENCE, animal science and veterinary educator; b. San Francisco, Mar. 14, 1930; s. George Clarence and Elizabeth Ann (Murphy) A.; m. Lorraine Aylmer Hughes, Aug. 17, 1957; children: Maryann A. Williams, Amy Elizabeth Schalk. BS with honors, Calif. State Poly. U., 1952; MS, Wash. State U., 1954, PhD, 1957. Rsch. asst. Wash. State U., 1952-54, 55-57, acting instr., 1954-55; instr. Calif. State Poly. U., 1955, 57-59; asst. prof. U. Ill., Urbana, 1959-63; assoc. prof. Purdue U., West Lafayette, Ind., 1963-66, prof. animal sci. Sch. Agr., 1966-96, prof. animal mgmt. and behavior Sch. Vet. Medicine, 1974-96, prof. emeritus animal sci. and vet. medicine, 1996—. Mem. Ctr. Applied Ethoiogy and Human-Animal Interactions, Human/Animal Bond Purdue U., 1982-96, Purdue Interdisciplinary Undergrad. Program in Animal Welfare and Societal Concerns, 1992-96, Purdue Animal Care and Use com., 1989-92, Ctr. for Rsch. on Livestock Behavior and Well-Being in Food Animals, 1992-96; vis. prof. U. Ariz., Tucson, 1995, N.Mex. State U., Las Cruces, 1995, U. Ill., Urbana, 1988-89; vis. prof. pure and applied zoology U. Reading, Eng., 1977-78; vis. scientist N.Z. Dept. Agr., Ruakura, Hamilton, 1971-72, Dairy Shrine, Ft. Atkinson, Wis., 1958—; cons., lectr. in field, animal mgmt., behavior, care and welfare; mem. Ind. Commn. Farm Animal Care, 1981-99; numerous invited lectures worldwide. Author more than 900 papers, revs., chpts., guidelines, and books; reviewer sci. jours. Vestryman St. John's Episcopal Ch., Lafayette, Ind., 1979-82; bellringer Salvation Army, 1964—; mem. judging teams Cal Poly Dairy Cattle, Dairy Products and Livestock; vol. Ind. Livestock Care Assistance Project Helpline, 1999—, Heifer Project Internat., Hoofed Animal Humane Soc. Fulbright scholar, N.Z., 1971-72; NSF Animal Behavior grantee, summer 1964; USDA/FAS/ICD Sci. and Tech. Exch. Program awardee to Rep. of Ireland, 1994; recipient Guardian award Ind. Vet. Med. Assn., 1995, Sci., Edn. and Tech. award dept. animal scis. Washington State U., 1996; one of 7 named to inaugural Renaissance Acad. Hall of Fame, Paso Robles H.S., 1998. Fellow AAAS, Am. Dairy Sci. Assn., Ind. Acad. Sci.; mem. Am. Dairy Sci. Assn. (sec. 1972-73, chmn. profl. coun. 1973-74, Dairy Mgmt. Rsch. award 1986, invited lectrs. ann. meeting, 1982, 86-87, 92, 94, found. charter 1992), Animal Behavior Soc. (charter), Am. Soc. Animal Sci. (chmn. animal behavior com. 1970, 76, 85, Animal Mgmt. Rsch. award 1988, Found. charter 1993, animal care com. 1994-96), Am. Registry Profl. Animal Sci. (dairy and animal behavior 1993—), Humane Slaughter Assn., Am. Coll. Animal Behavior Sci. (cert., charter, diplomate 1995), Am. Soc. Vet. Ethology (charter), Internat. Soc. Applied Ethology, Chillingham Wild Cattle Assn. (life), Soc. Study Ethics and Animals, Scientist's Ctr. Animal Welfare (corr.), Univs. Fedn. for Animal Welfare, Hooved Animal Humane Soc., Los Lecheros Dairy Club Calif. State Poly. U. (hon.), Kiwanis (pres. Lafayette Noon club 1969-70, bd. dirs., treas. found. 1971-75, sec. found. 1976-77, Tablet of Honor Internat. Kiwanis Found. 2000), Blue Key, Delta Soc., Sigma Xi, Alpha Zeta, Gamma Sigma Delta, Farm House. Home: 188 Blueberry Ln West Lafayette IN 47906-4810 Office: Purdue Univ Poul Bldg Dept Animal Scis West Lafayette IN 47907-1026 E-mail: jla9@juno.com, jackalbrig@aol.com.

ALBRIGHT, JOSEPH P., state supreme court justice; b. Parkersburg, W.Va., Nov. 8, 1938; s. M.P. and Catherine (Rathbone) A.; m. Patricia Ann Deem, 1958 (dec. 1993); children: Terri Albright Cavi, Lettie K., Joseph P. Jr., John Patrick (dec.); m. Nancie Gensert Divvens, 1995; stepchildren: Susan Divvens Bowman, Debbie Divvens Rake, Sandy Divvens Fox. BBA cum laude, U. Notre Dame, JD, 1962. Bar: W.Va. 1962, U.S. Dist. Ct. W.Va. 1962. Pvt. practice, Parkersburg, 1964-95; asst. prosecuting atty. Wood County, 1965-68; city atty. City of Parkersburg, W.Va., 1968; justice W.Va. Supreme Ct. of Appeals, Charleston, 1995—96, 2001—, chief justice, 2005; pvt. practice Parkersburg and Charleston, 1997—2000. Former mem. W.Va. State Ethics Commn.; bd. dirs. Albrights of Belpre (Ohio), Inc. Former clk. Charter Bd. of Parkerburg; mem. W.Va. Ho. of Dels., 1970-72, 74-86, mem. jud. com., chmn. com. on edn., 1977-78, chmn. com. on judiciary, 1979-84, 52d spkr. of Ho. of Dels., 1985-86; mem., former chmn. Blennerhassett Hist. Park Commn.; former co-chmn. Blennerhassett Hist. Commn.; mem. St. Francis Xavier Ch., Parkersburg, past pres. parish adv. coun. Named Freshman Legislator of Yr., Charleston Gazette, 1971. Office: WVa Supreme Ct Appeals State Capitol Complex Bldg 1 Room E308 1900 Kanawha Boulevard E Charleston WV 25305 Office Phone: 304-558-2605.

ALBRIGHT, JOSEPH WILLIAM, civilian military employee; b. Chillicothe, Ohio, Feb. 3, 1954; s. Herman LeRoy and Catherine Regina (Rieder) A.; m. Deanna Wells, Aug. 13, 1989; children: Andrea Lyn, Jason Michael; stepchildren: Jennifer Carlene, Tammy Darlene. BME, U. Dayton, 1976; M in Strategic Studies, U.S. Army War Coll., 2000; MS in Indsl. Engring., U. Tenn., 2001. Commd. 2nd lt. Ordnance br. U.S. Army, 1976; advanced through grades to col. Ordnance br. U.S. Army, 1999; accountable officer 9th ordnance co. 9th Ordnance Co., Germany, 1977-79, ops. officer, 1979-80; rsch. engr., chief integrated logistic support office large caliber weapon sys. lab., 1980-82; material officer 3rd ordnance bn. 59th ordnance brigade 3d Ordnance Bn., 59th Ordnance Brigade, 1982-85; Dept. of Army coord. for ammunition logistics Dept. of Army, 1985-87; asst. exec. officer to dep. commanding gen. Material Readiness Army Material Commd., 1987-88; commdr. 96th ordnance co. 96th Ordnance Co., 1988-90; inspector gen. Tech. Insp. divsn. Army Material Command Tech. Insp. divsn. Army Materiel Command, 1990-93, chief program mgmt. divsn., 1993-94; comdr. Milan Army Ammunition Plant Milan Army Ammunition Plant, Tenn., 1994-96; dep. support ops. officer 3rd corps support command V U.S. Army Corps, 1996-98; depot maintenance project chief Hdqrs., Dept. of Army, 1998-99, indsl. ops. project chief, office dep. chief staff logistics, 2000—02; sr. logistics analyst Office of Dep. Undersec. of Army, Washington, 2002—04; ret., 2004; sr. logistician Office of Sec. Army, Washington, 2004—. Decorated Legion of Merit, Meritorious Svc. medal 6 awards, Army Commendation medal 2 awards, Army Achievement medal; named Disting. Mil. Grad., 1976, Disting. Grad. Ordnance Officer Advanced Course, 1980. Mem. ASME, Pi Sigma Tau. Home: 220 Norva Ave Frederick MD 21701 Office Phone: 703-695-7612. E-mail: joseph.albright@us.army.mil.

ALBRIGHT, LAURIE JO, school psychologist; b. Toledo, Jan. 14, 1952; d. Lawrence Ray and Josephine Amelia (Knott) A.; m. Brian Lee Larson, Sept. 24, 1983; children: Timothy Martin, Bradley Roy. BA in Psychology magna cum laude, Cleve. State U., 1973, MA in Psychology, 1975. Lic. sch. psychologist, counselor with clin. endorsement, Ohio. Staff sch. psychologist Positive Edn. Program Early Intervention Ctr. East, Cleve., 1975-80, program coord., 1980—. Co-pres. Sch. Psychol. Ohio Polit. Action Com., 1987-89; treas. First Unitarian Ch. of Cleve., pres. bd. trustees, 2000-2001. Mem. Nat. Assn. Sch. Psychologists, Am. Psychol. Assn., Ohio Sch. Psychologist Assn. (pres. 1994-95), Cleve. Assn. Sch. Psychologists (pres. 1983-84), Ohio Assn. Masters in Psychology (founding bd. mem. 1994—). Office: Positive Edn Program 3100 Euclid Ave Cleveland OH 44115-2508

ALBRIGHT, LYLE FREDERICK, chemical engineering educator; b. Bay City, Mich., May 3, 1921; s. William Edward and Isabella (Sidebotham) A.; m. Jeanette Van Belle, Mar. 4, 1950; children: Christine, Diane. BS in Chem. Engring, U. Mich., 1943, MS in Chem. Engring, 1944, PhD in Chem. Engring, 1950. Lab. technician Dow Chem. Co., Midland, Mich., 1939-41; chem. engr. Manhattan Project E.I. duPont de Nemours & Co., Hanford, Wash., 1944-46; research chem. engr. Colgate-Palmolive Co., Jersey City, 1950-51; asst. prof. U. Okla., Norman, 1951-54, assoc. prof., 1954-55, Purdue U., West Lafayette, Ind., 1955-58, prof. chem. engring., 1958—. Cons. to numerous chem. petroleum cos., 1960— Author: Industrial and Laboratory Pyrolyses, 1976, Industrial and Laboratory Alkylations, 1977, Coke Formation on Metals, 1982, Pyrolysis: Theory and Industrial Practice, 1983, Processes for Major Addition Type Plastics and Their Monomers, 2d edit., 1985, Novel Production Methods for Ethylene, Light Hydrocarbons, and Aromatics, 1992, Nitrations: Recent Laboratory and Industrial Developments, 1996. Recipient Shreve prize Purdue U., 1960, 70, 88, Potter award for best instr. Schs. of Engring. Purdue U., 1988. Fellow AIChE (dir. 1982-84, Van Antwerpen award 2003); mem. Am. Chem. Soc., Internat. Brotherhood Magicians, Sigma Xi, Tau Beta Pi. Methodist. Home: 4750N N 250 W West Lafayette IN 47906-5525 Office: Purdue Univ Sch Chem Engring West Lafayette IN 47907 Office Phone: 765-494-4087. Business E-Mail: albright@ecn.purdue.edu.

ALBRIGHT, MADELEINE KORBEL, former secretary of state; b. Prague, Czechoslovakia, May 15, 1937; arrived in Am., 1950, naturalized, 1957; d. Josef and Anna (Speeglova) Korbel; m. Joseph Medill Patterson Albright, June 11, 1959 (div. 1983); children: Anne Korbel, Alice Patterson, Katharine Medill. BA with honors in Polit. Sci., Wellesley Coll., 1959; student, John's Hopkins U.; MA, cert.Russian Inst., Columbia U., 1968, PhD, 1976. Washington coord. Maine for Muskie, 1975-76; chief legis. asst. to U.S. Senator Muskie, 1976-78; mem. staff NSC, 1978-81, White House, 1978-81; sr. fellow in Soviet and Eastern European Affairs Ctr. for Strategic and Internat. Studies, Ctr. for Strategic and Internat. Studies, 1981; fellow Woodrow Wilson Internat. Ctr. for Scholars, Washington, 1981-82; Research prof. internat. affairs, dir. women in fgn. service Sch. Fgn. Service Georgetown U., 1982-93; pres. Ctr. for Nat. Policy, 1985-93; fgn. policy coord. Mondale for Pres. campaign, 1984, to Geraldine A. Ferraro, 1984; vice chmn. Nat. Dem. Inst. for Internat. Affairs, Washington, 1984-93; perm. rep. of the U.S. UN, N.Y.C., 1993-97; Sec. U.S. Dept. of State, 1997-2001; founder & principal The Albright Group LLC, Washington, 2001—; chair Nat. Dem. Inst., Washington, 2001—; Michael and Virginia Mortara Endowed prof. in practice of diplomacy Georgetown Sch. Fgn. Svc.; Disting. scholar William Davidson Inst., U. Mich. Bus. Sch. Sr. fgn. policy advisor Dukakis for Pres. Campaign, 1988; mem. Pres.'s Cabinet, NSC; bd. dirs. N.Y. Stock Exchange. Author: Poland: The Role of the Press in Political Change, 1983, Madam Secretary: A Memoir, 2003; contbr. articles to profl. jours., chpts. to books. Bd. dirs. Beauvoir Sch., Washington, 1968-76, chmn., 1978-83; trustee Black Student Fund, 1969-78, 82-93, Dem. Forum, 1976-78, Williams Coll., 1978-82, Wellesley Coll., 1983-89; mem. exec. com. D.C. Citizens for Better Pub. Edn., 1975-76; bd. dirs. Washington Urban League, 1982-84, Atlantic Coun., 1984-93, Ctr. for Nat. Policy, 1985-93, Chatham House Fedn., 1986-88. Mem. Council Fgn. Relations, Am. Polit. Sci. Assn., Czechoslovak Soc. Arts and Scis. Am., Atlantic Council U.S. (dir.), Am. Assn. for Advancement Slavic Studies. Democrat. Office Phone: 202-842-7222. Office Fax: 202-354-3888.

ALBRIGHT, RAYMOND JACOB, federal official; b. Reading, Pa., Apr. 7, 1929; s. Raymond Wolf and Mary Catherine (Sherr) A.; m. Ruthmarie Reich, Sept. 13, 1952; children: Raymond Jacob, David Reich. BA, Yale, 1951; Fulbright scholar, U. Vienna, Austria, 1951-52; MA, Harvard, 1954, PhD; in Polit. Sci., 1961. Fgn. affairs officer (Nat. Security Council affairs and policy planning) Office Asst. Sec. Def. (Internat. Security Affairs), 1954-61; with Office Asst. Sec. State (European affairs), 1961-62; nat. security affairs adviser Treasury Dept., 1962-67; asst. to sec. treasury (Nat. Security Affairs) Office Sec. Treasury, 1967-69; counselor for econ. affairs Am. embassy, Belgrade, Yugoslavia, 1969-72; fgn. service res. officer Dept. State, 1969-73; v.p. Export-Import Bank U.S., 1973-92, sr. v.p., 1992-95; mng. dir. GlobalNet Fin. Solutions, LLC. Lectr. Yale, 1959, George Washington U., 1960, George Mason U., 1997. Author (with others): Forging a New Sword, 1958. Pres. Fgn. Policy Discussion Group, Washington. Mem.: Yale Club (Washington) (bd. dirs., chmn. Yale and govt. com. 1966-69). Home: 3609 Dunlop St Chevy Chase MD 20815-5926 E-mail: rj.albright2@verizon.net.

ALBRIGHT, RICHARD SHELDON, II, literature educator; b. Harrisburg, Pa., July 11, 1951; s. Richard Sheldon and Iona Madrienne (Booth) A.; m. Marcia Anne Zimmers, Aug. 17, 1974; children: Christopher Erik, Courtney Elizabeth. BA in English, Lehigh U., 1973; MA in English, Millersville U., 1997; PhD in English, Lehigh U., 2002. Systems analyst U.S. Navy Fleet Material Support Office, Mechanicsburg, 1977—86, supervisory systems analyst, 1986—97; tchg. asst. Lehigh U., 1997—2000; adj. instr. Harrisburg Area C.C., 1998—, Elizabethtown Coll., 2002—04; vis. asst. prof. English Shippensburg U., 2004—. Contbr. articles to profl. publs. Avocations: photography, writing, personal computers, astronomy, music. Home: 67 Fleisher Rd Marysville PA 17053-9505

ALBRIGHT, TERRILL D., lawyer; b. Lebanon, Ind., June 23, 1938; s. David Henry and Georgia Pauline (Doty) A.; m. Judith Ann Stoelting, June 2, 1962; children: Robert T., Elizabeth A. AB, Ind. U., 1960, JD, 1965. Bar: Ind. 1965, U.S. Dist. Ct. (so. dist.) Ind. 1965, U.S. Dist. Ct. (no. dist.) Ind. 1980, U.S. Ct. Appeals (7th cir.) 1981, U.S. Ct. Appeals (3d and D.C. cirs.) 1982, U.S. Supreme Ct. 1972; cert. arbitrator for large complex cse program constrn. and internat. comml. cases; cert. mediator; on constrn. master arbitrator roster, Am. Arbitration Assn. Assoc. Baker and Daniels Law Firm, Indpls., 1965-72, ptnr., 1972—. Mem. panel of disting. neutrals. nat. panel for constrn. and regional comml. panel CPR Inst. for Dispute Resolution, N.Y.C. Pres. Christamore House, Indpls., 1979-86; bd. dirs. Greater Indpls. YMCA,

1980-82; chmn. Jordan YMCA, Indpls., 1982; pres. Community Ctrs. Indpls., 1987-90. 1st lt. U.S. Army, 1960—62. Fellow: Acad. Law Alumni, Ind. U. Sch. of Law (bd. dirs. 1974—80, pres. 1979—80), Am. Coll. Trial Lawyers, Ind. Bar Found, Indpls. Bar Found., Am. Bar Found.; mem.: Am. Arbitration Assn., Ind. State Bar Assn. (chmn. young lawyers sect. 1971—72, rep. 11th dist. 1983—85, bd. dirs., v.p. 1991—92, pres.-elect 1992—93, pres. 1993—94), Nat. Conf. Bar. Pres. (exec. coun. 1995—98). Democrat. Office: Baker & Daniels 300 N Meridian St Ste 2700 Indianapolis IN 46204-1782 Office Phone: 317-237-1262. Business E-Mail: terry.albright@bakerd.com.

ALBRIGHT, TOWNSEND SHAUL, brokerage house executive, consultant; b. Anderson, Ind., May 1, 1942; s. Townsend S. and Maxine Aree (Zimmerman) A.; m. Eileen Therese Argent, Aug. 30, 1968; children: Megan Eileen, Alexandra Michele. BA, Wabash Coll., 1964; MBA, U. Mich., 1966. With Mead Corp., Cin. and Chgo., 1966-69; mcpl. bond underwriter No. Trust Co., Chgo., 1969-71; v.p. Channer Newman Securities Co., Chgo., 1971-80; v.p., treas., dir. Croake Roberts, Inc., Chgo., 1980-86; v.p. instl. sales John Nuveen & Co., Chgo., 1986-90; with Fin. Forum, 1991—; sr. funding mgr. Ill. Fin. Authority, Chgo., 2004—; faculty mem. Loyola U., 1990—. Bd. dirs. Urban Gateways, Chgo., 1976—; dean Mcpl. Bond Sch. Chgo.; with Inst. Entrepreneurial Studies U. Ill., Chgo. Served with USAR, 1966-72. Mem. Chgo. Assn. Wabash Men, U. Mich. Alumni Assn., Mcpl. Bond Club Chgo., Phi Gamma Delta (Chgo. grad. chpt., former bd. dirs., Econ. Club. Presbyterian. Home: 2019 Beechwood Ave Wilmette IL 60091-1503 Office Phone: 312-496-1138. E-mail: talbright@il-fa.com.

ALBRINK, MARGARET JORALEMON, medical educator; b. Warren, Ariz., Jan. 6, 1920; d. Ira Beaman and Dorothy (Rieber) Joralemon; m. Wilhelm Stockman Albrink, Sept. 16, 1944 (dec. July 1991); children: Frederick Henry, Jonathan Wilhelm, Peter Varick (dec. March 2003). BA in Psychology cum laude, Radcliffe Coll., 1941; MS in Physiol. Chemistry, Yale U., 1943, MD, 1946, MPH, 1951. Cert. Diplomate Am. Bd. Med. Examiners, Diplomate Am. Bd. Nutrition, Diplomate Am. Bd. Physician Nutrition Specialists. Intern New Haven (Conn.) Hosp., 1946—47; NIH postdoctoral fellow Yale U., New Haven, 1947—49, fellow pub. health, 1950—51, instr. medicine, 1952—58, asst. prof. medicine, 1958—61; assoc. prof. W.Va. U., Morgantown, 1961—66, prof. medicine, 1966—90, prof. emerita, 1990—, mem. grad. faculty, 1977—92; mem. med. and dental staff W.Va. U. Hosp., Morgantown, 1961—2000. Vis. scientist Donner Lab., U. Calif., Berkeley, 1993—; assoc. physician Grace-New Haven Cmty. Hosp., 1952-61; cons. nutrition study sect. NIH; vis. scholar U. Calif., Berkeley, 1977-78; established investigator Am. Heart Assn., 1958-63. Guest editor: Clinics in Endocrinology and Metabolism, 1976; guest editor Am. Jour. Clin. Nutrition, 1968, mem. editorial bd., 1963-68; mem. editorial adv. bd. Jour. Am. Coll. Nutrition, 1988-89; reviewer jours.; contbr. articles, chpts. and abstracts to profl. jours. Recipient Rsch. Career award Nat. Heart, Lung and Blood Inst., 1963-90. Fellow: ACP, Am. Coll. Nutrition, Am. Heart Assn. (emeritus, fellow arteriosclerosis coun., fellow coun. epidemiology); mem.: LWV, ACLU, Am. Diabetes Assn. (epidemiology coun.), Am. Soc. Clin. Nutrition, Am. Soc. Clin. Investigation, Am. Fedn. Clin. Rsch., Phi Beta Kappa, Sigma Xi, Alpha Omega Alpha. Democrat. Avocations: music, archeology, computers, nature conservation. Home: 817 Augusta Ave Morgantown WV 26501-6237 Office: WVa U Dept Medicine PO Box 9159 Morgantown WV 26506-9159 E-mail: mjalbrink@aol.com.

ALBRITTON, ARTHUR DALLAS, lawyer; b. Jacksonville, Fla., June 16, 1928; s. Arthur Dallas and Grace Elizabeth (Pratt) Albritton; m. Frances Gail Kelley, Dec. 21, 1951; m. Ann Elizabeth Hill, Dec. 27, 1968; m. Grace Lovelace, Jan. 26, 1991; children: Gary Callan, Andrew Brian, Laura Elizabeth, Rachel Ann, Jacoba Lehane. BS, Fla. State U., 1950, MS, 1951; JD, Yale U., 1956. Bar: Fla. 1956, U.S. Dist. Ct. (so. dist.) Fla. 1956, U.S. Dist. Ct. (mid. dist.) Fla. 1959, U.S. Ct. Appeals (5th cir.) 1959, U.S. Supreme Ct. 1966, U.S. Ct. Appeals (11th cir.) 1981. Ptnr. Hardee & Ott, Tampa, Fla., 1956—60; sr. ptnr. Albritton & Sessums, Tampa, 1961—82; pres. Albritton & Assocs., P.A., Tampa, 1982—. Counsel Fla. Bd. Bar Examiners, 1958—68; asst. county solicitor Hillsborough County, 1960, asst. state atty., 1961—62; chmn., mem. Jud. Nominating Commn., 1972—79; pres. Albritton and Sebring, 1998—; arbitrator; lectr.; participant various seminars. Contbr. articles to legal publs. Sec.-treas., mem. Tampa Sports Authority, 1966—70; chmn. Mayor's Mgmt. Analysis Team, City of Tampa, 1962—66; pres. Agape Evangelistic Mission, 1980—. 1st lt. USAF, 1951—53. Recipient various awards of recognition for profl. svc. activities. Mem.: ATLA, ABA, Fla. Acad.Trial Lawyers, Hillsborough County Bar Assn. (pres. 1965, Outstanding Trial Lawyer award 2000), Fla. Bar, Univ. Club, Bay Area Yale Club. Democrat. Office: 100 E Madison St Ste 302 Tampa FL 33602-4703

ALBRITTON, WILLIAM HAROLD, III, federal judge; b. Andalusia, Ala., Dec. 19, 1936; s. Robert Bynum and Carrie (Veal) A.; m. Jane Rollins Howard, June 2, 1958; children: William Harold IV, Benjamin Howard, Thomas Bynum. AB, U. Ala., 1959, JD, 1960. Bar: Ala. 1960. Assoc. firm Albrittons & Rankin, Andalusia, 1962-66, ptnr., 1966-76; ptnr. firm Albrittons & Givhan, Andalusia, 1976-86; ptnr. Albrittons, Givhan & Clifton, Andalusia, 1986-91; judge U.S. Dist. Ct. (mid. dist.) Ala., Montgomery, 1991-97, chief judge, 1998—2004, sr. judge, 2004—. Mem. 11th Circuit Jud. Coun., 1998—2004. Pres. Ala. Law Sch. Found., 1988-91, Ala. Law Inst. Fellow Am. Coll. Trial Lawyers, Am. Bar Found.; mem. Fed. Judges Assn. (bd. dirs. 1999-2002, jud. conf. U.S. com. on ct. adminstrn. and case mgmt. 1999-2004), Ala. State Bar (commr. 1981-89, disciplinary commn. 1981-84, v.p. 1985-86, pres.-elect 1989-90, pres. 1990-91), Am. Judicature Soc., Am. Inns of Ct., Bluewater Bay Sailing Club, Bluewater Bay Country Club, Phi Beta Kappa, Phi Delta Phi, Omicron Delta Kappa, Alpha Tau Omega.

ALBRITTON, WILLIAM HOYLE, training and consulting executive, lecturer, writer; b. Cleveland, Tenn., May 29, 1942; s. Hoyle Franklin and Marie Arlene (Mount) Albritton; m. June Ellington, June 20, 1964; children: Elizabeth Anne, William Hoyle. BA, Tenn. Wesleyan Coll., 1964; postgrad. in bus. adminstrn., U. Chgo., 1974—75. Assoc. Lendman Assocs., L.A., 1969—70, dir. West Coast ops., 1970—71; ter. mgr. Baxter-Travenol, Deerfield, Ill., 1971—72, field sales trainer, 1972, sales edn. mgr., 1973; nat. sales recruiter The Kendall Co. divsn. Colgate-Palmolive, Boston, 1973—75, tng. and devel. mgr., 1975—76, dir. compensation, 1976—77, dir. staffing and mgmt. devel., 1978—81; pres. Tng. Concepts, Inc., Boston, 1981—86, chmn. bd. dirs., CEO, 1986—; ptnr. Ollinger Ptnrs. Mgmt. Cons., 1989—93, Choice Point, 1994—96, Duxbury, Mass., 1994—; v.p. Advt. Sys. Plus, 1994—96; sr. assoc. The Change Mgmt. Group, LLC, 1995—; v.p. Hamilton Cornell Assocs., 1996—. Host Bill Board TV Show. Author: Managing Yourself and Others, Internal Consulting for Results, Results-Oriented Selling, Results-Oriented Management, Presenting Technical Information. Team capt. Jordan Hosp. Spl. Funds, Plymouth, Mass., 1982; mem. pers. bd. Town of Duxbury, 1984—; mem. Bay Players Cmty. Theater. Officer USNR, 1966—69. Mem.: Instnl. Sys. Assn., South Shore C. of C., Am. Mgmt. Assn. (pres. assn.), ASTD, Old Colony Club, Rotary (v.p. local dist. 1978—79, pres. 1979—80, group exch. com. 1983—93), Duxbury Yacht Club (chmn. tournament com., Ouimet Scholarship Fund 1989, chmn. golf com. 1992—94), Exec. Club. Home: PO Box 2442 Duxbury MA 02331-2442 Office: PO Box 357 Duxbury MA 02331-0357 E-mail: walbritton@allianceresource.net.

ALBRIZIO, EILEEN MARIE, commentator, poet; b. Hartford, Conn., Sept. 18, 1963; d. Constance Claire Magnan-Albrizio and Francis John Albrizio; m. Wayne Edward Horgan, Sept. 22, 1989. Degree, Conn. Sch. Broadcasting, 1995; BFA in Theater, Ctrl. Conn. State U., 2004, student, 2005—. Owner/propr. Heroes and Hitters - Comic Book Store, Rocky Hill, Conn., 1989—; broadcast journalist and news host Newsradio WPOP, Hartford, Conn., 1995—97, WNPR Radio News, Hartford, Conn., 1997—2005; voice talent Conn. Pub. TV, Hartford, Conn., 1997—2005. Poetry tchr. Colleges, Universities and Cultural venues, Conn., 1998—; visual art dir. The Buttonwood Tree, Middletown, Conn., 2001—03. Author: Messy on the Inside, Alison's Weight, 2005, (plays) Rain - Dark as Water in Winter; narrator: albums On The Edge. Recipient Best Newscast, Conn. AP, 1996, Best News Feature, 1998, Best Spot News, Soc. of Profl. Journalists, 1999, Best News Feature, 1999, Hon. Mention for Stage Play, Writer's Digest Mag., 1996, 1997, Hon. Mention for Poetry, 1999, Poetry fellowship, Greater Hartford Arts Coun., 2003. Mem.: Artemis Rising (life). Independent.

ALBUM, JERALD LEWIS, lawyer; b. Monroe, La., Oct. 18, 1947; s. Natt B. and Rose Marie (Pickens) A.; m. Joan Abbey Lurie, July 30, 1983; children: Nicole, Jeffrey. BS, Tulane U., 1969, JD, 1973. Bar: La. 1973, Colo. 1990, Tex. 1992, U.S. Dist. Ct. (ea. dist.) La. 1975, U.S. Dist. Ct. (mid. dist.) La. 1980, U.S. Dist. Ct. (we. dist.) La. 1983, U.S. Ct. Appeals (5th cir.) 1976. Assoc. Mmahat, Gagliano, Duffy & Giordano, Metairie, La., 1973-79; assoc. to ptnr. Lemle, Kelleher, Hunley, Moss & Frilot, New Orleans, 1980-85; shareholder Abbott Simses, Album & Knister, New Orleans, 1985-96; ptnr. Album, Stovall, Radecker & Giordano, New Orleans, Reich, Meeks & Treadaway, Metairie, La., 2001—. Mem. La. Assn. of Def. Counsel, New Orleans Bar Assn., La. State Bar Assn. Avocations: golf, volleyball, gardening. Home: 4637 Southshore Dr Metairie LA 70002-1430 Office: Reich Meeks & Treadaway 3850 N Causeway Blvd Ste 1000 Metairie LA 70002-7247

ALBYN, RICHARD KEITH, retired architect; b. Detroit, Apr. 8, 1927; s. Walter Harris and Corrine Henrietta (Miller) A.; m. Nancy Jane Cosby; children: Keith Cosby, Lisa Benton Albyn Drummond. Student, U. Ill., 1945-49. Registered architect, Mich., Ohio, Fla., Md., W.Va., N.C. Prin. dir. Linn Smith Assocs., Inc., Birmingham, Mich., 1962-64, TMP Assocs., Inc., Bloomfield Hills, Mich., 1964-82, HEPY Assocs., Inc., Southfield, Mich., 1982-86; ret., 1986. Co-author: Buildings of Michigan, 1987; also articles in profl. jours. and hist. publs.; illustrator: A Handbook for the Amateur Archaeologist, 1967, The Archaeologists Coloring Book, 1964. Mem. Preservation N.C., Transylvania County Arts Coun., Asheville Art Mus.; bd. dirs. Asheville Pub. Radio Sta. WCQS, 2003—. Recipient citation Am. Assn. Sch. Adminstrs., 1964, 70, 1st pl. award Ch. Architects Guild, 1965, others. Fellow: AIA (lectr. 1961—65, treas. 1968, sec. 1969, pres. Detroit chpt. 1971, pres. Detroit archtl. found. 1971, host chpt. com. nat. conv. 1971, mem. past pres. com. 1971—86, mem. vocat.-tech. edn. svc. study com. 1976, honor award 1964, 1971, award of merit 1971, honor award 1977, 1st pl award Focus on Art Exhibit 1997, Viewer's Choice award 1997, Merchant's award 1998, Merit award 1999, Patrons award 2000, Hon. Men. 2001, 2002, Merit award 2003, 1st pl award Focus on Art Exhibit 2004); mem.: Brevard Music Ctr. Assn. (pres. 2001—02), Preservation N.C. (bd. advisors 1999—), Archaeol. Soc. N.C., Transylvania County Joint Hist. PreservationCommn. (chmn. 1993—96), Transylvania County Hist. Soc. (bd. dirs. 1919—94, bd. visitors 1999—), AIA N.C. Presbyterian. Avocations: painting, archaeology, geneology, photography, writing. Home: 60 Kentwood Ln Pisgah Forest NC 28768-9511

ALCALAY, ALBERT S., artist, design educator; b. Paris, Aug. 11, 1917; came to U.S., 1951, naturalized, 1956; s. Samuel and Lepa (Afar) A.; m. Vera Eskenazi, Nov. 11, 1950; children: Leor, Ammiel. Student in Paris, Rome. Lectr. design Carpenter Center, Harvard U., 1960—. One man shows, De Cordova and Dana Mus., Lincoln, Mass., 1968, Swetzoff Gallery, Pucker-Safrai Gallery, Pace Gallery, others; retrospective, Carpenter Ctr., Harvard U., 1982; group shows, Inst. Contemporary Art, Boston, 1960, Venice (Italy) Biennale, Mus. Modern Art., 1955, Whitney Mus. Am. Art, 1956, 58, 60, U. Ill., Urbana, Pa. Acad. Fine Arts, 1960; represented in permanent collections, Mus. Modern Art, N.Y.C., Boston Mus. Fine Arts, Fogg Art Mus., DeCordova and Dana Mus., Phillips Acad., Mus. Am. Art, Brandeis U. Rose Art Mus., U. Mass. Mus., Wellesley Coll. Mus., Colby Coll. Mus., Smith Coll., Rome Mus. Modern Art, U. Rome, Brockton Art Mus., Tufts U., Medford, Mass., Boston Pub. Library, Smithsonian Inst. Archives of Am. Artists; documentary fmil A.A. Self-Portraits. Guggenheim fellow, 1959-60; recipient prize Boston Arts Festival, 1960 Home: 66 Powell St Brookline MA 02446-3929 Office: Harvard U Carpenter Ctr Cambridge MA 01238

ALCALAY, EUGENE CHRISTIAN, pianist; b. Bucharest, Romania, Oct. 13, 1966; arrived in U.S., 1984; s. Alexander and Gina Alcalay; m. Ruth Elisabeth Mayers, July 19, 2003. Diploma, The Curtis Inst. Music, 1990; MusB, Ind. U., 1988; MusD, The Juilliard Sch., 1998. Instr. piano 6th Internat. Music Festival and Sch., Bogota, Colombia, 2000; sr. specialist Fundacion U. Juan N. Corpas, Bogota, Colombia, 2004; instr. U. Nacional de Colombia, Bogota, Colombia, 2003; mem. faculty piano and chamber music Masterworks Internat. Festival and Sch., London, 2004; asst. prof. piano Geneva Coll., Beaver Falls, Pa., 2004—. Adjudicator young artist competitions Duquesne U., 2000; adjudicator concerto competitions U. Nacional de Colombia, 2003; adjudicator Steinway Soc. We. Pa., 2005. Musician: Beethoven Sonata, 1998. Recipient award, Pro-Piano Recital Series, N.Y., 1997, winner, Pitts. Concert Soc. Maj. Auditions, 2001; scholar, Fulbright Found., 2003; The Leonard Bernstein Personal scholarship, 1982. Mem.: Pitts. Piano Tchrs. Assn., Pa. Music Tchrs. Assn., Music Tchrs. Nat. Assn., Mortar Bd., Pi Kappa Lambda (life). Home: 940 St James Cir Platteville WI 53818 Office: U Wis Platteville Dept Fine Arts 1 University Plz 175C Doudna Hall Platteville WI 53818 Office Phone: 724-847-6663. Personal E-mail: ealcalay@geneva.edu, acalcalay@yahoo.com.

ALCALDE, HECTOR, public relations executive; b. NYC; BA, U. Tampa; MA, Peabody Coll. Former educator, Fla.; chief of staff to former chmn. of ways and means com. U.S. Ho. of Reps., Washington, 1962—74; founder, chmn. Alcalde & Fay, Arlington, Va., 1973—. Bd. dirs. SAFLink, Inc. Fomer trustee Fairfax County Pub. Schs. Edn. Found. Office: Alcalde & Fay 2111 Wilson Blvd 8th Fl Arlington VA 22201 also: 400 N Capitol St NW Ste 475 Washington DC 20001 Office Phone: 202-783-6669, 703-841-0626.*

ALCANTARA, ANITA LUISA, community arts administrator; b. May 30, 1942; d. Francisco B. and Eleanor E. (Locke) A. AA, Wright City Coll., 1962; BEd, Northeastern Ill. U., 1964; cert. cmty. svc. mgmt., Roosevelt U., 1989; postgrad., Garrett Evangelical Theol. Sem. Tchr. 5th grade Chgo. Pub. Schs., 1964—65; libr. technician at main libr. Chgo. Pub. Libr., 1967—71; field dir., ednl. svcs. dir. Girl Scouts of Chgo., 1971-79; nat. tng. coord. Girl Scouts U.S.A., N.Y.C., 1979-84; mgmt. devel. cons. Equitable Corp., NYC, 1984; adminstr. United Ch. of Rogers Park, Chgo., 1985-86, min. of cmty. life, 1986—2000; dir. adminstrv. svcs. and cmty. life United C.h. of Rogers Park, 2000—03; coord. sr. program, adminstrv. asst. Insight Arts, 2003—. Cons. Contact Chgo., 1985-86; Yule Connection mgr., 1985-86. Author: You Make the Difference, Leaders' Guide: Council Guide, 1980. Leadership Let's Get Started print/video tng. program, 1981; coun. guide Daisy Girl Scouts Coun., 1983; exec. dir. Insight Arts, 1993-96; collaborator exhibn. Out of the Loop: Neighborhood Voices, Chgo. Hist. Soc., 2001; active Chgo. Hist. Soc.; mem. Parliament, World's Religion Project in Rogers Park; bd. mem. Rogers Park Cmty. Action Network; superintendency com. mem. United Meth. Ch. Recipient Chgo. Youth award Mayor's Commn. Youth Welfare, 1968, Chgo. Pub. Libr. award, 1970, Thanks Badge award, Girl Scouts Chgo., 1975; named Vol. of Yr. Chgo. Area Project, 1993 Office: 1545 W Morse Ave Chicago IL 60626-3306 Office Phone: 773-973-1521. Personal E-mail: rochafan@aol.com.

ALCH, MARK LEE, finance educator, researcher; b. Mpls., Oct. 21, 1945; s. Harry Brown and Dora Alch; m. Sharlene Rivi Eigen, June 22, 1969; children: Matthew Cary, Nikkie Shana. BA, U. Minn., 1967, MA, 1970; PhD, UCLA, 1977, C.Phil, 1973. cert. tchr., Calif., Calif. C.C. supr. credential, instr. credential; lic. real estate sales, Calif. Asst. mgr. Eagle Cleaners & Launderers, Mpls., 1961-72; grad. asst. U. Minn., Mpls., 1969-70; program coord., tchg. asst. UCLA, 1972-76, asst. to vice chancellor for student and campus affairs, 1976—77; tng. mgr. So. Calif. divsn. Fluor-Daniel, Irvine, 1977-80, project adminstr. advanced tech. divsn., 1980-81; v.p. Drake Beam Morin, Inc., Irvine, 1981—84, sr. v.p., mng. dir., offices in Orange County, San Diego, Phoenix, Tucson, Las Vegas, Riverside and San Bernardino, Calif., 1985-95; CEO, v.p. edn., tng. and devel. Uniben, Inc., Pasadena, Calif., 1996-99; instr. extension divsn. bus. mgmt. program U. Calif., Irvine, 1997—; nat. dir. edn. Am. Youth Soccer Orgn., Hawthorne, Calif., 2000—01, Kuykendall and Alch Real Estate Investments, 2000—; realtor Team Gage Realtors, 2002; dir., exec. v.p. Hall Career Svcs., 2003—, Ryness Co., San Diego, 2003—04. Adj. prof. Occidental Coll., Eagle Rock, Calif., 1977; instr. U.C. Irvine; cons. Mark Alch & Assocs., Irvine, 1996-2000; adj. Temps Plus, 2003-2004, Ryness Co., 2004; presenter in field Author: A Diplomatic Study of Anglo-German NavalTensions 1904-08, Including Kaiser Wilhelm's Year of Indiscretions, 1970, Germany's Naval Resurgeon, British Appeasement, and the Anglo-German Naval Agreement of 1935, 1977, A Financial Aid and College Planning System for Parents of High School Students, 1996, How to Become a Millionaire, 1999, Coaching for the New Century, 2004; contbr. more than 50 articles to profl. jours., internet and online broadcasts. Exec. com. Irvine, Newport Beach and Costa Mesa YMCA, 1992-93, fedn. chief, 1992-93; co-chmn. econ. devel. com. City of Irvine and Irvine C. of C., 1992-95; active Am. Youth Soccer Orgn., 1991—, referee com. region 213, Irvine, 1994—, area referee, 1995, sect. referee, 1996, referee assessor, 1996-, dir. referee instrn. region 213, 1997-98, sect. referee instr., trainer regional, area and sect. referee, 2000-, others; beadkeeper Indian Guides, YMCA, 1989-90, asst. chief, 1990-91, chief, 1991-92, fedn. chief, 1992-93, mem. exec. com. YMCA, 1992-94, national elder, 1999-93. Mem. ASTD (membership com. Orange County chpt. 1995-96), Assn. Profl. Cons., Med. Mktg. Assn., Profl. Coach and Mentors Assn. (dir. evaluations nat. conf. 2003), Nat. Human Resources Assn., Life Sci. Industry Coun., Nat. Assn. Realtors, Calif. Assn. Realtors, Orange County Assn. Realtors, Inland Empire (sales mktg. coun.), Orange County Indsl. League, Orange County Venture Network (sales and mktg. coun.), UCLA Alumni Assn. (life). Democrat. Jewish. Avocations: jogging, travel, high performance and muscle car restoration, music, public speaking. Office: 25 W Lucero Irvine CA 92620 Office Phone: 949-413-9511. E-mail: markalch@cox.net.

AL-CHALABI, SUHAIL ABDUL-JABBAR, transportation executive; b. Baghdad, Iraq, July 14, 1940; arrived in U.S., 1965; s. Abdul Jabbar and Wajeeha al-Chalabi; m. Margery Lee Pupach, Mar. 9, 1965. BArch, MIT, 1962; MSc, Athens (Greece) Tech. Inst., 1965. Planner, arch. Doxiadis Assocs., Athens, 1963-65, Skidmore Owings & Merrill, Chgo., 1965-67; rsch. dir. Northeastern Ill. Planning Commn., Chgo., 1967-74; exec. dep. dir. Chgo. Area Transp. Study, 1974-81; spl. advisor to mayor City of Chgo., 1981-82, commr. dept. econ. devel., 1982-83; exec. v.p., CFO The al Chalabi Group, Ltd., Chgo., 1983—. Mem. team planning 3d Chgo. airport, 1986—; adapted hwy. planning models for use in planning airports, commuter rail and interurban bus; initiated build/no-build analyses EIS; project mgr. for numerous transp. projects: rail, toll road, airport sys., bridges. Mem. rsch. and forecast adv. com. Northeastern Ill. Planning Commn., Chgo., 1992—. Mem.: Am. Assn. Airport Execs. (corp.), World Soc. Ekistics, Chgo. Southland C. of C., Lambda Alpha. Achievements include securing financing, overseeing restoration, operation of Chicago Theater, 1994-95. Home: 718 Wilson Ave Beverly Shores IN 46301-0232 Office: al-Chalabi Group Ltd 330 W Diversey Pkwy Ste 1403 Chicago IL 60657-6206 E-mail: acgtran@aol.com, suhail@al-chalabi.com.

ALCINDOR, LEWIS FERDINAND See ABDUL-JABBAR, KAREEM

ALCOCK, CHARLES ROGER, science educator; b. Windsor, Eng., June 15, 1951; arrived in US, 1973; BS in Physics and Math., U. Auckland, 1972; PhD in Astronomy and Physics, Calif. Inst. Tech., 1977. Long-term mem. Inst. for Advanced Study, Princeton, N.J., 1977-81; assoc. prof. dept. physics MIT, Cambridge, 1981-86; head Astrophysics Ctr., Inst. Geophysics & Planetary Physics Lawrence Livermore (Calif.) Nat. Lab., 1986-97, head Inst. Geophysics and Planetary Physics, 1994-98, dep. assoc. dir. for sci. in the physics directorate, 1998-2000; Reese W. Flower prof. astronomy and astrophysics Univ. Pa., 2000—04; dir. Harvard-Smithsonian Ctr. for Astrophysics, Smithsonian Astrophysical Observatory, Harvard Coll. Observatory, Cambridge, Mass., 2004—. Vis. prof. Niels Bohr Inst., Copenhagen, 1979; vis. fellow Australian Nat. U., Canberra, 1983; adj. prof. dept. astronomy U. Calif., Berkeley. Recipient R&D 100 award, 1993, E.O. Lawrence award, 1996, Beatrice M. Tinsley prize, AAS, 2000; fellow Earle C. Anthony, Caltech. U., 1973—79, Alfred P. Sloan rsch., MIT, 1983—86. Mem.: Nat. Acad. of Sci. Office: Harvard Smithsonian Ctr for Astrophysics Director's Office 60 Garden St Cambridge MA 02138*

ALCOCK, GEORGE LEWIS, JR., (PETER ALCOCK), investor, business strategist; b. Boston, Feb. 26, 1940; s. George Lewis and Louise Hall Alcock; m. Louise Stewart Bachelder, Sept. 29, 1984; children: Peter L., Caroline S. BS, Northeastern U., Boston, 1962. Prodn. supr. J.H. Winn, Winchester, Mass., 1963-65; sales staff Liberty Mutual Ins., Boston, 1966-68; fin. staff Nat. Med. Leasing, Cambridge, Mass., 1968-69; cons. Innovative Mgmt., Cambridge, Mass., 1970-73; treas. Devel. Mgmt. Consultants, Boston, 1973-80; chmn. M.B. Claff & Sons Inc., Brockton, Mass., 1980-2001; corp. fin. staff Alcock Investments, Watertown, Mass., 1980-87; pres., CEO U.S. Repeating Arms Co., New Haven, Conn., 1987-90; gen. ptnr. Alcock Ltd. Ptnrs., Weston, Mass., 1991—. Pres. Beckwood Svcs., Inc., Pliastow, N.H., 2001—. Dir. The Nat. Coun. Northeastern U., Boston, 1989—; trustee Fitchburg (Mass.) State Coll., 1999—, chmn. bd. trustees, 2001—; bd. mem. Mass. Bd. Higher Edn., 2003—. Mem.: Assn. for Corp. Growth, Nat. Assn. Corp. Dirs., Newcomen Soc. U.S. Avocation: outdoor sports. Office: Alcock Ltd Ptnrs 105 Cherry Brook Rd Weston MA 02493-1347 Office Phone: 781-894-4947. Personal E-mail: palcock@comcast.net.

ALCORN, WALLACE ARTHUR, minister, writer; b. Milw., Aug. 29, 1930; s. William Keith and Dora Mildred (Brazee) Alcorn; m. Ann Margaret Carmichael, June 5, 1958; children: John Mark, Allison Alcorn-Oppedahl, Stephen, Paul. Student, Marquette U., 1950; AB, Wheaton Coll., 1952; MDiv, Grand Rapids Bapt. Theol. Sem., 1959; AM, Wheaton Grad. Sch. Theology, 1959; postgrad., Mich. State U., 1959-60, U. Mich., 1960-61; ThM, Princeton Theol. Sem., 1965; PhD, NYU, 1974; cert. in clin. pastoral edn., Fitzsimons Army Med. Ctr., 1975; postgrad., U. Minn., 1980-81. Ordained to ministry Gen. Assn. Regular Bapt. Chs., 1957; cert. advanced mediator Am. Arbit. Assn. Program sec. Wis. Heart Assn., 1954—55; field program rep. Chgo. Heart Assn., 1955—56; pastor Caddy Vista Bapt. Ch., Caldonia, Wis., 1955-57; tchr. Wyoming (Mich.) Schs., 1958-60; pastor Bloomfield Hills (Mich.) Bapt. Ch., 1960-61; English tchr. Waterford-Kettering H.S., Drayton Plaines, Mich., 1961-62; pastor Cmty. Bapt. Ch. Shark River Hills, Neptune, NJ, 1962-67, 1st Bapt. Ch., Austin, Minn., 1976-83; prof. bible Moody Bible Inst., Chgo., 1967-73; assoc. prof. N.T. N.W. Bapt. Sem., Tacoma, 1974-76; clin. pastoral care specialist Madigan Army Med. Ctr., Tacoma, 1974-76; police chaplain Tacoma, 1974-76, Austin, 1976-90; pres. Faith Acad., Mpls., 1986; prin. Wallace Alcorn Assocs., Austin, 1983—; pastoral counselor New Life Family Svcs., Rochester, Minn., 1987-92. Cons. U.S. Dept. Edn., 1953—54, N.J. Dept. Edn., 1964—67; radio tchr. Moody Radio Network, 1968—74; chmn. Minn. Assn. Regular Bapt. Chs., 1980—83; radio commentator Sta. KTIS and Northwestern Coll. Network, 1987—98; syndicated newspaper columnist, 1993—; adj. faculty Riverland C.C., 1994—99;. Author: (book) The Bible as Literature, 1965, Elijah, Prophet of God, 1972, The Life of Christ Visualized, 1973, Knowing and Using the Bible, 1975, Momentum, 1986; nat. editor: Christian Life, 1956—60, Mil. Life, 1983—86, Ampersand, 1995—99, N.T. editor: Living Bible Commentary, 1974—76, The Book We Love, 1994; contbr. Wycliffe Bible Ency., 1974, Tyndale Family Bible Ency., 1976, New Commentary on the Whole Bible, 1990, Stones of Remembrance, 1995, articles to profl. jours. Mem. citizen's adv. coun. Neptune Bd. Edn., 1965—67; chair Austin Human Rights Commn., 1989—98; mem. profl. adv. coun. Pub. Edn. Relgion Studies Ctr., Wright State U., 1972—76; pub. mem. 10th Jud. Dist. Ethics Com., 1993—99; dir. Good News Hour, Austin, 1976—83, Minn. Human Rights Commn., 1990—98, Coop. Solutions Mediation Ctr., Austin, 1995—99. With USNR, 1947—52, with U.S. Army, 1952—54, with USAR, 1954—57, chaplain, col. USAR, 1957—90. Recipient Amy Writing award, Amy Found., 1988, Baptist Heritage award, 2003, 2004. Mem.: Am. Pub. Health Assn., Hist. Soc. Minn., Hist. Soc. S.C., Hist. Soc. Ohio, Hist. Soc. Wis., Mil. Chaplains Assn. (pres. Chgo. chpt. 1970—74), Assn. Former Intelligence Officers, Soc. Profl. Journalists, Nat. Religious Broadcasters, Evang. Press Assn., Evang. Theol. Soc. Office: 500 J Oakland Place NE Austin MN 55912

ALCOTT, COLIN C., prosecutor; b. Balt., June 26, 1945; Grad., Johns Hopkins U., 1967; grad. cum laude, Ohio State U., 1976. Bar: N.Mex. 1976, Md. 1989. Pvt. practice, 1976—91; pros., 1991—. Mem.: N.Mex. State Bar (pres. 2003). Office: 237 S Fourth St Santa Rosa NM 88435

ALCOTT, MARK HOWARD, lawyer; b. New York, Aug. 11, 1939; s. Harvey and Rose (Eigerman) A.; m. Susan M. (Bell), Sept. 3, 1961; children: Jill, Laura, Daniel, Elizabeth. AB, Harvard U., 1961, LLB, 1964. Bar: N.Y. 1965, U.S. Dist. Ct. (so. and ea. dists.) N.Y. 1966, U.S. Ct. Appeals (2d cir.) 1966, U.S. Ct. Appeals (9th and 10th cirs.) 1980, U.S. Ct. Internat. Trade 1980, U.S. Supreme Ct. 1982, U.S. Ct. Appeals (D.C. cir.) 1983, D.C. 1984, U.S. Tax Ct. 1985; U.S. Ct. Appeals (1st. cir.),2000; U.S. Ct. Appeals (11th. cir.), 2003, U.S. Ct. Appeals (7th cir.) 2004. Assoc. Paul, Weiss, Rifkind, Wharton, and Garrison, N.Y.C., 1964-73, ptnr., 1973—. Mediator Mandatory Mediation Program, U.S Dist. Ct. (so. dist.) N.Y.; spl. master, mediator commercial divsn. N.Y. Supreme Ct.; Spl. Master Appellate Divsn. first dept. Mem. Community Planning Bd., Riverdale, N.Y., 1970-72; comr. Larchmont, N.Y. Planning Commn., 1982-94; bd. dir. Mosholu-Montefiore Community Ctr., Bronx, N.Y., 1966-77. Fellow: Am. Bar Found., N.Y. Bar Found., Am. Coll. Trial Lawyers (chmn. downstate N.Y. com., 1994-1996, chmn. internat. com., 1998-2002); mem.: ABA (litigation sect. internat. litigation com.), Fed. Bar Coun., Internat. Bar Assn. (bus. law sect., internat. litigation com.), Assn. Bar: City of N.Y. (fed. legis. com. 1970—73, commn. campaign finance reform 1997—99), N.Y. State Bar Assn. (chmn. internat. litigation com. comml. and fed. litigation sect. 1989—92, sec. exec. com., exec. vice chmn. 1992—93, sect. chmn.-elect 1993—94, sect. chmn. 1994—95, chmn. spl. commn. on continuing legal edn. 1996—98, chmn. spl. commn. on admin. adjudication 1998—2001, mem. ho. of dels., mem. exec. com., v.p. 2001—05, exec. com. internat. law and practice sect., pres. elect 2005—). Avocation: sailing. Office: Paul Weiss Rifkind Wharton & Garrison 1285 Ave Americas New York NY 10019-6064

ALCOTT-JARDINE, SUSAN, artist, writer; b. L.A., June 7, 1940; d. William Kenneth and Hazel Stella (Pearson) Allin; m. Neal J. Jardine, 1996. Student, LA Harbor Coll., 1958—59, El Camino Coll., 1959—61, Calif. State U., 1961—64, Writers Guld Am. West, Inc., 1970—74, UCLA, 1993, U. Judaism, 2000—. Tchg. asst., lab. technician Calif. State U., LA, 1963—64; with Musifon, Inc., LA, 1965—69, Mickey Garrett & Assoc., LA, 1967—68; freelance reader Screen Gems TV, Burbank, Calif., 1972; corp. sec.-treas., adminstrv. asst., dir. Don Perry Enterprises, Inc., LA, 1969—80; owner Susan Alcott's Scribe Svcs. Ltd., Sherman Oaks, Calif., 1981—88; pub. rels. adminstr., editor, feature writer the Spl. Friends of Kenny Rogers Kenny Rogers Prodns. Inc., LA, 1981—87; with music pub. and copyright dept. Cooper, Epstein & Hurewitz, Beverly Hills, Calif., 1988—90; with Sta. KRCA-TV, Burbank, 1990—94, Fischbach, Perlstein, Lieberman & Yanny, LA, 1995—96; owner, fine artist ltd. edit. art prints Greendoor Edits., 1999—. Actress: theatres So. Calif., films, TV, commls; author: numerous poems; editor: Patterns, 1982; contbr. articles to popular mags.; Represented in permanent collections; lyricist: Nobody's Child. Recipient Writers Guild Found. award, 1972, Writers Guild Found. cert., 1974, Dorothy Daniels Hon. Writing award, Nat. League of Am. PEN Women, 1994, 1997, 1st place fiction, Nat. League Am. Pen Women-Simi Valley Br., 1988. Mem.: SAG, ASCAP, Nat. Writers Union (steering com. 1998—2000), Folk Art Soc. Am., Artist Co-Op 7, Friends of PEN Am. West. Office: PO Box 56839 Sherman Oaks CA 91413-1839 Office Phone: 818-906-9650. E-mail: susanajardine@greendooreditions.com.

ALDA, ALAN, actor, film director, scriptwriter; b. N.Y.C., Jan. 28, 1936; s. Robert and Joan (Browne) A.; m. Arlene Weiss; children: Eve, Elizabeth, Beatrice. BS, Fordham U., 1956, hon. degree, 1978, Drew U., 1979, Columbia U., 1979, Conn. Coll., 1980, Kenyon Coll., 1982. Ind. actor stage, screen, TV, 1956—. Tchr. Compass Sch. Improvisation. Actor: (Broadway plays) including The Apple Tree (nominated Tony award), The Owl and the Pussycat, Purlie Victorious, Fair Game for Lovers, Jakes Women (Tony award nominee), Art, (films) including Gone Are the Days, 1963, The Moonshine War, Paper Lion, 1968, The Extraordinary Seaman, 1968, Jenny, 1970, The Mephisto Waltz, 1971, To Kill a Clown, 1972, California Suite, 1978, Same Time, Next Year, 1978, The Seduction of Joe Tynan, 1979, Crimes and Misdemeanors, 1989 (D.W. Griffith award, N.Y. Film Critics award), Whispers in the Dark, 1992, Manhattan Murder Mystery, 1993, Canadian Bacon, 1995, Flirting With Disaster, 1996, Everyone Says I Love You, 1996, Murder at 1600, 1997, Mad City, 1997, The Object of My Affection, 1998, What Women Want, 2000, The Aviator, 2004; (TV movies) include The Glass House, 1972, Marlo Thomas and Friends in Free to be...You and Me, 1974, 6 Rms Riv Vu, 1974, Kill Me If You Can, And The Band Played On, 1993 (Emmy nomination, Supporting Actor - Special, 1994), White Mile, 1994, Club Land, 2001, The Killing Yard, 2001, (TV series) M*A*S*H, 1972-83 (also writer of 17 episodes, dir. 30 episodes, recipient 5 Emmy awards, 5 Golden Globe awards, Humanitas award for writing), The West Wing, 2004-; creator: (TV series) We'll Get By, 1975, The Four Seasons; writer, narrator Scientific American Frontiers, 1993—; actor, writer, dir.: (films) The Four Seasons, 1981, Sweet Liberty, 1986, A New Life, 1987, Betsy's Wedding, 1990; TV guest appearances include Route 66, 1963, The Nurses, 1963, The Carol Burnet Show, 1974, ER, 1999. Presdl. appointee Nat. Commn. for Observance of Internat. Women's Yr., 1976; co-chair Nat. ERA Countdown Campaign, 1982; trustee Mus. of TV and Radio, 1985, Rockefeller Found., 1989. Recipient Theatre World award for Fair Game for Lovers, 7 People's Choice awards; elected to TV Acad. Hall of Fame, 1994. Mem. AFTRA, Dirs. Guild Am. (awards 1977, 82), Writers Guild Am. (award 1977), Screen Actors Guild, Actors Equity Assn.*

ALDAG, RAMON JOHN, management and organization educator; b. Beccles, Suffolk, Eng., Feb. 11, 1945; came to U.S., 1947; s. Melvin Frederick and Joyce Evelyn (Butcher) A.; m. Hollis Maura Jellinek, June 11, 1977; children: Elizabeth, Katherine BS, Mich. State U., 1966, MBA, 1968, PhD, 1974. Thermal engr. Bendix Aerospace div., Ann Arbor, Mich., 1966-70; teaching asst., instr. Mich. State U., East Lansing, Mich., 1966-73; asst. prof. mgmt. U. Wis., Madison, 1973-78, assoc. prof., 1978-82, prof. mgmt. and orgn., 1982—, chmn. dept. mgmt., 1986-88, assoc. dir. Indsl. Rels. Rsch. Inst., 1977-83, co-dir. Ctr. for Study of Orgnl. Performance, 1982—, faculty senator, 1980-84, Pyle Bascom prof. leadership, 1992—, student advisor, 1979—, Glen A. Skillrud Family chair in bus., 2001—, chmn. dept. mgmt. and human resources Sch. Bus., 1995—, co-dir. Weinert Ctr. for Entrepreneurship, 2000—, exec. dir. Weinert Ctr. Entrepreneurship, 2002—. Mgmt. cons. various businesses and industries, 1973-. Author: Task Design and Employee Motivation, 1979, Managing Organizational Behavior, 1981, Introduction to Business, 1984, (now titled Business in a Changing World), 3d edit., 1993, 4th edit., 1996, Management, 1987, 2d edit., 1991, Leadership and Vision, 2000, Organizational Behavior and Management, 2002, Mastering Management Skills, 2005; contbr. articles to profl. jours.; cons. editor for mgmt. South-Western Pub. Co., 1987—; assoc. editor Jour. Bus. Rsch., 1988—, Decision Scis., 2002-; essays co-editor Jour. Mgmt. Inquiry. Bd. dirs. Family Enhancement Program, Madison, 1981- Grantee U. Wis., HEW, 1975-85; recipient Adminstrv. Rsch. Inst. award, 1976, Jerred Disting. Svc. award, 1993, NSF, 2000—; U. Wis. faculty rsch. fellow, 1985-88. Fellow. Acad. of Mgmt. (div. chmn. 1971—, bd. govs. 1986—, v.p. and program chair 1989—, pres. elect 1990, pres. 1991, past pres. 1992—, dep. dean 2003-05, dean 2005-, recipient Disting Svc. award, 1995); mem. Midwest Acad. Mgmt. (pres. 1973-), Decision Scis. Inst. (track chmn. 1975-), Indsl. Rels. Rsch. Assn. (elections commn. 1980-), Found. Adminstrn. Rsch. (pres. 1992—), Pi Tau Sigma, Tau Beta Pi, Sigma Iota Epsilon, Beta Gamma Sigma, Alpha Iota Delta. Avocations: gardening, reading, fishing. Home: 2818 Van Hise Ave Madison WI 53705-3620 Office: U Wis 3112 Grainger Hall 975 University Ave Madison WI 53706-1323 Office Phone: 608-263-3771. Business E-Mail: raldag@bus.wisc.edu.

ALDANA, PHILIPP ROQUE, neurosurgeon; b. Cebu, Philippines, July 3, 1966; s. Benigno Salcedo Aldana, Jr. and Estelita Roque Aldana; m. Carmina Montesa, Oct. 19, 1969; children: Carissa, Katrina. BS in zoology cum laude, U. Philippines, 1987; MD in rsch. with distinction magna cum laude, St. Louis U., 1994. Resident dept. surgery U. Miami, Fla., 1994—95; resident dept. neurosurgery U. Miami/Jackson Meml. Hosp., 1995—2001; pediatric neurosurgery fellow U. Utah, Primary Children's Hosp., Salt Lake City, 2001—02; asst. dir. divsn. neurosurgery Akron Children's Hosp., Ohio, 2002—. Dir. comprehensive traumatic brain injury program Akron Children's Hosp., 2003—; clin. asst. prof. neurosurgery Northeastern Ohio U. Coll. Medicine, Akron, 2002—. Contbr. chapters to books, articles to profl. jours. Recipient Mo. State Med. Assn. award, St. Louis U., 1994, Resident Day Rsch. award, U. Miami Dept. Neurosurgery, 2001; grantee Instl. grantee brain tumor rsch., Miami Children's Hosp., 1999; Akron Children's Hosp. Found. grantee for brain injury rsch., 2004. Mem.: Children's Oncology Group, Congress Neurol. Surgeons, Am. Assn. Neurol. Surgeons, Alpha Sigma Nu, Alpha Omega Alpha. Office: Akron Children's Hospital Neurosurgery One Perkins Square Akron OH 44308 Office Phone: 330-543-8661.

ALDAVE, BARBARA BADER, lawyer, educator; b. Tacoma, Dec. 28, 1938; d. Fred A. and Patricia W. (Burns) Bader; m. Rafael Aldave, Apr. 2, 1966; children: Anna Marie Alkin, Anthony John. BS, Stanford U., 1960; JD, U. Calif., Berkeley, 1966. Bar: Oreg. 1966, Tex. 1982. Assoc. law firm, Eugene, Oreg., 1967-70; asst. prof. U. Oreg., 1970-73, prof. Eugene, 2000—; vis. prof. U. Calif., Berkeley, 1973-74; from vis. prof. to prof. U. Tex., Austin, 1974-89, co-holder James R. Dougherty chair for faculty excellence, 1981-82, Piper prof., 1982, Joe A. Worsham centennial prof., 1984-89, Liddell, Sapp, Zivley, Hill and LaBoon prof. banking fin. and comml. law, 1989; dean Sch. Law, prof. St. Mary's U., San Antonio, 1989-98, Ernest W. Clemens prof. corp. law, 1996-98; Loran L. Stewart prof. corp. law, dir., Ctr. for Law and Entrepreneurship U. Oreg. Sch. Law, 2000—. Vis. prof. Northeastern U., 1985-88, 98, Boston Coll. 1999-2000, Cornell U., 2002; ABA rep. to Coun. Inter-ABA, 1995-99; NAFTA chpt. 19 panelist, 1994-96. Pres. NETWORK, 1985-89; chair Gender Bias Task Force of Supreme Ct. Tex., 1991-94; bd. dirs. Tex. Alliance Children's Rights, Lawyer's Com. for Civil Rights Under Law of Tex., 1995-2000; nat. chair Gray Panthers, 1999-2003. Recipient Tchg. Excellence award U. Tex. Student Bar Assn., 1976, Appreciation awards Thurgood Marshall Legal Soc. of U. Tex., 1979, 81, 85, 87, Tchg. Excellence award Chicano Law Students Assn. of U. Tex., 1984, Hermine Tobolowsky award Women's Law Caucus of U. Tex., 1985, Ethics award Kugle, Stewart, Dent & Frederick, 1988, Leadership award Women's Law Assn. St. Mary's U., 1989, Ann. Inspirational award Women's Advocacy Project, 1989, Appreciation award San Antonio Black Lawyers Assn., 1990, Spl. Recognition award Nat. Conv. Nat. Lawyers Guild, 1990, Spirit of the Am. Woman award J. C. Penney Co., 1992, Sarah T. Hughes award Women and the Law sect. State Bar Tex., 1994, Ann. Tchg. award Soc. Am. Law Tchrs., 1996, Legal Svcs. award Mexican-Am. Legal Def. and Ednl. Fund, 1996, Woman of Justice award NETWORK, 1997, Ann. Peacemaker award Camino a la Paz, 1997, Outstanding Profl. in the Cmty. award Dept. Pub. Justice, St. Mary's U., 1997, Charles Hamilton Houston award Black Allied Law Students Assn. St. Mary's U., 1998, Woman of Yr. award Tex. Women's Polit. Caucus, 1998, award Clin. Legal Edn. Assn., 1998, Lifetime Achievement award Jour. Law and Religion, 1998, Harriet Tubman award African-Am. Reflections, 2002. Mem.: ABA (com. on corp. laws, sect. banking and bus. law 1982—88, Latin Am. law initiative coun. 2004—), Inter-Am. Bar Assn., Tex.-Mex. Bar Assn., Stanford U. Alumni Assn., Order of Coif, Delta Theta Phi (Outstanding Law Prof award St. Mary's U. chpt. 1990, 1991), Omicron Delta Kappa, Iota Sigma Pi, Phi Delta Phi. Roman Catholic. Home: 86399 N Modesto Dr Eugene OR 97402-9031 Office: U Oreg Sch Law Eugene OR 97403-1221 Office Phone: 541-346-3985. Personal E-mail: balaw98@aol.com. Business E-Mail: aldave@law.uoregon.edu.

ALDAY, PAUL STACKHOUSE, JR., retired mechanical engineer; b. Camden, N.J., May 31, 1930; s. Paul Stackhouse and Amanda (Knocke) A.; m. Ethel Humes O'Connor, Nov. 29, 1952; children: Amy Jane, Paul Stackhouse III, Sarah Jean. BS in ME, Drexel U., 1953, MS in ME, 1957. Registered profl. engr., N.J. Engr. Naval Shipyard/Burroughs Corp., Phila., 1953-56; rsch. engr. Franklin Rsch. Labs., Phila., 1956-57, Univac, Phila., 1957-59; sr. engr. RCA Corp., Camden, 1959-68; sr. design engr. Univac/Burroughs/Control Data, southeastern Pa., 1968-74; project engr. Campbell Soup Co., Camden, 1974-90; cons. Budd Co., Phila., 1990-91; mail processing equipment U.S. Post Office, Phila., 1991-98; ret., 1998. Drexel U. scholar, 1948. Mem. Sigma Xi, Tau Kappa Epsilon Frat. Achievements include stress analysis, supports and preliminary bearing test on design of Enrico Fermi Nuclear Reactor; mechanical concept and design of digital data recorder for Gemini Spacecraft; concepts and designs of video recorder mechanisms used in surveillance satelites, digital computer input/output and memory devices, single position mail sorting machine for the U.S. Post Office. Home: 5759 Rogers Ave Pennsauken NJ 08109-2374

ALDCROFT, GEORGE EDWARD, guidance counselor; b. Toronto, Canada, Nov. 29, 1941; s. George and Margaret Aldcroft; m. Bernadette M. Cartoski, Nov. 27, 1971; children: Allison Marie, Bonnie Christine. BS in Edn., Wayne State U., 1966; MS in Guidance and Counseling, U. Mich., 1971; postgrad., Gestalt Ctr. L.I. Nat. cert. counselor, nat. cert. sch. counselor; cert. leader Developing Capable Young People. Elem. and jr. HS tchr. Center Line (Mich.) Pub. Sch. Sys., 1967-72; summer camp counselor, vol. worker Boys' Clubs Met. Detroit, 1967-69; guidance dir. Shelter Island Union Free Sch. Dist., NY, 1972-83; sch. counselor Westhampton Beach Union Free Sch. Dist., 1983-89, Mattituck Cutchogue Sch. Dist., 1989—2002. Part-time employee Mattituck Cutchogue Sch. Dist., Cutchogue, NY, 2002—; facilitator parenting program. Mem. Shelter Island Drug Edn. Com., 1974, Southold Union Free Sch. Dist. Bd. Edn., 1983-86; bd. dirs. Human Understanding and Growth Seminars, 1985—, pres. bd. dirs., 1991-92. Recipient Outstanding Vol. Leader award Boys' Clubs Detroit, 1968. Mem. N.Y. State Counseling Assn., N.Y. State Sch. Counselors Assn., East End Counselors Assn. (pres. 1995-97), Am. Sch. Counselors Assn., U. Mich. Aumni Assn., N.Y. State United Tchrs. Roman Catholic. Home and Office: PO Box 431 Peconic NY 11958-0431 Personal E-mail: galdcroft@aol.com.

ALDEA, PATRICIA, architect; b. Bucharest, Romania, Mar. 18, 1947; came to U.S., 1976; d. Dan Jasmin Negreanu and Sonia (Friedgant) Philip-Negreanu; m. Val O. Aldea, Feb. 17, 1971; 1 child, Donna-Dana. March, Ion Mincu, Bucharest, 1970. Registered architect, N.Y. Architect, project. mgr. The Landmark Preservation Inst., Bucharest, 1971-76; architect Edward Durell Stone Assn., N.Y.C., 1977-79; sr. assoc. architect, project mgr. Alan Lapidus P.C., N.Y.C., 1980-2001; assoc. project arch., mgr. HLW, N.Y.C., 2001—02; chief plan examiner DOB, N.Y.C., 2003—. Columnist Contemporanul art jour., 1969-73. Hist. landmarks study fellow Internationes Fed. Republic of Germany, 1974. Office: DOB 120-55 Queens Blvd Kew Gardens NY 11424

ALDEN, JOHN W., lawyer; BS, Stanford U., 1955, MS, 1956, JD, 1959. Bar: Calif. 1960. Assoc. Pillsbury, Madison & Sutro, 1959-67; assoc. gen. counsel Occidental Petroleum Corp., L.A., 1967—2004; ret., 2004. Office: Occidental Petroleum Corp 10889 Wilshire Blvd Ste 1500 Los Angeles CA 90024-4216 E-mail: john_w_alden@oxy.com.

ALDEN, STEVEN MICHAEL, lawyer; b. L.A., May 19, 1945; s. Herbert and Sylvia Zina (Hochman) A.; m. Evelyn Mae Subotky, Dec. 31, 1977; children: Carissa Louise, Bramley Marshall, Darym Alexander. AB, UCLA, 1967; JD, U. Calif., Berkeley, 1970. Bar: Calif. 1971, NY 1971. Assoc. Debevoise & Plimpton LLP, NYC, 1971-78, ptnr., 1979—, head Real Estate Dept. Lectr., seminar panelist Practising Law Inst., NYC, 1981—; panelist, lectr. NY State Bar, Albany, 1984. Contbr. articles to profl. jours. Chmn. bd. Symphony Space, Inc., N.Y.C. Mem. ABA (real estate fin. com.), Assn. of Bar of City of NY (com. real property law), Am. Land Title Assn. (assoc. lender's counsel group), Am. Coll. Real Estate Lawyers, Am. Coll. Mortgage Attys., Order of Coif, Phi Beta Kappa, Sky Club (N.Y.C.). Republican. Office: Debevoise & Plimpton LLP 919 3rd Ave Fl 42 New York NY 10022 Office Phone: 212-909-6481. Office Fax: 212-909-6836. E-mail: smalden@debevoise.com.

ALDEN, VERNON ROGER, bank executive; b. Chgo., Apr. 7, 1923; s. Arvid W. and Hildur Pauline (Johnson) A.; m. Marion Frances Parson, Aug. 18, 1951 (dec. Aug. 1999); children: Robert Parson, Anne Elizabeth, James Malcolm, David Douglas. AB magna cum laude, Brown U., 1945; MBA, Harvard, 1950; LLD (hon.), Brown U., 1964, Emerson Coll., 1957, Ohio Wesleyan U., 1964, R.I. Coll., 1965, William Jewell Coll., 1965, Loyola U., 1966, Wilberforce U., 1970, Ottawa U., 1970, Babson Coll., 1972; LHD, North Park Coll., 1965; LittD, Ohio U., 1969; DPS, Bowling Green U., 1969; LittD, Bethany Coll., 1970. Admission officer Brown U., 1946-48; asst. dir. admissions Northwestern U., 1950-51; dir. fin. aid Harvard Grad. Sch. Bus. Adminstrn., assoc. dean, faculty, 1951-61; ednl. dir. U. Hawaii Advanced Mgmt. Program, summer 1960, Keio U. Advanced Mgmt. Program, Tokyo, summers 1960-61; pres. Ohio U., Athens, 1961—69; chmn. bd., chmn. exec. com. Boston Co. and subsidiary Boston Safe Deposit & Trust Co., 1969-78. Bd. dirs. Colgate-Palmolive Co., Digital Equipment Corp., Mead Corp., McGraw Hill, Sonesta Internat. Hotels Corp., Tax-Free Trust Funds Hawaii, Oreg. and Rhode Island, ML-Lee Fund, Ind. Gen. Ptnrs.; hon. consul-gen. Kingdom of Thailand. Chmn. Pres.' Task Force Job Corps Program, com. Future of U. Mass, 1971, chmn. Mass. Coun. Arts/Humanities, 1972-84, Mass. Bus. Devel. Coun./Fgn. Bus. Coun., 1978-83; life trustee Boston Symphony Orch., Mus. Sci., Boston; chmn. arts facilities com. MIT; fellow emeritus Brown U.; life trustee French Libr., Boston; adv. com. Harvard Program Japan-U.S. Rels. Lt, USNR, 1943-46 Recipient Gov.'s award State Ohio, 1969; Founder's citation Ohio U., 1969; Bus. Statesman award Harvard Grad. Sch. Bus., 1975; named Hon. Consul-Gen. Kingdom of Thailand; decorated Order Rising Sun, Star (Japan), Most Noble Order of the Crown of Thailand, Disting. Civilian Svc. medal U.S. Army, Most Exalted Order of the White Elephant (Thailand). Mem. Nat. Assn. Japan-Am. Socs. (chmn.), Japan Soc. of Boston (chmn.), Somerset Club (Boston), Edgartown Yacht Club (Martha's Vineyard), Country Club (Brookline), Farm Neck Golf Club (Martha's Vineyard), Phi Beta Kappa, Phi Kappa Phi, Phi Delta Theta, Beta Gamma Sigma. Episcopalian. Avocations: golf, tennis, reading. Home: 37 Warren St Brookline MA 02445-5925 Office: 20 Park Plz Ste 414 Boston MA 02116-4308

ALDER, BERNI JULIAN, physicist, researcher; b. Duisburg, Germany, Sept. 9, 1925; came to U.S., 1941, naturalized, 1944; s. Ludwig and Ottilie (Gottschalk) A.; m. Esther Berger, Dec. 28, 1956; children: Kenneth, Daniel, Janet. BS, U. Calif., Berkeley, 1947, MS, 1948; PhD, Calif. Inst. Tech., 1951. Instr. chemistry U. Calif., Berkeley, 1951-54; theoretical physicist Lawrence Livermore Lab., Livermore, Calif., 1955-93; prof. dept. applied sci. U. Calif., Davis, 1987-93, prof. emeritus, 1993; van der Waals prof. U. Amsterdam, Netherlands, 1971; prof. associé U. Paris, 1972. G.N. Lewis lectr. U. Calif., Berkeley, 1984, Hinshelwood prof., Oxford, 1986, Lorentz prof., Leiden, 1990, Kistiakowsky lectr. Harvard U., 1990, Royal Soc. lectr., 1991. Author: Methods of Computational Physics, 1963; editor: Jour. Computational Physics, 1966-91. Served with USN, 1944-46. Recipient Boltzmann medal Internat. Union Pure and Applied Physics, 2001; Guggenheim fellow, 1954-55; NSF sr. postdoctoral fellow, 1963-64, Japanese Promotion of Sci. fellow, 1989; Berni J. Alder prize established by European Phys. Soc., 1999. Fellow: Am. Phys. Soc.; mem.: Rare Gas Dynamics Soc. (Grad lectr. 2000), Am. Chem. Soc. (Hildebrand award 1985), Nat. Acad. Scis. Republican. Jewish. Office: Lawrence Livermore Lab PO Box 808 Livermore CA 94551-0808 Office Phone: 925-422-4384. Business E-Mail: alder1@llnl.gov.

ALDERDICE, CYNTHIA LOU, artist; b. Des Moines, Mar. 16, 1932; d. Charles Lloyd and Marion Maxine (Hinn) Sandahl; m. Lee Edward Alderdice, Jan. 30, 1954; children: Cheryl Lynn, Kirk Bryan. BA, U. Tex., 1957. Pres. Am. Art Assocs., Inc., Bethesda, Md., 1966-92; v.p. Am. Art Make-A-Frame, Inc., Rockville, Md., 1972-97; pres. Am. Art Assocs, Inc., Annapolis, Md., 1997—. V.p., bd. dir. Pyramid Atlantic, Inc., Riverdale, Md., 1994—; com. mem. Jewelry from Walters Art Gallery and Zucker Family Collection, 1987, Greek Gold from Beenaki Mus., 1991; com. mem. tarnished vistas Hist. Annapolis, Md., 1988. One-woman shows include: Touchstone Gallery, Washington, 1993, 95, 97, 99, 2002, 2004, Marion Price Contemporary Fine Art Gallery, Centreville, Md., 1995, U. Md., University College, Annapolis, 1996, Md. Fedn. of Art, Annapolis, 1997, Robert C. Williams Am. Museum of Papermaking, Atlanta, 1998, Richards Gallery, Westbrook Gallery, Robert Ferst Ctr. for the Arts, Atlanta, 1998, Air Gallery, Annapolis, 1998, Zaruba Gallery, Rockville, Md., 1999, Ellen Noel Art Museum, Odessa, Tex., 1999, Mill River Gallery, Ellicott City, Md., 1999, 2000, Towson (Md.) U., 2000, The Morris Mechanic Theater, Balt., Md., 2002, Jane Voorhees Zimmerli Mus., N.J., 2004, Touchstone Gallery, Washington, 2004, Atlantic Invitational, 2005; exhibited in group shows Sandy Spring Mus., Md., 2005, Md. Fedn., Annapolis, 2005. Walters Art Mus., Balt. Jewlry Fair, 2004, Jane Voorhees Zimmer Mus., NJ, St. John's Coll. Greenland Libr. Annapolis, 2003, Ann Arndel CC, Arnold, Md., Md. Fedn. Art, Mus. Contemporary Art, Chamalieres, France, 1991, Walters Art Mus., Balt., 1991, 2004, 2005, Inst. of the Arts George Mason U., Fairfax, Va., 1995, Montpelier Cultural Arts Ctr., Laurel, Md., 1995, Tarrytown Gallery, Austin, Tex., 1995, Fairbanks Arts Assn., Alaska, 1997, Melvin Art Gallery, Lakeland, Fla., 1997, Towson State U., Md., 1997, Montgomery Coll., Rockville, Md., 1997, Corcoran Mus. Art, Washington, 1997, Fernbank Mus. of Natural History, Atlanta, 1997, 98, Ann Arundel C.C., Annapolis, Md., 1997, 98, 2003 Tallahassee Mus. of Natural History, 1998, Fed. Res. Bd., Washington, 1998, Washington Arts Club, 1998, Ellen Noel Art Museum, TX, 1999, American Swedish History Museum, 2000, Hanoi Coll. of Fine Art, 2000, Am. Swedish Hist. Mus., Phila., Pa., 2000, Red River Valley Museum, 2001, The Art Gallery at U. Md., Coll. Pk., Md., 2001, Kirkpatric Galleries at Omniplex, Okla. City, Okla., 2001, Hand Workshop Art Ctr., Richmond, Va., 2002, Carla Massoni Gallery, Chestertown, Md., 2002, St. Johns Coll. Greenfield Libr., Annapolis, Md., 2003, Md. Fedn. Art 40th Ann. Show, 2003; permanent collections include Musee d'Art Contemporain of Chamalieres, France, Artist Book Collection Balt. Mus. Art, Md. Fedn. Art, Internat. Monetary Fund Collection, Washington, Freedie Mac's Collection Honoring Washington Artists, U. Md., The Jane Voorhees Silmmerli Art Mus., N.J., Robert C. Williams Am. Mus. Papermaking, Ga. Tech. Univ., U. Md., Fisher Coll. Bus. Ohio State U., Columbus Ohio, D.C. Commn. for the Arts and Humanities, Washington, D.C., others; author: Best of Printmaking. Recipient individual artist award Md. Arts Coun., 1992, Annie award, Cultural Arts Found. Anne Arundel County, 2004. Mem. Md. Fedn. Art (pres., bd. dirs. 1985-87), Md. Printmakers, So. Graphics Art Coun., Friends Cardinal Gallery (hon.), Friends of Dard Hunter. Avocations: tennis, swimming, reading, working on computer. Studio: Annapolis Bus Pk 2104 Renard Ct Annapolis MD 21401-6748

ALDERETTE, BOB, art educator; b. Los Angeles, Calif., July 19, 1943; s. Augustine Alderette and Rose Landa; 1 child, Lauren. BA in art, Calif. State U. at Long Beach, 1969; MFA, Claremont Graduate, 1971. Art prof. Golden West Coll., Huntington Beach, Calif., 1969—83, Calif. State U., Long Beach, 1983—84; prof. U. of Southern Calif., Los Angeles, 1984—. Painting award NEA, 1984. Office: U Southern Calif University Park Los Angeles CA 90089 Business E-Mail: alderett@usc.edu.

ALDERFER, CLAYTON PAUL, psychologist, educator, writer; b. Sellersville, Pa., Sept. 1, 1940; s. Joseph Paul and Ruth Althea (Buck) A.; m. Charleen Judith Frankenfield, July 14, 1962; children: Kate, Benjamin. BS with high honors, Yale U., 1962, PhD, 1966. Cert. Am. Bd. Profl. Psychology. Asst. prof. Cornell U., Ithaca, NY, 1966-68, Yale U., New Haven, 1968-70, assoc. prof., 1970-78, prof. Sch. Orgn. Mgmt., 1978-92, assoc. dean Sch. Orgn. Mgmt., 1982-84; prof. II Grad. Sch. Applied and Profl. Psychology Rutgers U., 1992—, dir. Orgnl. Psychology program, 1992—2004. Author: Existence, Relatedness and Growth, 1972, Learning from Changing, 1975; mem. editl. bd. Jour. Applied Behavioral Sci., 1978-89, editor, 1990-2003; mem. editl. bd. Family Bus. Rev., 1987—, Jour. Orgnl. Behavior, 1988-92; editor: Advances in Experiential Social Processes, vol. 1, 1979, vol. 2, 1980; contbr. articles to profl. jours. Bd. dirs. NTL Inst., Arlington, Va., 1975-78, DATA, New Haven, 1989-92. Grantee Office Naval Rsch., 1970-74, 79-80, 82-86; recipient Cattell award, 1972, McGregor award, 1979, Levinson award, 1997, Helms award, 1999. Fellow Am. Psychol. Assn., Soc. Applied

Anthropology, Am. Psychol. Soc.; mem. Sigma Xi, Tau Beta Pi. Independent. Lutheran. Office: Rutgers Grad Sch Applied Profl Psychology 152 Frelinghuysen Rd Piscataway NJ 08854-8020 E-mail: claygray@aol.com.

ALDERMAN, AMY JOY SPIGEL, elementary school educator; b. Boston, May 16, 1961; d. Gerald David and Rosalind Natalie (Kisloff) Spigel; m. Wesley Lee Alderman, June 22, 1986; children: Adam Michael, Sara Elizabeth. BA, U. Mass., 1983. Cert. tchr. Mass., Tex. Tchr. Daniel Webster Elem. Sch., Dallas, 1983—88, T. C. Wilemon Elem. Sch., Waxahachie, Tex., 1991—97, E. B. Wedgeworth Elem. Sch., Waxahachie, 1997—99, Turner Mid. Sch., Waxahachie, 2000—. Chair lang. arts dept. Turner Mid. Sch., Waxahachie, 2000—01, chair math dept., 2005—, tchr. math., 2005—. Mem.: Newspapers in Edn., Assn. Tex. Profl. Educators. Avocations: assertive discipline, accelerated reading, philosophies. Home: 4230 Black Champ Rd Midlothian TX 76065

ALDERMAN, ANNABEL (ELSIE HIGGS GRINER JR.), writer; b. Nashville, Ga., July 15, 1924; d. Elsie Higgs Griner; m. Hugh Dorsey Alderman, July 20, 1952 (dec. Apr. 25, 1973); 1 child, Galen Alderman Mirate. Grad., high sch., Ga. Regional Police Acad., 1983. Stage performer Miss Peaches, Nashville, Ga., 1948—54; radio show host Miss Peaches Cafe, Moultrie, 1954—54, Houston, 1954—54; stage performer The Holy Notes, Nashville, 1954—62; editor, pub. The Nashville Herald, 1962—66; stage performer Chief Jesters of the South, 1966—75; legal investigator Griner & Alderman, 1981—95; novelist, poet The Write Pl., 1995—; polit. columnist The Valdosta Daily Times, Valdosta, 2000—01. Composer (performer): (songs) Callin' Moody Field, 1954; editor (pub.): The Nashville Herald (2nd Pl.; H. H. Dean Trophy for best editl., 1965, 2nd Pl.; James Cranston Williams Trophy for editl. page, 1965, 3rd Pl.; James Cranston Williams Trophy for editl. page, 1966, Otis Brumby Award for weekly column, 1964, 1966, Fearless Editl. Award, 1966, 3rd Pl., Gen. Excellence, 1965), author of short stories, Solemn in Gomorrah (Southeastern Writers' Assn.; Cappy Hall Award for So. Lit. Fiction, 1998), (novels) Family Man, 1999 (Nominated; Ga. Author of the Yr., 2000, Nominated; Townsend Prize for Fiction, 2000), limericks; composer (performer): (songs) It Is Well With My Soul; Holy Notes; composer: Brand New Star; composer: (performer) Focus On The South, Safari Down South; author: (book of poetry) Lost Loves Don't Count, 1997 (Writer's Digest Self Pub. award); composer: Gospel Music Catalogue, 1952-1975. Aide de camp Gov. Staff, Atlanta, 1963—67, 1971—74. Named Chief Jester of Ga., 1971; recipient citation Writing & Performing in Ann. Cracker Crumble Stage Prodn., Ga. Press Assn., 1963—75. Mem.: Internat. Soc. Poets, Ga. Poetry Soc., Southeastern Writers Assn., Mensa Soc. Republican. Episcopalian. Office Phone: 229-686-2496.

ALDERMAN, MINNIS AMELIA, psychologist, educator, small business owner; b. Douglas, Ga., Oct. 14, 1928; d. Louis Cleveland Sr. and Minnis Amelia (Wooten) A. AB in Music, Speech and Drama, Ga. State Coll., 1949; MA in Supervision/Counseling Psychology, Murray State U., 1960; postgrad., Columbia Pacific U., 1987. Tchr. music Lake County Sch. Dist., Umatilla, Fla., 1949—50; instr. vocal/instrumental music, dir. band, orch., choral Fulton County Sch. Dist., Atlanta, 1950—54; instr. English, speech, debate, vocal and instrumental music Elko County Sch. Dist., Wells, Nev., 1954—59, dir. drama, band, choral and orchestra, 1954—59; tchr. English and social studies Christian County Sch. Dist., Hopkinsville, Ky., 1960; instr. psychology, counselor critic prof. Murray State U., Ky., 1961—63, U. Nev., Reno, 1963—67; owner Minisizer Exercising Salon, Ely, Nev., 1969—71, Knit Knook, Ely, 1969—, Minimimeo, Ely, 1969—, Gift Gamut, Ely, 1977—; prof. dept. fine arts Wassuk Coll., Ely, 1986—91, assoc. dean, 1986—87, dean, 1987—90; counselor White Pine County Sch. Dist., Ely, 1960—68; dir. Child and Family Ctr. Ely Indian Tribe, 1988—93. Supr. testing Ednl. Testing Svc., Princeton, NJ, 1960-68, Am. Coll. Testing Program, Iowa, 1960-68, U. Nev., Reno, 1960-68; chmn. bd. White Pine Sch. Dist. Employees Fed. Credit Union, Ely, 1961-69; psychologist mental hygiene divsn. Nev. Pers., Ely, 1969-75, dept. employment secrity, 1975-80; sec.-treas. bd. dirs. Gt. Basin Enterprises, Ely, 1969-71; rep. Ely/East Ely Bus. Coun., 1997—; mem. Econ. Devel. Bd., 1998—; prof. Great Basin C.C., 1999—, pvt. instructor piano, violin, voice and organ, Ely, 1981—; spkr. in field Author: various news articles, feature stories, pamphlets, handbooks and grants in field. Dir. Family Resource Ctr. (Great Basin Rural Nev. Youth Cabinet), 1996—; bd. dir. band Sacred Heart Sch., Ely, 1982-99; active Gov.'s Mental Health State Commn., 1963-65, Nev. Hwy. Safety Leaders Bd., 1979-82, Ely Shoshone Tribal Youth Camp, 1991-92, Elys Shoshone Tribal Unity Conf., 1991-92, Tribal Parenting Skills Coord., 1991, White Pine Overall Econ. Devel. Plan Coun., 1992-2005, White Pine C. of C., 2000-; bd. dir. White Pine County Sch. Employees Fed. Credit Union, 1961-68, pres., 1963-68; 2d v.p. White Pine Cmty. Concert Assn., 1965-67, pres., 1967, 85—, treas., 1975-79, dr. chmn., 1981-85; chmn. of bd., 1984; bd. dir. White Pine chpt. ARC, 1978-82; mem. Gov.'s Commn. on Status Women, 1968-74, Gov.'s Nevada State Juvenile Justice Adv. Commn., 1992-94; dir. White Pine Legis. Coalition, 2002—; sec.-treas. White Pine Rehab. Tng. Ctr. for Retarded Persons, 1973-75, White Pine County Juvenile Problems Cabinet, 1994—; mem. Gov.'s Commn. on Hwy. Safety, 1979-81, Gov's. Juvenile Justice Program; dir. White Pine Cmty. Choir, 1962—; vice-chmn. Gt. Basin Health Coun., 1973-75, Home Ext. adv. Bd., 1977-80; sec.-treas. Gt. Basin chpt. Nev. Employees Assn.; bd. dir. United Way, 1970-76; vice-chmn. White Pine Coun. on Alcoholism and Drug Abuse, 1975-76, chmn., 1976-77, White Pine County Bus. Coun., 1998—; dir. White Pine Coalation; grants author 3 yrs. Indian Child Welfare Act, State Hist. Preservation, Fair and Recreation Bd. Centennial Fine Arts Ctr.; originator Cmty. Tng. Ctr. Retarded People, 1972, Ret. Sr. Vol. Program, 1974, Nutrition Program Sr. Citizens, 1974, Sr. Citizens Ctr., 1974, Home Repairs Sr. Citizens, 1974, Sr. Citizens Crafters Assns., 1976, Inst. Current World Affairs, 1989, Victims of Crime, 1990-92, grants author Family Resource Ctr., 1995; bd. dir. Family coalition, 1990-92, Sacred Heart Parochial Sch., dir. band, 1982—; candidate diaconal ministry, 1982-93; invited performer Branson Jubilee Nat. Ch. Choir Festival, Mo., Ely Meth. Ch. Choir, 1960-84; choir dir., organist Sacred Heart Ch., 1984—; Precinct reporter ABC News, 1966; bd. dir. White Pine Juvenile Cabinet, 1993—, Ely/East Ely Bus. Coun., 1997—, Econ. Devel. Bd., 1998— Named scholar, Nat. Trust for Hist. Preservation, 2000; recipient Recognition rose, Alpha Chi State Delta Kappa Gamma, 1994, Recognition Rose, 2002, Perserving America's Treasures in the 21st Century, 2001; grantee, Nat. Trust for Historic Preservation, L.A., 2000. Fellow Am. Coll. Musicians, Nat. Guild Piano Tchrs.; mem. NEA (life), UDC, DAR, Nat. Fedn. Ind. Bus. (dist. chair 1971-85, nat. guardian coun. 1985—, state guardian coun. 1987—), AAUW (pres. Wells br. 1957-58, pres. White Pine br. 1965-66, 86-87, 89-91, 93—, bd. dirs. 1965-87, rep. edn. 1965-67, implementation chair 1967-69, area advisor 1969-73, 89-91), Nat. Fedn. Bus. and Profl. Women (1st v.p. Ely chpt. 1965-66, pres. Ely chpt. 1966-68, 74-76, 85—, bd. dirs. Nev. chpt., 1st v.p. Nev. Fedn. 1970-71, pres. Nev. chpt. 1972-73,nat. bd. dirs. 1972-73), White Pine County Mental Health Assn. (pres. 1960-63, 78—), Mensa (supr. testing 1965—), White Pine C. of C. (bd. dirs.), White Pine Nuc. Waste Assn., Lincoln Hwy. Assn., Bus. Area Network Group, Delta Kappa Gamma (br. pres. 1968-72, 94-99, state bd. 1967—, chpt. parliamentarian 1974-78, 99—, state 1st v.p. 1967-69, state pres. 1969-71, nat. bd. 1969-71, state parliamentarian 1971-73, 95—, chmn. state nominating com. 1995-97, chmn. bylaws com. 2003—, workshop presenter on aging 1995, presenter 1998-99), White Pine Knife and Fork Club (1st v.p. 1969-70, pres. 1970-71, bd. dirs.), Soc. Descs. of Knights of Most Noble Order of Garter, Nat. Soc. Magna Charta Dames. Office: PO Box 150457 Ely NV 89315-0457 Office Phone: 775-289-2116. *My mission in this life: To use to the fullest good, the talents and abilities that have been given to me in order to productively help whenever and wherever the opportunity arises.*

ALDERMAN, WILLIAM FIELDS, lawyer; b. Hamilton, Ohio, 1945; AB summa cum laude, Miami U., 1967; JD, Yale U., 1970. Bar: Calif. 1971. Ptnr. Orrick, Herrington & Sutcliffe, San Francisco, 1976—. Ct. apptd. arbitrator, mediator and evaluator, 1988—. Dir. Lawyers Com. for Civil Rights of the San Francisco Bay Area, 1985—, St. Thomas More Soc. San Francisco, 1987-94, pres. 1993; dir. San Francisco Neighborhood Legal Assistance Found., 1995—. Mem. Phi Beta Kappa. Office: Orrick Herrington & Sutcliffe Old Federal Reserve Bank Bldg 400 Sansome St San Francisco CA 94111-3143

ALDERSLEY, STEPHANIE POLOWE, language educator; b. Sacramento, July 16, 1945; d. Joseph Polowe and Elizabeth Margaret Nowatka; m. Stephen Francis Aldersley, May 30, 1982; 1 child, Jordan Polowe; m. Edward Stafford Downey, Sept. 23, 1967 (div. Jan. 1981); children: Jennifer Victoria Rubens, Ian Edward Downey. Student, St. Lawrence U., 1963—66; BA in English and Am. Lit., Wayne State U., 1968; MA in English Lit., SUNY, Brockport, 1980; EdD in Psycholinguistics, U. Rochester, 1985. Tchr. Rochester City Sch. Dist., NY, 1971—72; instr. English Rochester Inst. Tech., 1974—83, asst. prof. English, 1983—90, assoc. prof. English, 1990—; legis. Monroe County Legis., 1998—, minority leader, 2002—. Sec. Conv. Am. Instrs. Deaf, Dallas, 1987—89, program chair, 1989—91, pres., 1991—93. Mem. West Irondequist Sch. Bd., 1986—92. Mem.: Rochester Yacht Club, Rotary. Democrat. Presbyterian. Avocations: running, painting, music, bicycling. Home: 169 Wisner Rd Rochester NY 14622 Office: NTID Rochester Inst Tech 1 Lomg Meml Dr Rochester NY 14623

ALDERSON, ARTHUR STANCLIFF, III, education educator; b. Washington, Pa., Dec. 15, 1965; s. Arthur Stancliff Alderson Jr. and Patricia Euginia Blanock; m. Indermohan Virk, Feb. 18, 1961; children: Meera Patrica Virk, Neal Virk. BA, Indiana U. of Pa., 1988; MA, U. N.C., 1992, PhD, 1997. Asst. prof. Ind. U., Bloomington, 1997—2004, assoc. prof., 2004—. Author: World Societies: The Evolution of Human Social Life; contbr. scientific papers pub. to profl. jour., chapters to books. Adv. bd. Prague Inst. for Global Urban Devel., Prague and Washington, Czech Republic, 2004. Recipient Carolina Soc. of Fellows dissertation fellow, 1995; Structure of the World City Sys. grantee, World Soc. Found., 2001. Mem.: Prague Inst. for Global Urban Devel. (subcom. on global urban devel.), So. Sociol. Soc., Internat. Sociol. Assn., Am. Sociol. Assn. Achievements include research in income distribution, globalization, and urban development. Office: Ind Univ Ballantine Hall 744 Bloomington IN 47405-6628 Office Phone: 812-856-5883.

ALDERSON, GLORIA FRANCES DALE, rehabilitation specialist; b. Rainelle, W.Va., May 11, 1945; d. Orval Rupert and Juanita Rose (Nelson) Dale; m. Grayson Raines Alderson, June 3, 1964; children: John Grayson, James Leslie. ADN, U. Charleston; BS, W.Va. U. DON Charleston Area Med. Ctr., Charleston, 1977-84; head nurse Eye & Ear Clinic, Charleston, 1981-84; owner, operator ABZ Nursing, Kanawha County, W.Va., 1983-87; rehab. specialist W.Va., 1983—. Bd. dirs. Profl. and Social Com. on Nursing. Bd. dirs. Urban Politics Symposium, Charleston, 1978; election campaign mgr. Rep. Party, Charleston. Bd. Regents scholar, W.Va. U., 1974-77; named Woman of Yr., Am. Biographical Assn., 1996-97, Internat. Ambassadore with hn. title HE, Cambridge, Eng. and the Crown, 1998. Mem.: AAUW, Internat. Platform Assn., Internat. Soc. Poets (Nominee Poet of Yr. 1997), Am. Rehab. Profls., Am. Bd. Disability Analysts (life; cert., diplomate), Menniger Soc., Order Ea. Star. Avocations: painting, writing. Home and Office: 1089 Highland Dr Saint Albans WV 25177-3675 Personal E-mail: GFA722@aol.com.

ALDERSON, JO BARTELS, writer, poet; b. Janesville, Wis., Sept. 21, 1930; d. Frederick Carl William and Rose Augusta Theresa (Griesbach) Bartels; m. James Michael Alderson, Sr., June 21, 1952; children: James Jr. (Mick), Kaye, Jaye, Ann, Erica. BA, Milton Coll., 1952. Part-time reporter Janesville Gazette, 1949—52; tchr. Oshkosh (Wis.) Area Schs., 1958—59, play dir., 1962—67; proofreader The Paper for Ctrl. Wis., Oshkosh, 1968—70; tchr. writing workshops Johnson Found., Racine, Wis., 1969—70; guide/publs. editor Paine Art Ctr. and Arboretum, Oshkosh, 1974—92; freelance writer, 1960—. Pres., editor, bd. mem. Wis. Fellowship Poets, 1960—; bd. mem. Coun. for Wis. Writers, Milw., 1962—78, pres., 1976—78; judge various state and nat. literary contests; judge H.S. forensic contests; treas., dir., actor, bd. mem. The Co. for Wis. Arts, Oshkosh, 1977—94. Author: (biography) The Man Mazzuchelli, 1974, Rain From a Clear Sky, 1991 (Nat. Fedn. Press Women award, 1993), (history book) Wisconsin's Early French Habitants, 1998 (Nat. Fedn. Press Women award, 1999), (poetry book) Owls, 1980, Owls Too and II, 1984, Tri-Owls, 1988 (1st place Nat. Fedn. Press Women, 1989), Rudd Owls (1st place Nat. Fedn. Press Women, 1996), From the Fairy Tales, 2003, numerous poems; editor: Poems Out of Wisconsin III, 1967, 30th Anniversary Book of Paine Art Center, 1981, inner-mission, 1983—92; contbr. articles to profl. jours. Dir., actor 4 cmty. theatre groups, Wis., 1953—95; founder, pres., bd. mem. The Grand Opera House Com., Oshkosh, 1965—80; mem. Oshkosh Found. Arts Com., 1997—98. Recipient 4th Pl., Nat. Legacies Contest, N.Y., 1994. Mem.: Coun. for Wis. Writers (newsletter editor), Wis. Regional Writers, Wis. Fellowship Poets (bd. mem. 1951—, newsletter editor), Nat. Fedn. Press Women, Wis. Press Women (treas. 2000—, newsletter editor). Avocations: travel, remodeling houses, art, sewing, exploring nature. Home: 1950 Georgia St Oshkosh WI 54902 Office Phone: 920-231-8646.

ALDERSON, PHILIP OTIS, radiologist, educator; b. San Francisco, Aug. 11, 1944; s. Lloyd I. and Helen A. (Boekemeier); m. Marjorie Jean Hawkins, June 13, 1970; children: Kelly Suzanne, Lisa Joanne. AB in Zoology, Washington U., St. Louis, 1966, MD, 1970. Cert. Diplomate Am. Bd. Nuclear Medicine, Am. Bd. Radiology (Diagnosis). Intern Jewish Hosp., Washington U. Med. Sch., St. Louis, 1970-71, resident in radiology and nuclear medicine, 1971-74; instr. in radiology Mallinckrodt Inst., Washington U. Med. Sch., St. Louis, 1974-75; from asst. to assoc. prof. dept. radiology Johns Hopkins Med. Inst., Balt., 1977-80; prof. radiology Columbia-Presbyn. Med. Ctr., N.Y.C., 1980—, James Picker prof., chmn. dept. radiology, 1990—. Trustee Am. Bd. Radiology, 1998—, sec.-treas., 2002—04, pres.-elect, 2004—; trustee Am. Bd. Nuc. Medicine, 1989—95. Author 4 books; contbr. articles to profl. jours. Maj. USAF, 1975—77. Recipient Alumni Achievement award, Washington U. Med. Sch., 1995; grantee, NIH, 1974—2001. Fellow: AAAS, Am. Inst. Med. and Biol. Engrs., N.Y. Acad. Medicine, Am. Coll. Radiology (bd. chancellors 1993—2000, v.p. 1999—2000), Am. Coll. Nuclear Physicians; mem.: Soc. Chmn. Acad. Radiology Depts. (rep. Coun. Acad. Socs. of Am. Assn. Med. Colls. 1990—95, pres. 1994—95), Acad. Radiology Rsch. (sec. 1998—99, v.p. 1999—2001, pres. 2001—03), Am. Roentgen Ray Soc. (chmn. exec. coun. 1997—98, v.p 2004—05, pres.-elect 2005—), Assn. Residency Program Dirs. in Radiology (sec.-treas. 1996—97, pres. 1998—99), Assn. Univ. Radiologists (sec.-treas. 1994—95, pres. 1996—97), Soc. Nuclear Medicine (v.p. 1984—85, chmn. sci. program com. 1984—86), N.Y. State Radiol. Soc. (sec.-treas. 1991—93, pres. 1993—94), N.Y. City Roentgen Soc. (v.p. 1989—90, pres. 1991—92), Fleischner Soc. (sec. 1989—92, treas. 1996—99, pres. 2000—01), Omicron Delta Kappa. Office: Columbia-Presbyn Med Ctr Dept Radiology 630 W 168th St New York NY 10032-3702 E-mail: poa1@columbia.edu.

ALDERSON, SANDY (RICHARD LYNN ALDERSON), major league baseball executive; b. Seattle, Nov. 22, 1947; s. John Lester and Gwenny (Parry) A.; m. Linda Lee Huff, Dec. 20, 1969; children: Catrin Gwennan, Bryn Garreth. BA, Dartmouth Coll., 1969; JD, Harvard U., 1976. Assoc. Farella, Braun & Martel, San Francisco, 1976-81; gen. counsel Oakland Athletics, Calif., 1981-83, v.p. baseball ops., 1983-93, pres., gen. mgr., 1993—95, 1997—98; exec. v.p., baseball ops. Major League Baseball, 1998—2005; CEO San Diego Padres, 2005—. Dir. Major League Scouting Bur., Newport Beach, Calif. Served to lt. USMC, 1969-73, Vietnam Office: 9449 Friars Rd San Diego CA 92108*

ALDINGER, WILLIAM F., III, diversified financial services company executive; b. 1947; BA, CUNY, 1969. With U.S. Trust Co., N.Y.C., 1969-75, Citibank Corp., N.Y.C., 1975-76; exec. v.p. Wells Fargo Bank NA, San Francisco, 1986-98; CEO HSBC N. Am. Inc. (Formerly Household Internat., Inc.), Prospect Heights, Ill., 1994—, chmn. bd. dirs., 1996—. Office: HSBC N America Inc 2700 Sanders Rd Prospect Heights IL 60070-2701

ALDISERT, RUGGERO JOHN, federal judge; b. Carnegie, Pa., Nov. 10, 1919; s. John S. and Elizabeth (Magnacca) Aldisert; m. Agatha Maria DeLacio, Oct. 4, 1952; children: Lisa Maria, Robert, Gregory. BA, U. Pitts., 1941, JD, 1947. Bar: Pa. 1947. Gen. practice law, Pitts., 1947—61; judge Ct. Common Pleas, Allegheny County, 1961—68, U.S. Ct. Appeals (3d cir.), Pitts., 1968—84, chief judge, 1984—87, sr. judge Pitts., Santa Barbara, Calif., 1987—. Adj. prof. law U. Pitts. Sch. Law, 1964—87; faculty Appellate Judges Seminar, NYU, 1971—85, assoc. dir., 1979—85; chmn. Fed. Appellate Judges Seminar, 1972—78; mem. Pa. Civil Procedural Rules Com., 1965—84, Jud. Conf. Com. on Adminstrn. Criminal Law, 1971—77; chmn. adv. com. on bankruptcy rules Jud. Conf. U.S., 1979—84; vis. prof. univs. in U.S. and abroad, 1965—99; intensive lectures at univs in, Italy, Germany, France, Poland, Croatia and Serbia. Author: Il Ritorno al Paese, 1966—67, The Judicial Process, Readings, Materials and Cases, 1996, 2d edit., 1996, Logic for Lawyers: A Guide to Clear Legal Thinking, 1997, 3d edit., 1997, Opinion Writing, 1990, Winning on Appeal, 2003, Road to the Robes: A Federal Judge Recollects Young Years and Early Times, 2005; contbr. over 30 articles to profl. publs. Allegheny dist. chmn. Multiple Sclerosis Soc., 1961—68; pres. ISDA, Cultural Heritage Found., 1965—68; trustee U. Pitts., 1968—; mem. bd. visitors Pitts. Sch. Law, 1968—, chmn., 1969—99. Maj. USMC, 1942—46, with USMC, 1946—51. Recipient Outstanding Merit award, Allegheny County Acad. Trial Lawyers, 1964. Mem.: Am. Law Inst., Italian Sons and Daus. Am. Fraternal Assn. (nat. pres. 1954—68), Omicron Delta Kappa, Phi Alpha Delta, Phi Beta Kappa. Democrat. Roman Catholic. Office: US Ct Appeals 120 Cremona Dr Ste D Santa Barbara CA 93117-5511

ALDOCK, JOHN DOUGLAS, lawyer; b. Washington, Jan. 20, 1942; s. Sam I. and Myrtle C. (Cohen) Aldock; m. Judy Robichek, May 18, 1969; children: Jessica Lauren, Stephanie Lisa. BS with honors, Northwestern U., Evanston, Ill., 1964; LLB cum laude, U. Pa., 1967. Bar: D.C. 1968, Md. 1973, U.S. Supreme Ct. 1972. Law clk., Hon. Luther W. Youngdahl U.S. Dist. Ct. D.C., 1967-68; asst. U.S. atty. Dept. of Justice, Washington, 1968-71; ptnr., chair, Wash. off. Shea & Gardner (now Goodwin Procter LLP), Washington, 1971—, and mem. exec. com. Vice-chmn. Unauthorized Practice of Law Com. to D.C. Ct. of Appeals, 1979-83; chmn. Adv. Com. on Rules to U.S. Dist. Ct. for D.C., 1987—; ind. counsel Meese Investigation, Adminstrv. Off. of U.S. Cts., Washington, 1984; mem. Dist. Ct. Civil Adv. Com., 1991—; bd. dir.Wash. Legal Clinic for the Homeless Mem. ABA, Jud. Conf. for D.C. Cir., Am. Law Inst., Am. Arbitration Assn. (arbitrator 1985—), D.C. Bar Assn., Asst. U.S. Attys. Assn. (pres. 1975); fellow, Am. Coll. Trial Lawyers, Am. Bar Found. Office: Goodwin Procter LLP 901 New York Ave NW Washington DC 20001 Office Phone: 202-346-4240. Office Fax: 202-346-4444. Business E-Mail: jaldock@goodwinprocter.com.

ALDONAS, GRANT D., lawyer, former federal agency administrator; b. Mpls. m. Pam Olson; children: Nicole, Kirsten, Noah. BA in Internat. Rels., U. Minn., 1975, JD, 1979. Spl. asst. Under Sec. of State for Econ. Affairs; dir. South Am. and Caribbean Affairs Office of the U.S. Trade Rep.; ptnr. Miller & Chevalier, Washington; chief internat. trade counsel Chmn. of the Senate Fin. Com.; under sec. for internat. trade adminstrn. US Dept. Commerce, Washington, 2001—05; ptnr. Akin Gump Strauss Hauer & Feld LLP, Washington, 2005—. Adj. prof. law Georgetown U. Law Ctr.; counsel Bipartisan Commn. on Entitlement and Tax Reform; adviser Commn. on U.S.-Pacific Trade and Investment. Mem.: ABA (chair task force on multilateral investment agreements, vice chair com. on trade and fgn. investment sect. internal law and pr). Office: Akin Gump Strauss Hauer & Feld LLP Robert S Strauss Bldg 1333 New Hampshire Ave NW Washington DC 20036

ALDOUS, CHARLA G., lawyer; b. Tex. 4 children. BA in Polit. Sci and History, Austin Coll., 1982; JD, So. Methodist U. Sch. Law, 1985. Bar: Tex., admitted to practice: US Dist. Ct. (Ea. Dist.) Tex., US Dist. Ct. (No. Dist.) Tex. Co-founder & ptnr. Aldous & McDougal LLP; spl. counsel Baron & Budd, Dallas, 2005—. Named a Tex. Super Lawyer; named one of Best Lawyers in Dallas, D Magazine, 2001, 2003, 2005, Best Lawyers in Am., 2003—04, 2005—06, Top 100 Dallas/Ft. Worth Super Lawyers, Top 50 Female Tex. Super Lawyers. Mem.: Tex. Trial Lawyers Assn., Tex. Bar Found., State Bar Tex., Dallas Trial Lawyers Assn., Dallas Bar Assn., Assn. Trial Lawyers Am., Am. Bd. Trial Advocates (exec. com., Dallas Chpt.), ABA. Office: Baron & Budd PC Ste 1100 3102 Oak Lawn Ave Dallas TX 75219 Office Phone: 214-521-3605. Office Fax: 214-520-1181.*

ALDOUS, DAVID J., statistics professor; b. July 13, 1952; BA in Mathematics, Cambridge U., 1973, PhD in Mathematics, 1977; ScD (hon.), U. Chicago, 2000. Rsch. fellow St. John's Coll., Cambridge, 1977—79; asst. prof. statistics U. Calif., Berkeley, 1979—82, assoc. prof. statistics, 1982—86, prof. statistics, 1986—, chair statistics, 1997—99. A.D. White prof.-at-large Cornell U., 2004—; mem. NSF Review Panel in Probability; assoc. editor Annals of Probability, 1982—87, 1994—2000, Annals of Applied Probability, 1989—96, Jour. Mathematical Analysis, 1986—91, Jour. Theoretical Probability, 1988—95, Electronic Jour. Probability, 1995—, Random Structures & Algorithms, 2001—. Recipient Rollo Davidson prize, 1980, Loeve prize in Probability, 1993. Fellow: Am. Acad. of Arts & Sciences, Royal Soc., Inst. of Mathematical Statistics (IMS Council 1987—89). Office: U Calif Dept Statistics 367 Evans Hall Berkeley CA 94720-3860

ALDREDGE, THEONI VACHLIOTIS, costume designer; b. Athens, Greece, Aug. 22, 1932; d. Gen. Athanasios and Meropi (Gregoriades) Vachliotis; m. Thomas E. Aldredge, Dec. 10, 1953. Student, Am. Sch., Athens, 1949—53, Goodman Theatre, Chgo.; LHD, De Paul U., 1985. Mem. design staff Goodman Theatre, 1951-53; head designer N.Y. Shakespeare Festival, 1962—91. Designer numerous Broadway and off Broadway shows, ballet, opera, TV spls.; films include Girl of the Night, You're a Big Boy Now, No Way to Treat a Lady, Uptight, Last Summer, I Never Sang for My Father, Promise at Dawn, The Great Gatsby (Brit. Motion Picture Acad. award 1976), Network, The Cheap Detective, The Fury, The Eyes of Laura Mars (Acad. Sci. Fiction Films award), The Champ, Semi-Tough, The Rose, Monsignor, Annie, Ghostbusters, Moonstruck, We're No Angels, Stanley and Iris, Other People's Money, Night and the City, Addams Family Values, Milk Money, Mrs. Winterbourne, The Mirror Has Two Faces, The First Wives Club; over 100 Broadway shows include A Chorus Line (Theatre World award 1976), Annie (Tony award 1977), Barnum (Tony award 1979), Dream Girls, Woman of the Year, Onward Victoria, La Cage Aux Folles (Tony award 1984), 42d Street, A Little Family Business, Merlin, Private Lives, The Corn Is Green, The Rink, Blithe Spirit, Chess, Gypsy (1989 revival), Oh, Kay, The Secret Garden, Nick and Nora, High Rollers, Putting It Together, Annie Warbucks, The Flowering Peach, School for Scandal, Taking Sides, The Three Sisters, St. Louis Woman, The Best Man, "EFX" MGM Grand, Follies 2001 Revival. Recipient Obie award for Disting. Svc. to Off-Broadway Theatre Village Voice, Maharam award for Peer Gynt, N.Y.C. Liberty medal, 1986, Career Achievement award Costume Designers Guild, 2000, DePaul U., 1999, TDF Irene Sharaff Lifetime Achievement award, 2002, numerous Drama Desk and Critic awards; inducted into Theatre Hall of Fame. Mem. United Scenic Artists, Costume Designers Guild, Acad. Motion Picture Arts Scis. (Oscar award Great Gatsby 1975).

ALDRICH, ANN, judge; b. Providence, June 28, 1927; d. Allie C. and Ethel M. (Carrier) A.; m. Chester Aldrich, 1960 (dec.); children: Martin, William; children by previous marriage: James, Allen; m. John H. McAllister III, 1986. BA cum laude, Columbia U., 1948; LLB cum laude, NYU, 1950, LLM, 1964, JSD, 1967. Bar: D.C. bar, N.Y. bar 1952, Conn. bar 1966, Ohio bar 1973, Supreme Ct. bar 1956. Research asst. to mem. faculty N.Y. U. Sch. Law; atty. IBRD, 1952; atty., rsch. asst. Samuel Nakasian, Esq., Washington, 1952-53; mem. gen. counsel's staff FCC, Washington, 1953-60; U.S. del. to Internat. Radio Conf., Geneva, 1959; practicing atty. Darien, Conn., 1961-68; asso. prof. law Cleve. State U., 1968-71, prof., 1971-80; judge U.S. Dist. Ct. (no. dist.) Ohio, Cleveland, 1980—. Bd. govs. Citizens' Comm. Ctr, Inc., Washington, mem. litigation com.; guest lectr. Calif. Inst. Tech., Pasadena, summer 1971. Mem. Fed. Bar Assn., Nat. Assn. of Women Judges, Fed.

Communications Bar Assn., Fed. Judge Assn. Episcopalian. Office: US District Court Ste 17B 801 W Superior Ave Cleveland OH 44113-1829 Office Phone: 216-357-7200. E-mail: Ann_Aldrich@OHNDUSCourts.gov.

ALDRICH, CLARENCE KNIGHT, physician, educator; b. Chgo, Apr. 12, 1914; s. L. Sherman and Bessie A. (Knight) A.; m. Julie H. Murphy, Feb. 4, 1942; children— Carol K., Michael S., Thomas K., Robert F. BA, Wesleyan U., 1935; MD, Northwestern U., 1940. Faculty U. Minn. Med. Sch., 1947-55, asst. prof., 1947-52, assoc. prof., 1952-55; prof. psychiatry U. Chgo. Sch. Medicine, 1955-70, chmn. dept. psychiatry, 1955-64; prof., chmn. dept. N.J. Med. Sch., Newark, 1970-73; prof. psychiatry Sch. Medicine, U. Va., Charlottesville, 1973-77, prof. psychiatry and family medicine, 1977-84, prof. emeritus, 1984—, mem. Ctr. Advanced Studies, 1981-84. Vis. prof. psychiatry U. Edinburgh, 1963-64; dir. Blue Ridge Mental Health Ctr., 1973-75; Mayne guest prof. U. Queensland, Australia, 1986. Author: Psychiatry for the Family Physician, 1955, Introduction to Dynamic Psychiatry, 1966, (with C. Nighswonger) A Casebook for Pastoral Counseling, 1968, The Medical Interview: Gateway to the Doctor-Patient Relationship, 1993, Quest for a Star, 2003. Served from asst. surgeon to surgeon USPHS, 1940-46. Fellow Am. Coll. Psychiatrists, Am. Orthopsychiat. Assn., Am. Psychiat. Assn.; mem. Group for Advancement Psychiatry. Home and Office: 250 Pantops Mountain Rd Apt 5115 Charlottesville VA 22911 Office Phone: 434-972-2414. Business E-Mail: cka3f@virginia.edu.

ALDRICH, FRANK NATHAN, banker; b. Jackson, Mich., June 8, 1923; s. Frank Nathan and Marion (Butterfield) A.; m. Edna Dora DeJan, Nov. 21, 1956; children: Marion Dolores, Clinton Pershing. Student, U. Md., 1943; AB in Govt, Dartmouth Coll., 1948; postgrad., Harvard U., 1948. Sub-mgr. First Nat. Bank of Boston, Havana, Cuba, 1949—60, Rio de Janeiro, 1961—62, Sao Paulo, Brazil, 1963—64, mgr., 1965, exec. mgr. Rio de Janeiro, 1966, v.p. Brazilian brs., 1966—69, v.p. overseas ops. Boston, 1969—70; v.p. Latin Am.-Asia-Africa-Middle East div., Boston, 1970—73; sr. v.p. Latin Am. div., Boston, 1973—88; pres., CEO McLaughlin Bank N.V., Netherlands Antilles, 1989; CEO Amicorp N.V., Netherlands Antilles, 1996—. Dir. Paradigm Fin. Svcs., Netherlands Antilles; prin. Mitan Capital Corp., N.Y.C. Trustee Pan Am. Devel. Found., Washington. With USAAF, 1943-46. Decorated Air medal with 4 oak leaf clusters, D.F.C. U.S.; Medalha Marechal Candido Mariano da Silva Rondon (Brazil); Ordem Nacional do Cruzeiro do Sul (Brazil). Fellow Brit. Interplanetary Soc.; mem. Air Force Assn., Res. Officers Assn., Confederate Air Force, Inst. Navigation, Royal Astron. Soc. Can., Soc. of the Cin., Sphinx Soc., Vets of Battle of the Bulge, Squadron A Assn. of N.Y., Disting. Flying Cross Soc., Harvard Club (Boston), Dartmouth Coll. Club, Yale Club (N.Y.C.), Army and Navy Club (Washington), Wellesley (Mass.), Country Club, Wellesley Coll. Club, Masons, Shriners., Beta Theta Pi. Home: 3 Indian Spring Rd Dover MA 02030-2331 Business E-Mail: amicorp@amicorp.com.

ALDRICH, FRANKLIN DALTON, medical researcher, consultant; b. Detroit, Jan. 25, 1929; s. George Franklin and Ruth Markham (Dalton) A.; m. Margaret Joan Pearson, Mar. 22, 1952; children: Allison R., Janet D., George P.; m. Gertrude Suydam Melsom, Mar. 24, 1984. BS, Mich. State U., 1950; MA, Oreg. State U., 1953, PhD, 1954; MD, Case Western Res. U., 1962. Diplomate Am. Bd. Med. Toxicology. Intern U. Iowa Hosps., Iowa City, 1962-63; fellow in medicine U. Colo., Denver, 1964-65; resident and chief resident Lemuel Shattuck Hosp., Boston, 1969-71; physician Colo. Dept. Pub. Health, Denver, 1966-69; asst. med. dir. MIT, Cambridge, 1971-76; med. dir. Climax (Colo.) Molybdenum Co., 1976-77; health effects research mgr. IBM, Boulder, Colo., 1977-92, ret., 1992; cons. Boulder, 1992—. Mem. com. mil. environ. rsch. Nat. Acad. Scis., 1976-80; mem. toxicology adv. com. U.S. Consumer Product Safety Com., 1982-85; clin. assoc. prof. medicine U. Colo. Health Scis. Ctr., Denver. Contbr. articles to profl. jours. Served with AUS, 1954-56. Case Meml. scholar, Mich. State U., 1948. Fellow ACP (Mead Johnson resident scholar 1970), Am. Acad. Clin. Toxicology (pres. 1980-82). Avocations: fishing, amateur radio.

ALDRICH, GARY O., singer, educator; b. Gloversville, N.Y., Apr. 12, 1947; s. Orville Bert and Maretta Hill Aldrich; life ptnr. Ronald J. Miller. MA, SUNY, Albany, 1970. Cert. permanent secondary English, drama and music N.Y. State Dept Edn., 1971. Founder and dir. Gary Aldrich Vocal Studios, Albany, NY, 1971—2000; asst. music dir. Empire State Inst. Performing Arts, 1978—79; teacher-artist The Theatre Inst., Troy, 1979—90; founder and artistic dir. N.Y. Concert Artists, Albany, 1996—2000, Lyric Opera Theatre, Reno, 2000—04; founder and dir. Gary Aldrich Vocal Studios, 2000—; vocal music faculty U. Nev., 2000—. Dir. Sierra Lyric Opera Studio, Reno, 2004—. Prodr.: (musical) M4M; composer: (songs) One Common Heartbeat; performer: Die Fleidermaus, 2004. Mem.: Nat. Assn. Tchrs. Singing (assoc.), Am. Guild Musical Artists (assoc.), Actor's Equity Assn. (assoc.), Phi Mu Alpha Sinfonia (assoc.). Avocations: gardening, travel. Office: Univ Nev 3565 Balboa Dr Reno NV 89557 Office Phone: 775-784-6145.

ALDRICH, GEORGE HOOVER, judge, arbitrator; b. St. Louis, Feb. 25, 1932; s. Emmett Porter and Hettie Barbara (Hoover) A.; m. Rosemary Margaret Balmforth Aldrich, June 6, 1959; children: Edward, Stephen, Robert. BA, DePauw U., 1954; LLB, Harvard Law Sch., 1957, LLM, 1958. Bar: Ind., 1958. Atty. Dept. Navy, Washington, 1959-60, Dept. Def., Washington, 1960-63; legal adv. U.S. Delegation to NATO, Paris, 1963-65; asst. legal adv. Dept. State, Washington, 1965-69, deputy legal adv., 1969-77, amb., deputy spl. rep. to pres., 1977-81; judge Iran-U.S. Claims Tribunal, The Hague, The Netherlands, 1981—; commr. Eritrea-Ethiopia Claims Commn, The Hague, The Netherlands, 2001—. U.S. amb. for Laws of War Negotiations, Geneva, Switzerland, 1974-77; mem. UN Internat. Law Commn., Geneva, Switzerland, 1981; bd. editors Am. Jour. Internat. Law, 1987—; prof. Leiden U., The Netherlands, 1990-97; comr. Eritrea-Ethiopia Claims Commn., The Hague, The Netherlands, 2001—. Author: The Jurisprudence of the Iran-United States Claims Tribunal, 1996; author, negotiator: The Protocols to the 1973 Vietnam Peace Agreement.; contbr. articles to profl. jours. Pres. Exec. com. of Am. Sch. of The hague, 1987-88. Named Disting. Sr. Exec. President Carter, 1980. Mem. Coun. on Fgn. Rels., Am. Soc. Internat. Law, Internat. Inst. Humanitarian Law. Avocations: tennis, sailing. Office: Iran-US Claims Trib Parkweg 13 2585 JH The Hague Netherlands Office Phone: 31 70 352 0064. E-mail: GAldrich@compuserve.com.

ALDRICH, JOHN HERBERT, political science professor; b. Pitts., Sept. 24, 1947; s. Herbert Canon and Ruth Eleanor (Taggart) A.; m. Cynthia Kay Aldrich, June 13, 1970; 1 child, David Shawn BA, Allegheny Coll., 1969; MA, U. Rochester, 1971, PhD, 1975. Asst. prof. polit. sci. Mich. State U., East Lansing, 1974-78, assoc. prof., 1978-81; assoc. prof. polit. sci. U. Minn., Mpls., 1981-83, prof., 1983-87, Duke U., Durham, NC, 1987—, chmn. dept. polit. sci., 1992—96, 1999—2000, Pfizer-Pratt univ. prof., 1997—. Vis. prof. Harvard U., 1996-97. Co-author: Change and Continuity in the 1980 Elections, 1982, rev. edit., 1983, Change and Continuity in the 1984 Elections, 1986, rev. edit., 1987, Change and Continuity in the 1988 elections, 1990, rev. edit., 1991, Change and Continuity in the 1992 Elections, 1994, rev. edit., 1995, Change and Continuing in the 1996 Elections, 1997, Change and Continuity in the 1996 and 1998 Elections, 1999, Change and Continuity in the 2000 and 2002 Elections; author: Before the Convention, 1980, Why Parties?, 1995; co-editor: Am. Jour. Polit. Sci., 1985-87; contbr. articles to profl. jours. Served with U.S. Army, 1970-72, Vietnam Ctr. for Advanced Study in Behavioral Scis. fellow, 1989-90; NSF rsch. grantee, 1977-79, 81-87; NEH teaching grantee, 1977-79; resident fellow Rockefeller Found., 2002. Fellow: Am. Acad. Arts and Scis.; mem.: Midwest Polit. Sci. Assn. (pres. 2004—05), So. Polit. Sci. Assn. (rec. sec. 1992—93, v.p. 1995—96, pres. 1998—99, Pi Sigma Alpha award 1997), Am. Polit. Sci. Assn. (sec. 1993—94, Eulau prize 1990, Kammerer prize 1996, CQ Press award 1996). Office: Duke U Dept Polit Sci Durham NC 27708 Office Phone: 919-660-4346. E-mail: aldrich@duke.edu.

ALDRICH, MICHAEL RAY, library curator, health educator; b. Vermillion, S.D., Feb. 7, 1942; s. Ray J. and Lucile W. (Hamm) A.; m. Michelle Cauble, Dec. 26, 1977. AB, Princeton U., 1964; MA, U. S.D., 1965; PhD, SUNY, 1970. Fulbright tutor Govt. Arts and Commerce Coll., Indore, India, 1965-66; founder Lemar Internat., 1966-71; mem. faculty Sch. Critical Studies Calif. Inst. Arts, Valencia, 1970-72; co-founder Amorphia The Cannabis Co-op, Mill Valley, Calif., 1969—74; curator Fitz Hugh Ludlow Meml. Libr., San Francisco, 1974—2003, curator Aldrich Archives, 1974—. Cons. Commn. of Inquiry into Non-Med Use of Drugs, Ottawa, Ont., 1973; rsch. aide select com. on control marijuana Calif. Senate, 1974; mem. Princeton working group Future of Drug Policy, 1990—93; asst. dir. Nat. Inst. on Drug Abuse AIDS Project Menu, Youth Environment Study, San Francisco, 1987—88; project adminstr. YES Tng. Ctr., 1989; program. coord. Calif. AIDS Intervention Tng. Ctr. Inst. for Cmty. Health Outreach, 1990—2001; bd. dirs. Exotic Dancers Alliance, San Francisco, 1997—, Calif. Helping Alleviate Med. Problems (CHAMP), 1997, exec. dir., 2001—02; cons. on drug rsch.; freelance writer, photographer; lectr. in field. Author: The Dope Chronicles 1850-1950, 1979, Coricancha, The Golden Enclosure, 1983; co-author: High Times Ency. of Recreational Drugs, 1978, Fiscal Costs of California Marijuana Law Enforcement, 1986, YES Tng. Manual, 1989, Methods of Estimating Needle Users at Risk for AIDS, 1990; editor: Marijuana Rev., 1968-74, Ludlow Libr. Newsletter, 1974-81; contbg. author: Cocaine Handbook, 1981, 2d edit., 1987, Cannabis in Medical Practice, 1997; mem. editl. rev. bd. Jour. Psychoactive Drugs, 1981—, marijuana theme issue editor, 1988; rsch. photographer Life mag., 1984; contbg. editor High Times, 1979-85; contbr. articles to prfl. publs. Office: PO Box 640346 San Francisco CA 94164-0346

ALDRICH, NANCY COOK, engineer; b. Ogden, Utah, Oct. 16, 1944; d. William Burford and Margaret (Spilker) Cook; m. Ralph E. Aldrich, Aug. 10, 1968. BA in Physics, Scripps Coll., 1966; MS in Physics, Tufts U., 1969. Physicist Naval Underwater Weapons Sta., Newport, R.I., 1966; engr. Microwave Assn., Burlington, Mass., 1967; assoc. engr. Honeywell Electro Optics (formerly Honeywell Radiation Ctr.) div. Honeywell Corp., Lexington, Mass., 1969-70, engr., 1970-71, sr. engr, 1971-72, prin. engr., 1972-75, sr. prin. engr., 1975-78, program mgr., 1978-81, bus. mgr., 1981-82, engring. mgr., 1982-84, sect. head, 1984-86; chief engr. Honeywell Electro Optics (formerly Honeywell Radiation Ctr.) div. Honeywell Corp. (name now Loral Infrared and Imaging Systems), Lexington, Mass., 1986—. Leader Girl Scouts U.S., Acton, Mass., 1972. Recipient Ed Lund Mgmt. award, 1987; named Disting. Alumna Scripps Coll., 1984. Mem. Profl. Council. Avocations: flying, wildlife photography, fly fishing. Office: Electro-Optics div Honeywell Corp 2 Forbes Rd Lexington MA 02421-7306

ALDRICH, PATRICIA ANNE RICHARDSON, retired magazine editor; b. St. Paul, Apr. 6, 1926; d. James Calvin and Anna Catherine (Eskra) Richardson; m. Edwin Chauncey Aldrich, July 31, 1948; 1 son, Mason Calvin. Student, Stout Inst., 1944-45; BS in Journalism; scholar, Northwestern U., 1948. Editor Child's World News, The Child's World, Inc., Chgo., 1952-57; assoc. editor Home Life mag. Advt. Div., Inc., Chgo., 1957-71, editor, 1971-90, ret., 1990; pres. Aldrich Enterprises, Inc., Chgo. Mem. steering com., publicity chmn. Evanston Urban League, 1961-64. Democrat.

ALDRICH, RICHARD JOHN, agronomist, educator; b. Fairgrove, Mich., Apr. 16, 1925; s. George and Eva Ann (Misner) A.; m. June Ellen Ellison, Apr. 5, 1943; children: Judith Allman, Sharon, Jeffrey. BS, Mich. State U., 1948; PhD, Ohio State U., 1950. Agronomist U.S. Dept. Agr., Rutgers U., New Brunswick, N.J., 1950-57; asst. dir. Agr. Exptl. Sta., Mich. State U., East Lansing, 1957-64; assoc. dir., dean agr. exptl. sta. U. Mo., Columbia, 1964-76; adminstr. CSRS, U.S. Dept. Agr., Washington, 1976-78; prof. agronomy U. Mo., Columbia, 1978-81; research agronomist, prof. SEA-ARS, Dept. Agr.-U. Mo., 1981-87; ret., 1987. Cons. OTA, U.S. Congress, 1979, The Standard Oil Co., 1983; mem. adv. com. Fed. Assistance Rev., 1970-71; pres. Agr. Research Inst., 1974-75 Author: Weed Crop Ecology, 1983; co-author: Principles in Weed Management, rev. edit., 1997; editor: Weed Sci. Jour., 1989-94; contbr. articles to profl. jours. Served to 1st lt. USAAF, 1943-46. Fellow AAAS, Weed Sci. Soc. Am.; mem. Am. Soc. Agronomy (dir. 1949-50), Agrl. Research Inst. (pres. 1974-75), Nat. Assn. State Univs. and Land Grant Colls. Home: PO Box 236 Marcell MN 56657-0236 also: 2663 S Fade Dr Green Valley AZ 85614-1151

ALDRICH, ROBERT ADAMS, agricultural engineer, consultant; b. Veteran Twp., N.Y., Apr. 25, 1924; s. Luman Woodbridge and Mabel Hastings (Gibbs) A.; m. Roberta Ann Bowlby, Aug. 27, 1946; children— Susan Carol, Gail Jessica, Kathleen Lois, Margaret Louise. BS in Agrl. Engring, Wash. State U., 1950, MS, 1952; PhD, Mich. State U., 1958. Instr., then asso. prof. agrl. engring. Wash. State U., 1951-58; asso. prof. U. Ky., 1958-59, Mich. State U., 1959-62; asso. prof., then prof. Pa. State U., 1962-79; prof. agrl. engring., head dept. U. Conn., Storrs, 1979-88, prof. dept. nat. rsch., mgmt. and engring., 1988-89, ret., 1989; prin. Aldrich Engring. Author papers in field. Served with C.E. AUS, 1942-46. Mem. Am. Soc. Agrl. Engrs., Nat. Soc. Profl. Engrs. Home: 72 Tressler Blvd Lewisburg PA 17837-1033 Office Phone: 570-522-0503.

ALDRICH, SANDRA PICKLESIMER, publications executive; b. Keith, Ky., Feb. 17, 1945; d. Mitchell and Wilma (Farley) Picklesimer, Sr.; m. Donald J. Aldrich, Feb. 5, 1966 (wid. Dec. 1982); children: Jay, Holly. BA, Ea. Mich., 1967, MA, 1970. Pub. sch. tchr. Garden City (Mich.) Pub. Schs., 1967-84; comm. svc. rep. Harris Funeral Homes, Detroit, 1985-86; assoc. editor Christian Herald Mag., Chappaqua, NY, 1986-90; sr. editor Focus on the Family Mag., Colorado Springs, 1990-94; exec. asst. for acad. rels. Focus on the Family, Colorado Springs, 1994-95; pres. Bold Words, Inc., Colorado Springs, 1995—; contbg. editor Today's Christian Woman Mag., Carol Stream, Ill., 1996-98. Author: From One Single Mother to Another, 2005, Husbands Read Newspapers, Not Minds, Bless Your Socks Off: Unleashing the Power of Encouragement, Will I Ever Be Whole Again?, Honey, Hang in There! Encouragement for Busy Mothers. Bd. dirs. Family Inn, Colorado Springs, 1994-96. Mem. Evangel. Press Assn. Avocations: Ky. history, quilting, gardening. Office: Bold Words Inc PO Box 51351 Colorado Springs CO 80949-1351 E-mail: boldwords@aol.com.

ALDRICH, THOMAS ALBERT, former brewing executive, consultant; b. Rosebud, Tex., Nov. 30, 1923; s. John Albert and Georgia Opal (Hilliard) A.; m. Virginia Elaine Peterson, Mar. 1, 1944; children: Sharon Aldrich Lingis, Pamela Aldrich Williams, Thomas Charles. Student, Tex. A&M U., 1942-43, U. Chgo., 1943-44; BA in Math., George Washington U., 1961, MS in Bus. Adminstrn., 1968; student, Air War Coll., 1960-61. Commd. 2d lt. USAF, 1944, advanced through grades to maj. gen., 1974, pilot, meteorologist, 1943-57; dep. dir. air ops. Air Weather Svc., Washington, 1957-60; comdr. 57th Weather Reconnaissance Squadron, Melbourne, Australia, 1962-65; chief mil. employment div. Air Command and Staff Coll., 1965-68; dir. war plans Hdqrs. Mil. Airlift Command, Scott AFB, Ill., 1968-69; comdr. 9th Weather Reconnaissance Wing, McClellan AFB, Calif., 1969-70; vice comdr. USAF Air Weather Svc., Scott AFB, Ill., 1970-71, comdr., 1973-74, U.S. Forces Azores, Portugal, 1971-73; dep. chief of staff plans Hdqrs. Mil. Airlift Command, 1974-75; comdr. 22d Air Force, Travis AFB, Calif., 1975-78; ret., 1978; v.p., corp. rep. Anheuser-Busch Cos., Inc., Sacramento, 1978-94, ret., 1994. Decorated D.S.M., Legion of Merit with oak leaf cluster, Meritorious Service medal. Mem. Nat. Honor Soc., Brewers Inst., Calif. Mfrs. Assn. (chmn.), Calif. C. of C. (bd. dirs.), Air Force Acad. Falcon Found. (bd. dirs.), No. Calif. Ret. Officers Cmty. (vice chmn.), Phi Theta Kappa. Republican. Presbyterian. Home: 659 Lake Wilhaggin Dr Sacramento CA 95864-7226 Personal E-mail: tomginnya@aol.com.

ALDRICH-BENNETT, FLORENCE ANNE, elementary school educator; b. Poughkeepsie, NY; d. Russell and Grace Marie (Burke) Aldrich; m. Craig Robert, Mar. 14, 1981. BA, Newton Coll. of the Sacred Heart, 1964; EdM, Lesley College, 1978. Tchr. Sudbury (Mass.) Sch. Dist., 1964—. Mem.NEA, Mass. Tchrs. Assn., Sudbury Edn. Assn. Office: Sudbury Schools 280 Old Sudbury Rd Sudbury MA 01742

ALDRIDGE, DONALD O'NEAL, military officer; b. Solo., Mo., July 22, 1932; BA in History, U. Nebr., Omaha, 1974; postgrad., Creighton U., 1975. Commd. 2d lt. USAF, 1958, advanced through grades to lt. gen., 1988, asst. dir. plans Washington, 1978-79; spl. asst. to dir. Joinr Chiefs of Staff, Washington, 1979-80; dep. dir. Def. Mapping Agy., Washington, 1980-81; dep. U.S. rep. NATO Mil. Com., Brussels, 1981-83; rep. Joint Chiefs of Staff, Geneva, 1983-86; comdr. 1st Strat. Aerospace Divsn. USAF, Vanderberg AFB, Calif., 1986-88, vice-CINC Strategic Air Command Offutt AFB, Nebr., 1988—91; mgmt. cons. Sacramento, 1991—. Chmn. bd. dir. Octus, Inc., 1995—98, Ceracon, Inc., 1996—2005. Office Phone: 402-293-0543. Personal E-mail: daldridge@cox.net.

ALDRIDGE, EDWARD CLEVELAND, JR., former federal agency administrator; b. Houston, Tex., Aug. 18, 1938; BS, Tex. A&M U., 1960; MS, Ga. Inst. Tech., 1962. Mgr. missile and space div. Douglas Aircraft Co., Santa Monica, Calif., 1962-67, Washington, 1962-67; dir. strategic def. div. U.S. Dept. Def., 1967-72, dep. asst. sec. for strategic programs, 1974-76; dir. planning and evaluation Office of Sec. Def., 1976-77; sr. mgr. LTV Aerospace Corp., Dallas, 1972-73; sr. mgmt. assoc. Office Mgmt. & Budget, Washington, 1973-74; v.p. Strategic Systems Group System Planning Corp., Arlington, Va., 1977-81; undersec. USAF, 1981-86, sec., 1986-88; pres. McDonnell Douglas Electronic Systems Co., McLean, Va., 1988-92; pres., CEO Aerospace Corp., El Segundo, Calif., 1992—2001; under sec. acquisition, tech. and logistics U.S. Dept. Def., Washington, 2001—03. Formerly advisor Strategic Arms Limitation Talks, Helsinki and Vienna Recipient George M. Low Space Transp. award AIAA, 1990. Mem.: bd. dirs., Alion Science & Tech, Lockheed Martin Corp., 2003-.

ALDRIDGE, JOHN, lawyer; b. Durham, N.C., Jan. 31, 1943; BA, Duke U., 1965; JD with honors, U. N.C., 1968. Bar: Ga. 1968, D.C. 1969. Mem. Long, Aldridge & Norman (now McKenna Long & Aldridge), Atlanta. Assoc. editor N.C. Law Rev., 1967-68. Mem. ABA, State Bar Ga., D.C. Bar, Atlanta Bar Assn., Lawyers Club Atlanta, Order of Coif. Office: Long Aldridge & Norman LLP One Peachtree Ctr 303 Peachtree St NE Ste 5300 Atlanta GA 30308-3264

ALDRIDGE, JOHN WATSON, language educator, writer; b. Sioux City, Iowa, Sept. 26, 1922; s. Walter Copher and Nell (Watson) A.; m. Leslie Felker, Dec. 10, 1954 (div. June 1968); 1 son, Geoffrey; children by previous marriages: Henry, Stephen, Leslie, Jeremy; m. Alexandra Bertash, July 13, 1968 (div. Dec. 1982); m. Patricia McGuire Eby, July 16, 1983. Student, U. Chattanooga, 1940-43; fellow, Breadloaf Sch. English, summer 1942; BA, U. Calif.-Berkeley, 1947. Lectr. English U. Vt., 1948-50, asst. prof., 1950-53, 54-55; lectr. Christian Gauss Seminars Criticism, Princeton, N.J., 1953-54; mem. lit. faculty Sarah Lawrence Coll., also New Sch. Social Research, 1957; prof. English Queens Coll., 1957; Berg prof. English NYU, 1958; Fulbright lectr. U. Munich, Fed. Republic of Germany, 1958-59; writer-in-residence Hollins Coll., 1960-62; Fulbright lectr. U. Copenhagen, Denmark, 1962-63; prof. English U. Mich., 1964-91, prof. emeritus, 1991; book critic N.Y. Herald Tribune Book Week, 1965-66, Saturday Review, 1970-79. Staff Bread Loaf Writers Conf., 1966-69; chief regional judge Book-of-the Month Writing Fellowship Program, 1966-67; spl. adviser for Am. studies U.S. Embassy, Germany, 1972-73; spl. adviser for Authors Am. Sta. WETA, 1990—; book commentator McNeil/Lehrer News Hour, 1983-84. Author: After the Lost Generation, 1951, Critiques and Essays on Modern Fiction, 1952, In Search of Heresy, 1956, The Party at Cranton, 1960, Time to Murder and Create, 1966, In the Country of the Young, 1970, The Devil in the Fire, 1972, The American Novel and the Way We Live Now, 1983, Talents and Technicians, 1992, Classics and Contemporaries, 1992; also articles.; editor: Selected Stories by P.G. Wodehouse, 1958. Served with AUS, 1943-45, ETO. Decorated Bronze Star; Rockefeller Humanities fellow, 1976-77 Mem. Authors Guild and League of Am., MLA, Nat. Book Critics Circle, P.E.N. Home: 381 N Main St Madison GA 30650 Office Phone: 706-752-0194.

ALDRIDGE, LINDA ANN, retired elementary education educator, librarian; b. Columbus, Ga., July 27, 1931; d. Carey Curry and Jimmie Allie (Brown) Willis; m. R. Franklynn Van Stralen, Aug. 5, 1950 (div. Mar. 1974); children: Errol, Daved, Cary; m. Charles Ray Aldridge, Dec. 22, 1974. BA, Calif. State U., L.A., 1966, MA, 1972. Tchr. Bellflower (Calif.) Unified Schs., 1966-71, L.A. Unified Schs., 1971-81, Pinellas Sch. Dist., St. Petersburg, Fla., 1983—2003; ret., 2003. Instr. St. Petersburg Jr. Coll., 1983—. Libr. info. specialist Pinellas County, 1997, 2003. Mem. Fla. Assn. Media Edn., Fla. Storytellers Guild, Pinellas Assn. Libr.-Media Specialists (Libr. Info. Specialist of Yr. 1998). Baptist. Avocations: composing and writing children's music and plays, storytelling, musician. E-mail: aldridge@aldridges.com.

ALDRIDGE, MELVIN DAYNE, engineering educator; b. Crab Orchard, W.Va., July 20, 1941; s. William Bert and Gladys Revelle A.; m. Nancy L. Dickinson, June 6, 1963; children: Kenrick Lee, Randal Jay. BSEE with high honors, W.Va. U., 1963; MEE, U. Va., 1965, D of Elec. Engring., 1968. Registered profl. engr., W.Va. Electronic engr. NASA, 1963-68; from asst. prof. to assoc. prof. elec. engring. W.Va. U., Morgantown, 1968-76, prof., 1976-84; dir. Energy Rsch. Ctr., 1978-84; asst. dean for rsch. Auburn (Ala.) U., 1984-87, dir. engring. expt. sta., 1984-89, prof. elec. engring., 1984-89, acting dean coll. engring., 1987-88, assoc. dean for rsch., 1988-90, assoc. dean for cross-disciplinary programs, 1989-99, dir. ctr. for tech. mgmt., 1989-99; dean, prof. Mercer U., Macon, Ga., 1999—, Kaolin chair engring., 2004—. Chmn., officer Engring. Accreditation Commn.; cons. tp pvt. and govtl. orgns. Contbr. articles to profl. publs. Thomas Walter Eminent scholar Auburn U., 1994-99; recipient Rufus A. West award, 1963; named Outstanding Young Engr. W.Va., 1977-78. Fellow IEEE (sr.), ASEE, Accreditation Bd. for Engring. and Tech. (officer); mem. Indsl. Applications Soc. of IEEE (officer). Baptist. Home: 669 River North Blvd Macon GA 31211-6333 Office: Macon U 1400 Coleman Ave Macon GA 31207-0001

ALDRIDGE, SANDRA, civic volunteer; b. Iowa, Apr. 22, 1939; d. Maurice D. and Maureen M. (Bennett) Anderson; m. Guy E. Seymour, Jan. 8, 1960 (div. Oct. 1966); m. Victor E. Aldridge, Jr., Nov. 11, 1970 (dec. May 1995); 1 child, Victor E. III. Student, Millikin U., Decatur, Ill., 1957-58. Pres. Crawford Sch. PTA, 1976-78, Terre Haute Lawyers Aux., 1979; pres., dir. Wabash Valley Assn. for Gifted and Talented Children, 1981-83, Vigo County Task Force for Alcohol and Drug Abuse, 1983-84; treas., dir. Union Hosp. Svc. League; bd. dirs. YWCA of Terre Haute, Inc., 1987-89; v.p., fin. chair, mem. exec. coun. Wabash Valley coun. Boy Scouts Am., Inc.; mem. Vigo County Tax Adjustment Bd., 1986-88; mem. Class IX Leadership Terre Haute, 1985; bd. trustees Vigo County Sch. Corp., Terre Haute, 1985-97, v.p., 1992-93, 96; sec. Ernie Pyle Chapter, The Ret. Officers Assn., 1998-2000; active Children's Theatre, United Way of Wabash Valley. Mem. Ind. Assn. Gifted Children, Swope Art Gallery, Vigo County Hist. Soc., Women's Dept. Club, Arts Illiana, Elks Women's Golf League. Democrat. Episcopalian. Home: 2929 Winthrop Rd Terre Haute IN 47802-3443

ALDRIN, BUZZ, retired astronaut; b. Montclair, NJ., Jan. 20, 1930; s. Edwin Eugene and Marion (Moon) Aldrin; m. Lois Driggs Cannon, Feb. 14, 1988; children from previous marriage: James Michael, Janice Ross, Andrew John. BS, U.S. Mil. Acad., 1951; ScD in Astronautics, MIT, 1963; ScD (hon.), Gustavus Adolphus Coll., 1967, Clark U., 1969, U. Portland, 1970, St. Peter's Coll., 1970; LittD (hon.), Montclair State Coll., 1969; HHD (hon.), Seton Hall U., 1970. Commd. officer USAF, 1951, advanced through grades to col.; served as fighter pilot in Korea, 1953; pilot Gemini XII orbital rendezvous space flight, Nov. 11-15, 1966; lunar module pilot on first manned lunar landing Apollo XI; comdr. Aerospace Rsch. Pilots Sch., Edwards AFB, Calif., 1971-72; ret. USAF, 1972; with Ctr. for Aerospace Scis. U. N.D., Grand Forks, 1989. Sci. cons. Beverly Hills Oil Co., Inforex Computer Co., Laser Video Corp., Mut. of Omaha Ins.; founder Starcraft Enterprises (Starcraft Boosters, Inc.), 1988-; created ShareSpace Found. to promote affordable space tourism for all people; lectr. in field. Author: Return to Earth, 1973, Men From Earth, 1989, Encounter with Tiber, 1996, The Return, 2000, (children's book) Reaching for the Moon, 2005. Decorated D.S.M., Legion of Merit, D.F.C. with oak leaf cluster, Air medal with 2 oak leaf clusters;

recipient Horatio Alger award, 2005, numerous other awards including Presdl. medal of Freedom, 1969. Fellow AIAA; mem. Nat. Space Soc. (chmn.), Soc. Exptl. Test Pilots, Royal Aero. Soc. (hon.), Sea Space Symposium; charter Internat. Acad. Astronautics (corr.), Sigma Xi, Tau Beta Pi. Clubs: Masons (33 degree). Shot down two MiG-15s during 66 combat mission in the Korean War; In November, 1966, established record over 7 hours and 52 minutes outside spacecraft in extra-vehicular activity on the Gemini XII orbital flight mission; On July 20, 1969, walked on moon along with Neil Armstrong during Apollo XI Mission, becoming the first two humans to set foot on another world. This heroic endeavor was witnessed by the largest worldwide television audience in history; In 1993, received US patent for permanent space station he designed. Legally changed name from Edwin E. Aldrin Jr.

ALDROW-LIPUT, PRISCILLA REESE, retired elementary education educator; b. Kingston, Pa., Apr. 10, 1951; d. Thomas Edward and Martha Mae (Hadsall) Reese; children: Colin Michael, Justin John; m. Willard C. Aldrow. BS, Bloomsburg U., 1973. Cert. instructional II. Tchr. grade 5 Dallas Sch. Dist., Pa., 1973—2001, ret., 2001; homebound tchr., pre-K-12 Williamsburg-James City County Sch. Dist., Va., 2002—. Homebound tchr. Williamsburg-James County Sch. Dist., Va. Mem. NEA, Pa. State Edn. Assn., Dallas Edn. Assn. Home: 109 Rondane Pl Williamsburg VA 23188 Office Phone: 757-565-3638. E-mail: aldrow@bznt.com.

ALEA, JORGE ANTONIO, physician; b. Cuba; came to U.S., 1949; m. Barbara Chandler; children: Craig, Karen. BS in Chemistry, U. Ga., 1953; MD, Med. Coll. Ga., 1957. Diplomate Am. Bd. Internal Medicine, Am. Bd. Gastroenterology, Nat. Bd. Med. Examiners. Staff physician State Hosp., Raleigh, NC, 1957—58; intern City Meml. Hosp., Winston-Salem, NC, 1958—59; resident in internal medicine Henry Ford Hosp., Detroit, 1959—62; resident VA Hosp.- Med. Coll. VA, Richmond, Va., 1962—63; chief of gastroenterology VA Hosp., Buffalo, 1963—69; asst. prof. medicine SUNY, Buffalo, 1963—69; chief med. svc. and charter mem. Doctor's Hosp., Lake Worth, Fla., 1969—; mem. staff JFK Med. Ctr., Lake Worth, Fla., 1969—. Contbr. articles to profl. jours. Deacon First Bapt. Ch., West Palm Beach, Fla. Capt. USAR. Fellow ACP, Am. Coll. Gastroenterology; mem. Am. Gastroenterologic Soc., Am. Soc. Gastrointestinal Endoscopy. Avocations: bicycling, golf, reading. Home: 904 Pine Ridge Rd Beech Mountain NC 28604-8156

ALEINIKOFF, THOMAS ALEXANDER, dean, law educator; b. 1952; BA, Swarthmore Coll., 1974; JD, Yale U., 1977. Bar: NY 1978, Mich. 1983. Law clk. to Judge Edward Weinfeld, 1977-78; atty., advisor Office Legal Counsel Dept. Justice, 1978-80; trail atty. wildlife sect. Land & Nat. Resources Dept. Justice, 1981; asst. prof. law U. Mich., 1981-84, assoc. prof., 1984-86, prof., 1984-86, 1986—94; gen. counsel US Dept. Justice Immigration and Naturalization Svc., 1994—95, exec. assoc. commr. for programs, 1995—97; prof. law Georgetown U. Law Ctr., 1997—, assoc. dean rsch., 2003—04, dean, 2004—; exec. v.p. law ctr. affairs Georgetown U., 2004—. Past rschr. in Internat. Migration Policy Carnegie Endowment for Internat. Peace. Co-author (with J. Garvey): Modern Constitutional Theory: A Reader, 1994; co-author: (with D. Martin and H. Motomura) Immigration: Process and Policy, 1995. Office: Georgetown U Law Ctr 600 NJ Ave NW Washington DC 20001 Office Phone: 202-662-9031.*

ALEINIKOV, ANDREI GRIGORYEVICH, linguist, art director; b. Sverdlovsk, Russia, Mar. 13, 1948; arrived in U.S., 1992, naturalized, 2002; s. Grigory Stepanovich Aleinikov and Nina Ivanovna Aleinikova; m. Elena Nikolayevna Kohn, Jan. 8, 1948; 1 child, Andrei Aleinikov-Kohn. BA and M.Ed, State Pedagogic U., Volgograd, Russia, 1967—72; PhD in Linguistics, State U., Tbilisi, Georgia, 1983; DSc, Mil. U., Moscow, 1992; postgrad., USAF Air War Coll., 1992—93. H.S. tchr. English and German, Volgograd, Russia, 1975; asst. prof., then assoc. prof. Mil. U., Moscow, 1984—92; lectr. in edn. Ctr. for Creative Rsch. Russian Acad. Scis., Moscow, 1989—92; adj. instr. Troy U., Montgomery, Ala., 1994—. Interpreter Russian Army and Indian Navy, Visakhapatnam and Bombay, India, 1990—91; internat. fellow USAF Air War Coll., Maxwell AFB, Ala., 1992—93; adj. instr. Auburn U., Montgomery, 1994—99; dir., innovative edn. divsn. Venturist, Inc, Montgomery, 1996—99; lectr. Ohio Wesleyan U., 2004; spkr., presenter in field. Author: (book) Grammar Creation and Creation Grammar, 1990, ALEANDR: Creativity Testing Program, 1990, Creativity in Teaching and Studying Theoretic Disciplines, 1990, Creating Creative Teachers, 1996, Make Your Child a Genius, 1996, Creative Problem Solving: Present, Past, and Future, 1997, Creating Yourself: Creative Compendium, 1999, Mega-Creator: From Creativity to Mega-, Giga-, and Infi-Creativity, 1999, MegaCreativity: Five Steps to Thinking Like a Genius, 2002; editor: Language Awareness: Stereotypes and Creativity, 1988, (5 volume book) Creative Management, 1991, (book) When will it be?, 1996, Soul Poem, 1997, Run with the Wind, 1997, Microdictionary of Foreign Words (Nine languages), 1997, Mighty Colloquial Pomposity Power Words, 1997, Designing a Genius, 1996, Future Geniuses of the Earth, 1996, Mega-Creator in the Non-Profit Universe: Launch to Excellence, 2000, The Future of Creativity, 2002; author: (audiotape) Nurturing the Genius in Your Child, 2000; contbr. numerous articles to profl. publs. Life time mem. Creative Edn. Found., Buffalo, 1999; mem. Internat. Coun. for Innovation in Higher Edn., Toronto, Canada, 1997. Col. Russian Army, 1973—93. Named Hon. Citizen of Ala., Gov. of Ala., 1992, Dr. E. Paul Torrance lectr., U. Ga., 2001; recipient 4 medals for Excellence in Svc., Supreme Soviet, USSR, 1980—90, numerous awards and certificates for excellence in svc., Russian Ministry of Def., 1975—92, Silver Medal for H.S. excellence, Russian Ministry of Edn., 1966, Guinness World Record for fastest written, printed and pub. book Making the Impossible Possible, 2001, Outstanding Educator award for Innovative and Creative Tchg., Acad. Ednl. Leadership, NC, 2003; vis. fellow, Woodrow Wilson Nat. Fellowship Found., Princeton, N.J., 2003—. Mem.: Am. Creativity Assn. (founding pres. Ala. chpt.), Internat. Acad. Genius (pres. 1995—), Air War Coll. Alumni Assn., Kiwanis, Phi Delta Kappa. Achievements include discovery of megacreativity; creator genius education methodology; founding of Novology, the science of newness; founding of Geniusology, the science of genius; founding of Organizology, the sci. of ogrn; founding of 4 new branches of science, including creative linguistics, creagogy, innovagogy and generagogy; invention of decorative lamp; device for accelerated learning of verbal expressions of time; device for accelerating symbol recognition and reading. Avocations: swimming, chess, travel, composing. Office: Internat Acad of Genius 2125 E 6th St Montgomery AL 36106 Office Phone: 334-263-3618. Personal E-mail: aleini13@aol.com. Business E-Mail: dr_andy@mega-creator.com.

ALEMAN, MARTHANNE PAYNE, environmental planner, consultant; b. Houston, Dec. 3, 1938; d. Charles Franklin and Evelyn Inez (Dudley) Payne; m. Samuel Garza Alemán, July 5, 1968. BS in Landscape Arch. magna cum laude, Tex. A&M U., 1988; MS in Interdisciplinary Studies, Tex. Tech. U., 1989; PhD in Urban and Regional Sci., Tex. A&M U., 1995. Engring. aide City of Austin, 1966-69, Bryant-Curington Engrs., Austin, 1969-72; entrepreneur Rio Verde Farm, San Benito, Tex., 1972-83; rsch. asst. Tex. Tech. U., Lubbock, 1988-91, Tex. A&M U., College Station, 1993-94; cons. Rio Verde Land & Investment Corp., Calvert, Tex., 1995—. Sec./treas., bd. dirs. Tex. Avocado Growers Assn., Weslaco, 1979-83. Author: Soil Salinity in the Texas Lower Rio Grande Valley: Cause for Concern, 1987, Export-Driven Development of Soil and Water Resources: Barrier to Sustainable Development and Inducement to Desertification, 1995. Mem. and active participant Robertson County Hist. Commn., Calvert, 1980-83. Smithsonian Instn. intern, Washington, 1987, Presdl. scholar U.S. Fed. Register, 1993; recipient Nat. Collegiate Archtl. and Design award, U.S. Achievement Acad., Lexington, Ky., 1989. Mem. Am. Planning Assn., Soil and Water Conservation Soc. of Am. (vol. Heart of Tex. chpt., Waco, Tex.). Avocations: breeding, showing, and training collies. Office: Rio Verde Land and Investment Corp 201 E Browning Calvert TX 77837 Office Phone: 979-364-2631.

ALEMANY, ELLEN, finance company executive; With Chase Manhattan Bank, 1977—87; various positions including sr. lender media and electronics dept., head N.Y. Leveraged Capital Group, sr. credit officer, customer group exec. N.Am. Citibank, 1987—; chmn., CEO Citibank Internat. plc, exec. v.p. Comml. Bus. Group; pres., CEO CitiCapital. Mem.: Equipment Leasing and Fin. Found. (bd. mem., treas. 2004). Office: CitiCapital 2d Fl 399 Park Ave New York NY 10103

ALEMAYEHU, BERHANU, health facility administrator, researcher; b. Debrebrhan, Ethopia, Aug. 15, 1958; arrived in U.S., 1985; s. Alemayehu Beyene and Bafena W. Berreyes; 1 child, Elena. BS in Math and Statis., Adois Azaba U., 1983; MS in Statis, U. Tex., 1986; DPh in Health Policy, U. Mich., 2001. Lectr. U. Tex., El Paso, 1985—87, Lansing C.C., Mich., 1990—91; sr. statistician Dept. Cmty. Health, 1988—96; mgr. Blue Cross Blue Shield, Detroit, 1996—99; dir. MEDCO Health Solution, Franklin Lakes, NJ, 1999—2005. Mem. exec. com. Soc. Against AIDS in Ethopoe, N.Y.C., 2000—. Fellow, PEW, 1995—2001. Mem.: Acad. Health, Am. Statis. Assn. Avocations: reading, running. Home: 200 McElroy Ave Fort Lee NJ 07024

ALESCH, DANIEL JAMES, social sciences educator, researcher; b. Appleton, Wis., Apr. 21, 1939; s. Roman William Alesch and Margaret Ella Danielsen; children: Kirsten Ann Muth, Greta Jane Liddell. BS, U. Wis., 1962, MS, 1964; MA, U. Calif., 1969, PhD, 1970. Post grad. fellow Inst. Pub. Adminstrn., N.Y., 1964—65; planner Exec. Chamber, Albany, NY, 1965—67; sr. rschr. U. So. Calif., L.A., 1967—68; prof. U. Wis., Green Bay, Wis., 1968—79, prof. emeritus, 2001—; sr. social scientist The RAND Corp., Santa Monica, Calif., 1968—79. Bd. dirs., v.p. Fox-Wolf Basin 2000, Green Bay, 1992—97; commr., pres. Green Bay (Wis.) Met. Sewerage Dist., 1992; bd. dirs. Brown County Planning Commn., Green Bay, Wis., 1980—87; chmn. bd. dirs. Housing Allowance Office of Brown County, Inc., Green Bay, 1973—95. Home: 909 Forest Hill Drive Green Bay WI 54311 Personal E-mail: dalesch@new.rr.com.

ALESCHUS, JUSTINE LAWRENCE, retired real estate broker; b. New Brunswick, N.J., Aug. 13, 1925; d. Walter and Mildred Lawrence; m. John Aleschus, Jan. 23, 1949; children: Verdene Jan, Janine Kimberley, Joanna Lauren. Student, Rutgers U. Dept. sec. Am. Bapt. Home Mission Soc., N.Y.C., 1947-49; claims examiner Republic Ins. Co., Dallas, 1950-52; broker Damon Homes, L.I., 1960-72; pres. Justine Aleschus Real Estate, Smithtown, NY, 1975—2002; ret. Exclusive broker estate of Kenneth H. Leeds, L.I., N.Y., 1980-90; past pres. S.C. Real Estate Bd. Past pres. Nassau-Suffolk Coun. of Hosp. Aux, 1981-82; hon. mem. aux. St. Catherine of Siena, Smithtown, N.Y., past pres., hosp. adv. bd.; past pres. L.I. Coalition for Sensible Growth, Inc.; past v.p. Suffolk County coun. Boy Scouts Am. Mem. Sky Island Club (gov.), S.C. Citizen Police Acad. (alumni). Republican. Lutheran. Address: 2261 The Woods Dr East Jacksonville FL 32246 Personal E-mail: landauntjay@aol.com.

ALESSANDRONI, VENAN JOSEPH, lawyer; b. N.Y.C., Mar. 1, 1915; s. Anthony P. and Andromeda (Rossini) A.; m. Alice Shaughnessy, Feb. 2, 1949 (dec. June 1973); m. Adelle Lincoln, Mar. 10, 1974. AB, Columbia U., 1937, JD, 1939. Bar: N.Y. 1941, also, Supreme Ct. of Korea 1946. Announcer CBS Artists Service, Inc., 1940; U.S. atty. Bd. Econ. Warfare, 1942; mem. U.S. Fgn. Econ. Adminstrn. Mission, Belgian Congo, 1943; sr. partner Wormser, Kiely, Alessandroni, Hyde & McCann (and predecessor firm), 1959—. Legal officer Mil. Govt. Korea, 1945-46; legal adviser to provincial gov. Kyunggi-Do, Korea, 1946; chief provost judge, City of Seoul, 1946; adj. prof., law sch. U. Miami, 1974—; lectr. various tax insts., univs., profl. assns. Author: The Executor, 1963, Applied Estate Planning, 1963, also articles.; Departmental editor: Jour. Taxation, 1955-56. Recipient U.S. Army Commendation award, 1946; regional award N.Y. Times, 1932; Curtis medal Columbia, 1936 Office: Wormser Kiely Galef & Jacobs 825 3d Ave New York NY 10017-4014

ALESSI, ROBERT JOSEPH, lawyer, real estate developer, pharmacist; b. Rome, NY, Aug. 22, 1958; s. William John and Mary Jean A.; m. Ellen Mary (Paczkowski), May 21, 1988; children: Laura C., and Grace E. BS in Pharmacy, Union Univ., 1982; JD cum laude, Albany Law Sch., 1985. Bar: N.Y. 1986; U.S. Dist. Ct. (no. dist.) N.Y. 1986; U.S. Dist. Ct. (we. dist.) N.Y. 1986; U.S. Dist. Ct. (ea. dist.) N.Y. 1993; U.S. Dist. Ct. (so. dist.) N.Y. 1993; U.S. Ct. Appeals (2d cir.) 1995; U.S. Supreme Ct. 1996; registered NY State Pharmacist. Assoc. Nixon, Hargrave, Devans, and Doyle, Albany, NY, 1985-90, LeBoeuf, Lamb, Greene, & MacRae LLP, Albany, NY, 1990-93, ptnr., 1994—, mng. ptnr., hiring ptnr. Albany office, 1999—; mng. dir. Hudson Heritage LLC, 1999—2005. Ad., prof. law Albany Law Sch., 1989—94; town atty. Bethlehem, NY, 2001—03. Co-author: Yr. 2000 Deskbook, 1998. Mem. master plan com. Town of Bethlehem, Delmar, N.Y., 1989-89; mem. planning bd. counsel, 1990-94. Mem. N.Y. State Bar Assn., Albany Law Sch., Environ. Alumni Group, Rockefeller Found., advisor Pocantico roundtable consensus on brownfields. Avocations: tennis, reading, exercise. Office: LeBoeuf Lamb Greene & MacRae LLP One Commerce Plz Ste 2020 99 Washington Ave Albany NY 12210 Office Phone: 518-626-9000. Office Fax: 518-626-9010. Business E-Mail: ralessi@llgm.com.

ALETTA, JOHN MICHAEL, neurobiologist; b. Teaneck, NJ, July 17, 1952; s. Michael Patrick Aletta and Mary Jane Minardi; m. Elvira Gomez Aletta, June 17, 1984; children: Gianmichael Gomez, Sofia Francesca. AB, Columbia U., 1974, MA, 1980, MPhil, 1981; PhD, Columbia P&S, 1984. With spl. chemistries of blood and bodily specimens Englewood Clin. Labs., NJ, 1974—76; rsch. asst. Lab. Lance L. Simpson, N.Y.C., 1976—78; tchg. asst. dept. pharm. Columbia P&S, 1980—83, asst. prof. dept. pathology, 1988—90; prin. investigator dept. pharmacology U. Buffalo Sch. Medicine, 1991—. Ad hoc reviewer NSF, NIH, NINDS; cons. in field., Lloyd A Greene fellow NYU Sch. Medicine, 1984—87. Mem.: N.Y. Acad. Sci., Soc. Neurosci. Achievements include invention of protein methylarginine-specific antibodies. Home: 12 Auden Ct Williamsville NY 14221-3529 Office: U Buffalo Sch Medicine 3435 Main St Buffalo NY 14214-3000 Office Phone: 716-829-2800. E-mail: jaletta@buffalo.edu.

ALEVIZOS, SUSAN BAMBERGER, lawyer, writer, musician; b. N.Y.C., May 19, 1936; d. L. Richard and Helen (Thatcher) Bamberger; m. Theodore George Alevizos, May 6, 1960; children— Gregory, L. Richard, Theodore. BA, Smith Coll., 1958; postgrad., Columbia, 1959-60, Women's Lyceum, Athens, Greece, 1967-68; Master classes with, Maestro Yannis Jovenos, Naxos, Greece, 1967-74; JD, Suffolk U., 1978; grad. tax program, Boston U., 1986. Bar: Mass. 1978, Fed. 1979, U.S. Supreme Ct. 1982, U.S. Tax Ct. 1986. Assoc. editor Condé Nast, 1958-60; assoc. Alevizos & Alevizos, Boston, 1978-94, ptnr., 1994—; pres. Gnision Music Company, 1999—. Cons. Greek divsn. MGM Records; rec. divsn. Nat. Geog. Soc.; mem. adv. coun. Ctr. for Greek Studies, U. Fla., Gainesville, 1995—. Santouri player, 1967—, performed concerts, UN, N.Y.C., 1969, Am. embassy, Athens, 1968, Boston Mus. Fine Arts, 1972, Gardiner Mus., Boston, 1971, also in, Phila., Milw. and Detroit, field work, Nat. Folklore Archives of Greece, 1956—; recs. include Songs of Greece, 1960, Folksongs of Greece, 1961, Greek Folksongs, 1969, Poetry and Song, 1973, Traditional Songs and Dances of Greece and the Grecian Islands, 1978; author: Folksongs of Greece, 1968; prodr. Greek Cultural Hour, Sta. WBCN-FM, Boston, 1965-67; legal columnist Hellenic Chronicle, Boston, 1979—; contbr. articles to profl. publs. prod., A Greek Byzantine Christmas, 2000, A Greek Byzantine Easter, 2002. Trustee Pro Arte Chamber Orch. Boston, 1990-94; mem. bus. com. for arts Palm Beach County Cultural Coun., 1993-97. Mem. ABA, NARAS, Mass. Bar Assn., Boston Bar Assn., Assn. Trial Lawyers Am., Am. Folklore Soc., Modern Greek Studies Assn. Office: Alevizos and Alevizos PO Box 391409 Cambridge MA 02139-1409

ALEWINE, BETTY, retired telecommunications executive; V.p. sales and marketing Comsat Internat., v.p. & gen. mgr., pres.; CEO, pres. Comsat (merged with Lockheed Martin), Bethesda, Md., 1996—2000; ret., 2000. Bd. dirs. Rockwell Internat. Corp., 2000. Dir. The Nat. Symphony Orchestra, The Brink's Co., NY Life Ins. Co., Rockwell Automation, 2000—. Mailing: The Brink's Co PO Box 18100 Richmond VA 23226-8100

ALEX, JOANNE DEFILIPP, elementary school educator; m. Joseph Alex; children: Jessica, Joel, Julianna. BA in Art and Edn., Colby Coll., 1976; grad./cert., Montessori Methods, 1982; MEd, U. Maine, 2001. Tchr., kindergarten, Montessori schs., various cities, 1979-83; founder, tchr. Montessori Sch., Stillwater, Maine, 1983—; instr. elem. sci. methods U. Maine, 2003. AMS Montessori intern supr., Univ. student tchr. placements (supr. tchr.); presenter numerous workshops and confs.; trained facilitator of Systematic Tng. for Effective Parenting; instr. parenting courses; ednl. cons.; facilitator Project Learning Tree, Project Wild, Project Aquatic, Project Wet workshops; coord 1st Maine Tchrs. Forum, 1998. Co-author: I Wonder What's Out There? A Vision of the Universe for Primary Classrooms, 2002. Selected to attend Nat. Geographic Soc. Summer Inst., 1993, Nat. Geographic Soc. Alliance Leadership Acad., 1999; named State Coord. Maine, Nat. Geographic Soc. Action 2003!, Outstanding Environ. Educator of Yr. (nat.), Am. Tree Found., 1994, Tchr. of Yr., Maine Audubon Soc., 1995, Maine Tchr. of Yr., 1998; recipient award for outstanding contbns. to child-care in Maine, 1996; state finalist Presdl. Award for Excellence in Elem. Sci. Tchg., 2002, 04. Mem. Am. Montessori Soc. (cert. tchr.), N. Am. Montessori Tchrs. Assn., Maine Montessori Assn. (treas.). Avocations: biking, hiking, wild flowers, children's books, children's resources. Office: Stillwater Montessori Sch 1024 Stillwater Ave Unit 1 Old Town ME 04468-5112 Office Phone: 207-827-2404. E-mail: jalex1@adelphia.net.

ALEX, PAULA ANN, foundation administrator; b. New Haven, May 1, 1945; d. Ralph P. and Louise A. (Pesanelli) A. Student, Conn. Coll., 1962-64; diploma, U. Paris, Sorbonne, 1966; BA, Am. U., 1967; cert. bus. mgmt., NYU, 1978. Exec. asst. Olin Corp., Stamford, 1968-72, Wheelabrator-Frye, N.Y.C., 1973-75; account exec. SSC & B: Lintas, N.Y.C., 1976-82; account supr. Lawrence Charles Free & Lawson, N.Y.C., 1982—84; v.p. Advt. Ednl. Found., N.Y.C., 1985-88, exec. v.p., 1989—, mng. dir., bd. dirs., 1992—, CEO, 2003—. Mem. exec. com. Murray Hill Aux. Lenox Hill Hosp., N.Y.C. Mem. Am. Acad. Advt., Am. Advt. Fedn. Bd., Advt. Women N.Y. Avocations: southeast asian art, opera, riding. Office: Advt Ednl Found 220 E 42d St Ste 3300 New York NY 10017-5806 Office Phone: 212-986-8060. E-mail: pa@aef.com.

ALEXANDER, ALONZO, III, music educator, composer; b. Cin., Sept. 4, 1956; s. Alonzo Alexander Jr. and Mamie (Comer) Alexander. MusB, U. Cin., Coll. Conservatory of Music, 1978, MusM, 1982, MusD, 1997. Music dir. St. Mark Cath. Ch., Cin., 1980—84, 1990—99; instr. Pasadena Conservatory of Music, Pasadena, Calif., 1985—90; adj. instr. Coll. Conservatory of Music, Cin., 1996—99, Antioch U., Yellow Springs, Ohio, 1996—97; asst. prof. music Morris Brown Coll., Atlanta, 1999—2003, Spelman Coll., Atlanta, 2004—. Accompanist Americolor Opera Alliance, Atlanta, 2000—05. Recipient Cert. of Honor award, Pi Kappa Lambda (Pi Chpt.), 1977, Recognition award, Phi Mu Alpha Sinfonia, 2004. Mem.: Phi Mu Alpha Sinfonia (faculty adv. 2001—04). Democrat. Cath. Avocations: poetry, singing, Greek mythology. Home: 1236 Anchor Terr SW Atlanta GA 30311 Office: Spelman Coll 350 Spelman Ln Atlanta GA 30314 Office Phone: 404-270-5494. E-mail: alonzoafricano@aol.com.

ALEXANDER, ANDREW NELSON, journalist; b. Rochester, N.Y., June 7, 1948; s. William Robert and Dorothy Marie (Stimple) A.; m. Beverly Eileen Jones, July 24, 1986. BS in Journalism, Ohio U., 1972. Reporter Dayton (Ohio) Jour.-Herald, 1971-76, Washington corr., 1976-83; nat. staff corr. Washington bur. Cox Newspapers, 1983-90, fgn. editor Washington bur., 1990—97, dep. bur. chief Washington bur., 1997—, bur. chief Washington bur. Mem. Nat. Press Club, Gridiron Club. Office: Cox Newspapers Washington Bur 400 N Capitol St NW Ste 750 Washington DC 20001-1536

ALEXANDER, ANNA MARGARET, artist, writer, educator; b. Greenville, Tex., Jan. 26, 1913; d. Samuel Jefferson and Elizabeth (Smith) Fooshee; m. Joseph C. Jake Alexander, Feb. 12, 1936 (dec. 1988); children: Joanna, Ellen Alexander Stein, Mardi. BA, Rice U., 1933. Cert. tchr. Tchr., Klein, Tex., 1933-38; fashion artist, writer, adv. mgr. Smart Shop, Houston, 1938-43; fashion artist, writer Kreeger's, New Orleans, 1943-45, Everitt Buelow Ralph Rupley, 1953-68; owner Ideas Ink, 1950—54; art tchr. Spring Branch, Houston, 1968-74. Founder Historic Outdoor Art Gallery, New Braunfels, Tex. Vol. literacy program, ch., hist. socs., sr. citizen groups, children's mus., food bank; leader, camp counselor Girl Scouts U.S.A., Houston, 1956-60; pres. Girl's Booster Club, Houston, 1966-68; bd. dirs. St. Francis Episc. Day Sch., 1965-70; Sunday sch. tchr. St. Francis Ch., Houston, 1958-62; active PTA. Mem. Advt. Club Houston, Univ. Women Houston, DAR, Colonial Dames New Braunfels, Garden Club, Ret. Tchrs. Assn., C. of C. Vis. Bur. (downtown design rev. commn., 45 Yrs. as Vol. award 1983), others. Avocations: ecology, church activities, gardening, volunteerism, travel, family activities. Home: 909 Allen Ave New Braunfels TX 78130-4903

ALEXANDER, ANTHONY J., electric power industry executive; m. Becky Alexander; 4 children. BS, U. Akron, 1972, JD, 1975. Bar: Ohio 1976. Sr. tax acct. Ohio Edison Co., Akron, 1972-76, atty., 1976-83, sr. atty., 1984-87, assoc. gen. counsel, 1987-89, sr. v.p., gen. counsel, 1898-91; exec. v.p., gen. counsel Ohio Edison Co. (merged with Centerior Energy to form FirstEnergy), Akron, 1996—97, FirstEnergy Corp., Akron, 1997—2000, pres., 2000—, COO, 2001—04, CEO, 2004—. Bd. dirs. Ohio Electric Utility Inst., Assn. of Edison Illuminating Companies, Inc. Bd. trustees Akron Gen. Health System, The NEOUCOM Found., Playhouse Square Found., Green Schools Found., U. Akron Found.; vice chmn. Greater Akron Chamber. Recipient Dr. Frank L. Simonetti Dist. Bus. Alumni award, U. Akron. Mem.: Nat. Assn. of Manufacturers (dir.-at-large). Office: FirstEnergy Corp 76 S Main St 18th Fl Akron OH 44308-1812*

ALEXANDER, ARTHUR JACOB, economist; b. Carbondale, Pa., Oct. 6, 1936; s. Howard R. and Sylvia (Eisner) A.; m. Elaine Averich, Aug. 25, 1963; children: Sarah, Jonathan. BS, Mass. Inst. Tech., 1958; MSc, London Sch. Econs., 1966; PhD, Johns Hopkins U., 1969. Sys. analyst IBM, Poughkeepsie, N.Y., 1960-63; rsch. economist Rand Corp., Santa Monica, Calif., 1968-90; pres. Japan Econ. Inst., Washington, 1990—2001. Vis. prof. UCLA, 1988-90, Johns Hopkins U., 1994-97, George Mason U., 1998—, Georgetown U., 2000—; mem. U.S. Army Sci. Bd., Washington, 1978-82; rsch. assoc. Internat. Inst. Strategic Studies, London, 1976-77. With U.S. Army, 1959-60. Avocations: photographica collections, running. Office: Japan Econ Inst 3517 Raymond St Chevy Chase MD 20815-3227 Office Phone: 301-652-4574. Business E-Mail: aalexander@jei.org.

ALEXANDER, BARBARA LEAH SHAPIRO, clinical social worker; b. St. Louis, May 6, 1943; d. Harold Albert and Dorothy Miriam (Leifer) Shapiro; m. Richard E. Alexander. B in Music Edn., Washington U., St. Louis, 1964; postgrad., U. Ill., 1964-66; MSW, Smith Coll., 1970; postgrad., Inst. Psychoanalysis, Chgo., 1971-73, grad., child therapy program, 1976-80; cert. therapist Sex Dysfunction Clinic, Loyola U., Chgo., 1975. Diplomate in Clin. Social Work. Rsch. asst., NIMH grantee Smith Coll., 1968-70; probation officer Juvenile Ct. Cook County, Chgo., 1966-68, 70; therapist Madden Mental Health Ctr., Hines, Ill., 1970-72; supr., therapist, field instr. U. Chgo., U. Ill. Grad. Schs. Social Work; therapist Pritzker Children's Hosp., Chgo., 1972-82; therapist, cons., also pvt. practice, 1973—; pres. On Good Authority, 1992—; intern Divorce Conciliation Svc., Circuit Ct. Cook County, 1976-77. Contbr. articles to profl. jours. Bd. dirs., Grant Park Concerts Soc.; sec. Art Resources in Teaching. Recipient Sterling Achievement award Mu Phi Epsilon, 1964. Mem. Nat. Fed. Soc. for Clin. Social Work (chmn. 20th ann. conf., exec. bd.), Ill. Soc. Clin. Social Work (pres. 1986-90, bd. dirs., chmn. svcs. to mems. com., dir. pvt. practitioners' referral service), Assn. Child Psychotherapists, Amateur Chamber Music Players Assn., Jewish Geneal. Soc., Smith Coll. Alumni Assn. (bd. dirs., v.p. 1992-94). Home and Office: 6 Horizon Ln Galena IL 61036-9258

ALEXANDER, BARBARA TOLL, financial consultant; b. Little Rock, Dec. 18, 1948; d. Lawrence Jesser and Geraldine Best (Proctor) Toll; m. Lawrence Allen Alexander, Jan. 25, 1969 (div. 1980); m. Thomas Beveridge

Stiles, II, Mar. 7, 1981; stepchildren: Thomas B. Stiles III, Jonathan E. Stiles. BS, U. Ark., 1969, MS, 1970. Asst. v.p. Wachovia Bank & Trust Co., Winston-Salem, NC, 1972—77; security analyst Investors Diversified Services, Mpls., 1977—78; 1st v.p. Smith Barney Inc., N.Y.C., 1978—84; mng. dir. Salomon Bros., N.Y.C., 1984—91, Dillon Read & Co., 1992—97, UBS Securities, 1997—99, sr. advisor, 1999—2004. Bd. dirs., mem. nominating and governing coms. Centex Corp.; bd. dirs., chmn. audit com. Harrah's Entertainment, Inc.; bd. dirs., mem. audit com. Burlington Resources; bd. dirs., mem. fin. and capital deployment, mission and sourcing coms. Freddie Mac; former chmn. policy adv. bd. Joint Ctr. for Housing Studies of Harvard U.; exec. fellow Harvard U.; mem., bd. dirs. HomeAid Am. Presbyterian. E-mail: barbara.alexander@cox.net.

ALEXANDER, BRUCE DONALD, real estate executive, educator; b. Hartford, Conn., May 11, 1943; BA, Yale U., 1965, MA (hon.), 1998; JD, Duke U., 1968. With Rouse Co., Balt., 1969-96, sr. v.p., dir. comml. devel. divsn., 1978-93, sr. v.p., dir. new bus., 1993-96; dir. Balt. Equitable Ins., 1987-89, Enterprise Social Investment Corp., 1995-2000, Balt. Devel. Corp., 1996-98; v.p., dir. New Haven and State Affairs Yale U., New Haven, 1998—, adj. prof. real estate, Yale Sch. Mgmt., 1998—. Trustee Goucher Coll., Balt., 1984-2001, chmn., 1991-96; trustee Columbia (Md.) Found., 1981-86, pres., 1983-85; trustee Balt. Ednl. Scholarship Trust, 1990-93, Conn. Pub. Broadcasting, 2002-; co-chair eastern region Yale U. Campaign, 1991-97; bd. dirs. Balt. Symphony Orch., 1986-91, Cmty. Found. Greater New Haven, 2003-. Recipient John Franklin Goucher medal. Office: Yale Univ 433 Temple St New Haven CT 06511-6803 Office Phone: 203-432-8623. E-mail: bruce.alexander@yale.edu.

ALEXANDER, C. ALEX, physician; b. Kerala, India, Mar. 1, 1935; came to U.S., 1962; naturalized, 1974; s. Chandy and Sarah (Yohannan) A.; m. Sudha Trivedi, July 1, 1982. MD, U. Madras (India), 1958; MPH, Johns Hopkins U., 1964, DPH, 1966. Diplomate Am. Bd. Preventive Medicine. Intern Muhlenburg Hosp., Plainfield, N.J., 1962-63; resident in preventive medicine Johns Hopkins U., Balt., 1964-66, asst. to assoc. prof. public health adminstrn., 1966-72; dir. med. affiars Provident Hosp., Balt., 1971-73; assoc. prof. social and preventive medicine Med. Sch. U. Md., Balt., 1972-75; chief of staff VA Med. Ctr., Castle Point, N.Y., 1983-90, Ft. Howard, Md., 1990-95; dir. John J. Pershing VA Med. Ctr., Poplar Bluff, Mo., 1995-96; chief med. officer Vets. Integrated Svc., Network #6, Durham, N.C., 1996—. Clin. prof. community medicine Wright State U., Dayton, 1975-83, asst. dean Sch. of Medicine, 1975-76; clin. prof. community medicine N.Y. Med. Coll., 1984-90, health svcs. adminstrn. uniformed svcs. U. Health Sci., Bethesda, Md., 1990-95; cons. WHO, 1969, USPHS, 1967-75. Col. M.C., U.S. Army Res. Recipient Disting. Service award Community Health Council Md., 1974; Leadership award VA, 1979; decorated meritorious svc. medal U.S. Army, 1991. Fellow Am. Coll. Preventive Medicine, Am. Public Health Assn., Am. Coll. International Physicians (pres. 1978-79, 90-91), Am. Coll. Healthcare Execs.; mem. Am. Legion. Syrian Orthodox. Office: Dept Vet Affairs Vets Integrated Svc # 1402 300 W Morgan St Durham NC 27701-2162

ALEXANDER, CARL ALBERT, ceramics engineer, educator; b. Chillicothe, Ohio, Nov. 22, 1928; s. Carl B. and Helen E. Alexander; m. Dolores J. Herrenstein, Sept. 4, 1954; children: Carla C., David A. BS, Ohio U., 1953, MS, 1956; PhD, Ohio State U., 1961. Mem. staff Battelle Columbus Labs., 1956—, rsch. leader, 1974—, mgr. physico-chem. systems, 1976—; mem. faculty Ohio State U., 1963—, prof. ceramic and nuc. engring., 1977—. Sr. rsch. leader, chmn. tech. coun. of Biol. and Chem. Scis. Directorate, 1987—, chief scientist, 1987; prof. materials sci. and engring., 1988—. Author; patentee in field. Served to lt. (j.g.) USNR, 1951-54. Recipient Merit award NASA, 1971, IR-100 award, 1987, R & D-100 award, 1988; citations Dept. Energy, citations AEC, citations ERDA. Mem. Am. Soc. Mass Spectrometry, Keramos, Sigma Xi Home: 4249 Haughn Rd Grove City OH 43123-3216 Office: 505 King Ave Columbus OH 43201-2696 Office Phone: 614-424-5233. E-mail: alexandc@battelle.org.

ALEXANDER, CECIL ABRAHAM, academic administrator, consultant, retired architect; b. Atlanta, Mar. 14, 1918; s. Cecil Abraham and Julia (Moses) A.; m. Hermione Weil, Jan. 20, 1943 (dec. 1983); children: Therese, Judith, Douglas; m. Helen Eisemann, 1985. Student, Ga. Inst. Tech., 1936; AB, Yale, 1940; student, Mass. Inst. Tech., 1941; M. Arch., Harvard, 1947. Partner Alexander & Rothschild (architects), Atlanta, 1949-58; chmn. bd. Finch, Alexander, Barnes, Rothschild & Paschal, Architects and Engrs., Inc., Atlanta, 1958-86; archtl. cons. Atlanta, 1986-90; coord. continuing edn. Ga. Inst. Tech. Coll. Architecture, Atlanta, 1994-96; prin.-in-charge Leo A. Daley Archtl. Engrs., Atlanta, 1996-97; ptnr. Alexander-Weiner Baker Architects, Atlanta, 1997—, Alexander Weiner Architects, 00—. Coord.; chmn. bd. A.S.D. Inc., interior design svc.; dir. Atlanta office Leo A. Daly Archtl. Engring. Internat.; chmn. Atlanta Citizens Adv. Com. Urban Renewal, 1958-60; vice chmn. Atlanta Met. Planning Commn., 1962—; past chmn. Ga. Fgn. Trade Zone Corp. Prin. works include Ga. Power Bldg., Atlanta, 1st Nat. Bank, Atlanta, Cin. Riverfront Stadium, Coca-Cola Internat. Hdqs., Sci. Atlanta Hdqs., U.S. Pavilion Expo '82, So. Bell. Hdqs.; designer new Ga. flag, 2001. Past vice chmn. Community Coun., Atlanta, Ga.; mem. Mayor's Adv. Com. Race Relations, Nat. Citizens Com. Community Rels.; chmn. Atlanta chpt. Am. Jewish Com., 1963; chmn. housing resources com. City of Atlanta; past chmn. com. Yale Sch. Architecture; pres., founder Resurgens Atlanta; past v.p. Atlanta Symphony Orch.; Mem. Yale Nat. Alumni Bd., 1963; bd. dirs. Atlanta U.; bd. dirs. emeritus, Clark Atlanta U.; past bd. dirs. Marist High Sch., Atlanta; chmn. Com. to Combat Drugged and Drunken Driving; past pres. Atlanta's Clifton Corridor Biomed. Rsch. Coun. Served to lt. col. USMCR, World War II. Decorated Air medal, D.F.C.; (2) Recipient Brotherhood award NCCJ, 1973; Archdiocesan medal of St. Paul, 1980, Yale medal, 1980. Fellow AIA (pres. Ga. 1957, Ivan Allen award); mem. Atlanta C. of C. (dir., Whitney Young award, Nat Am. Inst. Architects). Home: 2677 Rivers Rd NW Atlanta GA 30305-3549 Office Phone: 404-210-4365. E-mail: cecilalexander@comcast.net.

ALEXANDER, CLIFFORD JOSEPH, lawyer; b. New Orleans, Oct. 2, 1943; s. Charles Ernest and Lois Primus (Boley) A.; m. Elizabeth McAnany, June 11, 1966; children: Brian, Heather, Rachel. AB, Rockhurst Coll., 1966; JD, Georgetown U., 1969. Bar: Mass. 1970, D.C. 1977. Mem. staff SEC, Washington, 1967-70; assoc. Gaston Snow & Ely Bartlett, Boston, 1970-75; mem. staff U.S. Senate Banking Com., Washington, 1975-77; mem. Kirkpatrick & Lockhart Nicholson, Graham LLP, Washington, 1977—. Co-editor: Money Managers Compliance Manual. Mem. ABA (corp., banking and bus. law sect.), Boston Bar Assn., Fed. Bar Assn. (securities and banking law sects.), D.C. Bar Assn., Mass. Bar Assn., U.S. Supreme Ct. Bar. Home: 8721 Bluedale St Alexandria VA 22308-2307 Office: Kirkpatrick & Lockhart 1800 Massachusetts Ave NW Fl 2 Washington DC 20036-1806 Office Phone: 202-778-9068. Business E-Mail: calexander@klng.com.

ALEXANDER, DONALD CRICHTON, lawyer; b. Pine Bluff, Ark., May 22, 1921; s. William Crichton and Ella Temple (Fox) A.; m. Margaret Louise Savage, Oct. 9, 1946; children: Robert C., James M. BA with honors, Yale U., 1942; LLB magna cum laude, Harvard U., 1948; LLD (hon.), St. Thomas Inst., 1975, Capital U., 1989. Bar: D.C. 1949, Ohio 1954, N.Y. 1978. Assoc. Covington & Burling, Washington, 1948-54, Taft, Stettinius & Hollister, Cin., 1954-56, ptnr., 1956-66, Dinsmore, Shohl, Coates & Deupree, Cin., 1966-73; commr. IRS, 1973-77; mem. Commn. on Fed. Paperwork, 1975-77; ptnr. Olwine, Connelly, Chase, O'Donnell & Weyher, N.Y.C., Washington, 1977-79, Morgan, Lewis & Bockius, N.Y.C. and Washington, 1979-85, Cadwalader, Wickersham & Taft, Washington, 1985-93; ptnr., tax. practice group Akin, Gump, Strauss, Hauer & Feld, Washington, 1993—. Mem. adv. bd. NYU Tax Inst., 1969-73, 77-87, Tax Mgmt., Inc., 1968-73, 77—; mem. adv. Treas. Dept., 1970-72; mem. adv. group to commr. IRS, 1969-70, chmn. exempt orgns. adv. group, 1987-89; mem. adv. bd. Mertens, 1986-2002, Maxwell Macmillan fed. Taxes 2d, 1989-92; commr. Martin Luther King, Jr. Fed. Holiday Commn., 1993-96; mem. Harvard Bd. Overseers' vis. com. to law sch., 1999—; mem. com. on univ. resources Harvard U., 2002—; mem. interior dept. commn. on coal leasing, 1983-84. Author: The Arkansas Plantation, 1943; editor Harvard Law Rev., 1947-48; contbr. more than 50 articles on fed. taxation. Co-chmn. bd. advisors NYU/IRS Continuing Profl. Edn. Program, 1982-85; dir. Treasury Hist. Assn., 1996—. Served to maj. AUS, 1942-45. Decorated Silver Star, Bronze Star. Mem. ABA (vice chmn. taxation sect. 1967-68), Am. Law Inst. (tax adv. group), U.S. C. of C. (taxation com. 1981-91, bd. dirs. 1984-89, health and employee benefit com. 1989-94, regulatory affairs com. 1993-98), Chevy Chase Club (Md.), Met. Club, Nantucket Yacht Club (Mass.), Mill Reef Club (Antigua, B.W.I.), Yale Club N.Y. Office: Akin Gump Strauss Hauer & Feld Robert S Strauss Bldg 1333 New Hampshire Ave NW Washington DC 20036-1564 Office Phone: 202-887-4064. Office Fax: 202-887-4288. Business E-Mail: dalexander@akingump.com.

ALEXANDER, DONALD G., state supreme court justice; Grad., Bowdoin Coll.; JD, U. Chgo. Bar: Maine 1972, U.S. Supreme Ct. 1973. Former legislative counsel Nat. League of Cities; former mem. Sen. Edmund Muskie's staff; asst. Maine atty. gen., 1974-76; dep. atty. gen.; judge Dist. Ct., 1979, Maine Superior Ct., 1980-98; justice Maine Supreme Ct., 1998—. Ct. liaison Advisory Com. on Maine Rules of Civil Procedur, State Ct. Library Com., Maine State Bar Assn. Continuing Legal Education Com. Author: (books) The Maine Jury Instruction Manual, 2003, Maine Appellate Practice, 2003; editor: The Maine Rules of Civil Procedure with Advisory Committee Notes from 1981, Commentary and Recent Case Citations, 2003. Office: Cumberland County Courthouse 142 Federal St PO Box 368 Portland ME 04112-0368*

ALEXANDER, DRURY BLAKELEY, retired architecture educator; b. Paris, Tex., Feb. 4, 1924; s. Drury Blakeley and Katherine (Stone) Alexander. B.Arch., U. Tex., 1950, BS in Art, 1951; MA, Columbia U., 1953. Instr. Kans. State U., Manhattan, 1953-55; asst. prof. architecture U. Tex., Austin, 1955-60, assoc. prof., 1960-67, prof., 1967-84, Meadows Found. prof. architecture, 1984-94, emeritus prof., 1994—; ret., 1994. Eugene McDermott lectr. U. Tex., 1983—85. Author: Texas Homes of the 19th Century, 1966, Sources of Classicism, 1978. Chmn. Hist. Landmark Commn., Austin, 1975—85. With U.S. Army, ETO. Decorated Bronze Star medal; named a Arch. Archive in his name, The Arch. Libr. The U. Tex., Austin, 2002; recipient Disting. Svc. award, City of Austin, 1976, Svc. award for hist. preservation, Heritage Soc. Austin, 1976, Tex. Hist. Preservation award, Tex. Hist. Commn., 1986, Nat. Preservation Honor award, Nat. Trust for Hist. Preservation, 1991, Disting. Achievement award in archtl. edn., Tex. Soc. Architects, 1994, Disting. Prof. award, Assn. Collegiate Schs. of Arch., 1995, D.B. Alexander Lifetime Achievement award named in his honor, Heritage Soc. Austin, 2001. Mem.: Victorian Soc. Am., Assn. Preservation Technologists, Soc. Archtl. Historians (bd. dirs. 1979—82). Democrat. Presbyterian. Avocations: book collecting, travel. Home: 4100 Jackson Ave # 115 Austin TX 78731-6029 Office: U Tex Sch Architecture Austin TX 78712

ALEXANDER, DUANE FREDERICK, federal agency administrator, pediatrician, researcher; b. Balt., Aug. 11, 1940; s. Fred Lucas and Christiana H. (Showacre) A.; m. Marianne Ellis, June 23, 1963; children: Keith Duane, Kristin Marianne. BS, Pa. State U., 1962; MD, Johns Hopkins U., 1966. Diplomate: Am. Bd. Pediatrics. Intern Johns Hopkins Hosp., Balt., 1966—67, resident, 1967—68, fellow, 1970—71; commd. officer USPHS, 1968—2000, ret. rear adm.; clin. assoc. Nat. Inst. Child Health and Human Devel., NIH, Bethesda, Md., 1968—70, asst. to sci. dir., 1971—74, asst. to dir., 1978—82, dep. dir., 1982—86, dir., 1986—; staff pediatrician Nat. Commn. for Protection of Human Subjects of Research, 1974—78. Contbr. articles to profl. jours. Recipient Commendation medal USPHS, 1970, Meritorious Svc. medal USPHS, 1985, Spl. Recognition medal USPHS, 1985, Surgeon Gen.'s Exemplary Svc. medal, 1990, Irving B. Harris Lectureship award Soc. Behavioral Pediatrics, 1991, Pub. Svc. award Am. Coll. Ob-Gyn., 1992, Surgeon Gen.'s Medallion, 1993, Disting. Pub. Svc. award Am. Acad. Phys. Medicine and Rehab., 1993, Presdl. Citation, APA, 1992, Sec.'s Disting. Svc. award HHS, 1997, 98, Disting Alumnus award Pa. State U., 1999, Nathan Davis award AMA, 2004; alumni fellow Pa. State U. Alumni Assn, 1993. Fellow Am. Acad. Pediatrics (Excellence Pub. Svc. award 1998), Soc. Devel. Pediatrics, Am. Pediatric Soc., Assn. for Retarded Citizens. Methodist. Office: Nat Inst Child Health-Human Devel 31 Center Dr Msc 2425 Bldg 31 Bethesda MD 20892-0001 Office Phone: 301-496-3454. Business E-Mail: da43w@nih.gov, nichddir@mail.nih.gov.

ALEXANDER, EDWARD RUSSELL, retired epidemiologist, science administrator; b. Chgo., June 15, 1928; s. Russell Green and Ethelyn Satterlee (Abel) A. PhB, U. Chgo., 1948, BS, 1950, MD, 1953. Intern Cin. Gen. Hosp.; chief surveillance sect. Communicable Disease Center, Atlanta, 1955-57, 59-60; resident, instr. dept. pediatrics U. Chgo., 1954-55, 57-59; asst. prof. dept. preventive medicine and dept. pediatrics U. Wash., Seattle, 1961-65, assoc. prof., 1965-69, prof., 1969-79; chmn. dept. epidemiology U. Wash. Sch. Pub. Health, 1970-75; prof. dept. pediat. U. Ariz., Tucson, 1979-83; dir. rsch. br., venereal diseases control divsn. Ctrs. for Disease Control, Atlanta, 1983-89, asst. dir. sci. sexually transmitted diseases divsn., 1989; chief of epidemiology Seattle King County Dept. Pub. Health, Seattle, 1990-98; prof. dept. epidemiology U. Wash. Sch. Pub. Health, Seattle, 1990-98, prof. emeritus, 1998—. Contbr. articles to profl. jours. Markle scholar, 1962-67. Mem. Am. Acad. Pediatrics, Am. Pediatric Soc., Am. Pub. Health Assn. (Abraham Lilienfeld award 1988), Assn. Tchrs. Preventive Medicine, Am. Epidemiol. Soc. (pres. 1986-87), Soc. Epidemiol. Rsch., Internat. Epidemiol. Soc., Am. Venereal Disease Assn. (Thomas Parran award 1984, pres. 1985-87) Personal E-mail: erussa@comcast.net.

ALEXANDER, ELMORE ROSEBUR, III, business educator, dean; b. Florence, S.C., July 14, 1952; m. Pamela J. Carlson. BA, Wake Forest U., 1974; MA, U. Ga., 1976, PhD, 1978. Prof. mgmt. U. Memphis, 1977-89; prof. Am. U., Washington, 1989-96, chair mgmt. dept., 1989-93, assoc. dean Kogod Coll. Bus. Adminstrn., 1993-96; prof., dir. divsn. bus. mgmt. Johns Hopkins U., Balt., 1996-98; prof., dean Sch. Bus. Adminstrn. Phila. U., 1998—. Contbr. articles to profl. jours. Methodist. Avocations: golf, tennis. Home: 348 Valley Rd Merion Station PA 19066-1520 Office: Phila U School House Ln & Henry Ave Philadelphia PA 19144-5497 Fax: 215-951-2652. Office Phone: 215-951-2827.

ALEXANDER, ERROL DUANE, management consultant, educator, writer, artist; b. Sandusky, Ohio, July 11, 1941; s. Willis B. Alexander; divorced; children: Errol, Mia, Lorre, Penny; married; children: Kay, Doug, Jamie, Victoria. BS in Quality Control Methods, Strathclyde U., 1961, MBA with distinction, 1987; PhD in Strategic Mgmt. and Innovation, Glasgow U., 1990. Cert. mgmt. cons., 1975. Quality assurance tech. Sparton Electronics, Jackson, Mich., 1962-65; asst. project mgr. Bendix Aerospace Sys. Divsn., Ann Arbor, Mich., 1965-67; sr. project engr. Pratt & Whitney Aircraft, East Hartford, Conn., 1967-69; venture capitalist Hartford Nat. Bank, 1969-71; founder/CEO Profiles Rsch. & Cons. Groups, Hartford, 1971—. Lectr. bus. policy & strategy Univ. Edinburgh, Scotland; vis. fellow Univ. Cambridge Ctr. Internat. Studies. Bd. dirs., pres. Sandusky NAACP, 1962-64; chmn. Urban League of Hartford, 1976; treas. Am. Heart Assn., 1979; active United Way of Hartford, 1982; chmn. Internat. Ctr. Advance Mgmt. in Scotland, 1994-96; mem. Scottish Conservative Coun. Advisors, 1995; mem. UN Staff Coll., Turin, Italy, 1996. Recipient Disting. Svc. award U.S. Dept. Commerce, 1982, Disting. Scholar award Fortuna Soc., 1991, others; named Young Man of Yr., NAACP, 1963; Arden House fellow Columbia U., N.Y.C., 1974, Amos Tuck Bus. Sch. fellow Dartmouth Coll., 1989. Fellow Royal Soc. Art and Commerce (London), Inst. of Dirs. (U.K.); mem. Sigma Pi Phi. Avocations: golf, reading, oil and water color painting collection.

ALEXANDER, F. KING, academic administrator; b. Ky. BA in Polit. Sci., St. Lawrence U., N.Y.; MS in Comparative Edn. Policy, Oxford (Eng.) U.; PhD in Higher Edn. Adminstrn., U. Wis., Madison. Mgr. Liberty Nat. Bank, Louisville; postdoctoral rschr., office of the provost U. Wis., Madison, vice chancellor for acad. affairs, lectr. ednl. adminstrn.; adminstr., mem. faculty U. Ill., Urbana-Champaign; pres. Murray (Ky.) State U., 1997. Contbr. articles to profl. jours. and publs. Office: Murray State U 218 Wells Hall Murray KY 42071

ALEXANDER, FRED CALVIN, JR., lawyer; b. Abingdon, Va., Nov. 4, 1931; s. Fred C. and Mary F. (White) A.; m. Betsy Jones, May 17, 1957 (div.); children— Mitchell, Mary, Marjorie, Margaret; m. Janet Lee Hammond, Jan. 2, 1982 Student, Davidson Coll., 1950-52; BA, U. Va., 1954, LLB, 1959. Bar: Va. 1959, U.S. Dist. Ct. (ea. dist.) Va. 1959, U.S. Ct. Appeals (4th cir.) 1960. Assoc. Boothe, Prichard & Dudley, Alexandria, Va., 1959-64; ptnr. McGuire, Woods, Battle & Boothe LLP and predecessor firms, Alexandria, Va., 1964-97, ret. McLean, Va., 1997. Mem. jud. conf. U.S. Ct. Appeals (4th cir.), 1964-99; lectr. legal edn. Va. State Bar, 1970, 75-77, 89; chmn. adv. com. rules of ct. Supreme Ct. of Va., 1984-98; bd. dirs. Thomas Rutherfoord, Inc. Past bd. dirs. counsel to Alexandria Hosp., St. Stephens Sch. 1st lt. U.S. Army, 1954-56. Fellow: Am. Coll. Trial Lawyers (chmn. Va. com. 1994—96), Va. Law Found.; mem.: Alexandria Bar Assn. (pres. 1969—70), Va. Bar Assn. (chmn. civil litigation sect. 1989—92), Va. Assn. Def. Attys., Va. Trial Lawyers Assn., Nat. Assn. R.R. Trial Counsel, Def. Rsch. Inst. (chmn. railroad law com. 1989—92), Belle Haven Country Club (bd. dirs. 1997—2000, 2001—04), Wyndemere Country Club. Episcopalian. Home: 1313 Gatewood Dr Alexandria VA 22307-2033 Office: McGuire Woods LLP 1750 Tysons Blvd Ste 1800 Mc Lean VA 22102-4231

ALEXANDER, GARY R., lawyer, state legislator, lobbyist; b. Washington, Nov. 16, 1942; s. Orville I. and Ann Z. Alexander; m. Anita G. Alexander; children: Jennifer Paige, Cory Brooke. BA, U. Va., 1964; LLB, George Washington U., 1967. Pvt. practice, Washington, Md. and Va., 1967-69; ptnr. Giordano, Alexander, Haas, Mahoney & Bush, Oxen Hill, Md., 1970-78, Haas & Alexander, Md., 1978-82; prin. ptnr. Alexander & Cleaver, P.A., Ft. Washington, Md., 1982—. Bd. dirs., chmn. Prince George County bar legis. com., 1972-79; bd. vis. U. Md. Sch. Pub. Policy, 2002—. Del. Md. Ho. of Dels., 1983-94, spkr. pro tem, 1993-94; chmn. Dem. Cen. Com., Prince George County, 1978-86; people's counsel Md. Pub. Svc. Commn., 1974-78; apptd. Gov.'s Task Force to Study Gambling, Md., 1993; taxation com. Md. C. of C., 1995; bd. trustees U. Md. Found., 2002—. Recipient Outstanding Svc. award Md. Senate, 1976, Outstanding Svc. citation, 1976, Pub. Svc. cert. Prince George County Exec. and County Coun., 1976, Local Employer of Yr. award Bus. and Profl. Woman's Club, 1993, Outstanding Atty. award Washington mag., 1997. Mem. ABA (chmn. automobile law com. 1975-77, chmn. automobile ins. legis. com. 1977-80), Nat. Conf. State Legislatures, Md. Bar Assn. (chmn. fed. laws com. 1973-79), D.C. Bar Assn., Va. Bar Assn., Md. Govt. Rels. Assn. Jewish. Avocations: history, gardening, golf, cooking. Office: Alexander & Cleaver PA 11414 Livingston Rd Fort Washington MD 20744-5145 also: Alexander & Cleaver PA 54 State Cir Annapolis MD 21401-1906 Office Phone: 301-292-3300.

ALEXANDER, GEORGE JONATHON, lawyer, educator; b. Berlin, Mar. 8, 1931; s. Walter and Sylvia (Grill) A.; m. Katharine Violet Sziklai, Sept. 6, 1958; children: Susan Katina, George Jonathon II. AB with maj. honors, U. Pa., 1953, JD cum laude, 1969; LLM, Yale U., 1965, JSD, 1969. Bar: Ill. 1960, N.Y. 1961, Calif. 1974. Instr. law, Bigelow fellow U. Chgo., 1959-60; instr. internat. relations Naval Res. Officers Sch., Forrest Park, Ill., 1959-60; prof. law Syracuse U. Coll. Law, 1960-70, assoc. dean, 1968-69; prof. law U. Santa Clara (Calif.) Law Sch., 1970—, disting. univ. prof., 1994-95, Elizabeth H. and John A. Sutro prof. law, 1995—2005, pres. faculty senate, 1996-97, dean, 1970-85, dean emeritus, 2005—, dir. Inst. Internat. and Comparative Law, 1986—, dir. grad. programs, 1998-2001, co-dir., 2002. Dir. summer programs at Oxford, Geneva, Strasbourg, Budapest, Tokyo, Hong Kong, Beijing, Shanghai, Ho Chi Minh City, Singapore, Bangkok, Kuala Lumpur, Seoul, Munich, Sydney, 1986-2004; vis. prof. law U. So. Calif., 1963; vis. scholar Stanford (Calif.) U. Law Sch., 1985-86, 92; cons. in field. Author: Civil Rights, U.S.A., Public Schools, 1963, Honesty and Competition, 1967, Jury Instructing on Medical Issues, 1966, Cases and Materials on Space Law, 1971, The Aged and the Need for Surrogate Management, 1972, Commercial Torts, 1973, 2d edit. 1988, U.S. Antitrust Laws, 1980, Writing A Living Will: Using a Durable Power of Attorney, 1988, (with Scheflin) Law and Mental Disabilities, 1998; author, editor: International Perspectives on Aging, 1992; also articles, chpts. in books, one film. Dir. Domestic and Internat. Bus. Problems Honors Clinic, Syracuse U., 1966-69, Regulations in Space Project, 1968-70; ednl. cons. Comptroller Gen. U.S., 1977—; mem. Nat. Sr. Citizens Law Ctr., 1983-89, pres., 1986-90. With USN, 1953-56. U.S. Navy scholar U. Pa., 1949-52; Law Bds. scholar, 1956-59; Sterling fellow Yale, 1964-65; recipient Ralph E. Kharas Civil Liberties award, Syracuse U. Sch. Law, 1970, Owens award as Alumnus of Yr., 1984, Disting. prof. Santa Clara Univ. Faculty Senate, 1994-95, 2000 award for outstanding contbns. to cause of civil liberties Freedom of Thought Found.; named Disting. Vis. Prof. Krems Danube U., Vienna, 2001. Mem. Internat. Acad. Law Mental Health (mem. sci. com. 1997-99), Calif. Bar Assn. (first chmn. com. legal problems of aging), Assn. Am. Law Schs., Soc. Am. Law Tchrs. (dir., pres. 1979, Visionary Activist for Equality, Access and Diversity Throughout Law and Soc. award 2000), AAUP (chpt. pres. 1962), N.Y. Civil Liberties Union (chpt. pres. 1965, dir., v.p. 1966-70), Am. Acad. Polit. and Social Sci., Order of Coif (charter pres. 2004—), Justinian Honor Soc., Phi Alpha Delta (chpt. faculty adviser 1967-70) Home: 11600 Summit Wood Ct Los Altos Hills CA 94022 Office: U Santa Clara Sch Law Santa Clara CA 95053-0001 E-mail: gjalexander@scu.edu, georgealexander@email.com. *I think a primary purpose of law is the protection of individual rights. That requires disproportionate attention to the interests of groups not in the mainstream of our society.*

ALEXANDER, GERRY L., state supreme court justice; b. Aberdeen, Wash., Apr. 28, 1936; BA, U. Wash., 1958, JD, 1964; LLD (hon.), Gonzaga U., 2005. Bar: Wash. 1964, U.S. Supreme Ct. 2000. Pvt. practice, Olympia, Wash., 1964—73; judge Wash. Superior Ct., Olympia, 1973—85, Wash. Ct. Appeals Divsn. II, Tacoma, 1985—95; justice Wash. Supreme Ct., Olympia, 1995—2000, chief justice, 2000—. Lt. U.S. Army, 1958—61. Named Disting. Alumnus, U. Wash., 2000. Mem.: ABA, Statute Law Com., Washington Cts. Hist. Soc., Bench-Bar-Press (chair), Puget Sound Inn of Ct. (pres. 1996), Thurston-Mason County Assn. (pres. 1973), Wash. State Bar Assn., Am. Judges Assn. Office: Temple of Justice PO Box 40929 Olympia WA 98504-0929 Office Phone: 360-357-2029. E-mail: j_g.alexander@courts.wa.gov.

ALEXANDER, GREGORY STEWART, law educator, educator; b. Chgo., 1948; BA, Ill. U., 1970; JD, Northwestern U., 1973; postgrad., U. Chgo., 1974-75. Law clk. to chief judge U.S. Ct. Appeals, 1972-74; asst. prof. law U. Ga., 1975-78, assoc. prof., 1978-84; prof. Cornell U., Ithaca, N.Y., 1984—, A. Robert Noll prof. law, 2000—. Vis. prof. Harvard Law Sch., 1997—. Bigelow fellow U. Chgo., 1974-75; fellow Max-Planck Inst. (Germany), 1995-96, Ctr. for Advanced Study in Behavioral Scis., Palo Alto, Calif., 2003-2004, Inst. for Advanced Study, Stellenbosch, South Africa. Fellow Ctr. Advanced Study in Behavioral Scis., Stellenbosch, South Africa, 2004; mem. Am. Soc. Politics and Legal Philosophy, Am. Soc. Legal History. Office: Cornell U Law Sch Myron Taylor Hall Ithaca NY 14853 Office Phone: 607-255-3504. Business E-Mail: gsa9@cornell.edu.

ALEXANDER, HERBERT E., political scientist; b. Waterbury, Conn., Dec. 21, 1927; s. Nathan and Pearl (Shub) A.; m. Nancy Frances Greenfield, Dec. 5, 1953 (dec.); children: Michael David, Andrew Steven, Kenneth Bruce. BA, U. N.C., 1949; MA, U. Conn., 1951; PhD, Yale U., 1958. Asso. dir. adminstrn. officer money in politics research project U. N.C. at Chapel Hill, 1954-55; instr. Princeton U., 1956-58; dir. Citizens' Rsch. Found., Princeton, 1958-78, L.A., 1978-98, dir. emeritus, 1998—; prof. polit. sci. U. So. Calif., 1978—, prof. emeritus, 1998—. Exec. dir. Pres.'s Com. on Campaign Costs, Washington, 1961-62; cons. Pres. U.S., 1962-64, House Adminstrn. Com., 1966-67, Comptroller Gen. U.S. and Office Fed. Elections at GAO, 1972-73, Senate Select Com. on Presdl. Campaign Activities, 1973-74; vis. lectr. Princeton U., 1965, U. Pa., Phila., 1967-68, Yale U., 1977; cons. N.J. Election Law

Enforcement Commn., 1973-78, 82, 86, N.Y. State Bd. Elections, 1974-76, Ill. Bd. Elections, 1974-75, Gov. of R.I., 1987, others Author: Money in Politics, 1972, Financing the 1976 Election, 1979, Financing the 1980 Election, 1983, Financing Politics, 1976, 2d edit., 1980, 3d edit., 1984 4th edit., 1992, Campaign Money, 1976; (with Brian A. Haggerty) Financing the 1984 Election, 1987; editor: Studies in Money in Politics, vol. 1, 1965, vol. 2, 1970, vol. 3, 1974, Comparative Political Finance in the 1980s, 1989, (with Rei Shiratori) Comparative Political Finance Among the Democracies, 1994, (with Monica Bauer) Financing the 1988 Election, 1991, Reform and Reality: The Financing of State and Local Campaigns, 1991, (with Anthony Corrado) Financing the 1992 Election, 1995, Spending in the 1996 Elections, 1999, Financing the 1996 Election, 1999 Served with AUS, 1946-47. Mem. Am. Polit. Sci. Assn., Nat. Mcpl. League, Pi Sigma Alpha. Home: Unit 314 2904 N Leisure World Blvd Silver Spring MD 20906

ALEXANDER, ICIE M., communications executive; b. Knoxville, Tenn., Apr. 10, 1933; d. Jasper J. and Gracie L. (Taylor) Casey; m. William C. Alexander, July 14, 1954 (dec. 1982); 1 child, Billie Jean. Diploma in Supr., Ohio State Extension Studies, 1972. Instr. printing Columbus (Ohio) State Inst., 1967—70; supr. Dept. Printing Columbus (Ohio) Devel. Ctr., 1970—89; loan officer Columbus (Ohio) State Sch. Fed. Credit Union, 1982—89; sec. Labor Union Columbus (Ohio) Devel. Ctr., 1983—86; pres. Internat. Tng. in Comm., Columbus, 2002—03. Treas. Corban Comm. Rsch. Coun., Columbus, 2001—03. Performer: (play) Black to the Truth, 2000. Mentor Cassady Elem. sch., Columbus, 2000—02, Granville T. Woods Sch., Columbus, 2003—; vol. receptionist Corban Commons Sr. Cmty., 2004—. Mem.: Mt. Calvery Bapt. Dist. Assn. (gen. sec. 2001, Dedicated Svc. award 2002), East Columbus (Ohio) Civic Assn., East Columbus (Ohio) Dem. Club (chmn. fundraising 1995—2003), Cmty. Svc. Club. Democrat. Baptist.

ALEXANDER, JACK DUDLEY, III, natural resources consultant; b. Nashville, Apr. 8, 1962; s. Jack Dudley II and Linda Lee (Shackleford) A. BS, Texas A&M U., 1984; MS, Mont. State U., 1989. Ranch mgr. Caldwell Estate, McKinney, Tex., 1986-89; extension mgr. U. Nebr., Scottsbluff, 1989-90; natural resources cons. Resource Concepts, Inc., Carson City, Nev., 1990—. Editor: Drought Mgmt. Handbook, 1990; contbr. articles to jours. Mem. Soc. Range Mgmt. Avocation: running. Office: Resource Concepts Inc 340 N Minnesota St Carson City NV 89703-4152 Home: 1755 Hymer Ave Sparks NV 89431-5535

ALEXANDER, JACQUELINE PETERSON, librarian; b. NYC, Aug. 28, 1928; d. Stephen Edgar and Anna (Boehm) Peterson; m. Lewis McElwain Alexander, Dec. 30, 1950; children: Louise, Lance. AB, Hunter Coll., 1949; MS in Libr. Sci., U. RI, 1972. Asst. editor Law of the Sea Inst. Procs., 1966—71; ref. libr. U. RI, Kingston, 1971; rsch. libr. Internat. Ctr. Marine Resource Devel., 1973—79, 1988—92; tech. libr., head books, periodicals divsn. Nav. Underwater Systems Ctr., Newport, RI, 1971—72; regional libr. US Naval Edn. and Tng. Support Ctr., Groton, Conn., 1979—81; asst. chief acquisitions sect. Dept. Transp., 1983—84; libr. Edwards & Angell, Providence, 1984—88; pres. Offshore Cons., Inc., Wakefield, RI, 1992—96. Pres. South County Sr. Citizens Housing, 1974—82; active South Kingstown Citizens Adv. Bd., 1965—71; vol. AARP; vol. for tax aide, 1997—2003; vol. libr. Vis. Nurse Assn., 1992—95; bd. dirs., sec. South County Housing Improvement Found., 1966—83; bd. dirs. Washington County Vis. Nurse Assn., 1968—71. Mem.: RI Libr. Assn., Law Librs. of New Eng., Internat. Assn. Marine Sci. Librs. and Info. Ctrs., Am. Assn. Law Librs., Beta Phi Mu. Home: 66 Beech Hill Rd Wakefield RI 02879-2524

ALEXANDER, JAMES PATRICK, lawyer, educator; b. Glendale, Calif., Oct. 14, 1944; s. Victor Elwin and Thelma Elizabeth (O'Donnell) A.; m. Jeanne Elizabeth Bannerman, June 10, 1967; children: Rene Leigh, Amy Lynne. AB, Duke U., 1966, JD, 1969. Bar: Ala. 1969. Assoc. Bradley, Arant, Rose & White, Birmingham, Ala., 1969-75, ptnr., 1975—. Adj. lectr. employment discrimination law U. Ala. Sch. Law, 1981-2003; exec. adv. com. spl. studies program U. Ala., Birmingham, 1991-93; mem. local rules adv. com. U.S. Dist. Ct. (no. dist.) Ala., 1997—. Trustee Ala. chpt. Nat. Multiple Sclerosis Soc. (vice-chmn. 1987-89, chmn. 1990-91); bd. dirs. Birmingham Civil Right Inst. 1998-2004. Fellow Coll. Labor and Employment Lawyers; mem. Birmingham Bar Assn., Ala. State Bar, ABA, Am. Arbitration Assn. (comml. arbitrator, employment disputes arbitrator), Labor Employment Rels. Assn. (Ala. chpt.), Sigma Nu, Duke Law Alumni Assn. (pres. Ala. chpt. 1989-90). Home: 4309 Altamont Rd Birmingham AL 35213-2407 Office: Bradley Arant Rose & White LLP 1819 5th Ave N Birmingham AL 35203 Office Phone: 205-521-8348. Business E-Mail: jalexander@bradleyarant.com.

ALEXANDER, JAMES WESLEY, surgeon, educator; b. El Dorado, Kans., May 23, 1934; s. Rossiter Wells and Merle Lydia Alexander; m. Maureen L. Strohofer; children: Joseph, Judith, Elizabeth, Randolph, John Charles, Lori, Molly. Student, Tex. Technol. Coll., 1951-53; MD, U. Tex., 1957; ScD, U. Cin., 1958-64; postgrad., U. Minn., 1966-67. Diplomate Am. Bd. Surgery, Am. Bd. Thoracic Surgery, lic. physician Ohio. Intern Cin. Gen. Hosp., 1957-58; resident U. Cin.-Cin. Gen. Hosp., 1958-64; mem. faculty Coll. Medicine, U. Cin., 1962-64, 66—, prof. surgery, 1975—, dir. transplantation div., dept. surgery, 1967-99, dir. surg. immunology lab., 1967—2000; dir. research Shriners Burns Inst., 1979-90; practice medicine and surgery Cin., 1966—; dir. Ctr. for Surg. Weight Loss, 2001—. Mem. staff U. Cin. Hosp., Bethesda Hosp., Christ Hosp., Good Samaritan Hosp., Jewish Hosp.; mem. study sect. NIH, 1983—87, 1989—93, chmn. 1990—93, mem. ad hoc com., 1990—2005. Author (with R.A. Good): Fundamentals of Clinical Immunology, 1977; contbr. more than 650 articles to sci. jours. Capt. M.C. U.S. Army, 1964—66. Mem.: ACS, AAAS, Am. Soc. Bariatric Surgeons, Mont Reid Surg. Soc., Shock Soc., Transplantation Soc., Surg. Infection Soc. (sec. 1981—84, pres.-elect 1985—86, pres. 1986—87), Soc. Univ. Surgeons, Ohio Med. Assn., St. Paul Surg. Soc. (hon.), Internat. Soc. Surgery, Halsted Soc., Am. Surg. Assn., Am. Soc. Parenteral and Enteral Nutrition, Am. Soc. Transplant Surgeons (sec. 1985—87, pres.-elect 1987—88, pres. 1988—89), Am. Burn Assn. (pres.-elect 1983—84, pres. 1984—85), Am. Assn. for Surgery of Trauma, Peruvian Acad. Surgery (hon.; hon.), Colombian Coll. Surgeons (hon.; hon.), Surg. Biology Club, Phi Eta Sigma, Alpha Epsilon Delta, Alpha Chi, Alpha Omega Alpha. Home: 757 Riverwatch Dr Crescent Springs KY 41017-4480 Office: U Cin Coll Medicine 231 Albert Sabin Way Cincinnati OH 45267-0558 Office Phone: 513-558-6006, 513-585-2434. Business E-Mail: jwesley.alexander@uc.edu.

ALEXANDER, JANE, actress, retired federal agency administrator, theater educator, writer; b. Boston, Oct. 28, 1939; d. Thomas Bartlett and Ruth (Pearson) Quigley; m. Robert Alexander, July 23, 1962 (div. 1969); 1 child, Jason; m. Edwin Sherin, Mar. 29, 1975. Student, Sarah Lawrence Coll., 1957-59, U. Edinburgh, 1959-60; LHD, Wilson Coll., 1984; DFA (hon.), The Julliard Sch., 1994, N.C. Sch. Arts, 1994; PhD (hon.), U. Pa., 1995; DFA (hon.), The New Sch. Social Rsch., 1996; PhD (hon.), Duke U., 1996; LHD (hon.), The Coll. of Santa Fe, 1997; PhD, Sarah Lawrence Coll., 1998; DFA (hon.), Smith Coll., 1999, Pa. State U., 2000. Ind. TV, film and theatrical actress, 1962—; chmn. Nat. Endowment for Arts, Washington, 1993-97. Guest artist in residence Okla. Arts Inst., 1982, tchr. adult theatre workshop, 1984, 91, tchr. master class, 1990, Francis Eppes prof. Fla. State U., 2002-2004; bd. trustees Wildlife Conservation Soc., 1997—, Am. Bird Conservancy, 1995-98, The MacDowell Colony, 1997—, Arts Internat., 2000-2004. Author: (with Greta Jacobs) The Bluefish Cookbook, 5 edits., 1979-95,; translator: (with Sam Engelstad) The Master Builder (Henrik Ibsen), 1978; Command Performance, An Actress in the Theater of Politics, 2000; appeared in prodns.: Charles Playhouse Boston, 1964-65, Arena Stage, Washington, 1965-68, 70—, Am. Shakespeare Festival; plays include Major Barbara, Mourning Becomes Electra, Merry Wives of Windsor, Stratford, Conn., summers 1971-72; Broadway prodns. include The Great White Hope, 1968-69 (Tony award 1969, Drama Desk award, Theatre World award), 6 Rms Riv Vu, 1972-73 (Tony nomination), Find Your Way Home, 1974 (Tony nomination), Hamlet, 1975, The Heiress, 1976, First Monday in October, 1978 (Tony nomination), Goodbye Fidel, 1980, Monday After the Miracle, 1982, Night of the Iguana, 1988, Shadowlands, 1990-91, The Visit, 1992 (Tony nomination), The Sisters Rosensweig, 1993 (Drama Desk award 1992-93, Tony award nomination, Obie award 1993), Honour (Tony nomination), 1998; also appeared in plays The Time of Your Life, Present Laughter, 1975, The Master Builder, 1977, Losing Time, 1980, Antony and Cleopatra, 1981, Hedda Gabler, 1981, Old Times, 1984, Approaching Zanzibar, 1989, Mystery of the Rose Bouquet, 1989, The Cherry Orchard, 2000, Mourning Becomes Electra, 2002, Rose and Walsh, 2003, Ghosts, 2003, What of the Night, 2005; appeared in films The Great White Hope, 1970 (Acad. award nomination), A Gunfight, 1970, The New Centurions, 1972, All the President's Men, 1976 (Acad. award nomination), The Betsy, 1978, Kramer vs. Kramer, 1979 (Acad. award nomination), Brubaker, 1980, Night Crossing, 1981, Testament, 1983 (Acad. award nomination), City Heat, 1984, Sweet Country, 1986, Square Dance, 1987, Glory, 1989, The Cider House Rules, 1999, Sunshine State, 2001, The Ring, 2002, Carry Me Home, 2003; appeared in TV films Welcome Home Johnny Bristol, 1971, Miracle on 34th Street, 1973, Death Be Not Proud, 1974, This Was the West That Was, 1974, Eleanor and Franklin, 1976 (Emmy nomination), Eleanor and Franklin: The White House Years, 1977 (Emmy nomination, TV Critics Circle award), Lovey, 1977, A Question of Love, 1978, Playing for Time, 1980 (Emmy award 1980), Calamity Jane: The Diary of a Frontier Woman, 1981, Dear Liar, 1981, Kennedy's Children, 1981, In the Custody of Strangers, 1982, When She Says No, 1983, Multiverview, 1989, Daughter of the Streets, 1990, A Marriage: Georgia O'Keeffe and Alfred Stieglitz, 1991; appeared in TV spls. A Circle of Children, 1977, Blood and Orchids, 1986, Calamity Jane, 1984 (Emmy nomination), Malice in Wonderland, 1985 (Emmy nomination), In Love and War, 1987, Open Admissions, 1988, A Friendship in Vienna, 1988, Stay the Night, 1992, The Jenifer Estess Story, 2001; appeared in TV series: Law and Order Spl. Victims Unit, 2000, (Emmy nomination); Intimate Portrait, Lifetime TV Biography, 1998. Recipient Achievement in Dramatic Arts award St. Botolph Club, 1979, Israel Cultural award, 1982, Western Heritage Wrangler award, 1985, Helen Caldicott Leadership award, 1984, Living Legacy award Women's Internat. Ctr., San Diego, 1988, Environ. Leadership award Eco-Expo, 1991, Muse award N.Y. Women in Film, 1993, Torch of Hope award, 1992, Lectureship award NIH, 1994, Houseman award The Acting Co., 1994, medal UCLA, 1994, Outer Critics Circle award Disting. Voice in Theatre, 1994, Helen Hayes award Am. Express Tribute, 1994, Women of Achievement award Anti-Defamation League, 1994, Margo Jones award, 1995, Mass. Soc. award, 1995, N.Am. Mont Blanc de la Culture award, 1995, Common Wealth award, 1995, Creative Coalition: Christopher Reeve First Amendment award, 1998, Outstanding Leadership for Advancement in Arts, People for Am. Way, 1998, Lifetime Achievement award Americans for Arts and U.S. Conf. Mayors, 1999, Harry S. Truman award for pub. svc., Independence, Mo., 1999; Woman of Achievement Award, San Antonio, Tex., 2000. Director's Guild of Am. award, 2002; named to Theatre Hall of Fame, 1993. Mem. AFTRA, SAG, Actors Equity Assn., Acad. Motion Picture Arts and Scis., Acad. Arts and Scis., Actors Fund. Office: William Morris Agy c/o Samuel Liff 1325 Avenue of Americas New York NY 10019

ALEXANDER, JANET COOPER, law educator; b. 1946; BA in English Lit., with distinction, Swarthmore Coll., 1968; MA in English, Stanford U., 1973; JD, U. Calif., Berkeley, 1978. Bar: Calif. 1978, DC 1980, US Dist. Ct. Ctrl. Dist. Calif. 1978, US Dist. Ct. No. Dist. Calif. 1982, US Dist. Ct. Ea. Dist. Calif. 1985, US Supreme Ct. 1987. Jud. clk. to Hon. Shirley M. Hufstedler US Ct. Appeals 9th Cir., 1978—79; jud. clk. to Hon. Thurgood Marshall US Supreme Ct., 1979—80; assoc. Califano, Ross & Heineman, Washington, 1980—82, Morrison & Foerster, San Francisco, 1982—84, ptnr., 1984—87; assoc. prof. law Stanford Law Sch., Calif., 1987—94, prof., 1994—2002, Frederick I. Richman prof., 2002—, Justin M. Roach, Jr. faculty scholar, 1998—2002; prin. investigator Stanford Ctr. on Conflict and Negotiation, 1994—2002. Vis. prof. Toin U. of Yokohama, Japan, 1998. Alumni coun. Swarthmore Coll., 2001—, exec. com., 2003—, co-chair coll. advisory and support com., 2003—, acting chair, 2003; leadership coun. Castilleja Sch., Palo Alto, Calif., 2002—, athletic coun., 2002—, sch. assn. bd., 2002—03, co-chair parent edn., 2002—03, lead parent rep., 2002—03. Mem.: Am. Assn. Law Schools (sections on civil procedure, fed. courts, women and the law). Office: Stanford Law Sch Crown Quadrangle 559 Nathan Abbott Way Stanford CA 94305-8610 Office Phone: 650-723-2892. Business E-Mail: jca@stanford.edu.

ALEXANDER, JASON (JAY SCOTT GREENSPAN), actor; b. Newark, N.J., Sept. 23, 1959; s. Alexander and Ruth Minnie (Simon) Greenspan; m. Daena E. Title, May 31, 1982;1 child, Gabriel. Student, Boston U., 1977-80. N.Y.C. stage debut in Merrily We Roll along, Alvin Theatre, 1981; other theater appearances include America Kicks Up Its Heels, 1982, On Hold With Music, 1982, Fragments, 1982, Forbidden Broadway, 1983, The Rink, 1984, D, 1985, Personals, 1985-86 season, Broadway Bound, 1986-87 season, Jerome Robbins' Broadway, 1989 (Tony award for best performance by a leading actor in a musical), Accomplice, 1990, Light Up The Sky, 1990, Give 'Em Hell, Harry, 1993 (Drama-Loge award), The Producers (Los Angeles), 2003; film debut in The Burning, 1979; other film appearances include The Mosquito Coast, 1986, Brighton Beach Memoirs, 1986, Pretty Woman, 1989, Jacobs Ladder, 1989, White Palace, 1989, I Don't Buy Kisses Anymore, 1991, Coneheads, 1993, Sexual Healing, 1993, North, 1994, The Paper, 1994, Blankman, 1994; The Last Supper, 1995, Love! Valour! Compassion!, 1996, the Hunchback of Notre Dame, 1996, For Better or Worse, 1996, Dunston Checks In, 1996, Denial, 1998, Adventures of Rocky & Bullwinkle, 1999, On Edge, 2001, Shallow Hal, 2001, How to Go Out on a Date in Queens, 2003; TV films include Senior Trip, 1981, Rockabye, 1986, Favorite Son, 1988, Bye Bye Birdie, 1995, Cinderella, 1998, Love & Action in Chicago, 1998,; TV series: E/R, 1984-85, Everything's Relative, 1987, Seinfeld, 1990-98 (Emmy nomination, Supporting Actor - Comedy, 1993, 94), Duckman (voice only), 1994—97, Bob Patterson, 2001, Listen Up, 2004; guest appearances include Dream On, 1993 (Emmy nomination, Guest Actor - Comedy Series, 1994), Star Trek, Voyager, 1999, actor, dir. For Better or Worse, 1995. Office: William Morris Agy 151 S El Camino Dr Beverly Hills CA 90212-2775

ALEXANDER, JESSIE ARONOW, anesthesiologist; b. Beaumont, Tex., May 19, 1957; MD, U. Tex. Health Sci. Ctr., 1984. Diplomate Am. Bd. Anesthesiology. Resident in anesthesiology Med. U. S.C., Charleston, 1984-87, fellow in obstet. anesthesiology, pain mgmt., 1987-88; staff anesthesiologist Cape Fear Valley Med. Ctr., Fayetteville, N.C., 1989-98, Highsmith-Rainey Meml. Hosp., Fayetteville, 1988-98; pvt. practice Valley Anesthesia, P.A., Fayetteville, 1988-90; founding ptnr., sec. bd. dirs. Cumberland Anesthesia Assocs., P.A., Fayetteville, 1990-98; asst. prof. anesthesiology U. N.C., Chapel Hill, 1989-94; assoc. prof. divsn. anesthesia, symptom control and palliative care U. Tex. M.D. Anderson Cancer Ctr., Houston, 1998—2003; clin. prof. anesthesiology U. Tex. Health Sci. Ctr., San Antonio, 2003—. Lectr., author on dangers of nutraceuticals and on physician stress; owner art studio Alexander Studios. Contbr. articles to profl. jours.; exhibited art work in one-woman show, 2004. Active Fayetteville Area C. of C., 1988-98, Fayetteville Area Econ. Devel. Corp., 1996-98. Recipient 1st prize award Am. Soc. Anesthesiologists Art Exhbn., 1999, 2000. Mem. AMA, Am. Soc. Anesthesiologists, So. Med. Assn., N.C. Med. Soc., N.C. Soc. Anesthesiology (past pres.), Tex. Soc. Anesthesiologists, Tex. Med. Assn. (comms. com., legis. affairs com.). Office: 7703 Floyd Curl Dr MC 7838 San Antonio TX 78229-3900 E-mail: jleak@houston.rr.com.

ALEXANDER, JOHN CHARLES, pharmaceutical executive, preventive medicine physician; b. Perth Amboy, NJ, Dec. 28, 1943; s. Charles John and Agnes (Maloney) A.; m. Margaret Ann Kohler, July 19, 1969; children: Laurel, Jennifer, Anna. BS, St. Francis Coll., Loretto, Pa., 1965; MD, St. Louis U., 1970; MPH, Johns Hopkins U., 1972. Intern Barnes Hosp./Washington U., St. Louis, 1970-71; resident in gen. preventive medicine State of Va./Med. Coll. Va., Richmond, 1974-76; clin. rsch. dir. Squibb Inst. Med. Rsch., Princeton, NJ, 1976—82, v.p. cardiovascular clin. rsch., 1982-86, sr. v.p. med. affairs, 1986-90; v.p. rsch. Bristol-Myers-Squibb Pharm. Rsch. Inst., Princeton, 1990-91; sr. v.p. med. rsch. Searle, Skokie, Ill., 1991-93, exec. v.p. med. rsch., 1993-99; pres. Sankyo Pharma Devel., Edison, NJ, 1999—; global head R&D Sankyo Co. Ltd., Tokyo, 2003—; also. bd. dirs. Patentee in field. Lt. comdr. USN, 1972-74. Mem. Drug Info. Assn. (pres., bd. dirs.), Alpha Omega Alpha. Home: 86 Beech Hollow Ln Princeton NJ 08540-1235 Office: Sankyo Pharma Inc 399 Thornall St Edison NJ 08837-2236 Office Phone: 732-590-5000. E-mail: jalexander@sankyopharma.com.

ALEXANDER, JOHN DAVID, JR., college administrator; b. Springfield, Tenn., Oct. 18, 1932; s. John David and Mary Agnes (McKinnon) A.; m. Catharine Coleman, Aug. 26, 1956; children: Catharine McKinnon, John David III, Julia Mary. BA, Southwestern at Memphis, 1953; student, Louisville Presbyn. Theol. Sem., 1953—54; PhD, Oxford (Eng.) U., 1957; LLD, U. So. Calif., Occidental Coll., 1970, Centre Coll. of Ky., 1971, Pepperdine U., 1991, Albertson Coll. Idaho, 1992; LHD, Loyola Marymount U., 1983; LittD, Rhodes Coll., 1986, Pomona Coll., 1996. Assoc. prof. San Francisco Theol. Sem., 1957-65; pres. Southwestern at Memphis, 1965-69, Pomona Coll., Claremont, Calif., 1969-91. Am. sec. Rhodes Scholarship Trust, 1981—98; mem. commn. liberal learning Assn. Am. Colls., 1966—69, mem. commn. instl. affairs, 1971—74; mem. commn. colls. So. Assn. Colls. and Schs., 1966—69; mem. Nat. Commn. Acad. Tenure, 1971—72; bd. dirs. Children's Hosp., LA; trustee Tchrs. Inst. and Annuity Assn., 1970—2002, Woodrow Wilson Nat. Fellowship Found., 1978—99, Seaver Inst., 1992—, Fellows of Soc. Phi Beta Kappa, 1993—, v.p., 1998—; trustee Emeriti, Inc., 2004—; bd. dirs. Wenner-Gren Found. for Anthrop. Rsch., Webb Schs. Calif.; bd. overseers Huntington Libr., 1991—. Editor: The American Oxonian, 1997-2000. Pres. Am. Friends of Nat. Portrait Gallery (London) Found., 2004—. Decorated comdr. Ordèr Brit. Empire; named Disting. Friend of Oxford U., 2000; Rhodes scholar, Oxford U., 1955—57. Mem. Soc. Bib. Lit., Soc. Religion in Higher Edn., Phi Beta Kappa Alumni in So. Calif. (pres. 1974-76), Century Club, Calif. Club, Bohemian Club, Athenaeum (London) Phi Beta Kappa, Omicron Delta Kappa, Sigma Nu. Office: Pomona Coll 333 N College Way Claremont CA 91711-4429 Business E-Mail: dalexander@pomona.edu.

ALEXANDER, JOHN J., chemistry professor; b. Indpls., Apr. 13, 1940; s. John Gregory and Inez Helene (Snedaker) A. AB summa cum laude, Columbia U., 1962, MA, 1963, PhD, 1967. Postdoctoral fellow Ohio State U., Columbus, 1967-69, research assoc., 1977-78; asst. prof. chemistry U. Cin., 1969-73, assoc. prof., 1973-79, prof., 1979—, dir. undergrad. studies in chemistry, 1998—2001. faculty fellow, 1972-74. Vis. prof. Ohio State U., 1985-86, 94. Author: (with M.J. Steffel) Chemistry in the Laboratory, 1976, 2d edit., 1988, (with B.E. Douglas, D.H. McDaniel) Concepts and Models of Inorganic Chemistry, 3d edit., 1994, Problems for Inorganic Chemistry, 1994; column editor: Jour. Chem. Edn., 1976—; mem. editl. adv. team for chemistry Ency. Britannica, 1999-2001; contbr. chpts. to books, articles to profl. jours. Vestryman Calvary Episcopal Ch., 1999-2002. Woodrow Wilson fellow; NSF fellow Columbia U., 1963-65, faculty fellow, 1966; grantee NSF, Petroleum Rsch. Fund. Mem. Am. Chem. Soc. (past chmn., trustee), Phi Beta Kappa, Sigma Xi, Phi Lambda Upsilon. Democrat. Episcopalian. Office: U Cin Dept Chemistry Cincinnati OH 45221-0001 Home: 209 Hosea Ave #3 Cincinnati OH 45220-1705

ALEXANDER, JOHN KURT, history professor; b. Vancouver, Wash., Oct. 25, 1941; s. Eugene Victor and Marta T. Alexander; m. June Granatir, Dec. 29, 1973. BS in Edn. with honors, Western Oreg. U., Monmouth, 1964; MA in History, U. Chgo., 1965, PhD in History, 1973. From asst. prof. to prof. history U. Cin., 1969—81, Disting. tchg. prof., 2003—. Author: Render Them Submissive, 1980, The Selling of the Constitutional Convention, 1990, Samuel Adams, 2002; assoc. editor Am. Nat. Biography, Oxford U. Press, 1989-99; contbr. articles to profl. jours. Mem. Orgn. Am. Historians, Hist. Soc. Pa., Pa. Hist. Soc., Ohio Acad. History (Outstanding Tchr. award 2002), Soc. for Historians of Early Am. Republic. Home: 3410 Bishop St Cincinnati OH 45220-1831 Office: Univ Cin Dept History Ml 0373 Cincinnati OH 45221-0373 Business E-Mail: John.K.Alexander@uc.edu.

ALEXANDER, JOHN MACMILLAN, JR., chemistry professor; b. Columbia, Mo., Aug. 17, 1931; s. John Macmillan and Victoria (Holladay) A.; m. Betty Jo Linton, Aug. 1, 1953; children: Mary Jo, John Macmillan III, Frank Linton, James Holladay. BS, Davidson Coll., 1953; PhD, MIT, 1956. Research assoc. MIT, 1956-57; research chemist Lawrence Radiation Lab., Berkeley, Calif., 1957-63; assoc. prof. chemistry SUNY at Stony Brook, 1963-67, prof., 1968—96, leading prof., 1996—. Rscher. AEC-ARDA Dept. Energy, 1964—; rsch. collaborator Brookhaven Nat. Lab., 1964—, program adv. com. tandem Van De Graaff accelerator, 1977—83, rsch. collaborator E895 and PHEVIX, 1997—; chmn. Gordon Rsch. Conf. on Nuc. Chemistry, 1966; chmn. exec. com. faculty senate SUNY at Stony Brook, 1969, chmn. dept. chemistry, 1970—72; mem. exec. com. Berkeley Superhilac Accelerator, 1975—78, 1985—87; vis. scientist Centre d'Etudes Nucléaires, Bordeaux, France, 1974; vis. prof. Centre d'Etudes Nucléaires-Gradignan et Institut de Physique Nucléaire, Orsay, France, 1978; program adv. com. Heavy Ion Rsch. Facility Oak Ridge Nat. Lab., 1986—87, SARA accelerator Institut des Sciences Nucléaires, Grenoble, France, 1988. Assoc. editor: Am. Chem. Soc. Monographs, 1968-69; contbr. articles to profl. jours. Recipient Great Amer. Home award Nat. Trust for Historic Preservation, 1993; Dupont teaching fellow, 1955-56, Sloan fellow, 1964-67, Guggenheim fellow Laboratoire de Chimie Nucléaire, Orsay, France, 1969-70. Fellow Am. Phys. Soc.; mem. Am. Chem. Soc. (chmn. divsn. nuclear chemistry and tech. 1988, vice chmn. 1987, nuclear chemistry award 1991), Phi Beta Kappa. Democrat. Achievements include research on radioactivity, high-energy nuclear reactions: fission, spallation and fragmentation; heavy ion reactions: elastic scattering, complete and incomplete fusion and reaction cross sections; splintering central collisions; energy thermalization mechanisms from low to relativistic energies; hot nuclei; energy and spin dissipation, evaporative deexcitation; fragmentation; emission lifetimes; nuclear equation of state; statistical and dynamical models; hadron correlations driven by collective flow, source size and jet physics. Home: 14 Highwood Rd East Setauket NY 11733-1512 Office: SUNY Dept Chemistry Stony Brook NY 11794-3400

ALEXANDER, JOHN STONE, retired radiologist; b. Paris, 1929; s. Drury B. and Katherine (Stone) A. BA, U. Tex., 1950; MD, U. Tex., Galveston, 1954. Diplomate Am. Bd. Radiology. Intern DC Gen. Hosp., Washington, 1954-55; resident in radiology Scott-White Clinic, Temple, Tex., 1957-60; ret., 1989. Mem. staff Harris Hosp., Ft. Worth. Fellow Am. Coll. Radiology; mem. AMA, Radiol. Soc. N.Am. Presbyterian. E-mail: jsalex947@charter.net.

ALEXANDER, JOHN THORNDIKE, historian, educator; b. Cooperstown, N.Y., Jan. 18, 1940; s. Edward Porter and Alice Wagner (Bolton) A.; m. Maria Kovalak Hreha, June 13, 1964; children— Michal Porter, Darya Ann BA, Wesleyan U., Middletown, Conn., 1961; cert. regional specialization Russian Inst., MA, Ind. U., 1963, PhD, 1966. Asst. prof. U. Kans., Lawrence, 1966-70, assoc. prof., 1970-74, prof. history, 1974—. Fellow Inter-Univ. Com. on Travel Grants, 1964-65, Internat. Research and Exchanges Bd., 1971, 75, 96. Author: Autocratic Politics, 1969, Emperor of the Cossacks, 1973, Bubonic Plague in Russia, 1980, 2003, Catherine the Great, 1989 (Byron Caldwell Smith award for best book by a Kans. author pub. in 1987-88), reissued luxury edit., 1999; translator, editor: Platonov, Time of Troubles, 1970, Anisimov, Reforms of Peter the Great, 1993, Anisimov, Empress Elisabeth, 1995. Recipient Balfour Jeffrey Higuchi Endowment Rsch. Achievement award, 1992. Mem. Am. Assn. for Advancement Slavic Studies, Brit. Study Group on 18th Century Russia, So. Conf. on Slavic Studies (ann. sr. scholar award 2001). Democrat. Roman Catholic. Avocation: sports. Home: 2216 Orchard Ln Lawrence KS 66049-2706 Office: U Kans Dept History Wescoe Hall Rm 3001 1445 Jayhawk Blvd Lawrence KS 66045-7590 E-mail: jatalex@ku.edu.

ALEXANDER, JOSEPH KUNKLE, JR., physicist; b. Staunton, Va., Jan. 9, 1940; s. Joseph Kunkle and Charlotte (Harper) A.; m. Diana Lenore Titolo, Sept. 22, 1962; children: Kathryn, Stephen, David. BS in Physics, Coll. William and Mary, 1960, MA in Physics, 1962. Physicist Nat. Bur. Standards, 1960; research asst. Coll. William and Mary, Williamsburg, Va., 1960-62;

physicist Goddard Space Flight Ctr., NASA, Greenbelt, Md., 1962-85, head planetary magnetospheres br., 1976-84; dep. chief scientist NASA, Washington, 1985-87, asst. assoc. adminstr. space sci. and applications, 1987-93; assoc. dir. space scis. Goddard Space Flight Ctr., NASA, Greenbelt, Md., 1993-94; dep. asst. administr. R&D EPA, Washington, 1994-98; dir. space studies bd. Nat. Acad. Scis. Nat. Rsch. Coun., Washington, 1998—. Vis. scientist U. Colo., 1973-74; sr. policy analyst White House Office Sci. and Tech. Policy, Washington, 1984-85; assoc. chief Lab. Extraterrestrial Physics, 1985, acting dir. life scis. NASA, Washington, 1992-93; acting chief Lab. Extraterrestrial Physics, Goddard Space Flight Ctr., NASA, Greenbelt, Md., 1994. Contbr. articles to sci. and tech. jours. Mem. Am. Geophys. Union, Am. Astron. Soc., Internat. Astron. Union. Office: Nat Acad of Scis 500 Fifth St Washington DC 20001 Business E-Mail: jalexander@nas.edu.

ALEXANDER, JUDD HARRIS, retired paper company executive; b. Owatonna, Minn., Mar. 23, 1925; s. Mark Hastings and Veta Enola (Harris) A.; m. Theo Mary Paltzer, May 19, 1956; children: Morah Lee, Duncan McIndoe, Todd Stewart. BA, Carleton Coll., 1949, PhD (hon.), 2001; postgrad., Harvard U., 1967. Co-founder Nu-Bilt Co., Owatonna, dir., 1942-71; sec. in pres.'s office, salesman Marathon Corp., Rothschild, Wis., 1949-57; with Am. Can Co., Greenwich, Conn., 1957-82, v.p., gen. mgr. spl. products packaging, 1972-73, sr. v.p. group exec. packaging, 1974-75, sr. v.p. office of chmn., 1975-81, exec. v.p. paper sector, 1981-82; exec. v.p. James River Corp., Norwalk, Conn., 1982-89, ret., 1989; chmn. Paperboard Packaging Council, 1976-78, Can Mfrs. Inst., 1978-80, Solid Waste Coun. of Paper Industry, 1977-88. Bd. dirs. encore Paper Co., Inc., 1992-95; adj. prof. environ. sci. SUNY, Syracuse, 1979-84. Author: In Defense of Garbage, 1993; contbr. articles to profl. and bus. jours., including Wall Street Jour., N.Y. Times, Industry Week. Trustee Carleton Coll., 1973-2000, Am. Shakespeare Theater, 1980-82; bd. dirs. New Eng. Legal Found., 1979-82, Norwalk (Conn.) Hosp., 1985-88, Ctr. for Advanced Studies U. Va., 1988—; chmn. bd. trustees Keep Am. Beautiful (bd. dirs. 1979-90), 1986-88. Decorated Bronze Star medal; Woodrow Wilson vis. fellow, 1975-82 Mem. Conn. Bus. Industry Assn. (bd. dirs. 1976-80, 85-89), Quechee Club, The Boulders Club. Republican. Congregationalist. Home: PO Box 3034 3041 Ironwood Rd Carefree AZ 85377

ALEXANDER, KAREN, museum staff member; m. Walter Alexander. Vice chmn. bd. trustees Art Inst. Chgo., vol. Dept. European Decorative Arts and Sculpture and Ancient Art. Office: Art Inst Chgo 111 S Michigan Ave Chicago IL 60603*

ALEXANDER, KEITH B., federal agency administrator, career military officer; b. Syracuse, N.Y. BS, U.S. Mil. Acad., 1974; MBA, Boston U.; MS in Physics and Electronic Warfare, Naval Post Grad. Sch.; grad., U.S. Army Command Staff Coll., Nat. War Coll. Commd. 2d lt. U.S. Army, 1974, advanced through grades to lt. gen., 2003; platoon leader, B Co., 2nd Bn. 81st Armor, 1st Armored Divsn. U.S. Army Europe & 7th Army, Germany, 1975—76, asst. S-4 (logistics), later S-4, 511th mil. intelligence bn. 66th mil. intelligence group, 1976—77, comdr. field office, 511th mil. intelligence bn. 66th mil. intelligence group, 1977—78; electronic warfare staff officer 525th mil. intelligence group U.S. Army, Ft. Bragg, NC, 1979, comdr. 336th Amy Security Agy. Co., 319th mil. intelligence bn. (corps electronic warfare intelligence) 52th mil. intelligence group, 1979—81, asst. S-3 (ops.) 525th mil. intelligence group, 1981; ops. officer, later chief intelligence electronics warfare systems task force, later chief concepts & studies divsn. US Army Intelligence Ctr & Sch., Ft. Huachuca, Ariz., 1983—85; dep. dir. intelligence & electronics warfare master plan spl. task force, intelligence staff officer, Office Dep. Chief of Staff for Intelligence U.S. Army, Washington, 1986—88, S-3 ops. later exec. officer, 522nd mil. intelligence bn. 2nd armored divsn. Ft. Hood, Tex., 1988—90; asst. chief of staff, G-2 (intelligence), 1st armored divsn. US Army Europe & Seventh Army & Operation DESERT SHIELD/STORM Saudi Arabia, 1990—91; comdr. 204th mil. intelligence bn. US Army Europe & Seventh Army, Germany, 1991—93; chief, army intelligence initiative, Office of the Dep. Chief of Staff for Intelligence U.S. Army, Washington, 1994—95, exec. officer 522d mil. intelligence brigade Ft. Bragg, NC, 1995—97; dep. dir. for intelligence The Joint Staff, Washington, 1997—98; dir. intelligence (J-2) U.S. Ctrl. Command, MacDill AFB, Fla., 1998—2001; comdr. US Army Intelligence & Security Command U.S. Army, Ft. Belvoir, Va., 2001—03, dep. chief of staff (G-2) Washington, 2003—05; dir. Nat. Security Agy./Ctrl. Security Svc., Ft. George E. Meade, Md., 2005—. Decorated Disting. Svc. medal, Def. Superior Svc. medal with oak leaf cluster, Legion of Merit with four oak leaf clusters, bronze star, Meritorious Svc. medal with 4 oak leaf clusters, Air medal, Army Commendation medal, Army Achievement medal, . Office: Nat Security Agy 9800 Savage Rd Fort George G Meade MD 20755*

ALEXANDER, KENNETH SAUL, pharmaceuticals educator; b. Phila., Nov. 27, 1942; s. Martin R. and Ida Z. Alexander; m. Karen L. Haury, Aug. 18, 1968; children: Kimberly A., Kirsten R. (dec.), Kevin C. BSc, Phila. Coll. Pharmacy and Sci., 1965, MSc, 1970; PhD, U. R.I., 1972; EdS, U. Toledo, 1981. Instr. U. R.I., 1971-72; asst. prof. pharmacy U. Toledo, 1972-76, assoc. prof., 1977-92, prof. pharmacy, 1992—. Coord. indsl. pharmacy divsn., Coll. Pharmacy, U. Toledo; bd. dirs. MCO Fed. Credit Union, 1976-91, pres., 1981-84; cons. to pharm. and pharmacy industry. Mem. St. Mary's Sch. Bd., Monroe, Mich., 1985-89; mem. adv. com. Bedford Twp. Community Ctr., 1979-80; mem. Lucas County Hypertension Coordinating Com., 1985-89; mem. exec. coun. Boy Scouts Am., 1998—, troop com., 1990—. Mem. Am. Assn. Colls. aPharmacy (sec. tchrs. pharmacy sect. 1986, chmn.-elect 1987, chmn. 1988), Am. Chem. Soc., Ohio Pharm. Assn. (treas. 1986-89, v.p. 1989-90, pres. 1991), Ohio Pharmacists Assn. (pres. 1991-92), Toledo Acad. Pharmacy (bd. dirs. 1976-88, pres. 1990-91), pres. 1985-86), Toledo Area Soc. Hosp. Pharmacists (pres. 1986-87, 89-90). Home: 7924 Wiseman Rd Lambertville MI 48144-9682 Office: U Toledo Coll Pharmacy 280L W Bancroft St Toledo OH 43620-1832 Office Phone: 419-530-1988.

ALEXANDER, KENNETH SIDNEY, mathematician, educator; b. Seattle, Mar. 3, 1958; s. Stuart Murray and Elspeth (Dautoff) Alexander; m. Crystal Czarnecki, Aug. 21, 1982; 1 child, Glenn. BS in Maths., U. Wash., 1979; PhD in Maths., MIT, 1982. Mem. Math. Scis. Rsch. Inst., Berkeley, Calif., 1982-83; postdoctoral fellow U. Wash., Seattle, 1983-86; asst. prof. U. So. Calif., LA, 1986-90, assoc. prof., 1990—96, prof., 1996—. Editor: Spatial Stochastic Processes, 1991; assoc. editor: Probability Theory and Related Fields, 1987—94, Annals of Probability, 1994—2001; contbr. articles to profl. jours. Fellow: Inst. Math. Statis.; mem.: Am. Math. Soc., Phi Beta Kappa. Office: U So Calif Dept Math KAP 108 Los Angeles CA 90089-2532 Office Phone: 213-740-2400.

ALEXANDER, KENT B., lawyer; b. Atlanta, Nov. 7, 1958; BA in Polit. Sci. magna cum laude, Tufts U., 1980; JD, U. Va., 1983. Bar: Ga. 1983. Assoc. Long & Alridge, Atlanta, 1983-85; asst. U.S. atty. for no. dist. Ga., U.S. Dept. Justice, Atlanta, 1985-92, U.S. atty., 1994-97; of counsel, ptnr. King & Spalding, Atlanta, 1992-94, ptnr., 1997-99; sr. v.p., gen. counsel Emory Univ., 2000—. Co-founder Hands On Atlanta; pres. Am. Jewish Com., Atlanta. Office: Emory Univ 401 Administration Bldg Atlanta GA 30322-0001

ALEXANDER, LAMAR (ANDREW LAMAR ALEXANDER), state senator, former secretary of education, former governor, lawyer; b. Maryville, Tenn., July 3, 1940; s. Andrew Lamar and Geneva Floreine (Rankin) A.; m. Leslee Kathryn Buhler, Jan. 4, 1969; children: Andrew, Leslee, Kathryn, Will. BA, Vanderbilt U., 1962; JD, NYU, 1965. Bar: Tenn. 1965. Law clk. to Hon. John Wisdom U.S. Ct. Appeals (5th cir.), New Orleans; assoc. Fowler, Rountree, Fowler & Robertson, Knoxville, 1965; legis. asst. to Senator Howard Baker, 1967-68; exec. asst. to Bryce Harlow, White House Congl. Liaison Office, 1969-70; ptnr. Dearborn and Ewing, Nashville, 1970-76; gov. State of Tenn., Nashville, 1979-87; chmn. Leadership Inst. Belmont Coll., Nashville, 1987-88; pres. U. Tenn., 1988-91; sec. Dept. Edn., Washington, 1991-93; counsel Baker, Donelson, Bearman & Caldwell, Nashville, 1993-98; pvt. practice Nashville, 1999—2001; US senator from Tenn., 2003—; mem. fgn. rels. com. US Senate. Mem. Pres.'s Task Force on Federalism; chmn. Nat. Govs. Assn., 1985-86, Pres.'s Commn. on Ams. Outdoors, 1985-87; co-director Empower Am., 1994-95; Goodman vis. prof. practice of pub. svc. Harvard U., 2001. Author: Steps Along the Way, 1986, Six Months Off, 1988, We Know What To Do, 1995; co-editor: The New Promise of American Life, 1995, Friends, Japanese and Tennesseans: A Model of U.S.-Japan Cooperation, 1986, Lamar Alexander's Little Plaid Book, 1998. Mgr. Winfield Dunn for Gov. Campaign, 1970, chief transition, 1970-71; Rep. nominee for Gov. of Tenn., 1974; chmn. Rep. Exch. Satellite Network, 1993-95; Rep. Presdl. candidate, 1995-96. Recipient Nat. Disting. Svc. to Edn. award Burger King, 1988, James B. Conant award Edn. Commn. of the States, 1988, Disting. State Leadership award Am. Assn. State Colls. and Univs., 1989, Teddy Roosevelt award Nat. Coll. Athletic Assn., 1993, honored as Silver Anniversary scholar-athlete, 1987; NYU Law Sch. Root-Tilden scholar. Fellow (sr.) Hudson Inst.; mem. Phi Beta Kappa. Republican. Presbyn. Office: US Senate 302 Hart Senate Ofc Bldg Washington DC 20510 Office Phone: 202-224-4944.

ALEXANDER, LESLIE LEE, professional sports team owner; b. NYC, June 30, 1943; m. Nanci Alexander (div. 2002); 1 child, Jodi. BS, NYU, 1965; JD, Western State Coll., 1977. Owner, pres. Houston Rockets, 1993—; owner Houston Comets, WNBA, 1996—; former owner Houston ThunderBears, Arena Football League. Founder City Clutch Found., Houston, 1995—. Mem.: Calif. State Bar Assn. Office: Houston Rockets 1510 Polk St Houston TX 77002*

ALEXANDER, LLOYD CHUDLEY, author; b. Phila., Jan. 30, 1924; s. Alan Audley and Edna (Chudley) A.; m. Janine Denni, Jan. 8, 1946; 1 dau., Madeleine (Mrs. Zohair Khalil). Student, West Chester (Pa.) State Coll., 1942, Lafayette Coll., 1943, U. Paris, 1946. Free-lance writer and translator, 1946—; cartoonist, pianist, advt. writer, mag. editor, 1948—; author-in-residence Temple U., 1970. Author: And Let The Credit Go, 1955, My Five Tigers, 1956, Janine is French, 1958, August Bondi, 1958 (Isaac Siegel Meml. award 1959), My Love Affair with Music, 1960, Aaron Lopez, 1960, Time Cat, 1963, Fifty Years in the Doghouse, 1964, (with Dr. Louis J. Camuti) Park Avenue Vet, 1962, The Book of Three, 1964 (A.L.A. notable book 1964), The Black Cauldron, 1965 (A.L.A. notable book 1965), Coll and His White Pig, 1965, The Castle of Llyr, 1966 (A.L.A. notable book 1966), Taran Wanderer, 1967, The Truthful Harp, 1967, The High King, 1968 (Newbery medal 1969), The Marvelous Misadventures of Sebastian, 1970 (Nat. Book award 1971), The King's Fountain, 1971, The Four Donkeys, 1972, The Foundling, 1973 (A.L.A. notable book 1973), The Cat Who Wished to be a Man, 1973 (A.L.A. notable book), The Wizard in the Tree, 1975, The Town Cats, 1977 (ALA notable book 1977), The First Two Lives of Lukas-Kasha, 1978, Westmark, 1981 (Am. Book award 1982), The Kestrel, 1982, The Beggar Queen, 1984, The Illyrian Adventure, 1986, The El Dorado Adventure, 1987, The Drackenberg Adventure, 1988, The Jedera Adventure, 1989, The Philadelphia Adventure, 1990, The Remakable Journey of Prince Jen, 1991, The Fortune-tellers, 1992, The Arkadians, 1995, The House Gobbaleen, 1995, The Iron Ring, 1997, Gypsy Rizka, 1999, How the Cat Swallowed Thunder, 2000, The Gawgon and the Boy, 2001, The Rope Trick, 2002, The Xanadu Adventure, 2005, Dream-of-Jade the Emperor's Cat, 2005; translator from French: (Paul Eluard) Selected Writings, 1950, (Jean-Paul Sartre) The Wall, 1951, Nausea, 1953, (Paul Vialar) The Sea Rose, 1951. Bd. dirs. Carpenter Lane Chamber Music Soc., Phila. Served with AUS, World War II. Recipient Golden Cat award, 1984, Regina medal, 1986, Carolyn W. Field medal, 1987, Otter award, 1993, Horn Book-Boston Globe award 1993; World Fantasy Life Achievement award, 2003. Mem. Authors League Am., P.E.N. Address: 1005 Drexel Ave Drexel Hill PA 19026-3306 also: E P Dutton Pub Co 345 Hudson St New York NY 10014-4502 also: Dell Pub Co 1540 Broadway New York NY 10036-4039

ALEXANDER, LORA KAY, writer, composer; b. Campton, Ky. d. Dewey Raymond and Ada Ann (Bankenship) Tyra; m. James Kenneth Alexander; children: Kristi Eve, Eva Wynne, James Kenneth Jr. Student in video/films, Writers Digest Sch., Anacontes, Wash., 1985. Spl. writer Wolfe County News, Campton, Ky., The Times, Kettering, Oakwood; adminstrv. asst. Shawnee Kitchens, Centerville, Ohio; staff writer Blue Mountain Arts; owner Gift Shop, Roses in the Rain, 2001; prodr. and owner Country Unplugged, TV show. (films, ednl.) White Tigers, 1985; Wobbles World, 1985; Deer Daniel, 1985; author: (novels) By Appointment Only, 1985 (commonwealth publication, 1992), Until We're Free, 1986 (commonwealth publication, 1992), Roses In The Rain, 1987 (commonwealth publication, 1992), Until We're Free, 2004, (booklet) Strength of the Towers (award Pres. Bush); composer: (songs) Our People are Free (letter and award from Pres. Carter for song.), (video) She Won't Come Close/Trailblazer, 1992 (Video, 1992), (CD) Roses In the Rain (with Reba McIntire's band). Achievements include design of greeting card line-"Lovelines"; recorded and sang with Reba McIntire's band; two music videos; 1000 songs; 10-45rpm records; CD sales. Avocations: cooking, running, psychology. Office: Roses In The Rain Music Publishing Music Row Glen Manor 1700 18th Ave S # 15 Nashville TN 37212 E-mail: lorakay10@juno.com.

ALEXANDER, LYNN See MARGULIS, LYNN

ALEXANDER, MARJORIE ANNE, artist, art consultant; b. Chgo., Apr. 16, 1928; d. Alexander and Nancy Rebecca (Cordrey) Roberts; m. Harold Harman Alexander, June 13, 1948; children: Jeffrey C., Cassandra J., Peter B., Timothy C., Patrick J. Student, Wilson Jr. Coll., 1945-47; MFA in Painting, U. Ill., 1968, MA in Art Edn., 1972. cert. tchr. K-12, Ill., Minn. Graphic artist Barry Martin Studio, Rumson, N.J., 1963-65; instr. painting, drawing U. YMCA, Champaign, Ill., 1968-72; teaching asst. U. Ill., Urbana, 1968-72, rsch. assoc., 1972-76; instr. art Champaign High Sch., 1973-75, Urbana High Sch., 1976-80, Concordia Acad., St. Paul, Minn., 1982-84, U. Minn., Mpls., 1984-87, design, housing and apparel artist in residence St. Paul, 1984-88; craft cons. and educator tech. asstance program USAID, OAS, U. Minn., Kingtson, Jamaica, 1986—. Design cons. J.A.M. Corp., Mpls., 1988—; tech. cons. OAS, Kingston, 1990-91, Blandin Found. grantee, Minn., 1989—; rsch. and product devel. agrl. unilization rsch. inst., 1992-95; tech. cons. Zabbaleen Paper Project, Assn. for the Protection of the Environment, Cairo, 1993—, St. Lucia Paper project Weyerhauser Found., 1994—, paper project YMCA, Jamaica, W.I., 1997—; co-curator Paper Trivia and Treasure exhibit Goldstein Mus. Design/U. Minn., St. Paul, 2000. Works have appeared in more than 35 solo shows, 1960—, more than 80 invitational shows nationally and internationally, 1985—; work chosen for inclusion 1996 Internat. Calendar Papierfabak Schfufelen Lenningen, Germany; work chosen for poster paper exhibit Leopold-Hoesch Mus., Doren, Germany, 1999; traveling exhibit, Bavaria, Germany, Geneva; work chosen for exhibit Mus. Santa Maria Della Scala, Siena, Italy, 2003, Augsburg Coll. Mpls., 2003, Hist. Mus. Jeongju, South Korea, 2004; represented in permanent collections Imadate, Fukui, Japan, U. Ill., Weisman Art Mus., U. Minn., So. Cross U., NSW, Australia, Montclair (N.J.) Art Mus., Am. U. Cairo, Sori Arts Ctr., Jeonsu, Korea, Mus. Louvre It or Leavie It, Mpls., others; co-author: Selected Papers, 1994, Handcrafted paper and Paper Products Made from Indigenous Plant Fibers, 1997; contbr. articles to profl. jours, columns to newspaper. Vestry mem. St. John's Episcopal Ch., Champaign, 1975-78, St. Matthew's Episcopal Ch., St. Paul, 1989—. Recipient Celebrity award, Minn. State Fair, 1984, book First award, 1986, Honorable mention, 3d On/Off Paper Nat., Wis., 1984, 1st prize cmty. fine art exhibit, St. Paul, Minn., 2002, 2003; grantee, Blandin Found., U. Minn., 1989—90, OAS, 1990—91, Agrl. Utilization Rsch. Inst., 1992—95, Weyerhauser Found., 1997, Minn. Arts Bd., 1999. Mem.: Internat. Assn. Hand Papermakers and Paper Artists (pres. 2003—), Nat. League Am. Penwomen (state v.p. 1994—96, Minn. art chair 2002—), Friends of Dard Hunter Paper Mus. (com. chair 1990—95, adv. bd. 2001—). Episcopalian. Avocations: swimming, cooking, theater, travel.

ALEXANDER, MARTIN, microbiologist, educator; b. Newark, Feb. 4, 1930; s. Meyer and Sarah (Rubinstein) A.; m. Renee Rafaela Wulf, Aug. 26, 1951; children: Miriam H., Stanley W. BS, Rutgers U., 1951; MS, U. Wis., 1953, PhD, 1955. Asst. prof. Cornell U., Ithaca, N.Y., from 1955, now L.H. Bailey prof. Advisor agys. fed. govt., Washington, 1965—, UN agys., Kenya, France, Italy, 1963—; mem. coms. Nat. Acad. Sci., Washington, 1971—; cons. Author: Microbial Ecology, 1971, Introduction to Soil Microbiology, 1977, Biodegradation and Bioremediation, 1994; editor: Advances in Microbial Ecology, 5 vols., 1977-81. Recipient Indsl. Research 100 award, 1968, Fisher award Am. Soc. Microbiology, 1980, Superior Svc. award USDA, 1989. Fellow Am. Acad. Microbiology, AAAS, Internat. Inst. Biotechnology, Am. Soc. Agronomy (Soil Sci. award 1964) Home: 301 Winthrop Dr Ithaca NY 14850-1736 Office: Cornell U Bradfield Hall Ithaca NY 14853

ALEXANDER, MARY MELSON, secondary school educator; b. Carrollton, Ga., Mar. 24, 1938; d. O.C. and Mary Florence (Blunt) Melson; m. John Alexander, Jan. 2, 1971. BS, Albany State U., 1962; MA, NYU, 1976. Cert. secondary tchr., N.Y., cert. in social studies. Tchr. health edn. Bklyn. Schs., 1976—95, ret., 1995. Judge filmstrips awards competition Nat. Coun. Family Rels., 1974-75; vol. Pan Hellenic Cmty. Svc., 1990; v.p. Top Ladies of Distinction, Inc. Recipient Cmty. Svc. award, Alpha Kappa Alpha Sorority, Inc., 1986, Silver Star, 1986; Merit scholar York Rite Masons, 1956; named Soror of Yr., Pan Hellenic Coun. N.Y., 1999. Mem. AAHPERD, Am.Fedn. Tchrs., Nat. Coun. Negro Women (life), Ednl. Advancement Found. (charter 1988, life), Pan Hellenic Coun. Greater N.Y. (exec. com. award 1988-92), N.Y.C. ASCD, Albany State U. Nat. Alumni Assn. (life, N.Y. state chpt., pres. 1992-93), Kappa Delta Pi (life, v.p. Beta Pi chpt. 1989), Alpha Kappa Alpha (life).

ALEXANDER, MELVIN TAYLOR, quality assurance engineer, statistician; b. Greensboro, N.C., June 2, 1949; s. Melvin Taylor and Sabina Mae (Anglin) A.; m. Karen Gwendolyn Davenport, Aug. 22, 1973 (div. 1982); children: Asia Trinicia, Sabina, Melvin Taylor III; m. Lucia Antoinette Ward, Apr. 23, 1983. Student, Guilford Coll., 1967-70; BS in Math., N.C. A&T State U., 1972; MSPH in Biostats., U. N.C., 1979. Registered quality engr. Instr. math. N.C. A&T State U., Greensboro, 1975-77; grad. asst. biostatis. dept. U. N.C., Chapel Hill, 1977-79; rsch. assoc. Sch. Pub. Health, Chapel Hill, 1980-81, jr. statis. analyst, 1981-82; engring. staff asst. Westinghouse Electronic Systems Group, Balt., 1982-83, sr. engr., 1983-95; prin. quality analyst ARINC, Annapolis, Md., 1996-97; biostatistician GloboMax LLC, Hanover, Md., 1997—. Cons. N.C. Dept. Adminstrn., Raleigh, 1979-80, S.C. Conf. Black Mayors, Gifford, 1980. Co-author: Managing Industrial Processes, 1984. USPHS grantee, 1977; U. N.C. Minority Student fellow, 1978. Mem. Am. Statis. Assn., Am. Soc. Quality (sec. Balt. sect. 1990-91, vice chmn. 1991-92, chmn. 1996, health care div., chair-elect 1999—), Internat. Soc. for Hybrid Microelectronics. Democrat. Presbyterian. Avocations: music, photography, computers.

ALEXANDER, MICHAEL, conductor; b. Buffalo, Jan. 8, 1973; s. Gary and Marsha Alexander. B of Music Edn., U. Ga., 1995; MusM, U. Wis., 1997, D of Musical Arts, 2003. Assoc. lectr. U. Wis., Milw., 1997—2000; orch. dir. Ripon Coll., Wis., 2002—04; music dir./condr. Cobb Symphony Orch., Marietta, Ga., 2004—; orch. dir. Kennesaw State U., Ga., 2004—. Office Phone: 678-797-2141.

ALEXANDER, MICHAEL LEE, music educator, cellist; b. Houston, Sept. 11, 1959; s. Robert W. and Betty (Wood) A. MusB in Edn., Southwestern U., 1982; MusM, Sam Houston State U., 1984; MusD, U. Houston, 2000. Cert. music edn. all levels. Dir. orch. Stratford H.S., Houston, 1984—; music dir. Austrian Alps Performing Arts Festival, 1995—. Cellist, asst. condr. Houston Sinfonietta, 1984-87, also orch. dir.; chamber music dir. Sam Houston Summer Music, Huntsville, Tex., 1984—; dir. Summer Preparatory String Inst., U. Houston, 1996—; guest condr. Houston Civic Symphony, 1990, 2005; condr. Phila. orch. Houston Youth Symphony, 1994—; music judge, Houston, 1984—; tenor soloist DA Camera on Nat. Pub. Radio; guest conductor New Mex. All State Orchestra, 1996, La. All State Orchestra, 1997, All South Honor Orchestra, 1997, Fla. All State Orch., 1999, N.Mex. All-State Orch., 2000-03, N.D. All-State Orch., 2004 Music arranger youth musicals Music Man, Annie, 1983, 84; composer string orch. Soliloquy, 1985; condr. musicals: Barnum, Chorus Line, Annie Get Your Gun, Music Man, Annie, Into the Woods, Me and My Girl, 42nd Street, Oliver, West Side Story, Brigadoon. Mem. Trinity Episcopal Ch. Named Tchr. of Yr., Stratford H.S., 1994, Disting. Educator Houston Symphony, 1994 Mem. Am. String Tchrs. Assn. (Elizabeth Green Tchr. award), Tex. Mus. Edn. Assn. (bd. dirs.), Tex. Orch. Dirs. Assn. (bd. dirs.), Mu Psi Chi (outstanding alumni 1983), Phi Mu Alpha Sinfonia Office: Stratford High Sch 14555 Fern Dr Houston TX 77079-5405

ALEXANDER, MILES JORDAN, lawyer; b. Reading, Pa., Nov. 20, 1931; s. Abe Alexander and Sarah (Gold) Fidlow; m. Elaine Eve Barron, May 29, 1955; children: Kent, David, Michael, Paige. BA in Polit. Sci. with honors., Emory U., 1952; LLB cum laude, Harvard U., 1955. Bar: Ga. 1955, D.C. 1977. Assoc. Kilpatrick & Stockton, Atlanta, summers 1954-55; tchg. fellow Harvard U., Cambridge, Mass., 1957-58; assoc. Kilpatrick Stockton LLP, Atlanta, 1958-63; chmn. Kilpatrick & Stockton LLP, Atlanta, 1996—. Lectr. P.L.I., Internat. Trademark Assn., Am. Law Inst., ABA Internat. Franchise Assn., other seminars on trademarks and unfair competition, antitrust, franchising, dispute resolutions and litig. tactics; guest lectr. on trademark law NYU, U.Ga., Ga. State Law Sch., also bd. visitors; bd. visitors Emory U.; chmn. U.S. trademark pub. adv. com. Emory U., 2000-03. Editor-in-chief: The Trademark Reporter, 1978-80; contbr. numerous articles to jours. in trademark field. Mem. City of Atlanta Ethics Bd., chmn., vice-chmn., 1980-92, Emory U. and Harvard Law Sch. Alumni Funds; legal counsel to Mayor Maynard Jackson, 1974-82, 89-93; chmn. City of Atlanta Lic. Rev. Bd., 1976-79; former pres. Am. Jewish Com.; mem. Friends of Morehouse Coll.; adv. bd. Family Outreach Ctr.; mem. adv. coun. J. Thomas McCarthy Inst. Intellectual Property and Tech. Law, 2001--. Capt. USAF, 1955-57. Recipient Human Rels. award Anti-Defamation League, 1997, Disting. Alumni award Emory U., 2000. Fellow Am. Bar Found., Am. Coll. Trial Lawyers; mem. ABA, Internat. Trademark Assn. (counsel 1997-2000, chmn. trademark pub. com.), Ga. Bar Assn., Ga. State Bar Assn. (former chmn. antitrust sect., advisor to legal counsel 1997—), Atlanta Bar Assn., Lawyers Club Atlanta, Internat. Trademark Assn. (lectr., bd. dirs. 1980-82, rev. commn. 1986, legal counsel 1987-2000, Pres.'s Lifetime Achievement award 2003), Am. Law Inst. (adv. com. restatement of law of unfair competition 1986-95), 191 Club (bd. dirs.), Atlanta City Club (chmn. bd.), Commerce Club, Standard Club, Old War Horse Lawyers Club, Phi Beta Kappa. Avocations: reading, sports. Office: Kilpatrick Stockton LLP 1100 Peachtree St NE Ste 2800 Atlanta GA 30309-4530 Office Phone: 404-815-6410. Business E-Mail: malexander@kilpatrickstockton.com.

ALEXANDER, NANCY A., information technology manager, consultant; b. Kansas City, Kans., Mar. 31, 1957; d. Carl Glenn and Norma Louise Hanks; m. Steven Dale Alexander, May 20, 1981; 1 child, Anne Louise. AS in Computer Info. Systems summa cum laude, Kansas City (Kans.) C.C., 1989; BS in Computer Info. Systems with highest honors, Friends U., Wichita, Kans., 1999, MS in Mgmt. Info. Systems, 2001. Sec., a/c schedule control Trans World Airlines, Inc., Kansas City, Mo., 1976—79, coord. scheduling and planning group, 1979—80, planner, facilities and equipment engring., 1980—81, master planner, facilities and equipment programs, 1981—82, mgr., facilities and equipment programs, 1982—83; office mgr., info. tech. dir. Steven D. Alexander, Chtd., Overland Park, Kans., 1983—2004. Faculty adv. bd. Kansas City (Kans.) C.C., 1988—90; cons. Profl. Support, Inc., Shawnee, Kans., 1983—; real estate investor, 1978—; real estate agent, cons., 2002—. Software developer Legal Billing and Analysis System, 1989; author: Think of Your Future, 1992. Troop leader Girl Scouts Am., Shawnee, 1988—92; county coun. rep., project leader 4-H, Olathe, Kans., 1994—97, judge, 1995—97; youth group leader Master's Cmty. Ch., Kansas City, Kans., 1999—2001. Avocations: travel, racquetball, swimming, painting.

ALEXANDER, PATRICK BYRON, university administrator, consultant; b. Texas City, Tex., May 11, 1950; s. Alvin Wesley and Mabel Bernice Alexander; m. Linda Graham, May 7, 1975. BA in Econs., George Mason Coll., U. Va., 1972. Publs. dir. George Mason U., Fairfax, Va., 1973-75, U. Okla. Health Scis. Ctr., Oklahoma City, 1975-78, Presbyn. Hosp. Inc.,

Oklahoma City, 1978-79; mng. dir. Okla. Symphony Orch., Oklahoma City, 1979-88; exec. dir. Allied Arts Found., 1988-92, Okla. Zool. Soc., 1992—2001; exec. dir. advancement Oklahoma City U., 2001—03; planned giving dir. The Children's Ctr., 2003—. Dir. Planned Giving Children's Ctr.; bd. dirs. Okla. Philharm. Found., English-Speaking Union Okla., Red Earth Indian Ctr. Recipient Gov.'s award for excellence in arts, 1987, Okla. Fundraiser of Yr. award, 1991; English-Speaking Union Okla. Kerr Found. fellow, 1981. Home: 1515 Glenwood Ave Oklahoma City OK 73116-5206 Office: Oklahoma City U 2501 N Blackwelder Oklahoma City OK 73106 E-mail: palexander@okcu.edu.

ALEXANDER, PAUL RICHARD, illustrator; b. Richmond, Ind., Sept. 3, 1937; s. Fred and Olive (Phillips) A. BFA, Wittenberg U., 1959; BFA in Illustration, Art Ctr. Coll. Design, 1967. Archtl. delineator Forest Studios, Chgo., 1961-64; advt. illustrator Pitt Studios, Cleve., 1967-70; freelance illustrator Chgo., 1970-76, Mendola Artist's Rep., N.Y.C., 1976—. Contbg. artist: (anthologies) Tomorrow and Beyond, 1970s, Infinite Worlds—The Fantastic Visions of Science Fiction Art, 1997, Spectrum Sci. Ficton Annual, Vol. 1-4, 1990. With USAR, 1960-66. Mem. Mensa. Episc. Avocations: art, architecture, classical music, railfan. Home and Office: 1380 Oaktree Dr Greenville OH 45331-2730 Office Phone: 937-547-9568.

ALEXANDER, PETER HOUSTON, artist; b. L.A., Feb. 27, 1939; s. Richard Henry and Marion Celeste (Pluard) A.; m. Clytie Patricia Moore, June 8, 1964; children: Clytie Hope, Julia Pebrina. One man shows: Nicholas Wilder Gallery, L.A., 1970, Robert Elkon Gallery, N.Y.C., 1970, Art in Progress, Munich, 1973, U. Calif., Irvine, 1975, Calif. State U., Long Beach, 1976, Rico Mizuno, L.A., 1980, James Corcoran, L.A., 1981, Charles Cowles Gallery, N.Y.C., 1982, Arco Ctr., L.A., 1983, L.A. Mcpl. Art Gallery, 1983, Cirrus Gallery, L.A., 1983, Fuller Goldeen Gallery, San Francisco, 1984; group shows include Seattle Art Mus., 1968, Mus. Modern Art, N.Y.C., 1969, 83, 84, Walker Art Ctr., Milw., 1969, Whitney Mus. Am. Art, N.Y.C., 1969, Mus. Contemporary Art, Chgo., 1970, Locksley/Shea Gallery, L.A., 1971, Calif. State U., Long Beach, 1975, 78, San Francisco Mus. Modern Art, 1976, La Jolla (Calif.) Mus. Contemporary Art, 1981, Art Ctr. Coll. Design, Pasadena, Calif., 1981, Bklyn. Mus., 1983; retrospective exhbn. Orange County Mus. Art, Newport Beach, Calif., 1999; represented in permanent collections: Walker Art Ctr., Mpls., Mus. Modern Art, N.Y.C., La Jolla Art Mus., Vancouver (Can.) Mus. Art, Los Angeles County Mus. Art, Corcoran Gallery Art, Washington, Ft. Worth Art Mus., San Francisco Mus. Modern Art, Bklyn. Mus., Newport Harbor Art Mus., Walker Art Ctr., Fogg Mus., Harvard U., others. Served with USMC, 1961-66. Nat. Endowment for Arts artist fellow. Address: 1811 16th St Santa Monica CA 90404-4403 Business E-Mail: peter@peteralexander.com.

ALEXANDER, R. DAVID, retail executive; From sr. v.p. distbn. and transp. to exec. v.p., COO Family Dollar Stores, Charlotte, NC, 1995—2002, pres., COO, 2003—. Office: Family Dollar Store PO Box 1017 10401 Old Monroe Rd Charlotte NC 28201

ALEXANDER, RALPH WILLIAM, JR., physics professor; b. Phila., May 17, 1941; s. Ralph William and Gladys (Robin) A.; m. Janet Erdien Bradley, Sept. 4, 1965; children: Ralph III, Margaret. BA, Wesleyan U., Middletown, Conn., 1963; PhD, Cornell U., Ithaca, N.Y., 1968; postdoctoral study, U. of Freiburg, Fed. Republic Germany, 1968-70. From asst. to assoc. prof. physics U. Mo., Rolla, 1970-80, prof., 1980—, chmn. dept., 1983-92. Contbr. articles to profl. jours. Mem. Am. Phys. Soc., Assn. Am. Physics Tchrs. Office: U Mo Dept Physics Rolla MO 65409-0640 Office Phone: 573-341-4796. Business E-Mail: ralexand@umr.edu.

ALEXANDER, REBECCA, library director, artist; b. Mpls., June 25, 1960; d. Edward and Leah Rae Alexander; m. Carlo Levy, May 29, 1987. BA in Practice of Art, U. Calif., Berkeley, 1982; MFA in Painting, Pratt Inst., 1985; MLS in Libr. and Info. Sci., U. Wash., 1991. Cert. libr. Wash. Libr. dir. Temple De Hirsch Sinai Libr., Seattle, 1991—. Author (illustrator): Alef is Silent: A Hebrew Alphabet, 1997. Mem.: Assn. Jewish Libr. Jewish.

ALEXANDER, ROBERT JACKSON, economist, educator; b. Canton, Ohio, Nov. 26, 1918; s. Ralph S. and Ruth (Jackson) A.; m. Joan O. Powell, Mar. 26, 1949; children: Anthony, Margaret. BA, Columbia U., 1940; MA, Columbia U., 1941; PhD, Columbia U., 1950. Asst. economist Bd. Econ. Warfare, 1942, Office Inter-Am. Affairs, 1945—46; mem. faculty Rutgers U., 1947—, prof. econs., 1961—89, prof. emeritus, 1989—. Mem. Pres.-elect Kennedy's Latin Am. Task Force, 1960-61 Author 46 books including Juan Domingo Peron: A History, 1979, Romulo Betancourt and the Transformation of Venezuela, 1982, Bolivia: Past, Present and Future of Its Politics, 1982, Biographical Dictionary of Latin American and Caribbean Politics, 1988, Juscelino Kubitschek and the Development of Brazil, 1991, International Trotskyism 1929-85, 1991, The ABC Presidents, 1992, The Bolivarian Presidents, 1994, The Presidents of Central America, Mexico, Cuba and Hispaniola, 1995, Presidents, Prime Ministers and Governors of the English Speaking West Indies and Puerto Rico, 1997, The Anarchists in the Spanish Civil War, 1999, International Maoism in the Developing World, 1999, Hava de la Torre Man of the Millennium: His Life, Ideas and Continuing Relevance, 2001, A History of Organized Labor in Cuba, 2002, History of Organized Labor in Brazil, 2003, History of Organized Labor in Argentina in English Speaking West Indies, 2003, History of Organized Labor in Uruguay and Paraguay 2005 Mem. nat. bd. League Indsl. Democracy, 1955—; mem. nat. exec. com. Socialist Party-Social Dem. Fedn., 1957-66; bd. dirs. Rand Sch. Social Sci., 1951-56; mem. exec. com. Open Door Student Exch., 1970-94. Decorated officer Order Condor of the Andes Bolivia Mem. Am. Econ. Assn., Latin Am. Studies Assn., Mid. Atlantic Coun. Latin Am. Studies (v.p. 1986-87, pres. 1987-88), Coun. Fgn. Rels., Interam. Assn. Democracy and Freedom (chmn. N.Am. com. 1970-87), Phi Gamma Delta. Home: 944 River Rd Piscataway NJ 08854-5504 Office: Rutgers U Dept Econs New Brunswick NJ 08903 *I have sought to extend the bounds of knowledge through research and writing, and to pass on to my children and students not only what I have learned, but also, hopefully, some idea of how to behave in a civilized manner.*

ALEXANDER, RODNEY M., congressman; b. Jonesboro, La., Dec. 5, 1946; m. Nancy Sutton; children: Ginger, Rod, Lisa. Attended, La. Tech. U., 1965. Ins. agent; mem. La. Ho. of Reps., 1987—2002, US Ho. of Reps. from 5th La. dist., 2003—. Mem. Jackson Parish, La. Police Jury, 1970—85, pres., 1978—85. With USAF, 1965—71. Named Legis. of Yr., La. Rural Health Assn., 1997. Republican. Baptist. Office: 316 Cannon HOB Washington DC 20515 Mailing: District Office 1900 Stubbs Ave Ste B Monroe LA 71201 Office Phone: 202-225-8490, 318-322-3500. Office Fax: 318-322-3577, 202-225-5639.*

ALEXANDER, ROY, public relations executive, writer; b. Asheville, NC, Feb. 3, 1928; s. William Roy and Ruth (Upshaw) A. PhB, Northwestern U., 1954. Mng. editor Daily Northwestern, 1951-52; assoc. editor Food Retailing, 1951-55; dir. pub. relations Mid-States Corp., 1952-53; editor Splty. Salesman, 1953-56, Mobile Homes mag., 1953-54; account exec. Philip Lesly Co., 1956-58, sr. v.p. NYC, 1958—62; pres. Alexander Co., NYC, 1962—2004, Taggart & Alexander, NYC, 1993—. Mgr. N.Y. product publicity for Wurlitzer Co.; pub. relations counsel to Grad. Sch. Sales Mgmt. and Mktg., Lincoln Logs Ltd., Maleck Group, Barter Advantage, Inc., Mantis Mfg. Co., Huntingdon Valley, Pa.; Z-Flex, Manchester, N.H., Sales and Mktg. Mgmt., Sturm, Ruger & Co., Southport, Conn. Writer, exec. producer: (motion picture) The Greening of Augusta; dir.: (pub. edn. program) Iron Mountain Stoneware; creator: (pub. edn. program) W.Va. Coal Assn.; designer, creator (communications and promotion program) Nat. Pest Control Assn; author: Direct Salesman's Handbook, 1958, Mehdi: Story of Metlife's Top Salesman, 1977, Duke Medical Center's Ricer's Guide, 1984, Climbing the Corporate Matterhorn, 1985, Power Speech: Your Quickest Route to Success, 1986, Taking Your Company Public, 1990, Commonsense Time Management, 1992, More Mehdi: Everything Is Possible, 2000, Secrets of Closing Sales, 7th edit., 2004; editor Mktg. Times, 1970-80. Served with AUS, 1946-49; feature editor Armed Forces Press Service, 1948-49. Address: 430 E 20th St Ste 5C New York NY 10009-8203 Office Phone: 212-420-7767. Office Fax: 212-420-7768. Personal E-mail: 113streetman@msn.com. *My guiding principles: (1) Do something even if it's wrong - percentages favor the activist. (2) Don't waste words or time; both are in finite supply. (3) All generalizations are false, including these. (4) Assume most people will fail their responsibilities and plan accordingly. (5) Avoid all medication; solve health problem with diet and exercise. (6) Work is a chance to find yourself. (7) Never forget: The market economy makes it all possible.*

ALEXANDER, SHAUN, professional football player; b. Florence, Ky., Aug. 30, 1977; m. Valerie Alexander, May 18, 2002; 1 child, Heaven. BS in Marketing, U. Ala. Running back Seattle Seahawks, 2000—. Founder The Shaun Alexander Found. Named to NFC Pro Bowl team, 2003—04. Office: Seattle Seahawks 11220 NE 53rd St Kirkland WA 98033*

ALEXANDER, SHEILA A., education educator, nurse, researcher; b. Oil City, Pa., Sept. 15, 1966; d. John L. and Deanna L. McChesney; m. Damian F. Alexander, May 1, 1997. PhD, U. Pitts. Sch. of Nursing, Pitts., 2004. RN State of Pa., 1989. Asst. prof. U. Pitts. Sch. of Nursing, Dept of Acute and Tertiary Care, Pitts., 2005—; rsch. assoc. U. Pitts. Sch. of Nursing, Pitts., 1999—2004. Recipient Elizabeth Lloyd Norian Scholarship, U. Pitts., Sch. of Nursing. Mem.: Internat. Soc. of Nurses in genetics, Assn. of Clin. Rsch. Profls., Am. Assn. for Critical Care Nurses, Ea. Nursing Rsch. Soc., Soc. for Critical Care medicine, Am. Assn. for Neuroscience Nursing, Sigma Theta Tau. Business E-Mail: salexand@pitt.edu.

ALEXANDER, STEWART J., lawyer; b. Newark, July 6, 1939; s. Simon and Grace (Glikin) A.; m. Shirley Feingold, June 17, 1962; children: Brenda Alexander Schram, David I. BBA, LLB, St. Mary's U., San Antonio, 1962. Asst. city atty. City of San Antonio, 1964-66; judge mcpl. ct. City of Live Oak, San Antonio, 1975-83; pvt. practice San Antonio, 1966—. Guest lectr. St. Mary's U., U. Tex., San Antonio, San Antonio Coll., San Antonio Coll. Nursing. V.p. Cong. Rodfei Sholom, 1989-97; pres. B'nai B'rith, 1976-77. Capt. JAG U.S. Army, 1962-68. Named Boss of Yr., San Antonio Legal Sec's Assn., 1989-90. Office: 7718 Broadway St San Antonio TX 78209-3243 Office Phone: 210-828-6777.

ALEXANDER, SUE, writer; b. 1933; Student, Drake U., 1950—52, Northwestern U., 1952—53. Writer. Author: Small Plays for You and a Friend, 1973, Nadir of the Streets, 1975, Peacocks Are Very Special, 1976, Witch, Goblin and Sometimes Ghost, 1976, Small Plays for Special Days, 1977, Marc the Magnificent, 1978, More Witch, Goblin and Ghost Stories, 1978, Seymour the Prince, 1979, Finding Your First Job, 1980, Whatever Happened to Uncle Albert? and Other Puzzling Plays, 1980, Witch, Goblin and Ghost in the Haunted Woods, 1981, Witch, Goblin and Ghost's Book of Things to Do, 1982, Nadia the Willful, 1983, Dear Phoebe, 1984, World Famous Muriel, 1984, Witch, Goblin and Ghost Are Back, 1985, World Famous Muriel and the Scary Dragon, 1985, Lila on the Landing, 1987, There's More-Much More, 1987, America's Own Holidays, 1988, World Famous Muriel and the Magic Mystery, 1990, Who Goes Out on Halloween?, 1990, Sara's City, 1995, What's Wrong Now, Millicent?, 1996, One More Time, Mama, 1999, Behold the Trees, 2001. Home and Office: 6846 McLaren Ave Canoga Park CA 91307-2525 E-mail: suealexander@earthlink.net.

ALEXANDER, THOMAS BENJAMIN, historian, educator; b. Nashville, July 23, 1918; s. Thomas Benjamin and Mary Christine (Sanders) A.; m. Elise Hadley Pritchett, June 16, 1941; children: Wynne Hadley Alexander Guy, Elaine Elliston Alexander Gates, Carol Pope Alexander Gajek. BA, Vanderbilt U., 1939, MA, 1940, PhD, 1947. From asst. prof. to assoc. prof. history Clemson U., S.C., 1946-49; prof., chmn. div. social scis. Ga. So. U., Statesboro, 1949-57; from assoc. prof. to prof. history U. Ala., Tuscaloosa, 1957-69; prof. history U. Mo., Columbia, 1969-88, Middlebush prof. history, 1979-82, prof. emeritus, 1988—, Sesquicentennial prof., 1990. Author: Political Reconstruction in Tennessee, 1950, Thomas A.R. Nelson of East Tennessee, 1956, Sectional Stress and Party Strength, 1836-1860, 1967, The Anatomy of the Confederate Congress, 1972 (Sydnor award 1973, Jefferson Davis award 1972). Served to lt. USNR, 1943-46, ETO. Fellow Guggenheim Found., 1955-56; grantee Social Sci. Research Council, 1947, 67-68; fellow Inst. So. History, 1968-69 Mem. AAUP, So. Hist. Assn. (pres. 1980), Am. Hist. Assn., Orgn. Am. Historians, Social Sci. History Assn. (pres. 1986), S.C. Hist. Assn. (pres. 1958). Home: 2606 Summit Rd Columbia MO 65203-1336 Office: U Mo Dept History Columbia MO 65211-0001

ALEXANDER, THOMAS G., chemist, researcher; b. Washington, Sept. 9, 1928; s. Lyle Thomas and Helen Goodwin Alexander; m. Amy Turner, June 1, 1991; m. Eleanor Carol Harkness, Aug. 25, 1951 (dec. Jan. 15, 1990); children: Lyle Steven, Helen Ruth, Carol Anne. BS, U. of Md., College Park, MD, 1946—50; MS, George Wash. U., Washington, DC, 1953—57. Analytical chemist US FDA, Washington, 1956—93; chemist USDA, Washington, 1952—56; analyst NY Dept. of Agr., Ithaca, NY, 1950—. Gen. referee Assn. of Ofcl. Analytical Chemists, Arlington, Va., 1969—94. Contbr. chapters to books. Commr. Boy Scouts of Am., Washington, 1969—94; bd. mem. Assn. of Analytical Chemists, Arlington, Va., 1986—88. Pfc U.S. Army, 1950—52, Maryland. Recipient Outstanding Gen. Referee, 1988. Fellow: Assn. of Ofcl. Analytical Chemists. United Methodist. Achievements include Developed Methods For The Analysis Of Milk Products, Ergot Alkaloids And Antibiotics. Avocation: photography.

ALEXANDER, VERA, dean, marine science educator; b. Budapest, Hungary, Oct. 26, 1932; came to U.S., 1950; d. Paul and Irene Alexander; div.; children: Graham Alexander Dugdale, Elizabeth Alexander. BA in Zoology, U. Wis., 1955, MS in Zoology, 1962; PhD in Marine Sci., U. Alaska, 1965; LLD, Hokkaido U., Japan, 1999. From asst. prof. to assoc. prof. marine sci. U. Alaska, Fairbanks, 1965-74, prof., 1974—, dean Coll. Environ. Scis., 1977-78, 80-81, dir. Inst. Marine Sci., 1979-93, acting dean Sch. Fisheries and Ocean Scis., 1987-89, dean, 1989—2004; asst. to provost Fisheries and Oceans Policy, 2004—. Mem. adv. com. to ocean scis. divsn. NSF, 1980-84, chmn. adv. com., 1983-84; mem. com. to evaluate outer continental shelf environ. assessment program Minerals Mgmt. Svc., Bd. Environ. Sci. and Tech. NRC, 1987-91, mem. com. on geophys. and environ. Data, 1993-98; mem. adv. com. Office Health and Environ. Rsch., U.S. Dept. Energy, Washington, 1987-90; vice chmn. Arctic Ocean Scis. Bd., 1988-89; commr. U.S. Marine Mammal Commn., 1995—; U.S. del. North Pacific Marine Sci. Orgn., 1991-2002, vice-chmn., 1999-2002, chmn., 2002—; bd. dirs. Western Regional Aquaculture Ctr.; mem. sci. adv. bd. NOAA, 1998-2004; mem. ocean rsch. adv. panel Nat. Oceans Leadership Coun., 1998-2002; mem. internat. steering com. Census of Marine Life, 1999—; mem. Pres.'s Panel on Ocean Exploration, 2000; pres. Arctic Rsch. Consortium U.S., 2003-; chmn. Internat. Com. Sigma Xi, 2004-. Editor: Marine Biological Systems of the Far North (W.L. Rey), 1989. Sec. Fairbanks Light Opera Theatre Bd., 1987-88; chair Rhodes Scholar Selection Com., Alaska, 1986-95; pres. Arctic Rsch. Consortium U.S., 2003—. Research grantee U. Alaska. Fellow AAAS, Arctic Inst. N.Am., Explorers Club (sec., treas. Alaska/Yukon chpt. 1987-89, 91-99, pres. 1990-91); mem. Am. Soc. Limnology and Oceanography, Am. Geophys. Union, Oceanography Soc., Am. Fisheries Soc., Nature Conservancy of Alaska (bd. dirs.), Rotary (pres. 1999-2000). Avocations: classical piano, horsemanship. Home: 3875 Geist Rd Ste E Fairbanks AK 99709 Office: U Alaska PO Box 707220 Fairbanks AK 99775 Office Phone: 907-474-5071. Personal E-mail: veroniha@earthlink.net. Business E-Mail: vera@sfos.uaf.edu.

ALEXANDER, W. M., philosophy educator; b. Jacksonville, Fla., Dec. 5, 1928; s. Leon Wilson Alexander and Ruth Louise Chesebrough; m. Katherine Alice Fryer, June 5, 1953; children: John Edward, Susan Dorman, David Leon (dec.). AB, Davidson Coll., 1950; BD, Louisville Presbyn. Sem., 1953; STM, Harvard U., 1957; PhD, Princeton Theol. Sem., 1961. From asst. to assoc. prof. to prof. philosophy St. Andrews Coll., Laurinburg, N.C., 1961-83, disting. prof., 1983. Vis. prof. philosophy U. N.C., Pembroke, 1983-93 Author: (book) Johann Georg Hamann, Philosophy and Faith, 1966, (book chpts.) The Death of God Debate, The Philosophy of Sex; contbr. articles to profl. jours. and encys. Chaplain, 1st lt. U.S. Army, 1953-56. Rsch. grantee Am. Coun. Learned Socs., 1967; fellow Coun. for Philos. Studies, 1974. Mem. Am. Philos. Assn., Metaphys. Soc. Am., Soc. for Philosophy in Pub. Affairs, Soc. for Philosophy of Sex and Love. Avocations: foreign travel, racquetball. Home: 1105 Shepherd Ave Laurinburg NC 28352 Office: St Andrews Coll Laurinburg NC 28352

ALEXANDER, WILLIAM BROOKS, lawyer, former state senator; b. Boyle, Miss., Dec. 23, 1921; s. William Brooks and Vivien (Beaver) A.; m. Belle McDonald, Mar. 12, 1950; children— Brooks, Becky, John, Jason, Grace. Student, Miss. Coll., 1940-42; LL.B., U. Miss., 1948. Bar: Miss. 1948. Ptnr. Alexander, Johnston & Alexander, Cleveland, 0198—; mem. Miss. Senate, 1960-83, past pres. pro tem. Past pres. Miss. Heart Assn.; bd. dirs. Miss. Coll., Delta Coun., Miss. Econ. Coun.; founder Save a Life, Cleve. Served with AUS, 1942-46 Mem. Miss. Bar Assn. (Outstanding Legislator), Bolivar County Bar Assn., Am. Legion, VFW (past dep. comdr.), Exchange Club, Masons. Baptist. Office: PO Box 1737 Cleveland MS 38732-1737

ALEXANDER, WILLIAM HERBERT, business educator, former construction executive; b. Harrisburg, Pa., Apr. 17, 1941; s. Wallace Hale and Jeannette Kauffman (Hackenberger) A.; m. Marion Elizabeth Carey, Nov. 30, 1963; children: Charles, Elizabeth, Robert, Kathryn. BS, U.S. Mil. Acad., 1963; MBA, U. Pitts., 1969; D of Pub. Svc. (hon.), Harrisburg Community Coll., 1992. Registered profl. engr., Pa. Commd. 2d lt. U.S. Army, 1963, advanced through grades to capt., 1968; platoon leader, co. comdr. Kitzingen, Germany, 1963-66; capt., co. comdr. Officer Candidate Regiment, Ft. Belvoir, Va., 1966-67; staff officer, engr. constrn. battalion Cu Chi, Vietnam, 1968; resigned, 1968; project mgr. H.B. Alexander & Son, Inc., Harrisburg, 1970-77, chmn., 1977-94; dir. Pa. Blue Shield, Mchts. & Businessmen's Mut. Ins. Co., 1985—97; dir. family bus. programs Wharton Sch. U. Pa., 1988-94, mng. dir. Sol. C. Snider Entrepreneurial Ctr. Wharton Sch., 1994-98; chair Wharton Family Controlled Corp. Program, 1998—2002; dir. Gelsinger Health Sys., Danville, 1997—. Pres. Capital Region Econ. Devel. Corp., 1987—88; chmn. Hershey Trust Co., 1997—98; lectr. Mgmt. Dept. Wharton Sch. U. Pa., Phila., 1998—. Bd. dirs. AAA Ctrl. Penn Auto Club (chmn. 1991-93); pres. Tri County United Way, 1979-80, Ams. for Competitive Enterprise System, 1981-82; bd. dirs. Milton Hershey Sch., 1989-2002, chmn., 1997-98; chmn. Harrisburg C.C. Found., 1981-82. Decorated Bronze Star; recipient Whitney award for tchg. excellence undergrad. divsn., Wharton Sch., U. Pa., 2005. Mem. ASCE, Pa. Soc. Profl. Engrs. (Engr. of Yr. in Central Pa. 1986), Harrisburg C. of C. (bd. dirs., chmn. 1982-83), Harrisburg Rotary (pres. 1981-82), Beta Gamma Sigma, Delta Mu Delta. Presbyterian (elder). Home: 16 Wagner St Hummelstown PA 17036-9113 Office: 428 Vance Hall 3733 Spruce St Philadelphia PA 19104-6301

ALEXANDER, WILLIAM OLIN, finance company executive; b. Lexington, Ky., Aug. 2, 1939; s. Elby Olin and Louise (Watson) A.; m. Yvonne Davis, Jan. 26, 1961; children: Keith Davis, Hope. BS, U. Ky., 1961. CPA, Fla. Auditor Ring, Mahony & Arner (CPAs), Miami, Fla., 1961-62, sr. auditor, 1964-66; v.p., treas. Seabird Industries, Miami, 1966-70, exec. v.p., 1970-73; controller Belcher Oil Co., Miami, 1973-75, treas., 1976-83; sr. v.p., treas. Mitchell Co., Mobile, Ala., 1983-85; pres. Alexander & Co., PA, CPA, 1985—. Served to 1st lt. AUS, 1962-64. Mem. AICPA, Fla. Inst. CPAs, Porsche Club Am., Beta Alpha Psi, Delta Sigma Pi, Delta Tau Delta. Republican. Home: 10910 Juniperus Pl Tampa FL 33618-3818 Office: 14033 N Dale Mabry Hwy Tampa FL 33618-2401

ALEXANDER, WILLIAM POWELL, business advisor; b. Buffalo, June 16, 1934; s. James Nelson and Helen (Johnston) A.; m. Eunice Gail Elwood, May 8, 1981; 1 child from previous marriage, Christine Alexander Johnson. BA, Gettysburg Coll., 1956; postgrad., Temple U., 1960-62. With Aetna Casualty & Surety Co., 1956-57, RCA Corp., N.Y.C., 1960-86, asst. sec., 1968-73, sr. asst. sec., 1973-78, sec., 1978-86; also sec. NBC, Coronet Industries, RCA/Ariola, Hertz, Random House; sec. to office of chmn., asst. to chmn. Marine Midland Banks, Inc., 1987-88; adminstrv. dir. The Gt. Atlantic & Pacific Tea Co. Inc., 1988-89. Served to 1st lt. USAF, 1957-59. Mem. Am. Soc. Corp. Secs., Phi Kappa Psi. Clubs: Cavalier Golf and Yacht (Virginia Beach, Va.). Home and Office: 216 61st St Virginia Beach VA 23451-2117

ALEXANDER-GRAY, MARK ALLEN, music educator; s. Lee Roy and Phyllis Mariada Gray; m. Jessie Violet Alexander, July 29, 2001; children: Elizabeth, Caden. B in Music Edn., Ohio State U., 1983. Bank dir. Madison Sch. Dist., Mansfield, Ohio, 1983—87, Carlisle Area Sch. Dist., Pa., 1987—. Percussion instr. Bluecoats Drum and Bugle Corp, Canton, Ohio, 1984—87. Musician (percussionist): Harrisburg (Pa.) Opera, 1999—2003. Mem.: Pa. Music Edn. Assn. Democrat. Roman Catholic. Office: Lamberson Mid Sch 623 W Penn St Carlisle PA 17013

ALEXANDER-GUERRA, LYCIA LUCIA, psychiatrist; b. June 3, 1955; d. E. Holmes and Lilia Alexander. MD, Boston U., 1983; postgrad., N.Y. Psychoanalytic Inst., 1988-95. Diplomate Am. Bd. Psychiatry and Neurology. Intern U. Fla.-Shands Tchg. Hosp., Gainesville, 1983-84; chief resident in psychiatry U. South Fla., Tampa, 1986-87; chief teaching unit, acute adult svc. James A. Haley Vets.' Hosp., Tampa, 1987-88; unit chief, long-term young adult svc. Bronx (N.Y.) Children's Psychiat. Ctr., 1988-89; pvt. practice N.Y.C., 1989-95, Tampa, 1996—. Mem. Am. Psychiat. Assn., Am. Psychoanalytic Assn. Office: 14043 N Dale Mabry Hwy Tampa FL 33618-2401 Office Phone: 813-908-5080.

ALEXANDER-HAYNES, SANDRA, psychologist, educator; b. Cleve., Nov. 18, 1961; d. Winfield Edward Wright, Jr. and Mary Lee Alexander; m. Jeffery Orlando Haynes, June 27, 2003; 1 child, Michael A. Alexander-Leeks. BA cum laude, Cleve. State U., 1983, MA in Psychology, 1985, PhD in Urban Edn., 1997. Nationally cert. sch. psychologist 2003. Sch. psychology intern E. Cleve. Schs., 1985—86, summer sch. psychologist, 1986; sch. psychologist PSI Assocs., Inc., Akron, Ohio, 1986—87, Cleve. Mcpl. Schs., 1987—2000, lead psychologist, 1998—2000; sch. psychologist Orange City Schs., Pepper Pike, Ohio, 2000—03. Workshop co-facilitator Soc. for Prevention of Violence, 1997—2000; adj. prof. Kent State U., Kent, Ohio, 1999—2000, mem. sch. psychology program adv. com., 1999—2002; chair, multicultural com. Cleve. Mcpl. Schs., 1997—2000; thesis reader Notre Dame Coll., S. Euclid, Ohio, 2000—02, adj. prof., 2000—02. Bd. mem. Ratner Schs., Lyndhurst, Ohio, 1998—2000. Mem.: Ohio Sch. Psychology Assn. Office: Orange Schs 32000 Chagrin Blvd Pepper Pike OH 44124

ALEXANDRE, KRISTIN KUHNS, public relations executive, writer; b. Dayton, Ohio, July 15, 1948; d. James Edward and Faith (Colgan) Kuhns; m. DeWitt Loomis Alexandre, 1988; children: James Andrew, Cynthia Lenox Banks. BA, Sweet Briar, 1968. Editor C.I.T. Finance Corp., N.Y.C., 1970-73; newscaster Channel 5 News, N.Y.C., 1973-74, Channel 13 News, N.Y.C., 1974-75; editor Champion Internat., N.Y.C., 1975-76; copy editor House Beautiful, N.Y.C., 1975-76; pub. rels. officer Economic Devel. Adminstrn. Puerto Rico, N.Y.C., 1976-80; pres. Kristin Alexandre Pub. Rels., N.Y.C., 1980—. Bd. dirs. Kuhns Investment Corp., Dayton; pres. Robert Kuhns, Inc., Dayton. Bd. trustees Friends Clarence Dillo Libr. Mem. New York Jr. League. Home: PO Box 367 Far Hills NJ 07931-0367

ALEXANIAN, MOORAD, physics professor; b. Havana, Cuba, Dec. 28, 1936; came to U.S., 1954; s. Krikor and Noyemzar (Khimatian) A.; m. Mary Altounian, Aug. 21, 1960; children: Mariam, Sona, Aram. BA, U. R.I., 1960; PhD, Ind. U., 1964. Sr. scientist Lawrence Livermore (Calif.) Lab., 1964-70; prof. physics Centro De Investigacion, Mexico City, Mex., 1970-86; vis. prof. So. Ill. U., Carbondale, 1984-86; prof., chmn. U. N.C., Wilmington, 1986-89, prof. physics, 1989—. Contbr. articles to Physics Letters A, Physica A, Phys. Rev. Mem. Am. Phys. Soc., Am. Scientific Affiliation. Armenian Evangelical.

Achievements include rsch. on quantum optics, condensed matter physics, cosmology and particle physics. Office: U NC College Rd Wilmington NC 28403 Office Phone: 910-962-3463. Business E-Mail: alexanian@uncw.edu.

ALEXANIAN, RAYMOND, hematologist; b. N.Y.C., June 8, 1932; s. Hagop and Eleeza (Bynderian) A.; m. Lois Abbott, Jan. 16, 1960; 1 dau., Jane. BA with highest honors, Dartmouth Coll., 1952; MD, Harvard U., 1955. Diplomate: Am. Bd. Internal Medicine. Intern King County Hosp., Seattle, 1955-56; successively asst. resident in medicine, research fellow in hematology, instr. medicine U. Wash. Med. Sch., 1958-64; mem. faculty U. Tex. M.D. Anderson Hosp., Houston, 1964—, prof. medicine, 1975—. Contbr. numerous articles on myeloma and related disorders to med. jours. Served as capt. M.C. AUS, 1956-58. Mem. Am. Soc. Hematology, AMA, Tex. Med. Assn. (Waldenstrom award 1997). Home: 4082 Breakwood Dr Houston TX 77025-4033 Office: MD Anderson Hosp Dept Lymphoma-Myeloma 1515 Holcombe Blvd Houston TX 77030-4009 Office Phone: 713-792-2850.

ALEX-ASSENSOH, YVETTE MARIE, political scientist; b. Lafayette, La., Feb. 12, 1967; d. Livingston and Thelma Coleman A.; m. A.B. Assensoh, May 7, 1994; children: Kwadwo Stephen, Livingston. BA summa cum laude, Dillard U., 1988; postgrad., Columbia U., 1987-88; MA, Ohio State U., 1991, PhD, 1993. Asst. prof. Ind. U., Bloomington, 1994-2000, assoc. prof., 2001—, dir. grad. studies in polit. sci., 2003—. Rsch. assoc. Ohio State U., 1992-93; spkr. in field. Author: Neighborhoods, Family and Political Behavior, 1998; co-author: Afrian Military, 2001; co-editor: Black and Multiracial Politics, 2000; contbr. articles to profl. jours. Recipient Mays-Cook Sr. award Dillard U., New Orleans, 1998; NSF grantee, 1992-93, So. Regional Coun. grantee, 1994-95, Active Learning Teaching Strategies grantee, Ind. U., 1995, Multi Disciplinary Ventures grantee, 1997, Spencer Found. grantee, 2001; Benjamin E. Mays-Samuel DuBois Cook scholar, 1988; Ford Found. fellow, 1992-93, U. N.C. postdoctoral fellow, 1993-94, Nat. Acad. Edn./Spencer Found. postdoctoral fellow, 1999-2000, Fulbright fellow, 2001. Fellow Am. Polit. Sci. Assn.; mem. Assn. Third World Studies, Internat. PEN. Avocations: reading, tennis. Home: 4301 Cricket Knoll Dr Bloomington IN 47401 Office: Ind U Polit Sci Dept Bloomington IN 47405 Fax: 812-855-2027. E-mail: yalex@indiana.edu.

ALEXE, GABRIELA, research scientist; arrived in US, 1998; d. Gheorghe and Ecaterina Gheorghe; m. Sorin Alexe, Nov. 17, 1990. MSc in Math., U. Bucharest, 1986; MSc in Math. and Computer Sci. with honors, U. Galati, 1995; PhD of Ops. Rsch., Rutgers U., 2003. Asst. prof. U. Galati, Romania, 1990—98; rsch. asst. Rutgers U., NJ, 2000—03; mem. Ctr. Sys. Biology Inst. for Advanced Study, Princeton, NJ, 2003—. Postdoctoral fellow N.J. Commn. on Cancer Rsch., 2003—05, Computational Biology Ctr., TJ Watson IBM Rsch., Yorktown Heights, NY, 2005—. Contbr. articles to profl. jours. Recipient Nat. Math. Student Competition Spl. prizes, Ministry Edn., Romania; fellow Grad. Student Project, Discrete Math and Theoretical Computer Sci. Found., Rutgers U., 1998—2002; grantee, Office Naval Rsch.; Soros fellow, Rostock U., Rostock, Germany, 1997. Excellence fellow, Rutgers U., 1998—2001, TEMPUS fellow, Humboldt U., Berlin, 1998. Mem.: N. Y. Acad Sci., Internat. Soc. for Computational Biology, Inst. for Advanced Study, Inst. for Ops. Rsch. and Mgmt. Sci. (assoc.), Classification Soc. N.Am. Office: Inst for Advanced Study 1 Einstein Dr Princeton NJ 08540 Office Phone: 914-945-2354. E-mail: galexe@us.ibm.com.

ALEXEEV, DMITRI KONSTANTINOVICH, pianist; b. Moscow, Aug. 10, 1947; s. Konstantin and Gertrude (Bolotina) A.; m. Tatiana Sarkisova, 1970; 1 child. Studied with Dmitri Bashkirov, Moscow Conservatoire. Pianist performing USSR, U.K., Europe, U.S., touring Australia, Japan, Hong Kong, others; pianist London Philharm. Orch., Berlin Philharm., Berlin Radio Symphony Orchs., Chgo. Symphony Orch., Phila. Orch., London Symphony Orch., St. Petersburg Philharm. Orch., Royal Concertgebouw of Amsterdam, Munich Bavarian Radio Orch., Orchestre de Paris, City of Birmingham Symphony Orch., Royal Philharm. Orch., Hallé Orch., Balt. (Md.) Symphony Orch., Royal Flanders Philharm. Orch., Israel Philharm.; recordings include concertos by Schumann, Grieg, Rachmaninov, Prokofiev, Shostakovich, Scriabin, Medtner and solo works by Brahms, Rachmaninov, Schumann, Chopin, Liszt; performed at recitals in Munich, Florence, Rome, London, St. Petersburg, and Helsinki among others; worked with conductors such as Ashkenazy, Boulez, Dorati, Giulini, Muti, Rozhdestvensky, Tennstedt, Temirkanov, Tilson Tomas, and Jansons, among others. Recipient top honours Marguerite Long Competition, Paris, 1969, George Enescu Competition, Bucharest, 1970, Tchaikovsky Competition, Moscow, 1974, first prize 5th Leeds Internat. Piano Competition, Eng., 1975, Edison award The Netherlands, 1994. Office: IMG Artists/Lovell House 616 Chiswick High St London W4 5RX England Office Phone: 44-20-8-2335832. E-mail: cdyer@imgartistsworld.com.

ALEXEFF, IGOR, retired electrical engineering educator; b. Pitts., Jan. 5, 1931; s. Alexander and Tamara (Tchirkow) A.; m. Anne I. Fabina, Feb. 4, 1954; children: Alexander, Helen. BA with honors, Harvard U., 1952; MS, U. Wis., 1955, PhD, 1959. Registered profl. engr., Tenn. Research engr. Westinghouse Corp., Pitts., 1952-53; NSF postdoctoral fellow U. Zurich, Switzerland, 1959-60; group leader controlled thermonuclear fusion Oak Ridge Nat. Lab., 1960-71; prof. elec. engring. U. Tenn., 1971-96, prof. emeritus, 1996—; chief scientist Haleakala R&D Corp. Vis. prof. Inst. Plasma Physics, Nagoya, Japan, 1973, Phys. Rsch. Lab., Ahmedabad, India, 1975, physics dept. U. Natal, Durban, South Africa, 1976, U. Fed. Fluminense Niteroi, Brazil, 1978, Birla Inst. Tech., Ranchi, India, 1991; organizer Plasma Physics Workshop, U.S. and India, 1976; chmn. Gordon Rsch. Conf. on Plasma Physics, 1974; pres. So. Appalachian Sci. and Engring. Far, 1985-86. Co-author: High Power Microwave Sources, 1987; contbr. articles to profl. jours.; over 10 patents in field. Chancellor's rsch. scholar U. Tenn., 1984; recipient Advanced Tech. award Internat. Hall of Fame, 1989, 91, (with others) R&D 100 award R&D Mag., 1989, 91; named Most Outstanding Tchr. of Yr., U. Tenn. Elec. Engring. Dept., 1992. Fellow IEEE (assoc. editor Trans. on Plasma Sci., organizer 1st Internat. Conf. on Plasma Sci. 1974, former pres. Oak Ridge sect., Centennial medal 1987, Outstanding Engr. in S.E. award 1987), Am. Phys. Soc. (past sec.-treas. div. plasma physics); mem. ASI (co-founder), Tech. Corp., Tenn. Inventors Assn. (founding pres., Inventor of Yr. award 1988), Nuclear and Plasma Scis. Soc. of IEEE (chmn. plasma sect. 1983-84, v.p. 1998, pres. 1999-2000, Shea award for outstanding svc., Plasma Scis. and Applications award 2002). Home: 2790 Turnpike Oak Ridge TN 37830 Office: U Tenn Ferris 315 Knoxville TN 37996-2100 also: 1907 Holston River Rd Knoxville TN 37914-6144 Office Phone: 865-974-5467. Personal E-mail: ialexeff@comcast.net. Business E-Mail: alexeff@utk.edu.

ALEXIADES-ARMENAKAS, MACRENE RENEE, dermatologist, scientist, researcher, educator, consultant; d. Gregory and Sophia Alexiades; m. Noel Anthony Armenakas, Oct. 26, 1996; children: Sophia Stella Armenakas, Anthony Emmanuel Armenakas. BA, Harvard U., 1989; MD, Harvard Med. Sch., 1997; PhD, Harvard U., 1997. Cert. MD, PhD, lic. medicine & surgery N.Y., 1998, medicine and surgery Conn., 2004, Greece, 2004, credentialed in medicine and surgery European Union, 2004, diplomate Am. Bd. Dermatology, 2002. Rschr. Harvard U., Cambridge, 1984—91, tutor supr., 1985—89, tchg. asst., 1990—97, doctorate rschr. Boston, 1991—97; intern medicine Lenox Hill Hosp., N.Y.C., 1997—98; Fulbright scholar U. Heraklion, Crete, Greece, 1989—90; resident dermatology NYU Sch. Medicine, N.Y.C., 1998—2000, chief resident dermatology, 2000—01; dir. rsch. & laser dermatology Laser & Skin Surgery Ctr. N.Y., 2001—03; attending physician Lenox Hill Hosp., N.Y.C., 2001—; pres., dir. dermatology & laser surgery Macrene Alexiades-Armenakas, MD, PhD, PC, 2003—; clin. instr. Yale U. Sch. Medicine, 2003—; attending physician Yale/New Haven Hosp. Tutor supr. Harvard Bur. Study Coun., 1985—89; mem. MD/PhD program steering com. Harvard Med. Sch., 1993—94, mem. MD/PhD program retreat com., 1992—94, mem. minority recruitment com., 1992—95, mem. advanced biomed. scis. com., 1993—95, admissions interviewer com., 2002—. Editor: (jour.) Dermatologic Surgery, 2004—, The Harvard Polit. Rev., 1985—89; editor: (writer) The Biology Rev., 1986—89; mem. editl. bd.: The Harvard Crimson, 1985—89; author: abstracts, jour. articles, book chpts. Counselor rape crisis Response, Cambridge, 1988-89; counselor Harvard Med. Sch. peer counseling, 1990-92; yoga instr. Vanderbilt Hall Athletic Facility, Boston, 1990-92; vol. St. Francis House Soup Kitchen, 1990-94; solicitation coord. fundraising com. William Woodward Nursery Sch., 2001-02, chairperson, 2004-, bd. trustees, 2004-; mem. art com. The Chapin Sch., 2004-05, mem. Parents Assn., 2004-05. Recipient Husik prize, 2001, First Pl. award, Jour. Drugs in Dermatology Rsch. Competition, 2004; grantee, Nat. Eye Inst., 1995; scholar, Fulbright Found., 1989—90; Paul Dudley White scholar, Harvard U., 1991. Fellow: Hellenic Med. Soc.; mem.: Am. Soc. Laser Medicine and Surgery, Dermatology Found., Am. Acad. Dermatology, Harvard Hellenic Soc. (founder), Mass. Med. Soc., Am. Soc. Dermatologic Surgery (chmn. rsch. com. 2004—, councilman edn. and rsch. com. 2004—, editor, columnist jour. 2005), Harvard Greek Club. Greek Orthodox Christian. Achievements include numerous scientific discoveries, inventions, and patents. Avocations: portraiture, sculpting, drawing, painting, skiing, yoga, photography. Office: Macrene Alexiades-Armenakas MD PhD PC 800 Fifth Ave New York NY 10021 Office Phone: 212-570-2067. Office Fax: 212-861-7964. Business E-Mail: dralexiades@nyderm.org.

ALEXICK, DAVID FRANCIS, art educator; b. Phila., Jan. 25, 1942; s. John Francis Alexick and Katie Louise Gibbs; m. Anne Menin Gibson-Alexick, Mar. 27, 2004; m. Helen Cecelia Fecher (dec. 1996). BFA, Richmond Profl. Inst. of Coll. William and Mary, 1964; MFA, Va. Commonwealth U., 1966; PhD, Pa. State U., 1976. Instr. York Coll. Pa., 1966—68; grad. asst. Coll. of Edn., Pa. State U., University Park, 1969—71; asst. prof. Longwood Coll., Farmville, Va., 1971—78, Christopher Newport Coll., Newport News, Va., 1979—82, dir. art, asst. prof., 1982—86; assoc. prof. Christopher Newport U., Newport News, Va., 1986—2003, prof., 2003—. One-man shows include The Robinson House (Cert. Distinction), Va. Mus. Fine Arts (Cert. Distinction), exhibited in group shows at York Coll., Longwood Coll., Christopher Newport U., Charles Taylor Art Ctr., Hampton, Va. Founder, donor Alexick Family Scholarship for art students Christopher Newport U., Newport News, 1996. Recipient fellowship and tchg. assistantship, Va. Mus. Fine Arts, 1965. Mem.: Coll. Art Assn., Va. Art Edn. Assn. (extended bd. mem.). Avocations: painting, art. Home: 220 Crittenden Ln Newport News VA 23606 Office: Christopher Newport U 1 University Pl Newport News VA 23606

ALEXIOU, JAMES, electronics executive; b. Manchester, N.H., May 25, 1932; s. George Nicholas and Mary Alexiou; m. Elaine Alexiou, Feb. 4, 1962; children: Stephanie Alexiou Hubbard, Thomas James. BS in Bus. Mgmt., Boston U., 1954, MA in Econ., 1962. Prodn. mgr. Raytheon Co., Newton, Mass., 1962-65; plant mgr. Norton Co., Worcester, Mass., 1965-70; chmn., treas. New Eng. Rsch. Ctr., Sudbury, Mass., 1976-78; chmn., CEO Irvine Sensors Corp., Costa Mesa, Calif., 1970-97, chmn., 1970—, Novaloc, Inc., Costa Mesa, Calif., 1995—. Bd. dirs. Dycam Corp., Chatsworth, Calif. Bd. dirs. Phila. Soc. Orange County, Irvine, Calif. 1994—, chmn., 1999-2000, pres., 1997-99; pres. St. Paul's Greek Orthodox Ch. Found., Irvine, 1998-2001; founder, benefactor Orange County Performing Arts Ctr., Costa Mesa, 1984-2001. Recipient Disting. Svc. to Profession award Boston U. Sch. Mgmt., 1996. Mem. Center Club, Sigma Alpha Epsilon (past pres.). Avocations: hiking, movies, performing arts. Office: Irvine Sensors Corp 3001 Redhill Ave Costa Mesa CA 92626 E-mail: alexiou@aol.com.

ALEXIS, CARL ODMAN, lawyer, geologist; b. Valparaiso, Nebr., Aug. 8, 1918; s. Joseph Emmanual Alexander Alexis and Marjorie Edith Odman; m. May Britt Lennerup, 1954 (div. 1962); children: Carl Erik, Karin Frenze; m. Mildred Craig Bartos, 1966 (dec. 1996); m. Jeanette Strain, Apr. 24, 1999. BS, U. Nebr., 1937; MS, U. Ariz., 1940, PhD, 1949; postgrad., Calif. Inst. Tech., 1939-40, NYU, 1943-44; JD, U. Nebr., 1966. Bar: Nebr. 1966. Chemist Am. Potash and Chem. Corp., 1940-41; mucker Phelps Dodge Corp., Bisbee, Ariz., 1941; instrument man Stanolind Oil and Gas Co., Tulsa, 1941-42; sr. supr. Plum Brook Ordnance Works, Sandusky, Ohio, 1942-43; grad. asst. U. Ariz., Tucson, 1947-48; field engr. Anaconda Copper Corp., Salt Lake City, 1948-49; geologist U.S. Geol. Survey, Washington, 1949-50; phys. sci. adminstr. Office Naval Rsch., Washington, 1950-62; spl. asst. atty. gen. Atty. Gen.-Dept. Rds., 1967-71. Lt. comdr. USN, 1943-46, USNR, 1946-69, ret. Mem. Neb. Bar Assn., Lincoln Bar Assn., Audubon Soc., Am. Legion, Friends of Nebr. State Mus., Nebr. State Hist. Soc., Nebr. Art Assn., Gt. Plains Assn., Rotary (#14), Sigma Xi, Phi Kappa Phi. Home: 1811 S Pershing Rd Lincoln NE 68502-4840

ALEXIS, GERALDINE M., lawyer; b. N.Y.C., Nov. 3, 1948; d. William J. and Margaret Daly; m. Marcus Alexis, June 15, 1969; children: Marcus L., Hilary I., Sean C. BA, U. Rochester, 1971; MBA, JD, Northwestern U., 1976. Bar: Ill. 1976, Calif. 2001, U.S. Dist. Ct. (no. dist.): Calif. 1976, Ill. 1976, U.S. Trial Bar: 1985, U.S. Ct. Appeals (7th cir.): 1986, U.S. Ct. Appeals (5th cir.): 1996, bar: (U.S. Ct. Appeals (9th cir.)) 2002. Law clk. to Hon. John F. Grady, justice U.S. Dist. Ct. (no. dist.) Ill., Chgo., 1976-77; assoc. Sidley & Austin, Chgo., 1977-79, 81-83, ptnr., 1983-2000; advisor U.S. Dept. Justice Office Legal Counsel, Washington, 1979-81; ptnr. McCutchen, Doyle, Brown & Enersen (now Bingham McCutchen LLP), San Francisco, 2001—. Mem.: ABA (co-chair fin. mkts. and instns. com. antitrust sect.), Bar Assn. San Francisco (chair antitrust and trade regulation sect.). Democrat. Office: Bingham McCutchen LLP 3 Embarcadero Ctr San Francisco CA 94111

ALEXIS, NOEL RICHARD, mathematician, educator; arrived in U.S., 1976; s. William and Eileen Alexis; m. Jacqueline Jackman; children: Anthony, Whitney. BA, Wentworth Inst., 1991; MEd, Cambridge Coll., 1993; DEd, U. Sarasota, 2002. Instr. math. Roxbury C.C., Boston, 1991—93; asst. prof. Three Rivers Coll., Norwich, Conn., 1993—96; head dept. math. Carroll Sch., Lincoln, Mass., 1997—98; assoc. prof. Wentworth Inst., Boston, 1991—98; lectr. U. Mass., Boston, 1996—2002; chmn., prof. Lasell Coll., Newton, Mass., 1999—2001; pres. Inst. Advanced Math. Skills, Cambridge and Ocala, Fla., 1997—; mem. grad. faculty Regis Coll., Weston, 2000—02. Pres. Noel R. Alexis & Assocs., Cambridge, 1986—2002; dir. New Francise Inst., Newton, 1999—. Named to Order of Engr., Nat. Soc. Profl. Engrs., Boston, 1997; tng. scholar, Ctr. for Excellence, Boston, 1992. Mem.: Inst. Indsl. Engring. (sr.), Assn. Computing Machinery (sr.), Soc. Mfg. Engrs. (sr.). Office: Inst Advancement Math Skills PO Box 1511 Ocala FL 34478

ALEXOPOULOS, NICOLAOS GEORGE, electrical engineering educator; b. Athens, Greece, Apr. 14, 1942; arrived in US, 1959; s. Yeoryeos A. and Efstathia (Yiannopoulou) A.; m. Sue B. Bunting, June 25, 1966; children: Efstathia Nicole, Christina Ariadne, Theodore Andrew. BSEE, U. Mich., 1965, MSEE, 1967, PhD in elec. engring., 1968. Asst. prof. elec. engring. UCLA, 1969-75, assoc. prof., 1975-81, prof., 1981—96, chmn. dept., 1987—92, assoc. dean faculty affairs, 1986-87; dean The Henry Samueli Sch. Engring. U. Calif., Irvine, 1997—, prof. dept. elec. engring. and computer sci., 1997—. Pres. Phraxos R & D Corp., Santa Monica, Calif., 1986—; cons. aerospace industry, 1970—. Contbr. over 100 articles to profl. jours. NSF rsch. grantee, 1979—. Fellow: IEEE (S.E. Schelkunoff Prize Best Paper Award 1985, 1998, Orange County Sec. Engr. of Yr. 2001). Office: U Calif Irvine Box 2700 Irvine CA 92697-2700

ALEY, SHELLEY B., composition and rhetoric educator; b. Kansas City, Mo., Dec. 28, 1951; d. William Lewis Sellers and Gloria Jean (Shields) Sellers/Miller. BS in Edn., S.W. Mo. State U., 1981, MA in English, 1988; PhD in Composition Studies, Tex. Christian U., 1994. High sch. tchr. Forsyth (Mo.) H.S., 1981-86; lectr. S.W. Mo. State U., Springfield, 1988-91; asst. prof. Cottey Coll., Nevada, Mo., 1993-99; assoc. prof. James Madison U., Harrisonburg, Va., 1999—. Mem. English dept. adv. bd. S.W. Mo. State U., Springfield, 1993-99. Mem. MLA, Mo. Philological Assn., Am. Culture Assn., Coll. Composition & Comm., Modern Lang. Assn. Office: Writing Program James Madison Univ Harrisonburg VA 22807-0001 Office Phone: 540-568-2334.

ALF, MARTHA JOANNE, artist; b. Berkeley, Calif., Aug. 13, 1930; d. Foster Wise and Julia Vivian (Kane) Powell; m. Edward Franklin Alf, Mar. 17, 1951; 1 child, Richard Franklin. BA with distinction, San Diego State U., 1953, MA in Painting, 1963, jr. coll. teaching credential, 1969; MFA in Pictorial Arts, UCLA, 1970. Rsch. asst. Health and Welfare Assn., Seattle, 1956; tchg. asst. in drawing, instr. design San Diego State U., 1963; instr. drawing L.A. Valley Coll., 1970-73, El Camino Coll., Hawthorne, Calif., 1971; instr. drawing and painting L.A. Harbor Coll., Wilmington, Calif., 1971-75; instr. art UCLA Extension, 1971-79. Instr. contemporary art Brand Library Art Ctr., Glendale, Calif., 1973; vis. artist Calif. State Coll., Bakersfield, 1980; freelance art critic Artweek, Oakland, Calif., 1974-77; guest curator Lang Art Gallery, Scripps Coll., Claremont, Calif., 1974. Retrospective exhbn. Fellows Contemporary Art, L.A. Mcpl. Art Gallery, San Francisco Art Inst., 1984; represented in permanent collections L.A. County Mus. Art, Chem. Bank N.Y., Ga. Mus. Art., Israel Mus. Art, Jerusalem, L.A. County Mus. Art, McCrory Corp., N.Y., Metromedic, Inc., L.A., N.Y., San Diego Mus. Art, San Jose Mus., Santa Barbara Mus. Art, Southland Corp., Dallas, Spencer Mus. Art U. Kans., Lawrence, Met. Mus. Art., N.Y., Phoenix Art Mus., Fresno Art Mus., Grand Rapids Art Mus., Orange County Mus. Art, Newport Beach, Calif., Palm Springs Desert Mus., Laguna Art Mus., U. Calif. Santa Barbara Art Gallery, Eli Broad Collection, Santa Monica, U. Va. Bayley Art Mus., Charlottesville; one-woman shows include John Berggruen Gallery, San Francisco, 1977, Forth Worth Art Mus., 1988, Susan Caldwell Gallery, N.Y., 1980, Dorothy Rosenthal Gallery, Chgo., 1982, Eloise Pickard Smith Gallery Cowell Coll. U. Calif., Santa Cruz, 1983, Newspace Gallery, L.A., 1976-85, 90-2004, Henry Gardiner Gallery, Palm Beach, 1986, Tortue Gallery, Santa Monica, 1986, Jan Baum Gallery, L.A., 1988, Trabia Gallery, N.Y., 1990, 871 Fine Arts, San Francisco, 1991, Art Inst. of So. Calif., Laguna Beach, Calif., 1991, Fresno Art Mus., 1992, Mt. San Antonio Coll., Walnut, Calif., 1993; exhibited in group shows at San Diego Mus. of Art, 1964, 67-68, 70-71, 77-78, 83, Whitney Mus. Contemporary Art Biennial, 1975, Newport Harbor Art Mus., 1975, Marion Koogler McNay Art Inst., San Antonio, 1976, Long Beach Mus. Art, 1972, 82, 86, Am. Acad. Arts and Letters, N.Y., 1985, 96, Henry Art Gallery U. Wash., Seattle, 1985, L.A. County Mus. of Art, 1979 (Kay Neilson award 1979), 82, Womens Mus., Washington, 1994, Bakersfield Mus. Art, 1999, Santa Barbara Mus. Art, 2001, Calif. State U., L.A., 2001, Laguna Beach Art Mus., 2001, San Jose Mus. Art, 2003-2004, Pasadena Mus. Calif. Art, 2004, Contemporary Arts Ctr., New Orleans, 2004, Norton Mus. Art, West Palm Beach, Fla., 2004, Hudson River Mus., Yonkers, N.Y., 2004, arcadiana Ctr. for Arts, Lafayette, La., 2005, McDonough Mus. Arts, Youngstown (Ohio) State U., 2005. Nat. Endowment for Arts grantee, 1979, 89; recipient Richard Florsheim Art Fund award, 1996, Calif. Heritage Mus. print commn., 1998. Avocations: body building, walking, reading, keeping journal, bird study and videos. Home: 103 Brooks Ave Venice CA 90291-3254 Office Phone: 310-396-3031. Personal E-mail: alf1@earthlink.net.

ALFA, MICHELLE JOSEPHINE, microbiologist, educator; b. Winnipeg, Man., Canada, Dec. 9, 1953; d. Jim R. and Betty M. Foubert; m. Attahiru S. Alfa; children: Ismaila, Aisha. BSc, U. Man., 1975; MSC, U. NSW, Sydney, Australia, 1980; PhD, U. Alta., Edmonton, Can., 1986. Asst. prof. U. Man., 1989—96, assoc. prof., 1996—2000, prof., 2000—02; asst. dir. microbiology lab. St. Boniface Gen. Hosp., Winnipeg, 1989—2000, asst. dir., 2002—; assoc. prof. Wayne State U., Detroit, 2000—02. Contbr. articles to profl. jours. Bd. dirs., sec. Horace Patterson Found., Winnipeg. Studentship, Alta. Heritage Found., 1981—85, postgrad. fellow, Man. Health Rsch. Coun., 1986—88. Mem.: Assn. for Advancement of Med. Instrumentation., Am. Bd. Microbiology, Can. Coll. Microbiologists (mem. exec. com. 2003—, treas. 2003—). Achievements include invention of artificial test soil. Avocations: mentoring women in science, science education. Home: 51 Ravine Rd Winnipeg MB Canada R2M 5N4 Office: St Boniface Gen Hosp Microbiology Lab L4025 409 Tache Ave Winnipeg MB Canada R2H 2A6 E-mail: malfa@sbgh.mb.ca.

ALFANGE, DEAN, JR., academic administrator, educator; b. N.Y.C., May 6, 1930; s. Dean and Thalia (Perry) A.; m. Barbara Jean Vance, June 6, 1959. AB, Hamilton Coll., 1950; MA, U. Colo., 1960; PhD, Cornell U., 1967. Instr., then asst. prof. govt. Lafayette Coll., Easton, Pa., 1963-67; from asst. prof. to assoc. prof. polit. sci. U. Mass., Amherst, 1967-75, prof., 1975-99, prof. emeritus, 1999—, dean Faculty Social and Behavioral Scis., 1970-75, acting vice chancellor for acad. affairs, 1975-76, 83. Vis. scholar Yale Law Sch., 1977-78, Stanford Law Sch., 1986, 92. Served to 1st lt. USAF, 1952-57. Home: 5 Montague Rd Leverett MA 01054-9725 Office: U Mass Dept Political Science Amherst MA 01003

ALFANO, CHARLES THOMAS, SR., lawyer; b. Suffield, Conn., June 21, 1920; s. Dominick and Rosina (Dimartino) A.; m. Mary Ann Sinatro, Nov. 13, 1954; children: Diane Elizabeth, Andrea Rose, Charles Thomas Jr., Susan Marie. Student, Ill. Coll., 1939-40; BA cum laude, U. Conn., 1943; LL.B., JD, U. Mich., 1948. Bar: Conn. 1948. Since practiced in, Hartford; partner firm Alfano Halloran & Flynn; judge Town Ct. of Suffield, 1949-51, 55-59; mem. Conn. Senate, 1959-77, asst. majority leader, 1966, pres. pro tem, 1967-73, minority leader, 1973-75, v.p. pro tem, 1975-77; corp. counsel Town of Suffield, 1977-83. Dir., chmn. bd. Suffield Savs. Bank; dir. Conn. Water Co. Bd. dirs. Conn. Pub. TV. Served with USNR, 1942-47, PTO. Mem. ABA, ATLA, Conn. Bar Assn., Hartford County Bar Assn., Conn. Trial Lawyers Assn. (bd. dirs.), Hartford Club, Mystic Yacht Club, Mason's Island Yacht Club, N.Y. Athletic Club, KC, Sigma Nu. Home: 50 Marbern Dr Suffield CT 06078-1533 Office: 89 Oak St Hartford CT 06106-1515 also: 53 Mountain Rd Suffield CT 06078-2041 Office Phone: 860-668-0221.

ALFANO, MICHAEL CHARLES, dental school dean; b. Newark, Aug. 8, 1947; s. Michael Ferdinand and Anne Marie (Barrington) A.; m. JoAnn Mary Coletta, Mar. 30, 1969; children: Michael Anthony, Kristin Lynn. Student, Rutgers U., 1965-67; DMD, U. Medicine and Dentistry of N.J., 1971; postgrad. in periodontics, Harvard U., 1971-74; PhD, MIT, 1975. Asst. prof. dentistry Fairleigh Dickinson U., Hackensack, NJ, 1974-77, assoc. prof., 1977-80, prof. with tenure, 1980-82, dir. Oral Health Rsch. Ctr., 1977-82, asst. dean grad. affairs and rsch., 1981-82; v.p. dental rsch. Block Drug Co., Inc., Jersey City, 1982-84, sr. v.p. R&D, 1987-98, bd. dirs., 1988-98, pres. dental products divsn., 1985-88, cons. office of chief exec., 1990-98; dean Coll. Dentistry NYU, 1998—, prof. basic scis. & periodontology Coll. Dentistry, 1998—; bd. dirs. Dentsply Inc., 2001—. Cons. Nat. Inst. Dental Rsch., Bethesda, Md., 1976-82; apptd. nat. adv. dental rsch. coun. NIH, Bethesda, 1994-98; apptd. vis. prof. Nat. Dairy Coun., Chgo., 1981; vis. sr. scientist Fairleigh Dickinson U., 1982-88; adj. prof. U. Medicine and Dentistry of N.J., Newark, 1985-2003; mem. sci. adv. coun. Office of Gov., State of N.J., 1981-84. Editor: Symposium on Nutrition, 1976; contbr. articles to profl. jours. and chpts. to books; patentee in field. Trustee Found. of U. Medicine and Dentistry of N.J., 1988-98, N.Y. State Dental Found., 2004—; mem. adv. bd. Columbia U. Sch. Dental and Oral Surgery, 1990-98; mem. program com. Am. Fund for Dental Health, 1991-93; bd. overseers Forsyth Dental Ctr., Boston, 1992-99, U. Pa. Coll. Dental Medicine, 1992-2004; trustee Santa Fe Group, 1998—; founding dir. Friends of Nat. Inst. of Dental Rsch., 1998—; dir. Dentsply Internat., 2001—. Recipient Leadership citation Newark YMCA, 1966, Disting. Alumnus award U. Medicine and Dentistry of N.J., 1986, Harvard U. Sch. Dental Medicine, 1998; NIH rsch. grantee, 1974-82; NIH postdoctoral fellow, 1971-74. Fellow Am. Coll. Dentists, Am. Coll. of Prosthodontists (hon. fellow), Internat. Congress Oral Implantologists (hon. life 2002-); mem. Am. Acad. Oral Med. (hon. mem., 2003), ADA (cons., Future of Dentistry Commn. 1999-2001, bd. govs. student clinicians 2000—, Nat. Achievement award 1978), Internat. Assn. for Dental Rsch., Am. Assn. for Dental Rsch. (pres. N.J. chpt. 1985, Hein Pub. Svc. award 2004, Shils award 2004), Am. Inst. Nutrition. Independent. Roman Catholic. Achievements include 8 patents; discovery of role of Vitamin C in mucous membrane barrier function. Home: 29 Washington Sq W Apt 5C New York NY 10011-9132 Office: NYU Coll Dentistry 345 E 24th St New York NY 10010-4086 Business E-Mail: mca1@nyu.edu.

ALFANO, ROBERT R., science educator, engineering educator; BS, Fairleigh Dickinson U., Teaneck, N.J., 1963, MS, 1964; PhD, NYU, N.Y., 1972. Rschr. GTE, N.Y.C., 1964-72; from asst. prof. to prof. CUNY, N.Y.C., 1972-88, disting. prof. sci., 1988—; dir. N.Y. State Ctr. for Adv. Tech. in Ultrafast Photonics, 1992—; co-dir. NASA Ctr. for Optical Sensing and

Imaging, 2003—; dir. DOD Ctr. for Nanoscale Photonic Emitters and Sensors, 2003—. Dir. Ctr. on Laser in Medicine, Dept. Energy, 1998-2002. Editor: Biological Events Probed by Ultrafast Laser Spectroscopy, 1982, Semiconductors Probed by Ultrafast Laser Spectroscopy, 1985, The Supercontinuum Laser Source, 1989, Photonics: Nonlinear Optics and Ultrafast Phenomena, 1990; contbr. 680 articles to profl. jours.; 92 patents in field. A.P. Sloan fellow, OSA fellow, APS fellow. Fellow: IEEE. Office Phone: 212-650-5531. Business E-Mail: Alfano@sci.ccny.cuny.edu.

ALFARO, VICTOR, fashion designer; b. Mexico; s. Hector and Pilar A. Grad., Fashion Inst. Tech., 1987. Apprentice with Mary Ann Restivo, N.Y.C., 1987-90, with Joseph Abboud, 1990; designer Victor Alfaro collection, 1990—; sr. v.p., creative dir. Wet Seal, 2003—04. Recipient Perry Ellis award for new talent CFDA, 1994.

ALFERINK, LARRY ALLEN, psychology educator; b. Holland, Mich., May 26, 1948; s. Benjamin and Dorothy (DeVisser) A.; m. Laura Rae Lawrence, Aug. 29, 1970; children: Kristine Jennifer Mertens, Paul Raymond. BA, Western Mich. U., Kalamazoo, 1970; MS, Utah State U., 1973, PhD, 1975. Instr. psychology Drake U., Des Moines, 1974, asst. prof., 1975-79, assoc. prof., 1979-83, chair dept., 1981-83, assoc. prof., 1983—93; prof. Psychology Ill. State U., Normal, 1993—, chair dept. psychology, 1983-98, acting assoc. dean grad. studies, 1998-2000, asst. to the assoc. v.p. for undergrad. studies, 2000—03, interim dir. honors program, 2002—04. Chmn. exec. com. Coun. Applied Masters Programs in Psychology, exec. com. Coun. Grad. Depts. in Psychology, 1991-96; mem. Ill. Consortium Ednl. Opportunity Programs Adv. Bd., 1998-2004, chmn., 1999-2001. Mem. APA (sec.-treas. divsn. 25 1995-2004, chair Master's Edn. Working Group, mem. coalition for Psychology in the schs. and edn. 2002—, pres.-elect divsn. 25 2005), AAAS, Assn. Behavior Analysis, Mid-Am. Assn. Behavior Analysis (treas. 2001-2003, pres. 2003-2004). Office: Ill State U PO Box 4620 Normal IL 61790-4620 E-mail: alferink@ilstu.edu.

ALFERT, PETER WAYNE, lawyer; b. Oakland, Calif., July 12, 1953; s. Max F. and Elizabeth (Muller) A.; m. Nova Wallace, Aug. 6, 1982; children: Christopher, Erin, Marc. BA cum laude, St. Mary's, Moraga, Calif., 1975; JD cum laude, U. San Francisco, 1978. Bar: Calif. 1978; U.S. Dist. Ct. (no. dist.) Calif. 1978; U.S. Ct. Appeals (9th cir.) 1978. Assoc. Ginder, Kelly & McGray, Walnut Creek, Calif., 1978-82, Law Offices of Peter J. Hinton, Walnut Creek, 1982-83, Hinton & Pashkowski, Walnut Creek, 1983-87; ptnr. Hinton & Alfert, Walnut Creek, 1987—. Lectr. in field. Recipient Am. Jurisprudence awards, Evidence and Family Law. Mem. ABA, Calif. Bar Assn., Contra Costa County Bar Assn., Am. Trial Lawyers Assn., Calif. Trial Lawyers Assn., Alameda Contra Costa Trial Lawyers Assn. (bd. dirs. 1984-99, pres. 1999-2000). Office: Hinton & Alfert 1646 N California Blvd Ste 600 Walnut Creek CA 94596-4100

ALFIDI, RALPH JOSEPH, retired radiologist; b. Rome, Apr. 20, 1932; s. Luca and Angeline (Panella) A.; m. Rose Esther Senesac, Sept. 3, 1956 (div. 1991); children: Suzanne, Lisa, Christine, Katherine, Mary, John; m. Mariella Boller, Aug. 29, 1992. AB, Ripon (Wis.) Coll., 1955; MD, Marquette U., Milw., 1959. Intern Oakwood Hosp., Dearborn, Mich., 1959-60; resident, chief resident, A.C.S. fellow U. Va., 1960-63; practice medicine, specializing in radiology Cleve., 1965-2000; staff mem. Cleve. Clinic, 1965-78, head dept. hosp. radiology, 1968-78; dir. dept. radiology Univ. Hosps., Cleve., 1978-92; prof. radiology U. N.Mex., Albuquerque, 2000—03. Cons. VA Hosp., Cleve.; chmn. dept. radiology Case Western Res. U. Sch. Medicine, 1978-92; chmn. staff Cleve. Clinic Found., 1975-76. Author: Complications and Legal Implications of Special Procedures, 1972, Computed Tomography of the Human Body: An Atlas of Normal Anatomy, 1977; editor: Whole Body Computed Tomography, 1977; contbr. articles to radiology jours. Served to capt., M.C. U.S. Army Res., 1963-65 Picker Found. grantee, 1969-70; NRC grantee, 1969-70 Mem. Radiol. Soc. N. Am., Am. Roentgen Ray Soc., Am. Heart Assn., Soc. Cardiovascular Radiology, Soc. Gastrointestinal Radiology, Soc. Computed Body Tomography (pres. 1977-78), Eastern Radiol. Soc., Cleve. Radiol. Soc. (pres. 1976-77), Las Campanas Club. Roman Catholic. Achievements include discovery of renal splanchnic steal syndrome: aka Alfidi's Syndrome. Home: 81 Calle Ventoso W Santa Fe NM 87506-0141

ALFIERI, VINCENT, lawyer; BA, Fordham U., 1975; JD, NY Law Sch., 1980. Bar: NY, US Dist. Ct., So. and Ea. Dists. NY 1981, US Ct. Appeals, Second Cir. 1982, US Dist. Ct., No. Dist. NY. Ptnr., group leader Labor and Employment Bryan Cave LLP, NYC. Office: Bryan Cave LLP 1290 Ave of the Americas New York NY 10104 Office Phone: 212-541-2270. E-mail: valfieri@bryancave.com.

ALFINI, JAMES JOSEPH, dean, educator, lawyer; b. Yonkers, NY, Oct. 12, 1943; s. James Joseph and Olga (Genish) Alfini; m. Carol Miller, Dec. 23, 1966; children: David James, Michael Steven. AB, Columbia U., 1965; JD, Northwestern U., 1972. Bar: N.Y. 1973, Ill. 1976, U.S. Dist. Ct. (no. dist.) Ill. 1976, U.S. Ct. Appeals (7th cir.) 1982, U.S. Supreme Ct. 1977. Reginald Heber Smith cmty. lawyer Monroe County Legal Assistance Corp., Rochester, NY, 1972—73; asst. dir. rsch. Am. Judicature Soc., Chgo., 1973—77, dir. rsch., 1977—80, asst. exec. dir. programs, 1980—85; adj. prof. law IIT Chgo.-Kent Sch. Law, 1978—85; assoc. prof. law Fla. State U., Tallahassee, 1985—90, prof. law, 1990—91; dean, prof. No. Ill. U. Coll. Law, 1991—97, prof., 1997—2003; pres., dean South Tex. Coll. Law, Houston, 2003—. Co-author: (book) Making Jury Instructions Understandable, 1982, Judicial Conduct and Ethics, 1990, Judicial Conduct and Ethics, 2d edit., 1995, Judicial Conduct and Ethics, 3d edit., 2000, Mediation Theory and Practice, 2000; bd. editors: jour. Ohio State Jour. Dispute Resolution, 1994—98. Mem. governing bd. Cook County Legal Assistance Found., 1981—83; chmn. coord. coun. Nat. Ct. Orgns., 1982—83; arbitration and mediation rules com. Fla. Supreme Ct., 1988—91; mem. Ill. Jud. Ethics com., 1993—97; bd. govs. Chgo. Coun. Lawyers. 1st lt. U.S. Army, 1965—69. Decorated Commendation medal U.S. Army. Mem.: ACLU, ABA (sect. dispute resolution, chmn.), Law and Soc. Assn., Am. Law Inst. Democrat. Home: 3928 Southwestern Houston TX 77005 Office Phone: 713-646-1819.

ALFONE, JOHN R., school system administrator; b. New Haven, Conn., Sept. 13, 1952; s. Salvatore A. and Veronica Monahan M. Alfone; m. Christine (Tina) A. Balog, June 21, 1975; children: Carissa Ann, Nicole Maria. BS in Pharmacy, Bklyn. Coll. Pharmacy, 1975; MS in Elem. Edn., So. Conn. State U., 1992; EdD, U. Hartford, 1997. Cert. Conn. Prin. St. Vincent de Paul Sch., East Haven, Conn., 1990—97, St. Gabriel Sch., Milford, Conn., 1997—2001; coord. elem. edn. Diocese of Bridgeport, 2001—02, asst. supt. sch., 2002—. Parish coun. St. Pius X Ch., Fairfield, Conn., 2002—04. Mem.: Phi Delta Kappa (assoc.). Roman Catholic.

ALFONSO, ANTONIO ESCOLAR, surgeon; b. Manila, Nov. 25, 1943; came to U.S., 1968, naturalized, 1978; s. Ricardo Lagdameo and Marita (Escolar) Alfonso; m. Teresita Nazareno, Apr. 25, 1970; children: Margaretta, Roberto. AB cum laude, Ateneo U., 1963; MD cum laude, U. Philippines, 1968. Diplomate: Am. Bd. Surgery. Intern U. Philippines-Philippine Gen. Hosp., 1968; instr. surgery Temple U., Phila., 1968-72; sr. fellow surg. oncology Meml. Sloan-Kettering Cancer Ctr., N.Y.C., 1972-74; dir. head and neck surgery svc. SUNY Downstate Med. Ctr., Bklyn., 1974—, assoc. dir. divsn. surg. oncology, 1974—, asst. prof. surgery, 1974-77, assoc. prof., 1977-82, prof., 1982—, vice-chmn. dept. surgery, 1988—. Chmn. dept. surgery Bklyn. Hosp., 1982-88; chmn. Dept. Surgery L.I. Coll. Hosp., 1988—; cons. head and neck surgery Bklyn. VA Hosp., 1974— Author: Principles of Surgery Oncology; contbr. articles to profl. med. jours., chpts. in med. books. Recipient rsch. essay prize N.Y. Colon and Rectal Surg. Soc., 1973; grantee Am. Cancer Soc., 1978 Mem. ACS (bd. govs. Bklyn.-L.I. chpt., gov. 1998—), Assn. Acad. Surgeons, Am. Soc. Clin. Oncology, Am. Assn. Cancer Edn., Soc. Head and Neck Surgeons, N.Y. Surg. Soc. (treas. 1994, v.p. 1998, pres. 1999), Bklyn. Surg. Soc. (pres. 1986-87), N.Y. Cancer Soc. (v.p. 1986-87, pres.-elect 1987-88, pres. 1988-89), Soc. Surg. Oncology, N.Y. Head and Neck Soc. (sec. 1993-97, pres. 1998), N.Y. Soc. Colon and Rectal Surgeons, Triboro Dirs. of Surgery Assn. (pres. 1989—), Phi Kappa Phi. Roman Catholic. Home: 50 Olive Pl Flushing NY 11375-5938 Office: LI Coll Hosp Dept Surgery 340 Henry St Brooklyn NY 11201-5514 Office Phone: 718-875-3244.

ALFONSO, MARIANA, education educator, researcher; b. Córdoba, Argentina, 1975; arrived in U.S., 1999; d. Jorge Heraldo Alfonso and Maria Cristina Dalmagro; m. Ricardo Parodi, July 31, 2004. Licenciada in Econ., U. Nacional of Córdoba, 1997; MPhil, PhD, Columbia U., 2004. Lectr. econ. U. Nacional of Córdoba, 1997—99, Inst. U. Aeronautico, Cordoba, 1999; sr. rsch. asst. Cmty. Coll. Rsch. Ctr., N.Y., 2000—04; postdoctral rsch. assoc. Brown U., Providence, 2004—. Cons. The Coll. Bd., N.Y., 2003. Contbr. articles pub. to profl. jour. Scholar Fulbright Scholarship, Fulbright Commn., Argentina, 1999—2001. Mem.: Comperative Internat. Edn. Soc., Assn. for the Study of Higher Edn., Latin Am. Studies Assn. Achievements include orgn. com. ann. meeting Edn. Across the Am. Tchrs. Coll., Columbia Univ. 2003, 04. Avocations: tennis, reading, literature. Office: Taubman Ctr for Pub Policy Brown Univ 67 George St Providence RI 02912

ALFONSO, ROBERT JOHN, university administrator; b. NYC, Dec. 17, 1928; s. Robert Richard and Bertha Rose (Schmitt) A.; m. Martha Sue Ralston, June 9, 1956; children: Allison Denise, Robert John, Andrea Diane (dec.). BA, Roberts Wesleyan Coll., 1952; postgrad., N.Y. U., 1952-53; PhD, Mich. State U., 1962. High sch. English tchr. Syracuse, N.Y., 1956-58, Billings, Mont., 1958—59; asst. to dean Coll. Edn., Mich. State U., 1959-60; asst. prof. edn. Queens Coll., N.Y.C., 1962-64; assoc. exec. sec. Assn. for Supervision and Curriculum Devel., 1964-67; assoc. prof. curriculum and supervision Coll. Edn., U. Ala., 1967-68; asst. dean instrn. and grad. studies, prof. Coll. Edn., Kent State U. (Ohio), 1968-71; dean Coll. Edn. and Grad. Sch. Edn., also prof., 1971-80, assoc. v.p., dean faculties, 1980-82; v.p. acad. affairs East Tenn. State U., Johnson City, 1984-94, v.p. emeritus, 1994—. Vis. prof. U. Ga., 1982-83. Author: Instructional Supervision: A Behavior System, 1975, 2d edit., 1981; Asst. editor: Mich. Jour. Secondary Edn, 1959-62. Bd. dirs. Nat. Interagy. Coun. on Smoking and Health, 1964-67; Inter-Profl. Rsch. Commn. on Pupil Pers. Svcs., 1965-68. 1st lt. USMC, 1953—56, ret. lt. col. USMCR. Recipient Alumnus of Year award Roberts Wesleyan Coll., 1967 Mem. Assn. for Supervision and Curriculum Devel. (dir.), Am. Assn. Sch. Adminstrs., Nat. Council Tchrs. English (dir. 1965-68), Ohio Assn. for Supervision and Curriculum Devel. (pres.), Am. Ednl. Research Assn., Ohio Congress Sch. Adminstr. Orgns. (v.p.), Coun. Profs. Instrnl. Supervision (pres.), Phi Delta Kappa, Kappa Delta Pi, Phi Kappa Phi. Methodist. Home: 104 Ridgemont Rd Johnson City TN 37601-3940 Office: East Tenn State U Dossett Hall Johnson City TN 37614 E-mail: alfonso@xtn.net.

ALFORD, BOBBY RAY, otolaryngologist, educator, academic administrator; b. Dallas, May 30, 1932; s. Bryant J. and Edith M. (Garrett) A.; m. Othelia Jerry Dorn, Aug. 28, 1953; children: Bradley Keith, Raye Lynn, Alan Scott. AS, Tyler Jr. Coll., 1951; postgrad., U. Tex., 1951-52; MD, Baylor U., 1956. Diplomate Am. Bd. Otolaryngology (dir. 1972-90, pres. 1985-86, exec. v.p. 1986-90). Intern Jefferson Davis Hosp., Houston, 1956-57; resident Baylor U. Coll. Medicine Affiliated Hosps. Program, 1957-60; mem. faculty Baylor U. Coll. Medicine, 1962—, prof. otolaryngology, 1966—, chmn. dept., 1967-95, 96—, v.p. and dean acad. and clin. affairs, 1984-88, disting. service prof., 1985—, interim chmn. dept. surgery, 1983—84, exec. v.p., dean medicine, 1988—2004, chancellor, 2004—; pres., CEO BaylorMedCare, Houston, 1994-96; chmn., CEO Nat. Space Biomed. Rsch. Inst., 1997—. Rev. panel surgeon gen. on neurol. and sensory disease USPHS, 1965-67; cons. Nat. Inst. Neurol. Disease and Stroke, 1970-74; cons. to surgeon gen. U.S. Army, 1963-73; nat. adv. coun. Neurol. and Communicative Disorders and Stroke, NIH, 1977-80, Deafness and Other Communicative Disorders, 1991-95, NASA, 1992-95, chmn. aerospace medicine adv. com., 1993-94, chmn. life microgravity scis. and applications adv. com., 1993-95. Author: Neurological Aspects of Auditory and Vestibular Disorders, 1964, Electrophysiologic Evaluation in Otolaryngology, 1997; chief editor: A.M.A. Archives of Otolaryngology, 1970-79. Bd. dirs. Houston Acad. Medicine Tex. Med. Ctr. Libr., 1983-94. Recipient Herman Johnson award Baylor U. Coll. Medicine, 1956, NASA Disting. Pub. Svc. award, 1992, 95, Jeffries Aerospace Medicine and Life Scis. Rsch. award Am. Inst. Aeronautics and Astronautics, 2003; spl. NIH fellow Johns Hopkins Hosp., 1961-62. Fellow ACS (bd. govs. 1977-82); mem. AIAA (Jeffries Aerospace Medicine and Life Scis. Rsch. award 2003), NAS Inst. Medicine, Am. Laryngol. Assn., Soc. Univ. Otolaryngologists-Head and Neck Surgeons (sec. 1965-69), Am. Otol. Soc., Assn. Acad. Dept. Otolaryngology-Head and Neck Surgery, Am. Laryngol., Rhinol. and Otol. Soc., Am. Soc. Head and Neck Surgery (councillor 1978-80) Am. Acad. Otolaryngology-Head and Neck Surgery (pres. 1981), Am. Coun. Otolaryngology-Head and Neck Surgery (pres. 1980-81), Am. Bronchoesophagological Assn., Soc. Head and Neck Surgeons, Acoustical Soc. Am., Collegium Oto-Rhino-Laryngologicum Amicitiae Sacrum, Johns Hopkins U. Soc. Scholars, Univ. Space Rsch. Assn. (bd. dirs. 1991-95), Tex. Corinthian Yacht Club (bd. dirs. 1978-80, 94-95), Doctors Club (bd. govs. 1967-70, 91-93), Petroleum Club, Lakewood Yacht Club, Alpha Omega Alpha. Office: 6501 Fannin Ste NA102 Houston TX 77030 Office Phone: 713-798-5906. Business E-Mail: balford@bcm.edu.

ALFORD, FRANCES HOLLIDAY, artist, retired elementary school educator; b. Houston, Tex., Oct. 1, 1945; d. Samuel and Nancy Hayes Holliday; m. John R. Alford Jr., Oct. 25, 1996. MEd, U. of Ariz., 1970—72. Cert. Tchr. Tex., 1980. Tchr. Tex. Pub. Schools, 1989—94. Vol. U.S. Peace Corps, 1979—80; trustee The Congl. Ch. of Austin, Austin, Tex.; chair, director's cir., fund raising com. Nat. Peace Corps Assn., Washington, 2001—03; pres. Friends of Korea, Washington. Mem.: AAUW (assoc.), Coun. for Exceptional Children, Austin Area Textile Artists (assoc.), 1812 Club (assoc.). Non-Partisan. Protestant/ Congregational. Avocations: travel, art quilting, philanthrophy. Home: 8100 Hickory Creek Dr Austin TX 78735 Personal E-mail: francesholliday@aol.com.

ALFORD, REBECCA DIANNE, food products executive; b. Chatanooga, Ga., Oct. 3, 1967; d. Leslie Bentley and Gladys Irene Bean; m. Steve F. Alford, May 4, 1985; children: Rubin Cain, Sydni Leann. GED, Stephenville, Tex. Christian columnist Stephenville Empire Tribune, Tex., 1996—2000; mgr. Harmon & Creed, Lipan, 1999—, Jack in the Box, Palestine, 2001; gen. mgr. Dairy Queen, Tyler, 2002—03; brazer Snoke Spl. Products Co., Inc., 2003—. Contbr. poetry to anthologies, columns to papers. Sec. exec. com. Erath County Rep., Stephenville, 1999 Personal E-mail: droflab@yahoo.com.

ALFORD, RENEE MARIE, speech pathology/audiology services professional, educator; d. James, Jr. and Claudia Mae Alford, Aloysius (Stepfather) and Emily Patricia Chisley (Stepmother). BS in Speech and Lang. Pathology, U. DC, 1986, MS in Speech and Lang. Pathology, 1993. Cert. speech-lang. pathology Va., lic. speech/lang. disorders PreK-12 Va.; cert. early/primary edn. PreK-3 Va., devel. reading assessment Fairfax County Pub. Schs. Tchr. Fairfax County Pub. Schs., Alexandria, Va., 1990—, speech and lang. pathologist, 1990—2000, Chesapeake Ctr., Inc., Springfield, Va., 1998. Presenter mentoring program Fairfax County Pub. Schs., Alexandria, 2001—; presenter troops tchrs. program Old Dominion U., Ft. Belvior, Va., 2002—. Clinic team coord. Mid-Atlantic Pom and Dance Assn.; team coord. Mid Atlantic Poand Dance Assn. Named Outstanding Young Women of Am., 1988; scholar, U. DC, 1982, 1983; Dept. of Edn. Minority Tng. grantee, 1988—90. Mem.: Mid-Altantic Pomand Dance Assn. (team coord.), Am. Speech-Lang. Hearing Assn. (life cert. clin. competence in speech-lang. pathology), Nat. Allied Health Honor Soc., Delta Sigma Theta (life scholar 1984), Phi Delta Kappa (life). Avocations: dance choreography, pom pon coach. Personal E-mail: teachernva2000@aol.com.

ALFORD, WILLIAM LANIER, elementary school educator; b. Milledgeville, Ga., July 12, 1954; s. Mack Furman and Dorothy Lanier Alford; m. Roya Smith Alford, Feb. 27, 1977; children: William M., Tyler L. BMed, Ga. Coll., 1976; MMed, Shorter Coll., 1993; degree in ednl. adminstr., Columbus State U., 2003. Tchr. Staley Jr. HS, Americus, Ga., 1976—77, Perry Jr. HS, Perry, Ga., 1977—83, Model HS, Rome, Ga., 1983—87, Model Mid. Sch., Rome, 1987—90, Lafayette Mid. Sch., Lafayette, Ga., 1990—94, Northside Mid. Sch., Warner Robins, Ga., 1994—. Mem.: Profl. Assn. of Educators, Ga. Music Educators Assn. Bapt. Avocations: golf, church work. Home: 1201 Settlers Trail Warner Robins GA 31088 Office Phone: 478-329-2239. E-mail: b.alford@cox.net.

ALFORD, WILLIAM P., law educator; b. Brookline, Mass., May 29, 1948; s. Hyman and Rose B. (Glaser) Alford. BA in Am. Studies, Amherst Coll., 1970; LLB, St. John's Coll., Cambridge U., 1972; MA in Chinese Studies, Yale U., 1974, MA in Chinese History, 1975; JD, Harvard U., 1977. Bar: DC 1977, US Ct. Appeals DC Cir. 1978, US Supreme Ct. 1981. Assoc. Fried, Frank, Harris, Shriver & Jacobson, Washington, 1977-82; acting prof. law UCLA, 1982-86, prof., 1986-90; Henry L. Stimson prof. law Harvard Law Sch., Cambridge, Mass., 1990—, dir. East Asian legal studies, 1990—, assoc. dean. grad. program and internat. legal studies, 2002—03, vice dean, 2003—. Adj. prof. Georgetown U. Law Ctr., Washington, 1980-82; cons. Ford Found., NYC, 1982, Internat. Adv. Bd., Washington, 1986—; mem. exec. com. law Assn. Asian Studies, 1983—; cons. Assn. Am. Schs., 1983—; mem. legal edn. com. bd. dirs. Exch. with China, NYC; dispute resolution panelist U.S.-Can. Free Trade Agreement. Contbr. articles to profl. journals. O'Melveny & Myers grantee, 1986. Mem. Internat. Law Inst. (adv. bd. publs. 1985—, Kluwer prize newsletter 1985), Phi Delta Phi (hon.). Office: Harvard Law Sch 1563 Massachusetts Ave Cambridge MA 02138 Office Phone: 617-495-4693. Office Fax: 617-495-8129. Business E-Mail: alford@law.harvard.edu.*

ALFRED, R. See BEATTY, ROBERT

ALFRED, STEPHEN JAY, retired lawyer; b. N.Y.C., Aug. 15, 1934; s. George J. Alfred and Janet (Brenner) Miller; m. Nora Richman, June 24, 1956 (div. 1980); children: Deborah Susan, Lynda Beth, Bruce David, Julianne Richman; m. Lynne Belofsky Durchslag, Jan. 10, 1981 (div. 1992); m. Rita G. Hungate, Aug. 23, 1997. AB, Princeton U., 1956; JD, Harvard U., 1959. Bar: Ohio 1959. From assoc. to ptnr. Squire, Sanders & Dempsey, Cleve., 1959—97; councilman City of Shaker Heights, Ohio, 1972—79, 1981, mayor, 1984—91; exec. dir. Common Cause/Ga., 1998—2001; ret., 2001. Gen. chmn. Cleve. Tax Inst., 1981. Contbr. articles to profl. jours. Trustee Citizens League of Cleve., 1976-83, Com. for Sandy Springs, Atlanta, 1998-2001, vice-chair, 1999-2000; trustee Beech Brook Children's Home, Orange, Ohio, 1968-84, pres., 1971-72, treas., 1979-81; pres. Lomond Assn., Shaker Heights, 1965-67, Harvard U. Law Sch. Assn. of Cleve., 1982; active Peoria County Govt. Study Commn., Peoria, 2000-01; govt. vision task force Peoria Area C. of C., 2001-02; bd. dirs. Ill. Campaign for Polit. Reform, Chgo., 2000—, v.p., 2002—; bd. dirs. Mayors Vision 2020, Peoria, 2002—, Counseling and Family Svcs., Peoria, 2002—, v.p., 2003-04, pres. 2004-05; exec. dir. Ctrl. Ill. Biomed. Rsch. Group, 2000-02, vice-chmn., 2001-02; assoc. bd. dirs. WCBU, Peoria, 2001—, v.p., 2003-05, pres., 2005—. Democrat. Jewish. E-mail: sjalfred@aol.com.

ALFRED, SUELLEN, English education educator; b. May 2, 1941; d. Andrew and Freeda (Murray) A. BA, Carson-Newman Coll., 1963; MA, Ga. State U., 1969; EdD, U. Tenn., 1991. Cert. secondary English, gifted edn. Prof. curriculum and instrn. Tenn. Tech. U., Cookeville, 1990—. Pub. spkr. current issues in edn. Co-author: Teaching Through Stories: Yours, Mine, and Theirs, 1998; editor Tenn. English Jour.; co-editor: Southern Voices in Every Direction, 1996, English Jour.; contbr. articles to profl. jours.; author poems. NEH fellow Vanderbilt U., 1984. Mem. ASCD, NEA, Nat. Coun. Tchrs. English, Internat. Reading Assn., Tenn. Edn. Assn. (comms. com. 1978-79), Tenn. Tech. U. Edn. Assn., Tenn. Coun. Tchrs. English (pres. 1993-94, co-editor Tenn. English jour., Excellence in Tchg. of English award 1996). Office: Tenn Tech U PO Box 5042 Cookeville TN 38505-0001 Office Phone: 931-372-3824. E-mail: salfred@tntech.edu.

ALGEO, JOHN THOMAS, association executive, retired educator; b. St. Louis, Nov. 12, 1930; s. Thomas George and Julia Winifred (Wathen) A.; m. Adele Marie Silbereisen, Sept. 6, 1958; children: Thomas John, Catherine Marie. EdB cum laude, U. Miami, 1955; MA, U. Fla., 1957, PhD, 1960. Instr. Fla. State U., Tallahassee, 1959-61; from asst. to full prof. U. Fla., Gainesville, 1961-71, asst. dean grad. sch., 1969-71, dir. program in linguistics, 1969-71; prof. U. Ga., Athens, 1971-88, dir. program in linguistics, 1974-79, head dept. English, 1975-79, alumni found. disting. prof., 1988-94; nat. pres. Theosophical Soc. in Am., Wheaton, Ill., 1993—2002; internat. v.p. Theosophical Soc., Adyar, India, 2002—. Mem. gen. coun. Theosophical Soc., Adyar, India, 1993—; dir. Manor Found. Ltd., Sydney, Australia, 1995—; accreditation cons. So. Assn. Colls. and Schs., Atlanta, 1967-90; cons. NEH, Washington, 1974-94; dir. Commn. on the English Lang., Nat. Coun. Tchrs. of English, Urbana, Ill., 1976-82; del. Am. Coun. Learned Socs., N.Y.C., 1984-87; cons. in lang. and lexicography Cambridge Univ. Press, N.Y.C., 1987-93; cons. in Am. usage Kenkyusha Ltd., Tokyo, 1991-99; cons. Webster's New World Dictionary, 4th edit., Cleve., 1993-95. Author: Problems in the Origins and Development of the English Language, 1966, 5th edit., 2004, On Defining the Proper Name, 1973, Exercises in Contemporary English, 1974, Reincarnation Explored, 1987, Reincarnatie in Kaart gebracht, 1990, Fifty Years "Among the New Words": A Dictionary of Neologisms, 1941-91, 1991, Eigo no kigen to hatatsu, 1991, Reinkarnation: Evolution der Seele, 1991, 96, Reinkarnation i ny belysning, 1994, Investigando a reencarnacao, 1996, Unlocking the Door: Studies in The Key to Theosophy, 2001; co-author: English: An Introduction to Language, 1970, Spelling: Sound to Letter, 1971, The Origins and Development of the English Language, 1982, 5th edit., 2004, Elements of Literature, Sixth Course: Literature of Britain, 1989, The Power of Thought, 2001, Pensamento: Oque e e como usar, 2003; editor: American Speech, 1972-81, Thomas Pyles: Selected Essays on English Usage, 1979, Among the New Words, American Speech, 1987-97, Cambridge History of the English Language, vol. 6, English in North America, 2001, 02, The Quest, 1997-2003, The Letters of H.P. Blavatsky, vol. 1, 2003; assoc. editor: The Oxford Companion to the English Language, 1992; mem. editl. bd. Jour. of English Linguistics, 1970—, Internat. Jour. Lexicography, 1990-93, World Englishes, 1996—, Names, 1997—, Language Problems Language Planning, 1997-99, Studies in English Language, 1987—. Sgt. U.S. Army, 1951-54, Korea. Fellow Guggenheim Found., London, 1986-87; Fulbright scholar U. Coll. London, Eng., 1986-87. Mem. Am. Dialect Soc. (pres. 1979), Am. Name Soc. (pres. 1984), Internat. Assn. Univ. Profs. English, Internat. Linguistic Assn., Ea. Order Internat. Co-Freemasonry, Internat. Phonetic Assn., Linguistic Assn. of the U.S. and Can., Linguistic Soc. Am., Modern Lang. Assn. Am., Philological Soc., Southeastern Conf. on Linguistics (pres. 1970-71), Dictionary Soc. N.Am. (pres. 1995-97), Theosophical Soc. (nat. pres. 1993-2002, internat. v.p. 2002-), Ea. Order Internat. Co-Freemasonry (adminstr. 2002—). Democrat. Home: PO Box 80206 Athens GA 30608-0206 E-mail: johnalgeo@aol.com.

ALGER, CHADWICK FAIRFAX, political scientist, educator; b. Chambersburg, Pa., Oct. 9, 1924; s. Herbert and Thelma (Drawbaugh) A.; m. Elinor Reynolds, Aug. 28, 1948; children: Mark, Scott, Laura, Craig. BA, Ursinus Coll., 1949, LLD, 1979; MA, Johns Hopkins U., 1950; PhD, Princeton, 1958. Internat. relations specialist Dept. Navy, 1950-54; instr. Swarthmore Coll., 1957; faculty Northwestern U., Evanston, Ill., 1958-71, prof. polit. sci., 1966-71, dir. internat. relations program, 1967-71; Mershon prof. polit. sci. and pub. policy Ohio State U., 1971-95, emeritus prof., 1995—, dir. transnat. intellectual cooperation program, 1971-80, dir. world affairs program, Mershon Ctr., 1980-88, coord. working group on global rels. and peace studies, 1988-95, acting dir. univ. ctr. for internat. studies, 1990-91. Vis. prof. UN affairs N.Y.U., 1962-63 Author: Internationalization from Local Areas: Beyond Interstate Relations, 1987, Perceiving, Understanding and Coping with World Relations in Everyday Life, 1993, The United Nations System: Potential for the Twenty-First Century, 1998; co-author: Simulation in International Relations, 1963, You and Your Community in the World, 1978, Conflicts and Crisis of International Order: New Tasks for Peace Research, 1985, A Just Peace Through Transformation: Cultural, Economic and Political Foundations for Change, 1988, The United Nations System: The Policies of Member States, 1995; contbr. articles to profl. jours. Mem. Trade Coun., State of Ohio, 1984-87. Served with USNR, 1943-46. Recipient Disting. Scholar award Internat. Soc. for Ednl., Cultural and Sci. Interchanges, 1980, Golden Apple award Am. Forum for Global Edn., 1993. Mem. Am. Polit. Sci. Assn. (coun. 1970-72), Internat. Polit. Sci. Assn., Internat. Studies Assn. (pres. 1978-79), Internat. Studies Assn. Midwest (Quincy Wright disting. scholar award 2000), Internat. Peace Rsch. Assn. (coun. 1971-77, sec.-gen. 1983-87), Internat. Peace Rsch. Assn. Found. (v.p. 1998—), Midwest Conf. Polit. Scis. (recipient prize 1966), Consortium on Peace Rsch., Edn. and Devel. (exec. com. 1971-77, chmn. 1976-77), Hunger and Devel. Coalition of Cen. Ohio (bd. dirs. 1983-90), Columbus Coun. on World Affairs (bd. dirs. 1974-88), UN Assn. (pres. Columbus chpt. 1991-93). Home: 2674 Westmont Blvd Columbus OH 43221-3354 Office: Ohio State U Mershon Ctr 1501 Neil Ave Columbus OH 43201-2602 E-mail: Alger1@osu.edu.

ALGERMISSEN, S. T., geophysicist, consultant; b. St. Louis, May 9, 1932; s. S.C. Algermissen and Margaret A. Neary; m. Sandra J. Emery; children: Stephen, Catherine, Carl. BS, Mo. Sch. Mines, 1953; AM, Washington U., St. Louis, 1955, PhD, 1957. Supr., geophysicist NOAA, Boulder, Colo., Rockville, Md., 1963—73; supr. U.S. Geol. Survey, Golden, Colo., 1973—93, dep. chief Office of Internat. Geology Reston, Va., 1993—95; assoc. EQE Internat., Inc., Evergreen, Colo., 1995—96; dir. GeoRisk Assocs., Inc., Golden, 1997—. Author: Introduction to the Seismicity of the United States, 1984. Pres., CEO Jefferson Symphony Orch., Golden, 1998-99. Recipient Meritorious Svc. award U.S. Dept. Interior, 1984. Fellow AAAS; mem. Am. Geophys. Union, Seismological Soc. Am. Achievements include creation of earthquake ground motion maps that were the basis for seismic resistant building codes from 1970 to 1996. Home: 800 Meadow Run Golden CO 80403-1901 Office Phone: 303-215-0809. E-mail: STAGeoRisk@aol.com.

ALGIERE, DENNIS LEE, state legislator; b. Westerly, Rhode Island, July 30, 1960; s. Joseph L. and Ida R. (Vacca) A.; m. Leigh A. Williams, Nov. 7, 1992. BA, Providence Coll., 1982; MS, Northea. U., 1984; JD, So. New England Sch. Law, 1991. Town councilor Town of Westerly, R.I., 1990-92; mem. RI Senate, Dist. 38, 1993—; minority leader R.I. Senate, 1997—. Sr. v.p. Washington Trust Co.; mem. consumer adv. con. Fed. Res. Bd. Govs. Bd. dirs. Westerly Hosp., Chorus of Westbury; dir. adv. com. for the arts John F. Kennedy Ctr. for the Performing Arts, 2002—. Mem. Lions. Republican. Roman Catholic. Home: 6 Elm St Westerly RI 02891-2126 Office: RI Senate State House Rm 120 Providence RI 02908

ALHADEFF, DAVID ALBERT, economics professor; b. Seattle, Mar. 22, 1923; s. Albert David and Pearl (Taranto) A.; m. Charlotte Pechman, Aug. 1, 1948. BA, U. Wash., 1944; MA, Harvard U., 1948, PhD, 1950. Faculty U. Calif.-Berkeley, 1949-87, prof. bus. adminstrn., 1959-87, prof. emeritus, 1987—, assoc. dean Sch. Bus. Adminstrn., 1980-82, 85-86. Author: Monopoly and Competition in Banking, 1954, Competition and Controls in Banking, 1968, Microeconomics and Human Behavior, 1982; Contbr. articles to profl. jours., chpts. to books. Served with AUS, 1943-46. Recipient The Berkeley Citation U. Calif.-Berkeley, 1987. Home: 2101 Shoreline Dr Apt 456 Alameda CA 94501-6249 Office: Haas Sch Bus Berkeley CA 94720-0001

AL-HAFEEZ, HUMZA, minister, editor; b. NYC, Feb. 28, 1931; s. Asa Moss and Rosa May Danielson-Weir; children: Jacqueline, Yuhanna, Rasul, Bismillah, Habib, Wardi, Larry, Don, Mariama. Student, Food Trades Vocat. Sch., 1947-48. Patrolman N.Y.C. Police Dept., from 1959; chmn. Temple of Islam, Inc. Founder Nat. Soc. Afro-Am. Policemen Inc.; also past pres.; cons. community relations to chief insp. N.Y.C. Police Dept., to; U.S. Dept. Justice; investigator of corruption among N.Y.C. police officers Knapp Commn.; undercover narcotic officer, investigator Manhattan office Dist. Atty.; investigator Office of 1st Dep. Policy Commr.; undercover investigator U.S. Dept. Justice.; insp. N.Y. State Athletic Commn.; Lectr. Princeton U., Mich. State U., N.Y. State U., Pace Coll., Bklyn. Coll., U. Chgo., NYU, Satellite Acad., N.Y.C., Kinlock Mission for Blind, City N.Y. Police Acad., Nassau Community Coll.; others Appeared on radio and TV; editor-in-chief: Your Muhammad Speaks newspaper; author: The Slanderer, 1987, Some Things to Think About, 2003. Pastoral bd. Interfaith Hosp.; chaplain Frackville (Pa.) Correctional Facility, 1995—. Recipient Father of Yr. award Kinlock Freedom Found. for the Blind, 1973; Community Service award United Council of Chs., 1975; named Person of Yr. Nat. Assn. Black Policemen, 1982. Mem. Internat. Platform Assn. Mem. Nation of Islam; minister Muhammad's Temple of Islam, Bklyn. Home: 361 Clinton Ave Apt 12C Brooklyn NY 11238-1145 Office: 1211 Atlantic Ave Brooklyn NY 11216-2709 Office Phone: 718-789-7747. Personal E-mail: humzahafeez@msn.com. *To expect all of the people to cooperate is something that should be given some thought. Change comes through the efforts of a person, or a small group of people, not all of the people. However, all of the people may benefit, or suffer, from the action of a person, or a small group. History will bear me witness.*

ALHAKK, YUSEF, history educator; b. Buffalo, June 29, 1945; s. Abu Bakr and Lillian Ann (Daniels) Alhakk; m. Maryamma Foster (div.); children: Sadika, Daleylah, Shaheedah; m. Sally Ann Moran, July 11, 1998. BA in Am. studies, SUNY, Buffalo, 1990, EdM, 2001. Cert. tchr. NY, 2001. Sub. tchr. DePew Pub. Schs., NY, 1998—2001; 7th grade tchr. Greater Refuge Temple Christian Acad., Buffalo, 2001—02; social studies tchr. Buffalo Pub. Schs., 2002—. Bd. mem. N.Y.State Coun. for the Social Studies, 2001—. Author: To Serve the People, 2004. Activist Build Orgn., Buffalo, 1978—80. Mem.: Colored Musicians Club. Avocation: chess. Home: 147 Villa Ave Buffalo NY 14216 Personal E-mail: yusefalhakk@adelphia.net.

AL-HASHIMI, IBTISAM, oral surgeon, educator; b. Karbala, Iraq; d. Hadi A. and Rabab H. Al-H. B Dental Sci., Sch. Dentistry, Baghdad, 1973; MS, SUNY, Buffalo, 1985, PhD, 1989. Diplomate in Oral Surgery. Registrar Sch. Dentistry, Baghdad, 1975-81; postdoctoral assoc. SUNY, Buffalo, 1984-88, asst. prof., 1988-89, U. Pacific, San Francisco, 1989-90; dir. stomatology lab. Baylor Coll. Dentistry, Dallas, 1991—, dir. salivery dysfunction clinic, 1992—; clin. asst. prof. surgery U. Tex. Southwestern Med. Ctr., Dallas, 1996—. Adv. com. mem. SS Found. (we. N.Y. chpt.) Buffalo, 1985-89, Dallas-Ft. Worth chpt., 1992—; mem. med. adv. bd., organizer Sjogren's Multispecialty Referral Ctr., 1996; pres. Salivery Rsch. Group, Nat. Inst. Dental Rsch., 1999. Author: Proceeding of the Second Dows Symposium, 1987; contbr. articles to profl. jours. Mem. med. adv. bd. SS Found., 1995. Mem. AAAS, Am. Assn. Dental Schs., N.Y. Acad. Sci., Internat. Platform Assn., Internat. Assn. Dental Rsch., Libr. Congress Assn., Salivary Rsch. Group, Sigma Xi. Achievements include research on molecular mechanisms of salivary gland diseases, development of a laboratory test for the diagnosis of Sjogren's Syndrome using salivary protein electrophoresis; characterization of a major salivary enzyme inhibitor in the mouth; identification of the principal protein components that participate in the formation of the protective coat of the teeth of healthy subjects. Office: Baylor Coll Dentistry 3302 Gaston Ave Dallas TX 75246-2027

AL-HAWAMDEH, SULIMAN, education educator; PhD, U. Sheffield, Eng., 1989. Prof. Nanyang Technol. U., Singapore, 1998—2002, U. of Okla., Tulsa, 2003—. Mng. dir. ITC Info. Tech. Consultants, Singapore, 1992—97. Editor-in-chief: Jour. Info. and Knowledge Mgmt.; editor: (book series) Innovation and Knowledge Management. Mem.: Info. and Knowledge Mgmt. Soc. (pres. 2000—03, founder), Info. Resources Mgmt. Assn., Am. Soc. Info. Sci. & Tech. Achievements include founder and director of the first Master of Science in Knowledge Management in Asia; chmn. First and Second Internat. Conf. on Knowledge Mgmt. E-mail: suliman@hawamdeh.net.

ALI, AHMED HAIDER, geophysicist; b. Alexandria, Egypt, Sept. 20, 1968; s. Haider Ali and Karima Saleh; m. Manal Fawzy Hussein, Mar. 13, 1971; children: Ali Ahmed Haider, Fatema Ahmed Haider, Ali Ahmed Haider, Fatema Ahmed Haider, Amena Ahmed Haider. BS, U. of Alexandria, Egypt, 1991; MS, U. of Alexandria, 1996; PhD, U. of Del., Newark, 2001. Rsch. asst. Coastal Rsch. Inst., Alexandria, Egypt, 1991—96; vis. scholar U. of Del., Newark, 1996—97, rsch. asst., 1997—2001; scientist/engr. Raytheon, Pasadena, Calif., 2001—02, sr. scientist/engr., 2003—; tech. staff mem. NASA's Jet Propulsion Lab., Pasadena, Calif., 2002—03. Vis. scholar World Sci. Lab., Erice, Italy, 1995—96; cons. Calif. Dynamics Corp., L.A. Publication (research) Geophysical Research Letters, publicationn Proceeding of the IEEE International Symposium on Computational Intelligence for Measurement System and Applications; contbr. articles to profl. jours. Mem.: Am. Geophys. Union. Islam. Office: Raytheon 299 N Euclid Ave Pasadena CA 91101 Office Phone: 626-744-5441. Office Fax: 626-744-5523. Personal E-mail: masrauy@hotmail.com. E-mail: aali@pacific.jpl.nasa.gov.

ALI, ASHRAF, psychiatrist; b. Dhaka, Bangladesh, June 7, 1951; s. Wazed Ali and Noorjahan Khatoon; m. Shada Ali, Oct. 19, 1984; children: Sanah, Amir, Omar. MD, Rajshahi (Bangladesh) Med. Coll., 1974; diploma in child health, Nat. U. Ireland, Dublin, 1988. Cert. Am. Bd. Psychiatry and Neurology, Am. Bd. Adolescent Psychiatry. Resident psychiatry Brookdale U. Hosp., Bklyn., 1993—96; fellow in child and adolescent psychiatry SUNY, Bklyn., 1996—98; area dir. Camino Real Cmty. Mental Health Mental Retardation Ctr., Eagle Pass, Tex., 1998—2001; med. dir. Border Region Cmty. Ctr., Laredo, Tex., 2001—05; regional med. dir. Cigna Behavioral Health, Irving, Tex., 2005—. Fellow: Royal Soc. Health London; mem.: Am. Med. Soc. Vienna, Am. Soc. Addiction Medicine, Am. Soc. Clin. Psychopharmacology, Am. Psychiat. Assn. Moslem. Avocations: travel, fishing. Office: Cigna Behavioral Health 6601 E Campus Circle Dr Ste 110 Irving TX 75063 Home: 3013 Sheraton Dr Plano TX 75075 Office Phone: 972-465-7027. Personal E-mail: ashrafali80@hotmail.com.

ALI, FATIMA Z., physician; MD, Dow Med. Coll., Pakistan, 1978. Clin. dir. Linden Oaks Hosp., Naperville, Ill., 1995—; clin. asst. prof. Loyola U. Med. Sch., Maywood, Ill., 1995—. Office: DuPage Mental Health Svcs Ltd 1776 S Naperville Rd Bldg B Ste 203 Wheaton IL 60187 Office Phone: 630-690-2222.

ALI, LAYLAH, artist; b. Buffalo, NY, 1968; BA in Studio Art & English Lit., Williams Coll., 1991; attended, Whitney Mus. Ind. Study Program, NY, 1991—92, Skowhegan Sch. Painting & Sculpture, Maine, 1993; MFA in Painting, Washington U., 1994. One-woman shows include, 303 Gallery, NY, 2005, Mus. Contemporary Art, Chgo., Inst. Contemporary Art, Boston, Albright-Knox Art Gallery, Buffalo, NY, 2003, Project 75, Mus. Modern Art, NY, 2002, Atlanta Coll. Art Gallery, Ga., 2002, Indpls. Mus. Art, Iowa, 2002, Inst. Contemporary Art, Boston, 2001, Yerba Buena Ctr. Arts, San Francisco, 2001, 303 Gallery, NY, 2000, MassMOCA, North Adams, Mass., 2000, Mus. Contemporary Art, Chgo., 1999, Miller Block Gallery, Boston, 1998, Hallwalls Contemporary Arts Ctr., Buffalo, NY, 1994, exhibited in group shows at The 10 Commandments, KW Inst. Contemporary Art, Berlin, 2004, Whitney Biennial Am. Art, Whitney Mus. Am. Art, NY, 2004, Material Witness, Mus. Contemporary Art, Cleve., 2004, Crosscurrents at Century's End, Henry Art Gallery, Seattle, 2003, me and more, Kunstmusuem Lucerne, Switzerland, 2003, Fault Lines: Contemporary African Art & Shifting Landscapes, Venice Biennale, Italy, 2003, Splat, Boom, Pow, Contemporary Art Mus., Houston, Tex., 2003, Comic Release: Negotiating Identity for a New Generation, Carnegie Mellon U., Pitts., 2002, Fantasyland, D'Amelio Terras, NY, 2002, Painting in Boston, DeCordova Mus. & Sculpture Park, Mass., 2002, First Person Singular, Seattle Art Mus., 2002, Against the Wall: Painting against the Grid, Surface, Frame, U. Pa., 2001, A Work in Progress, New Mus., NY, 2001, Premio Regione Piemonte, Palazzo Re Rebaudengo, Italy, 2001, Freestyle, Studio Mus. Harlem, NY, 2001, FRESH: The Altoids Curiously Strong Collection 1998 - 2000, New Mus., NY, 2001, Art on Paper, Weatherspoon Art Gallery, U. NC, 2000, Bizzarro World, Cornell Fine Arts Mus., Fla., 1999, The 1999 DeCordova Ann. Exhbn., Decordova Mus. & Sculpture Park, Mass., 1999, Collectors Collect Contemporary, Inst. Contemporary Art, Boston, 1999, No Place Rather than Here, 303 Gallery, NY, 1999, Selections Summer '98, Drawing Ctr., NY, 1998, Posing, Boston Ctr. Arts, 1998, Paradise 8, Exit Art, NY, 1998, Telling Tales, Atrium Gallery, U. Conn., 1998. Mailing: c/o 303 Gallery 525 West 22nd St New York NY 10011*

ALI, MIR MASOOM, statistician, educator; b. Bangladesh, Feb. 1, 1937; arrived in U.S., 1969; s. Mir Muazzam and Azifa Khatoon (Chowdhury) Ali; m. Firoza Chowdhury, June 25, 1959; children: Naheed, Fahima, Farah, Mir Ishtiaque. BSc, U. Dhaka, 1956, MSc, 1957, U. Toronto, 1967, PhD, 1969. Rsch. officer, Ministry of Food and Agr., Ministry of Commerce, Ctrl. Pub. Svc. Commn. Govt. of Pakistan, 1958—66; tchg. asst. U. Toronto, Canada, 1966—69; asst. prof. math. scis. Ball State U., Muncie, Ind., 1969—74, assoc. prof., 1974—78, prof., 1978—2000, George and Frances Ball disting. prof. stats., 2000—. Vis. prof. U. Windsor, Canada, 1972—73, U. Dhaka, 1983—84, Purdue U., 1978, Jahangirnagar U., 1991, Indian Stats. Inst., Calcutta, 1991, Yeungnam U., Republic of Korea, 1993, King Saud U., 1999. Assoc. editor Jour. Statis. Rsch., Aligarh Jour. Stats., Pakistan Jour. Stats., Jour. Statis Mgmt. Systems, overseas exec. editor Jour. Statis. Studies; contbr. articles to profl. jours. Named Sagamore of the Wabash, State of Ind., 2002; recipient Q.M. Husain Gold medal, Bangladesh Stats. Assn., 1990. Fellow: Bangladesh Acad. Sci., Inst. Statisticians, Eng., Am. Statis. Assn. (meritorious svc. award from biopharm. sect. 1987, 1997, 2002), Royal Statis. Soc.; mem.: Inst. Math. Stats., Internat. Statis. Inst. Muslim. Home: 5200 W Deerbrook Dr Muncie IN 47304-3475 Office: Ball State U Dept Math Scis Muncie IN 47306-0490 Office Phone: 765-285-8670. Business E-Mail: mali@bsu.edu.

ALI, MUHAMMAD (CASSIUS MARCELLUS CLAY), retired professional boxer; b. Louisville, Jan. 17, 1942; s. Marcellus and Odessa (Grady) Clay; m. Sonji Roi, August 14, 1964 (div. Jan. 10, 1966); m. Kalilah Tolona (Belinda Boyd), Apr. 17, 1967 (div. 1977) children: Rasheeda, Jamilla, Maryum, Muhammed Jr.; m. Veronica Porshe, June 19, 1977 (div. 1986), children: Hana, Laila; m. Yolanda Williams, Nov. 19, 1986, 1 child, Asaad; two other children Miya, Khalilah. Ed. pub. schs., Louisville. Profl. boxer, 1960—79, 1980—81; ret., 1981. Film appearances: The Greatest, 1976, Freedom Road (TV), 1978; author: The Greatest: My Own Story, 1975, (with Thomas Hauser) Healing, 1996, (with Hana Ali) More Than a Hero, 2000, (with Hana Ali and Hana Yasmeen Ali) The Soul of a Butterfly: Reflections on Life's Journey, 2004. Named the greatest heavyweight champion of all time, Ring Mag., 1987, Muhammad Ali Mus., Louisville Galleria opened, 1995; named to U.S. Olympic Hall of Fame, 1983, World Boxing Hall of Fame, 1986, Internat. Boxing Hall of Fame, 1990, Sport in Soc. Hall of Fame, 1994; recipient 6 Kentucky Golden Gloves titles, Olympic gold medal in boxing, 1960, Nat. Golden Gloves titles, 1959—60, Jim Thorpe Pro Sports award, lifetime achievement, 1992, Essence award, 1997. Mem. World Community Islam. Achievements include being a light heavyweight champion AAU, 1959, 60; light heavyweight champion Golden Gloves, 1959, heavyweight champion, 1960; light heavy weight champion Olympic Games, 1960, world heavyweight champion, 1964-67, 74-78, 78-79.

ALI, MURAD CAJETAN, transportation executive, writer; b. Greenbay, Mich., Aug. 4, 1974; s. Karen Malmstead and Ernest Abel; m. Sadiya Ahmed; children: Abel Murad, Gabriel Murad. BS, Ctrl. Mich. U.; MBA in Human Resources, Davenport U., Dearborn, Mich., 2002—04. Hiring mgr. Metamerica, Southfield, Mich., 2003—. Pvt. first class USMC, 1992—94. Muslim. Avocations: writing, horseback riding. Office: MTS 4844 Lanyo Detroit MI 48210 Office Phone: 866-256-6900. Personal E-mail: murad_ali@excite.com.

ALI, NAGLAA, design educator; PhD, U. Fla., 2004. Instrnl. designer U. Fla., Gainesville, Fla., 1999—2004. Office: U Fla 2423 Norman Hall Gainesville FL 32608

ALI, TRACEE PAINTER, career management consultant; b. Mantistique, Mich., June 26, 1966; d. James L. and Jeanne F. Painter; m. Mir Hassan Ali, Aug. 15, 1997; 1 child, Sarah. EdS, MS, Fla. State U., 1993. master career counselor. Career advisor, job placement asst. Career Ctr. Fla. State U., Tallahassee, 1990-93; cooperative edn. coord. Career Placement Office U. New Orleans, 1994-96; career cons. Strategic Resumes, New Orleans, 1996-99; employment counselor Travelers Aid Soc., New Orleans, 1999; dir. MBA Career Mgmt. Office U. Dallas, Irving, Tex., 2000—. Mem. ACA, Nat. Assn. Colls. and Employers, Soc. Human Resource Mgmt., Nat. Career Devel. Assn., MBA Career Svcs. Coun. Office: U Dallas MBA Career Mgmt GSM Adm #216 1845 E Northgate Dr Irving TX 75062 Office Fax: 972-721-5254. E-mail: tali0626@hotmail.com, tali@gsm.udallas.edu.

ALIBER, ROBERT Z., economist, educator; b. Keene, N.H., Sept. 19, 1930; s. Norman H. and Sophie (Becker) A.; m. Deborah Baltzly, Sept. 9, 1955; children: Jennifer, Rachel, Michael. BA, Williams Coll., 1952, Cambridge U., 1954, MA, 1957, PhD, Yale U., 1962. Staff economist Commn. Money and Credit, N.Y.C., 1959-61; staff economist Com. on Econ. Devel., Washington, 1961-64; sr. econ. advisor AID, Dept. State, Washington, 1964-65; assoc. prof., then prof. internat. econs. and fin. U. Chgo., 1965—2004. Vis. prof. Brandeis U., 1987-93; vis. Bundesbank prof. Free U. Berlin, 1999; Houblon-Norman fellow, Bank of Eng., 1996, J.P. Morgan Internat. prize fellow, Am. Academy in Berlin, 2002. Author: The International Money Game, 1973, 76, 79, 83, 87, 2001, Exchange Risk and Corporate International Finance, 1978, Your Money and Your Life, 1982; co-author: Money, Banking, and the Economy, 1981, 84, 87, 90, 93, The Multinational Paradigm, 1993; editor: National Monetary Policies and the International Financial System, 1974, The Political Economy of Monetary Reform, 1976, The Reconstruction of International Monetary Arrangements, 1987, The Handbook of International Financial Management, 1989; co-editor Global Portfolios, 1991, Readings in International Business: A Decision Approach, 1993. With U.S. Army, 1954—56. Fulbright fellow, 1952-54. Fellow Woodrow Wilson Internat. Ctr. Scholars, 2004-05; mem. Am. Econs. Assn., Acad. Internat. Bus., Quadrangle Club, Williams Club of N.Y., Post Mills Soaring Club. Office Phone: 603-643-0107. Business E-Mail: rza@gsb.uchicago.edu.

ALIEV, ELDAR, artistic director, choreographer, educator; b. Azerbaijan; Grad. (hon.), Baku Choreographic Acad. CEO, artistic dir. Ballet Internationale, Indpls., 1994—. Former prin. ballet dancer with the Kirov Ballet appearing in more than 30 countries; guest star Bolshoi Ballet and the Australian Ballet; choreographer ballets 1001 Nights, 1995, The Nutcracker, 1996, The Firebird, 1999; choreographer operas Eugene Onegin, 1999, Samson and Deliah, 2000, Anoush, 2001; classics restaged Don Quixote, Giselle, La Sylphide, Paquita, Les Sylphides. Office: Ballet Internationale USA 502 N Capitol Ave Ste B Indianapolis IN 46204-1204

ALIEV, GJUMRAKCH, biomedical researcher; arrived in U.S., 1997; s. Mamed Aliyev and Simosh Aliyeva; 1 child, Galina Alieva. MD, Moscow State U., PhD, 1988. Dir. Microscopy Rsch. Ctr. Case Western Res. U., Cleve., 1998—99, asst. prof. pathology, 1999—. Mem. grant com. rev. bd. NIH, 2000—04. Grantee, Philip Morris USA Inc., Alzheimer's Assn., 1992, 1995, 2001—04. Mem.: Am. Fedn. Aging Rsch. Achievements include research in new theory relationship between the cardiovascular and neurodegenerative diseases. Office: Case Western Res U 2085 Adelbert Rd Cleveland OH 44106 Office Phone: 216-368-6605. Home Fax: 216-368-8649; Office Fax: 216-368-8649. Business E-Mail: gxa15@cwru.edu.

ALIG, FRANK DOUGLAS STALNAKER, retired construction company executive; b. Indpls., Oct. 10, 1921; s. Clarence Schirmer and Marjory (Stalnaker) A.; m. Ann Bobbs, Oct. 22, 1949; children: Douglas, Helen, Barbara. Student, U. Mich., 1939-41; BS, Purdue U., 1948. Registered profl. engr., Ind. Project engr. Ind. State Hwy. Commn., Indpls., 1948; pres. Alig-Stark Constrn. Co., Inc., 1949-57, Frank S. Alig, Inc., 1957-97—; ret. V.p., bd. dirs. Bo-Wit Products Corp., Edinburg, Ind.; pres., bd. dirs. Home Stone Realty, Inc. With AUS, 1943-46. Mem. Dramatic Club, Lambs Club. Republican. Presbyterian. Office Phone: 317-251-3600.

ALIGA, OLIVIA R., music educator, choral director; b. Manila, Philippines, Sept. 8, 1951; d. Fernando Bellapaz Rocha and Thelma Reyes Rocha; m. Norman Asis Aliga, Apr. 24, 1976; children: Norman Vincent, Ferdinand Alphonse, Chester. AM in Music, Pilar Coll., Zamboanga City, Philippines; B of Music, U. Philippines, 1974, postgrad., Vandercook Coll. Music, Chgo. Cert. in Kindermusik. Mem. faculty Vallejo (Calif.) Conservatory of Music, 1982-83; music tchr. New Life Christian Sch., Middleton, Wis., 1983-86; choral dir. Lombard (Ill.) Chorale, 1986—. Music dir. Winfield Cmty. United Meth. Ch., 1988—, trustee, 1995—; bd. dirs. U. Philippines Club Am., Chgo., 1996—, music dir., 1999; music dir., vocal coach U. of the East Med. Chorale, Chgo., 1990-95. Pianist, performed to benefit Marklund Found., Chgo., 1997, and the U. Philippines Club Am., Chgo., 1991. Named to Filipino Am. Chicago Hall of Fame, 1999. Mem. Ill. Music Assn., Ill. State Music Tchrs. Assn., Ill. Philippine Med. Soc. Aux., Philippine Med. Assn. Chgo. Aux., U. PHilippines Club Am. (pres. 2003). Methodist. Avocations: raising orchids, flower arrangements, collecting stamps and coins.

ALIMO, CRAIG, educational consultant; s. M.J. and Catherine Alimo. MS, Northeastern U., 1995; PhD, U. Md., 1999; CAGS, U. Mass., 1999. Resident dir. Centenary Coll., Hackettstown, NJ, 1992—93; grad. asst. Residence Life Northeastern U., Boston, 1993—95; residence dir. housing svcs. U. Mass., Amherst, 1995—99; coord. sexual harassment prevention program Office Human Rels. Programs U. Md., College Park, 1999—2001, diversity tng. specialist Office Human Rels. Program, 2001—03, grad. asst. for diversity initiatives dept. transp. svcs., 2003—. Ind. ednl. cons. Diversity Tng., 1995—. Contbr. articles to profl. publs. Mem.: Svc. Employees Internat. Union (steward 1997—99), Nat. Assn. Multicultural Edn., Nat. Assn. Student Pers. Adminstrs., Am. Coll. Pers. Adminstrn. Avocations: volleyball, music. Home: 6002 Kilmer St Cheverly MD 20785 Office: Univ Md 0123 Regents Drive Parking Garage College Park MD 20742 Home Fax: 301-386-9789; Office Fax: 301-314-7179. Personal E-mail: calimo@wam.umd.edu. Business E-Mail: calimo@umd.edu.

ALIN, ROBERT DAVID, lawyer; b. Mt. Vernon, NY, Oct. 10, 1952; s. Morris and Sylvia (Horowitz) A.; m. Arlene Susan Kerner, Feb. 14, 1988; children: Dustin, Lauren. BA in Math., U. Rochester, 1974; JD, NYU, 1977, LLM in Taxation, 1983. Bar: N.Y. Assoc. atty. Willkie Farr & Gallagher, NYC, 1977-79, Halperin Shivitz Eisenberg Schneider & Greenawalt, NYC, 1979-84, Berman Koerner Silberberg P.C., NYC, 1984-86; sr. v.p., sec., gen. counsel The Pentegra Group, White Plains, NY, 1986—. Mem. ABA, N.Y. State Bar Assn., Web Network. Democrat. Jewish. Avocations: tennis, bridge, music. Home: 7 Aspen Rd Scarsdale NY 10583-7301 Office: The Pentegra Group 108 Corporate Park Dr White Plains NY 10604-3805 E-mail: ralin@pentegra.com.

ALINDER, MARY STREET, writer, educator; b. Bowling Green, Ohio, Sept. 23, 1946; d. Scott Winfield and McDonna Matlock (Sitterle) Street; m. James Gilbert Alinder, Dec. 17, 1965; children: Jasmine, Jesse, Zachary. Student, U. Mich., 1964-65, U. N.Mex., 1966-68; BA, U. Nebr., 1976. Mgr. The Weston Gallery, Carmel, Calif., 1978-79; chief asst. Ansel Adams, Carmel, 1979-84; exec. editor, bus. mgr. The Ansel Adams Pub. Rights Trust, Carmel, 1984-87; freelance writer, lectr., curator, Gualala, Calif., 1989—; selector and writer biographies Focal Press Ency., 3d edit., 1993; ptnr. The Alinder Gallery, Gualala, 1990—2003; cultural expert U.S. State Dept., Guadalajara, Mexico, 2003. Curator Ansel Adams Centenial Celebration, 2002, Ansel Adams: 80th Birthday Retrospective, Friends of Photography, Carmel, Acad. Sci., San Francisco, Denver Mus. Natural History, Ansel Adams and the West, Calif. State Capitol, Sacto., 2001; co-curator One With Beauty, M.H. deYoung Meml. Mus., 1987, Ansel Adams: American Artist, The Ansel Adams Ctr., San Francisco; lectr. Nat. Gallery Art, Barbican Ctr., M.H. deYoung Meml. Mus., Stanford U., LA County Mus., U. Mich.; vis. artist and lectr. Nebr. Art Assn., 1997; Wallace Stegner meml. lectr. Peninsula Open Space Inst., Mountainview, Calif., 1998, Assn. Internat. Photographic Art Dealers, NYC, 1999, Cin. Art Mus., 2000, Eiteljorg Mus., Indpls., 2001, Internat. Wildlife Mus., Jackson Hole, 2003, Nat. Forestry Ctr., 2003, Telluride Mountain Film Festival, Nev. Mus. Art, Reno, 2004, U. Tex., Austin, 2005; faculty Stanford U., 2000 Author: Picturing Yosemite (Places), 1990, The Limits of Reality: Ansel Adams and Group f/64 (Seeing Straight), 1992, Ansel Adams, A Biography (Henry Holt), 1996, Mabel Dodge Luhan, 1997 (ViewCamera), Ansel Adams: Milestone, 2002; (with others) the Scribner Encyclopedia of American Lives, 1998; co-author: Ansel Adams: An Autobiography, 1985; co-editor: Ansel Adams: Letters and Images, 1988; columnist Coast and Valley Mag., 1993-98, Ansel Adams: Political Landscape, Focal Ency. Photography, 1993—; political landscape (Civilization), 1999; contbr. articles to profl. jours., popular mags. Business E-Mail: alinders@mcn.org.

ALIOTO, ANGELA MIA, lawyer; b. San Francisco, Oct. 20, 1949; m. Adolfo Veronese (dec. Sept. 1990); children: Angela Veronese, Adolfo Veronese, Joseph Veronese, Gian-Paolo Veronese. BA, Lone Mountain Coll., 1971; JD, U. San Francisco, 1983. Lawyer Alioto and Alioto, San Francisco, 1980—; mem. bd. supr. City and County of San Francisco, 1989—97, pres. bd. supr., 1993—95. Candidate for mayor City of San Francisco, 1991, 2003; first vice-chair Calif. State Dem. Party, 1991—93; co-chair Calif. del. Dem. Nat. Conv., 1992; mem. Golden Gate Bridge Dist., Outer-Continental Shelf Bd. Control; vice-chair San Francisco County Transp. Authority; mem. San Francisco Mental Health Bd. Author: Straight to the Heart. Chair bd. dir. Nat. Shrine St. Francis Assisi. Mem.: Soc. Profl. Journalists, Am. Trial Lawyers Assn., Bar Assn. San Francisco, NAACP (life), Dante Soc. Am. Democrat. Roman Catholic. Office: Alioto & Alioto 700 Montgomery St San Francisco CA 94111

ALIPIO, GARY GLYNN, writer, consultant; b. Jefferson, La., June 7, 1968; s. Glynn Phillip Alipio and Eloise Gidiere Faciane; m. Nicol J. Breaux Alipio, Nov. 8, 1997. BJ, La. State U., 1986—91. Ddb needham/focus agy. Project Mgr., Dallas, 1996—97; sr. copywriter Pierce, DeDitius & Galyean, Arlington, Tex., 1997—98, Saunders-Ream, Dallas, 1998—99, Ackerman-McQueen, Okla. City, 1999—2001; freelance writer Galipio, New Orleans, La., 2001—. Copywriter (advertising) Six Flags Subway & Are You Getting Enough? Campaigns (Advt. ADDYs., 2001). Mem.: Soc. of Children's Book Writers and Illustrators (assoc.). Mem. Christian Ch. Avocations: golf, fishing, bicycling, swimming, painting.

ALISETTI, EDWIN LUIS, engineer, corporate financial executive; b. Caracas, Venezuela, Aug. 10, 1969; s. Gualtiero Alisetti and Rina Esther Pacillo. BSCE, U. Catolica Andres Bello, Caracas, Venezuela, 1995; MSME, U. Miami, 1998, MBA, 2001. Pres. Casa Bella, Caracas, Venezuela, 1992-95; apt. adminstr. Miami, 1996-98; data analyst U. Miami Sch. Architecture, Coral Gables, Fla., 2000—; jr. analyst M&A dept. Royal Bank of Can., 2001; bus./fin. intern Merrill Lynch, Miami, 2001; eCommerce Latin Am. intern Fed. Express, Miami, 2000; cons. The Fin. Group, Fort Lauderdale, Fla., 2002—. Tutor econs. and fin. U. Miami Sch. Bus., 2000—; pres. KateMi Group Inc. Contbr. articles to sci. and tech. jours. Mem.: ASME. Avocations: martial arts, soccer, rugby. Home: 1217 NW 107th Terr Plantation FL 33322 Personal E-mail: ealisett@hotmail.com.

ALISKY, JOSEPH MARTIN, physician, medical researcher; s. Marvin and Beverly Alisky; m. Elena Lvovna Chertkova, Oct. 28, 2000; children: Michael, Peter. BS, U. Ariz., 1987; MD, PhD, St. Louis U. Sch. Medicine, 1996. Diplomate Am. Bd. of Internal Medicine. Resident in internal medicine U. Iowa Hosps. and Clinics, Iowa City, 1996—99, postdoctoral fellow in gene therapy rsch., 1999—2001, fellow in geriat., 1999—2002; gen. internal medicine Marshfield Clinic Thorp Ctr., Thorp, Wis., 2002—; med. rschr. Marshfield Clinic Rsch. Found., Marshfield, Wis. Contbr. articles to profl. jours. Grantee Nat. Rsch. Svc. award, NIH, 1999-2000. Mem.: AMA. Achievements include patents for transduction of neurons using retroviral vectors and cholera toxin subunit b. Office: Marshfield Clinic Thorp Ctr 704 South Clark Thorp WI 54771 Office Phone: 715-669-5536. E-mail: alisky.joseph@marshfieldclinic.org.

ALITO, SAMUEL ANTHONY, JR., federal judge; b. Trenton, NJ, Apr. 1, 1950; AB, Princeton U., 1972; JD, Yale U., 1975. Bar: NJ 1975, NY 1970. Law clk. to Hon. Leonard I. Garth U.S. Ct. Appeals (3d cir.), Newark, 1976—77; asst. U.S. atty. NJ US Dept. Justice, Newark, 1977—81, US atty., 1987—90, asst. to solicitor gen. Office of Solicitor Gen. Washington, 1981—85, dep. asst. atty. gen. Office of Legal Counsel, 1985—87; judge U.S. Ct. Appeals (3d cir.), Newark, 1990—. Office: US Courthouse Federal Sq & Walnut St PO Box 999 Newark NJ 07101-0999 Office Phone: 973-645-2424.

ALIVISATOS, ARMAND PAUL, chemist, educator; b. Chgo., Nov. 12, 1959; BA in Chemistry, U. Chgo., 1981; PhD of Chem. Physics, U. Calif. Berkeley, 1986. Postdoctoral fellow AT&T Bell Labs, 1986-88; asst. prof., assoc. prof. U. Calif., Berkeley, 1988-95, prof. chemistry, 1995—, vice chmn. dept. chemistry, 1995-98, Chancellor's prof., 1998—2001, prof. materials sci. and mineral engring., 1999—; dir, materials, sci. divsn. Lawrence Berkeley Nat. Lab., 2003—. Head Molecular Foundry LBNL, 1995—. Editor Am. Chem. Soc. Jour., Nano Letters; mem. editorial bd. Jour. Physical Chem., Chem. Physics, Jour. Chem. Physics, Advanced Materials Jour. Recipient Outstanding Scientific Accomplishment in Materials Chemistry award Dept. Energy, 1994, Coblentz award, 1994, Colloid and Surface Chemistry ACS award, 2004. Fellow Am. Phys. Soc., Am. Acad. Arts & Sci.; mem. AAAS, Am. Chem. Soc., Materials Rsch. Soc. (Outstanding Young Investigator award 1995), Nat. Acad. Scis. Office: U Calif Dept Chem Room 419 Latimer Hall Berkeley CA 94720-0001

ALIZADEH, KAVEH, plastic surgeon, educator; b. Tehran, Iran; s. Hossein and Mina Alizadeh. BA, Cornell U., 1988, MD, 1993; MS, Columbia U., 2000. Am. Bd. Plastic Surgery, 2001. Vice chmn. plastic surgery Winthrop U., Mineola, NY, 2003; chmn. microsurgery Winthrop U., Mineola, 2002—; ptnr. L.I. Plastic Surgery, Garden City, NY, 2001—; program dir., plastic surgery Nassau U. Med. Ctr., 2001—. Chief med. officer Advance Aesthetic Inst. Contbr. articles to jours. Recipient Disting. Alumni award, Dwight Englewood Sch., 2004; fellow, Meml. Sloan Kettering Cancer Ctr., 2000; Edn. grant, Smile Train. Fellow: Am. Coll. Surgeons; mem.: Assn. Acad. Chm. Plastic Surgery, Am. Soc. Aesthetic Plastic Surgery, Am. Soc. Plastic Surgeons. Office: 501 Madison Ave New York NY 10020 Office Phone: 516-742-3404.

ALIZOR, JOHN O., elementary school educator, director, editor; b. Otolokpo, Delta, Nigeria, Feb. 20, 1948; s. Okitia and Amikor (Mokuye) Alizor; m. Evelyn Matchen, Jan. 10, 1970 (div.); children: Alexis Ann, Ashley Elizabeth, Alyssa Eva; m. Connie Kay Emmons, Apr. 19, 2000. BA in Polit. Sci., Calif. State U. Dominguez Hills, Carson, MEd in Ednl. Adminstrn., 2003. Cert. tchr. State of Calif. Commn. Tchr. Credentialing. Resource coord. Title 1 programs Lynwood Unified Sch. Dist., Calif., 1998—. Collegiate All-Am. scholar, US Achievement Acad., Lexington, Ky., 2003, US Nat. Collegiate scholar, US Achievement Acad., Lexington, Bloomington, 2003. Mem.: Pi Lambda Theta. Home: 3412 Falcon Ave Long Beach CA 90807 Office Phone: 310-603-1515 ext. 22.

ALJIAN, JAMES DONOVAN, investment company executive; b. Oakland, Calif., Nov. 5, 1932; s. George W. and Marguerite (Donovan) A.; m. Marjorie L. Townsend, Oct. 17, 1959; children: Mark Donovan, Mary Anne, Reed Townsend. BS, U. Calif., Berkeley, 1955; MBA, Golden Gate U., 1965. Office mgr. Uniroyal Co., San Francisco, 1957-60; audit supr. Ernst & Ernst, San Francisco, 1960-65; sec.-treas. Tracy Investment Co., Las Vegas, 1965-73, Internat. Leisure Corp., Las Vegas, 1967-70; sr. v.p. fin. MGM, Culver City, Calif., 1973-79; pres. Tracinda Corp., Las Vegas, 1979-82; sr. v.p. fin. planning MGM/UA Entertainment Co., Culver City, Calif., 1982-85; exec. v.p., chief fin. officer, dir. Southwest Leasing Corp., Los Angeles, 1985-87, also bd. dirs.; with Tracinda Corp., Las Vegas, Nev., 1987—. Mem. shareholder com. Daimler Chrysler AG, 1998-2000; bd. dirs. MGM Grand, Inc. With AUS, 1955—57. Mem. Am. Inst. C.P.A.s, Calif. Soc. C.P.A.s, Acad. Motion Picture Arts and Scis.

ALJIAN, JOHN MITCHELL, ophthalmologist; s. Robert and Sonia Aljian; m. Sylvie Khorenian, July 1, 1995. BS in biology, Boston Coll., 1986; MS in human physiology, Georgetown U., 1988; MD, NJ Med. Sch., 1991. Cert. Am. Bd. Ophthalmology. Pvt. practice, NY, 1996—, 1996—; clin. prof. NY Med. Coll., Valhalla, NY, 1997—; chief eye trauma svc. The NY Eye and Ear Infirmary, N.Y.C., 1997—; intern Monmouth Med. Ctr. Internal Medicine, 1991—92; residency ophthalmology NY Eye and Ear Infirmary, 1992—95. Recipient Sigma XI honor, Scientific Rsch. Soc. Mem.: Alpha Omega Alpha Med. Honor Soc., Am. Acad. Ophthamology. Achievements include The NY Eye and Ear Infirmary was awarded the Outstanding Teaching and Svc. award, 1998. Office: John M Aljian MD PC 630 Palisade Ave Englewood Cliffs NJ 07632 also: Ste 618 45 Ludlow St Yonkers NY 10705 also: Ste 1501 425 Madison Ave New York NY 10017

ALKADI, IHSSAN S., adult education educator; b. Kuwait, Kuwait, Feb. 4, 1963; s. Ihssan Salim Alkadi, Mona Adelle Alkadi; m. Mona Addelle Jamell; children: Hanna, Rodwan. PhD, La. State U., 1999. Instr. Southeastern La. U., Hammon, 1992—2000; asst. prof. Nicholls State U., Thibodaux, La., 2000—. Named Sigma Tau Gamma Alumni of Yr., 1997. Mem.: ACM (advisor 2000—02). Office: Nicholls State Univ PO Box 2168 Thibodaux LA 70310 Personal E-mail: cmps-isa@nicholls.edu.

ALKALAY, ARIE L., pediatrician, neonatal/perinatal nurse practitioner; b. July 23, 1946; MD, Hadassah Sch. Medicine, Jerusalem, 1971. Intern Belinson Med. Ctr./Kaplan Hosp., Israel, 1971-72, Cedars Sinai Med. Ctr., L.A., 1984-85; resident in pediat. Kaplan Hosp., Israel, 1975-80, fellow in neonatal-perinatal medicine, 1980-82, Cedars Sinai Med. Ctr., L.A., 1982-84; assoc. dir. neonatology Cedars-Sinai Med. Ctr., L.A., 1992-97, dir. Well Baby Nursery, 1993-99, 2004—; prof. pediat. UCLA, 1997—. Contbr. over 40 articles to profl. jours. Recipient the Morris Press Humanism award Cedars-Sinai Med. Ctr., 1989. Office: 8700 Beverly Blvd Los Angeles CA 90048-1804

ALKANA, LINDA KELLY, history professor; b. Calgary, Alta., Can., Nov. 9, 1946; arrived in U.S., 1963; d. Bernard Joseph and Lorna Lucille (Sutherland) Kelly; m. Ronald Lee Alkana, Sept. 12, 1970; children: Alexander Philippe, Lorna Jane. BA, UCLA, 1969; MA, U. Calif., Irvine, 1975, PhD, 1985. Lectr. humanities U. Calif., Irvine, 1985-93; lectr. history Calif. State U., Long Beach, 1981—, lectr. internat. studies, 2000—. Affiliate scholar Ctr. Study Women UCLA, 1987—89. Assoc. editor: The History Teacher, 1987—; contbr. articles to profl. jours. Mem.: Western Assn. Women Historians, Am. Hist. Assn. Office: Calif State U Long Beach Dept History 1250 N Bellflower Blvd Long Beach CA 90840-0006

ALKASS, DALYA, Spanish educator; b. Beacon, N.Y., Sept. 1, 1970; d. Younis and Jean Diana (Brown) Alkass. BA, Drew U., 1992; MA, SUNY, Albany, 1994; postgrad., SUNY, Buffalo. Lectr. in Spanish SUNY, Buffalo, 1996—97, tchg. asst. in Spanish, 1997—98. Mem.: Spanish Grad. Assn., Sigma Delta Pi. Home: 7 Stearns Rd Binghamton NY 13905-1321

ALKER, HAYWARD ROSE, political scientist, educator; b. N.Y.C., Oct. 3, 1937; s. Hayward Rose and Dorothy (Fitzsimmons) Alker; m. Judith Ann Tickner, June 3, 1961; children: Joan Christina, Heather Jane, Gwendolyn Ann. BS, MIT, 1959; MS, Yale U., 1960, PhD, 1963. From instr. to assoc. prof. Yale U., New Haven, 1963-68; prof. polit. sci. MIT, 1968-95; John A. McCone prof. internat. rels. U. So. Calif., L.A., 1995—2005, prof., 2005—. Vis. prof. U. Mich., 1968; Olaf Plame vis. prof. U. Stockholm, U. Uppsala, 1989; vis. prof., scholar Brown U., 1996, 2003—04; chmn. Math. Social Scis. Bd., 1970—71; mem. exec. com. Internat. Social Sci. Coun., 1990—92. Author: (non-fiction) Mathematics and Politics, 1965; co-author: World Handbook of Political and Social Indicators, 1966; co-author: (with Russett) World Politics in the General Assembly, 1966; co-author: (with Bloomfield and Choucri) Analyzing Global Interdependence, 1974; co-author: (with Hurwitz) Resolving Prisoner's Dilemmas, 1981; co-editor, co-author: non-fiction Journeys Through Conflict, 2001; author: Rediscoveries and Reformulations, 1996; editor: Honors Theses in International Relations, 2003; editor: (mem. bd.) (jour.) Jour. Interdisciplinary History, 1969—71, Internat. Orgn., 1970—76, Quality and Quantitiy, 1974—, Internat. Studies Quar., 1980—89, European Jour. Internat. Rels., 1995—99, Internat. Rels. of Asia Pacific, 2000—, Internat. Rels., 2003—. Congl. intern Office of Chester Bowles, 1960. Fellow, Ctr. Advanced Studies in Behavioral Scis., 1967—68. Mem.: Internat. Studies Assn. (v.p. 1990—91, pres. 1992—93), Internat. Peace Rsch. Assn., Internat. Polit. Sci. Assn., Am. Polit. Sci. Assn. Business E-Mail: alker@usc.edu.

AL-KHATIB, TAREQ, surgeon; b. Jerusalem, June 11, 1945; Student, Damascus (Syria) U., 1964-65, MD, 1971. Diplomate Am. Bd. Emergency Medicine, Am. Bd. Surgery. Intern Yale Affiliated Hosp., New Haven, 1971-72; resident in surgery Albert Einstein Hosp., N.Y.C., 1973-77; surgeon Port Charlotte (Fla.) Hosps., 1977—; pvt. practice Port Charlotte, 1977—. Fellow ACS; mem. AMA, Am. Coll. Emergency Physicians. Office: Emerald Sq 2852 Tamiami Trl Ste 5 Port Charlotte FL 33952-5100 Fax: 941-625-9797. E-mail: alkhatibmd@aol.com.

ALKIRE, JOHN D., lawyer, arbitrator, mediator; b. Seattle, Nov. 15, 1948; s. Durwood Lee and Dorys (Maryon) A.; m. Karen A. Heerensperger, May 6, 1994; children: Lauren M., Kevin G. Student, U. Calif., Berkeley, 1967-68; BA, Principia Coll., Elsah, Ill., 1970; JD, U. Wash., 1975. Bar: Wash. 1975, Washington 1977, U.S. Dist. Ct. (we. dist.) Wash., U.S. Ct. Appeals (4th, 9th and D.C. cirs.), U.S. Supreme Ct. Budget analyst Office Mgmt. and Budget, Seattle, 1970-72; law clk 9th cir. Honorable Eugene A. Wright, Seattle, 1975-76; assoc. Jones, Grey & Bayley, Seattle, 1976-77, Steptoe & Johnson, Washington, 1977-80, Perkins Coie, Seattle, 1980-85, ptnr., 1985—. Mem. ABA, Wash. State Bar Assn. Avocations: outdoor sports, major league baseball, travel, volunteer mediation. Office: Perkins Coie 1201 3rd Ave Fl 40 Seattle WA 98101-3029

ALKON, ELLEN SKILLEN, physician; b. L.A., Apr. 10, 1936; d. Emil Bogen and Jane (Skillen) Rost; m. Paul Kent Alkon, Aug. 30, 1957; children: Katherine Ellen, Cynthia Jane, Margaret Elaine. BA, Stanford U., 1955; MD, U. Chgo., 1961; MPH, U. Calif., Berkeley, 1968. Diplomate Nat. Bd. Med. Examiners, Am. Bd. Pediat., Am. Bd. Preventive Medicine in Pub. Health. Chief sch. health Anne Arundel County Health Dept., Annapolis, Md., 1970-71; practice medicine specializing in pediat. Mpls. Health Dept., 1971-73, dir. MCH, 1973-75, commr. health, 1975-80; chief preventive and pub. health Coastal Region of Los Angeles County Dept. Health Svcs., 1980-81; chief pub. health West Area Los Angeles County Dept. Health Svcs., 1981-85; acting med. dir. pub. health Los Angeles County Dept. Health, 1986-87, med. dir. pub. health, 1987-93; med. dir. Coastal Cluster Health Ctrs. L.A. County Dept. Pub. Health Svcs., 1993-96, CEO, 1996-98, med. dir., 1998-2000; dir. Pub. Health Edn. in Medicine, 2000—. Adj. prof. UCLA Sch. Pub. Health, 1981—; adminstr. vis. nurses svc., Mpls., 1975-80. Fellow Am. Coll. Preventive Medicine, Am. Acad. Pediat.; mem. So. Calif. Pub. Health Assn. (pres. 1985-86, 2004), Minn. Pub. Health Assn. (pres. 1978-79), Am. Pub. Health Assn., Calif. Conf. Local Health Officers (pres. 1990-91), Calif. Ctr. for Pub. Health Advocacy (pres. 2002-03), Calif. Acad. Preventive Medicine (pres. 1988-92, 2003—), Delta Omega. Office: Los Angeles County DHS 241 N Figueroa St Rm 143 Los Angeles CA 90012 Office Phone: 213-250-8623. Business E-Mail: ealkon@ladhs.org.

ALKON, PAUL KENT, language educator; Grad., Phillips Acad., 1953; AB, Harvard U., 1957; PhD in English Lit., U. Chgo., 1962. Instr., asst. prof. English lit. U. Calif.-Berkeley, 1962-70; assoc. prof. U. Md., 1970-71; assoc. prof. English U. Minn., Mpls., 1971-73, prof., 1973-80; Leo S. Bing prof. English U. So. Calif., Los Angeles, 1980—. Vis. prof. English, Ben Gurion U. of Negev, Israel, 1977-78 Author: Samuel Johnson and Moral Discipline, 1967, Defoe and Fictional Time, 1979, Origins of Futuristic Fiction, 1987, Science Fiction Before 1900, 1994. Mem. Am. Soc. 18th Century Studies (pres. 1989-90), Sociètè française d'Etude du 18ème Siècle, Churchill Ctr. (bd. acad. advisers). Home: 17 Masongate Dr Palos Verdes Peninsula CA 90274-1560 Office: U So Calif Dept English Los Angeles CA 90089-0354 Office Phone: 213-740-2815. E-mail: alkon@usc.edu.

ALLABY, STANLEY REYNOLDS, clergyman; b. Providence, Dec. 28, 1931; s. Edwin T. and Hope (Swift) A.; m. Marion Arlene Johnson, Dec. 18, 1954; children— Norman R., Darlene R., Kimberly A., Stephen R. AB, Gordon Coll., 1953; M.Div., Gordon Conwell Sem., 1956; D.D., Barrington (R.I.) Coll., 1977; D.Min., Westminster Theol. Sem., 1978. Ordained to ministry, 1956; pastor Black Rock Conglist. Ch., Fairfield, Conn., 1956-97; dir. Sudan Interior Mission, N.C., 1970—, chmn. bd., 1985—2005, vice chmn. internat. bd. govs., 1985-90; vice chmn. Billy Graham New Haven Crusade, 1982; exec. com. Billy Graham Hartford Crusade, 1985; prof. practical theology Bethel Sem. of the East; Ockenga lectr. Gordon-Conwell Sem., 1983; sr. cons. Wilson Ctr. for Missions, Gordon-Conwell Sem., 2001—. Guest lectr. Tyndale Theol. Sem., Amsterdam, 1996; lectr. Bethel Seminary of the East, 1999—. Bd. dirs. United Neighbors for Self Devel., Bridgeport, Conn., 1963-64, Christian Freedom Found., 1960-70, Operation Hope, Fairfield, 1986-89; trustee Gordon Div. Sch., 1965-69. Recipient George Washington honor medal Freedoms Found., 1968, 69; Alumnus-of-Year award Gordon Coll., 1976 Mem. Gordon Coll. Alumni Assn. (past pres.), Nat. Assn. Evangelicals (dir. 1974-95, exec. com. 1980-82, nat. conv. coordinator 1981-82, (chmn. resolutions com. 1982-83), Bridgeport Pastors Assn. (past pres.), Greater Bridgeport Fellowship Evangelicals (past pres.) Home: 123 Lyon Rd Woodstock Valley CT 06282-2612 E-mail: stanreynolds6@juno.com.

ALLAIN, JEAN PAUL, research scientist; b. Bogota, Cundinamarca, Colombia, June 17, 1970; s. John Frederick Allain and Luz Patricia Allain De La Torre; m. Monica Marie Cortez, June 21, 1997; 1 child, Karina Rae Chavez. BS, Calif. State Poly. U., Pomona, 1996; MS, PhD, U. Ill., 2001. Co-op rsch. intern Intel Corp., Santa Clara, Calif., 1997—97; grad. rsch. assoc. U. Ill., Urbana, 1996—2001, postdoctoral rsch. assoc., 2001—02; nuclear engr. Argonne Nat. Lab., 2002—. Summer rsch. intern Gen. Atomics, La Jolla, Calif., 2000—00. Fellow SURGE, U. Ill., 1996—2001. Mem.: Am. Vacuum Soc., Am. Phys. Soc., Phi Kappa Phi, Sigma Chi (assoc.). Achievements include first to Low-Energy Sputtering of Liquid-Lithium. Avocations: soccer, writing, poetry, reading. Office: Argonne Nat Lab 9700 S Cass Ave Bldg 308 Argonne IL 60439 E-mail: allain@anl.gov.

ALLAIN, LOUIS, literature educator; b. Brest, France, June 28, 1933; s. Louis and Louise (Nicolas) A.; m. Annie Luc, May 21, 1964; children: Andree-Lise, Juliette, Laurence, Alexandre. B Degree, Ecole Normale Superieure, Paris, 1958, Agregation, 1957; Doctorate, Sorbonne, Paris, 1979. Sch. tchr. Lycee Lakanal, Paris, 1961; asst. lectr. Sorbonne, 1961-63, sr. lectr., 1963-69; mng. lectr. Univ. Lille, 1969-81, prof., head dept. Slavic langs., 1981-98, prof emeritus, 1998—. Contbr. Acad. Sci., Hungary, 1988, Russia, 1988, 90, 94, 96, 2000, Israel, 1994, Poland, 1995, 96, 97, 98, 2000, Montenegro, 1996, U. Houston, 1989, Cornell U., 1994, Columbia U., 1998, Dostoevsky Symposium, Cerisy-la-Salle, 1983, Ljubljana, 1989, Oslo, 1992, Kartause Gaming, 1995, N.Y. 1998, Gumilev Symposium I & II, Glasgow, 1986, St. Petersburg, 1996, Chekhov Symposium I & II, Badenweiler, 1985, 94, From Dissidence to Democracy, Paris, 1996., Jerusalem in Slavic cultures and religious traditions, 1996, others. Author: Dostoievski et Dieu, 1981, Dostoievski et l'Autre, 1984, Etiudy o russkoi literature, 1989, Dostoevsky i Bog, 1993, F.M. Dostoevsky: Poetika, mirooshchushchenie, bogoiskatel'stvo, 1996, Skvoz' prizmu vekov, 1998, Shtrikhi k portretu F.M. Dostoevskogo, 1998; editor: B. Poplavsky, I&II, 1993, N. Otsup, 1993-95, G. Adamovich, 1993, G. Ivanov, 1993, V. Vishnjak, 1993, V.V. Rozanov, (study), 1993, A. Remizov, 1994, N. Plevitskaya, 1994, N. Fedorova, 1994, V. Gippius, 1994, V. Zen'kovsky, 1994, I. Napelbaum, 1995, M. Voloshin (study), 1996, F. M. Dostoevsky: Poetika, mirooshchushchenie, bogoiskatel'stvo, 1996, Skvoz' Prizmu Vekov, 1998, Shtrikhi k portretu F.M. Dostoevskogo, 1998, D. Granin, Tajny znak Peterburga, 2000; co-editor: Jews and Slavs, vol. 2, 1994; contbr. articles to profl. jours. Lt. French Navy, 1958-61, France. Comdr. of Acad. Palms, French Ministry of Edn., 1990, medal City of Lille, 1994, Melanges offerts au Professeur Louis Allain, Lille, 1996, Am. Order of Excellence, 2000. Mem. Alumni Ecole Normale Superieure, Intra-Marine/France, Internat. Dostoevsky Soc., Inst. Slavic Studies, Paris. Avocations: cooking, gardening. Home: Rue Jules Guesde 408 Villeneuve d'Ascq 59650 France Office: Charles de Gaulle Univ BP 149 Villeneuve d'Ascq Cedex 59653 France

ALLAIRE, GASTON GEORGE, music educator, researcher; b. Berlin, NH, June 18, 1916; s. Francis Xavier Allaire and Mary Laura Pellerin; m. Fleurette Carmen Turcotte, July 1, 1963; children: Anne, Claud. MusB, U. Montreal, 1947; MA, U. Conn., 1956; PhD, Boston (Mass.) U., 1960. Organist, choirmaster Our Lady's, Holyoke, Mass., 1950—54, St. Joseph's, Belmont, Mass., 1954—56, Paulist Ctr., Boston, 1956—60; prof. music Loyola Coll., Montreal, Canada, 1962—67, U. Moncton, New Brunswick, 1967—84, prof. emeritus, 1984—. Mem. rsch. coun. U. Moncton, 1968; cons. Can. Coun. Arts, Ottawa, Canada, 1970—79. Editor: CFMS Newsletter, 1969—71; author: The Theory of Hexachords, 1972; contbr. articles to profl. jours. Nat. pres. Can. Folk Music Soc., 1968—71. Finalist, Can. Coun. Arts, 1961; fellow, Fulbright Found., 1962; grantee, Ministry Cultural Affairs, Quebec, Can., 1965. Mem.: Am. Musicological Soc. Avocations: swimming, walking, piano, music, reading. Home: 82 Markham E Deerfield Beach FL 33442-2757 E-mail: gallaire@bellsouth.net.

ALLAIRE, JOSEPH LEO, French educator; b. Detroit, Feb. 23, 1929; s. Leonel J. and Stella Marie (Latour) A.; m. Andrea Woodruf Jensen, June 19, 1974; 1 child, Joseph Arnold Leonel. AB, U. Detroit, 1952; MA, Wayne State U., 1957, PhD, 1966. Tchr. French U. Detroit High Sch., 1952-53; tchr. French, Latin, Spanish Detroit Pub. Schs., 1953-62; head fgn. lang. dept. Cody High Sch., Detroit Pub. Schs., 1962-67; asst. prof. to assoc. prof. French Fla. State U., Tallahassee, 1967—. Adj. French, Wayne State U., 1962-67. Editor: Le Miroir de l'Ame Pecheresse, 1972; contbr. (bibliography) Critical Bibliography of French Literature: 16th Century, 1984. Mem. MLA, Am. Assn. Tchrs. French (pres. Fla. chpt. 1974-75), South Atlantic MLA (v.p. 1975, pres. 1976), Soc. Internat. des Seiziemiste, Renaissance Soc. of Am. Home: 1004 Shalimar Dr Tallahassee FL 32312-3019 Office: Fla State U Dept Modern Langs Tallahassee FL 32306-1540 E-mail: jallaire@mailer.fsu.edu.

ALLAIRE, PAUL ARTHUR, former office equipment company executive; b. Worcester, Mass., July 21, 1938; s. Arthur E Allaire and Elodie (LePrade) Murphy; children: Brian, Christiana. BSEE, Worcester Poly. Inst., 60; MSIA, Carnegie-Mellon U., 1966. Fin. analyst Xerox Corp., Rochester, N.Y., 1966-70; dir. fin. analysis Rank Xerox Ltd., London, N.Y., 1970-73; dir. internat. ops. fin. Xerox Corp., Stamford, Conn., 1973-75; chief staff officer Rank Xerox Ltd., London, 1975-79, mng. dir., 1979-83; sr. v.p., chief staff officer Xerox Corp., Stamford, Conn., 1983-86, pres., 1986—97, CEO, 1990—99, 2000—01, chmn. bd., 1991—2001, chmn. exec. com., 2000—01. Bd. dirs. Segway, Nature Air. Bd dirs NY City Ballet, 2000—04; chmn. bd. dirs. Ford Found., 2000—; trustee Worcester Poly Inst, Carnegie Mellon Univ. Mem.: Nat. Acad. Engring., Eta Kappa Nu, Tau Beta Pi. Democrat. E-mail: p.all@xerox.com.

ALLAMON, KAREN HENN, minister; b. Jackson, Mich., Aug. 1, 1958; d. Richard Leonard and Lujean Lirones Henn; m. Randall M. Allamon, Nov. 26, 1983; children: Matthew B., Lucas A. BFA, Webster U., 1992; MDiv, Princeton Theol. Sem., 1994—96, post grad, 2002—. Crisis Counselor Life Crisis Services - St. Louis, 1992. Pastor Barre Ctr. Presbyn. Ch., Albion, NY, 1996—; interim spiritual care coord. Hospice of Orleans County, Albion, NY, 1998—99; critical incident stress debriefer COVA, Albion, NY, 1998—; instr., worship, sacraments, preaching Presbytery of Genesee Valley, Rochester, NY, 2001—04. Presbyn. worship coord. Presbyn. of Genessee Valley, Rochester, NY, 2001—04. Cmty. leadership participant Albion Sch. Sys., NY, 1996—; mem. Ministirial Alliance, Albion, NY, 1996—; Legacy of Love endowment com. ARC of Orleans County, Albion, 2003—. Recipient One of the Fastest Growing Congregations in the US: US Congl. Study, Eli Lilly Found., 2002, Excellence in Evangelism, Synod of the NE, Presbyn. Ch. (USA), 1998—99, Preaching prize, Princeton Theol. Sem., 1996, Bibl. Theology; Hebrew, Eden Theol. Sem., 1994; Synod Mission Partnership Grant: Leadership Devel., Synod of the NE, 2003. Mem.: Albion Area

Ministirium (treas. 2002, v.p. 2003). Achievements include development of family systems leadership group for pastors. Office: Barre Center Presbyterian Church 4706 Oak Orchard Albion NY 14411 E-mail: karen.allamon@ptsem.edu.

ALLAMONG, BETTY DAVIS, retired academic administrator; b. Morgantown, W.Va., Apr. 8, 1935; d. Lonnie R. and Jessie R. (Hoffman) Davis; m. Joseph K. Allamong, Sept. 12, 1954; 1 child, John Bradley. BS, W.Va. U., 1961, MA, 1964, PhD, 1971; student, Inst. for Ednl. Mgmt. Harvard U., 1984. Instr. biology Morgantown HS, W.Va., 1961-67; instr. edn. W.Va. U., Morgantown, 1965-67, instr. biology, 1967-72; asst. to full prof. biology Ball State U., Muncie, Ind., 1972-87, assoc. dean, scis. and humanities, 1981-86, dean, scis. and humanities, 1986-87; provost and v.p. acad. affairs Bloomsburg U., Pa., 1987-92, ret., 1992—. Mem. Ind. Corp. for Sci. & Tech., 1983-87. Co-author: Energy for Life, 1976; author numerous lab. manuals; contbr. articles to profl. jours. Recipient Women of Achievement edn. award Women in Comms. Inc., Muncie, 1981. Fellow Ind. Acad. Sci. Home: 253 Pixler Hill Rd Morgantown WV 26508-9541

ALLAN, ALEXANDER R.C. (SANDY ALLAN), food products executive; Joined The Coca-Cola Co., 1968, internal auditor, 1968, mem. Home Office traveling audit team, 1971, fin. controller So. Africa Divsn., 1978, asst. divsn. mgr. and fin. mgr. So. and Cent. Africa Divsn., mng. dir. NATBEV, 1987, pres. Middle East Divsn. (renamed Middle East and N. Africa Divsn. 1998), 1993, pres. Asia Pacific Group, 1999—2000, pres., COO Asia Group, exec. v.p., pres., COO Europe, Eurasai, and Middle East, 2001—. Office: The Coca-Cola Co PO Box 1734 Atlanta GA 30301

ALLAN, BARRY DAVID, research chemist, government official; b. Steubenville, Ohio, Jan. 20, 1935; s. John Young and Frances Lucy (Halbrunner) A.; m. Inge Elisabeth Bergeler, Aug. 5, 1961; children— Barbara Diane, Stephen Barry. BS, Ariz. State U., 1956; MS, U. Ala., 1964, PhD, 1968. Chemist White Sands Missile Range, N.M., 1956; aero. fuels research chemist Army Missile Command, Redstone Arsenal, Ala., 1958-62, research chemist-phys., 1962-96, research chemist, 1968-95; prof. J.C. Calhoun Coll., Decatur, Ala., 1969-73, Athens (Ala.) Coll., 1970-73, U. Ala., Huntsville, 1974-76; rsch. cons. Allan Cons., Huntsville, 1996—. Cons., 1965—; reviewer Nat. Sci. Found., 1973— Publs. in field. Active Huntsville Civic Assn., 1961— . Served to capt. AUS, 1956-58. Recipient Army Research And Devel. Achievement award, 1962, Navy commendation, 1968, Army commendation, 1971, 72 Mem. Am. Chem. Soc. (treas. 1969-73, pres. 1974-76), Combustion Inst., Pasteur Soc., Assn. U.S. Army, N.Y. Acad. Scis., Joint Army, Navy, NASA, Air Force Propellant Characterization Group on Fluids and Materials, Sigma Xi, Gamma Sigma Epsilon, Theta Chi. Office: Barry D Allan Cons 7803 Michael Cir SW Huntsville AL 35802-2900 Fax: 256-881-4101. Office Phone: 256-881-4088. E-mail: ballan@hiwaay.net.

ALLAN, COL, editor-in-chief; m. Sharon Bowditch; children: Michael, Tom, Mathew, Kate. NY corr. for Australian papers News Corp., 1978—80, London corr. for Australian papers, 1981—82; chief of staff Brisbane Sun, Australia, 1982—85; news editor The Australian, 1985—88; dep. editor Daily Telegraph, 1988—92, editor, 1992—99; editor-in-chief Daily Telegraph and Sunday Telegraph, Sydney, 1999—2001, NY Post, 2001—. Office: Editor in Chief New York Post 1211 Ave of Americas New York NY 10036*

ALLAN, GEORGE GRAHAM, fiber and polymer sciences educator, consultant; b. Glasgow, Scotland, Nov. 21, 1930; came to U.S., 1956; s. Frederick James and Margaret Graham (Wright) A.; m. Margaret Muir Allingham, Aug. 31, 1956; children: Frederick James, Lesley Allingham, George Graham, Robert Gordon, Ian Malcolm, Catherine Holly. Diploma, Royal Tech. Coll., Glasgow, 1951; BS with honors, U. Strathclyde, Glasgow, 1952, U. Glasgow, 1952, PhD, 1955; DSc, U. Strathclyde, 1970. Lectr. David Dale Tech. Coll., Glasgow, 1952-56, U. Paisley, Scotland, 1952-56; rsch. fellow U. Strathclyde, 1955-56; rsch. scientist DuPont Co., Wilmington, Del., 1956-61, Niagara Falls, N.Y., 1961-62; sr. scientist Weyerhaeuser Co., Seattle, 1962-66; assoc. prof. U. Wash., Seattle, 1966-70, prof., 1970—. Author 20 chpts. to books; contbr. over 300 articles to profl. jours.; 70 patents in field. Fellow Royal Inst. Chemistry; mem. AIChE, Am. Chem. Soc., Tech. Assn. Pulp and Paper Industry, Controlled Release Soc. Avocations: skiing, music. Home: 18411 60th Pl NE Kenmore WA 98028-8907 Office Phone: 206-543-1491.

ALLAN, JANET D., dean; BSN, Skidmore Coll., 1964; MS in Cmty. Health Nursing, U. Calif.-San Francisco, 1968; PhD in Med. Anthropology. Cert. adult nurse practitioner ANA. Former dean Health Sci. Ctr. U. Tex., San Antonio; dean Univ. of Maryland Sch. of Nursing, Baltimore, Md., 2001—. Recipient 2001 Distinguished Researcher Award. Office: Univ Maryland Sch Nursing 655 West Lombard St Baltimore MD 21201-1579

ALLAN, JONATHAN DAVID, autograph dealer, pop culture historian; b. Grasmere, N.H., July 23, 1948; s. David Nisbet and Natalie Mary (Chandler) A.; m. Barbara Lauderbach, 1966 (div.); 1 child, Jonathan David II; m. Nancy Page, 1982. BA magna cum laude, U. N.H., 1972. Registered dealer. Bookseller, book buyer, columnist, book reviewer, freelance writer, 1972-81; co-owner, pres. Elmer's Nostalgia, Inc., Sanford, Maine, 1981—. Author: The Rock Trivia Book, 1976; columnist; mem. adv. bd. Autograph Collector Mag., 1986-92. N.H. chmn. Nat. Com. to Reopen the Rosenberg Case, 1973-77; vol. York County Shelters, Alfred, Maine, 1993—. Served with USNR, 1966-67. Mem. ACLU, NAACP, Ams. United for Separation Ch. and State, Universal Autograph Collectors Club (Outstanding Autograph Dealer award 1998), Am. Polit. Items Collectors, Maine People's Alliance, Planned Parenthood, People for the Am. Way, So. Poverty Law Ctr., Amnesty Internat., McFarlane Clan Soc., Phi Beta Kappa. Mem. Green Party of Maine. Avocations: collecting autographs and historical ephemera, painting, gardening, doing historical research. Office: Elmer's Nostalgia Inc 3 Putnam St Sanford ME 04073-2024 Office Phone: 207-324-2166. E-mail: jon@elmers.net.

ALLAN, LARRY See BOERSMA, LAWRENCE

ALLAN, LIONEL MANNING, lawyer; b. Detroit, Aug. 3, 1943; AB cum laude, U. Mich., 1965; JD, Stanford U., 1968; student, U. Paris. Bar: Calif. 1969, U.S. Supreme Ct. 1972. Law clk. U.S. Dist. Ct. (no. dist.) Calif., 1969—70; pres. Allan Advisors, Inc., bd. governance and legal cons. firm. Spkr. and writer in field of corp. and bd. governance law; sec. adv. com. San Jose Fed. Ct., 1969-85; mem. bd. visitors Stanford Law Sch., 1985-88; mem. com. comml. code State Bar Calif., 1974-77, corps. com., 1983-86. Co-author: How to Structure the Classic Venture Capital Deal, 1983, Equity Incentives for Start-up Companies, 1985, Master Limited Partnerships, 1987. Bd. dirs. San Jose Mus. Art, 1983-87; trustee KTEH-TV Channel 54 Found., 1987—; dir. NCCJ, 1995-2001, Harker Sch., 1998—, chair 2002-. Served to capt. JAGC USAR, 1974. Mem. ABA (com. on small bus. 1980—, chmn. internat. bus. subcom. 1985-88, chmn. small bus. com. 1989-93), Santa Clara Bar Assn. (chmn. fed. ct. sect. 1971, 77), Internat. Bar Assn., Nat. Assn. Corp. Dirs. (chair no. Calif. chpt. 2004—), San Jose/Silicon Valley C. of C. (dir.), Pi Sigma Alpha, Phi Sigma Iota, Phi Delta Phi. Office: Allan Advisors Inc 18222 Seebree Ln Monte Sereno CA 95030-3135 Office Phone: 408-354-8854. Business E-Mail: lon@lonallan.com.

ALLAN, ROBERT MOFFAT, JR., corporate executive, educator; b. Detroit, Dec. 8, 1920; s. Robert M. and Jane (Christman) A.; m. Harriet Spicer, Nov. 28, 1942; children: Robert M. III, Scott, David, Marilee. BS, Stanford U., 1941; postgrad., Stanford Grad. Sch. Bus., 1941-42; MS, UCLA, 1943; postgrad., Loyola Law Sch., 1947-50. Economist rsch. dept. Security First Nat. Bank, 1942; exec. Marine Ins., 1946-53; asst. to pres., work mgr. Zinsco Elec. Products, 1953-55, v.p., dir., 1956-59; asst.to pres. The Times-Mirror Corp., 1959-60, corp. v.p., 1961-64; pres., dir. Cyprus Mines Corp., 1964-67; pres. Litton Internat., 1967-69, U.S. Naval Postgrad. Sch. Found., prof. internat. mgmt., 1969-85. Bd. dirs., advisor U.S. Naval Acad.; trustee Boys Republic, Pomona Grad. Sch., Claremont Grad. Sch., Del Monte Forest Homeowners; vis. prof. of internat. mgmt. grad. schs. of bus. MBA Stanford, Harvard, U. of Chgo., UCLA, USA and Internat. Inst. Fgn. Studies, Monterey; adv. trustee Monterey County Sheriff, 1982—. Capt. USAF, 1942-45. Recipient award Helms Athletic Found., 1947, 49, Navy Cross of Merit, 1976, Plaque of Merit USCG, 1990, Medal for Heroism, 1990; named Outstanding Businessman of Yr., L.A., Nat. Assn. Accts., 1966; elected to U.S. Intercollegiate Sailing Hall of Fame, 2000; named Monterey Inst. Fgn. Studies trustee and sr. fellow, 1976. Mem. Mchts. and Mfrs. Assn. (dir.), Intercollegiate Yachting Assn. (dir.), Intercollegiate Yachting Assn. (regional dir. 1940-55), Newport Harbor Yacht Club (commodore 1962), Trans-Pacific Yacht Club, Carmel Valley Country Club, Phi Gamma Delta, Phi Delta Phi.

ALLAN, RONALD GAGE, academic research coordinator; b. Cin., May 9, 1941; s. Robert Gage Allan, William Herbert (Stepfather) and Gladys (Mosier) Anderson; life ptnr. Miriam Scholar Clinton. BS in Indsl. Mgmt., U. Cin., 1966, MBA, 1968; PhD, George Washington U., 1977; MS in Taxation, Georgetown U., 1993. Rsch. economist U.S. Dept. Commerce, Bur. Econ. Analysis, Washington, 1972-79; tax analyst Congl. Budget Office, Washington, 1979-81; planning dir. and analyst Vanguard Techs., Fairfax, Va., 1982-88; rsch. coord. Georgetown U., Washington, 1988—. Mem. rsch. com. Nat. Assn. Student Fin. Aid Adminstrs. Contbr. articles to profl. jours. Mem. Nat. Economists Club, Data Warehousing Inst., Am. Taxation Assn., Assn. Instnl. Rsch., Omicron Delta Epsilon. Episcopalian. Home: Apt 406 7401 Eastmoreland Rd Annandale VA 22003 Office: Georgetown U Office of Student Fin Svcs Washington DC 20057 Office Phone: 202-687-8967. Business E-Mail: allanr@georgetown.edu.

ALLAN, WALTER ROBERT, lawyer; b. Detroit, Aug. 1, 1937; s. Walter Francis and Henrietta (Fairchild) A. AB, U. Mich., 1959, JD, 1962. Bar: Calif. 1964, U.S. Ct. Appeals (9th Cir.) 1964, U.S. Supreme Ct. 1972, U.S. Ct. Appeals (D.C. cir.) 1973, U.S. Ct. Appeals (5th cir.) 1977, U.S. Ct. Appeals (3d cir.) 1988. From assoc. to ptnr. Pillsbury, Madison & Sutro, San Francisco, 1963—98; sole practitioner Tiburon, Calif., 1998—. Office: PO Box 771 Belvedere Tiburon CA 94920-0771 Office Phone: 415-889-4048. Business E-Mail: walterallan@mac.com.

ALLAN, WILLIAM GEORGE, artist, educator; b. Everett, Wash., Mar. 28, 1936; BFA, San Francisco Art Inst., 1958. Instr. painting U. Calif., Davis, 1965-67, Berkeley, 1969; prof. art Calif State U., Sacramento, 1968—. Exhibited in group shows at Carnegie Internat. Exhbn., Pitts., 1975, Continuing Surrealism, La Jolla (Calif.) Mus. Art, 1971, Whitney Painting Ann., N.Y.C., 1972, 70th Ann. Exhbn. Art Inst. Chgo., 1972, Indpls. Mus. Art Exhbn., 1972, Whitney Mus. Am. Art, N.Y.C., 1973-74, Painting and Sculpture in Calif.: The Modern Era, San Francisco Mus. Modern Art, 1976, Chgo. Arts Club, 1978; represented in permanent collections at Dallas Mus. Art, San Francisco Mus. Art, Phila. Mus. Art, Whitney Mus. Am. Art, Mus. Modern Art, N.Y.C. Office: Calif State U Sacramento Dept Art 6000 J St Sacramento CA 95819-2605

ALLARD, CATHERINE, music educator, musician; b. Watertown, N.Y., Nov. 13, 1950; d. Joseph Ambrose and Sally (Phillips) Allard. BS in Music Edn., SUNY Coll.-Potsdam, 1972, MusM, 1974; D of Musical Arts, Peabody Conservatory Johns Hopkins U., 1991. Profl. singer, condr.; choral music tchr. Binghamton City Schs., 1974—78; condr. Binghamton Symphony Chorus, 1978—83; music dir. Summer Savoyards, Binghamton, 1976—87; prof. music Troy U., Ala., 1989—; condr. Ala. Jubilee Chorus, Troy, Ala., 2004—. Singer Opern Aachen, Germany, 1984—85; cons. SPEBSQSA, Troy, Ala., 1998—. Singer: (opera) From Winter Darkness (World Premiere Performance), Galileo Galilei (World Premiere), Requiem for the Victims of AIDS (World Premiere); prodr.(host): (TV series) Opus 3, 2000—. Pres. Pilot Club of Troy, Ala., 1994—95, 2003—04. Fellow Chancellor's Fellowship, Troy U., 2004; grantee Performance Enhancement grant, Ala. State Arts Coun., 1999, 2000, Summer Musical, Troy Arts Coun., 1996, 1997, 1998, 2000, 2001, 2002, Amahl and the Night Visitors, 2003, 2004. Mem.: Am. Musicological Soc., Music Educators Nat. Assn., Am. Choral Dirs. Assn., Nat. Assn. Tchrs. of Singing, Sigma Alpha Iota. Liberal. Office: 202 Smith Hall University Ave Troy AL 36082 Office Fax: 334-670-3858. E-mail: callard@troy.edu.

ALLARD, DEAN CONRAD, historian, retired historical center director; b. Kansas City, Mo., Oct. 19, 1933; s. Dean Conrad Sr. and Elizabeth Donaldson (Graves) A.; m. Constance Lynne Morgan, June 17, 1955; children: Scott, Hunt, Elizabeth. AB, Dartmouth Coll., 1955; MA, Georgetown U., 1959; PhD, George Washington U., 1967. Head Naval Operational Archives, Washington, 1958-82; sr. historian Naval Hist. Ctr., Washington, 1982-89; dir. naval history USN, Washington, 1989-95. Adj. prof. George Washington U., 1979-89, v.p. Internat. Commn. Mil. History, 2000—05. Author: The United States Navy and the Vietnam Conflict, Vol. I, 1976, Spencer Fullerton Baird: A Study in the History of American Science, 1978; also articles on naval and maritime history; editor: U.S. Naval History Sources in the United States, 1979. Chmn. Hist. Commn., Arlington, Va., 1978-80; pres. Arlington Hist. Soc., 1974-75; mem. coun. Woodlawn Plantation, Fairfax, Va., 1976-84; mem. French-U.S. Sci. Com. on CSS, Ala., 1991-95. Lt. (j.g.) USN, 1955-58. Recipient Superior Civil Svc. award U.S. Govt., 1995, Samuel Eliot Morison award for Disting. Svc., USS Constn. Mus. Found., Boston, 1995. Mem.: Internat. Commn. Mil. History (v.p. 2000—), Internat. Commn. Maritime History (mem. exec. coun. 1990—2002), U.S. Commn. Mil. History (pres. 1995—99), World War II Studies Assn. (bd. dirs.), Soc. for Mil. History (v.p. 1983—86), N.Am. Soc. for Oceanic History (pres. 1985—89), Cosmos Club (Washington), Phi Beta Kappa. Avocations: gardening, hiking. Home: 2701 N Quincy St Arlington VA 22207-5046 E-mail: allard@prodigy.net.

ALLARD, JUDITH LOUISE, secondary school educator; b. Rutland, Vt., Feb. 21, 1945; d. William Edward and Orilla Marion (Trombley) A. BA, U. Vt., 1967, MS, 1969. Nat. bd. cert. tchr. in adolescent and young adulthood sci., 1999. Tchr. math., sci. Edmunds Jr. H.S., Burlington, Vt., 1969-73, biology tchr., 1973-78, sci. dept. chair, 1975-78; biology tchr. Burlington (Vt.) H.S., 1978—; instr. edn. St. Michaels Coll., Winooski, Vt., 2001—02; lectr. in edn. U. Vt., 2002—. Bd. dirs. Vt. Creative Imagination, Inc., 1998—; instr. environ. studies U. Vt., Burlington, 1988-89; adviser Nat. Honor Soc., 1986—; mentor No. New Eng. Comentoring Network, 2002—05; leader Vt. Profl. Devel. Network, 2004—. Co-author Favorite Labs of Outstanding Tchrs., 1991. Active Amnesty Internat., 1985—; mem. Lake Champlain Com., Burlington, 1987—, Vt. Goals 2000 Panel, 1995—99, Vt. State Licensing Commn., 1995—96, Vt. Stds. Bd. for Profl. Educators, 1996—2002, co-vice chair, 2000—01, chmn., 2001—02; state bd. dirs. Odyssey of the Mind, 1986—98. Named Outstanding Vt. Educator, U. Vt., 1983, Outstanding Vt. Sci. Tchr., Sigma Xi Soc., 1984, Vt. Tchr. Yr., 1998, Outstanding Vt. Sci. Tchr., Vt. Acad. Sci. and Engring., 2000, Tandy Tech. scholar, 1990, Genentech Access Excellence fellow, 1995, 1996, Access Excellence Retro fellow, 1996, Tchr. of Yr., Biol. Scis. Curriculum Study, 2001; recipient Presdl. Sci. Tchg. award, NSF, 1983, Tech. award, Tandy, 1998, Siemens award for Advanced Placement, 2000. Mem. NEA (bd. dirs. Vt. chpt., 1990-98), Vt. Sci. Tchrs. Assn. (bd. dirs. 1980-92, treas. 1985-92), Burlington Profl. Stds. Bd. (chair 1991-2001), Parents and Friends of Edn. (trustee), Nat. Assn. Biology Tchrs. (dir. Vt. Outstanding Biology Tchr. award program 1977—, Outstanding Biology Tchr. award 1975), Assn. Presdl. Awardees in Sci., Phi Delta Kappa. Roman Catholic. Avocations: needlecrafts, fishing, music. Home: 221 Woodlawn Rd Burlington VT 05401-5722 Office Phone: 802-864-8411. Business E-Mail: jallard@bsdvt.org.

ALLARD, MICHAEL ALAN, music educator, conductor; b. Waynesboro, Pa., Dec. 6, 1953; s. Nicholas Leo and Lillian Lee Allard; m. Barbara Diane Mazzotta, Aug. 29, 1976; children: Allison, Kristen. BA, Colgate U., 1976; M of Music Edn., Fla. State U., 1978; PhD, U. Tex., 1992. Orch. tchr. Washoe County Sch. Dist., Reno, 1977—79; orch. coord. Clark County Sch. Dist., Las Vegas, 1979—87; asst. instr. U. Tex., Austin, 1987—88; orch. dir. Punahou Sch., Honolulu, 1988—91; orch. condr., assoc. prof. U. Pacific, Stockton, Calif., 1991—2000; orch. tchr. Porterville Unified Sch. Dist., Calif., 2000—; adj. prof. Porterville Coll., 2000—03; orch. condr. Ctrl. Valley Youth Symphony, Stockton, 1993—2000; nat. music edn. clinician The Selmer Co., Elkhart, Ind., 1978—. Musician (condr.): Carnegie Hall, Sydney Opera House. Recipient Robert G. Ingram Music Prize, Colgate U., 1976. Mem.: Am. Fedn. of Musicians, Music Educators Nat. Conf., Am. String Tchr. Assn. (pres. Calif. 1999—2000), Phi Kappa Lambda, Mu Phi Epsilon (U. Pacific chpt. adv. 1991—99).

ALLARD, WAYNE (A. WAYNE ALLARD), senator, veterinarian; b. Ft Collins, Colo., Dec. 12, 1943; m. Joan Malcolm, Mar. 23, 1967; children: Christie, Cheryl. DVM, Colo. State U., 1968. Veterinarian Allard Animal Hosp.; mem. Colo. State Senate, 1983-90, U.S. Ho. Reps., Washington, 1991-96; U.S. senator from Colo., 1996—; deputy maj. whip U.S. Senate, 2003—. Chmn. health, environment and instn. com., chmn. senate majority caucus; mem. 102nd-104th Congresses from 4th dist., Colo., 1991-96; mem. agrl. com., 1991-92, 93-94, 95-96, mem. small bus. com., 1991-92, mem. interior and insular affairs com., 1991-92, mem. com. on coms., 1991-92, 93-94, mem. budget com., 1993-94, 95-96, mem. natural resources com., 1993-94, 95-96, mem. joint com. on reorganization of Congress, 1993-94, 95-96, chmn. subcom. of agr. conservation, forest and water, 1995-96; senator 105th Congress, 1997—, mem. banking, urban affairs com., 1997—, environment and pub. works com., 1997—, intelligence select com., 1997—, Senate armed svcs. com., banking, housing and urban affairs com., select com. on intelligence; mem. select com. on intelligence, armed svcs. com., chmn. pers. subcom., banking, housing and urban affairs com., chmn. subcom. on housing and transp. 106th Congress; health officer, Loveland, Colo.; mem. regional adv. coun. on vet. medicine Western Interstate Commn. Higher Edn.; mem. Colo. Low-Level Radioactive Waste Adv. Com. Chmn. United Way; active 4-H Found. Mem. AVMA, Colo. Vet. Medicine Assn., Larimer County Vet. Medicine Assn. (past pres.), Bd. Vet. Practitioners (charter mem.), Am. Animal Hosp. Assn., Nat. Conf. State Legislatures (vice-chmn. human resources com. 1987—, healthcare cost containment com.), Loveland C. of C., Republican. Methodist. Home: PO Box 2405 Loveland CO 80539-2405 Office: US Senate 521 Dirksen Senate Office Bldg Washington DC 20510-0001*

ALLARD, WILLIAM KENNETH, mathematician; b. Lowell, Mass., Oct. 29, 1941; s. Frederic Pratt and Jeannette Edna (Perrault) A.; m. Priscilla Elaine May, Aug. 10, 1968; children: Felicia, Christopher. Sc.B., Villanova U., 1963; PhD in Math, Brown U., 1968. Asst. prof. math. Princeton U., 1971-75; prof. math. Duke U., Durham, N.C., 1975—, chmn. dept., 1985-86. Mng. editor Duke Math. Jour. 1983-85 Alfred P. Sloan fellow, 1970-72 Mem. Am. Math. Soc. Office: Duke U Dept Math Durham NC 27708 E-mail: wka@math.duke.edu.

ALLBRITTON, CLIFF, personal and organizational consultant; b. Aransas Pass, Tex., Aug. 19, 1931; BS, Okla. State U.; MDiv, Southwestern Sem.; MA, Baylor U.; PhD, Columbia Pacific U., 1994. Editor family ministry dept. Lifeway Christian Resources, Nashville, 1979-91; pres. Cliff Allbritton Rsch. Ctr., Nashville, 1991-96. V.p. Corp. Pers. Cons., Dallas, 1972-79; acct. exec. Beaver Assocs. Advt., Akron, Ohio, 1971-72. Author: How to Get Married and Stay That Way, 1982, Dare to Win-How to Live the American Dream, 1992, Personal Riches for Today's Singles, 1992, The Psychology of Grace, 1994; co-author: Solo Flight, 1981, Single Adult Ministry in Your Church, 1985. Min. 8 congregations, Tex., N.Mex., Ohio, Va., 1954-71. Named Internat. Man of Yr. by Internat. Biographical Ctr., Cambridge, Eng., 1992; recipient Presdl. Legion of Merit, 2003. Mem. Am. Assn. Christian Counselors, Am. Assn. Family Counselors, Internat. Platform Assn., Health Scis. Inst., Omicron Delta Kappa, Alpha Zeta, Kappa Tau Pi. Home: 865 Bellevue Rd U21 Nashville TN 37221-2794

ALLBRITTON, JOE LEWIS, diversified financial services company executive, director; b. D'Lo, Miss., Dec. 29, 1924; s. Lewis A. and Ada (Carpenter) A.; m. Barbara Jean Balfanz, Feb. 23, 1967; 1 son, Robert Lewis. LLB, Baylor U., 1949, LLD (hon.), 1964, JD, 1969; LHD, Calif. Bapt. Coll., 1973. Bar: Tex. 1949. Dir. Perpetual Corp., Houston, 1958—, pres., 1965—76, 1978—81, chmn. bd., 1973—. Chmn. Allbritton Comm. Co., 1974-98, chmn. exec. com., 1998-; chmn. Univ. Bancshares, Inc., Houston, 1975-97, Houston Fin. Svcs., Ltd., London, 1977-2003, Riggs Nat. Corp., Washington, 1981-2001, sr. chmn., 2001-04; dep. chmn. Riggs Bank Europe Ltd., London, 1986-92, chmn., 1992-2001; mem. Greater Washington Bd. Trade, 1983-88, 92-; trustee The Mitre Corp., Bedford, Mass., 1987-93. Trustee Fed. City Coun., Washington, 1975—, John F. Kennedy Ctr. for Performing Arts, Washington, 1985-90, Nat. Geog. Soc., 1986-99, trustee emeritus, 1999—; trustee The Ronald Reagan Presdl. Found., L.A., 1990—, George Bush Presdl. Found., College Station, Tex., 1993—; bd. dirs. Nat. Fund for U.S. Bot. Garden, 1992-95, The Lyndon Baines Johnson Found., 1989-2001, Georgetown U., Washington, 1990-96. With USN, 1943-46. Mem.: Bankers Roundtable, State Bar Tex.

ALLCOCK, HARRY R., chemistry professor; b. Loughborough, Eng., Apr. 8, 1932; naturalized U.S. citizen; s. Claud Leonard and Nora (Clarke) A.; m. Noreen Raworth, Nov. 14, 1959. BSc, U. London, 1953, PhD, 1956. Cert. chemist. Postdoctoral fellow Purdue U., West Lafayette, Ind., 1956-58, Can. Nat. Rsch. Coun., Ottawa, Ont., 1958-60; rsch. scientist Cen. Rsch. Labs. Am. Cyanamid Co., Stamford, Conn., 1961-66; assoc. prof. chem. Pa. State U., University Park, 1966-70, prof. chem., 1970-85, Evan Pugh Prof. Chem., 1985—. Author: (books) Heteroatom Ring Systems and Polymers, 1967, Phosphorus-Nitrogen Compounds, 1972, (monograph) Chemistry and Applications of Polyphosphazenes, 2003; author: (with F.W. Lampe) (books) Contemporary Polymer Chemistry, 1981; author: (with F.W. Lampe and J.E. Mark), 2003; author: (with M. Zeldin & K.J. Wynne) Inorganic and Organometallic Polymers, 1988; author: (with P. Wisian-Neilson and K.J. Wynne) Inorganic and Organometallic Polymers II, 1994, editor Inorganic Syntheses Vol. XXV, (jours.) Phosphorous, 1973—77, Macromolecules, 1974—79, Chem. Revs., 1974—79, Biomaterials, 1980—82, Jour. of Polymer Sci., 1987—, Inorganic Chem., 1988—91, Chem. of Materials, 1988—, Heteroatom Chem., 1988—93, Jour. Inorganic and Organometallic Polymers, 1990—. Guggenheim fellow 1986-87. Fellow Am. Inst. Chemists (Chem. Pioneer award 1989); mem. Am. Chem. Soc. (nat. award polymer chemistry 1984, nat. award chemistry of materials 1992, Herman Mark award polymer chemistry 1994), Royal Soc. Chemistry (various coms.), Corp. Inorganic Syntheses. Office: Pa State U Dept Chemistry 104 Chemistry Bldg University Park PA 16802-4615

ALLDAY, MARTIN LEWIS, lawyer; b. El Dorado, Ark., May 30, 1926; s. Martin L. Sr. and Bess (Kavanaugh) A.; m. Patricia Pryor, May 1, 1954; children: Katherine, Elizabeth, Martin III. JD, U. Tex., Austin, 1951. Bar: Tex. 1951. Examiner oil and gas div. R.R. Commn. of Tex., Austin, 1951-53; legal dept. Superior Oil Co., Midland, Tex., 1953-57, Houston, 1957-59; ptnr. Lynch, Chappell, Allday and Alsup, Midland, Austin & Dallas, 1959-89; past solicitor Dept. of Interior, Washington, 1989; chmn. Fed. Energy Regulatory Commn., Washington, 1989-93; of counsel Scott, Douglass and McConnico, Austin, Dallas, Tex., 1993—. Past pres. Midland Jaycees, C. of C., Indsl. Found.; past trustee, gov. Midland Meml. Hosp.; bd. trustees Petroleum Mus. Hall of Fame; presiding officer Tex. State Cemetery Commn., Austin, 1998-2004. With Inf. U.S. Army, 1944-46. Decorated Purple Heart, Bronze Star, Combat Infantry badge, 96th Presdl. Citation award; recipient Hard Hat award Ind. Producers Assn. Am., 1992, Disting. Alumni award Schreiner U., 2004; named Pioneer, Tex. R.R. Commn., 2003; named one of top 50 Oil and Gas Attys. Tex. Monthly Mag. Mem. ABA, Tex. Bar Assn. (chmn. oil, gas and mineral sect. 1970), Tex. Bar Found., Midland County Bar Assn. (pres. 1972-73), Ind. Prodrs. Assn. Am., Midland Country Club (pres.), Petroleum Club (bd. dirs.), Tex. Ind. Prodr. and Royalty Orgn. (Hats Off award 2004). Republican. Episcopalian. Avocations: fishing, hunting, golf. Office: 600 Congress Ave Ste 1500 Austin TX 78701-2976 Office Phone: 512-495-6354. E-mail: mallday@scottdoug.com.

ALLDREDGE, NOREEN S., librarian; b. Sacramento, Apr. 8, 1939; d. Harold and Cecelia (Doherty) Sunderland. BA, Mount St. Mary's Coll., L.A., 1961; MS, Columbia U., 1965; MA, Tex. A&M U., 1980. Film librarian N.Y. Pub. Library, N.Y.C., 1964-65; ref. librarian U. Nev., Reno, 1965-66, librarian

Desert Rsch. Inst., 1966-70, circulation librarian, 1970-74, collection devel. librarian, 1974-76; asst. dir. Tex. A&M U., College Station, 1976-81; dean libraries Mont. State U., Bozeman, 1981—. Accreditation visitor N.W. Assn. Schs. and Colls., 1985—, ALA, 1982—. Vol. Am. Hiking Soc., 1985-88; sr. assoc. N.S. Dept. Edn., 1990. Mem. ALA, Women Acad. Library Dirs., Am. Assn. Higher Edn. Home: 14574 Outrigger Dr San Leandro CA 94577-6415

ALLECTA, JULIE, lawyer; b. Worcester, Mass., Oct. 28, 1946; BA magna cum laude, U. N. Mex., 1973, MBA magna cum laude, JD, U. N. Mex., 1977. Bar: M. Mex. 1978, D.C. 1984, Calif. 1985, U.S. Supreme Ct., U.S. Ct. Appeals, fifth & tenth cir. Office gen. counsel SEC, Washington, 1977—81; ptnr. Paul, Hastings, Janofsky & Walker LLP, San Francisco, co-chmn. nat. investment mgmt. practice group. Editl. bd. Arlen Mutual Fund Handbook, Bd. IQ. Mem.: Am. Law Inst. ABA Com. Continuing Profl. Edn. (faculty mem.), Mutual Fund Dir. Forum (adv. dir.), ABA-Bus. Law Sect. (com. fed. regulation securities, sub. com. investment co. & investment advisors). Office: Paul Hastings Janofsky & Walker LLP 55 Second St 24th Floor San Francisco CA 94105 Office Phone: 415-856-7106. Office Fax: 415-856-7106. Business E-Mail: julieallecta@paulhastings.com.

ALLEE, NANCY JANE, reference librarian, library administrator; b. Greencastle, Ind. d. Walter L. and Peggy J. (Matlock) A. BA, DePauw U., 1985; MLS, Ind. U., 1986; MPH, U. Okla., 1994. Reference libr. Northeastern State U., Tahlequah, Okla., 1987-95; dir. Pub. Health Libr. and Informatics U. Mich., 1995—. Presenter, writer, cons. in field; mem. leadership fellows program Nat. Libr. Medicine/Assn. Acad. Health Scis. Librs., 2003—04. Reviewer (video reviews) Video Rating Guide for Libraries, 1990-95. Actress Tahlequah Community Playhouse, 1988-95 (Best Actress 1988); bd. dirs. Arts Coun. Tahlequah, 1992-93; chmn. pub. health tng. subcom. Ptnrs. in Info. Access, 1998—. Recipient Univ. Libr. ACE award, 1997. Mem. ALA, APHA, MLA (pub. health/health adminstrn. sect. chmn. 1997-98), Acad. Health Info. Profls., Phi Beta Kappa, Phi Delta Kappa (sec. Tahlequah chpt. 1988-89, pres. 1989-90). Office: Sch Pub Health Libr U Mich Ann Arbor MI 48109

ALLEGRA, FRANCIS M., federal judge, retired federal official; m. Regina Lynne Esposito. Student, Case We. Res. U.; BA magna cum laude, Borromeo Coll. Ohio, 1978; JD magna cum laude, Cleve. State U., 1981. Bar: D.C., Ohio, Ct. Fed. Claims, U.S. Ct. Appeals, U.S. Supreme Ct. Jud. clk. Chief Trial Judge Philip R. Miller, 1981-82; assoc. Squire, Sanders & Dempsey, Cleve., 1982-84; line atty., appellate sect. US Dept. Justice, 1984-88, counselor to the asst. atty gen., Tax Div., 1994, dep. assoc. atty. gen. Washington, 1996-98, counselor to the assoc. atty. gen., 1994-96; judge US Ct. of Fed. Claims, Washington, 1998—. Contbr. articles to profl. jours. Mem. Coun. 1000 Nat. Italian Am. Found., Sons of Italy of Am. Office: US Court of Federal Claims 717 Madison Pl NW Washington DC 20439-0002*

ALLEGRUCCI, DONALD LEE, state supreme court justice; b. Pittsburg, Kans., Sept. 19, 1936; s. Nello and Josephine Marie (Funaro) A.; m. Joyce Ann Thompson, Nov. 30, 1963; children: Scott David, Bowen Jay. AB, Pittsburg State U., 1959; JD, Washburn U., 1963. Bar: Kans. 1963. Asst. county atty. Butler County, El Dorado, Kans., 1963-67; state senator Kans. Legislature, Topeka, 1976-80; mem. Kans. Pub. Relations Bd., 1981-82; dist. judge Kans. 11th Jud. Dist., Pittsburg, 1982-87, adminstrv. judge, 1983-87; justice Kans. Supreme Ct., Topeka, 1987—. Instr. Pittsburg State U., 1969-72; exec. dir. Mid-Kans. Community Action Program, Inc.; mem. exec. com. Kansas Dist. Judges Assn., 1982-87; chmn. KDJA Legislative Coordinating Com., 1982-86; mem. Judicial Council Ct. Unification Advisory Com., 1984-85. Mem. Dem. State Com., 1974-80; candidate 5th Congl. Dist., 1978; past pres. Heart Assn.; bd. dirs. YMCA. Served in USAF, 1959—66. Mem. Kans. Bar Assn.; former mem. Crawford County Bar Assn. (past pres.), Butler County Bar Assn. (past pres.). Democrat. Office: Kansas Supreme Court 374 Kansas Judicial Ctr 301 SW 10th Ave Fl 3 Topeka KS 66612-1507*

ALLEMANG, ARNOLD A., chemicals executive; B in Chemistry, Sam Houston State U. Unit mgr. Dow Chem. Co., 1981—84, prodn. mgr. Terneuzen, Netherlands, 1984—88, mgr. hydrocarbon prodn. Freeport, Tex., 1988—89, dir. tech. ctrs. Midland, Mich., 1989—92, mfg. gen. mgr. Dow Benelux, 1992—93, regional v.p. mfg. and adminstrn. Dow Benelux, 1993, v.p. mfg. ops. Dow Europe, 1993—95, VP ops. Midland, 1995—, exec. v.p., 2000—. Bd. dirs. Dow Corning Corp., Liana Ltd., Dorinco Reinsurance Co., Mems. Com. of Dupont Dow Elastomers LLC, Cargill Dow, LLC. Adv. bd. President's Cir. of Sam Houston State. U.; adv. bd. Coll. Engring. Kans. State U. Mem.: Nat. Assn. Mfrs. (bd. dirs.), Am. Chem. Soc., Ctr. Chem. Process Safety (advisory bd.). Office: The Dow Chem Co 47 Building Midland MI 48667

ALLEN, A. WILLIAM, III, (BILL ALLEN), food service executive; CEO la Madeleine French Bakery and Cafe; pres. West Coast Concepts, 2004—05; CEO Outback Steakhouse, 2005—. Office: Outback Steakhouse Company 10001 E Pinnacle Rd Scottsdale AZ 85255*

ALLEN, ALICE, communications and marketing executive; b. N.Y.C., May 31, 1943; d. C. Edmonds and Helen (McCreery) A.; 1 child, Helen. Student, Conn. Coll., 1961. Pres. Alice Allen, Inc., N.Y.C., 1970—83; sr. v.p. Robert Marston, N.Y.C., 1983—84, Cunningham & Walsh, N.Y.C., 1984—86, Carl Byoir (acquired by Hill & Knowlton), N.Y.C., 1986; sr. v.p., dir. comms. and corp. mktg. Hill & Knowlton, N.Y.C., 1986—88; pres., owner Allen Comms. Group, Inc., N.Y.C., 1988—95, Alice Allen Comms., 1995—2003. Bd. dirs. Family Dymanics, N.Y.C., 1976-78, Veritas, 1980-85; v.p. Jr. League, N.Y.C., 1975-76; mem. adv. bd. Enterprise Found., 1992-2001. Mem. Pub. Rels. Soc. Am., Pub. Publicity Assn. (pres. 1969-71), Women's Media Group, Comm. Network. Office: Alice Allen Comms 320 E 72nd St New York NY 10021-4769

ALLEN, ANN SALATHE, social studies educator, researcher; d. Leonhard Francis, Jr. and Elaine Sorjonen Salathe; m. John Robert Allen, Nov. 23, 1968; 1 child, Christopher Michael. BA, U. New Orleans, 1964—68, MEd, 1970—72; PhD, Va. Commonwealth U., Richmond, 1997—2003. Cert. tchr. La. State Bd. Edn., 1968, Va. Bd. Edn., 2004. Classroom tchr. Grace King H.S., Metairie, La., 1968—71, L.W. Higgins H.S., Marrero, La., 1971—74, social studies dept. head, 1972—74; part-time rschr., rsch. asst. Richmond Pub. Schs., Va., 1974—79, 1979—90, coord., rsch. & evaluation, 1990—. Mem. Va. Commonwealth U. Sch. Edn. Search Coms., Richmond, 1999—, Va. Commonwealth U., Sch. Edn. Nat. Coun. for Accreditation of Tchr. Edn. Com., Richmond, 2004—. Vol., allocations & assessment United Way Svcs., Richmond, Va., 1979—97; mem., class of 1989 Leadership Metro Richmond, Va., 1989—2004; bd. mem. Teens Encounter Christ, Richmond, Va., 2000—04. Mem.: ASCD (assoc.), Richmond Assn. Sch. Adminstrs. (pres. 1985—86), Va. Ednl. Rsch. Assn. (pres. 1999—2000), Am. Ednl. Rsch. Assn. (assoc.), Richmond First Club (bd. dirs. 2004—), Phi Delta Kappa (bd. dirs. 2004—). Lutheran. Avocations: reading, bicycling, running, yoga, sewing. Office: Richmond Pub Schs 301 N 9th St Richmond VA 23219 E-mail: aallen@richmond.k12.va.us.

ALLEN, ANNE ELLIOTT, municipal official; b. Boston, June 27, 1951; d. William Augustus Allen II and Cynthia Gilbert Allen; children: Molly Macdonald Brown, Robert H. Macdonald II. BA, U. Maine, 1993, MPA, 1996. Mgr. fund accounts U. Maine, Orono; mcpl. ofcl. City of Bangor, Maine. Bd. dirs. Eastern Maine Devel. Corp. Mem. Bangor City Coun., 2001—04; mem. adv. com. Barker Area Comprehensive Traffic Sys. Transit; pres. Penobscot Valley Coun. Govt.; bd. dirs. Ea. Maine Devel. Corp.; bd. mem. Maine Comm. Sys. Policy Bd. Avocations: sailing, skiing, swimming. Home: PO Box 2323 Bangor ME 04402-2323 Office: 75 Harlow St Bangor ME 04401 Business E-Mail: annie.allen@unit.maine.edu.

ALLEN, ANNETTE, minister; b. Helena, Ga., Apr. 27, 1962; d. Raymond and Nonie Mae Allen; m. Tigen R. Griffith (div.); children: Erick Raphael Griffith, Leah Charisse Griffith. Student, Medgar Evers Coll., Bklyn., 1983—85; cert., Inst. Biblical Studies, Lynchburg, Va., 2000; diploma, Liberty U., Lynchburg, 2004; DD, World Christianship Ministry, Fresno, Calif., 2004. Program asst. Nat. Coun. Ch. World Svc., N.Y.C., 1981—90; cmty. activist Clergy Inc., Bklyn., 1990—92; office mgr. United Ch. of Christ, N.Y.C., 1992—93; freelance writer Bklyn., 1993—96; metaphysician Lady Solomon, McRae, Ga., 1997—; min. New Hope Deliverance Ctr., McRae. Motivational spkr., Ga., 2000—. Author: War Between Two Minds, 2003. Founder New Hope HIV/AIDS Outreach Ctr., 2005. Republican. Home: Rte 1 Box 26C Mc Rae GA 31055 Home Fax: 229-868-5886. Personal E-mail: ladysolomon@planttel.net.

ALLEN, BARRY MORGAN, corporate communications consultant; b. N.Y.C., June 3, 1939; s. Robert Mitchell and Edna B. (Feldman) A.; m. Reña Susan Garfinkle, June 16, 1974 children: Lynda Gicca, David Krasno, Sheri BS in Journalism, U. Md., 1961. Mng. editor Diamondback, 1959; assoc. editor Old Line, 1959; reporter Radio News Assocs., 1960, Hearst Metrotone News/ABC-TV, 1961; mgr. account Burson-Marsteller, Washington, 1967—71; dir. comm. Archon Pure Products Corp., Beverly Hills, Calif., 1971—73; v.p. comm. Glass Packaging Inst., Washington, 1973—77; 1st v.p., corp. comm. Bank of Boston, 1977—86; sr. v.p. corp. affairs Hartford Nat. Corp., Conn., 1986—88; sr. v.p., dir. pub. affairs Manning, Selvage & Lee, N.Y.C., 1988—94; pres. Barry Allen & Assocs., Inc., Boca Raton, Fla., 1994—. Charter mem. Evanston Group, 1985-87. Mem. adv. com. Boca Raton Resort and Club, 2001—03, bd. govs., 2003—; pres. Boca Golf and Tennis Property Owners Assn., 2001—04; mem. adv. bd. South Palm Beach County, Fla., 2000—; mem. Gov.'s Alliance Against Drugs, Mass., 1985—86, Boca Raton Airport Authority, 2003—04, chair pub. affairs com., 2003—04; bd. dirs. Morgan Meml. Good Will, Boston, 1986, Bay State Games, Mass., 1986. Lt. USNR, 1961—67, Vietnam. Scholar, Montgomery County, Md., 1960. Mem.: Union League Club N.Y.C., Pi Delta Epsilon. Avocations: golf, travel. Home and Office: 15378 Lakes of Delray Blvd #16 Delray Beach FL 33484

ALLEN, BARRY W., research scientist, writer; b. Chgo., Mar. 3, 1942; s. Joseph Garrott and Dorothy Olive (Travis) Allen; m. Nancy Carol Bates, June 7, 1974; children: Dorothy Jean, Peter Woodward. Diplome (Cert. of Exam.), Sorbonne, Universite de Paris, Cours de Civilisation Francaise, 1961—62; BA, Harvard Coll., 1966; PhD, Duke U. Med. Ctr., Durham, N.C., 1984. Rsch. asst. Dept. Biophysics, Harvard Med. Sch., Boston, 1964—65; archtl. draftsman and designer Robert Charles Assocs., Huygens and Tappe, Boston, 1968—71; asst. rsch. prof., dept. anesthesiology Ctr. Hyperbaric Medicine and Environ. Physiology, Duke U. Med. Ctr., Durham, NC, 1994—. Chief scuba instr. Harvard Coll., 1970—78, Boston U., 1970—78, Wellesley Coll., 1970—78; chief diver, chief surveyor Ancient Gythion Underwater Archaeology Expdn., Gythion, Greece, 1972; tchg. asst. Biology Dept., Harvard Coll., 1972—73; instr., expository writing Dept. English, Harvard Coll., 1977—78; post-doctoral rsch. assoc. Lab. G.G. Somjen, Duke U. Med. Ctr., Durham, 1984—86; instr., writing program Dept. English, Duke U., 1986—87; post-doctoral rsch. assoc., divsn. pulmonary diseases Sch. Medicine, U. NC, Chapel Hill, 1986—87. Author: (book) Sports Illustrated Skin Diving and Snorkeling, 1976, Beneath Cold Seas, 1983. Pres. Durham Inter-Neighborhood Coun., 1987—89; dir. Nat. Assn. Underwater Instrs., Calif., 1978—85; exec. bd. mem. LWV, 1990—92. Recipient Outstanding Contributions Sport of Diving, Nat. Assn. Underwater Instrs., 1975—76, Grad. Rsch. award, Duke U., 1980, Neighborhood and Cmty. award, Durham Inter-Neighborhood Coun. Democrat. Achievements include invention of device for long-term monitoring of blood ions; procedure for direct casting of collagen supports for cell culture; patents for electrochemical detection of a biologically-important molecule.

ALLEN, BELLE, management consulting firm executive, communications executive; b. Chgo. d. Isaac and Clara (Friedman) Allen., U. Chgo. Cert. conf. mgr. Internat. Inst. Conf. Planning and Mgmt., 1989. Reporter, spl. corr. The Leader Newspapers, Chgo., Washington, 1960—64; cons., v.p., treas., dir. William Karp Cons. Co. Inc., Chgo., 1961—79, chmn. bd., pres., treas., 1979—; pres. Belle Allen Comm., Chgo., 1961—; nat. corr. CCA Press, 1990—. Apptd. pub. mem., com. on judicial evaluation Chgo. Bar Assn., 1998—; v.p., treas., bd. dirs. Cultural Arts Survey Inc., Chgo., 1965-79; cons., bd. dirs. Am. Diversified Rsch. Corp., Chgo., 1967-70; v.p., sec., bd. dirs. Mgmt. Performance Systems Inc., 1976-77; cons. City Club Chgo., 1962-65, Ill. Commn. on Tech. Progress, 1965-67; hearing mem. Ill. Gov.'s Grievance Panel for State Employees, 1979—; hearing mem. grievance panel Ill. Dept. Transp., 1985—; mem. adv. governing bd. Ill. Coalition on Employment of Women, 1980-88; spl. program advisor President's Project Partnership, 1980-88; mem. consumer adv. coun. FRS, 1979-82; reporter CCA Press, 1990—; panel mem. Free Press vs. Fair Trial Nat. Ctr. Freedom of Info. Studies Loyola U. Law Sch., 1993, mem. planning com. Freedom of Info. awards, 1993; conf. chair The Swedish Inst. Press Ethics: How to Handle, 1993. Editor: Operations Research and the Management of Mental Health Systems, 1968; contbr. articles to profl. jours. Mem. campaign staff Adlai E. Stevenson II, 1952, 56, John F. Kennedy, 1960; founding mem. women's bd. United Cerebral Palsy Assn., Chgo., 1954, bd. dirs., 1954-58; pres. Dem. Fedn. Ill., 1958-61; pres. conf. staff Eleanor Roosevelt, 1960; mem. Welfare Pub. Rels. Forum, 1960-61; bd. dirs., mem. exec. com., chmn. pub. rels. com. Regional Ballet Ensemble, Chgo., 1961-63; bd. dirs. Soc. Chgo. Strings, 1963-64; mem. Ind. Dem. Coalition, 1968-69; bd. dirs. Citizens for Polit. Change, 1969; campaign mgr. aldermanic election 42d ward Chgo. City Coun., 1969; mem. selection com. Robert Aragon Scholarship, 1991; mem. planning com. mem. Hutchins Era reunion U. Chgo., 1995, 2000. Recipient Outstanding Svc. award United Cerebral Palsy Assn., Chgo., 1954, 55, Chgo. Lighthouse for Blind, 1986, Spl. Comms. award The White House, 1961, cert. of appreciation Ill. Dept. Human Rights, 1985, Internat. Assn. Ofcl. Human Rights Agys., 1985; selected as reference source Am. Bicentennial Rsch. Inst. Libr. Human Resources, 1973; named Hon. Citizen, City of Alexandria, Va., 1985; selected to be photographed by Bachrach nat. exhibit for Faces of Chicago, 1990. Mem. AAAS, NOW, AAAU, Affirmative Action Assn. (bd. dirs. 1981-85, chmn. mem. and programs com. 1981-85, pres. 1983—), Fashion Group (bd. dirs. 1981-83, chmn. Restrospective View of an Hist. Decade 1960-70, editor The Bull. 1981), Indsl. Rels. Rsch. Assn. (bd. dirs., chmn. pers. placement com. 1960-61), Sarah Siddons Soc., Soc. Pers. Adminstrs., Women's Equity Action League, Nat. Assn. Inter-Group Rels. Ofcls. (nat. conf. program 1959), Publicity Club Chgo. (chmn. inter-city rels. com. 1960-61, Disting. Svc. award 1968), Ill. C. of C. (cmty. rels. com., alt. mem. labor rels. com. 1971-74), Chgo. C. of C. and Industry (merit employment com. 1961-63), Internat. Press Club Chgo. (charter 1992—, bd. dirs. 1992—), Chgo. Press Club (chmn. women's activities 1969-71), U. Chgo. Club of Met. Chgo. (program com. 1993—, chair summer quarter programs 1994), Soc. Profl. Journalists (Chgo. Headline Club 1992—, regional conf. planning com. 1993, co-chair Peter Lisagor awards 1993, program com. 1992—), Assn. Women Journalists, Nat. Trust for Historic Preservation. Office: 111 E Chestnut St Ste 29J Chicago IL 60611

ALLEN, BENJAMIN J., academic administrator; b. Jan. 5, 1947; BS in Bus. Econs., Ind. U., 1969; MA in Econs., U. Ill., 1973, PhD in Econs., 1974. Asst. prof. Wash. State U., 1974—79, mem. grad. faculty, 1976—79, Iowa State U., 1979—90, 1991—, acting head transp. and logistics area, 1982—83, prof., 1984—88, 1991—, dir. Midwest Transp. Ctr., 1988—90, dean Coll. Bus., 1994—2001, interim v.p. external affairs, 2001—02, provost, 2002—; prof. U. Ark., 1990—91, mem. grad. faculty, 1990—91. Bd. dirs. Heartland Express, INc.; pres. Midwest Bus. Deans Assn., 1998—99. Mem. editl. rev. bd.: Jour. Bus. Logistics, 1986—94, Transp. Jour., 1988—, Jour. Advanced Transp., 1990—92, Transport Logistics, 1995—, Jour. Transp. Rsch. Forum, 1996—; contbr. articles to profl. jours. Bd. dirs. Ames (Iowa) C. of C., 1995—2000, pres.-elect bd. dirs., 1996, pres. bd. dirs., 1998; mem. exec. com., bd. dirs. Greater DesMoines C. of C. Fedn., 1998. Recipient Disting. Transp. Rsch. award, Transp. Rsch. Forum, 1996; NSF fellow, U. Ill., 1969—70, Univ. fellow, 1972—73, Brookings Econ. Policy fellow, 1976—77, Twin City Barge fellow in transp., 1980—81. Mem.: Transp. and Pub. Utilities Group, Am. Soc. Transp. and Logistics, Am. Econ. Assn., Golden Key Nat. Honor Soc., Phi Kappa Phi. Office: Iowa State Univ Office of the Provost 1550 Beardshear Hall Ames IA 50011-2021

ALLEN, BENNIE CARNEL, employee relations specialist; b. Detroit, Feb. 3, 1947; s. John Wilson and Rosella (Griffin) Allen; m. Janet Smith, 2005; 1 child, Daron K. BA in Hist., Wayne State U., 1968; Grad. Studies, Wayne State U., Detroit Mich., 1972—78, Hampton U., 1991. Employee relations spec. U.S. Army Tank-Automotive Command, Warren, Mich., 1982—2002; supr. pers. staff. spec. IRS, Detroit, 1979; pers. staff. spec. US. Vet. Admin., 1975—79. Adj. course mgr. instr. US Army Ctr. for Civil. Human Resource Mgmt., Lancaster, Pa., 1993—2002. Editor: (Regulations) Supr. Pers. Mgmt. Manual, 1987; author: (policy) Family Leave Update, 2000. Bd. mem. Detroit Fed. Exec. Bd., Detroit, 1975—79. Sgt. (E-5) USMC, 1968—71. Mem.: Detroit Instit. of Arts, Detroit Pub. Television, Marine Corps. League. Independent. Avocation: reading.

ALLEN, BERTRAND-MARC, lawyer; b. June 21, 1973; AB summa cum laude, Princeton Univ., 1995; JD, Yale Univ., 2002. Bar: Va. 2004. Law clk. U.S. Ct. Appeals (4th cir.), Alexandria, Va., 2002—03; law clk. to Hon. Anthony M. Kennedy U.S. Supreme Ct., Washington, 2003—04; assoc. Kellogg Huber Hansen Todd & Evans, Washington, 2004—. Contbr. articles in law jour. Mem.: N.Y. State Bar. Office: Kellogg Huber Hansen Todd & Evans Sumner Sq Suite 400 1615 M St NW Washington DC 20036

ALLEN, BETTY (MRS. RITTEN EDWARD LEE III), mezzo-soprano; b. Campbell, Ohio, Mar. 17, 1930; d. James Corr and Dora Catherine (Mitchell) A.; m. Ritten Edward Lee, III, Oct. 17, 1953; children: Anthony Edward, Juliana Catherine. Student, Wilberforce U., 1944-46; certificate, Hartford Sch. Music, 1953; pupil voice, Sarah Peck More, Zinka Milanov, Paul Ulanowsky, Carolina Segrera Holden; LHD (hon.), Wittenberg U., 1971; MusD (hon.), Union Coll., 1981; DFA (hon.), Adelphi U., 1990, Bklyn. Coll., 1991; LittD (hon.), Clark U., 1993; MusD (hon.), New Sch. Social Rsch., 1994. Faculty Phila. Mus. Acad., 1979, Manhattan Sch. Music, 1971, N.C. Sch. Arts, 1978-87; now faculty Harlem Sch. Arts. Tchr. master classes Inst. Teatro Colon, 1985-86, Curtis Inst. Music, 1987—; exec. dir. Harlem Sch. Arts, 1979, now pres.; vis. faculty Sibelius Akademie, Helsinki, Finland, 1976; mem. adv. bd. music panel Amherst Coll.; mem. music panel N.Y. State Council of the Arts, Dept. State Office Cultural Presentations, Nat. Endowment Arts.; bd. dirs. Arts Alliance, Karl Weigl Found., Diller-Quaile Sch. Music, U.S. Com. for UNICEF, Manhattan Sch. Music, Theatre Devel. Fund, Children's Storefront; mem. adv. bd. Bloomingdale House of Music; bd. vis. artists Boston U.; bd. dirs., mem. exec. com. Carnegie Hall, Nat. Found. for Advancement in the Arts; bd. dirs. Chamber Music Soc. of Lincoln Ctr., N.Y.C. Housing Authority Orch., Independent Sch. Orch., N.Y.C. Opera CO., Joy in Singing, Arts & Bus. Coun.; mem. Mayor's adv. commn. Cultural Affairs. Appeared as soloist: Leonard Bernstein's Jeremiah Symphony, Tanglewood, 1951, Virgil Thomson's Four Saints in Three Acts, N.Y.C. and Paris, 1952, N.Y.C. Light Opera Co., 1954; recitalist, also soloist with major symphonies on tours including ANTA-State Dept. tours, Europe, N. Africa, Caribbean, Can., U.S., S.Am., Far East, 1954-, S.Am. tour, 1968, Bellas Artes Opera, Mexico City, 1970; recital debut, Town Hall, N.Y.C., 1958, ofcl. debuts, London, Berlin, 1958, formal opera debut, Teatro Colon, Buenos Aires, Argentina, 1964; U.S. opera debut San Francisco Opera, 1966; N.Y.C. opera debut, 1973, Mini-Met. debut, 1973; Broadway debut in Treemonisha, 1975; opened new civic theaters in San Jose, Calif., and in Regina, Sask., Can., concert hall, Lyndon Baines Johnson Library, Austin, Tex., 1971; artist-in-residence, Phila. Opera Co.; appeared with Caramoor Music Festival, summer 1965, 71, Cin. May Festival, 1972, Santa Fe Opera, 1972, 75, Canadian Opera Co., Winnipeg, Man., 1972, 77, Washington Opera Co., 1971, Tanglewood Festival, 1951, 52, 53, 67, 74, Oslo, The Hague, Montreal, Kansas City, Houston and Santa Fe operas, 1975, Saratoga Festival, 1975, Casals Festival, 1967, 68, 69, 76, Helsinki Festival, 1976, Marlboro Festival, 1967-74, numerous radio and TV performances, U.S., Can., Mex., Eng., Germany, Scandinavia; rec. artist, London, Vox, Capitol, Odeon-Pathe, Decca, Deutsche Grammophon, Columbia Records, RCA Victor records; represented U.S. in Cultural Olympics, Mexico City, 1968. Recipient Marian Anderson award, 1953-54, Nat. Music League Mgmt. award, 1953, 52 St Am. Festival Duke Ellington Meml. award, 1989, Bowery award Bowery Bank, 1989, Harlem Sch. of the Arts award Harlem Sch. and Isaac Stern, 1990, Womans Day Celebration award St. Thomas Episcopal Ch., 1990, St. Thomas Ch. award St. Thomas Catholic Ch., 1990, Men's Day Celebration award St. Paul's Ch., 1990, Martell House of Segram award Avery Fisher Hall, 1990; named Best Singer of Season Critics' Circle, Argentina and Chile, 1959, Best Singer of Season Critics' Circle, Uruguay, 1961; Martha Baird Rockefeller Aid to Music grantee, 1953, 58; John Hay Whitney fellow, 1953-54; Ford Found. concert soloist grantee, 1963-64 Mem. NAACP, Urban League, Hartford Mus. Club (life), Am. Guild Mus. Artists, Actors Equity, AFTRA, Silvermine Guild Artists, Jeunesses Musicales, Gioventu Musicale, Student Sangverein Trondheim, Unitarian-Universalist Women's Fedn., Nat. Negro Musicians Assn. (life), Concert Artists Guild, Met. Opera Guild, Amherst Glee Club (hon. life), Union Coll. Glee Club (hon. life), Met. Mus. Art, Mus. Modern Art, Am. Mus. Natural History, Century Assn., Sigma Alpha Iota (hon.) Unitarian-Universalist. Clubs: Cosmopolitan, Second. Office: Harlem Sch of Arts 645 Saint Nicholas Ave New York NY 10030-1098 *To be able to combine childhood fantasies of self-expression, to travel and roam the world, to meet again and make new friends, to serve the demanding, yet fulfilling art of music - these are some of the wonderful joys of being a singer. I have been free to be me.*

ALLEN, BEVERLY E., medical librarian; Bachelor's Degree, U. Mo.; MSLS, Syracuse U. Joined Morehouse Sch. Medicine, Atlanta, 1976, dir. Multi-Media Ctr., ret., 2004. Mem. Nat. Mus. and Libr. Svcs. Bd., Washington, 2004—; past regent Nat. Libr. Medicine. Mem.: ALA, AAMC Group for Info. Resources, Am. Assn. Health Scis. Librs., Med. Libr. Assn. Avocations: travel, reading, classical music. Office: Inst Mus and Libr Svcs 1100 Pennsylvania NW Washington DC 20506

ALLEN, BLAIR HAMILTON, writer, poet, artist, editor, photographer; b. LA, Calif., July 2, 1933; s. Wendall Boyd and Ethel Rose Allen; m. Juanita Aguilar Raya, Jan. 27, 1968; children: Theresa, Geoffrey. AA in Social Studies, San Diego Jr. Coll., 1964; student, U. Wash., 1965—66; BA in Graphic Arts, San Diego State U., 1970. Book reviewer LA Times, 1977—78; assoc. editor, advisor Cerulean Press and Kent Publs., Northridge, Calif., 1982—2005. Author: Televisual Po-ums for Bloodshot Eyeballs, 1973, Malice in Blunderland, 1974, N/Z, 1979, The Atlantis Trilogy, 1982, Dreamwish of the Magician, 1983, Right Through the Silver Lined 1984 Looking Glass, 1984, Trapped in a Cold War Travelogue, 1991, May Burning into August, 1992, The Subway Poems, 1993, When the Ghost of Cassandra Whispers in my Ears, 1996, Ashes Ashes All Fall Down, 1997, Traveling Around the World in 56 Days, 1998, Jabberbanglamerkeltoy, 1999, Thunder-clouds from the Door, 1999, The Athens Cafe, 2000, The Day of the Jamberee Call, 2001, Assembled I Stand, 2002, Wine of Starlight, 2002; editor: The Magical World of David Cole, 1984, Snow Summits in the Sun, 1988, 3 poetry anthologies. Sgt. USMC, 1953—59. Recipient 1st prize poetry, Pacificus Found., LA, 1992, Literary prize for Lifetime Achievement in Poetry and Storytelling, 2003. Mem.: Poets and Writers, Am. Acad. Poets. Democrat. Roman Catholic. Avocations: travel, Santa Anita race tracks. Mailing: PO Box 162 Colton CA 92324

ALLEN, BRUCE, physicist; b. Boston, May 11, 1959; s. Steven and Malwina (Gerson) A.; m. Sylvie Debaisieux, Aug. 26, 1986 (div. 1992); m. Marialessandra Papa, Apr. 1, 2000; children: Daniel, Martin. BS in Physics, MIT, 1980; PhD in Gravitation/Cosmology, Cambridge U., Eng., 1984. Rsch. assoc. U. Calif., Santa Barbara, 1983-85, Tufts U., Medford, Mass., 1985-86; Chercheur Associe CNRS, Paris, 1986-87; rsch. asst. prof. Tufts U., Medford, 1987-89; asst. prof. physics U. Wis., Milw., 1989-92, assoc. prof. physics, 1992—. Vis. Isaac Newton Mat. Inst., 1994; vis. assoc. Calif. Inst. Tech., 1995-97. Contbr. over 70 articles to profl. jours. Recipient Knight prize Cambridge U., 1981, first prize Gravity Rsch. Found., 1990, Bessel prize Alexander Von Humboldt Found., 2003; named Marshall scholar, 1980-83; NSF rsch. grantee, 1987—. Fellow Inst. Physocs; mem. IEEE, Am. Phys.

Soc., Phi Beta Kappa. Avocations: swimming, french language and culture. Office: Univ of Wis Dept Physics 1900 E Kenwood Blvd Milwaukee WI 53211-3061 Office Phone: 414-229-6439. E-mail: ballen@uwm.edu.

ALLEN, BRUCE TEMPLETON, retired economics professor; b. Oak Park, Ill., Jan. 27, 1938; s. William Hendry and Harriet (Iverson) A.; m. Virginia Elizabeth Peterson, June 16, 1962; children: Elizabeth Rachel, Catherine Grace. AB, De Pauw U., 1960; MBA, U. Chgo., 1961; PhD, Cornell U., 1965. Asst. prof. econs. Mich. State U., East Lansing, 1965-75, assoc. prof., 1975-80, prof., 1980—2003; ret., 2003. Mem. Am. Econ. Assn., Indsl. Orgn. Soc. Avocation: railroads. Personal E-mail: allenb@msu.edu.

ALLEN, CAROLINE JAQUELENE, education educator, retired; b. Belton, Tex., May 31, 1925; d. William Warren and Beatrice (Pinkard) Baker; m. Samuel Alphonse Allen, Sr., June 5, 1946; children: Samuel A. Allen, Jr., Aljonia Beatrice Allen Porter. BS, Huston-Tillotson Coll., Austin, 1946; MEd, U. W. Fla., Pensacola, 1974; vocat. cert., Okaloosa-Walton C.C., Niceville, Fla. Tchr. Okaloosa County Sch. Sys., Baker, Crestview, Fla., 1949-79; owner, opr. Versatility Prodns., Crestview, Fla., 1984—. Notary pub. Versatility Prodns., Crestview, Fla., 1984-; pres. Carver-Hill Mem. and His. Soc., Crestview, Fla., 1969—. Author, editor: Family Tree, The Tex. Forest-Revised, 1975—; editor: Father's Autobiography, When God Was Near, 1974; contbr. newspaper articles in local papers, chpts. to books. Chairperson Delta Sigma Theta Social Action Com., Okaloosa County Fla., 1997—; chpt. rep. Delta Days At the Capitol, Tallahassee; mem. Okaloosa County, Fla.; Notary Pub., 1984- Recipient Cmty. Svc. award Okaloosa County, Fla., 1950—; inducted into Okaloosa County Women's Hall of Fame, 2001; nominated Vol. of Yr. award Okaloosa Ret. Educator's Assn., 2003. Mem. Delta Sigma Theta, Retired Educators, NAACP, Crestview C. of C. Democrat. Baptist. Avocations: jig saw puzzles, sewing, music, people, travel. Home: 649 McClelland St Crestview FL 32536-3949

ALLEN, CHARLES ETHELBERT, III, lawyer; b. Louisville, May 14, 1948; s. Charles Ethelbert and Elsie Kathryn (Liliequist) A. BA, Duke U., 1970; JD, U. Ky., 1977. Bar: Ky. 1977, U.S. Dist. Ct. (we. dist.) Ky. 1977, U.S. Dist. Ct. (ea. dist.) Ky. 1985, U.S. Ct. Appeals (6th cir.) 1985, U.S. Dist. Ct. (so. dist.) Ind. 1998. With Brown, Todd & Heyburn, Louisville, 1977—, ptnr., 1983—, vice chair labor & employment group, 1983—, assoc. coord., 1987-93. Dir. Louisville Regional Sci. Fair, 1994—, v.p., 1997-99, judge, 1993-99; dir. Internat. Sci. and Engring. Fair Ky., Inc., 1994-98, sec. 1995-98; vice chair ISEF 97, 1994-96, grand awards judge ISEF, 1995; dir. Ky. Sci. Fair Endowment, Inc., 1998—, sec., 1998—; presenter numerous programs, lectrs. astronomy, space sci., 1960—. 1st lt. USAF, 1971-74. Recipient Air Force Commendation medal, 1974; named to Waggener H.S. Hall of Fame, 1997. Mem. Am. Astronomical League (bd. dirs., v.p. 1994-98, pres. 1998—, chair Great Lakes Region, 1991-95, chair, founder Nat. Young Astronomer award 1991-98), Louisville Astronomical Soc. (bd. dirs., pres. 1991-94, v.p. 1990-91, 95-96, 97-98, sec. 1994-95, 96-97), Beta Omega Sigma, Pi Sigma Alpha. Republican. Presbyterian. Avocations: astronomy, pub. edn. astronomy, sci. fair orgn., ski racing, mountain climbing. Office: Brown Todd & Heyburn 400 W Market St Fl 32 Louisville KY 40202-3346 E-mail: cea@compuserve.com.

ALLEN, CHARLES EUGENE, university administrator, agriculturist, educator; b. Burley, Idaho, Jan. 25, 1939; s. Charles W. and Elsie P. (Fowler) A.; m. Connie J. Block, June 19, 1960; children: Kerry J., Tamara S. BS, U. Idaho, 1961; MS, U. Wis., 1963, PhD, 1965. NSF postdoctoral fellow, Sydney, Australia, 1966-67; asst. prof. agr. U. Minn., St. Paul, 1967-69, assoc. prof., 1969-72, prof., 1972—, dean Coll. Agr., assoc. dir. Agrl. Expt. Sta., 1984-88, acting v.p., 1988-90, v.p. agriculture, forestry and home econs., dir. Minn. Agr. Expt. Sta., 1990-95, provost profl. studies, dir. Minn. Agr. Expt. Sta., 1995-97, dir. global outreach, 1997-98, exec. dir. internat. programs, 1998—2004, assoc. v.p. for internat. programs, 2004—. Vis. prof. Pa. State U., 1978; cons. to industry; C. Glen King lectr. Wash. State U., 1981; Univ. lectr. U. Wyo., Laramie, 1984; adj. prof. Hassan II U., Rabat, Morocco, 1984. Recipient Horace T. Morse-Amoco Found. award U. Minn., 1984, Disting. Tchr. award U. Minn. Coll. Agr., 1984, Disting. Alumni award U. Idaho, 1989. Fellow AAAS, Inst. Food Tech.; mem. Am. Meat Sci. Assn. (bd. dirs. 1970-72, Rsch. award 1980, Signal Svc. award, 1985), Am. Soc. Animal Sci. (Exceptional Rsch. Achievement award 1972, Rsch. award 1977), Sigma Xi. Avocations: photography, reading, outdoor sports, golf. Business E-Mail: ceallen@umn.edu.

ALLEN, CHARLES FRANKLIN, music educator; b. Kingsport, Tenn., Mar. 1, 1964; s. Clarance Allen and Barbara Charlene Messick. MusB Edn., Union U., 1986. Cert. elem. tchr. Tenn, Orff-Schulwerk Level One. Elem. music tchr. McDowell County Schs., Welch, W.Va., 1989—96, Sarasota County Pub. Schs., Sarasota, Fla., 1996—; vocal instr. Venice (Fla.) Little Theatre, 2003—, musical theatre instr., 2004—. Dir. choral music competition Music USA Choral Festival, Universal Studios; dir. choral performance ABC 7 Sunrise Morning News program, Sarasota County Fair, W.Va. State Capital Showcase of Music Edn. Author: (musical) Rappin' Romantic, 1992, (book) Teaching Tolerance: A Handbook for Teachers, 1992, (play) It's the Chance You Take, 1995; composer: (opera) The Magical Friendship, 1997; musician: (PBS gulf coast TV show feature) Venice Little Theatre's Theatre Fest, 2002. Tech. staff vol. Player's Theatre, Sarasota, 2002—03; rep. W.Va. Edn. Assn., Charleston, 1992—95, state educator trainer, 1992—96, mem. minority affairs com., 1995—96; pres. McDowell County Music Edn. Assn., Welch, W.Va., 1995—96; sec. Polit. Com. of the Sarasota County Classified Teachers Assn., Sarasota, Fla., 2004—05, First Congl. United Ch. of Christ Bd. of Music and Fine Arts, Sarasota, Fla., 2005—05. Named Tchr. of the Yr., Panther Elem. Sch., 1993, Wal-Mart, 1999; recipient Outstanding Sch. Project award, Partnerships and Alliances Linking Schs., 1999. Mem.: Sarasota Classified Teachers Assn. (faculty representive 2002—05), Sarasota Assn. Music Edn. (pres. 2000—03, sec. polit. com. 2004—05, Music Tchr. of Yr. 2002), Fla. Elem. Music Educators Assn., Fla. Music Educators Assn., Phi Mu Alpha Sinfonia (life; v.p. 1984—85). Democrat. Mem. United Ch. Of Christ. Avocations: cooking, paranormal investigations, dog shows, reading. Home: 2713 Wells Ave Sarasota FL 34232 Office: Wilkinson Elem Sch 3400 Wilkinson Rd Sarasota FL 34232 Office Phone: 941-361-6477. Personal E-mail: defyinggravity2713@comcast.net.

ALLEN, CHARLES NORMAN, television, film and video producer; b. Miami, July 13, 1944; s. Claude Braswell and Virginia Lucille (Gravitt) A.; m. Susan Carole Dorn, May 1, 1970; children: Jennifer, Brian. BS, U. Miami, 1967. V.p. Tel-Air Interests Inc., Miami, 1967-79; pres. Cinema East Corp., Miami, 1979—, World Studios Corp., Atlanta, 1987—, ADR Internat., Miami, 1991—2001. Bd. dirs. World Studios Corp. Representer prodns. U.S. internat. film events CINE-Washington, 1974, 75, 80, 81, 87, 88, 89, 92. Trustee Dade County Pub. Health Trust; commr. Biscayne Park, Fla., 1974-76; active Dade County Dem. Exec. Commn., 1976-80, Dade Dem. Treas., 1976-79; mem. Gov.'s Fla. Motion Picture and TV Adv. Coun., 1978-80. Mem.: Greater Miami C. of C., Advt. Miami, Greater Miami Advt. Fedn., Nat. Advt. Fraternity, Internat. Cinematographers Guild (dir. photography), Assn. Ind. Comml. Producers, S. Fla. Film and Tape Producers Assn., Am. Advt. Fedn., Iron Arrow Hon. Soc., Alpha Delta Sigma, Sigma Chi. Democrat. Methodist. Office: Cinema East Corp 5859 Biscayne Blvd Miami FL 33137-2690 Office Phone: 305-757-5859. E-mail: callen@cinemaeast.com.

ALLEN, CHARLES WILLIAM, mechanical engineer, educator; b. Newbury, Eng., July 24, 1932; s. Isaac William and Emily (Butler) A.; m. Rita Joyce Pembroke, Dec. 28, 1957; children: Malcolm Charles, Verity Simone. BS, U. London, 1957; MS, Case Inst. Tech., 1962; PhD, U. Calif., Davis, 1966. Design engr. Lear Siegler, Cleve., 1957-62; group leader Aerojet Gen., Sacramento, 1962-63; assoc. engring. U. Calif., Davis, 1965-66; assoc. prof. Calif. State U., Chico, 1966-71, prof. engring., 1971-88, prof. emeritus, 1988—, head mech. engring., 1976-79, 82-84. Vis. fellow U. Leicester, Eng., 1974; vis. lectr., rschr. U. Guadalajara, Mex., 1986, guest prof., 1997. Contbr. articles to profl. jours. Fellow NASA, 1967, 68, 69 Mem. ASME. Home: 1691 Filbert Ave Chico CA 95926-1777 Office: Calif State U Dept Mech Engring Chico CA 95629 Personal E-mail: charleswilliamallen@yahoo.com.

ALLEN, CHARLOTTE, secondary school educator; BS in Edn., Athens State Coll. Tchr. sci. East Lawrence High Sch., Trinity, Ala., 1988—. Coach cheerleading; camp dir. Nat. Cheerleading Assn. Named Outstanding Sci. Tchr., 1992. Mem. Nat. Assn. Geology Tchrs. Avocations: church activities, hiking.

ALLEN, CHRISTOPHER C., publishing executive; V.p., pub. Cooking Light mag., Birmingham, Ala. Office: care Cooking Light PO Box 1748 2100 Lakeshore Dr Birmingham AL 35201*

ALLEN, CLARENCE RODERIC, geologist, educator; b. Palo Alto, Calif., Feb. 15, 1925; s. Hollis Partridge and Delight (Wright) A. BA, Reed Coll., 1949; MS, Cal. Inst Tech., 1951, PhD, 1954. Asst. prof. geology U. Minn., 1954-55; mem. faculty Calif. Inst. Tech., 1955—, prof. geology and geophysics, 1964-91, prof. emeritus, 1991—; interim dir. Seismological Lab., 1965-67, acting chmn. division of geological scis., 1967-68. Phi Beta Kappa Disting. lectr., 1978; chmn. cons. bd. earthquake analysis Calif. Dept. Water Resources, 1965-74; chmn. geol. hazards adv. com. for program Cal. Resources Agy., 1965-66; mem. earth scis. adv. panel NSF, 1965-68, chmn., 1967-68, mem. adv. com. environmental scis., 1970-72; mem. U.S. Geol. Survey adv. panel to Nat. Center Earthquake Research, Calif. Cal. Mining and Geology Bd., 1969-75, chmn., 1975; mem. task force on earthquake hazard reduction Office Sci. and Tech., 1970-71; mem. Can. Earthquake Prediction Evaluation Council, 1983-88; vice-chmn. Nat. Acad. Sci. Com. on Advanced Study in china, 1981-85; chmn. geology sect. Nat. Acad. Sci., 1982-85, Com. on Scholarly Communication with People's Republic China, 1984-89, chmn., 1987-89; mem. Nat. Acad. Sci. Commn. on Phys. Scis., Math. and Resources; mem. Pres.'s Nuclear Waste Tech. Rev. Bd., 1989-97. Served to 1st lt. USAAF, 1943-46. Recipient G.K. Gilbert award seismic geology Carnegie Instn., 1960. Fellow Am. Geophys. Union, Geol. Soc. Am. (counselor 1968-70, pres. 1973-74), Am. Acad. Arts Scis.; mem. Nat. Acad. Scis., Earthquake Engring. Research Inst. (bd. dirs. 1985-88, Housner medal 2001), Seismological Soc. Am. (dir. 1970-76, pres. 1975-76, medal 1995), Nat. Acad. Engring., Phi Beta Kappa. Office: Calif Inst Tech Dept Geology Pasadena CA 91125-0001 Office Phone: 626-395-6904. E-mail: allen@gps.caltech.edu.

ALLEN, CLAUDE ALEXANDER, federal official; b. Phila., Oct. 11, 1960; m. Jannese Mitchell; children: Claude Alexander III, Lila-Cjoan, Christian Isaiah. Degree in Polit. and Sci. and Linguistics, U. N.C., 1982; LLM in Internat. and Comparative Law, Duke U., JD, 1990. Bar: Pa. 1991, DC 1992, Va. 1995. Law clerk to Hon. David B. Sentelle U.S. Ct. Appeals (D.C. cir.), 1990—91; atty. Baker & Botts, L.L.P., Washington, 1991—95; counsel to atty. gen. Office of the Atty. Gen., Commonwealth of Va., 1995—97, dep. atty. gen. for civil litigation divsn., 1997—98; sec. health and human resources Office of Gov., Commonwealth of Va., 1998—2001; dep. sec. US Dept. Health & Human Svcs., Washington, 2001—05; asst. to the Pres. for domestic policy The White House, Washington, 2005—, dir. domestic policy coun., 2005—. Office: The White House 1600 Pennsylvania Ave Washington DC 20500 Office Phone: 202-690-6133.

ALLEN, CLAXTON EDMONDS, III, investment banker; b. NYC, Aug. 27, 1944; s. C. Edmonds and Helen (McCreery) A. BA, Washington and Lee U., 1964, JD, 1967. Bar: N.Y. 1969. Assoc. Simpson Thacher & Bartlett, N.Y.C., 1967-70; assoc. gen. counsel GE Credit Corp., N.Y.C., 1970-71; investment banker Merrill Lynch, Pierce, Fenner & Smith, Inc., N.Y.C., 1971-72; pres. Gloucester Internat. Ltd., N.Y.C., 1972-82, Comanche Exploration Corp., N.Y.C., 1981-86, Compass Internat. Corp., N.Y.C., 1982—, Horizon Coal Corp., Mineral Res. Corp., N.Y.C., 1982-85, Compass Coal Corp., N.Y.C., 1986-91, Overseas & Fgn. Investors, Inc., N.Y.C., 1990—. Bd. dirs. Purbrook Ltd., Cranbrook Investments Ltd., Lupton Estates Ltd., Morehead State U. Found., Inc., L&H Internat. Ltd. Mem. Met. Club. Home: 405 E 54th St New York NY 10022-5123 Office: 123 E 54th St 8th Fl New York NY 10022-4506 Office Phone: 212-308-0606. Business E-Mail: ceallen@compass1.com.

ALLEN, CRAIG ADAMS, lawyer, director; b. Ironton, Ohio, June 30, 1941; s. Enoch Stanely and Margaret (Adams) Allen; m. Carol Linda Brewster, Aug. 15, 1964; children: Laura, Kathy. BA cum laude, Denison U., 1963; JD, Ohio State U., 1966. Bar: Ohio 1966. Ptnr. Edwards, Klien, Compton & Allen, Ironton, Ohio, 1966—76; sole practice Ironton, 1976—77; ptnr. Allen & Anderson, Ironton, 1977—78, Allen, Anderson & Anderson, Ironton, 1978—82, Allen & Stillpass, Ironton, 1983—84, Allen & Payne, Ironton, 1985—; sole practice, 1985—. Served Ohio Nat. Guard, 1966—72. Mem.: Hosp. Atty. Assn., Lawrence County Bar Assn., Ironton C. of C., Lawrence County Democratic Ctrl Com., So. Ohio AAA, Elks, Lions. Episc. Office: 311 S 3rd St Ironton OH 45638-1630 Office Phone: 740-533-1700. Business E-Mail: alcaa@bright.net.

ALLEN, DAVID, systems engineer; b. York, Maine, May 15, 1942; s. Pliny Arunah and Tillie (MacQuinn) A.; m. JoAnn Moeckly, 1968 (div. 1975); children: Torrie, Heather; m. Robin Lee Perry, Mar. 11, 1983 (div. 2004); children: Rebecca, Patrick. BA, Lake Forest Coll., 1965; MA, U. Ariz., 1967, PhD, 1968. Asst. prof. dept. psychology S.D. State U., Brookings, 1968-71; rsch. psychologist CIA, Washington, 1971-78, chief rsch. br., 1978-85, dep. chief psychol. svcs. divsn., 1985-87, chief rsch. and info. systems divsn. Washington, 1987-90, trustee investment plan, 1988-92, investigator Office of Insp. Gen., 1990-92, chief info. systems Latin Am. divsn., 1992-95; chief electronic messaging divsn., program dir. Enterprise Messaging Svcs., Office of Comm. CIA, Washington, 1995-97; dir. program devel./mktg. for Ctr. for Sci. and Tech. Mitretek Sys., Inc., 1998—2000; program dir. SRS Technologies, 2002—. Contbr. articles to profl. jours. Rsch. fellow USPHS, 1967-68; rsch. grantee NSF, 1970-71; recipient U.S. Govt. Career Intelligence medal, CIA, 1997. Republican. Avocations: choral singing, amateur radio, cosmology, mathematics, information technology. Home: 905 N Emerson St Arlington VA 22205-2562 Office: DARPA 3701 N Fairfax Dr Arlington VA 22203 Personal E-mail: davidalle1@aol.com.

ALLEN, DAVID C., lawyer; b. Warwick, RI; BA cum laude, Providence Coll., 1981; JD, George Washington Univ., 1984. Bar: Va. 1984, Calif. 1987. Ptnr.-in-charge LA office and mem. mgmt. com. Akin Gump Strauss Hauer & Feld LLP, LA. Mem. George Washington Univ. Law Rev., 1983—84. Office: Akin Gump Strauss Hauer & Feld LLP Ste 2600 2029 Century Pk E Los Angeles CA 90067 Office Phone: 310-229-1010. Office Fax: 310-229-1001. Business E-Mail: dallen@akingump.com.

ALLEN, DAVID JAMES, lawyer; b. East Chicago, Ind. BS, Ind. U., 1957, MA, 1959, JD, 1965. Bar: Ind. 1965, U.S. Dist. Ct. (so. dist.) Ind. 1965, U.S. Ct. Appeals 1965, U.S. Tax Ct. 1965, U.S. Supreme Ct. 1965, U.S. Ct. Appeals (fed. and 7th cirs.) 1983. Of counsel Hagemier, Allen and Smith, Indpls., 1975—. Adminstrv. asst. Gov. of Ind. Mathew E. Welsh, 1961—65; counsel Ind. Gov. Roger D. Branigin, 1965—69; asst. to Gov. Edgar D. Whitcomb, 1969; univ. counsel Ind. State U., Terre Haute, 1969—70; legis. counsel Ind. Gov. Evan Bayh, 1989—90; spl. counsel Gov. Frank O'Bannon State of Ind., 1999—2002; mem. Spl. Commn. on Ind. Exec. Reorgn., 1967—69; commr. Ind. Utility Regulatory Commn., 1970—75; mem. Ind. Law Enforcement Acad. Bd. and Adv. Coun., 1968—85, Ind. State Police Bd., 1968—; commr. for revision Ind. Commn. Recommend Changes Ind. Legis. Process, 1990—2002; commr. Ind. Criminal Code Revision Study Commn., 1998—2002; nat. judge adv. Acacia Frat., 1980—86, 1992—2002, internat. pres., 2002—; chief counsel Ind. Ho. Reps., 1975—76, spl. counsel, 1979—89, Ind. Senate, 1990—97; adj. prof. pub. law Sch. Pub. and Environ. Affairs, Ind. U., Bloomington, 1976—. Author: (book) New Governor in Indiana: Transition to Executive Power, 1965. Mem.: ABA, Indpls. Bar Assn., Ind. State Bar Assn. (criminal justice law exec. com. 1966—72, mem. adminstrv. law com. 1968—77, chmn. adminstrv. law com. 1973—76, mem. law sch. liaison com. 1977—78). Office: Hagemier Allen & Smith 1170 Market Tower 10 W Market St Ste 1170 Indianapolis IN 46204-5924 Office Phone: 317-464-8110.

ALLEN, DAVID JOSEPH, music educator; b. Ottawa, Ill., Oct. 4, 1969; s. Elza Joe and Marie Elaine Allen; m. Betty Jane Hood, Jan. 2, 1993. BS in Music Edn., U. Ill., 1992, MusM, 1994. Dir. bands Salem (Ill.) Cmty. H.S., Salem, 1994—99, Centennial H.S., Champaign, Ill., 1997—. Coord. Ill. Summer Youth Music Band Camps, Urbana-Champaign, 2001—. Mem.: Champaign Fedn. Tchrs., Ill. Music Educators Assn. (dist. rep. 2002). Avocation: computers. Home: 1508 White Pine Dr Champaign IL 61822 Office: Centennial H S 913 S Crescent Champaign IL 61821

ALLEN, DEBBIE, actress, choreographer, dancer, television director; b. Houston, Jan. 16, 1950; d. Vivian Ayers; m. Win Wilford (div.); m. Norm Nixon; 2 children: Vivian, Norman, Jr. BA, Howard U. Appeared in Broadway musicals including Purlie, 1972, West Side Story (revival), Guys and Dolls, Raisin, Aint Misbehavin, Sweet Charity, 1986 (revival, Tony Award); appeared in (play) Sweet Charity, Los Angeles, 1985, choreographer Broadway prodn. Carrie, 1988; (TV spl.) Dancing in the Wings, 1985, (TV series) Fame, 1982-87 (3 Emmys for choreography), In the House, 1995; dir. TV series A Different World, 1988-92; dir. episodes TV series Family Ties; dir., producer films including The Fish That Saved Pittsburgh, 1979, Fame, 1980, Ragtime, 1981, JoJo Dancer, Your Life is Calling, 1986, Mona Must Die, 1994, Blank Check, 1994, Out-of-Sync, 1995, Everything's Jake, 1999, (TV movie) C Bear and Jamal (voice), 1996; star, dir., prod., co-writer, choreographer The Debbie Allen Special, ABC-TV, 1988; dir., choreographer Polly (mus. version Disney's Pollyanna), 1989; dir., appeared in CBS Stompin' at the Savoy, 1992; rec. album Special Look, MCA Records, 1989; dir. pilot and 1st episode NBC series The Fresh Prince of Bel Air, 1990; dir., choreographer NBC-Disney movie Polly II, 1990; choreographer of 63d Acad. Awards, 1991, 64th Acad. Awards, 1992, 65th Acad. Awards, 1993, 66th Acad. Awards, 1994; dir. (TV) Cool Women, 2000. Mem. exec. com. dean's adv. bd. UCLA Sch. Theatre, Film and TV, 1993. Office: William Morris Agency 151 S El Camino Dr Beverly Hills CA 90212-2775

ALLEN, DIOGENES, clergyman, theology studies educator; b. Lexington, Ky., Oct. 17, 1932; m. Jane Mary Billing, Sept. 8, 1958; children: Mary, George, John, Timothy. BA with high distinction, U. Ky., 1954; postgrad., Princeton U., 1954-55; BA with honors, Oxford U., 1957, MA, 1961; B.D., Yale U., 1959, PhD, 1965. Ordained to ministry Presbyn. Ch., 1959; ordained priest Episc. Ch., 2002. Minister Windham Presbyn. Ch., N.H., 1958-61; asst. prof. York U., Toronto, Ont., Can., 1964-66, assoc. prof. philosophy, 1966-67; assoc. prof. Princeton Theol. Sem., N.J., 1967-74, prof., 1974—, prof. philosophy, 1981—2002, Stuart prof. philosophy emeritus, 2002—. Author: The Reasonableness of Faith, 1968, Finding Our Father, 1974, reissued under title The Path to Perfect Love, 1992, Between Two Worlds, 1978, reissued under title Temptation, 1985, Traces of God, 1981, Three Outsiders: Pascal, Kierkegaard and S. Weil, 1983, Mechanical Explanations and Their Relation to the Ultimate Origin of the Universe According to Leibniz, 1983, Philosophy for Understanding Theology, 1985, Love, 1987, Christian Belief in a Postmodern World, 1989, Quest, 1990, Primary Reading in Philosophy for Understanding (with Eric Springsted), 1992, (with Eric Springsted) Nature, Spirit, Community: The Thought of Simone Weil, 1994, Spiritual Theology, 1997; editor: Theodicy (Leibniz), 1966, Steps Along the Way, 2002. Rhodes scholar, 1955-57, 63-64, Pew Evang. scholar, 1991-92; fellow Rockefeller Found., 1962-64, Ctr. Theol. Inquiry, Princeton, 1985-88, 94-95, Adv. Bd. Ctr. Theol. Inquiry, 1988-94. Mem. Soc. Christian Philosophers (bd. dirs.), Am. Weil Soc. (bd. dirs.), Leibniz Gellschaft, N.J. Com. for the Humanities, Phi Beta Kappa. Office: Princeton Theol Seminary Dept Theology Princeton NJ 08542 *In my life I have found there are many people who are glad to encourage and help another person in the pursuit of worthwhile tasks.*

ALLEN, DONALD VAIL, investment company executive, writer, musician; b. South Bend, Ind., Aug. 1, 1928; s. Frank Eugene and Vera Irene (Vail) A.; m. Betty Dunn, Nov. 17, 1956. BA magna cum laude, UCLA, 1972, MA, D (hon.), UCLA, 1973. Pres., chmn. bd. dirs. Cambridge Investment Corp.; music editor and critic Times-Herald, Washington; music critic L.A. Times. Lectr. George Washington U., Am. U., Washington, Pasadena City Coll. Transl. works of Ezra Pound from Italian into English; author of papers on the musical motifs in the writings of James Joyce; specialist in works of Beethoven, Chopin, Debussy, Liszt, and Scriabin; premiere performances of works of Paul Creston, Norman dello Joio, Ross Lee Finney, appearances in N.Y., L.A., Washington; represented by William Matthews Concert Agy., N.Y.C.; selected by William Steinway and Sascha Greiner of Steinway Piano Co. as an exclusive Steinway concert artist. Pres. Funds for Needy Children, 1974-76; mem. Am. Guild Organists. Mem. Ctr. for Study of Presidency, Am. Mgmt. Assn., Internat. Platform Assn., Nat. Assn. Securities Dealers, Am. Guild Organists, Chamber Music Soc., Am. Mus. Natural History. Avocations: languages, music, travel, writing, stock market.

ALLEN, DOROTHEA, secondary school educator; b. Rockaway, NJ, Apr. 30, 1919; d. Harrison Engleman and Caroline (Tierney) Allen. AB, Montclair U., 1941, MA, 1949. Cert. secondary, sci., math. tchr., counselor, supr., prin. N.J. Tchr. sci. and math. Denville (N.J.) Jr. High Sch., 1942-46; tchr. sci. Boonton (N.J.) High Sch., 1946-94, supr. sci. dept., 1978-94. Lab. technician Drew Chem. Corp., Boonton, 1942—47; tech. asst. Bell Telecom. Lab., Whippany, NJ, 1956; rsch. scientist Warner Lambert Rsch. Inst., Morris Plains, NJ, 1959—62; tchr. sci. enrichment Boonton Summer Sch., 1963—85; curriculum developer Morris County Vocat.-Tech. Sch., Denville, 1987; project evaluator Mid. States Assn., 1973, 79; facilitator Ptnrs. in Edn. Program; promoter Media Ctr. Open House; cons., reviewer Am. Biol. Tchr. Mag., 1975—; com. mem. Sch. Articulation Program Boonton Schs., 1991—94; media ctr. spkr. Meet the Author; sponsor Student Showcase of Excellence in Sci., 1990—94; faculty sponsor, mentor h.s. students, 1966—94; mentor Alt. Rt. Program Tchrs. N.J. Organizer Am. Dental Health Clinic, Boonton, 1968—72; presenter, spkr. in field. Author: Research Projects for High School Biology, 1971, Biology Teacher's Desk Book, 1979, Science Activities for Every Month of the School Year, 1981, Science Demonstrations for Elementary Classrooms, 1988, Hands-on Science, 1991; contbr. articles to profl. jours. including Am. Biology Tchr., The Sci. Tchr. Mem. career com. N.J. divsn. Theobald Smith Soc., 1975—76, mentoring program, 1992—; fundraiser Am. Hemophilia Found., Rockaway, NJ, 1985—, Am. Heart Assn., 1995—, Muscular Dystrophy Found., 1995—, Nat. Children's Cancer Soc., 1996—; mothers march vol. March of Dimes, 1990—; cons. Cmty. Mid. Sch. Planning Com., Boonton, 1988—90; bd. advisors ABI Rsch., 1995—. Named Outstanding Biology Tchr., Nat. Assn. Biology Tchrs., 1972, Outstanding Sci. Tchr., Rsch. Assn. N.Am., 1980, Woman of the Yr., 1993—98; named to Sci. Edn. Hall of Fame, 1994—98, Boonton H.S. Wall of Fame, 1996, 1997, 1998; recipient Disting. Citizen's award, Town of Rockaway, 1984, Gov.'s and Edn. award, N.J. Dept. Edn., 1984, Morris County Tchr. of the Yr. award, 1990, Presdl. award, NSF, 1984, Cert. of Honor, State of N.J., 1985, World Lifetime Achievement award, 1994, Internat. Order of Merit, 1994, Spotlight award, Boonton Bd. Edn., 1980—86, Tchr. of Yr., 1984, 1990, Women's Inner Cir. of Achievement award, 1995. Mem.: NSTA, ASCD, NEA, NEA Ret., Morris Area Sci. Alliance, N.J. Dept. Edn. Exec. Acad., N.J. Dept. Edn. Exec. Acad., N.J. Alliance for Math. and Sci., N.J. Prins. And Suprs. Assn., N.J. Edn. Assn., Assn. Presdl. Award Winners in Sci. Tchg., Nat. Assn. Secondary Sch. Prins., Morris County Ret. Educators Assn. Avocations: reading, propagating plants, collecting gold coins. Home: 115 Jackson Ave Rockaway NJ 07866-3039

ALLEN, DOROTHY JEAN, librarian; b. McComb, Miss., Oct. 4, 1952; d. John Lee and Mary Louise (Wells) A.; children: Gregory, Demetrious. BA, Southern U., Baton Rouge, 1978; MLS, U. Pitts., 1979. Reference libr. W.Va. U., Morgantown, 1980-81; sch. libr. Eva Gordon Elem. Sch., Magnolia, Miss., 1981-82, 85-86; libr. East La. State Hosp., Jackson, 1982-85; reference libr. Jackson (Miss.) Hinds Libr. Sys., 1986-88; circulation libr. Rowland Med. Libr., Jackson, 1988-94; acquisitions libr. Southern Univ. Law Ctr.

Libr., 1994—. Mem. Am. Assn. Law Librs. Democrat. Baptist. Office: Southern Univ Law Ctr Libr 56 Roosevelt Steptoe Dr Baton Rouge LA 70813 Office Phone: 225-771-2189. Business E-Mail: jallen@sulc.edu.

ALLEN, FRANCES MICHAEL, publisher; b. Charlotte, N.C., Apr. 7, 1939; d. Thomas Wilcox and Lola Frances (Horne) A.; m. Joseph Taylor Lisenbee, Feb. 24, 1955 (div. 1957); 1 child, Leslie Autice., Abilene (Tex.) Christian Coll., 1954-56, Chico (Calif.) State U., 1957-59. Art dir. B&E Publs., L.A., 1963-65, editor, 1969-70; art dir. Tiburon Corp., Chgo., 1970-75; founder, editor Boxers, Internat., L.A., 1970-76; editor The Hound's Tale, 1974, Saints, Incorp., 1974-76; founder, editor Setters, Incorp., Costa Mesa, Calif., 1975-85; founder, owner Michael Enterprises, Midway City, Calif., 1976—; editor Am. Cocker Rev., Midway City, 1980-81; editor, pub. Am. Cocker Mag., 1981-99; editor, co-pub. Sporting Life, 1991; editor, pub. The Royal Spaniels, 1995—. Author: The American Cocker Book, 1989; editor, pub. The Royal Spaniels, 1995— (Dogs Writer's Assn. awards 1995, 96, 99); illustrator: The First Five Years, 1970, The Aftercare of the Ear, 1975, The Shenn Simplicity Collection, 1976, The Miniature Pinscher, 1967; prin. works include mag. and book covers for USA, most widely published show dog artist world wide, past 30 yrs. Recipient Dog World Award Top Producer, 5 times, 1966-88, 10-time winner and nominee Dog Writers Assn. Am., winner best breed publ. World Congress Pet Publs., Ukraine, 1995, winner Kirk Paper Co. award of excellence. Mem. Dog Writers Assn. Am. Republican. Mem. Ch. of Christ. Avocations: dog breeding, ballooning, photography, art. Home and Office: 14531 Jefferson St Midway City CA 92655-1030 Office Phone: 714-893-0053. E-mail: baliwck@socal.rr.com.

ALLEN, FRANK CLINTON, JR., lawyer, chemical engineer; b. New Orleans, Apr. 14, 1934; s. Frank Clinton and Lucy Charlotte (Walters) A.; m. Cynthia Ann Church, June 7, 1958; children: Frank C. III, Thomas Church, C. Ann. BSChemE, Tulane U., 1955, LLB, 1964. Registered profl. engr., La.; bar: La. 1964, Miss. 1977, Tex. 1991, U.S. Supreme Ct. 1972. Process engr. Am. Oil Co., New Orleans, 1955-60, Chevron Oil Co., New Orleans, 1960-64; atty. Jones, Walker, Waechter, New Orleans, 1964-78; v.p., gen. counsel, corp. sec. McDermott Internat., Inc., New Orleans, 1978-99; atty. Jones, Walker, Waechter, Poitevent, Carrere, Denegre, New Orleans, 1999—2002; of counsel Killen & Assocs., P.C., Houston, 2002—. Mem. AIChE, ABA, La. Bar Assn., Miss. Bar Assn., Tex. Bar Assn. Avocation: sailing. Office: Graham, Arceneaux, & Allen Ste 2080 601 Poydras St New Orleans LA 70112 also: Killen & Assocs PC 8 Greenway Plz Ste 614 Houston TX 77046 Office Phone: 504-522-8256. Personal E-mail: fallen@datasync.net. Business E-Mail: fca@gra-arc.com.

ALLEN, FRANK DAVIS, JR., lawyer; b. Helena, Ark., Aug. 30, 1937; s. Frank Davis and Pauline Marie (Crabtree) A.; m. Mary Lee Campbell, Dec. 19, 1970; 1 child, Sean Greenhill Cruz. BS, Millsaps Coll., 1960; LLB, Vanderbilt U., 1964. Bar: D.C. 1964. Assoc. Woodson, Pattishall & Hofstetter, Washington, 1964-66; atty. Civil Rights divsn. U.S. Dept. Justice, Washington, 1966-70, atty.-in-charge New Orleans field office, 1970-72, dep. chief criminal sect. Civil Rights divsn. Washington, 1972-75, dep. chief appellate sect. Civil Rights divsn., 1975-77, sr. atty. appellate sect. Civil Rights divsn., 1977-87; sr. counsel, asst. gen. counsel Pension Benefit Guaranty Corp., Washington, 1987-95; sole practitioner law Washington, 1995—. Elder, Ch. of the Pilgrims, Washington, 1990-92, clk. of session, 1995-96. Mem. ABA, D.C. Bar Assn. Presbyterian. Office: PO Box 15539 Washington DC 20003-0539

ALLEN, G. ASHLEY, chemicals executive; With Milliken Rsch. Corp., 1969, from gen. mgr. chem. and packaging divsns. to pres. chem. and indsl. specialties, 1989—2002; pres., COO Milliken & Co., Spartanburg, SC, 2002—. Office: Milliken & Co PO Box 1926 920 Milliken Rd Spartanburg SC 29304

ALLEN, GARLAND EDWARD, biology professor, biologist, writer; b. Louisville, Feb. 13, 1936; s. Garland Edward and Virginia (Blandford) A.; children: Tania Leigh, Carin Tove. AB, U. Louisville, 1957; AMT, Harvard U., 1958, AM, 1963, PhD, 1966. Programmer, announcer WFPL-WFPK, Louisville, 1956-58; tchr. Mt. Hermon (Mass.) Sch., 1958-61; Allston-Burr sr. tutor, instr. history of sci. Harvard, 1965-67; asst. prof. biology Washington U., St. Louis, 1967-72, assoc. prof., 1972-80, prof., 1980—. Cons. Ednl. Rsch. Corp., Cleve., 1967-85; commr. Commn. Undergrad. Edn. in Biol. Scis., 1967-70; mem. NSF Panel for Social Scis., 1968-71; mem. ELSI rev. panel NIH, 2002; trustee Marine Biol. Lab., Woods Hole, Mass., 1985-93; Sigma Xi nat. lectr., 1973-74, bicentennial lectr., 1974-77; Watkins vis. prof. Wichita State U., 1984; vis. prof. dept. history of sci. Harvard U., 1989-91, Sarton Award Lecture, AAAS, 1998. Author: Life Sciences in the Twentieth Century, 1975, 1978, T.H. Morgan: The Man and His Science, 1978; author: (with J.J.W. Baker) Matter, Energy and Life, 1965, 1970, 1975, 1981; author: The Study of Biology, 1967, The Study of Biology, 4th edit., 1982, Hypothesis, Prediction and Implication, 1969, The Process of Biology, 1970, Biology: Scientific Process and Social Issues, 2001; co-editor: Mendel Newsletter, 1989—92, Jour. History of Biology, 1996—; mem. editl. bd.: San Josè Studies, —, Jour. History of Biology, 1968—91, 1998—, Folia Medeliana, History and Philosophy of the Life Scis., 1993—; co-editor: Science, History, and Social Activism: A Tribute to Everett Mendelsohn, 2002, Centennial History of the Carnegie Institution of Washington's Department of Embryology, 2005. Adv. bd. Holocaust Meml. Mus., 2000—01. Fellow Charles Warren Ctr. for Studies in Am. History, Harvard U., 1981-82; sr. fellow Dibner Inst. for the History of Sci. and Tech., MIT, 2002. Mem. AAAS (coun., sect. L exec. com. 1975, Sarton award lectr. 1998), History Sci. Soc. (chmn. Schumann Prize com. 1972, Pfizer prize com. 1977, 80, 91-94, HSS coun. 1994-96, vis. lectr. program 1985-87), Internat. Soc. for the History, Philosophy and Social Studies of Biology (pres.-elect 2003-05, pres. 05—), Sigma Xi. Home: 1526 Mississippi Ave Saint Louis MO 63104-2512 Office: Washington U Biology Dept Saint Louis MO 63130 Office Phone: 314-935-6808. Business E-Mail: allen@biology2.wustl.edu.

ALLEN, GARY CURTISS, geology educator; b. Stockton, Calif., July 18, 1939; s. Curtiss Wright and Helen Lucille (McElroy) A.; m. Ruth Lee Mayeux, June 5, 1965; children: Adrienne Lucille, Christopher Gary. BS in Chemistry, Stanford U., 1961; MA in Geology, Rice U., 1963; PhD in Geochemistry, U. N.C., 1968. Head geochemistry and petrology dept. Mineral Resources div. State of Va., Charlottesville, 1966-68; asst. prof. earth scis. La. State U., New Orleans, 1968-78; assoc. prof. earth scis. U. New Orleans, 1972-78, prof. geology, 1978—2003, prof. emeritus geology and environ. sci., 2004, dir. environ. tng. program, 1993-94, coord. environ. sci. and policy degree program, 2000—03. Coord. for radiation safety La. State U. System, 1989—2003, chair coun. faculty advisors, 1995-97; pres. Sunbelt Assocs. Inc., New Orleans 1978—; bd. dirs. Holocene Rsch. Inst.; pres. Assn. La. Faculty Senates, 1997-99; chair La. Bd. Regents Faculty Adv. Coun., 1997-2000 Contbr. articles to profl. jours. Mem. St. Frances Cabrini Sch. Bd., New Orleans, 1979-82. NASA fellow, 1963-66. Mem. Geol. Soc. Am., New Orleans Geol. Soc., U. New Orleans Fedn. Tchrs. (pres. 1985-87, treas. 1987—), Sigma Xi (pres. New Orleans chpt. 1977-78, v.p. 1991—). Home: 180 Devon Dr Mandeville LA 70448-3406 Office: U New Orleans Dept Geology And Geoph New Orleans LA 70148-0001 E-mail: gallen@uno.edu.

ALLEN, GEORGE CAPPS, lawyer; b. Atlanta, Sept. 11, 1949; s. Henry C. and Emalyn P. (Jones) A.; m. Nancy A. Busch, Aug. 7, 1971; children: Sarah R., Susannah C., Patrick R., G. William. Student, U. de Montpelier, France, 1969-70; AB, Davidson Coll., 1971; JD, U. N.C., 1977. Bar: Wash. 1977, U.S. Dist. Ct. (we. dist.) Wash. 1977. Atty. Bogle & Gates, Seattle, 1977-79; pvt. practice Seattle, 1979-80, 90—; atty. Devin, Hamlin & Erickson, Seattle, 1980-83, Powe, Housh, Bingham & Allen, Seattle, 1983-90. 1st lt. U.S. Army, 1971-73. Mem. Wash. Def. Trial Lawyers, Wash. State Trial Lawyers Assn., Wash. State Bar Assn., Def. Rsch. Inst. Office: 1301 5th Ave Ste 2600 Seattle WA 98101-2622 E-mail: georgecallen@worldnet.att.net.

ALLEN, GEORGE FELIX, senator, former governor; b. Whittier, Calif., Mar. 8, 1952; s. George H. and Henrietta Lumbroso A.; m. Susan M. Brown; children: Tyler, Forrest, Brooke. BA cum laude in History, U. Va., 1974, JD, 1977. Mem. Va. Ho. of Dels., Richmond, 1982—91, 102d Congress from 7th Dist. Va., 1991-93; gov. State of Va., 1994-98; ptnr. McGuire Woods Battle & Boothe, LLP, Richmond, 1998-2001; US senator from Va., 2001—. Mem. Fgn. Rels. Com. Chmn. Chesapeake Bay Exec. Coun., 1995—96, So. Gov.'s Assn., 1996—97. Republican. Presbyn. Office: 204 Russell Senate Office Bldg Washington DC 20510*

ALLEN, GEORGE SEWELL, neurosurgery educator; b. St. Louis, Jan. 10, 1942; BA in Chemistry, Wesleyan U., 1963; MD, Washington U., St. Louis, 1967; PhD, U. Minn., 1975. Diplomate Am. Bd. Neurol. Surgeons. Intern Duke U., Durham, NC, 1967-68; rsch. assoc. Nat. Inst. Neurol. Disease and Stroke, NIH, 1968-70; resident dept. neurol. surgery U. Minn., Mpls., 1970-75; asst. prof. neurol. surgery Johns Hopkins U. and Hosp., Balt., 1975-79, assoc. prof., 1979-83, prof., 1983-84; prof. neurol. surgery, chmn. dept. Vanderbilt U. Med. Ctr., Nashville, 1984—. Mem. med. staff Vanderbilt U. Hosp., Met. Nashville Gen. Hosp., VA Hosp., Nashville, St. Thomas Hosp., Nashville, all 1984—; A.W. Rogers lectr. Milw. Acad. Medicine, 1988, J. Jay Keegan Meml. lectr. U. Nebr. Med. Ctr., Omaha, 1988, J. Cochran lectr. Med. Assn. Ala., Montgomery, 1988, A.B. Baker lectr. U. Minn., Mpls., 1988. Contbr. articles to profl. jours. Comdr. USPHS, 1968-70. Mem. ACS, Am. Assn. Neurol. Surgeons, Congress of Neurol. Surgeons, Brain Surgery Soc., Soc. Neurol. Surgeons, H. William Scott, Jr. Soc., Soc. Neurosurg. Anesthesia and Neurologic Supportive Care Office: Vanderbilt U Med Ctr N Dept Neurosurgery Rm T 4224 Nashville TN 37232-2380 E-mail: george.allen@vanderbilt.edu.

ALLEN (IRVIN M.N.), GEORGIANNE LYDIA CHRISTIAN, writer, poet; b. Chgo., Apr. 30, 1943; d. George Aaron Irvin and Madeline Anandabai (Sobrian M.N.) Irvin Gordon, Earl Ovington Gordon (Stepfather); m. Ernest James Allen, Feb. 29, 1992; m. Hillard Roland Phillips, July 1, 1960 (div. June 16, 1977); children: Kellie Annette Phillips Mortley, Madeline Charlotte Phillips Kimmich, Matthew Roland Phillips. Secretarial cert., Chgo. Coll. Commerce, 1963; AA in Psychology, Southwestern Coll., Chula Vista, Calif., 1974; AS in Nursing, Mo. So. State Coll., Joplin, 1977; BSN, Pittsburg State U., Kans., 1979; clin. pastoral edn., St. Paul Sch. Theology and Ossawatomie State Hosp., Kans., 1984; MDiv, MRE, St. Paul Sch. of Theology, Kansas City, Mo., 1985; postgrad., Ga. State U., 2005. RN Mo., Ga., 1977; ordained to ministry Mo. West Conf., 1980; lic. practitioner Nambudripad Allergy Ellimination. Bd. dirs. United Meth. Ch. Black Meth. for Ch. Renewal, 1981—82; pastor Pitts Chapel United Meth. Ch., Springfield, Mo., 1984—85; founder, chairperson Matthew 25 Collaboration, Atlanta, 1998—99; pastor, CEO Ch. of the Creator Incarnate, Coverings, Creative Theol. Ministries, Stone Mountain, Ga., 1994—; nursing instr. Pacific Coast Coll., Chula Vista, Calif., 1990—91; mem. adv. bd. Nambudripad's Allergy Rsch. Found. Author: How to Study and Pass Tests (on line at Virtual University, www.vu.com), I Will Trust Him, Poetry of Faith, (book of poetry) Today (appeared in Poetry's Elite the Best Poets of 2000, 2000); composer: (songs) Atlanta, God Will See You Through, On this Our Wedding Day, The Gospel in Calypso, When I See a Rainbow et al.; prodr.: (radio broadcast) Creative Christian Living; prodr.: (motivational/relaxation cassette) How to Release Worry Anxiety and Stress; web site designer www.coverings.org;, author of poems. Participant Atlanta Taskforce for the Homeless, 1994—98; lectr. leadership classes Dekalb Hist. Soc., Decatur, Ga., 1999—2001; newsletter editor and organizer Stone Mountain Estates Cmty. Orgn., Ga., 2002—03; bd. dirs. Black Methodists for Ch. Renewal, 1981—82; chairperson Matthew 25 Collaboration, Atlanta, 1998—99; treas. Conf. Youth Coun. of Rock River Conf. of Meth. Episcopal Ch., 1959—60; designer, coord. Project Hope. Nominee Ga. Author Yr., Ga. Writers Assn., 2000; recipient Instr.'s Appreciation plaque, Nursing Students Pacific Coast Coll., 1991, Appreciation Cert., Bd. Dirs. Coverings Ministry, 1997, Internat. Poet of Merit award, Internat. Soc. Poets, 2000 - 2003; Betty Stephens Scholarship award for religious edn., St. Paul Sch. of Theology, 1980—81. Mem.: Sigma Theta Tau. Achievements include research in basis for harmonius race relations (100+ yrs) between residents of the Village of Stone Mountain, GA, former home of the Grand Imperial Wizard of the Ku Klux Klan, site of USAs largest Klan rallies; first African Am. woman to enter and grad. from both Mo. So. State Coll.'s Nursing Program and St. Paul Sch. of Theology. Avocations: travel, music (writing, playing and listening), sewing, writing, history. Home: 4965 Dantel Way Stone Mountain GA 30083 Office Phone: 770-469-6611.

ALLEN, GLORIA ANN, real estate broker, artist; b. Paterson, N.J., May 1, 1940; d. Victor and Anna (Nagorny) Borovoy; m. Byron Paul Allen, July 7, 1964 (div. Jan. 1986); children: Andreya Monica, Sarah Patricia. Student, Cir. in Sq. Acting Sch., N.Y.C., 1963-64; MA, Johns Hopkins U., 1962; MBA, Golden Gate U., 1986; art student, City Coll. of San Franciso, 2004—. Lic. real estate broker, Calif. Tchr. Elem. Sch., East Rutherford, N.J., 1963; social worker Bur. Child Welfare City of N.Y., 1964-68; social worker Dept. Social Svcs. City and County San Francisco, 1968-78; property mgr. San Francisco, 1981-91; broker assoc. Ritchie and Ritchie, San Francisco, 1992, Evans Pacific Realtor, San Francisco, 1993-94, Frank Howard Allen Realtors, San Francisco, 1994-97, Fred Sands City Properties, San Francisco, 1997-2001, Coldwell Banker, San Francisco, 2001—02, Merchant Real Estate Inc., 2003—. Fin. com. mem. St. Mary's Cathedral, San Francisco, 1993-94 Mem. Nat. Assn. Realtors, Nat. Network Comml. Real Estate Women (chief fin. officer 1987-89, co-chair facilities Nat. Conv. 1993). Democrat. Personal E-mail: gloria3@mindspring.com.

ALLEN, H. WILLIAM, lawyer; b. Nevada, Mo., Apr. 7, 1944; s. Henry W. and Betty Jeane (Grover) A.; m. Kay Willis, Sept. 22, 1944; children— West, Farrell, Lindsay BA, Rhodes Coll., 1966; JD, Washington U., St. Louis, 1969. Bar: Ark. 1969, Ill. 1969, Mo. 1969. Asst. U.S. atty., Chgo., 1969-70; spl. asst. to pres. ABA, 1970-71; assoc. Wright Lindsay & Jenninger, 1971-76, ptnr., 1976-80; spl. chief just. Ark. Supreme Ct., 1980; sr. ptnr. Allen Cabe & Lester, Little Rock, 1980-86; mng. ptnr. Allen Law Firm, P.C., Little Rock, 1986—. Mem. ABA (ho. of dels. 1991-00, chmn. com. on ethics and profl. responsibility 1978-84, bd. gov. 1975-78, 2002-05), Am. Bar. Found. (pres., bd. dirs.), Am. Judicature Soc. (bd. dirs. 1981-85); Pulaski County Bar Assn, (pres. 1984-85, Outstanding Lawyer award, 1991); Ark. Bar Assn. (chmn. Commn. Ethics 1989-92); Am. Law Inst. Office: Allen Law Firm 9th Floor 212 Center St Little Rock AR 72201-2425 Office Phone: 501-374-7100.

ALLEN, HARRY FRANKLIN, finance educator; b. Amersham, Eng., Mar. 6, 1956; came to U.S., 1980. s. Harry Cranbrook and Mary Kathleen (Andrews) A.; m. Sally Elizabeth Riley, July 9, 1977; children: James Franklin, Toby Thomas. BA, U. East Anglia, 1977; M of Philosophy, Oxford U., 1979, D of Phil., 1980; MA, U. Pa., 1987. Asst. prof. fin. Wharton Sch. U. Pa., Phila., 1980—86, assoc. prof. fin. and econs., 1986—90, prof., 1990—93; Nippon life prof. fin. and econs. Wharton Sch., U. Pa., Phila., 1994—; exec. editor Rev. of Fin. Studies Wharton Sch., 1993—95. Mem. Am. Fin. Assn. (pres. 2000). Home: 929 Merion Square Rd Gladwyne PA 19035-1509 Office: U Pa Wharton Sch Fin Philadelphia PA 19104 Office Phone: 215-898-3629. Business E-Mail: allenf@wharton.upenn.edu.

ALLEN, HENRY LEE, sociology educator, consultant; b. Joiner, Ark., July 7, 1955; s. John Henry Jr. and Mahalie (Moore) A.; m. Juliet Eugenia-Agnes Cooper, July 7, 1979; children: Jonathan, Jessica, Janice, Justin, Julia, Janel, Joseph, Judith. BA cum laude, Wheaton Coll., 1977; MA, U. Chgo., 1979, PhD, 1988. Sociology instr., adminstrv. asst. to pres. Bethel Coll., St. Paul, 1982—87; assoc. prof. sociology Calvin Coll., Grand Rapids, Mich., 1987—91; asst. prof. edn. Grad. Sch. Edn., U. Rochester, NY, 1991—97; assoc. prof. sociology Rochester Inst. Tech., 1997—98, Wheaton Coll., Ill., 1998—. Cons. NEA, Washington, 1992—, Am. Bible Soc., 2001—, Inst. for the Black Family, Detroit, 1984—, among others, FBI Acad., 2003—04; mem. Oxford U. Round Table, 2004—05. Contbr. articles to profl. jours. Bd. dirs. Genessee Settlement House, Rochester, 1993-96, Koinonia House, African-Am. Leadership Roundtable of Dupage County, 2000—; mem. Kettering Found. Cmty. Leadership Program, Oxford U. Roundtable, 2004-05; mem. adv. com. United Way, Rochester, 1995-96; African-Am. Leadership Roundtable, Rochester, 1993-96; mem. Jubilee Bapt. Ch., 2002. Fellow Danforth Found., 1978-81. Mem. Am. Acad. Polit. and Social Sci., Nat. Orgn. Black Law Enforcement Execs., Wilson Ctr. for Scholars, N.Y. Acad. Scis., Dupage Redn. Human Svcs. Reform, Game Theory Soc. Avocations: science fiction, archery, astronomy, football, museums. Home: 111 W Lincoln Ave Wheaton IL 60187-4114 Office: Wheaton Coll Dept Sociology Wheaton IL 60187 Office Phone: 630-752-7222. E-mail: henry.l.allen@wheaton.edu.

ALLEN, HENRY SERMONES, JR., lawyer; b. Bronxville, N.Y., Aug. 26, 1947; s. Henry S. and Cecelia Marie (Chartrand) A.; m. Patricia Stromberger, Nov. 26, 1988; children: David Beckman, Amy Louise, Jeffrey Roy. AB magna cum laude, Washington U., St. Louis, 1969; MPA, Cornell U., 1973, JD, 1974. Adminstrv. resident Montefiore Hosp. and Med. Ctr., Bronx, NY, 1971; rsch. trainee Nat. Ctr. Health Svcs. Rsch. HEW, 1974—75; assoc. Vedder, Price, Kaufman & Kammholz, Chgo., 1975—79; pvt. practice Springfield, 1979—81; ptnr. Allen & Reed, Chgo., 1981—86, McBride, Baker & Coles, 1986—2002, Holland & Knight LLC, Chgo., 2002—. Adj. asst. prof. hosp. law Ithaca (NY) Coll., 1974-75; adj. prof. Cornell U., 1995—, Northwestern U. Sch. Law, 2003—, Northwestern U. Kellogg Sch. Mgmt., 2003—. HUD fellow, 1969-71. Mem. Am. Health Lawyers Assn., Ill. Soc. Hosp. Attys., Nat. Health Lawyers Assn., Cornell U. Club Chgo., Phi Beta Kappa, Omicron Delta Epsilon Office: Holland and Knight 131 S Dearborn St Chicago IL 60603-5506 Office Phone: 312-715-5729. Business E-Mail: henry.allen@hklaw.com.

ALLEN, HENRY SOUTHWORTH, journalist, critic; b. Summit, N.J., May 23, 1941; s. Henry Southworth and Mary Darmour (Williams) A.; m. Deborah Etta Mandel, Mar. 25, 1972; children: Hannah Rose, Peter Griffith, Nicholas Isaac DeWolf. BA, Hamilton Coll., 1967. Copy editor New Haven (Conn.) Register, 1966; reporter N.Y. News, N.Y.C., 1967-70; reporter, editor, critic The Washington Post, 1970—. Tchr. in culture and meaning U. Md. Honors Program. Author: Glare, 1991, Fool's Mercy, 1982, Going Too Far Enough, 1994, What It Felt Like B Living in the American Century, 2000; writer (articles) New York Review of Books, New Yorker, Forbes, Paris Review, Smithsonian, Vogue, Wilson Quarterly. Cpl. USMC, 1963-66, Vietnam. Recipient Am. Soc. Newspaper Editors award for commentary, 1992, Am. Soc. of Sunday and Feature Editors prize for creative writing, finalist Pulitzer prize, 1994, Pulitzer prize Journalism for Criticism, 2000, Sherwood Media award, Blinded Americans Veterans Found., 2000; NEH fellowship for journalists, U. Mich., 1975-76. Mem. Marine Corps Hist. Assn. Avocations: windsurfing, squash. Home: 513 New York Ave Takoma Park MD 20912-4119 Office: The Washington Post 1150 15th St NW Washington DC 20071-0002*

ALLEN, HERBERT ELLIS, environmental chemistry educator; b. Sharon, Pa., July 19, 1939; s. Jacob Samuel and Florence (Safier) A.; m. Deena Wilner, 1962 (dec. 1983); children: Francine Joy, Julie Michelle; m. Ronnie Magil, 1984 BS in Chemistry, U. Mich., 1962; MS, Wayne State U., 1967; PhD, U. Mich., 1974. Chemist U.S. Bur. Comml. Fisheries, Ann Arbor, Mich., 1962-70; lectr. U. Mich., Ann Arbor, 1970-74; asst. prof. Ill. Inst. Tech., Chgo., 1974-76, assoc. prof., 1976-80, prof. environ. engring., 1980-83; dir. Environ. Studies Inst., Drexel U., Phila., also prof. chemistry, 1983-89; prof. civil engring. U. Del., Newark, 1990—, dir. Ctr. for Study of Metals in the Environment, 2002—; dir. Del. Waste Reduction Assistance Program, 1991-95. Vis. prof. Water Rsch. Ctr., Medmenham, Eng., 1980-81, Nankai U., Tianjin, People's Republic of China, 1993—; cons. WHO, U.S. EPA. Editor: Nutrients in Natural Waters, 1972, Analysis and Effects of Metal Speciation, Applications to Water, Waste, Soil, 1988, Metals in Groundwater, 1993, Metal Speciation and Contamination of Soil, 1994, Metal Contaminated Aquatic Sediments, 1995, Metals in Surface Water, 1998, Bioavailability of Metals in Terestrial Ecosystems, 2002, Solid Waste, 2004. Fellow, WHO, 1981. Mem. Am. Chem. Soc. (chmn. divsn. environ. chemistry 1972-75), Water Environment Fedn., Soc. for Environ. Toxicology and Chemistry, Internat. Water Assn. Home: 21 E Levering Mill Rd Bala Cynwyd PA 19004-2251 Office: Univ Delaware Dept Civil & Environ Engring Newark DE 19716 Office Phone: 302-831-8449. Business E-Mail: allen@ce.udel.edu.

ALLEN, JACQUELYN MAY, education educator, consultant; b. L.A., Nov. 6, 1943; d. John Richard and Ida May (Townsend) Hinson; m. James William Allen, Dec. 19, 1970; children: Julene May, Jason William. BA, U. Redlands, 1965; MA, Berkeley Bapt. Div. Sch., 1969; MS, Calif. State U., Hayward, 1972; DEd, U. San Francisco, 1990. Lic. marriage and family counselor, Calif; nat. cert. counselor, nat. cert. sch. counselor; cert. neuropsychology Fielding Inst. ESL tchr. U. Mexico, Mexico City, 1967; missionary Am. Bapt. Conv., El Salvador, Ctrl. Am., 1966-67; tchr. Foothill Intermediate Sch., Walnut Creek, Calif., 1968-72; marriage, family, child counselor Fremont Inst. Transactional Analysis, Fremont, Calif., 1977-78; career cons. Pvt. Sch. & Chronicle Guidance Project, Fremont, 1989-91; CEO, pres. Am. Sch. Counselor Assn., Alexandria, Va., 1993-94; cons. Allen Cons. Assocs., Fremont, 1985—; sch. psychologist, sch. counselor Fremont Unified Sch. Dist., 1972—; edn. program cons. Calif. Dept. Edn., 2001—04; assoc. prof. U. of La Verne, 2004—. Liaison Counseling for High Skills, De Witt Wallace Reader's Digest, Manhattan, Kans., 1994-95; liaison for Am. Sch. Counseling Assn., Nat. Bus. Adv. Bd., Alexandria, Va., 1993-95; project coord. Ednl. Devel. Ctr. Grant on Comprehensive Health and HIV, AIDS Prevention, Boston, 1994-95; pres., negotiator Fremont Counseling and Psychologists Assn., 1972-73, 75-77, 90-91; mem. retirement and bilingual spl. edn. coms. Fremont Unified Sch. Dist., 1994-95; adj. faculty Chapman U., 1995—. Editor: (compendium) Action-Oriented Desk Guide for Professional School Counselors, 1992; author, editor: School Counseling: New Perspectives and Practices. Treas. Antelope Hills Home Owners Assn., Fremont, 1984-85; leader troop 1382 Girl Scouts Am., Fremont, 1990-94. Named Outstanding Young Educator Fremont Jaycees, 1974; recipient H. B. McDaniel Individual award, 2002; inductee H. B. McDaniel Hall of Fame, 2005. Mem. ACA (governing coun. 1991-94, exec. com. 1993-94, pub. policy and legis. com. 1994-97), Am. Sch. Counselor Assn. (pres., CEO 1993-94, exec. and fin. com. 1992-95, grant 1990), Calif. Assn. Counseling and Devel. Edn. Found. (bd. dirs., v.p., editor CASC Monograph, 2001-05, pres., 1999-01), Calif. Assn. Counseling and Devel. (pres. 1991-92, editl. bd. jour. 1995-97), Calif. Alliance for Pupil Pers. Svc. Orgns., Calif. Career Devel. Assn. (conf. com., grant 1990), Calif. Assn. Sch. Counselors (newsletter editor), Coalition for Counselor Licensure (bd. dirs.), ASCA (life, CACD Clarion Modell Disting. Svc. award, 1998, H.B. McDaniel Individual award, 2003, H.B. McDaniel Hall of Fame, 2003, Delta Kappa Gamma (rsch. chair 1988-92, scholarships 1988-89, profl. devel. 1995-96). Avocations: reading, travel, writing, public speaking, photography. E-mail: jallen5@ulv.edu.

ALLEN, JAMES EDWARD, preventive medicine physician; b. Sterling, Ill., 1944; PhD, U. Iowa, 1971; MD, U. Miami, 1973. Cert. Am. Bd. Internal Medicine, 1989, in Infectious Diseases 1990. Resident, internal medicine Loyola U. Med. Ctr., Maywood, Ill., 1973—76; fellow, infectious disease U. Colo., Denver, 1976—78; physician Elmhurst Meml. Hosp., Ill. Office: Metro Infectious Disease Cons 500 E Ogden Ave Ste C Hinsdale IL 60521

ALLEN, JAMES LEE, lawyer; b. Lakewood, Ohio, Apr. 21, 1952; s. Frank M. and Dorothy S. (Stone) A.; m. Sue Eveline Goble, July 25, 1981. BA with high distinction, U. Mich., 1974, JD, 1977; LLM, Wayne State U., 1988. Bar: Mich. 1977, U.S. Dist. Ct. (ea. dist.) Mich. 1978, U.S. Ct. Appeals (6th cir.) 1982, U.S. Tax Ct. 1981, U.S. Supreme Ct. 1984. Assoc. Hardig, Goetz, Heath, Merritt & Reebel, Birmingham, Mich., 1977-83; ptnr. Plunkett & Cooney, P.C., Detroit, 1983—; instr. Walsh Coll., Troy, Mich., 1980. Vestryman Nativity Episcopal Ch., Birmingham, 1978-81; bd. dirs., treas. Common Ground, Birmingham, 1980; bd dirs. Birmingham Community House, 1983-86. Mem. U. Mich. Alumni Assn., Oakland County Bar Assn. (chmn. program com. (1979-82), Mich. Bar Assn. (mem. representation assembly 1978-90), Phi Beta Kappa. Republican. Home: 3755 Ledge Ct Troy MI 48084-1142

ALLEN, JAMES RICHARD, accountant; b. Columbus, Tex., Nov. 10, 1956; s. Jack Kenneth and Genola Marie (Gardner) A.; m. Melinda Lee Strong, Feb. 25, 1956; children: Benjamin, Ashley. BBA in Acctg., Tex. A&M U., 1979; postgrad., North Tex. State U., 1982. CPA, Tex. Tax mgr. Price Waterhouse, Ft. Worth, 1979-84; tax ptnr. Stiefel Lyles & Allen, P.C., Tyler, Tex., 1984—, also bd. dirs. Contbr. articles to profl. jours. Mem. com. Estate Planning Coun., 1985—; bd. dirs. Tyler Crime Stoppers, 1987-94; deacon, treas. Green Acres Bapt. Ch., chmn., 2004-05; pres. bd. dirs. Discovery Pl. Children's Mus., 1998-99, 2001—. Named One of Outstanding Young Men in Am., 1986. Mem. AICPA, Tex. Soc. CPAs (fed. tax com., treas. East Tex. chpt., chmn. taxation East Tex. chpt.), Tyler Jaycees (bd. dirs., dir. of quarter 1986, Key Man award 1986). Republican. Avocation: sports. Home: 605 Carriage Dr Tyler TX 75703-3688 Office: Stiefel Lyles & Allen PC 4710 Kinsey Dr Tyler TX 75703-1009 Office Phone: 903-581-3883.

ALLEN, JEFFERSON F., oil company executive; Pres., CEO, chmn. bd. dirs. Comfed Bancorp, Inc., Lowell, Mass.; exec. v.p., CFO Tosco Corp., Stamford, Conn., pres., 1997—, pres., CFO. Office: Tosco Corp # 500 1700 E Putnam Ave Old Greenwich CT 06870-1321*

ALLEN, JEFFREY MICHAEL, lawyer; b. Chgo., Dec. 13, 1948; s. Albert A. and Miriam (Feldman) A.; m. Anne Marie Guaraglia, Aug. 9, 1975; children: Jason M., Sara M. BA in Polit. Sci. with great distinction and distinction in honors, U. Calif., Berkeley, 1970, JD, 1973. Bar: Calif. 1973, U.S. Dist. Ct. (no. and so. dists.) Calif. 1973, U.S. Ct. Appeals (9th cir.) 1973, U.S. Dist. Ct. (ea. dist.) Calif. 1974, U.S. Dist. Ct. (cen. dist.) Calif. 1977, U.S. Dist. Ct. (so. dist.) Calif., U.S. Supreme Ct.; lic. real estate broker. Prin. Graves & Allen, Oakland, Calif., 1973—. Teaching asst. dept. polit. sci. U. Calif., Berkeley, 1970-73; lectr. St. Mary's Coll., Moraga, Calif., 1976-90; mem. faculty Oakland Coll. of Law, 1996-98, 2004-; bd. dirs. Family Svcs. of the East Bay, 1987-92, 1st v.p., 1988, pres., 1988-91; mem. panel arbitrators Ala. County Superior Ct.; arbitrator comml. arbitration panel Am. Arbitration Assn. Mem. editorial bd. U. Calif. Law Rev., 1971-73, project editor, 1972-73; mem. Ecology Law Quar., 1971-72; contbr. articles to profl. jours. Mem. U.S. Youth Soccer Constl. Commn., 1997—98, U.S. Youth Soccer Bylaws Com., 1998—; mem. region 4 regional coun. U.S. Youth Soccer, 1996—99, chmn. mediation and dispute resolution com., 1999—2000; bd. dirs. U.S. Futsal Fedn., 2000—; treas. Hillcrest Elem. Sch. PTA, 1984—86, pres., 1986—88; past mem. GATE adv. com., strategic planning com. on fin. and budget, dist. budget adv. com., instructional strategy counsel Oakland Unified Sch. Dist., 1986—91; mem. Oakland Met. Forum, 1987—91, Oakland Strategic Planning Com., 1988—90; mem. adv. com. St. Mary's Coll. Paralegal Prog.; commr. Bay Oaks Youth Soccer, 1988—94; asst. dist. commr. dist. 4 Calif. Youth Soccer Assn., 1990—92, also bd. dirs., pres. dist. 4 competitive league, 1990—93, sec. bd. dirs., 1993—96, chmn. bd. dirs., 1996—99; chmn. U.S. Soccer dateabase mktg. com. Calif. Soccer Assn., 1997—99; bd. dirs. Montera Sports Complex, 1988—89, Jack London Youth Soccer League, 1988—94, Calif. Soccer Assn., 1996—99. Mem.: Rotary (bd. dirs. Oakland 1992—94), Oakland C. of C., Assn. Conflict Resolution, Calif. North Referee Assn. (referee adminstr. dist. 4 1992—96, state bd. dirs. 1996—2000), U.S. Soccer Fedn. (nat. C lic. coach and state referee, state referee instr. and state referee assessor), Calif. Scholarship Fedn., U.S. Soccer Assn. (database mktg. com., constl. commn.), Alameda County Bar Assn. (past vice chmn. com. continuing edn., arbitrator, exec. com. alternative dispute resolution programs, panel mediator), Calif. Bar Assn. (mem. ADR com. 2001—04), ABA (chmn. subcom. on use of computers in real estate trans. 1985—86, chmn. real property com. gen. practice sect. 1987—91, mem. programs com. 1991—93, adv. coord. 1993—96, sect. coun. 1994—98, mktg. bd. 1996—98, mem. 1998—99, editor, columnist Tech. and Practice Guide 1998—, editl. bd. GP Solo 1999—, editor, columnist Tech. e Report 2002—). Avocations: reading, computers, photography, skiing, baseball, coaching and refereeing youth soccer. Office: Graves & Allen 436 14th St Ste 1400 Oakland CA 94612-2716 Office Phone: 510-839-8777. Personal E-mail: jallenlaw@aol.com. Business E-Mail: jallenlaw@gravesandallen.com.

ALLEN, JEFFREY RODGERS, lawyer; b. West Point, N.Y., Aug. 15, 1953; s. James R. and Kathryn (Lewis) A.; m. Cynthia Lynn Colyer, Aug. 10, 1975; children: Emily Rodgers, Elizabeth Colyer, Richard Byrd. BA in History, U. Va., 1975; JD, U. Richmond, 1978. Bar: Va. 1978, U.S. Ct. Mil. Appeals 1981, U.S. Ct. Appeals (4th cir.) 1982, U.S. Supreme Ct. 1982. Trial atty. Michie, Hamlett, Donato & Lowry, Charlottesville, Va., 1982-86; chief counsel Va. Dept. Mil. Affairs, Blackstone, Va., 1986-2000; U.S. property and fiscal officer for Va. Blackstone, 2001—. Atty., advisor U.S. Army Mobile Air Surg. Transport Team, Savannah, Ga., 1980-82; steering com. X-Car Litigation Group, 1983-85; lectr., organizer Law Everyone Should Know series Piedmont (Va.) C.C., Charlottesville, 1984-86; trial atty., of counsel Thorsen, Marchant & Scher, L.L.P., Richmond, 1986-98; mem. legal adv. com. Va. Gov.'s Mil. Adv. Commn., 1987-2000, judge advocate adv. coun. N.G. Bur., 1993-96, TJAG Air N.G. judge advocate adv. coun., 1997-, coord. strategic planning com.; mem. coun. futures com., USPFO, 2002—, chmn. edn. com., 2004—. Pres. Regency Woods Condominium Assn., Richmond, 1976-78, Ashcroft Neighborhood Assn., Charlottesville, 1983-86; treas. Va. N.G. Found., 1986-2002, mem. strategic planning coun. USPFO Coun., 2002—. Capt. U.S. Army, 1978-82, lt. col. JAGC, Va. Air N.G., 1982-2000, col. USAF, 2001—. Mem. Assn. Trial Lawyers Am., Va. Trial Lawyers Assn., Richmond Bar Assn. Avocations: jogging, mountain climbing, photography, fishing, swimming. Home: 2700 Cottage Cove Dr Richmond VA 23233-3318 Office: USPFO Bldg 316 Ft Pickett Blackstone VA 23824-6316 Office Phone: 434-298-6161. Business E-Mail: jeff.allen@va.ngb.army.mil.

ALLEN, JERE HARDY, artist; b. Selma, Ala., Aug. 15, 1944; s. Newton Erwin and Fannie Hardy Allen; m. Joe Ann Marshall Marshall, Nov. 11, 1946; children: Paige, Jeffrey Marshall. BFA, Ringling Sch. Art, 1970; MFA, U. Tenn., 1972. Prof. emeritus of art U. Miss., University, Miss., 1972—2000. Exhibitions include Carol Robinson Gallery, New Orleans, La., Washington, D.C., one-man shows include Contemporary Art Ctr., Peoria, Illinois, Builder AUS Am., Der Kunstkreis Hamely, Germany, Huntsville (Ala.) Mus. Art. With U.S. Army, 1964—70. Recipient Susan B. Herron award, Miss. Arts Commn., 1996; fellow, 1996; grantee, Fulbright Found., 1979. Home: 1103 Sourh 14th Street Oxford MS 38655 Office: Jere Hardy Allen 130 Alderson Road Oxford MS 38655 Office Phone: 662-816-3529. Personal E-mail: a_jere@bellsouth.net. E-mail: jere@jerehallen.com.

ALLEN, JESSE OWEN, III, organizational behavior specialist; b. Albany, Ga., Apr. 7, 1938; s. Jesse Owen Jr. and Erma Hazel (Pearson) A.; children by previous marriage: Charlotte Renee, Garrett Owen, Cheryl Hazel; m. Barbara Joanna Smith Ozment, May 23, 1987; 1 stepchild, Pamela Ozment Cartee. LLB, LaSalle Law Sch., 1967; AS, U. State N.Y., Albany, 1978, BS in History, Lit. and Bus., 1986; MA in Philosophy, Calif. State U., 1987; PhD in Organizational Behavior, The Union Grad. Sch., 1991; postgrad., Oxford U., England, 1997. Founder, pres. Specific Action Corp., Greensboro, N.C., 1971—; pres. Inst. for Christian Studies, Inc., Greensboro, N.C., 1987—. Bd. dirs. ECA Internat.; pres. Worldwide Travel, Greensboro, N.C., 1994—; lectr., cons. in field. Author: Weatherization Production Control, 1978, Personal Profile Labs, 1980, Management Power: The Specific Action Way, 1985, Personality Power: The Specific Action Way, 1988, Master of Personal Excellence Program, 1994; contbr. articles to profl. jours., Specific Action Management System, 1996, Specific Action Personality System, 1996, Specific Action Team System, 1997; patentee Allen valve, 1967. Named to Hon. Order of Ky. Cols., Commonwealth of Ky., 1978, Hon. Adm. State of Nebr., 1978. Mem. Am. Soc. Tng. and Devel. (pres. 1976, Best Chpt. award 1976), Nat. Speakers Assn. (cert. speaking profl. 1988), Greensboro City Club, Inst. Mgmt. Cons. (cert. 1989). Republican. Home: 520 Lindley Rd Greensboro NC 27410-4933 Office: Specific Action Corp PO Box 19125 Greensboro NC 27419-9125 Office Phone: 336-854-9494.

ALLEN, JOAN, actress; b. Rochelle, Ill., Aug. 20, 1956; m. Peter Friedman, Jan. 1, 1990; 1 child. Student, Ea. Ill. U., No. Ill. U. Founding mem. Steppenwolf Theatre Co., Chgo.; theater appearances include (debut) And A Nightingale Sang, N.Y.C. (Clarence Derwent award, Drama Desk award, Outer Critics Circle award 1984), Steppenwolf Theatre Co., also Hartford, 1983, The Marriage of Bette and Boo, N.Y. Shakespeare Festival, 1986, Burn This! (Tony awrd for Best Actress 1989) Mark Taper Forum, L.A., also NYC, 1987, The Heidi Chronicles, N.Y.C., 1988, 89; film appearances include Compromising Positions, 1985, Peggy Sue Got Married, 1986, Manhunter, 1986, Tucker: The Man and His Dream, 1988, In Country, 1989, Ethan Frome, 1993, Searching for Bobbie Fischer, 1993, Josh and S.A.M., 1993, Nixon, 1995 (Acad. award nominee for best supporting actress 1996), Mad Love, 1995, The Crucible, 1996, Ice Storm, 1997, Face/Off, 1997, Pleasantville, 1998, Veronica Guerin, 1999, All the Rage, 1999, When the Sky Falls, 2000, The Contender, 2000, Off the Map, 2003, The Notebook, 2004, The Bourne Supremacy, 2004, Yes, 2004, The Upside of Anger, 2005; TV appearances include The Twilight Zone, 1987, Am. Playhouse, PBS, 1987, Robert Frost, Voices and Visions, PBS, 1988, Fraiser, 1996, TV films All My Sons, 1986, The Room Upstairs, 1987, Without Warning: The James Brady Story, 1991, Say Goodnight, Gracie, PBS, TV miniseries Evergreen, 1985, The Mists of Avalon, 2001. Office: ICM care Brian Mann 8942 Wilshire Blvd Beverly Hills CA 90211-1934*

ALLEN, JOE BAILEY, III, lawyer; b. Oklahoma City, Okla., Oct. 18, 1951; s. Joe Bailey Jr. and Ann (Flesher) A.; m. Susan Katherine Elkins, Apr. 23, 1977; 1 child, Mark Robert. BA, U. Tex., 1973; JD, So. Meth. U., 1976. Bar: Tex. 1976, U.S. Ct. Appeals (5th cir.) 1977, U.S. Dist. Ct. (no. dist.) Tex. 1979, U.S. Dist. Ct. (ea. dist.) Tex. 1992. Assoc. Elliott, Churchill, Hansen, Dyess & Maxfield, Dallas, 1976-81; atty. Tex. Oil & Gas Corp., Dallas, 1981-82, sr. atty., 1982-85, asst. sec., sr. atty., 1985-86; mem., bd. dirs. Leithiser, Palmer & Allen, P.C., Dallas, 1986-93; ptnr. Palmer Allen & McTaggart, L.L.P., Dallas, 1993—. Mem. Tex. Bar Assn. Methodist. Office: Palmer Allen & McTaggart 8111 Preston Rd Ste 300 Dallas TX 75225-6329 Business E-Mail: jallen@pamlaw.com.

ALLEN, JOHN JAY, Spanish language educator; b. May 20, 1932; AB, Duke U., 1954; MA, Middlebury Coll., 1957; PhD, U. Wis., 1960; DLit (hon.), Middlebury Coll., 2004. Prof. Spanish, U. Fla., Gainesville, 1960-83, U. Ky., Lexington, 1983-2000. Home: 1153 Stirling Dr Danville KY 40422-2714 E-mail: jjallen@kih.net.

ALLEN, JOHN JEFFREY BECK, psychology educator; b. Northampton, Mass., Aug. 10, 1961; s. Ronald Royce and JoAnne Elizabeth (Kuehl) A; m. Connie J.A. Beck; 1 child, Gabrielle JoAnne Allenbeck. BS, U. Wis., 1986; MA, U. Minn., 1991, PhD, 1992. Lic. psychologist, Ariz. Instr. psychology U. Minn., Mpls., 1988-92; intern psychology VA Med. Ctr., Mpls., 1991-92; asst. prof. psychology U. Ariz., Tucson, 1992-98, assoc. prof., 1998—2002, prof., 2002—. Contbr. articles to profl. jours. Recipient Disting. Sci. award, 2000; grantee NIH, 1993—2005. Mem. APA, Am. Psychol. Soc., Soc. for Psychophysiol. Rsch., Cognitive Neurosci. Soc., Sigma Xi, Phi Beta Kappa, Phi Kappa Phi. Office: U Ariz Dept Psychology Tucson AZ 85721-0001 Office Phone: 520-621-4992. E-mail: jallen@u.arizona.edu.

ALLEN, JOHN L., JR., journalist, writer; m. Shannon Allen. Degree in Philosophy, Fort Hays State U., 1989; MA in Scripture, U. Kans. Opinion editor Nat. Cath. Reporter, 1997—2000, Rome corr., 2000—, author weekly internet column The Word from Rome, 2001—. Contbr. FOX News Channel; Vatican analyst CNN, NPR. Author: Cardinal Ratzinger: The Vatican's Enforcer of the Faith, 2000, Conclave: The Politics, Personalities and Process of the Next Papal Election, 2002, All the Pope's Men: The Inside Story of How the Vatican Really Thinks, 2004, The Rise of Benedict XVI: The Inside Story of How the Pope Was Elected and Where He Will Take the Catholic Church, 2005; Has contbd. to The Tablet, Jesus, Second Opinion, The Nation, The Miami Herald, Die Furche, The Irish Examiner. Office: Nat Cath Reporter Pub Co 115 E Armour Blvd Kansas City MO 64111-1203 Business E-Mail: jallen@natcath.org.*

ALLEN, JOHN LOGAN, geographer, department chairman; b. Laramie, Wyo., Dec. 27, 1941; s. John Milton and Nancy Elizabeth (Logan) Allen; m. Anne Evelyn Gilroy, Aug. 9, 1964; children: Traci Kathleen, Jennifer Lynne. BA (Gen. Motors Corp. scholar 1959-63), U. Wyo., 1963, MA, 1964; PhD (univ. grad. fellow 1964-67), Clark U., Worcester, Mass., 1969; PhD NSF postdoctoral fellow, 1970-71. Mem. faculty U. Conn., Storrs, 1967-2000, prof. geography, 1979-2000, head dept., 1976-94, dir. grad. program in geography, 1992-2000, mem. nat. exec. com. Faculty Athletic Rep. Assn., 1987-96; parliamentarian Faculty Athletic Rep. Assn., 1996—; prof., chair dept. geography U. Wyo., Laramie, 2000—. Non-resident fellow Ctr. Great Plains Studies; scholar-in-residence Nat. Lewis and Clark Trail Interpretive Ctr. Author: Passage Through the Garden: Lewis and Clark and the Geog. Lore of the Am. N.W., 1975, Jedediah Smith and the Mountain Men of the Am. West, 1991, Lewis and Clark and the Images of the Am. N.W., 1991, Student Atlas of World Politics, 1991, 2005, Atlas of Econ. Devel., 1997, Atlas of Environ. Issues, 1997, Student Atlas of World Geography, 1998, 4th edit., 2004, Student Atlas of Anthropology, 2003; editor (ann. edits.): Environment, 1982—, Reshaping Traditions, 1994—; mem. editl. bd.: Jour. Hist. Geography, —, project dir., gen. editor: North Am. Exploration: A Comprehensive History, 3 vols., 1997—; contbr. articles to profl. jours., chpts. to books. Pres. Mansfield (Conn.) Middle Sch. Assn., 1979-80; mem. Mansfield Conservation Commn.; vice chmn. Mansfield Zoning Bd. Appeals; mem. Mansfield Planning and Zoning Commn.; adv. bd. Nat. Lewis and Clark Bicentennial Commn. Recipient Meritorious Achievement award Lewis and Clark Trail Heritage Found., 1976, Excellence in Teaching award U. Conn. Alumni Assn., 1987, Outstanding Contbn. award UCONN Club, 1993, Outstanding Alumnus award U. Wyo. Coll. Arts and Scis., 1999, Spl. Recognition award U. Conn., 2000. Fellow Am. Geog. Assn., Royal Geog. Soc.; mem. Assn. Am. Geographers, Western History Assn.(hon. life), Soc. Historians Early Am. Republic, Soc. History Discovery (nat. councilor), AAAS, Phi Beta Kappa, Phi Kappa Phi, Omicron Delta Kappa. Clubs: Elks, Masons. Democrat. Congregationalist. Home: 2703 Leslie Ct Laramie WY 82072-2979 Office: Univ of Wyoming Dept Geography PO Box 3371 Laramie WY 82071-3371 Office Phone: 307-766-2836. Business E-Mail: jlallen@uwyo.edu. *As a scientist and educator, I have tried to abide by the principle that learning is necessary for the public good and that academicians should make their skills and knowledge available to society at large. Service to others is as important an educational function as the more frequently recognized components of teaching and research.*

ALLEN, JOHN RYBOLT L., chemist, biochemist; b. Indpls., Sept. 14, 1926; BA, Ball State Tchrs. Coll., 1949; PhD in Biochemistry, U. Ill., 1954. Rsch. assoc. biochemistry Northwestern U., 1953-56; asst. prof. Coll. Med. Baylor U., 1956-59; sr. scientist Warner-Lambert Pharm. Co., N.J., 1959-60; rsch. assoc. Dental Sch. Wash. U., 1960-62; prof. chemistry, head. dept. Union Coll., Ky., 1962-64; clin. assoc. clin. chemistry U. Hosp. Case Western Reserve U., 1964-65; asst. prof. pathology and radiology coll. medicine Ohio State U., 1965-68; clin. chemist St. John's Mercy Hosp., St. Louis, 1968-69, Decatur Meml. Hosp., Ill., 1969-70, San Diego Inst. Pathology, 1970, San Bernardino County Hosp., 1970-75; instr. chemistry Phoenix Coll., 1975-80. Recipient G.K. Warren prize Nat. Acad. Scis., 1990, Penrose medal Geol. Soc. Am., 1996. Fellow AAAS, Am. Assn. Clin. Chemistry, Am. Chemistry Soc., Acad. Clin. Lab. Physicians & Scientists, Am. Inst. Chemistry. Achievements include research in quality control and methods, creating phosphokinase, vitamin E deficiency, lipid metabolism and structure. Home: 9627 N 32nd St Phoenix AZ 85028-4832

ALLEN, JOSE R., lawyer; b. Panama, Sept. 8, 1951; arrived in US, 1956; s. Joseph R. and Grace A. (Osborne) A.; m. Irvenia E. Waters, July 20, 1986; 1 child, Jeffrey Richard Allen. BA, Yale U., 1973; JD, Boston Coll., 1976. Bar: Mass. 1977, Calif. 1986. Asst. atty. gen. Mass. Atty. Gen. Office, Boston, 1976-79; trial atty. US Dept. Justice, Washington, 1979-80, asst. sect. chief, 1980-82, sect. chief, 1982-85, chief, environ. def. sect., land, and natural resources divsn., 1981—84, chief, gen. litigation sect., land, and nat. resources divsn., 1984—85; of counsel Orrick, Herrington & Sutcliffe, San Francisco, 1985-88; ptnr., environment practice area Skadden, Arps, Slate, Meagher & Flom LLP, San Francisco, 1988—. Mem. adv. com. on environ. Practising Law Inst., NYC, 1992—; spkr. in the field. Contbr. articles in profl. jours. Bd. dirs. San Francisco Bay Area Lawyers' Com. Urban Affairs, 1990, Legal Aid Soc. San Francisco, 1993. Mem. ABA (mem. sect. on natural resources, energy and environ. law and lit. sect.), Bar Assn. San Francisco, Charles Houston Bar Assn., State Bar Calif. (mem. environ. law sect.). Office: Skadden Arps Slate Meagher & Flom LLP Four Embarcadero Ctr San Francisco CA 94111 Office Phone: 415-984-6442. Office Fax: 888-329-1260. Business E-Mail: jrallen@skadden.com.

ALLEN, JOSEPH HENRY, retired publishing company executive; b. Evanston, Ill., Nov. 9, 1916; s. Joseph Henry and Ann Eugenia (Jansen) A.; m. Eleanor Clark, June 14, 1941; children— David, Elisabeth Allen Adams, Melinda Allen Beardsley. BA, Kenyon Coll., 1938; advanced mgmt. program, Stanford Grad. Sch. Bus., 1953. Joined McGraw-Hill Inc., 1938, regional editor and advt. salesman, 1938-42, established S.W. office Dallas, also mgr., 1948, div. mgr. Los Angeles, 1951-55, v.p., dir. mktg. N.Y.C., 1955-63, v.p. ops., 1963-66; pres. McGraw-Hill Publs. Co., 1966-70; group pres. McGraw-Hill, Inc., 1970-74, dir., 1966-75; sr. v.p. United Techs. Corp., Hartford, Conn., 1974-77. Bd. dirs. Ronin Corp. Served as lt. USNR, 1942-45. Mem. Wee Burn Country Club. Home: 29 Tokeneke Trl Darien CT 06820-6129

ALLEN, JOYCE SMITH, librarian; b. Englewood, N.J., Aug. 1, 1939; d. Harold Willard and Mary Elizabeth Smith; m. Jim Frank Allen, Mar. 1974 (div. 1982); 1 child, Shani Jamilla. BA, Howard U., 1961; MLS, Atlanta U., 1966; cert. in advanced studies, U. Ill., 1974. Reference libr. Howard U., Washington, 1966-73; mgr. libr. Meth. Hosp. Ind., Indpls., 1974-94; libr., dir. distance learning Aenon Bible Coll., Indpls., 1994—; libr. Rowland Design Inc., 1995—2001. Instr. Ind. Vocat. Tech. Coll., 1979, 85, Med. Libr. Assn., 1982—95, Martin Ctr. Coll., Indpls., 1983—84. Author: career materials. Vol. Indpls. Police Dept. Libr., 1977, Children's Mus., Indpls., 1987—88, Children's Bur., 2001—, Black Expo, 1995—, Minority Health Fair, 1995—. Recipient Minority Bus. and Profl. Achiever award, Ctr. Leadership Devel., Indpls., 1981, Ctrl. Ind. Area Libr. Svcs. Authority cert. of Excellence, 1990. Mem.: ALA, Ch. and Synagogue Libr. Assn. (pres. 1992—93, 1995—96), Internat. Tng. Comm. Democrat. Avocations: travel, reading, needlepoint, bicycling. Home: 3815 N Bolton Ave Indianapolis IN 46226-4826 Office: Aenon Bible Coll 3919 Meadows Dr Indianapolis IN 46205-3113 Office Phone: 317-549-0255. Personal E-mail: jsaallen@hotmail.com.

ALLEN, JULIAN MYRICK, JR., industrial engineer; b. Mobile, Ala., Mar. 29, 1956; s. Julian Myrick and Sarah Jane (Scanlan) A.; m. Betty Jo Culpepper; children: Kiesha Monique, Jaron Myrick, Nathan Ryan. AA, Jones County Jr. Coll., 1976; BSBA, U. So. Miss., 1980; MBA, Miss. State U., 1985. Store mgr. Burger King Inc., Slidell, La., 1976-78; indsl. engr. Howard Industries, Laurel, Miss., 1978-80; plant indsl. engr. Fairbanks Scale div. Colt Industries, Meridian, Miss., 1980-86; sr. indsl. engr. COMM/TEC div. Reliance Electric, Greenville, Miss., 1986-88, William L. Bonnell div. Tredegar Industries, Newnan, Ga., 1988-91; engring. and maintenace mgr. Borden Foodsvc., Jackson, Miss., 1991-92, engring. and maintenace mgr. Chambersburg, Pa., 1992-93; plant mgr. seafood divsn. Borden, Cape May, N.J., 1993-94; ops. mgr. Bama Foods, Birmingham, Ala., 1994, Snow's Doxsee Inc., Cape May, N.J., 1994-99; dir. ops. Baumer Foods Inc., New Orleans, 1999-2000; materials mgr. Danfoss Maneurop Ltd., Lawrenceville, Ga., 2000—. Author: Welding Robotics Handbook, 1986; contbr. articles to profl. jours. Tchr. United Pentecostal Ch., Meridian, 1983-86, New Life Pentecostal Ch., Newnan, 1990-91. Mem. Soc. Mfg. Engrs. (speaker confs. 1984-86, Pres. Club 1985, Outstanding Paper Robotics Internat. 1985-86, sr. mem.), Inst. Indsl. Engrs. (sr. mem.). Republican. Office: Danfoss Comml Compressors 1775-G MacLeod Dr Lawrenceville GA 30043 E-mail: r.allen@danfoss.com.

ALLEN, LARRY CHRISTOPHER, professional football player; b. L.A., Nov. 27, 1971; m. Janelle Allen; 1 child, Jayla. Student, Butte Jr. Coll., Sonoma State U. Tackle Dallas Cowboys, 1994—. Named to NFC Pro-Bowl team, 1995-2001, 2003-2004, NFL all decade team, 1990's; Named NFL All-Pro, 1995-98, 1999-01 Achievements include third player in NFL history to be selected to the Pro Bowl at more than one offensive line position, 1998; mem. SuperBowl XXX Champion Dallas Cowboys, 1995. Office: care Dallas Cowboys 1 Cowboys Pkwy Irving TX 75063-4945*

ALLEN, LAYMAN EDWARD, law educator, research scientist; b. Turtle Creek, Pa., June 9, 1927; s. Layman Grant and Viola Iris (Williams) A.; m. Christine R. Patmore, Mar. 29, 1950 (dec.); children: Layman G., Patricia R.; m. Emily C. Hall, Oct. 3, 1981 (div. 1992); children: Phyllip A. Hall, Kelly C. Hairston; m. Leslie A. Olsen, June 10, 1995. Student, Washington and Jefferson Coll., 1945-46; AB, Princeton U., 1951; MPub. Admnstrn., Harvard U., 1952; LLB, Yale U., 1956. Bar: Conn. 1956. Fellow Ctr. for Advanced Study in Behavioral Scis., 1961-62; sr. fellow Yale Law Sch., 1956-57, lectr., 1957-58, instr., 1958-59, asst. prof., 1959-63, assoc. prof., 1963-66; assoc. prof. law U. Mich. Law Sch., Ann Arbor, 1966-71, prof., 1971—. Chmn. bd. trustees Accelerated Learning Found., 1998—; sr. rsch. scientist Mental Health Rsch. Inst., U. Mich., 1966-99; cons. legal drafting Nat. Life Ins. Co., Mich. Blue Cross & Blue Shield (various law firms); mem. electronic data retrieval com. Am. Bar Assn.; ops. rsch. analyst McKinsey & Co.; orgn. and methods analyst Office of Sec. Air Force.; trustee Ctr. for Study of Responsive Law. Editor: Games and Simulations, Artificial Intelligence and Law Jour., Theoria; author: WFF 'N Proof: The Game of Modern Logic, 1961, rev. edit., 1990, (with Robin B.S. Brooks, Patricia A. James) Automatic Retrieval of Legal Literature: Why and How, 1962, WFF: The Beginner's Game of Modern Logic, 1962, rev. edit., 1973, Equations: The Game of Creative Mathematics, 1963, rev. edit., 1994, (with Mary E. Caldwell) Reflections of the Communications Sciences and Law: The Jurimetrics Conference, 1965, (with J. Ross and P. Kugel) Queries 'N Theories: The Game of Science and Language, 1970, rev. edit., 1973, (with F. Goodman, D. Humphrey and J. Ross), On-Words: The Game of Word Structures, 1971, rev. edit., 1973; contbr. articles to profl. jours.; co-author/designer: (with J. Ross and C. Stratton) DIG (Diagnostic Instrnl. Gaming) Math; (with Charles Saxon) Normalizer Clear Legal Drafting Program, 1986, MINT System for Generating Dynamically Multiple-Interpretation Legal Decision-Assistance Systems, 1991, The Legal Argument Game of Legal Relations, 1997, (with Sandra Bartlett) LawToe: the Game to Learn the Game Rules of The Legal Argument Game of Legal Relations, 2003, (with Sandra Bartlett) The New Legal Argument Game of Legal Relations, 2003, (with Adam Trury) New MINT System for Dynamically Generating Multiple Interpretation Legal Analysis Systems, 2004. With USNR, 1945—46. Mem. ABA (coun. sect. sci. and tech.), AAAS, ACLU, Assn. Symbolic Logic, Nat. Coun. Tchrs. Math. Democrat. Unitarian Universalist. Home: 5353 Red Fox Run Ann Arbor MI 48105 Office: U Mich Sch Law 625 S State St Ann Arbor MI 48109-1215 Office Phone: 734-764-9339. Business E-Mail: laymanal@umich.edu.

ALLEN, (EDWIN) LEE, artist; b. Muscatine, Iowa, Sept. 16, 1910; s. Herman Clyde Allen and Loredo Robinson; m. Sally Boyce, Mar. 9, 1936 (divorced); children: Loredo Ann, Mary Lee, Elizabeth Jane. Student, U. Iowa, 1929-37. Mural painter Pub. Works of Art Project, Iowa City, 1933—36, US Treasury Dept., 1936—37; med. artist dept. ophthalmology U. Iowa, 1937—75, instr., 1940—75, ocularist, 1945—75, ret., 1975; co-owner Iowa Eye Prosthetics Inc., Coralville, 1975—82. Iowa post offices, 1937—38; inventor (Buried Motility Ocular Implant), 1945; exhibitions include painting Whitney Mus., 1999, one-man shows include U. of Iowa, Iowa City, 2000, Iowa State U., Ames, 2000; co-author: (book) The Hole in My Vision, 2000. Named Hall Fame, East Des Moines HS, Iowa, 2003—. Democrat. Episc. Home: Hawthorne Inn 1500 N 1st Ave # 74 Coralville IA 52241

ALLEN, LEE NORCROSS, historian, educator; b. Shawmut, Ala., Apr. 16, 1926; s. Leland Norcross and Dorothy (Whitaker) A.; m. Catherine Ann Bryant, Aug. 24, 1963; children— Leland Norcross, Leslie Catherine. BS, Auburn U., 1948, MS, 1949; PhD, U. Pa., 1955. From instr. to prof. history Ea. Bapt. Coll., St. Davids, Pa., 1952-61; prof. history Samford U., Birmingham, Ala., 1961-2001, grad. dean, 1965-86; dean Howard Coll. Arts and Scis., 1975-90, rsch. prof., 2001—. Author: (with Mrs. E.S. Bee) History of

Ruhama, 1969, The First One Hundred Fifty Years: First Baptist Church of Montgomery, 1979, Born for Missions, 1984; Southside Baptist Church: A Centennial History, 1985, Woodlawn Baptist Church: The First Century, 1886-1986, 1986; (with Catherine B. Allen) Courage to Care, 1988; Expanding the Dream, Montgomery Baptist Hospital, 1988, Notable Past, Bright Future: First Baptist Church 1893-1993, 1993, Born for Missions, 16th Decade, 1993, Outward Focus: Mountain Brook Baptist Church, The First Fifty Years, 1994, The First 150 Years Supplement: 1980-1995, 1996, (with Catherine B. Allen) Christ Is Our Salvation: Paul Piper, 1998, (with Catherine B. Allen) The Boaz Heritage: A Centennial History, Boaz, Alabama, 1897-1997, 1999, Ralph W. Beeson: A Biography, 2005. Served with AUS, 1944-46. Recipient Commendation cert. Am. Assn. State and Local History, Thomas Jefferson award, 1985, disting. svc. award Ala. Baptist Hist. Commn., 1996; Auburn U. rsch. fellow, 1948-49; Harrison fellow U. Pa., 1949-52. Mem. Am. Hist. Assn., Am. Bapt. Hist. Assn. (editor The Ala. Bapt. Historian 1989—), So. Bapt. Hist. Assn. (pres. 1987-88), So. Hist. Assn., Ala. Hist. Assn. (editor newsletter 1989-2001, pres. 1994-95), Rotary (pres. Shades Valley chpt. 1969-70), Omicron Delta Kappa, Phi Alpha Theta, Phi Kappa Phi, Pi Gamma Mu. Baptist. Home: 5025 Wendover Dr Birmingham AL 35223-1631

ALLEN, LEON ARTHUR, JR., lawyer; b. Springfield, Mass., July 15, 1933; s. Leon Arthur Sr. and Elsie (Shoemaker) A.; m. Patricia Mellion, June 23, 1961; 1 child, Christopher L. BEE, Cornell U., 1955; LLB, NYU, 1964. Bar: N.Y. 1964, U.S. Dist. Ct. (so. and ea. dists.) N.Y. 1965. Tech. editor McGraw Hill Pub. Co., N.Y.C., 1958-62; constrn. engr. Gilbert Assocs., N.Y.C., 1962-64; assoc. LeBoeuf, Lamb, Leiby & MacRae, N.Y.C., 1964-70; ptnr. LeBoeuf, Lamb, Leiby & MacRae (name changed to LeBoeuf, Lamb, Greene & MacRae), N.Y.C., 1971—. Served with U.S. Army, 1956-58. Mem. ABA, Assn. of Bar of City of N.Y. (chmn. adminstrv. law com. 1972-74). Clubs: Racquet & Tennis (N.Y.C.); Union (N.Y.C.), Tuxedo (Tuxedo Park, N.Y.). Home: 530 E 86th St New York NY 10028-7535 Office: LeBoeuf Lamb Greene MacRae 125 W 55th St New York NY 10019-5369 Business E-Mail: laallen@llgm.com.

ALLEN, LINDA S., editor, writer; d. Jim J. and Barbara J. Holland; children: Amy L. Cason, Mandy S. Devich, Jeremy S., Ethan M. BS in Journalism/News Editl., U. Colo., Boulder, 1992. Electronics technician AT&T, Denver, 1973—83, master prodn. scheduling specialist, 1983—89; intern reporter Longmont Times-Call, Longmont, Colo., 1991—92; rschr. The NY Times-Rocky Mountain Bur., Denver, 1992—94; staff reporter The Stuart News, Fla., 1994—97; pub. info. officer Big Bros. Big Sisters of Martin County, Stuart, Fla., 1997—99; editor/writer LRP Publs., Palm Beach Gardens, Fla., 1999—. Author: (non-fiction) You Don't Know Jack: The Tale of a Father Once Removed, WaveMaker. Victim advisor Thornton/Northglenn Police Depts., Colo., 1989—94. Mem.: Fla. Press Assn. (assoc.). Liberal. Christian. Avocations: wilderness hiking/backpacking, downhill skiing, travel. Personal E-mail: lindaallen@comcast.net.

ALLEN, LOIS ARLENE HEIGHT (MRS. JAMES PIERPONT ALLEN), musician; b. Kenton, Ohio, Sept. 2, 1932; d. Robert Harold and Frances (Sims) Height; m. James Pierpont Allen, June 14, 1953; children: Daniel Pierpont, Carole Elizabeth. BS, Ohio State U., 1954, MA, 1958. Tchr. jr. and sr. high music Upper Arlington H.S., Columbus, Ohio, 1954-56; h.s. music supr. Westerville, Ohio, 1956-57; tchr. music Ohio State U. Sch., 1957-59; pvt. tchr. music Columbus, 1960—. Exec. dir. Battelle Scholars Program Trust Fund, 1983-86; ch. organist, choir dir. Mountview Bapt. Ch., Upper Arlington, Ohio, 1960-77, moderator, 1996-97; ednl. radio interviewer WOSU, 1970, 71, 72. Mem. Project Hope, Ctrl. Ohio, 1967-73; mem. sustaining bd. Maryhaven House for Alcoholic Women, 1969-73, 1st v.p.; mem. women's bd. Columbus Symphony, 1965-79, 91—, bd. trustees edn. com., 1992-2004, co-chair edn. com. women's assn., 1992-2004, charter mem. trustee's cir., 2000, bd. dir., chmn. youth coun., 1965-68, pres.-elect women's assn., 1973, chmn. edn. com., 1991—, pres., 1974-76; pres. vol. coun. Am. Symphony Orch. League, 1987-89; organist, choir master The Ch. of St. Edwards, 1990-92; chmn. juried art competition Cen. Ohio Arts Festival, 1969, 70, chmn. fine and applied arts, 1971, gen. chmn. of festival, 1972; area chmn. United Appeals Franklin County, 1966-68, Heart dr., 1968-85; pres. Ohio State U. Soc. Friends Sch. Music, 1977-78; trustee Columbus Symphony Orch., 1973-81, Opera/Columbus, 1981-85; v.p. women's guild Opera/Columbus, 1986-94, pres., 1987-88; mem. vol. coun. Am. Symphny Orch. League, 1981—, v.p., 1983-84, mem. exec. com., 1986-88, mem. artistic affairs com., 1987-89, pres., 1987-88; organist, choir dir. North Congregational Ch., 1979-85; area leader Rep. Party, 1966-68; mem. Mayor's Award Coun. Com., 1981-84; active Connexions, Columbus Literacy Coun.; bd. dir., pres. Ohio Theatre Shop, 1995-96, publicity dir. 1996--; bd. dir., pres. Women's Bd. Columbus Mus. Art, 1991—; organist Glen Echo Presbyn. Ch., 2002-04. Recipient Columbus Symphony Advocate award, 2002, Music Educator award, Columbus Symphony Orch., 2005. Mem. Am. Guild Organists, Choristers Guild Am., Fedn. Am. Bapt. Musicians, Ctr. Sci. and Industry, Ohio State Hist. Soc., Ohio Orgn. Orchs. (treas. 1976-79, sec. 1979-82), Nat. Trust U.S.A., Mountview Bapt. Ch. (moderator 1996—), Rotary Club (Women of Yr. Upper Arlington Ohio 1995), Order Ea. Star, White Shrine of Jerusalem, Ohio State U. Alumnae of Franklin County Club (pres. 1962-64, 71-72), Tau Beta Sigma, Delta Omicron, Kappa Delta (Cen. Ohio Woman of Yr. 1970). Home: 3355 Somerford Rd Columbus OH 43221-1436 E-mail: jallen6@columbus.rr.com.

ALLEN, LOUIS ALEXANDER, management consultant; b. Glace Bay, N.S., Oct. 8, 1917; s. Israel Nathan and Emma (Greenberg) A.; m. Ruth Graham, Aug. 24, 1946; children: Michael, Steven, Ace, Terry Allen Beck, Deborah Allen. BS cum laude, Wash. State U., 1941. Cert. mgmt. cons. Asst. to dean of men Wash. State U., Pullman, 1940-42; tng. supr. Aluminum Co. Am., Pitts., 1946-49; mgr. pers. adminstrn. Koppers Co. Inc., Pitts., 1949-53; dir. rsch. projects The Conf. Bd., N.Y.C., 1953-56; dir. orgnl. planning Booz, Allen & Hamilton, Chgo., 1956-58; founder Louis Allen Assocs., Inc., Los Altos, Calif., 1958-92; ind. rschr., 1992-95. Lectr. on bus. mgmt. Stanford U., U. Chgo., NYU, Japan, China, Australia, Africa and Europe. Author: Improving Staff and Line Relationships, 1956, Preparing the Company Organization Manual, 1957, Organization of Staff Functions, 1958, Management and Organization, 1958, The Management Profession, 1964, Professional Management: New Concepts and Proven Practices, 1973, Time before Morning: Art and Myth of the Australian Aborigines, 1975, Making Managerial Planning More Effective, 1982, The Allen Guide for Management Leaders, 1989, Common Vocabulary for Management Leaders, 1989, The Louis Allen Leader's Handbook, 1995, The New Leadership, 1996; (mus. catalog) Australian Aboriginal Art, 1972; translated into Japanese, German, French, Finnish, Swedish, Dutch, Spanish, Portuguese, Bahasa; contbr. numerous articles and monographs to profl. jours. on mgmt., primitive art; exhibitor primitive art major mus. worldwide, 1969—. Maj. USAF, 1942-55, PTO. Decorated Legion of Merit; recipient McKinsey award Acad. Mgmt. Mem. Inst. Mgmt. Cons. (sr. assoc., regional pres. 1985). Achievements include first to fully classify human work into categories, a typology which facilities diagnosis and correction of organizational problems. Personal E-mail: laglaceby@aol.com.

ALLEN, LYLE WALLACE, lawyer; b. Chillicothe, Ill., June 17, 1924; s. Donald M. and Mary Ellen (McEvoy) A.; m. Helen Kolar, Aug. 16, 1947; children: Mary Elizabeth Watkins, Bryan James. Student, N.C. State Coll., 1943-44; BS, Northwestern U., 1947; postgrad., Columbia Law Sch., 1947-48; JD, U. Wis., 1950. Bar: Ill. 1950, Wis. 1950. Of counsel Heyl Royster Voelker & Allen, Peoria, Ill., 1951—. Served with 87th Inf. Div. U.S. Army, World War II. Decorated Purple Heart, Bronze star, Combat Infantry badge, Presdl. Unit Citation. Mem. ABA, Ill. State Bar Assn. (pres. 1972-73), Assn. of Ins. Attys. (pres. 1965-66), Illinois Valley Yacht Club, Wig and Pen Club (London). Democrat. Presbyterian. Office: 124 SW Adams St Ste 600 Peoria IL 61602-1392

ALLEN, MARC KEVIN, emergency physician, educator; b. Bedford, Ind., Sept. 2, 1956; s. Robert Edward and Edna Ruth (Little) A.; m. Marita Ann Volk, May 13, 1995. AB, Washington U., St. Louis, 1978; MD, Wright State U., 1982. Diplomate Am. Bd. Emergency Medicine. Intern Mt. Sinai Med. Ctr., Cleve., 1982-83, chief resident in emergency medicine, 1984-85, rsch. dir. emergency med. residency, 1986-96; attending physician Worcester (Mass.) City Hosp., 1985-86; flight physician Metro Lifeflight, Cleve., 1984—; attending physician Summa Health Sys., Akron, Ohio, 1999—, Lake County Hosp., Willoughby, Ohio, 2005—. Co-author: A Practical Approach Emergency Medicine, 1987. Co-chmn. Washington U. YWCA-YMCA, 1977—78; med. dir. Ohio Assn. EMS, 2004—, Aurora (Ohio) Fire Dept., 1997—, Six Flags Worlds of Adventure, 2001—03. Fellow Am. Coll. Emergency Physicians (councillor 1996-98, Star of Life Ohio chpt. 2005); mem. Assn. Air Med. Svcs., Assn. Air Med. Physicians, N.E. Soc. Emergency Med. (bd. dirs. 1992-99), Ohio Assn. Emergency Med. Svcs. (med. dirs. 2004—), South Ea. Area Law Enforcement (med. dir. 2004—), Phi Rho Sigma. Avocations: skiing, golf, cooking. Home: 485 Club Dr Aurora OH 44202-8564 Office: Summa Health Sys Akron City Hosp 525 E Market St Akron OH 44304-1619 Personal E-mail: ermarc@aol.com.

ALLEN, MARCUS, retired professional football player; b. San Diego, Mar. 26, 1960; Student, U. So. Calif. Running back with Los Angeles Raiders, NFL, El Segundo, Calif., 1982-92; with Kansas City Chiefs, NFL, 1993-97; nat. analyst, broadcaster CBS Sports, N.Y.C., 1998; co-host Marcus Allen Show KCTV 5, Kansas City, Mo., 1997-98; features/sideline reporter CBS Sports, 1999—. Co-owner Pro Ball Beverage Corp.; v.p. Marcus Allen's Broadway Ford, Kansas City, Mo. Author: (with Carlton Stowers) Marcus: The Autobiography of Marcus Allen, 1997. Recipient Heisman Trophy Downtown Athletic Club of N.Y.C., 1981; named Coll. Football Player of Yr., Sporting News, 1981, The Sporting News NFL Rookie of Yr., 1982, Player of Yr., 1985; named to Sporting News Coll. All-Am. Team, 1981. Achievements include playing in NFL championship game, 1984, Pro Bowl, 1983, 85, 86, 88; establishing NFL season record for most combined yards, 1985; holds NFL record for most consecutive games with 100 or more yards rushing (11), 1986. Office: Marcus Allen's Ford 3401 Broadway St Kansas City MO 64111-2403

ALLEN, MARILYN MYERS POOL, theater director, video specialist; b. Fresno, Calif., Nov. 2, 1934; d. Laurence B. and Asa (Griggs) Myers; m. Joseph Harold Pool, Dec. 28, 1955; children: Pamela Elizabeth, Victoria Anne, Catherine Marcia; m. Neal R. Allen, Apr. 1982. BA, Stanford U., 1955, postgrad., 1955—56, U. Tex., 1957—60, West Tex. State U., 1962—63, Odessa Coll., 1987—88. Free-lance radio and TV actress; adj. prof. theatre Midland Coll., 1997—98; dir. Globe Theater, Odessa, 1998, 2002; asst. mng. dir. Amarillo Little Theatre, 1964—66, mng. dir., 1966—68, Horseshoe Players, touring profl. theater, 1969—73; actress multi-media prodn. Palo Duro Canyon, 1971; dir. touring children's theatre, 1978—79; guest actress in Medea at Amarillo Coll., 1981; guest reciter Amarillo Symphony, 1972, Midland-Odessa Symphony, 1984. Pres. Tex. Non-Profit Theatres, 1972-77, bd. dirs., 1988-91; 1st v.p. High Plains Ctr. for Performing Arts, 1969-73; adv. dept. fine arts Amarillo Coll., 1980-82; adv. Tex. Constnl. Revision Commn., 1973-75; adv. coun. U. Tex. Coll. Fine Arts, 1969-72; cmty. adv. com. for women Amarillo Coll., 1975-79; conv. program com. Am. Theatre Assn., 1978, program participant, 1978-80, bd. dirs., 1980-83; bd. dirs. Amarillo Found. Health and Sci. Edn., 1976-82, program v.p., 1979-81; bd. dirs. Domestic Violence Coun., 1979-82, March of Dimes, 1979-81, Tex. Panhandle Heritage Found., 1964-82, Friends of Fine Arts, West Tex. State U. (now West Tex. A&M U.), 1980-82, Amarillo Pub. Libr., 1980-82, Amarillo Symphony, 1981-82; publicity chmn. Midland Cmty. Theatre, 1984-87, bd. govs., 1986-92, sec., 1987-88, v.p., 1988-92; bd. dirs. Globe of the Great S.W., Odessa, 1998—, v.p. media, 2000-02, v.p. vols., 2002-05; active Mus. of S.W., Midland Arts Assembly; bd. dirs. Midland County Rep. Women, Ways and Means Ch., 1991, 1st v.p., 1992, publicity chair, 1994; mem. Midland County Redistricting com., 1991; cultural exch. del. from Midland, Tex., to Dong Ying, China, 1993; Tex. UIL one act play adjudicator, 1974-99; mem. Diocesan Comm. Com., N.W. Tex., Mission Com., 2003—; co-chmn. Companion Diocese Com., Spain, 2003— Recipient cert. of appreciation Woman of Yr., Amarillo Bus. and Profl. Women's Club, 1966, Best Actress award for Hedda Gabler role Amarillo Little Theatre, 1965, Best Dir. award for Rashomon, 1967, 1st Pl. award for video spl. Tex. Press Conf., 1988, 1st Pl. award for news Tex. Press Conf., 1989, Disting. Svc. award Tex. Non-Profit Theatres, 1992; named Amarillo Woman of Yr., Beta Sigma Phi, 1980, Broadcaster of the Yr., Rocky Mountain Press Conf., 1988, Hamhock of Yr., Midland Cmty. Theatre, 1992, Outstanding Svc. award Midland Arts Assembly, 1992; Travel fellow AAUW, 1973, 78. Fellow Am. Assn. Cmty. Theatre (dir. 1969-72, 82-84, v.p. planning and devel. 1985-87, co-chair AACT/Fest '95), Internat. Amateur Theatre Assn. 23d World Congress (del. Monaco 1997); mem. USTA (sr. women's team sect. winner 1993, 94), S.W. Theatre Conf. (dir. 1973-76, 82-84, exec. com. 1982-84, Disting. Svc. award 1985), Tex. Theatre Coun. (dir. 1974-78, exec. com., pres. 1975-76), AAUW (br. pres. 1973-75, state chmn. cultural interests 1975-77, 86-88, state program v.p. 1977-79, state bd. dirs. 1984-88, program v.p. Midland 1988-89), Episc. Ch. Women (program v.p. Midland 1988-89, outreach chair 1996, 2005, program v.p., pres.-elect 1997-98, pres. 1999-2000), DAR (chpt. chaplain 1971-75, historian 1975-77), C. of C. (fine arts coun.), U.S. Tennis Assn. (sr. mixed doubles sect. winner 1999), U.S. Judo Assn., Symphony Guild, Amarillo Art Assn., Midland Symphony Guild (arrangements chmn. 1983-84), Act IX, Amarillo Law Wives Club (pres. 1976-77), Hamhocks (hon. life, v.p. 1985-86)

ALLEN, MARJORIE JOAN, librarian, educator; b. Austin, Tex., Feb. 11, 1931; d. Dwight Edward Sr. and Marguerite Faye (Jackson) Farr; m. Frank Morrell Jr., June 25, 1955 (dec.); children: Edward, Debra (dec.), David (dec.), Faye. BFA in Theatre, U. Tex., 1951; MLS, 1977, postgrad, 1976-78. Technician Tex. Touring Theatre, Austin, 1951-52; sec. to econs. dir. UN, Beirut, 1953-54; elem. and secondary tchr. Smithville (Tex.) Ind. Sch. Dist., 1954-74, theatre dir., 1962-74; tchr. San Marcos (Tex.) Consol. Sch. Dist., 1974-75; tchr., theatre dir. Wiemar (Tex.) Ind. Sch. Dist., 1975-76; tchr., theatre dir., libr. Tex. Sch. for Blind, Austin, 1976-82; theatre dir., dist. libr. Smithville Ind. Sch. Dist., 1982-92, secondary libr., 1992—2000, dir. high sch. theatre, 2003—. Cons. in field. Author: Hope Made A Window, 1991, Lady Alicia's Legacy, 2002; author poems. Del. to state conv. Rep. Com., Houston, Tex., 1988, Ft.Worth, 1990, San Antonio, 1996, precinct chmn. 1995, 96, alt. state conv., Dallas, 1992. Mem.: ALA (Tex. del. legis. day 1992), PEO (various offices 1987—92, pres. 1992—94), Tex. Ednl. Theatre Assn. Adjudicators Orgn. (critic judge 1992—), Tex. Assn. Secondary Librs. (bd. dirs. 1980—82), Tex. Libr. Assn. (sec.-treas. 1978—80), Tex. Ednl. Theatre Assn. (sec. 1974—76, bd. dirs. 1976—78, Achievement award 1980), Romance Writers Am. (editor newsletter 1993—), Univ. Interscholastic League (critic judge 1992—99). Republican. Methodist. Avocations: writing, needle point, quilting. Home: PO Box 660 Smithville TX 78957-0660

ALLEN, MARTIN, chemistry educator, consultant; b. N.Y.C., Mar. 26, 1918; s. Isidor and Frances (Gudowitz) A.; m. Sophie Parker, June 13, 1942; children: Susan, Scott, Barbara, Robert. AB, Bklyn. Coll., 1938; MS, U. Minn., 1941, PhD, 1944. Instr. U. Minn., Mpls., 1943-45; rsch. assoc. Alleghany Ballistics Lab., Cumberland, Md., 1945; sr. tech. mgr. B.F. Goodrich Co., Akron, Ohio, 1945-47; assoc. prof. Butler U., Indpls., 1947-56; prof. U. St. Thomas, St. Paul, 1956-84, chmn. chemistry dept., 1975-84, dir. scis. and math., 1977-84, ret., 1984. Vis. prof. dept. chem. engring. U. Minn., 1981-83, rsch. assoc., 1984-86; assoc. dir. Ctr. for Interfacial Engring., U. Minn., 1988-90, sci. cons., 1994-2002. Contbr. over 6 articles to profl. jours and 600 abstracts to Chem. Abstracts. Mem. Citizens Com. on Pub. Edn., Mpls., 1965-70. Fellow AAAS; mem. Am. Chem. Soc., Fedn. Am. Scientists, Phi Lambda Upsilon, Sigma Xi. Achievements include research in thermodynamics of solutions and surface chemistry. Home: 4620 Bassett Creek Ln Minneapolis MN 55422-3606 E-mail: martin2@mninter.net.

ALLEN, MARTIN T., music educator; b. Buffalo, Jan. 31, 1965; s. Robert Edward and Joan Mildred Allen; 1 child, Ryan Carter. B in Music Edn., SUNY, Buffalo, 1988; M in Music Edn., Vandercook Coll., 1992. Elem. band dir. Grand Island (N.Y.) Sch., 1988—92, h.s. band dir., 1992—. Named Outstanding Band Dir., Am. Sch. Band Dir., 1994, Buffalo Philharmonic Orch., Eric County Music Coordinators, 2004. Mem.: Nat. Band Assn. (exec. bd. 2003—05), Music Educators Nat. Conf., Erie County Music Educators (exec. bd. 2002—, bd. dirs. 2002—). Republican. Roman Catholic. Avocation: water-skiing. Home: 1911 Chreeside Dr Grand Island NY 14072 Office: Grand Island Sch 1100 Ranson Rd Grand Island NY 14072

ALLEN, MARYON PITTMAN, former senator, clothing designer, journalist; b. Meridian, Miss., Nov. 30, 1925; d. John D. and Tellie (Chism) Pittman; m. Joshua Sanford Mullins, Jr., Oct. 17, 1946 (div. Jan. 1959); children: Joshua Sanford III, John Pittman, Maryon Foster; m. James Browning Allen, Aug. 7, 1964 (dec. June 1978). Student, U. Ala., 1944—47, Internat. Inst. Interior Design, 1970. Office mgr. for Dr. Alston Callahan, Birmingham, Ala., 1959-60; bus. mgr. psychiat. clinic U. Ala. Med. Center, Birmingham, 1960-61; life underwriter Protective Life Ins. Co., Birmingham, 1961-62; women's editor Sun Newspapers, Birmingham, 1962-64; v.p., ptnr. Pittman family cos., J.D. Pittman Partnership Co., J.D. Pittman Tractor Co., Emerald Valley Corp., Mountain Lake Farms, Inc., Birmingham; mem. U.S. Senate (succeeding late husband James B. Allen), 1978; dir. pub. rels. and advt. C.G. Sloan & Co. Auction House, Washington, 1981; feature writer Birmingham News, 1964; writer syndicated column Reflections of a News Hen, Washington, 1969—78; feature writer, columnist Maryon Allen's Washington, Washington Post, 1979—81; columnist McCall's Needlework Mag., 1993—. Owner The Maryon Allen Co. (Restoration/Design), Birmingham. Contbg. editor: So. Accents Mag., 1976—78. Mem. Ladies of U.S. Senate unit ARC, Former Mems. of Congress, Ala. Hist. Commn., Blair House Fine Arts Commn.; charter mem. Birmingham Com. of 100 for Women; mem. steering com. Ala. Gov.'s Mansion; trustee Children's Fresh Air Farm; trustee, deacon, elder Ind. Presbyn. Ch., Birmingham; Dem. Presdl. elector, Ala., 1968. Recipient 1st place award for best original column Ala. Press Assn., 1962, 63, also various press state and nat. awards for typography, fashion writing, food pages, also several awards during Senate service; sponsor, U.S. Navy Nuclear submarine, U.S.S. Birmingham, S.S.N. 695, launched Newport News, Va., 1977, commissioned 1978. Mem.: Nat. Press Club, 1925 F St. Club, 91st Congress Club, Congl. Club, Birmingham Country Club. Home and Office: Creekstone Cottage 1551 Creekstone Cir Birmingham AL 35243 Office Phone: 205-822-9266. E-mail: maryonallenco@aol.com. *You have to believe in yourself, your talents and the premise that you were put here to contribute of yourself...not always to take.*

ALLEN, MATTHEW ARNOLD, physicist; b. Edinburgh, Scotland, Apr. 27, 1930; came to U.S., 1955; s. William Wolff and Clara (Bloch) A.; m. Marcia Harriet Katzman, Sept. 15, 1957; children: Bruce William, Peter Jonathan, David Michael. BSc in Physics, U. Edinburgh, 1951; PhD in Physics, Stanford U., 1959. Rsch. assoc. Hansen Labs., Stanford (Calif.) U., 1959-61; rsch. mgr. tube div. Microwave Assocs., Burlington, Mass., 1961-65; radio frequency group leader Stanford Linear Accelerator Ctr., 1965-82, head accelerator physics dept., 1982-84, head klystron microwave dept., 1984-90, asst. dir. for elec. and electronic systems, 1989-90, assoc. dir. lab., 1990—2003, emeritus, 2003—. Cons. Microwave Assocs. Inc., 1965-71, Aerojet Gen., Azusa, Calif., 1959-62, Bechtel Corp., San Francisco, 1965-67; mem. tech. rev. com. Synchotron Radiation Rsch. Ctr., Taipei, Taiwan, 1985-98; chmn. U.S.A. Particle Accelerator Conf., 1991. Contbr. articles to profl. jours.; patentee in field. Commr. Environ. Planning Commn., Mountain View, Calif., 1971-74; councilman Mountain View City Coun., 1974-82; mayor City of Mountain View, 1977, 81; pres. Mountain View Community TV, 1989. Lt. British Army, 1953-55. Fellow IEEE, Am. Phys. Soc.; mem. IEEE Nuclear and Plasma Scis. Soc. (adminstrv. com. 1978-84, 98-2001), Dem. Club (bd. dirs. 1980-84), Sigma Xi. Democrat. Avocations: skiing, running, tv producing. Home: 620 Sand Hill Rd # 318D Palo Alto CA 94304 Office: Stanford Linear Accelerator Ctr 2575 Sand Hill Rd Menlo Park CA 94025 Business E-Mail: matmar@pacbell.net.

ALLEN, MAURICE BARTELLE, JR., architect; b. Lansing, Mich., Mar. 20, 1926; s. Maurice Bartelle and Marguerite Rae (Stahl) A.; m. Nancy Elizabeth Huff, June 29, 1951; children— Robert (dec.), Katherine, David. Student, Western Mich. U., 1944, Notre Dame U., 1944-46; BArch, U. Mich., 1950. Registered profl. architect, Mich. Draftsman, designer Smith, Hinchman & Grylls (architects), Detroit, 1950-51; designer, assoc. Eero Saarinen & Assocs., Bloomfield Hills, Mich., 1951-61; v.p. design and planning TMP Assos. (architects, engrs. and planners), Bloomfield Hills, 1961-92, emeritus, 1993; design critic, lectr. Coll. Architecture and Urban Planning, U. Mich., 1958—. Cons. arch. Camelback Bible Ch., Paradise Valley, Ariz. Prin. archtl. works include Gen. Motors Inst. campus devel. and bldgs, Flint, Mich., Mackinac and Manitou halls, Grand Valley State Coll, O'Dowd Hall, Oakland U, Prototype Regional Correctional Facilities, Mich. Dept. Corrections, Fine Arts Ctr. and Theater, Allied Scis. Bldg., Macomb Community Coll., Scheide Music Ctr., Coll. of Wooster, Towsley Ctr. Sch. of Music, U. Mich., Performing Arts Ctr. and Student Ctr., Lake Superior State U., Art Music Humanities Ctr., Wabash Coll., Univ. Community Ctr., U. Western Ont., Drama Theater and Arts Bldg., Concordia Coll., St. Paul. Active Detroit Area council Boy Scouts Am., 1969—, Detroit Inst. Arts, Detroit Symphony; mem. environmental arts com. Mich. Council for Arts, 1970; vice chmn. Mich. Gov.'s Spl. Commn. on Architecture, 1971. Served with USNR, 1944-47. Recipient honor awards Detroit chpt. AIA, 1970-71, Gold medal, 1994, citation for design high rise structures Am. Iron and Steel Inst., 1971, citation of excellence Architecture for Justice Exhbn., 1982. Mem. Coll. of Fellows AIA (co-chair urban priorities Detroit chpt. 1995—), Mich. Soc. Architects (honor awards 1970-71), Sr. Men's Club Birmingham, Masons, Alpha Tau Omega. Republican. Episcopalian. Home and Office: 4325 Derry Rd Bloomfield Hills MI 48302-1835

ALLEN, MERRILL JAMES, marine biologist; b. Brady, Tex., July 16, 1945; s. Clarence Francis and Sara Barbara (Finlay) A. BA, U. Calif., Santa Barbara, 1967; MA, UCLA, 1970; PhD, U. Calif., San Diego, 1982. Cert. jr. coll. tchr., Calif. Asst. environ. specialist So. Calif. Coastal Water Rsch. Project, El Segundo, 1971-77; postdoctoral assoc. Nat. Rsch. Coun., Seattle, 1982-84; oceanographer Nat. Marine Fisheries Svc., Seattle, 1984-86; sr. scientist MBC Applied Environ. Scis., Costa Mesa, Calif., 1986-93; prin. scientist So. Calif. Coastal Water Rsch. Project, Long Beach and Westminster, Calif., 1993—. Tech. adv. com. Santa Monica Bay Restoration Project/Commn., L.A., 1989-2003; steering com. So. Calif. Bight Pilot Project, 1993-98, So. Calif. Bight 1998 and 2003 Regional Marine Surveys; affiliate asst. prof. sch. fisheries U. Wash., Seattle, 1985-89; mem. sci. rev. panel for marine ecol. reserves rsch. program Calif. Sea Grant Coll., 1996-97; adj. prof. dept. biology Calif. State U., Long Beach, 1996—. Mem. Calif. Marine Life Mgmt. Act Evaluation Com., 2000—, Fellow Am. Inst. Fisheries Rsch. Biologists (dir. So. Calif. dist. 1991-93); mem. AAAS, Am. Fisheries Soc., Am. Soc. Ichthyologists and Herpetologists, So. Calif. Acad. Sci. (bd. dirs. 2000—). Achievements include development of most comprehensive atlas of marine fishes from Bering Sea to Mexico; description of state of contamination of Santa Monica Bay. Office: So Calif Coastal Water Rsch Project 7171 Fenwick Ln Westminster CA 92683-5218 Business E-Mail: jima@sccwrp.org.

ALLEN, MICHAEL AUSTIN, language educator; b. Providence, R.I., Nov. 3, 1961; s. Raymond Benjamin and Barbara Foye Allen. BA in English, U. R.I., 1995, BS in Edn., 1996, MEd, 1999; postgrad., U. N.H., 2005—. Capt. Tiger Jo, Inc., Pt. Judith, RI, 1988—95; tchr. English South Kingston High Sch., 1996; mcht. mariner DiHerent Cos., 1995—; martime trainer U.S. Mcht. Marine Acad., Kings Point, 1998—; rsch. asst. Harvard U., Boston, 1998—99, U. Pa., Phila., 2000, U. N.H., Durham, 2004—. Pres., CEO Allen Maritime, Inc., Providence, 2001—. Tutor Dover Literacy Ctr., NH, 2004—. Mem.: The Glacier Soc., Coun. Master Mariners, The Nautical Inst., Phi Delta Kappa. Avocations: sailing, snowboarding, reading. Home: 27 Moharimet Dr Madbury NH 03823 Office: U NH Morrill Hall 3d Fl Durham NH 03823

ALLEN, MICHAEL JOHN BRIDGMAN, language educator; b. Lewes, Eng., Apr. 1, 1941; came to U.S., 1966; m. Elena Hirshberg; children: William, Benjamin. BA, Oxford (Eng.) U., 1964, MA, 1966, DLitt, 1987; PhD, U. Mich., 1970. Asst. prof. UCLA, 1970-74, assoc. prof., 1974-79, prof. English, 1979—, disting. prof., 2004, assoc. dir. Ctr. for Medieval and Renaissance Studies, 1978-88, dir., 1988—93, 2003—04; v.p. Renaissance Soc. Am., 2004—. Editor Renaissance Quar., 1993—2001; faculty rsch. lectr. UCLA, 1998. Author: Marsilio Ficino: The Philebus Commentary, 1975, Marsilio Ficino and the Phaedran Charioteer, 1981, The Platonism of Marsilio Ficino, 1984, Icastes: Marsilio Ficino's Interpretation of Plato's "Sophist," 1989, Nuptial Arithmetic, 1994, Plato's Third Eye: Studies in Marsilio Ficino's Metaphysics and Its Sources, 1995, Synoptic Art: Marsilio Ficino on the History of Platonic Interpretation, 1998; co-author: Sources and Analogues of Old English Poetry, 1976, Marsilio Ficino: Platonic Theology, Vol. I, Books I-IV, 2001, Vol. 2, Books V-VIII, 2002, Vol. 3, Books IX-XI, 2003, Vol. 4, Books XII-XIV, 2004, Vol. 5, Books XV-XVI, 2005, Vol. 6, Books XVII-XVIII; co-editor: First Images of America, 1976, Shakespeare's Plays in Quarto, 1984, Sir Philip Sidney's Achievements, 1990, Marsilio Ficino: His Theology, His Philosophy, His Legacy, 2002. Recipient Eby award for disting. tchg. UCLA, 1977; Guggenheim fellow, 1977; disting. vis. scholar Ctr. for Reformation and Renaissance Studies, U. Toronto, 1997, Ludwig Maximilians U., Munich, 1999, Ariz. Ctr. for Medieval and Renaissance Studies, 2002. Office: UCLA 2225 Rolfe Hall 405 Hilgard Ave Los Angeles CA 90095-9000 Business E-Mail: mjballen@humnet.ucla.edu.

ALLEN, MIKE, writer; b. Mpls., Feb. 1, 1969; s. Theodore Darrell and Shonna Lee Allen; m. Anita Devi Seth, June 26, 1992. BA in Liberal Arts, Va. Tech, Blacksburg, 1992; MA in Creative Writing, Hollins U., Roanoke, Va., 1994. Staff writer Roanoke Times, 1998—. Pres. Sci. Fiction Poetry Assn., Ocala, Fla., 2004—. Poetry mag., Mythic Delirium; editor: (fiction anthology) New Dominions: Fantasy Stories by Virginia Writers; co-editor: (poetry anthology) The Alchemy of Stars: Rhysling Award Winners Showcase; author: (poetry collection) Defacing the Moon and Other Poems, Petting the Time Shark and Other Poems, (poem) Disturbing Muses; co-author: Epochs in Exile: A Fantasy Trilogy (Rhysling Award for Long Poem, 2003); author: (poetry and fiction collection) Strange Wisdoms of the Dead. Named Fellow of the Knight Ctr., Knight Ctr. for Specialized Journalism, 2005. Home: 3514 Signal Hill Ave NW Roanoke VA 24017-5148 Personal E-mail: mythicd@infionline.net.

ALLEN, M(ILFORD) RAY, secondary school educator; b. Martin, Ky., July 7, 1941; s. Ralph Earl and Pauline (Hall) A.; m. Cherie Suzanne Davis, Aug. 5, 1973; children: Landon Ray, Jana Cherie, Amber Suzanne, Anmarie Rosalee. BA in English, Phys. Edn., Morehead State U., 1963, MA in Secondary Edn., 1965; MFA in Theater Arts, UCLA, 1980. Coach baseball, basketball Lewis County H.S., Vanceburg, Ky., 1963-65; coach baseball, cross country Fraser (Mich.) H.S., 1965-67; coach baseball, basketball Marina H.S., Huntington Beach, Calif., 1967-75; tchr. Fountain Valley (Calif.) H.S., 1976-78; coach basketball, golf Alleghany County H.S., Covington, Va., 1978-83, tchr., 1985—; coach golf Clifton Middle Sch., Clifton Forge, Va., 1983-85. Author: The Roads I Travel, 1990, Between the Thorns: Windcarver Songs of Appalachia, 1991, Beyond Star Bottom and Other Poems, 2000; co-author (with Robert Francis Campbell): (song) Home Sweet Home Virginia (top 20 finalist in Va. State Song competition, 1999); editor: Teach Me to Plow, 1988, Appalachian Legacy, 1999; sports editor Alleghany Highlander, 1981-85. Mem. adv. bd. Green River Writers, Louisville, 1990-97. Named to Morehead State U. Alumni Hall of Fame, 1991. Mem. Appalfolks Am. Assn. (founder, pres. 1985-2000), Appalachian Writer Assn., Appalachian South Writers Coop. (founder), Order Ky. Cols. Democrat. Avocations: fishing, bowling, swimming, jogging, golf. Home: 720 Callie Mines Rd Clifton Forge VA 24422-3714 Office: Appalfolks Am Assn PO Box 613 510 Main St Clifton Forge VA 24422-1167

ALLEN, NATALIE, cable news anchor; Postgrad., Memphis State U.; B in Radio, T.V. and film, U. So. Miss. News anchor, reporter Sta. WREG-TV, Memphis, 1985-88, Sta. WFTV-TV, Orlando, Fla., 1988-92; co-anchor CNN Today, News Stand, Atlanta, 1992—. Recipient Emmy award for Spot News Reporting, 1989, Edward R. Murrow award, 1990.

ALLEN, NEWTON PERKINS, lawyer; b. Memphis, Jan. 3, 1922; s. James Seddon and Sarah (Perkins) Allen; m. Malinda Lobdell Nobles, Oct. 4, 1947 (dec. Nov. 1986); children: John Lobdell, Malinda Nobles, Newton Perkins, Cannon Fairfax; m. Malinda Lobdell Crutchfield, June 23, 1990. AB, Princeton, 1943; JD, U. Va., 1948. Bar: Tenn 1947, NC 1990. Assoc. Armstrong, Allen, Prewitt, Gentry, Johnston & Holmes, Memphis, 1948, ptnr., 1950-95; assoc. Dann & Allen, 1996—2001; with Newton P. Allen Law Firm, Memphis, 2001—. Contbr. articles to profl jours. Mem Chickasaw coun Boy Scouts Am, 1958—60, mem exec bd, 1961—69; trustee LeBonheur Children's Hosp, Memphis, 1964—72, vice chmn bd, 1965; mem alumni coun Princeton, 1954—64, 1990—93; chmn Greater Memphis Coun Crime and Delinquency, 1976—80; bd dirs Memphis Orchestra Soc, pres, 1979—81; pres bd trustees St Mary's Episcopal Sch, 1966—67, vpres, 1972—73; co-chmn Memphis Conf Faith at Work, 1975, bd dirs, 1976—79. Mem.: ABA (ed bd sr lawyers div 1990, pub comt chair 1993—95, coun mem 1994—95, chair travel and leisure comt 1995—96, vice chair 1996—97, chair-elect 1997—98, chair 1998—99), Princeton Alumni Asn Memphis (pres 1992), NC Bar Asn, Tenn Def Lawyers Asn, Memphis Bar Asn, Tenn Bar Asn, Am Col Trust and Estate Coun, Memphis Lions (pres 1956). Office: Law Office 840 Valleybrook Dr Memphis TN 38120 Office Phone: 901-682-0555. Personal E-mail: lawmemphis@aol.com.

ALLEN, NORMA ANN, librarian, educator; b. Balt., Jan. 22, 1951; d. James Crawley and Thelma Agusta (Keaton) Ghee; children: Lamont Ricardo Ghee, Alissa S. Allen, Avery O. Allen. BA in Adminstrn. Mgmt., Sojourner Douglass Coll., Balt., 1987; MS in Instrnl. Tech., Towson State U., 1999. Instr. data processing PSI Inst., Balt., 1987-88; acquisition technician Social Security Adminstrn., Balt., 1987-89, reference librarian, 1989-91, acquisitions librarian, 1991—; librarian United Bapt. Membership Conv., Balt., 2002—. Instrnl. developer Computer Asst. Instrn., Towson U., 1995—; bus. computer tech. instr. Balt. City C.C., 2000—; freelance floral designer/arranger, freelance instr. basic writing skills and computer literacy; instr. bus. computer tech. Balt. City C.C., 2000—. Sec., bd. dirs. New Image Child Care Facility, Balt., 1992, chmn. bd. dirs., 2001-02; instr. active reading literacy program Enoch Pratt Libr., Balt., 1992; instr. United Missionary Bapt. Conv., 1997, libr., 2003. Multicultural scholar Towson U., 1995-96. Mem. ALA, Spl. Librs. Assn., Horizon User Group. Office: Social Security Adminstrn 6401 Security Blvd Rm 571 Baltimore MD 21235-0001 E-mail: norma.allen@ssa.gov.

ALLEN, OLIVER E., writer; b. Cambridge, Mass., June 29, 1922; s. Frederick Lewis and Dorothy Cobb Allen; m. Deborah Hutchison, May 8, 1948; children: Stephen(dec.), Frederick, Henry, Letitia, Jennie. AB, Harvard Coll., 1943. Writer, editor Life Mag., N.Y.C., 1947—60; editor Life World Libr. Time-Life Books, 1960—65, editor Time-Life Libr. Am., 1965—68, dir. editl. planning, 1968—76; freelance writer, 1976—. Author: Wildflower Gardening, 1977, Decorating With Plants, 1978, Pruning and Grafting, 1978, The Windjammers, 1978, Shade Gardens, 1979, Winter Gardens, 1979, The Pacific Navigators, 1980, The Airline Builders, 1981, Building Sound Bones and Muscles, 1981, Secrets of Good Digestion, 1982, The Atmosphere, 1983, The Vegetable Gardeners' Journal, 1985, Gardening With the New Small Plants, 1987, New York, New York, 1991, The Tiger, 1993, Tales of Old Tribeca, 1999. 1st lt. U.S. Army, 1943—46. Mem.: Century Club. Democrat. Home: 42 Hudson St New York NY 10013

ALLEN, PAGE RANDOLPH, artist; b. St. Charles, Ill., Sept. 6, 1951; d. Thomas Eliot and Ann Page (Platt) A.; m. W. Scott Morris, June 19, 1970 (div. May 1977); m. Nathaniel Otis Owings, July 26, 1981; 1 child, Maya Jehan. Student, Princeton U., 1969-70; BA, Hampshire Coll., 1974; MA, No. Ill. U., 1980; postgrad., Santa Fe Inst. Fine Arts. One woman shows include ARC Gallery, Chgo., 1980, Raw Space/ARC Gallery, Chgo., 1981, Fine Arts Gallery, U. Mont., Missoula, 1983, U. Club Gallery, Chgo., 1984, Northcutt Gallery, Ea. Mont. Coll., Billings, 1986, Owings-Dewey Fine Art, Santa Fe, 1987, 88, 90, 91, 94, CAFE Gallery, Albuquerque, 1992, DeWeese Gallery of Contemporary Arts, Bozeman, Mont., 1994, Danforth Gallery, Livingston, Mont., 1994, Meredith Long & Co., Houston, 1996; exhibited in group shows at Arvada (Colo.) Ctr. Arts and Humanities, 1992, Meredith Long & Co., 1993, Albuquerque Mus., 1994, Nora Eccles Harrison Mus. Art, Logan, Utah, 1994; represented in permanent collections Albuquerque Mus. Art, Arvada Ctr. Arts and Humanities, Eiteljorg Mus. Am. Indian and Western Art, Indpls., Missoula Mus. Arts, Mus. Fine Arts, Mus. N.Mex., Santa Fe, Pepsi Cola/Frito Lay Corp., Dallas, Telecomm. France Corp., N.Y.C., Temple (Tex.) Ctr. Contemporary Art. NEA grantee, 1981, Ill. State Arts Coun. grantee, 1981; named Artist in Edn., Mont. Arts Coun., NEA, 1982-84. Democrat. Avocations: travel, walking, gardening, reading. Office: Page Allen Studio 1229 Bishops Lodge Rd Santa Fe NM 87501-1002

ALLEN, PAUL GARDNER, computer company executive, professional sports team executive; b. Seattle, Wash., Jan. 21, 1953; s. Kenneth and Faye Allen. Student, Wash. State U., 1971—73. Co-founder Traf-O-Data Co., Seattle, 1972—73; progammer Honeywell Internat. Inc., Waltham, 1974—75; co-founder Microsoft Corp. (formerly Micro-Soft), Albuquerque, 1975; gen. ptnr. Microsoft Corp., 1975—77, v.p., 1977—81, exec. v.p. rsch. & new product devel., 1981—83, sr. strategy advisor, 2000—; founder Asymetrix Corp., Bellevue, Wash., 1985, Starwave Corp., Bellevue, 1992; co-founder Interval Rsch. Corp., Palo Alto, Calif., 1992; founder Vulcan Prodns.; founder, chmn. Vulcan Inc., Seattle; CEO Vulcan Ventures, Bellevue, 1987—; owner, chmn. bd. Portland Trail Blazers, 1988—; owner, chmn. Seattle Seahawks, 1997—; chmn. Charter Communications Inc., 1998—, Charter Investment, Inc., 1998—; owner TechTV; sponsor, funder SpaceShipOne Venture, Mojave, Calif., 2003; funder Allen Telescope Array, SETI Inst. U. Calif. Berkeley, 2004. Bd. dirs. Egghead Discount Software, Microsoft Corp., 1983—2000, Darwin Molecular, Inc.; founder Allen Inst. Brain Sci., 2003, Allen Brain Atlas Initiative, Experience Music Project, Seattle, Science Fiction Mus. and Hall of Fame, Seattle, 2004; ptnr. DreamWorks SKG. Exec. prodr.: (film series) The Blues. Named one of Top 15 Philanthropists in America, Top 200 Collectors, Artnews Mag., 2004; named to Computer Mus. Hall of Fame. Achievements include sponsoring and funding the record flights for Space ShipOne, which won the Ansari X prize on Oct. 4, 2004. Avocation: Collecting impressionism, Old Masters, pop art, tribal art. Office: Vulcan Inc 505 5th Ave S Ste 900 Seattle WA 98104 also: Seattle Seahawks 11220 NE 53rd St Kirkland WA 98033-7505 Office Phone: 425-453-1940, 206-342-2000. Office Fax: 206-342-3000.*

ALLEN, PINNEY L., lawyer; b. Marshalltown, Iowa, Jan. 26, 1953; d. Walker Woodrow and Doris (Pinney) A.; m. Charles C. Miller, III, Aug. 20, 1977; children: Linden, Doria. AB summa cum laude, Harvard U., 1976; JD cum laude, Harvard Law Sch., 1979. Bar: Ga., 1976; U.S. Tax Ct. 1984. Assoc. Alston & Bird, Atlanta, 1979-86; ptnr., co-chair, tax practice group Alston & Bird LLP, Atlanta, 1986—. Contbr. articles to profl. jours., 1981—. Mem. ABA, Nat. Soc. Accts. for Coops., Ga. Bar Assn., Atlanta Bar Assn., Atlant Tax Forum. Office: Alston & Bird 1 Atlantic Ctr 1201 W Peachtree St NW Atlanta GA 30309-3424 Office Phone: 404-881-7485. Office Fax: 404-881-7777. Business E-Mail: pallen@alston.com.

ALLEN, RACHEL LOREY, lawyer; b. Pitts., Oct. 23, 1964; d. Phillip Joseph and Patricia Grace (Mullen) L. BS, Allegheny Coll., 1986; JD, U. Va., 1989. Bar: Pa. 1989. Assoc. atty. Kirkpatrick & Lockhart, Pitts., 1989-96, Jones, Day, Reavis & Pogue, Pitts., 1996-99; v.p. DQE Enterprises, Pitts., 1999—2001; ptnr. Jones Day, Pitts., 2001—. Dir. PROGRAM for Female Offenders, Inc., Pitts., 1991-2005, Arc Washington County (Pa.), Inc., 1991-99 Bd. dirs. Women's Ctr. and Shelter Greater Pitts., 2000—; dir. Alpha Chi Omega Found., 2004-, Brothers Brother Found., 2004—. Mem. ABA, Allegheny County Bar Assn., Order of the Coif, Phi Beta Kappa. Office: Jones Day 31st Fl 500 Grant St Pittsburgh PA 15219 Office Phone: 412-391-3939. Business E-Mail: rlallen@jonesday.com.

ALLEN, RALPH DEAN, diversified company corporate executive; b. Stanhope, Iowa, July 3, 1941; s. Ralph Carlton and Arvella Ruth (Tade) A.; m. Joanne Johnson; children: June Ann, Lisa Renee, Jeffrey Carlton. BSBA, Drake U., 1964; postgrad., U. Rochester, N.Y.; Advanced Mgmt. Program, Duke U., 1989. With Eastman Kodak Co., 1964-80, dir. shareowner relations, 1976-80; dir. investor relations ITT Corp., N.Y.C., 1980-95, v.p., 1981-95; v.p., dir. investor rels. IIT Industries, White Plains, NY, 1995-99; prin. Allen Advisors, South Salem, NY, 1999—2003; mng. prin. Beacon Advisors, 2003—. Guest lectr. Fordham U. Grad. Sch. Mem. Investor Rels. Assn. (pres. 1981-82), Nat. Inst. Investor Rels. (bd. dirs.), Fin. Analysts Fedn. Office: ITT Industries 4 W Red Oak Ln Ste 2 White Plains NY 10604-3617 Office Phone: 914-763-9388. Business E-Mail: ralph@beaconadvisors.us.

ALLEN, RANDALL L., lawyer; b. Tullahoma, Tenn., Sept. 10, 1956; BA, Ga. State Univ., 1982, JD cum laude, 1986. Bar: Ga. 1986. Ptnr., co-chmn, litig. and trial practice group Alston & Bird LLP, Atlanta. Bd. visitors Ga. State Univ. Coll. of Law; bd. dir, gen. counsel Ronald McDonald Children's Charities. Mem.: ABA. Office: Alston & Bird LLP One Atlantic Ctr 1201 W Peachtree St NW Atlanta GA 30309-3424 Office Phone: 404-881-7196. Office Fax: 404-881-7777. Business E-Mail: rallen@alston.com.

ALLEN, RAY, professional basketball player; b. Merced, Calif., July 20, 1975; Student, Conn., 1996. Shooting guard Milw. Bucks, 1996—2002, Seattle SuperSonics, 2002—. Named Three-time Ea. Conf. All-Star, 2000—02; recipient Gold medal, Summer Olympics, 2000. Office: Bradley Ctr 1001 N 4th St Milwaukee WI 53203

ALLEN, REX WHITAKER, retired architect; b. San Francisco, Dec. 21, 1914; s. Lewis Whitaker and Maude Rex (Allen) A.; m. Elizabeth Johnson, Oct. 11, 1941 (div. 1949); children: Alexandra A., Frances Lambert (Mrs. Andrew Dunn); m. Ruth Batchelor, Apr. 1, 1949 (div. 1971); children: Mark B., Susan Moore (Mrs. Kofy Lechner); m. Bettie J. Crossfield, Nov. 6, 1971. AB, Harvard U., 1936, MArch, 1939; student, Columbia U. Archtl. Sch., 1936—37. With Rsch. and Planning Assocs., N.Y.C., 1939-42, Camloc Fastener Corp., N.Y.C., 1942-45, Isadore Rosenfield (arch.), N.Y.C., 1945-48, Blanchard and Maher (archs.), San Francisco, 1949-52; established pvt. practice San Francisco, 1953; pres. Rex Whitaker Allen & Assocs., San Francisco, 1961-71, Archtl. Prodns., Inc., 1971-76; prin. Hugh Stubbins/Rex Allen Partnership, 1968, Rex Allen Partnership, 1971-76; pres. Rex Allen-Drever-Lechowski, Archs., 1976-85, Rex Allen/Mark Lechowski & Assocs., 1985-87; cons. arch., health facility planner, 1987—. Mem. Calif. Bldg. Safety Bd., 1973-93. Author: (with Ilona von Karolyi) Hospital Planning Handbook, 1976; contbr. articles to profl. jours.; prin. works include French Hosp., San Francisco, Mercy Hosp., Sacramento, Roseville (Calif.) Dist. Hosp., Highland Hosp., Oakland, St. Francis Hosp., San Francisco, Dominican Hosp., Santa Cruz, Alta Bates Hosp., Berkeley, Calif., Boston City Hosp., Out-Patient bldg. Woodland (Calif.) Meml. Hosp., Stanislaus Meml. Hosp., Modesto, Calif., Madera (Calif.) Cmty. Hosp., Sacred Heart Hosp., Eugene, Oreg., St. Joseph Hosp., Mt. Clemens, Mich., Commonwealth Health Ctr., Saipan, Guam Meml. Hosp. and Nursing Facility. Chmn. Mill Valley Adv. Edn. Coun., 1956; mem. Blue Ribbon com. Sonoma Valley Unified Sch. Dist., 1997-2002. Fellow AIA (nat. pres. 1969-70, v.p. No. Calif. chpt. 1964, bd. dirs. Calif. coun. 1955-56, 1962-64), Royal Archtl. Inst. Can. (hon.), Am. Coll. Healthcare Archs. (Lifetime Achievement award 2003, Gold medal 2003); mem. Constrn. Specification Inst. (pres. San Francisco chpt. 1961), San Francisco Zool. Soc. (bd. dirs. 1974-86, 88-95, exhibits com. 1988—, chmn. design stds. com. Assn. Western Hosps., chmn. arch. sect. 1957-58), Calif. Hosp. Assn., Am. Hosp. Assn., Internat. Hosp. Fedn., Am. Assn. Hosp. Planning (pres. 1971-72), Union Internat. des Architectes Pub. Health Work Group (dir. 1979-80), La Sociedad de Arquitectos Mexicanos (hon. mem.), Federaciñn Panamericana de Asociaciones de Arquitectos (v.p. 1980-84), San Francisco Planning and Urban Renewal Assn., San Francisco Mus. Modern Art, Japanese Garden Soc. of Oreg., Portland Classical Chinese Garden, Asian Art Coun., Portland Art Mus., Sierra Club. Home and Office: 9946 SW 61st Ave Portland OR 97219 Office Phone: 503-977-2770. E-mail: rethmore@msn.com.

ALLEN, RICHARD BLOSE, legal editor, lawyer; b. Aledo, Ill., May 10, 1919; s. James Albert and Claire (Smith) A.; m. Marion Treloar, Aug. 27, 1949; children: Penelope, Jennifer, Leslie Jean. BS, U. Ill., 1941, JD, 1947; LLD, Seton Hall U., 1977. Bar: Ill. 1947. Staff editor ABA Jour., 1947-48, 63-66, exec. editor, 1966-70, editor, 1970-83, editor, pub., 1983-86; pvt. practice Aledo, 1949-57; gen. counsel Ill. Bar Assn., 1957-63; mng. editor Def. Counsel Jour., Chgo., 1987—2005. Editor Sr. Lawyer, 1986-90, 94-2000. Maj. Q.M.C., AUS, 1941-46. Mem. ABA (mem. ho. of dels. 1996-99, chair sr. lawyers divsn. 2000-01, mem. commn. on law and aging 2002—), Ill. Bar Assn. (mem. assembly 1972-74), Chgo. Bar Assn., Am. Law Inst., Selden Soc., Mich. Shores Club, Kappa Tau Alpha, Phi Delta Phi, Alpha Tau Omega. E-mail: rallen2304@sbcglobal.net.

ALLEN, RICHARD GARRETT, healthcare educator; b. St. Paul, July 8, 1923; s. John and Margaretta (Taggart) A.; m. Ida Elizabeth Vernon, July 5, 1944; children: Richard Garrett, Barbara Elizabeth, Julie Frances (dec.). BS cum laude, Trinity U., 1954; MHA, Baylor U., 1957; postgrad., Indsl. Coll. of Armed Forces, 1962, USAF Command and Staff Coll., 1962. Commd. 2d lt. Med. Svc. Corps USAF, 1948, advanced through grades to maj., 1961; served in U.S., Pacific, Germany; ret., 1964; asst. adminstr. U. Ala. Hosp. and Clinics; dir. Ctr. for Hosp. Continuing Edn., Sch. for Health Svcs., U. Ala., Birmingham, 1965-68; dir. edn. New Eng. Hosp. Assembly, Inc., New Eng. Ctr. for Continuing Edn., U. N.H., Durham, 1968-74; dir. Office Health Care Edn., 1970-74; exec. v.p. Edn. and Rsch. Found., San Francisco, 1974-77, Assn. West Hosps., 1974-77. V.p. health affairs M G & M Comm., Foster City, Calif.; pres. Calif. Coll. Podiatric Medicine; CEO Calif. Podiatry Hosp. and Outpatient Clinic, San Francisco, 1977-81; prof. health care adminstrn. St. Mary's Coll. of Calif., Moraga, 1982-85; cons. health care and edn., 1985—; owner Sleepy Hollow Books, 1985—; mem. Nat. Adv. Coun. on Vocat. Edn., 1969-71; also cons.; cons. Booz, Allen & Hamilton, Washington, Ops. Rsch., Inc., Silver Spring, Md., Republic of Korea Air Force Med. Svcs., Seoul, Bio-Dynamics, Inc., Cambridge, Mass., HEALTHSAT-Appalachia Cmty. Svcs. Network, Washington, 1980—. Pub.: Hosp. Forum, San Francisco, 1974-77; contbr. articles to profl. jours. Decorated Air Force Commendation medal with oak leaf cluster. Fellow Am. Coll. Hosp. Adminstrs.; mem. Am. Soc. for Health Manpower Edn. and Tng., Am. Hosp. Assn., AAUP, Am. Soc. Hosp. Edn. and Tng. (pres. 1972), Am. Assn. Colls. Podiatric Medicine (pres. 1979-81), Sherlock Holmes Soc. London, Masons. Episcopalian. Home and Office: Sleepy Hollow Books 1455 Camino Peral Moraga CA 94556-2018 E-mail: dick78@earthlink.net. *Uncertainty is a fact of life; there is no progress free of the risk of change. Sharpen your sense of timing and know when it is time to let go and when to hang on. Trials and defeats are inevitable elements of the committed life; welcome these conflicts for it is your principles that are involved. Appreciate the past, but focus on today's tasks— while realizing that tomorrow will be nothing like you expect it to be. Cultivate a cheerful acceptance of your own mortality, and its attendant limitations and blessings.*

ALLEN, RICHARD STANLEY (DICK ALLEN), literature and language professor, writer; b. Troy, N.Y., Aug. 8, 1939; s. Richard Sanders and Doris (Bishop) A.; m. Loretta Mary Negridge, Aug. 13, 1960; children: Richard Negridge, Tanya Angell. AB, Syracuse U., N.Y., 1961; MA, Brown U., 1963. Teaching assoc. Brown U., 1962-64; instr. English Wright State U., Dayton, Ohio, 1964-68; mem. faculty U. Bridgeport, Conn., 1968—, prof. English, 1976-79, Charles A. Dana prof. English, 1979—2001, also dir. creative writing, Dana prof. emeritus English, 2001—. Author: Anon and Various Time Machine Poems, 1971, Overnight in the Guest House of the Mystic, 1984, Regions with No Proper Names, 1975, Flight and Pursuit, 1987, Ode to the Cold War: Poems New and Selected, 1997, The Day Before: New Poems, 2003; also poems, articles, revs.; editor, poetry editor: Mad River Rev., 1964-68; co-editor: Detective Fiction: Crime and Compromise, 1974, Looking Ahead: The Vision of Science Fiction, 1975; book reviewer: Poetry, Hudson Rev., Am. Book Rev.; editor: Science Fiction: The Future, 1982, Crosscurrents Expansive Poetry: The New Formalism and the New Narrative, 1989. Recipient poetry prize Union Arts and Civic League, 1971, Disting. Tchg. award MLA-Assn. Depts. English, 1971, San Jose poetry prize, 1976, poetry prize Nassau Rev., 1995, Poetry award L.A. (Calif.) Times, 2004; Hart Crane Meml. poetry fellow, 1966, Robert Frost poetry fellow, 1972, Mellon rsch. fellow, 1981, poetry writing fellow Ingram Merrill Found., 1986; poetry writing grantee Nat. Endowment Arts, 1984, Nat. Millennium Survey Project, 2000; finalist Winship/PEN Am. award, W. Carlos Williams PSA 1st Finalist award, NBCC Poetry Book award, Conn. Poetry Book award, 2004, Sheila Motion Poetry prize, 2004, Pushcart prize, 2005. Mem. Associated Writers Programs, Poets and Writers, PEN, Poetry Soc. Am. (Carolyn Davies Meml. Poetry award 1986), Modern Poetry Soc. Republican. Unitarian Universalist. Home: 74 Fern Cir Trumbull CT 06611-4910 Personal E-mail: rallen285@earthlink.net.

ALLEN, RICHARD VINCENT, international business consultant, former national security advisor; b. Collingswood, N.J., Jan. 1, 1936; s. Charles Carroll and Magdalen (Buchman) A.; m. Patricia Ann Mason, Dec. 28,1957; children: Michael, Kristin, Mark, Karen, Kathryn, Kevin, Kimberly. BA, U. Notre Dame, 1957, MA, 1958; postgrad., U. Munich, W. Ger., 1958-61; hon. doctorate, Hanover Coll., Korea U., Pepperdine U. Instr. U. Md. Overseas Div., 1959-61; asst. prof. polit. sci. Ga. Inst. Tech., 1961-62; sr. staff mem. Center for Strategic and Internat. Studies, Georgetown U., 1962-66, Hoover Instn. on War, Revolution and Peace, Stanford U., 1966-69; fgn. policy coord. Richard Nixon Presdl. campaign, 1967-68; sr. staff mem. Nat. Security Council, White House, 1969; dep. asst. to Pres. The White House, Washington, 1971-72; pres. Potomac Internat. Corp., Washington, 1972-80; sr. fgn. policy to Pres. The White House, Washington, 1978-80; asst. to Pres. for nat. security affairs Nat. Security Coun., Washington, 1981-82; pres. Richard V. Allen Co., Washington, 1982-90, chmn., 1991—2003. Disting. fellow, chmn. Asian Studies Ctr. Heritage Found., 1982-98; sr. counselor for fgn. policy and nat. security Rep. Nat. Com., 1982-88; sr. fellow Hoover Instn., 1983—; vice chmn. Internat. Dem. Union, 1983-88; chmn. German-Am. Tricentennial Found., 1983; mem. Pres.'s Task Force on U.S. Govt. Internat. Broadcasting, 1991-92; mem. adv. bd. Cath. Campaign for Am., 1993-96; mem. Rep. Congl. Policy Adv. Bd., 1998-2001; mem. U.S. Def. Policy Bd., 2001—. Author: Peace or Peaceful Coexistence, 1966, (with others) Communism and Democracy: Theory and Action, 1967; editor: (with David M. Abshire) National Security: Political, Military and Economic Strategies in the Decade Ahead, 1963, Yearbook on International Communist Affairs, 1969. Chmn. com. on intelligence Republican Nat. Com., 1977-80; trustee St. Francis Prep. Sch., Spring Grove, Pa. Named Patriot of Yr. SAR, 1981; H.B. Earhart fellow Relm Found., 1958-61; decorated Order of Diplomatic Merit Republic of Korea, 1982, Knight Comdr.'s Cross Fed. Republic of Germany, 1983, Badge and Star of Order of Merit Fed. Republic of Germany, 1983, Order of Brilliant Star, Republic of China, 1986, Sovereign Mil. Order of Knights of Malta, 1987. Mem. Am. Polit. Sci. Assn., Coun. on Fgn. Rels., Intercollegiate Studies Inst. (trustee), Com. on Present Danger (dir. 1976-90), Univ. Club, Farmington Country Club (Charlottesville, Va.), Burning Tree Club (Bethesda, Md.), Met. Club, Cordillera Club (Colo.). Office: 1 Metro Ctr 700 12th St NW Washington DC 20005 Office Phone: 202-737-2824. E-mail: rvallen@aol.com.

ALLEN, ROBERT DEE, lawyer; b. Tulsa, Oct. 13, 1928; s. Harve and Olive Jean (Brown) A.; m. Mary Latimer Conner, May 18, 1957; children: Scott, Randy, Blake. BA, U. Okla., 1951, LLB, 1955, JD, 1970. Bar: Okla. 1955, Ill. 1979, U.S. Dist. Ct. (we., no. and ea. dists.) Okla. 1955, U.S. Dist. Ct. (no. dist.) Ill. 1979, U.S. Ct. Appeals (10th cir.) 1956, U.S. Ct. Appeals (7th cir.) 1980, U.S. Supreme Ct. 1985. Assoc. Abernathy & Abernathy, Shawnee, Okla., 1955; law clk. to judge 10th U.S. Ct. Appeals, Denver, 1956; to judge Western Dist. Okla., 1956-57; asst. ins. commr., gen. counsel Okla. Ins. Dept., 1957-63; partner firm Quinlan, Allen & Batchelor, Oklahoma City, 1963-65,

DeBois & Allen, 1965-66; counsel AT&T, Washington, 1966-67; gen. atty. Southwestern Bell Telephone Co., Okla., 1967-79; v.p., gen. counsel Ill. Bell Telephone Co., Chgo., 1979-83; sole practice law Chgo. and Oklahoma City, 1983—; mcpl. counselor Oklahoma City, 1984-89; of counsel Hartzog, Conger & Cason, 1983-90, Kimball, Wilson, Walker and Ferguson, 1990-93, Berry & Durland, 1993-94, Durland & Durland, 1994-96, White, Coffey, Galt & Fite, P.C., 1996-97, Phillips, McFall, McCaffrey, McVay & Murrah, P.C., 1997-2000; asst. gen. counsel Okla. Corp. Commn. Pub. Utilities Divsn., 2000—04, Roberrt D. Allen PC, 2004—; ret., 2004. Spl. counsel Okla. Mcpl. Power Authority, 1990-94, City of Altus, Okla., 1990-95; mem. Gov.'s Ad Valorem Tax Structure and Sch. Fin. Commn., 1972; bd. dirs. Taxpayers Fedn. Ill., 1980-83; adv. bd. dirs. Ctr. Am. and Internat. Law., 1985—; rsch. fellow Ctr. Am. and Internat. Law, 1994—; adj. prof. ins. law Oklahoma City U. Coll. Law, 1985—, agy. and partnership law, U. Okla. Coll. Law, 1989—; Okla. State chmn. Nat. Inst. Mcpl. Law Officers, 1984-89; apptd. mem. Legis Task Force on Okla. Adminstrv. Code, 1987; founding mem. U. Okla. Assocs., 1980. Bd. dirs. Oklahoma County Legal Aid Soc., 1973—; trustee Oklahoma City Riverfront Redevel. Authority, 1997-2003 With U.S. Army, 1946-48, 1st lt., 51-53; lt. col. USAR. Fellow Am. Bar Found., Okla. Bar Found. (charter benefactor); mem. ABA, Fed. Bar Assn. (v.p. Okla. chpt. 1977—), Okla. Bar Assn., Okla. County Bar Assn., Am. Judicature Soc., Okla. Assn. Mcpl. Attys. (bd. dirs. 1984-89), English Speaking Union (dir. 2001—), Order of Coif, Chgo. Club, Lions Club of Oklahoma City, The Econs. Club of Okla., Oklahoma City Golf and Country Club, Phi Delta Phi, Sigma Phi Epsilon (dir.) Presbyterian. Home: 8101 Glenwood Ave Oklahoma City OK 73114-1107 Office Phone: 405-840-0787. Personal E-mail: rdeeallen@sbcglobal.net.

ALLEN, ROBERT EUGENE BARTON, lawyer; b. Bloomington, Ind., Mar. 16, 1940; s. Robert Eugene Barton and Berth R. A.; m. Cecelia Ward Dooley, Sept. 23, 1960 (div. 1971); children: Victoria, Elizabeth, Robert, Charles, Suzanne, William; m. Judith Elaine Hecht, May 27, 1979 (div. 1984); m. Suzanne Nickolson, Nov. 18, 1995. BS, Columbia U., 1962; LLB, Harvard U., 1965. Bar: Ariz. 1965, U.S. Dist. Ct. Ariz. 1965, U.S. Tax Ct., 1965, U.S. Supreme Ct. 1970, U.S. Ct. Customs and Patent Appeals 1971, U.S. Dist. Ct. D.C. 1972, U.S. Ct. Appeals (9th cir.) 1974, U.S. Ct. Appeals (10th and D.C. cirs.) 1984, U.S. Dist. Ct. N.Mex., U.S. Dist. Ct. (no. dist.) Calif., U.S. Dist. Ct. (no. dist.) Tex. 1991, U.S. Ct. Appeals (fed. cir.) 1992, U.S. Dist. Ct. (ea. dist.) Wis. 1995. Spl. asst. atty. gen., 1978; judge pro-tem Ariz. Ct. Appeals, 1984, 92, 99; Ptnr., dir. Allen, Price & Padden, Phoenix, 2000—. Nat. pres. Young Dems. Clubs Am., 1971-73; mem. exec. com. Dem. Nat. Com., 1972-73, Ariz. Gov.'s Kitchen Cabinet working on a wide range of state projects; bd. dirs. Phoenix Bapt. Hosp., 1981-83, Phoenix and Valley of the Sun Conv. and Visitors Bur., United Cerebral Palsy Ariz., 1984-89, Planned Parenthood of Ctrl. and No. Ariz., 1984-87, Ariz. Heart Inst. Found., 1998-2003, Cordell Hull Found. for Internat. Edn., 1996—; trustee Environ. Health Found., 1994-97, Friends of Walnut Canyon, 1991-94; bd. dirs. Ariz. Aviation Futures Task Force, chmn. Ariz. Airport Devel. Criteria Subcom.; Am. rep. exec. bd. Atlantic Alliance of Young Polit. Leaders, 1973-77, 77-80; trustee Am. Counsel of Young Polit. Leaders, 1971-76, 81-85; mem. Am. delegations to Germany, 1971, 72, 76, 79, USSR, 1971, 76, 88, France, 1974, 79, Belgium, 1974, 77, Can., 1974, Eng., 1975, 79, Norway, 1975, Denmark, 1976, Yugoslavia and Hungary, 1985; Am. observer European Parlimentary elections, Eng., France, Germany, Belgium, 1979, Moscow Congressional, Journalist delegation, 1989, NAFTA Trade Conf., Mexico City, 1993, Atlantic Assembly, Copenhagen, 1993. Contbr. articles on comml. litig. to profl. jours. Mem. ABA, Ariz. Bar Assn., Maricopa County Bar Assn., N.Mex. State Bar, D.C. Bar Assn., Am. Judicature Soc., Fed. Bar Assn., Am. Arbitration Assn., Phi Beta Kappa, Harvard Club. Democrat. Episcopalian.

ALLEN, ROBERTA, writer, photographer, conceptual artist; b. N.Y.C., Oct. 6, 1945; d. Sol and Jeanette (Waldner) A. Student, Inst. Bellas Artes, Mex., 1971. Lectr. Corcoran Sch. Art, Washington, 1975, Kutztown State Coll., 1977, C.W. Post Coll., 1979. Instr. creative writing Parsons Sch. Design, N.Y.C., 1986; instr. The Writer's Voice, 1992—97, The New Sch., 1993—, Dept. Continuing Edn., NYU, 1993—99; Tennessee Williams fellow, writer-in-residence U. of the South, Sewanee, Tenn., 1998; adj. asst. prof. Columbia U. Sch. of the Arts, 1998—99, Eugene Lang. Coll., 2000. Author: Partially Trapped Lines, 1975, Pointless Arrows, 1976, Pointless Acts, 1977, Everything in The World There Is To Know Is Known By Somebody, But Not By the Same Knower, 1981, Amazon Dream, 1993; author: (fiction) The Daughter, 1992, The Dreaming Girl, 2000, The Traveling Woman, 1986, Certain People, 1997; author: (writing guide) Fast Fiction, 1997, The Playful Way to Serious Writing, 2002, (Personal Growth) The Playful Way to Knowing Yourself, 2003; one-woman shows include Galerie 845, Amsterdam, Netherlands, 1967, John Weber Gallery, N.Y.C., 1974—75, 1977, 1979, Inst. for Art and Urban Resources, 1977, 1980, Galerie Maier-Hahn, Dusseldorf, Germany, 1977, MTL Galerie, Brussels, 1978, C.W. Post Coll., Glenvale, N.Y., 1978, Galerie Walter Storms, Munich, 1981, Kunstforum, Stadt. Galerie in Lenbachhaus, 1981, Galeria Primo Piano, Rome, 1981, Perth Inst. Contemporary Arts, 1989, Art Resources Transfer, Inc., 2001, SUNY, Binghamton, 2001. Fellow, Va. Ctr. Creative Arts, 1985, 1994, 2005; McDowell Colony fellow, 1971—72, Yaddo fellow, 1983, 1987, 1993, LINE grantee, 1985. E-mail: roall@aol.com.

ALLEN, RONALD CARL, commissioner, state senator, computer company executive, consultant, artist; b. Salt Lake City, Mar. 25, 1953; s. Carl Franklin and Mary Jean (Benson) A.; m. Delia Ann Fordham, Nov. 15, 1974; children: Lisa, Cindy, Jeffrey. BS in Acctg., U. Utah, 1980, MA in Art History, 2004. Owner, bus. mgr. Alinco Mfg., Salt Lake City, 1977-79; owner, pres. Comics Utah Bookstores, Salt Lake City, 1984-86; adminstrv. supr. Am. Stores, Salt Lake City, 1978-89; pres. Cons. Svcs., Salt Lake City, 1989—2003; fire chief No. Tooele County Fire Dept., 1987-96; mem. Utah Senate, Dist. 12, Salt Lake City, 1998—, Dem. whip, 2001—. Adj. instr. Utah State U. Chmn., chief North Tooele County (Utah) Fire Dept., 1987—95; mem. adv. bd. Usute Found., Mus. Utah Art and History. Recipient over 40 awards for visual arts, 1981—. Mem., Tooele County Chamber of Commerce. Mem. Lds Ch. Avocations: photography, sailing, golf. Office: Cons Svcs 835 Lakeview Tooele UT 84074-9613 Office Phone: 801-538-1406. E-mail: rallen@vonallen.com.

ALLEN, RONALD JAY, law educator; b. Chgo., July 14, 1948; s. J. Matteson and Carolyn L. (Latchum) A.; m. Debra Jane Livingston, May 25, 1974 (div. 1982); children: Sarah, Adrienne; m. Julie O'Donnell, Sept. 2, 1984; children: Michael, Conor. BS, Marshall U., 1970; JD, U. Mich., 1973. Bar: Nebr. 1974, Iowa 1979, U.S. Ct. Appeals (8th cir.) 1980, U.S. Supreme Ct. 1981, Ill. 1986. Prof. law SUNY, Buffalo, 1974-79, U. Iowa, Iowa City, 1979-82, 83-84, Duke U., Durham, NC, 1982-83, Northwestern U., Chgo., 1984—, John Henry Wigmore prof., 1992—. Pres. faculty senate U. Iowa, 1980-81. Author: Constitutional Criminal Procedure, 1985, 91, 95, An Analytical Approach to Evidence, 1989, Evidence: Text, Cases and Problems, 1997, Arthritis of the Hip and Knee: The Active Person's Guide to Taking Charge, 1998, Comprehensive Criminal Procedure, 2d edit., 2005, Evidence: Text, Problems, Cases, 2002, Criminal Procedure: Investigation and Right to Counsel, 2005; contbr. articles to profl. jours. Bd. dirs. Continental Rights Found., 1992—, Joffrey Ballet, 2003—. Mem. ABA (rules com. criminal justice sect.), Am. Law Inst. Office: Northwestern U Sch Law 357 E Chicago Ave Chicago IL 60611-3059 Office Phone: 312-503-8372. E-mail: rjallen@northwestern.edu.

ALLEN, RONALD JOHN, astrophysics educator, researcher; b. Prince Albert, Sask., Can., Nov. 12, 1940; s. Arthur and Lillian May (Brown) A.; m. Janice Ruth Nielsen, Jan. 7, 1967; children: Melanie Ruth, Matthew John, Stefan Ronald. BA in Physics with honors, U. Sask., 1962; PhD in Physics, MIT, 1967. Postdoctoral fellow NRC Can., Paris, 1967-68; rsch. assoc. Kapteyn Astron. Inst., U. Groningen, The Netherlands, 1969-70, rsch. supr., 1971, lectr. in radio astronomy, 1972-80, prof. radio astronomy, 1980-85, chmn., 1982-85; prof. astronomy U. Ill., Urbana, 1985-90, head dept. astronomy, 1985-88; astronomer Space Telescope Sci. Inst., Balt., 1989—, head sci. computing divsn., 1989-95, head rsch. programs office, 1995-99, mgr. dirs. discretionary rsch. fund, 1995—; mission scientist NASA/JPL Space Interferometry Mission, 2000—. Vis. lectr. Cavendish Lab., Cambridge, Eng., 1971; mem. acad. council Ministry Edn. and Sci., The Netherlands, 1982-85; mem. vis. com. Nat. Radio Astronomy Obs., Charlottesville, Va., 1986-89; sr. scientist NATO, U.S., 1975-76; vis. prof. Kapteyn Astron. Inst., 1985-95; adjunct prof. Johns Hopkins U., 1991—; advisor NSF, NASA, Can. Nat. Sci. Engring. Rsch. Coun., Swedish Nat. Rsch. Bd., French Conseil Nat. Rsch. Sci., European Space Agy., U.K. Sci. Rsch. Coun., Academia Sinica Taiwan. Co-editor: Image Processing in Astronomy, 1979, The Milky Way Galaxy, 1985, The Restoration of HST Images and Spectra, 1991; contbr. numerous articles to sci. jours. Fellow Inst. des Hautes Etudes Scientifiques, Bures-sur-Yvette, France, 1974. Mem. Internat. Astron. Union, Am. Astron. Soc., Internat. Radio Sci. Union. Office: Space Telescope Sci Inst 3700 San Martin Dr Baltimore MD 21218-2464

ALLEN, ROSEMARY M., lawyer; b. 1948; BA, Ind. U., 1970; MEd, Boston U., 1979; JD, Northeastern U., 1986. Bar: Mass. 1987, RI 1995, US Ct. Appeals (1st Cir.). Law clk. to Hon. Bruce M. Selya US Ct. Appeals (1st Cir.), 1987; ptnr. Mintz, Levin, Cohn, Ferris, Glovsky & Popeo PC, Boston, coord., Intellectual Property Sect. Mem.: ABA, RI Bar Assn., Mass. Bar Assn., Boston Bar Assn. Office: Mintz Levin Cohn Ferris Glovsky & Popeo PC One Financial Center Boston MA 02111 Office Phone: 617-348-1601. Office Fax: 617-542-2241. Business E-Mail: rallen@mintz.com.

ALLEN, RUSSELL G., lawyer; b. Ottumwa, Iowa, Nov. 7, 1946; BA, Grinnell Coll., 1968; JD, Stanford U., 1971. Bar: Calif. 1971. Ptnr. O'Melveny & Myers LLP, Newport Beach, Calif., 1975-2001; wealth advisor J.P. Morgan Chase & Co., Newport Beach, Calif., 2001—04. Trustee Grinnell Coll. Capt. JAGC, USAF, 1971-75. Fellow Am. Coll. Trust and Estate Counsel; mem. ABA (real property, probate and trust law and taxation sects.), Orange County Bar Assn. (estate planning, probate and trust sects.) Office: 2101 East Coast Hwy Ste 215 Corona Del Mar CA 92625 Office Phone: 949-760-4090. E-mail: Russ@russallenlaw.com.

ALLEN, SHARON, accounting firm executive; B in acctg., U. Idaho, 1973, D (hon.) in adminstrv. sci., 2004. Mng. ptnr. Pacific Southwest practice Deloitte & Touche USA LLP, LA, 2003—; chmn. bd. Deloitte & Touche Tohmatsu USA LLP, 2003—. Mem. bd. United Way Greater LA; bd. mem. YMCA Met. LA; co-chair Nat. Campaign Com. Campaign for Idaho; bd. dirs. Malcolm Baldridge Found., Harvard U., John F. Kennedy Sch. Govt. Women's Leadership Coun.; chmn. bd. dirs. Independent Coll. So. Calif. (ICSC), 2003—; adv. bd. Coll. Bus. and Econ. Named one of Top 100 Most Influential People in 2003, Acctg. Today mag. Mem.: LA Area C. of C. (bd. mem.). Office: Deloitte & Touche USA LLP Two Calif Plz 350 S Grand Ave Ste 200 Los Angeles CA 90071-3492 Office Phone: 213-688-0800. Office Fax: 213-688-0100.

ALLEN, STACY DALE, historian, parks director; b. Independence, Kans., Apr. 23, 1958; s. Charles Bradley and Etta JoAnn Allen; m. Diane Elizabeth Woodford, July 14, 1992; children: Jennifer Elizabeth Harrison, Jonathan C. Morton. B in Anthropology, U. of Kans., 1983. Fed. Law Enforcement Commn. Fed. Law Enforcement Tng. Ctr., 1987, Ranger Skills Nat. Pk. Svc. Albright Tng. Ctr., 1989. Pk. ranger Nat. Pk. Svc. Vicksburg (Miss.) Nat. Mil. Pk., 1984—89; lead pk. ranger Nat. Pk. Svc. Shiloh (Tenn.) Nat. Mil. Pk., 1989—92, historian, 1992—2002; supervisory pk. ranger Shiloh (Tenn.) Nat. Mil. Pk. Nat. Pk. Svc., 2002—. Agy. Ea. Nat. coord. Ea. Nat. Bookstore Shiloh Nat. Mil. Pk., 1992—; historian, subject matter advisor Miss. Civil War Battlefield Commn., 2000—; historian NPS Core Study Team, Corinth Spl. Resource Study, Corinth, Miss., 2000—04, NPS Core Study Team: Vicksburg Campaign Trail Spl. Resource Study, Shiloh, 2000—04; historian, subject matter advisor Siege and Battle of Corinth (Miss.) Commn., 1992—; historian Lower Miss. Civil War Task Force, Shiloh, 1995—97; historian, site investigator Civil War Sites Adv. Commn., Shiloh, 1992—93. Author: (Blue & Gray Magazine) Corinth: Crossroads of the Western Confederacy, 2002, (audio cassette, CD tape tour) Battle of Shiloh (Nat. Silver Microphone award, 2001), (guidebook) Blue & Gray Magazine: Shiloh! A Visitor's Guide, 2001, (publn.) Blue & Gray Magazine: Shiloh! Campaign and First Day of Battle; Second Days Battle and Aftermath, 1997, (tour guide) A Guide to the Corinth Campaign of 1862, 1998, (publn.) The Tennessee Conservationist: Hell on the Hatchie, 1998; contbr. Atlas of the Civil War, James A. McPherson, ed.,1994, The Civil War Battlefield Guide, Francis Kennedy, Ed., 1998, Steven E. Woodworth, Ed., 2001. Recipient drama scholarship, Coffeyville C.C., Kans., 1976, Outstanding Achievement in Theater award, Field Kindley Meml. H.S., 1975. Mem.: The Civil War Fortification Study Group (assoc.; editor 1993—, pres. 1999—), Shiloh Battlefield Employees Assn. (assoc.; pres. 1990—2000, treas. 2000—02), NPS Employee and Alumni Assn. (assoc.), U. of Kans. Alumni Assn. (assoc.), Civil War Historians of the Western Theater (assoc.), Orgn. of Am. Historians (assoc.). Conservative. Achievements include research in Corinth/Battery Robinett Archaeological Investigations; Shiloh National Military Park Archaeological Investigations; Battlefield Investigations: Civil War Sites Advisory Commission; National Park Service, Corinth Special Resource Study; National Park Service, Vicksburg Campaign Trail Special Resource Study. Avocations: hunting, travel, drawing and painting, retriever training, reading. Home: 290 Residence Cir Shiloh TN 38376 Office: Shiloh Nat Mil Pk 1055 Pittsburg Landing Rd Shiloh TN 38376 Office Phone: 731-689-5275 x32. Business E-Mail: stacy_allen@nps.gov.

ALLEN, STANLEY T., architect, dean, educator; BA, Brown U.; BArch, Cooper Union Sch. Arch.; MArch, Princeton U. Dean, prof. Sch. Arch. Princeton U.; arch., prin. Field Ops. Recipient fellowship in arch., N.Y. Found. for Arts, 1986, fellowship in design arts, NEA, 1990, Graham Found. fellowship, 1993. Office: Princeton Univ School of Architecture Princeton NJ 08544

ALLEN, STEPHEN D(EAN), pathologist, microbiologist; b. Linton, Ind., Sept. 8, 1943; s. Wilburn and Betty Allen; m. Vally C. Autrey, June 17, 1964; children: Christopher D., Amy C. BA, Ind. U., 1965, MA, 1967; MD, Ind. U., Indpls., 1970. Diplomate Am. Bd. Pathology Anatomic and Clin. Pathology and Med. Microbiology. Intern in pathology Vanderbilt U. Hosp., Nashville, 1970-71, resident in pathology, 1971-74; clin. asst. prof. pathology Emory U., Atlanta, 1974-77; asst. prof. clin. pathology Ind. U., Indpls., 1977-79, asst. prof. pathology, 1979-81, assoc. prof. pathology, 1981-86, prof. pathology, 1986-92, prof. pathology and lab. medicine, 1992—, assoc. dir. div. clin. microbiology, dept. pathology, 1977-92, dir. grad. progam pathology, 1986—, sr. assoc. chmn. dept. pathology, 1990-91, dir. divsn. clin. microbiology dept. pathology/lab. medicine, 1992-98, assoc. chair dept. pathology and lab. medicine & dir. labs., 1996-99; dir. disease control lab. divsn. Ind. State Dept. Health, Indpls., 1994—; dir. divsn. clin. microbiology dept. pathology/lab. medicine Clarian-Meth.-Ind U.-Riley Hosps., 1998—. Mem. residency rev. com. for pathology Accreditation Coun. for Grad. Med. Edn., 1996—2004, mem. residency rev. com. for molecular genetic pathology, 1999—2004, vice chmn., 2003—04, mem. molecular genetic pathology policy com., 1999—; trustee Am. Bd. Pathology, 1995—, chmn. microbiology test devel. and adv. com., 1995—, sec. bd., 2001—02, v.p., 2002, pres., 03, immediate past pres., 04. Co-author: Introduction to Diagnostic Microbiology, 1994, Color Atlas of Diagnostic Microbiology, 1997, 2005, (CD-ROM) Direct Smear Atlas, 1998; contbr. With USPHS, 1974—77. Fellow: Binford-Dammin Soc. Infectious Disease Pathologists, Infectious Diseases Soc. Am., Am. Acad. Microbiology, Coll. Am. Pathologists; mem.: Anaerobe Soc. Ams. (mem. coun. 1994—2002, pres. 2002—04), Am. Soc. Clin. Pathologists (coun. microbiology 1983—89), Masons (32d deg.), Shriners, Sigma Xi. Avocations: musicial instruments, fly fishing. Office: Ind U Hosp Rm 4430 550 University Blvd Indianapolis IN 46202-5149 Business E-Mail: sallen@iupui.edu.

ALLEN, STEVEN GLEN, economics professor, business professor; b. Louisville, Mar. 17, 1952; s. Charles Freeman and Lois (Crask) A.; m. Linda L. Pattison, May 19, 1978. BA in Math., Mich. State U., 1973, MA in Econs., 1974; PhD in Econs., Harvard U., 1978. Asst. prof. econs. and bus. N.C. State U., Raleigh, 1978—83, assoc. prof., 1983—87, prof., 1987—, dir. MS mgmt. program, 1993—2002, dir. MBA program, 2002—, assoc. dean grad. programs and rsch., 2003—. Rsch. economist Nat. Bur. Econ. Rsch., Cambridge, Mass., 1983-86, rsch. assoc., 1986—; mem. bd. reviewers Indls. Rels., Berkeley, Calif., 1989—. Contbr. articles to profl. jours. Recipient Allyn Young award Harvard Coll., 1975, 76, Disting. Rsch. and Lit. Publ. award Sch. Humanities and Social Scis., N.C. State U., 1986, Outstanding Rsch. award Coll. Mgmt., 1993; NSF grantee, 1984-86, 87-92, five-time U.S. Dept. Labor grantee; Fulbright scholar, 1991, 93. Mem. Am. Econ. Assn., Soc. Labor Economists, Econometric Soc. Office: NC State U PO Box 7229 Raleigh NC 27695-7229

ALLEN, STEVEN JEFFREY, anesthesiologist, educator; b. Abilene, Tex., 1952; MD, U. Tex. Med. Br., Galveston, 1977. Diplomate Am. Bd. Anesthesiology, Am. Bd. Critical Care Medicine. Intern U. Utah Med. Ctr., Salt Lake City, 1977-78; resident in anesthesiology U. Wash., Seattle, 1980-82; fellow in critical care medicine U. Tex. Med. Sch., Houston, 1982-83, prof. anesthesiology, 1983—; med. staff Hermann Hosp., Houston, 1983—; med. dir. Meml. Hermann Hosp., 1996—. Mem. AMA, Am. Soc. Anesthesiologists, Soc. Critical Care Medicine. Office: U Tex HSC Anesthesiology 6431 Fannin MSMB 5 020 Houston TX 77030-1501

ALLEN, STUART (STUART ALLEN SUP), film and television company executive; b. N.Y.C., July 24, 1943; s. Rudolph and Rita Geraldine (Tellez) Sup; m. Carol Ann Terminelli, June 30, 1982. AA in Engring., NYU, 1961; BA in Communications, Pace U., 1963. Free-lance photographer, photojournalist, N.Y.C., 1963—; producer, dir. Stuart Allen Assocs., Iselin, N.J., 1967-76; pres., chief exec. officer Internat. Media Svcs., Inc., Plainfield, N.J., 1976—; pres., gen. mgr. The Legal Svcs. Group, Plainfield, N.J, 1976—. Mem. adj. faculty roundtable group IEEE. Spl. producer ABC-TV Evil Knievel Snake River Canyon Jump, 1974; author, producer Counterattack, 1978 (One to One Media award 1979), producer, dir. Eagle in the Wind, 1980 (Best Film award 1984); producer 2d unit The Girl Next Door, CBS TV Movie of the Week. Chmn. Plainfield (N.J.) Cultural and Heritage Commn., 1982-96; mcpl. liaison Union County (N.J.) Cultural and Heritage Adv. Bd., 1982-92; trustee Drake House Mus., Plainfield Hist. Soc., 1982-92; dir. Plainfield Econ. Devel. Corp., 1984—; trustee DeCret Sch. of Arts, 1990—; vice chmn. Plainfield City Coun. Budget Adv. Com., 1992-94. N.J. State Council Arts grantee, 1979, 86. Mem. Indsl. Photographers Assn. N.J. (pres. 1976-77, award of Excellence), Internat. TV Assn., Am. Film Inst., Cen. Jersey C. of C., Internat. Platform Assn., Am. Coll. Forensic Examiners, Am. Bd. Recorded Evidence, Soc. Motion Picture and TV Engrs., Marco Polo Club (Chgo.). Avocations: travel, exploration, fishing. Home and Office: 718 Sherman Ave Plainfield NJ 07060-2232 E-mail: stuart.allen1@att.net.

ALLEN, SUZANNE, financial planning executive, insurance agent, writer, educator; b. Santa Monica, Calif., May 31, 1963; d. Raymond A. and Ethel Allen; m. Steve Milstein Roth, Dec. 27, 1992, (div. 2000). BA, U. Calif., Santa Cruz, 1986; MA in Edn., Calif. State U., L.A., 1990; postgrad., Art Ctr. Sch. Design, 1994—. Cert. tchr., Calif.; lic. real estate agt., Calif. Interviewer LA Times Newspaper, 1986-88; educator LA Unified Sch. Dist., 1987-90, Burbank Unified Sch. Dist., Calif., 1990-94, 1994—2000; ptnr. fin. svc. Roth & Assoc./NY Life, LA, 1993-2000; educator Pasadena Unified Sch. Dist., 2001—02; ptnr. fin. svc. Pacific Life Ins. Co.; v.p. Jarvis & Mandell LLC Estate Planning Svc., Mass. Mut. Ins. Co., 2001—; agt. Mass. Mut. Ins., Beverly Hills, Calif. Ptnr. Retirement Educators Fin. Svc.; agt.-cons. Frasier Fin. Group, 2001—02; bilingual program coord. Amadeo Spanish Lang. Enrichment Sch., 2004—. Model, actor:, 1998—; author: End of Days, 2001—; author: (pen name Quinn Allen) (poems) I Will Serve You All My Days, Black Dahlia, Alone, 2002, I Miss Him, 2003, Waiting for Godot, 2003, The Pasadena Porch, 2004, I'm Sad You Went Away, 2004, DNA Destiny, 2004, Disclaimer, 2004, Bless the Church, 2005. Mem. PTA, United Tchr. Pasadena, Civil War Trust; vol. SPCA/Humane Soc., 1999—; mem. Nat. Trust Hist. Preservation, Honor Roll mem.; bd. mem. Bungalow Heaven Neighborhood Assn.; hon. mem. Top Bus. Rep. Party for Sen. Tom Delany. Recipient 4 Silver Cups, Internat. Poet of Merit, 8 Bronze medals, Internat. Poets Soc., Piece of the Roof award, N.Y. Life Ins. Co. for Roth & Assocs., 1994, Nat. Leadership award, Nat. Rep. Congl. Com., 2003, Silver trophy Outstanding Achievement in Poetry, 2003, Silver trophy outstanding achievement in poetry, 2004, 2005. Mem.: NEA, Libr. of Congress, Nat. Soc. for Hist. Preservation, Burbank Tchrs. Union, Internat. High IQ Soc., Abraham Lincoln Assn., Internat. Soc. Poets (hon.). Avocations: painting, illustrating, writing, weight training, quilting. Office: Jarvis & Mandell LLC 1875 Century Park E # 1550 Los Angeles CA 90067 also: Michael's Agy Mass Mut Beverly Hills Office 1875 Century Park E # 1550 Los Angeles CA 90067 Office Phone: 626-296-8479.

ALLEN, TED, television personality; b. 1965; life ptnr. Barry Rice. Co-author: Things a Man Should Know About Marriage: A Groom's Guide to the Wedding and Beyond, 1999, Things a Man Should Know About Style, 1999, Things a Man Should Know About Sex, 2001, Things a Man Should Know About Handshakes, White Lies and Which Fork Goes Where, 2001, Queer Eye for the Straight Guy: The Fab 5's Guide to Looking Better, Cooking Better, Dressing Better, Behaving Better, and Living Better, 2004; co-author and contbg. editor: Things a Man Should Know column Esquire mag., contbg. author: Conde Nast Traveler, Travel & Leisure, GQ, Nat. Geog. Adventure, Self, Men's Jour., Women.Com, Chgo. Sun-Times; sr. editor and restaurant critic Chgo. mag., food and wine specialist (TV series) Queer Eye for the Straight Guy, 2003—. Office: William Morris Agy One William Morris Pl Beverly Hills CA 90212

ALLEN, TERRY DEVEREUX, retired urologist; b. Dallas, Nov. 28, 1930; s. Lester E. and Gladys (McIver) A.; m. Carolyn Latham, June 26, 1955; children: Kevin, Kathleen, Cheryl, Robin. Student, Rice U., 1951; MD, Baylor Med. Sch., 1955. Diplomate Am. Bd. Urology. Intern Jefferson Davis Hosp., Houston, 1955-56; attending physician Terrell (Tex.) State Hosp., 1958-59; resident surgery Parkland Meml. Hosp., Dallas, 1959-60, resident urology, 1960-63; pvt. practice Dallas Med./ Surg. Clinic, 1963-70; faculty Southwestern Med. Sch., Dallas, 1971-98. Mem., chair Residency Rev. Com., 1977-83; exec. com. mem. Am. Bd. Med. Specialties, 1992-94; trustee Am. Bd. Urology, 1985-91. Assoc. editor Jour. Urology, Balt., 1983-93; contbr. numerous articles to profl. jours., chpts. to books. Capt. USAF, 1956-58. Fellow ACS (gov.), Am. Acad. Pediatrics (urology, pres. 1984-85, Pediat. Urology medal 2002); mem. Soc. Univ. Urologists (sec., pres. 1985-86), Soc. Pediatric Urology (sect. pres. 1977-79, 81-83), Am. Urol. Assn. (Edn. award 1985, Hugh Hampton Young award 1990), Am. Assn. Genitourol. Surgeons (Harry Spence award 2003), Clin. Soc. GU Surgeons (pres. 2003-). Avocations: sailing, languages. Home: 9829 Elmcrest Dr Dallas TX 75238-1831 Office: Children's Med Ctr Bank One Tower 14th Fl 6300 Harry Hines Blvd Dallas TX 75235-5259

ALLEN, THAD W., military officer; s. Clyde and Wilma Allen; m. Pamela A. Hess; children: Amanda, Meghan, Lucas. Grad., US Coast Guard Acad., 1971; MPA, George Washington U.; MS, Sloan Sch. Mgmt., MIT. Previous flag assignments include commdg. the Seventh Coast Guard Dist., directing all Coast Guard ops. in SC, Ga., Fla., and the Caribbean; dir. resources US Coast Guard; comdr. Coast Guard Atlantic Area, Fifth Coast Guard Dist.; operational comdr. US Maritime Def. Zone, Atlantic; serves as Coast Guard transition dir.; chief of staff, US guard and commdg. officer Coast Guard Hdqs., Washington, 2002—. Specialist for Coast Guard cutters ANDROSCOGGIN, GALLATIN, CITRUS; coastal ops. assignments include Capt. of the Port Group Long Island Sound, Conn., Group Atlantic City, NJ, and LORAN Sta., Thailand; search and rescue controller Greater Antilles Sect., San Juan, PR; intelligence watch officer DEA/INS El Paso Intelligence Ctr., Tex.; chief budget officer Maintenance and Logistics Command, Atlantic, Governors Island, NY; dep. project mgr. Fleet Modernization and Rehabilitation (FRAM) Project; asst. divsn. chief, programs divsn., office of the chief of staff Coast Guard Hdqs. Recipient Disting. Alumni award, George Washington U., 2000. Office: Coast Guard Hdqs 2100 Second St SW Washington DC 20593*

ALLEN, THERESA OHOTNICKY, neurobiologist, consultant; b. Torrington, Conn., Apr. 27, 1948; d. Frank Richard and Helen Theresa (Drozdenko) Ohotnicky; m. Thomas Atherton Allen, Aug. 12, 1972; children: Melanie Atherton, Abigail Baldwin. BA, U. Conn., 1970; MS, Villanova U., 1975; PhD, Duke U., 1978; cert. in bus. adminstrn., U. Pa., 1983. Realtor. Rsch. assoc. U. Pa., Phila., 1981-83; sci. dir. Drexel U., Phila., 1983-84; cons. on neurobiology to sci.-oriented cos., 1984—. Contbr. articles to profl. jours., also chpts. to books. Bd. dirs. Gladwyne (Pa.) Libr. League, 1986—, Athena Inst. for Women's Wellness, Haverford, Pa., 1989-93; trustee Gladwyne Libr., 1988—, pres., 1991-93; com. chmn. Jr. League Phila., 1989-90. Fellow Inst. Neurol. Scis., U. Pa., 1978-80, NIH, 1980-81. Mem.: Phila. Country Club, Humane Soc., Phila. Skating Club, Phi Beta Kappa. Episcopalian. Avocations: skiing, gardening, antiques. Home: 1433 Waverly Rd Gladwyne PA 19035-1224

ALLEN, THOMAS DRAPER, lawyer; b. Detroit, June 25, 1926; s. Draper and Florence (Jones) A.; m. Joyce M. Johnson, July 18, 1953; children—Nancy A. Bowser, Robert D., Rebecca A. Hubbard. BS, Northwestern U., 1949; JD, U. Mich., 1952. Bar: Ill. 1952, U.S. Supreme Ct. 1971. Assoc. Kirkland & Ellis, Chgo., 1952-60, ptnr., 1961-67, Wildman, Harrold, Allen & Dixon, Chgo., 1967-96, of counsel, 1997—. Chmn. Community Caucus, Hinsdale, Ill., 1960-61; mem. Hinsdale Bd. Edn., 1965-71, pres., 1970-71; pres. West Suburban coun. Boy Scouts Am., 1980-82, mem. nat. exec. bd., 1986—, chmn. internat. com., 1995-99, mem. world program com., 1983-93; moderator Union Ch., Hinsdale, 1983-84; trustee Chgo. Theol. Sem., 1988-97, chair, 1990-96, life trustee, 1997—. With USN, 1944-46. Recipient Silver Beaver award Boy Scouts Am., 1964, Silver Buffalo award, 1997, Bronze Wolf award World Scout Orgn., 1993. Fellow Am. Coll. Trial Lawyers (state chair 1984-85, chair internat. com. 1997-99); mem. ABA, Ill. Bar Assn., Chgo. Bar Assn. (bd. of mgrs 1989-91), Law Club of Chgo., Legal Club of Chgo., Jaycees Internat. (senator, 1965), Internat. Bar Assn., Hinsdale Golf Club. Mem. United Ch. of Christ. Home: 505 N Lake Shore Dr Chicago IL 60611-3427 Office: Wildman Harrold Allen & Dixon 225 W Wacker Dr Chicago IL 60606-1224 Office Phone: 312-201-2630. Business E-Mail: allen@whad.com.

ALLEN, THOMAS E., obstetrician, gynecologist; b. Bairdford, Pa., July 2, 1919; s. Emerson Ray and Lillie Mabel (McIntyre) A.; m. Ruth Jenkins, 1943 (dec. 1991); m. Judi Cannava, 1995; children: Catherine, Christine, Cynthia, Carolyn, Thomas J., Candace. BS, U. Pitts., 1940, MD, 1943. Diplomate Am. Bd. Ob-Gyn. Rotating intern U. Pitts., 1944, assoc. clin. prof. ob-gyn. Sch. Medicine; resident in gynegology Magee Hosp., Pitts., 1944-45, resident in ob-gyn., 1948-51; gen. practice medicine Oakmont, Pa., 1947-48; practice medicine specializing in ob-gyn. Pitts., 1951—. Med. dir., co-founder Women's Health Service, Inc., Pitts., 1973-94, cons., 1994—; cons. ob-gyn Russelton Med. Group, New Kensington, Pa., 1953-73. Pres. Oakmont Sch. Bd., 1962-71; pres. bd. dirs. Am. Waterways Wind Orch., Pitts., 1970-93, chmn. bd. dirs., 1993—; bd. dirs. ACLU, Pitts., 1972-90. Served to capt. U.S. Army, 1945-47. Am. Legion and Buhl scholar, 1937. Fellow ACS, Am. Coll. Obstetricians and Gynecologists, Pan Pacific Surg. Assn., Pitts. Ob-gyn. Soc.; mem. AMA, county and state med. assns. Democrat. Avocations: cooking, music, reading, golf. Home: 301 Halket St Pittsburgh PA 15213-3104 Office: Planned Parenthood 933 Liberty Ave Pittsburgh PA 15222-3783 Office Phone: 412-687-5785. Personal E-mail: ccann19601@aol.com.

ALLEN, THOMAS H., congressman, lawyer; b. Portland, Maine, Apr. 16, 1945; s. Charles and Genevieve A.; m. Diana Bell; children: Gwen, Kate. BA, Bowdoin Coll., 1967; BPhil, Oxford U., 1970; JD, Harvard U., 1971. Atty. Drummond, Woodsum, Plimpton and MacMahon, Maine, 1974—94; mem. Portland (Maine) City Coun., 1989-95; mayor City of Portland, 1991-92; mem. U.S. Congress from 1st Maine dist., 1997—, armed svcs. com., energy & commerce com., dep. whip-at-large, former mem. govt. reform and oversight com., co-chair, affordable medicines task force & bipartisan house oceans caucus. Dem. candidate for Gov., State of Maine, 1994; chair Clinton/Gore campaign, Maine, 1992; mem. Pres. Clinton's Agrl. Transition Team; bd. overseers Bowdoin Coll.; bd. dirs. Shalom House, United Way; chair Gov. Joseph Brennan Task Force on Foster Care for Children; pres. Portland Stage Co.; mem. exec. and legis. policy coms. Maine Mcpl. Assn. Rhodes scholar Oxford U. Mem.: Phi Beta Kappa. Democrat. Office: US Ho of Reps 1127 Longworth Ho Off Bldg Washington DC 20515-0001 also: Dist Off 57 Exchange St Ste 302 Portland ME 04101 Business E-Mail: rep.tomallen@mail.house.gov.*

ALLEN, THOMAS JOHN, finance educator; b. Newark, Aug. 20, 1931; s. Thomas John and Margaret Ann (Conley) A.; m. Joan Marie Gilmartin, Jan. 28, 1961; children: Thomas John, Susan Marie, Máirín. BS, Upsala Coll., East Orange, N.J., 1954; postgrad., U. Wash., 1957-58; SM, MIT, 1963, PhD, 1966, D (hon.) in Bus. Adminstrn., 1966; D Mgmt. (hon.), Rijkuniversiteit Gent, Belgium, 1990; ScD (hon.), Chalmers U. Tech., Gothenburg, Sweden, 1992; D in Engring. (hon.), Linkoping U., Sweden, 1998; PhD (hon.), Ramon Llull U., Spain, 2003. Design engr. Tung-Sol Electric Co., Bloomfield, NJ, 1956-57; research engr. Boeing Co., Seattle, 1957-64; research assoc. MIT, Cambridge, 1963-66, assoc. chmn. faculty, 1983-85, MacVicar faculty fellow Cambridge, 1993—, dep. dean, Howard W. Johnson prof. mgmt., 1994—98, co-dir. Leader for Mfg. program, system design mgmt. program, 2003—. Disting. vis. prof. U. Coll. Dublin, Ireland, 1993; hon. mem. of faculty Chalmers U. of Tech., Gothenburg, Sweden, 1992—. Author: Managing the Flow of Technology, 1977; co-author (with M.S. Scott Morton) Information Technology and the Corporation of the 1990s, 1993, Lean Enterprise Value: Insights from MIT's Lean Aerospace Initiative, 2002 (Engring. Sci. Book award Internat. Acad. Astronautics 2003). Chmn. Cath.-Jewish Com., Boston, 1977-79; chmn. bd. Rosary Acad., Watertown, Mass., 1976-79; trustee Mt. St. Joseph Acad., Boston, 1992-98, 99-04. Served USMC, 1954—56. Hon. sr. rsch. fellow U. Manchester, 1970—; Macvicar Faculty fellow, MIT, 1993—; named disting. vis. prof. U. Coll. Dublin, Ireland, 1993. Fellow AAAS; mem. IEEE, Am. Psychol. Assn., Irish Am. Cultural Assn., Sigma Xi Office: Mass Inst Tech 77 Massachusetts Ave E52-536 Cambridge MA 02142-1347 E-mail: tallen@mit.edu.

ALLEN, TIM (TIMOTHY ALLEN DICK), actor, comedian; b. Denver, June 13, 1953; s. Gerald and Martha Dick; m. Laura Diebel, 1978; 1 child, Kady. Grad., Western Mich. U., 1975. Appeared in numerous Showtime spls.; actor: (TV series) Home Improvement, 1991-99 (Emmy award nomination, Lead actor - comedy 1993), exec. prodr., 1996-99, also writer; (films) The Santa Clause, 1994; (voice) Toy Story, 1995, Meet Wally Sparks, 1997, Jungle 2 Jungle, 1997, For Richer or Poorer, 1997, (voice) Toy Story 2, 1999, Galaxy Quest, 1999, Who is Cletis Tout, 2001, Joe Somebody, 2001, Big Trouble, 2002, The Santa Clause 2, 2002, Christmas with the Kranks, 2004; (TV spls.) Comedy's Dirtiest Dozen, 1988, exec. prodr. Men Are Pigs, 1991; author: I'm Not Really Here, 1996, Don't Stand Too Close to a Naked Man, 1994; TV guest appearances The Flying Doctors, 1985, The Drew Carey Show, 1995, The Front, 1996, Soul Man, 1997, The Larry Sanders Show, 1992, Spin City, 1996, (voice) The Adventures of Jimmy Neutron: Boy Genius, 2004; exec. com. TV series Home Improvement, 1991. Recipient Golden Globe, 1995, Favorite Comedy Actor People's Choice award, 1995,97, 98, 99, TV Guide award 1999; nominated for Golden Globe awards 1993, 94, 96, 97, Blockbuster Entertainment award 1998. Office: William Morris Agy 151 El Camino Dr Beverly Hills CA 90212 Address: care Messina Baker 955 S Carillo Dr Ste 100 Los Angeles CA 90048

ALLEN, TONI K., lawyer; b. NYC, Aug. 6, 1940; d. Irving M. and Mary (Sackler) Schoolman; m. Robert W. Clark III, July 22, 1985. AB, Wellesley Coll., 1960; LLB, NYU, 1964. Bar: NY 1964, DC 1972. Atty. Office of Irving M. Wall, Esquire, N.Y.C., 1964-68; gen. counsel, asst. to pres. Nat. Econ. Rsch. Assocs., N.Y.C., 1968-71; atty., advisor Postal Rate Commn., Washington, 1971-72; assoc. Wald, Harkrader & Ross, Washington, 1972-73, ptnr., 1974-85, Piper & Marbury LLP, Washington, 1986-98, chmn. environ. dept., 1991-94, mem. policy and mgmt. com., 1992-94, ptnr. emeritus, 1999—. Adj. fellow Hudson Inst., 2001—. Trustee Levine Sch. Music, Washington, 1981—2004, pres., 1991-96; co-chair exec. bd. Environ. Lawyer, 1994-96, Leadership Washington, 1996-97; bd. dirs., 2003—, vice chair United Way of the Nat. Capital Area, 2003—05, treas. 2005- . Fellow Am. Bar Found.; mem. Order of Coif. Democrat. Avocations: sports, music, travel, cooking. E-mail: tka5640@aol.com.

ALLEN, VICKY L., secondary school educator; b. Enid, Okla., Jan. 8, 1954; d. Clyde and Carolyn Pollard Allen; children: Jeremey J. Phelan, Maleah L. Meloy. BS, Okla. State U., 1976, MS, 1981. Tchr. Covington (Okla.)-Douglas H.S., 1976—85, Hennessey (Okla.) H.S., 1985—87, Crescent (Okla.) H.S., 1987—97, Wylie (Tex.) H.S., 1997—99, Tonkawa (Okla.) H.S., 1999—2002, Kingfisher (Okla.) H.S., 2002—. Alt. No. Okla. Regional Speech Bd., Alva, 2003—; Oklahoma State Cross-Examination Debate Coach; Oklahoma All-State Academic Coach; Oklahoma All-State Speech Coach. Mem.: NEA (assoc.), Ctrl. Okla. Acad. Coaches Assn. (pres. 2004—), Nat. Music Educator's Assn. (assoc.), Okla. Music Educator's Assn. (assoc.), Okla. Edn. Assn. (assoc.), Sigma Alpha Iota (assoc.). Republican. Methodist. Avocations: music, reading, gardening. Home: RR 3 Box 49 Hennessey OK 73742 Office: Kingfisher Public Schools 1500 S 13th St Kingfisher OK 73750 Office Phone: 405-375-4191.

ALLEN, WALTER RECHARDE, sociology educator; b. Kansas City, Mo., Feb. 3, 1949; s. Grady Lee and Freddie Mae (Clayton) A.; m. Wilma Jean Sharber, Sept. 26, 1970; children: Rena Marie, Binti Tamarra, Bryan Recharde. BA, Beloit (Wis.) Coll., 1971; MA, U. Chgo., 1973, PhD, 1975. Asst. prof. sociology U. N.C., Chapel Hill, 1974-79; asst. prof. sociology, Afro-Am. and African studies U. Mich., Ann Arbor, 1979-84, assoc. prof. sociology, Afro-Am. and African studies, 1985-88, assoc. dir. Cen. for Afro-Am. Studies, 1987-89, dir. Nat. Study Black Coll. Students, 1979-89, prof. sociology Afro-Am. and African studies, 1989-91; prof. sociology UCLA, 1989—, assoc. dir. Robert Wood Johnson clin. scholars program, Sch. Medicine, 1992—. Co-author: The Colorline and the Quality of Life, 1987; co-editor: (book) Beginnings: Development of Black Children, 1985, College in Black and White, 1991; (bibliography) Black Families, 1965-80, 1986. Recipient distinguished leadership award United Negro Coll. Fund, 1985; Rockefeller Found. fellow, 1982-83, Fulbright scholar, 1984, 86-87; named Allerton Lectr. U. Ill., 1988. Mem. Internat. Sociol. Assn., Am. Sociol. Assn. (coun. 1991-94), Am. Ednl. Rsch. Assn. (disting. scholar 1987, rsch. excellence award, 1993), APHA, Assn. Black Sociologists (pres. 1992, disting. career award 1995), Population Assn. Am., Sociol. Rsch. Assn., Phi Delta Kappa. Baptist. Avocations: reading, travel, swimming, gardening. Office: UCLA Dept Sociology 405 Hilgard Ave Los Angeles CA 90095-9000

ALLEN, WILLIAM CECIL, physician, educator; b. LaBelle, Mo., Sept. 8, 1919; s. William H. and Viola O. (Holt) A.; m. Madge Marie Gehardt, Dec. 25, 1943; children: William Walter, Linda Diane Allen Deardeuff, Robert Lee, Leah Denise Rogers. AB, U. Nebr., 1947, MD, 1951; M.P.H., Johns Hopkins U., 1960. Diplomate Am. Bd. Preventive Medicine. Intern Bishop Clarkson Meml. Hosp., Omaha, 1952; practice medicine specializing in family practice Glasgow, Mo., 1952-59; specializing in preventive medicine Columbia, Mo., 1960—; dir. sect. chronic diseases Mo. Div. Health, Jefferson City, 1960-65; asst. med. dir. U. Mo. Med. Ctr., 1965-75; assoc. coordinator Mo. Regional Med. Program, 1968-73, coordinator health programs, 1969—, clin. asst. prof. community health and med. practice, 1962-65, asst. prof. community health and med. practice, 1965-69, assoc. prof., 1969-75, prof., 1975-76, prof. dept. family and community medicine, 1976-87, prof. emeritus, 1987—. Cons. Mo. Regional Med. Program, 1966-67, Norfolk Area Med. Sch. Authority, Va., 1965-66; governing body Area II Health Systems Agy., 1977-79, mem. coordinating com., 1977-79; founding dir. Mid-Mo. PSRO Corp., 1974-79, dir., 1976-84. Contbr. articles to profl. jours. Mem. Gov.'s Adv Coun. for Comprehensive Health Planning, 1970-73; trustee U. Mo. Med. Sch. Found., 1976—2004. Served with USMC, 1943-46. Fellow Am. Coll. Preventive Medicine, Am. Acad. Family Physicians (sci. program com. 1972-75, commn. on edn. 1975-80), Royal Soc. Health; mem. Mo. Acad. Family Physicians (dir. 1956-59, 76-82, alt. del. 1982-87, pres. 1985-86, chmn. bd. 1986-87), Mo. Med. Assn., Howard County Med. Soc. (pres. 1958-59), Boone County Med. Soc. (pres. 1974-75), Am. Diabetes Assn. (pres. 1978, dir. 1974-77), Mo. Diabetes Assn. (pres. 1972-73), Soc. Tchrs. Family Medicine, AMA, Mo. Public Health Assn., Am. Heart Assn. (program com. 1979-82), Am. Heart Assn. of Mo. (sec. 1980-81), Mo. Heart Assn. (sec. 1979-82, pres.-elect 1982-84, pres. 1984-86). Methodist. Office: U Mo M218 Medical Ctr Columbia MO 65203

ALLEN, WILLIAM HAYES, lawyer, educator; b. Palo Alto, Calif., Oct. 19, 1926; s. Ben Shannon and Victoria Rose (French) A.; m. Joan Webster Emmett, July 16, 1950; children: Edwin Hayes, Neal French, William Kent. Student, Deep Springs Coll., 1942-44; BA with gt. distinction, Stanford U., 1948, LLB, 1956. Bar: D.C. 1958. Corr. AP, Fresno, Calif., 1948-49, newsman Sacramento, 1950-53; law clk. to Chief Justice Earl Warren U.S. Supreme Ct., Washington, 1956-57; assoc. Covington & Burling, Washington, 1957-64, ptnr., 1964-92; ret., 1993—. Acting. prof. Stanford U. Law Sch., 1979; adj. prof. Howard U. Law Sch., 1981—83; lectr. George Mason U. Law Sch., 1983—86; practitioner-in-residence Cornell U. Law Sch., 1992; vis. prof. Deep Springs Coll., 1973, 96; chmn. jud. rev. com. Adminstrv. Conf. U.S., 1972—82, sr. conf. fellow, 1982—95; mem. steering com. Nat. Prison Project, 1975—93. Pres. Stanford Law Rev., vol. 8, 1955-56; contbr. articles to legal jours. Trustee Deep Springs Coll., 1984-92, chmn. bd. trustees, 1992; mem. Fair Housing Bd., Arlington County, Va., 1974-79. With U.S. Army, 1945-47. Mem. ABA (mem. coun. adminstrv. law sect. 1969-72, 79-81, chmn. 1982-83), D.C. Bar (chmn. legal ethics com. 1976-78), Am. Law Inst., Am. Acad. of Appellate Lawyers, Order of Coif, Cosmos Club. Democrat. Mem. United Ch. of Christ. Office: Covington & Burling 1201 Pennsylvania Ave NW Washington DC 20004-2401 Office Phone: 202-662-5420. Personal E-mail: billthedog2001@comcast.net. Business E-Mail: wallen@cov.com.

ALLEN, WILLIAM JERE, minister; b. Greenville, Miss., Apr. 23, 1934; s. Marion Goodman and Gradie Lee (Yates) A.; m. Lorena Faye Franklin, June 24, 1960; children: Lorena Lynn Brickson, Jennifer Dawn Moradi, William Jere Allen Jr. B of Bldg. Constrn., Auburn U., 1956; BDiv, So. Bapt. Theol. Sem., 1963; DMin, Union Theol. Sem., 1973. Ordained to ministry First Bapt. Ch., 1960. Pastor 45th Street Mission, Ashland, Ky., 1959-60, Rose Hill Bapt. Ch., Ashland, 1960-62, Colonial Ave. Bapt. Ch., Roanoke, Va., 1962-67, Bainbridge St. Bapt. Ch., Richmond, Va., 1967-71, Bainbridge Southampton Bapt. Ch., Richmond, 1972-75; cons., dir. spl. missions dept. Ala. Bapt. State Conv., Montgomery, 1975-79; assoc. then dir. met. mission dept. Home Mission Bd., So. Bapt. Conv., Atlanta, 1979-91; exec. dir., min. D.C. Bapt. Conv., Washington, 1992-2000; interim pastor Calvary Bapt. Ch., Washington, 2001—03. Mega focus cities cons. Home Mission Bd., So. Bapt. Conv., Atlanta, 1982—2002. Co-author: Shaping a Future for Church in Changing Community, 1981, Church and Community Diagnostic Workbook, 1986; author: (with others) Shooting the Rapids: Efective Ministry in a Changing World, 1990, Faith and Social Ministry: Ten Christian Perspectives, 1990. Capt. USAF, 1956—62. Baptist. Avocations: jogging, reading, family travel, golf. Home: 3041 Chestnut St NW Washington DC 20015-1407

ALLEN, WILLIAM L., editor; Student, Ga. Inst. Tech.; BA in Govt., La. State U. Intern Ctr. for Strategic & Internat. Studies, Washington, 1964—66; with Nat. Geog., 1969—, editor Washington, 1995—2005. Bd. dir. Inst. on Nautical Archaeology, Nat. Geog. Soc., Inst. of Nautical Archaeology, Teton Sci. Sch.; mem. Coun. on Fgn Rels. Mem. Cosmos Club, Washington; bd. dirs. Nat. Geog. Ednl. Found., Nat. Space Biomed. Rsch. Inst., World Wildlife Fund. Lt. U.S. Army, Korea. H.B. Earhart fellow, Georgetown U.

ALLEN, WILLIAM MARION, III, retired graphics designer, artist; b. Ft. Worth, July 10, 1927; s. William Marion and Lucile Beasley Allen. Student, Southwestern U., 1944-45, Tex. Christian U., 1945-46; BFA, U. Tex., 1950; postgrad., UCLA, 1954; MFA, U. So. Calif., 1955. Art tchr. El Paso Pub. Schs., 1950-51; illustrator Ramo Wooldridge Corp., L.A., 1956-58, Space Tech. Labs., L.A., 1958-60; graphic design coord. The Aerospace Corp., L.A., 1960-89; ret., 1989. One-man shows include Comara Gallery, L.A., 1975, 76, Art Gallery-The Aerospace Corp., L.A., 1982, Atrium Gallery, U. North Tex. Health Sci. Ctr., 1999; exhibited in group shows including Long Beach Mus. Art, Calif. State Fair, Chico State Coll., Tex. Fine Arts Assn., Butler Inst. Am. Art, Youngstown, Ohio, Ft. Worth Art Assn., L.A. Art Assn., also others. With U.S. Army, 1951-53, PTO. Recipient Cash award 18th Annual Artists Show, Ft. Worth, 1957, Purchase award 19th Annual Tex. State Fair, Dallas Mus. Art, 1957, Cash award 22nd Annual Local Artists Show, Ft. Worth, Award of Merit, Mus. N.Mex. Art Show, Santa Fe, 1959, Bertram M. Newhouse award 1st prize oil 27th Annual Local Artists Show, Ft. Worth, 1967, Third award contemporary So. Calif. Exbhn., Del Mar, Calif., 1967, Buza Cardoza Cash award 52nd Annual Calif. Nat. Watercolor Soc., 1972, Award of Merit, Templeton June Show, Ft. Worth, 1992, Award of Merit, 1996 Main St., 11th Annual Festival Exhbn., Ft. Worth, 1996, Cash award, Arches Paper award, Nat. Watercolor Soc. 77th Annual Exhbn., L.A., 1998, cash award 500X Gallery, Expo '98, Dallas, 1998. Mem. Nat. Watercolor Soc., Soc. Watercolor Artists (cash award 7th ann. membership exhbn. Ft. Worth 1998, 8th ann. juried exhbn. 1998, 18th juried exhcn. 1999, 1st place cash award mems. juried exhbn. 1999, 20th Anniversary Show Juried Competition Merit award 2001). Avocations: gardening, travel. Home: 3754 Somerset Ln Fort Worth TX 76109-3555 E-mail: dockwatch@home.com.

ALLEN, WILLIAM RICHARD, retired economist; b. Eldorado, Ill., Apr. 3, 1924; s. Oliver Boyd and Justa Lee (Wingo) A.; m. Frances Lorraine Swoboda, Aug. 15, 1948 (dec.); children: Janet Elizabeth, Sandra Lee. AB, Cornell Coll., Iowa, 1948; PhD, Duke U., 1953. Faculty, Washington U., St. Louis, 1951-52; faculty UCLA, 1952—, prof., 1963-91, prof. emeritus, 1991—. Vis. prof. Northwestern U., 1952, U. Wis., 1964, U. Mich., 1965, So. Ill. U., 1969, Tex. A&M, 1971-73; cons. Dept. Commerce, 1962; v.p. Found. Rsch. in Econs. and Edn., 1971-73; pres. Internat. Inst. Econ. Rsch., 1974-86; v.p. Inst. for Contemporary Studies, 1986-90; assoc. Reason Found., 1990-92; econs. corr. Calif. Polit. Rev., 1992-2002; newspaper, mag. columnist; nationally syndicated radio commentator, 1979-92. Author: (with others) Foreign Trade and Finance, 1959, Essays in Economic Thought, 1960, University Economics, 3d edit., 1972, Exchange and Production, 3d edit., 1983, International Trade Theory, 1965, Midnight Economist, 1981, vol. 2, 1989, vol. 3, 1997; mem. adv. bd.: History of Polit. Economy, 1969-84, Social Sci. Quar., 1975-2003; contbr. articles to profl. jours. Served with USAAF, 1943-46. Social Sci. Research Council grantee, 1950-51, 62; Ford Found. grantee, 1958-59, 72-74; NSF grantee, 1965-66; Earhart Found. grantee, 1972, 74-75 Mem. Western Econ. Soc. (pres. 1970-71), So. Econ. Assn. (v.p. 1978-79), History of Econs. Soc. (v.p. 1974-75), Phi Beta Kappa. Home: 11809 Allaseba Dr Los Angeles CA 90066-1112 Office Phone: 310-825-1011. Business E-Mail: allen@econ.ucla.edu. E-mail: midnightecon@cs.com.

ALLEN, WILLIAM SHERIDAN, retired social sciences educator; b. Evanston, Ill., Oct. 5, 1932; s. William S. and Rose (Brahm) Allen; m. Karen Miller, Jan. 9, 1982; children: Caitilyn, Jefferson, Rebecca, Claire. AB, U. Mich., 1955; MA, U. Conn., 1956; PhD, U. Minn., 1962. Instr. history Bay City (Mich.) Jr. Coll., 1957-58; instr. humanities MIT, Cambridge, Mass., 1960-61; asst. prof. history U. Mo., Columbia, 1961-65, assoc. prof., 1966-67, Wayne State U., Detroit, 1967-70; prof. SUNY, Buffalo, 1970-2001, chmn. history dept., 1987-90. Vis. prof. U. Mich., Ann Arbor, 1967; cons. Time-Life Books, Alexandria, Va., 1988—89. Author: (book) The Nazi Seizure of Power, 1984; editor, translator: book The Infancy of Nazism, 1976; contbr. articles to profl. jours. V.p. Holocaust Resources Ctr., Buffalo, 1985—90; publicity chmn. Buffalo Group Amnesty Internat., 1985—87; dir. Parkside Fed. Credit Union, Buffalo, 1986—87. Fellow, Alexander von Humboldt Found., 1965—66, NEH, 1979. Mem.: United Univ. Profs. (pres. Buffalo chpt. 1978—81), N.Y. State Assn. European Historians (pres. 1983—84), Am. Conf. Irish Studies. Avocations: sailing, gardening.

ALLEN, WILLIAM THOMAS, law educator; b. Phila., July 17, 1944; s. E. William and Mary E. (Graef) Allen; m. Ruth Horowitz, June 28, 1981. BS, NYU, 1969; JD, U. Tex., 1972; LLD (hon.), Dickinson Law Sch., Pa. State U. Law clk. to Hon. Walter King Stapleton US Dist. Ct. Dist. Del., Wilmington, 1972-74; assoc. Morris, Nichols, Arsht & Tunnell, Wilmington, 1974-79, partner, 1979-85; chancellor Ct. Chancery, State of Del., Wilmington, 1985-97; Nusbaum prof. law & bus. NYU Sch. Law & Stern Sch. Bus., NYC, dir. Ctr. for Law and Bus., 1997—; of counsel Wachtell, Lipton, Rosen & Katz, NYC, 1997—. Flegler vis. prof. Stanford Law Sch., 1989, 93; adj. prof. law U. Pa. Law Sch., 1991-93, 95; Raben lectr. Yale Law Sch., 1996. Trustee U. Del., Newark, 1997. Recipient Chief Justice Award for Jud. Svc., Del. Supreme Ct., 1997. Fellow Am. Acad. Arts & Sciences; mem. AICPA (chmn. Independence Standards Bd. 1997-2000), ABA, Del. Bar Assn., Am. Law Inst., Am. Economics Assn. Office: NYU Stern Sch Bus Kaufman Mgmt Ctr 44 W 4th St New York NY 10012-1126 also: NYU Sch Law Vanderbilt Hall Rm 336B 40 Washington Sq S New York NY 10012-1099 Office Phone: 212-998-6327. E-mail: allenw@juris.law.nyu.edu.*

ALLEN, WOODY (ALLEN STEWART KONIGSBERG), director, actor, writer; b. N.Y.C., Dec. 1, 1935; s. Martin and Nettie (Cherry) Konigsberg; m. Harlene Rosen, 1954 (div. 1960); m. Louise Lasser, 1964 (div. 1969); ptnr. Mia Farrow; 1 child, Satchel; adopted children: Moses, Dylan; m. Soon-Yi Previn, 1997; adopted children: Bechet, Manzie Tio Student, NYU, 1953, CCNY, 1953. Writer TV comedy for Sid Caesar, 1957, Art Carney, 1958-59, Herb Shriner, 1953; appeared in numerous nightclubs, TV shows, from 1961; author screenplay, also appeared in motion picture What's New Pussycat?, 1964-65; screenplay, dir., actor Take the Money and Run, 1969, Bananas, 1971, What's Up Tiger Lily?, 1966, Everything You Always Wanted to Know About Sex But Were Afraid to Ask, 1972, Sleeper, 1973, Love and Death, 1975, The Front, 1976, Manhattan (Brit. Acad. award 1979, N.Y. Film Critics award), Stardust Memories, 1980; writer, dir., prodr., actor films Annie Hall, 1977 (N.Y. Film Critics Circle award for Best Dir. and Best Screenplay 1977, Acad. awards for best film, best direction, Nat. Soc. Film Critics Screenwriting award), Zelig, 1983, Broadway Danny Rose, 1984, Hannah and Her Sisters, 1986 (Acad. award for best screenplay, D.W. Griffith award for best dir. Nat. Bd. Rev. of Motion Pictures), New York Stories (Oedipus Wrecks segment), 1989, Mighty Aphrodite, 1995 (Acad. award nominee for best screenplay 1996), Everyone Says I Love You, 1996, Deconstructing Harry, 1997, Count Mercury Goes to the Suburbs, 1997, Celebrity, 1998, Sweet and Lowdown, 1999, Small Town Crooks, 2000, The Curse of the Jade Scorpion, 2001, Hollywood Ending, 2002, Anytyhing Else, 2003; writer, dir., narrator film Radio Days, 1987; screenplay, dir. films Interiors, 1978, Purple Rose of Cairo, 1985, A Midsummer Night's Sex Comedy, 1982, September, 1987, Another Woman, 1988, Crimes and Misdemeanors, 1989, Alice, 1990, Shadows and Fog, 1992, Husbands and Wives, 1992, Manhattan Murder Mystery, 1993, Bullets Over Broadway, 1994, Mighty Aphrodite, 1995; dir. Melinda and Melinda, 2004; author play: Don't Drink the Water, 1966 (actor, dir. of TV movie, 1994), The Floating Lightbulb, 1981, (one act) Death Defying Acts, 1995, Sounds from a Town I Love (TV movie), 2001; play, screenplay Play It Again, Sam, 1969, film, 1972; actor, film King Lear, 1988, Scenes From a Mall, 1990, Cannes...les 400 coups, 1997, Waiting for Woody, 1998, Impostors, 1998, AFI's 100 Years...100 Movies, 1998, Antz, 1998, Wild Man Blues, 1998, Stuck on You, 1998, Company Man, 1999 Picking Up the Pieces, 1999; author: Getting Even, 1971, Without Feathers, 1975, Side Effects, 1980; guest appearances (TV) Just Shoot Me, The Tonight Show; writer, director (off broadway play) A Second Hand Memory, 2004; contbr. numerous pieces to Playboy, New Yorker, other mags. Recipient Sylvania award, 1957; Spl. award Berlin Film Festival, 1975; nominated for Emmy award as TV writer, 1957 Democrat.

ALLEN-CASTELLITTO, ANITA LAFRANCE, law educator; b. Ft. Warden, Wash., Mar. 24, 1953; d. Grover Cleveland Allen and Carrye Mae Cloud; m. Michael Kelly Williams, June 1982 (div. Mar. 1985); m. Paul Vincent Castellitto, June 7, 1985; children: Adam Peter Castellitto, Ophelia Anne Castellitto. BA, New Coll., 1974; MA, PhD, U. Mich., 1978; JD, Harvard U., 1984. Bar: NY 85, Pa. 85. Prof. philosophy Carnegie-Mellon U., Pitts., 1978—81; lawyer Cravath, Swaine & Moore, N.Y.C., 1984—85; prof. law U. Pitts., 1985—87; prof. Georgetown Law Ctr., Washington, 1987—96, assoc. dean, 1996—98; prof. U. Pa., Phila., 1998—2004, Henry R. Silverman Prof. Law, 2004—. Mem. adv. bd. Nat. Inst. for Human Genome Rsch., Washington, 1994—98, Electronic Privacy Info. Ctr., Washington, 1998—2002, Bazelon Ctr. for Mental Health Law, Washington, 2002—. Author: Uneasy Access: Privacy, 1988, Why Privacy Isn't Everything, 2003, The New Ethics: A Tour of the 21st Century Landscape, 2004; co-author: Privacy Law, 2002; co-editor: Debating Democracy's Discontent, 1998. Bd. dirs. Planned Parenthood, N.Y.C., 1992—97, Washington, 1992—97, New Coll. Found., Sarasota, Fla., 1990—95; mem. exec. com. Assn. Am. Law Schs., Washington, 1999—2002. Ford Found. fellow, N.Y., 1974—78, law and pub. affairs fellow, Princeton U., 2003—. Avocation: gardening. Office: Univ Pa Law Sch 3400 Chestnut St Philadelphia PA 19104 Office Fax: 215-573-2025.*

ALLENDER, JOHN ROLAND, lawyer; b. Boone, Iowa, Oct. 22, 1950; s. John S. and C. Corinne (Hayes) A.; m. Patti Allender; children: Susan A., Andrew J. BS, Iowa State U., 1972; JD, U. San Diego, 1975; LLM in Taxation, NYU, 1976. Bar: Calif. 1976, Tex. 1977, U.S. Ct. Claims 1977, U.S. Tax. Ct. 1977, U.S. Dist. Ct. (so. dist.) Tex. 1977. Assoc. Fulbright & Jaworski LLP, Houston, 1976-83, ptnr., 1983—, and head, tax dept. Mem. adv. commn. Tex. Bd. Legal Specialization, 1986-2000. Bd. dirs. Ronald McDonald House, Houston, 1991-, pres. 2003-05; adv. dir. Cath. Charities, Houston/Galveston. Mem. State Bar of Tex. (chmn. sect. taxation 1990), Houston Bar Assn. (chmn. sect. taxation 1979). Office: Fulbright & Jaworski Ste 5100 1301 McKinney St Houston TX 77010-3031 Office Phone: 713-651-5151. Office Fax: 713-651-5246. Business E-Mail: jallender@fulbright.com.

ALLEN-SCERBO, SUSAN LYNN, secondary education educator, counselor; b. Morristown, N.J., Apr. 15, 1950; d. Harry Moore and Rosemary (Griffin) A. BA, Monclair State U., 1972; MA, Fairleigh Dickinson U., 1978. Cert. drug and alcohol counselor; cert. tchr., N.J. Tchr. Bernards Twp. Bd. Edn., Basking Ridge, N.J., 1972—; mental health counselor St. Clares Hosp., Denville, N.J., 1987-93; pvt. practice counselor Mendham, N.J., 1991—. Mem. CORE team Ridge H.S., Basking Ridge, 1987—. Instr. ARC, Somerset County, N.J.; legis. chair Bernard Twp. Edn. Assn., Somerset County, N.J., 1994—, v.p., 1996-98, del., 1998, pres., 2001—. Gymnastics State Champion Tenn., 1970; named Counselor of yr., Somerset County, N.J., 1998. Mem. Nat. Assn. Alcohol and Drug Counselors, N.J. Assn. Alcohol and Drug Abuse Counselors. Avocations: softball, tennis, swimming, golf, gardening. Home and Office: 139 Mendham Rd E Mendham NJ 07945-3016 Fax: 973-543-1671.

ALLER, WAYNE KENDALL, psychologist, educator, computer company executive, property manager; b. Slyvia, Kans., Feb. 20, 1933; s. Alvin Ray and Florence Dorothy (Snowbarger) A.; m. Sharon Cecelia Forray, Aug. 21, 1962 (div.); children: Jay Ramzi, Joyce Amal; m. Sonia Y. Konialian, Apr. 8, 1969 BA in Physics, N.W. Nazarene Coll., Nampa, Idaho, 1955; MS in Psychology, U. Wash., 1960, PhD in Psychology, 1964. Asst. prof. psychology Pacific Lutheran U., 1962-64; asst. prof., chmn. divsn. behavioral scis. Beirut Coll. for Women, 1964-67; assoc. prof. Mankato State Coll., Minn., 1967-68, Ind. State U., Terre Haute, from 1968, prof., to 1985; pres. Learning Unlimited, 1983—, CompuLearn, 1983-87. Adj. prof. psychology Calif. State U., Northridge, 1984-2003; sr. rsch. adv. Ctr. Ednl. R&D, Ministry Planning, Republic Lebanon, Beirut, 1974-75; sr. rsch. assoc. Ctr. Behavioral Rsch., Am. U. of Beirut, 1974-75; vis. scholar dept. psychology UCLA, 1982-83; cons. English as fgn. lang. Vietnamese Affairs Ctr., Terre Haute, 1976-78. Author: Readings and Experiments in General Psychology, 1970, rev. edit., 1971 Pres. Knollwood Property Owners Assn., 2002—; bd. mem. Granada Hills North Neighborhood Coun., 2002—; sec., bd. trustees Knollwood United Methodist Ch., 2004; sec. City of L.A. Sunshine Canyon Landfill Tech. Adv. Com., 2004—. Ford Found. grantee, 1974-75 Mem. Western Psychol. Assn., N.Y. Acad. Scis., Soc. for Computers in Psychology, Computer Users Speech and Hearing, Wabash Valley Apple Byters Club (Terre Haute)(pres. 1981-82), Sigma Xi, Psi Chi, Sigma Phi Iota. Methodist. Home: 12045 Susan Dr Granada Hills CA 91344-2642 E-mail: wayneaaller07@hotmail.com.

ALLERHAND, JOSEPH S., lawyer; b. Bklyn., Aug. 10, 1953; BA, Columbia U., 1975; JD, Georgetown U. Law Ctr., 1978. Bar: NY 1979, US Dist. Ct. (Ea. and So. Districts NY) 1979, US Ct. Appeals (8th Cir.) 1984, US Ct. Appeals (2nd Cir.) 1985, US Ct. Appeals (3rd Cir.) 1986, US Ct. Appeals (6th Cir.) 1992. Law clerk ti Hon. David N. Edelstein, 1978—80; ptnr., co-head bus. and securities litigation dept. Weil, Gotshal & Manges LLP, NYC. Lectr. in field. Mem. Georgetown Jour., 1977—78; contbr. articles to profl. jours. Bd. dir. NY Legal Assistance Corp., Big Brother/Big Sisters NY, UJA Fedn. NY; pres. UJA Fedn. NY Lawyer's Divsn.; founder, bd. dir. Solomon Schechter Sch. Manhattan. Mem.: Fed. Bar Coun., ABA. Office: Weil, Gotshal & Manges LLP 767 Fifth Ave New York NY 10153 Office Phone: 212-310-8725. Office Fax: 212-310-8007. Business E-Mail: joseph.allerhand@weil.com.

ALLERTON, WILLIAM, III, public relations executive; b. New Orleans, June 20, 1951; s. William Jr. and Marion (Helmstetter) A.; m. Constance Rose Driscoll, Dec. 18, 1971; children: Amy Elizabeth, Timothy Daniel, Sean Patrick, Colleen Rose. Student, U. New Orleans, 1969-73; fellow, Loyola U. Inst. Politics, 1980-81. Pres. Capitol Pub. Rels., 1978-86; chmn., CEO Capitol Comm., New Orleans, 1986—; with office presdl. advance White House, 1990-93. Dir. Advertisers Legis. Action Council, Baton Rouge, 1985-86; bus. ptnr. Benjamin Franklin High Sch. New Orleans Pub. Schs., 1987—; bd. dirs. Inst. Politics Loyola U.; del. White House Conf. on Small Bus., Washington, 1995. Participant Met. Area Com. Tulane U., 1978; apptd. mem. nat. adv. com. U.S. SBA, 1989-93; mem. La. State Bd. Elem. and Secondary Edn. Non-Pub. Sch. Commn., 1986—, Nat. Coun. Trustees Freedoms Found. at Valley Forge, 1989—, La. Commn. on the Bicentennial of U.S. Constn., 1986-91; vice-chmn. Marine Corps Scholarship Fund Leatherneck Ball, 1986; vice chmn. 83d Anniversary Dinner of Navy League of U.S., 1987; mem. exec. com. Archbishops Cmty. Appeal, 1975-85; mem. U.S. adv. coun. SBA dist., La., 1973-76; mem. Mayor's Coun. Youth Opportunity, New Orleans, 1969-70; dist. chmn. New Orleans coun. Boy Scouts Am., 1992-93, mem. exec. bd., 1990—, chmn. centennial pledge of allegiance salute, 1992, coun. activities chmn., 1992—, mem. exec. com., 1992—, mem. nat. coun., 1994—, New Orleans coun. commr., 1995—; bd. dirs. La. State Mus., 1988-94; participant Columbia U. Am. Assembly, 1989; chmn. La. Com. George Washington Bicentennial, 1999; mem. La. State Mineral Bd., 1996—, La. State Tech. Adv. Com., 1997—. Recipient Addy award Am. Advt. Fedn., 1983, Tops award Dallas Advt. League, 1983, George Washington Honor medal Freedoms Found. at Valley Forge, 1989, Friends of Edn. award La. Fedn. Tchrs., 1989, Presdl. Recognition Office Nat. Svc., Points of Light Found., 1992, Silver Beaver award Boy Scouts Am., 1992; James E. West Fellowship award, 1994, Cathedral award Archdiocese of New Orleans Cath. Com. on Scouting, 1995. Mem. Am. Assn. Polit. Cons. (Media Excellence awards 1984, 86, 88, 98), So. Polit. Sci. Assn., Acad. Polit. Sci., Soc. for U.S. Constn., U.S. Capitol Hist. Soc., Ctr. for Study of the Presidency, Assn. Descendants Isaac Allerton Mayflower, Order of Arrow (Chilantakoba lodge). Office: Capitol Comm PO Box 791348 New Orleans LA 70179-1348

ALLEVA, PAULA SAVINO, principal, elementary school educator; b. N.Y.C., Mar. 17, 1924; d. Leonardo and Rosa (D'Amato) S.; m. Albert Alleva, July 1, 1951; children: Anthony A., Rosalinda. BA, Hunter Coll., N.Y.C., 1945; MS in Ednl. Adminstrn., Pace U., 1974; MA in Elem. Edn., Columbia U., 1983, EdD, 1984. Cert. ednl. adminstr., supr.; lic. prin. Tchr. in algebra and Italian Jr. H.S. 128 and 281, Bklyn., 1959—73; dist. coord. bilingual, ESL and fgn. langs. in 30 schs. Dist. 21, Bklyn., 1973-79; edn. cons./evaluator U.S. Office of Edn., Washington, 1973—95; edn. adminstr. Sch. Improvement Project, N.Y.C., 1979-82; asst. prin. P.S. 290 K, Bklyn., 1982-84; prin. P.S. 214 K, Bklyn., 1984—. Adj. prof. Bklyn. Coll., L.I. U., 1976—82; cons./evaluator HEW, Washington, 1976—96. Named to Hunter Coll. Hall of Fame, 1985; recipient Star of Solidarity award, Republic Italy, 1977, Ednl. Achievement award, Am. Commn. on Italian Migration, 1978, Italian Am. Nat. Hall of Fame award, 1977; Fulbright-Hays scholar, U. Rome, 1971. Mem.: AAUW, Columbia Assn. of Bd. Edn., Italian Tchrs. Assn. (treas.-sec.), Ret. Sch. Suprs. and Adminstrs. (exec. bd. 1987—), Assn. Italian Am. Educators (Lifetime Achievement in Edn. award 2004), Inst. Design and Constrn. (trustee 1987—), Italian Hist. Soc. Am. (exec. v.p. 1949—73, 1949—, Educator of Yr. in Ctrl. Park, NYC 1973, Antonio Meucci award 1998), Columbia Assn. Bd. Edn. (pres. 1977—79, Golden Anniversary award in edn. 2000), Nat. Italian Am. Found., Nat. Orgn. Italian Am. Women, UNICO Nat. (edn. liaison 1970—88, Civis Illustris award 1978). Home: 2062 81st St Brooklyn NY 11214-1807

ALLEY, ALLEN H., semiconductor company executive; BS in Mech. Engring., Purdue U. Product design engr. Ford Motor Co., 1976—79; lead mech. engr. Boeing Comml. Airplane Divsn., 1979—83; dir. mech. computer aided engring. Computervision Corp., 1983—86; gen. ptnr. Battery Ventures, 1986—92; v.p. corp. devel., engring. and product mktg. InFocus Sys., 1992—96; co-CEO Motif (joint venture with Motorola, Inc.) InFocus Sys.; co-founder, pres., CEO, chmn. bd. Pixelworks, Inc., Tualatin, Oreg., 1997—. Office: Pixelworks Inc Ste 300 8100 SW Nyberg Rd Tualatin OR 97062

ALLEY, GLENDA PAULINE, music educator; b. Boulder, Colo., June 28, 1946; d. Glen LeRoy Taylor and Hazel Pauline Reynolds; m. Robert Lynn Alley, Aug. 22, 1965; children: Faith, Joy, Timothy. Sec. Gen. Electric, San Leandro, Calif., 1969—70, Internat. Beef Breeders, Denver, 1973—75, Northglenn (Colo.) Sch. Dist., 1975—76; pvt. practice music tchr. Tacoma, 1986—; sec. Nat. Bank Am., Anchorage, 1980—82, Humana Hosp., Anchorage, 1982—86, Puget Sound Hosp. and Multicare, Tacoma, 1986—96. Mem.: Kindermusik Educators Assn., Kindermusik Internat. (mentor 2001—), Wash. State Music Tchrs. Assn. (newsletter editor 1996—). Avocations: scrapbooks, sewing, reading, playing with grandchildren. E-mail: rgalley65@msn.com.

ALLEY, KIRSTIE, actress; b. Wichita, Kans., Jan. 12, 1951; m. Parker Stevenson Dec. 22, 1983 (div. Dec. 1997); children: William True, Lillie. Student, U. Kans., Kans. State U. Actress: (stage prodns.) Cat on a Hot Tin Roof, Answers; (feature films) Star Trek II: The Wrath of Khan, 1982, Blind Date, 1984, Champions, 1984, Runaway, 1984, Summer School, 1987, Shoot to Kill, 1988, Look Who's Talking, 1989, Daddy's Home, 1989, One More Chance, 1990, Madhouse, 1990, Sibling Rivalry, 1990, Look Who's Talking Too, 1990, Look Who's Talking Now, 1993, Village of the Damned, 1995, It Takes Two, 1995, Sticks and Stones, 1996, For Richer of Poorer, 1997 (People's Choice award 1997), Deconstructing Harry, 1997 (People's Choice award 1997), Toothless, 1997, Drop Dead Gorgeous, 1999, The Mao Game, 1999, Back by Midnight, 2002; (TV mini-series) North and South Book I, 1985, North and South, Book II, 1986, The Last Don, 1997, The Last Don Part II, 1998 (Emmy nomination), Blonde, 2001, Salem Witch Trials, 2002; (TV movies) Sins of the Past, 1984, A Bunny's Tale, 1984, The Prince of Bel Air, 1985, Stark: Mirror Image, 1986, Infidelity, 1987, David's Mother, 1994 (Emmy award, Lead Actress - Special, 1994), Radiant City, 1996, Family Sins, 2004; (TV series) Masquerade, 1984-85, Cheers, 1987-1993 (Emmy award as Outstanding Lead Actress in a Comedy Series 1991); actress, exec. prodr.: Suddenly, 1996, Profoundly Normal, 2003; actress, co-prodr.: Nevada, 1997; prodr., actress: Veronica's Closet, 1997-2000; actress, writer, exec. prodr.: Fat Actress, 2005; TV appearances include The Match Game PM, 1979, The Hitchhiker, 1985, 87, Wings, 1993, Ink, 1997, Dharma & Greg, 2001, Without a Trace, 2004. Spokesperson for Narcanon Drug Rehab.; founder Ch. of Scientology, Mission of Wichita. Recipient People's Choice award, 1998. Mem.: Gamma Phi Beta.*

ALLEYNE, GEORGE A.O., public health administrator, educator; b. St. Philip, Barbados; DSc (hon.), Queens U., Ontario, Can., 2001. Dir. Pan Am. Health Org., Washington, dir. emeritus. Recipient Order of the Caribbean Community (O.C.C.). Office: Pan Am Health Org Regional Office WHO 525 TwentyThird St NW Washington DC 20037

ALLEYNE, MARK DACOSTA, communications educator, journalist; BA in Journalism, Howard U., 1984; MPhil in Internat. Rels., Oxford U., 1988, DPhil in Internat. Rels., 1991. Freelance corr. Caribbean ag. BBC, London, 1986-88; night support staffer Oxford (Eng.) Analytica Data Base, 1988; asst. prof. internat. communication Sch. Communication and Cognitive Sci., Hampshire Coll., Amherst, Mass., 1989-90; asst. prof. internat. svc. Am. U., Washington, 1990-93; asst. prof. comm. Loyola U., Chgo., 1993—98; vis. asst. prof. U. Ill., 1998—99, rsch. asst. prof., 1999—2003; assoc. dir. rsch. UCLA, 2003—. Vis. scholar program in internat. communication, Am. U., Washington, 1989. Co-author: Barbados, 1987; contbr. articles to profl. jours. and newspapers; columnist Barbados Adv., 1986-88; features editor The Bajan mag., 1984-86, corr., 1981-84; guest commentator CBC Radio, 1984-86; broadcaster WHUR Radio, 1981-82; author: International Power and International Communication, 1995, News Revolution: Political and Economic Decisions About Global Information, 1997, Global Lies?: Propaganda, the UN, and World Order, 2003. Winner Caribbean short story of yr. competition BBC, 1977; recipient U.S. Caribbean scholars award, 1983-84, Disting. Alumni award Howard U., 1991; Rhodes scholar, 1986; rsch. fellow Columbia U. Freedom Forum Media Studies Ctr., 1993-94. Mem. AAUP, Internat. Comm. Assn., Oxford Soc., Internat. Studies Assn., Barbados Assn. Journalists (pres. 1985), USTA, Met. Cricket Club (sec. 1984). Office: UCLA Ralph J Bunche Ctr 160 Haines Hall Box 95145 Los Angeles CA 90026

ALLGEIER, PETER FREDERICK, ambassador; b. Orange, NJ; m. Marsha Uehara; 2 children. AB in Internat. Rels., Brown U.; MA in Internat. Rels., Johns Hopkins U.; PhD in Internat. Economics, U. N.C. Internat. economist USAID, Washington; internat. economist Asia US Trade Reps., 1980—81, dir. Japanese affairs, 1981, dep. asst. US Trade Rep. Asia and the Pacific, 1981—85, asst. US Trade Rep. for Asia & the Pacific, 1985—89, asst. US Trade Rep. Europe & the Mediterranean, 1989—95, assoc. US Trade Rep. for western hemisphere Washington, 1995—2001; sr. dir. internat. econ. affairs Nat. Econ. Coun., Washington, 2001; dep. U.S. Trade Rep. Exec. Office of the Pres., Washington, 2001—05, acting U.S. Trade Rep., 2005. Vis. instr. econ. Duke U. Recipient Presdl. Disting. Rank award, 1988. Office: Exec Office of the Pres US Trade Rep 600 17th St NW Washington DC 20508-4801*

ALLIK, MICHAEL, manufacturing executive; b. N.Y.C., Aug. 28, 1935; s. Michael and Alma (Busch) A.; m. Deborah Dixon, Jan. 2, 1983; children—William Michael, Timothy John, Ryan Andrew, Lauren Alexandra. BS, MIT, 1957; MBA, Harvard U., 1961. V.p. Kondu Corp., Erie, Pa., 1961-66; assoc. Booz, Allen & Hamilton, Cleve., 1966-69; gen. mgr. Textile Friction Group H.K. Porter, Pitts., 1969-71; gen. mgr. transformer div. Allis Chalmers, Pitts., 1971-75; exec. v.p. Mead Paper Group, Dayton, Ohio, 1975-78; sr. v.p. strategy and adminstrn. Mead Corp., Dayton, 1978-81; sr. v.p. fin. and adminstrn. Dart & Kraft, Inc., Northbrook, Ill., 1981-83, pres. Splty. Products Group, 1984-86; pres., chief oper. officer, dir. RTE Corp., Milw., 1986-89; pres. Premier Aluminum, Inc., Racine, Wis., 1989—. Ptnr. Harvest Capital Mgmt., Inc., Vero Beach, Fla.; mem. coun. Grad. Sch. Bus., U. Chgo., 1985-92. Pres. bd. trustees Victory Theatre, Dayton, 1980-81; bd. dirs. Chgo. Hort. Soc., 1982-86, Milw. Repertory Theater, 1991-93. Served to 1st lt. C.E. U.S. Army, 1957-59. Mem. Wis. Taxpayers Alliance (bd. dirs. 1987). Clubs: Chgo. Economic. Home: 2260 Seaside St Vero Beach FL 32963-3131

ALLINGTON, MAYNARD, writer; b. Santa Cruz, Calif., Dec. 2, 1931; s. Francis Elden and Lee (Haverkamp) Allington; m. Esther Marie Anthony, Feb. 21, 1951 (div. Apr. 1966); children: John, Steve, Lance; m. Saundra Louise Johnson, Apr. 14, 1966; children: Lee Anne, Aleta Ann. BS in law enforcement and corrections, U. Nebr., 1968. Writer, novelist self employed, 1977—. Author: The Grey Wolf, 1986, The Fox in the Field, 1994, The Court of Blue Shadows, 1995. Lt. col. USAF, 1951—76. Mem.: Mystery Writers of Am. Republican. Catholic. Avocations: piano, composing music. Home: 336 lake Victoria Cl Melbourne FL 32940 E-mail: mallington@earthlink.net.

ALLIO, ROBERT JOHN, management consultant, educator; b. N.Y.C., Sept. 1, 1931; s. Albert Joseph and Helen (Gerbereux) A.; m. Barbara Maria Littauer, Oct. 3, 1953; children: Mark, Paul, David, Michael. BMetE, Rensselaer Poly. Inst., 1952; MS, Ohio State U., 1954; PhD, Rensselaer Poly. Inst., 1957. Mgr. advanced materials Gen. Electric Co., Schenectady, 1957-60; sr. staff AEC, Washington, 1962; engring. mgr. atomic power div. Westinghouse Corp., Pitts., 1962-68; dir. corp. planning Babcock & Wilcox, N.Y., 1968-75; v.p. Can. Wire Co., Toronto, Ont., 1975-78; pres. Canstar Communications, Toronto, 1976-78; sr. staff mem. Arthur D. Little Co., Cambridge, Mass., 1978-79; dean Rensselaer Poly. Inst. Sch. Mgmt., Troy, N.Y., 1981-83; pres. Robert J. Allio and Assoc., Providence, 1979—; prof. mgmt. Babson Coll, Wellesley, Mass., 1984—; mng. dir. Anasazi Group, 2000—. Bd. dirs. Fourth Shift, Springboard Software, GardenWay, NICON, TBS Funding Corp., Infantelligence; chmn. bd. TracRac Inc. Author: Corporate Planning: Techniques and Applications, 1979, Corporate Planning, 1985, The Practical Strategist, 1988, Leadership Myths and Realities, 1999, The Seven Faces of Leadership, 2003, Practical Strategy for Family Business, 2005; editor Planning Rev. Jour.; contbg. editor Strategy and Leadership Jour Mem.: Planning Forum (pres. 1976—77). Office: 150 Chestnut St Providence RI 02903

ALLIOT-MARIE, MICHÈLE, federal official; b. Villeneuve-le-Roi, France, Sept. 10, 1946; d. Bernard Marie; life ptnr. Patrick Ollier. M Ethnology, JD, Paris-I U. Mem. mcpl. coun. Ciboure, Pyrénées-Atlantiques, 1983—88, Biarritz, 1989—92, mem. gen. coun., 1994; MEP, 1989—92; Rassemblement pour Republique rep. Nat. Assembly, Pyrénées-Atlantiques, 1986, rassemblement pour republique, 1993, 1995; mayor St. Jean-de-Luz, 1992—; min. of state French Govt., 1986—88, min. for youth and sport, 1993—95, min. def., 2002—. Nat. sec. for civil svc. Rassemblement pur la Republic, 1981, dep. sec-gen for fgn. affairs, 91, ex-officio mem. polit. com., 1998—. Named one of most powerful women, Forbes mag., 2005. Achievements include being first French women to hold position Minister of Defense, and therefore control the nation's military. Office: Ministere de la Defense 14 rue St Domonique 00452 Armees France*

ALLISON, ANDREW MARVIN, church administrator; b. Long Beach, Calif., May 21, 1949; s. Howard C. and Wilma A. (Franks) A.; m. Kathleen L. Anderson, May 28, 1971; children: Rebecca, Nathan, Joanna, Spencer, Jacob, Camilla. AA, Glendale (Ariz.) C.C., 1972; BA in History, Brigham Young U., 1974; PhD of Polit. Sci., Coral Ridge U., 1993. Cert. secondary tchr., Ariz., Utah. Adminstrv. staff, editor Brigham Young U., Provo, Utah, 1972-74; adminstrv. asst. LDS Ch., Salt Lake City, 1977-79; prin., tchr. LDS Seminaries, Ariz.,Utah, 1974-77, 79-80; assoc. editor, art dir. Bookcraft Publs., Salt Lake City, 1983-85; dir. rsch. and publs. Nat. Ctr. for Constl. Studies, Salt Lake City, 1980-83, 85-91, chmn., pres. West Jordan, Utah, 1991-95; product devel. editor Deseret Book Co., Salt Lake City, 1995-96; supr. confidential applications LDS Ch., Salt Lake City, 1996-99, mgr. confidential records, 1999—. Adj. prof. polit. sci. George Wythe Coll., Cedar City, Utah, 1993—. Author: The Real Thomas Jefferson, 1982, The Real Benjamin Franklin, 1983, The Real George Washington, 1991; contbr. articles to profl. jours. Mem. West Jordan City Coun., Utah, 2000—03, mayor pro-tem, 2001. Mem.: Phi Kappa Phi.

ALLISON, ANNE MARIE, retired librarian; b. Oak Park, Ill., Oct. 3, 1931; d. Gerald Patrick and Anna Evelyn (Beam) Myers; m. James Dixon Alison, Aug. 28, 1954; children: Mark, Mary, Clare, Ruth, Edward. BA in French, St. Mary of the Woods Coll., 1951; postgrad., U. Fribourg, 1952-53; MLS, Rosary Coll., 1968. Asst. libr. Triton Coll., River Grove, Ill., 1967-68; asst. libr. tech. svcs. Moraine Valley Community Coll., Palos Hills, Ill., 1968-69; dir. learning resources, head libr. Coll. Lake County, Grayslake, Ill., 1969-71; asst. head catalog dept. Kent (Ohio) State U. Librs., 1971-73, head processing dept., 1973-79, asst. dir. libr. svcs., 1979-81; acting dir. Fla. Atlantic U. Libr., Boca Raton, 1980-81; asst. dir., head tech. svcs. Wayne State U. Librs., Detroit, 1981-83; dir. librs. U. Cen. Fla., Orlando, 1983-97, ret., 1997. Past chair, bd. dirs. Fla. Extension Libr., Tampa; bd. dirs. Ctr. for Libr. Automation, Gainesville, Fla., Cen. Fla. Holocaust Meml. Resource Ctr., Orlando; adj. prof. Libr. and Info. Sci., U. S. Fla., Tampa. Editor: OCLC: A National Library Network, 1979; contbr. articles to profl. jours. Arbitrator alternative dispute resolution program Better Bus. Bur. Cen. Fla., Maitland, 1985—; active Friends Winter Park Pub. Libr., Friends of Orlando Pub. Libr. Recognized for Outstanding Leadership in Edn. Cen. Fla. Ednl. Consortium for Women, 1990. Mem. ALA (chair profl. ethics com.), Fla. Libr. Assn., Fla. Assn. Coll. and Rsch. Librs. (pres. bd. dirs.). Avocations: fruit farming, collecting china. Office: U Cen Fla PO Box 25000 Orlando FL 32816-0001

ALLISON, BEVERLY GRAY, retired religious organization administrator, theology studies educator; b. La., May 7, 1924; s. John Richard Preston and Ora (Byram) A.; m. Voncille Cruse; children: Suzanne Grigsby, Charlotte Miller, Gray Maloy. BS, La. Polytech. Inst. (now La. Tech. U.), 1948; BD, New Orleans Bapt. Theol. Sem., 1952, ThD, 1954. Spl. agt. N.Y. Life Ins. co., Ruston, La., 1948-49; pastor New Prospect Bapt. Ch., Hilly, La., 1951-52, Sharon (La.) Bapt. Ch., 1951-52; assoc. pastor Temple Bapt. Ch., Ruston, La., 1952-54; pastor Southside Bapt. Mission, Ruston, 1953-54; asst. prof. church history New Orleans Bapt. Theol. Sem., 1954-56, assoc. prof. missions, 1955-60, prof. evangelism, 1964-66; evangelist Allison Evangelistic Assn., Ruston, 1960-72; assoc. dir. div. evangelism Home Mission Bd. So. Baptist Convention, 1966-67; pres. Mid-Am. Bapt. Theol. Sem., Memphis, 1972-97, pres. emeritus, 1997—, prof. evangelism, 1972—. Contbr. articles to profl. jours. With USAAF, 1943-45. Baptist. Office: Mid-Am Bapt Theol Sem PO Box 381528 Germantown TN 38183-1528

ALLISON, BROOKE HASTINGS, artist, educator; b. NYC, Feb. 12, 1940; s. Frederick Gay and Miriam Lorraine (Watkins) Hastings; m. John Borden Allison, Dec. 17, 1966 (dec. 1996); children: Brooke Allison Scannell, Jaime Joy; stepchildren: Jeffrey Clark, Jay Borden, Jerrianne Allison Anderson, Jane Sue. Student, Shimer Coll., 1957-58, Art Inst. Chgo., 1958-60, 81-82, Am. Acad. Art., 1960-61, Lake Forest Coll., 1961. Instr. Dunedin (Fla.) Fine Art Ctr., 1984-2001. Exhibited in groups shows at Tampa Mus. Art, 1997, Jacksonville (Fla.) Mus. Art, 1998, featured in 200 Great Painting Ideas, 1998, Artist Mag., 1998, St. Petersburg Arts Ctr., 1999 (J. Brown Meml. award), Ridge Art 50th Ann. Nat. Competition, 2000 (2d prize 2000), Broome St. Gallery, 1999-2001 (1st prize 2000), Butler Inst. Am. Art, Youngstown, Pa., 2003; curator Artists of the 3d Age, Octagon Gallery, Clearwater, Fla.; In Praise of Pastel curator Dunedin (Fla.) Fine Art Ctr., 2004; contbr. articles to profl. jours Recipient award, Catharine L. Wolfe Exhbn., 1993—94, Richwood Art Inst. award, Catharine Larillard Wolfe Open Internat. Exhbn., Nat. Arts Club, N.Y.C., 2001, Award of Excellence in Fine Arts, Ocala Art Festival, 2001, Award of Excellence for Mainsail, Art Festival of St. Petersburg, Fla., 2002, Distinction award, Fine Arts for Ocala, 2001, Excellence award, Mainsail Art Festival, 2002; grantee Pinellas County Artists Resource, 1991, 1999. Mem. Pastel Soc. Am. (profl. mem.), Pastel Soc. of West Coast, Midwest Pastel Soc., Profl. Assn. Visual Artists (past. pres. 1992-94), Fla. Artist's Group, Catherine Lorillard Wolfe Art Club, Butler Inst. Am. Art, Pastel Soc. Am. Presbyterian. Avocations: reading, service work. Home: 1654 Mckay Ct Dunedin FL 34698-3529 Office Phone: 727-734-4285. E-mail: brookeallison@earthlink.net.

ALLISON, CHRISTINE LYNN, optometrist, educator; d. Thomas Roger and Carol Elizabeth Allison; m. Gregory George Furman, Dec. 5, 1999; children: Thomas George Furman, Allison Ann Furman, Katrina Carolyn Furman. BS in Biology, U. Notre Dame, 1991; OD, SUNY, N.Y.C., 1995. Diplomate in binocular vision, perception and pediat. optometry Am. Acad. Optometry, 1995. Resident in pediatric optometry Ill. Coll. Optometry, Chgo., 1995—96, assoc. prof. optometry, 1996—; optometrist Ctrl. Optical, Chgo., 1996—. Clin. dir. Spl. Olympics Opening Eyes Program, Ill., 1999—; faculty advisor Coll. Optometrists in Vision Devel., Chgo.; residency program coord. Ill. Coll. Optometry, Chgo. Contbr. articles to profl. jours. Fellow: Coll. Optometrists in Vision Devel., Am. Acad. Optometry. Home: 3732 W Eddy St Chicago IL 60618 Office: Ill Eye Inst/Ill Coll Optometry 3241 S Michigan Ave Chicago IL 60616 E-mail: callison@eyecare.ico.edu.

ALLISON, DWIGHT LEONARD, JR., investor; b. Boston, Oct. 27, 1929; s. Dwight Leonard and Stella (DeGrasse) A.; m. Lyona G. Strohacker, June 19, 1954; children: Dwight Leonard III, Barbara Lynn, Laurie. AB, Dartmouth Coll., 1951, MBA, 1952; LLB, Harvard U., 1956; DCS (hon.), Suffolk U., 1989. Bar: Mass. 1956. Practiced in, Boston, 1956-66; assoc. Goodwin, Procter & Hoar, Boston, 1964-66, ptnr., 1965-66; v.p., dir. Gardner Assocs., Inc., Boston, 1966-68; chmn. fin. com. C.H. Sprague & Son Co., 1968-69; chmn. bd. Sprague Assoc., Inc., Boston, 1969-71; gen. ptnr. Sprague & Co., 1971-80; pvt. investor, 1973-77; pres., chief exec. officer Boston Co., 1977-81, chmn. bd., 1981-83, vice chmn., 1983-86; pvt. investor, 1986—. 1st lt. USAF, 1952—53. Address: 4228 Pine Cone Ln Boynton Beach FL 33436-3017 Home (Summer): 23782 Paseo Del Campo Laguna Niguel CA 92677 E-mail: DA1296@aol.com.

ALLISON, FRED, JR., internist, retired medical educator; b. Abingdon, Va., Sept. 8, 1922; s. Fred and Elizabeth Harriet (Kelly) A.; m. Clara Knox, Oct. 14, 1949; children: Rebecca Allison Parsley, Martha Allison Brown, Fred III, Robert Gardiner. BS, Ala. Poly. Inst., 1944; MD, Vanderbilt U., 1946. Diplomate: Am. Bd. Internal Medicine. Intern Vanderbilt Hosp., Nashville, 1946-47; resident Peter Bent Brigham Hosp., Boston, 1949-50; practice medicine specializing in internal medicine, 1946—; asst. prof. medicine Washington U., St. Louis, 1955; prof. medicine, head infectious disease divsn. U. Miss., Jackson, 1955—68; vis. scientist Rockefeller U., N.Y.C., 1966-67; Edgar Hull prof. medicine, head dept. medicine La. State U., New Orleans, 1968-87; chief medicine La. State U. div. Charity Hosp., 1968—87; prof. medicine emeritus La. State U., 1987—; prof. medicine Vanderbilt U., Nashville, 1987-96, prof. medicine emeritus, 1996—, med. cons. Zerfoss Student Health Svc., 1996-99; physician-in-chief Met. Nashville Gen. Hosp., 1987-93; chief, divsn. gen. internal medicine Vanderbilt U., 1993-96. Bd. dirs. La. State U. Health Network, 1995-01; vice chmn. bd. trustees Hosp. Authority of Metro. Nashville and Davidson County, 1999—. With US Army, 1943-46, 47-49. Home: 418 Fairfax Ave Nashville TN 37212-4009

ALLISON, GLORIETTA TRAVIS, music educator, soprano; b. Big Spring, Tex., July 8, 1932; d. Arthur Edwin Travis and Emma Jewel York; m. Grady Ned Allison, June 2, 1950; children: Carroll Edwin, Melissa Louise Allison Sherman. BRE, Southwestern Bapt. Theol. Sem., Ft. Worth, Tex., 1954. Vocal instr., Grand Falls, Tex., 1954—55, Munday, Tex., 1957—59, Baytown, Tex., 1959—66; performing artist, soprano, 1954—66, Houston, 1966—73, N.Y.C., 1973—92; vocal instr., performing artist Grand Junction, Colo., 1994—2001, Alachua, Fla., 2001—. Soloist Aims Orch., Graz, Austria, 1980; prin. role Salzburg Music Festival, Austria, 1980; soloist Beethoven Ninth Flint Symphony, Mich., 1981. Mem.: Gainesville Music Tchrs. Assn., Fla. Music Tchrs. Assn., Nat. Assn. Tchrs. Singing. Democrat. Unitarian Universalist. Avocations: gardening, reading, walking, bicycling, swimming.

ALLISON, GRAHAM TILLETT, JR., government professor; b. Charlotte, N.C., Mar. 23, 1940; s. Graham Tillett and Virginia (Wright) A.; m. Elisabeth Kovacs Smith, Aug. 23, 1968. AB, Harvard U., 1962, PhD, 1968; BA, MA, Hertford Coll., Oxford (Eng.) U., 1964. Asst. prof. John F. Kennedy Sch. Govt., Harvard U., Cambridge, Mass., 1968-70, assoc. prof., 1970-72, prof., 1972—, assoc. dean, 1975-77, dean, 1977-89, Douglas Dillon prof. govt., 1989—; dir., Belfer Ctr. for Science & Internat. Affairs John F. Kennedy Sch. Govt.; spl. adviser to Sec. of Def., 1985-87; dir. Project on Strengthening Dem. Instns., 1990-93; asst. sec. of def. for policy and plans U.S. Dept. Def., Washington, 1993—94. Fellow Ctr. for Advanced Studies, Stanford, Palo Alto, Calif., 1973-74; mem. Sec. Def.'s Policy Bd., 1985—; cons. Rand Corp., U.S. Dept. Def., others; mem. numerous NAS panels; mem. Trilateral Commn., 1974-84, Coun. on Fgn. Rels.; mem. Fgn. Affairs Task Force Dem. Adv. Com., 1974-80; mem. vis. com. on fgn. policy studies Brookings Instn., 1972-77. Author: Essence of Decision: Explaining the Cuban Missile Crisis, 1971, Remaking Foreign Policy: The Organizational Connection, 1976, Sharing International Responsibility Among the Trilateral Countries, 1983, Nuclear Terrorism: The Ultimate Preventable Catastrophe, 2004; co-author: (with Carnesale and Nye) Hawks, Doves and Owls: An Agenda for Avoiding Nuclear War, 1985, Fateful Visions: Avoiding Nuclear Catastrophe, 1988, (with W. Ury) Windows of Opportunity: From Cold War to Peaceful Competition, 1989, (with Grigory Yavlinsky) Window of Opportunity: The Grand Bargain for Democracy in the Soviet Union, 1991, (with Greg Treverton) Rethinking America's Security, 1992, (with Konstantin Sarkisov and Hiroshi Kimura) Beyond the Cold War to Trilateral Cooperation in the Asia-Pacific Region, 1992; contbr. articles to profl. jours. Democrat. Office: Belfer Ctr for Science & Internat Affairs 79 JFK St Cambridge MA 02138 E-mail: grahamallison@harvard.edu.*

ALLISON, HERBERT MONROE, JR., investment firm executive; b. Pitts., Aug. 24, 1943; s. Herbert M. Sr. and Mary B. (Boardman) A.; m. Simin N. Nazemi, May 9, 1974; children: John, Andrew. BA, Yale U., 1965; MBA, Stanford U., 1971. With Merrill Lynch & Co., Inc., NYC, Paris, London and Tehran, Iran, 1971-78, asst. to pres. NYC, 1978-80, mgr. market planning, 1980-83, treas., 1983-86, sr. v.p., dir. human resources, from 1986, CFO, pres., COO until 1999; pres., CEO AllLearn.org; chmn., pres., CEO TIAA-CREF, NYC, 2002—. Bd. dirs. NY Stock Exch., 2003—05, N.Y. Infirmary-Beekman Downtown Hosp. Served in USN, 1965—69. Mem. Wall Street Personnel Mgmt. Assn. Office: TIAA-CREF 730 Third Ave New York NY 10017

ALLISON, JOAN KELLY, music educator, pianist; b. Denison, Iowa, Jan. 25, 1935; d. Ivan Martin and Esther Cecelia (Newborg) K.; m. Guy Hendrick Allison, July 25, 1954 (div. Apr. 1973); children: David, Dana, Douglas, Diane. MusB, St. Louis Inst. of Music, 1955; MusM, So. Meth. U., 1976. Korrepetitor Corpus Christi (Tex.) Symphony, 1963-85; staff pianist Am. Inst. Mus. Studies, Graz, Austria, 1974-89; prof. Del Mar Coll., Corpus Christi, 1976—2002. Adj. prof. Del Mar Coll., 1959-75, Corpus Christi State U., 1978-93, Tex. A&M U., Corpus Christi, 1993-2004; program dir. Corpus Christi Chamber Music Soc., 1986—; piano chmn. Corpus Christi Young Artists' Competition, 1987—; chmn. Del Mar Coll. Student Programs Com., 1986-88, 91-92, 94-95, 2001-02; chmn. radio com., S.Tex. Pub. Broadcasting Svc., Corpus Christi, 1987-88; asst. mus. dir. Little Theater, Corpus Christi, 1970-74; judge, Houston Symphony Auditions, 1988, S.C. Young Artist Competition, Columbia, 1990; freelance accompanist, 1955—, adjudicator, 1960—; v.p. united fac., Del Mar Coll., 1986-88; pianist with Del Mar Trio, 1965-95, Young Audiences, Inc., 1975-83; recital tours in U.S., Mex., Austria, 1954-88. Piano soloist, St. Louis Symphony, 1956, 57, Bach Festival Orch., St. Louis, 1955, Corpus Christi Symphony; recipient Artist Presentation award, Artist Presentation Soc., St. Louis, 1956; contbr. articles to profl. jours., including Internat. Piano Quar. Co-chmn. Mayor's Com. on Recycling, Corpus Christi, 1989-91; bd. dirs. Corpus Christi Symphony; adv. bd. Corpus Christi Concert Ballet; mem. steering com. cultural devel. plan City of Corpus Christi, 1995-96. Recipient Women in Careers award YWCA, 1985. Mem. Corpus Christi Music Tchrs. Assn., Liszt Soc. (contbr. to jour.). Avocations: foreign travel, water-skiing, hiking, acting in community theatre. Home: 4709 Curtis Clark Dr Corpus Christi TX 78411-4801 Personal E-mail: Jallison@the-i.net.

ALLISON, JOHN ANDREW, IV, bank executive; b. Charlotte, N.C., Aug. 14, 1948; s. John Andrew III and Anne Allison; m. Elizabeth Mc Donald, Aug. 19, 1973; children: Eric, William, Sarah. BBA, U. N.C., 1971; M in Mgmt., Duke U., 1974; grad. Stonier Sch. Banking, Rutgers U., 1981. Chmn., CEO BB&T Corp.; mgr. fin. analysis Br. Banking & Trust Co., Wilson, N.C., 1971-72, mgr. loan officer devel. program, 1972-73, regional loan adminstr., 1973-80, mgr. bus. loan adminstrn., 1980-81, mgr. banking div. (now Br. Banking Group), 1981—, pres., 1987—, also bd. dirs.; vice chmn. BB&T Fin. Corp., Wilson, 1987—; chmn., CEO So. Nat. Corp., Winston-Salem, N.C., 1996—, BB&T & Branch Banking & Trust Co., Winston-Salem, NC. Bd. dirs., chmn. capital campaign Children's Svcs. Ea. N.C., Greenville, 1985—; bd. dirs. Diversified Opportunities, Inc., Wilson, 1980-87; mem. exec. com. state fin. com. Com. to Reelect Gov. Martin, Raleigh, N.C., 1988; mem. N.C. bus. adv. bd. Fuqua Sch. Bus., Duke U.; bd. dirs. Med. Found. East Carolina U., Brody Found.; mem. communications, agy. and pub. rels. subcom. United Way Wilson County, Inc., 1989—; mem. So. Growth Policies Bd. Mem. Am. Bankers Assn., N.C. Bankers Assn., Robert Morris Assocs. (past bd. dirs. Carolinas-Va. chpt.), N.C. Citizens for Bus. and Industry, Phi Beta Kappa. Office: BB&T Corp 200 W 2nd St Winston Salem NC 27101-4019

ALLISON, JOHN LANGSDALE, marine architect, marine engineer; b. Sutton Coldfield, Eng., Aug. 10, 1930; arrived in US, 1966; s. Herbert Mandall and Eva May (Langsdale) A.; m. Eunice Quick, Apr. 7, 1956; children; Christopher John, Nigel Mark, Katherine Sarah. BSc in Engring., U. Nottingham, Eng., 1954; postgrad., U. Nottingham; aero. engring. cert., Royal Naval Engring. Coll., Plymouth, Eng., 1955; profl. mgmt. cert., U. Aston, Birmingham, Eng., 1959. Chartered engr., U.K. Sr. rsch. engr. Birmingham Small Arms Co./Daimler Group Rsch., 1956-58; lectr. in engring. Bromsgrove Coll. of Further Edn., Worcestshire, Eng., 1958-66; sr. rsch. engr. Bell Aerospace Textron, Buffalo, 1966-71; chief engr. ship tech. Textron Marine Sys. Inc. divsn. Bell Aerospace Textron, New Orleans, 1971-87; chief engr. Band, Lavis & Assocs., Inc., Severna Park, Md., 1987—2002, CDI Marine Sys. Design & Devel. (formerly Band, Lavis & Assocs., Inc.), Severna Park, Md., 2002—. Student advisor George Washington U., Washington, 1991-92; cons. Outboard Motor Corp., Waukegan, Ill., 1994-97; presenter, cons. Inst. for Maritime Dynamics and Meml. U., St. Johns, Nfld., Can., 1995; cons. Kvaerner Mandal (Norway) A.S., 1995-99, UMOE, Mandal, Norway, 1999—; advisor H.S. students Hi-Frontiers Ann. Competition; presenter in field. Author (chpts. for): Ship Design & Construction, 2004; contbr. chpts. for Transactions of Learned Societies, articles to many profl. jours., reports to U.S. Navy and other armed svcs. Sub-lt. Royal Navy, 1954-56. Recipient Maritech award U.S. Govt./Advanced Rsch. Projects Agy., 1995. Fellow Inst. Mech. Engrs., Royal Instn. Naval Architects; mem. Am. Soc. Naval Engrs. Ret., Soc. Naval Architects and Marine Engrs. (Vice Adm. Cochrane award 1993), Navy League, US Naval Inst. (ret.). Republican. Presbyterian. Achievements include patents for waterjet steering and reversal for large ships, and design of heavy lift air cushion vehicle; inventor of low-profile thrusters for naval hovercraft, 2001. Home: 4119 Hummingbird Ct Lebanon OH 45036 Office: CDI Marine / Sys Design & Devel 900 Ritchie Hwy Severna Park MD 21146-4142 Office Phone: 513-696-8054. Personal E-mail: jaeqallison@aol.com.

ALLISON, JOHN ROBERT, lawyer; b. San Antonio, Feb. 9, 1945; s. Lyle (stepfather) and Beatrice (Kaliner) Forehand; m. Rebecca M. Picard; 1 child, Katharine. BS, Stanford U., 1966; JD, U. Wash., 1969. Bar: Wash. 1969, D.C. 1973, Minn. 1994, U.S. Supreme Ct. 1973. Assoc. Garvey, Schubert & Barer, Seattle, 1969-73; ptnr., 1973-86; prin. Betts, Patterson & Mines, P.S., 1986-94; sr. counsel 3M Co., 1994-2000, asst. gen. counsel, 2000—. Bd. dirs. So. Minn. Regional Legal Svcs.; bd. dirs., pres. Jewish Family Svc., St. Paul; pres., lectr. bus. law Seattle U., 1970, U. Wash., 1970-73; judge pro tem, King County Superior Ct., 1983-94 Mem. ABA (vice chmn. toxic and hazardous substances and environ. law com. 1986-91, chair elect 1991-92, chair 1992-93), Minn. Bar Assn., Seattle-King County Bar Assn. (chmn. jud. evaln. polling com. 1982-83), Wash. State Bar Assn. (bd. bar examiners 1984-94), D.C. Bar Assn., Nat. Inst. Pollution Liability (co-chmn. 1988), Order of the Coif. Office: 3M Co 3 M Ctr Saint Paul MN 55144-1000 Office Phone: 651-736-3993. Business E-Mail: jrallison@mmm.com.

ALLISON, LAIRD BURL, business educator; b. St. Marys, W.Va., Nov. 7, 1917; s. Joseph Alexander and Opal Marie (Robinson) A.; m. Katherine Louise Hunt, Nov. 25, 1943 (div. 1947); 1 child: William Lee; m. Genevieve Nora Elmore, Feb. 1, 1957 (dec. July 1994). BS in Personnel and Indsl. Relations magna cum laude, U. So. Calif., 1956; MBA, UCLA, 1958. Chief petty officer USN, 1936-51, PTO; asst. prof. to prof. mgmt. Calif. State U., L.A., 1956-83; asst. dean Calif. State U. Sch. Bus. and Econs., L.A., 1971-72, assoc. dean, 1973-83, emeritus prof. mgmt., 1983—. Vis. asst. prof. mgmt. Calif. State U., Fullerton, 1970. Co-authored the Bachelors degree program in mgmt. sci. at Calif. State U., 1963. Mem. U.S. Naval Inst., Navy League U.S. Ford Found. fellow, 1960. Mem. Acad. Mgmt., Inst. Mgmt. Sci., Western Econs. Assn. Internat., World Future Soc., Am. Acad. Polit. Social Sci., Calif. State U. Assn. Emeriti Profs., Calif. State U. L.A. Emeriti Assn. (program v.p. 1986-87, v.p. adminstrn. 1987-88, pres. 1988-89, exec. com. 1990-91, treas. 1991—), Am. Assn. Individual Investors, Am. Assn. Ret. Persons, Ret. Pub. Employees Assn. Calif. (chpt. sec. 1984-88, v.p. 1989, pres. 1990-92), Am. Legion, Phi Kappa Phi, Beta Gamma Sigma, Alpha Kappa Psi. Avocations: history, travel, photography, hiking. Home: 2176 E Bellbrook St Covina CA 91724-2346 Office: Calif State U Dept Mgmt 5151 State University Dr Los Angeles CA 90032-4226

ALLISON, MARY ANN, consulting company executive, writer, speaker; b. Sept. 27, 1949; d. David S. and Mary (McNaughton) Burnet; m. Eric William Allison, July 17, 1971. BA, Shimer Coll., 1971; MBA, L.I. U., 1977; PhD, NYU, 2005. Various positions Avis Rent-a-Car, Garden City, N.Y., 1971-80; v.p. Citicorp, N.Y.C., 1980-96; pres. Human Ordered Tech. LLC., 1996-97; chmn., chief cybernetics officer The Allison Group, LLC, 1996—; chmn. Allison-LoBue Group, LLC, 1999-2000. N.Y.C. artist in residence. Co-author: Through the Valley of Death, 1983, Managing Up, Managing Down, 1984, The Complexity Advantage: How the Science of Complexity Can Help Your Business Achieve Peak Performance, 1999; contbr. articles to profl. publs. and nat. mags. Bd. advisors Human Issues in Mgmt., N.Y.C. Artist in Residence. Mem. OD Network, Authors Guild. Episcopalian. Office: The Allison Group 100 Freeman St Ste F2 Brooklyn NY 11222-5899 E-mail: maa@allisongroup.com.

ALLISON, MICHAEL DAVID, space scientist, educator; b. Salem, Ill., Oct. 11, 1951; s. James M. and Claudine K. A.; m. Siri Wannamaker, Feb. 4, 1984; children: Hilary Kirstyn, Christopher Caleb. AB in Physics and English, Wittenberg U., 1973; SM in Physics, U. Chgo., 1976; PhD in Space Physics and Astronomy, Rice U., 1982. Resident rsch. assoc. Nat. Rsch. Coun. NASA/Goddard Inst for Space Studies, N.Y.C., 1981-83, space scientist, 1984—. Guest lectr. Am. Mus. Natural History, Hayden Planetarium, N.Y.C., 1984-88, 94-2003; mem. joint sci. working group for the NASA/ESA assessment study of the Cassini mission to Saturn and Titan, 1984-89; adj. prof. astronomy Columbia U., N.Y.C.- 1987—; co-investigator Huygens, Titan Doppler Wind Expt., U. Bonn., Germany, 1990—, team mem. Cassini Radar investigation, NASA, 2000—; rsch. assoc. Am. Mus. Dept. Astronomy, 1997-99. Co-editor: (conf. proceedings) The Jovian Atmospheres, 1986; contbr. articles to profl. jours. including Science, Icarus, Jour. of Atmospheric Scis., Geophys. Rsch. Letters, Planetary and Space Sci. Participating scientist Mars Observer and Surveyor '98 Missions, NASA, 1992-99. Mem. Am. Astron. Soc. (divsn. for planetary scis.), Am. Meteorol. Soc., Internat. Astronomical Union Achievements include research in planetary atmospheric dynamics and meteorology, application of potential vorticity homogenization to planetary zonal circulation studies, first identification of Saturn's polar hexagon as a planetary Rossby wave, inference of a probable super-solar abundance of water on Jupiter based on the diagnostic analysis of equatorial waves, development of efficient planetocentric solar timing algorithms for Mars and other planets. Home: 81 Teller Ave Beacon NY 12508-3067 Office: NASA/Goddard Inst Space Studies 2880 Broadway New York NY 10025-7848 E-mail: michael.d.allison@nasa.gov.

ALLISON, RICHARD CLARK, judge; b. N.Y.C., July 10, 1924; s. Albert Fay and Anice (Clark) A.; m. Anne Elizabeth Johnston, Oct. 28, 1950; children: Anne Sidney, William Scott, Richard Clark. BA, U. Va., 1944, LLB, 1948. Bar: N.Y. 1948. Practiced in, N.Y.C., 1948-52, 54-60; with CIA, 1952—54; ptnr. Reid & Priest, 1961-87; mem. Iran-U.S. Claims Tribunal, The Hague, 1988—. Lt. (j.g.) USNR, 1945—46. Fellow Am. Bar Found. (life), Ctr. for Am. and Internat. Law; mem. ABA (chmn. com. Latin Am. Law 1964-68, chmn. Internat. Law Sect. 1977, chmn. Nat. Inst. on Doing Bus. in Far East 1972, chmn. internat. legal exch. program 1981-85), Internat. Bar Assn. (chmn. 1986 Conf., ethics com. 1986-89), Société Internat. des Avocats, Inter-Am. Bar Assn., Am. Arbitration Assn. (internat. panel), Am. Soc. Internat. Law, Coun. on Fgn. Rels., Assn. Bar City N.Y., Raven Soc., SAR, St. Andrew's Soc. N.Y., Manhasset Bay Yacht Club, Phi Beta Kappa, Omicron Delta Kappa, Pi Kappa Alpha, Phi Delta Phi. Republican. Congregationalist. Home: 224 Circle Dr Manhasset NY 11030-1123 Office: c/o Iran-US Claims Tribunal Parkweg 13 2585 JH The Hague Netherlands

ALLISON, ROBERT JAMES, JR., retired oil and gas company executive; b. Evanston, Ill., 1939; married; 3 children. BS in Petroleum Engring., Kans. U., 1960. Engring. mgmt. Amoco Prodn. Co., U.S., Trinidad and Iran, 1960-73; v.p. ops. Anadarko Prodn. Co., Ft. Worth and Houston, 1973-76, pres., dir. Houston, 1976-79, pres., CEO, 1979-86; group v.p. Panhandle Eastern Corp., Houston, 1980-86, dir., 1986-93; CEO Anadarko Petroleum Corp., Houston, 1986—2001, 2002—03, pres., 2002—03, chmn., 1986—. Bd. dirs. Sam Houston Area Coun. Boy Scouts Am., Houston, 1985—; adv. coun. U. Tex. Engring. Found.; chmn. Spindletop Charities, Houston, Mr. Spindletop, 1991; mem. bd. visitors M.D. Anderson Cancer Ctr. Mem. IPAA, NGSA, Am. Petroleum Inst. (bd. dirs.), All Am. Wildcatters Assn., Tex. Mid-Continent Oil and Gas Assn., Nat. Gas Coun., Soc. Petroleum Engrs., River Oaks Club, Lochinvar Golf Club (pres. 1982-85), Houston Club, Petroleum Club (bd. dirs.), Pine Valley Golf Club, Champions Golf Club. Republican. Presbyterian. Avocations: golf, hunting, flying. Office: Anadarko Petroleum Corp 1201 Lake Robbins Dr The Woodlands TX 77380*

ALLISON, RON, oncologist, researcher; BS, Bklyn. Coll., 1983; MD, SUNY, 1987. Cert. radiation oncology Am. Bd. Radiology, 1992. Intern, resident, chief resident SUNY, 1987—91; prof., chmn. ECU/U. N.C., Greenville, 2001—, oncologist. Mem.: Phi Beta Kappa. Achievements include patents in field. Office: ECU 600 Moye Blvd Greenville NC 27834 Office Phone: 252-744-2900.

ALLISON, STEPHEN GALENDER, broadcast executive; b. Springfield, Mo., Dec. 11, 1952; s. Edgbert Allcorn and Naomi Louise (Chamless) A.; m. Linda Lavelle, June 6, 1974 (div. Dec. 1980); children: Julie Ann, Jennifer Erin; m. Tara Rae Foster, Aug. 20, 1986 (div. Aug. 1994); m. Sibel Galinda Pisken, Apr. 6, 2002; children: Fox Stephen, Jaz Sibel. Cert. radio mktg. cons. Radio Advt. Bur. On-air personality Sta. WSBB, New Smyrna, Fla., 1971-72, Sta. WMFJ-AM-FM, Daytona Beach, Fla., 1972-75, Sta. KADI-FM, St. Louis, 1975-76, Sta. KAUM-FM, Houston, 1976-79, Sta. WKYS-FM, Washington, 1979-81; gen mgr. Sta. KSTM-FM, Phoenix, 1981-85; pres. Allison Broadcasting Co., Inc., Phoenix, 1985—, Allison Broadcast Group, Inc., Dallas, Del Mar, Calif., 1987—; owner Stas. KGRX-FM/KIKO, Phoenix, 1986-91, Sta. KDGE-FM, Dallas, 1989-94, WLVX-FM, Gainesville, Fla., 1994-95; mgr. talk/bus./ESPN programming ABC Radio Networks, Dallas, 1996-97; dir. Clear Channel Comms., Tampa, 1997-98; nat. dir. mktg. Metro Networks, Phoenix, 1998-99; sr. exec. analyst George S. May Internat. Co., San Jose, Calif., 1999—2002; with SLGG Cons. LLC, 2002—; pres. Allison Group, Inc., 2004—. Mktg. cons. St. Louis Post-Dispatch, 1975-76, Houston Chronicle, 1976-79, Washington Star, 1980-81; advt. cons. Celebrity Theatre, Phoenix, 1985-86; pres. JFM Branson (Mo.) Inc., 1993—; owner Doc Severinsen Theater. Bd. dirs. Desert-Mt. Foothills Assn., Scottsdale, Ariz., 1981-91, 98—, Alwun House Cultural Ctr., Phoenix, 1982—, Film in Ariz., Phoeniz, 1985-93, Ariz. Commn. on the Arts, Phoenix, 1986-89; active Nat. Rep. Congl. Com., 1988-93, No. Tex. Commn. Mem. Nat. Assn. Broadcasters, Ariz. Broadcasters Assn., Tex. Assn. Broadcasters, Phoenix Active 20-30 Club, Internat. Platform Assn., Las Colinas Sports Club, Pointe Royale Country Club, Preston Trails Country Club, The Heritage Club. Avocations: collecting classic cars, travel, racquetball, golf, boating. Home: 205 Sebastians Run Austin TX 78738-6557 E-mail: sga@allisongrp.com.

ALLISON, STUART ANTHONY, chemistry professor, researcher; b. Kalispell, Mont., Mar. 26, 1951; s. Bruce Allan and Arretta Allison; m. Lenong Wang. BA Chemistry, U. Mont., 1973; MS Phys. Chemistry, U. Calif., Berkeley, 1975; PhD Phys. Chemistry, U. Wash., 1980. Postdoctoral fellow U. Oreg., Eugene, 1980—82, U. Houston, Houston, 1982—84; asst. prof. chemistry Ga. State U., Atlanta, 1984—90, assoc. prof. chemistry, 1990—2000, prof. chemistry, 2000—. Contbr. articles to profl. jours. Recipient Presdl. Young Investigator award, NSF, 1985. Mem.: Am. Biophysical Soc. Roman Catholic. Achievements include development of numerical methods for computing transport properties of complex model systems. Avocations: hiking, coin collecting/numismatics, stamp collecting/philately. Home: 978 Biltmore Dr Atlanta GA 30329 Office: Ga State U University Pl Atlanta GA 30303 Office Phone: 404-651-1986. Business E-Mail: sallison@gsn.edu.

ALLMAN, MARGARET ANN LOWRANCE, counseling administrator; b. Carmel, Calif., June 2, 1938; d. Edward Walton and Rhoda Elizabeth (Patton) Lowrance; m. Jackie Howard Hamilton, Dec. 21, 1959 (div. May 1976); children: John Scott Hamilton, David Lee Hamilton, Dennis Lynn Hamilton; m. Jack Fredrick Allman, Dec. 22, 1977; stepchildren: John Frederick, James Paul, Jeffrey Lee. AA, Christian Coll., 1958; BA in Spanish, U. Mo., 1960, MEd, 1971, EdD, 1994. Tchr. Spanish Neosho (Mo.) HS, 1961-62, asst. prin., 1974-77; florist Wallflower Shop and Greenhouse, Joplin, Mo., 1962-69; dean girls Joplin Sr. HS, 1967-69; florist, bookkeeper Mueller's Garden Ctr., Columbia, Mo., 1969-71; instr. edn., asst. dean of students Columbia Coll., 1971-74; dir. guidance Am. Cmty. Sch., Buenos Aires, 1978-81; tchr. Spanish, psychology Ava (Mo.) HS, 1982-84; tchr. Spanish, social studies McDonald County HS, Anderson, Mo., 1984-88; counselor, acad. advisor Mo. So. State U., Joplin, 1988—2003. Cons. Mo. So. State Univ., 1990—; mem. internat. task force Mo. So. State Coll., 1994—96; mem. adv. bd. Adult Basic Edn., Joplin, 1992—2003; presenter Ctr. Applications Psychol. Type Internat. Conf., 1996. Named to Outstanding Young Women Am., 1972; recipient William D. Phillips Music award, 1st Christian Ch., Columbia, 1956. Mem.: Southwest Mo. Sch. Counselor Assn. (sec. 1994—97, v.p. 1992—94, 1999—2001, mem. governing bd., chmn. publs. and rsch. com. 1997—99), Mo. Sch. Counselor Assn., Phi Theta Kappa, Sigma Delta Pi, Phi Sigma Iota (romance lang., pres. 1959—60), Delta Eta Chi, Sigma Phi Gamma, Kappa Delta Pi. Avocations: music, photographer, sketch artist, needlecrafts, jewelry crafts. Home: 1214 Circle Dr Neosho MO 64850-1301 Office Phone: 417-451-7633.

ALLMAN, MARGO HUTZ, sculptor, painter; b. NYC, Feb. 23, 1933; d. Werner H. and Avis (Newcomb) Hutz; m. William B. Allman, Feb. 19, 1954; children: Avis Louise, David Drue. Student, Smith Coll., 1950-51, Moore Coll. Art, 1952-55, Hans Hofmann Sch. Art, 1953, U. Del., 1967-70. Artist-in-residence Canakkale Seramik, Turkey, 1995. One-woman shows include Wallingford (Pa.) Art Ctr., 1964, Windham Coll., 1974, Bloomsburg State Coll., 1976—77, Moore Coll. Art and Design, 1979, Marian Locks Gallery, Phila., 1984, McKinney Gallery West Chester U., Pa., 1994, Gomez Gallery, Balt., 2002, Garrubbo Bazan Gallery, West Chester, 2005, Exhibited in group shows at Phila. Art Alliance, 1954, Del. Art Mus., Wilmington, 1958, 1965, 1967, 1993, 2000, Print Club, Phila., 1959, U. Del., 1977, Del. State Arts Coun., Wilmington, 1981, C. Grimaldis Gallery, Balt., 1983, Art in Form Gallery, Karlsruhe, Germany, 1984, Contemporary Women Artists Phila., 1986—87, Del. Ctr. Contemporary Arts, Wilmington, 1995, 2002, Long Beach Island Found. Arts and Scis., Loveladies, N.J., 1995, Cecil County Arts Coun., Elkton, Md., 1998—99, Chester County Art Assn., West Chester, 1999—2001, 2003, Regional Ctr. Women Arts, 2001, 2003, Moore Galleries Kimmel Ctr. Performing Arts, Phila., 2004, Represented in permanent collections Del. Mus., Phila. Mus., Tidewater Pub. Co., Centerville, Md., Hercules, Inc., Wilmington, Connolly Bove Lodge & Hutz LLP. Bd. dirs. Robert Small Dance Co., N.Y.C., 1979—80. Recipient Mildred Boericke prize, Print Club, 1958, Landscape prize, Wilmington Trust Bank, 1969, Disting. Alumnae award, Moore Coll. Art Design, 1998. Mem.: Phila. Mus. Art, Nat. Mus. Women Arts (charter), Del. Art Mus., Del. Ctr. Contemporary Arts, Moore Coll. Art and Design Alumnae Assn. Home: 202 State Rd West Grove PA 19390-8906

ALLMAND, LINDA F(AITH), retired library director; b. Port Arthur, Tex., Jan. 31, 1937; d. Clifton James and Jewel Etoile (Smith) Allmand. BA, North Tex. State U., 1960; MA, U. Denver, 1962. Clerical asst. Gates Meml. Libr., 1953-55; libr. asst. Houston Pub. Libr., 1955-58; children's libr. Denver Pub.

Libr., 1960-63; children's coord. Anaheim (Calif.) Pub. Libr., 1963-65; br. mgr. Dallas Pub. Libr, 1965-71, chief br. svcs., 1971-81; dir. Ft. Worth Pub. Libr., 1981-98; instr. North Tex. State U., Denton, 1967—2004, ret., 2004. Instr. Dallas County C.C., 1981; bldg. cons. Dallas Pub. Libr., 1974-80, Hurst Pub. Libr., 1977-78, Jacksonville (Tex.) Pub. Libr., 1976-79, Carrollton Pub. Libr., 1979-81, Haltom (Tex.) City Pub. Libr., 1984, Iowa Park (Tex.) Pub. Libr., 1985, S.W. Regional Libr., Ft. Worth, 1987. Author: 1981-2000, Ft. Worth Public Library-Facilities and Long-Range Planning Study, 1982; contbr. chpts. to books, articles to profl. jours. Bd. dirs. City of Dallas Credit Union, 1973-81, Sr. Citizen's Ctrs., Inc., 1982; com. chmn. Goals for Dallas, 1967-69; mem. Forum Ft. Worth, 1983; mem. Edn. Info. Task Force, Downtown Fort Worth, Inc., 1992-93; mem. women's health adv. bd. Harris Meth. Hosp., 1999-2004. Pilot Club of Port Arthur scholar, 1954, Libr. Binding Inst. scholar, 1958; recipient Disting. Alumnus award North Tex. State U., 1983, U. North Tex., 1998, Leadership Ft. Worth, 1982-83; named Tarrant County Newsmaker of Yr., 1984, Outstanding Leader Ft. Worth Star Telegram, 1989, Outstanding Woman of Yr. Mayor's Commn. on Status of Women, 1989. Mem. ALA, AAUP, AAUW (Tarrant County pres.-elect 1998, pres. 1999), Tex. Libr. Assn. (pres. pub. libr. divsn. 1980-81, chmn. planning com. 1982-84, pres.-elect 1985-86, pres. 1986-87, Libr. of Yr. award 1985, North Tex. Pub. Adminstr. of Yr. award 1990), Tarrant Regional Librs. Assn., Am. Mgmt. Assn., Dallas County Librs. Assn. (pres. 1968-69), Downtown Ft. Worth Rotary Club (mem. edn. info. task force 1992-93), Freedom to Read Found., Ft. Worth C. of C. (bd. dirs. 1993-95), Sister Cities, Inc., Ft. Worth Pub. Libr. Found. Home: 701 Timberview Ct N Fort Worth TX 76112-1715

ALLMON, MICHAEL BRYAN, financial consultant; b. Oceanside, Calif., July 14, 1951; s. William Bryan and Cecelia Audrey (Wright) A.; m. Monika Ann Arth, Sept. 15, 1979; children: Stefanie Michele, Danika Audrey. BBA, U. Tex., 1975; MBT, U. So. Calif., 1986. CPA, Calif., 1978; registered pvt. trusee, Calif. Dept. Justice, 2005. Acct. Alexander Grant & Co., LA, 1976—77, Laventhol & Horwath, CPAs, LA, 1977—85; dir. tax, fin. planning svcs. Zusman, Cameron and Allmon, CPAs, 1985-88; CEO, dir. Essential Profl. Svcs., Inc., 1985-86; ptnr. Michael B. Allmon & Assocs. LLP, CPAs, Manhattan Beach, Calif., 1988—; pres. MBA Group, Inc., Marina Del Rey, 1991—2004; pvt. practice, 1995—. Chmn., MBA Advisors, Inc., Manhattan Beach, 1999—; exec. bd. dirs. estate and gift com. of taxation sect. State Bar Calif Contbr. articles to profl. jours. Trustee Calif. Dept. Justicec, 2005—. Mem. AICPAs (fed. tax divsn.), Calif. Soc. CPAs (fin. planning com., tax com., v.p., bd. dirs. LA chpt. 1992-99, statewide bd. dirs. 1995-97, 2000-2003, chair LA estate planning com. 1992—, founding chair statewide estate planning com. 2000-2003, com. mem. 2000—), Am. Assn. Profl. Fin. Planners (LA chpt. pres.), Wall-Nuts Track Club (LA, pres. team), Manhattan Beach (Calif.) Country Club. Office: 1230 Rosecrans Ave Ste 102 Manhattan Beach CA 90266 Office Phone: 310-536-0200. Business E-Mail: mike@mbacpas.com.

ALLMON, MICHAEL W, SR., sales executive; b. Orange, Tex., Feb. 3, 1952; s. Paul James and Bobbie Jean Coe Allmon; m. Nancy Louise Ham Allmon, July 17, 1971; children: Jennifer Leigh, Michael Wayne Jr. BS, Southwest Tex. State U., 1986. Paramedic Houston Fire Dept., 1973—78; med. sales rep. Ross Labs, Sherman, Tex., 1978—79, Bristol Labs, Sherman and Temple, Tex., 1979—88; regional med. sales rep. Laborie Med. Technologies, Temple, Tex., 1992—96; regional sales mgr. Gen. Orthopedic, Temple, Tex., 1996—. Sales trainer Bristol Labs, Temple, Tex., 1983. Co-campaign chmn. Hugh Shine U.S. Congression Campaign, Temple and Waco, Tex., 1985. Mem.: Wildflower Country Club, Travis Masonic Lodge (3rd degree mason). Republican. Avocations: golf, photography, gardening, travel, stain glass. E-mail: mallmon1@hot.rr.com.

ALLNER, WALTER HEINZ, graphics designer, painter, art director; b. Dessau, Germany, Jan. 2, 1909; arrived in U.S., 1949, naturalized, 1957; m. Colette Vasselon, Mar. 8, 1938 (div. June 1951); 1 child, Michel; m. Jane Booth Pope, Apr. 4, 1954; 1 child, Peter. Student, Bauhaus-Dessau, 1927-30. Designer Gesellschafts-und Wirtschafts-Museum, Vienna, Austria, 1929; asst. to typographer Piet Zwart, Wassenaar, Holland, 1930; editorial, painting, and advt. designer Paris, 1932-49; ptnr. Omnium Graphique, Paris, 1933-36; art dir. Formes, Editions d'Art Graphique et Photographique, Paris, 1933-36; Paris editor Swiss art mag. Graphis, 1945-48; founder, editor Internat. Poster Ann., 1948-52; co-dir. Editions Paralleles, Paris, 1948-51; mem. staff Fortune mag., N.Y.C., 1951-74, art dir., 1962-74; mem. faculty Parsons Sch. Design, N.Y.C., 1974-86. Vis. critic, mem. Comite de Parrainage Ecole Superieure d'Arts Graphiques, Paris, 1979—; freelance designer, design cons.; lectr., Australia, 1983. Posters for traffic safety campaign, Outdoor Advt. Assn. Am., 1959—60, exhibitions include Salon des Surindependants, Paris, Salon des Réalités Nouvelles, Germany, Austria, U.S., Eng., France, The Netherlands, Switzerland, Latin Am., Japan, others; compiler, editor: A.M. Cassandre, Peintre d'Affiches, 1948; editor: Posters, 1952; corr.: Signes mag., 1990—92; contbg. editor: Design Jour., 1990—92; contbr. articles to profl. jours. Named Laureate 4th Block, Kharkov, Ukraine, 1997; recipient medal Bauhaus-Dessau, German Acad. Architecture, 1979, Bruno Biennale Hon. Membership, Henri award, Alliance Graphique Internat., 1998. Mem.: Alliance Graphique Internationale (internat. pres.), Assn. Italiana Creativi Comunicazione Visiva (hon.). Home: 110 Riverside Dr New York NY 10024-3715 Home (Summer): 5 Slade Hill Rd Truro MA 02666-0167

ALLNUTT, ROBERT FREDERICK, management consultant, lawyer; b. Richmond, Va., June 15, 1935; s. Robert Carhart and Evelyn Rosalie (Brooks) A.; m. Jan Latven, July 17, 1938; children: Robert David, Thomas Frederick. BS in Indsl. Engring, Va. Poly. Inst., 1957; JD with distinction, George Washington U., 1960, LLM, 1962. Bar: D.C. 1960, Va. 1960. Patent examiner U.S. Patent Office, 1957-60; with NASA, 1960-70, 78-83, asst. adminstr. legis. affairs, 1967-70, assoc. dep. adminstr., 1978-81, assoc. adminstr. external rels., dep. gen. counsel, 1981-83; legal counsel, corp. sec. U.S. Com. Energy Awareness, 1983-84; v.p. Communication Satellite Corp., 1984-85; exec. v.p. Pharm. Mfrs. Assn., 1985-95; sr. counselor APCO Worldwide, Washington, 1995—. Assoc. gen. counsel Commn. on Govt. Procurement, 1970-73; staff dir. com. aero. and space scis. U.S. Senate, 1973-75; dep. asst. adminstr. ERDA, 1975-78; lectr. law Am. U. Law Sch., 1964; bd. dirs. Cortex Pharms., Inc., Irvine, Calif., F. Dohmen Co., Inc., Germantown, Wis. Trustee Air and Space Heritage Coun.; bd. dirs. Nat. Health Coun., 1987-98, Nat. Coun. on Aging, 1990-98; mem. Com. of 100, Va. Poly. Inst., 1991—; mem. program coun. Internat. Ctr. for Sci. Lit., Chgo. Acad. Scis.; bd. dirs. Nat. Medals Sci. and Tech. Found., 1997—2005, Partnership for Caring, 1998-2001, Am. Hospice Found., 2003- . Recipient Superior Performance award U.S. Patent Office, 1959, Apollo Achievement award NASA, 1969, Meritorious Svc. medal ERDA, 1976, Exceptional Svc. medal NASA, 1981, Disting. Svc. medal NASA, 1983; named Meritorious Fed. Exec. with Presdl. Rank Office of Pres., 1981. Mem. Legal Aid Soc. D.C. (bd. dirs.), Nat. Space Soc. (bd. govs.), NASA Alumni League (v.p.), Edgemoor Tennis Club (Bethesda, Md., pres. 1987-89), Order of Coif. Home: 5415 Moorland Ln Bethesda MD 20814-1335 Office: APCO Worldwide 1615 L St NW Washington DC 20036-5610

ALLRED, ALBERT LOUIS, chemistry professor; b. Mount Airy, N.C., Sept. 19, 1931; s. Caleb Haynes and Bessie (Brown) A.; m. Nancy Jean Willis, Aug. 30, 1958; children— Kevin Scott, Gregg Warren, Sarah Elaine. BS in Chemistry, U. N.C., 1953; A.M., Harvard, 1955, PhD, 1956. Chemist E.I. du Pont de Nemours Co., Wilmington, Del., 1952, 55, Mallinckrodt Chem. Works, St. Louis, 1954, Argonne (Ill.) Nat. Lab., 1958, 76; mem. faculty Northwestern U., 1956—, prof., 1969-91, prof. emeritus, 1991—, assoc. dean Coll. Arts and Scis., 1970-74, chmn. dept. chemistry, 1980-86, acting dean Coll. Arts and Scis., 1987-88, acting v.p. for rsch. and dean Grad. Sch., 1992, acting provost, 1995. Vis. scholar Cambridge (Eng.) U., 1987. Alfred P. Sloan fellow, 1963-65; postdoctoral fellow U. Rome, Italy, 1967; hon. research assoc. Univ. Coll., London (Eng.), 1965 Mem. AAUP (pres. Northwestern U. 1968-69), Am. Chem. Soc., Chem. Soc. (London), Coun. Chem. Rsch. (gov. bd. 1985-88), Rotary Internat., Phi Beta Kappa, Phi Lambda Upsilon, Sigma Xi, Alpha Chi Sigma. Home: 820 Milburn St Evanston IL 60201-2450

ALLRED, BRADY RUSSELL, conductor, pianist; b. Provo, Utah, Mar. 18, 1961; s. Fred Russell and Arleen Harding Allred; m. Carol Ann Goodwin, Apr. 21, 1984; children: Loren Rachel, Megan Rose, Brennan Elaine, Karin Arleen. MusB in Flute Performance & Theory/Composition, Brigham Young U., Provo, Utah, 1985; MusM in Choral Conducting, Eastman Sch. of Music, Rochester, N.Y., 1987; performer's cert. in Flute, Eastman Sch. of Music, 1988, D of Mus. Arts in Conducting, 1990. Assoc. prof. of conducting and dir. of choral activities Duquesne U. Sch. of Music, Pitts., 1989—2003; assoc. prof. of music and dir. of choral conducting U. of Utah Sch. of Music, Salt Lake City, 2003—. Artistic dir. and condr. Bach Choir of Pitts., Pitts., 1993—2004, Utah Choral Artists, Salt Lake City, 2004—; artistic dir. N.Y. State Summer Sch. of the Arts, Sch. of Choral Studies, Fredonia, NY, 2002—; music dir. and condr. Butler Symphony Orch., Butler, Pa., 1995—97; singer Robert Shaw Festival Singers, N.Y.C., 1993—99. Condr. (compact disc recording (digital audio) Cantate Hodie: Sing Forth This Day (Clarion Label, 2001). Stake mission pres. Ch. of Jesus Christ of Latter-day Saints, Pitts., 2000—02. Recipient 1st prize and Condrs. prize, Martoberdorf Internat. Chamber Choir Competition, 1997, winner, Florilége Vocal de Tours, France, 1999, Guest Condr., Salt Lake Mormon Tabernacle Choir, 1993, 1998, Am. Choral Dirs. Nat. Conv., Lincoln Ctr., N.Y., Am. Choral Dirs. Assn., 2003, Karl G. Maeser scholar and Mayhew Composition prize, Brigham Young U., 1985. Mem.: Internat. Fedn. for Choral Music, Phi Kappa Lambda (life; pres. 1996—97), Phi Kappa Phi (life). Lds. Avocation: travel. Office: School of Music University of Utah 1375 East Presidents Cir Salt Lake City UT 84112 Office Phone: 801-587-9377. Office Fax: 801-581-5683. E-mail: brady.allred@music.utah.edu.

ALLRED, DAWN PETERMAN, education educator; b. Roscrea, Ireland, Aug. 15, 1952; arrived in U.S., 1958, naturalized; d. Eugene Vincent and Ruth Kavanaugh Peterman; children: Anne Kavanaugh, Brendan, James. BA in Speech and Comm., U. Mo., Columbia, 1973; MEd in Spl. Edn., U. Mo., St. Louis, 2000, postgrad. Cert. tchr. Mo. Rschr. comm. divsn. Marshall Field & Co., Chgo., 1979; tchr. ESL Parkway Sch. Dist., Creve Coeur, Mo., 1977—78; tchr. grade 3, primary grade coord. Annunziata Sch., St. Louis, 1974—77; tchr. grades 4, 5, 6, 7 St. Justin the Martyr Sch., St. Louis, 1979—82; grad. tchg. fellow U. Mo., 2000—, instr. Coll. Edn., 2001—04, student tchr. supr., 2004. Mem. com. Qualitative Rsch. Conf., St. Louis, 2001—. Pres. PTA The Miriam Sch., Webster Groves, Mo., 1993—95; mem. govt. rels. com. Parkway Sch. Dist., Chesterfield, Mo., 2000—05; bd. dirs. Spl. Edn. Transition Adv. Bd., St. Louis, 2001—. Recipient Meritorious Svc. commendation, U. Mo., 2004. Mem.: Mo. Assn. on Higher Edn. and Disability, Learning Disabilities Assn. Mo., Assn. for Study Higher Edn., Equestrian Order of the Holy Sepulchre of Jerusalem, Kappa Delta Phi, Phi Kappa Phi. Roman Catholic. Avocations: travel, Irish history and culture, hiking. E-mail: dpa340@umsl.edu.

ALLRED, GLORIA RACHEL, lawyer; b. Phila., July 3, 1941; d. Morris and Stella Bloom; m. William Allred (div. Oct. 1987); 1 child, Lisa. BA, U. Pa., 1963; MA, NYU, 1966; JD, Loyola U., LA, 1974; JD (hon.), U. West LA, 1981. Bar: Calif. 1975, U.S. Dist. Ct. (ctrl. dist.) Calif. 1975, U.S. Ct. Appeals (9th cir.) 1976, U.S. Supreme Ct. 1979. Ptnr. Allred, Maroko, Goldberg & Ribakoff (now Allred, Maroko & Goldberg), LA, 1976—. Former host KABC TalkRadio, Los Angeles. Contbr. articles to profl. jours. Pres. Women's Equal Rights Legal Def. and Edn. Fund, LA, 1978—, Women's Movement Inc., LA. Recipient Commendation award City of LA, 1986, Mayor of LA, 1986, Pub. Svc. award Nat. Assn. Fed. Investigators, 1986, Vol. Action award Pres. of U.S., 1986, Women of Distinction award Nat. Coun. on Aging, 1994, The Judy Jarvis Meml. award, 2001; Named to Millennium Hall of Fame, Nat. Assoc. Women Bus. Owners, LA Chapter, 2000. Mem. ABA, Calif. Bar Assn., Nat. Assn. Women Lawyers, Calif. Women Lawyers Assn., Women Lawyers LA Assn., Friars (Beverly Hills, Calif.), Magic Castle Club (Hollywood, Calif.) Office: Allred Maroko & Goldberg 6300 Wilshire Blvd Ste 1500 Los Angeles CA 90048-5217 Office Phone: 323-653-6530.

ALLRED, NANCY CAROL, music educator; b. L.A., May 6, 1960; d. John Loraine and Carol Janice Larson; m. John David Allred, May 25, 1991 (dic. Oct. 1998); children: Spencer David, Benjamin William, Rebecca Susan, Preston Matthew. B in Music, Brigham Young U., 1986, M in Music, 1988; D in Musical Arts, U. Mo., Kansas City, 1999. Class piano instr. Dixie Coll., St. George, Utah, 1993-94, piano instr., 1993-95, Tuacahn Ctr. for the Arts, Ivins, Utah, 1993-96, chair piano dept., 1994-96; piano instr. Allred Piano Studio, St. George, Utah, 1993—; music instr. Dixie State Coll., St. George, Utah, 2000—; piano instr., 2000—; class piano instr., 2001—. Adj. asst. prof. pedagogy U. Mo. Kansas City Conservatory of Music, 1991-92, piano instr. divsn. continuing edn., 1988-93. Contbr. author: Gina Bachauer: A Pianist's Odyssey, 1999. Mem. Music Tchrs. Nat. Assn., Utah Music Tchrs. Assn. (pres. St. George chpt. 1994-95). Republican. Mem. Lds Ch.

ALLSBROOK, JAMES T., music educator; b. Franklin, Va., Feb. 18, 1971; s. James Carter and Linda McAuley Allsbrook. MusB in Edn., Old Dominion U., 1993. Cert. Educator Va. Dept. Edn., 2001. Grad. asst. trombone Fla. State U., Tallahassee, 1993—95; stage crew leader Va. Symphony, Norfolk, 1995—96; lead web designer Georgi Enterprises, Portsmouth, Va., 1996—97; dir. bands Bayside HS, Virginia Beach, Va., 1997—. Bd. mem. Bayside Band Boosters, Virginia Beach, 1997—2005. Recipient Cmty. Star, Sta. WTKR-TV, 2005; Grad. assistantship, Fla. State U., 1993-1995. Mem.: Va. Music Educators Assn., Va. Beach Edn. Assn., VA Band and Orch. Dirs. Assn., Phi Mu Alpha Sinfonia (life; alumni sec. 1995—97). D-Conservative. Avocations: travel, music, web design. Home: 528 Chapel Lake Dr 102 Virginia Beach VA 23454 Office: Bayside HS Va Beach City Pub Schs 4960 Haygood Rd Virginia Beach VA 23455 Office Fax: 757-473-5123. Personal E-mail: jtallsbrook@aol.com. Business E-Mail: james.allsbrook@vbschools.com.

ALLSBROOK, OGDEN OLMSTEAD, JR., retired economics professor; b. Wilmington, NC, July 1, 1940; s. Ogden Olmstead Sr. and Elizabeth Barringer (Warren) A. BA, Wake Forest U., 1962; PhD, U. Va., 1966. Ops. rsch. analyst Dep. Def., Washington, 1966-68; asst. prof. econs. U. Ga., Athens, 1968-73, dir. grad. studies econs., 1971-81, assoc. prof., 1974-96, ret., 1996. Author: Utilization of Military Resources, 1969; contbr. articles to profl. jours. Capt. U.S. Army, 1966-68. Mem. AAUP, Nat. Soc. SAR (pres. Athens chpt. 1992-94), Cape Fear Club, So. Econ. Assn. Lutheran. Avocations: motor sports, stamp collecting/philately, turned wood objects, coin collecting/numismatics, Japanese cloisonne. Home: 115 Tillman Ln Athens GA 30606-4115 E-mail: ooalls1@wmconnect.com.

ALLSHOUSE, MERLE FREDERICK, educational organization administrator; b. Pitts., Pa., Apr. 26, 1935; s. Merle Lawrence and Helen (Frederick) A.; m. Myrna Mansfield, Apr. 1, 1956; children: Frederick Scott, Kimberly Dawn. BA (Rector fellow), DePauw U., 1957; MA (Rockefeller Theol. fellow), Yale, 1959, PhD (Rockefeller fellow 1959-61, Kent fellow 1961), 1965. Instr. philosophy Dickinson Coll., 1963-65, asst. prof., 1965-68, assoc. dean of coll., asso. prof. philosophy, 1968-70; dean of coll., prof. philosophy Bloomfield (N.J.) Coll., 1970-71, pres., 1971-86, Myron Stratton Home Found., Colorado Springs, Colo., 1986-88; prof. publ adminstr. Grad. Sch. Pub. Affairs, U. Colo., 1988; v.p. U. Colo. Found., 1989-94; exec. dir. Acad. Sr. Profls., Eckerd Coll., St. Petersburg, Fla., 1994—2002. Mem. adv. bd. U. South Fla. Sch. Bus.; mem. N.J. Student Assistance Bd. Bd. dirs. Presbyn. Career and Counseling Ctr., N.J. Coll. Fund, Inc., Colo. Children's Campaign-The Goodwill of Colorado Springs, The Colorado Springs Symphony Orch., Coun. Ind. Colls., N.E. region Boy Scouts Am., Colorado Springs Symphony Orch., The Broadmoor Improvement Soc.; pres., Beth El Coll. Nursing, Goodwill of Colorado Springs; moderator Broadmoor Community Ch.; div. chmn. United Way; mem. Da Vinci Quartet; trustee Montclair Kimberley Acad.; pres. Presbyn. Coll. Union. HEW fellow, 1979-80, U. South Fla. fellow. Mem. Metaphys. Soc. Am. (chair 2004), Am. Philos. Assn., Am. Acad. Religion, Assn. Ind. Colls. and Univs. in N.J. (dir., chmn. bd.), Nat. Assn. Ind. Colls. and Univs. (chmn. secretariat 1983-86, bd. dirs.), Council Ind. Colls. (bd. dirs.), St. Petersburg Rotary. Home: Marina Bay 15 Crescent Pl S Saint Petersburg FL 33711-5118 Office Phone: 727-365-0160. Personal E-mail: Allshouse@ureach.com.

ALLUMS, JAMES A., retired surgeon; b. Kountze, Tex., Sept. 28, 1937; m. Elizabeth Dee Walton, June 24, 1961; children: Ann Elizabeth, Sarah Dee, Benjamin Walton. BA, U. Tex., 1959; MD, U. Tex. Med. Br., 1962. Diplomate Am. Bd. Med. Examiners, Am. Bd. Surgery, Gen. Vascular Surgery, Am. Bd. Thoracic Surgery. Rotating intern Phila. Gen. Hosp., 1962-63; resident gen. surgery Med. Br. U. Tex., Galveston, 1963-66, 68-69; resident thoracic surgery Med. Branch U. Tex., Galveston, Tex., 1969—71; ptnr. Thoracic and Cardiovasc. Surg. Assocs., Beaumont, Tex., 1971-97; clin. asst. prof. dept. thoracic and cardiovasc. surgery U. Tex. Med. Br., Galveston, ret., 1997. Active physician St. Elizabeth Hosp., chief of staff 1976-77, 87-88; active Beaumont, Bapt. Hosp. of S.E. Tex., Beaumont, Beaumont Regional Med. Ctr., Beaumont Regional Med. Ctr., Park Place Hosp.; courtesy staff St. Mary Hosp., Port Arthur, Mid Jefferson Hosp., Nederland, Tex.; cons. staff U. Tex. Med. Br. Hosp., Galveston; mem. cardiovasc. com. Bapt. Hosp., 1991-93, 1996, physician, nurse ad hoc com., 1992; clin. asst. prof. Dept. of Surgery U. Tex. Med. Br. Hosp., 1993-94; OR com. St. Elizabeth Hosp., Beaumont, 1990-91, 93-94, cardiovasc. quality assurance subcom., 1991-92, cardiovasc./coronary care com., 1990-91, 92-93, CCU quality assurance subcom. Contbr. articles to profl. jours. Capt. US Army, 1966-68. Recipient J.C. Crager award Am. Heart Assn., 1992, Mr. East Tex. award Tyler County Dogwood Festival, 1993. Fellow ACS (gov. 1989-94, pres. South Tex. chpt. 1987), Am. Coll. of Angiology, Am. Coll. of Cardiology, Am. Coll. of Chest Physicians, Beaumont Acad. of Medicine; mem. AMA, Assn. of Am. Physicians and Surgeons, Bapt. Hosp. P.H.O., Beaumont Regional P.H.O., Jefferson County Med. Soc., Singleton Surg. Soc., Soc. of Thoracic Surgeons, So. Assn. for Vascular Surgery, So. Med. Assn., So. Thoracic Surg. Assn., St. Elizabeth Hosp. P.H.O., Tex. Med. Assn. (coun. on med. edn. 1985-92), Tex. Surg. Soc., Alumni Assn. of the U. of Tex. Med. Br. (pres. 1984-85)Phi Eta Sigma, Alpha Epsilon Delta.

ALLY, MOONIS R., chemical engineer; b. Karachi, Pakistan; s. Mehboob and Parveen Ally; m. Nafis Ally; children: Tanya, Faiz, Nadya, Alia. MS, Ill. Inst. Tech., 1977; PhD, U. Pitts., 1981. Group leader Energy Divsn., Oak Ridge Nat. Lab., Oak Ridge, Tenn., 1985—91, Chem. Tech. Divsn., Oak Ridge, Tenn., 1991—2000. Sr. rsch. staff Engring. Sci. and Tech. Divsn., Oak Ridge Nat. Lab., Oak Ridge, Tenn., 2000—. Reviewer State Textbook Commn., Nashville, 2002; mentoring U. Tenn., Knoxville, 1997—2004. Recipient Dist. Scientist award, Lockheed Martin Energy Sys., Inc., 1998, Technical Achievement award, U. Tenn.-Battelle, LLC, 2000, Clinton Stryker Dist. Svc. award, Ill. Inst. Tech., 1977. Mem.: Am. Chem. Soc. Achievements include patents for electrolyte solutions; detection of minute quantitites of explosives. Home: 1 Bethel Valley Rd Oak Ridge TN 37831-6070 Office: Oak Ridge Nat Lab PO Box 2008 MS-6070 Oak Ridge TN 37831 Office Phone: 865-576-8003. Personal E-mail: allymr@ornl.gov.

ALM, JOHN RICHARD, beverage company executive; b. Jamestown, NY, Feb. 25, 1946; s. Carl Raymond and Erma Grace (Williams) A.; m. Cheryl D. Van Marter; Apr. 26, 1969; children: Lara, Richard. BS in Acctg., SUNY, Buffalo, 1972. Sr. auditor Price Waterhouse, N.Y.C. and Los Angeles, 1974-77; sr. v.p. fin., controller Johnston Coca-Cola Bottling Group, Inc., 1977—, v.p., CFO Atlanta, pres., COO; pres., CEO Coca-Cola Enterprises Inc., Atlanta, 2004—. CPA, Minn. Served with USAF, 1969-72. Mem. Fin. Execs. Inst., Am. Inst. CPA's, Minn. Soc. CPA's. Office: Coca-Cola Enterprises Inc 2500 Windy Ridge Pkwy SE Atlanta GA 30339-5677*

ALMAGUER, FRANK, ambassador; m. Antoinette Gallegos, 1970; children: Francisco Daniel, Nina Suzanne. BA in Polit. Sci., U. Fla., 1967; MS in Govt. and Bus. Adminstrn., George Washington U., 1974. Vol. Peace Corps, Orange Walk Town, Belize, 1967-69; mgmt. analyst Office of Auditor Gen., USAID; mgmt. analyst for health affairs Office of Econ. Opportunity; assoc. country dir. U.S. Peace Corps, Belize City, 1974-76, country dir. Tegucigalpa, Honduras, 1976-79; dep. mission dir. USAID, Panama City, 1979-83, dir. Office of S.Am. and Mex. Affairs Washington, 1983-86, mission dir. Quito, Ecuador, 1986-90; mem. Sr. Seminar Fgn. Svc. Inst., 1990-91; regional mission dir. Eastern Europe USAID, Washington, 1991-93, acting asst. adminstrn. Bur. for Europe, 1993, dep. asst. adminstr. human resources Bur. of Mgmt., 1993-96, mission dir. La Paz, Bolivia, 1996-99; amb. Republic of Honduras Dept. State, Tegucigalpa, 1999—2002; internat. cons. and lectr. on L.Am. and social and econ. devel. issues, 2003—. U.S. del. UN Commn. on Human Rights, 2004; sr. advisor Pan Am. Devel. Found., 2004—05; dir. for fin. and adminstrn. OAS, 2005—. Recipient Meritorious award U.S. Peace Corps, 1979, Disting. svc. award USAID, 1989, Spl. Act award, 1992, Presdl. Meritorious awards, 1988, 99, Roger W. Jones Exec. Leadership award, 1996, State Dept. Superior Honor award, 1999, Sec. of State's Career Achievement award, 2002, AID Adminstr.'s Disting. Career award, 2002. Home: 1503 Dulcimer Ct Vienna VA 22182-1607 Office: 1889 F Street NW Washington DC 20006 Office Phone: 202-458-3436. Personal E-mail: falmaguer@oas.org.

AL MALIK, AMIR ISA, entrepreneur, consultant, musician; b. Shreveport, La., Apr. 2, 1951; s. Samuel Leroy and Evelyn Cynthia (Jones) K.; m. Sannah N. Parkies. AA Arts and Humanities, Laney Coll., 1981, AA Social Sci., 1983, AA Language Arts, 1985, AA Theater Arts, 1989, AA in Music, 1995; student, Columbia Sch. Broadcasting, Radio & T.V. Announcing, 1986; male modeling student, Barbizon Sch. Modeling, 1994; cert., Founds. of Faith Theology, 1994. Assoc. The Heritage Group, Walnut Creek, Calif., 1974—; pres., CEO Magnetic Phi Artists, Oakland, Calif., 1988—; supr. Loomis Armored Inc., Oakland, Calif., 1991—; coach San Francisco Generals; coord.-backfields and lineman Am. Athletic League; coach Alameda County Knights. Musician, poet free-lance, Oakland, 1970—; model, actor, Laney Coll., Yosson Enterprises, Oakland, San Francisco, 1981—; actor, dir. The Mahdi Theater, Oakland, 1989—; rschr., dir., The Oil Bandana, Oakland, 1989—. Author: (book of poetry) Africa Sweet Africa Me Africa Me, 1991, (short story) Three Coins for the Fisherman, 1990; composer: Tally of the Leaves, 1994, Clown Cloud, 1999; musician: Ben Oni Orch. Min. Imam Nation of Islam, San Francisco, 1975—; min.-in-tng. Allen Temple Bapt. Ch., 1981; fruit of Islam, Nation of Islam Mosque 26; asst. coach Peralta Coll. Dist., Oakland, 1986-87; active spl. svcs. Rainbow Coalition Calif., 1984; del. Students for Jesse Jackson Campaign, Calaif., 1989; candidate for mayor City of Oakland, 1994. With U.S. Army, 1975-76. Named Citizen of Yr., recipient Ambassador award Principality of the Hutt River Province, Queensland, Australia. Mem. Internat. Platform Assn., Pre-Paid Legal Svcs. (assoc., license), The Fed. Bear Sports Club (diploma), Nirvana Found. for Psychic Rsch. (life), Am. Legion (life), Smithsonian Inst., Knight of the Realm (ambassador, Citizen of Yr. 1995, Principality of Hutt River Province Australia), Phi Beta Lambda, Epsilon Alpha Phi (past pres., past v.p. state chpt.). Republican. Moslem. Avocations: martial arts, weightlifting, yoga, wrestling. Home and Office: 9437 Olive St Oakland CA 94603-1725 E-mail: amir6.2@netzero.net.

ALMAN, EMILY ARNOW, lawyer, sociologist; b. N.Y.C., Jan. 20, 1922; d. Joseph Michael and Cecilia (Greenstone) Arnow; B.A., Hunter Coll., 1948; Ph.D., New Sch. for Social Research, 1963; J.D., Rutgers U., Newark, 1977; m. David Alman, Aug. 1, 1940; children: Michelle Alman Harrison, Jennifer Alman Michaels. Bar: N.J. 1978, U.S. Supreme Ct. 1987. Probation officer, N.Y.C., 1945-48; assoc. prof. sociology Douglass Coll. Rutgers U., Newark, 1960-86, prof. emeritus, 1986—; sr. ptnr. Alman & Michaels, Highland Park, N.J., 1978—. Candidate for mayor, City of East Brunswick, 1972; chmn. Concerned Citizens of East Brunswick, 1970-78; pres. bd. trustees Concerned Citizens Environ. Fund., East Brunswick, 1977-78. Mem. ABA (com. family law) N.J. Bar Assn. (bd. dirs. legal svcs), Middlesex County Bar Assn. (Ann. Aldona Appleton award women lawyers sect. 1990, Ann. Svc. to Families award 1993), Am. Sociol. Assn., Assn. Fed. Bar State of N.J., Assn. Trial Lawyers Am., Trial Lawyers Assn. Middlesex County, Law and Soc. Assn., Am. Judicature Soc., Nat. Assn. Women Lawyers, N.J. Assn. Women Lawyers, ACLU, AAUP, Women Helping Women. Author: Ride The Long Night, 1963; screenplay, The Ninety-First Day, 1963. Home: 48 Timber Trace Ballston Spa NY 12020-3720

ALMASAN, ALEXANDRU, geneticist; b. St. Petersburg, Russia, Mar. 15, 1954; came to U.S., 1984; s. Horia and Paraschiva (Elekes) A.; m. Carmen Pricajan, July 28, 1978 BS, U. Brasov, Romania, 1977, MS, 1979; PhD, U. S.C., 1989. Rsch. assoc. Cen. Inst. for Forest Rsch., Bucharest, Romania, 1979-83; rsch. asst. U. S.C., Columbia, 1984-89, postdoctoral fellow, 1989, Salk Inst., San Diego, 1990, rsch. assoc., 1991-94; mem. asst. staff Cleve. Clinic Found., 1995—. Contbr. articles to profl. jours. Recipient NRSA award NIH, 1991, Am. Cancer Soc., 1995, 97; Gordon Bellser fellow U. S.C., 1989. Mem. AAAS, Am. Assn. Cancer Rsch., Radiology Rsch. Soc., Sigma Xi. Achievements include research on role of tumor supressor genes p53 and R6 in genetic instability and cell cycle control; molecular mechanisms of radiation sensitivity. Home: 10358 Hanford Ln Twinsburg OH 44087-1471 Office: Cleve Clinic Found 9500 Euclid Ave Rm T28 Cleveland OH 44195-0001

ALMEIDA, ARTIE N., music specialist; Music spec. Bear Lake Elem. Sch., Apopka, Fla., 1985—; tchr. U Ctrl. Fla., 1997—98, Seminole Cmty. Coll., 1995—, Valencia Cmty. Coll., 1992; dir. U. Ctrl. Fla., 1997—98. Music instr. four-day seminar, Taiwan. Author various music instruction books. Finalist Fla. Tchr. of Yr., 1998; named Music Educator of Yr., Fla., 1999, Seminole County Tchr. of Yr., 1999, School Level Tchr. of Yr., six times. Mem.: nat. Bd Profl. Tchg. Standards. Office: Bear Lake Elem Sch Music Dept 3399 Gleaves Ct Apopka FL 32703

ALMEIDA, DEBRA HANSON, elementary school educator; b. New Bedford, Mass., Jan. 31, 1955; d. John Henry and Delores Mary (Rose) Hanson; m. Dana B. Almeida, Aug. 31, 1973; children: Tara, Shana, Derek. BS, Bridgewater State, Mass., 1977, MEd, 1986; cert. Advanced Grad. Credit, Fitchburg State, Mass., 2003. Cert. tchr. k-6 Mass., prin. k-6 Mass., reading specialist Mass., nat. bd. cert. mid. childhood generalist. Tchr. grade 4 and 5 Sippican Elem. Sch., Marion, Mass., 1982—; workshop presenter sci. and math. Ctr. Innovation in Edn., Calif., 1992—. Title I tchr. math. Freetown Elem. Sch., Mass., 1976—78; workshop presenter math. inservice Old Rochester Regional Schs., 1998, New Bedford area schs., 1998—; author and presenter Newspapers in Edsn., 2002. Treas.and host Fairhaven-New Bedford/Tosashimizu Sister City Com., 1992—. Named Excellence on Inclusive Edn., Family Connections, 2001; recipient Tchr. Recognition award, Marion Sch. Com., 2004. Mem.: Mass. Tchrs. Assn., Marion Tchrs. Assn. (treas.), Nat. Tchrs. Assn., Fairhaven Colonial Club (program activities chmn., v.p., pres.), Delta Kappa Gamma (v.p. ETA chpt. 1996—2000). Roman Catholic. Avocations: travel, art museums, musical theater. Home: 3 Kacy Ln Fairhaven MA 02719

ALMEIDA, JOSÉ AGUSTIN, romance languages educator; b. Waco, Tex., Aug. 28, 1933; s. Jesse M. and Teodora (Mancillas) A.; m. Maritza Barros, Sept. 5, 1964; 1 son, José Rodolfo BA, Baylor U., 1961; MA, U. Mo., 1964, PhD, 1967. Teaching asst. U. Mo., Columbia, 1961-66; instr. Baylor U., Waco, 1962-63; asst. prof. dept. Romance langs. U. N.C., Greensboro, 1966-77, assoc. prof., 1977-99, chmn. Latin Am. studies, 1979-81, emeritus, 1999. Vis. prof. Elmira (N.Y.) Coll., summer 1967; asst. prof. Inst. in Mid. Am., summers 1968-69, Cali, Colombia, summer 1973; assoc. prof. study abroad program U. N.C.-Greensboro-Guilford Coll., Madrid, 1980, dir. grad. studies in Spanish, 1991-95; cons. verbal-active teaching method Hampton Inst., 1976, 77, U. N.C.-Charlotte, 1984; lectr. 1st Internat. Conf. Picaresque Lit., Madrid, 1976, 6th Conf. Internat. Assn. Hispanists, 1977, 1st Internat. Conf. on Lope de Vega, 1980. Author: (with Stephen C. Mohler and Robert R. Stinson) Descubrir y crear, 1976, 3d edit., 1986; La crítica literaria de Fernando de Herrera, 1976 With USAF, 1953-57 Nat. Endowment for Humanities fellow, 1970 Mem. MLA, Am. Assn. Tchrs. Spanish and Portuguese, Internat. Assn. Hispanists, Cervantes Soc. Am., Hispanic Soc. Am. (hon.), Asociación de Cervantistas, Sigma Delta Pi (faculty sponsor 1989—). Democrat. Roman Catholic.

ALMEIDA, RICHARD JOSEPH, finance company administrator; b. N.Y.C., Apr. 29, 1942; s. Caetano Escudero and Grace (Maya) A.; m. Jill Farris, Mar. 17, 1979; 1 child, Alexis Farris. BA in Internat. Affairs, George Washington U., 1963; MA in Internat. Adminstrn., Maxwell Sch. Syracuse U., 1965. Comml. and internat. banker Citibank, N.Y. and South Am., 1966; area head comml. and internat. banking Citicorp/Citibank, Chgo., 1976, L.A., 1978-84, dep. strategic planning N.Y.C., 1984; head fin. inst. and investment banking origination Citicorp Investment Bank, N.Y.C., 1985-87; CFO Heller Fin., Inc., Chgo., 1987—2002, chmn., CEO, 1995—2002. Bd. dirs. Corn Products Internat., E-funds Corp., Care-USA, Old Masters Soc. of Art Inst. Chgo. High Jump. Trustee The Latin Sch. of Chgo. With USCG, 1966-72. Mem. Chgo. Coun. on Fgn. Rels., Chgo. Club, The Casino Club, The Racquet Club, Econ. Club. Chgo., Comml. Club Chgo. Roman Catholic.

ALMEKINDER, DANIEL WAYNE, secondary school educator, theater educator; s. Donald Walter Almekinder and Debbie Jean Florack. BS in Theatre Arts, SUNY, New Paltz, N.Y., 1998, MS in Edn., 2004. Cert. tchr. N.Y. State Edn. Dept., 2004. Drama tchr. Rondout Valley (N.Y.) Mid. Sch., 1998; counselor Camp Hillcroft, Millbrook, NY, 1999; tchr. english Beacon (N.Y.) H.S., 1999—. Adj. instr. theatre Dutchess C.C., Poughkeepsie, NY, 2003—. Actor: (films) The Road Ahead, 2004, Fall to the Son, 2005, Demon Resurrection, 2005. Mem.: N.Y. State English Coun. Office Phone: 845-838-6900. Personal E-mail: almekinder@yahoo.com.

ALMEN, LOWELL GORDON, church official; b. Grafton, N.D., Sept. 25, 1941; s. Paul Orville and Helen Eunice (Johnson) A.; m. Sally Arlyn Clark, Aug. 14, 1965; children: Paul Simon, Cassandra Gabrielle. BA, Concordia Coll., Moorhead, Minn., 1963; MDiv, Luther Theol. Sem., St. Paul, 1967; LittD (hon.), Capital U., 1981; DD (hon.), Carthage Coll., 1989, Concordia Coll., 1994. Ordained to ministry Luth. Ch., 1967. Pastor St. Peter's Luth. Ch., Dresser, Wis., 1967-69; asso. campus pastor, dir. communications Concordia Coll., Moorhead, Minn., 1969-74; mng. editor Luth. Standard ofcl. publ. Am. Luth. Ch., Mpls., 1974-78; editor Luth. Standard, 1979-87; sec., officer Evangelical Luth. Ch. Am., Chgo., 1987—. Author: Old Songs for a New Journey, 1990, One Great Cloud of Witnesses, 1997; author, co-editor: The Many Faces of Pastoral Ministry, 1989; editor: World Religions and Christian Mission, 1967, Our Neighbor's Faith, 1968. Recipient Disting. Alumnus award Concordia Coll., 1982; Bush Found. grantee, 1972 Lutheran. Office: Evang Luth Ch 8765 W Higgins Rd Chicago IL 60631-4101

ALMES, JUNE, retired education educator, librarian; b. Pitts., Feb. 14, 1934; d. Donald John Rowbottom and Marie Catherine (Linz) Douglas; widowed; children: Lawrence John, Douglas Alan. BS in Edn., Indiana U. of Pa., 1955; MLS, U. Pitts., 1969. Tchr. Shippensburg (Pa.) Area High Sch., 1964-68; assoc. prof. Lock Haven (Pa.) U., 1971-94; ret., 1990. Instr. Changsha U. Electric Power, Hunan, China, 1989-90, 95. Co-author: A Survey of the United Kingdom and the United States of America, 2004. Trustee Ross Pub. Libr., Lock Haven, 1975-88, community story programs, 1973-86; tutor Clinton City Literacy Found., Lock Haven, 1979; pres. Ea. Clinton Co. Democratic Women's Club, 2003—. Mem. Am. Assn. Sch. Librs., Pa. Assn. Sch. Librs., ACLU, Phi Kappa Phi, Phi Delta Kappa. Democrat. Avocations: playing bridge, reading, travel, literacy. Home: 228 East Hillside Dr Lock Haven PA 17745-1733 Personal E-mail: jalmes@lhup.edu.

ALMÉSTICA, JOHANNA LYNNETTE, mental health counselor, administrator; b. Ponce, P.R., Aug. 4, 1970; arrived in U.S., 1988; d. Joaquin Alméstica and Margarita Bracero. BA in Psychology, U. Mass. Boston, 1993; MS in counseling Psychology, Our Lady of Lake U., 1999. Counselor, case mgr. supr. Acute Treatment Ctr. Dimock Cmty. Health Ctr., Roxbury, Mass., 2000—. Mem.: APA. Roman Catholic. Avocation: reading. Office: Dimock Cmty Health Ctr Acute Treatment Ctr 41 Dimock St Roxbury MA 02119

ALMJELD, PAUL F., conductor, music educator; b. Wabasso, Minn., June 2, 1942; s. Floyd J. and Frances M. Almjeld; m. Susan J. Gartman; children: Karin, Kristin, Karl. BS, Mankato State Coll., 1964, MusM, 1973; D in Musical Arts, U. Ill., 1988. Music tchr. Taylor Jr. HS, Eielson AFB, Alaska, 1965—67; dir. choral music New London (Wis.) Pub. Schs., 1970—74, Sheboygan (Wis.) South HS, 1974—82; assoc. prof. music Lakeland Coll., Sheboygan, 1982—92, Dakota Wesleyan U., Mitchell, SD, 1997—. Founder, condr. Lakeshore Chorale, Sheboygan, 1982—97; condr. Dakota Chorale, Mitchell, 1997—. Author: (book) The Madrigals of Horatio Faa, 1988; composer: (choral music) Amazing Grace, 2002, Praise the Lord, 2002. Sgt. U.S. Army, 1967—70. Mem.: Music Educators Nat. Conf., S.D. Choral Dirs. Assn., Wis. Choral Dirs. Assn. (pres. 1987—89, bd. dirs. 1985—91), Am. Choral Dirs. Assn. (life; bd. dirs. north ctrl. divsn. 1985—89), Phi Delta Kappa. Avocations: restoring british sports cars, fishing. Home: 1509 S Miller Ave Mitchell SD 57301 Office: Dakota Wesleyan Univ 1200 W University Ave Mitchell SD 57301 Personal E-mail: palmjeld@mit.midco.net. Business E-Mail: paalmjel@dwu.edu.

ALMODOVAR, PEDRO, filmmaker; b. Calzada de Calatrava, Spain, Sept. 25, 1949; s. Francisca Caballero. Co-founder El Deseo S.A. prodn. co., 1987. Theater group actor: Los Goliardos; short films include: Salome, 1978-83; films: Pepi, Luci, Bom y otras chicas del monton, 1980, Laberinto de pasiones, 1980, Dark Habits, 1983, What Have I Done to Deserve This?, 1985, Matador, 1986, Law of Desire, 1987, Women on the Verge of a Nervous Breakdown, 1988 (Felix award 1988), Tie Me Up, Tie Me Down, 1990, High Heels, 1991, Kika, 1993, The Flower of My Secret, 1995, Live Flesh, 1997, All About My Mother, 1999 (Best Dir., Cannes Film Festival, 1999, Best Fgn. Lang. Film, Acad. Awards 2000), Talk To Her, 2002 (Best Original Screenplay Academy award, 2003, Best Screenplay-Original, British Acad. Film Award (BAFTA), 2003), Bad Education, 2004; pub. Fuego en las entrañas, 1982, Patty Diphusa and Other Stories, 1992. Address: El Deseo SA Ruiz Perello 15 Madrid 28028 Spain

ALMON, LORIE, lawyer; b. NYC, Feb. 19, 1969; d. William Scott and Margaret Elise (Erickson) A. BA, U. Vt., 1991; JD, U. Va., 1994. Bar: N.Y. 1995, U.S. Dist. Ct. (so., ea. no. and we. dists., NY, Conn.), US Ct. of Appeals 2d Cir. Asst. corp. counsel Office Corp. Counsel, NYC, 1994—98; co-mng. ptnr. Seyfarth, Shaw, LLP, NYC, 1998—. Named one of Top 40 Under 40 Lawyers, Nat. Law Jour., 2005. Mem. ABA, NYC Bar Assn., Soc. Human Resource Mgmt. Office: Seyfarth Shaw LLP 1270 Avenue Of The Americas Ste 2500 New York NY 10020-1801 Office Phone: 212-218-5517. Office Fax: 212-218-5526.

ALMOND, CARL HERMAN, surgeon, physician, educator; b. Latour, Mo., Apr. 1, 1926; s. Hugh Herman and Sylvia (Morrison) A.; m. Nancy Ginn, June 18, 1964 (div. 1990); children: Carrie, Callie, Carl, Christopher. BS, Washington U., St. Louis, 1949, MD, 1953. Diplomate Am. Bd. Surgery, Am. Bd. Thoracic Surgery. Rotating intern Los Angeles County Gen. Hosp., 1953-54; resident surgery U. Mich., Ann Arbor, 1954-56, jr. clin. instr. surgery, 1956-57, sr. clin. instr., 1957-58; fellow surg. pathology Barnes Hosp.-Washington U., St. Louis, 1956; sr. surg. resident in urology Baylor U. Affiliated Hosps., 1958-59; resident thoracic surgery U. So. Calif., Los Angeles, 1959, fellow thoracic surgery, 1962-63; staff surgeon Univ. Hosp., Columbia, Mo., 1959-78, dir. thoracic and cardiovascular surgery, 1968-77, VA Hosp., Columbia; fellow Brompton Hosp., London, Eng., 1961; asst. prof. surgery U. Mo. Sch. Medicine, Columbia, 1959-64, asso. prof., 1964-69, prof., chief thoracic and cardiovascular surgery, from 1969; prof. and chmn. dept. surgery Sch. Medicine, U. S.C., Columbia, 1978-85, dir. gen. surgery residency program, 1979-85, assoc. dean clin. research and devel., 1986-90. Vis. prof. U. Geneva, Switzerland, 1972—73; mem. med. adv. panel FAA, 1970—75; mem. U.S. Commn. on UNESCO, 1983. Contbr. articles to profl. jours. Served with USNR, 1944—52. Fellow ACS; mem. AMA, Boone County Med. Soc., Columbia Med. Soc., S.C. Med. Assn., S.C. Thoracic Soc., Am. Assn. Med. Colls., Frederick H. Coller Surg. Soc., St. Louis Surg. Soc., Am. Coll. Cardiology, Am., S.C. heart assns., Am. Soc. Artificial Internal Organs, Soc. Med. Cons. to Armed Forces, Am. Coll. Chest Physicians, So. Thoracic Surg. Assn., Central Surg. Soc., Am. Assn. Thoracic Surgery, So. Surg. Assn., S.C. Surg. Soc., Chest Club, Soc. Surg. Chairmen, Marion S. DeWeese Surg. Soc., Southeastern Surg. Soc., So. Surg. Soc., Internat. Cardiovascular Soc., Soc. Thoracic Surgeons, Sigma Xi, Nu Sigma Nu, Sigma Chi. Home: 1829 Senate St 4E Columbia SC 29201 Office: U SC Sch Medicine Dept Surgery Two Medical Park Ste 402 Columbia SC 29203 Office Phone: 803-254-4158.

ALMOND, HARRY DON, vocational school educator; b. Milan, Mo., May 16, 1953; s. Harley Edward and Peggy Gertrude (Head) Almond; m. Paula Sharon Shaw, Aug. 10, 1973; children: Nathan Edward, Ryan Earl. B, U. Ozarks, 1975; M, U. Ark., 2001. Vocat. bus. tchr. Gravette (Ark.) Pub. Sch., 1991—2005. Mem.: ASCD, ABEA, NBEA, SBEA, Ark. Edn. Assn. Mem. Church Of Christ. Avocations: reading, softball, gardening, farming. Home: 40 Brentwood Dr Bella Vista AR 72715

ALMOND, LINCOLN, national lobbyist, retired lawyer, former governor; b. Central Falls, R.I., 1936. BS, U. R.I., 1959; LLB, J.D., Boston U. Bar: R.I., 1962. Adminstr. Town of Lincoln, R.I., 1963-69; U.S. atty. R.I., Dept. Justice, Providence, 1969-78, 81-93; pvt. practice, 1978-81; vice chmn., chmn. Blackstone Valley Devel. Found., 1969-95; gov. State of R.I., Providence, 1995-2003; mem. adv. com. Atty. Gen., 1971-78.

ALMOND, PAUL, film director, film producer, scriptwriter, writer; b. Montreal, Que., Can., Apr. 26, 1931; s. Eric and Irene Clarice (Gray) Almond; m. Joan Elkins, Sept. 11, 1976; 1 child, Matthew James. Student, McGill U., Montreal, 1948-49; BA, Balliol Coll., Oxford, 1952, MA, 1954. TV producer-dir. CBC, Toronto, also in Los Angeles, N.Y.C., London, 1954-67; pres. Quest Films, Montreal, 1967—2002. Writer, producer, dir: (films) Isabel, 1968 (DGA nomination Best Feature Dir); Act of the Heart, 1970 (Genie for Best Feature Dir., 1970); Journey, 1972; Ups & Downs, 1982; The Dance Goes On, 1991; dir.: Captive Hearts, 1984; author: La Vengeance des Dieux, 1999; author: (with M Ballantyne) High Hopes, 1999. Decorated officer Order of Can.; recipient Liberty All Can. TV award for best drama dir., 1958, Spec Diploma of Merit, Prague for Seven Up, 1963, Genie for Best Can TV Drama Dir, 1980. Mem.: Writers Union of Can., Royal Can. Acad. Arts, Dirs. Guild Am., Dirs. Guild Can. (hon.). Anglican. Home: 54 Malibu Colony Malibu CA 90265-4637

ALMONY, ROBERT ALLEN, JR., librarian; b. Charleston, W.Va., Oct. 14, 1945; s. Robert Allen and Margaret Elizabeth A.; m. Carol A. Krzeminski, May 6, 1972; children— Rob, Michael, Chandra, Rachel. AA, Grossmont Coll., 1965; BA, San Diego State U., 1968; M.L.S., U. Calif.-Berkeley, 1977. Sr. div. clk. San Diego State U. Library, 1965-68; acct. Calif. Tchrs. Fin. Services, Orange County, 1968-70, v.p., gen. mgr., 1971-76; research asst. library sch. U. Calif.-Berkeley, 1976-77; reference librarian Oberlin Coll. Library, Ohio, 1977-79; asst. dir. libraries U. Mo., Columbia, 1980—; owner Almony & Assocs. Tax and Fin. Planning, Columbia, 1980—; distbr. USA Today, Columbia, 1984-88. Guest lectr. libr. budgeting, personal fin. planning; spkr. on fin. planning, U. Mo. HR seminars, 1999—; cons. libr. copy svcs.; faculty coun. exec. bd., 1994-2000, recorder Mo. U., 1994-98, chair fiscal affairs, 1998-2000, learning strategies tchr., 1986—, adj. faculty Libr. Sch., 1997—. Contbr. articles to profl. jours. Treas. Bahai's of Columbia, 1982-86, 95-97, 2003-, sec., 1987-89, 93-95, 1998-2001, 2001-2002, chmn., 1989-93; coach Columbia Youth Soccer League, 1981-92; cubmaster Boy Scouts Am., Columbia, 1983-85; asst. scoutmaster, 1985-91; hon. warrior Mic-O-Say, 1986-, treas. Mo. U. Soccer Boosters, 1996—2003; mem. Daniel Boone Regional Libr. Devel. Bd., 1999-2000. Mem. ALA, Mo. Libr. Assn. (treas. 1996-97, 98-99), Assn. Coll. and Rsch. Librs. (exec. com. 1983-86), Libr. Adminstrn. and Mgmt. Assn. (chmn. mem. 1991-93, 2000-01, Outstanding Svc. award 1994, B & F Officers Group Libr. Adminstrn. and Mgmt. (chmn. 1987-91), Nat. Commn. on Edn. Stats. Integrated Post-Secondary Edn. Data Sys. Acad. Librs. (coord. Mo. 1992-2003, 2005, Mo. Assn. Coll. and Rsch. Librs. (vice chmn., chmn. 1982-84), Hickman Athletic Boosters (pres. 1991-94), Maplewood Barn Theater (bd. dirs. 1993-2000, sec., treas. 1998-2000), COE Coll. Parents (bd. dirs. 1993-95). Home: 301 Rothwell Dr Columbia MO 65203-0257 Office: U Mo 104 Ellis Libr Columbia MO 65201-5149 Office Phone: 573-882-4701. Personal E-mail: ralmony@aol.com. Business E-Mail: almonyr@missouri.edu. *Be of service to others in everything you do. Become a person of value to others.*

ALMORE-RANDLE, ALLIE LOUISE, special education educator, academic administrator; b. Jackson, Miss, Apr. 20; d. Thomas Carl and Theresa Ruth (Garrett) Almore; m. Olton Charles Randle, Sr., Aug. 3, 1974. BA, Tougaloo (Miss.) Coll., 1951; MS in Edn., U. So. Calif., L.A., 1971; EdD, Nova Southeastern U., 1997. Recreation leader Pasadena Dept. Recreation, Calif., 1954-56; demonstration tchr. Pasadena Unified Sch., 1956-63; cons. spl. edn. Temple City Sch. Dist., Calif., 1967; supr. tchr. edn. U. Calif., Riverside, 1971; tchr. spl. edn. Pasadena Unified Sch. Dist., 1955-70, dept. chair spl. edn. Pasadena H.S., 1972-98, also adminstrv. asst. Pasadena HS, 1993-98; ind. rep. Am. Comm. Network, Inc., 1997—. Supr. Evelyn Frieden Ctr., U. So. Calif., LA, 1970; mem. Coun. Exceptional Children, 1993—; ednl. cons. Shelby Renee Ednl. Ctr., Gardena, Calif., 2000—. Organizer Northwest Project, Camp Fire Girls, Pasadena, 1963; leader Big Sister Program, YWCA, Pasadena, 1966; organizer, dir. March on The Boys' Club, the Portrait of a Boy, 1966; organized Dr. Allie's Book Mobile Project, 2002; pub. souvenir journ. Women's Missionary Soc., AME Ch., State of Wash. to Mo.; mem. Ch. Women United, Afro-Am. Quilters LA;, established Dr. Allie Louise Almore-Randle Scholarship Award, Pasadena HS, 1998, Tougaloo Coll., 2005, First AME Ch., Pasadena, 2005; co-established Theressa Garrett Almore Music Scholarsip award Jackson State U., Jackson, Miss., 1989; co-founder Cmty. Women of San Gabriel Valley, 1998, Women of Pasadena, 2002. Recipient Cert. of Merit, Pasadena City Coll., 1963, Outstanding Achievement award Nat. Coun. Negro Women, Pasadena, 1965, Earnest Thompson Seton award Campfire Girls, Pasadena, 1968, Spl. Recognition, Outstanding Cmty. Svc. award Tuesday Morning Club, 1967, Dedicated Svc. award AME Ch., 1983, Educator of Excellence award Rotary Club of Pasadena, 1993, Edn. award Altadena NAACP, 1994; named Tchr. of Yr., Pasadena Masonic Bodies, 1967, Woman of the Yr. Zeta Phi Beta, 1992, Commendation, City of Pasadena, 1998, Outstanding Educator, Phi Delta Kappa, 1998; Grad. fellow U. So. Calif., LA, 1970, recognition Uniformly Excellent Work and Exceptional Commitment and Dedication to Altadena/Pasadena Communities, Pasadena African Amer. Sch. Administr., 1998, Cert. Achievment award First AME Ch., 1998, Fran Cook Salute Great Inspiring Educator Award, United Tchr. of Pasadena, 1998; named Dr. Allie Louis Almore-Randle scholar in her honor Tougaloo Coll., Miss., 2005, First AME Ch., Pasadena, Calif., 2005 Mem. NAACP (life; bd. dirs., chmn. ch. workers com. 1955-63, Fight for Freedom award West Coast region 1957, NAACP Edn. award Altadena, Calif. chpt. 1994), ASCD, Calif. Tchrs. Assn., Calif. African Am. Geneal. Soc., Nat. Coun. Negro Women, African Pan Am. Doctoral Scholars, L.A. World Affairs Coun., Phi Delta Gamma (hospitality chair 1971—), U. So. Calif. Alumni Assn. (life), Tougaloo Coll. Nat. Alumni Assn. (life), Phi Delta Kappa, Alpha Kappa Alpha (life, membership com.), Phi Delta Phi (founder, organizer 1961), Phi Delta Kappa, Phi Gamma Sigma. Democrat. Mem. Ame Ch. Avocations: wedding director, photography, gardening, family history. Personal E-mail: akainger@sbcglobal.net.

ALMQUIST, DON, illustrator, artist; b. Hartford, Conn., July 21, 1929; s. Nils Herbert and Jeannette Theresa (Perrow) A.; m. Kerstin Rigmor Jesslen, May 21, 1955; children: Kristina, Jan Christian BFA, RI Sch. of Design, 1951. Staff artist Esquire, Inc., N.Y.C., 1951; creative dir. Ahlen & Akerlund, Stockholm, 1963-66; adj. prof. Paier Coll. of Art, Hamden, Conn., 1979-84; graphic advisor U.S. Dept. of Fish and Wildlife, Washington, 1981-83. Illustrator: Christmas With Ed Sullivan, 1960, Doomed Road of Empire, 1962, What Did I See?, 1961, Loudmouse, 1962, (new illustrations) 1967, (new edit./illustrations) 1982, Spring is Like the Morning, 1964, Summer is a Very Busy Day, 1967, Dolls from Cheyenne, 1968, Some Animals Are Vary Small, 1968, When Grandmother was Young, 1970, When Great Grandmother was Young, 1971, Getting to Know New York State, 1971, Den Förtrollade Lådan, 1967, It Never Is Dark, 1967, Not Very Much of a House, 1967, Cathy Uncovers a Secret, 1969, Ginnie and the Mystery Light, 1973, Libby Shadows a Lady, 1974, Season at the Point, 1991, The Little Red Hen, 1991, Dragged Aboard, 1998; one-man shows include Galleri Z, Ystad, Sweden, 2000, Carolynn Roberts Gallery, Hockessin, Del., 2002, 2005; exhibited paintings and drawings in group and one-man shows New Castle (Del.) Arts Gallery, Ltd., 1991, Springfield Art Mus., 1993, Soc. Devel. en Arts Contemporains, Montreal, Que., Can., 1994; one-man shows include Askersund, Sweden, 1993, Miriam Schiell Fine Arts, Toronto, 1994, Gallery M2, Stockholm, 1995, Gallery Vattern Askersund, Sweden, 1996, Montchanin (Del.) Arts, 1996, New Castle Arts, 1998, Galleri Cafe Lucas, Stockholm, 1999, Carolynn Roberts Gallery, Yorklyn, Del., 2002, 04, Rosenfield Gallery, Phila., 2003, Am. Swedish Hist. Mus., Phila., 2004; juried exhbns. include Miss. Watercolor Soc., Miss. Mus. Art, Hoyt Inst. Fine Arts, 1993, Nat. Art Show, New Castle, Pa., La. Art & Artists Guild and River Show, 1993, Aqueous '95 Show, Louisville (Grumbacher gold medal), Charlotte County Art Guild, Punta Gorda, 1997, 98, New Castle Hist. Soc., Kent. Watercolor Soc., 1997, Pleiades Gallery, N.Y.C., 2002, Md. Fedn. Art Am. Landscapes, Annapolis, Md., 2002, Rosenfeld Gallery, Phila., 2003, Pleiades Gallery, N.Y.C., 2003. Served as sgt. U.S. Army, 1951-53, Korea. Recipient numerous awards of merit Soc. of Illustrators, N.Y.C., 1953-84, Silver medal Phila. Art Dirs., 1955, Gold medal Milw. Art Dirs., 1963, Gold medal Grumbacher, 1997, numerous awards of merit N.Y. Art Dirs., N.Y.C. Episcopalian. Avocation: horticulture. Home and Office: 103 The Strand New Castle DE 19720-4827 Office Phone: 302-322-1609. E-mail: almquistart@aol.com, don@almquistart.com.

ALMQVIST, PELLE, singer; With band The Hives, 1995—. Music tchr., Skinnskatteberg, Sweden. Singer: (albums) Barely There, 1997, A.K.A. I-D-I-O-T, 1998, Veni Vidi Vicious, 2000, Your Favorite New Band, 2002, Tyrannosaurus Hives, 2004. Co-recipient Best Nordic Act, MTV Europe awards, 2004. Mailing: Interscope Records 2220 Colorado Ave Santa Monica CA 90404

AL-MUSAWI, MUHSIN JASSIM, education educator, writer; b. Nasr, Iraq, Sharjah, United Arab Emirates; s. Jassim Ali Al-Musawi and Malika Haydar; m. Bahira S. Hijab, Nov. 1, 1941; children: Zainab Ali, Adnan Alghourabi, Rawa Jassem, Wafa Muhsin. PhD with distinction, Dalhousi U., Canada, 1978. Prof. Am. U., Sharjah, United Arab Emirates, 2000—, Columbia U., N.Y.C., 2003—. Pres. Iraqi Critics Assn., Baghdad, 1983—88. Editor: Jour. Arabic Lit. (Owais award in Scholarship and Criticism, 2002); author: Scheherazade In England, 1981, The Anglo-Orient, 2000, Brill, 2003, over 20 other books. Recipient Venzewellian award of the Arts, Latin Am. Writers, 1987; scholar Fulbright, Fulbright Commn., 1998—2001. Mem.: MESA, Iraqi Writers, ACCUTE, ACAIA. Office: American Univ HO5 26666 Sharjah United Arab Emirates also: Columbia Univ Kent Hall 5 Amsterdam Ave New York NY 10027 Office Fax: 971 6 5585011, 212-854-5517. Business E-Mail: mmusawi@ausharjah.edu, ma2188@columbia.edu.

ALMY, EARLE VAUGHN, JR., (BUDDY ALMY), real estate executive; b. July 29, 1930; s. Earle Vaughn and Minnye Ruth (Rounsaville) A.; m. Gorden Yetive McGowan, July 31, 1964 (div. 1967). BS in Animal Husbandry, Tex. Tech. U., 1952; postgrad., Am. Inst. Banking, 1956-62; grad., Realtors Inst. Cert. real estate brokerage mgr.; accredited land cons.; cert. real estate appraiser, Tex. State Cert. Gen. Real Estate Appraiser. Credit analyst First Nat. Bank, Fort Worth, 1956-62; dir. finance and poultry feed sales Burrus Feed Mills, Saginaw, Tex., 1963-69; pres., mgr. Almy and Co., Hurst, Tex., 1970-79, Granbury, Tex., 1979—; v.p., dir. Northeast Tarrant County Bd. of Realtors, Hurst, Tex., 1972-74; pres. Almy and Co. Realtors, Weatherford, Tex., 1973-78; instr. appraisal of farms and ranches Weatherford Coll., 1986-89. Dir. Fort Worth Farm and Ranch Club, 2004-; usher Acton United Meth. Ch.; pres. Rep. Club Hood County, 1991. With USAF, 1952-56. Sears Roebuck scholar, 1951. Mem. Nat. Assn. Realtors, Tex. Assn. Realtors, Granbury Assn. Realtors, Nat. Realtors Land Inst., Tex. Realtor's Land Inst. (state dir.), Nat. Assn. Real Estate Appraisers (cert. real estate appraiser), Pecan Plantation Country Club. Republican. Avocations: golf, hunting, fishing, boating, swimming. Home: PO Box 129 Granbury TX 76048-0129 E-mail: almyco@hcnews.com.

ALOFF, MINDY, writer; b. Phila., Dec. 20, 1947; d. Jacob and Selma (Album) A.; m. Martin Steven Cohen, June 16, 1968 (div. June 2000); 1 child, Ariel Nikiya. AB in English, Vassar Coll., 1969; MA in English, SUNY, Buffalo, 1972. Asst. prof. English U. Portland, Oreg., 1973-75; editor Encore Mag. of the Arts, Portland, 1977-80, Vassar Quar., Poughkeepsie, NY, 1980-88; dance critic New Republic, Bklyn., 1993—2001; cons. The George Balanchine Found., 2000—; editor Dance Critics Assn. Newsletter, 2003—. Coord. Portland Poetry Festival, 1974—75; adj. assoc. prof. Barnard Coll., 2000—. Author: (poems) Night Lights, 1979; contbr. articles to mags. and jours. Recipient Whiting Writers award Mrs. Giles Whiting Found., N.Y.C., 1987; Woodrow Wilson Found. fellow, 1969, Woodburn fellow SUNY-Buffalo, 1972, Am. Dance Festival Dance Critics Inst. fellow, New London, Conn., 1977, John Simon Guggenheim Meml. Found. fellow, 1990. Mem. PEN Am. Ctr., Nat. Book Critics Circle (bd. dirs. 1988-91), Phi Beta Kappa. Personal E-mail: MindyAloff@aol.com.

ALOFSIN, ANTHONY, art historian, writer, educator; b. Memphis, June 22, 1949; s. Frederick Benjamin and Eleanor (Brodsky) A.; m. Patricia Tierney, June 5, 1993. AB magna cum laude, Harvard U., 1971, MArch with distinction, 1981; MPhil, Columbia U., 1983, PhD, 1987. Assoc. chmn. divsn. hist. preservation Columbia U., N.Y.C., 1983-84, adminstrv. dir., founder Ctr. Preservation Rsch., 1984-85; scholar-in-residence The Frank Lloyd Wright Found., 1984-85; asst. prof. architecture Columbia U., N.Y.C., 1984-86; from assoc. prof. to prof. architecture U. Tex., Austin, 1987—99, prof. art and art history, Roland Roessner Centennial prof., 1999—. Rsch. dir. A Tense Alliance: Arch. Cen. Europe, Internat. Travelling Exhbn., 1993-96; consulting curator: Frank Lloyd Wright, Arch., Mus. Modern Art, 1994; guest curator Prairie Skycraper, 2005; dir. MS in archtl. studies, history and theory program and PhD program, U. Tex., Austin, 1987-97; cons., lectr., spkr. in field. Author: Frank Lloyd Wright: Lost Years 1910-1922, 1993, The Struggle for Modernism: Architecture Landscape Architecture and City Planning At Harvard, 2002, When Buildings Speak: Architecture as Language in the Late Habsburg Empire and Its Aftermath, 1867-1933, 2005; editor: Frank Lloyd Wright: An Index to the Taliesin Correspondence, 1988, Frank Lloyd Wright: Europe and Beyond, 1999, Prairie Skyscraper, 2005; contbr. articles to lit. and profl. jours. Recipient Vasari award Dallas Mus. Art, 1989; Graham Found. for Visual Arts grantee, 1993; Santa Fe Workshop Contemporary Art scholar, 1971; Fulbright Professorship fellow Acad. Fine Arts, Vienna, Austria, 1989-90, fellow Internationales Forschungzentrum Kulterwissenshaften, Vienna, 1995, Ailsa Mellon Bruce Sr. fellow Casva Nat. Gallery Art, Washington, 2003-04. Mem. Soc. Archtl. Hists., (nat. chpt., NY chpt., Tex. chpt., nat. bd. 2005-), Coll. Art Assn., Harvard Grad. Sch. Design Alumni Coun., Fulbright Assn., US Internat. Coun. Monuments and Sites, Phi Kappa Phi. Avocation: gardening. Home: 2207 Camino Alto Austin TX 78746-2436 Office: U Tex Sch Arch 1 University Sta B7500 Austin TX 78712-0222 Office Phone: 512-471-8156. Business E-Mail: alofsin@mail.utexas.edu.

ALOI, MICHAEL JOHN, lawyer; b. Apr. 1958; BA, W.Va. Wesleyan Coll.; JD, W.Va. U. Bar: W.Va. 1983. Pntr. Manchin & Aloi, PLLC, Fairmont, W.Va. Mem.: W.Va. State Bar (pres. 2002). Address: Manchin & Aloi Ste 203 1543 Fairmont Ave Fairmont WV 26554 Office Phone: 304-367-1862. E-mail: maloi@manchin-aloi.com.

AL-OMARI, RA'ED M., computer engineer, consultant, computer scientist, researcher; b. Irbid, Jordan, June 3, 1971; s. Mohammad Sh. Al-Omari, Mariam M. Al-Skran; m. Maisaa W. Hawana, May 10, 1974; 1 child, Param. BSEE, Jordan U. Sci. and Tech., Irbid, 1994, MS in Computer Engring., 1997; PhD in Computer Engineering, Iowa State U., 2001. Registered engr. Tchr.'s asst. Jordan U. Sci. and Tech., Irbid, 1994—96; sys. engr. Yarmouk U., Irbid, 1996—97; rsch., tchr.'s asst. Iowa State U., Ames, 1997—2001; simulation software engr. Levetate Design System Inc., Portland, Oreg., 2000; adv. engring., scientist IBM Inc., Austin, 2001—. Recipient Distinction Acad. award, Jordan U. Sci. and Tech., 1991-1992. Independent. Moslem. Avocation: travel. Office: IBM Inc Bldg 45 11400 Burnet Rd Austin TX 78758 Office Phone: 512-838-6996. Office Fax: 512-838-7694. Personal E-mail: raedomari@hotmail.com. Business E-Mail: alomari@us.ibm.com.

ALONEFTIS, ANDREAS, financial analyst; b. Nicosia, Cyprus, Aug. 24, 1945; BA, Sch. Accountancy and Bus. Studies, Glasgow, Scotland, 1973; MBA, So. Meth. U., 1978; postgrad., N.Y. Inst. Fin., 1982, Henley Mgmt. Coll., U.K., 1996—2000, Middlesex U., 2002. Acct. Cyprus Devel. Bank, Nicosia, 1966—72, chief acct., 1972—76, mgr. fin., 1976—78, sr. mgr. investments, 1978—82; gen. mgr., chief executive officer Cyprus Investment and Securities Corp., Nicosia, 1982—88; minister of def. Republic of Cyprus, 1988—93; chief exec. Am. Life Ins. Co., Nicosia, Cyprus, 1993—95; mng. dir. CypriaLife Ins., Nicosia, Cyprus, 1995—99, group gen. mgr. ins., 1999—2000; mng. dir., CEO Lambousa Venture Capital and Olympos Investments, Nicosia, 2000—01; exec. chmn. Allied Capital, 2001—; exec. vice chmn. Alliance Internat. Reinsurance, 2001; chmn. Cyprus Broadcasting Corp., 2003—. Contbr. articles to profl. jours. and newspapers. 2nd lt. Cyprus N.G., 1964-66. Fulbright Found. grantee, 1977-78; So. Meth. U. fellow, 1977-78, Salzburg Seminaz fellow, 1984. Fellow Assn. Internat. Accts. (vice chmn.). Clubs: Propeller Club of the U.S. Lodges: Rotary. Greek Orthodox. Avocations: music, reading, cinema, jogging. Home: 10 Kastellorizo St Nicosia 2108 Cyprus Office: Allied Capital ltd 5 Prometheus St n Nicosia 1065 Cyprus Office Phone: 357-22873620. E-mail: alonefan@cytanet.com.cy, andreas.aloneftis@alliancereinsurance.com.

ALONZO, JULIE ANN, secondary school educator, researcher; b. Mountain View, Calif., Oct. 16, 1968; d. Gerald John and Claudie Bourne Alonzo. Postgrad., U. Oreg., 2002. Cert. tchr. Nat. Bd. Proft. Tchg. Stds. H.S. tchr. Los Gatos, Anzar, and Mt. Pleasant High Schs., Los Gatos, San Juan Bautista, and San Jose, Calif., 1990—2002; rsch. asst. Behavioral Rsch. and Tchg. U. Oreg., Eugene, 2002—. Asst. to area head Ednl. Leadership, Eugene, 2004—. Stafford student scholar, Nat. Inst. on Leadership, Disability, and Students Placed at Risk, 2003—05. Mem.: Am. Ednl. Rsch. Assn. Home: 2314 Compton St Eugene OR 97404 Office: U Oreg Behavioral Rsch and Tchg Eugene OR 97403 Office Phone: 541-346-0119. Personal E-mail: jalonzo@uoregon.edu.

ALONZO, MARTIN VINCENT, mining and aluminum company executive, investor, financial consultant; b. N.Y.C., Apr. 8, 1931; s. Mariano and Mary (Traina) A.; m. Sabina Gallucci, June 7, 1952; children: Martin Vincent, Marlene, Sabrina. BBA in Acctg. cum laude, Baruch Coll., CUNY, 1952, MBA in Fin. and Investments, 1971. CPA, N.Y. Acct. Eisner and Lubin CPAs, N.Y.C., 1952-57; treas., contr. Credit-Am. Corp., N.Y.C., 1957-60; asst. v.p. indsl. time sales, financing and leasing A.J. Armstrong Co., Inc., N.Y.C., 1960-65; treas., sec. So. Nitrogen Co., Savannah, Ga., 1965-67; asst. to v.p. fin. AMAX Inc., Greenwich, Conn., 1967-68, mgr. fin. planning, 1968-69, asst. contr., 1969, contr., 1970, v.p. and contr., 1973-78, sr. v.p. controls and adminstrn., 1978-80, sr. v.p. and pres. indsl. minerals div., 1981-82, exec. v.p. and pres. splty. and light metals ops., 1982-83, exec. v.p., chief fin. officer, 1983-87; pres. MVA Fin. Corp., 1987—; chmn., pres., CEO Chase Industries, Inc., 1990—2001; ptnr. Tri-Artisan Capital Ptnrs., LLC, Mcht. Bankers, 2002—. Mem. Am. Copper Coun.; bd. dirs. Copper & Brass Fabricators Coun., Inc., Copper Devel. Assn.; pres.'s coun. MAPI, 1993; mem. Internat. Wrought Copper Coun., 1999-2002. Bd. dirs. Greenwich Health Assn., 1978-90, Am. Found., 1993-95; active Greenwich Bd. Health, 1982-92, U.S. Nat. Com. Pacific Econ. Cooperation, 1993-99; trustee Baruch Coll. Fund, 2004. Recipient Freedom of the Human Spirit award, Internat. Ctr. for the Disabled, 1999, Alumni Achievement award, Bernard M. Baruch Coll., 2002. Mem. Nat. Assn. Accts. (chmn. mgmt. acctg. practices com. 1976-79), Conf. Bd., Coun. Fin. Execs., Fin. Adv. Coun. (exec. com. 1984-87), Extractive Industries Luncheon Group (chmn. 1978-79), Am. Mining Congress (chmn. acctg. com. 1980-82, mem. pension com. 1978-82), Internat. Magnesium Assn. (bd. dirs. 1983-84), AICPA, Fin. Execs. Inst., AIME, Phosphate Rock Export Assn. (dir. 1982-83), Mining Club N.Y.C. (dir.), Econ. Club N.Y., Westchester Country Club, Sky Club, Roundtable of Greenwich, Beta Alpha Psi, Beta Gamma Sigma, Am. Assn. Sovereign Mil. Order of Malta, Legatus. Republican. Office: 2 Sound View Dr Ste 100 Greenwich CT 06830 Office Phone: 203-622-1340. Personal E-mail: mvalonzo1@aol.com.

ALOSH, MAHDI, Arabic language educator, translator; b. Damascus, Syria, Oct. 15, 1943; came to U.S., 1982; 010s. Abulfaraj and Falak Alosh; m. Ibtissam Alama, June 20, 1971. BA, Damascus U., 1967; MA, Ohio U., Athens, 1984; PhD, Ohio State U., 1987. English tchr. Ministry of Edn., Damascus, 1964-67, Kuwait City, Kuwait, 1968-82; lectr. Ohio State U., Columbus, 1987-89, asst. prof. Arabic studies, 1989-95, assoc. prof. Arabic studies, 1995—, dir. Arabic lang. program, 1989—. Author: Learner, Text and Context, 1997, Ahlan wa Sahlan, 2000. Mem. MLA, Am. Assn. Tchrs. of Arabic (pres. 1998-99), Am. Coun. Tchg. Fgn. Langs. Avocations: walking, reading, travel. Office: Ohio State U 203 B&Z 1735 Neil Ave Columbus OH 43210 E-mail: alosh.1@osu.edu.

ALOU, FELIPE ROJAS, professional baseball manager; b. Santo Domingo, Dominican Republic, May 12, 1935; Player San Francisco Giants, 1958-62, Milw. Braves, 1964-65, Atlanta Braves, 1966-69, Oakland Athletics, 1970-71, N.Y. Yankees, 1971-73, Montreal Expos, 1973, Milw. Brewers, 1974; coach Montreal Expos, 1979-80, 84, mgr., 1992—2001; bench coach Detroit Tigers, 2002; mgr., S.F. Giants, 2002—. Named to Nat. League All-Star team Sporting News, 1966; named Nat. League Mgr. of Yr. Sporting News, 1994, Baseball Writers' Assn. Am., 1994. Office: San Francisco Giants Pacific Bell Pk 24 Willie Mays Plz San Francisco CA 94107*

ALOU, MOISES, professional baseball player; b. Atlanta, July 3, 1966; s. Felipe Alou. Outfielder Pitts. Pirates, 1990, Montreal Expos, 1990, 1992—96, Fla. Marlins, 1997, Houston Astros, 1998—2001, Chgo. Cubs, 2002—04, San Francisco Giants, 2005—. Named to Nat. League All-Star Team, 1994, 1997, 1998, 2001, 2004; recipient Buck Canel award for Top L. Am. Player, 1994. Achievements include mem. World Series Champion Florida Marlins, 1997. Office: San Francisco Giants Pac Bell Park 24 Willie Mays Plaza San Francisco CA 94107

ALPEN, EDWARD LEWIS, biophysicist, educator; b. San Francisco, May 14, 1922; s. Edward Lawrence and Margaret Catherine (Shipley) A.; m. Wynella June Dosh, Jan. 6, 1945; children: Angela Marie, Jeannette Elise. BS, U. Calif., Berkeley, 1946, PhD, 1950. Br. chief, then dir. biol. and med. scis. Naval Radiol. Def. Lab., San Francisco, 1952-68; mgr. environ. and life scis. Battelle Meml. Inst., Richland, Wash., 1968-69, assoc. dir., then dir. Pacific N.W. div., 1969-75; dir. Donner Lab., U. Calif., Berkeley; also assoc. dir. Lawrence Berkeley Lab., 1975-87; prof. biophysics emeritus U. Calif., Berkeley, 1975—, prof. radiology emeritus San Francisco, 1976—, dir. U. Calif. Study Ctr. London, 1988-90; councillor, dir. Nat. Coun. Radiol. Protection, 1969-92; exec. v.p., tech. dir. Neutron Tech. Corp., Berkeley, 1990-93. Mem. Gov. Wash. Council Econ. Devel., 1973-75; bd. dirs. Wash. Bd. Trade, 1973-76. Author books, papers, abstracts in field. Served to capt. USN, 1942-64. Recipient Navy Sci. medal, 1962, Disting. Service medal Dept. Def., 1963, Sustaining Members medal Assn. Mil. Surgeons, 1971; fellow Guggenheim Found., 1960-61; sr. fellow NSF, 1958-59 Fellow: Calif. Acad. Scis.; mem.: Biophys. Soc., Radiation Rsch. Soc., Am. Philat. Soc., Bioelectromagnetics Soc. (pres. 1979—80), Sigma Xi (nat. lectr. 1994—96). Episcopalian. E-mail: e.alpen@comcast.net.

ALPER, HOWARD, chemistry professor; b. Montreal, Oct. 17, 1941; s. Max and Frema (Weinstein) A.; m. Anne Elizabeth Fairhurst, June 4, 1966; children: Lara, Ruth. BS, Sir George Williams U., Montreal, 1963; PhD, McGill U., 1967. From asst. prof. to assoc. prof. SUNY, Binghamton, 1968-74; assoc. prof. U. Ottawa, 1975-77, prof., 1977—. Chmn. dept. chemistry U. Ottawa, 1982-85, 88-94, asst. v.p. rsch., 1995-96, v.p. rsch., 1997—; co-chair Interacad. Network of Acads. of Scis., 2004-. Contbr. articles to profl. jours. Mem. adv. coun. Order of Can., 2001—03. Decorated officer Nat. Order of Merit (France); recipient Alfred Bader award in organic chemistry, 1990, Commemorative medal for significant contbns. to Can., 125th Anniversary of Can., 1992, E.W.R. Steacie award for disting. contbns. to chemistry, Can. Soc. for Chemistry, 1993, Urgel-Archambault prize in phys. scis., math. and engring., 1996, Bell Can. Forum award, 1998, Gerhard Herzberg Gold medal, 2000, Nat. Merit award, Life Scis. Coun., 2001, Le Seuer meml. award, Soc. Chem. Industry, 2002, Montreal medal, Can. Soc. Chemistry, 2003; fellow, NATO, 1967—68, Killam Found., 1986—88; Steacie fellow, Nat. Sci. Engring. Rsch. Coun., 1980—82, Guggenheim fellow, 1985—86. Fellow: Acad. of Sci. (v.p. 1995—98, pres. 1999—2003, co-chmn. interam. network 2004—, chair partnership group sci. and engring. 1995-99), Royal Soc. Can. (former pres.), 3d World Acad. Scis. (assoc.); mem.: Order of Can. (officer 1999), European Acad. Arts Sci. Humanities (titular mem.), Chem. Inst. Can. (Alcan award 1980, Catalysis award 1984, CIC medal 1997, Montreal medal 2003), Royal Soc. Chemistry (London), Am. Chem. Soc., Natural Scis. and Engring. Rsch. Coun. Can. (group chmn. chemistry 1987-90). Jewish. Achievements include patents in field. Office: U Ottawa Dept Chemistry 10 Marie Curie Ottawa ON Canada K1N 6N5 Office Phone: 613-562-5270. Business E-Mail: howard.alper@uottawa.ca.

ALPER, MERLIN LIONEL, corporate financial executive; b. Bklyn., May 25, 1932; s. James B. and Rose (Mellis) Alper; m. Elaine R. Honig, Dec. 21, 1957; children: Jerome Eric, Alyssa Ellen. BBA, Adelphi U., 1955. CPA N.Y. With Arthur Andersen & Co., N.Y.C., 1955-68, comml. audit mgr., 1963-68; dir. fin. controls ITT, N.Y.C., 1968-73, asst. comptr., 1973-93, corp. v.p., 1979; v.p., contr. ITT Europe, Inc., 1978-84; corp. v.p., comptr., dir. ITT Telecom. Corp., 1984-85; v.p., dep. contr. ITT Corp., N.Y.C., 1993-95; exec. v.p., CFO Madison Sq. Garden, N.Y.C., 1995-98; mng. dir. Ind. Coll. Fund N.Y., 1999—, also chmn. bd. dirs., 2003—. Mem. emerging issues task force Fin. Acctg. Stds. Bd., 1990—95. With Chem. Corps U.S. Army, 1956—58. Named to Acad. of Distinction, Adelphi U. Alumni, 1984. Mem.: AICPA, Fin. Execs. Internat. (mem. com. on corp. reporting), Inst. Mgmt. Accts. (dir. NY chpt. 1965—66), N.Y. State Soc. CPAs. E-mail: malper@prodigy.net.

ALPERIN, GOLDIE GREEN, consulting librarian, lawyer; b. Des Moines, Aug. 16, 1905; d. Morris and Bessie (Miliwer) Green; LL.B., Drake U., 1927; m. Moses Alperin, Dec. 25, 1930 (dec. 1950); children: Herschel Burton, Judith Miriam. Admitted to Iowa bar, 1927, U.S. Supreme Ct. bar, 1959; practice in Des Moines, 1927-30; law librarian Chgo. Bar. Assn., 1951-63; dir. Def. Information Office, Chgo., 1963-65; librarian book selections Northwestern U. Law Sch. Library, 1966-72; ret., 1972. Named one of 20 rep. U.S. women lawyers of various phases practice Women's Adjustment Bd., London, Eng., 1957; One of Outstanding Women of Am. Bicentennial, Austin (Tex.) Bicentennial Com., 1976; cert. religious sch. tchr. Bd. Jewish Edn., Chgo., 1951. Mem. Am. (sec. 1960-65), Chgo. (past exec. bd., editor 1958-59) assns. law libraries, Nat. Assn. Women Lawyers (regional) dir. 1960-64). Jewish religion. Asst. editor Women Lawyers Jour., 1961-67, exec. bd., 1961-67. Home: 3100 N Lake Shore Dr Apt 1512 Chicago IL 60657-4953

ALPERIN, RICHARD MARTIN, social worker, psychoanalyst; b. Mt. Vernon, N.Y., Oct. 16, 1946; s. Israel and Sara A.; children: Heather Nicole, Alexander Scott. BBA, We. Mich. U., 1968; MSW, Fordham U., 1974; DSW, Columbia U., 1982; postdoctoral diploma in psychotherapy and psychoanalysis, Adelphi U., 1988. Lic. clin. social worker, N.Y., N.J.; diplomate Am. Bd. Examiners in Clin. Social Work; cert. group psychotherapist Nat. Registry Cert. Group Psychotherapists. Cons. Mt. Vernon Youth Bd., 1972-76; adj. faculty Marymount Manhattan Coll., N.Y.C., 1974-76; psychotherapist Riverdale Mental Health Clinic, N.Y.C., 1974-77; psychol. counselor, psychotherapist Ctr. Counseling and Psychol. Svcs. Ramapo Coll. of N.J., 1976-81, adj. faculty, 1977-86, moderator evening forums, 1978, 80; counselor, psychotherapist Ctr. Counseling and Psychol. Svcs. SUNY, Purchase, 1981-82, 84-85, acting dir., 1982-84; clin. cons. Westside Ctr. for Family Svcs., N.Y.C., 1985-87; pvt. practice psychotherapy and psychoanalysis Riverdale, N.Y., 1977—, Teaneck, N.J., 1980—, N.Y.C., 1984—. Lectr. Cabrini Med. Ctr., 1979; guest lectr. grand rounds dept. psychiatry, Brookdale Hosp. Med. Ctr., 1996; field instr. Sch. Social Work-Columbia U., 1983-85; adj. assoc. prof. Sch. Social Svc.-Fordham U., 1985-98; adj. asst. prof. Grad. Sch. Social Work-NYU, 1989-91; mem. faculty, dean curriculum Rockland Inst. for Psychoanalysis and Psychotherapy, 1990-95; mem. faculty Advanced Inst. Analytic Psychotherapy, 1992-95, Object Rel. Inst. Psychoanalysis and Psychotherapy, 1992—, Psychoanalytic Psychotherapy Study Ctr., 1994—, N.J. Inst. for Tng. in Psychoanalysis, 1994—. Co-editor: The Impact of Managed Care on the Practice of Psychotherapy: Innovation, Implementation, and Controversy, 1996; contbr. articles to profl. jours.; rsch. on psychotherapy, suicide and provision of preventative svcs. Nat. Jewish Welfare Bd. fellow Fordham U., 1972-74. Trainee NIMH Columbia U., 1978. Mem.: NASW, Nat. Acads. Practice (disting. practitioner), N.J. Coalition Mental Health Profls. and Consumers (mem. adv. bd.), Nat. Study Group on Social Work and Psychoanalysis, Alliance for Universal Access to Psychotherapy (founder, membership chair, mem. steering com. 1994-96), Nat. Membership Com. Psychoanalysis Clin. Social Work (treas. 1991—93, chair NY-NJ area 1992—94), Nat. Fedn. Soc. Clin. Social Work, Acad. Cert. Social Workers (cert.), Ea. Group Psychotherapy Soc., Am. Group Psychotherapy Assn., Adelphi Soc. Psychoanalysis and Psychotherapy, N.Y. State Soc. Clin. Social Work (chair com. on psychoanalysis 1991—96, diplomate). Office: 175 Cedar Ln Teaneck NJ 07666-4315 Office Phone: 201-836-5050. Business E-Mail: ralperin@aol.com.

ALPERIN, STUART N., lawyer; b. Bklyn., 1953; BA, SUNY, Binghamton, 1973; JD, Syracuse U., 1976; LLM in Taxation, NYU, 1980. Bar: NY 1977. Assoc. Skadden, Arps, Slate, Meagher & Flom LLP, NYC. Contbr. articles to profl. jours. Mem. Order of Coif, Phi Beta Kappa, NY Bar Assn. (co-chair, Committee on Employee Benefits, Tax Section, 1990, Committee on Qualified Plans, Tax Section, 1991-96). Office: Skadden Arps Slate Meagher & Flom LLP 4 Times Sq New York NY 10036 Office Phone: 212-735-3920. Office Fax: 917-777-3920. Business E-Mail: salperin@skadden.com.

ALPERN, ANDREW, lawyer, architect, historian; b. NYC, Nov. 1, 1938; s. Dwight K. and Grace M. (Michelman) Alpern. BArch, Columbia U., 1964; DSc, London Coll. Applied Sci., 1971; JD magna cum laude, Benjamin N. Cardozo Sch. Law, 1992. Registered arch., N.Y.; bar: N.Y. 1993, U.S. Dist. Ct. (so. and ea. dists.) N.Y. 1994. With Haines Lundberg Waehler, archs., NYC, 1962—67; project dir. Saphier, Lerner, Schindler, Environetics, NYC, 1968—72; v.p., dir. arch. Environ. R&D, Inc., Space Planning & Design, NYC, 1972—75; dir. rsch. Corp. Planners & Coord., NYC, 1973—75; project mgr. Hellmuth, Obata & Kassabaum, P.C., NYC, 1977—78; mgr. real estate and facilities planning Coopers & Lybrand, NYC, 1978—88; cons. arch., hist. arch. NYC, 1988—. Mem. adv. bd. Inst. Applied Psychotherapy, 1969—72; nat. panel arbitrators Am. Arbitration Assn., 1971—86; cons. lawyer, 1993; spl. counsel Hughes Hubbard & Reed LLP, 1994—2002; exec. v.p., counsel Peter Kimmelman Asset Mgmt. LLC, 2002—; lectr. CUNY, Inst. Architecture and Urban Studies, Grolier Club, Mcpl. Art Soc., Sotheby's Art Inst. Author: Apartments for the Affluent: A Historical Survey of Buildings in New York, 1975, Garret Ellis Winants: 1813-1890, 1976, Alpern's Architectural Aphorisms, 1979, Handbook of Specialty Elements in Architecture, 1981, In the Manor Housed, 1982, Holdouts!, 1983, Fifth Avenue, 1986, New York's Fabulous Luxury Apartments, 1987, Statutes of Repose and the Cons. Industry: A Proposal for New York, 1991, Luxury Apt. Houses of Manhattan: An Illus. History, 1993, Hist. Manhattan Apt. Houses, 1996, New York's Arch. Holdouts, 1997, 101 Questions About Copyright Law, 1999, The New York Apartment Houses of Rosario Candela and James Carpenter, 2001; editor-in-chief: Legal Briefs for the Cons. Industry, 1978—92, pub.: F.M.R.A. (Edward Gorey), 1980; contbg. editor: NY Habitat, 1985—92; mem. bd. adv. Profl. Office Design Mag., 1986—89; contbg. columnist: Avenue Mag., 2000—02. Recipient Presdl. citation, N.Y. State Assn. Archs., 1991. Mem.: AIA, Friends Cast Iron Architecture, Mcpl. Art Soc., N.Y. Hist. Soc., Bklyn. Hist. Soc., Soc. Archtl. Historians.

ALPERN, ROBERT J., dean, medical educator; b. Nov. 3, 1950; m. Patricia Ann Preisig; chilren: Rachelle, Kyle. BA in Chemistry with honors and highest distinction, Northwestern U., 1972; MD with honors, U. Chgo., 1976. Diplomate Am. Bd. Internal Medicine; bd. cert in nephrology. Intern in internal medicine Columbia U., N.Y.C., 1976-77, resident in internal medicine, 1977-79; fellow in nephrology and renal physiology U. Calif. Cardiovascular Rsch. Inst., San Francisco, 1979-82, asst. prof. medicine divsn. nephrology, 1982-87; assoc. prof. medicine U. Tex. Southwestern Med. Ctr., Dallas, 1987-90, chief nephrology, 1987-98, prof. medicine, 1990—2004, Ruth W. and Milton P. Levy, Sr. chair in molecular nephrology, 1994—2004, dean, 1998—2004, Atticus James Gill M.C. Chair in Med. Sci., 2000—04; dean Yale U. Sch. Medicine, New Haven, 2004—. Max Martin Salick vis. prof., UCLA Sch. Medicine, 1994; mem. Med. Sch. Admissions com. U. Calif. San Francisco, 1985-87, general clin. rsch. ctr. adv. com. U. Tex. Southwestern Med. Ctr., 1987-91, search com. for chief of cardiology, 1989, search com. for chmn. urology, 1993, search com. for chief of hematology/oncology, 1997, Med. Sch. Admissions com., 1994-96, chmn. 1996-98; chmn. general clin. rsch. ctr. adv. com. U. Tex. Southwestern Med. Ctr., 1988-90, search com. for chief of infectious diseases U. Tex. Southwestern Med. Ctr., 1994-96; adv. coun. Nat. Inst. Diabetes and Digestive and Kidney Diseases; presenter, lectr. in field. Editl. bd: Kidney Internat., 1989-90, Renal Physiology and Biochemistry, 1989-95, Am. Jour. Physiology, 1992-94, Internat. Yearbook of Nephrology, 1989-92, Seminars in Nephrology, 1990—, Am. Jour. Kidney Diseases, 1991-96, Kidney and Blood Pressure Research, 1996—, Am. Jour. Med. Scis., 1996—, Am. Jour. Medicine, 1997—; cons. editor: Jour. Clin. Investigation, 1993-99, Kidney Internat., 1990—; editl. com. Jour. Clin. Investigation, 1988-93; assoc. editor Am. Jour. Physiology, 1989-92, Hospital Practice: Physiology in Medicine, 1991-94; section editor: Annual Review of Physiology, 1993-97, Current Opinion in Nephrology and Hypertension, 1997-99; contbr. papers, chaps., articles to profl. pubs. Recipient NSF award for rsch. in developmental biology, 1971, NIH Merit award, 1996-2003. Mem. Am. Soc. Nephrology (mem. coun. 1995-2002, pres.-elect 2000, pres. 2001), Internat. Soc. Nephrology, Am. Physiological Soc., Am. Heart Assn., Am. Soc. Clin. Investigation, Assn. Am. Physicians, Alpha Omega Alpha, Sigma Xi, Phi Beta Kappa. Office: Yale U Sch Medicine Physicians Bldg 800 Howard Ave New Haven CT 06520

ALPEROVITZ, GAR, author, educator; b. Racine, Wis., May 5, 1936; s. Julius and Emily (Bensman) A.; m. Sharon Sosnick, Aug. 29, 1976; children by previous marriage: Kari Fai, David Joseph. BS in History, U. Wis., 1958; MA in Econs, U. Cal. at Berkeley, 1960; PhD in Polit. Economy, U. Cambridge, Eng., 1964. Congl. legis. asst., 1961-62; Senate legis. dir. U.S. Senate staff, 1964-65; spl. asst. Dept. State, 1965-66; fellow King's Coll., Cambridge (Eng.) U., 1964-68, Inst. Politics Harvard, 1965-68, Brookings Instn., 1966, Inst. Policy Studies, 1968-69, 89-99; co-dir. Cambridge (Mass.) Inst., 1968-71; dir. Exploratory Project Econ. Alternatives, 1973—; pres. Nat. Center Econ. and Security Alternatives, 1978—. Guest prof. Notre Dame U., 1982-83; sr. rsch. scientist, dept. govt. and politics U. Md., College Park, 1993-96, Harrison rsch. prof. dept. govt. and politics, 1996-99, Lionel R. Bauman prof. polit. economy, 1999—. Author: Atomic Diplomacy: Hiroshima and Potsdam, 1965, rev., 1985, 1994, Cold War Essays, 1970, Strategy and Program, 1973, Rebuilding America, 1984, American Economic Policy, 1985, The Decision to Use the Atomic Bomb, 1995, Making a Place for Community, 2002, America Bayond Capitalism, 2004; also articles. Home: 2317 Ashmead Pl NW Washington DC 20009-1413 also: Univ Md 3140 Tydings Hall College Park MD 20742-7215 E-mail: garalper@ncesa.org.

ALPERS, DAVID HERSHEL, internist, educator; b. Phila., May 9, 1935; s. Bernard Jacob and Lillian (Sher) A.; m. Melanie Goldman, Aug. 12, 1977; children: Ann, Ruth, Barbara. BA, Harvard U., 1956, MD, 1960. Intern Mass. Gen. Hosp., Boston, 1960-61, resident in internal medicine, 1961-62; instr. medicine Harvard U., 1965-67, assoc. in medicine, 1967-68, asst. prof., 1968-69; asst. prof. medicine Washington U., St. Louis, 1969-72, assoc. prof., 1972-73, prof., 1973—, William B. Kountz prof., 1997—, dir. gastrointestinal divsn., 1969-97, asst. dir. clin. nutrition rsch. unit, 1999—; sr. cons. R&D

GlaxoSmithKline, 1999—. Author: (with others) Manual of Nutritional Therapeutics, 4th edit., 2002; assoc. editor: Textbook of Gastroenterology, 4th edit., 2003, Physiology of the Gastrointestinal Tract, 4th edit., 1997; assoc. editor Jour. Clin. Investigation, 1977-82; editor Am. Jour. Physiology, Gastrointestinal and Liver Physiology, 1991-97; contbr. articles and revs. to profl. jours., chpts. to books. With USPHS, 1962-64. Mem. Am. Soc. Clin. Investigation, Assn. Am. Physicians, Am. Gastroent. Assn. (pres. 1990-91, Friedenwald medal 1997), Am. Soc. Biochem. Molecular Biology (editl. bd. 1998-2003), Am. Fedn. Clin. Rsch., Am. Soc. Clin. Nutrition. Office: Washington U Med Sch Dept Internal Medicine PO Box 8031 Saint Louis MO 63110-1010 Office Phone: 314-362-8943. E-mail: DAlpers@im.wustl.edu.

ALPERS, EDWARD ALTER, history professor; b. Phila., Apr. 23, 1941; s. Bernard Jacob and Lillian (Sher) A.; m. Ann Adele Dixon, June 14, 1963; children: Joel Dixon, Leila Sher. AB magna cum laude, Harvard U., 1963; PhD, U. London, 1966. Lectr. history Univ. Coll., Dar es Salaam, Tanzania, 1966-68; from asst. prof. to prof. history UCLA, 1968—, dean divsn. honors Coll. Letters and Sci., 1985-87, dean honors and undergrad. programs, 1987-96, chair dept history, 2005—. Author: Ivory and Slaves in East Central Africa, 1975; editor: Walter Rodney: Revolutionary and Scholar, 1982, History, Memory and Identity, 2001, Africa and the West, 2001, Sidis and Scholars: Essays on African Indians, 2004, Slavery and Resistance in Africa and Asia, 2005; (newsletter) Assn. Concerned Africa Scholars, 1983-85; contbg. editor: Comparative Studies of South Asia, Africa and the Middle East, 1997—; bd. editors The American Historical Rev., 2002-2005; contbr. articles to profl. jours. Fellow Ford Found., 1972-73, NEH, 1978-79, Fulbright Found., 1980; Conf. fellow Humanities Rsch. Ctr., Nat. Australia U., Canberra, 1998; Fundacao Calouste Gulbenkian grantee, Lisbon, Portugal, 1975. Mem. Am. Hist. Assn. (mem. com. Joan Kelly Meml. prize 1998-99, chair 2000), Africa Studies Assn. (bd. dirs. 1985-88, v.p. 1992-93, pres. 1993-94), Assn. Concerned Africa Scholars (bd. dirs. 1983-93), Alliance for Undergrad. Edn. (UCLA rep. 1987-95, co-chair 1989-92), Hist. Abstracts (adv. bd. 1994—). Office: UCLA Dept History Los Angeles CA 90095-1473 Office Phone: 310-825-2347. Business E-Mail: alpers@history.ucla.edu.

ALPERS, JOHN HARDESTY, JR., financial planner, retired military officer; b. Richmond, Va., Sept. 7, 1939; s. John Hardesty and Laura Elizabeth (Gaylor) A.; m. Sharon Kay Kurrle, May 1, 1971; 1 child, John Hardesty III. BS, U. Colo., 1963; MBA, InterAm. U., 1969; postgrad., USAF Squadron Officers Sch., 1968-69, USAF Command and Staff Coll., 1976-78, USAF Air War Coll., 1978-79; CFP, Nat. Endowment for Fin. Edn., 1989; CFS, Inst. Bus. & Fin., 1994. Registered investment adv. svc. exec. Commd. 2d lt. USAF, 1964; advanced through grades to lt. col., 1979; SAC B-52 navigator, select radar bombardier Ramey AFB, PR, 1967-70; squadron weapon systems officer Ubon RTAFB, Thailand, 1970-71; radar strike officer Linebacker II strike plans officer, 1972; prisoner of war Hanoi, North Vietnam, 1972-73; asst. wing weapons officer Seymour-Johnson AFB, N.C., 1971-72, wing command post contr., 1973-74; asst. prof. aerospace studies AFROTC U. Ariz., Tucson, 1974-78; asst. div. chief aviation sci. USAF Acad., Colorado Springs, 1978-79, spl. asst. to commandant, 1979-80; divsn. chief plans, policy and standardization/evaluation, 1980-83; ret., 1983; reg. rep. Waddell & Reed, Inc., 1986-90, Fin. Network Investment Corp., 1990-97; vice pres. Fln. Planning & Mgmt., Inc., Boulder, CO, 1990-97; chmn. Gateway Fin. Strategies LLC, Erie, Colo.; registered rep., registered investment adv. Royal Alliance Assocs., Inc., 1997—; pres. GFS Mgmt., Inc., 2000—; mng. mem. GFS Properties, LLC, 2001—. Lectr., spkr. in field. POW/MIA Activist. With USCG, 1961-63. Decorated Legion of Merit, DFC (2), Bronze Star for Valor, Purple Heart (2), Air Medal (9), Air Force Commendation medal (2), Vietnamese Cross of Gallantry; recipient ceremonial sabre U.S. Air Force Acad. Cadet Corps., 1983. Mem. Air Force Assn., Ret. Officers Assn., U.S. Strategic Inst., Am. Def. Inst., Red River Valley Fighter Pilots Assn., Arnold Air Soc., Nam-POWS, Inc., Inst. CFPs, CFP Bd. Stds., Registry Fin. Planning Practitioners, Internat. Platform Assn., Sports Car Club Am., Rocky Mountain Vintage Racing, HSR-West Racing Club, Vintage Auto Racing Assn., Nostalgia Racing, Pi Kappa Alpha. Republican. Avocations: vintage race car owner, driver and enthusiast (Can-Am thunder series). Home: 12600 N Como Dr Tucson AZ 85742 Office: Gateway Fin Strategies LLC 526 Briggs St Ste D Erie CO 80516 Address: PO Box 957 Erie CO 80516-0957 Office Phone: 303-828-0077.

ALPERS, ROJANN RENEE, nursing educator, curator; b. Dallas, Jan. 20, 1955; d. Ralph William Alpers and Miriam Marguerite Russell-Alpers. BSN, Ariz. State U., 1977, MS in Cmty. Health Nursing, 1983; PhD, U. Iowa, 1992. Cert. advanced practice nurse, Tex., 1994, alternative and complementary care, U. Phoenix, 1997. Staff nurse Good Samaritan Hosp., Phoenix, 1977—79; maternal/child clin. specialist Mesa (Ariz.) Gen. Hosp. Med. Ctr., 1979—83; lectr. U. Iowa Coll. Nursing, Iowa City, 1983—92; asst. prof. U. Iowa, Iowa City, 1992—93, Tex. Christian U., Ft. Worth, 1993—95, Ariz. State U., Tempe, 1996—99, assoc. prof., chair, 1999—, curator Am. Mus. Nursing, 2000—. Mus. dir., curator Am. Mus. Nursing, Tempe, 2000; ind. legal cons., Scottsdale, Ariz., 1996—; presenter in field. Curator (museum displays and exhibits) Nursing History; contbr. articles to profl. jours. Task force mem. Scottsdale Unified Sch. Dist., 2004. Lillian Sholtis-Brunner fellow, U. Pa., 2004. Mem.: APHA, ANA, Mus. Assn. Ariz., Ctrl. Ariz. Mus. Assn., Am. Assn. for the History Nursing, Sigma Theta Tau (officer 1985—, com. mem. 1995—2001, Excellence in Nursing Journalism award 1999), Ariz. Adolescent Health Coalition, Ariz. Nurses Assn. Republican. Avocations: travel, collecting nursing memorabilia. Home: 3815 North 85th Pl Scottsdale AZ 85251 Office: Arizona State Univ ASU Box 3008 Tempe AZ 85287-3008 Office Phone: 480-965-7618. Business E-Mail: rojann@asu.edu.

ALPERT, BARRY MARK, insurance company and banking executive; b. Chgo., Apr. 17, 1941; s. Isadore Daniel and Betty Shane A.; m. Judith Rae Schwartz, Dec. 24, 1969; children: Daniel Ian, Jason Bradley, Stephanie Ann. Student, Ind. U., 1958-60; BBA, Roosevelt U., 1961; MBA in Banking, U. Wis., 1965. V.p. Exch. Nat. Bank, Chgo., 1961-72; pres., CEO Belleair Bluffs Corp., Largo, Fla., 1973-77; chmn., CEO Orange State Life and Health Ins. Co., Largo, 1977-87, Home Life Fin. Assurance Corp., 1982-88; pres., CEO United Ins. Cos., Inc., Largo, 1988-89; pres. Pioneer Western Corp., Largo, 1989-91; vice chmn. Western Res. Life Assurance Co. of Ohio, Largo, 1989-91, Colony Savs. Bank, Clearwater, 1989-92. Chmn. bd., CEO Alpert Fin. Group Inc., 1988; sr. v.p. Robert W. Baird & Co., Inc., Tampa, Fla., 1991-97; chmn. bd., founder Life Savs. and Loan Assn., Clearwater, Vla., 1979-83; asst. prof. fin. Roosevelt U., Chgo., 1965-69; host radio program Ask a Banker, Sta. WBBM/CBS, Chgo., 1966-67; mng. dir. Raymond James, 1997—. Founding dir., chmn. Ruth Eckerd Hall-Pact Inc., Clearwater, 1980-86, Fla. Holocaust Mus., 1995—; founder North Suncoast Symphony Guild, Clearwater, 1974; bd. dirs. Fla. Orch., Clearwater, 1974-80, St. Petersburg (Fla.) chpt. United Way, 1975; trustee Fla. House Washington, 1984—, Tampa Bay Rsch. Inst., 1993—. Served with USAFR, 1961-65. Home and Office: Alpert Fin Group Inc 239 Bath Club Blvd N Redington Beach FL 33708 Office Phone: 727-567-5029. Business E-Mail: barry.alpert@raymondjames.com.

ALPERT, DANIEL, broadcast executive; b. Chgo., June 20, 1952; s. Herbert and Miriam Florence (Nemiroff) A.; m. Doreen Marie Podolski, Apr. 30, 1976; children: Hilary Marie, Neil Andrew. BA, Mich. State U., 1973, postgrad., 1974-76. News reporter, disk jockey Sta. WITL-AM-FM, Lansing, Mich., 1973; audio producer Instructional Media Ctr. Mich. State U., East Lansing, 1973-74; dir. pub. info. Sta. WKAR-TV, East Lansing, 1974-76; v.p., dir. pub. info. Sta. WTVS Detroit Pub. TV, 1976-82, sr. v.p., acting gen. mgr., 1983, sr. v.p., asst. gen. mgr., 1983-96, sr. v.p. sta. mgr., 1996-2000, COO, Sta. mgr., 2000—. Contbr. articles on travel and sci. local newspapers. Trustee Karmanos Cancer Inst., Detroit, 1984-2004. Recipient Devel. award Corp. for Pub. Broadcasting, 1976, Promotion award Broadcast Promotion Assn., 1978, Pub. Broadcasting Svc., 1981, Govt. Rels. awards Nat. Assn. Pub. TV Stas., 1989, 96, ACE award Mich. Assn. Broadcasters, 1991. Mem. NATAS (gov. Detroit chpt. 1980-97, Silver Circle award Mich. chpt. 2000), Mich. Assn. Broadcasters, Mich. Pub. Broadcasters (exec. com. 1995—). Office: Sta WTVS 7441 2nd Ave Detroit MI 48202-2796 Business E-Mail: alpert@dptv.org.

ALPERT, HERB, composer, recording artist, producer, painter; b. Los Angeles, Mar. 31, 1935; s. Louis and Tillie (Goldberg) A.; m. Sharon Mae Lubin, Aug. 5, 1956 (div.); children: Dore, Eden; m. Lani Hall. Co-owner, founder A&M Record Co., 1962-94, Rondor Music Internat., 1994—. Band leader, trumpeter, arranger producer music group Herb Alpert & The Tijuana Brass, 34 recs. including The Lonely Bull, Whipped Cream & Other Delights, Going Places, Rise, Under A Spanish Moon, Colors, 1999 (14 Platinum recs., 15 gold recs., 7 Grammy awards); prodr. Broadway shows, including Angels in America, Jelly's Last Jam, Seven Guitars. Founder Herb Alpert Found. Office: c/o No Bull Inc 1414 6th St Santa Monica CA 90401-2510

ALPERT, HOLLIS, writer; b. Herkimer, NY, Sept. 24; s. Abram and Myra (Carroll) A.; m. Joan O'Leary (dec.). Student, New Sch. Social Research, 1947-49. Book reviewer Sat. Rev., N.Y. Times, others, 1947-59; film critic Sat. Review, after 1950, Woman's Day, 1953-60; assoc. fiction editor New Yorker, 1950-56; contbg. editor Woman's Day, 1956-69; mng. editor World Mag., after 1972, film editor, lively arts editor, after 1973; editor in chief Am. Film Mag., Washington, 1975-80; Algur Meadows Disting. vis. prof. So. Meth. U., 1982; freelance author, 1980—. Past dir. Edward MacDowell Assn.; vis. lectr. Yale U., 1972; lectr. film and writing Philharm. Ctr., Naples, Fla., 1995—. Author: The Summer Lovers, 1958, Some Other Time, 1960, The Dreams and the Dreamers, 1962, For Immediate Release, 1963, The Barrymores, 1964, The Claimant, 1968, The People Eaters, 1971, Smash, 1973, (under name Robert Carroll) A Disappearance, 1974, The Life and Times of Porgy and Bess, 1990, Broadway! 125 Years of Musical Theatre, 1991; editor: The Actors Life—Journals, Charlton Heston, 1978, Burton, 1986, Fellini, 1986; contbr. numerous short stories to mags. including Harper's Bazaar, The New Yorker. Served to 1st lt. AUS, 1942-46, ETO. Recipient Critic's award Screen Dirs.' Guild Am., 1957. Mem. Nat. Soc. Film Critics (chmn. 1972-73) Home: 1710 SW Health Pkwy 305 Naples FL 34109 Personal E-mail: halpert109@aol.com.

ALPERT, JOEL JACOBS, medical educator, pediatrician; b. New Haven, May 9, 1930; s. Herman Harold and Alice (Jacobs) A.; m. Barbara Ellen Wasserstrom, July 13, 1957; children: Norman, Mark, Deborah. AB, Yale U., 1952; MD, Harvard U., 1956. Diplomate Am. Bd. Pediatrics. Intern in medicine Children's Hosp. Med. Ctr., Boston, 1956-57, jr. asst. resident in medicine, 1957-58, chief resident for ambulatory svcs., fellow in medicine, 1961-62, from asst. to sr. assoc., 1962-72; exch. registrar St. Mary's Hosp. Med. Sch., London, 1958-59; from instr. to assoc. prof. Med. Sch., Harvard U., Boston, 1962-72, lectr., 1972; pediatrician in chief Boston City Hosp., 1972-92; prof. pediatrics and pub. health Boston U. Sch. Medicine, 2002—02, chmn. dept. pediatrics, 1972-93, also prof. sociomed. scis. and pub. health law, 1980—2002, prof. emeritus pediats. cmty. medicine and sociomed. scis., chmn. pediats., 2002—, prof. emeritus pub. health and health law, 2002—. Dozer vis. prof. Ben. Gurion Sch. Medicine, Beersheva, Israel, 1979; Raine Found. vis. prof. U. Western Australia, Perth, 1983; James and Jean Davis Prestige visitor U. Otago, Dunedin, New Zealand, 1995; cons. USPHS, 1972—, Children's Hosp., Boston, 1972; spl. cons. pres. N.Y.C. Health and Hosps. Corp., 1989; vis. prof. pediatrics Columbia Coll. Phys. and Surg., NYU Sch. Medicine; mem. med. adv. com. N.Y.C. Health and Hosps. Corp., 1989—. Author books, including: The Education of Physicians For Primary Care, 1974; also numerous papers Mem. Town Meeting, Winchester, Mass., 1970-72; mem. exec. com. Mass. Com. for Children and Youth, Boston, 1975-82; chmn. adv. com. Mass. Poison Info. System, Boston, 1980-92; bd. dirs. Med. Found., Boston, 1992—; cons. Commonwealth Fund and MEM Assocs., 1996—. Capt. U.S. Army, 1959-61. Recipient lifetime achievement award Mass. Poison Info. System, 1992, Hon. Mention Pub. Health Svc. award Pew Found., 1999, Pew Found. award for Achievement in Primary Care Edn.; numerous grants, 1965—; spl. fellow Nat. Ctr. Health Svcs. Rsch., London, 1971. Fellow: Royal Coll. Pediat. and Child Health (hon. 2000, U.K.), Am. Acad. Pediat. (v.p. 1997—98, pres. 1998—99, Job Lewis Smith award 1992); mem.: Mass. Assn. Pediat. Dept. Chmn. (chmn. 1976—78, 1981—93), Ambulatory Pediat. Assn. (pres. 1969, George Armstrong medal 1989, Lifetime Career Achievement award 2000, Pub. Policy and Advocacy award 2002), Philippine Ambulatory Pediat. Assn. (hon.), Soc. Pediat. Rsch., Am. Pediat. Soc., Inst. Medicine NAS (mem. governing coun. 1993—95, mem. bd. families and children 1993—95, mem. task force on future of primary care 1994—96), St. Botolph Club, Aescalapian Club, Harvard Club, Yale Club, Lancet Club, Alpha Omega Alpha. Jewish. Office: Boston U Sch Medicine Boston Med Ctr 91 E Concord St Boston MA 02118-2335 Home: 1802 Wisteria Way Wayland MA 01778 Office Phone: 617-414-5938.

ALPERT, JOSEPH STEPHEN, cardiologist, educator; b. New Haven, Feb. 1, 1942; s. Zelly Charles and Beatrice Ann (Kopsofsky) A.; m. Helle Mathiasen, Aug. 6, 1965; children: Eva Elisabeth, Niels David. BA magna cum laude, Yale U., 1963; MD cum laude, Harvard U., 1969. Diplomate internal medicine and cardiovasc. disease Am. Bd. Internal Medicine. Successively intern, resident in internal medicine, fellow in cardiovascular disease Peter Bent Brigham Hosp.-Harvard U. Med. Sch., Boston, 1969-74, dir. Samuel A. Levine cardiac unit, asst. prof. medicine, 1976-78; prof., dir. divsn. cardiovascular medicine U. Mass. Med. Sch., Worcester, 1978-92, vice-chm. dept. medicine, 1990—, Edward Budnitz prof. of cardiovascular medicine, 1988-92; Robert W. and Irene P. Flinn prof., chmn. dept. medicine U. Ariz., 1992—. Cons. West Roxbury VA Hosp., Boston, VA Med. Ctr., Tucson; sec., treas. med. staff U. Mass. Med. Ctr., 1979-81, pres. med. staff, 1981-82; bd. dirs. Am. Bd. Internal Medicine. Author: The Heart Attack Handbook, 1978, 3d edit., 1993, Cardiovascular Physiopathology, 1984; co-author: Manual of Coronary Care, 1977, 1980, 1984, 1987, 1993, 2000, Manual of Cardiovascular Diagnosis and Therapy, 1980, 1984, 1988, 1996, 2003, Valvular Heart Disease, 1981, 1987, 2000, Intensive Care Medicine, 1985, 2d edit., 1991, The Clinician's Companion, 1986, Modern Coronary Care, 1990, 2d edit., 1996, Diagnostic Atlas of the Heart, 1994, Cardiology for the Primary Care Physician, 1996, 2d edit., 1998, Primary Care of Native American Patients, 1999, American Heart Association's Clinical Cardiology Consult, 2001; editor-in-chief Current Cardiology Reports, 2001—, Am. Jour. Medicine, 2005—; co-editor: Cardiology in Rev., 2001—; assoc. editor Jour. History of Medicine and Allied Scis., 1977—80, editl. cons. Little, Brown & Co., Appleton-Century Crofts, mem. editl. bd. Am. Jour. Cardiology, 1985—, Archives Internal Medicine, 1987—, Heart and Lung, 1987—90, Geriatric Cardiovascular Medicine, 1988—89, Am. Jour. Noninvasive Cardiology, 1987—95, Am. Heart Jour., 1992—97, Internat. Jour. Cardiology, 1992—, European Heart Jour., 1995—, Heart Disease, 1999—2004, Cardiology, 1985—, assoc. editor, 1987—, editor-in-chief, 1991—2005, Am. Jour. Medicine, 2005—; contbr. articles to profl. jours. Lt. comdr. USNR, 1974—76. Recipient Gold medal U. Copenhagen, 1968, Edward Rhodes Stitt award San Diego Naval Hosp., 1976, George W. Thorn award Peter Bent Bingham Hosp., 1977, Outstanding Tchr. award U. Mass. Med. Sch., 1981, 86, 87, 90, U. Ariz. Med. Sch., 1995, 97-2002; Fulbright scholar Copenhagen, 1963-64; USPHS-Mass. Heart Assn. fellow, 1971-72, NIH spl. rsch. fellow, 1972-73 Fellow ACP, Am. Coll. Cardiology (jour. editl. bd. 1983-86, chmn. tng. dirs. com. 1991—, trustee 1996-2001, Gifted Tchr. award 2004), Am. Coll. Chest Physicians (gov. for Mass. 1983-85); mem. AAAS, Am. Heart Assn. (fellow coun. clin. cardiology, vice chmn. 1991-92, chmn. 1993-95, exec. com. 1986—, Disting. Achievement award 2001), Am. Assn. History of Medicine, Am. Fedn. Clin. Rsch., Assn. Univ. Cardiologists, New Eng. Cardiovascular Club, Assn. Profs. of Medicine, Danish Cardiology Assn. (hon.), Argentine Heart Assn. (fgn. corr.), Israeli Heart Soc. (hon.), Aesculapian Club, Phi Beta Kappa, Sigma Xi, Alpha Omega Alpha. Office: U Az Coll Medicine 1501 N Campbell Ave Tucson AZ 85724-0001 Business E-Mail: jalpert@email.arizona.edu. *I have lived my life following 3 rules: (1) maintain enthusiasm for living and learning; (2) love family and friends; and (3) work hard.*

ALPERT, MARK IRA, marketing educator; b. Duluth, Minn., Nov. 6, 1942; s. Isadore L. and Lillian Alpert; m. Judith Itzkovits, Sept. 3, 1967; 1 child, Nicole Deborah. BS, MIT, 1964; MBA, U. So. Calif., 1965, MS, 1967, D of Bus. Adminstrn., 1968. Asst. prof. mktg. Calif. State U., Long Beach, 1967-68, U. Tex., Austin, 1968-72, assoc. prof., 1972-76, prof., 1976—, La Quinta Motor Inns Centennial prof. bus., 1982-87, Foley's Federated prof. in retailing, 1987—. Vis. prof. bus. U. Pitts., 1978; cons. Zenith Mgmt. Co., Duluth, 1980—. Author: Pricing Decisions, 1971; co-author: Managerial Analysis Marketing, 1970; also articles in profl. jours.; mem. editl. rev. bd. Jour. of Mktg., 1979—, Jour. of Retailing, 1979—, Jour. Mktg. Rsch., 1985-91, Jour. of Bus. Rsch., 1988—95. Mem. exec. com. Congregation Agudas Achm, Austin, 1977, 78, bd. dirs., 1977-79, 85-88; bd. dirs. B'nai Brith Hillel, Austin, 1980-85; adv. coun. Shattuck-St. Mary's Sch., 2004— Mem. Am. Mktg. Assn. (track chmn. 1976, 87), Assn. for Consumer Research, Am. Psychol. Assn. Avocations: tennis, golf, water-skiing, music. Office: U Tex Austin McCombs Sch Business, Dept Mktg 1 Univ Sta B6700 Austin TX 78712-0218 Office Phone: 512-471-5417.

ALPERT, MARTIN JEFFREY, chiropractic physician; b. NYC, Apr. 22, 1951; s. Sheldon Lee and Beatrice (Ostrager) Alpert; m. Gilberta Joachim, May 4, 2000; children: Chad, Mitchell, Eva. BA, Syracuse U., 1972; DC, N.Y. Chiropractic Coll., 1976; MS, U. Bridgeport, 1979. Diplomate Am. Bd. Disability Analysts, Am. Acad. Pain Mgmt., Am. Bd. Profl. Disability Cons., Am. Acad. Experts Traumatic Stress, Am. Assn. Integrative Medicine, Coll. Pain Mgmt. Pvt. practice, Yonkers, NY, 1977-84, Hollywood, Fla., 1985, Coconut Creek, Fla., 1987-92, Miami, Fla., 1992-95, Ft. Lauderdale, Fla., 1985—, Orlando, Fla., 1994—. Lt. col. USAR, 1970—, 11th Bn (CGSOC), Concord, NC. Fellow: Am. Acad. Experts in Traumatic Stress, Am. Assn. Integrative Medicine (diplomate), Am. Back Soc., Internat. Biog. Assn.; mem.: U.S. Sports Chiropractic Fedn., Fla. Chiropractic Assn., Fla. Chiropractic Soc., Am. Acad. Spine Physicians, Am. Acad. Chiropractic Physicians, Internat. Fedn. Sports Chiropractic, World Fedn. Chiropractic, Am. Pub. Health Assn., N.Y. Acad. Scis., Am. Coll. Sports Medicine, Internat. Chiropractors Assn., Am. Chiropractic Assn. Democrat. Avocations: jogging, chess, basketball, piano. Home: 19674 Black Olive Ln Boca Raton FL 33498 Office: Third Ave Chiropractic Ctr Inc 300 W Sunrise Blvd Ste 7 Fort Lauderdale FL 33311-6200 also: Colonial Chiropractic Ctr 1310 W Colonial Dr Ste 21 Orlando FL 32804 Office Phone: 954-524-1416. Business E-Mail: doctorofchiropractic@hotmail.com.

ALPERT, NORMAN, chemical company executive; b. Phila., May 5, 1921; s. Barnet and Celia A.; m. Adeline Edna Gushman, Apr. 9, 1948; children: Rosalind Alice, Barbara Naomi. AB in Chemistry, Temple U., 1942, MA, 1947; PhD (AEC research fellow 1948-49), Purdue U., 1949. Devel. engr. Publicker Industries, Phila., 1942-45; group head Texaco, Inc., Beacon, N.Y., 1949-59; div. mgr. Exxon Research, Linden, N.J., 1959-79; v.p., dir. research Hooker Chem. Co., Grand Island, N.Y., 1979-82; v.p. spl. environ. projects Occidental Chem. Corp., Niagara Falls, N.Y., 1982-84, v.p. corp. environ. affairs, 1984-86. Environ. cons. Author; patentee in field. Mgr. Career Explorer Post local Boy Scouts Am., 1981. Mem. Am. Chem. Soc., Soc. Automotive Engrs., Niagara Frontier Assn. Research and Devel. Dirs. Home: 4060 Lower River Rd Youngstown NY 14174-9739 E-mail: naalp@aol.com.

ALPERT, SEYMOUR, anesthesiologist, educator; b. N.Y.C., Apr. 20, 1918; s. Louis and Ida (Freedman) Alpert; m. Cecilia Bernadine Cohen, Sept. 7, 1941. AB, Columbia U., 1939; MD, SUNY, Bklyn., 1943; LLD (hon.), George Washington U., 1984. Diplomate Am. Bd. Anesthesiology. Intern Beth Israel Hosp., N.Y.C., 1943-44; resident in anesthesiology Gallinger Mcpl. Hosp., Washington, 1946-47; mem. faculty dept. anesthesiology George Washington U. Sch. Medicine and Hosp., Washington, 1948—, prof., 1961-83, prof. emeritus, 1983—; v.p. for devel. George Washington U., 1969-83, v.p. emeritus for devel., 1983—. Cons. in anesthesiology Walter Reed Army Hosp., Washington, 1948-83, VA Hosp., Washington, 1948-70, D.C. Gen. Hosp., 1948-69, Mead Dental Hosp., 1949-69; dir. Jefferson Fed. Savs. and Loan Assn., 1979-82; adv. bd. Washington Fed. Savs. & Loan, 1982-89. Contbr. articles to med. jours. Bd. govs. Hebrew U., Jerusalem, 1968-; bd. govs. State of Israel Bonds, 1964—, nat. chmn. med. divsn., 1969-86; bd. dirs. Israel Investors Corp., 1965-82, exec. com., 1974-82; bd. dirs. Am. Friends of Hebrew U., 1966—, chmn. med. divsn., 1969-86, v.p., 1969-90, hon. v.p. 1990—; examining physician Met. Police Boys Clubs, 1952-76; pres. United Jewish Appeal Greater Washington, 1966-67, exec. com., 1955—; bd. dirs. United Givers Fund, 1972-74; exec. com. Jewish Community Council, 1958-75; bd. mgrs. Adas Israel Congregation, 1963—; bd. dirs. Kaufmann Camp for Boys and Girls, 1964-78, Council Jewish Fedn. and Welfare Funds, 1966-73, Jewish Cmty. Found., 1966—, v.p., 1968-69; trustee United Jewish Endowment Fund D.C. 1984-98, trustee emeritus, 1998—, vice chmn., 1984-98, 1984-86, pres. 1986-88; found. com. Jewish Fedn. Palm Bch., Fla., 1990—. Capt. AUS, 1944-46. Recipient Man of Yr. award State of Israel Bonds, 1964; Freedom award, 1970; Disting. Svc. award Phi Delta Epsilon, 1971, 73; Torch of Learning award Am. Friends of Hebrew U., 1975; Med. award United Jewish Appeal, 1980; Achievement award Profl. Fraternity Assn., 1995; State of Israel Bonds Salvador Dali Menorah award, 2001. Fellow Am. Coll. Anesthesiology; mem. Am. Soc. Anesthesiologists (dir. 1963-66, trustee Wood Lib. Mus. Anesthesiology 1968-74, v.p. 1970-74), Md.-D.C. Soc. Anesthesiologists (pres. 1968-69), AMA, Med. Soc. D.C. (mem. numerous coms.), Jacobi Med. Soc., Pan Am. Med. Soc. (pres. 1967), Assn. Am. Med. Colls. (co-dir. nat. med. lib. study 1965-66), Assn. Univ. Anesthetists, Phi Delta Epsilon (nat. pres. 1961-62, exec. com. 1961—, exec. sec. 1963-72, v.p. bd. trustees 1972-73, pres. bd. trustees 1973-74), Cosmos Club (Washington), Woodmont Country Club (Rockville, Md.). Home: Brighton Gardens 5555 Friendship Blvd Apt 424 Chevy Chase MD 20815

ALPERT, WARREN, oil industry executive, foundation administrator; b. Chelsea, Mass., Dec. 2, 1920; s. Goodman and Tena (Horowitz) Alpert. BS, Boston U., 1942; MBA, Harvard U., 1947; DBA (hon.), Bryant Coll. Mgmt. trainee Std. Oil Co. of Calif., 1947—48; financial specialist The Calif. Oil Co., 1948—52; pres. Warren Petroleum Co., 1952—54; now chmn. bd.; founder, pres., chmn. bd. Warren Equities, Inc., 1954. Chmn. emeritus Ritz Tower Hotel, 1995—; chmn. bd. Kenyon Oil Co., Inc., Mid-Valley Petroleum Corp., Puritan Oil Co., Inc., Drake Petroleum Co., Inc.; mem. U.S. Com. for UN, 1958; exec. com. Small Bus. Adminstrn., 1958; adminstr. for adminstrn. U.S. AID, 1962; former trustee, mem. exec. com. Boston U.; trustee Emerson Coll.; former v.p. Petroleum Mktg. Edn. Found.; bd. dirs., life mem. Assocs. of Harvard Bus. Sch., Mass.; mem. com. for resource and devel. Harvard Med. Sch. bd. fellows. Bd. dirs. World Coun. Synagogues; bd. overseers Albert Einstein Med. Sch.; founder Warren Alpert Found.; bd. fellows Harvard Med. Sch.; former trustee Boston U., Emerson Coll. Named Harvard Med. Sch. Rsch. Ctr. Bldg. named in his honor, 1993; recipient Andrew Wellington Cordier fellow Sch. Internat. Affairs, Columbia U. Mem.: Am. Petroleum Inst. (dir. mktg. divsn.), Young Pres. Orgn. (past dir.), Univ. Club, Met Club, Marco Polo Club, Harvard Club (N.Y.C. mem. house com.), Am. Petroleum Industry 25 Yr. Club, Harvard Bus. Sch. Club (exec. com., dir., bd. govs., pres. 1960—61). Office: Warren Equities Inc 375 Park Ave Ste 2502 New York NY 10152-2595

ALPERT, WILLIAM HAROLD (BILL ALPERT), artist, painter; b. Bronx, NY, Dec. 21, 1934; s. Jacob Joseph and Fannie (Leff) Alperovicz. PharmD, U. So. Calif., 1958; BA, UCLA, 1963, MA, 1965. Adj. prof. painting Cooper Union Sch. Art, N.Y.C., 1979-82; adj. instr. drawing Parsons Sch. Design, N.Y.C., 1981-82, Pratt Inst. Summer Program, 1981; prof. painting, drawing and watercolor Sch. Visual Arts, 1989-, The Dactyl Found. for Arts & Humanities, 2005; guest lectr. and studio visitor Yunnan Art Inst., Kunming, China, 1993, Ctrl. Acad. Fine Arts, Bejing, China, 1993, The Green Horse Coll. Art, Ulaanbaatar, Mongolia, 1998. Exhbns. include Constructs Orgn. Ind. Artists, Bleecker Renaissance, NY, 1978, OIA: 6 Artists View Devel., N.Y. Acad. Sci., Orgn. Ind. Artists Postcard Show, Bologna Art Fair, Italy, 1978, Indpls. Mus. Art, 1978, Albright-Knox Mus., 1978, Joe & Emily Lowe Art Gallery, Syracuse U., 1980, W. Paterson Collection of NJ, 1981, Coll. Charleston (S.C.), 1987, 89, The N.Y. Bot. Garden, Bronx, 1993, Yunnan Art Inst., Kunming, China, 1993; pub. collections include Power

Gallery Contemporary Art, Sydney, Australia, The Dactyl Found. for Arts and Humanities, N.Y.C.; contbr. to NY Art Yearbook, 1975-76, The Sciences, NYAS, 1978, Antinf Arte Informa, 1981. Avocations: pharmacy, photography, travel. Home: 64 Grand St # 5 New York NY 10013-2267 Office Phone: 212-966-1715.

ALPHER, RALPH ASHER, physicist, educator; b. Washington, Feb. 3, 1921; s. Samuel and Rose (Maleson) Alpher; m. Louise Ellen Simons, Jan. 28, 1942; children: Harriet Alpher Lebetkin, Victor. BS, George Washington U, 1943, MS, 1945, PhD, 1948; ScD (hon.), Union Coll., 1992, Renssalaer Poly. Inst., 1993. Physicist Bur. Ordnance and Naval Ordnance Lab., USN, Washington, 1940-44, Applied Physics Lab., Johns Hopkins U., Silver Spring, Md., 1944-55, GE R&D Ctr., Schenectady, NY, 1955-86; disting. rsch. prof. physics Union Coll., Schenectady, 1986—2004, emeritus, 2004—. Adj. prof. aero engring. Renselaer Poly. Inst., 1958—63, adj. prof. physics, 1986—92. Contbr. chapters to books, articles to profl. jours. Bd. dirs. Mohawk-Hudson Coun. Ednl. TV, 1974—80, 1982—87, chmn., 1978—80, 1986—87; bd. dirs. Dudley Obs., Union U., Albany, NY, 1968—72, 1980—86, v.p., 1983—86, adminstr., disting. sr. scientist, 1987—. Recipient Magellanic Premium, Am. Philos. Soc., 1975, Georges Vanderlinden prize, Belgian Royal Acad. Scis., Letters and Fine Arts, 1975, John Price Wetherill medal, Franklin Inst., 1980, Phys. and Math. Scis. prize, N.Y. Acad. Scis., 1981, Disting. Alumnus award, George Washington U., 1987, Henry Draper medal, NAS, 1993. Fellow: AAAS (sect. B physics steering com. 1982—86), Am. Acad. Arts & Scis., Am. Phys. Soc. (councillor-at-large 1979—82, mem. exec. com. 1980—81); mem.: Internat. Astron. Union, Am. Astron. Soc., Fedn. Am. Scientists, Internat. Torch Club, Sigma Xi. Personal E-mail: alpherr@aol.com.

ALPHER, VICTOR SETH, clinical psychologist, consultant; b. Washington, Oct. 20, 1954; s. Ralph Asher and Louise Ellen (Simons) A. BA, U. Pa., 1976; PhD, Vanderbilt U., 1985. Diplomate in clin. psychology Am. Bd. Profl. Psychology. Grad. fellow Vanderbilt U., Nashville, 1981-85; asst. prof. U. Tex. Health Sci. Ctr., Houston, 1986-88, clin. asst. prof., 1989-96; ret., 1996. Cons. Rsch. Inst. on Addictions, Buffalo, 1990—, Meml. Geriatric Evaluation and Resource Ctr., Houston, 1991-95; bd. cons. Fla. Inst. Psychology, 1994—. Cons. reviewer Jour. Cons. and Clin. Psychology, 1996; contbr. articles to profl. jours., including Jour. Cons. and Clin. Psychology, Jour. Personality Assessment, Jour. Psychopathology and Behavioral Assessment, Psychotherapy, and Jour. Applied Physiology. Fellow Am. Acad. Clin. Psychology; mem. Sigma Xi. E-mail: valpher@aol.com.

ALPHIN, J. STEELE, bank executive; b. Windsor, Va. BS in Mil. History, U. N.C., Chapel Hill. With consumer bank Bank of Am., Chapel Hill, NC, 1977—80, compensation analyst, personnel Charlotte, NC, 1980—84, regional personnel mgr. Tampa, Fla., 1984—85, personnel dir., 1985—88, corp. personnel divsn. exec. Charlotte, NC, 1988—92, Atlanta, 1992—94, exec., consumer & comml. bank and wealth mgmt. Charlotte, NC, 1994—99, corp. personnel exec., 1999—. Bd. mem. Bank Adminstrn. Inst.; mem. U. N.C. Bd. Visitors, Class of 2006. Office: Bank of America Corp 100 N Tryon St Charlotte NC 28255 Office Phone: 800-432-1000. Office Fax: 704-386-6699.*

ALPI, KRISTINE MARKOVICH, librarian, educator; m. Jeffery A. Alpi, 1999. BA, Ind. U., 1995, MLS, 1996; MPH, CUNY, 2003. Assoc. fellow Nat. Libr. Medicine, Bethesda, Md., 1997—98; edn. coord. Nat. Network Librs. Medicine, N.Y. Acad. Medicine, N.Y.C., 1998—99; info. svcs. libr. Weill Med. Coll., Cornell U., N.Y.C., 2000—02, lectr. in pub. health, 2002—; libr. mgr. NYC Dept. Health & Mental Hygiene, N.Y.C., 2002—05; assoc. libr. dir. Weill Med. Coll., Cornell U., N.Y.C., 2005—. Ednl. collaborator Nat. Ctr. for Biotechnology Info., Bethesda, Md., 2001—. Contbr. chapters to books. Scholar, NE Pub. Health Leadership Inst., 2004—05. Mem.: Med. Libr. Assn. (bd. mem. N.Y.-N.J. chpt. 2003—05, chair pub. health/health adminstrn. sect. 2004—05, David A. Kronick Traveling fellow 2005), Beta Phi Mu (assoc.), Phi Beta Kappa (assoc.). Office: Weill Cornell Med Libr 1300 York Ave New York NY 10021 Office Phone: 212-746-6068. Office Fax: 212-746-8374. Personal E-mail: kalpi@att.net.

ALPINI, GIANFRANCO D., medical educator; b. Rome, Jan. 15, 1955; m. Aliza Tasimowicz-Alpini; children: Sarah, Helene Rosalia Francesca, Sally Filomena Olga. PhD in Chemistry & Pharm. Tech., U. Studies of Rome, 1984. Postdoctoral fellow divsn. Hematology Mt. Sinai Med. Ctr., N.Y.C.; rsch. assoc. Albert Einstein Coll. Medicine, Bronx, N.Y., 1988—91; sr. postdoctoral fellow GI Basic Rsch. Digestive Diseases, Mayo Clinic, Rochester, Minn., 1991—94; asst. prof. Scott & White Meml. Hosp./Tex. A&M U. Health Sci. Ctr., Temple, 1994—2000, assoc. prof. med. physiology, 2000—03, prof. internal medicine and med. physiology, 2003—. Career rsch. scientist Ctrl. Tex. Vets. Adminstrn., Temple, 2004—; endowed chair holder gastroenterology Scott & White Meml. Hosp./Tex. A&M U. Health Sci. Ctr., 2004—. Recipient VA Rsch. award, NIH and Vets. Adminstrn.; grantee NIH RO1 grant awards (2). Mem.: Am. Assn. Study Liver Diseases, Am. Soc. Cell Biology, European Assn. Study of the Liver, Italian Liver Found. (internat. mem.), Am. Physiol. Soc., Am. Gastroenterol. Assn. Avocations: tennis, soccer, bicycling, travel. Office: Scott & White Meml Hosp Tex A&M Univ 702 SW HK Dodgen Loop Temple TX 76504 Office Fax: 254-724-5944. Business E-Mail: galpini@tamu.edu.

AL-SABAH, SHEIKH JABIR AL-AHMAD AL-JABIR AL-AHMED, Emir of Kuwait; b. Kuwait City, Kuwait, June 29, 1928; s. His Highness Sheikh Ahmad Al-Jabir Al-Sabah; married. Student, Al-Mubarakiyyah Sch. Chief of pub. safety in the Oil Regions, Kuwait, 1949-59; head Dept. Fin. (then Ministry of Fin. and Economy) Govt. of Kuwait, 1959—62, dep. prime min., 1962—65, prime minister, 1965-67; crown prince, 1966-77; Emir of Kuwait, 1978—. Chmn. Supreme Def. Council, Kuwait, Supreme Petroleum Coun.; chmn. 5th session Orgn. of Islamic Conf., 1987-; chmn. Supreme Com. for Master Plan and Major projects, Kuwait; delivered speech before the 43rd session of the US General Assembly, September 28, 1988. Chmn. bd. dirs. Kuwait Fund for Arab Econ. Devel.; chmn. Kuwait Found. for Sci. Advancement; chmn. Supreme Com. for Master Plan and Maj. Projects, Kuwait. Home: Sief Palace Amiry Diwan Kuwait Office: care of Press Attache Embassy State Kuwait 2600 Virginia Ave NW Ste 404 Washington DC 20037 Office Fax: 202-338-0957, 202-965-3463.

ALSAUD, PRINCE ALWALEED BIN TALAL BIN ABDULAZIZ, investment company executive, investor, entrepreneur; b. Riyadh, Saudi Arabia, Mar. 1955; s. Prince Talal Bin AbdulAziz Alsaud and Princess Mona El-Solh; divorced; children: Khalid, Reem; m. Princess Kholood Alsaud. BSc, Menlo Coll., 1979; MA, Syracuse U., 1985, LLD (hon.), 1999; DHL (hon.), U. New Haven, 1992; D in bus. adminstrn. (hon.), Kyungwon U., 1998; LLD (hon.), Exeter U., 2002, Am. U., 2002. Chmn. Kingdom Holding Co., Saudi Arabia, Azizia Commercial Investment Co., Rotana Video and Audio Visual Co.; pvt. entrepreneur; investor Four Seasons Hotel and Resorts, Fairmount Hotels and Resorts, Mövenpick Hotels and Resorts, US, Middle East, and Africa, Citigroup, 1991—, News Corp, Time Warner, Motorola, Apple Computers, Ballast Nedam, Canary Wharf, Disneyland Paris, Saks Inc., Kingdom Ctr. Recipient Arab Bankers Assn. of Am. Lifetime Achievement award, 2000. Avocations: exercise, reading. Office: Kingdom Holding Co PO Box 2 Riyadh 11321 Saudi Arabia

ALSBERG, DIETRICH ANSELM, electrical engineer, consultant; b. Kassel, Germany, June 5, 1917; came to U.S., 1939, naturalized, 1943; s. Adolf and Elisabeth (Hofmann) A.; m. Glenna Rose Le Baron, Nov. 6, 1942; children: Peter Allyn, Ronald Ashley, Terry Wayne, David James (dec.). BS in E.E, Tech. U., Stuttgart, 1938; postgrad., Case Sch. Applied Sci., Cleve., 1939-40. Engr. Wright Tool and Forge Co., Barberton, Ohio, 1940-41, Bridgwater Machine Co., Akron, Ohio, 1941-43; with Bell Labs., Holmdel, Murray Hill, Whippany (N.J.) and N.Y., 1945-82, head various depts., 1965-82. Author: (autobiography) A Witness to a Century, 1999; contbr. articles to profl. jours. and books; patentee in field of comms., electromagnetic waves, missile and space guidance and civil engring. Mem. Berkeley Heights (N.J.) Bd. Edn., 1955-58; chmn. Environ. Commn., Berkeley Heights, 1971-76; various office positions local Meth. Ch. With U.S. Army, ETO, 1943-45. Fellow IEEE (life). Lutheran. Home: 8545 Carmel Valley Rd Carmel CA 93923-9556 E-mail: dalsberg@ieee.org.

ALSBERG, FRED GAINES, literature educator; s. Henry Alsberg and Frances Mary Gaines; m. Thangeswari Maia Kesnan, Jan. 23, 2003; children: Mesha, Naveenah. MFA in Creative Writing, U. Ark., 1988. Asst. prof. Southwestern Okla. State U., Weatherford, Okla., 1991—. Author: (poem) Waiting for That Day; editor: Westview, 1992—2004. Avocation: jazz.

ALSCHULER, AL, freelance/self-employed writer; b. Gary, Ind., Jan. 27, 1934; s. Harold Morris and Sarah N. Alschuler; m. Joy Van Wye, June 28, 1956 (div. 1986); children: Mari Lynn, David Van, Mark Jonathan; m. Jacqulyn Yde, Oct. 7, 2000. BA in Journalism with honors, U. Okla., 1955. Exec. v.p. Vanleigh Furniture Showrooms, N.Y.C., 1958-71, Miami, Fla., 1971-79; advt. and pub. rels. cons., Miami Beach, Fla., 1979-82; mng. editor Fla. Designer Quar., Miami, 1982-84, Design South, Miami Beach, 1984-87; freelance writer, pub. rels. counsel Miami, 1987—. Cons. interior design adv. bd. Fla. Internat. U., Miami, 1988—, Art Inst. Ft. Lauderdale, 1991—. Editor: I.D.E.A.S., 1994—95; contbg. editor: South Fla., 1996—97, Gables Living mags., Mass Media, Inc., 2004—; guest expert on design WFOR-TV; contbr.: publs. including articles U.S. Architecture, Casa and Estilo Internat.; contbr. articles to profl. jours. Founding chmn. Players State Theatre Conservatory, Coconut Grove, Fla., 1975; mem. Metro Dade Performing Arts Dist. Commn., 1976—77, Miami Com. Beautification, 1977; trustee Miami Design Preservation League, 1988—98, Interior Design Guild Found., 1999—; bd. dirs. Skyline Theatre Co.; committeeman East Rockaway (N.Y.) Dem. Com., 1968—69; bd. dirs. City Theatre, 1999—. Recipient Rachline Comm. award, 1996. Fellow: Interior Design Guild (past pres., Comm. award 1996); mem.: Miami Internat. Press Club (pres. 1994), Soc. Profl. Journalists, Mensa, Phi Beta Kappa. Avocations: theater, travel. Home and Office: 2430 Brickell Ave Apt 104A Miami FL 33129-2455 Office Phone: 305-860-0730. E-mail: alal34@aol.com.

ALSCHULER, ALBERT W., law educator; b. Aurora, Ill, Sept. 24, 1940; s. Sam and Winifred (King) Alschuler; m. Louise Evans Alschuler, Mar. 21, 1970 (div.); 1 child, Samuel Jonathan. AB in History, cum laude, Harvard U., 1962, LLB magna cum laude, 1965. Bar: Ill. 1965. Law clk. to Hon. Walter V. Schaefer Ill. Supreme Ct., 1965—66; fellow Ctr. for Studies in Criminal Justice U. Chgo., 1967—68; spl. asst. to Hon. Fred M. Vinson, Jr. Asst. Atty. Gen. criminal divsn., 1968—69; asst. prof. law U. Tex., Austin, 1966—67, assoc. prof., 1969—70, prof., 1970—76, U. Colo., Boulder, Colo., 1976—84, U Pa., Phila., 1984, U. Chgo. Law Sch., 1985—88, Wilson-Dickinson prof., 1988—2002, Julius Kreeger prof. law and criminology, 2002—. Author: Law Without Values: The Life, Work and Legacy of Justice Holmes, 2000; co-author: The Privilege Against Self-Incrimination: Its Origins and Development, 1997. Fellow: Am. Bar Found. Office: U Chgo Law Sch 1111 E 60th St Chicago IL 60637-2776 Office Phone: 773-702-3586. E-mail: awaa@midway.uchicago.edu.

ALSCHULER, SAM, retired lawyer; b. Aurora, Ill., June 16, 1913; s. Benjamin P. and Lillian (Reinheimer) A.; m. Winifred King, Feb. 8, 1939 (dec. Dec. 1998); children: Albert W., Therese Alschuler Hale. AB, U. Wis., 1933; JD, U. Chgo., 1935. Bar: Ill. 1935, U.S. Supreme Ct. 1953. Pvt. practice, Aurora, 1935; ptnr. Alschuler & Funkey, 1935-84, counsel, 1984-96; ret. Bd. dirs. Weslin Properties, Inc., 1982-93. Mem. Aurora Spl. Svc. Area Com., 1976; pres. bd. dirs. United Cmty. Svc., Aurora, 1959-68; chmn. United Fund Gen. Campaign, 1966; mem. Citizens Cmty. Survey Com., 1964; vice chmn., dir. Kane County Coun. for Equal Opportunity, 1966-69; corp. counsel City of Aurora, 1961-65; pres., trustee Ill. Assn. for the Crippled, 1948-63, pres., 1963; governing mem. Copley Meml. Hosp., dir. Rush-Copley Meml. Hosp., 1942-2004; past pres., hon. bd. dirs. Rehab. Ctr. for So. Kane, Kendall and DeKalb Counties. With AUS, 1944-45. Recipient Copley Caring award Copley Healthcare Found., 1991. Mem. ABA, Ill. Bar Assn., Kane County Bar Assn. (Community Svc. award 1993), Am. Judicature Soc., Greater Aurora C. of C. (pres. 1953-55, dir.), Elks, Moose, Rotary, Sigma Delta Chi, Zeta Beta Tau. Democrat. Home: 119 S Buell Ave Aurora IL 60506-4603 E-mail: samanedwini@webTV.net.

ALSCHULER, STEVEN, public relations executive, writer, consultant; b. NYC, Feb. 12, 1958; s. Robert and Caroline (Benjamin) A. BA, Queens Coll., CUNY, 1979. Press sec. State Senator Roy Goodman, NYC, 1979-86, NY State Senate Com. Investigations, Taxation and Govt. Ops., NYC, 1979-86; sr. v.p. Howard Rubenstein Assoc., Inc., NYC, 1986-93; pres. Linden Alschuler & Kaplan, Inc., NYC, 1993—. Pub. rels. cons. corporations and private sector clients, pub. affairs, fin. svcs. cos., founds., candidates and elected officials, nat., state and local offices, 1993—. Co-author: Lethal Medicine, 1993. Pub. rels. advisor N.Y. Rep. County Com., 1981-86. Mem. Pub. Rels. Soc. of Am. Office: Linden Alschuler & Kaplan Inc 1251 Ave of the Americas New York NY 10020 Office Phone: 212-575-4545. Business E-Mail: salschuler@lakpr.wn.

ALSDORF, ROBERT HERMANN, lawyer; b. Ashland, Ohio, Mar. 5, 1946; s. Howard Alton and Henrietta (Bulleit) A.; m. Sarah Jane Schlick, Nov. 27, 1970; children: Matthew William, Paul August. B.A. magna cum laude, Carleton Coll., 1967; M.A. in U.S. History, Yale U., 1973, J.D., 1973. Bar: D.C. 1973, Wash. 1975, U.S. Dist. Ct. (we. dist.) Wash. 1975, U.S. Ct. Appeals (9th cir.) 1975, U.S. Dist. Ct. (ea. dist.) Wash. 1981, U.S. Supreme Ct. 1984. Trial atty. Dept. Justice, Washington, 1973-75; assoc. Culp, Dwyer, Guterson & Grader, Seattle, 1975-79; ptnr. Armstrong, Alsdorf, Bradbury & Maier P.C. and predecessor Armstrong & Alsdorf, Seattle, 1979-84, pres., 1984—; speaker continuing legal edn. seminars; pvt. arbitrator of disputes. Author continuing legal edn. materials. Bd. dirs. Stevens Neighborhood Housing Improvement Program, Seattle, 1979-82, pres., 1980-81. Mem. ABA (antitrust sect.), Wash. State Bar Assn. (franchise law revision subcom. corp. bus. and banking com. 1985—, exec. com., sec.-treas. consumer protection antitrust and unfair bus. practices sect. 1987—), Seattle-King County Bar Assn. (com. mem. young lawyers sect. 1978-80, continuing legal edn. 1984-87), Phi Beta Kappa. Home: 952 12th Ave E Seattle WA 98102-4516 Office: Armstrong Alsdorf Bradbury & Maier 1300 Hoge Bldg Seattle WA 98104

ALSENTZER, WILLIAM JAMES, JR., lawyer; b. Ravenna, Ohio, Mar. 15, 1942; s. William J. Alsentzer and Vivian (Guy) Soash; children: Lesley Joan, Michelle Guy. AB, Duke U., 1964, JD, 1966. Bar: Del. 1966, U.S. Dist. Ct. Del. 1967, Ariz. 1980, U.S. Dist. Ct. Ariz. 1980. Assoc. Wilson & Lynam, Wilmington, Del., 1967-70; ptnr. Bayard, Brill & Handelman, Wilmington, 1970-79; v.p., gen. counsel Bapt. Hosps. and Health Systems, Phoenix, 1979-2000; legal counsel BHHS Legacy Found., Phoenix, 2000—. Mem. Maricopa County Bar Assn., Am. Health Lawyers Assn., Fedn. Def. and Corp. Counsel. Office: 2999 N 44th St Ste 530 Phoenix AZ 85018

AL SNIH, SOHAM, rheumatologist, researcher; d. Maaza Snih and Yasmin Al Sneih. MD, Ctrl. U. Venezuela, 1986; MS, U. Tex., 2001, PhD, 2005. Intern U. Hosp. of Caracas, Venezuela, 1986—88, resident in internal medicine, 1989—91, fellow in rheumatology, 1992—93, faculty dept. internal medicine, divsn. of rheumatology, 1994—98; postdoctoral fellow Sealy Ctr. on Aging, Galveston, Tex., 1998—. Recipient Pub. Recognition award, U. Hosp., Caracas, Venezuela, 1998, Best Student Poster, Forum on Aging, 1999, 2000, 2001, 2002, 2003, 2004, Grad. Student award, Sealy Ctr. on Aging, 2000, Rose and Harry Walk Rsch. award, 2004; Don W. Micks scholarship in preventive medicine and cmty. health, 2004. Mem.: Venezuelan Soc. of Rheumatology, Venezuelan Soc. of Internal Medicine, Gerontol. Soc. of Am., Am. Geriat. Soc. Office: Sealy Ctr on Aging 301 University Blvd Galveston TX 77555-0460 Office Phone: 409-747-3580. Business E-Mail: soalsnih@utmb.edu.

ALSOBROOK, HENRY BERNIS, JR., lawyer; b. New Orleans, Nov. 9, 1930; s. Henry Bernis and Ethel (Smith) A.; m. Carey Turner Mackie; children: Eugenie Alsobrook Burglass, John Gleason, Emily Alsobrook. BA, Tulane U., 1952, JD, 1957. Bar: La. 1957. Since practiced in, New Orleans; sr. partner firm Adams & Reese. Past mem. faculty Tulane U. Law Sch.; bd. dirs. Def. Research Inst., 1978-81, 85-88, chmn. med.-legal com., 1967-72; lectr. in field. Author articles in field;: editorial bds. legal jours. Chmn. dean's coun. Tulane U., 1983-88; elder St. Charles Ave. Presbyn. Ch., New Orleans; 1st pres. Les Compagnons du Barreau de La Louisiane, 1985—; treas., bd. dirs. La. State Mus.; bd. dirs. New Orleans Symphony Soc., New Orleans Opera.; mem. La. Gov.'s Commn. on Med. Malpractice, 1989—; mem. Audubon Inst. Aquarium Capital Campaign Commn. With USNR, 1953. Fellow Am. Bar Found., Am. Coll. Trial Lawyers (state chmn.); mem. ABA (past chmn. standing com. commerce, ho. of dels. 1984-89), La. Bar Assn. (pres. 1982-83), New Orleans Bar Assn., Internat. Assn. Def. Counsel (exec. com. 1982-88, pres. 1986-87), Fedn. Ins. Counsel, New Orleans Assn. Def. Counsel (pres.), La. Assn. Def. Counsel (gov. 1965), La. Law Inst. (council 1984-89), Soc. Med. Assn. Counsel (charter), Soc. Hosp. Attys. (charter), AMA (hon.), Confrerie des Chevaliers du Tastevin (grand cellerier 1990-2001), New Orleans Country Club, Avoca Duck Club, Lakeshore Club, Pickwick Club, La. Club. Office: Adams & Reese 4500 One Shell Sq New Orleans LA 70139-4501 Office Phone: 504-585-0211. Business E-Mail: alsobrookhb@arlaw.com.

ALSOP, DONALD DOUGLAS, federal judge; b. Duluth, Minn., Aug. 28, 1927; s. Robert Alvin and Mathilda (Aaseng) A.; m. Jean Lois Tweeten, Aug. 16, 1952; children: David, Marcia, Robert. BS, U. Minn., 1950, LLB, 1952. Bar: Minn. 1952. Pvt. practice, New Ulm, Minn.; ptnr. Gislason, Alsop, Dosland & Hunter, 1954-75; judge U.S. Dist. Ct. Minn., St. Paul, 1975—, chief dist. judge, 1985-92, sr. dist. judge, 1992—. Mem. 8th cir. jud. coun., 1987-92, Jud. Conf. Com. to Implement Criminal Justice Act, 1979-87; mem. exec. com. Nat. Conf. Fed. Trial Judges, 1990-94. Chmn. Brown County (Minn.) Republican Com., 1960-64, 2d Congl. Dist. Rep. Com., 1968-72, Brown County chpt. ARC, 1968-74. Served with AUS, 1945-46. Mem. 8th Cir. Dist. Judges Assn. (pres. 1982-84), New Ulm C. of C. (pres. 1974-75), Order of Coif. Office: US Dist Ct 754 Fed Bldg 316 Robert St N Saint Paul MN 55101-1495

ALSOP, MARIN, conductor; d. LaMar and Ruth A. Student, Yale Univ., Julliard Sch. Debut with Symphony Space, N.Y.C., 1984; founder, artistic dir. Concordia Chamber Orchestra, N.Y.C., 1984—; asst. condr. Richmond Symphony, Va., 1987; music dir. Eugene Symphony Orchestra, Oreg., 1989—96, Long Island Philharmonic, 1989—96, Colorado Symphony Orchestra, Denver, 1993—; principal guest condr. City of London Sinfonia, 1999—; principal condr. Bournemouth Symphony Orchestra, England, 2003—. Guest condr. San Francisco Symphony Orchestra, Boston Pops, Los Angeles Philharmonic Orchestra, 1991, City Ballet Orchestra, 1992; dir. Cabrillo Music Festival, Calif., 1991—; concertmaster Northeastern Pennsylvania Philharmonic, Scranton; founder, mem. String Fever (swing band), 1980—. Recipient Koussevitzky Conducting prize Tanglewood Music Festival, 1988. Office: Colo Symphony Orch Denver Place N Tower 999 18th St Ste 2055 Denver CO 80202*

ALSOP, REESE FELL, medical educator; b. N.Y.C., Feb. 24, 1913; s. Reese Denny and Julia Chapin Alsop; m. Elise Coates, Nov. 7, 1947; children: Brooke, Elise, Jane, Anne, Penn. BA, Harvard U., 1936; MD, Columbia U., 1944. Diplomate Am. Bd. Internal Medicine. Resident Mary Imogene Bassett Hosp., Cooperstown, NY, 1944—45, Bellevue Hosp., N.Y.C., 1947—48, Bronx VA Hosp., 1948—50; asst. prof. medicine NYU, N.Y.C., 1950—60; chmn. dept. medicine Huntington Hosp., NY, 1968—98; clin. prof. medicine SUNY, Stonybrook, 1990—. Cons. in medicine Northport VA Hosp., NY, 1990—. Articles editor New Eng. Jour. Medicine, 1952—; author: (poetry) Back Talk, —, (book) George and His Horse Bill, 1948—; contbr. articles to profl. jours. Reader Episcopal Ch., Cold Spring Harbor, NY, 1970—. Capt. Med. Corps U.S. Army, 1942—47. Mem.: Century Assn. (hon.). Achievements include patents for on audiocatheter; examining glove; return envelope. Avocations: reading, tennis, writing. Home: Lloyd Neck 33 Fort Hill Dr Huntington NY 11743

ALSOP, THOMAS WALTER, secondary education educator; b. Indpls., July 27, 1942; s. Russell and Carolyn (Alberti) A.; m. Jill E. DeShon, Aug. 24, 1968; children: Daniel, Nicole. BA in Spanish, Marian Coll., 1965; MA in Spanish Lit., Ind. U., 1968. Cert. secondary edn. tchr., Ind. Spanish tchr.-coach Scecina High Sch., Indpls., 1965-66, Brebeuf Prep. Sch., Indpls., 1968-69; instr. Spanish Kent (Ohio) State U., 1969-70; Spanish tchr., fgn. lang. chair Cathedral High Sch., Indpls., 1970-73, South Wayne Jr. High Sch., Indpls., 1973-82; Spanish tchr. Ben Davis High Sch., Indpls., 1982—. Coach state champion Spanish Acad. Competition Team, 1985-94, 10 consecutive State Acad. Competition Championships. Author: Mi Diario Español, 1990, Feliz Cumpleaños, 1992, Permiteme Hablar, 1992, Explorando España por Sus Matriculas, 1992, Mi Diario Español Intermedio, 1993, Alsop's Lesson Plan Enrichment Guide for Foreign Language Teachers, 1994, Spanish Conversation in Pairs, 1994, Telecocina Mexicana, 1995; author over 50 supplemental publs. for Spanish tchrs.; contbr. articles to profl. jours. Rockefeller fellow Rockefeller Found., 1986, Lilly Creative Tchr. fellow Lilly Found., 1988; finalist State Tchr. Yr., 1989; recipient Golden Apple award for Use of Tech. Indpls. Power and Light Co., 1993. Mem. Am. Assn. Tchrs. of Spanish (pres. Ind. chpt. 1988-92, mem. exec. bd. Ind. chpt. 1986—), Soc. Hon. Tchrs. of Spanish (regional dir. 1994—), Ctrl. States Conf. Fgn. Lang. Assn. (mem. adv. coun., bd. dirs.), Am. Coun. Tchrs. of Fgn. Lang. (Excellence in Tchg. of Culture Nelson Brooks award 1994), Ind. Fgn. Lang. Tchrs. Assn. (mem. exec. bd. 1985—, v.p., pres.-elect 1993—, bd. dirs. 1994—, internat. baccalaureate Spanish Oral Examiner, nominee AATSP Nat. Spanish Tchr. of Yr. 1994). Roman Catholic. Avocations: writing, softball, tennis, music, golf. Home: 6707 Yorkshire Pl Avon IN 46123-8812

ALSPACH, PHILIP HALLIDAY, manufacturing executive; b. Buffalo, Apr. 19, 1923; s. Walter L. and Jean E. (Halliday) A.; m. Jean Edwards, Dec. 20, 1947 (dec.); children: Philip Clough, Bruce Edwards (dec.), David Christopher; m. Loretta M. Hildebrand, Aug. 1982. B in Mech. Engring., Tulane U., 1944. Registered profl. engr., Mass., Wis., La. With GE, 1945-64, mgr. indsl. electronics divsn. planning, 1961-64; v.p., gen. mgr. constrn. machinery divsn. Allis Chalmers Mfg. Co., Milw., 1964-68; exec. v.p., dir., mem. exec. com. Jeffrey Galion, Inc., 1968-69; v.p. I.T.E. Imperial Corp., Springhouse, Pa., 1969-75; pres. E.W. Bliss divsn. Gulf & Western Mfg. Co., Southfield, Mich., 1975-79; group v.p. Katy Industries, Inc., Elgin, Ill., 1979-85; pres. Intercon Inc., Irvine, Calif., 1985—, also bd. dirs.; pres. Intercon Publ., Irvine, 1991—. Bd. dirs. Fortifiber Corp.; adv. bd. Diamond Stainless, Inc. Author: Swiss-Bernese Oberland, 1992, 3d edit., 2004; contbr. articles to profl. jours. Mem. pres.'s coun. Tulane U., 1982-90. Mem. IEEE, Soc. Automotive Engrs. (sr.), Soc. Mfg. Engrs., Internat. Forum Corp. Dirs., Inst. Dirs. (U.K.), Am. Mgmt. Assn., Chaîne des Rotisseurs (officier). Home: 23 Alejo Irvine CA 92612-2913 Office: Intercon Inc 2500 Michelson Dr Ste #125 Irvine CA 92612-1529 Office Phone: 949-955-2344. E-mail: intercon@att.net.

ALSTADT, LYNN JEFFERY, lawyer; b. Erie, Pa., Dec. 27, 1951; s. Willis Harry and Norma Margaret (Linn) A.; m. Nancy Ann Weiz, Apr. 16, 1977. BS, BA, U. Pitts., 1973, JD, 1976. Bar: Pa. 1976, U.S. Dist. Ct. (we. dist.) Pa. 1976, U.S. Patent and Trademark Office 1979, U.S. Ct. Appeals (3d cir.) 1980, U.S. Ct. Appeals (6th and Fed. cirs.)1983, U.S. Supreme Ct. 1982, U.S. Ct. Internat. Trade 1983. Assoc. Blenko, Buell, Ziesenheim & Beck, Pitts., 1976-79; ptnr. Buell, Blenko, Ziesenheim & Beck, Pitts., 1979-84, Buell, Ziesenheim, Beck & Alstadt, Pitts., 1984-88, Buchanan Ingersoll, Pitts., 1988—. Adj. prof. U. Pitts. Sch. Law, 1988—, Duquesne U. Sch. Law, 1995—; dir. Internat. Congress on Tech., Pitts., 1983-84. Contbr. articles to legal jours. Treas. Moon Twp. Planning Agy., 1984; mem. Moon Twp. Vol. Fire Dept., 1981—. Recipient Samuel G. Wagner prize U. Pitts. Law Sch., 1976. Mem. ABA, Pa. Bar Assn., Allegheny County Bar Assn., Pitts. Intellectual Property Law Assn. (chmn. pub. rels. 1982-83, treas. 1993, chmn.

ethics grievences and membership coms. 1994-95, dir. 2000-01, 2003— v.p. 2001-02, pres. 2002-03), Rivers Club, Phi Alpha Delta. Republican. Home: 1918 Franklin Pl Moon Township PA 15108-3531 Office Phone: 412-562-1632. E-mail: alstadtlj@bixc.com.

ALSTON, BETTYE JO, minister, nursing administrator; b. Memphis, Dec. 17, 1938; d. Thomas L. and Bettie Marie (Golden) Harris; m. Neasbie Alston, Nov. 29, 1980; children: Donna, Robin, Bernetta, Lissa, Karen, Nataline, Rebecca, Neasbie Jr. AA, Memphis State U., 1969; MDiv cum laude, Memphis Theol. Sem., 1984; D Ministry, St. Paul Sch. Theology, Kansas City, Mo., 1986; PhD in Counseling Psychology, Emmanuel Bapt. U., 1990. RN, Tenn. Nursing supr. John Gaston Hosp., Memphis, 1969-78; nurse recruiter W.F. Bowld Hosp., U. Tenn. Coll. Health Scis., Memphis, 1978-81; dir. nursing Collins Chapel Health Care Ctr., Memphis, 1981-82; asst. adminstr. North Memphis Home Health Agy., 1982-84; pastor Brown Chapel A.M.E. Ch., Memphis, 1977-88; pastor, founder New Beginning Ch., Memphis, 1988—; staff adviser, counselor Regional Med. Ctr., Memphis, 1987-89, dir. nursing spl. svcs., 1989—; pres., CEO Inside and Out Wellness Ctr., Memphis. With West Tenn. Audit Conf., Memphis, 1974-78. Author poetry and devotionals. Mem. Leadership Memphis, 1990-91. Named Outstanding Pastor Memphis A.M.E. Ch., 1982, Disting. African Am. Alumnae, Memphis Theol. Sem., 1990. Mem. Tenn. Nurses Assn., Exec. Female, Interdenominational Women Ministerial Alliance (pres. 1989—), Alston Family Evangelistic Assn. (v.p., exec. dir. 1981—), Nat. Coun. Negro Women, Ch. Women United, Toastmasters. Democrat. Avocations: writing, swimming, reading. Office: Inside and Out Wellness Ctr 1024 Cooper St Memphis TN 38104

ALSTON, GOLDIE VENESSA, early childhood educator; b. Long Branch, N.J., Apr. 5, 1970; d. Helen Clanton. BA, Rutgers U., 1992; postgrad. in MA program, Kean U. Pre-kindergarten tchr. Urban League Presch., Newark, 1994-96; tchr. Cleveland Sch. Pub. & Tech., Newark, 1996—. Workshop presenter Newark Pub. Schs.; critical friends coach mentoring program. Avocation: reading. Home: 1617 Monroe Ave Neptune NJ 07753-4521 E-mail: toldiereads@al.com.

ALSTON, JAMETTA O., lawyer; 1 child. Grad., Temple U.; JD, Howard U. Bar: D.C., RI 1987, Fed., Dist. and Cir. Cts. Asst. atty. gen. civil divsn., RI, 1993—2002; city solicitor Cranston, RI, 2002—. Mem. jud. nom. com., RI, 2003—; mem. exec. com. Edinburgh U.; gov. attys. com. women and minority involvement McGeorge U., 1985; spkr. in field. West Elmwood devel. Supreme Ct. com., 2003—; city solicitor Providence Shelter for Colored Children. Recipient Pro Bono award, Edinburgh, Scotland, 1989. Mem.: RI Bar Assn. (pres. 2004—, pres.-elect 2003). Office: 869 Park Ave Cranston RI 02910 Office Phone: 401-780-3133. Office Fax: 401-780-3179. E-mail: jalston@cranstonri.org.

ALSTON, WALLACE KEMPER, physician; b. N.Y.C., Nov. 28, 1958; s. William Watson and Frances (Kemper) A.; m. Catherine Gollner, Oct. 27, 1990. BS, Tulane U., 1980; MD, N.Y. Med. Coll., 1987. Physician U. Vt., Burlington, 1993—. Office: Fletcher Allen Health Care Brown 338A MCHV Burlington VT 05401

ALSTON, WILLIAM PAYNE, philosophy educator; b. Shreveport, La., Nov. 29, 1921; s. William Payne and Eunice (Schoolfield) A.; m. Mary Frances Collins, Aug. 15, 1943 (div.); 1 dau., Frances Ellen; m. Valerie Tibbetts Barnes, July 3, 1963. B.M., Centenary Coll., 1942; PhD, U. Chgo., 1951; LHD (honoris causa), Ch. Div. Sch. Pacific, 1988. Instr. philosophy U. Mich., 1949-52, asst. prof., then asso. prof., 1952-61, prof., 1961-71, acting chmn. dept., 1961-64; prof. philosophy Rutgers U., 1971-76, U. Ill., Champaign, 1976-80, chmn. dept., 1977-80; prof. philosophy Syracuse (N.Y.) U., 1980-99, prof. emeritus, 1999. Vis. asst. prof. UCLA, 1952-53; Austin Fagothey vis. prof. philosophy Santa Clara U., 1991; vis. lectr. Harvard U., 1955-56; fellow Ctr. for Advanced Study in the Behavioral Scis., 1965-66; dir. summer seminars for coll. tchrs. NEH, 1978-79, NEH Summer Inst. in Philosophy of Religion, 1986, NEH Fellowship for Univ. Tchrs., 1988-89, Vatican Obs. Project on Divine Action in the Light of Contemporary Sci., Symposium of Chinese-Am. Philosophy and Religious Studies, 1994; dir. Calvin Coll. Summer Seminar in Christian Scholarship, 1999. Author: Religious Belief and Philosophical Thought, 1963, (with G. Nakhnikian) Readings in Twentieth Century Philosophy, 1963, Philosophy of Language, 1964, (with R.B. Brandt) The Problems of Philosophy: Introductory Readings, 1967, 3d edit., 1978; Divine Nature and Human Language, 1989, Epistemic Justification, 1989, Perceiving God, 1991, The Reliability of Sense Perception, 1993, A Realist Conception of Truth, 1996, Illocutionary Acts and Sentence Meaning, 2000, A Sensible Metaphysical Realism, 2001, Realism and Antirealism, 2002, Beyond "Justification," 2005; editor: Philos. Rsch. Archives, 1974-77, Faith and Philosophy, 1982-90, Cornell Studies in Philosophy of Religion, 1987—; contbr. articles to profl. jours., chpts. in books. Served with AUS, 1942-46. Recipient Chancellor's Exceptional Acad. Achievement award Syracuse U., 1990. Fellow Am. Acad. Arts and Scis.; mem. Am. Philos. Assn. (pres. Western divsn. 1978-79), Soc. Christian Philosophers (pres. 1978-81), Scholarly Engagement Anglican Doctrine, Am. Theol. Soc., Soc. for Philosophy Religion (pres. 2001-02). Home: 1301 Nottingham Rd #A224 Jamesville NY 13078 Office: Syracuse U Dept Philosophy Syracuse NY 13244-1170 Business E-Mail: wpalston@mailbox.syr.edu.

ALSTOTT, MICHAEL JOSEPH (MIKE ALSTOTT), professional football player; b. Joliet, Ill., Dec. 21, 1973; Student, Purdue U. Fullback Tampa Bay Buccaneers, 1996—. Office: Tampa Bay Buccaneers 1 Buccaneer Pl Tampa FL 33607-5797*

ALSTROM, ERIC CARL, conservator, educator; b. Farmington, Mich., June 8, 1966; s. James W. and Jane Zaebst Alstrom; m. Katharine Stevens, May 29, 1995; 1 child, Katharine Sarah. BA in History, Kalamazoo Coll., Mich., 1984—88; MILS, U. Mich., Sch. Info. and Libr. Studies, Ann Arbor, 1988—89. Asst. conservator James Craven and Assocs., Ann Arbor, Mich., 1989—94; bookbinder Bessenberg Bindery, Ann Arbor, Mich., 1990—92; collections conservator Ohio U., Athens, 1994—98, Dartmouth Coll., Hanover, NH, 1998—2004, Mich. State U., East Lansing, 2004—. International bookbinding exhibition, Il Cantico delle Creature, L'Infinito, 1998, guild of book workers exhibition, Three Flights, A Box Containing Dreams, 1998, Paper Bound: A Collection of Paper Samples, 1996. Bd. mem. Upper Valley Humane Soc., Lebanon, NH, 1999—2000; pres. Dartmouth Coll. Libr. Staff Assn., Hanover, NH, 2001—02. Mem.: Ohio Preservation Coun. (sec. 1996—97), Am. Inst. for Conservation, Guild of Book Workers (publicity chair, webmaster 1998—2004). Avocation: web page design. Office: Mich State Univ Librs 100 Library Mich State Univ East Lansing MI 48824 Office Phone: 517-432-8828. Office Fax: 517-353-8969. E-mail: alstrom@msu.edu.

ALSTROM, SVEN ERIK, architect; b. Emporia, Kans., July 27, 1951; Buddhist. s. William E. and Willa M. (Russell) A.; m. Lynn M. Mathews, June 22, 1974 (div. June 1983). B. in Gen. Studies, U. Kans., 1975; postgrad., U. Denver, 1984. Registered Calif., Colo., Kans., Mo., N. Mex., cert. Nat. Coun. Archtl. Registration Bds. Arch. PGAV Archs., Kansas City, Mo., 1972-74, Horner Blessing, Kansas City, 1977-79, MSFS Archs., Kansas City, 1979-80, Urban Design, Denver, 1981-82, Dominck Assocs., Denver, 1983-84; with C. Welton Anderson & Assocs., Aspen, Colo., 1989-90; pvt. practice Alstrom Group, Aspen, 1990-99; arch. Ecol. Archs., Aspen, 1999—. Mem. AIA (Colo.). Buddhist. Office: 842 W 21st St Lawrence KS 66046 Office Phone: 785-749-1018. E-mail: alstrom@sbcglobal.net.

ALT, BETTY L., sociology educator; b. Walsenburg, Colo., Nov. 12, 1931; d. Cecil R. and Mary M. (Giordano) Sowers; m. William E. Alt, June 19, 1960; 1 child, Eden Jeanette Alt Murrie. BA, Colo. Coll., 1960; MA, NE Mo. State U., 1968. Instr. sociology Indian Hills Community Coll., Centerville, Iowa, 1965-70; dept. chmn. Middlesex Community Coll., Bedford, Mass., 1971-75; instr. sociology Auburn U., Montgomery, 1975-76; div. chmn. Tidewater Community Coll., Virginia Beach, Va., 1976-80; program coord. Pikes Peak Community Coll., Woomera, Australia, 1980-83; instr. sociology Hawaii Pacific Coll., Honolulu, 1983-86, U. Md., Okinawa, Japan, 1987-88, Christopher Newport Coll., Newport News, Va., 1988-89, U. Colo., Colorado Springs, 1989-96, Colo. State U., Pueblo, 1992—. Co-author: Uncle Sam's Brides, 1990, Campfollowing: A History of the Military Wife, 1991, Weeping Violins: The Gypsy Tragedy in Europe, 1996, Slaughter in Cell House 3, 1997, Wicked Women, 2000, Black Soldiers-White Wars, 2002, Keeper of the Keys, 2003, Fleecing Grandma and Grandpa, 2004, Police Women: Life with The Badge, 2005. Active Pueblo County Planning comm., Colo. Mem. AAUW, LWV, Pen Women, N.E. Mo. State U. Alumni Assn. (bd. dirs. 1993-97) Home: 2460 N Interstate 25 Pueblo CO 81008-9614 Office: Colo State U - Pueblo 2200 Bonforte Blvd Pueblo CO 81001-4901

ALT, CAROL A., actress, model, entrepreneur, writer; d. Anthony Ted and Muriel B. Alt; m. Ronald John Greschner, Nov. 21, 1983 (div. Mar. 12, 2001). Student, Hofstra U., LI, NY. Model Ford Models, NYC; actress Moress Nanas Hart Enterprises, LA; spokesperson QVC, Westchester, Pa. Reporter Fox News, 2002. Author: Eating In the Raw, 2004. Vol. Tribeca Performing Arts Ctr., NYC, MS, NYC, Am. Cancer Soc., NYC, Cerebral Palsy. With U.S. Army, 1978—79. Recipient Model Woman of Yr., CFDA, 1981, Female Model of Yr., 1986, Oscar Moda New Actress of Yr., Moda Mag., 1986, European Emmy, Berlosconi Group, 1987, Cert. of the Arts, European Artistic Cmty., 1988, European Emmy, Berlosconi Group, 1990, Mont Blanc award, 1991, Golden Box Office Ticket, Fedn. of European Theater Owners, 1993, European Emmy, Berlosconi Group, 1994. Avocations: amateur race car driver, interior decorating, marketing. Office: Just Simplicity c/o Assante 280 Park Ave New York NY 10010 Office Phone: 818-342-9800. Personal E-mail: altie1A@aol.com.

ALT, FREDERICK W., geneticist, pediatrician; BS, Brandeis U., 1971; PhD in Biological Scis., Stanford U., 1977. Resident fellow MIT, Cambridge, Mass., 1977-82; from asst. prof. to prof. in Biochemistry Columbia U., N.Y.C., 1982-91, prof. Microbiology, 1986-91; prof. in Genetics and Pediatrics Harvard Med. Sch., Boston, 1991—; investigator Howard Hughes Med. Inst. Children's Hosp., Boston, 1991—; sr. investigator Ctr. Blood Rsch., 1991—, Charles A. Janeway prof. Genetics and Pediatrics, 1991—. Contbr. articles to profl. jours. Recipient Stephen J. Fox. Meml. award, Stanford U., 1973, Irma T. Hirschl Career Scientist award, 1983, Searle Scholars award, 1983, Mallinckrodt Schoolar, 1984, Clowes Meml. award, Am. Assn. Cancer Rsch., 2004. Mem. Nat. Acad. Scis. (pres., 1994), Am. Acad. Microbiol. (pres., 1994), AAAS (pres., 1994). Office: Howard Hughes Med Inst Childrens Hosp 300 Longwood Ave Boston MA 02115-5724

ALT, JAMES EDWARD, political science professor; b. N.Y.C., Aug. 16, 1946; s. Franz Leopold and Alice (Modern) A.; m. Elaine Fiore, June 26, 1968; children: Rachel, Adam. AB, Columbia U., 1968; MSc in Econs., London Sch. Econs., 1970; PhD, Essex U., Eng., 1978. Lectr. U. Essex, Wivenhoe Park, Eng., 1971-79; assoc. prof. Washington U., St. Louis, 1978-82, prof., 1982-86, Harvard U., Cambridge, Mass., 1986—; dir. Ctr. for Basic Rsch. in Social Sci., 1998—2004. Author: Politics of Economic Decline, 1979, (with K. Chrystal) Political Economics, 1983; editor: (with K. Shepsle) Perspectives on Positive Political Economy, 1990, (with M. Levi and E. Ostrom) Competition and Cooperation, 1999; contbr. articles to profl. jours. Rsch. grantee, NSF, 1980, 1985, 1991, 1993, 2001, 2002, Guggenheim fellow, 1997—98. Fellow Am. Acad. Arts and Scis.; mem. Brit. Politics Group (pres. 1983-85), Am. Polit. Sci. Assn. (coun. 1996-97), Midwest Polit. Sci. Assn. (exec. coun. 1985-88). Office: Harvard U Dept Govt Cambridge MA 02138 Business E-Mail: james_alt@harvard.edu.

ALTABE, JOAN AUGUSTA BERG, artist, writer, art and architecture critic; b. N.Y.C., Apr. 27, 1935; d. Harold and Evelyn (Cooperman) Berg; m. David F. Altabe, Sept. 28, 1958; children: Richard Jonathan, Madeline Nissa. Studied with Robert Motherwell; BA, Hunter Coll., 1956, postgrad., 1956-57. Tchr. fine art N.Y.C. secondary schs., 1957-72. Vol. sculpture tchr. N.Y. Lighthouse For Blind, 1950-53; curator Bicentennial exhibit Long Beach (N.Y.) Mus. Art, 1975-76; architecure columnist Bradenton Herald, 2001-. Artist and muralist, 1982—; prin. work includes 6 stained glass window murals N.Y. Synagogue, 1973, heraldic deisgn Smithsonian Instn. Bicentennial Travelling Exhibit, 1976-78; represented in permanent collection at Santa Barbara (Calif.) Mus.; author: (art history) Behind the Scenes, 2004, 100 Art Works That Shaped Art History, 2005; book reviewer: Leonardo, Pergamon Press, Eng., 1980-94; feature writer Art Press, Paris, 1992; art writer Art & Antiques mag., 1998, 99; art and architecture critic, feature writer Sarasota Herald Tribune, 1986-2001, Robb Report, 2001-05; columnist Bradenton Herald, 2001-05; book reviewer Western Humanities Rev., N.Y. Times; contbr. Art: Behind The Scenes, 2005; contbr. articles and illustrations to profl. jours. Recipient Fla. Press award, 1990, 1991, 1996, Chmn. award, N.Y. Times, 1997, Fla. Press Club award, 2004. Mem. Soc. Profl. Journalists (award in criticism 1995, 96, 97, 99, Tampa Bay chpt., citation for excellence in journalism criticism 1990, 95-99, 2001, 02, 03), Fla. Soc. Newspaper Editors (columns and criticism 1997, 99, 2003 criticism award 1996, 98-2000, Sunshine State award 1999, 2002). Home: 604 Avenida De Mayo Sarasota FL 34242-1502 Office Phone: 813-404-7385. Personal E-mail: jaltabez@msn.com. *To transcend my life through painting, teaching or writing, with loyalty to my individual spirit and dedication to communication.*

ALTABEF, PETER ANTHONY, lawyer; b. NYC, June 13, 1959; s. Isaac and Dolores (Cristiani) A.; m. Jennifer Leigh Burr, Aug. 10, 1985; 2 children, Hayley, Will. BA, SUNY, Binghamton, 1980; JD cum laude, U. Chgo., 1983. Bar: Tex. 1985. Law clk. U.S. Ct. Appeals, Dallas, 1983-84; assoc. Simpson, Thacher & Barlett, NYC, 1984-85, Hughes & Luce, Dallas, 1985-90, ptnr., 1991-93; assoc. gen. counsel Perot Systems Corp., Dallas, 1993-94, v.p., gen. counsel, secy., 1994—2004, pres., CEO, 2004—. Mem. ABA, Dallas Bar Assn., Tex. Bar Assn. Office: Perot Systems Corp 2300 W Plano Pkwy Plano TX 75075 Office Phone: 972-577-6692. E-mail: peter.altabef@ps.net.*

ALTABET, MARK AASDA, oceanographer, educator; b. New York, Nov. 22, 1957; s. Simon and Gatelle Altabet; m. Lisa A. Michael, June 16, 1985; children: Elia, Meira Naomi, Ezra Simon, Eitan Raphael. BS, SUNY, Stony Brook, 1979; PhD, Harvard U., 1984. Scientist Woods Hole (Mass.) Oceanog. Inst., 1986—95; prof. Sch. for Marine Sci. and Tech. U. Mass. Dartmouth, New Bedford, Mass., 1995—. Assoc. editor Jour. of Marine Chemistry, Miami, Fla., 1991—, Organic Geochemistry Jour., Bristol, United Kingdom, 2001—; adj. prof. dept. geol. scis. Brown U., Providence, 2001—; spkr. in field. Contbr. more than 55 articles to profl. jours. Grantee, NSF, 1985—, Dept. Energy, 2001—, 2004, EPA, 2004—, Dept. Def., 1985—, Camile and Henry Dreyfus Found., 1999; scholar, Fulbright Found., 1993; Postdoctoral fellow, Woods Hole Oceanog. Inst., 1984, NSF Grad. fellow, 1979—83. Mem.: European Union Organic Geochemistry, Am. Soc. Limnology and Oceanography, Am. Geophys. Union, Phi Beta Kappa. Achievements include development of fundamental understanding of marine nitrogen isotope biogechemistry; research in sensitivity of the marine nitrogen cycle to past climate change; marine nitrogen cycle may influence on atmospheric CO2. Avocations: hiking, camping, birdwatching. Office: Sch Marine Science and Technology 706 S Rodney French Blvd New Bedford MA 02744-1221 Office Phone: 508-999-8622. Office Fax: 508-999-8197.

ALTAMURA, MAURO A., artist, educator; b. Hoboken, N.J., June 8, 1954; s. Angelo and Theresa (Calabrese) Altamura; m. Leslie Kippen, Nov. 12, 1997. BA, Ramapo Coll. N.J., 1976; MFA, SUNY Buffalo, 1981. Vis. prof. John Cabot U., Rome, 1990—98; asst. prof art N.J. City U., Jersey City, 1991—. One-man shows include photography Jersey City Mus., 1996, N.J. State Mus., Trenton, 1998, Vertedu St., Bklyn., 2004, Hudson Valley C.C., Troy, NY, 2005, exhibited in group shows at City Without Walls, Newark, 2005, exhibitions include Pub. Sch. 122, 1992, N.J. State Mus., 1998, Jersey City Mus., 2000, Vertex List, 2004. Fellow, N.Y. State Coun. on Arts, 1982, N.J. State Coun. on Arts, 1985, 1988, 1989, 1998, NEA, 1988; grantee Artist in Residence, Mid Atlantic Arts Coun., 2001. Avocation: fiction writing. Office: New Jersey City University 2039 Kennedy Blvd Jersey City NJ 07305 Office Phone: 201-200-3285. Personal E-mail: maltamura@njcu.edu.

ALTAMURA, MICHAEL VICTOR, physician; b. Bklyn., Sept. 28, 1923; s. Frank and Theresa (Inganamorte) A.; m. Emily Catherine Wandell, Sept. 21, 1948; children: Michael Victor, Robert Frank BS, LIU, 1949; MA, Columbia U., 1951; DO, Kirksville Coll., 1961; MD, Calif. Coll. Medicine, 1962. Diplomate Am. Bd. Family Practice. Intern Los Angeles County Gen. Hosp., 1961-62; practice medicine specializing in family practice Sunnyvale, Calif., 1962—. Aviation med. examiner, 1969-94; staff El Camino Hosp., chief family practice dept., 1972-73; preceptor family practice Stanford Sch. Medicine, 1972-73, clin. asst. prof., 1974-81, clin. assoc. prof., 1982—; assoc. prof. family medicine Calif. Coll. Osteo. Medicine, 1985—; preceptor family practice Davis (Calif.) Sch. Medicine, 1974-75; adj. asst. prof. Midwestern U., Ariz. Coll. Osteo. Medicine, 2000—. Author: (with Mary Falconer and Helen Behnke) Aging Patients: A Guide for Their Care. Served to 1st lt. AUS, 1942-45, 51-53; ETO. Recipient Order of Golden Sword, Am. Cancer Soc., 1973 Fellow Am. Acad. Family Physicians (pres. Santa Clara County chpt. 1972-73, Calif. del. Santa Clara chpt. 1991), Calif. Acad. of Family Physicians (bd. dirs. 1987-90), Royal Soc. Health, Am. Geriatric Soc.; mem. AMA, Calif., Santa Clara County socs., Internat. Platform Assn. Republican. Lutheran.

ALTAN, TAYLAN, engineering educator, director; b. Trabzon, Turkey, Feb. 12, 1938; arrived in US, 1962; s. Seref and Sadife (Baysal) Kadioglu; m. Susan Borah, July 18, 1964; children: Peri Michele, Aylin Elisabeth Diploma in engring., Tech. U., Hannover, Fed. Republic Germany, 1962; MS in Mech. Engring., U. Calif.-Berkeley, 1964, PhD in Mech. Engring., 1966. Research engr. DuPont Co., Wilmington, Del., 1966-68; research scientist Battelle Columbus Labs, Ohio, 1968-72, research fellow, 1972-75, sr. research leader, 1975-86; prof. mech. engring., dir. engring. rsch. ctr. Ohio State U., Columbus, 1985—. Chmn. sci. com. N.Am. Mfg. Rsch. Inst. Soc. Mfg. Engrs., Detroit, 1982-86, pres., 1987; dir. Ctr. for Net Shape Mfg. Co-author: Forging Equipment, 1973, Metal Forming, 1983, Metal Forming and the Finite Element Method, 1989, Cold, Warm and Hot Forging, 2004; assoc. editor Jour. Materials Processing Tech., Eng., 1978-99; contbr. over 400 tech. articles to profl. jours. Fellow: ASME, Am. Soc. Metals (chmn. forging com. 1978—87), Soc. Mfg. Engrs. (Gold medal 1985). Avocations: languages, travel. Office: Ohio State U 210 Baker Bldg 1971 Neil Ave Columbus OH 43210-1210 Business E-Mail: altan.1@osu.edu.

ALTBACH, PHILIP, director, educator; b. Chgo., May 3, 1941; s. Milton and Josephine (Huebsch) A.; m. Edith Hoshino, June 16, 1962; children: Eric, Frederick Gabriel. BA, U. Chgo., 1962, MA, 1964, PhD, 1966. Lectr. Harvard U., Cambridge, Mass., 1967-68; from asst. prof. to assoc. prof. U. Wis., Madison, 1968-75; prof., chmn. dept. ednl. orgn., adminstrn. and policy SUNY, Buffalo, 1976-80, 86-92, dir. Comparative Edn. Ctr., 1978-94; prof. sch. edn. Boston Coll., 1994—, dir. Ctr. Internat. Higher Edn., 1995—, J. Donald Monan SJ prof. higher edn., 1996—. Fulbright rsch. prof. U. Bombay, 1968; cons. Regional Inst. Higher Edn., Singapore, 1979, 81, 82, Carnegie Found. Advancement Tchg., 1990-94, Rockefeller Found., 1991—; vis. prof. Moscow State U., 1981, Stanford U., 1989; Fulbright cons. U. Singapore, 1982; sr. assoc. Carnegie Found. Advancement Tchg., 1992-96; sec.-gen. Bellagio Publ. Network, 1992-98; guest prof. Peking U.; leader New Century Scholars, Fulbright Inst. Program, 2005. Author: Student Politics in America, 1975, rev., 1997, Higher Education in Third World, 1982, Knowledge Context, 1987, International Higher Education: An Encyclopedia, 1991, Publishing and Development in the Third World, 1994, Higher Education in the 21st Century, 1999, rev. edit., 2005, Private Prometheus: Private Higher Education and Development, 2000, Comparative Higher Education, 2000, In Defense of American Higher Education, 2001, The Decline of the Guru, 2003, Asian Universities, 2004, others; editor: Comparative Edn. Rev., 1979—89, Rev. of Higher Edn., 1996—2004, Ednl. Policy, 1989—2004, Internat. Higher Edn., various newsletters and publs. Mem. capital budget rev. com. City of Buffalo, 1980. Grantee, NEH, 1976, Exxon Edn. Found., 1982, 1984, NSF, 1987, Rockefeller Found., 1993, 1994, 1995, Ford Found., 1998, 2001—04, MacArthur Found., 2003, Toyota Found., 2003, Carnegie Corp. N.Y., 2003; scholar, Fulbright Found. Mem. Comparative Edn. Soc. (editor jour. 1980-89), Assn. Study Higher Edn. (editor jour. 1996-2004). Office: Boston Coll 207 Campion Hall Chestnut Hill MA 02467 Office Phone: 617-552-4236. E-mail: altbach@bc.edu.

ALTBERGS, JON M, school system administrator, educator; b. Willimantic, Conn., Apr. 8, 1971; s. Martin Altbergs and Elizabeth Anne Cassidy; m. Deborah Wodzinski, June 25, 1994. BA, Allegheny Coll., 1989—93; MA in tchg., U. of NH., 1994—96. Curriculum coord. Epping Middle-H.S., Epping, NH, 2004—, program coord., tchr., 1997—2004. Mem.: Nat. Assn. of Secondary Sch. Principals, Assn. for Supervision and Curriculum Devel. Progressive. Buddhist. Home: 82 Elm St Epping NH 03042-2407 Office Phone: 603-679-5472. Personal E-mail: altbergs@altbergs.net.

ALTEKRUSE, JOAN MORRISSEY, retired preventive medicine physician; b. Cohoes, N.Y., Nov. 15, 1928; d. William T. Dee and Agnes Kay (Fitzgerald) Morrissey; m. Ernest B. Altekruse, Dec. 17, 1950; children—Philip, Clifford, Lisa, Janice, Charles, Sean, Lowell, Patrick, E. Caitlin. AB, Vassar Coll., N.Y., 1949; MD, Stanford U., Calif., 1960; MPH, Harvard U., Cambridge, 1965; DPH, U. Calif., Berkeley, 1973; MPS, Loyola U., New Orleans, 1999. Cons., program dir. Calif. State Health Dept., 1966-69; vis. mem. faculty U. Heidelberg, Germany, 1970-72; med. dir. regional office Fla. State Health Dept., 1972-75; prof., dir. health adminstrn. Sch. Pub. Health, U. S.C., Columbia, 1975-77; prof. preventive medicine Univ. S.C. Sch. of Medicine, Columbia, 1975-94, chmn. dept., 1979-89, disting. prof. emerita, 1994—. Fellow, assoc. dir. Irish Peace Inst., U. Limerick, Ireland, 1990; vis. scholar Ctr. for Rsch. in Disease Prevention, Stanford U., 1992; women in medicine liaison officer Assn. Am. Med. Colls., 1980-94; mem. editl. bd. Aspen Publs. Mem. editorial bd. Family and Community Health Jour., Jour. Community Health; editorial adv. bd. VA Practitioner. Sr. docent chair, vol. bd. mem. Hunter Mus. Am. Art, Chattanooga; activist in social justice, peace and health advocacy orgns. Lt. USMC, 1949—51, sr. surgeon USPHS, 1960—64, capt. USPHS. Recipient Adminstrn. award Women in Higher Edn., 1989, Achievement award S.C. Commn. on Women, 1990, Ann. award, 1991, Life Achievement award Emma Willard Sch., 1996; WHO travel fellow, Eng., 1974; grantee NIH, NCI, Ctr. for Disease Control, pvt. founds; recipient Alumni award of merit Harvard Sch. Pub. Health, 1997. Fellow: APHA (mem. emerita), Assn. Tchrs. Preventive Medicine (pres. 1986, Spl. Recognition award 1995), Am. Coll. Preventive Medicine; mem.: Nat. Bd. Med. Examiners (comprehensive test com. 1986—92), Am. Heart Assn. (SC affiliate pres. 1986, mem. nat. agenda planning com. 1987—89, women and minorities leadership com. 1989—92, Lifetime Achievement award 1992), Am. Bd. Med. Specialties, Am. Bd. Preventive Medicine (trustee 1983—92), Emma Willard Sch. Alumni Assn. (bd. dirs. 2003—), Am. Womens Med. Assn., Harvard Sch. Pub. Health Alumni Assn. (pres. 1999—2001, leadership coun. 2003—), Harvard Alumni Assn. (bd. dirs. 2001—03). Democrat. Roman Catholic.

ALTEMOSE, MARK KENNETH, lawyer; b. Easton, Pa., July 21, 1965; s. Richard and Constance Irene (Silfies) Altemose; m. Jennifer Lou Abram, Nov. 24, 1995; children: Rachel Rebecca, Meghan Grace, Abigail Lynne. BA in Econ., Lafayette Coll., 1987; JD, Villanova, 1990. Bar: Pa. 1990, N.J. 1990, U.S. Dist. Ct. N.J. 1991, U.S. Dist. Ct. (ea. dist.) Pa. 1991, U.S. Ct. Appeals (3rd cir.) 1991, cert.: Nat. Bd. Trial Advocacy. Assoc. Korn, Kline & Kutner, Phila., 1990-91, Brown, Brown, Solt & Ferretti, Allentown, Pa., 1991-94, Knafo Law Offices, Allentown, Pa., 1994—2003, jr. ptnr., 2004—. Hearing com. mem. Disciplinary Bd. Supreme Ct. of Pa., Harrisburg, 1995-2000, chmn., 1999-2000. Mem.: ATLA, Northampton County Bar Assn., Pa. Bar Assn., Pa. Trial Lawyers Assn. (bd. govs. 1998—), Lehigh County Bar Assn.

(co-chmn. Law Day 1995—, bd. dirs. 2001—). Democrat. Presbyterian. Avocations: weightlifting, running, golf. Office: Knafo Law Offices 4201 W Tilghman St Allentown PA 18104-4448 Office Phone: 610-432-2221. E-mail: maltemose@knafo.com.

ALTENBURG, JOHN D., JR., career military officer, lawyer; b. Phila., June 10, 1944; m. Diane Sedler, 1970. BA, Wayne State Univ., 1966; JD, Univ. Cincinnati, 1973; M Mil. Art & Sci., U.S. Army Command & Staff Coll.; graduate, Nat. War Coll. Bar: Ohio, D.C., U.S. Army Ct. Criminal Appeals, U.S. Ct. Appeals Armed Forces, U.S. Supreme Ct. Commd. U.S. Army, advanced through grades to maj. gen., 1973—2001, asst. judge advocate gen. Rosslyn, Va., 1997—2001; cons. Office of Pres., World Bank Group, 2002; of counsel Greenberg Traurig LLP, Washington, 2002—; appointing authority U.S. Office of Military Commissions for military tribunals at Guantanamo Bay, Cuba, Washington, 2003—. Contbr. articles to profl. jour. V.p. & mem. bd. dir. Nat. Coalition for Homeless Vets.; pres. & mem. bd. gov. VII Corps Desert Storm Vet. Assn.; U.S. rep., experts panel Internat. Inst. Humanitarian Law; trustee Joseph House Homeless Vets. Decorated Disting. Svc. medal, Legion of Merit (2), Bronze Star (2); recipient Disting. Alumnus award, Univ. Cincinnati Coll. Law, 2003. Office: Office of Military Commissions The Pentagon Washington DC 20301 also: Greenberg Traurig LLP Suite 500 300 Connecticut Ave NW Washington DC 20006

ALTENBURGER, KARL MARION, allergist; b. Coral Gables, Fla., Nov. 13, 1949; s. Karl and Carol Altenburger; m. Carol Bauer, May 25, 1974; children: Laura Alyson, Ashley Carolyn, Elizabeth Ann, Allison Nicole. BA in Zoology, U. South Fla., 1971, MD, 1974. Diplomate Am. Bd. Pediatrics, Am. Bd. Allergy and Immunology, Nat. Bd. Med. Examiners. Intern in pediatrics U. Colo. Med. Ctr., Denver, 1975-76, resident, 1976-78, fellow in allergy and immunology, 1978-81, Nat. Jewish Hosp. and Rsch. Ctr.-Nat. Asthma Ctr., Denver, 1978-81; pvt. practice, Ocala, Fla., 1981—. Instr. dept. pediatrics U. Colo. Sch. Medicine, 1980-81; bd. dirs. Fla. Med. Polit. Action Com., 1991-2003, pres., 1998-2001. Contbr. articles to profl. jours. Trustee Am. Lung Assn. Ctrl. Fla., 1985—93. Fellow Am. Acad. Allergy, Asthma and Immunology, Am. Coll. Allergy Asthma and Immunology; mem. AMA, Fla. Med. Assn. (bd. dirs. 2002—, v.p. 2004—),Southeastern Allergy Assn., Am. Assn. for History Medicine, Fla. Med. Assn. (Marion County del. 1990—), Fla. Allergy Asthma and Immunology Soc. (exec. com. 1990-96, pres. 1993-94), Marion County Med. Soc. (bd. dirs. 1983-88, pres. 1985-86, editor Bull. 1986-89), U. South Fla. Coll. Medicine Alumni Assn. (pres. 1983-87), Alpha Omega Alpha. Roman Catholic. Avocations: faith, family, friends. Office: 1800 SE 17th St Ste 300 Ocala FL 34471-4173 Office Phone: 352-622-1126. Personal E-mail: altenburge@aol.com.

ALTENKIRCH, ROBERT A., academic administrator; b. St. Louis; m. Beth Harsch Altenkirch; 2 children. BS in Mech. Engring., Purdue U., 1970; MS, U. Calif., Berkeley, 1971; PhD, Purdue U., 1975. Grad. instr. rsch. Sch. Mech. Engring. Purdue U., West Lafayette, Ind., 1971—75; asst. prof. mech. engring. U. Ky., Lexington, 1975—80, assoc. prof. mech. engring., 1980—85, prof. mech. engring., 1984—88, chmn. mech. engring., 1985—88; prof. mech. engring., dean Coll. Engring. Miss. State U., Mississippi State, 1988—95, v.p. for rsch., prof. mech. engring., 1998—2002; prof. mech. and materials engring., dean Coll. Engring. and Arch. Wash. State U., Pullman, 1995—98; pres. N.J. Inst. Tech., Newark, 2002—, disting. prof. mech. engring., 2002—. Mem. NASA Microgravity Combustion Discipline Working Group, 1992—; mem. com. on microgravity rsch. Space Studies Bd. NRC Commn. on Phys. Scis., Math. and Applications, 1995—99, mem. bd. on assessment of NIST, 2000—04; vice-chair governing coun. Partnership for Natural Disaster Relief, 1998—2002; mem. rev., planning and implementation steering com. Govs. Commn. on Health Sci., Edn. and Tng., NJ, 2002—; trustee Prosperity N.J., 2002—; mem. Govs. Commn. on Job Growth and Econ. Devel., NJ, 2003—, Govs. Blue Ribbon Commn. on Transp., NJ, 2003—04, NJ Amistad Commn., 2004—, Mayor's Blue (Newark) Ribbon Commn. on downtown core redevelopment, 2004—; bd. dirs. Golden Triangle Enterprise Ctr., EPSCoR Found., R&D Coun. N.J. Recipient Ralph R. Teetor award, Soc. Automotive Engrs., 1979, Outstanding Mech. Engr. Alumnus award, Purdue U. Sch. Mech. Engring., 2001. Fellow: ASME (bd. govs. task force on electronic networking 1993—96, member-at-large coun. on edn. 1993—97, Gustus L. Larson Meml. award 1984); mem.: NSPE, Miss. Engring. Soc., Am. Soc. for Engring. Edn., Combustion Inst., Phi Kappa Phi, Sigma Xi, Tau Beta Pi, Pi Tau Sigma, Phi Eta Sigma. Office: NJ Inst Tech 310 East Bldg University Heights Newark NJ 07102

ALTER, EDWARD T., treasurer; b. Glen Ridge, NJ, July 26, 1941; s. E. Irving and Norma (Fisher) A.; m. Patricia R. Olsen, 1975; children: Christina Lyn, Ashly Ann, Darci Lee. BA, U. Utah., 1966; MBA, U. Utah, 1967. CPA Calif., Utah. Sr. acct. Touche Ross & Co., LA, 1967—72; asst. treas. U. Utah, Salt Lake City, 1972-80; treas. State of Utah, Salt Lake City, 1981—. Bd. dirs. Utah Housing Corp., Utah State Retirement Bd., pres., 1984-93, 2003-04; mem. Utah State Rep. Ctrl. Com., 1981—, Anthony Com. on Pub. Fin., 1988-92. Sgt. USAR, 1958-66. Named to All-pro Govt. Team, City and State Mag., 1988; recipient Adminstr. of Yr. award Romney Inst. Pub. Mgmt., Brigham Young U., 2003. Mem. AICPA, Nat. Assn. State Treas. (past sr. v.p., pres. 1987-88, Harlan E. Boyles Disting. Svc. award 2003, Jesse M. Uhruh award svc. to state treas. 1989), Utah Assn. CPAs (Outstanding CPA 2000), Utah Bond Club (pres. 1981-82), Delta Sigma Pi, Delta Phi Kappa. Republican. Office: State Capitol 215 State Capitol Bldg Salt Lake City UT 84114-1202 Office Phone: 801-538-1042. Business E-Mail: ealter@utah.gov.

ALTER, ELEANOR BREITEL, lawyer; b. N.Y.C., Nov. 10, 1938; d. Charles David and Jeanne (Hollander) Breitel; children: Richard B. Zabel, David B. Zabel. BA with honors, U. Mich., 1960; postgrad., Harvard U., 1960-61; LLB, Columbia U., 1964. Bar: N.Y. 1965. Atty., office of gen. counsel, ins. dept. State of N.Y., 1964-66; assoc. Miller & Carlson, N.Y.C., 1966-68, Marshall, Bratter, Greene, Allison & Tucker, N.Y.C., 1968-74, mem. firm, 1974-82, Rosenman & Colin, 1982-97, Kasowitz, Benson, Torres & Friedman, N.Y.C., 1997—. Fellow U. Chgo. Law Sch., 1988; adj. prof. law NYU Sch. Law, 1983-87; vis. prof. law U. Chgo., 1990-91, 93; lectr. in field. Mem. editl. bd. N.Y. Law Jour.; contbr. articles to profl. jours. Trustee Lawyers' Fund for Client Protection of the State of N.Y., 1983—, chmn., 1985—; bd. visitors U. Chgo. Law Sch., 1984-87. Mem. Am. Law Inst., Am. Coll. Family Trial Lawyers, N.Y. State Bar Assn., Assn. of Bar of City of N.Y. (libr. com. 1978-80, com. on matrimonial law 1977-81, 87-88, 2002-05, judiciary com. 1981-84, 94, 95, 96, exec. com. 1988-92), Am. Acad. Matrimonial Lawyers, Internat. Acad. Matrimonial Lawyers. Office: Kasowitz Benson Et Al 1633 Broadway New York NY 10019 Office Phone: 212-506-1760. Business E-Mail: ealter@kasowitz.com.

ALTER, HARVEY J., hematologist, educator; b. N.Y.C. BA, U. Rochester, MD, 1960. Internship, first-yr. resident Strong Meml. Hosp., Rochester, NY, 1960—61; clin. assoc. NIH, Bethesda, Md., 1961—64; second-yr. resident U. Wash. Hosp. Sys., Seattle, 1964—65; hematology fellow Georgetown U. Hosp., Wash., DC, 1965—66; instr. medicine Georgetown U. Sch. Medicine, Wash., 1966—68; dir. hematology rsch. Georgetown U. Hosp., Wash., 1966—69; asst. prof. medicine Georgetown U. Sch. Medicine, Wash., 1968—69, clin. asst. prof. medicine, 1969—71, clin. assoc. prof. medicine, 1969—71; sr. investigator NIH, Bethesda, Md., 1969—, chief infectious disease sect. clin. ctr., 1972—, assoc. dir. rsch. clin. ctr. dept. transfusion medicine, faculty clin. rsch., 1988—; clin. prof. medicine Georgetown U. Hosp., Wash., 1988—. Adj. prof. S.W. Found. Biomed. Rsch., San Antonio, 1986—. Contbr. articles to profl. jours. Recipient Disting. Svc. Medal, U.S. Pub. Health Svc., 1977, Karl Lansteiner award, Am. Assn. Blood Banks, 1992, Lab. Pub. Svc. Nat. Leadership award, 1999, World Health Day award, Am. Assn. World Health, 2000, Albert Lasker award Clin. Med. Rsch., 2000. Master: ACP; fellow: Am. Soc. Internal Medicine; mem.: Nat. Acad. Scis., Inst. Medicine, Am. Bd. Pathology. Achievements include first to conduct work leading to the discovery of the virus that causes hepatitis C; development of screening methods that reduced the risk of blood transfusion-associated hepatitis in the U.S. from 30% in 1970 to virtually zero. Office: NIH Warrem G Magunson Clin Ctr Dept Transfusion Medicine 10/1C711 10 Center Dr MSC-1184 Bldg 10 Room 1C711 Bethesda MD 20892

ALTER, JONATHAN HAMMERMAN, journalist; b. Chgo., Oct. 6, 1957; s. James M. and Joanne (Hammerman) A.; m. Emily Lazar, Oct. 18, 1986; children: Charlotte Helen, Thomas Beck, Molly Cecelia. AB in History cum laude, Harvard U., 1979. Mem. staff speech writing office The White House, 1978; editor The Washington Monthly, 1981-82; sr. editor, columnist, media critic Newsweek, NYC, 1983—; on-air analyst, corr. NBC News, 1996—. Ferris vis. prof. Princeton U., 1997, Minow vis. prof., Northwestern U., 2003. Author: The Defining Moment: FDR's First Hundred Days and the Triumph of Hope, 2006; co-author: Selecting A President, 1980; editor: (with Charles Peters) Inside the System. 5th edit., 1984. Bd. dirs. Donors Choose, 2003—. Recipient Gerald Loeb award 1987, Lowell Mellett award for Improving Journalism, 1987, Clarion award, 1994, N.Y. Press Club award, 2001, ABA Silver Gavel award, 2001, John Bartlow Martin award Northwestern U., 2001; fellow U.S.-Japan Leadership program, 1992-93, Nat. Headliners Best Column award, 1997, 2001, Mentoring USA award, 1999; named 1 of Top 10 Media Critics in U.S., Columbia U., 1991. Office: care Newsweek Magazine 251 W 57th St New York NY 10019-1802 Business E-Mail: jalter@newsweek.com.

ALTER, MARIA POSPISCHIL, language educator; b. Vienna; came to U.S., 1947; d. Karl and Ludmilla (Von Adamovic) Pospischil; divorced; children: Assunta, Sylvia, Nora. BA, U. Okla., 1948, MA, 1950; PhD, U. Md., 1961. Instr., asst. prof. Howard U., Washington, 1955-66; asst. prof. Case Western U., Cleve., 1966-70; acad. cons. Am. Assn. Tchrs. German, Phila., 1970-73; prof. Villanova (Pa.) U., 1974—. Author: The Role of the Physicians in Schnitzler's and Corossa's Work, 1961, A Modern Case for German, 1971. Mem. Assn. German, Modern Lang. Assn. Home: 830 Montgomery Ave Bryn Mawr PA 19010-3343

ALTER, MILTON, retired neurologist; b. Buffalo, Nov. 11, 1929; s. Samuel and Rose (Schaffer) Alter; m. Reina Rolnick, Aug. 31, 1952; children: David S., Daniel M., Michael A., Naomi T., Joel A. BA, U. Buffalo, 1951, MD, 1955; PhD, U. Minn., 1966. Diplomate Am. Bd. Psychiatry and Neurology. Intern U. Minn., Mpls., 1955-56; sr. surgeon USPHS, Bethesda, Md., 1956-62; fellow Med. Coll. S.C., Charleston, 1956-57, Dalhousie U., Halifax, 1957, Columbia U. Coll. Physicians and Surgeons, N.Y.C., 1957-58, Hebrew U., Jerusalem, 1960-62; mem. faculty, chief neurology svc. U. Minn., Mpls., 1962—67, Mpls. VA Hosp., 1967-76; chmn. dept. neurology Temple U., Phila., 1976-87, prof. neurology, 1987—89; prof., dir. residency tng. Med. Coll. Pa., Phila., 1989-91; clin. prof. Allegheny U., 1995—2004, ret., 2004. Mem. sci. adv. bd. Nat. Multiple Sclerosis Soc., N.Y.C., Dystonia Med. Rsch. Found., Alzheimer Disease Assn.; peer reviewer Epidemiology and Disease Control 1 and 2 NIH, Bethesda, Md.; adj. prof. Ctr. Clin. Epidemiology and Biostats. U. Pa., 1995—2004; adj. prof. Thomas Jefferson U., 1999. Guest editor: numerous profl. jours., editor-in-chief: Neuroepidemiology, 1989—96; editor emeritus Neuroepidemiology; contbr. articles to profl. jours., chapters to books. Capt. USPHS, 1962. Grantee, NIH, Multiple Sclerosis Soc. Mem.: AMA, World Fedn. Neurol. (chair rsch. group epidemiology 1998—2001), Am. Epidemiology Soc., Assn. Rsch. Nervous and Mental Diseases, Am. Neurol. Assn., Am. Acad. Neurology. Democrat. Jewish. Home: 236 Indian Creek Rd Wynnewood PA 19096-3404 also: Lankenau Med Rsch Ctr 100 E Lancaster Ave Wynnewood PA 19096-3404 Office Phone: 610-649-2095. Personal E-mail: malter5280@aol.com.

ALTER, NELSON TOBIAS, retail executive, wholesale distribution executive; b. San Antonio, July 14, 1926; s. William and Celia (Tobias) A.; m. Shirley Ann Jacobs, June 12, 1949; children: Dennis Ira, Keith Alan, Brian Reid, Wendy Ilene. BBA in Acctg., U. Tex., 1948, JD, 1950. Mgr. 9 coin-operated washeterias, 1960-67; mgr. Sta. KOGT radio, Orange, Tex., 1950-65; ptnr. Calder Properties, 1977—; mng. ptnr. Crow Road Devel. Co., Beaumont, Tex., 1976-77, Normandy Townhomes, Beaumont, 1978—, Griffing Devel. Co., Beaumont, 1978—, Griffing Realty Joint Venture, Beaumont, 1983—; comptroller Gem Jewelry Cos., Beaumont, 1950-58; pres. Gem Jewelry Co. of Beaumont, Inc., 1958—, chmn. of bd., 1991—; mng. ptnr. Gem Distbg. Co. Wholesale Jewelry, Beaumont, 1958—; gen. ptrn. Alter's Gem Jewelry, Ltd. (formerly Gem Jewelry Corp.), Beaumont. Also pres., chmn. of bd. Gem Jewelry Co. of Port Artur, Inc., 1991—, Gem Jewelry C. of Orange, Inc., 1991—, Gem. Jewelry C. of Alexandria (La.), Inc., 1991—, Gem. Jewelry C. of Rapides (La.) Inc., 1991, Gem Jewelry Distbg. Co. Inc., 1991—; U.S. rep. Tex. region Habsbourg-Feldman Fine Art Auctioneers, Geneva, 1986, 87, 88, 89; real estate developer Normandy Townhomes, Griffing Devel. Co., Joint Venture, Griffing Realty Joint Venture, Partner Calder Properties. Past pres. Downtown Beaumont Unltd.; co-chmn. Beaumont Urban Renewal; drive chmn. United Jewish Appeal, Beaumont, 1954, 67; pres. Temple Emanuel, 1974-75, pres., 1981; mem. Beaumont Heritage Soc., Beaumont Music Commn., Beaumont Symphony Soc., Am. Cancer Soc.; co-founder, mem. BBB S.E. Tex.; bd. dirs. A.W. Schlesinger Geriatric Ctr., 1996-2003. Recipient Paul Harris Fellow, Rotary Internat. Found., 2002. Mem. Tex. Retail Jewelers Assn. (v.p. 1974-75), Jefferson County Bar Assn., Tex. Bar Assn., Edna Gladney Aux., Beaumont Jewish Fedn., Buckner Benevolences, Tower Club, Masons, B'nai Brith, Phi Eta Sigma, Beta Gamma Sigma, Phi Alpha Delta, Sigma Alpha Mu. Jewish. Avocations: art collecting, swimming, golf. Office: Alter's Gem Jewelry Ltd 3155 Dowlen Rd Beaumont TX 77706 Office Phone: 409-861-3005.

ALTER, PAUL R., lawyer; b. NYC, June 22, 1941; AB, Columbia Univ., 1962; JD, Cornell Univ., 1965. Bar: NY 1965. Shareholder, real estate, bd. dir. Greenberg Traurig LLP, NYC. Mem.: ABA, NY State Bar Assn., Assn. Bar NYC, NY Assn. New Americans (dir., past pres.), UJA Fedn. NY (chair, real estate lawyers divsn.). Office: Greenberg Traurig LLP MetLife Bldg 200 Park Ave New York NY 10166 Office Phone: 212-801-9292. Office Fax: 212-801-6400. Business E-Mail: alterp@gtlaw.com.

ALTER, ROBERT BERNARD, literature educator, critic; b. N.Y.C., Apr. 2, 1935; s. Harry and Tillie (Zimmmerman) A.; m. Judith Berkenbilt, June 4, 1961 (div. 1973); children: Miriam, Dan; m. Carol Cosman, June 17, 1973; children: Gabriel, Micha. BA, Columbia U., 1957; MA, Harvard U., 1958, PhD, 1962; LHD (hon.), Hebrew Union Coll., 1985. Instr., then asst. prof. English Columbia U., 1962-66; mem. faculty U. Calif.-Berkeley, 1967—, prof. Hebrew and comparative lit., 1969—, chmn. dept. comparative lit., 1970-73, 88-89, class of 1937 prof., 1989—; columnist Commentary mag., 1965-73, contbg. editor, 1973-86. Author: Rogue's Progress: Studies in the Picaresque Novel, 1964, Fielding and the Nature of the Novel, 1968, After the Tradition, 1969, Partial Magic: The Novel as a Self-Conscious Genre, 1975, Defenses of the Immagination, 1977, A Lion for Love, 1979, The Art of Biblical Narrative, 1981, Motives for Fiction, 1984, The Art of Biblical Poetry, 1985; co-editor: The Literary Guide to the Bible, 1987, The Invention of Hebrew Prose, 1988, The Pleasures of Reading in an Ideological Age, 1989, Necessary Angels, 1991, The World of Biblical Literature, 1992, Hebrew and Modernity, 1994, Genesis: Translation and Commentary, 1996, The David Story: A Translation with Commentary of 1 and 2 Samuel, 1999, Canon and Creativity, 2000, The Five Books of Muses: A Translation with Commentary, 2004; contbg. editor: Tri Quarterly mag., 1975—. Recipient essay prize English Inst., 1965, Nat. Jewish Book award for Jewish thought, 1982, Present Tense award for Jewish thought, 1986, Bay Area Book Reviewers Transl. award, 1997, Koret Book award, 2005; Guggenheim fellow, 1966-67, 78-79, sr. fellow NEH, 1972-73, fellow Inst. for Advanced Studies, Jerusalem, 1982-83; scholar Nat. Found. for Jewish Culture, 1995. Fellow Am. Acad. Arts and Scis., Am. Philosoph. Soc.; mem. Council of Scholars of Library of Congress, Assn. Lit. Scholars and Critics (pres. 1996-97). Jewish. Home: 1475 Le Roy Ave Berkeley CA 94708-1911 Office: U Calif Dept Comp Lit 4408 Dwinelle Hall Berkeley CA 94720-2510 E-mail: altcos@uclink4.berkeley.edu.

ALTERMAN, ERIC ROSS, writer, journalist; b. Queens, N.Y., Jan. 14, 1960; s. Carl J. and Ruth N. (Weitzman) A.; m. Patricia Ann Caplan, Aug. 10, 1992. BA, Cornell U., 1982; MA, Yale U., 1986; AB, Stanford U., 1993. Assoc. for pub. policy Bus. Execs. for Nat. Security, Washington, 1983-84; sr. fellow World Policy Inst., N.Y.C., 1985—; peace studies fellow Stanford (Calif.) U., 1992; critic-at-large World Policy Jour., Stanford, 1992—. Author: Sound and Fury: The Washington Punditocracy and the Collapse of American Politics, 1992, Who Speaks for America?: Why Democracy Matters in Foreign Policy, 1998, It Ain't No Sin to Be Glad You're Alive: The Promise of Bruce Springsteen, 1999, What Liberal Media? The Truth About Bias and the News, 2003, The Book on Bush: How George W. (Mis)leads America, 2004, When Presidents Lie: A History of Official Deception and Its Consequences, 2004; columnist Mother Jones, 1992—. Home and Office: 151 W 74th St Apt 1B New York NY 10023-2203*

ALTERMAN, IRWIN MICHAEL, lawyer; b. Vineland, N.J., Mar. 4, 1941; s. Joseph and Rose A.; m. Susan Simon, Aug. 6, 1972 (dec. Apr. 1997); 1 son, Owen. AB, Princeton U., 1962; LLB, Columbia U., 1965. Bar: N.Y. 1966, Mich. 1967. Law clk. to chief judge Theodore Levin U.S. Dist. Ct. (ea. dist.) Mich., 1965-67; assoc. Kaye, Scholer, Fierman, Hays & Handler, N.Y.C., 1967-70, Hyman, Gurwin, Nachman, Friedman & Winkelman, Southfield, Mich., 1970-74, ptnr., 1974-88, Kaufman and Payton, Farmington Hills, Mich., 1988-89, Kemp, Klein, Umphrey, Endelman & May, Troy, Mich., 1989—. Author: Plain and Accurate Style in Court Papers, 1987; founding editor: Mich. Antitrust, 1975—92; editor: Mich. Antitrust Digest, 3d edit., 2001; contbr. articles to profl. jours. Bd. gov. Jewish Fedn. Detroit, 1990—; mem. nat. young leadership cabinet United Jewish Appeal, 1978-79, mem. nat. exec. com., 1980; past pres. Adat Shalom Synagogue, Farmington Hills, Mich. Mem. ABA, Am. Law Inst., State Bar Mich. (past chmn. com. on plain English, past. chmn. antitrust sect.), Princeton Club (past pres. Mich.). Office: Kemp Klein Umphrey & Endelman 201 W Big Beaver Rd Ste 600 Troy MI 48084-4136 Office Phone: 248-528-1111. Business E-Mail: irwin.alterman@kkue.com.

ALTERMAN, MICHAIL A., biochemist, researcher; b. Moscow, Apr. 29, 1951; s. Aron and Blyuma Alterman; m. Marina V Shegai, Dec. 26, 1983; children: Julia M, Elina M, Jonathan Aron. MS in bioorganic chemistry, Lomonosov Moscow State Acad. of Fine Chem. Tech., Russia, 1974; PhD in biol. scis., Russian State Med. U., Moscow. Sr. rschr. dept. of biochemistry Russian State Med. U. (formerly 2nd Moscow Med. Inst.), Moscow, 1976—90; asst. rsch. prof. dept. of vet. anatomy and pub. health Tex. A&M U. Coll. of Vet. Medicine, Coll. Sta., 1991—93; lab. dir. and sr. scientist U. of Kans., Lawrence, 1994—. Contbr. articles to profl. jours. Sr. lt. Russian Army, 1974—76. Grantee, NIH, 1989, U. Kans., Russian Acad. of Scis. Independent. Jewish. Achievements include patents for membrane-associated methane monooxygenase from methylococcus capsulatus. Avocations: reading, travel. Office: U Kans 1251 Wescoe Hall Dr Lawrence KS 66045 E-mail: malterman@ku.edu.

ALTFEST, LEWIS JAY, financial planner; b. NYC, Oct. 14, 1940; s. Sam and Ruth (Zwang) A.; m. Karen Caplan, Dec. 25, 1966; children: Ellen Wendy, Andrew Gamer. BBA with honors, CCNY, 1962; MBA, NYU, 1970; PhD, CUNY, 1978. CPA NY; CFA, CFP, cert. personal fin. specialist. Sr. investment analyst Wertheim and Co., NYC, 1969-75, Lehman Bros., 1975-76; dir. rsch., gen. ptnr. Lord Abbett and Co., 1976-82; pres. L.J. Altfest and Co., Inc., 1982—; assoc. prof. fin. Pace U. Grad. Sch. Bus., 1984—; dir. fin. planning and investments program New Sch. for Social Rsch., 1988—2005. Arbitrator Nat. Assn. Securities Dealers, Am. Arbitration Assn., 1985-88; bd. dirs. Consumer Fin. Edn. Found., 1994-95. Author: (with others) Introduction to Business, 1978, Capital Budgeting Handbook, 1986; author: Lew Altfest Answers Almost All Your Questions About Money, 1992, rev. edit., 1994; contbr. articles to profl. jours. Pres. 240 E. 79th Coop. Bd., NYC, 1983-86; bd. dirs. Consumer Fin. Edn. Found., 1993-97. With U.S. Army, 1962-63. Named One of Best Fin. Planners in U.S., Money Mag., 1987, One of Best Fin. Advisors, Worth Mag., 1996, 97, 98, One of Best Advisers for Physicians, Med. Econs., 1998, 2000, 02, 04, One of 100 Gt. Fin. Planners, Mut. Funds Mag., 2001, One of Top Wealth Mgrs. (Bloomberg), firm L.J. Altfest & Co., 2003, 05; recipient Disting. Alumni award PhD Alumni Assn. CUNY, 1992. Mem. Nat. Assn. Personal Fin. Advisors (bd. dirs. 1985-89, Outstanding Leadership award 1989), AICPA, Internat. Assn. for Fin. Planning (bd. dirs. NY chpt. 1987-93), Inst. Chartered Fin. Analysts, Am. Fin. Assn., Fin. Analysts Fedn., Fin. Mgmt. Assn., NY Soc. Security Analysts, Registry Fin. Planning Practitioners, CCNY Bus. Alumni Assn. (bd. dirs. 1983-87), Acad. Fin. Svcs. Office: LJ Altfest & Co Inc 116 John St Rm 1120 New York NY 10038-3305 Office Phone: 212-406-0850.

ALTHAVER, LAMBERT EWING, manufacturing executive; b. Kansas City, Mo., May 18, 1931; s. Edward William and Dorothy Lambert (Ewing) A.; m. Holly Elizabeth Walpole, Feb. 28, 1953; children: Brian, Lauren BA, Principia Coll, 1952; LLD honoris causa, Northwood U., 2003. Account exec. Walbro Corp., Cass City, Mich., 1954-58, asst. to pres., 1958-65, v.p. fin., 1965-70, exec. v.p., 1970-77, pres., chief ops. officer, 1977-82, pres., CEO, 1982-87, chmn., pres., CEO, 1987-96, also bd. dirs., chmn., CEO, 1996-98, chmn. emeritus, 1998-2000. Councilman Village of Cass City, 1963—65, pres., 1965—84, 1987—2000, 2004—; mem. Tuscola County Planning Commn., Caro, Mich., 1966—94; chmn. Cass City Econ. Devel. Corp., 1983—96, Tuscola Area Airport Authority, 1994—2004; co-founder, v.p. Village Bach Festival, 1979—; mem. Mich. Jobs Commn., 1996—99; bd. dirs. Tuscola Econ. Devel. Corp., 1985—2004; vice-chmn., sec., dir. Artrain, Inc., 1975—96, chmn., 1996—2003; v.p., bd. dirs. Lake Huron area Boy Scouts Am., 1988—94; dir. Am. Bus. Conf. Found., Washington, 1998—, Mich. Mcpl. League Found., Ann Arbor, 1999—2002; trustee Jordan Coll., 1990—95, Northwood U., 2000—, Hills & Dales Hosp., Cass City, 1998—. Served with U.S. Army, 1952—54. Recipient Dr. of Laws Honoris Causa, Northwood U., 2003, Silver Beaver award Boy Scouts Am., 1995, Disting. Eagle Scout award, 1989; named Citizen of Yr. Cass City C. of C., 1978; Paul Harris fellow Rotary Internat., Evanston, Ill., 1979, 94, 99, 2002, 04; named Outstanding Bus. Leader, Northwood U., 1997. Mem. Mich. C. of C. (bd. dirs. 1986-92), Cass City C. of C. (bd. dirs. 1985-2004), Detroit Athletic Club, Rotary. Avocation: golf. Office: PO Box 27 Cass City MI 48726-0027 Office Phone: 989-872-8183. E-mail: althaver@tband.net.

ALTHEIMER, BRIAN P. See TUTASHINDA, KWELI

ALTHOFF, J(AMES) L., construction company executive; b. McHenry, Ill., June 9, 1928; s. William H. and Eleanor M. (Smith) A.; m. Joan E. Andreen, June 18, 1949; children: Tim, Betsy, Kate, Tod, Patti, Jim Jr., Karyn. Grad., McHenry (Ill.) High Sch., 1947. Owner, pres. Althoff Gas Svc., McHenry, 1949-60, Fox Valley Propane, 1952-60, No. Equip. Corp., McHenry, 1958-72; CEO Althoff Industries, Crystal Lake, Ill., 1961—, Althoff & Assocs., McHenry, 1962—, Brookside Indsl., McHenry, 1991—. Trustee Plumbers Welfare Fund, Chgo., 1972—; dir. McHenry Bank. Pres. McHenry High Sch. Bd. Edn., 1967-79, Fire Protection Dist., McHenry, 1964-92; chmn. bd. govs. Ill. Univs., 1980-91; commr. Ill. State Lottery, 1991—. Recipient award for outstanding leadership Chgo. State U., 1986, Leadership award No. Med. Ctr., McHenry, 1984, Ea. Ill. U., 1987. Mem. Contrs. Assn. No. Ill. (pres. 1969-72), Bradley Dads' Assn., Kiwanis. Home: 508 N Green St Mchenry IL 60050-5684 Office: Althoff Industries 8001 S State Route 31 Crystal Lake IL 60014-8184

ALTIER, JAMES EDWARD, JR., martial arts professional; b. Warren, Ohio, June 10, 1966; s. James Edward Altier, Sr. and Edith Altier; m. Michelle Marie Leatherherry, Oct. 10, 1987; children: James Edward III, Christopher Allan, Michael Vincent. BA in Labor Rels., Youngstown State U., 1994. Assembler Delphi, 1985—89, customer svc. rep., 1989—2000, quality engr., 1989—2000, mfg. supr., 2000—02, master black belt (six sigma) Warren, Ohio, 2002—. Capt. Am. Cancer Soc. Relay for Life, Niles, 2003—05. Mem.: Am. Soc. for Quality, Moose. Avocations: golf, motorcycling.

ALTIER, WILLIAM JOHN, management consultant; b. Drexel Hill, Pa., July 22, 1935; s. William John and Gertrude (Soule) Altier; m. Mileen Rishel Bower, June 21, 1958; children: William Clark, Dwight Douglas. BA, Lafayette Coll., 1958; MBA, Pa. State U., 1962. Assoc. Kepner-Tregoe Inc., Princeton, N.J., 1964-68, Applied Synergetics Ctr., Waltham, Mass., 1968-69; dir. mktg. Comstock & Wescott Inc., Cambridge, Mass., 1969-70; gen. mgr. divsn. Princeton Rsch. Press, 1970-75, sr. assoc., 1975-76; pres. Princeton Assocs. Inc., Buckingham, Pa., 1976—. Grad. asst. Dale Carnegie Courses; lectr. Assn. Media-Based Continuing Edn. Engrs.; guest lectr. Grad. Sch. Mgmt., New Sch. Social Rsch., Wharton Sch., U. Pa., Pa. State U.; bd. dirs., vice chmn. Inst. Mgmt. Cons., exec. editor IMC newsletter. Author: The Thinking Manager's Toolbox, 1999; editor, pub.: PA Perspective, abstractor: Jour. Product Innovation Mgmt.; mem. editl. rev. bd. Jour. Managerial Issues; co-author: Management Consulting, 3d edit., 1996, The Art of M&A Integration: A Guide to Merging Resources, Processes, and Responsibilities, 1997; contbr. articles to profl. jours.; patentee in field. Co-chmn. indsl. divsn. United Cmty. Fund, Carlisle, Pa., 1963; exec. v.p. Bucks County br. ARC, planning com. southeastern Pa. chpt.; vol. worker civic orgns.; elder Doylestown Presbyn. Ch. Fellow: Inst. Mgmt. Cons. (participative process cons. spl. interest group, cert.); mem.: Am. Creativity Assn., Pa. Innovation Network, Tech. Coun. Greater Phila., Assn. Mng. Cons. (trustee, editor newsletter UPDATE II), Am. Arbitration Assn., Inst. Mgmt. Cons., Liberty Bell Spkrs. Assn., Nat. Spkrs. Assn., Product Devel. and Mgmt. Assn. (v.p.), Am. Mgmt. Assn., Am. Vacuum Soc., Am. Chem. Soc., Acad. Mgmt., Doylestown Toastmasters (v.p.), Ctrl. Bucks C. of C., U. So. Calif. Ctr. Futures Rsch., Armed Forces Comm. and Electronics Assn., Mensa, World Affairs Coun. Phila., 1000 Club, Exch. Club (bd. control 1960—64), Indsl. Mgmt. Club, Union League Phila., Kappa Sigma Alumni Corp. (chpt. pres.). Office: PO Box 820 Buckingham PA 18912-0820 Office Phone: 215-794-5626. Business E-Mail: princetoninc@cs.com.

ALTIERI, JAMES M., lawyer; b. Dumont, NJ, 1949; BS magna cum laude, Univ. Md., Balt., 1971; JD, Fordham Univ., 1975. Bar: NJ 1975, NY 1976, Ariz. 1987. Atty. Simpson Thacher & Bartlett, NYC; joined Drinker Biddle & Reath LLP, 1985, mng. ptnr., head, insurance practice group Florham Park, NJ. Mem.: ABA, Assn. Bar City NY, Assn. Fed. Bar, NJ Bar Assn. Office: Drinker Biddle & Leath LLP 500 Campus Dr Florham Park NJ 07932-1047 Office Phone: 973-549-7060. Office Fax: 973-360-9831. Business E-Mail: james.altieri@dbr.com.

ALTMAN, ARNOLD DAVID, manufacturing executive; b. South Bend, Ind., Dec. 10, 1917; s. David and Goldie (Mooren) A.; children: Daniel Blair, Jonathan Estes. BSEE, U. Notre Dame, 1941. With Newman and Altman, Inc., South Bend, 1946-64; pres. Avanti Motor Corp., South Bend, 1976-82, Nat. Inventory Res., Inc., South Bend, 1980—; pres., CEO Rosenstein & Co., South Bend, 1985—. Lt. USN, 1942-46. Democrat. Jewish. Home: 1527 E Colfax Ave South Bend IN 46617-2601 Office: PO Box 603 Mishawaka IN 46546 Office Phone: 574-255-9639. E-mail: nir603@aol.com.

ALTMAN, BRIAN DAVID, pediatric ophthalmologist; b. Temple, Tex., Feb. 29, 1944; s. Harold and Alice A. BA, Adelphi U., 1965; MD, Yale Med. Sch., 1969. Diplomate Am. Bd. Pediatrics, Am. Bd. Opthalmologists. Pediatric ophthalmologist pvt. practice, Huntington Valley, Pa., 1976-98, Plymouth, Pa., 1976-98, Ocean City, N.J., 1992—, Cape May Courthouse, 1992—. Cons. in pediatric ophthalomogy several hosps. in Pa. and N.J., 1977—. Co-author: (with others) Medications in Pediatric Ophthalmology, 1975. Lt. cmmdr. USPHS, 1970-72. Fellow Am. Acad. Opthalmology, Am. Acad. Pediatrics, Am. Assn. Pediatric Ophthalmologists. Office: 315 Rt 9 S Cape May Court House NJ 08210 Home and Office: PO Box 1259 Ocean City NJ 08226-7259 Office Phone: 609-398-1100.

ALTMAN, DOROTHY JEWELL, language educator; b. Gloversville, N.Y. d. Albert Edward and Irene Fitch Jewell; m. Eric H. Altman, May 10, 1969; children: Brian, Michael, Sara. BA magna cum laude, SUNY, Albany, 1963; MA English, CUNY, 1970; PhD, SUNY, Albany, 1979. Adj. instr. Ramapo Coll., Mahwah, NJ, 1979—80, Bergen C.C., Paramus, NJ, 1980—94; gifted & talented coord. Rutherford Pub. Schs., NJ, 1994—96; instr. Bergen C.C., 1996—2001, asst. prof., 2002—. Mem.: N.J. Writing Alliance, N.E. Modern Lang. Assn., Two-Year Coll. Assn., Nat. Coun. Tchrs. English. Home: 10 Strawberry Ln Upper Saddle River NJ 07458 Office Phone: 201-493-3544. E-mail: daltman@bergen.edu.

ALTMAN, DREW E., foundation executive; b. Boston, Mar. 21, 1951; s. George and Harriet A.; m. Pamela Koch; children: Daniel, Jessica. BA magna cum laude, Brandeis U., 1973; MA, Brown U., 1974; PhD in Polit. Sci., MIT, 1983. Postdoctoral fellow, rsch. assoc. Harvard U. Sch. Pub. Health, Boston, 1975-76, 78-80; prin. rsch. assoc. Codman Rsch. Group, Boston, 1976-80; spl. asst. office of adminstr. Health Care Fin. Adminstrn. Dept. HHS, Washington, 1979-81; v.p. Robert Wood Johnson Found., Princeton, N.J., 1981-86; commr. N.J. Dept. Human Svcs., Trenton, 1986-89; program dir. health and human svcs. The Pew Charitable Trusts, Phila., 1989-90; pres., CEO Henry J. Kaiser Family Found., Menlo Park, Calif., 1990—. Contbr. articles to profl. jours. Mem. Inst. of Medicine, Nat. Acad. of Soc. Ins., Assn. for Health Svcs. Rsch. Office: Henry J Kaiser Family Found 2400 Sand Hill Rd Menlo Park CA 94025-6941

ALTMAN, EDITH G., sculptor; b. Altenberg, Germany, May 23, 1931; arrived in U.S., 1939; BA, Wayne State U., 1949; student, Marygrove Coll., 1956-57. Instr. visual arts and printing project U. Omaha, 1984; asst. prof. painting, grad. advisor U. Chgo., 1984-85; vis. asst. prof. painting Sch. Art Inst. Chgo., 1985-86. Lectr. painting U. Ill., Columbia Coll., Oakton C.C., Chgo. One-woman shows include NAME Gallery, 1987, Spertus Mus. Gallery Contemporary Art, 1988, Rockford Art Mus., 1989, State of Ill. Mus. Gallery, Chgo., 1992, Loyola U. Fine Arts Gallery, 1993, Peace Mus., Chgo., 1993, Mitchell Mus., Ill., 1995, Minn. Mus. Am. Art, 1995, Lindeau Mus., Altenburg, Germany, 2001, Frauen Mus., Bonn, Germany, 2001, Contextual Cultural Ctr., Chgo., 2001, Natl. Museum of Szczecin, Poland, 2002-. Hyde Park Art Ctr., 2002. others; exhibited in group shows Art Inst. Chgo., 1975, 79, 81, 85, Mus. Contemporary Art, Chgo., 1976, 81, 83, 97, Acad. Kunst, Berlin, 1987, Barbicon Ctr., London, 1990, Knoxville Mus. Art, Tenn., 1998, N.J. State Mus., 1999, Okla. City Art Mus., 1999, Decordova Mus., 2000; represented in permanent collections Standard Oil Co., Mus. Contemporary Art, Chgo., 1997, State of Ill., Yale U. Mus., Holocaust Mus., Peace Mus., Gallery 312, Chgo., 2003; contbr. articles to profl. jours., newspapers. Named Art Matters fellow, 1994; Individual Artist fellow, Ill. Arts Coun., 1984, 1994, Internat. grantee, 2003, Individual Artist Fellow grantee, NEA, 1990—91. Mem. Chgo. Artist Coalition (founding mem., mem. com. artists rights, 1988). Address: 811 W 16th St Chicago IL 60608-2222 Office Phone: 312-421-2881. E-mail: ealtman3@aol.com.

ALTMAN, HEIDI ZIMMERHANZEL, educational administrator educator, educational specialist; d. Paul Peter and Jaime Leah Zimmerhanzel; m. Brett Andrew Altman, Oct. 14, 2000; 1 child, Ryan James. BS in Elem. Edn., Tex. A&M U., College Station, 1996; MEd in Elem. Edn., U. North Tex., Denton, 1998, MEd in Edn. Adminstrn., 2002. Cert. prin. Tex., gifted and talented tchr. Tex., ESL and spl. edn. tchr. Tex. Tchg. fellow, adj. prof. U. North Tex., Denton, 1996—99; elem. tchr. Richardson I.S.D., Richardson, 1996—99, gifted and talented tchr., 1999—2002, instrnl. specialist, 2002—03; instrnl. specialist, tchr. Highland Pk. Presbyn. Day Sch., Dallas, 2003—05, staff developer, 2003—05. Author: (curriculum writing) Richardson I.S.D., 1996—2003. Named Oustanding Grad., Tex. A&M U.; Grad. fellow, U. North Tex. Mem.: ACSD, Tex. Assn. Gifted and Talented. Avocations: reading, crafts, writing. Office Phone: 214-559-5353. Office Fax: 214-559-5357. Business E-Mail: hzaltman@msn.com.

ALTMAN, IRWIN, psychologist, educator; BA, NYU, 1951; MA, U. Md., 1954, PhD, 1957. Asst. prof. psychology Am. U., Washington, 1957-58, sr. rsch. scientist, assoc. prof., 1960-62, adj. prof., 1962-69; rsch. scientist in human scis. Arlington, Va., 1958-60; rsch. psychologist Naval Med. Rsch. Inst., Bethesda, Md., 1962-69; adj. prof. U. Md., 1968-69; prof. U. Utah, Salt Lake City, 1969-79, chmn. dept. psychology, 1969-76, dean Coll. Social and Behavioral Sci., 1979-83, v.p. for acad. affairs, 1983-87, disting. prof., 1987—2005, disting. prof. emeritus, 2005—. Author: (with J.E. McGrath) Small Groups, 1966, (with D.A. Taylor) Social Penetration, 1973, Environment and Social Behavior, 1975; (with M. Chemers) Culture and Environment, 1980; (with J. Wohlwill) Human Behavior and Environment: Vol. I, 1976, Vol. II, 1977, Vol. III, 1978, Vol. IV, 1980, Vol. V, 1981, Vol. VI, 1983, Vol. VII, 1984, (with C. Werner) Vol. VIII, 1985, (with A. Wandersman) Vol. IX, 1987, (with E. Zube) Vol. X, 1989, (with K. Christensen) Vol. XI, 1990, (with S. Low) Vol. XII, 1992, (with A. Churchman) Women and the Environment, Vol. XIII, 1994; (with D. Stokols) Handbook of Environmental Psychology, Vols I and II, 1987; (with J. Ginat) Polygamous Families in Contemporary Society, 1996; mem. editl. bds.: Small Groups, 1970-79, Man-Environment Systems, 1969-73, Jour. Applied Social Psychology, 1973-85, Sociometry, 1973-76, Environment and Behavior, 1975, Jour. Personality and Social Psychology, 1974-83, Contemporary Psychology, 1975-86, Environ. Psychology and Nonverbal Behavior, Psychology, 1976-90, Am. Jour. Cmty. Psychology, 1978-81, Population and Environment, 1979, Jour. Environ. Psychology, 1982, Computers and Human Behavior, 1985, Internat. Jour. Applied Social Psychology, 1984, Communication Monographs, 1992-95; assoc. editor Am. Jour. Cmty. Psychology, 1988-92; co-editor Jour. Environ. Psychology, 1990-98; contbr. articles to profl. jours. 1st lt. Adj. Gen. Corps, AUS, 1954-56. Mem. APA (pres. divsn. population and environment), AAAS, Soc. Exptl. Social Psychology, Soc. Psychol. Study of Social Issues, Soc. Personality and Social Psychology (pres.), Environ. Design Rsch. Assn., Am. Psychol. Soc. Office Phone: 801-581-7109. Business E-Mail: irwin.altman@m.cc.utah.edu.

ALTMAN, JAMES WAYNE, music educator; b. Hialeah, Fla., June 27, 1963; s. James Nelson and Rosella Altman; m. Lisa Ann Blalock; children: James, Amber, Haley. MusB in Edn., U. Ga., 1988, MusM in Edn., 1998; cert. edn. specialist in adminstrn. and supervision, Clemson U., 2001. Cert. tchr. Ga. Sys. wide music tchr. Hart County Sch. Sys., Hartwell, Ga., 1988—89; band dir. Elbert County HS, Elberton, Ga., 1989—. Choir dir. LDS Ch., Elberton, 1985—. Mem.: PAGE, Nat. Band Assn., Music Educators Nat. Conf., Ga. Music Educators Assn. Mem. Lds Ch. Office: Elbert County Comprehensive HS 600 Abernathy Cir Elberton GA 30635 Personal E-mail: jwaltman3@yahoo.com.

ALTMAN, LAWRENCE GENE, biologist, educator; b. July 4, 1952; s. Mark Eugene and Roberta Mercedes (Baron) Altman. BA in Biology, Fordham U., 1972, MS, 1974, PhD, 1982. Rsch. biologist VA, West Haven, Conn., 1982-85; asst. prof. divsn. sci. and math. Fordham U., N.Y.C., 1986-87; postdoctoral assoc. in pathology Yale U. Med. Sch., New Haven, 1982-85; cons. Coll. New Rochelle, N.Y., 1980-81, Polyscis., Inc., Warrington, Pa., 1985-89, Columbia U. Coll. Physicians and Surgeons Dept. Microbiol., N.Y.C., 1986-88; asst. prof. biology Western Conn. State U., Danbury, 1992-93, 94-95, 98, CUNY, 1998-2000, Naugatuck Valley C.C., 2000—. Mem. part-time faculty Fordham U., N.Y.C., mem. dean's adv. coun. Grad. Sch. Arts and Scis., 2003—; mem. part-time faculty Western Conn. State U., Danbury, 1990—91, Danbury, 1996—98; pres. Cider Mill Pond Assn., Greenwich, Conn., 1994—96. Contbr. articles to profl. jours. Recipient Excellence award, Nat. Inst. Staff and Orgnl. Devel., U. Tex., 2003, 2004; fellow, Fordham U., 1975—77. Mem.: AAAS, Conn. Microscopy Soc. (pres. 2005—), Microscopy Soc. Am., Am. Soc. Cell Biology, Sigma Xi. Avocations: theater, travel, educational technology.

ALTMAN, LAWRENCE KIMBALL, physician, journalist; b. Quincy, Mass., June 19, 1937; s. William S. and Esther (Kimball) A. AB cum laude, Harvard U., 1958; MD, Tufts U., 1962. Diplomate: Am. Vet. Epidemiology Soc. Intern Mt. Zion Hosp., San Francisco, 1962-63; USPHS epidemic intelligence service officer CDC, Atlanta, 1963-66; med. resident, fellow U. Wash. Hosp., Seattle, 1966-69; med. corr., columnist The Doctors World NY Times, 1969—; clin. prof. medicine NYU, 1970—. Vis. physician Serafimer Hosp., Karolinska Inst., Stockholm, Sweden, 1973; vis. scientist U. Wash., 1971; Chancellor's Disting. Lecture for Pub. Understanding of Sci., U. Calif., San Francisco, 1989; Ida Beam Disting. vis. prof. U. Iowa, 2000. Author: Science of The Times, 1981, Who Goes First? The Story of Self-Experimentation in Medicine, 1987, 98; contbr. chpts. to books, articles to profl. jours.; contbr. Ency. Brit., 1979, Grolier Ency., 1972-87. Recipient Claude Bernard award, Nat. Soc. Med. Rsch., 1971, 1974, Pub. Svc. award, Nat. Kidney Found., 1977, Walter C. Alvarez award, Am. Med. Writers Assn., 1980, journalism award, Am. Acad. Pediat., 1982, Pub. Svc. award, Nat. Kidney Found., 1983, Howard W. Blakeslee award, Am. Heart Assn., 1982—83, 1994, Journalism award, Coll. Am. Pathologists, 1985, George Polk award, 1986, Vincent Downing award, 1988, Med. Media Excellence award, Friends Nat. Libr. Medicine, 1993, Victor Cohn prize, Coun. for the Advancement of Sci. Writing, 2000, Howard Lewis Career award, Am. Heart Assn., 2001, medal, U. Calif., San Francisco, 2004, Walsh McDermott award, Associated Med. Schs. N.Y., 2004. Master ACP; fellow Am. Coll. Epidemiology, NY Acad. Medicine; mem. Inst. Medicine, NAS, Am. Soc. Tropical Medicine and Hygiene, Soc. Epidemiology, Am. Bd. Med. Spltys. (pub. 1986-88), Alpha Omega Alpha, Century Club (NYC), Harvard Club (NYC). Home: 140 W End Ave New York NY 10023-6131 Office: New York Times 229 W 43rd St New York NY 10036-3959

ALTMAN, PETER A., theater director; b. Washington, June 3, 1943; s. Oscar Louis and Alberta Petrie (Smith) Altman; m. Anne Devereux Emerson; children: Katherine Ann Farrell, Josephine Burr, Hannah Burr. BA, U. Calif., Berkeley, 1963; MA, U. Pa., 1964; postgrad., Harvard U., 1968, postgrad., 1973—74, U. Urbino, Italy, 1969, Goethe Inst., Passau, Germany, 1976. Theatre critic, arts editor Mpls. Star, 1966—75; lectr. U. Minn., Mpls., 1965—76; lit. mgr. Guthrie Theatre, Mpls., 1971; exec. officer for the arts Boston U., 1977—82, prof. theatre, 1978—2000; producing dir. Huntington Theatre, Boston, 1982—2000; producing artistic dir. Mo./Kansas City Repertory Theatre, 2000—. With U.S. Army, 1964—65, with USAR, 1965—70. Recipient Elliott Norton award, Boston Critics, 1983, Chevalier Arts and Letters, Govt. France, 2002; Critics fellow, Nat. Endowment Arts, 1971, Leaders fellow, Bush Found., 1973. Office: Kansas City Repertory Theatre 4949 Cherry St Kansas City MO 64110

ALTMAN, ROBERT, lawyer; b. St. Paul, Feb. 21, 1949; s. Milton and Helen (Horwitz) A.; m. Margo Geller, Mar. 28, 1998; children: (by previous marriage: Jesse, David, Aaron. BA, U. Calif., Berkeley, 1970; JD, U. Minn., 1973. Bar: Minn. 1975, Ga. 1978, U.S. Ct. Appeals (5th cir.) 1978, U.S. Ct. Appeals (11th cir.) 1981, U.S. Supreme Ct. 1981; registered mediator Ga. Supreme Ct., 2003—. Atty. Team Def. Project, Atlanta, 1976-77; assoc. dir. So. Prisoners Def. Com., New Orleans, 1978-79; exec. dir. Fed. Defender Program, Inc., 1980-84; pvt. practice Atlanta, 1984—; judge Mcpl. Ct. City of Atlanta, 1988-96; mediator/arbitrator JAMS, Atlanta. Pres. Fed. Defender Program, Inc., 1990-91; instr. Nat. Inst. Trial Advocacy, Emory U., Atlanta, 1983-2000; com. to rev. the criminal justice act U.S. Jud. Conf., 1991-93; mediator/arbitrator Atlanta office JAMS. Contbr. articles to profl. jours. Mem. ATLA, Ga. Bar Assn., Atlanta Bar Assn. (Blue Ribbon commn.), Ga. Trial Lawyers Assn. (chair bad faith ins. litigation group, mem. exec. com. 1999-2004), Ga. Assn. Criminal Def. Laywers, Phi Beta Kappa. Office: Hughes & Altman LLP 1842 Independence Sq Atlanta GA 30338 also: JAMS 235 Peachtree St Ste 600 Atlanta GA 30303 Office Phone: 404-892-8766. Personal E-mail: altlaw@mindspring.com.

ALTMAN, ROBERT ALAN, lawyer; b. Washington, Feb. 23, 1947; s. Norman S. and Sophie B. (Robinson) A.; m. Lynda J. Carter, Jan. 29, 1984; children: James Clifford, Jessica Carter. BA, U. Wis., 1968; JD, George Washington U., 1971. Bar: D.C. 1971. Ptnr. Clifford & Warnke, Washington, 1971—91; chmn., CEO ZeniMax Media, Inc., Washington, 1999—2000. Pres. 1st Am. Corp., Washington, 1982-91; bd. dirs. 1st Am. Bankshares Inc., Washington, 1st Am. Bank N.Y., N.Y.C. Avocations: tennis, skiing.

ALTMAN, ROBERT B., film director, writer, producer; b. Kansas City, Mo., Feb. 20, 1925; s. B.C. and Helen Altman; m. LaVonne Elmer, 1947 (div.), 1 child, Christine; m. Lotus Corelli, 1954 (div.), children Stephen, Michael; m. Kathryn Altman, 1959, children Robert, Matthew Student, U. Mo., 3 years. Owner Sandcastle 5 Prodns. Writer, prodr., dir.: (TV) Kraft Theatre; writer, prodr., dir.: (TV pilot) The Long Hot Summer; co-prodr.: (film) The James Dean Story, 1957; dir.: (films) The Delinquents, 1957, Countdown, 1968, That Cold Day in the Park, 1969, M*A*S*H, 1970 (Grand Prix award Cannes Film Festival 1970, Best Film, Nat. Soc. Film Critics 1970), Popeye, 1980, Come Back to the 5 & Dime, Jimmy Dean, Jimmy Dean, 1982, Streamers, 1983, Beyond Therapy, 1987, The Gingerbread Man, 1997, (TV series) Gun, 1997; producer: The Late Show, 1977, Welcome to L.A., 1977, Rich Kids, 1979, Remember My Name, 1979, Mrs. Parker and the Vicious Circle, 1994; prodr. and dir.: A Wedding, 1978, Quintet, 1979, A Perfect Couple, 1979, Secret Honor, 1985, The Player, 1992 (Best Dir. citation Cannes Film Festival, 1992), After Glow, 1997, The Company, 2003; prodr., dir., screenwriter: Three Women, 1977, Health, 1979, Gosford Park, 2001 (nominee Best dir. and Best Picture Acad. award 2002, Best dir. in Motion Picture Golden Globe award 2002, Dir. of Yr. AFI. Film Award 2002, BAFTA award, Evening Std. Brit. Film award NSFC award NYFCC award, Best Dir./Best Film Silver Ribbon award 2002), Paint, 2005; dir., screenwriter: Brewster McCloud, 1970, McCabe and Mrs. Miller, 1971, Images, 1972, The Long Goodbye, 1973, Thieves Like Us, 1974, California Split, 1974, Buffalo Bill and the Indians, 1976, Fool for Love, 1985, Short Cuts, 1993 (nominee Best Dir. Acad. award 1993), Ready to Wear (Prêt-à-Porter), 1994, Kansas City, 1996, Cookie's Fortune, 1999; dir. for stage: (Broadway) Come Back to the 5 & Dime, Jimmy Dean, Jimmy Dean, 1982, (Lyric Opera of Chgo.) McTeague, 1993; prodr., dir.: (TV) The Laundromat, 1984, The Dumb Waiter, 1987, The Room, 1987, Caine Mutiny Court Martial, 1987, Tanner '88, 1988, Tanner on Tanner, 2004; dir. film Vincent and Theo, 1990; prodr., dir. Nashville, 1976; actor: (TV movie) Frank Capra's American Dream, 1997; exec. prodr. Roads & Bridges, 2000; actor Dr. T & The Women (Golden Lion award 2000). Served with AUS, 1943-47. Named 17th Greatest Director of all time, Entertainment Weekly; recipient Lifetime Achievement award, 2000, Hon. Golden Berlin Bear award, 2002. Mem. Dirs. Guild Am. Office: Sandcastle 5 Prodns 502 Park Ave Ste 15G New York NY 10022-1108 also: ICM 8942 Wilshire Blvd Beverly Hills CA 90211-1934*

ALTMAN, ROY PETER, pediatric surgeon; b. N.Y.C., Apr. 13, 1934; s. Charles and Sue (Solomon) A.; m. Hanna Diamond, Aug. 22, 1964; children: James David, Robert Ross. AB, Colgate U., 1955; MS, U. Rochester, 1958; MD, N.Y. Med. Coll., 1961. Diplomate Am. Bd. Surgery, Am. Bd. Thoracic Surgery, Am. Bd. Pediatric Surgery. Intern Mount Sinai Hosp., N.Y.C., 1961-62; surg. resident Tufts-New Eng. Med. Ctr, Boston, 1962-66, chief resident, 1966-67; postdoctoral fellow NIH, Dept. Surgery Tufts-New Eng. Med. Ct., 1964-65; chief resident in thoracic surgery George Washington U. Hosp., Washington, 1967—68; chief resident in pediatric surgery Children's Hosp. Nat. Med. Ctr., Washington, 1967-69; spl. fellow clin./rsch. surgery (transplantation) U. Colo. Health Scis. Ctr., Denver, 1974; prof. surgery in surgery and pediatrics Coll. Physicians and Surgeons, Columbia U., N.Y.C., 1980—; surgeon in chief Children's Hosp. N.Y. Presbyn. Hosp., N.Y.C., 1980—; v.p. med. affairs, physician in chief Children's Health System, 1998. Prof. surgery and child health George Washington Sch. Medicine, 1977-80; sr. attending surgeon Children's Hosp., Nat. Med. Ctr., Washington, 1973-80, dir. surg. rsch., 1975-80, surg. dir. clin. rsch. ctr., 1975-80, dir. organ transplantation, 1975-80; cons. surgeon Walter Reed Army Hosp., 1974-80, Dewitt Army Hosp., Ft. Belvoir, Va., 1973-80, The Hosp. for Sick Children, Washington, 1974-80; asst. prof.surgery and child health George Washington U. Sch. Medicine, 1970-73, Tufts U. Sch. Medicine, Editl. cons. Pediat. Surgery Internat., 1985—; editl. adv. bd. Surgery Ann., 1986—, Surgery, 1992-98, Jour. Pediat. Surgery, 1996. Bd. dirs. Ronald McDonald House and Found. Children's Oncology Soc., N.Y. C.V. Mosby Scholar, N.Y. Med. Coll., 1961. Fellow: ACS, Am. Acad. Pediats.; mem.: Am. Pediat. Surg. Assn. (gov. 1996, bd. govs. 1996—99, pres. 2002—, bd. govs. 2003, pres. elect 2002, pres. 2003, bd. govs. 2004), Internat. Coll. Surgery, Soc. Univ. Surgeons, Am. Surg. Assn., Alpha Omega Alpha. Avocations: skiing, golf, tennis, music. Home: 15 W 81st St New York NY 10024-6022 Office: Children's Hosp of NY Presbyn-Columbia Univ Med Ctr 3959 Broadway 116 S New York NY 10032-1590 Office Phone: 212-305-5804. Business E-Mail: RPA1@columbia.edu.

ALTMAN, SCOTT, law educator, dean; b. 1962; BA, Univ. Wis., Madison, 1983; JD cum laude, Harvard Univ., 1987. Law clerk U.S. Ct. Appeals 9th cir., 1987—88; asst. prof. Univ. So. Calif. Law Sch., 1988—90, assoc. prof., 1990—93, prof., 1993—97, assoc. dean, 1995—, Virginia S. & Fred H. Bice prof., 1997—. Contbr. articles prof. law jour. Mem.: Phi Beta Kappa. Office: The Law Sch Univ So Calif Los Angeles CA 90089

ALTMAN, SIDNEY, biology professor; b. Montreal, Que., Can., May 7, 1939; s. Victor Altman and Ray Arlin; m. Ann Korner, 1972; children: Daniel, Leah. BS, MIT, 1960; PhD in Biophys., U. Colo., 1967; DSc (hon.), McGill U., Montreal, 1991, York U., U. Colo., U. Montreal, U. B.C. Teaching asst. Columbia U., 1960—62; Damon Runyon Meml. Fund cancer rsch. fellow in molecular biology Harvard U., 1967—69; Anna Fuller Fund fellow, then Med. Rsch. Coun. fellow Med. Rsch. Coun. Lab. Molecular Biology, 1969—71; from asst. to assoc. prof. Yale U., New Haven, 1971—80, prof. molecular cellular and devel. biology, 1980—, Sterling prof. biology, 1990—, prof. biophysical chemistry, 1994—, chmn. dept., 1983—85; dean Yale Coll., 1985—90. Tutor Radcliffe Coll., 1968—69. Author: Transfer RNA, 1978. Recipient Nobel Prize in Chemistry, 1989, Merit Award, Nat. Inst. Health, 1989, Yale Sci. and Engring. Assn. Award, 1990. Fellow: AAAS; mem.: Am. Philos. Soc. (Rosenstiel award 1989), Nat. Acad. Scis., Genetics Soc. Am., Am. Soc. Biol. Chemists. Achievements include research in on effects of acridines on T4 DNA replication, mutants, precursors of tRNA processing by catalytic RNA and ribonuclease function. Office: Yale U Kline Biology Tower 402 New Haven CT 06520-8103*

ALTMAN, STEVEN LAWRENCE, lawyer; b. Far Rockaway, N.Y., Oct. 2, 1961; s. Allan and Marcia Ann (Edelman) A.; children: Natalie Rose, Zachary Aaron. BSBA, Boston U., 1983; JD, N.Y. Law Sch., 1986. Bar: N.Y. 1987, U.S. Dist. Ct. (so. and ea. dists.) N.Y. 1987, U.S. Ct. Appeals (5th cir.) 1989, U.S. Ct. Appeals (fed. cir.) 1993, U.S. Ct. Appeals (2d cir.) 1995, 9th cir., 2005. Law clk. Poskauer Rose Goetz & Mendelsohn, N.Y.C., 1985-86, assoc., 1986-93; ptnr. Ziegler, Ziegler & Altman, LLP, N.Y.C., 1994—2002, Altman & Co., N.Y.C., 2002—. Home: 265 E 66th St New York NY 10021-6404 Office: Altman & Co PC 260 Madison Ave New York NY 10016 Office Phone: 212-683-7600.

ALTMAN, STUART HAROLD, economist, educator; b. N.Y.C., Aug. 8, 1937; s. Sidney and Florence A.; m. Diane Kleinberg, June 7, 1959; children: Beth, Renee, Heather. BBA, CCNY; MA in Econs; PhD, UCLA. Asso. prof. econs. Brown U., 1966-71; dep. asst. sec. health and planning HEW, 1971-76; dep. dir. for health (Cost of Living Council), 1973-74; dean Florence Heller Grad. Sch., Brandeis U., Waltham, Mass., 1977-92; Sol C. Chaikin prof. Nat. Health Policy, 1992—. Chmn. bd. Univ. Health Policy Consortium; chmn. U.S. Prospective Payment Assessment Commn.; mem. Inst. Medicine, Nat. Acad. Scis., 1978— Author, editor govt. publs., reports. Bd. dirs. Beth Israel Hosp., Brookline, Mass., 1979— . Mem. Am. Public Health Assn. Office: Inst for Health Policy Heller Grad Sch PO Box 9110 Waltham MA 02454-9110

ALTMAN, WILLIAM CARL, health facility administrator, industrial relations specialist, investment company executive, consultant; b. La Grange, Tex., Nov. 11, 1957; s. Lester Arthur and Goldie Bertha (Kretzschmar) A.; m. Danguole Julia Spakevicius, Sept. 2, 1989; children: Darius, Indre, Ilona, Isabella. BS, Tex. A&M U., 1979; BA, MA, Oxford U., Eng., 1982; MBA, Harvard U., 1984. Project dir. Trammell Crow Co., Houston, 1984-85; cons. McKinsey & Co., Inc., Houston, N.Y.C., 1985-89; v.p. Capital Guidance Corp., Houston, 1989-93, sr. v.p., 1993-94; COO Obstet. and Gynecol. Assocs., PA, Houston, 1994-97; exec. v.p. acquistions FemPartners, Inc., Houston, 1997—, also bd. dirs.; mng. dir. Interlaken Ventures, Inc., 2000—.

Bd. dirs. Tredex Tile Corp., Houston, 1991-94, pres., 1993-94. Devel. bd. dirs. Tex. A&M U. Coll. Liberal Arts, College Station, 1987—; bd. dirs. U.S.-Baltic Found., Washington, 1990—, chmn., 1993-96, 2001—; mem. N.Y. coun. on Fgn. Rels., 2000—; mem. Houston com. Coun. on Fgn. Rels., 1990—; co-chair Houston com. Campaign for Oxford, 1990-91; mem. Tex. Rhodes Scholarship Selection com., 1990-91. Recipient Rhodes scholarship Rhodes Scholarship Trustees, Oxford, Eng., 1980. Mem. Harvard Bus. Sch. Club. Republican. Avocations: scouting, politics. Office: Interlaken Ventures Inc 4030 Case St Houston TX 77005-3606

ALTMANN, JEANNE, zoologist, educator; b. N.Y.C., Mar. 18, 1940; BA in Math., U. Alta., Can., 1962; MAT, Emory U., 1970; PhD, U. Chgo., 1979. Rsch. assoc., co-investigator U. Alta., Canada, 1963-65, Yerkes Regional Primate Rsch. Ctr., Atlanta, 1965-67, 69-70; rsch. assoc. dept. biology U. Chgo., 1970-85, assoc. prof. dept. ecology and evolution, 1985-89, prof., dept. ecology & evolution, 1989—98; rsch. curator, assoc. curator primates Chgo. Zool. Soc., 1985—; prof., dept. ecology & evolutionary biology Princeton U., NJ, 1998—, faculty assoc., Office of Population Rsch., 1999—. Hon. lectr. dept. zoology U. Nairobi, Africa, 1989-90; chair com. evolutionary biology U. Chgo., 1991—; bd. sci. dirs. Karisoke Rsch. Ctr., Rwanda, 1980-82, 86-89, acting chairperson, 1980; mem. biosocial perspectives on parent behavior and off-spring devel. com. Social Sci. Rsch. Coun., 1984-91; mem. adv. coun. dept. ecology and evolutionary biology Princeton (N.J.) U., 1991—; mem. rev. com. dept. zool. rsch. Nat. Zool. Park, Smithsonian Inst., Washington, 1992; mem. com. Internat. Ethol. Congress, 1992—; mem. vis. com. dept. anatomy and biol. anthropology Duke U., Durham, N.C., 1993; reviewer manuscripts various jours. Author: (with S. Altmann) Baboon Ecology: African Field Research, 1970, Baboon Mothers and Infants, 1980; editor: Animal Behaviour, 1978-82; consulting editor: Am. Jour. Primatology, 1981—; mem. editorial panel: Monographs in Primatology, 1982-90; mem. editorial bd. Bioscience, 1983-88, ISI Reviews in Animal Science, 1988, Human Nature, 1989-92, Internat. Jour. Primatology, 1990—, Am. Naturalist, 1991—; contbr. articles to profl. jours. Fellow Ctr. Advanced Study in Behavioral Scis., 1990-91. Fellow Animal Behavior Soc. (mem. exec. com 1978-82, 84-87, mem, nominating com. 1987-89, pres. 1985-86), Animal Behavior Soc.; mem. NSF (mem. sci. adv. panel psychobiology program 1983-86, mem. adv. panel for vis. professorships for women 1987, 88, mem. adv. panel conservation and restoration biology 1990, mem. task force behavioral, biol. and social scis. Looking Toward the 21st Century 1990-91, mem. adv. coun. directorate for social, behavioral and econ. scis. 1992—), Internat. Primatol. Soc. (v.p. conservation, mem. exec. com.). Home: 54 Hardy Dr Princeton NJ 08540-1211

ALTMANN, STUART ALLEN, biologist, educator; b. St. Louis, June 8, 1930; s. Maurice Walter and Deborah (Freedman) A.; m. Jeanne Glaser, June 19, 1959; children: Michael Alexander, Rachel Ann BA in Zoology, UCLA, 1953, MA, 1954; PhD in Biology, Harvard U., 1960. Asst. prof. zoology U. Alta., Can., 1960-65, assoc. prof., 1965; sociobiologist Yerkes Regional Primate Rsch. Ctr., 1965-70; prof. anatomy U. Chgo., 1970-80, prof. biology, 1970-88, prof. ecology and evolution, 1988-95, prof. emeritus, 1995—; lectr., prof. ecology and evolutionary biology Princeton (N.J.) U., 1998—. Hon. rsch. assoc. Haile Sellaissie I U., Ethiopia, 1971; exptl. psychology sci. adv. panel NIMH, 1969-73; primate conservation com. NAS-NRC, 1970-72; grant reviewer NSF, NIH, NIMH, Spencer Found., Nat. Geog. Soc., Smithsonian Instn., others Mem. editl. bd. Behavioral Ecology and Sociobiology, 1976-79, Am. Naturalist, 1977-79, Animal Behavior, 1978-79, Ethology, Ecology and Evolution, 1989—; mem. bd. editl. commentators The Behavioral and Brain Scis., 1977-82 Fellow AAAS, Am. Acad. Arts and Scis., Animal Behavior Soc. (pres. 1977, exec. com. 1975-78); mem. Comparative Nutrition Soc., Internat. Primatol. Soc. Avocations: making pottery, orchard farming. Office: Princeton U Dept Ecology Evol Biology Princeton NJ 08544-1003 Office Phone: 609-258-4520. E-mail: salt@princeton.edu.

ALTMEJD, DAVID, artist; b. Can., 1974; BFA, Université du Québec à Montréal, 1998; MFA, Columbia U., 2001. One-man shows include, Andrea Rosen Gallery, NY, 2004, The University 2, 2005, Sarah Altmejd, Galerie SKOL, Montreal, 2003, Galerie Optica, Montreal, 2003, Galerie SKOL, Montreal, 2003, Pointe de chute, Galerie de l'UQAM, Montreal, 2002, Interval, Sculpture Ctr., NY, 2002, Clear Structures for a New Generation, Ten in One Gallery, NY, 2002, Modèles d'esprit et jardins intérieurs, Galerie B-312, Montreal, 1999, Jennifer, Galerie Clark, Montreal, 1998, exhibited in group shows at SCREAM, Anton Kern Gallery, NY, 2004, Whitney Biennial Am. Art, Whitney Mus. Am. Art, 2004, Material Eyes, LFL Gallery, NY, 2003, 8th Istanbul Biennial, Turkey, 2003, Corp. Profits vs. Labor Costs, D'Amelio Terras Gallery, NY, 2003, Demonclownmonkey, Artist Space, NY, 2002. Mailing: c/o Andrea Rosen Gallery 525 West 24th St New York NY 10011*

ALTOMARE, ERICA VON SCHEVEN, psychologist; b. Trenton, N.J., Jan. 11, 1950; d. Eric Kurt and Lorraine (Seabridge) Von Scheven; m. Joseph E. Altomare, Aug. 14, 1971; children: Mikal Melissa, Damon Joseph, Reice Eric. RN, Helene Fuld Sch. Nursing, 1970; BSN, Clarion U., 1986; MA in Clin. Psychology, Edinboro U., 1988; PhD in Counseling Psychology, U. Pitts., 2001. Lic. psychologist; cert. clin. specialist in child and adolescent psychiatry and mental health nursing, cognitive behavioral therapist. Staff nurse N.Y. Hosp., N.Y.C., 1970-71; instr. Northeastern Hosp., Phila., 1971-74, Venango County Vocat. Tech. Sch., Oil City, Pa., 1974-81; psychology intern Meadville (Pa.) Mental Health Clinic, 1988-89; rsch. asst. Cleft Palate Clinic, Erie, Pa., 1987-89; psychotherapist, psychologist PSY Svcs., Titusville, Pa., 1989—96, asst. prof. psychology, 2001—. Instr. U. Pitts., 1989—2000, rsch. asst. Pitt. Mother and Child Project, 1997—99; psychology intern U. Buffalo Counseling Ctr., 2000—01; presenter, counselor Ctrs. N.Y. Conf., 2001. Contbr. articles to various prof. jours. Bd. dirs. Forest/Warren (Pa.) Mental Health Svcs., 1975-78, Forest/Warren Children Svcs., 1975-78, Tionesta (Pa.) Area Health Svcs., Inc., 1976-78, Western Pa. Behavioral Health Network, 1994—; producer Miss Crawford County Scholarship Pageant, Meadville, 1986-89; workshop presenter Titusville Area Hosp., 1989-91. Mem. APA (assoc.), Learning Disabilities Assn. (adv. bd. 1993-2000), Pa. Psychol. Assn., N.W. Pa. Psychol. Assn., Pa. Soc. Behavioral Medicine and Biofeedback, Alliance Mentally Ill of Pa., Soc. Rsch. in Children (writer, rsch. presenter 2003), Am. Cleft Palate Assn. (writer, rsch. presenter 1994). Democrat. Avocations: travel, downhill skiing, racquetball, horseback riding. Home: 700 Rockwood Dr Titusville PA 16354-1244 Office: Univ Pitts Broadhurst Sci Ctr Titusville PA 16354 Office Phone: 814-827-4430. E-mail: altomar@pitt.edu.

ALTON, ANN LESLIE, judge, lawyer, educator; b. Pipestone, Minn., Sept. 10, 1945; d. Howard Robert, Jr. and Camilla Ann (DeMong) A.; m. Gerald Russell Freeman Sr.; children: Brady Michael Alton Freeman, Matthew Alton Freeman (dec.). BA, Smith Coll., 1967; JD, U. Minn., 1970; postgrad., Nat. Jud. Coll., U. Nev., 1989. Bar: Minn. 1970, U.S. Dist. Ct. Minn. 1972, U.S. Supreme Ct. 1981. Apptd. gen. jurisdiction state trial ct. judge civil and criminal jurisdiction Dist. Ct., 4th Jud. Dist., Hennepin County, Minn., 1989—, elected, 1990, 2002—, mem. exec. com. Hennepin County, 1995—98, chair psychol. svcs. com., 1996, vice chair adminstrv. com., 1989-94, asst. county atty. Mpls., 1970-89, felony prosecutor, criminal divsn., 1970-75, acting chief citizen protection divsn., 1975-76, chief citizen protection/econ. crime divsn., 1976-79, chief econ. crime unit, 1979-85, sr. atty. civil divsn. handling labor and employment law, 1989-89, mem. civil com., 1989—, presiding judge probate/mental health div., 1995-98, mem. exec. com., 1995-98, chair psychol. svcs. to ct. com., 1997-2000, 2002. Adj. prof. law Hamline U. Law Sch., St. Paul, 1973-77, 2004—; adj. prof. law William Mitchell Coll. Law, St. Paul, 1977—; adj. prof. U. Minn. Law Sch., 1978-82; lectr. in field, 1970—; sr. faculty Minn. Advocacy Inst., Minn. CLE, 1988—; mem. faculty Nat. Inst. Trial Advocacy, U. Notre Dame Law Sch., 1989—, asst. team leader North Ctrl. Regional Jury Trial Advocacy Course, 1991—; sr. critiquing judge Jud. Trial Skills Tng. Program Minn. Supreme Ct. Continuing Edn. Program for State Cts., 1993—; mem. faculty intensive trial advocacy program Widener U. Sch. of Law, Wilmington, Del., 1993-96; bd. dirs. Pan-O-Gold Realty Co., 1986-89, Alton Realty Co., 1986-89, Alton Found., 1999—. Author articles, pamphlet, manual. Vice-chmn. bd. dirs. Minn. Program on Victims of Sexual Assault, 1974-76; bd. dirs. Physician's Health Plan (now Allina), Health Maintenance Orgn., 1976-80, exec. com., 1977-80; mem. legal drug abuse subcom. Gov. Minn. Adv. Com. Drug Abuse, 1972-74; bd. visitors U. Minn. Law Sch., 1979-85; mem. child abuse project coordinating com. Hennepin County Med. Soc., 1982-83, chmn. corp., labor, ins. subcom., 1982; commr. corrections task force sex offenders, 1999-2001. Recipient Honorable Mention Roscoe Pound award for Excellence in Tchg. Trial Advocacy, Roscoe Pound Inst., Washington, 2000. Mem. ABA (jud. adminstrn. divsn.), Minn. Bar Assn. (criminal law, labor and employment law, civil litigation sects.), Hennepin County Bar Assn. (ethics com. 1973-76, criminal law com. 1973—, vice chmn. 1979-80, 83-84, unauthorized practice law com. 1977-78, individual rights and responsibilities com. 1977-78, labor and employment law com. 1985—, civil litigation com. 1985—), Minn. Dist. Judges Assn. (benefits com. 1991—, mem. program and edn. com. 1993—, mem. worker compensation risk mgmt. com. 1995-97), U. Minn. Law Sch. Alumni Assn. (bd. dirs. 1979-85), Nat. Women Judges, Douglas K. Amdahl Inn of Ct. (master, exec. bd. 2003-). Achievements include pioneering achievement first woman prosecuting felony jury trials for Hennepin County; first to changing state-wide systems for sexual assault and child abuse victims and for battered women. Office: 1251-C Hennepin County Govt Ctr 300 S 6th St Minneapolis MN 55487 Office Phone: 612-348-8105. E-mail: ann.alton@courts.state.mn.us. *The greatest joy and biggest challenge of my life has been the privilege of loving, nurturing and guiding my son. Motherhood is my most rewarding accomplishment. The most important lesson I've learned is that one person with vision, perseverance, and energy can cause significant changes in government, in an organization, in society. My great-grandmother told me, "You can do anything you want to do if you're willing to work hard for it, and don't let anyone tell you otherwise". She was right.*

ALTON, HOWARD ROBERT, JR., lawyer, food company executive, real estate executive; b. Pipestone, Minn., May 12, 1927; s. Howard Robert Sr. and Vera Edna (Boehmke) A.; m. Camilla Ann DeMong; children: Ann, Jeanine, Howard R. III, Patricia, Michelle. BBA, U. Minn., 1950; JD cum laude, Hamline U., 1975. Bar: Minn., 1975, U.S. Ct. Appeals (8th cir.) 1975, U.S. Dist. Ct. Minn. 1976. Founder Hamline Sch. Law, 1972-74, Alton, Severson & Sovis, Apple Valley, Minn., 1978-86, Freeman, Alton & Dodd, Mpls., 1987-88; sr. counsel, chief exec. officer Pan-O-Gold Baking Co., Wayzata and St. Cloud, Minn.; now chmn. With U.S. Marines, 1945-46. Mem. Minn. Young Pres. Orgn. (past chmn.), Minn. Execs. Orgn. Forum (past chmn.), The Mpls. Club, Old Port Cove Yacht Club, North Palm Beach City Club, Gt. Lakes Cruising Club, Wayzata Country Club, Ocean Reef Club, Madaline Island Yacht Club (LaPointe, Wis.), Madaline Island Golf Club. Avocations: conservation, wildlife preservation, power boating. Home and Office: PO Box 619 Wayzata MN 55391-0619

ALTON, N. KIRBY, health facility administrator; B in Zoology, U. Ga., 1974, D in Molecular Genetics, 1981. Joined Amgen, 1981—, dir. therapeutic product devel., 1986, v.p. therapeutic product devel., 1988-92, FDA contact, 1989, sr. v.p. devel., 1992—. Achievements include research in expression of eucaryotic genes in E.coli.

ALTSCHAEFFL, ADOLPH GEORGE, retired civil engineering educator; b. Passaic, N.J., July 20, 1930; s. Ludwig and Crescenz (Liebl) A.; m. Martha Anne Filiatreau, Aug. 6, 1966. BSC.E., Purdue U., 1952, MSC.E., 1955, PhD, 1960. Instr. civil engring. Purdue U., West Lafayette, Ind., 1952-60, asst. prof. civil engring., 1960-64, assoc. prof., 1964-74, prof., 1974-2000, asst. head dept., 1983-91, head geotech. engring., 1994-2000; with Waterways Expt. Sta., C.E., Vicksburg, Miss., 1955, U.S. Geol. Survey, Indpls., 1956. Cons. civil engring. with various architect and contractor firms. Contbr. articles to profl. jours. Served with USAR, 1950—61. Mem.: ASCE, Nat. Soc. Profl. Engrs., Am. Soc. Engring. Edn. Office: Purdue U Civil Engring Bldg West Lafayette IN 47907 E-mail: altsch@ecn.purdue.edu.

ALTSCHUL, ALFRED SAMUEL, airline executive; b. Chgo., Oct. 16, 1939; s. Herman and Lillian (Ginsburg) A.; m. Lynn Silverman, Sept. 8, 1968; children: Howard, Steven, Mark. BS, U. Wis., 1961; MBA, U. Chgo., 1963. CPA Ill. With G.A.T.X. Corp., Chgo., 1965-69, asst. treas., 1967-70, treas., 1970-81; v.p. fin., chief fin. officer Midway Airlines, Chgo., 1981-90, sr. v.p., chief fin. officer, 1990-92; CFO Sage Enterprises, Des Plaines, Ill., 1993-95; exec. v.p., CFO A. Epstein and Sons Internat., 1995-96; v.p., CFO Amtrak, 1996-99, Airlines Reporting Corp., 1999—. Lectr. in field. Served with AUS, 1963—69. Mem. AICPA, Fin. Execs. Inst., Alpha Epsilon Pi. Clubs: Standard (Chgo.). Jewish. Home: 3909 Highwood Court NW Washington DC 20007-2268 Personal E-mail: bigchief@aol.com.

ALTSCHUL, B J, public relations counselor; b. Jan. 28, 1948; d. Lemuel and Sylva (Behr). Student, Goucher Coll., 1965-67; BA, U. South Fla., 1970; MA, U. Md., 1995. Reporter St. Petersburg (Fla.) Times, 1973—74; dir. pub. rels. Valkyrie Press, Inc., St. Petersburg, 1974—77; founding editor Bay Life, Clearwater, Fla., 1977—79, Tampa Bay Monthly, Clearwater, 1977—79; mng. editor Fla. Tourist News, Tampa and Orlando, 1981; founder Capital Comms. of Tampa, 1981; owner, prin. b j Altschul & Assocs. (formerly Capital Comms. of Tampa), 1985—. Mgr. editl. and info. svcs. Va. Pt. Authority, Norfolk, 1985-88; dir. pub. rels. Va. Dept. Agr. and Consumer Svcs., Richmond, 1988-93; adj. faculty Old Dominion U., Norfolk, 1986-88, U. Richmond, 1990, 94, Washington Ctr. for Internships, 1995-96; mgr. pub. rels. U. Md. Biotech. Inst., 1997-99; lectr. dept. comm. U. Md., 1999-2001; asst. prof. Am. U., 2001—. Author: Cracker Cookin' & Other Favorites, 1984; contbg. author: Virginia: A Commonwealth Comes of Age, 1988. Bd. dirs. Pinellas County Big Bros.-Big Sisters, 1980-82, Fla. Folklore Soc., 1984-85. Mem. Fla. Motion Picture and TV Assn. (treas. 1976-78), Hampton Rds. C. of C. (co-chmn. pub. rels. Internat. Azalea Festival 1986, chmn. publs. 1987), Va. Conf. on World Trade (chmn. pub. rels. com.), Downtown Norfolk Devel. Corp. (chmn. urban living com.), Pub. Rels. Soc. Am. (chmn. Mid.-Atlantic Dist. 1988, chmn. govt. sect. 1989, bd. dirs., chmn. chpt. accreditation, chmn. Univ. Rels. Nat. Capital chpt., 2002-), Va. State Agy. Pub. Affairs Assn. (pres. 1990), Internat. Assn. Bus. Communicators (v.p. mem. svcs. Richmond chpt. 1996), Nat. Assn. Sci. Writers, D.C. Sci. Writers Assn. (bd. dirs. 2004—), Forum Agr. and Consumer Topics (founder, chmn. 1992), Sierra Club (mem. Montage Co. environ. edn. com. 2004—). Avocations: piano, Irish set dancing, sailing, classical, folk, and jazz music. Office: b j Altschul & Assocs 14100 Beechvue Ln Silver Spring MD 20906 Personal E-mail: sunrises111@hotmail.com.

ALTSCHULER, BRUCE ROBERT, research dentist; b. Bklyn., Feb. 17, 1947; s. Frank Philip and Sarah Gertrude (Cloder) A.; m. Ruth Phyllis Gass, Oct. 27, 1974; children: Joan Ellen, Wendy Karen, Cheryl Miriam. BA, Bklyn. Coll., 1967; DDS, Temple U., 1971. Lic. dentist Md., Pa., Conn., Maine, N.Y. Commd. capt. USAF, 1971, advanced through grades to col., 1986; project scientist dental holography Dental Scis. Br., Brooks AFB, Tex., 1971-74, chief dental consultation, 1975-76; chief dental laser holography USAF Dental Investigation Svc., Brooks AFB, Tex., 1976-80; chief dental computer/laser tech. USAF Aerospace Medicine, Brooks AFB, Tex., 1980-82; chief avionics advanced systems rsch. group Info. Processing Br., Wright-Patterson AFB, Ohio, 1982-84; dep. optical processing Systems Avionics Div., Wright-Patterson AFB, 1985; dental resident Advanced Clin. Dentistry Residence Program, Eglin AFB, Fla., 1985-86; Air Force rsch. liaison, chief laser imaging U.S. Army Inst. Dental Rsch., Ft. Meade, Md., 1986-94; chief imaging robotics lab. Walter Reed Army Inst. Rsch. Dental Rsch. Detachment, Ft. Meade, Md., 1995-97; dir. rsch. devel. Cobalt Rsch. LLC, 1997—2003, CEO, 2004—. Clin. asst. prof. dept. diagnosis/roentgenology U. Tex. Health Sci. Ctr., San Antonio, 1976-80, dept. dental diagnostic svc., 1980-82; mem. dental x-ray subcom. 26 Am. Nat. Standards Inst., Washington, 1980-85; reviewer NIH Computer Aided Dentistry, Washington, 1987. Editor 3-D Machine Perception; patentee in field. Bd. dirs. Am. Cancer Soc., Bexar County, Tex., 1980-82, mem. pub. edn. com., 1980-82; campaign coord. Avionics Lab. Combined Fed. Campaign, Dayton, Ohio 1984; spl. award judge Alamo Regional Sci. Fair, San Antonio, 1980-82. Mem. ADA, Internat. Assn. Dental Rsch., Soc. Photo Optical Instrumentation Engrs., Air Force Assn., Armed Forces Communications, Electronics Assn., Nat. Def. Indsl. Assn., Md. State Dental Assn., Tex. Dental Assn., Am. Mensa. Republican. Jewish. Avocations: photography, electronics, computers. Home: PO Box 458 Simpsonville MD 21150-0458 Office: Cobalt Rsch LLC PO Box 458 Simpsonville MD 21150-0458 Office Phone: 410-309-6089. E-mail: cobalt-research@starpower.net.

ALTSCHULER, STEVEN M., health facility executive, pediatrician, gastroenterologist; m. Robin L. Altschuler. degree, MD, Case Western. Bd. cert. pediatrician, gastroenterologist. Pediat. residency tng. Children's Hosp., Boston; subspecialty tng., pediat. gastroenterology and nutrition Children's Hosp. Phila.; prof. pediat. U. Penn. Sch. Med., chmn. pediat. dept., 1997; fellow Children's Hosp. Phila., 1982, joined, 1985, physician-in-chief, chmn. dept. pediat., 1997, pres. & CEO, 2000—. Faculty mem. Harvard Med. Sch.; Leonard and Madlyn Abramson endowed chair, pediat. med. Children's Hosp. Phila., chmn. exec. com. Joseph Stokes Jr. Rsch. Inst.; spkr. in pediat. healthcare, gastroenterology, and rsch. Contbr. articles to med. jours., chapters to books. Recipient Janssen award, Janssen Pharmaceutica, 1999. Mem.: No. Am. Soc. Pediat. Gastroenterology, Am. Gastroent. Assn. Sect. on Motility and Nerve/Gut Interaction. Office: Children's Hosp Phila 34th St and Civic Ctr Blvd Philadelphia PA 19104-4399

ALTSHULER, ALAN ANTHONY, dean, political scientist, educator; b. Bklyn., Mar. 9, 1936; s. Leonard M. and Janet A. (Sonnenstrahl) A.; m. Julie C. Maller, June 15, 1958; children: Jennifer, David. BA, Cornell U., 1957; MA, U. Chgo., 1959, PhD, 1961. Instr. Swarthmore Coll., 1960-61; Smith-Mundt vis. asst. prof. Makerere (Uganda) Coll., 1961-62; asst. prof. Cornell U., 1962-66; assoc. prof. MIT, 1966-69, prof. polit. sci. and urban studies and planning, 1969-71, 1975-83, head dept. polit. sci., 1977-82; dean Grad. Sch. Pub. Adminstrn. NYU, 1983-88, dir. Urban Research Ctr., 1986-87; prof. urban policy and planning Kennedy Sch. Govt. and Grad. Sch. Design Harvard U., 1988—; dir. Taubman Ctr. State and Local Govt. Harvard U., 1988—2004, acad. dean Kennedy Sch. Govt., 1993-95; dir. Rappaport Inst. Greater Boston, 1999—2004; dean Grad. Sch. Design Harvard U., 2004—. Sec. transp. and constrn. Commonwealth Mass., 1971-75; dir. Boston Transp. Planning Rev. (part-time), 1970-71. Author: The City Planning Process: A Political Analysis, 1965, Community Control: The Black Demand for Participation in Large American Cities, 1970, The Urban Transportation System: Politics and Policy Innovation, 1979; co-author: The Future of the Automobile, 1984, Regulation for Revenue: The Political Economy of Land Development Exactions, 1993, Mega-Projects: The Changing Politics of Urban Public Investment, 2003; editor: Current Issues in Transportation Policy, 1979; co-editor: The Politics of the Federal Bureaucracy, 1977, Innovation in American Government, 1997, Governance and Opportunity in Metropolitan America, 1999; contbr. articles to profl. jours. Mem. Nat. Acad. Pub. Adminstrn., Am. Acad. Arts and Scis. E-mail: alan_altshuler@harvard.edu.

ALTSHULER, KENNETH Z., psychiatrist, educator; b. Paterson, NJ, Apr. 11, 1929; s. Jacob and Altie (Freedman) A.; m. Gloria Seigel, June 14, 1952 (div. 1981); children: Steven, Lori, Dara; m. Ruth Collins Sharp, Dec. 5, 1987. BA, Cornell U., 1948; MD, U. Buffalo, 1952; DSc (hon.), Gallaudet Coll., 1972. Intern Kings County Hosp., Bklyn., 1952-53; resident NY State Psychiat. Inst., NYC, 1955-58; asst. in psychiatry Columbia U., 1958-59, instr., 1959-63, rsch. assoc., 1963-67, asst. clin. prof., 1967-71, assoc. clin. prof., 1971-75, prof., 1975-77; tng. analyst Columbia U. Psychoanalytic Clinic for Tng. and Rsch., 1969-77; project dir. Essential Aspects of Deafness, 1972-76, Trauma and Sleep Physiology, 1975-77; Stanton Sharp prof., chmn. psychiatry U. Tex.-Southwestern Med. Sch., Dallas, 1977-2000, Stanton Sharp prof. psychiatry, 2000—; tng. analyst New Orleans Psychoanalytic Inst., 1979-86, Dallas Psychoanalytic Inst., 1986—. Chief of deafness unit Rockland State Hosp., Orangeburg, NY, 1966-77; cons. to NIH; dir. Am. Bd. Psychiatry and Neurology, 1990-97, pres., 1996; mem. Nat. Bd. Med. Examiners, 1986-89, chmn. Part II psychiatry com., 1988-89; dir. Tex. Dept. Mental Health and Mental Retardation, 1999-2004; mem. Am. Assn. Chmn. Depts. Psychiatry, 1977-2000, pres. 1990-91. Co-author: Managing Sleep Complaints, 1982; co-editor: Family and Mental Health Problems in a Deaf Population, 1963, Comprehensive Mental Health Svc. for the Deaf, 1966, Psychiatry and the Deaf, 1968, Expanded Mental Health Care for the Deaf, 1970, Depression: Mechanisms, Diagnosis and Treatment, 1986; others.; Contbr. articles to profl. jour. Mem. governing bd. Tex. Sch. for the Deaf, 1986-90; bd. dir. Tex. Dept. Mental Health and Mental Retardation, 1999-2004. Served with USNR, 1953-55. Recipient Wilson award in genetics and preventive medicine, 1961, Disting. Cmty. Svc. award Dallas County Mental Health Assn., 1986, Prism award, 1992, Disting. Alumnus award SUNY, Buffalo, 1993, 1st Trailblazer award named in his honor, Dallas County Mental Health and Retardation Ctr., 1996, Tex. Star award for Outstanding Cmty. Svc. Tex. Mental Health Assn., 1997; named Outstanding Psychiatrist, Tex. Soc. Psychiat. Physicians, 1996, Alumnus of the 1960s Decade Columbia U., 1996; Kenneth Z. Altshuler Clinic named in his honor by the Dallas County Mental Health and Mental Retardation Ctr., 1997; Cert. of Achievement Bd. of Hosp. Psychiatry, Cert. of Significant Achievement for Deafness Program, NY State, 1976, Cert. of Significant Achievement for Mental Health Connections Program, 1995. Fellow Am. Psychiat. Assn., Am. Coll. Psychiatrists, Am. Coll. Psychoanalysts; mem. AAAS, AMA, Am. Psychoanalytic Assn., Assn. for Psychoanalytic Medicine (Merit award 1965), Tex. Med. Soc., Dallas County Med. Soc., Am. Psychopathol. Assn., Assn. Dir. Med. Student Edn. in Psychiatry (founder, v.p. 1976-77), So. Assn. Rsch. Psychiatry (pres. 1993-94). Office Phone: 214-648-5588. E-mail: kenneth.altshuler@utsouthwestern.edu.

ALTSHULER, MIRIAM R., literary agent; d. Bernard and Lillian Altshuler; m. Thomas C. Mansfield, Sept. 6, 1986; children: Caleb Mansfield, Erica Mansfield. BA, Middlebury Coll., Vt., 1983. Asst. Russell & Volkening, N.Y.C., 1983—86, literary agt., 1986—94; pres., literary agt. Miriam Altshuler Literary Agy., Red Hook, NY, 1994—. Mem.: Assn. of Author's Reps. (bd. dirs. 2000—, mem. contracts com. 1989—). Avocations: theater, skiing, horseback riding, reading. Office: Miriam Altshuler Literary Agy 53 Old Post Rd N Red Hook NY 12571 Office Phone: 845-758-9408.

ALTURA, BURTON MYRON, physiologist, educator; b. NYC, Apr. 9, 1936; s. Barney and Frances (Dorfman) A.; m. Bella Tabak, Dec. 27, 1961; 1 child, Rachel Allison. BA, Hofstra U., 1957; MS, NYU, 1961, PhD, 1964. Diplomate Am. Bd. Forensic Med., Am. Coll. Forensic Medicine, Am. Bd. Forensic Examiners, Coll. Pharm. and Apothecary Scis., Am. Assn. Integrative Medicine. Tchg. fellow in biology NYU, 1960—61, instr. exptl. anesthesiology Sch. Medicine, 1964—65, asst. prof. Sch. Medicine, 1965—66; rsch. fellow Bronx Mcpl. Hosp. Ctr., 1967—76; asst. prof. physiology and anesthesiology Albert Einstein Coll. Medicine, N.Y.C., 1967—70, assoc. prof., 1970—74, vis. prof., 1974—78; prof. physiology SUNY Health Sci Ctr., Bklyn., 1974—, prof. medicine, 1992—; mem. Ctr. Cardiovasc. and Muscle Rsch., 1995—; prof. pharmacology SUNY Health Sci. Ctr., Bklyn., 1998—. Mem. spl. study sect. on toxicology Nat. Inst. Environ. Health Scis., 1977—78, 2001; mem. Alcohol Biomed. Rsch. Rev. Com. Nat. Inst. Alcohol Abuse and Alcoholism, 1978—83, mem. spl. study sect. medications, 2002; mem. panel CNF bd. Inst. Med., NAS, 1996—97; adj. prof. biology Queens Coll., CUNY, 1983—84; pres. (hon.) Internat. Symposium on Interactions of Magnesium and Potassium on Cardiac and Vascular Muscle, Montbazon, France, 1984; pres. (hon.), lectr. (hon.) Hungarian Soc. Electrochemistry, Budapest, 1995; organizer, condr. symposia; organizer workshop Nat. Inst. Alcohol Abuse and Alcoholism, 1992; condr., chmn. Gordon Rsch. Conf. on Magnesium in Biochem. Processes and Medicine, 1984; v.p. Internat. Symposium on Magnesium, Blacksburg, 1985; organizer Internat. Workshop Unique Magnesium Sensitive Ion Selective Electrodes, Orlando, Fla., 1993, Crete, 97; judge Am. Inst. Sci. and Tech., 1984—86, 1988—91, 1993, Jr. Acad. N.Y. Acad. Scis., 1987, 1989—90; mem. adv. coun. Nat. Found. Addictive Drugs, 1986—; vis. prof. Yamaguchi U., Japan, 1988, 93, Beijing Coll. Traditional Chinese Medicine, China, 1988, Harvard U. Med. Sch., 1988, U. Tokyo, 1993, Kyoto U. Sch. Medicine, 1993, Kumamoto U., 1993,

U. Copenhagen, 1994, U. Florence, 1994, Humboldt Univ., Berlin, 1995, U. Birmingham, England, 1996, Self Med. Def. Coll., Japan, 1996, U. Calif., Riverside, 1998, Fla. Atlantic U., 1998, Inst. Water, Soil and Air Hygiene, Fed. Health Inst., Berlin, 1991, Max Planck Inst., Dortmund, Germany, 1992, 94, British Min. Defense, Porton Down, Salisbury, England, 2004, Naval Med. Rsch. Ctr., Walter Reed Med. Ctr., Bethesda, Md., 2004, U.S. Def. Threat Reduction Agy., Ft. Belvoir, Va., 2005; vis. prof., lectr. Navy Med. Rsch. Ctr., Walter Reed Med. Hosp. Med. Ctr., NJ, 2004, Def. Threat Reaction Agy., Ft. Belvoir, Va., 2005; CEO, pres. Bio-Defense Sys., Inc., Rockville Center, NY; cons. NSF, Va. Grants Rev. Com., Nat. Heart, Lung, and Blood Inst., Nat. Inst. Drug Abuse; lectr., spkr. in field. Author: Microcirculation, 3 vols., 1977—80, Vascular Endothelium and Basement Membranes, 1980, Pathophysiology of the Reticuloendothelial System, 1981, Ionic Regulation of the Microcirculation, 1982, Handbook of Shock and Trauma, Vol. 1: Basic Science, 1983, Magnesium and the Cardiovascular System, 1985, Cardiovascular Actions of Anesthetic Agents and Drugs Used in Anesthesia, vol. I, 1986, vol. II, 1987, Magnesium, Stress and the Cardiovascular System, 1986, Magnesium in Biochemical Processes and Medicine, 1987, Magnesium in Clinical Medicine and Therapeutics, 1992, Unique Magnesium-Sensitive Ion Selective Electrodes, 1994; editor-in-chief: Physiology and Patho-physiology Series, 1976—81, Microcirculation, 1980—84, Magnesium: Exptl. and Clin. Rsch., 1981—89, Microcirculation, Endothelium and Lymphatics, 1984—, Magnesium and Trace Elements, 1990—, mem. editl. bd.: Jour. Circulatory Shock, 1973—85, Advances in Microcirculation, 1976—92, Jour. Cardiovasc. Pharmacology, 1977—84, Prostaglandins, Leukotrienes and Fatty Acids, 1978—2001, Substance and Alcohol Actions/Misuse, 1979—84, Alcoholism: Clin. and Exptl. Rsch., 1982—87, assoc. editor: Jour. Artery, 1974—, Microvasc. Rsch., 1978—85, Agts. and Actions, 1981—88, Biogenic Amines, 1985—88, Jour. Am. Coll. Nutrition, 1982—94, Frontiers in Biosci., 1996—, Internat. Jour. Cardiovasc. Medicine, Surgery and Biomechanics, 1997—; contbr. over 900 articles to profl. jours.; patentee in field. Recipient Rsch. Career Devel. award USPHS, 1968-72, Silver medal for furthering French-U.S. sci. rels. Mayor of Paris, 1984, Medaille Vermeille, French Nat. Acad. Medicine, 1984, Travel awards NIH, 1968, Am. Soc. Pharm. and Exptl. Therapeutics, 1969, Golden Hippocrates award, Haifa, Israel, 2002, Chancellor's Outstanding Inventor of Yr. award SUNY, 2002, Medal for Lifetime of Basic Med. Rsch. and Tchg., Haifa, Israel, 2002, Seelig award Gordon Rsch. Conf. on Magnesium, 2005; grantee NIH, 1968—, NIMH, 1974-78, Nat. Heart Lung Blood Inst., 1974-86, Nat. Inst. Drug Abuse, 1979-83, Nat. Inst. Alcohol Abuse and Alcoholism, 1990-; named Eminent Fellow, Wisdom Hall of Fame, 1999, Winston Churchill Fellow, Wisdon Hall of Fame, 2000. Fellow: AAAS, Molecular Medicine Soc., Royal Australian Chem. Inst., Am. Soc. Angiology, Nat. Acad. Clin. Biochemistry, Am. Heart Assn. (coun. basic sci. 1969—, coun. on thrombosis 1971—, coun. on stroke 1973—, cardiovasc. A study sect. 1978—81, coun. on circulation 1978—, coun. on high blood pressure 1978—, coun. on cardiopulmonary circulation 1987—, coun. on arteriosclerosis, thrombosis, and vascular biology 1997—, coun. on cardiovascular basic scis. 2001—, fellow coun. on high blood pressure rsch. 2002, rsch. grants rev. com. N.E. 2004—), Am. Coll. Angiology, Am. Bd. Forensic Examiners (life), Am. Soc. Integrative Medicine (life), Am. Coll. Forensic Examiners (life), Internat. Coll. Angiology, Am. Inst. Chemists, Am. Coll. Nutrition (Seelig award 2002), Assn. Clin. Scientists, Am. Physiol. Soc. (circulation group 1971—, pub. info. com. 1980—84); mem.: APHA, AAUP, AHA N.E. Study Section, AM Physiol. Soc., Internat. Soc. Free Radical Rsch., Am. Soc. Biochemistry and Molecular Biology, Am. Inst. Biol. Sci., Internat. Soc. Police Surgeons, Am. Med. Writers Assn., Nat. Coun. for Magnesium and Cardiovasc. Disease, Am. Assn. Pharm. Scis., Inter-Am. Soc. Hypertension, Am. Soc. Hypertension (founder), Internat. Soc. for Hypertension, Internat. Anesthesia Soc., Coun. Biology Editors, N.Y. Soc. Electron Microscopy, N.Y. Heart Assn., N.Y. Acad. Scis. (com. mem.), Am. Soc. Magnesium Rsch. (exec. dir. 1984—, founder, pres., symposium chmn. and organizer), Am. Soc. Bone and Mineral Rsch., Am. Soc. Cell Biology, The Oxygen Soc., Am. Soc. Zoologists, Am. Microscopical Soc., Am. Assn. Lab. Animal Sci., Soc. for Xenobiotics, Internat. Platform Assn., Soc. Scholarly Pub., Soc. Nutrition Edn., Soc. of Parenteral and Enteral Nutrition, Liposome Soc., Internat. Soc. Exposure Analysis, Reticuloendothelial Soc., Soc. Cardiovasc. Pathology, Soc. Environ. Geochemistry and Health (hon lectr., symposium organizer), Soc. Leukocyte Biology, Internat. Soc. Biorheology, Biomed. Optics Soc., Internat. Soc. Biomed. Rsch. on Alcoholism (founder), Am. Soc. Microbiology, Am. Inst. Nutrition, Fedn. Am. Soc. Exptl. Biology (pub. info. com. 1981—86), Internat. Anesthesia Rsch. Soc., Neurotrauma Soc., European Conf. Microcirculation (symposium organizer), Microscopy Soc. Am., Am. Fedn. Clin. Rsch., Shock Soc. (founder, hon. lectr., symposium organizer), Soc. for Neurosci., Am. Thoracic Soc., Soc. for Critical Care Medicine, Rsch. Soc. on Alcoholism, Am. Oil Chemists Soc., Rsch. Soc. on Alcoholism (hon lectr., symposium organizer), Am. Coll. Toxicology, Harvey Soc., Endocrine Soc., Am. Soc. Nutritional Scis., Am. Soc. Pharm. and Exptl. Therapeutics (symposium organizer, Hon. lectr.), Am. Chem. Soc., Am. Soc. Headache, Am. Assn. for Clin. Chemistry (hon. lectr.), Soc. Exptl. Biology and Medicine (editl. bd. 1976—83), Microcirculatory Soc. (nominating com. 1973—74, past exec. coun., hon. lectr.), Am. Soc. Investigative Pathology, Soc. for Magnetic Resonance, Sigma Xi. Office: 450 Clarkson Ave Brooklyn NY 11203-2056 Office Phone: 718-270-2194. E-mail: baltura@downstate.edu.

ALUMBAUGH, JOANN MCCALLA, magazine editor; b. Ann Arbor, Mich., Sept. 16, 1952; d. William Samuel and Jean Arliss (Guy) McCalla; m. Lyle Ray Alumbaugh, Apr. 27, 1974; children: Brent William, Brandon Jess, Brooke Louise. BA, Ea. Mich. U., 1974. Cert. elem. tch., Mich. Assoc. editor Chester White Swine Record Assn., Rochester, Ind., 1974-77; prodn. editor United Duroc Swine Registry, Peoria, Ill., 1977-79; dir., pres. Nat. Assn. Swine Records, Macomb, Ill., 1979-82; free-lance writer, artist Ill. and Nat. Specific Pathogen Free Assn., Ind. producers, Good Hope, Emden, Ill., 1982-85; editor The Hog Producer Farm Progress Publs., Urbandale, Iowa, 1985-99; exec. editor Nebr. Farmer, Kans. Farmer, Mo. Ruralist, We. Beef Prodr., Beef Prodr., Farm & Fireside, 1999—2003; dir. comms. Farms.Com, 2003—. Family Living Program, Farm Progress Show, 1985-2004, Master Farm Homemaker Program, 1989-99; mem. U.S. Agrl. Export Devel. Coun., Washington, 1979-82, apptd. mem. Blue Ribbon Com. on Agr., 1980-81. Contbr. numerous articles to profl. jours. Precinct chmn. Rep. Party, Linden, Iowa, 1988; mem. Keep Improving Dist. Schs., Panora, Iowa, 1990-91; v.p. Sunday sch. com. Sunset Circle, United Meth. Ch., Linden, 1990-91; pres. PTA, Panorama Schs., Panora, 1993-94; coach Odyssey of Mind Program World Competition, 1994—. Mem.: Iowa Master Farm Homemakers, Guthrie County Prok Prodrs., McDonough County and Ill. Porkettes (county pres. 1978—79, Belleringer award 1979), Nat. Pork Prodrs. Coun., Iowa Pork Prodrs. Assn. (legis. com. 1990—95, hon. master pork prodr.), U.S. Animal Health Assn., Am. Agrl. Editors Assn. (chmn. dist. svc. com. 1991, master writer 1997, pres.-elect 1998, pres. 1999, chmn. adv. coun. 1999—2002, co-chmn. comm. clinic, chmn. comms. clinic, trustee 2002—, World of Difference award 1995, Oscar in Agr. 1999), Internat. Platform Assn. Avocations: reading, painting, flower gardening. Home: 2644 Amarillo Ave Linden IA 50146-8029 Office: PigChamp Aspen Business Park 426 S 17th Ames IA 50010 Office Phone: 641-744-2114.

ALUMBAUGH, RONALD P, music educator; b. Joplin, Mo., Apr. 25, 1961; s. Alfred Paul and Barbara Lucille Alumbaugh; m. Terri Jo Alumbaugh, Nov. 10, 1984; 1 child, Lauren Madison; children: Logan Paul, Taylor Jo. BS in music edn., Mo. So. State U.; MS in choral conducting, Mo. State U. Vocal music tchr. Couch R-1 H.S., 1984—87; dir. choral activities and condr. El Dorado Springs R-2 H.S., 1987—. Nominee Disney Tchr. of the Year; recipient Dist. Tchr. of the Yr. Mem.: Cmty. Teachers Assn., Am. Choral Dir. Assn., Mo. Music Educators Assn., Music Educators Assn., Optimist Internat., Hazel Dell Missionary Bapt. Ch., Scottish Rite Mason, Tri-M Honor Soc. Mailing: 3320 S 315 Rd El Dorado Springs MO 64744

ALUTTO, JOSEPH ANTHONY, dean, management educator; b. Bronx, N.Y., June 3, 1941; s. Anthony and Concetta (Del Prete) Alutto; m. Carol Newcomb, Sept. 9, 1948; children: Patricia, Christina, Kerrie, Heather. BBA, Manhattan Coll., Riverdale, N.Y., 1962; MA, U. Ill., 1965; PhD, Cornell U., 1968. Asst. prof. orgnl. behavior SUNY, Buffalo, 1966-72, assoc. prof., 1972-75, prof., 1975-91, dean Sch. Mgmt., 1976-91, Clarence S. Marsh chair mgmt., 1991; dean Fisher Coll. of Bus. Ohio State U., Columbus, 1991—, exec. dean for profl. coll., 1998—. Bd. dirs. United Retail Group, Inc., Nationwide Fin. Svcs.; pres., bd. dirs. M/I Homes. Author: (with others) Theory Testing in Organizational Behavior: The Varient Approach, 1983; contbr. 65 articles to profl. jours. United Way, Buffalo, 1982—91; pres. Amherst Cen. Sch. Bd., 1982—86. Mem. APA, AAAS, Acad. Mgmt. (pres. Ea. divsn. 1980-81), Am. Sociol. Assn., Capital Club, Athletic Club. Office: Ohio State U Fisher Coll of Bus 201 Fisher Hall 2100 Neil Ave Columbus OH 43210-1309 Office Phone: 614-292-2666. Business E-Mail: alutto.1@osu.edu.

ALVA, SALVADO, food products executive; b. 1951; With Pepsico Inc., 1973—; Pres., Pepsico. Internat. Foods Latin Am. Former pres. Mexican Assn. for Electronic Commerce; mem. Bd. dirs. Maxicom Telecomunicaciones, 2001-02. Office: Pepsico Internat Avenue Lazaro Cardenas 2404 Pte Garza Garcia Mexico

ALVARADO, LINDA G., construction executive; Doctorate (hon.), Dowling Coll. Pres., CEO Alvarado Constrn., Inc., Denver, 1976—. Owner Colorado Rockies franchise; corp. dir. 3M, Pepsi Bottling Group, Pitney Bowes and Lennox Industries. Chmn. bd. dirs. Denver Hispanic C. of C.; commrs. White House Initiative for Hispanic Excellence in Edn. Named Revlon Bus. Woman of Yr., 1996, Bus. Woman of Yr., U.S. Hispanic C. of C., 1996, 100 Most Influential Hispanics in Am., Hispanic Bus. Mag., others; recipient Nat. Minority Supplier Devel. Coun. Leadership award, 1996, Sara Lee Corp. Frontrunner award, 2001, Horatio Alger award, others; inducted into Nat. Women's Hall of Fame, Colo. Women's Hall of Fame. Office: Alvarado Construction 1266 Santa Fe Dr Denver CO 80204-3546

ALVARADO, PABLO, day laborer organizer & immigrant rights activist; b. El Salvador; married; 2 children. High Sch. teaching credential, Universidad de El Salvador, 1989. Prog. coord. Inst. of Popular Edn. of So. Calif., 1991—95; lead coord., day labor project Coalition for Humane Immigrant Rights, LA, 1995—2002; nat. coord. Nat. Day Laborer Organizing Network, LA, 2002—. Named one of 25 Most Influential Hispanics, Time Mag., 2005; recipient Leadership for a Changing World award, 2004. Office: National Day Laborer Organizing Network Ste 101 2533 W Third St Los Angeles CA 90057*

ALVARE, CHARLES DAGUERRE, television producer; s. Carlos J. and Mary J. H. Erskine Alvare; m. Carrie Rudolf, Oct. 10, 1999. BA, Columbia Coll., 1979; MPhil, Cambridge U., 2003. Mktg. dir. Praxis Film Works, North Hollywood, Calif., 1983—86; exec. prodr. EUE/Screen Gems, Burbank, Calif., 1986—88; ind. prodr. LA., N.Y.C., London, 1989—99; pres. Sanctuary Media, Hollywood, 2000—02. Lectr. Los Angeles City Coll., 2004—. Mem.: ATAS (Emmy Awards) (judge), Delta Psi. E-mail: sanctuarymedia@hotmail.com.

ALVAREZ, AIDA, former federal agency administrator; b. Aguadilla, P.R., July 22, 1949; BA cum laude, Harvard U., 1971; LLD (hon.), Iona Coll., 1985. News reporter, anchor Metromedia TV, N.Y.C.; reporter N.Y. Post, N.Y.C.; mem. N.Y.C. Charter Revision Commn.; v.p. N.Y.C. Health and Hosps. Corp., 1984—85; investment banker 1st Boston Corp., N.Y.C., San Francisco, 1986-93; dir. Office Fed. Housing Enterprise Oversight, Washington, 1993-97; adminstr. Small Bus. Adminstrn., 1997-2001. Mem. bd. dirs. PacifiCare Health Systems Inc., 2003-, Former mem. bd. dirs. Nat. Hispanic Leadership Agenda, N.Y. Cmty. Trust, Nat. civic League; former chmn. bd. Mcpl. Assistance Corp./Victim Svcs. Agy., N.Y.C.; N.Y. State chmn. Gore Presdl. Campaign, 1988; nat. co-chmn. women's com. Clinton Presdl. Campaign, 1992; mem. President's Econ. Transition Team, 1992. Recipient Front Page award, award for excellence AP, 1982, Emmy nomination for reporting guerrilla activities in El Salvador. Democrat. Home: 3051 New Oak Ln Bowie MD 20716-1349

ALVAREZ, BRYAN, newsletter editor, writer; b. Seattle, June 12, 1975; s. Carlos Moya Alvarez, Valerie Gibson. Co-host, Wrestling Observer Live Radio www.eyada.com, www.sportsbyline.com, N.Y.C., 1999—; Editor, publisher Figure Four Weekly Newsletter, Woodinville, Wash., 1995—; Wrestling Columnist Penthouse Magazine, New York, NY, 2000—01, Wrestlingobserver.com, San Jose, Calif., 1998—. Editor: (Newsletter) Figure Four Weekly, 1995; author: (Penthouse wrestling articles) Mat Max!, 2000. Gymnastics coach Cascade Elite Gymnastics, Leading Edge Gymnastics, Lynnwood, WA, 1989—2001. Avocation: Wrestling, bodybuilding, gymnastics. Office: Figure Four Weekly PO BOX 426 Woodinville WA 98072 Office Phone: 425-485-0384. E-mail: bryan@wrestlingobserver.com.

ALVAREZ, CESAR L., lawyer; b. Havana, Cuba, June 17, 1947; arrived in US, 1960; m. Kathleen Alvarez; children: Elizabeth, Christopher, Kathryn, Colleen. AA, Miami-Dade CC; BS, U. Fla., 1969, MBA, 1970, JD with high honors, 1972. Bar: Fla. 1973. Joined Greenberg Traurig LLP (Greenberg Traurig Hoffman Lipoff Rosen & Quentel until 1998), Miami, Fla., 1973, pres., CEO, 1997—; exec. v.p. Air Fla., 1981—82. Mem. U. Fla. Legal Aid and Defender Clinic, 1971-72. Editor U. Fla. Law Rev., 1972. Participant Guardian Ad Litem Program, Miami; trustee Vizcaya Found., Our Kids Inc., Nat. Found. for Advancement in the Arts, Miami Art Mus., Manhattanville Coll., NY, Fla. Internat. U. Found., John S. and James L. Knight Found., 2000—; mem. exec. com. New World Symphony; bd. dirs. Holocaust Documentation and Edn. Ctr. Inc.; chair adv. bd. Fla. Internat U. Law Sch.; chmn. bd. dirs. United Way of Miami-Dade, 2003—04. Named one of 100 Most Influential Hispanics, Hispanic Bus., 1996, 1998, 100 Most Influential Lawyers in Am., Nat. Law Jour., 1997, 2000, 100 Most Powerful People in Miami, Miami Bus. Mag., 2001, 100 Most Powerful People in So. Fla., So. Fla. CEO Mag., 2002, 50 Most Powerful People in So. Fla., Poder Mag., 2003, 2004, 100 Most Powerful Latinos, 2003, 2004, 2004 Legal Elite, Fla. Trend mag., Top Lawyers in So. Fla., So. Fla. Legal Guide, 2004; named to Miami-Dade CC Hall of Fame, 2003; recipient Humanitarian of Yr. Award, Women's Internat. Zionist Orgn., 1997, Atty. of Yr. Award, Hispanic Nat. Bar Assn., 2001, Golden Castanets Award, Ballet Hispanico, 2002, Silver Medallion for Svc. to Humanity Award, Nat. Conf. for Cmty. and Justice, 2003, New Am. Award, Archdiocese of Miami, Inc., 2003, Diversity Works! Advocate-Individual Award, So. Fla. Bus. Jour., 2004. Mem.: Miami Bus. Forum, Fla. Coun. of 100, Dade County Bar Assn., Fla. Bar, Cuban-Am. Bar Assn. (Pro-Bono Award), ABA, Cuba Study Group, Order of Coif. Office: Greenberg Traurig LLP 1221 Brickell Ave Miami FL 33131

ALVAREZ, GOAR N., pharmacist; arrived in U.S., 1962; s. Manuel A. Alvarez and Maura E. Perez; m. Alina M. Roiz, May 27, 1983; 1 child, Nicole M. BS in Pharmacy, Fla. A&M U., 1975; PharmD, Nova Southeastern U., 1994. Lic. pharmacist Fla., Ala. Staff pharmacist Pasteur Clinics Pharmacy, Hialeah, Fla., 1976—77, Budget Pharmacy, Miami, 1976—77; pres. Mega Profl. Pharmacy, Miami, 1977—96, Mega Pharmacy II, Miami, 1982—87; freelance cons. pharmacy Fla., 1996—99; dir. Pharmacy Svcs. Coll. Pharmacy Nova Southeastern U., Ft. Lauderdale, Fla., 1999—, asst. prof., 1999—, asst. dean pharmacy svcs., 2002—; dir. pharmacy South Fla. State Hosp., Pembroke Pines, Fla., 2001—. Cons. in field; mem. pharmacy network com. Broward County Health Dept., 1999—; mem. adv. com. Agy. Health Care Adminstrn., 2001; numerous coms.; expert witness in field; presenter, lectr. in field. Contbr. articles to profl. jours. Active in numerous cmty. health fairs and events, 2000—. Scholar, Pfizer, 2004, Scholastic Achievement and Cmty. Pharmacy Svc., 2004. Fellow: Am. Soc. Consultant Pharmacists; mem.: Broward County Pharmacy Assn., Dade County Pharmacy Assn. (mem. exec. com. 1992—, chmn. exec. com. 1998—99, chmn. contg. edn. com. 1993—96, pres. 1997—98, chmn. membership com. 1999—2001, mem. legis. com. 2002—04), Am. Coll. Clin. Pharmacists, Am. Assn. Colls. Pharmacy, Nat. Assn. Cmty. Pharmacists, Am. Pharmacy Assn., Fla. Pharmacy Assn. (Dade county del. 1996—, mem. exec. com. 1997—99, chmn. various councils 1999—, mem. exec. com. 2002—, mem. James H. Beal award com. 2003—04, mem. nominations com. 2003—, James H. Beal award 2002, Pharmacist of Yr.), Mortar and Pestle Soc., Alpha Kappa Mu, Phi Lambda Sigma. Office: 3200 S University Dr Fort Lauderdale FL 33328

ALVAREZ, JULIA, writer; b. NYC, 1950; Attended, Conn. Coll., Bread Loaf Sch. English, Middelbury Coll.; BA summa cum laude, Middlebury Coll., 1971; MFA, Syracuse U., 1975. Poet-in-the-schools, Ky., 1975—78, 1975—78, 1975—78; prof. creative writing and English Phillips Andover Acad., Mass., 1979—81, U. Vt., 1981—83, U. Ill., 1985—88; prof. English Middlebury Coll., 1988—. Jenny McKean Moore vis. writer George Wash. U., 1984. Author: (novels) How the Garcia Girls Lost Their Accents, 1991 (selected as notable book Am. Libr. Assn., 1992), In the Time of Butterflies, 1994, The Other Side, 1995, YO!, 1997, Something to Declare, 1998, In the Name of Salomé, 2000, The Secret Footprints, 2000, How Tia Lola Came to Stay, 2001, A Cafecito Story, 2001, Before We Were Free, 2002, (poetry) The Woman I Kept to Myself, Homecoming: New and Collected Poems. Recipient Benjamin T. Marshall Poetry Prize, Conn. Coll., 1968, 1969, prize, Acad. Am. Poetry, 1974, poetry award, La Reina Press, 1982, Third Woman Press award, first prize in narrative, 1986, award for younger writers, Gen. Elec. Found., 1986, syndicated fiction prize for "Snow" grant from Ingram Merrill Found., PEN, 1990, Josephine Miles award, PEN Oakland, 1991; grantee, Nat. Endowment Arts, 1987—88; creative writing fellow, Syracuse U., 1974—75, Robert Frost Poetry fellowship, Bread Loaf Writers' Conf., 1986, Kenan grant, Phillips Andover Acad., 1980, exhbn. grant, Vt. Arts Coun., 1984—85. Office: Susan Berghol Literary Svcs 17 W 10th St 5B New York NY 10011 Office Phone: 212-387-0545. Office Fax: 212-387-0546.

ALVAREZ, MARIANNE, artist, photographer, educator; b. Miami, Nov. 27, 1930; d. Walter Knox and Irma Margaret (Rempe) Payne; m. Jack Alvarez, Dec. 19, 1969. B in Art Edn., U. Fla., 1959; MA, U. South Fla., 1967; postgrad., S.E. Ctr. for Photographic Studies, Daytona Beach, 2001. Adminstrv. sec. Walter Reed Army Med. Ctr., Washington, 1952-58; art tchr. Sligh Jr. H.S., Tampa, 1959-60, Tyrone Jr. H.S., St. Petersburg, 1960-61, Dunedin (Fla.)-Highland Jr. H.S., 1961-66; media specialist Volusia County Secondary Schs., Daytona Beach, Fla., 1967-90. One-woman shows include The Capitol, Tallahassee, 1997, two-person show, Art League of Daytona Beach, 2002, exhibited in group shows at Art League Daytona Beach, 1986—, exhibitions include Carnegie Mus. Natural History, Pitts., 1992, 1994, 1996, Cork Gallery, Lincoln Ctr., N.Y.C., 1994, U. Mobile, Ala., 1995, Charles Summer Sch. Mus., Washington, 1995, Mobile Mus. Art, 1996, Walter Greer Gallery, Hilton Head, S.C., 1997, Cen. Arts Collective, Tucson, 1998, S.E. Mus. Photography, Daytona Beach, Fla., 1999, Harris House, New Smyrna Beach, Fla., 1999, William Benton Mus. Art, U. Conn., Storrs, 2000, Ormond Meml. Art Mus., 2002, Represented in permanent collections Fla. Art in State Bldgs. program, Fla. State Capitol, William Benton Mus. Art, U. Conn., Storrs, S.E. Mus. Photography, Daytona Beach, Fla., Halifax Collection, ArtHaus Found., Port Orange, Fla., work on display, Nassau County Health Dept., Fernandina Beach, Yulee, also pvt. collections. Mem. Jr. League Daytona Beach. Recipient Grumbacher Gold Medallion award, 1995, numerous others. Mem. Nat. League Am. Pen Women (pres. 2000-02), Fla. Ret. Educators Assn., Volusia County Ret. Educators Assn., Beaux Arts Volusia, Ormond Meml. Art Mus., Ormond Beach, Daytona Beach, Mus. Arts and Scis., Art League of Daytona Beach, Delta Kappa Gamma Soc. Internat., Alpha Delta Pi Alumnus. Democrat. Roman Catholic. Home and Studio: 2727 N Atlantic Ave Apt 611 Daytona Beach FL 32118-3047 Personal E-mail: jamaimages@aol.com.

ALVAREZ, OFELIA AMPARO, medical educator; b. Havana, Cuba, Mar. 29, 1958; BS, U. Puerto Rico, 1978, MD, 1982. Diplomate Nat. Bd. Med. Examiners, Am. Bd. Pediat., Sub-bd. Pediatric Hematology-Oncology. Pediatric residency Univ. Children's Hosp., San Juan, P.R., 1982-85; fellow pediatric hematology, oncology Children's Hosp. L.A., 1985-88; asst. prof. pediat. Loma Linda (Calif.) U., 1988-95, assoc. prof., 1995-2000; assoc. prof. clin. pediats. Univ. Miami, 2001—. Med. advisor Candlelighters, Inland Empire, 1988-2000. Contbr. articles to profl. jours. Bd. mem., med. advisor Make-A-Wish Found., Inland Empire, 1994-95. Clin. oncology fellow Am. Cancer Soc., 1985-86; pediatric rsch. fund Loma Linda U., 1993-95. Fellow: Am. Acad. Pediat.; mem.: AAUW, Histiocyte Soc., Am. Soc. Hematology, Am. Soc. Pediatric Hematology/Oncology, Am. Soc. Clin. Oncology, Beta Beta Beta. Roman Catholic. Office: Univ Miami Divsn Pediats Hematology Oncology Dept Pediats PO Box 016960 Miami FL 33101 E-mail: oalvarez2@med.miami.edu.

ALVAREZ, RALPH, food service executive; BBA cum laude, U. Miami, Fla. Various pos., including mng. dir. Burger King Spain, pres. Burger King Can., regional v.p. Fla. region Burger King Corp., 1977—89; divsn. v.p.-Fla. to corp. v.p. Wendy's Internat. Inc., 1990—94; dir. devel. for No. Calif. McDonald's Corp., 1994, regional v.p., Sacramento region, regional dir., Chipotle Mex. Grill, pres. McDonald's Mex., pres., ctrl. divsn., McDonald's USA, 2001—03; COO, exec. v.p. McDonald's USA, Oak Brook, Ill., 2003—04, pres., 2004—05, McDonald's N. Am., 2005—. Office: McDonald's USA 1 McDonald's Plz Oak Brook IL 60523*

ALVAREZ, RODOLFO, sociology educator, consultant; b. San Antonio, Oct. 23, 1936; s. Ramon and Laura (Lobo) A.; m. Edna Rosemary (Simons), June 25, 1960 (div. 1984); children: Anica, Amira. Cert. European Studies, Inst. Am. Univ., Aix en Provence, France, 1960; BA, San Francisco State U., 1961; MA, U. Wash., 1964, PhD, 1966. Tchg. fellow U. Wash., Seattle, 1963—64; asst. prof. Yale U., New Haven, 1966—72; dir. Chicano Studies Rsch. Ctr. Univ. Calif. at Los Angeles, 1972—74, assoc. prof. sociology, 1972—80, prof., 1980, chair under grad. coun., 1995—97. Vis. lectr. Wesleyan Univ., Middletown, Conn., 1970; founding dir. Spanish Speaking Mental Health Rsch. Ctr., 1973-75. Author: Discrimination in Organizations: Using Social Indicators to Manage Social Change, 1979; Racism, Elitism, Professionalism: Barriers to Cmty. Mental Health, 1976; mem. editorial bd. Social Sci. Quar., 1971-86. Pres. ACLU So. Calif., 1980-81, sec., treas. 1999, pres. Westwood Dem. Club, Calif., 1977-78, v.p. 2003-; trustee Inst. for Am. Univ., Aix en Provence, France, 1968—; bd. dir. Mex. Am. Legal Def. and Ednl. Fund, 1975-79, 88-92; mem. adv. commn. on housing 1984 Olympic Organizing Com., 1982-84; chmn. bd. dir. Narcotics Prevention Assn., L.A., 1974-77; mem. bilingual adv. com. Children's TV Workshop, N.Y.C., 1979-82; candidate rep. Nat. Dem. Platform Com., Washington, 1976; alt. del. Nat. Dem. Conv., N.Y.C., 1976; bd. dir. Univ. Credit Union, 1985-92, chmn. strategic plan com., 1987-92. Sgt. USMC, 1954-57. Pres. Mgmt. Fellow U. Calif., 1994-95; recipient citation meritorious svc. for devel. of Nat. Fed. Offenders Rehab. and Rsch. Program, State of Wash., 1967. Mem. Internat. Sociol. Honor Soc. (pres. 1976-79), Am. Sociol. Assn. (mem. coun. 1982-85, chair person sect. racial and ethnic minorities 1989-90, assoc. editor Am. Sociol. Rev. 1989-91, chairperson sect. on sociol. practice 1990-91), Soc. Study of Social Problems (bd. dir. 1982-87, pres. 1985-86), Pacific Sociol. Assn. (mem. coun. 1979-83, 87-89, v.p. 1991-93, pres. 1996-97), Architectural Rev. Bd. City of Santa Monica, Calif., 2002-, Marines Meml. Club, Village Rotary Club (pres. 2004-2005), Rotary Internat. (exec. aide, 2005—) Office: UCLA Dept Sociology 405 Hilgard Ave Los Angeles CA 90095-1551 Business E-Mail: alvarez@soc.ucla.edu.

ALVAREZ, SCOTT G., lawyer; b. 1955; BA in Econ., Princeton U., 1977; JD cum laude, Georgetown U., 1981. Joined bd. as staff attorney Fed. Res. Sys., Washington, 1981—85, bd. sr. attorney, 1985, asst. gen. counsel, 1989—91, assoc. gen. counsel, 1991—2004, legal divsn./gen. counsel, 2004—. Office: Fed Res Sys Legal Divsn Rm 1046A 20th & C Sts NW Office Washington DC 20551-0001 Office Phone: 202-452-3000. Office Fax: 202-452-3101. Business E-Mail: scott.alvarezs@frb.gov.

ALVAREZ, THOMAS, foundation administrator, writer, consultant; b. Ft. Wayne, Ind., Jan. 1, 1948; s. Raul and Felicitas (Vargas) A. Student, Purdue U., 1965-69. Prodr., dir. McGraw-Hill Broadcasting Co. Inc./WRTV-TV, Indpls., 1973-88; pres. The Alvarez Group Inc., Indpls., 1988-98; mng. dir. Edyvean Repertory Theatre, 1998-99; pres. Alvarez Resource Group, Indpls., 1999-2001; mng. dir. Ballet Internationale, 2000-2001; exec. dir. Freetown Village Living History Mus., 2001—02, Mundo Latino, 2002, Beacon Health

Found., 2002—03; dir. devel. Fairbanks, 2003—05; prodr. Ideavenue, 2005—. Freelance journalist Indpls. Star, Indpls. Monthly, Nuvo, Arts Inc., Ind. Bus. Mag., Indpls. New Times, Mundo Latino, La Guia; arts reporter Across Ind., WFYI-TV, 1991-93, mem. adv. coun.; cmty. adv. coun. Sta. WRTV, 1993-96, Sta. WFYI-FM, 1991-93; adj. faculty dept. journalism Ind. U., Indps., 1995-97. Prodr., dir. (documentaries) A Portrait of La Gente, 1975, Dave Baker: A Medley, 1976, Concord Today, 1977, Nine Leaves on a Sprig: The Story of Madame C.J. Walker, 1977, Domestic Violence, 1977, 500 Miles: Yesterday and Today, 1979, Tuckaway, 1982, Under the Influence, 1983, Rag to Bop: A Memoir of Indianapolis Jazz, 1984, A Woman's Story, 1985, Indiana State Museum: Living the Legend, 1986, Indiana Repertory Theatre: The First Fifteen Years, 1986, Solid Gold Years, 1987; prod. James Dean & Me: Nineteenth Star, 1995 (Telly award 1997, Emmy award 1997), The Rythm Makers: A Chronicle of Indiana Jazz, 1996. Bd. dirs. Phoenix Theatre, Indpls., 1982-85, First Step, Inc., 1988-90, Ind. Film Soc., 1988-90, ARC, 1989, United Way Cen. Ind., Greater Indpls. Coun. on Alcoholism, 1993, Damien Ctr., 1996-98, Indpsl. Animal Care and Control, 2004—, Madame Walker Theatre Ctr., 2005; founder, chair Festival of New Can. Cinema, 1988-89; active Ind. Cares, Inc., 1991-93, Indpls. Men's Chorus, 1992-96; adv. com. Arts. Coun. Indpls., 1996. Recipient Casper award Cmty. Svc. Coun. Indpls., 1974, CEBA award of merit Advt. and Comm. to Black Cmty. Inc., 1981, Nat. Coun. on Family Rels. award, 1984, Arti award, 1991, Minority Bus. and Profl. Achievers award, 1999; Hispanic Am. Svc. Achievement award, 2003, Hispanic Edn. Ctr. Lifetime Acheivement award (HASA), 2003; Links Celebrity Barbecue & Grille, 2003, fellow media arts Ind. Arts Commn. Avocations: travel, cinema, running, gardening, photography. Home and Office: 850 Broadway St Indianapolis IN 46202 E-mail: talvarez@gmail.com.

ALVAREZ, TIRSO REYES, JR., engineer; b. San Antonio, Dec. 26, 1948; s. Tirso and Casimira (Reyes) A.; m. Melinda Marie Jaurequi, May 12, 1975 (div. Feb. 1998); children: Sonya Marie, Tirso Adrian. With electro-motive divsn. GM, Commerce, Calif., 1970-82, 92-97; electronic motors technician A/R Delco, Signal Hill, Calif., 2000—; with G.M.C./U.A.W. Nat. Employee Placement Ctr. Svs. Parts Ops., Rancho Cucamonga, Calif., 2003—. Democrat. Roman Catholic. Avocations: fishing, automotive repairs, hiking, boating. Home: 2599 Walnut Ave Unit 229 Signal Hill CA 90755-3672 Mailing: PMB 337 2201 E Willow St Ste D Signal Hill CA 90755-2148 Office: GMC/UAW Nat Employee Placement Ctr Svc Parts Ops 9150 Hermosa Ave Rancho Cucamonga CA 91730 Office Phone: 800-886-3913, 909-477-5804. Personal E-mail: tralvarezjr@aol.com. E-mail: signalmailboxplus@yahoo.com.

ALVAREZ-BORLAND, ISABEL, Spanish educator; b. Sagua la Grande, Cuba, Apr. 8, 1949; came to U.S., 1962, naturalized, 1969. B.A. in Spanish and French, Lycoming Coll., 1970; M.A., Middlebury Coll., 1972; Ph.D., in Spanish Am. Lit., Pa. State U., 1980. Tchr. Spanish, French, Watchung Hills Regional High Sch., 1970-74; teaching asst. Pa. State U., 1974-79; instr. French and Spanish, Dubois Campus, Pa. State U., 1979-80, asst. prof. Spanish, 1980-81; asst. prof. Spanish Coll. Holy Cross, Worcester, Mass., 1981-84, assoc. prof., 1985— . Author: Discontinuidad y ruptura en Guillermo Cabrera Infante, 1982. Contbr. articles to profl. jours. Grantee Coll. Liberal Arts, 1980, Dubois Ednl. Found., 1980, Southland Corp., 1985; fellow Coll. of Holy Cross, 1982, 85, NEH, 1983. Mem. Am. Assn. Tchrs. Spanish Portuguese, MLA, NE Modern Lang. Assn., Asociacion Internacional de Hispanistas, Istituto Internacional de Literatura Iberoamericana, Sigma Delta Pi, Phi Sigma Iota.

ALVAREZ DE DECLARIS, MARIA CLEMENCIA, writer, educator; b. Santafe de Bogota, D.C., Dec. 14, 1944; d. Luis Maria and Stella (Botero) A. de DeC.; m. Nicholas DeClaris. AA in Tchrs. Edn. cum laude, AA in Gen. Studies cum laude, Howard C.C., 1977, AA in Tchrs. Edn. cum laude, 1978; cert. translation, Georgetown U., 1978; BA cum laude, U. Md., 1982, MA in Spanish and Latin Am. Lit., 1986; PhD in Modern Langs. and Lit., Cath. U. of Am., 1995. Adj. prof. Spanish U. Md., College Park, 1983-86, 96, Montgomery Coll., Rockville, Md., 1987-95, The Cath. U., Washington, 1989, 1992, 1996—98, The Am. U., Washington, 1997—. ESL coord. Comfenalco, Santa Fe de Bogota, 1979; course designer to teach practical Spanish, 1987, 87, 88. Mem. organizing com. Internat. Book Fair, Gaithersubrg, 1998—; mem. large treasury Magdalena Found., Alexandria, 1993; vosl. translator, collaboratory Colombian Assn. of Vol. Work, 1997—; vol. broadcaster, literary segment Colombia canta para el mundo, Radio Borinquen WILC, 1996-2000. Mem. MLA, Instituto Cultural Hispano, Mid. Atlantic Coun. of Latin Am., Asociacion Internat. Colombianistas. Avocations: travel, music, ancient history, arts. Home: 8518 Beaufort Dr Fulton MD 20759-9632 Office: Am Univ 4400 Massachusetts Ave Washington DC 20016 E-mail: Alvarez@american.edu.

ALVAREZ-GALLOSO, ROBERTO C., mental health professional; b. Akron, Ohio, Mar. 5, 1962; m. Marlene de la Caridad Melendez, July 25, 1992; 1 child, Veronica Maria. Student, U. Akron, 1980-81; MD, U. Cen. del Este, Dominican Republic, 1985. Cert. profl. in utilization rev. Observer VA Med. Ctr., Miami, Fla., 1990-92, mental health assoc., 1992—; office mgr. E. G. Hernandez, MD, PA, Miami, 1998-99. Author: (book) Defensive Documentation and More/Documentation Preventiva, 2004. Mem. Nat. Assn. for Health Care Orgns. Avocations: stamps, coins, dxing, ping pong/table tennis, swimming. Personal E-mail: AlvarezGalloso@terra.com.

ALVARIÑO DE LEIRA, ANGELES (ANGELES ALVARIÑO), biologist, oceanographer; b. El Ferrol, Spain, Oct. 3, 1916; came to U.S., 1958, naturalized, 1966; d. Antonio Alvariño-Grimaldos and Carmen Gonzalez Diaz-Saavedra; m. Eugenio Leira-Manso, Mar. 16, 1940; 1 child, Angeles. BS Letters and Humanities summa cum laude, U. Santiago de Compostela, Spain, 1933; M in Natural Scis., U. Madrid (now U. Complutense), 1941, Doctorate cert., 1951, DSc summa cum laude, 1967. Cert. biologist-oceanographer, 1951, Spanish Inst. Oceanography. Prof. biology Univ. Coll., El Ferrol, Spain, 1941-48; fishery rsch. biologist dept. Sea Fisheries Spain, 1948-52; histologist Superior Coun. Sci. Rsch., 1948-52; biologist, oceanographer Spanish Inst. Oceanography, 1952—57; biologist Scripps Inst. Oceanography-U. Calif. San Diego, LaJolla, 1958—69; fishery rsch. biologist Nat. Marine Fisheries Svc. S.W. Fisheries Sci. Ctr., NOAA, U.S. Dept. Commerce, La Jolla, 1970-87; emeritus scientist Nat. Marine Fisheries Svc. S.W. Fisheries Ctr., NOAA, U.S. Dept. Commerce, La Jolla, 1987—; assoc. prof. U. Nat. Autonomous Mexico, 1976, San Diego State U., 1979-82; rsch. assoc. U. San Diego, 1982—84. Vis. prof. Inst. Poly. Tech. Mexico, 1982—, U. Parana, Brazil, 1982. Author: Spain and the First Scientific Oceanic Expedition (1789-1794) Malaspina and Bustamante with the Corvettes "Descubierta" and "Atrevida", 2000, 2d deluxe edit., 2003; contbr. over 100 articles to profl. jours., chpts. to books; discovered 22 new species of oceanic animals and the indicator species for various oceanic currents, ocean dynamics, and the study of the biotic environment of fish spawning grounds, study of plankton predators and the impact in fisheries, bunch of plankton populations carried by ships into exotic oceanic areas and throughout interoceanic canals, studies on Chaetognatha and Siphonophora in all world oceans and of Hydromedusae in the Atlantic, Pacific and Indian oceans; studies on the reproductive processes in Chaetognatha, others. Brit. Coun. fellow, 1953-54, Fulbright fellow, 1956-57; NSF grantee, 1961-69, U.S. Office Navy grantee, 1958-69, Calif. Coop. Oceanic Fishery Investigations grantee, 1958-69, UNESCO grantee, 1979; recipient Great Silver Medal of Galicia, Spain, presented by King Juan Carlos and Queen Sofia of Spain, 1993. Fellow Am. Inst. Fishery Rsch. Biologists, Natural History Assn.; mem. Am. Assn. Rschrs. on Marine Scis. Achievements include discovery of biotic differences in the habitat of various fishes; sci. work on the fauna represented in about 100 color plates from specimens of plankton, fishes, turtles, birds. It includes a total of near 200 species collected along the South Atlantic and Pacific (up to Alaska, western Pacific Islands, the Philippines, Australia and back to Spain), during oceanic sci. expedition of 1789-1794 with specific identification, description, behavior and distribution; scientist in British, U.S., Mexican and Spanish research vessels in cruisers and expeditions in the Atlantic and Pacific Oceans. Home: 7535 Cabrillo Ave La Jolla CA 92037-5206

ALVERSON, ELIZABETH M., writer, media consultant; b. Philadelphia, Pa., Sept. 14, 1961; d. Charles T and Nancy H. McAllister; m. Dean Alverson; 1 child, Joshua T. Flowers. Pub. policy mgr. YWCA Greater Atlanta, Atlanta, 1989—92; exec. dir. Georgians for Choice, Atlanta, 1992—95; v.p., pub. affairs and mktg. Planned Parenthood LA, Los Angeles, Calif., 1995—97; exec. dir. Ga. Network to End Sexual Assault, Atlanta, 1997—2000; cons. The Alverson Group, Alpharetta, Ga., 2000—. Author: (short fiction) Flea Market (Georgia's Newest and Most Promising Writers, 2004). Trainer, edn. for global responsibility YWCA, New York, NY, 1991—92; mem. Foster Care Jud. Rev. Panel, Atlanta, 1993—93, Greene Fund Adv. Com., Atlanta, 2000—00; pres. LWV, Norcross, Ga., 1985—87; mem. Hadassah-Nes Harim, Alpharetta, Ga., 2004—; pres. of bd. Ga. Abortion & Reproductive Rights Action League, Atlanta, 1998—2000; participant, uganda, africa travel study: the feminization of poverty YWCA of the USA, New York, NY, 1991—91; com. mem. Nat. Family Planning and Reproductive Health Assn., Washington, 1996—97; co-producer Atlanta Women's Voices Pub. TV Series, Atlanta, 1991—92. Recipient Commendation Pub. Svc., Calif. Bd. Equalization, 1997, Pro-Choice Woman Achievement, Nat. Coun. of Jewish Women - Atlanta, 1995, 20 Women Making a Mark on Atlanta, Atlanta Mag., 2000. Independent. Jewish. Avocations: reading, gardening, sewing. Office: The Alverson Group 11585 Jones Bridge Rd Ste 420-303 Alpharetta GA 30022 Office Phone: 770-416-8315. Personal E-mail: liz@lizalverson.com.

ALVERSON, WILLIAM H., lawyer; b. Rockford, Ill., July 23, 1933; AB, Princeton U., 1955; LL.B., U. Wis., 1960. Bar: Wis. 1960. Currently mem. firm Godfrey & Kahn. Pres. Milw. Profl. Sports and Services, 1972-76; chmn. Houston Rockets basketball team, 1977-79; chmn. bd. govs. Nat. Basketball Assn., 1975-76. Mem. Milw., Am. bar assns., State Bar Wis., Phi Delta Phi. Office: 780 N Water St Milwaukee WI 53202-3512

ALVES, DONALD W., emergency physician, educator; b. Ariz., 1968; s. L. and E. Alves; m. Michele Alves, 1998; 1 child, Kaitlyn Marie. BS, Calif. State U., Sacramento, 1990; MD, Ea. Va. Med. Sch., Norfolk, 1997; BS, Madison U., Gulfport, Miss., 2003; MS, U. Md., Balt., 2005. Diplomate Am. Bd. Emergency Medicine. Internal medicine intern Ea. Va. Med. Sch., Norfolk, 1997—98; resident in emergency medicine Morristown, NJ, 1998—2001; fellow in EMS U. Md., Balt., 2001—03; tactical physician Md. State Police, Balt., 2003—; adj. asst. prof. U. Md., Balt., 2004—; basic trauma life support med. dir. State of Md., Balt., 2004—; asst. prof. U. Md. Sch. Medicine, Balt., 2004—, EMS fellowship dir., 2004—. Recipient EMS Fellowship Recognition Award, NAEMSP, 2004. Fellow: Am. Coll. Emergency Physicians; mem.: AMA, Internat. Tactical EMS Assn., Nat. Assn. of EMS Educators, Nat. Collegiate EMS Found. (life), Am. Coll. of Forensic Examiners (life), Law Enforcement Alliance of Am. (life), Am. Criminal Justice Association-LAE. Episcopalian. Avocations: swimming, reading, antiques, wood working, model trains. Office: University Maryland School of Medicine 419 West Redwood Street Ste#280 Baltimore MD 21201 Office Fax: 410-328-8028. Personal E-mail: Border1099@aol.com.

ALVES, KYRIN JEAN, cultural organization administrator, educator; b. Milw., Sept. 5, 1949; d. Donald Eugene Bailey and Lila Anna Monday; m. David Vierra Alves, Dec. 9, 1967 (div. 1973); children: Sean David, Kyle Vierra. AS in Bus. Adminstrn., Pima CC, 1977, AAS in Computers, 1987; BA in Philosophy and Classics, U. Ariz., 1980; MEd, Northern Ariz. U., 1997. Cert. CC tchr. Ariz. Project controls adminstrn. Hughes Aircraft Co., Tucson, 1973-79; prin., co-owner Computers for People, Tucson, 1983-84; sr. budget rsch. analyst Pima County Govt., Tucson, 1981-82, 85-88, info. sys. mgr., 1989-94; prof. Kazakh State Acad. Arch. and Construction, Almaty, Kazakhstan, 1994; pres., CEO Rebuilding Together Tucson, 1994—. Instr. Pima CC, 1987—96. Mem. Met. Housing Commn., Tucson, 1994—96, Almaty Sister City Com., Tucson, 1993—95; dir. Vets. Transitional Housing Project, 1993—95; mem. adv. bd. Homeless Mgmt. Info. Sys. Project, 2004—. Recipient Women on the Move award, YWCA, Tucson, 1995, Exemplary Mgmt. award, Booz Allen Hamilton, Washington, 1999, Dynamic Duo award, Compass Health Care, Tucson, 1999, Best of Pima award, Pima Coll., Tucson, 1992, 2002, Outstanding Svc. award, Old Pueblo Rotary, Tucson, 2003. Mem.: Housing Rehab. Collaborative (co-chair 1999), Southern Ariz. Home Bldrs. Assn. (remodelors coun., sec. 1995—2001). Democrat. Avocations: travel, reading, learning. Business E-Mail: kyrin@rebuildingtogethertucson.org.

ALVINE, ROBERT, industrialist, philanthropist, entrepreneur; b. Newark, Aug. 25, 1938; s. James C. and Marie Alvine; m. Diane C. Marzulli, May 6, 1961 (div. 1995); children: Robert James, Laurie Anne. BA, Rutgers U., 1960; postgrad., Syracuse U., 1968-69; grad. PMD, Harvard Bus. Sch., 1972; DHL (hon.), U. New Haven, 2000. With Celanese Corp., 1960-77; bus.gen. mgr. nylon products Celanese Plastics Co., Newark, 1967-69, bus. gen. mgr. polyolefin products, 1969-72; sr. dir. mktg. and ops. Celanese Piping Systems and Fabricated Products Co., Hilliard, Ohio, 1972-75; v.p., gen. mgr. comml. Celanese Polymer Spltys. Co., Louisville, 1975-77; v.p gen. mgr. Uniroyal Tire Co., 1977—80; pres., CEO Uniroyal Merchandising Co., 1977—82, Uniroyal Development and Internat., 1980—82; sr. v.p. strategic planning, corp. devel. mktg. and capital planning Uniroyal, Inc. Worldwide, 1977—82; CEO, COO Uniroyal Engineered Products & Svcs., Worldwide, 1982-87; founder, chmn., CEO I-Ten Mgmt. Corp., Woodbridge, Conn., 1987—; founder, chmn., CEO, I-Ten Capital Corp., Woodbridge, 1987, Aim Capital Group, Woodbridge, 1987—; chmn., CEO, prin. shareholder Charter Power Sys. (now C&D Techs. Inc.), Blue Bell, Pa., 1988—95; entrepreneur, prin., sr. oper. bus. leader Charterhouse Group Internat., Inc., N.Y.C., 1988—96; vice-chmn., CEO, major shareholder AP Parts Mfg. Co., Toledo, 1989—94; prin., dir. Internat. Automobile Products Holdings Corp., N.Y.C., 1990—96; prin. owner, chmn. Premier Subaru, Bradford, Conn., 2001—. Prin. Uniroyal Holdings, Waterbury, Conn., 1985—; trustee Uniroyal Liquidating Trust, 1985—; sr. oper. ptnr., mem. investment com. Desai Capital Pvt. Equity Investors, 1999—; chmn. compensation com., strategic com., exec. com., chmn. spl. com., chmn. pension com., bd. EDO Corp., 1995—; trustee Jackson Labs., Bar Harbor, Maine, 1997—, mem. exec. com. capital campaign, chmn. rsch. resources com., mem. devel. com., 1998—; adv. bd. Polaris Fund, N.Y.C., 1996-99; bd. govs. U. New Haven, 1998, chmn. audit com., chmn. exec. com., chmn. commn. on future of U. New Haven, 1998-2000, bd. govs., 2000—, chmn. bd. govs., 2000—, chmn. bd. govs., chmn. exec. com., 2000—, chair Presdl. search com., 2003; chmn. Henry Lee Inst. Forensic Scis., 1998—; sr. oper. 1999—. Bd. dirs., trustee Nat. Theater of the Deaf, Chester, Conn., 1994—, chmn. bd. dirs., 1995—98, hon. chmn., 1999—2002; bd. dirs. Wildlife Conservation Soc., NY, 1994—2002; trustee Long Wharf Theatre, New Haven, 1993—, exec. fin. com., chmn. bus. devel. com., strategy com.; mem. adv. bd. Arts Scis. Coun., Rutgers U., NJ; mem. Navy War Coll. Found.; mem. sch. bus. adv. bd. U. New Haven; mem. Assn. Governing Bds. of Univs. and Colls.; state chmn. United Way Campaign, 1975; hon. trustee Parent's TV Coun., 2001—; chmn. state campaign United Way, 1975; mem. Rep. Presdl. Task Force, Pres.'s Roundtable, Citizens Against Govt. Waste, Presdl. Legion of Merit; Conn. state chmn. Congl. Bus. Adv. Coun., 2002. With U.S. Army, 1961—68, active duty Cuban Missile Crisis, 1962. Recipient citations, awards and recognitions including Disting. Leadership award proclaimed by Congl. Bus. Adv. Coun., 2002, Man of Yr. for Outstanding Accomplishments, 1991, Disting. Bus. Achievement and Svcs. to the Nations award, 1984, Presdl. Legion Merit, Honor grad. Southeastern Signal Sch., 1962, Proclamation for Supreme Achievement Within the Internat. Cmty., 1986; named Ky. Col., Gov. Ky., 1976. Mem.: VFW, Nat. Paint and Coatings Assn, Soc. Chemie Industriale, Mfg. Chemists Assn, Soc. Plastics Engrs. (past dir.), Battery Coun. Internat., Rubber Mfrs. Assn., Nat. Assn. Corp. Growth, Nat. Planning Inst., World Affairs Coun.-Conn., Am. Inst. Mgmt., Assn. Governing Bd. of Univ. and Coll., Nat. Adv. Coun., Pres.'s Assn., Nat. Assn. Corp. Dirs., Soc. Plastics Industry (sr.; past dir., Industry Legend Honor for plastic milk, juice and water bottles 1971), Nat. Campaign for Tolerance and Wall of Tolerance (founding mem.), New Haven Colony Hist. Soc., Newcomen Soc. Am. (Conn. com.), Coun. of Ams., Nat. Maritime Hist. Soc., Nat. Trust for Hist. Preservation, So. Conn. Ellis Island Found. (charter mem.), U.S. Naval Inst., WWII Meml. Found. (charter founding mem., founder Nat. Law Enforcement Officers Meml.), U.S. Senatorial Inner Circle, U.S. Navy Meml. Found. (charter founding mem.), Commanders Club, Harvard Bus. Sch. Club Conn., Columbus House, Rutgers Alumni Assn., Renaissance Club, Harvard Bus. Sch. Club Greater N.Y., Harvard Bus. Sch. Alumni Assn., U. New Haven Legacy Soc., Oaklane Country Club, Am. Legion, Chi Phi. Achievements include leading corporate officer for world's largest management led leveraged buyout of Uniroyal Inc. in 1985. Home: 55 N Racebrook Rd Woodbridge CT 06525-1407 Office Phone: 203-387-1550. Office Fax: 203-389-5153.

ALVING, BARBARA, federal agency administrator, hematologist, oncologist; BS with highest distinction, Purdue U.; MD cum laude, Georgetown U., 1972. Joined dept. hematology and vascular biology Walter Reed Army Inst. Rsch., 1980, chief dept. hematology and vascular biology; dir. hematology/med. oncology sect. Washington Hosp. Ctr., 1997—99; rsch. investigator Divsn. Blood and Blood ProductsFDA Bur. Biologics; leader divsn. blood diseases and resources Nat. Heart, Lung and Blood Inst. NIH, Bethesda, Md., 1999—2001, dep. dir. Nat. Heart, Lung and Blood Inst., 2001—03, acting dir. Nat. Heart, Lung and Blood Inst., 2003—. Editor 3 books; contbr. articles to profl. jours. Achievements include patents in field. Office: Nat Heart Lung and Blood Inst Bldg 31 31 Center Dr MSC 2486 Bethesda MD 20892-2846

ALVIS, JOEL LAWRENCE, JR., minister; b. Memphis, Nov. 12, 1955; s. Joel Lawrence Sr. and Martha Jean (Lowe) A.; m. Vicki Lynn Welch, Aug. 12, 1978; children: Joel Lawrence III, Mark Thomas. BA, Samford U., 1977; MA, U. Miss., 1980; PhD, Auburn U., 1985; MDiv, Louisville Presbyn. Theol. Sem, 1989. Ordained to ministry Presbyn. Ch. (U.S.A.), 1989. Local ch. history and records adminstr. Presbyn. Hist. Found., Montreat, N.C., 1982-86; rsch. assoc. Louisville Presbyn. Sem., 1986-89; pastor St. Pauls (N.C.) Presbyn. Ch., 1989-97; assoc. pastor St. Luke's Presbyn. Ch., Dunwoody, Ga., 1998—2003, interim ministry spec., 2003—. Mem. com. on ministry Coastal Carolina Presbytery, 1990-93, moderator of Presbytery, 1997. Author: (with others) Diversity of Discipleship, 1991, Religion and Race: Southern Presbyterians, 1946-1983, 1994. Mem. congl. ministry team Greater Altanta Presbyn. Ch., com. preparation of ministry, 2005—. Recipient Nelson R. Burr prize Hist. Soc. of Episcopal Ch., 1981, Book award N.C. Presbyn. Hist. Soc., 1995; Univ. fellow U. Miss., 1977-78, Anderson fellow Louisville Presbyn. Theol. Sem., 1991.

ALVORD, JOEL BARNES, retired bank executive; b. Manchester, Conn., Nov. 29, 1938; s. Martin Earl and Elizabeth (Barnes) A.; m. Anne Stilson, June 23, 1962; children: Sarah, Seth. AB, Dartmouth Coll., 1960, MBA, 1961. Joined Hartford Nat. Corp., Conn., 1963, exec. v.p. investments and exec. v.p., 1976-78, pres., 1978-88, chief exec. officer, 1986-88, chmn., 1988—95, also bd. dirs.; chmn. Conn. Nat. Bank subs. Shawmut Nat. Corp., 1986—96; chmn., chief exec. officer Shawmut Nat. Corp., 1988-95; chmn. Fleet Fin. Group, Boston, 1995-98, chmn. exec. com., 1998-99. Dir. Hartford Steam Boiler Inspection and Ins. Co. Bd. dirs. Inst. of Living, Hartford; dir. Jobs for Mass.; active Mass. Bus. Roundtable, Mus. Fine Arts, Boston, the Backers Roundtable the Wadsworth Atheneum Hartford, Wang Ctr. for the Performing Arts, Boston. Congregationalist.

ALWANI, AHMED J., dean, consultant; b. Dec. 17, 1964; arrived in U.S., 1984; s. Taha Jabir and Saadia Al Alwani; m. Ilham Ahmad Totonji, June 19, 1990. BSME, King Saud U., Saudi Arabia, 1987; M in Engring. Adminstrn., George Washington U., 1990; PhD in Human Resources Develop., Va. Tech., 2003. Plant supt. Piedmont Poultry, Lumber Bridge, NC, 1990—95, Mountaire Corp., Lumber Bridge, 1995—97; exec. dean GSISS, Leesburg, Va., 1998—. Bd. trustees Heritage Edn. Trust, Va., 2002—, GSISS, 2002—. Tchrs. evaluation and selection com. Adam Ctr., Herndon, Va., 2002—03; edn. and workforce develop. com. Loudoun County Econ. Develop. Commn., Va., 2000—. Mem.: Acad. Human Resource Develop., Assn. Expl. Edn., Assn. Supervision and Curriculum Develop., Phi Kappa Phi. Office: GSISS Ste 303 45150 Russell Branch Pkwy Ashburn VA 20147 E-mail: aalwani@siss.edu.

ALWARD, RUTH ROSENDALL, nursing consultant; d. Henry Rosendall and Freda Jonkman; m. Samuel Alward, Jan. 17, 1976. RN, Butterworth Hosp. Sch. Nursing, Grand Rapids, Mich.; BSN summa cum laude, Hunter Coll./CUNY, N.Y., 1980; MA Tchrs. Coll., Columbia U., 1982, EdM, 1983, EdD, 1986. Sr. clin. nurse Wadsworth VA Hosp., L.A., 1966-68; exec. dir. nursing Care Corp, Grand Rapids, Mich., 1968-71; nursing cons. Humana Inc., Louisville, 1972-76; asst. prof., dir. nursing adminstrn. grad. prog. Hunter Coll., CUNY, N.Y.C., 1986-90; pres. Nurse Exec. Assocs., Inc., Washington, 1990—; series editor Delmar Pubs. Inc., Albany, 1993-96. Co-author: The Nurse's Shift Work Handbook, 1993, The Nurse's Guide to Marketing, 1991; contbr. articles to profl. jours.; mem. editorial adv. bd. Jour. of Nursing Adminstrn. Bd. dirs., past pres. James Lenox House Assn.; bd. dirs. IONA Sr. Svcs., 1998-2004. Mem. Va Nurses Assn. (mem. fin. com.), Nat. League Nursing (treas. D.C. chpt.), Am. Orgn. Nurse Execs., Sigma Theta Tau. Home and Office: 2011 N St NW Washington DC 20036-2301 Office Phone: 202-728-2956. E-mail: ruthalward@aol.com.

ALWES, CHESTER LEE, JR., music educator; b. Lousville, Nov. 5, 1947; s. Chester Lee and Myra (Pound) Alwes; m. Martha Anne Lafferty, Aug. 21, 1971 (div. Jan. 13, 2000); children: Christopher Michael, Jonathan David, Benjamin Andrew. BA, Hanover Coll., 1969; SMM, Union Theol. Sem., N.Y.C., 1971; DMA, U. Ill., 1980. Tchg. asst. U. Louisville, 1972—73; instr. Coll. Wooster, Ohio, 1973—77; asst. prof. U. Rochester, NY, 1980—82; from asst. prof. to assoc. prof. U. Ill., Urbana, 1982—. Music dir. Baroque Artists Champaign, Ill., 1996—. Dir. music Grace Luth. Ch., Champaign, 1983—. Named Disting. Alumnus, Hanover Coll., 1989. Mem.: Music Tchrs. Nat. Assn., Am. Choral Dirs. Assn. (bd. dirs. 1983—98, Julius Herford Dissertation prize 1982). Avocations: fishing, golf, travel, reading. Office: U Ill Sch Music 1114 W Nevada Urbana IL 61801 Home: 101 Peacock Dr Mahomet IL 61853-9112 Business E-Mail: c-alwes@iuc.edu.

ALY, ALAA H., environmental engineer, consultant; b. Giza, Egypt, Sept. 28, 1965; s. Hassan Aly and Monira Abd El-Naby; m. Ghada F Saad, May 19, 1969; children: Noor, Sarah. BSc in Civil Engring., Cairo (Egypt) U., 1987; MS with hons. in Stats., PhD with hons. in Irrigation Engring., Utah State U., 1998. Registered profl. engr., Colo., 2000, Fla., 2000, cert. ground water profl., Nat. Ground Water Assn., 2000. Asst. rsch. prof. Utah State U., Logan, Utah, 1997—98; dir. water resources Waterstone Environ. Engring., Boulder, Colo., 1999—2001; sr. engr. INTERA, Niwot, Colo., 2001—. Contbr. articles to profl. jours. Mem.: ASCE, Am. Water Resources Assn., Phi Kappa Pi. Achievements include development of demand forecasting approach for municipalities; design of groundwater remediation systems; development of software for integrated hydrologic systems; optimal management software. Office: Intera 137 2nd Ave Niwot CO 80544 Office Phone: 303-652-8899.

ALYKOVA, VALENTINA, musician, music educator; b. Moscow, June 22, 1949; arrived in U.S., 1991; d. Trifon Alykov and Zoya Alykova; m. Vladimir Binevitch, Jan. 19, 1991. M in Musical Arts, Moscow Conservatory, 1973; postgrad., Gnessin Musical Pedagogical Inst., Moscow, 1980. Violin instr. Music Sch. for Gifted Children, Moscow, 1973—77; asst. prof. Gnessin Musical Pedagogical Inst., Moscow, 1978—82; violinist Moscow String Quartet, 1973—96; artist-in-residence Lamont Sch. Music, Denver U., 1991—96; violin instr. Forte Acad. Music, Littleton, Colo., 1997—. Recipient Second prize, Internat. Quartet Competition, Budapest, Hungry, 1978, Grand Prix and First prize, Internat. Quartet Competition, Evian, France, 1979; grantee, Colo. Coun. on the Arts, Denver, 1999, 2000. Mem.: Music Tchrs. Nat. Assn. Russian Orthodox. Avocations: reading, travel, mahjong. Home: 14299 E Arizona Ave Aurora CO 80012 Office: Forte Acad Music Ste 15 10143 W Chatfield Ave Littleton CO 80127-4245 E-mail: walter2B@aol.com.

AL-ZUBAIDI, AMER AZIZ, physicist, researcher; b. Najaf, Iraq, June 10, 1945; came to U.S., 1974; s. Aziz Allawi and Shahai Ali (Al Fartousi) A.; m. Haifa M. Al-Zubaidi, Aug. 24, 1972; children: Samer, Akrum. BS in Physics,

U. Baghdad, Iraq, 1966; MS in Physics, Pa. State U., 1976, postgrad., 1977, 81, Va. Poly. Inst. and State U., 1977-82. bd. dirs. KCIK. High sch. tchr. Inst. for Tchrs., Riyadh, Suadi Arabia, 1966-68; high sch. tchr. physics, math., and related scis. Saudi Ministry of Edn., Riyadh, 1966-68; high sch. tchr. physics, math., mem. phys. lab. supplies and equipments com. Agrl. Vocat. Sch., Iraqi Ministry Edn., Baghdad, 1968-74; grad. teaching asst. Va. Poly. Inst. and State U., Blacksburg, 1976-82, rsch. sci. nuclear physics, 1982—; owner Al's Internat. Editor-in-chief Al-Kufa, 1994. Chmn. bd. dirs. Kufa Ctr. of Islamic Knowledge, editor-in-chief newsletter; min. Mem. Union of Concerned Scientists, Sigma Xi. Home: 2319 10th St NW Roanoke VA 24012-3929 Office Phone: 540-563-8471. Personal E-mail: aal_zubaidi@hotmail.com.

AMABILE, JOHN LOUIS, lawyer; b. N.Y.C., Oct. 13, 1934; s. John A. and Rose (Singer) A.; m. Christina M. Leary, Nov. 23, 1963; children: Tracy Ann, John Christopher. BS cum laude, Coll. Holy Cross, 1956; LLB, St. John's Sch. Law, 1959. Bar: N.Y. 1959, U.S. Dist. Ct. (so. and ea. dists.) N.Y. 1961, U.S. Supreme Ct. 1964, U.S. Ct. Claims 1964, U.S. Ct. Appeals (2d cir.) 1970, U.S. Tax Ct. 1984, U.S. Ct. Appeals (9th cir.) 1984. Assoc. Law Office of Allen Taylor, N.Y.C., 1959-62; assoc. Schwartz & Frohlich, N.Y.C., 1963-69, ptnr., 1969, Summit, Solomon & Feldesman (and predecessor firms), N.Y.C., 1971-93, Putney, Twombly Hall & Hirson, N.Y.C., 1993-2000, of counsel, 2001—04. Faculty mem. ann. seminar Practising Law Inst., 1987-91; mediator so. dist. U.S. Dist. Ct. N.Y., comml. divsn. Supreme Ct., N.Y.; arbitrator ea. dist. U.S. Dist. Ct., Bklyn.; panel chair appellate divsn. Disciplinary Com., 1980-85, 87-92; lectr. in field. Author: Responses to Complaints: Commercial Litigation in New York State Courts, 1995, 2d edit., 2005, Warranties: Business and Commercial Litigation in Federal Courts, 1998, 2d edit., 2005, The City of New York as a Major Institutional Litigant: A Follow-up on the Price Waterhouse Study, The Record of the Association of the Bar of the City of New York, vol. 54, no. 5, 1999; editor St. John Law Rev. 1958-59. Regional commr. Am. Youth Soccer Orgn., Chappaqua, N.Y., 1975-84; mem. New Castle Recreation and Parks Commn., 1984-90, chairperson, 1987-89, dir. Aiken Area Coun. on Aging, 2003—. Mem. ABA, N.Y. State Bar Assn., Assn. Bar City N.Y. (mem. com. on state legis. 1971-74, chair 1975-78, com. on grievances 1979-80, com. on women in cts. 1988-94, com. on judiciary 1989-92, interim mem. 1992, 93, 94, 96, 97, 98, 99, 2000, chair com. on gender bias in fed. cts. 1991-93, coun. judicial adminstrn. 1996-2001, com. on symposium 1997-2000, chair 1998-2000), Fed. Bar Coun., Practising Law Inst. (chair winning strategies for depositions in corp. litigation 1991-92, co-chair seminars on art of taking and defending depositions in corp. litigation 1982-85). Democrat. Roman Catholic. Home: Woodside Plantation 308 Willow Lake Ct Aiken SC 29803

AMACHER, RICHARD EARL, retired literature educator; b. Ridgway, Pa., Dec. 13, 1917; s. Albert and Emma (Luchs) A.; m. Cordelia Anne Ward, Aug. 26, 1953; 1 child, Alice Marie. AB, Ohio U., 1939; postgrad., U. Chgo., 1939-42; PhD, U. Pitts., 1947. Instr. English Yale U., New Haven, 1944-45; instr. Rutgers U., New Brunswick, N.J., 1945-47, asst. prof., 1947-53, lectr., 1953-54; chmn. English dept. Henderson State Tchrs. Coll., Arkadelphia, Ark., 1954-57; asso. prof. English Auburn (Ala.) U., 1957-65, prof., 1965-78, Hargis prof. Am. Lit., 1978-84, prof. emeritus, 1984—; ret., 1984. Fulbright prof., Würzburg, Fed. Republic Germany, 1961-62, Konstanz, W. Ger., 1969-70 Author: Franklin's Wit and Folly, 1953, Practical Criticism, 1956, Benjamin Franklin, 1962, Edward Albee, 1969, rev. edit., 1982, (with Margaret Rule) Edward Albee at Home and Abroad, 1973, (with Victor Lange) New Perspectives in German Literary Criticism, 1979, American Political Writers, 1588-1800, 1979; editor: (with G. Polhemus) J.G. Baldwin's The Flush Times of California, 1966. Chmn. Auburn Chamber Music Soc., 1980-82, 85-86, 88-89; elder Presbyterian Ch. Am. Coun. Learned Socs. grantee, 1972 Mem. Am. Studies Assn. (pres. southeastern sec. 1977-79), Société Historique d'Auteuil et de Passy, Nat. Soc. Lit. and Arts. Democrat. Home: 515 Auburn Dr Auburn AL 36830-5547

AMADA, GERALD, retired psychotherapist; b. Newark, Aug. 13, 1938; s. Samuel and Rose Amada; m. Marcia Rae Hirshberg, Aug. 9, 1962; children: Robin, Naomi, Laurie, Eric. BA, Rutgers U., Newark, 1960; MSW, Rutgers U., 1962; PhD, Wright Inst., Berkeley, Calif., 1977. Psychotherapist Mercer County Mental Health Clinic, Trenton, NJ, 1962—64, Dept. Mental Hygiene, Modesto, Calif., 1964—66, Homewood Terrace, San Francisco, 1966—68; staff devel. supr. Solano County Dept. Social Svcs., Vallejo, Calif., 1968—70; dir. Mental Health program City Coll. of San Francisco, 1970—2000; psychotherapist Mill Valley, Calif., 1980—2003; ret., 2003. Cons. KPIX-TV, San Francisco, 1980—82, Mass. Mutual Life Ins. Co., San Francisco, 1980—83. Author (and book rev. editor): (jour.) Jour. of Coll. Student Psychotherapy, 1988—; book reviewer Am. Jour. Psychotherapy, 1983—; author: 9 books; contbr. articles to profl. jours. Commr. Marin County Human Rights Commn.; facilitator Alzheimer's Orgn., San Rafael, Calif., 1998—2003. Recipient Award of Excellence, Nat. Assn. of Vocat. Edn. Spl. Needs Pers., 1984. Mem.: Am. Fedn. Tchrs., NASW, Freedom for Individual Rights in Edn. Avocations: tennis, writing, reading, travel, classical music. Mailing: 185 Mount Lassen Dr San Rafael CA 94903 Office Phone: 415-479-8889. Personal E-mail: mgamada@earthlink.net.

AMADEI, DEBORAH LISA, librarian; b. Jersey City, June 13, 1952; d. Joseph and Thelma (Pugach) Irgon; m. Albert E. Amadei, July 19, 1987. BA, Northeastern U., 1975; MS, Pratt Inst., 1985. Cert. profl. librarian. Tech. libr. asst. Tracor Jitco, Dover, N.J., 1977-84, lead tech. libr. asst., 1984-85; sr. libr. East Orange (N.J.) Pub. Libr., 1986—. Mem. ALA, N.J. Libr. Assn. Avocations: writing, hiking, movies. Office: East Orange Pub Libr 21 S Arlington Ave East Orange NJ 07018-3804 Office Phone: 973-266-5204. E-mail: damadei@hotmail.com.

AMADO, DAVID, conductor; b. Merion, Pa. m. Meredith Rodig. BA in piano performance, Juilliard School of Music; MA in orchestral conducting, Indiana U.; postgrad. studies with Otto-Werner Mueller, Juilliard School of Music. Founder, mng. dir. Sequitur, 1996; asst. conductor St. Louis Symphony, 1997—2003, assoc. conductor, 1999—2004; music dir., conductor St. Louis Symphony Youth Orchestra, 1997—2004; music dir. Del. Symphony Orchestra, 2003—. Prodr.: St. Louis Symphony's own recording label, Arch Media. Recipient Bruno Walter Meml. award. Office: Delaware Symphony Orch PO Box 1870 Wilmington DE 19899 Business E-Mail: davida@desymphony.org.

AMADO, JOSEPH S., information technology executive; Bachelors Degree, Winston-Salem State U. With Nestle, NY; computer analyst Philip Morris USA, Richmond, Va., 1986—89; systems supervisor Philip Morris USA Inc., Louisville, 1989—92, information technology mgr., 1992—94, with SAP Competency Ctr. Richmond, Va., 1994—97, information technology dir., Information Svcs. Sales Orgn., 1997—98, information technology dir. ops., 1998, information tech. dir. ops. (Richmond, Louisville, and Cabarrus Facilities), v.p., chief information officer Richmond, Va., 2000—. Exec. sponsor for coll. recruiting efforts for Philip Morris USA Information Technology Orgn. Bd. dir. Greater Richmond Technology Coun.; trustee bd. dirs. Winston-Salem State U., GRTC, Greater Richmond Found., FRIENDS, Assn. for Children, Richmond, Va. Office: Philip Morris USA Inc 6601 W Broad St Richmond VA 23230-1701 Office Phone: 804-274-2000. Office Fax: 804-484-8231.*

AMADOR, MIRANDA BARBARA, artist; b. London, Sept. 4, 1957; came to U.S., 1960; d. Stefan I. and Barbara (Kownacka) Ulankiewicz; m. Luis Valentine Amador, June 14, 1980 (div. 1987). AD in Fine Art, Am. Acad. Art, Chgo., 1978; AD in Comml. Art, Am. Acad. Art, 1978; BFA, Sch. Art Inst. Chgo., 1983. Med. illusrator, graphic artist Qually & Co., Chgo., 1980-82; art dir. Playboy Erotic Fantasies Videos Playboy Mag., Chgo., 1981-83; creative dir. Santa Monica (Calif.) Propellor, 1984-85; art dir., prodn. designer L.A., 1985—. Judge Cable Ace Awards in art direction, 1994-95. Illustrator (book) Brain Tumors in the Young, 1981-82; art dir. CA Lottery for Spanish Channel, 1996, CLIO award; co-editor, cons. History of Neurosciences, L.A. Mem. AFI, Art Inst. Chgo. (life.). Avocations: photography, writing, drawing, sports, travel. Home and Office: 9312 1/2 W Olympic Blvd Beverly Hills CA 90212-4510

AMAECHI, BENNETT TOCHUKWU, dentist, prosthodontist; b. Obosi, Anambra state, Nigeria, Dec. 23, 1959; s. Christian and Henrietta Amaechi; m. Adaorah Ezife Adibe, Feb. 3, 1964; children: Chikaosolu, Adaiba, Chukwubinyelum, Chizaramepkere. BSc in Health Scis., U. Ife, Nigeria, 1983, B in Dental Surgery, 1986; MSc in Prosthodontics, U. London, 1993; PhD in Cariology, U. Liverpool, Eng., 1999. Cert. in dental implantology Guy's Dental Hosp., London and Branemark Inst., Gotenborg, Sweden. Dental house officer U. Ife Tchg. Hosp., Ile-Ife, Nigeria, 1986—87; prosthodontics sr. house officer Guy's Dental Hosp., London, 1993—94; rsch. assoc. cariology U. Liverpool, 1995—2001; asst. prof. cmty. dentistry U. Tex. Health Sci. Ctr., San Antonio, 2001—, clin. tchr. in preventive dentistry, 2001—, dir. cariology, 2001—. Presenter in field. Contbr. book Tooth Wear and Sensitivity: Clinical Advances in Restorative Dentistry, 2000, articles to profl. jours. Recipient Rsch. in Prevention award, Internat. Assn. for Dental Rsch./Colgate-Palmolive, 1998. Mem.: CommonWealth Dental Assn., Am. Assn. for Dental Rsch., Internat. Assn. for Dental Rsch., European Orgn. for Caries Rsch. (Young Investigators Travel award 1998). Avocation: travel. Home: 2011 Encino Alto St San Antonio TX 78259 Office: Univ Tex Health Sci Ctr 7703 Floyd Curl Dr San Antonio TX 78229 Personal E-mail: amaechi2011@sbcglobal.net. Business E-Mail: amaechi@uthscsa.edu.

AMAISMEIER, DAWN AIMEE, psychologist; b. Arlington, Va., Oct. 24, 1974; BS with honors, Old Dominion U., 1996; MA in Exptl. Psychology, Towson U., 2002. Intern Victim/Witness Asst. Program, Norfolk, Va., 1995; psychiat. tech. No. Va. Mental Health Inst., 1997; rsch. asst. Towson (Md.) U., 1997—98, Hotspots Initiative, 1998—99; sr. rsch. data coord. epidemiology Johns Hopkins U., Balt., 1999—2000. Comm. program asst. CIA, Va., 1993, 96. Vol. Cross Cultural Health Program, Towson, Md., 2002. Scholar, U. Canterbury, New Zealand, 2005. Mem.: Golden Key (life). Avocations: aerobics, body sculpting, dance, travel, gourmet cooking. Home: 500 Horn Ln Eugene OR 97404 Office: Univ Canterbury Campus New Zealand Mailing: 701 NW Coast St 112 Newport OR 97365 Personal E-mail: media01@earthlink.net.

AMALDOSS, WILFRED, marketing educator; b. Madras, India, Nov. 15, 1961; s. Aea Doss; m. Nirmala Amaldoss, May 3, 1963; children: Bernard, Nicole. PhD, U. Pa., 1998. Instr. Wharton Sch. Bus. U. Pa., Phila., 1998; asst. prof. Purdue U., West Lafayette, Ind., 1998—2002, Duke U., NC, 2002—. Author: Collaborating to Compete, 2000, David Vs. Goliath, 2002. Office: Duke U A337 Fuqua Bus Sch Durham NC 27708

AMAN, ALFRED CHARLES, JR., law educator; b. Rochester, N.Y., July 7, 1945; s. Alfred Charles Sr. and Jeannette Mary (Czebatul) Aman; m. Carol Jane Greenhouse, Sept. 23, 1976. AB, U. Rochester, 1967; JD, U. Chgo., 1970. Bar: (D.C.) 1971, Ga. 1972, N.Y. 1980. Law clk. U.S. Ct. Appeals, Atlanta, 1970—72; assoc. Sutherland, Asbill & Brennan, Atlanta, 1972—75, Washington, 1975—77; assoc. prof. Sch. Law, Cornell U., Ithaca, NY, 1977—82, prof. law, 1983—91, exec. dir. Internat. Legal Studies Program, 1988—90; dean Sch. Law, Ind. U., Bloomington, 1991—2002, prof. law, 1991—, Roscoe C. O'Byrne chair in law, 1999—, disting. Fulbright chair in comparative constitutional law, 1998; vis. prof. law U. Paris II, 1998; vis. fellow law and pub. affairs program Princeton U., 2002—03. Cons. U.S. Adminstrv. Conf., Washington, 1978—80, Washington, 1986—; trustee U. Rochester, 1980—; vis. fellow Wolfson Coll., Cambridge U., 1983—84, 1990—91. Author: Energy and Natural Resources, 1983, Administrative Law in a Global Era, 1992, Administrative Law Treatise, 1992, 2d edit., 2001. Chmn. Ithaca Bd. Zoning Appeals, 1980—82. Mem.: ABA, N.Y. State Bar Assn., Ga. Bar Assn., D.C. Bar Assn., Am. Assn. Law Schs., Phi Beta Kappa. Avocations: music, jazz drumming, piano, composition and arranging. Office: Ind U Sch Law 211 S Indiana Ave Bloomington IN 47405-7001*

AMAN, GEORGE MATTHIAS, III, lawyer; b. Wayne, Pa., Mar. 2, 1930; s. George Matthias and Emily (Kalbach) A.; m. Ellen McMillan, June 20, 1959; children: James E., Catherine E., Peter T. AB, Princeton U., 1952; LL.B., Harvard U., 1957. Bar: Pa. 1958. Assoc. Townsend Elliot & Munson, Phila., 1960-65; ptnr. Morgan Lewis & Bockius, Phila., 1965-93; of counsel High, Swartz, Roberts & Seidel, Norristown, Pa., 1993—. Commr. Radnor Twp., Pa., 1976-80, 86-92, planning commr., 1981-86; pres. bd. trustees Wayne Presbyn. Ch., Pa., 1981-84. Served to 1st lt. U.S. Army, 1952-54. Mem. ABA, Pa. Mcpl. Authorities Assn., Nat. Assn. Bond Lawyers, Pa. Assn. Bond Lawyers; Clubs: Merion Cricket (Haverford, Pa.); Princeton (Phila.) (dir 1977-79, treas. 1985-86). Republican. Home: 246 Upland Way Wayne PA 19087-4859 Office: High Swartz Roberts Seidel 40 E Airy St Norristown PA 19401-4803 Office Phone: 610-275-0700. Personal E-mail: george.aman@verizon.net. Business E-Mail: gaman@highswartz.com.

AMAN, MOHAMMED MOHAMMED, dean, library and information science professor; b. Alexandria, Egypt, Jan. 3, 1940; came to U.S., 1963, naturalized, 1975; s. Mohammed Aman and Fathia Ali (al-Maghribi) Mohammed; m. Mary Jo Parker, Sept. 15, 1972; 1 son, David. BA, Cairo U., 1961; MS, Columbia U., 1965; PhD, U. Pitts., 1968. Libr. Egyptian Nat. Libr., 1961-63, Duquesne U., Pitts., 1966-68; asst. prof. libr. sci. Pratt Inst., N.Y.C., 1968-69; from asst. prof. to assoc. prof. St. John's U., Jamaica, NY, 1969-73, prof., dir. divsn. libr. and info. sci., 1973-76; prof. libr. sci., dean Palmer Grad. Libr. Sch., C.W. Post Ctr., L.I. U., 1976-79; dean Sch. Info. Studies U. Wis., 1979—2003, prof., dean, interim dean Sch. Edn. Milw., 2001—02, dean emeritus, prof. Sch. Info. Scis., 2003—. Cons. UNESCO, U.S., AID and UNIDO; USIA acad. specialist, Germany, 1989; Fulbright lectr. Cairo U., 1990-91; USIA-sponsored lectr. Mohamed V. Univ., Rabat, Morocco, 1997. Author: Librarianship and the Third World, 1976, Cataloging and Classifications of Non-Western Library Material: Issues, Trends and Practices, 1980, Arab Serials and Periodicals: A Subject Bibliography, 1979, Online Access to Databases, 1983, On Developing Computer-Based Library Systems (Arabic), 1984, Information Services (Arabic), 1985, Trends in Urban Library Management, 1989, The Bibliotheca Alexandrina: A Link in the Chain of Cultural Continuity, 1991, Information Technology Use in Libraries (Arabic), 1998, Internet Use in Libraries, 2000, The Gulf War in World Literature, 2002; editor: Digest of Middle East Studies. Chmn. Black Faculty Coun., U. Wis., Milw.; mktg. com. Milw. Art Mus.; bd. dirs. Clara Mohammed Sch., 2001-. Recipient Outstanding Achievement award, Egyptian Libr. Assn., 1997. Mem. NAACP, ALA (chmn. internat. rels. com. 1984-86, standing com. on libr. edn., internat. subcom. 1990-91, chmn. 1991-93, internat. rels. Round Table 1993-94, John Ames Humphry/Online Computer Libr. Ctr. Outstanding Contbn. award 1989, Leadership award black caucus 1994, Excellence award black caucus 1995), Assn. Libr. and Sci. (Svc. award 1988), Am. Soc. for Info. Sci. (chmn. spl. interest group in internat. info. issues, internat. rels. com.), Egyptian Libr. Assn. (life, Outstanding Achievement award 1997), Arab/Jewish Dialogue, Egyptian-Am. Scholars Assn., Assn. for Libr. and Info. Sci. Edn. (chmn. internat. rels. com. 1983-85), Wis. Libr. Assn. (Svc. award 1992, P.N. Kaula Internat. award and medal 1996, Wis. Libr. of Yr. 1998), Libr. Svcs. and Constrn. Act. (adv. com. 1986-89), Internat. Archtl. Jury for Bibliotheca Alexandrina, Internat. Fedn. Libr. Assns. and Insts. (sec. on edn. and tng. 1983-92), Coun. on Egyptian Am. Rels., The Gamaliel Chair (bd. dirs. 1995-97), Leaders Forum (bd. dirs. 1995—), America's Black Holocaust Mus. (bd. dirs. 1999—), Islamic Social Family Svcs. (bd. dirs. 1999—), Milw. Tchr.'s Edn. Ctr. (bd. dirs.). Democrat. Moslem. Office: U Wis-Milw Sch Info Studies PO Box 413 Milwaukee WI 53201-0413 Office Phone: 414-229-3315. Business E-Mail: aman@sois.uwm.edu.

AMAN, REINHOLD ALBERT, philologist, writer; b. Fuerstenzell, Bavaria, Apr. 8, 1936; came to U.S., 1959, naturalized, 1963; s. Ludwig and Anna Margarete (Waindinger) A.; m. Shirley Ann Beischel, Apr. 9, 1960 (div. 1990); 1 child, Susan. Student, Chem. Enging. Inst., Augsburg, Germany, 1953-54; BS with high honors, U. Wis., 1965; PhD, U. Tex., 1968. Chem. engr., Munich and Frankfurt, Ger., 1954-57; petroleum chemist Shell Oil Co., Montreal, Que., Can., 1957-59; chem. analyst A. O. Smith Corp., Milw., 1959-62; prof. German U. Wis., Milw., 1968-74; editor, pub. Maledicta Jour., Maledicta Press Publs., Santa Rosa, Calif., 1976—; pres. Maledicta Press, Santa Rosa, 1976—. Dir. Internat. Maledicta Archives, Santa Rosa, 1975— Author: Der Kampf in Wolframs Parzival, 1968, Bayrisch-oesterreichisches Schimpfwoerterbuch, 1973, 86, 96, Talking Dirty, 1993, Opus Maledictorum, 1996, Hillary Clinton's Pen Pal, 1996; gen. editor Mammoth Cod (Mark Twain), 1976, Dictionary of International Slurs (A. Roback), 1979, Graffiti (A. Read), 1977; editor Maledicta: The Internat. Jour. Verbal Aggression, 1977—, Maledicta Monitor, 1990-92; contbr. articles to profl. jours. U. Wis. scholar, 1963-65; U. Wis. research grantee, 1973, 74; NDEA Title IV fellow, 1965-68 Mem. Internat. Maledicta Soc. (pres.), Am. Dialect Soc., Am. Name Soc., Dictionary Soc. N.Am. Home and Office: PO Box 14123 Santa Rosa CA 95402-6123 Office Phone: 707-795-8178. E-mail: aman@sonic.net.

AMANN, CHARLES ALBERT, mechanical engineer, researcher; b. Thief River Falls, Minn., Apr. 21, 1926; s. Charles Alois and Bertha Ann (Oetting) Amann; m. Marilynn Ann Reis, Aug. 26, 1950; children: Richard, Barbara, Nancy, Julie. BS, U. Minn., 1946, MSME, 1948. Instr. U. Minn., Mpls., 1946-49; rsch. engr. GM Rsch. Labs., Detroit, 1949-54, supervisory rsch. engr. Warren, Mich., 1954-71, asst. dept. head, 1971-73, dept. head, 1973-89, rsch. fellow, 1989-91; prin. engr. KAB Enging., 1991—. Spl. instr. Wayne State U., Detroit, 1952—55; guest lectr. Mich. State U., 1980—; outside prof. U. Ariz., 1983; mem. adv. com. Gas Rsch. Inst., 1992—98, Oak Ridge Nat. Lab., 1996—98; invited lectr. Inst. Advanced Enging., Seoul, Republic of Korea, 1994. Author (with others): (book) Automotive Engine Alternatives, 1986, Advanced Diesel Engineering and Operations, 1988; co-editor: Combustion Modeling in Reciprocating Engines, 1980. Lt. (j.g.) USNR, 1944—46. Recipient James Clayton prize, Inst. Mech. Engrs., 1975, Outstanding Achievement award, U. Minn., 1991. Fellow: Soc. Automotive Engrs. (Arch T. Colwell merit award 1972, Disting. Spkr. award 1981, Arch T. Colwell merit award 1984, Disting. Spkr. award 1991, Forest R. McFarland award 2001); mem.: ASME (Richard S. Woodbury award 1989, Soichiro Honda lectr. 1992, Spkr. award Internal Combustion Engine Divsn. 1997, Internal Combustion Engine award 2000, Disting. lectr. 2002—04), NAE, Tau Beta Pi, Tau Omega, Sigma Xi. Presbyterian. Achievements include patents in field. Avocation: music. E-mail: mcamann@juno.com.

AMANPOUR, CHRISTIANE, news correspondent; b. London, Jan. 12, 1958; m. James Rubin, 1998; 1 child, Darius John Rubin. BA in Journalism, summa cum laude, Rhode Island U. Reporter, anchor, prodr. WBRU-Radio, Providence, 1981—82; asst. internat. assignment desk CNN, Atlanta, 1983, correspondent Frankfurt, 1989, Kuwait, 1990; contbr. 60 Minutes CBS News, 1996—. Named Woman of Yr., Women in Cable and Telecommunications, NY Chpt., 1994; named one of most powerful women, Forbes mag., 2005, 2005; recipient News & Documentary Emmy, George Foster Peabody award, 1994, 1997, Courage in Journalism award, Worldfest-Houston Internat. Film Festival Gold award, Livingston award for young journalists, Breakthrough award, Women, Men and Media, 1991, Sigma Chi award, Edward R. Murrow award for disting. achievement in broadcast journalism, 2002. Fellow: Soc. of Profl. Journalists. Fluent in English and Farsi (Persian). Mailing: CNN One CNN Center Atlanta GA 30303*

AMAON, GARY P., lawyer; b. Lubbock, Tex., Nov. 18, 1945; BS, Abilene Christian Coll., 1966; JD, U. Tex., 1969. Bar: Tex. 1969. Mem. Vinson & Elkins L.L.P., Houston. Mem. Chancellors, Order of Coif, Phi Delta Phi. Office: Vinson & Elkins LLP 2500 First City Tower 1001 Fannin St Ste 3300 Houston TX 77002-6706 Address: 7897 Broadway, Apt #601 San Antonio TX 78209

AMAR, A. D., business educator, management consultant; b. Bhakkar, India; s. Prem Dutt and Kaushlya Devi Shakir; m. Sneh Lata Chopra, Mar. 16, 1975; children: Harpriye Amar Juneja, Januj Amar Juneja. Advanced Diploma, Punjab Engring. Coll., Chandigarh, India, 1966; BS Prodn. Engring., Panjab U., Chandigarh, India, 1969; MS Indsl. & Mgmt. Engring., Mont. State U., 1973; MBA, Baruch Coll., 1980; PhD, CUNY, N.Y.C., 1980. Asst. prof. Punjab Engring. Coll., Chandigarh, India, 1969—72; asst. engr. Teledyne Pacific Indsl. Controls, Oakland, Calif., 1972; design engr. Vornado-Store Decor, Fairfield, NJ, 1973—76; asst. prof. fin. & quantitative methods Montclair State U., Upper Montclair, NJ, 1978—83; dir.-editor The Mid-Atlantic Jour. Bus. Seton Hall U., South Orange, NJ, 1991—2002, prof. mgmt. Sch. Bus., 1983—. V.p. publs. & pub. rels. Am. Prodn. & Inventory Control Soc.--Ctrl. Jersey Chpt., Woodbridge, NJ, 1989—91; mem. editl. adv. bd. Computers & Ops. Rsch., Potomac, 1998—2002. Author: Managing Knowledge Workers: Unleashing Innovation & Productivity, 2001. Recipient Tech. Incubator at Seton Hall U.-Feasibility Study award, State of N.J., 2001. Mem.: Inst. Ops. Rsch. and Mgmt. Scis. (track chair 1975). Republican. Hindu. Avocation: travel. Office: Seton Hall U Stillman Sch Bus South Orange NJ 07079

AMAR, AKHIL REED, law educator; b. Ann Arbor, Mich., Sept. 6, 1958; s. Arjan D. and Kamla (Chabra) A.; m. Vinita Parkash, Sept. 3, 1989. BA summa cum laude, Yale U., 1980, JD, 1984; LLD (hon.), Suffolk U., 1997. From asst. prof. to assoc. prof. Yale Law Sch., New Haven, Conn., 1985-90, prof. law, 1990-93, Southmayd prof. law, 1993—. Samuel Rubin vis. prof. law Columbia Law Sch., NYC, 1993; vis. prof. Stanford U., 2001. Author: The Constitution and Criminal Procedure, 1997, The Bill of Rights, 1998, Processes of Constitutional Decisionmaking, 2000; co-author: For the People, 1998; contrib. articles to law jours. Recipient Paul M. Bator award Federalist Soc., 1993; named 36th Ann. Coen lectr. U. Colo., 1992, Dillard lectr. U. Va., 1994, 7th ann. Barrett lectr. U. Calif., Davis, 1994, 57th Cleveland-Marshall lectr., 1994, Rutgers-Camden U., 1995, Suffolk U., 1996, Tuft lectr. U. Cin., 1998, Seegers lectr. Valparasio, 1998; DePaul Coll. Law Disting. scholar, 1991. Mem. United Ch. of Christ. E-mail: akhil.amar@yale.edu.*

AMARA, LUCINE, vocalist; b. Hartford, Conn., Mar. 1, 1925; d. George and Adrine (Kazanjian) Armaganian; married, Jan. 7, 1961 (div. June 1964). Student, Music Acad. of West, 1947, U. So. Calif., 1949-50. Artistic dir. N.J. Assn. Verismo Opera, Ft. Lee. Tchr. master classes, U.S., Mex., Can. Appeared at Hollywood Bowl, 1948, soloist, San Francisco Symphony, 1949-50; career includes over 1000 operatic performances; with Met. Opera, N.Y.C., from 1950, sang 800 performances, 9 new prodns., 5 opening nights, 57 radio broadcasts, 4 telecasts including appeared on Met. Opera: In Performance, 1982, 83, 84, 85, 86, 87, 88, 90, 91; recorded Pagliacci, 1951, 60; singer with New Orleans, Hartford, Pitts., Central City operas, 1952-54, appeared Glyndebourne Opera, 1954, 55, 57, 58, Edinburgh Festival, 1954, singer, Aida, Terme Di Caracalla, Rome, 1954, also Stockholm Opera, N.Y. Philharm., St. Louis Civic Light Opera, 1955-56; has appeared in leading or title roles in several operas including: Tosca, Aida, Amelia in Un Ballo in Maschera, Turandot, Riverside Opera Assn., 1986, others; appeared with St. Petersburg (Fla.) Opera, Venezuela Philharm. Orch., 1988, 93; opera and concert tour, USSR, 1965, 91, Manila, 1968, Paris, Mex., 1966, Hong Kong and China, 1983, Yugoslavia, 1988; rec. artist, Columbia, RCA, Victor, Angel records, Met. Opera Record Club; albums include: Beethoven's Symphony No. 9, Leoncavallo's, I Pagliacci, Puccini's La Bohème, Verdi Requiem. Recipient 1st prize Atwater-Kent Radio Auditions, 1948; inducted to Acad. Vocal Arts Hall Fame, 1989. Office: PO Box 3024 Fort Lee NJ 07024-9024 E-mail: lamara@nyc.rr.com. *My life has been filled with new experiences. I have been most fortunate to have achieved a career that has introduced me to so many wonderful people. Some have become close friends; others, because of time and distance, have become warm acquaintances. I am humbly grateful for all God's blessings.*

AMARA, SUSAN, neuroscientist; BS, Stanford U.; PhD in physiology and pharmacology, U. Calif., San Diego, 1983. Sr. scientist Vollum Inst.; investigator Howard Hughes Med. Inst.; prof. Oreg. Health Sci. U.; Thomas Detre prof., chair, dept. neurobiology Pitts. Sch. Medicine, U. Pitts., 2003—. Mem.: Dana Alliance Brain Initiatives, Soc. Neurosci., Nat. Acad. Scis. Office: Univ Pitts Dept Neurobiology E1440 Biomedical Sci Tower 3500 Terrace Pittsburgh PA 15261 Business E-Mail: amaras@pitt.edu.

AMARAL, JOSEPH FERREIRA, surgeon; b. Pawtucket, R.I., Aug. 9, 1955; s. Joseph and Rosa (Ferreira) A.; m. Linda Watson, June 6, 1981; children: Courtney, Ashley, Gregory. BS in Biology summa cum laude, Providence Coll., 1977; MD, Brown U., 1981. Diplomate Am. Bd. Surgery, Am. Bd. Med. Examiners. Intern R.I. Hosp., Providence, 1981-82, resident, 1982-83; surg. rsch. fellow Brown U./R.I. Hosp., Providence, 1983-86; sr. surg. resident R.I. Hosp., Providence, 1986-88, adminstrv. chief surg. resident, 1988-89, ccord. surg. residency, asst. surgeon, asst. prof. Brown U., 1989-91, coord. surg. residencey, dir. laparoscopic surgery, 1991-92, dir. laparoscopic surgery, asst. surgeon, asst. prof., 1991-93, assoc. prof., surgeon, 1993-98, prof., 1998—, pres., CEO, 2000—. Treas. R.I. Hosp. Staff Assn., 1991-93; sec. R.I. Hosp. Surg. Found., 1992—; bd. dirs. R.I. Hosp. PHO; vis. surgeon hosps. in Australia, Argentina, Portugal, Austria, Rome, Singapore and Brazil. Contbr. articles to numerous profl. jours.; numerous internat., nat. and regional presentations; various scientific exhibits. Recipient Merck Clin. Achievement award, 1981, Haffenraffer Surg. Rsch. fellowship, 1983-85, 16th ACS scholarship, 1984-86, Young Investigators award Shock Soc., 1986, Residents Rsch. award Surg. Infection Soc., 1986. Fellow ACS, Internat. Coll. Surgeons; mem. AMA, AAAS, R.I. Med. Soc., Providence Surg. Soc., New Eng. Surg. Soc., Soc. Laproendoscopic Surgeons, Assn. Surg. Edn., Ctrl. N.Y. Surg. Soc. (hon.), Soc. Minimally Invasive Therapy, Am. Soc. Gastrointestinal Endoscopy, Am. Biatric Soc., Surg. Infection Soc., N.Y. Acad. Scis., Wound Healing Soc., Am. Soc. Eternal and Parenteral Nutrition, Shock Soc., Assn. Acad. Surgeons, Brown Med. Alumni Assn., Sigma Xi, Phi Sigma Tau, Sigma Pi Sigma. Office: Univ Surg Assn Ste 470 2 Dudley St Providence RI 02905-3236 Business E-Mail: jfamaral@lifespan.org.

AMARATUNGA, KEVIN SAMANTHE, computer engineer, researcher; b. Colombo, Sri Lanka, Dec. 9, 1965; arrived in U.S., 1991; s. Milton and Patricia Amaratunga; m. Alexandra Houck, Sept. 18, 2004. BS with hons. in Engring., U. Southampton, England, 1991; MS, MIT, 1993, PhD in Computational Engring., 1996. Software engr. Netscape Comm. Corp., Mountain View, Calif., 1996—97; asst. prof. MIT, Cambridge, Mass., 1997—2002, assoc. prof., 2002—05. Contbr. articles to profl. jours. Grantee, NSF, 2000. Mem.: IEEE, Soc. for Indsl. and Applied Math. Achievements include patents for method and apparatus for eliminating artifacts in data processing and compression systems. Avocations: music, travel, bicycling. Personal E-mail: kevin@alum.mit.edu.

AMARAVADI, CHANDRA SEKHAR, information scientist, educator; b. Vijayawada, Andhra Pradesh, India, Jan. 28, 1960; arrived in U.S., 1981; s. Venkata Rama Sastry and Prabhavathi Devi Amaravadi; m. Saraswathi Sathya Vyakarnam, May 29, 1993; children: Sankhya Krithi, Sankalp Purva. B Engring., Andhra U., Vizag, India, 1981; MBA, U. Minn., 1984; PhD, U. Ariz., 1989. IT cons. Wellspring Computer Svcs., Mpls., 1983—84; prof. Western Ill. U., Macomb, 1989—; IT cons. Dun & Bradstreet Sathyam Software, Madras, India, 1995—97. Contbr. articles to profl. publs. (Best Paper Prize, 2001). Named Tchr. of Week, Delta Sigma Pi, 2001; recipient State Farm Disting. Prof. award, State Farm Inc., 1992, Faculty Excellence award for Outstanding Rsch., Coll. of Bus. and Tech., Western Ill. U., 2001; summer rsch. grantee, U. Rsch. Coun., 1992. Republican. Hindu. Avocations: fitness, science fiction, travel, investing, World War II history. Office: Western Ill U 1 University Cir Macomb IL 61455 E-mail: c-amaravadi@wiu.edu.

AMARI, SUPRASAD V., mechanical engineer; b. Nellore, Andhra Pradesh, India, Nov. 11, 1967; s. Joseph and Sugunamma Amari; m. Srujana Vadde, Jan. 16, 1979. B. Tech in Mech. Engring., S.V. U., Tirupati, 1985—89; M. Tech in Reliability, Indian Inst. of Tech., Kharagpur, India, 1990—92, Ph.D. in Reliability Engring., 1992—96. Info. tech. analyst Tata Consultancy Svcs., Mumbai, India, 1996—2001; sr. reliability engr. Relex Software Corp., Greensburg, Pa., 2001—. Adv. bd. mem. 2nd Internat. Conf. on Quality, Reliability and IT, Indian Nat. Sci. Acad., Delhi, India, 2003—; program vice chair Reliability and Maintainability Symposium, Alexandria, Va., 2005—; tech. adv. bd. mem. Internat. Conf. on Reliability and Safety Engring., Bhubhneswar, Orisa, India, 2005—; editor Internat. Jour. oPerformability, Jaipur, Rajasthan, India, 2005—. Contbr. over 35 articles to profl. jours. Scholar Grad. Aptitude Test in Engring., Ministry of Human Resources Devel., Govt. of India., 1990—96. Mem.: IEEE, Assn. for Computing Machinery, Reliability and Maintainability Symposium (vice chair 2005—05), Am. Statis. Assn., Am. Soc. for Quality. Achievements include research in development of SEA algorithm; design of Relex OpSim and Markov. Office: Relex Software Corporation 540 Pellis Road Greensburg PA 15601

AMATANGELO, NICHOLAS S., retired printing company executive, finance educator; b. Monessen, Pa., Feb. 12, 1935; s. Sylvester and Lucy Amatangelo; m. Kathleen Driscoll, May 16, 1964; children: Amy Kathleen, Holly Megan. BA, Duquesne U., 1957; MBA, U. Pitts., 1958. Indsl. engr. U.S. Steel Co., Pitts., 1959—61; indsl. engr. mgr. Anaconda Co., N.Y.C., 1961—63; mgmt. cons. The Stanley Works, Conn., 1963—65; product mktg. mgr. Xerox Corp., N.Y.C., 1965—68; dir. mktg. Macmillan Co., N.Y.C., 1968—70; dir. product planning Philco-Ford Corp., Phila., 1970—72; pres., CEO Bowne & Co., Inc., Subsidiaries, 1972—97, Bowne of San Francisco, 1972—79, Bowne Houston, Inc., Houston, 1979-87, Bowne Chgo., Inc., 1983-96, corp. cons., advisor, 1996-97; pres., CEO Bowne Detroit, Inc., 1987-96; ret., 1997. Instr. U. Pitts., Pitts., 1959—61; asst. prof. Westchester CC, N.Y.C., 1961—64, N.Y.C., 1970—72; ad. prof. grad. sch. bus. mgmt. and mktg. Roosevelt U. Grad Sch. Exec. MBA program, Chgo., 1996—2004. Contbr. articles to profl. jours. Mem. pres.'s coun. Houston Grand Opera, 1980—86; mem. adv. bd. Chgo. Coll. Performing Arts, 1997—; bd. dirs. San Francisco Boys Club, 1974—79, Boys Town Italy, 1973—79, Alley Theatre, Houston, 1982—86; bd. dirs. exec. bd. Auditorium Theatre, Chgo., 2001—; mem. adv. bd. bus. sch. Roosevelt U., 1996—, vice chair, 1996—99. With U.S. Army, 1958—59, with U.S. Army, 1961—62. Mem.: Assn. Colls. Ill. (trustee 1993—), Pres. Assn., Am. Mgmt. Assn., Am. Soc. Corp. Secs., Printing Industries Am. (bd. dirs.), Duquesne U. Century Club (chmn. exec. com.), Union League Club Chgo., Econs. Club Chgo., Exec. Club Chgo. (bd. dirs.).

AMATO, DEBORAH DOUGLASS, aerospace engineer; b. Mo. d. Clyde and Wilma Douglass; m. Michael Amato, 1996. BS, MIT, 1994; MS, U. Md., 1998. Programmer Orbital Scis. Corp., Va., 1993; aerospace engr. NASA-Goddard Space Flight Ctr., Greenbelt, Md., 1993—. Mem.: AIAA. Avocations: music, swimming. Office: NASA Goddard Space Flight Ctr Greenbelt MD 20771-0001

AMATO, VINCENT VITO, computer engineer; b. Bklyn., Oct. 14, 1929; s. Anthony and Josephine (Maniscalco) A.; m. Marie Dioguardi, Apr. 24, 1955; children— Stephanie, Janine, Anthony, Christopher. BBA, CCNY, 1951, MBA, 1958. Liaison to div. contr. Allied Chem. Corp., N.Y.C., 1951-59; acctg. systems rep. Olivetti-Underwood, N.Y.C., 1958-61; v.p. planning, contr., acquisitions exec. Ingredient Tech. SuCrest Corp., N.Y.C., 1961-72, v.p. planning, treas., 1972-73, pres. splty. products, 1973-78; pres., owner Market Makers Inc., Woodbridge, NJ, 1978-97; owner Animated Computer Engring. Inc., Woodbridge, NJ, 1991-97; founder imadeadifference.com. Adj. asst. prof. NYU; presenter seminars Am. Mgmt. Assn.; mem. food sci. adv. bd. Rutgers U., 1988—, also adv. bd. Cook Coll. Rutgers U. Pres. Lakeridges Civic Assn. Mem. Fin. Execs. Inst., Assn. for Corp. Growth, Am. Mgmt. Assn. (tech. adviser) Home and Office: Vincent V Amato Mktg Consulting 7 Alder Ct Matawan NJ 07747-3717 Office Phone: 732-583-2599. Personal E-mail: vincemarie@aol.com.

AMATO CHIARAMONTE BORDONARO, BARON CARLO CAMILLO, ambassador, consultant; s. Giuseppe Michele Amato and Fernanda Giannini Paolini; m. Lorraine Manville-Dresselhouse, Feb. 22, 1959 (dec. June 1998); m. Irela Fabiola Lopez Fonseca, Nov. 16, 2003. Diploma in Archaeology, Mex. U., Mexico, U. of Barcelona, Spain. Appraiser Assn. of Am., N.Y., 1978. Pres., founder Old World Internat., Canada, 1968—; asst. prof. biology Ga. State U., Athens, 1971—81; amb. Soverign Mil. Order of Malta, Saint Vincent and the Grenadines, 1983—; pres., founder Old World Galleries, N.Y.C., 1977—84; editor-at-large Conde.Nast Publs., Milan and Paris, Italy, 1984—91; dir. fgn. rels. Gesfid, Lugano, Switzerland, 1984—98, fin. mgr., 1984—94; mng. dir. Canouan Resort Devel. Co. Ltd, Saint Vincent and the Grenadines, 1994—98; min. plenipotentiary at large Republic of San Marino, San Marino, 1983—2000. Author: (book) The Wild Boar: History Husbandry The Hunt; editor: (mag.) Artequia Internat., Harper-Bazaar. Named Man of Yr., World Inst. for Sci. Humanism, Fordham U., 1982; recipient Cert. of Appreciation, City of N.Y., 1977, Order of the Trinity, Imperial Ho. of Ethiopia, 1997, Knight of Real Cuerpo de la Nobleza de Madrid, Nobility of Castilla, 1998, Knight Comdr. of St. Maurice and Lazarus, The Savoy Order, 1999, Knight of Grace and Devotion of the Sacred Mil. Order of Malta, 2000. Fellow: Explorer Club; mem.: Knickerbocker Club. Roman Catholic. Avocations: landscaping, ecological research, cooking, gardening, enology.

AMATULI, ROBERT ALEXANDER, architect; b. NYC, May 30, 1957; s. A. James and Catherine Amatuli; m. Jeanne Marie Amatuli, Apr. 19, 1985; children: Robert Alexander II, Nicholas Brandon. BS in Archtl. Tech., NY Inst. Tech., 1979. Registered architect N.Y., Conn.; registered interior design, Conn. Dir. archtl. dept. United Artists Comm., Dallas, 1979—85, dir. east coast constrn. N.Y.C., 1982; assoc., asst. office mgr. Page Southerland Page, Ft. Worth, 1985—87, assoc., prodn. coord. Dallas, 1987—95; v.p., dir. healthcare Gideon Toal Inc., Ft. Worth, 1995—99; sr. v.p., dir. ops., telecomm. Gideon Toal Fulwiler Oates, Ft. Worth, 1997—99; assoc., unit mgr. Carter & Burgess Inc., Hartford, Conn., 1999—2001; dir. health care design Tecton Archs., PC, Hartford, 2001—. Cons. JPS Archtl. Cons., Ft. Worth, 1996—. Recipient craftsmenship award Knights of Pythius, N.Y.C., 1972. Mem. AIA (design award Ft. Worth 1999). Avocations: golf, auto racing, hockey, basketball, ambulist. Office: Tecton Architects pc One Hartford Sq W Hartford CT 06106

AMBACH, DWIGHT RUSSELL, retired foreign service officer; b. Highland Park, Ill., Jan. 9, 1931; s. Russell William and Ethel (Repass) A.; m. Betsy Hunter, Aug. 27, 1955; children: Hunter MacKay, Nancy Cole, James Gordon. AB, Brown U., 1952; MA, Fletcher Sch., 1953; postgrad., MIT, 1963-64. Dep. dir. Office Regional Econ. Policy, Bur. Inter-Am. Affairs Dept. State, Washington, 1971-74; exec. asst. to chmn. Export-Import Bank, Washington, 1974-76, 84-86; counselor for econ. and comml. affairs Am. Embassy, Vienna, 1976-80; dean Fgn. Service Inst., Washington, 1980-84; office dir. Bur. Adminstrn. and Info. Services, 1986-88; cons., 1988-96; mem. Fgn. Svc. Res. Corps, 1995—2001. Pres. Montgomery County chpt. Md. Mcpl. League; bd. dirs. Mathews County Cmty. Found. Recipient Superior Honor award Dept. State, 1973; Disting. Service award Export-Import Bank, 1985 Mem. Am. Fgn. Service Assn., Am. Econ. Assn., Phi Beta Kappa Home: Aldendale PO Box 26 Susan VA 23163-0026

AMBACH, GORDON MAC KAY, educational association executive; b. Providence, Nov. 10, 1934; s. Russell W. and Ethel (Repass) A.; m. Lucy DeWitt Emory, Mar. 9, 1963; children: Kenneth Emory, Alison Repass, Douglas Mac Kay. BA, Yale U., 1956; MA, Harvard U. Grad. Sch. Edn., 1957, cert. advanced study, 1966. Tchr. social studies 7th and 8th grades East Williston Sch. Dist., L.I., NY, 1958-61; asst. program planning officer U.S. Office Edn., Washington, 1961-62, asst. legis. specialist, 1962-63, exec. sec. Higher Edn. Facilities Act Task Force, 1963-64; adminstrv. asst. to mem. Boston Sch. Com., 1964-65; staff seminar mgr., mem. staff Harvard U. Grad. Sch. Edn., Cambridge, Mass., 1966-67; spl. asst. to commr. for long range planning NY State Edn. Dept., Albany, 1967-69, asst. commr. for long range planning, 1969-70, exec. dep. commr., 1970-77; commr. edn. and pres. U. of the State of N.Y., Albany, 1977-87; exec. dir. Coun. Chief State Sch. Officers, Washington, 1987—2001; ret., 2001. Del., chmn. resolutions com. The White House Conf. on Librs. and Info. Scis., 1991; mem. Nat. Coun. on Edn. Stds. and Testing, 1993; mem. edn. com. Nat. Alliance for Bus., 1994-2001; mem. Nat. Bd. Internat. Comparative Studies in Edn., U.S. rep. to Internat. Assn. for Evaluation of Edn. Achievement, mem. standing com., 1990-2001; bd. dirs. Wallace Found., Newspaper Assn. Am. Found., Ctr. for Naval Analysis Corp.; mem. edn. bd. NAS. With USAR, 1957-63. Mem. Acad. Polit. Scis., Am. Assn. Sch. Adminstrs., PEW Forum on Edn. Reform, Phi Delta Kappa.

AMBADY, NALINI, social psychologist, educator, researcher; b. Calcutta, India; came to U.S., 1983; d. Shanker and Viji Ambady; m. Raj Marphatia, June 8, 1988; children: Maya Mallika, Leena Anupama. PhD, Harvard U., 1991. Asst. prof. Holy Cross Coll., Worcester, Mass., 1993-94, Harvard U., Cambridge, Mass., 1994-99, Ruth and John Hazel assoc. prof. social sci., 1999—2004; prof., social psychology Tufts U., Medford, Mass., 2004—. Recipient, Behavioral Sci. Rsch. prize AAAS, 1993, Presdl. Early Career award U.S. Govt., 1998, Excellence in Mentoring Award, Harvard U., 2000. Office: Tufts U The Psychology Bldg 490 Boston Ave Medford MA 02155 E-mail: naliniambady@tufts.edu.

AMBALAVANAN, NAMASIVAYAM, neonatologist, educator; m. Priya Prabhakaran, May 25, 1995; 1 child, Aarthi Namasivayam. MBBS, Jawaharlal Inst. Post Grad. Med. Edn. and Rsch., Pondicherry, India, 1990; MD in Pediat., Post Grad. Inst. Med. Edn. and Rsch., Chandigarh, India, 1993. Diplomate Am Bd. Pediat., subsplty. in Neonatology. Intern Jawaharlal Inst. Post Grad. Med. Edn. and Rsch., 1984—90; resident in pediat. Post Grad. Inst. Med. Edn. and Rsch., 1990—93; fellow in neonatology U. Ala., Birmingham, 1994—97, asst. prof. pediat., 2000—. Office: U Ala Birmingham 619 South 19th St 525 New Hillman Bldg Birmingham AL 35233

AMBALAVANAN, SIVA, nephrologist, educator; b. Madras, India, Nov. 26, 1962; arrived in U.S., 1993; d. A. and Sundari Sivasankaran; m. Geetha Ambalavanan, Aug. 22, 1991; children: Anita, Manoj. MB, BS, Madras Med. Coll., 1985. Cert. nephrology, internal medicine, Fed. Lic. Exam., Ednl. Commn. Fgn. Med. Grads. Tutor in medicine U. Aberdeen, Scotland, 1990—92; fellow Med. Ctr. Stanford U., 1993—95; physician VA Med. Ctr., Salt Lake City, 1996—97; resident Med. Ctr. U. Utah, Salt Lake City, 1996—97, asst. prof. medicine, cons. nephrologist Sch. Medicine, 1996—98. Asst. prof. medicine Wright State U., Dayton, Ohio, 1998—; adj. prof. U. Utah; mem. transfusion com. Fransiscan Med. Ctr., 1999—2000; mem. transplant com. Miami Valley Hosp. Contbr. articles to profl. jours. Active Hindu Cmty. Orgn., Dayton, Ohio, 1999. Recipient Trainee Investigator award for excellence in sci. rsch., Clin. Rsch. Meeting, 1995; grantee, Allan Evan. Fellow: Royal Coll. Physicians; mem.: AMA, ACP. Avocations: golf, travel, cooking, music. Office: Renal Physician Inc 1427 Business Ctr Dayton OH 45410

AMBER, DOUGLAS GEORGE, lawyer; b. East Chicago, Ind., Apr. 15, 1956; s. George and Margaret (Watson) A. BA in Polit. Sci., Ind. U., 1978; JD, U. Miami, 1985. Bar: Fla. 1985, US. Ct. Claims 1986, U.S. Ct. Internat. Trade 1986, U.S. Tax Ct. 1986, U.S. Ct. Appeals (11th cir.) 1986, U.S. Dist. Ct. (mid. and so. dists.) Fla. 1987, U.S. Ct. Mil. Appeals 1987, U.S. Ct. Appeals (fed. cir.) 1987, Ind. 1988, U.S. Dist. Ct. (no. and so. dists.) Ind. 1988, U.S. Ct. Appeals (7th cir.) 1989, U.S. Supreme Ct. 1989; Ind. Registered Civil Mediator. Dep. prosecutor 31st Jud. Cir. Ind., Crown Point, 1988-93; pvt. practice Munster, 1993—. Adj. prof. polit. sci. Purdue U., 1997—. Mem. exec. bd. dirs. Calumet coun. Boy Scouts Am., 1994-96; apptd. Ind. State Pub. Defenders Coun., 2001—. Mem. Ind. State Bar Assn., Lake County Bar Assn. (bd. dirs. 1990-96), Mensa, Delta Theta Phi. Avocations: bicycling, weight training. Office: Amber Golding & Hofstetter 9250 Columbia Ave Ste E-2 Munster IN 46321-3530 Office Phone: 219-836-8530. E-mail: amber@calumet.purdue.edu.

AMBERG, DEBORAH ANN, lawyer; b. 1965; BA, U. Minn., 1987, JD cum laude, 1990. Bar: Minn. 1990. Staff atty. Allete, Inc., Duluth, Minn., 1990—98, sr. atty., 1998—2004, gen. counsel, v.p., corp. legal svcs. corp. sec., 2004—. Mem.: ABA, Minn. State Bar Assn., Minn. Women Lawyers. Office: Allete Inc 30 W Superior St Duluth MN 55802-2093 Office Phone: 218-723-3930. Office Fax: 218-723-3996. E-mail: damberg@allete.com.

AMBERG, THOMAS L., public relations executive; b. Glen Cove, N.Y., Apr. 13, 1948; s. Richard Hiller Amberg and Janet Law Volkman; m. Tauna Urban, June 19, 1971 (div. Jan. 1980); children: Edward, Robert; m. Kathy Stewart, Oct. 9, 1982; 1 child, Thomas Jr. BA, Colgate U., 1971; MBA, U. Mo., St. Louis, 1980. Reporter, editor St. Louis Globe-Democrat, 1971-83; pres., coo Aaron D. Cushman and Assocs., Chgo., 1991—; pres. Cushman Amberg Comms., Chgo. Mem. adv. bd. Salvation Army, St. Louis, 1986-91, Chgo., 1992—, pres., 1995-2003; bd. dirs. Wishing Well Found., St. Louis, 1985-91, Hope Ctr., St. Louis, 1985-91; bd. trustees St. Patrick's Sch., Chgo., 1994-2001. Recipient Disting. Achievement award Inland Daily Press Assn., 1978, 82, Frank Kelly Meml. award, 1980, Gavel award ABA, 1983, Unity awards in Media Lincoln U., 1984. Mem. Mental Health Assn. St. Louis (pres. 1987-88), Pub. Rels. Soc. Am., Press. Club Met. St. Louis (pres. 1981-83), Internat. Assn. Bus. Communicators, Soc. Am. Travel Writers. Presbyterian. Home: 1783 Bowling Green Dr Lake Forest IL 60045-3559 Office: Cushman Amberg Comms 180 N Michigan Ave Ste 1600 Chicago IL 60601-7478

AMBERS, ANN, bishop, educator; b. Brusly, La., Feb. 26, 1948; d. Fannie Mae Jones and Eddie Elmore, Sr., Oliver Jones, Jr. (Stepfather); m. Jackie Roy Ambers, Sept. 3, 1994; m. Lester Moore Jackson, Feb. 11, 1967 (dec. May 24, 1987); children: Gregory, Felita, Lindsey. B, Golden State Sch. Theology, 1989; M, Bell Grove Theol. Sem., 1993, DD (hon.), 1998. Cert. Ordination New St. Paul Missionary Bapt. Ch., 1988, Missionary Lic.-Exec. Sec. Nat. Bapt. Women Min. Conv., 1988. Substitute tchr. Iberia Parish Sch. Bd., New Iberia, La., 1998—; assoc. min. New St. Paul Missionary Bapt. Ch., Oakland, Calif., 1987—93; acctg. clk. Iberia Parish Sheriff's Dept., New Iberia, 1998—2000; pastor True Vine Full Gospel Ch., Oakland, 1990—93, Port Allen, La., 1993—; exec. sec. J. Bryant Aids Found., Oakland, 1991—93; exec. dir. True Vine Ministries, Oakland, 1988—93. Nat. pres. Nat. Bapt. Women Min. Conv., New Iberia, 2003; assoc. min. Union Bapt. Ch., Brusly, La., 1999—2003; state mission pres. La. Freewill Bapt. Assn., Baton Rouge, 1999—2003; nat. amb. #1 Nat. Bapt. Women Min. Conv., Berkeley, Calif., 1990—2003. Recipient Cert. Of Award, Nat. Bapt. Women Min. Conv., 1989, Cert. Of Honor, Alpha Tron Task Force, 1990, Alphatron Christian Task Force, 1990, Disting. Achievement Award, Greater Resurrection Bapt. Ch., 1996, Disting. Svc. award, J. Bryant Aids Found., 1991, Disting. Achievement Award, New St. Paul Missionary Bapt. Ch., 1988, Disting. Achievement, One True Vine Outreach Ministries, 1997.

AMBORSKI, LEONARD EDWARD, retired chemist; b. Buffalo, Aug. 23, 1921; s. Nicholas Leon and Angeline (Laskowska) A.; m. Irene Kazmierczak, Oct. 3, 1944; children: Donna Marie, David Paul. BS, Canisius Coll., 1943; MA, SUNY, Buffalo, 1949, PhD, 1951. Cert. indsl. hygienist Am. Bd. Indsl. Hygiene; cert. EPA instr. in lead abatement and hazardous materials worker tng. Instr. physics Canisius Coll., 1943-44; physicist Carnegie Mellon Inst., Washington, 1944-45; with E.I. DuPont de Nemours & Co., Buffalo, 1945-90, staff scientist, 1973-90, environ. health cons., 1973-90; cons. in environ. health, 1990—. Rsch. assoc. Toxicoloty Rsch. Ctr., SUNY, Buffalo. Patentee in field. Bd. dirs. Am. Lung Assn. of N.Y. State, Buffalo, 1985—; chmn. Tonawanda (N.Y.) Citizen Pre-Treatment Program, 1985-86, Tonawanda Hazardous Materials Adv. Com., Buffalo, 1985-88; chmn. local emergency planning commn. Buffalo and Erie County, N.Y., 1988—; mem. citizens adv. com. Remedial Action Plan for Niagara River Recipient Indsl. and Hazardous Waste award N.Y. State Water Pollution Control Assn., 1989. Mem. Air Pollution Control Assn. (chmn. 1983-84, Svc. award 1984), Am. Chem. Soc., Am. Indsl. Hygiene Assn., Am. Bd. Indsl. Hygiene, Am. Pub. Health Assn., Am. Soc. Safety Engrs., Water Pollution Control Fedn. Republican. Roman Catholic. Avocations: photography, swimming, bicycling. Home: 62 Wedgewood Dr Buffalo NY 14221-1469 E-mail: lamborski@webtv.net.

AMBRO, THOMAS L., federal judge; b. Cambridge, Ohio, Dec. 27, 1949; BA, Georgetown U., 1971, JD, 1975. Bar: Del. 1976. Clk. Hon. Daniel L. Herrmann Del. Supreme Ct., 1975—76; assoc. Richards, Layton and Finger, 1976—82, ptnr., 1982—2000; judge U.S. Ct. Appeals (3d cir.), 2000—. Mem. State Del. Gov.'s Com. on Major Comml. Litig. Reform, 1993, N.Y. TriBar Opinion Com., 1988—. Author: Third Party Legal Opinions in Asset Based Financing: A Transactional Guide, 1990; contbr. articles to profl. jours. Mem.: ABA (vice-chair com. on programs 1987—90, chair com. on meetings 1988—90, participant Silverado Conf. on Legal Opinions 1989, mem. drafting subcom. third-party legal opinion report 1989—91, chair subcom. on opinion letters 1989—95, mem. com. on comml. fin. svcs. 1989—95, chair com. on meetings 1990—94, chair or co-chair com. on publs. 1994—97, chair com. on legal opinions 1994—98, mem. coun. sect. bus. law 1994—98, editl. bd. The Bus. Lawyer 1998—99, editor The Bus. Lawyer 1999—2000, vice-chair sect. bus. law 1999—2000, chair elect bus. law 2000—01, chair sec. bus. law 2001—02, sec. sect. bus. law 1998-99, immediate past chmn. 2002—03, mem. com. on uniform comml. code, mem. com. on negotiated acquisitions, mem. bus. bankruptcy com.), Am. Coll. Comml. Fin. Lawyers, Am. Coll. Bankruptcy, Del. State Bar Assn. (chmn. 1979—82, vice-chmn. 1982—83, comml. law sect., chair subcom. on uniform comml. code 1983—2003), Phi Beta Kappa. Office: Lockbox 32 5300 Fed Bldg 844 N King St Wilmington DE 19801

AMBROSE, ANTHONY, business owner, chef; Chef Marlborough Inn, Montclair, NJ, 1979, Bay Twr. Rm., Boston, 1984, Jasper's, Boston, Rarities, Boston; chef de cuisine Julien, Hotel Meridien; exec. chef Seasons Restaurant, Bostonian Hotel, Boston, 1991—93; co-owner Ambrosia on Huntington, Boston, 1993—. Named USA Chef of Yr., Am. Tasting Inst., 1999. Office: Ambrosia on Huntington 116 Huntington Ave Boston MA 02116

AMBROSE, BRADLEY SCOTT, physics educator, researcher; b. Lewisburg, Pa., Oct. 7, 1969; s. Alfred Anthony and Janice Marie (Hescox) A.; m. Alice Anita Bass, Feb. 14, 1998. BS in Physics cum laude, Yale U., 1991; MS in Physics, U. Wash., 1993, PhD in Physics, 1998. Tchg. asst., rsch. asst. in physics U. Wash., Seattle, 1991—99; assoc. prof. physics Grand Valley State U., Allendale, Mich., 1999—. Contbr. Physics by Inquiry, 1996, Tutorials in Introductory Physics, 1998. Recipient Prof. Howard L. Schultz Physics prize Yale U., 1991; fellow U.S. Armed Forces Comms. and Electronics Assn., 1987. Mem. Am. Assn. Physics Tchrs., Am. Phys. Soc. Lutheran. Office: Grand Valley State U Dept Physics 125 Padnos Hall Allendale MI 49401 Business E-Mail: ambroseb@gvsu.edu.

AMBROSE, DANIEL MICHAEL, publishing executive; b. Salem, Oreg., Nov. 1, 1955; s. Franklin Burnell and Jean Marie (Crakes) A.; m. Cynthia Barbara Friedman, Mar. 26, 1983; children: Robert Grant, Michael Bruce. BS in Polit. Sci., Lewis and Clark Coll., 1977. Mktg. mgr. Washington Monthly, 1978-79; advt. promotion mgr. Am. Film Mag., Washington, 1979-80, advt. mgr., 1980-81, advt. dir., 1981-83, Backpacker Mag., N.Y.C., 1983-84; advt. salesman House Beautiful, Hearst Mag., N.Y.C., 1984-85; corp. advt. dir. mag. div. Hearst Pub. Corp., N.Y.C., 1985-87; pub. Fathers Mag., N.Y.C., 1987-89; advt. dir. Cahners Pub. Co., N.Y.C., 1989-92; pub. Child Mag. Network Women's Mag. div. N.Y. Times Co., N.Y.C., 1992-94; mng. dir. ambro.com., N.Y.C., 1994—, DeSilva & Phillips Media Investment Bankers, N.Y.C., 1998—2003. Media cons., investments and sales, N.Y.C., 1994—; presenter Mag. Pubs. Am. Contbr. articles on mag. mgmt. to Folio mag. Chmn. bd. Kidsports, 2002—03. Avocations: book collecting, skiing, tennis.

AMBROSE, DONETTA W., federal judge; b. New Kensington, Nov. 5, 1945; m. J. Raymond Ambrose Jr., Aug. 19, 1972; 1 child. BA, Duquesne U., 1963-67, JD cum laude, 1967-70. Law clerk to Hon. Louis L. Manderino Commonwealth Ct. Pa., 1970-71, Supreme Ct. Pa., 1972; asst. atty. gen. Pa. Dept. Justice, 1972-74; pvt. practice atty. Ambrose & Ambrose, Kensington, Pa., 1974-81; asst. dist. atty. Westmoreland County, Pa., 1977-81; judge Ct. Common Pleas Westmoreland County, 1982-93, US Dist. Ct. (We. Dist.) Pa., Pitts., 1994—, chief judge. Resident advisor Duquesne U., 1967-70. Scholar Pa. Conf. State Trial Judges, 1992, State Justice Inst., 1993. Mem. ABA, Nat. Assn. Women Judges, Am. Judicature Soc., Pa. Bar Assn., Women's Bar Assn. Western Pa., Pa. Conf. State Trial Judges (sec. 1992-93), Westmoreland

County Bar Assn., Italian Sons and Daus. Am., William Penn Fraternal Assn., New Kensington Women's Club, Delta Kappa Gamma. Office: US Courthouse Office 700 Grant St Rm 307 Pittsburgh PA 15219-1906*

AMBROSE, JUDITH ANN, interior designer; b. San Jose, Calif., Oct. 22, 1940; d. Howard Linse and Beula May (Russell) Shannon; m. James Paul Ambrose, Apr. 17, 1965; children: Sheryl Ann Beckey, James Paul Jr. BS, Salem Coll., Winston-Salem, NC, 1962; postgrad., Purdue U., 1963—64. Lic. home econs. tchr. Fla., NC. Home econs. tchr. Broward County, Ft. Lauderdale, Fla., 1962—67; owner Decorative Accents, Ft. Lauderdale, 1984—99; wedding coord. Christ Ch. United Meth., Ft. Lauderdale, 1990—2004. Home econs. curriculum dir. Broward County Schs., Ft. Lauderdale, 1965—66. Pres. Parent Tchr. Fellowship Westminster Acad., 1982—83; mem. resource group Children's Diagnostic and Treatment Ctr., Ft. Lauderdale, 1997—2003, bd. dirs., 2001—, sec. bd. dirs., 2003—, interim co-chair Sunflower Cir. of Friends, 2004; founder Friends of Jack & Jill Nursery, Ft. Lauderdale; organizer shoe fund for children in cmty. Christ Meth. Ch., 1992—; mem. Pres's Coun. Ft. Lauderdale, 1989; bd. dirs. Jack & Jill Nursery Sch., Ft. Lauderdale, 1974—2000; mem. Beaux Arts, 1986—90. Recipient Outstanding Cmty. Svc. award, Jr. League of Ft. Lauderdale, 1989, Golden Rule award, J C Penney, Ft. Lauderdale, 1995, Heart of the Cmty. Vol. of Yr. award, Children's Diagnostic and Treatment Ctr., Broward, Fla., 2002, 2005. Mem.: AAUW, Charity Guild (chmn. fall function 1992, publicity chmn. 1993—96, chmn. fall function 1997, pres. 1998—99, bd. dirs. 2001—03, rep. to Kids in Distress), Coral Ridge Jr. Women's Club (hon.; past pres., Clubwoman of Yr. 1975—76). Republican. Methodist. Avocations: growing orchids, volunteer work. Home: 4720 NE 25th Ave Fort Lauderdale FL 33308-4811

AMBROSE, LAUREN, actress; b. New Haven, Conn., Nov. 16, 1978; d. Frank and Annie Ambrose; m. Sam Handel, 2001. Attended, Conn. Ednl. Ctr. Arts, Yale U., Tanglewood Inst., Boston U. Actor(guest appearances): (TV series) Law & Order, 1992—98, Party of Five, 1999, Saving Graces, 1999, Six Feet Under, 2001—05 (Emmy nom. Supporting Actress Drama, 2003); (plays, off-Broadway) Soulful Scream of a Chosen Son, 1992; (films) In & Out, 1997, Can't Hardly Wait, 1998, Summertime's Calling Me, 1998, Psycho Beach Party, 2000, Swimming, 2000. Office: c/o United Talent Agency 9560 Wilshire Blvd Ste 500 Beverly Hills CA 90212

AMBROSE, MYLES JOSEPH, lawyer; b. N.Y.C., July 21, 1926; s Arthur P. and Ann (Campbell) A.; m. Elaine Miller, June 26, 1948 (dec. Sept. 1975); children: Myles Joseph, Kathleen Anne, Kevin Arthur, Elise Mary, Nora Jeanne, Christopher Miller; m. Lorraine Genovese, June 3, 1994. Grad., New Hampton Sch., N.H., 1944; BBA, Manhattan Coll., 1948, LLD (hon.), 1972; JD, N.Y. Law Sch., 1952. Bar: N.Y. 1952, U.S. Supreme Ct. 1969, D.C. 1973, U.S. Ct. Appeals (fed. cir.) 1970, U.S. Ct. Internat. Trade 1970, D.C. Ct. Appeals 1973. Pers. mgr. Devenco, Inc., 1948-49, 51-54; adminstrv. asst. U.S. atty. So. dist., N.Y., 1954-57; instr. econs. and indsl. rels. Manhattan Coll., 1955-57; asst. to sec. U.S. Treasury, 1957-60; exec. dir. Waterfront Commn. of N.Y. Harbor, 1960-63; pvt. practice law N.Y.C., 1963-69; chief counsel N.Y. State Joint Legislative Com. for Study Alcoholic Beverage Control Law, 1963-65; U.S. commr. customs Washington, 1969-72; spl. cons. to Pres., spl. asst. atty. gen., 1972-73; ptnr. Spear & Hill, 1973-75, Ambrose & Casselman, P.C., 1975—78, O'Connor & Hannan, Washington, 1978—88, Ross and Hardies, Washington, 1988—98; of counsel Arter & Hadden, Washington, 1998—2002; currently sr. advisor Sandler Travis Trade Adv. Svc. U.S. observer 13th session UN Commn. on Narcotics, Geneva, Switzerland, 1958; chmn. U.S. del. 27th Gen. Assembly, Internat. Criminal Police Orgn., London, 1958, 28th Extraordinary Gen. Assembly, Paris, 1959; U.S. observer 29th Gen. Assembly, Washington, 1960; mem. U.S. del., Mexico City, 1969, Brussels, 1970, Ottawa, 1971, Frankfurt, 1972; chmn. U.S.-Mexico Conf. on Narcotics, Washington, 1960, mem. confs., Washington and; Mexico City, 1969, 70, 71, 72; chmn. U.S.-Canadian-Mexican Conf. on Customs Procedures, San Clemente, Calif., 1970; chmn. U.S. del. Customs Cooperation Coun., Brussels, 1970; chmn., Vienna, 1971, U.S.-European Customs Conf. Narcotics, Paris and; Vienna, 1971; organized Drug Enforcement Adminstrn. (DEA), 1973; hon. consul Principality of Monaco, Washington, 1973-98; mem. adv. com. on customs comml. ops. U.S. Treasury Dept., 1988-91; past chmn. ABA standing com. on customs law. Author: Primer on Customs Law. Bd. dirs. U. Coll. of Dublin-Grad. Bus. Sch., 1996-2001; bd. mem. Daytop Village, 1973—; vice-chmn. Reagan-Bush Inaugural Com., 1980; mem. adv. bd. Eisenhower Inst. of World Affairs. Decorated chevalier Order of Grimaldi (Monaco), knight comdr. Order of Merit Italian Republic, knight Holy Sepulchre; recipient Presdl. Mgmt. Improvement cert. Pres. Nixon, 1970, Sec. Treasury Exceptional Svc. award, 1970, Disting. Alumnus award N.Y. Law Sch., 1973, Alumni award for pub. svc. Manhattan Coll., 1972 Fellow Am. Bar Found.; mem. Friendly Sons of St. Patrick, Univ. Club (D.C.), Alpha Sigma Beta, Phi Alpha Delta (hon.) Republican. Roman Catholic. Home: #912 19375 Cypress Ridge Ter Leesburg VA 20176-5182 Office: Sandler Travis Trade Adv Svc 1300 Penn Ave Washington DC 20004-9307 Office Phone: 202-216-9307. Personal E-mail: ballyeagna@aol.com.

AMBROSE, SAMUEL SHERIDAN, JR., retired urologist educator; b. Jacksonville, N.C., Oct. 2, 1923; s. Samuel Sheridan and Beatrice (Collins) A.; m. Betty Stuart Stansbury, Oct. 7, 1950; children: Charles Stuart, Ann Collins, Samuel Bruce. AB in Chemistry, Duke U., 1943, MD, 1947. Diplomate: Am. Bd. Urology, Nat. Bd. Med. Examiners. Intern surgery, then asst. resident urology Duke U. Hosp., 1947—50, resident urology, 1953; instr. physiology Duke U. Med. Sch., 1947, instr. urology, 1953; mem. faculty Emory U. Med. Sch., Atlanta, 1954—, prof. urology, 1972—92, prof. urology surgery emeritus, 1992—, chmn. divsn. urology, 1985—89; mem. staff Emory U. Hosp., 1972—92, chief urology, 1972—91; pvt. practice medicine specializing in urology Atlanta, 1954—71; mem. staff Piedmont Hosp., 1954—72, chief urology, 1960; mem. staff Grady Meml. Hosp., 1954—82, Henrietta Egleston Hosp. for Children, 1956—92; retired, 1992. Contbr. numerous articles to med. jours. Served as officer M.C. USNR, 1950-52. Fellow Royal Soc. Medicine; mem. AMA, ACS, Am. Urol. Assn. (hon. S.E. chpt., pres. S.E. sect. 1974-75, chmn. nat. sci. exhibits com. 1974-83, exec. com. 1983-90, Disting. Svc. award 1990, Gold Cane award 1995, hon. 1996—), Soc. Pediatric Urology (pres. 1971-72), Am. Assn. Clin. Urologists, Am. Acad. Pediat., Am. Assn. Genito-Urinary Surgeons, Soc. Internat. D'Urologie, Pan-Pacific Surg. Assn., Med. Assn. Ga., Ga. Urol. Assn. (pres. 1967), So. Med. Soc. (chmn. urology sect. 1970-71), Fulton County Med. Soc., Atlanta Clin. Soc. (v.p. 1964), Soc. Univ. Urologists, Piedmont Driving Club, Cherokee Town and Country Club (pres. 1968-69), Univ. Yacht Club (commodore 1973), Homosassa Fishing Club (v.p. 1980-81, 92-94). Presbyterian. Home: 1014 Nawench Dr NW Atlanta GA 30327-1340 E-mail: sam@maclanta.com.

AMBROSE, SHERRY L, principal, elementary school educator; b. Orefield, Pa., Jan. 18, 1970; d. Arlan Stewart and Dorothy Helen Stahley; 1 child, Alisa. BA in elem. edn., student, Wilkes U., 1999—. Cert. tchr. Pa., 1999. Computer sci. tchr. Transfiguration Elem. Sch., West Hazelton, Pa., 1999—2001, tchr., 2001—02, tchr. lang. arts, 2002—03, prin., 2003—. Mid. states accreditation chairperson Transfiguration Elem. Sch., 2002—03, pastoral coun. mem., 2003—, sci. fair chairperson, 1999—2002, social studies fair chairperson, 2002—03, religion fair adv., 2003—04, sch. newspaper adv., 1999—2001, sch. column adv., 1999—2001, leadership team mem., 2003—, tech. com. mem., 1999—, student coun. founder/leader, 2003—, sch. adv. bd. co-founder and ex-officio mem., 2003—; Parent Guild ex-officio mem., 2003—. Leader Carbon County 4-H, Weatherly, Pa., 2002—03. Recipient David Cudney scholarship, Wilkes U., 1995, Celebration of Tchg. Participant, 1995. Cath. Avocations: reading, writing, gardening. Office: Transfiguration Elem Sch 217 W Green St Hazleton PA 18202

AMBROSE, TOMMY W., chemical engineer, engineering executive; b. Jerome, Idaho, Oct. 14, 1926; s. Fines M. and Avice (Barnes) A.; m. Shirley Ann Ball, June 23, 1951; children: Leslie Ann, Julie Lynn, Pamela Lee. BS, U. Idaho, 1950, MS, 1951, PhD (hon.), 1981; PhD, Oreg. State U., 1957. Registered profl. engr., Wash., Ohio, Idaho. Engr. GE, Richland, Wash., 1951-54, 57-60, supr. reactor fuels, 1960-63, mgr. process and reactor devel., 1963-65, mgr. rsch. and engring., 1965; mgr. for rsch. and engring. Douglas United Nuclear Co., Richland, 1969-71; asst. dir. Battelle Seattle Rsch. Ctr., 1969-71, exec. dir., 1971-75; dir. Battelle Pacific N.W. Labs., Richland, 1975-79; corp. dir. multicomponent ops. Battelle Meml. Inst., Columbus, Ohio, 1979-88, dir. Battelle Edn. and Tng. Bus., 1988-90, v.p., 1975-90; liaison officer Lawrence Livermore (Calif.) Nat. Lab., 1990-91; spl. asst. lab. affairs U. Calif., Oakland, 1992-96. Adj. prof. grad. level Idaho State U. Coll. Engring., 1998—. Mem. adv. bd. Coll. Engring., U. Idaho, Moscow, 1974-83, 85-91, chmn. adv. bd., 1988-91, 96—; mem. vis. com. Coll. Engring., U. Wash., 1974-83; adj. prof. grad. level Idaho State U. Coll. Engring., 1998-, mem. adv. coun., 1999—; mem. gov.'s adv. coun. Dept. Commerce and Econ. Devel., 1975-79; mem. Wash. State Coun. Postsecondary Edn., 1977-79; chmn. bd. trustees Columbia Basin Coll., 1967-69; bd. dirs. N.W.Coll., U. Assn. for Sci., 1976-79; v.p., trustee, mem. exec. com. Pacific Sci. Ctr. Found.; trustee, mem. exec. com. Columbus Symphony Orch., 1980-84; trustee Ohio Wesleyan U., 1987-91; bd. dirs. Idaho State Civic Symphony, 1999—, pres., 2000-01; mem. Gov.'s Sci. and Tech. Coun. for Idaho, 1999—; mem. adv. bd. Natural Heritage Ctr., 1998—2002; bd. dirs. U. Idaho Found., 1996—2002. Recipient Profl. Achievement award Idaho State U. Coll. Engring., 2000; inductee Oreg. State U. Coll. Engring. Hall of Fame, 2001. Fellow AICE (chmn. comms. com. mgmt. divsn. 1981-87, program evaluator and mem. Accreditation Bd. for Engring. and Tech. engring. accreditation commn. 1989-96); mem. Am. Nuclear Soc., Ohio Acad. Sci., Sigma Xi, Pi Lambda Upsilon. Methodist. Home: 2500 Spider Creek Inkom ID 83245-1740

AMBROSINI, ARMAND ANTHONY, music educator; b. New Haven, Ct., Sept. 11, 1949; s. Armand and Dina Ambrosini. BFA, Calif. Inst. of Arts, 1972, MFA, 1974; MusM, Yale Sch. of Music, 1976; MusD, SUNY, 1995. Vis. asst. prof. U. Nebr., Lincoln, Nebr., 1989—90; lectr. Humboldt State U., Arcata, Calif., 1990—93; vis. asst. prof. U. Okla., Norman, Okla., 1993—. Performing artist, coach Sequoia Chamber Music Workshop, Arcata, Calif., 1992—; artist, coach Ashland Chamber Music Workshop, Ashland, Oreg., 1995—, Humboldt Chamber Music Workshop, Arcata, 2004—; performing artist, coach Chamber Music Conf., Composer's Forum of East, Bennington, Vt., 2001—. Author, recording artist: book and cd Ned Rorem's Song Cycle Areil: A Musical Dramatization of Five Poems by Sylvia Plath, 2001; co-author: Introduction To Western Concert Music, 2003, rev. edit., 2005. Treas. Chamber Musicians' Alliance of Greater New Haven, New Haven, 1979—80; bus. mgr. Cordier Ensemble, 1974—. Mem.: Coll. Music Soc., Alpha Lambda Chpt. of Pi Kappa Lambda Nat. Music Honor Society. Achievements include founding mem. Cordier Ensemble. Avocations: sailing, hiking, camping. Home: 709 S Flood Ave Norman OK 73069 Office: U Okla 500 W Boyd St Rm 138 Norman OK 73019-3130 Office Phone: 405-325-0434. E-mail: aambrosini@ou.edu.

AMBROSINO, RALPH THOMAS, JR., retired telecommunications executive; b. Gloversville, N.Y., Aug. 5, 1940; s. Ralph Thomas and Mary Agnes (Peters) A.; m. Roberta Joy Goldman, Nov. 1, 1970; children: Robin, Jill. BS in Acctg., U. Buffalo, 1961. With Gen. Telephone Co., 1968-74; gen. comml. mgr. Upstate N.Y., Johnstown, 1968-70, gen. service office mgr., 1970-74; regulatory matters mgr. GTE Service Corp., Stamford, Conn., 1974-76, revenues and earnings mgr., 1976-78; dir. regulatory affairs Gen. Telephone Co. of Calif., Santa Monica, 1979-81; dir. regulatory matters GTE Service Corp., Stamford, 1981-84, v.p. investor relations, 1984-87, v.p. external affairs, 1987. Mem. Investor Relations Assn. Home: 154 Southport Woods Dr Southport CT 06890

AMBROSIO, JOSEPH MICHAEL, secondary school educator, composer; s. James Vincent and Margaret Rita Ambrosio; m. Constance Ann Rast, Nov. 9, 1969; children: Joseph Michael, John, Jean. BA, Manhattan Sch. Music, 1976; M of Liberal Arts, Stony Brook U., 1999. Cert. tchr. NY. Composer, arranger Chappell Music, NYC, 1977—81; pvt. practice East Northport, NY, 1981—92; tchr. Islip (NY) HS, 1992—. Cons. Hauppauge (NY) HS, 2003—04. Composer: (songs) Raggedy Rosie, March for John, The Strasburg Railroad, Clowntown, Nature's Serenade, A Valiant Procession, Royal Blue Procession. With N.G. U.S. Army, 1960. Recipient Composer award, New Music for Young Ensembles, 1985—2004. Mem.: ASCAP (Std. Publ. award 1985—). Republican. Avocations: reading, gardening.

AMBROZIC, ALOYSIUS CARDINAL (HIS EMINENCE ALOYSIUS CARDINAL AMBROZIC), archbishop; b. Gabrje, Slovenia, Jan. 27, 1930; s. Aloysius and Helen (Pecar) Ambrozic. Student, St. Augustine Sem., 1955; STL, U. San Tommaso, Rome, 1958, Sacrae Scripturae Licentiatus, Biblicum, Rome, 1960; ThD, U. Wurzburg, 1970. Ordained priest Roman Cath. Ch., 1955. Ordained aux. bishop of Roman Cath. Ch., Toronto, 1976; appointed coadjutor archbishop of Toronto, 1986; archbishop of Toronto, 1990—; created cardinal, 1998. Faculty St. Augustines Sem., Scarborough, Ont., Canada, 1956—76, dean studies, 1971—76; rep. Synod on the Formation of Priests, Rome, 1990, Synod on Religious Life, Rome, 1994; prof. N.T. exegesis Toronto Sch. Theology, 1970—76; apptd. to Pontifical Coun. for Pastoral Care of Migrants and Itinerant People, 1990, Vatican Congregation for Clergy, 1991, Pontifical Coun. for Culture, 1993, Vatican Congregation for Divine Worship and Discipline of Sacraments, 1999, Congregation for Oriental Chs., 1999. Author: The Hidden Kingdom: A Redaction-Critical Study of the References to the Kingdom of God in Mark's Gospel, 1972, Remarks on the Canadian Catechism, 1974; past columnist: Cath. Register. Roman Catholic.

AMBRUS, CLARA MARIA, physician; b. Rome, Dec. 28, 1924; arrived in U.S., 1949, naturalized, 1955; d. Anthony and Charlotte (Schneider) Bayer; m. Julian Lawrence Ambrus, Feb. 17, 1945; children: Madeline Ambrus Lillie, Peter, Julian, Linda Ambrus-Broenniman, Steven, Katherine Ambrus-Cheney, Charles. Student, U. Budapest (Hungary), 1943—47; MD, U. Zurich, Switzerland, 1949; postgrad., U. Paris, 1949; PhD, Jefferson Med. Coll., 1955. Diplomate Am. Bd. Clin. Chemists. Research asst. Inst. Histology, Embryology and Biology U. Budapest, 1943-45; demonstrator in pharmacology U. Budapest Med. Sch., 1946-47; asst. dept. pharmacology U. Zurich Med. Sch., 1947-49; asst. dept. therapeutic chemistry and virology Inst. Pasteur, Paris, 1949; asst. prof. pharmacology Phila. Coll. Pharmacy and Sci., 1950-52, assoc. prof., 1952-55; research assoc. Roswell Park Meml. Inst., Buffalo, 1955-58, sr. cancer research scientist, 1958-64, assoc. scientist, 1964-69, prin. cancer research scientist, 1969-85; prof. pharmacology State U. N.Y., Buffalo Med. and Grad. Schs., 1955—, assoc. prof. pediatrics, 1955-76, prof. pediatrics, 1976, research prof. ob-gyn, 1983—; chmn., founder, chief of R&D Hemex Inc., 1984—. Contbr. articles to med. and sci. jours. Trustee Nichols Sch., Buffalo, Cmty. Music Sch. Decorated lady comdr. Equestrian Order of the Holy Sepulchre of Jerusalem; named Outstanding Woman of Western N.Y., Cmty. Adv. Coun., SUNY, Buffalo, 1980, Med. Woman of Yr., Buffalo Gen. Hosp., 2000; recipient award for excellence in clin. care, d'Youville Coll., 2004, George F. Koepf, MD award, Hauptman-Woodward Med. Rsch. Inst., Buffalo, 1997. Fellow: ACP, Internat. Soc. Hematology; mem.: Hungarian Acad. Sci. (fgn. mem.), Am. Med. Women's Assn., Buffalo Acad. Medicine, Am. Soc. Hematology, Am. Physiol. Soc., Am. Fedn. Clin. Rsch., Am. Soc. Cancer Rsch., Am. Soc. Pharmacology and Exptl. Therapeutics, Saturn Club, Clarksburg Country Club, Garrett Club, Sigma Xi. Home: 143 Windsor Ave Buffalo NY 14209-1020 also: West Hill Farm Boston NY 14025 Office: Buffalo Gen Hosp 100 High St Buffalo NY 14203-1154 Office Phone: 716-859-1512. Personal E-mail: jlambrus@netscape.net.

AMBRUS, JULIAN L., physician, medical educator; b. Budapest, Hungary, Nov. 29, 1924; arrived in U.S., 1949, naturalized, 1955; s. Alexander and Elizabeth Ambrus; m. Clara M. Bayer, Feb. 18, 1945; children: Madeline Lillie, Peter, Julian, Linda Broenniman, Steven, Katherine Cheney, Charles. Student, U. Budapest, 1942—47; MD, U. Zurich, 1949; postgrad., Sorbonne U., 1949—50; PhD in Med. Sci, Jefferson Med. Coll., 1954; ScD (hon.), Niagara U., 1984. Diplomate Am. Bd. Clin. Chemistry, Am. Acad. Pain Mgmt. Rsch. asst., instr. histology and med. biology U. Budapest, 1943-45, demonstrator pharmacology, 1946-47; asst. pharmacology U. Zurich, 1947-49; asst. dept. therapeutic chemistry, virology and tropical medicine Inst. Pasteur, Paris, 1949; asst. prof., assoc. prof., prof. Phila. Coll. Pharmacy and Sci., 1950-55; prin. cancer rsch. scientist Roswell Park Meml. Cancer Inst. and Hosp., 1955-65; asst. to dir. Roswell Park Meml. Inst. and Hosp., 1961-65; dir. Springville Labs., 1965-75, dir. cancer rsch., head dept. pathophysiology, 1975-89, mem. dept. medicine, 1989-92; asst. prof. pharmacology U. Buffalo Med. Sch., 1955-61, assoc. prof. pharmacology, 1961-65, prof., 1965-72; chmn. Roswell Park divsn. exec. com. Grad. Sch., 1955-65; assoc. in internal medicine SUNY, Buffalo, 1961-64, asst. prof. internal medicine, 1964-66, prof. biochem. pharmacology, 1964-80, assoc. prof. internal medicine, 1966-71, prof., 1971—, prof., chmn. dept. exptl. pathology Grad. Sch., 1972-92, prof. emeritus, 1992—. Attending physician Roswell Park Meml. Cancer Hosp., 1955-92, prof. emeritus Roswell Park Cancer Inst., 1992—; attending physician Buffalo Gen. Hosp., Erie County Med. Ctr., Children's Hosp. Buffalo, 1983—; cons. Millard Fillmore Hosp., Sisters of Charity Hosp., Buffalo, 1983—; dir. Instnl. Cancer Tng. Program, USPHS, 1956-65; mem. com. Thrombolytic agts. USPHS-NIH, 1960-66; cons. adv. com. on thrombosis AMA Coun. Drugs; Blood Coagulation Components, Protein Found., Cambridge, Mass.; Bur. Drugs FDA, WHO, Geneva; commr. Lake Erie chpt. U.S. Pony Clubs, mem. intercollegiate polo com. Editor-in-chief: Revs. of Hematology Jour. Medicine; contbr. articles to profl. jours. Trustee Calasanctius Prep. Sch. for Academically Gifted, 1964-92; bd. trustees Elmwood Franklin Sch., 1967-79, v.p., 1978-79. Decorated Order of Alexander the Great (France), knight comdr. Equestrian Order Holy Sepulcher of Jerusalem; recipient first prize med. student paper Hungarian Med. Sch., 1947, 1st prize surgery U. Budapest, 1947, Nelson lectureship and medal U. Calif. Davis, 1972, George F. Koepf award in biomed. rsch. Hauptman-Woodward Med. Rsch. Inst., 1997, Heart and Hand award EUA, 1997, Louis A. and Ruth Siegel award SUNY Buffalo Sch. Medicine, 1997, Achievement award in health care D'Youville Coll., 2004; named Disting. Alumnus Thomas Jefferson U., 1990. Fellow ACP, AAAS, Am. Coll. Nuc. Physicians, Am. Coll. Angiology, Royal Soc. Medicine, Am. Coll. Pharmacology and Chemotherapy, Coun. on Clin. Cardiology, Am. Heart Assn., Internat. Coll. Angiology, Am. Geriat. Soc., NY Acad. Sci., Internat. Soc. Hematology; mem. NAS (fgn. mem. Hungary), Am. Soc. Hematology, Am. Soc. Pathologists, Am. Soc. Nuc. Medicine, Am. Soc. Pharmacology and Exptl. Therapeutics, Am. Soc. Physiology, Am. Assn. Cancer Rsch., Am. Soc. Clin. Oncology, Fedn. Clin. Rsch., Soc. Exptl. Biology and Medicine, Assn. Am. Med. Colls., Cath. Physicians Guild (pres. 1985-86, 93-96), Sigma Xi, Rho Chi, Physiol. Soc. Phila., Radiation Rsch. Soc., Buffalo Zool. Soc. (chmn. sci. com. 1965-66), Buffalo Acad. Medicine (pres. 1976-77). Home: 143 Windsor Ave Buffalo NY 14209-1020 also: West Hill Farm Emmerling Rd Boston NY 14025 Office: Buffalo Gen Hosp Kaleida Health Sys SUNY/B 100 High St Buffalo NY 14203-1154 Fax: 716-859-1491. Office Phone: 716-859-1399. Personal E-mail: jl.ambrus@netscape.net.

AMDAHL, DOUGLAS KENNETH, retired state supreme court justice; b. Mabel, Minn., Jan. 23, 1919; BBA, U. Minn., 1945; JD summa cum laude, William Mitchell Coll. Law, 1951, L.L.D. (hon.), 1987. Bar: Minn. 1951, Fed. Dist. Ct. 1952. Ptnr. Amdahl & Scott, Mpls., 1951-55; asst. county atty. Hennepin County, Minn., 1955-61; judge Mcpl. Ct., Mpls., 1961-62, Dist. Ct. 4th Dist., Minn., 1962-80, chief judge, 1973-75; assoc. justice Minn. Supreme Ct., 1980-81, chief justice, 1981-89; of counsel Rider, Bennett, Egan & Arundel, Mpls., 1989-99; ret. Asst. registrar, then registrar Mpls. Coll. Law, 1951-65; moot ct. instr. U. Minn.; faculty mem. and advisor Nat. Coll. State Judiciary; mem. Nat. Bd. Trial Advocacy; chmn. Nat. Ctr. for State Cts. Delay Reduction Adv. Com., 1986-88, Nat. Ctr. for State Cts. Coordinating Coun. on Life-Sustaining Decisionmaking by the Cts., 1989-93. Mem. ABA (chmn. com. on stds. of jud. adminstrn. 1987-96), Minn. Bar Assn., Hennepin County Bar Assn., Internat. Acad. Trial Judges, State Dist. Ct. Judges Assn. (pres. 1976-77), Conf. of Chief Judges (bd. dirs. 1987-88), Delta Theta Phi (assoc. justice supreme ct.). Home: 6600 Lyndale Ave S 905 Richfield MN 55423 Personal E-mail: dougamdahl@aol.com.

AMDUR, ARTHUR R., lawyer; b. Houston, Jan. 19, 1946; s. Paul S. and Florence Amdur; m. Dora B. Amdur; children: Josh, Jonny. BA, 1967, JD, 1970, LLM, 1974. Bar: Tex. 1970, D.C. 1974, cert.: Tex. Bd. Legal Specialization (in immigation law) 1988. Pvt. practice, Houston, 1970—76, Washington, 1970—76; asst. U.S. atty. Houston, 1976—82; pvt. practice, 1982—. Lectr. on immigration law; adj. prof., law S. Tex. Coll. Law, Houston. Spl. asst. to gen. counsel Republican Nat. Com., Washington, 1974; bd. dirs. YMCA Internat. Refugee Ctr., 1985—. Named Adj. Prof. Yr., S. Tex. Coll. Law, 1983. Mem.: Immigration Law Examiner, Am. Immigration Lawyers Assn., Tex. State Bar Assn. (bd. legal specialization 1997—2001), Fed. Bar Assn., Georgetown U. Alumni (pres., Houston chpt. 1984). Jewish. Office: Amdur Law Office 6161 Savoy Dr Ste 450 Houston TX 77036-3379 Office Phone: 713-268-1000. Business E-Mail: visas@amdurlaw.com.

AMDUR, MARTIN BENNETT, lawyer; b. N.Y.C., Aug. 19, 1942; s. Charles and Helen (Freedman) A.; m. Shirley Bell, May 25, 1975; children: Richard J., Stephen B. AB, Cornell U., 1964; LLB, Yale U., 1967; LLM in Taxation, NYU, 1968. Bar: N.Y. 1968, U.S. Tax Ct. 1970, U.S. Dist. Ct. (so. and ea. dists.) N.Y. 1971. Assoc. Weil, Gotshal & Manges LLP, N.Y.C., 1968-75, ptnr., 1975—. Lectr. various tax insts. Contbr. articles to legal jours. Mem. ABA, Am. Coll. Tax Counsel, N.Y. State Bar Assn., Assn. Bar City N.Y. Home: 983 Park Ave Apt 6B New York NY 10028-0808 Office: Weil Gotshal & Manges LLP 767 Fifth Ave New York NY 10153-0119 Office Phone: 212-310-8224. Business E-Mail: Martin.Amdur@Weil.com.

AMELAN, BJORN G., sculptor, set designer; Ptnr. Fashion Designer Patrick Kelly, 1983—90; choreographer Bill T. Jones/Arnie Zane Dance Co., N.Y.C., 1993—. Office: Bill T Jones/Arnie Zane Dance Co Found for Dance Promotion 853 Broadway Ste 1706 New York NY 10003

AMELAR, RICHARD DANIEL, urologist; b. N.Y.C., July 9, 1927; m. Alice Zinman, 1952; children: Jessica, Sarah, Susanna. BA, NYU, 1946, MD, 1950. Intern in urology French Hosp., 1950-51, resident in urology, 1951-54, attending urologist, 1956—68, dir. urology, 1968—77; pvt. practice urology, N.Y.C., 1956-96; mem. faculty NYU, 1956—, prof. clin. urology, 1977—; dir. Male Infertility Clinic, Bellevue Hosp., 1958-72, dir. Free Vasectomy Clinic, 1970-72, attending urologist, 1972—96; expert urol. cons. NY State Dept. Health, Office Profl. Med. Conduct, 2001—. Dir. male infertility svcs. Margaret Sanger Rsch. Bur., 1959-68; cons. WHO, Nat. Inst. Child Health and Human Devel., drug evaluation sect. AMA, NSF. *Clinical research began in 1958 with studies on patients with congenital absence of the vasa deferentia and seminal vesicles, determining that their semen lacked fructose and failed to coagulate upon ejaculation. Has made several contributions to the understanding of male infertility and is known for publications on sperm and semen analysis, the diagnosis and surgery of varicoceles and congenital anomalies of the male reproductive tract and studies which laid the foundation of knowledge for assisted reproductive technology methods in the treatment of infertility. Current interests are in the field of Public Health, serving as an expert consultant to the New York State Department of Health.* Cons. editor Urology; assoc. editor Internat. Jour. Fertility; editl. bds. Fertility and Sterility, Jour. Andrology Internat. Jour. Nephrology, Urology, Andrology. Capt. M.C., USAF, 1954-56. Grantee Irene Heinz Given and John La Porte Given Found. and N.Y. Found., 1970; recipient Disting. Andrologist award Am. Soc. Andrology, 1999; recipient Disting. Svc. award Am. Soc. Reproductive Medicine, 2002. Fellow ACS; mem. Am. Soc. Andrology, Soc. Sci. Study Sex (pres. 1970-71), Soc. Reproductive Surgeons, Am. Soc. for Study of Male Reprodn., Am. Urol. Assn., Am. Fertility Soc., Endocrine Soc., Pacific Coast Fertility Soc., NYU Sch. Medicine Alumni Ass. (pres. 1984-85, named Disting. Alumnus 2005), Alpha Omega Alpha (alumni mem. 1991) Home: 526 Bull Mill Rd Chester NY 10918-4706 Office Phone: 845-783-6768. Personal E-mail: ramelar@frontiernet.net.

AMEMIYA, KOICHI, motor vehicle company executive; Pres. Am. Honda Motor Co., Torrance, Calif., 1989—; COO, Automobile Operations/N. Am. Honda Motor Co., 1992—94, exec. v.p. Office: Am Honda Motor Co 1919 Torrance Blvd Torrance CA 90501-2722*

AMEN, ROBERT M., paper company executive; b. NYC, 1949; BA, Boston Coll., 1971; MBA, Columbia U., 1973. From v.p., contr. to v.p. Bleached Bd., Folding Carton and Label, 1988—94; v.p. Consumer Packaging, 1994—96; pres. Internat. Paper-Europe, Brussels, 1996—2000; exec. v.p. Internat. Paper Co, Stamford, Conn., 2000—03, pres., 2003—. Office: Internat Paper Co 400 Atlantic St Stamford CT 06921

AMENABAR, ALEJANDRO, film director, film producer, actor; b. Santiago, Chile, Mar. 31, 1972; Actor: (films) Al lado del Atlas, 1994, Allanamiento de morada, 1998, Butterfly Tongues, 1999, Nobody Knows Anybody, 1999; dir., actor, writer: Himenoptero, 1991; Luna, 1995; Open Your Eyes, 1997; The Others, 2001; prodr., dir., actor, writer Thesis, 1996; Mar adentro, 2004 (Acad. award Best Fgn. Lang. Film, 2005); prodr.: (films) El Sonador, 2004. Office: c/o Dimension Films 375 Greenwich St New York NY 10012*

AMEND, JAMES MICHAEL, lawyer; b. Chgo., July 19, 1942; s. Nathan and Edith (Greenberg) A.; m. Sheila Rae Cohen, Apr. 4, 1971; children: Allison, Anthony. BSE, U. Mich., 1964, JD, 1967. Bar: Ill. 1968, U.S. Dist. Ct. (no. dist.) Ill. 1968, U.S. Ct. Appeals (7th cir.) 1969, U.S. Supreme Ct. 1970, U.S. Ct. Appeals (9th cir.) 1985. Ptnr. Kirkland & Ellis, Chgo., 1968—. Prof. Stanford U. Law Sch., 1996-97. Editor U. Mich. Law Rev., 1966, Patent Law: A Primer for Federal District Court Judges, 1998; author: Intellectual Property Law, 1982. Chmn. Chgo. Lawyers Com. for Civil Rights Under Law, 1985-86. Fulbright scholar, 1967. Mem. ABA, U.S. Trademark Assn., Mid-Am. Club (Chgo.). Jewish. Avocations: running, skiing, golf. Office: Kirkland & Ellis 200 E Randolph St Fl 54 Chicago IL 60601-6636 Office Phone: 312-861-2154. E-mail: jamend@kirkland.com.

AMEND, JOSEPH H., III, military officer; BS in Civil Engring., Va. Poly. Inst. and State U., 1971, MS in Civil Engring., 1972, PhD in Civil Engring., 1973. Commd. 2d lt. USAF, 1971, advanced through grades to col., 1996; assoc. prof. civil engring., vice commandant and dean Civil Engr. and Svcs. Sch., Air Force Inst. Tech., 1997—98, assoc. prof. civil engring., dean Civil Engr. and Svcs. Sch., 1998—2001, vice commandant, 2001—. Decorated Meritorious Svc. medal with 4 oak leaf clusters, Commendation medal with one oak leaf cluster, Achievement medal, Outstanding Unit award with 3 oak leaf clusters, Organizational Excellence award with 3 oak leaf clusters, Def. Svc. medal with svc. star, Armed Forces Expeditionary medal; named Air Force Mil. Engr. of Yr., Nat. Soc. Profl. Engrs., 1984. Fellow: ASCE; mem.: Chi Epsilon, Tau Beta Pi, Phi Kappa Phi. Office: Air Force Inst Tech Office of Pub Affairs Wright Patterson Afb OH 45433-7765

AMEND, STEPHEN J., musician; b. Bay Shore, NY, Dec. 23, 1957; s. Anthony John and Matilda Teresa Amend; m. Patti Thompson, Oct. 29, 1983; 1 child, Tyler. Master guitar tchr. Music Services, Deer Park, NY, 1980—; record prodr. Photon Records, Deer Park, 1994—; music cons. O.D.O.L. Inc., New York, 2001—; recording guitarist Photon Records, Deer Park, 1980—. Talent judge Nationals Inc., Melville, NY, 2003; voting mem. Grammy Acad., N.Y.C., 2002—. Achievements include four NMW Top 40 Spin credits, two Gavin Top 40 Spin credits, three commercial endorsements, prod. wing-Grammy Acad. Avocations: racquetball, dogs, WWI planes. Home: 222 West 21st Street Deer Park NY 11729 Office: Photon Records 222 West 21st Street Deer Park NY 11729 Office Phone: 631-243-2941. Office Fax: 631-243-2941. E-mail: pattia@optonline.net.

AMEND, WILLIAM JOHN CONRAD, JR., physician, educator; b. Wilmington, Del., Sept. 17, 1941; s. William John Conrad and Catherine (Broad) A.; m. Constance Roberts, Feb. 3, 1962; children— William, Richard, Nicole, Mark BA, Amherst Coll., 1963; MD, Cornell U., 1967. Diplomate Am. Bd. Internal Medicine. Asst. clin. prof. U. Calif. Med. Ctr., San Francisco, 1974-76, assoc. clin. prof., 1977-82, prof. clin. medicine and surgery, 1982—2005, prof. emeritus medicine, 2005—; chief divsn. nephrology U. Calif., San Francisco, 1998—2003; physician Falmouth Med. Assocs. Contbr. articles to med. jours. Chmn. med. adv. com. No. Calif. Kidney Found., 1987-88; mem. stewardship com. 1st Presbyn. Ch., Burlingame, Calif., 1983, 84, elder, 1982-85, 93-96. Maj. U.S. Army, 1969-71. Simpson fellow, 1963; recipient Gift of Life award No. Calif. Kidney Found., 1993 Fellow: ACP; mem.: Amherst Coll. Alumni Fund (class agt. 1973-83, reunion chmn. 2003, class pres. 2003—). Avocations: golf, gardening, hiking. Home: 2860 Summit Dr Burlingame CA 94010-6257 Office: U Calif Med Ctr 3rd & Parnassus San Francisco CA 94143-0001

AMENOFF, GREGORY, artist, educator; b. St. Charles, Ill., 1948; BA, Beloit Coll., 1970; DFA (hon.), Mass. Coll. Arts, 1994. Pres. Nat. Acad. Mus. & Sch. Fine Arts, NYC, 2001—05; Eve and Herman Gelman prof. visual arts Columbia U., NYC. One-man shows include Galerie Marie-Louise Wirth, Zurich, 1990, Hirchl & Adler Modern, NYC, 1990, Kirchgemeinde Aussersihl, Kohn, Germany, 1991, Gerald Peters Gallery, Santa Fe, 1991, Galerie Bernard Vidal, Paris, 1991, Victoria Munroe Gallery, NYC, 1992, Nielsen Gallery, Boston, 1992, Tampa Mus. Art, Tampa, Fla., 1993, Norton Gallery Art, West Palm Beach, Fla., 1993, Galerie Vidal-Saint-Phalle, Paris, 1994, Oestreicher Fine Arts, New Orleans, 1994, Betsy Senior Gallery, NYC, 1995, Stephen Wirtz Gallery, San Francisco, 1995, Allen Priebe Gallery U. Wis.-Oshkosh, Wis., 1996, Schick Art Gallery Skidmore Coll., NY, 1997, U. Tenn., 1997, Calif. Ctr. for Arts, Escondido, Calif., 1997, Maier Art Mus., Lynchburg, Va., 1998, Lowe Art Mus., Coral Gables, Fla., 1998, Silvermine Guild Arts Ctr., New Cannan, Conn., 1999, others, exhibited in group shows at Atkins Mus. Art, Kans. City, Mo., 1990, Dalsheimer Gallery, Balt., 1990, Whitney Mus. Am. Art, NY, 1991, Adair Margo Gallery, El Paso, Tex., 1991, L.A. County Mus. Art, L.A., 1992, Pratt Manhattan Gallery, NYC, 1992, Cute-des-Neiges, Montreal, 1993, Centre Culturel Pierrefonds, France, 1993, Elvehjem Mus. Art, Madison, Wis., 1994, Gallery Camino Real, Boca Raton, Fla., 1994, Fletcher/Priest Gallery, Worcester, Mass., 1995, Columbia U., NYC, 1995, Boston U. Art Gallery, 1996, Ark. Arts Ctr., Little Rock, 1996, Newhouse Ctr. Contemporary Art, Staten Island, NY, 1997, Calif. Mus. Art, 1997, Butler Inst. Am. Art, Youngstown, Ohio, 1998, Cleve. Mus. Art, Ohio, 1998, Philbrook Mus. Art, Tulsa, 1999, U. Colo. art Galleris, Boulder, 1999, Represented in permanent collections Mus. Fine Arts, Boston, Bklyn. Mus. Art, NY, Mpls. Inst. Art, Minn., Whitney Mus. Am. Art, NYC, San Francisco Mus. Art, Phoenix Art Mus., NY Pub. Libr., Nat. Mus. Am. Art, Washington, Mus. Modern Art, NYC, Albright-Knox Art Gallery, Buffalo, NY, Francis and Sidney Lewis Found., Richmond, Va., Phoenix Art Mus., others; author (with Donald Kuspit and William Corbett): Sky Below: 18 Paintings by Gregory Amenoff, 1997; exhibitions include Salander O'Reilly Gallery, N.Y., —, exhibited in group shows at Whitney Biennials, 1981—85. Recipient Purchase award, AAAL, 1993, 1995, 1996. Office: Columbia U Sch of the Arts 305 Dodge Hall Mail Code 1808 2960 Broadway New York NY 10027 Office Fax: 212-426-1711.*

AMENTA, PETER SEBASTIAN, pathologist; b. Middletown, Conn., Feb. 21, 1953; s. Sebastian Peter and Mary Veronica (Branciforte) Am. m. Edna A. Salvo, Aug. 26, 1978; children: Peter S., Katherine D. BS, Trinity Coll., 1975; MS, MD, Hahnemann U., 1980, PhD, 1984. Cert. anatomic and clin. pathologist. Asst. prof. pathology Hahnemann U., Phila., 1984-89, Robert Wood Johnson U. Hosp., New Brunswick, N.J., 1989-93, assoc. prof. clin. pathology, 1993, residency program dir. pathology, chief pathology svc., 1999—, chmn. pathology and lab. medicine, 2002—, interim chief of staff, 2002—05, chief of staff, 2005—. Mem. Am. Assn. Anatomists, Am. Soc. Cell Biology, Hahnemann Club, Alpha Omega Alpha. Achievements include research in extracellular matrix pathobiology. Home: 2 Cartwright Dr Princeton Junction NJ 08550-1928 Office Phone: 732-235-8120. E-mail: amenta@umdnj.edu.

AMERIN, CANDEE LYNN-CRONIN, pre-school educator; b. Garden City, Kans., Oct. 17, 1967; d. Jon Kent and Sylvia Ann-Richard Cronin; m. Bill J. Amerin, Nov. 20, 1993; children: Jeremy Scott, Shae Lynn, Jenny Christine. AA, Dodge City CC, 1987; BS in Elem. Edn., Ft. Hays State U., 1989; MS in Edn. with ESL, Newman U., 2004. ESL cert. Newman U., 2004, cert. in Bldg. Leadership Newman U., 2005. First grade tchr. Johnson Grade Sch., Kans., 1989—93, second grade tchr., 1993—2000, first grade tchr., 2003—04, chairperson site based coun., 2004—05; owner, operator Candee Cares Daycare, Johnson, 2000—03; at-risk pre-sch. tchr. Stanton County Elem. Sch., Johnson, 2004—, coord. after-sch. reading program, 2003—04. Trumpet instr., Johnson, 1991—93; mem. health ins. com. Stanton County, Kans., 1994—99; profl. tutor, Johnson, 2000—02; prof. Newman U. Western Outreach Ctr., Dodge City, Kans., 2004—. Pre-sch. religion tchr. St. Bernadette's Cath. Ch., Johnson, 1999—2000. Mem.: Stanton County Tchrs.' Assn. R-Conservative. Roman Catholic. Avocations: walking, swimming, reading, gardening. Office: Stanton County Elem Sch 200 N Long St Johnson KS 67855 Personal E-mail: candle@pld.com.

AMERINGER, CHARLES D., history educator; b. Milw., Sept. 19, 1926; s. Carl and Pearl (Nelson) A.; m. Jean Stewart McNicol; children— Carl, William BA, U. Wis., Madison, 1949; MA, Fletcher Sch. Law and Diplomacy, Medford, Mass., 1951, PhD, 1958. Asst. prof. history Bowling Green State U., Ohio, 1959-64; assoc. prof. history Pa. State U., University Park, 1964-74, prof. history, 1974-95; prof. history emeritus, 1995—; head dept. history Pa. State U., University Park, 1985-90. Author: The Democratic Left in Exile: The Antidictatorial Struggle in the Caribbean, 1945-59, 1974, Don Pepe: A Political Biography of Jose Figueres of Costa Rica, 1979, Democracy in Costa Rica, 1982, U.S. Foreign Intelligence: The Secret Side of American History, 1990, The Caribbean Legion: Patriots, Politicians, Soldiers of Fortune, 1996, The Cuban Democratic Experience: The Auténtico Years, 1944-1952, 2000; editor: Political Parties of the Americas, 1980s to 1990s: Canada, Latin America and the West Indies, 1992. Capt. USAFR, 1951-69. Mem. Conf. Latin Am. History, Middle Atlantic Coun. Latin Am. Studies, Phi Beta Kappa. Office: Pa State U Dept History 108 Weaver Bldg University Park PA 16802-5500 E-mail: cdal@psu.edu.

AMES, ADELBERT, III, neuroscientist, educator; b. Boston, Feb. 25, 1921; MD, Harvard U., 1945. Intern, then resident in internal medicine Presbyn. Hosp., 1945-52; rsch. assoc. Med. Sch. Harvard U., Boston, 1955-69, prof. physiology, dept. surgery, 1969-91, Charles Anthony Pappas prof. neurosci. Med. Sch., 1983-91, prof. emeritus, 1991—; neurophysiologist in neurosurgery Mass. Gen. Hosp., Boston, 1983—. Recipient Rsch. Scientist award NIMH, 1968-80. Mem. Am. Physiol. Soc., Am. Soc. Neurochemistry, Soc. Neurosci., Internat. Soc. Neurochemistry. Home: 84 Jenckes Rd Brattleboro VT 05301-9258 E-mail: delames@sover.net.

AMES, ALLEN LEONARD, musician, composer; b. Greeley, Colo., Apr. 21, 1953; s. Leonard Justice and Rowena June (Griep) Ames; m. Maryanne Barbara Kremer-Ames, Oct. 22, 1989. Student, U. Ariz., 1973—76, Ariz. State U., 1992—94; studied violin with Max Mandel, studied with Phoenix, studied with Theodora McMillan, studied with James Buswell Tucson, studied with William Majors and Frank Spinoza, studied composition with Janne Irvine, studied with James DeMars, studied violin making with Carl Reiter. Concertmaster Scottsdale (Ariz.) Symphony Orch., 1976—80, Biltmore Strings, 1980—84, Phoenix (Ariz.) String Quartet, 1985—87, Nouveau West Chamber Orch., 1985—88; asst. concertmaster Ariz. Opera Orch., 1985—91; musician Lyra, 1987—, Chamber Music Consort, 1990—92; asst. concertmaster William Eaton Ensemble, 1990—; musician Camerata Sonora, 1993—96, Esteban, 1993—96, Meadowlark, 1996—, Mosaico Flamenco, 2000—. Mem. composers forum, Ariz., 1985—88; summer resident Briar Patch Inn, Sedona, Ariz., 1989—; mem. touring roster Ariz. Commn. Arts, 1998—2002; judge Young Musicians Competition Phoenix (Ariz.) Symphony Guild, 2001. Musician: (albums) Spirit Horses, 1991 (Grammy nominee), Lyra: Violin and Guitar, 1992, Music From the Magnificent Seven, 1993, Where Rivers Meet, 1994 (named Billboard Critics Choice, Downbeat 4-star rev.), Children of the Sun, 1994, Touch The Sweet Earth, 1995 (Indie award), Luna Trece, 1996, Naked in Eureka, 1996 (ranked #1 Nat. New Age Airplay), Songs for my Ancestors, 1996, Legend of the Land, 1998 (named Top 100 Internat. Airplay), Colors of My Heart, 1999 (Native Am. Music award Album of Yr.), Way Back Tomorrow, 1999, Mosaico, 2000, Free Fall, 2000, Wolves at my Door, 2000, Four Hands, One Heart, 2002, Amor, 2003, Sparks and Embers, 2003 (ranked #2 New Age Airplay, named Echoes 25 Essential CDs); contbr. poems to jours. and mags. Mem.: Chamber Music Am., Am. Soc. Composers and Performers. Avocations: hiking, writing, poetry, violinmaking.

AMES, DONALD PAUL, retired air transportation executive; b. Brandon, Man., Can., Sept. 13, 1922; came to U.S., 1932; s. Paul and Della Johanna (Hebel) A.; m. Doris Elizabeth Ubbelohde, Dec. 30, 1949; children: Elizabeth Carol Ames Herbert, Barbara Louise Ames Jones. BS in Chemistry, U. Wis., 1944, PhD in Phys. Chemistry, 1949; LLD (hon.), U. Mo., St. Louis, 1978. AEC postdoctoral fellow, 1949-50; staff chemist Los Alamos Sci. Lab., 1950-52; asst. prof. physical chemistry U. Ky., Lexington, 1952-54; staff chemist DuPont Co., Aiken, S.C., 1954-56; sr. rsch. chemist, scientist/fellow Monsanto, St. Louis, 1956-61; from scientist to sr. scientist rsch. div. McDonnell Aircraft Co., St. Louis, 1961-68; from dep. dir. rsch. to dir. rsch. McDonnell Douglas Rsch. Labs., St. Louis, 1968-71, dir., 1971-76, staff v.p., 1976-86, staff v.p., gen. mgr., disting. fellow, 1986-89, cons., 1989—; pres. Fluotech Inc., 1991—. Adj. prof. physics U. Mo., St. Louis, 1989—2000, Washington U., St. Louis, 1989-99; mem. vis. com. dept. mech. engring. Lehigh U., 1984-90; mem. adv. bd. Coll. Engring., U. Ill., Urbana, 1986-89; mem. spl. com. U. Chgo. 7 GeV Synchrotron Light Source, 1984-89; adv. com. U. Mo. Rsch. Reactor, Columbia, 1985-92; mem. indsl. adv. coun. dept. chemistry U. Mo., St. Louis, 1985-95; mem. subcom. on materials sci. and engring. needs and opportunities in aerospace industry NAS, 1985-86; bd. dirs. St. Louis Tech. Ctr., 1983-95; participant Manhattan Project U.S. Army, 1944-46. Contbr. articles to profl. jours.; patentee in field. With U.S. Army, 1944-46. Recipient Civic award St. Louis sect. AIAA, 1985, James B. Eads award Acad. Sci. St. Louis, 2003; Wis. Alumni Rsch. fellow, 1946-48, AEC fellow, 1948-49, Monsanto fellow, 1959-61, McDonnell Douglas Disting. fellow, 1986-89. Mem. Am. Phys. Soc., Am. Chem. Soc., Soc. Engring Sci., Combustion Inst., Mo. Acad. Sci., Phi Beta Kappa, Sigma Xi, Phi Eta Sigma, Phi Kappa Phi, Phi Lambda Upsilon, Gamma Alpha, Alpha Chi Sigma. Office Phone: 314-984-8846. E-mail: dpa922@cs.com.

AMES, FRANK ANTHONY, musician, film producer; b. Wheeling, W.Va., Oct. 12, 1942; s. Louis Higgins and Camille (O'Brien) A.; m. Susan Whalley, June 14, 1966 (div. 1971); 1 child, Kristan; m. Annette Ruth Beck, 1980; 1 child, Angharad Elisabeth. MusB, Eastman Sch. Music, Rochester, N.Y., 1964; MFA, Carnegie Mellon U., 1966. Percussionist Pitts. Symphony, 1964-66, Balt. Symphony, 1966-68; prin. percussionist Nat. Symphony, Washington, 1968—; exec. dir. 20th Century Consort, Washington, 1975-83, Millennium Inc., Washington, 1979—; pres. Potomac Prodns., Washington, 1982—; ind. film producer Washington, 1982—. Assoc. prof. percussion U. Md. Sch. Music, 2003—04; adj. prof. percussion U. Md., 2003—. Producer, performer various recs., producer (film) Music of the 12th Century, 1986 (1st prize Houston Film Festival 1986), (music) Arrangements for children's musical Red Shoes, 1993, showcased in Arlington, Va., 1993, Wheeling, W.Va., 1994; author; (script) Petrushka, 1987. Founder, dir. Nat. Symphony outreach program In Your Neighborhood, 1992-94. Recipient Mayor's Achievement award, Washington, 1982. Mem. Chamber Music Am., Cosmos Club Washington. Avocations: sailing, squash. Home and Office: 1235 Potomac St NW Washington DC 20007-3230

AMES, RAYMOND ALVIN, middle school band director; b. Elkhorn, Wis., Mar. 24, 1956; s. John D and Isabelle Ames; m. Sherri L Hopkins; children: Amanda L, Benjamin R. B.Music Edn., U. Wis., Eau Claire, 1978. Band dir. Lake Geneva Schs., Lake Geneva, Wis., 1978—2005. Capt. Lake Geneva Cruise Line, 1979—2005. Recipient Tchr. of the Yr. award, Lake Geneva Schs., 1995. Mem.: Wis. Band Masters Assn. Home: 603 Center St Lake Geneva, WI 53114 Office: Lake Geneva Middle School 600 Bloomfield Rd Lake Geneva WI 53114 Office Phone: 262-348-3000 3327. Home Fax: 262-248-2164.

AMES, RICHARD POLLARD, physician, educator, lecturer; b. Northampton, Mass., Aug. 4, 1932; s. Harold Leslie and Effie Melissa (Crowley) A.; m. Janet Ann Shaw, Oct. 7, 1961; children: Patricia Jean, Brian Shaw. BA cum laude, Williams Coll., 1954; MD, Columbia U., 1958. Diplomate Am. Bd. Internal Medicine, Am. Bd. Nephrology, Am. Bd. Med. Oncology, Am. Bd. Hematology, Am. Soc. of Hypertension Specialist in Clin. Hypertension. Intern Boston City Hosp., 1958-59, resident, 1959-61; fellow N.Y. Heart Assn. Presbyn. Hosp., N.Y.C., 1961-63; clin. assoc. Nat. Cancer Inst., Bethesda, Md., 1963-65; investigator Nat. Inst. Arthritis Metab., Paris, 1965-66, Whitehall Found., N.Y.C., 1967-70; nephrologist St. Luke's Roosevelt Hosp., N.Y.C., 1970—, chief hypertension clinic, 1973-94, dir. phys. diagnosis, 1981-94, assoc. dir. nephrology, 1990-93; chief nephrology St. Clare's Hosp., N.Y.C., 1998-2000. Dir. hypertension Am. Health Found., N.Y.C., 1972-82; clin. prof. Columbia U., N.Y.C., 1989—. Contbg. author: Topics in Hypertension, 1980, Frontiers in Hypertension Res., 1981, Clinical Cardiovascular Therapeutics, 1989, Hypertension, 1995, Messerli's Cardiovascular Drug Therapy, 1996; co-editor: Medical Symposium Drugs, 1988. Asst. surgeon USPHS, 1963-65. Fellow ACP, AHA (mem. Coun. For High Blood Pressure Rsch., Kidney Coun.); mem. Am. Soc. Hypertension (charter), Phi Beta Kappa. Office: 1886 Broadway New York NY 10023- Office Phone: 917-224-4270.

AMES, ROBERT G., lawyer; b. Buffalo, Feb. 24, 1949; BBA, Temple U., 1970; JD with honors, George Washington U., 1973. Bar: Ga. 1973, DC 1976, Md. 1980. Ptnr. Labor & Employment Dept. Venable LLP, Washington, DC. Mem.: ABA (mem. Labor Law Sect.), State Bar Ga., DC Bar, Fed. Bar Assn., Md. State Bar Assn., Bar Assn. of Balt. City, Order of the Coif. Office: Venable LLP 575 7th St NW Washington DC 20004 Office Phone: 202-344-4840. Office Fax: 202-344-8300. E-mail: rgames@venable.com.

AMES, STEVEN, management consultant; Pres. Steven Ames & Assoc. Adv. bd. Gugenheim Mus.; trustee Whitney Mus. Am. Art. Mailing: BCE Place 181 Bay St Heritage Bldg Fl 2R Toronto ON M5J 2T3 Canada also: c/o Whitney Mus Am Art 945 Madison Ave New York NY 10021 E-mail: stevenames@shaw.ca.*

AMES, STEVEN REEDE, financial planner; b. Washington, Aug. 15, 1951; s. Reede Maughan and Mary (Soderberg) A.; m. Marsha M. Ames, Sept. 1994. BS in Bus. Administrn., U. Md., 1973; MPA, Am. U., 1976; MS, Coll. Fin. Planning, 1994. Cert. fin. planner; registered investment advisor; enrolled agt. IRS. Specialist bus. financing Gov.'s Office State Del., Dover, 1978-83; exec. v.p. Econ. and Bus. Devel. Corp. Montgomery County, Rockville, Md., 1983-85; owner, operator Scarborough Ames and Assocs., Annapolis, Md., 1986-92; owner, prin. Ames Fee-Only Fin. Planning, Annapolis, 1993—. Instr. Anne Arundel Community Coll., Annapolis, 1987-98; bd. arbitrators Nat. Assn. Securities Dealers. Bd. dirs. Md. Hall for Creative Arts; mem. charitable gift planning adv. com. Anne Arundel Med. Ctr., Chesapeake Cmty. Found. Fin. and Asset Mgmt. com. Named among best fin. advisors Worth Mag., 1996-2002, one of 100 Gt. Fin. Planners, Mut. Funds Mag., 2001, 02. Mem. Nat. Assn. Personal Fin. Advisors (regional chmn. bd.), Nat. Assn. Securities Dealers (bd. arbitrators 1996—), Annapolis C. of C. (Mem. of Yr. 1990), Md. Soc. Accts., Kiwanis (bd. dirs. Annapolis club 1986-97, pres. 1989-90), Greater Annapolis C. of C. (bd. dirs.). Avocations: sports, travel, financial reading. Office Phone: 410-280-2390. Personal E-mail: steve.ames@comcast.net.

AMES, WILLIAM FRANCIS, mathematician, educator; b. Brandon, Man., Can., Dec. 8, 1926; s. Paul Main and Della Johanna (Hebel) A.; m. Theresa Danielson, May 29, 1951; children: Karen Anne, Susan Lynn, Pamela Margaret. MS, U. Wis., 1950. Instr. U. Wis., Racine, 1953-55; sr. engr. DuPont Co., Wilmington, Del., 1955-59; prof. U. Del., Newark, 1959-67, U. Iowa, Iowa City, 1967-75, Ga. Inst. Tech., Atlanta, 1975—, Regents prof., 1980-91, prof. emeritus, 1991—, dir., 1981-87; research prof. U. Ga., Athens, 1977-79. Cons. in field. Author: Nonlinear Partial Differential Equations in Engineering, Vol. I, 1965, Vol. II, 1972, Nonlinear Ordinary Differential Equations in Transport Processes, 1968, Numerical Methods for Partial Differential Equations, 1970, 77, 92, Nonlinear Boundary Value Problems in Science and Engineering, 1989; book and jour. editor for Academic Press; editor 9 books.; contbr. articles to profl. jours. Served with USNR, 1944-46, 51-52. NSF faculty fellow, 1963-64, NATO sr. fellow, 1972-73; grantee, 1964-67, 76-79, 79-81, 83-85, 89-91, 92-95, NBS grantee, 1967-71, USPHS grantee, 1961-63, EPA grantee, 1978-81, U.S. Army grantee, 1968-75, 81-87; Humboldt sr. scientist, 1974-75. Home: 125 Tamarisk Dr NE Atlanta GA 30342-1421 Office: Ga Inst Tech Sch Math Atlanta GA 30332-0001 Personal E-mail: williamames@hotmail.com.

AMESTOY, JEFFREY LEE, law educator, former state supreme court chief justice; b. Rutland, Vt., July 24, 1946; s. William Joseph and Diana (Wood) Amestoy; m. Susan Claire Lonergan, May 24, 1980; children: Katherine Leigh, Christina Elizabeth, Nancy Claire. BA, Hobart Coll., 1968; JD, U. Calif., San Francisco, 1972; MPA, Harvard U., 1982; D of Pub. Adminstrn. (hon.), Norwich U., 1994; LLD (hon.), Vermont Law Sch., 2002. Bar: Vt. 1973, U.S. Dist. Ct. Vt. 1973. Assoc. Mahady & Klevana, Windsor, Vt., 1973—74; legal counsel Gov.'s Justice Commn., Montpelier, Vt., 1974—77; asst. atty. gen., chief of Medicaid fraud div. State of Vt., Montpelier, 1978—81, commr. labor and industry, 1982—84, atty. gen., 1985—97; chief justice Supreme Ct. Vt., 1997—2004; fellow John F. Kennedy Sch. of Govt. Harvard U., 2004—. Pres. Nat. Assn. of Attys. Gen., 1992—93. Trustee Thomas Waterman Wood Gallery, Montpelier, 1986—92. With USAR, 1968—74. Mem.: Conf. Chief Justices, Vt. Bar Assn., Kennedy Sch. Govt. Harvard U. Alumni Exec. Coun. Republican. Congregationalist.

AMEZCUA, CHARLIE ANTHONY, social science counselor; b. L.A., Sept. 1, 1928; s. Carlos and Inez (Nunez) Amezcua; m. Kathleen Joyce Greene, Mar. 7, 1964; children: Colleen Alvita, Charles Anthony. BA, UCLA, 1958; MS, Calif. State U., L.A., 1961. Cert. cmty. coll. counselor, supr-adminstrn., jr. coll. tchg. in psychology. Student psychologist Rancho Los Amigos Hosp., Downey, Calif., 1959—60; instr. in psychology East Los Angeles Coll., 1962—72, asst. prof. counseling, 1972—74, assoc. prof. counseling, 1974—, prof. psychology, 1980—, spl. edn. counselor, 1981—, coord. vet. affairs, 1972—. Personnel asst. L.A. City Sch. Dist., 1963—64; counselor Youth Tng. and Employment Project, L.A., 1965—66, project dir., 1966—67; counseling psychologist VA, L.A., 1967—70; dir. Head Start, L.A. County Edn. and Youth Opportunities Agy., 1970—71; bd. dirs. Tng. and Rsch. Found., Child and Family Resources Ctrs.; lectr. counselor edn. Calif. State U., L.A.; guest lectr. John F. Kennedy U., 1987—. Mem. Calif. Gov.'s Adv. Com. on Children and Youth, 1966—67; judge blue ribbon panel NATAS, 1966—76. With USN, 1948—52, Korea. Mem.: APA, Western Psychol. Assn., Calif. Assn. Post-Secondary Educators of Disabled, Calif. State Psychol. Assn. Democrat. Home: 8348 Fable Ave Canoga Park CA 91304-3036 Office: East Los Angeles Coll 1301 Brooklyn Ave Monterey Park CA 91754-6001

AMFT, ROBERT ERNEST, artist, photographer; b. Chgo., Dec. 7, 1916; s. Fred and Elizabeth (Koopman) Amft; m. Marian J.Schmeling, Jan. 18, 1940 (dec. 1985); children: Peter, Sally, Joseph, Mark. Grad., Sch. Art Inst. Chgo., 1940; student Francis Chapin. Represented by Corbett vs. Dempsey, Chgo. One man shows include We. Ill. U., 1979, Hammer & Hammer Gallery, Chgo., 1981, Joy Horwich Gallery, Chgo., 1981, Kans. State U., 1985, U. Ill. Ctr., Chgo., 1985, Ill. Painters, 1989, Houston Ctr. Photography, 1990, Intuit Gallery, 1996; group shows include Pa. Acad., 1958, Butler Inst. Art, Youngstown, Ohio, 1958 (Purchase prize), Art U.S.A., Tacoma Mus., 1965, Art Inst. Chgo., 1986, New Horizons, 1990, Alverо Coll., Milw., 1993, R.H. Love Gallery, Chgo., 1993, Mus. Art, Lafayette, Ind., 1997, Osaka Triennale,

Japan, 1997, Internat. Print Triennial, Krakow, 2000, Anti-Cruelty Soc., Chgo. (1st prize sculpture), 2003, Hyde Park Art Ctr., 2005. Mem. Alumni Assn. Art Inst. Chgo., Arts Club Chgo. C.A.C. Home: 7340 N Ridge Blvd Chicago IL 60645-6900

AMGOTT, MADELINE, television producer, consultant; b. N.Y.C., Aug. 31, 1921; d. Samuel and Rose (Kanter) Barotz; m. David Karr, Sept. 5, 1942 (div. 1956); children: Andrew, Katharine Karr-Kaitin; m. Milton Amgott, Dec. 15, 1962; 1 child, Seth; 1 stepchild, Margo. BA cum laude, Bklyn. Coll., 1942. Feature coordinator CBS News, N.Y.C. Prodr. WNBC-TV Not for Women Only, CBS News 60 Minutes, Morning Show, 30 Minutes, Bill Moyers' Constitution Hours, Phil Donahue spl. documentary The Human Animal, Good Housekeeping A Better Way, Today Show, CNBC Home and Family Hour, Real Story, Hans Hofmann, Artist/Teacher, Teacher/Artist, PBS, 2003; cons. Times Mirror, N.Y.C., King Features Entertainment, TBM; bd. dirs. Am. Jour. Nursing Pub. Co., N.Y.C. Co-author: Teenage Gangs, 1957. Mem. West Pride, W. 86th St. Tenants Assn.; co-founder 168 W 68th St Tenants Assn.; mem. N.Y.C. Bicentennial Commn., 1987-89. Recipient Emmy Nat. Acad. TV Arts, 1981, 82, 83; Ohio State award, 1976. 78; Peabody award, 1976; Matrix award, 1976, award Greater Miami Film Festival, Internat. Film Festival of N.Y., others. Mem. Women's Forum, Women in Communications, Inc. Avocations: gardening, tennis, bicycling.

AMHOWITZ, HARRIS J., lawyer, educator; b. N.Y.C., Mar. 19, 1934; s. Samuel and Ruth Amhowitz; m. Melanie Leigh Gale; children: Jennifer Ann, Joshua Seth. AB, Brown U., 1955; LLB, Harvard U., 1961. Bar: N.Y. 1961, U.S. Supreme Ct. 1967. Law clk. to judge U.S. Dist. Ct. N.Y., 1961-63; assoc. Hughes Hubbard & Reed, N.Y.C., 1963-69; gen. counsel Coopers & Lybrand, N.Y.C., 1970-96, dep. chmn., 1991-95, mem. internat. exec. com., 1991-95; of counsel Hughes Hubbard & Reed, 1996—2003. Adj. prof. NYU Sch. Law, 1975-83; receiver, spl. master U.S. Dist. Ct., 1963-70; pres. bd. dirs. Prosher Group, Ltd., 1970-71; trustee Citizens Budget Commn., Inc., 1983-97. Lt. comdr. USN, 1955—58. Mem. Assn. Bar City N.Y. (spl. com. on lawyers' role in securities transactions 1975-77, com. profl. and jud. ethics 1983-86, com. profl. discipline 1987-91), Harmonie Club. Home: 5150 N Windsong Canyon Dr Tucson AZ 85749

AMICK, STEVEN HAMMOND, state legislator, lawyer; b. Ithaca, N.Y., May 13, 1947; s. Arthur Hammond and Marolyn Dee (Hollingshead) A.; m. Helen Louise Masten, Aug. 9, 1969. BA, Washington Coll., 1969; JD, Dickinson Sch. of Law, 1972. Bar: Del. 1972, U.S. Dist. Ct. Del. 1973. Assoc. Daley & Lewis, Wilmington, Del., 1972-74; atty. E.I. Dupont De Nemours and Co., Wilmington, 1974-85, counsel, 1986-96; mem. Del. Ho. of Reps., Dover, 1986-94; spl. counsel Cooch and Taylor, 1996—2002; mem. Del. Senate, Dover, 1994—, minority leader, 1998—2002. Pres. Com. of 39, Wilmington, 1978, Civic League for New Castle County, Wilmington, 1984-86. Mem. Del. Bar Assn. Republican. Presbyterian. Avocation: antique cars. Home: 449 W Chestnut Hill Rd Newark DE 19713-1132 Office: Legislature Hall PO Box 1401 Dover DE 19901 Office Phone: 302-744-4138.

AMICK, WILLIAM WALKER, golf course architect; b. Scipio, Ind., June 16, 1932; s. George Ellsworth Sr. and Myrtle (Walker) A.; m. Sara Dell Rogers, Apr. 6, 1957; 1 child, David Walker. BA, Ohio Wesleyan U., 1954. Registered landscape architect, Fla. Golf course archt. asst. William H. Diddel, GCA, Carmel, Ind., 1954-55, Charles Adams, GCA, Atlanta, 1957-58; golf course architect Daytona Beach, Fla., 1959—. Capt. USAF, 1955-57. Fellow Am. Soc. Golf Course Architects; mem. Am. Soc. of Golf Course Architects (treas., v.p., pres. 1975-77). Avocation: low handicap golf. Office: PO Box 1984 Daytona Beach FL 32115-1984 Office Phone: 386-767-1449. E-mail: amick@iag.net.

AMIDEI, SHIRLEY ANN, music educator; b. Hannibal, Mo., Oct. 10, 1961; d. Lawrence Wesley and Catherine Ann Wiseman; m. Lawrence John Amidei, July 4, 1998; children: Ashton Lake, Tyler Lake. B in Music Edn., Truman U., 1987. Band, vocal tchr. Winston (Mo.) Sch., 1987—90; vocal tchr. Louisiana (Mo.) Sch., 1990—94; band, vocal tchr. Atlanta (Mo.) Sch., 1994—98, Bevier (Mo.) Sch., 1999—2000; vocal tchr. Westran H.S., Huntsville, Mo., 2000—. Mem.: Music Educators Nat. Conf., Mo. Choral Dir. Assn., Mo. State Tchrs. Orgn. (legis. chairperson 1997—98). Baptist.

AMIDON, PAUL CHARLES, publishing executive; b. St. Paul, July 23, 1932; s. Paul Samuel and Eleanor Ruth (Simons) A.; m. Patricia Jean Winjum, May 7, 1960; children: Karen, Michael, Susan. BA, U. Minn., 1954. Bus. mgr. Paul S. Amidon & Assocs., Inc., St. Paul, 1956-66, pres., 1966—. Served with AUS, 1954-56. Home: 1582 Hillcrest Ave Saint Paul MN 55116-2147 Office: 1966 Benson Ave Saint Paul MN 55116-3214 Business E-Mail: paul@amidongraphics.com.

AMIDON, ROGER LYMAN, public health service officer, educator; b. Burlington, Vt., Apr. 8, 1938; s. Ellsworth L. and Mae (Liddle) A.; m. JoAnn Reiland, Aug. 1, 1968. BA, U. Vt., 1960; MA in Hosp. and Health Adminstrn., U. Iowa, 1965, PhD (USPHS trainee), 1968. Asst. prof. hosp. and health adminstrn. U. Iowa, 1968-73, asso. prof., 1973-77; prof., chmn. dept. health adminstrn. U. Okla., 1977-81; prof., chmn. dept. health svcs. policy and mgmt. U. S.C., 1981-88, on sabbatical, 1988-89, prof., grad. dir., 1989—2002, disting. prof. emeritus, 2002—. Exec. sec. Nat. Ctr. Health Svcs. Rsch., 1975-76; dir. Am. Indian Grad. Program in Health Adminstrn., U. Okla., 1977-81; cons. China Med. U. Hosp., 1999—, vis. scholar, Nat. Def. Med. Ctr., Taiwan, 2003. Contbr. articles to profl. jours. Chair S.C. Ctr. for Gerontology, 1999-01; exec. coun., SC AARP, 2004-. Lt., M.S.C. U.S. Army, 1961—62, exec. officer and platoon leader, 418 Med. Co. (Ambulance), XVIII Airborne Hdqs. Mem. APHA, AARP (exec. coun. 20042), Am. Coll. Healthcare Execs., Am. Hosp. Assn. (life), Vermont Soc. Colonial Wars. Home: 234 Saluda Ave Columbia SC 29205-3031 Office: Arnold SPH U SC Health Svcs Policy and Mgmt Columbia SC 29208-0001 Business E-Mail: amidon@sc.edu.

AMIGONI, MICHAEL, information technology executive; MBA, U. Ill., Chgo. Cons. in field for small co. including ARO Inc., Kansas City, Mo.; managed operations and info. tech. ARO's Contact Ctr., Kansas City, 1992—; head architect remote bus. model ARO, Inc., Kansas City, 1997, CIO, COO. Office: ARO Contact Ctr 3100 Broadway Ste 100 Kansas City MO 64111

AMIN, MOENESS GAMAL, education educator, director; b. Cairo, Mar. 11, 1955; s. Mohamed Amin and Nahed Sadek; m. Ebtehal M. Afifi; children: Nariman Moeness, Gamal Moeness, Amro Moeness. BSc, Cairo U., Egypt, 1976; MSc, U. Petroleum, Saudi Arabia, 1980; PhD, U. Colo., Boulder, Colo., 1984. Asst. prof. Villanova U., Villanova, Pa., 1985—88, assoc. prof., 1988—91, assoc. prof. - tenured, 1991—94, prof. - tenured, dir., ctr. for advanced comm., 2002—. Cons. ELCOM Tech. Corp, Malvern, Pa., VIZ Mfg. Co., Phila., Micronetics Wireless, Hudson, NH. Contbr. chapters to books, over 300 articles to profl. jours. Fellow: IEEE (IEEE Third Millennium Medal, Outstanding Intellectual and Orgnl. Contributions IEEE, Phila. Sect., IEEE Signal Processing Soc. Disting. Lectr.); mem.: Phi Kappa Phi, Sigma Xi, Eta Kappa Nu. Achievements include patents for US Patent, smart antenna channel simulator, and test sys., 5, 973, 638, 1999 and no. 6, 236, 363, 2001. Office: Villanova Univ 800 Lancaster Ave - Tolentine 119 Villanova PA 19085 Business E-Mail: moeness.amin@villanova.edu.

AMIN, MOHAMMAD, urology educator; b. Sargodha, Pakistan, Jan. 1, 1942; came to U.S., 1964; s. Mohammad and Gulzar (Begum) Nawaz; m. Elizabeth Anne Howarth, May 25, 1973; children: Daniel, Omar. MB, BS, King Edward Coll., Lahore, Pakistan, 1963. Diplomate Am. Bd. of Urology. Intern Muhlenberg Hosp., Plainfield, N.J., 1964-65; resident in surgery Norton Hosp., Louisville, 1965-66; asst. prof. urology U. Louisville, 1971-74, assoc. prof., 1974-80, prof. urology, 1980—, resident in urology, 1966-69; med. officer Social Security, Pakistan, 1969-70; house officer urology Southmede Hosp., Bristol, Eng., 1970-71. Contbr. articles and book chpts. to profl. jours. Recipient Health Advancement award Nat. Kidney Found., 1981. Mem.: ACS, Soc. Internat. d'Urologie, Am. Urol. Assn. Democrat. Islamic. Address: VA Med Ctr 800 Zorn Ave Louisville KY 40206 Office Phone: 502-287-4000.

AMIRKHANIAN, YURI ALBERTOVICH, sociologist, researcher; b. St Petersburg, Russia, July 10, 1973; PhD, St. Petersburg State U., 1991—99. Fogarty postdoctoral fellow CAIR, Med. Coll. of Wis., 1999—2002, asst. prof., 2002—. Assoc. dir., internat. aids rsch. core CAIR, Med. Coll. of Wis., 2002—. Fogarty fellowship, Fogarty Ctr., NIH, 1999—2002. Office: CAIR Med Coll of Wis 2071 North Summit Ave Milwaukee WI 53202 Office Phone: 414-456-7784. Office Fax: 414-287-4209. E-mail: yuri@mcw.edu.

AMIS, EDWARD STEPHEN, JR., radiologist, retired military officer; b. Baton Rouge, June 23, 1941; s. Edward Stephen and Annie Velma (Birdwhistell) Amis; m. Anne Schneider, Sept. 2, 1984. Student, U. Rochester, 1959-61; BS, U. Ark., 1963; MD, Northwestern U., 1967. Diplomate Am. Bd. Urology, Am. Bd. Radiology. Commd. ensign USN, 1966, advanced through grades to capt., 1980; resident in urology Naval Hosp., San Diego, 1968-72, resident in radiology, 1975-78, staff radiologist, 1978-80, 81-82, staff urologist Great Lakes, Ill., 1972-75; radiology fellow Mass. Gen. Hosp., Boston, 1980-81; chmn. radiology Naval Hosp., Bethesda, Md., 1982-84, exec. officer, 1984-85, comdg. officer, 1985-87; head sect. uroradiology dept. radiology Columbia U., N.Y.C., 1987-91, vice chmn. dept. radiology, 1990-91; chmn. dept. radiology Albert Enstein Coll. Medicine and Montefiore Med. Ctr., Bronx, N.Y., 1991—. Co-author: Essentials of Uroradiology, 1990, Textbook of Uroradiology, 2000; contbr. chapters to textbooks. Leadership council Montgomery County Heart Assn., Bethesda, 1986-87. Bausch and Lomb scholar, 1959. Mem.: Am. Coll. Radiology (bd. chancellors 1995—, vice chair 2000—02, chair 2002—04, pres. 2004—05), Am. Roentgen Ray Soc., Soc. Uroradiology, Assn. Univ. Radiologists, Radiol. Assn. N.Am. Republican. Avocations: stamp collecting/philately, modern art, antique British cars. Business E-Mail: amis@aecom.yu.edu.

AMIS, MARTIN LOUIS, author; b. Oxford, Aug. 25, 1949; s. Kingsley and Hilary (Bardwell) A.; m. Antonia Phillips, 1984 (div. 1996); 5 children; Isabel Fonseca, 1998; m. Isabel Fonseca, 1998; 2 children. BA in English with honors, Oxford U., 1971. Editorial asst. Times Literary Supplement, London, 1972-75; asst. literary editor New Statesman, London, 1975-79; spl. writer The Observer, 1980—, The Guardian, 1997—. Actor: (film) A High Wind in Jamaica, 1965; author: The Rachel Papers, 1973 (Somerset Maugham award 1974), Dead Babies, 1975 (pub. as Dark Secrets, 1977), Success, 1978, Other People, 1981, Invasion of the Space Invaders, 1982, Money: A Suicide Note, 1984, The Moronic Inferno and Other Visits to America, 1986, Einstein's Monsters, 1987, London Fields, 1989, Time's Arrow, 1991, Visiting Mrs. Nabokov and Other Excursions, 1994, The Information, 1995, Heavy Water and Other Stories, 1998, State of England: And Other Stories, 1998, Amis Omnibus, 1999, Experience, 2000, Koba the Dread: Laughter and the Twenty Million, 2002, Yellow Dog, 2003; co-author: (with others) My Oxford, 1977, night Tain, 1997, Heavy Water & Other Stories, 1998, Experience, 2000, The War Against Cliche, 1971-2000, 2001; screenwriter: Saturn 3, 1980. Address: The Wylie Agy 17 Bedford Square London WCIB 3JA England

AMIS, ROBERT WRIGHT, lawyer; b. Dallas; s. Walter Hogan and Marjorie Sue Amis; m. Dorothy Johnston, Sept. 5, 1958; children: Sahron Marie, Cynthia Ann Franklin, Marilyn Elaine Chladil. BS in Geology, U. Okla., 1958; JD, U. Tex., 1962. Bar: Tex. 1962, Okla. 1967. Asst. county atty., asst. dist. atty. State of Tex., Denton, 1962—64; mcpl. ct. judge City of Lewisville, Tex., 1964—66; adj. prof. law Oklahoma City U., 1967—68; pvt. practice Plano, Tex. Mem.: Rotary. Methodist. Avocation: music. Home: 7065 Helsem Way Dallas TX 75230 Office: 555 Republic Dr Ste 200 Plano TX 75074

AMLING, FREDERICK, economist, educator, investment advisor; b. Cleve., Dec. 23, 1926; s. Gustav and Elsie (Fischer) Amling; m. Gwendolyn Stewart, Feb. 17, 1951; children: Jeffrey, Scott, Terrance. BA, Baldwin Wallace Coll., 1948; MBA, Miami U., Oxford, Ohio, 1949; PhD, U. Pa., 1957. Instr. U. Maine, 1948-50, U. Pa., 1950- 52, U. Conn., 1952—; prof. finance and investment chmn. dept. Miami U., Oxford, 1955-66; prof. finance U. R.I., Kingston, 1966-69, dean Coll. Bus. Adminstrn., 1966-69; prof. fin. Grad. Sch. Bus. and Pub. Mgmt. George Washington U., 1970-2000, prof. emeritus, 2000—; pres. Frederick Amling & Assocs., computer models, Amling & Co. Investment Advisers. Cons. fin. and investment, 1959—; cons. Riggs Nat. Bank, 1970—90, Am. Psychiat. Assn., 1975—91; bd. advisers Rsch. Ctr. Credito Emiliano, Milan, 1991—93. Author: (book) Investments: An Introduction to Analysis and Management, 1963, Investments: An Introduction to Analysis and Management, 7th edit., 2000, Plaid on Investments, 1983, Dow Jones Irwin Guide to Personal Financial Planning and Personal Financial Management, 1986; author: (with Bill Droms) Investment Fundamentals, 1994; editor, contbr.: articles on fin. to profl. jours., newspapers and mags. Chmn. local Cancer Crusade, 1964; trustee Georgetown Prebyn. Ch., 1977—79; elder Presbyn. Ch., 1962—. With USNR, World War II, lt. (j.g.) USNR, 1955. Recipient Alumni Merit award, Baldwin Wallace Coll., 1973, Sch. Bus. and Pub. Mgmt. George Washington U., 1982. Mem.: Eastern Fin. Assn. (v.p. 1979), Am. Fin. Assn. (membership chmn. 1973—90), Fin. Mgmt. Assn., Washington Soc. Fin. Analysts (treas.), Colett Club, Cosmos Club, Turks Head Club (Providence), Univ. Club (Miami U., Oxford), George Washington U. Club, Congl. Country Club, Lambda Chi Alpha, Delta Sigma Pi, Beta Gamma Sigma (pres. George Washington U. chpt. 1985). Home: Apt 312 3555 S Ocean Blvd Palm Beach FL 33480-5765 Office Phone: 301-299-3935. E-mail: tigerfred@aol.com. *To work for family and society with God's help.*

AMMANN, JEAN-CHRISTOPHE, art director; b. Berlin, Jan. 14, 1939; PhD, U. Fribourg, Switzerland, 1966. Asst. Kunsthalle Bern, Switzerland, 1967-68; dir. Kunstmuseum, Lucerne, Switzerland, 1968-77, Kunsthalle, Basle, Switzerland, 1978-88, Mus. für Moderne Kunst, Frankfurt, Germany, 1989—2001, prof., 1998—. Commr. German Pavillion of Biennial of Venice, Italy, 1995; lectr. U. Frankfurt/M. and Giessen, 1992—, U. Heidelberg, 2001—02. Author: Rèmy Zaugg—Discussion with Jean-Christophe Ammann, 1994, (with Harald Szeemann) Von Hodler zur Antiform, 1968, Louis Moilliet: Das Gesamtwerk, 1972, Bewegung im Kopf. Vom Umgang mit der Kunst, 1993, Kulturfinanzierung, 1995, Annäherung. Über die Notwendigkeit von Kunst, 1996, Remy Zaugg-Conversation with Jean Christophe Ammann, French edit., 1990, German edit., 1994, Das Glück Zu Sehen, 1998; co-organizer of documenta 5, Kassel, 1972; curator: 9th Triennial small sculptures, Fellbach-Stuttgart, Germany; organizer (with Natalie De Ligt): Ninth Triennial of Small Sculptures, Fellbach-Stuttgart, 2004. Decorated Officier Des Arts et Des Lettres, Goethe-medal City of Frankfurt, Germany; recipient Culture award, Wormland Found., 2001. Office: Klettenbergstrasse 11 60322 Frankfurt Germany Office Phone: 0049/69/5963 160.

AMMANN, LILLIAN ANN NICHOLSON, writer, editor, small business owner; b. Pearsall, Tex., June 20, 1946; d. Harvey Franklin and Annie Laura (Matthews) Nicholson; m. Jack Jordan Ammann Jr., May 31, 1967; 1 child, William Erik. BA magna cum laude, Southwestern U., 1968. Mgr. inventory Kelly AFB, San Antonio, 1967-70; employment counselor Tex. Employment Commn., San Antonio, 1970-75; owner, operator Lillie's Lovely Little Gardens, San Antonio, 1975-77, Lillie's Interior Landscapes, San Antonio, 1980-82, pres., 1983-96; sec. Jack Ammann Inc., 1983-87; pres. Lillie's & Sherry's Plants & Pottery, San Antonio, 1977-80; ind. bus. owner Rexall Showcase Internat., 1996—; editor-in-chief Our Mail Network, 2000—. Author: Lillie's Lovely Gardening Book, 1976, Look Beyond Tomorrow: The Carola Spencer Story, 1998, Stroke of Luck, 1999, How to Get Started in Network Marketing from Home, 2001; editor: A Bouquet of Recipes from the Diocese of the Southwest of the Anglican Church in America; author: Dream or Destiny, 2005. Vol. All Saints Anglican Ch. Mem.: San Antonio Writers Guild (past pres.), Electronically Published Internet Connection. Home and Office: 603 Mauze Dr San Antonio TX 78216-3711 Fax: 210-344-1958. Office Phone: 210-344-5554. E-mail: lillie@lillieammann.com.

AMMAR, RAYMOND GEORGE, physicist, researcher; b. Kingston, Jamaica, July 15, 1932; arrived in US, 1950, naturalized, 1965; s. Elias George and Nellie (Khaleel) A.; m. Carroll Ikerd, June 17, 1961 (dec. 2004); children: Elizabeth, Robert (dec.), David AB, Harvard U., 1953; PhD, U. Chgo., 1959. Rsch. assoc. Enrico Fermi Inst., U. Chgo., 1959-60; asst. prof. physics Northwestern U., Evanston, Ill., 1960-64, assoc. prof., 1964-69; prof. physics U. Kans., Lawrence, 1969—, chmn. dept. physics and astronomy, 1989—2003; (on sabbatical leave Fermilab and Deutsches Elektronen Synchrotron, 1984-85). Cons. Argonne (Ill.) Nat. Lab., 1965-69, vis. scientist, 1971-72; vis. scientist Fermilab, Batavia, Ill., summers 1976-81, Deutsches Elektronen Synchrotron, Hamburg, Germany, summers 1982-88, lab. of nuclear studies Cornell U., summers 1989-98; project dir. NSF grant for rsch. in high energy physics, 1962-2001. Contbr. articles to sci. jours. Fellow Am. Phys. Soc.; mem. AAUP. Home: 1651 Hillcrest Rd Lawrence KS 66044-4525 Office: U Kans Dept Physics And Astronomy Lawrence KS 66045-0001 Business E-Mail: ammar@ku.edu.

AMMARI, HABIB, computer science educator, researcher; b. Kairouan, Tunisia, Nov. 24, 1966; s. Mokhtar and Mbarka Ammari; m. Fadhila Oueslati, Aug. 8, 1999; children: Leena, Muath, Mohamed-Eyed. U. Diploma Sci. Studies, Faculty of Scis., Tunis, Tunisia, 1988; diploma engring. in Computer sci. (equivalent to BS and MS in Computer Science), Faculty of Sci., Tunis, Tunisia, 1992; Doctorat De Specialite in Computer sci. (equivalent to PhD in Computer Science), Faculty of Scis., Tunis, Tunisia, 1996. Prin. engr. computer sci. Superior Sch. Comm. (Sup'Com Tunis), Tunisia, 1992—93, asst. lectr. computer sci., 1993—97, asst. prof. computer sci., 1997; vis. faculty Inst. Sci. Rsch., Fairmont, 1999; vis. scientist U. W.Va., Morgantown, 1999—2001; PhD grad. student So. Meth. U., Dallas, 2001—04. Coord. dept. computer sci. and networks Superior Sch. Comm. (Sup'Com Tunis), Tunisia, 1995—96. Author: (rsch. paper) 30th Annual Hawaii Internat. Conf. on System Scis., 4th Workshop on Applications and Svcs. in Wireless Networks, 2004, Internat. Workshop on Wireless, Mobile, and Ad Hoc Networks, 2004, (book chpt.) Relational Methods in Computer Science. Recipient Laureat in Physics and Chemistry, Faculty of Scis. and Ministry of Superior Edn., Tunis, Tunisia, 1988, Ericsson First Prize ($500), 2004, Nokia First Prize ($500), Nokia Rsch. Lab. Elec. Engring. Dept., So. Meth. U., 2004; scholar Vis. Faculty Inst. Sci. Rsch., Ministry Superior Edn., 1999, PhD Student in Computer Sci., CSE Dept. So. Meth. U., 2001-2004. Mem.: ACM (corr.), IEEE (corr.). Avocations: travel, soccer, swimming. Home: 4676 Amesbury Dr Apt 1070 Dallas TX 75206 Office: Southern Meth Univ Dallas TX 75275 Business E-Mail: hammari@engr.smu.edu.

AMMER, CHRISTINE, writer; b. Vienna, May 25, 1931; arrived in U.S., 38; d. Herbert Henry and Helen Parker; m. Dean S. Ammer, Mar. 3, 1960 (dec. Nov. 4, 1999); children: Karen, John, David. Student, Swarthmore Coll., 1952. Editor Parents' Mag. Cultured Libr., N.Y.C., 1956—59, Harvard U. Press, Cambridge, Mass., 1965—68. Author: Getting Help: A Consumer's Guide to Therapy, 1982, Unsing: A History of Women in American Music, 1980, The A to Z of Investing, 1986, It's Raining Cats and Dogs and Other Beastly Expressions, 1989, paperback edit., 1990, Have A Nice Day - No Problem!, 1992, Seeing Red or Tickled Pink, 1993, Southpaws and Sunday Punches and Other Sporting Expressions, 1993, paperback edit., 1994, Fruitcakes and Couch Potatoes and Other Delicious Expressions, 1995, Dictionary of Business and Economics, 2d edit., 1984, The A to Z of Foreign Musical Terms, 1989, The Harper/Collins Dictionary of Music, 3d edit., 1995, The American Heritage Dictionary of Idioms, 1997, Fighting Words from War, Rebellion and Other Combative Capers, 2d edit., 1999, Cool Cats, Top Dogs and Other Beastly Expressions, 1999, The New A to Z of Women's Health, 4th edit., 2000, Unsing: A History of Women in American Music, 2d edit., 2001, The Facts on File Dictionary of Cliches, 2001. Mem.: Dictionary Soc. N.Am., Soc. for Am. Music, Am. Dialect Soc., Internat. Alliance of Women in Music, Nat. Writers Union. Avocations: hiking, tennis, choral singing, swimming, travel.

AMMER, WILLIAM, retired judge; b. Circleville, Ohio, May 21, 1919; s. Moses S. and Mary (Schallas) A. BS in Bus. Adminstrn., Ohio State U., 1941, JD, 1946. Bar: Ohio 1947. Atty., examiner Ohio Indsl. Commn., Columbus, 1947-51; assty. atty. gen. State of Ohio, Columbus, 1951-52; pvt. practice Circleville, 1953-57; pros. atty. Picaway County, Circleville, 1953-57, common pleas judge, 1957-95; ret., 1995. Judge by assignment Supreme Ct. Ohio, 1995—; asst. city solicitor Circleville, 1955-57. Past. pres. Pickaway County ARC, Am. Cancer Soc. Served with inf., AUS, 1942-46. Mem. ABA, Ohio Bar Assn. (chmn. criminal law com. 1964-67), Pickaway County Bar Assn. (pres. 1955-56), Ohio Common Pleas Judges Assn. (pres. 1968), Masons, K.T., Shriners, Kiwanis (Ohio dist. chmn., past lt. gov.). Methodist. Home: PO Box 87 Circleville OH 43113-0087 Office: 113 1/2 South Court St PO Box 87 Circleville OH 43113-0087

AMMIRATO, VINCENT ANTHONY, lawyer; b. Somerville, N.J., Dec. 6, 1942; s. Vincent Salvatore and Elizabeth L. (Masiello) A.; m. Anna Maria Cook, June 19, 1965 (div. Apr. 1994); children: Lisa Maria, Vincent Salvatore II; m. Nancy Lieggi. BA, Long Beach (Calif.) State U., 1968; JD, U. San Diego, 1971. Bar: Calif. 1971, U.S. Supreme Ct. Atty. Buck, Ammirato, and Rutter, Long Beach, 1972-73, 73-88; dep. prosecutor Long Beach Prosecutor, 1973; atty. Burns, Ammirato, Palumbo, Milam & Baronian, Pasadena, Calif., 1989-99; Ammirato & Palumbo, LLP, 1999—. V.p. Shadow Park Home Owners Assn., Cerritos, Calif., 1978-83; mem. adv. coun. John Crowley for City Coun., Cerritos, 1988; advisor YMCA, Sacramento, 1993—; bd. dirs., pres. Cerritos-Artesia Little League, 1986-89. With U.S. Army, 1966-68, Germany. Named Super Lawyer of So. Calif., 2004. Mem. Am. Bd. Trial Advocates, Los Angeles County Bar Assn., Italian/Am. Lawyers of L.A., Forty-Niner Athletic Assn., Pasadena Bar Assn., Assn. Trial Lawyers Am., Consumer Atty. Calif., The Order of Barristers. Avocations: golf, racquetball, swimming. Home: 2031 Buckingham Pl Glendale CA 91206-1402 Office: Ammirato & Palumbo LLP 99 N Lake Ave Pasadena CA 91101-1825 Fax: 626-432-5182. E-mail: vince@ammiratopalumbo.com.

AMMON, GARY D., lawyer; b. Frederick, Md., 1947; BA, Allegheny Coll., 1969; JD, Duquesne Univ., 1977; LLM in Taxation, Temple Univ., 1992. Bar: Pa. 1977. Law clerk, Judge Aldisert Ct. of Appeals (3d cir.); assoc., employee benefits group Drinker Biddle& Reath LLP, Phila., 1981—88, ptnr., employee benefits group, 1988—, now chair, employee benefits group. Office: Drinker Biddle & Reath LLP One Logan Sq 18th & Cherr Sts Philadelphia PA 19103-6996 Office Phone: 215-988-2981. Office Fax: 215-988-2757. Business E-Mail: gary.ammon@dbr.com.

AMMON, HARRY, history professor; b. Waterbury, Conn., Sept. 4, 1917; s. Grover and Lena Mary (Pyne) Amman. BS, Georgetown U., 1939, MA, 1940; PhD, U. Va., 1948. Editor Md. Hist. Mag., Balt., 1948-50; asst. prof. So. Ill. U., Carbondale, 1950-57, assoc. prof., 1957-66, prof. history, 1967—, prof. emeritus, 1984—, chmn. dept., 1977-1983. Fulbright lectr. U. Vienna, Austria, 1954-55, Seoul Nat. U., Korea, 1984-85; vis. prof. U. Va., Charlottesville, 1968-69; guest lectr. Northeast Normal and Liaoning Univs., People's Republic of China, 1986, 88. Author: James Monroe: The Quest for National Identity, 1971, new edit. 1990, The Genet Mission, 1973, James Monroe A Bibliography, 1991. Mem.: Phi Beta Kappa. Office: So Ill U History Dept Carbondale IL 62901 Home: 2950 Westridge Pl Apt 222 Carbondale IL 62901-1090 Business E-Mail: harryam@siu.edu. E-mail: harryam@verizon.net.

AMMON, JOHN RICHARD, anesthesiologist; b. N.Y.C., 1948; MD, U. Pa., 1974. Cert. in anesthesiology. Intern Crozer Chester Med. Ctr., 1974—75; resident in anesthesiology Mass. Gen. Hosp., Boston, 1975—77; fellow in cardiac anesthesiology Stanford (Calif.) Med. Ctr., 1977—78; dir., v.p. Am. Bd. Anesthesiology, Phoenix, 1988—99; pvt. practice Valley Anesthesiology Ltd., Phoenix, 1999—. Mem.: Am. Soc. Anesthesiology, Alpha Omega Alpha. also: Am Bd Anesthesiology 4101 Lake Boone Trl Ste 510 Raleigh NC 27607-7506 Office: Valley Anesthesiology Consultants 2901 N Central Ave Ste 500 Phoenix AZ 85012-2700

AMMONS, JAMES H., academic administrator; s. James Henry and Agnes Ammons; m. Judy Riffin; 1 child, James III. BS in Polit. Sci., Fla. A&M State U., 1974; MS in Pub. Adminstrn., Fla. State U., 1975, PhD in Govt., 1977. Faculty program cons. State U. Sys. Fla., Tallahassee, 1987—88; asst. v.p. acad. affairs Fla. A&M State U., 1984—89, assoc. v.p. acad. affairs, 1989—95, provost, v.p. acad. affairs, 1995—2001; chancellor N.C. Ctrl. U., Durham, 2001—. Contbr. articles to profl. jours. Mem. adv. commn. Habitat for Humanity, Durham, 2004—; mem. Leadership N.C., 2003; bd. dirs. Greater Durham C. of C., 2001, Ctrl. Carolina Bank, 2002. Named Disting. Alumni, Fla. A&M State U., 1999, Citizen of Yr., BEta Phi chpt. Omega Psi Phi, Durham, 2002; fellow, Am. Coun. Edn., 1986—87, CIGNA Found., 1986—87; Am. Coun. Edn. fellow, Fla. State U., Tallahassee, 1986—87, Booth Ferris fellow, U. Wis., Madison, 1993. Mem.: Commn. Colls., Coun. Advancement & Support Edn. (chair compliance and report com.). Office: NC Ctrl U 1801 Fayetteville St Durham NC 27707

AMOLSCH, ARTHUR LEWIS, publishing executive; b. L.A., Nov. 28, 1939; s. Arthur Bruce Amolsch and Mildred Vivian (Guyott) Fry; m. Judith Ann Marolda, Aug. 27, 1963 (div. 1982); children: Christopher Bryan, Kira Leigh; m. Imelda Marie Moore Madden, Mar. 27, 1983. BS, Ea. Mich. U., 1963. Tchr. Edmondson Jr. High Sch., Ypsilanti, Mich., 1963-66; fgn. svc. officer Dept. State, Washington, 1971-72; head speech writer Com. for Re-election of the Pres., Washington, 1972; dep. dir., press rels. Presdl. Inaugural Com., Washington, 1973; dir. pub. info. FTC, Washington, 1973-76; pres., pub. Washington Regulatory Reporting Assocs., 1976—. Capt. USAF, 1967-71. Home: PO Box 356 Basye VA 22810-0356 Office Phone: 202-639-0581. E-mail: ftcwatch@usa.net.

AMON, CAROL BAGLEY, federal judge; b. 1946; BS, Coll. William and Mary, 1968; JD, U. Va., 1971. Bar: Va. 1971, D.C. 1972, N.Y. 1980. Staff atty. Communications Satellite Corp., Washington, 1971-73; trial atty. U.S. Dept. Justice, Washington, 1973-74; asst. U.S. atty. Ea. Dist. N.Y., 1974-86, U.S. magistrate, 1986-90, dist. ct. judge, 1990—. Recipient John Marshall award U.S. Dept. Justice, 1983. Mem. ABA (joint commn. evaluate model code judicial conduct 2004-05), Va. State Bar Assn., D.C. Bar Assn. (chair codes of conduct com. of jud. conf. 1998-2001). Office: US District Court 225 Cadman Plz E Brooklyn NY 11201-1818

AMONETT, LARRY, accountant; b. 1952; s. Marvin Earl and Jewell Maude (Anderson) A.; m. Dixie Lee Rector, Aug. 5, 1972; children: Laura Lee, Kristin Nicole BS in acctg., BS in Gen. Bus. Adm., Ball State U., 1975. Auditor Ind. State Bd of Accounts, 1974-78, asst. auditor, supr., 1978-81, supr., 1981-84; asst. bus. mgr. Anderson (Ind.) Community Sch., 1984-95; asst. bus. mgr., dep. treas. Metro. Sch. Dist. of Lawrence Twp., Indpls., 1996—. Recipient Awarded Sagamore of the Wabash Gov. Evan Bayh, 1996. Mem. Ind. Assn. Sch. Bus. Ofcls. (treas. 1992-93, sec. 1993-94, pres.-elect 1994-95, pres. 1995-96), Assn. Sch. Bus. Ofcls., Ind. Govtl. Fin. Officers Assn. (bd. dirs.), Registered Sch. Bus. Offcl., Ind. Registered Sch. Bus. Offcls. Democrat. Avocations: computers, sports, woodworking. Office: Met Sch Dist of Lawrence Twp 7601 E 56th St Indianapolis IN 46226-1310 E-mail: larryamonett@msdlt.k12.in.us.

AMONETTE, REX. A., physician; b. Ozan, Ark., June 17, 1939; MD, U. Ark., 1966. Intern Ark. Bapt. Med. Ctr., Little Rock, 1966-67; resident U. Tenn., Memphis, 1969-71; physician Balt. Meml. Hosp., Memphis, 1974—. Mem. AMA, Am. Dermatology Assn. Office: Memphis Dermatology Clinic 1455 Union Ave Memphis TN 38104-6727

AMONTE, ANTHONY LEWIS, professional hockey player; b. Weymouth, Mass., Aug. 2, 1970; Student, Boston U. Profl. hockey player N.Y. Rangers, NY, 1988—94, Chgo. Blackhawks, 1994—2002, Phoenix Coyotes, 2002—03, Philadelphia Flyers, 2003—05, Calgary Flames, 2005—. Named NCAA All-Tournament Team, 1990—91; named to NHL All-Rookie Team, 1992, NHL All-Star Team, 1997—2001. Office: c/o Calgary Flames PO Box 1540 Stn M T2P 3B9 Calgary Al Canada*

AMORES, JOSE E., director; b. Mexico City, Mar. 10, 1919; m. Alicia Salinas, July 10, 1947; 1 child, Beatriz. Degree in chem. engring., Nat. U., Mexico. Sch. dir. Monterrey (Mexico) Tech., 1947-59, v.p., 1960-70; social dir. Alfa Group, Monterrey, 1970-84; cultural dir. State Govt., Monterrey, 1984-87; mus. dir. Monterrey Art Mus., 1988-90; dir. Cultural Ctr., Monterrey, 1991-94, Nuevo León Pub. Broadcast System, 1996-98, Mex. History Mus., 1998—2002. Bd. trustees several univs., 1980—. Author of poems. Pres. Artistic Soc., Monterrey, 1948-80, Chem. Engring. Inst., Monterrey, 1974-76. Recipient Chemistry Nat. prize, 1970. Mem. Sembradores Internat. (pres. 1961-62, 70-72). Home: Rio Presas 305 66220 Garza Garcia Mexico Office: Ctr Cultural Alta PO Box 1177 64000 Monterrey Mexico

AMORIM, CELSO LUIZ NUNES, Brazilian government official; b. June 3, 1942; m. Ana Maria Amorim; children: Vincente, Anita, Joao, Pedro. Student, Rio-Branco Inst., Diplomatic Acad. Vienna, London Sch. Econs. Dir. gen. EMBRAFILME (Brazilian Film Corp.), 1979—82; amb. UN, Geneva, 1991-93; min. fgn. affairs Brazil, 1993—94; permanent rep. Brazil UN, N.Y.C., 1995-99, Geneva, 1999—; min. foreign affairs, 2003—. Spl. asst. to Ministry Sci. & Tech.; asst. prof. dept. polit. sci. and internat. rels. U. Brasilia, permanent mem. dept. internat. affairs Inst. Advanced Studies; pres. UN Security Coun., 1999; chmn. ILO Govt. Body, 2000; amb. Brazil to Ct. of St.James's, 2001-2002. Contbr. articles to profl. jours. Office: Ministry of Foreign Affairs Esplanada Dos Ministerios Bloco H 70170-900 Brasília Brazil

AMOROS, GRIMANESA, multimedia artist; b. Lima, Perú, Apr. 21, 1962; arrived in U.S., 1984; d. Carlos Amoros Heck and Gladys Amoros Marquina; m. William Grant Fleischer, Sept. 24, 1988; 1 child, Shammiel Fleischer-Amoros. Studied, Pvt. Ateliers, Lima, Peru, 1981—84, The Art Students League, N.Y.C., 1985—88. Guest lectr. SUNY, Stony Brook, 1990, Stockton State Coll., Pomona, NJ, 1990, Fine Arts U., Cuenca, Ecuador, 1992, Spruill Ctr. for Arts, Atlanta, 1997, Colgate U., Hamilton, NY, 2000, Sweet Briar Coll., Va., 2002. One-woman shows include Gayo Gallery, Lima, Peru, 1982, Warike Gallery, 1984, Ollantay Ctr. for the Arts, Flushing, N.Y., 1986, Union Gallery, SUNY, Stony Brook, 1987, Art Soc., Internat. Monetary Fund, Washington, D.C., 1988, Atlantic City Art Ctr., N.J., 1989, Mus. Nagin Isaias, Guayaquil, Ecuador, 1991, Mus. Mod. Art, Cuenca, Ecuador, 1992, Porter Randall Gallery, San Diego, 1993, Carolyn J. Roy Gallery, N.Y.C., 1994, Mus. Mod. Art, Santo Domingo, Dominican Rep., 1995, Art Renaca Gallery, Valparaiso, Chile, 1997, Artco Gallery, Lima, Peru, 2003, R&F Gallery, Kingston, N.Y., 2003, Maxwell Fine Arts, Artspace, Raleigh, N.C., 2004, exhibited in group shows at Nat. Art Club Gallery, N.Y.C., 1986, El Bohio Gallery, 1986, Arthur Ross Gallery, U. Pa., Phila., 1987, Mus. New Art, Detroit, 2001, Santa Fe Art Inst., 2002, The Times Sq. Lobby Gallery, N.Y.C., 2003, Mus. Ams., Washington, D.C., 2004, Athens Inst. for Contemp. Art, Ga., 2004, Abrons Arts Ctr., N.Y.C., 2005; contbr. articles to profl. jours.; Represented in permanent collections U. Vt., Burlington, Mus. Contemp. Drawings, Santo Domingo, Dominican Rep., Santa Fe Art Inst., Va. Ctr. for Creative Arts Fellowship Residency, Lynchburg, Va., Mus. Mod. Art, Santo Domingo, Dominican Rep., Doro Prodns., Vienna, Winslow Adv. Group Ltd., N.Y.C., Aurobora Press, San Francisco, Advance Ins. Svcs., N.Y.C., Intergraphic Found., Berlin. Fellow, Bronx Mus. Art, 1986, NEA, 1993, Santa Fe Art Inst., 2002, Centrum Artist Residency, 2004. Avocations: travel, yoga. Home: 117 Hudson St New York NY 10013 Business E-Mail: grimanesa@grimanesaamoros.com.

AMOROSO, FRANK, retired communication system engineer, consultant; b. Providence, July 31, 1935; s. Michele and Angela Maria Barbara (D'Uva) A. BSEE, MSEE, MIT, 1958; postgrad., Purdue U., 1958-60, U. Turin, Italy, 1964-65. Registered profl. engr., Calif. Instr. elec. engring. Purdue U., West Lafayette, Ind., 1958-60; rsch. engr. Melpar Inc., Roxbury, Mass., 1959, MIT Instrumentation Lab., Cambridge, Mass., 1960, Litton Sys. Advanced Devel. Lab., Waltham, Mass., 1960-61; engr. Melpar Applied Sci. Divsn., Watertown, Mass., 1961; mem. tech. staff RCA Labs. David Sarnoff Rsch. Ctr., Princeton, N.J., 1962-64, Mitre Corp., Bedford, Mass., 1966-67; sr. applied mathematician Collins Radio Co., Newport Beach, 1967-68; comm. sys. engr. N.Am. Rockwell Corp., El Segundo, Calif., 1968-71, Northrop Electronics Divsn., Palos Verdes Peninsula, 1971-72; comm. sys. engr., sr. staff engr. Hughes Aircraft Co., Fullerton, 1972-89; ret., 1989; cons., developer, presenter ednl. seminars, 1989—. Cons. Lincom, Inc., L.A., 1994—96, Omnipoint Corp., Price Comms., 2004—; cons. client Sklar Comm. Engring., 1996—, Mascarell Microones, S.L., Tarragona, Spain; instr. continuing engring. edn. program George Washington U., San Diego, 1993; instr. ext. short courses UCLA, 1987—89, 1998—; cons. Mobile Elec. Tracking Sys., Boca Raton, Fla., 1992, Word Works, Newport Beach, Calif., 2003—. Co-author: (book) Power Amplifier Design, 2002. 1st lt. U.S. Signal Corps, 1961-62. Recipient Outstanding Achievement award RCA Labs., 1964; grad. study scholar Italian Govt., 1964-66. Mem. IEEE (sr. mem., session organizer, chmn. conf. on mil. com., presenter). Achievements include patents in field. Home and Office: Digital Data Modulation Studies 271 W Alton Ave Apt D Santa Ana CA 92707-4171 Office Phone: 714-557-1061.

AMOROSO, RICHARD LOUIS, psychologist, educator; b. Medford, Mass., Apr. 24, 1946; s. Louis Raymond and Marjorie Lou (McCathie) Amoroso; m. Juliette Noble Sherer, Oct. 1982 (div. 1986); 1 child, Juliette Rachael. BS in Psychology, U. Mass., 1972; postgrad., Stanford U., 1972—74, Harvard U., 1980—82; PhD in Cosmology, Internat. Noetic U., 1992; MA in Consciousness Studies, J.F.K. U., 1994. Computer engr. Harvard Smithsonian Astrophys. Obs., Cambridge, Mass., 1980-82; instr. Peralta Coll., Oakland, Calif., 1987-88; dir. Mus. Robotics, Berkeley, Calif., 1989—, Noetic Advanced Studies Inst., Orinda, Calif., 1992—; pres. Cereroscopic Sys., Inc., Provo, Utah; CFO Elec. Corp., Oakland, 1992-94; prof. philosophy of mind Internat. Noetic U., Oakland, 1995—. Founding editor: Noetic Jour., 1997—; editor: (book) Science and the Primary of Consciousness, 1998, The Scientific Origins of Sexual Preference, 2000, Gravitation and Cosmology: From the Hubble Radius to the Planck Scale, 2001, The Complementarity of Mind and Body, 2003, What is Conciousness? Introducing the Cosmology of Being, 2003, Shifting the Medical Paradigm, 2004, A Revolucao da Consciencia, 2005; editor: (with B. Lehnert and J.-P. Vigier) The Search for Unity in Physics: Extending the Standard Model, 2005. Mem.: AAAS, N.Y. Acad. Sci., Romanian Acad. Sci. (hon.). Republican. Mem. Lds Ch. Achievements include having the 1st comprehensive theory of dualism in history. Avocations: meditation, scuba diving, robotic sculpture, reading, sailing. Office: Noetic Inst 120 Village Sq # 49 Orinda CA 94563-2502 E-mail: noeticj@mindspring.com.

AMOS, BETTY GILES, food service executive, accountant; b. Lebanon, Mo., July 18, 1941; d. Clarence Edgar and Clara Mae (Gann) Giles; m. E.L. Amos, Sept. 18, 1959 (div. Oct. 1965); 1 child, Jeffrey Lee; m. Thomas R. Righetti, Jan. 2, 1983 (dec. Sept. 18, 2002). BBA magna cum laude, U. Miami, Coral Gables, Fla., 1973, MBA, 1976; D of Bus. Adminstrn. honoris causa, Johnson & Wales U., 1990. CPA, Fla. Sec. City of Lebanon, 1959-63; dept. head Empire Gas Co., Lebanon, 1963-68; fin. analyst asst. Biscayne Assocs., Ltd., Miami, Fla., 1968-73; investment mgr. Universal Restaurants Inc., Miami, 1973-77; pvt. practice acct., investment mgr. Miami, 1977-83; pres. The Abkey Cos., Miami, 1983—. Founder Mega Bank, Miami, 1983-94; mem. adv. com. Fuddruckers, Inc., Boston, 1986-2002. Trustee Miami Project, 1986-89, United Fund of Dade County, 1992—; pres. Humane Soc. Greater Miami, 1994-2000, bd. dirs., 1993-2000; mem. pres. coun. U. Miami, 1994—, mem. founder's soc., 1994—, bd. trustees, 1997—; mem. presdl. search com. U. Miami, 2000; dir. Wings Over Miami Aviation Mus., treas., 2002-03, pres., 2004—; bd. dirs. IVAX Corp., 2003—; mem. audit com. Miami-Dade County Sch. Bd., 2004—. Recipient Philip J. Romano Founders award, 1988. Mem. AICPA, Fla. Inst. CPAs, Am. Women's Soc. CPAs, Coconut Grove C. of C. (trustee 1988-2001), Nat. Assn. Women Bus. Owners (Outstanding Woman Bus. award 1993), U. Miami Alumni Assn. (nat. pres. 1999-2001), Iron Arrow, Internat. Women's Forum, Women of Tomorrow (Orange Bowl com. 2002-), Women's Exec. Leadership (adv. bd. 2005—). Republican. Roman Catholic. Avocations: skiing, water-skiing, scuba diving, tennis. Home: 7330 SW 165th St Palmetto Bay FL 33157 Office: The Abkey Cos 9275 Coral Reef Dr Ste 107 Miami FL 33157 Office Phone: 305-278-4422. Business E-Mail: bgamos@bellsouth.net.

AMOS, DANIEL PAUL, insurance company executive; b. Pensacola, Fla., Aug. 13, 1951; s. Paul Shelby and Mary Jean (Roberts) A.; m. Mary Shannon Landing, Sept. 12, 1972; children: Paul Shelby, Lauren Alyse BS in Risk and Ins. Mgmt., U. Ga., 1973. Co-state mgr. Am. Family Life Assurance Co., Columbus, Ga., 1973-78, state mgr., 1978-83, pres., 1983-96; dep. CEO Am. Family Corp., Columbus, Ga., 1996; vice-chmn., pres., CEO AFLAC Inc., Columbus, Ga., 1996—, CEO, 1990—, chmn., 2001—, pres., 1983—2001. Dir. Columbus Bank & Trust Co., Synovus Fin. Corp., So. Co. Bd. trustees Children's Healthcare of Atlanta, House of Mercy of Columbus. Methodist. Avocation: bridge. Office: AFLAC Inc 1932 Wynnton Rd Columbus GA 31999-0001*

AMOS, JAMES LYSLE, photographer; b. Kalamazoo, Jan. 25, 1929; s. George Elsworth and Lois Hazel (Noffsinger) A.; m. Martha Imogene (Holbrook), Sept. 1975. Student, U. Idaho, 1947-49; AAS, Rochester Inst. Tech., 1951. Trainee Eastman Kodak Co., 1951-53, salesman Des Moines, 1956, tech. sales rep. Balt., 1957-67. Free lance photographer, 1967-69, 93—; staff photographer, Nat. Geog. Soc., Washington, 1969-89, contract photographer, 1989-93; prin. photographer (books) on Hawaii and America's Inland Waterway. Served with AUS, 1953-55. Named Mag. Photographer of Yr., Nat. Press Photographers Assn., 1969, 70. Mem. N.Am. Nature Photography Assn., Internat. Assn. Panoramic Photographers. Home: PO Box 807 Chestertown MD 21620-0607 E-mail: jlapix@dmv.com. *To achieve success we must love what we are doing, be willing to take risks and trust our instincts.*

AMOS, JOSEPH GLENN, media specialist; b. Topeka, Aug. 22, 1953; s. Glenn Michael and La Verda Mavis Amos; m. Renee Diane Kilgore, Dec. 17, 1983; children: Brooke Rachelle, Michael Joseph, William Clark. BA in Phys. Edn., Ottawa U., Kans., 1971—75; MS in Phys. Edn., Emporia State U., Kans., 1976—80, MLS, 2000—03. Cert. tchr. State of Kans., 2003. Social studies tchr. Blue Valley North H.S., Overland Park, Kans., 1987—2001, libr. media specialist, 2001—. Com. mem. Summer Inst. for Sch. Librs., Kans., 2002—05. Contbr. articles to profl. jours. Named an Honored Tchr., The Kans. City Star Newspaper. Mem.: NEA, ALA, Kans. Assn. Sch. Librs. (editor 2003—05), Am. Assn. Sch. Librs. Liberal. Avocations: reading, backpacking, hunting, fishing. Home: 16209 W 126th Terr Olathe KS 66062 Office: Blue Valley North HS 12200 Lamar Overland Park KS 66209 Office Phone: 913-239-3026. Office Fax: 913-345-7370. Personal E-mail: amosj@sbcglobal.net. E-mail: jamos@bluevalleyk12.org.

AMOS, LINDA K., academic administrator; b. Findlay, Ohio, Sept. 7, 1940; d. Blond G. and Dorotha (Brinkman) A. BS, Ohio State U., 1962, MS, 1964; EdD, Boston U., 1977. Asst. dean of baccalaureate affairs Boston U. Coll. Nursing, 1971-74, dean, prof., 1975-80, U. Utah Coll. Nursing, Salt Lake City, 1980—2000; assoc. v.p. for health scis. U. Utah, Salt Lake City, 1998—, Dorthie & Keith Barnes presdl. chair, prof. nursing. Cons. Social Sci. Rsch. Inst., Boston; chmn. Commn. on Collegiate Nursing Edn., 1998-2000; bd. dirs. Univ. Health Network. Contbr. articles to profl. jours. Chmn. Presdl. Commn. on Status of Women, U. Utah, 1995—99; bd. dirs. Utah Heart Assn.; trustee U. Utah Hosp. Served as cons. with USPHS. Named for Outstanding Contbns. to the Nursing Profession, Utah Citizen's League for Nursing, 1989; recipient VA Chief Nurse award for promoting unity between edn. and practice, Lawrence and Delores Weaver Coll. Pharmacy Recognition award, 2002, Disting. Woman prize Salt Lake Jr. Assistance League, 2004. Fellow Am. Acad. Nursing (governing coun. 1986-90, selection com. 1995—98); mem. ANA, Am. Assn. Colls. of Nursing (pres. 1984-86, Sister Bernadette Armiger award 2000), Nat. Adv. Coun. on Nurse Tng., Utah Women's Forum, Internat. Women's Forum, Salt Lake City Rotary, Sigma Theta Tau (internat. nominating com. 1995-97, Mary Tolle Wright award for excellence in leadership 1991).

AMOS, THERESA ANN, marketing professional; BA in Comm., U. Colo., Colorado Springs, 1985. Cert. sailing. Mktg. mgr. Subway Devel. Corp. San Diego, 1990—94; dir. bus. devel. and account supr. Janis Brown and Assocs., San Diego, 1996—99; dir. corp. mktg. Boxlot, San Diego, 1999—2001; dir. Marcom Bidland Sys., San Diego, 2001; v.p. bus. devel. and mktg. Computer Market Rsch., San Diego, 2001—02; v.p. comm. techs. The Dakota Group, San Diego; v.p. mktg. comm. Path Network Techs., San Diego, 2001—02; dir. comm. strategies Four Sq., San Diego, 2002—. Mem. adv. bd. Cmty. Options, San Diego, 2003; mem. adv. bd. cord blood options Stem Cell Consortium, Calif., 2003. Vol. Am.'s Cup, San Diego, 1992, Am. Diabetes Assn., San Diego, 1994. Mem.: NAFTA, AMA, Health Care Communicators, Nat. Acad. TV Arts and Scis., Am. Mktg. Assn., Nat. Home Builders Assn., Bldg. Industry Assn., Biocom. Avocations: sailing, running, bodybuilding, writing, dance. Office: Four Square 5205 Kearny Villa Way San Diego CA 92123

AMOS, TORI, musician, singer; b. N.C. d. Edison and Mary Ellen A. Student, Peabody Conservatory. Albums: Y Kant Tori Read, 1988, Little Earthquakes, 1992, Under the Pink, 1994 (Grammy nomination, Best Alternative Music Performance, 1995), Boys for Pele, 1996, From the Choirgirl Hotel, 1998, To Venus and Back, 1999, Strange Little Girls, 2001, Scarlet's Walk, 2002, Tales of a Librarian: Tori Amos Collection, 2003; author: (with Ann Powers) Tori Amos: Piece By Piece, 2005. Office: Atlantic Records 1290 Avenue Of The Americas New York NY 10104-0184

AMOSS, WALTER JAMES, III, (JIM AMOSS), editor; b. New Orleans, Oct. 22, 1947; s. Walter James Jr. and Berthe Lathrop (Marks) A.; m. Nancy Brooks Monroe, Apr. 5, 1975; children: Adam Brooks, Sophia Philomene. BA magna cum laude, Yale U., 1969. Reporter The States-Item, New Orleans, 1974-79, The Times-Picayune, New Orleans, 1980-82, city editor, 1982-83, met. editor, 1983-88, assoc. editor, 1988-90, editor, 1990—. Bd. vis. La. State U. Manship Sch. Mass. Comms.; trustee Trinity Episcopal Sch.; mem. Pulitzer Prize bd., 2003-, juror, 1994-95, 99-2000. Mem. La. Com. of Selection for Rhodes Scholarships, 1982—. Rhodes scholar Oxford (Eng.) U., 1970-71; Journalistes en Europe grantee, 1979-80; named Nat. Press Found.'s Editor of Yr., 1997. Mem. Am. Soc. Newspaper Editors, AP Mng. Editors, Phi Beta Kappa. Roman Catholic. Office: The Times-Picayune 3800 Howard Ave New Orleans LA 70125-1429

AMOURY, RAYMOND ANTHONY, retired surgeon, educator; b. S.I., N.Y., Feb. 9, 1928; s. Alphonse Alfred and Mary Lorena (Balish) A.; m. Mary Frances Byrne, Sept. 21, 1957; children: Mary Patricia, Peter Anthony, Anne Veronica, Gerard Joseph, Jane Frances. BS, Wagner Coll., 1951; MD, SUNY, Bklyn., 1955. Diplomate Am. Bd. Thoracic Surgery, Am. Bd. Surgery, cert. spl. competence in pediat. surgery, recert. pediat. surgery. Instr. surgery Columbia U. Coll. Physicians and Surgeons, N.Y.C., 1960-64, asst. prof., 1964-68; assoc. prof. U. Mo., Columbia, 1968-70; prof. U. Mo. Kansas City Sch. Medicine, 1970-72, Katharine Berry Richardson prof., 1973-94, prof. emeritus, 1994—. Assoc. dir. for surg. affairs Children's Mercy Hosp., Kansas City, Mo., 1969-94, surgeon-in chief, 1968-94, emeritus, 1994—. Contbr. articles to profl. jours. and publs. Pfc. U.S. Army, 1946-47. Roman Catholic. Office: The Childrens Mercy Hosp 2401 Gillham Rd Kansas City MO 64108-4698

AMPARADO, KEITH D., communications company executive; b. Bklyn., Oct. 5, 1952; m. Arcadeo and Sadie J. (Browne) A. BS, SUNY, Empire State Coll. Supr. data processing Franklin Nat. Bank/European Am. Bank, 1974-78; mgr. Ctr. for Computing Activity Columbia U., N.Y.C., 1978-80; systems analyst Morgan Guaranty Trust Co., 1980-81; programmer, analyst Europen Am. Bank, 1981-83; sr. tech editor Mfrs. Hanover Trust, 1983-85; founder, pres. KDA Comm, Bklyn., 1985—. Cons. Siloam Presbyn. Ch., Bklyn., 1988—. Mem. Soc. for Tech. Communication (sr.), Am. Mgmt. Assn., Am. Mktg. Assn., Mktg. Rsch. Assn., Nat. Assn. Desktop Pubs., Qualitative Rsch. Cons. Assn., Internat. Assn. of Bus. Communicators.

AMPY, FRANKLIN ROOSEVELT, zoologist; b. Dinwiddie, Va., June 22, 1936; s. Preston and Beatrice Tucker A.; B.S., Va. State Coll., 1958; M.S., Oreg. State U., 1960, Ph.D., 1962. Asst. prof. Am. U. Beirut, 1962-68; NIH fellow U. Calif., Davis, 1968-71; assoc. prof. zoology Howard U., Washington, 1971—90; prof. biology, 1990-, acting chmn. dept. zoology, 1973-75, 84-86, 90-92, now acting chmn. dept., dir. undergrad. edn., dept. biology, 2003-; geneticist Lebanese del. to World Poultry Conf., 1966; cons. NIH, 1981, 83. NASA-Ames faculty fellow, 1976; dir. undergraduate edn. biology, 2003-04; NIH grantee, 1978—; NSF grantee, 1978,95. Mem. Bd. dirs., Project 30, Am. Genetic Assn., Am. Soc. Genetics, Environ. Mutagenesis Soc., Am. Soc. Cell Biologists, Smithsonian Assocs., Sigma Xi (pres. Howard U. cptr., 1993-94), Beta Kappa Xi, Alpha Phi Alpha. Democrat. Episcopalian. Home: PO Box 91886 Washington DC 20090-1886 Office: Dept Biology Howard Univ 415 College St Washington DC 20001

AMRON, CORY M., lawyer; b. NYC; BA, U. Rochester, 1974; JD, Harvard U., 1977. Ptnr. Vorys, Sater, Seymour and Pease, LLP. Mem.: Commercial Real Estate Women Fellows of the Am. Bar Found. (state chair 2001—), Women's Bar Assn. DC (tres. 1982—83, mem., bd. dirs. 1994—97, Woman Lawyer Yr. 2004), Am. Bar Assn. (mem., Task Force Law Schools and Profession: Narrowing the Gap 1988—92, chair, Commn. Women Profession 1991—94, mem., Commn. Domestic Violence 1998—2002), Bar Assn. DC (chair, Young Lawyers Sect. 1983—84, mem., bd. dirs. 1985—87, mem., Out of Box Com., Sect. Legal Edn. 2001—), DC Bar (editor, DC Practical Manual 1985—87, chair, Commerical Real Estate Com. 1986—89, mem., Steering Com., Real Estate Housing and Land Use Sect. 1989—94, mem., Reproductive Cancer Task Force 1994—96). Office: Vorys Sater Seymour and Pease LLP 11th Fl 1828 L St NW Washington DC 20036-5109 Business E-Mail: cmamron@vssp.com.

AMSDEN, TED THOMAS, lawyer; b. Cleve., Dec. 11, 1950; s. Richard Thomas and Mary Agnes (Hendricks) A.; m. Ruth Anna Rydstedt, May 1, 1982; children: Jennifer Rydstedt, Matthew Lars, Alexis Linnea. BA, Wayne State U., 1972; JD, Harvard U., 1975. Bar: Mich. 1975, U.S. Dist. Ct. (ea. dist.) Mich. 1975, U.S. Ct. Appeals (6th cir.) 1975, U.S. Supreme Ct. 1979. From assoc. to ptnr. Dykema Gossett PLLC and predecessor firm, Detroit, 1975—. Chmn. Baha'i Justice Soc., 1986-88, corr. sec., 1988-92, bd. dirs., 1986-93, 95—; bd. dirs. Internat. Inst., Detroit, 1989-97, 99—, v.p. legal affairs, 1991-94, v.p., 1994-95, pres.-elect 1995-96, pres., 1996-97, co-chair Ethnic Summit '96; bd. dirs. Racial Justice Ctr., Grosse Pointe, Mich., 1992-94, Greater Detroit Interfaith Roundtable, 1994—, bd. dirs. Model of Racial Unity, Inc., 1995-97, treas., 1997—, chmn., 1998—, vice chmn.; mem. Mich. Bar Rep. Assembly, 1988-94. Recipient Detroit Principles award of Race Relations Coun. of Metropolitan Detroit, 1993, Spirit of Detroit award City of Detroit Common Coun., 1996, 97. Mem. ABA, Mich. Bar Assn., Wolverine Bar Assn., Detroit Bar Assn., Detroit Bar Assn. Found. (bd. dirs. 1992-98, sec., 1993-95, pres. 1995-97), Macomb County Bar Assn., Assn. Def. Counsel, Civic Searchlight (Macomb County steering com., jud. com. 1990-91, Wayne County jud. com. 1992-95). Home: 987 Lake Shore Rd Grosse Pointe Shores MI 48236-1171 Office: Dykema Gossett 400 Renaissance Ctr Ste 3800 Detroit MI 48243-1603

AMSLER, DARLENE C, elementary school educator; b. Bklyn., May 10, 1957; d. Leslie Earle and Dorothy Louise Clarke; m. Joseph Amsler (dec.); children: Joshua, Rachel. B, Bloomsburg State Coll., 1978. Cert. PA Dept. Edn. Tchr. Newport Sch. Dist., Newport, Pa., 1978—. Tchr., liason mem. Newport Elem. Leader Girl Scouts, Newport, Pa., 1970—87, 1998—; dir., bd. mem. Perry County Day Camp, Pa., 1984—2001. Mem.: Nat. Edn. Assn., Newport Edn. Assn. Episc. Avocation: quilting. Office: 272 Creek Rd Newport PA 17074 also: Newport Sch Dist 420 Fickles Lane PO Box 9 Newport PA 17074

AMSLER, LAURIE VIAL, voice educator; d. Robert Vial and Eulice Hoke Vial; children: Christopher, Elizabeth, Jonathan. BS in Music Edn., Tex. Woman's U., 1977. Cert. music edn. Tex. Edn. Agy., 1977, Kodaly Certification Sam Houston State U., Tex., 1986. Tchr. elem. music and movement Fairview Elem. Sch., Copperas Cove, Tex., 1984—95; tchr. choral and music Smith Mid. Sch., Fort Hood, 1995—99; choral educator Cedar Bayou Jr. Sch., Baytown, 1999—2003, S.P. Waltrip H.S., Houston, 2003—. Ch. musician, accompanist various chapels, chs., civic orgns. and univs. Mem. German Cmty. Ch. Choir, Ansbach, Germany, 1981—84. Mem.: Am. Choral Dirs. Assn., Tex. Choral Dirs. Assn., Tex. Music Educators Assn. Office: Waltrip High Sch 1900 West 34th St Houston TX 77018 Office Phone: 713-688-1361. Personal E-mail: lvamsler@hotmail.com. E-mail: lamsler@houstonisd.org.

AMSTADT, NANCY HOLLIS, retired language educator; b. Chgo., Ill., Mar. 1, 1932; d. James George and Agnes Green Hollis; m. Ervin Carl Amstadt, Dec. 27, 1952; children: Elaine, Joan, Steven, Carolyn. BA, De Paul U., 1952; MA, San Diego State U., 1966. English & history tchr. Sweetwater H.S. Dist., Chula Vista, Calif., 1957—59; tchr., counselor Santa Clara City Schs., Santa Clara, Calif., 1959—63; secondary English tchr. San Diego City Schs., San Diego, 1966—91; English instr. San Diego C.C., San Diego, 1993—95; ret., 1995. Chmn. dept. English Kearny H.S., San Diego, 1985—91. Exhibitions include San Diego Art Inst., 1984—2003. Mem. U.N. Gender Equity, San Diego, 2001—04; docent art gallery U. Calif., San Diego, 1998—2004; program dir. San Diego Mus. Art, San Diego, 1968—2003. Democrat. Avocations: tennis, women refugees, art history, classical music, Chinese exercise. Home: 1097 Alexandria Drive San Diego CA 92107

AMSTADTER, LAURENCE, retired architect; b. Chgo., Apr. 9, 1922; s. Frank J. and Irene B. (Black) A.; m. Erma Jacqueline Kallen, Mar. 8, 1948; children: John Kallen, Marc Robert. BA in Architecture, Chgo. Tech. Coll., 1948; postgrad., Northwestern U., Evanston, Ill., 1948-49. Registered architect, Ill., 20 other states. Architect Ford Bacon & Davis Inc., Chgo., 1949-50, Skidmore Owings & Merrill, Chgo., 1950-51, Sidney Morris & Assocs., Chgo., 1951-52, Chgo. Housing Authority, 1952-53; sr. v.p. A. Epstein and Sons Inc., Chgo., 1953-87; cons., 1987—. Mem. Exec. Svc. Corps of Chgo. With Air Corps, U.S. Army, 1941-45, ETO. Mem. AIA (corp.), Svc. Corps Ret. Execs., Soc. Am. Registered Architects, Chgo. Com. on High Rise Bldgs. Democrat. Home: 1633 Cambridge Ave Flossmoor IL 60422-2127 Office: Amstadter Architects 360 N Michigan Ave Chicago IL 60601 E-mail: lekamstadter@aol.com.

AMSTER, LINDA EVELYN, newspaper executive, consultant; b. N.Y.C., May 21, 1938; d. Abraham and Belle Shirley (Levine) Meyerson; m. Robert L. Amster, Feb. 18, 1961 (dec. Feb. 1974). BA, U. Mich., 1960; M.L.S., Columbia U., 1968. Tchr. English Stamford High Sch., Conn., 1961-63; research librarian The Detroit News, 1965-67, The N.Y. Times, N.Y.C., 1967-69, supr. news research, 1969-74, news research mgr., 1974—2004, dir. news research, 2004—. Bd. dirs. Council for Career Planning, N.Y.C., 1982— Editor: The New York Times Passover Cookbook, 1999, Kill Duck Before Serving, 2002, The New York Times Jewish Cookbook, 2003, The New York Times Chicken Cookbook, 2005; contbr. articles to books, N.Y. Times and other publs. Mem. adv. com. N.Y.C. 100 Greater N.Y. Centennial Celebration. Mem.: Spl. Librs. Assn., Coffee House. Home: 336 Central Park W New York NY 10025-7111 Office: The NY Times 229 W 43rd St New York NY 10036-3959

AMSTERDAM, ANTHONY GUY, law educator; b. Phila., Sept. 12, 1935; s. Gustave G. and Valla (Abel) A.; m. Lois P. Sheinfeld, Aug. 29, 1968. AB, Haverford Coll., 1957; LLB, U. Pa., 1960; LLD (hon.), John Jay Coll. Criminal Justice, 1987, Haverford Coll., 1993. Bar: D.C. 1960. Law clk. to U.S. Supreme Ct. Justice Felix Frankfurter, 1960-61; asst. U.S. atty., 1961-62; prof. law U. Pa., 1962-69, Stanford U., 1969-81, Montgomery prof. clin. legal edn., 1980-81; prof. law, dir. clin. programs and trial advocacy NYU, 1981—2001, univ. prof., 2001—. Cons. litigating atty. numerous civil rights groups; cons. govt. commns.; mem. Commn. to Study Disturbances at Columbia, 1968; trustee Death Penalty Info. Ctr., Lawyers Constl. Def. Com., NAACP Legal Def. Fund, Nat. Coalition to abolish the Death Penalty, So. Poverty Law Ctr., mem. Calif. Fed. Jud. Selection Com., 1976-80; mem. coord. coun. on lawyer competence Conf. of Chief Justices; gen. counsel N.Y. Civil Liberties Union; adv. counsel Civil Liberties Union No. Calif.; mem. ABA task force. Author: The Defensive Transfer of Civil Rights Litigation From State to Federal Courts, 1964, Trial Manual for Defense of Criminal Cases, 5th edit., 1989, (with Hertz and Guggenheim) Trial Manual for Defense Attorneys in Juvenile Court, 1991, (with Bruner) Minding the Law, 2000; editor-in-chief: U. Pa. Law Rev., 1959-60; contbr. articles to profl. jours. Named Outstanding Young Man of Year Phila. and Pa. Jaycees, 1967; recipient First Disting. Service award U. Pa. Law Sch., 1968; Haverford award Haverford Coll., 1970; Arthur V. Briesen award Nat. Legal Aid and Defender Assn., 1972, 76; named Lawyer of Year Calif. Trial Lawyers Assn., 1973; recipient 1st Earl Warren Civil Liberties award No. Calif. chpt. ACLU, 1973, Citizen of Merit award Sun Reporter, 1974, Walter J. Gores award Stanford U., 1977, William O. Douglas award Pub. Counsel, 1977, 2d ann. award Calif. Attys. Criminal Justice, 1978, award for enhancement human dignity Durfee Found., 1982, Francis Rawle award ALI-ABA, 1984, 3d ann. Civil Liberties award Pa. ACLU, 1985, clinical legal edn. award AALS Sect. on Clinical Legal Edn., 1986, August Vollmer award Am. Soc. Criminology, 1986, Disting. Tchr. award NYU, 1988, award N.Y. Criminal Bar Assn., 1989, Tchg. Achievement award Soc. Am. Law Tchrs., 1999, Kutak award ABA, 2002; named MacArthur fellow, 1989; hon. fellow for pub. interest svc. U. Pa. Law Sch., 2001. Fellow Am. Acad. Arts and Scis. Home: 68 Middle Line Hwy Southampton NY 11968-1645 Office: NYU Sch Law Clinical Ctr 245 Sullivan St 5th Fl New York NY 10012 Business E-Mail: aa1@nyu.edu.

AMSTERDAM, MARK LEMLE, lawyer; b. N.Y.C., June 10, 1944; s. Leonard M. and Erica (Lemle) A.; children: Lauren, Matthew. AB, Columbia U., 1966; JD cum laude, Columbia Law Sch., 1969. Bar: N.Y. 1969, U.S. Dist. Ct. (so., ea. and no. dists.) N.Y. 1972, U.S. Supreme Ct. 1973. Assoc. Fried, Frank, Harris, N.Y.C., 1969-70; staff atty. Ctr. Constl. Rights, N.Y.C., 1970-75; atty. pvt. practice, N.Y.C., 1975-76, 81—; ptnr. Rubin Hanley & Amsterdam, N.Y.C., Amsterdam & Lewinter LLP, N.Y.C., 1990—. Instr. N.Y. Law Sch., 1982-83. Contbr. articles to profl. jours. Fellow: N.Y. State Bar Assn.; mem.: Columbia Coll. Alumni Assn. (bd. dirs.), Columbia Law Sch. Alumni Assn. (bd. dirs.), Columbia Club (bd. govs.), Gardiners Bay Country Club. Home: 1220 Park Ave New York NY 10128-1733 Office: 9 E 40th St New York NY 10016-0402

AMSTERDAM, MILLICENT, manufacturing executive; Pres. MAF Mech. Svc. Corp., 1968—. Former bd. dirs. Long Island Ctr. for Bus. and Profl. Women, Advancement Commerce, Industry & Tech.; apptd. mem. Nassau County Panel for Home Improvement Industry. Recipient Small Bus Adv. Women in Bus. award, 1988. Mem.: Nat. Assn. Remodeling Industry, Long Island Builders Inst., Nat. Assn. Women in Constrn., Nat. Assn. Women Bus. Owners, Long Island Assn., Women Econ. Developers Long Island (bd. dirs.), Air Conditioning Contractors Am. (bd. dirs.). Office: MAF Mechanical-Air Cond Corp 168 Irving Ave Port Chester NY 10573-4144 E-mail: mafmech@erols.com.

AMSTUTZ, DANIEL GORDON, agricultural products executive, consultant, retired federal agency administrator, retired grain company executive; b. Cleve., Nov. 8, 1932; s. Gordon M. and Elizabeth (Kiss) Amstutz. BS, Ohio State U., 1954. Trainee Cargill, Inc., Mpls., 1954-55, grain mcht. Ft. Worth, 1959, sr. grain mcht. Mpls., 1960-72; grain mcht. Tradax Can., Ltd., Montreal, 1955-56, Tradax Geneva S.A., 1956-57; mgr. Deutsche Tradax GMBH, Hamburg, Germany, 1957-58; pres. Cargill Investor Svcs., Inc., Chgo., 1972—78; ptnr. Goldman, Sachs & Co., N.Y.C., 1978-82; undersec. Dept. Agr., Washington, 1983-87; pres. Cmty. Credit Corp., Washington, 1983-87; amb., chief trade negotiator for agr. USDA, Washington, 1987-89; exec. dir. Internat. Wheat Coun., London, 1992-95; pres., CEO N.Am. Export Grain Assn., Inc., Washington, 1995-2000; pres. Amstutz & Co., Washington, 2000—; sr. ministry adv. agrl. Iraq, 2003—04. Mem. U.S. Agrl. Policy Adv. Com., 1998—2003, U.S.-Russian Joint Commn. Econ. and Tech. Coop., 1996—2000; bd. dirs. U.S. Feed Grains Coun., 1967—72. Mem.: Nat. Grain and Feed Assn. (bd. dirs. 1973—82), Ohio State U. Found. (bd. dirs. 1998—), Ohio State U. Alumni Assn. (v.p. 1989, co-chair fund raising campaign 1990—99). Business E-Mail: dan@amstutzandcompany.com.

AMSTUTZ, HAROLD EMERSON, veterinarian, educator; b. Barrs Mill, Ohio, June 21, 1919; s. Nelson David and Viola Emma (Schnitzer) A.; m. Mabelle Josephine Bower, June 26, 1949; children: Suzanne Marie, Cynthia Lou, Patricia Lynn, David Bruce. BS in Agr, Ohio State U., 1942, DVM, 1945. Diplomate Am. Coll. Vet. Internal Medicine (pres. 1972-73, chmn. bd. regents 1973-74); hon. diplomate Am. Coll. Theriogenology. Pvt. practice vet. medicine, Orrville, Ohio, 1946-47; instr. vet. medicine Ohio State U., 1947-52, asst. prof., 1952-54, asso. prof., 1954-56, prof., 1957-61, prof., head dept. vet. medicine, 1956-61; head dept. vet. clinics Purdue U., West Lafayette, Ind., 1961-75, prof. large animal clinics, 1975-89, prof. emeritus, 1989—. Editor: Bovine Medicine and Surgery Book, 1979; contbg. editor: Modern Veterinary Practice, 1979-84; mem. editorial bd. The Merck Vet. Manual, 6th, 7th and 8th edits.; contbr. to books on diseases of large domestic animals. Mem. exec. bd. Ind.-Ky. synod Luth. Ch. Am., 1986-88; pres. World Assn. for Buiatrics, 1972-84. Served with U.S. Army, 1945-46. Recipient Borden award for outstanding research in diseases of dairy cattle, 1978; named Disting. Alumnus Ohio State U. Coll. Vet. Medicine, 1974; recipient Alumni Faculty award Sch. Vet. Medicine, Purdue U., 1989, Sagamore of the Wabash Ind. Gov., 1990, Ark. Traveler award Ark. Gov., 1969, Gustav Rosenberger Meml. award Dutch Veterinary Assn., 1992, Alumni Recognition award Vet. Medicine Alumni Soc. Ohio State U., 1998. Mem. AVMA (12th Internat. Congress prize for contributing to internat. understanding of vet. medicine 1995), Am. Assn. Vet. Clinicians (pres. 1972), Am. Assn. Bovine Practitioners (exec. sec. 1971-89, exec. v.p. 1989-93, hon. mem. 1993), World Assn. Buiatrics (pres. 1972-84), Am. Coll. of Theriogenologists (hon. diplomate 1993), Sigma Xi, Phi Zeta, Gamma Sigma Delta (award of merit), Omega Tau Sigma (nat. Gamma award). Republican. Office: Purdue Univ Dept Veterinary Sci West Lafayette IN 47907 Office Phone: 765-494-8560. Business E-Mail: amstutzh@purdue.edu.

AMTOFT, TORBEN, adult education educator, researcher; b. Copenhagen, June 6, 1963; s. Henning Hansen and Tove Amtoft. PhD, U. of Aarhus, Denmark, 1989—93. Rsch. assoc. U. of Aarhus, 1992—98, Boston U., 1999—2002, Heriot-Watt U., Edinburgh, Scotland, 2002—02; asst. prof. Kans. State U., 2002—. Avocations: reading, theology, travel. Office: Kansas State U 234 Nichols Hall Manhattan KS 66506

AMUGHAN, KENNEDY ABBA KEDAY, lawyer; s. Activity Thompson and Juliana Omajuwatan Amughan; m. Grace Okpongu, Nov. 6, 1993; children: Ebitie Thomasina, Juliana Perebotie, Ceth Tamaranpreye. LLB with honors, U. Maiduguri, 1988; Barrister-at-Law, Nigerian Law Sch., 1989. Bar: Nigeria 1990, cert.: Barrister-at-Law 1990. Tchr. State Tchg. Svc. Commn., Borno, Nigeria, 1983; sr. counsel Legal Aid Counsel, Katsina, Katsina (NYSC), Nigeria, 1989—90; dep. prin. counsel Taiwo Kupolati & Co, Lagos, Nigeria, 1990—92; prin. coun. Kennedy Amughan & Co, Lagos, 1996—. Legal cons. Savannah Bank Plc, Lagos, Nigeria, 1994—; external solicitors Union Bank PLC, Lagos, 1994—, Broad Bank PLC, Lagos, 1996—; sec., legal adviser Korea Machinery Co Ltd, Lagos, 1998—2002, head of chambers legal dept, 1998. Author: (book) Directors Under The Nigerian Companies Act 1968, 1988. Mem.: U. Maiduguri Alumu Assn. (assoc.), Nigerian Bar Assn. (exec. official 1997, Merit award 1996), Nat. Ijaw Lawyers Assn. (pres. 1997), Young Internat. Lawyers Assn. (assoc.), Internat. Bar Assn. (assoc.), U. Maidugar Alumni Assn. (sec.gen. 1994, Disting. Alumnus award 1994, Merit award 1995). Democrat-Npl. Roman Catholic. Avocations: soccer, poetry, lawn tennis, drama, reading. Home: #221 12721 W Buckeye Rd Avondale AZ 85323

AMUNDSON, JOHN KAY, electrical engineer; b. Glasgow, Mont., Aug. 28, 1925; s. Fred K. Amundson and Grace Ethel Westerman; m. Catherine M. Sutherland, June 12, 1951; children: Lynn M., Michael K. BS in electrical engring., Mont. State U., 1951. Sr. engr. IBM, San Jose, Calif., 1951—84; ret., 1984. With Conflict Resolution Program, Santa Cruz, Calif., 1985—90; special advocate Silver Haired Legislature, 1999—2002; founder, mem. Kiwanis Key Club Douglas HS, 2000—05; with Purple Ribbon Coalition Abused Adults & Children; ct. apptd. spl. advocate for children CASA, 1994—2005. With USN, 1945—50, Hawaii. Mem.: TRIAD (sec. 2000—05), Partnership of Cmty. Resources (pres., v.p., treas. 2003—05), Douglas County Sheriffs Dept. (Citizen of Yr. 2003), Elks Club (Citizen of Yr. 2001), Carson Valley Kiwanis Club (Kiwanis Dist. Svc. award 2000). Avocations: car restoration, photography, travel. Personal E-mail: jkcma@charter.net.

AMUNDSON, JOY A., pharmaceutical and health products executive; V.p. corp. hosp. mktg. Abbott Labs., Abbott Park, Ill., 1993-94, v.p. Abbott HealthSys., 1994-95, sr. v.p. chem. and agrl. products, 1995-98, sr. v.p. Ross Products, 1998—; corp. officer, 1990.

AMUNDSON, KRISTEN JANE, communications executive, writer; b. Brainerd, Minn., Dec. 3, 1949; d. Grant O. and Patricia L. (McGivern) A.; m. Craig W. Conrath, Sept. 18, 1971 (div. 1991); 1 child, Sara. BA, Macalester Coll., 1971; MA, Am. U., 1978. English tchr. Hopkins (Minn.) Pub. Schs., 1971-75, Montgomery County Pub. Schs., Rockville, Md., 1975-76; asst. dir. humanities program John F. Kennedy Ctr., Washington, 1976-77; dir. pub. rels. Nat. Assn. Elem. Sch. Prins., Arlington, Va., 1977-80; pres. KJA Comm., Alexandria, Va., 1980—. Mt. Vernon rep. Fairfax County Sch. Bd., Va., 1991-99, chmn. 1996-97. Author: Linking Up, 1991, Teaching Values and Ethics, 1991. Pres. Rt. One Corridor Housing, Alexandria; pres. Va. Sch. Bds. Assn., 1999—; elected Va. Ho. of Dels., 44th dist., 1999. Recipient Good Neighbor award, New Hope Housing, 2005, Stennis Ctr. for Pub. Svc., 2002, 2003; Flemming Fellow, 2001, Roosvelt Fellow, 2002. Office: PO Box 143 Mount Vernon VA 22121-0143

AMUSSEN, SUSAN DWYER, history educator; b. N.Y.C., Aug. 24, 1954; d. Robert Martin and Diane (Duke) Amussen. AB, Princeton U., 1976; MA, Brown U., 1977, PhD, 1982. Mellon postdoctoral fellow Cornell U., Ithaca, N.Y., 1982-83; asst. prof. history Conn. Coll., New London, 1984-91; prof. interdisciplinary studies Union Inst. and Univ., 1990—. Author: An Ordered Society: Gender and Class in Early Modern England, 1988; contbr. articles to profl. jours. Alice Freeman Palmer fellow Wellesley Coll., 1981-82; fellow Shelby Cullom Ctr. Historical Studies Princeton U., 1988-91; rsch. fellow Henry E. Huntington Libr., 2002-03, Yale Ctr. for Brit. Art, 2004. Mem. Am. Hist. Assn., Women in Hist. Profession (coordinating com.), N.Am. Conf. on Brit. Studies (regional co-program chmn., regional pres.), Berkshire Conf. Women Historians (co-chmn. book prize com., chmn. article prize com.). Business E-Mail: susan.amussen@tui.edu.

AMY, JONATHAN WEEKES, scientist, educator; b. Delaware, Ohio, Mar. 3, 1923; s. Ernest Francis and Theresa Louise (Say) A.; m. Ruthanna Borden, Dec. 20, 1947 (dec. Apr. 1999); m. Betty Joy Flood, July 2, 2000; children— Joseph Wilbur, James Borden, Theresa BA, Ohio Wesleyan U., 1948; MS, Purdue U., 1950, PhD, 1955. Rsch. assoc. dept. chemistry Purdue U., West Lafayette, Ind., 1954-60, assoc. prof., 1960-70, prof., 1970—, assoc. dir. labs., 1960—, dir. instrumentation, 1970-84, emeritus, 1988. Cons. chem. instrumentation; sec.-treas. Technometrics, Inc., 1968-2001; mem. adv. panels AAAS, Assn. Am. Univs., NSF, Am. Chem. Soc.; vis. scholar Stanford U., 1992. Assoc. editor Ind. Chem. News; patentee elec. measuring equipment and chem. instrumentation Pres. Wabash Twp. Vol. Fire Dept., 1970-86. Served with U.S. Maritime Service, 1943-46. Recipient George award Lafayette Jour. and Courier, 1978, Sagamore of the Wabash award State of Ind., 1999. Mem. AAAS, Am. Chem. Soc. (Chem. Instrumentation award), Sigma Xi, Sigma Chi. Episcopalian. Office: Purdue U Dept Chemistry West Lafayette IN 47907 E-mail: jamychemst@aol.com.

AMYES, EDWIN WESTBY, neurosurgeon; b. Edinburgh, Scotland, Nov. 2, 1920; came to U.S., 1921; s. Herbert Westby and Ruth Frieda Amyes; children: Nina, Christopher. BS, Pacific Union Coll., 1941; MD, Loma Linda U., 1944. Diplomate Am. Bd. of Neurosurgery. Intern White Meml. Hosp., Loma Linda, 1943, resident in psychiatry and neurology, 1944; staff physician St. Francis Hosp., Lynwood, Calif., 1946-48; pvt. gen. practice Huntington Park, Calif., 1946-48; resident, sr. resident in neurology U. So. Calif.-Loma Linda U., 1948-50; resident in neurosurgery L.A. County Hosp./White Meml. Hosp., 1950-53; with Rancho Los Amigos, 1955-65, organizer, designer neurosci. svcs., chief of neurosurgery, chief of staff; neurosurgeon Loma Linda U./White Meml. Hosp., St. Francis Hosp., Lynwood; staff neurosurgeon Hoag Meml. Hosp. Presbyn., Newport Beach, Calif., 1972—2000. Asst. prof. neurol. surgery Loma Linda U., L.A.; chief of neurosurgery Loma Linda U. at L.A. County Hosp., 1953-56; assoc. clin. prof. neurol. surgery U. Calif./Irvine Med. Ctr., 1972—; cons. in neurosurgery; pres., CEO Bioelectronics, Inc., Lynwood. Contbr. articles to profl. jours. 1st lt. U.S. Army, 1944-46. Recipient award for exceptional and disting. svc. Congress Neurol. Surgeons, 1980. Mem. Coun. of State Neurol. Socs. (founder, 1st chmn. 1975-80), Am. Assn. Neurol. Surgeons. Achievements include chair Calif. com. which developed the relative value scale for neurosurg. fees; development of the first edition of national guidelines for practice of neurosurgery, 1975. Home: 1220 Colony Plz Newport Beach CA 92660- Office: 320 Superior Ave Ste 310 Newport Beach CA 92663-2742 Office Phone: 949-642-6320. Office Fax: 949-642-6326. Business E-Mail: ljacobs@nmadl.com.

AN, HONG, engineer; arrived in U.S., 1989; s. Yimin An and Xiulan Huang; m. Xiangwei Zhang, Oct. 22, 1988; 1 child, Miranda Bonnie. B in Engring., Tsinghua U., Beijing, 1982; MS, U. Iowa, 1991, Wayne State U., 1993; PhD, Columbia U., 1999. Engr. Chongqing (China) Inst. Steel, 1982—85, Sichuan Inst. Antibiotics, Chengdu, China, 1985—87; rschr. Tsinghua U., Beijing, 1987—89; engr. Millipore, Bedford, Mass., 1999—. Grad. student adv. coun. mem. Columbia U. Grad. Sch., N.Y.C., 1996—97; mem. Scienceboard.net, 2002. Internat. com. mem. AIChE, N.Y.C., 1995—2000; press marshal Atlanta Olympics Com., 1996; active Hist. Dist. Com. Recipient Atlanta Olympics Vols. Recognition award, Internat. Olympic Com., Juan A. Samaranch, 1996, Fellowship award, Am. Soc. Artificial Internal Organs, 1997. Mem.: Am. Chem. Soc., Internat. Soc. for Pharm. Engring., Sigma Xi. Achievements include patents pending for Protein Aggregates Removal; research in mathematical analysis of a flame front inside a combustion chamber; cell deformation in an asymmetric thin liquid film. Avocations: swimming, painting, golf. Home: 5 Reeve St Acton MA 01720 Office: Millipore 80 Ashby Rd Bedford MA 01730 Personal E-mail: ha13@columbia.edu.

ANACKER, EDWARD WILLIAM, retired chemistry educator; b. Chgo., June 2, 1921; s. Edward Frederick and Nellie Adelaide (Adolfs) A.; m. Stella Evelyn Lillo, Jan. 16, 1945; children: Steven Edward, David Carlyle, Eric Roland, John William. BS, Mont. State Coll., 1943; PhD, Cornell U., 1949. Instr. Mont. State Coll., Bozeman, 1949-52, asst. prof., 1952-58, assoc. prof., 1958-63, prof. chemistry, 1963-91, prof. emeritus, 1991—, head chemistry dept., 1972-77. Participant Oak Ridge (Tenn.) Inst. Nuclear Studies, 1957; vis. prof. NSF Sci. Faculty Fellowship, U. Oreg., Eugene, 1964-65 Contbr. articles to profl. jours. Ensign USN, 1944-46, PTO. Named one of 100 Soc. Centennial Alumni, Mont. State U., Bozeman, 1993; grantee Rsch. Corp., 1950-56, Petroleum Rsch. Fund, 1957-60, Bur. of Reclamation, 1961-66, NSF, 1960-72, Mont. State U., 1981. Mem. Am. Chem. Soc. (chmn. Mont. sect. 1952-53, 67-68, 98-99), Mont. Acad. Scis. (pres. 1959-60), Sigma Xi (pres. Mont. chpt. 1973-74, faculty rsch. award 1967), Phi Kappa Phi, Alpha Chi Sigma. Lutheran. Avocations: running, hiking, bicycle racing. Office: Montana State U Bozeman MT 59717-3400

ANAGNOST, DINO, artistic director; b. Manchester, NH; Grad., The Juilliard Sch., Boston U. Music dir., condr. Little Orch. Soc. NY, 1979—; dean music Greek Orthodox Archdiocesan Cathedral of North and South America. Adj. prof. music Columbia U. Founder Chance for Children, 1980. Named Commendatore Order of Merit, Italian Republic. Mem.: Park Ave. Chamber Symphony, Inc. Office: Little Orch Soc 330 W 42nd St Fl 12 New York NY 10036-6902

ANAGNOSTIS, ANTHE, principal; b. Ft. Worth, July 29, 1958; d. Homer James and Thespa Anagnostis. BSEd, Tex. Christian U., 1980, MEd, 1985. Cert. prin. 1994. Tchr. Eagle-Mt. Saginaw Ind. Sch. Dist., Ft. Worth, 1980—2000, asst. prin., 2000—04, prin., 2004—. Mem. edn. com. Saginaw C. of C., 2004—05. Named Educator of Yr., Saginaw C. of C., 1995. Mem.: Kiwanis, Phi Beta Kappa, Kappa Delta Pi. Avocations: photography, reading. Office: Creekview Mid Sch 6717 Bob Hanger Fort Worth TX 76179

ANAGNOSTOPOULOS, CONSTANTINE EMMANUEL, venture capitalist, former company executive; b. Athens, Greece, Nov. 1, 1922; came to U.S., 1946; s. Emmanuel Constantine A. and Helen (Michaelides) Kefalas; m. Maria Tsagarakis, July 10, 1949; 1 son, Paul Constantine. Sc.B. in Chemistry, Brown U., 1949; MS in Chemistry, Harvard U., 1950, PhD in Chemistry, 1952; postgrad. in bus. adminstrn., Columbia U., 1964. Dir. research and devel. organic div. Monsanto Co., St. Louis, 1962-67, research scientist, 1952-61, bus. dir., 1967-71, gen. mgr. New Enterprise div., 1971-75, gen. mgr. rubber chem. div., 1975-80; v.p. mng. dir. Monsanto Europe-Africa, Brussels, 1980-82; corp. v.p., vice chmn. corp. devel. and growth com. Monsanto Co., St. Louis, 1982-85; cons., 1986-87; mng. gen. ptnr. Gateway Venture Ptnrs., L.P., St. Louis, 1987—. Bd. dirs. Advent Capital Ltd., London, U.S.A., Advent Internat. Corp., Genzyme Corp., Biotage Corp., CytoMed, Inc., Virus Rsch. Inst., Inc.; chmn. bd. Monsanto Europe S.A., Brussels, 1980-82; mem. com. on patent system Nat. Acad. Engring., 1971; mem. nat. inventors coun. Dept. Commerce, 1964-72. Patentee in organic and polymer chemistry, 1953-67; contbr. articles to profl. jours. Bd. dirs. Am. C. of C., Brussels, 1981-82; mem. European Govt. Bus. Coun., Strasbourg, France, 1981-82; pres. United Fund Belgium, 1982; mem. presdl. com. prizes for innovation, Washington, 1972, U.S.-USSR Trade and Econ. Coun., 1980-82; chmn. bd. St. Louis Tech. Ctr. Served to capt. Brit. Army, 1944-46. Recipient chemistry prize Brown U., 1949, teaching award Harvard U., 1950, 51, 52, St. Louis Tech. award Regional Comml. and Growth Assn., 1987. Mem. Rsch. Soc. Am., Comml. Devel. Assn., Am. Chem. Soc., St. Louis Art Mus. Clubs: Bellerive Country (St. Louis). Republican. Episcopalian. Office: Gateway Assocs LP 8000 Maryland Ave Ste 1190 Saint Louis MO 63105-3910 Home: 213 N Bemiston Ave Clayton MO 63105-3827

ANAND, JAIDEEP, management educator, consultant; b. Delhi, India, Aug. 13, 1966; arrived in U.S., 1998; s. Krishan Kumar and Nirmal Anand; m. Seema Monga, Feb. 27, 1997; children: Alvin Shiv, Audrey Nirmal. BS in Tech., Indian Inst. of Tech., 1987; PhD, U. Pa., 1994. Asst. prof. Ivey Bus. Sch. U. Western Ont., London, Canada, 1994—98; asst. prof. Bus. Sch. U. Mich., Ann Arbor, Mich., 1998—2004; assoc. prof. Fisher Coll. of Bus. Ohio State U., Columbus, Ohio, 2004—. Contbr. articles to profl. jours. Recipient Cert. Excellence in Rsch. award, ANBAR, 1997; Alliance Edge Rsch. fellowship, Queen's U., 2003. Mem.: Strategic Mgmt. Soc. (Booz, Allen and Hamilton fellowship 2001), Acad. Mgmt. (Outstanding Rev. award 2000, Best Paper award 2001). Office: Ohio State Univ 2100 Neil Avenue Columbus OH 43210-1144 Office Fax: 614-292-7062. Business E-Mail: anand.18@osu.edu.

ANAND, RAJEN S., physiologist, educator; b. Kohat, India, June 8, 1937; came to U.S., 1963; s. Dial Singh and Daya Kaur (Kohli) A.; m. Asha Angela Bawa, Oct. 29, 1969; children: Sunjay, Shabeen. BS, Meerut U., 1956; DVM, M.P. Vet. Coll., 1960; PhD in Physiology, Biochem. & Nutrition, U. Calif., 1969. Demonstrator M.P. Vet. Coll., Mhow, India, 1960-63; research asst. U. Calif., Davis, 1963-68, P.G. research physiologist, 1968-69; prof. physiology Calif. State U., Long Beach, 1970—, chmn. dept. anatomy and physiology, 1970-95, chmn. dept. communicative disorders, 1990-92; exec. dir. Ctr. for Nutrition Policy & Promotion USDA, Washington, 1995—2001; prof. emeritus Calif. State U., Long Beach, Calif., 2002—. Freelance journalist; apptd. to Nat. Com. on Accreditation Fgn. Med. Schs., 1994—. Contbr. articles to profl. jours. Mem. state Dem. ctrl. com., 1982-97; vice chmn. Coun. Asian and Pacific Am. Dems., 1988-91, del. to Dem. Nat. Conv., 1988,

92; mem. exec. bd. Calif. Dem. Party, chair Asian and Pacific caucus, 1991-93. Named Outstanding Prof., Calif. State U., Long Beach, 1983, Outstanding Student, U. Calif., Davis, 1967, 68; recipient Hertzendorf prize in physiology, 1969; postdoctoral fellow UCLA Harbor Med. Ctr., Torrence, 1977-78, Meritorious Performance and Profl. Promise award Calif. State U., Long Beach, 1986, 88. Mem. Am. Physiol. Soc., AAAS, Sigma Xi, Fedn. Indian Assns. (sec. 1981-84, pres. 1984-86, chmn. 1986-88), Nat. Fedn. Indian-Am. Assns. (exec. dir. 1990-92, sec. 1996—), Indo-Am. Polit. Assn. (chair 1986—). Avocations: writing, hiking. Home: 6912 Winter Ln Annandale VA 22003-6162 Office: Ctr for Nutrition Policy & Promotion #200 North Lobby 1120 20th St NW Washington DC 20036-3406*

ANAND, SANJAY, training services executive, consultant, entrepreneur, educator; s. Ram Dhan and Sudarshan Anand; m. Jennifer Tran, Mar. 22, 2003. MSc in Tech., Birla Inst. Tech. and Sci., Pilani, India, 1990, MSc in Computers, 0192; MBA summa cum laude, Boston Coll., 1995, MS in Fin., 2002. Instr. cert. profl. J.D. Edwards, 1998, cert. webmMaster profl. NJ. Inst. Tech., 2001; export mgmt. cert. Nat. Export Programmes, 1993. Software engr. Ctr. Devel. Advanced Computing, Pune, India, 1991—92; software designer Yojana Sys., Pune, India, 1992—93; sr. cons. J.D. Edwards, Rutherford, NJ, 1995—98, global enterprise mgr. Denver, 1998—2001; v.p., internat. bus. devel. HyperSpace Comm., Denver, 2001—02; founder, chmn., pres., CEO The CLA Group of Cos., Clifton, NJ, 2002—. Tech. cons. InterPrint, CALS, SAC, DCM, New Delhi, 1986—90; adj. faculty Maharashtra Inst. of Tech., Pune, Maharashtra, 1992—93; rschr. ops. and strategic mgmt. Boston Coll., Chestnut Hill, Mass., 1993—95, cons. small bus. devel. ctr., 1994—95; dir. CLA Solutions Assurance Systems, New Delhi, 2003, ASPL, Pune, 2002—03. Contbr. articles to profl. jours. Vol. cons. UN Assn. Greater Boston, Boston, 1994—95; young leader United Way of Essex and West Hudson, Newark, 2000—03; team leader Nat. Multiple Sclerosis Soc., Jersey City, 2000—01; founder Career Path Work Team, Woodcliff Lake, NJ, 2002. Recipient Ann. Gold medal, Birla Inst. of Tech. and Sci., 1992. Fellow: Inst. Electronics and Telecom. Engrs. (life Elected Fellow 1999); mem.: Fast Co.-Co. of Friends. Achievements include patents for Watch with Therapeutic Metal Strap; design of standard Point-to-Point Protocol network; development of X.25 wide area network; iterative network based logic emulator. Avocations: motorcycling, music, poetry, swimming, travel. Personal E-mail: sanjay@anands.com.

ANAND, SURESH CHANDRA, physician; b. Mathura, India, Sept. 13, 1931; arrived in U.S., 1957, naturalized, 1971; s. Satchit and Sumaran Bai Anand; m. Wiltrud Anand, Jan. 29, 1966; children: Miriam, Michael. MB, BS, King George's Coll., U. Lucknow (India), 1954; MS in Medicine, U. Colo., 1962. Diplomate Am. Bd. Allergy and Immunology. Fellow pulmonary diseases Nat. Jewish Hosp., Denver, 1957-58, resident in chest medicine, 1958-59, chief resident allergy-asthma, 1960-62; intern Mt. Sinai Hosp., Toronto, Ont., Can., 1962-63, resident in medicine, 1963-64, chief resident, 1964-65, demonstrator clin. technique, 1963-64, U. Toronto fellow in medicine, 1964-65; rsch. assoc. asthma-allergy Nat. Jewish Hosp., Denver, 1967-69; clin. instr. medicine U. Colo., Denver, 1967-69; internist Ft. Logan Mental Health Ctr., Denver, 1968-69; pres. Allergy Assocs. & Lab., Ltd., Phoenix, 1974—. Mem. staff Phoenix Bapt. Hosp., chmn. med. records com., 1987; mem. staff St. Joseph's Hosp., St. Luke's Hosp., Human Hosp., John C. Lincoln Hosp., Good Samaritan Hosp., Phoenix Children's Hosp., Tempe St. Luke Hosp., Desert Samaritan Hosp., Mesa Luth. Hosp., Scottsdale Meml. Hosp., Chandler Regional Hosp., Ariz., Valley Luth. Hosp., Mesa, Ariz.; mem. staff. Phoenix Meml. Hosp., mem. med. com.; pres. NJH Fed. Credit Union, 1967—68; adj. assoc. prof. medicine Midwestern U., 2004—. Contbr. articles to profl. jours. Mem. citizens adv. bd. Camelback Hosp. Mental Health Ctr., Scottsdale, Ariz., 1974—80; mem. Phoenix Symphony Coun., 1973—90, Ariz. Opera co., Boyce Thompson Southwestern Arboretum, Ariz. Hist. Soc., Phoenix Arts Mus., Smithsonian Inst. Fellow: ACP, Am. Coll. Allergy and Immunology (pub. edn. com. 1991—94, aerobiology com., internat. com.), Am. Assn. Cert. Allergists, Am. Coll. Chest Physicians (crit. care. com.), Am. Acad. Allergy (pub. edn. com.); mem.: AMA, AAAS, Ariz. Thoracic Soc., Assn. Care of Asthma, Internat. Assn. Asthmology, World Med. Assn., N.Y. Acad. Sci., Greater Phoenix Allergy Soc. (v.p. 1984—86, pres. 1986—88, med. adv. team sports medicine Ariz. State U.), West Coast Soc. Allergy and Immunology, Maricopa County Med. Soc. (bd. dirs. 1996—98, exec. com. 1996—98, pres.-elect 2002, pres. 2003, del. Ariz. Med. Assn.), Ariz. Allergy Soc. (v.p. 1988—90, pres. 1990—91), Ariz. Med. Assn., Internat. Assn. Allergy and Clin. Immunology, Ariz. Wild Life Assn., Nat. Geog. Soc., Phoenix Zoo, Village Tennis Club. Office: 1006 E Guadalupe Rd Tempe AZ 85283-3047 also: 4901 N 44th St Phoenix AZ 85018 also: 6553 E Baywood Ave Ste 201 Mesa AZ 85206-1754 also: 7331 E Osborn Dr Ste 340 Scottsdale AZ 85251-6435 also: 4901 N 44th St Phoenix AZ 85018 also: 2248 N Alma School Rd Chandler AZ 85224-2488 Office Phone: 480-838-4296. E-mail: sanand1@aol.com.

ANANIA, ANDREA, information technology executive; Grad., Queens Coll.; MBA, U. Pa. Various positions Unisys Corp., 1975—95; sr. v.p., divsn. sys. info. officer Cigna Corp., 1995—98, chief info. officer, 1998—, exec. v.p., chief info. officer Phila., 2001—. Office: Cigna Corp 1 Liberty Pl Philadelphia PA 19192-1550

ANANIAS, JOSÉ, retired school system administrator; b. N.Y.C., Aug. 17, 1929; s. Jose A. and Inez Beatrice Johnson; m. Mamie Seymour, Dec. 30, 1953 (div. Feb. 1978) children: Jose III, Antonio, Ersell; m. Wilhemina Wright, June 17, 1978 (dec. June 1992); m. Ivanete do Nascimento Pena Lins, May 24, 1994. *America imploded into the Great Depression on October 29, 1929. Jose A. died in 1932. "Mommy Inez" never faltered. She lined up daily with Harlem mothers in the Bronx along Prospect and Westchester Avenues in the "Bronx Slave Market" niggling with garrulous, mercenary females for a day's wages (from 12 cents to $1) for food. My sister, Thelma, and I were "home alone" learning to live as adults instead of learning to live as children. The Federal Nursery Program refused to service Harlem mothers. Home relief was late and inequitable. This inflamed my passion for welfare work with the downtrodden, the impoverished, and those without hope. Sister, Thelma, BA 1952 Spelman; MSLS 1957, Atlanta U., Librarian 42 years Public Libraries: Brooklyn, NY, Library of Congress, San Diego, CA, Sunnyvale, CA, Assistant. Director, Binghamton, NY (1974-1988); Los Angeles, CA Public 1988 until retirement in 1999. Daughter, Ersell, BA Hunter 1983, M.S. Ed, City College 1984, Teacher, NYC Board of Education 1984 to present. Jose III, BA Morehouse 1977, Teacher, NYC Bd. of Education 1997-1978. U.S. Postal Service 1977 until retirement in 2005 (25 years).* BA, Morehouse Coll., 1951; postgrad., NYU, 1957-59; MEd, CUNY, 1968. Cert. sch. adminstr. and supr., attendance tchr., English tchr., phys. edn. and recreation tchr., subst. attendance tchr. Social investigator St. Nicholas Welfare Ctr. N.Y.C. Dept. Welfare, 1955-60; attendance tchr. N.Y.C. Bd. Edn., 1965-67; adminstrv. asst. to supr. recreation Cmty. Sch. Dist. # 7, Bronx, 1969-75; supr. Office of High Sch. SPARK program Drug Abuse Prevention Citywide, Bronx, 1971-77; borough supr., asst. coord. Office of High Sch. SPARK program, Bklyn., 1971-77; tchr. English High Sch. Redirection, Bklyn., 1977-78, asst. prin., 1978-79; dist. supervising attendance officer Chancellor's Task Force on Attendance, Bklyn., 1978-79; dist. supervising attendance officer Evander Childs High Sch Bronx High Sch. Attendance Dist., 1979; dist. supervising attendance officer office of dir. pupil personnel svcs., 1979-84; ret., 1984. *"Mommy Inez" (a Spelman College graduate) infused us with the belief that education is not a gift. It has to be earned. The price is ambition, desire, initiative, perseverance, and hard work. Of these, attendance is most frequently neglected. The body has to be in the classroom. In the 1960's I was known as "the attendance officer who went after and retrieved absentees and placed them in school in his Rolls Royce automobile. "While some considered this odd, it fell within my belief that I had to use every lawful means to enforce the law while safeguarding the student's right to an education. I was also reluctant to leave my car unattended too long, and the kids enjoyed the ride.* Mem. Borough Pres. Sutton's Adopt a Child com., edn. com.; mem. bd. mgr. Harlem br. YMCA, 1974-96, mem. adv. com., editor, compiler brochure; founder Dist. 7 Scholarship Awards Fund, 1971-78; Dem. county committeeman 71st A.D.; edn. chmn. Com. to Rebuild Harlem, 1978; mem. parish coun. St. Charles Borromeo Cath. Ch., 1979; mem. PTA John F. Kennedy High Sch., DeWitt Clinton High Sch.; svc. officer VFW Post 1753, Las Vegas, 2000—; mem. Our Lady of Las Vegas Ch. Served with USN, 1951-55, Korea. Recipient Citation, Gov. Mario Cuomo, 1984, Citation, Mayor Edward I. Koch, 1984, Cert. Recognition Sec. of Def., Cert. Appreciation, Harlem Bd. Mgrs., 1996, Lifetime Achievement award World Congress of Arts, Scis. and Comms., 2005; named Vol. of Yr., YMCA Greater N.Y., 1995; José Ananias Day proclaimed in his honor. Mem. VFW (Cmmdr.'s Spl. Merit award 2003), Assn. Black Educators N.Y., Am. Legion, USN Meml., Holy Name Soc. St. Charles Borromeo Cath. Ch., So. Nev. Alumni Chpt. CCNY, Kappa Alpha Psi. Democrat. Roman Catholic. Home: 11-1074 1600 S Valley View Blvd Las Vegas NV 89102-1869

ANANIASHVILI, NINA, ballerina; b. Tbilisi, Republic of Georgia; Student, Choreographic Sch. of Georgia; grad., Bolshoi Ballet Sch., 1981. Ballerina Bolshoi Ballet, 1981—. Guest artist Am. Ballet Theatre, N.Y.C.; performed with Kirov Ballet, N.Y.C. Ballet, Royal Ballet, The Royal Danish Ballet, Royal Swedish Balltet, others. Roles include La Bayadere (Nikiya), Don Quixote (Kitri), Giselle, The Golden Age (Rita), Mlada, Raymonda, Romeo and Juliet, Swan Lake (Odette-Odile), The Dying Swan, A Dream of the Rose, Balanchine's Apollo, Raymonda Variations, Symphony in C, The Prince of the Pagodas, The Nutcracker. Recipient Gold medal Varna Competition, 1980, 5th Moscow Competition, 1985, Grand prix 4th Moscow Competition 1981, 3rd Jackson Competition, 1986, Outstanding Achievements in Fine Arts award Russia State, 1992, STate prize Georgia, 1993. Office: Am Ballet Theatre 890 Broadway New York NY 10003-1211

ANANTH, JAMBUR, psychiatrist, educator; b. Hassan, Mysore, India, Apr. 27, 1932; s. Venkata Subbaiah and Gundamma (Nanjundaiah) A.; m. Kamala Maroor, Apr. 23, 1971; 1 child, Kartik. MD, Kasturba Med. Sch., 1960; Diploma in Psychol. Medicine, Nat. Inst. Mental Health, India, 1963. Diplomate Am. Bd. Psychiatry and Neurology. Asst. prof. McGill U., Montreal, Canada, 1969—74, assoc. prof., 1974—81; prof. UCLA, 1981—. Chief clin. investigations dept. psychiatry McGill U., 1969-71, dir. edn. and research dept. psychiatry, 1971-72; dir. edn. and research St. Mary's Hosp., Montreal, 1972-76; dir. biol. psychiatry Allan Meml. Inst., Montreal, 1976-81. Contbr. articles to profl. jours.; adv. editor: Psychosomatics, 1978-87. Grantee Dept. Mental Health State of Calif., 1983. Fellow Collegeum Internat. Neuropharmocologicum, Royal Coll. Psychiatrists, Am. Psychiat. Assn. (pres. Que. dist. br. 1978-79). Avocations: photography, stamps. Home: 2709 Via Pacheco Palos Verdes Peninsula CA 90274-4351 Office: Harbor-UCLA Med Ctr Dept Psychiat PO Box 2910 Torrance CA 90509-2910 Office Phone: 562-651-4505. Business E-Mail: Jananth@rei.edu, jananth@labiomed.com, Jananth@dmhmsh.state.ca.us.

ANASTACIA, (ANASTACIA LYN NEWKIRK), singer; b. Chgo., Ill., Sept. 17, 1973; Grad., Profl. Children's Sch. Of Manhattan. Former dancer Club MTV. Singer: (songs-single) I'm Outta Love, 2000, Not That Kind, 2000, One Day In Your Life, 2002, Left Outside Alone, 2004 (nominated for best song, MTV Europe Music Awards, 2004), (albums) Not That Kind, 2001, Freak of Nature, 2002, Anastacia, 2004; singer, performer (DVD Video) The Video Collection, 2002, One Day In Your Life, 2003, (DVD Video (single), 2002; singer: (TV) Party in the Park 2001, 2001, Double Bill, 2003, (films) Coyote Ugly, 2000, Chicago, 2002, (TV series) Um Anjo Caiu do Céu, 2001; composer, performer (TV) VH1 Divas Las Vegas, 2002, guest singer Elton John: One Night Only-Greatest Hits Live, 2001; performer: (TV) Pavarotti & Friends for Afghanistan, 2001, Nobel Peace Prize Concert, 2001, Danish Music Awards, 2001, Brit Awards, 2002, Royal Variety Performance, 2002, 95.8 Capital FM's Party in the Park for the Prince's Trust, 2004; presenter (TV) MTV Europe Music Awards, 2002, special guest appearences I Love the 80's, Tops of the Pops, 2000, 2001, 2004, Ally McBeal, 2001, Wetten, dass...?, 2002, 2004, and several others. Her trademark: rose-colored glasses. Office: Sony Music Entertainment Inc 550 Madison Ave New York NY 10022 Address: Club Anastacia PO Box 7149 San Francisco CA 94120-7149

ANASTASI, MICHAEL ANTON, journalist; b. Kitzbuhel, Tirol, Austria, Sept. 15, 1965; s. Antone Frank and Waltraud (Salinger) A; m. Julie Hibbs Anastasi, Nov. 18, 1995; children: Grace Antonia, Alexandra Renee. BA in Internat. Rels., U. Calif., Davis, 1988; Journalism, Calif. State U., Long Beach, 2001. Reporter The Daily Democrat, Woodland, Calif., 1984-85, dep. sports editor, 1985-87; sports editor The Davis (Calif.) Ent., 1987-93; asst. sports editor L.A. Daily News, 1993-95, sports editor, 1995—2004; mng. editor The Salt Lake (Utah) Tribune, 2004—. Recipient 1st prize best sports sect., Calif. Newspaper Pubrs. Assn., 1990, 1992, 2001, 2002, Best sports columns award, Nat. Newspaper Assn., 2d place award, 1992, hon. mention, 1993, Best Daily Sports section, APSE, 1995, hon. mention Best spl. section over 175,000, 1993, 1st place and honorable mention, Best Enterprise reporting, under 50,000, 1993, 4th place columnist under 50,000, honorable mention, 1989, Best Daily sect., 2000, 2001, 2002, 2004, Best Sunday sect., 2000, 2001, 2002, 2004, Top 10 100,000-250,000, 2d place best sports column, Nat. Newspaper Assn., 1992, hon. mention best sports column, 1993, 3d place best sports pages, 1993. Mem. Soc. Profl. Journalists (1st place best columnist, 1991, 93, 94,), AP Sports Editors. Roman Catholic. Office: Salt Lake Tribune 90 South 400 West Salt Lake City UT 84101

ANASTASI, WILLIAM JOSEPH, artist; b. Aug. 11, 1933; s. Joseph Anthony and Jeanette (Corona) A.; m. Irene Ierardi, Aug. 15, 1951 (div. 1964); children: William, Lawrence, Jean. Student, U. Pa., 1953-61. Tchr. painting Sch. Visual Arts, N.Y.C., 1971-86; co-artistic advisor Merce Cunningham Dance Co., N.Y.C., 1984—. Presenter in field. One-man shows include Dwan Gallery, N.Y.C., 1966, 67, 70, Witherspoon Gallery, U. N.C., Greensboro, 1965, Washington Sq. Gallery, N.Y.C., 1964, PS 1 Mus., L.I., N.Y., 1977, Hetzler and Keller Gallery, Stuttgart, Germany, 1979, Whitney Mus. Am. Art, N.Y.C., 1979, 81, Kuntsmuseum Dusseldorf, Fed. Republic Germany, 1979, Bess Culter Gallery, N.Y.C., 1987, 88, The New Mus., N.Y.C., 1987, Stalke Gallery, Copenhagen, Denmark, 1988, 96, Scott Hanson Gallery, 1989, Ball State U., Muncie, Ind., 1990, Sandra Gering Gallery, N.Y.C., 1991, 93-95, Krister Fahl Gallery, Stockholm, 1994, The Sorbonne, Paris, 1994, Rosenbach Mus. & Libr., Phila., 1995, Brown U., Providence, R.I., 1995, Pier Gallery, Orkney, Stromness, Scotland, 1995, Moore Coll. Art and Design, Phila., 1995, Anders Tornberg Gallery, Lund, Sweden, 1996, Hubert Winter Gallery, Vienna, Austria, 1998, The Mus. of Judaica, Phila., 1998, Stalke Gallery, Copenhagen, 1999, 2004, Specta Gallery, Copenhagen, 1999, Galerij S65, Aalst, Belgium, 1999, Gary Tatintsian Gallery, N.Y.C., 1999, Art Agents Gallery, Hamburg, Germany, 2000, 04, Niels Borch Jensen Gallery Berlin, 2000, Nikolaj Comtemporary Art Ctr., Copenhagen, 2001, Hubert Winter Gallery, Vienna, 2001, Thomas Rehbein Gallery, Cologne, 2002, 04, Gary Tatintsian Gallery, N.Y.C., 2003, The Annex, N.Y.C., 2003, Quadrum Gallery, Lisbon, Portugal, 2003, Slought Found., Phila., 2004, Solway Gallery, L.A., Reykjavik Art Mus., 2004, Stalke Gallery, Copenhagen, 2004, 05, Bayly Mus. U. Va., 2005, Stefanie Hering Gallery, Berlin, 2005, Thomas Rehbein Gallery, Cologne, 2005, Art Agts. Gallery, Hamburg, 2005, others; represented in permanent collections Neuberger Mus., Purchase, N.Y., Met. Mus. Art, N.Y.C., Bklyn. Mus. Art, Phila. Mus. Art, Phoenix Mus. Art, Ga. Mus. Art, Walker Art Ctr., The Getty Ctr., Santa Monica, Calif., The Mus. Contemporary Art, L.A., Davison Art Ctr., Wesleyan U., Middletown, Conn., Des Moines Art Ctr., Mus. Modern Art, N.Y.C., Art Inst. of Chgo., Nat. Gallery Art, Washington, Fogg Art Mus., Harvard Univ. Art Mus., Cambridge, Mass., Contemporary Mus., Honolulu, Musee Moderne, Stockholm, Sweden, Whitney Mus. Am. Art, Denver Art Mus., Chrysler Mus., Norfolk, Va., J.B. Speed Art Mus., Louisville, Ky., Le Witt Collection, Chester, Conn., Jewish Mus., N.Y.C., Statensmuseum for Kunst, Copenhagen, Rooseum, Ctr. Contemporary Art, Malmo, Sweden, Phila. Mus. Jewish Art, Guggenheim Mus., N.Y.C., Ark. Art Ctr., Okla. City Art Mus., Milw. Art Mus., Museet for Samtidskunst, Roskilde, Denmark, Contemporary Arts Mus., Houston, Balt. Mus. Art, Md., Mus. Ludwig Koln, Cologne, Wadsworth Athenaeum, Hartford, Conn., Rubin Mus. Art, N.Y.C., Birmingham (Ala.) Mus. Art, U. Va. Art Mus., others; artist in residence Sirius Art Ctr., Ireland, 2000, Statens Vaerksteder for Kunst, Copenhagen, 2000, Deutscher Akademischer Austauschdienst, Berlin, 2002. Home: 924 W End Ave New York NY 10025-3534 Office Phone: 212-666-4133. Personal E-mail: wanastasi@nyc.rr.com.

ANASTASIO, MICHAEL R., science foundation director; m. Ann Anastasio; children: Alison, Alexandra. B in Physics, Johns Hopkins U.; MA, PhD in Theoretical Nuclear Physics, SUNY, Stony Brook. Physicist Lawrence Livermore Nat. Lab., Calif., 1980, assoc. dir. def. and nuclear techs., dep. dir. strategic ops., dir., 2001—. Sci. advisor Dept. of Energy. Recipient Weapons Recognition of Excellence award, Dept. of Energy, 1990. Mem.: Sigma Pi Sigma. Avocations: sports, cello. Office: Lawrence Livermore Nat Lab 7000 East Ave Livermore CA 94550-9234

ANASTOLE, DOROTHY JEAN, retired electronics company executive; b. Akron, Ohio, Mar. 26, 1932; d. Helen (Sagedy) Dice; children: Kally, Dennis, Christopher. Student, De Anza Jr. Coll., Cupertino, Calif., 1969. Various secretarial positions in mfg., 1969-75; office mgr. Sci. Devices Co., Mountain View, Calif., 1975-76; exec. adminstrv. sec. corp. office Cezar Industries, Palo Alto, Calif., 1976-77; office and pers. mgr. AM Bruning Co., Mountain View, 1977-81; dir. employee rels. Consol. Micrographics, Mountain View, 1981-83; pers. mgmt. cons., 1983-84; mgr. adminstrn./employee rels. Mitsubishi Electronics Am., Inc., Sunnyvale, Calif., 1984-89, sr. mgr., 1989-91, corp.-nat. v.p., 1991-96, ret., 1996. Nat. adv. Field Philanthropy, 1992-96. Bd. dirs. Agnew State Hosp., San Jose, Calif., 1966-72, div. chmn. program mentally retarded, 1966-72, staff tutor, 1966-72; bd. dirs. Project Hired, Sunnyvale, 1991-93; bd. advisors The Senior Staff, 1994-96. Recipient Svc. award Agnew State Hosp., 1972.

ANAWALT, PATRICIA RIEFF, anthropologist, researcher; b. Ripon, Calif., Mar. 10, 1924; d. Edmund Lee and Anita Esto (Capps) Rieff; m. Richard Lee Anawalt, June 8, 1945; children: David, Katherine Anawalt Arnoldi, Harmon Fred. BA in Anthropology, UCLA, 1957, MA in Anthropology, 1971, PhD in Anthropology, 1975. Cons. curator costumes and textiles Mus. Cultural History UCLA, 1975-90, dir. Ctr. for Study Regional Dress, Fowler Mus. Cultural History, 1990—; trustee S.W. Mus., L.A., 1978-92; rsch. assoc. The San Diego Mus. Man, 1980—, UCLA Inst. Archaeology, 1994—. Trustee Archaeol. Inst. Am., U.S., Can., 1983-95, 98—; traveling lectr., 1975-86, 1994-2000, Pres.'s Lectureship, 1993-94, Charles E. Norton lectureship, 1996-97; cons. Nat. Geog. Soc., 1980-82, Denver Mus. Natural History, 1992-93; apptd. by U.S. Pres. to Cultural Property Adv. Com., Washington, 1984-93; fieldwork Guatemala, 1961, 70, 72, Spain, 1975, Sierra Norte de Puebla, Mex., 1983, 85, 88, 89, 91. Author: Indian Clothing Before Cortés: Mesoamerican Costumes from the Codices, 1981, paperback edit., 1990; co-author: The Codex Mendoza, 4 vols., 1992 (winner Archaeol. Inst. Am. 1994 James Wiseman Book award), The Essential Codex Mendoza, 1996; mem. editl. bd. Ancient Mesoamerica; contbr. articles to profl. jours. Adv. com Textile Mus., Washington, 1983-87. Grantee NEH, 1990, 96, J. Paul Getty Found. 1990, Nat. Geog. Soc., 1983, 85, 88, 89, 91, Ahmanson Found., 1996; Guggenheim fellow, 1988. Fellow Am. Anthrop. Assn.; mem. Centre Internat. D'Etude Des Textiles Anciens, Am. Ethnol. Soc., Soc. Am. Archaeology, Soc. Women Geographers (Outstanding Achievement award 1993), Textile Soc. Am. (bd. dirs. 1992-96, co-coord. 1994 biennial symposium). Avocations: ballet, reading, hiking. Office: Fowler Mus Cultural History Ctr Study Of Regional Dress Los Angeles CA 90095-0001 E-mail: panawalt@arts.ucla.edu.

ANAYA, RICHARD ALFRED, JR., accountant, brokerage house executive; b. N.Y.C., Dec. 19, 1932; s. Ricardo Martinez and Clara (Chamarro) A.; m. Ninette Calandra, Sept. 8, 1957; children: Suzanne, Richard J. BBA, CCNY, 1958. CPA, N.Y. Tax acct. C.I.T. Fin. Corp., N.Y.C., 1964-67; asst. treas. Mut. Broadcasting System, Inc., N.Y.C., 1967-72; treas. Host Internat., Inc., Santa Monica, Calif., 1972-85; dir. fin. Windsor Fin. Corp, Encino, Calif., 1985; ind. cons. mergers and acquisitions A&I Investments, Inc, Century City, Calif., 1986-87, Anaya Assocs., Century City, Calif., 1987-90, CPA cons. mergers and acquisitions Woodlands Hills, Calif., 1990—. Founder retail store chain, Clear Connect Comms., LLC, 1995. Served with U.S. Navy, 1952-54. Mem. AICPA, Calif. State Soc. CPAs, N.Y. State Soc. CPAs. Roman Catholic. E-mail: anayaassociates@pacbell.net.

ANAYA, RUDOLFO, writer, educator; b. Pastura, N.Mex., Oct. 30, 1937; s. Martin and Rafaelita (Mares) A.; m. Patricia Lawless, July 23, 1966. BA, U. N.Mex., Albuquerque, 1963, MA, 1968; PhD (hon.), U. Albuquerque, 1982; PhD, Mary Crest Coll., 1984; LLD (hon.), U. N.Mex., 1996. Prof. U. N.Mex., Albuquerque, 1974—. Author: (novels) Bless Me Ultima, 1972 (Premio Quinto sol) Heart of Aztlan, 1976, Tortuga, 1979 (Before Columbus Found. award), Alburquerque, 1992 (Pen West award for fiction), Zia Summer, 1995, The Farolitos of Christmas, 1995, Jalamanta, 1996, Rio Grande Fall, 1996, Jemez Spring, 2005, (children's picture books) Maya's Children, 1997, Shaman Winter, 1999, Roadrunner's Dance, 2000, Elegy for Cesar Chavez, 2000, Farolitos for Abuelo, 2000, The Santero's Miracle, 2004, (young adult) Serafina's Stories, 2004. NEA fellow, Nat. Medal of Arts (lit.), 2001. Home: 5324 Canada Vista Pl NW Albuquerque NM 87120-2412 Office: U NMex English Dept Albuquerque NM 87131-0001

ANBAR, MICHAEL, biophysics professor; b. Danzig, June 29, 1927; came to U.S., 1967, naturalized, 1973; s. Joshua and Chava A.; m. Ada Komet, Aug. 11, 1953; children: Ran D., Ariel D. MSc, Hebrew U., Jerusalem, 1950, PhD, 1953. Instr. chemistry U. Chgo., 1953-55; sr. scientist Weizmann Inst. Sci., 1955-67; prof. Frienberg Grad. Sch., Rehovoth, Israel, 1960-67; sr. rsch. assoc. NASA Ames Rsch. Ctr., 1967-68; dir. phys. sci. SRI Internat., Menlo Park, Calif., 1968-72, dir. mass spectrometry research ctr., 1972-77; prof. biophysical sci., chmn. dept. Sch. Medicine, SUNY, Buffalo, 1977-90, rsch. prof. dental materials, rsch. prof. ophthalmology, 1990—, exec. dir. Health Instrument and Device Inst., 1983-85, assoc. dean applied research, 1983-85; v.p. R&D AMARA Inc, Amherst, NY, 1992—; rsch. prof. surgery Sch. Medicine, SUNY, 1998—. Author: The Hydrated Electron, 1970, The Machine of the Bedside: Strategies for Using Technology in Parient Care, 1984, Clinical Biophysics, 1985, Computers in Medicine, 1986, Quantitative Dynamic Telethermometry in Medical Diagnosis and Management, 1994; editor-in-chief: Thermology, 1993; contbr. articles to profl. jours. With Israeli Air Force, 1947-49. Fellow, AIMBE, 2001; grantee in field. Fellow Am. Inst. Biomed. Engrs.; mem. IEEE, AAAS, IEEE Computer Soc., IEEE Engrng. in Biology and Medicine Soc., Assn. Am. Med. Colls., Am. Inst. Physics, Am. Chem. Soc., Am. Inst. Ultrasound in Medicine, Am. Assn. Clin. Chemistry, Am. Assn. Dental Rsch., Am. Assn. Mass Spectrometry, Am. Acad. Thermology, Am. Assn. Med. Systems Informatics, N.Y. Acad. Scis., Internat. Assn. Dental Rsch., Radiation Rsch. Soc., Internat. Med. Informatics Assn., Internat. Soc. Optical Engrng., Radiol. Soc. N.Am., Am. Soc. Clin. Oncology. Office: SUNY 118 Cary Hall Buffalo NY 14214-3023 *Any scientist should first try to understand nature and then to utilize knowledge for the betterment of the quality of life. Even a single modest contribution to medicine can help thousands, making it a worthwhile cause for any scientist. My research and teaching focus, therefore, is on the application of the physical sciences to medicine.*

ANBINDER, PAUL, publishing company executive; b. Bklyn., Apr. 19, 1940; s. Tulea Herzel and Gussie (Dandeshane) A.; m. Helen Rabinowitz, Feb. 16, 1964; children: Mark Harris, Jeffrey Todd. BA, Cornell U., 1960; postgrad., Columbia U., 1960—61. Editor Dover Publs., N.Y.C., 1961-64; editor-in-chief Shorewood Pubs., N.Y.C., 1964-69; with Harry N. Abrams, Inc., N.Y.C., 1969-71, sr. v.p., 1972-73, pres., 1974-75; v.p., editor trade paperbacks Ballantine Books, N.Y.C., 1975-78; dir. spl. projects Random House/Alfred A. Knopf, N.Y.C., 1975-78; pres., pub. Hudson Hills Press, N.Y.C., 1978—2002, chmn., founding pub., 2002—. Bd. dirs. Friends of the Neuberger Mus. of Art, Purchase, N.Y., 1986-96; vol. Westchester Med. Ctr., 2003-. Mem. Assn. Am. Pubs. (bd. dirs. N.Y.C. and Washington chpts. 1987-91), Century Assn. Democrat. Jewish. Avocations: opera, collecting art, travel. Office: 144 Southlawn Ave Dobbs Ferry NY 10522 Personal E-mail: panbinder@14850.com.

ANCELL, ROBERT MANNING, leadership organization executive; b. Phoenix, Oct. 16, 1942; s. Robert Manning and Alice (Lovett) A.; m. Janet Claire Neuber, Dec. 21, 1966 (div. Oct. 1984); children: Kevin Robert, Kristin Deann; m. Christine M. Miller, Mar. 30, 1995. BA, U. N.Mex., 1971. Lic. pvt. pilot. Reporter KOB Radio and TV, Albuquerque, 1966-72; sr. sales rep. Xerox Corp., Albuquerque, 1972-78; pub. Colo. Bus. mag., Denver, 1978-83; publ. mgr. Denver Bus. mag., 1983-84; pub. Endless Vacation mag., Indpls., 1985-88; mktg. mgr. World Pub. Co., Evanston, Ill., 1989-92; writer, 1962—; founder, exec. dir. Soc. for 4-Star Leadership, Alexandria, Va., 1998—. Cons. Cowles Mags., Harrisburg, Pa., 1994-95, Exec. Books, Mechanicsburg, Pa., 1996-98. Author: The Biographical Dictionary of World War II Generals and Flag Officers, 1997; co-author: Who Will Lead?, 1996, Four-Star Leadership for Leaders, 1997, Vol. I and II, 1999. Lt. comdr. USNR, 1971-93. Recipient 1st pl. TV Documentary award N.Mex. Broadcasters Assn., Albuquerque, 1968, UPI, Albuquerque, 1968, Washington Ind. Writers. Mem. Naval Order of U.S. (v.p. pub. affairs 1997—), Soc. for Mil. History, U.S. Naval Inst., Ret. Officers Assn., Assn. of U.S. Army, Air Force Assn., Am. Turkish Soc., Washington Ind. Writers, Christian Businessmen's Com., Surface Navy Assn., USN Pub. Affairs Alumni Assn. Republican. Presbyterian. Avocations: flying, photography, outdoors activities. Home: 11419 South Lakes Dr Reston VA 20191 E-mail: rmancell@comcast.net.

ANCES, BEAU M, neurologist; b. Balt., Md., Feb. 24, 1972; s. I.G. and Marlene Ances; m. Elizabeth Z. Wheeler, May 22, 2004. MSc, London Sch. of Economics, 1993—94; PhD, U. of Pa., 1994—2000, MD, 1994—2001, BA, 1989—93. Neurologist Hosp. of U. of Pa., 2001—. Editor Neurology. Achievements include research in Neuroimaging and NeuroAIDS. Office: Hosp of the Univ of Pennsylvan 3400 Spruce St Philadelphia PA 19103-4283 Office Phone: 215-662-2700. Personal E-mail: beau.ances@uphs.upenn.edu.

ANCES, I. G(EORGE), obstetrician, gynecologist; b. Balt., July 3, 1935; s. Harry and Fanny A.; m. Marlene Roth, Oct. 23, 1966; 1 son, Beau Mark. BS, U. Md., 1956, MD, 1959. Diplomate Am. Bd. Ob-Gyn. Intern Ohio State U. Hosp., 1959-60; resident in ob-gyn. Univ. Hosp., Balt., 1960-61, 63-65; faculty U. Md. Med. Sch., Balt., 1966—, prof. ob-gyn., 1975-83, dir. labs. obstetrics and gynecol. rsch. and clin. labs., 1967-83, dir. divsn. adolescent ob-gyn. and family planning, 1981-83; prof. ob-gyn., chmn. dept. Rutgers U. Sch. Medicine, Camden, N.J., 1983—. Contbr. chpts. to books, articles to profl. jours. Capt. sustaining fund drive Balt. Symphony Orch., Opera Co. Phila.; med. adv. com. Fire Dept. Balt. City. With USAF, 1961-63. Recipient of Outstanding Tchg. and Edn. award Robert-Wood Johnson Sch. of Medicine-Cooper Hosp., 1989, 92, 96, 2000, 01, 02, Appreciation Coverage award, 1999, 2000, 2002, Nat. Faculty award for excellence in resident edn., 1996. Fellow Am. Coll. Obstetrics and Gynecology; mem. Endocrine Soc., Soc. Gynecol. Investigation, Soc. Study Reprodn. (charter), Internat. Soc. Rsch. in Biology Reprodn. (charter), Md. Obstetrics and Gynecol. Soc. (sec. 1978-81, dir. 1979—), Med. and Chirurgical Soc. Md., Soc. Adolescent Medicine, Douglas Obstet. and Gynecol. Soc. (pres. 1984—), N.J. State Med. Soc. (chmn. neo-natal coop. So. Jersey 1986—), Phila. Ob-Gyn. Soc., English Speaking Union, Cooper Found., N.J. Conservation Coun., Harbour League Club, Md. Club, Towson Golf and Country Club, Sigma Xi. Clubs: Maryland, Towson Golf and Country. Home: 1 Lane Of Acres Haddonfield NJ 08033-3504 Office: Rutgers U Sch Medicine Dept Ob-Gyn 3 Cooper Plz Camden NJ 08103-1438

ANCIER, GARTH RICHARD, television broadcast executive; b. Perth Amboy, N.J., Sept. 3, 1957; s. Sherman and Jean Ancier. BA, Princeton U., 1979. Exec. prodr. syndicated program Am. Focus, 1975—79; v.p. comedy programs NBC Entertainment, N.Y.C. and Burbank, Calif., 1979—86; pres. entertainment Fox TV Network, L.A., 1986—89; pres. network TV shows Walt Disney Studios, Burbank, 1989—90; corp. officer, prodr. Fox, Inc., L.A., 1991—92; pres. The Warner Bros. TV Network, 1994—99, NBC Entertainment, Burbank, Calif., 1999—2000; exec. v.p. programming Turner Networks, 2001—03; co-chmn. The Warner Bros. TV Network, 2003—04, chmn., 2004—, CEO, 2004—. TV cons. Dem. Nat. Com., Washington, 1991—92; trustee Nat. Coun. Families and TV, 1991—; creator, exec. prodr. (TV show) Ricki Lake The Garth Ancier Co., 1992—97, exec. cons., 1997—. Mem.: Hollywood TV and Radio Soc. (trustee 1996—99). Democrat. Office: The WB Network 4000 Warner Blvd Burbank CA 91522

ANCKER, SUSAN WEIR, ceramics artist, educator; b. Ogden, Utah, Dec. 25, 1946; d. Ralph Leon and Barbara Ann (Barber) Weir; m. Leif Erickson Ancker, Aug. 23, 1971; children: Hilary (dec.), Eric. BAE, Wayne State U., 1969; BFA, Cleve. Inst. Art, 1985; MA, Ursuline Coll., Pepper Pike, Ohio, 1995. Art tchr. S. Weir Art Studio, Cleveland Heights, Ohio, 1972-91; instr. Eastern N.Mex. U., Ruidoso, 1997—2003; instr. ceramics, art history, art appreciation SWAN Ceramic Studies, Lincoln, N.Mex., 1997—. Pres. Art Loop, 2003. Recipient 1st place in design competition Cleve. Inst. Art, 1970; recipient Art Therapy Clin. award Ursuline Coll., 1996. Mem. NCECA. Office: SWAN Ceramic Studio PO Box 201 Lincoln NM 88338-0201

ANCKER-JOHNSON, BETSY, physicist, engineer, retired automotive executive; b. St. Louis, Apr. 29, 1927; d. Clinton James and Fern (Lalan) Ancker; m. Harold Hunt Johnson, Mar. 15, 1958; children: Ruth P. Johnson, David H. Johnson, Paul A. Johnson (dec.), Marti H. Johnson. BA in Physics with high honors (Pendleton scholar), Wellesley Coll., 1949; PhD in Exptl. Physics magna cum laude, U. Tuebingen, Germany, 1954; D.Sc. (hon.), Poly. Inst. N.Y., 1979, Trinity Coll., 1981, U. So. Calif., 1984, Alverno Coll., 1984; LL.D. (hon.), Bates Coll., 1980. Instr., jr. research physicist U. Calif., Berkeley, 1953-54; physicist Sylvania Microwave Physics Lab., 1956-58; mem. tech. staff RCA Labs., 1958-61; rsch. specialist Boeing Co., 1961-70, exec., 1970-73; asst. sec. U.S. Dept. Commerce for Sci. and Tech., 1973-77; dir. phys. rsch. Argonne Nat. Lab., Ill., 1977-79; v.p. for environ. activities GM, Warren, Mich., 1979-92. Affiliate prof. elec. engring. U. Wash., 1961-73; mem. Energy Rsch. Adv. Bd., 1983-87, adv. com. on inertial confinement fusion Dept. Energy, 1992-94, US Safety Rev. Panel NSF, 1987-88; cons. Inland Steel Inc., 1991-96; adv. com. Rowan Sch. Engring., 1993-96; Regents vis. prof. U. Calif., Berkeley, 1988-89; dir. Acad. Medicine, Engring. and Sci. of Tex., 2004—. Contbr. articles to profl. jours. Mem. staff Inter-Varsity Christian Fellowship, 1954-56; mem. vis. com. elec. and computer divsn. MIT, U.S. Dept. Def. Sci. Bd.; mem. adv. bd. Stanford U. Sch. Engring., Fla. State U., Fla. A&M U., Congl. Caucus for Sci. and Tech.; trustee Wellesley Coll., 1971-77; chair bd. dirs. World Environ. Ctr., 1988-93, dir., 1988-99; founding trustee Johnson Scholarship Found., 1991-2001; founding dir. Work Place Influence, 1997—, dir. Enterprise Devel. Internat., 1992—; mem. faculty adv. coun. U. Tex. Sch. Engring., 1998—; bd. dirs. Tex. Environ. Forum, 2000-01. AAUW fellow, 1950-51; Horton Hollowell fellow, 1951-52; NSF grantee, 1967-72; recipient Chmn's. award Am. Assn. Engring. Socs., 1986, Award of Honor, Licensing Execs. Soc. Fellow AAAS, IEEE, Am. Phys. Soc. (councillor-at-large 1973-76); mem. NRC (bd. engring. edn. 1991-95, com. on women in sci. and engring. 1990-96, office sci. and engring. pers. adv. com. 1993-96), Nat. Acad. Engring. (councillor 1995-2001), Air Pollution Control Assn., Soc. Automotive Engrs. (bd. dirs. 1979-81), Acad. Medicine, Engring. and Sci. Tex. (founding dir. 2004—), Phi Beta Kappa, Sigma Xi. Achievements include patents in field. Business E-Mail: bancker-johnson@austin.rr.com.

ANCONA, GEORGE EFRAIN, photographer, author; b. N.Y.C., Dec. 4, 1929; s. Ephraim Jose and Emma Graziana (Diaz) A.; m. Helga Von Sydow, July 20, 1968; children: Lisa, Gina, Tomas, Isabel, Marina, Pablo. Student, Academia de San Carlos, Mexico, 1949, Art Students League, 1950, Cooper Union Sch. Design, 1950. Art dir. Esquire Inc., N.Y.C., 1951-53, Seventeen mag., N.Y.C., 1953-54, Grey Advt. Agy., N.Y.C., 1954-58, Daniel & Charles Advt. Agy., N.Y.C., 1958-60; free lance photographer, film producer N.Y.C., 1960—. Lectr. graphic design, photography Rockland Community Coll., 1973—, Parsons Sch. Design, 1974—, Sch. Visual Arts, 1978— Author-illustrator: Handtalk, 1974, Monsters on Wheels, 1974, What Do You Do?, 1976, I Feel, 1977, Growing Older, 1978, It's a Baby!, 1979, Dancing Is, 1981, Bananas, from Manolo to Margie, Team Work, 1983, Monster Movers, Sheepdog, Helping Out, Freighters, 1985, Handtalk Birthday, 1986 (NY Times 10 Best Illustrated Children's Books of Yr.), Turtle Watch, 1987, Handtalk Zoo, 1989, Riverkeeper, 1990, Handtalk School, 1991, The Aquarium Book, 1991, Man and Mustang, 1992, Pow Wow, 1992, My Camera, 1992, Pablo Remembers, 1993, The Pinatamaker, 1994, The Golden Lion Tamarin Comes Home, 1994, Fiesta U.S.A., 1995, Cutters, Carvers & the Cathedral, 1995, Earth Daughter, 1995, Mayeros, 1997, Fiesta Fireworks, 1998, Barrio, 1998, Let's Dance, 1998, Charro, The Mexican Cowboy, 1999, Carnaval, 1999, Cuban Kids, 2000, Harvest, 2001, Viva Mexico, the Food, The Fiestas, The Folk Arts, The People, The Past, 2001, Murals: Walls That Sing, 2002, Somos Latinos: Mi Casa-My House, 2004, Mis Amigos-My Friends, 2004, Mi Escuela-My School, 2004, Mi Barrio-My Neighborhood, 2004, Mi Familia-My Family, 2004, Mis Bailes-My Dances, 2004, Mis Fiestas-My Festivals, 2005, Mis Quehaceros-My Chores, 2005, Mi Musica-My Music, Mis Comidas-My Foods, Mis Juegas-My Games, Mis Abuelos-My Grandparents. Office Phone: 505-471-8755. E-mail: geoancona@cybermesa.com. *Curiosity is the biggest element in my work. Watching people and making contact through my photographs have given me a sense of myself. My work keeps me in touch with the world around me. Whether a person bakes, builds, sings, or drives, people reach one another in their own way. Mine is taking pictures. Reaching out to others...I think that's what living is all about.*

ANCU, EDWARD FLORIN, veterinarian; b. Galati, Romania, Oct. 14, 1969; s. Vasile and Haiganush Ancu-Gheorghiu; m. Jennifer Ann Marvel, Aug. 2, 2003. BSc, U. Calif. San Diego-Revelle, 1991; DVM, U. Wis., Madison, 1996. Intern small animal surgery and medicine Calif. Animal Hosp., L.A., 1996—97; relief Dr. self-employed, 1997—2000; pvt. practice Big Tujunga Vet. Hosp., Calif., 2000—. Mem.: Lions Club (Tujunga chpt.). Avocations: travel, reading. Office: Big Tujunga Vet Hosp 6934 Foothill Blvd Tujunga CA 91042

ANDELA, VALENTINE BISANGENA, medical researcher; b. Yaounde, Center, Cameroon, July 5, 1974; s. John Balinga and Blanche Rose Andela. MD, U. of Yaounde I, Cameroon, 1999. Wilmot cancer rsch. fellow U. of Rochester Med. Ctr., Rochester, NY, 2001—, postdoctoral fellow NY, 1999—2000. Founding mem. www.Cancer-Africa.org, Yaounde, Cameroon, 2002. Author: (rsch.) Modulation of Tumor Metastasis (Wilmot Fellowship award, 2000). Mem.: Assn. UICC Fellows, Am. Assn. Cancer Rsch. Achievements include research in AACR-AFLAC Young Investigator Award; International Cancer Research and Technology Transfer (ICRETT) award. E-mail: valentine_andela@urmc.rochester.edu.

ANDEREGG, KAREN KLOK, cosmetic company executive; b. Council Bluffs, Iowa; d. George J. and Hazel E. Klok; m. George F. Anderegg Jr., Aug. 27, 1970 (div. Dec. 1993); m. William Drake Rutherford, Jan. 2, 1994. BA, Stanford U., 1963. Copywriter Vogue Mag., NYC, 1963-72; copy editor Mademoiselle Mag., NYC, 1972-77, mng. editor, 1977-80; assoc. editor Vogue Mag., NYC, 1980-85; editor-in-chief Elle Mag., NYC, 1985-87; pres. Clinique USA, 1987-92; bus. cons. Portland, Oreg., 1993—. Bd. dirs. Oreg. Dental Svcs. Health Plans, Ethicspoint. Bd. dirs. Oreg. Hist. Soc.

ANDERER, JOSEPH HENRY, textile company executive; b. Phila., Oct. 12, 1924; s. Joseph L. and Catherine (Fleck) A.; m. E. T'Lene Brinson, Apr. 4, 1948; children: Joseph D., Mark H., Nancy T. B.M.E., Ga. Inst. Tech., 1947, B.I.E., 1948. Chem. engr. Atlantic Richfield Corp., 1947-55; asst. prof. mech. engring. Drexel Inst., Phila., 1949-56; fiber rsch. mgr., textile devel. lab. mgr. Am. Viscose Corp., 1955-62; with Celanese Corp., 1962—68, exec. v.p. textile mktg., 1967-68; pres. cosmetic and fragrance div., also dir. Revlon, N.Y.C., 1968—72; pres., chief operating officer dir. M. Lowenstein, 1972-77; dir. Aloe Creme Labs., Ft. Lauderdale, Fla., 1974-78, Fairfax Mills, N.Y.C., 1977-78; chmn. bd., chief exec. officer Warren Corp., Stafford Springs, Conn., 1978-89, Grendel Corp., Greenwood, S.C., 1979-88; v.p., dir. Trivest Corp., Sarasota, Fla., 1989-92. Trustee Lincoln Savs. Bank, N.Y.C., 1973-86, N.Y. Ocean Sci. Lab., Montauk, 1973-80, Mus. Am. Textile History, 1986-93; bd. dirs. U.S. Shoe Corp., Cin., 1980-95, Cleyn & Tinker Ltd., St. Laurent, Que., Can., 1990-94, Soundwaters, Stamford, Conn., 1990-93, Gen. Clutch Corp., Stamford, 1991-95, Storage Sol'ns, Inc., Stamford, 1993-95; chmn. nat. adv. bd. Ga. Inst. Tech., 1976-82; chmn. Emergency Med. Svcs., New Canaan, Conn., 1991-94. Patentee fiber technology. Asst. dist. mgr. SBA, Score, Conn., 1992-93, dist. mgr., 1993-94; bd. dirs. S.W. Heritage Found., 2003—. Served to lt. USMCR, 1943-47. Named to Hall of Fame Ga. Tech. Coll. of Engring., 1997. Mem. Wool Mfg. Council (exec. com.), No. Textile Assn. (dir., v.p. 1986-88, chmn. 1988-90), Lugano Condominium Assn. (pres. 1997-98), N.Y. Yacht Club, Stamford Yacht Club (dir., comdr.), N.Am. Sta of Royal Scandinavian Yacht Clubs, Tau Beta Pi, Pi Tau Sigma. Congregationalist. Personal E-mail: Wolfeboro@Juno.com.

ANDERHALTER, OLIVER FRANK, educational organization executive; b. Trenton, Ill., Feb. 14, 1922; s. Oliver Valentine and Catherine (Vollet) A.; m. Elizabeth Fritz, Apr. 30, 1945; children: Sharon, Stephen, Dennis. B.Ed., Eastern Ill. State Tchrs. Coll., 1943, Ped.D. (hon.), 1956; A.M., St. Louis U., 1947, PhD, 1949. Mem. faculty St. Louis U., 1947—, prof. edn., 1957—; dir. Bur. Instl. Research, 1949-65, 1949-65, Univ. Computer Center, 1961-69, chmn. research methodology dept., 1968-76; v.p. Scholastic Testing Service, Chgo., 1951-89; pres. Scholastic Testing Svc., Chgo. and St. Louis, 1989—. Chmn. finance com. Greater St. Louis Campfire Girls Orgn., 1958-59 Author, editor standardized tests. Served as pilot USNR, 1943-46. Mem. Am. Ednl. Research Assn., Nat. Council Measurement, Am. Statis. Assn., N.E.A. Home: 12756 Whispering Hills Ln Saint Louis MO 63146-4449 Office: Scholastic Testing Svc 4320 Green Ash Dr Earth City MO 63045-1208 Office Phone: 314-739-3650. E-mail: budbetty@sbcglobal.net.

ANDERLINI, P. TERRY, lawyer; m. Regan Anderlini; children: Gina, Andy. BA, Tulane U., 1965; JD, San Francisco Law Sch., 1969. Ptnr. Anderlini, Finkelstein & Emerick, San Mateo, Calif. Mem. State Bar Commn. on Future of State Bar and Legal Profession, 1993-94; mem. Calif. Commn. on Jud. Performance, 1989-90; Calif. State Bar ABA del., 1989-92; chair San Mateo Bar Pro-Bono Project; chair San Mateo County Bench and Bar Com.; mem. San Mateo Pub. Defender Com.; dir. Legal Aid Soc. San Mateo County; guest lectr. San Mateo Trial Lawyers Assn. and Calif. Trial Lawyers Assn. Seminars, Stanford U., Santa Clara Law Sch., U. San Diego Law Sch., U. San Francisco Law Sch., 1993-2001; seminar spkr. San Francisco Law Sch., 1993, Stanford Law Sch., 1994-2002. Contbr. articles to profl. jours. Past dir. Poplar Ctr. for Retarded Adults and Children; mem. Svc. League San Mateo County; past pres. Italian Am. Fedn. San Mateo County; bd. dirs. Redwood Shores Homeowners Assn., also pres. Mem. Italian Am. Bar Assn. (pres. 1993), State Bar Calif. (pres. 1987-88, bd. govs. 1984-87), San Mateo County Bar Assn. (pres. 1982), Calif. Trial Lawyers Assn. (bd. govs. 1978), San Mateo County Trial Lawyers Assn. (pres. 1977), San Mateo Barristers Club (pres. 1975), Peninsula Social Club (dir.), San Francisco Bay Knarr Sailing Assn. (past pres.), St. Francis Yacht Club (staff commodore), San Francisco Law Sch. Bd. (pres. 2003-2005). Office: 400 S El Camino Real Ste 700 San Mateo CA 94402-1744 Office Phone: 650-348-0102.

ANDERS, BRENDA MICHELLE, communications professional; b. Washington, July 9, 1971; d. Stephen R. and Mary (Phillips) A. BA, Smith Coll., 1993. Mem. advance staff Clinton/Gore '92, Little Rock, 1992; confidential asst. Sec. U.S. Dept. Edn., Washington, 1993—94; dir. scheduling and advance Alan Wheat for U.S. Senate, Kansas City, Mo., 1994; splty. press coord. The White House, Washington, 1995—96; press sec. to Tipper Gore Clinton/Gore '96, Washington, 1996; coord. radio and spl. projects The White House, Washington, dir. TV prodn., 1998—; dir. pub. affairs Lifetime TV, N.Y.C., 2000—. Democrat. Home: Apt D 302 W 105th St New York NY 10025 E-mail: brendaanders@yahoo.com.

ANDERS, DAVID BRIAN, prosecutor; b. NYC, 1969; AB, Dartmouth Coll., 1991; JD cum laude, Fordham U., 1994. Assoc. Simpson, Thacher & Bartlett, 1994—95; law clerk US Dist. Ct., 1995—96; assoc. Davis Polk & Wardwell, 1996—98; asst. US atty. (So. dist.) NY US Dept. Justice, NYC, 1998—. Named one of Top 40 Lawyers Under 40, Nat. Law Jour., 2005. Mem.: Order of Coif. Office: US Attys Office So Dist NY One St Andrews Plz Rm 619 New York NY 10007 Office Phone: 212-637-2200. Office Fax: 212-637-2239.

ANDERS, EDWARD, chemist, educator; b. Liepaja, Latvia, June 21, 1926; came to U.S., 1949, naturalized, 1955; s. Adolph and Erica (Leventals) Alperovitch; m. Joan Elizabeth Fleming, Nov. 12, 1955; children: George Charles, Nanci Elizabeth. Student, U. Munich, Germany, 1946—49; MA in Chemistry, Columbia U., 1949—51, PhD in Chemistry, 1950—54; ChD, Latvian Acad. Scis., 2000. Instr. U. Ill., 1954-55; mem. faculty U. Chgo., 1955—, prof. chemistry, 1962-73, Horace B. Horton prof. chemistry, 1973-91, Horace B. Horton prof. emeritus, 1991—; vis. prof. Calif. Inst. Tech., 1960, U. Berne, Switzerland, 1963-64, 70, 78, 80, 83, 87, 89-90; research asso. Field Mus. Natural History, Chgo., 1968-91; resident research asso. NASA, 1961. Cons. NASA, 1961—69, mem. lunar sample analysis planning team, 1967—69. Assoc. editor: Geochimica et Cosmochimica Acta, 1966-73, Icarus, 1970-91, Earth, Moon and Planets, 1974-91; contbr. articles to profl. jours. Mem. hon. bd. Mus. Occupation Latvia. Recipient Univ. medal for excellence Columbia U., 1966; Quantrell award for excellence in undergrad. tchg. U. Chgo., 1973; NASA medal for exceptional sci. achievement, 1973; Guggenheim fellow, 1973-74; Fairchild disting. scholar Calif. Inst. Tech., 1992-93. Fellow: AAAS (Newcomb Cleveland prize 1959), Am. Geophys. Union (Harry H. Hess medal 1995), Am. Acad. Arts and Scis., Meteoritical Soc. (v.p. 1968—72, 1989—90, pres. 1991—92, Leonard medal 1974); mem.: Acad. Creative Endeavors (fgn. mem.), Geochem. Soc. (hon., v.p. 1987—88, Goldschmidt medal 1990), Royal Astron. Soc. (assoc.), Internat. Astron. Union (pres. com. on moon 1976—79), NAS (J. Lawrence Smith medal 1971), Am. Astron. Soc. (chmn. divsn. planetary scis. 1971—72, Kuiper prize 1991). Achievements include research in the origin, age, composition of meteorites and lunar rocks, interstellar grains in meteorites, origin moon and planets; development of recovering names of Holocaust victims, which are now represented on a wall with names of 6400.

ANDERS, GEORGE CHARLES, journalist, writer; b. Chgo., Nov. 12, 1957; s. Edward and Joan Elizabeth (Fleming) Anders; m. Elizabeth Anne Corcoran, Aug. 27, 1988. BA in Econs., Stanford U., 1978. Nat. copyreader Wall St. Jour., N.Y.C., 1978—81, Heard on the St. columnist, 1981—82, London bur. chief European edit., 1982—85, news editor, 1985—89, sr. spl. writer, 1988—2000; sr. editor Fast Company Mag., 2000—03; news editor Wall St. Jour., 2003—. Contbg. editor: SmartMoney mag., 1992—95; author: Merchants of Debt, 1992, Health Against Wealth, 1996, Perfect Enough, 2003. Co-recipient Pulitzer Prize for nat. reporting, 1997; recipient Janus award, Am. Mortgage Bankers Assn., 1987.

ANDERS, GERALD RANDOLPH, music educator; b. Jacksonville, Fla., Sept. 3, 1943; s. Gerald Randolph Anders and Hortense Alma Webster; m. Bruce Bennett Castellano. MusB, Carson-Newman Coll., 1965; MusM, Ohio State U., 1972. Asst. dir. publications Cleve. Orch., 1970—72; chmn. music dept. Columbia Grammar and Prep. Sch., NYC, 1972—82, St. Ann's Sch., Bklyn., 1983—91; dir. of arts in edn. Teatro dell'Opera, Bklyn, 1991—92; chmn. fine and performing arts Dwight Englewood Sch., Englewood, NJ, 1992—2002; organist/condr. Cmty. Ch.of Douglaston, Queens, 2001—; artistic dir. Douglaston Concerts, Queens, 2001; condr. Bayside Men's Glee Club, NY, 2002—. Author: (book) Music: A College Appreciation Text, 1975. Mem.: Chamber Music of Am., Am. Guild of Organists, Am. Choral Directors Assn., Pi Kappa Lambda. Avocations: travel, cooking, gardening, reading. Home: 119 Glen Ave Sea Cliff NY 11579

ANDERS, HARLEY DILLON, SR., retired federal agency administrator; b. Clarita, Okla., Nov. 9, 1918; s. Harley Anders and Malsey Fay Simmons; m. Eleanor J. Fitzwater, July 17, 1941 (div. Nov. 12, 1963); children: Harley, Vicki. Enlisted U.S. Army, 1939; advanced through grade to 2d lt. U. S. Army, 1942; claims examiner U.S. Dept. VA, Muskogee, 1944—66, chief claims svc. Juneau, Alaska, 1966—72, dir. Alaska region, 1972—74; ret., 1974. Cons. comprehensive health State of Alaska, Juneau, 1972—74. Author: (genealogy) The Ancestors and Descendants of Elias M. Anders of Missouri, 1985; editor: (book) Genealogical Gleanings in Southeast United States, 1997; author: The Life and Times of John Turnbull, Indian Trader, 1997. Avocations: genealogy, archaeology. Home: 17543 102nd Ave NE #224 Bothell WA 98011

ANDERS, JERROLD P., lawyer; b. Wilkes-Barre, Pa., Sept. 21, 1953; m. Joan Anders, June 28, 1975; children: Jessica, Douglas. AB magna cum laude, Franklin & Marshall Coll., 1975; JD cum laude, U. Pitts., 1978. Jud. law clk. to Hon. Martin J. Coyne Lehigh County Ct. of Common Pleas, 1978-79; ptnr. White and Williams, LLP, Phila., 1979—. Mem. Phi Beta Kappa, Order of Coif. Office: White and Williams LLP 1 Liberty Pl 1650 Market St Ste 1800 Philadelphia PA 19103-7304 E-mail: andersj@whiteandwilliams.com.

ANDERSEN, ANTON CHRIS, lawyer; b. Salina, Kans., Oct. 3, 1960; s. Anton Jay and Mary Louise (Breitweiser) A. BS in BA, U. Kans., 1983; JD with honors, Washburn U., Topeka, Kans., 1986. Bar: Kans. 1986, U.S. Dist. Ct. Kans. 1986. Ptnr. McAnany Van Cleave & Phillips P.A., Lenexa, Kans., 1991—. Active Leadership Lenexa, 1987. Mem. Kans. Bar Assn., Phi Delta Phi. Republican. Presbyterian. Avocations: golf, reading, basketball. Office: McAnany Van Cleave & Phillips PA PO Box 1300 Kansas City KS 66117

ANDERSEN, BURTON ROBERT, immunologist, educator; b. Chgo., Aug. 27, 1932; s. Burton R. and Alice C. (Mara) A.; children: Ellen C., Julia A., Brian E. Student, Northwestern U., 1950—51; BS, U. Ill., 1953; MS, U. Ill., Chgo., 1957; MD, U. Ill., 1957. Intern Mpls. Gen. Hosp., 1957-58; resident and fellow U. Ill. Hosp., 1958-61; clin. assoc. NIH, Bethesda, Md., 1961-64; asst. prof. U. Rochester, NY, 1964-67; assoc. prof. Northwestern U., 1967-70; prof. medicine and microbiology U. Ill., Chgo., 1970—, chief infectious diseases, 1986-99, West Side VA Med. Ctr., 1970-90. Contbr. sci. rsch. articles to profl. jours. Served as sr. surgeon USPHS, 1961-63. Grantee Rsch. grantee, NEH, 2000—03. Fellow ACP; mem. Am. Assn. Immunologists, Am. Soc. for Clin. Investigation, Ctrl. Soc. for Clin. Rsch. Achievements include research in infectious diseases, white blood cells and ancient Mesopotamian medicine. Office: U Ill Sect Infectious Diseases 808 S Wood St Chicago IL 60612-7300 Business E-Mail: branders@uic.edu.

ANDERSEN, IB, performing company executive; b. Denmark; Prin. dancer N.Y.C Ballet, 1980—90; tchr. various companies in Belgium, Norway, Japan, Can. and U.S., 1990—2000; artistic dir. Ballet Ariz., 2000—. Avocations: cooking, painting, music, poetry, literature. Office: Ballet Arizona 3645 E Indian Sch Rd Phoenix AZ 85018 E-mail: ib@balletaz.org.

ANDERSEN, JAMES A., retired state supreme court justice; b. Auburn, Wash., Sept. 21, 1924; s. James A. and Margaret Cecelia (Norgaard) A.; m. Billiette B. Andersen; children: James Blair, Tia Louise. BA, U. Wash., 1949, JD, 1951. Bar: Wash. 1952, U.S. Dist. Ct. (we. dist.) Wash. 1957, U.S. Ct. Appeals 1957. Dep. pros. atty. King County, Seattle, 1953-57; assoc. Lycette, Diamond & Sylvester, Seattle, 1957-61; ptnr. Clinton, Andersen, Fleck & Glein, Seattle, 1961-75; judge Wash. State Ct. of Appeals, Seattle, 1975-84; justice Wash. State Supreme Ct., Olympia, 1984-92, chief justice, 1992-95; ret., 1995. Chair Legis. Ethics Bd. Mem. Wash. State Ho. of Reps., 1958-67, Wash. State Senate, 1967-72. Served with U.S. Army, 1943-45, ETO. Decorated Purple Heart; recipient Disting. Alumnus award U. Wash. Sch. of Law, 1995. Mem. ABA, Wash. State Bar Assn., Am. Judicature Soc. Home: 3008 98th Ave NE Bellevue WA 98004-1817

ANDERSEN, K(ENT) TUCKER, investment executive; b. Manchester, Conn., June 5, 1942; s. Alfred Hans and Dorothy Emily (Ray) A.; m. Karen Ann Kirchofer, Oct. 11, 1963; children: Heather Michele, Kristen Eileen. Student, Phillips Exeter Acad., N.H., 1957-59; BA, Wesleyan U., 1963. Chartered fin. analyst. Actuarial student Travelers Ins. Co., Hartford, Conn., 1963-66; security analyst Smith Barney & Co., N.Y.C., 1968-69; ptnr. Rudman Assocs., N.Y.C., 1969-72, Cumberland Assocs. LLC, N.Y.C.,

1972—, mng. ptnr., 1982-96, chief investment strategist, 1997—. Bd. dirs. Cato Inst., Washington, 1987—, exec. com., 1992—; trustee YWCA of Montclair, North Essex, N.J., 1980—, 1st United Meth. Ch., Montclair, 1976-94, Martin Luther King Scholarship Fund Montclair, 1989-94, Phillips Exeter Acad., 1989—, chmn. investment com., 1992—, bd. v.p. and chmn. exec. com., 1993—, admissions rep. N.J. area, 1983-93; exec. com. GOPAC, 1993—, bd. dirs., 1995—. With USPHS, 1966-68. Recipient Disting. Alumnus award Wesleyan U., 1988. Mem. Soc. Actuaries, N.Y. Soc. Security Analysts, Inst. Chartered Fin. Analysts, Polit. Club for Growth (mem. exec. com. 1984-94), Kappa Nu Kappa (pres. 1963). Republican. Avocation: marathon running. Office: Cumberland Assocs 38th Fl 1114 Avenue Of The Americas New York NY 10036-7703

ANDERSEN, KURT BYARS, writer; b. Omaha, Aug. 22, 1954; s. Robert and Jean (Swarr) A.; m. Anne (Kreamer), May 9, 1981; children: Katherine, and Lucy. AB magna cum laude, Harvard U., 1976. Writer NBC-TV, N.Y.C., 1976-80, Time Mag., N.Y.C., 1981-84, arch. critic, 1984-93, columnist, 1993-94; co-founder, co-editor Spy Mag., N.Y.C., 1986-93; editor-in-chief New York Mag., N.Y.C., 1994-96; columnist The New Yorker, N.Y.C., 1996-99; co-founder, co-chmn. Inside, N.Y.C., 1999—. Author: The Real Thing, 1980; Turn of the Century, 1999; co-author: Tools of Power, 1980; (off-Broadway revue and book) Loose Lips, 1994-95, 98; exec. prodr. TV pilots After Hours, 1987; Zero Hour; 1991, Pranks, 1992; exec. prodr., co-writer TV spl. How To Be Famous, 1990; The Hit List, 1992; host TV spl. Comedy Spotlight, 1996; radio show Studio 360, 2000—. Recipient journalism award ABA, 1983; Page One Award Newspaper Guild N.Y., 1984. Mem.: bd. of trustees Pratt Inst.

ANDERSEN, LEONARD CHRISTIAN, former state legislator, real estate investor; b. Waukegan, Ill., May 30, 1911; s. Lauritz Frederick and Meta Marie (Jacobsen) A.; m. Charlotte O. Ritland, June 30, 1937; children: Karen Schneider, Paul R., Charlene Olsson, Mark Luther. BA, Huron (S.D.) Coll., 1933; MA, U. S.D., 1937. Tchr. Onida (S.D.) H.S., 1934-35; dir. bus. tng. Waldorf Coll., Forest City, Iowa, 1935-39; ins. salesman, 1939-41; tchrs. econs., current history Morningside Coll., Sioux City, Iowa, 1941-43; ins., real estate investor Sioux City, 1943-76. Mem. Iowa Ho. of Reps., Woodbury County, 1961-64, 66-71; mem. Iowa Senate, 26th Dist., 1972-76, chmn. rules and adminstrn. com.; former mem. Iowa Commn. on Aging; former mem. investment adv. bd. IPERS; former mem. cen. com. Woodbury County Reps., del. county, dist. and state convs.; former mem. Simpco Projects Rev. Com.; former pres., chmn. bd. Siouxland Rental Assn.; past mem. Sioux City Housing Appeals Bd., Siouxland Com. on Alcoholism; bd. regents Augustana Coll., Sioux Falls, S.D., 12 yrs., mem. Augustana Fellows, 2003—; mem. fin. com. Morningside Luth. Ch., co-chair call com. 2003—; active Rep. Party Campaigns, del. to state, dist. and county Rep. convs., Iowa, 1998, 2000; bd. dirs. Human Rights Commn., Sioux City, 1997-2003. Del. Evang. Luth. Ch. Conv., 1999, 2000, 2001, 2002, promoter Wordalone movement; apptd. anti-violence com. Siouxland Area. Mem. Masons, Lions. Home: 3112 Nebraska St Apt 2 Sioux City IA 51104-3948 E-mail: lande11211@aol.com.

ANDERSEN, MARGO K., federal agency administrator; BA, Gettysburg Coll.; M in Mgmt., George Washington U. Program mgr. for arts programs Nat. Endowment for the Arts, Am. Correctional Assn.; dir. Office Fin. Mgmt. and Performance Measurement, Office Innovation and Improvement U.S. Dept. Edn., Washington. Office: US Dept Edn IES Rm 500F 555 New Jersey Ave NW Washington DC 20208

ANDERSEN, MARK, musician; m. Lynn Rowley, July 5, 2002. PhD, Paris Conservatory, 1971. Concert organist, composer Internat. Artists Records, 1971—; host, performer Crescendo TV Program, Oneonta, NY, 2003—. Composer: (music composition and performance) Fantasie Francais. Recipient Internat. Composer's award, Fedn. of World Music, 1976, 1999. Fellow: Am. Guild of Organists. Episcopalian. Achievements include design of Digital Pipe Organ Voices; development of Pipe Organ Control System; Hospital Data Management Program; Over 200 Classical Compositions Published. Office: Internat Artists 350 5th Ave New York NY 10019 Office Phone: 607-847-9496. Personal E-mail: emarka@mac.com. E-mail: internationalartists@mac.com.

ANDERSEN, MELVIN ERNEST, toxicologist, educator; b. Providence, Dec. 13, 1945; s. Magnus and Mildred Elaine (Petersen) A.; m. Christine Ann Jaeger, Aug. 3, 1968; children: Kathryn Louise, Heidi Lynn, Rebecca Arline. BSc in Chemistry, Brown U., 1967; PhD in Biochemistry, Cornell U., 1971. Diplomate Am. Bd. Indsl. Hygiene, Am. Bd. Toxicology. Civil svc. staff Dept. of Def., Dayton, Ohio, 1979-88; dept. head, sr. scientist Chem. Ind. Inst. Toxicology, Research Triangle Park, N.C., 1989-92; rsch. prof. Duke U., Durham, N.C., 1992-93; sr. scientist U.S. EPA, Research Triangle Park, 1993-94; v.p. The KS Crump Group, ICF Kaiser Internat., Research Triangle Park, N.C., 1994-98; prof. dept. environ. health Colo. State U., 1998—2002; divsn. dir. CIIT Ctrs. for Health Rsch., Morrisville, NC, 2002—. Mem. sci. adv. panel Chem. Industry Inst. Toxicology, Research Triangle Park, 1984-88; adj. prof. Wright State U., Dayton, 1979-89; adj. prof. medicine Duke U., 1994-95; adj. assoc. prof. U. N.C., Chapel Hill, 1993-97. Contbr. articles to profl. jours., chpts. to books. Lt. comdr. USN, 1971-78. Recipient Kenneth Morgareidge award Internat. Life Scis. Inst., 1989, George Scott award Toxicology Forum, 1993, Harry G. Armstrong award Aerospace Med. Rsch. Lab., 1982, Outstanding Profl. Achievement award Engring./Sci. Found. of Dayton, 1985. Mem. Soc. Toxicology (Frank Blood award 1982, Achievement award 1984), Soc. Risk Analysis, Am. Bd. Toxicology (bd. dirs. 1991-94), Am. Conf. Govtl. Indsl. Hygienists (Herbert Stokinger award 1988). Methodist. Avocations: birding, astronomy, blues harmonica. Home: 30148 Walser Chapel Hill NC 27517-8063 E-mail: manderson@ciit.org.

ANDERSEN, NIELS HJORTH, chemistry professor, consultant, biophysicist, researcher; b. Copenhagen, Oct. 9, 1943; came to U.S. 1949; s. Orla and Inger (Larsen) A.; m. Sidnee Lee (div. 1986); children: Marin Christine, Beth Arkady; m. Susan Howell, July 21, 1987. BA, U. Minn., 1963; PhD, Northwestern U., 1967. Rsch. assoc and fellow Harvard U., Cambridge, Mass., 1966-68; asst. prof. U. Wash., Seattle, 1968-72, assoc. prof., 1972-76, prof., 1976—; prin. scientist ALZA Corp., Palo Alto, Calif., 1970-75. Cons. Genetic Systems, Seattle, 1984-86, Bristol-Myer Squibb, Princeton, N.J., 1984-95, Amylin Pharmaceutics, San Diego, 1992-2001 Receptron Corp., Mountain View, Calif., 1995—2001, Chiron, Seattle, 1997—2003. Mem. adv. bd. Biopolymers; contbr. articles to profl. jours. Recipient Teacher-Scholar award Dreyfus Found., 1974-79, Career Devel. award NIH, 1975-80. Mem. AAAS, Am. Chem. Soc., Am. Peptide Soc., Protein Soc. Democrat. Avocations: contemporary folk music and swing, dulcimer playing. Office: U Wash Dept Chem PO Box 351700 Seattle WA 98195-1700 Office Phone: 206-543-7099. E-mail: andersen@chem.washington.edu.

ANDERSEN, ROBERT, health products, business executive; b. Bklyn., Oct. 9, 1937; s. Ingulf Bertel Andersen and Helen Jane Akin (McDowell) Miller; m. Elaine Marie Wood, June 13, 1958; children: Susan Marie, Robert Alan, Dori Ann. Grad. h.s., La Mesa, Calif. Area sales mgr. Golden Arrow Dairy, San Diego, 1958-66; retail sales mgr. Hollandia Dairy, San Marcos, Calif., 1966-69; pres. Health Best Inc., San Marcos, 1969-98; founding ptnr. Escondido Mills, San Marcos, 1980—; owner, operator Andersen Trading Co., Valley Center, Calif., 1984—; ptnr. Earth Products, Valley Center, 1989—; founding ptnr. Elaina's Snacks, San Marcos, 1991-94; owner, operator Andersen Gallery, Valley Center, 1992-98; pres. Gisé LLC, 1997—2001. Bd. dirs. Russian Art Guild, San Diego, 1992-96; pres. Kamut Assn. N.Am., San Marcos, 1997—. Republican. Avocation: poetry. Home: 30126 Castlecrest Dr Valley Center CA 92082-4923

ANDERSEN, ROBERT ALLEN, retired state official; b. Denver, Aug. 27, 1936; s. Emmett Christian and Margaret Irene (Maupin) A.; m. Jane Eng (dec.), May 13, 1967. AB in Polit Sci., U. S.C., 1958, MA in Polit Sci., 1961; postgrad. in law, U. Colo., 1958-59; PhD in Internat. Relations, Am. U., 1973. Area coordinator for econ. devel. Area Redevel. Adminstrn., Commerce Dept., 1962-64; acting dir. urban projects div., program officer, chief Project Adminstrn. VISTA (OEO), Washington, 1964-66; implementation programming, planning and budgeting system Office Program Planning and Evaluation, Office Edn., 1966-67; staff asst. to dep. postmaster gen. Postal Service, 1967-72, sr. planning officer, 1972-74; dir. evaluation Immigration and Naturalization Service, Washington, 1974-86, dir. Office of Program Inpection, 1986-88; dir. mgmt., planning and review Office Inspector Gen., Dept. Justice, Washington, 1988-90, dir. quality assurance rev., 1990-97; ret., 1997. Past pres. bd. dirs. D.C. Assn. Retarded Citizens; past. sec. The Arc. Episcopalian. Home: 5701 Nebraska Ave NW Washington DC 20015-1221

ANDERSEN, RONALD MAX, public health service officer, educator; b. Omaha, 1939; s. Max Adolph and Evangeline Dorothy (Wobbe) Andersen; m. Diane Borella, June 19, 1965; 1 child, Rachel. BS, U. Santa Clara, 1960; MS, Purdue U., 1962, PhD, 1968. Rsch. assoc. Purdue U., West Lafayette, Ind., 1962—63; assoc. study dir. Nat. Opinion Rsch. Ctr., Chgo., 1963—66; rsch. assoc. U. Chgo., 1963—77, from assoc. prof. to prof. Grad. Sch. Bus., 1974—90, dir. Program in Health Adminstrn. and Ctr. for Health Adminstrn. Studies, 1980—90; Wasserman prof. dept. health svcs. and sociology UCLA, 1991—, prof. emeritus, 2004—, chmn. dept. health svcs., 1993—96, 2000—03. Com. mem. Agy. for Health Care Policy and Rsch., Rockville, Md., 1970—. Mem. editl. bd.: Health Adminstrn. Press, 1980—83, 1988—98, Med. Care Rsch. & Rev., 1994—; author: A Decade of Health Services, 1967, Two Decades of Health Service, 1976, Total Survey Error, 1979, Health Services in the U.S., 1980, Ambulatory Care and Insurance Coverage in an Era of Constraint, 1987, Training Physicians, 1994, Changing the U.S. Health Care System, 1996, 2001. Fellow, NIH, 1960—62; grantee, Agy. for Health Care Policy and Rsch, 1982, Robert Wood Johnson Found., 1983, Kaiser Family Found., 1983, WHO, 1990. Mem.: APHA, Assn. for Health Svcs. Rsch. (dir. 1981—83, 1997—99, Disting. Career award 1996), Assoc. Univ. Program in Health Adminstrn. (Baxter Allegiance prize 1999), Inst. Medicine NAS, Am. Sociol. Assn. (chmn. med. sociology sect. 1980—81, Disting. Med. Sociologist 1994). Roman Catholic. Home: 10724 Wilshire Blvd Apt 312 Los Angeles CA 90024-4453 Office: UCLA Sch Pub Health Los Angeles CA 90024 Office Phone: 310-206-1810. Business E-Mail: randevse@ucla.edu.

ANDERSEN, SUSAN MARIE, psychologist, educator; b. Santa Monica, Calif., June 6, 1955; BA in Psychology with honors, U. Calif., Santa Cruz, 1977; PhD in Psychology, Stanford U., 1981. Lic. psychologist Calif., N.Y. Asst. prof. psychology Univ. Calif., Santa Barbara, 1981-87; assoc. prof. NYU, N.Y.C., 1987-94, prof., 1994—, dir. grad. studies in psychology, 1993—97, 2000—02, dir. doctoral program in social psychology. Dir. doctoral program social psychology, cons. Edn. Commn. of the States; Grantmaker Forum for Cmty. and Nat. Svc., Common Cents N.Y.; bd. dirs. Common Cents, N.Y.; grants panel, social and group processes rev. panel NIMH, 1992-94, 96, Integrative Grad. Edn. and Rsch. Tng. rev. panel NSF, 2003; other panels. Assoc. editor Jour. Social and Clin. Psychology, 1987-92; Social Cognition, 1993; Jour. Personality and Social Psychology: Attitudes and Social Cognition, 1994-95, Psychol. Rev., 1998-2000, Self and Identity, 2004—; mem. editl. bd. Jour. Personality and Social Psychology, 1990-93, 2000-01, Nouvelle Revue de Psychologie Sociale, 2002—; ad hoc reviewer Jour. Comm. Rsch., Jour. Exptl. Psychology: Learning, Memory & Cognition, Jour. Exptl. Social Psychology, Jour. Personality, Jour. Rsch. in Personality, Motivation and Emotion, Personality and Social Psychology Bull., Psychol. Sci., NSF, Australian Social Sci. Rsch. Coun., Social Sci. and Human Rsch. Coun. Can., Brit. Jour. Clin. Psychology, Brit. Jour. Social Psychology, Jour. Abnormal Psychology; contbr. articles to profl. jours. Chair svc. learning task force White House Congl. Conf. on Character Bldg.; mem. rsch. and evaluation com. Character Edn. Partnership; rsch. adv. bd. Kellogg Found. Nat. Initiative on Cmty. Svc. in Edn.; Learning in Deed; edn. policy task force Inst. for Comm. Policy Studies, George Washington U.; mem. Russell Sage Found.'s Social Identity Consortium; bd. dirs. Common Cents, NY. Grantee NIMH, 1985-86, 92-98; Sr. fellow Inst. for Comm. Policy Studies, George Washington U. Fellow: APA, Soc. Psychol. Study of Social Issues, Soc. Personality and Social Psychology (mem. exec. com.), Am. Psychol. Soc.; mem.: Soc. Advancement of Socio Econ., Soc. Exptl. Social Psychology, Internat. Soc. Self and Identity. Office: Dept Psychology NY Univ 6 Washington Pl 7th Fl New York NY 10003-6603 Business E-Mail: andersen@psych.nyu.edu.

ANDERSEN, TORBEN BRENDER, optical researcher, astronomer, software engineer; b. Naestved, Denmark, May 17, 1954; came to U.S., 1983; U.S. citizen, 1994; s. Bjarne and Anna Margrethe (Brender) Andersen; m. Olga Pedina, June 2004; children: Iris, Erik, Maxim. PhD, Copenhagen U., Denmark, 1979. Rsch. fellow Copenhagen U., 1980-82, sr. rsch. fellow, 1982-85; optical cons. Nordic Optical Telescope Assn., Roskilde, Denmark, 1985; optical systems analyst Telos Corp., Santa Clara, Calif., 1985-88; rsch. scientist Lockheed Martin Missiles and Space, Palo Alto, Calif., 1988-93, staff scientist, 1993-95, sr. staff scientist, 1995-96, staff software engr., 1996—. Vis. scholar Optical Scis. Ctr., U. Ariz., Tucson, 1983-85. Editor: Astronomical Papers Dedicated to Bengt Strömgren, 1978; contbr. articles to Jour. Quantitative Spectroscopy Radiation Transfer, Applied Optics, Astronomische Nachrichten. Mem. Optical Soc. Am., Internat. Astron. Union, Soc. Photo-Optical Instrumentation Engrs. Achievements include development of method for computing optical aberration coefficients to arbitrarily high orders; discovery of set of differential equations for the Voigt function; contributing to optical design software. Office: Lockheed Martin Advanced Tech Ctr O/ABDS 3251 Hanover St # B201 Palo Alto CA 94304-1121 Office Phone: 650-424-3305. Business E-Mail: torben.andersen@lmco.com.

ANDERSLAND, ORLANDO BALDWIN, engineering educator; b. Albert Lea, Minn., Aug. 15, 1929; s. Ole Larsen and Brita Kristine (Okland) A.; m. Phyllis Elaine Burgess, Aug. 15, 1958; children: Mark, John, Ruth BCE, U. Minn., 1952; MSCE, Purdue U., 1956, PhD, 1960. Registered profl. engr., Minn., Mich. Staff engr. NAS, Am. Assn. State Hwy. Ofcls. Road Test, Ottawa, Ill., 1956-57; rsch. engr. Purdue U., West Lafayette, Ind., 1957-59; mem. faculty Mich. State U., East Lansing, 1960—, prof. civil engring., 1968—, prof. emeritus, 1994—. Co-author: Geotechnical Software for the IBM, PC, 1987, Geotechnical Engineering and Soil Testing, 1992, An Introduction to Frozen Ground Engineering, 1994, 2d edit., 2004; sr. editor: Geotechnical Engineering for Cold Regions, 1978; contbr. chpt. Ground Engineer's Handbook, 1987; contbr. articles to profl. jours.; patentee in field. 1st lt. C.E., U.S. Army, 1952-55. Decorated Nat. Def. Svc. medal; UN Svc. medal; Korean Svc. medal; recipient Best Paper award Assn. Asphalt Paving Technologists, 1956; postdoctoral fellow Norwegian Geotech. Inst., 1966; grantee NSF, EPA, Dept. of Energy. Fellow ASCE (best paper award Cold Regions Engring. Jour. 1991); mem. ASTM (sr.), Internat. Soc. Soil Mechanics and Found. Engring., Am. Soc. Engring. Edn. (life), Sigma Xi, Chi Epsilon, Tau Beta Pi. Lutheran. Office: Mich State U Dept Civil/Environ Engring East Lansing MI 48824 Office Phone: 517-355-5107.

ANDERSON, AL H., JR., communications executive; b. Winston Salem, N.C., May 4, 1942; s. Al H. Sr. and Gladys (Harris) A.; m. Jeanette R., Nov. 25, 1971; children: April, Albert III. BS, Morehouse Coll., 1964; MBA, Rutgers U., 1970; MS (hon.), Ga. State U., 1972. Mgmt. trainee Allstate Ins. Co., Atlanta, 1968-70; loan officer C&S Bank, Atlanta, 1970-72; v.p. Citizens Trust Bank, Atlanta, 1972-73; pres. Triangle Assocs., Atlanta, 1972-75; chmn., founder Anderson Communications Media, Atlanta, 1975—; pres. The Shiloh Inst., Atlanta, 1979—. Cons. Small Bus. Adminstrn., Atlanta, 1978-85. Dir. Sickle Cell Found. of Ga., Atlanta, 1984, United Way of Atlanta, 1987; pres. Cascade Youth Orgn., Atlanta, 1986. Mem. Black Pub. Relations Soc. (v.p. 1986—), Atlanta Bus. League, Atlanta Advt. Club, Pub. Relations Soc. of Am. Democrat. Avocations: classic cars, grand prix racing. Office: Anderson Communications Media 2245 Godby Rd Atlanta GA 30349-5012 Office Phone: 404-766-8000.

ANDERSON, ALBERT SYDNEY, III, lawyer; b. Atlanta, July 7, 1940; s. Albert S. Jr. and Constance S. (Spalding) A.; children: Judith, William. BA in Math., Emory U., 1962; MS in Physics, Stanford (Calif.) U., 1964, PhD in Physics, 1968, JD, 1977. Bar: Ga. 1978, U.S. Patent and Trademark Office 1980, U.S. Supreme Ct. 1981. Assoc. Stokes & Shapiro, Atlanta, 1978-81, Kutak, Rock & Huie, Atlanta, 1981-84; ptnr. Jones & Askew, Atlanta, 1984-96; pvt. practice Norcross, Ga., 1996—. Asst. atty. gen. State of Ga., Atlanta, 1984-88. Elder Trinity Presbyn. Ch., Atlanta, 1978-81; chmn. bd. trustees Trinity Sch., Atlanta, 1971-74. Mem. Am. Phys. Soc. Avocations: golf, hiking, music. Office: Patent Law Offices 35 Technology Pkwy S Ste 170 Norcross GA 30092-2928 E-mail: aanderson@andersonpatent.com.

ANDERSON, ALFRED OLIVER, mathematician, consultant; b. Marmon, N.D., May 18, 1928; s. Frederick Gustav and Minnie Petrine (Jensen) Anderson. BS, Oreg. State U., 1953. Sys. programmer U.S. Army Ballistics Rsch. Lab., Aberdeen, Md., 1953-83; cons. Aberdeen, 1983—. Investment specialist, Palermo, Maine, 1983—. Mem.: Mensa, Pi Mu Epsilon. Democrat. Lutheran. Avocations: wood working, investment analysis. Home and Office: 107 Banton Rd Palermo ME 04354-6521 Office Phone: 207-993-2042.

ANDERSON, ALLAMAY EUDORIS, health educator, home economist; b. N.Y.C., July 18, 1933; d. John Samuel and Charlotte Jane (Harrigan) Richardson; m. Edgar Leopold Anderson, Jr., Apr. 14, 1957 (div. Apr. 14, 1963); 1 child, David Lancelot; m. Diane Kay Swartz, July 19, 2003. B.A., Queens Coll., CUNY, 1975; profl. mgmt. cert. Adelphi U., 1978; M.S. in Edn., Fordham U., 1984. Mem. staff sch. food svc. dietitian Bd. Edn., N.Y.C., 1968-88; tchr. home and career skills Louis Armstrong Mid. Sch., 1988; spl. edn. tchr. Manhattan H.S., N.Y.C., 1989-95, coord AIDS resource, 1995, ret. 1995; profl. devel. cons., N.Y.C., 1978—; ptnr. Masiba Bldg. Corp., Corona, N.Y., 1975-82; adj. lectr. home econs. Queens Coll., 1987; owner AEA Devel. Svc., 1987-97; mem. exec. bd. Ssch. Edn. Alumni Assn., Fordham U., 1997—. Devel. coord. League for Better Cmty. Life, Inc., 1977; treas. exec. bd., 1970-76; officer N.Y.C. Cmty. Devel. Agy., 1980-83; mem. Kwanzaa Adv. Com. (P.R.) Urban Coalition, 1983, L.I. # 28 Episcopal Cursillo, 1991; vestry mem. youth ministries Grace Episcopal Ch., 1982-85, vestry mem., 1996-99; mem. NAACP (local Women's History Month honoree); asst. presiding ptnr. Dynamic Investors Club, 1996—; Bridges chairperson Srs. of Dorie Miller, 2003. Recipient Elmcor Cmty. Svc. award Elmcor Youth and Adult Activities, Inc., 1989, Alumni Achievement award Fordham U. Sch. Edn., 2000, Cmty. Svc. award N.Y. State United Tchrs., 2001, Concourse Village Br. Positive Image award Key Women Am., Inc., 2005. Mem. Assn. Fundraising Profls. (Greater N.Y. chpt.), Nat. Assn. Investment Clubs, Langston Hughes Libr. Action Com. (bd. dirs. 1987—, treas. 1989, Kwanza chair 1994-97), Queens Coll. Home Econs. Alumni Assn. (v.p., chmn. bylaws com. 1982), United Fedn. Tchrs. (Ret. Tchrs. chpt.), Negro Bus. and Profl. Women's Clubs (Profl. award 1998), Phi Delta Kappan (Fordham U. chpt.).

ANDERSON, ANTHONY LECLAIRE, lawyer; b. Davenport, Iowa, Sept. 15, 1938; s. Frederic Nielsen and Marie Louise (LeClaire) A.; m. Beulah M. Bassham, July 3, 1963; children: Timothy LeClaire, Mark LeClaire, Jonathan Frederic LeClaire. BS with final honors, Washington U., St. Louis, 1967; JD, St. Louis U., 1971. Bar: Mo. 1972, U.S. Dist. Ct. (we. dist.) Mo. 1972, U.S. Dist. Ct. (ea. dist.) Mo. 1972, U.S. Ct. Appeals (8th cir.) 1974, U.S. Ct. Appeals (7th cir.) 1992, U.S. Tax Ct. 1976, U.S. Supreme Ct. 1976. Dir. pub. affairs Key Comm., Inc., St. Louis, 1973-74, Anderson, Wollrab & Wilson, St. Louis, 1974-76, Anderson, Preuss, Mooney & Eickhorst, St. Louis, 1976-82, Anderson, Preuss & Bachman, St. Louis, 1982-87, Anderson & Preuss, St. Louis, 1987—. Dir. Shield Fire Ins. Co., St. Louis, 1976-83. Panel atty. Lawyers Reference Svc., St. Louis, 1972-92; mem. Nat. Rep. Congrl. Com., 1998. Served with U.S. Army, 1962-64. Recipient Law Enforcement Assistance cert. Bd. Police Commrs., 1967, Bi-Centennial Commn., Davenport, Iowa, 1976. Mem. ABA, ATLA, Am. Judicature Soc., Ill. Trial Lawyers Assn., Bar Assn. Met. st. Louis, Press (editor 1968-69), Phi Alpha Delta. Episcopalian. Home: 2919 Moniteau Dr Saint Louis MO 63121-4518 Address: 7260 Pershing Ave Apt 1E University City MO 63130-4251

ANDERSON, ARTHUR ALLAN, management consultant; b. Grand Rapids, Mich., Apr. 16, 1939; s. Alvin Alexander and Mildred Jane (Grice) A. AB in History, ScB in Chemistry, Brown U., 1962; LLB, Yale U., 1965. Bar: N.Y. 1966. Assoc. Fish & Neave, N.Y.C., 1965-69; co-founder, pres. Source Securities Corp., 1970-72; gen. counsel Teleprompter Corp., N.Y.C., 1973-74; ptnr. Anderson & Rubin, N.Y.C., 1975-82, Choate, Moore, Hahn & McGarry, N.Y.C., 1982-85; sole practice N.Y.C., 1985-87; prin., bd. dirs. Morgan, AndersonConsulting, N.Y.C., 1988—. Bd. dirs. Woodstock Artists' Assn.; mem. exec. bd. Samuel Dorsky Mus. of Art, SUNY, New Paltz. Mem. Nat. Arts Club, Explorers Club. Home: Moonhaw Rd West Shokan NY 12494 Office: Morgan Anderson Cons 1123 Broadway New York NY 10010 Business E-Mail: consultants@morgananderson.com.

ANDERSON, ARTHUR OSMUND, pathologist, immunologist, military officer; b. N.Y.C., Mar. 12, 1945; s. Arthur Edmund and Florence Ranveig (Osmundsen) A.; m. Julane Kay Pynn, Oct. 4, 1969; 1 child, Phoebe MacDonald Anderson. BS, Wagner Coll., 1966; MD, U. Md., 1970; PhD (hon.), Wagner Coll., 2003. Diplomate Am. Bd. Pathology. Intern in pathology Johns Hopkins Hosp., Balt., 1970-71, fellow in exptl. pathology, 1970-74, resident in pathology, 1971-73; commd. 2d lt. U.S. Army, 1974, advanced through grades to col., 1988; asst. prof. biology and pathology U. Pa., Phila., 1980-83; prin. investigator pathology div. U.S. Army Med. Rsch. Inst. Infectious Diseases, Ft. Detrick, Md., 1974-80, chief respiratory immunity, 1983—, chmn. human investigational rev. bd., 1976-80, 84—. Appeared in (History Channel) Suicide Missions: Human Guinea Pigs, 2000; contbr. numerous articles to profl. jours., chpts. to immunology text books and websites. Decorated Meritorious Svc. medal; N.Y. State Regents scholar, 1962-66; recipient Order of Mil. Med. Merit award, 2002. Mem. Found. for Advanced Edn. in Scis., Am. Assn. Immunologists, Am. Assn. Pathologists, Applied Rsch. Ethics Nat. Assn. (treas. 2000-04), Kiwanis (pres. Frederick 1988-89), Beta Beta Beta, Omicron Delta Kappa. Republican. Achievements include first documented role of endothelium in immunity; first showed evidence in vivo that lymphocytes adhered to endothelial cells in lymph nodes, first showed that adjuvants could enhance mucosal secretion of IgA; contributed to medical ethics as chronicled in the book Undue Risk: Secret State Experiments on Humans, 1999. Office: US Army Med Rsch Inst Infectious Diseases Fort Detrick Frederick MD 21702 Office Phone: 301-619-4723. Personal E-mail: artnscience@yahoo.com.

ANDERSON, ARTHUR STEPHEN, lawyer; b. Vienna, Apr. 4, 1947; came to U.S., 1947; s. F. M. Anderson and Catherine Jane (Algee) Davis; m. Rebecca Lynn Olsen Roth, June, 1968 (div. Aug. 1973); 1 child, Jeffrey Martin Roth; m. Barbara Ellen Uszak, Mar. 25, 1983; children: Lauren Nicole, Alexa Yurianna. BS in Psychology cum laude, U. Wash., 1974, JD, MBA, 1978. Bar: Wash. 1978, U.S. Dist. Ct. (we. dist.) Wash. 1978, Alaska 1979. Assoc. McCutcheon, Groshong, Geisness & Day, Seattle, 1978-80, McCutcheon & Groshong, Seattle, 1980-82; ptnr. Groshong Lehet & Anderson, Seattle, 1982-84; pvt. practice Seattle, 1984-92, 95-99; ptnr. Nelson Anderson Krafchick, Seattle, 1992-94; assoc. Law Office of Ron Perey, Seattle, 1999—. Sgt. U.S. Army, 1967-69, Vietnam. Recipient Courageous award Wash. State Bar Assn., 1998. Mem. ATLA, Wash. State Trial Lawyers Assn. (bd. dirs. 1984-91), King County Bar Assn. (chair young lawyers sect. 1981-82). Avocations: reading, sailing, skiing. Office: 2025 1st Ave Ste 250 Seattle WA 89121-2147 E-mail: asa@pereylaw.com.

ANDERSON, AUSTIN GOTHARD, lawyer, consultant, academic administrator; b. Calumet, Minn., June 30, 1931; s. Hugo Gothard and Turna Marie (Johnson) A.; m. Catherine Antoinette Spellacy, Jan. 2. 1954; children: Todd, Susan, Timothy, Linda, Mark. BA, U. Minn., 1954, JD, 1958. Bar: Minn. 1958, Ill. 1962, Mich. 1974. Assoc. Spellacy, Spellacy, Lano & Anderson, Marble, Minn, 1958-62; dir. Ill. Inst. Continuing Legal Edn., Springfield, 1962-64; dir. dept. continuing legal edn. U. Minn., Mpls., 1964-70, assoc. dean gen. extension divsn., 1968-70; ptnr. Dorsey, Marquart, Windhorst, West & Halladay, Mpls., 1970-73; assoc. dir. Nat. Ctr. State Cts., St. Paul, 1973-74; dir. Inst. Continuing Legal Edn. U. Mich., Ann Arbor, 1973-92; dir. Inst. on Law Firm Mgmt., 1992-95; prin. AndersonBoyer Group, Ann Arbor, 1995—; pres. Network of Leading Law Firms, 1995—. Adj. faculty U. Minn., 1974,

Wayne State U., 1974-75; mem. adv. bd. Ctr. for Law Firm Mgmt. Nottingham Trent U., Eng.; draftsman ABA Guidelines for Approval of Legal Asst. Programs, 1973, Model Guidelines for Minimum Continuing Legal Edn., 1988; chair law practice mgmt. sect. State Bar Mich., 2000-2001; mem. Task Force on Court Filing, State Bar of Mich., 2000—; mem. Com. on Quality of Life, 2000-2001; cons. in field. Co-editor, contbg. author: Lawyer's Handbook, 1975, co-editor 3d edit., 1992; author: A Plan for Lawyer Development, 1986, Marketing Your Practice: A Practical Guide to Client Development, 1986; cons. editor, contbg. author: Webster's Legal Secretaries Handbook, 1981; cons. editor Merriam Webster's Legal Secretarial Handbook, 2d edit., 1996; co-author: The Effective Associate Training Program-Improving Firm Performance, Profits and Prospective Partners, 2000, Associate Retention: Keeping Our Best and Brightest, 2002; author, co-editor: The Effective Training Program, revised edit., 2005; contbr. chpt. to book and articles to profl. jours. Chmn. City of Bloomington Park and Recreation Adv. Commn., Minn., 1967-72; chmn. Ann Arbor Citizens Recreation Adv. Com., 1981-89, Ann Arbor Parks Adv. Com., 1983-92, chair, 1991-92; rep. Class of '58 U. Minn. Law Sch., 1996-2004. Recipient Excellence award CLE sect. Assn. of Am. Law Schs., 1992. Fellow Am. Bar Found. (Mich. chmn. 2002-), State Bar Mich. Found.; mem. ABA (vice chmn. continuing legal edn. com. sect. legal edn. and admission to bar 1988-93, standing com. continuing edn. of bar 1984-90, 2000—, chmn. law practice mgmt. sect. 1981-82, Am. Law Inst.-ABA com. on continuing profl. edn. 1993-96, Am. Law Inst.-ABA com. on continuing profl. edn. 1999—2002, spl. com. on rsch. on future of legal profession 1998-2000, sec. Coll. of Law Practice Mgmt. 1993-97, house of dels. 1993-99, commn. on lawyer advt. 1994-97, mem. task force Lawyer Ctr. on pers. legal svcs. and client devel. 2002-03, spl. advisor to standing com. on continuing edn. of the bar 2002—, chair cmty. on econ. of law practices, 2002-, torts, trial and ins. practice sect.), Internat. Bar Assn., Mich. Bar Assn., Ill. Bar Assn., State Bar of Mich. (chair law practice mgmt. sect. 2000-01), Minn. Bar Assn., Internat. Bar Assn., Assn. Continuing Legal Edn. Adminstrs. (pres. 1969-70), Laurel Gardens Condominium Assn. (pres. 2004—), Ann Arbor Golf and Outing Club. Home: 4660 Bayberry Cir Ann Arbor MI 48105-9762 Office: AndersonBoyer Group 118 E Mich Ave Ste 200 Saline MI 48176 Office Phone: 734-944-6040. E-mail: aga@andersonboyer.com.

ANDERSON, BARBARA JEANNE, music educator; b. Berkeley, Calif., Aug. 25, 1928; d. Hermanq Eston Mathis and Betty Jayne Baumann; widowed; children: Geoffrey P., Steven M., Cheryl I. Devlin, Donna Van Soelen. BA in Music, U. Calif., 1973; MusM, Holy Names Coll., 2000. Dic. sacred music 1st Presbyn. Ch., San Leandro, Calif., 1972—82; substitute tchr. Acalanes, Md. Daiblo High Sch. Dist., Contro Costa County, 1974—79; staff asst., dir. youth music Orinda Cmty. Ch., 1982—92; tchr. piano pvt. practice, 1979—; instr. Las Positas Coll., Livermore, 2001—. Mem.: Music Tchrs. Assn. (Contra Costa bd. bd. dirs., Contra Costa bd. program chmn. 2001—03), Nat. Guild Piano Tchrs., Music Tchrs. Nat. Assn. Avocations: photography, piano. Home and Office: 6 Van Tassel Ln Orinda CA 94563 E-mail: bandersonpiano@aol.com.

ANDERSON, BARBARA MCCOMAS, lawyer; d. Ben C. Jr. and Elsa A. McComas; m. Roy Ryden Anderson Jr., Dec. 11, 1982; 1 child, Ryden McComas Anderson. BA, Trinity U., San Antonio, 1972; JD, U. Tex., 1978. Bar: Tex. 1978; cert. in estate planning and probate Tex. Bd. Legal Specialization. From assoc. to ptnr. Locke Purnell Rain Harrell, Dallas, 1978-97; of counsel Locke Liddell & Sapp, LLP, Dallas, 1997—2003; pvt. practice Dallas, 1997—. Fellow: Coll. of State Bar of Tex., Tex. Bar. Found., Am. Coll. Trusts and Estates Counsel; mem.: Tex. Acad. Probate and Trust Lawyers (charter) (charter, bd. dirs., bd. dirs.), Dallas Bar Assn., Tex. Bar Assn. (chair real estate, probate and trust law sect. 2003—04). Avocations: reading mysteries, gardening. Office: PO Box 181147 Dallas TX 75218-8147

ANDERSON, BASIL L., retail executive; b. Jamaica; BS in Engring., Israeli Inst. Tech., 1968; MS in Engr., U. Ill., 1969; MBA, U. Chgo., 1971. With Scott Paper Co., 1975-93, US treas., 1985-87, worldwide treas., 1987-92, CFO, 1993-96; sr. v.p. fin., CFO, treas. Campbell Soup Co., 1996-97, exec. v.p., 1997-2001; vice chmn. Staples, Inc., Framingham, Mass., 2001—. Bd. dir. Staples, Inc., Hasbro, Inc. Office: Staples, Inc 500 Staples Dr Framingham MA 01702

ANDERSON, BERNARD E., economist; b. Phila. s. William and Dorothy (Gideon) Anderson; children: Melinda D., Bernard E. II. BA with highest honors, Livingstone Coll., 1959; MA, Mich. State U., 1961; PhD, U. Pa., 1969; LHD (hon.), Shaw U., 1984, Livingstone Coll., 1995; LLD (hon.), Benedict Coll., 2002. Economist U.S. Bur. Labor Stats., Washington, 1963-65; successively asst. prof., assoc. prof., prof. Wharton Sch. U. Pa., Phila., 1969-79; dir. social sci. Rockefeller Found., N.Y.C., 1979-86; mng. ptnr. Urban Affairs Partnership, Phila., 1987-91; pres. Anderson Group, Phila., 1991-93; asst. sec. U.S. Dept. Labor, 1994-2001; chmn. Pa. Intergovernmental Cooperation Authority, Phila., 1991-93; Whitney M. Young prof. mgmt. Wharton Sch., U. Pa., Phila., 2001—. Vice chmn., bd. dirs. Manpower Demonstration Rsch. Co., N.Y.C., 1977—93, Pa. Econ. Devel. Partnership, Harrisburg, Provident Mut. Life Ins. Co., 1988—2002; vis. fellow Woodrow Wilson Sch., Princeton (N.J.) U., 1985; bd. dirs. United Bank Phila. Co-author: (book) Impact of Government Training and Employment Programs, 1975, Black Managers in American Business, 1978, Soul in Management, 1996; author: Youth Employment and Public Policy, 1980; mem. editl. bd. Rev. Black Polit. Economy, 1977—89. Mem. Pres.'s Commn. Employment/Unemployment Stats., Washington, 1979; trustee Livingstone Coll., Salisbury, NC, 1980—94; chmn. bd. trustees Lincoln U., Oxford, Pa., 1987—93; mem. Com. Fgn. Rels., Phila., 1983—94; bd. dirs. Franklin Inst., Phila., Opportunities Industrialization Ctrs. Am., 2001—, Leon H. Sullivan Found., 2002—, Phila. Orch., 2004—. With U.S. Army, 1961—63. Recipient Disting. Educator award, Citizens Urbanism, 1987, Cmty. Svc. award, Delaware Valley Housing Assn., 1989, Disting. Svc. award, A. Philip Randolph Inst., 1990, Bayard Rustin Humanitarianism award, 1996. Mem.: Nat. Econ. Assn. (pres. 1982, Samuel Z. Westerfield award 2003), Indsl. Rels. Rsch. Assn. (mem. exec. com. 1979—82), Am. Econ. Assn., Union League, U. Pa. Faculty Club. Democrat. A.M.E. Zion.

ANDERSON, BO I., automotive executive; b. Oct. 16, 1955; Grad, Sweden's Military Acad.; BBA, Stockholm U.; post grad., Harvard U., 1999. Mgr. Saab, 1987, v.p. purchasing, 1990; exec. dir. worldwide purchasing GM Corp Elec. Commodity Group, 1993; exec. dir. GM Chem. Commodity Group, 1994; v.p. purchasing GM Europe, 1997; exec. worldwide purchasing GM Corp., 1997, v.p. worldwide purchasing, 2001—. Bd. dirs. New United Motors Mfg. Inc. Chmn. bd. dirs. Mich. Minority Bus. Devel. Coun., Mich. With Swedish Army. Mem.: HOPE (adv. bd.), St. Joseph Mercy Oakland Hosp. (bd. trustees).

ANDERSON, BOB, state legislator, retired small business owner; b. Wadena, Minn, Jan. 16, 1932; s. Alfred Emmanuel and Frances Agnes (Hassler) A.; m. Janet Lynn Hemquist, Aug. 3, 1967 BBA, U. Miami, 1959; student, US Army War Coll., 1996. Owner small bus., Minn., 1954-96; mem. Minn. Ho. of Reps., 1976-96; mem. steering com. House DFL Caucus, 1993-94. Vice chair, sec., mem. exec. com. Legis. Commn. on Waste Mgmt., 1980—96; chair NCSL com. Agrl., 1985; chair human svc. fin. divsn., 1985—86; dir. NCSL Found. for State Legislatures, 1987—93; mem. ways and means com., 1993—96; chair health and housing fin. divsn., 1993—94; chair health and human svc. com., 1995—96; legis. cons., 1997—; past pres. Viking-Land USA; bd. dir. West Ctrl. Minn. Emergency Med. Svc., Inc., chair, 2005—, mem. exec. com., 2000—; mem. Minn. Emergency Med. Svc. Regulatory Bd., 2001—02; assoc. chair Senate Dist. 10, 2002—04, chmn., 2004—, DFL Ho. Dist. 10A, 2004—; mem. 7th Congl. Dist. DFL Ctr. Com., 2002—. Past pres. Otter Tail Lake Property Owners Assn.; mem. Fergus Falls N.G. Citizens Com.; mem. state ctrl. com. Minn. Dem.-Farmer-Labor Party, 2002—; bd. dir. Friends of History Mus. of East Otter Tail County, 2002—. With U.S. Army, 1952—54. Decorated D.S.M.; named Hon. Citizen, City of Winnipeg, Chief Author Glendalough State Pk., Fergus Falls Vets. Home, Prairie Wetlands Environ. Learning Ctr.; recipient Highroad Explorer award, Hon. Viking award, Svc. award Minn. Assn. Rehab. Facilities, West Cen. Emergency Med. Corp, Minn. Ambulance Assn., Nat. Fedn. Ind. Bus., Minn. Head Start Assn., Econ. Justice award MNCAP, Ctr. For Ind. Living, Minn. Cmty. Action award, Pub. Ofcl. Yr. award Minn. Nurses Assn., 1994, Food First Coalition award, 1995, Arrowhead Friends of EMS award, 2003. Mem. NRA (life), Nat. Conf. State Legislatures (exec. com. 1986-88, commerce, labor and regulation com. 1991-94), Nat. Parks Conservations Assn., Nat. Wild Turkey Fedn., Minn. Meat Processors Assn. (past pres.), Rocky Mountain Elk Fedn., Pioneer Heritage Conservation Trust, Nature Conservancy, Friends of Prairie Wetlands Learing Ctr., Otter Tail County Hist. Soc. (life), Am. Legion (life), VFW (life; Ladies Aux. Vet. of Yr. award 1994), Minn. Outdoor Heritage Caucus, Fergus Falls Fish and Game Club, Millerville Sportsmen Club, Evansville Sportsmen Club, Ottertail Rod and Gun Club, Knob Hill Sportsmen, Sons of Norway, Elks, Masons, Shriners, Theta Chi, Alpha Kappa Psi. Democrat. Home: PO Box 28 Ottertail MN 56571-0028

ANDERSON, BRADBURY H., retail executive; m. Janet Anderson; 2 children. AS, Waldorf Coll.; BA, U. Denver. Bd. dirs. Best Buy, 1986—; pres., COO Best Buy Co., Inc., Richfield, Minn., 1991—2002, CEO, vice chmn., 2002—, mem. Long-Range & Strategic Planning Com. Bd. dirs. Minn. Public Radio, Am. Film Inst., Best Buy Children's Found., Internat. Mass Retail Assn., Waldorf Coll. Bd. Regents. Office: Best Buy 7601 Penn Ave S Richfield MN 55423-3645*

ANDERSON, BROOKS DORAN, II, geologist, consultant; b. Auburn, NY, June 18, 1941; s. Brooks Doran and Violet (Risley) Anderson; m. Maria de Los Angeles Antuna, Aug. 16, 1963; 1 child, Loani. BSc in Geology, Bowling Green State U., 1963, MA in Geology, 1965; PhD in Ocean and Environ. Affairs, Heed U., 1977. Geologist Geolabs, Inc., Honolulu, 1972—74; project geologist Dames & Moore, Inc., Honolulu, 1974—76; pvt. practice Honolulu, 1976—77; prof. geology U. Baja Calif., Ensenada, Mexico, 1977—78; pvt. practice Saltillo, Mexico, 1982—86, 1991—2001; info. officer Securitas, San Antonio, 2001—. Cons. in field. Contbr. articles to profl. jours. Capt. U.S. Army, 1968—70. Grantee, U. Nuevo Leon, Guatemala, 1986; Australian Commonwealth scholar, Australian Fed. Govt., 1971. Achievements include development of grain size analysis method for nuclear craters costing 1% of previous methods; conceptual model of Hawaiian coral cmty. structure; conceptual model of faults for finding groundwater in impermeable shale in Northeastern Mexico. Avocation: writing. Home: Colonia Doctores 204 Dr Miguel Farias 25250 Saltillo Coahuila Mexico Office: Brooks Anderson Cons 320 Avondale Ave San Antonio TX 78223-2546

ANDERSON, BRUCE EDWIN, lawyer; b. Greeley, Colo., June 21, 1948; s. Maxwell Edward and Anne (Koss) A.; m. Cheryl A. Quinlan, Aug. 30, 1969; 1 child, Nathan Douglas. BA, U. Mo., 1970, JD, 1975. Bar: Mo. 1975, Tex. 1980; cert. in civil trial law and personal injury law Tex. Bd. Legal Specialization. Law clk. to Hon. Albert L. Rendlen, Mo. Ct. Appeals, St. Louis, 1975-76; asst. atty. gen. Mo. Atty. Gen.'s Office, Jefferson City, 1976-79; pvt. practice Austin, Tex., 1980-84; assoc. Davis & Davis, Austin, 1984-89, Brin & Brin, San Antonio, 1990, owner, 1991—. Adj. prof. St. Mary's Univ. Lt. (j.g.) USNR, 1970-72. Avocations: running, science fiction, genealogy, political history. Office: 10999 W Ih 10 #800 San Antonio TX 78230-1349 E-mail: banderson@brinandbrin.com.

ANDERSON, CARL ALBERT, fraternal organization administrator, lawyer, dean; b. Torrington, Conn., Feb. 27, 1951; s. Carl August and Louise Joanna (Giorcelli) A.; m. Dorian Jean Lounsbury Anderson, Aug. 19, 1972; children: Carl, Matthew, Teresa, Katherine, Clare. BA in Philosophy, Seattle U., 1972; JD, U. Denver, 1975. Bar: D.C. 1979. V.p. John Paul II Inst. for Studies on Marriage and Family, Cath. U. Am., Washington, 1999—; dir., bd. dirs. Basilica of the Nat. Shrine of Immaculate Conception, Washington, 2001—; corp. CEO KC, New Haven. Legis. asst. U.S. Senate, Washington, 1976-81; counsellor to the Undersec. U.S. Dept. Health and Human Svcs., Washington, 1981-83; staff mem. White House Office of Policy Devel., Washington, 1983-85; spl. asst. to the Pres., 1985-87; acting dir. White House Office of Pub. Liaison, 1987; commr. U.S. Commn. on Civil Rights, Washington, 1990-2000. Contbr. articles to profl. jours. Mem. transition team Office of the Pres.-Elect, Washington, 1980, 88; trustee Cath. U. Am., 2002—; consultor Pontifical Coun. for the Family, Pontifical Coun. Justice and Peace. Recipient Thomas Linacre award Nat. Fedn. Cath. Physicians' Guilds, 1992; Knight of the Equestrian Order of the Holy Sepulchre of Jerusalem, Knight of St. Gregory the Great, Pontifical Acad. for Life, Pontifical Coun. for the Laity, consultor Pontifical Coun. for the Family, and Pontifical Coun. for Justice and Peace. Mem. D.C. Bar Assn., KC (v.p. pub. policy 1987-97, state dep. for D.C. 1995-97, asst. supreme sec. 1997—). Roman Catholic. Address: KC One Columbus Plz New Haven CT 06510-3326 Business E-Mail: carl.anderson@kofc.org.

ANDERSON, CARMA ROSE DE JONG, artist, poet, actress; b. Provo, Utah, Mar. 6, 1930; d. Gerrit and Rosabelle (Winegar) de Jong; m. Richard L. Anderson, May 22, 1951; children: Roselle, Nathan Richard, Gerrit Lloyd, Chandelle Jeannette. Student, Brigham Young U., 1948-92, Harvard U., 1952, Coll. So. Utah, 1954-55, U. Calif., Berkeley, 1960-61; BA in Art and Modern Langs., Brigham Young U., 1976, PhD in Hist. Costume and Art History, 1992. English tchr., librarian Centro Cultural, Brasil/Estados Unidos, Santos, Brazil, 1947-48; set designer, choreographer, dancer BYU Opera Workshops, 1944, 48; dancer Mt. Timpanogos festivals, 1948-49; founding officer, choreographer, costumer Nat. Orchesis Brigham Young U., 1949; actress cmty., ch., univ. theaters. Cons., prodr., demonstrator Utah Centennial This Is the Place State Park, Salt Lake City; hist. costumer KUED PBS documentaries, Salt Lake City; demonstrator culinary crafts KBYU TV, Provo, 1984—; design and textile cons., collector of muti-thousands of costumes, costumer, interior designer of permanent exhibits, living history docents Mus. Ch. History and Art, LDS Ch., Salt Lake City; hist. costumer of manikins and actors at U.S. hist. sites, for hist. films, illustrators, painters, sculptors, doll-makers and re-enactment groups; tchr. of costume Brigham Young U.; rschr. in field. One woman performances of hist. characters across U.S., poetic dramas; actress KBYU FM documentaries; paintings exhibited at Utah State exhibits; permanent collection exhibited at Utah State Bldg., Provo; also one-woman shows. Bd. dirs. Brigham Young U. Academy. Recipient prizes for parade floats. Mem. Utah Valley Poetry Soc. (founder), Costume Inst. Utah (founder). Avocations: religious history research, garden designing (award winner), compassionate service to the sick. Office: Costume Inst Utah 3736 Little Rock Dr Provo UT 84604-5235

ANDERSON, CAROL ANN, retired secondary school educator, lawyer, political organization worker; b. Glendive, Mont., Oct. 2, 1934; d. Richard William and Gertrude Elizabeth (Carey) Johnson; m. Roger J.W. Anderson, Dec. 29, 1954; children: Leslie Anderson Cornejo, Kevin Roger, Jeffrey Richard. BA in English, Fresno State U., 1970; MA in English, Bakersfield State U., 1978; JD, Santa Barbara (Calif.) Coll. Law, 1989. Bar: Calif. 1989; life secondary sch. credential Calif., edn. adminstr. credential Calif. English tchr. Kern H.S. Dist., Bakersfield, Calif., 1971—78; supr., adj. lectr. Calif. State U., Bakersfield, 1978—82; pvt. practice lawyer Montecito, Calif., 1990—97; chmn. Santa Barbara (Calif.) County Rep. Party, 2000—05; dist. chmn. Channel Islands Dist. Calif. Rep. Party. Active Calif. Rep. Party, Burbank, 1997—, Channel Island dist. chmn., 2002—; bd. dirs. Earl Warren Showgrounds, Santa Barbara, Calif., 1996—98. Mem.: Calif. Bar Assn., New Horizons Band Assn. (mem. organizing com.), Prime Time Band (pres. 2000—, v.p., bd. mem. 2005). Avocations: flute, reading, snorkeling, swimming. Office: Santa Barbara County Rep Party 3887 State St #11 Santa Barbara CA 93105

ANDERSON, CAROL LEE, communications executive; b. Sharon, Pa., Nov. 5, 1943; d. James W. and Charlene Helen (Lang) Thomas; m. Duane A. Anderson, Dec. 16, 1978; children: Mark Powell, Steve Anderson. Student, Youngstown (Ohio) State U., 1961, Pa. State U., Sharon, 1964. Field mgr. Welcome Wagon Internat., Memphis, 1975-78; dir. Merrill Chase Gallery, Naperville, Ill., 1978-80; br. mgr. CONTEL/Executone, Burr Ridge, Ill., 1980-84; major mkt. account exec. Ill. Bell Comm., Westbrook, 1984-90; strategic account exec. govt. accounts Ameritech Custom Bus., Westbrook, Ill., 1990-93, sales mgr. fed., mil. and civilian, 1993-97, regional dir. govt. and edn., 1997-98; dir. bus. sales Ameritech Gen. Bus., 1998—. Mem. Internat. Orgn. Women in Telecommunications, Delta Chi Epsilon. Home: 213 Pfaff Dr Frankfort IL 60423-1624 Office: Ameritech Enhanced Bus Two Westbrook Corp Westchester IL 60154

ANDERSON, CAROLE ANN, nursing educator, academic administrator; b. Chgo., Feb. 21, 1938; d. Robert and Marian (Harrity) Irving; m. Clark Anderson, Feb. 14, 1973; 1 child, Julie. Diploma, St. Francis Hosp., 1958; BS, U. Colo., 1962, MS, 1963, PhD, 1977. Group psychotherapist Dept. Vocat. Rehab., Denver, 1963-72; psychotherapist Prof. Psychiatry and Guidance Clinic, Denver, 1970-71; asst. prof., chmn. nursing sch. U. Colo., Denver, 1971-75; therapist, coordinator The Genessee Mental Health, Rochester, N.Y., 1977-78; assoc. dean U. Rochester, N.Y., 1978-86; dean, prof. Coll. Nursing Ohio State U., Columbus, 1986-2001, prof., 2001—, vice provost acad. and faculty offices, 2001—, interim dean grad. sch., 2005. Lectr. nursing sch. U. Colo., Denver, 1970-71; prin. investigator biomed. rsch. support grant, 1986-93, clin. rsch. facilitation grant, 1981-82; program dir. profl. nurse traineeship, 1978-86, advanced nurse tng. grant, 1982-85. Author: (with others) Women as Victims, 1986, Violence Toward Women, 1982, Substance Abuse of Women, 1982; editor Nursing Outlook, 1993-2002. Pres., bd. dirs. Health Assn., Rochester, 1984-86; mem. north sub area council Finger Lakes Health Systems Agy., 1983-86, longrange planning com., 1981-82; mem. Columbus Bd. Health; dir. Netcare Mental Health Ctr. Am. Acad. Nursing fellow. Mem. ANA, Ohio Nurses Assn., Am. Assn. Colls. Nursing (bd. dirs. 1992-94, pres.-elect 1994-96, pres. 1996-98), Sigma Theta Tau. Home: 406 W 6th Ave Columbus OH 43201-3137 Office: The OH State U Office Acad Affairs 203 Bricker Hall 190 N Oval Mall Columbus OH 43210-1358 Business E-Mail: anderson.32@osu.edu.

ANDERSON, CHARLES ARTHUR, retired science administrator; b. Columbus, Ohio, Nov. 14, 1917; s. Arthur E. and Huldah (Peterson) A.; m. Elizabeth Rushforth, Oct. 27, 1942; children: Peter C., Stephen E., Julia E. AB, U. Calif. at Berkeley, 1938; MBA, Grad. Sch. Bus. Adminstrn., Harvard U., 1940; LHD, Colby Coll., 1975. Asst. prof. Grad. Sch. Bus. Adminstrn., Harvard U., Boston, 1945-48; v.p. Magna Power Tool Corp., Menlo Park, Calif., 1948-58; prof., asso. dean Stanford Grad. Sch. Bus., 1959-61; v.p. Kern County Land Co., San Francisco, 1961-64; pres. Walker Mfg. Co., Racine, Wis., 1964-66, J.I. Case Co., Racine, 1966-68; pres., chief exec. officer SRI Internat., Menlo Park, 1968-79. Bd. dirs. KRI Internat., Japan, Eaton Corp., Conoco, Owens-Corning Fiberglas, NCR, Boise Cascade, Saga; mem. adv. council Bus. Sch., Stanford, 1966-72, 74-79; mem. industry adv. council Dept. Def., 1971-73 Author (with Anthony) The New Corporate Director. Mem. Menlo Park Planning Commn. and City Coun., 1955-61, Govs. Commn. on Reorgn. Wis. State Govt., 1965-67; bd. dirs. Calif. State C. of C., 1972-77, Internat. House, U. Calif., Berkeley, 1979-90; bd. dirs. Lucile Salter Packard Children's Hosp., Stanford, 1979-95, chmn., 1992-94. With USNR, 1941-45. Recipient Exceptional Service award USAF, 1965 Mem. Palo Alto Club, Pacific-Union Club, Menlo Country Club. Presbyterian. Office: 555 Byron St Apt 207 Palo Alto CA 94301-2037 E-mail: caacaa@pacbell.com.

ANDERSON, CHARLES DAVID, lawyer; b. Balt., Aug. 4, 1943; s. Charles Quentin and Enid Ruth A.; m. Alison Grey, Apr. 15, 1972 (div. Oct. 1990); children: Charles Thomas, Patrick Grey; m. Kathleen McGuinness, June 8, 1991 (div. Dec. 2001); 1 child, Alexander James McGuinness. BA, Yale Coll., 1964; JD, U. Chgo., 1967. Capt. USAF, Pentagon, 1967-70; assoc. Caplin & Drysdale, Washington, 1970-72; from assoc. to ptnr. Tuttle & Taylor, L.A., 1972-2000; ptnr. Loeb & Loeb, L.A., 2000—. Lectr. Harvard Law Sch., Cambridge, Mass., 1983, U. So. Calif. Law Sch., L.A., 1976, 78, UCLA Law Sch., 1979, 81, 85. Pres. L.A. Soccer Found., 1994—. Avocations: pens, skiing. Home: 1375 Linda Vista Ave Pasadena CA 91103-2347 Office: Loeb & Loeb LLP 10100 Santa Monica Blvd Los Angeles CA 90067 E-mail: danderson@loeb.com.

ANDERSON, CHARLES HILL, lawyer; s. Ray N. and Lois M. Anderson; (div.); children: Eric S., Alicia L., Burton H. JD, U. Tenn., 1953. Bar: Tenn. 1953, U.S. Dist. Ct. Tenn. 1953, U.S. Ct. Appeals (6th cir.) 1956, U.S. Supreme Ct. 1956, U.S. Ct. Mil. 1964. Pvt. practice, Chattanooga, 1953-59, 2001—; assoc. gen. counsel Life & Casualty Ins. Co. Tenn., Nashville, 1960-69; dist. atty. U.S. Dept. Justice, Nashville, 1969-77; pvt. practice Nashville, 1977-79, 87—; asst. adj. gen. State of Tenn., Nashville, 1979-87. Mem. U.S. Atty. Gen. Adv. Com., Washington, 1973-77; del. Tenn. Constl. Conv., Nashville, 1965-66; dir. Nashville Pub. TV Coun., 1994-99; chmn. Met. Bd. of Equalization, 1998-2001. Brig. gen. AUS, ret., 1987. Mem. ABA, Tenn. Bar Assn., Nashville Bar Assn., Fed. Bar Assn. (pres. Nashville chpt. 1972), Assn. Life Ins. Counsel, Cumberland Club (pres. 1981-82), The Federalist Soc. Presbyterian. Home: 1515 Woodbine Ct Columbia SC 29206-4403

ANDERSON, CHARLES ROSS, civil engineer; b. N.Y.C., Oct. 4, 1937; s. Biard Eclare and Melva (Smith) A.; m. Susan Breinholt, Aug. 29, 1961; children: Loralee, Brian, Craig, Thomas, David. BSCE, U. Utah, 1961; MBA, Harvard U., 1963. Registered profl. engr. Owner, operator AAA Engring. and Drafting, Inc., Salt Lake City, 1960—. Acad. adv. com. U. Utah, 1990-91, chmn. civil engring. adv. bd., 1995—, U. Utah nat. engring. adv. coun., 2001—. Mayoral appointee Housing Devel. Com., Salt Lake City, 1981-86; bd. dirs., vice chmn. Met. Water Dist., Salt Lake City, 1985-99; bd. dirs., pres., v.p., sec. bd. Utah Mus. Natural History, Salt Lake City, 1980-92; asst. dist. commr. Sunrise dist. Boy Scouts Am., Salt Lake City, 1985-86; fundraising coord. architects and engrs. United Fund; mem. Sunstone Nat. Adv. Bd., 1980-88; bd. dirs. Provo River Water Users Assn., 1986—, Salt Lake Convention & Visitor Bur., 2001-03; mgmt. bd. U. Utah Hosp. and Clinic, 2000—. Recipient Hamilton Watch award U. Utah Nat. Adv. Coun., 2001-, Merit of Honor award U. Utah Alumni Assn., 2001; fellow Am. Gen. Contractors, Salt Lake City, 1960. Mem.: ASCE, Harvard U. Bus. Sch. Club (pres. 1970—72), U. Utah Alumni Assn. (bd. dirs. 1989—92), U. Utah Crimson Club (bd. dirs. 1996—99), The Country Club (bd. dirs., v.p. 1998-2001), Rotary (pres. 1998—99, v.p. Club 24 1990-91, chmn. election com. 1980-81, vice chmn. and chmn. membership com. 1988-90, Salt Lake Rotary Club Found. bd. dirs. 2000-, 1st v.p. 1997-98), Tau Beta Pi, Chi Epsilon, Phi Eta Sigma, Pi Kappa Alpha (internat. pres. 1972-74, trustee endowment fund 1974-80, Outstanding Alumnus 1967, 72, mem. Hall of Fame 1995). Avocations: fly fishing, golf, foreign travel. Home: 2689 Comanche Dr Salt Lake City UT 84108-2846 Office: AAA Engring & Drafting Inc PO Box 58171 Salt Lake City UT 84158-0171 Office Phone: 801-583-0311. E-mail: ross@uofu.net.

ANDERSON, CHESTER GRANT, language educator; b. River Falls, Wis., Dec. 8, 1923; s. C.A. Chester and Inga Amelia (Grant) A.; m. Carole Nygard, Apr. 23, 1945; children: Stephen, Mark, Jonathan. Student, St. Olaf Coll., 1941-43; MA, U. Chgo., 1948; PhD, Columbia U., 1962. Asst. prof. English Creighton U., Omaha, 1948-50, asst. prof., 1954-57, Fordham U., N.Y.C., 1951-52; dir. State Soc. Services, AICPAs, 1952-54; assoc. prof. Western Conn. State U., 1957-63; asst. prof. Columbia U., 1963-68; prof. English U. Minn., Mpls., 1963-96, prof. emeritus, 1996—; Fulbright prof. Helsinki (Finland) U., 1963-64. Semester-at-Sea prof., 1987; W.B. Yeats Internat. Summer Sch. prof., Sligo, Ireland, 1987; vis. prof. Odense U., Denmark, 1977-78, Curtin U., Australia, 1989. Author: James Joyce and His World, 1967, translation in Portugese and Italian, 1989, Spanish, 1990, Chinese, 1999, Critical Edit. of James Joyce's A Portrait of the Artist, 1968, corrected 1992, Growing Up in Minnesota, 1976. Ensign AC, USNR, 1943-45. Mem. MLA, MLA Helsinki, Acad. Am. Poets, James Joyce Found. Home: 660 S Sandlake Ct Mount Dora FL 32757-6085 E-mail: chestergan@aol.com.

ANDERSON, CHRISTINE MARLENE, software engineer; b. Washington, D.C., Nov. 19, 1947; 2 children. BS in Math., U. Md., 1969. Mathematician Naval Oceanographic Office, Suitland, Md., 1969-71; sr. analyst, fgn.

tech. divsn. Planning Rsch. Corp., Ohio, 1971-72; computer scientist USAF Avionics Lab., Wright-Patterson Air Force Base, Dayton, Ohio, 1971-74; sr. analyst USAF C3 Ctr., Cheyenne Mountain, Colorado Springs, Colo., 1974-76; chief computer tech. section USAF Wright Lab./Armament Directorate, Eglin Air Force Base, Fla., 1982-92; ADA 9X project mgr. Office Sec. Defense, 1987-94; chief software tech. br. Phillips Lab., Kirtland Air Force Base, N.Mex., 1992-93, chief, space soperations and simulation divsn.oftware rsch. ctr., 1993-96, dir. space and missiles tech. directorate, 1996; mem. sr. exec. svcs., dir. space vehicles directorate Phillips Lab., Kirtland Air Force Base, Air Force Rsch. Lab., N.Mex., 1996—. Co-chmn. on Ada computer programming lang. Am. Nat. Standards Inst., 1989—; editor Ada standard Internat. Standards Orgn., 1991—. Co-author: Aerospace Software Engineering, 1991; contbr. articles to profl. jours. Recipient Engr. of the Year USAF Armament Lab., 1989, Software Engring. award Am. Inst. Aeronautics, 1991, Program Mgr. of the Year award USAF Armament Lab., 1992, Sec. of Defense medal for Meritorious Civilian Svc., 1996. Fellow AIAA (chair software systems tech. com. 1987-89, bd. dirs. 1989—, Aerospace Software Engring. award 1991).

ANDERSON, CHRISTOPHER JAMES, lawyer; b. Chgo., Nov. 26, 1950; s. James M. and Margaret E. (Anderson) A.; m. Lyn R. Buckley, Jan. 3, 1976; children: Vaughn Buckley, Weston Buckley. BA, Grinnell Coll., 1972; JD with highest distinction, U. Iowa, 1975. Bar: Mo. 1975. From assoc. to ptnr. Armstrong Teasdale LLP, Kansas City, Mo., 1975—. Mem. ABA, Mo. Bar Assn., Kans. City Bar Assn., Lawyers Assn. Kansas City, Estate Planning Soc. Office: Armstrong Teasdale, et al 2345 Grand Blvd Ste 2000 Kansas City MO 64108-2617 Office Phone: 816-221-3420. E-mail: canderso@armstrongteasdale.com.

ANDERSON, CLARENCE AXEL FREDERICK, retired mechanical engineer; b. Muskegon, Mich., Dec. 14, 1909; s. Axel Robert and Anna Victoria (Wikman) A.; m. Frances K. Swem, Apr. 9, 1934; children: Robert Curtis, Clarelyn Christine Anderson Schmelling, Stanley Herbert. Student, Muskegon Jr. Coll., 1929, Internat. Corr. Schs., 1934. With Shaw-Walker Co., Muskegon, Mich., 1928-78, mech. engr., 1940-65, project engr., 1965-70, chief engr., 1970-78, ret., 1978. Mem. Forest Park Covenant Ch., 1953—, Christian edn. bd. Forest Park Covenant Ch., 1959-61, 67-73, usher, 1953-86, trustee, 1985, 86, chmn. bd. trustees 1986; co-chmn. Jackson Hill Oldtimers Reunion, 1982, 83, 85. Mem. Holland (Mich.) Beagle Club (life, pres. 1966-96). Home: 5757 Sternberg Rd Fruitport MI 49415-9740

ANDERSON, CLARENCE GLEN, dean; b. Galahad, Alta., Can., Nov. 20, 1955; arrived in U.S., 1993; s. Andrew Anselm and Marilyn Clarissa Anderson; m. Judy Pearlene Newell, June 4, 1978; children: Cordel, Talea. BA, Walla Walla Coll.; PhD, U. Alta., Edmonton, 1996. Dean Walla Walla Coll., College Place, Wash., 1993—. Office: Walla Walla Coll 204 S College Ave College Place WA 99324 Office Phone: 509-527-2368. Business E-Mail: andecl@wwc.edu.

ANDERSON, CLAUDIA SMITH, lawyer; b. Peoria, Ill., Mar. 21, 1953; d. Lester Berry and June Edda (Kopal) Smith; m. Curtis Allan Anderson, Aug. 26, 1972; children: Breda Thorn, Celia Allana, Keira June. Student, Stephens Coll., 1971-72; BS in Elem. Edn., Rockford Coll., 1976; JD cum laude, Gonzaga U., 1979. Bar: Ill. 1979, U.S. Dist. Ct. (cen. dist.) Ill. 1979. Assoc. Acton, Acton, Meyer & Smith, Danville, Ill., 1979-83; ptnr. Acton, Meyer, Smith, Miller & Anderson, Danville, 1984-86, Anderson & Anderson, 1986-99. Apptd. mem. Danville Plan Commn., 1984—, judge Ill. Cir. Ct., 1998—; bd. dirs. YWCA, Danville, 1984—; adv. bd. dirs. St. Elizabeth Hosp., 1987—. Recipient Am. Jurisprudence award, 1979. Mem. AAUW (life), Ill. Bar Assn., Vermilion County Bar Assn. (pub. relations chmn. 1984—), Assn. Trial Lawyers Am., Ill. Trial Lawyers Assn., Danville C. of C. (bd. dirs. 1985—, v.p. 1988—), DAR. Republican. Roman Catholic. Club: Executive (Danville) (pres. 1981-82). Office: Vermilion County Court House 7N Vermilion St Danville IL 61832

ANDERSON, CRAIG ALLEN, retired art educator, artist; b. Chgo., July 28, 1947; s. Elmer Albert and Roseanne Marie (Werner) A.; m. Mary Susan Scarnato, Apr. 23, 1971. BFA, Bradley U., 1970; MA in Art Edn., U. Ill., 1972; MFA, No. Ill. U., 1978. Cert. art specialist Ill. State Bd. Certification. Tchr., rsch. asst. U. Ill., Champaign, 1970-72; art tchr. Oliver W. Holmes Jr. H.S., Wheeling, Ill., 1972; art instr. Countryside Art Ctr., Arlington Heights, Ill., 1972-74, Harper Coll., Palatine, Ill., 1975-80; art tchr. Palatine H.S., 1972—2003, chmn. dept. art, 1996—2003, dist. art chair, 2000—03. Cons. Ill. Art Coun., Harvey, Ill., 1990; guest lectr. U. Ill. Commencement, Champaign, 1993, Temple U., 1985; mem. adv. bd. Masters program Sch. Art Inst. Chgo., 2000; mem. steering com. Chgo. Artists' Month, Chgo. Cultural ctr., 2001-03. One person shows include Gilman Galleries, Chgo., 1978-85, Heuser Art Ctr., 1989, 100 Paintings/100 Drawings Project, Chgo., 2004-05; exhibited in group shows at Abstract Chgo., 1993, Klein Art Gallery, 1993, 98, New Sch., N.Y.C., 2000. Co-dir. NAB Gallery, Chgo., 1977—; guest curator Gallery 400, Chgo., 1994, Wooden Gallery, Chgo., 1989; cultural exch. NAB Gallery Palais des Expo, Nice, France, 1987, NAB Gallery Diewand Gallery, Hamburg, Germany, 1983. Recipient Binney & Smith Inc. Tchrs. Portfolio award Nat. Scholastic Art awards, Washington, 1995, Art in Architecture award State of Ill., 1982, 88, Outstanding Art Tchr. award Nat. Scholastic Art, 2003, Outstanding Tchr. award U. Chgo., 1996; Pougialis fellow Columbia Coll., 1990; named Ill. Painter, Ill. Arts Coun., 1980. Mem. Nat. Art Edn. Assn., Ill. Art Edn. Assn. (H.S. Art Tchr. of Yr. 1994, 2000), Palatine/Inverness Arts Coun. (pres. 2001-04), Chgo. Artists Coalition, Soc. Aesthetics, Soc. Rsch. in Art Edn., Internat. Assn. Emirical Aesthetics. Avocation: volunteering for arts advocacy organizations. Home: 108 N Oak St Palatine IL 60067-5229 Office: 1117 W Lake St Chicago IL 60607 Office Phone: 312-738-1620. Business E-Mail: craig@craigaanderson.com.

ANDERSON, CURTIS THORWALD, II, military officer; b. Ft. Bragg, N.C., Jan. 11, 1969; s. Curtis Thorwald, Sr. and Wanda Lee Anderson; m. Faye Renee Ide, Aug. 7, 2004. BA in Polit. Sci., Bemidji State U., 1991. Advanced through grade to maj. U.S. Army, 1992; platoon leader C & B Batteries, 3-4 Air Def. Arty. Bn., 82nd Airborne Divsn., Ft. Bragg, 1992—94; battery exec. officer D Battery, 3-4 Air Def. Arty. Bn., 82nd Airborne Divsn., Ft. Bragg, 1994—95; asst. divsn. air def. officer 3-4 Air Def. Arty. Bn., 82nd Airborne Divsn., Ft. Bragg, 1995—96; bn. intelligence officer 5-5 Air Def. Arty. Bn., 2nd Inf. Divsn., Camp Stanley, Republic of Korea, 1996—97; co. comdr. Hdqs. Svc. Co., 313th M.I. Bn., 82nd Airborne Divsn., Ft. Bragg, 1998—2000; civil affairs team leader Joint Spl. Ops. Task Force North (Task Force Dagger), Herat, Afghanistan, 2001—02, C Co., 96th Civil Affairs Bn., Ft. Bragg, NC, 2002, theater ops. officer, 2002—03; civil affairs officer Joint Spl. Ops. Task Force West, Jordan, 2003; civil mil. ops. officer Coalition Land Component Command, Camp Doha, Kuwait, 2003—04, Mulit-National Forces Iraq, Baghdad, Iraq, 2004; civil affairs detachment comdr. E Co., 96th Civil Affairs Bn. (Airborne), Ft. Bragg, 2004—. Decorated Army Commendation medal with 2 oak leaf clusters, Master Parachutist badge, Can. Jump Wings, Meritorious Svc. medal, Bronze Star with 1 oak leaf cluster, Joint Svc. Commendation medal, German Jump Wings. Mem.: NRA (life), VFW (life), Civil Affairs Assn. (life), 82nd Airborne Divsn. Assn. (life), Assn. U.S. Army (life), Res. Officers Assn. (life), Future Farmers Am. Alumni (life), Am. Legion (life). Presbyterian. Avocations: hunting, softball. Home: 8440 Foxtrail Dr Fayetteville NC 28311 Office: E Co 96th Civil Affairs Bn Fort Bragg NC 28310 Office Phone: 910-907-3124. Personal E-mail: curtis.anderson@us.army.mil.

ANDERSON, DALE C., state agency professional, travel consultant; b. Grinnell, Iowa, Sept. 13, 1953; s. Clifford Simon and Wilma Grace (Grunhaupt) A. AAS in Indsl. Mktg., Des Moines Area C.C., Ankeny, Iowa, 1973; BA in Comm. and Theatre, Cen. Coll., 1978. Asst. buyer Ardan Wholesaler, Des Moines, 1979; office mgr. Moingona Girl Scout Coun., Des Moines, 1979-82, dir. adminstrv. svcs., 1982-88, property/purchasing dir., 1988-96; travel cons. Al Travel, Des Moines, 1989-90, First Tours, Des Moines, 1990-95; clk. typist Iowa State Dept. Transp., Des Moines, 1996-97; acctg. clk. II Iowa Dept. Revenue and Fin., Des Moines, 1997-98; acct./auditor 1 Iowa Dept. Corrections, Des Moines, 1998—2003, acct. 2, 2003—. Chmn. Des Moines Purchasing Agts., 2004—; camp visitor for camp accreditation State of Iowa, 1990—99. Campaign co-chmn. Kellogg (Iowa) Cmty. Chest, 1983-85, pub. rels. chmn., 1982; leader local club Jasper County 4-H, Kellogg, 1971-76, state leadership conf. del., 1971, nat. citizenship del., Washington, 1971, instr. county officers tng. sch. Jasper County, 1970-71, Jasper County v.p., 1970, state conv. del., Ames, Iowa, 1970, state counselor Des Moines Area 4-H, Madrid, Iowa, 1970; local club pres. Kellogg Club 4-H, 1970-71. Recipient State Leadership award Jasper County 4-H, 1970, named Outstanding 4-H'er of Yr., 1971; named Kellogg's Outstanding Citizen, 1983. Mem. Am. Camping Assn. (stds. chair for camp accreditation Iowa chpt. 1992-95, state of Iowa sec. 1996), Am. Camping Assn. (stds. camp accreditation com. Iowa chpt. 1996-99), Iowa State Grange (lectr. 1983-85, 91-93, state youth com. 1981-82, Iowa state youth rep. 1976), Richland Grange (state del. 1980, 83, sec. 1980-84, steward 1970-73, 77-79, overseer 1973-77, youth chmn. 1973, 75-76). United Methodist. Avocations: collecting horse figures, gardening, community service work, travel. Office: 686 Highway 224 S Kellogg IA 50135-8579

ANDERSON, DARRELL EDWARD, psychologist, educator; b. Coleridge, Nebr., May 2, 1932; s. Roy Blenton and Ruby Grace (Cisney) A.; m. Violeta Salazar, Sept. 3, 1951; children: Robert, James, Timothy. AB, York Coll., 1953; PhD, U. Nebr., 1958. Counselor, asst. prof. U. Nebr., Lincoln, 1957-59; asst. prof. psychology Wittenberg U., Springfield, Ohio, 1959-61; chief psychologist Weld County Mental Health Ctr., Greeley, Colo., 1961-62; asst. prof. U. No. Colo., Greeley, 1962-66, assoc. prof., 1966-70, prof., 1970-77, chmn. dept. psychology, 1972-77; prof. counselor edn. U. N.Mex., Albuquerque, 1977-87, chmn. dept., 1977-85, prof. counseling and family studies, 1987-92, prof. emeritus, 1992—. Cons. psychologist Dulce (N.Mex.) Pub. Schs., 1984-85. Contbr. articles to profl. jours. Mem. APA, N.Mex. Psychol. Assn. Democrat. Avocation: golf. Home: 4 Latir Ct Santa Fe NM 87508

ANDERSON, DAVID ALLEN, military officer, educator; b. Springfield, Minn., Aug. 24, 1960; s. Allen John and Donna Marie Anderson; m. Julia Anne Campbell, Feb. 23, 1984; children: Jennifer Blair children: David Allen, Ashley Elizabeth, Lauren Kate. BS in Geography, U. Wis., River Falls, 1983; MA in Bus. Adminstrn and Mgmt., Webster U., St. Louis, 1987; DBA, Alliant Internat. U., San Diego, 1993. Commd. 2d. lt., 1983; advanced through grades to lt. col., 2000; commdg. officer, combat svc. support detachment-21 Marine Corps Air Sta., Cherry Point, NC, 1995—98; econs. prof. US Naval Acad., Annapolis, Md., 1998—2001; head logistics, strategic force planning Supreme Hdqs. Allied Powers Europe, NATO, Mons, Belgium, 2001—04; logistics, ops. and plans officer II Marine Expeditionary Force, USMC, Camp Lejeune, NC, 2004—; assoc. prof. Dept. Jt. Multinational Ops., Army Command and Gen. Staff Coll., Fort Leavenworth, Kans., 2005—. Adj. prof. bus. Campbell U., Buies Creek, NC, 1994—98; adj. prof. bus., mgmt. Pk. U., Parkville, Mo., 1995—98; adj. prof. bus. Webster U., St. Louis, 1998. Contbr. articles marine and naval publs. Conductor fin. planning seminars USMC, Camp Lejeune, 1987—; vol. coord. Adopt a Sch. Program, NC, Havelock, 1995—98; tchg. vol. West Annapolis Elem., 1998—2001; coach, track and field boys and girls secondary sch. teams Supreme Hdqs. Allied Powers Europe, Am. H.S., Mons, 2004; officer rep. men's track and field team U.S. Naval Acad., Annapolis, 1998—2001. Decorated Naval Commendation medal USMC, Meritorious Svc. medal (Gold Star in Lieu of fourth award), Def. Meritorious Svc. medal Supreme Hdqs. Allied Powers Europe, NATO; recipient tchg. and rsch. excellence award, U.S. Naval Acad., 2001. Mem.: Mil. Officers Assn. of Am., Marine Corps Assn. Republican. Roman Catholic. Avocations: fishing, running, antique stained glass restoration, softball, writing. Office Phone: 910-451-8258. Personal E-mail: profusmc@hotmail.com.

ANDERSON, DAVID ARNOLD, law educator; b. 1939; AB, Harvard U., 1962; JD, U. Tex., 1971. Bar: Tex. 1972. Reporter, bur. chief United Press Internat., Austin, Tex., 1963-69; chief counsel Tex. Civil Jud. Coun., Austin, 1972; asst. prof. law U. Tex., Austin, 1972-75, prof., 1975-78, Thompson and Knight Centennial prof., 1987—2003, Fred and Emily Wulff Centennial chair in law, 2005—. Vis. Lee prof. William and Mary U., 1983, Queen Mary Coll. U. London, 1988, 92; vis. scholar Trinity Coll. Cambridge U., 1988; vis. prof. U. New South Wales, 1998, Univ. Coll. London, 2003. Fellow Gannett Ctr. Media Studies. Mem. Assn. Am. Law Schs. (mass communications law sect.), Order of Coif, Phi Delta Phi. Office: U Tex Sch Law 727 Dean Keeton St Austin TX 78705-3224

ANDERSON, DAVID BOWEN, lawyer; b. Seattle, Sept. 19, 1948; s. Gordon Browne and Elizabeth Josephine (Bowen) A.; m. Laura Ann Jorgensen, May 23, 1975; children: Elizabeth Christine, Christina Louise. BA with great distinction, Stanford U., 1970; JD, U. Mich., 1974; MBA, Western Wash. U., 1982. Bar: Wash. 1974, Alaska 2000, Oreg. 2002, U.S. Dist. Ct. (we. dist.) Wash. 1974. Clk. Ctr. for Law and Social Policy, Washington, 1973; assoc. Bogle & Gates, Seattle, 1974-77; ptnr. Anderson, Connell & Murphy, Bellingham, Wash., 1977—; pres. San Juan Tug & Barge Co., 1979-85. Arbitrator Whatcom County, Am. Arbitration Assn.; instr. Pacific N.W. Admiralty Law Inst., Seattle, 1983, Nat. Fishery Law Symposium, Seattle, 1984; lectr. constnl. law Western Wash. U., 1996. Mem. adv. com. Bellingham Sch. Bd., 1981-82, Bellingham Vocat. Tech. Inst., 1986; mem. Bellingham Pub. Sch. Found. Bd., 1992, pres., 1992-93; bd. dirs. Interfaith Coalition, 1999-2002; mem. exec. com. Primorsky-Washington Russian Rule of Law Partnership. Mem. ATLA, ABA, Wash. State Bar Assn. (spl. dist. counsel, rules of profl. practice com.), Alaska Bar Assn., Oreg. State Bar, Whatcom County Bar Assn. (pres. 1986), Maritime Law Assn. U.S. (proctor), Wash. Atheltic Club (Seattle), Bellingham Rotary Club. Presbyterian. Home: 500 16th St Bellingham WA 98225-6315 Office: Anderson Connell & Murphy 1501 Eldridge Ave Bellingham WA 98225-2801 E-mail: boatlaw@boatlaw.com.

ANDERSON, DAVID BOYD, lawyer, metal products executive; b. Moorhead, Minn., Mar. 10, 1942; children: Kimberly, Erik, Jonathan, Caroline J. BA, U. Minn., 1964, JD, 1967; LLM, DePaul U., 1983. Bar: Minn. 1967, Ill. 1978. Labor rels. supr. Continental Can Co., NYC, 1970—72; asst. gen. counsel Am. Hosp. Supply Co., Evanston, Ill., 1972—83; v.p. planning and gen. counsel Inland Steel Industries, Inc., Chgo., 1983—2001; active adv. com. LISC, planning com. Northwestern U. Corp. Counsel Inst. Capt. USAR, 1967—70. Mem.: Minn. Bar Assn., Ill. Bar Assn., ABA. Office: 16th Fl 30 W Monroe St Fl 16 Chicago IL 60603-2495

ANDERSON, DAVID CHARLES, librarian, writer; b. Oakland, Calif., Apr. 27, 1931; s. Charles Emil Sr. and Alice P. (Smith) A.; m. Jean Lynn Hess, June 8, 1957; children: Alan R., David Christian, Gregory Leon, Bradley Ross, Lisa Louise. BA in Liberal Arts, U. Calif., Berkeley, 1952, BLS, 1953. Libr. State Office of Local Planning, Sacramento, 1957-62, Calif. State Dept. of Fin., Sacramento, 1960-62; serials cataloger gen. libr. U. Calif., Davis, 1962-69, head health scis. cataloging pool, 1969-71, head tech. svcs. Carlson Health Sci. Libr., 1971-91, part-time info. specialist Ctr. Animal Alternatives Sch. Vet. Medicine, 1992-98; owner Rocky Dell Resources, 1989—. Editor: Veterinary Serials, A Union List, 2d edit., 1988, Humans and Other Species (quar. resource jour. on the human-animal relationship), 1990-1999; author poetry; author Guide To Pet Loss Resources, 3d edit., 2005; contbr. articles to profl. jours. Served with U.S. Army, 1953-56. Mem. Med. Libr. Assn. (chair vet. med. librs. sect. 1988-89, chair union list com. 1981-95, chair pub. and info. industries rels. com. 1984-85), No. Calif. Med. Libr. Group, Spl. Librs. Assn. E-mail: rockydell@digitalpath.net.

ANDERSON, DAVID DANIEL, retired humanities educator, writer, editor; b. Lorain, Ohio, June 8, 1924; s. David and Nora Marie (Foster) A.; m. Patricia Ann Rittenhour, Feb. 1, 1953. BS, Bowling Green State U., 1951, MA, 1952, DLitt, 2005; PhD, Mich. State U., 1960; DLitt, Wittenberg U., 1986. From instr. to prof. dept. Am. thought and lang. to univ. disting. prof. Mich. State U., East Lansing, 1957-90; lectr. Am. Mus., Bath, Eng., 1980; editor U. Coll. Quar., 1971-80; Fulbright prof. U. Karachi, Pakistan, 1963-64. Am. del. to Internat. Fedn. Modern Langs. and Lit., 1969-93, Internat. Congress Orientalists, 1971-79, European Am. Studies Assn., 1994. Author: Louis Bromfield, 1964, Critical Studies in American Literature, 1964, Sherwood Anderson's Winesburg, Ohio, 1967, Sherwood Anderson, 1968 (Book Manuscript award, 1961), Brand Whitlock, 1968, Abraham Lincoln, 1970, Suggestions for the Instructor, 1970, Robert Ingersoll, 1972, Woodrow Wilison, 1978, Igantius Donnelly, 1980, William Jennings Bryan, 1981, Route Two, Titus, Ohio, 1993, The Path in the Shadow, 1998, Command Performances, 2003, Ohio in Myth, Memory, and Imagination, 2004, Ohio in Myth, Memory and Imagination, 2004, Ohio in Fact and Fiction, 2005; editor: The Black Experience, 1969, The Literary Works of Abraham Lincoln, 1970, Sunshine and Smoke: American Writers and the American Environment, 1971; editor: (with others) The Dark and Tangled Path, 1971; editor: Mid America, 1974—, 27th edit., 2000, Sherwood Anderson: Dimensions of His Literary Art, 1976, Sherwood Anderson: The Writer at His Craft, 1979, Critical Essays on Sherwood Anderson, 1981, Michigan: A State Anthology, 1983, Myth, Memory and the American Earth: The Durability of Raintree County, 1998, Midwestern Miscellany, 1974—, Lieutenant William E. Slight and the 102nd Regiment, U.S. Colonial Infantry, in the Civil War, 2003, numerous articles, essays, short stories, poems. Served with USN, 1942-45; with AUS, 1952-53. Decorated Silver Star, Purple Heart; recipient Disting. Alumnus award Bowling Green State U., 1976, Disting. Faculty award Mich. State U., 1974, Disting. Faculty award Mich. Assn. Governing Bds., 1988, Disting Research award Mich. State U., 1988. Mem. ASA, AAUP, MLA, Popular Culture Assn., Soc. Study Midwestern Lit. (founder, exec. sec., Disting. Service award 1982), Assn. Gen. and Liberal Edn. Am. Assn. Advancement Humanities, Internat. Assn. U. Profs. English, Univ. Club. Home: 6555 Lansdown Dr Dimondale MI 48821-9428 Office: Mich State U Dept Am Thought and Lang East Lansing MI 48824

ANDERSON, DAVID J., corporate financial executive; Grad., Ind. U., 1971; MBA, U. Chgo., 1977. Sr. fin. positions Kraft, Inc., Quaker Oats Co.; sr. v.p., chief fin. officer RJR Nabisco, Newport News Shipbuilding, ITT Industries, mem. exec. com.; sr. v.p., chief fin. officer Honeywell Internat. Inc., Morristown, NJ, 2003—. Office: Honeywell Inernat Inc 101 Columbia Rd Morristown NJ 07962

ANDERSON, DAVID J., manufacturing executive; Pres., dir., CEO Sauer-Danfoss, Ames, Iowa. Office: Sauer-Danfoss Ste 270 250 Parkway Dr Lincolnshire IL 60069 Office Phone: 515-239-6000. Office Fax: 515-239-6318.*

ANDERSON, DAVID LAWRENCE, lawyer; b. Balt., Oct. 29, 1948; s. Robert L. and Ruth (Hahn) A. BS, Towson U., 1970; JD, U. Md., 1973. Bar: Md. 1973, U.S. Dist. Ct. Md. 1976, D.C. 1979, U.S. Dist. Ct. D.C. 1979, U.S. Ct. Appeals (D.C. cir.) 1976. Asst. revisor Gov.'s Commn. to Revise Md. Annotated Code, Annapolis, Md., 1973-74; counsel Gov.'s Task Force on Campaign Financing, Annapolis, Md., 1974-75; atty. Fed. Election Commn., Washington, 1975-77, Federal Energy Adminstrn., Washington, 1977; asst. chief counsel, trial atty. U.S. Dept. Energy, Washington, 1977-85; sr. trial atty., leader litigation team environ. enforcement sect., environment and natural resources div. U.S. Dept. Justice, Washington, 1986-90; lead counsel for Love Canal, Rocky Mountain Arsenal and New Bedford Harbor Superfund cases; sr. assoc. Shea & Gould, Washington, 1990-91, Arent Fox Kintner Plotkin & Kahn, Washington, 1992-93; ptnr. O'Connor & Hannan, Washington, 1993-95; mgr. regulatory and legis. svcs. group Waste Policy Inst., Arlington, 1995-99; sr. environ. counsel, sr. project mgr. Parsons, Fairfax, Va., 1999—. Adj. prof. polit. sci. Towson State U., 1971-73; adj. prof. legal rsch. and writing Am. U., 1985-87, 93-94. Recipient Outstanding Performance award Dept. Energy, 1981, medal and award Dept. Energy, 1983, spl. commendation Dept. Justice, 1989. Mem. ABA (environment, energy and resources law sect.), D.C. Bar Assn., Environ. Law Inst. Home: 25299 Diligence Ct Aldie VA 20105 Office: Parsons 10521 Rosehaven St Fairfax VA 22030-2839 E-mail: david.l.anderson@parsons.com.

ANDERSON, DAVID LOUIS, academic administrator, history professor; b. Pampa, Tex., Aug. 10, 1946; s. Benjamin Louis and Ruby Lucille (Baird) A.; m. Helen Esther Fleischer, June 9, 1973; 1 child, Hope Mindy. BA cum laude, Rice U., Houston, 1968; MA, U. Va., 1971, PhD, 1974. Vis. asst. prof. of history U. Mont., Missoula, 1974-75, 76-77, Tex. Tech. U., Lubbock, 1975-76; asst. prof. of history Sam Houston State U., Huntsville, Tex., 1977-80; lectr. in history Calif. Poly. State U., San Luis Obispo, 1980-81; asst. prof. history U. Indpls., 1981-84, assoc. prof. history, 1984-90, prof. history, 1990—2004, dept. chair, 1988-2000, assoc. dean arts and scis., 1999—2001, dean arts and scis., 2001—04; dean univ. studies and programs Calif. State U. Monterey Bay, Seaside, Calif., 2004—. Author: (book) Imperialism and Idealism, 1985, Trapped By Success: The Eisenhower Administration and Vietnam, 1991 (Robert H. Ferrell Book prize Soc. for Historians of American Fgn. Rels. 1992), Shadow on the White House: Presidents and the Vietnam War, 1993, Facing My Lai, 1998, The Human Tradition in the Vietnam Era, 2000, The Columbia Guide to the Vietnam War, 2002 (Best of Best prize Am. Lib. Assn.), The Human Tradition in America Since 1945, 2003, The Vietnam War, 2005. Sgt. U.S. Army, 1968—70. Named Ind. Prof. of the Yr. Coun. for Advancement and Support of Edn., 1991. Mem. Am. Hist. Assn., Orgn. Am. Historians, Soc. for Historians of Am. Fgn. Rels. (coun. mem. 1995-97, v.p. 2004, pres. 2005). Avocation: magic. Office: Calif State U Monterey Bay 100 Campus Ctr Bldg 58 Seaside CA 93955-8001 Office Phone: 831-582-3818. Business E-Mail: david_anderson@csumb.edu.

ANDERSON, DAVID MARK, research scientist; b. LaCrosse, Wis., Dec. 29, 1954; s. Warren Sanford and Dorothy Ann Anderson; m. Katarina Anderson, Dec. 28, 1990; children: Max David, Benjamin Luke. BS in math, U. Minn., 1979, MS in math, 1982, PhD in chem. engring., 1986. Post doctoral rschr. U. Mass. at Amherst, Polymer Sci., 1986—87; guest rschr. U. Lund, Phys. Chemistry, Lund, Sweden, 1987—91; asst. prof. SUNY Buffalo, Bio Materials, 1991—96; v.p. sci. affairs Select Release, LLC, Richmond, Va., 1996—99; founder, v.p. sci. affairs Lyotropic Therapeutics, Ashland, Va., 1999—. Contbr. articles various profl. jours. Finalist Innovation Cup award, Dagens Industries, 1988, Niagara Frontier Inventor of the Yr. award, Consortium, 1993. Mem.: Am. Chem. Soc., Am. Assn. Pharm. Sci., Tau Beta Pi. Achievements include patents for controlled pore nanoporous materials; coated liquid crystalline microparticles (LyoCells). Avocations: guitar, baseball, superstring theory, compose music. Office: Lyotropic Therapeutics Inc 10487 Lakeridge Pkwy Ste 400 Ashland VA 23005 Office Phone: 804-550-1280. Business E-Mail: danderson@lyotropics.com.

ANDERSON, DAVID MARTIN, environmental engineer, consultant; b. Boston, July 19, 1930; s. Martin Jens and Dorothy (Finnin) A.; m. Marjorie Gilbert, July 19, 1958; children: David, Michael, Anne, Stephen. Grad., Boston Latin Sch., 1948; BS, Northeastern U., 1953; SM, Harvard U., 1955, PhD, 1958. Registered profl. engr., Pa., diplomate, Am. Acad. Environ. Engrs., cert. Am. Bd. Indsl. Hygiene. Rsch. fellow Harvard Sch. Pub. Health, 1953-58; pub. health engr. USPHS, Cin., 1958-60; indsl. health engr. Bethlehem Steel Corp. (Pa.), 1960-67, asst. mgr. environ. quality control, 1967-71, mgr., 1971-80, corp. dir. environ. affairs, 1980-84, dir. environ. and govtl. affairs, 1984-87, gen. mgr. environ. affairs, 1987-94, cons. environ. health, 1994—. Vis. lectr. Pa. State U., 1966-71, Harvard U., 1969-81; chmn. coun. tech. advisers Pa. Dept. Health, 1964-70, N.Y. Dept. Environ. Conservation, 1974-75; co-chmn. OSHA/Am. Iron and Steel Inst. Task Force on coke oven emission stds., 1975-76; mem. Pa. Gov.'s Task Force on Occupl. Health and Safety, 1975-76; mem. com. on biol. effects of atmospheric pollutants NAS, 1971-74; mem. nat. air quality criteria adv. com. EPA, 1971-76; mem. Sec. Health, Edn. and Welfare Coal Mine Health Rsch. Adv. Coun., 1972-76; mem. U.S. Dept. Commerce Adv. Com. on Indsl. Innovation, 1978-79, mem. adv. com. Ctr. for Risk Analysis Harvard U., 1989-94; mem. negotiated rulemaking com. U.S. EPA, 1992-93. Contbr. articles to profl. jours. Mem. Am. Iron and Steel Inst. (com. on environ. 1971-94, chmn. 1978-80, 87-89), Internat. Iron and Steel Inst. (com. on environ. 1980-94), Am. Chem. Soc., Am. Indsl. Hygiene Assn. (dir. 1968-71), Air and Waste

Mgmt. Assn. (dir. 1971-74), Sigma Xi, Delta Omega. Achievements include research in and critical evaluation of the epidemiology and control of dust disease. Home and Office: 1037 Westgate Cir Bethlehem PA 18017-3637 E-mail: DMAenvhealth@aol.com.

ANDERSON, DAVID POOLE, sportswriter; b. Troy, N.Y., May 6, 1929; s. Robert P. and Josephine (David) A.; m. Maureen Ann Young, Oct. 24, 1953; children: Stephen, Mark, Mary Jo, Jean Marie. BA, Holy Cross Coll., 1951. Sports writer Bklyn. Eagle, 1951-55, New York Jour.-Am., 1955-66, New York Times, 1966—. Author: Countdown to Super Bowl, 1969; (with Ray Robinson) Sugar Ray, 1970; (with Larry Csonka and Jim Kiick) Always On The Run, 1973; Pancho Gonzalez, 1974; (with Frank Robinson) Frank: The First Year, 1976; Sports Of Our Times, 1979; The Yankees, 1979; (with John Madden) Hey, Wait a Minute, I Wrote a Book, 1984; (with John Madden) The Story of Football, 1985; One Knee Equals Two Feet, 1986; (with John Madden) One Size Doesn't Fit All, 1988; The Story of Basketball, 1988; In The Corner, 1991; Pennant Races, 1994; The Story of the Olympics, 1996; (with John Madden) All Madden, 1996; The Story of Golf, 1998; editor: The Red Smith Reader, 1981. Named to Nat. Sportscasters and Sportswriters Assn. Hall of Fame, 1990, N.Y. Sports Mus. and Hall of Fame, 1991; recipient Pulitzer prize for disting. commentary, 1981, Red Smith award, 1994, PGA of Am. Lifetime Achievement award in journalism, 1998, McCann Meml. award for disting. pro football reporting, Pro Football Hall of Fame, 1998, William D. Richardson award, Golf Writers Assn. of Am., 2003, Peter Kihss award, Soc. of Silurians, 2003. Office: NY Times 229 W 43rd St New York NY 10036-3959

ANDERSON, DAVID TREVOR, law educator; b. Winnipeg, Man., Can., Oct. 25, 1938; s. David and Mary (Irwin) A. BA, U. Man., 1959; BA in Jurisprudence, U. Oxford (Eng.), 1961, B in Civil Law, 1962. Asst. prof. law U. Alta., Edmonton, Can., 1962-66, assoc. prof., 1966-69, prof., 1969-71; prof. law U. Man., Winnipeg, 1971—, assoc. dean faculty of law, 1972-77, dean, 1984-89. Bd. dirs. Alta. Inst. Law Rsch. and Reform, Edmonton, 1968-71; mem. Man. Law Reform Commn., Winnipeg, 1981-84, Man. Pub. Utilities Bd., 1988-2000. Named Queen's Counsel, Province of Man., 1985; Rhodes scholar, 1959. Mem. Law Soc. Man. (dir. edn. 1977-80, bencher 1984-89), Can. Bar Assn. Presbyterian. Office: U Man Faculty of Law Robson Hall Winnipeg MB Canada R3T 2N2

ANDERSON, DAVID WAYNE, federal agency administrator; married. MPA, Harvard U., 1986. Chmn., CEO Famous Dave's of Am., Inc., Eden Prairie, Minn., 1994—2003, chmn. emeritus, 2003—; asst. sec. Bur. Indian Affairs US Dept. Interior, Washington, 2003—. Mem. National Task Force on Reservation Gaming, Bur. Indian Affairs, 1983, Am. Indian Edn. Found., 2003; mem. presdl. adv. coun. Tribal Colls. and Univs., 2001; founder LifeSkills Ctr. for Leadership, 2001. Named Emerging Entrepreneurof Yr., Ernst and Young, NASDAQ, USA Today, Restaurateur of Yr., Mpls.-St. Paul (Minn.) Mag., 1998, Olympic Torch Carrier, 2002. Office: US Dept Interior 1849 C St NW Rm 4160 Washington DC 20240

ANDERSON, DEAN WILLIAM, educational association administrator; b. Mpls., Aug. 28, 1946; s. Edward Marvin and Mabel (Gilland) A.; m. Elaine Heumann Gurian; children: Erik Wheeler, Matthew Edward. BA, Macalester Coll., 1968; MA, U. Calif.-Berkeley, 1970. Examiner Office Mgmt. and Budget, Washington, 1970-73; adminstrv. officer Smithsonian Instn., Washington, 1973-84, asst. sec. history and art, 1984-85, under sec., 1985-90; dep. dir. mgmt. and planning Woodrow Wilson Ctr., Washington, 1990—2001, acting dir., 1997-99; vis. lectr. Grad. Program Goteborg U., 2002—; ptnr. Interim Mus. Svcs. LLC, 2005—. Trustee Interlochen Ctr. for Arts. Recipient Robert Brooks award Smithsonian Instn., 1983; Minn. SPAN Assn. scholar, Israel, 1967; MacPherson Found. scholar, Mpls., 1967. Mem. Interlochen Alumni Orgn. (pres. 1994-98, nat. bd. dirs.), Phi Beta Kappa, Pi Sigma Alpha. Avocation: golf. E-mail: danderson@ix.netcom.com.

ANDERSON, DEBORAH GAIL COOK, secondary school educator, special education educator; b. San Antonio, Dec. 26, 1956; d. Clarence Edward Cook, Sr. and Dorothy Mae (Colvin) Phillips; m. Dwight Edward Anderson, June 22, 1980 (div. Sept. 1981). BS, Tex. Woman's U., 1979; MEd in Ednl. Psychology, Spl. Edn., U. Houston, 1989. Tchr. classroom, 1979—80; substitute tchr. Marshall Elem. Sch., Detroit, 1980—81; tchr. spl. edn. resource, cons. Ashford Elem. Sch. Houston Ind. Sch. Dist., 1981—95, tchr. spl. edn., program pre-sch. children with disabilities Ashford Primary Sch., 1996—. Tutor spl. edn., Houston, 1982—; tutor Denton Assn. Student Helpers, Tex., 1977; vol. behavior technician Behavior Studies Ctr. North Tex. State U., Denton, 1976—77; vol. Spl. Olympics, Denton, 1978, Lowry Hall, Denton, 1978. Mem. Young Women's Aux. Mt. Calvary Bapt. Ch., Denton, 1977—79, pres. Young Women's Aux., 1978—79, mem. usher bd. Young Women's Aux., 1977—79, youth worker, 1978—79; youth worker, outreach com., Christian debutante com. Sara Cir. Liberty Bapt. Ch., pres. Gen. Mission Sara Cir., 1991—92. Named Outstanding Young Educator, Ashford Elem. Sch., 1985, Tchr. of Yr., 1987; recipient Dedicated Christian Svc. and Christian Leadership award, Liberty Bapt. Ch., 1990—92, Loyal and Dedicated Svc. award, 1995, Faithful Cornerstone Plaque, Angel of Faith award, Dedicated Missionary Svc. and Labor award. Mem.: NAACP (named most prominent black woman Tex. Woman's U. chpt. 1979), NEA, Houston Coun. Edn., Houston Tchrs. Assn., Tex. State Tchrs. Assn., Nat. Assn. Black Social Workers, Assn. Childhood Edn. Internat., Coun. Exceptional Children, Mortar Bd., Delta Sigma Theta, Alpha Chi. Democrat. Home: 1919 S Kirkwood Rd Apt 249 Houston TX 77077-6233 Office: Ashford Primary Sch 1815 Shannon Valley Dr Houston TX 77077-4998 Office Phone: 281-368-2120.

ANDERSON, DON LYNN, geophysicist; b. Frederick, Md., Mar. 5, 1933; s. Richard Andrew and Minola (Phares) Anderson; m. Nancy Lois Ruth, Sept. 15, 1956; children: Lynn Ellen, Lee Weston. BS, Rensselaer Poly. Inst., 1955; MS, Calif. Inst. Tech., 1959, PhD, 1962; DSc (hon.), Rensselaer Poly. Inst., 2000. With Chevron Oil Co., Mont., Wyo., Calif., 1955—56; with Air Force Cambridge Research Center, Boston, 1956—58, Arctic Inst. N.Am., Boston, 1958; mem. faculty Calif. Inst. Tech., Pasadena, 1962—, assoc. prof. geophysics, 1964—68, prof., 1968—, dir. seismol. lab., 1967—89, Eleanor and John R. McMillan prof. of geophysics, 1990—. Prin. investigator Viking Mars Seismic Expt.; mem. various coms. NASA; chmn. geophysics rsch. forum NAS; chmn. Arthur L. Day award com. NSF, chmn. Geosci. adv. com., 1994; chmn. adv. bd. for Sch. of Earth Scis. Stanford U., 1995; mem. adv. com. Purdue U., U. Chgo., U. Tex., Stanford U., U. Calif. Berkeley, Carnegie Instn., Washington, U. Paris, Yale U., Rice U.; Consortium for High Pressure Rsch. U. Calif.-Riverside; co-founder Inc. Rsch. Insts. for Seismology. Assoc. editor Jour. Geophys. Rsch., 1965—67, Tectonophysics, 1974—77; editor: Physics of the Earth and Planetary Interiors, 1984—94. Recipient Exceptional Sci. Achievement award, NASA, 1977, Emil Wiechert medal, German Geophys. Soc., 1986, Crafoord prize, Royal Swedish Acad. Scis., 1998, Nat. medal of Sci., 1998; fellow Guggenheim, 1998, Sloan Found., 1965—67. Fellow: AAAS (pres. tectonophysics sect. 1971—72, chmn. Macelwane award com. 1975, mem. Bowie medal com. 1985, pres.-elect 1986—88, pres. 1988—90, chair 1994, James B. Macelwane award 1966, Bowie medal 1990), Geol. Soc. Am. (assoc. editor bull. 1971—, mem. Penrose medal com. 1989, mem. Arthur L. Day medal com. 1989—90, mem. long range planning com. 1990—, Arthur L. Day medal 1987), Am. Geophys. Union; mem.: NAS (chmh. seismology com. 1975, chmn. Geophysics Rsch. Forum 1984—86), Seismol. Soc. Am., Royal Astron. Soc. (Gold medal 1988), Am. Philos. Soc., Sigma Xi. Home: 669 Alameda St Altadena CA 91001-3001 Office: Calif Inst Tech Seismol Lab 252 21 Pasadena CA 91125-0001*

ANDERSON, DONALD BERNARD, oil industry executive; b. Chgo., Apr. 6, 1919; s. Hugo August and Hilda (Nelson) A.; m. Patricia Gaylord, 1945 (dec. 1978); m. Sarah Midgette, 1980. BS in Mech. Engring, Purdue U., 1942. Vice pres. Hondo Oil & Gas Co. (formerly Malco Refineries, Inc.), Roswell, N.Mex.; vice pres. Hondo Oil & Gas Co. and subs. corps., Roswell, N.Mex., 1946-63; pres. Anderson Oil Co., Roswell, 1963—, Cotter Corp., 1966-70, chmn. bd., 1966-74; founder, pres. Anderson Drilling Co., Denver, 1974—, pres., chmn. bd., 1977—. Curator fine arts, mem. acquisitions com. Roswell Mus. and Art Center, 1949-56, trustee, 1956-85, pres. bd., 1960-85, 87—, trustee, pres. 1987-90; bd. dirs. Sch. Am. Rsch., Santa Fe, chmn. bd., 1985-88, bd. dirs. 1989—; bd. dirs. Jargon Soc., Penland, N.C.; regent Ea. N.Mex. U., 1966-72; commr. Smithsonian Instn., Nat. Mus. Am. Art, 1980-88. Lt. USNR, 1942-46. Office: PO Box 1 Roswell NM 88202-0001

ANDERSON, DONALD GORDON MARCUS, mathematics professor; b. Sarnia, Ont, Can., Jan. 4, 1937; s. Gordon Lincoln and Jean Merritt (McNaughton) A. BS, U. Western Ont., 1959; A.M., Harvard, 1960, PhD, 1963. Lectr., research fellow Harvard, 1963-65, asst. prof. applied math., 1965-69, Gordon McKay prof. applied math., 1969—. Mem. AAAS, Soc. for Indsl. and Applied Math. Office: Maxwell Dworkin 137 33 Oxford St Cambridge MA 02138-2901

ANDERSON, DONALD H., gas industry executive; b. 1948; Grad., U. Colo., Boulder, 1970. Acct. Peat, Marwick, Mitchell Y Co., Denver, 1970—78, Western Crude Oil Inc., Denver, 1978—82; with Lantern Petroleum Corp., Denver, 1983—; chmn, pres., ceo Pan Energy, Houston; vice-cmn. & CEO TransMontaigne Inc., Denver, 1999—, pres., vice-chmn. & CEO, 2000—. Office: Trans Montaigne Inc 1670 Broadway Ste 3100 Denver CO 80217-5660*

ANDERSON, DONALD KENNEDY, JR., language educator; b. Evanston, Ill., Mar. 18, 1922; s. Donald Kennedy and Kathryn Marie (Shields) A.; m. Kathleen Elizabeth Hughes, Sept. 11, 1949; children: David J., Lawrence W. AB, Yale U., 1943; MA, Northwestern U., 1947; PhD, Duke U., 1957. Instr. Geneva Coll., Beaver Falls, Pa., 1947-49; from instr. to asst. prof. Rose Poly. Inst., Terre Haute, Ind., 1952-58; asst. prof., assoc. prof. Butler U., Indpls., 1958-65; assoc. prof. U. Mo., Columbia, 1965-67, prof. dept. English, 1967-92, prof. emeritus Columbia, 1992—, assoc. dean Grad. Sch. Columbia, 1970-74. Author: John Ford, 1972; editor: John Ford's Perkin Warbeck, 1965, John Ford's The Broken Heart, 1968, Concord in Discord, The Plays of John Ford, 1586-1986, 1987. Served to lt. (j.g.) USNR, 1943-46. Folger fellow, 1965; U. Mo. Summer Research fellow, 1966, 68, 76, 79, 84 Mem. MLA (midwest regional del. 1972-75), AAUP (sec.-treas. 1962-63) Democrat. Methodist. Home: Apt 224 1800 Riverside Dr Columbus OH 43212-1804

ANDERSON, DONALD MEREDITH, bank executive; b. Milan, Minn., Feb. 19, 1928; s. Meredith A. and Lydia (Helseth) A.; m. Christine Skorupa; 1 child, Karen. Student, St. Olaf Coll., Northfield, Minn., 1946-48; BA, U. Minn., 1948-50; MBA, Harvard U., 1952; postgrad. Grad. Banking Sch., U. Wis.-Madison, 1965-67. Factory rep. Congoleum-Nairn, Inc., 1953-56; stockbroker J.M. Dain & Co., Mpls., 1956-58; v.p. comml. lending and corr. banking Northwestern Nat. Bank of Mpls., 1958-69; v.p. lending Santa Barbara Nat. Bank, Calif., 1969-71; pres. Santa Barbara Bank & Trust, 1971-89, chmn., 1989—. Dir. Gen. Telephone Calif., 1976—, mem. audit com., 1982—; mem. regional adv. com. Comptroller of Currency, 1975-76 Bd. dirs. Blue Cross So. Calif., 1981—; bd. dirs. Mission council Boy Scouts Am., 1977—, v.p. 1977-80, pres. 1985; bd. dirs. Goleta Valley Hosp., 1978—, pres., 1979-80; mem. Industry Edn. Council, 1975—, chmn., 1984—; trustee U. Calif.-Santa Barbara, 1984—; mem. comdr.'s adv. bd. Vandenberg AFB, 1978—; mem. adv. bd. Vis. Nurses Assn., 1983—; past pres. bd. dirs. Trinity Lutheran Ch., United Way; bd. dirs. Santa Barbara Zoo, 1985— . Served to 1st lt. USAF, 1952-53 Mem. Calif. Bankers Assn. (dir. 1982—, chair comml. lending com. 1977), Santa Barbara C. of C. (v.p. 1979, dir. 1972, 78—, Western Ind. Bankers Assn. (pres. 1985, sec. 1983, dir. 1981—), Am. Bankers Assn. (bank investments com. 1976-79) Republican. Home: 485 Via Hierba Santa Barbara CA 93110-2214 Office: Santa Barbara Bank & Trust 1021 Anacapa St Santa Barbara CA 93101-2102

ANDERSON, DONALD MORGAN, entomologist, researcher; b. Washington, Dec. 27, 1930; s. John Kenneth and Alice Cornelia (Morgan) A. BA, Miami U., Oxford, Ohio, 1953; PhD, Cornell U.I, 1958. Grad. teaching asst. Cornell U., 1954-57; asst. prof. sci. SUNY-Buffalo, 1959-60, rsch. fellow, 1960; rsch. entomologist Dept. Agrl., Washington, 1960-90, rsch. collaborator, 1990—; rsch. assoc. Buffalo Mus. Sci., 1972—, Smithsonian Instn., 1978—. Contbr. articles to profl. jours., chpts to books. Sigma Xi grantee, 1959 Mem. Entomol. Soc. Washington (corr. sec. 1963-65, pres. 1985, hon. mem. 1999—), Entomol. Soc. Am., Coleoperists Soc., Am. Inst. Biol. Sci., St. Andrews Soc. Washington, Clan Anderson Soc. (editor 1979-84, treas. 1985-90, pres. 1990-92), Sigma Xi, Phi Kappa Phi. Office: Nat Mus Natural History Dept Agr Systematic Entomology Lab Washington DC 20560-0001

ANDERSON, DONNA KAY, musicologist, educator; b. Underwood, ND, Feb. 16, 1935; d. Freedolph E. and Olga (Mayer) A. PhD, Ind. U., 1966. Instr. piano MacPhail Sch. Music, 1956-59, Summit Sch., 1959-61; asst. prof. music history SUNY, Cortland, 1967-70, assoc. prof., 1970-78, prof., 1978—, chmn. dept. music, 1985-92, 95-97, faculty rsch. fellow, 1967-69, prof. emerita, 1997—. Author: Charles T. Griffes: Annotated Bibliography, Discography, 1977, The Works of Charles T. Griffes: A Descriptive Catalogue, 1983, Charles T. Griffes: A Life in Music, 1993; editor: Three Preludes for Piano, 1967, Four Impressions, 1970, Legend for Piano, 1972, De Profundis, 1978, Song of the Dagger, 1983, Seven English Songs, 1986, Rhapsody, 1992, The Pleasure Dome of Kubla Khan, 1993, The War-Song of the Vikings, 1995, Hampelas, 1995, Kinanti, 1995, Djakoan, 1995, Pieces for Children, 1995; editor, translator: Four German Songs, 1970, Nachtlied, 1983, Six German Songs, 1986, Three German Songs, 1995, A Winter Landscape, 1996, Belle Nuit, 2000, Three Japanese Melodies, 2000. Bd. dirs. YMCA, 1998—; mem. Brooks outstanding tchrs. award com. SUNY, 1999—. Recipient N.Y. State/United U. Professions Excellence award, 1991; summer grantee, 1972. Mem. Am. Musicol. Soc., Coll. Music Soc., Soc. Am. Music, Music Library Assn., Tri-M, Mu Phi Epsilon, Pi Kappa Lambda, Alpha Psi Omega, Phi Kappa Phi. Office: SUNY Performing Arts Cortland NY 13045 Business E-Mail: andersond@cortland.edu.

ANDERSON, DOROTHY S., literature educator; d. Verner J. and Margaret S. Swanson; m. Donald R. Anderson, June 10, 1952 (dec. Sept. 1994); children: Elizabeth, Arthur, Ann, Sara, Steven(dec.). BA in English, Oberlin Coll., 1952; postgrad., Harvard U., 1952; MA in English, Boston U., 1954. English tchr. Howe Jr. HS, Billerica, Mass., 1953—56, North Shore Tech. HS, Beverly, Mass., 1979—92; vis. prof. English Salem (Mass.) State Coll., 1986—. Author: John Jacob Astor, 1962, Junior Science Book of Sound, 1962; contbr. short stories to mags. Bd. dirs. North Shore Tech. H.S., Middleton, Mass., 1995—98, North Shore Horticultural Soc., Manchester, Mass., 2001—. Grantee NEH, Horace Mann, Mass. Dept. Edn. Avocations: gardening, reading.

ANDERSON, DOUGLAS RICHARD, ophthalmologist, educator, researcher; b. Memphis, Apr. 7, 1938; s. William Arnold Douglas and Hariott Isabel (Gates) A.; m. Wirtley Anne Raine, Nov. 28, 1964; children: John Douglas, Wendy Anne, Michael Allen Scott. AB magna cum laude, U. Miami, Coral Gables, Fla., 1958; MD, Washington U., St. Louis, 1962. Diplomate Am. Bd. Ophthalmology (bd. dirs. 1988-95). Rotating intern U. Hosp. Cleve., 1962-63; staff assoc. Nat. Cancer Inst., Bethesda, Md., 1963-65; resident in ophthalmology U. Calif. Med. Ctr., San Francisco, 1965-68; rsch. fellow Howe lab. Mass. Eye and Ear Infirmary, Boston, 1968-69; asst. prof. U. Miami (Fla.) Sch. Medicine, 1969-75, assoc. prof., 1975-82, prof., 1982—. Mem. nat. eye adv. coun. NIH, Bethesda, 1982-86, visual sci. study sect. A, 1972-76, chmn., 1975-76; bd. govs. Anne Bates Leach Eye Hosp., Miami, 1987-93, 98-2004, outpatient med. dir., 1993-95. Author: Testing the Field of Vision, 1982, Perimetry With and Without Automation, 1987, Automated Static Perimetry, 1992, 2d edit., 1999; contbr. over 200 sci. articles and book chpts.; co-editor: Discussions on Glaucoma, 1977, Automatic Perimetry in Glaucoma, 1985, Encounters in Glaucoma Research I: Receptors, 1994, Optic Nerve in Glaucoma, 1995, How to Ascertain Progression and Outcome, 1996; assoc. editor Am. Jour. Opthalmology, Chgo., 1973-90. Mem., active med. staff Jackson Meml. Hosp., 1969--, Anne Bates Leach Eye Hosp., active med. staff, 1976-, v.p., 1983-84, pres., 1984-86. Surgeon USPHS, 1963-65. Recipient William and Mary Greve Internat. Scholars award Rsch. to Prevent Blindness, Inc., 1978, Sr. Sci. Investigator award, 1986, 93, 99, Recognition award Alcon Rsch. Inst., Ft. Worth, 1986, Georg von Bartisch Medal for contributions to Glaucoma Rsch., 2002, Global Glaucoma Special Recognition Internat. Glaucoma Review, 2002, Hans Goldmann Medal Glaucoma Soc. of Internat. Congress Ophthalmology, 2003; rsch. grantee Nat. Eye Inst., 1969-91, 93-97, Am. Health Assistance Found., 1978-95, Glaucoma Rsch. Found., 1993-94. Fellow Am. Acad. Ophthalmology (councillor 1984-86, Gold medal 1972, Honor awards 1978, 83, Sr. Honor award 1992, Secretariat award 2004); mem. Am. Glaucoma Soc. (v.p. 1988-90, pres. 1990-92), Assn. for Rsch. in Vision and Ophthalmology (trustee 1983-88, pres. 1987, Mildred Weisenfeld award 1997), Am. Ophthal. Soc., Internat. Perimetric Soc. (hon. lectr. 2004). Home: 11880 SW 63rd Ave Miami FL 33156-4802 Office: Bascom Palmer Eye Inst PO Box 016880 900 NW 17th St Miami FL 33101-6880 Fax: 305-326-6306.

ANDERSON, E. KARL, lawyer; b. Huntington, W. Va., Mar. 30, 1931; s. Earle Karl and Helen Emrie (Johnson) A.; m. Mary Elizabeth Williams, Nov. 13, 1953; children: Sharon Elizabeth, Charles Wesley. BBA, So. Methodist U., 1953, LLB, 1960. Bar: Tex. 1960, U.S. Dist. Ct. (no. dist.) Tex. 1963, U.S. Supreme Ct. 1971. Field supr. Travelers Ins. Co., Dallas, 1956-57; claim mgr. Allstate Ins. Co., Dallas, 1958-62; practiced in Dallas, 1963—; pntr. Lastelick, Anderson and Arneson, Dallas, 1968—. 1st lt. USAF, 1954—56. Fellow Tex. Bar Found.; mem. Am. Bar Assn., Dallas Assn. Trial Lawyers (dir. 1964-65, 74-75), Tex. Trial Lawyers Assn., Assn. Trial Lawyers Am., Dallas Country Club, Delta Theta Phi, Sigma Iota Epsilon, Sigma Alpha Epsilon. Presbyterian. Home: 3111 Drexel Dr Dallas TX 75205-2910 Office: Univ Twr Bldg S-402 6440 N Central Expy Dallas TX 75206-4123 Office Phone: 214-363-0555.

ANDERSON, EDGAR RATCLIFFE, JR., career officer, physician, health facility administrator; b. Baton Rouge, Mar. 13, 1940; m. Sandra Caston; children: Melisa, Edward, Mark. MD, La. State U., 1964; grad., Industrial Coll. Armed Forces, 1972, Air War Coll., 1982. Diplomate Am. Bd. Family Practice, Am. Bd. Dermatology, Am. Bd. Preventive Medicine. Commd. 2d lt. USAF, 1965, advanced through grades to lt. gen., 1994, flight surgeon 464th Troop Carrier Wing Pope AFB, N.C., 1965-68, chief aerospace medicine 33d Tactical Fighter Wing Eglin AFB, Fla., 1968-69, undergrad. pilot tng. Williams AFB, Ariz., 1969-71, completed F-4 combat crew tng. MacDill AFB, Fla., 1971, aircraft comdr. 336th Tactical Fighter Squadron Seymour Johnson AFB, N.C., 1971, asst. ops. officer Ubon Royal Thai AFB, chief aeromed. svcs. USAF Regional Hosp. MacDill AFB, 1973-75, comdr. USAF Hosp. Seymour Johnson AFB, 1975-77, staff dermatologist USAF Med. Ctr. Keesler AFB, Miss., 1980-81, chief flight test ops. USAF-RAF exchange program Royal Air Force Station, Farnborough, Eng., 1981-83, comdr. USAF Regional Hosp. Langley AFB, Va., 1983-84, dir. profl. svcs. Office of Command Surgeon Tactical Air Command, 1984, command surgeon HQ Pacific Air Forces Hickam AFB, Hawaii, 1984-86, command surgeon SAC Offutt AFB, Nebr., 1986-90, comdr. Wilford Hall USAF Med. Ctr. Lackland AFB, Tex., 1990, surgeon general Washington, ret., 1996; CEO Truman Health Sys., Kansas City, Mo., 1996-98. Dean, prof. Sch. Med. U. Mo., Kansas City, 1996-97; exec. v.p., CEO AMA, Chgo., 1998-2001; pres., CEO Anderson Med. Consulting, LLC, 2001-; prof. medicine Loyola U. Med. Ctr., Chgo., 2002-. Decorated D.S.M. with oak leaf cluster, Legion of Merit with oak leaf cluster, D.F.C. with oak leaf cluster, Meritorious Svc. Medal with two oak leaf clusters, Air medal with nine oak leaf clusters, Air Force Commendation Medal.

ANDERSON, EDWARD RILEY, state supreme court justice; b. Chattanooga, Aug. 10, 1932; BS, U. Tenn., 1955, JD, 1957. Bar: Tenn. 1958, U.S. Dist. Ct. (ea. dist.) Tenn. 1965, U.S. Ct. Appeals (4th cir.) 1985, U.S. Ct. Appeals (6th cir.), U.S. Supreme Ct. 1988. Assoc. Joyce & Wilson, Oak Ridge, Tenn., 1957—61; ptnr. Joyce, Anderson & Meredith, Oak Ridge, 1961—87; judge Tenn. Ct. Appeals, Knoxville, 1987—90; justice Tenn. Supreme Ct., Knoxville, 1990—, chief justice, 1994—2001. Mem. Tenn. Jud. Conf., 1987—; bd. dirs. Conf. of Chief Justices, 1999-2000, vice chair children and the family com., 1998-99; chmn. Tenn. Jud. Coun., 1990-95, Select Senate/House Com. on Ct. Automation,1990-94. Past commr. Oak Ridge City Charter. Recipient Vocat. Svc. award Oak Ridge Rotary Club, 2000; named Judge of Yr. Am. Bd. Trial Advocates, 1998. Fellow Am. Bar Found., Tenn. Bar Found.; mem. ABA, Am. Bd. Trial Advocates (pres. Tenn. chpt. 1987-88), Tenn. Bar Assn. (William M. Leech Jr. Pub. Svc. award 2001), Anderson County Bar Assn. (pres. 1961), Tenn. Def. Lawyers Assn. (pres. 1980-81), Am. Inns of Ct. (pres. Tenn. chpt. 1988-90). Avocations: reading, golf, tennis. Office: Tenn Supreme Ct Supreme Court Bldg 505 Main St Ste 200 Knoxville TN 37902-2512

ANDERSON, EDWARD VIRGIL, lawyer; b. San Francisco, Oct. 17, 1953; s. Virgil P and Edna Pauline (Pedersen) A.; m. Kathleen Helen Dunbar, Sept. 3, 1983; children: Elizabeth D., Hilary J. AB in Econs., Stanford U., 1975, JD, 1978. Bar: Calif. 1978. Assoc. Pillsbury Madison & Sutro, San Francisco, 1978—, ptnr., 1987-94; chmn. mng. ptnr., mem. firm mgmt. com. Skjerven Morrill LLP, San Jose, 1994—2003; ptnr. Sidley Austin Brown & Wood, San Francisco, 2003—. Editor IP Litigator, 1995—; mem. bd. editors Antitrust Law Devel., 1983-86. Trustee Lick-Wilmerding H.S., San Francisco, 1980—, pres.; trustee Silicon Valley Law Found., 1995—; trustee, v.p. Hamlin Sch. for Girls, San Francisco, 1998—, v.p. Mem. ABA, Calif. Bar Assn., San Francisco Bar Assn., Santa Clara Bar Assn., City Club San Francisco, Stanford Golf Club, Phi Beta Kappa. Republican. Episcopal. Home: 330 Santa Clara Ave San Francisco CA 94127-2035 Office: Sidley Austin Brown & Wood Ste 5000 555 Calif St San Francisco CA 94104 Office Phone: 415-772-7420. E-mail: evanderson@sidley.com.

ANDERSON, ELIZABETH CARMAL (BETTE ANDERSON), librarian, writer; b. Henagar, Ala., Jan. 20, 1925; d. Buren Martin and Evelyn Vashtie (Keys) Farr; m. G. Kenneth Anderson, Aug. 23, 1947; 1 child, Merrill Clinton. BA in English, Wayne State U., 1946, MA in English, 1955, MLS, 1966. Cert. secondary edn. tchr., Mich., Calif. Copywriter Mich. Bell Tel. Co., Detroit, 1947-52; sch. libr. Bloomfield Hills (Mich.) Schs., 1964-68; libr. coord., media cons. West Bloomfield Schs., 1968-86; reference libr. Newport Beach (Calif.) Libr., 1988-95. Instr. adult edn. West Bloomfield Schs., 1975; instr. part-time Oakland Community Coll., Farmington, Mich., 1980. Author: Close-Ups, 2001, (stories) Faces You Meet, 2005; contbr. articles and short stories to profl. and lit. publs. Mem. Laguna Canyon Conservancy, Laguna Beach, Calif., 1988—; vice chmn. Laguna Beach Telecomm. Com., 1988-98, Laguna North Cmty. Assn., 1990—, v.p., 1995; pres. Village Laguna, 2000-02. U. Mich. grant, 1979. Mem. ALA, NEA (v.p. West Bloomfield chpt. 1985, union rep. 1986—), LWV (pub. rels. dir. Orange Coast 1990-92), PEN USA-West, Detroit Inst. Art, Laguna Art Mus., Orange County Art Mus., Laguna Festival Arts. Democrat. Presbyterian. Avocations: photography, jogging, reading. Home: 611 High Dr Laguna Beach CA 92651-1555 E-mail: bookpwr@cox.net.

ANDERSON, ELLIS BERNARD, retired lawyer, pharmaceutical executive; b. Michigan City, Ind., Aug. 30, 1926; s. A.B. and Esther Anderson; m. Adrienne Scotchbrook, Aug. 6, 1955 (dec. Aug. 1991); children: Rebecca J., Katherine V.; m. Jermain Johnson Andrews, May 22, 1993. AB cum laude, Ind. U., 1949, JD, 1952; grad., Advanced Mgmt. Program, Harvard U., 1970. Bar: Ind. 1952. Ptnr. Butt, Bowers & Anderson, Evansville, Ind., 1952-60; with Baxter Labs. Inc., Morton Grove, Ill., 1961-65; sr. v.p., gen. counsel, dir., mem. exec. com. Hoffmann-La Roche Inc., Nutley, N.J., 1965-88. With AUS, World War II. Mem. Nassau Club, Bay Head Yacht Club, Springdale Golf Club, Phi Beta Kappa. Home: 1 Larch Way Princeton NJ 08540-5053

ANDERSON, ERIC ANTHONY, city manager; b. June 2, 1946; s. Eric Albert and Edna (Barrie) Anderson; m. Linda Jane Briefstein, June 22, 1967; children: Eric Scott, Stacy Alissa. BA, Syracuse U., 1967; MPA, SUNY, Albany, 1968; MA, Maxwell Sch., Syracuse U., 1970, Harvard U., 1994. Adminstrv. intern City of Phoenix, 1970—71; asst. dir. Rsch. and Devel. Ctr. Internat. City Mgmt. Assn., Washington, 1971—73; asst. town mgr. Town of

Windsor, Conn., 1973—78; town mgr. Munster, Ind., 1978—83; city mgr. Eau Claire, Wis., 1984—91, Evanston, Ill., 1991—95, Des Moines, 1995—2005, Tacoma, 2005—. Mem. fed. graphic data com. U.S. Dept. Interior, 1998—; mem. local leaders for GIS, 1998—; trustee Geodata Alliance, 2001—02. Bd. mgrs. Windsor-Bloomfield YMCA, 1976—78; adv. coun. Urban League N.W. Ind., 1979. NEH fellow, Princeton Univ., 1977. Fellow: Nat. Acad. Pub. Adminstrn.; mem.: Internat. City Mgmt. Assn. (v.p. midwest 1987—89, trustee retirement corp. 1989—92), Conn. City Mgmt. Assn. (treas. 1977—78), Ind. Mcpl. Mgmt. Assn. (pres. 1979—80), Nat. Resource Coun. (mem. mapping sci. com. 2000—02), N.W. Mcpl. Conf. (exec. bd. 1991—92), League of Wis. Municipalities (com. on fin. and taxation 1984—90, bd. dirs. 1991), Nat. League of Cities (cmty. and econ. devel. policy com. 1984—91). Home: 3309 Wolcott Ave Des Moines IA 50321-1949 Office: Office of the City Manager City Hall 400 E 1st St Des Moines IA 50309-1809

ANDERSON, ERIC EDWARD, psychologist, consultant, health facility administrator; b. Mpls., Jan. 24, 1951; s. Charles Eric and Elizabeth Blanche (Engstrand) A.; m. Florence Kaye, June 18, 1978; children: Cara Elizabeth, Evan Travis. BA summa cum laude, U. Minn., 1973; MA, Fuller Theol. Sem., 1977, PhD in Clin. Psychology, 1978. Lic. psychologist Minn., Calif., Pa.; cert. community coll. teaching credential in psychology and philosophy Calif. Postdoctoral intern U. Minn., Mpls., 1978-79, asst. prof., coord. tng. in aging, 1979-83; group v.p. Kiel Profl. Svcs., Inc., St. Paul, 1983-84; pres. Primary Mental Health Care, Inc., Bloomington, Minn., 1984-86; sr. v.p. Treatment Ctrs. Am., Inc., Pasadena, Calif., 1986-88, LifeLink, Inc., Laguna Hills, Calif., 1988-89, chief operating officer, 1989-91; v.p., managed healthcare Columbia Gen., Laguna Hills, 1990-91; sr. v.p. managed health care Coll. Health Enterprises, Huntington Beach, Calif., 1991-94; exec. v.p. Medco. Behavioral Care/Merck Medco., 1994-96; pres. Anderson Health Strategies, LLC, 1996-97; pres., CEO Integra, Inc., 1997—2001, Anderson Health Strategies, LLC, 2001—; assoc. clin. prof. Widener U., 2000—. Cons. Ebenezer Soc., Mpls., 1979-82, Wilder Found., St. Paul, 1981-84; rsch. advisor Walden U., Mpls., 1982-86; assoc. prof. Sch. Psychology, Fuller Theol. Sem., Pasadena, 1989; adj. prof. Chestnut Hill Coll., Phila. Contbr. articles to profl. jours. Mem.: Am. Mgmt. Assn., Soc. Psychologists in Mgmt., Am. Psychol. Assn. (conf. participant 1981), Union League, Phi Beta Kappa. Avocations: tennis, gardening, bicycling, photography, golf. Address: 715 S Bryn Mawr Ave Bryn Mawr PA 19010-2005 Office Phone: 610-519-1793. Personal E-mail: eanderh@aol.com.

ANDERSON, ERIC SCOTT, lawyer; b. Grand Forks, N.D., Aug. 26, 1949; s. Lyle William and Norma Sylvia (Lundeby) A.; children: Peter Scott, Nathan William. BSChemE, U. Wis., 1971, JD, 1977. Bar: Wis. 1977, Minn. 1977, U.S. Dist. Ct. (we. dist.) Wis. 1977, U.S. Dist. Ct. Minn. 1978. Assoc. Fredrikson & Byron, P.A., Mpls., 1977-83, shareholder, 1983—. Mem. Wis. Bar Assn., Minn. Bar Assn., Hennepin County Bar Assn., Phi Eta Sigma, Tau Beta Pi, Phi Kappa Phi, Order of Coif. Avocations: golf, running, music. Office: Fredrikson & Byron PA 200 S 6th St Ste 4000 Minneapolis MN 55402-1425 Office Phone: 612-492-7030. E-mail: eanderson@fredlaw.com.

ANDERSON, ERIC SEVERIN, lawyer; b. N.Y.C., Dec. 16, 1943; s. Edward Severin and Dorothy Elvira (Ekbloom) A. BA in History summa cum laude, St. Mary's U., San Antonio, 1968; JD cum laude, Harvard U., 1971. Bar: Tex. 1971. From assoc. to of counsel Fulbright & Jaworski, L.L.P., Houston, 1971—. Served with USAF, 1961-65. Mem. ABA, State Bar Tex., Houston Bar Assn. Clubs: Houston Ctr., Houston City. Democrat. Avocations: classical music, theater, sports. Home: 14 E Greenway Plz Unit 21-O Houston TX 77046-1406 Office: Fulbright & Jaworski LLP 1301 Mckinney St Houston TX 77010-3031 Office Phone: 713-651-5265. Business E-Mail: eanderson@fulbright.com.

ANDERSON, ERNEST FREDERICK, social worker, educator; s. Ernest A. and Marie H. Anderson; m. Del Marie Neely, Mar. 31, 1968 (div. Feb. 11, 1985); 1 child, Pamela (dec.). BA in Sociology/Social Welfare, Calif. State U., 1965; MSW, San Diego State U., 1967; PhD, U. So. Calif., 1976. Diplomate NASW, Am. Bd. Examiners in Clin. Social Work, lic. clin. social worker Calif., designated services credential Calif. Dept. Edn., credential in child welfare and attendance Pasadena Unified Sch. Dist., 1969; lic. marriage, family and child counselor Calif. Clin. social worker Calif. Youth Authority, Norwalk; cons. in child welfare and attendance Pasadena Unified Sch. Dist., 1969; asst. dean Coll. Health and Human Svcs. San Diego State U., 1982—91; adj. assoc. prof. social work U. So. Calif., L.A., 1982—91, clin. assoc. prof. pediat., 1984—91; prof. Calif. State U., L.A., 1991—96, chmn. dept. social work, 1991—96, founding dir. Sch. Social Work, 1997—2001; assoc. prof. social work San Diego State Coll., 1969—76. Contbr. articles to profl. publs., chpt. to book. Cons. Region IX USPHS, San Francisco, 1995—2001; cons. to dependency ct. L.A. County, 1999—2000. Recipient Inter-University Consortium award, L.A. County, 1999—2001, Cert. Appreciation for Outstanding Leadership on the Curriculum Com. of the Geriatric Social Work Consortium, Grad. Social Work Edn. Consortium, 2003; grantee, Calif. Social Work Educators Consortium, 1999—2001. Mem.: Coun. on Social Work Edn. (cons., com. chair 1972—80). E-mail: fanders@cslanet.calstatela.edu.

ANDERSON, EUGENE ROBERT, lawyer; b. Portland, Oreg., Oct. 24, 1927; s. Andrew E. and Ruth Beatrice (White) A.; m. Jenny Morgenthau, Nov. 8, 1986: children: Matthew, Martin. BS, UCLA, 1949; student, Oreg. State Coll., 1945; JD, Harvard U., 1952; LLM, NYU, 1960. Bar: N.Y. bar 1953, Mass., So. and Eastern dists. N.Y., Second Circuit, D.C. Circuit, U.S. Ct. Claims, U.S. Supreme Ct. bars 1953. Asso. firm Chadbourne & Parke, N.Y.C., 1953-61, partner, 1965-69; asst. U.S. atty. So. Dist. N.Y., Foley Square, 1961-65, chief civil div., 1963-65; ptnr. firm Anderson Kill & Olick, P.C., N.Y.C., 1969—; asst. dist. atty. N.Y. County, 1977. Spl. hearing officer U.S. Dept. Justice, 1965-68; arbitrator Am. Arbitration Assn., 1965—, Small Claims Ct., 1970-76; mem. com. on trial practice and technique Second Circuit, 1967-73 Mem. N.Y.C. Mayor's Bus. Adv. Com., Mayor's Task Force Auto. Ins. Served with AUS, 1945-46. Mem. ABA, Fed. Bar Assn., Assn. Bar City N.Y., Police Athletic League (dir., gen. counsel). Office: Anderson Kill & Olick PC 1251 Avenue of the Americas New York NY 10020-1182 E-mail: eanderson@andersonkill.com.

ANDERSON, EVELYN LOUISE, elementary teacher; b. Abilene, Tex., Apr. 10, 1943; d. Dexter W. and Hattie M. Armstrong; m. E. Wade Anderson, Dec. 22, 1962; children: Cynthia Gail, Tresa Lynet. BA magna cum laude, Sul Ross State U., 1985. Kindergarten tchr. Socorro Ind. Sch. Dist., El Paso, Tex., 1985-86; tchr. kindergarten through 3d grade, resource rm. Ft. Stockton Ind. Sch. Dist., 1986-90; tchr. kindergarten Lydia Rippey Elem. Sch., Aztec, N.Mex., 1990—. Organizer Children's Libr., Ft. Stockton (Tex.) Pub. Libr., 1980-84, pre-school tchr. First Bapt. Ch., Ft. Stockton, Tex., 1979-84. Nominee Disney Tchr. awrd, 2000. Mem.: Coun. Exceptional Children, Kappa Delta Pi. Democrat. Avocations: writing, reading, travel, painting, crocheting. Home: 1709 Winter Ct Farmington NM 87401-2086

ANDERSON, FRANCILE MARY, secondary school educator; b. Poland, Ind., Nov. 10, 1926; d. Matthew Henry and Emma Alvina (Dettinger) Worthman; m. Robert Charles Anderson, Aug. 23, 1953; children: Sally Quick, Sue Wilkinson, Robert Charles, Russell. BA, U. Mich., 1948. Tchr. Pontiac (Mich.) Sch. Dist., 1948-54. Co-organizer Mich. Law Related Edn. Conf., Lansing, 1978; mem. exec. bd. North Ctrl. Assn. Commn. on Schs., Tempe, Ariz., 1996-99. Trustee North Oakland Med. Ctrs., Pontiac, 1994—; campaign chair United Way of Oakland County, 1995. Recipient Disting. Svc. award Mich. Assn. Secondary Sch. Prins., 1987; named to Mich. Edn. Hall of Fame, 1990. Mem. Oakland County Hosp. Assn. (pres.), Oakland County Bar Law Libr. Found., North Ctrl. Assn. Mich., North Oakland Med. Ctrs. Found. (pres.), Delta Kappa Gamma. Republican. Presbyterian. Home: 2570 Silverside Dr Waterford MI 48328-1760 Personal E-mail: franan@famvid.com.

ANDERSON, FRANK GIST, JR., ophthalmologist, educator; b. College Station, Tex., Aug. 17, 1928; s. Frank Gist Anderson and Helen Arnett Salyer; m. Velma Cartwright Gilmore, June 10, 1953 (dec. Jan. 15, 2002); children: Edith Anderson Wakefield, Frank Gist III; m. Jane Nugent Hafner, Nov. 8, 2003. BS, Tex. A&M U., 1950; MD, U. Tex., Galveston, 1954. Intern Kans. U. Med. Ctr., Kansas City, 1954-55; resident Mayo Found., Rochester, Minn., 1958-61; ophthalmologist Kelsey-Seybold Clinic, Houston, 1961-64; pvt. practice Bryan, Tex., 1964-93. Core investigator FDA Intraocular Lens Investigations, 1978; clin. prof. ophthalmology Tex. A&M U. Coll. Medicine, College Station, 1981-2001; vis. ophthalmologist King Khalid Eye Specialist Hosp., Riyadh, Saudi Arabia, 1983; prof. humanities in medicine Tex. A&M U., College Station, 1996-2001; pres. med. staff St. Joseph Hosp., Bryan, 1974, Humana Hosp., Bryan-College Station, 1983-84; chief of surgery St. Joseph Hosp., Bryan, 1968, 88, Humana Hosp., Bryan-College Station, 1978-79, 83-84. Author: (book) History of Medicine in Brazos County, 2001; contbr. articles to profl. jours. Pres.Friends of Med. Scis. Libr. Tex. A&M U., College Station, 1987—88; mem. chancellor's coun. Tex. A&M U. Sys., College Station, 1996—2003; del. Tex. Rep. Party Conv., Ft. Worth, 1990. Capt. U.S. Army, 1955—57. Fellow ACS, Am. Acad. Ophthalmology, Tex. Soc. Ophthalmology and Otolaryngology; mem. AMA, Tex. Med. Assn. (hon., del. for ophthalmology, ho. of dels. 1989), Tex. A&M Univ. Assocs., Brazos-Robertson County Med. Soc. (pres. 1978), Tex. Longhorn Breeders Assn. Am. Home: 828 S Rosemary Dr Bryan TX 77802

ANDERSON, FRANK J., JR., retired career officer; BA in Bus. Mgmt. and Econ., Chapman Coll., 1972; student, Office Tng. Sch., Lackland AFB, Tex., 1973, Squadron Officer Sch., 1975; M in Mgmt., Ctrl. Mich. U., 1982; student, Air Command and Staff Coll., 1984, Def. Sys. Mgmt. Coll., 1987, Indsl. Coll. Armed Forces, 1992. Cert. lead assessor ISO 9000 quality sys., total quality mgmt. facilitator, program mgmt. level III, contracting level III. Commd. 2d lt. USAF, 1973, advanced through grades to brig. gen., 1997; base contracting officer, chief constrn. br. Washington Area Contracting Ctr., Andrews AFB, Md., 1973-76, chief specialized contracting br., 1973-76; with Edn. With Industry Program Boeing Co., Phila., 1976-77; chief subcontractor mgmt. div. then dep. chief contract adminstrn. divsn. GE Air Force Plant Rep. Office, Phila., 1977-79; stationed at Andrews AFB, Md., 1979-83, 89-91; comdr. Air Force Plant Rep. Office Rockwell Internat., Columbus, Ohio, 1984-87; dir. contracting Electronic Combat and Reconnaissance Sys. Program Office, Wright-Patterson AFB, Ohio, 1987-89; sys. program dir. Sys. Program Office Aero. Sys. Ctr., Eglin AFB, Fla., 1992-94, dir. Weapons, Air Base and Range Product Support Office, 1994-95, mgr. armament product group, 1995-96, dir. contracting Wright-Patterson AFB, 1996-97; dep. asst. sec. contracting Office Asst. Sec. Acquisition, adv. gen. Air Force Competition Hdqs. USAF, Pentagon, Washington, 1997-2000; comdt. Def. Sys. Mgmt. Coll., Ft. Belvoir, Va., 1999—2000; ret., 2001; pres. Def. Acquisition Univ., Va. Decorated Legion of Merit. Recipient Air Force Professionalism in Contracting award, 1988; named Career Broadening Personnel Officer of Yr., Air Force Sys. Command, 1980, Co. Grade Officer of Yr., Air Force Sys. Command, 1982. Office: Def Acquisition Univ 9820 Belvoir Rd Fort Belvoir VA 22060-5565

ANDERSON, FRANK J(OHN), retired librarian; b. Chgo., Jan. 29, 1919; s. Charles Emil and Alida (Solomon) Anderson; m. Jeanette Irene Rioux, Feb. 17, 1944; 1 child, Maria Alida Anderson King. AB in Am. and English lit., Ind. U., 1950; MS in Libr. Sci., Syracuse U., 1951. Dir. libr. Kansas Wesleyan U., Salina, 1952—56; dir. branch libr. E. Chgo., 1956—57; dir. libr. Kansas Wesleyan U., Salina, 1960—66; dir. libr. and mus. Submarine Libr., Groton, Conn., 1957—60; dir. libr. Wofford Coll., Spartanburg, SC, 1966—84, libr. emeritus, 1984—; propr. Kitemaug Press, Spartanburg, 1965—. Author: Submarines, Diving and the Underwater World - A Bibliography, 1975, Private Presswork, 1977; contbr. numerous articles and revs. to profl. publs.; printer, pub.: more than 100 miniature books. With USN, 1943—45, PTO, with USN, 1951—52. Mem.: Guild of Book Workers, Amalgamated Printers' Assn., Am. Printing History Assn., Miniature Book Soc. Avocations: printing, book making, travel. Home and Office: 229 Mohawk Dr Spartanburg SC 29301 E-mail: kitemaugpresswhq@msn.com.

ANDERSON, FRANK LAWLER, physician; b. Hartford, Ct., July 21, 1955; s. Fred Andrew and Ruth (Messer) A.; m. Jennifer Angilitt Anderson, June 23, 1990; children: Christopher John, Dylan Martin. BS, Tufts U., 1977; MD, Boston U., 1981. Diplomate Am. Bd. Internal Medicine, Am. Bd. Gastroenterology. Trustee New London County Med. Soc., 1999—. Mem.: Am. Law Found. (adv. bd., Conn. chpt.), Conn. State Med. Soc. (councilor), New London County Med. Assn. (pres. 2002). Democrat. Protestant. Avocations: photography, golf, birding, kayaking, book clubs. Office: 118 New London Tpke Norwich CT 06360-2616

ANDERSON, FRED RICHARD, minister, writer; b. San Bernardino, Calif., Dec. 27, 1941; s. Elmer Duffield and Gladys Lucile (Lawlace) A.; m. Questa Lucile Donnelly, Sept. 4, 1965; children: Larra Anne, Rebecca Lucile; 1 foster child, James Gordon Cushman. BM in Voice, U. Redlands, 1963; MDiv, Princeton Theol. Sem., 1973, D in Ministry, 1981. Pastor Pompton Valley Presbyn. Ch., Pompton Plains, N.J., 1973-78; sr. pastor Pine St. Church, Harrisburg, Pa., 1978-92, Madison Ave. Presbyn. Ch., N.Y.C., 1992—. Bd. dirs. Liturgical Conf., 1990-94; bd. trustees Princeton Theol. Sem., 1992—; chair edn. bd. Reformed Liturgy and Music, 1983-89. Author: Singing Psalms of Joy & Praise, 1986, The Presbyterian Hymnal, 1990; assoc. editor: Book of Common Worship, 1993; contbr. articles to profl. jours.; opera, concert singer, 1963-64. Trustee Harrisburg Hosp., 1990-92, Chilton Meml. Hosp., Pompton Plains, 1976-78; pres. Pequennock (N.J.) Sr. City Housing, 1974-78; v.p. YMCA, Harrisburg, 1987-92, v.p., 1987-92. Capt. USAF, 1964-69. Recipient Fine Arts award Bank Am., 1959. Mem. Appeal Conscience Found. (trustee), N.Am. Acad. Liturgy, Presbyn. Assn. Musicians, Union League Club (N.Y.C.), The Pilgrims. Avocations: jogging, boating, fishing, hymntext writing, hiking the white mountains. Office: Madison Ave Presbyn Ch 921 Madison Ave New York NY 10021-3508

ANDERSON, FREDERICK RANDOLPH, JR., lawyer, educator; b. Rutherfordton, NC, June 28, 1941; s. Frederick Randolph and Ophelia (Meeler) A.; m. Barbara Alison Rose, Nov., 1991; 1 child, Molly Elizabeth. BA with highest honors, U. N.C., 1963; BA in Jurisprudence, Oxford (Eng.) U., 1965; JD, Harvard U., 1968. Bar: DC 1969, US Supreme Ct. 1980, US Ct. Appeals (DC cir.) 1995, US Ct. Appeals (9th cir.) 1999, US Ct. Appeals (3rd cir.) 2002. Teaching fellow Harvard U., Cambridge, Mass.; editor in chief Environ. Law Reporter, Washington, 1970-73; exec. dir. Environ. Law Inst., Washington, 1973-78, pres., 1978-80; prof. law U. Utah Coll. Law, Salt Lake City, 1980-85; dean Washington Coll. Law Am. U., 1985-88, Ann Loeb Bronfman Prof. Law, 1988-91; mem. firm Cadwalader, Wickersham & Taft, Washington, 1991-93, ptnr., 1993—2004, McKenna Long & Aldridge, Washington, 2004—. Mem. congl. study of common law relief for hazardous waste injuries, 1980-82; mem. Adminstrv. Conf. U.S., 1978-80, cons., 1983-84, 89-91; chmn. adv. working group on environ. sanctions U.S. Sentencing Commn., 1992-94. Author: NEPA in the Courts, 1973, Environmental Improvement Through Economic Incentives, 1978, Environmental Protection: Law and Policy, 1984, 4th edit., 2003; contbg. author: Federal Environmental Law, 1974, Occupational and Environmental Health, 1982, The Southwest under Stress, 1981. Chmn. bd. dirs. Ctr. for Internat. Environ. Law, 1993—; v.p. Western Network, 1986-89; mem. Harvard Group on Risk Mgmt. Reform, 1994-96; bd. dirs. René Dubos Ctr., 1994—. Morehead scholar, Nat. Merit scholar U. N.C., Marshall scholar Oxford U. Mem. ABA (chmn. standing com. on environ. law 1980-82, chmn. commn. on inter-Am. affairs 1986-88), NAS (mem. Comm. on Life Scis. 1995-2001, bd. environ. studies and toxicology 1988-94, com. on sci., tech. and law 2000—, bd. on atmospheric sci. and climate 2003—), Am. Law Inst. (life), NatureServe (bd. dirs. 2000—). Office: McKenna Long & Aldridge LLP 1900 K St NW Washington DC 20006 Business E-Mail: fanderson@mckennalong.com.

ANDERSON, G. BARRY, state supreme court justice; b. Mankato, Minn., Oct. 24, 1954; m. Louise Helleoid, June 30, 1884; 3 children. BA magna cum laude, Gustavus Adolphus Coll., 1976; JD, U. Minn., 1979. Bar: Minn. 1979, U.S. Dist. Ct. Minn. 1979, U.S. Ct. Appeals (8th cir.) 1980; cert. civil trial specialist. Partner Arnold, Anderson & Dove; city atty. City of Hutchinson, Minn., 1987-88; gen. counsel Minn. Rep. Party, 1987-97; chair Minn. Ethical Practices Bd., 1997-98; judge Minn. Ct. Appeals, St. Paul, 1998—2004; justice Minn. Supreme Ct., 2004—. Bd. dirs. Hutchinson Cmty. Video Network, pres., 1984-98. Mem. Alpha Kappa Psi, Rotary (pres. Hutchinson chpt. 1997-98). Lutheran. Avocations: golf, historical and biographical works. Office: Minn Supreme Ct 305 Minn Jud Ctr 25 Rev Dr Martin Luther King Jr Blvd Saint Paul MN 55155

ANDERSON, GARY F., sales executive; BA in Econ. with dept. honors, MBA in Fin., Oakland U., Rochester, Mich. System analyst IT dept. Kmart Corp., Troy, Mich., 1987—89, mem. exec. mgmt. training program, 1989—91, asst. to exec. v.p., 1991—92, gen. store mgr., 1992—95; store mgr. Svc. Mdse., Mishawaka, Ind., 1995—97; mgr. sales and store operations Centennial Wireless, Mishawaka, 1997—2001; account exec. Yellow Book USA, Mishawaka, 2002—03; dir. merchandising V-Mobile Inc., Bradenton, Fla., 2004—05. Home: 1025 Villagio Cir #101 Sarasota FL 34237

ANDERSON, GARY GENE, music educator; b. Hampton, Va., Apr. 17, 1953; s. Arthur Hobert (Stepfather) and Phyllis Hartman Carmony, Harold G. Anderson; m. Melinda Ann McClain; children: Eric, Mary Beth Harley. B in Music Edn., James Madison U., 1977. Cert. tchr. Ariz., 1991. Dir. bands & gen. music Norton (Va.) City Schs., 1977—78; dir. bands Spratley Jr. HS, Hampton, Va., 1979—80, Tabb Intermediate Sch., Yorktown, Va., 1980—85, Ferguson HS, Newport News, Va., 1985—90, Ctrl. HS, Phoenix, 1990—96, North Canyon HS, Phoenix, 1996—. Adjudicator/Clinician Arizona Band and Orchestra Directors Association, AZ, United States, 2000—02; Trombonist Superjazz Band, Yorktown, VA, United States, 1980—90, Pat Curtis Big Band, Virginia Beach, VA, United States, 1983—90. Musician: Ariz. Symphic Wind Ensemble; trombonist: Superjazz Band, 1980—90, Pat Curtis Big Band, 1983—90. Mem.: Ariz. Band and Orch. Dir.'s Assn. (band chair west region 1999—2001, instrumental chair ctrl. region 1993—95, O.M. Hartsell Excellence in Tchg. Music award 1999), Music Educators Nat. Conf., Phi Mu Alpha Sinfonia (life). Avocations: music, woodworking, gardening. Office: North Canyon High Sch Band 1700 E Union Hills Dr Phoenix AZ 85024 Office Phone: 623-780-4256. Office Fax: 623-780-4304.

ANDERSON, GARY WILLIAM, physician; b. NJ, 1951; divorced; 1 child, Eric William George. BA, Seton Hall U., 1974; MA in Psychology, Fairleigh Dickinson U., 1977; MD, Autonomous U. Guadalajara, Mex., 1983. Intern Rutgers Med. Sch., New Brunswick, N.J., 1984; resident St. Joseph's Med. Ctr., Paterson, N.J., 1985; med. dir. Sandoz Rsch. Inst., East Hanover, N.J., 1985-96, Pfizer Pharms., N.Y.C., 2000—; global dept. exec. dir. clin. safety dept. Novartis Pharms., East Hanover, 1996-2000. Vol. med. dir., bd. trustees, exec. com. Sussex County (N.J.) Domestic Abuse Program, 1986-98. Mem.: N.J. Acad. Medicine, Am. Acad. Family Physicians, AMA, Nat. Honor Soc. Psychology. Republican.

ANDERSON, GAVIN, finance company executive, consultant; b. Melbourne, Victoria, Australia, Sept. 12, 1945; came to U.S., 1974; s. George and Dulcie A.; m. Valia Olita Beldaus, Sept. 7, 1972; children: Tegwyn, Kylie, George. Student, Monash U., Melbourne, 1965-66. Mgr. Sydney area Pan Pub. Rels., Sydney, Australia, 1968-69; dir. Europe region Hill and Knowlton Inc., London, Eng., 1970-74, sr. v.p. internat. N.Y.C., 1974-81; chmn. Gavin Anderson & Co., N.Y.C., 1981—2003; pres., CEO, Governance Metrics Internat., N.Y.C., 2003—. Mem. Am. Australian Assn. (bd. dirs. 1986—), Internat. Pub. Rels. Assn., Econs. Club of N.Y. Office: Governance Metrics Internat 521 Fifth Ave New York NY 10175

ANDERSON, GEORGE See WEISSMAN, JACK

ANDERSON, GEORGE KENNETH, surgeon, retired military officer, foundation administrator; b. Providence, Feb. 17, 1946; s. George Raymond and Mildred (Caster) A.; m. Kimberly Kay Baker, May 18, 1968; children: George D., Ginger K. MD, U. Mich., 1971; MPH, Tulane U., 1973; postgrad., Nat. War Coll., Ft. McNair, Va., 1982-83. Diplomate Am. Bd. Preventive Medicine (chmn. 1991-95), Am. Bd. Med. Mgmt. (bd. dirs.). Intern Wilford Hall USAF Med Ctr., 1971-72; resident USAF Sch. Aerospace Medicine, 1973-75; commd. 2d lt. USAF, 1967, advanced through grades to maj. gen., 1993; comdr. USAF Hosp., Kunsan, Republic of Korea, 1975-76, 86th Tactical Hosp., Germany, 1976-79; mem. faculty USAF Sch. Aerospace Medicine, Brooks AFB, Tex., 1979-82; div. chief Office Surgeon Gen., Bolling AFB, Md., 1983-85, dep. dir., 1985-87; command surgeon Air Force Systems Command, Andrews AFB, Md., 1987-88; dir. med. inspection Air Force ISC, Norton AFB, Calif., 1988-90; comdr. Human Systems Ctr., Brooks AFB, 1990-94; dep. asst. sec. def. Health Svcs. Ops. and Readiness, Washington, D.C., 1994; ret. USAF, 1996; pres., CEO Koop Found. Inc., Rockville, Md., 1997-98; exec. v.p. Oceania Corp., Falls Church, Va., 1998-99; pres., CEO Oceania, Inc., Redwood City, Calif., 1999—. Bd. dir. New World Healthcare Solutions, Washington. Decorated Legion of Merit, Disting. Svc. medal; Koop Found. fellow. Fellow Am. Coll. Preventive Medicine (pres.), Am. Coll. Physician Execs. (disting.), Aerospace Med. Assn. (Julian Ward award 1975); mem. AMA, Air Force Assn. (life).

ANDERSON, GEORGE ROSS, JR., federal judge; b. Anderson, S.C., Jan. 29, 1929; s. George Ross and Eva Mae (Pooler) A.; m. Dorothy M. Downie, Dec. 2, 1951; 1 son, G. Ross. B.Comml. Sci., Southeastern U., 1949; postgrad., George Washington U., 1949-51; LL.B., U. S.C., 1954, LLD (hon.), 1984, Anderson Coll., 1998. Bar: S.C. 1954. Mem. identification div. FBI, Washington, 1945-47; clk. to U.S. Senator Olin D. Johnston, Washington, 1947-51, Columbia, S.C., 1953-54; individual practice law Anderson, S.C., 1954-79; U.S. dist. judge Dist. Ct. of S.C., Anderson, 1980—. Asst. editor: U. S.C. Law Rev, 1953-54. Bd. dirs. Salvation Army, 1968, YMCA, 1968-79, Anderson Youth Assn., 1978-80. Served with USAF, 1951-52. Recipient War Horse award So. Trial Lawyers Assn., 1990, Dist. Judicial Svc. award The Civil Justice Found., Am. Trial Lawyers Assn., 1997, Ernest F. Hollings Pub. Svc. award, 2002, Order of the Palmetto award, 2002; named for Federal Bldg. Courthouse in Anderson, SC, 2002. Fellow Internat. Acad. Trial Lawyers (dir. 1979-81), Internat. Soc. Barristers; mem. S.C. Bar Assn. (dir. 1977-80, past cir. v.p.), Assn. Trial Lawyers Am. (bd. govs. 1969-71), S.C. Trial Lawyers Assn. (v.p. 1970-71, pres. 1971-72, Outstanding Trial Judge of Yr. 1984), hon. doctor of Laws, U. SC, 1984, bd. dirs. Federal Judges Assn., 1993-97. Democrat. Baptist. Office: US Dist Ct PO Box 2147 Anderson SC 29622-2147

ANDERSON, GERALD DWIGHT, history educator; b. Dale, Minn., Nov. 18, 1944; s. Wilferd Dean and Violet Caria-Maria (Heigg) A.; m. Rhonda Waldahl, July 8, 1967 (div. June 1975); 1 child, Carmen Nell; m. Barbara Ann Thill, May 13, 1978; children: Karl August, Paul Martin. BA, Concordia Coll., Moorhead, Minn., 1965; MA, N.D. State U., 1966; PhD, U. Iowa, 1973. Asst. prof. history Waldorf Coll., Forest City, Iowa, 1966-70, Drake U., Des Moines, 1973, Iowa Wesleyan Coll., Mt. Pleasant, 1974; instr. Austin (Minn.) C.C., 1974-75; rschr. Minn. State Senate, St. Paul, 1976-79; asst. prof. Luther Coll., Decorah, Iowa, 1979-85; assoc. prof. history N.D. State U., Fargo, 1985—. Cons. history textbooks Harper Collins, N.Y.C., 1988-97, West Pub., St. Paul, 1988-97; cons. various hist. socs. Author: Fascists, Communists, The National Government, 1983, The Uffda trial, 1994, The Western Perspective Study Guide, Vols. I and II, 1999. Precinct chair Moorhead DFL Party, 1986-97; v.p. Gooseberry Park Players, Moorhead, 1994-97. Recipient Robert Odney Excellence in Tchg. award N.D. State U., 2005; named Outstanding Tchr., N.D. State U., 1992; Fulbright scholar U.S. State Dept., 1991, Internat. Seminar scholar Com. for Internat. Edn., Moscow, 1994, Berlin, 1996, Budapest, 1999, Madrid, 2002. Lutheran. Avocations: reading and writing detective fiction, scandinavian ethnic studies, acting in community theater. Home: 1320 5th St S Moorhead MN 56560-3420 Office: North Dakota State Univ Minard Hall 412H Fargo ND 58105 Office Phone: 701-231-7709. E-mail: gerald.anderson@ndsu.nodak.edu.

ANDERSON, GERALD EDWIN, utilities executive; b. Boston, Apr. 9, 1931; s. Clarence Gustav and Lela Pauline (Kelley) A.; m. Mary Elizabeth Iverson, May 21, 1955; children: Todd K., Timothy J., Kristin E. May. AA, Worthington (Minn.) Jr. Coll., 1950; BBA, U. Minn., 1952. C.P.A., Minn. Staff accountant, audit mgr. Arthur Andersen & Co., Mpls., 1953-65; asst. comptroller Commonwealth Energy System (formerly New Eng. Gas & Electric Assn.), Cambridge, Mass., 1966, system comptroller, 1967-71, v.p., comptroller, 1971-72, treas. parent co., financial v.p. system, 1972-74, pres., 1974-91, chief exec. officer, 1975-91; ret., 1992. Trustee parent co., 1974-91; also dir. operating subs. Commonwealth Energy Sys., 1972-91, dir. Liberty Mutual Ins. Co., Liberty Mutual Fire Ins. Co., 1980-2001, Liberty Life Assurance Co. of Boston, 1984-95, Liberty Fin. Cos., Inc., 1995-2001. Vice chmn. United Ways Ea. New Eng., 1986; mem. town fin. com., Carlisle, Mass., 1968-73, chmn., 1972-73; dir. Swedish Coun. Am., 1987-2003; mem. Corp. of Mass. Gen. Hosp., 1988-95. 1st lt. USAF, 1952-53. Mem. AICPA, Minn. Soc. CPAs, Fin. Execs. Inst., Oyster Harbors Club, The Lakes Country Club, Somerset Club, Comml. Club of Boston, Beta Alpha Psi, Beta Gamma Sigma. Episcopalian. Home: 75 Hornbeam Ln Centerville MA 02632-3521 also: 245 Wild Horse Dr Palm Desert CA 92211-3220 Personal E-mail: ganderso3@aol.com.

ANDERSON, GERALD LESLIE, finance company executive; b. Washington, May 24, 1940; s. Paul Hash and Edith (Hathaway) A.; m. Margaret Marie Curley, June 8, 1974; children: Paul Charles, Laura Marie. BS in Indsl. Mgmt., Carnegie Mellon U., 1961, MS in Indsl. Adminstrn., 1962. Econ. analyst Sun Oil Co., Phila., 1962-66; asst. treas. Selas Corp. Am., Dresher, Pa., 1966-74; treas. Midrex Corp., Charlotte, N.C., 1974-76; v.p., treas. Georgetown Industries, Inc., Charlotte, 1976-85, v.p. fin., chief fin. officer, 1985-95; prin. Anderson Investments, Charlotte, NC, 1995—2000. Active Ch. at Charlotte Evangelical Free Ch. Republican. Home and Office: 4519 N Parview Dr Charlotte NC 28226-3450

ANDERSON, GERALDINE LOUISE, medical researcher; d. George M. and Viola Julia-Mary (Abel) Havrilla; m. Henry Clifford Anderson, May 21, 1966; children: Bruce Henry, Julie Lynne. BS med. tech., U. Minn., 1959—63. Cert. med. technologist ASCP, clin. lab. sci. NCA. Med. technologist Swedish Hosp., Mpls., 1963-68; hematology supr. lab. Glenwood Hills Hosp., Golden Valley, Minn., 1968-70; assoc. scientist pediats. U. Minn. Hosps., Mpls., 1970-74; instr. health occupations, med. lab. asst. Suburban Hennepin County Area Vocat. Tech. Ctr., Brooklyn Park, Minn., 1974-81, 92-95, St. Paul Tech. Vocat. Inst., Brooklyn Park, 1978-81; rsch. med. technologist Miller Hosp., St. Paul, 1975-78; rsch. assoc. Children's and United Hosps., St. Paul, 1979-88; sr. lab. analyst Cascade Med. Inc., Eden Prairie, Minn., 1989-90; lab. mgr. VAMC, Mpls., 1990; tech. support scientist INCSTAR Corp., Stillwater, Minn., 1990-94; mem. network staff Clin. Design Group, Chgo., 1992-98; regulatory affairs product analysis coord. Medtronic Neurol., Mpls., 1995; quality assurance documentation coord. Lectec Corp., Minnetonka, Minn., 1995; clin. rsch. monitor Eli Lilly Rsch. Labs., Indpls., 1995-98; sr. clin. rsch. assoc. Covance, Inc., Princeton, N.J., 1998-99. Sr. clin. rsch. assoc. Parexel Internat., Inc., Chgo., 1999—2000; clin. rsch. assoc. AAI Internat., Boston, 2000—01; regional clin. rsch. assoc. Wyeth, Collegeville, Pa., 2001—02; health occupations adv. com. Hennepin Tech. Ctrs., 1975—90, chairperson, 1978—79; mem. hematology slide edn. rev. bd. Am. Soc. Hematology, 1977—96; mem. flow cytometry and clin. chemistry quality controll subcoms. Nat. Com. for Clin. Lab. Stds., 1988—92; cons. FCM Specialists, 1989—99, 2002—. Clin. Design Group, 1992—98; mem. rev. bd. Clin. Lab. Sci., 1990—91, The Learning Laboratorian Series, 1991; presenter in field. Contbr. articles to profl. jours. Charter orgns. rep. Viking Coun. troop 534 Boy Scouts Am., 1988—90; resource person lab. careers Robbinsdale (Minn.) Sch. Dist., 1970—79; active Women Scientists Spkrs. Bur., 1989—92, Helping Hands, 2002—. Med. Lab. Tech. Polit. Action Com., 1978—99; observer UN 4th World Conf. on Women, Beijing, 1995; del. Crest View Home Assn., 1981—; sci. and math. subcom. Minn. High Tech. Coun., 1983—88; bd. dirs. Big Pine Lake Property Owners, 1996—. Recipient Svc. awards and honors, Omicron Sigma. Mem.: NAFE, AAUW, AAAS, Grad. Women in Sci., Inc., Great Lakes Internat. Flow Cytometry Assn. (charter mem. 1992), Internat. Soc. Analytical Cytology, Am. Soc. Hematology, Minn. Med. Tech. Alumni, Assn. Clin. Rsch. Profls., World Future Soc., Assn. Women in Sci., Twin Cities Hosp. Assn. (spkrs. bur. 1968—70), Am. Soc. Clin. Lab. Sci. (del. to ann. meetings 1972—, chmn. hematology sci. assembly 1977—79, nomination com. 1979—81, bd. dirs. 1986—88), Soc. Clin. Rsch. Assocs., Am. Soc. Profl. and Exec. Women, Minn. Soc. Med. Tech. (sec. 1969—71), Minn. Emerging Med. Orgns., Nat. Assn. Women Cons., Inc., Soc. Tech. Comm., Soc. Clin. Rsch. Assocs., Assn. Clin. Rsch. Profls. (cert. clin. rsch. assoc., cert.), Women in Comm., Inc., Am. Med. Writers Assn., Nat. Ch. Libr. Assn., Alpha Mu Tau, Sigma Delta Epsilon (corr. sec. XI chpt. 1980—82, pres. 1982—84, nat. membership com. 1990—92, nat. nominations chair 1991—92, nat. v.p. 1992—93, nat. pres.-elect 1993—94, nat. pres. 1994—95, bd. dirs. 1996—2001, chmn. bd. dirs. 2000—01). Personal E-mail: gerrylou@comcast.net.

ANDERSON, GERARD FENTON, economist, academic administrator; b. Mariemont, Ohio, June 24, 1951; s. Harry C. and Dorothy C. (Fenton) A.; m. Judith Rae Peres; 1 child, Anna. BA in Econs., Haverford Coll., 1973; PhD in Pub. Policy, U. Pa., 1978. Spl. asst. Cost of Living Coun. Exec. Office of the Pres., Washington, 1972; research analyst Fed. Reserve Bank, Washington, 1973-74; prin. investigator Phila. Health Mgmt. Corp., 1974-78; economist Office of the Sec. HHS, Washington, 1978-83; assoc. dir. Ctr. for Hosp. Fin. and Mgmt. Johns Hopkins U., Balt., 1983-87, dir., 1987—; co-dir. Johns Hopkins Program for Med. Tech. and Practice Assessment, Balt., 1986-94, 1994—. Cons. Blue Cross Greater Phila., 1978, World Bank, Washington, 1988; adj. prof. Grad. Sch. Pub. Adminstrn. Am. U., Washington, 1978-82; presenter to Congl. coms. over 30 times. Author: Health Care Cost Containment, 1990, Providing Hospital Services, 1989; contbr. over 120 articles to profl. jours. Fellow U. Pa., Phila., 1978. Mem. Am. Econ. Assn., Am. Pub. Health Assn., Assn. for Health Svcs. Rsch., Phi Beta Kappa, Delta Omega. Democrat. Mem. Soc. Of Friends. Home: 8022 Glendale Rd Chevy Chase MD 20815-5903 Office: Johns Hopkins U 624 N Broadway # 300 Baltimore MD 21205-1900 E-mail: ganderso@jhsph.edu.

ANDERSON, GILLIAN, actress; b. Chgo., Aug. 9, 1968; d. Edward and Rosemary A.; m. Errol Clyde Klotz, Jan. 1, 1994 (div. 1997); 1 child, Piper; m. Julian Ozanne, Dec. 29, 2004. BFA, DePaul U., 1990; grad., Goodman Theatre Sch., Chgo. Appeared on TV series, X-Files, 1993-2002 (Emmy award for Outstanding Lead Actress in a Drama Series, 1997, Golden Globe award for Best Actress in a Drama Series, 1997); stage appearance in Absent Friends, Manhattan Theatre Club, 1991 (Theatre World award 1991), The Philanthropist, Along Wharf Theater, 1992, The Vagina Monologues, 1999, 2000, What the Night is For, 2002-03, The Sweetest Swing in Baseball, 2004; appeared in films Three at Once, 1986, A Matter of Choice, 1988, The Turning, 1992, X-Files the Movie, 1998, The Mighty, 1998, Playing By Heart, 1998, Hellcab, 1998, Princess Mononoke, 1999, The House of Mirth, 2000 (British Independent Film award for Best Actress, 2000); TV appearances Class of '96, 1993, Reboot, 1995, The Simpsons, 1997, Frasier, 1999, Harsh Realm, 1999.

ANDERSON, GORDON LOUIS, foundation administrator; b. St. Croix Falls, Wis., Nov. 16, 1947; s. Erwin Louis and Eunice Arlene (Johnson) A.; m. Mary Jane Evenson, July 1, 1982; children: Tamara, Jayna, Greta, Evan. BME, U. Minn., 1975; MDiv in Ethics, Union Theol. Sem., N.Y.C., 1980; MA in Religion, Claremont Grad. Sch., 1985, PhD Philosophy Religion, 1986. Engr. Gull Engring. Inc., Mpls., 1974-80, also bd. dirs.; owner, mgr. Aerograph Aerial Photography, Claremont, Calif., 1981-84; sec. gen., bd. dirs. Profs. World Peace Acad., N.Y.C., 1984-93, sec. gen. St. Paul, 1993—; sec., gen., bd. dirs. Internat. Cultural Found., Washington, 1986—. Lectr. Unification Theol. Sem., Barrytown, N.Y., 1987-96, bd. dirs., 1988-96; lectr. 40 countries including Europe, Africa, Asia and South America. Author: The Philosophy of the United States, 2004; assoc. editor Internat. Jour. World Peace, 1985—94; editor: Internat. Jour. World Peace, 1994—2000; pub. Internat. Jour. World Peace, 2000—, assoc. editor Morality and Religion in Liberal Democratic Societies, 1992, Worldwide State of the Family, 1995, Family in Global Transition, 1997; contbr. articles to profl. jours., chapters to books. Mem. Citizens for Better N.J., 1986-92; bd. dirs. Paragon House Pubs., 1993—, exec. dir., 1996—; trustee U. Bridgeport, Conn., 1994—. With U.S. Army, 1969-72, Vietnam. Mem. World Future Soc., Am. Acad. Religion, Am. Polit. Sci. Assn., Internat. Studies Assn., Consortium on Peace Rsch. Mem. Unification Ch. Office: Paragon House 1925 Oakcrest Ave Saint Paul MN 55113-2619 Office Phone: 651-644-3087. E-mail: gla@paragonhouse.com. *Religion or culture has always defined manhood, womanhood, the relation to our neighbor, the government, the spiritual world and God. This has yet to take place in a normative way for the modern world.*

ANDERSON, GREGG W., minister; b. Cin., Oct. 11, 1953; s. William M. and Julia J. Anderson. AA in Liberal Arts, St. Catharine Jr. Coll., Springfield, Ky., 1972; BS in Psychology and Communications, Trevecca Nazarene Coll., Nashville, 1976; MA in Relgion, Trinity Coll. & U., 2002; DD (hon.), Chaplain Fellow Ministries Bible Inst., 2003. Ordained to ministry Evang. Ch., 1990. Dir. no. Ky. region Fellowship Christian Athletes, Highland Heights, 1984-86; dir. pub. rels. Christian Leaders and Sunday Sch., Cin., 1990—; dir. publicity Full Gospel Bus. Men's, Covington, Ky., 1990—; exec. dir. 70x7 Evangelistic Ministry, Highland Heights, 1990—; exec. bd. Jesus 1990's, Cin., 1991—. Vis. instr. Cin. Christian Coll., 1990—; bd. dirs. Action Unltd. News Svc., Hightland Heights, Ky. Mem. No. Ky. Teen Com., Covington, 1987, Highland Heights Planning and Zoning, 1990. Named Ky. Col., Gov. of Ky., 1989; Gregg Anderson Day established in his honor Mayor of Cin., 1987. Fellow: European Broadcasters; mem.: Ky. Chaplins Assn., Chaplain Fellowships Ministries, Am. Special Chaplians Assn. Office Phone: 513-557-2931. Business E-Mail: gregga@fox7ministry.com. *After spending 15 years as a radio or TV news reporter God has given me a new "News Assignment." He wants me to report the good news of Jesus Christ.*

ANDERSON, GREGORY THOMAS, secondary school educator, researcher, historian; s. Ralph Curtis (Stepfather) and Darlene Dolores Miley, Thomas Lyle Anderson; m. Suzanne Marie Anderson, July 30, 1988; 1 child, Kathryn Michelle. BA, Calif. State U., 1999. Secondary Profl. Clear Tchg. Credential Calif. Commn. on Tchr. Credentialing, 1999. Asst. regional mgr. U.S. Dept. of Commerce, Bur. of the Census, San Pedro, Calif., 1988—90; tchr. Redondo Beach Unifed Sch. Dist., Calif., 1991—2000, Torrance Unifed Sch. Dist., Torrance, Calif., 2000—. Author: (book) Index to the Mayors of Redondo Beach, California, 1991; editor: (newsletter) 1812 Overtures, Golden State Patriot. Mem. Gen. Plan Adv. Com., Redondo Beach, Calif., 1989—92, South Bay Union HS Dist. Hist. Com., Redondo Beach, Calif.; state pres. Soc. of the War of 1812 in the State of Calif., 1989—92; state sec. SR in the State of Calif., 1989—92; state dep. gov. Soc. of Mayflower Descendants in the State of Calif., 1989—2003; mem. Redondo Beach Hist. Soc., Calif., 1993—95. Recipient Games of the XXIII Olympiad, LA Olympic Organizing Com., 1984, Ky. Col. Commn., Commonwealth of Ky., 1989. Mem.: New Eng. Geneal. Libr., Orgn. of Am. Historians, Sons and Daughters of the Colonial and Antebellum Bench and Bar 1565-1861, Order of the Crown of Charlemagne in the U.S., Flagon and Trencher, SAR in the State of Calif., Soc. of the War of 1812 in the State of Calif. (state pres. 1991—92, Pres's. Commendation 1990), Sons the Revolution in the State of Calif. (state sec. 1989—92, Pres's. Commendation 1992), The Soc. of the Descendants of the Colonial Clergy, Soc. of Mayflower Descendants in the State of Calif. (colony gov. 1999—2003). Democrat. Congregationalist. Avocations: genealogy, travel, local politcs. Personal E-mail: anderson@bnet.org.

ANDERSON, HARRISON CLARKE, pathologist, educator, biomedical researcher; b. Louisville, Sept. 2, 1932; married, 1961. BA in Zoology, U. Louisville, 1954, MD, 1958. Diplomate Am. Bd. Pathology. Pathology intern Mass. Gen. Hosp., Boston, 1958-59; NIH rsch. trainee U. Louisville, Ky., 1959-60; resident in pathology Sloan Kettering Meml. Hosp. N.Y.C., 1960-62; postdoctoral fellow Sloan Kettering Inst., Rye, N.Y., 1962-63; from asst. prof., assoc. prof. to prof. pathology SUNY Downstate Med. Ctr., Bklyn., 1963-78; prof. pathology, chmn. dept. U. Kans. Med. Ctr., Kansas City, 1978-90, Harrington prof. orthopedic rsch., 1990—. Mem. study sect. NIH, Bethesda, Md., 1977—81, Bethesda, 1999—2005; chmn. Gordon Rsch. Conf. on Bone, Meriden, NH, 1981. Edit. bd. Am. Jour. Pathology, others, 1981—; contbr. articles to profl. jours. Recipient Biol. Mineralization Research award Internat. Assn. Dental Research, 1985, Sr. Faulty Research award U. Kans. Med. Ctr., 1986, Kappa Delta Orthopedic Rsch. award Orthopedic Rsch. Soc., 1982, Higuchi Biomed. Rsch. award U. Kansas, 1991; NIH rsch. fellow Strangeways Lab., Cambridge, Eng., 1971-72, NIH sr. rsch. fellow in cell biology Yale U., New Haven, 1984-85; grantee NIH, 1967—. Mem. Am. Soc. Investigative Pathologists, Assn. Pathology Chmn. (pres. 1988-90), Am. Soc. Cell Biology, Am. Soc. Bone and Mineral Research, Orthopaedic Research Soc. Clubs: Am. Yacht (Rye); Carriage (Kansas City). Avocations: tennis, skiing, sailing. Office: U Kansas Dept Pathology 39th & Rainbow Kansas City KS 66160-0001 Office Phone: 913-588-7474. Business E-Mail: handerso@kumc.edu.

ANDERSON, HARRY W. (HUNK), retired food service executive; b. Corning, NY, 1922; m. Mary Margaret Ransford, 1950. B, Hobart Coll., 1949, LLD (hon.), 1967, Mount St. Scholastica Coll., 1968. Co-founder Saga Corp. food svc., NY, 1948, v.p., 1957—62, v.p., personnel, 1962—68, sr. v.p., vice-chmn. of bd., 1968—77; ret., 1978. Charter mem., v.p. Coun. Personnel Officers. Co-founder Harry W. and Mary Margaret Anderson Charitable Found., Atherton, Calif.; trustee Mount St. Scholastica Coll., Kans. Named one of Top 200 Collectors, ARTnews Mag., 2004. Avocation: Collecting NY Sch. contemporary art. Office: Harry W and Mary Margaret Anderson Charitable Found 62 Faxon Rd Atherton CA 94027-4046

ANDERSON, HERBERT G., marine biologist, researcher; b. Roanoke, Ala., Dec. 29, 1931; s. Herbert Godwin and Ethel Blanche Anderson. BS, Auburn U., Auburn,Al, 1958; MS, Auburn U., Auburn, L, 1960; PhD, U. Of Miami, Miami, Fl, 1965. Prof. of biol. sci. Ctrl. Ct State U., New Britain, Conn., 1964—89, prof.of biogical sci. emeritus, 1989. Chair,univ,graduate studies comm. Ctrl. Ct State U., New Britain, Conn., chair, univ. termination, appeals.com., chair grad. scholarship subcom., secr.for state univ.marine studies com. Solo classical piano recital Jacksonville State U., Jacksonville, Ala., 1951; mem. of bd. of directors Westbay Pt.mooringsll, Holmes Beach, Fla., 1996; recipient of recognition for my Art Abstract Installed As A Stained Glass, Ann Maria, Fla., 2002. Petty officer 3rd u.s.navy, 1951—55, Lake Champlain (Cva) Korea. Recipient Rsch. Fellowship, F & W-l Bur. Of Sport Fisheries,Sandy Hook Nj, 1962 to 1964; grantee Rsch. Grant, Rsch. Dept. Ctrl. Ct State Univ. New Britain,ct, 1976. Mem.: Marquis Whos Who In The East (assoc.), The Am. Soc.of Parasitologists (assoc.), Sigma Xi) The Sci. Rsch. Soc. (assoc.). Episcopalian. Achievements include research in Meristic charactistics and marine fish parasites do not confirm color differen. Avocations: piantist(classical), artist(geomerical cubist abstract). Home: 6308 5th Ave NW Bradenton FL 34209-1611

ANDERSON, HERBERT HATFIELD, lawyer, farmer; b. Rainier, Oreg., Aug. 2, 1920; s. Odin A. and Mae (Hatfield) A.; m. Barbara Stuart Bastine, June 3, 1949; children: Linda, Catherine, Thomas, Amy, Elizabeth, Kenneth BA in Bus. Adminstrn., U. Oreg., 1940; JD, Yale U., 1949. Exec. trainee U.S. Steel Co., San Francisco, 1940-41; assoc. Koerner, Young, McColloch & Dezendorf, Portland, Oreg., 1949—54; ptnr. Spears, Lubersky, Bledsoe, Anderson, Young & Hilliard, 1954-90, Lane, Powell, Spears & Lubersky, Portland, 1990—. Instr. law Lewis and Clark Coll., Portland, 1950-70. Mem. planning adv. com. Yamhill County, Oreg., 1974-82; bd. dirs. Emanuel Hosp., 1967—; bd. dirs. Flyfisher Found., 1972—, pres., 1972-84; bd. dirs. Multnomah Law Libr., 1958—, sec. 1962-68, 77-94, pres., 1964-74. Served to maj., parachute inf. U.S. Army, 1942-46, ETO. Fellow Am. Bar Found. (chmn. Oreg. chpt. 1988—); mem. ABA (chmn. governing com. forum on health law 1984-89, chmn. standing com. on jud. selection, tenure and compensation 1978-80, Lawyer's Conf., exec. com. 1980-94, chmn. 1989-90, jud. adminstrn. divsn. coun. 1988-94, sr. lawyer's divsn. coun. 1987-89), Am. Judicature Soc. (bd. dirs. 1981-85), Soc. Law and Medicine, Nat. Health Lawyers Assn., Am. Acad. Hosp. Attys., Oreg. Soc. Hosp. Attys. (pres. 1984-85), Multnomah Bar Found. (bd. dirs. 1955—, pres. 1959-64, 87—), Nat. Bankruptcy Conf. (conferee 1964—, exec. com. 1976-79, chmn. farmer insolvency com. 1985-88), Nat. Assn. R.R. Trial Counsel, Oreg. Bar Assn. (del. to ABA 1966-68), Multnomah Bar Assn. (pres. 1955), Western States Bar Conf. (pres. 1967), Oreg. Asian Pear Coun. (pres. 1989-91), Multnomah Athletic Club, Michelbook Country Club, Flyfishers Oreg. Club (pres. 1972), Flyfisher Found. (pres. 1957-67), Willamette Amateur Field Trial Club (pres. 1966-72), Amateur Field Trial Clubs of Am. (trustee 2002-), Masons, Sigma Chi. Democrat. Lutheran. Home: River Meadow Farm 19289 SE Neck Rd Dayton OR 97114-7815 Office Phone: 503-226-3601. E-mail: hhanderson@verizon.net.

ANDERSON, HERBERT W., consumer products company executive; b. Indpls., Oct. 1, 1939; BS in Bus. Mgmt., U. Wis. Sr. mgmt. positions McGraw-Edison, Eaton Cos.; corp. v.p., mgmt. info. svcs. Western Gear Corp.; v.p., info. rescource mgmt. Northrop Grumman Corp., 1984-90, corp. v.p., ctr. mgr., 1990-94, dep. gen. mgr., DSSD, 1994-95, corp. v.p., gen. mgr., DSSD, 1995-98, pres., CEO, Logicon, 1998—2001, corp. v.p., pres. Information Technology, 2001—04, corp. v.p., special projects, 2004. With U.S. Army 1958-61. Office: Northrop Grumman Corp 1840 Century Park E Los Angeles CA 90067-2101

ANDERSON, HERSCHEL VINCENT, retired librarian; b. Charlotte, N.C., Mar. 14, 1932; s. Paul Kemper and Lillian (Johnson) Anderson. BA, Duke U., 1954; MS, Columbia U., 1959. Library asst. Bklyn. Public Library, 1954-59; asst. bookmobile librarian King County Public Library, Seattle, 1959-62; asst. librarian Longview (Wash.) Public Library, 1962-63; librarian N.C. Mus. Art, Raleigh, 1963-64; audio-visual cons. N.C. State Library, Raleigh, 1964-68; dir. Sandhill Regional Library, Rockingham, N.C., 1968-70; asso. state librarian Tenn. State Library and Archives, Nashville, 1970-72; unit dir. Colo. State Library, Denver, 1972-73; state librarian S.D. State Library, Pierre, 1973-80; dir. Mesa (Ariz.) Public Library, 1980-99. Founding mem., chief officers State Libr. Agys., 1973—80, bd. dirs.; dir. Bibliog. Ctr. Rsch., Denver, 1974—80, v.p., 1977; founding mem. Western Coun. St. Librs., 1975—80, v.p., 1978, pres., 79; mem. libr. technician tng. adv. com. Mesa CC, 1982—85, mem. commn. excellence, 1993—2003; chmn. Serials On-Line Ariz. Consortia, 1985—86; mem. Ariz. Libr. Devel. Coun., 1991—93, Ariz. State Libr. Adv. Coun., 1998—, chair, 1999—; mem. Libr. Facilities Adv. Bd., Gilbert, Ariz., 1999—. Mem., treas. Maricopa County Libr. Coun., 1981—99, pres., 1983, 1993; mem. hist. preservation com. City of Mesa, 2000—; mem. Valley Citizens League, 1991—; jr. warden St. Mark's Episcopal Ch., Mesa, 1985—87, vestryman, 1987—90, 1995—98, sr. warden, 1996—98, archivist, 2000—; del. ann. conv. Episcopal Diocese Ariz., 1989—92, 1994—98, mem. archives com., 1990—97, mem. Diosecan Coun. Episcopal, 1996—98; mem. steering com. N.E. Regional Parish, 1994—2004, chair Native Am. com., 1999—2004. With U.S. Army, 1955—57. Recipient Emeritus Honors, Ariz. Libr. Friends, 1987. Mem.: ALA, Heard Mus., Ariz. Hist. Found., N.C. Literary and Hist. Assn., Nat. Trust for Hist. Preservation, Ariz. Hist. Found., Ariz. Libr. Assn. (mem. exec. com. 1986—87), Mountain Plains Libr. Assn. (pres. 1974, bd. dirs. 1974—77, 1986—87, Intellectual Freedom award 1979), S.D. Libr. Assn. (life Libr. of Yr. award 1977), Kiwanis (bd. dirs. Mesa 1981—86, v.p. 1983, pres. 1985—86), Phi Kappa Psi. E-mail: andersonvince@aol.com.

ANDERSON, HOWARD WAYNE, JR., training company executive; b. Sharon, Pa., Oct. 29, 1957; s. Howard Wayne Anderson Sr and Judith Kathleen Anderson; m. Mary Elizabeth Santo, July 11, 1981; children: Jennifer, Ryan. BA in Criminal Justice, Mercyhurst Coll., 1980; MS in Sys. Mgmt., U. So. Calif., 1989; MEd in Tng. and Devel., Pa, State U., 2000; PhD in Mgmt., Madison U., 2003. Commd. 2d lt. USMC, 1980, advanced through grades to maj., exec. officer 2d marine divsn. Camp Lejeune, NC, 1982—84, commdg. gen. aide de camp Quantico, Va., 1986—88, commdg. officer air ground task force Twentynine Palms, Pa., 1989—91; sr. ops. mgr. Schneider Nat. Carriers, Inc, Carlisle, Pa., 1991—99; dir., N.E. tng. and loss prevention Schneider Tng. Acad., Carlisle, 1999—. Contbr. articles to profl. jours. Mem. Compassion Internat., Colorado Springs, Colo., 1989. Recipient 32 letters of appreciation, various civic groups, 1986—88. Mem.: Pa. Interscholastic Athletic Assn., Nat. Assn. of Sports Officials. Avocations: weightlifting, exercise, reading, writing. Office: Schneider National Carriers Inc 1 Schneider Drive Carlisle PA 17013 Personal E-mail: hwajr@aol.com. E-mail: wayne_anderson/schneider@schneider.com.

ANDERSON, HUGH GEORGE, bishop; b. L.A., Calif., Mar. 10, 1932; s. Reuben Leroy and Frances Sophia (Nielsen) A.; m. Synnøve Anna Hella, Nov. 3, 1956 (dec. Apr. 1982); 1 child, Erik; m. Jutta Ilse Fischer, July 2, 1983; children: Lars, Niels; 1 child, Kristi. AB, Yale U., 1953; BD, Luth. Theol. Sem., Phila., 1956, STM, 1958; MA, U. Pa., 1957, PhD, 1962; LittD, Lenoir Rhyne Coll., 1971; DD, Roanoke Coll., 1971, Wagner Coll., 1987, Gen. Theol. Sem., N.Y.C., 1996, Luther Coll., Decorah, Iowa, 1996; LHD, Newberry Coll., 1979, Columbia (S.C.) Coll., 1981. Ordained Luth. min. Tchg. fellow Luth. Theol. Sem., Phila., 1956—58; prof. ch. history Luth. Theol. So. Sem., Columbia, SC, 1958—70, dir. grad. studies, pres., 1970—82, Luther Coll., Decorah, Iowa, 1982—95; presiding bishop Evang. Luth. Ch. Am., Chgo., 1995—2001; ret., 2001. Chair Pub. House of the Evang. Luth. Ch. Am., 1987—93; co-chmn. U.S. Luth.-Roman Cath. Dialogue, 1979—90; mem. Commn. for a New Luth. Ch., 1982—86; v.p. Luth. World Fedn., 1996—. Author: Lutheranism in the Southeastern States, 1969, A Good Time to be the Church, 1997; co-author: Lutherans in North America, 1975; translator: I Believe (H. Thielicke), 1968, Historical Commentary on the Augsburg Confession (W. Maurer), 1986. Bd. dirs. Minn. Pub. Radio, St. Paul, 1983—91. Mem.: Luth. World Fedn. (commn. on studies 1984—90). Lutheran. Avocations: astronomy, sailing. Home: PO Box 719 Prospect Heights IL 60070-0719 E-mail: hgeorgea@earthlink.net.

ANDERSON, ILSE JANELL, clinical geneticist; b. Elmhurst, Ill., May 3, 1959; d. Lowell Leonard and Avis Janell Anderson; m. Nicholas Thomas Potter, June 24, 1989; children: Nils Andrew, Anders Matthew. BS in Biology, Lehigh U., 1981; MD, N.Y. Med. Coll., 1985. Diplomate Nat. Bd. Med. Examiners, Am. Bd. Pediatrics, Am. Bd. Med. Genetics. Resident pediatrics U. Conn., Farmington, 1985-88, fellow human genetics, 1988-91; clin. geneticist Med. Ctr. U. Tenn., Knoxville, 1991—. Mem. Phi Beta Kappa. Office: Univ Tenn Med Ctr 1930 Alcoa Hwy Ste 435 Knoxville TN 37920-1520

ANDERSON, J. TRENT, lawyer; b. Indpls., July 22, 1939; s. Robert C. and Charlotte M. (Pfeifer) Anderson; m. Judith J. Zimmerman, Sept. 8, 1962; children: Evan M., Molly K. BS, Purdue U., 1961; LLB, U. Va., 1964. Bar: Ill. 1965, Ind. 1965. Tchg. asst. Law Sch. U. Calif., Berkeley, 1964-65; assoc. Mayer, Brown & Platt, Chgo., 1965-72; ptnr. Mayer, Brown, Rowe & Maw LLP, Chgo., 1972—. Instr. Loyola U. Law Sch., Chgo., 1985. Mem.: Mich. Shores Club, Union League Club, Law Club. Home: 3037 Iroquois Rd Wilmette IL 60091-1106 Office: Mayer Brown Rowe & Maw LLP 71 S Wacker Dr Chicago IL 60606-4637 Office Phone: 312-701-7365. Business E-Mail: janderson@mayerbrown.com.

ANDERSON, JACK NORTHMAN, newspaper columnist; b. Long Beach, Calif., Oct. 19, 1922; s. Orlando N. and Agnes (Mortensen) A.; m. Olivia Farley, Aug. 10, 1949; children: Cheri, Lance F., Laurie, Tina, Kevin N., Randy N., Tanya, Rodney V., Bryan W. Student, U. Utah, 1940-41, Georgetown U., 1947-48, George Washington U., 1948. Reporter Salt Lake City Tribune, 1939-41; missionary in So. states for Mormon Ch., 1941-44; war corr. Deseret News, 1945; mem. staff Washington Merry-go-Round column, 1947—2004, co-writer, 1965—69, writer, 1969—2004; Washington editor Parade mag., 1954-68, bur. chief, from 1968. Host, panelist UPI Roundtable. Author: (with Ronald May) McCarthy the Man, the Senator, The Ism, 1952, (with Fred Blumenthal) The Kefauver Story, 1956, (with Drew Pearson) U.S.A. Second Class Power? 1958, Washington Expose, 1966, Case Against Congress, 1968, (with Carl Kalvelage) American Government-Like It Is, 1972, (with George Clifford) The Anderson Papers, 1973, (with James Boyd)

Confessions of a Muckraker, 1979, (with Bill Pronzini) The Cambodia File, 1981, (with John Kidner) Alice in Blunderland, 1983, (with James Boyd) Fiasco, 1983, Stormin' Norman, 1991, The Japan Conspiracy, 1993. Sec., trustee Chinese Refugee Relief, from 1962. Served with U.S. Mcht. Marine, 1944-45; with AUS, 1946-47. Recipient Pulitzer Prize for Nat. Reporting, 1972 Mem. White House Corr. Assn. Clubs: National Press (Washington). Office: United Features 200 Madison Ave Fl 4 New York NY 10016-3911

ANDERSON, JACK ROY, health care company executive; b. Mansfield, Ohio, Feb. 14, 1925; s. Roy L. and Katherine (Munson) A.; m. Rose-Marie J. Garcia, June 24, 1950; children— Gail Ellen, Neil Robert, Barbara Ann BS, Miami U., Oxford, Ohio, 1947; MS, Columbia Bus. Sch., 1949. Acctg. mgr. Time, Inc., N.Y.C., 1950-59; asst. to controller W.R. Grace & Co., N.Y.C., 1959-62; v.p., treas. Hartford Publs., Inc., N.Y.C., 1962-65; controller McCall Corp., N.Y.C., 1965-68; v.p. Reliance Group, Inc., N.Y.C., 1968-70; pres., dir. Hosp. Affiliates Internat., Inc., Nashville, 1970-76, chmn. bd., dir., 1977-81; chmn. INA Health Care Group, Dallas, 1978-81; pres. Manor Care, Inc., Silver Spring, Md., 1981-82, Calver Corp., Dallas, 1982—. Adj. faculty Vanderbilt Owen Grad. Sch. Mgmt., 1978—79. Author: The Road to Recovery, 1976. Trustee Nat. Com. for Quality Health Care, 1979—87, vice chmn., 1979—82; mem. bus. adv. coun. Miami U., 1975—78, chmn., 1978; mem. bd. overseers Hoover Instn. on War, Revolution and Peace, Stanford U.; mem. Pres.'s Cir., NAS, NAE, Inst. Medicine. Lt. (j.g.) USNR, 1943—46. Mem.: Montaigne Club, Reform Club, Greenwich Country Club, Met. Club, Double Eagle Club, Clove Valley Rd and Gun Club, Blind Brook Club, Desert Forest Golf Club, Beta Alpha Psi, Sigma Chi, Beta Gamma Sigma (hon.). Office: 16475 Dallas Pkwy Addison TX 75001-6821

ANDERSON, JACK W., historian, consultant, state representative; b. Augusta, Maine, Dec. 20, 1947; m. Diane Pepka; 1 child. BA, U. Maine, Orono, 1970; MA in Tech., Assumption Coll., 1975; MS, U. Vt., 1995. Historic preservation cons.; rep. Vt. State Ho. Reps., 1999—. Instr. history. Mem. Woodstock (Vt.) East End Study Group; active The Ctr. for Rsch. on Vt.; mem. Civil War Preservation Trust; trustee The Calvin Coolidge Meml. Found.; founder Green Mountain Civil War Round Table. Mem.: Woodstock Hist. Soc. (v.p.), Vt. Hist. Soc., Rotary. Independent. Home: 2812 Westerdale Cut Off Rd Woodstock VT 05091

ANDERSON, JACQUELINE ANNETTE, information technology manager; b. Balt., Jan. 20, 1962; d. Edward Anderson and Beatrice Ward. AA in Bus. Adminstrn., cert. in Office Skills, C.C. of Balt., 1984; BA in Mgmt. sci., Coppin State Univ., 2001. Sec. Social Security Adminstrn., Balt., 1982—86, computer asst., 1986—99, computer specialist, 1999—. Election judge voting polls Bd. Election, Balt., 1996—99; interviewer Senatorial Scholarship Com., Balt., 1996—2000. Mem.: Black Affairs Adv. Coun., Toastmasters Club (v.p. #7046 1999—2000, treas. #7046 2000—, Trophy 2000). Avocations: sewing, movies, reading, tennis. Personal E-mail: jcdarius@aol.com.

ANDERSON, JAMES, senator; b. Douglas, Wyo., Mar. 17, 1943; m. Pamela Anderson. BS in Edn., Chadron State Coll., 1996; postgrad., U. Wyo. Tchr.; logging and sawmill operator; precinct committeeman; Rep. rep. dist. 2 Wyo. Ho. of Reps., 1996-2000; senator Wyo. State Senate, 2000—. Mem. appropriations com. Wyo. State Senate, corps., elections and polit. subdivsns. Mem. Converse County Group Home. Mem. Nat. Coun. Tchrs. Math., NRA, Wyo. Reading Coun., Ducks Unltd., U. Wyo. Alumni, Glenrock C. of C. also: Wyo State Senate State Capitol Cheyenne WY 82002 Office: 92 Running Dutchman Dr Glenrock WY 82637-9512 E-mail: jamesda@msn.com.

ANDERSON, JAMES ALFRED, psychology professor, linguist; b. Detroit, July 31, 1940; s. Courtney Alfred and Catherine (Bullock) A.; m. Diana De Vincenzi, Nov. 1, 1969; 1 child, Eric David. BS, MIT, 1962, PhD, 1967. Postdoctoral fellow UCLA, 1967-71; research assoc. Rockefeller U., N.Y.C., 1971-73; asst. prof. cognitive and neural scis. Brown U., Providence, 1973-78, assoc. prof., 1978-85, prof., 1985—, chmn. dept. cognitive and linguistic scis., 1993—2002. Chmn. cognitive functional neurosci. rev. panel NIMH, 1992-94; mem. adv. bd. Social, Behavioral and Econ. Scis. Directorate, NSF, 1996-99; co-founder QCD Associates Inc., 1997-2003; founder Artemis Assocs., Inc., 1989-2004. Editor: (with G. Hinton) Parallel Models of Associative Memory, 1981, (with S. Lehmkuhle and W. Levy) Synaptic Modification, Neuron Selectivity and Nervous System Organization, 1985, (with E. Rosenfeld) Neurocomputing: Some Important Papers, 1988, (with E. Rosenfeld and A. Pellionisz) Neurocomputing 2, 1990, An Introduction to Neural Networks, 1995; (with E. Rosenfeld) Talking Nets, 1998. Recipient Info. Sci. award, Joint Conf. on Info. Sci., 2002; grantee, NSF, 1979, 1985, 1991, 1997, Office Naval Rsch., 1986, 1991, 1996, Def. Advanced Rsch. Projects Agy., 2002. Mem. Cognitive Sci. Soc., Psychonomic Soc., Soc. for Neurosci., Soc. for Math. Psychology, Internat. Neural Network Soc. (governing bd. 1987-95), Sigma Xi. Avocation: amateur radio. Home: 1 Mathewson Rd Barrington RI 02806-4414 Office: Brown U Dept Cognitive & Linguistic Scis 190 Thayer St Providence RI 02912-9067 Office Phone: 401-863-2195. Business E-Mail: James_Anderson@Brown.edu.

ANDERSON, JAMES E., lawyer; b. Jan. 31, 1965; BA, Univ. Utah, 1988; JD magna cum laude, Brigham Young Univ., 1992. Bar: Utah 1992, DC 1995. Staff atty. Office of Investment Co. Regulation SEC; ptnr., co-chmn. Investment Mgmt. group Wilmer Cutler Pickering Hale & Dorr, Washington, 1994—. Co-author: Investment Advisers: Law & Compliance; author (contbr.): Mutual Fund Regulation. Office: Wilmer Cutler Pickering Hale & Dorr 2445 M St NW Washington DC 20037 Office Phone: 202-663-6180. Office Fax: 202-663-6363. Business E-Mail: james.anderson@wilmerhale.com.

ANDERSON, JAMES E., JR., lawyer, information technology executive; BA, Stanford U., 1969, JD, 1972; attended, U. Calif. at Berkeley Grad. Sch. Bus. Bar: Calif. 1972, Tex. 1973, Tenn. 1985. Assoc. Akin, Gump, Strauss, Hauer & Feld, Dallas, 1972-74, 76-78, ptnr., 1979-83, Wald, Harkrader & Ross, 1983-84, Dearborn & Ewing, Nashville, 1984-91; v.p., gen. counsel Ingram Industries Inc., Nashville, 1991-96; sr. v.p., sec., gen. counsel Ingram Micro Inc., Santa Ana, Calif., 1996—2004; ret., 2004.

ANDERSON, JAMES FRANCIS, lawyer; b. Glen Ridge, NJ, June 13, 1965; BA, Seton Hall U., 1987, JD, 1990. Bar: N.J. 1991, U.S. Supreme Ct. 1995. Pvt. practice, Spring Lake, NJ, 1991—2001; staff atty. Ocean-Monmouth Legal Svcs., Freehold, NJ, 2001—. Pro bono atty. Ocean-Monmouth Legal Svcs., Freehold, N.J., 1991-2001; mentor Manasquan (NJ) HS, 1994. Office: 25-13 Broad St Freehold NJ 07728 E-mail: janderson@monmouth.com.

ANDERSON, JAMES FREDERICK, clergyman; b. Elizabeth, N.J., Aug. 23, 1927; s. Fred and Hazel Minerva (Brown) A.; m. Bette Dillensnyder, Sept. 8, 1951; children: Judith (Mrs. Wayne Westbury) (dec.), James Frederick, Mark, Rebecca (Mrs. Patrick Williams). BA, Princeton U., 1948; BD, Princeton Theol. Sem., 1952; DD, Alma Coll., 1974. Ordained to ministry Presbyn. Ch., 1952; chaplain Hun Sch. for Boys, Princeton, 1953; instr. religion Lafayette Coll., Easton, Pa., 1954-55; pastor Presbyn. chs., Catasauqua, Pa., 1956-61, Narberth, Pa., 1961-66, Second Presbyn. Ch., Richmond, Va., 1966-72, Kirk in the Hills, Bloomfield Hills, Mich., 1972-94, pastor emeritus, 1994—. Trustee emeritus Alma (Mich.) Coll. With USNR, 1945-46. Home: 3808 Haylor's Beach Way Glen Allen VA 23060-7232

ANDERSON, JAMES GEORGE, sociologist, educator, communications educator; b. Balt., July 24, 1936; s. Clair Sherrill and Kathryn Ann (Plovanich) A.; m. Marilyn Anderson, 1984; children: Robin Marie, James Brian, Melissa Lee, Derek Clair. B in Engring. Scis. in Chem. Engring, Johns Hopkins U., 1957, MSE in Ops. Rsch. and Indsl. Engring., 1959, MAT in Chemistry and Math., 1960, PhD in Edn. and Sociology, 1964. Adminstrv. asst. to dean Eve. Coll., Johns Hopkins U., 1964-65, dir. divsn. engring., 1965-66; rsch. prof. ednl. adminstrn. N.Mex. State U., 1966-70; mem. faculty Purdue U., Lafayette, Ind., 1970—, prof. sociology, 1974—, prof. com., 2004—; asst. dean for analytical studies Sch. Humanities, Social Sci. and Edn., Lafayette, Ind., 1975-78. Assoc. dir. AIDS Rsch. Ctr., Purdue U., 1991—, co-dir. Rural Ctr. for AIDS/STD Prevention, 1993—; adj. prof. med. sociology grad. med. edn. program Meth. Hosp. Ind., 1991—; dir. Social Rsch. Inst., Purdue U., 1995-98; cons. in field. Guest editor spl. issue on simulation in health sci.: Simulation, Apr., 1996, spl. issues on modeling epidemics: guest editor spl issue on simulation in med. informatics, Jour. of the Am. Med. Informatics Assn, 2002; issue in simulation in health care mgmt., Health Care Mgmt. Sci., 2002. Mem. Am. Assn. for Med. Systems and Informatics Del. to the Peoples Republic of China, 1985; mem., citizens amb. People to People Med. Informatics Del. to Hungary and Russia, 1993. USPHS grant; recipient award for outstanding paper Am. Assn. Med. Sys. and Informatics, 1983, Gov. award State of Ind., 1987, T. Hale New Investigators award Assn. Am. Med. Coll., 1988, Wyeth-Ayerst/William Campbell Felch, MD award Alliance for Continuing Med. Edn., 1995, Seeds of Excellence award, Purdue U., 2005. Fellow: Am. Coll. Med. Informatics; mem.: APHA, AAUP, AAAS (rep. soc. for computer simulation biol. scis. sect. 1992—99), Social Sci. Computing Assn. (chair life scis. 1991—), Am. Sociol. Assn. (chair sect. sociology and computers 2000—01), Internat. Soc. Sys. Sci. in Health Care, Internat. Network for Social Network Analysis (chair life scis. 1997—), Soc. Modeling and Computer Simulation (sr.; assoc. v.p. simulation in health care 1992—), Am. Med. Informatics Assn. (internat. affairs com. 1993—96, chmn. sect. ethical, legal and social issues 1997—2000, sci. program com. ann. conf. 1999, mem. editl. bd. 2000—, chmn. sect. on quality improvement 2002—04, guest editor 2002, Best Theoretical Paper award 1997), Am. Ednl. Rsch. Assn. (treas. spl. interest group 1969—71), Am. Sociol. Assn., Assn. for Computing Machinery. Business E-Mail: andersonj@soc.purdue.edu.

ANDERSON, JAMES GILBERT, chemistry professor; BS, physics, U Washington, Seattle, 1966; PhD, physics, astrogeophysics, U Colorado, Boulder, 1970. Prof. Harvard U., Cambridge, Mass., 1978—, now Philip S. Weld prof. atmospheric chemistry, chmn. dept. chemistry and chem. biology. Recipient Am. Chem. Soc. award, 1989, Gustavus John Esselen award, 1993, Earth Day Internat. award UN, 1992, Arts and Scis. Disting. Alumnus Achievement award U. Wash., 1993, E.O. Lawrence award in environ. sci. and tech., 1993. Fellow Am. Geophysical Union, Am. Assn. for the Advancement of Sci., Am. Acad. of Arts and Sci.; mem. NAS (Arthur Lay prize and lectureship 1996). Achievements include research in stratospheric physics and chemistry central to the understanding of atmospheric ozone and the ozone hole above the Antarctic. Office: Harvard U Dept of Chem & Chem Biology 12 Oxford St Cambridge MA 02138-2902

ANDERSON, JAMES M., pathologist; BS in Chemistry, U. Wis., Eau Claire; PhD in Chemistry, Oreg. State U. Prof. pathology, macromolecular sci. and biomed. engring. Inst. of Pathology, Case Western Res. U., Cleve. Cons. NIH, FDA. Contbr. over 300 articles to profl. jours.; editor: Jour. of Biomed. Materials Rsch. Mem.: Soc. for Biomaterials (past pres.), Controlled Release Soc. (pres.), Inst. of Medicine, 2004 (life). Office: Case Western Reserve Univ Inst of Pathology 2085 Adelbert Rd Cleveland OH 44106

ANDERSON, JAMES MILTON, lawyer; b. Chgo., Dec. 29, 1941; s. Milton H. and Eunice (Carlson) A.; m. Marjorie Henry Caldwell, Jan. 22, 1966; children: James Milton, Joseph H., Hilding F., Marjorie II. BA, Yale U., 1963; JD, Vanderbilt U., 1966. Bar: Ohio 1967. Assoc. rifm Taft, Stettinius & Hollister, Cin., 1968-75, ptnr., 1975-77, 82-96, mem. exec. com., 1975-77, 91-96; pres. U.S. ops., dir. Xomox Corp., Cin., 1977-81; sec. Access Corp., 1984-96; asst. sec. Carlisle Cos., 1985-90; bd. dirs. Nat. Stock Exch., 1978—, chmn., 1980-89. Bd. dirs. Command Sys. Inc., 1986—2002; trustee, chmn. Monarch Found., 1988—; assoc. sr. v.p. med. affairs U. Cin., 1997—; bd. adminstrs. Coun. Tchg. Hosps., 2000—04; dir. Nat. Assn. Children's Hosps. and Related Instns., 2002—; bd. dirs. 3CDC Inc., 2003—, Uptown Consortium, 2004—; chmn. bd. dirs. Cin. br. Fed. Res. Bank Cleve., 2005—; bd. dirs. Union Ctrl. Life Ins. Co.; chmn. bd. dirs. Cin. br. Fed. Res. Bank of Cleve. Mem. Indian Hill Coun., 1981-89, vice-mayor, 1985-87, mayor, 1987-89; mem. Hamilton County Airport Authority, 1980-85; trustee Children's Hosp. Med. Ctr., Cin., 1979—, chmn. bd. trustees, 1991-96, pres., CEO, 1996—; trustee The Children's Hosp. Found., 1990—, chmn. bd. trustees, 1990-93; trustee Cin. Ctr. for Devel. Disorders, 1969—, pres., 1974-80; trustee Dan Beard coun. Boy Scouts Am., 1982—, chmn., 1984-87, area pres. Ea. Ctrl. Region, 1989-91; trustee Cin. Mus. Natural History, 1984-87, Coll. Mt. St. Joseph, 1990-98; trustee Joy Outdoor Edn. Ctr., 1984-2000, pres., 1991-93, chmn., 1993-95. Capt. AUS, 1966-68. Decorated Bronze Star with two oak leaf clusters, Air medal. Mem. ABA, Ohio Bar Assn., Cin. Bar Assn., Valve Mfrs. Assn., Young Pres. Orgn., Camargo Club, Queen City Club, Commonwealth Club, Yale Club of N.Y., Cin. Yale Club, Order of Coif, Comml. Club. Avocation: sailing. Office: 3333 Burnet Ave Cincinnati OH 45229-3026

ANDERSON, JAMES WINGO, physician; b. Hinton, W.Va., Aug. 6, 1936; s. Fred Wingo and Georgia Lee (Whittaker) A.; m. Gay Veree Gilbert, June 7, 1957; children: Katherine, Steven. BS, W.Va. U., 1957; MD, Northwestern U., 1961; MS, Mayo Clinic, 1965. Intern Presbyn. Med. Ctr., Denver; resident, fellow Mayo Clinic, Rochester, Minn.; asst. prof. medicine U. Calif., San Francisco, 1968-73; prof. medicine, clin. nutrition U. Ky. Coll. Medicine, Lexington, 1973—; pres., founder HCF Nutrition Found., Lexington, 1979—. Author: Diabetes-A Practical Guide to HEalty Living, 1981, Dr. Anderson's High Fiber Fitness Plan, 1994, Dr. Anderson;s Antioxident Antiaging, 1996. Trustee Georgetown (Ky.) Coll., 1988—, chmn. bd. trustees, 1994-96. Capt. U.S. Army, 1965-68. Fellow Am. Coll. Physicians. Republican. Baptist. Home: 913 Taborlake Ct Lexington KY 40502-3032 Office: VA Med Ctr 2250 Leestown Rd Lexington KY 40511-1052 Office Phone: 859-257-4058.

ANDERSON, JANICE M., freelance/self-employed photojournalist; b. Muncie, Ind., Oct. 19, 1938; d. John A. and Iva May McCreary; m. Jack W. Anderson, Dec. 1, 1974; m. Joe Bill Ewing (div.); children: Greg A. Ewing, Kathy L. Buesink, Gary J. Ewing. Student, Ball State U., 1990. Notary pub.: Ind.; Cert. Profl. Sec. Reporter, photographer Brownsburg Guide, Ind., 1964—68; reporter, circulation asst., photographer, writer Frankfort Times, 1969—71; reporter Lafayette Jour. Courier, Lafayette, 1971—72; reporter, broadcaster Kaspar Broadcasting (WILO Radio), Frankfort, 1972—75; sec. City Engr. Frankfort, Ind., 1975—83; baliff Clinton Circuit Ct., 1983—84; sec. to dean Ball State U., Muncie, 1985—2002. Freelance photojournalist, Muncie, 1969—. Sec. to city engr., asst. secy to mayor City of Frankfort, 1976—83, sec. plan commn., sec. to zoning bd.; sec., radio operator Clinton County CD, 1977—83; apptd. mem. Clinton County Area Plan Commn., sec., co-director, 1975—76; writer, coach puppet ministry First Bapt. Ch., 1977—84; bd. dirs., sec., treas. Am. Bapt. Campus Ministry at Ball State U., Muncie, 1987—2002; writer, prodr., camera, bd. operator First Bapt. Ch. TV Ministry, Frankfort, 1976—84; pub. rels. coord. Ctrl. Ind. Coun. of Campfire Girls, Indpls., 1963—68; bd. mem. Clinton County Boys Club, Frankfort. Nominee Woman of the Yr., 1995, 1997, A. Jane Morton award Excellence Staff Performance, Ball State U., 1996; named Poet of Yr. and Internat. Poet of Merit, Internat. Soc. Poets, 2005; named to Internat. Poetry Hall of Fame, 1996; recipient Top News Story in Ind., 1972, Key to the City, Hon. Mayor of Frankfort, 1983, Meritorious Svc. award, Ball State U., 1992, Best Poems and Poets of Yr., The Internat. Libr. of Poetry, 1995—2004, Internat. Profl. and Bus. Women's Hall of Fame, 1995—2001, Pres.'s award, Iliad Press, 1995. Mem.: Am. Women Radio & TV (state conf. chair 1975), Internat. Assn. Adminstrv. Profls. (chpt. pres. 1995—97, ind. divsn. historian 1995—2000, editor, historian local chpt. 1996—2000, ind. divsn. ann. meeting registration chair 2001). American Baptist. Achievements include Star Lecturer, Conway Diet Institute. Avocations: writing, travel, antiques. Personal E-mail: janderso@bsu.edu.

ANDERSON, J.C., oil industry executive, gas industry executive, rancher; b. Oakland, Nebr. Student, Midland Coll., Fremont, Nebr., 1949-51; BSc in Petroleum Engring., U. Tex., 1954. With Amoco Prodn. Co., various locations; chief engr. Amoco Can., Calgary, Alta., 1966-68; founder, chmn. bd., CEO Anderson Exploration Ltd., Calgary, 1968—2001; rancher Anderson Ranch; pvt. practice. With Counter-Intelligence Corps, U.S. Army, 1954-56. Mem. Assn. Profl. Engrs., Geologists and Geophysicists of Alta., Soc. Petroleum Engrs., Can. Soc. Petroleum Geologists. Office: Ste 239 132-250 Shawville Blvd SE Calgary AB Canada T2Y 2Z7 Office Phone: 403-256-7550. E-mail: husker@telus.net.

ANDERSON, JEAN BRADLEY, writer; b. Phila., June 1, 1924; d. William Nathaniel and Marion Agnes (Butsch) Bradley; m. Carl Lennart Anderson, June 30, 1952; children: William Bradley, Julian Augusta. BA in English, U. Pa., 1946, MA in English, 1948, postgrad., 1948-52. Rschr. N.C. Divsn. of Archives and History, Raleigh, 1976-80. Author: Piedmont Plantation, 1985, The History of Durham County, 1990, The Kirklands of Ayr Mount, 1990, North Carolinian on the Hudson, 1996. Apptd. mem. Orange County (N.C.) Hist. Preservation Commn., 1991—, Hist. Hillsborough Commn., 1998—. Mem. Hist. Soc. N.C. (elected), Hist. Stagville Found. (bd. mem., pres. 1998—), North Caroliniana Soc. (elected), Friends of the N.C. Archives (bd. mem. 1996-2002), Eno River Assn. (bd. mem. 1966-77), Hillsborough Hist. Soc. (bd. mem. 1965-87, Engstrom award 1986), Hist. Preservation Soc. Durham (charter, bd. mem.), Phi Beta Kappa (Beta chpt.Pa.). Democrat. Avocations: genealogy, antiques, biographical and historical reading, historic preservation. Home: 2701 Pickett Rd #4044 Durham NC 27705 E-mail: jean.anderson1@verizon.net.

ANDERSON, JEAN R., women's health physician; b. 1953; MD, Vanderbilt U. Intern and resident in obstetrics and gynecology Vanderbilt U.; attending physician Met. Nashville Gen. Hosp., 1983—86; assoc. prof. dept. population and family health sci. Johns Hopkins Sch. Pub. Health, Balt., assoc. prof. gynecology and obstetrics; founding dir. Johns Hopkins HIV Women's Health Program, Balt., 1987—; faculty Johns Hopkins U., Balt., 1987—. Cons. to Brazilian Ministry of Health, 1998. Author, editor: The Manual for the Clinical Care of Women with HIV, 2001; contbr. articles to profl. jour. Recipient CIBA award for cmty. svc., Vanderbilt U. Sch. Medicine, 1977. Fellow: Am. Coll. Obstetricians and Gynecologists; mem.: Am. Acad. HIV Medicine. Office: Johns Hoplins Divsn Gynecologic Specialties Harvey 319 600 N Wolfe St Baltimore MD 21287

ANDERSON, JEFFREY LEE, physician, anesthesiologist, consultant; b. Fontana, Calif., Feb. 3, 1959; s. Earle R. and Joyce E. Anderson; m. Crystal G. Anderson, Dec. 18, 1987; children: Kimberly, Kristin. BS, USAF Acad., 1981; MD, Loma Linda U., 1985. Cert. in anesthesiology. Resident in anesthesiology Loma Linda (Calif.) U. Med. Ctr., 1985-89; chief anesthesiologist USAF Hosp., Mather AFB, Calif., 1989-93; staff anesthesiologist Mercy Hosp. of Folsom, Calif., 1990—, Mercy Gen. Hosp., Sacramento, 1992—, Mercy San Juan Hosp., Carmichael, Calif., 1997—; chief anesthesiologist Folsom Surgery Ctr., 2001—. Medicolegal cons. Med. Bd. Calif., Sacramento, 1995—; clin. faculty U. Calif. Davis Sch. Medicine, 1993-96; anesthesia cons. Blue Shield of Calif., 1998—. Co-author: (textbook) Manual of Postanesthesia Care, 1993. Instr., course dir. ACLS, Am. Heart Assn., Sacramento, 1992—; physician Mercy White Rock Free Clin., 1994—. Mem. Calif. Soc. Anesthesiologists, C. of C. Office: 1650 Creekside Dr Folsom CA 95630-3400 Office Phone: 916-983-7490. Personal E-mail: folsomlakeortho@aol.com.

ANDERSON, JEFFREY LYNN, music educator; b. Lexington, Ky., Nov. 14, 1976; s. George Fox and Linda Kay Anderson; m. Katherine Ann Anderson, Aug. 31, 2003. B of Music Edn., U. Louisville, 2000, MusM, 2002. Tchr. music, band, chorus Beth County High Sch, Owingsville, Ky., 2000—01; rep. band & orch. Don Wilson Music, Inc., Louisville, 2002—03; trombone soloist The Top Brass, 2002—; children's min. Buckner Bapt. Ch., La Grange, 2003—; tchr. band Henry County Pub. Schs., New Castle, 2003—. Instr. North Woods High Sch. Band, Radcliff, Ky., 1999—2003, Western Hills High Sch. Band, Frankfort, 2000—02. Performer: (albums) Music for the Holidays, 2001. Vol. musician Buckner Bapt. Ch., La Grange, 2003—, Burgass Christian Ch., Louisville, 2002—03; vol. Parkwood Bapt. Ch., 1996—97. Scholar, Brevard Music Ctr., N.C., 1995—96. Mem.: Ky. Music Educators Assn. (membership dist. rep. 2003), Phi Mu Alpha (pres. 1998—2002). Republican. Baptist. Avocations: cooking, history.

ANDERSON, JERRY LEE, pianist, music educator; b. St. Louis, Dec. 24, 1941; m. Joanne Jones, Aug. 24, 1963. BS, diploma in Piano, S.W. Mo. State U., 1962; MusM, U. Wichita, 1964; postgrad., U. N.C., U. Iowa. Prof. music Augustana Coll., Rock Island, Ill., 1969-70; dir. music First Luth. Ch., Moline, Ill., 1970-72; prof., dir. keyboard studies Mo. Western State U., St. Joseph, 1972—; dir. music First Presbyn. Ch., St. Joseph, 1974—. Mem. Music Tchrs. Nat. Assn. (chmn. west-cen. div. auditions 1980-82), Mo. Music Tchrs. Assn. (editor Notes 1976-79, chmn. piano div. for Mo. 1984-92, univ. faculty 1996—, Mo. Music Tchr. of Yr. 2004). Business E-Mail: anderson@missouriwestern.edu.

ANDERSON, JERRY MAYNARD, retired speech educator; b. Deronda, Wis., Sept. 16, 1933; s. Jens B. and Mamie P. (Hanson) A.; m. Betty Lou Schultz, Feb. 7, 1959; children: Gregory J., Timothy B. BS, Wis. State U. at River Falls, 1958; MS, No. Ill. U., 1959; PhD, Mich. State U., 1964; postgrad., U. Minn., 1987, U. Ariz., 1997. Instr. speech U. Maine, 1959-61; asst. prof. speech, dir. forensics Mich. State U., 1961-68; prof., chmn. dept. speech and dramatic arts Central Mich. U., Mt. Pleasant, 1968-72, vice provost, 1972—73; provost, v.p. acad. affairs and prof. speech Western Wash. U., 1973-75; vice chancellor, prof. speech U. Wis., Oshkosh, 1975-79; pres., prof. speech Ball State U., Muncie, Ind., 1979-81; sr. cons. Am. Assn. State Colls. and Univs., Washington, 1981-82; rsch. adminstr. U. Wis., Stout, 1982—85; v.p. devel. Concordia Coll., Minn., 1985-88, prof. speech comm., 1988-99, prof. emeritus, 2000—; pres. Anderson and Assoc. Cons., 2000—. Author: Handbook for Forensic Students, 1963, Readings in Argumentation, 1968, Essays in Forensics, 1970, Case Studies in Public Relations: The 1994 U.S. West Crisis in Fargo, 1998; contbr. articles to profl. jours., chapters to books. Trustee Lake Wapogasset Assn.; bd. dirs. Radio Sta. WPCA. With USN, 1952—54. Recipient 1st Sr. Disting. Professionalism award Central Mich. U., 1971; Research fellow Harry S Truman Found., 1965; fellow Am. Council on Edn. Acad. Adminstrn. Internship Program, 1971-72; Recipient Disting. Alumnus award Delta Sigma Rho-Tau Kappa Alpha, 1980; Sagamore of Wabash Public Service award Gov. of Ind., 1980 Mem. Ctrl. States Speech Assn. (pres. 1973, Outstanding Young Tchr. award 1966), Mich. Speech Assn. (pres. 1967-68), Am. Forensic Assn. (pres. 1972-74, Disting. Svc. award 1994), Midwest Forensic Assn. (pres. 1969-72), Speech Comm. Assn. (legis. coun. 1967, legis. assembly 1975), Kiwanis, Rotary. Office Phone: 715-268-8494. Personal E-mail: jandbander@amerytel.net. *During my adult years the aphorism attributed to the late Senator Robert M. laFollette, Sr., has guided my work with others: "Give the people the facts and freedom to discuss and all will go well.".*

ANDERSON, JERRY WILLIAM, JR., diversified financial services company executive, educator; b. Stow, Mass., Jan. 14, 1926; s. Jerry William and Heda Charlotte (Petersen) A.; m. Joan Hukill Balyeat, Sept. 13, 1947; children: Katheleen, Diane. BS in Physics, U. Cin., 1949, PhD in Econs., 1976; MBA, Xavier U., 1959. Rsch. and test project engr. Wright-Patterson AFB, Ohio, 1949-53; project engr., electronics divsn. AVCO Corp., Cin., 1953-70, program mgr., 1970-73; program dir. Cin. Electronics Corp., 1973-78; pres. Anderson Industries Unltd., 1978—. Chmn. dept. mgmt. and mgmt. info. svcs. Xavier U., 1980-89, prof. mgmt., 1989-94, prof. emeritus, 1994—; lectr. No. Ky. U., 1977-78; tech. adviser Cin. Tech. Coll., 1971-80; co-founder, exec. v.p. Loving God "Complete Bible" Christian Ministries, 1988—. Contbr. articles on radars, lasers, infrared detection equipment, air pollution to govt. pubs. and prof. jours.; author: 3 books in field; reviewer, referee: Internat. Jour. Energy Sys., 1985—86. Mem. Madeira (Ohio) City Planning Commn., 1962-80; founder, pres. Grassroots, Inc., 1964; active United Appeal, Heart Fund, Multiple Sclerosis Fund. With USNR, 1943-46. Named Man of Yr., City of Madeira, 1964. Mem. MADD, VFW (life), Am. Mgmt. Assn., Assn. Energy Engrs. (charter), Internat. Acad. Mgmt. and Mktg., Nat. Right to Life, Assn. Cogeneration Engrs. (charter), Assn. Environ. Engrs. (charter), Am. Legion (past comdr.), Acad. Mgmt., Madeira Civic

Assn. (past v.p.), Cin. Art Mus., Cin. Zoo, Colonial Williamsburg Found., Omicron Delta Epsilon. Republican. Home and Office: 7208 Sycamorehill Ln Cincinnati OH 45243-2101 Office Phone: 513-561-7685.

ANDERSON, JEWELLE LUCILLE, musician, educator; b. Alexandria, La., Jan. 4, 1932; d. William Andrew and Ethel Dee (Hall) Anderson. Student, Springfield Coll., 1981-82; MusB, Boston U., 1984; postgrad., Harvard U., 1995-96. Cert. tchr. music and social studies Mass. Soloist Ch. of the Redeemer Episcopal Ch., Chestnut Hill, Mass., 1964-69, St. James Episcopal Ch., Cambridge, Mass., 1970-75; kindergarten tchr. and music dir. Trinity Episcopal Ch., Boston, 1984-86; chorus music dir. Spencer for Hire, Boston, 1986; music dir. Days in the Arts summer program Boston Symphony Orch., Tanglewood, Mass., summer 1991, 92; chorale dir. Boston Orch. Chorale, 1996-97; tchr. scholar Harvard Grad. Sch. of Edn., 1998-99. Founder Jewelle Anderson Found., Inc., Boston, 1996. Vol. ARC, Boston, 1994—; bd. dirs. Mattapan Cmty. Health Ctr., Boston, 1990—92; founder, pres. Dr. William and Ethel Hall Anderson Scholarship, 1989—. Recipient Am. Music award, Nat. Fedn. Music, 1970, Spl. Individual award, 1969, Outstanding Contbn. to Humanity award, Alexandria Civic Improvement Coun., 1967, Outstanding Achievement award, Boston Tchrs. Union, 2000, Cope Plaque for Outstanding Achievement, 2000, Action for Boston Cmty. Devel. award, 2003. Mem.: AAUW, Black Educators Alliance of Mass., Amnesty Internat., Women Svc. Club (head youth group 1989—, 1st v.p. 2002), Alpha Kappa Alpha. Democrat. Baptist. Avocations: walking, boating. Office: PO Box 124 Boston MA 02117-0124

ANDERSON, JOAN BALYEAT, theology studies educator, minister; b. Cin., Apr. 14, 1926; d. Hal Donal and Myrtle (Skinner) Hukill Balyeat; m. Jerry William Anderson, Jr., Sept. 13, 1947: children: Katheleen, Diane. AA, Stephens Coll., 1946. Ordained Christian minister Ohio, 1988. Christian ch. bible tchr., Cin., 1944—; Christian counselor, advisor, 1964—; founder, pres., dir., ruling elder, and pastor Loving God "Complete Bible" Christian Ministries and First Ch., Cin., 1988—. Christian Bible tchr., preacher, pastor daily and Sunday radio throughout the east and midwest, 1988—. Mem. Am. Conservative Cause, 1998—2001, Capitol His. Soc., 2000—; legacy leader supporter George Washington's Mt. Vernon, 2001—; coord., collector Heart Fund, T.B., 1948—90; civic assn. officer, rep. edn. com. to all Madeira Schs., 1960—62; co-founder, officer Grassroots, Inc., Cin., 1962—65; mem. Cin. Art Mus., 1972—, Cin. Zoo, 1974—, Colonial Williamsburg Found., 1979—, Nat. Right to Life, 1980—, MADD, 1985—, Heritage Found., 1996—, Am. Conservative Union, 1998, Ronald Reagan Presdl. Found., 1998—, Parents TV Coun., 1998—2001, Am. Policy Ctr., 1998—2001, U.S. Justice Found., 1998—, Nat. Right to Work Legal Def. Found., 1998—, Nat. Security Ctr., 1998—, U.S. Intelligence Ctr., 1998—, Jud. Watch, 1999—, Young Ams. Found., 2000—; supporter The Liberty Com., 2001—; lifelong activist for preservation of U.S. Constn. and Bill of Rights; mem. U.S. Rep. Senatorial Adv. Com., Washington and Cin., 1987—88; mem. Rep. Senatorial Commn., Washington & Cin., 1996—2000; mem. Am. Prayer Network, 1998—. Master: Blue Book of Cin. Avocation: touring america by car. Home: 7208 Sycamorehill Ln Cincinnati OH 45243-2101 Office: Loving God Complete Bible Christian Mins/1st Ch PO Box 43404 Cincinnati OH 45243-2101

ANDERSON, JOHN ALBERT, physician; b. Ashtabula, Ohio, Jan. 25, 1935; s. Albert Gunnard Anderson and Martha Anetta (Bieshline) White; m. Nicole Jeanne Anderson, July 10, 1963; children: Carole Beno, John-Marc, Christopher B. BS, U. Ill., 1958, MD, 1960. Diplomate Am. Bd. Pediat., Am. Bd. Allergy and Immunology. Intern U. Ill., 1960-61, resident in pediat. Chgo., 1961-62, U.S. Naval Hosp., Bethesda, Md., 1964-65; fellow in allergy and immunology Children's Hosp., Washington, 1967-69; mem. sr. staff Henry Ford Hosp., Detroit, 1969-99, dir. pediat. allergy fellowship program, 1969-77, dir. allergy and immunology program, 1977-99, head divsn. allergy and immunology, dept. pediatrics, 1977-99, chmn. dept. pediatrics, 1982-90; physician Vivra Asthma and Allergy, Tucson, 1999-2000; with Vivra Asthma and Allergy, Inc., 2000—02; physician Allergy and Asthma Ctr. Ariz., Tucson, 2001—03, Aspen Med. Ctr., Fort Collins, 2003—. Clin. prof. U. Mich., Ann Arbor, 1985—94; prof. pediat. Case Western Res. U., 1994—99; dir. Am. Bd. Allergy and Immunology, 1990—96, sec., 1995—96. Contbr. articles Contbr. more than 60 articles to profl. jours. Lt. comdr. USN, 1962-66. Fellow Am. Acad. Allergy and Immunology (pres. 1990-91), Am. Acad. Pediat. (chmn. allergy sect. 1979-82), Mich. Allergy Soc. (pres. 1978-79); mem. Asthma and Allergy Found. Am. (dir. 1992-99, v.p. med. affairs 1992-95, v.p. rsch. 1995-99), Coun. Med. Splty. Socs. (bd. dirs. 1992-94), Am. Bd. Med. Specialists, Sci. Advisors Internat. Life Scis. (allergy sect. 1990-2003). Home: 7368 Tamarisk Dr Fort Collins CO 80528 Office: 2001 S Shields Bldg H Fort Collins CO 80526 Office Phone: 970-498-9226. Personal E-mail: jonicoleanderson@msn.com.

ANDERSON, JOHN DAVID, architect; b. New Haven, Dec. 24, 1926; s. William Edward and Norma Vere (Carson) A.; m. Florence A. Van Dyke, Aug. 26, 1950; children— Robert Stewart, David Carson. AB cum laude, Harvard U., 1949, M.Arch., 1952. Draftsman John K. Monroe, Architect, Denver, 1952-54; draftsman, designer, assoc. Wheeler & Lewis, Architects, Denver, 1954-60; pvt. practice Denver, 1960-64; ptnr. Anderson, Barker Rinker, Architects, Denver, 1965-69, A-B-R Partnership, Architects, Denver, 1970-75; prin., CEO Anderson Mason Dale P.C., Denver, 1975-96, sr. v.p., 1997—. Vis. lectr. U. Colo., U. N.Mex., U. Nebr., U. Cape Town, Colo. State U., Plymouth Polytech., Eng.; chmn. Colo. Gov.'s Task Force on Removal of Archtl. Barriers, 1972-74; vice chmn. Colo. Bd. Non-Residential Energy Conservation Stds., 1978-80. Prin. works include: Front Range Community Coll., Westminster, 1977, Solar Energy Rsch. Inst., Golden, 1980 (award winning solar heated structures). Served with USNR, 1944-46. Fellow AIA (pres. Colo. chpt. 1967, Western Mountain region dir. 1995-97, Silver medal, 1984, Firm of Yr. award 1986 Western Mountain region); mem. AIA (Arch. of Yr. award 1987, pres. 1971, nat. v.p. 1999, 1st v.p. 2000, pres. 2001), Internat. Solar Energy Soc., Council Ednl. Facility Planners (internat. chmn. energy com. 1980). Democrat. Congregationalist. Home: 57 S Rainbow Trail Golden CO 80401-8341 Office: Anderson Mason Dale Architects 1615 17th St Denver CO 80202-1293 Office Phone: 303-294-9448. Business E-Mail: janderson@amdarchitects.com.

ANDERSON, JOHN DAVID, JR., aerospace engineer; b. Lancaster, Pa., Oct. 1, 1937; s. John David and Esther Pearl (Stoneback) A.; m. Sarah Allen West, Sept. 11; children: Katherine Josephine, Elizabeth Esther. B.Aero. Engring. with honors (Gen. Motors scholar, J. Hillis Meml. scholar), U. Fla., 1959; PhD in Aero. Engring., Ohio State U. Chief hypersonics group Naval Ordnance Lab., White Oak, Md., 1966-73; prof., chmn. dept. aerospace engring. U. Md., College Park, 1973-99; prof. emeritus U. Md., College Park, 1999—; Charles Lindbergh prof. Nat. Air Space Mus. Smithsonian Instn., 1986-87; curator for aerodynamics Nat. Air Space Mus., Smithsonian Instn., 1998—. Author: Gasdynamic Lasers: An Introduction, 1976, Introduction to Flight: Its Engineering and History, 1978, 4th edit., 2000, Modern Compressible Flow: with Historical Perspective, 1982, 3d edit., 2003, Fundamentals of Aerodynamics, 1984, 3d edit., 2001, Hypersonic and High Temperature Gasynamics, 1989, Computational Fluid Dynamics, 1995; History of Aerodynamics, and Its Impact on Flying Machines, 1997, Aircraft Performance and Design, 1999, The Airplane: A History of Its Technology, 2003, Inventing Flight, 2004; contbr. articles to profl. jours. Served with USAF, 1959-62. Named disting. scholar/tchr. U. Md., 1981-82; NSF fellow, NASA fellow Ohio State U., 1966; recipient Meritorious Civilian Service award Naval Ordnance Lab., 1972 Fellow Washington Acad. Scis. (Engring. Sci. award 1975), AIAA, Royal Aeronaut. Soc.; mem. Am. Soc. Engring. Edn., Am. Phys. Soc., Sigma Xi, Tau Beta Pi, Sigma Tau, Phi Kappa Phi, Phi Eta Sigma. Roman Catholic. Office: U Md Dept Aerospace Engring College Park MD 20742-0001 also: Aeronautics Dept Nat Air and Space Mus Smithsonian Inst Washington DC 20560-0312 Office Phone: 202-633-2632. Business E-Mail: andersonja@si.edu. *A prescription for success in professional life involves a proper balance of hard work, long hours, awareness and clear thinking, with a goal-oriented philosophy and outright love of one's profession. In addition, one must have the desire, abilities and opportunities to accomplish his goals.*

ANDERSON, JOHN EDWARD, mechanical engineering educator; b. Chgo., May 15, 1927; s. Claus Oscar and Ruth Melvina (Engstrom) A.; m. Cynthia Louise Howard, May 24, 1975; children: Candice, James, Stanley. BME, Iowa State U., 1949; MSME, U. Minn., 1955; PhD, MIT, 1962. Registered profl. engr., Minn., Ill. Aero. research scientist Nat. Adv. Com. for Aeros., Langley Field, Va., 1949-51; devel. engr. Honeywell, Inc., Mpls., 1951-53, research engr., 1953-55, prin. research engr., 1955-58, research project engr., 1954-58, sr. staff engr., 1958-62, mgr. space systems, 1963; mem. faculty U. Minn., Mpls., 1963-86, prof. mech. engring., 1971-86, Boston U., 1986-94. Cons. Colo. Regional Transp. Dist., 1974-75, Raytheon Co., 1975-76, Mannesmann Demag, 1978-79, Arthr D. Little, Inc., 1981, Indpls. Transit Commn., 1979-81, Davy McKee Corp., 1984-85; founder, pres., CEO Taxi 2000 Corp. (formerly ATS Inc.), 1983-2004, PRT Internat., LLC, 2005-. Author: Magnetohydrodynamic Shock Waves, Magnetogasdynamics of Thermal Plasma, Transit Systems Theory; editor: Personal Rapid Transit II. With USN, 1945-46. Recipient Outstanding Inventor in Am. award Intellectual Property Owners Found., 1989; Convair fellow. NAS, 1967-68 Fellow: AAAS; mem.: ASME, Union Concerned Scientists, World Federalists Assn., Mensa. Unitarian Universalist. Home: 5164 Ranier Pass NE Minneapolis MN 55421-1338 E-mail: jeanderson01@msn.com.

ANDERSON, JOHN ERLING, chemical engineer; b. Quincy, Mass., Mar. 12, 1929; s. Victor Emanuel and Elin Helen (Nelson) A.; m. Karin Henrietta Thornberg, Feb. 3, 1951; children: Mark David, Lynn Karin, Kristin Leslie, Claire Martha. BSCE, MIT, 1950, DSc in Chem. Engring., 1955; MSCE, Ill. Inst. Tech., 1951. Sr. corp. fellow Praxair, Inc., Tarrytown, NY, 1954-99; ret. Lectr. chem. engring. dept. MIT, 1977; mem. adv. com. Solar Energy Rsch. Inst., Golden, Colo., 1985-87; mem. combustion program work group DOE Office of Indusl. Programs, Wash., 1986-88. Contbr. articles to profl. jours.; patentee in field. Recipient Personal Merit award Chem. Engring. mag., 1974, Kirkpatrick Chem. Engring. award Chem. Engring. mag., 1989; named Inventor of Yr., N.Y. Patent Assn., 1989. Mem. NAE, Combustion Inst., Am. Inst. Chem. Engrs., Am. Chem. Soc. Democrat. Mem. Unitarian Ch. Avocations: hiking, reading. Home: 476E Heritage Hills Somers NY 10589-1920

ANDERSON, JOHN FIRTH, retired religious organization administrator, retired librarian; b. Saginaw, Mich., Oct. 5, 1928; s. Harlan Firth and Irene Martha (Bowser) Anderson; m. Patricia Ann Goble, June 18, 1950 (dec. Oct. 1995); children: Douglas Firth, Elizabeth Ann; m. Barbara Peterson Smith, May 18, 1996. BA, Mich. State U., 1949; MS in L.S, U. Ill., 1950. Young people's librarian Enoch Pratt Free Library, Balt., 1950-52; with Baltimore County Pub. Libr., 1952-58, supr. adult work, 1955- 56, asst. county libr., 1956-58; dir. Knoxville Pub. Libr. Sys., 1958-62, Tucson Pub. Libr., 1962-68, 73-82; city libr. San Francisco Pub. Libr., 1968-73; exec. presbyter, stated clk. Presbytery of Santa Barbara, Calif., 1982-91; ret., 1991; interim exec. presbyter Presbytery de Cristo, 1993, stated clk., 1993-2000. Mem. Presbyn. Churchwide Adminstr. Coordinating Cabinet, 1987—89; cons. libr. bldgs., devel. and mgmt. Contbr. articles to profl. publs. Mem. Ariz. Libr. Adv. Coun., 1975—81; bd. dirs. Amigos Bibliographic Coun., 1977—81, vice-chmn., 1977—79, sec., 1980—81; charter mem. Freedom to Read Found.; bd. dirs. Ariz. Theatre Co., 1978—82. Recipient Disting. Citizen award, U. Ariz., 1981. Mem.: ALA (mem. at large coun. 1961—65, bd. dirs. pub. libr. assn. 1961—65, bd. dirs. libr. adminstrn. divsn. 1964—65, chmn. libr. orgn. and mgmt. sect. 1964—65, mem. at large coun. 1966—70, pres. libr. adminstrn. divsn. 1968—69), Ariz. Assn. County Librs. (pres. 1979—80), Ariz. Libr. Assn. (pres. pub. librs. divsn. 1964—65, pres. 1967—68, Libr. of the Yr. 1968, Rosenzweig award 1981), Southwestern Libr. Assn. (pres. 1976—78), Calif. Libr. Assn. (coun. 1970—71), World Alliance Reformed Chs. (mem. Caribbean and N.Am. area coun. 1991—93, rec. clk. 1992—93), Ariz. China Coun. (pres. 1979—80), Beta Phi Mu. Presbyterian.

ANDERSON, JOHN FREDRIC, science administrator, entomologist, researcher; b. Fargo, ND, Feb. 25, 1936; s. Oscar Fredric and Eleanor Birdee (Fiskum) A.; m. Marilynn Joy Robinson, June 30, 1958; children: Linda, John Jr., Kristin. BS, N.D. State U., 1957, MS, 1959; PhD, U. Ill., 1963. NSF postdoctoral fellow Dept. Entomology U. Ill., Urbana, 1963-64; asst. entomologist Conn. Agrl. Expt. Sta., New Haven, 1964-66, assoc. entomologist, 1966-69, chief entomologist, 1969-87, dir., 1987—2004, disting. scientist, 2004—. Mem. Conn. Tree Examining Bd., New Haven, 1969-79. Author: (with others) Biology of Sex, 1967, Diseases Transmitted from Animals to Man, 6th edit., 1975, Perspectives in Forest Entomology, 1976, Preventing Lyme Disease, 1989, Ecology and Environmental Management of Lyme Disease, 1993, The Natural History of Ticks, 2002; editor: Perspectives in Forest Entomology, 1976; contbr. articles to profl. jours. 2d lt. Med. Svc. Corp. U.S. Army, 1959, capt. Res., 1969. Recipient award of Merit Conn. Tree Protective Assn., 1976, Bronze medal Fed. Garden Clubs Conn., 1981, Author Citation award Internat. Soc. Arboriculture, 1983, award of Merit Conn. Nurserymen's Assn., 1994, cert. recognition Conn. Nurserymen's Found., 2000, Environ. Industry Coun. Outstanding Svc. award, 2000, Conn. Friend of Floristry award, 2002, Federated Garden Clubs Conn. presdl. citation, 2004, Conn. Farm Bureau Recognition award, 2004. Mem. AAAS, Entomol. Soc. Am., Am. Mosquito Control Assn., Am. Soc. Microbiology, Am. Soc. Parasitologists, Am. Soc. Tropical Medicine and Hygiene, Soc. Invertebrate Pathology, Conn. Acad. Sci. and Engring., (hon.) Conn. Tree Protective Assn., New Haven, 1976-84, (dir., pres.), Phi Kappa Phi. Office: Conn Agrl Expt Sta 123 Huntington St PO Box 1106 New Haven CT 06504-1106 Office Phone: 203-974-8564. Business E-Mail: John.F.Anderson@PO.state.ct.us.

ANDERSON, JOHN GASTON, electrical engineer, consultant; b. Dante, Va., Aug. 21, 1922; s. Harvey Ellis and Lenora (Ingram) A.; m. Elizabeth Amelia Weller, Sept. 18, 1948 (dec. Mar. 1993); 1 son, David John; m. Avery Emma Weymouth, Sept. 24, 1994. BS with honors in Elec. Engring., Va. Poly. Inst., 1943. Registered profl. engr., Mass. With Gen. Electric Co., 1946-84, mgr. AC transmission studies Schenectady, 1972-74, mgr. high voltage lab. Pittsfield, Mass., 1974-80, cons. engr. transmission systems Schenectady, 1980-84. Sr. cons. Power Techs., Inc., 1984-92; profl. cons. engr., 1992-95; cons., lectr. on high voltage and power transmission; mem. U.S. USSR Tech. Exch. for High Voltage Transmission. Co-author books in field; contbr. articles to profl. publs.; editor: GE Transmission Mag., 1972-74; patentee in field. Active Boy Scouts Am., 1960-79. Served to capt. USAAF, 1943-45. Recipient Nat. prizes for papers Am. Inst. Elec. Engrs., 1957 Fellow IEEE (chmn. transmission and distbn. com. 1980-82, Centennial medal 1984, Halperin award 1991, Excellence Engring. medal 1997, Excellence in Power Distbn. Engring. award 1999, Millennium medal 2000); mem. NAE, Power Engring. Soc. (chmn. nat. pub. affairs subcom. 1979, chmn. tech. coun. 1982-85), Tau Beta Pi, Eta Kappa Nu, Phi Kappa Phi.

ANDERSON, JOHN MURRAY, operations research specialist, consultant, retired academic administrator; b. Toronto, Ont., Can., Sept. 3, 1926; s. Murray Alexander and Eleanor Montgomery (Valentine) A.; m. Eileen Anne McFaul, Nov. 3, 1951 (dec. Nov. 1983); children: Nancy, Susan, Peter, Katherine; m. Sylvia Richard, May 10, 1986 B.Sc.F., U. Toronto, 1951, PhD, 1958; LL.D., St. Thomas U., 1974, Dalhousie U., 1979; D.Ped., U. Maine, Orono, 1976; DSc, U. N.B., Can., 2001. Asst. prof. U. N.B., Can., 1958-63; assoc. prof. Carleton U., 1963-67; dir. Fisheries Research Bd. Can. Biol. Sta., St. Andrews, N.B., 1967-72; dir. gen. Canadian Research and Devel., Fisheries and Marine Service, Dept. Environment, Ottawa, Ont., 1972-73; pres. U. N.B., 1973-79, J.M. Anderson Consultants Inc., 1980—; v.p. ops. Atlantic Salmon Fedn., 1984-96. Pres., chmn. bd. dirs. Huntsman Marine Lab., St. Andrews, N.B., 1973-77, bd. dirs., 1985—, chmn. bd. dirs., 1995-99; mem. Huntsman Adv. Bd., 2004—, chmn. adv. bd., 2004-2005; bd. govs. Rothesay (N.B.) Collegiate Sch., 1976, Kenya Tech. Tchrs. Coll., Nairobi, 1977-79; chmn. Assn. Atlantic Univs., 1978-79; v.p. Biol. Coun. Can., 1977-79; mem. Sci. Coun. of Can., 1988-92; sci. advisor Nature Conservancy of Can., 2003—. Contbr. numerous articles on fish physiology to profl. jours. Bd. dirs. Internat. Atlantic Salmon Found., 1979-83, J.R. Bradfield Edn. Fund, Noranda, 1979-86, Aquaculture Assn., N.B., 1981—; pres., chmn. bd. trustees Sunbury Shores Arts and Nature Ctr., Inc., 1982-84; chmn. bd. trustees Mackenzie King Scholarship Trust, 1986—; trustee Nature Trust N.B., Inc., 1987-91; v.p. Atlantic Aquaculture Fair, 1993, pres., 1994; bd. dirs. St. Croix Estuary Program, 1990-2002, vice chmn. sci., 2001-02, bd. dirs. Fundy Cmty. Found., 2004-. Recipient Happy Fraser award Atlantic Salmon Fedn., 2001. Fellow Royal Can. Geographic Soc.; mem. Inst. Can. Bankers (gov. 1974-79), Can. Soc. Zoologists (pres. 1973-74), Aquaculture Assn. Can. (pres. 1984-85), Assn. Univs. and Colls. Can. (dir. 1975-79, chmn. McCain Scholarship Group 1997—), Sigma Chi. Anglican. Office: Atlantic Salmon Fedn Saint Andrews NB Canada E0G 2X0 E-mail: atlsal@nbnet.nb.ca.

ANDERSON, JOHN ROBERT, retired mathematics professor; b. Stromsburg, Nebr., Aug. 1, 1928; s. Norris Merton and Violet Charlotte (Stromberg) A.; m. Bertha Margery Nore, Aug. 27, 1950; children: Eric Jon, Mary Lynn. Student, Midland Coll., 1945-46; AA, Luther Jr. Coll., 1949; BS (Regents scholar), U. Nebr., Lincoln, 1951, MA in Math, 1954; PhD, Purdue U., 1970. Tchr. math., coach Bloomfield (Nebr.) High Sch., 1951-52; control systems analyst, Allison div. Gen. Motors Corp., Indpls., 1954-60; prof. math. Depauw U., Greencastle, Ind., 1960, asst. dean, dir. grad. studies, 1973-76, dir. grad. studies, 1976-84, chmn. math. dept., 1984-90, prof. math., 1990-92, ret., 1992; adj. prof. math. IVTC, Greencastle, 1996—; resident dir. W. European studies program Depauw U., Germany, 1975, resident dir. Mediterrenean Studies program, 1982, 90; dir. NSF Coop. Coll. Sch., Sci. Inst., 1969-70; instr. NSF summer inst., 1972; instr. Challenge sci. and math. program U.S. Students in Europe, 1976, 77, 78, 80, 82. Bd. dirs. Law Focused Edn., Indpls., 1975-77, Ind. Regional Math. Consortium, 1977-92; adj. prof. math. IVTC Coll., Greencastle, 1997-2003. Bd. dirs. Luth. Brotherhood br. 8746, 1967-2002, pres. Thrivent for Luth. chpt. 30903, 2002-, United Way of Greencastle, Ind., 1992-98, treas., Putnam Co. Food Pantry, 1993-98; officer Peace Evangel. Luth. Ch., 1960—. Served with U.S. Army, 1946-48. Danforth Tchr. fellow, 1963-64; NSF sci. faculty fellow, 1964-65; Lilly Found. edn. grantee, summers 1961-63 Mem. Math. Assn. Am., Nat. Council Tchrs. Math., North Central Assn. (commr. 1974-78), Sigma Xi, Pi Mu Epsilon, Kappa Delta Pi, Beta Sigma Psi. Clubs: Rotary Internat. (sec. 1976-77, v.p. 1977-78, pres. 1978-79, 1998-99). Home: 1560 S Bloomington St Greencastle IN 46135-2212 E-mail: johnanderson@depauw.edu, jranderson28@hotmail.com. *When you work with people, always keep in mind: "If I were in their place, is this the way I would like to be treated by someone in my position?".*

ANDERSON, JOHN S., art educator, sculptor; b. Seattle, Wash., Apr. 29, 1928; s. Ralph and Susan Elizabeth Anderson; m. Marlyn J. Anderson, Jan. 15, 1960; 1 child, Susan E. Degree, Pratt Inst., 1957. Instr. Pratt Inst., N.Y.C., NY, 1963—64; vis. prof. U. N. Mex., Alarverque, N.Mex., 1969; prof. Sch. of Visual Arts, N.Y.C., NY, 1969—70; prof. in sculptor Cooper Union, N.Y.C., 1970—75; vis. prof. U. Conn., Storrs, Conn., 1978. One-man shows include Allan Stone Gallery, N.Y.C., 1962, 1964—67, 1970, 1972, 1975, 1977, 1981, 1985, 2002, Coliseum Show, 1962, Pk. Synagogue Art Fest., Cleve., 1965, Whitney Mus. of Am. Art, 1965—68, Maeght Found., France, 1971, Allan Stone Gallery, N.Y.C., 2000—01, Represented in permanent collections Mus. of Modern Art, Whiney Mus. of Am. Arts; contbr. articles various profl. jours. Pvt. U.S. Army, 1951—53, El Paso, Tex. Grant to Mexico, Guggenheim Found., 1965, grant to Norway, 1965. Democrat. Avocations: swimming, sci. fiction, Brazilian Music. Home: 12 Sch St Asbury NJ 08802

ANDERSON, JOHN THOMAS, lawyer; b. Gary, Ind., July 13, 1930; s. Jack and Dorothy Genevieve (Gustafson) A.; m. Marvel Nancy Filkey, Aug. 15, 1953; children: Kirsten E. Teevens, Katherine L., Eric M. AB, DePauw U., 1952; LLB, Harvard U., 1955. Bar: Ind. 1955, Ill. 1956. Assoc. Lord, Bissell & Brook, Chgo., 1958-66, ptnr., 1966-95, of counsel, 1996-98. Trustee DePauw U., Greencastle, Ind., 1982—; chmn. bd. dirs. Joyce Found., Chgo., 1979—; Lt. USNR, 1955-58. Methodist. Home and Office: 2313 Cassia Ct Naples FL 34109-3370

ANDERSON, JOHN THOMAS, librarian, historian; b. Burlington, Iowa, Feb. 7, 1955; s. Alvin Jay and Margaret Ann (Thomas) A. BA, U. No. Iowa, 1976; MA, Coll. William and Mary, 1979; PhD, U. Va., 1982; M in Info. and Libr. Studies, U. Mich., 1987. Cert. substitute tchr. Temp. asst. prof. history Chadron (Nebr.) State Coll., 1984; asst. libr. pub. svcs. Mid. Ga. Coll., Cochran, 1989-91; temp. reference libr. U. No. Iowa, Cedar Falls, 1991; reference libr. Palm Beach County Libr. Sys., Boca Raton, Fla., 1992, Salve Regina U., Newport, R.I., 1992-93, catalog libr., 1993-94; media cataloger libr. Tex. A&M U., Commerce, 1997-98; libr. I info. svcs. Abilene (Tex.) Pub. Libr., 1998—2002. Catalog libr. Abilene Christian U., 1999—2002; rare book cataloger UB Found., SUNY, Buffalo, 2002—03; catalog libr. St. Bonaventure (NY) U., 2003—. Exhibits judge Nat. History Day Competition, Chadron, Nebr., 1984. Philip Francis du Pont fellow Coll. William and Mary, 1976; Philip Francis du Pont fellow U. Va., 1977; Virginia Mason Davidge fellow U. Va., 1978, 79. Mem. Soc. Historians Am. Fgn. Rels. Republican. Unitarian Universalist. Avocations: collecting postage stamps and first-edition books, public radio. Office: St Bonaventure Univ Tech Svcs Dept Friedsam Libr Buffalo NY 14778 Home: 1501 Pleasant St Apt 6D Olean NY 14760-1579 Office Phone: 716-375-2340. Personal E-mail: janderso@adelphia.net.

ANDERSON, JON MAC, lawyer, educator; b. Rio Grande, Ohio, Jan. 10, 1937; s. Harry Rudolph and Carrie Viola (Magee) A.; m. Deborah Melton, June 1, 1961; children: Jon Gordon, Greta. AB, Ohio U., 1958; JD, Harvard Law Sch., 1961. Bar: Ohio 1961. Law clk. Hon. Kingsley A. Taft Ohio Supreme Ct., Columbus, 1961-62; assoc. Wright, Harlor, Morris & Arnold, Columbus, 1962-67, ptnr., 1968-76, Porter, Wright, Morris & Arthur, Columbus, 1977—. Adj. prof. law Ohio State U. Law Sch., Columbus, 1975-83; bar examiner State of Ohio, 1971-76, chmn., 1975-76; lectr. tax and estate planning insts.; bd. dirs. White Castle System, Inc. Trustee Columbus Mus. of Art, 2003—, Berea Coll, Ky., 1976-2000, Pro Musica Chamber Orch., Columbus, 1980-98, Opera Columbus, 1985-88, 1st Congl. Ch., Columbus, 1979-83, Greater Columbus Arts Coun., 1989-99; chmn., 1996-98; mem. adv. coun. The Textile Mus., 1996-2002. Mem. ABA, Ohio State Bar Assn., Columbus Bar Assn., The Columbus Club, Rocky Fork Hunt and Country Club. Democrat. Avocations: music, art, textiles, literature, antique collections. Office: Porter Wright Morris & Arthur 41 S High St Ste 2800 Columbus OH 43215-6194 Office Phone: 614-227-2154. Personal E-mail: jander18@columbusrr.com. Business E-Mail: janderson@porterwright.com.

ANDERSON, JON STEPHEN, newswriter; b. Montreal, Que., Can., Mar. 13, 1936; arrived in U.S., 1963; s. William Howard and Dorothy Beatrice (Ryan) A.; m. Gail Rutherford, Feb. 20, 1960 (div. 1966); 1 child, Jon Gregory (dec.); m. Abra Prentice, Sept. 14, 1968 (div. 1976); children: Ashley Prentice Norton, Abra Cantrill Williams, Anthony Ryan; m. Pamela Sherrod, Sept. 23, 2001. BA, Mt. Allison U., Sackville, Can., 1955; BCL, McGill U., Montreal, 1959; MAW, U. Iowa, 1991. Reporter Montreal Gazette, 1957-60; chief bur. Time Mag., Montreal, 1960-63, staff corr. Chgo., 1963-66; staff writer Chgo. Sun-Times, 1967-69; columnist Chgo. Daily News, 1969-72; pub. Chicagoan Mag., 1972-74; staff writer Chgo. Tribune, 1978—; writing instr. U. Iowa, 1989—2002. Author: City Watch: Discovering the Uncommon Chicago, 2000; contbr. articles to Readers Digest, 1977—, Chgo. Mag., 1977, Clothesline Rev., 1986. Gen. mgr. Second City Ctr. Pub. Arts, 1966-67; bd. dirs. Chgo. Internat. Film Festival, 1975-78 Recipient Stick o' Type award, Newspaper Guild Am., 1969, Studs Turkel Journalism award, 1999. Mem.: Order Ky. Cols. Roman Catholic. Office: Chgo Tribune 435 N Michigan Ave Chicago IL 60611-4066 Business E-Mail: jsanderson@tribune.com.

ANDERSON, JONATHAN WALFRED, lawyer; b. New Haven, May 13, 1957; s. Robert W. Anderson and Dorothy (Partington) Barker; m. Leslie D. Vanderveen, Oct. 17, 1981; children: Jeffrey W., Theodore M. BA, Calvin Coll., 1979; JD cum laude, U. Notre Dame, Ind., 1982. Bar: Mich. 1982. Assoc. Varnum, Riddering, Schmidt & Howlett, Grand Rapids, Mich., 1982-88, ptnr., 1988—, mem. mgmt. com., 2000—03. Lectr. Inst. of Continuing Legal Edn., Ann Arbor, Mich., 1988—, Nat. Bus. Inst., Grand Rapids, 1988—. Bd. dirs. Dwelling Place Grand Rapids, Inc., 1988-93, pres.,

1993; bd. dirs. Habitat for Humanity Grand Rapids, Inc., 1988-92, pres. bd. dirs., 1990-91; bd. dirs. Cherry St. Health Svcs., 1995-98, Legal Aid Western Mich., 1998-2002. Mem. ABA, Internat. Coun. Shopping Ctrs., Bldg. Owners and Mgrs. Assn. Grand Rapids (treas. 1991-92), Constrn. Fin. Mgrs. Assn., State Bar Mich., Grand Rapids Bar Assn. Presbyterian. Avocations: genealogy, running, opera. Office: Varnum Riddering Schmidt & Howlett PO Box 352 Grand Rapids MI 49501-0352

ANDERSON, JOSEPH ANDREW, JR., retired apparel executive; b. Logan, Utah, Nov. 1, 1921; s. Joseph Andrew and Melicent H. (Willmore) A.; m. Gwen Elsie Smith, Sept. 29, 1954; children: Brian, Jodi, Paul, Bradley, Stacey, Jeffrey, Tiffani. BS, Utah State U., 1947; postgrad., Stanford U., 1949-50. With Zion's Coop. Mdse. Inst. Dept. Store, Salt Lake City, 1950-86, various positions, 1950-82, pres., chief exec. officer, 1982-84, vice chmn. bd., 1984-86, ret., 1986. Chmn. bd. Mr. Mac Clothiers, Inc.; ret., 1988; retail cons., Salt Lake City, 1988-90; mem. consumer bd. Utah Dept. Commerce, 1985-92; bd. dirs. Zions 1st Nat. Bank, Salt Lake City. Chmn., bd. dirs. Salt Lake City, 1985-88, Westminster Coll. Found., Salt Lake City, 1985-86, Utah Opera Co., 1998—; bd. dirs. Westminster Coll. Bus. Sch., 1985—; trustee Westminster Coll., 1988-96, L.D.S. Hosp.-Deseret Found., 1987-88, Salt Lake Visitor Bur., 1987-89; corp. solicitation state chmn. Am. Cancer Soc. of Utah, 1989-90; pres., bd. dirs. AMICUS-Deseret Found., Salt Lake City, 1986-89; adv. bd. Sta. KSL-TV, 1985-88; mem. dean's adv. coun. Bus. Sch. Utah State U., 1982-89; mem. Utah Employer Support of the Guard and Res. Com. Area # 3, 1986-91; bd. dirs. Utah Youth Village, Salt Lake City, 1990-94, chmn., 1994-96; chmn. Fitness Inst. L.D.S. Hosp., Salt Lake City, 1991-93, bd. of fitness inst., 1994-97; chmn. Utah Youth Village, 1994-96; bd. dirs. Utah Symphony, 2002—; lifetime trustee Utah Symphony and Opera, 2002—; dist. chmn. Area Emergency Preparedness Com., 2003—. 1st lt. U.S. Army, 1943-46, ETO. Named Outstanding Boss of Yr. Salt Lake Nat. Bus. Women's Club, 1972; recipient Block "A" award, 1947, Outstanding Alumnus award Utah State U., 1984, Outstanding Svc. award L.D.S. Hosp. Desert Found., 1990, Profl. Achievement award Utah State U. and Coll. Bus., 2005. Mem. Utah Retail Mchts. Assn. (dir., sec. 1983-87, bd. dirs. nat. assn. 1983-87), Execs. Assn. Salt Lake City (bd. dirs. 1990-91), Sons of Utah Pioneers (pres. 1976-77), Rotary, Lions (1st v.p. Salt Lake City club 1990-91, pres. 1991-92). Republican. Mem. Lds Ch. Avocations: jogging, fishing, golf, tennis. Home: 4394 Adonis Dr Salt Lake City UT 84124-3433

ANDERSON, JOSEPH NORMAN, retired food products executive, retired academic administrator; b. Mpls., May 12, 1926; s. Joseph E. and Helen (Larson) A.; m. Ruth E. Anderson, Sept. 6, 1952; children: Peter, Timothy, Paul, Matthew, Robin, Kathryn, Charles. BBA with distinction, U. Minn., 1947. With Sears, Roebuck & Co., 1947-49, Gamble-Skogmo, Inc., 1950-64; v.p. fin., dir. Nat. Bellas Hess, Inc., 1964-67, pres., chief exec. officer, dir., 1967-69, chmn. bd., pres., chief exec. officer, 1969-75; pres. Jamestown (N.D.) Coll., 1975-83, Dakota Bake-n-Serv, Inc., 1979-86; exec. cons. Gladstone, Mo., 1986-90, Edwardsville, Ill., 1990—. Pres. Mchts. Rsch. Coun., 1961-62. With AUS, 1953-55. Mem. Phi Beta Kappa, Beta Gamma Sigma. Republican. Presbyterian.

ANDERSON, JUDITH HELENA, English language educator; b. Worcester, Mass., Apr. 21, 1940; d. Oscar William and Beatrice Marguerite (Beaudry) A.; m. E. Talbot Donaldson, May 18, 1971 (dec. Apr. 1987). AB magna cum laude, Radcliffe Coll., 1961; MA, Yale U., 1962, PhD, 1965. Instr. English Cornell U., Ithaca, N.Y., 1964-66, asst. prof. English, 1966-72; vis. lectr. Coll. Seminar Program, Yale U., New Haven, 1973; vis. asst. prof. English U. Mich., Ann Arbor, 1973-74; assoc. prof. Ind. U., Bloomington, 1974-79, prof., 1979—, Chancellor's prof., 1999—, dir. grad. studies, 1986-90, 93, mem. governing bd. univ. Inst. for Advanced Study, 1983-85, 86-88. Morris W. Croll lectr. Gettysburg Coll., 1988, Kathleen Williams lectr., 89, 95; dir. Folger Inst. Seminar, 1991-, 1991. Author: The Growth of a Personal Voice, 1976, Biographical Truth, 1984, Words that Matter, 1996, Translating Investments, 2005; editor: (with Elizabeth D. Kirk) Piers Plowman, 1990; (with Donald Cheney and David A. Richardson) Spenser's Life and the Subject of Biography, 1996; mem. editl. bd. Spenser Ency., 1979-90, Duquesne Studies in Lang. and Lit., 1976-2004, Spenser Studies, 1986—, Medieval and Renaissance Literary Studies, 2004—; adv. bd. Textbase of Women Writers, Brown U., 1989-2000; contbr. articles to profl. jours. Woodrow Wilson fellow, 1961-62, 63-64, NEH summer fellow and sr. rsch. fellow, 1979, 81-82, Dulin fellow Folger Libr., 1991; Huntington Libr. rsch. grantee, 1978, 97, NEH fellow, 1985-86, Mayers Found. fellow, 1990-91, Nat. Humanities Ctr. fellow, 1995-96, Newberry-NEH fellow, 2002-03; recipient Outstanding Scholar award Office of Women's Affairs Ind. U., 1996. Mem. MLA (exec. com. Renaissance divsn. 1973-78, 86-90, del. to assembly 1991-93, publs. com. 1999-2002), AAUP, internat. Spenser Soc. (pres. 1980, 88, Lifetime Achievement award 2004), Renaissance Soc. Am. (rep. for English to coun. 1991-93), Milton Soc., Donne Soc. (exec. com. 2004—), Shakespeare Assn., Chaucer Soc., Phi Beta Kappa. Home: 2525 E 8th St Bloomington IN 47408-4214 Office: Ind U Dept English Bloomington IN 47405 Office Phone: 812-855-8224. Business E-Mail: anders@indiana.edu.

ANDERSON, KARL See KORS, MICHAEL

ANDERSON, KARL RICHARD, aerospace engineer, consultant; b. Vinita, Okla., Sept. 27, 1917; s. Axel Richard and Hildred Audrey (Marshall) Anderson; m. Jane Shingeko Hiratsuka, June 20, 1953; 1 child, Karl Richard. BS, Calif. Western U., 1964; MA, 1966; PhD, U.S. Internat. U., 1970. Registered profl. engr., Calif. Engr. personnel subsystems Atlas Missile Program, Gen. Dynamics, San Diego, 1960-63; design engr. Solar divsn. Internat. Harvester, San Diego, 1964-66, sr. design engr., 1967-69, project engr., 1970-74, product safety specialist, 1975-78, aerospace engring. cons., 1979-86; cons. engring. San Diego, 1979—. Lectr. Am. Indian Sci. and Engring. Soc. Served to maj. USAF, 1936—60. Recipient Spl. Commendation award, San Diego City Coun., 1985, Spl Commendation award, City of San Diego, 1994, Grace "Peter" Sargent award, San Diego City Natural Pk., 1994. Home and Office: 5886 Scripps St San Diego CA 92122-3212

ANDERSON, KATHRYN D., retired surgeon; b. Ashton-Under-Lyne, Lancashire, Eng., Mar. 14, 1939; came to U.S., 1961; m. French Anderson, June 24, 1961. BA, Cambridge (Eng.) U., 1961, MA, 1964; MD, Harvard U., 1964. Diplomate Am. Bd. Surgery with cert. in spl. competence in pediat. surgery. Intern in pediat. Children's Hosp., Boston, 1964-65; resident in surgery Georgetown U. Hosp., Washington, 1965-69, chief resident in surgery, 1969-70, attending surgeon, 1972-74; chief resident in pediat. surgery Children's Hosp., Washington, 1970-72, sr. attending surgeon, 1974-92, surgeon-in-chief L.A., 1992—2004; vice chmn. surgery George Washington U., Washington, 1984-92; ret., 2004. Prof. surgery U. So. Calif. Fellow: ACS (sec. 1992—2001, first v.p. 2001—02), Royal Coll. Surgeons (Eng.); mem.: Soc. Univ. Surgeons, Am. Surg. Assn., Am. Pediat. Surg. Assn. (sec. 1988—91, pres. 1999—2000), Am. Acad. Pediat. (sec. surg. sect. 1982—85, chmn. 1985—86). Avocations: opera, yoga.

ANDERSON, KATHRYN PARKS, music educator; b. Trenton, Mo., Nov. 30, 1951; d. Carroll Lloyd and Viva Jean (Landes) Parks; m. Leander Albert Anderson, May 31, 1977; children: Lindsay Anderson Guerriere, Kirsten Joy. MusEdB in applied organ, Ctrl. Mo. State U., 1972, MusM in applied organ, 1974. Cert. Mo. Life Tchg. Cert., Conn. Standard Tchg. Cert. Vocal, instrumental music tchr. Plainville Pub. Schs., Plainville, Conn., 1978—80; dir. music, organist Grace Bapt. Ch., Bristol, Conn., 1977—87; vocal, instrumental music tchr. Archdiocese of Hartford, Sacred Heart Sch., New Britain, Conn., 1986—2001; dir. music, organist Mill Plain Union Ch., Waterbury, Conn., 1987—92, First Bapt. Ch., Meriden, Conn., 1992—2001, Ch. of St. Mary, Newington, Conn., 2001—. Music cons. small Christian cmtys. Archdiocese of Hartford, Bloomfield, Conn., 2003—. Recorded choral and handbell music: various CD's. Mem.: Am. Guild of English Handbell Ringers, Nat. Assn. of Pastoral Musicians, Am. Guild of Organists (registrar Greater Hartford Conn. chpt. 1984—87), Phi Kappa Phi, Pi Kappa Lambda Honor Music Fraternity. Avocations: walking, fitness training, poetry. Home: 112 Butternut Ln Bristol CT 06010-8049 Office: Ch of St Mary 626 Willard Ave Newington CT 06111 Office Phone: 860-666-1858, 860-666-1591. Office Fax: 860-666-5720. E-mail: kathrynparksanderson@hotmail.com.

ANDERSON, KEITH, retired lawyer, retired banker; b. Phoenix, June 21, 1917; s. Carl and Helen (Fairchild) A.; m. Grace R. VanDenburg, 1941 (div. 1957); m. Catherine Huber, 1960; children: Fletcher F., Warren, Nicholas H. AB, Dartmouth Coll., 1939; LLB, Harvard U., 1942. Bar: N.Y. 1942, Ariz. 1946, Colo. 1950. Ret. lawyer. Mem. Univ. Club of Denver, Cactus Club. Democrat.

ANDERSON, KENNETH ALLEN, lawyer, hotel executive; b. Grand Junction, Colo., Sept. 16, 1962; s. Lila Marie and Norling Wayne A. AB in Polit. Sci., U. So. Calif., L.A., 1985; JD, Yale U., 1989. Bar: Calif. 1989, U.S. Dist. Ct. (ctrl. dist.) Calif. 1989, U.S. Ct. Appeals (9th cir.) 1989. Assoc. Irell & Manella, L.A., 1989-91; sr. assoc. Pettit & Martin, Newport Beach, Calif., 1991-94, O'Melveny & Myers, Newport Beach, 1994—98; v.p., sr. counsel Hilton Hotels Corp., Beverly Hills, Calif., 1998—. Author: White Bird, 1981. Mem. ABA, Beverly Hills Bar Assn., Assn. Corp. Counsel. Avocations: reading, hiking, travel. Home: 24934 Vista Verenda Woodland Hills CA 91367 Office: Hilton Hotels Corp 9336 Civic Ctr Dr Beverly Hills CA 90210 Office Phone: 310-205-4572. E-mail: allen_anderson@hilton.com.

ANDERSON, KENNETH CARL, physician, educator; b. Worcester, Mass., Oct. 3, 1951; s. Kenneth R. and Helen L. Anderson; m. Cynthia Ellen Bird; children: Emily, David, Peter. BA summa cum laude, Boston U., 1973; MD, Johns Hopkins U., 1977. Lic. physician, Md., Mass.; diplomate Am. Bd. Internal Medicine. Intern medicine Johns Hopkins Hosp., Balt., 1977-78, asst. resident medicine, 1978-79, sr. resident, 1979-80, clin. fellow medicine, 1977-80, Harvard Med. Sch., Boston, 1980-83, instr. medicine, 1983-84, asst. prof., 1985-91, assoc. prof., 1992—, Kraft Family Prof. Medicine, 2002—; clin. fellow med. oncology Dana-Farber Cancer Inst., Boston, 1980-83, fellow tumor immunology, 1981-83; clin. fellow medicine Brigham and Women's Hosp., Boston, 1980-83, jr. assoc. physician, 1983—85, attending physician bone marrow transplantation, 1984—88; clin. assoc. med. oncology Dana-Farber Cancer Inst., 1983—85, med. dir. Blood Component Lab., 1984—, attending physician med. oncology, 1984—, attending physician bone marrow transplantation, 1984—, asst. physician, 1985—; dir. Jerome Lipper Multiple Myeloma Ctr. Dana Farber Cancer Inst., med. dir. Kraft Family Donor Ctr. Rsch. assoc. Ctr. for Blood Rsch., Boston, 1994—; vis. prof. dept. pathology U. Pa. Sch. Medicine, 1991; Joseph R. Bove transfusion medicine vis. prof. Yale U. Sch. Medicine, 1994; prin. investigator Cancer and Leukemia Group B, 1993—; mem. blood product adv. com. U.S. FDA, 1993—; mem. med. adv. com. ARC Blood Svcs., N.E. Region, 1985—; med. dir. Donor Ctr. Nat. Marrow Donor Program, 1987—; mem. sci. rev. com. Dana Farber Cancer Inst., 1984-90, 92—, clin. exec. com., 1984—, utilization rev. and quality assurance com., 1984—, clin. lab. com., 1984—, chmn. transfusion com., 1984—; mem. sci. adv. bd. Internat. Myeloma Found., 1991—, Multiple Myeloma Rsch. Found.; editorial bd., Transfusion Science, Medical Oncology, American Journal of Hematology, and American Association of Blood Banks Press; assoc. editor, Transfusion and European Journal of Hematology; lectr. various orgns. Reviewer New Eng. Jour. Medicine, Blood, Cancer Rsch., Annals Internal Medicine, Jour. Clin. Oncology, Jour. Immunology, Procs. NAS, Jour. Clin. Investigation, European Jour. Cancer and Clin. Oncology, Transfusion, Procs. Exptl. Biology and Medicine, Transfusion Sci., Intensive Care Medicine, Leukemia, Acta Hematologica; editl. bds. Transfusion Sci., 1990—, Jour. Clin. Oncology, 1990-93, Blood, 1991—, Transfusion, 1994; editor: (with P.M. Ness) Scientific Basis of Transfusion Medicine: Implications for Clinical Practice, 1994; contbr. articles to profl. jours. Bd. dirs. Internat. Myeloma Found., 1993—. Recipient CIBA Cmty. Svc. award, 1975, Jr. Faculty Rsch. award Am. Cancer Soc., 1986-89; Med. Found. fellow, 1984-86, spl. fellow Leukemia Soc. Am., 1986-89. Mem. AMA (Physician's Recognition award), ACP, AAAS, Am. Soc. Hematology (coordinating reviewer in transfusion 1994, reviewer in lymphomas and myelomas 1993), Am. Assn. Blood Banks (chmn. transfusion practice com. 1992-93), Mass. Assn. Blood Banks (Morten Grove-Rasmussen Meml. award 1994), Mass. Med. Soc., Soc. Hemopheresis Specialists, Sigma Xi, Phi Beta Kappa, Alpha Phi Omega. Achievements include research on monoclonal antibodies defining B cell differentiation antigens and B cell malignancies in man, clinical and laboratory aspects of bone marrow transplantation, developing and validating new targeted therapies for myeloma, clinical and laboratory aspects of blood component therapy in patients with malignancy. Office: Dana Farber Cancer Inst 44 Binney St Boston MA 02115-6084

ANDERSON, KENNETH PAUL, nephrologist, administrator; b. Council Bluffs, Iowa, June 17, 1952; s. Kenneth Paul and and Kathleen Marie (Wyckoff) A.; children: Jennifer, Cassie, Zach. BS with honors, U. Iowa, 1974; DO, Coll. Osteo. Medicine, Des Moines, 1978; MS, U. Wis., 1996; cert., Harvard U., 1993. Diplomate Am. Bd. Family Practice. Resident, chief resident Luth. Hosp.-U. Iowa, Des Moines, 1978-81, Norwalk (Conn.) Hosp.-Yale U., 1981-83; fellow in nephrology, clin. instr. U. So. Calif., L.A., 1983-85; med. dir. Mercy Hosp., Iowa Luth. Hosp., Des Moines, 1985-96; clin. instr. Coll. Osteo. Medicine, Des Moines, 1986-96; chief of staff Mercy Hosp. Med. Ctr., Des Moines, 1992-94; sec., bd. officers Iowa Luth. Hosp., Des Moines, 1989-90; chief med. officer Ptnrs. Nat. Health Plans, South Bend, Ind., 1996—2000; v.p. Meml. Hosp., South Bend, 2000—. Chmn., mem. ESRD Network # 12 of HCFA, Kansas City, 1984-95; pres., CEO Nephrology and Internal Medicine Specialists, Des Moines, 1985-96; med. dir. SecureCare of Iowa, Des Moines, 1992-96. Contbr. articles to profl. jours. Bd. dirs. Iowa State Bd. of Health, Des Moines, 1993-96; cons. Nat. Health Policy Adv. Team, Washington, 1989-94, Ind. Perinatal Task Force, 1997-2000. Fellow Am. Acad. Family Practice; mem. AMA, Am. Soc. Hypertension, Am. Coll. Physician Execs., Am. Soc. Nephrology, Iowa Osteo. Med. Assn. Democrat. Roman Catholic. Avocations: camping, blues music, fishing, biking, writing short stories. Home: 11034 Birch Lake Dr E Granger IN 46530-6013 Office: Meml Hosp and Health System 615 N Michigan St South Bend IN 46601-1033 Office Phone: 574-647-3104. Business E-Mail: kanderson@memorialsb.org.

ANDERSON, KENNETH WARD, investor, consultant; b. Evanston, Ill., Dec. 14, 1931; s. Sydney Cleminson and Grey (Simpson) A.; m. Jean Jensen, Mar. 21, 1953; children: Kenneth Ward, Richard Scott, Wendy Lynn. BSBA, Northwestern U., 1953; postgrad. in fin., UCLA, 1955-56, U. So. Calif., 1956-58. Asst. v.p. United Calif. Bank, L.A., 1956-63; v.p. fin., asst. sect. T.I.M.E.-DC, Lubbock, Tex., 1963-70; sr. v.p. fin. Campbell-Taggart, Dallas, 1970-80; sr. v.p., CFO Galveston-Houston Co., Houston, 1980-82; pres., CFO, dir. Cook Data Svcs., Dallas, 1983-85; pres., dir. Blockbuster Entertainment Corp., Dallas, 1985-87; pres., dir., chmn. bd. Amtech Credit Corp., Dallas, 1987-90; chmn. exec. com., dir. Amtech Corp., 1987-92; bd. dirs. Lake Area Health Ctr. Found., 1993—, Fossil, Inc., 1993—, MarketQuiz, Inc., 2000—. Bd. dirs. Ch. at Horseshoe Bay Endowment Fund, 1996—2003; trustee Ch. at Horseshoe Bay, 1999—2002. With U.S. Army, 1953—55, Japan. Mem. Preston Trail Golf Club (Dallas), Horseshoe Bay Country Club. Republican. Methodist. Address: PO Box 8189 Horseshoe Bay TX 78657-8189

ANDERSON, KERRII B., food service executive; b. 1957; BS, Elon Coll., 1978; MBA, Duke U., 1987. CPA. With Peat, Marwick, Mitchell & Co., Greensboro, N.C., 1978-84, RJ Reynolds Corp., Winston-Salem, N.C., 1984-85, Key Co., Greensboro, N.C., 1985-87; sr. v.p., CFO, chmn. bd. M/I Schottenstein Homes Inc., Columbus, 1987—2000; exec. v.p., CFO Wendy's Internat., Dublin, Ohio, 2000—, also bd. dirs. Bd. dirs. The Lancaster Colony Corp., M/I Schottenstein Homes, Inc. Mem. fin. com. The Columbus Found.; bd. mem. Grant-Riverside Hosp.; mem. dean's adv. com. Fisher Coll. Bus., Ohio State U. Office: Wendys Internat Inc One Dave Thomas Blvd Dublin OH 43017

ANDERSON, KIMBALL RICHARD, lawyer; b. San Antonio, Aug. 20, 1952; s. Richard John and Martha (Bishop) A.; m. Karen Gatsis, Aug. 18, 1974; children: Alexis Katrina, Melissa Martha, Sophia Diane. BA, U. Ill., 1974, JD, 1977. Bar: Ill. 1977, U.S. Ct. Appeals (7th cir.) 1979, U.S. Supreme Ct. 1987; CPA, Ill. 1974. Assoc. Winston & Strawn LLP, Chgo., 1977-84, ptnr., 1984—, chmn. pro bono com., 1984—, mem. exec. com., 1994—, gen. counsel, 2000—. Disting. neutral CPR Inst. for Dispute Resolution; adj. prof. trial advocacy Northwestern U; pres. CBA TV Prodns., Inc., 1989-1991, CBA Ins. Adminstrs., 1993-; spkr. in field. Contbr. articles to profl. jours. V.p. Pub. Interest Law Initiative, 2002—; chmn. bd. AIDS Legal Coun. Chgo.; bd. dirs. De Paul U. Coll. Law Ctr. Justice in Capital Cases, pres., 2003—. Named Person of Yr. 1996 Chgo. Lawyer Mag., laureate Ill. Acad. Lawyers, 2005. Fellow Am. Coll. Trial Lawyers, Am. Bar Found.; mem. ABA (mem. ethics 2000 adv. coun. 1998-, mem. Ctr. Profl. responsibility, Pro Bono Publico award 2003), Ill. Bar Assn., Chgo. Bar Assn. (bd. mgrs. 1990-92), Ill. CPA Soc., Chgo. Bar Found. (2d v.p. 2001-02, 1st v.p. 2003-). Home: 2045 N Seminary Ave Chicago IL 60614-4109 Office: Winston & Strawn 35 W Wacker Dr Ste 4200 Chicago IL 60601-1695 Office Phone: 312-558-5858. Business E-Mail: kanderson@winston.com.

ANDERSON, LARRY, media specialist, consultant; b. Sydney, NSW, Australia, Apr. 27, 1956; arrived in U.S., 1999; s. Keith Anderson and Shirley Evelyn (May) Slater; m. Tamara Anne Graham, Sept. 29, 1990; children: River, Tassia, Xavier. BA, Australian Nat. U., 1983. Acting chief staff ABC Radio News, Barwin, Australia, 1986—88; media advisor Senator Ted Robertson, 1984—85; pres. Seal Enterprises, Perth, 1990—94; media dir. Pub. & Broadcasting, Sydney, 1994—96; dir. internat. television Murdoch Media, 1996—98; pres., CEO Masthead Media, N.Y.C., 1998—. Cons. Am. Media, Inc., NY, 2004, 20th Television, Calif., 2004, Conde Nast, NY, 2004. Editor: Westside News Mag., 1994, Internat. Women's Surfing Mag., 1995. Media advisor Australian Labor Party, 1980—90; pres. Surfrider Found., 1985—87; speech writer Sen. Ted Robertson, Australia, 1983. Mem.: Assn. Surfing Profls. Avocations: surfing, rugby, bicycling, yoga. E-mail: larry@mastheadmedia.com.

ANDERSON, LARRY WAYNE, language educator; b. St. Joseph, Mo., May 22, 1951; s. Jack Clarence and Helen Bond Anderson; m. Marcha Lynn Rankin. BS in Seconday Edn., N.W. Mo. State U., 1973, MA in Lang., 1977. Cert. secondary en. Lang. instr. Craig (Mo.) R-III H.S., 1974—77, Nodaway-Holt R-VII Sch. Dist., Skidmore, Mo., 1977—84, Savannah (Mo.) R-III Sch. Dist., 1984—. Editor: (poetry anthology) Field Stones, (lit. booklet) Look Who's Writing in Northwest Missouri, 1981; contbr. poetry to anthologies. Chmn. Lit. divsn. Nodaway Arts Coun., Maryville; com. mem. and commr. Zoning Com., Maryville. Recipient Poetry award, Nodway Arts Coun., 1979—81. Mem.: NEA (Savannah Edn. Assn. br.), Lions Club (pres. Maryville Pride club). Avocation: writing. Office Phone: (816) 324-3126.

ANDERSON, LAURIE MONNES, state senator; b. Coronado, Calif., Dec. 31, 1945; 2 children. BA, Willamette U., 1968; MA, U. Colo., 1972; BSN, Radford U., 1982. Rsch. biologist, 1972—78; pub. health nurse, 1982—2000; state rep., 2001—05. Sch. bd. Gresham-Barlow Sch. Dist., 1991—2001. Mem.: Oreg. Sch. Bd. Assn. (dir. 1996—). Democrat. Office: 900 Court St North East S 310 Salem OR 97301

ANDERSON, LAWRENCE KEITH, electrical engineer, consultant; b. Toronto, Ont., Can., Oct. 2, 1935; came to U.S., 1957; s. Wallace Ray and Irene Margaret (Linn) A.; m. Katherine Florence Drechsler, Sept. 21, 1963; children— Susan Barbara, Robert Keith. B. in Engring. Physics, McGill U., 1957; PhDEE, Stanford U., 1962. With Bell Labs., 1961-85, dir. electronic components and Subsystems lab. Allentown, Pa., 1981-85; v.p. component devel. Sandia Nat. Labs., Albuquerque, 1985-88; exec. dir. AT&T Bell Labs. Interconnection and Power Tech. Div., Parsippany, NJ, 1988-89; prof., dir. Alliance for Photonic Tech., Albuquerque, 1990-91; dir. Colo. Inst. Tech. Transfer and Implementation, U. Colo., Colorado Springs, 1991-95. Bd. dirs. N.M. Inst. for Lifelong Learning, 2002—. Bd. dirs. Inst. for Lifelong Learning for New Mexicans, 2003—. Fellow IEEE (pres. Electron Devices Soc. 1976-77, bd. dir. 1979-80), Engring. Mgmt. Soc. (bd. govs. 1999-02, v.p. confs. 2001-02). Home: 150 Whitetail Rd NE Albuquerque NM 87122-1921 Personal E-mail: andersnm@aol.com.

ANDERSON, LAWRENCE OHACO, United States magistrate judge, lawyer; b. Phoenix, Sept. 7, 1948; s. Jack M. and Viola (Ohaco) A.; m. Aimee. BS, U. San Francisco, 1971; JD, Ariz. State U., Tempe, 1974. Bar: Ariz. 1975. Prosecutor City of Phoenix, 1973-75; assoc. Jack M. Anderson, Phoenix, 1975-78; sole practice Phoenix, 1978-90; judge Superior Ct. of Ariz., Phoenix, 1990-92, judge, criminal calender, 1992-95, judge, juvenile ct., 1995-98, magistrate judge, 1998—. Natl. Wheelchair Weightlifting Championship, Spokane, Wash., 1974; Victory Achievement Award, State of Ariz., 1990; Outstanding Citizens award, Nat. Counil on Disability, 1992. Mem. ABA, Assn. Trial Lawyers Am., Ariz. Trial Lawyers Assn. (bd. dirs. 1985-90). Republic. Roman Catholic. Avocations: fishing, sports. Office: 401 W Washington SPC11 Phoenix AZ 85003-2120

ANDERSON, LEA E., lawyer; b. Clarksburg, W.Va., May 25, 1954; d. Jackson Lawler and Barbara Jean (Sanford) A.; m. Templeton Smith Jr., Aug. 2, 1980; children: Templeton Smith III, Suzanne Lea Smith. BA, W.Va. U., 1976, JD, 1979. Bar: W.Va. 1979, U.S. Dist. Ct. (so. dist.) W.Va. 1979, Pa. 1981, U.S. Supreme Ct. 1982. Assoc. Bowles, McDavid, Graff & Love, Charleston, W.Va., 1979-80, Goehring, Rutter & Boehm, Pitts., 1980-84, ptnr., 1984-89, mem., 1990—, sec., shareholder, 1993—. Mem. credit com. Alcobar Fed. Credit Union, 1985-87, mem. supervisory com., 1981; mem. vis. com. W.Va. Coll. Law, 1986-89, mem. W.Va. U. student affairs vis. com., 1996-99, chmn.; course planner and spkr. Estate Planning for Subsequent Marriages, 2002; spkr. Estate Planning in Divorce and Remarriage in Pa., 2001. Vol. March of Dimes, 1986, neighborhood coord., 1987-91; chmn. fundraising com. Southminster Nursery Sch., 1989; chmn. Windy Ridge, 1991-93; mem. Performing Arts for Children, South, 1991-94, v.p., membership com. 1993-94; mem. bd. deacons Southminster Presbyn. Ch., Mt. Lebanon, Pa., 1990-93, vice chmn. bd. deacons, 1993, session mem., elder, trustee, 1993-97, 2001—, v.p. trustees, 2002—, assoc. min. search com., 1997, dir. Christian edn. search com., 2002—; active Foster Sch. PTA, 1993-97. Mem. W.Va. Bar Assn., Pa. Bar Assn., Allegheny County Bar Assn. (chmn. edn. com. of young lawyers 1983-84, treas. 1984-85, mem. rules com. family law sect. 1993-94), Child Study Club of Mt. Lebanon (pres. 1989-91), Mt. Lebanon Aqua Club (treas. 1996-98, nominating com. 1997, 98, sec. 1999-2001), Phi Beta Kappa, Phi Kappa Phi, Phi Delta Phi. Republican. Office: Goehring Rutter & Boehm 1424 Frick Bldg 437 Grant St Ste 437 Pittsburgh PA 15219-6002

ANDERSON, LELA M, music educator, composer; b. Houston, Sept. 01; d. Archie and Florence. BA in Music Edn., Prairie View A&M U., 1972, MA in Music Edn., 1979. Piano tchr. Prairie View A&M U., Tex., 1974—75; choir tchr. Aldine Ind. Sch. Dist., Tex., 1975—78, Crockett Ind. Sch. Dist., Tex., 1980—85; gen. music tchr. Houston (Tex.) Ind. Sch. Dist., 1985—87, tchr. piano, 1987—2004. Musician, dir. various chs., Houston, 1975—; founder, pres. Grace Publ., Houston, 1998, composer, 1998—. Mem.: Am. Choral Dir. Assn., Nat. Guild of Piano Tchrs., Am. Soc. Composers, Authors, and Pub. Baptist. Avocation: coin collecting/numismatics. Home: PO Box 38434 Houston TX 77238

ANDERSON, LENNART, artist; b. Detroit, Aug. 22, 1928; B.F.A., Art Inst. Chgo., 1950; M.F.A., Cranbrook Acad. Art Mich., 1952. Instr. art Chatham Coll., Pitts., 1961-62, Pratt Inst., N.Y.C., 1962-69, Skowhegan Sch., 1965, 67, Art Students League, NY, Yale U., 1967, Finch Coll., N.Y.C.; prof. painting and drawing Bklyn. Coll., 1974—2003. One man shows include Tanager Gallery, NYC, 1962, Graham Gallery, 1963, 67, 69, 70, Davis & Long Co., 1976, Davis & Langdale Co., 1981, 84, 85, 91, 92, William Crapo Gallery, New Bedford, Mass., 1982, Darien Libr., Darien, Conn., 1984, Delaware Art Mus., Wilmington, 1992, Salander-O'Reilly Galleries, 1995, 97, 99, 2002,

Rider Univ. Gallery, Lawrenceville, NJ, 2000, others; group shows include March Gallery, NYC, 1957, 58, Palazzo dell'Esposizione, Rome, 1958, 59, 60, Kans. City Art Inst., 1962, Carnegie Internat., Pitts., 1964, 67, Am. Fedn. Arts, NYC, 1965, Yale Univ., 1967, Cleve. Mus. Art, Ohio, 1972, Mus. Fine Arts, Boston, 1975, 1982-83, Art Inst. Chgo., 1976, Harold Reed Gallery, NYC, 1978, Pa. Acad. Fine Arts, Phila., 1981 Robert Schoelkopf Gallery, 1984, 85, Nat. Acad. Design, NYC, 1988, Meml. Art Gallery, Rochester, NY, 1989, Oglethorpe Univ. Art Gallery, Atlanta, 1990, Gerald Peters Gallery, Santa Fe, N.Mex., 1993, Salander-O'Reilly Galleries, Inc., NYC, 1994, 95, Aspen Art Mus., Aspen, Colo., 1996, Art Inst. So. Calif., Laguna Beach, Calif., 1999, Bates Coll. Mus. Art, 2000, Widener Gallery Trinity Coll., Hartford, Conn., 2003, others; represented in permanent collections, Whitney Mus. Am. Art, Bklyn. Mus., Hirschorn Mus., Washington, Mus. Fine Arts, Boston, Cleve., Yale Univ., New Haven, Conn., Delaware Art Mus., Wilmington, Mellon Bank, Pitts., Bklyn. Mus., NY, others. Recipient Prix de Rome, 1958-60; Raymond A. Speiser Meml. prize Pa. Acad. Fine Arts, 1966; Nat. Council on Arts prize, 1966, Emil & Dines Carlson award Nat. Acad. Design, 1988, Benjamin Altman prize, 2005; Mus. Tiffany Found. grantee, 1957, 61, Guggenheim fellow, 1986; grantee Nat. Endowment for Arts, Tiffany Found. Am. Acad. and Inst. Arts and Letters; assoc. Am. Acad. Design. Home: 877 Union St Brooklyn NY 11215-1401

ANDERSON, LESLIE J., lawyer; b. 1953; BA in English Lit. magna cum laude, Allegheny Coll., 1975; MA in English and Comparative Lit., Columbia Univ., 1976, MPhil, 1979; JD cum laude, Univ. Mich., 1983. Bar: Minn. 1983. Assoc. Dorsey & Whitney LLP, Mpls, 1984—91; ptnr., litig. group Dorsey & Whitney, Mpls., 1991, now ptnr., co-chair, employee benefits group. Staff mem. Mich.Yearbook of Internat. Legal Studies, 1981—82, editor-in-chief, 1982—83. Bd. dir. Greater Twin Cities Youth Symphonies, 2003—. Mem.: Minn. Women Lawyers, Minn. Advocates for Human Rights, Phi Beta Kappa. Office: Dorsey & Whitney LLP Ste 1500 50 S Sixth St Minneapolis MN 55402-1498 Office Phone: 612-343-7960. Office Fax: 612-340-2868. Business E-Mail: anderson.leslie@dorsey.com.

ANDERSON, LISA D., graphics designer, educator; d. Robert Boston Wilson and Fanny Ruth Dickey. Degree in Mech. Drafting, Mid-Florida Tech. Inst., 1982, Degree in Tech. Illustration, 1983; B in Graphic Design, U. Ctrl. Fla., 1986; MS in Edn., Nova Southeastern U., 1998; PhD, U. South Fla., 2000. Cert. web page design U. South Fla., 2003, web devel. U. South Fla., 2002, Train The Trainer Dvd Sonic, 2002. Mktg. graphic designer east coast Hansen Lind Meyer, Orlando; sr. graphic designer Harris Corp., Orlando, 1991—93; sr. illustrator Westinghouse, Orlando, 1992—95; sr. imager CGS, Tampa, 1995—98; chair advt. and computer graphics IADT, Tampa, 1998—2000, chair graphic design, 1998—. Presenter, rschr. and cons. in field. Named Media Arts Employee Of The Yr., IADT, 2001; recipient Outstanding Contributions To Academic Excellence award, 2003. Mem.: ASCD (assoc.), Soc. For Instrnl. Tech. in Edn. and Tchr. Tng. (assoc.), Internat. Digital Media Assn. (assoc.), Am. Assn. for Computers in Edn. (assoc.), Easter Ednl. Rsch. Assn. (assoc.). Office: Ednl Interactive Group 31739 Hedgerow Dr Zephyrhills FL 33543

ANDERSON, LLOYD LEE, zoology educator; b. Nevada, Iowa, Nov. 18, 1933; s. Clarence and Carrie G. (Sampson) A.; m. Janice G. Peterson, Sept. 7, 1958 (dec. Dec. 1966); m. JaNelle R. Hall, June 15, 1970; children: Marc C., James R. Student, Simpson Coll., 1951-52, Iowa State U., 1952-53, BS in Animal Husbandry, 1957, PhD in Animal Reproduction, 1961; DSc (hon.), Georgian Acad. Scis., Tbilisi, 2003. NIH postdoctoral fellow Iowa State U., Ames, 1961-62, asst. prof., 1961-65, assoc. prof., 1965-71, prof. animal sci., 1971—, Charles F. Curtiss Disting. prof. agr., 1992—, chmn. com. on coms., faculty senate, 2000—02, prof. biomed. sci., 2002—. Lalor Found. fellow Sta. Recherches Physiologie Animale, Inst. Nat. Recherche Agronomique, Jouy-en-Josas, France, 1963—64; rschr. physiology of reprodn. and ctrl. nervous sys.-pituitary regulation of growth for increased prodn. efficiency of farm animals; mem. reproductive biology study sect. NIH, 1984—88, NIH Reviewers Res. (NRR), 1988—92; mem. peer rev. panel animal health spl. rsch. grants on beef and dairy cattle reproductive diseases USDA, 1986—88; Honor lectr. representing Iowa State U. Mid-Am. State Univs. Assn., 1989—90; mem. sustainable growth agrl. panel USDA, Agrl. Rsch. Svc., Nat. Program Staff to rev. rsch. projects, 1993; mem. referees panel for sponsored rsch. Kuwait U., 1998—; mem. Janice Peterson Anderson Excellence award and scholarship Coll. of Design Iowa State U., chair com. on coms., Faculty Senate, 2000—02; trustee Asian Inst. Nanobiosci. and Tech., Busan, Republic of Korea, 2002—. Mem. editl. bd. Biology Reprodn., 1968-70, 86-90, Jour. Animal Sci., 1982-87, 98-2001, Animal Reprodn. Sci., 1978—, Inst. for Sci. Info. Atlas of Sci., 1987-90, Domestic Animal Endocrinology, 1992-95, 2004—, Endocrinology, 1993-97; contbr. articles to profl. jours. Mem. 4-H Club. With Constrn. Engrs., U.S. Army, 1953-55, Germany, Signal Corps USAR, 1955-61. Recipient Cert. Recognition, Cold War, 1991, disting. Achievement award, Iowa State U. Alumni Assn., 2005; grantee, USDA, 1978—. Fellow AAAS, Am. Soc. Animal Sci. (hon. Animal Physiology and Endocrinology award 1988, Nat Pork Prodrs. Coun. Innovation award in basic rsch. 1993, Outstanding Achievement in Rsch. award 2001, Animal Growth and Devel. award 2004); mem. ACLU, NRA, VFW, Endocrine Soc., Am. Physiol. Soc., Iowa Physiol. Soc., Am. Assn. Anatomists, Am. Soc. Cell Biology, Soc. for Study of Reprodn., Soc. for Exptl. Biology and Medicine (mem. coun. 1980-83), Brit. Soc. for Study of Fertility, Soc. for Neurosci., Iowa Acad. Sci., Pituitary Soc., Asian Inst. of Nanobioscience and Tech., Busan, Korea (trustee 2002—), Am. Legion, Nat. Block and Bridle Club, Osborn Rsch. Club (chair 1994), Faculty Citation Iowa State Univ. Alumni Assn. 2003, Sigma Xi, Gamma Sigma Delta (Mission award in rsch. 2002, Alumni Award of Merit 2004), Alpha Tau Omega (Gold Cir. award 2002). Methodist. Home: 2812 Valley View Rd Ames IA 50014-4506 Office: Iowa State U Dept Animal Sci 2356 Kildee Hl Ames IA 50011-3150 Office Phone: 515-294-5540.

ANDERSON, LORRAINE PEARSON, dean; b. Orlando, Fla., Mar. 12, 1956; d. Embree Jones and Marilyn (Meckstroth) Pearson; m. Steve W. Smith; m. Dale A. Anderson; children: Brandon, Alexandra. BA, U. Fla., 1978; MBA, Marshall U., Huntington, W.Va., 1991; EdD, W.Va. U., 2000. Coll. rels. coord. Walt Disney World, Huntington, W.Va., 1973—85; owner, mgr. Premier Travel Co., Huntington, 1991—94; instr. Marshall U., Huntington, 1991—93, dir. undergrad. studies, 1993—96, assoc. dean, 1996—. Developer leadership tng. program U.S. Army C.E. Contbr. articles to profl. jours. Recipient EntrePrep award, Kauffman Found., 1996—2003, Mini-Soc. award, 1999—2004. Mem.: NAFE, Acad. of Mgmt., Nat. Soc. Human Resource Mgmt., TriState Soc. for Human Resource Mgmt. (bd. dirs. 2002—), Beta Alpha Psi, Phi Beta Kappa. Office: Marshall Univ Lewis Coll of Bus One John Marshall Dr Huntington WV 25755-2300 E-mail: lorraine.anderson@marshall.edu.

ANDERSON, LOUIS WILMER, JR., physicist, researcher; b. Houston, Dec. 24, 1933; s. Louis Wilmer and Margaret Quarles (Brockett) A.; m. Marguerite Gillespie, Aug. 30; children— Margaret Mary, Louis Charles, Elizabeth Brockett BA, Rice U., 1956; A.M., Harvard U., 1957, PhD, 1960. Asst. prof. U. Wis.-Madison, 1960-63, assoc. prof., 1963-68, prof. physics, 1968-94, Julian E. Mack prof. physics, 1994—. Cons. U. Calif.-Berkeley Lawrence Lab. Author 2 textbooks. Contbr. articles to profl. jours. Patentee type of N2 laser, collisional pumping ion source. Fellow U. Wis. Tchg. Acad.; co-recipient IEEE Particle Accelerator Conf. Tech. award for invention and devel. of optically pumped polarized H-Ion source, 1993. Fellow Am. Phys. Soc.; mem. Sigma Xi Home: 1818 Chadbourne Ave Madison WI 53726 Office: U Wis Dept Physics Madison WI 53706 Office Phone: 608-262-8962. Business E-Mail: lwanders@wisc.edu.

ANDERSON, LYLE ARTHUR, retired manufacturing company executive; b. Jewell, Kans., Dec. 29, 1931; s. Arvid Herman and Clara Vera (Herman) A.; m. Harriet Virginia Robson, June 12, 1953; children— Brian, Karen, Eric. BS, U. Kans., 1953; MS, Butler U., 1961. C.P.A., Mo., Kans. Mgmt. trainee, internal auditor RCA, Camden, N.J. and Indpls., 1955-59; auditor Ernst & Ernst (C.P.A.'s), Kansas City, Mo., 1959-63; v.p. fin. and adminstrn., treas., dir. Affiliated Hosp. Products, Inc., St. Louis, 1963-71; sr. v.p. Sara Lee Corp., Deerfield, Ill., 1971-74; exec. v.p. fin. Consol. Foods Corp., Chgo., 1974-76. Pres. Autotrol Corp., Crystal Lake, Ill. Bd. dirs. Crystal Lake Civic Ctr. Authority, Raue Ctr. for the Arts. With U.S. Army, 1953-55. Mem. Omicron Delta Kappa. Republican. Methodist. Home: 9804 Partridge Ln Crystal Lake IL 60014-6627

ANDERSON, LYNN (RENE ANDERSON), singer; b. Grand Forks, N.D., Sept. 26, 1947; d. Casey and Liz Anderson; m. Glenn Sutton (div.); 1 child, Lisa; m. Harold Stream III (div.); children: Gray, Melissa. Singer, rec. artist, 1966—; appeared on Lynn Anderson Spls. Appearances on Lawrence Welk Show, 1967-70, Grand Old Opry, 1967, Ed Sullivan Show, Bob Hope Spls., Starsky and Hutch, (NBC Movie of the Week); TV guest appearances L. Frank Baum's The Marvelous Land of Oz, 1981, Country Gold, 1982, Law and Order, 1991, XXX's and OOO's, 1994, Babylon 5, 1994; rec. artist: (songs) I Never Promised You a Rose Garden, Cry, Listen to a Country Song, Your're My Man, Top of the World, Rocky Top, (albums) Encore, Under the Boardwalk, Greatest Hits, Rose Garden, What She Does Best, 1988, (duet with Gary Morris) You're Welcome to Tonight, 1983, What She Does Best, 1988, Country Spotlight, 1991, (with Emmylou Harris and Marty Stuart) Cowboys' Sweetheart, 1992; discs include Latest and Greatest, 1998, Anthology: The Columbia Years, 1999, Anthology: The Chart Years, 1999, Live at Billy Bob's Texas, 2000, Christmas, 2002, Pure Country, 2004, Heart Songs, 2004. Recipient Grammy award; named Female Artist of the Decade by Record World, 1971, Best Female Vocalist, CMA Awards, Most Promising, Best Female Vocalist, Acad. Country Music Awards, Best Country Performance-Female, People's Choice awards.

ANDERSON, LYNN D., telecommunications industry executive; BA, Kans. State U.; MBA, U. Tex. With GE Capital; CFO Optical Capital Group, Broadwing Comms., Austin, Tex. Office: Broadwing Communications LLC 1122 Capital of Texas Hwy S Austin TX 78746-6426

ANDERSON, LYNN L., bank executive; B in B in Bus., JD, U. Kans. Various positions Frank Russell, 1987; chmn. Frank Russell Trust Co., Tacoma, Frank Russell Investment Mgmt. Co., Tacoma. Vice chmn. Frank Russell Co. Office: Frank Russell Co 909 A St Tacoma WA 98402 Office Phone: 253-439-3510.

ANDERSON, MARILYN JUNE, retired secondary school educator; b. Aldrich, Mo., July 3, 1935; d. Lafayette and Helen Louise (Cheek) A. BS in Edn., S.W. Mo. State U., Springfield, 1958; MEd, U. Mo., 1966. Vocal, instrumental music Licking (Mo.) High Sch., 1958-62; vocal music, English I and English II Sullivan (Mo.) High Sch., 1962-65; vocal music Willard (Mo.) High Sch., 1965-67, Hillcrest High Sch., Springfield, Mo., 1967-92; substitute tchr. Springfield R-12 Schs., 1992-95. Sponsor Future Nurses Am., Licking, 1958-62; chpt. organizer and sponsor Hillcrest Tri-M, 1988-92; pvt. piano and voice tchr., music contest adjudicator; singer Mid. Am. Singers, Springfield, 1969-76. Chmn. of drive March of Dimes, Licking, Mo., 1961; edn. chmn. Am. Cancer Soc., Texas County, 1961-62; Bible sch. tchr. Ch. of Christ, Springfield, Mo., 1968-71, 80-2000; singer S.W. Mo. State U., Collegiate Chorale, 1992-99. Mem. NEA, Mo. Music Educators Assn. (dist. vocal v.p. 1986-87), Music Educators Nat. Conf., Am. Choral Dirs. Assn., Springfield Area Ret. Tchrs. Assn., Mo. Ret. Tchrs. Assn., Nat. Fedn. of State H.S. Assn., Delta Kappa Gamma (chpt. rec. sec. 1992—). Republican. Avocations: needlecrafts, reading, walking, flower gardening, writing.

ANDERSON, MARK ALEXANDER, lawyer; b. Santa Monica, Calif., Nov. 15, 1953; s. William Alexander and Christina (Murray) A.; m. Rosalie Louise Movius, Nov. 28, 1986; 1 child, Morgan Anderson Movius. AB, U. So. Calif., 1974; JD, Yale U., 1978. Bar: Calif. 1979, U.S. Dist. Ct. (no. dist.) Calif. 1979, U.S. Ct. Appeals (9th cir.) 1979, Oreg. 1982, U.S. Dist. Ct. Oreg. 1982, Wash. 1985, U.S. Dist. Ct. (we. dist.) Wash. 1986, U.S. Supreme Ct. 1989. Law clk. U.S. Ct. Appeals (9th cir.), San Francisco, 1978-79, U.S. Dist. Ct. Oreg., Portland, 1980-82; atty. Miller, Nash, Wiener, Hager & Carlsen, Portland, 1983-92; gen. counsel, asst. sec. Dark Horse Comics, Inc., Milwaukie, Oreg., 1992-98; sr. asst. atty. gen. Oreg. Dept. Justice, Salem, Oreg., 2002—04. Chair Raleigh Hills-Garden Home Citizen Participation Orgn., 1992-93. Mem. N.W. Lawyers and Artists (pres. 1988-90), State Bar Calif., Wash. State Bar Assn., Oreg. State Bar (chair antitrust, trade regulation and unfair bus. practices sect. 1991-92), City Club of Portland (chair arts and culture standing com. 1990-92, rsch. bd. 1999-2002). Home: PO Box 8154 Portland OR 97207-8154

ANDERSON, MARTIN CARL, economist; b. Lowell, Mass., Aug. 5, 1936; s. Ralph and Evelyn (Anderson) A.; m. Annelise Graebner, Sept. 25, 1965 AB summa cum laude, Dartmouth Coll., 1957, MS in Engring., MSBA; PhD in Indsl. Mgmt., MIT, 1962. Asst. to dean, instr. engring. Thayer Sch. Engring. Dartmouth Coll., Hanover, N.H., 1959; research fellow Joint Ctr. for Urban Studies MIT and Harvard U., Cambridge, 1961-62; asst. prof. fin. Grad. Sch. Bus. Columbia U., N.Y.C., 1962-65, assoc. prof. bus., 1965-68; sr. fellow Hoover Inst. on War, Revolution and Peace Stanford (Calif.) U., 1971—; spl. asst. to Pres. of U.S. The White House, 1969-70, spl. cons. for systems analysis, 1970-71, asst. for policy devel., 1981-82. Mem. Pres.' Fgn. Intelligence Adv. Bd., 1982-85, Pres.' Econ. Policy Adv. Bd., 1982-88, Pres.' Gen. Adv. Com. on Arms Control and Disarmament, 1987-93; pub. interest dir. Fed. Home Loan Bank San Francisco, 1972-79; mem. Commn. on Crucial Choices for Ams., 1973-75, Def. Manpower Commn., 1975-76, Com. on the Present Danger, 1977—. Author: The Federal Bulldozer: A Critical Analysis of Urban Renewal, 1949-62, 1964, Conscription: A Select and Annotated Bibliography, 1976, Welfare: The Political Economy of Welfare Reform in the U.S., 1978, Registration and the Draft, 1982, The Military Draft, 1982, Revolution, 1988, Impostors in the Temple, 1992, Reagan in his Own Hand, 2001, Reagan: A Life in Letters, 2003, Reagan's Path to Victory, 2004; columnist Scripps-Howard News Svc., 1993-94. Dir. research Nixon presdl. campaign, 1968; policy adviser Reagan presdl. campaign, 1976, 80; del. Rep. Nat. Conv., 1992-2000; policy adviser Dole Presdl. Campaign, 1996; sr. adviser Bush presdl. campaign, 1998-2000; trustee Ronald Reagan Presdl. Found., 1985-92; mem. Calif. Gov.'s Coun. Econ. Advisors, 1993-98, chmn. Congl. Policy Adv. Bd., 1998-2001. 2d lt. AUS, 1958-59. Mem. Mont Pelerin Soc., Phi Beta Kappa. Clubs: Bohemian. Office: Stanford U Hoover Instn Stanford CA 94305-6010

ANDERSON, MARY ANN GRASSO, theater association executive; b. Rome, NY, Nov. 3, 1952; d. Vincent and Rose Mary (Pupa) Grasso; m. J. Wayne Anderson, Feb. 14, 2004. BA in Art History, U. Calif., Riverside, 1973; MLS, U. Oreg., 1974. Dir. Warner Rsch. Collection, Burbank, Calif., 1975-84; mgr. CBS TV/Docudrama, Hollywood, Calif., 1984-88; v.p., exec. dir. Nat. Assn. Theatre Owners, North Hollywood, Calif., 1988—. Instr. theatre arts UCLA, 1980-85, Am. Film Inst., L.A., 1985-88. Screen credits: The Scarlet O'Hara Wars, This Year's Blonde, The Silent Lovers, A Bunnies Tale, Embassy. Apptd. commr. Burbank Heritage Commn. Recipient Friend award, Tripod Sch., 1999, Stace award, Dolby, 2002, Intersoc. Ken Mason award, 2004. Mem.: Found. of the Motion Picture Pioneers, Acad. Motion Picture Arts and Scis., Retinitis Pigmentosa Internat. (The Vision award 1996), Bus. and Profl. Women's Assn. (Woman of Achievement award 1983), Phi Beta Kappa. Avocation: traditional music and dance. Office: Nat Assn Theatre Owners 750 1st St NE Ste 1130 Washington DC 20002 Office Phone: 202-962-0054.

ANDERSON, MARY JANE, library director, consultant; b. Des Moines, Jan. 23, 1935; d. William Kenneth and Margaret Louise (Snider) McPherson; m. Charles Robert Anderson, Oct. 21, 1965 (div. Oct. 24, 1989); 1 child, Mary Margaret. BA in Edn., U. Fla., 1957; MLS, Fla. State U., 1963. Elem. sch. librarian Dade County Schs., Miami, Fla., 1957-61; children's/young adult librarian Santa Fe Regional Library, Gainesville, Fla., 1961-63; br. librarian Jacksonville (Fla.) Pub. Library, 1963-64, chief of children's services, 1964-66, head of circulation, 1966-67; pub. library cons. Fla. State Library, Tallahassee, 1967-70; dir. tech. processing St. Mary's Coll. of Md., St. Mary's City, 1970-72; coordinator children's services Balt. County Pub. Library, Towson, Md., 1972-73; exec. dir. young adult services div. ALA, Chgo., 1973-75, exec. dir. assn. for library service to children, 1973-82; pres. Answers Unltd., Inc., Deerfield, Ill., 1982-92; dir. Wilmington (Ill.) Pub. Libr., 1993-97; dir. media svcs. Newark (Ill.) County Sch. Dist., 1997-98; dir. Maud P. Palenske Pub. Libr., St. Joseph, Mich., 1998-2000; coord. Sr. Net Learning Ctr., Ariea IV Agy. Aging, St. Joseph, 2000—03; libr. cons., 2000—. Instr. and cons. in field; part-time faculty No. Ill. U., 1985-86, Nat. Coll. Edn., Evanston, Ill., 1989; head youth svcs. Waukegan (Ill.) Pub. Libr., 1988-93; mem. exec. com. U.S. sect. Internat. Bd. on Books for Young People, 1973-82; mem. adv. bd. Reading Rainbow, TV series, 1981-84; mem. sch. bd. Avoca Sch. Dist. 37, 1985-87; mem. ALSC Newbery Medal Com., 1991. Editor: Top of the News, 1971-73, Fla. State Library Newsletter, 1967-70, Nor'Easter (North Suburban Library System Newsletter), 1984-88; contbr. articles to profl. jours. Bd. dirs. Child Devel. Assocs. Consortium, 1975—83, Coalition for Children and Youth, 1978—80; downtown redevel. commn. City of Wilmington, 1996—98; coun. mem. Episcopal Diocese Chgo. Diocese, 1988—94, standing com., 1994—97, dep. to gen. conv., 1997, Bishop's search com., 1997—98, province V rep., 1998—99; mem. vestry St. Thomas' Episcopal Ch., Morris, Ill., 1996—98; active Episcopal Diocese West, Mich., Diocesan cons. team, 1999—, alt. dep. to gen. conv., 2003; deanery rep. St. Paul's Episc. Ch., St. Joseph, Mich., 2000—01, lay eucharistic min., 1999—, mem. vestry, 2003—05. Mem. ALA (coun. 1992-2000, com. on orgn. 1999-01), Rotary (sec.-treas. 1994-96, pres. 1996-97), Wilmington C. of C. (bd. dirs. 1996-97, sec. 1997), Caxton Club (Chgo.), Beta Phi Mu, Sigma Kappa. Episcopalian. E-mail: mjanderson@mich.com.

ANDERSON, MARY JANE, music educator; b. St. Louis, Oct. 9, 1954; d. William Edward and Katherine Ruth Anderson. Student, The Juilliard Sch., 1967—72; BFA in Piano Performance, Stephens Coll., 1976; MM in Piano Performance, So. Ill. U., Edwardsville, 1991. Piano faculty mem. St. Louis Conservatory and Schs. for the Arts, St. Louis, 1977—81, So. Ill. U., Edwardsville, 1984—; pvt. piano instr. St. Louis, 1975—. Adjudicator state and local piano competitions, Mo. and Ill.; soloist St. Louis Symphony, St. Louis Philharmonic; recitalist, orchestral soloist numerous performances throughout Midwest U.S., Pa, NY. Recipient 1st pl. Profl. Debut Recital, Artist Presentation Soc., 1975, 1st pl. Dimitri Mitropoulos Nat. Piano Competition, Stephens Coll., 1972; scholar, Dimitri Mitropoulos Piano Competition; Piano scholar, Am. Acad. Arts in Europe, 1975. Mem.: St. Louis Area Music Tchrs. Assn. (pres. 2002—), Mo. Music Tchrs. Assn., Music Tchrs. Nat. Assn. Avocations: reading, fishing, crossword puzzles. Office: So Ill U Edwardsville Music Dept PO Box 1771 Edwardsville IL 62026-1771 Office Phone: 618-650-2022. Business E-Mail: manders@siue.edu.

ANDERSON, MAUREEN ANNE, librarian; b. Fresno, Calif., Aug. 9, 1935; d. Harry Burney and Edna Grace (Jacobsen) Thorpe; m. Edward Dan Anderson, Sept. 15, 1964; 1 child, David Burke. BA, U. Calif., Santa Barbara, 1957, MA in History, 1960; MSLS, U. So. Calif., 1963. Asst. librarian Coll. of Sequoias, Visalia, Calif., 1959-62; librarian U.S. Army Spl. Services, Babenhausen and Aschaffenburg, Republic of Germany, 1963-64, Mt. Whitney High Sch., Visalia, Calif., 1966—94; ret., 1994. Contbr. articles pub. to profl. jour. Mem. adv. bd. Tulare County Libr Mem. NEA, Visalia Unified Tchrs. Assn. (chmn. bd. dirs. 1975-76, sec. 1984-85), Tulare County Ret. Tchrs. Assn., Tulare County Hist. Soc. (editor Los Tulares newsletter 1995—), Calif. Ret. Tchrs. Assn Democrat. Avocations: history, writing, needlecrafts. Home: 1201 W Westcott Ave Visalia CA 93277-2456

ANDERSON, MAYNARD CARLYLE, security firm executive; b. Hesper, Iowa, Aug. 6, 1932; s. Carl Adolph and Mathilda Theodora (Wold) A. BA, Luther Coll., 1954. Mem. spl. ops. group Hqrs. Dept. of Navy, Washington, 1966-68, supervising agt. Naval Investigative Svc. Office Guantanamo Bay, Cuba, 1968-69, asst. head internal security divsn. hqrs. Washington, 1969-73, dir. spl. security and spl. activiites, 1973-78, dir. spl. security, 1978-79; dep. security policy Dept. of Def., Washington, 1979-82, dir. security plans and programs, 1982-88, asst. dep. under sec., 1988-93, acting dep. under sec. def., 1993-94; pres., mng. dir. Arcadia Group Worldwide, Inc., Chantilly, Va., 1994—; founder Arcadia Inst., Chantilly, 1997; prin. Strategic Trade Adv. Group, Inc., Washington, 1997—. Dir. Nat. Intellectual Property Law Inst., Washington, 1994; chmn. policy com. Security Affairs Support Assn., Washington, 1988—94; former chmn. adv. com. Dept. of Def. Security Inst., Dept. of Def. Polygraph Inst., Def. Pers. Security Rsch. and Edn. Ctr.; chmn. Nat. Adv. Group/Security Countermeasures; hon. faculty mem. Def. Security Inst.; lectr. Sch. Criminal Justice, Coll. Social Sci. Mich. State U., mem. rsch. task force; lectr. Luther Coll., Decorah, Iowa; del. UN Econ. Commn. for Europe, Com. on Sustained Devel., 1999—; dir. VT Griffin Svcs., Inc., Atlanta, 2002—, mng. dir. multi-sector crisis mgmt. consortium, Arlington, Va., 2003—. Author/contbr.: Citizen Espionage: Studies in Trust and Betrayal, 1994; contbr. articles to profl. jours. Mem. pres. coun. Luther Coll., Decorah, Iowa, 1990—. Recipient Meritorious Exec. Presdl. Rank award, Washington, 1985, 92, Disting. Svc. award Luther Coll., Decorah, 1989, Donald B. Woodbridge award of excellence Nat. Classification Mgmt. Soc., Washington, 1990, Def. Disting. Svc. medal, 1992. Lutheran. Avocations: tennis, writing, lecturing, travel. Home: 205 S Yoakum Pky Apt 721 Alexandria VA 22304-3818 Office: Arcadia Group Worldwide Inc PO Box 222245 Chantilly VA 20153-2245 E-mail: arcadiagwi@iopener.net. *Sometimes it seems that significant achievements have been realized by accident. Actually, they have resulted from taking advantage of opportunities.*

ANDERSON, MELISSA JOELL, sales executive, educator; b. Arlington Heights, Ill., Apr. 23, 1972; d. Thomas Robert and Rebecca Jo Anderson. BA, UCLA, 1995; MA, Columbia U., 1997, MBA, 1999; EdD, Pepperdine U., 2005. Dir. programs Friends HSES, N.Y.C., 1995—99; dir. corp. programs Kaplan, Inc., N.Y.C., 1999—2000; dir. ednl. tech. NYU Stern Sch., N.Y.C., 2000—03; dir. instrnl. tech. Pepperdine U., Malibu, Calif., 2003—04, adj. faculty, 2004—; sales engr. Blackboard, Inc., Washington, 2004—05. Author: Students' Guide to Blackboard, 1999. Avocations: ballroom dancing, cooking, snowboarding. Office: Blackboard Inc 1899 L St NW Washington DC 20036

ANDERSON, MICHAEL CURTIS, computer industry analyst; b. Belton, Tex., Nov. 19, 1953; s. Curtis Raymond Anderson and Joan Evelyn (Sievers) Bleuer; m. Debra Beth Shlaes, June 7, 1975; children: Sara Joyce, John Michael, Ethan Michael. BA cum laude, Augustana Coll., 1975; postgrad., U. Iowa, 1982—. Mgmt. sci. analyst Deere & Co., Moline, Ill., 1975-80, mgr. office automation, 1980-88; sr. planner office systems IBM, Roanoke, Tex., 1988-89, mgr. strategy and requirements, planning-office systems, 1989-90; program dir. office info. systems Gartner Group, Stamford, Conn., 1990-93; dir. mkt. rsch. & competitive analysis Ameritech, Chgo., 1993-94; v.p., rsch. dir. adv. techs. Gartner Group, Stamford, Conn., 1994-99, v.p., rsch. area dir. Distributed Electronic Workplace, 1999-2000, v.p. rsch. ops., 2000—, v.p., dir. rsch., 2000—03, mng. v.p. rsch. quality Stamford, 2003—. Ill. State scholar, 1971, I.B. McGladrey Accountancy award McGladrey-Hendrickson, 1974. Avocations: tennis, golf, bicycling, exercise, coaching. Home: 1644 Byron Nelson Pkwy Southlake TX 76092 Office: Gartner Inc 125 E John Carpenter Fwy Ste 550 Irving TX 75062

ANDERSON, MICHAEL R., elementary school educator, writer; b. Washington, Ill., Jan. 2, 1952; s. Roy Robert and Mildred Louise Anderson; m. Martha Elizabeth Ward; children: Samuel Ward, Anna Louise. BA, Ill. Coll., 1974; MA, St. Xavier U., 2002. Cert. tchr. K-9 Ill. Educator Sch. Dist. 117, Jacksonville, Ill., 1974—. Cons. Ill. State Bd. Edn., Springfield, Ill., 1999—2001. Author: (children's book) Construction of the Classical Whanger, 1981, The Phantom Teacher, 2001; musician: (audio recording) Solo: Not Alone, 1990, Ice Out, 1998; author: The Great Sled Race, 2000 (Parents' Choice Silver Honor award, 2000). Dir. Lincoln's New Salem Storytelling Festival, Petersburg, 1986—2002; artist dir. Claville Music and Storytelling Festival, Pleasant Plains, 1981—86. Named Ten Outstanding Young Persons, Ill. Jaycees, 1989; recipient Outstanding Young Educator, Jacksonville Jaycees, 1987—88, Innovative Instrnl. Initiative award, West Ctrl. Ill. Assn. for Supervision and Curriculum, 1994, Disting. Alumni award,

Ill. Coll., 2003. Mem.: Jacksonville Ednl. Assn. (mem. chmn. 1986—90), Riverwinds Storytelling Guild, Prairie Grapevine Folklore Soc. (pres. 1985—88), Nat. Storytelling Network, Kappa Delta Pi. Home: PO Box 35 Jacksonville IL 62651 Office: MW Prodn PO Box 35 Jacksonville IL 62651 Home Fax: 217-245-9752; Office Fax: 217-245-9752. E-mail: mworks@fgi.net.

ANDERSON, MICHAEL THOMAS, mathematics professor, researcher; b. Boulder, Colo., Nov. 17, 1950; s. Julian Thompson and Elinor Elizabeth (Uhl) A.; m. Myong Hu Kim, Aug. 15, 1986; 1 child, Steven. BA, U. Calif., Santa Barbara, 1975; MA, U. Calif., Berkeley, 1977, PhD, 1981. Rsch. instr. Rice U., Houston, 1981-84; from asst. to assoc. prof. Calif. Inst. Tech., Pasadena, 1984-88; assoc. prof. SUNY, Stony Brook, 1988-91, prof., 1991—. Invited spkr. Internat. Congress Maths., Zurich, 1994. Assoc. editor: Duke Math. Jour., 1991—, mem. editl. bd.: Jour. Geometric and Functional Analysis, 1991—2000; contbr. articles to profl. jours. Recipient Annales Henri Poincare prize, 2000; NSF grantee, 1981—; NSF postdoctoral fellow, 1984-86. Mem. Am. Math. Soc. (rsch. fellow 1990-91). Democrat. Office: SUNY Dept Math Stony Brook NY 11794-3651 Office Phone: 631-632-8269. E-mail: anderson@math.sunysb.edu.

ANDERSON, MONICA LUFFMAN, school librarian, educator, real estate broker; b. Ramsgate, Kent, U.K., Sept. 28, 1914; arrived in U.S., 1952; d. Percy Victor Luffman and Rosalind Dismorr; m. Howard Richmond Anderson, Dec. 22, 1951 (dec.); children: Monica Jane, James Stewart. BA in English with honors, London U., 1936; MS in Libr. Sci., Simmons Coll., 1968; EdM in Ednl. Media, Boston U., 1970. Evacuation officer London Borough of Acton, 1940—41; dir. Coun. for Edn. in World Citizenship, London, 1941—47; from asst. to head of sect. with diplomatic status UNESCO, Paris, 1947—50; H.S. libr. Holliston, Mass., 1968—70; coord. libr. svcs. Lincoln-Sudbury (Mass.) Regional H.S., 1970—81; real estate broker Coldwell Banker Residential Brokerage, Wayland, Mass., 1982—. Author brochures. Troop leader Girl Scouts Am., Weston, Mass., 1963—65; tutor in English Laotian Refugees, Weston, Mass., 1981—82, Literacy Unltd., Framingham, Mass., 1998—. Democrat. Avocations: gardening, reading, Boston Annual Walk for Hunger. Home: 2214 Heatherwood at Kings Way Yarmouth Port MA 02675

ANDERSON, N. CHRISTIAN, III, newspaper publisher; b. Montpelier, Idaho, Aug. 4, 1950; s. Nelson C. and Esther Barbara Anderson; m. Sara Ann Coffenberry, Dec. 11, 1971 (div.); children: Ryan, Erica; m. Aletha Ann Yurewicz, May 3, 1986; children: Paul, Amanda. BA in Liberal Studies with honors, Ore. State U., 1972. From asst. city editor to city editor Albany (Oreg.) Democrat-Herald, 1972—75; mng. editor Walla Walla (Wash.) Union Bulletin, 1975—77; assoc. mng. editor Seattle Times, 1977—80; from editor to exec. v.p., assoc. publisher The Orange County Register, Santa Ana, Calif., 1980—94; pub. Gazette Telegraph, Colorado Springs, 1994—98; pub., CEO, Orange County Register, Santa Ana, 1999—; sr. v.p. Freedom Comm., Inc., Irvine, Calif., 1999, pres., metro divsn. Instr. Calif. State U., Fullerton, 1983, Fullerton, 87; Pulitzer Prize juror, 87, 88, 96; exec. editor Freedom Newspapers, Inc., Irvine, Calif., 1990—94; exec. v.p., CEO Golden West Publ., Irvine, 1991—94; mem. adv. bd. Poynter Inst. for Media Studies, St. Petersburg, Fla., 1994—99, also past chmn. adv. bd.; former chmn. bd. dirs. New Directions for News, newspaper think tank; mem. nominating com. AP; bd. dirs. Robert C. Maynard Inst. for Journalism Edn. Chmn. Orange County Bus. Com. for Arts; past mem., bd. dirs. Calif. First Amendment Coalition; bd. dirs. Santa Ana Rotary Found., 1984, Colorado Springs Fine Arts Ctr., 1994—98, Colorado Springs Non-Profit Ctr., 1994—98, Colorado Springs Sports Corp., 1994—98, Pike's Peak United Way, 1994—98, South Coast Repertory, Econ. Devel. Corp., Colorado Springs, chmn. bd., 1996. Named Nat. Newspaper Editor of Yr., 1989, Calif. Newspaper Exec. of Yr., Calif. Press Assn., 1993; recipient George D. Beveridge award, Nat. Press Found., 1989. Mem.: Calif. Soc. Newspaper Editors (founder, former bd. dirs. and pres.), Soc. Newspaper Design (co-founder), Am. Soc. Newspaper Editors (bd. dirs. 1996, treas. 1996, sec. 1997, v.p. 1998, pres. 1999). Office: Orange County Register 625 N Grand Ave Santa Ana CA 92701-4347 also: Freedom Communications 17666 Fitch Irvine CA 92614-6022

ANDERSON, NANCY DIXON, librarian; b. Clarkesville, Ga., Oct. 7, 1938; d. Sherman Allen and Willie Mae (Black) Dixon; m. David Morris Anderson, Nov. 23, 1958 (div. June 1978); children: Wendy, Laurie, David Jr. BS in Mid. Grades Edn., Brenau Coll., 1981; MEd in Ednl. Media, U. Ga., 1985. Asst. prof. humanities, libr. Brenau Coll., Gainesville, Ga., 1979-87; also acad. tutor Learning Disability Ctr., 1985-87; head libr. Hightower Libr. Gordon Coll., Barnesville, Ga., 1987—. Children's ch. dir. 1st Presbyn. Ch., Gainesville, 1983-87; v.p. Friends of Libr., Barnesville/Lamar County, 1991; pres. Newcomers Club, Gainesville, 1974, Phoenix Soc., Ga. Fedn. Women's Club, Gainesville, 1978; pub. chmn. Barnesville Women's League, 1992-94; pres. Barnesville Garden Club, 1992; mem. Community Svcs. Bd., Barnesville, 1994—. Mem. Ga. Libr. Assn., Ctr. Ga. Associated Librs. Consortium (pres. 1992-93). Avocations: gardening, travel, reading. Home: 236 Harrell Cir Barnesville GA 30204-1751 Office: Gordon Coll Hightower Libr 419 College Dr Barnesville GA 30204-1746

ANDERSON, NED, SR., Apache tribal chairman; b. Bylas, Ariz., Jan. 18, 1943; s. Paul and Maggie (Rope) Anderson; m. Delphina Hinton; children: Therese Kay, Linette Mae, Magdalene Gail, Ned, Sean. AA, Ea. Ariz. Coll., 1964, AAS in Computer Sci., 1989; BS, U Ariz., 1967, JD, 1973. Field dir. Nat. Study Indian Edn. dept. anthropology U. Ariz., Tucson, 1968-70, dir. Jojoba Project, Office of Arid Land Studies, 1973-76; tech. asst. Project Head Start Ariz. State U., Tempe, 1970; ethnographer Smithsonian Instn., Washington, 1970-73; with Jojoba devel. project San Carlos (Ariz.) Apache Tribe, 1976-78, tribal councilman, 1976-78, 93-98, tribal chmn., 1978-86, gen. mgr. spl. housing projects, 1991-99, coord. Ctrl. Ariz. project, 1999—. Contbr. articles to profl. jours. Mem. affirmative action com. City of Tucson, 1975—76; mem. study panel NAS, 1975—76; mem. supervisory bd. Ariz. Justice Planning Commn., 1978; mem. county govt. study commn. State of Ariz., 1981—84; mem. reinvention mgmt. lab. workgroup Nat. Housing Improvement Program, 1995—96; mem. Indian adv. bd. Intergovernmental Pers. Program, 1978; mem. adv. bd. Am. Indian Registry Performing Arts, 1985, San Carlos Fish and Game Commn., 1975, chmn., 1976; pres. Intertribal Coun. Ariz., 1979—85, 1992; pres. bd. dirs. Ft. Thomas HS Unified Dist., 1977, clk., 1987, clk. bd. dirs., 1989; bd. dirs. Southwestern Indian Devel., Inc., 1971, Indian Enterprise Devel. Corp., 1976—78, San Carlos Lake Devel., 1994—98, We. Apache Constrn. Co., 1994—98, Apache Gold Resort Pub. Authority, 1997—99, vice chmn., acting chmn., 2002—03; mem. adv. bd. Gila Pueblo CC ext. Ea. Ariz. Coll., 1979, Indian Edn., Ariz. State U., Tempe, 1978—86, U. Ariz., Tucson, 1978—86; trustee Bacone Coll.; enterprise bd. chmn. Apache Gold Casino Resort, 2003—. Recipient Outstanding CC Alumni award, Ariz. CC Bd./Ea. Ariz. Coll., 1982, Outstanding Coop. award, U.S. Secret Svc., 1984, Univ. Rels. award, AT&T, 1989; A. T. Anderson Meml. scholar, 1989. Mem.: Ariz. Acad., Globe C. of C., Nat. Tribal Chmn.'s Assn. (mem. bd. edn., mem. adv. bd. 1978—86), Phi Theta Kappa. Office Phone: 928-475-3832.

ANDERSON, NICK, editorial cartoonist; b. Toledo, Ohio; m. Cecilia Anderson; 2 children. Grad in Polit. Sci., Ohio State Univ., 1991. Summer intern Louisville Courier-Journal, Ky., assoc. editl. cartoonist, 1991—95, chief editl. cartoonist, 1995—. Syndicated cartoonist Wash. Post Writers Group, 1996—. Recipient Charles M. Schulz award for best coll. cartoonist in US, Canada, Mexico, 1989, John Fischetti award for editl. cartooning, 1999, Sigma Delta Chi Mark of Excellence award, 2001, Pulitzer Prize for editl. cartooning, 2005. Avocations: kayaking, mountain biking. Office: Louisville Courier-Journal 525 W Broadway PO Box 740031 Louisville KY 40201-7431 Office Phone: 502-582-4011.*

ANDERSON, NORMA V., state legislator; b. Elyria, Ohio, July 6, 1932; Student, Denver U., Jones Real Estate Coll. Owner, operator KBJ Stables; office mgr. Capitol Solar; supr. Time, Inc.; mem. Colo. Ho. of Reps., Dist. 30, 1986-98, Fin. & State Affairs Coms., Legis. Coun., Colo. Senate, Dist. 22, Denver, 1998—, Judiciary, Appropriations Coms., Legis. Coun., State Compensation Bd., Colo. Uninsurable Health Ins. Bd.; majority leader, chair Legis. Audit, Edn., Trans. & Energy Coms.; vice-chair Health, Environ., Welfare & Inst. Com., Legis. Audit Com., Judiciary Com., Assembly on Fed. Issues; chair Minority Caucus, Bus. Affairs & Labor Com.; mem. labor dept. State Adv. Coun.; exec. com., chair Energy & Trans.; co-chair Social Security Task Force, DC. Mem. state adv. coun. labor dept.; bd. dir. state compensation, regional transp. dist., Foothills Found.; mem. West Chamber; mem. numerious senate coms. including most recently jud. com., appropriations com. Vice-chair Health Environ. Welfare Insts.; bd. dirs. Foothills Found.; mem. budget com. R-1 Sch. Dist; exec. com. Nat. Conf. State Legis.; vice-chair Arapahow House; adv. bd. Drug Control Systems Improvement, Com. Corrections; mem. Am. Cancer Soc., Bear Creek Jr. Sports Assn., Great Outdoors Colo. Republican. Office: State Capitol 200 E Colfax Ave Ste 274 Denver CO 80203-1716 Office Phone: 303-866-4859. E-mail: norma.anderson.senate@state.co.us.

ANDERSON, PAMELA DENISE, actress; b. Ladysmith, BC, Can., July 1, 1967; d. Barry and Carol Anderson; m. Tommy Lee, Feb. 19, 1995 (div. Feb. 28, 1998); children: Brandon Thomas Lee, Dylan Jagger Lee. Syndicated columnist Jane, 2002—, Marie Claire, 2002—, Can. Elle, 2002—; launched clothing line "The Pamela Collection", 2003—. Actor: (TV series) Home Improvement, 1991—93, Baywatch, 1992—97; actor, exec. prodr.: (TV series) V.I.P., 1998; actor(voice): Stripperella, 2003—, Stacked, 2005—; (TV films) Baywatch: River of No Return, 1992, Come Die with Me: A Mickey Spillane Mike Hammer Mystery, 1994, Baywatch: Forbidden Paradise, 1995, Naked Souls, 1996, Baywatch: Hawaiian Wedding, 2003, (guest appearances): (TV series) Charles in Charge, 1990, Married...with Children, 1990, 1991, Top of the Heap, 1991, Days of Our Lives, 1992, The Nanny, 1997, Home Improvement, 1997, Just Shoot Me, 2001, Less Than Perfect, 2002, (guest appearances, voice) Futurama, 1999,: (films) Snapdragon, 1993, Raw Justice, 1994, Naked Souls, 1995, Barb Wire, 1996, Scary Movie 3, 2003, (music videos for) Aerosmith, Lit, Cinderella, Vince Neil, Bree Sharp, Methods of Mayhem, Jaz-Z, Kid Rock; author: (novels) Star, 2004. Activist PETA; participant Nat. Conf. Viral Hepatitis, Can. Liver Found.; founder Pamela Anderson Found.; grand marshall S.O.S. ride Am. Liver Found., 2002. Recipient Linda McCartney award for animal rights, 1999. Achievements include has appeared a record twelve times on the cover of Playboy. Office: William Morris Agy 151 El Camino Dr Beverly Hills CA 90212*

ANDERSON, PARKER LYNN, columnist, playwright; b. Wickenburg, Ariz., Apr. 19, 1964; s. Harry Milton and Darla Raejean (Hangartner) A. Mem. prodn. com. Prescott (Ariz.) Fine Arts Assn., 1993-95, 98—, adv. mem., 1987—; columnist, theatre critic The Prescott News, 1995-96; with Cath. Social Svc. of Yavapai, 1983—. Mem. adv. com. The Blue Rose Theatre Co., Prescott, 1994—; guest on talk shows Sta. KUSK-TV, 1991—. Author: (plays) The Startled Cowboys, 1991, Voices From the Past, 1995, The Sleeping Toad, 1997, Virgil Earp, 1998, Until the Last Dog is Hung, 2000, Murder Dismissed, 2001; co-author: (plays) Lady with a Gun (with Jody Drake), 2002; freelance guest columnist and letters of comment in numerous Ariz. publs., 1990—. Home: PO Box 1285 Prescott AZ 86302-1285 E-mail: parkerr86302@yahoo.com.

ANDERSON, PATRICIA FRANCIS, librarian; b. Ames, Iowa, Oct. 20, 1956; d. Arthur Raymond and Rose Ann (Cooper) Anderson; m. Patrick Henry Veninga, Apr. 27, 1991 (div. 2002); children: Zera Esther Ruth Anderson, Luke Robert Morris Veninga. BS, Iowa State U., 1979; M in Info. and Libr. Sci., U. Mich., 1987. Media libr. Galter Health Sci. Libr. Northwestern U., Chgo., 1987—98; libr. assoc. Engring Librs. U. Mich., Ann Arbor, 1985-87, head libr. Dentistry Libr., 1998—. Cons., Consensus Devel. Conf. Diagnosis, Mgmt. Dental Caries Throughout Life NIH, 2001, program planning com., Working Conf. Dental Informatics, Dental Rsch., 03. Author: (guide book) The Medical Library Encyclopedic Guide to Searching and Finding Health Information on the Web, 2004. Chairperson for design working group HealthWeb, 1994—2001; Editor HealthWeb: Dentistry, 1998—. Recipient Wallace H. Bonk award U. Mich., 1987, James Neubacher award, 2004, Beta Phi Mu Essay award, 1987. Mem. Am. Soc. for Info. Sci. (Nat. Student Paper award 1986), Health Scis. Comms. Assn. (biomed. librs. interest group sec. 1992-93), Med. Libr. Assn. (sec., treas. dental sect. 2000-03, centennial exhibit coord. ednl. media and techs. sect., Rittenhouse award 1989, Harriet L. Steuernagel award 2004), Feminist Writers Guild (bd. dirs. 1990-93, newsletter editor 1990-94). Democrat. Roman Cath. Avocations: poetry, music composition, fiber art, jewelry making, Aikido. Office: Univ of Mich Dentistry Libr 1100 Dental Bldg Ann Arbor MI 48109-1078 Office Phone: 734-764-1526. Business E-Mail: pfa@umich.edu.

ANDERSON, PATRICIA JEAN, elementary school educator; b. Grand Forks, Nd, Aug. 14, 1953; d. Donald H. and Ardyce Frigstad Anderson; 1 child, Kayla Jennifer. BS in Elem. Edn., Delta State U., 1975; EdD, U. Ga., 1980. 4th grade tchr., Greenville, Miss., 1975—78; asst. prof. Iowa Wesleyan Coll., Mt. Pleasant; prof., grad. dir. dept. curriculum and instrn. East Carolina U., Greenville, NC, 1982—. Cons. elem. schs. and sch. sys. Contbr. articles to profl. jours.; co-author: Facilitating the One-Stop Process, 1999, Raising Achievement: Project Evenesis, A Significan School Model, 2003. Recipient Tchg. award, East Carolina U., 1984—85. Mem.: Internat. Reading Assn., Nat. Coun. Tchrs. English, Assn. Tchr. Educators. Home: 2902 Hunter's Run Greenville NC 27858 Office: E Carolina Univ Dept Curriculum and Instrn Greenville NC 27858 Home Fax: 252-328-2585; Office Fax: 252-328-2585. Personal E-mail: andersonp@mail.ecu.edu.

ANDERSON, PATRICIA SUE, writer; b. San Springs, Okla., July 14, 1940; d. John Monroe and Annabelle A. BA in Psychology, Okla. State U., 1963. Co-owner, CEO River's West Prodns. CEO River's Bend Literary Agy., Cleveland, Okla., 1984-99. Author: Organizational Handbook, 1985, Campaign Organization, 1990, Getting Women to Participate, 1991; (screenplays) Nightmares Do Come True, Desert Conspiracy, Mriqtrishna; (novels) A Cold Wind in August, Surviving Toxic Parents. Democrat. Methodist. Home and Office: RR 1 Box 272 Cleveland OK 74020-9723 E-mail: pande86245@aol.com.

ANDERSON, PAUL HOLDEN, state supreme court justice; b. May 14, 1943; m. Janice M. Anderson; 2 children. BA cum laude, Macalester Coll., 1965; JD, U. Minn., 1968. Atty. Vols. in Svc. to Am., 1968—69; spl. asst. atty. gen. criminal divsn. dept. pub. safety Office Minn. Atty. Gen., 1970—71; assoc., ptnr. LeVander, Gillen & Miller, South St. Paul, Minn., 1971—92; chief judge Minn. Ct. Appeals, 1992—94; assoc. justice Minn. Supreme Ct., 1994—. Mem. PER coms. Ind. Sch. Dist. 199, 1982—84, chmn. cmty. svcs. adv. com., bd. dirs., chmn. bd.; deacon, ruling elder, clk. of session House of Hope Presbyn. Ch., St. Paul. Mem.: Dakota County Bar Assn. (bd. dirs., pres.), South St. Paul/Inver Grove Heights C. of C. (bd. dirs., exec. com.). Avocations: tennis, gourmet cooking, bike riding. Office: 425 Minn Judicial Ctr 25 Rev Dr Martin Luther King Jr Blvd Saint Paul MN 55155-0001 Fax: 651-282-5115. Office Phone: 651-296-3314. Business E-Mail: paul.anderson@courts.state.mn.us.

ANDERSON, PAUL MARTIN, music educator, musician; b. Hammond, Ind., Feb. 8, 1955; s. Robert Lawrence and Grace Louise Anderson; m. Nancy Ruth Carter, Aug. 16, 1986; children: Nichole Marie, Michael Paul. MusB, Butler U., 1977; MusM, Bowling Green (Ohio) State U., 1981. Band dir. Whiting (Ind.) Jr. Sr. H.S., 1977—79, Donald E. Gavit Jr. Sr. H.S., Hammond, 1981—86; dir. of bands Thornwood H.S., South Holland, Ill., 1994—. Mem.: Ill. Music Educators Assn. (assoc.), Music Educators Nat. Conf. (assoc.), Pi Kappa Lambda (life), Phi Kappa Psi (life), Phi Mu Alpha Sinfonia (life). Home: 7143 Northcote Ave Hammond IN 46324 Office: Thornwood HS 17101 S Park Ave South Holland IL 60473 Office Phone: 708-225-4777.

ANDERSON, PAUL MAURICE, electrical engineering educator, researcher, consultant; b. Des Moines, Jan. 22, 1926; s. Neil W. and Buena Vista (Thompson) A.; m. Virginia Ann Worswick, July 8, 1950; children: William, Mark, James, Thomas. BSEE, Iowa State U., 1949, MSEE, 1958, PhD, 1961. Registered profl. elec. engr., Ariz., Calif., Iowa, Guam; registered control sys. engr., Calif. Elec. engr. Iowa Pub. Service Co., Sioux City, 1949-55; prof. elec. engring. Iowa State U., Ames, 1955-75; program mgr. Electric Power Research Inst., Palo Alto, Calif., 1975-78; pres., prin. engr. Power Math Assocs. Inc., Palo Alto, Tempe, Del Mar and San Diego, 1978-99; prof. elec. engring. Ariz. State U., Tempe, 1980-84. Schweitzer vis. prof. elec. engring.97 Wash. State U., 1996. Author: Analysis of Faulted Power Systems, 1973; (with others) Power System Control and Stability, 1977, 3d edit., 2003, Subsynchronous Resonance in Power Systems, 1990, Series Compensation of Power Systems, 1996, Power System Protection, 1999; cons. editor: Ency. Sci. and Tech., 1979-92; contbr. articles to profl. jours. NSF faculty fellow, 1960-61; recipient Faculty citation Iowa State U. Alumni Assn., 1973, Profl. Achievement citation Iowa State U., 1981 Fellow IEEE (life mem., chmn. Iowa sect. 1959-60), Conf. Internat. des Grands Reseaux Electriques, Sigma Xi, Phi Kappa Phi, Eta Kappa Nu, Pi Mu Epsilon. Republican. Home: 13335 Roxton Cir San Diego CA 92130-1841 Personal E-mail: p.anderson@ieee.org.

ANDERSON, PAUL MILTON, energy executive; b. Richland, Wash., Apr. 1, 1945; s. Paul Milton and Elfrieda (Blehm) A.; m. Kathleen Sue Kinzel, Feb. 25, 1984; children: Wendy Christine, Heather Colleen. BSME, U. Wash., 1967; MBA, Stanford U., 1969. Mgr. product planning Ford Motor Co., Dearborn, 1969-77; various positions Tex. Eastern Corp., Houston, 1977-85, v.p., 1985-87, sr. v.p., 1987-89; v.p. fin., chief fin. officer Inland Steel Industries, Chgo., 1990-91; exec. v.p. Panhandle Eastern Corp., 1991-94, pres., 1994—, Panhandle Eastern Pipe Line Co., 1991—; pres., CEO Panenergy (named changed Duke Energy), Houston, 1991-97; pres., COO Duke Energy, 1997-99; CEO, mng. ptnr. BHP Ltd., Melbourne, Australia, 1998—2002; chmn., CEO Duke Energy, 2003—. Mem. Interstate Natural Gas Assn. Am., Inst. Gas Tech. Office: Duke Energy 526 South Church St Charlotte NC 28202

ANDERSON, PAUL NATHANIEL, oncologist, educator; b. Omaha, May 30, 1937; s. Nels Paul E. and Doris Marie (Chesnut) A.; m. Dee Ann Hipps, June 27, 1965; children: Mary Kathleen, Anne Christen. BA, U. Colo., 1959, MD, 1963. Diplomate Am. Bd. Internal Medicine, Am. Bd. Med. Mgmt., Am. Bd. Med. Oncology. Intern Johns Hopkins Hosp., Balt., 1963-64, resident in internal medicine, 1964-65, fellow in oncology, 1970-72; rsch. assoc., staff assoc. NIH, Bethesda, Md., 1965-70; asst. prof. medicine, oncology Johns Hopkins U. Sch. Medicine, 1972-76; attending physician Balt. City Hosps., Johns Hopkins Hosp., 1972-76; dir. dept. med. oncology Penrose Cancer Hosp., Colorado Springs, Colo., 1976-86; clin. asst. prof. dept. medicine Colo. Sch. Medicine, 1976-90, clin. assoc. prof., 1990—. Dir. Penrose Cancer Hosp., 1979-86, chief dept. medicine, 1985-86; founding dir. Cancer Ctr. of Colorado Springs, 1986-95, Pikes Peak Forum for Health Care Ethics, 1996—, Rocky Mountain Cancer Ctr., Colorado Springs, 1995—; med. dir. So. Colo. Cancer Program, 1979-86; pres., chmn. bd. dirs. Preferred Physicians, Inc., 1986-92; mem. Colo. Found. for Med. Care Health Stds. Com., 1985, sec., exec. com., 1990, bd. dirs., pres., 1992-93; mem., chmn. treatment com. Colo. Cancer Control and Rsch. Panel, 1980-83; prin. investigator Cancer Info. Svc. of Colo., 1981-87; pres., founder Timberline Med. Assocs., 1986-87, Oncology Mgmt. Network, Inc., 1985-95. Editor Advances in Cancer Control; editl. bd. Jour. Cancer Program Mgmt., 1987-92, Health Care Mgmt. Rev., 1988—; contbr. articles to med. jours. Mem. Colo. Gov.'s Rocky Flats Employee Health Assessment Group, 1983-84; mem. Gov.'s Breast Cancer Control Commn. Colo., 1984-89; founder, dir. So. Colo. AIDS project, 1986-91; mem. adv. bd. Colo. State Bd. Health Tumor Registry, 1984-87; chmn., bd. dirs. Preferred Physicians, Inc., 1986-92; bd. dirs. Share Devel. Co. of Colo. Share Health Plan of Colo., 1986-90, vice chmn., 1989-91; bd. dirs., chmn. Preferred Health Care, Inc., 1991-92; mem. health care stds. com., trustee colo. Found. for Med. Care (PRO); mem. nat. bd. med. dirs. Fox Chase Cancer Ctr. Network, Phila., 1987-89; mem. tech. expert panel Harvard Resource-Based Relative Value Scale Study for Hematology/Oncology, 1991-92. With USPHS, 1965-70. Mem. AMA (mem. practice parameters forum 1989-97, adv. com. to HCFA on uniform clin. data set), AAAS, Am. Coll. Forensic Examiners, Am. Soc. Clin. Oncology (chmn. subcom. on oncology clin. practice stds., mem. clin. practice com., rep. to AMA 1991—, mem. healthcare svcs. rsch. com., chmn. clin. guidelines subcom. 1993—), Am. Assn. Cancer Rsch., Am. Assn. Cancer Insts. (liaison mem. bd. trustees 1980-82), Am. Coll. Physician Execs., Am. Hospice Assn., Am. Soc. Internal Medicine, Nat. Cancer Inst. (com. for cmty. hosp. oncology program evaluation 1982-83), Colo. Soc. Internal Medicine, Assn. Cmty. Cancer Ctrs. (chmn. membership com. 1980, chmn. clin. rsch. com. 1983-85, sec. 1983-84, pres.-elect 1984-85, pres. 1986-87, trustee 1981-88), N.Y. Acad. Scis., Johns Hopkins Med. Soc., Colo. Med. Soc., Am. Mgmt. Assn., Am. Assn. Profl. Cons., Am. Soc. Quality, Am. Acad. Med. Dirs., Am. Coll. Physician Execs., El Paso County Med. Soc., Rocky Mountain Oncology Soc. (chmn. clin. practice com. 1989-94, pres.-elect 1990, pres. 1993-95), Acad. Hospice Physicians, Coalition for Cancer, Colorado Springs Clin. Club, Alpha Omega Alpha. Office: Rocky Mountain Cancer Ctr 3027 North Circle Dr Colorado Springs CO 80909 also: 32 Sanford Rd Colorado Springs CO 80906-4233 Office Phone: 719-577-2555. E-mail: paul-anderson@usoncology.com.

ANDERSON, PAUL WAYNE, assistant principal; b. Cullman, Ala., May 24, 1958; s. Paul Ray Anderson and Edna Faye Carey; m. Kelli Shawn Fox, Mar. 10, 1985; 1 child, Joshua Paul. A in Sci. Music Edn., Wallace State C.C., Hanceville, Ala., 1979; BS in Music Edn., U. North Ala., 1981, MA in Music Edn., 1986; cert. in sch. adminstrn., U. Ala., 1998. Band dir. Lawrence County H.S., Moulton, Ala., 1981—82, Wallace State C.C., Hanceville, Ala., 1982—91, Hanceville H.S., 1991—2004, asst. prin., 2004—, Hanceville Mid. Sch., 1998—2004. Chmn. accrediting com. So. Assn. Colls. and Schs., Hanceville, 1998—99. Mem.: NEA (assoc.), Ala. Music Educators Assn. (assoc.), Music Educators Nat. Conf. (assoc.), Ala. Edn. Assn. (assoc.).

ANDERSON, PAULETTE ELIZABETH, investment company executive, retired elementary school educator; b. Los Angeles, Calif., 1942; d. John Paul and Frances Lillian Ross; m. Kenneth Jerome Anderson, Mar. 27, 1997; children: Melody Ann Helland, Edward Michael Helland. D of Ministry, Christian Internat. Grad., Pointe Washington, Fla., 1989—2001; BA Elem. Edn., Calif. State U. LA, Los Angeles, 1970; AA, Pasadena City Coll., Calif., 1960—63; MA in Elem. Edn., Ariz. State U., Tempe, 1975—76; Ms of Div., Christian Internat., Pointe Washington, Fla., 1977—88. Standard tchg. credential State of Calif., 1972, cert. standard elem. Ariz., 1977. Certification com. mem. Florence Mid. Sch., Florence, Ariz., 1978—79; advisor Wonderful Wonders, Phoenix, 1993—94; kindergarten & first grade Long Beach Hebrew Acad., Calif., 1969—70; fifth grade self contained Bullhead City Elem. Sch., Ariz., 1971—72; reading tchr. mid. sch. Florence Mid. Sch., Ariz., 1977—81; first grade tchr. Murphy Sch. Dist. -Sullivan, Phoenix, 1985—87; elem. tchr. grades 2, 5, 8 Roosevelt Sch. Dist.-Valley View, Phoenix, 1993—99, ret., 1999—. Curriculum guideline's com. mem. Roosevelt Sch. Dist., 1994—98; dist. scheduling com. mem. Rooselvelt Sch. Dist., 1997. Author: (non fiction) Evidence of Holy Spirit GIven Glossolalia, (children's nonfiction) Polycarp. Organizer/pres. Nevitt Neighborhood Assn., Phoenix, 1987—99; elected precinct committeeman Rep. Party, Phoenix, 1988—99, chmn. dist. 23, 1994—96; chmn. Christian Coalition, Pasadena, 2000—01; v.p. God Provides Ministry, 2004. Recipient Cert. of Appreciation, Nat. Rep. Senator Com., 1996, Lincoln Bust Award, Maricopa County Rep. Party, 1993, Vol. of the Yr., Dist. 23, 1998. R-Consevative. Christian. Achievements include organizing Nevitt Neighborhood Assn.:Rid Neighborhood of Graffiti; organizing 8th graders from low income area to go to Washington, DC; organized VCC Cares for food to be distributed each Wednesday to the needy, 2001-; development of Spanish Ch., 2004. Avocations: travel, archeological dig in Israel, 1994. Home: PO Box 686 Temple City CA 91780-0686 Office Phone: 626-442-4273. Personal E-mail: openportels@msn.com.

ANDERSON, PAULINE HARRIET, library consultant; b. Broadalbin, N.Y., Nov. 27, 1918; d. Donald and Bertha (Brooks) Anderson. BA, Keuka Coll., 1939; BLS, NYU, 1943. Libr. Abbot Acad., Andover, Mass., 1945-50; dir. Andrew Mellon Libr. Choate Rosemary Hall, Wallingford, Conn., 1950-73, sch. libr. cons., 1963—2000, dir. of edni. devel., 1973-83, holder of the Leinbach chair, 1981-83. Pres. bd. mgrs. Wallingford Pub. Libr., 1979-82. Contbr. articles to profl. jours. and hist. newsletters; author: (Books) The Library in the Independent School, 1968, 1980, Library Media Leadership in Academic Secondary Schools, 1985, Planning School Library Media Facilities, 1990. Archivist First Presbyn. Ch., Broadalbin, 1983—; mem. Kennyetto Hist. Soc., Broadalbin, 1987—; bd. dirs. Amsterdam (N.Y.) Free Pub. Libr., 1991-98, Montgomery Co. Historical Soc., 1999—, vol. at hosps and hist. sites. Named Braitmeyer fellow, Nat. Assn. Ind. Schs., 1966—67. Mem.: ALA, N.Y. State Libr. Assn., Assn. Ind. Sch. Libraries, Friends Saratoga Springs Pub. Libr., Friends of Keuka Coll. Libr., Friends of Wallingford Pub. Libr., Friends of Saratoga Battlefield, Friends of Amsterdam (N.Y.) Pub. Libr. Avocations: book collector, local history, needlecrafts. Home: 156 Lawrence St Apt 118 Saratoga Springs NY 12866-1350

ANDERSON, PEGGY REES, accountant; b. Casper, Wyo., Sept. 8, 1958; d. John William and Pauline Marie (Harris) Rees; m. Steven R. Anderson, May 26, 1984 (div. Sept. 1990). BS in Acctg. with honors, U. Wyo., 1980. CPA. Audit staff to sr. Price Waterhouse, Denver, 1980-84; asst. contr. to contr. Am. Investments, Denver, 1984-88; cons. ADI Residential, Denver, 1988-89; contr., treas. Plante Properties, Inc., Denver, 1989-92; acctg. mgr. Woodward-Clyde Group, Inc., Denver, 1992-96; internat. fin. mgr. USWest, Inc., Denver, 1996-98, Media One Group, Denver, 1998—2000; internat. fin. cons. Orica Inc., Denver, 2001—02; internat. acctg. coord. Newmont Mining Corp., Denver, 2003—04; assoc. mgr. Great-West Fin. Svcs., Denver, 2004—. Diving scholar U. Wyo., 1976-78. Mem. Colo. Soc. CPAs. Roman Catholic. Avocations: skiing, swimming, aerobics, needlepoint, golf. Office Phone: 303-737-4081.

ANDERSON, PETER D., pharmacist, forensic specialist; b. Stoughton, Mass. BS in Pharmacy, U. R.I., 1989, PharmD, 1998. Diplomate Am. Bd. Forensic Examiners; cert. psychiat. pharmacist Bd. Pharm. Spltys. Lab. asst. U. R.I., Kingston, 1988—89; staff pharmacist Mass. Eye & Ear Infirmary, Boston, 1991—2000; clin. pharmacist pvt. practice, Boston, 1994—, forensic pharmacist, 1995—; criteria mgr., Drug Utilization Rev. Program, U. Mass. Med. Sch., 1999—2000; clin. pharmacist Mass. Eye & Ear Infirmary, 2000—01, McKesson Med. Mgmt., Inc., Taunton, Mass., 2001—. Clin. asst. prof. Northeastern U. Sch. Pharmacy, Boston, 2000—; adj. instr. med. imaging Bunker Hill C.C., 1999—; adj. assoc. prof. pharmacy U. R.I., 2001—; clin. instr. psychiatry Harvard Med. Sch., Boston, 2003—; acting chmn. pharmacy and therapeutics com. Taunton (Mass.) State Hosp., 2002. Biomed. comms. and informatics rev. sect. editor: Jour. Pharmacy Practice, 2000—; contbg. editor: The ADHD Challenge, 1997—2002. Chmn. rsch. steering com. Taunton State Hosp., Mass., 2001—. Grantee Am. Pharm. Assn. Found., Washington, 1994-95. Fellow: Am. Coll. Forensic Examiners (dir. divsn. of pharmacology 2003—), Am. Soc. Cons. Pharmacists; mem.: Mass. Tchrs. Assn., U. R.I. Emergency Med. Svcs. (vet. mem.), Nat. Space Soc., Mass. Pharmacists Assn., Coll. Psychiat. and Neurologic Pharmacists (founding mem.), Assn. Cert. Fraud Examiners (assoc.), Am. Coll. Clin. Pharmacology, Am. Acad. Clin. Toxicology, Am. Med. Writers Assn., Am. Coll. Clin. Pharmacy, Am. Soc. Health System Pharmacists, Am. Acad. Experts Traumatic Stress, Kappa Psi. Avocations: volleyball, space flight, juggling, computers. Home and Office: 1035 Southern Artery Apt 301 Quincy MA 02169-8304 Office: Taunton State Hosp PO Box 4007 Taunton MA 02780-0997 E-mail: PAnder7291@aol.com.

ANDERSON, PETER DAVID, lawyer; b. Wadena, Minn., Aug. 21, 1940; s. Alfred Parnell and Emma (Stevens) A.; m. Jacqueline Juanita Kent, Sept. 16, 1963; children: Peter K., Amy E., Seth E. BA, U. Minn., 1965, JD, 1967. Bar: Calif. 1968, U.S. Supreme Ct. 1995. Atty. Hutton, Foley & Anderson, King City, Calif., 1968-95, Anderson & Bolles, King City, Calif., 1995—. Jud. candidate Mcpl. Ct., Monterey County, Calif., 1995; county chmn. Dem. Ctrl. Com., Monterey County, 1976. Recipient Silver Beaver award Boy Scouts Am., 1986. Mem. ABA, Masons, King City Rotary (pres. 1992-93). Democrat. Unitarian Universalist. Home: 433 Park Pl King City CA 93930-2976 Office: Anderson & Bolles 523 Broadway St King City CA 93930-3230 Office Phone: 831-385-5428. E-mail: pandersen@redshift.com.

ANDERSON, PETER JOSEPH, lawyer; b. Camden, N.J., Mar. 15, 1951; s. Lester Ryan and Rose Helen; m. Sheila K.; children: Elizabeth Rose, Hannah Louise. BA, Dickinson Coll., 1972; JD, Dickinson Sch. of Law, 1975. Bar: Pa. 1975, Ga. 1978, U.S. Dist. Ct. (ea. dist.) Pa. 1978, U.S. Dist. Ct. (no. dist.) Ga. 1978, U.S. Ct. Appeals (11th cir.) 1978, U.S. Tax Ct. 1986, U.S. Supreme Ct. 1989. Dep. dist. atty. Dist. Attys. Office, Harrisburg, Pa., 1974-77; ptnr. Peterson, Dillard, Young, Self & Asselin, Atlanta, 1977-92, Sutherland, Asbill & Brennan, Atlanta, 1992—. Bd. dirs. CADEF-Childhood Autism Found., 1986—; chmn. bd. trustees The Paideia Sch., Atlanta, 1997-2000. Mem. ABA (subcom. securities litigation 1978—), State Bar Ga., Pa. Bar Assn., Atlanta Bar Assn. Republican. Roman Catholic. Home: 1503 Emory Rd NE Atlanta GA 30306-2429 Office: Sutherland Asbill & Brennan 999 Peachtree St NE Ste 2300 Atlanta GA 30309-3996 Office Phone: 404-853-8414. Business E-Mail: peter.anderson@sablaw.com.

ANDERSON, PETER MACARTHUR, lawyer; b. New Castle, Ind., July 15, 1937; s. Earl Canute and Catherine Elizabeth (Schultz) A.; m. Ann Warren Gibson, Sept.1, 1962; children: David, Karen. AB, Dartmouth Coll., 1959; LLB, Stanford U., 1962. Bar: Calif. 1963, Wash. 1970. Assoc. O'Melveny & Myers, L.A., 1966-70, Bogle & Gates, Seattle, 1970-74, mem., 1974-99; ptnr. Preston Gates & Ellis, Seattle, 1999—2002, sr. counsel, 2003—. Co-chmn. equal employment law com. ABA, 1983-86. Mem. Ecumenical Commn. for Seattle Archdiocese, St. Petersburg-Seattle Sister Chs. Com. Capt. U.S. Army, 1963-65. Fellow Coll. Labor and Employment Lawyers; mem. Phi Beta Kappa. Roman Catholic. Home: 9200 SE 57th St Mercer Island WA 98040-5005 Office: Preston Gates & Ellis LLP 925 4th Ave Ste 2900 Seattle WA 98104-1158 Office Phone: 206-623-7580.

ANDERSON, PHILIP SIDNEY, lawyer; b. Little Rock, May 9, 1935; s. Philip Sidney and Frances (Walt) Anderson; m. Rosemary Gill Wright, Sept. 26, 1959; children: Sidney Walt Kenyon, Philip Wright, Catherine Gill Askew. BA, LLB, U. Ark., 1959. Bar: Ark. 1960, U.S. Supreme Ct. 1966. Assoc. Wright, Lindsey & Jennings, Little Rock, 1960—65, ptnr., 1965—88, Williams & Anderson PLC, Little Rock, 1988—. Lectr. Ark. Law Sch., 1963—66; mem. com. on jury instrns. Ark. Supreme Ct., 1962—97; mem. panel for 8th cir. U.S. Cir. Judge Nominating Commn., 1978—79; mem. fed. adv. com. U.S. Ct. Appeals 8th cir., 1983—88, co-chmn., 1987—88; bd. dirs. WEHCO Media, Inc., Ark. Dem.-Gazette, Inc. Co-author: Arkansas Model Jury Instructions, 1965, 1974, 1989. Pres. Friends of Little Rock Pub. Libr., 1968—69, Little Rock Unltd. Progress, Inc., 1973—74; trustee Ctrl. Ark. Libr. Sys., 1981—87, pres., 1984; trustee George W. Donaghey Found., 1976—, pres., 1979—80; trustee Lawyers' Com. for Civil Rights Under Law, 2001—. 2d lt. U.S. Army, 1959—60. Fellow: Ark. Bar Found. (pres. 1973—74), Am. Bar Found.; mem.: ABA (chair ho. of dels. 1992—94, pres. 1998—99), Am. Law Inst. (mem. coun. 1982—), Ark. Bar Assn. (spl. award meritorious svc.), The Grolier Club of the City of N.Y. Episcopalian. Home: 4716 Crestwood Dr Little Rock AR 72207-5436 Office: Williams & Anderson PLC 111 Center St Ste 2200 Little Rock AR 72201-4429 Office Phone: 501-372-0800.

ANDERSON, PHILIP W., physicist; b. Indpls., Ind., Dec. 13, 1923; s. Harry W. and Elsie (Osborne) Anderson; m. Joyce Gothwaite, July 31, 1947; 1 child, Susan Osborne. BS, Harvard U., 1943, PhD, 1949; DSc (hon.), U. of Ill., 1978, Rutgers U., 1991, Gusavus Adolphus, 1992, Ecole normale Superieure, 1992, Sheffield U., 1995, U. Tokyo, 2002. With Naval Rsch. Lab., Washington DC, 1943—54; chmn. Theoretical Physics dept. Bell Labs., Madison, Wis., 1959—61; vis. fellow Cambridge U., England, 1961—62, prof., 1967—75, fellow Jesus Coll., 1969—75; asst. dir. of physical rsch. lab. Bell Labs., 1974—76; Joseph Henry prof. in physics Princeton U., 1975—97; cons. dir. of physical rsch. lab. Bell Labs., 1976—84; Joseph Henry chair in physics Princeton U., 1978; vice chmn., sci. bd. external prof. Sante Fe Inst., 1985—; prof. emeritus of physics Princeton U., 1997—. Mem. steering com. Santa Fe Inst., 1989—97. Author: (book) Concepts in Solids, 1963, Basic Notions of Condensed Matter Physics, 1984, A Career in Theoretical Physics, 1994, The Theory of Superconductivity in High-Tc Cuprates, 1997. Chmn. bd. trustees Aspen Ctr. Physics, 1982—87. Recipient Oliver E. Buckley prize, Am. Physical Soc., 1964, Loeb lectr., Harvard U., 1965, Regents lectr., U. of Calif., 1967, Dannie Heinemann prize, Acad. of Sci. at Gottingen, 1975, Centennial medal, Harvard U., 1977, nobel prize in physics, 1977, Guthrie medal and prize, 1978, London lectr., Duke U., 1980, Abigail and J.H. Van Vleck lectr., U. of Wis., 1983, Nat. medal of sci., 1983, Bethe lectr., 1985, George Eastman prof. of physics, Oxford U., 1993—94, John Bardeen prize; honorary fellow, Jesus Coll., Cambridge U., 1977. Fellow: Inst. of Physics (hon.), Indian Acad. of Sci. (hon.; fgn. fellow); mem.: Am. Acad. Arts and Sci., Nat. Acad. Sci. (coun. mem.), Royal Soc. (fgn. mem.), Acad. Lincei (fgn. assoc.), Japan Acad. Sci. (fgn. fellow), Am. Philos. Soc., Russian Acad. Sci. (fgn.mem.), Wash. Acad. Sci., N.Y. Acad. of Sci. (hon.; life mem. 1992). Office: Dept of Physics Joseph Henry Labs Princeton U 339 Jadwin Hall POB 708 Princeton NJ 08544

ANDERSON, PHILLIP V., lawyer; b. Danville, Va., Mar. 22, 1958; s. Verne D. and Joyce (Worley) A.; m. Mary Elizabeth Hankins, Aug. 14, 1982; children: Benjamin, Jordan, William. BA, Hampden-Sydney Coll., 1980; JD, U. Va., 1984. Bar: Va. 1984. Clk. Hon. Jackson L. Kiser U.S. Dist. Ct., Roanoke, Va., 1984-85; ptnr. Gentry Locke Rakes & Moore, Roanoke, Va., 1985—97, Frith, Anderson & Peake, Roanoke, Va., 1997—. Bd. dirs. Jr. Achievement South We. Va.; mem. steering com. Hidden Valley H.S., 2000—02, pres., founding mem. athletic booster club, 2001—02; grad. leadership Roanoke Valley Roanoke Regional C. of C., 1997. Mem. Va. State Bar (8th dist. disciplinary com. 1992-93, standing com. on professionalism 1992—95, professionalism course faculty 1995-98, bd. govs. young lawyers conf., 1989-92, former chmn., sec. 1993-96, mem. lawyer malpractice ins. com. 2000-03, budget and fin. com. 2000-03, mem. exec. com. 2002-, pres.-elect 2004-), Va. Assn. Def. Attys., Def. Rsch. Inst., Va. Trial Lawyers Assn., Roanoke Bar Assn. (sec., treas. 2001-02, pres.-elect 2003). Baptist. Office: Frith Anderson & Peake PC 29 Franklin Rd SW PO Box 1240 Roanoke VA 24006-1240

ANDERSON, PORTER WARREN, JR., retired pediatrics educator; b. Corinth, Miss., Jan. 1, 1937; BA, Emory U., 1958; MA, Harvard U., 1962, PhD, 1967. Rsch. trainee Oak Ridge Nat. Lab., Tenn., 1957; asst. chemist tropical rsch. dept. Uited Fruit Co., Lima, Honduras, 1959-61; faculty mem. dept. chemistry Stillman Coll., Tuscaloosa, Ala., 1966-68; rsch. assoc. infectious diseases The Children's Hosp. Med. Ctr., Boston, 1968-77; asst. prof. microbiology & molecular genetics Harvard U., Cambridge, Mass., 1972-75, assoc. prof., 1975-77; assoc. prof. dept. pediatrics & microbiology U. Rochester (N.Y.) Sch. Medicine & Dentistry, 1977-87, prof., 1987-95, prof. emeritus, 1995-96; ret., 1996. Recipient Albert Lasker Clinical Med. Rsch. award, 1996. Office: U Rochester Sch Medicine & Dentistry Dept Pediatrics 601 Elmwood Ave # 690 Rochester NY 14642-0001

ANDERSON, PT (PAUL THOMAS IV), film director; b. Studio City, Calif., Jan. 1, 1970; s. Ernie Anderson. Dir., writer: The Dirk Diggler Story, 1988, Cigarettes and Coffee (short film), 1993, Sydney/Hard Eight, 1996 (Boston Soc. Film Critics award 1997, nominated Grand Spl. prize Deauville Film Festival, 1996, nominated Ind. Spirit awards, best 1st feature, best 1st screenplay, 1996); dir., writer, prodr.: Boogie Nights, 1997 (New Generation award L.A. Film Critics Assn., 1997, Metro Media award Toronto Internat. Film Festival, 1997, Boston Soc. Film Critics Best New Filmmaker award, 1997, nominated Oscar, best writing, screenplay written directly for screen, 1998, nominated Brit. Acad. award, best screenplay-original, 1998, nominated Five Continents award, European Film awards, 1997, nominated Golden Satellite awards, best dir. motion picture, best motion picture-drama, 1998, nominated Writers Guild Am. Screen award, best screenplay written directly for screen, 1997), Magnolia, 1999 (awards for best dir. and best screenplay, best picture, Toronto Film Critics Assn.), Punch-Drunk Love, 2002 (Cannes Film Festival Best Dir. award), (TV) SNL Fanatic, 2000.*

ANDERSON, RACHAEL KELLER (RACHAEL KELLER), retired library director; b. N.Y.C., Jan. 15, 1938; d. Harry and Sarah Keller; m. Howard D. Goldwyn; children: Rebecca Anderson, Michael Goldwyn, Bryan Goldwyn, David Goldwyn. AB, Barnard Coll., 1959; MS, Columbia U., 1960. Librarian CCNY, 1960-62; librarian Mt. Sinai Med. Ctr., N.Y.C., 1964-73, dir. library, 1973-79; dir. Health Scis Libr. Columbia U., N.Y.C., 1979-91, acting v.p., univ. libr., 1982; dir. Ariz. Health Scis. Libr., U. Ariz., Tucson, 1991-2001; assoc. dir. Ariz. Telemedicine Program, 1996—2001; ret., 2001. Bd. dirs. Med. Libr. Ctr. of N.Y., N.Y.C., 1983-91; mem. biomed. libr. rev. com. Nat. Libr. Medicine, Bethesda, Md., 1984-88, chmn., 1987-88; mem. bd. regents Nat. Libr. Medicine, 1990-94, chmn., 1993-94; pres. Ariz. Health Info. Network, 1995. Contbr. articles to profl. jours. Mem. Med. Libr. Assn. (pres.-elect 1996-97, pres. 1997-98, bd. dirs. 1983-86, 98-99), Assn. Acad. Health Scis. Libr. Dirs. (bd. dirs. 1983-86, 90-93, pres. 1991-92). E-mail: rachaela@ahsl.arizona.edu.

ANDERSON, RALPH ROBERT, endocrinologist, educator; b. Fords, N.J., Nov. 1, 1932; s. Harry Walter and Johanna Katherine (Damgaard) Anderson; m. LaVeta Ann Phillips, Jan. 28, 1961; children: Richard, Laura. BS, Rutgers U., 1953, MS, 1958; PhD, U. Mo., 1961. Cert. animal scientist. Rsch. asst. Rutgers U., 1957-58, U. Mo., Columbia, 1958-61, instr. dairy sci. (endocrinology), 1961-62, from asst. prof. to assoc. prof., 1965—72, prof., 1976—97, prof. emeritus, 1997—. Asst. prof. Iowa State U., Ames, 1962—64; rschr. in field. Editor, co-editor: 6 books; contbr. articles to profl. jours., chapters to books. With U.S. Army, 1954—56. Recipient Grad. Tchg. Merit award, U. Mo. chpt. Gamma Sigma Delta, 1982, Rsch. award, 1994, Cook Disting. Alumni award, Rutgers U., 1997; NIH Endocrinology Postdoctoral fellow, 1964—65, Endocrinology fellow, U. Wis., 1964—65, Fulbright-Hays Sr. Rsch. fellow, New Zealand, 1973—74. Mem.: Sigma Xi (sec.-treas. U. Mo. chpt. 1981—83, pres. 1984—85). Presbyterian. Home: 2517 Shepard Blvd Columbia MO 65201-6131 Office: U Mo Animal Sci Rsch Ctr Columbia MO 65211-0001

ANDERSON, RAYMOND QUINTUS, diversified company executive; b. Jamestown, N.Y., Nov. 27, 1930; s. Paul N. and Cecille (Ogren) A.; m. Sondra Rumsey, June 5, 1954; children: Heidi, Kristin, Gerrit, Mitchell, Tracy, Brooks. Grad., Phillips Acad., Andover, Mass., 1949; BS in Engring., Princeton U., 1953; postgrad., Sloane Sch., MIT, MIT. With Dahlstrom Corp., Jamestown, 1957-76, exec. v.p., 1965, pres., 1968-76; founder, pres. Aarque Steel Corp., Jamestown, 1976-78, Aarque Mgmt. Corp., Jamestown, 1978-96; founder, chmn. Aarque Cos., Jamestown, 1980-96, Aarque Capital Corp., 1996—. Bd. dirs. Oneida Ltd., Bus. Coun. N.Y. State, Inc., Cold Metal Products Co., Inc., Aarque Steel Group, Kardex Sys., Inc.; trustee Northwestern Mut. Life Ins. Co. Patentee in field. Chmn. Jamestown United Fund drive, 1964, 74; bd. dirs. N.Y. State Dept. Environ. Conservation; dir. Oneida, Ltd.; trustee Roger Tory Peterson Inst., Chautauqua Found. Inc.; civilian aide to Sec. of the U.S. Army; mem. adv. bd. World Econ. Forum. Served with USNR, 1954-57. Mem. Mfrs. Assn. Jamestown Area (pres. 1967-68), Empire State C. of C. (pres. 1974-76), Royal Round Table of Swedish Coun. Am., U.S. Can. Trade Coun., U.S. Dept. Commerce Ind. Sector Adv. Com., Tau Beta Pi. Clubs: Moon Brook Country (Jamestown); Sportsmen's (Chautauqua, N.Y.); Union League Met. (N.Y.C.). Republican. Episcopalian. Address: 20 W Fairmont Ave Lakewood NY 14750-0109

ANDERSON, REBECCA MARIE, piano teacher, administrative assistant; b. Franklin, Pa., Oct. 14, 1974; d. Martin Wells and MaryJane (McConally) A. A in Specialized Bus., The Art Inst., 1995. Videographer Investigative Photography, Pitts., 1996-97; piano tchr. Pitts. Music Acad., Carnegie, 1997—; co-owner Pitts. Music Acad., Inc., Pitts., 2001—. Ballet rehersal accompanist S.W. Ballet, Carnegie, 1998—99. Prodr., scriptwriter, co-editor, cameraperson: (video documentary) The Mighty Wurlitzer, 1995. Ch. sec. Ross Cmty. Prebyn. Ch., Pitts., 1997—. Mem. Suzuki Assn. Ams. (cert. tchr.). Home: 4046 Ellwood Rd New Castle PA 16101-6424

ANDERSON, REID BRYCE, performing company executive; b. New Westminister, B.C., Can., Apr. 1, 1949; s. Warren Nels and Phyllis Jessie Bryce (Purser) Anderson. Student dance, Dolores Kirkwood, Burnaby, B.C., Royal Ballet Sch., 1967, 68. Dancer Stuttgart (Fed. Republic Germany) Ballet, 1969-86, prin. dancer, 1975-86, ballet master, 1982-86; artistic dir. Ballet B.C., Vancouver, 1987-89, Nat. Ballet Can., Toronto, Ont., 1989—, Stuttgart Ballet, 1996—. Choreographer numerous works for performing cos. Decorated Order of Fed. Republic Germany; recipient John Cranko prize for svc. to Art of Classical Ballet and in particular teaching, coaching and maintaining the work of the late John Cranko, 1995. Office: The Stuttgart Ballet Obere Schlossgarten 6 70173 Stuttgart Germany

ANDERSON, RICHARD A., telecommunications industry executive; b. Ky. BS in Mktg. magna cum laude, Murray State U., 1980, MBA, 1981. Acct. exec. South Ctrl. Bell, Nashville, 1981—88; v.p. product mgmt., exec. v.p., chief operating officer Universal Comm. Sys., 1988—93; pres. interconnection svcs. Bellsouth Corp., 1993—99, pres. customer markets Atlanta, 1999—. Bd. dirs. Cingular Wireless, Adtran, Inc., SciTrek. Mem. dean's adv. coun. Murray State U. Coll. Bus. and Pub. Affairs; bd. dirs. Camp Twin Lakes. Mem.: Atlanta C. of C. (bd. dirs.), Lambda Chi Alpha (bd. dirs.). Office: Bellsouth Corp 1155 Peachtree St NE Atlanta GA 30309-3610

ANDERSON, RICHARD CARL, geophysical exploration company executive; b. Pontiac, Mich., June 6, 1928; s. Earling Adolph and Blenda Maria (Johnson) A.; m. Georgia L. Carnahan, Aug. 14, 1949; children— Laurie Ann, Gary Carl, Curtis Murray, Denise Carla BS in Mining Engring., N.Mex. Inst. Mining & Tech., 1950, MS in Geophysics, 1953. Engr. Allis Chalmers, Milw., 1949-51; geophysicist, v.p. Geophys. Service, Inc., Dallas, 1953-71; v.p., then exec. v.p. Digicon, Houston, 1971-75; sr. v.p., exec. v.p. Seismograph Service Corp., Tulsa, from 1975, pres., 1981-85; ret., 1985-88; pres. Fairfield Industries, Houston, 1988-91, vice chmn., chief exec. officer, 1991-93; ret., 1993. Mem. Energy Advocates, Tulsa, 1981-93, coordinator, 1983, 86. Served with U.S. Army, 1946-47 Recipient Disting. Achievement award N.Mex. Inst. Mining and Tech., 1984 Mem. Soc. Exploration Geophysicists, Internat. Assn. Geophys. Contractors (hon. life mem., bd. dirs. 1977-85, 89-94, chmn. 1978-79). Home: 1111 Hermann Dr Unit 11F Houston TX 77004-6929

ANDERSON, RICHARD CHARLES, geology educator; b. Moline, Ill., Apr. 22, 1930; s. Edgar Oscar and Sarah Albertina (Olson) A.; m. Ethel Irene Cada, June 27, 1953; children: Eileen Ruth, Elizabeth Sarah, Penelope Cada. AB, Augustana Coll., Rock Island, Ill., 1952; SM, U. Chgo., 1953, PhD, 1955. Geologist Geophoto Svcs., Denver, 1955-57; from asst. prof. to prof. geology Augustana Coll., Rock Island, 1957-96; prof. emeritus, 1996—. Rsch. affiliate Ill. State Geol. Survey, Champaign, 1959—. Editor: Earth Interpreters, 1992; author reports. Recipient Neil Miner award Nat. Assn. Geology Tchrs., 1992. Fellow Geol. Soc. Am. (sect. co-chair 1990). Lutheran. Home: 2012 24th St Rock Island IL 61201-4533 Office: Augustana Coll Dept Geology 639 38th St Rock Island IL 61201-2210 E-mail: glanderson@augustana.edu.

ANDERSON, RICHARD EDMUND, city manager, management consultant; b. Ferndale, Mich., Dec. 23, 1938; s. Richard H. and Carolyn Jeanne (Figg) A.; m. Kay Clarke, Nov. 6, 1961 (div.); children: Pam, Mark, Linda; m. Linda (Hawk)Jenkins, Sept. 11, 1997; stepchildren: Travis, Todd. BA, Mich. State U., 1962; postgrad. in advanced mgmt., Harvard U., 1979. Aide to mgr. City of St. Petersburg, Fla., 1962-64; adminstrv. asst. City of Ft. Lauderdale, Fla., 1964-67, dep. mgr., 1967-75, city mgr., 1975-80; v.p. Fla. Innovation Group, Tampa, 1980-81; pres. Intragrated Systems Assocs., Inc., Ft. Lauderdale, 1981-90; city mgr. City of Florida City, Fla., 1990-94, City of Brooksville, Fla., 1995—. Contbr. articles to profl. jours. Mem. Internat. City Mgmt. Assn. Office: 201 Howell Ave Brooksville FL 34601-2041 Office Phone: 352-544-5435. Business E-mail: citymgr@cl.brooksville.fl.us.

ANDERSON, RICHARD ERNEST, agricultural engineer, consultant, rancher; b. North Little Rock, Ark., Mar. 8, 1926; s. Victor Ernest and Lillian Josephine (Griffin) A.; m. Mary Ann Fitch, July 18, 1953; children: Vicki Lynn, Lucia Anita. BSCE, U. Ark., 1949; MSE, U. Mich., 1959. Registered profl. engr., Mich., Va., Tex., Mont. Commd. ensign USN, 1952, advanced through grades to capt., 1968, ret., 1974; v.p. Ocean Resources, Inc., Houston, 1974-77; mgr. maintenance and ops. Holmes & Narver, Inc., Orange, Calif., 1977-78; pres. No. Resources, Inc., Billings, Mont., 1978-81; v.p. Holmes & Narver, Inc., Orange, Calif., 1981-82; owner, operator Anderson Ranch, registered Arabian horses, Pony, Mont., 1982—; pres., dir. Carbon Resources Inc., Butte, Mont., 1983-88, Agri Resources, Inc., Butte, Mont., 1988-95, Anderson Holdings, Inc., Pony, Mont., 1995—. Trustee Lake Barcroft-Virginia Watershed Improvement Dist., 1973-74; pres. Lake Barcroft-Virginia Recreation Center, Inc., 1972-73. With USAAF, 1944-45. Decorated Silver Star, Legion of Merit with Combat V (2), Navy Marine Corps medal, Bronze Star with Combat V, Meritorious Service medal, Purple Heart; Anderson Peninsula in Antarctica named in his honor. Mem. ASCE, Soc. Am. Mil. Engrs. (Morrell medal 1965). Republican. Methodist. Office: Anderson Holdings Inc PO Box 266 Pony MT 59747-0266

ANDERSON, RICHARD H., health insurance company executive, former air transportation executive; b. Galveston, Texas; BS, U. of Houston; JD, South Texas Coll. of Law. Various positions Harris County Dist. Atty.'s office, Houston, 1978—87; staff v.p., dep. gen. counsel Continental Airlines, 1987—90; v.p., dep. gen. counsel Northwest Airlines Corp, Eagan, Minn., 1990—94, sr. v.p. labor rels., state affairs, law, 1994—96, sr. v.p. tech. ops. and airport affairs, 1997—98, exec. v.p. tech. ops. and airport affairs, 1998, exec. v.p., COO Eagan, Minn., 1998—2001, CEO, 2001—04; exec. v.p. UnitedHealth Group, Mpls., 2004—. Bd. dirs. Northwest Airlines, Minn. Life Ins. Co., Mpls. Inst. Arts, Mpls. Downtown Coun.; chmn. Min. Bus. Leadership Network; dir. Medtronic, Inc. Office: UnitedHealth Group Inc PO Box 1459 Minnetonka MN 55343

ANDERSON, RICHARD LOUIS, electrical engineer; b. Mpls., Feb. 4, 1927; s. Ben Walter and Anna Elizabeth (Zitcowicz) Anderson; m. Claire Louise Petersen, Sept. 15, 1951; children: Gretchen, Betty Lise, Karl. BS, U. Minn., 1950, MS, 1952; PhD, Syracuse U., 1960; DSc (hon.), U. Sao Paulo, Brazil, 1969. Research asst. U. Minn., 1950-52; research engr. IBM Corp., Poughkeepsie, N.Y., 1952-60; from. instr. to prof. elec. and computing engring. Syracuse U., 1954-79; prof. elec. engring. U. Vt., Burlington, 1979-95, prof. emeritus elec. engring. and materials sci., 1995—, dir. materials sci. program, 1981-91. Fulbright-Hayes prof. U. Madrid, 1960—61, U. Sao Paulo, 1967—69; cons. in field. Author: 2 textbooks; contbr. articles to profl. jours. With USNR, 1944—47. Recipient 1st Brazilian prize microelectronics, 1980; fellow, Ford Found., 1967—69; grantee, NSF, 1974—85, N.Y. State Sci. and Tech. Found., 1974—75, 1977—78, Dept. Energy, 1979—83. Fellow: IEEE; mem.: AAUP, Am. Phys. Soc., Sigma Xi. Achievements include patents in field. Home: 601 Wake Robin Dr Shelburne VT 05482-7580 Personal E-mail: vze4v7r5@verizon.net.

ANDERSON, RICHARD MCLEMORE, internist; b. Gainesville, Fla., Mar. 3, 1930; s. Montgomery Drummond and Myrtle (McLemore) A.; m. Leewood Shaw, Mar. 21, 1959; children: Richard McLemore Jr., Bruce Dexter. BS, U. Fla., 1951; MD, Emory U., 1958. Diplomate Am. Bd. Internal Medicine. Chief of staff Alachua Gen. Hosp., Gainesville, Fla., 1973-75; internist Gainesville, Fla., 1962—. Chmn. of bd. Santa Fe Health Care, Gainesville, 1984-91, bd. dirs. Pres. Rotary Club of Gainesville, 1980-81. Capt. USAF, 1951-54. Mem. AMA, ACP, Alachua County Med. Soc. (v.p. 1972), Fla. Med. Assn. Presbyterian.

ANDERSON, RICHARD THEODORE, trade association administrator, urban planner; b. Bklyn., Oct. 11, 1940; s. Charles Theodore and Lillian Elizabeth (Holmlin) Anderson; m. Anasta Frank, Oct. 3, 1970; children: Erik Theodore, Leslie Elisabeth. AB, Rutgers U., 1962; M in Regional Planning, Cornell U., 1964; postgrad., NYU, 1964-67. Pres. Regional Plan Assn., N.Y.C., 1964-92; exec. dir. Dallas Plan, 1993-94; pres., CEO N.Y. Bldg. Congress, N.Y.C., 1994—; pres. N.Y. Bldg. Found., N.Y.C., 1998—. Vis. assoc. prof. dept. city and regional planning Pratt Inst., N.Y.C., NY, 1974—92; chmn. Pres.'s Coun. N.Y.C. Planning & Design Orgns., 1982—92. Co-chmn. NY chpt. Rebuild Am. Coalition; v.p., trustee Big Bros./Big Sisters, NYC, 1969—, Audrey Cohen Coll., 1998—2001; bd. dirs. Water Resources Assn. Delaware River Basin, 1977—80, United Way, Pelham, NY, 1977—79, Friends of Hudson River Park, 2001—03; active Times Sq. Adv. Coun., NYC, 1985—89, Bus. Coun. N.Y. State, NYC Partnership, Archtl. League NY, NYC and Co., Citizens Union, Citizens Housing and Planning Coun., Nat. Bldg. Mus., Met. Mus. Art, Mus. City NY, Village Planning Bd., Pelham, 1977—80, Whitney Mus. Am. Art; adv. coun. Cornell U. Coll. Architecture, Art and Planning, 1984—94; bd. dirs. Regional Alliance Small Contractors, 1994—, ACE Mentorship Program, 1997—, Bklyn. Sports Found., 1998—. Named Pub. Sector Mentor of Yr., ACE Mentorship Program, 2005; recipient Ellis Island medal of honor, 1995, Disting. Svc. award, N.Y. Bldg. Congress, 2004; vis. scholar, N.Y. U., 1992. Fellow: Inst. Urban Design, Am. Inst. Cert. Planners (chmn. Coll. Fellows 2003); mem.: AIA (pub. dir. NY chpt. 2003—05, NY chpt. George S. Lewis award 2001), Soc. Mktg. Profl. Svcs. (N.Y. chpt. Honor award 2004), Archtl. League N.Y., Gen. Soc. Mechanics and Tradesmen City of N.Y., Met. Leadership Network, N.Y. Acad. Scis., Urban Land Inst., N.Y. Soc. Assn. Execs., Am. Soc. Planning Ofcls. (bd. dirs. 1977—78), Am. Planning Assn. (dir., treas. 1978—80, pres. 1980—81, Disting. Svc. award 1985), Nat. Trust Hist. Preservation, Empire State Transp. Alliance, Rutgers Alumni Assn. (Loyal Son award 1989), Ellis Island Medal of Honor Soc., Bklyn. C. of C., Van Alen Inst., Assn. for a Better N.Y., Club 101, Sloane Gardens Club. Lutheran. Home: 9 Highview Cir Dobbs Ferry NY 10522 Office: NY Bldg Congress 44 W 28th St New York NY 10001-4212 Office Phone: 212-481-9230.

ANDERSON, ROBERT ALEXANDER, portrait artist; b. Wyandotte, Mich., Jan. 26, 1946; s. Donald Eugene and Janet Linn (Alexander) A.; m. Francesca Florence Waring Schager, June 19, 1976 (div.); 1 child, Julianne Humphrey; m. Margaret Colton Hand, May 26, 1990. BA, Yale U., 1968; Diploma, Sch. Mus. Fine Arts, Boston, 1975. Exhibited in group shows at: John F. Kennedy Presdl. Libr., Boston, 1981, Symphony Hall, Boston, 1982, Beaux Arts Gallery, Houston, 1983, Soc. of Illustrators, N.Y.C., 1987, Boston Atheneum, 1989, Norman Rockwell Mus., Stockbridge, Mass., 2000; represented in pub. collections Boston Pub. Libr., Mass. Gen. Hosp., duPont Inst., Wilmington, Del., Dana-Farber Cancer Inst., Boston Coll., Phillips-Exeter Acad., Yale U., Harvard U., Mt. Sinai Hosp., city Bar Assn. N.Y., Commonwealth of Mass., Mass. Inst. Tech., others; represented in numerous pvt. family collections; pastel artist for John H. Breck Co. advt., 1976-91; designed cover rec. You Don't Have To Take What You Get (Karen Kayen); also currently painting stamp portraits for U.S. Postal Service "Great Ams." series including John Harvard and Chief Red Cloud; recently selected by Pres. George W. Bush to paint his portrait for the Yale Club of N.Y.C. Bd. dirs. Munroe Ctr. for the Arts, Mass., 1994—; trustee Schwamb Mill Hist. Preservation, Arlington, Mass., 1985—. Served to lt. USNR, 1968-71, including Vietnam. Recipient First prize N.E. Competition Nat. Portrait Seminar, N.Y.C., 1981, Best of Show Nat. Competion Grand prize, 1982. Home: 27 Brush Island Rd Darien CT 06820-5706 Office Phone: 203-655-9724. E-mail: robander@optonline.net.

ANDERSON, ROBERT FRANCIS, academic administrator; b. Madison, Wis., Feb. 1, 1974; s. Richard Charles Anderson and Patricia Kay Nachreiner. MusB in Applied Vocal Performance, Viterbo U., 1992; MSc in Student Devel. Adminstrn., U. Wis., La Crosse, Wis., 2003. Asst. property mgr., leasing cons. Nat. Realty Mgmt. Inc., Madison, Wis., 1996—99; office mgr. Anchor Property Mgmt., Madison, 1999; area coord., dir. grad. housing, coord. orientation Viterbo U., La Crosse, 1999—2003; asst. dir. residence life Melrose Mpls., 2003; coord. residence hall U. Iowa, Iowa City, 2003—, ednl. programmer, 2003—. Chmn. La Crosse (Wis.) Area Pride Along The Miss. Festival, 2001—02. Recipient Bldg. A Found. For Our Cmty. Philanthropy award, La Crosse Cmty. Found., 2002, I Dare You Danforth Leadership award, U. Wis. Extension, Sauk County 4-H, 1990; scholar David And Cis Hogue Student Devel. Adminstrn. award, U. Wis., La Crosse, Wis., 2002. Mem.: Nat. Assn. Coll. and U. Residence Halls (Top Program award 2004), Wis. Coll. Personnel Assn. (mem. exec. bd. 2001—03, State Showcase Program award 2002), Assn. Of Coll. And U. Housing Officers Internat., Nat. Orientation Directors Assn. (mem. conf. com. 2000—02, 2004, chmn. GLBTA network 2005—05, Regional Showcase Program award 2003, Best Overall Case Study Presentation award 2001, named Outstanding Chairperson 2004), Am. Coll. Pers. Assn. (mem. core coun. profl. devel. 2003—05, mem. standing com. lesbian, gay, bisexual and transgender awareness 2003—05, scholarship 2002), Viterbo U. Alumni Assn. (mem. exec. bd. 2001—03). Avocations: travel, fashion, cooking, films, music. Office Phone: 319-335-9576. Personal E-mail: bobbysworlds80@hotmail.com.

ANDERSON, R(OBERT) GREGG, real estate company executive; b. St. Joseph, Mo., Oct. 3, 1928; s. Clarence William and Marie Louise (Newman) A.; m. Janice Kimrey, May 6, 2001; 1 child, Robert Gregg Jr. Student, U. Okla., 1948-49, U. Tulsa, 1950. Pres. Gregg Anderson Realty, San Diego, 1959-63; v.p. Trousdale Constrn. Co., L.A., 1963-67; pres. Amfac Properties div. Amfac, Inc., Honolulu, 1967-69; v.p. Amfac, Inc., Honolulu, 1967-69, sr. v.p., 1969-74; pres., chmn. bd. Accent Enterprises, Inc., Amfac Communities, Inc., Amfac Silverado Corp., Neilson Way Corp., 745 Fort St. Corp., Cen. Oahu Land Corp., L.A. Environ. Structures, Inc., 1969-74; chmn. bd. West Maui Properties, Inc., 1969-74; v.p. Silverado Country Club & Resort, Inc., 1969-74; pres. Gregg Anderson Realty & Devel., Inc., 1974—, Villa Pacific Bldg. Co., 1980—; gen. ptnr. Rancho Vista Devel. Co., Palmdale, Calif., 1980—; pres. Videocable, Inc., Palmdale, 1984-87; gen. ptnr. ProRep Assocs., 1991—. Bd. dirs. Antelope Valley Bd. Trade, 1991—. With USNR, 1950-54. Named Builder of Yr., Calif. Bldg. Industry Assn., 1998; inductee Calif. Bldg. Industry Hall of Fame, 1999. Mem. Bldg. Industry Assn. (bd. dirs. 1984-94), Rotary (hon.), Kiwanis (hon.). Republican. Avocations: tennis, golf, bowling. Office: Rancho Vista Devel Co 3011 Rancho Vista Blvd Ste F Palmdale CA 93551-4823 Business E-Mail: ranchvista@qnet.com.

ANDERSON, ROBERT LANIER, III, federal judge; b. Macon, Ga., Nov. 12, 1936; s. Robert Lanier II and Helen Anderson; m. Nancy Briska, Aug. 18, 1962; 3 children. AB magna cum laude, Yale U., 1958; LLB, Harvard U., 1961. Assoc. Anderson, Walkert, Reichert, Macon, Ga., 1963—79; judge U.S. Ct. Appeals (5th cir.), 1979—81, U.S. Ct. Appeals (reassigned to 11th cir.), 1981—; chief judge U.S. Ct. Appeals (11th cir.), Macon, Ga., 1999—2002. With USAR, 1958—61, capt. U.S. Army, 1961—63. Mem.: ABA, Am. Judicature Soc., State Bar of Ga., Macon Bar Assn., Ga. Bar Assn. Office: US Ct Appeals PO Box 977 Macon GA 31202-0977

ANDERSON, ROBERT MORRIS, JR., electrical engineer; b. Crookston, Minn., Feb. 15, 1939; s. Robert Morris and Eleanor Elaine (Huotte) A.; m. Janice Ilene Pendell, Sept. 3, 1960; children— Erik Martin, Kristi Lynn. BEE, U. Mich., 1961, MEE, 1963, MS in Physics, 1965, PhD in Elec. Engring, 1967. Asst. research engr. U. Mich., Ann Arbor, 1963-67; research engr. Conductron Corp., Ann Arbor, summer 1967; asst. prof. elec. engring. Purdue U., West Lafayette, Ind., 1967-71, assoc. prof., 1971-79, prof., 1979, engring. coordinator for continuing edn., 1973-79, Ball Bros. prof., 1976-79; mgr. engring. edn. and tng., corp. cons. services GE, Bridgeport, Conn., 1979-82, mgr. tech. edn. operation, corp. engring. and mfg., 1982-88; mgr. tech. edn., corp. mgmt. devel. Gen. Electric Co., Bridgeport, Conn., 1988-90; vice provost, dir. coop. extension Iowa State U., Ames, 1990-95, prof. elec. engring., 1990-2000, prof. emeritus, elec. engring., 2000—. Author: (multimedia learning packagE) Fundamentals of Vacuum Technology, 1973; author: (with others) Divided Loyalties, 1980; contbr. with others articles to profl. jours. Chmn. bd. dirs. Lincoln Way Chapter, Am. Red Cross, 2003—04; bd. trustees Ames Pub. Libr., 2005—. Recipient Dow Outstanding Young Faculty award, 1974, Ky. Col. award, Jullian M. Carroll, Gov., Commonwealth Ky., 1977. Fellow Am. Soc. Engring. Edn. (cert. of merit 1977, Joseph M. Biedenbach Disting. Svc. award 1986), IEEE (Meritorious Achievement award in continuing edn. activities 1987), Rotary Club (Unsung Hero award, 2002, pres. 2005-. Conservative. Lutheran. Office: Iowa State U 2218 Coover Hall Ames IA 50011-0001 Home: 4038 Stone Brook Rd Ames IA 50010-2900

ANDERSON, ROBERT ORVILLE, oil and gas company executive; b. Chgo., Apr. 13, 1917; s. Hugo A. and Hilda (Nelson) A.; m. Barbara Phelps, Aug. 25, 1939; children: Katherine, Julia, Maria, Robert Bruce, Barbara Burton, William Phelps, Beverley. BA, U. Chgo., 1939. With Am. Mineral Spirits Co., Chgo., 1939-41; pres. Malco Refineries, Inc., Roswell, N.Mex., 1963-86; with Atlantic Richfield Co., Los Angeles, retired chmn. bd., chief exec. officer. Mem. Com. Econ. Devel., Washington. Hon. coun. trustees Aspen Inst.; trustee Calif. Ins. Tech., U. Chgo.; chmn. Lovelace-Anderson Endowment Found. Mem. Nat. Petroleum Coun., Am. Petroleum Inst. Clubs: Century (N.Y.C.); California (Los Angeles); Pacific-Union (San Francisco). Office Phone: 505-625-6801.

ANDERSON, ROBERT RAYMOND, artist, consultant; b. Orange, N.J., Nov. 9, 1945; s. Walter Edmund Anderson and Althea (Weimer) Casler; m. June Elizabeth Giardino, June 8, 1968. Student, N.J. Inst. Tech., 1964-66; BS, SUNY, Brockport, 1969; MFA, Pratt Inst., 1972. Represented by OK Harris Gallery, N.Y.C. Instr. Art Ctr. N.J., Summit, 1974-79, Newark (N.J.) Mus. Arts Workshop, 1976-79, County Coll. Morris, Dove, N.J., 1978-79; tech. cons. Binney & Smith, Easton, Pa., 1991-2000, Colart, 2000—. Co-author: Art of the Dot/Advanced Airbrush Techniques, 1985; one man shows include Park Gallery, N.Y.C., 1972, Newark Mus., 1975, N.J. State Mus., 1978, Jack Gallery, N.Y.C., 1984, Littlejohn-Smith Galery, N.Y.C., 1986, 89, OK South Gallery, Bay Harbor Isle, Fla., 1989, Robin Hutchins Gallery, Maplewood, N.J., 1990, Wetherholt Gallery, Washington, 1992, OK Harris Gallery, N.Y.C., 2001-02; exhibited in group shows at Montclair (N.J.) Mus., 1972, Hartwick Coll., N.Y.C., 1975, Morris Mus., N.J., 1976, Temple U., Pa., 1980, San Jose State U., 1982, N.J. State Mus., 1984, Noyes Mus., N.J., 1986, Schering Plough, Inc., 1988, Ea. Wash. U., 1988, Tex. A&M U., 1989, Gallery and hasting-on-Hudson, N.Y., 1989, Fairleigh Dickinson U., N.J., 1990, Trenton City Mus., N.J., 1991, Newark Mus., N.J., 1992, Marlboro Art Gallery, Md., 1993, First St. Gallery, N.Y.C., 1993, County Coll. Morris, Dover, N.J., 1994. Trustee Oakeside Cultural Ctr., Bloomfield, N.J., 1988-89; mem. Bloomfield (N.J.) Cultural Commn., 1988-89. Recipient fellowship grants N.J. State Coun. on the Arts, Trenton, 1976, 84, 2004, Nat. Endowment for the Arts, Washington, 1985. Mem. Trenton Artists Workshop Assn., Studio Montclair. Avocations: running, cross country skiing. Home: 46 Glen Rock Rd Cedar Grove NJ 07009-1638 Personal E-mail: bob@arttekstudios.com.

ANDERSON, ROBERTA JOAN See MITCHELL, JONI

ANDERSON, ROBIN LOUISE, music educator; b. Wewoka, Okla., Jan. 8, 1962; d. Herbert Napoleon and Janet Faye Rainbolt; m. Roger Kelly Anderson, July 31, 1982; children: Hillary, Hayley. MusB, Okla. Baptist U., Shawnee, 1984. Lic. educator Kindermusik. Pvt. practice piano instr., Durant, Okla., 1984—86, Ardmore, 1986—88, Bartlesville, 1988—92; piano tchr. and accompanist Borger (Tex.) H.S., 1992—2000; accompanist local schs. Wichita Falls, 2000—; Kindermusik tchr. FBC Music Acad., 2003—04, piano tchr., 2001—. Coord. and dir. handbell program FBC Music Acad., Borger, Tex., 1993—2000; contest adjudicator, 1990—. Mentor young women; vol. vocal and instrumental coach jr. and sr. H.S.; mem. and vol. Highland Park Baptist Ch., Bartlesville, Okla., 1988—92, First Baptist Ch., Borger, Tex., 1992—2000, West Side Baptist Ch., Wichita Falls, 2000—; Bible study tchr. Avocation: music arranging.

ANDERSON, ROLPH ELY, finance educator; b. Buchanan, Mich., Aug. 27, 1936; s. Eugene Jefferson and Susanna (James) Anderson; m. Sallie Durkee Warner; children: Rachel Elizabeth, Stuart James. BA, Mich. State U., 1958, MBA, 1964; PhD, U. Fla., 1971. Inventory mgr. Shell Oil Co., Detroit, 1958-59; contract adminstr. Westinghouse Elec. Corp., Pitts., 1962-63; mgr. new product devel. Quaker Oats Co., Chgo., 1964-67; prof., chmn. dept. bus. mgmt. Old Dominion U., Norfolk, Va., 1971-75; chmn. dept. mktg. Drexel U., Phila., 1975-97, Royal H. Gibson prof. bus. adminstrn., 1991—. Mem. sales com. Fin. Svcs. Advisor mag., 2000—; disting. fellow LeBow Coll. Ctr. for Tchg. Excellence, 2003—. Author: Professional Personal Selling, 1991, Essentials of Personal Selling: The New Professionalism, 1995; co-author: Introduction to Multivariate Data Analysis, 1974, Multivariate Data Analysis, 1979, 5th edit., 1998;: Personal Selling: Achieving Customer Satisfaction and Loyalty, 2004, Sales Management, 1983, Professional Sales Management, 3d edit., 1999; translator: Analisis Multivaricate 5th edit., 1990, Administración De Ventas 2d edit., 1995, Professionalini Manažment Prodaje, 1998, Análise Multivaiada De Dados 5th edit., 2005. Mem. faculty adv. bd. Fisher Inst. Profl. Selling, 1998—. Served to capt. Supply Corps. USN. Recipient award for best publ. article, Jour. Pers. Selling and Sales Mgmt., 1988, Excellence in Reviewing award, 1996, Rsch. Excellence award, LeBow Coll., 2000—01; fellow, LeBow Coll. Ctr. Tchg. Excellence, 2003—. Mem.: Internat. Am. Mktg. Assn. (Sales Interest Group Inaugural Excellence in Sales Rsch award 1998), N.E. Am. Inst. Decision Scis. (bd. dirs. 1977—78), Acad. Mktg. Sci. (sec., mem. exec. coun. 1984—86), So. Mktg. Assn., Sales and Mktg. Execs. Internat., Am. Mktg. Assn. (internat. conf. co-chmn. 1978, v.p. programming Phila. chpt. 1984—85, bd. dirs. 1986—87, 1992—93), Am. Inst. Decision Scis. (nat. coun. 1977—79), S.E. Am. Inst. Decision Scis. (pres. 1977—78), Res. Officers Assn., Naval Res. Assn., Beta Gamma Sigma. Office: Drexel U LeBow Coll Bus Philadelphia PA 19104 E-mail: ralph.e.anderson@drexel.edu.

ANDERSON, RON JOE, health facility administrator, internist, educator; b. Chickasha, Okla., Sept. 6, 1946; s. Ted J. and Ruby (Harston) Anderson Benjamin; m. Sue Ann Blakely, Apr. 12, 1975; children: Sarah Elizabeth, Daniel Jerrod, John Charles. BS in Pharmacy, Southwest U. Okla., 1969; MD, U. Okla., 1973. Diplomate Am. Bd. Internal Medicine, Am. Bd. Geriatrics. Intern U. Tex. Southwestern Med. Sch., Parkland Meml. Hosp., VA Hosp., Dallas, 1973-74, resident and chief resident in internal medicine, 1974-76; asst. prof. internal medicine U. Tex. Health Sci. Ctr., Dallas, 1976-81, asst. dean clin. affairs, 1979-82, prof. internal medicine, 1981—; med. dir. ambulatory-emergency services Dallas County Hosp. Dist., 1979-82, acting. med. dir., 1981-82, CEO, 1982—; chmn. Tex. Bd. Health, 1991-93. Mem. task force on teaching hosps. Tex. Hosp. Assn., 1982—, task force on indigent health care, 1983-86; cons. on high blood pressure Am. Heart Assn., 1981-83; advisor Tex. Assn. Physician Assts.; chmn. Neighborhood Clinic Cooperating Com., Dallas, 1980-82; bd. dirs. Children's Oncology Services Tex., Dallas, 1982-86, Addison, Carrollton, Coppell, Farmers Branch chpt. Am. Heart Assn., 1978-80; mem. Tex. Gov.'s Task Force on Indigent Health Care, 1983-86, Tex. Health and Human Services Coordinating Council, 1983-86, Tex. Cancer Council, 1985-87, Spl. Task Force on Future of Long-Term Health Care for Tex., Mayor's Task Force on Internat. Devel., Dallas AIDS Planning Commn.; mem. Tex. Bd. Health, 1983—, chmn., 1983-87, 91—; mem. Dallas Council on Alcoholism and Drug Abuse, 1982, bd. dirs., 1982—, v.p., 1986, pres., 1987-88; mem. adv. com. program to improve maternal and infant care in South Robert Wood Johnson Found. Contbr. articles to profl. jours. Bd. dirs. Project Independence, Greater Dallas Ahead, 1985—, Kaiser Found. Health Plan Tex., 1991, Interfaith Housing Coalition; preceptor Dallas Ind. Sch. Dist. Talented and Gifted Program, 1977; mem. Dallas Commrs. Ct. Task Force on Mental Patients, 1979, Dallas Alliance, 1986—, Dallas Assembly, 1984—, Hogg Found. for Mental Health Commn. on Community Care of Mentally Ill, 1987—; adv. bd. Dallas Challenge, 19846; co-chmn. Tex. Response, 1985—; chmn. mission bd. 1st Bapt. Ch. of Oak Cliff, and others. Recipient Tex. Aging Leadership award, 1987, Community Service award Community and Migrant Health Ctrs. Tex., 1986, Tex. Leadership in Aging award Tex. 6th Annual Joint Conf. on Aging, 1987, Disting. Alumnus award S.W. U. Okla., 1987, James E. Peavy Meml. award Tex. Pub. Health Assn., 1988, Dallas Hist. Soc. award, Headliner award Dallas Press Club, Health Care Profl. of Yr. award Tex. Nurses Assn., 1990; named to Disting. Alumni Hall of Fame Southwestern Okla. State U., 1987. Fellow ACP; mem. AMA, Inst. Medicine NAS, Nat. Assn. Pub. Hosps. (bd. dirs., exec. com., chmn.-elect 1991, Safety Net awrd 1990, Safety NEt Leadership award 2004), Nat. Pub. Health and Hosp. Inst. (bd. dirs., chmn. devel. com., chmn. 1991), Tex. Med. Assn., Tex. Hosp. Assn. (chmn. 1999—), Dallas County Med. Soc., Am. Soc. Internat. Medicine, Soc. Gen. Internal Medicine, Dallas-Ft. Worth Hosp. Coun. (chmn.-elect 1991), Salesmanship Dallas Club. Democrat. Baptist. Office: Dallas County Hosp Dist Parkland Meml Hosp 5201 Harry Hines Blvd Dallas TX 75235-7708

ANDERSON, RONALD DELAINE, education educator; b. Poplar, Wis., Aug. 25, 1937; s. Leslie A. and Linnea A. (Bergsten) A.; m. Sandra Jean Wendt, June 1, 1963; children— Debra Jean, Timothy James, Nathan David. BS, U. Wis., 1959, PhD, 1964. Asst. prof. edn. Kans. State U., Manhattan, 1964-65; mem. faculty U. Colo., Boulder, 1965—, prof. edn., 1971—, asso. dean edn., 1972-78. Cons. to numerous ednl. agys. Author: Religion and Spirituality in the Public School Curriculum, 2004; co-author: Developing Children's Thinking Through Science, 1970, Issues of Curriculum Reform, 1994, Local Leadership for Science Education Reform, 1995, Portraits of Productive Schools, 1995, Study of Curriculum Reform, 1996; contbr. articles to profl. jours. Program dir. NSF, 1989—90. Fulbright scholar, 1986-87. Fellow AAAS (chair edn. sect. 1998-99, mem. Assn. Coun. 2002-05); mem. Nat. Assn. Rsch. Sci. Tchg. (pres. 1975-76), Assn. Edn. Tchrs. in Sci. (pres. 1972-73), Nat. Sci. Tchrs. Assn., Phi Delta Kappa. Home: 4800 North Creek Rd Beulah CO 81023-9601 Office: Univ Colo Sch Edn Boulder CO 80309-0001 Office Phone: 303-492-7738.

ANDERSON, RONALD TRENT, artist, educator; b. Madison, Wis., Oct. 10, 1938; s. Delmar LeRoy and Violet (Doering) A.; m. Barbara Groffman, June 9, 1962; 1 child, Brett Erland. BS in Art Edn., U. Wis., 1961, MS in Art, 1962, MFA in Art, 1963. Tchr. Waupun (Wis.) High Sch., 1961; tchg. asst. rural art program U. Wis., Madison, 1961-63; tchr. Bloom Twp. High Sch., Chgo. Heights, Ill., 1963-67; asst. prof. art edn. Nova Scotia Coll. of Art and Design, Halifax, Nova Scotia, 1967-69; tchr. Springfield (Mass.) Pub. Schs., 1969—2000. Represented in permanent collections U. Wis., Dalhousie U., Halifax, Westfield (Mass.) Coll., Walter J. Kohler, Jr., family, work reproduced in, Prize-Winning Watercolors Book I, 1963, Prize-Winning Watercolors Book II, 1964, The Art of Written Forms, 1969, one-man shows include Arts Unlimited Gallery, Milw., Wis., 1965, Bradley Gallery, 1967, Burnett Gallery, Amherst, Mass., 2005, exhibited in group shows at Smithsonian Instn., Washington, D.C., 1962, Ill. State Mus., Springfield, Ill., 1965, 1967, Nat. Design Ctr., Chgo., Ill., 1967, Dalhousie U., 1967, Montreal (Can.) Mus. Fine Arts, 1968, Boston Symphony Hall, 1992, Colo. Coll., Colo. Springs, Colo., 1998, numerous others. Recipient Beacon award for excellence in edn., Springfield Sch. Com., 1992, 20 awards for painting and printmaking in juried art exhbns. U.S. and Can., Mass. Art Educator of Yr. award, Mass. Art Edn. Assn., 1999, Sch. Edn. Alumni Achievement Award, U. Wis. Madison, 2001; fellow Tchr.-Artist Program, The Marie Walsh Sharpe Art Found., 1998. Mem.: NEA, Internat. Platform Assn. (First Prize for Graphics Exhbn. 1995, Best of Show award 2001), Nat. Art Edn. Assn., Salmagundi Club (Rita Duis Meml. award 2003, Gene Magazzini Meml. award traditional oil 2003, Joseph DiMare award 2005), Phi Delta Kappa. Lutheran. Avocations: studying the arts and humanities, foreign travel, bicycling, photography, fishing. Home: 9 Autumn Ln Amherst MA 01002-3316 Personal E-mail: Ronbarb8@aol.com.

ANDERSON, ROSE L. DYESS, elementary school educator, poet; b. Laurel, Miss., Dec. 24, 1941; d. James Lamar and Mildred Josephine (Moore) Dyess; m. Rushel Talmadge Anderson, May 13, 1965; 1 child, Joel Alan. BE, William Carey Coll., Hattiesburg, Miss., 1964; grad., Univ. So. Miss., Hattiesburg, Miss. Elem. tchr. Natchez-Adams Pub. Sch., Natchez, Miss., 1968—. Author: (poetry) Lifes Fleeting Days, 1996, The Winds of Change Keep on Blowing, 1997. Facilitator numerous workshops and conf. within dist., Miss. Early Childhood Conf, Summer Math and Sci. Conf., Miss. Univ. for Women; mentor tchr. for numerous student tchrs. Alcorn State Univ., Univ. So. Miss. Nominee Disney Tchr of the Yr., 1995; recipient Golden Apple award, Covington Rd. Ch. of Christ, Miss., 1996, Tchr. of the Yr., Frazier Primary Sch., Miss., 2002. Mem.: Miss. Edn. Assn., Nat. Libr. of Poetry, Alpha Delta Kappa (chaplin, treas., historian). Republican. Ch. Of Christ. Achievements include design of and edited a children's activity page for a religious newspaper, The Magnolia Messenger; movtivantional spkr. for ch. ladies day activites. Avocations: writing, painting, interior decorating, gardening, travel. Home: 505 Lindberg Ave Natchez MS 39120 Office: Frazier Primary Sch 1445 George F West Blvd Natchez MS 39120

ANDERSON, ROSS CARL, mayor, lawyer; b. Logan, Utah, Sept. 9, 1951; s. E. LeRoy and Grace (Rasmussen) Anderson; 1 child, Lucas Craig Arment. BS in Philosophy magna cum laude, U. Utah, 1973; JD with honors, George Washington U., 1978. Bar: U.S. Dist. Ct. Utah 1978. Assoc. Berman & Giauque, Salt Lake City, 1978-80; v.p., ptnr. Berman & Anderson, Rooker Larsen Kimball & Parr, Salt Lake City, 1980-82; ptnr. Berman & Anderson, Salt Lake City, 1982-85; ptnr., v.p. Hansen & Anderson, Salt Lake City, 1986-89, Anderson & Watkins, Salt Lake City, 1989-92; pres. Anderson & Karrenberg, Salt Lake City, 1992-98, of counsel, 1999; mayor Salt Lake City, 1999—. Columnist: Enterprise, 1997—98, I-15 Mag., 2000—01, Catalyst, 2002—. Pres. bd. dirs. Citizens Penal Reform, 1991—94, Guadalupe Ednl. Programs, Salt Lake City, 1985—96, 1997—99, ACLU Utah, 1980—85; bd. dirs. Common Cause Utah, 1987—89, Planned Parenthood Utah, 1979—83; mem. Salt Lake Com. Fgn. Rels., 1983—95; Dem. candidate for Congress Utah 2d Congl. Dist., 1996. Mem.: Utah State Bar Assn. Avocations: history, skiing. Home: 418 Douglas St Salt Lake City UT 84102-3231 Office: Office Mayor 451 S State St Rm 306 Salt Lake City UT 84111-0005 Office Phone: 801-535-7704. Business E-Mail: rocky.anderson@slcgov.com.

ANDERSON, ROSS S., architectural firm executive; Grad., Harvard Grad. Sch. of Design, 1977; BA Human Biol., Art, and Arch., Stanford Univ., 1973. Registered licensed, New York, Calif., Ohio. Pres. Anderson Arch., New York, NY, 1996—; vis. prof. in arch. Advanced Studios, Yale Univ., 1992; ptnr. Anderson/Schwartz Arch., New York, NY, 1984—96, San Francisco, 1984—96; vis. critic in arch. Yale Univ., 1987; head of second year Studio Parsons Sch. of Des., 1984—85; ptnr. Anderson-Wheelwright Assoc., New York, NY, 1981—84; project arch. John Carl Warnecke, New York, NY, 1980—81, Turner Brooks, Starksboro, Vt., 1979—81, MLTW/Turnbull Assoc., San Francisco, 1977—80. Exhibitions include Negotiating Domesticity, The Greenwich Arts Coun., Greenwich, Ct., 2003, Small Firms, Gt. Projects, AIA/SF Gallery, San Francisco, CA, 1992, Ann. Exhbn., Am. Acad. in Rome, Rome, Italy, 1990, exhibitions include Thumbnail Sketches AIA/SF Gallery, San Francisco, Calif., 1989, exhibitions include Arch. Art, Am. Crafts Mus., New York, NY, 1988. Recipient EDRA/Places Design Award, Abercrombie & Fitch Office campus, 2003, Build. Team Project of the Yr.- Grand Award, Abercrombie & Fitch Office campus, Build. and Des. & Construct. Mag., 2003, Good Des. is Good Bus. Award, Abercrombie & Fitch, Bus. wk/Arch. Record, 2002, Hollister Co., Bus. wk./arch. design, 2002, Project Award, Hudson River Pk., 2000 Design Awards, AIA NY Chapt. Interior Des., 2000, Interior Arch. Award, AIA NY Chapt., Design Awards, 1998, SMA Video, AIA NY Chapt., 1995, Western Home Award, Citation, Napa Valley House, 1991, AIA, 1991, Sunset Mag., 1991, 40 Under 40, Interiors Mag., 1986—87. Office: Anderson Arch 555 W 25th St New York NY 10001

ANDERSON, ROY EVERETT, retired electrical engineer; b. Batavia, Ill., Oct. 30, 1918; s. Elof and Nellie Amanda Anderson; m. Gladys Marie Nelson, Aug. 22, 1943; children: Paul V., David L., Barbara J. Anderson Wald, Dorothy M. Anderson Presser. BA in Physics, Augustana Coll., Rock Island, Ill., 1943; MSEE, Union Coll., Schenectady, 1952. Instr. physics Augustana Coll., 1943-44, 46-47; cons. engr. GE, Schenectady, 1947-83; co-founder, v.p. Mobile Satellite Corp., Malvern, Pa., 1983-88; owner, mgr., cons. Anderson Assocs., Glenville, NY, 1988—99; pres. Rega Assocs., Glenville, 1993—2000; ret., 2000. Cons. Am. Mobile Satellite Corp., Washington, 1988-91; participant nat. and internat. regulatory and stds. orgns. leading to establishment generic mobile satellite svc. Contbr. over 125 articles to profl.

jours.; patentee indsl. electronic measurement and quality control instruments, tone code ranging technique for position surveillance using satellites; developer Doppler radio direction finder. Trustee Dudley Obs., Schenectady, 1975-83, 90-2002, chmn. bd. trustees, 1980-83, 90. With USN, 1944-46. GE Coolidge fellow, 1970. Fellow IEEE, AAAS, Radio Club Am., Inst. Navigation; mem. AIAA. Home and Office: PO Box 2531 Glenville NY 12325-0531 Personal E-mail: regainc@aol.com.

ANDERSON, RUDOLPH J., JR., lawyer; b. Bklyn., Apr. 15, 1924; s. Rudolph John and Nora (Cawley) A.; m. Helen O'Donnell, May 28, 1949; children: Mary Josephine Anderson Coughlin, Rudolph John III, Peter, Thomas, Michael, Rosemary, Christopher, Terrence. BS in Naval Sci., U. Notre Dame, 1945, BS in Chem. Engring., 1947; JD, Georgetown U., 1951. Bar: Va. 1950, D.C. 1955, N.J. 1963, Mo. 1985, Vt. 1989. Asst. to pres. Permacel div. Johnson & Johnson, 1955-60; assoc. gen. counsel, dir. patents Merck & Co., Inc., Rahway, N.J., 1960-83; gen. patent counsel Monsanto Co., St. Louis, 1984-87; of counsel Fitzpatrick, Cella, Harper & Scinto, N.Y.C., 1987-89. Former committeeman Scotch Plains Twp. Com., N.J. Served to lt. USNR, 1943-46, PTO. Mem. ABA (chmn. patent trademark and copyright law sect. 1984-85), Assn. Corp. Patent Counsel, Am. Intellectual Property Law Assn. Roman Catholic. Home and Office: PO Box 416 811 Pinnacle Rd Stowe VT 05672-0416 Personal E-mail: helenrudy1@aol.com.

ANDERSON, RUSSELL A., state supreme court justice; b. Bemidji, Minn., May 28, 1942; m. Kristin Anderson; children: Rebecca, John, Sarah. BA, St. Olaf Coll., 1964; JD, U. Minn., 1968; LLM, George Washington U., 1977. Pvt. practice, 1976-82; atty. Beltrami County, 1978-82; dist. ct. judge 9th Jud. Dist., 1982-98; assoc. justice Minn. Supreme Ct., 1998—. Mem. Jud. Edn. Adv. Com., Sentencing Guidelines Commn., Supreme Ct. Adv. Com. on Rules of Criminal Procedure, Supreme Ct. Gender Fairness Implementation com., Connect U.S.-Russian Domestic Violence Delegation to Russia, 1995, 97. Lt. comdr. USN, 1968—76. Mem.: Minn. Dist. Judges Assn., 14th Dist. Bar Assn., Minn. State Bar Assn. Office: Minn Supreme Ct 305 Minn Judicial Ctr 25 Rev Martin Luther King Jr Blvd Saint Paul MN 55155

ANDERSON, RUTH NATHAN, columnist, television personality, writer, lyricist, poet; b. N.Y.C., Jan. 28; d. Solomon and Anna (Cornick) Gans; m. Arthur Aksel Anderson Jr., Sept. 11, 1971 (dec.); stepchildren—Jack Anderson, Barbara Anderson-Rouse, Terri Anderson-Sarli. Student, NYU, George Washington U. Feature editor Crusade for Freedom, Radio Free Europe, N.Y.C.; feature-series reporter N.Am. Newspaper Alliance, Women's News Svc., N.Y.C., 1961-79; writer, originator Doctor's Grapevine column Nat. Features Syndicate, Chgo., 1969-73; author-owner syndicated column VIP Med. Grapevine/Celebrity Health News, Round Lake, Ill., 1973-2001. Newsletter editor Washington Post; chief med. writer, press officer Nat. Multiple Scierosis Soc., N.Y.C.; feature news corr. Waukegan (Ill.) News-Sun, 1977-82; writer, host Celebrity Health News, Cablenet TV, Chgo., 1985-89; feature writer Ind. News Alliance, Chgo.; Chgo. contbg. editor Music City Entertainer, Nashville, 1976-2002; writing projects dir. Comedy Hall of Fame, Chgo., 1989-2001; ethics writer, Chicago Journalist, 1998-04, internet's Doctor Who's Who, 1999, chief lyricist Anderson-Fejer Musicals, 1995—; lifestyle editor, columnist Emerald Coast Insider, 2003—; tchr. journalism, creative writing, speech arts Fla. State Bd. Adult Edn., 1968-79; writing instr. Bay Country Dist. Schs., 2002—; lectr. writing seminars for faculty U. Ill. at Chgo. Circle Campus, 1970-80. Author: (poetry) Naked Brunch, 1996, (booklet) How You Can Be a Part of Your United Nations, Intimate Travels, 2005, (book and lyrics for musical play) Menage a Trois, 1997; contbr. articles to various mags. including Parents, Pagent Mademoiselle, Science Digest, Reader's Digest, TV Guide, TV Radio Mirror, This Week, Am. Weekly, Am. Home, others; CD release Love Songs for Lovers, 2002; contbr. poems to (book) Nat. Libr. Poetry (Best Poems of 1990, 2000, 2001, 2003, 2004); features on U.S. Presidents in archives of Hoover, Truman, Eisenhower, Kennedy and Johnson Presdl. Librs.; contbr. poem to Theatre of the Mind anthology, 2003. Trustee, v.p. bd. Round Lake Pub. Library, 1977-86; mem. Nat. Trust for Hist. Prservation; Right=to-Read vol. tutor jr. high schs., Round Lake, 1977-86; singer ARC entertainment com. Beside Network, 1974-80; citizen amb. to South Africa with Creative Women of the Arts Del. under People-to-People Amb. Programs, 1999. Recipient Golde Poet Trophy award, Internat. Soc. Poets, 1990, Silver Cup award, 2004, Editor's Choice award, Nat. Libr. Poetry, Rec. artist mus. comedy songs, pop for Am. Sound label. Mem. NARAS, NATAS, Chgo. Women in Broadcasting, Am. Med. Writers Assn. (Beth Fonda award, 1984), Am. Mus. Women in Arts (charter), Lake County Assn. Journalist, NAFE, Chgo. Unltd., Press Vets. Assn., Internat. Platform Assn., Future Physicians Am. (hon.) Soc. Profl. Journalists Headline Club, Panhandle Writers Guild, P.C. Profl. Writers Assn., Gulf Coast Jazz Soc., Authors League Am., Dramatists Guild. Chgo. Press Club, Chgo. Advt. Club. Home and Office: Writing/Entertainment Arts 1836 N East Ave Lot 24 Panama City FL 32405 Fax: 850-215-9058. Office Phone: 850-215-3409. E-mail: ruthswritings@aol.com.

ANDERSON, RUTH T., retired air traffic controller; b. Bartow, Fla., July 2, 1935; d. John Benjamin Thompson and Susan Ettie Scott; m. Malcolm Edward Jack Anderson; m. Perry Brannon, Jr. (div. Oct. 29, 1973); children: Glenda Brannon Parrish, Ronald Allen Brannon. AA Computer Acctg. Technology, SE Coll. of Tech., Mobile, Ala., 1992. Air traffic control specialist FAA, Dothan, Ala., Gulfport, Miss., Mobile, Ala., 1972—89. EEO investigator FAA, Atlanta, 1985—89. Methodist. Avocation: reading, writing, sewing and crafting, fishing. Home: 1983 Powell Tr Abbeville AL 36310

ANDERSON, SARA SHUTTLEWORTH, artist, educator; b. Davenport, Iowa, Aug. 6, 1934; d. Thomas Henderson and Eloise Dorothy (Thompson) Shuttleworth; m. Theodore Charles Anderson; children: Andrew, Dale, Eric, Tod. BA in Edn., Mills Coll., 1956; cert. in painting, Royal Acad. Fine Arts, Brussels, 1969; BA in Fine Arts, Calif. State U., Northridge, 1970. Cert. primary and elem. tchr. fine arts to jr. coll., life early childhood credential, Calif. Tchr. art Triton Mus. Art, Santa Clara, Calif., 1985-89; tchr. art, contract art cons., classroom facilitator Rose Avenue Sch., Oxnard, Calif., 1995—. Owner, coord. Ventura Harbor Village Art Gallery, 1992-95; vol., pres., cons. Art Docents Los Gatos, Calif., 1976-82. One-woman shows Leamington Coll., Eng., 1972, Western Instruments, 1993; 2-person show Doubletree Inn, 1994; exhibited in group shows Los Gatos Fellowship Gallery, 1983, Fremont Hub Shows, 1984, Santa Cruz Art League, 1984, San Jose, 1988, Los Gatos Art Assn., 1991, Triton Mus., 1992, Ventury Harbor Village Art Gallery, 1992-94, Ventura County Fair, 1993, City Hall, Ventura, Calif., 1995; author: (sketchbook) Seeing the Seaside, 1991; illustrator: Sword of the Teacher, 1996. Mem. Los Gatos Heritage Preservation Soc., 1978-90; pres. Los Gatos Friends of Arts, 1985-90. Named Arts Citizen of Yr., Town of Los Gatos, 1987; recipient awards for art, 1984—. Mem. Calif. Gold Coast Watercolor Soc. (signature mem.), Los Gatos Art Assn. Anglican. Avocations: grandchildren, husband, boating. Home: 607 Carpenteria Rd Aromas CA 95004-9718

ANDERSON, SCOTT A., electronics executive; BA in Elec. Engring. magna cum laude, U. Utah. Joined Motorola, Inc., 1978, microprocessor product engr. Semiconductor Products Sector, 1978, v.p., gen. mgr. custom specified integrated cir. microcontroller divsn., 1991—96, mng. dir., dep. gen. mgr. semiconductor products divsn. Nippon Motorola Ltd., 1996, corp. v.p., dir. Semiconductor Products Sector transition mgmt. orgn., 1998—99, sr. v.p., gen. mgr. Semiconductor Products Sector transp. and std. products group, exec. v.p., pres., CEO semiconductor products sector, 2003—. Mem.: Semiconductor Industry Assn. (bd. dirs.).

ANDERSON, SCOTT RICHARD, geologist, consultant; b. State College, Pa., Dec. 7, 1972; s. Richard Anderson and Marjorie Price, Denny Price (Stepfather) and Sarah Anderson (Stepmother); m. Heidi Renee Sykes, June 17, 1995; children: Kelly Rae children: Megan Rachel, Tyler Ryan, Julie Rosemary. BS with honors and high distinction, Pa. State U., 1995. Sr. geologist GeoTrans Inc., Sterling, Va., 1996—2003; earth scientist iii, project geologist Tetra Tech NUS, Inc., Pitts., 2003—. Geology mentor Geol. Soc. of Am., Seattle, 2003—03. Recipient A.P. Honess Geology award, Coll. Earth and Mineral Scis. Pa. State U., 1995, Geosci. Dept. Marshall, Coll. of Earth and Mineral Scis., 1995, Undergraduate Rsch. award, Pa. State U., 1995, Daniel E. Weber Math. award, 1993, Evan Pugh Scholar award, 1994. Mem.: Geol. Soc. Am. (assoc.). Achievements include discovery of soft tissue tongue containing bite mark and multiple insect meals from a 23 million year old tree frog preserved in Dominican Amber; research in frozen insect interactions and behaviors caught in amber; currently compiling and researching scientifically important mid-Cretaceous Burmite (amber from Myanmar) collection (over 600 specimens in 17 insect orders); emphasis is on social insects (evolutionarily primitive ants, termites and wasps). Avocation: golfing. Home: 609 Fieldstone Dr Moon Township PA 15108 Office: Tetra Tech NUS Inc 661 Andersen Dr Foster Plaza #7 Pittsburgh PA 15220-2700 Office Phone: 412-921-7090. Office Fax: 412-921-4040. Personal E-mail: scottranderson72@msn.com. Business E-Mail: andersons@ttnus.com.

ANDERSON, SCOTT ROBBINS, hospital administrator; b. Fargo, N.D., Mar. 25, 1940; BA, U. N.D., 1962; M Health Adminstrn., U. Iowa, 1964. Adminstrn. res. St. Luke's Methodist Hosp., Veteran's Adminstrn. Med. Ctr., Cedar Rapids, Iowa City, 1963-64; adminstrv. asst. North Meml. Med. Ctr., Robbinsdale, Minn., 1964-65, asst. dir., 1965-69, adminstr., 1969-76, v.p., 1976-81, pres., 1981—; pres., ceo North Meml. Med. Ctr. (now North Meml. Health Care), Robbinsdale, Minn., 1981—. Adj. prof. in field. Office: N Meml Health Care 3300 Oakdale Ave N Robbinsdale MN 55422-2926

ANDERSON, STANFORD OWEN, architect, architectural historian, educator; b. Redwood Falls, Minn., Nov. 13, 1934; s. Carl Alfred and Dora Helena (Paulson) A. BA, U. Minn., 1957; MA in Arch., U. Calif., Berkeley, 1958, postgrad., 1958-59; PhD, Columbia U., 1968. Registered arch., Mass. Tchr. Archtl. Assn., London, 1962-63, 74-78; co-dir. research project Inst. for Architecture and Urban Studies, N.Y.C., 1970-72, fellow, 1971-81; asst. prof. history and architecture MIT, 1963-69, assoc. prof., 1969-72, prof., 1972—, head dept. architecture, 1991—2005. Co-dir. archtl. transl. project Am. Acad. Arts and Scis., 1977-80; mem. adv. council Mcpl. Art Soc., City N.Y., 1972-78. Author: Hermann Muthesius: Style-Architecture and Building-Art, 1994, Peter Behrens: A New Architecture for the Twentieth Century, 2000; editor: Planning for Diversity and Choice, 1969, On Streets, 1978, Eladio Dieste: Innovation in Structural Art, 2004. Mem. Boston Landmarks Commn., 1980—87, Massport Designer Selection Panel, 1993—97; bd. dirs. Boston Preservation Alliance, 1989—91, Batuz Found. USA, 1997—, pres., 2000—04; bd. dirs. Fulbright Assn., 1998—2004, Boston Soc. Architects, 1992—2004; mem. Nat. Register Peer Profls., U.S. Gen. Svcs. Adminstrn., 2002—. Named AIA/ACSA Topaz Laureate, 2004, Hon. Citizen, Montevideo, Uruguay, 2004; Fulbright scholar, 1961-62; John Simon Guggenheim fellow, 1969-70; Graham Found. fellow, 1971; ACLS fellow, 1977-78; festschrift pub. in his honor, 1997. Mem. AIA, Assn. Collegiate Schs. Architecture, Boston Soc. Architects, Brit. Soc. for Philosophy of Sci., Coll. Art Assn., Soc. Archtl. Historians (dir. 1969-72, 76-77). Home: 63 Commercial Wharf Boston MA 02110-3814 Office: MIT Dept Architecture 77 Massachusetts Ave Cambridge MA 02139-4307 Office Phone: 617-253-1351. Business E-Mail: soa@mit.edu.

ANDERSON, STANTON DEAN, lawyer; b. Portland, Oreg., Oct. 18, 1940; s. Lloyd T. and Ruth M. (Bruns) A.; children: Stanton D. Jr., Mamie D. BA, Westmont Coll., 1962; JD, Willamette U., 1969. Bar: D.C. 1969. Staff asst. to pres. The White House, Washington, 1971-73; dep. asst. sec. US Dept. State, Washington, 1973-74; assoc. Surrey & Morse, Washington, 1975-76, ptnr., 1977-81, Anderson, Hibey & Blair, Washington, 1981—95, McDermott, Will & Emery, Washington, 1995—; exec. v.p., chief legal officer US C. of C., Washington, 2003—. Assoc. editor Willamette U. Law Rev. Mem. D.C. Reps. Cen. Com.; del. Rep. Nat. Conv. 1984. Mem. ABA, D.C. Bar Assn., City Club (Washington), Congl. Country Club (Bethesda, Md.), Robert Trent Jones Golf Club (Lake Manassas, Va.), Bear Lakes Country Club (West Palm Beach, Fla.). Office: McDermott Will & Emery 600 13th St NW Washington DC 20005-3096

ANDERSON, STASIA ANN, medical researcher; children: Erica Ann, Helen Elise, Ian Andrew. BS, Drexel Univ., Phila., 1992; PhD, Pa. State U., Univ. Pk., 1992—97. Postdoctoral rschr. Wash. U., St. Louis, 1997—99, Pharmacia Corp., St. Louis, 1999—2001; staff scientist NIH, Nat. Inst. Neurol. Disorders and Strokes, Bethesda, Md., 2001—05; head Mouse Imaging Core NIH, Nat. Heart Lung and Blood Inst., Bethesda, Md., 2005—. Recipient Top Basic Sci. Abstract, Acad. Molecular Imaging, 2002. Mem.: Soc. for Molecular Imaging, Internat. Soc. for Magnetic Resonance in Medicine. Achievements include research in cellular magnetic resonance imaging of stem cells and immune cells in cancer and autoimmune disease. Office: NIH 10 Center Dr B1N256 Bethesda MD 20892 Office Phone: 301-402-0908.

ANDERSON, STEFAN STOLEN, banker; b. Madison, Wis., Apr. 15, 1934; s. Theodore M. and Siri (Stolen) A.; m. Joan Timmermann, Sept. 19, 1959; children: Sharon Jill, Theodore Peter. AB magna cum laude, Harvard, 1956; MBA, U. Chgo., 1960; PhD (hon.), Ball State U., 1993. With Am. Nat. Bank & Trust Co. of Chgo., 1960—74, exec. v.p., 1969—74, 1st Mchts. Bank, Muncie, Ind., 1974, pres., 1979—98, chmn. bd. dirs., 1987—2005; pres., dir. First Mchts. Corp., Muncie, 1983—98, chmn. bd. dirs., 1987—2005; dir. Fed. Res. Bank of Chgo., 1991—97. Bd. dirs. Maxon Corp., 1985-2004, Techpoint Inc., Pub. Radio Capital Fund, 2000-03. Past pres. Delaware County United Way, Muncie Symphony Orch.; trustee Roosevelt U., 1970-74, George Francis Ball Found., BMH Found., Ziegler Found., Ind. State Mus. Found.; trustee, chmn. Minnitrista Cultural Found.; past chair Ind. Nature Conservancy; past pres. Cmty. Found. of Muncie and Delaware County. Mem. Ind. Acad., Skyline Club (Indpls.), Rotary (past pres.), Phi Beta Kappa, Beta Gamma Sigma. Home: 2705 W Twickingham Dr Muncie IN 47304-1050 Office: 1st Mchts Bank 200 E Jackson St Muncie IN 47305-2800

ANDERSON, STEPHEN HALE, federal judge; b. Salt Lake City, Jan. 12, 1932; m. Shirlee Gehring; 2 children. Student, Eastern Oreg. Coll. Edn., LaGrande, 1951, Brigham Young U., Provo, 1956; LLB, U. Utah, 1960. Bar: Utah 1960, U.S. Claims Ct. 1963, U.S. Tax Ct. 1967, U.S. Ct. Appeals (10th cir.) 1970, U.S. Supreme Ct. 1971, U.S. Ct. Appeals (9th cir.) 1972. Tchr. South H.S., Salt Lake City, 1956—57; trial atty. tax divsn. U.S. Dept. Justice, 1960—64; ptnr. Ray, Quinney & Nebeker, 1964—85; judge U.S. Ct. Appeals (10th cir.), Salt Lake City, 1985—. Spl. counsel Salt Lake County Grand Jury, 1975; mem. Nat. Jud. Coun. State and Fed. Cts., 1992—96; chmn. fed.-state jurisdiction com. Jud. Conf. U.S., 1995—98; ad hoc. com. on bankruptcy appellate panels 10th Cir. Jud. Coun., 1995—97; com. mem. U.S. Ct. Appeals (10th cir.). Editor (in chief): Utah Law Rev. With U.S. Army, 1953—55. Mem.: Am. Bar Found., Salt Lake County Bar Assn. (pres. 1977—78), Utah State Bar (pres. 1983—84), U. Utah Coll. Law Alumni Assn. (trustee 1979—83, pres. 1982—83), Salt Lake Area C. of C. (bd.govs. 1984), Order of Coif. Office: US Ct Appeals 4201 Fed Bldg 125 S State St Salt Lake City UT 84138-1102*

ANDERSON, SUSAN LEIGH, philosophy educator; b. Portland, Oreg., Nov. 13, 1944; d. Paul Lynge and Viola Fern (Malm) Smith; m. J. Brooks Colburn, Aug. 1969 (div. Mar. 1974); m. Michael Edward Anderson, Mar. 11, 1974; 1 child, Alexander Scott. AB, Vassar Coll., 1966; MA, UCLA, 1971, PhD, 1974. Teaching assoc. UCLA, 1968-70; instr. Calif. State U., Northridge, 1970-71; instr., asst. prof., assoc. prof. philosophy U. Conn., Stamford, 1972-91, prof., 1991—. Vis. asst. prof. Mt. Holyoke Coll., South Hadley, Mass., 1977. Author: On Kierkegaard, 2000, On Mill, 2000, On Dostoevsky, 2001; contbg. author: Falling in Love with Wisdom, 1993; editor: Guidebook for Publishing Philosophy, 1986; co-author logic software: Proof Reader 1986, 88; also articles. Fellow NEH, Princeton U., 1975, Brown U., 1978, U. Calif., Santa Cruz, 1992, Lilly fellow, Yale U., 1976, vis. faculty fellow Yale U., 1990-91; NSF grantee, 2005. Mem. Am. Philos. Assn. (Centenniel award 2002). Avocations: book collecting, antiquing. Office: U Conn Philosophy Dept One University Pl Stamford CT 06901-2315 Business E-Mail: susan.anderson@uconn.edu.

ANDERSON, TAD STEPHEN, landscape architect, consultant, photographer; b. Mpls., June 9, 1955; s. Rudolph Dennis and Verna Aurora (Young) A.; m. Kay Ann Weber, Jan. 22, 1987; children: Lena Mialisa, Rachel Aurora. Student, Utah State U., 1973-75, U. Minn., 1975-77. Landscape draftsman Minn. Valley Landscape, Bloomington, 1975-76; engring. dratfsman Temple Assoc. Civil Engrs., Wayzata, Minn., 1976; landscape designer Minn. Valley Landscape, Shakopee, Minn., 1976-78; owner, landscape designer, landscape archtl. cons. Anderson Design Svcs., Minnetonka, Minn., 1978—; artist, owner Anderson Editions Fine Art Prints, Minnetonka. Creative devel., designer "The Anderson Horticultural Series" of copyrighted horticultural design plans; pin. projects include U. Minn. Landscape Arboretun, Mpls., Anderson Arboretum, Litchfield, Minn., U. Minn. Landscape Aboretum, Chanhassen, Minn., 2003; designer several projects in nat. pubIs. Mem. Nat. Landscape Assn., Am. Soc. Media Photographers, N.Am. Native Photographers Assn., Garden Writers Assn. of Am., Am. Assn. Nurserymen, Am. Soc. Landscape Architects, Assn. Profl. Landscape Designers, Minn. State Horticultural Soc., Minn. Builders Assn., Minn. Nursery and Landscape Assn. (award of excellence 1989, 97, 98, 99, 2000, 04, 05, award of merit 1989, 94, 95, 97, 98, 99, 2000, 03, 04, award of design excellence 2003), Mpls. Builders Assn. (Roma award of excellence 1990), Internat. Sculpture Ctr. Independent. Avocations: photographer, sailor, sculptor, illustrator, skiing. Office: Anderson Design Svcs/Landscape & Anderson Photography PO Box 5264 Minnetonka MN 55343-2264 also: Anderson Editions Fine Art Prints Studio PO Box 5264 Minnetonka MN 55343-2264 E-mail: andersondesigns@cs.com.

ANDERSON, TERENCE JAMES, law educator; b. Chgo., Feb. 26, 1940; s. James E. and Charlotte (Flatley) A.; m. Carolyn Bugh; children: Michael, Kathleen, Jamie, Andrew. BA, Wabash Coll., 1961; JD, U. Chgo., 1964. Bar: Ill. 1967, D.C. 1973, Fla. 1977. Local cts. commr. Zomba, Malawa, Africa, 1964-66; assoc. Goldberg, Weigle, Mallin & Gitles, Chgo., 1966-69, ptnr., 1970-73; att. prof. Antioch Sch. of Law, Washington, 1973-78, acad. dean, 1975-76; vis. prof. U. Miami Sch. of Law, Coral Gables, Fla., 1976-78, prof., 1978—. Spl. counsel to gen. counsel SEC, Washington, summers 1980-81; dir. Legal Svcs. of Greater Miami, Inc., 1977-83. Author (with William Twining and David Schum): Analysis of Evidence, 1991, 2d edit., 2005; author: The Battles of Hastings: Four Stories in Search of a Meaning, 1996. Bd. dirs. ACLU of South Fla., 1981-85; mem. dist. admissions com. U.S. Dist. Ct. (so. dist.) Fla.; counsel to former U.S. Judge Alcee L. Hastings and now mem. Ho. of Reps., 1982—. Netherlands Inst. Advanced Studies fellow, 1994-95. Mem. ABA, Am. Assn. Law Schs. Office: Univ Miami Sch Law PO Box 248087 Miami FL 33124-8087 Office Phone: 305-284-2253.

ANDERSON, THEODORE ROBERT, physicist, small business owner; b. Lodi, Ohio, Jan. 30, 1949; s. Robert Anderson and LaVaughn (Mitchell) Gillotti. BS in Physics, Fla. State U., 1971; postgrad. in math. physics, U. Geneva, 1973, postgrad. in math. physics, 1975; MS in Physics, NYU, 1979, MS in Applied Sci., 1983, PhD in Physics, 1986. Nuc. engr. Gibbs & Hill Inc., NYC, 1980—83; rsch. physicist elec. boat divsn. Gen. Dynamics, Groton, Conn., 1983—88; rsch. physicist Naval Underwater Systems Ctr., New London, Conn., 1988—; co-founder, CEO Haleakala R & D Inc., Brookfield, Mass., 2002—; prin., owner Smart Bond Technologies Inc. Adj. prof. mech. engring., astronomy U. Conn., Storrs, Groton, 1983—; adj. prof. math. Mitchell Coll., New London, 1985, U. Hartford, 1990—; adj. prof. mech. and aero. engring., mgmt. and mech. engring. U. Bridgeport, 1989—; adj. prof. mech. and aero. engring. Hunter Coll.; adj. prof. physics and astronomy CUNY, 1979-83; adj. prof. physics L.I. Univ., 1980-83; adj. prof. elec. and mech. engring. Rensselaer Poly. Inst., Hartford, 1986—; adj. prof. Sch. Bus. U. New Haven, 1989—, mech. engring., 1983—, elec. engring., 1983—; rsch. prof. Rensselaer Poly. Inst., Troy, NY, U. Tenn. Elec. Engring. dept., Knoxville; instr. Cooper Union Sch. Engring., NYC, 1980; prin. investigator ASI Tech. Corp.; founder, CEO, chief tech. officer Haleokala Rsch. and Devel., Inc. Active Met. Opera Guild, NYC, 1986—, Mus. Modern Art, NYC, 1985—, Met. Mus. Art, NYC, 1984—, Am. Mus. Natural History, NYC, 1987—, NY Shakespeare Festival, 1987—, NY Zool. Soc., 1988—, Ea. Nat. Pk. and Monument Assn., 1990—; founder and CEO Haleakala Rsch. and Devel., Inc. Recipient Spl. Achievement award, USN, 1989, 1990. Mem. IEEE, Electromagnetic Compatibility Soc., Nat. Geog. Soc., Nat. Parks and Conservation Assn., Am. Phys. Soc., Soc. Rheology, Nat. Parks and Conservation Assn., The Adirondack Coun., The Nature Conservancy, The Smithsonian Assocs., World Powerlifting Alliance, Amnesty Internat., Wilderness Soc., World Wildlife Fund, Sierra Club, Greenpeace. Achievements include research in fluid dynamics, plasma physics, acoustics and atomic physics, electromagnetic interference, nuclear engineering solar cells; patents for plasma antenna, plasma waveguides and plasma frequency selective surfaces. Home and Office: 7 Martin Rd Brookfield MA 01506 Office Phone: 508-867-3918. Business E-Mail: anderdrted@aol.com, tedanderson@haleakala-research.com.

ANDERSON, THEODORE WELLINGTON, portfolio strategist; b. Napa, Calif., Apr. 30, 1941; s. Theodore William and Donna Elorita (Dove) A.; children: Thomas Wellington, Hilary Dove. Student, Princeton U., 1959-60; BA, Stanford U., 1963; MBA, U. Calif., Berkeley, 1966. Portfolio mgr., v.p. John W. Bristol Inc., N.Y.C., 1968-77; assoc. rsch. dir., sr. v.p Argus Rsch., N.Y.C., 1977-82; portfolio strategist The Ford Found., N.Y.C., 1982—. Mem. Fin. Analysts Fedn., N.Y. Soc. Security Analysts, DeBruce Fly Fishing Club, Angler's Club of N.Y., St. George's Soc. Episcopalian. Avocations: flyfishing, foreign languages and history, tennis, bamboo rod building. Home: PO Box 432 Chappaqua NY 10514-0432 Office: The Ford Found 320 E 43rd St New York NY 10017-4890 Personal E-mail: theodoreand@msn.com. Business E-Mail: t.anderson@fordfound.org.

ANDERSON, THEODORE WILBUR, statistics educator; b. Mpls., June 5, 1918; s. Theodore Wilbur and Evelynn (Johnson) A.; m. Dorothy Fisher, July 8, 1950; children: Robert Lewis, Janet Lynn, Jeanne Elizabeth. BS with highest distinction, Northwestern U., 1939, DSc, 1989; MA, Princeton U., 1942, PhD, 1945; LittD, North Park U., 1988; PhD (honoris causa), U. Oslo, 1997; D (hon.), U. Athens, 1999. Asst. dept. math. Northwestern U., 1939-40; instr. math. Princeton U., 1941-43, rsch. assoc., 1943-45, Cowles Commn., U. Chgo., 1945-46; staff Columbia U., 1946-67, successively instr. math. stats., asst. prof., assoc. prof., 1946-56, prof., 1956-67, chmn. math. stats. dept., 1956-60, 64-65, acting chmn., 1950-51, 63; prof. stats. and econs. Stanford U., 1967-88, prof. stats. and econs. emeritus, 1988—. Dir. project Office Naval Rsch., 1950-82; prin. investigator NSF project, 1969-92, Army Rsch. Office project, 1982-92; vis. prof. math. U. Moscow, 1968; vis. prof. stats. U. Paris, 1968; vis. prof. econs. NYU, 1983-84; acad. visitor math. Imperial Coll. Sci. and Tech., U. London, 1967-68, London Sch. Econs. and Polit. Sci., 1974-75, U. So. Calif., 1989; C.G. Khatri Meml. lectr. Pa. State U., 1992; rsch. visitor Tokyo Inst. Tech., 1977; sabbaticant IBM Systems Rsch. Inst., 1984; rsch. assoc. Naval Postgrad. Sch., 1986-87; cons. RAND Corp., 1949-66; mem. com. on basic rsch. adv. Office Ordnance Rsch., Nat. Acad. Scis.-NRC, 1955-58; mem. panel on applied math. adv. Nat. Bur. Standards, 1964-65; chmn. com. on stats. NRC, 1961-63; mem. exec. com. Conf. Bd. Math. Scis., 1963-64; com. on support rsch. in math. scis. NAS, 1965-68; mem. com. Pres.'s Statis. Socs., 1962-64; sci. dir. NATO Advanced Study Inst. on Discriminant Analysis and Its Applications, 1972. Author: An Introduction to Multivariate Statistical Analysis, 1958, 3d edit., 2003, The Statistical Analysis of Time Series, 1971, (with Somesh Das Gupta and George P.H. Styan) A Bibliography of Multivariate Statistical Analysis, 1972, (with Stanley Sclove) Introductory Statistical Analysis, 1974, An Introduction to the Statistical Analysis of Data, 1986, (with Jeremy D. Finn) The New Statistical Analysis of Data, 1996; editor: (with Krishna B. Athreya and Donald L. Iglehart) Probability, Statistics and Mathematics: Papers in Honor of Samuel Karlin, 1989, (with Kai Tai Fang) Statistical Inference in Elliptically Contoured and Related Distributions, 1990; (with K.T. Fang and I. Olkin) Multivariate Analysis and Its Applications, 1994; editor Anns. of Math. Stats., 1950-52; assoc. editor jour. Time Series Analysis, 1980-88; mem. adv. bd. Econometric Theory, 1985—, Jour. Multivariate Analysis, 1988—; mem. editl. bd. Psychometrika, 1954-72. Recipient R.A. Fisher award Pres.'s Statis. Socs., 1985, Disting. Alumnus award North Park Coll. and Theol. Sem., 1987, Minnehaha Acad., 1992, Award of Merit Northwestern U. Alumni Assn., 1989; named Wesley C. Mitchell Vis. Prof. Columbia U., 1983-84; Guggenheim fellow, 1947-48, fellow Ctr. for Advanced Study in Behavioral Scis., 1957-58; vis. scholar, 1972-73, 80; Sherman Fairchild disting. scholar Calif. Inst. Tech., 1980; vis. disting. prof. Norwegian Coun. Sci. and Indsl. Rsch. U. Oslo; Abraham Wald Meml. lectr., 1982; S.S. Wilks lectr. Princeton U., 1983, P.C. Mahalanobis Meml. lectr., 1985, S.N. Roy Meml. lectr. Calcutta U., 1985, Allen T. Craig lectr. U. Iowa, 1991, C.G. Khatri Meml. lectr. Pa. State U., 1992, George Zyskind Meml. lectr. Iowa State U., 1995. Fellow AAAS (chmn. sect. 1990-91), Am. Statis. Assn. (v.p. 1971-73, Samuel S. Wilks Meml. medal 1988, R.A. Fisher lectr. 1985), Econometric Soc., Royal Statis. Soc., Inst. Math. Stats. (pres. 1963), Am. Acad. Arts and Scis.; mem. NAS, Am. Math. Soc., Internat. Statis. Insts., Bernouilli Soc. for Math. Stats. and Probability, Norwegian Acad. Sci. and Letters (fgn.), Phi Beta Kappa. Achievements include research in multivariate statistical analysis, time series analysis, and econometrics. Home: 746 Santa Ynez St Stanford CA 94305-8441 Office: Stanford U Dept Stats Stanford CA 94305-4065 Office Phone: 650-723-4732. Business E-Mail: twa@stanford.edu.

ANDERSON, THOMAS DUNAWAY, retired lawyer; b. Oklahoma City, Mar. 9, 1912; s. Frank Ervin and Burdine (Clayton) A.; m. Helen Sharp, Feb. 21, 1938; children: Helen Shaw, Lucille Streeter, John Sharp. Student, Rice Inst., 1930-31; LLB, Washington and Lee U., 1934; LLD (hon.), Lambuth Coll., 1967. Bar: Va. 1933, Tex. 1934. Assoc. Andrews & Kurth, 1934-41, 46-47; sr. v.p., trust officer Tex. Commerce Bank, Houston, 1947-51, 60-65; co-founder Tex. Fund, 1949; pres. Tex. Fund Mgmt. Co., Houston, 1952-60; ptnr. Anderson Brown & Jones, Houston, 1965-93; ret. Trustee emeritus Washington and Lee U.; life mem., past pres. bd. visitors M.D. Anderson Cancer Ctr.; past pres., chmn. Kelsey Rsch. Fedn., Protestant Episcopal Ch. Coun., Diocese of Tex., Washington-on-Brazos State Park Assn., Mus. Fine Arts Houston, Houston Grand Opera; bd. dirs. Bayou Bend Gardens Endowment, Retina Rsch. Found., Harris County Hist. Commn. First recipient Leon Jaworski award for vol. cmty. svc., 1988. Mem. ABA, Tex. Bar Assn., Philos. Soc. Tex., Bayou, Eagle Lake Rod and Gun Club, Houston Country Club, Petroleum Club of Houston, River Oaks Garden Club (hon.), SAR, Omicron Delta Kappa, Phi Delta Phi. Episcopalian. Office: River Oaks Bank Bldg 2001 Kirby Dr Houston TX 77019-6033

ANDERSON, TIMOTHY CHRISTOPHER, educational association administrator; b. Hinsdale, Ill., Dec. 27, 1950; s. Paul Eugene and Mary Agnes (Donnell) Anderson. BA in Polit. Sci. with honors, Boston Coll., 1973; MPA, Harvard U., 2000. Rsch. asst. to Rep. Thomas P. O'Neill U.S. Ho. Reps., Washington, 1973; ednl. cons. E. F. Shelly Co., 1973—74; assoc. dir. Boston Zool. Soc., 1974—76, exec. dir. and adminstr. Boston's two zoos, 1976—81; New Eng. regional v.p. Nat. Alliance Bus., 1981—83; pres. Dovetail Cons., Hull, Mass., 1983—2001, Boston Harbor Assocs., 1983—87; ecology coord. Hull Pub. Schs., 1992—93; dir. Hull Environment and Svc. Corps, 1992—94; founder, CEO South Shore Charter Sch., 1994—99, headmaster, 1994—97; founder and pres. World Computer Exch., Hull, 1999—. Bd. dirs. VSAarts Mass., 1997—, chmn. bd. dirs., 1998—2001, 2005—, vice chmn. bd. dirs., 2004—05; spl. projects dir. South Shore Edn. Collaborative, 1993—94; cons. NEH, 1977—78; trustee, chmn. bd. dirs. South Shore Charter Sch., 1994—95; chmn. bd. dirs. W. Seavey Joyce SJ Award, 1988—. Mem. woring group on access UN ICT Task Force, 2003—; mem. Global Digital Divide Task Force World Econ. Forum, 2001—03. Named Hon. Prof. Tbilisi Orbeliani, State Pedagogical U., 2002, Hon. Citizen, Kutaisi, Georgia; recipient Cmty. Svc. award, Girl Scouts Greater Boston, 1978, Leadership Commendation award, Nat. Alliance Bus., 1983, Leadership award, Mass. Cultural Alliance, 1986, Pres.'s award, 1986, Leadership award, Franklin Pk. Coalition, 1987, Boston Mgmt. Consortium, 1992, John Ames award, Boston Harbor Assocs., 1987, Mayor's cert. of recognition, 1992, Supts. Leadership award, 1992, Excellence award, South Shore Charter Sch. Students, 1999, badge of honor, Republic of Georgia, 2002. Office: World Computer Exch 936 Nantasket Ave Hull MA 02045-1453 Office Phone: 781-925-3078. E-mail: tanderson@worldcomputerexchange.org.

ANDERSON, TIMOTHY J., chemical engineering professor; Prof., assoc. dean rsch. and grad. programs U. Fla., Gainsville. Recipient Charles M.A. Stine award in Materials Engring. and Sci. Am. Inst. Chem. Engrs., 1994. Office: U Fla Dept Chem Engring 229 Che Bldg/Box 116005 Gainesville FL 32611-6005 Office Phone: 352-392-0946.

ANDERSON, URTON LIGGETT, accounting educator; b. Salem, Ohio, Dec. 10, 1951; s. Urton and Alice (Kenrich) A.; m. Deborah Mary Johnson, June 12, 1973; children: Bryony, Urton. BA in Greek and Philosophy magna cum laude, St. Olaf Coll., 1974; MA in Classics, U. Minn, 1977; PhD in Bus. Adminstrn., U. Minn., 1985. Instr. dept. acctg. U. Tex., Austin, 1984-85, asst. prof. dept. acctg., 1988-89, assoc. prof. dept. acctg., 1989-95, prof. dept. acctg., 1995—, assoc. dir. C. Aubrey Smith Ctr. for Auditing Edn. and Rsch., 1989-92, dir. C. Aubrey Smith Ctr. for Auditing Edn. and Rsch., 1992-93, acting dept. chair, 1996, assoc. dean ubdergrad. programs Coll. Bus., 1997—. Clark W. Thompson Jr. prof. in acctg. edn. U. Tex., Austin, 1997—. Author: Quality Asurance for Internal Auditing, 1983; co-editor: Internal Auditing, 1990—2001; contbr. articles to profl. jours.;: Implementing the Professional Practices Framework, 2002. Rsch. fellow KPMG Peat Marwick Found., 1988-89, faculty fellow, 1990-92, Rsch. Opportunities in Auditing grantee, 1991, 94, Ernst & Young faculty fellow, 1988-93, Atlantic Richfield Centennial fellow in acctg., 1993-97. Mem. Inst. Internal Auditors Rsch. Found. (bd. rsch. advisors 1985-94), Inst. Internal Auditors (bd. regents 1994-99, 2003—, chmn. 2003—, internal auditing standards bd. 1999-2003, chair 2002-03, cert. internal auditor, cert. control self-assessment, cert. govt. audit profl). Office: U Tex Austin Dept Acctg CBA 4M 202 Austin TX 78712-1172 Office Phone: 512-471-9481. E-mail: urton@mail.utexas.edu.

ANDERSON, VERA STRONG, retired dentist; b. Mound Bayou, Miss., Aug. 5, 1931; d. Will Clarence and Charlotte Montgomery Strong; m. Arthur Ray Anderson, Apr. 21, 1955; children: Arthur Ray Jr., Lisa LaMarr. BS, Tenn. State U., 1953; DDS, Meharry Med. Coll., 1957. Practiced dentistry, Memphis, 1960—65; intern Cambridge State Hosp.; pres., founder An-Strong Symbols, Inc., nonprofit corp., Richmond, Calif., 1992—. Designer African Am. flag, motivational spkr. in promotion of racial harmony. Recipient Offcl. Citation, Gary Common Coun., 1993, Commendation award, County of Alameda 4th Dist., 1993, Cert. Recognition, Calif. Legis. Assembly, 1994, Cert. Appreciation, Golden Gate U. NAACP, 1997. Democrat. Office: An-Strong Symbols Inc PO Box 2725 Richmond CA 94801

ANDERSON, VINTON RANDOLPH, bishop; b. Somerset, Bermuda; came to U.S., 1947; m. Vivienne Louise Cholmondeley, 1952; children: Vinton Jr., Jeffrey, Carlton, Kenneth. BA, Wilberforce U., HHD (hon.), 1973; MDiv, Payne Theol. Sem., 1952; MA in Philosophy, Kans. U., 1962; postgrad., Yale U. Div. Sch.; DD (hon.), Paul Quinn Coll., Payne Theol. Sem., Temple Bible Coll., Interdenom. Theol. Sem., Eden Theol. Sem.; LHD (hon.), Morris Brown Coll., ITC Seminary, Eder Theol. Ordained to ministry A.M.E. Ch., 1952, bishop, 1972. Pastor various chs. in Kans. and Mo., 1952-72; presiding bishop A.M.E. Ch., Ala., 1972-76, presiding bishop, chief pastor, 1976-84, dir. Office of Ecumenical Rels. and Devel., 1984-88, presiding bishop 5th Episcopal dist., 1988-96; presiding bishop 2nd Episcopal district A.M.E. church, Washington D.C., 1996—. Chmn. bd. dirs. Payne Theol. Sem., Xenia, Ohio; preacher, lectr. in Caribbean, Republic of South and West Africa, Middle East, Europe, South Pacific; del. World Meth. conf., Nairobi, Kenya, 1986; mem. exec. com. World Meth. Coun., 1981—, 1st v.p. N.Am. region; v.p. Consultation on Ch. Union; mem. Gen. Commn. Christian Unity and Interreligious Concern, United Meth. Ch.; pres. World Coun. Chs., 1991—, del. 7th assembly, moderator liaison com. of hist. black chs.; mem. governing bd., faith and order Nat. Coun. Chs.; charter mem., v.p. Congress Nat. Black Chs. Founder, editor Connector, info. publ.; editor A Syllabus for Celebrating the Bicentennial; contbr. articles to profl. jours. Mem. nat. adv. com. on the black population 1990 U.S. Census; mem. Nat. Commn. on Sch./Community Role in Improving Adolescent Health; mem. nat. adv. bd. Schomburg Ctr. for Rsch. in Black Culture; immediate past chairperson bd. trustees Wilberforce U.; chairperson bd. dirs. Payne Theol. Sem. Recipient Ann. Religion award Ebony mag., 1988, Disting. Alumni Honoree award Nat. Assn. for Equal Opportunity in Higher Edn., 1991. Home: 1134 11th St NW Washington DC 20001 Office: AME Ch 2562 Martin Luther King Jr Ave Washington DC 20020-5247

ANDERSON, W. FRENCH, biochemist, physician; b. Tulsa, Okla., Dec. 31, 1936; m. Kathryn D. Anderson, June 24, 1961. AB magna cum laude, Harvard U., 1958, MD magna cum laude, 1963; MA, Cambridge U., 1960; LHD (hon.), U. Okla., 1992; DSc (hon.), U. Tulsa, 1996, SUNY, 2002. Diplomate Nat. Bd. Med. Examiners, 1964, lic. DC, 1963. Intern pediatric medicine Children's Hosp. Med. Ctr., Boston, 1963—64; rsch. fellow Harvard Med. Sch., Boston, 1964—65; rsch. assoc. lab. biochem. genetics Nat. Heart, Lung & Blood Inst., 1965-67, rsch. med. officer, 1967-68, head sect. human biochem., 1968-71, head sect. molecular hematology, 1971-73, chief molecular hematology br., 1973-92; cons. in rsch., genetics program George Wash. U., 1975—78; prof. biochemistry and pediatrics, dir. gene therapy labs. U. So. Calif. Norris Cancer Ctr., 1992—, program coord. for gene therapy, 1995—; adj. prof., grad. genetics program George Wash. U., 1978—92. Rsch. fellow bacteriology and immunology med. sch. Harvard U., 1964—65; prof. lectr. sch. medicine George Washington U., 1967—75; mem. faculty dept. genetics Grad. Program, NIH, 1967—92; mem. dept. medicine & physiology NIH, 1981—92, chmn. dept. medicine & physiology, 1984—92; mem. heart fellow bd. Nat. Heart & Lung Inst., NIH, 1968—70; mem. task force hemoglobinopathies Nat. Heart, Lung and Blood Inst., NIH, 1972, mem. nat. task group on Cooley's anemia, 1977—78; pres. Assembly of Scientists, Nat. Heart, Lung and Blood Inst., NIH, 1982; chmn., inter-agy. coord. com. on Cooley's anemia NIH, 1972—77, chmn. inter-agy. coord. com. on Cooley's anemia, HEW, 1975—77; mem. exec. com. & bd. dirs. Found. Adv. Educ. in Scis., Inc., nih, 1984—92; mem. working group human gene therapy, recombinant DNA adv. com. NIH, 1984—86, mem. working group on viruses, recombinant DNA adv. com., 1985—86; hematology program dir. Lab Molecular Hematology, NIH, 1985; mem. coord. com. human genome NIH, 1988—92; mem. sr. exec. sci. svc. Dept. Health and Human Svc., 1980—92; cons. Pres. Commn. Study Ethical Problems Medicine & Biomed. Behavior Rsch., 1981—82, Human Gene Therapy Ctr. for Bioethics, Kennedy Inst. Ethics, Wash., DC, 1982—92; chmn. sci. adv. bd. Genetic Therapy Inc., Gaithersburg, Md., 1986—87; mem. sci. adv. bd. S/L Health Care Ventures, N.Y.C., 1986—88, N.Y.C., 1993—; cons. human gene therapy St. Jude Childrens Rsch. Hosp., Memphis, 1990—92, U. Pitt., 1990—92, Baylor Coll. Medicine, Houston, 1990—92, M.D. Anderson Hosp., Houston, 1990—92; chmn. scientific adv. com. Children's Nat. Med. Ctr., Wash., DC, 1990—92; lectr. Mider Lecture, NIH, 1992, Timely Topics Lecture, U.S. and Can. Acad. Pathology, 1992, Frontiers in Clin. Sci. Lecture, Am. Fedn. Clin. Rsch., 1992, Myron Karon Meml. Lectureship, Children's Hosp., L.A., 1992, Disting. Sci. Lecture, Internat. and Am. Assns. Dental Rsch., 1993, Plenary Lecture, 17th Internat. Congress of Genetics, 1993, Martin Meml. Lecture, 79th Ann. Clin. Congress, Am. Coll. Surgeons, 1993, Plenary Lecture, Am. Acad. Pediatrics, 1993, others; bd. dirs. various; mem. Inst. Genetic Medicine, U. So. Calif. Sch. Medicine, 1992—; vis. assoc. in applied physics Calif. Inst. Tech., 2001—. Co-editor: Fifth Cooley's Anemia Symposium, 1985; mem. editl. bd. various publs. Mem. med. resources coun. Cooley's Anemia Blood & Rsch. Found for Children, 1974-77; mem. adv. bd. Cooley's Anemia Found., Inc., 1977—; mem. sci. adv. com. Children's Hosp. Rsch. Found., Cin., 1985-88; commd. officer USPHS, 1965-67. Recipient Thomas B. Cooley award Sci. Achievement Cooley's Anemia Blood & Rsch. Found. for Children, 1977, Mary Ann Liebert Biotherapeutic award, 1991, Pres. Award lectr. Am. Thoracic Soc., 1991, Maude L. Menten award U. Pitts., 1991, Ralph R. Braund award U. Tenn., 1991, Presdl. Meritorious Exec. Rank award HHS, 1991, Fed. Lab. Consortium award for Excellence in Tech. Transfer, 1992, Disting. Svc. award Nat. Ctr. Infectious Diseases, 1993, Dr. Murray Thelin award Nat. Hemophilia Found., 1993, Drew award lectr., 1993, King Faisal ibn Abdul Aziz Internat. Prize for Medicine, 1994, NORD Leadership award Nat. Orgn. Rare Disorders, 1996, Am. Assn. Clin. Chemistry award, 2001; named BioPharm Person of Yr. Biopharm Mag. editl. adv. bd., 1994. Fellow AAAS; mem. Assn. Am. Physicians, Am. Soc. Clin. Investigation, Am. Soc. Hematology, Am. Soc. Human Genetics, Am. Soc. Biol. Chemists, Am. Fedn. Clin. Rsch., Am. Soc. Gene Therapy, Internat. Soc. Stem Cell Rsch., Peripatetic Club. Achievements include research in regulation of RNA and protein synthesis, hemoglobin biosynthesis, thalassemia and hemoglobinopathies, gene expression in mammalian cells, genetic engineering of mammalian cells, human gene therapy. 10 patents issued. Office: U So Calif Keck Sch Medicine Norris Cancer Ctr Rm 6316 1441 Eastlake Ave Los Angeles CA 90033 E-mail: sdiaz@genome2.hsc.usc.edu.

ANDERSON, WALTER HERMAN, editor, educator; b. Mt. Vernon, NY, Aug. 31, 1944; s. Walter Henry and Ethel Magdalena (Crolly) Anderson; m. Loretta Gritz, Sept. 9, 1967; children: Eric Christian, Melinda Christe. AA, Westchester C.C., 1970; BS summa cum laude, Mercy Coll., 1972; DHL (hon.), St. Ambrose U., 1988, Clemson U., 1990, Mercy Coll., 1989, U. of the Pacific, 1990. Reporter Reporter Dispatch, White Plains, NY, 1967—68, night city editor, 1968—69, editor, gen. mgr., 1975—77; police reporter Westchester Rockland Newspapers, White Plains, NY, 1969—70, help editor for action line, 1970—71, investigative reporter, 1971—72, mng. editor, 1973—74; editor, gen, mgr. Standard Star, New Rochelle, NY, 1974—75; sr. editor Parade mag., N.Y.C., 1977—78, mng. editor, 1978—80, editor-in-chief, 1980—2000, chmn., CEO, 2000—. Author: Courage is a Three-Letter Word, 1986, The Greatest Risk of All, 1988, Read With Me, 1990, The Confidence Course, 1997, Meant to Be, 2003; actor(one-man show): Talkin' Stuff, 1992. Chmn. bd. trustees Mercy Coll, Dobbs Ferry, NY, 1980—88; bd. dirs. St. Vincent Hosp., 1975—80, N.Y. Vietnam Vets. Leadership Program Inc., 1984—89, Dropout Prevention Fund, 1987—, Nat. Ctr. for Family Literacy, 1990—, Very Spl. Arts, 1990—; bd. advisors Naval Postgrad. Sch., 1988—; mem. nat. adv. bd. Lit. Vols., 1990—2002; apptd. to U.S. Commn. on Librs. and Info. Sci., Pres. Clinton, 1995—2001. With USMC, 1961—66. Recipient Frank Tripp Meml. award, Gannett Group, 1971, Tree of Life award, Jewish Nat. Fund, 1988, Spirit of Am. award, 1988, Napoleon Hill Gold award, 1989, Horatio Alger award, 1994, Literacy Vols. of Am. Stars in Literacy cert., 1990, others. Mem.: Soc. Silurians, Overseas Press, Psi Chi, Sigma Delta Chi. Office: Parade Publs Inc 711 3rd Ave New York NY 10017-4014 *I hope a single driving desire remains with me always— that is, to encourage talented people. To share, even in the least of ways, in the growth of a creative talent is the highest goal of an editor, if his career is to matter at all.*

ANDERSON, WARREN MATTICE, lawyer; b. Bainbridge, N.Y., Oct. 16, 1915; s. Floyd E. and Edna (Mattice) Anderson; m. Eleanor C. Sanford, June 28, 1941 (dec. Sept. 1996); children: Warren David, Lawrence, Richard, Thomas; m. Ruth W. Bennett, Aug. 25, 2001. BA, Colgate U., 1937; JD, Albany Law Sch., 1940, LLD (hon.), 1979, Hartwick Coll., 1976, Coll. of New Rochelle, 1979, Fordham U., 1980, Union Coll., 1981, Colgate U., 1982, Hamilton Coll., 1985, Clarkson U., 1987, St. Lawrence U., 1988, Elmira Coll., 1989, St. Francis Coll., 1991; LHD (hon.), Hofstra U., 1987. Bar: N.Y., 1940. Practice in, Binghamton; asst. county atty. Broome County, N.Y., 1940-42; assoc. Hinman, Howard & Kattell LLP, 1949-52; ptnr. Hinman, Howard & Kattell, 1952—; mem. N.Y. State Senate, 1953-88, chmn. fin. com., 1966-72, pres. pro tem, majority leader, 1973-88. Del. Rep. Nat. Conv., 1972, 76, 80, 84, 88, mem. platform com., 1972; trustee Colgate U., 1964-70, Cornell U., 1973-88, Elmira Coll., 1989-95; mem. N.Y. State Commn. on Jud. Nominations; mem. Hartwick Coll. Coun.; mem. adv. com. Govt. Law Ctr., Albany Law Sch.; mem. bd. overseers Nelson A. Rockefeller Inst. Govt. With AUS, 1943-45, lt. JAGD, 1945-46. Recipient Alumni award Colgate U., 1972 Fellow Am. Bar Found.; mem. ABA, Broome County Bar Assn. Clubs: Binghamton; Oteyokwa Lake (Hallstead, Pa.). Presbyterian. Home: 34 Lathrop Ave Binghamton NY 13905-4343 Office: Hinman Howard & Kattell 700 Security Mut Bldg Binghamton NY 13902-5250 Office Phone: 607-723-5341.

ANDERSON, WARREN RONALD, electrical engineering educator; b. July 31, 1914; s. Wallace Roy and Helen Adelia (Abrahamson) A.; m. Dantza Peinovich, May 28, 1945; children: Richard Godfrey, John Warren, Deborah Annete. AA, Bethel Coll., 1935; BS, U. Minn., 1939; BSEE, La. State U., 1944. Registered profl. engr., Calif. Design engr. Plant Engring. Agy., Phila., 1945-46; circuits engr. Automatic Electric, Chgo., 1946; prof. elec. engring. Calif. Polytech. State U., San Luis Obispo, 1946-76, head elec. engring. dept., 1976-79, prof. emeritus, 1979—. Design engr. GE, Ft. Wayne, Ind., 1951; rsch. analyst Northup Aircraft, Hawthorne, Calif., 1952; sys. engr. Western Gear Corp., Lynwood, Calif., 1955; edn. cons. GE, Schenectady, 1956. Leader Boy Scouts Am., San Luis Obispo, 1958-64. With U.S. Army, 1942-45. Recipient Cert of Appreciation AIEE, 1963. Mem. IEEE, NSPE, Am. Soc. Engring. Edn., Calif. Soc. Profl. Engrs. (dir. 1949-55), Calif. State Employees Assn. (dir. 1955-59), Eta Kappa Nu. Democrat. Baptist. Home: 573 Jeffrey Dr San Luis Obispo CA 93405-1003 Office: Calif Poly State Univ Elec Engring Dept San Luis Obispo CA 93407 Office Phone: 805-543-1326. Personal E-mail: wanderso@charter.net. Business E-Mail: wanderso@calpoly.edu.

ANDERSON, WAYNE CARL, public information officer, retired corporate financial executive; b. Sheboygan, Wis., May 5, 1935; s. Chester Phillip and Mabel Mary (Edler) A.; m. Joan Dorothy Staranick, May 18, 1963; children: David Wayne, Steven Michael, Karen Colleen. BS in Bus. Adminstrn., Upsala Coll., 1977. Cert. arbitrator, mediator. Dir. state govt. rels. Nabisco Brands Co., Parsippany, N.J., 1974-78, dir. fed. govt. rels., 1978-79, dir. govt. rels., 1979-81, v.p. govt. rels., 1981-84, v.p. govt. and cmty. rels., 1984-87, v.p. pub. affairs, 1987; non-lawyer exec. Evans Kitchel & Jenckes, P.C., 1988-89; pres., CEO Ariz. C. of C., 1990-95; exec. v.p. Americare, 1996-98; exec. emeritus Thunderbird--The Am. Grad. Sch. Internat. Mgmt., 1999—. Guest lectr. in field. Editl. adv. bd. Pub. Affairs in Rev., 1980; contbr. articles to profl. jours. Mem. Roseland (N.J.) Planning Bd., 1978—79, Roseland Citizens Adv. Com., 1977—78; trustee State Govt. Rsch. and Edn. Found., 1981—82; mem. gov.'s adv. coun. on quality, 1991—95, gov.'s commn. econ. devel., 1991—95, Ariz. Space Commn., 1992—2000, commr. emeritus, 1996; bd. dirs. Ariz. Quality Alliance, 1992—95, NCCJ, Fiesta Bowl Com., Ariz. Econ. Forum, Ariz. Utility Investors, Philos. Soc. Ariz., 2001—04; statewide com. chmn. Superbowl XXX, 1995—96; chmn. adv. bd. NYU, Baruch Coll., U. N.Y.; pres. Grace Luth. Ch., Livingston, NJ, 1980—81, chmn. bd. elders, 1981—82; trustee Evang. Luth. Synod, 2003—; elder Redeemer Luth. Ch., Scottsdale, Ariz., 1997—98, v.p., 1998—; pres. State Govtl. Affairs Coun. Served with U.S. Army, 1958—60. Mem. Internat. Jaycees (senator 1989—), U.S. Jaycees (nat. dir. 1964-65), Pub. Affairs Coun. (exec. com. 1986, bd. dirs. 1988—), Nat. Fgn. Trade Coun. (dir. 1986), State Govt. Affairs Coun. (past pres. 1978-79), Ford's Theatre (bd. govs.), Acad. Polit. Sci., Pub. Affairs Profls. Ariz. (founder 1987—), World Affairs Coun. (pres. 1994-95), Thunderbird Am. Grad. Sch. Internat. Mgmt., Thunderbird Global Coun. E-mail: wayneanderson@cox.net.

ANDERSON, WAYNE LEROY, music educator; b. Superior, Wisc., Aug. 19, 1949; s. Marvin Wayne and Margaret LaVerne Anderson; m. Lois Helen Kolzow, May 27, 1972; children: Jennifer, Katherine. MusB, U.Wisc., 1971. Choral dir. Cashton Pub. Schools, 1971—73, Antigo Pub. Schools, 1973—2004; voice instr. Wausau Conservatory Music, 2004—. Co-author: (audio tape) Fly Fishing the Wolf River. Home: N 4324 Highland Dr White Lake WI 54491

ANDERSON, WES (WESLEY WALES ANDERSON), film director; b. Houston, May 1, 1969; BA in Philosophy, U. Tex., 1991. Writer, dir.: (films) Bottle Rocket, 1994; writer, prodr., dir. Rushmore, 1998; The Royal Tenenbaums, 2001; The Life Aquatic with Steve Zissou, 2004. Office: UTA 5th Fl 9560 Wilshire Blvd Beverly Hills CA 90212*

ANDERSON, WILLIAM, JR., (WILLIAM ALBION ANDERSON JR.), management consultant; b. Paris, Ark., July 12, 1939; s. William A. and Maud (Rodgers) A.; m. Patricia P. Puterbaugh, July 5, 1968; stepchildren— Charles L. Kuehn, Cynthia P. Robinson. BSBA, U. Ark., 1961; MBA, Harvard U., 1963. With Blyth Eastman Dillon & Co., Inc., N.Y.C., 1963-75, exec. asst. to chief exec. officer, dir. planning, 1973-74, sr. v.p., 1974-75; sr. v.p., chief fin. officer ENSTAR Corp., Houston, 1975-84; pres. Farmers Oil Co., 1987-96; ltd. ptnr. Weller, Anderson, & Co., Ltd., Houston, 1988—2003. Mng. trustee J. G. Puterbaugh Trust.; cons. Eastman, Dillon Oil & Gas Assocs. Mem. River Oaks Country Club (Houston), The Houston Club. Office: 2001 Kirby St Ste 1300 Houston TX 77019 Personal E-mail: banderson@lucianmorrison.com.

ANDERSON, WILLIAM BANKS, JR., ophthalmology educator; b. Durham, NC, June 14, 1931; s. William Banks and Mildred Ursula (Everett) A.; m. Nancy Eldridge Walker, Sept. 17, 1960; children: Mary Banks, Mark Eldridge, Elizabeth Perry. AB, Princeton U., 1952; MD, Harvard U., 1956. Diplomate: Am. Bd. Ophthalmology (dir. 1986-92). Intern Duke U. Med. Ctr., Durham, N.C., 1956-57, resident, 1959-62, asst. prof. ophthalmology, 1962-67, assoc. prof. ophthalmology, 1967-76, prof. ophthalmology, 1976—, acting chmn., 1991-92. Mem. profl. adv. com. N.C. Div. Services to the Blind, Raleigh, 1972-84 Chmn. bd. trustees Durham Acad., 1975-77. Served to capt. M.C. U.S. Army, 1957-59. Fellow ACS; mem. Am. Ophthalmol. Soc. (sec.-treas. 1989-98, v.p. 1998-99, pres. 1999-2000), Am. Acad. Ophthalmology (bd. dirs. 1986-89), Am. Bd. Ophthalmology (bd. dirs. 1986-93). Episcopalian. Home: 2401 Cranford Rd Durham NC 27705-1011 Office: Duke U Eye Ctr Box 3802 Erwin Rd Durham NC 27710

ANDERSON, WILLIAM CARL, association executive, environmental engineer, consultant; b. Vinton, Iowa, Sept. 24, 1943; s. Ivan D. and Lois B. (Schlotterback) A.; m. Elizabeth A. Dingman, Nov. 12, 1966; children: William Carl III, Erica Dawn. BSCE, Iowa State U., 1967. Registered profl. engr., N.Y., N.J., Pa., Iowa; diplomate Am. Acad. Environ. Engrs. Dir. environ. health Cayuga County Health Dept., Auburn, N.Y., 1969-73; owner Pickard & Anderson, Auburn, 1973—; trustee Am. Acad. Environ. Engrs., Annapolis, Md., 1982-85, exec. dir., 1985—2003, Coun. Engring. & Sci. Specialty Boards, 1992—. Dir. CLC Mus. & Rsch. Ctr., 2000—; v.p. Buick Alliance, 2004—. Editor: Environ. Engr., 1985—2004; author: Restoration Facts, 1941. Gen. chmn. Cayuga County United Way, 1982, exec. com., 1982-84, bd. dirs., 1981-84; exec. dir. Coun. Engring. and Scientific Specialty bds.; health and safety com. Cayuga County council Boy Scouts Am., 1969-83; parish council Sacred Heart Parish, 1981-82; bd. dirs. YMCA-WEIU Cayuga County, 1982-85. With USNR, 1967—69. Recipient Recognition award United Way, 1982; named Honorable Conceptor, Mich. Cons. Engrs. Council, 1983. Fellow ASCE (Outstanding Service award 1981, 86); mem. Assn. Environ. Engring. Profs., NSPE, N.Y. Soc. Profl. Engrs., N.Y. Water Pollution Control Assn. (Lewis Van Carpenter award 1974), Water Environment Fedn. (Philip F. Morgan medal 1973), Buick Club Am. (bd. dirs. 1996-99), Chi Epsilon, Tau Chi Alpha. Republican. Roman Catholic.

ANDERSON, WILLIAM CORNELIUS, III, lawyer; b. Haddonfield, N.J., Dec. 1, 1947; s. William Cornelius Jr. and Madelyn Anna (Penny) A.; m. Christine Joan Keck, June 20, 1970; children: William C. IV, Teresa, Stephen, Geoffrey, Thomas, Matthew. BA, Georgetown U., 1969; JD, Villanova U., 1975. Bar: Del. 1975, Ill. 1979. Atty. Morris, Nichols, Arsht & Tunnell, Wilmington, Del., 1975-77, Biggs & Battaglia, Wilmington, 1978, Lord, Bissell & Brook, Chgo., 1979-85, ptnr., 1985-2000; founding ptnr. Anderson, Bennett & Ptnrs., Chgo., 2000—. Contbr. chpt. to book, articles to law jours. Capt. USAR, 1969-72. Fellow Am. Coll. Trial Lawyers; mem. ABA, Internat. Assn. Def. Counsel, Am. Acad. Healthcare Attys., Soc. Trial Attys., North Shore Country Club, Kenilworth Club. Home: 717 Kent Rd Kenilworth IL 60043-1031 Office: Anderson Bennett & Ptnrs 55 E Monroe St Ste 3650 Chicago IL 60603-5713 E-mail: w.anderson@abandpartners.com.

ANDERSON, WILLIAM H., architect; b. Conroe, Tex., July 28, 1933; s. William hartford and Lena Mattie A.; m. Kay W., Sept. 10, 1982; children: Linda, Susan, William, Francis. BArch, Tex. A&M U., 1956. Cert. architect, Tex., S.C. Intern architect George Dahl, Dallas, 1959-60, Caudill Rowlett & Scott, Houston, 1960-61, Howard Barnstone, Houston, 1961-62; architect Houston, 1962-66, Pearlstine Anderson, Columbia, S.C., 1966-74, Anderson Assocs., Columbia, 1975—. Past chmn. S.C. Bldg. Code Coun., Columbia,

1974—; mem. Hist. Columbia Foundation Properties Co., 1997—. Dir. Architects Bicentennial Com., Columbia, 1976. Served to capt. USAFR, 1956-59. Recipient design & environ. award Army Corps Engrs., 1990. Mem. AIA (bldg. and& performance regulations com. 19770—, bd. dirs. S.C. chpt. 197), Nat. Trust Historic Preservation. Office: Anderson Assocs Architects PO Box 6203 Columbia SC 29260-6203

ANDERSON, WILLIAM HENRY, psychobiology educator; b. Phila., 1940; s. William Henry Schoen and Elizabeth Winifred (Laverty) A.; m. Catherine Sacchetti, Oct. 7, 1967 (dec. Sept. 1991); 1 child, Jennifer Ann Gist; m. Claudia Winkler, July 25, 2005 BS, MIT, 1962; MA, U. Pa., 1967; MD, Thomas Jefferson U., 1967; MPH, Harvard U., 1977. Diplomate Am. Bd. Psychiatry and Neurology. Intern. Pa. Hosp., Phila., 1967-68; resident in psychiatry Mass. Gen. Hosp., Boston, 1968-71, assoc. psychiatrist dept. psychiatry, 1976-97, sr. psychiatrist, 1998—, dir. postgrad. edn., 1976-81; instr. psychiatry Harvard U., Boston, 1973-75, asst. prof., 1975-81, asst. clin. prof., 1981-82, lectr., 1982—; chmn. psychiatry St. Elizabeths Hosp., Boston, 1981-92. Dir. clinical svcs. Augusta Mental Health Inst., 1993-96; asst. attending psychiatrist Mclean Hosp., Belmont, Mass.; Cons. Scientists' Inst. Pub. Info.; mem. Carnegie Coun. Ethics and Internat. Affairs. Contbg. editor: The New Physician, 1977-79; editorial bd. Topics in Geriatrics, 1981-87, Jour. Geriatric Psychiatry and Neurology; co-author: (with M.T. McGuire) The U.S. Healthcare Dilemma, 1999. Lt. comdr., M.C. USNR, 1971-73. Fellow Am. Psychiat. Assn., Human Biology coun.; mem. AAAS, Am. Acad. Clin. Psychiatrists, Internat. Soc. Polit. Psychology, Coun. on Fgn. Rels. (lectr. to coms.), Med. Assn. P.R. (hon.), Mass. Med. Soc., Soc. Ethnobiology, U.S. Naval Inst., Boston Athenaeum (proprietor), Harvard Club of Boston, Union Club, Sigma Xi. Office: 34 Coolidge Hill Rd Cambridge MA 02138-5527 Office Phone: 617-492-8090. Business E-Mail: wander@post.harvard.edu.

ANDERSON, WILLIAM HOPPLE, lawyer; b. Cin., Feb. 28, 1926; s. Robert Waters and Anna (Hopple) A.; m. Jean Koop, Feb. 3, 1951; children: Susan Hopple, Nancy, Barbara, William Hopple Jr., Francie. Student, Carleton Coll., 1946; LL.B., U. Cin., 1952. Bar: Ohio bar 1952, U.S. Supreme Ct 1964. Mem. firm Becker, Loeb, & Becker, Cin., 1952-54; asst. pros. atty. Hamilton County, Ohio, 1953-57; of counsel Graydon, Head & Ritchey, Cin.; judge Wyoming (Ohio) Mcpl. Ct., 1960-67. Mem. Ohio Ho. of Reps., 1967-69. With USMC, 1944-46. Republican. Presbyterian. Home: 297 Mount Pleasant Ave Wyoming OH 45215-4212 Office: 511 Walnut St Cincinnati OH 45202-3115

ANDERSON, WILLIAM MAXWELL, artist, educator; b. July 31, 1941; s. Robert Arthur and June Anderson; m. Augma Edite Leipins; children: Kerri, Craig. BS, Mankato State U., 1963. Tchr. art Long Beach Unified Sch. Dist., Calif., 1963—69, Appleton Unified Sch. Dist., Wis., 1969—73, Anaheim Union High Sch. Dist., Calif., 1973—80, Los Alamitos Unified Sch. Dist., Los Alamitos, 1980—2001, Orange County High Sch. for Arts, L.A., 1985—96, East L.A. Coll., 2001—02; owner Anderson Art Gallery, Sunset Beach, 1994—. Author: The Work of Bill Anderson, 1984,·Painter, 2003; 3 murals, Mankato State U., 1990, mural, East L.A. Coll., 2001—02, exhibitions include Nat. Mus. Watercolor, Mexico City, 1994, Luckman Art Ctr., L.A., 1995, Vincent Price Mus., 2000, Millard Sheets Art Ctr., Pomona, Calif., 2004, Ontario Mus., 2004—05. Mem., pres. Allied Art Bd., Huntington Beach, Calif., 1979—91. Office: Anderson Art Gallery 16812 Pacific Coast Hwy Sunset Beach CA 90742 Business E-Mail: yannis@billandersonartgallery.com.

ANDERSON, WILLIAM ROBERT, career naval officer; b. Bakerville, Tenn., June 17, 1921; s. David Hensley and Mary (McKelvey) A.; m. Yvonne Etzel, June 10, 1943 (div. Apr. 1979); children: Michael David, William Robert; m. Patricia Walters, Dec. 26, 1980; children: Jane Hensley, Thomas McKelvey Grad., Columbia Mil. Acad., 1939; BSEE, U.S. Naval Acad., 1942; DSc, Defiance Coll., 1958. Commd. ensign USN, 1942, advanced through grades to capt., 1960; assigned submarines Tarpon, Narwhal, Trutta and 11 Pacific combat patrols, World War II; postwar service submarine Trutta, Sarda; comdr. attack submarine USS Wahoo, Pearl Harbor, 1953-55; head tactical dept. Submarine Sch., 1955-56; staff naval reactors br. AEC, Washington, 1956-57; comdr. USS Nautilus, 1957-59; ret. USN, 1962. Cons. to Pres. J.F. Kennedy, until 1963; mem. 89th-92d Congresses from 6th Tenn. Dist.; pvt. bus. exec., 1973—; co-founder Pub. Office Corp., database mgmt. firm. Author: Nautilus 90 North, 1959, First Under the North Pole, 1959, The Useful Atom, 1966; Contbr. articles to nat. mags. and profl. publs. Decorated Bronze Star, Legion of Merit; recipient Stephen Decatur prize Navy League U.S., Distinguished Service award N.Y.C., Christopher Columbus Internat. Communications award Genoa, Italy; Elisha Kent Kane medalist Geog. Soc. Phila., 1959; Patron's medal Royal Geog. Soc., 1959; Leadership award Freedoms Found., 1960, Lowell Thomas award The Explorers Club, N.Y.C., 1997; featured in Greatest Adventures of All Times spl. edit. Life mag.

ANDERSON, WILLIAM SCOVIL, classics educator; b. Brookline, Mass., Sept. 16, 1927; s. Edgar Weston and Katrina (Brewster) A.; m. Lorna Candee Bassette, June 12, 1954 (dec. Dec. 1977); children: Judith, Blythe, Heather, Meredith, Keith; m. Deirdre Burt, May 28, 1983. BA, Yale U., 1950, PhD, 1954; AB, Cambridge U., (Eng.), 1952; MA, Cambridge (Eng.) U., 1955. Prix de Rome fellow Am. Acad. in Rome, 1954-55; instr. classics Yale U., 1955-59; resident in Rome, Morse fellow, 1959-60; mem. faculty U. Calif., Berkeley, 1960-94, prof. Latin and comparative lit., 1966-94, prof. charge Intercollegiate Ctr. Classical Studies, 1967-68, chmn. classics, 1970-73. Rsch. prof. U. Melbourne, 1984; Robson lectr. Victoria Coll., Toronto, 1987; Blegen rsch. prof. Vassar Coll., 1989-90, vice chair comparative lit., 1990-93; vis. disting. prof. Fla. State U., spring 1995; Gail Burnett lectr. San Diego State U., 2001; vis. prof. Ohio State U., 2003. Author: The Art of the Aeneid, 1969, Ovid, Metamorphoses, Critical Text, 1977, Essays on Roman Satire, 1982, Barbarian Play: Plautus' Roman Comedy, 1993, Ovid's Metamorphoses 1-5 and 6-10 Text and Commentary, 1972, 2d edit., 1997, Why Horace?, 1998; co-editor (with L.N. Quartarone) Approaches to Teaching Vergil's Aeneid, 2002. Served with U.S. Army, 1946—48, Korea. Recipient Berkeley citation, 1994; NEH sr. fellow, 1973-74. Mem.: Danforth Assocs., Am. Philol. Assn. (pres. 1977), Soc. Religions. Episcopalian. Office: Univ Calif Dept Classics Berkeley CA 94720 Business E-Mail: wsand@berkeley.edu.

ANDERSON, WILLIAM WALLACE, financial executive; b. Balt., Apr. 8, 1958; s. Joseph Merryman II and Ann Marie (Moran) Anderson; m. Marian A. Gannon, July 24, 1987; children: Ciara Ann, Deirdre Christine. BA in Acctg., U. West Fla., 1980. CPA, Md., Calif. Audit staff to supr. Coopers & Lybrand, Balt., 1980-85, audit mgr. Dublin, 1985-87, Sacramento, 1987—92; dir. acctg. Raley's Supermarkets, Sacramento, 1992—97, v.p., contr., 1992—97, exec. v.p., CFO, 1997—. Bd. dirs., CFO Food for Families, Sacramento, 1990—. Mem. AICPA. Avocations: travel, basketball, tennis. Office: Raleys Supermarkets 500 W Capitol Ave West Sacramento CA 95605

ANDERSON-SPIVY, ALEXANDRA, news correspondent, editor, writer; b. Boston, Mass, May 14, 1942; d. Henry and Marion Ruth (Thompson) Fuller; m. Samuel O.J. Spivy; children: Lafcadio, Genevieve, Oscar. BA, Sarah Lawrence Coll., 1961. Art editor Paris Rev., 1972-76, Village Voice, NYC, 1973-76; features assoc. Vogue mag., NYC, 1976-78; sr. editor Portfolio mag., NYC, 1979-83; editor-in-chief Arts and Antiques mag., NYC, 1983-85; exec. editor Am. Photographer, NYC, 1985-87; arts editor Smart mag., NYC, 1988-90; contbg. arts editor Esquire mag., NYC, 1990-94; NY editor The Argonaut, 1992-96; reviews editor The Art Jour., 1995-2000; editor-in-chief The Craftsman on CD-ROM, 1996—; projects editor Interactive Bur., 1996-99; editl. dir. Circle.com, 1999-2001; corr. Bloomberg.com, 2004—. Chair bd. dirs. Franklin Furnace; bd. govs. Colby Coll. Art Mus.; profl. fellow Morgan Libr. Author: Anderson and Archer's SoHo: The Essential Guide to Art and Life in Lower Manhattan, 1979, Living With Art, 1988, Portraits of Olga, 1992, Keith Haring, Last Works, 1995, Gardens of Earthly Delight: The Art of Robert Kushner, 1997, Foliage: Photographs by Harold Feinstein, 2001; mem. adv. bd. Rev. Mag., 1998-2000. V.p., Mus. Modern Art, Contemporary Arts Coun.; pres., Bd. of Dir., Exhibitions Internat., 2000-. Recipient Art Critics' award NEA, 1978; Travel grant Japan Found., 1976. Mem. Internat. Assn. Art Critics (pres. Am. sect. 1997-2001).

ANDERSON-THOMPKINS, SIBBY ELLEN, dean; d. William Howard and Dorothy Beatrice (Thompson) Anderson; m. James Norwood Thompkins, Sept. 30, 1989; 1 child, Austin Spencer Thompkins. BA in Speech Comm., U. NC, 1987, MA in Speech Comm./Performance Studies, 1990; MS in Ednl. Rsch., Stats. and Measurements, postgrad., Ga. State U., 2001—. Asst. dean U. NC, Chapel Hill, 1991—96; assoc. dean Hampshire Coll., Amherst, Mass., 1996—97; program devel. cons. Ga. Human Rels. Commn., Office of Gov., Atlanta, 1999—2000; asst. dean coll., dir. office acad. advising Agnes Scott Coll., Decatur, Ga., 2004—. Co-author (with Marybeth Gasman): Fund Raising from Black College Alumni: Successful Strategies for Supporting Alma Mater, 2003; contbr. articles to profl. jours., chapters to books. Vol. Orange County Rape Crisis Ctr., 1991—93; mem. Orange County Inter-Agy. Domestic Violence Com., 1993—94; vol. DeKalb Rape Crisis Ctr., 1997—2003; mem. youth diversion bd. DeKalb County Juvenile Justice Dept., 2000—03; mem. task force on domestic violence and sexual assault Chapel Hill Town Coun., 1992—94. Named to Atlant Met. chpt. Nat. Coalition of 100 Black Women; recipient Harvey E. Beech Outstanding Black Alumni award, U. NC, 1987, award for Outstanding Svc. in Support of Professoin, NC Coll. Pers. Assn., 1995, Oustanding Ga. Citizen award, Office of Sec. of State, 1999, Unsung Heroine award, 1999, H.S. Warrick Rsch. award, 2004; grantee, Ford Found., 1995—96, Hewlett Found., 1995—96. Fellow: Alpha Kappa Alpha; mem.: Assn. for Study of Higher Edn., Am. Ednl. Rsch. Assn., Philanthropic Ednl. Orgn. Internat., Order of Golden Fleece, Pi Lambda Theta, Kappa Delta Pi. Home: 15 Grayson Ln Covington GA 30016 Office: Agnes Scott Coll 41 E College Ave 30030

ANDERSSON, CRAIG REMINGTON, retired chemical company executive; b. Winnipeg, Man., Can., June 16, 1937; came to U.S., 1937; s. Anders Einar and Doris (Pearson) A.; m. Dawn Marie Traver, June 13, 1959; children— Lee Erik, Karin Ingrid, Jon Kristien, Jenni Kate BS in Chem. Engring., U. Minn., 1960; postgrad., U. Del., 1960-66. Rschr. Sun Oil, 1960-67; v.p. ops. Custom Chems., Inc., 1967-68; Engr., supr. U.S. Steel Chems., Haverhill, Ohio, 1968-76, product mgr. Pitts., 1976-80, gen. mgr. Cin., 1980-82, v.p. Pitts., 1982-85, pres., 1985-86; pres., COO Aristech Chem. Corp., Pitts., 1986-93; vice chmn. Aristech Chem. Co., Pitts., 1994-95; ret., 1995. Cons.; bd. dirs. Albemarle Corp., ret., 2002; bd. dirs. RTI Internat. Metals, Inc.; former bd. dirs. Duquesne U. Contbr. articles to profl. jours. Mem. citizen's sponsoring com. Allegheny Conf. Cmty. Devel. Mem. AIChE, Alpha Chi Sigma. Lutheran. Achievements include patents in field. Avocations: golf, hunting, fishing, auto racing.

ANDERSSON, HELEN DEMITROUS, artist; b. Kotzebue, Alaska, Sept. 9, 1958; d. Thomas Wade Sr. and Rose (Koonook) Sours; children: Jason Ray, Gwendolyn Joyce Field. Student, U. Fairbanks, 1980, U. Hilo, Hawaii, 1981. Exhibited works in Anchorage Mus. History and Arts Show, Stephan Fine Arts, 1984. Recipient 1st pl. Alaska Silver Anniversary Juried Arts Show. Avocations: painting, drawings, carvings, sewing, beadwork.

ANDERTON, JAMES FRANKLIN, IV, real estate development executive; b. Lansing, Mich., Aug. 2, 1943; s. James Franklin III and Florence Ethel (Bear) A.; m. Deborah Anne Garlock, Apr. 2, 1966 (div.); 1 child, James Franklin, V.; m. Denise Marie Thelen, July 6, 1985; 1 child, Sarah Elizabeth. BA, Hobart Coll., Geneva, N.Y., 1965; MBA, Cornell U, 1967; PhD, Mich. State U., 1997. Controller Summit Steel Processing Corp., Lansing, 1967-69, exec. v.p., 1970, pres., 1971-90, Processed Plastics Co., Ionia, Mich., 1986-90, Universal Steel Co. of Mich., Lansing, 1988-90; chmn., pres., CEO, Summit Holdings Corp., East Lansing, Mich., 1986—2001; pres. Lansing C.C., 1999-2000; mng. gen. ptnr. Summit Holdings Ltd. Partnership, 1996—; mng. mem. Maplegrove Property Mgmt., LLC, 2001—. Pres. Inst. Scrap Recycling Industries, Washington, 1982-83, bd. dirs.; v.p. Bur. Internat. de la Recuperation, Brussels, 1984-85; bd. dirs. Auto-Owners Ins. Co., Lansing; mem. Mich. Resource Recovery Com., 1975-77, Mich. Job Devel. Authority, 1977-79, nat. adv. coun. Mich. State U. Coll. Edn., 1998—; mem. Mich. com. on financing postsecondary edn., 1999-2001; bd. dirs. Tchr. Edn. Accreditation Coun. Pres. Lansing Met. Devel. Authority, 1971-72, Delta Twp. Econ. Devel. Authority, 1975-76; campaign chmn. Capital Area United Way, Lansing, 1976; chmn. Lansing Regional C. of C., 1977; chmn. Montessori Children's House, Lansing, 1982-85, St. Lawrence Hosp., Lansing, 1985-86, Capital Region Cmty. Found., Lansing, 1992-93; trustee Hobart and William Smith Colls., Geneva, NY, 1993-98. Staff sgt. USNG, 1968-74 Recipient Am. Spirit Honor medal. Episcopalian. Avocations: reading, hiking, piano, tennis, golf. Home: 1618 Stanlake Dr East Lansing MI 48823-2018

ANDES, LARRY DALE, minister; b. Warrenton, Va., June 7, 1947; s. William Christian and Hilda Elizabeth (Beach) A.; m. Bobbi E. Stephens, July 16, 1966; 1 child, Joshua Dale. BS in Pastoral Studies, North Ctrl. U., 1970; student, U. Richmond, 1991, Bethel Theol. Sem., 1992. Ordained to ministry Assembly of God Ch., 1975, non-denominational, 1987. Assoc. pastor Calvary Assembly of God, Staunton, Va., 1971-72; youth min. Arlington (Va.) Assembly of God, 1972-75; assoc. pastor West End Assembly of God, Richmond, Va., 1975-76; founder, pres., festival dir. Fishnet Ministries Inc., Richmond, Front Royal, Va., 1976—; sr. pastor Fishnet Christian Ctr., Front Royal, 1992—. Named one of Outstanding Young Men of Am., 1984. Office: Fishnet Ministries Inc PO Box 1919 Front Royal VA 22630-1919 Office Phone: 540-636-2961. Personal E-mail: larryandes@hotmail.com. Business E-Mail: fishnet@fishnetministries.org.

ANDES, REV. DONNA M., adult education educator, community health nurse; BS in Nursing, Marquette U., Milw., 1964; Masters, Life Ch. Univ., Milw., 1999; PhD in Theology, Life Ch. Univ., Va., 2001. Lic. min. Supr. oper. rm. Gabriels Hosp., Little Falls, Minn., 1956; dir. home health Sr. Citizen Agy., Thomas, W.Va., 1969—71; tchr. LCU, Warrenton, Va., 1999, 2004—, nutritional advisor, 2004. Contbr. articles Breakthrough Mag.; author: Know thy Enemy. Mem. Women Prisoners Fellowship, Warrenton, Va., 1993—2001. Home: PO Box 188 Midland VA 22728 Office Phone: 540-439-8510. Home Fax: 540-439-8510. E-mail: d.andes@juno.com.

ANDJABA, MARTIN, ambassador; Permanent rep. of Republic of Namibia UN, N.Y.C., 1996—; pres. UN Security Council. Office: 360 Lexington Ave RM 1502 New York NY 10017-6552

ANDO, KUNITAKE, consumer products company executive; Grad., Sch. of Economics, U. Tokyo, 1969. With Sony Corp., 1969—; mng. dir. Sony Life Ins. Co., Ltd. (formerly Sony Prudential Life Ins. Co.), 1979—85, dep. pres., 1985—90; gen. mgr., corp. planning Sony Electronics, Inc. (formerly Sony Corp. of Am.), 1976—79; pres. and COO Sony Engring. and Mfg. of Am. (now part of Sony Electronics Inc.), 1990—94; exec. v.p., sr. gen. mgr., corp. planning, consumer A & V Products Co. Sony Corp., 1994—96, pres., Divisional Info. Tech. Co., 1996—99, pres. and COO, Personal IT Network Co., 1999—2000, pres. and group COO (formerly COO), rep. corp. exec. officer, 2000—05, advisor, 2005—. Avocations: golf, swimming, tennis. Office: Sony Corp 6-7-35 Kitashinagawa Shinagawa 141-0001 Japan

ANDOLSEN, ALAN ANTHONY, management consultant; b. Cleve., Feb. 19, 1943; s. Lloyd Anthony and Helen Mae (Kozinski) A.; m. Barbara Hilkert, Jan. 20, 1968; children: Daniel, Ruth. AB magna cum laude, Borromeo Coll., 1964; MA, U. Dayton, 1967; postgrad., Vanderbilt U., 1967-69. Cert. mgmt. cons.; cert. records mgr. V.p. Bergamo East, Marcy, N.Y., 1969-71; dir. Met. Health Dept., Nashville, 1971-76; prin. Naremco Svc., Inc., N.Y.C., 1976-79, v.p., 1979-86, pres., 1986—. Bd. dirs. Assn. Mgmt. Cons. Firms., N.Y.C. Editor: Management Consulting-A Model Course, 1989, 96; contbr. articles to profl. jours. V.p. Inst. Cert. Records Mgrs. Mem. Inst. Mgmt. Cons., Assn. Records Mgrs. and Adminstrs., Assn. Image and Info. Mgmt., Am. Mensa Ltd. Roman Catholic. Avocations: music, bicycling, reading. Office: Naremco Svcs Inc 60 E 42nd St New York NY 10165-0006 Office Phone: 212-697-0290.

ANDORKA, FRANK HENRY, lawyer; b. Lorain, Ohio, July 25, 1946; s. Frank Henry and Sue (Parham) A.; m. M. Jean Deliman, Aug. 10, 1968; children: Frank Henry Jr., Claire E. AB, Ohio U., 1968; postgrad., Ind. U., 1968-69; JD, Cornell U., 1975. Bar: Ohio 1975, U.S. Dist. Ct. (no. dist.) Ohio 1975. From assoc. to ptnr. Baker & Hostetler, Cleve., 1975—. Author: A Practical Guide to Copyrights and Trademarks, 1989, What is a Copyright?, 1992. Served to 1st lt. U.S. Army, 1969-72. Mem. ABA (chmn. internat. copyright laws and treaties com. 1984-86, chmn. govt. rels. to copyright com. 1986-88, chmn. broadcasting, sound rec. and performing artists com. 1988-90, chmn. divsn. III copyrights 1990-92, chmn. divsn. IX publs. 1992-93), Ohio Bar Assn., Greater Cleve. Bar Assn. Avocations: bowling, tennis. Home: 31000 Clinton Dr Cleveland OH 44140-1500 Office: Baker & Hostetler 3200 Nat City Ctr 1900 E 9th St Ste 3200 Cleveland OH 44114-3475 E-mail: fandorka@bakerlaw.com.

ANDRABI, IMRAN AMJAD, physician; b. Dhaka, Bangladesh, June 1, 1967; came to U.S., 1991; s. Javaid Amjad and Shireen Amjad (Adil) A.; m. Reema Ali, July 4, 1991; children: Maaz A., Moeed A., Maira A. BS, U. Punjab, Lahore, Pakistan, 1988; MBBS, King Edward Med. Coll., Lahore, Pakistan, 1990. Diplomate Am. Bd. Family Practice; bd. cert. managed care medicine. Intern in medicine, surgery Mayo Hosp., Lahore, Pakistan, 1991; transitional intern Mercy Hosp., Toledo, 1992—93, resident in family practice, 1993—95, chief resident, 1994—95; med. dir. ACLS edn., 1995—; pvt. practice St. Vincent's Med. Ctr., Toledo, 1995—96; asst. dir. residency program Mercy Health Ptnrs. Family Practice, Toledo, 1995—, dir. inpatient svcs., 1995—, assoc. program dir., 1998—2000, program dir., 2000—, v.p., chief acad. officer, 2002—. Project dir. Islamic Ctr. Directory, 1996-97; pres. Friends of Pakistan, 2001—. Fellow Am. Acad. Family Practice, Nat. Inst. Program Dir. Devel.; mem. AMA, Am. Coll. Physician Execs., Am. Assn. Pakistani Physicians N.Am., Am. Acad. Family Practice, Am. Coll. Physician Execs., Assn. Internat. Physicians N.W. Ohio (pres. elect), AAPNA, Ohio State Med. Assn., Pakistan Med. and Dental Coun., King Edward Alumni Assn., Toledo Lucas County Acad. Medicine, Soc. Tchrs. Family Medicine, Assn. Internat. Physicians of N.W. Ohio (pres.). Avocations: music, golf, computers. Home: 2840 Squirrel Bnd Toledo OH 43617-1363 Office: 2200 Jefferson Ave Toledo OH 43624-1117 E-mail: imran@sev.org.

ANDRADE, ANDRES, vocalist, educator; BA in Vocal Performance, U. So. Fla., 1987; MusM in Vocal Performance, New Eng. Conservatory of Music, 1995. Tchg. asst., vocal music New Eng. Conservatory of Music, Boston, 1993—94; vocal instr., opera theatre dir. LaGuardia H.S. Music & Art and Performing Arts, N.Y.C.; pvt . vocal instr. N.Y.C.; freelance singer. Prodr.: (Operas) Alcina, Orfeo ed Euridice, Dido and Aeneas, Orpheus in the Underworld; contbr. articles to profl. jours. Founder Citywide Youth Opera, Inc.; instr. voice and diction First Ch. Congregational, Malden, Mass., 1991—97; music dir., cantor St. Patrick's Old Cathedral, N.Y.C., 1999—2001. Fellow, New Eng. Conservatory, 1993. Mem.: Nat. Assn. Tchrs. Singing, N.Y. Singing Tchrs. Assn. Home: PO Box 20498 Columbus Circle Sta New York NY 10023 Office Phone: 212-539-3561. Personal E-mail: andradeten@aol.com.

ANDRADE, EDNA, artist, art educator; b. Portsmouth, Va. d. Thomas Judson and Ruth (Porter) Wright; m. C. Preston Andrade, Jr., July 12, 1941 (div. 1960). BFA, Pa. Acad. Fine Arts/U. Pa., 1937. Supr. art elem. schs., Norfolk, Va., 1938-39; instr. drawing and painting Newcomb Art Sch., Tulane U., 1939-41; lectr. U. N.Mex., 1971; prof. Phila. Coll. Art, 1957—72, 1973—82, prof. emeritus, 1982—; prof. art Temple U., 1972-73. Adj. prof. art Ariz. State U., 1986—; critic Pa. Acad. Fine Arts, 1988—89. Artist, designer, OSS, 1942-44, free-lance designer, Washington, 1944-46, free-lance painter, designer, muralist, Phila. and, N.Y.C., 1946—, artist-in-residence, Hartford Sch. Art and Tamarind Inst., 1971, U. Sask., Can., 1977, U. Zulia, Maracaibo, Venezuela, 1980, Ariz. State U., Tempe, 1981, 83, Fabric Workshop, Phila., 1984, Hollins Coll., Va., 1985; vis. artist, Skidmore Coll., 1973, 74, one-woman shows, Phila. Art Alliance, 1954, Beaver Coll., 1963, East Hampton Gallery, N.Y.C., 1967, Peale Galleries Pa. Acad., 1967, Rutgers U., 1971, U. Hartford, 1977, Marian Locks Gallery, 1969, 1971,74, 77, 83, 1989, Phila., Hollins Coll., 1985; retrospective Pa. Acad. Fine Arts, 1993, Locks Gallery, Phila., 1993-94, 97, 99, 2002-03, Inst. Contemporary Art, Phila., 2003; group shows include AAAL, In This Acad., Pa. Acad. Fine Arts, Phila., William Penn Meml. Mus., Harrisburg, Three Centuries Am. Art, Phila. Collects Art Since 1940, Phila. Mus. Art, Bklyn. Mus., Ft. Worth Art Ctr., Des Moines Art Ctr., Philbrook Art Ctr., Tulsa, Contemporary Phila. Artists, 1990, Phila. Mus. Art, Artists Choose Artists, Inst. of Contemporary Art, Phila., 1991, Klein Gallery, Univ. City Sci. Ctr., Phila., 1998, Phila. Mus. Art, 2000, others; represented in permanent collections, Phila. Mus. Art, Pa. Acad. Fine Arts, Print Club, Balt. Mus. Art, Addison Gallery Am. Art, McNay Art Inst., San Antonio, Montclair (N.J.) Art Mus., Nat. Collection Fine Arts, Libr. of Congress, USIA, Albright-Knox Art Gallery, Buffalo, Tamarind Collection, U. N.Mex. Mus., Woodmere Art Mus., Phila., Yale Art Gallery, Am. Tel. & Tel. Co., Bell of Pa., Phila., Fed. Res. Bank, Phila., Price-Waterhouse, Phila., Edwin A. Ulrich Mus. Wichita State U., Pepsi-Cola, Leeway Found., Phila., Please Touch Mus., Phila., Va. Mus. Fine Arts, Richmond, Dallas Mus. Art, Mus. Fine Arts, Houston. Mem. Mayor's Cultural Adv. Coun., Phila., 1984—85. Recipient 1st and 2d Cresson European Traveling scholarships Pa. Acad., 1936, 37, Eyre medal Phila. Water Color Club, 1968, Mary Smith prize Pa. Acad. Fine Arts, 1968, Childe Hassam Meml. purchases AAAL, 1967, 68, Hazlett Meml. award in arts, 1980, Honor award Women's Caucus for Art, 1983, Hunt award visual arts Phila. Women's Way, 1984, Roland Gallimore Meml. award Interior Design Coun., Phila. Mayor's Arts and Culture award, 1991, Founders award Samuel S. Fleisher Art Meml., 1993, Disting. Daughter Pa. award, 2002 Mem. Coll. Art Assn. (Disting. Tchr. of Art award 1996).

ANDRAKE, NANCY CAROLYN, retired secondary school educator; b. Elmira, NY, Jan. 12, 1944; d. Stephen Francis Andrake and Theresa Ida Skoreski; m. Edward J. Jeziorski Jr., July 4, 1970 (div. Feb. 1984); children: Jennifer Granger, Carolyn Jeziorski, Edward Jeziorski, Patrick Jeziorski. BA cum laude, Coll. Misericordia, Dallas, 1965; MA, Fla. State U., 1967; postgrad., SUNY Stonybrook, Elmira Coll., SUNY Cortland, U. Del. Latin/English tchr. Hammondsport Sch. Dist., NY, 1966—70; Latin/Greek/English tchr. Horseheads Sch. Dist., NY, 1970—; English/study skills tchr. Elmira Summer Sch., NY, 1984—; ret. Horseheads Sch. Dist., 2005; English tchr. Taejon Christian Internat. Sch., Republic of Korea, 2005—; ret. Sales assoc. Kaufmann's Dept. Store, Horseheads, 1995—; cons. Latin Regents Exam NY State Dept. Edn., Albany, 1985—. Leader Girl Scouts Am., Hammondsport, 1965—70, Elmira, 1980—90; mem., pres. St. Casimir's Parish Coun., Elmira, 1984—90. Fellow Rockefeller Found., Am. Sch., Athens, 1989; grantee NEH, 1982; scholar Corning Sister Cities, to teach in Poland, 1999. Mem.: Nat. Jr. Classical League, NY State Jr. Classical League (co-chair 1986—96), Classical Assn. Empire State (bd. dirs. 1986—96), Am. Fedn. Tchrs., NY State United Tchrs., Horseheads Tchrs. Assn. (rep. 1985—90, 2002—), Lambda Iota Tau, Sigma Phi Sigma, Kappa Gamma Pi. Roman Catholic. Avocations: European travel, reading, music, taking students on trips. Home: 51 Ashland Ave Elmira NY 14903 Office: Horseheads High Sch 401 Fletcher St Horseheads NY 14845 E-mail: magistrahhds@yahoo.com.

ANDRASICK, JAMES STEPHEN, transportation executive; b. Passaic, NJ, Mar. 27, 1944; s. Stephen Adam and Emily (Spolnik) A.; children: Christopher J., Gregory O.; m. Ginger Michael Simon, Feb. 22, 1997. BS, USCG Acad., 1965; MS, MIT, 1971. Commd. ensign USCG, 1965, advanced through grades to lt., 1968; assigned to Vietnam, 1967-68; sys. analyst Jamesbury Corp., 1970; corp. fin. and product devel. staffs Ford Motor Co., 1971-74; mgr. corp. devel. IU Internat. Corp., Phila., 1974-78; from v.p. planning, contr. to exec. v.p. C. Brewer & Co., Ltd., Honolulu, 1978-92, pres., 1992-2000; sr. v.p., CFO, treas. Alexander & Baldwin, Inc., Honolulu,

2000—02, exec. v.p., 2002; pres., CEO Matson Navigation Co., 2002—. Chmn. bd., mng. gen. ptnr. ML Macadamia Orchards LP, 1986-88; chmn. bd. HCPC, Olokele Sugar Co., Hawaiian Sugar and Transp. Coop., 1993-96; chmn. Hawaiian Sugar Planters Assn., 1992-93; bd. dirs. Wailuku Agribus. Co., C. Brewer Co., Ltd., Honolulu. Bd. dirs. Aloha United Way, Honolulu, 1983-89, Hawaii Opera Theater, 2001-03; treas., bd. dirs. ARC, Hawaii, 1983-94, 96-2002, chmn., 1989-90; bd. dirs. Hawaii Employers Coun., 1992-98, chmn., 1995-98; trustee UH Found., 1988-94, vice chmn., 1992-93, chmn., 1993-94; trustee Hawaii Maritime Ctr., 1993-98; bd. dirs. Coast Guard Found., Honolulu Symphony, 2002-05; trustee Mills Coll., 2004-. Mem.: San Francisco (Calif.) Maritime Pk. Assn. (bd. dirs.), Standard Club. Office: Matson Navigation Inc 555 12th St Oakland CA 94607 Business E-Mail: jandrasick@matson.com.

ANDRÉ, JOY LARAE, elementary school educator, adult education educator, language educator; b. L.A., Apr. 29, 1936; children: Scott, Brent. BA in Music and Edn., Pepperdine U., 1957, postgrad., 1958—75. Life tchg. credential Calif., cert. lang. devel. specialist Calif. Tchr. elem. and adult edn. L.A. Unified Sch. Dist., 1957—93; tchr. adult edn. Saddleback Valley Unified Sch. Dist., Mission Viejo, Calif., 1993—. Mentor tchr. selection com. L.A. Unified Sch. Dist., 1984, bilingual coord., 1985—91, master tchr., 1987—88, ESL coord., 1990—91. Recipient Govt. Studies Program award, Close Up Found., 1998; scholar, Pepperdine U., 1980; Coe fellow. Mem.: AAUW, United Tchrs. L.A., Calif. Ret. Tchrs. Assn., Orange County Natural History Assn., L.A. Conservancy, Laguna Niguel Women's Club (participant/vol. sec. 2002—03). Republican. Presbyterian. Avocations: photography, scrapbooks, collecting Indian art and miniature boxes, reading, travel. Home: 9 Killini Laguna Niguel CA 92677 E-mail: jandreln@hotmail.com.

ANDRE, MICHAEL (KENNETH ANDRE), editor-in-chief; b. Halifax, N.S., Can., Aug. 31, 1946; s. Kenneth Bailey and Kathleen Mary (Warburton) A.; m. Erika Rothenberg, 1974 (div. 1983); m. Jane Adler (div. 1995); 1 child, Benjamin Eyton. BA, McGill U., 1968; MA, U. Chgo., 1969; PhD, Columbia U., 1973. Lectr. CCNY, N.Y.C., 1973, Baruch Coll., N.Y.C., 1974; editorial assoc. Art News, N.Y.C., 1973-77; treas. SoHo Baroque Opera Co., N.Y.C., 1980—; exec. dir. Unmuzzled Ox, N.Y.C., 1971—. Author: Experiments in Banal Living, 1990; edited W.H. Auden libretto for opera to be produced in spring 2004. Grantee Nat. Endowment Arts, Coordinating Coun. Lit. Mags., N.Y. State Coun. on Arts; grad. fellow Can. Coun. Fellow PEN; mem. MLA. Office: Unmuzzled Ox 105 Hudson St New York NY 10013-2331 Office Phone: 212-226-7170. Personal E-mail: mandre0x@aol.com.

ANDRE, MICHAEL PAUL, physicist, educator; b. Des Moines, Apr. 25, 1951; s. Paul Leo and Pauline (Vermie) A.; m. Janice Joan Hanecak, Mar. 12, 1988. BA, Cen. U. Iowa, 1972; postgrad., U. Ariz., 1972-73; MS, UCLA, 1975, PhD, 1980; cert., Am. Bd. Radiology, 1999. Rsch. assoc. Inst. Atmospheric Physics, Tucson, Ariz., 1972-73; mem. tech. staff Hughes Aircraft Co., L.A., 1973-74; postgrad. researcher UCLA, 1974-77; cons. L.A., 1975-84; med. radiologic physicist LACO/UCLA Olive View, L.A., 1977-81; sr. radiation physicist Cedars-Sinai Med. Ctr., L.A., 1979-84; chief med. physicist Dept. Vet. Affairs, San Diego, 1981—; prof. radiology, chief divsn.Physics and Engring. sch. medicine U. Calif., La Jolla, 1981—; chief scientific officer Radco Corp., 1996—; chief med. officer Almen Labs., Inc., 1999—. Qualified expert Calif. Radiol. Health Dept., Berkeley, 1979—; chmn. Nat. Physics Conf., San Diego, 1984-89; mem. U. Calif.-San Diego Cancer Ctr., 2004— Editor: Physics and Biology of Radiology, 1988, Investigative Radiology, 1990—; guest editor: Internat. Jour. Imaging Sci. & Tech., 1997; contbr. articles to profl. jours. Mountain guide Sierra Club, L.A., 1977-80; dir. Ariz. PIRG, Tucson, 1973; mountain guide Am. Alpine Inst., Peru, 1987-90. Rsch. grantee U. Calif.-San Diego Found., 1989—, NIH, Nat. Cancer Inst., 1986—, VA, 1989—, U.S. Army, 1994—, Pfeiffer Rsch. Found., 2002—. Mem. Am. Assn. Physicists in Medicine, Am. Inst. Ultrasound in Medicine, San Diego Radiol. Soc., Am. Inst. Physics, Soc. Photo-Optical Inst. Engrs., Am. Coll. Radiology, Soc. of Breast Imaging. Avocations: himalayan and andean expeditions, BMS motorsports racing. Office: U Calif Dept Radiology 9114 La Jolla CA 92093 E-mail: mandre@ucsd.edu.

ANDRE, PATRICK GERARD, electronics engineer, sound recording engineer; b. Mpls., Minn., May 13, 1958; s. Gerard Alexander and Rita Therese Andre; m. Therese Ann Blazina, Sept. 23, 1983; 1 child, Cherylin Jessica. BS Physics, Seattle U., Seattle, Wash., 1982. Cert. EMC Engr., NARTE, 1990, ESD Engr., NARTE, 1995. Mgr., tech. adviser CKC Lab., Redmond, Wash., 1996—2001; emc engr. NW EMC, Bothell, Wash., 1995—96; sr. environ. engr. ELDEC Corp., Lynnwood, Wash., 1983—95; electromagnetic compatibility engring. cons. Andre Consulting, Inc., Bothell, Wash., 2001—, electrostatic discharge engring. cons., 2001—, sound designer, 2001—. Pres. Andre Consulting, Inc., Bothell, Wash., 2001—. Dir.: (sound design) Seattle Gilbert and Sullivan Soc.; contbr. articles pub. to profl. jour., scientific papers (Customer Svc. All Star, 1994, 1995). Sound designer Evergreen Cmty. Ch., Bothell, Wash., 1996—2005; chmn., vice chmn. IEEE EMC Soc., Seattle, Wash., 1999—2005. Mem.: IEEE (chmn. 2002—). Office: Andre Consulting Incorp 12812 NE 185th Court Bothell WA 98011-3121 Office Phone: 425-485-7019. Business E-Mail: pat@andreconsulting.com.

ANDRÉ 3000, See BENJAMIN, ANDRE

ANDREACCI, JOSEPH L., education educator; b. Williamsport, Pa., May 22, 1974; s. John V. Andreacci and Lynne M. Lowe, Linda Andreacci (Stepmother) and James Lowe (Stepfather). BS Natural Sci. Pre-PT, Ind. U. Pa., Ind., Pa., 1997; MS Exercise Sci. & Adult Fitness, Bloomsburg U., Bloomsburg, Pa., 2000; PhD Exercise Physiology, U. Pitts., Pitts., Pa., 2003. Grad. student asst. Bloomsburg U., Bloomsburg, Pa., 1998—2000; grad. student rschr. U. Pitts., Pitts., 2000—01, grad. student asst., 2001—03; instr. C.C. of Alleghney County, Pitts., 2001—03; asst. prof. Bloomsburg U., Bloomsburg, Pa., 2003—. Contbr. articles pub. to profl. jour. Adv. bd. mem. Columbia County Children & Youth, Bloomsburg, Pa., 2003—05. Recipient MARC President's Award, Mid-Atlantic Regional Chpt. Am. Coll. of Sports Medicine, 2002, Student Rsch. Award, North Am. Soc. of Pediatric Exercise Medicine, 2002; Health Sci. Fellowship, Jewish Healthcare Found., 2003, Owens Fellowship, U. Pitts., 2000-2003. Mem.: North Am. Soc. of Pediatric Exercise Medicine (assoc.), Am. Coll. of Sports Medicine (assoc.). Home: PO Box Bloomsburg PA 17815 Office: Bloomsburg Univ 130 Centennial Hall Bloomsburg PA 17815 Office Phone: 570-389-5340. Office Fax: 570-389-5047. Business E-Mail: jandreac@bloomu.edu.

ANDREADIS, CONSTANTINE, art educator, art therapist; b. N.Y.C. s. George Andreadis and Rita Papatsos; m. Susan Andreadis, June 15, 1990; children: Justin, Zachary. BFA, N.Y. Inst. Tech., 1971; MA, Lehman Coll., 1976; MS, Coll. of New Rochelle, N.Y., 1990; EdD, Nova Southea. U., 2000. Program coord. Riverdale (N.Y.) Mental Health Orgn./Riverdale Neighborhood Ho., 1971—76; cmty. worker, tchr. Sch. Dist. 10, Bronx, NY, 1976—80; tchr. Allen-Stevenson Sch., N.Y.C., 1980—87; tchr., coord. Greenburgh Sch. Dist. #7, Hartsdale, NY, 1987—; adj. prof. Westchester C.C., White Plains, NY, 1992—, Fordham U., Tarrytown, NY, 1999—. Program coord. Woodlands Individualized Sr. Experience, Hartsdale, 2000—. Mem.: Am. Art Therapy Assn., Hellenic Am. Educators Assn., Westchester Art Therapy Assn. (bd. dirs. 1995—, past pres., award for significant contbn. to art therapy 1998—99). Avocations: photography, art, writing, web site creation, music. Office: Ctr for Growth and Edn Through the Arts PO Box 406 Dobbs Ferry NY 10522 Office Phone: 914-761-6052 ext 3029. E-mail: arteducator@usa.net, doctorcostas@yahoo.com.

ANDREADIS, TIM D., physicist, researcher; s. Dimitri and Irene Andreadis; m. Kimberly Anastasia Andreadis; children: Tanya, Anastasia. PhD, U. Md., 1981. Rsch. physicist Naval Rsch. Lab., Washington, 1984—92, sect. head high power microwave sect., 1992—. Dep. mgr. high power microwave program Naval Rsch. Lab., 2002; chmn. AMEREM, High Power Microwave Conf., Annapolis, Md., 2000—02, Small Boat Threat Workshop, Washington, 1999. V.p. Hellenic Am. Acad., Potomac, Md., 1993—95. Fellow, Nat. Rsch. Coun./Nat. Bur. Stds., 1981. Mem.: Directed Energy Profl. Soc., Assn. Old Crows. Greek Orthodox. Achievements include research in high power microwave effects on electronics; discovery of cause of atomic-like spectra from ion-bombardment induced Auger emission; development of EVOLVE, a time dependent ion bombardment simulation program. Avocations: computers, travel, politics. Office: Naval Rsch Lab 4555 Overlook Ave Washington DC 20375-5000 Personal E-mail: andreadi@bellatlantic.net. E-mail: tim.andreadis@nrl.navy.mil.

ANDREAE, CHRISTINE EWING, writer; b. Stamford, Conn., July 13, 1942; d. William and Mary (Challinor) Ewing; m. Frederick Shedd Andreae, Aug. 19, 1967; children: Morgan MacKenzie, Timothy Ewing. BA, Manhattanville Coll., 1964; MAT, Yale U., 1967. Author: Seances and Spiritualists, 1974, Trail of Murder, 1992, Grizzly, 1994, A Small Target, 1996, One Woman's Death, 1996, Smoke Eaters, 2000, When Evening Comes, 2000. Bd. dirs. Blue Ridge Hospice, 1989-95, vol., 1990—. Recipient Founder's award Blue Ridge Hospice, 1994, Lit. award Shenandoah Arts Coun., 1996. Mem. Mystery Writers Am., Sisters in Crime, Internat. Assn. Crime Writers, Women Writing the West.

ANDREANO, RALPH LOUIS, economist, educator; b. Waterbury, Conn., Apr. 11, 1928; s. John and Loretta (Creasia) A.; m. Carol Jean Wessbecher, Sept. 5, 1955; children: Maria Carol, Nicholas George. AB, Drury Coll., 1952; MA, Washington U., St. Louis, 1955; MA Fulbright scholar, U. Oslo, Norway, 1952-53; PhD, Northwestern U., 1961. Instr. econs. Northwestern U., 1959-60; asst. prof. econs. Earlham Coll., 1961, asso. prof., chmn. dept., 1962-65; asst. prof. bus. adminstrn. Harvard Bus. Sch., 1961-62; Brookings Nat. Research prof., 1964-65; asso. prof. econs., dir. undergrad. program econs. U. Wis., 1965-67, prof., 1967—, dir. Health Econs. Research Ctr., 1969-87, chmn. dept. econs., 1980-83, dir. Ctr. for Devel.; emeritus prof. econs., 1994—. Ofcl. del. Am. Econ. Assn. to Am. Council Learned Socs., 1964-70; adminstr. Div. Health State of Wis., 1976-78; economist WHO, Geneva, 1973-74. Author: (with H.F. Williamson and others) A History of American Petroleum Industry, 2 vols., 1959, 63, No Joy in Mudville: The Dilemma of Major League Baseball, 1965, Student Economists Handbook, 1967, (with B.A. Weisbrod and others) Disease and Economic Development, 1973, (with B.A. Weisbrod) American Health Policy, 1973; editor, author: New Views on American Economic Development, 1965; editor: Economic Impact of the Civil War, 1963, rev., 1967, The New Economic History: Papers on Methodology, 1971, (with J. Siegfried) Economics of Crime, 1981, Essays on International Health, 2001, The International Health Policy Program: An Internal Assessment, 2001; editor, founder: Explorations in Entrepreneurial History, 2d series, 1963-71, Explorations in Economic History 1971-78; editor: Jour. Econ. History, 1974-75; sr. editor (econs.): Social Sci. and Medicine, 1983-87; contbr. articles to profl. jours. Ford Faculty Research fellow, 1968-69 Mem. Inst. Medicine of Nat. Acad. Scis. Democrat. Home: 1815 Vilas Ave Madison WI 53711-2231 E-mail: rlandrea@wisc.edu.

ANDREAS, DAVID LOWELL, retired banker; b. St. Paul, Minn., Mar. 1, 1949; s. Lowell Willard and Nadine B. (Hamilton) A.; m. Debra Kelley, June 20, 1985; 2 children. BA, U. Denver, 1971; MA, Mankato State U., 1976. Credit mgmt. trainee United Calif. Bank, Los Angeles, 1976-77; comml. loan officer Nat. City Bank of Mpls., 1977-80; from v.p., sr. vp., to chmn., chief exec. officer to pres. & CEO Nat. City Bancorp., Mpls., 1980—2001. Chmn. ADAPA, Inc., Mpls., 1986-93; chmn. bd. Nat. City Bank, Mpls., 1991-94; pres., CEO Nat. City Bank, Mpls., 1994-2001. Bd. mem. Minn. Ctr. Victims of Torture, Marshall & Ilsley Corp., Milwaukee; mem. exec. com., dir. Children's Heart Link, 1988—, Ctr. Ethical Bus. Cultures, Minn. State U., Mankato Coll. Bus. Adv. Coun., Bus. Adv. Coun.; mem. Minn. State U. Mankato Coll. bus. adv. coun.; mem. Coll. of Social and Behavioral Scis. adv. bd.; trustee Breck Sch., Golden Valley, Minn., 1997, Mpls. Coll. Art and Design. With U.S. Army, 1971-73. Mem.: Golden Valley Golf & Country Club. Avocations: swimming, snowboarding. E-mail: 5033@usinternet.com.

ANDREAS, G(LENN) ALLEN, JR., agricultural company executive; b. Cedar Rapids, Iowa, June 22, 1943; s. Glenn Allen and Vera Irene (Yates) A.; m. Toni Kay Hibma, June 19, 1964; children: Bronwyn Denise, Glenn Allen III, Shannon Tori. BA, Valparaiso U., 1965, JD, 1968. Bar: Colo. 1969. Atty. U.S. Treas. Dept., Denver, 1969-73, Archer Daniels Midland Co., Decatur, Ill., 1973-75, asst. treas., 1975-86, treas., 1986—, v.p., chief fin. officer Europe, 1986-94, v.p., counsel to chief exec., 1994-96, mem. office of chief exec., 1996-97, pres., CEO, 1997-99, chmn., CEO, 1999—. Bd. dirs. Nat. City Bancorp., Mpls., Oelmühle Hamburg A.G, Hamburg, Federal Republic of Germany. Mem. ABA, Colo. State Bar Assn., Decatur Bar Assn. Clubs: Country of Decatur, Decatur. Democrat. Avocation: golf. Office: Archer Daniels Midland Co 4666 E Faries Pkwy Decatur IL 62526-5666*

ANDREASEN, NANCY COOVER, psychiatrist, educator, neuroscientist; d. John A. Sr. and Pauline G. Coover; children: Robin, Susan. BA summa cum laude, U. Nebr., 1958, PhD, 1963; MA, Radcliffe Coll., 1959; MD, U. Iowa, 1970. Instr. English Nebr. Wesleyan Coll., 1960—61, U. Nebr., Lincoln, 1962-63; asst. prof. English U. Iowa, Iowa City, 1963—66, resident, 1970—73, asst. prof. psychiatry, 1973—77, assoc. prof., 1977—81, prof. psychiatry, 1981—82, Andrew H. Woods prof. psychiatry, 1992-97, Andrew H. Woods chair psychiatry, 1997—. Dir. Mental Health Clin. Rsch. Ctr., 1987—, The MIND Inst., Albuquerque, 2002-; sr. cons. Northwick Pk. Hosp., London, 1983; acad. visitor Maudsley Hosp., London, 1986; adj. prof psychiatry U. N.Mex., Albuquerque. Author: The Broken Brain, 1984, Introductory Psychiatry Testbook, 1991; editor: Can Schizophrenia be Localized to the Brain?, 1986, Brain Imaging: Applications in Psychiatry, 1988, Brave New Brain: Conquering Mental Illness in the Era of the Genome, 2001, The Creating Brain: The Neuroscience of Genius, 2005, Am. Jour. Psychiat., 1988—, 1989—93; editor-in-chief:, 1993—; contbr. articles to profl. jours. Recipient Rhonda and Bernard Sarnat award NAS, 1999, C. Charles Burlingame award, 1999, Arthur P. Noyes award in schizophrenia, 1999, Lieber prize Nat. Alliance for Rsch. on Schizophrenia and Depression, 2000, Pres.'s Nat. Medal Sci., 2000, Interbrew Baillet-Latour Health prize, 2003; Woodrow Wilson fellow, 1958-59, Fulbright fellow Oxford U., London, 1959-60. Fellow Royal Coll. Physicians Surgeons Can. (hon.), Am. Psychiat. Assn. (Adolf Meyer award 1999, Disting. Svc. award 2004), Am. Coll. Neuropharmacologists, Royal Soc. Medicine; mem. Am. Acad. Arts and Scis., Am. Psychopathol. Assn. (pres. 1989-90), Inst. Medicine of NAS (coun. 1996—). Office: U Iowa Hosps and Clinics 200 Hawkins Dr Iowa City IA 52242-1057

ANDREASON, JOHN CHRISTIAN, lawyer; b. Marysville, Calif., Nov. 18, 1924; s. John Christian and Sadie Louisa (Duus) A. BA, JD, Stanford U., 1958. Bar: Calif. 1958. With Aerojet-Gen. Corp., La Jolla, Calif., 1958-87, v.p., gen. counsel, 1980-87. Mem. ABA, Nat. Contract Mgmt. Assn., Am. Corp. Counsel Assn. Lodges: Masons. Republican. Home: PO Box 39 Plymouth CA 95669-0039

ANDREASSI, JOHN LAWRENCE, psychologist, educator; b. N.Y.C., Oct. 23, 1934; s. Croce and Agnes Marie Andreassi; m. Gina Maria Andreassi, Mar. 29, 1969; children: John II, Jeanine, Cristina. BA, CCNY, 1956; MA, Fordham U., 1959; PhD, Case Western Res. U., Cleve., 1964. Lic. psychologist, N.Y. Psychologist Dunlap & Assocs., Stamford, Conn., 1958-61; USPHS fellow Case Western Res. U., Cleve., 1961-64; assoc. prof. NYU, N.Y.C., 1967-73; prof. psychology CUNY, 1973—. Author: Psychophysiology, 1980, 4th edit., 2000; editor-in-chief Internat. Jour. Psychophysiology, 1988—. With USN, 1964-67. Disting. Faculty scholar Baruch Coll., CUNY, 1978; Office of Naval Rsch. grantee, 1969-73, Air Force Office of Sci. Rsch. grantee, 1973-85. Mem. APA, Internat. Orgn. Psychophysiology (v.p. 1984-94, bd. govs. 1996—, bd. dirs. 1982-94), Assn. for Applied Psychophysiology and Biofeedback, Sigma Xi. Avocations: tennis, golf, chess. Office: City Univ of New York Baruch Coll Dept Psychology Box B8-215 One Bernard Baruch Way New York NY 10010 Office Phone: 646-312-3790. Business E-Mail: john_andreassi@baruch.cuny.edu.

ANDREASSON, KIM J., writer, consultant; b. Varberg, Sweden, Feb. 17, 1976; s. Kenth and Gullvi Andreasson. BA (hon.), NYU, 2000; MIA, Columbia U., 2002. Web editor Goteborgs-Posten, Sweden, 1997—98, asst. editor, 1998—98; forum coord. Fgn. Policy Assn., N.Y.C., 2001—01. Contbr. articles to profl. jours. Assoc. Civic Resource Group, L.A., 2003—. Recipient, Am.-Scandinavian Found., 2005; scholar, The Marcus Wallenberg Found., 2001. Mem.: Internat. Inst. Strategic Studies. Conservative. Personal E-mail: kim@kimandreasson.com.

ANDREEN, AVIVA LOUISE, dentist, researcher, academic administrator, educator; b. Frankfurt, Germany, Jan. 6, 1952; (parents Am. citizens); d. Robert Benjamin Andreen and Margie Corinne (LaPointe) Marshall; m. Merrill R. Penn, Nov. 8, 1987 (div.); 1 child from previous marriage, Robert Morton Salkin. BA, NYU, 1975; student, Westchester C.C., 1976; DDS, NYU Coll. Dentistry, 1996; postgrad., Laser Inst. Am., 1980. Cert. mobile laser operator, N.Y. Tchr. Kibbutz Regavim, D.N. Menasche, Israel, 1975-76; account rep. Traveler's Ins. Co., N.Y.C., 1976; spl. projects coord. Sapan Engring. Co., N.Y.C., 1976-78; sec., treas. founder J. Sapan Holographic Studios, N.Y.C., 1979; owner, pres. Universal Media Cons., White Plains, NY, 1980-84; dir. edn., owner Am. Ctr. for Laser Edn., Bronx, NY, 1984-96; pres. Penn Laser Systems Inc., 1994-96; chief dental resident St. Barnabas Hosp., Bronx, 1997—98; fellow in spl. patient care Helen Hayes Hosp., West Haverstraw, NY, 1998-99; clin. instr. spl. patient care, oral medicine and pathology NYU Coll. Dentistry, N.Y.C., 1999; dentist Marvin Family Dentistry, Nanuet, NY, 1999—2001; owner, ptnr. Dental Arts of Suffern, LLP, NY, 2001—02; assoc. Dr. Gerald B. Greitzer, Tarrytown, NY, 2002—04. Attending dentist Bronx Park Dental; faculty practice St. Barnabas Hosp., 2003-04; attending dentist Helen Hayes Hosp.; lectr. Hudson River Mus., Yonkers, N.Y., 1986-87; prodr. laser light show, Andrus Planetarium; tchr. 1st laser safety course in Am. H.S., 1980; designed laser safety course for Westchester C.C., 1992; cons.in field. Curator Holography A New Dimension White Plains Mus. Gallery, Hudson River Mus., Yonkers, Troster Hall Sci.; vol. forensic dentist for World Trade Ctr. attack N.Y.C. Med. Examiner's Office, 2001—02. Lt. comdr. Dental Corps USNR, 2001—03. Mem. Acad. Gen. Dentistry, Alpha Omega. Avocations: reading, dental laser research, crocheting, embroidery. Office: Special Care Treatment Ctr D880 UMDNJ 110 Bergen St Newark NJ 07106

ANDREESSEN, MARC, software company executive, internet innovator; BS in Computer Sci., U. Ill., 1993. Founder Mosaic Comm. Corp. (now Netscape Comm. Corp.), Mountain View, Calif., 1994; v.p. tech. Netscape Comm. Corp., Mountain View, Calif., 1994-97, exec. v.p., 1997-99; chief tech. officer AOL, 1999; co-founder, chmn. Opsware Inc. (formerly Loudcloud), 1999—. Achievements include development of Mosaic graphical browser for the World Wide Web. Office: Opsware Inc 599 N Mathilda Ave Sunnyvale CA 94085-3545

ANDREOFF, CHRISTOPHER ANDON, lawyer; b. Detroit, July 15, 1947; s. Andon Anastas and Mildred Dimitry (Kolinoff) A.; m. Nancy Anne Krochmal, Jan. 12, 1980; children: Alison Brianne, Lauren Kathleen. BA, Wayne State U., 1969; postgrad. in law, Washington U., St. Louis, 1969-70; JD, U. Detroit, 1972. Bar: Mich. 1972, U.S. Dist. Ct. (ea. dist.) Mich. 1972, U.S. Ct. Appeals (6th cir.) 1974, Fla. 1978, U.S. Supreme Ct. 1980. Legal intern Wayne County Prosecutor's Office, Detroit, 1970-72; law clk. Wayne County Cir. Ct., Detroit, 1972-73; asst. U.S. atty. U.S. Dept. Justice, Detroit, 1973-80; asst. chief criminal divsn. U.S. Atty.'s Office, 1977-80; spl. atty. organized crime and racketeering sect. U.S. Dept. Justice, 1980-84, dep. chief Detroit Organized Crime Strike Force, 1982-85, mem. narcotics adv. com., 1979-80; ptnr. Evans & Luptak, Detroit, 1985-93, Jaffe, Raitt, Heuer & Weiss, Detroit, 1995—. Lectr. U.S. Atty. Gen. Advocacy Inst., 1984. Recipient numerous spl. commendations FBI, U.S. Drug Enforcement Adminstrn., U.S. Dept. Justice, U.S. Atty. Gen. Mem. ABA, FBA (spkr. trial adv. and criminal law sect. Detroit 1983—, bd. dirs. 1989-91, chmn. criminal law sect. 1990-91), Mich. Bar Assn., Fla. Bar Assn., Nat. Assn. Criminal Def. Lawyers, Detroit Bar Assn. Greek Orthodox. Home: 4661 Rivers Edge Dr Troy MI 48098-4161 Office: Jaffe Raitt Heuer & Weiss One Woodward Ave Ste 2400 Detroit MI 48226

ANDREOLI, KATHLEEN GAINOR, nurse, educator, dean; b. Albany, NY, Sept. 22, 1935; d. John Edward and Edmunda Elizabeth (Ringlemann) Gainor; children: Paula Kathleen, Thomas Anthony, Karen Marie. BSN, Georgetown U., 1957; MSN, Vanderbilt U., 1959; DSN, U. Ala., Birmingham, 1979. Staff nurse Albany Hosp. Med. Ctr., 1957; instr. St. Thomas Hosp. Sch. Nursing, Nashville, 1958—59, Georgetown U. Sch. Nursing, 1959—60, Duke U. Sch. Nursing, 1960—61, Bon Secours Hosp. Sch. Nursing, Balt., 1962—64; ednl. coordinator, physician asst. program, instr. coronary care unit nursing inservice edn. Duke U. Med. Ctr., Durham, NC, 1965—70; ednl. dir. physician asst. program dept. medicine U. Ala. Med. Ctr., Birmingham, 1970—75, clin. assoc. prof. cardiovasc. nursing Sch. Nursing, 1970—77, asst. prof. nursing dept. medicine, 1971, assoc. prof., 1972—, assoc. prof. nursing Sch. Pub. and Allied Health, 1973—; assoc. dir. Family Nurse Practitioner Program, 1976, assoc. prof. cmty. health nursing Grad. Program, 1977—79, assoc. prof. dept. pub. health, 1978—79; prof. nursing, spl. asst. to pres. for ednl. affairs U. Tex. Health Sci. Ctr., Houston, 1979—82, acting dean Sch. Allied Health Scis., 1981, v.p. for ednl. svcs., interdisciplinary edn., internat. programs, 1983—87; v.p. nursing affairs Rush-Presbyn.-St. Lukes's Med. Ctr., Chgo., 1987—; dean Rush U. Coll. Nursing, 1987—2005, Kellogg emeritus dean, 2005—. Mem. nat. adv. nursing coun. VHA, 1992; adv. bd. Nursing Spectrum, midwest region, 1995—2005; cons. in field. Editor: Heart and Lung, Jour. of Total Care, 1971; editl. bd. Nursing Consult, Elsevier Publs., 2004—05; contbr. articles to profl. jours.; author, editor: Comprehensive Cardiac Care, 1983. Active Internat. Nursing Coalition for Mass Casualty Edn., 2002—; mem. adv. bd. Robert Wood Johnson Clin. Nurse Sch. Program; mem. vis. com. Vanderbilt U. Sch. Nursing; mem. Leadership Ill., 1991; mem. nat. nursing asdv. com. Voluntary Hosp. Am., 1991; mem. governing coun. Inst. for Hosp. Clin. Nursing Edn., Am. Hosp. Assn., 1993; bd. dirs. Ill. League for Nursing, 1994, Lyric Opera Chgo. Guild; adv. bd. Hospice Ptnrs. Recipient Founder's award, N.C. Heart Assn., 1970, Disting. Alumni award, Vanderbilt U. Sch. Nursing, 1985, Leadership Tex. award, 1985, Disting. Alumni award, U. Ala. Sch. Nursing, 1991, Henry Betts MD Employment Advocacy award, Rehab. Inst. Chgo., 2004. Fellow: Am. Acad. Nursing; mem.: ACNA, ANA, Internat. Nursing Coalition for Mass Casualty Edn., Inst. Medicine Chgo. (bd. govs. 2004—), Nat. Nursing Adv. Coun. Hosps. Am., Am. Heart Assn. Coun. Cardiovasc. Nursing, Coun. Family Nurse Practitioners and Clinicians, Ala. Heart Assn., Nat. League Nursing, Inst. Medicine of NAS, Am. Assn. Colls. Nursing, Rotary One Club Chgo., Phi Kappa Phi, Alpha Eta, Sigma Theta Tau (Dreher Outstanding Dean award 2003, Rehab. Inst. of Chgo. Henry Setts Disability Advocacy award 2004). Roman Catholic. Home: 1212 N Lake Shore Dr Apt 10AN Chicago IL 60610-2359 Office: 1212 N Lake Shore Dr Chicago IL 60610-2359 Office Phone: 312-266-8338. Business E-Mail: kathleen_g_andreoli@rush.edu.

ANDREOLI, THOMAS EUGENE, physician; b. Bronx, NY, Jan. 9, 1935; BA cum laude, St. Vincent Coll., Latrobe, Pa, 1952—56; ScD (hon.), St. Vincent Coll., 1987; MD magna cum laude, Georgetown U., 1956—60; PhD (hon.), Univ. Paris, 1993; MD (hon.), Aristotle U., Thessaloniki, Greece, 2000, Semmelweis U., Budapest, Hungary, 2003. Diplomate: Am. Bd. Internal Medicine and subspecialty in nephrology. Intern, resident in medicine Duke U., Durham, N.C., 1960-61, 64-65, assoc. prof. medicine and asst. prof. physiology, 1965-70; prof. medicine and physiology, dir. nephrology research and tng. center U. Ala. Sch. Medicine, Birmingham, 1970-78; prof., chmn. dept. internal medicine U. Tex. Med. Sch., Houston, 1979-87, Edward Randall III prof., chmn. dept. internal medicine, 1986-87; chief medicine Hermann Hosp., Houston, 1979-87; Nolan prof. and chmn. dept. internal medicine U. Ark. Coll. Medicine, Little Rock, 1988—2004, Disting. prof. dept. internal medicine, dept. physiology and biophysics, 2004—. Author: Disturbances in Body Fluid Osmolality, 1977, Physiology of Membrane Disorders, 1978, 86, Cecil Essentials of Medicine, 1986, 90, 93, 97, 2001, 04, Molecular Biology of Membrane Transport Disorders, 1996; Editor Am. Jour. Physiology: Renal, Fluid and Electrolyte Physiology, 1976-83, Kidney

Internat., 1984-97; assoc. editor Annual Rev. Physiology, 1977-83, Am. Jour. Medicine, 1979-86; mem. editorial bd. Jour. Clin. Investigation, 1976-81, Mineral and Electrolyte Metabolism, 1977-80, Tex. Health Letter, 1980-88, Seminars in Nephrology, 1980-92, Kidney Internat., 1981-85, Physiol. Revs., 1982-84. Recipient Louis Pasteur medal U. Louis Pasteur Strasbourg, France, 1995, Hume award Nat. Kidney Found., 1997, Making Lives Better award, 2004. Fellow Royal Coll. Physicians; mem. ACP (master)(Disting. Teacher award, 2000), Assn. Am. Physicians, Assn. Profs. Medicine (Robert H. Williams Disting. Chair of Med. award, 1998), Am. Soc. Clin. Investigation, Am. Physiol. Soc. (Robert W Berliner award for excellence in Renal Physiology, 2000), Am. Soc. Nephrology (coun. 1988-95, pres. 1993-94, Homer W. Smith award 1995), Internat. Soc. Nephrology (hon.)(exec. com. 1985-2003, v.p. 1995-97, pres.-elect 1997-99, pres. 1999-2001).

ANDREOPOULOS, SPYROS GEORGE, writer; b. Athens, Greece, Feb. 12, 1929; came to U.S., 1953, naturalized, 1962; s. George S. and Anne (Levas) A.; m. Christiane Loesch Loriaux, June 6, 1958; 1 child, Sophie. AB, Wichita State U., 1957. Pub. info. specialist USIA, Salonica, Greece, 1951-53; asst. editorial page editor Wichita (Kans.) Beacon, 1955-59; asst. dir. info. svcs., editor The Menninger Quar., The Menninger Found., Topeka, 1959-63; info. officer Stanford U. Med. Ctr., 1963-83; dir. comm., editor Stanford Medicine, 1983-93, dir. emeritus comm., editor emeritus, 1993—. Editor Sun Valley Forum on Nat. Health, Inc. (Idaho), 1972-83, 85-95, editor emeritus, 1995—. Co-author, editor: Medical Cure and Medical Care, 1972, Primary Care: Where Medicine Fails, 1974, National Health Insurance: Can We Learn from Canada? 1975, Heart Beat, 1978, Health Care for an Aging Society, 1989; contbr. articles to newspapers and profl. jours. With Royal Hellenic Air Force, 1949-50. Mem. AAAS, Assn. Am. Med. Colls., Nat. Assn. Sci. Writers, Am. Med. Writers Assn., Am. Hosp. Assn., Am. Soc. Hosp. Mktg. and Pub. Rels., Coun. for Advancement and Support of Edn. Home: 1012 Vernier Pl Stanford CA 94305-1027 Office Phone: 650-723-6911.

ANDREOTTI, LAMBERTO, pharmaceutical executive; Former exec. Farmitalia Carlo Erba, Pharmacia AB; former sr. v.p., pres. oncology divsn. Pharmacia & Upjohn; v.p., gen. mgr. Italy and European oncology, Worldwide Medicines Group Bristol-Myers Squibb Co., Paris and Rome, 1998—2002, sr. v.p. Europe, Asia-Pacific and Africa, 2002—. Office: Bristol-Myers Squibb Co 345 Park Ave New York NY 10154-0037

ANDREOZZI, LOUIS JOSEPH, lawyer; b. N.J., 1959; m. Lisa Marie Clark, Apr. 12, 1987. BS in Bus. Adminstrn. with hons., Rutgers U., 1981; JD, Seton Hall U., 1984. Bar: N.J. 1984. Asst. gen. counsel Gordon Pub., Inc., Randolph, NJ, 1984—93; dep. gen. counsel Elsevier U.S. Holdings, Morris Plains, NJ, 1985—93; v.p., sec., gen. counsel Reed Elsevier Med. Pub., Belle Mead, NJ, 1994—95; v.p., gen. counsel, sec., head ops. support and svcs., purchasing, sales force homeworking project, customer svc. integration project Lexis-Nexis, Miamisburg, Ohio, 1994—97; pub. Martindale-Hubbell, 1996; chief legal counsel Lexis-Nexis, 1997—98; COO Martindale-Hubbell, New Providence, NJ, 1997—99, Marquis, NRP, New Providence, NJ, 1998—99; vice-chmn. Reed Tech. and Info. Svcs., Inc., 1999—2000; pres., CEO Martindale-Hubbell, Marquis, NRP, New Providence, 1999—2000, LexisNexis North American Legal Markets, 2000—; global officer, mktg. and technology LexisNexis Group, 2001—. Mem. legal adv. bd. Lexis-Nexis, 1994—, exec. bd., 1994—; mem. Friends of the Law Libr. of Congress; bd. dirs. Am. Assn. of Pub. Named to Dept. Distinction in Bus., Rutgers U., 1981, Nat. Honor Soc. in Econs. and Bus., 1981. Mem.: ABA, N.J. Employment Law Assn., Am. Corp. Counsel Assn., Internat. Bar Assn., N.J. Bar Assn. Roman Catholic. Office: Lexis Nexis Group 9443 Springboro Pike Miamisburg OH 45342-4425*

ANDRES, GREG D., prosecutor, lawyer; b. 1967; m. Ronnie Abrams, 2001. BA, U. Notre Dame; JD, U. Chgo., 1995. Bar: 1996. Assoc. Davis, Polk & Wardwell, NYC, 1997—99; asst. U.S. atty. (ea. dist.) NY US Dept. Justice, Bklyn., 1999—, dep. chief organized crime sect., 2005—. Vol. Peace Corps, Benin, 1989—92. Named one of Top 40 Lawyers Under 40, Nat. Law Jour., 2005. Office: 1 Pierrepont Plz Brooklyn NY 11201*

ANDRES, RONALD PAUL, chemical engineer, educator; b. Chgo., Jan. 9, 1938; s. Harold William and Amanda Ann (Breuhaus) A.; m. Jean Mills Elwood, July 15, 1961; children: Douglas, Jennifer, Mark. BS, Northwestern U., 1959; PhD, Princeton U., 1962. Asst. prof. Princeton U., 1962-68, assoc. prof., 1968-76, prof. chem. engring., 1976-81, Purdue U., West Lafayette, Ind., 1981—, head Sch. Chem. Engring., 1981-87, engring. rsch. prof., 1987—2004, emeritus prof. chem. engring., 2004—. Mem. Sigma Xi, Tau Beta Pi, Pi Mu Epsilon, Phi Lambda Upsilon, Phi Eta Sigma. Office: Purdue U Sch Chem Engring West Lafayette IN 47907-2100 Office Phone: 765-494-4047. Business E-Mail: ronald@ecn.purdue.edu.

ANDRESEN, LINDA SKEEN, academic administrator; b. Charleston, W.Va., Feb. 21, 1951; 1 child, Peter Joseph. BS in Secondary Edn., W.Va. State Coll., 1972; MA in Adult Edn., Marshall U., 1979. Learning ctr. coordinator Kanawha County Adult Basic Edn. Program, Charleston, 1975-86; basic skills instr. lead tchr. for W.Va. C&P Telephone Co., Charleston, 1983—; adult basic edn. staff devel. coordinator Marshall U., Huntington, W.Va., 1986—, Regional Edn. Svc. Agy. III, Dunbar, W.Va., 1986—. Sec. W.Va. Adv. Council on Reading, Charleston, 1978; tutor recruitment chmn. and workshop leader Literacy Vols. of Kanawha County, 1981-82; staff devel. dir. RESA III, 1998—, adminstrv. asst., 2001--; dir. Project TEACH, 2001-05 Mem. adv. bd. Nat. Adult Literacy and Learning Disabilitis Ctr., bd. dirs.; bd. dirs. Nat. Assn. Adults with Spl. Learning Needs. Named an Outstanding Young Woman St. Alban's Jaycettes, 1983. Mem. Am. Assn. for Adult and Continuing Edn., W.Va. Adult Edn. Assn. (pres. 1983-84, legis. chairperson 1984-86, bd. dirs. 1986—, Adult Educator of Yr. 1984, W.Va. Adult Edn. Adminstr. of Yr. 1990). Home: 2703 Lincoln Ave Saint Albans WV 25177-2151 Office: RESA III 501 22nd St Dunbar WV 25064-1711

ANDRESEN, MALCOLM, lawyer; b. Medford, Wis., July 26, 1917; s. Thomas Whelen and Ethel (Malkson) A.; m. Ann Kimball, 1942 (div. 1968); children: Anthony M., Susan A. Bridges, Abbott K.; m. Barbara Brown, 1971 (div. 1976); m. Nigi Sato, 1979. BA, U. Wis., 1940, LLB, 1941. Bar: Wis. 1941, N.Y. 1946, U.S. Supreme Ct. 1958. Acct. J.D. Miller & Co., N.Y.C., 1946-47; jr. tax acct. Peat Marwick Mitchell & Co., N.Y.C., 1947-48; assoc. Davis Wagner Hallett & Russell, N.Y.C., 1948-52; tax counsel, then sr. tax counsel, sr. govt. rels. adviser Mobil Oil Corp., N.Y.C., 1952-70; dir. tax legal affairs Nat. Fgn. Trade Coun., N.Y.C., 1970-73; of counsel Delson & Gordon, N.Y.C., 1973-77, Whitman & Ransom, N.Y.C., 1977-86; pvt. practice N.Y.C., 1986—. Trustee, fin. v.p. Nat. Urban League, 1959-65; trustee, treas. Cathedral Ch. of St. John the Divine, N.Y.C., 1977-84. Capt. USMCR, 1942-46. Decorated Bronze Star medal. Mem. Assn. of Bar City of N.Y., Internat. Fiscal Assn. (coun. U.S.A. br. pres. 1971-72), Univ. Club (coun. mem. 1985-89, co-chair com. women mem. admission 1988). Democrat. Episcopalian. Home: 2 Lincoln Sq Apt 24D New York NY 10023-6218 Office: 60 E 42nd St Ste 764 New York NY 10165-0799

ANDRE-STARK, CARRIE BETH, farm management extension agent, educator; d. Philip H. and Cheryle Eileen Andre; m. James Todd Stark, Aug. 23, 1969; 1 child, Kody Archer Stark. BS, U. Idaho, 1993, MS, 2002. Asst. ext. educator 4-H U. Idaho Coop. Ext. Sys., Twin Falls, Idaho, 1994—97; county ext. 4-H youth devel. agt. Mich. State U. Ext., Sault Ste. Marie, 1997—2002; 4-H youth devel. specialist N.D. State U. Ext. Svc., Fargo, 2002—. Mem.: Mich. Assn. Ext. 4-H Youth Staff (treas. 2000—02), Nat. Assn. Ext. 4-H Agents (chair-character edn. task force 2004—, Achievement in Svc. Award 2001). Roman Catholic. Achievements include research in learning styles versus teaching styles. Office: ND State Univ Ext 219 FLC Fargo ND 58105 Office Phone: 701-231-5923. Office Fax: 701-231-8568. E-mail: cstark@ndsuext.nodak.edu.

ANDRETTI, JOHN, professional race car driver; b. Bethlehem, Pa., Mar. 12, 1963; s. Aldo and Carolyn (Stofflet) A.; m. Nancy Ann Summers, Sept. 7, 1987; children: Jarett John, Olivia Elizabeth. BA in Bus. Mgmt., Moravian Coll. Vehicle maintenance Paul E. Smith Plumbing, 1977-78; gen. maintenance Firestone Tire & Rubber Co., 1978-81; sportsman stock cars, 1982; formula super vee, 1982; USAC midgets, 1983-85, 87-89, 93; sprint cars (USAC & CRA), 1983-87; IMSA GTP, 1986, 87, 89, 93; SCCA Can Am, 1984; IMSA showroom stock, 1986-87; CART Indy cars, 1987-94; chmn. bd. Andretti-Helmling Automotive Corp., 1991—. Shareholder Andretti-Laird Racing, 1997, Andretti-Laird Helmling Mfg., 1997. Winner U.S. Auto Club Midget Championship, 1983, 24 Hours of Daytona, 1989, 1st Indy car win in Australia, 1991, USAC Championship Dirt Cars, 1985, Group A, 1988, Group C, 1988-89, NHRA Top Fuel Dragster, 1993, British F2, 1993, Land Speed Record, Subaru Legacy, 1993, Nascar Winston Cup, 1993-98, first Nascar Winston Cup pole position, 1995, first win Nascar Winston Cup, 1997, many others; only driver to compete in Indy 500 and World 600 in same day, 1994; named USAC Midget rookie of yr., 1983, Dorney Park rookie of yr., 1982. Roman Catholic. Office: c/o Petty Enterprises 311 Branson Mill Rd Randleman NC 27317-8008

ANDRETTI, MARIO, retired race car driver; b. Montona, Italy, Feb. 28, 1940; came to U.S., 1955, naturalized, 1964; s. Alvise and Rina (Benvegnu) A.; m. Dee Ann Hoch, Nov. 25, 1961; children: Michael, Jeffrey, Barbra. Began racing career at age 19, Nazareth, Pa. Champ Car Nat. Champion, 1965, 66, 69, 84; Daytona 500 winner, 1967; 12 Hrs. of Sebring winner, 1967, 70, 72; Indpls. 500 winner, 1969; Indy 500 pole winner, 1966, 67, 87; USAC Nat. Dirt Track Champion, 1974; Formula One World Champion, 1978; Internat. Race of Champions titlist, 1979; Driver of the Yr., 1967, 78, 84, Driver of the Quarter Century, 1992, Driver of the Century, 1999-00; all-time leader in Champ Car Pole Positions won (67); all-time Champ Car lap leader (7,587); all-time record holder for Champ Car starts (407); oldest race winner in recorded Champ car history (53 years 34 days, Phoenix, 1993); only driver to win Champ Car races in four decades; had 12 Formula One victories and captured 18 Formula One pole positions.

ANDREU, HELENE C., dancer, educator; b. N.Y.C., Nov. 8, 1930; d. Gaston Andreu and Clotilde Jaureguibéhère. BA, CUNY, 1953; student, Sch. Am. Ballet, 1948—54; MA in Dance Edn., Columbia U., 1971. Lic. tchr. of dance early childhood, recreational, jr. H.S., H.S. performing arts N.Y.C. Bd. Edn. Singer, dancer, choreographer Am. Savoyards, N.Y.C., 1957—68; dance instr. pvt. dance studios Bklyn., N.Y.C., 1959—92; dance instr., substitute Bd. Edn. After Sch. Ctrs., N.Y.C., 1963—73; singer, dancer, choreographer Ephrata (Pa.) Star Playhouse, 1964—67; part-time adj. lectr. dance CUNY, N.Y.C., 1973—2002; dance instr., choreographer Bd. Edn. Adult Edn., N.Y.C., 1975—92; dance instr. Henry Street Settlement, N.Y.C., 1989—98. Speech/English tutor CUNY, 1989—98. Author, choreographer Jazz Dance: An Adult Beginners Guide, 1983, author, photographer, choreographer Aerobic Razzmatazz, 2000, Jazz Dance Styles and Steps, 2003. Vol. Bklyn. Pub. Libr. Literacy Program. Mem.: Actors Equity Assn. Avocations: gardening, cats, singing, photography.

ANDREULA-ORTIZ, JO-ELLEN, hospital administrator, cosmetics executive; b. Hoboken, NJ, Mar. 19, 1958; d. Peter Albert and Gilda Rosemary A.; m. Carlos Ruben Ortiz, Nov. 29, 1997; children: Krista-Rae, Kortney-Lyn, Kerrin Marie, Carlos II. Ptnr. Vinny's Confectionary Store, Hoboken, NJ, 1976-84; with Washington Savs. Bank, Hoboken, 1990-92; bus. bank svcs. Bank of N.Y., Weehwken, N.Mex., 1992; brand product dir. adminstr. Roche (Labs.) Pharm. Co., Nutley, NJ, 2000—; med. adminstr. Christ Hosp., Jersey City. Bus. and beauty cons. Jo-Ellen's Collectables, Hoboken, 1997—. Mem. Jehovah's Witness. Office: Roche Pharms 360 Kingsland Ave Nutley NJ 07110 also: Christ Hosp Bon Secours of Canterbury 176 Palisade Ave Jersey City NJ 07306 E-mail: Jo_ellen.ortiz@roche.com.

ANDREW, GIACCIA A., lawyer; b. Reading, Pa., Aug. 31, 1959; AB magna cum laude, Georgetown U., 1981, JD, 1984. Bar: Pa. 1984, NJ 1984, DC 1987, US Dist. Ct. (Dist. NJ), US Dist. Ct. (Dist. DC), US Dist. Ct. (Ea. Dist.) Pa., US Ct. Appeals (DC Cir.). Ptnr. Chadbourne & Parke LLP, Washington, chmn, Environ. Practice Group, resident mng. ptnr. Washington Office. Contbr. articles to profl. jour.; spkr. in field. Mem.: DC Bar, ABA, Phi Beta Kappa. Office: Chadbourne & Parke LLP 1200 New Hampshire Ave NW Washington DC 20036 Office Phone: 202-974-5652. Office Fax: 202-974-5602. Business E-Mail: agiaccia@chadbourne.com.

ANDREW, JOHN HENRY, lawyer; b. Duluth, Minn., May 23, 1936; s. Frederick William and Florence Elizabeth (Phillips) A.; m. Floretta Claudette Townsend; children: Sean Townsend, Brett Townsend. BA cum laude with distinction, U. Minn., Duluth, 1958; JD, Northwestern U., 1961. Bar: Ill. 1961, Calif. 1975, N.Y. 1980. Assoc. Pattishall, McAuliffe & Hofstetter, Chgo., 1961-71; sr. atty. J.C. Penney Co., Inc., N.Y.C., 1971-74, sr. counsel legis. and regional ops., Western regional coun. L.A., Buena Park, Calif., 1974-93, sr. govt. rels. counsel Sacramento, 1993-97, chief counsel govt. rels., 1997. Author: The Hanging of Arthur Hodge: A Caribbean Anti-Slavery Milestone. Chmn. pub. affairs com. Planned Parenthood Assn. Chgo., 1970-71; mem. Calif. State Dem. Cen. Com., 1976-82. Mem.: ABA, Sacramento County Bar Assn. (co-chmn. history com. 2001—02), Calif. State Bar (com. on consumer fin. svcs. 1982—84, 1990—93), Ill. State Bar Assn. (chmn. internat. law sect. 1969—70), Calif. C. of C. (regulatory, consumer and legal affairs com. 1974—86, mem. air and waste mgmt. com. 1994—97), Sullivan County (Pa.) Hist. Soc. (life), Renaissance Soc. Calif. State U. Sacramento (v.p. 2003—05, pres. 2005—), Cornwall Family History Soc., No. Calif. Pubs. and Authors (Best Gen. Non-Fiction award 2000—01), JCPenney Retirees Club (regional pres. 2003—04). Home: 11359 Mother Lode Cir Gold River CA 95670-3025 Personal E-mail: jandrew523@sbcglobal.net.

ANDREW, JOSEPH JERALD, lawyer; b. Poe, Ind., Mar. 1, 1960; s. Jerald Lee Andrew and Sylvia Huss Hanselmann; m. Anne Slaughter, Sept. 9, 1989. BA, Yale U., 1982, JD, 1985. Bar: Ind. 1986, DC 2002, NY 2002, US Ct. Appeals 7th Cir. 1986, US Dist. Ct. No. & So. Districts Ind. 1986. Law clk to Judge Flaum US Ct. Appeals 7th Cir., Chgo., 1985-86; assoc. Baker & Daniels, Indpls., 1986-89; chief dep. sec. of State of Ind., Indpls., 1989-91; with Bingham, Summers, Welsh & Spilman, Indpls., 1991-95, ptnr., 1992-95; chmn. Ind. Dem. Party, 1995-99; ptnr. Johnson Smith Pence, Indpls., 1997-99; nat. chmn. Dem. Nat. Com., Washington, 1999-2001; ptnr. Cadwalader, Wickersham & Taft, Washington, 2001—03, McDermott, Will & Emery, Washington, 2003—04, Sonnenschein Nath & Rosenthal, LLP, Washington, 2004—. Chmn. adv. bd. New Dem. Network. Author: (book) The Disciples, 1993. Glen Peters Legal Scholar, 1983—85. Democrat. Office: Sonnenschein Nath & Rosenthal LLP Ste 600, E Tower 1301 K St NW Washington DC 20005 Office Phone: 202-408-5210. Office Fax: 202-408-6399. Business E-Mail: jandrew@sonnenschein.com.

ANDREW, KENNETH L., physicist, researcher, physics professor; b. Wichita, Kans., June 14, 1919; s. I(saac) Ernest and Hulda (Cox) A.; m. Lois Renner, Sept. 1, 1940; children— Ralph K., Dale Ernest, Nancy Lee AB, Friends U., 1940; MA, Johns Hopkins U., 1942; PhD, Purdue U., 1951. Head dept. physics Friends U., Wichita, 1942-56; chmn. dept. physics Dickinson Coll., Carlisle, Pa., 1956-57; assoc. prof. physics Purdue U., West Lafayette, Ind., 1957-68, prof. physics, 1968-89; prof. emeritus, 1989—. Exchange prof. Lab. Aimé-Cotton, Orsay, France, 1968-69; cons. Los Alamos Nat. Lab., 1965-72, 77-99, Argonne Nat. Lab. Ill., 1977-83; prin. investigator research grants in atomic emission spectroscopy NSF, 1958-83, research grants in atomic spectroscopy NASA, 1963-75, contracts in spectroscopy Office Naval Research, 1959-66; mem. com. on line spectra of elements NRC, 1961-73, chmn., 1966-68 Contbr. numerous articles to profl. jours. Recipient Disting. Alumnus award Friends U., 1971. Fellow Optical Soc. Am. (assoc. editor 1980-83); mem. European Group Atomic Spectroscopists, Am. Phys. Soc., Am. Assn. Physics Tchrs., Internat. Astron. Union, Sigma Xi. Home: 1637 May St # 1002 Wichita KS 67213-3503

ANDREW, LUCIUS ARCHIBALD DAVID, III, bank executive; b. Mar. 5, 1938; s. Lucius Archibald David Jr. and Victoria (Rollins) A.; m. Susan Ott, June 1, 1963 (div. 1973); children: Ashley W., L.A. David IV; m. Phoebe Haffner Kellogg, Dec. 21, 1974; children: Gaylord M., Charles H., Matthew K., Louise K. BS, U. Pa., 1962; MBA, NYU, 1965. Asst. treas. The Bank of N.Y., N.Y.C., 1962-68; instl. salesman Drexel, Harriman, Ripley, N.Y.C., 1968-70; v.p., br. mgr. Drexel, Firestone, Inc., Chgo., 1970-72; ptnr., br. mgr. Fannestock & Co., Chgo., 1972-74; pres. N.E.A., Inc., 1975-85; dir. First Am. Bank Corp., Seattle, 1985—. Vice chmn. Viner's, Ltd., Sheffield, Eng., 1981-82; chmn. exec. com. Cert. Mfg. Co., Shelton, Wash., 1975-85; bd. dirs. First Am. Bank, Chgo., 1965-91, chmn., 1982-91; bd. dirs. First Am. Data Corp.; chmn. FGI, Inc., Forest Grove, Oreg., 1985-86, Union St. Capital Corp., Seattle, Wash., 1986-87, Brudi Inc., Seattle, 1988-90. Trustee Brooks Sch.; past trustee Seattle Repertory Theatre; bd. dirs. Swedish Met. Ctr. Found. Mem. The Brook, Racquet and Tennis Club (N.Y.C.), Racquet Club (Chgo.), Rainier Club, Univ. Club, Golf Club (Seattle), Tennis Club (Seattle). Home: The Highlands Seattle WA 98177 Office: 200 1st Ave W Ste 400 Seattle WA 98119-4219

ANDREWS, ARCHIE MOULTON, retired federal official; b. Greenwich, Conn., July 29, 1919; s. Archie M. and Eleanor (Underwood) A.; m. Margaret Jane Jones, Mar. 3, 1944 (dec. Sept. 1977); children: Archie Moulton III, Peter Underwood, Duncan Trumbull; m. Nike Smith Middleton, Oct. 3, 1978 (dec. Mar. 1987); m. Dorothy Johnson Conley, Sept. 30, 1989. AB, Princeton U., 1941. Exec. trainee W.R. Grace & Co., 1941-42; econ. analyst State Dept., 1942-43; U.S. rep. blacklist com. Ministry Econ. Warfare, Am. embassy, London, 1943-45; with Dictograph Products, Inc., Danbury, Conn., 1946-63, pres., 1962-63; also dir.; pres. Acousticon-Dictograph Co. Ltd., Can., 1963, dir., 1958-63, Gen. Acoustics Ltd., Eng., 1950-63; dep. dir. Bur. Internat. Commerce, Dept. Commerce, 1964-69; dir. U.S. trade mission to N. Africa, 1966; comml. counsellor Am. embassy, London, 1970-75; dir. bus. services Office Internat. Affairs, HUD, Washington, 1976-77; dir. exporters service Office Export Adminstrn., Dept. Commerce, Washington, 1978-86; sr. policy analyst Office of Tech. and Policy Analysis, 1986-88, ret., 1988. Mem. SAR Clubs: Princeton (Washington and N.Y.C.); Pilgrims; Diplomatic and Consular Officers Ret. Home: 7101 Bay Front Dr #325 Annapolis MD 21403 Personal E-mail: aandrews@friend.ly.net.

ANDREWS, BENNY, artist; b. Madison, Ga., Nov. 13, 1930; s. George Clevel and Viola (Perryman) A.; children: Christopher, Thomas Michael, Julia Rachael; m. Nene Humphrey, June 14, 1986. Student, Ft. Valley State Coll., 1948-50, U. Chgo., 1956-58; BFA, Chgo. Art Inst., 1958. Instr. art New Sch. Social Rsch., NYC, 1967-70, Queens Coll., NYC, 1969—; dir. visual arts program Nat. Endowment for Arts, Washington, 1982—84. Vis. artist Calif. State Coll. Hayward, 1969; vis. art critic Yale U., 1974. Author: Between the Lines, 1978; illustrator: Applachee Red (Raymond Andrews), 1978, Rosebell Lee Wildcat Tennessee (Raymond Andrews), 1980; contbr. articles on black art, culture to profl. jours.; assoc. editor (art): Encore mag.; one man shows Kessler Gallery, Provincetown, Mass., 1960-70, Forum Gallery, N.Y.C., 1962-64-66, Henri Gallery, Alexandria, Va., 1963-64, Studio Mus., N.Y.C., 1970, ACA Gallery, N.Y.C., 1972, U. Md., 1972, Aronson-Midtown Gallery, Atlanta, 1973, Lerner-Heller Gallery, N.Y.C., 1979, 80, 81, Gallery of Sarasota, 1979, Savannah Coll. Art and Design, 1983, Sid Deutsch Gallery, N.Y.C., 1983, Merida Galleries, Louisville, 1984, Michael Rosenfeld Gallery, N.Y.C., 1997-98, ACA Galleries, 2000-01, others; exhibited in group shows at Detroit Inst., 1959, Phila. Acad. Art, 1960, Bklyn. Mus., 1963, Butler Inst. Am. Art, 1967, Mus. Modern Art, N.Y.C., 1968-71, High Mus., Atlanta, 1971, Wadsworth Atheneum, 1979, Art Inst. Chgo., 1979, Los Angeles County Mus. Art, 1982, ACA Galleries, N.Y.C., 1995-97, 2000-01, Wichita Art Mus., Wichita, Kans., 1996-97, others; represented in permanent collections Mus. Modern Art, N.Y.C., High Mus., Atlanta, African Mus., Washington, Norfolk Mus., Va., Butler Inst. Am. Art, Youngstown, Ohio, Chrysler Mus., Provincetown, Mass., La Jolla (Calif.) Mus., NYU, N.Y.C., Detroit Inst. Art, U. Kans. Art Mus., Lawrence, U. Wyo. Art Gallery, Laramie, Joslyn Mus. Art, Omaha, Bklyn. Mus., Joseph H. Hirschhorn Mus., Ohara Mus., Japan, Edwin A. Ulrich Mus., Wichita, Kans. Co-chmn. Black Emergency Cultural Coalition, 1969—; bd. dirs. Children's Art Carnival, MacDowell Colony, Artists Talk on Art, Provincetown Work Ctr., Creative Drama Soc., Atlanta Bur. Cultural Affairs Gallery. staff sgt. USAF, 1950-54. John Hay Whitney fellow, 1965-67; Dorne Professionship U. Bridgeport, Conn., 1970; N.Y. Council Arts grantee, 1971; fellow Nat. Endowment for Arts, 1974-81, NY Coun. on Arts, 1971-1981, MacDowell Colony fellow, 1973-73, 75-78. Office: 564 Sackett St Brooklyn NY 11217-3019 *My whole existence as a person and as an artist rests on how I relate to my principles. It is very important for me to keep those principles high, and in so doing, I hope to inspire others to do the same.*

ANDREWS, BETTY BAUSERMAN, retired secondary school educator, property manager; b. Luray, Va, Dec. 29, 1935; d. Raymond Edgar Bauserman and Elizabeth Elaine Houser; m. George Norman Andrews, July 26, 1964 (dec. Apr. 1996). BS, Madison Coll., 1958; postgrad., U. Va., 1964—68, George Mason U., 1969. Cert. coll. profl. cert., Va. Classroom tchr. Clarke County H.S., Berryville, Va., 1958—64, Loudoun Valley H.S., Purcellville, Va., 1964—68; proofreader Missles and Rockets mag., Washington, 1964, Loudoun County H.S., Leesburg, Va., 1968—69; head libr. media specialist Broad Run H.S., Ashburn, Va., 1969—2000. Cons., libr. reorganizer Logetronics Corp., Springfield, Va., 1974; mem. sch. improvement team Broad Run HS, Ashburn, 1996-2000. Adv. bd. Sterling (Va.) Pub. Libr., 1998—. Mem. NEA, AAUW, James Madison U. Alumni Assn., Va. Edn. Assn. (life), Loudoun Edn. Assn. (life), Loudoun Educators Media Assn. (life), Nat. Soc. DAR, Sparlandria Investment Club, Alpha Gamma Delta. Democrat. Methodist. Avocations: antique collecting, gardening, investing, sailing, reading. Home: 821 Golden Arrow St Great Falls VA 22066-2517 Personal E-mail: striperstripes@aol.com.

ANDREWS, BILLY FRANKLIN, pediatrician, educator; b. Graham, NC, Sept. 22, 1932; s. Dean Franklin and Arlee (Byers) A.; m. Faye Rich, Dec. 25, 1953; children: Ann Elizabeth Feigenbaum, Billy Franklin Jr., David Ashley. Student, Brevard (N.C.) Coll., 1950, Elon Coll., 1951; BS cum laude, Wake Forest Coll., 1953; MD, Duke U., 1957. Diplomate Am. Bd. Pediat., 1963. Commd. 2d lt. U.S. Army, 1956, advanced through grades to maj., 1962; intern Ft. Benning U.S. Army Hosp., Ga., 1957—58; resident pediat. Walter Reed Gen. Hosp., Washington, 1958—60; with mil. med. and allied scis. course Walter Reed Army Inst. Rsch., Washington, 1960—61; chief pediat. svc. Rodriguez U.S. Army Hosp., Ft. Brooke, PR, 1961—63; chief pediat. Tropical Med. Rsch. Lab., Ft. Brooke, 1963—64; ret. U.S. Army, 1964; dir. newborn svcs. U. Louisville, 1964—76, from asst. prof. pediat. to chmn., 1964—93, chmn. emeritus, 1993—, dir. Comprehensive Health Care Ctr. for High Risk Infants and Children, 1968—98; chief of staff Kosair Children's Hosp., Louisville, 1969—93, chief-of-staff emeritus, 1993—. Cons. divsn. adult and child health Ky. Dept. Pub. Health, 1966—2003; lectr. Jour. Pediat. Found., 1972; Staley Disting. Christian scholar Mary Baldwin Coll., Washington and Lee U., Sch. Medicine of U.Va., 1990; vis. scholar in med. history and ethics Green Coll., Oxford (Eng.) U., 1993, vis. fellow, 98. Author: Children's Bill of Rights, 1968; editor: Small-for-Date Infants, 1970, The Newborn, Pediatric Clinics of North America, 1977, Aphorisms, Tributes and Tenets of Billy F. Andrews: In Walls, M.E., 1986, Ideals and Inspiration (F.R. Andrews), 1993, Words to Live By (F.R. Andrews), 1993, A Statement on Transplantation and Organ Donors, 1994; contbr. numerous articles to profl. publs.; inventor, poet. Pres. Kornhauser Libr., Health Scis. Ctr., 1981-82, 90-91; mem., tchr., deacon, elder United Ch. of Christ. Recipient Helen B. Fraser award for Leadership in Ocontalogy, 1978, Norton-Children's Hosp. award for Leadership in Neonatology, 1978, Award of Recognition, XVII Internat. Congress Pediat., Manila, 1983, Wisdom award of honor, eminent fellow The Wisdom Soc., 1991, The Billy F. Andrews, M.D. Endowed Chair in Pediat., U. Louisville, 1993, Winston Churchill medal of Wisdom Soc., Eminent Churchill Fellow of Wisdom Soc., 1993, Disting. Alumnus award Wake Forest U., 1983, The Billy F. Andrews, M.D. scholarship for pediat. U. Louisville Sch. Medicine, 1986, Festschrift to Billy F. Andrews, M.D., Jour. of Perinatology, 1995; Billy F. Andrews, MD, Lectureship in Neonatology

Dept. Pediat., U. Louisville, 2002. Fellow ACP, Am. Acad. Pediat., Royal Soc. Medicine (London), Internat. Biog. Assn.; mem. AMA, Am. Pediat. Soc., Am. Osler Soc. (pres. 1996-97), Am. Soc. for Bioethics and Humanities, Soc. for Pediat. Rsch., So. Soc. Pediat. Rsch. (founding), Southeastern Perinatal Soc. (founding), Nat. Assn. Children's Hosps. and Related Instns. (founding), Ky. Med. Assn. (faculty Sci. Achievement award 1971, del. 1981-82, Ednl. Achievement award 1997), Jefferson County Med. Soc., Ky. Pediat. Soc., Louisville Pediat. Soc., U. Louisville Sch. Medicine Alumni Assn. (bd. govs. 1972-75), Univ. Pediatric Found. Inc. (pres. 1982-93), Internat. Assn. Bioethics, Am. Soc. Law, Medicine and Ethics, Order of Internat. Fellowship (Cambridge), Internat. Order of Merit (Cambridge), Alpha Omega Alpha. Achievements include invention of infant oxygen hood, iontophoresis sweat induction apparatus, radiant open infant warmer, infant blood warmer, diagnostic and treatment table with warmer and position changes, infant transport incubator, others. Office: Kosair Charities Pediat Ctr 571 S Floyd St Ste 449 Louisville KY 40202-3830 Business E-Mail: sahabb01@gwisonlouisville.edu. *Personal philosophy: "The level of civilization attained by any society will be determined by the attention it has paid to the welfare of its infants and children." Also, "The responsibility of the physician is to prevent, to diagnose, to prognosticate, to treat when and if necessary, and always to keep foremost in mind 'Primum Non Nocere'".*

ANDREWS, CAESAR, editor; BA, Grambling State U., La., 1979. Sr. mgr. Florida Today, Melbourne, Fla., The Reporter, Lansdale, Pa., Rockland Jour.-News, West Nyack, NY, Gannett Suburban Newspapers, White Plains, NY; various positions, including dep. mng. editor, special sect. & chief states editor USA Today, 1982—86; editor Gannett News Svc., Arlington, Va., 1997—. Lectr. Am. Press Inst. Mem.: Am. Soc. Newspaper Editors, Nat. Assn. Minority Media Exec., Nat. Assn. Black Journalists, AP Mng. Editors (mem. bd., v.p.). Office: Gannett News Services 7950 Jones Branch Dr Mc Lean VA 22108-0001*

ANDREWS, CHARLES ROLLAND, library administrator; b. Scranton, Pa., July 5, 1930; s. Edgar W. and Margaret (Machenry) A.; m. Harriet Williams, Dec. 27, 1954 (dec. 1985); m. Dorothy Kramer, Dec. 10, 1988. BS in Edn., Bloomsburg U., 1954; MA in English Lit., U. Okla., 1959; MS in L.S., Case Western Res. U., 1964, PhD, 1967. Head reference dept. Cleve. Pub. Library, 1966-68, Case Western Res. Univ. Libraries, Cleve., 1968-69, librarian Freiberger Library, 1969-72, asst. dir. pub. services, 1972-74; univ. librarian Southeastern Mass. Univ. Library, North Dartmouth, 1974-76; dean library services Hofstra U. Library, Hempstead, NY, 1976-96, prof. emeritus, 1997—. Lectr. Hofstra U., U. Coll. Continuing Edn., 1997—. Editor: Reference Books for Small and Medium-Sized Libraries, 1973; contbr. articles, revs. to profl. jours. Bd. trustees Unitarian Universalist Congregation, Garden City, NY, 1998—2004, chair art exhibits com., 1999—2002, newsletter editor, 2000—. Mem. ALA, Assn. Coll. and Rsch. Librs., Archons of Colophon, L.I. Libr. Resources Coun. (chair regional automation com. 1986-92, bd. trustees 1990-94), Am. Express (sr. adv. bd. mem. 1998-99). Democrat. Avocations: calligraphy, word processing, graphics. Home and Office: 305 Hillside Ave Bellmore NY 11710-3519

ANDREWS, DAVID RALPH, lawyer; b. Oakland, Calif., Jan. 4, 1942; m. Rozan McCurdy, July 1, 1962; children: David, Linda. BA, U. Calif., Berkeley, 1968; JD, U. Calif., 1971. Bar: Calif. 1971, D.C. 1986, U.S. Dist. Ct. (no. dist.) Calif. 1971, U.S. Dist. Ct. Hawaii 1991, U.S. Supreme Ct. 1980. Assoc. McCutchen, Doyle, Brown & Enersen, San Francisco, 1971-75; regional counsel Reg. IX U.S. EPA, San Francisco, 1975-77; legal counsel and spl. asst. for policy US EPA, Washington, 1977-79; dep. gen. counsel US Dept. Health & Human Svcs., Washington, 1980-81; ptnr. McCutchen, Doyle, Brown & Enersen, San Francisco, 1981-97, chmn., 1991-95; legal adviser US Dept. State, Washington, 1997-2000; ptnr. McCutchen, Doyle, Brown & Enersen, San Francisco, 2000—02; sr. v.p., govt. affairs, gen. counsel & sec. Pepsi Co. Inc., Purchase, NY, 2002—05. Amb., spl. negotiator U.S./Iran Claims, 2000—; bd. dirs. Union Bank Calif., Kaiser Permanente, NetCel360 Holdings Ltd., PG&E Corp. Trustee San Francisco Mus. of Modern Art, 1988-97; bd. trustees Golden Gate Nat. Park Assn., 1992-95, Marin Cmty. Found., 1996-97; mem. U.S. Agy. for Internat. Devel. Energy Tng. Program Adv. Com. of the Inst. Internat. Edn.; mem. bd. dirs. Union Bank Calif., Kaiser Permanente and NetCel360 Holdings Ltd., 2000—. Fellow Max Planck Inst. of Pub. Internat. Law, Heidelberg, Fed. Republic of Germany, 1974. Mem. ABA (natural resources sect.), Calif. Bar Assn.), San Francisco Bar Assn. Avocations: photography, tennis, running.

ANDREWS, DONNA L., professional golfer; b. Lynchburg, VA, Apr. 12, 1967; d. James Barclay and Helen Louise (Munsey) Andrews. BBA, U. N.C., 1989. Qualified golfer LPGA Tour, Fla., 1990; winner Ping-Cellular One Golf Tounament, Portland, Oreg., 1993, Ping-Welch's Golf Tournament, Tucson, Ariz., 1994, Dinah Shore Major Golf Tournament, Palm Springs, Calif., 1994, Longs Drugs Challenge, Lincoln, CA, 1998. Office: LPGA 100 International Golf Dr Daytona Beach FL 32124-1092

ANDREWS, DUDLEY JO, geophysicist; b. Harrisonburg, Va., Oct. 29, 1935; s. Dudley Charles Andrews and Margaret Jean Gilchrist; m. Judith Helen Bourdon, Aug. 23, 1969; 1 child, Brian Charles. BS, Tulane U., 1957; MS, Yale U., 1959; PhD, Wash. State U., 1970. Geophysicist U.S. Geol. Survey, Menlo Park, Calif., 1973—. Contbr. articles to profl. jours. Fellow: Am. Geophys. Union; mem.: Seismol. Soc. Am. Office: US Geological Survey Mail Stop 977 345 Middlefield Rd Menlo Park CA 94025 Office Phone: 650-329-5606.

ANDREWS, E. WYLLYS, archaeologist, educator; b. Phila., Oct. 10, 1943; s. Edward Wyllys and Ann (Wheeler) Andrews IV; m. Patricia Antell Andrews, June 15, 1965; children: Dwen Hardy Andrews-Cita, Edward VI Wyllys, Ruth Wheeler. AB, Harvard U., 1964; PhD, Tulane U., 1971. Asst. prof. anthropology No. Ill. U., DeKalb, 1970-75; dir. Mid. Am. Rsch. Inst., Program Rsch. in Yucatan Tulane U., New Orleans, 1972-74, dir. Mid. Am. Rsch. Inst., gen. editor publs., 1975—, assoc. prof. anthropology, 1975-80, prof. anthropology, 1980—. Dir. excavations at Quelepa, El Salvador, Tulane U., 1967—69, dir. excavations at Komchen, Yucatan, Mex., 1980—84, dir. excavations Copan Royal Residence, Honduras, 1990—94. Author: The Archaeology of Quelepa, El Salvador, 1976, Excavations at Dzibilchaltun, Yucatan, Mexico, 1980; co-editor: Late Lowland Maya Civilization: Classic to Postclassic, 1986, Five Hundred Years After Columbus, 1994, Copan: The History of an Ancient Maya Kingdom, 2005; mem. editl. bd. Rsch. and Exploration, 1984-95, Latin Am. Antiquity, 1989-95. Grantee NEA, 1978, NSF, 1980, Nat. Geog. Soc., 1992. Mem. Am. Anthrop. Assn., Soc. for Am. Archaeology, Sociedad Mexicana de Antropologia. Avocations: photography, backpacking, cross country skiing, downhill skiing, canoeing. Office: Tulane U Mid Am Rsch Inst New Orleans LA 70118 Office Phone: 504-862-3104. Business E-Mail: wandrews@tulane.edu.

ANDREWS, FRANK LEWIS, lawyer; b. Rhinebeck, N.Y., June 8, 1950; s. William Fisher and Merna Louise (Lewis) A.; m. Barbara Della Chapman, Aug. 30, 1980; children: William Chapman, S. Ross Chapman. Student, U. Vienna, Austria, 1971; BS magna cum laude, Mich. State U., 1973; JD cum laude, Harvard U., 1976. Bar: Mich. 1976. Sr. prin. Miller, Canfield, Paddock & Stone PLC, Troy, Mich., 1983—. Avocations: skiing, sailing.

ANDREWS, GAYLEN, public relations executive; Pres. Blitz Media-Direct, Middle Island, NY. Office: Blitz Media-Direct Communications Bldg PO Box 102 Middle Island NY 11953-0102 Office Phone: 631-924-8555. Business E-Mail: blitz4pr@att.net.

ANDREWS, GEORGE EYRE, mathematics professor; b. Dec. 4, 1938; s. Raymond Leslie and Rovena Pearl (Eyre) A.; m. Joy Margaret Brown, Sept. 2, 1960; children: Amy Beth, Katherine Yvonne, Derek George. BS, MA, Oreg. State U., 1960; postgrad., Cambridge (Eng.) U., 1960—61; PhD, U. Pa., 1964; Doctorate in Physics (hon.), Parma (Italy) U., 1998; DSc (hon.), U. Fla., 2002; DMath (hon.), Waterloo (Can.) U., 2004. Asst. prof. math. Pa. State U., University Park, 1964-67, assoc. prof. math., 1967-70, prof. math., 1970-81, Evan Pugh prof. math., 1981—, math. dept. head, 1980-82, 95-97. Hedrick lectr. Math. Assn. Am., 1980, J.S. Frame lectr., 1993; adj. prof. U. Waterloo, Ont., Can., 1982-92, regional conf. lectr., NSF-Conf. Bd. Math. Scis., 1985. Author: Number Theory, 1971, Theory of Partitions, 1976, Partitions: Yesterday and Today, 1979, q-Series, 1986, (with R. Askey and R. Roy) Special Functions, 1998, (with K. Eriksson) Integer Partitions, 2004; editor: Collected Papers of P.A. MacMahon, Vol. I, 1978, Vol. II, 1986, Ramanujan Revisited, 1988, The Rademacher Legacy to Mathematics, 1994, (with S. Ahlgren and K. Ono) Topics in Number Theory in Honor of B. Gordon and S. Chowla, 1999. Recipient Disting. Univ. Tchg. award Allegheny Mountain sect. Math. Assn. Am., 1993, Centennial award U. Pa., 1999; Guggenheim fellow, 1982-83. Mem.: NAS, Am. Acad. Arts and Scis. Avocation: boogie-woogie piano. Home: 119 Meadow Ln Centre Hall PA 16828-8515 Office: Pa State U Dept Math 410 Mcallister Bldg University Park PA 16802-6404 Office Phone: 814-865-6642. Business E-Mail: andrews@math.psu.edu.

ANDREWS, GERALD BRUCE, SR., textiles executive; b. Valley, Ala., Sept. 17, 1937; s. Bruce and Sara Andrews; m. Claire Smith; children: Gerald Bruce Jr., Benjamin G., Suzanne Andrews Smith. Diploma in textile mfg., Auburn U., 1956; BS in Mgmt. and Indsl. Engring., Auburn U., 1958; postgrad., Harvard U., 1979. Various positions WestPoint Pepperell, Inc., 1954-67, mgr. Opelika (Ala.) Mill, 1967-68, gen. mgr. no. ops. Biddeford, Maine, 1968-70, dir. indsl. engring. West Point, Ga., 1970-72, gen. mgr. towels ops. Valley, 1972-74, v.p. mfg., 1974-80, sr. v.p. merchandising and mktg. N.Y.C., 1980-87; pres. Stores div. N000, West Point, 1987-92; exec. v.p. merchandising WestPoint Pepperell, Inc., N.Y.C., 1992—; pres., COO Johnston Industries Inc., N.Y.C., 1992—, pres., CEO Columbus, Ga., 1995-97, ret., 1997; exec.-in-residence, vis. prof. Auburn U., 1998-99. Chmn. com. to evaluate Sch. Textile Engring., Auburn (Ala.) U., also lay speaker Guest Speakers Bur.; mem. president's adv. com. So. Union Coll.; chmn. Westpoint Pepperell Polit. Action Com., West Point; bd. dirs. Ala. Textile Edn. Found., Johnston Industries Inc., Tapistron Internat., Tech. Textiles U.S.A.; instr. textile mfg. and indsl. engring. Pres. bd. trustees Lanier Meml. Hosp., Valley; chmn. Chattahoochee Valley Health Care Found., Valley; mem. Ala. Gov.'s Adv. Coun., Montgomery; trustee Christian City, Atlanta; chmn. bd. trustees Atlanta Christian Coll., 1995-96; chmn. bd. dirs. Lanier Health Care Found., 2000-01. Named Citizen of Yr., Valley-Lanett C. of C.; recipient President's award Geo. H. Lanier Coun. Boy Scouts Am.; inducted Engring. Hall of Fame, 1995. Fellow Textile Inst. (Manchester, Eng.); mem. Am. Inst. Indsl. Engrs., Am. Textile Mfg. Assn. (dir. 1995, textile leader of yr. in Am. 1995), Ala. Textile Mfg. Assn. (pres.), Harvard Bus. Sch. Assn., Spring Wood Athletic Club (pres.), Rotary (pres. West Point), Harvard Club (N.Y.C.). Avocations: travel, golf, reading, architecture, painting. Home: 111 Highland Dr West Point GA 31833-6100 E-mail: gandrews@knology.net.

ANDREWS, GORDON CLARK, lawyer; b. Boston, Mar. 25, 1941; s. Loring Beal and Flora Spencer (Hinckley) A.; m. Deborah M. Devere, July 9, 1966; children: Christine Leigh, Cynthia Lyn, Carey Loring. BA, Dartmouth Coll., 1963; JD, NYU, 1969. Bar: N.Y. State bar 1970, Conn. bar 1971. Assoc. Morgan Lewis & Bockius (and predecessor), N.Y.C., 1969—72; asst. sec., asst. gen. counsel Howmet Corp., Greenwich, Conn., 1973—75; sec., asst. gen. counsel Beker Industries Corp., Greenwich, 1976—, v.p., 1978—81; gen. counsel M&T Chems., Inc., Woodbridge, NJ, 1982—86, v.p. law dept., 1986—90, sec., 1987—90; v.p., sec. Atochem Inc., Glen Rock, NJ, 1987—; gen. counsel, sec. ESSROC Corp., Bath, Pa., 1990—, sr. v.p., 1993—; ptnr. Epstein, Becker & Green, N.Y.C., 1995—; gen. counsel Troy Corp., Florham Park, NJ, 2000—. Bd. dir. San Juan Cement Co., Inc., Essroc Cement Corp.; chmn. legal counsel com. Portland Cement Assn., 2003—. Mem. exec. com. Cement Kiln Recycling Coalition, 2001—. Lt. USNR, 1963—69. Recipient Am. Law award, 1969. Mem. ABA, N.Y. State Bar Assn., Conn. Bar Assn., Am. Soc. Corp. Secs., Westchester-Fairfield Corp. Counsel Assn., Greenwich Country Club. Republican. Home: 46 Club Rd Riverside CT 06878-2034 Office: Epstein Becker & Green 250 Park Ave Ste 1201 New York NY 10177-0001

ANDREWS, GROVER JENE, adult education educator, administrator; b. Batesville, Ark., June 1, 1930; s. Grover Jones and Ruth Burlie (Ruble) A. BA, Vanderbilt U., 1963, MA, 1964; EdD, N.C. State U., 1972. Dir. univ. rels. Baylor U., Waco, Tex., 1955-61; asst. to pres. Peabody Coll. Vanderbilt U., Nashville, 1961-64; asst. prof. English, asst. acad. dean U. Ark., Little Rock, 1964-66; dir. of devel. Meredith Coll., Raleigh, N.C., 1966-67; asst. to dean of extension N.C. State U., Raleigh, 1967-68, assoc. vice chancellor for extension, assoc. prof. adult edn, 1979-89; assoc. exec. dir. commn. on colls. So. Assn. Colls. and Schs., Atlanta, 1968-79; assoc. dir. for instrn. U. Ga. Ctr. for Continuing Edn., 1989—, sr. pub. svc. assoc., chair sr. pub. svc. faculty, 1989—, adj. assoc. prof. adult edn., 1989—, asst. v.p. pub. svc. and outreach, 1998-99, interim dir., 1998—, assoc. v.p. pub. svc. and outreach, 1999—2001; ret., 2001. Bd. dirs. Am. Tech. Inst., Memphis, 1985-98; trustee Coun. for Adult and Exptl. Learning, Chgo., 1985-91; dir. rsch. Internat. Assn. for Continuing Edn. and Tng., Washington, 1987-92, pres., 1992-96. Member Raleigh Lions, 1967-68, 79-89; chair Christmas pageant Waco Jaycees, 1956-60; patron Atlanta Arts Ctr., 1968-79. With USN, 1948-50. Named Educator of the Yr., Fedn. of Women's Clubs, 1966; recipient Nat. Leadership award Assn. for Continuing Higher Edn., 1984, Gruman award N.C. Adult Edn. Assn., 1985, Pinnacle award for outstanding leadership Internat. Assn. for Continuing Edn. and Tng., 1996; named to Internat. Hall of Fame for Adult and Continuing Edn., 1996; Grover J. Andrews Rsch. Endowment established by Internat. Assn., for Continuing Edn. and Tng., 1996. Mem.: So. Assn. Colls. and Schs. (chair accrediting coms. 1980—, Meritorious Svc. award 2003), Ga. Adult Edn. Assn., Nat. Univ. Continuing Edn. Assn. (chair elect rsch. divsn. 1996—97, chair rsch. divsn. 1997—98, 1998—99, M. Nolte award 1995), Pi Kappa Alpha, Sigma Tau Delta, Phi Delta Kappa. Democrat. Baptist. Avocations: gardening, arts, antiques. Home: 243 Ashbrook Dr Athens GA 30605-3956

ANDREWS, HOLDT, investment banker; b. NYC, May 2, 1946; s. William Lloyd and Edna (Faulconer) A.; m. Nina Lawrence, Sept. 16, 1982; 1 child, Kelli. BS, U. Fla., 1968; MBA, Fla. Atlantic U., 1971. Asst. to v.p. mktg. Eltra Corp., Wilmington, Mass., 1972-74; v.p. Bank of Am., N.Y.C., 1974-81; group v.p. Amrobank, N.Y.C., 1981-84; exec. v.p. CenTrust Savs. Bank, Miami, Fla., 1984, KMC Group, Miami, 1985-86; sr. mng. dir. J.W. Charles Capital Corp.-Bush Securities, Boca Raton, Fla., 1986-89; v.p. corp. fin. dept. Internationale Nederlanden Bank N.V., N.Y.C., 1989-94; sr. v.p. S.N. Phelps and Co., Greenwich, Conn., 1994; chief oper. officer VHC, Ltd., West Palm Beach, Fla., 1994-99; sr. exec. mng. dir. The March Group, LLC, Nashville, 1999—. Mem. adv. bd. Tucker State Bank, Jacksonville, Fla., 1987-88; bd. dirs. Qilu-Maul, Shandong, Peoples Republic China, 1997-99. 1st lt. U.S. Army, 1968-70. Mem. Blue Key. Avocations: tennis, sailing, skiing. Office: The March Group 1900 Church St Nashville TN 37203-2234 Office Phone: 570-620-2773. Business E-Mail: andrews@marchgroup.com. E-mail: haimpact@msn.com.

ANDREWS, J. DAVID, lawyer; b. Decatur, Ill., July 5, 1933; s. Jesse D. and Louise Glenna (Mason) A.; m. Helen Virginia Migely, July 12, 1958; children: Virginia, Robert, Michael, Betsy. BA magna cum laude, U. Ill., 1955, JD with honors, 1960. Bar: Wash. 1961. Ptnr. Perkins Coie, Seattle, 1960-96, sr. counsel, 1997—. Bd. dirs., v.p. Am. Bar Ins. Plans Cons., Inc., 1991—; pres. Wash. Law Fund, 1997—98; bd. dirs. Am. Bar Endowment, 1981—94, pres., 1985—87; bd. visitors U. Puget Sound Law Sch., 1976—94, Ill. Coll. Law, 2005—; trustee AEF Pension Fund, 1975—79. Contbr. articles to profl. jours. Bd. dirs. Leukemia Soc. Wash., 1984-99, pres. 1985-91; nat. bd. dirs. Leukemia Soc. Am., 1992-96. Capt. USAF, 1955-57. Fellow Am. Bar Found. (bd. dirs., former treas.), Am. Coll. Trial Lawyers; mem. ABA (ho. of dels. 1967-69, 75—, asst. treas. 1972-74, treas. 1975-79, bd. govs. 1975-79, fed. judiciary standing com. 1985-90), Wash. Bar Assn. (chmn. pub. rels. com. 1971-73), Seattle-King County Bar Assn., Am. Judicature Soc. (bd. dirs. 1985-89), Phi Beta Kappa, Phi Kappa Phi, Phi Eta Sigma. Home: 9413 SW Quartermaster Dr Vashon WA 98070-7081 Office: Perkins Coie 1201 3rd Ave Ste 4000 Seattle WA 98101-3029 Office Phone: 206-359-8423. Business E-Mail: andrj@perkinscoie.com.

ANDREWS, JAMES R., orthopedic surgeon; m. Jenelle Andrews; children: Andy, Any, Archie, Ashley, Amber, Abby. Grad., La. State U., 1963, MD, 1967; LLD, Livingston U.; DSc, Troy State U., La. State U. Orthopedic resident Tulane Med. Sch., 1972; surgical fellow in sports medicine U. Va. Med. Sch., 1972, U. Lyon, Lyn, France, 1972; co-founder Ala. Sports Medicine and Orthopedic Ctr., Healthsouth Med. Ctr., Birmingham, Ala.; co-founder, chmn., med. dir. Am. Sports Medicine Inst., Healthsouth Med. Ctr., Birmingham, Ala. Nat. med. dir. Healthsouth Corp.; med. dir. Healthsouth Sports Medicine Coun.; clin. prof. orthopedic surgery U. Ala. Birmingham Med. Sch., Ala. Med. Sch., U. Va. Sch. Medicine, U. Ky. Med. Ctr., U. SC Med. Sch.; co-medical dir., intercollegiate sports Auburn U.; sr. orthopedic cons., intercollegiate athletics U. Ala.; orthopedic cons. for athletic teams Troy State U., U. West Ala., Tuskegee U., Grambling U.; spl. med. cons., dept. athletics Ala. A&M U.; med. dir. Tampa Bay Devil Rays; sr. orthopedic cons. Washington Redskins, Cin. Reds; team physician Birmingham Barons Double A, affiliate Chgo. White Sox; co-medical dir. PGA Tour, Sr. PGA Tour, Ladies Profl. Golf Assn.; mem., sports medicine com. US Olympic Com.; served on NCAA Competitive Safeguards in Medical Aspects of Sports Com.; current mem. med. and safety adv. com. USA Baseball; co-founder, bd. dir. Fast Health Corp.; bd. dir. HealthTronics Corp., Am. Club Systems, Banc Corp., Robins Morton Construction Co.; lectr. in field. Author numerous sci. articles and books. Pres., chmn. bd. Aloha Racing Found.; mem. bd. trustee Troy State U. Named to Ala. Sports Hall of Fame, La. State U. Alumni Hall of Distinction, 1996; recipient Disting. Sportsman award, Ala. Sports Hall of Fame, 1992. Mem.: Internat. Knee Soc. (bd. dir.), Arthroscopy Assn. N.Am. (bd. dir.), Am. Orthopedic Soc. Sports Medicine (bd. dir., sec. bd. dir.), Am. Acad. Orthopedic Surgeons, Am. Bd. Orthopedic Surgery. Widely recognized for his role in advancing the field of shoulder, knee and elbow surgery; mentored over 125 fellows throughout the course of his academic career; considered one of the foremost orthopedic surgeons and sports doctors in the world; and operated on a remarkable number of prominent athletes, including Troy Aikman, Roger Clemens, and Jack Nicklaus. Office: Ala Sports Medicine & Orthopedic Ctr 1201 11th Ave S Ste 200 Birmingham AL 35205 Office Phone: 205-939-3000. Office Fax: 205-930-9011.*

ANDREWS, JEAN, artist; b. Kingsville, Tex., Dec. 23, 1923; d. Herbert and Katharine Andrews; divorced; children: Robert Fleming Wasson Jr., Jean Andrews Wasson(dec.). BS in Home Economics, U. Tex., 1944; MS in Edn., Tex. A & I Univ., 1966; PhD in Fine Arts, U. North Tex., 1976. Cert. home economist. Artist, writer, Austin, Tex. Vis. scholar dept. integrative biology U. Tex., Austin, adv. coun. Coll. Natural Sci., 1983-, past mem. exec. com., 1986-97, chmn. botany dept. vis. com., 1985-1993; presenter to seminars and confs. in field. Author: Sea Shells of the Texas Coast, 1971, Shells and Shores of Texas, 1977, Texas Shells: A Field Guide, 1981, Peppers: The Domesticated Capsicums, 1984, rev. edit., 1995, The Texas Bluebonnet, 1985, rev. edit., 1993, An American Wildflower: Florilegium, 1992, Texas Monthly Field Guide to Shells of the Texas Coast, 1992, Red Hot Peppers, 1993, Texas Monthly Field Guide to the Shells of the Florida Coast, 1994, The Peppers Lady's Pocket Pepper Primer, 1998, The Pepper Trail, 2000, The Peppers Cookbook, 2005, also articles; one-woman shows include RGK Found. Gallery, Austin, 1993, numerous others. Nat. adv. bd. Leadership Am., 1988-95; trustee Laguna Gloria Art Mus., 1985-91, Nat. Wildflower Rsch. Ctr., 1987-94, adv. coun. 1995—; past trustee Art Mus. of S. Tex.; past bd. dirs. Planned Parenthood; mem. Austin Symphony Soc., Friends of Huntington Gallery/Univ. Tex., others. Recipient Disting. Alumna award U.North Tex., 1991, Hall of Honor award U. Tex. Coll. Natural Sci., 1991, Disting. Alumna award U. Tex. Austin, 1997; endowments include Jean Andrews vis. professorship in human nutrition, and vis. professorship in tropical and econ. botany, endowed scholar Tex. Found. for Women's Resources, U. Tex.; endowed scholar in art U. North Tex., others; named Tex. Inst. Letters. Mem. DAR, Am. Malacol. Union, Tex. Pepper Found. (life), Tex. State Tchrs. Assn. (life), U. Tex. Alumni Assn. (life), U. North Tex. Alumni Assn. (life), Colonial Dames of 17th Century, Nat. Soc. Ams. of Royal Descent, Nat. Soc. Colonial Dames in Am., Nat. Soc. Magna Charta Dames, Daus. of Cin., Huguenot Soc., Order of Descendants of Ancient Planters, Daus. of the Confederacy, Descendents of Ancient Planters, Jamestowne Soc., Descendants of Colonial Govs. E-mail: thepepperlady@sbcglobal.net.

ANDREWS, JENNIFER LEE, secondary school educator; b. York, Pa., Feb. 18, 1971; d. Samuel Ray and Mary Lee Andrews. BS, Towson State U., 1995; MEd, Pa. State U., 2005. Itenerant adaptive physical edn. instr. Howard County Pub. Sch., Md., 1995—97; health and physical edn. instr. South Ea. Sch. Dist., Fawn Grove, Pa., 1997—. Jr. HS field hockey coach Dallastown Sch. Dist., Pa., 2000—. Tobacco Grant, York City, 2004. Mem.: Pa. State Health, Physical Edn. and Dance, Nat. Edn. Assn. Office: Kennard Dale HS 393 Main St Fawn Grove PA 17321

ANDREWS, JOHN FRANK, civil and environmental engineering educator; b. Cave City, Ark., July 10, 1930; s. Frank Ferd and Ruth Lanell (Puckett) A.; m. Margery Ann Hall, June 21, 1952; children: John Patrick, Carol Ann, Laurie Lanell. BS in Civil Engring., U. Ark., 1951, MS, 1953; PhD, U. Calif., Berkeley, 1964. Instr. civil engring. U. Ark., 1953-55, asst. prof., 1955-59, assoc. prof., 1959-60; project engr. U. Calif. at Berkeley, 1962-63; assoc. prof., assoc. dir. water resources engring. program Clemson U., 1963-66, prof., dir. environmental systems engring., 1966-68, prof., dept head, 1968-74; prof. civil and environmental engring. U. Houston, 1975-81; prof. environ. sci. and engring. Rice U., 1981-91, prof. emeritus, 1991, ret., 1991. Vis. prof. McMaster U., Can., Kyoto U., Japan, 1988; vis. rschr. Water Pollution Rsch. Lab., Eng., 1970, Wastewater Tech. Ctr., Can., 1988; hon. prof. Harbin Inst. Archtl. and Civil Engring., People's Republic of China, 1990; cons. water pollution control Engring.-Sci., Inc., Los Angeles, Phila., Chgo., Mpls.; cons. U.S. Army, Bacardi Distilleries, Pan Am. Health Orgn., UN Devel. Program, Greeley & Hansen Engrs., Shell Devel. Co., Weyerhauser Co., Woodlands Devel. Co. Gulf Coast Waste Disposal Authority, Met. Sanitary Dist. Greater Chgo., others. Research, publs. in field. NSF grantee Mem. ASCE, AIChE, Am. Chem. Soc., Am. Water Works Assn., Water Environ. Fedn. (Harrison Prescott Eddy award 1975), Internat. Assn. Water Quality (U.S. editor Water Research 1974-84, vice chmn. Vienna conf. 1971, 75, 79, 83, program chmn. London conf. 1973, Stockholm conf. 1977 Munich conf. 1981, Houston conf. 1985, Kyoto conf. 1990, hon. mem. 1986), Am. Soc. Engring. Edn., Am. Acad. Environ. Engrs. (emeritus), Assn. Environ. Engring. Profs. (dir. 1967-70, chmn. workshops 1968-70, chmn. nat. conf. 1977, v.p. 1984-85, pres. 1985-86), Sigma Xi, Tau Beta Pi, Phi Kappa Phi. Methodist. Home: 1719 E Rayview Dr Fayetteville AR 72703-2625 E-mail: jand109090@aol.com.

ANDREWS, JOHN FRANK, editor, author, educator; b. Carlsbad, N.Mex., Nov. 2, 1942; s. Frank Randolph and Mary Lucille (Wimberley) A.; m. Vicky Roberta Anderson, Aug. 20, 1966 (div. 1983); children: Eric John, Lisa Gail; m. Janet Ann Denton, Oct. 15, 1994. AB, Princeton U., 1965; MAT, Harvard U., 1966; PhD, Vanderbilt U., 1971. Instr. English U. Tenn., Nashville, 1969-70; asst. prof. Fla. State U., Tallahassee, 1970-74, dir. grad. studies in English, 1973-74; dir. acad. programs Folger Shakespeare Library, Washington, 1974-84; chmn. Folger Inst., Washington, 1974-84; exec. editor Folger Books, Washington, 1974-84; dep. dir. div. edn. programs NEH, Washington, 1984-88; editor The Guild Shakespeare, 1988-92; pres. The Shakespeare Guild, 1992—; editor The Everyman Shakespeare, 1993—; exec. dir. Washington br. English-Speaking Union, 2001—. Cons. Time-Life TV, WNET/Thirteen, Corp. for Pub. Broadcasting, Pub. Broadcasting Svc., Nat. Pub. Radio, U.S. Dept. Edn., others; chmn. Nat. Adv. Panel for the Shakespeare Plays, 1979-85; core advisor The Shakespeare Hour, 1985-86; mem. adv. bd. Theatre for a New Audience, Humanities Coun. of Washington, Ctr. for Polit. and Strategic Studies, Ctr. for Renaissance and Baroque Studies, U. Md., others; cons. Shakespeare: The Globe and the World, touring exhbn., 1978-81; adminstr. program grants NEH, Andrew W. Mellon Found., Exxon

Corp., Met. Life, Surdna Found., others; founder of the Guild's Gielgud Award for Excellence in the Dramatic Arts, 1994. Asst. editor: Shakespeare Studies, 1972-74; editor: Shakespeare Quar., 1974-85; editor-in-chief, contbr.: William Shakespeare: His World, His Work, His Influence, 1985; editor-in-chief: Shakespeare's World and Work, 2001; contbr. numerous articles to mags. and scholarly jours. Decorated officer Order Brit. Empire; recipient rsch. awards Folger Shakespeare Libr., Fla. State U., NEH. Fellow Royal Soc. Arts; mem. AAUP (sec. chpt. 1972-74), Modern Lang. Assn., Milton Soc. Am., Nat. Council of Tchrs. of English, Renaissance Soc. Am. (mem. council 1975-84), Internat. Shakespeare Conf., Shakespeare Assn. Am. (trustee 1979-82), The Lit. Soc., Cosmos Club. Home and Office: 2141 Wyoming Ave NW Apt 41 Washington DC 20008-3916 Office Phone: 202-234-4602. Personal E-mail: shakesgmild@msn.com.

ANDREWS, JONATHAN BRITTON, art educator; b. Mpls., Apr. 29, 1977; s. Robert M. and Sharon K. Andrews. BS, Bob Jones Univ., 2000, MA, 2002. Asst. graphic designer Bob Jones U. Art Agy., Greenville, SC, 1997—2002; graphic designer self-employed, 1998—; art educator Bob Jones U., 2002—; graphic designer Athyns, 2004—, Little Red Book, Rochester, NY, 2004—. Cofounder Athyns, Greenville, SC, 2004—; stage artist Bob Jones Univ., 2003. Exhibition, Alphabetic Alchemy; musician: (published music cd) Sketches. Pro bono graphic designer Beth Eden Bapt. Sch., Wheat Ridge, Colo., 2003—04, Upstate Visual Arts, Greenville, SC, 2004—04. Mem.: Met. Arts Coun., Upstate Visual Arts. Avocations: writing, composing music, arranging music, reading. Home: Cva B410 Greenville SC 29614 Office: Bob Jones Univ 1700 Wade Hampton Blvd Greenville SC 29614 Office Phone: 864-271-5000.

ANDREWS, JOSEPH LYON, JR., internist, pulmonologist; b. N.Y.C., Mar. 19, 1938; s. Joseph Lyon and Katherine Louise (New) A.; m. Margareta Langert, Apr. 18, 1969 (dec. Mar. 1994); children: Joe, Sara, Jennifer. BA cum laude, Amherst Coll., 1959; MD, U. Rochester, 1963. Diplomate Am. Bd. Internal Medicine, Am. Bd. Pulmonary Medicine. Intern, resident Boston City Hosp., 1963-65, Tufts Med. Sch., Boston, 1963-65; resident, fellow Harvard Med. Sch., Boston, 1967-70; pulmonary fellow Mass. Gen. Hosp., 1967-68; sr. resident Boston VA Hosp., 1968-69; cardiology fellow West Roxbury VA Hosp., 1969-70; internist, pulmonologist Lahey Clinic, Boston, Burlington, Mass., 1971-90; dir. ambulatory care Bedford (Mass.) VA Med. Ctr., 1999-2000; internist Harvard Vanguard Health Care, Boston, 2003; internist, pulmonary cons. New Eng. Allergy, Asthma and Immunology PC, North Andover, 2004—05, Cmty. Med. Professionals, North Andover, Mass., 2005—. Clin. tchg. staff Harvard Med. Sch., 1971-90, Tufts Med. Sch., 1971—, Boston U. Med. Sch., 1999-2000; chief pulmonary dept. New Eng. Deaconess Hosp., Boston, 1972-82. Author: Revolutionary Boston, Lexington and Concord, 1999; freelance writer Boston Globe Newspaper, 1971—; contbr. articles to profl. jours. Pres.'s assoc. World Learning, Inc., Brattleboro, Vt., 1987—; mem., social action com. Temple Shalom, Newton, Mass., 1988-93; mem. Human Rights Com., Newton, 1983-88; bd. dirs. Am. Lung Assn. Boston, 1977-90; lic. guide Town Concord, 1995—; mem. Concord Mill Brook Task Force, 1995—, Concord Hist. Commn., 1996-99; mem. social action com. Kerem Shalom, Concord, 1996—; mem. Am. Friends Neve Shalom, Israel, 1996—. Capt. USAF, 1965-67. Traveling fellow Am.Jewish Congress, Israel, 1959, Am. Cancer Soc., Mendoza, Argentina, 1962. Fellow Am. Coll. Physicians, Am. Coll. Chest Physicians; mem. AMA, Am. Thoracic Soc., Mass. Med. Assn., Mass. Thoracic Soc., Am. Jewish Hist. Soc., Sons Am. Revolution, Thoreau Soc., Concord Visitors Guide, Concord Guides and Press (founder, dir.). Avocations: writing, photography, swimming, hiking, tour guiding. Home: 28 Center Village Dr Concord MA 01742-2900 Personal E-mail: joelandrew@aol.com.

ANDREWS, DAME JULIE (JULIA ELIZABETH WELLS), actress, singer; b. Walton-on-Thames, Eng., Oct. 1, 1935; d. Edward C. and Barbara Wells; m. Tony Walton, May 10, 1959 (div.); 1 child, Emma Walton; m. Blake Edwards, 1969; adopted children: Amy Edwards, Joanna Edwards stepchildren: Jennifer Edwards, Geoffrey Edwards. studied with pvt. tutors, studied voice with Mme. Stiles-Allen. Debut as singer, Hippodrome, London, 1947; appeared in pantomime Cinderella, London, 1953; appearances include (Broadway prodns.) The Boy Friend, NYC, 1954, (& Conn., 2005), My Fair Lady, 1956-60 (NY Drama Critics award 1956), Camelot, 1960-62, Putting It Together, 1993, Victor/Victoria, 1995 (Tony award nominee Best Actress in a Musical); films include Mary Poppins, 1964 (Acad. award for Best Actress 1964), The Americanization of Emily, 1964, Torn Curtain, 1966, The Sound of Music, 1966, Hawaii, 1966, Thoroughly Modern Millie, 1967, Star!, 1968, Darling Lili, 1970, The Tamarind Seed, 1973, 1979, Little Miss Marker, 1980, S.O.B, 1981, Victor/Victoria, 1982, The Man Who Loved Women, 1983, That's Life!, 1986, Duet For One, 1986, A Fine Romance, 1992, Relative Values, 2000, The Princess Diaries, 2001, Unconditional Love, 2002, Shrek 2 (voice), 2004, The Princess Diaries 2: The Royal Engagement, 2004; TV debut in High Tor, 1956; star TV series The Julie Andrews Hour, 1972-73 (Emmy award for Best Variety Series), Julie, 1992; also spls.; TV movies include Our Sons, 1991, One Special Night, 1999, Eloise at the Plaza, 2003; author: (as Julie Edwards): Mandy, 1971, The Last of the Really Great Whangdoodles, 1974; recs.: The King and I, 1992. Named World Film Favorite (female), 1967; named to 100 Great Britons, 2002; recipient Golden Globe award, Hollywood Fgn. Press Assn., 1964, 1965, Lifetime Achievement award, Kennedy Ctr., 2001. Achievements include knighted by Queen Elizabeth, 1999.*

ANDREWS, KELLY SHAWN, ecologist; b. Altus, Okla., May 24, 1974; s. William Howard Andrews and Doris Jean Campbell; m. Megan Elizabeth Boyer, Aug. 2, 2002; 1 child, Jackson David. BS in Marine Biology, Western Wash. U., 1996; MS in Biology, Ecology, San Diego State U., 2003. Cert. NOAA working diver Nat. Oceanic & Atmospheric Adminstrn., NOAA Dive Ctr., Wash., 2003. Rsch. trainee San Diego State U., 2000—03; rsch. scientist NOAA Fisheries, Seattle, 2003—. Recipient Best Paper, So. Calif. Acad. of Sciences, 2003, Above and Beyond award, NW Fisheries Sci. Ctr., 2004; grantee Calif. SeaGrant Student Rsch. Traineeship, Calif. SeaGrant, 2001-2003. Independent. Avocation: stimulating the growing mind of my son. Office: NOAA Fisheries 2725 Montlake Blvd Seattle WA 98112 Business E-Mail: kelly.andrews@noaa.gov.

ANDREWS, KENNETH RICHMOND, retired business administration educator; b. New London, Conn., May 24, 1916; s. William John and Myrtle (Richmond) A.; m. Edith May Platt, Apr. 29, 1945 (div. 1969); children: Kenneth Richmond, Carolyn; m. Carolyn Erskine Hall, Feb. 14, 1970 (dec. 2002). AB, Wesleyan U., 1936, MA, 1937; PhD, U. Ill., 1948; MA (hon.), Harvard U., 1957. Tchr. English U. Ill., 1937-41; instr. bus. adminstrn. Harvard Grad. Sch. Bus. Adminstrn., 1946-47, asst. prof., 1947-52, assoc. prof., 1952-57, prof., 1957-65, Donald K. David prof. bus. adminstrn., 1965-86, emeritus, 1986—, faculty chmn. Advanced Mgmt. Program, 1967-70, master Leverett House, 1971-81, chmn. gen. mgmt. faculty, 1981-83. Cons. on mgmt. devel. and policy problems; dir. Xerox Corp. and other cos., 1972-86. Author: Nook Farm, 1950, (with others) Problems of General Management, 1962, Business Policy Text and Cases, 1965, rev. edit., 1969, 73, 77, 79, 87, 90, The Effectiveness of University Executive Development Programs, 1966, The Concept of Corporate Strategy, 1971, rev. edit., 1980, 3d edit., 1987; editor: The Case Method of Teaching Human Relations and Administration, 1953; chmn. editorial bd.: Harvard Bus. Rev, 1972-79; editor in chief, 1979-85. Trustee Wesleyan U., 1955-72. Served from pvt. F.A. to maj. USAAF, 1941-46. Recipient Harvard medal, 1986. Disting. Alumnus award, Wesleyan U., 1986, Disting. Svc. award, Harvard Bus. Sch., 1990; Wesleyan U. scholar, 1967. Mem. Phi Beta Kappa. Office: Soldiers Field Boston MA 02163 E-mail: ceakra@aol.com.

ANDREWS, LEWIS MARSHALL, writer, educator; b. N.Y.C., July 17, 1946; s. Lewis M. and Katherine (Englehart) A. AB, Princeton U., 1968; MA, Stanford U., 1970; PhD, Union Inst., Cin., 1976. Author: (with others) Bio Feedback, 1972, Psychology: What's In It For Us?, 1975, To Thine Own Self Be True, 1987. Chmn. Children's Ednl. Opportunity Found. Conn.; exec. dir. Yankee Inst. for Pub. Policy. Avocation: walking. Office: PO Box 459 Redding Ridge CT 06876-0459 E-mail: lew@lewisandrews.com.

ANDREWS, M. DEWAYNE, internist, educator, dean; b. Enid, Okla., May 24, 1944; s. Mitchell S. and Truel Eva (Melton) A.; m. Rebecca Ellen Meltzer, Aug. 26, 1984. BS, Baylor U., 1966; MD, U. Okla., 1970. Diplomate Am. Bd. Internal Medicine. Resident internal medicine Johns Hopkins Hosp., Balt., 1970-71, U. Okla. Health Sci. Ctr., Oklahoma City, 1971-72, 74-76; asst. prof., assoc. prof., dir. residency program dept. medicine U. Okla., Oklahoma City, 1976-84, vice chmn., chief gen. internal medicine, prof. dept. medicine, 1986—, assoc. dean grad. med. edn. Coll. Medicine, 1994—2000, sr. assoc. dean, 1996—2002, v.p. health affairs, exec. dean, 2002—; chief of medicine regional med. ctr., vice chmn. dept. medicine U. Tenn. Coll. Medicine, Memphis, 1984-86; chief of staff U. Hosp., Oklahoma City, 1992-94, med. dir., 1994-96. Bd. dirs. Nat. Commn. Certification Physician Assts., 1995—2003. Editor: Jour. Okla. State Med. Assn., 1991—; contbr. numerous articles to profl. jours. Bd. dirs. Chamber Orch. Oklahoma City, 1982-84, Lyric Theatre, Oklahoma City, 1996-2000, Oklahoma City Philharm. Found., 2003—; del. Okla. State Leadership Initiative to Soviet Union, 1988. Surgeon CDC, USPHS, 1972-74. Recipient Stollermen Award U. Tenn., 1986, Aesculapian award U. Okla. Coll. Medicine, 1989; ACP tchg. and rsch. scholar, 1976-79. Master ACP (bd. govs. Okla. 1995-99); mem. AMA, Alpha Omega Alpha. Episcopalian. Avocation: photography. Office: U Okla Coll Medicine RM 357 BMSB PO Box 26901 Oklahoma City OK 73126-0901

ANDREWS, MARK JOSEPH, lawyer; b. Chgo., July 27, 1944; s. Mark Lewis and Elizabeth (Glendening) A.; m. Martha Jo Shipman, Nov. 29, 1969(div. 2002); children: Eliza, Jonathan. AB, Harvard Coll., 1966; JD, Harvard U., 1969. Bar: U.S. Dist. Ct. D.C. 1970, U.S. Ct. Appeals (D.C. cir.) 1970, U.S. Ct. Appeals (5th and 11th cirs.) 1981, U.S. Ct. Fed. Claims 1983, U.S. Supreme Ct. 1990. From assoc. to ptnr. Verner, Liipfert, Bernhard, McPherson & Hand, Washington, 1969-91; ptnr. Barnes & Thornburg, Washington, 1991—2001, Strasburger & Price, LLP, Washington, 2001—. Co-chmn. federal govt. sponsored task force on regulatory aspects of transp. ins. crisis, 1986-87; vis. lectr. logistics Sturm Coll. Law, U. Denver, 2005. Contbr. articles to profl. jours. Pres. Amadeus Concerts (formerly Gt. Falls Va. Concert Series), 1985-87, bd. dirs., 1984-2000. Mem. ABA (founding mem. internat. transp. com. of sect. internat. law), Transp. Lawyers Assn. (Disting. Svc. 1985, exec. com. 1986-99, 2003-05, pres. 1992-93, Lifetime Achievement award 2005), Assn. Transp. Law, Logistics and Policy, Can. Transport Lawyers Assn., Conf. Claims Counsel, Am. Law Inst. Avocations: photography, hiking, collecting native american artifacts, music. Office: Strasburger & Price LLP 1101 Pennsylvania Ave NW Fl 7 Washington DC 20004-2514 Office Phone: 202-756-3629. Business E-Mail: mark.andrews@strasburger.com.

ANDREWS, MASON COOKE, mayor, obstetrician, gynecologist, educator; b. Norfolk, Va., Apr. 20, 1919; s. Charles James and Jean (Cooke) A.; m. Sabine Goodman, Sept. 24, 1949; children: Jean, Mason. BA, Princeton U., 1940; MD, Johns Hopkins U., 1943; LLD (hon.), Ea. Va. Med. Sch., 1987. Diplomate: Am. Bd. Ob-Gyn. Intern ob-gyn Johns Hopkins U., Balt., 1944, resident ob-gyn, 1946-50; pvt. practice ob-gyn Norfolk, Va., 1950-70; lectr. Johns Hopkins U. Sch. Medicine, Balt., 1971-72; prof. dept. ob-gyn. Eastern Va. Med. Sch., Norfolk, 1974—90, chmn. dept. ob-gyn., 1974-90; mayor City of Norfolk, 1992-94. Bd. dirs. First Va. Bank of Tidewater, Chesapeake and Potomac Telephone Co.; mem., dir. Norfolk City Planning Commn., 1963-65, twice chmn., commr., exec. com. mem. Hampton Rds. Planning Dist. Commn., pres. (1971) Planning Coun. of United Communities, Norfolk City Coun., 1974-2000; chmn. Ea. Va. Med. Authority, 1964-70; pres. Am. Assn. Obstetricians Found., 1986-89. Contbr. (numerous articles to sci. jours.). Councilman City of Norfolk, 1974-2000, vice mayor, 1978-82, mayor, 1992-94. Recipient First Citizen citation Norfolk Cosmopolitan Club, 1968, Norfolk citation for outstanding svc., 1964, award for cmty. svc. Med. Soc. Va., AMA, Nat. Brotherhood award Norfolk Conf. Christians and Jews. Fellow Am. Gynecol. and Obstet. Soc. (v.p. 1982-83, pres. 1992-93); mem. South Atlantic Assn. (pres. 1972), Va. Obstet. and Gynecol. Soc. (pres. 1975), Norfolk Acad. Medicine (pres. 1961), Johns Hopkins Soc. Scholars, Harbor Club, Norfolk Yacht and Country Club. Presbyterian. Home: 1011 N Shore Rd Norfolk VA 23505-3119 Office: Eastern Va Med Sch Dept Ob-Gyn 601 Colley Ave Norfolk VA 23507-1627 Business E-Mail: andrewsmc@eums.edu.

ANDREWS, MELINDA WILSON, human development researcher; b. N.Y.C., Aug. 12, 1956; d. William Maurice and Natalie Maxine (Amos) Wilson; m. James Robert Andrews, Dec. 3, 1977; children: Christopher Wilson Andrews, William James Andrews. BBA in Mgmt./Mktg., Abilene (Tex.) Christian U., 1977; MS in Human Devel., U. Tex., Dallas, 1988, postgrad., 1994—. Logics adminstr. Texas Instruments, Dallas, 1977-79, contract adminstr., 1979-81, 82-83; grocery mgr., co-asst. store dir. Tom Thumb, Dallas, 1981-82; teaching asst. U. Tex. at Dallas, Richardson, Tex., 1988-91, rsch. asst., 1991—. Dir. creative presch. coop., Richardson, 2000-02; dir. Waterview Christian Presch., 2002—; validator Nat. Assn. Edn. of Young Children, 2002—; presenter in field. Contbr. articles to profl. jours. Mem. Richardson Symphony Orch., 1977-79, bd. advs. Canyon Creek Elem. PTA, 2004-, 5th v.p., 1994-95, libr. rep., 1992-94, Canyon Creek PTA bd., 2004-; treas. exec. bd. Creative Presch. Coop., 1998-99, sec. ex. bd. 1999-2000, dir., 2000-02; Cub Scout leader, com. chmn., Pack 1001, 2002—; Girl Scout leader 2004-; asst. dir. English as second lang. sch. Waterview Ch. of Christ Mem. Soc. for Rsch. in Child Devel. (co-author paper-poster session 1991, 93 confs.), Southwest Soc. for Rsch. in Child Devel., Psi Chi. Mem. Ch. of Christ. Avocations: music, animals, carpentry. Home and Office: 1089 Edith Circle Richardson TX 75080-2331 E-mail: andrewsm1089@comcast.com.

ANDREWS, MICHAEL WILLIAM, library and information scientist; b. Rome, N.Y., Mar. 22, 1948; s. Martin Joseph and Mary (Dublanica) A.; m. Karen Lynn Mauro, July 23, 1982. AB in History, Cornell U., 1970; MS in Libr. Sci., Syracuse U., 1972. Libr. govt. documents SUNY, Plattsburgh, 1971-76, L.I. U., Bklyn., 1977-79; rsch. asst. Health Info. Sharing Project, Syracuse (N.Y.) U., 1979-80; readers svcs. libr. Elizabethtown (Pa.) Coll., 1980-85; online data base libr. U. D.C., Washington, 1986-87; dir. rsch. Korn/Ferry Internat., Washington, 1987-2001; owner Andrews Consulting, Woodbridge, Va., 2001—; libr., selection svcs. Prince William (Va.) Pub. Libr. Sys., 2001—03, libr., grants and spl. projects, 2003—. Editor: Proceeding of the Second Annual Government Documents Workshop, 1976. Bd. dirs. Friends Chinn Pk. Regional Libr., 1998-2004. Mem.: ALA, Va. Libr. Assn, Pub. Libr. Assn. Avocations: reading, photography, travel, coaching youth soccer. Home: 3825 Wagon Wheel Ln Woodbridge VA 22192-6441 Office: PWPLS 13083 Chinn Park Dr Woodbridge VA 22192-5073 Business E-Mail: mandrews@pwcgov.org.

ANDREWS, MICHELE C., patient safety specialist; d. Bernard R. and Michele Hurst; m. James E. Andrews, Nov. 15, 1975; children: Meghan C. Andrews Carnegie, Dominic J. AA, U. Md., England, 1990; BS in Biology cum laude, La. State U., Shreveport, 2000. Cert. clin. lab. compliance profl. Nat. Credentialing Agy., 2003. Lab. quality assurance coord. U.S. Dept. Defense, Barksdale AFB, La., 2002—03; asst. patient safety program Anteon, Fairfax, Va., 2003—. Publicity chmn. and mem. at large Shreveport Soc. Nature Study Bird Study Group. Recipient Style and Grace award, 81st MDG Keesler AFB, 1996. Mem.: Phi Theta Kappa, Phi Kappa Phi. Office: Patient Safety Anteon contractor Ste 100 243 Curtiss Rd Barksdale AFB LA 71110

ANDREWS, OAKLEY V., lawyer; b. Cleve., Apr. 15, 1940; BA, Yale U., 1962; JD, Western Reserve U., 1965. Bar: Ohio 1965, U.S. Tax Ct. 1968, U.S. Dist. Ct. (no. dist.) Ohio 1968, U.S. Ct. Appeals (6th cir.) 1968. Ptnr. Baker & Hostetler, LLP, Cleve. Fellow Am. Coll. Trust and Estate Coun.; mem. Ohio State Bar Assn., Estate Planning Coun. Cleve. (pres. 1982-83), Cleve. Bar Assn. (chmn. Estate Planning, Probate and Trust law sect. 1984-85), Phi Delta Phi Office: Baker & Hostetler LLP 3200 Nat City Ctr 1900 E 9th St Ste 3200 Cleveland OH 44114-3475 Office Phone: 216-861-7568. E-mail: oandrews@bakerlaw.com.

ANDREWS, RAYMOND DOUGLAS, financial executive; b. Phila., Mar. 17, 1953; s. David S. and Viola ED. (Wiehsner) A.; m. Melanie Szymanski; children: Raymond D. Jr., Jessica F. BS in Acctg., U. Del., 1976. CPA, Tex. Auditor E.I. du Pont de Nemours, Wilmington, Del., 1976-79, audit supr., 1979-81, mgr. accounts payable, 1981-84, fin. mgr., 1984-91; fin. dir. R&D DuPont Merck Pharm. Co., Wilmington, 1991-94, sr. dir. R&D, 1994-98; contr. DuPont Pharm. Co., Wilmington, 1998—2001; controller Invista, 2002—05; v.p., chief acctg. officer Checkpoint Sys., Inc., 2005—. Dir. Civic League Newcastle County, Wilmington, 1981-83; bd. trustees Del. Hospice, Inc., 1993—, pres., 1997-99; mem. Del. Gov.'s Coun. on Sci. and Tech., 1995-00. Mem. AICPA, Del. Soc. CPAs, Tex. Soc. CPAs, Sigma Nu. Home: 5 E Mozart Dr Wilmington DE 19807-1942 Office: Checkpoint Sys Inc PO Box 188 101 Wolf Dr Thorofare NJ 08086 Office Phone: 856-384-2448. E-mail: andrewsr103@aol.com.

ANDREWS, RICHARD NIGEL LYON, public information officer, educator, environmental services administrator; b. Newport, R.I., Dec. 6, 1944; s. Nigel Lyon and Constance Doane (Young) A.; m. Hannah Page Wheeler, June 7, 1969; children: Sarah Huntington, Christopher Page Monteith AB, Yale U., 1966; M in Regional Planning, U. N.C., 1970, PhD, 1972. Vol. U.S. Peace Corps, Bharatpur, Nepal, 1966-68; budget examiner U.S. Office of Mgmt. and Budget, Washington, 1970-72; prof. U. Mich., Ann Arbor, 1972-81; prof. pub. policy U. N.C., Chapel Hill, 1981—, dir. U. N.C. Inst. Environ. Studies, 1981-91, dir. environ. mgmt. and policy program, 1990-94, mem. exec. com. faculty coun., 1994-97, chair of faculty, 1997-00, Thomas Willis Lambeth disting. prof. pub. policy, 2004—. Cons. NSF, Washington, 1982-85, AID, Yaounde, Cameroon, 1983, U.S.-Asia Environ. Partnership, 2000—, Kenan Inst. Asia, 2000—; mem. N.C. Natural Heritage Adv. Com., Raleigh, 1982-87; sr. staff mem. Commn. on Future of N.C., Raleigh, 1982-84; mem. Bd. Environ. Studies and Toxology, NAS, 1986-88; chmn. study com. on opportunities in applied environ. R&D, NAS, 1988-90; mem. risk reduction subcom. Sci. Adv. Bd., EPA, 1989-90, AID, Czech and Slovak Republics, 1991-94; mem. adv. com. Pew Conservation Scholars Program, 1991-94; mem. adv. com. EPA Decisionmaking, Nat. Acad. of Pub. Adminstrn., 1994-95; chmn. adv. panel new approach to environ. regulation Office Tech. Assessment U.S. Congress, Washington, 1993-95; mem. Multi-State Working Group Environ. Mgmt. Systems, 1997—2004; chmn. adv. panel U.S. registration practices for ISO 14001 environ. mgmt. sys. Nat. Acad. Pub. Adminstrn., 2000-01; mem. adv. com. Environ. Stewardship N.C. dept. environ. and natural resources, 2002-, mem. study com. on environ. decision making, NAS, 2003-2005. Author: Environmental Policy and Administrative Change, 1976, Managing the Environment, Managing Ourselves: A History of American Environmental Policy, 1999; editor: Land in America, 1979, Environmental Change and Public Health-The Next Fifty Years, 1990; contbr. articles to profl. jours. Vestry Episcopalian Ch., Chapel Hill, 1986-89. Resources for the Future Inc. fellow, 1971-72, Rockefeller Found. fellow, 1977-78, Fulbright fellow Vienna U. Econs., 1990, Salzburg Seminar faculty fellow, 1990, fellow Nat. Acad. of Pub. Adminstrn., 1996. Fellow AAAS (nominating com. sect. on societal impacts of sci. and engring. 1987-90, chmn. 1989-90, 96-97, ann. meeting program com. 1988-90, com. on sci. engring. and pub. policy 1997-2003, com. sect. social, econ. and polit. scis. 1998-2002); mem. Assn. Pub. Policy and Mgmt. (ann. meeting program com. 2003), Soc. For Policy Scis., Golden Key, Sigma Xi, Delta Omega. Democrat. Avocations: tennis, sailing, camping, photography, squash. Office: U NC Dept Public Policy CB3435 Abernethy Chapel Hill NC 27599-3435 Office Phone: 919-843-5011.

ANDREWS, RICHARD OTIS, museum director; b. LA, Nov. 8, 1949; s. Robert and Theodora (Hammond) A.; m. Colleen Chartier, Jan. 3, 1976; 1 child, Bryce. BA, Occidental Coll., LA, 1971; BFA, U. Wash., 1973, MFA, 1975. Project mgr. Art in Pub. Places, Seattle Arts Commn., 1978-80, coord., 1980-84; dir. visual arts program Nat. Endowment for Arts, Washington, 1985-87; dir. Henry Art Gallery, U. Wash., Seattle, 1987—. Co-curator Art Into Life: Russian Constructivism 1914-1932; curator James Turrell: Knowing Light, 2003; cons. pub. art program devel., 1982-84; bd. trustees Assn. Art Mus. Dirs., 1997-2000. Author: Insights/On Sites, 1984, James Turrell: Sensing Space, 1992; editor Artwork/Network, 1984; contbg. editor Going Public, 1988. Mem. Seattle Arts Commn., 2004—. Office: U Wash Henry Art Gallery PO Box 351410 Seattle WA 98195-1410

ANDREWS, RICHARD VINCENT, physiologist, educator; b. Arapahoe, Nebr., Jan. 9, 1932; s. Wilber Vincent and Fern (Clawson) A.; m. Elizabeth Williams, June 1, 1954 (dec. Dec. 1994); children: Thomas, William, Robert, Catherine, James, John; m. Wyoma Upward, Oct. 18, 1997. BS, Creighton U., 1958, MS, 1959; PhD, U. Iowa, 1963. Instr. biology Creighton U., Omaha, 1958-60; instr. physiology U. Iowa, 1960-63; asst. prof. Creighton U., Omaha, 1963-65, assoc. prof., 1965-68, prof. physiology, 1968-97, asst. med. dean, 1972-75, dean grad. studies, 1975-85, dean emeritus, 1995—, prof. emeritus, 1997—. Vis. prof. Naval Arctic Rsch. Lab., 1963-72, U. B.C., 1985-86, U. Tasmania, 1993-94; cons. VA, NSF, NRC, ARS; plenary speaker USSR Symposium on Environment, 1970, Internat. Soc. Biomet., 1972. Contbr. articles to profl. jours. Mem. Gov.'s task force on fatigue State Nebr. Served with M.C. U.S. Army, 1951-54. NSF fellow, 1962-63; NSF-NIH-ONR-AINA grantee, 1963— Fellow Explorers Club, Arctic Inst. N.Am.; mem. Am. Physiol. Soc., Am. Mammal Soc., Endocrine Soc., Soc. Exptl. Biology and Medicine, Internat. Soc. for Biometeorology, Sigma Xi.

ANDREWS, ROBERT E., congressman, lawyer; b. Bellmar, N.J., Aug. 4, 1957; m. Camille Spinello, Nov., 1993; 2 children. BA summa cum laude, Bucknell U., 1979; JD magna cum laude, Cornell U., 1982. Bar: NJ 1982. Assoc. Archer & Greiner, Haddonfield, N.J., 1982-84, Charles J. Clarke & Assocs., Haddonfield, 1984-85, Kenney & Kearney, Cherry Hill, N.J., 1985-88; mem. Camden County (N.J.) Bd. Chosen Freeholders, 1987-90, freeholder dir., 1988-90; mem. U.S. Congress from 1st N.J. dist., Washington, 1991—, mem. edn. and workforce com., armed svcs. com., homeland sec. com., ranking mem., employer-employee relations subcom. Former adjunct prof. Rutgers U. Sch. of Law. Contbr. Bd. dirs. Camden County March of Dimes; mem. Task Force on Govt. Waste. Mem.: Phi Beta Kappa. Democrat. Episcopalian. Avocation: jogging. Office: US House of Reps 2439 Rayburn House Office Bldg Washington DC 20515-0001*

ANDREWS, SALLY MAY, healthcare administrator; b. Westfield, Mass., Feb. 29, 1956; d. Roger N. and Dorothy M. (Goodhind) A. Student, U. Conn., 1974-76; BA, Simmons Coll., Boston, 1978; MBA, Boston U., 1986. Payroll clk. Children's Hosp., Boston, 1978-79, asst. payroll supr., 1979-81, staff analyst dept. medicine, 1981-83, asst. adminstr. dept. medicine, 1983-86, adminstr. dept. medicine, 1986-97, vice chair adminstrn. and strategic planning dept. medicine, 1998-01; exec. dir. divsn. for rsch. and edn. in complementary and integrative med. therapies Harvard Med. Sch., Boston, 2002—. Mem. bd. overseers Lasell Coll., Newton, Mass., 1993-2001, trustee, 2001—. Mem. Adminstrs. Internal Medicine, Assn. Adminstrs. in Acad. Pediat. (pres. 1996-97). Congregationalist. Office: Osher Inst Harvard Med Sch Landmark Ctr Ste 22A 401 Park Dr Boston MA 02215 Business E-Mail: sally_andrews@hms.harvard.edu.

ANDREWS, SALLY S., lawyer; BA, Duke U.; MAT, Harvard U., U. N.C.; JD, U. Tex., 1984. Bar: Tex., U.S. Tax Ct., U.S. Dist. Ct. (so., no., ea. and we. dists.) Tex., U.S. Ct. Appeals (5th Cir.), U.S. Supreme Ct., 2003. With Rockefeller Bros. Fund; faculty assoc. Duke U. Med. Ctr., Tex. Med. Ctr. Sch. Pub. Health; pvt. practice Houston. Author: Elder Law Handbook Houston Bar, 1999, 2003, 2005; case editor: Tex. Internat. Law Jour., 1983—84. Adv. mem. tech. adv. com. Greater Houston YMCA, mem. endowment devel. com.; vol. Peace Corps, Ethiopia, mem. U.S. govt. selection and tng. staff; bd. dirs. Women's Bus. Support Network Found., 2003—, treas., 2004—, chair fin. com., 2004—. Recipient, 1996 Women on The Move award, Houston

Chronicle, Star award Assn. Women Attys.; named Woman of Excellence, Houston Fedn. Profl. Women, 2005 Mem.: Houston Bar (bd. mem. Houston Lawyer Referral Svcs. 2003—), State Bar Tex. (4-C Grievance Comm. 1991—95, chair 1994—95), Houston Estate Fin. Forum, Houston Bus. and Estate Coun., Tex. Acad. Probate and Trust Lawyers (fellow 1996—), Coll. State Bar Tex., Houston Bar Found, Christian Legal Soc., Tex. Exec. Women, Rotary (pres. Galleria area club 1995—96, asst. gov. 1996—98, 2001—02), Phi Beta Kappa, Phi Delta Phi, Phi Kappa Delta, Pi Sigma Alpha. Office: 2 Bering Pk 800 Bering Dr Ste 200 Houston TX 77057-2130 Office Phone: 713-787-6648. E-mail: andrews_nelson@compuserve.com.

ANDREWS, TERRENCE MICHAEL, senior policy advisor; s. Terrence Willard and Ann Bonnie Andrews; m. Lisa Tarsi, Oct. 12, 2002. BS, Morgan State U., Balt., 1992, MA, 1994; JD, Roger Williams U., Bristol, R.I., 1997. Bar: Ariz. 1997, DC 2001, U.S. Supreme Ct. 2001, Va. 2005. Dep. atty. Pima County Atty., Tucson, 1997—2002; chief prosecutor Pascua Yaqui Tribe, Tucson, 2002—04; spl. asst. U.S. atty. Dept. of Justice, Tucson, 2002—04; sr. policy advisor Dept. of Homeland Security, Washington, 2004—. Firearms instr. Old Pueblo Firearms Acad., Tucson, 2000—04. Soccer referee Ariz. Interscholastic Assn., Tucson, 1998—2004; nat. del. Rep. Party, Tucson, 2004, dist. chmn., 2000—04. Named Govt. Lawyer of Yr., State Bar Ariz., 2004, Animal Prosecutor of Yr., Humane Soc. Ariz., 1999; named to Academic All- Am., Mid Ea. Athletic Conf., 1990, 1991; recipient Native Am. DV Prosecutor award, Native Am. Alliance, 2003, Pres. Fellowship award, Morgan State U., 1992, Academic All- Am., Mid Ea. Athletic Conf., 1992. Mem.: Mason (life 32nd degree). Republican. Roman Catholic. Avocations: soccer referee, pistol shooting, baseball. Office: Dep Homeland Security Ste 5623 7th and D Washington DC 20045 Office Phone: 202-205-9513. Personal E-mail: mandrewsgop@yahoo.com.

ANDREWS, THEODORA ANNE, retired librarian, educator; b. Carroll County, Ind., Oct. 14, 1921; d. Harry Floyd and Margaret Grace (Walter) Ulrey; m. Robert William Andrews, July 18, 1940 (div. 1946); 1 child, Martin Harry. BS with distinction, Purdue U., 1953; MS, U. Ill., 1955. Asst. reference libr. Purdue U., West Lafayette, Ind., 1955—56, pharmacy libr., 1956—79, instr. libr. sci., 1956—60, asst. prof., 1960—65, assoc. prof., 1965—71, prof., 1971—79, 1991—92, prof. libr. sci., pharmacy, nursing and health scis. libr., 1979—90, spl. bibliographer, 1991—92, prof. emeritus libr. sci., 1992—. Del. Ind. Gov.'s Conf. Librs. and Info. Svcs., 1978. Author: A Bibliography of the Socioeconomic Aspects of Medicine, 1975, A Bibliography of Drug Abuse Including Alcohol and Tobacco, 1977, A Bibliography of Drug Abuse, Supplement, 1977-80, 1981, Bibliography on Herbs, Herbal Remedies and Natural Foods, 1982, Substance Abuse Materials for School Libraries, An Annotated Bibliography, 1985, Guide to the Literature of Pharmacy and the Pharmaceutical Sciences, 1986; sect. editor Advances in Alcohol and Substance Abuse, 1981-92; contbr. articles to profl. jours. Mem. Purdue Women's Caucus, 1973—, v.p., 1975-76, pres., 1976-77, Internat. Women's Yr. Regional Planning Com., 1977. Grad. fellow, U. Ill., 1954—55. Mem. ALA, AAUP, Spl. Libr. Assn. (John H. Moriatry award Ind. chpt. 1972), Med. Libr. Assn., Am. Assn. Colls. Pharmacy, Kappa Delta Pi, Delta Rho Kappa. Baptist. Office: Purdue U Sch Pharmacy West Lafayette IN 47907

ANDREWS, WILLIAM COOKE, physician; b. Norfolk, Va., June 7, 1924; s. Charles James and Jean Curry (Cooke) A.; m. Elizabeth Wight Kyle, Nov. 10, 1951; children— Elizabeth Randolph, William Cooke, Jr., Susan Carrington. AA, Princeton U., 1946; MD, Johns Hopkins U., 1947. Diplomate Am. Bd. Obstetrics and Gynecology. Intern N.Y. Hosp., 1947, resident in obstetrics and gynecology, 1948-50, 52-53; practice medicine specializing in obstetrics and gynecology Norfolk, Va., 1953-95; asst. in obstetrics and gynecology Cornell U. Med. Sch., 1948-50, 52-53; mem. attending staff Med. Ctr. Hosp.; prof. ob-gyn. Ea. Va. Med. Sch., Norfolk, 1975-95, prof. emeritus, 1995—, pres. faculty senate, 1976-77. Mem. fertility and maternal health drug adv. com. FDA, 1979-83, chmn., 1982-83, cons., 1983-87; mem. sci. adv. bd. Alan Guttmacher Inst., 1992-94; co-chair women's health measurement adv. panel Nat. Com. Quality Assurance, 1996—. Contbr. articles in field to profl. jours. Chmn. Norfolk Bicentennial Commn., 1969-71; mem. Community Facilities Commn., 1971-73, chmn., 1973-79; bd. dirs. Va. League for Planned Parenthood, 1966-68; pres. Norfolk chpt. Planned Parenthood, 1966-68; bd. govs. The Jacobs Inst. Women's Health, 1997—. With M.C., USN, 1950-52. Named Hon. Officer of the Most Excellent Order of the Brit. Empire, Queen Elizabeth II, 1967; presented Order of Andres Bello, Pres. Carlos Andres Perez of Venezuela, 1992. Fellow Am. Coll. Obstetricians and Gynecologists (vice chmn. dist. IV 1985-88, chmn. 1988-91, v.p. 1992-93, pres.-elect 1993, pres. 1994-95, exec. bd. 1988-96), Am. Assn. Obstetricians and Gynecologists, Am. Gynecol. and Obstet. Soc., Royal Coll. Obstetricians and Gynecologists (hon.); mem. AMA, Am. Fertility Soc. (bd. dirs. 1970-73, pres. 1977, med. dir. 1986-88, exec. dir. 1988-92), Nat. Osteoporosis Found. (interspecialty med. coun. 1995—), Med. Soc. Va., Norfolk Acad. Medicine, Va. Tidewater Obstetricians and Gynecologists Soc., Continental Gynecol. Soc., South Atlantic Assn. Obs.-Gyns., Norfolk C. of C. (chmn. armed forces com. 1966-68, v.p. 1968-69, pres. 1970), Internat. Fedn. Fertility Socs. (asst. treas. 1974-80, pres. 1983-86, chmn. sci. program com. 1986-89, exec. com. 1974-92), Navy League U.S. (pres. Hampton Roads coun. 1968-70, nat. dir. 1970-74), English Speaking Union U.S. (pres. Norfolk-Portsmouth br. 1964-66), Planned Parenthood Fedn. Am. (cons. nat. med. com. 1975-85, chmn. 1981-83), Norfolk Yacht and Country Club (commodore 1966). Presbyterian. Personal E-mail: wca3@aol.com.

ANDREWS, WILLIAM DOREY, law educator; b. NYC, Feb. 25, 1931; s. Sidney Warren and Margaret (Dorey) Andrews; m. Shirley May Herrman, Dec. 26, 1953; children: Helen Estelle (Noble), Roy Herrman, John Frederick, Margaret Dorey (Davenport), Susan Louise, Carol Mary (Reid). BA in English, Amherst Coll., 1952; LLD, 1977; LLB, Harvard U., 1955. Bar: Mass. 1959. Practice, Boston, 1959—63; assoc. Ropes & Gray, 1959—63; lectr. Harvard Law Sch., Cambridge, Mass., 1961—63, asst. prof., 1963—65, prof., 1965—. Eli Goldston prof. law, 1984—. Cons. Sullivan & Worcester, 1964—, US Dept. Treasury, 1966—68, 1984. Lt. USNR, 1955—58. Mem.: ABA, Am. Law Inst. Office: Harvard U Law Sch 1545 Massachusetts Ave Cambridge MA 02138-2903*

ANDREWS, WILLIAM FREDERICK, manufacturing executive; b. Easton, Pa., Oct. 7, 1931; s. William Frederick and Lydia Nielson (Cross) Andrews; children: William Frederick III, Whitney, Carter, Clayton, Sloane. BS, U. Md., 1953; MBA, Seton Hall U., 1961. Product mgr. Scovill Mfg. Co., Waterbury, Conn., 1965-68, v.p., gen. mgr. Raleigh, N.C., 1968-73, group v.p. Nashville, 1973-79, pres. Waterbury, 1979-81, chmn., pres., CEO, 1981-86, Singer Sewing Machine Co., 1986-89; pres., CEO, chmn. Massey Investment Co., 1989—90; pres., CEO, UNR Industries Inc., 1990—92; CEO, chmn. bd. Amdura Corp., Conn., 1992-94; chmn. bd. Utica Corp., Utica, N.Y., 1992-94, Schrader Bridgeport, 1995—98, Scovill Fasteners, Nashville, 1996—2001, Northwestern Steel and Wire Co., Nashville, 1998—2001, Corrections Corp. of Am., Nashville, 2000—, Katy Industries, Middlebury, Conn., 2001—, Allied Aerospace, Newport News, Va., 2000—, Singer Co., 2004—. Bd. dirs. Corrections Corp., Katy Industries, Black Box, Inc., Trex Industries, O'Charleys' Inc. Capt. USAF, 1953-56. Recipient Silver Beaver award Boys Scouts Am., 1979, Significant Sig award Sigma Chi, 1992. Mem.: Litchfield (Conn.) Country Club, The Golf Club of Tenn., Univ. Club (N.Y.C.), Chgo. Club, Highfield Country Club (Conn.), Bellemeade Country Club (Nashville). Republican. Episcopalian. Office: 1409 Moran Rd Franklin TN 37069-6301 Office Phone: 615-370-0098, 615-370-0098. Personal E-mail: wmfandrews@aol.com.

ANDREYCHUK, DAVID, professional hockey player; b. Hamilton, Ont., Can., Sept. 1963; m. Sue Andreychuk; children, Taylor, Caci. Player Buffalo Sabres, 1982—93, Toronto Maple Leafs, 1993—96, N.J. Devils, Rutherford, 1996—99, Boston Bruins, 1999—2000, Colorado Avalanche, 2000, Buffalo Sabres, 2000—01, Tampa Bay Lightning, 2001—. Named to NHL All Star Game, 1990, 94. Achievements include mem. Stanley Cup Championship Team, Tampa Bay Lightning, 2004. Office: c/o Tampa Bay Lightning St Pete Times Forum 401 Channelside Dr Tampa FL 33602

ANDREYEV, SERGEY V., language educator; b. Riga, Latvia, June 18, 1970; MEd, MA, U. Buffalo, 1997. Instr. English for specific purposes Riga Maritime Coll., 1990—93; asst. lectr. U. Latvia, Riga, 1993—2000; ESL specialist Mass. Coll. Pharmacy and Health Scis., Worcester, 2001—. Pres. Poseidon Publ., Worcester, 2001—, Poseidon Internat., Pireaus, Greece, 1990—93. Recipient Outstanding Achievement in Poetry Silver Cup, Internat. Soc. Poets, 2004. Mem.: TESOL. Office: MCPHS 19 Foster St Worcester MA 01608

ANDRIANO, KIRK PATRICK, pharmaceutical executive; b. Boise, Idaho, Nov. 10, 1956; s. Donald and Fae Andriano. BS, Utah State U., 1975—79; MS, U. of Utah, 1981—85, PhD, 1985—90. Post-doctoral fellow U. of Utah, 1990—91; nih - fogarty internat. rsch. fellow Tampere U. of Tech., Finland, 1991—92; post-doctoral fellow APS Rsch. Inst., Advanced Polymer Systems, Inc., Redwood City, Calif., 1994—95; vis. rsch. scholar Kyoto U., 1995—97; scientist ii Atrix Laboratories, Inc., Fort Collins, Colo., 1997—99; sr. scientist MacroMed, Inc., Sandy, 1999—2001, exec. dir., preclinical devel., 2002—03; v.p. rsch. & devel. Inion Ltd., Tampere, Finland, 2003—. Indsl. mentor, soc. for biomaterials Johns Hopkins U., Balt. Fogarty Internat. Rsch. fellow, NIH and Acad. of Finland. Master: Nat. Ski Patrol Sys.; mem.: Biomedical Engrng. Soc., Soc. for Biomaterials, Controlled Release Soc., ASTM, Am. Assn. of Pharm. Scientists, Tissue Engrng. Soc. Home: PMB 31102302 PO Box 311 Mendham NJ 07945-0311 Office: Inion Ltd Loakarinkatu 2 33520 Tampere Finland Office Phone: +352-3-230-6600. Office Fax: +358-3-230-6602. Personal E-mail: kandriano@aol.com. E-mail: kirk.andriano@inion.com.

ANDRIANO-MOORE, RICHARD COUNT, retired military officer, secondary school educator, elementary school educator; b. Petaluma, Calif., May 25, 1932; s. Norvel and Thelma Elizabeth Koch-Andriano (Cook) Moore; m. Janice Lynn Hironaka, Jan. 10, 1976 (div. Feb. 1990); children: Erika Lynn, Stephen Albert. BA, San Jose State U., 1956; MBA, Pepperdine U., 1977; B in Metaphysical Sci., U. Metaphysics, 1993. Commd. ensign USNR, 1957, advanced through grades to comdr.; 1st lt., gunnery officer USS Jefferson Count LST1068, 1957—60; tchr. 7th grade Oasis Sch., Riverside County, Calif., 1960—63; pers. and legal officer USS Maury AGS-16, 1963—65; commdg. officer Naval & Marine Corps Res. Tng. Ctr., Port Arthur, Tex., 1965—68; ops. officer USS Muliphen LKA 61, 1968—69; ASW & surface program officer 11th Naval Dist., San Diego, 1970—74; commdg. officer Naval Res. Ctr., Hunters Point, Calif., 1974—75, Army, Navy & Marine Corps Res. Ctr., San Bruno, Calif., 1975—79; dir. adminstrn. Nat. Com. Employer, Washington, 1979—82; comdr., recruiting coord. 10 we. states Alameda, Calif., 1982—84; chief staff N. Readiness comdr., Treasure Island, Calif., 1984—85; tchr. Shoreline Unified Sch. Dist., Tomales, Calif., 1985—92, 1994—. Editor-in-chief: California Compatriot, 1976—80. Insp. Precinct Bd., Petaluma, 1987—90; scoutmaster Boy Scouts Am., 1989—92, dist. exec., 1992—94; alumni mem. Naval War Coll. Found., Newport, RI, 2002—. Decorated Def. Meritorious Svc. medal Sec. Def., Washington, Ancestral Title and Coat of Arms Counts of Andriano Wappenrolle, Austria, Rome, knight comdr. Order St. John of Jerusalem Knights Hospitaller; recipient Disting. Alumni award, San Jose State U., 1991, Scoutmaster award of Merit, Boy Scouts Am., 1992, numerous Best of Show and 1st place ribbons for acrylic paintings, Sonoma-Marin County Fair, 1989—2003, Polish Silver Cross Merit, 1990. Mem.: Soc. of Colonial Wars, Noble Co. of the Rose (lt. magister rosae 1998—), Naval Order U.S., Mil. Order Loyal Legion U.S. (Calif. comdr. 1982—88), Calif. Soc. SAR (pres. San Francisco chpt. 1976—77, state pres. 1986—87, Silver Good Citizenship medal 1978, Patriot medal 1985, Meritorious Svc. medal 1987, oak leaf cluster 1996, Citation of Merit 2001, oak leaf cluster 2004), Augustan Soc. Inc. (v.p. 1995—). Avocations: reading, hiking, bicycling, travel, abstract artist. Office: 2920 Carissa Ct Santa Rosa CA 95405 E-mail: cteandriano@netscape.net.

ANDRIANOPOULOS, CHRISTINA I., marketing executive, consultant; BS in Bus. Mgmt. with honors, Worcester State Coll., Mass.; MBA in Mktg., Washington U., King of Prussia, Pa. Cert. bilingual med. interpreter U. Mass. Med. Sch., 2004. Dept. mgr. to divsnl. sales mgr. Jordan Marsh/Allied Stores, New England; regional sales mgr. Bugle Boy Industries, N.Y.C.; nat. sales mgr. Liz Claiborne, Inc., 1994—96; dir. mktg. and ops. Memory Ctrs. Am., Inc.; v.p. mktg. SilverCarrot, Inc., NY; dir. mktg. Profilics-IBM Advanced Bus. Ptnr.; cons. Omega Group, Inc. Contbr. articles columns and editorials to newspapers. Vol. Lupus Found., Mass. Adoption Resource Exch., Mason's Dyslexic Ctr.; mem. cmty. devel. com. County and City of Worcester; mem. gov. bd. St. Spyridon Greek Cathedral. Mem.: Worcester C. of C., Am.-Hellenic C. of C. Avocations: reading, writing, running. Address: 111 Amherst St Worcester MA 01602

ANDRIANOV, ALEXANDER K., polymer chemist; b. Moscow, Mar. 24, 1958; came to U.S., 1991; s. Kuzma and Irina Andrianova; m. Svetlana P. Andrianova, Apr. 6, 1979; 1 child, Liza. BS in Chemistry, Moscow State U., 1980, PhD in Polymer Chemistry, 1985. Rsch. scientist Moscow State U., 1985-92; vis. scientist MIT, Cambridge, 1991-93; dir. polymer rsch. devel. Virus Rsch. Inst., Cambridge, 1993—. Contbr. chpts. to books, numerous articles to profl. jours.; patentee in field. Mem. Am. Chem. Soc., AICE, Controlled Release Soc. Avocations: reading, travel, gardening. Office: Virus Rsch Inst 61 Moulton St Cambridge MA 02138-1127

ANDRIAS, RICHARD THOMPSON, state supreme court judge; b. NY, 1943; married; 2 children. BA, Bowdoin Coll., 1965; JD, Columbia U., 1970. Bar: N.Y. 1971, U.S. Dist. Ct. (so. and ea. dists.) N.Y., U.S. Ct. Appeals (2d cir.). Assoc. Gilbert, Segall & Young, N.Y.C., 1970-71; lawyer Legal Aid Soc., N.Y.C., 1971-75; assoc. Davis & Davis, N.Y.C., 1975-81, Gordon & Shechtman, N.Y.C., 1981-83; judge Criminal Ct. of City of N.Y., N.Y.C., 1983-87, Supreme Ct. of the State of N.Y., N.Y.C., 1988—; adj. prof. trial practice Pace Law Sch., White Plains, N.Y., 1991—; assoc. justice Appellate Divsn. First Dept. Supreme Ct. N.Y., 1996—. Vis. scholar London (Eng.) Sch. of Econs. Law Sch., 1974; chair N.Y. Task Force on Civilian Complaints, N.Y.C., 1987-90); mem. N.Y. State Gov.'s Task Force on Rape and Sexual Violence, 1989-90. Contbr. articles to profl. jours. Chair Cmty. Bd. 12, NYC, 1972-76; bd. dirs., chair Bronx (NY) Legal Svc., 1980-83; bd. dirs. NY Vietnam Vets. Leadership Program, NYC, 1984-97, NYC Audubon, 2003—. 1st lt. U.S. Army, 1965-67. Decorated Bronze star U.S. Army, Vietnam, 1967, Air medal U.S. Army, Vietnam, 1967. Fellow Am. Bar Found.; mem. ABA (chair AIDS in the criminal justice system 1987-89, victims com. 1995-97), CEELI Russian Program, 1995-96, Assn. of Bar of City of N.Y. (chair victims com. 1992, exec. com. 1998-2002, nominating com. 2004-), Am. Law Inst. Office: Appellate Divsn First Dept 27 Madison Ave Rm 406 New York NY 10010-2201 Office Phone: 212-340-0436.

ANDRICA, JOHN DEAN, management consultant; b. Canton, Ohio, Sept. 17, 1946; s. John and Diane C. A.; m. Diane Cherney, Aug. 2, 1980; 1 child, Stephanie N. BS, Indsl. Engrng. Coll., 1969; student, Allied Inst. Tech. Dir. engrng. Wilson Sporting Goods, Chgo., 1974-77; v.p. A.T. Kearney, Chgo., 1977-87, mng. dir., 1987-91, sr. v.p., 1991—; with Prin. Cleve. Investment Ptnrs. LLC., 1997—; dir. Union Ptnrs. LLC., 2000—. Candidate Ill. 9th dist. U.S. Congress, 1980; candidate city treas. City of Chgo., 1977; mem. exec. com., bd. trustees Bus. Volunteerism Unltd., Cleve., 1994—; mem. corp. coun. Cleve. Mus. Art, 1996—; bd. dirs. Cleve. Playhouse Square Found., Shaker Heights, Ohio, 1994—, Hathaway Brown Sch. Girls, Shaker Heights, 1998—. Named Young Rep. of Yr. Cook County Rep. Party, 1978. Mem. Inst. Mgmt. Cons., Shaker Country Club, Shaker Skating Club, The Club, Union Club. Republican. Avocations: skiing, skeetshooting, golf, boating, tennis. Office: A T Kearney 222 W Adams St #2500 Chicago IL 60606-5312

ANDRIEUX, RUTH ENID, music educator, composer; b. Riverside, Calif., Apr. 6, 1954; d. Carl Joseph and Carmen Marie Neugebauer; m. Clestian John Andrieux; children: Clestian John Jr., Matthew Joseph. MusB, Pacific Union Coll., Angwin, Calif., 1988. Pvt. practice piano instr. Napa County, Calif., 1979—; composer Andrieux House Music Pub. Co., Angwin, 1979—. Composer, singer, arranger, performer: albums Only Me, Celebrating Him, In The Beginning God, God's Gift of Love, Thy Word Have I Hid In My Heart, Let's Get Wild for Jesus (ASCAP's Plus award, 2004). Mem.: Music Tchrs. Assn. Independent. Seventh-Day Adventist. Avocations: walking, travel, gardening, sewing, cooking. Home and Office: PO Box 593 Angwin CA 94508 E-mail: ruthandrieux@mindspring.com.

ANDRIL, DAVID T., lawyer; b. Elizabeth, NJ, Aug. 5, 1956; BS, Georgetown U., 1977; JD, U. Va., 1980. Bar: DC 1980. Ptnr., co-head Energy Sect. Vinson & Elkins LLP, Washington, DC. Mem.: Energy Bar Assn. Office: Vinson & Elkins LLP Willard Office Building 1455 Pennsylvania Ave NW, Ste 600 Washington DC 20004 Office Phone: 202-639-6542. E-mail: dandril@velaw.com.

ANDRIOLA, MARY R., neurologist, pediatrician; b. NYC, Sept. 13, 1942; d. Anthony Francis Repole and Florence Elizabeth Elliott; m. Micheal John Andriola, July 21, 1962 (div. Jan. 1982); children: Margaret Mary Danao, Joseph Anthony, James Michael; m. Jordan I. Levine, Feb. 24, 1990. Student, Vassar Coll., 1958-60; AB, Johns Hopkins U., 1962; MD, Duke U., 1965. Diplomate Am. Bd. Pediatrics, Am. Bd. Psychiatry and Neurology, with spl. competence in child neurology and added qualification in clin. neurophysiology, subspecialty neurodevel. disabilities, 2005. Resident in pediatrs. Duke U. Sch. Medicine, Durham, N.C., 1965-66, U. Fla., Gainesville, 1966-67, resident in neurology, 1967-70; asst. prof. neurology and pediats. La. State U. Sch. Medicine, New Orleans, 1970-72; dir. electroencephalography and fellowship program U. Fla. Coll. Medicine, Gainesville, 1975-88, assoc. prof. neurology, 1975-88, assoc. prof. pediats., 1978-88; dir. pediat. neurology All Children's Hosp. U. S. Fla., St. Petersburg; assoc. prof. neurology SUNY, Stony Brook, 1988-98, dir. clin. neurophysiology, 1990-97, dir. divsn. clin. neurophysiology, 1997, prof. neurology and pediats., 1998—, dir. divsn. pediat. neurology, 2001—. Assoc. examiner Am. Bd. Qualification in EEG, 1976-85, Am. Bd. Psychiatry and Neurology, 1983—, Am. Bd. Clin. Neurophysiology, Inc., 1991—; mem. adv. com. Pinellas county Sch. Bd. Health, 1979-88; reviewer Neurology, 1997—; appeared in TV interviews; mem. People to People Women Specialist Med. Exch. to China, 1991; mem. profl. adv. bd. Epilepsy Found L.I., 1991—; mem. team to Russia, Physicians for Social Responsibility, 1992; lectr. in field. Author: Introduction to EEG and Evoked Potentials, 1983; contbr. numberous articles, abstract, revs. to profl. jours., chpts. to books. Grantee Abbott Labs., 1992, 96, Burroughs Wellcome, 1993, NIH, 1993, Parke-Davis, 1994, BECTS, 1995, Hoechst Marion Roussel, 1995, Warner Lambert, 1995, Cyberonics, 1998. Fellow: Am. Clin. Neurophysiology Soc. (program com. 1980—81, practice com. 1980—82, EEG lab. accreditation bd. 1980—90, liaison Child Neurology Soc. 1982—88), Am. Acad. Pediats.; mem.: So. Clin. Neurol. Soc. (bd. dirs.), Suffolk County Pediat. Soc., Tri-State Child Neurology Soc., Ea. Assn. Electroencephalographers, Child Neurology Soc., Am. Epilepsy Soc., So. EEG Soc. (sec.-treas. 1975—78, program chmn. 1979, pres. 1980, edn. chmn. 1981—89), Women's Am. Med. Assn. (sec.-treas. Suffolk County chpt. 1992). Office: SUNY Stony Brook Sch Medicine Dept Neurology Stony Brook NY 11794-0001 Office Phone: 516-444-2599. Business E-Mail: mandriol@notes.cc.sunysb.edu.

ANDRIOLA, ROCCO F., lawyer, diversified financial services company executive; b. Astoria, NY, Mar. 24, 1958; s. Pasquale and Lena (Dituri) A.; m. Susan A. Andriola; children: Patrick Nicholas, Mark Vari. BA summa cum laude, Fordham U., 1979; JD, NYU, 1982, LLM (corp. law), 1986. Bar: N.Y. 1983, D.C. 1985, U.S. Dist. Ct. (so., ea., no. and we dists.), U.S. Ct. Appeals (2d cir.) 1983, U.S. Ct. Internat. Trade 1983, U.S. Ct. Claims 1983, U.S. Supreme Ct. 1986; lic. real estate broker. Legal asst. Am. Clerical Svcs., N.Y.C., summers 1978-79; assoc. Ford Marrin Esposito & Witmeyer, N.Y.C., summer 1980, Donovan Leisure Newton & Irvine, N.Y.C., summer 1981, corp. and securities assoc., 1982-86; v.p., assoc. gen. counsel Shearson Lehman Bros., Inc., N.Y.C., 1986-89, 1st v.p. Capital Preservation and Restructuring Group, 1989-91; sr. v.p. diversified asset group Lehman Bros., N.Y.C., 1991-96, mng. dir. diversified asset group, 1996—2004, mng. dir., dir. global corp. svcs., 1998—2004, mng. dir. fixed income divsn., 2004—. Projects editor NYU Moot Ct. Bd., 1981-82. Bd. dirs. Symphony for UN, 1985-89, Playing-to-Win, 1988-94; mem. bd. advisors Fordham U., 1987-97, chmn. bd. advisors, 1996-97; founder, exec. dir. St. Francis Home Visitors Program, Astoria, 1983-85; v.p. St. Francis Parish Coun., Astoria, 1983-84; mem. Queens Citizens Orgn., 1979-86, Astoria Civic Assn., 1983-86, Residents for a More Beautiful Port Washington, 1992—, Am. Liver Found., bd. dirs. 1993-97, mem. exec. com., 1994-97, acting chmn. bd. dirs. 1995-96, Transplant Recipients Internat. Org., Transplant Living Ctr., Am. Tinnitus Assn., Urban Land Inst.; mem. L.I. chpt. MADD, 1991—; fellow David Rockefeller Fellowship Program, 1995-96; mem. bd. dirs. United Network for Organ Sharing, 1996, 97; bd. dirs. N.Y. Organ Donor Network, 1997—, chmn. governance com., 2000-03, vice-chmn., 2002-03, chmn. bd., 2004-05; mem. fundraising com. St. Peter of Alcantara Parish, 2000; bd. dirs. Monsignor McClancy Meml. H.S. Alumni, 2000-02; mem. N.Y.C. Partnership Borough Devel. Task Force, 2002. Mem. ABA (lt. gov. law student divsn. 1981-82), N.Y. State Bar Assn. (rep. 1980-82), Am. Corp. Counsel Assn. (bd. dirs. 1988-92, v.p. 1989-90, chmn. mergers and acquisitions com. N.Y. chpt. 1987-89), Order of Barristers, Homeowners Assn. Port Washington (pres. gen. coun. 1992-93), Fordham U. Pres. Coun., Morewood Oaks Homeowners Assn. (pres. 1991-93, 2004—), Order Sons of Italy in Am. (trustee 1995-97), Am. Israel Pub. Affairs Com., Republican Nat. Lawyers Assn., Combined Health Appeal Greater N.Y. (vice chmn., bd. dirs. 1992-95), Port Washington Rep. Club, KC. Republican. Roman Catholic. Home: 45 Morewood Oaks Port Washington NY 11050-1603 Office: Lehman Bros Inc 745 7th Ave New York NY 10019-1000 Office Phone: 212-526-3177.

ANDRIOLE, GERALD LOUIS, urologist; b. Hazelton, Pa., Aug. 31, 1955; s. Gerald Louis and Irene Dorothy (Serratore) A.; m. Dorothy Potter, June 1, 1985; children: Gerald, Nicholas, Philip. BS summa cum laude, Pa. State U., 1976; MD, Jefferson Med. Coll., Phila., 1978. Diplomate Am. Bd. Urology, Nat. Bd. Med. Examiners; lic. physician, Md., Mo. Intern, resident in surgery Strong Meml. Hosp./U. Rochester, N.Y., 1978-80; resident in urology Brigham and Women's Hosp./Harvard Med. Sch., Boston, 1980-83; expert in urologic oncology Nat. Cancer Inst./NIH, Bethesda, Md., 1983-85; asst. prof. urologic surgery Washington U. Sch. Medicine, St. Louis, 1985-90, assoc. prof., 1990—; chief urology sect. St. Louis VA Med. Ctr., 1985-95. Mem. staff Jewish Hosp., St. Louis, Children's Hosp., St. Louis, VA Hosp., St. Louis, St. Louis Regional Med. Ctr., Barnes Hosp., St. Louis. Author, editor, reviewer jours. Recipient 1st prize Radiol. Soc. N.Am., 1990, CIAO award for medicine, others; grantee Am. Cancer Soc., Nat. Cancer Inst., NIDDKD, NIH, Am. Found. for Urologic Disease/Nat. Kidney Found., others. Mem. ACS, Am. Assn. for Cancer Rsch., Am. Soc. Clin. Oncology, Am. Urol. Assn., Soc. Univ. Urologists, Soc. Urologic Oncology, Soc. for Basic Urologic Rsch., Nat. Urologic Forum. Office: Washington U Sch Medicine 4960 Childrens Pl Saint Louis MO 63110-1002 Office Phone: 314-362-8212. Business E-Mail: andrioleg@wustl.edu.

ANDRISANI, JOHN ANTHONY, editor, writer; b. Bayshore, NY, Sept. 24, 1949; s. Pat and Gwendoline Mary (Rose) A. Student, SUNY, Stony Brook, 1968—71. Instr. golf in country club, NY, 1971-78; freelance writer golf mags., 1977—; asst. editor Golf Illus. mag., London, 1980-82; sr. editor instrn. Golf mag., N.Y.C., 1982-98; pres. John Andrisani Assoc. Inc. Co-author: (with Sandy Lyle) Learning Golf: The Lyle Way, 1986, (with Seve Ballesteros) Natural Golf, 1987 (Book of Month Club 1987), (with Chi Chi Rodriguez) 101 Supershots, 1990, (with Robin McMillan) The Golf Doctor, 1990 (Brentanos bestseller 1990), (with Mike Dunaway) Hit It Hard!, 1991, (with Phil Ritson) Golf Your Way, 1992, (with John Daly) Grip It, and Rip It!, 1992, (with Fred Couples) Total Shotmaking, 1994, (with Craig Stadler) I Am The Walrus, 1995, (with Claude "Butch" Harmon Jr.), The Four Cornerstones of Winning Golf, 1996, (with Jim McLean) The X-Factor Swing, 1996, The Tiger Woods Way, 1997, The Short Game Magic of Tiger Woods, 1998, (with Mark Russell) Golf Rules Plain and Simple, 1999, The Hogan Way, 2000, (with John Anselmo) "A-Game" Golf, 2001, The Bobby Jones Way, 2002, Think Like Tiger, 2002, Everything I Learned about People, I Learned From a Round of Golf, 2002, The Nicklaus Way, 2003, Play Like Sergio Garcia,

2004, (with Jim Hardy) The Plane Truth for Golfers, 2005; contbr. articles to jours. and mags. Mem. Golf Writers Assn. (assn. champion 1985), Ballybunion Golf Club (life, Ireland). E-mail: jagolf3238@aol.com.

ANDRIST, DEBRA DIANE, Spanish language and literature educator; b. Goodland, Kans., Nov. 14, 1950; d. Bill Lee and Gerre Danleia (Ingamells) A.; m. A.L. Freeman, Jr., Aug. 26, 1989. BA, Ft. Hays Kans. State U., 1972; MA, U. Utah, 1979; PhD, SUNY, Buffalo, 1985. Instr. Spanish Grosse Pointe (Mich.) Pub. Schs., 1972-73, Westside Pub. Schs., Omaha, 1975-77; teaching asst. U. Utah, Salt Lake City, 1977-79, SUNY, Buffalo, 1979-82; assoc. prof. Spanish Baylor U., Waco, Tex., 1982-96; Cullen prof., chair modern and classical langs. dept. U. St. Thomas, Houston, 1996—2003. Evening Spanish instr. Maryvale Pub. Adult Sch., Cheektowaga, N.Y., 1981-82; instr. Spanish, Lorena (Tex.) Meth. Pre-Sch., 1985-87, Lakewood Bapt. Pre-Sch., waco, 1985-87; book reviewer D.C. Heath, Heinle & Heinle, Holt, Rinehart and Winston, Prentice Hall, Houghton Mifflin, Arte Publico Press, HarperCollins, W.B. Saunders; owner/operator Panache. Author: Deceit Plus desire Equals Violence, 1989, Charlemos un poco, 3d edit., 1994, Ahora leamos, 3d edit., 1994; contbr. numerous articles and revs. to profl. jours.; presenter numerous papers nat. and internat. scholarly confs. Bd. dirs. Ctrl. Tex. Women's Alliance, 1993, pres., 1994; mem. Historic Waco Found., 1992—; vol. Am. Heart Assn.; mem. Dallas Mus. Art, 1982—, Ft. Worth Mus. Art, 1984—, Kimball Mus., Ft. Worth, 1982—, Waco Art Ctr., 1982—, Tex. Arts Coun. Assn., exhbn. hostess, 1992; sec.-treas. Mackey Ranch Property Owners Assn., Eddy, Tex., 1987-88, pres., 1988-89; bilingual teaching vol. Utah Shriners Hosp., Salt Lake City, 1977-79; vol. Omaha Ballet, 1975-77, Joslyn Art Mus., Omaha, 1975-77, others. Named Multicultural Campus Community Creator of the Yr., Baylor U. Multicultural Alliance, 1992-93; Mellon fellow, 1989; recipient numerous grants and fellowships. Mem. AAUP, MLA (South Ctrl. chpt. pres. 2000), Rocky Mountain MLA, Midwest MLA, Am. Assn. Tchrs. Spanish and Portuguese, Internat. Imagery Assn., Women's Studies Assn., Medieval Feminist Scholars, L.Am. Studies Assn., Instituto Literario y Cultural Hispanico, S.W. Coun. L.Am. Studies, Feministas unidas, Asociacion de literatura femenina, PEO. Avocations: art history, antiques. Office: U St Thomas 3800 Montrose Blvd Houston TX 77006-4626 Fax: 713-525-6997. E-mail: andrist@stthom.edu.

ANDRITZKY, JOSEPH GEORGE, law educator; b. Milw., Jan. 15, 1947; s. George Joseph and Emma (Schreiner) A. AAS, Milw. Inst. Tech., 1967; BS, Calif. State U., Long Beach, 1971; MPA, U. So. Calif., L.A., 1978; PhD, Claremont Grad. Sch., 1984. Vis. prof. criminal law Calif. State U., Long Beach, 1979; adj. prof. criminal law Milw. Area Tech. Coll., 1980—81; instr. law and criminal justice Moraine Park Tech. Coll., Fond du Lac, Wis., 1985—88; asst. prof. criminal law Marquette U., Milw., 1988—89; asst. prof./dir. law enforcement-criminal justice U. Wis., Oshkosh, 1989—90; assoc. prof. criminal law/dir. justice/pub. policy Concordia U. Wis., Milw., 1990—; dir. counterintelligence nat. security law 1st Army Intelligence Sch., Ft. McCoy, Wis., 1988—95; strategic intelligence officer 400th Strategic Intelligence Group, 1995—98, European Command, Ft. Sheridan, Ill., 2000—; chief intelligence G-2 U.S. Army Corps Engrs., Baghdad, Iraq, 2003—04, gen. staff G-2 HQ Washington, 2004—05. Sr. instr. mil. law U.S. Army Command and Gen. Staff Coll.; mem. accredited evaluation team Am. Coun. on Edn., N.Y.C., 1992. Author: Civil Rights Law, 1984; editor: Criminal Law, 1990-2001; contbr. articles to profl. jours. Bd. dirs. Waukesha County Law Enforcement Adv. Bd., 1992-2000; elder Trinity Luth. Ch., Milw., 1989-2000; sec. judiciary com. Concordia U. Wis., Milw., 1991—. Lt. col. USAR, 1974—. Mem. ABA (criminal justice assoc.), Res. Officers Assn., Assn. U.S. Army, Nat. Assn. Scholars, Wis. Criminal Justice Edn. Assn. (bd. dirs., pres.), Am. Law Enforcement Trainers Assn. (founder), Pi Sigma Alpha, Alpha Delta Pi. Republican. Lutheran. Avocations: automobile restoration, antique toys and collectables, baseball. Home: 440 N 40th St Milwaukee WI 53208-3741 Office: Concordia U Wis 12800 N Lake Shore Dr Mequon WI 53097-2418 Office Phone: 202-761-1267. E-mail: jandritzky@aol.com.

ANDRUK, MARJORIE DEAN, artist, educator; b. Norfolk, Va., Aug. 11, 1922; d. Carl Chadbourne and Bessie Jane (Overman) Dean; m. Richard Andruk, June 5, 1944; children: Richard Dean (dec.), Kenneth Francis. BA, Md. Inst. Coll. Art, 1942; postgrad., Eastman Sch. Photography, Winona Lake, 1943, Inst. Allende, San Miguel de Allende, Guanajuato, Mex., 1968-72; MFA, U. S.C., 1976. 1st woman press photographer Balt. Sun, 1943-45; organizer art dept. Cath. Diocese St. Petersburg, St. Petersburg, Fla., 1957-58; prof. art Gertrude Herbert Art Inst., Augusta, Ga., 1972-76; tchg. assoc. U. S.C., Aiken, 1975-76. Panelist DSAC Grant Rev. Panel, 1984-85; condr. workshops Inst. Allende and Centro cultural El Nigromante. One-woman shows include Coyle & Richardson Gallery, Charleston, W.Va., Learning Founds. Gallery, Athens, Ga., Town and Gown Gallery, Athens, Arts and Sci. Mus., Macon, Ga., The Augusta (Ga.)-Richmond County Mus., 1973, 74, Quinlan Art Ctr., Gainesvile, Ga., La Galeria Gaudi, Maracaibo, Venezuela, 1973, Huntington Gallery, U. S.C., 1976, Gertrude Herbert Art Inst., Augusta, 1976, Grande Gallery, Wilmington, Del., 1978, Ware Gallery, Arden, Del., 1979, 81, Casa Carmen Gallery, San Miguel de Allende, 1980, 84, Rodney Square Gallery, Wilmington, Del., 1981, Longwood Gardens Gallery, 1983, The Highland Gallery, Atlanta, 1983, Del. Ctr. for Contemporary Arts, Wilmington, 1983, Evelyn Cobb Gallery, St. Petersburg, Fla., 1994, Lighthouse Gallery, Tequesta, Fla., 1995, St. Petersburg Art Ctr., 1999, many others; group shows include Corcoran Mus., Washington, 1974, Inst. Allende, Russell House Gallery, U. S.C., 1975, Ware Gallery, Rodney Square Gallery, Upham Gallery, St. Petersburg Beach, Fla., 1989, The Arts Ctr., St. Petersburg, Arts on Pk., Lakeland, Fla., 1995, Ridge Art Assn., Winter Haven, Fla., Northwood U., West Palm Beach, 1996, Venice Art Ctr., 1997, Vero Ctr. Arts, 1997, Northwood U., 1997, Southern Coll., Lakeland, Fla., 1999, and many others; permanent collections include Centro Cultural "El Nigromante," San Miguel de Allende, Cathedral Ch. of St. John, Wilmington, Del., Gertrude Herbert Art Inst., Augusta, Augusta-Richmond County Mus., Venice (Fla.) Golf and Country Club., also pvt. collections. Active mem. Suntan Art Ctr., St. Pete Beach, Fla., The Ctr. for the Arts, St. Petersburg, World Art Workshop, Ocean Hills, Calif. Mem. Nat. Assn. Women Artists, Del. State Arts Coun., Fla. Artist Group, Studio 1212. Episcopal. Avocations: world travel, swimming, flower arranging. Studio: 1620 Pelican Creek Xing Saint Petersburg FL 33707-3980 E-mail: www.mdandruk@aol.com.

ANDRUS, CECIL DALE, academic administrator; b. Hood River, Oreg., Aug. 25, 1931; s. Hal Stephen and Dorothy (Johnson) A.; m. Carol Mae May, Aug. 27, 1949; children: Tana Lee, Tracy Sue, Kelly Kay. Student, Oreg. State U., 1948-49; LLD (hon.), Gonzaga U., U. Idaho, U. N.Mex., Coll. Idaho, Idaho State U., Whitman Coll. State gen. mgr. Paul Revere Life Ins. Co., 1969-70; gov. State of Idaho, 1971-77, 87-95; sec. of interior, 1977-81; chmn. Andrus Ctr. for Pub. Policy, Boise (Idaho) State U., 1995—. Bd. dirs. Coeur d'Alene Mines; mem. Idaho Senate, 1961-66, 69-70; mem. exec. com. Nat. Gov.'s Conf., 1971-72, chmn., 1976; chmn. Fedn. Rocky Mountain States, 1971-72. Author: Cecil Andrus: Politics Western Style, 1998. Chmn. bd. trustees Coll. of Idaho, 1985-89; bd. dirs. Sch. Forestry, Duke U. With USN, 1951-55. Recipient Disting. Citizen award Oreg. State U., 1980, Collier County Conservancy medal, 1979, Ansel Adams award Wilderness Soc., 1985, Audubon medal, 1985, Statesman of the Yr. award Idaho State U., 1990, Torch of Liberty award B'nai B'rith, 1991, William Penn Mott award, Nat. Parks Conservation Assn., 2000; named Conservationist of Yr. Nat. Wildlife Fedn., 1980, Idaho Wildlife Fedn., 1972, Man of Yr., VFW, 1959. Mem. VFW, Idaho Taxpayers Assn. (bd. dirs. 1964-66). Democrat. Office: Boise State U Andrus Ctr Pub Policy 1910 University Dr Boise ID 83725-0399

ANDRUS, JOYCELON MARIE, art educator; b. Duluth, Minn., June 21, 1939; d. James W. and Rufina C. (Appert) A.; adopted children: Kimberly, Lisandra, Theresa, Tamara, Jacqueline, Cecilia, Michella, Antonya, Stephanie, Chandler, Michael, Kenneth, Austin, Halistin, Valerie, Kalanthe, Anton, Jamila, Lucas, Loveasha, Jasira, Takara, Mikias, RoseCeline; sponsored Young Soo Kim, John Weiwen Porter. BA in Art, Mont. State U., 1964; MA in Art, U. Mont., 1966. Cert. elem. and secondary tchr., Washington. Tchr. 7th grade St. Joseph's Sch., Mandan, ND, 1960—61, tchr. 7th and 8th grades, 1964—65; tchr. elem. art sch. dist. 405, Bellevue, Wash., 1966—71; tchr. art Stevens Jr. H.S., Port Angeles, Wash., 1971—76, Port Angeles H.S., 1976—96. Nun Sisters for Christian Cmty., 1979-91. Chmn. Port Angeles art com., 1976-86. Mem. NEA, Wash. Edn. Assn., Port Angeles Edn. Assn. Republican. Mem. Baha'i Faith. Avocations: art, stained glass. Home: 3012 Porter St Port Angeles WA 98362-2749 Office Phone: 360-452-3214. E-mail: jandrus@olypen.com.

ANDRUS, ROGER DOUGLAS, lawyer; b. Floral Park, N.Y., Dec. 3, 1945; s. Winfield and Julia Margaret (Arduino) A.; m. Patricia Ann McDonough, Oct. 4, 1986; children: Justin, Sarah, Michael, David, Molly. AB cum laude, Wagner Coll., 1966; JD, NYU, 1969. Bar: N.Y. 1970, U.S. Dist. Ct. (ea. and so. dists.) 1975, U.S. Ct. Appeals 2d cir.) 1975. Assoc. Cahill Gordon & Reindel, N.Y.C., 1970-78, ptnr., 1978—. Mem. N.Y. State Bar Assn., Canoe Brook Country Club, Grand Harbor Club, Down Town Assn., Omicron Delta Kappa. Office: Cahill Gordon & Reindel 80 Pine St New York NY 10005-1790

ANDRZEJEWSKI, PAT See BENATAR, PAT

ANDSNES, LEIF OVE, concert pianist; b. Karmoy, Norway, Apr. 7, 1970; Student, Bergen Music Conservatory. Concert pianist Oslo Philharm., Edinburgh Festival, 1989, Cleve. Orch. Philharm., Berlin Philharm., London Philharm., Chgo. Symphony, N.Y. Philharm., Boston Philharm., Kirov Orch., London Symphony Orch., Vienna Symphony Orch., L.A. Philharmonic, City of Birmingham Symphony, Brahms Piano Concerto No. 1 with CBSO and Simon Rattle, 1998; records for EMI classics, including Schumann Pianoworks and the Long Long Winter Night (a collection of Norwegian music), 1997, Haydn Piano Sonatas, 1999, Britten Piano Concerto and Shostakovich Concerto for Piano, Trumpet and Strings, 1999, Haydn Piano Concertos, 2000, Liszt Piano Pieces, 2001; recs. Virgin Classics include: Grieg: A minor and Liszt A major, Janacek: Piano Works (Deutschen Schallplaten award), Chopin: Sonatas, Nielsen Piano Works, Grieg Piano Works; maj. tours in Australia, Japan, Europe, U.S. Recipient First prize Hindemith Competition, Frankfurt-am-Main, prizewinner others, Dorothy Chandler award, L.A.; named The 1998 Gilmore Artist by Irving S. Gilmore Internat. Keyboard Festival of Kalamazoo. Home: IMG Artists Lovell House 616 Chiswick High Rd London London W4 2TH England W4 SRX

ANDUJAR, NORMA BURGOS, former state official; b. Chgo., Oct. 29, 1954; children: Roberto, Norman. BA in Econs. cum laude, U. P.R., 1976, MPA, 1982. Cert. mgr. of housing. Pres., exec. dir. Codevisa, Inc., 1986-90; cons. Dept. Transp. and Pub. Works, 1990; cons. Strategic Planning project P.R. Planning Bd., P.R. 2005, 1990-92; pres., assoc. mem. P.R. Planning Bd., 1993-98; sec. of state P.R., 1998-99. Chmn. bd. Old San Juan Corp. Recipient Spl. Recognition award Govt. of P.R., 1994, Exemplary Pub. Servant award, 1994, others. Mem. Am. Planning Soc., P.R. Planning Soc., Soc. for Internat. Devel., U. P.R. Alumni (pub. adminstrn. chpt.), Internat. Downtown Assn., P.R. C. of C. (transp. andurban coms.), U.S. Tennis Assn., P.R. Tennis Assn., P.R. Economists Assn. Mem. New Progressive Party. Roman Catholic. Office: Sec of State PO Box 3271 San Juan PR 00902-3271

ANESH, MARK K., lawyer; b. Bklyn., Sept. 8, 1954; BA, Bklyn. Coll., CUNY, 1975; JD, Rutgers U., Camden, 1978. Bar: NY 1979, US Dist. Ct. So. Dist. NY, US Dist. Ct. Ea. Dist. NY, US Ct. Appeals 2nd Cir. Ptnr. Wilson, Elser, Moskowitz, Edelman & Dicker LLP, NYC. Adj. prof. law Touro Law Sch.; asst. adj. prof. Hofstra Law Sch. Founding pres. Woodbury Jewish Ctr. Mem.: ABA (torts & ins. practice sect., sports & entertainment practice sect.), NY State Bar Assn. (ins. com.), Pine Hollow Country Club (bd. governors). Office: Wilson Elser Moskowitz Edelman & Dicker LLP 23rd Fl 150 E 42nd St New York NY 10017-5639 Office Phone: 212-490-3000 ext. 2517. Office Fax: 212-490-3038. Business E-Mail: aneshm@wemed.com.

ANG, ALFREDO HUA-SING, civil engineering educator; b. Davao, The Philippines, July 4, 1930; came to U.S., 1955; s. Tiong Ang and Khio Tan; m. Myrtle Mae Ang; children: Evelyn, Irene, James. BSCE, Mapua Inst. Tech., Manila, 1954; MS, U. Ill., 1957, Phd, 1959. Registered structural engr., Ill. From asst. prof. to prof. U. Ill., Urbana, 1959-65, prof., 1965-88, U. Calif., Irvine, 1988—. Cons. NRC, Washington, 1979—, Ea. Internat. Engrs., Lafayette, Calif., 1983-90, Internat. Civil Engring Cons., Berkeley, Calif., 1992—; sr. tech. adviser Kajima Corp., Tokyo, 1984—, Tokyo Elec. Power Svcs. Co., 1987—; MCA engr. Mobil Offshore Base. Author: Probability Concepts in Engineering Planning and Design, Vol. I, 1975, Vol. II, 1984; editor Jour. Structural Engring., 1986—; co-editor-in-chief Internat. Jour. Computational Structural Engring., 2000—; mem. editorial bd. Jour. Structural Mechanics, 1971-84, Structural Safety, 1982—, Probabilistic Engring. Mechanics, 1985—, Reliability Engring. and System Safety, 1992—, Internat. Jour. Structural Engring. and Mechanics, 1992—; contbr. numerous articles to profl. jours. Recipient Sr. Rsch. award Am. Soc. Engring. Edn., 1983, Disting. Rsch. award U. Calif.-Irvine Alumni Assn., 1993, Disting. Engring. Alumni award, U. Ill., 2003. Fellow ASME, ASCE (chmn. STD EXCOM, internat. dir. 1998—, rsch. prize 1968, State-of-Art award 1973, Freudenthal medal 1982, Newmark medal 1988, hon. mem. 1991, Ernest Howard award 1996), AIAA (assoc.); mem. NAE, Earthquake Engring. Rsch. Inst., Seismol. Soc. Am., Soc. Naval Architects and Marine Engrs., Internat. Assn. for Structural Safety and Reliability (pres. 1985-89, Rsch. prize 1993). Home: 5311 154th Ave SE Bellevue WA 98006-5151 Office: U Calif Dept Civil Engring Irvine CA 92697-0001 E-mail: ahang2@aol.com.

ANGEL, ALBERT D., research and development company executive; JD, Yale U., 1960. Assoc. Hughes Hubbard Blair & Reed; Latin Am. atty. Merck and Co., Inc., European counsel, internat. counsel, v.p. Merck Sharp and Dohme (Europe), Inc., regional dir. Merck Sharp and Dohme (Europe), Inc., chmn. and mng. dir. Merck Sharpe & Dohme Ltd., v.p. pub. affairs; ptnr. Naimark & Assocs.; pres. Angel Cons.; chmn. bd. dirs. Axonyx Inc., 1997—. Vice chair Nat. Bd. Trustees Nat. Jewish Med. and Rsch. Ctr., Denver. With U.S. Army. Office: 500 Fashion Ave FL 10 New York NY 10018-0805

ANGEL, ARTHUR RONALD, lawyer, consultant; b. Long Beach, Calif., May 10, 1948; s. Morris and Betty Estelle (Unger) A.; 1 child, Jamie Kathryn. BA, U. Calif.-Berkeley, 1969; JD, Harvard U., 1972. Bar: Mass. 1972, D.C. 1975, Okla. 1979, Calif. 2001, U.S. Dist. Ct. (we. dist.) Okla. 1980, U.S. Dist. Ct. (no. dist.) Okla. 1981, U.S. Dist. Ct. (ctrl. dist.) Calif. 2001, U.S. Supreme Ct. 1983. Atty. FTC, Washington, 1972-78; pvt. practice Oklahoma City, 1978-87; ptnr. Angel & Ikard, Oklahoma City, 1987-93; of counsel Abel, Musser Sokolosky & Assoc., L.A., 1994-2000; ptnr. Carrick Law Group, L.A., 2001—02; atty. Nagler & Assocs., L.A., 2002—04; of counsel Lee, Angel & Kent, L.A., 2004—. Mem. adv. panel on cardiovascular devices, Washington, 1979-82; cons. FTC, 1978-79; adminstrv. law judge Okla. Dept. Labor, 1999-2000; spl. mcpl. judge City of Oklahoma City, 1999-2001. Recipient Meritorious Service award FTC, Washington, 1978. Fellow: Inst. Law and Social Scis.; mem.: Calif. Bar Assn., Mass. Bar Assn., D.C. Bar Assn., Assn. Trial Lawyers Am., Am. Arbitration Assn. Democrat. Jewish. Home: 1305 N Poinsettia Pl Los Angeles CA 90046 E-mail: artang@adelphia.net.

ANGEL, AUBIE, endocrinologist, academic administrator; b. Winnipeg, Man., Can., Aug. 28, 1935; m. Esther-Rose Newhouse; children: Jennifer, Jonathan, Suzanne, Steven, Michael. BSc in Medicine, MD, U. Man., 1959; MSc, McGill U., 1963. Speciality resident in diabetes and endocrinology Montreal Gen. Hosp., 1961-62; postgrad. dept. exptl. medicine McGill U., 1962-63; asst. resident in medicine Royal Victoria Hosp., Montreal, 1963-64; asst. prof. pathology McGill U., Montreal, Que., Can., 1965-68; staff physician Royal Victoria Hosp., Montreal, 1965-68; sr. physician and staff endocrinologist Toronto Gen. Hosp., 1968-90; asst. prof. medicine U. Toronto, Canada, 1968-72, assoc. prof., 1972-81, prof. medicine, 1981-90, dir. Inst. Med. Sci. and clin. scis. divsn., 1983-90; prof., head dept. medicine U. Man., Canada, 1991-95, sr. fellow Ctr. for Advancement ofMedicine, 2002—; physician in chief Health Sci. Ctr., Winnipeg, Man., 1991-95. Vis. scientist U. Calif., San Diego, 1977—78, Hammersmith Hosp., London, 1978; founding pres. Diabetes Rsch. and Treatment Ctr., Winnipeg, 1991—; founding pres., chmn. bd. dirs. Friends of CIHR, 1994—; scholar-in-residence MRC, Canada, 1996; pres. 7th Internat. Congress on Obesity, 1994; co-chair Internat. Conf. Diabetes and Cardiovascular Disease, 1999. Editor (with C.H. Hollenberg and D.A.K. Roncari): The Adipocyte and Obesity: Cellular and Molecular Mechanisms, 1983; editor: (with J. Frohlich) Lipoprotein Deficiency Syndromes: Advances in Experimental Medicine and Biology, 1986; editor: (with N. Sakamoto and N. Hotta) New Directions in Research and Clinical Works for Obesity and Diabetes Mellitus, 1991; editor: (with H. Anderson, C. Bouchard, D. Lau, L. Leiter, R. Mendels) Progress in Obesity Research, 1996; editor: (with N. Dhalla, G. Grant, P. Singal) Diabetes and Cardiovascular Disease, 2001. Project dir. Can. Internat. Devel. Agy., Toronto and Costa Rica, 1987-94. Recipient Outstanding Svc. award Heart and Stroke Found. Ont., 1985; U. Toronto Med. Rsch. Coun. scholar, 1965-71; Trinity Coll. fellow, Toronto, 1989—; sr. fellow Massey Coll. U. Toronto, 2005—. Fellow Royal Coll. Physicians and Surgeons Costa Rica (hon.), N.Am. Assn. Study Obesity (pres. 1986-87), Can. Soc. Clin. Investigation (councillor 1977-80), Am. Soc. Clin. Investigation, Can. Inst. Acad. Medicine (founding pres. 1990-92), Internat. Assn. Study Obesity (bd. govs. 1986—), Internat. Acad. Cardiovasc. Scis., Juvenile Diabetes Found. Internat. (hon. bd. dirs. 1987-90), Obesity Canada (founding bd. dirs. 1999-2001). Office: 585 Huron St Toronto ON M5R 2R6 Canada

ANGEL, DENNIS, lawyer; b. Bklyn., Feb. 14, 1947; s. Morris and Rosalyn (Sobiloff) A.; m. Linda Marlene Lobel, May 15, 1977; children: Stephanie Lee, Michele Bari, Rebecca Jo. Diplome d'etudes françaises, U. Rouen, France, 1967; BA, St. Lawrence U., 1968; JD, Washington and Lee U., 1972. Cert. pratique de langue française ler Degre U. Rouen, France, 1967; bar: N.Y. 1972, U.S. Dist. Ct. (so. dist.) N.Y. 1977. Assoc. Johnson & Tannenbaum, N.Y.C., 1972-77; sole practice N.Y.C., 1978—. Contbr. articles to profl. jours. With USAR, 1969-75. Mem. ABA (subcommittee chmn. 1977-82), N.Y. State Bar Assn., Copyright Soc. U.S.A., Phi Alpha Delta. Home: 8 High Point Ln Scarsdale NY 10583-3122 Office: 1075 Central Park Ave Ste 306 Scarsdale NY 10583-3232 Office Phone: 914-472-0820. Business E-Mail: dangelesq@aol.com.

ANGEL, JAMES ROGER PRIOR, astronomer; b. St. Helens, Eng., Feb. 7, 1941; came to U.S., 1967; s. James Lee and Joan (Prior) A.; m. Ellinor M. Goonan, Aug. 21, 1965; children: Jennifer, James. BA, Oxford (Eng.) U., 1963, D.Phil., 1967; MS, Calif. Inst. Tech., 1966. From rsch. asst. to assoc. prof. physics Columbia U., 1967-74; prof. astronomy U. Ariz., 1975—, prof. optical sci., 1984—, Regents prof., 1990—. Sloan fellow, 1970-74; hon. fellow St. Peter's Coll., Oxford U.; MacArthur fellow, 1996. Fellow Royal Soc., Royal Astron. Soc., Am. Acad. Arts and Scis.; mem. NAS, Am. Astron. Soc. (v.p. 1987-90, Pierce prize 1976). Achievements include research on white dwarf stars, quasars, the search for extra-solar planetary systems, astronomical mirrors, telescopes and their instruments, and adaptive optics. Office: Univ Ariz Steward Obs Tucson AZ 85721-0001 Business E-Mail: rangel@as.arizona.edu.

ANGEL, MARINA, law educator; b. N.Y.C., July 21, 1944; BA, Barnard Coll., N.Y.C., 1965; JD magna cum laude, Columbia U., 1969; LLM, U. Pa., Phila., 1977. Bar: N.Y. 1969, Pa. 1971, U. S. Dist. Ct. (ea. dist.) Pa. 1971, U.S. Dist. Ct. (so. and ea. dists.) N.Y. 1973, U.S. Supreme Ct. 1974. Law clk. NAACP Legal Def. & Edn. Fund; atty. Phila. Voluntary Assn.; assoc. prof. Hofstra U. Law Sch., L.I., N.Y., 1971-78; assoc. Gordon & Shectman, PC, N.Y.C., 1973-75; prof. Temple U. Law Sch., Phila., 1979—, assoc. dean grad. legal studies, 1983-84, dir. summer sessions abroad Greece Athens, 1981-83, 85, 87, 89. Vis. prof. Queensland Inst. Tech.and Wollongong U., Australia, 1992, Tel Aviv Univ., 2001, Univ. Puerto Rico, 2002; gen. counsel Modern Greek Studies Assn., 1995—, Greek Am. Women's Network, 1995—; steering com. Temple U. Faculty Senate, 1996—. Author of numerous articles in profl. jours.; developed statistics for Pa. Bar Assn. Annual Report Card. Sec. bd. St. George Sr. Housing Corp., Phila., 1980-88; mem. exec. com. Community Legal Svcs., Phila., 1979-88. Named Most Outstanding Prof., Temple Law Sch., Phila., 1989. Mem. ABA (Margaret Brent Women Lawyers of Achievement award 2004), Penn. Bar Assn. (Anne X. Alpern award, 1998, Spl. Achievement award, 2003), Phila. Bar Assn. (Sandra Day O'Connor award 1996, mem Gender Bias Task Force), Assn. of Bar of City of N.Y., Assn. Am. Law Sch. (chair Women in Legal Edn. sect.). Office: Temple U Law Sch 1719 N Broad St Philadelphia PA 19122-6098

ANGEL, MICHAEL GONZALEZ, cultural organization administrator; b. Seattle, Dec. 21, 1960; s. Jose Vincente Gonzalez and Maria (del Carmen Romero de Villa) A.; m. Leni Alcantara Alonzo, May 1, 1992; 1 child, Catherine Isabella. BS in Bus. Adminstrn. magna cum laude, Creighton U., 1981; MBA, Harvard Bus. Sch., 1983. Project mgr. Harvard Group Devel., Manchester, NH, 1984-85, sales, leasing and mktg. mgr., 1986-87, gen. mgr., 1988-90; export product line mgr. Otto GmbH and Gebr. Otto KG, Cologne, Germany, 1991-92; export sales mgr. Latin Am. Otto Industries, Inc., Charlotte, NC, 1991-95; dir. N.Am. mktg. and sales Hyundai, San Diego, 1995-96; dir. wireless sales and internet applications Digital Sound Corp., Santa Barbara, CA, 1996-97; v.p. internat. bus. devel. and sales Messer/Hoechst AG, L.A., 1998-2000; v.p. technology devel. and investment Verizon Comms., N.Y.C., 2000-01; pres., CEO Nat. Assn. Advancement Hispanic People, 2001—. Mem. Harvard Club (N.Y. and Boston). Republican. Roman Catholic. Office: PO Box 893460 Temecula CA 92589-3460 E-mail: mgangel@adnc.com.

ANGEL, STEVEN, musician; b. Bklyn., Aug. 2, 1953; s. Morris and Rosalyn (Sobiloff) A. Grad. H.S., L.I. Pres. Daystar Records, Santa Monica, Calif., 1991—98. Profl. drummer, 1960—; lectr. The Whole Life Expo, Pasadena, 1992-95, Inst. for the Advanced Studies of Human Sexuality, San Francisco, 1993—; founder Drumming For Your Life Inst., 2002—; creator Rhythm of Learning, Rhythm of Connection for elem. schs. in L.A.; facilitator drum therapy workshops; leader profl. devel. rhythm of learning workshops, So. Calif. Author (music and book) Angels Rejoice, 1976-80; wrote music for tv show Another World, 1987-91; writer, recorder, prodr.: three songs for album Music for Lovers, 1993, album The Erotic God, 1993; editor Unity and Difference Jour., 1994-97; began program on CNN, Drumming For Your Life; featured on KNBC-TV Stop the Violence, KCBS Hometown Heroes, 1998, BBC Radio; creator Reading and Rhythm after sch. program, Life Skills Drumming Program for detention camps, 1999. Avocations: tennis, hiking, running. Home and Office: Drumming for Your Life Inst 2132 Montana Ave Ste B Santa Monica CA 90403-2017 Office Phone: 310-453-2348. E-mail: sangel@adelphia.net.

ANGEL, TRAVIS L., religious organization administrator, musician; b. Snyder, Tex., Jan. 8, 1953; s. Lloyd E. and Roxie Angel; m. Charlotte A. Crowell, Mar. 27, 1953; children: Courtney A., Holland T., Kevin Bryce. MA, West Tex. State U., 1975. Choral dir. Spearman Ind. Sch. Dist., Tex., 1976—82, A&M Consol. H.S., College Station, 1982—. Min. music First Bapt. Ch., Madisonville, Tex., 2003—. Singer soloist. Mem.: Am. Choral Dirs. Assn., Tex. Music Adjudicators Assn., Tex. Choral Dirs. Assn., Tex. Music Educators Assn. (region sec. 1995—2005). Southern Baptist. Avocations: water sports, woodworking, construction. Office: A&M Consolidated High Sch 1801 Harvey Mitchell Pky S College Station TX 77840 Office Phone: 979-764-5500. Office Fax: 979-693-0212. Personal E-mail: tlangel@tca.net. E-mail: tangel@csisd.org.

ANGELI, ROBERT JOSEPH, assistant principal; b. New Britain, Conn., Jan. 30, 1964; s. Angelo Robert and Rosemary Angeli; m. Christine Ruscik, Apr. 1, 1989; children: Silvana Rose, Vincent Robert, Olivia Grace. BA in Biol. Sciences, DePauw U., 1986; MS in Ednl. Leadership, Ctrl. Conn. State U., 1995, cert. in Ednl. Leadership, 1997; student in Edn., U. Hartford, 2002—. Lic. tchr. Conn. State Dept. of Edn. Tchr. sci. Granby (Conn.) Meml. H.S., 1992—97; dir. athletics Granby (Conn.) Pub. Schs., 1994—97; dean students Old Saybrook (Conn.) H.S., 1997—2001; asst. prin. Lyme-Old Lyme (Conn.) H.S., 2001—. Cons. Conn. State Dept. Edn., Hartford, Conn.,

1995—, test scorer, 2003—. Mem.: NRA (life), Nat. Assn. Secondary Sch. Prins., Conn. Assn. Secondary Sch. Prins., Assn. Supr.and Curriculum Devel. (assoc.), Niantic Sportsmen's Club, Kappa Delta Pi, Alpha Tau Omega. Avocations: weightlifting, motorcycling, fishing, hunting, gardening. Home: 24 Browns Lane Old Lyme CT 06371 Office: Lyme-Old Lyme High School 69 Lyme Street Old Lyme CT 06371 Office Phone: 860-434-1651. Office Fax: 860-434-8234. Personal E-mail: bbangeli@netscape.net. E-mail: rangeli@region18.org.

ANGELINE, MICHAEL E., social worker, educator; divorced; 1 child. BA, U. Cin., 1979. Cert. forensic counselor, sports counselor. Case mgr. AIDS Vols. of Cin. Mem. exec. com. Ryan White Consortia, Cin.; chair Cmty. Adv. Bd. Holmes Hosp., Cin.; mem. Sovereign Queen City Ct. of the Buckeye Empire, Cin.; mem. Ohio Drug Adv. Coun. Office: AVOC 2183 Central Pkwy Cincinnati OH 45214

ANGELINI, MARCELLO, artistic director; b. Naples, Italy, Feb. 11, 1962; Grad., Kiev Inst. Dance, 1980-81. Dancer Maggio Musicale Fiorentino, 1979, soloist, 1981; prin. dancer Deutsche Oper Berlin, 1983-84, No. Ballet Theater, Eng., 1984-87, Ballet West, Salt Lake City, 1988-89, Les Grands Ballets Danadiens, Montreal, 1991-94, Cin. Ballet, 1983-95; artistic dir. Tulsa Ballet, 1995—. Guest prin. dancer San Carlo Opera House, Rome Opera House, the Arena of Verona, Italy, Basler Ballet, Switzerland, English Nat. Ballet, Scottish Ballet, Ballet Ariz., Santiago Teatro Mcpl., Chile. Performer (leading roles in classical repertoire including): Giselle, Sleeping Beauty, Romeo and Juliet, Cinderella; choreographer leading role in Death and the Maiden. Recipient Golden Rose award, Internat. Ballet Competition, Rome, 1982, Leonide Massine Positano prize, 1989, Gov.'s Arts Award, 2002. Office: Tulsa Ballet 4512 S Peoria Ave Tulsa OK 74105-4563*

ANGELINI, MICHAEL P., insurance company executive; BA, Wesleyan U., 1964; JD, Duke U., 1968. Bar: (Mass.) 1968. With Bowditch & Dewey and predecessor firm Bowditch, Gowetz & Lane, 1968—2002, mng. ptnr., 1990—96, chmn., 1997—, Allmerica Fin. Corp., 2002—. Fellow: Am. Coll. Trial Lawyers; mem.: ABA, Worcester County Bar Found., Worcester County Bar Assn. (pres. 1983—84, bd. dirs.). Office: 440 Lincoln St Worcester MA 01653

ANGELL, ELLEN, interior designer; b. Centralia, Mo., Mar. 16, 1927; d. Robert Loren and Margaret Amanda Jane (Smith) A. Cert., N.Y. Sch. Design, 1946. Interior designer Denver Dry Goods, 1946-49; cons. home furnishings Barker Bros., Los Angeles, 1950-52; interior designer Joske's, Houston, 1952-55, Showroom Finer Furniture, Corpus Christi, Tex., 1955-66, Braslau's, Corpus Christi, 1966-70, Browning Bros., Corpus Christi, 1970—. Lectr. in field. Author: The Layman's Handbook of Interior Design, 1972. Fellow Am. Soc. Interior Designers (long range planning nat. com. 1987-89, nat. bd. dirs. 1984-86, regional v.p., Medalist award 1984, Commendation for Outstanding Service 1986); mem. Am. Inst. Interior Designers (sec., chmn., bd. dirs. Tex. chpt. 1959-75, Outstanding Interior Designer 1974). Democrat. Avocations: meditation, writing. Home: 346 Southern St Corpus Christi TX 78404-1853 Office: Browning Bros 2001 S Staples St Corpus Christi TX 78404-3000

ANGELL, KENNETH ANTHONY, bishop; b. Providence, Aug. 3, 1930; s. Henry L. and Mae T. (Cooney) Angell. AB in Philosophy, St. Mary's Sem., Balt., 1952, STB, 1954; STD (hon.), Our Lady of Providence Sem., 1975; JCD (hon.), Providence Coll., 1975; DHL (hon.), St. Michael's Coll., 1999, Salve Regina, 2000. Ordained priest Roman Cath. Ch., 1956, consecrated bishop Roman Cath. Ch., 1974. Vicar St. Mark Ch., Jamestown, RI, 1956; parochial vicar Sacred Heart Ch., Pawtucket, RI, 1956—60; asst. pastor St. Mary Ch., Newport, RI, 1960—68; asst. chancellor and sec. to bishop Diocese of Providence, 1968—72, chancellor, 1972—74, titular bishop Settimunicia, aux. bishop, 1974—92; pastor St. John Ch., Providence, 1975—81; bishop Diocese of Burlington (Vt.), 1992—. Trustee Wadhams Hall Sem. Coll., 1995—2002, Champlain Coll., 1995—98; v.p. Vt. Ecumenical Coun. & Bible Soc., 1997—99, pres., 1999—2000; bd. dirs. Sr. Thea Bowman Black Cath. Ednl. Fund, 1995—99. Mem.: U.S. Cath. Conf., Nat. Conf. Cath. Bishops. Roman Catholic. Office: Diocese of Burlington 351 North Ave PO Box 489 Burlington VT 05402-0526*

ANGELL, LOIS LOUISE, writer, comedienne, poet; b. Riceville, Iowa; d. Kenneth Edwin and Marie E. (Dynes) A.; 1 child, Jim Barrett. Student, Am. U., 1959—60, student, 1962—63, U. Alta., 1978. Staff dir. Justice Rehnquist U.S. Supreme Ct., Washington, 1971-80; pub. rels. dir. Better Comm. Found., Silver Spring, Md., 1984; freelance writer and performer Arlington, Va. Numerous appearances on talk and news shows; spkr. Washington's Angell. Performer at comedy and supper clubs, radio and TV. Recipient Spl. Achievement award U.S. Dept. Justice, 1971, Outstanding Svc. to the Arts in Comm. award Capitol Hill Arts Workshop, 1984 Mem. NAFE, Washington Ind. Writers, The Capitol Hill Club, Internat. Platform Assn., Capitol Hill Poetry Group (founder), Nat. Conf. Rsch. on Women, Nat. Capitol Spkrs. Assn., Washington Conv. and Visitors Assn., World Affairs Coun., The Cato Inst. Episcopalian. Home: The Georgetown 2512 Q St NW #314 Washington DC 20007-4310

ANGELL, MARCIA, pathologist, editor-in-chief; b. Knoxville, Tenn., Apr. 20, 1939; BS, James Madison U., 1960; MD, Boston U., 1967. Resident in internal medicine Mt. Auburn Hosp.; resident in pathology; resident in internal medicine Univ. Hosp.; resident in pathology New Eng. Deaconess Hosp.; with New Eng. Jour. Medicine, Boston, 1979—, exec. editor, 1988, interim editor-in-chief, 1999—. Lectr. Harvard U. Author: Science on Trial: The Clash of Medical Evidence and the Law in the Breast Implant Case; co-author: Basic Pathology. Named One of 25 Most Influential Ams. Time Mag., 1997. Mem. ACP, Inst. Medicine, Assn. Am. Physicians, Mass. Med. Soc. Office: New Eng Jour Medicine 10 Shattuck St Boston MA 02115-6011

ANGELL, MARY FAITH, federal magistrate judge; b. Buffalo, May 7, 1938; d. San S. and Marie B. (Caboni) A.; m. Kenneth F. Carobus, Oct. 27, 1973; children: Andrew M. Carobus, Alexander P. Carobus. AB, Mt. Holyoke Coll.; MSS, Bryn Mawr Coll.; JD, Temple U. Bar: Pa. 1971, U.S. Dist. Ct. (ea. dist) Pa. 1971, U.S. Ct. Appeals (3rd cir.) Pa. 1974, U.S. Supreme Ct. 1979; Acad. Cert. Social Workers. Dir. social work, vol. svcs. Wills Eye Hosp., Phila., 1961-64, 65-69; dir. soc. work dept. juvenile divsn. Defender Assoc., Phila., 1969-71; asst. dist. atty. City of Phila., 1971-72; asst. atty. gen. Commonwealth of Pa., Phila., 1972-74, deputy atty. gen., 1974-78; regional counsel ICC, Phila., 1978-80, regional dir., 1980-88; administrv. law judge Social Security Administrn., Phila., 1988-90; U.S. magistrate judge U.S. Dist. Ct. (ea. dist.) Pa., Phila., 1990—2004, chief U.S. magistrate judge, 2004—. Adj. prof. Temple U. Law Sch., Phila., 1976-94, clin. instr., 1973-76; co-chmn. Commn. on Gender, 3d Cir. Task Force on Equal Treatment in Cts., 1994—99; mem. com. on racial and gender bias in the justice sys. Supreme Ct. of Pa., 2000-02; bd. adv. Grad. Sch. Social Work and Social Rsch. Bryn Mawr Coll., 2004. Federal trustee Defender Assn. Phila., 1985-90; bd. dirs. Child Welfare Adv. Bd., Phila., 1984-90, Federal Cts. 200 Adv. Bd., Phila., 1987-88, Phila. Woman's Network, 1986-88. Recipient Sr. Exec. Svc. award U.S. Govt., 1980. Mem. NASW, FBA (chair exec. com., pres. 1990-92, recognition 1992), Nat. Assn. Women Judges, Fed. Magistrate Judges Assn. (dist. dir. 1994-98), Phila. Bar Assn. (chmn. com. 1976-77), Temple Am. Inn of Cts. (master 1993-98), Third Circuit Task Force on Equal Treatment in the Courts (co-chair Commn. on Gender 1994-97), Temple Law Alumni Exec. Bd. (Women's Law Caucus Honoree 1996). Office: US District Court 601 Market St 3030 US Courthouse Philadelphia PA 19106 Office Phone: 215-597-6079. Business E-mail: chambers_of_chief_magistrate_judge_m_faith_angell@paed.uscourts.gov.

ANGELL, RICHARD BRADSHAW, philosophy educator; b. Scarsdale, N.Y., Oct. 14, 1918; s. Stephen LeRoy and Alice (Angel) A.; m. Imogene Lucille Baker, June 4, 1949; children: John Baker, Paul McLean, James Bigelow, David Bradshaw, Kathryn Elizabeth. BA, Swarthmore Coll., 1940; M in Govt. Adminstrn., U. Pa., 1948; PhD in Philosophy, Harvard U., 1954. Acting asst. prof. Fla. State U., 1949-51; asst. prof. Ohio Wesleyan U., 1954-58, asso. prof., 1958-63, prof., 1963-68; chmn. philosophy dept. Wayne State U., 1968-73, 76-78, prof., 1968-89, prof. emeritus, 1989—. Author: Reasoning and Logic, 1964, A-Logic, 2002. Mem. AAUP, Am. Philos. Assn., ACLU., Mem. Soc. of Friends. E-mail: rbangell@bellatlantic.net.

ANGELO, CHRISTOPHER EDMOND, lawyer, consultant; b. L.A., Dec. 19, 1949; s. Edmond James and Shirley Ann (Richards) A.; m. Patrice Lonnette Brown, Apr. 26, 1980; 1 child, Alexander Bradshaw. BA, U. Calif., Riverside, 1972; JD, Loyola U., 1975. Bar: Calif. 1976, U.S. Dist. Ct. Calif. 1976. Trial atty. Spray, Gould & Bowers, L.A., 1976-78, Harrington, Foxx, Dubrow & Canter, L.A., 1978-83, Gage & Mazursky, Beverly Hills, Calif., 1983-85; trial atty., ptnr. Gage, Mazursky, Schwartz, Angelo & Kussman, Beverly Hills, Calif., 1986-88; trial atty., gen. ptnr. Mazursky, Schwartz & Angelo, L.A., 1988—. Faculty lectr. Calif. Judges Assn., 1989; mem. Loyola Law Sch. Law Review, L.A., 1974-75. Author books and articles in field of tort and ins. bad faith liability. Cons. Bet Tzedak Legal Aid Found., L.A., 1992; counsel Christopher Sampson Non-Profit Found. for Catastrophically Injured, L.A., 1991, dir., founder; trustee U.C.R. Found., Inc., 1998—. Recipient Highlander scholarship U. Calif., 1968-72. Mem. ABA, Italian Am. Lawyers Assn. (bd. govs. 1979-83), Calif. Trial Lawyers Assn. (lectr. 1983—, Cert. of Appreciation), Calif. Bar Assn., Consumer Attys. Assn. L.A. (lectr. 1983—, Cert. of Appreciation), Autism Soc. Am. (mem. adv. bd.). Office: Mazursky Schwartz & Angelo 10990 Wilshire Blvd Ste 1200 Los Angeles CA 90024-3919

ANGELO, E. JOANNE, child, adolescent and adult psychiatrist; b. Boston, Feb. 11, 1936; d. Gaspar and Eda (Polcari) A. AB, Mt. Holyoke Coll., 1957; MD, Tufts U., 1961. Diplomate Am. Bd. Psychiatry and Neurology. Pvt. practice, Boston, 1969—; med. dir. Canarsie Mental Health Ctr., Bklyn., 1967—69; staff psychiatrist Cmty. Mental Health Svc. Ctr., Boston, 1969—73; psychiat. dir. Laboure Ctr., South Boston, Mass., 1974—78. Cons. Chandler Sch. for Women, Boston, 1971-72, Kennedy Meml. Hosp., Boston, 1971-74, St. Margaret's Hosp., Boston, 1976-83, North Suffolk Health Ctr., Boston, 1978-79; mem. staff St. Elizabeth's Hosp., Boston, Good Samaritan Hospice Boston. Mem. editl. bd. (Jour.) Nat. Cath. Bioethics Quar. Mem. Pontifical Acad. for Life (corr.). Office: 403 Commonwealth Ave Boston MA 02215-2326

ANGELO, JIM, construction company executive; b. Detroit, June 23, 1956; s. Richard James and Edith Marlene (Schaefflin) A.; m. Brenda Angelo Wood, Sept. 15, 1985; 1 child, Nathan Miller. BS, Ctrl. Mich. U., 1978; AAS in Bldg. Constrn. Tech., Ferris State U., Big Rapids, Mich., 1982. Lic. home builder, Mich. Laborer, then carpenter Vail (Colo.) Valley Constrn., 1978-80; home builder Canadien Lakes, Mich., 1980-82; supt. Sikes Constrn., Denver, 1982-85; project mgr. Bronco Constrn., 1985-87, Ashwood Homes, Hampstead, NH, 1987-90; constrn. mgr. Lincoln Labs., Lexington, Mass., 1990-95; project mgr. Elzinga and Volkers Constrn., Holland, Mich., 1995-96, Triangle Assoc., Inc., Grand Rapids, Mich., 1997—2002, sr. project mgr., 1998—2002; project mgr. Skanksa USA, Kalamazoo, 2002—03; retail devel. constrn. mgr. Gen. Growth Properties, Chgo., 2003—. Author: My Thoughts, 1978 Chmn. Hwy. Bldg. Com., Hampstead, N.H. 1988; cons. Hampstead Bd. Edn., 1990-95, Hampstead Bd. Selectmen, 1990-95; officer Hampstead Civic Club, 1991; chmn. Hampstead Libr. Bldg. Com., 1992; chmn. Nat. Youth Sports Coaches Assn., Hampstead, 1993-95, Hampstead Capital Needs Com., 1994-95; clk. of works Hampstead Pub. Works Projects, 1994. Mem. Am. Inst. Constructors (cert. profl. constructor), Assoc. Builders and Contractors (polit. action com. 1999-2001), NRA, Theta Chi. Republican. Avocations: hunting, fishing, golf, skiing, fly tieing. Office: Gen Growth Properties Inc 110 Wacker Dr Chicago IL 60606 Office Phone: 312-960-2869. Business E-Mail: jangelo@generalgrowth.com.

ANGELOFF, DANN VALENTINO, brokerage house executive; b. Hollywood, Calif., Nov. 15, 1935; m. Jo Jeanne Ahlstrom, Sept. 26, 1964; children: Jennifer J., Dann V., Julie A. BS in Fin., U. So. Calif., 1958, MBA, 1963. Trainee Dean Witter & Co., Inc., L.A., 1957-60; v.p. Dempsey-Tegeler & Co., Inc., L.A., 1960-70; mng. dir. West Coast corp. fin. dept. Reynolds Securities, Inc., L.A., 1970-76; pres., bd. dirs. The Angeloff Co., L.A., 1976—. Bd. dirs. Softbrands Inc., Mpls., SunCal Cos., Newport Beach, Calif., Bjurman Barry Funds, Inc., Century City, Calif., Ready Pac Foods, Irwin Dale, Calif., Pub. Storage, Glendale, Calif., Nicholas-Applegate Fund, San Diego, Retirement Capital Corp., San Diego; chmn. bd. Marshall Assocs./U. So. Calif. Trustee U. So. Calif., 1979-86, univ. counselor; bd. dirs., chmn. Trojan Bd. Govs., 1990-92. Mem. Bond Club L.A., Commerce Assocs. U. So. Calif., Skull and Dagger, Cardinal and Gold, Calif. Club, Pacific Club, Valley Hunt Club, San Marino City Club, Kappa Beta Phi. Office: The Angeloff Co 727 W 7th St Los Angeles CA 90017-3707

ANGELOS, PETER, medical educator; b. Plattsburgh, N.Y., Aug. 9, 1962; BA, MD, Boston U., 1989, PhD in Philosophy, 1995. Diplomate Am. Bd. Surgery. Asst. prof. surgery Northwestern U., Chgo., 1996—, asst. prof. med. ethics and humanities, 1997—. Office: Northwestern U Dept Surgery Galter 10-105 201 E Huron St Chicago IL 60611

ANGELOS, PETER G., professional sports team executive, lawyer; b. Pitts., July 4, 1929; LLB, U. Balt. Bar: Md. 1961, D.C. 1974, Tenn. 1990, U.S. Dist. Ct. Md. 1964, U.S. Supreme Ct. 1974, U.S. Tax Ct. 1975, U.S. Ct. Appeals 1990. Pvt. practice atty., Balt., 1961—; mng. ptnr. Baltimore Orioles, 1993—; chmn., CEO Balt. Orioles, 1993—. Mem. Balt. City Coun., 1959—63; trustee Loyola Coll., Md. Mem.: Bar Assn. Balt. City, Tenn. Bar Assn., Md. Trial Lawyers Assn., Md. Trial Lawyers Assn., N.Y. State Trial Lawyers Assn., Criminal Def. Lawyers Assn., Assn. Trial Lawyers Am., Am. Judicature Soc. Office: 100 N Charles St # 22D Baltimore MD 21201-3805 also: Baltimore Orioles 333 W Camden St Baltimore MD 21201-2435*

ANGELOU, MAYA (MARGUERITE ANNIE JOHNSON), writer, actress; b. St. Louis, Missouri, Apr. 4, 1928; d. Bailey and Vivian (Baxter) Johnson; m. Tosh Angelos, 1950, (div. 1952); m. Vusumzi Make, 1960 (div. 1963), m. Paul Du Feu, 1973 (div. 1981) 1 child Guy Johnson. Studied dance with Pearl Primus, N.Y.C.; degrees (hon.), Smith Coll., 1975, Mills Coll., 1975, Lawrence U., 1976, Portland State U., 1973, Occidental Coll., 1979, Atlanta U., 1980, U. Ark., 1980, U. Minn., 1980, Austin Coll., 1980, Wheaton Coll., 1981, Kean Coll., 1982, Spelman Coll., 1983, Boston Coll., 1983, Winston-Salem U, 1984, U. Brunesis, 1984, Howard U., 1985, Tufts U., 1985, Va. Commonwealth U., 1985, Northeastern U., 1992, Academy of Southern Arts & Letters, 1993, Brown U., 1994, U. Durham, UK, 1995, Hope Coll., 2001, Columbia U., 2003, Eastern Conn. U., 2003. Taught modern dance The Rome Opera House and Hambina Theatre, Tel Aviv; writer-in-residence U. Kans., Lawrence, 1970; disting. vis. prof. Wake Forest U., 1974-, Wichita State U., 1974, Calif. State U., Sacramento, 1974; apptd. mem. Am. Revolution Bicentennial Council by Pres. Ford, 1975-76; 1st Reynolds prof. Am. Studies, Wake Forest U. 1981-, a lifetime appointment. Author: I Know Why the Caged Bird Sings, 1970, Just Give Me A Cool Drink of Water 'Fore I Die, 1971, Georgia, Georgia, 1972, Gather Together in My Name, 1974, Oh Pray My Wings are Gonna Fit Me Well, 1975, Singin' and Swingin' and Gettin' Merry Like Christmas, 1976, And Still I Rise, 1978, The Heart of a Woman, 1981, Shaker, Why Don't You Sing?, 1983, All God's Children Need Traveling Shoes, 1986, Now Sheba Sings the Song, 1987, I Shall Not Be Moved, 1990, On the Pulse of Morning: The Inaugural Poem, 1993, Lessons in Living, 1993, Wouldn't Take Nothing for My Journey Now, 1993, My Painted House, My Friendly Chicken, and Me, 1994, The Complete Collected Poems of Maya Angelou, 1994, Phenomenal Women: Four Poems for Women, 1995, A Brave and Startling Truth, 1995, From a Black Woman to a Black Man, 1996, Kofi and His Magic, 1996, Extravagant Spirits, 1997, Making Magic in the World, 1998, Even the Stars Look Lonesome, 1997, A Song Flung Up To Heaven, 2002, Angelina of Italy, 2004, (cookbooks) Hallelujah! The Welcome Table: A Lifetime of Memories with Recipes, 2004; (plays) Cabaret for Freedom, 1960, The Least of These, 1966, Gettin' Up Stayed On My Mind, 1967, Ajax, 1974, Moon On a Rainbow Shawl, 1988; (screenplays) Georgia, Georgia, 1972, All Day Long, 1974; author/prodr. Three Way Choice, Afro-American in the Arts (Golden Eagle award); wrote and presented Trying to Make it Home, 1988; writer for Oprah Winfrey's Harpo Prodns.; poetry writer for film Poetic Justice, 1993; appeared in plays: Porgy and Bess, 1954-55 (Europe), 1957 (U.S.), Calypso, 1957, The Blacks, 1960, Mother Courage, 1964, Medea, Look Away, 1973, Ajax, 1974, And Still I Rise, 1976, Moon on a Rainbow Shawl, 1988; (films) Porgy and Bess, 1959, Poetic Justice, 1993, How to Make an American Quilt, 1995, The Journey of August King, 1995; dir. (films) Down in the Delta, 1998; (TV minseries) Roots, 1977 (Emmy Nom. best sup. actress), TV appearances include The Richard Pryor Special, Sister, Sisters, 1982, There Are No Children Here, 1993, Touched By An Angel, 1995, Moesha, 1999, Runaway, 2000; spoken word albums include The Poetry of Maya Angelou, 1969, Women in Business, 1981, Been Found, 1996; contbd. articles, short stories, poems to Black Scholar, Chgo. Daily News, Cosmopolitan, Harper's Bazaar, Life Mag., Redbook, Sunday N.Y. Times, Mademoiselle Mag., Essence, Ebony Mag., Calif. Living Mag, Ghanaian Times. Apptd. by Dr. Martin Luther King Jr. No. Coord., SCLC, 1959-60, apptd. by Pres. Ford to Bicentennial Commn., by Pres. Carter to Nat. Commn. on Observance of Internat. Women's Yr., ambassador, Unicef Internat., 1996. Chubb fellowship award Yale U., 1970, named Woman of Yr. in Comm., 1976; Ladies Home Jour. Top 100 Most Influential Women, 1983, The Matrix award, 1983, Living Legacy award, Women's Internat. Ctr., 1986, The North Carolina Award in Lit., 1987, Woman of the Yr. Essence Mag., 1992, Disting. Woman of N.C., 1992, Horatio Alger award, 1992, Grammy award best spoken word or non-traditional album, 1994 (for recording of "On the Pulse of the Morning"), Grammy award best spoken or non-traditional album, 1994 (for recording of "Phenomonal Woman"), NAACP Image Award for Outstanding Literary Work for "Even the Stars Look Lonesome", 1997, National Medal of Art, 2001; inducted into the Women's Hall of Fame, 1998 Mem. AFTRA, Dirs. Guild Am., Equity, Harlem Writers Guild, Am. Film Inst. (trustee), Women's Prison Assn., Horatio Alger Assn. Dist. Americans, Nat. Soc. Prevention of Cruelty to Children (Maya Angelou Ctr. opened 1992), W.E.B. duBois Found., Nat. Soc. Collegiate Scholars, Nat. Soc. High School Scholars. Office: c/o Dave La Camera Lordly and Dame Inc 51 Church St Boston MA 02116-5417*

ANGELSON, MARK A., printing company executive; m. Lynn Angelson; 3 children. BA, Rutgers Coll., NJ; JD, Rutgers Law Sch. Atty. Sullivan & Cromwell, 1975; co-chair Intern. Ops. & resident mng. ptnr. Sidley & Austin, 1982—95; various positions to exec. dep. chmn. Big Flower Holdings, 1996—2001; CEO Moore Wallace Inc., 2001—03, R.R. Donnelley & Sons Co. (merge with Moore Wallace Inc.), 2003—. Past dep. chmn. Chancey Lane Capital; trustee Northwestern U. Fellow: Royal Soc. for Encouragement of Arts; mem.: Chgo. Coun. Fgn. Rels., Coun. Fgn. Rels., Comml. Club Chgo., Chgo. Club, Econ. Club Chgo., Pilgrims Great Britain, Yale Club (NYC), Phi Beta Kappa. Office: RR Donnelley & Sons Co 111 S Wacker Dr Chicago IL 60606

ANGELUCCI, TONY, marketing professional; B of Bus. in Mkgt., Western Ill. U. V.p. new bus. devel. Bernard Hodes Advt., LA, 1984—94; mng. dir. J. Walter Thompson Specialized Comm., Phoenix, 1994—96; v.p. Howard Marquis Advt., Westlake Village, Calif., 1996—98, 2000—04; nat. classified mgr. LA Times, 1998—2000; human resources spl. projects coord. Good Samaritan Hosp., LA, 2004; staffing specialist Cedars-Sinai Med. Ctr., LA, 2004—. Mem.: So. Calif. Assn. Healthcare Recruiters, Nat. Human Resources Assn. (v.p. mktg. Ventura County chpt. 2001—02), Employment Mgmt. Assn. (founding steering com. 2001, publicity chmn., co-chmn., sr. adv.), Soc. Human Resource Mgmt. Home: 1957 N Bronson #111 Los Angeles CA 90068

ANGER, PAUL, newspaper editor; m. Vickie Dahlman-Anger. Graduate, Univ. Wis., Oshkosh. Sports copy editor, page designer Miami Herald, 1972—77, sports editor, 1977—89, page 1A duty officer, 1989—95, Broward editor Hollywood, Fla., 1995—98, v.p., pub., Broward edition, 1998—2001; v.p., editor Des Moines Register, Iowa, 2002—05; Washington bur. news editor Knight Ridder, 2001; editor Detroit Free Press, 2005—. Office: Detroit Free Press 600 W Fort St Detroit MI 48226 Office Phone: 989-752-3023.*

ANGERS, WINSTON THOMAS, lawyer, publishing executive; b. Franklin, La., June 21, 1952; s. Robert John, Jr. and Geraldine Beaulieu Angers; 1 child, Austen John. BA in Polit. Sci. cum laude, U. La., 1974; JD, La. State U., 1976. Bar: La. 1977. Rsch. asst. Inst. for Civil Law Studies La. State U. Law Ctr., Baton Rouge, 1975—76; law clk. 15th Jud. Dist. Ct., New Iberia, La., 1976—77; pvt. practice Lafayette, La., 1977—; pres. Beau Bayou Pub. Co., Lafayette, 1985—. Author: Cajun Cuisine, 1986; editor: History of the Louisiana Society of the Sons of the American Revolution, 1997; contbr. articles to mags.; co-author: My Wars: Nazis, Mobsters, Gambling and Corruption: Colonel Francis C. Greuemberg Remembers, 2004. Bd. dirs. Coun. Devel. of French in La.; past chmn. bd. zoning adjustments City of Lafayette; pres. Acadiana Arts Coun., Lafayette, 1990—91; co-founder Citizens of S. Lafayette; pres. Attakapas chpt. SAR, 1994; pres. Acadian Civitan Club, Lafayette, 1997—98; del.-attendee Young Rep. Nat. Fedn. Conv., 1971; alt. del. Rep. Nat. Conv., Dallas, 1984, del. Houston, 1992, 7th district elector for pres. La., 2004; past chmn. by laws com. La. Rep. State Ctrl. Com.; chmn. Lafayette Parish Rep. Exec. Com., 1995—96; past chmn. Lafayette Parish Rep. Polit. Action Coun.; del. numerous state convs. La. Rep. Party; chair U. La. at Lafayette Coll. Reps., 1971—72. Recipient Bronze Good Citizenship medal, Attakapas Chpt. SAR, 1992, Oak Leaf Cluster, 1993, Meritorious Svc. medal, 1994, Oak Leaf Cluster, 1995, Oak Leaf Cluster for Meritorious Svc. medal, La. Soc. SAR, 1996. Mem.: ABA, Civitan Internat., Rotary Internat., Phi Eta Sigma, Phi Delta Phi. Republican. Avocation: collecting rare documents and political memorabilia. Home: 116 Teche Dr Lafayette LA 70503 Office: 1126 Coolidge St Lafayette LA 70503 Office Phone: 337-233-3268. Personal E-mail: tomangers@aol.com.

ANGEVINE, ROGER LEE, mathematician, educator; b. Columbus, Ohio, July 21, 1946; s. Ruth Sannan and Thomas Walls Angevine; m. Janice Sue Prather. B Math. and Physics, Western Ky. U., 1968; M in Math., U. Ill., 1974. Instr. math. Bates Coll., Lewiston, Maine, 1974—76; asst. and assoc. prof. Houston Bapt. U., 1976—91; assoc. prof., prof. of math. Somerset C.C., Ky., 1991—. Dir. acad. computing Houston Bapt. U., 1985—91; sacs steering com. chair Somerset C.C., 1999—2003, divsn. chair math. and phys. sciences, 1996—2002, divsn. chair math. and computer sci., 2002—, Perkins grant coord. Fellow, Woodrow Wilson Nat. Fellowship Found., 1968—69. Mem.: Am. Math. Assn. Two Yr. Colleges, Assn. Computing Machinery, Ky. Math. Assn. Two Yr. Colleges, Math. Assn. Am., Alpha Phi Omega (pres. 1967—68), Sigma Pi Sigma (hon.). Avocations: travel, birdwatching, hiking, fishing. Office: Somerset CC 808 Monticello St Somerset KY 42501 E-mail: roger.angevine@kctcs.edu.

ANGHELESCU, DORALINA LUCIA, anesthesiologist; b. Bucharest, Romania, Aug. 1, 1961; d. Liviu Veneriu and Aurelia Niculina (Arseni) Gontea; m. Mircea Vladimir Anghelescu, June 6, 1987 (div. July 1991); 1 child, Andrei. MD, Bucharest Sch. Medicine, 1985. Intern Elias Found. Hosp., Bucharest, 1985—87; staff physician in anesthesiology Inst. Endocrinology, Bucharest, 1987—93; resident in anesthesiology U. N.Mex., Albuquerque, 1993—97, fellow in pain mgmt., 1998—99; fellow in pediat. anesthesia Childrens Nat. Med. Ctr., Washington, 1997—98; pediat. anesthesiologist, dir. pain mgmt. svc. St. Jude Children's Rsch. Hosp., Memphis, 1999—. Co-author: The Pain Clinic Manual, 2d edit., 2000; contbr. articles to profl. jours. Grantee, Jenssen Found., 2001. Mem.: Internat. Assn. for the Study Pain, Am. Acad. Pain, Soc. Pediat. Anesthesia, Am. Soc. Anesthesiologists. Office: St Jude Childrens Rsch Hosp 332 N Lauderdale St Memphis TN 38105 Office Phone: 901-495-4034.

ANGINO, ERNEST EDWARD, retired geology educator, retired engineering educator; b. Winsted, Conn., Feb. 16, 1932; s. Alfred and Filomena Mabel (Serluco) A.; m. Margaret Mary Lachat, June 26, 1954; children— Cheryl Ann, Kimberly Ann. BS in Mining Engring., Lehigh U., Bethlehem, Pa.,

1954; MS in Geology, U. Kans., 1958, PhD in Geology, 1961. Instr. geology U. Kans., Lawrence, 1961-62, prof. civil engring., 1971-99, prof. geology, 1972-99, prof. emeritus, 1999—, chmn. dept. geology, 1972-86, dir. water resources ctr., 1990-99; asst. prof. Tex. A&M U., College Station, 1962-65; chief geochemist Kans. Geol. Survey, Lawrence, 1965-70, assoc. state geologist, 1970-72. Cons. on water chemistry and pollution to various cos. and govt. agys. including Dow Chem. Co., Ocean Mining Inc., Envicon, Oak Ridge Lab., Fisheries Rsch. Bd. Can., Midwest Rsch. Inst., Coast and Geodetic Survey, U.S. Geol. Survey. Author: (with G.K. Billings) Atomic Absorption Spectrometry in Geology, 1967; author, editor: (with D.T. Long) Geochemistry of Bismuth, 1979; editor: (with R.K. Hardy) Proc. 3d Forum Geol. Industrial Minerals, 1967, (with G.K. Billings) Geochemistry Subsurface Brines, 1969; contbr. more than 125 articles to sci. and profl. jours. Sec. Geochem. Soc., 1970-76; mem. Lawrence City Police Rels. Commn., 1970-76, Lawrence City Commn., 1983-87, mayor, 1984-85; pres. Soc. Environ. Geochemistry and Health, 1978-79; treas. Internat. Assn. Geochemistry and Cosmochemistry, 1980-94; mem. Lawrence 2020 Planning Commn., 1992-94, Police Adv. Coun., 1994—, Crimestoppers Bd., 1994-2003, Lawrence Tax Abatement Commn., 2001-02, Lawrence-Douglas County Planning Commn. 2002-05, Health Care Access Bd., 1997-2002. With U.S. Army, 1955-57. NSF fellow Oak Ridge Lab., 1963; recipient Antarctic Service medal Dept. Def., 1969; Angino Buttress in Antarctica named in his honor, 1967. Mem. Am. Philatelist Soc., Meter Stamp Soc., Forum Club (Factotum 1978-79), Rotary (pres. 1993-95). Republican. Roman Catholic. Avocations: philately, Western history, Indian lore. Home: 4605 Grove Dr Lawrence KS 66049-3777 Office: U Kans Dept Geology Lindley 120 1475 Jayhawk Blvd Lawrence KS 66045-0001 Personal E-mail: rockdoc@sunflower.com. *Knowledge is what really counts. The world does not owe anyone anything!.*

ANGINO, RICHARD CARMEN, lawyer; b. McKeesport, Pa., May 2, 1940; s. Carmen and Filomena (Lombardi) A.; m. Alice K. Angino, May 2, 1976; children: Elizabeth, Richard, William. BA in English, Franklin and Marshall Coll., Lancaster, Pa., 1958-62; JD, Villanova Law Sch., Pa., 1965. Bar: Pa. 1965, U.S. Supreme Ct. 1968, U.S. Ct. Appeals (3rd cir.) 1975, U.S. Dist. Ct. (ea. and cen. dist.) 1966. Ptnr., civil litigation specialist Angino & Rovner PC, Harrisburg, Pa., 1965—. Pres. Pa. Trial Lawyers Assn., Pa., 1982-83. Co-author: The Pennsylvania No-Fault Motor Vehicle Insurance Act, 1979, Pennsylvania Personal Injury Evidence, 1990. Pres. Leukemia Soc. Am., Ctrl. Pa., 1989-92; v.p. Am. Horticulture Soc., Alexandria. Va., 1990-92, Friends of Wildwood, Harrisburg, Pa., 1989-96; assoc. trustee Franklin and Marshall, 1979—; bd. cons. Villanova Univ. Sch. Law, 1994—, govs. residence preservation com., 1997-2002. Mem. Internat. Soc. Barristers, Dauphin County Bar Assn., Pa. Bar Assn., Pa. Trial Lawyers Assn., Assn. Trial Lawyers Am. Republican. Roman Catholic. Avocation: ornamental horticulture. Home: 2040 Fishing Creek Valley Rd Harrisburg PA 17112-9245 Office: Angino & Rovner PC 4503 N Front St Harrisburg PA 17110-1799 Office Phone: 717-238-6791. Business E-Mail: rca@angino-rovner.com.

ANGIONE, ELLEN V., counselor, therapist, management consultant; b. Glen Cove, N.Y., Oct. 26, 1965; d. Clark Peter and Vita Theresa (Buongiorno) Barnett, stepmother Mary Agnes (Walsh) Barnett; m. Brett Mitchell Angione, Sept. 23, 1989; children: Andrew, Eric. BA in Comm. and Pub. Rels., New Eng. Coll., Henniker, N.H., 1987; MA in Counseling/Psychology, Notre Dame Coll., Manchester, N.H., 1997. Pub. rels. specialist VA Med. Ctr., Manchester, 1987-88; dept. mgr. Jordan Marsh Co., Bedford, N.H., 1988-93; counselor therapist Cath. Med. Ctr., Manchester, 1995-96, Capital Region Family Health, Concord, N.H., 1996—. Vol. N.H. chpt. Nat. Multiple Sclerosis Soc., Manchester, 1988, 89, 90. Mem. ACA, N.H. Mental Health Counelors (pub. rels. com. 1996, chair 1997). Avocations: theatre acting, horseback riding, cross country skiing. Home: 20 Juniper Dr Goffstown NH 03045-2938

ANGIONE, HOWARD FRANCIS, lawyer, retired editor; b. N.Y.C., Aug. 3, 1940; s. Charles Francis Angione and Genevieve Rita (McCarthy) A.; m. Maryann Allgaier, June 24, 1971; children: Charles Francis, Mary Christine, Kathleen Elizabeth. BA in History, Holy Cross Coll., 1962; MA in Internat. Relations, Clark U., 1966; JD cum laude, St. John's U., Jamaica, N.Y., 1989. Bar: Conn. 1989, N.Y. 1990, D.C. 1991. Reporter, sci. writer Worcester Telegram, Mass., 1961-65; writer, day editor, sci. writer AP, Boston, 1965-69, editor, shift supr. Gen. Desk N.Y.C., 1969-77; tech. editor N.Y. Times, 1977-87; assoc. Weil, Gotshal & Manges, N.Y.C., 1989-93; pvt. practice, 1997—. Pub. N.Y. Region Lawyers Coop. Practice Guides, 1993-96; editor AP Stylebook, 1977; editor-in-chief N.Y. State Bar Jour., 1998—2004. Sec. Class of 1962 Holy Cross Coll., 1966-80. Mem. Harris Users Group (pres. 1980-84) Roman Catholic. Home and Office: 80-47 192d St Jamaica NY 11423-1042 Office Phone: 718-468-7700. Personal E-mail: angione@att.net, Business E-Mail: angione@nyelderlaw.com.

ANGLAND, JOSEPH, lawyer; b. N.Y.C., Sept. 1, 1949; s. Patrick and Josephine (Woods) A.; m. Ida Wolff, Aug. 4, 1984. BS, MIT, 1972; JD, Harvard U., 1975. Bar: N.Y. 1977, D.C. 1988, U.S. Dist. Ct. (so. and ea. dists.) N.Y. 1978, U.S. Ct. Claims 1983, U.S. Tax Ct. 1985, U.S. Ct. Appeals (2d cir.) 1982, U.S. Ct. Appeals (D.C. cir.) 1988, U.S. Dist. Ct. D.C. 1988, U.S. Ct. Appeals (3d cir.) 1990, U.S. Ct. Appeals (D.C. cir.) 1992, U.S. Ct. Appeals (5th cir.) 1993, U.S. Ct. Appeals (7th cir.) 1993, U.S. Supreme Ct. 1990. Law clk. to presiding justice Calif. Supreme Ct., San Francisco, 1975-76; assoc. Dewey, Ballantine, Bushby, Palmer & Wood, N.Y.C., 1976-83; ptnr. Dewey Ballantine, N.Y.C., 1984—2005; shareholder Heller Ehrman LLP, N.Y.C., 2005—. Bd. dirs. Legal Aid Soc., 1993—2001. Chmn. editl. bd. Antitrust Law Devel. Mem. ABA (chmn. elect antitrust sect.), N.Y. State Bar Assn., Assn. of Bar of City of N.Y. (com. on antitrust and trade regulation). Home: 292 Stanwich Rd Greenwich CT 06830-3528 Office: Heller Ehrman LLP 7 Times Square New York NY 10036-6524 Office Phone: 212-847-8730. Business E-Mail: joseph.angland@hellerehrman.com.

ANGLE, CINDY K., elementary school educator; b. Troy, Ohio, Apr. 10, 1966; d. Terry L. and Jane E. Byers; m. Timothy A. Angle, Mar. 21, 1987; children: Ashley, Alyssa, Austin. AA, Edison State C.C., Piqua, Ohio, 1986; BS, Wright State U., Dayton, Ohio, 1988; MS, U. Dayton, Ohio, 1995. Scholar, Martha Holden Jennings Com. Mem.: NEA. Avocations: volleyball, reading, church activities, outdoor activities. Home: 307 N Grant St Covington OH 45318 Office: Bradford Exempted Village Schs 940 Railroad Ave Bradford OH 45308 Office Phone: 937-448-2811. E-mail: cangle@woh.rr.com.

ANGLE, COLIN, electrical engineer, robotic company executive; BSEE, MS in Computer Sci., MIT. Co-founder ISRobotics (now iRobot Corp.), Burlington, Mass., 1990—; CEO iRobot Corp., Burlington, Mass. Named (with Helen Greiner) Ernst and Young New England Entrpreneur of Yr., 2003; recipient DEMO God award, IDG Exec. Forum, 2001. Achievements include pioneer in the field of mobile robots, designing the behavior-controlled rovers for NASA that led to the Sojourner exploring Mars in 1997. Office: iRobot Corp 63 South Ave Burlington MA 01803 Office Phone: 781-345-0200. Office Fax: 781-345-0201.*

ANGLE, JIM, political correspondent; Corr. politics and economy CNN; worked in pub. radio Am. Pub. Radio, Nat. Pub. Radio, sr. White House corr.; anchor, mng. ptnr. nat. program, Marketplace, 1990—93; corr. on econ. policy ABC News, contbr. World News Tonight, Nightline, Good Morning America; joined FOX News Channel, 1996—, sr. White House corr., chief Washington corr., 2005—, substitute host for Special Report with Brit Hume. Recipient Excellence in Financial Journalism award, 1994, 1995, Merriman Smith Meml. award, White House Corr. Assn., 2001, 2003. Office: FOX News Channel 1211 Avenue of the Americas New York NY 10036*

ANGLEMAN, SHARON ANN, journalist; b. Houston, Apr. 14, 1961; d. Hildred Bruce Lockhart and Elizabeth Ann Davis; children: Justin Angleman, Thomas Angleman, Robert Angleman. BS in Journalism magna cum laude, Ark. State U., Jonesboro, 1998. Freelance journalist NobleInk Co., Jonesboro, 1997—. Chair diversity SPJ, Jonesboro, 1997-98. Author numerous poems; photo editor Herald, 1997-98; contbr. articles to profl. jours. Recipient Udell Smith award Nat. Assn. Retired Employees, 1995, Foy Howard award Housing and Devel., 1996, 97, award Ark. Assn. Press, 1996, 97, 98. Mem. Ark. Press Photographer's Assn., Photographic Soc. (pres. 1998, Outstanding Sr. 1997), Bus. Profl. Women (Scholarship award 1997). Home: 111 Woodside Ln Rogers AR 72756-0711 Office: 111 Woodside Ln Rogers AR 72756-0711 E-mail: sharon@jrily.com.

ANGLIN, BETTY LOCKHART, artist, educator; b. Greenwood, SC, Apr. 23, 1937; d. Malcolm Mabry and Dorothy (Roessler) Lockhart; m. Ernie LaRue Anglin, June 10, 1957; children: Nancy Louise, Malcolm Lawrence. BA, Coll. William and Mary, 1972. Instr. Hampton Arts and Humanities, Va., 1967—73, Cecil Rawls Mus., Courtland, Va., 1973—84; tchr. Trinity Luth. Sch., Newport News, Va., 1972—88; prof. Christopher Newport U., Newport News, 1988—, dir. dept. fine arts, 2002—. One-woman shows include Va. Wesleyan Coll., 1972, Peninsula Arts Assn., Newport News, 1972, Arts Internat. Gallery Ltd., Norfolk, Va., 1973—74, Kirn Meml. Libr., Norfolk, 1976, Jr. League of Hampton Rds. Hdqrs., 1981, Coliseum Mall, Hampton, 1982, Mary Immaculate Hosp., 1983, Jr. League Offices, Newport News, 1983, Village Gallery, 1983, Hampton Arts and Humanities, 1986, exhibited in group shows at Va. Mus., Richmond, Chrysler Mus., Norfolk, Parthenon, Nashville, High Mus., Atlanta, Portsmouth Mus., Cecil Rawls Mus., Suffolk Mus., Represented in permanent collections Hampton Sch. System, City of Hampton, Newport News Shipbuilders, Va. State Fair Collection, Cecil Rawls Mus., Peninsula Arts Assn., Riverside Hosp., City of Stoney Creek, Va., Corning Glass, Anderson, S.C., Eastman Kodak, Phila., Hosp. of Kings Daus., Virginia Beach, Va., others. Active Hidenwood Presbyn. Ch., Newport News. Recipient Va. Gov.'s award, 1979, 1985; grantee, NEA, Va. Mus., 1991—92. Mem.: PEO (state pres. 1984), Am. PEN Women, Gallery on the York (Yorktown), Rawls Mus., Suffolk Art Mus., Smithfield Cultural Art Ctr., This Century Gallery (Williamsburg), Watercolor Soc., Tidewater Artists Va., Va. Mus. Assn., Hampton Arts and Humanities, Peninsula Arts Assn., Va. Watercolor Soc. Home: 213 Parkway Dr Newport News VA 23606-3651 Office: Christopher Newport Univ 1 University Pl Newport News VA 23606-2942 Office Phone: 757-594-7446. Business E-Mail: banglin-@cnu.edu.

ANGLIN, LINDA MCCLUNEY, retired elementary school educator; b. Turrell, Ark., Apr. 20, 1929; d. Denton Sims and Helen Louise (Davis) McCluney; m. Joe Van Anglin, Aug. 30, 1952; children: Van, Cheryl, Dent, George. BA magna cum laude, Millsaps Coll., 1951; MEd, Miss. Coll., 1970; Edn. Specialist, Miss. State U., 1974. Cert. tchr., Miss. Tchr. St. Andrew's Episcopal. Sch., Jackson, Miss., 1952-53; Carthage Elem. Sch., 1956-57, Jackson Pub. Schs., 1957-94. Founder Miss. Profl. Educators, 1979, pres., 1979-82; dir. Pub. Edn. Forum Miss., Jackson, 1989-93; classroom cons. Scholastic Tchr.; bd. dirs. 1st Am. Bank, Jackson. Lobbyist for edn. and children's issues State of Miss., 1980—; charter mem. Jackson Assn. for Children with Learning Disabilities, bd. dirs., historian, mem. adv. bd. Miss. chpt.; active many civic groups. Recipient Book of Golden Deeds award Exch. Club North Jackson, 1989, Disting. Tchr. award White House Commn. Presdl. Scholars, 1996. Mem. Jackson Profl. Educators (pres. 1988-90), Jackson Area Reading Coun. (pres. 1975-76, Outstanding Svc. award 1987), Miss. Hist. Soc. (bd. dirs. 1998-2000), Jackson-Hinds Ret. Tchrs. Assn., Miss. Ret. Tchrs. Assn., Sigma Lambda, Kappa Delta Pi, Phi Kappa Phi, Delta Kappa Gamma (workshop presenter 1985, pres. Tau chpt. 1986-88, Woman of Distinction 1990, Disting. Svc. to Edn. award 1984). Methodist. Avocations: volunteer activities, church activities, reading. Home: 785 Cedarhurst Rd Jackson MS 39206-4954

ANGLIN, MICHAEL WILLIAMS, lawyer; b. Chelsea, Mass., Dec. 3, 1946; s. John M. and Lillian Rogene (Williams) A. BS, Tex. A&M U., Commerce, 1969; JD, U. Tex., 1976. Bar: Tex. 1976, U.S. Dist. Ct. (no. dist.) Tex. 1979, U.S. Dist. Ct. (we. and ea. dists.) Tex. 1987, U.S. Dist. Ct. Ariz. 1992, U.S. Ct. Appeals (5th and 11th cirs.) 1981, U.S. Supreme Ct. 1986. With Passman & Jones, Dallas, 1976-87; sr. ptnr. Fulbright & Jaworski, LLP, Dallas, 1987—. Trustee Ofcl. Panel Bankruptcy Trustees for No. Dist. Tex., 1980—. Corp. mem. Dallas Mus. Fine Arts, 1984; ct. apptd. spl. advocate, 1990-95; bd. dirs. Dallas Opera, 1992-95; active Greater Dallas Planning Coun., 1994—, Greater Dallas Crime Commn., 1994—, Youth Crime Coun., 1994—; chair bd. dirs. Kessler Sch., 2001—; chair Dallas Tax Increment Fin. Bd., 2003—. Mem. ABA, Tex. Bar Assn., Dallas Bar Assn., Am. Bankruptcy Inst. Office: Fulbright & Jaworski LLP 2200 Ross Ave Ste 2800 Dallas TX 75201-2784 Office Phone: 214-855-8000. Business E-Mail: anglin@fulbright.com.

ANGOFF, GERALD HARVEY, cardiologist; b. Cambridge, Mass., Feb. 6, 1944; s. Nathan Robert and Evelyn (Kanter) A.; m. Rosalind Norma Tarko, Nov. 23, 1975; children: Elizabeth, Rebekah. AB, Harvard Coll., 1966; MD, Harvard U., 1970. Diplomate Am. Bd. Internal Medicine, Am. Bd. Cardiovascular Disease, Nat. Bd. Echocardiography; cert. physician exec. Resident internal medicine Cleve. Met. Gen. Hosp., 1970-72; fellow in cardiology Harvard Med. Sch., Peter Bent Brigham Hosp., Boston, 1975-77, Harvard Sch. Pub. Health, Boston, 1977-78; cardiologist The Heart Ctr., Manchester, N.H., 1978-99; dir. noninvasive cardiology New England Heart Inst., 1999—2002. Chief cardiology Elliot Hosp., Manchester, 1979-82, 86-93; instr. Harvard Med. Sch., Boston, 1978-96; pres. The Heart Ctr., 1995-99. Bd. dirs. Jewish Fedn. Greater Manchester, 1984-94; v.p. Temple Adath Yeshurun, Manchester, 1994-96, pres., 1996-98. Maj. U.S. Army, 1975-78. Recipient award of acad. achievement in med. mgmt., Am. Coll. Physician Execs. Fellow Am. Coll. Cardiology, Am. Heart Assn. (Coun. on clin. cardiology). Avocations: computers, skiing. Office: Cerner Corp 2800 Rockcreek Pkwy Kansas City MO 64117-2551 Office Phone: 816-201-7574, 603-669-0413. Personal E-mail: angnh@aol.com. Business E-Mail: gerry.angoff@cerner.com.

ANGOTTI, CATHERINE MARIE, occupational health director; b. Arlington, Va., Nov. 9, 1946; d. Frank William and Catherine Jeannette (Kolakoski) Poos; 1 child, Heather Jeannette. BS, James Madison U., 1968; RD, Med. Coll. Va., 1969. Home economist Washington Gas Light Co., 1968; clin. dietitian Fairfax (Va.) Hosp., 1969-73; pvt. practice as nutrition cons. Va., 1972-98; nutrition cons. Manassas (Va.) Manor Nursing Home, 1973-74, Bio-Tech., Inc., Falls Church, Va., 1977-78; nutrition surveyor JWK Internat., Annandale, Va., 1980-81; nutrition cons. NASA, Washington, 1977-92, program exec. occupl. health, 1992—2000, dir. occupl. health, 2000—03, adminstrv. dept. to chief health and med. officer, 2003. Pres. Nutrition Cons., Inc., 1980—98; nutrition lectr. Contbr. articles to profl. jours. Mem. com. Pub. Regional Diet Manual, 1971—73. Recipient Spl. Svcs. award, NASA, 1989, 1994, Exceptional Performance awards, 1996—2004, Space Flight Awareness award, 1996, Spl. Achievement award, 1997, Superior Accomplishment award, 2003, Exceptional Performance medal, 1999, Sr. Exec. Fellowship award, 2000, Outstanding Leadership medal, 2005. Mem.: NAFE, Cons. Nutritionists Chesapeake Bay Area (mem. nominating com. 1983, sec. 1986—87), Fairfax County Nutrition Com., No. Dist. Dietetic Assn. (exec. bd. 1977—86, treas. 1980—82, pres. 1983—84, chmn. nominating com. 1984—85, mem. awards com. 1988, exec. bd. 1988—95, Dietetic Appreciation award 1987), DC Dietetic Assn., Cons. Nutritionists (Va. state coord. 1976—79), Va. Assn. Allied Health Profls. (del. 1974—79, bd. dirs. 1975—77), Am. Dietetic Assn. (state rep. nutrition svcs. payment sys. 1984—87, del. 1987—90, chmn. dels. 1988—90, Recognized Young Dietitian of the Yr. award 1975, Outstanding Svc. award 1990, Occupation and Health award 1990, Disting. Dietitian award 1992), Va. Dietetic Assn. (del. Va. Coun. State Legis. 1974—76, exec. bd. 1974—76, legis. chmn. 1974—76, mem. nominating com. 1982—84, exec. bd. 1982—96, mem. licensure com. 1983—89, chmn. nutrition svcs. com. 1983—97, mem. payment sys. 1984—87, del., pres.-elect 1993—94, pres. 1994—95, chmn. nominating com. 1995—96, mem. disting. dietitian selection com. 2003—05, bd. dirs. 2004—, coord. outreach divsn. 2004—05, spl. advisor pub. policy 2005—). Home: 2727 Oak Valley Dr Vienna VA 22181-5339 Office: 300 E St SW Washington DC 20546 Business E-Mail: cangotti@hq.nasa.gov.

ANGOTTI, JOHN B., musician, director; b. Philipi, W.Va., Aug. 20, 1963; s. John Baptista and Mary Ann Angotti; m. Tracy Hopwood, Oct. 15, 1994; children: Dominica Marie, John Batista. Degree in Mktg., W.Va. U., 1985. Cert. in music U.S. Mil. Sch. Music, 1987. Ops. mgr. W.Va. U. Found., Morgantown, W.Va., 1994—97; dir. music St. Ann's Cath. Ch., Bartlett, Tenn., 2000—. Composer: (albums) Testify, Common Ground, Rise Up, Angels Cry Aloud with Joy, On This Journey. With U.S. Army, 1986—88. Mem.: Grammy Assn. (assoc.). Home: 3644 Wythe Road Memphis TN 38135 Office: St Ann's Church 6529 Stage Road Bartlett TN 38134 Office Phone: 901-266-5211. Home Fax: 901-373-9030; Office Fax: 901-373-9030. Personal E-mail: john.angotti@stann.cdom.org.

ANGST, GERALD L., lawyer; b. Chgo., Dec. 29, 1950; s. Gerald L. Sr. and Audrey M. (Hides) A.; m. Candace Simning, Jan. 29, 1983. BA magna cum laude, Loyola U., Chgo., 1972, JD cum laude, 1975. Assoc. Sidley Austin Brown & Wood, Chgo., 1975-82, ptnr., 1982—. Mem.: ABA (constrn. litigation com. litigation sect.), Chgo. Bar Assn. (civil practice com.). Office: Sidley Austin Brown & Wood Bank One Plz 47th Fl 10 So Dearborn St Chicago IL 60603-2000 Office Phone: 312-853-7757. Business E-Mail: gangst@sidley.com.

ANGSTROM, WAYNE RAYMOND, communications executive; b. Chgo., Mar. 26, 1939; s. Raymond Harry and Dorothy Louise (Dixon) A.; m. Sandra Sue Weber, Oct. 5, 1963; children: Mark, Carl, David, Kristina. AA in Bus. Adminstrn., Chgo. City Coll., 1962; student, Northwestern U., 1963-68. Mfg. mgr. R.R. Donnelley & Sons Co., Chgo., 1962, div. dir., v.p., 1981-87; exec. v.p. Maxwell Communications Corp., St. Paul, 1987-90, Quebecor Printing Inc., Boston, 1990-91; pres., CEO, St. Ives Inc. U.S.A., 1992—; also bd. dirs. Home: 7082 Valencia Dr Boca Raton FL 33433-7404 Office: Saint Ives Inc 2025 Mckinley St Hollywood FL 33020-3139

ANGUIANO, LUPE, advocate; b. La Junta, Colo., June 12, 1929; d. Jose and Rosario (Gonzalez) A. Student, Ventural (Calif.) Jr. Coll., 1948, Victory Noll Jr. Coll., Huntington, Ind., 1949-52, Marymount Coll., Palos Verdes, Calif., 1958-59, Calif. State U., L.A., 1965-67; MA, Antioch-Putney, Yellow Springs, Ohio, 1978. S.W. regional dir. NAACP Legal Def. and Ednl. Fund, L.A., 1965-69; civil rights specialist HEW, Washington, 1969-73; S.W. regional dir. Nat. Coun. Cath. Bishops, Region X, San Antonio, 1973-77; pres. Nat. Women's Employment and Edn. Inc., L.A., 1979-91; cons. Cisco Sys. Inc., 1998-99; pres., cons. Lupe Anguiano & Assocs., 1981—; dir. devel. La Jolla Inst., Van Nuys, Calif., West Valley Alliance; fund devel. dir. Girl Scouts of the San Fernando Valley, Chatsworth, Calif.; rep. Primerica, Valencia, Calif.; mktg. and fund devel. cons. self employed. Cons. Tex. Dept. Human Resources, Dept. Labor, Women's Bur., U.S. Office Pers. Mgmt., USCG, Washington, 1990-92; tech. cons. Cisco Sys. Inc.; developer regional networking acad., Oxnard Coll.; part-time faculty mem. Ventura (Calif.) Coll.; proposal reader U.S. Office Edn., Women's Equity Act; mem. Tex. Adv. Coun. on Tec.-Vocat. Edn., Calif. del. White House Conf. on Status of Mex.-Ams. in U.S., 1967; founding mem. policy coun. Nat. Women's Polit. Caucus, 1971—; Tex. and nat. del. Intrnat. Women's Yr., 1976-77; chmn. Nat. Women's Polit. Caucus Welfare Reform Task Force, 1977—; co-developer Cisco Networking Acad. in Ventura County high schs. Author (with others): U.S. Bilingual Edn. Act, 1967, Tex. AFDC Employment and Edn. Act, 1977; manuals for Women's Employment and Edn. Model program. Co-chmn. Nat. Peace Acad. Campaign, 1977-81; founder, bd. dirs. Nat. Chicana Found. Inc., 1971-78; bd. dirs. Calif. Coun. Children and Youth, 1967, Rio Grande Fedn. Chicano Health Ctrs., S.W. rural states, 1974-76, Women's Lobby, Washington, 1974-77, Rural Am. Women, Washington, 1978—, Small Bus. Coun. Greater San Antonio; mem. Pres.'s Coun. on Pvt. Sector Initiatives, 1983. Recipient Cmty. award Coalition Mex.-Am. Orgns., 1967, Outstanding Svc. award Washington, 1968, Thanksgiving award Boys' Club, 1976, Outstanding Svc. award Tex. Women's Polit. Caucus, 1977, Liberty Bell award San Antonio Young Lawyers, 1981, Vista award for Exceptional Svc. to end poverty, 1980, Headliner award San Antonio Women in Comm., 1978, Woman of Yr. award Tex. Women's Polit. Caucus, 1978, Pres.'s Vol. Action award 1983, Leadership award Nat. Network Hispanic women, 1989; named Outstanding Woman of Yr., L.A. County, 1972, Woman of the 80's, Ms. Mag., 1980, Nat. Pres.'s award Nat. Image Inc., 1981, Wonder Woman Found. award, 1982, Pres.'s Vol. Action award, 1983, Adv. of Yr., San Antonio SBA, 1984; selected one of Am.'s 100 Most Important Women, Ladies Home Jour., 1988, 89; featured in CBS TV series An American Portrait, 1985, Leadership award Nat. Network Hispanic Women, 1989. Mem. Nat. Assn. Female Execs., Pres.'s Assn., Am. Mgmt. Assn. Republican. Roman Catholic. Office: Primerica 25060 Stanford Ave Valencia CA 91355-3411 Home: 1031 Kumquat Pl Oxnard CA 93036-1533 Office Phone: 805-983-8517. Office Fax: 805-983-8519. Personal E-mail: languian@gte.net.

ANGULA, HELMUT KANGULOHI, Namibian government official; b. Ontananga, Oshikoto, Namibia, Nov. 11, 1945; s. Onesmus and Adda (Thomas) A.; div. Nov. 1992; children: Adda Kaone, Vita, Priscilla, Magdalena, Monica. Cert., Nikumbi Internat. Coll., 1969; MSc in Biology, Voronezh State U., USSR, 1975. Cert. Tchr. Biology and Chemistry. Tchr. SWAPO Edn. Ctr., Nyango, Zambia, 1975-76, adminstr., 1976-77; head of diplomatic mission SWAPO Mission, Havana, Cuba, 1977-86; head of mission SWAPO Observer Mission, UN, N.Y.C., 1986-89; deputy min. Ministry Mines and Energy, Republic of Namibia, 1990-91; min. Fisheries and Marine Resources, Republic of Namibia, 1991-95; min. of fin., 1995-96; min. Agr., Water and Rural Devel., 1997—. Author: Haimbodi Ya Haufiku 1000 Days, 1991. Activist South West Africa People's, Windhoek, 1964; youth activist Organization SWAPO, Zambia, 1966. Mem. Revival Volley Ball Club (patron), Parliamentary Football Team (capt. 1993—). Office: Embassy of Republic of Namibia 1605 New Hampshire Ave NW Washington DC 20009-2511

ANGULO, CHARLES BONIN, foreign service officer, lawyer; b. NYC, Aug. 6, 1943; s. Manuel R. and Carolyn C. (Bonin) A.; m. Penelope Snare, June 28, 1986. BA, U. Va., 1966; cert., U. Madrid, 1966; JD, Tulane U., 1969. Bar: Va. 1969. Assoc. Michael & Dent, Charlottesville, Va., 1969-73; assoc. editor The Michie Pub. Co., Charlottesville, 1973; fgn. svc. officer U.S. Dept. State, Washington, 1973-75, Am. Embassy U.S. Dept. State, Brussels, 1976-78, Santo Domingo, 1981-85, Office of the Legal Advisor, U.S. Dept. State, Washington, 1978-81; exec. dir. office of insp. gen. U.S. Dept. State, Washington, 1985-86; asst. chief protocol U.S. State Dept., Washington, 1986-88, Am. Consulate Gen. U.S. Dept. State, Jeddah, Saudi Arabia, 1988-93; fgn. svc. officer Am. Embassy U.S. Dept. State, Quito, Ecuador, 1993—. Home and Office: Ste 701 2320 Terra Ceia Bay Blvd Palmetto FL 34221

ANGULO, GERARD ANTONIO, publishing executive, investment company executive; b. Havana, Sept. 24, 1956; arrived in U.S., 1960; s. Ricardo A. and Rosario (Mestas) Angulo. BA, Princeton U., 1978; MBA, Harvard U., 1980. With office of pres. Consol. Mining & Industries, N.Y.C., 1980—84; prof. grad. bus. sch. Columbia U., N.Y.C., 1988—90, NYU, 1989—90; host TV show Capital Gains, 1990—91; owner, pub. San Juan STAR, 1994—. Cons. in field. Bd. dirs. YMCA of San Juan, PR, Salvation Army, Ballet Concierto; pres., bd. dirs. Better Bus. Bur.; pres. Harvard Bus. Sch. Assn., PR. Mem.: New Eng. Soc. (bd. dirs. 1986—91, v.p., Achievement award 1979—80). Roman Cath.

ANGULO, SKYE ELIZABETH, music educator, director; b. Torrance, Calif., May 31, 1974; d. James Phair O'Neil and Carolynn Joan Morel; m. Adrian Sean Angulo, Aug. 4, 2001. MusB magna cum laude, Chapman U., Orange, Calif., 1996; MusM, U. So. Calif., L.A., 1998. Music prof. Cypress Coll., Calif., 1999—2005; dir. choral studies Long Beach City Coll., 2004—.

Choir dir. Bellflower First Christian Ch., Calif., 1996—98; music dir. Christ Lutheran Ch., Long Beach, 1998—2001; pvt. voice instr., 1998—; performer musical theatre and opera, So. Calif.; featured soloist Cypress Masterworks Chorale. Singer: Disneyland Carolers, Definitely Dickens Carolers. Recipient Third pl., Musical Arts Competition Orange County, 1996, Dean's award Highest Standards, Chapman U., 1996, Gray Key, 1996; Dean's Scholarship award, U. So. Calif., 1996—98. Mem.: Music Assn. Calif. Cmty. Colleges (life), Am. Choral Dirs. Assn. (life), Gamma Beta Phi (life). Office: Long Beach City Coll 4901 E Carson St Long Beach CA 90808 E-mail: sangulo@lbcc.edu.

ANGUS, JOHN COTTON, chemical engineering educator; b. Grand Haven, Mich., Feb. 22, 1934; s. Francis Clark and Margaret (Cotton) A.; m. Caroline Helen Gezon, June 25, 1960; children: Lorraine Margaret, Charles Thomas. BSChemE, U. Mich., 1956, MS, 1958, PhD in Engring, 1960; DSc (hon.), Ohio U., 1998. Registered profl. engr., Ohio. Research engr. Minn. Mining & Mfg. Co., St. Paul, 1960-63; prof. Case Inst. Tech. (now Case Western Res. U.), Cleve., 1963-67, prof. chem. engring., 1967—2004, prof. emeritus, 2004—, chmn. dept., 1974-80, interim dean engring., 1986-87. Vis. lectr. U. Edinburgh, Scotland, 1972-73; vis. prof. Northwestern U., 1980-81; pres. Angus Engring., Inc. Trustee Ohio Scottish Games. NSF fellow, 1956-57; NATO sr. fellow, 1972-73 Fellow AIChE, Electrochem. Soc. (Pioneer award); mem. NAE, Am. Chem. Soc., Sigma Xi, Tau Beta Pi, Phi Lambda Upsilon. Achievements include research in fields of crystal growth, diamond synthesis, conducting diamond, electrochemical devices, thermodynamics. Office: Case Western Res U Dept Chem Engring Cleveland OH 44106-7217

ANGUS, W. DAVID, Queen's Counsel; AB cum laude, Princeton, 1959; BCL, McGill Univ., 1962. Mem. Senate of Can., 1993—; sr. ptnr. Stikeman Elliott LLP. Pres., bd. dirs. Turner's Grant Holdings, Inc.; bd. dirs. AON Reed Stenhouse, Inc., McGill U. Health Ctr., Montreal Gen. Hosp. Corp., Air-Canada, Autoskill Internat. Inc., Security Biometrics, Inc. Mem. St. Andrews Presbyn. Homes Found. Office: The Senate of Canada 903 Victoria Bldg Ottawa ON K1A 0A6 Canada

ANIMA, ROBERTO J., geologist, marine biologist; b. Tulare, Calif., Mar. 8, 1947; s. Marcos E. Anima; children: Jesus Chuey, Christina E. Pino, Beatrice E. Damaso, Leticia D. PhD in Earth Scis., U. Calif., Santa Cruz, Calif., 1999. Rsch. geologist US Geol. Survey, Menlo Park, Calif., 1972—. Contbr. articles to profl. jours. With USN, 1966—70. Mem.: Am. Geophys. Union. Achievements include research in coastal and nearshore geologic and sedimentologic processes. Avocations: sailing, swimming, music, scuba diving, travel. Home: PO Box 2242 Menlo Park CA 94026 Office: United States Geological Survey 345 Middlefield Road Menlo Park CA 94025 Office Phone: 650-329-5212. Office Fax: 650-329-5190. Business E-Mail: ranima@usgs.gov.

ANINAT, EDUARDO, international banking official; b. 1948; m. Maria Teresa Sahli; six children. BA in Econs., Pontificia U. Catolica, Chile; MA in Econs., PhD in Econs., Harvard U. Former asst. prof. econs. Boston U.; prin. Aninat, Mendez y Asociados, 1981-94; fin. min. Govt. of Chile, 1994—99; chmn. bd. govs. IMF and World Bank, 1995-96, former mem. devel. com.; Latin. Am. coord. internat. tax program Harvard U., 1989; deputy mng. dir. IMF, Washington, 1999—. Cons. various internat. instns. including the World Bank, Inter-Am. Devel. Bank; adv. various governments on tax policy matters; bd. dirs. various pvt. cos.; dep. mng. dir. IMF, Washington.

ANISE, NADER, lawyer; Pres., CEO Nader Anise Lawyer Mktg., Boca Raton, Fla.; ptnr. Anise & Anise Attys. at Law, Boca Raton, Fla. Adj. prof. managerial mktg. and entrepreneur law Nova SE Univ., Fort Lauderdale, Fla. Mem.: Am. Mktg. Assn., Legal Mktg. Assn., Nat. Speakers Assn., Am. Lawyers Public Image Assn. (founder, pres. 2000—), Fla. Bar. Office: Anise & Anise Attys Ste 358 1900 Glades Rd Boca Raton FL 33431 also: Lawyer Mktg Inc PO Box 11138 Fort Lauderdale FL 33339 Office Phone: 561-417-2324, 888-510-1520. Business E-Mail: nader@naderanise.com.

ANISTON, JENNIFER, actress; b. Sherman Oaks, Calif., Feb. 11, 1969; d. John and Nancy (Dow) Aniston; m. Brad Pitt, July 29, 2000. Attended, Fiorello La Guardia School of Music, Art & Performing Arts, N.Y.C. Actor: (TV series) Ferris Bueller, 1990, Molloy, 1990, The Edge, 1992, Muddling Through, 1994, Friends, 1994—2004 (Screen Actors Guild outstanding ensemble performance in comedy series, 1995, Emmy award best actress, 2002, Golden Globe award best actress, 2003, People's Choice award favorite female television performer, 2001, 2002, 2003, 2004), (guest appearances) Herman's Head, 1992—93, Quantum Leap, 1992, Burke's Law, 1994; host (TV Documentary) Growing Up Grizzly 2, 2004; actor: (TV films) Camp Cucamonga, 1990, Sunday Funnies, 1993; (films) Leprechaun, 1993, She's the One, 1996, Dream for an Insomniac, 1996, Til There Was You, 1997, Picture Perfect, 1997, The Thin Pink Line, 1998, The Object of My Affection, 1998, The Iron Giant (voice), 1999, Office Space, 1999, Rock Star, 2001, The Good Girl, 2002, Bruce Almighty, 2003, Along Came Polly, 2004, (off-broadway play) For Dear Life, Dancing on Checkers' Grave, (music videos) I'll Be There For You, 1995, Walls, 1996, I Want To Be In Love, 2001. Named Most Intriguing People, People Weekly, 1995; named one of Most Beautiful People in the World, People, 1999, 50 Most Beautiful People, 2002. Office: PMK/HBH 8500 Wilshire Blvd Ste 700 Beverly Hills CA 90211*

ANITESCU, MIHAI, computer scientist, mathematician; b. Bals, Romania, Aug. 10, 1968; arrived in U.S., 1993; s. Ilie and Marioara Anitescu; m. Magdalena Anitescu, Nov. 14, 1992; 1 child, Julia Christine. MS, Poly. U., Bucharest, Romania, 1992; PhD, U. Iowa, 1997. Asst. prof. math. U. Pitts., 1999—; computer scientist Argonne (Ill.) Nat. Lab., 2002—. Contbr. articles to profl. jours. Sgt. Inf. Romanian Mil., 1986—87. Fellow Wilkinson fellow, Argonne Nat. Laboratoty, 1997. Office: Argonne Nat Lab MCS Bdg 221 9700 S Cass Avenue Lemont IL 60439 E-mail: anitescu@mcs.anl.gov.

ANJULIS, STANLEY JOSEPH, retired church administrator; b. Jersey City, Feb. 4, 1948; s. Stanley and Lorraine Anjulis; m. Alane Hope Berney, Oct. 30, 1982. B of Bible Theology, Internat. B of Bible Theology, M of Bible Theology, Internat. Bible Inst., Plymouth, Fla., 1987; M of Ministry, Internat. Sem., Plymouth, Fla., 1988—90; DD (hon.), Internat. Bible Inst., Plymouth, Fla., 1988; PhD, Carolina Christian U., Linwood, N.C., 1988—90. Clin. Pastoral Counselor Acad. Prof. Clin. Therapists, 1991, Marriage & Family Therapist Acad. Prof. Clin. Therapists, 1992. Asst. regional dir. Servants of The Good Shepherd, N.Y.C., 1984—85; vicar-gen. Ecumenical Orthodox Ch., Balt., 1985—87, oeconomus, 1985—87; provost Am. Orthodox Ch., Balt., 1987—87, diocesan ordinary L.A., 1991—2000; superior gen. (ex-officio) Comm. Order of St. Benedict, L.A., 1991—2000; ret. with full faculties Am. Orthodox Ch./O. St. Benedict, Hudson, Wis., 2001—. CEO Ecumenical Orthodox Ch., Balt., 1985—87, dean of pesbyterium, 1985—87, dean of sem., 1985—87. Orthodox Catholic.

ANKER, BEVERLY ELAINE, retired elementary school educator; b. Buffalo, N.Y. d. George Chester Anker and Dorothy Beatrice Kelsey. EdB, SUNY U. at Buffalo, 1963; MS, SUNY Buffalo State, 1967. 1st grade tchr. Thomas Marks Elem. Sch., Wilson, NY, 1962—63; 1st and 2nd grade tchr. Wurlitzer Elem. Sch., North Tonawanda, NY, 1963—95; 3rd, 4th, and 5th grade tchr. Meadow Elem. Sch., North Tonawanda, NY, 1963—95, ret., 1995. Mem.: N.Y. State Retirees of Western N.Y. (rec. sec. 1998—), Delta Kappa Gamma (state sec. 1999—2001, state 1st v.p. 2001—03, state pres. 2003—05). Avocations: bridge, theater, museums, movies, opera. Home: 57 Princeton Blvd Buffalo NY 14217-1715 Personal E-mail: ankerdkgpi@aol.com.

ANKERMAN, WILLIAM LEWIS, lawyer; b. Lima, Ohio, Jan. 12, 1947; s. Fred Lewis and Mary Ola (Hilton) A.;m. Darcy Evelyn Wilson, Sept. 6, 1969; children: Justin Lewis, Amanda Darcy. BA, Ohio No. U., 1969; MA, Ohio State U., 1971; JD, Georgetown U., 1974. Bar: Ohio 1974, Conn. 1975, U.S. Dist. Ct. Conn. 1975, U.S. Ct. Appeals (2d cir.) 1975, U.S. Tax Ct. 1976, U.S. Dist. Ct. (no. dist.) Ohio 1982, U.S. Dist. Ct. (so. dist.) Ohio 1983, U.S. Ct. Appeals (6th cir.) 1982. Law clk. Judges of Hartford (Conn.) Superior Ct., 1974-75; assoc. Parakilas and Mack, Enfield, Conn., 1975-79; temporary asst. clk. Hartford Superior Ct., 1978-79; asst. prof. law Ohio No. U. Coll. Law, Ada, 1979-84; police prosecutor City of Bellefontaine (Ohio), 1980-82, civil service commr., 1983-84; pvt. practice West Hartford, 1978—. Justice of the peace Town of West Hartford, Conn., 1990—, mem. personnel bd., 1993—. Co-author: Wright, FitzGerald & Ankerman, Connecticut Law of Torts, 3d edit., 1991, Wright and Ankerman, Connecticut Jury Instructions, 4th edit., 1993. Chair West Hartford Pers. Commn., 1998—. Mem. ABA, Conn. Bar Assn., Hartford County Bar Assn. (lawyer referral panel com. 1988), West Hartford Rotary Club (pres. 1995-96, Paul Harris fellow 1997). Baptist. Avocations: history, genealogy. Office: PO Box 270684 West Hartford CT 06127-0684

ANKRAH, SHAWN B., secondary school educator; b. Paterson, N.J., Dec. 24, 1972; d. Robert Howard Gray and Terry Patricia Bannister; m. NiiAryoe Ankrah, Aug. 14, 2001. B, Rutgers U., 1997; M, Columbia U., 2000. Tchr. Paterson Pub. Sch., instrnl. coach. Mem.: Assn. Supr. and Curriculum Devel. Democrat. Baptist.

ANKROM, CHARLES FRANKLIN, golf course architect, consultant; b. Parkersburg, W.Va., Nov. 7, 1936; s. Donsel and Elva Dale (Cale) A.; m. Alice Lynell Glass, Aug. 24, 1968; children: Steven Charles, Cheryl Lyn, Jan Ellen Lambert, Beverly Lyn Webster. Student, W.Va. U., 1955, Eli Frank Sch. Design Arts, Tampa, Fla., 1956, Indian River C.C., Stuart, Fla., 1993—94. Exec. dir. golf, corp. golf course arch. Gen. Devel. Corp., Miami, Fla., 1964-70; exec. dir. golf, golf course arch. Boise Cascade Recreation Communities Group, Palo Alto, Calif., 1970-73; pres. Charles F. Ankrom, Inc., Internat. Golf Course Archs., Cons. & Planners, Stuart, Fla., 1973—, ptnr. Palm City, Fla., 2003—. Prin. works include Panther Woods Country Club, Ft. Pierce, Fla., Sabal Trace C.C., Port Charlotte, Fla., Sun 'N Lake Country Club, Turtle Run Golf Course, Sebring, Fla., Cocoa Beach Mcpl. Golf Course, Cocoa Beach City, Fla., Ft. Lauderdale (Fla.) Country Club, Boca Raton (Fla.) Mcpl. Golf Course, The Cypress Golf Course at Woodmont Country Club, Tamarac, Fla., The Club at Emerald Hills, Hollywood, Fla., The Habitat Golf Course, Brevard County, Fla., Aquarina Country Club, Melbourne, Fla., Crane Creek C.C., Palm City, Fla., Indian River Plantation Resort, Hutchinson Island Marriott Beach Resort and Marina, Jensen Beach, Fla., Metro Country Club Resort, Dominican Republic, Osprey Creek Golf Course, Palm City, Fla., San Miguel Country Club, Venezuela, numerous others; over 60 planned cmtys. including Indian River Plantation Marriott Resort, Hutchinson Island, Fla., Joe's Point, Hutchinson Island, Stuart West, Martin County, Fla., Pinecrest Lakes, Jensen Beach, Crystal Lakes, Okeechobee, Fla., Panther Woods, Ft. Pierce, Crane Creek, Palm City, Fla., River Ridge, Tequesta, Fla., River Landing, Palm City. Donated design & adminstrv. svcs. for Bulldog Sportsturf Complex, Martin County (Fla.) Schs. Recipient Outstanding Achievement by Ind. in Bus. or Industry award State of Fla. Coun. on Vocat. Edn., 1992, Bus. Ptnr. award Martin County Sch. Dist., 1991. Achievements include profl. svc. multi-disciplinary cons. assignments provided to clients in 28 states and 9 countries or territories, including approxmamtely 300 assignments to both the govt. and pvt. sectors, profl. orgns., coll. and univ. and the edn. industry, natl. and internat. conf. as the lectr. for seminars, including svcs. to resort ops., pvt. amenities and public ops., 2001; formed AMI (Ankrom and Miartus Internat.) for the internat. design of golf course projects, with offices in Fla. and Venezuela. Office: Charles F Ankrom Inc PO Box 898 Stuart FL 34995-0898

ANKRUM, DENNIS R., ergonomist, consultant; b. Webster City, Iowa, June 05; s. Homer R. and Ethel B. Ankrum; m. Sharon Godbey, July 11, 2003; m. Mildred J. Allen; 1 child, Carl R. BA, Northeastern Ill. U., 1995. Cert. indsl. ergonomist Oxford Rsch. Inst., Md., 1996. Pres. Ankrum Assocs., Chgo., 1990—93, Oak Park, Ill., 2003—; dir. human factors rsch. Nova Solutions, Effingham, Ill., 1993—2003. Mem. ANSI-HFES-100 Computer Workstation Stds. Com., San Jose, Calif., 1992—2002, ANSI-IESNA RP-1 Office Lighting Stds. Com., N.Y.C., 1998—; chmn. ASTM Ergonomics Com., West Coshohocken, Pa., 2001—. Contbg. author: Work With Display Units 94, 1995, Applied Ergonomics, 1995. Mem.: ASTM, Illuminating Engring. Soc. of N.Am., Human Factors and Ergonomics Soc. Achievements include first study to show tipping a computer monitor downward increases postural and visual discomfort. Home and Office: Ankrum Assocs 949 Lake St 3-G Oak Park IL 60301 Office Phone: 708-386-5753. Business E-Mail: ankrum@aol.com.

ANKRUM, DOROTHY DARLENE, elementary school educator; b. Wessington Springs, SD, Feb. 23, 1933; d. Clifford Lee and Ella Martha A. BA, Colo. State Coll., 1957; MEd, Black Hills State U., 1974. Cert. elem. tchr., SD. Tchr. Mitchell Ind. Sch. Dist., SD, 1953-56, Santa Ana Pub. Sch., Calif., 1957-58, Greybull Pub. Sch., 1958-62, Douglas Sch. Sys., Ellsworth AFB, SD, 1962-69, kindergarten coord., 1963-67; tchr. Rapid City Area Sch., SD, 1969-94; ret., 1994. Unit leader Individually Guided Edn., Rapid City, 1969-74. Author: Sit Up, Line Up, and Shut Up, 1987; contbr. articles to profl. jour.; artist oil painting (best of show 1987). Chair lit. divsn. Ctrl. States Fair, Rapid City, 1987-90; mem. choir, chair bd. edn. 1st Congl. Ch., 1962-92, chair bd. music, 1996-97; chair Altar Guild 1st Congl. Ch., 2003-05. Mem. AAUW (life, sec., bd. dir. 1970-92, state corr. sec. 1992-94, br. pres. 1996-98, named Woman of Worth 1989, Gift fellow 1994), NEA, Greybull Classroom Tchr. Assn. (sec. 1960-62), Douglas Edn. Assn. (past sec.). Avocations: art, sewing, reading, writing. Home: 255 Texas St #F 333 Rapid City SD 57701

ANLAGE, STEVEN, physics professor; BS in Physics, Rensselaer Polytech Inst., 1982; PhD, Calif. Inst. Tech., Pasadena, 1988. Postdoctoral rschr. Stanford U., Stanford, Calif., 1988—90; prof. of physics U. of Md., College Park, 1991—. Grantee Numerous rsch. grants, NSF, Air Force Office of Sci. Rsch., 1991-2006. Mem.: IEEE, Am. Phys. Soc. Achievements include research in superconductivity, near-field microwave microscopy, quantum chaos nano-science; patents for surface impedance measurement and near-field microscopes. Office: University of Maryland CSR Physics Department College Park MD 20742-4111

ANLIAN, STEVEN JAMES, urban planner, consultant; b. Jersey City, N.J., Sept. 18, 1953; s. Haig Anlian and Virginia Catherine States; m. Nune Vaganovna Anlian, Apr. 10, 1990; children: David Steven, Tigran John. BS in Environ. Sci., Syracuse U., 1975; B of Land Arch., SUNY, Syracuse, 1976; MPA, Harvard U., 1998. Internat. advisor Internat. City/County Mgmt. Assn., Washington, 1992-97; v.p. HOH Assocs. Inc., Alexandria, Va., 1976-92; sr. assoc. The Urban Inst., Washington, 1998—. Advisor to govt. of Republic of Armena, U.S. Agy. for Internat. Devel., Yerevan, 1992—. Grants bd. mem. Eurasia Found., Washington, 1995-96. Fulbright fellow Coun. for Internat. Exch. of Scholars, 1989. Mem. Am. Inst. Cert. Planners, Am. Planning Assn., Fulbright Assn. Office: The Urban Inst 2100 M St NW Washington DC 20037 E-mail: Anlian@alumni.ksg.harvard.edu.

ANLYAN, WILLIAM GEORGE, surgeon, educator, academic administrator; b. Alexandria, Egypt, Oct. 14, 1925; s. Armand and Emmy (Nazar) A.; children: William George, John Peter, Louise. BS magna cum laude, Yale U., 1945, MD, 1949; DSc (hon.), Rush Med. Coll., 1973. Diplomate Am. Bd. Surgery, Am. Bd. Thoracic Surgery. Intern, resident, instr., assoc. in surgery Duke Hosp., Durham, NC, 1949-53, asst. prof. surgery, 1953-58, prof. surgery, 1961-89; assoc. dean Duke U. Sch. Medicine, 1963, dean, 1964-69, v.p. health affairs, 1969-83, chancellor health affairs, 1983-88, exec. v.p., 1987—89; chancellor Duke U., 1989—90, chancellor emeritus, 1990—. Chmn, Durham VA Chancellor's Com., 1963—89; chmn. Pearle Health Svcs., Inc., 1983—85; surg. cons. Durham VA Hosp.; Markle scholar med. sci., 1953—58; bd. regents Nat. Libr. Medicine, 1971—72; trustee N.C. Sch. Sci. and Math., 1978—85, chmn. phys. facilities com., 1979, vice-chmn. bd. trustees, 1981—84; mem. bd. visitors The U. Tex. Health Sci. Ctr. at Houston, 1980—88, Stanford U., 1985—87; chmn. Yale U. Coun. Com. on Med. Affairs, 1985—93. Mem. editl. bd. Pharos, 1968-93. Trustee The Duke Endowment, 1990—, Commn. on Future Structure of Vet. Health Care, 1990-92; chmn. Gov.'s Task Force on Better Health for N.C. in 2000, 1991-97; mem. White House Sci. Coun., 1988-89. Recipient Disting. Achievement award Modern Medicine, 1974; Gov.'s Disting. Meritorious Svc. award, 1978; Abraham Flexner award, 1980, Disting. Surgeon Alumnus award Yale U. Sch. Medicine, 1979, Award of Merit Duke U. Hosp. and Health Adminstrn. Alumni Assn., 1987, Lifetime Achievement award Duke U. Med. Alumni, 1995, Lifetime Achievement award Rsch. Am., 1997, Disting. Meritorius Svc. medal, Duke Univ., 2002, N.C. award in sci., presented by the gov., 2002, Lifetime Achievement award City of Medicine, 2003. Fellow ACS; mem. AMA (adv. com. med. sci. 1972—), Soc. Univ. Surgeons, Soc. Vascular Surgery, Internat. Cardiovasc. Soc., Soc. Clin. Surgery, Am. Heart Assn., Soc. Med. Adminstrs. (pres. 1983-85), Inst. Medicine of NAS, Coun. Deans (chmn. 1968-69), AAMC (exec. com. 1965-71, chmn. 1970-71), AAMC Coun. Deans (chmn. 1968-69), So. Med. Assn., Coord. Coun. Med. Edn. (chmn. 1973-74), Surg. Biology Club II, Am. Surg. Assn., So. Surg. Assn., Halsted Soc., Allen O. Whipple Surg. Soc., Assn. Am. Med. Colls. (chmn. 1970-71), Ind. Rsch. Roundtable NAS, Assn. Acad. Health Ctrs. (pres. 1975), Rsch. Am. (bd. dirs. 1989-2005, chmn. 1992-96), Rotary, Phi Beta Kappa, Sigma Xi, Alpha Omega Alpha. Home: 1516 Pinecrest Rd Durham NC 27705-5817 Office: Duke Med Ctr PO Box 3626 Durham NC 27710-0001 Office Phone: 919-684-3438. E-mail: anlya001@mc.duke.edu.

ANMA, SO, engineer, consultant; b. Hamamatsu, Shizuoka, Japan, Nov. 7, 1936; s. Yu and Chie (Matsumoto) A.; m. Fumie Kishikawa, Mar. 15, 1964; children: Ryo, Akitsu, Mizuho, Yashima. *Wife, Fumie received a BA, Ferris Women's College of Music, Yokohama, 1958. She taught piano for children privately for 40 years. Son Ryo received a BS and MS from Ryukyu University and a PhD from Uppsala University, Sweden, 1997. He's working for Tsukuba University, Ibaraki and married to Yoriko Yokoo. Daughter Akitsu, received a BA from the Toho-Gakuen School of Music, Tokyo, 1989. She was granted Diplome Superieur d'Execution, Ecole Normal de Musique de Paris 1993. She performs piano in France, Spain and Japan. She is married to Kiyofumi Suzuki. Daughter Mizuho received a BS, MS and a PhD from Hokkaido University, Sapporo, 2001. She studies volcanology of the Izu-Bonnin Islands. She married Hiroki Miyasaka. Daughter Yashima, who married Itaru Ogasawara received a BJ from Hokkaido University, Sapporo 1997.* BS, Hokkaido U., Sapporo, Japan, 1959; DEng, Tokai U., Tokyo, 1987. Registered engring. geologist; profl. civil engr. Rschr. Hukada Chisitsu Inst., Tokyo, 1959-67; pres. Kisokogaku Co., Tokyo, 1967-70; exec. Kensetsu Kiso Chosa Sekkei Co., Shizuoka, Japan, 1970-91, pres., 1991—2002. Lectr. Tokai U., Shizuoka, 1988-; bd. dirs. Shizuoka Environ. and Resources, 1989-. Co-author: The First Ascent of Mt. Chamlang, 1965, Geology of Nepal Himalaya, 1967 (Chichibunomiya prize 1968), Patagonian Mountain Climb, 1968, Mt. Dhaulagiri-I Midwinter, 1985. Hazard reduction adviser Shizuoka Prefecture, 1984—. Recipient Chichibunomiya prize Chichibunomiya Meml. Found., Tokyo, 1968, Hokkaido prize Hokkaido Regional Govt., 1983, Asahi Sports prize Asahi Newspaper Inc., Tokyo, 1984. Fellow Japan Soc. Civil Engrs.; mem. Internat. Geosynthetic Soc., Internat. Soc. Soil Mechanics and Found. Engring., Internat. Assn. Engring. Geology and Environment, Geol. Soc. Japan, Japanese Soc. Snow and Ice, Japanese Alpine Club (chpt. chmn. 1986-95). Avocations: mountain climbing, forest watching. Office: 241-7 Shimizu-Kusunokishinden Shizuoka 424-0882 Japan Office Phone: 81-543-45-2415. Business E-Mail: anma.sf@tx.thn.ne.jp.

ANNABLE, CHARLES ROY, pathologist; b. Hastings, Mich., Mar. 3, 1932; s. Charles Roy and Verta Irene (Metster) A.; m. Toni Marie Pohl, June 8, 1985; children: Beverly, Rolf, Irene, Kelley, Monica, James, Jane, Sara. BS, U. Mich., 1957, MD, 1961; postgrad., Walter Reed Army Inst. Rsch., Washington, 1969-70, U. Conn., 1970-73, PhD, 1982. Cert. Am. Bd. Pathology, Surgery and Thoracic Surgery. Commd. 2d lt. U.S. Army, 1960, advanced through grades to col., 1974, ret., 1980; intern Womack Army Hosp., Fort Bragg, N.C., 1961-62; resident gen. surgery Walter Reed Army Med. Ctr., Washington, 1962-66, resident thoracic surgery, 1967-69, staff surgeon, dir. rsch. lab. transplantation svc., 1973-79; chief surgery 85th Evacuation Hosp., Qui Nhon, Vietnam, 1966-67; asst. chief medicine and surgery divsn. Acad. Health Scis., Fort Sam Houston, Tex., 1979-80; resident instr. dept. pathology U. Tex. Health Sci. Ctr., San Antonio, 1980-87; asst. prof. dept. pathology U. Tex. Med. Br., Galveston, 1987-90; dir. dept. pathology Driscol Children's Hosp., Corpus Christi, Tex., 1990-99; ret., 1999. Mem. Phi Beta Kappa, Alpha Omega Alpha, Phi Kappa Phi. Home: 31345 River Pines Dr Springfield LA 70462-8881

ANNAKIN, KENNETH COOPER, film director, writer; b. Beverly, Yorkshire, Eng. came to U.S., 1979; s. Edward C. and Hannah J. (Gains) A.; m. Pauline Mary Carter, 1960; children: Jane, Deborah. DLitt (hon.), Hull U., 1935. Writer, dir. 14 documentaries, 1941-46; movie dir. Holiday Camp, 1946, Miranda, 1948, Quartette, 1948, Trio, 1950, Hotel Sahara, 1951, Planter's Wife, 1952, Robin Hood and Hist Merry Men, 1952, Sword and the Rose, 1953, Loser Takes All, 1956, Three Men in a Boat, 1956, Across the Bridge, 1957, Third Man on the Mountain, 1959, The Swiss Family Robinson, 1960, A Very Important Person, 1961, The Hellions, 1961, Crooks Anonymous, 1962, The Fast Lady, 1962, The Longest Day, 1962, Those Magnificent Men in Their Flying Machines, 1965, The Battle of the Bulge, 1965, The Biggest Bundle of Them All, 1967, Those Daring Young Men in Their Jaunty Jalopies, 1969, Call of the Wild, 1972, Paper Tiger, 1974, The Fifth Musketeer, 1977, The Pirate Movie, 1982, Pippi Longstocking, 1986, 99; screenwriter Coco Chanel, 1999, Chiffon, 2001, Fair Play, 2001, Redwing, 2002; author (autobiography): So You Wanna Be A Director?, 2001. Decorated Order Brit. Empire. Office: 9233 Swallow Dr West Hollywood CA 90069-1145 E-mail: flyingmachines@earthlink.com.

ANNAN, KOFI A., Secretary General of the United Nations; b. Kumasi, Ghana, Apr. 8, 1938; m. Nane Lagergren (div.); 3 children. Grad., U. Sci. and Tech., Kumasi, Macalester Coll., St. Paul, 1961; grad. studies, Inst. des Hautes Etudes Internationales, Geneva, 1961—62; MS in mgmt., MIT, 1971-72. Held posts UN Econ. Commn. for Africa, Addis Ababa, Ethiopia, UN, NYC, WHO, Geneva, 1962-71; adminstrv. mng. officer UN, Geneva, 1972-74; chief civilian pers. officer UN Emergency Force, Cairo, 1974; mng. dir. Ghana Tourist Devel. Co., 1974-76; dep. chief staff svc. Office Pers. Svc., Office of UN High Commn. for Refugees, Geneva, 1976-80, dep. dir. divsn. adminstrn., head pers. svc., 1980-83; dir. adminstrn. mgmt. svc., dir. budget Office Fin. Svcs. UN, NYC, 1984-87; chmn. bd. trustees UN Internat. Sch., 1987-95; asst. sec-gen. Office Human Resources Mgmt., security coord. UN, NYC, 1987-90, asst. sec-gen. & contr. Office Program Planning., 1990-92, asst. sec.-gen. dept. peace-keeping ops., 1992—93, under-sec.-gen., 1993—96, spl. rep. of sec.-gen. to former Yugolslavia, 1995-96, sec.-gen, 1997—. Recipient Nobel Peace Prize, 2001. Office: UN Pub Inquiries Unit Rm GA-57 UN Plz 46th St at First Ave New York NY 10017*

ANNANDALE, GEORGE WILLIAM, engineer; b. Kimberly, South Africa, Aug. 2, 1951; s. George and Bernice Martha A.; m. Itha Mentz, Nov. 1970 (div. Jan. 1979); m. Linda Mouton, Dec. 12, 1980 (dec. Jan. 1985); m. Nicolene Maree, Jan. 11, 1986; children: Jacques, Graham, Lahne. BSCE, U. Pretoria, South Africa, 1974; MS in Engring., U. Witwatersrand, Johannesburg, South Africa, 1979; D of Engring., U. Pretoria, 1984. prof. engr. Engr. van Wyk & Louw, Pretoria, South Africa, 1975-76, Indsl. Devel. Corp., Johannesburg, 1976-77; sr. lectr. U. Pretoria, South Africa, 1979-81; prof., dept. head Rand Afirkaans U., South Africa, 1981—85; specialist engr. Bruinette Kruger Stoffberg, Pretoria, South Africa, 1986—87; ptnr. Steffen Roberston and Kirsten, Inc., Denver, 1988-93; mgr. water resources HDR Engring., Sacramento, 1993-95; assoc., dir. water resource engring. Golder Assocs., Lakewood, Colo., 1995-2001; pres. Engring. and Hydrosystems, Inc., Highlands Ranch, Colo., 2001—. Author: Reservoir Sedimentation, 1987; contbg. author: Guidelines for the Retirement of Dams and Hydroelectric Facilities, 1997, Reservoir Sedimentation Handbook, 1997, Stream Stability and Scour at Highway Bridges, 1999, Rock Scour due to High Velocity Falling Jets, 2002; mem. editl. bd. Internat. Assn. Hydraulic Rsch., 1985—; contbr. over 100 articles to profl. jours.; inventor in field. Bd. dirs. Arapahoe/Douglas Mental Health Network, Littleton, Colo., 1998-2000.

Mem. ASCE (sedimentation com. 1993--), Internat. Assn. Hydraulic Rsch. (editl. bd. 1985—), U.S. Soc. Dams (hydraulics com. 1995—). Achievements include developer of the erodibility index method, known as Annandale's method. Home: 2374 E Lansdowne Pl Littleton CO 80126 Office: Engring & Hydrosystems Inc 8122 South Park Lane 208 Littleton CO 80120

ANNAUD, JEAN-JACQUES, film director, film producer, scriptwriter; b. Juvisy, France, Oct. 1, 1943; s. Pierre and Madeleine (Tripoz) A.; m. Monique Rossignol, 1970 (div. 1980); 1 child, Mathilde; m. Laurence Duval; 1 child, Louise. Student, Ecole Louis Lumière, Institut Des Hautes Etudes Cinematographiques, Paris, 1966; Lic. Lettres, The Sorbonne, Paris, 1967. Freelance film dir., screenwriter, Paris, 1967—. Sreenwriter, dir.: Black and White in Color, 1976 (Oscar award Best Fgn. Film 1977), Hot head, 1978, Quest for Fire, 1981, (César award 1982), Name of the Rose, 1986 (César award 1987, Donatello award), The Bear, 1988 (César award best dir. 1988), The Lover, 1991 (Best Dir. award Japan Critics Assn., 1992); screenwriter, dir., prodr.: Wings of Courage, 1994 (in IMAX 3D), Seven Years in Tibet, 1997 (Best Fgn. Film Gilde Filmpreis, Germany, 1998), Enemy at the Gates, 2000, Two Brothers, 2004. Decorated commandeur Ordre des Arts et Lettres; recipient Grand Prix Nat. du Cinema, prix du Cinéma de L'Académie Française. Home: 9 rue Guénégaud 75006 Paris France also: Repérage SAS 10 rue Lincoln 75008 Paris France also: ICM care Jeff Berg 8899 Beverly Blvd Los Angeles CA 90048-2412 Office Phone: 33 140769411. E-mail: reperage@teaser.fr.

ANNE, LOIS, artist, educator; b. Buffalo, Oct. 15, 1950; BFA, Alfred (N.Y.) U., 1972. Working and exhibiting artist, 1972—; arts program coord. Coastal Workshop, Camden, Maine, 1989—. Tchr. privately, in pub. schs., galleries, museums and univs., 1968—. Exhibited in shows at Albright-Knox Art Gallery, 1975, U. Maine at Augusta, 1977, 78, 86, 89, Wm. A. Farnsworth Art Mus., Rockland, Maine, 1980, Maine Coast Artists Gallery, Rockport, 1979, 81, 83, 90, 91, Portland (Maine) Sch. Art, 1981, 83, U. Maine at Orono, 1982, Fine Art Ctr., Taos, N.Mex., 1985, Waterville (Maine) Gallery Fine Arts, 1986, Ogunquit (Maine) Art Ctr., 1990, 94, Maine Crafts Assn., Deer Isle, 1990-94, Bensons Fibre & Wood, Camden, 1993, 94, White House, Washington, 1993, Colby Coll., Waterville, Maine, 1995. Mem. Maine Crafts Assn., Union of Maine Visual Artists (newsletter editor 1986-87), Mid Coast Graphic Artists Network. Avocations: gardening, hiking, dance, travel, writing. Studio: 407 Main St Rockland ME 04841-3305

ANNENBERG, LEONORE A., foundation administrator; m. Walter H. Annenberg; 2 children. BA, Stanford U.; PhD (hon.), Pine Manor Coll., LaSalle U., U. Pa., Brown U.; DHL (hon.), U. So. Calif., 1998. Former chief of protocol for U.S.A. Pres., chair, sole dir. Annenberg Found.; founding mem. governing bd. Annenberg sch. comm. U. Pa., Annenberg sch. comm. U. So. Calif.; founder Am. Friends Covent Garden; past chmn., hon. chmn. Friends Art and Preservation Embassies; mem. trustee's coun. Nat. Gallery Art; mem. Com. Preservation White House; mng. dir. Met. Opera; mem. Acad. Music Com.; past pres., hon. trustee Palm Springs Desert Mus.; hon. trustee performing arts coun. L.A. Music Ctr.; trustee emeritus U. Pa.; former bd. dirs. Pa. Acad. Fine Arts, Phila. Orch. Assn.; bd. dirs. Met. Mus. Art, Phila. Mus. Art. Decorated Cavaliere Dell'Ordine Al Merito Della Repubblica Italiana, Grand Officio Order of Orange-Nassau (The Netherlands); recipient Wagner medal Robert F. Wagner grad. sch. pub. svc. NYU, Colonial Williamsburg Churchill Bell award, Nat. Medal of Arts, NEA, 1993. Fellow Am. Acad. Arts and Scis.; mem. Disting. Daus. Pa. Office: The Annenberg Found St Davids Ctr 150 Radnor Chester Rd Ste A-200 Wayne PA 19087-5293

ANNESE, DOMENICO, retired landscape architect; b. N.Y.C., June 9, 1919; s. Fedele and Antonia (Angelini) A.; m. Serafina Villanova, July 16, 1944; children: Donald F., Loretta S. Ed., SUNY Coll. Environ. Sci. and Forestry, 1942; BS in Landscape Architecture, Syracuse U., 1942. Registered landscape architect, N.Y., Pa., Conn., Mass., Ohio, Tenn. Landscape architect Clarence C. Combs, N.Y.C., 1946-50, asso., 1955-56; asst. chief landscape architect Nat. Capital Parks, Washington, 1950-55; asso. Clarke and Rapuano, Inc., N.Y.C., 1956-72, v.p., 1972-91. Vice chmn. N.Y. State Bd. Landscape Architects, 1961-67, chmn., 1967-71; mem. Pleasantville (N.Y.) Parks and Recreation Bd., 1974-83; adj. prof. urban landscape architecture CCNY, 1975-76; vis. prof., lectr. in landscape architecture Sch. Planning and Architecture, New Delhi, India, 1977; pres. Landscape Architecture Found., 1973-1975; dir. N.Y. State Coun. Landscape Architects; dir. coll. environ. sci. and forestry ESF Found., 1987-2000; dir. N.Y. Parks and Conservation Assn., 1991-1995 Served with Coast Arty., F.A. U.S. Army, 1942-46, ETO. Fellow Am. Soc. Landscape Architects, Sigma Lambda Alpha. Lutheran. Home: 315 Bedford Rd Pleasantville NY 10570-2212

ANNESI, ADELE MARY, editor, writer; b. Bayshore, NY, July 21, 1957; d. John Carmine and Adele (Frattini) Annesi. BA with honors, Bentley Coll., Waltham, Mass., 1981; Cert. Computer Graphics, Fairfield U., 1993; Cert., Wesleyan Writers Conf., 1999; Cert. Writing, Fairfield U., 2000. Adminstr. Mass. Fin. Svcs., Boston, 1981—82; asst. mgr. C-Systems, Ridgefield, Conn., 1982—83; advt. prodn. mgr. Christian Herald Mag., Chappaqua, NY, 1983—86; p.r. mgr. Housetronic Area Regional Transit, Danbury, Conn., 1986—87; mktg. mgr. Digitech, Danbury, 1987—2000; editor Scholastic Pub., Danbury, Conn., 2001—; writer Hersam Acorn Newspapers, Conn., 2000—. Writers residency Wisdom House, Harwinten, Conn., 2001. Meals provider Dorothy Day Hospitality House, Danbury, Conn., 1994—98; contbr. Cir. Lit. Jour., 2002—. Recipient Editor's Choice award, Nat. Libr. of Poetry, Md., 1998. Mem.: Conn. Authors and Pub. Assn., Shepaug River Writer's Group, Conn. Authors and Publishers Assn., Wellspring Writers' Group (coord. 2002—03). Democrat. Presbyterian. Avocations: hiking, reading, singing, travel. Office: Scholastic Publishing 90 Old Sherman Tpk Danbury CT 06816 Office Phone: 203-797-3486.

ANNESLEY, THOMAS MICHAEL, clinical chemist, pathology educator; b. Kewanee, Ill., Nov. 21, 1953; s. Charles Louis and Betty Jane Elsbecker; m. Linda Meeker, June 21, 1975. BA, Gustavus Adolphus, 1975; PhD, Rice U., 1979. Diplomate Am. Bd. Clin. Chemistry. Resident Mayo Clinic, Rochester, Minn., 1979-81; asst. prof. pathology U. Mich., Ann Arbor, Mich., 1981-87, lab. dir., 1981—, assoc. prof. pathology, 1988-94, prof. pathology, 1995—. Assoc. editor Clin. Chemistry; mem. editorial bd. sci. reviewer; contbr. articles to profl. jours. Ch. sch. tchr. St. Clare Ch., Ann Arbor, 1982-84, 88-91, vestry mem., 1985-88, 2001—. Recipient Young Investigator award Acad. Clin. Lab. Physicians, 1981, 1st Decade award Gustavus Adolphus Coll., 1985. Fellow Nat. Acad. Clin. Biochemistry (bd. dirs. 1999—); mem. Am. Assn. Clin. Chemistry (chmn. Mich. 1986, exec. com. TDM div. 1988, sec. TDM div. 1991—, nat. awards com. 1990, 91, clin. Chemist Recognition award 1985, Young Investigator award 1987, house of del. 1999—), Assn. Clin. Scientists, Clin. Ligand Assay Soc. (nat. meeting planning vol. 1990-91), Am. Bd. Clin. Chemists (bd. dirs. 1991-97). Avocations: scuba diving, golf. Home: 2530 Powell Ave Ann Arbor MI 48104-6467 Office: U Mich Hosp 1500 E Med Ctr Dr Ann Arbor MI 48109 E-mail: annesley@umich.edu.

ANNEXSTAD, AL, insurance company executive; s. Alice Annexstad. Graduated Minn. State Univ. Pres., CEO Federated Ins., 1999, also chmn. Office: Federated Mutual Insurance PO Box 328 121 E Park Sq Owatonna MN 55060-0328

ANNING, ROBERT DOAN HOPKINS, brokerage company executive; b. Cin., Apr. 16, 1940; s. Robert H. and Marjorie Thuma Anning; m. Sydney Ann Fish, July 6, 1963; children: Sydney M., Robert H. II, John H. II, Elizabeth M. BA, Trinity Coll., 1963. 1st v.p. investments Merrill Lynch Global Pvt. Client Group, 1967—. Bd. trustees Convalescent Hosp. for Children, 1985—2005, emeritus trustee, 2005—, chmn., 1988—94; bd. trustees The Children's Hosp., Cin., 1989—, pres., 2004—, chmn., 2003—; bd. trustees Cin. Children's Hosp. Med. Ctr., 1990—, Cerebral Palsy Svcs. Ctr., United Cerebral Palsy Cin., 1994—2003, Cin. Parks Found., 1995—, pres., 1999—2000; bd. trustees Found. Family Svc., 1997—, Family Svc. Cin. Area, 1998—99. Lt. USNR, 1963—67. Named one of All-Pro Stockbrokers Money mag., 1990, All-Star Brokers, 1994-96, Blue-Chip Brokers Town and Country mag., 1992. Mem.: Commonwealth Club, Queen City Club, Univ. Club, Camargo Club, Cin. Country Club. Home: 25 Weebetook Ln Cincinnati OH 45208-3330 Office Phone: 513-579-3673.

ANNIS, CARL ROBERT, music educator; b. Chgo., Oct. 7, 1958; s. Robert Richard and Phyllis L. Annis; m. Patricia Ann Annis, July 24, 1988. BA in Music Edn., Northeastern Ill. U., 1982. Profl. trombonist, 1976—; mem. staff Schurz H.S., Chgo., 1983—86, instrumental music instr., 1986—92, band dir., 1992—. Arranger, composer: 50 titles, 1976—. Mem.: Internat. Assn. Jazz Educators, Music Educators Nat. Conf., Chgo. Fedn. Musicians. Avocation: cooking. Home: 5353 W Pensacola Ave Chicago IL 60641-1309

ANNIS, PATRICIA ANNE, textile scientist, researcher, educator; b. Council Bluffs, Iowa; d. Maurice Hamilton and Margaret Jean (Parquet) Wilson; m. Michael Clifford Annis; 1 child, Paul Michael. MS, U. Ark., 1980; PhD, Kans. State U., 1988. Instr. Keokuk (Iowa) Community Schs., 1974-77; rsch. and teaching asst. U. Ark., Fayetteville, 1978-80, instr., 1980-81; rsch. asst. Kans. State U., Manhattan, 1982-87; asst. prof. textile scis. U. Ga., Athens, 1988-93, assoc. prof., 1993—. Expert witness on textile trace evidence; rsch. cons. to corp. and fed. orgns. related to the textile industry, 1987—. Contbg. author: (chpt.) Microstructural Characterization of Fibre Rainforced Composites; contbr. articles to Textile Rsch. Jour., Jour. Forensic Scis., AATCC Review, Can. Textile Jour., Jour. of Textile Inst., and others Recipient Faculty Rsch. Commercialization award Advanced Tech. Devel. Ctr., 1993; named Advisor or Yr., U. Ga., Tchr. of Yr., U. Ga.; Kappa Omicron Nu fellow, 1986, Phi Upsilon Omicron fellow, 1986, 87; grantee Hoechst-Celanese Corp., 1992, 93, Milliken Rsch. Corp., 1993, 94, Consortium for the Competiveness of the Carpet Apparel & Textile Industries, 1996—, DuPont, 1997-98, Cotton Inc., 1997-99, Absormex, 2000-02, Carpet and Rug Inst., 2002, Aquafil SPA, 2004— Mem. ASTM, INDA, Am. Assn. Textile Chemists and Colorists (first place tech. paper competition 1995), South Eastern Microscopy Soc., Sigma Xi, Gamma Sigma Delta. Achievements include patents for material wear testing devices and techniques; author 2 ASTM stds., 2003. Office: U Ga 309 Dawson Hall Athens GA 30602

ANN-MARGRET, (ANN-MARGRET OLSSON), actress, performer; b. Stockholm, Apr. 28, 1941; came to U.S., naturalized, 1949; d. Gustav and Anna Olsson; m. Roger Smith, 1967. Student, Northwestern U. Performer radio shows, band tours; appeared with: George Burns, Las Vegas, 1961; headliner numerous appearances, Las Vegas, 1961—; made NYC debut Radio City Music Hall, 1991; actress numerous films including Pocketful of Miracles, 1961, State Fair, 1961, Bye Bye Birdie, 1962, Viva Las Vegas, 1963, The Pleasure Seekers, 1964, Kitten With a Whip, 1964, Bus Riley's Back in Town, 1964, Once A Thief, 1965, Cincinnati Kid, 1965, Stagecoach, 1966, Made in Paris, 1966, The Swinger, 1966, Murderers' Row, 1967, The Tiger and the Pussycat, 1967, R.P.M., 1970, C.C. & Company, 1971, Carnal Knowledge, 1971, Train Robbers, 1972, Outside Man, 1972, Tommy, 1975, Joseph Andrews, 1976, The Last Remake of Beau Geste, 1977, Magic, 1978, The Cheap Detective, 1978, Lookin' To Get Out, 1978, The Villain, 1979, Middle-Age Crazy, 1980, The Return of the Soldier, 1982, I Ought To Be in Pictures, 1982, Twice in a Lifetime, 1985, 52-Pick-up, 1987, A Tiger's Tale, 1988, A New Life, 1988, Something More, Newsies, 1992, Grumpy Old Men, 1993, Grumpier Old Men, 1995, Seduced by Madness, 1996, The Limey, 1999, Any Given Sunday, 1999, The Last Producer, 2000, Interstate 60, 2002; several TV spls., 1975-76; TV films Who Will Love My Children, 1983, A Streetcar Named Desire, 1984, Our Sons, 1991, Nobody's Children, 1994, Seduced by Madness: The Diane Borchardt Story, 1996, Blue Rodeo, 1996, Life of the Party: The Pamela Harriman Story, 1998, Happy Face, 1999, The 10th Kingdom, 2000, Perfect Murder, Perfect Town, 2000, A Woman's a Helluva Thing, 2001; mini-series The Two Mrs. Grenvilles, 1987, Alex Haley's Queen, 1993, Scarlett, 1994, Blonde, 2001; TV series Four Corners, 1998; author: (with Todd Gold) Ann-Margret: My Story, 1994. Recipient 2 Acad. award nominations, 4 Emmy nominations, 5 Golden Globes. Office: William Morris Agy 151 S El Camino Dr Beverly Hills CA 90212-2775

ANNOTICO, RICHARD ANTHONY, legal administrator, real estate investor; b. Cleve., Sept. 17, 1930; s. Anthony and Grace (Kovarik) A. AB in Bus. with hons., Ohio U., 1953; LLB, Southwestern Law Sch., 1963; JD, UCLA, 1965. Dir. internat. sales then v.p. Liberty Records, L.A., 1957-64; real estate investment counselor Calif. Land Sales, Beverly Hills, 1964-66, R.A. Annotico & Assocs., L.A., 1966-68, real estate investor, 1969—. Spkr. in field.; mem. Bd. of Governors State Calif.; expert witness State Legis. Calif. Contbr. numerous articles to profl. jours. Commr. L.A. Transp. Commn., 1984-88, v.p. 1985-87; commr. L.A. Human Rels. Comm n., 1977-84, pres. 1983-84; mem. Calif. State Senate Small Bus. Adv. Bd., 1978-82, L.A. City County Adv. Commn. on Consolidation, 1976-77; pres. Federated Italian-Americans So. Calif., 1975-76; mem. Mayors Exec. Com. Christopher Columbus Quincentenary 1992. Lt. USAF, 1954-55. Decorated Cavaliere Ufficiale Order of Merit (Italy), Comdr. St. Lazarus Internat. Chivalric, Hospitaller and Mil. Order. Mem. Calif. State Bar Assn. (bd. govs., 1983-86, 86-89, 89-92, v.p. 1986, 89, 92). Office: Admiralty Suites 4170 Admiralty Way # 1G Marina Del Rey CA 90292

ANNS, ARLENE EISERMAN, publishing company executive; b. Pearl River, NY; d. Frederick Joel and Anna (Behnke) Eiserman. Student, Fairleigh Dickinson U., 1946—48; BS, Utah State U., 1950; postgrad., Traphagen Sch. Design, 1957, NYU, 1958, Hunter Coll., 1959—60. Rsch. and promotion asst. Archtl. Record, N.Y.C., 1952-56; asst. rsch. dir. Esquire Mag., N.Y.C., 1956-62; rsch. mgr. Am. Machinist publ. McGraw-Hill, Inc., N.Y.C., 1962-67, mktg. svc. mgr., 1967-69, 69-71, sales mgr., 1976-77, dir. mktg., 1977-78; v.p. mktg. svcs. Morgan Gramplan, Inc., N.Y.C., 1971-72; mktg. dir. Family Health and Diversion mag., 1972-74; dist. sales mgr. Postgrad. Medicine, 1974-76; advt. sales mgr. Contempory Ob/Gyn, 1976-78, dir. profl. devel., 1978-80; pub. graduating engr., dir. mktg. Aviation Week Group, 1980-90; pub. World Aviation Directory; dir. comms. Aviation Week Group, 1990-92; v.p. Phase, Ltd., 1993—. Mem. Am. Mktg. Assn., Pharm. Advt. Club, Advt. Women N.Y., Advt. Club N.Y., Sales Exec. Club, Employment Mgmt. Assn., Am. Soc. Pers. Adminstrs., Nat. Orgn. Disability (bd. dirs.), Internat. Platform Assn., Coll. Placement Coun., U. Va. Libr. Assoc. Bd., Svc. Corps Ret. Execs. (chair), Wings Club, Dir. Assn., Pi Sigma Alpha. Home: Barnahill Farm 6653 Celt Rd Stanardsville VA 22973-3638 Personal E-mail: theanns@earthink.net.

ANNS, PHILIP HAROLD, brokerage house executive, pharmaceutical executive; b. London, Eng., June 24, 1925; came to U.S., 1950; s. Harold Falkner and Dorothy Louise (Torckler) A.; m. Jacqueline Estelle Wyrtzen, Dec. 27, 1952 (div. 1975); 1 child, Jean Anns; m. Arlene Claire Eiserman, Apr. 1, 1978. BA in Econs., Christ Coll., Cambridge, Eng., 1948, MA in Econs., 1950. Asst. to pres. BASF Inc., N.Y.C., 1954-58; gen. mgr. Squibb Australia E.R. Squibb and Sons, Princeton, N.J., 1958-68, dir. animal health New Brunswick, N.J.; gen. mgr. animal health Am. Hoechst, Kansas City, Mo., 1968-72; exec. v.p. Lakeside Labs., Milw., 1972-75; sr. v.p., gen. mgr. internat. div. A.H. Robins Co., Inc., Richmond, Va., 1975-85, sr. v.p. corp. govt. relations Washington, 1986-90; pres. Phase Ltd., Arlington, Va., 1990—. With Va. Dist. Export Coun.; mem. Congl. staff U.S. Ho. of Reps., 1990—. Mem. Indsl. Devel. Authority, Greene County, Va. Served to lt. Brit. Royal Navy, 1943-46, ETO. Mem. Rotary. Republican. Episcopalian. Home and Office: 6653 Celt Rd Stanardsville VA 22973-3638 Personal E-mail: theanns@earthlink.net.

ANNULIS, JOHN THOMAS, mathematics professor; b. Cin., Nov. 13, 1945; s. John James and Vivian Marie (Jaeger) A.; m. Elizabeth Bruce, Jan. 25, 1969; children: Laura Elizabeth, Leah Catherine. BA, Grand Valley State Coll., 1966; MA, U. N.Mex., 1968, PhD, 1971. Asst. prof. math. U. Wis., Whitewater, 1971-72, U. Ark., Monticello, 1972-75, assoc. prof., 1975-81, prof., 1981—, head dept. math. and physics, 1979-82, dean, Coll. of Gen. Studies, 1993-97, dean Sch. Math. and Scis., 1997—. Contbr. articles to profl. jours. Named Disting. Alumnus, Grand Valley State Coll., 1985. Mem. Math. Assn. Avocations: gardening, reading. Home: 158 Glenwood Dr Monticello AR 71655-5544 Office: Univ Ark Sch Math & Natural Scis Monticello AR 71656-3480 Office Phone: 870-460-1016. Business E-Mail: annulisj@UAMont.edu.

ANNUNZIATA, ROBERT, fiber optics company executive; Pres. AT&T, until 1999; CEO, dir. Global Crossongs Ltd., Beverly Hills, Calif., 1999—.

ANNUS, JOHN AUGUSTUS, artist; b. Riga, Latvia, Oct. 25, 1935; U.S., 1949; s. Augustus and Irma (Gustavs) A.; m. Edite Zeile, Oct. 18, 1981; 1 dau., Aurelia 1 dau., by previous marriage, Fabiola. B.F.A., Pratt Inst., 1958; postgrad., Art Students League, 1958-59, Nat. Acad. Design, 1958-59, Academia de Belli Arti, Rome, 1962-64. One-man shows include Am. Acad. in Rome, 1960, Arte al Berge, Palermo, 1963, Archtl. League, N.Y., 1965, Vendo Nubes, Phila., 1965, 70, 76, Galleria del Vantaggio, Rome, 1962, 71, 73, 74, Galerie Clasing, Germany, 1982, T.L.C. Gallery, Toronto, 1985, Jacobi Gallery, Hamburg, 1987, 92, Raitern Gallery, Riga, Latvia, 1989, Gallery K. Munster, Germany, 1992, Internat. Mus., Riga, 1993, Jannus Image, Munster, 1993, 95, Design Technik GmbH Gallery-Verlag, Hamburg, 1995, Kunsthaus Schone, Anderhach, Germany, 2002-03; group shows include Spectrum 5, N.Y.C., 1972, 73, Skidmore Coll., N.Y.C., 1975, U. Pa., 1976, NAD, 1958, 59, 64, 67, 68, 75, 80, 91, Nat. Acad. Design Mems., 1993, Nat. Acad. Design Academician, 1995, Images Photokina, Cologne, Germany, 1996, 2nd internat. HRS Exhibition-Riga Latvia, 1998, Nat. Acad. Design, 2003; represented in permanent collections NAD, Balt. Mus., Collection of the Italian Govt., Henry Ranger Fund, Am. Acad. in Rome. Recipient Gold medal for oil painting Labyrinth, 1962; recipient Wallace Truman prize for oil painting Agrigento, 1967, Ranger Purchase prize for By the Sea, 1965, Reflection, 1965, award of Excellence for By the Sea, 1982; Nat. Acad. Design grantee, 1958-59, Albert Hallgarten traveling grantee, 1958-59; Prix de Rome Am. Acad. in Rome, 1959-60; Italian Govt. grantee, 1962— Mem. Nat. Acad. Design (academician), Soc. Fellows, Am. Acad. Rome (Centennial Directory listee), Nat. Soc. Mural Painters, others Lutheran. Office Phone: +49 (0)341 4980371. Personal E-mail: johnaugustusannus@hotmail.com.

ANOATUBBY, BILL, governor of Chickasaw Nation; b. Nov. 8, 1945; m. Janice Marie Loman, Dec. 23, 1967; children: Chris, Brian. AS, Murray State Coll., 1970; BS, East Ctrl. State Coll., 1972. Acct., office mgr. Am. Plating Co., 1972-74; acct., systems & budgetary contr. Little Giant Corp., 1974-75; dir. health svcs. The Chickasaw Nation, Ada, Okla., 1975-76, dir. acctg., 1976-78, spl. asst. to gov., 1978-79, lt. gov., 1979-87, gov., 1987—. Trustee Morris K. Udall Scholarship and Excellence in Nat. Environ. Policy Found., 1994-2000. Mem. adv. com. Okla. Dept. Commerce, 1990; mem. Trail of Tears Nat. Historic Adv. Com., 1990-92; trustee Oklahoma City U., 1991-98; trustee Native Am. Cultural Edn. Authority, 1998—. Recipient Gov.'s ARTS award, 1997; named Okla. Minority Bus. Advocate of Yr., U.S. SBA, 1995; named to Okla. Hall of Fame, 2004, Honored One and Friend of the Ct., Supreme Ct. Okla., 2005. Mem. Inter-Tribal Coun. of Five Civilized Tribes (past v.p., pres.), Ada Area C. of C. (bd. dirs.), Okla. Indian Affairs Commn. Democrat. Office: Chickasaw Nation PO Box 1548 Ada OK 74821-1548 Office Phone: 405-436-2603. Business E-Mail: bill.anoatubby@chickasaw.net.

ANONIA, FRANCIS, music educator; b. Danville, Pa., May 9, 1981; s. Charlotte Nicole and Robert Herman Kluge. MusB, Susquehanna U., 1999—2003. Choir mgr. Susquehanna U. Choir, Selinsgrove, Pa., 2000—03; dir. of choral activities Whitehall H.S., Whitehall, Pa., 2003—. Musical dir. Whitehall H.S., 2003—, chorale dir., 2003—. Mem.: MENC, Am. Choral Director's Assn., Pa. Music Educators Assn., Kappa Delta Pi (pres. 2002—03), Phi Mu Alpha Sinfonia (frat. edn. officer 2001—03). Office: Whitehall HS 3800 Mechanicsville Rd Whitehall PA 18052 Office Phone: 610-437-5081. Personal E-mail: anoniaf@cliu.org.

ANSAR, SABAH, toxicologist, research scientist; d. Ansar Ahmad and Shahnaz Ansar; m. Feroze Farhat, Jan. 19, 2002; 1 child, Sarah Farhat. PhD, AU, India, 2000; BS Toxicology, A. U. Cert. Toxicologist UP, 2000. Rsch. asst. HU, Delhi, India, 1998—2000; post doctoral rsch. assoc. KU, Lawrence, Kans., 2002—. Ednl. mentor KU, Lawrence, Kans., 2004—. Scientist U. Kans., Lawrence, Kans., 2002—04. Recipient Scientist travelling award, 1999. Mem.: Soc. of Neuroscience. Achievements include research in Alzheimers research; Graduate research scholarship; Honorary Research fellowship. Office: Dept Pharmacology and Toxicology 5064 Malot Hall 1251 Wescoe Hall Dr Lawrence 66044 Business E-Mail: sabah@ku.edu.

ANSARI, MOHAMMED RAFIULLAH, surgeon; b. Gokaram, India, Oct. 10, 1935; came to U.S., 1967, naturalized, 1977; s. Mohammed Mahboob Ali and Abbas (Bibi) A.; m. Raoof Yasmin, June 2, 1962; 1 child, Farrah Yasmin. BS, Osmania U., 1957, MB, BChir, 1962. Asst. surgeon Dist. Hosp., Karimnagar, India, 1963—67; intern St. Luke Hosp., St. Paul, 1967—68; resident Henry Ford Hosp., Detroit, 1968—73, staff surgeon, 1973—; clin. instr. surgery U. Mich., Detroit, 1976—80, clin. asst. prof., 1980—. Recipient Roy D. McClure Surg. award Henry Ford Hosp.-McClure Surg. Soc., 1971. Mem. AMA, ACS, Midwest Surg. Assn., Mich. State Med. Soc., Acad. Surgery Detroit. Republican. Moslem. Home: 3016 Westman Ct Bloomfield Hills MI 48304-2062 Office: 2799 W Grand Blvd Detroit MI 48202-2608 Office Phone: 248-644-2654. Personal E-mail: mransari@aol.com.

ANSART, GUILLAUME, French language educator; b. Paris, Dec. 10, 1960; s. Etienne and Jacqueline (Renié) A.; m. Dorothy Tilenis, July 26, 1986. BA, U. Paris VII, 1982, MA, 1983; PhD, Princeton U., 1995. Asst. prof. French Ind. U., Bloomington, Ind., 1995-2001, assoc. prof. French, 2001—. Author: Réflexion utopique et pratique romanesque au siècle des Lumières, 1999; contbr. articles to profl. jours. Mem. MLA, Am. Soc. 18th Century Studies, Am. Assn. Tchrs. of French. Office: Indiana U Dept French & Italian 1020 E Kirkwood Ave Bloomington IN 47405 E-mail: gansart@indiana.edu.

ANSARY, CYRUS A., investment company executive, lawyer; b. Shoraz, Oram, Nov. 20, 1933; s. A. R. and Jamali (Mostmand) Ansary; m. Janet C. Hodges, Aug. 1, 1970; children: Douglas C., Pary Ann, Jeffrey C., Bradley C. BS, Am. U., 1955; LLB, Columbia U., 1958. Bar: Md. 1959, D.C. 1960, Va. 1961. Pvt. practice, Washington, 1959-72; sr. ptnr. firm Ansary, Kirkpatrick and Rosse, 1964-72; chmn. bd. Industry Reports, Inc., Washington, 1960-72; organizer, 1st chmn. bd., pres. Woodland Nat. Bank, Alexandria, Va., 1963-67; lectr. Sch. Bus. Adminstrn., Am. U., 1967-71; chmn. bd. Fin. Dynamics Corp., Washington, 1967-72, Campbell Music Co., Washington, 1968-72, John L. Lindstrom and Assocs., Inc., Washington, 1962-86; pres. IK Investment A.G., Zurich, Switzerland, 1974-79, Investment Svcs. Internat. Co., Washington, 1973—; chmn. MACO Bancorp, Washington, 1988—95. Bd. dirs. Washington Mut. Investors Fund, J. P. Morgan Value Opportunities Fund, Am. Funds Tax-Exempt Series I, Fort Knox Nat. Co. Trustee Am. U., 1968—96, chmn. bd., 1982—91; trustee Internat. Law Inst., 1976—88, Wolf Trap Found., Vienna, Va., 1977—82, Fried Krupp Found., Essen, Germany, 1977—79, Washington Opera Soc., 1982—89; pres. Ansary Found., Washington, 1983—; mem. Woodrow Wilson Coun., Washington, 2000—. With USMCR, 1959—64. Mem.: Nat. Economists Club, Washington Assn. Money Mgrs., Nat. Press Club, Econ. Club Washington, Washington Soc. Investment Analysts, City Club, Chevy Chase Country Club (Bethesda), Met. Club (Washington), Rotary. Office: 1725 K St NW Ste 410 Washington DC 20006-1401 E-mail: cansary@isicollc.com.

ANSARY, MIR TAMIM, writer; b. Kabul, Afghanistan, Nov. 4, 1948; s. Mir Amanuddin Ansary and Terttu Maria Palm; m. Deborah Gale Krant, Sept. 11, 1981; children: Jessamyn Sylvie, Elina Marie. BA, Reed Coll., 1970. Writer Portland Scribe, Portland, Oreg., 1973—76; editor The Asia Found., San Francisco, 1976—79, Harcourt Brace Jovanovich, Orlando, Fla., 1980—84; freelance writer, 1989—; writer, columnist Encarta, Seattle, 2000—. Author: Holiday Histories, 1998, Native Americans, 1999, West of Kabul, East of

New York, 2002. Dir. San Francisco Writers Workshop, San Francisco, 1997—. Achievements include 900 word email "An Afghan American Speaks" written after 9/11. E-mail: tamim@mirtamimansary.com.

ANSBACHER, BARRY BARNETT, lawyer; b. Jacksonville, Fla., Jan. 7, 1963; s. Lewis and Sybil Ansbacher; m. Elaine Kenny, Aug. 30, 1992. BA, U. Fla., 1985, JD, 1988. Bar: Fla. 1989, D.C. 1989; bd. cert. real estate atty. Fla. Atty. Ansbacher & Schneider PA, Jacksonville, 1989-97; pvt. practice law Jacksonville, 1997—. Pres. Attys. Real Property Coun. NE Fla., Inc., Jacksonville; pub. rep. on Pvt. Provider Task Force Fla. Bldg. Commn., 2004. Author: Complex Real Estate Transactions-Subdivisions, 1997, 98, Issues of Transboundary Pollution in North America, 1988. Named Outstanding Young Men of Am., 1986. Mem. Fla. Bar Assn. (exec. coun. cir. rep. real property, probate and trust law sect. 1998), Jacksonville Bar Assn. Jewish. Avocation: equestrian sports. Office: 1301 Riverplace Blvd Ste 2540 Jacksonville FL 32207-9032 Office Phone: 904-396-8050. Business E-Mail: Info@ansbacher.net.

ANSBACHER, RUDI, physician; b. Sidney, N.Y., Oct. 11, 1934; s. Stefan and Beatrice (Michel) A.; m. Elisabeth Cornelia Vellenga, Nov. 19, 1965; children— R. Todd, Jeffrey N. Grad., Harvard Coll., 1951; BA, Va. Mil. Inst., 1955; MD, U. Va., 1959; MS, U. Mich., 1970. Diplomate Am. Bd. Ob-Gyn. Staff ob-gyn, chief clin. investigation Brooke Med. Ctr., San Antonio, 1971-75, asst. chief ob-gyn, 1975-77; chief dept. ob-gyn Letterman Army Med. Ctr., San Francisco, 1977-80; from prof. ob-gyn to prof. emeritus U. Mich., Ann Arbor, 1980—2001, prof. emeritus, 2002—. Cons. Biomed. Adv. Com. Population Resource Ctr., 1978-81; bd. dirs. Health Policy Internat. Contbr. articles to profl. jours., chpts to books; mem. editorial bds., reviewer jours. Served to col. U.S. Army, 1960-80. Named Disting. Mil. Grad. Va. Mil. Inst., Lexington, Va., 1955; NIH grantee, 1973-78 Fellow ACOG (Chmn.'s award 1970), AAAS; mem. Am. Fertility Soc. (dir. 1979-82), Am. Soc. Andrology (sec. 1978-80, pres. 1984-85), Central Assn. Ob-Gyn, Assn. Mil. Surgeons U.S., Soc. for Study Reprodn., Mich. State Med. Soc. (bd. dirs. 1995-2005, sec. 2005—), Mich. State Med. Soc. Found. (bd. dirs. 2003—), Physician's Rev. Orgn. Mich. (bd. dirs. 2000-). Republican. Presbyterian. Avocations: tennis, softball, gardening, skiing. Home: 3755 Tremont Ln Ann Arbor MI 48105-3022 Office Phone: 734-763-4344. Business E-Mail: ansbache@med.umich.edu.

ANSBACHER, SIDNEY FRANKLYN, lawyer; b. Jacksonville, Fla., May 28, 1961; m. Theresa Marie Rooney; stepchildren: Emily Matchett, Katelyn Matchett; 1 child from previous marriage, Benjamin Alexander. BA, U. Fla., 1981; JD, Hamline U., 1985; LLM in Agrl. Law, U. Ark., 1989. Bar: Fla., U.S. Dist. Ct. (mid. dist.) Fla., U.S. Ct. Appeals (D.C. cir.). Atty. Fla. Dept. Natural Resources, Tallahassee, 1986-87; assoc. Turner, Ford, Buckingham, Jacksonville, Fla., 1987-90; ptnr., assoc. Brant, Moore et al, Jacksonville, Fla., 1990-95; ptnr. Mahoney Adams & Criser, Jacksonville, Fla., 1995-97, Upchurch Bailey & Upchurch, St. Augustine, Fla., 1997—. Contbr. articles to profl. jours.; mng. editor Fla. Bar Environ. and Land Use CLE Manual, 1998—. Bd. dirs. Fla. Forestry Found., 1993-96. Recipient Outstanding Achievement award Fla. Wildlife Fedn., 1990. Mem.: Jacksonville Bar Assn. (chair environ. and land use law sect. 1994—96), Fla. Bar (bd. dirs. 1994—, chair environ. and land use law sect. 2001—02), Judy Florence Outstanding Svc. award 1992, 2000). Office: Upchurch Bailey & Upchurch PA 780 N Ponce De Leon Blvd Saint Augustine FL 32084-3519 Office Phone: 904-829-9066. Business E-Mail: sfansbacher@ubulaw.com.

ANSBRO, JOHN JOSEPH, philosopher, educator; b. NYC, Nov. 16, 1932; s. Thomas and Katherine (Reilly) Ansbro. BA, St. Joseph's Sem., Yonkers, N.Y., 1954, postgrad., 1955; MA, Fordham U., 1957, PhD, 1964. Lectr. philosophy Manhattan Coll., Riverdale, NY, 1958-59, instr., 1959-63, asst. prof., 1963-68, assoc. prof., 1968-79, prof., 1979-96; ret., 1996; writer, 1996—. Curriculum guidance supr. faculty counselors Sch. Arts & Scis. Manhattan Coll., 1962—73, chmn. co-curricular interdisciplinary arts program, 1962—70, chmn. com. faculty rsch. projects and grants, 1976—78, 1989—92, chmn. dept. philosophy, 1977—81, chmn. sabbatical leave com., 1989—91, dir. rsch. peace studies program, 1990—91, com. faculty rsch. projects, mem. instnl. rev. bd. human subjects, task force acad. programs, liaison officer Danforth Found., others; adj. asst. prof. philos. resources contemporary problems program Grad. Sch. Arts & Scis., Fordham U., 1975; chmn. Met. Round Table Philosophy, 1972—75; project field coord. N.Y. State Dept. Edn., 1965—67; founder, pres. Manhattan Coll. Coun. World Hunger, 1977—85. Author Martin Luther King, Jr.: The Making of a Mind, 1982, Martin Luther King, Jr.: The Making of a Mind, Mex. trans., 1985, Martin Luther King, Jr.: Nonviolent Strategies and Tactics for Social Change, 2d edit., 2000, The Credos of Eight Black Leaders: Converting Obstacles into Opportunities, 2004; contbr. 40 articles in philos., ednl. and civil rights jours. US, Europe, Asia, numerous philos. reviews. Grantee Travel and Study, Ford Found., 1973, Summer, Am. Can. Co. Found., 1985, Samuel Rubin Found., 1985; scholar, Fordham U. Grad. Sch., 1956—57. Mem.: AAUP, Gandhi-King Soc., Soren Kierkegaard Soc., Soc. Ancient Greek Philosophy, Hegel Soc. Am., Am. Philos. Assn., Soc. Advancement Am. Philosophy.

ANSCHER, MITCHELL STEVEN, physician, educator; b. N.Y.C., June 15, 1955; MD, Med. Coll. Va., Richmond, 1977—81. Diplomate Am. Bd. Radiology, 1987. Prof., radiation oncology Duke U. Med. Ctr., Durham, NC, 2000—. Fellow: Am. Coll. Radiation Oncology. Office: Duke Univ Med Ctr Box 3085 DUMC Durham NC 27710 Office Phone: 919-668-5637. Office Fax: 919-668-7345. E-mail: ansch001@notes.duke.edu.

ANSCHUTZ, PHILIP F., transportation executive, communications executive; b. Russell, Kans., 1939; m. Nancy Anschutz. BS, Univ. Kans., 1961. Dir. chair. QCC, 1993—; founder Anschutz Corp., Denver, 1965; dir. chair. Anschutz Co., Denver, 1991—; CEO, dir. Anschutz Corp., Denver, 1992—; dir. So. Pacific Rail Corp., San Francisco, 1988-96; chair. So Pacific Rail Corp., 1988-96; vice chmn. (merger with So Pacific Rail Corp) Union Pacific, San Francisco, 1996—; dir. Forest Oil Corp., 1995—, Qwest Comm., 1997—, chmn., 1997—2002; co-owner L.A. Kings, 1995—; owner L.A. Galaxy, 1996—; investor-operator Major League Soccer, 1995—; owner San Francisco Examiner, The Ind., Grant Printing Co., San Francisco, 2004—. Board Mem: Am. Petroleum Inst., Nat. Petroleum Council, Nat. Hockey League, Kansas Univ. Endowment Assoc., Regal Entertainment Group. Named one of 200 Top Collectors, ARTnews Mag., 2004. Avocation: Collecting 19th and 20th century Am. art, especially Western. Address: 555 17th St Ste 2400 Denver CO 80202-3941 also: Quest Communications 1801 California St Inglewood CA 80202*

ANSELL, EDWARD ORIN, lawyer; b. Superior, Wis., Mar. 29, 1926; s. H. S. and Mollie (Rudnitzky) A.; m. Hanne B. Baer, Dec. 23, 1956; children: Deborah, William. BSEE, U. Wis., 1948; JD, George Washington U., 1955. Bar: D.C. 1955, Calif. 1960. Electronic engr. FCC, Buffalo and Washington, 1948-55; patent atty. RCA, Princeton, NJ, 1955-57; gen. mgr. AeroChem. Rsch. Labs., Princeton, 1957-58; patent atty. Aerojet-Gen. Corp., La Jolla, Calif., 1958-63, corp. patent counsel, 1963-82, asst. sec., 1970-79, sec., 1979-82, assoc. gen. counsel, 1981-82; dir. patents and licensing Calif. Inst. Tech., Pasadena, Calif., 1982-92; pvt. practice Claremont, Calif., 1992—; co-founder Gryphon Pharms., South San Francisco, 1993, Ciphergen BioSystems, Fremont, Calif., 1993. Adj. prof. U. La Verne (Calif.) Coll. Law, 1972-78; spl. advisor, task force chmn. U.S. Commn. Govt. Procurement, 1971 Editor: Intellectual Property in Academe: A Legal Compendium, 1991; contbr. articles to profl. publs. Recipient Alumni Svc. award George Washington U., 1975. Mem. Am. Intellectual Property Law Assn., Assn. Corp. Patent Counsel, Ea. Bar Assn. Los Angeles County, L.A. Intellectual Property Law Assn., Assn. Univ. Tech. Mgrs., State Bar Calif. (exec. com. intellectual property sect. 1983-86), Athenaeum Club Pasadena, Univ. Club Claremont. Office: 427 N Yale Ave # 204 Claremont CA 91711 Office Phone: 909-621-1985. Personal E-mail: anselaw@verizon.net.

ANSELL, JOSEPH PAUL, director, art educator; b. Bethesda, Md., July 19, 1949; s. Leonard Raymond and Shirley Wolfson Ansell. BA, Knox Coll., 1971; MFA, George Washington U., 1975. From instr. to asst. prof. U. Md., College Park, 1979—91; prof. and chair dept. art Otterbein Coll., Westerville, Ohio, 1991—96; dean of faculty and instnl. programs Sch. Mus. Fine Arts, Boston, 1996—99; prof. and head dept. art Auburn U., Ala., 2001—, interim dir. Jule Collins Smith Mus. Fine Art, 2003—04, interim dean Coll. Liberal Arts, 2004—05. Exhbn. cons. U.S. Holocaust Meml. Mus., Washington, 2000—03. Author: Arthur Szyk: Artist, Jew Pole, 2004; contbr. articles to profl. jours. Art auction chair E. Ala. AIDS Outreach, Auburn, 2002, 2003. Mem.: Coll. Art Assn. (chair edn. com. 1992—96, chmn. diversity com. 2004—05). Home: 1309 Gatewood Dr # 408 Auburn AL 36830 Office: Dept Art Auburn U 108 Biggin Hall Auburn University AL 36849

ANSELL, JULIAN S., urologist, educator; b. Portland, Maine, June 30, 1922; s. Jacob M. and Anna Gertrude (Fieldman) A.; m. Eva Ruth Ballin, June 17, 1951; children: Steven, Jody, Carol, Ellen, Peter. BA, Bowdoin Coll., 1946; MD, Tufts U., 1951; PhD, U. Minn., 1959. Intern in surgery U. Minn. Hosps., Mpls., 1951-52, resident in urology, 1952-54; NIH fellow U. Minn., Mpls., 1954, instr., 1956-59; asst. prof., head urology U. Wash., Seattle, 1959-62, assoc. prof., head urology, 1962-64, prof., chair urology, 1965-87, prof. urology, 1987-92, prof. emeritus, 1992—. With U.S. Army, 1943-46. Mem. Am. Alpine Club. Office: 3827 49th Ave NE Seattle WA 98105-5233

ANSELM, WILLAM, aerospace engineer; s. William and Evelyn Anselm; m. Nancy Snell, Aug. 1974; children: Monica, Mark, Maxwell. BS in Engring., Syracuse U., 1974; MA in Bus., Ctrl. Mich. U., 1981. Practice lead Booz-Allen & Hamilton, Rockville, Md., 1981—90; obs. mgr. NASA Goddard Space Flight Ctr., Greenbelt, Md., 1990—. Sec.; pres. Indian Hills Cmty. Assn., Arnold, Md., 1986—2005. With US Army, 1968—72, Germany, Korea. Mem.: IEEE. Achievements include development of EOS/ICESat, Global Geospace Science WIND and POLAR satellites. Avocations: concert music, renaissance music, romantic art. Home: 7 Chautauqua Rd Arnold MD 21012-2506 Office: Goddard Space Flight Ctr Code 429 Greenbelt MD 20771 Personal E-mail: banselm@ieee.org.

ANSELME, JEAN-PIERRE LOUIS MARIE, chemist; b. Port-au-Prince, Haiti, Sept. 22, 1936; came to U.S., 1955, naturalized, 1960; s. Pierre F. and Jeanne (Kieffer) A.; m. Marie-Celine Carrie, Dec. 31, 1960; children: Fabienne, Veronika, Vanessa. BA, St. Martial Coll., Haiti, 1955; BS, Fordham U., 1959; PhD, Poly. Inst., Bklyn., 1963. Research asso. Poly. Inst. Bklyn., 1963, 65, sr. instr., 1965. NSF fellow Institut fur Organische Chemie, Munich, 1964; asst. prof. chemistry U. Mass. at Boston, 1965-68, asso. prof., 1968-70, prof., 1970—; pres. Organic Preparations and Procedures, Inc., Newton, Mass.; vis. prof. Research Inst. Indsl. Sci., Kyushu U., Fukuoka, Japan, 1972, U. Miami, Coral Gables, Fla., 1979 Author: (with others) Organic Compounds with Nitrogen-Nitrogen Bonds, 1966, N-Nitrosamines, 1979; founder, editor: Organic Preparations and Procedures, 1969-70, Organic Preparations and Procedures Internat, 1971—; contbr. (with others) articles to profl. jours. Recipient Seymour Shapiro award as outstanding grad. student organic chemistry Poly. Inst. Bklyn., 1963; Sloan fellow, 1969-71 Fellow Japan Soc. for Promotion Sci.; mem. Am. Chem. Soc., Chem. Soc. London, Sigma Xi, Phi Lambda Upsilon. Office: U Mass Dept Chemistry Harbor Campus Boston MA 02125-3393 Office Phone: 617-287-6141. Business E-Mail: jp.anselme@umb.edu.

ANSELMO, ROBERT LOUIS, writer; b. Yonkers, N.Y., Sept. 22, 1953; s. Albert Peter and Anna Marie (Zegarelli) Anselmo; 1 child, Jason. Florist, designer, East Meadow, NY, 1971—93; fed. govt. Manhaset (N.Y.) P.O., 1993—95; author Levittown, NY. Author: I Will Always Love My Grandma and Grandpa Too, 2004. Avocation: collect sports memorabilia.

ANSETH, KRISTI S., engineering educator; BS in Chem. Engring., Purdue U., 1992; PhD in Chem. Engring., U. Colo., 1994. Rsch. assoc. Purdue U., West Lafayette, Ind., 1995; rsch. fellow Mass. Inst. Tech., Cambridge, Mass., 1995—96; asst. prof. chem. engring. U. Colo., Boulder, Colo., 1996—98, Patten asst. prof. chem. engring., 1998—99, Patten assoc. prof. chem. engring., 1999—2002, asst. investigator Howard Hughes Med. Inst., 2000—; assoc. prof. surgery U. Colo. Health Sci. Ctr., Denver, 2000—; prof. chem. engring. U. Colo., Boulder, 2002—03, Tisone prof. chem. and biol. engring., 2003—, assoc. faculty dir. initiative in molecular biotech., 2003—, prof. (by courtesy), 2004—. Vis. rschr. Ecole Nationale Superieure de Chimie, Mulhouse, France, 1994. Recipient Career award, NSF, 1998—2002, First award, NIH, 1998—2003, Dow Outstanding New Faculty award, Am. Soc. Engring. Edn., 1999, Outstanding Young Investigator award, Materials Rsch. Soc., 2001, Curtis W. McGraw award, Am. Soc. Engring. Edn., 2003, Allan P. Colburn award, AIChE, 2003, Alan T. Waterman award, NSF, 2004, others; fellow, Am. Inst. Med. and Biol. Engring., 2001. Office: Dept Chem and Biol Engring ECCH 128 Univ Colo Boulder CO 80309-0424 Office Phone: 303-492-3147. Office Fax: 303-492-4341. E-mail: kristi.anseth@colorado.edu.

ANSHAW, CAROL, writer; b. Grosse Pointe Shores, Mich., Mar. 22, 1946; d. Henry G. and Virginia (Anshaw) Stanley; m. Charles J. White III, Mar. 15, 1969. BA, Mich. State U., 1968. Book reviewer, Voice Literary Supplement. Author: They Do It All With Mirrors, 1978, Aquamarine, 1992, Seven Moves, 1996. Tutor Literacy Council of Chgo., 1989—. Recipient Nat. Book Critics Circle citation for excellence in reviewing, 1989. Mem. Nat. Book Critics Cir., Nat. Writers Union. Democrat. Avocation: swimming.

ANSLEY, SHEPARD BRYAN, lawyer; b. July 31, 1939; s. William Bonneau and Florence Jackson (Bryan) A.; m. Boyce Lineberger, May 9, 1970; children: Anna Ansley Davis, Florence Bryan. BA, U. Ga., 1961; LLB, U. Va., 1964. Bar: Ga. 1967. Assoc. Carter & Ansley and predecessor firm Carter, Ansley, Smith & McLendon, Atlanta, 1967-73, ptnr., 1973-84, of counsel, 1984-91; with Attkisson Carter & Akers Inc., Atlanta, 1997—2000, Attkisson Carter & Co., Atlanta, 2001—04, Carter, Terry and Co., Inc., Atlanta, 2004—. Bd. dirs. Prime Bancshares, Inc., Prime Bank, FSB; chmn. bd. dirs., pres. Sodamaster Co. Am.; exec. v.p. Woodridge Realty, Inc.; sr. v.p., ACA Consulting, Inc.; fin. cons. Carter, Terry and Co. Inc.; bd. dirs., sec. CRM Co., LLC, L.A. County, Calif., bd. dirs., sec. CRM of America, LLC, Queen Creek, Ariz. Vestry mem. St. Luke's Episcopal Ch., Atlanta, 1971-74; treas., exec. com., bd. dirs. Alliance Theatre Co., Atlanta, 1974-85; trustee Atlanta Music Festival Assn., Inc., 1975—; v.p., bd. dirs. Atlanta Preservation Ctr. Inc., pres., 1988-90; bd. vis. Lineberger Cancer Rsch. Ctr. U. N.C., Chapel Hill, 1987-92; pres., Study Hall at Emmaus House, Inc., 1988-1992, bd. 1992—; bd. dirs. Margaret Mitchell House, Inc.; bd. govs. Ga. Pub. Policy Found., Inc., 1999-2001. Capt. U.S. Army, 1965-67. Mem. ABA, Ga. Bar Assn., Atlanta Bar Assn., Piedmont Driving Club. Office Phone: 404-364-2040. Personal E-mail: sbansley@bellsouth.net.

ANSORGE, IONA MARIE, retired real estate agent, musician, educator; b. Nov. 3, 1927; d. Edgar B. and Marie Louise (Bleeke) Bohn; m. Edwin James Ansorge, Sept. 13, 1949; children: Richard, Michelle. BA, Valparaiso U., 1949; cert. teaching, Drake U., 1964; MA, U. Iowa, 1976. Min. of music Our Savior Luth. Ch., Des Moines, 1949-63; dir. chorus, concert choir Johnston (Iowa) HS, 1964—75; instr. Iowa Meth. Sch. Nursing, Des Moines, 1978-87; owner, pres. Bed and Breakfast in Iowa, Ltd., 1982-86; realtor Better Homes and Gardens First Realty, Des Moines, 1986-92. Dir.: Valparaiso U. Glee Club, 1948—49, Luth. Hour Mass Children's Choir, Johnston Concert Choir European concert tour, 1972; piano soloist: Grieg Piano Concerto, 1947; composer: If Winter Comes, 1949, The Moldau, 1948. Pres. Des Moines Jaycee-ettes; spearheaded drive Des Moines Zoo; founder Messiah Luth. Ch., Des Moines, 1978; started Iowa Bed and Breakfast Industry, 1982; owner, pres. Bed and Breakfast in Iowa, Ltd.; mem. First Luth. Ch.; permanent sec. Class of 1949, Valparaiso U. Mem. LWV, AAUW, Am. Choral Dirs. Assn., Des Moines Bd. Realtors, Women's Coun. Realtors, Realtor's Million Dollar Club, Jaycee-ettes (pres. Des Moines chpt. 1957-58), Valparaiso U. Guild (charter mem. Des Moines chpt.), Mortar Bd. Lutheran. Avocations: playing piano and organ, tennis, bridge, reading, painting. Home: 8345 Twinberry Pt Colorado Springs CO 80920-5394

ANSPACH, ROBERT MICHAEL, lawyer; b. Tiffin, Ohio, Feb. 29, 1948; s. William Charles and Evelyn Helen (Smith) A.; m. Jane Evelyn Friedman, Oct. 29, 1983; children: Michael Robert, Robert Joseph, John William. BA, Cornell U., 1970, JD, 1973. Bar: Ohio 1973, U.S. Dist. Ct. (no. dist.) Ohio 1974, U.S. Ct. Appeals (6th cir.) 1976, U.S. Supreme Ct. 1976, U.S. Tax Ct. 1985. Assoc. Shumaker, Loop & Kendrick, Toledo, 1973-79, ptnr., 1979-83, mng. ptnr., 1984, adminstr. trial dept., 1985; founder, mng. ptnr. Anspach, Meeks & Nunn, L.L.P. and predecessor firm, Toledo, 1986—. Co-author: Winning in Court—The Accountant's Role in Litigation, Arbitration and Dispute Resolution, 1986. Trustee Toledo Repertoire Theatre, 1993—96, Boys and Girls Clubs Toledo, 1993—, Historic Perrysburg, Inc., 1998—99, pres., 1998—2000; trustee Toledo Cultural Arts Commn. at the Valentine Theatre, bd. chmn., 2001—. Recipient award of merit Ohio Legal Ctr., 1986. Fellow: Am. Bar Found., Ohio State Bar Found.; mem.: ABA, Def. Rsch. Inst., Nat. Assn. R.R. Trial Counsel, Toledo Bar Assn., Ohio Bar Assn. (vice chmn. jud. adminstrn. and legal reform com. 1982, lawyer's assistance com. 1986—). Avocations: singing, piano, art collecting, musical composition, tennis. Home: 535 E Front St Perrysburg OH 43551-2135 Office: Anspach Meeks & Nunn LLP Ste 1600 300 Madison Ave Toledo OH 43604-2633

ANSPACHER, JEFFREY CRAIG, international economist; b. Washington, Aug. 9, 1951; s. William Beverly and Helen (Klein) A.; m. Marion Story. BA in Econs., Lycoming Coll., 1973; MA in Econs., U. Md., 1976, MBA, 1987. Internat. economist U.S. Dept. Commerce, Washington, 1977-83, U.S. Internat. Trade Commn., Washington, 1984-91; sr. economist Law & Econs. Cons. Group, Washington, 1991—94, FCC, 1995—2002; dir. office export trading co. affairs U.S. Dept. Commerce, 2002—. Avocations: bicycling, literature. Home: 7206 Holly Ave Takoma Park MD 20912-4224 Office: US Dept Commerce Washington DC 20230 Office Phone: 202-482-6015. Personal E-mail: janspacher@hotmail.com.

ANSPACHER, STEPHEN JOHN, university official; b. Washington, Aug. 31, 1952; s. John M. and Ellinor J. (Feigl) Anspacher; m. Joanna Gould, Dec. 13, 1998; 1 child, James. BA, Columbia U., 1974, MA, 1992. Assoc. dir. intercultural rsch. Washington Internat. Ctr., 1974-76; cons. in internat. comm., Washington, 1976-83; dir. undergrad. rsch. U. N.C., Asheville, 1983-85; assoc. dir. Info. Tech. Inst., NYU, N.Y.C., 1985-89; mgr. acad. and career devel. AICPA, N.Y.C., 1989-93; dir. distance learning The New Sch., N.Y.C., 1993—96, assoc. provost, 1996—2004; v.p., dean Sch. Continuing Edn., Chauham Coll., Pitts., 2005—.

ANSPAUGH, LYNN RICHARD, research biophysicist; b. Rawlins, Wyo., May 25, 1937; s. Solon Earl and Alice Henrietta (Day) A.; m. Barbara Anne Corrigan, Nov. 2, 1965 (div.); children: Gregory, Heidi; m. Larisa Fedorovna Kornushina, Sept. 27, 1993. BA, Nebr. Wesleyan U., 1959; M in Bioradiology, U. Calif., Berkeley, 1961, PhD, 1963. Biophysicist Lawrence Livermore (Calif.) Nat. Lab., 1963-74, group leader, 1974-75, sect. leader, 1976-82, div. leader, 1982-92, dir. Risk Scis. Ctr., 1992-95, dir. Dose Reconstruction program, 1995-96; rsch. prof. radiobiology divsn. Univ. Utah, Salt Lake City, 1997—. Tchr. extension U. Calif., Berkeley, 1966-69; lectr. San Jose (Calif.) State U., 1975; guest lectr. UCLA, Stanford U., U. Calif., Davis, 1992-96; faculty affiliate Colo. State U., Ft. Collins, 1979-83; cons. EPA, Washington, 1984-85, U. Utah, Salt Lake City, 1983-88, NAS/NRC, 1998; mem. U.S. del. UN Sci. Com. on Effects of Radiation, Vienna, 1987—; mem. Nat. Coun. on Radiation Protection and Measurements, 1989-2001, hon. mem., 2002—; mem. radiation adv. com. EPA, 1999—. Contbr. articles to profl. jours. AEC fellow, 1959-61; fellow NSF, 1961-63. Fellow Health Physics Soc. (pres. environ. radiation sect. 1984-85, pres. No. Calif. chpt. 1986-87); mem. AAAS, Soc. for Risk Analysis, Internat. Union Radioecology, Radiation Rsch. Soc., Sigma Xi. Office: U Utah 729 Arapeen Dr Ste 2334 Salt Lake City UT 84108-1218 E-mail: LAnspaugh@aol.com.

ANSTATT, PETER JAN, marketing services executive; b. Haworth, N.J., Feb. 9, 1942; s. Herman E. and Margaret (Dunham) A.; m. Jean Ann Sorchiotti, Aug. 13, 1966; children: Christopher Ryan, Holley Elizabeth. BS in Printing Mgmt., Carnegie Mellon U., 1963; grad. program for mgmt. devel., Harvard U. Bus. Sch., 1977. Estimator Einson Freeman Inc., N.Y.C., 1963, project mgr., 1965-66, account exec. Fairlawn, N.J., 1966-71, gen. mgr., 1971-76, pres., chief exec. officer, 1977-78, chmn., chief exec. officer Paramus, N.J., 1978-93; pres. Enterprise Comms., Inc., Wyckoff, N.J., 1994-95; exec. dir. Buehler Challenger & Sci. Ctr., Paramus, 1995-2000; mem. Ednovations, LLC, Morristown, NJ, 2000—01, Wilmington, NC, 2002—. V.p. ops. EAC Industires, Paramus, 1978 Mem. alumni bd. govs. Blair Acad., 1974-77; bd. dirs. Ridgewood YMCA, 1981-90, bd. trustees, 1991—. Served with C.E., U.S. Army, 1963-65, Korea. Recipient Jacob Van Dyke award for Outstanding Service, Ridgewood YMCA, 1985. Mem. Point of Purchase Advt. Inst. (chmn. trade ethics com. 1973-78, chmn. ann. exhibit com. 1979, dir. 1973-81, vice chmn. bd. 1979, chmn. 1980, speaker ann. industry seminar 1977-88, Producer/Supplier of Yr. 1984, inducted into Hall of Fame, 1994), Beta Theta Pi (pres. 1962-63). Republican. Methodist. Home: 603 Gunston Ln Wilmington NC 28405-5317 E-mail: janstatt@ednovations.com. *Undying belief in God, country and the free enterprise system. Adherence to the principles of respect, fairness, achievement through teamwork, and happiness.*

ANSTEAD, HARRY LEE, state supreme court justice; b. Jacksonville, Fla., Nov. 4, 1937; m. Sue Anstead; children: Chris, Jim, Laura, Amy, Michael. BA, JD, U. Florida; grad., Nat. Coll. of State Judiciary. With Nat. Security Agency, Wash., DC; trial and appellate lawyer Fla., 1963—76; judge, then chief judge Fla. Ct. Appeals. (4th dist.), Fla., 1976—94; justice Fla. Supreme Ct., Tallahassee, 1994—, chief justice, 2002—04. Mem. Supreme Ct. Commn. on Structure of Florida's Courts; mem., vice-chair Supreme Ct. Com. on Civil Jury Instructions; mem. bd. governors Shepard Broad Law Ctr. Nova Southeastern U., St. Thomas U. Law Sch.; former chair Fla. Supreme Ct. Commn. on Professionalism. Published numerous articles relating to legal education, constitutional law, appellate practice. Founder, mem. Urban League of Palm Beach County, Beautiful Palm Beaches, Inc. Named to Hall of Fame, Boys and Girls Clubs of Am. Mem.: Fla. Bar Assn. (mem. steering com. for continuing legal education), ABA, Sons of the Am. Revolution. Office: Fla Supreme Ct 500 S Duval St Tallahassee FL 32399-6556*

ANSTICE, DAVID W., pharmaceutical executive; B of Econs., U. Sydney, Australia, 1970. Economist Australian Pharm. Mfrs. Assn., 1969—74; various positions Merck Sharp & Dohme Australia, 1974—81; with corp., domestic divsn. Merck Rsch. Labs., 1981—82; dir. mktg. and sales Merck Sharp & Dohme South Africa, 1982—84; dir. sales Merck Sharp & Dohme Australia, 1984—85, dir. mktg. and sales, 1985—86, mng. dir., 1986—88; v.p. internat. human health mktg. Merck Sharp & Dohme Internat., 1988—89; v.p. mktg. Merck Sharp & Dohme USA, 1989—91; sr. v.p. human health divsn., pres. human health Merck & Co., Inc., 1991—92, sr. v.p. Europe human health divsn., 1993, pres. human health U.S./Can., 1994—97, pres. human health for the Americas Whitehouse Station, NJ, 1997—2002, pres. human health, 2003—. Bd. dirs. Am. Found. Pharm. Edn.; bd. dirs., exec. com. Biotech. Industry Orgn., Washington; bd. dirs. Nat. Pharm. Coun., Reston, Va., chmn., 1997; bd. trustees U. Scis., Phila., Found. for Managed Care Pharmacy, Alexandria, Va., U.S. Found. of U. of Valley of Guatemala; mem. pres.'s coun. Gwynedd-Mercy Coll., Ambler, Pa.; mem. corp. adv. coun. COSSMHO, Nat. Coalition Hispanic Health and Human Svcs. Orgn., Washington; mem. corp. exec. bd. Phila. Mus. Art; mem. corp. coun. Children's Health Fund., Pitts. Chmn. steering com. Merck United Way, 1995—97. Office: Merck and Co Inc One Merck Dr Whitehouse Station NJ 08889-0100

ANSTROM, DECKER, broadcast executive; Grad., Macalester Coll., 1972; post grad., Princeton U. Sr. staff mem. Office Mgmt. and Budget, 1977—79; asst. dir. White House Office Presdl. Pers., 1979—81; pres. Pub. Strategies, Washington; exec. v.p. Nat. Cable TV Assn., 1987—93, pres., CEO, 1993—94, The Weather Channel, Atlanta, 1999—, Landmark Comm.; pres. The Weather Channel Companies. Recipient Am. Horizon Award, The Media Inst., 1999. Office: The Weather Channel 300 Interstate N Pkwy SE Atlanta GA 30339-2403

ANTAL, JOHN J., retired physicist, consultant; b. Taylor, Pa., Apr. 23, 1926; s. Joseph J. and Anna Mary (Belensky) A.; m. Berniece Baumann, Jan. 8, 1955; children: Anita, Christopher. BS, U. Scranton, 1948; MS, St. Louis U., 1949, PhD, 1952. Guest assoc. physicist Brookhaven Nat. Lab., Upton, NY, 1952—57; physicist Watertown Arsenal Lab., Mass., 1957—61; rsch. physicist Army Materials Rsch. Ctr., Watertown, 1962—94; cons. U. Mass., Harvard U. Mus. Natural History, 1997—. Lectr. NATO Summer Sch., Rhodes, Greece, 1962. Contbr. numerous articles to profl. jours. Sgt. U.S. Army, 1948. Sec. of Army Rsch. and Study fellow U.S. Dept. Army, Ispra, Italy, 1961-62. Mem. AAAS, Am. Phys. Soc., Am. Soc. Non-Destructive Testing. Achievements include patent on method of recording fast neutron images. Home: 116 Lake Rd Framingham MA 01701-4244 E-mail: johnantal@cs.com.

ANTALEK, EILEEN ELIZABETH, educational psychologist, consultant; b. Burtonwood, Eng., Jan. 16, 1957; d. Henry and Sarah Louise O'Connor; m. Michael Antalek, Feb. 16, 1980; children: Peter, Sarah. BA, Framingham State Coll., 1991; M in English, Clark U., 1994, EdD, 2004. House maintenance, Grafton, Mass., 1989-90; tutor Framingham (Mass.) State Coll., 1990-91, Clark U., Worcester, 1991-93, asst. dir. spl. needs, 1993-94, tchg. asst., 1994-95; asst. dir. Educational Directions, Westborough, Mass., 1995—. Cable access prodr. Grafton Cable Network, 1986—88. Publicity dir. North Grafton United Meth. Ch., 1986—88, Sunday sch. tchr., 1989—95, Sunday sch. supt., 1992—95, chair bd. edn., 1988—92, chair pastor parish rels., 1999—2003, chair space needs com., 2000—03. Scholar Resident, Clark U., 1991—96, Nat. Merit, 1975, 1976, David O. Wilson, Anderson Coll., 1976. Mem.: Ind. Edn. Cons. Assn., Internat. Dyslexia Assn., Consortium for Learning Disabilities, Sigma Tau Delta, Phi Eta Sigma. Avocations: textile art, motorcycling, painting, music, hiking. Office: Educational Directions 57 E Main St Ste 220 Westborough MA 01581 Fax: 508-870-1505. Office Phone: 508-870-1515 ext. 12. Business E-Mail: eileen@educationaldirections.com.

ANTALFFY, LESLIE PETER, mechanical engineer; b. Budapest, Hungary, Oct. 31, 1942; came to U.S., 1973; s. Vilmos Leslie and Margo (Simay) A.; m. Barbara Ann Clark, Jan. 19, 1970; children: Julie, Michael, Nicole. B in Mech. Engring., U. Adelaide, Australia, 1970; MBA, Sam Houston State U., 1980. Registered profl. engr., Tex.; chartered profl. engr. Instn. Engrs. Australia. Mech. engr. T. O'Connor & Sons, Adelaide, 1968-69; vessel engr. Lummus Co. Can., Toronto, 1970-71, A.G. McKee Co. Can., Toronto, 1972; sr. vessel engr. Lummus Co. Can., Toronto, 1972-73, Fluor Daniel, Houston, 1973-75, prin. engr., 1975-80, supervising mech. engr., 1980-89, mech. engring. dir., 1989-95, sr. mech. engring. dir., 1995—, sr. tech. fellow, 1996—. Contbr. articles to profl. jours.; presenter tech. papers at internat. confs. Fellow ASME (spl. working group on high pressure vessels, task group chmn. fabrication, examination testing of ASME VIII divsn. 3, 1992—, chmn. high pressure tech.-design 1993—). Republican. Roman Catholic. Achievements include patents in field of (6) delayed coking in petroleum refining with an additional four applications made for patents. Home: 11946 Summerdale St Houston TX 77077-3022

ANTELL, DARRICK EUGENE, plastic surgeon, educator; b. Cleve., Feb. 22, 1951; s. E. James and Wanda H. (Kociecki) A.; m. Elizabeth Ann Sobottka, July 14, 1984; children: Gillian Elizabeth, Darrick Eugene Jr., Leslie Jane, Helen Greer, Meredith James. BS in Biology, Hobart Coll., 1973; DDS, Case Western Res. U. Dental, 1978; MD, Med. Coll. of Ohio, 1982. Diplomate Am. Bd. Plastic Surgery. Surgery intern Stanford (Calif.) U. Med. Ctr., 1982-83, surgery resident, 1983-85; plastic surgery resident N.Y. Hosp. Cornell, N.Y.C., 1985-87; plastic and reconstructive surgeon St. Luke's/Roosevelt, N.Y.C., 1987—; asst. clin. prof. plastic surgery Columbia U., N.Y.C., 1989—; med. dir., founder 850 Park Surg. Ctr., N.Y.C. Author: Plastic Surgery, 1991; contbr. articles to profl. jours. Trustee East Side House Settlement, N.Y.C., 1991, Hist. Soc. of the Town of Greenwich, 1999, Univ. Sch. Cleve., 2000; trustee adv. Girl Scouts U.S.A., N.Y.C., 1991. Facial Proportions grantee Am. Soc. for Aesthetic Plastic Surgery, 1987; Maliniac fellow Plastic Surgery Edn. Found.; recipient Pres. Citizenship award N.Y. State Med. Soc., 1992. Fellow: ACS, Plastic Surgery Ednl. Found.; mem.: AMA, Lipoplasty Soc., Interplast, Am. Acad. Cosmetic Dentistry, Internat. Acad. Dental Facial Aesthetics (founding), Internat. Soc. for Aestheic Plastic Surgery, N.Y. Regional Soc. Plastic and Reconstructive Surgeons, Am. Soc. Maxillofacial Surgeons Parliamentarian, Am. Soc. Aesthetic Plastic Surgery, Am. Soc . Plastic and Reconstructive Surgeons, Univ. Sch. Alumni Adv. Coun., Herbert Conway Soc., Greenwich Skating Club, Mill Reef Club (Antigua, W.I.), Cleve. Skating Club, Fishers Island Yacht Club, Stanwich Country Club, Union Club. Avocations: squash, fly fishing, golf, skiing. Office: 850 Park Ave New York NY 10021-1845 E-mail: dea@antell-md.com.

ANTEZZO, MATTHEW J., artist; b. Hartford, Conn., 1962; Attended, U. Utah, 1982—84; degree, Parsons Sch. Design, NYC, 1985—88. One-man shows include Randy Alexander, NYC, 1991, Galerie George-Philippe Vallois, Paris, 1991, 1993, Basilico Fine Arts, NYC, 1993, 1994, Interim Art, London, 1994, Gian Enzo Sperone, Rom I, Galerie Georges Philippe Vallois, Paris, 1995, Blum & Poe, Santa Monica, Calif., 2000, Eleni Koroneou Gallery, Athens, 2001, Spüth Magers Projekte, Münich Arena, Mexico, 2003, Michele Maccarone Inc., NYC, 2005, exhibited in group shows at Am. Fine Arts, 1989, Galerie Georges-Philippe Vallois, Paris, 1990, Home For Contemporary Theatre and Art, NYC, 1991, John Post Lee Gallery, 1991, Andrea Rosen Gallery, 1993, Backstage, Kunstverein, Hamburg, Germany, 1993, ghost-limb, Basilico Fine Arts, NYC, 1993, Desire and Loss, Carl Solway Gallery, Cin., 1994, Crash, Thread Waxing Space, 1994, When Attitudes Become Form, Monclair Art Mus., NJ, 1994, I Love New York, Edinburgh Internat. Arts Festival, 1997, Influence, Anxiety and Gratitude, MIT List Visual Arts Ctr., Cambridge, 2002, Living with Duchamp, The Tang Teaching Mus. and Art Gallery, Skidmore Coll., 2003, Reanimation, Kunstmuseum Thun, 2004. Office: Basilico Fine Arts 26 Wooster St New York NY 10003

ANTHOINE, ROBERT, lawyer, educator; b. Portland, Maine, June 5, 1921; s. Edward S and Sara B (Pinkham) Anthoine; m. Rebecca S Rudnick, Dec. 2, 1990; children from previous marriage: Alison, Robert Neal, Nelson, Nina. AB, Duke U., 1942; JD, Columbia U., 1949. Bar: NY 1949, US Ct Appeals (2d cir) 1956, US Supreme Ct 1970. Rsch. assoc. Am. Law Inst. fed. income tax project Columbia U., N.Y.C., 1949—50; assoc. Cleary, Gottlieb, Friendly and Cox, 1950—52; assoc. prof. law Columbia U., 1952—56, prof. law, 1956—64, adj. prof., 1964—93; ptnr. Winthrop, Stimson, Putnam and Roberts, 1963—86, sr. counsel, 1987—2000, in charge London office, 1972—76; sr. counsel Pillsbury Winthrop Shaw Pittman LLP, N.Y.C., 2001—. Vis. prof. Law Sch. Ind. U., Bloomington, Ind., 1986; vis. prof. Law Sch. U. Tex., Austin, 1988; vis. prof. Law Sch. U. N.C., Chapel Hill, 1991, U. Pa., Philadelphia, 1996, Seattle U., 1997. Author, editor: survey Tax Incentives for Investment in Developing Countries, 1979; contbr. articles to profl jours. Active Coun Fgn. Rels.; chmn. emeritus, bd. dirs. Aperture Found.; pres. Lucid Art Found., S K Yee Found.; dir. Hazen Polsky Found.; hon. gov. Royal Shakespeare Theatre, Stratford-upon-Avon, England; vice-chmn, bd dirs Am. Friends Theater; trustee, dir. Grosvenor Gallery (Fine Arts) Ltd., London; vice chair, trustee Int. Photog. Coun., Royal Shakespeare Theatre Trust, Sevenarts, Ltd., London; bd. dirs. emeritus Eric and Salome Estorick Found. Vol. Lawyers Arts; bd. dirs., v.p. Morris Graves Found. Lt. USN, 1942—46. Mem.: ABA, Asn Litèraire et Artistique Int (US), Int. Fiscal Assn., Assn. Bar City NY, Am. Law Inst. (life), Queen's, Hurlingham Club (London), River Club (New York, NY), Century Assn. Club. Democrat. Office: Pillsbury Winthrop Shaw Pittman LLP 1540 Broadway New York NY 10036-4039 Office Phone: 212-858-1127. Business E-Mail: robert.anthoine@pillsburylaw.com.

ANTHONISEN, GEORGE RIOCH, sculptor, artist; b. Boston, July 31, 1936; s. Niels Landmark and Margaret (Rioch) A.; m. Ellen Friedman, Feb. 16, 1966; children: Rachel, Daniel. BA, U. Vt., 1961; postgrad., Nat. Acad. Design, N.Y.C., 1961—62, Art Students League, 1962—64, Dartmouth Coll. Med. Sch., 1967. One-man shows include Hopkins Ctr. Dartmouth Coll., 1966, Ctr. Art Gallery, N.Y.C., 1969, Moody Gallery, Pasadena, Calif., 1979, Bjorn Lindgren Gallery, N.Y.C., 1981, 82, U. Scranton (Pa.) Art Gallery, 1986, Rotunda Cannon House Office Bldg., U.S. Capitol, Washington, 1989, The Woodmere Art Mus., Phila., 1992, Bianco Gallery, Buckingham, Pa., 1994, 98, Phila. Flower Show-Gale Nurseries, 1995, Berman Mus. Art, Collegeville, Pa., 1996, Festival of Faiths, The Gardens of Louisville, 1999; exhibited in group shows NAD, N.Y., 1971, Port of History Mus., Phila., 1987, James A. Michener Art Mus., Doylestown, 1988, 00, Millersville (Pa.) U., 1991, Nat. Sculpture Soc., 1993, Morani Gallery, Med. Coll. Pa., 1994, Monuments Conservancy, Samuel Dorsky Symposium on Pub. Monuments/Time and Life Bldg., N.Y.C., 1997, Bianco Gallery, Buckingham, Pa., 1995-2002, Salmagundi Club, N.Y.C., 2000, Phila. Sketch Club, Travis Gallery, 2002, 03, 04, 05, Sculpture Along Bear Creek, Keller, Tex., 2005; represented in permanent collections at WHO, Geneva, U.S. Capitol Bldg. Hall of Columns, Washington, Carnegie Hall, N.Y.C., Rittenhouse Hotel, Phila., Cathedral Heritage Found., Louisville, Please Touch Mus., Phila., Dartmouth-Hitchcock Med. Ctr., Lebanon, N.H., Washington Sch. Psychiatry, Keneseth Israel, Elkins Park, Pa., Doylestown (Pa.) Hosp., Pa. Acad. Music, Lancaster, Atlanta U. Trevor Arnett Libr., Trevor Arnett Libr., U. Alaska, Fairbanks, James Michener Art Mus., Doylestown, Phila. Coll. Osteo. Medicine, Berman Mus. Art, Collegeville, Pa., Martin Art Gallery, Muhlenberg Coll., Allentown, Pa. With U.S. Army, 1955-57. Sculptor-in-residence Augustus St. Gaudens Nat. Hist. Site, U.S. Dept. Interior, 1971; recipient James Augustus Suydam bronze medal, 1968, Sen. Ernest Gruening award Alaska State Coun. on Arts, 1976, Exemplary Achievement in Arts award Bucks County (Pa.) C. of C., 1985. Fellow Nat. Sculpture Soc. (bd. dirs. 1993-94), hon. mem. Phila. Sketch Club, 2002. Avocations: fishing, baseball. Home and Office: PO Box 147 Solebury PA 18963-0147 Studio: c/o Peter Aaronson 22 Cassway Rd Woodbridge CT 06525 Fax: 215-297-5162. Office Phone: 215-297-5318. E-mail: ellena@voicenet.com.

ANTHONY, ANDREW JOHN, lawyer; b. Newark, Jan. 26, 1950; s. Andrew and Mary (Norton) A.; children: Nicholas, Natalie. BA, Kean Coll., 1973; JD cum laude, U. Miami, 1976. Bar: Fla. 1977, U.S. Dist. Ct. (so. dist.) Fla. 1977. Assoc. Knight, Peters, Hoeveler, Pickle, Niemoeller & Flynn, Miami, Fla., 1977-79, Vernis & Bowling, Miami, 1979, Ligman, Martin, Shiley & McGee, Coral Gables, Fla., 1979-86; sole practice Coral Gables, 1986—. Mem.: ABA, Fla. Bar Assn. Democrat. Roman Catholic. Avocations: coin collecting/numismatics, fishing, reading. Home: 90 Edgewater Dr 202 Coral Gables FL 33133 Office: The Law Offices of Anthony & Associates PA Ste 505 250 Catalonia Ave Coral Gables FL 33134 Office Phone: 305-444-8927 ext. 11. Business E-Mail: ajanthony@ajalaw.com.

ANTHONY, ART MICHAEL, military officer, English educator; b. San Antonio, Feb. 17, 1957; s. Alfred M. and Lydia (Uriegas) A.; m. Luise Kaindl, Mar. 23, 1995; 1 child, Suzanna Lydia. BA in English and History, Incarnate Word Coll., San Antonio, 1985; postgrad., Troy State U., 1988, Boston U., 1988, U. Md. Pvt. U.S. Army, 1975, advanced through grades to 1st lt., 1987; capt. USAR, 1992, U.S. Active Guard Res., 1998, maj., 2000; tchr. ESL AEG Tech. Co., Vienna, 1995-96; rear detachment comdr. Bamberg, Germany, 1996-97; field rep. U. Md. Univ. Coll. Austria, Vienna, 1997-98; tchr. ESL Nat. Def. Acad., Vienna, 1997-98; asst. prof. mil. sci. Truman State U., Kirksville, Mo., 1998-2000; AGR-USAR adjutant 38th Ordnance Group, Charleston, W.Va., 2000—. Workshop leader U. Kent, Canterbury, Eng., 1991, 93, Truman State U., 1999. Tchr. Sunday Sch., San Antonio, 1980-85, Frankfurt, 1986-90, Vienna, 1995-96; leader Boy Scouts Am., Frankfurt, 1990-95; coach little league, Vienna, 1995; participant Operation Enduring Freedom, Iraq, 2003. Recipient Army Good Conduct medal, 1978, NCO Profl. Devel. Ribbon, 1978, Army Svc. Ribbon, 1981, Overseas Svc. Ribbon, 1981, Army Achievement medal, 1988, Nat. Def. Svc. medal, 1990, Army Res. Components Achievement medal, 1995, Armed Forces Svc. Ribbon, 1996, NATO medal, 1996, Superior Unit award, 1996, Armed Forces Expeditionary medal, 1999, Global War on Terrorism Svc. medal, Citizen Warrior award Mem. KC, Res. Officers Assn., Assn. of U.S. Army. Avocations: sports, travel, home activities. Office: Ft Mc Pherson 38th Ordnance Group 101 Lakeview Dr Charleston WV 25313

ANTHONY, BARBARA COX, foundation administrator; b. Dec. 1922; m. Garner Anthony; children: Blair, James Cox Kennedy. Controller Cox Enterprises, Inc. Bd. dirs. Cox Enterprises, Atlanta; founder Barbara Cox Anthony Found., Hawaii; rancher, cattle breeder, Australia. Named one of World's Richest People, Forbes, 1999—2004. heiress to James M. Cox founder of Cox Enterprises, Inc. Office: Cox Enterprises Inc 6205 Peachtree Dunwoody Rd Atlanta GA 30328 also: Barbara Cox Anthony Foundation PO Box 4316 Honolulu HI 96813 Office Phone: 678-645-0000. Office Fax: 678-645-1079.

ANTHONY, CARMELO F., professional basketball player; b. May 29, 1984; Student, Syracuse U. Player Denver Nuggets, 2003—. Mem. US Men's Basketball Team, Athens Olympic Games, 2004. Vol. Family Resource Ctr., Denver. Named NBA Rookie of the Month (6 Times), 2003—04, NCAA Final Four Most Outstanding player, 2003; named to NBA All-Rookie Team, 2004. Office: Denver Nuggets 1000 Chopper Cir Denver CO 80204

ANTHONY, CAROLYN ADDITON, librarian; b. Pitts., Nov. 27, 1949; d. Elwood Prince and Elizabeth Martha (Gruginskis) Additon; m. William W. Anthony, III, July 7, 1973; children: Margaret Susan, Lauren Elizabeth. AB, Colby Coll., 1971; MLS, U. R.I., 1973. Reference libr. Enoch Pratt Free Lib., Balt., 1973-75, head info. and referral svc., 1975-78; head info. svcs. Balt. County Pub. Libr., Towson, Md., 1978-80, head, info. and program svcs., 1980-85; dir. Skokie (Ill.) Pub. Libr., 1985—. Pres. Libr. Adminstr. Conf. No. Ill., 1988—89; chair adv. bd. Pub. Librs., 1986—89. Pres. women's bd. Rush North Shore Hosp., 2004—05, bd. dirs., 2004—. Recipient Libr. of Yr., North Suburban Libr. Sys., 2004. Mem.: ALA (mem. coun. 1993—97), Ill. Libr. Assn. (pres. 1999—2000, award, Libr. of the Yr. 2003), Am. Libr. Trustee Assn. (bd. dirs.), Pub. Libr. Assn. (new task stds. force com. 1984—87, bd. dirs. 1987—89), Met. Libr. Assn. (exec. com. 1990—93), Chgo. Libr. Club (pres. 1991—92), Rotary (pres. Skokie chpt. 1992—93). Democrat. Soc. Of Friends. Office: Skokie Pub Libr 5215 Oakton St Skokie IL 60077-3680 Business E-Mail: canthony@skokielibrary.info.

ANTHONY, DONALD BARRETT, engineering executive; b. Kansas City, Kans., Jan. 28, 1948; s. Donald W. and Marjorie (Lifsey) A.; m. Darla S. Donovan, Dec. 16, 1972; children: Jennifer L., Danielle S. BSChemE, U. Toledo, 1970; MS, MIT, 1971, DSc, 1974. Asst. prof., practice sch. dir. dept. chem. engring. MIT, Cambridge, Mass., 1974-75; group supr. coal R&D Std. Oil Co. Ohio, Cleve., 1976-77, mgr. marine planning, 1978-79, mgr. synthetic fuels devel., 1980-83, v.p., gen. mgr. Pfaudler Divsn. Rochester, N.Y., 1983-85; v.p. R&D Std. Oil Co., Cleve., 1985-87, BP Am., Inc., Cleve., 1987-88, BP Exploration, Inc., Cleve., 1989-90; v.p. tech. Bechtel, Inc., Houston, 1990-94, v.p. ops., 1994-95, v.p. ref., 1995-96; pres. Bailey Controls Co., 1996-98, Process Ind. Group, ABB Automation, 1999—2000; pres., CEO NineSigma, Inc., Cleve., 2001—03; pres. Coun. for Chem. Rsch., Wash., DC, 2004—. Contbr. articles to profl. jours.; patentee in field. Capt. AUS, 1970-78. MIT Esso fellow, 1970-71, Little rsch.-devel. fellow, 1971-72, Procter & Gamble fellow, 1972-73, Bechtel fellow, 1992. Mem. AIChE, Am. Chem. Soc., Sigma Xi, Phi Kappa Phi, Tau Beta Pi, Pi Mu Epsilon, Phi Eta Sigma. Lutheran. Home: 122 Portofino Dr North Venice FL 34275 Office: Council for Chem Research Ste 302 1730 Rhode Island Ave Washington DC 20036 Office Phone: 202-429-3971. Business E-Mail: danthony@ccrhq.org.

ANTHONY, DONALD CHARLES, librarian, educator; b. N.Y.C., Mar. 29, 1926; s. Charles and Margaret Evelyn (Gleason) A.; m. Mary Miserez, Apr. 18, 1957; children— Stephen, Sheila, Irene. BA, U. Wis., 1951, MA, 1954; postgrad., U. Geneva, Switzerland, 1952-53. Library asst. Enoch Pratt Free Library, Balt., 1954-55; librarian Eleutherian Mills-Hagley Found., Wilmington, Del., 1955-59; dir. Fargo (N.D.) Pub. Library, 1959-61; asso. librarian N.Y. State Library, Albany, 1961-66; asst. dir. Columbia Libraries, 1966-69, acting dir., 1969, asso. dir., 1970-74; dir. Syracuse U. Libraries, 1974-85; cons. on preservation of library materials, 1986—; pres. Donmar Assocs., Clinton, NY, 1987—2004. Adj. faculty Mohawk Valley Community Coll., Utica, N.Y., 1989-97; docent Munson-Williams-Proctor Arts Inst., Utica, 1999—; cons. N.Y. State Edn. Dept., 1967-97. Producer; host: TV Museum, KXGO-TV, Fargo, 1960; Contbr. articles to profl. jours. Trustee N.Y. Met. Reference and Research Library Agy., 1969-74, Cen. N.Y. Library Resources Council, 1983-86; chmn. bd. dirs. Five Asso. U. Libraries, Syracuse, 1975-76, 77-79; trustee Bd. Edn., Dobbs Ferry, N.Y., 1971-74, v.p., 1973-74. Served with USNR, 1944-46. Fellow Coun. on Libr. Resources. Home: 120 Paris Rd New Hartford NY 13413-2433

ANTHONY, EDWARD MASON, linguistics educator; b. Cleve., Sept. 1, 1922; s. Edward Mason and Elsie (Haas) A.; m. Ann Louise Terbrueggen, Sept. 18, 1946; children: Lynn Diane Anthony Higgins, Janice Louise, Edward Mason, 4th. AB, U. Mich., 1944, MA, 1946, PhD, 1954. From instr. English to prof. linguistics U. Mich., 1945—64; prof. U. Pitts., 1964—90, prof. emeritus, 1990—, chmn. dept. gen. linguistics, 1964—74; dir. Lang. Acquisition Inst., 1970, dir. lang. orientation programs, 1974—82, dir. Asian Studies program, 1977—82, dir. Lang. and Culture Inst, 1982—90. Vis. lectr., Afghanistan, 1951, Thailand, 1955-57, Mexico, 1964, 65, Poland, 1977, Greece and Yugoslavia, 1981, Singapore and Thailand, 1984, Hong Kong, 1985, 86; dir. S.E. Asian English Project, Thailand, Laos, Vietnam, 1958-61, Rockefeller Found. Thai Project, 1967-72; vis. prof. Regional English Lang. Centre, Singapore, 1974-75, Peking Inst. Fgn. Lang., 1979-80; cons. in field; mem. Nat. Adv. Coun. Tchg. English as Fgn. Lang.; resource person Detroit Bd. Edn., 1964, Pitts. Bd. Edn., 1965; mem. adv. screening com. in linguistics Coun. for Internat. Exch. Scholars, 1976; mem. adv. panel in English tchg. to dir. USIA, 1987-93. Author: Reading Thai Syllables, 1962, (with others) Foundations of Thai, 2 vols, 1968, Towards a Theory of Lexical Meaning, 1975, About Thai, 2001; book rev. editor: Lang. Learning, 1948; editor, 1949. Mellon fellow Nat. Fgn. Lang. Ctr. Washington, 1990; Smith-Mundt grantee, 1951, Lang. Rsch. grantee NDEA, 1965-67, grantee State Dept., 1964, 65, 77, 81, 84, 90; recipient Fulbright award, 1955-57, Plaque of Honor Ramkhamhaeng U., Bangkok, Thailand, 1986, Cert. Appreciation USIA, 1992. Mem. Linguistic Soc., Am. Assn. Applied Linguistics, Assn. Asian Studies, Siam Soc. (life), Assn. Tchrs. English to Speakers of Other Langs. (pres. 1967, Alatis award 1991), Nat. Coun. Tchrs. English. Democrat. Presbyterian. Home: 4118 Northampton Dr Allison Park PA 15101-1532 Office: Dept Linguistics U Pitts Pittsburgh PA 15260 Business E-Mail: emal@pitt.edu.

ANTHONY, ETHAN, architect; b. Iowa City, Oct. 14, 1950; s. Frank and Carol (Kessler) A.; m. Luz Eugenia Rey, Feb. 18, 1984; children: Winston Eugene, Alexandra Luce, Edward Rey. Student, Boston Architecture Ctr., 1971-77; BArch, U. Oreg., 1980. Project architect Payette Assocs., Boston, 1980-83; prin. Anthony Assocs., Boston, 1983-90; pres. HDB/Cram & Ferguson Inc., Boston, 1998—; cons. architect Phillips Exeter Acad., 1998—2003, St. George's Sch., 1999—2001, The Canterbury Sch., Greensboro, NC, 1999—2003, Syon Abbey, Roanoke, Va., 2001—, Casady Sch., Oklahoma City, 2001—; pres. Kalmia Woods Corp., 2001—. Cons. N.E. Worldcom, 1994-2000; instr. design Roger Williams U., Bristol, R.I., 1984-89; thesis advisor Boston Archtl. Ctr., 1985-87; speaker in field. Author: The Architecture of Ralph Adams Cram and His Firm, 2005. Cons. architect Russell Sage First Presbyn. Ch., N.Y.C., 1994-98, All Saints Ch., Peterborough, N.H., 1998-2001. Recipient honor award Interfaith Forum on Religion, Art and Arch., 1993. Mem. AIA, Boston Soc. Archs. Avocations: painting, history, professional speaking. Office: HDB/Cram and Ferguson Inc 264 Beacon St Boston MA 02116 Office Phone: 617-424-6200.

ANTHONY, FRANCIS POLIPNICK (FRANCIS ANTHONY POLIPNICK), poet, writer; b. Breckenridge, Minn., June 6, 1922; s. Alois Howard Polipnick and Loretta Pauline Mikschе; m. Carol Louise Kessler, 1950 (div.); children: Ethan, Karen, Bryan, Leslie; m. Susan Carter Hall, June 30, 1985; 1 child, Frederick. BA, U. Minn., 1950; MALS, Dartmouth Coll., 1984; PhD, Fla. State U., 1990. TV prodr. Sta. KKTV, Colorado Springs, Colo., 1953-54; specifications engr. Douglas Aircraft, El Segundo, Calif., 1954-55; pers. mgr. Raytheon Co., Waltham, Mass., 1955-60; columnist, editor Beacon Publs., Acton, Mass., 1960—70; owner Small Cars of Stow, Mass., 1960-76; prodr. Vt. Pub. Radio, Windsor, 1977-80; pres. New Eng. Writers, Windsor, 1986—. Interviews of celebrities archived in spl. collections Dartmouth Coll., 1980—. Author: Terminus, 1976, books of poetry, essays and interviews, 1980—. Mem. nat. adv. bd. Boy Scouts Am., Boston, 1960—62; fund raiser State Red Feather, Boston, 1962—64; Windsor Planning Commn., 1995—; mem. Windsor Zoning Bd., 1995—, S.W. Regional Transp. Adv. Bd., 1995—; Rep. nominee to U.S. Ho. of Reps. Mass., 1964. Staff sgt. USAF, 1942—46. Arts coun. grantee State of Minn., 1982; recipient Lit. award Lambda Iota Tau, 1988, Hon. award Paradox Internat., 1999. Mem. Acad. Am. Poets, New Eng. Poetry Club, Bay Area Poetry Coalition (Poets prize 1996). Avocations: flying, painting, guns, interviewing. Home and Office: 151 Main St Box 5 Windsor VT 05089 Office Phone: 802-674-2315. E-mail: newvtpoet@aol.com.

ANTHONY, GENEVA JO, poet, writer; b. Minden, La., Apr. 10, 1946; Student, La. Polytech.Inst., 1964. Author: (poetry) Sweet Southern Dreams, 1990, short stories. Named Poet of Yr., Pascagoula, Miss., 1998; recipient, 1992, 2000, award, Magnolia Quarterly, 2003. Mem.: Gulf Coast Writers Assn., United Daus. of Confederacy (so. poets officer), Miss. Poetry Soc. (v.p. 1984—). Methodist. Avocations: sewing, writing. Home: 8417 Shady Rest Rd Vancleave MS 39565 E-mail: ganthony@datasync.com.

ANTHONY, HARRY ANTONIADES, retired city planner, architect, educator; b. Skyros, Greece, July 28, 1922; arrived in U.S., 1951, naturalized, 1954; s. Anthony G. and Maria G. (Ftoulis) Antoniades; m. Anne C. Skoufis, Sept. 23, 1950; children: Mary Anne Anthony Smith, Kathryn Harriet. B.Arch., Nat. Tech. U., Athens, Greece, 1945; student, Ecole Nat. Supérieure des Beaux Arts, Paris, 1945-46; M.City Planning, U. Paris, 1947; Docteur de l'Université, Sorbonne, Paris, 1949; PhD in Arch. and Urban Planning, Columbia, 1955. Architect-planner with Constantinos A. Doxiadis, Athens, 1943-45, LeCorbusier, Paris, 1946-47, ECA, Paris, 1949-51; city planner with Maurice E.H. Rotival, N.Y.C., 1951-52; chief planner Brown & Blauvelt, N.Y.C., 1952-54; city planner, urban designer Skidmore, Owings & Merrill, N.Y.C., 1954-56; prin. planning cons. Brown Engrs. Internat., N.Y.C., 1956-60; prin. Brown & Anthony City Planners, Inc., N.Y.C., 1960—69; v.p. Doxiadis Assocs., Inc., Washington, 1971—72; mem. faculty Columbia U., 1953-72, from asst. to assoc. prof., 1956-63, prof. urban planning, 1963-72, dir. grad. div. urban planning Grad. Sch. Architecture and Planning, 1962-65; prof. urban planning Calif. State Poly. U., Pomona, 1972-83, prof. emeritus urban and regional planning, 1983—, chmn. dept., 1972-76. Vis. prof. urban design Tulane U., 1967-68; vis. lectr. U. Calif. at Berkeley, Stanford U., Dartmouth, San Diego State U., CUNY, U. Okla., Ohio U., Auburn U., Salk Inst. Biol. Studies, U.S. Internat. U.; lectr. urban studies and planning U. Calif., San Diego, 1980-82, Chancellor's Assoc., 2001—; scholar-in-residence U. B.C., Vancouver, 1978; planning, zoning, urban renewal and urban design cons. to several cities, U.S. and abroad; also cons. to UN, Am. Med. Bldg. Guild, corps. and pvt. firms, to govts. and univs.; planning commr., Leonia, N.J., 1958-64; master planner, cons. arch. for Ss. Constantine and Helen Greek Orthodox Ch. and Village for the Elderly, Cardiff-by-the-Sea, Calif., 1983-97 (AIA design awareness program orchid award 1997). Author, co-author, contbr.: Four Great Makers of Modern Architecture: Gropius, Le Corbusier, Mies Van Der Rohe, Wright, Dictionary of American History, The Challenge of Squatter Settlements-With Special Reference to the Cities of Latin America, La Défense à Paris et le Quartier d'Affaires de Vancouver: Une Comparaison Urbaine, New Orleans Air Rights Study,

Woodstock Growth Plan and Land Use Controls, Mt. Vernon Planning Study, Corning Area, N.Y.: Conditions and Prospects, Corning Region: Development Plans, Metairie Shore, La.: Lakefront Recreation and Comty. Devel., U.S. Navy Multiple Activity Master Plan: Norfolk Complex, Aqaba, Jordan: Future Devel., Lands of Kapua, Hawaii: Feasibility Study for Urban, Agricultural and Recreational Devel.; several master plans, city and regional planning reports, urban design plans and programs, environ. impact reports, zoning ordinances, educational videocassettes on urban planning subjects; contbr. articles to profl. jours., mags., newspapers; acad. profl. writings, awards, plans, designs and reports included in Spl. Collections Libr., U. Calif. (San Diego), 1998. Recipient Premier Grand Prix Internat. Exhbn. Housing and City Planning, Paris, 1947, St. Paul's Gold Medal award Greek Orthodox Archdiocese Am., 2003; William Kinne Fellows travelling fellow in planning N.Am., 1956, French Govt. fellow, 1945-47; research award Urban Center of Columbia U., 1969; named Outstanding Prof. Calif. State Poly. U., 1975; founder Met. Opera House, Lincoln Ctr. for the Performing Arts, N.Y.C. Mem. AIA (Arnold W. Brunner scholar 1958), Am. Inst. Cert. Planners (bd. examiners), Am. Planning Assn. (Disting. Svc. award 1984, San Diego Cmty. Design Awareness Program Orchid award 1997), Order of Am. Hellenic Ednl. Progressive Assn., Hellenic Cultural Soc. (Dedication to Perpetuating the Greek Lang. award 2003), Internat. Soc. Greek Writers (Architecture and Poetry award 2004), Internat. Land Econs. Soc. of Lambda Alpha (Richard T. Ely Disting. Educator award 1988), U. Calif. San Diego Faculty Club. Home: 7665 Caminito Avola La Jolla CA 92037-3956 Business E-Mail: hanthony@ucsd.edu.

ANTHONY, JOAN CATON, administrative judge; b. South Bend, Ind., July 28, 1939; d. Joseph Robert and Margaret Catherine (McMeel) Caton; m. Robert Armstrong Anthony, Jan. 3, 1980; 1 child, Peter. BA, Marquette U., 1961; MA, Northwestern U., 1963; JD, Catholic U. Am., 1979. Bar: D.C. 1980, Va. 1982. Instr. English Marquette U., Milw., 1963-65, George Washington U., Washington, 1965-69, asst. prof., 1969-70; spl. asst. student affairs HEW, Washington, 1970-72; dir. Office Student and Youth Affairs U.S. Office Edn., Washington, 1972-74, legis. specialist, 1974-78; chief mgmt. ops. br. Fed. Wildlife Permit Office U.S. Fish and Wildlife Svc., Washington, 1978-81; assoc. Cate and Goodbread, Washington, 1981—85; atty., advisor office legis. counsel U.S. Dept. Interior, 1991-95; staff atty. Interior Bd. Land Appeals, 1995—2003; adminstrv. judge Def. Office of Hearings and Appeals, U.S. Dept. Def., 2003—. Mem. U.S. del. to 2d meeting Conf. Parties to Conv. on Internat. Trade in Endangered Species of Wild Fauna and Flora, San Jose, Costa Rica, 1979. Contbr. lit. revs., essays and articles on univ.-cmty. rels., western settlement and internat. negotiations to various publs. Pres. Franklin Forest Frolickers, 1985—86; den leader Cub Scouts, mem. com. Boy Scouts Am., 1990—2000; parent vol. Fairfax County Pub. Schs., 1987—2001; treas. Greater McLean Rep. Women's Club, 1987—88; bd. dirs. McLean Citizens Assn., 1982—83, Fairfax County Humane Soc., 1983. Recipient Spl. Achievement award U.S. Fish and Wildlife Svc., 1981. Mem.: DAR (Fauquier Courthouse chpt.), Va. Bar Assn., D.C. Bar Assn. Roman Catholic.

ANTHONY, JULIAN DANFORD, JR., lawyer; b. Boston, Oct. 23, 1935; s. Julian Danford and Eleanor Caroline (Hopkins) A.; m. Ellen Nora Brown, Apr. 8, 1961; children: Julian Danford III, Sarah Dodge, David Campbell. AB, Wesleyan U., 1957; LLB, Harvard U., 1960. Bar: Minn. 1961, Conn. 1965. Atty.-advisor U.S. Tax Ct., Washington, 1962-64; assoc. Day, Berry & Howard LLP, Hartford, Conn., 1965-70, ptnr., 1971—2004, of counsel, 2004—. Chmn. Conn. Red Cross Blood Svcs., Farmington, 1981—82; bd. dirs. J. Walton Bissell Found., Hartford, 1987—2004; pres., CEO J. Walton Bissell, 2004—; mem. adv. bd. dirs. Salvation Army, Hartford, 1990—96; elector Wadsworth Atheneum, Hartford, 1986—95; corporator Hartford Hosp., 1988—; trustee Amistad Found., Hartford, 1997—; bd. dirs. Hartford Symphony Orch., 1993—99, Conn. Children's Med. Ctr., 1994—2005, chmn., 1999—2002; bd. dirs. Conn. Children's Med. Ctr. Found., 1998—2004, Coordinating Coun. for Founds., Hartford, 1994—99. Mem. ABA, Fed. Tax Inst. New Eng. (exec. com. 1987—). Office: Day Berry & Howard LLP Cityplace Hartford CT 06103

ANTHONY, LEONARD MORRIS, steel company administrator, consultant; b. Allentown, Pa., July 28, 1954; s. Leonard M. and Gladys (Davies) A.; m. Pamela Ann Leon, Nov. 3, 1976; 1 child, Lindsay C. BS in Acctg., Pa. State U., 1976; MBA in Fin., U. Pa., 1993. Comml. lender Meridian Bancorp., Allentown, 1977-78; credit analyst Bethlehem Steel Corp., Bethlehem, Pa., 1979-82, adminstrv. mgr. credit, 1982-84, treasury analyst, 1984-85, credit mgr., 1985-86, dir. fin. svcs., 1986-90, dir. risk mgmt., 1990-93, mgr. fin. planning, 1993—95, asst. treasurer, 1995—99, treasurer, 1999—2001, senior vice president finance, CFO, 2001—03; CFO Internat. Steel Group, Richfield, Ohio, 2003—. Prin. MMC Cons., Phila., 1993—. Avocations: scuba, golf, personal investing, wine collecting. Home: 2224 Summit Dr Hellertown PA 18055-2948 Office: International Steel Group 3250 Interstate Dr Richfield OH 44286

ANTHONY, MARC (MARCO ANTONIO MUNIZ), singer, composer, actor; b. NYC, Sept. 16, 1969; s. Felipe and Guillermina Muniz; m. Dayanara Torres Delgado, 2000 (div. 2004); children: Cristian Anthony Muniz, Ryan Anthony Muniz; m. Jennifer Lopez, June 5, 2004; 1 child from previous marriage, Ariana. Singer, composer: (albums) When the Night is Over, 1991, Otra Nota, 1993, Todo a Su Tiempo, 1995, Contra La Corriente, 1997 (Grammy award for best tropical Latin album, 1998), The Best of Marc Anthony, 1997, March Anthony, 1999, When I Dream at Night, 2000, Libre, 2001, Mended, 2002, Amar Sin Mentiras, 2004 actor: (films) East Side Story, 1988, Carlito's Way, 1993, Natural Causes, 1994, Hackers, 1995, Big Night, 1996, The Substitute, 1996, Bringing Out the Dead, 1999, Con la musica por dentro, 1999, In the Time of the Butterflies, 2001, Man on Fire, 2004; (Broadway plays) The Capeman, 1998. Recipient award for Outstanding Performance Song for Feature Film (for The Mask of Zorro), Am. Latino Media Arts, 1999, award for Outstanding Performance in a Music, Variety or Comedy Spl., 2002, award for Most Performed Songs for Motion Picture (for Runaway Bride), ASCAP Film and TV Music Awards, 2001, Favorite Artist-Latin Music, Am. Music Awards, 2004.

ANTHONY, MARGARET LOUISE, nurse; b. Springfield, Mass., Feb. 11, 1960; d. Emmagean Lillus and James Cunningham Fettes; m. John Christ Anthony, July 14, 1990; children: Victoria Jean, John Stephen. BSN, Am. Internat. Coll., Mass., 1982; M in Health Scis., Med. U. SC, 2000. Clin. nurse Hartford Hosp., Conn., 1982—85; RN coord. Johnson Meml. Hosp., Johnson Ambulatory Surgery Ctr., Enfield, Conn., 1985—88; don svcs. Americare Health Svcs., Worcester, Mass., 1988—89; oper. room, ambulatory care nurse mgr. Clinton Hosp., Mass., 1989—92; clin. nurse iii main oper. room Med. U. SC, Charleston, SC, 1992—98; clin. nurse coord. MUSC Ambulatory Care, Charleston, SC, 1998—2000; clin. nurse mgr. MUSC Hollings Cancer Ctr., Charleston, SC, 2000—. Director's consumer liaison group Nat. Cancer Inst., Bethesda, 2004—. Contbr. chapters to books, articles to profl. jours. Pres. Oncology Nursing Soc., Charleston, SC, 2004—04. Recipient Excellence in Rsch., Dept. of Health Adminstrn. and Policy, College of Health Professions, MUSC, 2000. Mem.: Oncology Nursing Soc. (pres., pres. elect 2003—04). Greek Orthodox. Office: MUSC Hollings Cancer Ctr 86 Jonathan Lucas St Charleston SC 29425 Office Phone: 843-792-1628.

ANTHONY, MICHAEL FRANCIS, lawyer; b. Chgo., Dec. 19, 1950; s. Rudolph A. and Margaret M. (Shea) Anthony; m. Megan P. O'Connell; children: Erin Christine, Ian O'Connell, Connor Cullerton, Madeline Shea, McKenzie Galligan. BS cum laude, Xavier U., Cin., 1972, MHA, 1974; JD, U. Balt., 1978. Bar: Md. 1978, Fla. 1979, Ill. 1980, DC 1989. Various adminstrv. positions Johns Hopkins Hosp., Balt., 1973-78; assoc. Ober Kaler Grimes & Shriver, Balt., 1978-80; from assoc. to ptnr. McDermott, Will & Emery, Chgo., 1980-87, 1989—91, nat. head health law dept., 1991—2001; sr. v.p. for legal affairs Am. Hosp. Assn., Chgo., 1987-89. Contbr. articles to profl. jours. Mem. adv. bd. De Paul Inst. Health Law. Fellow: Am. Health Lawyers Assn. (past pres.), Am. Coll. Healthcare Execs. (various coms.). Office: McDermott Will & Emery 227 W Monroe St Ste 5300 Chicago IL 60606-5096 Office Phone: 312-984-7635. Business E-Mail: manthony@mwe.com.

ANTHONY, MICHELE, recording industry executive; b. 1956; BA with distinction, George Washington U.; JD, U. So. Calif. Bar: 1981. Ptnr. Manatt, Phelps, Rothenberg & Phillips; sr. v.p. Sony Music, N.Y.C., 1990—93, exec. v.p., 1993-94, Sony BMG Music Entertainment, N.Y.C., 1994—; COO Sony Music Label Group, U.S., 2004—. Bd. dirs. Recording Industry Assn. Am., Nat. Ctr. for Missing and Exploited Children; exec mem. bd. dirs. Rock and Roll Hall of Fame Found., The Vote. Recipient Norma Zarky Entertainment Law award; named one of 100 Most Powerful Women in Entertainment, Hollywood Reporter. Mem. State Bar Calif., Beverly Hills Bar Assn., L.A. County Bar Assn., Order of Coif. Office: Sony Music Entertainment 550 Madison Ave New York NY 10022-3211*

ANTHONY, RICHARD E., bank executive; b. May 6, 1946; BS in Fin., U. Ala., 1968; MBA, U. Va., 1971. Various position including exec. v.p. AmSouth Bank, N.A., Birmingham, 1971—85; pres. First Comml. Bancshares, Inc., 1985; chmn. bd., CEO First Comml. Bank, 1985; chmn. First Comml. Bank. (acquired by Synovus), Birmingham, 1985—93; pres. Synovus Finl. Corp., Ala., 1993—95; vice chmn. Synovus, Columbus, Ga., 1995—, COO, 2003—05, pres., 2003—, CEO, 2005—. Dir. Econ. Develop. Partnership Ala.; mem. Fin. Svc. Roundtable, U. Ala. Nat. Adv. Coun., U. Ala. Pres.'s Cabinet; mem. bd. vistors U. Ala. Sch. Commerce and Bus. Adminstrn.; bd. dirs. Bux. Coun. Ala. Mem.: Country Club Birmingham (pres. 1991), Ala. Golf Assn. (pres. 1985), Kiwanis (pres. Birmingham club 1996—97), Morning Quarterback Club (capt. 1993). Office: Synovus Finl Corp PO Box 120 Columbus GA 31902*

ANTHONY, ROBERT ARMSTRONG, lawyer, educator; b. Washington, Dec. 28, 1931; s. Emile Peter and Martha Graham (Armstrong) Anthony; m. Ruth Grace Barrons, Feb. 7, 1959 (div.); 1 child, Graham Barrons; m. Joan Patricia Caton, Jan. 3, 1980; 1 child, Peter Christopher Caton. BA, Yale U., 1953; BA in Jurisprudence, Oxford U., 1955; JD, Stanford U., 1957. Bar: Calif. 1957, N.Y. 1971, DC 1972. Assoc. Pillsbury, Madison & Sutro, San Francisco, 1957-62, Kelso, Cotton & Ernst, San Francisco, 1962-64; assoc. prof. law Cornell U. Law Sch., 1964-68, prof., 1968-75, dir. internat. legal studies, 1964-74; chief counsel, later dir. Office Fgn. Direct Investments, Dept. Commerce, 1972-73; cons. Adminstrv. Conf. U.S., Washington, 1968-71, chmn., 1974-79; ptnr. McKenna, Conner & Cuneo, Washington, 1979-82; pvt. practice Washington, 1982-83; prof. law George Mason U., Arlington, Va., 1983—2002, prof. emeritus, 2002—. Fulbright lectr., Slovenia, 1994; lectr. Acad. Am. and Internat. Law, Southwestern Legal Found., Dallas, 1967—72; instr. Golden Gate U., 1961; cons., chmn. pubs. adv. bd. Internat. Law Inst., 1984—2004; cons. Inst. Pub. Adminstrn., Slovenia, 1994—. Mem. editl. bd. Jour. Law and Tech., 1986—91; contbr. articles to profl. jours. Active Pres.'s Inflation Program Regulatory Coun., 1978—79; chmn. panel U.S. Dept. Edn. Appeal Bd., 1981—83; commr. Sausalito (Calif.) City Planning Commn., 1962—64; active Fairfax County (Va.) Rep. Com., 1984—86; bd. dirs. Nat. Ctr. Adminstrv. Justice, 1974—79, Marin Shakespeare Festival, San Rafael, Calif., 1961—64, Va. Assn. Scholars, 1990—98. Mem.: ABA (coun., sec. sect. adminstrv. law and regulatory practice 1988—94), Washington Inst. Fgn. Affairs, Stanford U. Law Soc. Washington (pres. 1982), Am. Law Inst., Assn. Am. Rhodes Scholars, Cosmos Club. Home: 275 Roebling St Warrenton VA 20186 Office: George Mason U Law Sch 3301 N Fairfax Dr Arlington VA 22201-4426 Personal E-mail: ranthonys@aol.com. Business E-Mail: ranthony@gmu.edu.

ANTHONY, ROBERT NEWTON, retired management educator; b. Orange, Mass., Sept. 6, 1916; s. Charles H. and Grace (Newton) A.; m. Gretchen Lynch, Aug. 28, 1943; children: Robert N., Victoria Stewart; m. Katherine Worley, Aug. 4, 1973. AB, Colby Coll., 1938, MA (hon.), 1959, LHD (hon.), 1963; MBA, Harvard U., 1940, DCS, 1952. Mem. faculty Bus. Sch., Harvard U., 1940-42, 46-67, 68-83, Ross Graham Walker prof. mgmt. control, prof. emeritus, 1983—. Pres. Mgmt. Analysis Ctr., Inc., 1955-63; asst. sec., contr. Dept. Def., 1965-68; prof. Mgmt. Devel. Inst., Switzerland, 1957-58; with Stanford Exec. Devel. Program, 1962; mem. adv. com. IMEDE, Switzerland, 1961-65, 68-77; spl. asst. to chmn. Price Commn., 1971-73; mem. educators cons. com. GAO, 1973-87; dir., chmn. audit com. Carborundum Co., 1971-77; dir. Warnaco, Inc., 1971-86; mem. adv. com. Kyoto Rsch. Inst., 1987-90, IPMI (Jakarta), 1983-90. Author: Management Controls in Industrial Research Organization, 1952, (with Dearborn and Kneznek) Shoe Machinery: Buy or Lease?, 1955, (with Reece) Accounting, Text and Cases, 1956, 11th edit. (with Hawkins and Merchant), 2004, Office Equipment, Buy or Rent?, 1957, Essentials of Accounting, 1964, 8th edit., 2003, (with Leslie Breitner) Accounting Principles, 1965, 7th edit., 1995, Planning and Control Systems: A Framework for Analysis, 1965, (with Govindarajan) Management Control Systems, (With Vijay Govindarajan) 11th edit., 2004, (with Hekimian) Operations Cost Control, 1967, Plaid in Management Accounting, (with Welsch) Fundamentals of Financial Accounting, 1974, Fundamentals of Management Accounting, 1974, (with Young) Management Control in Nonprofit Organizations, 1975, 7th edit., 2003, Accounting for the Cost of Interest, 1976, Financial Accounting in Nonbusiness Organizations, 1978, Tell It Like It Was, 1983, Future Directions for Financial Accounting, 1984, Teach Yourself the Essentials of Accounting (computer software), 1999; (with Anderson) The New Corporate Director, 1986, The Management Control Function, 1988, Should Business and Nonbusiness Accounting Be Different?, 1989, Rethinking the Rules of Financial Accounting, 2003; editor Richard D. Irwin, Inc.; mem. bd. Harvard Bus. Rev., 1947-60; contbr. articles to profl. jours. Trustee Colby Coll., 1959-74, 75—, chmn., 1978-83; trustee Dartmouth Hitchcock Med. Ctr., 1983-93, treas., 1993; town auditor Town of Waterville Valley, N.H., 1976-92; mem. audit com. City of N.Y., 1977-85. Lt. comdr. USNR, 1941-46. Recipient Disting. Leadership award Fed. Govt. Accts. Assn., Disting. Pub. Svc. medal Dept. Def., Disting. Svc. award Harvard Bus. Sch., Marriner Disting. Svc. award Colby Coll., Meritorious Svc. award Exec. Office of Pres., CINPAC Letter of Commendation, Baker Scholar; named to Acctg. Hall of Fame. Fellow Acad. Mgmt.; mem. Am. Acctg. Assn. (v.p. 1959, pres. 1973-74, Outstanding Acctg. Educator of Yr. 1989, acctg. sect. Lifetime Achievement award 2003), Fin. Exec. Inst., Inst. Mgmt. Accts. (chmn. cost concepts subcom., mgmt. acctg. practices com.), Assn. Govt. Accts., Am. Soc. Mil. Compts., Cosmos Club, Phi Beta Kappa, Pi Gamma Mu, Beta Alpha Psi. Home: 80 Lyme Rd Box 1 Hanover NH 03755-1233 Personal E-mail: rnanthony@valley.net.

ANTHONY, ROY SANFORD, JR., secondary school educator; b. L.A., Oct. 21, 1939; s. Roy Sanford and Phylis Dorthea Anthony; m. Catherine Opal Huggins, July 18, 1987; children: Roy Anthony, III, Ryan. BA, Whittier Coll., 1961. Cert. tchr. Calif. Tchr. Lowell Joint Sch. Dist., La Habra, Calif., 1961—62, East Whittier Sch. Dist., Whittier, Calif., 1962—65, La Serna H.S., Whittier, 1965—69, Mt. Miguel H.S., Spring Valley, Calif., 1985—97, Valhalla H.S., El Cajon, Calif., 1997—2003. Mentor Grossmont H.S. Dist., La Mesa, Calif., 1997—. Named Calif. Tchr. of Yr., 1995; recipient Disting. Tchr. award, NEA, 1987, Nat. Educator award, Milken Family Found., 1996. Mem.: Calif. Music Educators Assn., Music Educators Nat. Conf., Calif. Band Dirs. Assn., So. Calif. Band and Orch. Assn. Avocation: travel. Home: 11762 Monte View Ct El Cajon CA 92019 Office: Valhalla HS 1725 Hillsdale Rd El Cajon CA 92019 Personal E-mail: royband@aol.com. Business E-Mail: ranthony@guhsd.com.

ANTHONY, STEPHEN PIERCE, lawyer; b. Concord, Mass., Aug. 30, 1961; s. Reed Pierce and Barbara (Beatley) Anthony; m. Lisa Ann Battalia, June 2, 1990; children: Matthew William, Caroline Grace. AB, Dartmouth Coll., 1983; JD, Columbia U., 1988. Bar: Md. 1989, D.C. 1991, U.S. Dist. Ct. D.C. 1991, U.S. Dist. Ct. Md. 2000, U.S. Ct. Appeals (D.C. Cir.) 1991, U.S. Ct. Appeals (3rd Cir.) 2003. Law clk. to Hon. Patricia M. Wald, U.S. Ct. Appeals for D.C. Cir., Washington, 1988—89; assoc. Wilmer, Cutler & Pickering, Washington, 1989—91; asst. U.S. atty. U.S. Atty.'s Office for D.C., Washington, 1991—96; trial atty. pub. integrity sect. criminal divsn. U.S. Dept. Justice, Washington, 1996—2000; with Covington & Burling, Washington, 2000—, ptnr., 2003—. Barrister Edward Bennett Williams Am. Inn of Ct., Washington, 1997—. Notes and comments editor Columbia Law Rev., 1987-88. Harlan Fiske Stone scholar Columbia U., 1985-86, 87-88, James Kent scholar, 1986-87. Office: Covington & Burling 1201 Pennsylvania Ave NW Washington DC 20004 Office Phone: 202-662-5105. E-mail: santhony@cov.com.

ANTHONY, SYLVIA, social welfare organization executive; b. Boston, Oct. 5, 1929; d. Charles and Josephine (Guastaferro) Caccamesi; children: Lyn Newbury, Edward Charles Souza Jr., Dean Souza. Student, Northeastern U., Boston, 1968-69, Lee Inst., 1966, 86-87. Lic. real estate broker, Mass. Founder, pres. Life for the Little Ones, Inc., Everett, Mass., 1987-94, Sylvia's Haven, Everett, 1994—2005, Devens, Mass., 1997—. Recipient Arthur L. Whitaker award Am. Bapt. Ch. of Mass., 1992, Recognition award Commonwealth of Mass. State Senate, Ho. of Reps., Gov. of Mass., 1997, 99, Mass. Gov.'s Hwy Safety Bur., 1998, Mayor Dean J. Mazzarella City of Leominster, 1999, named Hometown Hero WBZ TV, Boston, 2001; Daily Point of Light award Points of Light Found., 2002, Amb. for Peace award The Interreligious and Internat. Fedn. for World Peace, 2002; Commendation from Pres. George Bush, 2002. Address: PO Box 1166 Groton MA 01450 Office Phone: 978-772-0925.

ANTHONY, THOMAS DALE, lawyer; b. Cleve., July 23, 1952; m. Susan Shelly; children: Lara, Elizabeth. BS, Miami U., Oxford, Ohio, 1974; JD, Case Western Res. U., 1977. Bar: Ohio 1977. Tax specialist Ernst & Young, Cleve., 1977—79; ptnr. Benesch, Friedlander, Coplan and Aronoff, Cin., 1979—89, Frost and Jacobs, Cin., 1989—98; exec. v.p., chief legal officer, sec. Choice Care, 1996—98; pres., CEO PacifiCare of Ohio, 1998—2002; mem., vice chair corp. dept. Frost Brown Todd LLC, 2001—. Speaker various orgns. Mem. Cin. Coun. on World Affairs, 1980-82; vol. fundraising drive Sta. WVIZ, 1978-79, Sta. WCET, 1980-82; legal counsel Children's Internat. Summer Villages, 1979—; account capt. United Way of Hamilton County, 1986-88, cabinet mem., 1993; pres. State Libr. Bd., Ohio, 1987-89; mem. bus. adv. coun., subcom. ednl. legis. Mariemont City Schs. and Bd. of Edn.; bd. dirs. Greater Cin. Ctr. for Econ. Edn., Am. Heart Assn. (Cin. chpt.), Juvenile Diabetes Found. Mem. ABA (taxation sect., tax acctg. problems com., tax shelter subcom., small bus. com., mem. health law forum), Ohio State Bar Assn. (health law com., ins. sect.), Cin. Bar Assn. (chmn. tax. inst. com. 1990, adminstrn. and fin. com. 1991-93, chmn. tax sect. 1993, health law com.), Cin. C. of C., Miami U. Alumni Assn. (bd. dirs., treas. 1989-91, v.p. 1991-92), Nat. Health Lawyers Assn., Rotary (co-chair youth in city govt. program), Omicron Delta Kappa, Sigma Phi Epsilon. Home: 4337 Ashley Oaks Dr Cincinnati OH 45227-3947 Office: PacifiCare 11260 Chester Rd Ste 800 Cincinnati OH 45246-4096 Office Phone: 513-651-6191. Business E-Mail: tanthony@fbtlaw.com.

ANTHONY, VIRGINIA QUINN BAUSCH, medical association executive; b. Odessa, Tex., June 9, 1945; d. William Francis and Florence Elizabeth (Decker) Quinn; m. E. James Anthony; 1 child, Justin. BA, Mt. Holyoke Coll., 1967. Exec. dir. Am. Acad. Child and Adolescent Psychiatry, Washington, 1973—, Recipient Spl. Presdl. citation Am. Psychiat. Assn., 1995, Exec. Achievement award AMA, 1999. Office: Am Acad Child & Adolescent Psychiatry 3615 Wisconsin Ave NW Washington DC 20016-3007 Business E-Mail: vqanthony@aacap.org.

ANTHONY, WILLIAM GRAHAM, artist; b. Ft. Monmouth, N.J., Sept. 25, 1934; s. Emile Peter and Martha Graham (Armstrong) A.; m. Norma Neuman, Jan. 16, 1983. BA in European History, Yale U., 1958; student, San Francisco Art Inst., 1959. Author: A New Approach to Figure Drawing, 1965, Bible Stories, 1978, Bill Anthony's Greatest Hits, 1988, War is Swell, 2000; exhibited in one-man shows: Legion of Honor, San Francisco, 1962, Stuart Katz Gallery, Laguna Beach, Calif., 1992, Cokkie Snoie Gallery, Rotterdam, 1995, 99, Dorfman Gallery, N.Y.C., 2002, 04, Stalke Gallery, Copenhagen, 2004, others; exhibited in group shows: San Francisco Mus. Modern Art, Art Inst. Chgo., Whitney Mus. Am. Art, N.Y.C., Allan Stone Gallery, N.Y.C., St. Paul Art Center; works represented in collections: Art Inst. Chgo., Bklyn. Mus., Cleve. Mus. Art, Corcoran Gallery Art, Washington, Detroit Inst. Arts, Mus. Fine Arts, Houston, Met. Mus. Art, N.Y.C., Seattle Art Mus., Whitney Mus. Am. Art, N.Y.C., Guggenheim Mus., N.Y.C., others. Served with U.S. Army, 1953-55. Republican. Home: 463 West St Apt 903 New York NY 10014-2010 Office Phone: 212-255-0379.

ANTHONY, WILLIAM PHILIP, management educator; b. Chgo., Ill., Jan. 30, 1943; s. Philip and Amelia (spina) A.; m. Roselyn Griest, Apr. 20, 1968; children: Catherine Eilzabeth, Sarah Elaine. BBA, Ohio U., 1965; MBA, Ohio State U., 1967, PhD, 1971. Carl DeSantis prof. bus. adminstrn., prof. mgmt., dir. Ctr. Exec. Mgmt. Fla. State U., Tallahassee, 1970—. Author: Managing Your Boss, 1984, Strategic Planning, 1985, Envisionary Management, 1988, Organization Theory, 6th edit., 2003, Strategic Human Resource Management, 4th edit., 2003. Mem. Acad. Mgmt., So. Mgmt. Assn., Soc. for Human Resource Mgmt. (cert. sr. profl.in human resource mgmt.). Office: Fla State U Coll Business Tallahassee FL 32306-1110 Office Phone: 850-644-7844. Fax: 850-644-0588. Business E-Mail: banthon@cob.fsu.edu.

ANTHONY-PEREZ, BOBBIE COTTON MURPHY, retired psychology educator, researcher; b. Macon, Ga., Nov. 15, 1923; d. Solomon Richard and Maude Alice (Lockett) Cotton; m. William Anthony, Aug. 22, 1959 (dec.); 1 child, Freida; m. Andrew Silviano Perez, June 20, 1979. BS, DePaul U., 1953, MS, 1954, MA, 1975; MS, U. Ill., 1959; PhD, U. Chgo., 1967. Tchr. Chgo. Pub. Schs., 1954-68; math. coord. U. Chgo., 1965; prof. Chgo. State U., 1968-95, coord. Black Studies Program, 1982-83, 90-94, prof. emeritus, 1985—; with psychol. svcs. Chgo. Pub. Schs., 1971-72; rsch. coord. Urban Affairs Inst. Howard U., Washington, 1978; coord. higher edn., careers counseling, campus ministry Ingleside Whitfield Parish, 1978-84, comm. chmn., 1991-92, 95. Contbr. numerous articles to profl. jours., chpts. to books. V.p. Cmty. Affairs Chatham Bus. Assn., 1981-85, asst. sec., 1985-86, sec., 1986-87, directory com., 1987, 88; bus. rels. chmn. Chatham Avalon Pk. Cmty. Coun., 1984—, newsletter editor, 1993-2001; bd. dirs. United Meth. Found. at U. Chgo., 1980-84, Cmty. Mental Health Coun. Inc., 1979-83; pub. edn. chairperson Chatham Avalon unit Am. Cancer Soc., 1977-88, 90-97, pub. info. chairperson, 1988-94; pres. Aux. Chgo. chpt. Tuskeegee Airmen, Inc., 1994-95, rec. sec., 1998-99, parliamentarian, 1991-95, newsletter feature writer, 1999—. NSF fellow, 1957, 58, 59; recipient numerous awards religious, civic and ednl. instns. and assns. Mem. APA, Internat. Assn. Applied Psychology, Internat. Assn. Cross-Cultural Psychology, Internat. Assn. Ednl. and Vocat. Guidance, Assn. Black Psychologists (elder 1995—, pres. Chgo. chpt. 1995-96, past pres.), Chgo. Psychol. Assn., Nat. Coun. Tchrs. Math., Am. Ednl. Rsch. Assn., Midwest Ednl. Rsch. Assn., Am. Soc. Clin. Hypnosis, Midwestern Psychol. Assn., Chgo. Soc. Clin. Hypnosis. Methodist.

ANTHONY-SMITH, MARY ANNE, mathematics professor; b. N.Y.C., Oct. 19, 1952; d. Harry Antoniades and Anne (Skoufis) Anthony; m. John LeRoy Smith, June 17, 1978; children: Alexander, Anastasia, Jeannette. BS in Math., U. Calif., San Diego, 1973; MS in Stats., San Diego State U., 1975; MS in Ednl. Computing, Pepperdine U., Malibu, Calif., 1984. Prof. math. Santa Ana (Calif.) Coll., 1976—, chair math. dept., 1993-96, acting dean, sci. and math., 1996; cmty. coll. coord. UC/CSU, Math. Diagnostic Testing Project, 2003—. Co-author: Developing Mathematically Promising Students, 1999; author, prodr. video: Classroom Voices, 1993. Mem. sch. site coun. Stone Creek Elem., Irvine, Calif., 1991-2000; Sunday sch. tchr. St. Paul's Greek Orthodox Ch., Irvine, 1987—. Recipient Disting. Faculty award Rancho Santiago C.C. Dist., Santa Ana, 1993, profl. devel. award, 1993. Mem. Nat. Coun. Tchrs. Math., Calif. Math. Coun. Cmty. Colls. Home: 1 Caraway Irvine CA 92604-3217 Office: Santa Ana Coll 1530 W 17th St Santa Ana CA 92706-3398

ANTIN, DAVID, poet, critic; b. Bklyn., Feb. 1, 1932; s. Max and Mollie (Kitzes) A.; m. Eleanor Fineman, Dec. 16, 1961; 1 son, Blaise BA, CCNY, 1955; MA, NYU, 1966. Prof. visual arts U. Calif., San Diego, 1968—99, prof. emeritus visual arts, 2000—. Author: Definitions, 1967, Autobiography, 1967, Code of Flag Behavior, 1968, Meditations, 1971, Talking, 1972, Talking at the Boundaries, 1976, Tuning, 1984, Selected Poems 1963-73, 1991, What It Means to be Avant Garde, 1993, (with Charles Bernstein) A Conversation with David Antin, 2002, I Never Knew What Time it Was, U.C.Press, 2005, John Cage Uncaged is Still Cagey, Singing Horse Press, 2005; contbg. editor: Alcheringa, 1972-80, New Wilderness, 1979-; mem. editl. com. U. Calif. Press, 1972-76. Recipient Creative Arts award U. Calif., 1972; Herbert Lehman fellow NYU, 1966; Guggenheim fellow, 1976-77; NEH fellow, 1983-84, Getty Rsch. fellow, 2002. Home: PO Box 1147 Del Mar CA 92014-1147 Office: U Calif San Diego Visual Arts Dept La Jolla CA 92037 E-mail: dantin@ucsd.edu.

ANTIN, ELEANOR, artist; b. N.Y.C., Feb. 27, 1935; d. Sol and Jeanette (Efron) Fineman; m. David Antin, Dec., 1961; 1 son, Blaise BA, CCNY, 1958; student, Tamara Daykarhanova Sch. for Stage, N.Y.C., 1954-56. Prof. visual arts U. Calif., San Diego, prof. emeritus. Artist producer videotapes Representational Painting, 1971, King Tape, 1972, Caught in the Act, 1973, Little Match Girl Ballet, 1975, Adventures of a Nurse, 1976, The Nurse and the Hijackers, 1977, The Angel of Mercy, 1980, from the Archives of Modern Art, 1987; writer, dir. producer films Loves of a Ballerina, 1986, The Last Night of Rasputin, 1988, The Man Without a World, 1991, Vilna Nights, 1993, Minetta Lane, 1995; co-writer, dirs. film The Hunger Artist, 1997; one-woman exhbns. include Mus. Modern Art, N.Y.C., 1973, Whitney Mus., N.Y.C., 1978, 97, L.A. County Mus. Art, 1999, Ronald Feldman Gallery, N.Y.C., 1977, 79, 80, 83, 86, 95, 98, 2002, 05, Marella Arte Contemporanea, Milan, 2002, 05, LA Mus. Art, 1999; group shows include, São Paulo Biennal, Brazil, 1975, Hirschhorn Mus., Washington, 1979, 84, Mus. Modern Art, N.Y.C., 1990, 98, 2000, 02, Whitney Mus., N.Y.C., 1989, 99, 2005, Mus. Contemporary Art, L.A., 1995, 98, Biennale of Sydney, 2002, Kunsthalle Wein, Museumsplatz, Vienna, 2002; performances include Battle of the Bluffs, 1975-80, The Angel of Mercy, 1977-80, Before the Revolution, 1979, Recollections of My Life with Diaghilev, 1980-86, El Desdichado (The Unlucky One), 1983, Help! I'm in Seattle, 1986, 87, Who Cares About a Ballerina?, 1987, 88, The Last Night of Rasputin, 1988-2002; represented in permanent collections, Mus. Modern Art, N.Y.C., Whitney Mus., N.Y.C., San Francisco Mus. Modern Art, Wadsworth Atheneum, Hartford, Conn., Jewish Mus., N.Y., Art Inst. Chgo., L.A. County Mus. Art, Wash. U. Gallery Art, Witherspoon Art Mus., Walker Art Ctr.; artist performer at Venice Bienale, 1976, Mus. Contemporary Art, Chgo., 1978, Contemporary Arts Mus. Houston, 1978, 80, Kitchen Ctr. for Music, Video, Dance, N.Y., 1979, LACE, L.A., 1982, 86, Sydney Opera House, 2002; film festivals include Berlin, 1992, U.S.A., 1992, Women in Film, 1992, San Francisco Jewish, 1991, London Jewish, 1991; author: Being Antinova, 1983, Eleanora Antinova Plays, 1995, 100 Boots, 1999, (screenplay) The Man Without a World, 2002. Recipient Pushcart prize VI, Best of the Small Presses, 1981-82, Vesta award for performance L.A., 1984, 16th Annual Crystal award Women in Film, 1992, Nat. Found. for Jewish Culture Media Achievement award, 1998, AICA Centennial Art Cities Assn. Best Show of Mid-Career award, 2001-2002; Nat. Endowment for Arts grantee, 1979; Guggenheim fellow, 1997.

ANTIN, MICHAEL, lawyer; b. Milw., Nov. 30, 1938; s. David Boris and Pauline (Mayer) A.; m. Evelyne Judith Hirsch, June 19, 1960; children: Stephanie, Bryan, Randall BS, Univ. Calif., 1960; JD, U. Calif., 1963. Bar: Calif. 1963; cert. tax specialist. Tax atty. Cruikshank, Antin & Grebow, Beverly Hills, Calif., 1963-81, Antin, Litz & Grebow, Beverly Hills, 1981-91, Antin & Taylor, L.A., 1993—99; sole practice L.A., 1999—. Bd. dirs. Small Bus. Counsel Am., Washington, The Group, Inc.; speaker in field; instr. Solomon S. Heubner Sch. CLU Studies, 1977-86; vis. prof. law U. Latvia, 2005. Author: How to Operate Your Trust or Probate, 1983; contbr. articles to profl. jours. With U.S. Air Force, 1959-67. Fellow Am. Coll. Tax Counsel, Am. Coll. of Trust and Estate Counsel, L.A. County Bowlers Assn. (bd. dirs. 1996-99). Avocations: jogging, tennis, cross country skiing, bowling. Office: Ste 2000 1925 Century Park East Blvd Fl 20 Los Angeles CA 90067-2721 Office Phone: 310-788-2733.

ANTIOCO, JOHN F., entertainment company executive; b. Brooklyn, Nov. 1, 1949; Grad. in Bus. adminstrn., N.Y. Inst. of Tech., 1970. Mgr. tng., v.p. of mktg., sr. v.p. oper. Southland Corp., 1970—90; CEO Pearle Vision, Dallas, 1990; pres., CEO Cir. K Corp, Phoenix, 1991-96, Taco Bell Corp., 1996-97; chmn., CEO Blockbuster Entertainment, Dallas, 1997—. Recipient Phoenix Award, Pub. Rel. Soc. of Am., Valley of the Sun Chap. Office: Blockbuster Entertainment Renaissance Tower 1201 Elm St Ste 3000 Dallas TX 75270-2187

ANTLE, CHARLES EDWARD, statistics educator; b. East View, Ky., Nov. 11, 1930; s. Bayard Pierpoint and Mary Elizabeth (Blaydes) A.; m. Elna Thomas Hall, Nov. 25, 1953; children— James, Rebecca, Susan Hall, Mark Edward. AA, Lindsey Wilson Coll., 1950; BS, Eastern Ky. State U., 1954, MA, 1955; postgrad., U. Ky., 1954-55; PhD (NDEA fellow), Okla. State U., 1962. Sr. aerophysics engr. Gen. Dynamics Corp., Fort Worth, 1955-57; mem. faculty U. Mo., Rolla, 1957-60, 62-68, prof. math., 1966-68; asso. prof. statistics Pa. State U., University Park, 1968-70, prof., 1970-92, prof. emeritus of stats. University Park, 1992—. Contbr. articles to profl. jours. Served with AUS, 1951-52. Decorated Bronze Star medal. Mem. Am. Statis. Assn. Home: 2303 W Branch Rd State College PA 16801-8043 Office: Pa State U Dept Stats University Park PA 16802 Business E-Mail: cea@psu.edu.

ANTMAN, KAREN, oncologist; b. N.J., July 26, 1948; MD, Columbia U. Coll. Physicians and Surgeons, 1974. Diplomate Am. Bd. Internal Medicine, Am. Bd. Med. Oncology. Intern Columbia Presbyn. Med. Ctr., N.Y.C., 1974—75, resident, 1975—77; fellow Dana Farber Cancer Inst., Boston, 1977—79; chief med. oncology Columbia U., N.Y.C.; attending physician N.Y. Presbyn. Hosp., 1993—; dir. Herbert Irving Cancer Ctr.; Wu prof. of medicine and prof. pharmacology Columbia U., N.Y.C., 1993—.

ANTMAN, STUART SHELDON, mathematician, educator; b. Bklyn., June 2, 1939; s. Mitchell and Gertrude (Siegel) A.; m. Wilma Gail Richlin, Mar. 24, 1968; children: Rachel Alexandra, Melissa Dora. BS, Rensselaer Poly. Inst., 1961; MS, U. Minn., 1963, PhD, 1965. Lectr. U. Minn., 1965; vis. mem. Courant Inst. of NYU, 1965-67; asst. prof. math. and aeros. NYU, 1967-69, assoc. prof. math., 1969-72; sr. vis. fellow U. Oxford, 1969-70, Heriot-Watt U., Edinburgh, 1972, 77; prof. math. U. Md., College Park, 1972—2001, disting. prof., 2001—. Prin. investigator NSF grants, 1972—; mem. Applied Math. Summer Inst., Dartmouth Coll., 1973; prof. Ecole d'Eté d'Analyse Numérique, Bréau, France, 1974; vis. prof. U. Paris-Sud, Orsay, 1975, Brown U., Providence, 1978-79, Ecole Polytechnique, Palaiseau, France, 1979, U. Nacional Autónoma de México, 1981, Math. Scis. Rsch. Inst., Berkeley, Calif., 1983, Univ. P. and M. Curie, Paris, 1983, 92, Math. Rsch. Ctr., U. Wis., 1984, Inst. Math. and Applications, U. Minn., 1985, U. Bonn, Germany, 1987, U. Leipzig, Germany, 1995, Tech. U. Darmstadt, Germany, 1999, Max Planck Inst., Leipzig, 1999, City Univ. of Hong Kong, 2000, U. Dortmund, Germany, 2001; mem. U.S. Nat. Com. on Theoretical and Applied Mechanics, 1980-88. Author: The Theory of Rods, 1972, Nonlinear Problems of Elasticity, 1995, 2d edit., 2005; co-editor: Bifurcation Theory and Nonlinear Eigenvalue Problems, 1969, Metastability and Improperly Posed Problems, 1987, Analysis and Continuum Mechanics, 1989; mem. editl. bd. Archive for Rational Mechanics and Analysis, 1972-89, 99—, editor in chief, 1989-99; editor The Non-Linear Field Theories of Mechanics, 3d edit., 2004; mem. editl. bd. Springer Tracts in Natural Philosophy, 1972-80, Acta Applicandae Mathematicae, 1982—, Jour. Elasticity, 1996—, Electronic Rsch. Announcements of Am. Math. Soc., 1997—, Quar. of Applied Math., 1999—, assoc. editor Notices of Am. Math. Soc., 1985-87; mem. editl. com. Proc. of Symposia on Applied Math, 1986-88; mem. editl. bd. (Springer series) Applied Math. Scis., 1998-2001, co-editor-in-chief, 2001—; mem. editl. bd. Interdisciplinary Applied Math., 1998-2001, co-editor-in-chief, 2001—; co-editor-in-chief Texts in Applied Math, 2001. Recipient D. Alcaraz medal, Nat. Autónoma U. Mex., 1997; John S. Guggenheim Meml. Found. fellow, 1978—79. Mem. Am. Math. Soc., Soc. Indsl. and Applied Math. (T. von Kármán prize 1999), Soc. for Natural Philosophy (sec. 1974-76), Soc. for Interaction of Mechanics and Math. (mem. exec. com. 1986-90), Math. Assn. Am. (L.R. Ford award 1987), Pi Mu Epsilon. Office: U Md Dept Math College Park MD 20742-0001 Business E-Mail: ssa@math.umd.edu.

ANTMANN, MICHAEL, music educator, director; b. Bay Shore, N.Y., Jan. 23, 1979; s. Leonard and Mary Ann Antmann; m. Ruthie Stant, May 25, 2002. MusB Edn., Fla. State U., 2001. Cert. Tchr. Music K-12 Fla., 2002. Band dir. Swift Creek Mid. Sch., Tallahassee, Fla., 2001—. Recipient Tchr. of Yr., Swift Creek Mid. Sch., 2004—05, Citation of Excellence, Nat. Band Assn., 2004, Eagle Scout, Boy Scouts of Am., 1995. Mem.: Internat. Assn. Jazz Educators, Nat. Band Assn., Music Educators Nat. Conf., Fla. Music Educators Assn., Fla. Bandmasters Assn. (sec. 2004—05). Office: Swift Creek Middle School Band 2100 Pedrick Rd Tallahassee FL 32317 Office Phone: 850-487-4868. Office Fax: 850-414-2650. Personal E-mail: antmann525@comcast.net. E-mail: antmannm@swiftcreek.leon.k12.fl.us.

ANTOINE, JANET ANNE, social worker; b. Chgo., Nov. 1, 1945; d. Karl Frederick Abrath and Aniela Domitilda Chappas; m. Lawrence Verne Antoine Sr., Sept. 4, 1964 (dec.); children: Lawrence V. Jr., Dennis Patrick. BA, Loyola U., Chgo., 1969; MPS, Western Ky. U., 1977; MS in Social Work, U. Louisville, 1981. Social worker Cabinet for Human Resources, Brandenburg, Ky., 1977-79, Louisville, 1979-81, Cath. Charities, Louisville, 1981-82, dir. maternity svcs., 1982-84; social worker Cabinet for Human Resources, Louisville, 1984-86, Dept. of Vet. Affairs, U.S. Govt., Louisville, 1986—. Site supr. Sr. Companion program, Louisville, 1987—. Cmty. vol. Army Com Svc., Ft. Knox and Ft. Gordon, 1968-77, 2d St. Neighborhood Assn., 1979-96, Old Louisville Neighborhood Assn., 1982-92. Recipient VA Sec. Hand & Heart award, 1998-99. Mem. NASW, AAUW, NOW. Roman Catholic. Avocations: needlepoint, gardening, reading, painting, tennis. Home: 1840 Fleming Rd Louisville KY 40205-2420 Office: VA Med Ctr Louisville 800 Zorn Ave Louisville KY 40206-1433 E-mail: Antoine.Janet@Louisville.Va.Gov.

ANTOINE, RICHARD L., human resources specialist, consumer products company executive; m. Dorothy O'Brien; 1 child. BS, U. Wis., 1969. Various positions including soap process supr. and plant mgr. Procter & Gamble Co., mgr. N.Am. supply sys., engring., and purchasing divsn., 1992—99, dir. global supply sys., 1999—2001, global human resources officer, 2001—. Bd. dirs. Cinn. Ballet Co. Avocations: travel, golf. Office: Procter & Gamble Co 1 Procter & Gamble Plz Cincinnati OH 45202 Office Phone: 513-983-1100. Office Fax: 513-983-9369.*

ANTOKOLETZ, ELLIOTT MAXIM, music educator; b. Jersey City, Aug. 3, 1942; s. Jack and Esther (Leiter) A.; m. Juana Canabal, May 28, 1972; 1 child, Eric. Student, Juilliard Sch. Music, 1960-65; BA in Musicology, Hunter Coll., 1968, MA in Musicology, 1970; PhD in Musicology, CUNY, 1975. Instr. violin Brearley Sch., N.Y.C., 1970-76; theory lectr., instr. chamber music Queens Coll., N.Y.C., 1973-76; prof. musicology U. Tex., Austin, 1976—. Author: The Music of Béla Bartók, 1984, Béla Bartók: A Guide to Research, 1988, Twentieth-Century Music, 1992, Musical Symbolism in the Operas of Debussy and Bartok, 2004; editor: Bartók Perspectives, 2000, Georg Von Albrecht Memoirs, 2004, Internat. Jour. of Musicology; contbr. articles to prof. jours. and mags. Recipient Béla Bartók Memorial award Hungarian Govt., 1981, Tacquard Endowed Centennial Chair, U. Tex., 1983-84, Tching. Excellence award U. Tex., 1981, Achievement PhD Alumni award CUNY, 1987. Mem. Am. Musicol. Soc. (Subvention award 1982), Coll. Music Soc., Internat. Alban Berg Soc., Sonneck Soc., Internat. Musicol. Soc. Avocation: oil and water-color painting. Office: U Tex Music Dept Austin TX 78712 Business E-Mail: antokoletz@mail.utexas.edu.

ANTON, BARBARA, writer; b. Pocono Pines, Pa., Apr. 3, 1926; d. Walter B. and Emma Agnes (Hess) Miller; m. Albert Anton, June 23, 1949. Grad. Gemologist, Gemol. Inst. of Am., 1964. Fashion and design editor Nat. Jeweler Mag., N.Y.C., 1956-58; freelance writer novels/plays, 1956—; staff writer Writer's Guidelines and News Mag.; instr. sr. divsn. U. South Fla., 2000—. Writing instr. Sr. Acad./Elderhostel U. South Fla., 1999—. Contbr. articles to numerous nat. mags. including Cosmopolitan, Family Circle, Bride's Mag., Saturday Evening Post, Thera Lit. Mag.;, author plays, (novels) Egrets to the Flames (Top Ten/Fla. Writers Festival, 1995), short stories, 13 plays produced off-Broadway, 1995—2003. Recipient First Prize Humor, Manatee Writers Contest, 2000—01, 1st prize, Father's Hall of Fame Contest, 2000—01, over 100 awards for various writings, 14 awards, Fla. Studio Theatre Shorts Contest. Mem. Dramatists Guild.

ANTON, BRYAN LARRY, music educator, musician; b. Fort Riley, Kans., Mar. 22, 1963; s. Larry Irving and Dorothy Judith Anton; m. Lori Elizabeth Henderson, Dec. 30, 1988. B in Music Edn., U. No. Iowa, 1985; MusM, Pa. State U., 1988. Music instr. Wise County Schs., Big Stone Gap, Va., 1985—86; grad. asst. Pa. State U., University Park, 1986—88; band dir. Concord (Mich.) Schs., 1988—90; mgr. Pizza Hut, Lansing, Mich., 1990—92; Cook Dante's Inc., State College, Pa., 1992—93; music instr. Windber (Pa.) Area Elem., 1993—. Free-lance bass trombonist, 1992—2002; bass trombonist Williamsport (Pa.) and Altoona (Pa.) Symphony, 1992—2002, Laurel Brass, 1997—2002. Band dir. Windber Town Band, 1995—98; soloist Johnstown Civic Band-Blue Topaz; ch. musician Mid-Pa. Ch., 1992—2002. Named Tchr. of Autistic Children, Cambria Chpt. Autism Soc. Am., 1997. Mem.: NEA (rep. Windber, mem. exec. com.), Pa. Music Educators, Internat. Trombone Assn. Republican. Methodist. Avocations: running, gardening, tropical fish, reading.

ANTON, DAVID L., research and development company executive, biotechnologist, researcher; b. Seattle, Mar. 20, 1953; s. Hector R. and Lois M. Anton; m. Johanna Kahalley, Sept. 2, 2000; children: Christopher D, Steven M, Kahalley M. PhD, U. Minn., 1980. From prin. investigator to mgr. rsch. DuPont Ctrl. Rsch., Wilmington, Del., 1983—94, mgr. rsch., 1994—2001; mgr. strategic R&D planning DuPont Crop Protection, Newark, Del., 2001—04; program mgr. biochemical products DuPont ConAgra Visions, LLC, Wilmington, 1991—93; mgr. biofuels devel. DuPont BioBased Materials, Wilmington, Del., 2004—; vp R&D DuPont Tate & Lyle BioProducts LLC, Wilmington, 2004—. Chmn. biocatalysis Gordon Rsch. Conf., 1990; chmn. enzyme engring. conf. Engring. Found., 1999. Editor: Jour. Molecular Catalysis B: Enzymatic, 1994—97. Recipient Bacaner Basic Sci. award, Minn. Med. Found., 1981, Presdl. Green Chemistry Challenge award, U.S. EPA, 2003; fellow, NIH, 1980—82. Mem.: Am. Chem. Soc. (nominating com. 1995—99, biotech rep. 1995—99), Am. Assn. Biochemistry and Molecular Biology, Del. Valley Enzymology Club (founder 1986—89, chmn. 1986—89). Achievements include development of and commercialization of a biological process for 1, 3Propanediol, DuPont's first bioprocess. Avocation: scuba diving. Office: DuPont Bio-Based Materials PO Box 80728 Wilmington DE 19880-0728 Business E-Mail: david.l.anton@usa.dupont.com.

ANTON, HARVEY, textile company executive; b. NYC, Nov. 10, 1923; s. Abraham J. and Byrdie (Casin) A.; student Western State Coll. Colo., 1941, Savage Sch. Edn., 1941-42; BS, NYU, 1949; m. Betty L. Weintraub, Dec. 18, 1949; children: Bruce Norman, Lynne Beth. Pres., Anton Yarn Corp. (merged with Robison Textile Co. to form Robison-Anton Textile Co. 1959), NJ, 1949-50, chmn. bd., 1989—; v.p. Arrow Spinning, Susquehanna, Pa.; adv. bd. 1st Jersey Nat. Bank; v.p. Mid-Valley Textile; sec. Bloomsburg Dye; chmn. bd. Robison-Anton Textile Co. Trustee Erza Charitable Found.; pres. Anton Found.; bd. dirs. Pascock Valley Hosp., Westwood, NJ Served to 1st lt. AUS, 1943-46. Clubs: Masons, KP; Leonia Tennis; NY Univ. Letter (NYC). Home: 41 Longview Dr Emerson NJ 07630-1507 Office: Robison Anton Textile Co 175 Bergen Blvd Fairview NJ 07022-1684

ANTON, JOHN PETER, philosopher, educator; b. Canton, Ohio, Nov. 2, 1920; s. Peter C. and Christine (Giannopoulos) A.; m. Helen Vezos, Nov. 26, 1955; children: James, Christopher, Peter. BS, Columbia U., 1949, MA, 1950, PhD, LHD, U. Athens, 1992; PhD, doctor humanities, U. Patras, 2004. Instr. Pace Coll., 1953-54; vis. lectr. U. N.Mex., 1954-55; asst. prof. U. Nebr., 1955-58; assoc. prof. Ohio Wesleyan U., 1958-62; prof. SUNY, Buffalo, 1962-67, assoc. dean grad. sch., prof., 1967-69; Fuller E. Callaway prof. Emory U., 1969-81, chmn. dept. philosophy, 1969-76; prof., provost New Coll., U. South Fla., Tampa, 1982-83, disting. prof. Greek philosophy and culture, 1983—, dir. Ctr. Greek Studies. Woods vis. prof. Mills. Coll., 1981; vis. prof. Columbia U., 1966. Author: Aristotle's Theory of Contrariety, 1957, Science, Philosophy and Educational Tasks, 1966, Naturalism and Historical Understanding, 1967, Philosophical Essays, 1969, Essays in Ancient Greek Philosophy (5 vols.), 1971-92, Science and the Sciences in Plato, 1980, Critical Humanism as a Philosophy of Culture, 1981, Upward Panic: The Autobiography of Eva Palmer-Sikelianos, 1993, The Poetry and Poetics of C.P. Cavafy, 1995, Categories and Experience, 1996, Archetypal Principles and Hierarchies, 2000, American Naturalism and Greek Philosophy, 2005; co-editor (jour.) Diotima: editl. cons. Jour. History of Philosophy, 1968—, The Humanist, 1967—; mem. editl. bd. So. Jour. Philos., 1974—, Eidos, 1974—, Ancient Philosophy, 1979, Idealistic Studies, 1981, Philos. Inquiry, 1981; founding editor (jours.) Jour. of Neoplatonic Studies, 1991, Revue de Philosophie Ancienne, 1984—, Skepsis, 1997, Phronimos, 2004. Bd. govs. St. Lawrence Coll., 1989. With U.S. Army, 1946—47. Mem. Am. Philos. Assn., Soc. Advancement of Am. Philosophy (founding mem.), Am. Philol. Assn., Am. Soc. Aesthetics (trustee 1973-76, 81-84), Ga. Philos. Soc. (v.p. 1972, pres. 1973), Internat. Soc. Neoplatonic Studies (chmn. exec. com., pres. 1997—2004), Soc. Ancient Greek Philosophy (sec., treas. 1973-81, pres. 1981-83), Internat. Assn. Sports Law (hon.), Modern Greek Studies Assn. (v.p. 1969—72), Soc. Macedonian Studies (hon.), Acad. Athens (corr.), Internat. Assn. Greek Philos. (hon. pres. 1993), Soc. Internat. pour l'Etude de la Philosophie Mediévale, Parnassos Lit. Soc. (hon.), Phi Beta Kappa, Eta Sigma Phi, Phi Sigma Tau. Home: 10012 Oxford Chapel Dr Tampa FL 33647-2870 Office: U South Fla Dept Philosophy Tampa FL 33620 Office Phone: 813-974-3670. E-mail: hanton1@tampabay.rr.com.

ANTON, RICHARD HENRY, lawyer; b. Ft. Worth, Aug. 30, 1946; s. Abe and Faye (Gernsbacher) A.; m. Merriessa Ratkin, June 23, 1968; children: Lane Elliot, Shirra Navit. BA with honors, U. Tex., 1968, JD, 1976; MS, Harvard U., 1973. Bar: Mo. 1976, U.S. Dist. Ct. (we. dist.) Mo. 1976, U.S. Ct. Appeals (10th cir.) 1978, U.S. Ct. Appeals (8th cir.) 1979, U.S. Supreme Ct. 1982, Tex. 1985, U.S. Dist. Ct. (we. dist.) Tex. 1985. Assoc. Koenigsdorf Kusnetzky, Kansas City, Mo., 1976-80; sole practice Kansas City, Mo., 1980-82; assoc. Law Offices of Gerald Rosen, Kansas City, Mo., 1982-84, Hancock Piedfort, Austin, Tex., 1985-87; ptnr. Hancock, Piedfort, Austin, 1987—94; sole practitioner Austin, 1995—. Served with USN, 1968-72. Mem. ABA, State Bar Assn. Tex., Assn. Trial Lawyers Am., Tex. Trial Lawyers Assn., Phi Beta Kappa. Democrat. Jewish. Avocations: golf, running. Home: 5005 Lodge View Ln Austin TX 78731-2674 Office: PO Box 26797 Austin TX 78755-0797 Office Phone: 512343.

ANTON, THOMAS JULIUS, political science and public policy educator, consultant; b. Worcester, Mass., Sept. 28, 1934; s. Julius and Irene (Dupsha) A.; m. Barbara Jane Lindblom, June 22, 1957; children: Lynn Allison, Leslie Carol, Thomas Rolf. AB, Clark U., 1956; MA, Princeton U., 1959; PhD, Prnceton U., 1961. Lectr. U. Pa., Phila, 1960-61; asst. prof. U. Ill., Urbana, 1961-63, assoc. prof. Urbana, Chgo., 1964-67; from assoc. prof. to prof. U. Mich., Ann Arbor, 1967-83, dir. PhD program in urban planning, 1977-80; prof. polit. sci., dir. A. Alfred Taubman Ctr. for Pub. Policy and Am. Instns. Brown U., Providence, 1983—, dean of faculty, 1990-91. Vis. prof. U. Stockholm, 1968, 71; cons. State of Ill., Springfield, Chgo., 1963-70, State of Mich., Lansing, 1972-83, HEW, Washington, 1976-80, Brookings Instn., Washington, 1970—; cons. NAS, Washington, 1976-80, panel mem., 1981-82; mem. Swedish Fulbright Commn., Stockholm, 1971; vice chmn., bd. trustees Clark Univ., 1995-2001. Author: The Politics of State Expenditure in Illinois, 1966, Governing Greater Stockholm, 1975, Moving Money, 1980, Administered Politics, 1980, American Federalism and Public Policy: How the System Works, 1989; editor: Policy Scis., Amsterdam, 1977-80. Commr. Providence Housing Authority, 1986—, chmn., 1990—. J.F. Kennedy fellow Gov. of Sweden, 1977; NSF grantee, 1980; recipient Individual Recognition award HUD, 1992. Mem. Am. Polit. Sci. Assn. (Gladys M. Kammerer award 1989, Disting. Federalism scholar award 2000), Assn. Pub. Policy and Mgmt., Midwest Polit. Sci. Assn., Nat. Acad. Pub. Adminstrn. (panel on info. mgmt. 1993—), Princeton Club (N.Y.C.), Phi Beta Kappa. Democrat. Home: 11 Gull Ln Orleans MA 02653 Office: Brown Univ Pub Policy Ctr PO Box 1977 Providence RI 02912-1977

ANTONACCI, ANTHONY EUGENE, engineer; b. Sept. 21, 1949; s. Salvatore Natali and Odile Estella (Stanton) A.; m. Sherry Lee Kessler, Mar. 6, 1971; children: Don Warren, Lance Anthony. Cadet, USAF Acad., 1968-69; AS, Forest Park Coll., 1971. Lic. power engr. Asst. supr. data processing ops. 1st Nat. Bank, St. Louis, 1969-71; engr. Installation & Svc. Engring. (Mech. & Nuclear) divsn. Gen. Electric Corp., St. Louis, 1971-76; engr. Anheuser-Busch Corp., St. Louis, 1976—. Author software. Trustee, treas. Antonette Hills Trusteeship, Affton, Mo., 1976-80. Mem. Brewers and Maltsters Local 6 (del. 1982-83), Nat. Aerospace Edn. Coun., Apple Programmers and Developers Assn., Am. Legion. Republican. Roman Catholic. Avocations: classic auto restoration, trumpet music. Home: 8971 Antonette Hills Dr Saint Louis MO 63123-6503 Personal E-mail: TonyA2@aol.com.

ANTONAKOS, STEPHEN, sculptor; b. So., Greece, Nov. 1, 1926; came to U.S., 1930; Ed., Bklyn. C.C. Lectr. Yale, New Haven, 1968; sculptor, working primarily in neon; vis. artist; artist-in-residence (U. Wis.), Madison, 1971, U. Calif.-Fresno, 1972. One-man shows U. Maine, 1958, Avant-Garde Gallery, N.Y., 1958, Miami Mus. Modern Art, 1964, Schramm Gallery, Ft. Lauderdale, 1964, Byron Gallery, N.Y.C., 1964, Fischbach Gallery, N.Y.C., 1967, 68, 69, 70, 72, John Weber Gallery, N.Y.C., 1974, 75, 76, 77, Ft. Worth Art Mus., 1970, 74-75, Contemporary Art Mus., Houston, 1971, SUNY, Albany, 1973, Bernier Gallery, 1977, Young Hoffman Gallery, Chgo., 1978, U. Mass., 1978, Bernier Gallery, 1977, Gillespie/de Laage Gallery, Paris, 1979, Albright-Knox Art Gallery, Buffalo, 1975, Wright State U., Dayton, Ohio, 1975, Galleria Marilena Bonomo, Bari, Italy, 1975, Galerie 26, Paris, 1975, Galleriaforma, Genoa, Italy, 1975, Galerie December, Dusseldorf, Germany, 1976, Art & Project, Amsterdam, 1976, Galerie Bonnier, Geneva, 1976, Nancy Lurie Gallery, Chgo., 1976, Galerie Aronowitsch, Stockholm, 1977, Galerie Tanit, Munich, 1978, 80, Lowe Art Mus., Miami, Fla., 1980, Nassau County Mus. Fine Art, Roslyn, N.Y., 1982, Maison de Culture de Nevers (France), 1983, Le Coin du Miroir, Dijon, France, 1983, Bonnier Gallery, N.Y.C., 1983, Jean Bernier Gallery, Athens, 1983, La Jolla (Calif.) Mus. Contemporary Art, 1984, Davenport (Iowa) Art Gallery, 1985, Ileana Tounta Contemporary Art Ctr., Athens, Greece, 1988, Rose Art Mus., Brandeis U., 1986, Elvehjem Mus. Art U. Wis., Madison, 1986, Burnett Miller Gallery, L.A., G.H. Dalsheimer Gallery, Balt., 1987, Kouros Gallery, N.Y.C., 1989, Galerie d'Art Contemporain, Geneva, 1990, Ileana Tounta Gallery, Athens, Greece, 1992, Carpenter Ctr., Harvard U., 1992-93, Rhodes (Greece) Contemp. Art Space, 1993, Mus. Contemporary Art, Salonika, 1993, Malibu (Calif.) Internat. Sculpt. Exhibition, 1993, Macedonian Mus. Modern Art, Salonika, Greece, 1993, The New Fort, Corfu, Greece, 1995, The Art Inst. Boston, 1996, Smith Coll. Mus. Art, Northampton, Mass., 1997, The Harn Mus., Gainesville, Fla., 1997, Stux Gallery, Athens Greece, 1997, Lucas Gallery Princeton U., 1998, Mitchell Algus Gallery, 1998, Gallery Camino Real, Boca Raton, Fla., 1999, St. Peter's Ch., 1999, Pub. Sch. 1, Long Island City, N.Y., 1999, Found. for Hellenic Culture, N.Y., Rose Art Mus., Brandeis U., Waltham, Mass., 2000, State Mus. Contemp. Art, Thessaloniki, 2000, Salonica, Greece, 2000, Neuberger Mus. Art, SUNY, Purchase, 2000, Corpus Christie Ch., N.Y., 2001, Galerie Denise Rene, Rive Gauche, Paris, 2002, Astrolavos Gallery, Athens, 2003, Macedonian Mus. Contemp. Art, Salonika, 2003, Alexander S. Onassis Pub. Benefit Found., N.Y., 2003, Lafayette Coll., Easton, Pa., 2004, The Kydoniefs Found., Andros, Greece, 2004, The Chapel of St. George, Mystra, Greece, 2004, Gallery of the Graduate Ctr., CUNY, 2005, others; exhibited in group shows Miami Mus. Modern Art, 1958, Martha Jackson Gallery, N.Y., 1960, Allan Stone Gallery, 1961, 62, 64, Byron Gallery, 1963, 64, PVI Gallery, N.Y., 1964, 65, Whitney Mus. Am. Art, 1966, 68, 69, 73, Newark Coll. Engring., 1968, U. N.C., 1968, R.I. Sch. Design, 1969, Worcester Art Mus., 1965, Nelson Gallery of Art, Kansas City, Mo., 1966, 68, Stedelijk von Abbemuseum, Eindhoven, 1966, Walker Art Ctr., Mpls., 1967, L.A. County Mus., 1987, N.J. State Mus. Cultural Ctr., 1967, Carnegie Internat. Mus., Pitts., 1967, Wadsworth Atheneum, Hartford, Conn., 1968, Fort Worth Art Mus., 1969, Smithsonian Instn., 1970, Portland Mus., Maine, 1971, Anne-Marie Verna Gallery, Zurich, 1972, San Francisco Mus. Art, 1973, Indpls. Mus. Art, 1974, Stadtischen Mus., Leverkusen, Federal Republic of Germany, 1975, MIT, Arts on the Line, 1980, Aldrich Mus., Ridgefield, Conn., 1979, 84, Corcoran Gallery of Art, Washington, 1987, Am. Craft Mus., N.Y.C., 1988, UCLA Art Gallery, 1969, U. Nebr., Lincoln, 1969, 70, Documenta 6, Kassel, W.Ger., 1977, Galerie Nancy Gillespie/Elisabeth de Laage, Paris, 1979, Wellesley (Mass.) Coll. Mus., 11th Internat. Sculpture Conf., Washington, 1980, Creative Time Inc., N.Y.C., Mus. Mod. Art, N.Y.C., 1981, Europalia, Brussels, 1982, Mus. Mod. Art of the City of Paris,1983, 24th Annual Print Exbn. Bklyn. Mus., 1986, Sao Paulo Internat. Biennale, Brazil, 1987, Rose Art Mus. Brandeis U., 1987, archtl. show Montreal, 1988, Boston Atheneum, 1988, Ileana Tounta Contemporary Arts Ctr., Athens, Greece, 1988, Artec, Nagoya, Japan, 1989, Fawbush Gallery, N.Y.C., 1990, Nat. Gallery, Athens, 1992, Harn Mus. Art, Gainesville, Fla., 1998, Chrysler Mus. Art., Norfolk, 1999; represented in permanent collections Fed. Bldg., Dayton, Ohio, Hampshire Coll., Amherst, Mass., U. Mass., Amherst, Atlanta Internat. Airport, Whitney Mus. Am. Art, Mus. Modern Art,N.Y.C., Wadsworth Atheneum, Hartford, Conn., Phoenix Art Mus., Weatherspoon Art Gallery, U. N.C., Greensboro, Newark Mus., Milw. Art Center, Guggenheim Mus., La Jolla Mus. Contemporary Art; pub. commns. include Fed. Bldg., Dayton, Ohio, U. Mass., Amherst, Harstfield Internat. Airport, Atlanta, The Atheneum, U. Dijon, France, 14th Dist. Police Sta., Chgo., Hampshire Coll., U. Mass., 42d St, N.Y.C., Bagley Wright Theatre, Seattle, Tacoma (Wash.) Dome, La Jolla Mus. Contemporary Art, Rose Art Mus., Columbus (Ohio) Mus. Arts, Greektown Sta., Detroit, 59th St. Marine Transfer Sta., N.Y., 7475 Wis. Ave., Bethesda, Md., Back Bay/South Sta., Boston, Exch. Pl. Sta., Jersey City, 5th/Hill Sta. L.A., Lawrence St., Denver, Southwestern Bell, Dallas, Davenport (Iowa) Transit Ctr., Charles St. Sta., Balt., South Campus Sta., Buffalo, York Coll., Jamaica, N.Y., Embassy Stes., San Diego, Neon for the 59th St. Marine Transfer Station, N.Y., 1990, Neons for Buttonwood, Phila., 1990, Neons and Drawings Galerie d'Art Contemporain, Geneva, 1990, Neons for Pershong Square, 1991, Neons for Momoci, Fukuoka, Japan, 1992, Neons for Messe Turm Frankfurt, Ger., 1993, Neons for the Stadtsparkasse, Cologne, 1993, Neons for Tachikawa, Tokyo, 1994, San Antonio Pub. Libr., 1995, Neons for Providence Convention Ctr., 1995, Neon for Granpark, Tokyo, 1996, Neon for William Paterson Coll., Wayne, N.J., 1995, Neuberger Gallery SUNY, Purchase, 1997, Neons for the Reading Power Plant, Tel Aviv, 1998—, Hot Glass, Flat Glass & Neon, Chrysler Mus., Norfolk, Va., 1999, Blue Cross: Meditation Chapel, Courthouse Gallery, Portsmouth, Va., 1999, Once Again, Smith Coll. Campus, Northampron, Mass, 2001, Six Incomplete Circles, Bati, Italy, 2002, Tria, Macedonian Mus. Contemp. Art, Thessaloniki, Greece, 2002, Double Sequence, Gen. Mitchell Internat. Airport, Milw., 2002, Ascension, Nat. Bank of Greece, Athens, 2003, Three Gates, Tsumari, Japan, 2003, Two Entrances, Athena Atrium, Odessa, Ukraine, 2004, Orizzonte, Aeroporto di Bari, Italy, 2005, Presence, European Cult. Ctr., Delphi, Greece, 2005. Recipient award NEA, 1973, N.Y. Creative Artists Pub. Svc. Program, Lifetime Achievement award Neuberger Mus. Art, 2000. Home: 435 W Broadway New York NY 10012-5902 Office Phone: 212-925-5956.

ANTONELLI, JOSEPH K., musician, educator; b. Chicago, Ill., Jan. 15, 1944; s. Joseph Antonelli and Concetta Chodur; m. Patricia Nelson, Aug. 0, 1969 (div. Oct. 0, 1980); children: Colleen, Jeffrey. BM, DePaul U., Chicago, IL, 1969; Masters Music Edn., Vander Cook Music Coll., Chicago, IL, 1973. Band dir. Lisle Sch. Dist., Lisle, Ill., 1969—70; music dir. jazz band Broadview Pk. Dist., Broadview, Ill., 1973—77; music dir. Lindop Sch. Dist. #92, Broadview, Ill., 1970—99; pres. Sound Cir. Inc., Villa Park, Ill., 1980—. Treas. Midwest Suburban Music Fest Assn., Broadview, Ill., 1970—99; music cons. SCI Inc., Villa Park, Ill., 1980—90; editor / pub. Music Lovers' Network, Oak Brook, Ill., 1993—95. Contbr. articles to profl. jours. Mem. Rotary Internat., Glen Lo Park, Ill., 1984, Iea, Nea, Broadview, Ill., 1970—99, M.E.N.C., 1980—89. Recipient Best in Class Jazz Band, Chgo. Area Jazz Festival, 1974, Wright Coll. Merit Award, Wright Coll. Music Dept., 1965. Mem.: Phi Mu Alpha Symphonia. Avocations: creating stained glass projects, continuing education, psychology, philosophy. Home: 1136 S Euclid Villa Park IL 60181 Personal E-mail: josepha334@aol.com.

ANTONELLI, PATTIE ELLEN, public relations executive; b. Cambridge, Mass., Nov. 1, 1953; d. Mary Frances (Keane) Collins; m. Joseph F. Antonelli, May 22, 1983. BS in Journalism, Suffolk U., 1975. Pub. relations dir. Foodmaster Supermarkets, Cambridge, 1975-77; pub. info. specialist Somerville (Mass.) Community Devel., 1978-80; adminstrv. asst. Middlesex County, Cambridge, 1980; dir. pub. affairs and vols. J.B. Thomas Hosp., Peabody, Mass., 1980-89; dir. pub. rels. Waltham-Weston (Mass.) Hosp. & Med. Ctr., 1989-91; pres. Antonelli Profl. Resources, Medford, Mass., 1991—. Bd. dirs. Bay Colony Devel. Corp., Newton. Bd. dirs. ACR, Lynn, Mass., 1981-83. Recipient Excellence in Pub. Relations award Pub. Relations Casebook, 1983, Merit award Healthcare Mktg. Report, 1985. Mem. Pub. Rels. Soc. Am. (accredited award 1985), New Eng. Hosp. Pub. Rels. Assn. (Excellence award 1983, '86, 1st Place 1984), Am. Soc. Hosp. Pub. Rels. and Mktg., New Eng. Devel. Soc. Roman Catholic. Avocations: travel, boating, horses, golf. Home and Office: Antonelli Profl Resources 1 Summit Rd Medford MA 02155-3010 Office Phone: 781-391-4528. E-mail: pcajfa@msn.com.

ANTONELLI, ROSEMARY, writer; b. Hazleton, Pa. d. Dominic A. and Carmella Antonelli. BA in Journalism, Pa. State U. Newspaper reporter Hazleton (Pa.) Standard-Speaker, Inc.; writer, pub. rels. cons. Orlando, Fla. Contbr. articles to consumer mags., newspapers, and profl. jours. including Design Times, Health Facilities Mgmt., Bldr./Arch., Orbus, Hosp. News of Fla., Fla. Design, Orlando Mag., Orlando Bus. Jour., The Lion, Hazleton (Pa.) Standard-Speaker. Recipient Newswriting award Pa. affiliate Nat. Fedn. Press Women; named Woman of the Yr., Soroptimist Internat. of Greater Hazleton, 1979; featured in Editor and Pub. mag., 1979.

ANTONIC, JAMES PAUL, international marketing consultant; b. Milw., Mar. 29, 1943; s. George Paul and Betti Ware (Littler) A.; m. Irene Robson, Dec. 26, 1970; 1 child, Glenn. BS in Psychology, U. Wis., 1964; MBA, Boston U., 1976. Owner JPA Supply and Warehouse Co., Milw., 1966—68; product mgr., market mgr. Delta Oil Products, Milw., 1968—74, v.p. internat. ops. Brussels, 1974—2003; pres. Internat. Market Devel. Group, Barrington, Ill., 1976—2003; CEO Internat. Market Devel. Group, LLC, Ft. Myers, Fla., 1998—; pres., COO, Advanced Composite Tech., Inc., Ft. Myers, 2003—04; pres., CEO CBS-Homes Fla. LLC, 2004—. Bd. dirs. ASG LLC, Schaumburg, Ill.; lectr. Cast Metals Inst., Am. Mgmt. Assn., U.S. Dept. Commerce, Ga. World Congress Inst., various colls.; dir., chmn. Compsite Bldg. Structures, Ltd., 2004—. Contbr. articles to profl. jours. With U.S. Army Combat Engrs., 1964-66. Fellow Anglo-Am. Acad.; mem. Licensing Execs. Soc., Internat. Trade Club Chgo., MIT Enterprise Forum, World Trade Assn., Japan Mgmt. Cons. Assn., Am. Foundrymen's Assn. (chair legis. task force), Oak Brook Hounds (pres.). Home: 9111 Southmont Cv Apt 406 Fort Myers FL 33908-6298 Office: Ste 102 1500 Colonial Blvd Fort Myers FL 33908 Office Phone: 941-870-4413. Business E-Mail: james.antonic@cbs-homes.com.

ANTONINO, LAUREN SLEPIN, lawyer; b. Norfolk, Va., Feb. 4, 1962; d. William Raymond Slepin and Carol Mae (Gross) Levin; m. Tom L. Antonino, Aug. 18, 1990; children: Tommy, Matthew, Jamie, David. AB, Duke U., 1984; JD, U. Va., 1987. Fed. law clk. Hon. Oliver Koelsch, U.S. Ct. Appeals (9th Cir.), Seattle, 1987—88; assoc. Long, Aldridge & Norman, Atlanta, 1988—92; ptnr. Meadows Ichter & Trigg, Atlanta, 1992—2000, Chitwood & Harley, Atlanta, 2000—. Adv. bd. Atlanta Legal Aid, 1998; pres., mem. bd. Legal Aid for Homeless, Atlanta, 1992—97. Contbr. articles to profl. publs. Mem.: Am. Mensa Soc., Phi Beta Kappa. Home: 1116 Santa Fe Station Dunwoody GA 30338 Office: Chitwood & Harley 1230 Peachtree St Ste 2300 Atlanta GA 30305 E-mail: lsa@classlaw.com.

ANTONIOU, ANDREAS, electrical engineering educator; b. Yerolakkos, Nicosia, Cyprus, 1938; immigrated to Can., 1969; s. Antonios and Eleni Hadjisavva; m. Rosemary C. Kennedy, 1964 (dec.); children: Anthony, David, Constantine, Helen BSc with honors, U. London, 1963, PhD, 1966; Dr honoris causa, Nat. Tech. U. Greece, Athens, 2002. Mem. sci staff GEC Ltd., London, 1966; sr. sci. officer P.O. Rsch. Dept., London, 1966-69; sci. staff in R & D No. Electric Co., Ottawa, Canada, 1969-70; from asst. prof. elec. engring. to prof., dept. chmn. Concordia U., Montreal, Canada, 1970-83; founding chmn. elec. and computer engring. dept. U. Victoria, Canada, 1983-90, prof., 1983—2003, prof. emeritus, 2003—. Author: Digital Filters: Analysis, Design, and Applications, 1979, 2d edit., 1993, Digital Signal Processing: Signals, Systems, and Filters, 2005; co-author: Two-Dimensional Digital Filters, 1992; contbr. articles to profl. jours. Recipient Chmn.'s award for Career Achievement, B.C. Sci. Coun., 2000. Fellow: IEEE (assoc. editor Trans. on Cirs. and Sys. 1983—85, editor 1985—87, bd. govs. Cirs. Sys. Soc. 1995—97, gen. chair, internat. symposium on circuits & sys. 2004, Golden Jubilee award Cirs. Sys. Soc. 2000, Disting. Lectr. Sig. Proc. Soc. 2003, Tech. Achievement award Sys. Soc. 2005), Instn. Elec. Engrs. (Ambrose Fleming premium 1969); mem.: Assn. Profl. Engrs. and Geoscientists B.C. (councilor 1988—90). Greek Orthodox. Home: 4058 Jason Pl Victoria BC Canada V8N 4T6 Office: U Victoria Dept Elec & Computer Engring PO Box 3055 STN CSC Victoria BC Canada V8W 3P6 E-mail: aantoniou@ieee.org.

ANTONOVICH, MICHAEL DENNIS, county official; b. L.A. m. Christine Hu; children: Michael Dennis, Jr., Mary Christine. BA, Calif. State U., LA, 1963, MA, 1967; secondary tchg. cert., Calif. State U., 1966; grad., Pasadena Police Acad., 1967; postgrad., Stanford U., 1968—70, Harvard U., 1984, postgrad., 1987. Cert. secondary tchr. 1966. Govt. and history instr. LA Unified Sch. Dist., 1966-72; Rep. whip Calif. State Assembly, 1976-78, assemblyman, 1972-78; mem. bd. suprs. 5th Dist. LA County, 1980—; mem. Gov. George Bush-Cheney State Steering Com., 2000, Bush-Cheney Re-election Com., 2004. Instr. Calif. State U., 1979, 85, Pepperdine U., 1979; trustee L.A. C.C.'s Dist., 1969-72. Mem. Tournament of Roses Com., Glendale Symphony, L.A. Zoo. Assn., South Pasadena Police Dept. Res., Good Shepherd Luth. Home for Retarded Children; mem. Met. Transp. Authority, 1993—, chmn., 1994-95; mem. L.A. County Transp. Commn., 1980-93, chmn., 1984, 92; chmn. Calif. State Rep. Party, 1985-86; mem. LA Coliseum Commn., South Coast Air Quality Mgmt. Dist.; presdl. appointee U.S. Del. to UN Internat. Conf. on Indo-Chinese Refugees, Geneva, 1989, Com. on Privatization, 1987-88, U.S.-Japan Adv. Com., 1984, J. Fulbright Fgn. Scholarship Bd., 1991-93; mem. adv. bd. Atty. Gen.'s Missing Children, 1987-88; mem. del. Rep. Nat. Com., 1972-76, 84-88, 92-96, 2000, mem. platform com., 1976, co-chmn. human resources com. With U.S. Army, 1957—65, lt. col. Calif. State Mil. Res., 2004—. Recipient Pub. Ofcl. Yr., Nat. Fedn. Indian-Ams., 1989, Outstanding and Invaluable Svc. award Home Visitation Ctr., 1990, Brother's Keeper award Chaplain's Eagles, 1990, Responsible Citizen award Thomas Jefferson Rsch. Ctr., 1990, Outstanding Citizen award Internat. Footprint Assn., 1991, Recognition award Salvation Army, Leadership awards United Way, 1987, 91, 93, Hon. Svc. award PTA, 1991, San Fernando Valley Outstanding Leadership award Min.'s Fellowship and Focus 90s, 1991, Mental Health Assn. award of appreciation Antelope Valley Social Ctr., 1991, Recognition award MADD, 1992, Appreciation award Soc. Hispanic Profl. Engrs., L.A. chpt., 1992, awards Boy Scouts Am., 1992, 93, 2001, Recognition award Mex. Am. Correctional Assn., 1996, Outstanding Leader award SER/Jobs Progress, 2002, Michael D. Antonovich Open Space Preserve dedicated, 2002, Person of Yr. award Met. News-Enterprise, 2002, Counties Care Kids award Nat. Assn. Counties, 2003, Friend of Youth award Glendale Youth Alliance, 2003, Humanitarian award Castaic Area Town Coun., 2004, Calif. Commendation medal Calif. N.G., 2004, 7 Seals award Dept. Def./Employee Support of Guard and Res., 2004, Spirit of Lincoln award L.A. Lincoln Club, 2004, Disting. Civic award Western Diocese of Armenian Ch., 2004, Humanitarian award Iranian Am. Parents Assn. Beverly Hills, 2005, Foster Parent of Yr. award Hilltoppers Aux. Assistance League of So. Calif., 2005, Presdl. Vol. Svc. award Points of Light Found., 2005, others; Michael D. Antonovich Antelope Valley Courthouse dedicated in his honor, 2003; Michael D. Antonovich Reg. Pk. dedicated, 2003; named Man of Yr. Pasadena NAACP, 1999. Mem. County Suprs. Assn. Calif. (bd. dirs.), Phila. Soc., Glendale C. of C., Blue Key, Elks, Sigma Nu. Lutheran. Office: LA County 5th Dist 869 Hall of Adminstrn 500 W Temple St Los Angeles CA 90012-2713

ANTONSEN, ELMER HAROLD, Germanic languages and linguistics educator; b. Glens Falls, NY, Nov. 17, 1929; s. Haakon and Astrid Caroline Emilie (Sommer) A.; m. Hannelore Gertrude Adam, Mar. 24, 1956; children: Ingrid Carol, Christopher Walter. BA, Union Coll., Schenectady, N.Y., 1951; postgrad., U. Vienna, 1951-52, U. Goettingen, 1956; MA, U. Ill., 1957, PhD, 1961. Instr. German, Northwestern U., Evanston, Ill., 1959-61; asst. prof. U. Iowa, Iowa City, 1961-64, assoc. prof., 1964-67, U. Ill., Urbana, 1967-70, prof. Germanic langs. and linguistics, 1970—, head dept. Germanic langs., 1973-82, head dept. linguistics, 1990-96, assoc. Ctr. for Advanced Studies, 1984. Vis. prof. U. N.C., Chapel Hill, 1972-73, U. Goettingen, 1988. Author: A Concise Grammar of the Older Runic Inscriptions, 1975, Runes and Germanic Linguistics, 2002; editor: The Grimm Brothers and the Germanic Past, 1989, Studies in the Linguistic Sciences, 1995—2002; co-editor: Staefcraeft: Studies in Germanic Linguistics, 1991; contbr. articles to profl. jours. Served with AUS, 1953-56. Fulbright scholar, 1951—52. Mem. Linguistic Soc. Am., Royal Norwegian Soc. Scis. and Letters, Soc. Advancement of Scandinavian Study, Institut für Deutsche Sprache (corr. mem.), Selskab for nordisk filologi, Soc. for Germanic Linguistics, Phi Beta Kappa. Home: 2210 Plymouth Dr Champaign IL 61821-6542 Office: Univ Ill 4088 Flb Urbana IL 61801 Personal E-mail: elmer.antonsen@insightbb.com.

ANTONUCCI, PETER A., lawyer; b. N.Y.C., Oct. 11, 1959; BA in English, U. Rochester, 1982; JD, Bklyn. Law Sch., 1990. Bar: N.Y., Conn., U.S. Dist. Ct. (ea. dist.) Wis., U.S. Dist. Ct. (so. dist.) N.Y., U.S. Dist. Ct. (ea. dist.) N.Y., U.S. Supreme Ct. Mng. clk. Martin, Clearwater & Bell, N.Y.C., 1982—87; law clk. to Chief Judge Paul P. Rao U.S. Ct. Internat. Trade, 1988; assoc. Weil, Gotshal & Manges LLP, N.Y.C., 1990—98, counsel, 1999—. Spkr. various confs. Co-author: A Punitive Damages Primer: Legal Principles and Constitutional Challenges, 1994; contbr. chapters to books; editor: numerous articles for ABA publs., 1993—; contbr. articles to profl. publs.; commentator CNN Headline News, 1996—, Fox TV Network, 1999. Pres. St. David's Sch. Alumni Assn., 1995—98; mem. exec. com. East Sixties Properties Owners' Assn., 1995—2002. Mem.: ABA (pub. rels. com. sect. tort and ins. practice 1999—2002, chair com. toxic substances and environ. law 1999—2000, mem. Yr. 2000 task force 1998—2000, co-chair subcom. on policy 1998—99, editor-in-chief newsletter 1993—98, sect. vice chair 1993—98, mem. ann. mtg. com. 1996—98, numerous other offices). Avocations: public speaking, skiing, golf, travel. Office: Weil Gotshal & Manges LLP 209 E 61st St New York NY 10021

ANTONUCCI, RON, librarian, editor; b. Akron, Ohio, Apr. 16, 1951; s. Dominic and Louisa (Conti) A.; m. Katherine Jean Lambert, Oct. 18, 1973 (div. Dec. 1991); four children. BS in Journalism, Ohio U., 1973; MLS, Kent State U., 1998. Owner, operator The Old Book Store, Akron, 1978-85; editor, reporter Maple Heights (Ohio) Press, 1985-89; mng. editor City Express Publs., Bklyn., 1989-90; cataloguer, bibliographer Strand Bookstore, N.Y.C., 1990-91; asst. dir. Hudson (Ohio) Libr. and Hist. Soc., 1991—2004; fiction editor Artful Dodge, 2001—; mgr. Middlefield Pub. Libr., Ohio, 2004—. Editor Ohio Writer Mag., 1996-2001. Mem. lit. jury Cleve. Arts Prize. Mem. ALA, Ohio Libr. Coun. (mem. intellectual freedom com.), Nat. Book Critics Cir., Poets League Greater Cleve., Ohiana Libr. Assn. (bd. dirs.). Home: 2431 Demington Cleveland Heights OH 44106 E-mail: owren@yahoo.com.

ANTONUCCIO, JOSEPH ALBERT, management consultant; b. San Pier Niceto, Sicily, Italy, Apr. 25, 1932; came to U.S., 1935, naturalized, 1941; s. Joseph and Nancy (Calogero) A.; m. Patricia B. Damon, June 1, 1957 (div. 1987); children— Joseph Russell, Louise Shaffer, Timothy Damon AB, Rutgers U., 1954. Vice pres. Deluxe Reading Corp., Elizabeth, N.J., 1962-67; ptnr. Peat, Marwick, Mitchell & Co., N.Y.C., 1967-88; exec. v.p. Lex Electronics Inc., Westbury, N.Y., 1988-90; v.p. Princess Hotels Internat., N.Y.C., 1990-98; mng. ptnr. Veritas Cons., N.Y.C., 1998—. Contbr. atricles on computers to profl. jours. Vice pres., bd. dirs. Sutton-Area Community, Inc., N.Y.C., 1983—; mem. N.Y.C. Bd. Elections task force N.Y.C. Partnership, Inc., 1985. Served to sgt. U.S. Army, 1954-56 Mem. Data Processing Mgmt. Assn. (bd. dirs. 1962-67), Computer Security Inst. (lectr. 1979—), Assn. Systems Mgmt. (project chmn. 1972-79) Clubs: University (N.Y.C.). Avocations: hiking, skiing. Home and Office: 405 E 56th St New York NY 10022-2412 Office Phone: 212-754-6202. Personal E-mail: jantonuccio@msn.com.

ANTOSCA, STEVE, composer, educator; b. Washington, Oct. 2, 1955; s. Joseph and Phyllis Antosca; m. Mary Schoenberger, Jan. 21, 1955; children: Nicholas, Gianmarco. Masters, Johns Hopkins U. Faculty George Mason U., Fairfax, Va., 2001—. Office: George Mason Univ 4400 University Dr MSN 3E3 Fairfax VA 22030-4422

ANTOUN, ANNETTE AGNES, editor, publisher; b. Franklin, Pa., Mar. 7, 1927; d. Adrien Uriel and Charlotte Mary (McMullen) Adelman; m. Frederic George Antoun, July 19, 1947 (dec.); children: Frederic G., Gregory S., Lawrence J., Mark J. (dec.), Laureace A., Scott J., Jonathan M., Lisa A. Student, Allegheny Coll., Meadville, Pa. Founder, editor-pub. Paxton Herald, Harrisburg, Pa., 1960—; founder, owner Graphic Svcs., advt. and graphics, Harrisburg, 1972—; owner Comms. Sys. Design, 1978—; pres. Susquehanna Valley Assocs., Inc., 1978—. Co-editor French Creek Patriot, cmty. newspaper, Cochranton, Pa., 1972. Mem. comms. com. Tri-County United Fund, 1973, mem. com. children's svcs., 1975-79; bd. dirs. Pa. Am. Lung Assn., 1973-98, treas., 1976, sec., 1979-80, v.p., 1980-81, treas., 1996-98; counselor to bd. Am. Lung Assn., 1989-90; bd. dirs. Harris Commn., 1975-79, Cath. Social Svc. Harrisburg, 1972-76; mem. extension planning com. YMCA, 1975-79; mem. bd. govs. Camp Curtin YMCA, 1980-85; mem. exec. bd. Lower Paxton Coalition Cmty. Groups, 1973-93; mem. comms. bd. Cath. Diocese Harrisburg, 1971-80; co-chmn. Dauphin County Ethics Com., 1979-81; chmn. bldg. com. Juvenile Detention Home, 1976-80; chmn. fund raising com. Greater Harrisburg Arts Coun., 1977-79; mem. Dauphin County bd. com. children and youth, 1982-85; vice chmn. Dauphin County Election Voting Machine Com., 1982—; mem. Tri-County Solid Waste Mgmt. Com., 1983-87; bd. dirs. Salvation Army Rehab. Svcs., 1992—, Capitol Pavilion Rehab., 1992—; mem. exec. com. spl. events United Negro Coll. Fund, 1993-98; spl. events chmn. Ctrl. Pa. UNCF, 1993-94, bd. dirs. H. John Heinz Ctr., 1994—; vice chmn. Millenium comm. City of Harrisburg, 1999—. Recipient Advocate award Paxton Area Jaycees, 1969, 73, citation Am. Legion Pa., 1971, 74, CAP, 1972, medallion Am. Legion Pa., 1972; award Am. Cancer Soc., 1969-89, March of Dimes award, 1969-89, AARP award, 1988, MADD award Hist. Preservation award, All Am. City Participation award, Nat. award Am. Lung Assn., 1992, Am. Legion REgional award, 1994, Pioneer award John Heinz Ctr., 1996, Cmty. Svc. award VFW, 1996, award for historic rehab. City Harrisburg, 1992, Cit of Harrisburg award, 1998, Gettysburg Monument Preservation award, 1998; numerous others. Mem. Am. Lung Assn. Pa. (treas. 1995-98), Internat. Platform Assn. Home: 4910 Earl Dr Harrisburg PA 17112-2123 Office: 101 Lincoln St Harrisburg PA 17112-2543

ANTOUN, MIKHAIL, medicinal chemistry and pharmacognosy educator; b. Khartoum, Sudan, Aug. 20, 1946; came to U.S., 1979; s. Daoud and Badia (Boulos) A.; m. Slavomira Kucerova, Sept. 14, 1973; children: Helena, David Emmanuel, Anna Maria. B in Pharm. with distinction, U. Khartoum, 1968; PhD, U. London, 1974. Asst. prof. pharm. U. Khartoum (Sudan), 1974—78, assoc. prof., 1978—81; sr. rsch. scientist Purdue U., West Lafayette, Ind., 1981—86; assoc. prof. medicinal chemistry and pharmacognosy U. P.R. Sch. Pharm., San Juan, 1986—92, prof. medicinal chemistry and pharmacognosy, faculty chairprof., dept. head, 1993—. Vis. prof., rsch. assoc. Sch. Pharmacy & Pharm. Sci. Purdue U., West Lafayette, 1979-81. Contbr. articles to profl. jours. Sr. scholar U. Khartoum, 1968-69; teaching fellow U. London, 1969-73. Fellow Linnean Soc.; mem. Am. Assn. Colls. Pharmacy, Am. Soc. Pharmacognosy, Sigma Xi. Avocations: piano, classical music, reading, chess, swimming. Office Phone: 787-758-2525 ext 5410. Personal E-mail: anto285@aol.com.

ANTREASIAN, GARO ZAREH, artist, lithographer, art educator; b. Indpls., Feb. 16, 1922; s. Zareh Minas and Takouhie (Daniell) A.; m. Jeanne Glascock, May 2, 1947; children: David Garo, Thomas Berj. BFA, John Herron Sch. Art, 1948; DFA (hon.), Ind. U.-Purdue U. at Indpls., 1972. Instr. Herron Sch. Art, Indpls., 1948—59, 1961—64; tech. dir. Tamarind Lithography Workshop, Los Angeles, 1960-61; prof. art U. N.Mex., 1964-87, chmn. dept. art, 1981-84; tech. dir. Tamarind Inst., U. N.Mex., 1970-72; vis. lectr., artist numerous univs. Bd. dirs. Albuquerque Mus., 1980-90; printmaker emeritus Southern Graphics Coun., 1994; Fulbright vis. lectr. U. São Paulo and Found. Armando Alvares Penteado, Brazil, 1985. Prin. author: The Tamarind Book of Lithography: Art and Techniques, 1970; one-man shows include Malvina Miller Gallery, San Francisco, 1971, Marjorie Kauffman Gallery, Houston, 1975-79, 84, 86, U. Colo., Boulder, 1972, Calif. Coll. Arts & Crafts, Oakland, 1973, Miami U., Oxford, Ohio, 1973, Kans. State U., 1973, Atlanta Coll. Art, 1974, U. Ga., Athens, 1974, Alice Simsar Gallery, Ann Arbor, 1977-79, Elaine Horwich Gallery, Santa Fe, 1977-79, Mus. of N.Mex., Santa Fe, 1979, Robischon Gallery, Denver, 1984, 86, 90, Moss-Chumley Gallery, Dallas, 1987, Rettig-Martinez Gallery, Santa Fe, 1988, 91, 92, U. N.Mex. Art Mus., 1988, Albuquerque Mus., 1988, Louis Newman Gallery, L.A., 1989, Expositum Gallery, Mexico City, 1989, State U. Coll., Cortland, N.Y., 1991, Mus. Art, U. Ariz., Tucson, 1991, 2004, Indpls. Mus. Art, 1994, Ruschmon Gallery, Indpls., 1994, Mitchell Mus. Art, Vernon, Ill., 1995, Cline-Lewallen Gallery, Santa Fe, 1997, 2002, Anderson Gallery, Albuquerque, 1997, Fenix Gallery, Taos, NM State U., Las Crucis, 1998, Lewallen Gallery, Santa Fe, 2002, Cline Gallery, Scottsdale, 2002, 03, 04, Cline Fine Art, Scottsdale, Ariz., 2002, Santa Fe, 2003, Fresno Art Mus., 2005, others; exhibited group shows Phila. Print Club, 1960-63, Ind. Artists, 1947-63, White House, 1966, Nat. Lithographic Exhbn. Fla. State U., 1965, Library Congress, 1961-66, Bklyn. Mus., 1958-68, 76, U.S. Pavilion Venice Biennale, 1970, Internat. Biennial, Bradford, Eng., 1972-74, Internat. Biennial, Tokyo, 1972, City Mus. Hong Kong, 1972, Tamarind UCLA, 1985, Roswell Mus., 1989, Pace Gallery, 1990, Worcester (Mass.) Art Mus., 1990, Amon Carter Mus., Ft. Worth, 1990, Albuquerque Mus., 1991, 92, Art Mus. U. N.Mex., 1991, 92, 99, 2001, Norton Simon Mus., Pasadena, Calif., 1999, U. N.H., 1999, Cline Fine Art, Scottsdale, Ariz., 2002, 03, Fenix Gallery, Taos, 2003, others; represented in permanent collections: Albuquerque Mus., Bklyn. Mus., Guggenheim Mus., N.Y.C., Cin. Mus., Chgo. Art Inst., Ind. State Mus., Mus. Modern Art, N.Y.C., Library of Congress, Met. Mus., N.Y.C., N.Y. Pub. Libr., Mus. Fine Arts, Santa Fe, also, Boston, Indpls., Seattle, Phila., San Diego, Dallas, N.Mex., Worcester Art Museums, Los Angeles County Mus., Roswell Mus. and Art Ctr., Tucson Mus., murals, Ind. U., Butler U., Ind. State Office Bldg., Smithsonian Inst., So. Ill. U., U. Nev., Cinn. Mus. Art, others. Combat artist with USCGR, World War II, PTO. Recipient Distinguished Alumni award Herron Sch. Art, 1972, N.Mex. Annual Gov.'s award, 1987; Grantee Nat. Endowment for Arts, 1983; fellow Nat. Acad. Design, NYC, 1993. Fellow NAD; mem. World Print Coun. (bd. dirs. 1980-87), Nat. Print Coun. Am. (co-pres. 1980-82), Coll. Art Assn. Am. (bd. dirs. 1977-80). Home: 11128 Malaguena Ln NE Albuquerque NM 87111-6861

ANTRIM, MINNIE FAYE, residential care facility administrator; b. Rochester, Tex., June 30, 1916; d. Charles C. Montandon and Myrtle Caldona (Brown) Montandon Taylor; m. Cecil C. Antrim, Jan. 1, 1938; children— Linda Faye Antrim Hathway, Cecil C. Student Central State Tchrs. Coll., Edmond, Okla., 1937. Asst. purchasing agt. Scenic Gen. Hosp., Modesto,

Calif., 1955-68, Health Dept., Probation Dept., Stanislaus, Calif., 1955-68; owner, adminstr. Sierra Villa Retirement Home, Fresno, Calif., 1968-77, Mansion Home, Fresno, 1977— . Mem. Am. Coll. Health Care Adminstrs., Calif Bus. and Profl Club. Methodist. Club: Garden. Avocation: glee clubs. Home: 6070 E Townsend Ave Fresno CA 93727-5617

ANTUNES, DANIEL L., sales consultant, camera operator; b. Portugal, June 24, 1971; came to U.S., 1986; s. Jose A. and Judite C. Antunes. AA, Union County Coll., 1991; BA, N.J. City U., 1994. Cameraman RTP-USA TV, Newark, 1988-90, tech. dir. news, 1990-93; actor, editor NBP Prodns., Lisbon, 1993; cameraman, robotics CN8, Union, N.J., 1997—; sales rep. Bell Atlantic Mobile, Paramus, N.J., 1994—. Avocations: snow boarding, tennis, soccer, online stock trading, video productions. Home: 9 Radley St Kearny NJ 07032-5915 E-mail: dantunes@aol.com.

ANTUNES, XANA, business journalist; BA in comm. and pub. media, Leeds U.; post grad. diploma in journalism, City U., London. Wall St. corr. London Evening Standard, 1993—95; dep. bus. editor NY Post, 1995—96, bus. editor, 1996—98, dep. editor, 1998—99, editor, 1999—2001; exec. editor Fortune Mag., 2003—. Cons. Office: Fortune Mag 1271 Ave of the Americas New York NY 10020 Business E-Mail: xana_antunes@fortunemail.com.

ANTWEILER, DENNIS FRANCIS, mechanical engineer; b. Cleve., June 16, 1949; s. Ralph Joseph and Marie Leola (Freeman) A.; m. Karen Lisa Porter, Feb. 27, 1971 (div. Feb. 2000); children: Christopher J., Brandon D., Jamie A. BSME, U. Calif. Berkeley, 1972. Mech. engr. Altare Sys., Inc., Oakland, Calif., 1973; controls and instrumentation engr. Exxon, USA Corp., Benicia, Calif., 1973-78, Hess Oil Virgin Islands Corp., St. Croix, V.I., 1978-79, Union Camp Corp., Savannah, Ga., 1979-81; mgr. ops. Stanford (Calif.) U., 1981-86; v.p. Cascade Controls, Inc., Sunnyvale, Calif., 1986—2005; mech. coord. Rudolph and Shetter, Foster City, Calif., 2005—. Mem. ASME, Instrument Soc. Am. Avocation: windsurfing. Office: Rudolph and Shetter 989 East Hillsdale Blvd Ste100 Foster City CA 94404

ANTWI, EBENEZER YAW, education educator; b. Bomeng, Ghana, Jan. 12, 1936; s. Kwasi Ofori and Akua Nyame; 7 children, Mavis, Salome, Stella, Beverly, Kwadwd, Kwame. BA, Kans.Wesleyan U., 1978; MA, PhD, Ohio State U., 1981. Pres., CEO MEDCO, Inc., Bronx, NY. Avocation: fishing. Office: 2240 E Tremont Ave 7D Bronx NY 10462 also: MEDCO Inc 2240 E Tremont Ste 7D Bronx NY 10462 E-mail: medco@optonline.net.

ANTZELEVITCH, CHARLES, research and development company executive; b. Israel, Mar. 25, 1951; arrived in US, 1959, naturalized; s. Chaim and Frida (Hassman) A.; m. Brenda Reisner, June 24, 1973; children: Daniel Avi, Lisa Rachel. BA, Queens Coll., 1973; PhD, SUNY, Syracuse, 1977. Postdoctoral fellow Masonic Med. Rsch. Lab., Utica, NY, 1977-80, rsch. scientist, 1980-83, sr. rsch. scientist, 1984, exec. dir., dir. rsch., 1984—; asst. prof. SUNY Health Scis. Ctr. Pharmacology, Syracuse, 1980-83, assoc. prof., 1983-86; prof. pharmacology SUNY Health Scis. Ctr., Syracuse, 1987—. Mem. editl. bd. Jour. Cardiovasc. Electrophysiology, 1990, NASPETAPES, Jour. Cardiovasc. Pharmacology and Therapeutics, Circulation, Current Cardiology Revs., Heart Rhythm, others; contbr. articles to profl. jours. Com. mem. N.Y. State Heart Assn., Syracuse, 1982-87; bd. dirs. Clin. Med. Network, Utica, 1987-94, Jewish Cmty. Ctr., Utica, 1987-92, Royal Arch Masons Med. Rsch. Found., 1989, Ctrl. N.Y. Heart Assn., 1989; v.p. Temple Beth El, Utica, v.p., 1993-95, pres., 1995-97, mem. com., 1991—; mem. instnl. rev. bd. Faxton Hosp., Utica, 1990—2002. Recipient Van Horne award Ctrl. N.Y. Heart Assn., 1981-84, numerous grants; Gordon K. Moe scholar chair in exptl. cardiology Masonic Med. Rsch. Lab., 1987—, Disting. Svc. award RAM Med. Rsch. Found., 1994, Charles Henry Johnson medal Grand Lodge Free and Accepted Masons N.Y., 1996, Disting. Achievement medal, 2001, Disting. Scientist award, Heart Rhythm Soc., 2002. Fellow: Am. Coll. Cardiology (editl. bd. jour. 1989—92, program com. 2001—); mem.: N.Am. Soc. Pacing and Electrophysiology (chmn. sci. com. 1995—98, long range planning com. 1995—98, nominations com. 1997—99, bd. dirs. 1997—2003, program com. 1998—2002, sec. 2000—03, exec. com. 2000—03, fin. com. 2000—03, Disting. Scientist award 2002), Internat. Cardiac Electrophysiology Soc. (sec.-treas. 1994—96, pres. 1996—98, sec.-treas. 1998—), Cardiac Electrophysiol. Soc., Internat. Soc. for Heart Rsch., N.Y. Acad. Scis., Am. Heart Assn. (chmn. peer rev. com. 1997—, Excellence in Cardiovasc. Sci. award 2003). Avocation: swimming. Office: Masonic Med Rsch Lab 2150 Bleecker St Utica NY 13501-1738 Business E-Mail: ca@mmrl.edu.

ANUSZKIEWICZ, RICHARD JOSEPH, artist; b. Erie, Pa., May 23, 1930; s. Adam Jacob and Victoria (Jankowski) A.; m. Sarah Feeney, Nov. 26, 1960; children: Adam John, Stephanie, Christine. B.F.A., Cleve. Inst. Art, 1953; M.F.A., Yale U., 1955; BS in Edn., Kent State U., 1956. Represented by David Pindlay Jr. Gallery, NYC. One-man shows at Butler Art Inst., Youngstown, Ohio, 1955, The Contempories, N.Y.C., 1960, 61, 63, Sidney Janis Gallery, N.Y.C., 1965-67, Dartmouth Coll., 1967, Cleve. Mus. Art, 1967, Kent State U., 1968, Andrew Crispo Gallery, N.Y.C., 1975, 77, La Jolla (Calif.) Mus. Contemporary Art, 1976, Univ. Art Mus., Berkeley, Calif., 1977, Columbus (Ohio) Gallery of Fine Arts, 1977, Charles Foley Gallery, Columbus, 1982, Graham Modern, N.Y.C., 1984, Heckscher Mus., Huntington, N.Y., 1984, Schweyer-Galdo Galleries, Pontiac, Mich., 1985, Tampa (Fla.) Mus., 1986, Richard Green Gallery, N.Y.C., 1987, Galleria Sagittaria, Pordenone, Italy, 1988, Charles Foley Gallery, Columbus, 1988, Galleie Civiche D'Arte Moderna, Ferrara, Italy, 1989, Newark Mus., 1990, Maruzen Co., Ltd., Tokyo, 1990-91, Abante Fine Art, Portland, Oreg., 1992, Ctr. fro Arts, Vero Beach, Fla., 1993, others; exhibited in group shows at Mus. Modern Art, 1960-61, 63, 65, U. Ill., 1961, NYU, 1961, Pa. Acad. Design, 1962, Whitney Mus. Am. Art, 1962, 63-64, 70, 71, Inst. Contemporary Arts, Boston, 1962, Columbus Gallery Fine Arts, 1962, City Art Mus., St. Louis, 1962, Munson-Williams-Proctor Inst., Utica, N.Y., 1962, Tweed Gallery U. Minn., 1962, Silvermine (Conn.) Guild Artists, 1962-63, Atheneum Sch., Helsinki, Finland, 1962, Mus. Modern Art, Sarasota, Fla., 1962, J.B. Speed Art Mus., Louisville, 1962, Meml. Art Gallery, Rochester, N.Y., 1962, Allentown (Pa.) Art Mus., 1963, Krannert (Ill.) Art Mus., 1963, De Cordova Mus., Lincoln, Mass., 1963, Washington Gallery Modern Art, 1963, U. Mich. Mus. Art, 1964, Sidney Janis Gallery, N.Y.C., 1964, 65, Art Inst., Chgo., 1964, 71, Tate Gallery, London, 1964, Far Gallery, 1964, Carnegie Inst., Pitts., 1964, Corcoran Gallery Art, Washington, 1965, Art Fair Cologne, Germany, 1967, Larry Aldrich Mus., Ridgefield, Conn., 1968, 71, Hopkins Center Art Galleries Dartmouth Coll., Hanover, N.H., 1969, Denver Art Mus., 1969, Va. Mus. Fine Arts, Richmond, 1970, Ind. State U., Terre Haute, 1970, Masur Modern Art, Monroe, La., 1970, Birmingham (Ala.) Mus., 1971, Whitney Mus. Am. Art, N.Y.C., 1972, Hirshhorn Mus. and Sculpture Garden, N.Y.C., 1974, Bklyn. Mus., 1977, Albright-Knox Gallery, Buffalo, 1979, Met. Mus. Art, N.Y.C., 1982, Museo de Arts Moderno, Ciudad Bolivar, Venezuela, 1984, Tel Aviv Mus., 1986, Paris-New York-Kent Gallery, Kent, Conn., 1987, Guggenheim Mus., N.Y.C., 1987-88, Marilyn Pearl Gallery, N.Y.C., 1988, James A. Michener Arts Ctr. Bucks County, Doylestown, Pa., 1988, Centre d'Art Contempora, Geneva, 1989, Provincaal Mus., Hasselt, Belgium, Ctr. d'Art en Sante Monica, Barcelona, Spain, 1989, Galleri Civiche D'Arte Moderna, 1989, Samuel P. Harn Mus. Art, Gainesville, Fla., 1990, 92, DeCordova Mus., Lincoln, Mass., 1991, Nat. Gallery Art, Washington, 1991, Cummer Gallery Art, Jacksonville, Fla., 1992, Harmon Meek Gallery, Naples, Fla., 1993, Nat. Acad. Design, Washington, 1993, Camino Real Gallery, Boca Raton, Fla., 1993, 96, 98, Center for the Arts, Vero Beach, Fla., 1993, Intermission Gallery, John Harms Ctr. Arts, Englewood, N.J., 1993, Williams Center Arts, Lafayette Coll., Easton, P.A., 1994, N.J. State Mus., Trenton, 1994, Harmon Meek Gallery, Naples, Fla., 1995, 2000, OK Harris Gallery, N.Y.C. 2002, ACA Gallery, N.Y.C., 2003others; represented in permanent collections, Mus. Modern Art, Whitney Mus. Am. Art, Cleve. Mus. Art, Corcoran Gallery Art, Allentown Art Mus., Albright-Knox Art Gallery, Butler Art Inst., Akron (Ohio) Art Inst., Yale Art Gallery, Chgo. Art Inst., Larry Aldrich Mus., Ridgefield, Conn., Fogg Art Mus. of Harvard U., Hirshhorn Mus. and Sculpture Garden, artist-in-residence, Dartmouth Coll., 1967, U. Wis., 1968, Cornell U., 1968, Kent State U., 1968; contbr. articles to profl. jours. Home and Office: 76 Chestnut St Englewood NJ 07631-3045 Office Phone: 201-567-9404. E-mail: sa22@earthlink.net.

ANVARIPOUR, M. A., lawyer; b. Tehran, Iran, Jan. 23, 1935; arrived in U.S., 1957; s. Ahmed and Monir (Georgi) A.; m. Patricia Matson Lynch (div. 1971); 1 dau., Sandra M.; m. Guilda Eshtehardi, Mar. 31, 1978 (div. 1984); 1 son, Cyrus Ramsey; m. Tess Temel, May 15, 1995 (div. 2002). LLB, U. Tehran, 1956; BS, U. San Francisco, 1959; student, U. Calif. Hastings Coll. Law, San Francisco, JD, 1973. Bar: Ill. 1973, Fed. cts. Asst. field dir. Am. Friends of Middle East, Inc., Iran, 1962-64, field dir., 1964-66; asst. dean students, dean internat. students and faculty affairs Ill. Inst. Tech., Chgo., 1966-81; practiced in Chgo., 1973—, in San Francisco, 1985—; ednl. and legal adviser Consulate Gen. Iran, Chgo., 1973-79; aux. lawyer NAACP, Chgo., 1973-74. Lectr. immigration and law seminar Ill. Inst. Tech.-Chgo.-Kent Coll. Law Sch., 1974 Mem. Am., Iran-Am. (sec.-gen. 1964-66), Chgo. Bar Assn. (chmn. immigration com. 1982-83), Iran Am. Alumni Assn. (sec. 1964-66), Nat. Assn. Fgn. Student Affairs (Ill. chmn. 1968-69), U. Tehran, U. San Francisco, Idaho State U. (hon.), Ill. Inst. Tech., Chgo.-Kent Coll. Law alumni assns., Am. Immigration Lawyers Assn. (sec.-treas. Chgo. chpt. 1976-78, v.p. 1978-80, pres. 1980-81), Armour Faculty Club (pres. 1977-78), Phi Delta Phi. Office: 180 N La Salle St Chicago IL 60601-2501 Office Phone: 312-750-0558. E-mail: anvaripourlaw@yahoo.com. *My biases have made my life extremely rewarding. I have several. I have a strong bias against intolerance. I have a deep-seated bias against hate and bigotry, a bias against war, a bias for peace, and a bias which guides me to have faith in the basic goodness of my fellow human beings.*

ANVERSA, PIERO, medical educator; s. Giuseppe Anversa and Maria Folzani; m. Sandra Zanelli, Sept. 16, 1968; 1 child, Matteo. MD, Med. Sch., Parma, Italy, 1959—65; MD (hon.), Med. Sch., Bologna, Italy, 2002. Prof., medicine N.Y. Med. Coll., Valhalla, 1984—, v.chmn., medicine, 2000—; vis. prof. Albert Einstein Coll. Medicine, N.Y.C., 1992—, Sacred Heart U., Rome, 1989—, U. Vita-Salute, Milan, 2003—, San Diego State U., 2003—. Fellow: Am. Heart Assn. (Rsch. Achievement award 2004, Disting. Scientist 2003). Achievements include research in the identification of cell death in the heart. Avocation: travel. Office Phone: 914-594-4168. Office Fax: 914-594-4406. E-mail: piero_anversa@nymc.edu.

ANYALEWECHI, PATRICK OKECHUKWU, psychology professor; b. Umunevo, Nvosi, Abia State, Nigeria, Mar. 4, 1955; came to U.S., 1983; s. John Ija and Hannah (Nma) A.; m. Ifeyinwa Anyalewechi, Aug. 26, 1989. BA, God's Bible Sch. & Coll., Cin., 1986, ThB, 1987; MEd, U. Cin., 1987, EdD, 1994. Lectr. Calvery Coll. of theology, Port Harcourt, Nigeria, 1982-83; tchg. asst. Coll. of Edn. U. Cin., 1987-89, adj. prof. dept. humanities and social sci., Summer 1992, asst. to assoc. dean Coll. Edn., 1990-92, asst. to asst. dean, 1992-93; asst. prof. psychology Wilberforce (Ohio) U., 1993-98, assoc. prof., 1998—. Author: A Comparative Study of Teachers and Principals, 1994. Mem.: AAUP, Am. Psychol. Soc., Am. Edn. Studies Assn., Am. Edn. Rsch. Assn., Phi Delta Kappa. Avocations: reading, travel, music, games, soccer. Office: PO Box 1001 Wilberforce OH 45384-1001 Office Phone: 937-708-5677. E-mail: panyalew@wilberforce.edu.

ANYANWU, CHUKWUKRE, alcohol/drug abuse services professional; b. Ogbor-Ugiri, Nigeria, Apr. 14, 1943; came to U.S., 1963; s. Peter Ebo and Eunice Ikwuaha (Madu) A.; m. Ngozi G. Nwaike, Jan. 10, 1980; children: Okechukwu-Pat, Adaku Cathy, Ikechukwu-Uzo, Uremegbulem, Kingsley-Ugo, Ucheckukwu. BS in Biology and Chemistry, St. Joseph's Coll., 1971; MS in Biochemistry, Fairleigh Dickenson U., 1972; postgrad., Temple U., 1979; MD, Cetec U., Dominican Republic, 1981. Internationally cert. alcohol and other drug counselor. Postdoctorate Temple Hosp.; diplomatic envoy Nigeria, 1973-75; extern various hosps., Phila. area, 1977-79; obstetrician-gynecologist, cons. Lagos U. Teaching Hosp., Nigeria, 1983-84; cons. psychiatry St. Mary's Hosp., Phila., 1981-82; rsch. nuclear medicine Temple U. Hosp., Phila., 1980-81; chmn. A-B Assocs. Inc., Phila., 1970—; CEO, owner, founder A-B Assocs., Inc., Phila., 1989—; virolog rsch. A-B Assocs. Inc., Phila., 1979-82; mem. staff dept. of psychiatry JFK Mental Health/Retardation, Phila., 1985-88; mem. staff dept. of drug and alcohol addiction Giuffré Med. Ctr., 1988-89; counselor in psychiatry Misericordia Hosp., Phila., 1987-88; mem. staff addiction svcs. Guiffre Med. Ctr., Phila., 1988—; founder, CEO AB Assocs. Am. Beats Addiction, Inc., Phila., 1989—. Paper rev. cons. NIH, Alcohol, Drug Abuse and Mental Health Adminstrn.; mem. com. peer rev. Dept. HHS, USPHS, NIH; mem. healthy start-reduction of infant mortality Pub. Policy Phila. Dept. Pub. Health; panelist Phila. Empowerment Zone for HealthCare Providers; founder, chmn., CEO African Congress U.S.A., Inc., 1995. Author numerous poems; contbr. articles profl. jours. Senate candidate Imo State Govt., Nigeria, 1983; mem. free standing steering com, pub. policy com. and providers com. Health Start Initiative-Phila. Dept. Pub. Health, vice chmn. programs, federally funded programs for maternal infant child care; Olympian athlete competing in pole vault, 1500 meters and 400 meter hurdles, Mex., 1968; bd. dirs. March of Dimes Birth Defects Found.; mem. adv. bd. Mayor's Office of Cmty. Svcs., City of Phila., 1994—; founder African Congress, 1995, chmn.; founder State Our Family Unity, 1999; rep. Area D., Phila.; treas. Phila. Health Consortium; candidate for City Coun., City of Phila., 1999; candidate city coun. City of Phila., 1999. First African immigrant of 20th century to run for City Council-at-Large, Phila., 1999. Mem. AAAS, Am. Coll. Healthcare Execs., Pa. Cert. Addiction Counselors, Orgn. Nigerian Profs. USA (chmn. jud. com.), Fedn. Police Law Enforcement, Phila. Fraternal Order of Police, Interagy. Coun. Homeless. Democrat. Roman Catholic. Office Phone: 215-228-4848. Personal E-mail: afcongress@aol.com.

ANZAI, EARL I., former state attorney general; b. Honolulu; Student, Emroy U., Oreg. State U.; BA, U. Hawaii, 1964, MA, 1966. Planning prog. coord. Oahu Metropolitan Planning Org., 1967—77; mgmt. analyst/investigator U.S. Gen. Accounting Office, 1968—70; sr. legislative analyst Hawaii state Office of the Legislative Auditor, 1970—75; special asst. exec. dir. Comprehensive Planning Org. San Diego, 1975—76; chief clerk/staff dir. state senate Ways and Means Com., 1979—81; com. clerk Hawaii com. on environment, agriculture, conservation and land, constitution convention of 1978, 1978; atty./chief investigator special senate com. investigating the pesticide heptachlor in milk, 1982—83; law clk. First Cir. Ct., Honolulu, 1982—83; sr. assoc. Schutter & Glickstein, 1983—88; ptnr. Anzai & Evangelista fka Anzai Ahn Holt & Evangelista fka Anzai Holt & Evangelitsta; dir. Dept. Budget and Fin., Honolulu, 1995—99; atty. gen. State Senate Hawaii, Honolulu, 1999—2002; com. clerk state senate Com. on Health, 1981—82; chief coun. com. on judiciary state senate, 1987.

ANZISKA, BRIAN JEFFREY, neurologist, researcher, educator; b. Cape Town, Republic South Africa, Jan. 2, 1946; came to U.S., 1970; s. Harry Hyman and Naomi Miriam (Kahn) A.; m. Rochelle Deborah Jaskoll, Dec. 10, 1971; children: S. Yaacov, Daniel, David. B.M., B.S., U. Cape Town, 1968. Diplomate Am. Bd. Psychiatry and Neurology. Intern, Groote Schuur Hosp., Cape Town, 1968; resident in neurology Pa. Hosp., Phila., 1970-73; hon. house physician Nat. Hosp., London, 1973; attending neurologist Kings County Hosp., Bklyn., 1973-85; assoc. prof. neurology SUNY-Bklyn., 1981— . Contbr. articles to profl. jours. Mem. Physicians for Social Responsibility, Am. Acad. Neurology, Am. EEG Soc., N.Y. Acad. Scis., Am. Soc. Law and Medicine. Democrat. Jewish. Avocations: history, philosophy, religious studies. Home: 75 Elizabeth Rd New Rochelle NY 10804-3211 Office: Downstate Med Ctr Dept Neurology 450 Clarkson Ave # 35 Brooklyn NY 11203-2098 Office Phone: 718-270-2734.

AO, XU, science educator; b. Xinjiang, China, Aug. 10, 1959; s. Zouqi Cao and Zaixou Li; m. Liming Zhang, Apr. 7, 1985; children: Yang Janet Cao, David Cao. BS, Xinjiang U., 1982; PhD, U. S.C., 1991. Instr. Washington U., St. Louis, 1994—96; asst. prof. U. Ala., Birmingham, 1996—2000, assoc. prof., 2000—04, prof., 2004—. Mem.: Am. Soc. Bone and Mineral Rsch. (Merck Young Investigator award 1993, Sandoz award 1993, John Hadded Young Investigator award 1999), Internat. Chinese Hard Tissue Soc. Office: U Ala 1670 Univ Blvd VH G003 Birmingham AL 35294

AOKI, MASANAO, economics professor; b. Hiroshima, Japan, May 14, 1931; came to U.S. 1956; BS, U. Tokyo, 1953, MS, 1955; PhD, UCLA, 1960; DSc, Tokyo Inst. Tech., 1966. Prof. elec. engrng. and econs. UCLA, 1963-73, 75-81, 85-92; prof. U. Ill., 1973-75, U. Osaka, Japan, 1981-85. Author: Optimization of Stochastic Systems, 1967, 2d edit., 1989, State Space Modeling of Time Series, 1987, 2d edit., 1996, New Approaches to Macroeconomic Modelings: Evolutionary Stochastic Dynamics, Multiple Equilibria, and Externalities as Field Effects, Modeling Aggregate Behavior and Fluctuations in Economics, 2002. Mem.: Soc. Econ. Dynamics and Control (pres. 1982—83), Soc. Instrument and Control Engrng. Japan, Japanese Econ. Assn. Office: UCLA Dept Econs 405 Hilgard Ave Los Angeles CA 90095-1477 Office Phone: 310-825-2630. Business E-Mail: aoki@econ.ucla.edu.

AOYAMA, KATSURA, linguist; MA, U. Hawaii, Manoa, 1997, PhD, 2000. Postdoctoral scholar U. of Ala. at Birmingham, 2000—02; asst. prof. Tex. Tech. Univ. Health Sci. Ctr., 2002—. Office: Texas Tech Univ Health Sci Ctr 3601 4th St Lubbock TX 79430-6073 Office Phone: 806-743-5660 239.

APANASOV, BORIS N., mathematics professor, researcher; b. Sukhobuzimskoe, Russia, Oct. 24, 1950; s. Nikolay Aleksandrovich and Aleksandra Mikhailovna A.; children: Tatyana, Anton, Nikolay. Magister, Novosibirsk State U., Russia, 1973; PhD in Math., Inst. Math. USSR Acad. Sci., 1976. Spl. researcher Inst. Math. Acad. Sci. USSR, Novosibirsk, 1973, sci. researcher, 1974-80; asst. prof. math. Novosibirsk State U., 1975-80, assoc. prof., 1980-82, Novosibirsk Elektro-Tech. Inst., 1982-88; sr. researcher Inst. Math., Acad. Sci. USSR, Novosibirsk, 1981—; prof. Inst. Math. Kl. Ohridski U., Sofia, Bulgaria, 1986. Mem. Math Sci. Rsch. Inst., Berkeley, Calif., 1989, 96-97; prof. math. Ohio State U., Columbus, 1990, Mittag-Leffler Inst. of Sweden Royal Acad., 1989, U. Autonoma de Barcelona, 1990-91, U. Okla., Norman, 1991—, Tokyo U., 1997, Paris-Sud U. at Orsay, 1998, Centre de Recerca Matematica at Barcelona, 2004. Co-author: Kleinian Groups and Uniformization in Examples and Problems, 1981; author: Discrete Transformation Groups and Manifold Structures, 1983, Discrete Groups in Space and Uniformization Problems, 1991, Geometry of Discrete Groups and Manifolds, 1991, Conformal Geometry of Discrete Groups and Manifolds, 2000; co-editor: Topology 90, 1992, Geometry, Topoloty and Physics, 1997. Mem. Am. Math. Soc., Siberian Math. Soc., Japanese Soc. Promotion of Sci. Office: Univ of Okla Dept Math Norman OK 73019-0001

APAP, ANTONIO, finance educator, portfolio manager; b. N.Y.C., Apr. 15, 1936; s. Emmanuel Charles and Josephine Dolores (Spagna) A.; m. Anna Frances Bradley, July 28, 1990. BS, U. West Fla., 1970; MBA, Tex. A&I U., 1976; MS, Naval Postgrad. Sch., 1977; DBA, U.S. Internat. U., 1982. Real estate license. Commd. ensign USN, 1957, advanced through grades to comdr., 1972, served in Vietnam, ret., 1980; CFO Sand Land Devel. Corp., Pensacola, Fla., 1981-85; pres. Denton Devel. Corp., San Diego, 1985-89; prof. fin. U. West Fla., Pensacola, 1990—. Dir. Acad. Econ. and Fin., Hattiesburg, Miss., 1997-01. Contbr. articles to acad. and profl. jours. Dir. Pace (Fla.) Water Sys., 1995-97, 2002-04; dir., pres. Solana Shores Owners Assn., Pensacola, 1992-93. Recipient Golden Apple award Found. for Excellence in Edn., Pensacola, 1997, 98, Disting. Tchg. award Student Govt. Assn., Pensacola, 1997. Mem. Am. Acad. Acctg. and Fin., Am. Soc. Bus. and Behavioral Sci., Acad. Econ. and Fin. (dir. 1997-01), Optimists (bd. dirs. West Pensacola 1992-93). Avocations: golf, fishing, travel. Office: Univ West Fla Acctg & Fin 11000 University Pky Pensacola FL 32514-5732 E-mail: aapap@uwf.edu.

APASSA, CYRIL OMO-OSAGIE, clergyman, educator; b. Aba, Abbia, Nigeria, Feb. 4, 1944; s. Emmanuel Agbonfiro and Agnes (Amobo) A. BD, Urban U., 1971; diploma in edn., U. Nigeria, 1977, MEd, 1986; EdD, U. San Francisco, 1996. Ordained to ministry, Roman Cath. Ch., 1971. Tchr. govt. h.s., Nigeria, 1964, 73-77; pastor Roman Cath. chs., Nigeria, 1971-81; prin. Govt. H.S., Nigeria, 1981-90; assoc. pastor Our Lady of Lourdes Parish, Aba, Nigeria, 1990-91, Holy Angel's Parish, Arcadia, Calif., 1991, St. John Eudes Parish, Chatsworth, Calif., 1991-92, St. Theresa Little Flower Ch., Reno, 1996—. Sch. counselor, chmn. disciplinary com. St. Ephrem's Secondary Sch., Owerrinta, Nigeria, 1975-79; mem. bd. govs. Mbutu Ngwa (Nigeria) Secondary Sch., 1984-89; mem. grad. coun. U. San Francisco, 1995-96. Bd. dirs. Scholz Found. and Project Restart, 1998—. Mem. ASCD, K.C. (chaplain 1991—, Svc. award 1991, 96, 99), Phi Delta Kappa. Avocations: photography, ping pong/table tennis, travel, soccer. Office: St Therese Ch of the Little Flower 875 E Plumb Ln Reno NV 89502-3507 Fax: 775-322-0196.

APATOFF, DAVID B., lawyer; b. Sept. 28, 1952; BA, Sarah Lawrence Col., 1974; JD, Univ. Chgo., 1977. Bar: Ill. 1977, D.C. 1979, US Ct. Fed. Claims 1983. Ptnr., Intellectual Property & Tech. Practice Group Arnold & Porter, Washington. Contbr. articles to profl. jours. Office: Arnold & Porter 555 Twelfth St NW Washington DC 20004-1206 Office Phone: 202-942-5556. Office Fax: 202-942-5999. Business E-Mail: david.apatoff@aporter.com.

APATOFF, MICHAEL JOHN, entrepreneur; b. Harvey, Ill., June 12, 1955; s. William and Frances (Brown) A; m. Monique Van Blitter, 2005. BA, Reed Coll., 1980. Chief legis. asst. to U.S. Congressman Al Ullman, Chmn. Ways and Means Com., Washington, 1978-80; spl. asst. to U.S. Congressman Tom Foley, Majority Whip, Washington, 1981-85; exec. v.p., COO Chgo. Merc. Exch., 1986-90; pres., COO Dresdner RCM Global Investors, San Francisco, 1991-98, fin. entrepreneur, 1999—. Democrat. Office: 11 Edwards Ave Sausalito CA 94965 Personal E-mail: mapatoff@msn.com.

APATOW, JUDD, scriptwriter, television producer, film producer; b. 1968; m. Leslie Mann. Exec. prodr., writer (TV series) The Ben Stiller Show, 1992—93 (Emmy award for best writing, 1993), Freaks and Geeks, 1999—2000, co-exec. prodr., writer, dir. The Larry Sanders Show, 1992—98 (Cable ACE award, 1994, 1995), exec. prodr., writer, dir. Undeclared, 2001—02, prodr., writer (TV films) Life on Parole, 2003, Sick in the Head, 2003, assoc. prodr. (films) Crossing the Bridge, 1992, exec. prodr., writer Heavy Weights, 1995, Celtic Pride, 1996; prodr.: (films) The Cable Guy, 1996, Anchorman: The Legend of Ron Burgundy, 2004; exec. prodr.: Kicking & Screaming, 2005; prodr., dir., writer (films) The 40 Year Old Virgin, 2005. Office: United Talent Agy 9560 Wilshire Blvd Ste 500 Beverly Hills CA 90212*

APEL, HARRY JAMES, music producer, entertainer, composer; b. Mitchel Field, N.Y., Apr. 17, 1946; s. Harold Robert Apel and Santa Sarah Falcone; 1 child, Angelica Valentino. Student, Miricosta Coll., 1969—70, Western Bible Coll., 1971—73; AA, Pima Coll., 1978; student, U. Ariz., 1979, student, 1984—85. Cert. substitute tchr. grades K-12 Ariz., martial arts instr. Japan. Substitute tchr. Ariz. Schs., 1973—2001; publicity dir. Kids Ind. of Drugs, Oceanside, Calif., 1987—88; actor, comedian Fosi's Talent Agy., Tucson, 1987—2003; instr. martial arts YMCA and Marana (Ariz.) Schs., Tucson, 1993—97. Founder Am. Shu-do-Kan, Tucson, 1993—. Composer: songs (APEL Music), 1993—; entertainer (CD) Hilarity with Vulgarity Armed Forces Radio, 2004—05; prodr.: (CD) Hilarity with Vulgarity Armed Forces Radio; entertainer (CD) Mama's Rose Garden; prodr.: (CD) Mama's Rose Garden, 2004—05; entertainer (comml.) AMC movie classics; prodr.: (comml.) AMC movie classics, 2004. Sgt. USAF, 1964—68. Avocations: reading, horseback riding, guitar, music. Home: 1681 W Prince Rd #7 Tucson AZ 85705-3036

APEL, ROBERT WILLIAM, actor; b. Elmont, NY, May 5, 1948; s. Harold Robert and Sally Santa (Falcone) Apel; m. Eula Rae Harris, Feb. 14, 1976; children: Shawn, Tina Barley, Dakota. Lic. CNA 1993. Stuntman Old Tucson Movie Location, Tucson, 1970—72, Fosi's Talent Agency, Tucson, 1975—2005; student Pima Coll., Tucson, 1984. Writer, singer, producer: CD

Country Girl, 2004; prodr.: (CD) Good bye to Jesse James, 2004, (comedy CD) Hilarity Without Vulgarity, 2004—05; writer: standup comedy; performer: Kids Against Drugs, 1988, Adopt Wild Mustang Program, 1985, (TV films) Outlaw Josey Wales, Last Hard Man, A Star is Born, Pursuit, Red Rock West, (Television) The Ascension, Father Murphy, Young Riders, Young Pioneers, Desperado, various TV commercials. Mem.: Nat. Rifle Assn., Screen Actors Guild. Avocations: guitar, music, horseback riding, swimming. Office Phone: 520-395-3534.

APELBAUM, PHYLLIS L., delivery messenger service executive; 1 child, Mark. Instr. Am. United Cab Co., Chgo., 1957-65; gen. mgr. City Bonded Messenger Svc., Chgo., 1960-74; founder, pres. Arrow Messenger Svc., Inc., Chgo., 1974—. 1st chair Affirmative Action Adv. Bd. of Chgo., 1991-92; chair Variety Club Children's Carnival, Chgo., 1990-94; mem. bicycle com. City of Chgo., 1992-95, parking task force, 1993-95; gov. Ill. Coun. on Econ. Edn., Chgo., 1995—; mem. Lakefront SRO Adv. Bd., Chgo., 1989-94; mem. Chgo. Police bd., 1995—. Recipient Small Bus. Innovative Mgmt. award Bank of Am., 1994; named Entrepreneur of the Yr., Ernst & Young, 1992, Nat. Small Bus. Person of the Yr., Small Bus. Assn., 1990; named to Entrepreneurship Hall of Fame, U. Ill., Chgo., 1993. Mem. Messenger Courier Assn. of Am. (bd. dirs. 1989—), Messenger Svc. Assn. Ill. (co-founder, pres.), Nat. Assn. Women Bus. Owners, The Chgo. Network. Office: Arrow Messenger Svc Inc 1322 W Walton St Chicago IL 60622-5340

APESOS, ANTHONY, art educator; b. Newark, Jan. 6, 1953; s. John Dimitrious and Helen Cotrotsos Apesos; m. Carolyn Smyth (div.); m. Natasha Therese Seaman, July 26, 1997; 1 child, Helen. AB, Vassar Coll., 1975; cert., Pa. Acad. Fine Arts, Phila., 1979; MFA, Bard Coll., 1991. Asst. prof. fine arts Moore Coll., Phila., 1986—92; chair fine arts Art Inst. Boston, 1992—2000, assoc. prof. fine arts, 1992—, dir. master's program, 2003—05. Critic New Art Examiner, Chgo., 1980—96; lectr., panelist fine arts numerous orgns., 1980—. Exhibitions include Scenes from the Bernadine Order, Mt. Alvernia Coll., 1984, Life of St. Francis, Sacred Heart Hosp., Chester, Pa., 1988, numerous others. Fellow, New Eng. Found. for Arts, 1996; grantee, Art Inst. Boston, 1999, 2003; Kress traveling fellow, Phila. Coll. Art, 1998. Mem.: Coll. Art Assn., Copley Soc. Democrat. Greek Orthodox. Avocations: botany, gardening, collecting skulls. Home: 306 Arborway Jamaica Plain MA 02130 Office: Art Inst Boston @ Lesley U 700 Beacon St Boston MA 02215 Business E-Mail: aapesos@aiboston.edu.

APFEL, CHRISTIAN C., anesthesiologist, consultant; MD, U. Giessen, Germany, 1995; Pvt. Docent (Lehrbefugnis), U. Wuerzburg, 2002. Lic. German Bd. of Anesthesiology Bavarian State Med. Chamber, Germany, 2001. Asst. prof. Dept of Anesthesiology, Louisville, Ky., 2003—. Asst. dir. Outcomes Rsch. Inst., Louisville, 2004—. Contbr. articles pub. to profl. jour. Achievements include research in Design and conduct of clin. trials related to perioperative outcome. Home: 501 Colonel Anderson Pw Louisville KY 40222 Office: Outcomes Rsch Inst 501 E Broadway Ste 210 Louisville KY 40202 Home Fax: 502-425-7712. Personal E-mail: apfel@ponv.org. Business E-Mail: christian.apfel@louisville.edu.

APFEL, GARY, lawyer; b. NYC, June 2, 1952; s. Willy and Jenny (Last) A.; m. Serena Jakobovits, June 16, 1980; children: Alyssa J., I. Michael, Alanna J., Stephen J., Alexander. BA, NYU magna cum laude, 1973; JD, Columbia U., 1976. Bar: N.Y. 1977, Calif. 1988, U.S. Dist. Ct. (so. and ea. dists.) N.Y. 1977, U.S. Dist. Ct. (cen. dist.) Calif. 1988, U.S. Ct. Appeals (9th cir.) 1988. Assoc. Sullivan & Cromwell, NYC, 1976-80, LeBoeuf, Lamb, Leiby & MacRae, NYC, 1980-84, ptnr., 1985-88, Kaye, Scholer, Fierman, Hays & Handler LLP, LA, 1988-97, Akin, Gump, Strauss, Hauer & Feld, L.L.P., LA, 1997—2000; chmn. bd. ELSA, Inc., 2000—01; co-mng. ptnr. LA office LeBoeuf, Lamb, Greene & MacRae LLP, 2001—, chmn. corp. dept. Kent scholar Columbia U., 1976. Mem. ABA, Calif. State Bar Assn. (bus. law sect. corps. com.), Phi Beta Kappa. Office: LeBoeuf Lamb Greene & MacRae 725 S Figueroa St Ste 3100 Los Angeles CA 90017 Office Phone: 213-955-7350. Office Fax: 213-955-7399. Business E-Mail: gapfel@llgm.com.*

APGAR, KENNETH EDWARD, lawyer; b. Tampa, Fla., Aug. 12, 1946; s. Charles F. and Mary E. (Camp) A.; m. Karen Lynn Von Nida, Apr. 11, 1970; children: Jennifer, Vanessa. BA, U. Fla., 1968, JD, 1970. Bar: Fla. 1971; U.S. Dist. Ct. (mid. dist.) Fla. 1977, U.S. Dist. Ct. (so. and no. dists.) Fla. 1984; U.S. Ct. Appeals (5th and 11 cirs.) 1981; U.S. Supreme Ct., 1975; cert. civil trial advocate, civil trial lawyer. Asst. state atty. State Atty.'s Office, 13th Jud. Cir., Tampa, Fla., 1976-79; assoc. de la Parte & Butler, Tampa, 1979-82; ptnr. Butler & Apgar, Tampa, 1982-90; pvt. practice Tampa, 1990—. Capt. USAF, 1971-76, Fed. Republic of Germany. Mem. ABA, Fla. Bar Assn., Nat. Bd. Trial Advocacy, Assn. of Trial Lawyers of Am., Acad. of Fla. Trial Lawyers, Hillsborough County Bar Assn. Methodist. Avocation: computers. Office: 3907 N Boulevard Tampa FL 33603-4627

APICELLA, MICHAEL ALLEN, physician, educator; b. Bklyn., Apr. 4, 1938; s. Anthony D. and Fay (Kahn) A.; m. Agnes Dengler, Aug. 19, 1961; children: Michael P., Christopher A., Peter N. AB, Holy Cross Coll., 1959; MD, SUNY, Bklyn., 1963. Diplomate Am. Bd. Internal Medicine, Am. Bd. Infectious Disease. Postdoctoral fellow Johns Hopkins Hosp., Balt., 1966-68; asst. prof. microbiology SUNY, Buffalo, 1970-74, assoc. prof., 1974-78, prof., 1981-92; prof., chmn. dept. microbiology Coll. Medicine U. Iowa, Iowa City, 1993—. Contbr. over 150 articles to profl. jours. Maj. USAF, 1968-70. Office: U Iowa Coll Medicine Dept Microbiology Coll Medicine 3-403 Science Bldg Iowa City IA 52242 E-mail: michael.apicella@uiowa.edu.

APJOHN, NELSON GEORGE, lawyer; b. N.Y.C., June 21, 1956; s. George N. and Catherine A.; m. Mary Joan Greene, June 3, 1978; children: Andrew, Eric, Allan. AB in Polit. Sci., Syracuse U., 1978; JD, Boston Coll., 1981. Bar: Mass. 1981, U.S. Dist. Ct. Mass. 1981, U.S. Ct. Appeals (1st cir.) 1984. Ptnr. Nutter, McClennen & Fish LLP, Boston, 1981—. Mem. ABA, Mass. Bar Assn., Boston Bar Assn., Phi Beta Kappa, Order of Coif. Home: 28 Homeward Ln Walpole MA 02081-2210 Office: Nutter McClennen & Fish LLP World Trade Ctr West 155 Seaport Blvd Boston MA 02210-2604

APLAN, FRANK FULTON, metallurgical engineering educator; b. Boulder, Colo., Aug. 11, 1923; s. Frank Fulton Sr. and Helen Elizabeth (Fischer) A.; m. Clare Marie Donaghue, July 30, 1955; children: Susan M., Peter D., Lucy A., Margaret Ann (dec.). BS, S.D. Sch. Mines and Tech., 1948; MS, Mont. Sch. Mines, 1950; ScD, MIT, 1957; hon. degree in mineral engring., Mont. Tech. of U. of Mont., 1968. Mill engr. Climax Molybdenum Co., Climax, Colo., 1950-51, 53; asst. prof. U. Wash., Seattle, 1951-53; sr. scientist Kennecott Copper Corp., Salt Lake City, 1957; group mgr. mineral engring. R & D Mining and Metals div., Union Carbide Corp., Niagara Falls, Tuxedo, N.Y., 1957-67; prof. metallurgy and mineral processing Pa. State U., University Park, 1968—, Disting. prof., 1990, head dept. mineral preparation, 1968-71, chmn. mineral processing sect. University Pk., 1971-77, chmn. metallurgy sect. University Park, 1973-75. Bd. dirs. Engring. Found., N.Y.C., 1977-90, chmn. 1985-87. Contbr. articles to profl. jours.; patentee in field. T/Sgt. U.S. Army, 1942-46, ETO. Decorated Bronze Star; recipient Engring. Found. award, 1989, Percy H. Nicholls award AIME/ASME Joint Soc., 1998; inductee S.D. Hall of Fame, 1998. Mem. Nat. Acad. Engring., AIME (hon. mem. 1991, Robert H. Richards award 1978, Mineral Industry Edn. award 1992), AIChE, ASM Internat., Archaeol. Inst. Am., Am. Filtration Soc., Am. Chem. Soc., Soc. Mining, Metallurgy & Exploration Engrs. (bd. dirs. 1973-76, chmn. mineral processing divsn. 1972-73, Arthur F. Taggart award 1985, Disting. Mem. award 1978, Antoine M. Gaudin award 1991), Minerals, Metals & Materials Soc., Mining History Assn. Home: 432 W Fairmount Ave State College PA 16801-4612 Office: Pa State U Dept Energy & Geo-Environ Engring 155 Hosler Bldg University Park PA 16802-5000 E-mail: ffa1@psu.edu.

APLAN, PETER DONAGHUE, pediatric oncologist; b. Salt Lake City, Aug. 10, 1957; s. Frank Fulton and Clare Marie (Donaghue) A.; m. Debra J. Hoffman, May 2, 1987; children: Kurt Matthew, Melissa Paige. BS in Biophysics, Pa. State U., 1979, MD, 1983. Diplomate, Am. Bd. Pediatrics. Resident, then chief resident in pediatrics Children's Hosp. Buffalo, 1983-87; pediatric oncologist NIH, Bethesda, Md., 1987—. Contbr. articles to med. jours. NIH grantee, 1989, 95, 96. Mem. AMA, AAAS, Am. Assn. Cancer Rsch., Am. Soc. Pediatric Hematology-Oncology (named Young Investigator of the Yr. 1991). Roman Catholic. Avocations: classical guitar, personal computers, literature. Home: 12519 Gooderham Way North Potomac MD 20878-3417

APONE, CARL ANTHONY, journalist; b. Brownsville, Pa., July 9, 1923; s. Peter P. and Carmela (Puglia) A.; m. Kathleen King, Jan. 23, 1965; 1 dau., Elizabeth. BA cum laude, U. Notre Dame, 1949; MA, Boston U., 1950. Dir. pub. rels., lectr. journalism and Am. lit. St. Mary's Coll., Notre Dame, Ind., 1950-53; staff writer UP, Detroit, 1953; city editor Brownsville Telegraph, 1953-57; staff writer Pitts. Sun- Telegraph, 1958-60; music editor Pitts. Press, 1960-89; mem. faculty journalism Duquesne U., 1967-72; free-lance writer, 1950—; artistic dir. Music for Mt. Lebanon, Pitts., 1989—. Mem. St. Vincent DePaul Soc., 1963—. Served with inf. AUS, 1943-46. Recipient Golden Quill Journalism awards; Pa. Newspaper Pubs. Assn. awards. Home: 2016 Worcester Dr Pittsburgh PA 15243-1542 Office: Music for Mt Lebanon 2016 Worcester Dr Pittsburgh PA 15243-1542

APONTE, ABRAHAM, secondary school educator; b. NYC, Aug. 6, 1953; s. Abraham and Gladys (Ayala) Aponte; m. Ana María Acevedo, June 15, 1985; children: Amitza, Abie. BA, Fordham U., 1975; MA, NYU, 1976. Tchr. NYC Pub. Sch., 1977—79, Colegio San José pvt. sch., Rio Piedras, PR, 1980—83, Ramey Sch., Aguadilla, PR, 1983—. EEO counselor Dept. Def. Ednl. Activity, Aguadilla, 1989—92. Mem.: Orgn. Am. Historians, Am. Hist. Assn., Phi Delta Kappa. Democrat. Mem. Christian Ch. (Disciples Of Christ). Avocations: photography, basketball, reading. Office: Ramey Sch 201 Arch Rd Ramey PR 00603

APONTE MARTINEZ, LUIS CARDINAL, retired archbishop; b. Lajas, P.R., Aug. 4, 1922; s. Santiago E. Aponte and Rosa Martinez. Student, San Ildefonso Sem., San Juan, P.R., 1944, St. John's Sem., Boston, 1950; LLD (hon.), Fordham U., 1965. Ordained priest Roman Cath. Ch., 1950. Asst. in Patillas, PR; pastor in Maricao, PR, Sta. Isabel, PR, 1953—55; sec. to bishop of Ponce, PR, 1955—57; pastor in Aibonito, PR, 1957—60; from aux. bishop to bishop of Ponce, 1960—64; archbishop of San Juan, 1964—99; archbishop emeritus, 1999—; created cardinal, 1973. Chancellor Cath. U., Ponce, 1963—64; pres. Puerto Rican Episcopal Conf. Chaplain P.R. N.G., 1957—60. Mem.: Lions. Roman Catholic. Mailing: Archdiocese of San Juan Apartado 901967 Calle San Jorge 201 Santurce San Juan PR 00902-1967*

APONTE-RIVERA, VIVIANNE RUTH, psychiatrist; b. San Juan, P.R., Jan. 16, 1977; d. Orlando Aponte-Aponte and Ruth P. Rivera-Torres. BS in Biology, U. P.R., 1998, MD, 2002. Diplomate Bd. Med. Examiners P.R., 2002. Intern Lincoln Nat. Forest USDA Forest Svc., Ruidoso, N.Mex., 1996; asst. Herbarium U., Rio Piedras, PR, 1996; summer rsch. fellow Molecular Genetics Lab. Robert Wood Johnson Med. Sch., Piscataway, NJ, 1997; rsch. asst. Plant Reproductive Biology Lab. U. P.R., Rio Piedras, PR, 1997—98, rsch. asst. Dept. Psychiatry San Juan, PR, 2001, resident - gen. psychiatry Dept. Psychiatry, 2002—. Health workshops in various prisons, San Juan, PR, 2001—01; delivery of food to the homeless Ch. Sponsored Program, San Juan, PR, 1998—98; sunday sch. tchr. San Juan, PR, 1992—98. Mem.: Assn. Physicians Grad. U. P.R. Sch. of Medicine, Am. Psychiatry Assn. Achievements include research in anorexia and bulimia in Puertorrican women; marital satisfaction in the resident physicians of the University of Puerto Rico system. Avocations: reading, tai chi. Home: Estancias del Parque calle A #10-E Guaynabo PR 00969

APOSTOLAKIS, GEORGE E., engineering educator, researcher; Diploma in Elec. Engring., Nat. Tech. U., 1969; MS in Engring. Sci., Calif. Inst. Tech., 1973, PhD in Engring. Sci. and Applied Math. Prof. nuc. engring. and engring. systems Mass. Inst. Tech. Founder, sec. Internat. Assn. Probabilistic Safety Assessment and Mgmt.; mem. adv. com. reactor safeguards U.S. Nuc. Regulatory Commn., chmn., 2001—02; chmn. peer rev. panel Internat. Space Sta. Probabilistic Risk Assessment NASA, 2002. Editor-in-chief: Reliability Engineering and System Safety, mem. editl. bd.: Process Safety and Environmental Protection, 1991—, Risk Analysis, 1997—; contbr. articles to profl. jours. Fellow: Soc. Risk Analysis, Am. Nuc. Soc. (Tommy Thompson award Nuc. Installations Safety Divsn. 1999, Mark Mills award 1974); mem.: Internat. Nuc. Tech. Commn. Office: Mass Inst Tech Dept Nuc Engring 77 Massachusetts Ave Bldg 24-221 Cambridge MA 02139-4307 Office Phone: 617-252-1570. Office Fax: 617-258-8863. Business E-Mail: apostola@mit.edu.

APOSTOLAKIS, JAMES JOHN, shipping company executive, pharmaceutical executive; b. N.Y.C., May 31, 1942; s. John George and Ann (Lampros) A. AB, U. Pa., 1962; LLB, Harvard U., 1965. Bar: N.Y. 1965. Atty. Dewey, Ballantine, Bushby, Palmer & Wood, N.Y.C., 1965-67; pres. Transoceanic Tank Ship Mgmt. Group, N.Y.C., 1968-72, Koplik Group Ltd., N.Y.C., 1983-84, A.G. Palmer & Co., Inc., N.Y.C., 1976—, Bradford Shipping, Inc., N.Y.C., 1973—, Bradmar Trading Corp., N.Y.C., 1975—; mng. dir. Poseidon Capital Corp., N.Y.C., 1998—; vice chmn., pres. Columbia Labs, Inc., Miami, Fla., 1999—; pres. Columbia Labs., Inc., Fla., 2000—. Pres. Lexington Shipping and Trading Corp., N.Y.C., 1980—, Bedford Capital Corp., N.Y.C., 1989—93; vice chmn. Koplik Group Ltd., N.Y.C., 1988—93, Columbia Labs. Inc., Livingston, NJ, 1999—; bd. dirs. Macmillan, Inc., Grow Group, Inc., Columbia Labs., Inc. Mem. Union Club, Met. Club, Phi Beta Kappa. Home: 150 E 69th St New York NY 10021-5704 Office Phone: 212-588-1900. Personal E-mail: apostolak@aol.com.

APOSTOLOPOULOS, JOHN, computer scientist; BS, MIT, 1989, MS, 1991, PhD, 1997. Prin. rsch. scientist Hewlett-Packard Lab., 1997—. Cons. asst. prof. elec. engring. Stanford U. Named one of 100 Top Young Innovators, MIT's Tech. Review, 2003; recipient Emmy award cert. for digital TV standard. Office: Hewlett Packard Lab 1501 Page Mill Rd M/S 1181 Palo Alto CA 94304

APPAREDDY, VIJAYA L., psychiatrist; b. India; came to US, 1983; d. Balakrishna Reddy; m. Ramesh Appareddy; 2 children. Grad., St. Francis Coll. for Women, Hyderabad, India; MD, Osmania U. Med. Sch., Hyderabad, India. Cert. General Psychiatry, Child and Adolescent Psychiatry. Fellow, child and adult psychiatry Mount Sinai Med. Sch., NYC; residency in adult psychiatry Elmhurst Gen. Hosp.; clinical asst. prof. Brown U. Med. Sch., RI; med. dir., residential unit Columbia Valley Hosp., Chattanoog, Tenn.; mem. President's Com. on Mental Retardation, 2003—. Bd. mem. HCA Valley Psychiatric Hosp., Chattanooga. Co-author: The Siblings of the Psychiatrically Disordered Child, Normal Sleep in Neonates and Children. Mem.: Chattanooga Psychiatric Network (sec., treasurer), Am. Med. Women's Assn. (pres. Chattanooga chapter), Am. Assn. of Physicians of Indian Origin (former vice chmn. & mem. bd. of trustees). Office: Admin Children and Families 370 L'Enfant Promenade SW Washington DC 20447*

APPEADU, CHARLES EDWARD, finance educator, researcher; b. Kwasibuokrom, Brong Ahafo Region, Ghana, Mar. 27, 1959; s. Kwame Ampomah and Grace Akosuah Kyeremaah; m. Christina Agyeiwaa; children: Edward, Michael, Sarah. BSc in Civil Engring., U. Sci. and Tech., Kumasi, Ghana, 1984; MASc, U. B.C., Vancouver, Can., 1989; PhD in Fin., U. Wash., 1996. CFA. Full time tchg. asst. U. of Sci. and Tech., Kumasi, 1984—86; asst. rsch. officer BRRI, Coun. for Sci. and Indsl. Rsch., Kumasi, 1986—87; tchg./rsch. assoc. Sch. Bus. Adminstrn. U. Wash., Seattle, 1991—94; asst. prof. fin. U. of Wis., Milw., 1994—98; U.S. equity rsch. mgr./portfolio mgr. Parametric Portfolio Assocs., Seattle, 1998—2000; asst. prof. of fin. Ga. State U., Atlanta, 2000—. CFA exam. grader/sr. grader CFA Inst., Charlottesville, 2000—05. Contbr. articles to scholarly jours. Asst. sr. prefect St. Augustine's Coll., Cape Coast, Ghana, 1978—79. Fellow Michael G. Foster fellow, U. of Wash., 1993—94; scholar Commonwealth scholar, Can. Govt., 1987—89. Mem.: Ghana Engring. Students Assn. (pres. 1982—84), CFA Inst. Home: 525 Meadows Creek Dr Alpharetta GA 30005 Office: Ga State U 35 Broad St Atlanta GA 30303 Business E-Mail: cappeadu@gsu.edu.

APPEL, ALBERT M., lawyer; b. N.Y.C., May 26, 1945; s. Morris and Belle (Kaplan) A.; m. Irena Uhl, June 10, 1979; 1 child, Elliott. BS in Econs., U. Pa., 1966; JD, NYU, 1969. Bar: N.Y. 1969, U.S. Dist. Ct. (so. and ea. dists.) N.Y. 1971, U.S. Ct. Appeals (2d cir.) 1974, U.S. Ct. Appeals (4th cir.) 1979, U.S. Ct. Appeals (11th Cir.) 2002. Assoc. Spear and Hill, N.Y.C., 1969-75, Webster & Sheffield, N.Y.C., 1976-80, ptnr., 1981-91; spl. counsel Stroock & Stroock & Lavan LLP, N.Y.C., 1991-97, ptnr., 1998—. Mem. ABA, Am. Health Lawyers Assn., N.Y. State Bar Assn., Assn. of Bar of City of N.Y., Beta Alpha Psi. Home: 670 W End Ave New York NY 10025-7313 Office: Stroock & Stroock & Lavan LLP 180 Maiden Ln New York NY 10038-4925 Office Phone: 212-806-6625. Business E-Mail: aappel@stroock.com.

APPEL, BERNARD SIDNEY, marketing professional, consultant, retired electronics executive; b. Boston, Jan. 10, 1932; s. Max and Sophie (Altshuler) A.; m. Ellen Carey, July 1988; children: Ann, Sharon; children by previous marriage: Arlene R., Gerald I. AA Commercial Sci., Boston U., 1959; D Comml. Sci. (hon.), McKenzie Coll., 1991. Store mgr., buyer S & W Distbg. Co., Boston, 1949-59; buyer Radio Shack Co., Boston, 1959-66, mdse. mgr., 1966-70, v.p. merchandising Ft. Worth, 1970-78, sr. v.p. merchandising and advt., 1978-80, exec. v.p. mktg., 1980-84, pres., 1984-92, chmn., 1992-93; sr. v.p. Tandy Corp., 1992-93; bd. dirs. Uniview Corp., 1995—; pres. Appel Assocs., Mktg. Cons., 1993—; vice chmn., bd. dirs. Integrated Tech. Inc., 1994-99. V.p. Holbrook (Mass.) Jewish Cmty. Ctr., 1958-59; bd. dirs. Dan Danciger Jewish Cmty. Ctr., Ft. Worth, 1989-98; v.p., founder Temple Aliyah, Needham, Mass., 1969-70; pres. Congregation Ahavath Sholom, Ft. Worth, 1979-81, bd. dirs., 1972—; bd. dirs. Jewish Fedn. Ft. Worth, 1975-97, v.p., 1981-85, pres., 1985-87; bd. dirs. Casa Manana Mus., 1978-79; mem. adv. bd. Arts Coun. Ft. Worth, 1985—; project renewal cluster chmn. Acco-East, Israel, 1981-94; mem. exec. com. so. regional campaign cabinet United Jewish Appeal, 1980-89; so. regional chmn. United Jewish Appeal's Passage to Freedom Campaign for Soviet Jewry, 1989; co-chmn. fin. rels. United Jewish Appeal Western Region, Jewish Agy. Com., 1992-93, United Jewish Appeal Ctrl. Region, Jewish Agy Com., 1993; mem. exec. com. Network of Ind. UJA Coms., 1994—; bd. dirs. Family Svcs., Inc., 1990—; mem. internat. bd. visitors M.J. Neeley Sch. Bus., Tex. Christian U., 1990—; hon. life mem. nat. commn. Anti-Defamation League, 1992. With USCG, 1951-54. Recipient Torch of Liberty award Anti-Defamation League of B'nai B'rith, 1988, Defender of Jerusalem award, 1990, Alumni award Boston U. Sch. Mgmt., 1994; named Man of Yr., B'nai B'rith Ft. Worth Jewish, 1984, Anti-Defamation League Ft. Worth, 1990; named to Consumer Electronics Hall of Fame, 2002. Mem. Electronic VIP Club, Ft. Worth C. of C. (bd. dirs. 1981-84), Masons, Shriners, Frog Club (Tex. Christian U.), Colonial Country Club, City Country Club, Ft. Worth. Home: 4917 Ranch View Rd Fort Worth TX 76109-3117 Office: Appel Assocs 301 Commerce St Ste 1415 Fort Worth TX 76102-4114 Office Phone: 817-338-9579. E-mail: bappel@flash.net.

APPEL, BRENT ROBERT, lawyer; b. Dubuque, Iowa, July 13, 1950; s. Herbert John and Janice Emily (Bardill) A. BA, MA, Stanford U., 1973; JD, U. Calif., Berkeley, 1977. Bar: Calif. 1978, Iowa 1979, U.S. Ct. Appeals (8th cir.), U.S. Dist. Ct. (no. and so. dists.). 1st asst. atty. gen. State of Iowa, Des Moines, 1979-80; campaign mgr. U.S. Sen. John Culver, Des Moines, 1980; dep. atty. gen. State of Iowa, Des Moines, 1981-82, 83-86; shareholder Dickinson, Mackaman, Tyler & Hagen, PC, Des Moines, 1987—, pres., 1991—. Contbr. articles to profl. jours. Dem. nominee for U.S. Congress, 2d dist. Iowa, 1982. Mem. ABA, ATLA, Iowa Trial Lawyers Assn., Iowa Bar Assn., Polk County Bar Assn. Democrat. Methodist. Office: Dickinson Mackaman Tyler & Hagen PC 1600 Hub Tower Des Moines IA 50309-3944 E-mail: bappel@dickinsonlaw.com.

APPEL, GERALD, investment advisor; b. N.Y.C., June 2, 1933; s. Samuel and Vivian (Adlerstein) A.; m. Judith Kane, May 26, 1956; children: Marvin Laurence, Marion Fran. BA, Bklyn. Coll., 1954; MSW, NYU, 1956. Adminstr. social agy. Jewish Family Svc., Bklyn., 1958-73; pvt. practice as psychoanalyst Great Neck, N.Y., 1963-95; pres. Signalert Corp., Great Neck, 1973—, Appel Asset Mgmt. Corp., 1995—. Author: Winning Market Systems, 1972, Double Your Money Every Three Years, 1973, 99 Ways to Make Money in a Depression, 1974, Stock Option and No-Load Switch Fund Scalpers Manual, 1979, Winning Stock Selection Systems, 1979, The Big Move, 1981, Time-Trend III, 1988, Portraits of Nature, 1992, American Photographers at the Turn of the Century, Travel and Trekking, 1994, (with others) The Art of the Human Form, 1995, New Directions in Technical Analysis, 1976, Stock Market Trading Systems, 1980, Far Away Faces-A Guide to Better Travel Portraits, 1998; (video) The MACD Trading System, 1990, Day Trading, 1990, Power Tools, 1992, Technical Analysis - Power Tools for the Active Investor, 2005; contbr. articles to profl. jours. Bd. dirs. Keystone Ctr. of Music and Arts, 1998-2000, Mountain Laurel Ctr. Performing Arts, 2000-2004, The Great Neck Ctr. Performing Arts, 2000—. Mem.: Nat. Psychol. Assn. for Psychoanalysis (bd. dirs., v.p.), Am. Assn. Media Photographers. Avocations: photography, tennis, sailing, music. Home: 97 Myrtle Dr Great Neck NY 11021-1805 Office: Signalert Corp 150 Great Neck Rd Ste 301 Great Neck NY 11021-3339 Office Phone: 516-829-6444. E-mail: gappel6@optonline.net, gappel@signalert.com.

APPEL, JACOB M., political scientist, educator, writer; b. Bronx, N.Y., Feb. 21, 1974; s. Gerald Bernard and Alice Sue Appel. BA, MA, Brown U., 1995; MFA, NYU, 1999; MPhil, Columbia U., 2000; JD, Harvard Law Sch., 2003. Instr. polit. science Brown U., Providence, 1996—; instr. creative writing NYU, N.Y.C., 1998—2000; instr. Gotham Writer's Workshop N.Y.C., 1998—. Adj. asst. prof. Brown Univ., 2001—; vis. faculty Columbia Univ., 2005. Contbr. numerous short stories to lit. publs. Recipient Dana award, Dana Awards Found., 2000, Hon. Mention, O'Henry Prize, 2001. Home: 140 Clarmont Apt 3D New York NY 10027-4632 Office Phone: 212-663-3643. Personal E-mail: jma38@columbia.com.

APPEL, JOEL, household cleaner manufacturing executive; With mktg. dept. Quaker Oats; pres. Orange Glo Internat., Greenwood Village, Colo. Office: Orange Glo International 8200 E Maplewood Ave Greenwood Village CO 80111-4822

APPEL, KENNETH I., mathematician, educator; b. Bklyn., Oct. 8, 1932; s. Irwin and Lillian (Sender) A.; m. Carole Stein, June 21, 1959; children—Andrew, Laurel, Peter BS, Queens Coll., 1953; MA, U. Mich., 1956, PhD, 1959. Mem. tech. staff Inst. for Def. Analyses, Princeton, N.J., 1959-61; asst. prof. math U. Ill., Urbana, 1961-67, assoc. prof., 1967-77, prof., 1977-93, prof. emeritus, 1993; prof. U. N.H., 1993—2003, chair dept. math., 1993—2002, prof. emeritus, 2003. Alderman, City of Urbana, 1971-75, mem. zoning bd. of appeals, 1975— . Served as pfc. U.S. Army, 1953-55 Recipient Delbert Ray Fulkerson prize Am. Math. Soc. and Math. Programming Soc., 1979, Disting. Alumnus award Queens Coll., 1979 Mem. Am. Math. Soc., Math. Assn. Am., Assn. Symbolic Logic Democrat. Jewish. Office: Univ New Hampshire Dept Math Kingsbury Hall Durham NH 03824 Business E-Mail: kia@oregano.unh.edu.

APPEL, KENNETH MARK, lawyer; b. N.Y.C., May 24, 1949; s. Jesse and Rose (Boyarsky) A.; m. Janis Lowe, May 21, 1982; children: Rachael, Matthew. BA with honors in history, NYU, 1972; JD, Cath. U., 1975. Pvt. practice St. Albans, Vt., 1981—. Office: 232 N Main St Saint Albans VT 05478-1554 E-mail: vtlaw@bellatlantic.net, kappel@together.net.

APPEL, LAURENCE BRUCE, lawyer, retail executive; b. 1961; m. Caren Appel; children: Molly, Rebecca, Michael. BA, U. Va., 1983; JD, U. Pa., 1989. Bar: Ga. 1989. Lawyer King & Spalding, Atlanta, Altman, Kritzer & Levick, Atlanta, 1995—97; sr. corp. counsel for strategic bus. devel. Home Depot Inc., 1997, sr. v.p. legal, 1997—2002; sr. v.p., gen. counsel Winn-Dixie

Stores, Inc., Jacksonville, Fla., 2002—, sec., 2003—. Mem.: Atlanta Bar Assn., State Bar Ga., ABA, Order of the Coif. Office: Winn-Dixie Stores Inc 5050 Edgewood Ct Jacksonville FL 32254-3699

APPEL, MARSHA CEIL, advertising executive; b. NYC, Dec. 3, 1953; d. Albert and Stella Joy (Glaser) A.; m. Mark D. Marcellus, Sept. 10, 1978; children: Sam, Jill. BA, SUNY, Albany, 1974; MSLS, Syracuse U., 1975. Info. specialist Am. Assn. Advt. Agys., NYC, 1976-79, mgr. member info. svc., 1979-89, v.p., 1989-97, sr. v.p., 1997—. Author: Illustration Index IV, 1980, Illustration Index V, 1984, Illustration Index VI, 1988, Illustration Index VII, 1993, Illustration Index VIII, 1998; editor What's New in Advertising and Marketing, 1978-80; mem. adv. bd., contbr. Ency. Advt., 2002; contbr. Super Searchers Madison Avenue, 2003. Mem.: Advt. Women of N.Y., Spl. Librs. Assn. (chmn. advt. mktg. divsn. 1982—83). Office: Am Assn Advt Agys 405 Lexington Ave New York NY 10174-0002

APPEL, NINA SCHICK, law educator, dean, academic administrator; b. Feb. 17, 1936; d. Leo and Nora Schick; m. Alfred Appel Jr.; children: Karen Oshman, Richard. Student, Cornell U.; JD, Columbia U., 1959. Instr. Columbia Law Sch., 1959-60; adminstr. Stanford U., mem. faculty, prof. law, 1973—, assoc. dean, 1976-83; dean Sch. Law Loyola U., 1983—2004, dean emerita, prof. law, 2004—. Mem. Am. Bar Found., Ill. Bar Found., Chgo. Bar Found., Chgo. Legal Club, Chgo. Network. Jewish. Office: Loyola U Sch Law 1 E Pearson St Chicago IL 60611-2055 Office Phone: 312-915-7128. E-mail: nappel@luc.edu.

APPEL, STANLEY HERSH, neurologist, educator; b. Boston, May 8, 1933; married; 4 children. AB, Harvard U., 1954; MD, Columbia U., 1960. Diplomate Am. Bd. Psychiatry and Neurology. Intern medicine Mass. Gen. Hosp., 1960-61; resident neurology Mt. Sinai Hosp., 1961-62; rsch. assoc. Lab. Molecular Biology NIH, 1962-64; chief rsch. assoc. Sch. Medicine U. Pa., 1965-66, asst. prof., 1966-67; assoc. of neurology Med. Ctr. Duke U., 1964-65, from assoc. prof. to prof. neurology, 1967-77, assoc. prof. biochemistry, 1968-77, chief divsn. neurology, 1969-77; prof. neurology Baylor Coll. Medicine, 1977—2004, prof., chmn. dept. neurology, 1977—2004, chmn. program neurosci., 1977-89, dir. Jerry Lewis Neuromuscular Disorder Rsch. Ctr., 1977—2004; dir. Vicki Appel MDA/ALS Ctr., 1977—2004; chair dept. neurology Meth. Hosp. Neurol. Inst., Houston, 2005—, dir. MDA/ALS Rsch. and Clin. Ctr., 2005—; prof. neurology Weill Med. Coll. Cornell U., NYC, 2005—. Recipient Rsch. Career Devel. award USPHS, 1965-70. Mem. Am. Acad. Neurology, Am. Soc. Biol. Chemistry, Am. Soc. Clin. Investigation, Am. Neurol. Assn. Achievements include research in etiology of amyotrophic lateral sclerosis, Parkinson's disease, and Alzheimer's disease. Office: Meth Neurological Inst Dept Neurology 6560 Fannin St #802 Houston TX 77030 Office Phone: 713-441-3760.

APPEL, WILLIAM FRANK, pharmacist; b. Mpls., Oct. 8, 1924; s. William Ignatius and Elna Antonia (Mulzahn) A.; m. Louise D. Altman, Sept. 24, 1949; children— Nancy, Peggy, James, Elizabeth. BS in Pharmacy, U. Minn., 1949; D.Sc. (hon.), Phila. Coll. Pharmacy and Sci., 1978. Intern in pharmacy Northwestern Hosp., Mpls.; pres., pharmacist, mgr. Appel Com-Pharm, Inc., Mpls., 1949—; pres. Pharm. Cons. Services, P.A., St. Paul, 1960—. Mem. Minn. Bd. Pharmacy, 1960-65, pres., 1965; preceptor internship requirement program; chmn. Minn. Gov's. Commn. on Drug Abuse, 1971-73; mem. Mpls. Health Dept. Task Force on Pub. Health Approaches to Chem. Dependency; clin. instr. U. Minn. Coll. Pharmacy, 1970—; cons. HEW; long term care facilities; rep. Nat. Pharmacy/Industry Com. on Nat. Health Ins.; mem. revision com. U.S. Pharmacopeial Conv., 1980— Served with USN, 1942-46. Recipient Good Neighbor award, Sta. WCCO, Mpls., 1973. Mem. Twin City Met. Drug Assn., Minn. Pharm. Assn. (v.p., Harold R. Popp award 1974, mem. continuing edn. faculty 1970—), Am. Pharm. Assn. (pres. N.W. br., nat. pres. 1976-77, Daniel B. Smith award 1970, treas. 1979—) pharm. assns), Minn. Gerontol. Soc., U. Minn. Coll. Pharmacy Alumni Assn. (v.p., Distinguished Pharmacist award 1971) Home: 7204 Trillium Ln Minneapolis MN 55435-4020 Office: Preferred Choice Pharmacy 900 Long Lake Rd #150 New Brighton MN 55112

APPELBAUM, ANN HARRIET, lawyer; b. Decatur, Ill., 1948; d. Irving and Cecelia (Hecht) A.; m. Neal Borovitz, July 4, 1982; children: Abby, Jeremy. BA, Barnard Coll., 1970; JD, Boston U., 1973. Bar: N.Y. 1974, U.S. Dist. Ct. (so. dist.) N.Y. 1975, U.S. Ct. Appeals (2nd cir.) 1975, U.S. Supreme Ct. 1978. Assoc. Hart & Hume, N.Y.C., 1974-76, Warshaw, Burstein, N.Y.C., 1976-80; counsel Jewish Theol. Sem. & Jewish Mus., N.Y.C., 1980—. Mem. Nat. Assn. Coll. and Univ. Attys. Office: The Jewish Theological Seminary 3080 Broadway New York NY 10027-4650 Office Phone: 212-678-8804.

APPELBAUM, DIANA KARTER, author; b. Ft. Belvoir, Va., Nov. 9, 1953; d. Peter and Elizabeth Carmen (Whitman) Karter; m. Paul Stuart Appelbaum, Mar. 31, 1974; children: Binyamin, Yonatan, Avigail. AB, Columbia U., 1975. Author: Thanksgiving, An American Holiday, 1984, The Glorious Fourth, 1989, Giants in the Land, 1993, Cocoa Ice, 1997. Recipient Booklist Mag. Top of the List prize, 1993. Mem. Author's Guild. Home: 100 Berkshire Rd Newton MA 02460-2404 Office: care Houghton Mifflin Co 222 Berkeley St Boston MA 02116-3748

APPELBAUM, ELIZABETH BERMAN (ELIZABETH BERMAN), mathematician; d. Reuben and Isabel Rosenstein Berman; m. Bradley Edward Appelbaum, Aug. 8, 1957; children: James Steven, Sharon Appelbaum Hoffmann. BA magna cum laude, U. Minn., 1958, MA, 1959; PhD, U. Mo., Kans. City, 1970. Asst. prof. math. Rockhurst Coll., Kans.City, 1970—75; faculty math. U. Mo. Kans. City, 1975—80; programmer-analyst AT&T Comm., Kans. City, 1981—85; tutor math. self-employed, Overland Park, 1985—; assoc. prof. math. Baker U., Baldwin, Kans., 1985—86; faculty, computer sci. and math. Johnson County CC, Overland Park, 1988; faculty math. Kans. City Acad., 1988—89, Longview CC, Lee's Summit, Mo., 1989—90; faculty economics Avila Coll., Kans. City, 1990—94; assoc. prof. math. Pk. Coll., Mo., 1995—96; cmty. liaison for math. Blue Valley Sch. Dist., Overland Park, Kans., 1997—. Reviewer Mcgraw-Hill, NY, 1973—75, Wiley, Boston, 1980—81, Addison-Wesley, Boston, 1979—80; cons. Donnelly Coll., Kans. City, 1975—75. Author: Mathematics Revealed; contbr. articles to profl. jours., chapters to books. With Olathe Civic Band; musician Temple Bnai Jehudah, Overland Park, Mo., 1966—. Fellow Grad. Fellowship, NSF, 1958-1959, Grad. Fellowships, 1967-1970. Mem.: Nat. Orgn. for Women (pres. Kans. City chpt. 1988—90), Nat. Coun. Tchrs. Math. (coll. rep. to Kans. City chpt. 1988—90), Kans. Assn. Tchrs. Math., Assn. For Women in Math. (spkr. 1984—86), Math. Assn. Am. (pub. info. officer Mo. sect. 1979—80), Phi Beta Kappa. Jewish. Achievements include research in abstract algebra. Avocations: piccolo, flute. Home: 8275 W 116 Terr Overland Park KS 66210

APPELBAUM, FREDERICK RAY, oncologist; b. Canton, Ohio, Sept. 2, 1946; s. Samuel and Evelyn (Shapiro) A.; m. Janet Wynn Schwarz, Feb. 3, 1980; children: Jacob, David. AB, Dartmouth Coll., 1968; MD, Tufts U., 1972. Intern, resident U. Mich., Ann Arbor, 1972-74; clin. assoc. NIH, Bethesda, Md., 1974-76, investigator, 1976-78; asst. prof. U. Wash., Fred Hutchinson Cancer Rsch. Ctr., Seattle, 1978-83, assoc. prof., 1983-88, prof., 1988—, dir. clin. rsch., 1993—; dept. head divsn. med. oncology U. Washington, 1998—. Mem. bd. sci. advisors Nat. Cancer Inst. Assoc. editor: Blood, 1993-2002; contbr. articles to profl. jours. Grantee NIH, 1980—. Mem. Am. Soc. Clin. Oncology (bd. dirs. 1990-93), Am. Soc. Hematology (bd. councillors 1994-98). Jewish. Office: Fred Hutchinson Cancer Rsch 1100 Fairview Ave N D5 310 Seattle WA 98109-1024

APPELBAUM, PAUL STUART, psychiatrist, medical educator, department chairman; b. Bklyn., Nov. 30, 1951; s. Isidore W. and Celia (Bressler) A.; m. Diana Muir Karter, Nov. 9, 1953; children: Binyamin, Yonatan, Avigail. AB, Columbia U., 1972; MD, Harvard U., 1976. Diplomate Am. Bd. Psychiatry and Neurology. Intern Soroka Med. Ctr., Beersheva, Israel, 1976-77; resident Mass. Mental Health Ctr., Boston, 1977-80; clin. fellow psychiatry Harvard Med. Sch., Boston, 1977-80; from asst. prof. to assoc. prof. psychiatry and law U. Pitts., 1980-84; assoc. prof. psychiatry Harvard Med. Sch., Boston, 1984-85; Zeleznik prof. psychiatry, dir. law and psychiatry program U. Mass. Med. Sch., Worcester, 1985—, chmn. dept., 1992—; vis. interdisciplinary prof. Law Ctr. Georgetown U., Washington, 1988-89. Mem. commn. on mentally disabled ABA, Washington, 1982-87; task force on involuntary civil commitment Nat. Ctr. for State Cts., Williamsburg, Va., 1984-89, Rsch. Network on Mental Health and Law, John D. and Catherine T. Macarthur Found., Chgo., 1988-96; fellow Ctr. for Advanced Study in the Behavioral Scis., Stanford, Calif., 1996-97; rsch. network on mandatory outpatient treatment John D. and Catherine T. MacArthur Found., Chgo., 2000--; bd. dirs. neurosci. and behavioral health Inst. Medicine of NAS, 2001-. Author: Clinical Handbook of Psychiatry and the Law, 1982 (M.F. Guttmacher award 1982), 3d edit., 2000, Informed Consent: Legal Theory and Clinical Practice, 1987, 2d edit., 2001, Paul Appelbaum on Law and Psychiatry, 1989, Almost A Revolution: Mental Health Law and Limits of Change, 1994 (M.F. Guttmacher award 1996), Trauma and Memory: Clinical and Legal Controversies, 1997, Assessing Patients' Capacities to Consent to Treatment, 1998 (M.F. Guttmacher award 2000), Rethinking Risk Assessment, 2001 (M.F. Guttmacher award 2002); contbr. articles to profl. jours. Nat. coord. Med. Mobilization for Soviet Jewry, Waltham, Mass., 1974-80; bd. dirs. Action for Soviet Jewry, Waltham, 1984-85, Torah Ctr., Sharon, Mass., 1987-88, Cmty. Health Link, Worcester, Mass., 1992—, Am. Psychiat. Press, 2001-03, Am. Psychiat. Inst. on Rsch. and Edn., 2001-03. Recipient Rsch. Scientist Devel. award NIMH, 1983; Rsch. grantee Pres.'s Commn. on Ethical Problems in Medicine, Washington, 1982, John D. and Catherine T. MacArthur Found., 1988, 2003; fellow Ctr. for Advanced Study in Behavioral Scis., Palo Alto, Calif., 1996-97. Mem.: NAS (elected to Inst. Medicine 2000), Mass. Psychiat. Soc. (pres. 1992—93), Am. Soc. Law and Medicine, Am. Acad. Psychiatry and the Law (councillor 1987—90, pres. 1995—96, Seymour Pollock award 2001), Am. Psychiat. Assn. (bd. dirs. 1997—, chair commn. on jud. action 1984—90, joint reference com. 1984—94, chair coun. on psychiatry and law 1990—94, 2004—, sec. 1997—99, v.p. 1999—2001, pres. 2002—03, Isaac Ray award 1990), Internat. Acad. Law and Mental Health (Philippe Pinel award 2000). Jewish. Avocation: writing for popular mags. Office: U Mass Med Sch Dept Psychiatry Worcester MA 01655 Office Phone: 508-856-3066. E-mail: appelbap@ummhc.org.

APPELL, LOUISE SOPHIA, retired consulting company executive; b. Northampton, Mass., Sept. 22, 1930; d. Romeo Edward and Phyllis Teresa (Szynal) Fortier; m. Melville Joseph Appell, July 26, 1953 (div. 1975); children: Melissande Foglio, David Maxcim; m. Clifford Harding Querolo, June 1, 1991 (dec. 1992). BA, Smith Coll., 1951; MA, U. Ky., 1966, PhD, 1972. Instr. U. Ky., 1966-68; dir. spl. edn. grad. program Catholic U. Am., Washington, 1969-76; assoc. dir. nat. com. Arts for the Handicapped, Washington, 1976-80; owner, pres. Louise Appell Cons. Svcs., Washington, 1980-82; assoc. Macro Systems, Inc., Silver Spring, Md., 1982-84, dir. edn. product devel., 1984-85, dir. ednl. product devel., 1985—, v.p., 1985—, ret., 1996. Personal E-mail: lsappell@verizon.net.

APPELLO, KATHY, English as a second language educator; b. Jersey City, N.J., Aug. 4, 1965; d. August and Anna (Schettino) Appello. AS, Katherine Gibb Sch., 1988; BA, Pace U., 1995. ESL lab. counselor, instr. LaGuardia C.C., NY, 1995—97. Mem. ESL coun. CUNY, 1997—; mem. N.Y. State TESOL, 1996—. Author: (poetry) Journey of Heart and Soul. Recipient Poetry award, Amherst Soc., 1996, Judith Grant Editor's award, 1997. Mem.: Acad. Am. Poets. Home: 90 Gold St Apt 13H New York NY 10038-1842 Office Phone: 212-714-6016.

APPELMAN, EVAN HUGH, retired chemist; b. Chgo., June 6, 1935; s. Harry Louis and Mollie Sarah (Hirsch) A.; m. Mary Frances Goold, Sept. 2, 1960; children: Harold Stewart, Hilary Louise. AB, U. Chgo., 1953, MS, 1955; PhD, U. Calif. at Berkeley, 1960. With Argonne (Ill.) Nat. Lab., 1960-95, chemist, 1963-76, sr. chemist, 1976-95, ret., 1995. Contbr. articles to profl. jours. Guggenheim fellow, 1973-74; Recipient award for service at Argonne Nat. Lab., U. Chgo., 1975, E.O. Lawrence award ERDA, 1976, Alexander von Humboldt Research award Fed. Republic Germany, 1988-89; vis. sr. rsch. fellow Brit. Sci. Rsch. Coun.-U. Oxford, 1983-84. Fellow AAAS; mem. Am. Chem. Soc., Phi Beta Kappa, Sigma Xi. Jewish. Home: 224 Lake Dr Kensington CA 94708-1132 E-mail: evhap@anl.gov.

APPENZELLER, OTTO, neurologist, researcher; b. Czernowitz, Romania, Dec. 11, 1927; came to U.S., 1963; s. Emmanuel Adam and Josephine (Metsch) A.; m. Judith Bryce, Dec. 11, 1956; children: Timothy, Martin, Peter. MBBS, Sydney U., Australia, 1957, MD, 1966; PhD, U. London, 1963. Diplomate Am. Bd. Psychiatry and Neurology. Prof. U. N. Mex., Albuquerque, 1970-90; vis. prof. McGill U., Montreal, Canada, 1977; hon. rsch. fellow U. London, 1983; vis. scientist Oxygen Transport Program Lovelace Med. Found., Albuquerque, 1990-92; pres. N.Mex. Health Enhancement and Marathon Clinics Rsch. Found., Albuquerque, 1992—; prof. exptl. neurobiology Bogomoletz Inst. Ukrainian Acad. Sci., Kiev, 1995-2000. U.S.-India exch. scientist NSF, 1992; Fogarty internat. exch. scientist, Kiev, Ukraine, 1993; rsch. com. UNESCO Internat. Coun. Sports and Phys. Edn., 1978-99; ref. Med. Rsch. Coun. New Zealand, 1986-99, reviewer, 1988-99; participant individual health scientist exch. program Fogarty Internat. Ctr., NIH to A.A. Bogomoletz Inst. Physiology, Kiev, 1993. Author: The Autonomic Nervous System, 5th edit., 1997; co-author: Headache, 1984; editor: Pathogenesis and Management of Headache, 1976, Health Aspects of Endurance Training, 1978, Sports Medicine, 3d edit., 1988, Jour. Headache, 1975-77, Annals of Sports Medicine, 1984-88; translator: Neurologic Differential Diagnosis (M. Mumentaler), 2nd edit., 1992; vol. editor: Handbook of Clinical Neurology: The Autonomic Nervous System, Parts I and II, 1998-2000; mem. editl. bd. numerous med. jours. Grantee Diabetes Rsch. and Edn. Found., 1988, Inst. C. Mondino, U. Pavia, Italy, 1992, 95-96, 2000, NMHEMC Rsch. Found., 1992-2005. Fellow ACP (sr.), Am. Acad. Neurology (sr.), Royal Australasian Coll. Physicians (sr.). Achievements include discovery of disease affecting peripheral nerves of Navajo children, of release of opioids and endothelin in human circulatory system after exercise, of chronic neurodegenerative disease in human T-lymphotropic viral II (HTLV II) infection, of peptidergic innervation of blood vessels supplying blood to peripheral nerves in present day and ancient mummified tissues of neurologic dis. in mummy portraits, of neuropathy in chronic pulmonary disease and chronic mountain sickness of human fossilized biological rhythm in ancient human teeth, and teeth of extinct archosaurs; leader of Mt. Everest rsch. expedition, 1987, Khachenjunga rsch. expedition, 1989, Stock Kangri rsch. expedition, 1992, Tso Moriri Lake (Ladakh) rsch. expedition, 1994, Cerro de Pasco rsch. expedition, 1997, 99-2000, 03, rsch. expedition Simen Mountains, Ethiopia, 2005. E-mail: ottoarun12@aol.com, o.appenzeller@comcast.net.

APPERSON, JACK ALFONSO, retired army officer, management executive; b. Fredericksburg, Va., Dec. 21, 1934; s. Claude Heywood and Mary Louise (Farmer) A.; m. Alexandra Maynard, Aug. 31, 1957 (dec. Aug. 1992); children: Melissa Heywood, Amy Alexandra, Robert Randall (dec.), Eric Edward; m. Marguerite M. Legin, Nov. 25, 1995. BS, U.S. Mil. Acad., 1957; MS in Nuclear Physics, U. Ala., 1962; AA (hon.), Texarkana C.C., 1979. Commd. 2d lt. U.S. Army, 1957, advanced through grades to brig. gen., platoon leader Ft. Bragg, N.C., 1957-58, Ft. Knox, Ky., 1958-59; comdg. officer 546th Ordnance Co. U.S. Army-Europe, 1963-64, materiel officer 66th Maintenance Bn., 1964-65, exec. officer bn., 1965-66; asst. prof., instr. dept. ordnance U.S. Mil. Acad., 1967-69; bn. comdr. and materiel officer 801st Maintenance Bn., Vietnam, 1969-70; assignment officer ordnance br. Office of Personnel Ops., Dept. Army, Washington, 1970-71, chief co. grade assignments, 1971-72; bn. comdr. 1st Inf. Div., Ft. Riley, Kans., 1973-74; office dep. chief of staff for logistics Dept. Army, Washington, 1974-75; chief war res. office Office Dep. Chief of Staff for Logistics, Dept. Army, Washington, 1975-76; exec. to asst. sec. Army Installations and Logistics, Washington, 1976-77; comdr. Red River Army Depot, Texarkana, Tex., 1977-79; dep. comdg. gen. U.S. Army Missile Materiel Readiness Command, Redstone Arsenal, Ala., 1979-81; comdg. gen. U.S. Army Depot System Command, Chambersburg, Pa., 1981-82; sr. v.p. ops. mgmt. div. Day & Zimmermann, Phila., 1982-83, also bd. dirs.; pres. Govt. Systems Group Day and Zimmerman, Phila., 1991-95, Systems Engring. Assocs. Corp., Mt. Laurel, NJ, 1983-91. Bd. dirs. Redstone Fed. Credit Union; vestryman Sharon Chapel Episcopal Ch., Alexandria, Va., 1975-77, St. Paul's Episcopal Ch., Phila., 1984-1988. Decorated DSM, Legion of Merit, Bronze Star (2), Meritorious Svc. medal, others; inducted into U.S. Army Ordnance Hall of Fame, 1994. Mem. Assn. Grads. U.S. Mil. Acad., West Point Soc. Phila. (bd. dirs.), Assn. U.S. Army (pres. chpt. 1983-85), Am. Def. Preparedness Assn., Alumni Assn. U.S. Army War Coll., Phila C. of C., Cherry Hill C. of C., Narragansett C. of C. (pres. 1996—2000), South County Hosp. Found.; trustee R.I. State Investment Commn., Rotary (pres. West Bay Rotary Coun. 2000), Rehoboth-Lewes Rotary, Sigma Pi Sigma. Republican. Home: 272 E Main St Moorestown NJ 08057

APPERSON, JEAN, psychologist; b. Durham, N.C., June 8, 1934; d. James Harry and Dorothy Elizabeth (Johnson) Apperson; m. Calvin Adams Pope, Mar. 23, 1956 (div. 1967); 1 child, Richard Allan. BA, U. S. Fla., 1966; MA, Mich. State U., 1970, PhD, 1973. Cert. in psychoanalysis Mich. Psychoanalytic Coun., 1990. Teaching asst. Mich. State U., E. Lansing, 1968-69; psychiatric technician St. Lawrence Community Mental Health Ctr., Lansing, Mich., 1968-69, psychology intern, 1969-71, Mich. State U. Counseling Ctr., 1971-73; clin. psychologist U. Mich. Counseling Ctr., Ann Arbor, 1973-81; pvt. practice psychology and psychoanalysis Ann Arbor, 1974—. Mem., chmn. Mich. Bd. Psychology, Lansing, 1984-91. Contbr. articles to profl. jours.; cons. editor Am. Psychol. Assn. Catalog of Selected Documents, 1975-80. USPHS grantee, 1969-70; NIMH grantee, 1970-71. Fellow Mich. Psychol. Assn. (chmn. women's issues com. 1981-83); mem. APA (com. on sci. and profl. ethics and conduct 1977-80), Mich. Soc. Psychoanalytic Psychology (treas. 1982-86), Mich. Psychoanalytic Coun. (tchg. and supervising analyst, mem. at large 1991-93, tng. com. 1992-2001, pres. 1995-97, v.p. for edn. and tng. 1998-2001), Assn. for Advancement of Psychology, Am. Women in Psychology, Mich. Women Psychologists. Democrat. Unitarian Universalist. Avocations: french language and culture, gardening, nature study, music. Home: 7224 Chelsea Manchester Rd Manchester MI 48158-9443 Office: Ste 23E 555 E William St Ann Arbor MI 48104-2428 Office Phone: 734-428-9110. E-mail: jeanatapp@aol.com.

APPIAH, JOSEPH YAW, historian, educator; b. Duayaw-Nkwanta, Ghana, May 6, 1954; arrived in U.S., 1983; s. Daniel Kwadwo and Grace Dufie Appiah; m. Lydia Pokuah, July 6, 1978; children: Amma, Daniel, Grace, Stephanie, Josephine. BA with honors, U. Ghana, Legon, 1979; MA, SUNY, Albany, 1984, MA, DA, SUNY, Albany, 1989. Instr. history Horry Georgetown Tech. Coll., Conway, SC, 1990—93; prof. history J. Sargeant Reynolds C.C., Richmond, Va., 1993—. Presiding elder Ch. of the Living God, Richmond, 2001—. Recipient 5 Yr. Svc. award, Commonwealth of Va., 1998, 10 Yr. Svc. award, 2003, Svc. award, Ch. of the Living God, 2004. Mem.: Delta Omicron, Phi Alpha Theta, Phi Theta Kappa (Horizon award 1993). Mem. Full Gospel Ch. Avocations: tennis, jogging, bicycling, swimming. Home: 9111 Medley Mill Ct Mechanicsville VA 23116 Office: J Sargeant Reynolds CC PO Box 85622 Richmond VA 23285 Business E-Mail: Jappiah@jsr.uccs.edu.

APPLBAUM, RONALD LEE, academic administrator; b. Charleroi, Pa., Dec. 14, 1943; s. Irwin and Marion (Caplan) A.; m. Susan Joy Stone, July 4, 1968; 1 child, Lee. BA, Calif. State U., Long Beach, 1965, MA, 1966; PhD, Pa. State U., 1969. Prof. Calif. State U., Long Beach, 1969-76, assoc. dean, 1976-77, dean, 1977-82; v.p. U. Tex.-Pan Am., Edinburg, 1982-90; pres. Westfield (Mass.) State Coll., 1990-96, Kean U., Union, NJ, 1996—2002, Colo. State U., Pueblo, 2002—. Mem. bd. examiners Dept. Edn., 1997—; dir. N.J. Alliance, Inc., 1998—. Author: Fundamentals of Human Communication, 1973, Process of Group Communication, 1979, Organizational Communication, 1981, Business and Professional Speaking, 1982; co-author 7 textbooks; editor textbook series ModComm, MassCom, ProCom, 1973-80; contbr. articles to profl. jours. Bd. dirs.Temple Emanuel, McAllen, Tex., 1983-90, pres., 1987-89; v.p. McAllen chpt. B'nai Brith, 1984-89. Mem. Internat. Comm. Assn., World Comm. Assn. (sec.-gen. 1982-91, pres. 1991-95), Ea. Comm. Assn. (reviewer 1991-93, exec. coun. 1994-96), Speech Comm. Assn., Mass Comm. Assn., Assn. Comm. Adminstrs. (editor JACA 1992—), Westfield C. of C. (bd. dirs. 1991-96, vice-chair 1992-94, chair 1994-95), Westfield Cmty. Devel. Corp. (pres. 1994, 95), Westfield Kiwanis (v.p. 1992-95, pres. 1995-96), Phi Kappa Phi (pres. Calif. State U. Long Beach chpt. 1976-77, Westfield State Coll. chpt. 1992-93), Union County Alliance (exec. bd. 1997—), Union County Twp. C.C. (bd. dirs. 1997—). Office: Kean U Office of Pres 1000 Morris Ave Union NJ 07083-7131

APPLE, D. JOHN, musician, writer; b. Ann Arbor, Mich., Apr. 9, 1953; s. Clyde Apple Jr and Ruth Vivian Swanson Apple. AA, Concordia Luth. Jr. Coll., 1975; MusB, Houghton Coll., 1978; MusM, Westminster Choir Coll., 1981. Organ & choral advisor Brodt Music Co, Charlotte, NC, 1983—94; organist, music assoc. St. Gabriel Cath. Ch., 1993—2004; organ music editor, cons. Michael's Music Svc., 2000—. Author: (book: annotated compendium) Pipe Organs of Charlotte; contbr. reference book for classical music; author: (festschrift) Richard M & Betty Peek. Basic oper. grants advisor Arts and Scis Coun., Charlotte, 1998—2000; v.p. Carolina Theatre Preservation Soc., 1997—2005. Mem.: Metrolina Theatre Organ Soc. (pres., founder 1989—), Organ Hist. Soc., Am. Theatre Organ Soc. (bd. dirs. 2003—05), Am. Guild Organists (Charlotte chpt. archivist, historian 1984—), Theatre Hist. Soc. Home: 4146 Sheridan Dr Charlotte NC 28205 Office: Michaels Music Svc 4146 Sheridan Dr Charlotte NC 28205 Office Phone: 704-567-1066. E-mail: john@michaelsmusicservice.com.

APPLE, DAINA DRAVNIEKS, federal agency administrator; b. Kuldiga, Latvia, July 6, 1944; came to U.S., 1951; d. Albins Dravnieks and Alina A. (Bergs) Zelmenis; divorced; 1 child, Almira Moronne; m. Martin A. Apple, Sept. 2, 1986. BSc, U. Calif., Berkeley, 1977, MA, 1980. Economist Pacific S.W. Rsch. U.S. Forest Svc., Berkeley, 1976-85, mgr. regional land use appeals San Francisco, 1986-88, program analysis officer, engring., 1988-90, asst. regulatory officer, 1990-95, strategic planner nat. forest sys. resources program, 1995-98, policy analyst, 1998—2002; adminstr. workplace rels. Pacific Southwest Region, Vallejo, Calif., 2002—03, staff asst. to dep. chief programs and legislation, 2004—05, staff asst. to the dep. chief for R&D, 2005—. Author: Public Involvement in the Forest Service-Methodologies, 1977, Public Involvement, Selected Abstracts for Natural Resource Managers, 1979, The Management of Policy and Direction in the Forest Service, 1982, An Analysis of the Forest Service Human Resource Management Program, 1984, Organization Design-Abstracts for Natural Resources Users, 1986, Social and Legal Forces Changing the Management of National Forests, 1996, Water and the Forest Service, 2000, The Forest Service as a Learning Organization, 2000, Evolution of U.S. Water Policy, 2001; contbg. editor Jour. Women in Natural Resources, 1987—. Fellow Soc. Am. Foresters (chair Nat. Capital Soc. 2000), Phi Beta Kappa Soc.; mem. AAAS, ESA, N.Y. Acad. Sci., Washington (D.C.) Acad. Scis., Am. Water Resources Assn., Am. Forestry Assn., Am. Latvian Assn. (bd. dirs. 1995-97), Phi Beta Kappa Assocs. (nat. sec. 1985-88, pres. No. Calif. 1982-84), Commonwealth Club of Calif., Exch. Club of Capitol Hill, Sigma Xi. Avocations: organization and political theory, ballroom dancing, tennis, film. Office: USDA Forest Svc PL&C PO Box 9288SW Arlington VA 22219 Office Phone: 202-205-1422. E-mail: dapple@fs.fed.us.

APPLE, JACKI (JACQUELINE B. APPLE), artist, educator, writer; b. NYC; Student, Syracuse U.; BFA, Parsons Sch. Design. Curator exhbns. and performance Franklin Furnace, N.Y.C., 1977—80; prodr., host Sta. KPFK-FM, North Hollywood, Calif., 1982—95; adj. prof. Art Ctr. Coll. Design, Pasadena, Calif., 1983—. Mem. faculty adv. com. Art Ctr. Coll. Design, Pasadena, 1993, Faculty Coun. rep., 2000-; vis. faculty UCSD, LaJolla, 1995-99. Contbg. writer: L.A. Weekly, 1983-89; contbg. editor: Artweek, 1983-90, High Performance Mag., 1984-95; performance works include The Garden Planet Revisited, 1982, The Amazon, the Mekong, the Missouri and the Nile, 1985, Palisade, 1987, Fluctuations of the Field, 1989, (with J. Adler) A Stone's Throw..., 2000, Kokoro No Mai, 2003, After the Fall...A Prophecy,

2004; writer, performer, dir., prodr.: (record) The Mexican Tapes, 1979-80, (performance/installation/audio work) Voices in the Dark, 1989-97, (radio art work) Swan Lake, 1989; artist, prodr.: (installations and audio work) The Culture of Disappearance, # 1-5, 1991-95; author, designer: (book, installation) Trunk Pieces, 1975-78, (cd) Thank You for Flying American, 1995, Ghost Dances/On the Event Horizon 1996; six part radio art series Redefining Democracy in America Parts, 1991-92; (site specific installation) Zeitghosts: Angels in the Architecture, 1996, Sanctuary, 1996, Hidden Desires, 1998, A Stone's Throw...The Last Witnesses, 2001; (photowork) ghost.dance series 1995—, (installation) Aviary of the Lost. 1994/2004, (photo/audio performance) You Don't Need a Weatherman, 1999; pub. art projects Aliso-Pico Cmty. Ctr., 1997-2000, Venice Oakwood Cmty. Ctr., 2000-03, Martin Luther King Rehab Ctr., 2000-03, Little Tokyo br. L.A. Pub. Libr., 2002-05; author: Doing It Right in L.A., 1990; prodr. EarJam Music Festival, 2000, 01, 02, 04. Recipient Vesta award Media Arts Women's Bldg., 1990, Faculty Enrichment grant Art Ctr. Coll. Design, 2001; NEA visual artists fellow, 1979, 81; InterArts program grantee NEA, 1984-85, 91-92; Calif. Arts Coun. Visual Arts/New Genres fellowship, 1996; grantee Durfee Foundation, 2003. Mem.: Internat. Art Critics Assn., Nat. Writers Union, Coll. Art Assn. (edn. com. 2005—), Am. Composers Forum. Home: 3532 Jasmine Ave Los Angeles CA 90034-4947 E-mail: jaworks@sprintmail.com.

APPLE, JAMES GLENN, lawyer, educator; b. Huntington, W.Va., Sept. 20, 1937; s. David French and Bernice (Stewart) A.; m. Emory O'Shee, June 9, 1959 (div. May 15, 1990); children: Meredith Ellen, Miles Stewart; m. Elizabeth Fitzpatrick Jones, Nov. 10, 1990. BA (with honors), U. Va., 1959, JD, 1962; LLM, U. Edinburgh, Scotland, 1990. Bar: Va. 1962, Ky. 1962, U.S. Dist. Ct. (ea. and we. dists.) Ky., U.S. Ct. Appeals (6th cir.), U.S. Supreme Ct. Pvt. practice law Wheeler & Marshall, Paducah, Ky., 1964-67; adminstrv. asst. Gov. of Ky., Frankfort, 1967-69; exec. asst. Ky. Commr. of Hwys., Frankfort, 1969-70; assoc. Stites & Harbison Law Firm, Louisville, 1970-72, ptnr., 1972-90; spl. asst., counsel to dir. Fed. Jud. Ctr., Washington, 1990-92; chief Interjudicial Affairs Office, Fed. Jud. Ctr., 1992-99; chmn., pres. Internat. Jud. Acad., Washington, 1999—. Adj. prof. Bellarmine Coll., Louisville, 1988-90; adj. prof. internat. law dept. polit. sci. George Washington U., 1995, Am. U., 1996; adminstr. justice program George Mason U., 2004. Comments and projects editor Va. Law Rev., 1961-62; editor State-Fed. Jud. Observer, 1993-99, Internat. Jud. Observer, 1994-98; co-author: A Primer on the Civil Law System (Fed. Jud. Ctr.), Manual for Cooperation Between State and Federal Courts (Fed. Jud. Ctr.); contbr. articles to profl. jours. Bd. dirs. Ky. Authority for Ednl. TV, Lexington, 1971-75; chmn. bd. Transit Authority of River City, Louisville, 1981-85; pres. Louisville Bar Found., 1986-87; mem. Leadership Louisville, 1983-84; bd. dirs, treas. Jud. Leadership Devel. Coun., Washington, 2001—. Lt. USAR, 1963-68. Recipient Award of Merit, Louisville Bar Assn., 1980, Pres.'s award Washington Combined Fed. Campaign, 1990, 91, Spl. Svc. award, 1990; first prize Brit. Red Cross Essay Contest, 1990; resident fellow Henri Dunaut Inst., GEneva, 1990. Fellow Am. Coll. Trial Lawyers; mem. Am. Law Inst., Am. Soc. Internat. Law (chair, tillar house com.), Am. Bd. Trial Advocates, Nat. Press Club, Univ. Club of Washington. Avocations: reading, writing, gardening, travel, walking. Office: Internat Jud Acad 1616 H St NW Ste 204 Washington DC 20006 Fax: 202-628-7803. Office Phone: 202-628-7801. E-mail: jgapple@verizon.net.

APPLE, MARTIN ALLEN, science executive, scientist, educator; b. Duluth, Minn., Sept. 17, 1938; m. M. Daina; children: Deborah Dawn, Pamela Ruth, Nathan, Rebeccah Lynn AB, ALA, U. Minn., 1959, MSc, 1962; PhD, U. Calif., 1968. Chmn. Multidisciplinary Drug Rsch. Group U. Calif., San Francisco, 1974-78; pres. IPRI, San Carlos, Calif., 1978-81; with EAN-Tech., Inc., Daly City, Calif., 1982-84, chmn. bd., 1983-84; with Adytum Internat., Mountain View, Calif., 1982-90, CEO, 1983-90, LEADERS, Washington, 1989—; pres., Coun. Sci. Soc. Presidents, Washington, 1993—; CEO Sci. Watch, Inc., 1996-98. With Hon. Doug Walgren co-chair Leadership Network, 1995-97; adj. prof. U. Calif., San Francisco, 1982-84; cons. SRI Internat. Dept. Edn., EPA, NIH, NSF, The Network, Hughes-GM, Nat. Cancer Inst., AAAS, Nat. Sci. Tchrs. Assn., others; adj. rsch. prof. George Mason U., Fairfax, Va., 1991-92; vis. scholar Nat. Humanities Ctr., 1990-91; nat. project mgr. NSTA Scope Sequence and Coordination Project, 1991-92; bd. dirs. Am. Med. Progress Ednl. Found.; bd. dirs. ACCTION, Inc., chmn. trustees, 1995-96; expert advisor Dept. of Edn., 1996-2001; mem. blue ribbon panel USDA, 2000-01; chmn. bd. trustees Ctr. Advanced Rsch. Behavioral Neurobiology U. Ill., Chgo., 2002-03; chmn. bd. visitors U. Md./U. Md. Biotech. Inst., 1999-2003. Author: (with F. Myers) Review Medical Pharmacology, 1976; (with M. Fink) Immune RNA in Neoplasia, 1976; (with F. Becker et al) Cancer: A Comprehensive Treatise, 1977; (with M. Keenberg et al) Investing in Biotechnology, 1981; (with F. Ahmad et al) From Genes to Proteins: Horizons in Biotechnology, 1983; (with J. Kureczka) Status of Biotechnology, 1987; (with M. Baum) Business Advantage, 1987 (winner Excellence award Software Pubs. Assn. 1987), (with R. Yager) Translating and Using Research for Improving Teacher Education in Science and Mathematics, 1998; mem. editl. bd. Computers in Medicine Mem. Calif. Coun. Indsl. Innovation, 1982. Recipient citation, East West Ctr. Bd. of Govs., 1988, Leadership citation, Coun. Sci. Soc. Pres., 1995, Support of Sci. award, 2002. Fellow Am. Coll. Clin. Pharmacology, Am. Inst. Chemists, Phi Beta Kappa Assocs. (Disting. Svc. award 1984, 85); mem. Assn. Venture Founders (bd. govs. 1982-83), East-West Ctr. Assn. (trustee 1982-88, vice chmn. 1983-85), Profl. Software Programmers Assn., Leaders of Tomorrow (chmn. 1987-88), Commonwealth Club Calif., Phi Beta Kappa, Sigma Xi (bd. dirs., chmn. long-range strategic planning com. 1988-92). Office: Coun Sci Soc Presidents PO Box 33999 Washington DC 20033-0999 also: PO Box 905 Benicia CA 94510-0905 E-mail: cssp@acs.org.

APPLE, RAYMOND WALTER, JR., journalist; b. Akron, Ohio, Nov. 20, 1934; s. Raymond Walter and Julia (Albrecht) A.; m. Betsey Pinckney Brown, July 14, 1982; stepchildren: Catherine Brown Collins, John Preston Brown. Student, Princeton U., 1952-56; AB, Columbia U., 1961; LHD (hon.), Denison U., 1989; LLD, Knox Coll., 1993, Gettysburg Coll., 1995, Marquette U., 2000; LittD (hon.), U. of the South, 2004. Reporter Wall St. Jour., 1956-57, 59-61; writer, corr. NBC News, 1961-63; mem. staff N.Y. Times, 1963—, Albany bur. chief, 1964-65, Vietnam corr., 1965-66, Vietnam bur. chief, 1966-68, Africa bur. chief, 1969, nat. polit. corr., 1970-76, London bur. chief, 1977-80, 81-85, Moscow bur. chief, 1980-81, Washington bur. chief, 1992-97, chief Washington corr., 1985-97, chief corr., 1998—. Assoc. edit. Theodore H. White Meml. lectr. Harvard U., 1989, Joe Alex Morris Jr. Meml. lectr., 1993; Herzberg lectr. Columbia U.; Kent Meml. lectr. Johns Hopkins U., 1990. Author: Apple's Europe, 1986, Apple's America, 2005; contbr. to nat. mags., books. Bd. visitors Western Res. Acad.; chmn. Rhodes Scholarship Com., Mid-Atlantic States. With AUS, 1957-59; judge James Beard Restaurant Awards. Recipient Krout prize history Columbia U., 1961, award NATAS, 1963, George Polk Meml. award, 1967, Overseas Press Club award, 1967, Outstanding Alumnus award Columbia U., 1988, Western Res. Acad., 1976, Weintal award for diplomatic reporting, 1993, Lowell Thomas award for travel writing, Am. Soc. Travel Writers, 1999; Chubb fellow Yale U., 1998. Mem. AFTRA, Am. Inst. Wine and Food, Gridiron Club, Princeton Club, Century Assn. N.Y., Met. Club (Wash.) Office: NY Times Washington Bur 1627 I St NW Washington DC 20006-4007 E-mail: rwappl@nytimes.com.

APPLEBAUM, ANNE, journalist, writer; b. Washington, D.C., 1964; m. Radek Sikorski; children: Alexander, Tadeusz. Grad, Yale U., 1986. Correspondent The Independent, London, 1988—90; journalist Economist, London, 1988—92; fgn. editor Spectator Mag., London, 1993—94, deputy editor, 1994—; columnist The Daily Telegraph, London, 1994—; columnist, mem. editl. bd. Wash. Post, 2002—. Author: (book) Between East and West: Across the Borderlands of Europe, 1995, Gulag, A History, 2004 (Nat. Book award nominee, 2003, Pulitzer Prize for general nonfiction, 2004), several writings have appeared in The Wall St. Jour., the Fin. Times, The Internat. Herald Tribune, Fgn. Affairs, Boston Globe, The Ind., The Guardian, Commentaire, Suddeutsche Zeitung, Newsweek, The New Criterion, others. Recipient Charles Douglas Home Meml. Trust award, 1992; Marshall Scholar, London Sch. Economics, St. Antony's Coll., Oxford. Office: Washington Post 1150 15th St NW Washington DC 20071*

APPLEBAUM, CHARLES, lawyer; b. Newark, May 19, 1947; s. Harry I. and Francis (Gastwirth) A.; m. Patricia (Gyurko) Applebaum; children: Matthew, David, Michael, Amanda. BA, U. Pa., 1969; JD, Rutgers U., 1973; LLM, NYU, 1978. Bar: U.S. Dist. Ct. N.J. 1973. Law clk. to Hon. Samuel A. Larner, Jersey City, 1973-74; assoc., then ptnr. Greenbaum, Rowe, Smith, Ravin, Davis & Himmel LLP, Woodbridge, N.J., 1974-89; gen. counsel Alfieri Orgn., Edison, NJ, 1989—2002, Kara Homes Inc., East Brunswick, NJ, 2002—. Adj. prof. Rutgers Law Sch., Newark, 1985-88. Co-author: New Jersey Real Estate Forms, 1988; contbr. articles to profl. jours. Mem. ABA (real property probate and trust, chmn. significant lit. and publs. 1985-97, co-editor The Acrel Papers 1992-94), Am. Coll. Real Estate Lawyers (editor publs. 1991—). Office: Kara Homes Inc 197 Rte 18 Ste 101N East Brunswick NJ 08816 Office Phone: 732-565-0720. Business E-Mail: capplebaum@karahomes.com.

APPLEBAUM, EDWARD LEON, otolaryngologist, educator; b. Detroit, Jan. 14, 1940; s. M. Lawrence and Frieda (Millman) A.; m. Eva Redei; children: Daniel Ira, Rachel Anne. AB, Wayne State U., 1961, MD, 1964. Diplomate: Am. Bd. Otolaryngology. Intern Univ. Hosp., Ann Arbor, Mich., 1964-65; resident Mass. Eye and Ear Infirmary Harvard Med. Sch., Boston, 1966-69; practice medicine specializing in otolaryngology Chgo., 1972—; assoc. prof. Northwestern U. Med. Sch., 1972-79; prof., head dept. otolaryngology, head and neck surgery Coll. Medicine, U. Ill., 1979-2000; acting chmn. dept. otolaryngolgoy Northwestern U. Med. Sch., Chgo., 2000—02, prof., 2002—, chmn. dept. otolaryngolgoy, 2002—. Mem. staff Northwestern Meml. Hosp. Author: Tracheal Intubation, 1976; mem. editorial bd. Am. Jour. Otolaryngology, Laryngoscope. Served as maj. U.S. Army, 1969-71. Recipient Anna Albert Keller Rsch. award Wayne State U. Coll. Medicine, 1964, Disting. Alumni award, 1989, William Beaumont Soc. Original Rsch. award, 1964, Disting. Faculty award, U. Ill. Coll. Medicine, 1996. Fellow ACS, Am. Soc. for Head and Neck Surgery, Surgery, Am. Acad. Otolaryngology, Head and Neck Surgery, Am. Laryngol., Rhinol. and Otol. Soc. (v.p. 1993, pres. 2000), Am. Laryngol. Assn., Am. Otol. Soc., Soc. Univ. Otolaryngologists, Head and Neck Surgeons (pres. 1988), Assn. Acad. Depts. Otolaryngology-Head and Neck Surgery (pres. 1995-96). Office Phone: 312-503-0458. Business E-Mail: eapple@northwestern.edu.

APPLEBAUM, STUART S., public relations executive; b. N.Y.C., Sept. 19, 1949; s. Jack and Anne (Miller) A. BA, Queens Coll., 1971. Publicist Alfred A. Knopf Inc., N.Y.C., 1971-73, MGM Pictures, N.Y.C., 1973, Bantam Books Inc., N.Y.C., 1974-77, mgr. publicity, 1977-79, dir. publicity, 1979-87, v.p., dir. pub. rels. and publicity, 1983-90, v.p., dir. pub. rels., 1990-91, v.p., dir. publicity and pub. rels., 1991—; sr. v.p., dir. pub. rels. Bantam Doubleday Dell Pub. Group, N.Y.C., 1987-98, Random House, Inc., N.Y.C., 1998—, exec. v.p. comms., 2002—. Named as one of the People Who Shaped the Book Bus., Pubs. Weekly, 1997. Mem. Publishers Publicity Assn. (bd. dirs. N.Y.C. chpt. 1979-84) Office: Random House Inc 1745 Broadway New York NY 10019 Business E-Mail: sapplebaum@randomhouse.com.

APPLEBEE, ARTHUR NOBLE, English education researcher; b. Sherbrooke, Que., Can., June 20, 1946; m. Judith A. Langer. BA cum laude, Yale U., 1968; MA in Teaching, Harvard U., 1970; PhD, U. London, 1973. Cert. tchr., U.S., England, Wales. Staff asst. Nat. Coun. Tchrs. of English, staff assoc., 1976-80; psychologist Child Devel. Lab. Mass. Gen. Hosp., 1969-71; resident tutor Goldsmiths Coll., U. London, 1971-73; evaluator Internat. Microteaching Unit U. Lancaster, Eng., 1973-74; tchr. English and drama Tarleton High Sch., Lancashire, Eng., 1974-76; assoc. prof. Sch. Edn. Stanford U., 1980-87; dir. Nat. Rsch. Ctr. on Lit. Teaching and Learning, 1987-95; prof. Sch. Edn. SUNY, Albany, 1987—2003, Leading prof., 2003—. Vis. lectr. U. Calif., Berkeley, summer, 1978; assoc. dir. ERIC Clearinghouse on Reading and Comm. Skills, 1978-80; dir. Ctr. on English Learning and Achievement, 1996—; lectr. in field. Author: The Child's Concept of Story: Ages Two to Seventeen, 1978, 2d edit., 1989, Contexts for Learning to Write: Studies of Secondary School Instruction, 1984, Literature in the Secondary School, 1993, (with J. Langer) How Writing Shapes Thinking: A Study of Teaching and Learning (Richard A. Meade award 1989), Curriculum as Conversation, 1996 (David H. Russell award 1998); editor: (with J. Langer) Research in the Teaching of English, 1984-91; contbr. articles, editorials and revs. to profl. jours. Grantee Spencer Found., 1986-87, Office of Ednl. Rsch. and Improvement, 1986-87, 87-88, 87-90, 91-95, 95—; recipient Outstanding Young Men of Am. award, 1978; named to Reading Hall of Fame, 2004. Fellow Nat. Conf. on Rsch. in English (pres. 1986); mem. Am. Ednl. Rsch. Assn., Conf. Coll. Composition and Comm., Conf. English Edn., Internat. Reading Assn., Nat. Assn. for the Tchg. of English (U.K.), Nat. Coun. Tchrs. English (com. on rsch., Promising Rschr. award 1974), Nat. Reading Conf., Soc. for the Study of Curriculum History (founder), Reading Hall of Fame. Office: SUNY Sch of Edn 1400 Washington Ave Albany NY 12222-1000

APPLEBERRY, JAMES BRUCE, educational association administrator; b. Waverly, Mo., Feb. 22, 1938; s. James Earnest and Bertha Viola (Lane) A.; m. Patricia Ann Trent, June 5, 1960; children: John Mark, Timothy David. BS, Central Mo. State Coll., 1960; MS, Cen. Mo. State Coll., 1963, EdS, 1967; postgrad., U. Kans., 1967; Ed.D., Okla. State U., 1969. Tchr. Knob Noster (Mo.) Pub. Sch., 1960-62; prin. Knob Noster Elem. Sch., 1962-63, Knob Noster Jr. High Sch., 1963-64; minister edn. Wornall Rd. Bapt. Ch., Kansas City, Mo., 1964-65; grad. fellow Cen. Mo. State Coll., Warrensburg, 1965-66, asst. dir. field service, 1966-67; grad. asst. Okla. State U., 1968-69, asst. prof. ednl. adminstrn., 1969-71, assoc. prof., 1971-73, prof., head dept. adminstrn. and higher edn., 1972-75; Am. Council on Edn. fellow acad. adminstrn. internship program U. Kans., Lawrence, 1973-74, dir. planning, prof. adminstrn., founds. and higher edn., 1975-76, asst. to chancellor, prof., 1976-77; pres. Pittsburg (Kans.) State U., 1977-83, No. Mich. U., Marquette, 1983-91, Am. Assn. of State Coll. and Univs., Washington, 1991-99, Appleberry Enterprises, 1999—; sr. cons. Acad. Search Consultation Svc., 2001—. Plenary rep. Univ. Council for Ednl. Adminstrn., 1968-72, mem. exec. com., 1973-76; ednl. adminstrn. rep. Council on Tchr. Edn., 1968-75; chmn. Am. Council Edn. Commn. Leadership Devel. and Acad. Adminstrn.; abstracter Univ. Council for Ednl. Adminstrn., Columbus, Ohio, 1969-75; asst. state liaison rep. to Am. Assn. Colls. for Tchr. Edn., 1971; coordinator Interested Profs. Ednl. Adminstrn.; cons. North Cen. Okla. Assn. Sch. Adminstrs.; vice chmn. adv. council Nat. Council Edn. Stats., 1980-83; Kans. rep. to Am. Assn. State Colls. and Univs., 1980-81; pres. Nat. Coll. Athletics Assn. Pres.'s Commn., 1988-89; chmn. bd. dirs. Thoroughbred Techs., 2000-02. Contbr. articles to ednl. jours. Trustee Marquette Gen. Hosp.; bd. dirs. Actor's Theatre, 2003—. Named Outstanding Alumnus Cen. Mo. State U., 1987, Disting. Alumnus Okla. State U., 1987. Mem. NEA, Am. Assn. for Higher Edn., Am. Assn. State Colls. and Univs. (chmn. policy and purposes com.), Am. Ednl. Rsch. Assn., Nat. Conf. Profs. Ednl. Adminstrn., Exec. Club Louisville, Mace and Torch, Rotary, Masons (33 deg.), Phi Delta Kappa, Phi Kappa Phi, Kappa Delta, Phi Sigma Phi, Kappa Mu Epsilon, Alpha Kappa Psy. Home: 504 Jarvis Ln Louisville KY 40207-1313

APPLEBERRY, PATRICIA TRENT, artist; b. Waverly, Mo., Dec. 16, 1939; d. Ryland Stewart and Lucile Fern Trent; m. James Bruce Appleberry; children: J. Mark. Timothy. BS in Edn., Ctrl. Mo. State U., 1961, postgrad., 1962. Tchr. Knob Nester (Mo.) Pub. Schs., 1961-64; interior design cons. Interiors by Design, Marquette, Mich., 1989-90; artist P. Trent Watermedia, Chevy Chase, Md., 1993-99, Louisville, 1999—. Spkr. in field. Bd. dirs. Arts and Crafts Coun., Pittsburg, Kans.; jr. mem. Women's City Club, Kansas City, Mo.; bd. dirs. Heart Fund, Pittsburg, 1979, Lawrence, 1995, United Way, 1980, Hospice, Pittsburg, 1979-81, Propolon, Marquette, 1984-85; vol. events planner No. Mich. U., Marquette, 1983-91, Pitts. State U., 1977-83. Recipient numerous art awards. Mem. Philanthropic Edn. Orgn., Women of Washington. Home: 504 Jarvis Ln Louisville KY 40207-1313

APPLEBY, ANNE L., artist; b. Harrisburg, Pa., Aug. 22, 1954; d. James Howard and Mary Louise Ellis Appleby. BFA, U. Mont., 1977; MFA, San Francsico, 1989. Pres. of bd. of dirs. Mountain Artist Refuge, Basin, Mont., 2002—04. Panza Collection, 2000—02, Henry Art Gallery, 2004. Recipient Pollocal Krasner Found. award, Soc. for the Encouragement of Contemporary Art, 1989, Louis Tiffany prize, Louis Comfort Tiffany Found., 1999.

APPLEBY, JOYCE OLDHAM, historian, educator; b. Omaha, Apr. 9, 1929; d. Junius G. and Edith (Cash) Oldham; children: Ann Lansburgh Caylor, Mark Lansburgh, Frank Bell Appleby. BA, Stanford U., 1950; MA, U. Calif., Santa Barbara, 1959; PhD, Claremont Grad. Sch., 1966. With Mademoiselle mag., 1950-52; asst. prof. history San Diego State U., 1967-70, asso. prof., 1970-73; prof. history, asso. dean Coll. Arts and Letters, 1973-75, prof., 1976-81. Vis. asso. prof. U. Calif., Irvine, 1975-76; vis. prof. UCLA, 1978-79, prof. history, 1981—; vis. fellow St. Catherine's Coll., U. Oxford, 1983; Harmsworth prof. Am. History, U. Oxford, 1990-91; Bd. fellows Claremont Grad. Sch. and U. Center, 1970-73 Author: Economic Thought and Ideology in Seventeenth-Century England, 1978, Capitalism and a New Social Order, 1983, Liberalism and Republicanism in the Historical Imagination, 1992; co-author: Telling the Truth about History, 1994; co-editor: Knowledge and Postmodernism in Historical Perspective, Inheriting the Revolution, 2000; mem. bd. editors Democracy, 1980-83, William and Mary Quar., 1980-83, 18th Century Studies, 1982-87, Ency. Am. Polit. History, Am. Hist. Rev., 1988—, Jour. Interdisciplinary History, 1989—, The Papers of Thomas Jefferson, 1988—, The Adams Papers, 1990—; contbr. articles to profl. jours.; mem. adv. bd. Am. Nat. Biography. Mem. Am. Acad. Arts and Scis., Am. Philos. Soc., Smithsonian Inst. (coun.), Am. Hist. Assn. (pres.), Orgn. Am. Historians (pres.), Inst. Early Am. History and Culture (coun. 1980-86, chmn. 1983-89). Home: 615 Westholme Ave Los Angeles CA 90024-3209 Office: UCLA Dept History Los Angeles CA 90024

APPLEBY, R(OBERT) SCOTT, history educator; b. Shreveport, La., Dec. 3, 1956; s. John and Joanne (Jackson) A.; m. Margaret Calhoun; children: Benjamin, Paul, Clare, Tony. BA, U. Notre Dame, 1978; MA, U. Chgo., 1979, PhD, 1985. Asst. prof., chair dept. religious studies St. Xavier Coll., Chgo., 1985-87; rsch. assoc. U. Chgo., 1988-94; assoc. dir. The Fundamentalism Project Am. Acad. Arts and Scis., Chgo., 1988—; dir. Cushwa Ctr. for Study of Am. Catholicism U. Notre Dame, Ind., 1994—, assoc. prof. history, 1994—. Cons. Lilly Endowment, 1994—, William Benton Broadcast Project, U. Chgo., 1989-92. Editor: (with Martin E. Marty) Fundamentalisms Observed, 1991. Mem. Am. Acad. Religion, Am. Hist. Assn., Am. Cath. Hist. Assn., Am. Soc. Ch. History, Coll. Theology Soc., Religious Rsch. Assn. (nominations com. 1993—). Office: U Notre Dame 614 Hesburgh Ctr Notre Dame IN 46556-5677

APPLEGARTH, PAUL VOLLMER, investment and finance executive; b. Wilkinsburg, Pa., Apr. 21, 1946; s. William Francis and Alice (Vollmer) A.; m. Linda Davis, Dec. 28, 1971; children: Katharine Davis, Coraline Elizabeth. MBA, JD, Harvard U., 1974; BA, Yale U., 1968. Bar: D.C. 1974, Mass. 1975. Various positions with The World Bank, Washington, 1974-83; sr. v.p. Bank Am., San Francisco, 1983-86, Am. Express/Lehman Bros., N.Y.C., 1987-94; mng. dir. Emerging Markets Corp., Washington, 1994—2003; CEO Millennium Challenge Corp., 2004—. Bd. mem. No. Calif. Resolve, 1985-87, Sales/Svc. Am., 1993-94; CFO United Way Am., Alexandria, Va., 1992-94. Capt. AUS, 1968-70. White House fellow, 1981-82. Mem. Mass. Bar Assn., D.C. Bar Assn., Belle Haven Club (bd. dirs. 1991-95, vice commodore 1993-94), Congl. Country Club, White House Fellows Alumni Assn. Office Phone: 202-521-3600.

APPLEGATE, CHRISTINA, actress; b. L.A., Calif., Nov. 25, 1971; d. Nancy Priddy; m. Johnathon Schaech, Oct. 20, 2001. Film appearances include: Jaws of Satan, 1980, Streets, 1990, Don't Tell Mom the Babysitter's Dead, 1991, Across the Moon, 1994, Vibrations, 1995, Wild Bill, 1995, Mars Attacks!, 1996, Nowhere, 1997, Claudine's Return, 1998, The Big Hit, 1998, Mafia!, 1998, The Giving Tree, 2000, Just Visiting, 2001, The Sweetest Thing, 2002, Heroes, 2003, View from the Top, 2003, Wonderland, 2003, Grand Theft Parsons, 2003, Employee of the Month, 2004, Anchorman: The Legend of Ron Burgundy, 2004, Surviving Christmas, 2004; TV appearances include: (series) Days of Our Lives, 1974, Washingtoon, 1985, Heart of the City, 1986, Married...With Children, 1987-97, All My Life, 1998, Jesse, 1998-2000, Friends, 2002, (TV movies) Grace Kelly, 1983, Dance 'til Dawn, 1988, Prince Charming, 2001. Off-broadway appearances include: Sweet Charity, 2005 (Theatre World award, 2005).*

APPLEGATE, K(ARL) EDWIN, lawyer; b. Cicero, Ind., July 21, 1923; s. Karl Raymond and Gladys Mae (Worley) A.; m. Elizabeth Ann Dilts, June 10, 1944; children: Eric Edwin, Raymond Alan, Robert Dale, Beth Ann. BS, Ind. U., 1946, JD, 1948. Bar: Ind. 1949, Fed. Ct. (7th cir.), U.S. Supreme Ct. 1968, U.S. Tax Ct. 1983. U.S. commr. So. Dist., Ind., 1953—58; cert. family and civil mediator Indiana, Fla., 1992; dep. prosecutor Monroe County, Ind., 1959; mcpl. judge Bloomington, Ind., 1960—63; mem. Ind. Ho. Reps., 1965—66; U.S. atty. So. Dist. Ind., 1967—70; sr. ptnr. Applegate Law Offices, Bloomington, 1970—92, sr. mem., 1991—93, Applegate, McDonald, Koch & Arnold, Bloomington, 1993—2005, Applegate, McDonald & Assocs. PC, Bloomington, 2005—. Legal cons. Ind. Masonic Home, Franklin, 1981-82. Trustee 1st United Meth. Ch., 1962-65. Staff sgt. AUS, 1941-44, ETO. Decorated Purple Heart; named Outstanding Young Man of Bloomington, Jaycees, 1956; recipient Disting. Svc. award, U.S. Jr. C. of C., 1956, Good Govt. award, 1961, 50 Yr. award, Ind. State Bar Found. Mem.: ABA, Tri-County Bar Assn., Monroe County Bar Assn., Ind. Bar Assn. (co-chair com. assistance to lawyers program 1990—94, mem. sr. coun.), Fed. Bar Assn., Kiwanis, Masons, Elks, Alpha Kappa Psi. Home: 509 S Swain Ave Bloomington IN 47401-5129 Office: Applegate McDonald & Assocs PO Box 2627 Bloomington IN 47402-2627

APPLEGATE, WILLIAM BROWN, dean, medical educator, researcher, physician; b. Louisville, July 28, 1946; s. Henry Lovelace and Margaret (Whitesides) A.; m. Gail Reekers, July 31, 1982; children: Elizabeth Marie, Jennifer Michelle. BA, U. Louisville, 1968, MD, 1972; MPH, Harvard U., 1973. Intern Boston City Hosp., 1973—74, resident in internal medicine, 1974—75; R.W. Johnson clin. scholar U. NC, Chapel Hill, 1975-77; asst. prof. medicine U. N.Mex., Albuquerque, 1977-79; chief divsn. geriatric medicine U. Tenn., Memphis, 1979-93, dir. gen. clin. rsch. ctr., 1993-99, chmn. dept. preventive medicine, 1994-99; chmn., prof. dept. internal medicine Wake Forest U., Winston-Salem, NC, 1999—, dean sch. medicine, sr. v.p. health scis., 2002—. Mem. coun. Nat. Inst. Aging, 1989-93, nat. adv. bd. Johnson Found. Clin. Scholars Program. Contbr. articles to med. jours., including Jour. AMA, Archives Internal Medicine, others. Recipient Alex Haley Gerontology award; named Alumni Fellow, U. Louisville, 2003; grantee. Mem. Am. Geriatrics Soc. (editor-in-chief jour. 1993-2000), Rotary. Democrat. Avocation: bicycling. Office: Wake Forest Med Ctr Medical Center Blvd Winston Salem NC 27157-0001

APPLEGET, TERRI LYNN, elementary school educator; b. Racine, Wis., Dec. 3, 1952; d. Richard Louis and Joan Elizabeth (Seatter) Tobias; m. Patrick R. Appleget, Dec. 26, 1971 (div. May 1997); children: Brooke Elizabeth, Patrick Justin-Shaun, Katherine Bethany Anne Aisling, Keir Michael James. BA, U. Wis., 1973; MA in Tchg., Coll. of Charleston, S.C., 1991; postgrad., Trinity Coll., Dublin, Ireland, 1994. Dir. extended day Ashley Hall, Charleston, 1993; founder, dir. The Children's Ctr., Summerville, S.C., 1993-97; tchr. mid. sch. lit., grammar, history Pinewood Preparatory, Summerville, 1993-97; tchr. kindergarten, early childhood diagnostic, 1st and 3d grade inclusion Charleston County Sch. Dist., 1997—2001; tchr. Charlestowne Acad. Magnet Sch., 2001—02, Ronald McNair Elem., 2002—03, N. Charleston Elem. at McNair, 2003—04; tchr. B-GAP (sci., math., English, social studies) Brentwood Mid. Sch., 2004—, Homesch. tchr. Charleston Preparatory Sch., 1998—; freelance tutor, 1997—; homebound tchr., 2004—. Tchr. ptnr. Jr. Achievement, Charleston, 2000; sponsor Jr. Beta Club, Summerville, 1993—97; docent Historic Charleston Soc., 1988—98; v.p. Oakleaf Officers Wives Club, Orlando, Fla., 1986—87; pres. Fellowship Wartburg Spouses,

Dubuque, Iowa, 1982—83; tchr. adult Sunday ch. sch. St. John's Luth. Ch., Charleston, 1988—, chair social ministry, 1989—2005, mem. vestry, 1989—2005. Mem. NEA, Nat. Assn. for Edn. of Young Children, Nat. Trust, Internat. Reading Assn. (S.C. coun.), Palmetto State Tchrs. Assn., Brentwood Sewing Soc. (life). Republican. Avocations: writing, studying irish history, reading. Home: 141 Palmetto Bluff Ct Charleston SC 29418-3017 Office Phone: 843-937-6300. Personal E-mail: tlabpkk@aol.com.

APPLER, THOMAS L., lawyer; b. Washington, Oct. 12, 1943; m. Nancy J. Babb, Dec. 3, 1967; children: Alexandra Whitney. AB in Politics, Princeton U., 1965; JD, George Washington U., 1968. Bar: Va. 1968. Atty. Office of Judge Adv., Surgeon Gen. of Army, 1969-70; ptnr. McGuire, Woods, Battle & Boothe (and predecessor firms), McLean, Va., 1970-99, Crews & Hancock, PLC, Fairfax, Va., 1999—2002, Hancock, Daniel, Johnson & Nagle, P.C., 2002—04, Wilson, Elser, Moskowitz, Edelman & Dicker LLP, McLean, 2005—. Co-author: Damages for Plaintiff and Defense Attorneys, 1987. USAR, 1970-76. Fellow Am. Coll. Trial Lawyers; mem. No. Va. Def. Attys. Assn. (pres. 1975), Va. Assn. Def. Attys. (v.p., bd. dirs. 1977-83), Va. Bar Assn. (bd. dirs. young lawyers sect. 1974-76, appellate judges com. 1989-91, Boyd-Graves Conf. com. 1988—), Va. State Bar (coun. 1985-92, malpractice ins. com. 1989-99), Fairfax Bar Assn. (pres. 1984-85, bd. dirs. 1983-86), No. Va. Young Lawyers Assn. (pres. 1974). Home: 9717 Meadowlark Rd Vienna VA 22182-1951 Office: Wilson Elser Moskowitz Edelman & Dicker LLP 8444 Westpark Dr Ste 510 Mc Lean VA 22102 Office Phone: 703-245-9300. Office Fax: 703-245-9301. Business E-Mail: Vapplert@wemed.com.

APPLETON, R. O., JR., lawyer; b. San Francisco, Aug. 17, 1945; s. Robert Oser and Leslie Jeanne (Roth) A.; m. Susan Frelich, June 3, 1971; children: Jesse David, Seth Daniel. AB, Stanford U., 1967; JD, U. Calif., San Francisco, 1970; postgrad., NYU, 1971. Bar: Calif. 1971, U.S. Dist. Calif. (no. dist.) Calif. 1971, Mo. 1973, U.S. Dist. Ct. (ea. dist.) Mo. 1974, U.S. Ct. Appeals (8th cir.) 1975, U.S. Ct. Internat. Trade, 1980. Assoc. Dinkelspiel & Dinkelspiel, San Francisco, 1971-73, Schramm & Morganstern, St. Louis, 1973-75; pvt. practice, 1975-77; ptnr. Braun, Newman, Stewart & Appleton, St. Louis, 1977-82, Appleton, Newman & Kretmar, St. Louis, 1982-84, Appleton, Newman & Gerson, St. Louis, 1984-89, Appleton & Kretmar, St. Louis, 1989—, Appleton, Kretmar & Beatty. Adj. prof. pre-trial litigation Washington U. Sch. Law, St. Louis, 1985-88. Arbitrator, vol. Better Bus. Bur. of St. Louis, 1980—; St. Louis Gymnastic Centre, 1984—; bd. dirs. St. Louis Friends of Tibet, 1991-94. Mem. ABA, Calif. Bar Assn., Met. Bar Assn. of St. Louis, St. Louis County Bar Assn., Am. Arbitration Assn. (arbitrator comml. panel, arbitrator mass claims appeals com. 1999), Stanford Club (pres. 1991—). Democrat. Jewish. Avocations: jogging, swimming, cooking, model trains, reading. Home: 8317 Cornell Ave Saint Louis MO 63132-5025 Office: Appleton Kretmar Beatty & Stolze 8000 Maryland Ave Ste 900 Saint Louis MO 63105-3911 Office Phone: 314-721-8685. E-mail: roajratty1@aol.com.

APPLETON, RICHARD NEWELL, lawyer; b. Bronx, N.Y., Sept. 1, 1941; s. Harry Newell Appleton and Catherine (Burke) Haddon; m. Kathleen Pauline Sheehan Morrell, Oct. 5, 1963 (div. Apr. 1974); children: Heather, Cheryl; m. Alene Marie Appleton, Aug. 31, 1990; children: Brennan, Adriana. BA, Rutgers Coll., 1964; JD, Western State U., 1983. Bar: Calif. 1984, U.S. Dist. Ct. So. Calif. 1984. Time study engr. E.R. Squibb & Sons, New Brunswick, N.J., 1963-65; plant indsl. engr. Anaconda Wire and Cable, Anderson, Ind., 1965-69; budget analyst Marcona Mining Co., San Juan, Peru, S.A., 1969-73, dir. adminstrv. svcs., 1973-76; internal cons. Iron Ore Can., Sept Iles, Que., 1976-78; mgr. adminstrn. Mullen Engring., Casper, Wyo., 1978-79; consulting engr. Woodward Assocs., San Diego, 1979-81; law clerk Stutz, McCormick, Mitchell & Verlasky, San Diego, 1981-84; assoc. McCormick & Mitchell, San Diego, 1984-91, ptnr., 1991-93, mng. ptnr., 1993-99, ptnr., 1999-2001; prin. Appleton Dispute Solutions, Chula Vista, Calif., 2001—. Arbitrator and mediator San Diego County Mcpl. and Superior Ct., 1989—; judge pro tem Small Claims Ct., 1995—. Contbr. articles to profl. jours. and book revs. Precinct committeeman Rep. Party, Anderson, 1966-68. Recipient Cert. Merit award NASA, 1962, Amjur in Evidence award The Lawyers Co-Op Bancroft Whitney, 1983, Most Valuable Reporter award Stats, Inc., 1994. Mem. ATLA, Assn. So. Calif. Def. Counsel, Soc. Profls. in Dispute Resolution. Roman Catholic. Avocations: golf, baseball, statistical analysis, fiction and non-fiction writing. Office: PO Box 212132 Chula Vista CA 91921-2132 Address: 1261 Crystal Springs Dr Chula Vista CA 91915-2154 E-mail: rna9141@aol.com.

APPLETON, SHELDON LEE, education educator; b. NYC, Sept. 17, 1933; s. Simon and Edith (Gutstein) Applebaum; m. Elizabeth Green, June 24, 1956; children: Vikki Susan, Kevin Daniel, Laura Michelle, Bradford David. BA in English and History, NYU, 1954, MA in History, 1956; PhD in Polit. Sci., U. Minn., 1961. Newswriter U.S. Agy. for Internat. Devel., Washington, 1955—56; fgn. svc. officer U.S. Dept. State, Washington, 1956—57; instr. U. Minn., Mpls., 1957—58, Ford found. fellow, 1958—60; asst. prof. Oakland U., Rochester, Mich., 1960—64, assoc. prof., 1964—69; vis. prof. U. Hawaii, Honolulu, 1969—70; prof. polit. sci. Oakland U., Rochester, Mich., 1970—, assoc. dean arts and scis., 1979—87, assoc. provost for undergrad. studies, 1987—93, assoc v.p. for undergrad. studies, 1993, disting. prof., 2002—05, disting. prof. emeritus, 2005—. Author: The Eternal Triangle, 1961, U.S. Foreign Policy, 1968; contbr. articles to profl. jours.; editorial bd.: American Journal of Political Science, 1976-82. Fulbright-Hays fellow, 1967. Mem. AAUP (chpt. pres. 1968-69. state exec. com. 1976-77), Soc. for Am. Baseball Rsch. Unitarian Universalist. Avocations: baseball research, theater. Personal E-mail: slappleton@sbcglobal.net. Business E-Mail: appleton@oakland.edu.

APPLETON, STEVEN R., electronics executive; b. Mar. 1960; BBA, Boise State U., 1982. Fab supr., prodn. mgr., dir. mfg., v.p. mfg. Micron Tech., Inc., Boise, Idaho, 1983—91, pres., COO, 1991, chmn., CEO, pres., 1994—; chmn., CEO Micron Semiconductor, 1992. Bd. dirs. St. Luke's Hosp.; trustee Boise State U.; mem. Coll. Bus. Adv. Coun., Semiconductor Tech. Coun. Mem.: Semiconductor Industry Assn. (bd. dirs.). Office: Micron Tech PO Box 6 8000 South Federal Way Boise ID 83707

APPLEWHITE, HARRIET BRANSON, political science educator; b. Cleve., June 5, 1940; d. Robert Lees and Eleanor (Verdier) Branson; m. Philip B. Applewhite, Aug. 10, 1963; children: Eleanor, Kate, Douglas. AB, Smith Coll., Northampton, Mass., 1962; MA, Stanford U., 1964, PhD, 1972. Lectr. Smith Coll., Northampton, Mass., 1965-66; asst. prof. So. Conn. State Coll., New Haven, 1967-76; assoc. prof. So. Conn. State Coll. (now So. Conn. State U.), New Haven, 1976-82, prof. polit. sci., 1982-95, Conn. State U. prof., 1995—. Author: Political Alignment in the French National Assembly, 1789-1791, 1993; co-editor: Women in Revolutionary Paris, 1979, Women and Politics in Age of Democratic Revolution, 1990; contbr. articles to profl. jours. Rockefeller Found. grantee, 1985; Am. Coun. Learned Socs. fellow, 1983-84; NEH fellow, 1973-74. Mem. AAUP, Am. Polit. Sci. Assn., Phi Beta Kappa. Democrat. Avocation: playing piano. Office: So Conn State U Dept Polit Sci New Haven CT 06515

APPLEWHITE, KIM, music company executive, educator; b. Atlantic City, N.J., Feb. 2, 1961; s. Paul C. and Ida B. Applewhite. AA specializing in tech. in video prodns., Art Inst. Phila., 2000; BA in Theology, Jameson Christian Coll., 2001; BS in Mgmt., U. Phoenix, 2002; MBA in Music Bus. Mgmt., Northwestern Internat. U., Denmark and Sweden, 2003; postgrad., Audrey Cohen Coll., 2003—. Lic. internat. evangelistic lic. Jameson Christian Coll., 1999. Pres., CEO Applewhite Entertainment Group, LLC, Atlantic City, 1995—; radio engr. WUSS 1490 Rejoice Radio, Linwood, NJ, 2002—. Author: (music bus. adminstrn. solutions) Recobizworks, 2002; contbr. poetry to anthologies. Pastor TriUnity Worship and Praise Ctr., Absecon, NJ, 2001—02. Home: PO Box 73 Pleasantville NJ 08232 Office: Prophete Music Group Inc 849 Cedar Ln Pleasantville NJ Office Phone: 609-641-3815. Personal E-mail: K_applewhite@yahoo.com.

APPLEY, MORTIMER HERBERT, psychologist, retired academic administrator; b. N.Y.C., Nov. 21, 1921; s. Benjamin and Minnie (Albert) A.; m. Dee Gordon, June 5, 1942 (div. Oct. 1969); children: Richard Gordon, John Benton; m. Mariann B. Hundahl, Jan. 10, 1971; stepchildren: Scott, Eric, Heidi Hundahl. BS, CCNY, 1942; MA, U. Denver, 1946; PhD, U. Mich., 1950; DSc (hon.), York U., 1975; DHL (hon.), Northeastern U., 1983; LittD (hon.), Am. Internat. Coll., 1984; LLD (hon.), Clark U., 1984. Instr. U. Denver, 1945-47; instr. U. Mich., 1947-49; asst. prof. Wesleyan U., Middletown, Conn., 1949-52; prof., chmn. psychology Conn. Coll., New London, 1952-60, So. Ill. U., Carbondale, 1960-62, York U., Toronto, Ont., Can., 1962-67, dean faculty grad. studies, 1965-68; prof., chmn. psychology U. Mass., Amherst, 1967-69; dean Grad. Sch., 1969-74, asso. provost, 1973-74; pres. Clark U., Worcester, Mass., 1974-84; vis. scholar psychology Harvard U., 1984-88, lectr., extension, 1985-95, vis. prof., 1985-86; exec. dir., Commn. on the Future of the Univ. U. Mass., Boston, 1988-89. Cons. NSF, NIMH, NRC of Can., Can. Council, VA., AAAS, MacArthur Found. Author: (with C.N. Cofer) Motivation: Theory and Research, 1964, (with R. Trumbull) Psychological Stress, 1967, (with J. Rickwood) Psychology in Canada, 1967, (with R. Trumbull) Dynamics of Stress, 1986, (with L. Lasagna) Who are the Elderly, 1986, (with W.B. Maher) Social and Behavioral Sciences, 1989, Learning to Lead, 1989; editor: Adaption Level Theory: A Symposium, 1971, Motivation and Emotion, 1976-88; assoc. editor Psychol. Abstracts, 1961-62; editor, contbr. Internat. Ency. Neurology, Psychology, Psychoanalysis and Psychiatry; contbr. articles to profl. jours. Chmn. bd. mgrs. Unitarian Fellowship, Toronto; vestryman King's Chapel, Boston; trustee Nantucket Atheneum. With USAAF, 1942-45. NSF Sci. Faculty fellow, 1959-60, Fulbright fellow, Germany, 1973-74. Fellow AAAS, APA (past chmn. edn. and tng. bd.), Can. Psychol. Assn. (bd. dirs.); mem. Conn. Psychol. Assn. (past pres.), New Eng. Psychol. Assn. (past pres.), St. Botolph Club (Boston, pres. 1997-2000), Worcester Econ. Club (pres. 1980-81), Wharf Rats (Nantucket), Sigma Xi, Psi Chi, Phi Sigma. Democrat. Unitarian Universalist. Home: Two Commonwealth Ave Boston MA 02116 Office Phone: 617-266-7272. Personal E-mail: mappley@comcast.net.

APPLEYARD, DAVID FRANK, mathematics professor; b. South Haven, Mich., July 13, 1939; s. Edwin Ray and Hortense Ruth (Guilford) A.; m. Joey Hierlmeier, Aug. 5, 1967; children: David Wayne, Gregory Jay, Robert James. BA, Carleton Coll., 1961; MS, U. Wis., 1963, PhD, 1970. Teaching asst. in math. U. Wis., Madison, 1961-66; prof. math. and computer science Carleton Coll., Northfield, Minn., 1966—. Lloyd P. Johnson Norwest Found. prof. liberal arts, 1993—, dean students Northfield, Minn., 1977-83, faculty pres., 1988-91. Carleton Coll. faculty athletic rep. to Midwest Collegiate Athletic Conf., 1975-83, pres., 1982-83 Trustee United Ch. Christ, Northfield, 1969—72. Recipient Cowling Cup for career achievement, 2002; NSF fellow, 1964, grantee prin. investigator, 1993—; NASA traineeship, 1965-66; Sloan Found. grantee, 1969, 73, 84. Mem. Math. Assn. Am., Nat. Coun. Tchrs. Math., Sigma Xi. Avocations: running, canoeing. Home: 6450 134th St E Northfield MN 55057-4611 Office: Carleton Coll 1 N College St Northfield MN 55057-4021 Office Phone: 507-646-4450. Business E-Mail: dappleya@carleton.edu.

APPLEYARD, DIANE PAIGE, human service administrator; b. Sept. 23, 1947; BA, Birmingham-So. Coll., 1969; MA in English, Vanderbilt U., 1973. Asst. editor Meth. Pub. Co., 1971-73; secondary sch. tchr. Escambia County, Fla., 1973-78; tchr. Dept. Def., Germany, 1973-78; dir. John Appleyard Agy., Inc., 1984—, v.p., 1989—; pres. Healthcare R&D Inst., Inc., Pensacola, Fla. Bd. dirs. U.S. Girls Scout Coun., W. Fla., v.p., 1988-95; bd. dirs. N.W. Fla. Rehab. Found., 1989-95, Pensacola Jr. Coll. Found., 1990—, Pensacola Jr. Coll., 1993—; trustee Nat. Com. Quality Health Care, 1995—, mem. exec. com., 1995—. Office: Healthcare R&D Inst Inc 4400 Bayou Blvd Pensacola FL 32503-2673 Fax: 850-494-0289.

APPS, JEROLD WILLARD, writer; b. Wild Rose, Wis., July 25, 1934; s. Herman E. and Eleanor S. (Witt) A.; m. Ruth Ellen Olson, May 20, 1961; children: Susan, Steven, Jeffrey. BS, U. Wis., 1955, MS, 1957, PhD, 1967. Extension agt. U. Wis., Green Lake, 1957-60, Green Bay, 1960-62, asst. prof. Madison, 1962-67, assoc. prof., 1967-69, prof. adult and continuing edn., 1969-94; prof. emeritus, 1994—. Vis. prof. N.C. State U., Raleigh, 1979, U. Guelph, Ont., Can., 1980, U. Alta., Can., 1982, 89, U. Man., Can., 1986, U. Victoria, Can., 1991, U. Alaska, 1995, 97, No. Ill. U., 1996. Author: The Land Still Lives, 1970, How to Improve Adult Education in Your Church, 1972, Cabin in the Country, 1972, Toward a Working Philosophy of Adult Education, 1973, Ideas for Better Church Meetings, 1975, Barns of Wisconsin, 1977, rev. edit., 1995, Problems in Continuing Education, 1979, Spanish edit., 1983, Mills of Wisconsin and the Midwest, 1980, The Adult Learner on Campus: A Guide for Instructors and Administrators, 1981, Study Skills: For Adults Returning to School, 1981, Improving Your Writing Skills, 1982, Improving Practice in Continuing Education, 1985, Skiing into Wisconsin: A Celebration of Winter, 1985, Higher Education in a Learning Society, 1988, Study Skills for Today's College Student, 1990, Mastering the Teaching of Adults, 1991, Breweries of Wisconsin, 1992, rev. 2004, Leadership for the Emerging Age, 1994, One-Room Country Schools, 1996, Rural Wisdom, 1997, Traveler's Companion, 1997, Cheese: The Making of a Wisconsin Tradition, 1998, When Chores Were Done, 1999, Symbols: Viewing a Rural Past, 2000, Humor from the Country, 2001, The People Came First: A History of Wisconsin Cooperative Extension, 2002, Eat Rutabagas, 2002, Stormy, 2002, The Travels at Increase Joseph, 2003, Ringlingville USA, 2004, Every Farm Tells A Story, 2005. Capt. U.S. Army, 1956. Recipient Non-Fiction Book award of merit Wis. Hist. Soc., 1978, 81, 93, 99, 2003, Wis. Idea award, 1994, Robert E. Gard Excellence in Lit. award, 1996, Wis. 4-H Alumni award, 1998, Midwest Favorite Book award Upper Midwest Booksellers, 1999, 2000, 02, Pride of Wis. award Barnes and Noble Booksellers, 2001, 02; recognized for Outstanding Lit. Achievement, Wis. Libr. Assn. Mem. Am. Assn. Adult and Continuing Edn. (mem. exec. com. 1975-76, Rsch. to Practice award 1982), Commn. Profls. of Adult Edn. (pres. 1972-74), Wis. Acad. Scis., Arts and Letters (pres. 1987), Wis. Assn. Adult and Continuing Edn. (pres. 1969, Outstanding Adult Educator of Yr. award 1986), Wis. Coun. Writers (pres. 1978-80, Best Non-Fiction Book award 1977, Scholarly Book award 1988, 2003). Business E-Mail: jwapps@wisc.edu.

APRISON, MORRIS HERMAN, experimental and theoretical neurobiology educator; b. Milw., Wis., Oct. 6, 1923; s. Henry and Ethel Aprison; m. Shirley Reder, Aug. 21, 1949; children— Barry, Robert. BS in Chemistry, U. Wis., 1945, tchrs. cert., 1947, MS in Physics, 1949, PhD in Biochemistry, 1952. Grad. teaching asst. in physics U. Wis., Madison, 1947-49; grad. research asst. in pathology Sch. Medicine, 1950-51, grad. research asst. in biochemistry, 1951-52; tech. asst. in physics Inst. Paper Chemistry, Appleton, Wis., 1949-50; biochemist, prin. investigator, head biophysics sect. Galesburg (Ill.) State Research Hosp., 1952-56; prin. research investigator in biochemistry Inst. Psychiat. Research; asst. prof. depts. biochemistry and psychiatry Ind. U. Med. Sch., Indpls., 1956-60, asso. prof., 1960-64, prof. biochemistry, 1964-78, distinguished prof. neurobiology and biochemistry, 1978-93, disting. prof. emeritus, 1993—, chief neurobiology sect., 1969-74. Mem. exec. com. dept. psychiatry, exec. adminstr. Inst. Psychiat. Rsch., 1973-74, dir. inst., 1974-78, chief sect. applied and theoretical neurobiology, 1978-93; co-chmn. session on neurotransmitters 23d Internat. Physiol. Congress, 1965; chmn. session neurochemistry and neuropharmacology 25th Congress, 1971; ad hoc mem. study sect. psychopharmacology NIMH, 1967-71, mem. neuropsychology study sect., 1970-74; mem. molecular and cellular neurobiology program adv. panel NSF, 1984-86; mem. com. recommendations U.S. Army sci. rsch. Nat. Rsch. Coun. Bd. Physics and Astronomy, 1987-89; mem. gov. bd. Inst. for Advanced Study Ind. U., Bloomington, 1989-92; vis. prof. 4th ASPET Workshop, Vanderbilt U., 1972; guest scholar Grad. Sch., Kans. State U., 1973. Adv. editor Neurosci. Rsch., 1968-73, Jour. Biol. Psychiatry, 1968-83, Neuropharmacology, 1969-93, Jour. Neurochemistry, 1972-75, Pharmacology, Biochemistry and Behavior, 1973-89, Jour. Comparative and General Pharmacology, 1974-75, Jour. Gen. Pharmacology, 1975-93, Jour. Developmental Psychobiology, 1974-77; regional editor Life Scis., 1970-73; co-editor Advances in Neurochemistry, 1973-92; mem. editorial bd. Jour. Neurochemistry, 1975-79, dep. chief editor, 1980-83; mem. editorial bd. Neurochem. Rsch., 1975-82, Jour. Neurosci. Rsch., 1984-92; co-editor 10 books; contbr. more than 355 rsch. articles and abstracts to profl. jours., chpts. to books, including one in History of Neuroscience in Autobiography, vol. 3, 2001. Mem. Ind. regional adv. bd. Anti-Defamation League, 1973-76; bd. overseers St. Meinrad Sem., 1974-77. Served with USNR, 1944-46. Prof. M.H. Aprison awards for best rsch. toward PhD in med. neurobiology at dept. psychiatry Ind. U. Sch. Medicine created in his honor, 1999. Mem. Am. Physiol. Soc., Biophys. Soc., Soc. Biol. Psychiatry (program com. 1974-75, co-chmn. 1975-76, gold medal 1975), Internat. Brain Rsch. Orgn., Internat. Soc. Neurochemistry (co-chmn. session 1st internat. meeting Strasbourg, France 1967, 4th meeting Tokyo 1973, 7th meeting Jerusalem 1979, coun. 1973-75, sec. 1975-79, chmn. 1979-81, publicity com. 1975-83, nominating com. 1983-87, policy adv. com. 1985-98, ad hoc and founding rules com. 1998-2000, standing rules com., 2000—), Am. Soc. Neurochemistry (co-chmn. sci. program com. 1972, mem. 1973), Soc. for Neurosci. (pres. Indpls. chpt. 1970-71), Sigma Xi. Home: 9268 Spring Forest Dr Indianapolis IN 46260-1266 Personal E-mail: maprison@iupui.edu.

APSEL, ALYSSA, electrical engineer, computer engineer; BS Electrical Engineering, Swarthmore College, 1995; MS Electrical Engineering, California Institute of Technology, 1996; PhD Electrical Engineering, Johns Hopkins University, 2002. Undergraduate research fellow U. of Pa, SUNFEST, 1994; grad. research asst., electrical engineering Calf. Institute of Technology, 1995—97; grad. research asst., electrical and computer engineering Johns Hopkins U., 1998—; grad. research asst., army research lab Adelphi, 2000—. Teaching asst., engineering methodology Swarthmore College, 1993; teaching asst., integrated electronics Johns Hopkins U., 1998, teaching asst., lab asst., Advanced Integrated Circuits, 99. Fellow Caltech Institute Fellowship, California Institute of Technology, 1995—96, Abel Wolman Fellowship, Johns Hopkins University, 1997—98. Achievements include patents for Integrated electronic-optoelectronic devices and method of making the same, 2000; Low Power, Differential Optical Receiver in Silicon on Sapphire, 2001. Office: Johns Hopkins U Dept Computer & Electrical Engineering 3400 N Charles St Baltimore MD 21218

APT, CHARLES, artist; b. NYC, Dec. 10, 1933; s. Gustav Lee and Tami (Vera Salzman) A.; m. Ursula Edith Betz, July 24, 1959; children— Gregory, Sam. B.F.A., Pratt Inst., 1956. Exhibited in group shows at Mus. Fine Art, Springfield, Mass., 1966, Expn. Intercontinentale, Monaco, France, 1966, 68, NAD, 1965, 68, 77-81, 83, 85, 87, 99, 2001, 03, 05, Am. Watercolor Soc., 1965-66, 68-69, Allied Artists Am., 1964-65, 67, 69-70, 72, Nat. Mus. Racing, Saratoga, N.Y., 1967, Atlantic City Race Track, 1967, Nat. Arts Club, 1967; one-man shows Ground Floor Art Gallery, N.Y.C., 1967-69, Aqueduct Race Track Art Gallery, N.Y.C., 1967, Grand Central Art Galleries, 1969, Far Gallery, N.Y.C., 1972, 78, Palm Beach (Fla.) Galleries, 1973, Talisman Gallery, Bartlesville, Okla., 1976, Gallery 52, South Orange, N.J., 1976-77, Lorings Gallery, Cedarhurst, N.Y., 1985, 87, Dassin Gallery, LA, Loring Gallery, Sheffield, Mass., Off the Wall Gallery, Savannah, Ga., Chapellier Fine Arts, Winston-Salem, N.C. Served with AUS, 1956-58. Recipient Gold medal Am. Vets. Soc. Artists, 1965; Best in Show award Saratoga Mus. Racing Ann., 1967; 2d Benjamin Altman award for figure painting NAD, 1968; Le Prix Prince Souverain Monaco, 1968; Bronze medal Nat. Arts Club, 1971; Sutherland prize Annual Open Oil Exhbn., 1972; Ject-key prize Salmagundi Club, 1972, prize, 1966, 68-69, 71, Williams award Salmagundi Club, 1966, 68, 1st prize Product Design award for Aquarelle fabric collection Resource Coun., 1984, 1st prize Am. Artists Profl. League, 1965, Talens award, 1966 Mem. NAD (academician, Briggs Meml. award 1989), Artists Equity Assn. N.Y. Studio: 152 South Almont Dr Los Angeles CA 90048

APT, LEONARD, physician; AB with highest honors, U. Pa., 1942; MD with highest honors, Jefferson Med. Coll., 1945. Diplomate Am. Bd. Pediat., Am. Bd. Ophthalmology. Intern Jefferson Med. Coll. Hosp., Phila., 1945-46; rsch. fellow in pathology-hematology Children's Hosp., Detroit, 1946-49, resident in pediat. Cin., 1949—50, Children's Med. Ctr., Boston, 1950-52, chief med. resident, 1952-53, asst. physician, 1953-55; resident in ophthalmology Wills Eye Hosp., Phila., 1955-57; first spl. fellow in pediat. ophthalmology NIH, Bethesda, and Children's Hosp., Washington, 1957—59; first fellow in Pediat. Ophthalmology Wills Eye Hosp., Phila., 1959—61; from asst. prof. to prof. ophthalmology Sch. Medicine, UCLA, 1961—72, prof., 1972—; disting. prof. UCLA, 1993—; attending surgeon Jules Stein Eye Inst., UCLA, founding dir. divsn. pediat. ophthalmology, 1961—81, founder, 1966, dir. emeritus, 1981—. Tchg. fellow in pediat. Harvard U. Med. Sch., Boston, 1950—52, instr. pediat., 1953—55; sr. physician radioisotope unit Boston VA Hosp., 1953—55; cons. pediat. ophthalmology Cedars-Sinai Med. Ctr., L.A., St. John's Hosp., Santa Monica, Calif., Bur. Maternal and Child Health, Dept. Pub. Health Calif., Dept. Health, L.A. *Dr. Apt is recognized as the founder of academic pediatric opthalmology. He is the first physician to be board-certified in both pediatrics and ophthalmology. At UCLA, Dr. Apt established the first full-time division of pediatric ophathalmology at a medical school in the United States. Dr. Apt authored one of the first books devoted to the new subspecialty. He is the originator of the Apt test-widely known especially to pediatricians and obstetricians. Dr. Apt helped develop a new antiseptic eyedrop that has appreciably reduced the incidence of pediatric blindness in developing countries.* Author: Diagnostic Procedures in Pediatric Ophthalmology, 1963; mem. editl. bd.: numerous med. jours.; contbr. articles to profl. jours., chapters to books. Founder L.A. Philharmonic Assn.; presdl. circle mem. L.A. County Mus. of Art; v.p. fin. UCLA Grunwald Ctr. for Graphic Arts, Hammer Mus.; bd. dirs. Royce Ctr. Cir., UCLA Performing Arts Dept.; founder John Wooden UCLA Athletic Ctr.; exec. coun. mem. UCLA Divsn. of Humanities; founder UCLA Acosta Athletic Tng. Complex; judge Wines of Am. Ann. Competition. 1st lt. M.C. U.S. Army, 1943—46. Recipient F.T. Stewart Surgery prize, Jefferson Med. Coll., 1945, Arthur J. Bedell Resident Rsch. prize, Wills Eye Hosp., Phila., 1957, Disting. Alumnus Achievement award, Jefferson Med. Coll., 1992, 1st Escalon Sci. award, 1992, Hall of Fame Distinction award, Cin. Pediat. Hist. Soc., 1994, 1st Disting. Alumni award, Sch. Arts and Scis. U. Pa., 1995, Alumni Univ. Svc. award, UCLA, 1996, William Feinbloom 1st Disting. Achievement award, 1999, Profl. Achievement award, UCLA Med. Alumni Assn., 1999, 1st Disting. Achievement award, Ethicon Inc.-Johnson & Johnson Co., 1999, S. Rodman Irvine prize, Jules Stein Eye Inst., UCLA, 2005. Mem.: AMA, Am. Med. Writers Assn., Pacific Coast Oto-Ophthal. Soc., Internat. Strabismol. Assn., Am. Assn. Pediat. Ophthalmology and Strabismus (1st Disting. Achievement award 1996, Honor award 1995), Soc. Pediat. Rsch., Assn. for Rsch. Ophthalmology, Am. Ophthal. Soc., Am. Acad. Pediats. (Lifetime Achievement award 2000, Ann. Leonard Apt Lectureship named in his honor 2000), Am. Acad. Ophthalmology (Honor award 1968), L'Ordre Mondial des Gourmets Deguistaeurs, Confrerie de la Chaine des Rotisseurs, Internat. Wine and Food Soc., Shriner, Masons (32d deg.), Alpha Omega Alpha. Avocations: sports, art, theater, gourmet food, oenology. Office: UCLA Sch Medicine Jules Stein Eye Inst 100 Stein Plz Los Angeles CA 90095-7000 Office Phone: 310-825-3986. Office Fax: 310-206-3652.

APTE, SOURABH VASANT, research scientist; b. Pune, India, Jan. 23, 1973; s. Vasant Mahadeo and Rajani Vasant Apte; m. Archana Balwant Habbu, July 24, 2000; 1 child, Tanvi Sourabh. PhD, Pa. State U., 2000. Intern Tata Rsch. Devel. and Design Ctr., Pune, 1996; grad. rsch. asst. Pa. State U., State College, 1996—2000; engring. rsch. assoc. Stanford (Calif.) U., 2000. Contbr. articles to profl. jours., chapters to books. Mem.: ASME, AIAA, Am. Phys. Soc. Office: Stanford U Bldg 500 ME/FPC 488 Escondido Mall Stanford CA 94305-3030

APTEKAR, KEN, painter; b. Detroit, May 13, 1950; BFA, U. Mich., 1973; MFA, Pratt Inst., 1975. Studio artist, N.Y.C. Solo shows include Jack Shainman Gallery, N.Y.C., 1994, 96, Palmer Mus. Art Pa. State U., 1995, Corcoran Gallery of Art, 1997, Cummer Mus. of Art, Jacksonville, Fla., 1998, Steinbaum-Krauss Gallery, N.Y.C., 1999, Victoria and Albert Mus., London, 2001, Meml. Art Gallery, Rochester, N.Y., 2002, Kemper Mus., Kansas City, 2001, Coll. of Wooster, Ohio, 2002, Pamela Auchincloss Projects, N.Y.C., 2001, Contemporary Art Ctr. of Va., 2001-02, Bernice Steinbaum Gallery,

2001, 03;, Douglas Coley Gallery, Reed Coll., Portland, Oreg., 2004, Espace Camille Lambert, Javisy, France, 2005; exhibited in group shows at Carnegie-Mellon U. Mus., Pitts., 1991, Corcoran Gallery, Washington, 1993-94, 97-98, Flint (Mich.) Inst. Art, 1993, Wight Gallery UCLA, 1994, Yerba Buena Ctr. Contemporary Art, San Francisco, 1994, Walters Art Gallery, Balt., 1995, Calif. Ctr. Contemporary Art, Escondido, 1996, Kohler Arts Ctr., Wis., 1996, Jewish Mus., N.Y.C., San Francisco, 1996, Armand Hammer Mus., L.A., 1996, Islip Art Mus., N.Y., 1998, Ashville Mus. Art, 2003; represented in permanent collections Kemper Mus., Kansas City, Mo., Corcoran Gallery Art, Washington D.C., Victoria & Albert Mus., London, Meml. Art Gallery, Rochester, Niagara U., Denver Mus. Art, Progressive Corp., Jewish Mus., Bell Atlantic Corp., Nat. Mus. Am. Art, Washington, Harvard U. Recipient Pollock-Krasner Found. award, 1989; NEA fellow, 1987, 95, Bellagio residency Rockefeller Found., 1992, artist residency Ucross Found., Wyo., 1992, painting residency Resident Artists Program Djerassi, 1991, 94, Mid Atlantic Arts Found. award, 1998. Home: 201 W 85th St Apt 7E New York NY 10024-3909 E-mail: kenaptekar@verizon.net.

APTER, EMILY, language educator; BA in History and Lit., Harvard U., 1977; PhD in Comparative Lit., Princeton U., 1983. Prof. French NYU, N.Y.C. Recipient Guggenheim fellowship, 2003, Mellon fellowship, Rockefeller fellowship, ACLS fellowship, NEH fellowship, Coll. Art Assn. fellowship. Office: 19 University Pl 634 New York NY 10003

APUD, JOSE ANTONIO, psychiatrist, educator; b. San Miguel de Tucuman, Argentina, May 25, 1948; came to U.S., 1987; s. Jose and Emelin (Chagra) A.; m. Graciela Varela, Jan. 25, 1979; children: Maria Macarena, Jose Sebastian. MD, U. Tucuman, 1975; degree in pharmacology, U. Milan, 1980, degree in exptl. endocrinology, 1983; PhD, U. Buenos Aires, 1985. Diplomate Am. Bd. Psychiatry and Neurology. Investigator CONICET, Buenos Aires, 1985—98; prof. pharmacology U. Buenos Aires, 1985-93; psychiatrist in residence St. Elizabeth's Hosp., Nat. Inst. of Mental Health, Washington, 1991-95; clin. assoc. neuropsychiatry br. Nat. Inst. of Mental Health, Washington, 1995-98; faculty psychiatry residency tng. program Commn. on Mental Health Svcs., Washington, 1998—2000; dir. psychopharmacology divsn. St. Elizabeths Hosp.-Commn. on Mental Health Svcs., Washington, 1998-2000; med. dir. Schizophrenia Inpatient Rsch. Program NIMH, 2000—. Cons. Farmitalia Carlo Erba Labs, Milan, 1979-83; vis. prof. pharmacology Georgetown U., Washington, 1987-91, instr. dept. psychiatry, 1995-98, prof. psychiatry, 1998-2004, adj. prof. neuroscis.; mem. editl. bd. Endocrinologia Clinica y Metabolism, 1982—, Neuroendocrinologia Latinoamericana, 1982—. Contbr. numerous articles to profl. jours. Fellow Nat. Atomic Energy Commn., 1976, Dept. Endocrinology French Hosp., 1978, Inst. Pharmacology U. Milan, 1978-84, sr. staff fellow St. Elizabeth's Hosp. NIMH, 1994-98; recipient Cediquifa award in pharmacology, 1992, Upjohn award NIMH, 1993. Mem. AMA, Am. Psychiat. Assn. (sci. com. 1993-95, Burroughs Wellcome award 1993), Am. Soc. Clin. Psychopharmacology, Washington Psychiat. Soc., Italian Soc. Neurosci., Italian Soc. Pharmacology, Soc. for Neurosci., Sociedad Argentina de Farmacologia Exptl., Internat. Soc. Psychoneuroendocrinology, Internat. Soc. Neuroendocrinology, Argentina Soc. Biology and Nuclear Medicine, Serotonin Club. Roman Catholic. Achievements include identification of Gabaergic system in rats; study of the mechanism of action of psychotropic drugs; studies on schizophrenia and tardive dyskinesia, pharmacogenomics in schizophrenia; identification of an endogenous ligand for the serotonin-2 receptor in the rat brain. Office: NIMH Clin Brain Disorders Br Bldg 10 Rm CRC 7-3350 10 Center Dr Bethesda MD 20892 E-mail: apudj@intra.nimh.nih.gov.

APURON, ANTHONY SABLAN, archbishop; b. Agana, Guam, Nov. 1, 1945; s. Manuel Taijito and Ana Santos (Sablan) P. BA, St. Anthony Coll., 1969; MDiv, Maryknoll Sem., 1972, M in Theology, 1973; MA in Liturgy, Notre Dame U., 1974; LHD, U. Guam, 1998. Ordained priest Roman Catholic Ch., 1972, bishop, 1984, installed archbishop, 1986. Chmn. Diocesan Liturgical Commn., Agana, 1974—86; vice-chmn. Chamorro Lang. Commn., Agana, 1984—86; aux. bishop Archdiocese of Agana, 1984—85, archbishop, 1986—. Chmn. Interfaith Vols. Caregivers, Agana, 1984—; active Civilian Adv. Com., Agana, 1986—, Post-Synod of Bishops of Oceania, 1998—; pres. Cath. Bishops' Conf. of Pacific, 1990—96; v.p. Cath. Bishops' Conf. of Oceania, 1990—98. Author: A Structural Analysis of the Content of Myth in the Thought of Mircea Eliade, 1973. Chmn. Cath. Ednl. Radio. Named Most Outstanding Young Man, Jaycees, Guam, 1984. Roman Catholic. Avocations: jogging, walking, swimming. Office: Archbishop's Office 196 B Cuesta San Ramon Agana Heights GU 96910-4334

APUZZO, MICHAEL LAWRENCE JOHN, neurological surgeon; b. New Haven, Conn., 1940; BA, Yale U., 1961; MD, Boston U., 1965. Intern in neurosurgery Yale U.; resident in surgery McGill U., 1966; resident in neurosurgery Yale U., New Haven, 1967-73; prof. neurol. surgery, radiation oncology, biology and physics U. So. Calif. Sch. Medicine, L.A. Editor Neurosurgery on-line; contbr. over 500 articles to profl. jours. Office: U So Calif Sch Medicine Ste 5046 1200 N State St Los Angeles CA 90033-1029 Office Phone: 323-226-7421.

AQUADRO, JEANA LAUREN, graphic designer, educator; b. Key West, Fla., June 10, 1957; d. Charles Frasure and Geraldine Ferguson (Norton) A.; m. John A. Crawford; 1 dau., Lauren Olya Crawford. B Environ. Design magna cum laude, N.C. State U., 1979; MFA, Yale U., 1984. Graphic designer various projects for Cooper-Hewitt Nat. Mus. Design, Whitney Mus. Am. Art, Shearson Lehman Bros., Citicorp Investment Bank, Abbeville Press, UNICEF, others, N.Y.C., 1984-91; asst. dir. graphic design dept. Mus. Modern Art, 1988-89; design cons. Solomon R. Guggenheim Mus., 1989-91; prof. Savannah Coll., Savannah, Ga., 1991—2001; graphic design cons., 2001—. Bd. dirs. Wilderness S.E. Recipient The Am. Fedn. of Arts award of Excellence, 1988, Fed. design achievement award Nat. Endowment for Arts, 1992, Presidential award for design excellence Fed. Govt., 1994. Avocations: aquatic sports, travel, gardening. Studio: 3 Pinewood Ave Savannah GA 31406

AQUILA, FRANCIS JOSEPH, lawyer; b. NYC, Feb. 3, 1957; s. Frank Joseph and Evelyn Jane (Farrell) A.; m. Catherine Spinella, June 10, 1984; children: Jessica Lynn, Jillian Rose, Elaina Kathryn. AB, Columbia U., 1979; JD summa cum laude, Bklyn. Law Sch., 1983. Bar: NY 1984. Ptnr. mergers and acquisitions Sullivan & Cromwell, NYC, 1991—, and dep. coord. intellectual property practice area. Exec. dir. Young Dems. of Am., Washington, 1981-83; v.p. US Youth Coun., Washington, 1982-84; mem. Dem. Nat. Com., 1979-81; Trustee exec. com. St. Peter's Univ. Hosp. and Health System, New Brunswick, NJ, 1998—; mem. Nat. Adv. Bd., NALP Found. for Edn. and Training, Washington, 1997—, Adv. Bd. Salavation Army of Greater NY, 2001—. Mem. ABA, NY State Bar Assn., Assoc. of the Bar of the City of NY Roman Catholic. Office: Sullivan & Cromwell 125 Broad St Fl 28 New York NY 10004-2489 Office Phone: 212-558-4048. Office Fax: 212-558-3588. Business E-Mail: aquilaf@sullcrom.com.

AQUILINO, DANIEL, banker; b. Needham, Mass., Feb. 4, 1924; s. Michael Aquilino and Anna (Bruno) A.; m. Theresa H. Barberio, Nov. 9, 1946; children: Donna Lee, Daniel C., Michael D. BS magna cum laude, Northeastern U., 1949; grad., Stonier Grad. Sch. Banking, Rutgers U., 1962. With Fed. Res. Bank Boston, 1949-85, exec. v.p., 1970-85, Bank of New Eng., Boston, 1985-89; cons. Boston, 1990—. Served with AUS, 1943-45. Recipient Sears B. Condit award Northeastern U., 1947, 49; recognition award Italian-Am. Soc., Inc., 1972. Home: 3 N Bennet Ct Apt 1 Boston MA 02113-1904

AQUILINO, THOMAS JOSEPH, JR., federal judge, law educator; b. Mt. Kisco, N.Y., Dec. 7, 1939; s. Thomas Joseph and Virginia Burr (Doughty) A.; m. Edith Luise Berndt, Oct. 27, 1965; children: Christopher T., Philip A., Alexander B. Student, Cornell U., 1957-59, U. Munich, 1960-61; BA, Drew U., 1962; postgrad., Free U., Berlin, 1965-66; JD, Rutgers U., 1969. Bar: N.Y. 1972, U.S. Dist. Ct. (so., ea. and no. dists.) N.Y. 1973, U.S. Ct. Appeals (2nd cir.) 1973, U.S. Supreme Ct. 1976, U.S. Ct. Appeals (3rd cir.) 1977, Interstate Commerce Commn. 1978, U.S. Ct. Claims 1979, U.S. Ct. Internat. Trade 1984. Law clk. to judge U.S. Dist. Ct. (so. dist.) N.Y., NYC, 1969-71; atty. Davis Polk & Wardwell, NYC, 1971-85; judge U.S. Ct. Internat. Trade, NYC, 1985—2005, sr. judge, 2005—. Adj. prof. law Benjamin N. Cardozo Sch. of Law, 1984-95; mem. bd. visitors Drew U., 1997—. With U.S. Army, 1962-65. Mem. N.Y. State Bar Assn., Fed. Bar Coun. Roman Catholic. Avocations: sports, travel, linguistics, cinema. Office: US Ct Internat Trade 1 Federal Plz New York NY 10278-0001

AQUINO, JOSEPH MARIO, clinical psychologist; b. NYC, Nov. 21, 1947; s. Joseph and Rose (Nasi) A.; m. Kathleen Ann Ryan, Oct. 6, 1990; children: Joseph Patrick, Ryan Thomas, Erin Rose. BA in English, So. Ill. U., 1969, MS in Secondary Edn., 1976; PhD in Clin. Psychology, St. John's U., Jamaica, N.Y., 1987. Lic. psychologist, N.Y. Tchr. English Wappingers Cen. Schs., Wappingers Falls, N.Y., 1969-79; intern psychology Maimonides Med. Ctr., Bklyn., 1983-84; specialist in applied behavior sci. Builders for Family and Youth, Bklyn., 1984-85; trainee psychology and psychologist St. Vincent's Svcs., Bklyn., 1984-89; psychologist St. Christopher-Ottilie Svcs., Sea Cliff, N.Y., 1989-96; pvt. practice psychology N.Y.C. area, 1989—. Guest lectr. St. John's U., 1990. Co-author: Situational Leadership for Principals, 1983; mem. editl. bd. Jour. Urban Psychiatry, 1982-84; guest The Women's Line, WVOX 1460 AM, 1994; cited in newspaper articles; contbr. articles to profl. jours. Recipient citation VFW, Wappingers Falls, N.Y., 1977; Bethany House Achievement award Bethany House II, 1991; psychology teaching fellow St. John's U., 1981; cited in article Emergency mag., 1991. Mem. APA, N.Y. State Psychol. Assn., Westchester County Psychol. Assn., Nat. Register of Health Svc. Providers in Psychology, Am. Coll. of Advanced Practice Psychologists (founding fellow). Office: 10 Rye Ridge Plz Ste 213 Rye Brook NY 10573-2857 Personal E-mail: werpsyched@aol.com.

AQUINO, VICTOR MICHAEL, pediatrician, educator; b. Bklyn., Oct. 20, 1964; m. Deborah Ballard; 1 child, Samantha. MD, SUNY, Syracuse, N.Y., 1989. Diplomate Am. Bd. Pediat., 1992. Assoc. prof. of pediat. U. Tex. Southwestern Med. Ctr., Dallas, 1997—. Office: UT Southwestern Medical Center at Dallas 5323 Harry Hines Blvd Dallas TX 75390-9063 Office Phone: 214-648-3074. Office Fax: 214-648-3122. E-mail: victor.aquino@utsouthwestern.edu.

ARABAS, JAN, artist, art educator; b. Buffalo, N.Y., June 6, 1958; d. Paul F. and Barbara M. (Skoupa) Arabas; m. Rick Ochberg, 2004; 1 child from previous marriage, Theodore Aaron. BA cum laude, SUNY, Binghamton, 1979; diploma, Sch. Mus. Fine Arts, Boston, 1983. Program dir. Cmty. Art Ctr., Cambridge, Mass., 1985-87, Jamaica Plains (Mass.) Multi-Cultural Arts Ctr., 1987-89; dir. Hand Press Workshop, Somerville, Mass., 1987—2002; assoc. prof. art Middlesex C.C., Bedford, Mass., 2000—; instr. art Decordova Mus. Sch. Art, Lincoln, Mass., 1993, Arnold Arboretum of Harvard U., Boston, 1997—; asst. prof. art North Shore C.C., Lynn, Mass., 1996—2000. Mem. Graphic Design Adv. Bd., Lynn, 1999—; artist in residence Mass. Cultural Coun., Boston, 1983-92. Artist: Basic Printmaking Techniques, 1992; contbg. editor Exhibition of Works on Paper, 1997; one-person shows include Roberson Ctr. for Arts, 1988, Lionheart Gallery, 1994, Middlesex C.C., 1995, Bricksbottom Gallery, 2000; exhibited in group shows at Brickbottom Gallery, 1990, 92, 94, 95, 97, 98, New Eng. BioLabs., 1997, Berkshire Mus., 1997, Aidekman Ctr., Tufts U., 1997, Grossman Gallery, Sch. Mus. Fine Arts, 1997, 98, Boston Pub. Libr., 1998, Higgins Art Gallery, Cape Cod C.C., 1998, Hobson Gallery, 1999, Laura Knott Art Gallery, Bradford Coll., 1999, Boston Pub. Libr., 2000, Rau U., Johannesburg, South Africa, 2000, WGBH, Boston, 2000, Middlesex C.C. Faculty Show, 2002, The Drawing Ctr., 2002, Havana, Cuba, 2003, Amsterdam Whitney Gallery, 2003, 2004 Silvermine Guild Nat. Print Show, 2003, Boston Pub. Libr., 2003, others; represented in permanent collections at The Mus. of Fine Art, Boston, The Drawing Ctr., N.Y.C., Boston Pub. Libr., Bank of Boston; also pvt. collections. Recipient award in fine arts SUNY Found., 1979, Juror's awards Boston Printmakers Nat., 1986, 87, support grant Somerville Arts Coun., 1990, project grant Mass. Cultural Coun., 1994, project grant Somerville Art Coun., 1996, grants North Shore C.C., 1997-98, Middlesex C.C., 1997-98, C.C. Humanities Assn., 1999; Artists Found. fellow in printmaking, 1987, Nat. Endowment for Arts/New Eng. Found. for Arts fellowship in printmaking, 1990, Berkshire Taconic Found., 2003. Mem.: FATE (Carnegie Coll. program), SIGGRAPH, Adobe Photoshop Profl. Users Group, Coll. Art Assn., Monotype Guild of New Eng., C.C. Humanities Assn., Boston Printmakers Soc. (juror awards 1985, 1986, 1987), N.E. Hist. Assn., Brickbottom Artists Assn. Avocations: skiing, sailing, scuba diving. Home: 18 Willard St Melrose MA 02176 E-mail: jarabas@comcast.net.

ARABATZIS, CONSTANCE ELAINE, lawyer; b. Dania, Fla., Jan. 23, 1961; BS in Health Services Adminstrn., summa cum laude, CUNY, 1986; JD, NYU, 1989. Bar: Conn. 1990, NY 1991, DC 1991, US Dist. Ct. (so. dist.) NY 1992, Fla. 1993. Asst. dist. atty. King's County Dist. Atty. Office, Bklyn., 1989—92; assoc., comm. real estate litig. Finkelstein Borah Schwartz Altschuler & Golstein, 1992—94; in-house counsel Investments Ltd., Fla., 1994—95; sr. assoc. Stephens Lynn Klein & McNicholas, Fla., 1995—98; assoc. Baer Marks & Upham, 1998—2001; sr. assoc., Litig. & Dispute Resolution Group Dickstein Shapiro Morin & Oshinsky LLP, NYC, 2001—, diversity/pro bono coun. Mem.: Fla. Bar, DC Bar, Soc. Human Resource Mgrs., Phi Alpha Delta. Office: Dickstein Shapiro Morin & Oshinsky LLP 1177 Avenue of the Americas New York NY 10036-2714 Office Phone: 212-896-5430, 212-997-9880. Business E-Mail: arabatzisc@dsmo.com.

ARABIAN, ARMAND, arbitrator, mediator, lawyer; b. NYC, Dec. 12, 1934; s. John and Aghavnie (Yalian) A.; m. Nancy Arabian, Aug. 26, 1962; children: Allison Ann, Robert Armand. BSBA, Boston U., 1956, JD, 1961; LLM, U. So. Calif., L.A., 1970; LLD (hon.) (hon.), Southwestern Sch. Law, 1990; LLD (hon.), Pepperdine U., 1990, U. West L.A., 1994, We. State U., 1997, Thomas Jefferson Sch. of Law, 1997, Am. Coll. Law, 2001. Bar: Calif. 1962, U.S. Supreme Ct. 1966. Dep. dist. atty. L.A. County, 1962-63; pvt. practice law Van Nuys, Calif., 1963-72; judge Mcpl. Ct., L.A., 1972-73, Superior Ct., L.A., 1973-83; assoc. justice Calif. Ct. Appeal, L.A., 1983-90, Supreme Ct. Calif., San Francisco, 1990-96. Adj. prof. sch. law Pepperdine U., 1996—. Contbr. articles to profl. jours. 1st lt. U.S. Army, 1956-58. Recipient Stanley Lintz Meml. award San Fernando Valley Bar Assn., 1986, Lifetime Achievement award San Fernando Valley Bar Assn., 1993; Outstanding Jurist of the Yr., Malibu Bar Assn., 1996, Mesrob Mashdots medal Aram I Catholicos, Beirut, Lebanon, 1999, Mekhitar medal Brotherhood in Venice, Italy, 1999, Gold medal of honor of Peter the Great, Russian Acad. Sci., 1999, Mekhitar Gosh medal Pres. of Armenia Robert Kocharian, 2001, St. James the Apostle medal Beatitude Torkom Manoogian, Jerusalem, 2001, Albert Einstein Gold medal of honor, Russian Acad. Natural Scis., 2003, Ellis Island Medal Honor award, 2004, St. Gregory the Illuminator medal Karekin II Catholicos Yerevan, Armenia, 2004, Women of LA Highlight award, 2005; Pappas Disting. scholar Boston U. Sch. Law, 1987; Justice Armand Arabian Resource and Comm. Ctrs. named in honor of Van Nuys and San Fernando Calif. Courthouses, 1999. Republican. Office: 6259 Van Nuys Blvd Van Nuys CA 91401-2711 Fax: 818-781-6002. Office Phone: 818-997-8900. Business E-Mail: honarabian@aol.com.

ARABIE, PHIPPS, marketing educator, researcher; b. Mar. 13, 1948; s. Wade Joseph and Betty Jo (Thomason) A.; m. Terry Feldstein, Feb. 24, 2000. Diploma, Phillips Acad., Andover, 1966; AB, Harvard U., 1970; PhD, Stanford U., 1974. Asst. prof. psychology U. Minn., Mpls., 1974-77, assoc. prof., 1977-80; prof. psychology and sociology U. Ill., Champaign-Urbana, 1980-90; prof. Rutgers U. Sch. Mgmt., Newark, 1990—; chair mktg. Rutgers U. Bus. Sch., Newark, 1990-96, 2000—02. Cons. AT&T Bell Labs, Murray Hill, N.J., 1975-82; Fulbright vis. prof. computer sci. U. Coll., Dublin, Ireland, 1986-87; vis. prof. psychology U. Santiago de Compostela, Spain, 1993; mem. adv. panel on methods, measures and stats. NSF, 1996-97. Co-author: Three-way Scaling and Clustering, 1987, Combinatorial Data Analysis: Optimization by Dynamic Programming, 2001; co-editor: Clustering and Classification, 1996, Clustering Classification, 2004, Data Mining Applications, 2004.; editor Jour. Classification, 1983-2002; contbr. articles to profl. jours.; author computer programs for multidimensional analysis of data. Grantee, NSF, Office Naval Rsch., Nat. Inst. Justice, AT&T; Beckman assoc., U. Ill., 1983—84. Fellow: AAAS, APA, Am. Statis. Assn., Am. Psychol. Soc.; mem.: INFORMS, Am. Mktg. Assn., Soc. Math. Psychology, Psychonometric Soc. (trustee 1987—89, pres. 1990—91), Classification Soc. N.Am. (bd. dirs. 1983—, pres. 2004—). Office: Rutgers U Business Sch 180 University Ave Newark NJ 07102-1893 Office Phone: 973-353-1020.

ARAC, JONATHAN, language educator; b. NYC, Apr. 4, 1945; s. Benjamin and Evelyn (Charm) A. AB, Harvard U., 1967, MA, 1968, PhD, 1974. Jr. fellow Soc. Fellows Harvard U., Cambridge, Mass., 1970-73; asst. prof. English Princeton U., 1973-79; assoc. prof. U. Ill., Chgo., 1979-85, prof., 1985-86; prof. grad. program lit. Duke U., 1986-87; prof. English and comparative lit. Columbia U., 1987-90; prof. English U. Pitts., 1989-2000, Mellon prof. English, 2000-01; Harriman prof. English and comparative lit. Columbia U., 2001—. Assoc. dir. Inst. for Humanities, U. Ill., Chgo., 1983-84, dept. chair, 2001—; Drue Heinz disting. vis. prof. Oxford U., 2000, 05; Avalon disting. vis. prof. humanities Northwestern U., 2000. Author: Commissioned Spirits, 1979, Critical Genealogies, 1987, Huckleberry Finn as Idol and Target, 1997, The Emergence of American Literary Narrative, 2005; editor: The Yale Critics: Deconstruction in America, 1983, Postmodernism and Politics, 1986, After Foucault, 1988, Consequences of Theory, 1990, Macropolitics of 19th Century Literature, 1991; mem. editl. bd. Comparative Lit., 1989—, Am. Lit., 2000-02, Boundary 2: Jour. Postmodern Lit. and Culture, 1979—. Am. Coun. Learned Socs. fellow, 1978-79, NEH fellow, 1986-87, 94-95. Mem. MLA (mem. publs. com. 1997-2000), Soc. Critical Exch. (bd. dirs. 1983-90), English Inst. (mem. supervisory com. 1985-88, chmn. 1987-88), PMLA (mem. adv. com. 1990-94). Office: Columbia U Dept English & Comp Lit 602 Philosophy Hall New York NY 10027 Office Phone: 212-854-3215. Business E-Mail: ja2007@columbia.edu.

ARAD, MICHAEL SAHAR, architect; b. Israel, 1969; arrived in U.S., 1991; s. Moshe and Rivka Arad; m. Melanie Ann Fitzpatrick, 2001; 1 child, Nathaniel. BA, Dartmouth Coll., 1991; MA, Ga. Inst. Tech., 1999. Arch. Kohn Pedersen Fox, 1999—2002; arch. design dept. N.Y.C. Housing Authority, 2002—. With Israeli Def. Force. Named co-winner, World Trade Ctr. Site Meml. Competition, 2003. Office: NYC Housing Authority 250 Broadway New York NY 10007

ARAGON, MANNY M., academic administrator, former state legislator, lawyer; b. Albuquerque, 1948; BA, JD, U. N. Mex. Bar: N.Mex. 1973. State senator 14th dist. N.Mex., 1975—2004; pres. pro tempore N.Mex. State Senate, 1988—2000; pres. N.Mex. Highlands Univ., 2004—. Mailing: New Mexico Highlands Univ Office of the President PO Box 9000 Las Vegas NM 87701*

ARAI, TOSHIHIKO, retired microbiology and immunology educator; b. Niigata, Japan, Sept. 12, 1937; s. Hachiro Sisido and Kazue Arai; m. Hatsue Aoki, Dec. 1, 1963; children: Masako, Tomoko, Kazuhiko. MD, Keio U., Tokyo, 1962; PhD, Keio U., 1968. Instr. dept. microbiology Keio U. Sch. Medicine, 1967-73, asst. prof., 1973-85, assoc. prof., 1985; prof. microbiology and immunology Meiji Coll. Pharmacy, Tokyo, 1985-97; ret., 1997. Rsch. assoc. U. Tex., Dallas, 1970—72; lectr. Ochanomizu U. Sch. Sci., Tokyo, 1978—79, Chiba (Japan) U. Sch. Medicine, 1978—82, Josai Dental U., Sakado, Japan, 1978—87, Aoyama Gakuin U., Tokyo, 1988—2003; cons. Kitasato Inst., Tokyo, 1981—84. Author (15 books); contbr. Mem.: N.Y. Acad. Scis., Am. Soc. Microbiology, Japan Antibiotic Rsch. Assn., Japan Soc. Chemotherapy, Japan Soc. Bacteriology. Zen Buddhist. Home: 5-1-23 Yatsu Narashimo-shi Chiba 275-0026 Japan Office: Kaiyu Clinic #205 Spur 3-3-6 Saginomiya Nakano-ku Tokyo 165-0032 Japan Office Phone: 81-3-5373-0254. E-mail: ya5-1-23@mxm.mesh.ne.jp.

ARAIZA, FRANCISCO (JOSÉ FRANCISCO ARAIZA ANDRADE), opera singer; b. Mexico City, Oct. 4, 1950; s. José and Guadalupe (Andrade) A.; m. Vivian Jaffray, Sept. 30, 1977 (div. 1995); children: José Riccardo, Maria del Carmen Cecilia; m. Ethery Inasaridse, children: Abessalom Rodrigo, Laura Imeda. Grad. in Bus. Adminstrn., U. Mexico City, 1972; grad., Nat. Sch. Music, Mexico City, 1974, Nat. Conservatory, 1974, Musikhochschule, Munich, 1975. Tenor roles (lyric repertory as well as dramatic parts till Wagner's Lohengrin in 1990) include performances in opera hos. Zurich, Munich, Vienna, Rome, Hamburg, Berlin, Milan, London, Parma, Florence, Venice, Barcelona, Madrid, Tokyo, Mexico City, Chgo., San Francisco, N.Y.C.; performed at Salzburg Festival, Bayreuth Festival; numerous recordings include works by Mozart, Rossini, Beethoven, Donizetti, Offenbach, Schubert, Verdi, Puccini, Gounod, Massenet, Weber and others; also six solo albums including opera arias, lieder, popular songs. Recipient Orphée d'Or, 1984, Deutscher Schallplattenpreis, 1984, Otello d'Oro performer prize, 1995, Golden Merkur best performance award, 1996, Mozart medal of Mex., 1991; named Kammersänger of Vienna State Opera, 1988, prof. of the Music and Art Hochschule Stuttgart, Germany, 2003. Address: c/o Elene Tschaidse Opern-und Konzertagentur Tal 28 80331 Munich Germany E-mail: faraiza@aol.com.

ARAKAWA, KASUMI, physician, educator; b. Toyohashi, Japan, Feb. 19, 1926; came to U.S., 1954, naturalized, 1963; s. Masumi and Fayuko (Hattori) A.; m. Juen Hope Takahara, Aug. 27, 1956; children: Jane Riet, Kenneth Luke, Amy Kathryn. MD, Tokyo Med. Coll., 1953; PhD, Showa U., Tokyo, 1984. Diplomate Am. Bd. Anesthesiology. Intern Iowa Meth. Hosp., Des Moines, 1954-56; resident in internal medicine U. Kans. Med. Ctr., Kansas City, 1956-58, instr. anesthesiology, 1961-64, from asst. prof. to prof., 1964-94; prof. emeritus, 1994—; Arakawa Disting. prof. anesthesiology U. Kans. Med. Ctr., Kansas City, 1990, Kasumi Arakawa professorship, 1994, prof. emeritus, 1994—. Clin. assoc. prof. U. Mo.-Kans. City Sch. Dentistry, 1973—; dir. Kansas City Health Care, Inc. Fulbright scholar, 1954; nat. cons. to surgeon gen., USAF, 1990—. Recipient Outstanding Faculty award Student AMA, 1970 Fellow Am. Coll. Anesthesiology; mem. Assn. Univ. Anesthetists, Acad. Anesthesiology (pres. 1986-87), Japan-Am. Soc. Midwest (v.p. 1965, 71). Office: Univ Med Ctr 3901 Rainbow Blvd Kansas City KS 66160-0001 Home: 2190 Rosa Vista Terr Camarillo CA 93012 E-mail: kcarakawa9@aol.com.

ARAKKAL, ANTONY LONA, engineering executive, researcher; b. Kattoor, Kerala, India, Dec. 15, 1937; came to U.S., 1969; s. Lona Joseph and Catherine N. A.; m. Bridget F. Fernandez, Feb. 4, 1967; 1 child, Antony, Jr. BS in Mech. Engring., U. Kerala, 1964; MS, Ill. Inst. Tech., Chgo., 1972. Mgr. mfg. engring. Black & Decker, Tarboro, N.C., 1977-86; pres. Arakkal Enterprises, Inc., Carlisle, Pa., 1986-93; v.p. advanced engring. Airtex Products, Inc., Fairfield, Ill., 1993—. Cons. Fasco, Ozark, Mo., 1986-87, Ametek, Gram, N.C., 1990-91, Penn Ventilator, Phila., 1991, Fawn Industries, Middlesex, N.C., 1992. Mem.: Inst. Indsl. Engrs. (pres. Tri-state chpt.), Soc. Mfg. Engrs. (N.C. chmn. 1985—86), Soc. Auto Engrs. (chmn. St. Louis chpt.), Lions Club (v.p. 1985), Internat. Rotary. Roman Catholic. Achievements include patent for Unipole Motor. Home: RR 3 Box 611E Fairfield IL 62837-9565 Office: Airtex Divsn UIS Fairfield IL 62837

ARAMBEL, PABLO OSCAR, electronics engineer; b. Olavarria, Buenos Aires, Argentina, May 24, 1963; arrived in US, 1991; s. Juan Gabriel Arambel and Elvira Maria Volpi; m. Maria Fernanda Quinteros Rivero, Mar. 30, 1990; children: Andres Fernando, Paula Agustina. Degree in Electronics Engring., U. Nacional de La Plata, 1987; MS, Northeastern U., 1993, PhD, 1995. Asst. lectr. U. Nacional de La Plata, Argentina, 1987—91, rsch. asst., 1988—91, rsch. fellow - asst. prof., 1995—97; rsch. asst. Northeastern U., Boston, 1992—95; rsch. engr. Sci. Sys. Co. Inc., Woburn, Mass., 1997—2002; lead engr. BAE Sys. Advanced Info. Technologies, Burlington, Mass., 2002—, sect. leader, 2002—. Contbr. articles to profl. jours. Fellow, U. Nacional de La Plata - Argentina, 1988—90, Comision de Investigaciones Cientificas - Buenos Aires - Argentina, 1990—91, Consejo Nacional de Investigaciones Cientificas y Tecnicas - Argentina, 1991—93; scholar, Northeastern U.,

Boston, Mass., 1992—95. Mem.: IEEE (mem. exec. com. robotics, power electronics, and control chpt. 1996—97). Office: BAE Systems Advanced Information Tech 6 New England Executive Park Burlington MA 01803 Office Phone: 781-273-3388 349. Office Fax: 781-273-9345. E-mail: pablo.arambel@baesystems.com.

ARAMBURUZABALA, MARIA ASUNCION, food products executive; b. Mexico, May 2, 1963; d. Pablo Aramburuzabala Ocaranza; m. Tony Garza, Feb. 26, 2005; 2 children. BA in Accounting, Technological Inst. of Mexico. Chairwoman Grupo Modelo (brewer of Corona), 1996—; bd. dir. Grupo Televisa, 2000—. Named one of most powerful women, Forbes mag., 2005. Achievements include being Mexico's richest woman. Mailing: Grupo Modelo Campos Elíseos #400 8th Fl Colonia Lomas de Chapultepec 11000 Mexico City Mexico*

ARAMS, FRANK ROBERT, electronics company executive; b. Danzig; came to U.S., 1939, naturalized, 1945; s. Richard and Alice (Frank) A.; m. Edith Knoll, July 24, 1952; children: Mark, Ronald. BEE, U. Mich., 1947; MS in Applied Physics, Harvard U., 1948; MS in Bus. Mgmt, Stevens Inst. Tech., 1953; PhD in Electrophysics, Poly. U. N.Y., 1961. Group leader RCA Microwave div., Harrison, N.J., 1948-56; cons. AIL div. Eaton Corp., Melville, N.Y., 1956-65, head electrooptics and infrared dept., 1965-71; v.p. LNR Communications, Inc., Hauppauge, N.Y., 1971-99, also bd. dirs.; mgmt. cons., patent tech. expert, 2000—. Author: Infrared-to-Millimeter Wave Detectors, 1972; contbr. articles to profl. jours. Served with AUS, 1942-44. Fellow IEEE. Home: 37 School House Ln Great Neck NY 11020-1322

ARANCHUK, VYACHESLAV, research scientist; b. Rashkov, Moldova, Sept. 22, 1958; s. Michail and Lidya Aranchuk; m. Ina Aranchuk, Sept. 11, 1983; 1 child, Tatsiana. BS in Engring., Inst. of Radio Engring., Minsk, 1980; PhD in Engring. Sci., Inst. Applied Physics, Nat. Acad. Scis., Minsk, Belarus, 1989. Sr. scientist Nat. Acad. Sci. Belarus, Minsk, 1989—2001, MetroLaser, Inc., Irvine, Calif., 2002—. Contbr. articles to profl. jours. and conf. proceedings. Achievements include patents for laser Doppler vibrometry. Office: MetroLaser Inc 1 Coliseum Dr Rm1101 University MS 38677

ARAND, FREDERICK FRANCIS, accountant, finance company executive; b. Chgo., Mar. 14, 1954; s. Bernard Anthony and Millicent Catherine (Schweizer) A.; m. Judith Mary Utz, May 22, 1982; children: Joseph, Diana, Thomas, Amanda, Laura. AB, Dartmouth Coll., 1976; MBA, U. Mich., 1978. CPA Mich. Staff acct. Ernst & Young, Chgo., 1978-79, advanced staff acct., 1979-80, sr. staff acct., 1980-82, supr., 1982-85, sr. mgr., 1985—94; contr. Ancilla Sys., Inc., Hobart, Ind., 1994—97, v.p. fin. svcs., 1997—. Bd. dirs. Simmons Ambulance Co., treas., 2004—; bd. dirs. L. Gilbraith SPC Ltd. Leader Jr. Achievement, Wheaton, Ill., 1981-83; mgr., coach Niles Baseball and Soccer Leagues, 1989-94, Park Ridge Softball and Soccer Leagues, 1993-94, Schererville Soccer League, 1994-2004, St. John Softball League, 1996, CYO Soccer League, 1997-2004; adv. bd. St. John Evangelist Sch.; bd. dirs. Schererville Soccer Club, treas., 1998-99; bd. dirs. Gary Cmty. Devel. Corp., treas., 2004-; bd. dirs. PHJC Cmty. Support Trust, St. Joseph Med. Ctr. of Ft. Wayne, St. Mary's Hosp. Health Found., Sisters of Providence Cmty. Support Trust, Gary Cmty. Health Found., Ancilla Ins. Trust, Catherine Kasper Life Ctr., treas. 2004-; bd. dirs. Linden House of Mishowaka, treas. 2004-; bd. dirs. Simmons Ambulance Co., treas. 2004-. Mem. AICPA (grassroots panel, 2003-), Math. Assn. Am., Ill. CPA Soc., Ind. CPA Soc. (leadership cabinet, 2003-), Fin. Mgr. Soc. (mem. fin. mgmt. com. 1986-91, vice chmn. 1987-88, chmn. 1988-90, mem. accounting issues com. 1991-92), Dartmouth Alumni Club, Met. Club, Toastmasters (area gov. 1985-86). Avocations: soccer, golf, tennis, softball. Home: 9123 Olcott Ave Saint John IN 46373-9729 Office: Ancilla Systems Inc 1000 S Lake Park Ave Hobart IN 46342

ARANDA, SANDRA LOUISE, speech pathology/audiology services professional; b. San Jose, Calif., Oct. 7, 1970; d. Peter Mora and Jerry Louise Aranda. BA in Speech-Lang. Pathology, San Jose State U., 1994, MA in Edn. Speech Pathology and Audiology, 1996; cert. in early childhood edn. infants and preschoolers with disabilities, 1996. Speech-lang. pathologist George Mayne Elem. Sch., Santa Clara, 1996—97, Mariano Castro Elem. Sch., Mountain View, 1996—97, Santa Clara Sch. Dist., 1997—98, Mountain View Sch. Dist., 1998—2000, Oak Grove Sch. Dist., San Jose, 2000—. Mem. support staff com. Santa Teresa Elem. Sch., 2000—. Mem.: AAUW, Calif. Speech Hearing Assn. (adv. bd. com. dist. 4 2001—02, Outstanding Achievement award 2003), Santa Clara Speech Hearing Assn. (co-social chair 1997—98, rec. sec. 1999—2000, v.p. 2000—01, pres. 2001—02, past pres. 2002—03), Am. Speech Hearing Assn. Roman Catholic. Avocations: reading, painting, cardio circuit training, animals, aqua aerobics. Home: PO Box 667 Morgan Hill CA 95038 E-mail: cccslplic@aol.com.

ARANGO, JORGE SANIN, architect; b. Bogota, Colombia, Nov. 29, 1916; s. Fernando Arango and Maria Sanin A.; m. Elizabeth Leighton, 1944; 1 child, Peter; m. Judith Brooks Wolpert, Dec. 14, 1951; children: Richard, Virginia; m. Penelope Corey, Aug. 18, 1976. Student, Universidad Catolica de Chile Sch. Architecture, 1935-42, Harvard Grad. Sch. Design, 1942-43. Head archtl. firm Arango & Murtra, Bogota, 1946-59; prof. architecture and urban design Nat. U., Bogota, 1945-47; vis. prof. Sch. Architecture U. Calif., Berkeley, 1956, 58; Pub. bldgs. dir. Colombia, 1948-49; pres. Colombian Soc. Architects, 1946-51, Colegio Engrs. and Architects of Colombia, 1955. Co-creator (with Le Corbusier) basic plan for devel. Bogota, 1948. Author: (with C. Martinez) Architecture in Colombia, 1951, The Urbanization of the Earth, 1970, Segunda Edad Media, 1994, Ecophila: The Future is Waiting, 2000, Villa Sofia, 2003, Jorge Arango-Architect, 2003; mem. bd. contbrs. Miami Herald, 1984-91. Recipient Excellence in Design awards Miami and Fla. chpts. AIA, 1967. Mem. AIA (mem. emeritus). Achievements include being invited to U.S. by State Dept. and Mus. Modern Art, N.Y.C. Home: 5153 SW 71st Pl Miami FL 33155-5640 E-mail: jorge.arango@gte.net.

ARANHA, ASHOK JOSEPH, management consultant; s. Ernest Francis and Stella Aranha. BA in Econs. with hons., York U., 1980; MA in Econs., York U., Toronto, 1983; MBA, U. Chgo., Grad. Sch. Bus., 2004—. Rsch. cons. CIBC World Markets, Toronto, Canada, 1987; sr. economist Ministry Fin., 1988—96; sr. risk analyst Can. Derivatives Clearing Corp., 1996—97; prin. cons. PricewaterhouseCoopers Consulting, Arlington, NYC, 1997—2001; sr. mgr. Arthur Andersen, NYC, 2001—03; mgmt. cons. Fifth Third Bank, Cin., 2003—. Ont. Grad. scholar, York U. Admission scholar, York U. Mem.: Fin. Execs. Networking Group (life), Profl. Risk Mgrs. Internat. Assn. (life). Avocations: travel, fitness, classical music, investing. Office Phone: 513-534-7422.

ARANI, ARDY A., marketing professional, sports association administrator; b. Bklyn., July 14, 1954; BBA, U. Miami, 1975; JD, Loyola U., New Orleans, 1978. Mktg. dir. Internat. Sports Mktg. Ltd., London, 1978-80; mng. dir., CEO Championship Group Inc., Atlanta, 1980—; exec. prodr. Race Day Fox Sports Radio, 2003—. Mem. editl. bd. Sport Mktg. Quar.; contbr. articles to profl. jours. Bd. dirs. Atlanta Sports Coun., 1986-97, Atlanta Olympic Organizing Com., 1988-96; chmn. TEAM Ga. Recipient Reggie Promotions award, Promotion Mktg. Assn. Am., 1999. Mem. Am. Mktg. Assn., Sports Car Club of Am. (Recognition award 1988), Nat. Assn. Stock Car Auto Racing, Am. Motorcycle Assn., Internat. Motor Sports Assn. Home: PO Box 80489 Atlanta GA 30366-0489 Office: Championship Group Inc 1954 Airport Rd Ste 2000 Atlanta GA 30341

ARANOFF, SHARA L., federal agency administrator; m. David Korn; 2 children. BA, Princeton U.; JD, Harvard U. Atty. Steptoe & Johnson LLP; atty. advisor Office Gen. Counsel U.S. Internat. Trade Commn., Washington, 1993—2001, sr. internat. trade counsel, 2001—05, commr., 2005—; mem. senate com. on fin. U.S. Senate, Washington, 2002—05. Office: US Internal Trade Commn 500 E St SW Rm 704 Washington DC 20436 Office Phone: 202-708-2880. Office Fax: 202-205-2798.*

ARANSON, ROBERT, physician; b. Portland, Maine, Dec. 18, 1953; s. Albert and Golde Leah (Rodman) A. BS in Biology, Trinity Coll., 1976; MD, Tufts U., 1980. Diplomate Am. Bd. Internal Medicine-Pulmonary Diseases, Critical Care Medicine. Resident in internal medicine Maine Med. Ctr., Portland, 1980-83; fellow in pulmonary and critical care medicine Albert Einstein Med. Ctr. & Temple U. Hosp., Phila., 1983-85; clin. instr. of medicine Temple U. Sch. of Medicine, Phila., 1983-85, asst. prof. of medicine, 1985-88, Tufts U. Sch. of Medicine, Boston, 1988-93; asst. prof. medicine Emory U. Sch. Medicine, Atlanta, 1993—2000; dir. med. ICU and respiratory care dept. Grady Meml. Hosp., Atlanta, 1993—2000; assoc. prof. cardiopulmonary care scis. Ga. State U., Atlanta, 1993—2000, med. dir. Sch. Respiratory Therapy, 1993—2000; pvt. practice Maine, 2000—04; chief pulmonary critical care and sleep medicine, dir. ICU and respiratory care dept. Parkview Adventist Med. Ctr., Brunswick, Maine, 2005—. Dir. med. respiratory ICU Temple U. Hosp., Phila., 1985-88, St. Elizabeth Hosp., Boston, 1988-93, dir. pulmonary fellowship program; med. physician Phila. Seventy-Sixers Profl. Basketball Team, Phila., 1987-88. Contbr. articles to profl. jours. Fellow ACP, Am. Coll. Chest Physicians; mem. Am. Thoracic Soc., Soc. Critical Care Medicine, Nat. Assn. for Med. Direction of Respiratory Care. Jewish. Avocations: basketball, sailing, skiing. Home: 20 Lookout Dr Freeport ME 04032-6272 Office Phone: 207-373-2303. Business E-Mail: raranson@parkviewamc.org.

ARANT, EUGENE WESLEY, lawyer; b. North Powder, Oreg., Dec. 21, 1920; s. Ernest Elbert and Wanda (Haller) A.; m. Juanita Clark Flowers, Mar. 15, 1953; children: Thomas W., Kenneth E., Richard W. BS in Elec. Engring, Oreg. State U., 1943; JD, U. So. Calif., 1949. Bar: Calif. 1950. Mem. engring. faculty U. So. Calif., 1947-51; pvt. practice L.A., 1950—51; patent atty. Hughes Aircraft Co., Culver City, Calif., 1953-56; pvt. practice L.A., 1957—2001, Lincoln City, Oreg., 2001—. Contbr. articles to profl. jours. Mem. La Mirada (Calif.) City Coun., 1958-60; trustee Beverly Hills Presbyn. Ch., 1976-78. Served with AUS, 1943-46, 51-53. Mem. ABA, Am. Intellectual Property Law Assn., State Bar Calif. Democrat. Home: 100 NE Indian Shores Lincoln City OR 97367 Office: PO Box 269 Lincoln City OR 97367 Office Phone: 541-557-1716. E-mail: gwapat@charterinternet.com.

ARAOZ, DANIEL LEON, psychologist, educator; b. Buenos Aires, Apr. 23, 1930; came to U.S., 1951, naturalized, 1967; s. Jose Daniel and Maria Lia (Suarez) A.; m. Marie Carrese, July 27, 1991; m. Dorita Catherine Smyth, July 17, 1964 (div. 1984); children: Leon Daniel, Nadine Victoria. BA, Gonzaga U., 1953, MA, 1954; MST., U. Santa Clara, 1961; MA, Columbia U., 1964, EdD, 1969; Psychoanalysis Diploma, Am. Inst. for Psychotherapy and Psychoanalysis, 1972. Clin. psychologist, Ill., Pa. Diplomate in counseling psychology and family psychology Am. Bd. Profl. Psychology; diplomate in clin. hypnosis Am. Bd. Psychol. Hypnosis. Asst. chaplain Coll. Mt. St. Vincent, Bronx, N.Y., 1962-64; psychotherapist Cmty. Guidance Svc., N.Y.C., 1965-72, supr., 1972-82; faculty Am. Inst. Psychotherapy and Psychoanalysis, N.Y.C., 1972-82; assoc. prof. counseling L.I. U., 1973-82, prof., 1982—, chmn. dept. counseling and devel., 1995-97. Dir. L.I. Inst. Ericksonian Hypnosis, 1992-97. Editor-in-chief Am. Jour. Family Therapy, 1973-76, jour. adv., 1977—; author: Hypnosis and Sex Therapy, 1982, 98; Hypnosex, 1982; Self-Transformation Through the New Hypnosis, 1984; The New Hypnosis, 1985, 95, The New Hypnosis in Family Therapy, 1987; Selbst Hypnose: Kreative Imagination in Beruf und Alltag, 1992, Reengineering Yourself, 1994, Solution-Oriented Brief Therapy for Adjustment Disorders, 1996, Power Over Stress at Work, 1998, The Symptom is not the Whole Story, 2006; co-editor: Hypnosis Questions & Answers, 1986; contbr. articles to profl. jours. Named Hon. Prof. U. peruana Cayetano Heredia, Lima, Peru. Fellow APA, Am. Inst. Psychotherapy and Psychoanalysis, Am. Soc. Psychosomatic Dentistry and Medicine, Acad. Counseling Psychology, Acad. Family Psychology; mem. Am. Assn. Sex Educators, Counselors and Therapists (diplomate), Am. Assn. Marriage and Family Therapy (supr. 1973—), Pa. Psychol. Assn., Ill. Psychol. Assn., Nassau County Psychol. Assn., Am. Mgmt. Assn. (unit trainer 1987-94), Soc. Clin. and Exptl. Hypnosis Home: 66 Gates Ave Malverne NY 11565-1912 Office: LI U CW Post Northern Blvd Greenvale NY 11548-1207 Office Phone: 516-299-2213. Business E-Mail: daniel.araoz@liu.edu.

ARASAKESARI, SUBRAMANIAM, chemical engineer, research scientist, consultant; US, 1987; s. S. and Chittal Arasakesari. BE Pulp & Paper, Indian Inst. of Tech., Roorkee, India, 1987; MS Paper Sc, Western Mich. U., Kalamazoo, Mich., 1990; PhD, U. Wash., Seattle, Wash., 1994. Lead developer Andritz Inc., Atlanta, 1995—2000; process tech. cons. MeadWestvaco Corp, Chillicothe, Ohio, 2000—02; process modeling cons. Procter & Gamble Corp, W. Chester, Ohio, 2002—. Contbr. articles pub. to profl. jour. Recipient Creative Rsch. Scholar, Western Mich. U., 1990, Outstanding Contr., Procter & Gamble Corp, 2004. Mem.: IPPTA, TAPPI (chmn., process engg 2000—). Achievements include first to Advanced pulping model & digester optimizer. Home: 8332 Landmark Ct Apt 101 West Chester OH 45069 Office: Procter & Gamble Corp 8256 Union Ctr Blvd Mail stop IP352 Wset Chester OH 45069 Office Phone: 513-627-0968. Office Fax: 513-634-9439. Personal E-Mail: mani287@gmail.com. Business E-Mail: arasakesari.s@pg.com.

ARAUJO, ILKA VASCONCELOS, musicologist, educator; arrived in U.S., 1997; d. Jose Mario and Maria Cleomar Vasconcelos Araujo; m. Aleksa Jovanovic, Sept. 18, 2004; 1 child, Isabella Araujo. Tech. Level, Conservatory Music Alberto Nepomuceno, Fortaleza, CE, Brazil, 1989; BMus in Piano Performance, State U. Ceara, Fortaleza, Brazil, 1995; MMus in Piano Performance and Pedagogy, U. Fla., Gainesville, 2001, PhD in Musicology, 2005. Piano and theory tchr. Juvenal de Carvalho H.S., Fortaleza, Brazil, 1993—94; piano tchr. Conservatory Music Alberto Nepomuceno, 1994—95, State U. Ceara, 1994—95; pianist and accompanist Maninha Mota Voice Sch., 1996—97; grad. tchg. asst. U. Fla., Gainesville, 1997—. Choir dir. Friends of Music Soc., Fortaleza, Brazil, 1992—93; co-director and cofounder Brazilian choir Brazilian Student Assn., Gainesville, Fla., 1997—2000; asst. mgr. Prague Internat. Piano Master Classes, Czech Republic, 1998—2001; pvt. instr. piano and accompanist, Gainesville, 1998—; co-organizer events, hostess and translator U. Fla. Sch. Music, 1998—, rep. grad. student coun., 2002—03. Composer: Instants, 2001— (3rd prize Fla. Juried Arts Exhbn., 2002); musician (pianist and lectr.): The Subjective Nationalitic Aspects in Liszt, Villa-Lobos and Ginastera, 2003, 20th Century Compositional Vocabulary featuring works by Villa-Lobos, Ginastera, and Ilka Araujo, 2004, Works of Schubert, Liszt, and Ginastera, 2004; musician: (pianist) Sonata No. 4 by Prokoviev, 2001, Works by Scriabin, Liszt, Villa-Lobos and Ilka Araujo, 2003, Vallee D'Obermann by Liszt, 2004, Works by Schubert, Liszt, Villa-Lobos, and Ginastera, 2004, Works by Villa-Lobos and Ginastera, 2004, Works by Liszt, Villa-Lobos, and Ginastera, 2004; musician: (master class presenter) Conservatory of Music and State Univ. Ceara, 2004, Music Acad.; performer: Programa do Jo, 2004; contbr. scientific papers in musicology. Vol. pianist The Village, Gainesville, Fla., 1999—2000, The Atrium; pianist Lochloosa United Meth. Ch., Hawthorne United Meth. Ch., Hawthorne, Fla., 2000, Dunnellon Presbyn. Ch., 2003; pres. Brazilian Student Assn., Gainesville, Fla., 1998—99, v.p., 1999—2000. Named an Internat. Female Leader, Women's Leadership Conf., Gainesville, 2005; recipient First prize, Piano Competition Young Instrumentalists Festival, Brazil, 1994, Paurillo Barrozo Piano Competition, Brazil, 1995, Alec Courtelis Award, 2004, Presdl. award Outstanding Achievement and Contibn., U. Fla., 1999, 2000, Oustanding Student Recognition, U. Fla. Ctr. Internat. Studies, 1998, 2000, Student Academic award, U. Fla. Coll. Fine Arts, 1998, 2000; Grad. Tchg. assistantship, U. Fla., 1997—. Mem.: Nat. Guild Piano Teachers Assn., Soc. Composers Inc., Coll. Music Soc., Am. Music Soc., Phi Lambda Beta, Pi Kappa Lambda. Avocations: swimming, travel, reading. Office Phone: 352-392-0223.

ARAUJO-PRADERE, EDUARDO A., geophysicist, researcher; b. Havana, Cuba, May 9, 1960; s. Leopoldo E. Araujo-Bernal and Elsa R. Pradere-Campos; m. Alma V. Fernandez-Cabral, Mar. 28, 1995; children: David R. Araujo-Gonzalez, Victor E. Araujo-Fernandez. MSc, UNAM, 1995, PhD, 1998. Physics instr. Front Range C.C., Boulder, 1999—; rsch. scientist CIRES-U. Colo., Boulder, 1996—. Cons. U. Corp. Atmospheric Rsch., Boulder, 2003—. Mem. Boulder Coun. Internat. Vis., 2003. Recipient Gabino Barreda Meml. medal, Academic Merit, Regents of UNAM, 1997, Hon. Mention award, 1995. Mem.: Latin Am. Assn. of Space Geophysics, Am. Geophys. Union. Achievements include research and development of the Storm Time Ionospheric Empirical Model. Office: CIRES-U Colo 325 Broadway R/SEC Boulder CO 80305

ARBABI, SAMAN, surgeon, researcher; b. Aug. 28, 1966; s. Esmail and Shahnaz Arbabi; m. Sielen S. Namdar, Aug. 16, 1998; 1 child, Kavon. BA, U. Calif., 1988, MD, 1992; MPH, U. Wash., 2001. Diplomate in gen. surgery and in surg. critical care Am. Bd. Surgery. Resident in surgery U. of Wash., Seattle, 1992—97, rsch. fellow, 1997—2001; fellow critical care and trauma Harborview and U. Wash., Seattle, 1999—2001; asst. prof. surgery U. Mich. Health Sys., Ann Arbor, Mich., 2002—. Mem.: Am. Assn. for Surgery Trauma (Jr. Faculty Rsch. award 2003, 2004), Am. Bd. Surgery (Best Regional Paper award 2001), Surg. Infection Soc. (assoc. Jr. Faculty Rsch. award 2003). Office: University of Michigan Health System 1C421 UH Box 0033 1500 E Medical Driv Ann Arbor MI 48109 Office Phone: 734-936-9666. E-mail: sarbabi@med.umich.edu.

ARBELBIDE, C(INDY) L(EA), historian, author; b. Stockton, Calif., Aug. 4, 1949; d. Garrett Walter and Fern Mable (Lea) A. AA in History, Santa Barbara City Coll., Calif., 1969; BS in Health & Phys. Edn., Oreg. State U., 1972; M in Libr. Sci., Emporia State U., 1980; cert., Nat. Crisis Response Team Tng. Inst., 1991. Tchr. Petersburg (Ala.) Sch. System, 1972-73, Santa Barbara (Calif.) Sch. System, 1973-74, Linn Benton Community Coll., Oreg. State U., Albany, Corvallis, 1974-75, Can. Acad., Kobe, Japan, 1975-76; tchr., libr. Wichita (Kans.) Pub. Schs., 1976-81; mgr. Geol. Info. Libr., Dallas, 1982-84; coord., cons. North Tex. Libr. System, Ft. Worth, 1984-86; dir. libr., rsch. svcs. Nat. Victim Ctr., Ft. Worth, 1986-91; dir. tng., coord. tng. all insts. Nat. Orgn. for Victim Assistance, Washington, 1991-95. Cons. Nat. Cmty. Response Team, N.J., Tex., 1992, FBI, Washington, 1994, NOVA, 1995. Author: Librarian's PLanning Handbook, 1986, National Library Resource Project on Crime Victimization, 1988, 89, Child Safety Curriculum Standards, 1989, The Story of Presidential Christmas Cards and Gift Prints, 1996, Diary of a White House Squirrel, 1996, The White House Easter Egg Roll, 1997. Named Woman of the Month Ladies Home Jour., 1973; recipient Yellow Rose of Tex. award Gov. Tex., 1992, Outstanding Contbn. letter U.S. Army, 1993, Recognition and Appreciation cert. Concerns of Police Survivors, 1994. Mem. ALA, Am. Assn. Law Librs., Spl. Librs. Assn. (chairperson catalog com. 1990-91, chairperson social sci. div. roundtable health and human svcs. 1990), Nat. Victim Ctr., Tex. Libr. Assn. (vice chairperson div. spl. librs. 1987-88, chairperson 1988-89), Critical Incident Stress Debriefing Soc. Internat. Assn. Trauma Counselors, Nat. Cmty. Crisi Response Team. Home and Office: 147 Dogwood Blossom Ln Front Royal VA 22630 Office: PO Box 55 Washington VA 22747

ARBER, WERNER, microbiologist; b. Gränichen, Switzerland, June 3, 1929; married; 2 children. Ed., Aargau (Switzerland) Gymnasium, Eidgenössische Technische Hochschule, Zurich, 1949—53. Asst. Lab. Biophysics, U. Geneva, 1953—58, docent, then extraordinary prof. molecular genetics, 1962—70; research assoc. dept. microbiology U. So. Calif., 1958—59; vis. investigator dept. molecular biology U. Calif., Berkeley, 1970—71; prof. microbiology U. Basel, Switzerland, 1971—96, rector, 1986—88. Co-recipient Nobel Prize for physiology or medicine, 1978. Mem.: Internat. Coun. Sci. (pres. 1996—99), Nat. Acad. Scis. (assoc.). Office: Biozentrum der Universität 70 Klingelbergstrasse CH-4056 Basel Switzerland E-mail: Werner.Arber@unibas.ch.

ARBIQUE, DEBBIE ANITA, emergency nurse practitioner; b. Halifax, N.S., Can. arrived in U.S., 1992; d. George Robert and Anita Marie (Jeannette) Renner; m. Gary Michael Arbique, Oct. 14, 1978; 1 child, Matthew Paul. RNA, Dartmouth Regional Vocat. Sch., N.S., 1976; RN, Algonquin Coll., Pembroke, Ont., Can., 1987; student in Nursing, Tex. Women's U., 2004—. Cert. chemotherapy treatment Parkland Hosp., instr. Am. Heart Inst., lic. emergency nursing pediats. course Emergency Nurses Assn., CPR instr. Am. Heart Inst., radiation surveyor Atomic Energy of Can. Ltd., oper. rm. technician Victoria Gen. Hosp., diplomate Am. Bd. Forensic Nursing; RN State of Tex., critical care, Algonquin Coll., cert. competence, Ont. Nursing asst. Halifax Infirmary Hosp., 1976—78; oper. rm. technician Victoria Gen. Hosp., Halifax, 1978—80; nursing asst. Deep River (Ont.) and Dist. Hosp., 1980—86, nurse, 1987—89, Pembroke Civic Hosp., 1988—90; radiation surveyor Atomic Energy of Can. Ltd., Chalk River, 1990—92; emergency dept. mgr., hosp. nursing supr., emergency dept. coord., emergency dept. nurse level III Charlton Meth. Hosp., Dallas, 1992—96; emergency dept. nurse, CPR and ACLS instr., med. tech. cons., hosp. nursing supr., with nursing edn. dept. St. Pauls Med. Ctr., Dallas, 1996—; agy. nurse USA Pers. Inc., Dallas, 1998—2001; ind. legal nurse cons., 1997—; rsch. nurse U. Tex. Southwestern Med. Ctr. at Dallas, 1996—98, clin. case mgr., rsch. nurse, rsch. coord., 1998—. Com. mem. Dallas Nursing Leadership Orgns. Coalitions, St. Paul Emergency Dept. Improvement Team, U. Tex. Southwestern Nursing Peer Rev. Com.; mem. ad hoc com. St. Paul Univ. Hosp. Contbr. articles to med. jours. Named Clin. Nurse Category finalist for Tex. Nursing Excellence award, HealthWeek Publ., 2000; recipient Nursing Excellence award, St. Paul Med. Ctr., 2001. Mem.: Tex. Nurse Practioners Assn., Case Mgmt. Soc. Am., Tex. Nurses Assn., Internat. Assn. Forensic Nurses, Am. Heart Assn. (CV nursing sci. coun.), Am. Coll. Cardiovasc. Nursing, Am. Assn. Legal Nurse Consultants (mem. Dallas chpt.), Emergency Nurses Assn. (cert. trauma nurse), Phi Kappa Phi, Phi Theta Kappa. Home: 613 Deer Creek Dr Desoto TX 75115 Office: U Tex Southwestern Med Ctr at Dallas 5323 Harry Hines Blvd Dallas TX 75390-8586

ARBISSER, ATON, lawyer; AB magna cum laude, Princeton U., 1978; MA in Economics, JD, U. Calif., Berkeley, 1982. Bar: NY 1984, Calif. 1990. Assoc., antitrust practice Kaye Scholer, Los Angeles, Calif., 1983—, now ptnr., antitrust & product liability groups. Mem.: ABA (ed. bd. mem., antitrust law devel., antitrust section 1989—92, vice-chmn. Robinson-Patman act com., antitrust section 1993—94), Los Angeles County Bar Assn. (exec. com., trade regulations section 1992—93), Calif. State Bar Assn. Office: Kaye Scholer 1999 Ave of Stars Ste 1700 Los Angeles CA 90067-6048 Office Phone: 310-788-1000. Office Fax: 310-788-1200. Business E-Mail: aarbisser@kayescholer.com.

ARBIT, BRUCE, direct marketing executive, consultant; b. Milw., Nov. 16, 1954; s. Saul B. and Naomi (Chase) A.; m. Tanya Arbit; children: Oren, Carmiel, Eugene. Student, U. Haifa, Israel, U. Wis. Founder, co-mgr., dir. A B Data, Ltd., Milw., 1977—. Chmn., bd. dirs. Integrated Mail Industries Ltd., Asset Devel. Group, Inc.; bd. dirs. State Fin. Bank, Integrated Mail Industries Israel, Ltd.; chmn. Fox Point Capital, LLC, Fox Point Credit Corp Pres., gen. campaign chmn., bd. dirs. Milw. Jewish Fedn. Keshet, Milw. Jewish Day Sch., Habonim Dror Found.; mem. United Jewish Appeal Young Leadership Cabinet; mem. Wexner Heritage Found., United Israel Appeal., Non-profit Mailers Fedn., Campaign Cabinet Devel. Corp. for Israel; trustee United Israel Appeal; bd. dirs., Jewish Telegraphic Agy.; bd. govs. Jewish Agy. for Israel; mem. nom. com. United Jewish Communities. Recipient Benjamin E. Nickoll Young Leadership award Milw. Jewish Fedn., 1989. Mem. Direct Mktg. Assn., Israel Direct Mktg., Wis. Direct Mktg. Assn. (Direct Marketer of Yr. award 1997), Am. Assn. Polit. Cons. Office: AB Data Ltd 8050 N Port Washington Rd Milwaukee WI 53217-2600 Business E-Mail: barbit@abdata.com.

ARBOGAST, GORDON WADE, systems engineer, educator, consultant, retired military officer; b. Charleston, S.C., May 24, 1942; s. Valentine and Teresa Louise Arbogast; m. Dorothy Sheryl Blackwell, Mar. 5, 1966; children: Annette Marie, Christina Theresa, Valentine Scott. BS, U.S. Mil. Acad., 1963; MSEE, MSIM, Ga. Inst. Tech., 1971; PhD, Clemson U., 1986. Commd. 2d lt. U.S. Army, 1963, advanced through grades to col., 1983, ret., 1990; head, assoc. prof. dept. engring. U.S. Mil. Acad., 1986-89; assoc. dir. engring. and tech. Def. Comm. Agy., 1989-90; v.p. sys. tech. Pacific Bell, San

Ramon, Calif., 1991—94; prof. Jacksonville (Fla.) U., 1994—. Prin. scientist Contel, Chantilly, Va., 1990; instr., cons. Miller Electric, Jacksonville, 1999—2000; instr., cons., ednl. advisor Scott McCrae Group, Jacksonville, 2003—; instr., cons. Jacksonville Jaguars, Jacksonville, 2004—05. Contbr. articles to profl. jours. Lector, eucharistic min. Cursillo Cath. Ch., 1988—2004. Decorated Legion of Merit, Bronze Star, Air medal, Def. Superior Svc. medal. Mem.: Armed Forces Comm.-Electronics Assn. (pres. West Point chpt. 1987—89), Inst. Indsl. Engrs. (sr.), West Point Soc. of North Fla. (pres. 1998—2001). Achievements include initiating systems engineering at U.S. Military Academy and major work in transforming Defense Communications Agency to Defense Information Systems Agency. Home: 9937 Orchard Hills Rd Jacksonville FL 32256 Office: Jacksonville U Davis Coll Bus 2800 University Blvd N Jacksonville FL 32211-3394 Business E-Mail: garboga@ju.edu.

ARBUTHNOT, ROBERT MURRAY, lawyer; b. Montreal, Quebec, Can., Oct. 23, 1936; s. Leland Claude and Winnifred Laura (Hodges) A.; m. Janet Marie O'Keefe, Oct. 6, 1968; children: Douglas, Michael, Mary Kathleen, Allison Anne. BA, Calif. State U., San Francisco, 1959; JD, U. Calif., San Francisco, 1966. Bar: Calif. 1967, U.S. Dist. Ct. (no. and cen. dists.) Calif. 1967, U.S. Ct. Appeals (9th cir.) 1967, U.S. Supreme Ct. 1975. Assoc. trial lawyer Rankin & Craddick, Oakland, Calif., 1967-69; assoc. atty. Ericksen, Arbuthnot, Brown, Kilduff & Day, Inc., San Francisco, 1970-73, ptnr., 1973-80, chmn. bd., mng. dir., 1980—. Gen. counsel CFS Ins. Svcs., San Francisco, 1990—; pro tem judge, arbitrator San Francisco Superior Ct., 1990—; lectr. in field. Bd. regents St. Mary's Coll. High Sch., Berkeley, Calif., 1988-91. With U.S. Army, 1959-62. Recipient Honors plaque St. Mary's Coll. High Sch., 1989. Mem. Internat. Assn. of Ins. Counsel, No. Calif. Assn. of Def. Counsel, Def. Rsch. Inst., Assn. Trial Lawyers Am., San Francisco Lawyers Club. Avocations: boating, family activities. Office: Ericksen Arbuthnot Kicduff Et Al 111 Sutter St #575 San Francisco CA 94104 E-mail: eakdlsf@aol.com.

ARBUZ, JOSEPH ROBERT, lawyer; b. N.Y.C., Nov. 23, 1949; s. Jose Hernan Cortes and Rachel Dweck Arbuz; m. Millicent Luck Fornah July, 1978 (div.); 1 child, Christina. BA, Fla. State U., 1972, MS in Pub. Adminstrn., 1975; JD, Howard U., 1977; MDiv, Southwestern Bapt. Sem., 1981; postgrad. in theology, Westminster Theol. Sem., 1995; D Divinity, Cohen U. & Theol. Sem., 2000. Bar: Fla. 1978, U.S. Ct. Mil. Appeals 1983, U.S. Dist. Ct. (so. dist.) Fla. 1986, U.S. Ct. Appeals (11th cir.) 2000, U.S. Supreme Ct., 2000; lic. min. So. Bapt. Ch., 1982—. EEO investigator Smithsonian Instn., Washington, 1985; asst. atty. gen. Atty. Gen., Miami, Fla., 1986; pvt. practice Miami, Fla., 1987-90, Miami Beach, Fla., 1994—. Evangelism Gambrell St. Bapt. Ch., Ft. Worth, 1980; pastor Biscayne Bapt. Ch., Miami, 1989; choir mem. U. Bapt. Ch., Coral Gables, Fla., 1994-97; performer Miami Christmas Pageant, Miami, 1994, 96; asst. staff judge advocate. 1st lt. Signal Corps., U.S. Army, 1972-74; capt. USAF, 1982-84. J.F.K. Tchg. scholar Miami-Dade C.C., Miami, 1969. Mem. Atty. Title Ins. Fund, South Fla. Hispanic C. of C., Dade County Bar Assn. Democrat. Presbyterian. Avocations: exercise, theater, reading, church activities. Office: PO Box 398843 Miami Beach FL 33239-8843 Office Phone: 305-673-2695. E-mail: joearbuz@aol.com.

ARCANGEL, CORY, computer technician, artist; B in Tech. in Music & Related Arts, Oberlin Coll. Founding mem. BIEGE Programming Ensemble, The 8-bit Construction Set. Curator (distributed on floppy disk, group shows) 1.44 Megs, with Moving Image Gallery & Rhizome.org, (web exhibitions) Low Level All Stars, Kingdom of Piracy; exhibitions include, NY Underground Film Festival, Fassbender Gallery, Chgo., Deadtech Gallery, Chgo., Foxy Production, Eye Beam, Am. Mus. Moving Image, NY, Royal Acad., London, Guggenheim, New Mus. Contemporary Art, Mus. Modern Art, NY, Lothringer13, Make-World Festival, Munich, Leroy Neiman Gallery, Columbia U., 2004, Migros Mus., Zurich, 2004, exhibited in group shows at Whitney Biennial Am. Art, Whitney Mus. Am. Art, 2004, exhibitions include, Deitch Projects, 2005. Grantee, turbulence.org, NY State Coun. Arts. Mailing: c/o Team Gallery 527 West 26th St New York NY 10001 E-mail: cory@gmail.com.*

ARCE, A. ANTHONY, psychiatrist, educator; b. San Juan, P.R., June 13, 1923; s. Angel and Juana (Baez) A.; m. Malvene Balkind, Oct. 7, 1971; children— Alan I. Scheer, Judith Ann Scheer, Michael Anthony Arce. BS, Washington and Jefferson Coll., 1942; MD, Temple U., 1946. Diplomate: Am. Bd. Psychiatry and Neurology; certified in adminstrv. psychiatry. Intern Mercy Hosp., Bay City, Mich. and; Frankford Hosp., Phila., 1946-47; dir. Aguadilla (P.R.) Dist. Hosp., 1947-48; chief health officer Utuado, P.R., 1950-51; physician U.S. Mil. Acad., West Point, N.Y., 1951-52; med. officer Pa. R.R., 1952-53; practice medicine Yonkers, N.Y., 1953-59; resident psychiatrist Payne Whitney Clinic, N.Y.C., 1959-62; assoc. dir. psychiatry Grasslands Hosp., Valhalla, N.Y., 1962-67; dir. psychiatry Lincoln Hall Sch., Lincolndale, N.Y., 1967-68; dir. Bur. Aftercare Services N.Y. State Dept. Mental Hygiene, 1968-71; dir. Manhattan Psychiat. Center, Ward's Island, N.Y., 1971-76, Hahnemann Community Mental Health and Mental Retardation Center, Phila., 1976-84; pvt. practice medicine specializing in psychiatry, 1962—; prof. psychiatry, dep. chmn. dept. mental health svcs. Hahnemann U., 1976-85, prof., chmn., 1985-87, prof., dir. amb. svcs., 1987-91; prof., dep. chmn. dept. psychiatry Med. Coll., U. Pa., Phila., 1991-96; chmn. dept. behavioral medicine Girard Med. Ctr., Phila., 1996—. Mem. president's council N.Y. U. Sch. Social Work, 1963-66; bd. dirs. P.R. Family Inst., N.Y.C., 1970-72. Served with AUS, 1943-46, 48-50. Mem. Am. Coll. Mental Health Adminstrs., Am. Coll. Psychiatrists, Am. Psychiat. Assn. (chmn. task force continuing care), Phila. Psychiat. Soc., Am. Assn. Psychiat. Adminstrs. (treas., pres.). Home: 1416 Academy Ln Elkins Park PA 19027-2515 Office: Girard Med Ctr 2ADC 8th St & Girard Ave Philadelphia PA 19122-9999 Office Phone: 215-787-2410. Business E-Mail: aarce@nphs.com.

ARCE, PHILLIP WILLIAM, hotel and casino executive; b. N.Y.C., June 25, 1937; s. Joseph F. and Margaret (Degnan) A.; m. Dorothy Fiss, June 25, 1966; children: Joseph, William, Serena. Student, U. Notre Dame, 1955-56; AA, San Diego Jr. Coll., 1958; student, San Diego State U., 1958-60, San Diego U., 1960-62, LaSalle Law Sch., 1963-65. Various positions Del Webb Corp., Las Vegas and Reno, Nev., Oahu, Hawaii, 1963-75; exec. Caesars Palace, Las Vegas, 1975-78; pres. Frontier Hotel, Las Vegas, 1978-84; corp. v.p., v.p. mktg., sr. v.p. Dunes Hotel & Country Club, Las Vegas, 1985-88; hotel and gaming specialist Arce Cons., Las Vegas, 1988—. Tchr. hotel div. U. Nev., Las Vegas, 1966-67, 1976-77 Mem. exec. com. Boulder Dam Area coun. Boy Scouts Am., 1976-88; vice chmn. United Way So. Nev., 1968-70; founder, chmn. Las Vegas Events, Inc., 1980-89; pres. Easter Seals Nev., 1974-76, pres. first nat. telethon, 1975; bd. dirs. Air Force Acad. Found., 1982-89. Served with USMC, 1962. Recipient numerous awards including Appreciation awards Easter Seals, 1972, 73, United Way, 1975, Silver Beaver Boy Scouts Am., 1984 Mem. Am. Hotel and Motel Assn. (bd. dirs. 1979-82), Nev. Hotel and Motel Assn. (founder, pres. 1980, Hotelier of Yr. award 1981), Las Vegas C. of C. (dir. 1979-85, pres. 1984). Republican. Roman Catholic. Home: 4243 Ridgecrest Dr Las Vegas NV 89121-4949 also: Colo Belle Hotel & Casino PO Box 77000 Laughlin NV 89028-7000 Office Phone: 702-298-4000.

ARCENEAUX, WILLIAM, historian, educator, educational association administrator; b. Scott, La., Aug. 19, 1941; s. Teddy and Regina (Begnaud) A.; m. Patricia Boozman; children: Ted, Angelle, Leah, Scott. BA, U. La., Lafayette, 1962; MA, La. State U., 1965, PhD, 1969; LHD, Loyola U., 1982. Instr. La. State U., 1966-67; asst. prof. Northwestern State U., Natchitoches, La., 1967-69; assoc. prof., chmn. dept. history So. U., New Orleans, 1969-72; exec. dir. La. Coordinating Council for Higher Edn., 1972-75; commr. higher edn. La. Baton Rouge, 1975-87; pres. La. Assn. Ind. Colls. and Univs., 1987—. Chmn. CSLA, Inc., Lajeunesse & Assocs., Inc. Author: Acadian General-Alfred Mouton and the Civil War, 1972, 2d edit., 1981, No Spark of Malice: The Murder of Martin Begnaud, 1999; editor: Postsecondary Education in Transition: Planning for Change in Louisiana, 1975. Bd. dirs., chmn. Student Loan Mktg. Assn., 1979-97; chmn. La. Found. La., 1993—; exec. com. La. Pub. Broadcasting, chair La. Bicentennial Com. of Baton Rouge. Decorated chevalier L'Ordre de la Pleiade, Association Internationale des Parlementaires de Langue Francaise, L'Ordre des Palmes Academique (France); named one of 100 Young Leaders of Academy Change mag., 1978; recipient Jefferson Davis medal UDC, E.T. Dunlap medal Southeastern Okla. State U. Mem.: La. Hist. Assn., World Trade Ctr. New Orleans, Am. Hist. Assn., Nat. Assn. Ind. Coll. and Univ. State Execs., Plimsol Club, City Club of Baton Rouge (bd. govs.), Country Club of La., Phi Alpha Theta, Omicron Delta Kappa. Roman Catholic. Office: La Assn Ind Colls and Univs Ste 104 320 Third St Baton Rouge LA 70801 Business E-Mail: bill@laicu.org.

ARCHABAL, NINA M(ARCHETTI), historic site director; b. Long Branch, N.J., Apr. 11, 1940; d. John William and Santina Matilda (Giuffre) Marchetti; m. John William Archabal, Aug. 8, 1964; 1 child, John Fidel. BA in Music History cum laude, Radcliffe Coll., 1962; MAT in Music History, Harvard U., 1963; PhD in Music History, U. Minn., 1979. Asst. dir. humanities art mus. U. Minn., Mpls., 1975-77; asst. supr. edn. divsn. Minn. Hist. Soc., St. Paul, 1977-78, dep. dir. for program mgmt., 1978-86, acting dir., 1986-87, dir., 1987—. Bd. dirs. U.S. nat. com. Internat. Coun. Mus. V.p. Friends of St. Paul Pub. Libr., 1983-93; Minn. state hist. preservation officer, 1987—; chair State Hist. Records Adv. Bd., 1987—, St. Anthony Falls Heritage Bd., 1988—; trustee, bd. dirs. Am. Folklife Ctr., Libr. of Congress, 1989-98; bd. dirs. N.W. Area Found., 1989-98, St. Paul Acad. and Summit Sch., 1993-2002, St. Paul Riverfront Corp., 2000-03, Rsch. Librs. Group, 2004—; bd. regents St. John's U., Collegeville, Minn., 1997-2004; overseer Harvard Coll., Cambridge, Mass., 1997—; mem. bd. overseers Hill Mus. and Manuscript Libr., 2004—. NDEA fellow U. Minn., 1969-72, U. Minn. grad. fellow, 1974-75; recipient Nat. Humanities medal The White House, 1997. Mem. Am. Assn. State and Local History (sec. 1986-88), Am. Assn. Mus. (v.p. 1991-94, chair bd. dirs. 1994-96). Office: Minn Hist Soc 345 Kellogg Blvd W Saint Paul MN 55102-1906 Office Phone: 651-296-6126.

ARCHAMBAULT, NICOLE MARIE, speech pathology/audiology services professional, consultant; b. Anaheim, Calif., Nov. 24, 1973; d. Guy Rene and Donna Jean Archambault. BA in Speech and Hearing Scis., Wash. State U., 1996; MS in Speech and Hearing Scis., U. N.Mex, 1999. Cert. clin. competence speech-lang. pathology Am. Speech-Language Hearing Assn., 2000, lic. speech-lang. pathologist Calif. Speech-Language Pathology and Audiology Bd., 2000, Nev. Bd. of Examiners for Audiology and Speech Pathology, 1999, cert. Hanen Centre, 2002, interior decorator Decorator Tng. Inst., 2005. Speech-language pathologist The Continuum, Reno, 1999—; pediatric speech-language pathologist Cedars Sinai Med. Ctr., L.A.; owner, dir. Talk For Tots, Santa Monica. Cons. Step By Step Early Childhood Devel. Ctr., Benjamin Links; sr. cons. Little Lima Bean Prodns.; co-owner Kids Places & Spaces Integrative Develop. Design Co., 2005—. Maynard Lee Daggy scgikar, Wash. State U., 1995, All-Am. scholar, U.S. Achievement Acad., 1996. Mem.: Internat. Mind, Brain, & Edn. Soc., Nat. Coalition Auditory Processing Disorders, Calif. Speech and Hearing Assn., Am. Speech-Lang. Hearing Assn. (Continuing Edn. award 2003), Acad. Neurological Comm. Disorders and Sci. (assoc.), Soc. Children's Book Writers and Illustrators (assoc.), Golden Key Nat. Honor Soc. Office: Talk For Tots 1814 14th St Ste 210 Santa Monica CA 90404

ARCHANGELSKY, DMITRY A., application developer, researcher; b. Kharkov, Ukraine, Nov. 29, 1960; s. Cecilia V and Avenir L Archangelsky; m. Svetlana V Loganova; 1 child, Alexander D. PhD, St.Petersburg State U., 1993. Assoc. prof. Tver State U., Tver, Russia, 1995—99; cons. Global Consulting Group, Haverhill, Mass., 1999—. Contbr. articles to profl. jours. Grant, Internat. Sci. Fund, Russian Fund of Fundamental Researches. Mem.: Am. Math. Soc. (assoc.), NY Acad. Of Sciences (assoc.). Achievements include invention of algorithm of person identification using blood vessel picture; algorithm of understanding of a natural language in a given context; development of a system for computer text book development; research in polinomial algorithm for BR-nets. Home: S Apt 2 10604 16th Ave Ct S Tacoma WA 98444-7013 Personal E-mail: dm_ar@hotmail.com.

ARCHBOLD, MICHALE G., transportation executive; BSc in Acctg., Fairfield U. Various fin. positions Woolworth Corp., 1988—96; v.p., CFO Booksellers Divsn. Barnes & Noble, Inc., 1996—2002; sr. v.p. Autozone, Memphis, 2002—, CFO, 2002—. Office: Autozone PO Box 2198 Memphis TN 38101-9842

ARCHER, ANNE, actress; b. L.A., Aug. 25, 1947; d. John and Marjorie (Lord) A.; m. Terry Jastrow; children: Thomas, Jeffrey. Actor: (theatre) A Coupla White Chicks Sitting Around Talking, 1981, Les Liaisons Dangereuses, 1988, The Poison Tree, (films) The Honkers, 1972, Cancel My Reservation, 1972, The All-American Boy, 1973, Trackdown, 1976, Lifeguard, 1976, Paradise Valley, 1978, Good Guys Wear Black, 1978, Raise the Titanic, 1980, Hero At Large, 1980, Green Ice, 1981, Waltz Across Texas, 1983 (also writer), Too Scared to Scream, 1985, The Naked Face, 1985, The Check Is in the Mail, 1985, Fatal Attraction, 1987 (Golden Globe nominee 1987, Acad. award nominee 1988), Love at Large, 1990, Narrow Margin, 1990, Eminent Domain, 1991, Patroit Games, 1992, Body of Evidence, 1993, Short Cuts, 1993 (Golden Globe award Best Ensemble Cast 1994), Clear and Present Danger, 1994, Mojave Moon, 1996, Nico the Unicorn, 1998, Dark Summer, 1999, (voice) Whispers: An Elephant's Tale, 2000, Rules of Engagement, 2000, The Art of War, 2000, The Gray in Between, 2002, Uncle Nino, 2003, November, 2004, The Iris Effect, 2004, Man of the House, 2005; (TV series) Bob and Carol and Ted and Alice, 1973, The Family Tree, 1983, Falcon Crest, 1985, (TV movies) The Blue Knight, 1973, The Mark of Zorro, 1974, The Log of the Black Pearl, 1975, A Matter of Wife...and Death, 1976, The Dark Side of Innocence, 1976, Seventh Avenue, 1977, The Pirate, 1978, The Sky's No Limit, 1984, A Different Affair, 1987, A Leap of Faith, 1988, The Last of His Tribe, 1992, Nails, 1992, Jane's House, 1994, Because Mommy Works, 1994 (also co-prodr.), The Man in the Attic, 1995, Present Tenes, Past Perfect, 1995, Jake's Women, 1996, Almost Forever, 1996, Indiscretion of an American Wife, 1998, My Husband's Secret Life, 1998, Jane's House, 2000, Night of the Wolf, 2002, (voice) 2004: A light Knight's Odyssey, 2004; TV appearances include Storefront Lawyers, 1970, Hawaii Five-O, 1970, The FBI, 1971, The Mod Squad, 1971, Ironside, 1971, Alias Smith and Jones, 1971, Love American Style, 1971, Mannix, 1973, Harry O, 1974, 76, Little House on the Prairie, 1975, Switch, 1975, 76, McCloud, 1976, Petrocelli, 1975, 76, Beggars and Choosers, 2000, Boston Public, 2003, The L Word, 2004. Office: care Ilene Feldman Agency 8730 W Sunset Blvd Ste 490 Los Angeles CA 90069-2248*

ARCHER, CHALMERS, JR., retired education educator; b. Tchula, Miss., Apr. 21, 1938; s. Chalmers Sr. and Eva Alcola (Rutherford) A. AS, Saints Jr. Coll., 1969; BS, Tuskegee Inst., 1972, MEd, 1974; post doctorate, U. Ala., 1980; cert., MIT, 1980; PhD, Auburn U., 1979. Asst. to the pres. Saints Coll., Lexington, Miss., 1968-72; asst. v.p. Tuskegee (Ala.) Inst., 1972-83; prof. No. Va. C.C., Manassas, 1983-2001, prof. emeritus, 2001. Author: Growing Up Black in Rural Mississippi (recipient Miss. Inst. of Arts and Letters award for Nonfiction), Green Berets in the Vanguard: Inside Special Forces, 1953-1963; contbg. editor: The Jackson Advocate; contbr. articles to profl. jours. and newspapers. Mem. Dem. Spkr.'s Bur. for Clinton/Gore Re-election Campaign. Recipient Nat. Edn. Articulation Model, Conf. on Blacks in Higher Edn., Washington, 1986. Mem. Rotary (county transportation commnr.). Democrat. Baptist. Avocations: writing, motivational speaking, academic/community program development. Home: 7885 Flager Cir Manassas VA 20109-7435 Office Phone: 703-335-5289. Personal E-mail: drarcher97@aol.com.

ARCHER, CRISTINA LOZEJ, meteorologist; b. Como, Italy, Apr. 21, 1970; d. Alessandra Bonfanti; m. Scott Mckinley Archer, Nov. 4, 2000; children: Emma Tiffany, Clara Maria. MS, Politecnico di Milano, 1995, San Jose (Calif.) State U., 1998; PhD, Stanford (Calif). U., 2004. Post doctoral scholar Stanford U., 2004—05; atmospheric modeler Bay Area Air Quality Mgmt. Dist., San Francisco, 2005—. Contbr. articles to profl. jours. Recipient Best thesis in environ. field award, Regione Lombardia, Milano, Italy, 1995. Mem.: Am. Meteorol. Soc. (assoc.). Roman Catholic. Achievements include research in first study on global wind power potential; discovery and study of an atmospheric vortex. Avocations: bicycling, beach, reading, knitting. Office: Bay Area Air Quality Dist 939 Ellis St San Francisco CA 94109 Personal E-mail: lozej@stanford.edu.

ARCHER, CYNTHIA DIANE, artist; b. New Martinsville, W.Va., Mar. 28, 1953; d. William Jr. Archer and Mabel Garnet Barney. BA, Goucher Coll., Towson, Md., 1975; MFA, W.Va. U., Morgantown, 1978. Curator and hand lithographer Plucked Chicken Press, Evanston, Ill., 1978—2000. Art cons. Jane Meyer Fine Art, Geneva & Elburn, Ill., 1985—; cons. in field. Stained glass window design, The Sun's Candle (Art in Architecture Award, So. Ill. U., Carbondale, 1995), painted bench, (Collection of The Chgo. Children's Mus., 1995), original hand printed lithograph, Lydian Cypher (Percent for Art Chgo. Pub. Libr. West Lawn Br., 1988), fine art commission, 4 Original Lithographs (permanent exhibit The U. of Chgo. Bus. Sch., 1995), original lithograph, The Plucked Chicken Press Permanent Memorial Exhbn. (Permanent Collection, 1997). Recipient The Pres.s Purchase award, Bradley U., 1990. Mem.: The U.S. Dressage Fedn. Office: Cynthia Archer Fine Art and Design 1604 Greenleaf St Evanston IL 60202 Office Phone: 847-475-0530. E-mail: cynthia@cynthiaarcher.com.

ARCHER, DENNIS WAYNE, lawyer, former mayor; b. Detroit, Jan. 1, 1942; s. Ernest James and Frances (Carroll) A.; m. Trudy Ann DunCombe, June 17, 1967; children: Dennis Wayne, Vincent DunCombe BS, Western Mich. U., 1965; JD, Detroit Coll. Law, 1970; LLD (hon.), Western Mich. U., 1987, Detroit Coll. Law, 1988, U. Detroit, 1988, John Marshall Law Sch., 1991, Gonzaga U., 1991, U. Mich., 1994; D in Pub. Svc. (hon.), Ea. Mich. U., 1994; LLD (hon.), Aquinos Coll., 1996, Marygrove Coll., 1997, Hamline U., 2001, Wayne State U., 2002, U. Balt., 2002, Stetson U., 2003, Temple U., 2004, U. Conn., 2004. Bar: Mich. 1970. Tchr. spl. edn. Detroit Bd. Edn., 1965-70; assoc. Gragg & Gardner, 1970-71; ptnr. Hall, Stone, Allen, Archer & Glenn, P.C., 1971-73, Charfoos, Christensen & Archer, P.C., 1973-85; assoc. justice Mich. Supreme Ct., 1986-90; ptnr. Dickinson, Wright, Moon, Van Dusen & Freeman, Detroit, 1991-93; chmn. Dickinson Wright PLLC, 2001—, Detroit, 2002—; mayor City of Detroit, 1994—2001. Assoc. prof. Detroit Coll. Law, 1972-78; adj. prof. Wayne State U. Law Sch., Detroit, 1984-85; mem. Mich. Bd. Ethics, 1979-83; mem. adv. bd. U.S. Conf. Mayors, 1994—; bd. dirs. Nat. Conf. Black Mayors, 1994—; mem. intergovtl. policy adv. com. U.S. Trade Rep.; bd. dirs. Compuware, Johnson Controls, Inc. Contbr. articles to legal jours. Bd. dirs. Legal Aid and Defenders Assn., Detroit, 1980-82, Nat. Conf. Black Mayors, 1994, CATCH, Henry Ford Health Sys.; co-chmn. Met. Detroit Cmty. Coalition for Dems., 1979-80; bd. trustees Olivet Coll., 1991-93; active numerous local Dem. campaigns, 1970-85; host local pub. svc. radio programs; co-chair platform com. Dem. Conv., 1996; pres. Nat. Conf. Dem. Mayors, 1996; mem. Nat. Com. on Crime Control and Prevention, 1995. Named Most Respected Judge in Mich. Mich. Lawyers Weekly Jour., 1990. Mem. ABA (ho. dels. 1979-93, chmn. drafting com. 1986-88, com. on scope and correlation of work sect. officers liaison 1987-90, chmn. gen. practice sect. 1987-88, chair commn. on opportunities for minorities in the profession 1987-91, sect. legal edn. and admissions to the bar, coun. mem. 1989-95, task force on profl. skills instrn. 1989-91, task force on law schs. and the profession, Narrowing The Gap, 1989-91, chmn. spl. com. prepaid legal svcs. 1981-83, chmn. sect. officers conf. 1988-90, resource devel. coun. 1988-91, bd. editors ABA Jour. 1988-94, bd. editors The Practical Litigator 1989-94, chmn. rules and calendar com. 1990-92, state del. 1990-96, pres. 2003-2004), ATLA, Nat. Bar Assn. (pres. 1983-84), Am. Judicature Soc. (bd. dirs 1977-81), State Bar Mich. (pres. 1984-85), Wolverine Bar Assn. (pres. 1979-80), Detroit Bar Assn. (bd. dirs. 1973-75), Mich. Trial Lawyers Assn. (exec. bd. 1973-74), Econ. Club, Alpha Phi Alpha. Roman Catholic. Office: Dickinson Wright Ste 4000 500 Woodward Ave Detroit MI 48226-3425 Office Phone: 313-223-3500. Office Fax: 313-223-3598. Business E-Mail: darcher@dickinsonwright.com.

ARCHER, GLENN LEROY, JR., federal judge; b. Densmore, Kans., Mar. 21, 1929; s. Glenn LeRoy and Ruth Agnes (Ford) A.; m. Carole J. Thomas, 1990; children: Susan, Sharon, Glenn, Thomas. BA, Yale U., 1951; JD with honors, George Washington U., 1954. Bar: D.C. 1954. Assoc. Hamel, Park, McCabe & Saunders, Washington, 1956—60, ptnr., 1960—81; asst. atty. gen. US Dept. Justice, Washington, 1981-85; circuit judge US Ct. Appeals (fed. cir.), Washington, 1985-94, chief judge, 1994-97, sr. cir. judge, 1997—. First lt. JAG Corps USAF, 1954—56. Republican. Methodist. Office: US Ct of Appeals Fed Circuit 717 Madison Pl NW Washington DC 20439-0002

ARCHER, JAMES ELSON, engineering educator; b. Hedley, Tex., Dec. 1, 1922; s. James M. and Mary Minerva (Bolles) A.; m. Reta Faye Turner, Nov. 8, 1942; 1 son, James Elson. BS, Tex. Tech. U., 1947; PhD, Mass. Inst. Tech., 1950. Instr. Mass. Inst. Tech., 1950-52, Sloan fellow in indsl. mgmt., 1963-64; researcher Pitts. Plate Glass Co., Pitts., 1952-53, asst. dir., 1953-54, asso. dir., 1954-56, dir. research, 1956-62; mng. partner Archer Assos., Dallas, 1962-64; corporate dir. mgmt. systems Tex. Instruments, Dallas, 1964-68; prof. Tex. Tech U., Lubbock, 1968-95, prof. emeritus, 1995—. Served with USAAF, 1943—46. Home: 6208 Lynnhaven Dr Lubbock TX 79413-5332

ARCHER, JAMES G., retired lawyer; b. San Antonio, Tex., Jan. 16, 1936; BA, U. Ill., 1957, LLB, 1959. Bar: Ill. 1960, N.Y. 1994. Ptnr. Sidley & Austin Brown & Wood, N.Y.; ret. Mem. State bd. acctg. examiners, 1976-78. Mem. Order of Coif. Office: Sidley Austin Brown & Wood 10 S Dearborn St Chicago IL 60603

ARCHER, JOAN M., trade association administrator; b. Sioux Falls, S.D., Aug. 7, 1953; d. Wilbur Lewis and Beverly Jane Archer. BA in Econ., U. S.D., 1974; MA in Urban Studies, Mankato State U., 1978. Cert. assn. exec. Inst. Orgn. Mgmt. City planner City of Redfield, S.D., 1974-76; planning cons. S.M.S.Q., Northfield, Minn., 1977-78; city planner City of New Brighton, Minn., 1978-82; exec. v.p. Minn. Mfr. Housing Assn., St. Paul, 1983-88, Builders Assn. Minn., St. Paul, 1988-96; v.p. govt. rels. Minn. Bankers Assn., St. Paul, 1996-98; pres. Minn. Soft Drink Assn., St. Paul, 1998—. Bd. dirs. Minn. Govt. Rels. Coun., pres., 1998, 99; bd. dirs. coun. Girl Scouts Am., St. Croix Valley, 2d v.p., 1993-95; bd. dirs. Youth in Govt., 1998-2000. Mem. Minn. Soc. Execs. Assn. (bd. dirs., pres. 1995-96), Green Haven Women's Golf League (pres. 2001). Office: Ste 830 161 Saint Anthony Ave Saint Paul MN 55103-2300 E-mail: joan@mn.state.net.

ARCHER, JULIAN PRATT WATERMAN, history educator; b. Fayetteville, Ark., Nov. 30, 1938; s. Julian S. and Evangeline (Pratt) W.; m. Jane Gochenour, June 15, 1962; children: Jane, Elisabeth, Laird. BA, U. Ark., 1960; MA, U. Colo., 1963; PhD, U. Wis., 1970. Instr. history U. Ark., 1964, U. Wis., Whitewater, 1967-68; asst. prof. Drake U., Des Moines, 1968-73, assoc. prof., 1973-85, prof., 1985—. Pres. Lucullan Travels, Ltd., Des Moines, 1978—. Author: The First International in France, 1864-1872. Its Origins, Theories, and Impact, 1997. Pres. Greater Des Moines Youth Symphony, 1977-80, Owl's Head Nat. Register Hist. Dist., 1974-91; mem. Hist. Dist. Commn., Des Moines, 1983-88, Des Moines Com. Fgn. Rels., 1980-95, hon. consul of France, 1984-2004. Capt. USAR, 1960-66. Decorated chevalier Ordre des Palmes Académiques, chevalier Confrérie des Chevaliers du Tastevin, chevalier Ordre Naional Du Merite; named Mentor of Yr. Drake U., 2000; Am. Philos. Soc. grantee, 1970; Drake Rsch. Coun. grantee, 1970, 74; Theodore J. Oseau fellow, 1966. Mem. Soc. French Hist. Studies, Western Soc. French History (coun. 1992-95), Pow Wow Club (pres. 1986-87), Des Moines Power Squadron (comdr. 1987-88), Aliance Francaise of Ctrl. Iowa (pres. 1994-96). Home: 402 29th St Des Moines IA 50312-4412 Office: Drake U Des Moines IA 50311

ARCHER, LILLIAN PATRICIA, academic administrator; b. Lawrenceville, Va., Oct. 31, 1952; d. Wyatt and Marian Lee Archer; m. James Leroy Drewery, July 7, 2000. BSBA, Morgan State U., 1976; MA in Human Resources, Coll. of Notre Dame of Md., 1990; EdD in Higher Edn., Morgan State U., 2002. Counselor CC of Balt. County, Balt., 1992—99, interim dir.

of human rels., 1998—99, dir. of counseling, 1999—2001, sr. dir. of student support svcs., 2001—02, sr. dir. of counseling, acad. advisement and entry svcs., 2002—04, sr. dir. of acad. and adminstrv. svcs., 2004—. Sys. appraiser Higher Learning Commn. of North Ctrl. Assn. of Colls. and Schs., Chgo., 2004—. Vol. Wigs for Kids, Cleve., 2004—04, South Balt. Emergency Relief (SOBER), Balt., 1999—2001; mem bd. dirs. Balt. Med. Sys.; mem. Balt. Med. Systems (BMS), Balt., 1992—93. Fellow, Am. Coun. on Edn., 2003—04. Mem.: Am. Coll. Pers. Assn. (ACPA), Am. Assn. of Women in Cmty. Colleges (AAWCC). Avocations: reading, travel, writing. Office Phone: 410-455-4222. Personal E-mail: archerfellow@yahoo.com.

ARCHER, LLOYD DANIEL, communications educator; b. Cromwell, Ind., May 15, 1942; s. Dallas Lloyd and Wilma Christine (Halsey) A.; m. Carol Sue Bonney, May 15, 1966; 1 child, Elisa Carol. BS, Ind. U., 1971, MS, 1973; EdS, U. Ga., 1992. Dir. media Ind. U. Sch. Edn., Bloomington, 1971-73; media cons. U.S. Agy. for Internat. Devel., Mali, Africa, 1982; dir. media and prof. edn. Ft. Valley (Ga.) State Coll., 1973-87, dept. chmn. mass communication, 1987-89, prof. mass communications, 1989—, dept. chmn. mass comm., 2000—. TV rsch. cons. Rsch. Comm.'s Ltd., Boston, 1989, 95; mem. evaluation team NCATE, U. N.Fla., 1986, U. N. Ala., 1986; mem. faculty devel. seminar, Zimbabwe and S. Africa, 1998; mem. Journalistic Tour Kenya, 1999. Photographer postcard views, Ft. Valley State Coll., 1981. Active Spl. Olympics, Warner Robins, Ga., 1981-87; panelist Reg. Minorities Conf., Atlanta Jour. and Const., 1988; dir. music/choir dir. Christ United Meth. Ch., Warner Robins, Ga., 1988-95. Named State Photographer of Yr., Ga. Spl. Olympics, 1986. Mem. Ga. Assn. Inst. Tech. (bd. dirs. 1986-88), Assn. for Ednl. Communications Tech., AAUP (v.p. 1975-88), Broadcast Edn. Assn. Avocations: photography, graphics, computers. Office: Mass Comm Dept Ft Valley State U Fort Valley GA 31030

ARCHER, MADOLIN B., art educator; d. Bernard and Jeanne Wallace Brown; children: Devon D., Palin G., Kier N., Breck B. BA, Adelphi U., 1968, MA, 1970. Art tchr. Harborfields Dist. Schs., Greenlawn, NY, N.Shore Schs., Sea Cliff, NY. Avocation: athletics. Home: 14 Barracuda Rd East Quogue NY 11942

ARCHER, RICHARD JOSEPH, lawyer; b. Virginia, Minn., Mar. 24, 1922; s. William John and Margaret Leanore (Duff) A.; m. Kristina Hanson, Jan. 29, 1977 (dec.); children: Alison P., Cynthia J. AB, U. Mich., 1947, JD, 1948. Bar: Calif. 1949, U.S. Supreme Ct. 1962, Hawaii 1982. Partner firm Morrison and Foerster, San Francisco, 1954-71, Sullivan, Jones and Archer, San Francisco, 1971-81, Archer Rosenak & Hanson, San Francisco, 1981-85, Archer & Hanson, San Francisco, 1985—. Served with USN, 1942-45. Decorated Bronze Star. Mem. ABA, Am. Bar Found. (life), Am. Law Inst. (life). Home: 3110 Bohemian Hwy Occidental CA 95465-9113 Office Phone: 707-874-3438. Personal E-mail: archerdic@aol.com.

ARCHER, RONALD DEAN, chemist, educator; b. Rochelle, Ill., July 22, 1932; s. Don Adam and Irma Cecil (Olson) Archer; m. Joyce Hilder Carlson, Jan. 31, 1954; children: Paul Dean, Lynn Sue, Sharon Jean, Julie Anne. BS, Ill. State U., 1953, MS, 1954; PhD, U. Ill., 1959. Tchr. Larson Jr. High Sch., Elgin, Ill., 1954; asst. prof. U. Calif., Riverside, 1959-63, Tulane U., New Orleans, 1963-65, assoc. prof., 1965-66, U. Mass., Amherst, 1966-70, prof. chemistry, 1970-99, prof. emeritus, 1999—, head chemistry dept., 1977-83. Cons., 1960—63, 1964—70, 1972—; vis. prof. Tech. U., Denmark, 1972, U. Vienna, 1987; rsch. scientist Naval Rsch. Lab., Washington, 1980; chief chemistry reader advanced placement program Ednl. Testing Svc., 1985—88. Author: (book) Inorg. Organomet Polymass, 2001; contbr. articles to profl. jours. With U.S. Army, 1956—56. Recipient Alumni Achievement award, Ill. State U., 1989; grantee, USAF, Rsch. Corp., NSF, Am. Chem. Soc., NIH, Army Rsch. Office, Office Naval Rsch. Fellow: AAAS; mem.: New Eng. Assn. Chemistry Tchrs., Am. Chem. Soc. (chmn. Conn. Valley sect. 1979, councilor 1981—, chmn. com. edn. 1987—89, nominating and election com. 1990—94, exec. com. divsn. chem. edn. 1995—98, coun. policy com. 1996—98, chair-elect, chair, past chair divsn. chem. edn. 1996—98, chair adv. bd. gen. chem. curriculum project 1997—2004, com. econ. profl. affairs 1999—2000, chair 2000, sci. com. 2001—03, com. on com. 2001—), Rotary Internat. (chpt. bd. dirs. 2005—), Sigma Xi, Phi Lambda Upsilon. Lutheran. Home: 19 Lantern Ln Amherst MA 01002-3222 Office: U Mass Dept Chemistry Grad Rsch Towers # A Amherst MA 01003-9336 Business E-Mail: archer@chem.umass.edu. *Nothing surpasses the joy in the eyes of a student who has just synthesized a new chemical compound, especially if it has unique properties or may benefit the human endeavor.*

ARCHERD, ARMY (ARMAND A. ARCHERD), retired columnist, retired television commentator; b. Bronx, Jan. 13, 1919; m. Selma Archerd. Grad., UCLA, 1941, U.S. Naval Acad. Postgrad. Sch., 1943. With Hollywood bur. AP, 1945—2005; columnist Herald-Express, Daily Variety, 1953—2005; ret. Master of ceremonies numerous Hollywood premieres, Acad. Awards shows; co-host People's Choice Awards shows. Served to lt. USN. Recipient awards Masquers, L.A. Press Club, Hollywood Fgn. Press Club, Newsman of Yr. award Publicists Guild, 1970. Mem. Hollywood Press Club (founder). Office: care Daily Variety 5700 Wilshire Blvd Ste 120 Los Angeles CA 90036-5804

ARCHIBALD, GEORGE, reporter; b. Newmarket, Eng., 1944; BA in Polit. Sci. and History, Old Dominion U., 1967. Editl. writer, columnist Ariz. Republic, Phoenix, 1971—73; congrl. aide Washington, 1973—75, 1977—81; assoc. staff Ho. Appropriations Com., 1979—81; dep. asst. sec. edn. Washington, 1981—82; nat. corr. Washington Times, 1982—93, 1995—; editor, gen. mgr. The Warren Sentinel, Front Royal, Va., 1993—94; nat. reporter Washington Times, 1995—; assoc. prof. Washington Grad. Journalism Ctr., Regent U., 2000—03. Press sec., legis. asst. Rep. John B. Conlan, 1973—75; adminstrv. asst. Rep. Eldon Rudd, 1977—78; exec. dir. Am. Legis Exch. Coun., Washington, 1976. With USAF, 1967—71. Office: Washington Times 3600 New York Ave NE Washington DC 20002-1996 Office Phone: 202-636-3166. E-mail: g_archi@yahoo.com.

ARCHIBALD, JAMES KENWAY, lawyer; b. Greenfield, Mass., Mar. 29, 1949; s. John Lawrence and Jean (Kenway) A.; m. Joanne Mary Ricciuti, Aug. 16, 1975; children: Kathryn, John. BA, Johns Hopkins U., 1971; JD, U. Md., 1975. Bar: Md. 1975, DC 1985, U.S. Dist. Ct. Md. 1976, US Ct. Appeals (4th cir.) 1978, US Supreme Ct. 1979, U.S. Ct. Appeals (9th cir.) 1984, Maine 1998. Assoc. Venable LLP, Balt., 1975-83, ptnr., 1983—. Co-author: Pleading Causes of Action in Maryland, 1990, Model Witness Examinations, 1997. Chmn. bd. trustees Md. State Colls. and Us., 1984-86; trustee Johns Hopkins U., 1997-2000; bd. dirs. Roland Park Country Sch., Inc., Balt., 1989-94; pres. Homeland Assn., Inc., Balt., 1990. Recipient Disting. Svc. award Litigation Sect. Md. State Bar, Md., 1981, Disting. Svc. Award, Md. Inst. for Continuing Edn. of Lawyers. Mem. ABA (litigation sect., co-chair com. 1987-2002), Internat. Assn. Def. Counsel, Def. Rsch. Inst. (Exceptional Performance award 1989, Md. state chair 1989-93), Md. Assn. Def. Trial Counsel (pres. 1988-89), Bar Assn. of Balt. City, Product Liability Adv. Coun., DC Bar, Md. State Bar., U. Md. Law Sch. Alumni Assn. (bd. mem.), Johns Hopkins Alumni Coun. (v.p. 1996-98, pres. 1998-2000), Johns Hopkins Second Decade Soc. (nat. chair 1989-91), Am. Law Inst. Avocation: running. Home: 13037 Jerome Jay Dr Cockeysville MD 21030-1523 Office: 1800 Mercantile Bank Bldg 2 Hopkins Plz Ste 2100 Baltimore MD 21201-2982 also: Venable LLP 575 7th St NW Washington DC 20004 Office Phone: 410-244-7525, 202-344-4901. Office Fax: 202-344-8300, 410-244-7742. E-mail: jkarchibald@venable.com.

ARCHIBALD, NOLAN D., household and industrial products company executive; b. Ogden, Utah, June 22, 1943; m. Margaret Hafen, June 8, 1967. AA, Dixie Coll., 1966; BS, Weber State Univ., 1968; MBA, Harvard U., 1970. Exec. v.p., gen. mgr. Sno Jet, Inc. div. Conroy, Inc., Burlington, Vt., 1970-77; sr. v.p., and pres. non-foods cos. Beatrice Foods, Chgo., 1977-85; chmn., pres., chief exec. officer The Black & Decker Corp., Towson, Md., 1985—. Former All Am. basketball player.; mem. bd. dir Huntsman Corp. Named one of 10 Most Wanted Execs in U.S., Fortune Mag.; recipient Six Best Mgrs. in U.S., Bus. Week Mag. Avocation: theater.*

ARCHIBALD, REGINALD MAC GREGOR, pediatrician, endocrinologist, chemist, educator; b. Syracuse, N.Y., Mar. 2, 1910; s. Eben Henry and Minnie (Archibald) A.; m. Evelyn Stroh, June 12, 1948; children: Ruth, Lawrence. BA, U. B.C., 1930, MA, 1932; PhD, U. Toronto, Ont., Can., 1934, MD, 1939. Tchr., rsch. asst. U. B.C., 1930-32; tchg. and rsch. asst. U. Toronto, 1932-33, fellow pathol. chemistry, 1933-35; intern pathology Hosp. for Sick Children, Toronto, 1937, surgery, 1938, medicine, 1939; intern Toronto Gen. Hosp., 1939-40; fellow divsn. med. scis. NRC, 1940-42; asst. resident physician Rockefeller Inst. Hosp., 1941-46; assoc. Rockefeller Inst. Med. Rsch., 1946, mem., 1948—; prof. Rockefeller U., 1955-80, prof. emeritus, 1980—; sr. physician Rockefeller Hosp., 1955-80. Prof. biochemistry Sch. Hygiene and Pub. Health Johns Hopkins U., 1946-48; mem. adv. bd. Hosp. of Rockefeller U., 1992-93. Mem. editl. bd.: Jour. Biol. Chemistry, 1948-58, Jour. Clin. Endocrinology and Metabolism, 1952-60, Child Devel., 1954-56; adv. bd.: Analytical Chemistry, 1957-60. Mem. Am. Chem. Soc., Am. Soc. Biol. Chemists, Harvey Soc., Med. and Chirug. Faculty Md., Endocrine Soc., Soc. Rsch. in Child Devel., Brit. Biochem. Soc., Lawson Wilkins Soc. Pediatric Endocrinology, Soc. Adolescent Medicine, Nat. Acad. Clin. Biochemistry, N.Y. Met. Pediatric Endocrine Soc., Internat. Assn. for Adolescent Medicine, Explorers Club, Sigma Xi. Achievements include medical research in pediatric endocrinology and biochemistry; development of clinical laboratory methods; study of influence of hormones on enzymes, problems of physical growth and maturation of children. Home: Apt 1810 211 Second St NW Rochester MN 55901 E-mail: archibald@charter.net.

ARCHULETA, KEITH ANTHONY, entrepreneur, business and management consultant; b. Denver, Mar. 13, 1955; s. Willie M. and Judith Ruth (Archuleta) Suggs; m. Iris Curtis, May 27, 1995; 1 child, Dorian. BA in Comm., BA in African and African Am. Studies, Stanford U., 1978; MA, U. San Francisco, 1992. Founder, bus. mgr. Stanford Black Media Inst., 1976; dir. So. Africa Media Ctr., San Francisco, 1979-80; program coord. Student Arts at Stanford (Calif.), 1982-84; asst. dir. Stanford Residential Edn., 1984-88; founder/dir. Black Cmty. Svcs. Ctr., Stanford, 1987-92; exec. dir. Oakland (Calif.) Youth Chorus, 1993; project adminstr. Arts Edn. Funders Collaborative, San Francisco, 1994-99; site adminstr. Young African Am. Achievers Program, San Francisco, 1995-97; interim exec. dir. LEAP...Imagination in Learning, San Francisco, 1996, Oakland Asian Cultural Ctr., Oakland, 1998; founder, CEO Ur At Work, Inc., 1999—2001; cons. East County Bus.-Edn. Alliance, 2000—; exec. dir. CASA Contra Costa County, 2001—. Founder/pres. Emerald Consulting, Antioch, Calif., 1992—; mem. adv. bd. CIIS MBA Program, San Francisco, 1994-97; mem. bd. devel./mktg. chair LEAP...Imagination in Learning, San Francisco, 1995-97; mem. bd. emeritus Theatre Works, 1992-; rev. panelist Arts Coun. Santa Clara County, San Jose, Calif., 1996-97, NEA, Washington, 2001-02; bd. dirs. Micro Credit Loan Fund, Inc., Regional Tng. Inst., Bd. of Legends, John F. Kennedy Univ., 2005. Author: (play) Their Spirits are Free, 1982; prodr., editor (ednl. video) Song for Melvin Truss, 1986. Fellow Calif. State Legislature, Sacramento, 1978-79; vol. Crossroads Africa, Liberia, West Africa, 1979, San Francisco Sch. Vols., 1995-99; founder Kuumba Arts Ensemble, 1979, East Palo Alto Youth Theatre Project, 1985; congrl. dist. coord./del. Jesse Jackson for Pres., Santa Clara County, Calif., 1984, 88; bd. regents JFK U., 2005; v.p. bd. Calif. CASA Assn. Mem. ASCD, Calif. Alliance Arts Edn., Calif. Assn. Non-Profits, PowerPac, Co-Op Am. Bus. Network, Fellowship Cos. Christ Internat., Bus. Social Responsibility (founding mem.), Antioch Christian Ctr., Am. Assn. Christian Counselors, Youth for Christ (mem. nat. adv. bd. 1997-99), Nat. Alliance of Bus., Calif. CASA Assn. (bd. dirs. 2003—). Avocations: poetry writing, theater, music, cinema, travel. Office: 1883 Mt Conness Way Antioch CA 94531-7492 Office Phone: 925-755-9291. Personal E-mail: emeraldk@aol.com.

ARCILLA, DEMETRIO BALLARES, JR., health facility administrator, rehabilitation services professional, writer, genealogist; b. Philippines, July 2, 1934; arrived in U.S., 1974; s. Demetrio F. Arcilla, Sr. and Justa M. Ballares; m. Juanita R. Arcilla; 1 child, Jeandell R. AA, Ateneo U., 1956; BS in Bus. Adminstrn., U. of the East, Manilla, Philippines, 1960. Acct. clk. Nat. Shipyard & Steel Corp., Manilla, 1956—58; internal auditor Manila (Philippines) Music Ctr., Inc., 1958—64; admin. Philrock, Inc., Manilla, 1964—74; chief bookkeeper Electroplating Co., Chgo., 1974—77; bookkeeper Bank of Am., Houston, 1977—79; acct. Kerr Steamship Co., Inc., Houston, 1979—85; pres. Adult & Children Rehab. Ctr., Houston, 1987—. Author: Pictoral Roster of Arcilla Clan-USA/Canada, 2000, Genealogy of Arcilla Clan-International, 2002; contbr. Philrock Mag., 1964—74, articles to newspapers. Co-coord. Feed the Hungry Ops. TAPP, Inc., 1998; founder BICOL USA, Houston, 1984—; chmn. White Cane Fund Raising, Houston; active Tex. Asian Rep. Caucus, Houston, 1989—; bd. trustees CIA Charitable Found., Chgo., 2000—. Mem.: Bicol Nat. Assns. Am. (v.p. 1986—88, adviser 1988—90), Tex. Assn. Philippine Physicians Alliance, Inc. (pres. 1995, 1998), Assn. Profl. Genealogists, Nat. Geneal. Soc., Tex. Med. Assn. Alliance, Harris County Med. Soc. Alliance, Fil-Am. Coun. South Tex., Catanduanes Internat. Assn. (v.p. 1991—, vol. med. and surg. missions 1993, 2002), Houston Fil-Am. Lion's Club (v.p., dir. 1987—96). Avocations: travel, dance, genealogy, gardening, movies. Home: 5630 Auden St Houston TX 77005-2008 Office: Adult & Children Rehab Ctr PO Box 270301 Houston TX 77277-0301

ARCILLA, JUANITA R., physical therapist; b. Manila City, Phillippines, June 24, 1942; d. Eliseo Rivera and Dominga Dimla; m. Denny B. Arcilla Jr., Mar. 25, 1973; 1 child, Jeandell R. BA in English, U. St. Tomas, Manila City, Phillipinnes, 1966; MD, Far Eastern U., Manila City, Phillipinnes, 1970. Lic. physician Pa., Tex., R.I. Rsch. assoc. Northwestern U., Chgo., 1975—77, U. Tex., Houston, 1977—80; resident in phys. medicine and rehab. La. State U., New Orleans, 1980—81, Baylor Coll. Medicine, Houston, 1981—83; fellow in pediat. rehab. Tex. Children's Hosp., Houston, 1983—84; staff physiatrist Profl. Rehab. Outpatient Svcs., Pitts., 1985—86; clin. dir. Phys. Handicap Offender Program, Jester III, Tex. Dept. Correction, Hunsville, Tex., 1986—87; cons. Tex. Dept. of Mental Health and Mental Retardation (MHMR), Richmond, 1987; med. cons. Phys. Handicap Offender Program, Jester III, Tex. Dept. Corrections, 1987—89; med. dir. Richmond State Sch., Richmond, 1987—97; med. staff Tex. Dept. of Mental Health & Mental Retardation (TDMHMR), Richmond, 1997—. Clin. instr. Baylor Coll. Medicine, Houston, 1981—83; asst. prof. U. Tex., Galveston, 1987—; faculty position appt. Tex. A&M U., 1988—94; med. dir. Adult & Children Rehab. Ctr., Houston, 1987—; med. cons. Total Care Med. Clinic, Houston, 1994—; designated Phys. with Tex. Dept. Worker Compensation Comm., Austin, 1994—; WC patient's phys. of Richmond State Sch., Richmond. Contbr. articles to profl. jour., med. mission vol. Catanduanes Internat. Assoc., Inc. (Academic Scholarship Award, 2002). Med. mission vol. Catanduanes Internat. Assn. Inc., 1993, Catanduanes Internat. Assoc. Inc., 2002; mem. fund raising Tex. Asian Rep. Caucus, Houston, 1989—. Named Outstanding Career Woman Yr., IC Metro Houston, Inc., 1996; fellow, United Cerebral Palsy Rsch. Edn. Found., 1983—84. Mem.: Am. Acad. Phys. Medicine and Rehab., Internat. Rehab. Medicine Assn., Am. Cong. Rehab. Medicine, Harris County Med. Soc., Tex. Med. Assn., Tex. Assn. Phillipinnes Physicians Inc. (pres. 1997—98, past v.p., coord. Feed the Hungry Opn. 1998, plaques for charity work 1997, 1998). Roman Catholic. Avocations: gardening, cooking, home decorating, travel, crocheting, winner of Trophy 1st. of Tango Compet. Office: Adult & Children Rehab Ctr PO Box 270301 Houston TX 77277-0301

ARCINIEGA, TOMAS ABEL, university president; b. El Paso, Tex., Aug. 5, 1937; s. Tomas Hilario and Judith G. (Zozaya) Arciniega; m. M. Concha Ochotorena, Aug. 10, 1957; children: Wendy H. Heredia, Lisa Gannon, Judy Shackleton, Laura. BS in Tchr. Edn., N. Mex. State U., 1960; MA, U. N. Mex., 1966, PhD, 1970; postdoc., Inst. for Ednl. Mgmt., Harvard U., 1989. Asst. dean Grad. Sch. U. Tex.-El Paso, 1972-73; co-dir. Southwestern Schs. Study, U. Tex.-El Paso, 1970-73; dean Coll. Edn. San Diego State U., 1973-80; v.p. acad. affairs. Calif. State U., Fresno, 1980-83, pres. Bakersfield, 1983—. Prof. ednl. adminstrn. and supervision U. N.Mex., U. Tex.-El Paso, San Diego State U., Calif. State U., Fresno, Calif. State U., Bakersfield; cons. in edn. to state and fed. agys., instns.; USAID advisor to Dominican Republic U.S. Dept. State., 1967-68; dir. applied rsch. project U. N.Mex., 1968-69, dep. chief party AID Project, Colombia, 1969-70; cons. in field. Author: Public Education's Response to the Mexican-American, 1971, Preparing Teachers of Mexican Americans: A Sociocultural and Political Issue, 1977; co-author: Chicanos and Native Americans: The Territorial Minorities, 1973; guest editor: Calif. Jour. Tchr. Edn., 1981; editor Commn. on Hispanic Underrepresentation Reports, Hispanic Underrepresentation: A Call for Reinvestment and Innovation, 1985, 88. Trustee emeritus Carnegie Corp. N.Y.; trustee Ednl. Testing Svc., Princeton, N.J., The Aspen Inst.; bd. dirs. Math., Engring., Sci. Achievement, Berkeley, Calif.; mem. bd. dirs. Air U., Hispanic Scholarship Fund; mem. Am. Coun. on Edn.; founding mem., trustee Tomas Rivera Policy Inst.; dir. Civic Kern Citizens Effective Local Govt.; mem. adv. bd. Beautiful Bakersfield; advisor Jr. League Bakersfield. Vis. scholar Leadership Enrichment Program, 1982; recipient Legis. commendation for higher edn. Calif. Legislature, 1975-78, Meritorious Svc. award Am. Assn. Colls. Tchr. Edn., 1977-78, Meritorious Svc. award League United L.Am. Citizens, 1983, Svc. award Hispanic and Bus. Alliance for Edn., 1991, Pioneer award Nat. Assn. Bilingual Edn., 1994; named to Top 100 Acad. Leaders in Higher Edn. Change Mag., 1978, Top 100 Hispanic Influentials Hispanic Bus. Mag., 1987, 97. Mem. Am. Ednl. Rsch. Assn. (editl. com. 1979-82), Am. Assn. State Colls. and Univs. (bd. dirs.), Hispanic Assn. Colls. and Univs. (bd. dirs.), Assn. Mexican Am. Educators (various commendations), Am. Assn. Higher Edn. (instl. rep.), Western Coll. Assn. (past pres.), Rotary, Stockdale Country Club, Bakersfield Petroleum Club. Democrat. Roman Catholic. Home: 2213 Sully Ct Bakersfield CA 93311-1560 Office: Calif State U 9001 Stockdale Hwy Bakersfield CA 93311-1022 *Ensuring the right of every American youngster to a first-rate public education has been a driving interest in my life. I consider myself extremely fortunate in having had numerous opportunities to become involved in meaningful efforts to ensure that basic right in our country.*

ARCOS, CRESENCIO S., ambassador; b. San Antonio, Nov. 10, 1943; m. Patricia Cordova; 2 children. BA, U. Tex., 1966; MA, Johns Hopkins U., 1973. Various pub. and cultural affairs positions, Leningrad, USSR, Sao Paulo, Brazil; consulate gen. Leningrad, Russia; various pub. and cultural affairs positions Am. Embassy, Lisbon, Portugal, from 1973, counselor pub. affairs Tegucigalpa, Honduras, 1980-85; dep. dir. Nicaraguan Humanitarian Assistance Office, Dept. State, Washington, 1985-86, dep. coord. Latin Am. and Caribbean pub. diplomacy, 1986-87, dep. asst. sec. state for Cen. Am., 1988-89; coord. pub. diplomacy White House Office Communications and Planning, Washington, 1987-88; amb. to Honduras, Am. Embassy, Tegucigalpa, 1990-93; sr. dep. asst. sec. state for internat. narcotics and crime Dept. State, 1993-95; v.p. for L.Am. and Can. AT&T Corp, IPA, Coral Gables, Fla., 1995—2002; Dir. Internat. Affairs Dept. Homeland Security, 2003—. Mem. White House Pres.'s Fgn. Intelligence Adv. Bd., 1999-2003; mem. res. forces policy bd. Dept. Def. Mem. Hispanic Coun. on Internat. Rels., Washington; bd. dirs. Caribbean-Latin Am. Action, Coun. of the Americas, N.Y.C., Pan Am. Devel. Found., Visit Fairfax; adv. com. Fla. Internat. Univ. Latin Am. Carribean Ctr.; bd. visitors Zamorano Agr. Sch., Honduras; dir. United Negro Coll. Fund Inst. Internat. Pub. Policy; bd. dirs. Fla. Foster Care Rev., 1999-02; mem. corp. adv. bd. Pacific Coun. on Internat. Policy; mem. corp. bd. Cuban-Am. Nat. Coun. Decorated Orden de Morazan (Honduras); recipient awards USIA, Superior Honor awards State Dept.; Regents' fellow U. Calif., 1998-99. Mem. Coun. Fgn. Rels., Am. Fgn. Svc. Assn., Coun. of Ams. (bd. dirs.), Interam. Dialogue, Pacific Coun. Internat. Policy. (mem. corp. adv. bd.), Pan Am. Devel. Found. Personal E-mail: arcoscs@yahoo.com.

ARCOT, PRAKASH KUMAR B, engineer, consultant; s. Bashyam Sarangapani and Shantha Arcot. Masters, Okla. State U., Stillwater Oklahoma, 1993—94. Professional Engineer, Minn., 1997, Certified Energy Manager, IEE, 1995. Sr. design engr. Fischtner Consulting Engineers, Chennai, India, 1988—93; rsch. engr. Okla. State U., Stillwater, Okla., 1993—94. Sr. software engr. Siemens Power Systems and Control, Minneapolis, Minn., 1995—2001; consulting engr. (cockpit avionics upgrade) United Space Alliance, Houston, 2002—. Author: (ieee paper) Screening Technique for Optimally Locating Phase Shifters in Transmission Systems (Selected as Top Ten Finalist, 1995). Fellow Govt. of India Merit Scholar, Govt. of India, 1984 - 1988. Mem.: IEE (Sr. Mem.). Achievements include research in Optimally Locating Phase Shifters in Power Systems; development of Software Architecture for Connecting Real Time Systems with Business Applications (Enterprise Integration); Object Oriented Architecture for Real Time Systems; Senior Member IEE; Government of India Merit Scholar. Personal E-mail: prakashkumar_a@yahoo.com.

ARCURI, LEONARD PHILIP, elementary school educator; b. Bklyn., Apr. 28, 1947; s. Leonard James And Elizabeth Eleanor (Jaeger) A.; m. Lillian Campo, Aug. 11, 1979. BA, St. John's U., Jamaica, N.Y., 1969; MS, St. John's U., 1974; profl. diploma, C.W. Post, Greenvale, N.Y., 1980. Sci. educator St. Agnes Parish Sch., Bklyn., 1969-73; narcotics coord. Dist. 32 Drug Prevention Program, Bklyn., 1973-74; common branches tchr. P.S. 86 K, Bklyn., 1974-75; narcotics coord. Dist. 32 Drug Prevention Program, Bklyn., 1975-77; sci. educator P.S. 123 K, Bklyn., 1977—. Tutor biology Empire State Coll., SUNY, N.Y.C., 1988-89; instr. sci. Coll. New Rochelle, N.Y., 1988-89; instr. camping St. John's U. Sch. Continuing Edn., Jamaica, 1989-91; del. to Assembly of United Fedn. Tchrs., 1996—. Pres. Greater Ridgewood (N.Y.) Hist. Soc., 1983-84; coun. commr. Boy Scouts Am., (Queens, N.Y.), N.Y.C. 1979-80; mem. nat. coun. Boy Scouts Am., Tex., 1979-80; scout master troop 154, Boy Scouts Am., Goldens Bridge, N.Y., 1994—. Recipient Energy Conservation Achievement award Dept. of Gen. Svcs. City of N.Y., 1983, Silver Beaver, 1980. Mem. Elem. Sch. Sci. Assn. N.Y., Planetary Soc., Astron. Soc. of the Pacific, Nat. Sci. Tchrs. Assn., Kiwanis. Democrat. Roman Catholic. Avocations: canoeing, hiking, camping, flyfishing. Office: PS 123 K 100 Irving Ave Brooklyn NY 11237-2952

ARCUS, SAM GEORGE, social worker, educator, writer; b. Bklyn., Oct. 19, 1921; s. Nathan Louis and Mollie (Srulowitz) Arcus; m. Adele Rosenthal, Jan. 27, 1946; children: Norman Louis, Rochelle Linda Arcus/Ting. B.Social Sci., CCNY, 1947; MSW, Columbia U., 1949. Supr. Pride of Judea Children's Home, Bklyn., 1942—44; casework counselor Jewish Family Svc., N.Y.C., 1949—50; program dir. Jewish Cmty. Ctr., Albany, NY, 1950—52, YM-YWHA, Elizabeth, NJ, 1952—53; asst. dir. Jewish Cmty. Ctr., Houston, 1953—56; exec. dir. Jewish Cmty. Alliance, Jacksonville, Fla., 1956—57; area dir. Niles Twp. Jewish Cmty. Ctr., Skokie, Ill., 1957—61, exec. dir. Dallas, 1961—66, exec. dir. North Shore Marblehead, Mass., 1966—79, exec. dir. Tucson, 1979—86; coord. Ct. Visitor's Program, Superior Ct., Tucson, 1986—89; coord. long-term care advocacy program, Ariz. ombudsman program Pima Coun. on Aging, Tucson, 1989—. Faculty Albany Tchrs. Coll., NY, 1950—52; field work supr. Columbia U., Elizabeth, NJ, 1952—53; faculty sociology U. Houston, 1953—55; field work supr. Lady of Lake Coll., San Antonio, 1962—65; instr. Bishop Coll., Dallas, 1963—65; field work supr. Brandeis U./Heller Sch. Communal Svc., Waltham, Mass., 1967—69; part-time faculty North Shore C.C., Beverly, Mass., 1970—73; overall supr. field work students Salem State Coll., 1973—74, asst. prof., 1974—79; field work supr. Ariz. State U. Sch. Social Work, Tucson, 1981—86, field work superior, 1987—93. Author: Deja Views of An Ag'ng Orphan, 2000, Journeys, 2002, Journeys: Sequel to Deja Views of an Aging Orphan, 2003, Kola: Episodes in the Life of A Siberian Husky, 2005; author: (editor) HNOH: Memories of Orphanage Life, 2001; author: Handbook for Volunteers in LTC Ombudsman Program, 1998; contbr. An Orphan Has Many Parents, 1999; contbr. numerous articles to profl. jours.; editor: alumni newsletter. Life mem. Jewish Cmty. Ctr.; mem. Jewish Hist. Soc. of So. Ariz. Recipient Ward medal in sociology, CCNY, 1947. Mem.: Columbia U. Alumni Assn., CCNY/Hunter Coll. Alumni Assn. Avocations: reading, walking, classical music. Office: PIMA Coun on Aging 8467 E Broadway Tucson AZ 85710 Office Phone: 520-790-7262.

ARD, HAROLD JACOB, library administrator; b. Herrick, Ill., Aug. 26, 1940; s. Jacob S. and Hazel E. (Taylor) A.; m. Erma Chapman, Jan. 30, 1960 (div. June 1974); children— Teri Ann, Mark Alan. BS in Edn, Ill. State U., 1962, MS in Psychology, 1964; M.L.S., Rosary Coll., River Forest, Ill., 1968.

Tchr., materials cons. Decatur (Ill.) Pub. Schs., 1962-64; head librarian Barrington (Ill.) Pub. Library, 1964-68; exec. librarian Arlington Heights (Ill.) Meml. Library, 1968-72; library system dir. Jackson (Miss.) Met. Library System, 1972-77; assoc. dir. Rowland Med. Library, U. Miss. Med. Ctr., Jackson, 1978-84; mgr. bus., sci. and tech. units Fort Worth Pub. Libr., 1985-91; mgr. Wedgwood Libr., Ft. Worth, 1991-94; dir. S.W. Regional Libr., Ft. Worth, 1994-97; ret., 1997; part-time instr. U. Tex., Arlington, 2001—. Owner Antiques, Etc., Arlington; cons., lectr. in field. Mem. ALA, Tex. Library Assn., Med. Library Assn., Beta Phi Mu. Clubs: Rotary. Methodist. Home: 1125 Clara St Fort Worth TX 76110-1026 Personal E-mail: hard730939@aol.com.

ARD, KENNETH PAUL, music educator; s. Mabel Loretta and Angus James Ard. M of Musical Arts (MMA), (MusM), U. of So. Miss., 1977. Adj. prof. Grossmont Coll., El Cajon, Calif., 1988—, Southwestern Coll., Chula Vista, Calif., 1991—99. Jazz choral dir. Southwestern Coll., Chula Vista, Calif., 1996—99. Composer: (musical theater) The Delta Queen. V.p. Music teachers' Assn. of Calif., 1995—96. Mem.: Music Teachers' Assn. of Calif. (Calif. plan chair 2000—02). Democrat-Npl. Science Of Mind. Avocations: travel, exercise, bicycling, swimming.

ARDAI, CHARLES E., online services executive; b. N.Y.C., Oct. 25, 1969; s. Tibor and Vera Ardai. BA, Columbia U., 1991. Mktg./subsidiary rights assoc. Davis Publs., Inc., N.Y.C., 1986-91; sr. v.p. D.E. Shaw & Co., L.P., N.Y.C., 1992—; pres. Juno Online Svcs., L.P., N.Y.C., 1995—, pres. & CEO, 2000—. Editor: Great Tales of Madness and Themalabre, 1990, Kingpins, 1992, Futurecrime, 1991, High Adventure, 1992; contbr. articles, revs. and stories to profl. publs. Mem. Phi Beta Kappa.

ARDAIOLO, FRANK P., academic administrator; b. Bklyn., Oct. 21, 1948; m. Joleen Phifer, Mar. 18, 1978; children: Shannon Gabriela, Michael Palma, Matthew Eric. BA, Assumption Coll., Worcester, Mass., 1970; MS, Ind. U., 1974, EdD, 1978. Dir. of residence life/assoc. dean Belmont Abbey Coll., NC, 1974—76; assoc. dean students U. S.C., Columbia, 1978—82; v.p. for student life, assoc. prof. Winthrop U., Rock Hill, SC, 1989—; dean students, asst. v.p. U. Conn., Storrs, 1982—89. Contbr. articles to profl. jours., chapters to books. Chair Friends of Liberia, Washington, 2002—05, Com. on Human Rels., Rock Hill, SC, 1999—2002, Internat. Ctr. of York County, Rock Hill, SC, 2002—05. Recipient Greenleaf Disting. Alumni award, Ind. U. Dept. of Higher Edn., 1990, Teele Award for Significant Contbn. to Knowledge, Am. Coll. Pers. Assn. Commn. XV, 1996. Mem.: Am. Coll. Pers. Assn. (chair Commn. XV (legal issues) 1981—83), Nat. Assn. Student Pers. Adminstrs. (v.p. (Region III), bd. dirs. 1998—2000). Roman Catholic. Office: Winthrop University 209 Dinkins Rock Hill SC 29733 Office Phone: 803-323-2251. Office Fax: 803-323-2395.

ARDALAN, ABOL, management consultant; b. Oct. 21, 1929; BSc, USN Postgrad. Sch., Monterey, Calif., 1966; MSc, USN Postgrad. Sch., 1967; DSc, George Washington U., 1993. Pres. Iran Electronic Industries, Teheran, 1972-79; dir. tech. ventures Westinghouse, Balt., 1981-92; pres. AAA Consulting Inc., Vienna, Va., 1992—. Adj. prof. Univ. Coll., U. Md. Home: 8703 Westwood Forest Ln Vienna VA 22182-5055

ARDALAN, PEZHMAN CHRISTOPHER, lawyer; b. Tehran, Iran, Aug. 26, 1973; arrived in U.S., 1977; s. Ali and Jessica Ardalan; m. Anavelle Ardalan, July 3, 1996; children: Ethan, Devin. BA cum laude, Calif. State U. Northridge, 1996; JD cum laude, Order of Coif, Loyola Law Sch., L.A., 2000. Bar: Calif. 2000, U.S. Dist. Ct. (cen., ea., so. and no. dists) Calif. 2000, U.S. Ct. Appeals 2000. Paralegal, counsel Law Offices of Robert J. Vars, Encino, Calif., 1996—2000; counsel, pres. Vars & Ardalan PLC, Encino, 2001—02, Ardalan & Assocs. PLC, Sherman Oaks, Calif., 2002—. Commr. San Fernando Valley Pub. Safety Commn., Van Nuys, Calif., 2001—. Mem.: ATLA, ABA, Consumer Attys. Assn. L.A. Avocations: basketball, dance, tutoring. Office: Ardalan & Assocs PLC 15060 Ventura Blvd Ste 201 Sherman Oaks CA 91403

ARDANS, ALEXANDER ANDREW, veterinarian, educator, lab administrator; b. Ely, Nev., June 6, 1941; s. Jean Baptiste and Eleanora (Campbell) A.; m. Janice Gae Sanford, Dec. 23, 1961; children: Tamara Marie, Stephanie Marie, Melanie Alexandra, Angela Rosanne, Jeanette Alison. Student, U. Nev., 1959-61; BS, U. Calif., Davis, 1963, DVM, 1965; MS, U. Minn., St. Paul, 1969. Instr. Colo. State U., Ft. Collins, 1965-66, U. Minn., St. Paul, 1966-69; asst. prof., Sch. Vet. Medicine U. Calif., Davis, 1969-74, assoc. prof., 1974-80, prof., 1980—, chmn. dept. medicine, 1983-87; dir. Calif. Animal Health and Food Safety Lab Sys., Davis, 1987—. Recipient Outstanding Tchr. award U. Calif.-Davis Sch. Vet. Medicine, 1970, 73, Alumni award Sch. Vet. Med. U. Calif. Davis, 2000. Mem. Nat. Acad. Practitioners, AVMA, Am. Assn. Vet. Lab. Diagnosticians (Pope award 2000), Calif. Vet. Med. Assn., Conf. Rsch. Workers in Animal Disease. Republican. Roman Catholic. Avocations: swimming, fishing, hunting. Office: Univ Calif Sch Vet Medicine CAHFS Davis CA 95617 Office Phone: 530-752-8709. Business E-Mail: aaardans@ucdavis.edu.

ARDASH, GARIN, mechanical engineer; b. Detroit, July 14, 1963; s. Berge and Lucy Alice (Souldourian) Ardash. BSME, U. Mich., 1986, MME, 1988. Grad. rsch. asst. U. Mich. Coll. Engring., Ann Arbor, 1986-87, Los Alamos (N.Mex.) Nat. Lab., 1987; analysis engr. Naval Reactors Facility, Idaho Falls, Idaho, 1989-92, rsch. analysis engr. materials tech. dept., 1992—94, sr. rsch. analysis engr. materials tech. dept., 1994—2001; sr. analysis engr. refueling engring. Bechtel Bettis Inc., Bettis Atomic Power Lab., West Mifflin, Pa., 2001—. Fellow U. Mich. Coll. Engring. 1986-87; scholar State Mich. Coop. 1982-83; recipient Best Landscape Photograph, Pittsburgh Salon 2002 Mem. AAAS, ASTM, ASME, Internat. Legion Intelligence, Photog. Soc. Am., Acad. Sci. and Art of Pitts. (photog. sect.), Mensa, Pitts. South Soccer Assn. Avocations: soccer, photography, skiing, chess. Office: Bettis Atomic Power Lab Central Office Bldg 2 / REO PO Box 79 West Mifflin PA 15122-0079 Home: 111 Maple Ave #6 Pittsburgh PA 15218 Office Phone: 412-476-6534. Personal E-mail: garinard7@netscape.net.

ARDEHALI, HOSSEIN, physician, researcher; b. Tehran, Iran, Dec. 21, 1968; s. Ali Ardehali and Masoumeh Toti; m. Fatemeh Majlessi; children: Mariam Mina, Ali Sam. MD, Vanderbilt U., 1990—98. Instr. of medicine Johns Hopkins U., Balt., 1998—2004; asst. prof. of medicine Northwestern U., 2004—. Mem.: Am. Heart Assn. (mem. of dirs. 2004—). Office: Johns Hopkins Univ 720 Rutland Ave Baltimore MD 21205 Office Phone: 410-955-2776. Office Fax: 410-955-9753. Personal E-mail: hardehal@jhmi.edu.

ARDEN, BRUCE WESLEY, retired computer scientist, retired engineering educator; b. Mpls., May 29, 1927; s. Wesley and Clare Montgomery (Newton) A.; m. Patricia Ann Joy, Aug. 25, 1951; children: Wayne Wesley, Michelle Joy. Student, U. Del., 1944; BS in Elec. Engring., Purdue U., 1949; postgrad., U. Chgo., 1949; MA, U. Mich., 1955, PhD, 1965. Detail engr. Allison div. Gen. Motors Corp., Indpls., 1950-51; asst. prof. dept. computing and communication scis. U. Mich., Ann Arbor, 1965-67, assoc. prof., 1967-70, prof., 1970-73, chmn. dept., 1971-73, from research asst. to assoc. dir. Computing Facilities, 1951-73; prof., chmn. dept. elec. engring. and computer sci. Princeton U., 1973-85, Arthur Le Grand Doty prof. engring., 1981-86; prof. elec. engring., computer sci., dean engring. and applied sci. U. Rochester, 1986-94, vice provost computing, 1992-94, William F. May Prof. Engring., 1993-95, dean emeritus, 1994—; William F. May Prof. Engring. Emeritus, 1995—. Vis. prof. U. Grenoble, France, 1971-72; guest prof. Siemens Research, Munich, Germany, 1983, also cons.; cons. to Gen. Motors Corp., Ford Corp., Westinghouse Co., RCA, Xerox Data Systems, IBM.; mem. sci. council USRA Inst. for Computer Applications in Sci. and Engring., 1973-79, 82-88; mem. sci coun. USRA Inst. Advanced Computer Sci., 1982-88; chmn. com. on anti-ballistic missile data processing Nat. Acad. Sci., 1966-71; mem. panel Inst. Computer Sci. and Tech., 1980-86; mem. acad. adv. council Wang Inst., 1978-87; mem. study sect. NIH, 1985-88; reviewer Guggenheim Found., 1985-91. Author: An Introduction to Digital Computing, 1963; (with K. Astil) Numerical Algorithms: Their Origins and Applications, 1970; editor: What Can Be Automated?, 1980. Served with USNR, 1944-46, 49-50. Fellow AAAS; mem. IEEE (sr.), Assn. for Computing Machinery, Univs. Space Research Assn. (bd. dirs. 1982-88), Sigma Xi, Tau Beta Pi, Eta Kappa Nu.

ARDEN, EUGENE, retired university provost; b. N.Y.C., June 25, 1923; s. Harry and Gussie (Shevach) A.; m. Sandra E. Rose, July 11, 1948; children: Stacey, Jonathan. BA, NYU, 1943; MA, Columbia U., 1947; PhD, Ohio State U., 1953. Mem. faculty Ohio State U., Columbus, Queen's Coll., Hofstra U., 1947-56; from asst. prof. to prof., chmn. dept. English and humanities div. C.W. Post Coll., Greenvale, N.Y., 1956-62, dean, 1962-64; dean grad. faculties L.I. U., 1964-70, dean Conolly Coll., 1970-71, exec. dean Bklyn. Ctr., 1971; vice chancellor, dean acad. affairs U. Mich., Dearborn, 1972-89, provost, 1989-91, ret., 1991. Editor: Boca Chase Newsletter, 1995—; contbr. articles to profl. jours., mags. Bd. dirs. Mid-Island YM and YWHA, 1962-64, Temple Beth Hillel, Margate, Fla; mem. nat. exec. com. Hillel Founds.; asso. chmn. civil liberties com. Jewish Cmty. Coun. Met. Detroit. Served with AUS, 1943-46, ETO. Mem. AAUP (editor Academe jour. 1991-93), B'nai Brith (pres. Ctrl. Nassau lodge 1966-68). Home: 18102 Clear Brook Cir Boca Raton FL 33498-1943

ARDEN, SHERRY W., publishing executive; b. N.Y.C., Oct. 18, 1923; d. Abraham and Rose (Bellak) Waretnick; m. Hal Marc Arden (div. 1974); children: Doren, Cathy; m. George Bellak, Oct. 20, 1979. Student, Columbia U. Publicity dir. Coward-McCann, N.Y.C., 1965-67; producer Allan Foshko Assoc., ABC-TV, N.Y.C., 1967-68; sr. v.p., pub. William Morrow & Co., N.Y.C., 1968-85, pres., pub., 1985-89; owner Sherry W. Arden Lit. Agy., 1990—. Mem. Assn. Am. Pubs. (dir.) Clubs: Pubs. Lunch.

ARDERY, PHILIP PENDLETON, lawyer; b. Lexington, Ky., Mar. 6, 1914; s. William Breckenridge and Julia (Spencer) A.; m. Anne Stuyvesant Tweedy, Dec. 6, 1941; children: Peter Brooks (dec.), Philip Pendleton, Jr., Joseph Lord Tweedy, Julia Spencer. AB, U. Ky., 1935; JD, Harvard U., 1938; MBA, U. Louisville, 1957. Bar: Ky. 1938. Practice law, Frankfort, 1938-40, 45-50, Louisville, 1952—; ptnr. Frost Brown Todd, 1972—. Sec. Ky. Aero. Commn., 1946-48; commr. Jefferson County, 1958-61 Author: Bomber Pilot: A Memoir of World War II, 1978, Heroes and Horses, Tales of the Bluegrass, 1996; also articles. Bd. dirs. Frazier Rehab. Ctr., 1953-93, Schizophrenia Found., Ky., 1981—, Thomas D. Clark Found., 1994—, Nat. Alliance Rsch. in Schizophrenia and Depression, 1985-92, Norton Hosp. Found., 1985-94, Ky. Mental Health Assn., 1985—, Jewish Hosp. Healthcare Svcs., 1986—, Ky. Shakespeare Festival, 1989-90, Ky. Humanities Coun., 1989-94; pres. Ky. Heart Assn., 1955, chmn. bd., 1956; incorporator, dir. Ballet Español, 1984—; chmn. bd. Am. Heart Assn., 1966-69; dep. Episcopal Gen. Convs., 1970, 73, 76, 79; mem. exec. com. Ky. Hist. Soc., 1983-95; trustee U. of South, 1977-80, Episcopal Theol. Sem. in Ky., 1985-90; sec. Ky. Horse Park Found., 1985—. Col. USAAF, 1940-45, col. USAF, 1950-52, maj. gen. USAFR, ret., 1974—. Decorated Silver Star, D.F.C. (2), Air medal (4); Croix de Guerre with palm (France) Mem. ABA, Ky. Bar Assn., Louisville Bar Assn., Soc. Cin., Order First Families of Va. (Burgess), Pendennis Club, Filson Club (bd. dirs. 1986-96), Phi Beta Kappa. Democrat. Episcopalian. Home: 448 Swing Ln Louisville KY 40207-1444 Office: 3200 Providian Ctr Louisville KY 40202-2873 Office Phone: 502-895-5400. Personal E-mail: pardery1@aol.com.

ARDISON, MATTHEW TANNER, physician assistant; b. York, Pa. s. Gary Winship and Linda (Tanner) Ardison. BS, Hampden-Sydney Coll., 1991; MA, Gordon-Conwell Theol. Sem., 1994; MHS, Duke U. Sch. Medicine, 1996; MPH, Johns Hopkins U. Bloomberg Sch. Pub. Health, 2003. Cert. physician asst. Duke U. Med. Ctr., N.C., 1996. Physician asst. family medicine Navajo Health Found., Sage Meml. Hosp., Ganado, Ariz., 1996—99; physician asst. internal medicine Yale-New Haven Hosp., 1999—2002; physician asst. family medicine Dartmouth-Hitchcock Med. Ctr. Cmty. Health Ctr., Lebanon, N.H., 2003—04; physician asst. cardiology Mass. Gen. Hosp., Boston, 2004—. Scholar Nat. Health Svcs., Nat. Health Svc. Corps., U.S. Dept. Health and Human Svcs., 1994—99. Fellow: Am. Acad. Physician Assts.; mem.: Am. Pub. Health Assn. Office: The Mass Gen Hosp 55 Fruit St Gray/Bigelow 852-J Boston MA 02114 Home: 61 Hancock St Apt 2 Boston MA 02114 Personal E-mail: matthewardison@yahoo.com. Business E-Mail: mardison@partners.org.

ARDITI, OLIVIA LYDIE, information technology executive, French educator; b. Paris, Nov. 5, 1958; d. Adrien Marc and Claude Gisele (Hugues) Benhaim; 1 child, Chloe. BA in Sociology, U. Haifa, Israel, 1982; MA in French Lit., SUNY, Stony Brook, 1984; MPhil in French Lit., NYU, 1992; M in Libr. and Info. Sci., San Jose State U., 1996. French tchr. Alliances Francaises, Berkeley, Calif. and Buffalo, 1992—; dir. western N.Y. regional info. network Inst. for Local Governance & Regional Growth, U. Buffalo, 1997—. Web cons. Fedn. of Alliances Francaises USA, Milw., 2003—. Recipient Best Mgr. of Yr. in Tech., U. Buffalo Sch. of Mgmt., 2002. Mem.: Fedn. of Alliances Francaises USA (bd. mem. 2004—05), Alliance Francaise de Buffalo (pres. 1998—2005). Achievements include design of online regional information system for Western New York, used daily by thousands of people. Home: 115 Niagara Falls Blvd Buffalo NY 14214 Office: Inst Univ Buffalo Beck Hall 3435 Main St Buffalo NY 14214 Office Phone: 716-829-3777. Office Fax: 716-829-3776. Personal E-mail: oarditi@yahoo.com.

ARDITI, RALPH, lawyer; b. NYC, 1948; BA, Yale Coll., 1970; JD, Yale Law Sch., 1973. Bar: NY 1974. Law clerk Hon. Morris E. Lasker, US Dist. Ct. for Southern Dist., NY, 1973—75; ptnr., mergers and acquisitions, securities and general corporate matters Skadden, Arps, Slate, Meagher & Flom LLP, NYC. Editor: Yale Law Jour., 1972—73. Mem.: Phi Beta Kappa. Office: Skadden Arps Slate Meagher & Flom LLP Four Times Sq New York NY 10036 Office Phone: 212-735-3860. Office Fax: 917-777-3860. Business E-Mail: rarditi@skadden.com.

ARDITTI, FRED D., economist, educator; b. N.Y.C., Jan. 30, 1939; s. David A. and Marie A.; children: Elizabeth Marie, Anne Sarah, David Frederick. BS in Elec. Engring., MIT, 1960, MS in Indsl. Mgmt., 1962, PhD in Econs., 1966. Economist Rand Corp., Santa Monica, Calif., 1965-67; lectr., asst. prof. fin. U. Calif., Berkeley, 1967-71; from assoc. prof. to prof. fin. U. Fla., Gainesville, 1971—73, Walter J. Matherly chair fin. and econs., 1974-80, chmn. dept. econs., 1977-80; v.p. research, chief economist Chgo. Merc. Exchange, 1980-82; pres. GNP Fin. Inc., 1982-86, GNP Commodities Inc., 1984-86, Drexel, Burnham, Lambert Quantitative Asset Mgmt. Group, Chgo., 1986-89; fin. cons. Chgo., 1989—; prof. fin. DePaul U., Chgo., 1990-97; sr. exec. v.p. for planning and devel. Chgo. Merc. Exch., 1997-2000; prof. fin. DePaul U., Chgo., 2000—. Vis. prof. Hebrew U., 1973, U. Toronto, 1976—77, U. Chgo., 1981—83, 1990. Author: Derivatives: A Comprehensive Resource for Options, Futures, Interest rate Swaps and Mortgage Securities, 1996; contbr. articles to profl. jours., chpts. in books. NSF fellow; Ford Found. rsch. grantee; NDEA fellow, other fellowships; Fred Arditti Innovation award created Chgo. Merc. Exhc., 2003.

AREEN, JUDITH CAROL, law educator, dean; b. Chgo., Aug. 2, 1944; d. Gordon Eric and Pauline Jeanette (Payberg) A.; m. Richard M. Cooper, Feb. 17, 1979; children: Benjamin Eric (dec.), Jonathan Gordon. AB, Cornell U., 1966; JD, Yale U., 1969. Bar: Mass. 1970, D.C. 1972. Program planner for higher edn. Mayor's Office City of N.Y., 1969-70; dir. edn. voucher study Ctr. for Study Pub. Policy, Cambridge, Mass., 1970-72; mem. faculty Georgetown U., Washington, 1972—, assoc. prof. law, 1972-76, prof., 1976—, prof. cmty. and family medicine, 1980-89, assoc. dean Law Ctr., 1984-87, dean, exec. v.p. for law affairs, 1989—2004, emeritus, 2004—, Paul Regis Dean endowed chair, 2004—. Gen. counsel, project coord. Office Mgmt. and Budget, Washington, 1977—80; spl. counsel White House Task Force on Regulatory Reform, Washington, 1978—80; cons. NIH, 1984, NRC, 1985; bd. dirs. Equal Justice Works, Pro Bono Inst.; pres.-elect Assn. Am. Law Schs., 2005. Author: Youth Service Agencies, 1977, Cases and Materials on Family Law, 4th edit., 1999, Law, Science and Medicine, 1984, 3d edit., 2005. Mem. Def. Adv. Com. Women In Svcs., Washington, 1979-82; trustee Cornell Univ., 1997-01. Woodrow Wilson Internat. Ctr. Scholars fellow, 1988-89, Kennedy Inst. Ethics Sr. Rsch. fellow, Washington, 1982-98. Mem. ABA, DC Bar Assn., Am. Law Inst. Business E-Mail: areen@law.georgetown.edu.

AREF, HASSAN, fluid mechanics educator; b. Alexandria, Egypt, Sept. 28, 1950; s. Moustapha and Jytte (Adolphsen) A.; m. Susanne Eriksen, Aug. 3, 1974; children: Michael, Thomas. Cand.Sci., U. Copenhagen, Denmark, 1975; PhD, Cornell U., 1980. Asst. prof. Brown U., Providence, 1980-85, assoc. prof., 1985; assoc. prof. fluid mechanics U. Calif., San Diego, 1985-88, prof. fluid mechanics, 1988-92; chief scientist San Diego Supercomputer Ctr., 1989-92; prof., head dept. theoretical and applied mechanics U. Ill., Urbana-Champaign, 1992—2003; Reynolds Metals prof., dean engring. Va. Tech., 2003—05. Corrsin lectr. Johns Hopkins U., Baltimore, 1988; Westinghouse disting. lectr. U. Mich., Ann Arbor, 1991; lectr. Midwest Mechanics, 1991. Editor Cambridge Texts in Applied Math., 1987-94, Advances in Applied Mechanics, 2001—; assoc. editor Jour. Fluid Mechanics, 1984-93; contbr. articles to profl. jours. Recipient Presdl. Young Investigator award, NSF 1985, Otto Laporte award, Am. Physical Soc., 2000. Fellow: World Innovation Found., Am. Acad. Mechanics, Am. Phys. Soc. (Otto Laporte award 2000); mem.: Soc. Indsl. and Applied Math. Office: Va Polytech Inst 320 Norris Hall Coll Engring Blacksburg VA 24061 Office Phone: 540-231-5626. Business E-Mail: haref@vt.edu.

AREGOOD, RICHARD LLOYD, editor; b. Camden, N.J., Dec. 31, 1942; s. Lloyd Samuel and Ruby Odell (Trousdale) A.; m. Barbara Sue Wittenberger, Oct. 6, 1962 (div. June 1978); children: Laurie, Christopher; m. Doris Joan Sampieri, Apr. 21, 1979 (div. July 1992); children: Deborah, David, Jennifer, William Sampieri; m. Kathleen Shea, Feb. 20, 1993; 1 child, James. BA in English, Rutgers U., 1965. Reporter, editor Burlington County Herald, Mount Holly, N.J., 1964-65; reporter Burlington County Times, Willingboro, N.J., 1965-66, Phila. Daily News, 1966-71, features editor, 1971-73, news editor, 1973-74, editor editorial page, 1975-95, dep. sports editor, 1976; editor the editl. page The Star Ledger of Newark (N.J.), 1995—. Co-author: Beyond Argument: A Handbook for Editorial Writers, 2001, The Journalist's Craft: A Guide to Writing Better Stories, 2002. Pres. local 10 Newspaper Guild, Phila., 1978-79, v.p., 1973-77. Recipient Pulitzer prize for editorial writing, 1985, Walker Stone award Scripps-Howard Newspapers, 1993; inducted into Rutgers Hall of Disting. Alumni, 1993. Mem. Am. Soc. Newspaper Editors (dir. 1996-2002, disting. writing award 1984, 90, 94), Nat. Conf. Editl. Writers. Episcopalian. Office: The Star Ledger Star Ledger Pla Newark NJ 07102-1200 Personal E-mail: raregood@yahoo.com. Business E-Mail: raregood@verizon.net.

AREM, LAWRENCE JAY, lawyer; b. Bklyn., Feb. 2, 1950; s. Gilbert and Renee (Rothman) A.; m. Marcia Susan Clark, May 4, 1980; children: Nathaniel, Hannah, Jacob. BS, NYU, 1972, LLM in Taxation, 1978; JD, U. Pa., 1975. Bar: Pa. 1975, U.S. Dist. Ct. (ea. dist.) Pa. 1975, U.S. Tax Ct. 1976. Assoc. Eilberg, Carson, Getson & Abramson, Phila., 1975-76, Krekstein, Wolfson & Krekstein, Phila., 1977-79, Klehr, Harrison, Harvey, Branzberg & Ellers, Phila., 1979—83, ptnr., 1983—, chmn. tax dept. Mem. ABA, Pa. Bar Assn., Phila. Bar Assn. Democrat. Jewish. Home: 645 Hazelhurst Ave Merion Station PA 19066-1406 Office: Klehr Harrison Harvey Branzberg & Ellers 260 S Broad St 3d Fl Philadelphia PA 19102 Office Phone: 215-569-4142. Business E-Mail: larem@klher.com.

ARENA, ALBERT A., museum director; b. Waltham, Mass., Nov. 12, 1929; s. John Giovanni and Jennie (Inferrera) A.; m. Jean Marie MacDonald, Dec. 29, 1935; children: Albert A. Jr., Andrew A., Arthur A. BS, Mass. Maritime Acad., 1952. Licensed Chief Marine Engr. Marine engr. Gulf Oil Co., N.Y.C., 1952, Farrell Lines, Inc., Bklyn., 1952-54; naval engr. officer USS New Jersey, Norfolk, Va., 1954-56; engr. Commonwealth of Mass., various locations, 1957-59, Harvard U., Roxbury, Mass., 1960; marine engr. SS America, N.Y.C., 1960-62; boiler and machine inspector Factory Mutual Ins., Norwood, Mass., 1963-70; assoc. prof. Mass. Maritime Acad., Buzzards Bay, Mass., 1970-72; engr. instr. Raytheon Co., Lexington, Mass., 1973-74; chief stationary engr. Allied Maintenance Corp., Boston, 1974-80; museum dir. Waltham (Mass.) Museum, 1971—. Producer, narrator This Was Waltham for Waltham Cable Access TV, 1989—. Recipient Ship Safety Achievement award Am. Merchant Marine Inst., 1962, Citation of Svc. for efforts associated with Waltham Mus. Mass. Ho. of Reps., 1994. Roman Catholic. Home: 17 Noonan St Waltham MA 02453-4212 Office: Waltham Mus 196 Charles St Waltham MA 02453-4206 Office Phone: 781-893-8017. Personal E-mail: aaarena@hotmail.com.

ARENA, BRUCE, professional soccer coach; b. Brooklyn, NY, Sept. 21, 1951; m. Phyllis Arena; 1 child, Kenny. Student, Nassau (N.Y.) C.C., 1969-71; BS in Bus., Cornell U., 1971-73. Asst. lacrosse coach, asst. soccer coach Cornell U., Ithaca, N.Y., 1973-76; head soccer coach U. Puget Sound, Tacoma, Wash., 1976-78; head soccer coach, asst. men's lacrosse coach U. Va., Charlottesville, 1978-95; head coach DC United, Washington, 1995-98, U.S. Nat. Soccer Team, Chgo., 1998—. Mem. U.S. nat. teams in both soccer and lacrosse and competed professionally in both sports; past chmn. ACC soccer coaches, ISAA Divsn. I nat. poll; "A" coaching lic. from U.S. Soccer Fedn.; mem. NCAA Divsn. I soccer com., 1989-95. Named ACC Coach of Yr., 1979, 84, 86, 88, 89, 91, South Atlantic Region Coach of Yr., 1982, 83, 87, nat. Coach of Yr. by Lanzera, 1993. Inducted into Cornell Athletic Field Hall of Fame, 1986, Long Island Lacrosse Hall of Fame, 1990. Head coach U.S. under-23 nat. team for 1996 Olympics; MLS Coach of Year, 1997. Achievements include career record of 295-58-32 (.808) in 18 yrs. at U. Va., leading U. Va. to NCAA titles in 1989, 91, 92, 93, 94, taking U. Va. to 6 or the last 7 NCAA semi-finals and 8 straight quarter finals, directing U. Va. to 15 straight NCAA tournament appearances (longest active streak in U.S.), Major League Soccer Cup Championships, 1996, 97, U.S. Open Cup Championship, 1996. Office: US Soccer 1801 S Prairie Ave Chicago IL 60616-1319

ARENA, KELLI, news correspondent; b. Bklyn., N.Y., Dec. 17, 1963; d. Melvin Mullins and Mary Ann (Scafa) Tracy. BFA, NYU, 1985. Prodr. various shows CNN, N.Y.C., 1985-89, prodr. spl. reports, 1988-89, line prodr., 1989-90, supervising prodr., 1990-92, exec. prodr. London, 1992, news editor N.Y.C., 1992-93, reporter, anchor, 1993—. Youth dir. St. George's Ch., N.Y.C., 1989-93. Recipient Peabody award U. Ga., 1987, Cable Ace award, 1987, Gold award Houston Internat. Film Festival, 1987, Nat. Headliner award Atlantic City Press Club, 2002, Emmy award for Sept. 11th coverage, CNN, 2002; named Top ten Fin. Journalist Jour. Fin. Reporting, 1989-92; named Best Corr. N.Y. Festivals, 2002. Mem. Soc. Am. Bus. Editors and Writers, Internat. Womens Media Found. Office: CNN 820 1st St NE Washington DC 20002-4243 E-mail: kelli.arena@turner.com.

ARENAL, JULIE (MRS. BARRY PRIMUS), choreographer; Tchr. Herbert Berghof Studio; asst. on tng. program Lincoln Center Repertory Theatre. Dancer with cos. of Anna Sokolow, Sophie Maslow, John Butler, Jack Cole, Jose Limon; choreographer: Marat/Sade for, Theatre Co. of Boston, Harvard U. Loeb Theatre, Municipal Theatre, Atlanta, Hair, on Broadway (Most Original Choreographer of Year award Sat. Rev. 1968), also London; dir., choreographer Hair, Stockholm (Best Dir.-Choreographer of Year award 1969); choreographer, dir. Isabel's a Jezebel; choreographer: Indians on Broadway, Fiesta for Ballet Hispanico, 1972, 20008 1/2, Boccaccio, 1975, A Private Circus, 1975, Free to Be You and Me, 1976, The Referee, 1976, El Arbito, 1978; choreographer for San Francisco Ballet, Nat. Ballet de Cuba, (film) King of the Gypsies, Great Expectations, Fur. Friends, 1980, Mistress, 1991, Once Upon a Time in America, Houston Grand Opera Co., Porgy and Bess, 1995, Great Expectations, 1997; dir., choreographer (stage) Funny Girl, Tokyo, 1979-80; dir. N.Y. Express Hip Hop Dance Co., commd. by Spoleto Festival of the Two Worlds, N.C. and Italy; toured 7 cities in People's Republic of China. N.E.A. grantee for A Puerto Rican Soap Opera, Ballet

Hispanico, 1973, Oreg. Shakespeare Festival, 1997, Porgy and Bess City Opera, N.Y.C. Opera, 2000, Am. Family PBS TV Series, 2002, Hair Downtown Cabaret, Bridgeport, Conn., 2005. Office Phone: 213-300-7416. E-mail: borbos@aol.com.

ARENBERG, IRVING KAUFMAN KARCHMER, otolaryngologist; b. East Chicago, Ind., Jan. 10, 1941; s. Harry and Gertrude (Field) Kaufman; divorced; children: Daniel Kaufman, Michael Harrison, Julie Gayle. BA in Zoology, U. Mich., 1963, MD, 1967. Diplomate Am. Bd. Otolaryngology. Intern Chgo. Wesley Meml. Hosp., 1967-68; resident Barnes and Allied Hosps., St. Louis, 1969-74; asst. prof. surgery U. Wis., Madison, 1976-80; chief otolaryngology VA Hosp., Madison, 1976-80; CEO Ear Ctr. PC, Englewood, Colo., 1989—96; chmn. bd., CEO IntraEar, Neurobiometrix Inc., Inc., 1994—99; pres., CEO, chmn. Arenberg and Assocs. Ltd., LLC, 2000—04. Dir., founder Internat. Meniere's Disease Rsch. Inst., Denver, 1971—; guest of honor 39th Chinese Nat. ENT Congress, Taipei, 1985, U. Antwerp, 1995, West German ENT Soc., 1996; vis. scientist Swedish Med. Rsch. Coun., 1975-76; vis. prof. U. Mich., Ann Arbor, 1988, 94, St. Mary's Hosp. and Med. Sch., London, 1988, U. Verona (Italy) Med. Sch., 1989, U. N.C., Chapel Hill, 1989, U. Wurzburg (Germany) Med. Sch., 1989, 90, 92, U. Ark., Little Rock, 1990, 95, U. Innsbruck, Austria, 1991, U. Sydney, Australia, 1992, U. Tex., Dallas, 1993. Editor: Meniere's Disease, 1983, Inner Ear Surgery, 1991, Dizziness and Balance Disorders, 1993; assoc. editor AMA Archives of Otolaryngology, 1968-81; mem. editorial bd. Am. Jour. Otology, 1978-91, Head and Neck Surgery Jour., 1992—; guest editor Otolaryngologic Clinics N.Am., 1980, 83, Neurologic Clinics N.Am., 1990; editor Inner Ear Surgery, 1991; mem. rev. bd. Rev. de Laryngologie et Otology (France), 1984—; contbr. over 400 articles to profl. peer-reviewed jours. Recipient Pietro Caliceti prize and Gold Medal Honor award U. Bologna, Italy, 1983, Spl. Tchr. Investigation Tng. award NIH, 1970-1975; fellow Barnes and Allied Hosps., 1968-69, 75, NIH, 1971-76, U. Uppsala-Royal Acad. Hosp., Sweden, 1975-76; grantee NIH, 1971-77, Deafness Rsch. Found., 1971-73. Fellow ACS, Am. Acad. Otolaryngology; mem. AMA, Am. Neurotology Soc., N.Y. Acad. Scis., Colo. Otologic Rsch. Ctr. (founder, pres., bd. dirs. 1980-88), Internat. Meniere's Disease Rsch. Inst. (dir. 1971—), Assn. Rsch. in Otolaryngology, Barany Soc., Triological Soc., Politzer Soc., Prosper Meniere Soc. (founder, exec. dir. 1981-99), Acoustical Soc. Am., Ogura Soc., Sigma Xi. Achievements include 10 U.S. and fgn. patents in field. Avocations: skiing, golf, biking, tennis.

ARENBERG, JULIUS THEODORE, JR., retired accounting company executive; b. Chgo., May 29, 1923; s. Julius Theodore and Ellen A. (Foran) A.; m. Jean E. Young, June 19, 1948; children— Robert, Thomas, Mary, James, Michael, Douglas. BS in Acctg, U. Ill., 1947. C.P.A., Ill. With Arthur Andersen & Co., Chgo., 1947—, ptnr., 1962—, head fin. services div., 1975—; chmn. C.P.A. adv. com. Nat. Assn. Ins. Commrs., 1974-75. Mem. faculty Bank Adminstrn. Inst. Sch., U. Wis., 1966-69, Nat. Installment Credit Sch., U. Chgo., 1965-70 Mem. Lombard (Ill.) Elementary Bd. Edn., 1960-66, pres., 1962-66. Served with USNR, 1943-46. Mem. Am. Inst. C.P.A.'s (chmn. com. ins. acctg. and auditing 1966-73), Ill. Soc. C.P.A.'s. Clubs: St. Charles Country, Bay Hill, Isleworth Golf. Roman Catholic. E-mail: payde369@aol.com.

AREND, ANTHONY CLARK, social studies educator, academic administrator; b. Balt., Oct. 24, 1958; s. Paul Joseph and Cora Allen (Clark) A. BSFS magna cum laude, Georgetown U., 1980; MA, U. Va., 1982, PhD, 1985. Rsch. asst. U. Va. Sch. Law, Charlottesville, Va., 1981-84, sr. fellow, 1985-86; professorial lectr. dept. govt. Georgetown U., Washington, 1986, asst. prof., 1988-93, assoc. prof., 1993-2000, chair main campus exec. faculty, 1997-2001, prof., 2000—, co-dir. Inst. for Internat. Law and Politics, 2003—, v.p. univ. faculty senate main campus, 2001—. Vis. asst. prof. Pa. State U., Harrisburg, 1987, Georgetown U., 1987—88; co-dir. Inst. for Internat. Law and Politics. Author: Pursuing a Just and Durable Peace: John Foster Dulles and International Organization, 1988, Legal Rules and International Society, 1999; co-author: International Law and the Use of Force: Beyond the United Nations Charter Paridigm, 1993; editor: The United States and the Compulsory Jurisdiction of the International Court of Justice, 1986; co-editor: The Falklands War: Lessons for Strategy, Diplomacy and International Law, 1985, International Rules: Approaches from International Law and International Relations, 1996; mem. bd. advisors Va. Jour. Internat. Law, 1992—; contbr. chpts. to books, articles to profl. jours. Chmn. adminstrv. coun. Severn United Meth. Ch., 1984-89, lay leader, 1990—; gov. bd. govs. Georgetown U. Alumni Assn., 2001-. Margaret Nils Butler Meml. DACOR fellow, 1980-81, Richard M. Weaver fellow, 1982-83, Lassen fellow, 1983-84, Philip Francis du Pont fellow, 1983-84. Mem. Am. Soc. Internat. Law, Georgetown U. Alumni Assn. (bd. govs. 2001—), Coun. on Fgn. Rels., Phi Beta Kappa Democrat. Avocations: golf, squash. Home: 1301 33rd St NW Apt 1 Washington DC 20007-2850 Office: Georgetown U Dept Govt Washington DC 20057-0001 Office Phone: 202-687-6237. Business E-Mail: arenda@georgetown.edu.

ARENDALL, CHARLES STEVEN, management consultant, educator; b. Warringon, Lancashire, Eng., Aug. 3, 1955; arrived in U.S., 1956, permanent resident; s. Charles Lewis and Pamela (Read) Arendall; m. Elizabeth Ann Kern, Dec. 13, 1980 (div. Apr. 3, 1984); m. Vivian Elizabeth Taylor, May 2, 1985; children: Dena Elizabeth, Charles Henry II. BBA U. Memphis, 1977; MBA, U. Memphis, 1980; PhD, U. Tenn., 1986. Mgr. territory Burroughs Corp., Memphis, 1977—79; grad. tchg. asst. U. Tenn., 1980—84; asst. prof. La. State U., Baton Rouge, 1985—88; mng. ptnr. Qualimetrics, Inc., Maryville, Tenn., 1987—90; asst. prof. Union U., Jackson, Tenn., 1990—93, assoc. prof., 1993—97, prof., dir. MBA program, 1997—. Cons. stats. process control Qualimetrics, Maryville, Tenn., 1982—87; cons. job safety Jaws Offshore, Baton Rouge, 1985—87; cons. total quality Jackson (Tenn.) Gen. Hosp., 1992—. Contbr. articles to profl. jours., 1995. Fellow Found. La. State U., 1986. Mem.: So. Mgmt. Assn., Decision Scis. Inst. (presenter 1990—), Acad. Mgmt. (reviewer, session pres. 2002). Episcopalian. Avocations: camping, golf, hiking, skiing, water-skiing. Office: Union Univ 2735 Hacks Cross Rd Germantown TN 38138 Home: 5860 Kesswood Ct Memphis TN 38119 E-mail: sarendal@uu.edu.

ARENDS, HERMAN JOSEPH, former insurance company executive; b. 1945; M of Math., Mich. State U., 1967. Tchr. Laningsburg (Mich.) H.S., 1967-72; chmn., CEO Auto-Owners Ins. Co., Lansing, Mich., 1972—2004. Office: Auto-Owners Insurance Co 6101 Anacapri Dr Lansing MI 48917-3994*

ARENDT, BRIAN BERNARD, historian, educator; b. St. Louis, Sept. 21, 1961; s. Bernard Charles and Isabelle Rita Arendt. BA, U. Mo., St. Louis, 1979—83; MA, SUNY, Stony Brook, 1983—84; PhD, Georgetown U., Washington, D.C., 1985—93. Prof., history Concordia U. Wis., St. Louis, 1994—. Cabinet mem. Corpus Christi Parish, Jennings, Mo., 2002—04, vol., 2002—03. Fellow, DAAD, 1990—91. Mem.: Am. Hist. Assn. Home: 7505 Calvin Ave Saint Louis MO 63136-1201 Office: Concordia Univ Wis 10825 Watson Rd Saint Louis MO 63127 Personal E-mail: barendt@ix.netcom.com.

ARENELLA, PETER LEE, law educator; b. Boston, Nov. 28, 1947; s. Nicholas Peter and Joanne (Issacson) A.; children: David Mack, Katherine Mack; m. Mia Arenella, July 1, 2002; children: Mara, Paloma. BA magna cum laude, Wesleyan U., 1969; JD cum laude, Harvard U., 1972. Bar: Mass. 1972. Law clk. to presidng chief justice Mass. Supreme Jud. Ct., Boston, 1972-73; atty. Mass. Pub. Defender's Office, Boston, 1973; sole practice Boston, 1974-75; asst. prof. law U. Mass., Boston, 1974-75, Rutgers U., Camden, N.J., 1975-78, assoc. prof., 1978-80, prof., 1980-82, Boston U., 1982-87, UCLA, Los Angeles, 1987—. Cons., expert witness Congress Hearings on Grand Jury Reform Insanity Def., Washington, 1982, 85; legal cons. ABC News (O.J. Simpson Case), 1994-97. Contbr. articles to profl. jours. Recipient Metcalf Tchg. Excellence prize Boston U., 1984, Rutter Tchg. Excellence award UCLA, 1999; Woodrow Wilson fellow, 1969. Mem. ABA (grand jury com. 1979-85, reporter model grand jury act 1980), Soc. Am. Law Tchrs. Unitarian Universalist. Avocations: swimming, tennis, softball, jogging. E-mail: arenella@law.ucla.edu.

ARENOWITZ, ALBERT HAROLD, psychiatrist; b. N.Y.C., Jan. 12, 1925; s. Louis Isaac and Lena Helen (Skovron) A.; m. Betty Jane Wiener, Oct. 11, 1953; children: Frederick Stuart, Diane Helen. BA with honors, U. Wis., 1948; MD, U. Va., 1951. Diplomate Am. Bd. Psychiatry, Am. Bd. Child Psychiatry. Intern Kings County Gen. Hosp., Bklyn., 1951-52; resident in psychiatry Bronx (N.Y.) VA Hosp., 1952-55; postdoctoral fellow Youth Guidance Ctr., Worcester, Mass., 1955-57; dir. Ctr. for Child Guidance, Phila., 1962-65, Hahnemann Med. Service Eastern State Sch. and Hosp., Trevose, Pa., 1965-68; dir., tng. dir. Child and Adolescent Psychiat. Clinic, Phila. Gen. Hosp., 1965-67; asst. clin. prof. psychiatry Jefferson Med. Coll., Phila., 1974-76; exec. dir. Child Guidance and Mental Health Clinics, Media, Pa., 1967-74; med. dir. Intercommunity Child Guidance Ctr., Whittier, Calif., 1976—. Cons. Madison Pub. Schs., 1957-60, Dane County Child Guidance Ctr., Madison, 1957-62, Juvenile Ct., Madison, 1957-62; clin. asst. prof. child psychiatry Hahnemann Med. Coll., Phila., 1966-74; asst. clin. prof. psychiatry U. Wis., Madison, 1960-62, clin. asst. prof. psychiatry, behavioral scis. and family medicine U. So. Calif., L.A., 1976—; mem. med. staff Presbyn. Intercommunity Hosp., Whittier, 1976—. Pres. Whittier Area Coordinating Coun., 1978-80; chmn. ethics com. Presbyn. Intercommunity Hosp. Flight officer, navigator USAF, 1943-45. Decorated Air medal, POW medal. Fellow Am. Psychiat. Assn. (disting. life), Am. Acad. Child Psychiatry; mem. AAAS, Los Angeles County Med. Assn., So. Calif. Psychiat. Soc., So. Calif. Soc. Child Psychiatry, Phila. Soc. Adolescent Psychiatry (pres. 1967-68), Peace Sci. Soc. Avocations: study of violence and aggression, ethnic travels, ethnic folk music, photography. Office: Intercommunity Child Guidance Ctr 10155 Colima Rd Whittier CA 90603 Office Phone: 562-692-0383.

ARENSON, GREGORY K., lawyer; b. Chgo., Feb. 11, 1949; s. Donald L. and Marcia (Terman) A.; m. Karen H. Wattel, Sept. 4, 1970; 1 child, Morgan Elizabeth. BS in Econs., MIT, 1971; JD, U. Chgo., 1975. Bar: Ill. 1975, U.S. Dist. Ct. (no. dist.) Ill. 1975, N.Y. 1978, U.S. Dist. Ct. (so. and ea. dists.) N.Y. 1978, U.S. Supreme Ct. 1985, U.S. Ct. Appeals (2nd cir.) 1987, U.S. Dist. Ct. (ctrl. dist.) Ill. 1995, U.S. Ct. Appeals (7th cir.) 1997. Assoc. Rudnick & Wolfe, Chgo., 1975-77, Schwartz, Klink & Schreiber P.C., N.Y.C., 1977-81, ptnr., 1982-87, Proskauer, Rose, Goetz & Mendelsohn, N.Y.C., 1987-93, Kaplan Fox & Kilsheimer LLP, N.Y.C., 1993—. Mediator U.S. Dist. Ct. (so. dist.) N.Y., 1993—; mem. MIT Corp., 1997—2002; mem. corp. devel. com. MIT, 1994—, mem. alumni/ae fund bd., 1989—, chair, 1994—96; mem. adv. bd. Fed. Discovery News, 1999—. Co-editor: Federal Rules of Civil Procedure, 1993 Amendments, A Practical Guide, 1994; contbr. articles to profl. jours. Mem. ABA, N.Y. State Bar Assn. (comml. and fed. litigation sect., chair com. on discovery 1989-97, chair com. fed. procedure 1997—), N.Y. Bar Found., Assn. Bar City N.Y Home: 125 W 76th St Apt 2A New York NY 10023-8334 Office: Kaplan Fox & Kilsheimer LLP 805 3d Ave New York NY 10022-7513 Office Phone: 212-687-1980. Business E-Mail: garenson@kaplanfox.com.

ARENSON, NATHAN, retired radiologist; b. N.Y.C., 1912; MD, N.Y. Med. Coll., 1937. Intern Metro Hosp., N.Y.C., 1937-39; resident radiology Hines VA Hosp., Chgo., 1940, Va. Hosp., Roanoke, 1940-41; assoc. radiologist Watts Hosp., Durham, N.C., 1945-47, Touro Infirm, New Orleans, 1947-48; chief radiologist Sacred Heart Hosp., Pensacola, Fla., 1948-75; radiologist chmn. West Fla. Regional Med. Ctr., Pensacola, ret. Recipient Gold medal Fla. Radiology Soc., 1992. Fellow Am. Coll. Radiology; mem. AMA, Am. Coll. Nuc. Medicine, Radiol. Soc. N.Am. E-mail: narenson@aol.com.

ARENT, ALBERT EZRA, retired lawyer; b. Rochester, N.Y., Aug. 25, 1911; s. Hyman J. and Sarah (Weller) A.; m. Frances Feldman, Nov. 23, 1939; children: Stephen Weller, Margery Arent Safir. AB, Cornell U., 1932, LL.B., 1935. Bar: N.Y. 1935, D.C. 1945. Rsch. asst. N.Y. State Law Revision Commn., 1934; atty. U.S. Bur. Internal Revenue, 1935-39; spl. asst. to Atty. Gen. U.S., 1939-44; chief trial atty. Alien Property Unit, U.S. Dept. Justice, 1942-44; pvt. law practice specializing in taxation; ptnr. firm Arent, Fox, Kintner, Plotkin and Kahn and (predecessor firms), Washington, 1944-86; counsel, 1986—2003; lectr. taxation Am. U., 1948-52; prof. taxation Georgetown Law Sch., 1951-73; ret. Also lectr. tax subjects before Practising Law Inst., NYU, U. Chgo. tax insts., Am., Fed., various local and state bar assns.; prosecuted leading fgn. agt. registration act cases, World War II.; chmn. adv. coun. Cornell Law Sch., 1979-82 Contbr. articles to legal pubs. Vice pres. Jewish Cmty. Coun. of Greater Washington, 1953-57, pres., 1957-61; chmn. Commn. on Social Action of Reform Judaism, 1973-77; chmn. Cornell Law Sch. Fund, 1975-77; mem. steering com. Nat. Urban Coalition, 1970-77, mem. exec. com., 1970-72; mem. governing bd. and exec. com. Common Cause, 1970-72; bd. dirs. Overseas Edn. Fund of LWV, 1961-79; vice chmn. Nat Jewish Cmty. Rels. Adv. Coun., 1967-70, chmn., 1970-73; vice chmn. Conf. Pres.'s Major Jewish Orgns., 1970-73; trustee Cornell U., 1978-83, trustee emeritus, 1983—; 1st v.p. Washington Hebrew Congregation, 1978-80; v.p. United Jewish Appeal Fedn. Greater Washington, 1979-81. Recipient Stephen S. Wise medallion award Nat. Capital chpt. Am. Jewish Congress, 1965, Vicennial medal Georgetown U., 1971, Humanitarianism award B'nai Brith, 1975, Disting. Alumnus award Cornell U. Law Sch., 1982, award for outstanding svc. Overseas Edn. Fund, 1983, Disting. Svc. award Washington Lawyers Com. for Civil Rights Under Law, 1987, Judge Learned Hand award Am. Jewish Com., 1991. Mem. ABA, Am. Law Inst., Fed. Bar Assn., D.C. Bar Assn., Telluride Assn., Phi Beta Kappa, Phi Kappa Phi. Home: 6620 Boca Del Mar Dr Apt 608 Boca Raton FL 33433-5718

ARES, MANUEL, JR., biology professor, research scientist; BS in biology, Cornell Univ., Ithaca, NY; PhD, U. Calif., San Diego, 1982; post doctorate studies, Yale Univ. Sch. Medicine. Asst. prof. U. Calif., Santa Cruz, 1987—98, prof., 1998—, chmn. Dept. Molecular Cell & Devel. Biology, 2000—02. Prin. investigator Ares Lab, Santa Cruz, Calif.; prof. Howard Hughes Med. Inst. Office: UC Santa Cruz 225 Sinsheimer Laboratories Santa Cruz CA 95064 Office Phone: 831-459-4628. Office Fax: 831-459-3139. E-mail: ares@biology.ucsc.edu.

ARESTY, JEFFREY M., lawyer; b. Framingham, Mass., Dec. 31, 1951; s. Victor Joseph and Pola (Granek) A.; m. Ellen Louise Gould, Aug. 15, 1976; children: Joshua, Abigail, Joanne. BA, Johns Hopkins U., 1973; JD, Boston U., 1976, LLM in Taxation, 1978, LLM in Internat. Banking, 1993. Bar: Mass. 1977, D.C. 1982. Tax specialist Coopers & Lybrand, Boston, 1976-78; assoc. Meyers, Goldstein & Crossland, Brookline, Mass., 1978-79; ptnr. Crossland, Aresty & Levin, Boston, 1979-87, Aresty & Levin, Boston, 1987-91, Aresty Internat. Law Offices, Boston, 1992—. Cons. editor Tax Shelter Investment Rev., 1981-85. Recipient Disting. Achievement award Boston Safe Deposit and Trust, 1976, Grad. Banking Alumni Achievement award Boston U. Law Sch., 1993. Mem. ABA (membership chmn. 1981-84, coun. 1985-91, vice chmn. computer divsn. 1985-90, reporter e lawyering 1999—, chmn. internat. interest group 1992-96, chmn. internat. negotiations task force 1992-96, chmn. Mass. membership com. 1985-91, internat. law sect., chair law practice com. 1995-98, co-editor ABA Guide Internat. Bus. Negotiations 1994-00, prodr. ABA/AT&T CD-Rom on Cross-Cultural Comm. 1997, chmn. task force on e-commerce, 2002—), Am. Bar Found. (standing com. tech. and info. systems 1998-99, pub. bd. gen. practice 1998—), Mass. Bar Assn. (bd. dels., exec. com. 1981-83, chmn. law practice sect. 1983-85), Mass. Bar Found. (chmn. bar website 2005), Internat. Bar Orgn. (pres. 2005). Home: 35 Three Ponds Rd Wayland MA 01778-1732 Office: Aresty Internat Law Offices Bay 107 Union Wharf Boston MA 02109 Personal E-mail: jaresty@cyberspaceattorney.com.

ARFMANN, DENNIS L., lawyer; BA, U. Nebr., 1974, JD, 1979; LLM, George Washington U., 1991. Bar: Nebr. 1980, Colo. 1988. Ptnr. Winner Nichols, Douglas, Kelly & Arfmann, Scottsbluff, Nebr., 1980-91, Bradley Cmapbell, Carney & Madsen, Golden, Colo., 1991-95, Holme Roberts & Owen LLP, Denver, 1995—2003, Hogan & Hartson, 2003—. Chair air quality com. Colo. Assn. Commerce and Industry; chair air subcom. Rocky Mtn. Oil and Gas Assn., 1992-95; adv. bd. Clean Air Act Reporter; mem. Denver Regional Air Coun., Western Regional Air Partnership's Market Trading Forum. Mem. ABA (natural resources, environ. & energy law sect.). Office: Hogan & Hartson 1470 Walnut St Ste 200 Boulder CO 80302 Office Phone: 720-406-5374. E-mail: darfmann@hhlaw.com.

ARGERS, HELEN, writer, playwright; b. Valisburg, N.J. BA; graduate studies, Europe. Writer advt. copy. Workshop lectr. 6th Ann. Metro. Writers Conf. Seton Hall U., South Orange, N.J., 1996; lectr. hist. sociol. view of Am., 1876 N.J. Hist. Soc., 1998. Author: A Lady of Independence, 1982, Noblesse Oblige, 1994, (play) The Home Visit, 1986 (Winner Nat. One-Act-Play Competition 1986, Weisbrod award 1987), A Scandalous Lady, 1991, A Captain's Lady, 1991, An Unlikely Lady, 1992, The Gilded Lily, 1998, (short story) The Ozymandias Bush (Nelson Algren award finalist 1990), Repossession (Writer's Digest Short Story Competition award); author (under pseudonym Helen Archery) The Age of Elegance, 1992, The Season of Loving, 1992, Lady Adventuress, 1994, Duel of Hearts, 1994; humor columnist Worrall Newspapers, 2003-05; classical and popular reviewer Arts and Entertainment for some 20 newspapers; contbr. articles to profl. jours. Recipient Resolution of Honor, State of N.J., 1994, 97. Mem.: Nat. Hist. Soc., Jane Austen Soc. N. Am.

ARGIE, JENNY LYNN, artist; b. Kansas City, Mo., July 4, 1970; d. David Lee and Kay Ellen Argie; m. Andrew Farrar Thornton; 1 child, David Farrar Thornton. Studied at, Kans. City Art Inst., 1990—92, Lacoste Sch. of the Arts, France, 1991; BFA, Calif. Coll. of Arts, 1992—94; MFA, Pa. Acad. of the Fine Arts, 1998—2001. Instr. for children ages K-12 Visible Horizons, Kans. City, Mo., 1996—98; instr. for adults Communiversity Drawing Class, 1996—98; vis. artist coord. Pa. Acad. of the Fine Arts, 1998—2001; asst. curator to Judith E. Stein Pa. Convention Ctr., 1999—; tchg. asst. Pa. Acad. of the Fine Arts, 2000—01; pres. Argington, Inc., 2004—. Exhibitions include Isabel Percy West Gallery, Calif. Coll. of Arts, 1993—94, Celsius Smith Gallery, 1998, New Works Gallery, Kans. City Artists Coalition, 1999, Pa. Acad. of the Fine Arts Student Gallery, 2000, Impact Gallery, Buffalo, N.Y., 2000, Claire Oliver Fine Art Gallery, Phila., Pa., 2000, Coll. Art Gallery, Pa., 2001, Kenise Barnes Fine Art, N.Y., 2001, Metaphor Gallery, 2002, Berlin Kunstproject, Berlin, Germany, 2002, LaGuardia Cmty. Coll., 2002, DC Arts Ctr., Washington, DC, 2004, exhibited in group shows at Spa Studio Pl. Arts, Barre, Vt., 2003. Recipient Ida Bruns Meml. prize, St. Louis Guild, 1998. Democrat. Greek Orthodox. Office: Argington Inc 766 Metropolitan Ave No3 Brooklyn NY 11211 Office Phone: 718-218-8508. Business E-Mail: jenny@argington.com.

ARGIRION, MICHAEL, editor; b. Chgo., May 2, 1940; s. Gus and Angela A.; m. Sherrie Berlant, Feb. 10; children: Carrie, Glen. Student, DePaul U., 1958-59, Northwestern U., 1959-60, U. Chgo., 1961-62. Copy editor Chgo.'s Am., 1959-68, wire editor, 1969; news editor Chgo. Today, 1970-71, Sunday and features editor, 1971-74; asst. Sunday editor Chgo. Tribune, 1974-75, features editor, 1975-79, asst. mng. editor features, 1979-81, asst. mng. editor news editing, 1981-82, exec. news editor, 1982-83, assoc. editor, 1983; editor Tribune Media Services, 1984, v.p., editor, 1985-93. Co-creator internationally syndicated newspaper word puzzle Jumble, That Scrambled Word Game, 1994—. Editor: History of Your World, 1969. Served with U.S. Army, 1962. Mem. Legacy Club Alaqua Lakes. Office: Argirion 1212 St Albans Loop Heathrow FL 32746

ARGIRIS, ATHANASSIOS, oncologist, researcher; b. Athens, Oct. 7, 1966; s. Stavros and Anna Argiris; m. Nektaria Koulaki. MD, Athens Med. Sch., 1990. Diplomate Am. Bd. Internal Medicine, Am. Bd. Med. Oncology. Resident in radiation oncology Areteion U. Hosp., Athens, 1992—94; resident in internal medicine Beth Israel Med. Ctr., N.Y.C., 1994—97; fellow in hematology-oncology Yale U., New Haven, 1997—2000; attending physician Northwestern Meml. Hosp., Chgo., 2000—05; asst. prof. medicine Northwestern U., Chgo., 2000—05; assoc. prof. medicine U. Pitts., 2005—. Attending physician Shadyside Hosp., 2005—, Presbyn. Hosp., 2005—, U. Pitts. Med. Ctr., 2005—; co-dir. head and neck program U. Pitts. Cancer Inst./Hillman Comprehensive Cancer Ctr., 2005—. Recipient Young Investigator award, Am. Assn. Cancer Rsch., 2000. Fellow: ACP; mem.: AMA, Am. Soc. Clin. Oncology. Business E-Mail: argirisae@upmc.edu.

ARGO, R. TRENT, academic administrator; s. Bobby Lee and L. Voncille Argo; m. Peggy Jean Reece, June 4, 1988; children: Chelsea Nicole, Lucas Trent, William Alexander, Rachel Lynn. MusB, Campbellsville Coll., Campbellsville, Ky., 1988; MusM in Music Edn., Campbellsville U., 1997—99. Security specialist USAF, Bellevue, Nebr., 1979—83; admissions counselor Campbellsville Coll., 1989—90; dir. of admissions Campbellsville U., 1990—2003; dean of enrollment mgmt. Okla. Bapt. U., Shawnee, Okla., 2003—. Cons. The Learning Ho., Louisville, 2005—; assoc. Paul Crippan and Assocs., Palm Springs, Calif., 2000—. Den leader Boy Scouts of Am., Campbellsville, 1999—2003, Webelos den leader Shawnee, Okla., 2003; deacon Campbellsville Bapt. Ch., Campbellsville, Ky., 1992—2003; v.p. Ky. Jr. MIss, Lexington, 2000—03. Staff sgt. USAF, 1979—83. Decorated Air Force Commendation Medal, Good Conduct Medal USAF; named Hon. Ky. Col., Gov. of the State of Ky., 1993; recipient Outstanding Den Leader award, Boy Scout Am., 2002. Mem.: Ky. Assn. of Collegiate Registrars and Admissions Officers (com. chair 2001—02), So. Assn. of Collegiate Registrars and Admissions Counselors, Assn. of So. Bapt. Admissions Profls., Nat. Assn.of Collegiate Admisssions Cousnelors, Am. Assn. of Collegiate Registrars and Admissions Officers (com. mem. 1995—2000). Avocations: golf, travel, music. Home: 4403 Bryant Via Shawnee OK 74804 Office: Oklhaoma Baptist University 500 W University Shawnee OK 74804 Office Phone: 405-878-2023. Personal E-mail: trent.argo@okbu.edu.

ARGUE, DON HARVEY, college president, minister; b. Winnipeg, Man., Can., July 12, 1939; came to U.S., 1948; s. Andrew Watson and Hazel Bell (May) A.; m. Patricia Jean Opheim, Sept. 23, 1961; children: Laurie, Lee, Jonathan. BA, Cen. Bible Coll., Springfield, Mo., 1961; MA, Santa Clara U., 1967; EdD, U. of the Pacific, 1969; postdoctoral study, Gordon-Conwell Theol. Sem., 1990, Regent Coll., Vancouver, Can., 1990. Ordained to ministry Assemblies of God, 1964. Pastor 1st Assembly of God, Morganville, Calif., 1965-67; dean of students/men Bethany Coll., Santa Cruz, Calif., 1967-69; asst. prof., dean of student life, dean of students Evangel Coll., Springfield, 1969-74; dean, v.p. North Cen. Bible Coll., Mpls., 1974-79; pres. North Ctrl. Bible Coll., Mpls., 1979—2002, Northwest Univ., 1998—. Gen. presbyter Assemblies of God, Springfield. Recipient Decade of Growth award Christianity Today, 1990. Mem. Nat. Assn. Evangs. (1st v.p.), Soc. for Pentecostal Studies (pres.), Rotary. Home: PO Box 579 Kirkland WA 98083-0579 Office: Northwest University 5520 108th Ave NE Kirkland WA 98033

ARGUEDAS, CRISTINA C., lawyer; b. 1953; BA, U. N.H.; JD summa cum laude, Rutgers U., 1979. Bar: Calif. Supreme Ct. 1979, U.S. Dist. Ct., No. Dist. Calif. 1979, So. Dist. Calif. 1983, Ctrl. Dist. Calif. 1982, Ea. Dist. Calif. 1982, Dist. Ariz. 1991, U.S. Ct. Appeals: Ninth Cir. 1980, Tenth Cir. 1985, U.S. Supreme Ct. 1983, U.S. Tax Ct. 1994. Dep. fed. defender U.S. Dist. Ct. (no. dist.) Calif.; ptnr. Cooper, Arguedas & Cassman, Emeryville, Calif., 1982—. Lawyer rep. U.S. Ct. Appeals (9th cir.) Jud. Conf.; adj. prof. Benjamin N. Cardozo Sch. Law, Yeshiva U., Boalt Hall Sch. Law. Named one of 50 Top Lawyers, Nat. Law Jour., 1998, Top Ten Lawyers in Bay Area, San Francisco Chronicle, 2003. Fellow: Am. Coll. Trial Lawyers; mem.: Am. Bd. Criminal Lawyers, Am. Inns of Ct. (master 1999—), Internat. Acad. Trial Lawyers, Calif. Attys. for Criminal Justice (past pres.). Office: Cooper Arguedas & Cassman 5900 Hollis St Ste N Emeryville CA 94608-2008 Office Phone: 510-654-2000.*

ARGYROS, GEORGE L., former ambassador, former development company executive, former professional sports team owner; b. Detroit; m. Judie Argyros. Student, Mich. State U.; BS in Bus. and Econs., Chapman Coll., 1959. Pres. Arnel Devel. Co.; chmn. bd. Arnel Mgmt.; chmn., dir. Air Cal,

1981—87; dir. comml. financing services Newport bancorp and Coast Thrift and Loan Co.; prin. owner Seattle Mariners Baseball Team, 1981-89; U.S. amb. to Spain & Andorra U.S. Dept. State, 2001—04. Mem. Baseball's Revenue sharing Com., Restructuring Com., Commr. Selection Com.; bd. dirs. Am. League Chmn. Western Wash.'s United Cerebral Palsy Telethon; chmn. fundraising Nat. Multiple Sclerosis Soc., Puget Sound chpt.; active NCCJ, Boy Scouts Am., World Affairs Council, Young Pres.'s Orgn.; chmn. bd. trustees Chapman Coll, 1976-.

ARGYROS, IOANNIS K., mathematics professor, researcher; b. Athens, Greece, Feb. 20, 1956; came to U.S., 1981; s. Konstantinos Ioannis and Anastasia Vassilios (Armaou) A.; m. Dianna Mihallaq Mina, Nov. 12, 1998; children: Gus, Michael, Christopher. BSc in Math., U. Athens, 1979; MSc in Math., U. Ga., 1983, PhD in Math., 1984. Tchr. and rsch. asst. U. Ga., Athens, 1982-84; vis. asst. prof. math. U. Iowa, Iowa City, 1984-86; asst. prof. dr. math. N.Mex. State U., Las Cruces, 1986-90; prof. Cameron U., Lawton, Okla., 1990—. Author: The Theory and Applications of Iteration Methods, 1993, A Unified Approach for Solving Nonlinear Operator Equations and Applications, 1997, The Theory and Application of Abstract Polynomial Equations, 1998, Dictionary of Comprehensive Dictionary of Mathematics: Analysis, Calculus and Differential Equations, 1999, Computational Methods for Abstract Polynomial Equations, 1999, A Survey of Efficient Numerical Methods for Solving Equations and Applications, 2000, A Unified Approach for Solving Equations, Part I: On Infinite-Dimensional Spaces, 2000, A Unified Approach for Solving Equations, Part II: On Finite-Dimensional Spaces, 2000, Two Contemporary Computational Aspects of Numerical Analysis, 2000, Advances in the Efficiency of Computational Methods and Applications, 2001, Herative Methods for Solving Equations Appearing in Engineering and Economics, 2001, Newton Methods, 2005; editor Advances Nonlinear Variational Inequalities, 1999, Internat. Jour. Computational Numerical Analysis Applications, 2000—, Internat. Jour. Pure and Applied Math., 2001, Math. Sci. Rsch. Jour., 2002, Internat. Review of Pure and Applied Math., 2004, Commns. Applied Nonlinear Analysis, 2005, Internat. Jour Applied Math. Sci., 2005, Internat. Jour. Theoretical and Applied Math., 2005; contbr. over 450 articles to profl. jours. With Greek Army, 1980-82. Mem. Am. Math. Soc. Avocations: fishing, sailing, scuba diving, tennis, reading. Home: 1307 NW 75th St Lawton OK 73505-4205 Office: Cameron U Dept Math 2800 W Gore Blvd Lawton OK 73505-6320 Office Phone: 580-581-2908.

ARHONDITSIS, GEORGE B., research scientist; b. Mytilene, Lesvos, Greece, May 8, 1970; s. Vasileios George Arhonditsis and Kiriaki Spanelli-Arhonditsi. BSc, MS, Agrl. U. Athens, 1993; PhD, U. of the Aegean, Mytilene, 1998. Cert. environ. scis. Greece, 1998. Lab mgr. U. of the Aegean, Mytilene, 2000—01; postdoctoral fellow U. Wash., Seattle, 2001—04; with Duke U., Durham, NC. Contbr. articles to profl. jours. Lance cpl. Arty., 1998—2000, Mytilene, Greece. Mem.: Am. Inst. Biol. Scis., Am. Geophys. Union, Ecol. Soc. Am., Am. Soc. Limnology and Oceanography. Office: Duke University Nicholas Sch of Environ/Earth Sci Durham NC Office Phone: 919-613-8105. Office Fax: 919-684-8741. Business E-Mail: georgear@duke.edu.

ARICI, AYDIN, gynecologist, reproductive endocrinologist; s. Ramiz and Muruvvet Arici; m. Ayse Dino, June 24, 1983; children: John, Jim. BS, Galatasaray Lyceum, Istanbul, Turkey, 1973; MD, Istanbul Med. Sch., 1979; MA Privatim (hon.), Yale U., 2002. Diplomate Am. Bd. Ob-Gyn. Dir., reproductive endocrinology and infertility fellowship program Yale U. Sch. Medicine, New Haven, 1999—, dir., oocyte donation program, 2000—, prof. and head, sect. of reproductive endocrinology and infertility, 2001—. Rsch. grantee, Endometriosis Assn., 2001—03, Clin. Investigator grantee, NIH, 1993. Fellow: ACOG (Parke-Davis award 1996); mem.: Conn. Assn. Reproductive Endocrinologists (pres. 2002—), European Soc. Human Reproduction and Embryology, Soc. Reproductive Endocrinologists, Am. Soc. for Reproductive Medicine (chair, reproductive immunology spl. interest group 1995—96), Endocrine Soc., Soc. Study of Reproduction, Soc. Gynecologic Investigation (mem. of edn. com. 2002, Mentor award 2003, Pres.'s Presenter award 1998—2001), Am. Bd. of Obstetrics and Gynecology. Office Phone: 203-785-3581. Business E-Mail: aydin.arici@yale.edu.

ARIEFF, ALLEN IVES, physician; b. Chgo., Sept. 30, 1938; BS in Math. and Chemistry, U. Ill., 1960; MS in Physiology, MD, Northwestern U., 1964. Intern Phila. Gen. Hosp., 1964-65; resident SUNY, Bklyn., 1967-68; renal fellow U. Colo., Denver, 1968-69; rsch. and edn. assoc., clin. investigator Wadsworth VA Med. Ctr., L.A., 1970-74; asst. prof. medicine, rsch. scientist UCLA Med. Ctr., 1971-74; asst. prof. medicine, dir. hemodialysis U. Calif. VA Med. Ctr., San Francisco, 1975-76, assoc. prof. medicine, dir. nephrology sect., 1976-83, prof. medicine, chief clin. nephrology, 1983-86, prof. medicine, dir. rsch. & edn. geriatrics, 1986—. Cons. and spkr. in field. Author: 6 books; contbr. 82 chpts. med. textbooks, over 400 articles to profl. jours. Fellow: ACP; mem.: Soc. Neurosci., Internat. Soc. Nephrology, We. Soc. Clin. Rsch., We. Assn. Physicians, Assn. Am. Physicians, Am. Soc. Bone and Mineral Rsch., Am. Soc. Clin. Investigation, Am. Soc. Neurochemistry, Am. Physiol. Soc., Am. Diabetes Assn., Am. Fedn. Med. Rsch., Am. Soc. Nephrology. Office: Penthouse 9400 Brighton Way Ph Beverly Hills CA 90210-4712 Office Phone: 310-276-2033. Business E-Mail: aarieff@itsa.ucsf.edu.

ARIENS, KARLA RAE, library director; b. Tremonton, Utah, July 3, 1966; d. Paul Elias and Lorna May Adams; m. Thaddeus William Ariens, Mar. 17, 1988; children: Talia Louise, Tori May, Terese Claire. BS in Elem. Edn., Utah State U., 1988. Tchr. asst. Children's Home, Logan, Utah, 1988-89; music specialist Hilltop Sch., Logan, Utah, 1988-89; chpt. I aide Adams Elem. Sch., Logan, Utah, 1989-90; gifted/talented specialist Cache County Sch. Dist., Logan, Utah, 1989-90; libr. dir. Brookville (Ind.) Town-Twp. Libr., 1991—2002. Sec. Franklin County Cmty. Network Com., Brookville, 1995. Mem. Lds Ch. Avocations: music, cooking, reading, piano, singing.

ARIETI, JAMES ALEXANDER, classics educator, writer; b. N.Y.C., May 12, 1948; s. Silvano and Jane (Jaffe) A.; m. Barbara Ann Mapes, May 23, 1976; children: Samuel Abraham, Ruth Sophia. BA, Grinnell Coll., 1969; MA, PhD, Stanford U., 1972. Asst. prof. Stanford (Calif.) U., 1972-74, Pa. State U., University Park, 1974-75, Cornell Coll., Mt. Vernon, Iowa, 1975-77; prof. dept. classics Hampden-Sydney (Va.) Coll., 1978—. Author: Love Can Be Found, 1975, Longinus on the Sublime, 1985, Interpreting Plato: The Dialogues as Drama, 1991, Discourses on the First Book of Herodotus, 1995, The Scientific and the Divine: Conflict and Reconciliation from Ancient Greece to Today, 2003, Philosophy in the Ancient World: An Introduction, 2005; editor: Hamartia, 1983; contbr. articles to profl. jours. Woodrow Wilson fellow, 1969; NEH fellow, 1977-78. Mem. Am. Philol. Assn., Classical Assn. Middle West and South, Classical Assn. Va., Phi Beta Kappa, Phi Alpha Theta, Eta Sigma Chi. Jewish. Home and Office: Hampden Sydney Coll PO Box 746 Hampden Sydney VA 23943-0746 Office Phone: 434-223-6252.

ARIEVITCH, IGOR, psychology professor; b. Moscow; s. Michael and Maria Arievitch; m. Anna Stetsenko; children: Ilia, Maria. MS in psychology, Moscow State U., 1972, PhD in psychology, 1976. Rsch. scientist Moscow State U., 1976—81, sr. rschr., 1981—93; vis. prof. U. Leiden, Netherlands, 1993—94, U. Bern, Switzerland, 1994—99, Grad Ctr., CUNY, 1999—2001; prof. Coll. S.I., NY, 2001—. Contbr. articles to over 50 publs. Recipient S.I. Presdl. award, Coll. S.I., 2003; Rsch. grant, Dutch Sci. Found., 1993, Swiss Sci. Found., 1995. Mem.: Internat. Soc. for Cultural Rsch. and Activity Theory, Am. Ednl. Rsch. Assoc. Office: Coll S I 2800 Victory Blvd Staten Island NY 10314 Office Phone: 718-982-4006. Business E-Mail: arievitch@mail.csi.cuny.edu.

ARIFI, FATANA BAKTASH, artist, educator; arrived in U.S., 2000; d. Mohammed Arif and Bibishreen Arifi. Diploma in art, Women Orgn. of Afghanistan, 1983; diploma in painting, Maimanagi Art Inst., Kabul, Afghanistan, 1983; MFA, Kabul (Afghanistan) U., 1987. Art instr. Kabul (Afghanistan) U., 1989—92; freelance artist, designer Afghan Internat. Orgn., 1994—99; dir. Maimanagi Fine Arts Ctr., Peshawar, Pakistan, 1995—99; art instr. Inst. of Fine Arts, Peshawar, 1996; founder, editor Art and Culture Jour., Peshawar, 1997—99; art instr. Hunarkada Acad. Visual and Performance Arts, Peshawar, 1998; sr. cert. framer Michael's Art and Crafts, Alexandria, Va., 2001—, instr. drawing, 2005—; freelance artist, 2001—. Mem. selection com. Afghan Artistic Competitions, Peshawar, Pakistan; dir. Afghan Musaic, 1999; artist mem. Gallery West, Alexandria, Va.; class instr. Michaels Arts and Craft Store, Springfield, Va. Author: Drawing and Painting, 1988, Painting and it's Status in Afghanistan, 1998, Drawing Technical Metodes, 1999. Recipient award, Artist Festival, Japan, 1981, Nat. Painting award, Ministry of Culture, Afghanistan, 1983, 1985, 1987, award, Women Orgn., Afghanistan, 1983, Army Mus., Afghanistan, 1986, Nat. Assn. Artists of Afghanistan, 1986, Youth Orgn. Afghanistan, 1985. Mem.: Gallery West (Old Town Alexandra) (artist mem.). Achievements include development of Handasism. Avocations: writing, poetry, cooking, music. Personal E-mail: fatana_ba@hotmail.com.

ARIMURA, AKIRA, biomedical research laboratory administrator, educator; b. Kagoshima, Japan, Dec. 26, 1923; arrived in U.S., 1965; s. Jyojiro and Kiyoko (Kajiwara) A.; m. Katsuko Yamashita, July 31, 1957; children: Jerome J., Mark M., Margaret M. BS, 7th Nat. Coll., Kagoshima, 1943; MD, Nagoya (Japan) U., 1951, PhD, 1957; diploma (hon.), Pécs Med. Sch., Hungary, 1995. James Hudson Brown postdoctoral fellow Yale U., New Haven, 1956-58; instr., rsch. assoc. Hokkaido U., Sapporo, Japan, 1961-65; instr. Tulane U., New Orleans, 1958-61, asst. prof., 1965-68, assoc. prof., 1968-73, prof. medicine, 1973—, dir. U.S.-Japan Biomedical Rsch. Lab. Belle Chasse, La., 1985—. Rsch. physician VA Hosp., New Orleans, 1965-80; mem. Endocrine Study Sect., NIH, 1978-82; adj. prof. anatomy Tulane U., New Orleans, 1979—, Physiology, 1989—, founder, dir. clin. RIA Lab., Tulane U. Med. Ctr., 1980-87, molecular neuroendo and diabetes lab. Belle Chasse, 1980-85, dir., 1985; vis. prof. Keio U., Tokyo, 1990—; founder U.S.-Japan Biomed. Rsch. Labs., Belle Chasse, 1985—; reviewer Jour. Clin. Endocrinology and Metabolism, Am. Jour. Physiology, Jour. Clin. Investigation, Sci., Life Sci., Procs. Soc. Exptl. Biology and Medicine, others. Mem. editorial bd. Peptides, Turkish Jour. Med. and Endocrine Jour.; contbr. articles to scholarly and profl. jours. Planner, initiator student exch. program Tulane U. and Keio U., New Orleans and Tokyo, 1986, Tulane U. and Nagoya (Japan) U., Showa U. Decorated with Order of Rising Sun, Gold Rays with Neck Ribbon, Govt. of Japan, 1995; named Fulbright scholar 1956. Mem. AAAS, Internat. Soc. Neuroendocrine, Endocrine Soc. U.S., Japan Endocrinology Soc. (hon.), Hungarian Soc. for Endocrinology and Metabolism (hon.), Am. Physiology Soc., Am. Soc. Neurosci., Soc. Exptl. Biology and Medicine, N.Y. Acad. Scis., Japan Physiol. Soc. (hon.), Japan Neuroenscience Soc. (hon.). Achievements include co-development of LHRH, somatostatin, Interleukin-1, pituitary adenylate cyslau activating polypeptide; discovery of PACAP. Office: Tulane U Herbert Rsch Ctr US-Japan Biomed Rsch Labs 3705 Main St Belle Chasse LA 70037-3001 Business E-Mail: arimura@tulane.edu.

ARING, MONIKA KOSMAHL, policy economist, consultant, researcher; b. Gablonz, Germany, Mar. 14, 1945; d. Heinrich G. and Gisela Ilse (Zelder) Kosmahl; m. Roomet Joost Aring, June 19, 1965 (dec.); children: Antje, Emily. BA, Bklyn. Coll., 1972; MPA, Harvard U., 1989. Dir. Pro Portsmouth Inc., Portsmouth, N.H., 1976-80; cons. Monika Aring Assocs., Portsmouth, 1980-88; v.p. pub. rels. Internt. Hotels, Portsmouth, 1980-82; v.p. mktg. Am. Leadership Forum, Denver, 1989-91; dir. Inst. for Edn. and Employment, Edn. Devel. Ctr. Inc., Newton, Mass., 1991-96, dir. CTr. for Workforce Devel., 1996—; exec. dir. Ctr. Edn. and Tng. Employment Ohio State U., Columbus, Ohio, 2002—03; sr. policy analyst workforce and econ. develop. RTI Internat., Wash., DC, 2003—. Project dir. Options for a New Downtown, Portsmouth, 1976-78, N.H. Blue Ribbon Commn. on Edn. and Employment, 1986-88; advisor Edn. Commn. of U.S., 1999—; mem. UNESCO Forum on Lifelong Learning, 1999; tech. advisor U.S Dept. Edn., 1995; keynote spkr. Asian Pacific Econ. Commn., 1999; bd. trustees Global Abundance Alliance. Author: Global Best Practice in Workforce Development, 1996, also other studies. Social entrepreneur/cons. N.H. Coun. for Humanities, 1977, Somersworth (N.H.) Children's Festival, 1980, Asia Devel. Bank, 1999, U.S. AID, Peru, India, Africa, 1997. Recipient Mayor's award City of Portsmouth, 1978, Leadership award C. of C., 1980; guest of German Parliament, Bonn, 1993. Mem. Knowledge Navigators Found. Avocations: outdoor sports, music, designing, foreign languages (german, russian, french, spanish). Home: Apt 26 350 9th St SE Washington DC 20003-2168 Office Phone: 202-728-2045. E-mail: monikakaring@yahoo.com, maring@rti.org.

ARION, DOUGLAS NORMAN, physicist, researcher; b. N.Y.C., Jan. 27, 1957; s. Gilbert Roger and Barbara Diane (Swinkin) A. AB, Dartmouth Coll., 1978; MS, U. Md., 1980, PhD, 1984. Physicist U.S. Army Cold Regions Rsch. Engring. Lab., Hanover, N.H., 1978-79; grad. rsch. fellow NASA-Goddard Space Flight Ctr., Greenbelt, Md., 1982-84; sr. scientist Sci. Applications Internat. Corp., McLean, Va., 1984-89, divsn. mgr. Albuquerque, 1989-93, asst. v.p., 1993—, cons., 1994—; prof. physics, Hedberg Disting. prof. entrepreneurship Carthage Coll., Kenosha, Wis., 1994—2000. Tech. dir. Ctr. for Advanced Tech. and Innovation, Racine, Wis. Mem. AAAS, Am. Phys. Soc. Appalachian Mountain Club, Appalachian Trail Conf. Republican. Avocations: bicycle racing, astronomy-astrophysics, architectural design, instrumentation development, music. Office: Carthage Coll Kenosha WI 53140 E-mail: ariond1@carthage.edu.

ARIOSTO-OILL, LYNN CAROL, music educator; m. Joseph Oill, June 22, 1984; children: Kevin, Christopher, Matthew. MusB, SUNY, Potsdam, 1974; M in Liberal Arts and Sci., SUNY, Stony Brook, 1987. Cert. tchg. Music tchr. Smithtown Ctrl. Sch. Dist., NY, 1974—2005. Mem.: Am. Choral Dirs. Assn., Music Educator's Nat. Conf., Am. Fedn. Tchrs. Office: Smithtown HS 100 Central Rd Smithtown NY 11787 Office Phone: 631-382-2900.

ARIS, RUTHERFORD, applied mathematician, educator; b. Bournemouth, Eng., Sept. 15, 1929; came to U.S., 1955, naturalized, 1962; s. Algernon Pollock and Janet (Elford) A.; m. Claire Mercedes Holman, Jan. 1, 1958. B.Sc. (spl.) with 1st class honours in Math, London (Eng.) U., 1948, PhD, 1960, D.Sc., 1964; student, Edinburgh (Scotland) U., 1948-50; D.Sc. (hon.), U. Exeter, 1984, Clarkson U., 1985; DEng honoris causa, U. Notre Dame, 1990; Ch.M., fellow, Inst. Math. Appications, 1992; D Engring. honoris causa, Tech. U., Athens, Greece. Tech. officer Billingham div. I.C.I. Ltd., 1950-55; research fellow U. Minn., 1955-56; lectr. tech. math. Edinburgh U., 1956-58; mem. faculty U. Minn., 1958—, prof. chem. engring., 1963—, Regents' prof., 1978-96, Regents prof. emeritus, 1996—. O.A. Hougen vis. prof. U. Wis., 1979; Sherman Fairchild Disting. scholar Calif. Inst. Tech., 1980-81; cons. to industry, lectr., 1961—; IXth Centennial lectr. in chem. engring. U. Bologna, 1988; mem. Inst. for Advanced Study, Princeton, 1994. Author: Optimal Design of Chemical Reactors, 1961, Vectors, Tensors and the Basic Equations of Fluid Mechanics, 1962, reprint edit., 1989, Discrete Dynamic Programming, 1964, Introduction to the Analysis of Chemical Reactors, 1965, Elementary Chemical Reactor Analysis, 1969, reprint edit., 1990, (with N.R. Amundson) First-Order Partial Differential Equations with Applications, 1973, reprint 1999, (with W. Strieder) Variational Methods Applied to Problems of Diffusion and Reaction, 1973, The Mathematical Theory of Diffusion and Reaction in Permeable Catalysts, 1975, Mathematical Modelling Techniques, 1978, 2d edit., 1994, Chemical Engineering in the University Context, 1982; co-editor: Springs of Scientific Creativity, 1982, An Index of Scripts for E.A. Lowe's Codices Latini Antiquiores, 1982, (with Amundson and Rhee) First-order Partial Differential Equations, Vol. I Theory and Applications of Single Equations, 1986, Vol. II Theory and Applications of Systems of Quasilinear Hyperbolic Equations, 1986, 2d edit., 2002, Explicatio Formarum Litterarum*The Unfolding of Letterforms, 1990, (with K. Alhumaizi) Surveying A Dynamical System: The Gray/Scott Reaction In A Two-Phase Reactor, 1995, Mathematical Modeling--A Chemical Engineer's Perspective, 1999. Recipient E. Harris Harbison award for disting. teaching, 1969, Alpha Chi Sigma award Am. Inst. Chem. Engrs., 1969, Chem. Engring. lectr. award Am. Soc. Engring. Edn., 1973, Damköhler medal Deutsche Vereinigung fur Chemie und Verfahrenstechnik, 1991, Richard E. Bellman Control Heritage award Am. Automatic Control Coun., 1992, N.R. Amundson award Internat. Symposium on Chem. Reaction Engring., 1998; sr. rsch. fellow NSF, 1964-65, Guggenheim fellow, 1971-72. Fellow Am. Acad. Arts and Scis., Inst. Math. and Applications, Instn. of Chem. Engring. (hon.); mem. NAE, Soc. Nat. Philosophy, Soc. Indsl. and Applied Math., AIChE (R.H. Wilhelm award 1975, Inst. lectr. 1997, Founders award 1999), Mediaeval Acad. Lutheran. Office: Univ Minn Dept Chem Engring & Materials Sci Minneapolis MN 55455 Business E-Mail: aris@umn.edu.

ARISON, MICKY, cruise line company executive, sports team executive; b. Tel Aviv, June 29, 1949; Student, U. Miami. Reservations mgr. Carnival Corp., 1974-76, v.p. passenger traffic, 1976-79, pres., CEO, 1979-90, chmn., CEO, 1990—; mng. gen. ptnr. Miami Heat, Miami. Office: Carnival Cruise Lines Inc 3655 NW 87th Ave Miami FL 33178-2428

ARISON, SHARI, investment company executive; m. Ofer Glazer; 4 children. Grad., U. Fl. Chmn. Arison Holdings, 1999—, Arison Investments, 1999—; chmn., pres. Ted Arison Family Foundation, 1999—; controller Bank Ha'poalim, Israel. Named one of world's 100 richest people, Forbes Magazine, 2004. Achievements include Israel's wealthiest citizen, 1999-2004; shareholder, Carnival Cruise Lines. Office: c/o Carnival Corp 3655 NW 87th Ave Miami FL 33178

ARISTIDES, SISMANIS, education educator, department chairman; b. Athens, Greece, Nov. 6, 1949; s. Dimitrios and Stella Sismanis; m. Anna Rozaki, Apr. 10, 1949; children: Stamatina Sismanis, Dimitrios Sismanis. MD, Med. Schol U. Athens, Athens, Greece, 1973. Md ECFMG, 1973. Prof. and chmn. of otolaryngology-head and neck surgery Va. Commonwealth U. Med. Ctr., Richmond, Va., 1996—. Mem.: Am. Neurotologic Soc., Am. Coll. Surgeons, Am. Otologic Soc. (life). Office: Va Commonwealth Univ Med Richmond VA 23298-0146 Office Phone: 804-828-3965. Office Fax: 804-828-5779.

ARKILIC, GALIP MEHMET, mechanical engineer, educator; b. Sivas, Turkey, Mar. 10, 1920; came to U.S., 1943, naturalized, 1960; s. Sabir Mehmet and Zahra Fatima (Hocazade) A.; m. Ann A. Bryan, Mar. 31, 1956. BME, Cornell U., 1946; MS, Ill. Inst. Tech., 1948; PhD, Northwestern U., 1954. Registered profl. engr., Va. Mech. engr. Miehle Printing Press and Mfg. Co., Chgo., 1948-49, analyst, 1954-56; research and devel. engr. Mech. and Chem. Industries, Turkey, 1949-52; asst. prof. Pa. State U., University Park, 1956-58; assoc. prof. dept. civil engring. George Washington U., Washington, 1958-63, prof. engring. and applied sci., 1963—, prof. emeritus, 1990—, chmn. dept. engring. mechanics, 1966-69, asst. dean, 1969-74. Contbr. articles to sci. jours. Vice pres. Courtland Civic Assn., Arlington, Va., 1965-66; pres. Am. Turkish Assn., Washington, 1967-71. Served to 2d lt. Turkish Army, 1939-41 Recipient Disting. Leadership award Am. Turkish Assn., 1972; Recognition of Service award Sch. Engring. and Applied Sci., George Washington U., 1976, Spl. Appreciation award Engring. Alumni Assn., George Washington U., 1990; Air Force Office of Sci. Research grantee, 1963-69 Mem. ASME, AAUP, Am. Acad. Mechanics, Math. Assn. of Am., Am. Math. Soc., Wash. Soc. Engrs., Sigma Xi. Clubs: George Washington U. (Washington). Home: 8403 Camden St Alexandria VA 22308-2111 Office: George Washington Univ Sch Of Engringand Applied Sc Washington DC 20052-0001 Office Phone: 202-994-1000. E-mail: gmarkilic@aol.com.

ARKIN, ADAM, actor; b. NYC, Aug. 19, 1956; s. Alan Arkin; m. Phyllis Lyons, Aug. 21, 1999. Actor, dir.: (TV series) Chicago Hope, 1994—2000; dir.: Monk, 2002—; (TV films) My Louisiana Sky, 2001 (Daytime Emmy for Oustanding Directing in a Children's Spl., 2002); (films) Pristine Books, 2003—; writer: Improper Channels, 1981; actor: (TV films) It Couldn't Happen to a Nicer Guy, 1974, All Together Now, 1975, Tom Edison: The Boy Who Lit Up the World, 1979, The Fourth Wise Man, 1985, Necessary Parties, 1988, Heat Wave, 1990, A Promise to Keep, 1990, In the Line of Duty: Hunt for Justice, 1995, Not in This Town, 1997, A Slight Case of Murder, 1999, Off Season, 2001, Roughing It, 2002, Damaged Care, 2002; (TV series) Busting Loose, 1977, Teachers Only, 1982, Tough Cookies, 1986, A Year n the Life, 1987—88, Big Wave Dave's, 1993, Baby Bob, 2002—03; (films) Under the Rainbow, 1981, Full Moon High, 1981, Chu Chu and the Philly Flash, 1981, Personal Foul, 1987, The Doctor, 1991, Halloween H20: 20 Years Later, 1998, With Friends Like These..., 1998, Dropping Out, 2000, Hanging Up, 2000, East of A, 2000, Mission, 2001, Stark Raving Mad, 2002, Kids in America, 2004, Marilyn Hotchkiss' Ballroom Dancing and Charm School, 2005, Hitch, 2005. Office: care CBS Entertainment 7800 Beverly Blvd Los Angeles CA 90036-2112*

ARKIN, MICHAEL BARRY, lawyer, arbitrator, writer; b. Washington, Jan. 11, 1941; s. William Howard and Zenda Lillian (Liebermann) A.; children and stepchildren: Tracy Renee, Jeffrey Harris, Marcy Susan, Chatom Callan, Michael Edwin, Samuel Hopkins, Brandon Maddox, Jessica Remaley, Brandi Remaley Arkin, Casey Remaley Arkin; m. Laura Dorene Haynes, Aug. 16, 1998. AA, George Washington U., 1961; BA in Psychology, U. Okla., 1962, JD, 1965. Bar: Okla. 1965, U.S. Ct. Claims 1968, U.S. Supreme Ct. 1968, Calif. 1970, U.S. Tax Ct. 1970, U.S. Ct. Appeals (3d, 5th, 6th, 9th, 10th cirs.) 1970, U.S. Dist. Ct. (cen. dist.) Calif. 1970, U.S. Dist. Ct. (so. dist.) Calif. 1970, U.S. Dist. Ct. (ea. dist.) Calif. 1987. Trial atty. tax divsn. U.S. Dept. Justice, 1965-68, appellate atty., 1968-69; ptnr. Surr & Hellyer, San Bernardino, Calif., 1969-79; mng. ptnr. Wied, Granby Alford & Arkin, San Diego, 1979-82, Lorenz Alhadeff Fellmeth Arkin & Multer, San Diego, 1982, Finley, Kumble, Heine, Underberg, Manley & Casey, San Diego, 1983; pvt. practice Sacramento and San Andreas (Calif.), 1984-86; ptnr. McDonough Holland & Allen, Sacramento, 1986-87; pvt. practice San Andreas, Calif., 1987—; chief counsel Calaveras County Child Protective Svcs., 1996—2002; hearing officer Calif. Spl. Edn. Hearing Office, McGeorge Sch. Law, U. Pacific, 2002—. Judge pro-tem Calaveras County (Calif.) Consol. Cts., 1999-2002. Author: History of the Bench and Bar of Calaveras County California, 1997—. Bd. dirs. San Bernardino County Legal Aid Soc., 1971-73, sec., 1971-72, pres., 1973; mem. Calaveras County Adv. Com. on Alcohol and Drug Abuse, 1985-94, pres., 1991-92; treas. Calaveras County Legal Assistance Program, 1987—; trustee Calaveras County Law Libr., 1987-98; bd. dirs. Mark Twain Hosp. Dist., 1990-2003, treas., 1994—; mem. Calaveras County Rep. Ctrl. Com., 1990-92, 94-96; Calaveras County chmn. Wilson for Gov., 1994. Named to Hon. Order of Ky. Cols., 1967. Mem. ABA, Calif. Bar Assn. (Wiley F. Manuel pro bono pub. svc. award 1991), San Diego County Bar Assn., San Bernardino County Bar Assn. (bd. dirs., sec.-treas. 1973-75, pilot drug abuse program 1970), Calaveras County Bar Assn. (bd. dirs., v.p. 1988-90, pres. 1990-95), Am. Arbitration Assn. (arbitrator 1987—). Jewish. Home: 16193 Hillaire Rd Rough And Ready CA 95975 Office: McGeorge Sch Law U of Pacific 3200 5th Ave Sacramento CA 95817 E-mail: markin2500@aol.com.

ARKIN, STANLEY S., lawyer; b. L.A., Feb. 28, 1938; s. Jerome and Lillian (Rogo) A.; m. Suzanne Arkin, Mar. 3, 1963; children: Adam Arkin, Alexander Arkin, Anthony Arkin. AB magna cum laude, U. So. Calif., 1959; JD cum laude, Harvard U., 1962. Bar: N.Y. 1964, Calif. 1977, D.C. 1982. Sr. ptnr. Stanley S. Arkin, P.C., N.Y.C., 1969-90, Chadbourne & Parke, N.Y.C., 1990-93, Arkin Kaplan, LLP (formerly Arkin Kaplan & Cohen LLP), N.Y.C., 1994—; chmn. Arkin Group LLC (pvt. intelligence agy.), 2000—. Author: (with Matthew Bender) Business Crime, 1982, (with Matthew Bender) Hi Tech Crimes, 1989; columnist, contbr. articles to newspapers and profl. jour. With JAGC U.S. Army, 1962—68. Fellow Am. Coll. Trial Lawyers; mem. Coun. on Fgn. Rels., Phi Beta Kappa. Office: Arkin Kaplan LLP 590 Madison Ave 35th Fl New York NY 10022 Office Phone: 212-333-0200. Business E-Mail: sarkin@arkin-law.com.

ARKING, LUCILLE MUSSER, nurse, epidemiologist; b. Centre County, Pa., Jan. 26, 1936; d. Boyd Albert and Marion Anna (Merryman) Musser; m. Robert Arking, May 8, 1958; children: Henry David, Jonathan Jacob. RN,

Episcopal Sch. Nursing, 1958; BSN, U. Pa., 1968; MSN, Wayne State U., 1986, postgrad., 1991—96. Psychiat. rsch. nurse Boston City Hosp., 1958; hosp. supr. Phila. Psychiat. Ctr., 1959-61; pub. health nurse Cmty. Nursing Svc., Phila., 1961-64; DON Green Acres Nursing Ctr., Phila., 1966-67; head nurse U. Va., Charlottesville, 1967-68; asst. DON U. Ky., Lexington, 1968-70; asst. dir. nursing edn. Rio Hondo Hosp., Downey, Calif., 1973-75; DON Bellwood Hosp., Bellflower, Calif., 1974-75; nurse epidemiologist Henry Ford Hosp., Detroit, 1975-84, dir. hosp. epidemiology, 1984-89, sr. clin. epidemiologist, 1990-94; v.p. clin. svcs. Great Lakes Rehab. Hosp., Southfield, Mich., 1994-96; adminstr. Cadillac Nursing Ctr., Detroit, 1997-99; exec. dir. St. Anthony Nursing Care Ctr., Warren, Mich., 1999—2001; with office of internat. affairs Pusan (South Korea) Nat. U., 2001; with St. James Nursing Ctr., Detroit, 2002—03, Arking Cons. Assocs., 2003—. Lectr. drug abuse Fountain Valley, Calif., 1970-75; instr. Santa Ana Coll., 1971-73. Contbr. articles to profl. jours. Co-founder Parents and Friends Learning Disabilities Orgn., 1968-70; dean leader Cub Scouts, Fountain Valley, 1968-75; bd. dirs. Wellness Networks, Detroit, 1982-86; mem. Mich. Gov. AIDS Task Force, 1985-86, Mich. Med. Soc. AIDS Task Force, 1986. Women's Club of Centre County scholar, 1954-58; grantee Cmty. Nursing Svc. Ednl., 1963-64; USPHS nursing trainee, 1965. Mem. APHA (mem. epidemiology sect. 1975-99), ANA, Mich. Nurses's Assn. (AIDS task force 1987-89, HIV adv. com. 1989-90), Assn. Practitioners Infection Control, Sci. Rsch. Soc., Assn. Women in Sci., Sigma Xi. Home: 4705 Stoddard Dr Troy MI 48085-3504 Office Phone: 248-689-5286. Personal E-mail: brkac@aol.com.

ARLEDGE, CHARLES STONE, former aerospace executive, entrepreneur; b. Bonham, Tex., Oct. 20, 1935; s. John F. and Mary Madeline (Jones) A.; m. Barbara Jeanne Ruff, June 18, 1966; children: John Harrison, Mary Katherine. BS, Stanford U., 1957, MS (Standard Oil Co. Calif. scholar 1958), 1958, MBA, 1966. Engr. Shell Oil Co., Los Angeles, 1958-64; with Signal Cos., La Jolla, Calif., 1966-86, v.p., 1970-79, group v.p., 1979-83, sr. v.p., 1983-86; v.p. Aerojet Gen. Corp., La Jolla, Calif., 1986-90; ptnr. Signal Ventures, 1990—2004. Mem.: California; La Jolla Beach and Tennis. Republican. Presbyterian. Home: PO Box 957 Rancho Santa Fe CA 92067-0957

ARLEDGE, DAVID A., energy executive; b. 1944; BBA, U. Tex., 1965, JD, 1968. With Touch Ross & Co., CPA's, 1968-72, ptnr., 1975-80, Penfold & Arledge, 1972-75; pres., CEO, COO Coastal Corp., West Memphis, Ark., 1980—2001; vice chmn. bd. dirs. El Paso Energy Corp. (formerly Coastal Corp.), 2001; dir. Enbridge Inc., Calgary, Canada, 2002—, chmn., 2005—. Bd. dir. AmerUS Group, Realty Group of Naples LLC, Fla. Office: Enbridge Inc 3000 Fifth Ave Pl 425 W 1st St SW Calgary AB T2P 3L8 Canada Office Phone: 713-420-2600. Office Fax: 713-420-4417.*

ARLEN, JENNIFER HALL, law educator; b. Berkeley, Calif., Jan. 7, 1959; d. Michael John and Ann (Warner) A.; m. Robert Lee Hotz, May 21, 1988; children: Michael Arlen Hotz, Robert Arlen Hotz. BA, Harvard U., 1982; JD, NYU, 1986, PhD in Econ., 1992. Bar: NY 1987, US Ct. Appeals (11th cir.) 1987. Summer clk. US Dist. Ct. (ea. dist.), Bklyn., 1984; summer assoc. Davis Polk & Wardwell, NYC, 1985; law clk. US Cir. Judge, 11th cir., Savannah, Ga., 1986-87; asst. prof. law Emory U., Atlanta, 1987-91, assoc. prof. law, 1991-93; prof. law U. So. Calif., LA, 1994—2002, Ivadelle and Theodore Johnson prof. law and bus., 1997—2002; prof. law NYU, 2002—03, Norma Z. Paige prof. Law, 2003—. Vis. prof. law U. So. Calif., 1993; dir. U. So. Calif. Ctr. Law, Econs. Orgn., 2000—02; vis. prof. law Calif. Inst. Tech., 2001, Yale U., 2001—02; mem. acad. bd. NYU Ctr. Law, Bus., 2003—. Olin fellow, U. Calif. Sch. Law, Berkeley, 1991. Mem. ABA, Am. Assn. Law Schs. (chair remedies sect. 1994, chair elect 1993, exec. com. 1990-91, 95, chair torts sect. 1995, chair-elect 1994, treas. 1991, sec. 1992-93, exec. com. bus. assns. sect. 1995-96, 2000—, chair law and econ., sect. 1996, chair-elect law and econs. sect. 1995, chair 1996), Am. Law and Econ. Assn. (bd. dirs. 1991-93, program com. 1999), Am. Econ. Assn., Order of Coif, Am. Law Inst. Democrat. Office: NYU Law Sch 40 Washington Square S New York NY 10012

ARLEN, MICHAEL J., writer; b. London, Dec. 9, 1930; s. Michael and Atlanta (Mercati) A.; m. Ann Warner, 1957 (div. 1971); children— Jennifer, Caroline, Elizabeth, Sally; m. Alice Albright Hoge, 1972; stepchildren— Alicia, James Patrick, Robert Hoge. Grad., St. Paul's Sch., Concord, N.H., 1948, Harvard U., 1952; LLD (hon.), Colby Coll., 1984. Reporter Life mag., 1952-56; contbr., TV critic The New Yorker mag., 1957-82; juror Columbia U.-Dupont awards for broadcast journalism, 1969-72, 78-80; faculty Bread Loaf Writers Conf., 1980. Bd. dirs. Nat. Arts Journalism Program. Author: Living-Room War, 1969, Exiles, 1970, An American Verdict, 1973, Passage to Ararat, 1975, The View from Highway 1, 1976, Thirty Seconds, 1980, The Camera Age, 1981, Say Goodbye to Sam, 1984. Recipient award for television criticism Screen Dirs. Guild, 1968; Nat. Book award for contemporary affairs, 1976; Le Prix Brémond, 1976 Mem. Authors Guild (exec. coun.), PEN Am. Ctr., Knickerbocker Club, Century Assn., Harvard Club of N.Y.

ARLEN, PHILIP MARTIN, medical researcher; s. Myron and Susan Arlen; m. Jodi Arlen, Apr. 24, 1999; children: Sydney, Jordan. MD, Coll. Ga., 1991. Diplomate Am. Bd. Internal Medicine, 1998. Clin. expert NCI, NIH, Bethesda, Md., 1999—2001, staff clinician, 2001—. Dir. clin. rsch. group LTIB, CCR, NCI, Bethesda, Md., 20817. Achievements include research in cancer vaccines. Home Fax: 301-480-1779. Personal E-mail: pa52s@nih.gov.

ARLIDGE, JOHN WALTER, retired utilities executive; b. Rochester, N.Y., Feb. 4, 1933; s. Harold Wesley and Grace Edith (Kempshall) A.; m. Sandra Marie Koswar, Feb. 4, 1955; children: James William, Edward John. BS, L.A. State Coll., 1962. Registered profl. engr., Calif., Nev., Utah. Comm. sys. engrng. design and purchase City of L.A., 1961-62, power sys. resource planning R & D, 1962-74; asst. to v.p. Nev. Power Co., Las Vegas, 1974-82, v.p. resource planning and power dispatch, 1982-89, sr. v.p. govt. affairs, 1989-93; v.p., dir. Nev. Electric Investment Co., Las Vegas, 1982-89; cons. on energy resources and regulation, Las Vegas, 1995—. Advisor electric-lignite sector Ministry Industy and Trade, Warsaw, Poland, 1992-95; mem. Nev. Engr.'s Adv. Com. on Geothermal Devel., 1974-76, Nev. Solar Energy Devel. Adv. Group, 1976-86; mem. energy task force WEST, 1972-84, mem. energy engrng. planning com., 1978; mem. advanced energy sys. divsnl. com. Electric Power Rsch. Inst., 1973-92; mem. Western Utility Group on Fed. Land, 1977; mem. endangered species subcom., rail issues group Edison Elec. Inst., 1977; cons. on air, land and water Western Regional Coun., 1977; mem. Nev. adv. bd. U.S. Bur. Land Mgmt., 1975-77, mem. adv. coun. Las Vegas dist., 1980-92; mem. rsch. adv. bd. U. Nev.; trustee Corp. Devel. Sci. Tech. Nev. Contbr. articles on energy resources to various publs. Mem. Nev. adv. bd. Nature Conservancy; mem. Sec. Energy's Nat. Coal Coun., 1988-93. With USMC, 1950-54. Mem. IEEE, Geothermal Resources Coun. (dir.), utility Coal Gasification Assn. (chmn.), Internat. Solar Energy Assn., Nat. Coal Coun. (advisor to sec. energy), Pacific Coast Elec. Assn., So. Nev. Off-Road Vehicle Assn., Slurry Transp. Assn. (dir. 1979), Masons.

ARLING, DONNA DICKSON, social worker; b. Jersey Shore, Pa., July 8, 1945; d. Eugene Robert and Helen (Bardo) Dickson; m. Bryan Jeremy Arling, Aug. 28, 1969; children: Elissa, Jeremy, Timothy. BS, Pa. State U., 1967; MSW, Smith Coll., 1969; PhD, Clinical Social Work Inst., Wash., DC, 2003. Bd. cert. diplomate in clin. social work; cert. social worker, Md.; cert. ind. clin. social worker, D.C. Clin. social worker N. County Mental Health Ctr., Palo Alto, Calif., 1969-71, VA Hosp., Washington, 1971-77; pvt. practice clin. social work Washington, 1978—. Mem. Nat. Assn. Social Workers, Greater Washington Soc. Clin. Social Work, Smith Coll. Sch. Social Work Alumni Assn. (nat. exec. com. 1979-82, Washington exec. com. 1976-86). Home: 3803 Taylor St Chevy Chase MD 20815-4117 Office: 1015 33rd St NW Washington DC 20007-3523 Office Phone: 202-337-7115.

ARLINGHAUS, SANDRA JUDITH LACH, mathematical geographer, educator; b. Elmira, N.Y., Apr. 18, 1943; d. Donald Frederick and Alma Elizabeth (Satorius) Lach; m. William Charles Arlinghaus, Sept. 3, 1966; 1 child, William Edward. AB in Math., Vassar Coll., 1964; postgrad., U. Chgo., 1964-66, U. Toronto, 1966-67, Wayne State U., 1968-70, MA in Geography, 1976; PhD in Geography, U. Mich., 1977. Vis. instr. math. U. Ill., Chgo., 1966; vis. asst. prof. geography Ohio State U., Columbus, 1977-78, lectr. math., 1978-79, Loyola U., Chgo., 1979-81, asst. prof. math., 1981-82; lectr. math. and geography U. Mich., Dearborn and Ann Arbor, 1982-83; founding dir. Inst. Math. Geography, Ann Arbor, 1985—; pres. Arlinghaus Enterprises, Ann Arbor, 1998—. Guest lectr. U. Chgo., 1979, 87, 2000-01, U. Calif., 1979, Syracuse U., 1991, U. No. Iowa, 1991; guest lectr. U. Mich., Ann Arbor, 1983, 90-93, adj. prof. math. geography, population-environ. dynamics Sch. Natural Resources and Environ., 1994—, adj. prof. Coll. Architecture and Urban Planning, 1997, 2001—; cons. Transp. Rsch. Inst., Coll. Architecture, 1985-86, Coll. Edn., 1992, Cmty. Sys. Found., 1993—; prodr. Ann Arbor Cmty. Access TV, 1988-90; dir. spatial analysis divsn. Cmty. Systems Found., 1996—, dir. fellowship tng. divsn., 1996—; co-founder Arlinghaus Enterprises, 1997, pres. 2000-02, mgr., 2003—, pres., 2004—. Author: Down the Mail Tubes: The Pressured Postal Era, 1853-1984, Essays on Mathematical Geography, 1986, Essays on Mathematical Geography-II, 1987, An Atlas of Steiner Networks, 1989, Essays on Mathematical Geography-III, 1991; co-author: Population-Environment Dynamics, Sectors in Transition, 1992 and later editions through 1998, Mathematical Geography and Global Art, 1986, Environmental Effects on Bus Durability, 1990, Fractals in Geography, 1993, Graph Theory and Geography: An Interactive View, Ebook 2002, Wiley, Spatial Synthesis; founder, editor, co-author Solstice, 1990—, Image Interactive Atlases, Image Game Series, Image Discussion Papers, Internat. Soc. Spatial Scis., 1995—; author, editor-in-chief Practical Handbook of Curve Fitting, 1994; co-author: (book chpt.) Handbook of Engineering, 2004; co-author, editor-in-chief Practical Handbook of Digital Mapping: Terms and Concepts, 1994; editor-in-chief Practical Handbook of Spatial Stats., 1995; editor internat. monograph series; reviewer Mathematical Reviews, 1992—; contbr. articles, book reviews to profl. jours. in field of geography, psychology, math., biology, history, philately. Mem. City of Ann Arbor Planning Commn., 1995-2003, sec., 1997-2002, chair, 2002-2003, vice-chmn., 2003; mem. City of Ann Arbor Environ. Commn., 2000-03; bd. dirs., chmn. Bromley Homeowners Assn., Ann Arbor, 1989-93, pres., 1990-93, 95-96; mem. ordinance revisions com. City of Ann Arbor, 1996-2003, mem. master planning com., 2002-03; donation GIS analysis City of Ann Arbor, 2003-, 3D virtual reality models downtown devel. task force, 2004; bd. dirs. World Jr. Bridge Championships, Ann Arbor, 1990-91, Dolfins Inc., 1993-96; artist Math. Awareness Week, Lawrence Tech. U., 1988; trustee Cmty. Sys. Found., 1995-2001; co-vice chair citizens adv. com. NE Ann Arbor master plan revision, 1999-2000; adv. bd. City of Ann Arbor Police Dept. Neighborhood Watch, 2001-05; mem. exec. com. Comty. Sys. Found., 2003—, sec. bd. trustees, 2003—; donation GIS analysis Am. Contract Bridge League, 2005—. Finalist Pirelli Internat. award, 2002; recipient Cmty. Svc. award, City of Ann Arbor, 1999, Pres.'s Vol. Svc. award, Pres. Bush's Coun. Svc. and Civic Participation, 2003—, Pirelli Internat. award semifinalist, 2001, 2003. Fellow Am. Geog. Soc. (rep. search com. for curator of collection in Golda Meir Libr. U. Wis.-Milw. Libr. 1993-94); mem. AAAS, Am. Math. Soc., Math. Assn. Am., Assn. Am. Geographers, Internat. Soc. Spatial Scis. (founder), Regional Sci. Assn. Achievements include discovery of exact fractal characterization of the geometry of central place theory and its electronic interpretation; alignment of earth marking sculptures to solstices and equinoxes in Minnesota, Washington, Alaska, New Brunswick, Canada, and USSR; creator of one of world's first refereed electronic journals; creator of applications of chaos theory in geography and population environment dynamics, maps for major international projects for Syria and Pakistan; creator of spatial synthesis materials. Office: U Mich Sch Natural Resources Ann Arbor MI 48109 Business E-Mail: sarhaus@umich.edu.

ARLITT, MARTIN FRASER, computer scientist, researcher; B of Edn., U. Sask., 1993, BS, 1994, MS, 1996. Rschr. Hewlett-Packard Labs., Palo Alto, Calif., 1997—. Mem.: ACM, IEEE. Achievements include patents for Web cache performance by applying different replacement policies to the web cache; Caching protocol method and system based on request frequency and relative storage duration. Office: Hewlett-Packard Labs 1501 Page Mill Rd MS 1125 Palo Alto CA 94304 Office Phone: 650-236-2162. E-mail: martin.arlitt@hp.com.

ARLOOK, IRA ARTHUR, advocate, communications executive; b. N.Y.C., Apr. 7, 1943; s. George G. and Shirley (Meyers) A.; m. Karen Beth Nussbaum, July 9, 1978; children: Gene, Jack, Eleanor. BA, Tufts U., 1964; MA in History, Stanford U., 1966; PhD in Pub. Policy, Union Inst., 1978. Asst. prof. Cleve. State U., 1975-80; exec. dir. Ohio Pub. Interest Campaign, Cleve., 1976-93, Citizen Action, Cleve., Chgo. and Washington, 1980-97; mng. dir. Fenton Comms., Washington, 2004—. Exec. dir. New Economy Comms., 1998—. Woodrow Wilson Nat. fellow, 1965, NSF fellow, 1980. Mem. Citizens for Tax Justice (pres. 1980-97), Nat. Conf. Alternative State and Local Pub. Policies (bd. dirs. 1976-80), Citizen Labor Energy Coalition (bd. dirs. Washington 1978-90), Nat. Campaign Against Toxic Hazards (bd. dirs. 1983-87). Avocations: sports, music. Office: New Economy Comm 1320 18th St NW 5th fl Washington DC 20036-1811 E-mail: ira@neweconomy.org.

ARLOTTA, JOHN J., pharmaceutical executive; BS mktg., Univ. Notre Dame. With Baxter Internat.; pres., COO Caremark Pharmaceutical Services; vice-chmn. Genesis Health Ventures; pres., chmn., CEO NeighborCare Inc. Office: NeighborCare Inc 3rd Fl 601 E Pratt St Baltimore MD 21202 Office Phone: 410-528-7300. Office Fax: 410-528-7447.*

ARLOW, ARNOLD JACK, advertising executive, artist; b. Bklyn., Sept. 29, 1933; s. Louis and Sylvia (Spitzberg) A.; m. Phyllis Banschick, Apr. 20, 1958 (div. 1990); children: Susan, Noah; m. Susan Gray, Nov. 22, 1992. B.F.A., Cooper Union, 1954. Art dir. N.Y. Times, 1958-61, Altman Stoller Advt., N.Y.C., 1961-65, Daniel & Charles Advt., N.Y.C., 1965, McCaffrey McCall Advt., N.Y.C., 1965-66; partner, creative dir. Martin Landey, Arlow Advt., N.Y.C., 1966-80; exec. v.p., creative dir. Geers Gross Advt., 1980-83; cons. communications industry, 1983-84; exec. v.p., creative dir. TBWA Advt., 1984-94; ptnr., creative dir. Margeotes, Fertitta & Ptnrs., N.Y.C., 1994—2003; creative cons., painter Amagansett, NY, 1998—99; sr. v.p., dir. luxury mktg. Berenter Greenhouse & Webster, N.Y.C., 2000—01. Tchr. design Wagner Coll., Staten Island, 1964-69 Alumni trustee Cooper Union, 1982-85. Served with USAF Res., 1961-66. Recipient Augustus Saint-Gaudens award for profl. achievement in art Cooper Union, 1995; Fulbright-Hays grantee Paris, 1954-55; Kelly award MPA for Absolut Vodka Campaign, 1988, 90. Democrat. Jewish. Home: 31 W 12th St New York NY 10011-8500 E-mail: arniearlow@aol.com.

ARM, THEODORE E., music educator, musician; b. Bklyn., May 18, 1945; s. Murray David and Helen Arm; m. Marilyn Lampert Arm, Nov. 25, 1983; children: Manya, Heather. BS, Julliard Sch., N.Y.C., 1967, MS, 1970, DMusA, 1976. Prof. music U. Conn., Storrs, Conn., 1968—; concert violinist. Violinist TASHI Chamber Ensemble, 1976—; guest artist Chamber Music Now, Portland, Oreg., 1976—, Chamber Music Soc. Lincoln Ctr., N.Y.C., 1980—2000, Music from Angel Fire, N.Mex., 1980—; vis. artist U. Ill., Champaign, Ill., 1979—80. Office: Music Dept Unit 1012 U Conn Storrs Mansfield CT 06269-1012 Home: 9 Norwich Salem Rd East Haddam CT 06423

ARMACOST, BARBARA ELLEN, law educator; b. Balt., 1954; BS, U. Va., 1976, JD, 1989; MTS, Regent Coll., U. BC, 1984. Bar: Va. 1989. Head nurse cardiovasc. unit U. Va. Hosp.; vol. mission hospital, La Pointe, Haiti; jud. clk. to Hon. J. Harvie Wilkinson III US Ct. Appeals 4th Cir., 1989—90; atty. adviser Office Legal Counsel US Dept. Justice, 1990—92; asst. prof. U. Va. Sch. Law, 1992—97, assoc. prof., 1997—98, prof., 1998—. Office: U Va Sch Law 580 Massie Rd Charlottesville VA 22903-1789 Office Phone: 434-924-3413. E-mail: bea4k@virginia.edu.

ARMACOST, MARY-LINDA SORBER MERRIAM, retired academic administrator; b. Jeannette, Pa., May 31, 1943; d. Everett Sylvester Calvin and Madeleine (Case) Sorber; m. E. William Merriam, Dec. 13, 1969 (div. 1975); m. Peter H. Armacost, July 10, 1993. Student, Grove City Coll., 1961-63; BA, Pa. State U., 1963-65, MA, 1965-67, PhD, 1967-70; HHD (hon.), Carroll Coll., 1991; LLD (hon.), Wilson Coll., 1994. Rsch. assoc. Pa. State U., University Park, 1970-72; asst. prof. speech Emerson Coll., Boston, 1972-79, dir. continuing edn., 1974-77, spl. asst. to pres., 1977-78, v.p. adminstrn., 1978-79; asst. to pres. Boston U., 1979-81; pres. Wilson Coll., Chambersburg, Pa., 1981-91, Moore Coll. Art and Design, Phila., 1991-93; sr. fellow Office of Women in Higher Edn. Am. Coun. on Edn., 1994—; interim pres. Moore Coll. Art and Design, Phila., 1998-99; pres. emerita, 2000. Cons. Govt. Edn. and Secondary Edn. Act Title III, Alameda County, Calif., 1968; adj. prof. U. Pa. Grad. Sch. Edn., 2003—. Bd. govs. New Eng. chpt. NATAS, 1980-81; bd. dirs. Sta. WITF, Inc., Harrisburg, Pa., 1982-91, chmn. bd., 1988-91; bd. dirs. Chambersburg Hosp., 1984-89, vice chmn. bd., 1987-89; bd. dirs. Elderhostel, 1997-2002; vice-chmn., 2000-2002; trustee Monmouth U., N.J., 1994-99, Sta. WHYY-FM-TV, Phila., 1992-93, Boston Zool. Soc., 1980-81, Arts Boston, 1979-81, Scotland Sch. Vets. Children, Pa., 1984-90, Randolph-Macon Woman's Coll., Lynchburg, Va., 2001-02; bd. dirs. Fla. Orch., 1993-97, co-chair edn. com., 1995-97, exec. com., 1995-97; exec. com. Found. for Ind. Colls., 1989-91, WEDU-TV, 1998-2002, chair planning com., exec. com., bd. dirs., 1998-2002; pres. Chambersburg Area Coun. Arts, 1988-90; chmn. higher edn. com. Gen. Assembly Presbyn. Ch., 1987-90; elder Falling Spring Presbyn. Ch., 1988-90; fellow Am. Coun. Edn., 1977-78, commn. on govtl. rels., 1985-89, commn. on women, 1992-93; exec. com. Pa. Assn. Colls. and Univs., 1984-90, Assn. Presbyn. Colls. and Univs., 1983-88, pres., 1986-87; edn. adv. com. John S. and James L. Knight Found., 1998-2000; bd. dirs., exec. com. Presbyn. Edn. Bd., Lahore, Pakistan 2003—. Recipient Disting. Alumna award Pa. State U., 1984, Disting. Dau. of Pa., 1986, Athena award Chambersburg C. of C., 1988, Outstanding Alumnae award Sch. Dist. Jeannette, 1991. Mem.: Phi Kappa Phi. E-mail: mlsma@cs.com.

ARMACOST, PETER HAYDEN, academic administrator; b. N.Y.C., July 12, 1935; s. George Henry and Verda Gay (Hayden) A.; m. Suzanne Lee Sadosky, June 22, 1957 (dec. Feb. 1991); children: Martha Hayden, David Keys, Sarah Jane, Rebecca Ann; m. Mary-Linda Merriam, July 10, 1993. BA, Denison U., 1957; PhD, U. Minn., 1963. Dean students, chmn. dept. psychology Augsburg Coll., Mpls., 1959-65; program dir. Assn. Am. Colls., Washington, 1965-67; pres., prof. psychology Ottawa U., (Kans.), 1967-77; pres. Eckerd Coll., St. Petersburg, Fla., 1977—2000, pres. emeritus, 2000—; sr. adviser Coun. Ind. Colls., 2001—; pres., prin. Forman Christian Coll., 2002—. Author materials in field. Chmn. Kansas City (Mo.) Regional Coun. Higher Edn., 1972-74; pres. Am. Bapt. Chs. U.S., 1974-75, So. Univ. Conf., 1997; bd. dirs. United Way of Pinellas County, 1995—. Recipient Disting. Alumnus citation Denison U.; Woodrow Wilson fellow; Danforth fellow; named to Tampa Bay Bus. Hall of Fame, 1999. Mem. Assn. Am. Colls. (bd. dirs.), Am. Coun. Edn., Nat. Assn. Student Pers. Adminstrs. (bd. dirs. divsn. rsch., publs. and conf. chmn. Disting. Svc. award), Assn. Ind. Colls. Kans. (pres. 1970-72), Young Pres. Orgn. (chmn. Fla. chpt. 1983-84), So. Assn. of Colls. and Schs. (appeals com.), Am. Assn. Higher Edn., Soc. Values in Higher Edn., Nat. Assn. Ind. Coll. and U. Pres., Fla. Assn. Colls. and Univs. (pres. 1989-90), Ind. Colls. and Univs. Fla. (sec. 1984-86, treas. 1986-88, vice chmn. 1990-91, chmn. 1991-93), Coun. Ind. Colls. (bd. dirs. 1993—, sec. exec. com.), Nat. Assn. Ind. Colls. and Univs. (bd. dirs. 1995-98), Suncoast C. of C. (chmn. 1984-85), Pinellas Econ. Devel. Coun. (bd. dirs. 1989—), Fla. Coun. of 100, St. Petersburg C. of C. (bd. dirs. 1995—), St. Petersburg Yacht Club, Suncoasters Club, Rotary, SunTrust Bank of Tampa Bay (bd. dirs. 1983—), Blue Key, Phi Beta Kappa, Omicron Delta Kappa, Pi Gamma Mu, Psi Chi. Republican. Home: 555 5th Ave NE #914 Saint Petersburg FL 33701 Office: Eckerd Coll 4200 54th Ave S Saint Petersburg FL 33711-4744 Office Phone: 92-42-587-4312. E-mail: peterarma@brain.net.pk.

ARMACOST, SAMUEL HENRY, bank executive; b. Newport News, Va., Mar. 29, 1939; s. George Henry and Verda Gae (Hayden) A.; m. Mary Jane Levan, June 16, 1962; children: Susan Lovell, Mary Elizabeth. BA, Denison U., 1961; MBA, Stanford U., 1964. With Bank of Am. NT & SA, San Francisco, 1961-81, v.p. mgr. London br., 1972-74, sr. v.p., mgr. San Francisco, 1975-77, exec. v.p. Europe, Middle East and Africa div. London, 1977-79, exec. v.p., cashier San Francisco, 1979-81; pres., chief exec. officer Bank of Am. and Bank Am. Corp., San Francisco, 1981-86; chmn., chief exec. officer Bank of Am., San Francisco, 1986-87; mng. ptnr. Merrill Lynch and Co., San Francisco, from 1987; mng. dir. Merrill Lynch Capital Markets, San Francisco, 1988-90; ptnr. Weiss Peck & Greer, San Francisco, Calif., 1990—. Bd. dirs. Chevron Corp. Bd. dirs. The Failure Group, The James Irvine Found., Calif. Acad. Scis. Mem. Bus. Coun., Bus. Roundtable, Bohemian Club, Pacific Union Club, San Francisco Golf Club, Augusta (Ga.) Nat. Golf Club. Republican. Presbyterian.

ARMAINGAUD, FRANCK, engineer; b. Marseille, France, July 3, 1939; s. Maurice Armaingaud and isabelle Marguerite Lourde-Rocheblave; m. Claude Alice Heer, May 25, 1963; children: Patrick, Yves, Agnes. Baccaloreat, Lycee Toulon, France, 1959. Field engr. and European support, Switzerland, France, Tunisia, Belgium, 1962-73; tng. mgr. Burroughs, France, Europe, 1973-75, internat. product mgr. Detroit, 1975-77, internat. tng. mgr., 1977-79; country svc. mgr. Burroughs, Columbia and Equador, Bogota, 1979-80, Data Gen., France, 1980-81; gen. mgr. SFR/Ins., Monaco, 1981-83; country svc. mgr. Prime Computer, France, 1983-85, country sales mgr., 1985-87; v.p. svc. South Europe ICL, Paris, France, 1987-89; pres. ICL-Sorbus, Europe, London, 1994-97; v.p. Jane Pannier, Marseille, 1998—2001. Mem. AFSMI (chmn., pres. 1992), Lions Club (pres. 2000-01). Avocations: gardening, sailing. E-mail: franck.armaingaud@wanadoo.fr.

ARMAND, SUSANNE MARIE, pharmaceutical executive; b. Houston, Jan. 20, 1952; d. Edward and Alice Ruth (Brown) A.; children: Jaime Susanne, Ken Coleman II. AAS in Biotech. summa cum laude, Kingwood Coll., 1994; student, Tex. A&M U., 1969-72. Office mgr. Scientific Time Sharing, Spring, Tex., 1975-77; electrologist Tomball (Tex.) Electrolysis, 1984-86; owner, v.p. Stevenson Enterprises, Spring, Tex., 1986-98; metrology specialist, quality control scientist Aronex Pharms. Inc., The Woodlands, Tex., 1994-99; quality control supr. Mill Biopharm., Inc., Okla. City, Okla., 1999-2000; quality mgr., quality improvement process mgr. Internat. Isotopes Inc., Denton, Tex., 2000—01; quality cons. Alcon Labs, Abbott Labs, 2001—02; mgr. quality control lab. PharmaFab, 2002—03; dir. ops. and quality CPM Lab., Inc., 2003—. Marathon runner Leukemia Soc. Fund Raiser, Houston, 1999; competitive runner Susan Koenig Breast Cancer Fund Raiser, Oklahoma City, 1999, Gulf Assn. of the Athletics Congress, 1982-99. Recipient first Aronex Chmn.'s award Aronex Pharms. Inc., 1997. Mem. Am. Soc. for Quality. Republican. Methodist. Avocations: rollerskating, calligraphy, long distance running, cake decorating. Home: 3820 Burr Oak Ct Bedford TX 76021-6180 Office: 2300 Valley View Ln Ste 230 Farmers Branch TX 75234 Office Phone: 972-241-8374. E-mail: susanne@cpmlab.com.

ARMAN GELENBE, DENIZ, concert pianist; b. Ankara, Turkey, Oct. 8, 1944; came to U.S., 1962; d. Abdul Kerim and Ayse Medina (Raif) A.; m. Erol Gelenbe, June 8, 1968; 1 child, Pamir Emre. Student, Eastman Sch. Music, 1962-64; MusB, Juilliard, 1967, MusM, 1968; postgrad., U. Mich., 1970-71. Founder, artistic dir., prof. piano Paris U., 1979-90; founder, artistic dir. Arman Ensemble, N.C., 1994—, Arman Ensemble, Arman Trio, Paris, 1994—. Dir. summer music program, Normandy, France, 1999—; vis. assoc. prof. piano U. Ctrl. Fla., Orlando, 1998—2003, artist in residence, assoc. prof. piano, 2001—03; sr. lectr., keyboard coord. for collaborative performance Trinity Coll. Music, London, 2003—. Musician (recitals): Carnegie Weill Hall, Salle Gaveau, Nat. Gallery Art, Tonhalle, Wigmore Hall, Concerts de Midi; musician: (soloist) Ensemble Orchestral Paris, New Japan Philharm., Ankara Presdl. Symphony Orch., Presdl. Symphony Orch., N.C. Symphony; musician: (CD) with Haydn Quartet, 1994, 2000, Arman Ensemble, 1996, Arman Trio, 2000, 2004. Emerging Artist grantee, Durham, N.C., 1984. Mem. European Piano Tchrs. Assn., Chamber Music Am., Coll. Music Soc.

Avocations: painting, reading, walking. Home: Flat 67 Campbell Ct 1-7 Queens Gate Gardens London SW7 4PD England Office: Trinity Coll Music KIng Charles Ct Old Royal Naval Coll, Greenwich London SE10 9JF England Personal E-mail: dgelenbe@aol.com.

ARMANI, FRANK HENRY, retired lawyer; b. Sept. 12, 1927; s. Ezzelin M. and Edvige A.; m. Natalie Mary Mozo, July 1, 1950; children: Deborah M., Dorina A. AB, Syracuse U., 1950, JD, 1956. Bar: N.Y. 1956, U.S. Dist. Ct. (no. dist.) N.Y. 1958, U.S. Ct. Appeals (2d cir.), 1962, U.S. Supreme Ct. 1964. Counsel Legal Aid, Onondaga County, N.Y., 1956-57; pvt. practice, Syracuse, 1957-62m 68-88; ptnr. Armani, Welch & Welch, Syracuse, 1962-68; asst. dist. atty. Onondaga County, 1961-70; ptnr. Armani, Fitzpatrick, Snyder & Armani, P.C., Camillus, N.Y., 1988-89; ret., 1989. Lectr. legal ethics, Syracuse U., Detroit Law Sch., U. Va., U. La.; participant profl. confs. and symposia.; prodn. and tech. advisor to movie Sworn to Silence, 1987; lectr. Syracuse U. Law, St. John's Law Sch. Membership chmn. Onondaga County Young Reps., 1948-50, chmn. Law Day com., 1970; bd. dirs. Onondaga Coun. on Alcoholism, 1979—; del. Rep. Nat. Conv., 1980; com. mem. VA Med. Ctr.; del. U.S.-China Joint Session on Trade, Investment and Econ. Law, Beijing, 1987. Recipient Law Day award Catharagus County Bar Assn., 1985, commendation La. Senate. Mem. ATLA, N.Y. State Bar Assn., Onondaga County Bar Assn. (bd. dirs. 1979-81, chmn. alcohol and drug abuse com. 1977—), Upstate Trial Lawyers Assn. Roman Catholic. Featured on Sta. WETA-TV documentary Ethics on Trial. Home and Office: 121 Munro Dr Camillus NY 13031-1934 Personal E-mail: farmani926@aol.com.

ARMAOU, ANTONIOS, chemical engineer, educator, researcher; arrived in U.S., 1996; Diploma in chem. engring., Nat. Tech. U., Athens, Greece, 1996; PhDChemE, UCLA, 2001. Registered profl. engr., Greece. Post doctoral rschr. UCLA, Calif., 2001, Princeton U., NJ, 2001—02; asst. prof. Penn State U., University Park, 2002—. Invited spkr. dept. chem. engring. Nat. Tech. U. Athens, Greece, 2003; invited spkr. Model Reduction and Coarse-Graining Approaches for Multiscale Phenomena, Internat. Workshop, Leicester, England, 2005—; workshop co-organizer 16th IFAC World Congress, Prague, Czech Republic, 2005—. Contbr. articles to jours. and conf. proceedings. Recipient Best Presentation award, Am. Control Conf., 1999, 2000, O. Hugo Schuck Best Paper Award, 2000, Outstanding PhD in Chem. Engring. award, UCLA, 2001; fellow, 2000—01. Mem.: AAAS, AIChE (session chair 1998—2005), IEEE Control Systems Soc. (assoc. editor, program com. mem., session chair 2000—05). Office: Penn State Univ 170 Fenske Lab University Park PA 16802-4400 Office Phone: 814-865-5316. Office Fax: 814-865-7846. E-mail: armaou @engr.psu.edu.

ARMARIO, JOSE, restaurant executive; b. Cuba; m. Mary Armario; 3 children. M in profl. mgmt., U. Miami. Joined McDonald's Corp., 1996, sr. v.p., relationship ptnr., pres., latin am. ops., 2003—. Office: McDonalds Corp McDonalds Plaza Oak Brook IL 60523

ARMBRECHT, WILLIAM HENRY, III, retired lawyer; b. Mobile, Ala., Jan. 13, 1929; s. William Henry and Katherine (Little) A.; m. Dorothy Jean Taylor, Sept. 1, 1951; children— Katherine Handley, William Taylor, Alexander Paterson. BS, U. Ala., 1950, JD, 1952. Bar: Ala. 1952, U.S. Supreme Ct. 1972. Assoc. Inge, Twitty, Armbrecht & Jackson, Mobile, 1952-56; ptnr. Armbrecht, Jackson, McConnell & DeMouy, Mobile, 1956-65, Armbrecht, Jackson & DeMouy, Mobile, 1965-75, Armbrecht, Jackson, DeMouy, Crowe, Holmes & Reeves, Mobile, 1976-94, Armbrecht, Jackson, DeMouy, Crowe, Holmes & Reeves, LLC, 1994-96. Served to 1st lt. JAGC, AUS, 1952-54. Mem. ABA, Ala. Bar Assn. (chmn. grievance com. 1973-74, chmn. sect. corp. banking and bus. law 1976-78), Mobile Bar Assn., Mobile Area C. of C. Found. (bd. dirs. 1990-92), Southeastern Corp. Law Inst. (mem. planning com. 1967-96), Phi Delta Phi, Delta Kappa Epsilon Episcopalian. Home: 600 Fairfax Rd E Mobile AL 36608-2931

ARMBRISTER, DOUGLAS KENLEY, surgeon; b. Emory, Va., Feb. 20, 1934; s. Victor Stradley and Naomi Lucile (Byrd) A.; m. Nancy Sheri Douglas, Apr. 30, 1960 (div. Sept. 1995); children: Valere Lynn, Victor Kenley, Christopher Douglas, Karen Leigh; m. Barbara Ann Atwell, Sept. 9, 2000. BA in English/German, BS in Chemistry/Biology, Emory and Henry Coll., 1955; MD, U. Va., 1959, MS in Surg. Rsch., 1962. Diplomate Am. Bd. Surgery. Intern surgery U. Va., 1959—60, resident surgery, 1960—62, 1964—67; pvt. practice Marion, Va., 1967—. Regional adv. group Va. Regional Med. Program, 1971; subarea coun. chmn. Health Systems Agy.; bd. dirs. Va. Health Quality Ctr.; pres. Smyth County Cmty. Hosp. Med Staff, 1973, chair surg. svcs., 1978—. Bd. visitors Emory and Henry Coll., 1982—. Capt. USAF, 1962-64. Fellow Am. Coll. Surgeons: mem. Va. Surg. Soc. (malpractice review panel mem. 1972—), Med. Soc. Va. (review bd. dirs. 1985-95), Southwest Va. Med. Soc., Muller Surg. Soc., Nat. Eagle Scout Assn., Blue Key Nat. Honor Soc. (pres. 1953). Methodist. Avocations: tennis, classical music, singing, piano. Office: 592 Radio Hill Rd Marion VA 24354-4224 Office Phone: 276-783-7226.

ARMBRUST, JOSEPH W., JR., lawyer; b. 1943; BS, Boston Coll., 1965; LLB, Univ. Va., 1968. Bar: NY, Va. Ptnr. Sidley Austin Brown & Wood LLP, 1976—, now ptnr. corp. securities group and co-head NYC office NYC. Mem. mgmt. and exec. committees Sidley Austin Brown & Wood LLP; lectr. on securities laws and corp. governance Univ. Va., Univ. Texas, Univ. Md. Mem.: ABA, Assoc. of the Bar of the City of NY, Am. Bar Found. Office: Sidley Austin Brown & Wood LLP 787 Seventh Ave New York NY 10019 Office Phone: 212-839-5390. Office Fax: 212-839-5599. E-mail: jarmbrust@sidley.com.

ARMBRUSTER, PAULA, social worker, director, child mental health educator; b. N.Y.C., June 30, 1935; d. William and Anna Bertha Armbruster; children: K. Levni, Elif-Lale A., Murat A. Student, Smith Coll., Geneva, 1954—55; BA, U. Conn., 1956, MSW, 1974; MA, Yale U., 1964. Intelligence analyst Nat. Security Agy., Washington, 1956—62; Nat. Def. Act fellow Yale U., New Haven, 1962—66; clin. instr. social work Yale Child Study Ctr., Sch. Medicine, Yale U., New Haven, 1974—80, assoc. clin. prof., 1980—, dir. social work tng., 1984—, dir. outpatient svcs., 1985—. Fellow Pierson Coll., Yale U., 1976—; assoc. project dir. HEW tng. grant, asst. prof. residence U. Conn. Sch. Social Work, West Hartford, 1979-80; mem. adv. coun. U. Conn. Sch. Social Work, So. Conn. State U. Sch. Social Work; Johnson Wax fellow, vis. prof. U. Surrey, Eng., 1984. Author, editor works in field. Founder The Neighborhood Place, New Haven; founder, bd. dirs Leadership, Edn. Athletics in Partnership for Youth of Conn.; dir. children's programs Yale Behavioral Health, 1997; nat. steering coun. Habitat for Humanity Mental Health Partnership; rep. of the Nat. Assn. Social Worker to the Nat. Consortium on Children's Mental Health Svcs., Washington, sec., 1994—96, pres., 1996—98; chmn. regional adv. coun. Conn. Dept. Children and Youth Svcs., chmn. regional adv. couns.; bd. dirs. YWCA, New Haven, Sylvan House, VISTA, New Haven Dept. Edn. Sch. Based Clinics Bd., Arts Coun., New Haven, New Haven Land Trust; mem. Yale Sch. Medicine Adv. Com. on Sch. Based Clinics, adv. faculty, Yale Child Study Ctr.; mem. manage care/med. oversight coun. Conn. Legis., chair quality assurance, 1995—, mem. behavioral health oversight com.; nat. task force managed care implementation U. Pa.; nat. task force Sch. Bd. Mental Health Svcs. U. Pa.; expert adv. panel Office Adolescent Medicine; bd. dirs. New Haven Colony Hist. Soc., Inst. for Victims of Trauma, Summerbridge, New Haven; cons. Robert Wood Johnson Found., Bur. Maternal & Child Health, Substance Abuse and Mental Health Svcs. Adminstrn. Mem.: NASW (sec. Conn. chpt.), Conn. Soc. Clin. Social Work, Nat. Acad. Cert. Social Workers, Mory's Assn., New Haven Lawn Club, Yale Club N.Y.C., Yale Club New Haven. Office: Yale Child Study Ctr 230 S Frontage Rd New Haven CT 06519-1124 Office Phone: 203-785-6252. Business E-Mail: Paula.Armbruster@Yale.edu.

ARMELLINO, MICHAEL RALPH, retired portfolio manager; b. Jersey City, Jan. 30, 1940; s. Ralph Michael and Florence (Arturo) A.; m. Patricia Ann Beckett, Mar. 3, 1963; children: Tracy, John, Joseph, Peter. BS in Econs., U. Pa., 1961; MBA, NYU, 1963. Chartered Fin. Analyst. Jr. analyst F.I. DuPont, N.Y.C., 1963-64; transp. analyst Standard & Poors, N.Y.C., 1964-67, Goodbody & Co., N.Y.C., 1967, Lord, Abbett & Co., N.Y.C., 1967-69; sr. transportation analyst Goldman, Sachs & Co., N.Y.C., 1970-90, dir. rsch., 1984-88, ptnr. in charge rsch., 1989-90; chmn., chief exec. officer Goldman Sachs Asset Mgmt., 1991-94; ret. ptnr. GS & Co., 1995—. Mem. N.Y. Stock Exch. (allied); bd. dirs., chmn. strategic planning com. Canadian Nat. Ry. Bd. Trustee Peddie Sch., 1996—, also mem. investment com., fin. com., exec. com. Mem. Benjamin Franklin Soc., U. Pa. Alumni Assn., Soc. Airline Analysts (pres. 1983-84). Roman Catholic. Home: Apt 2301 900 Palisade Ave Fort Lee NJ 07024 E-mail: mrarmellino@aol.com.

ARMEN, GARO H., research and development company executive; BA in Chem., Queens Coll.; PhD in Physical Chem., CUNY. Rsch. fellow Brookhaven Nat. Lab., Long Island, NY; sr. v.p. rsch. Dean Witter Reynolds, 1986—89; mng. gen. ptnr. Armen Ptnrs. LP, 1990—; assoc. prof. Merchant Marine Acad.; first v.p. rsch. E.F. Hutton & Co.; co-founder, chmn., CEO Antigenics Inc. (formerly Antigenics LLC), NYC, 1994—, pres., 1994—2002. Dir. Color Kinetics Inc.; bd. dir. Elan Corp. plc (non-exec. chmn. 2002-), Dublin, 1994—; founder and pres. Children of Armenia Fund. Office: Antigenics Inc Ste 2100 630 Fifth Ave New York NY 10111

ARMEN, MARGARET MEIS, lawyer; d. Joseph John and Florence Catherine Meis. BA, Carlow Coll., 1969; JD, Cleveland State U., 1978. Bar: Ohio 1978, Washington, DC 1980. Tchr. Pitts. City Sch., 1969—70, Archdiocese of Washington, DC, 1970—73; pers. adminstr. Stouffer Foods Corp., Cleve., 1973—75, Hospitality Motor Inns, Inc., Cleve., 1976—78; atty. adv. US Govt. Accountability Office, Washington, 1978—, sr. atty., 1986—. Dir. Am. Assn. for Budget and Program Analysis, Washington, 1986—93, pres., 1993—94; dir. Pub. Fin. Pub., Inc., Washington, 1990—2002, pres., 2003—. Exec. editor: Cleve. State U. Law Rev., 1977—78; contbr. articles to profl. jours. Mem.: Exec. Women in Govt. (v.p. 2002—03), Internat. Alliance for Women (sec. 2004—). Office: US Govt Accountability Office 441 G St NW Washington DC 20548 Business E-Mail: armenm@gao.gov.

ARMEN, ROBERT N., federal judge; b. Pa., 1947; BA, Duquesne, U., 1973; JD, Georgetown U., 1973, M in Taxation (MLT), 1984; LLM, Cleve. State U., 1979. Bar: Ohio 1973, US Tax Ct. 1973, DC 1999. With Office of Chief Counsel, Cleve. Dist. Counsel, IRS, 1973—78, Criminal Tax Divsn., 1978—79, Wash. Dist. Counsel, 1979—81; law clk. to Hon. Howard A. Dawson, Jr. US Tax Ct., 1981—83, asst. clk., 1983—85, dep. counsel to the chief judge, 1986—93, spl. trial judge, 1993—. Adj. prof. No. Va. Cmty. Coll., 1981—89, U. Balt. Law Sch., 1988—90. Office: US Tax Ct 400 Second St NW Washington DC 20217

ARMENAKAS, ANTHONY EMMANUEL, aerospace educator; b. Mytilene, Greece, Aug. 23, 1924; came to U.S., 1946; s. Emmanuel Anthony and Efterpe (Sakis) A.; m. Stella Dimitri Petroutsa, Jan. 3, 1950 (dec. Jan. 1988); children: Alexandra Daphne, Noel Anthony, Melina Cybel. BSCE, Ga. Inst. Tech., 1950; MSCE, Ill. Inst. Tech., 1952; PhD in Applied Mechanics, Columbia U., 1959. Registered profl. engr., N.Y., N.J., Greece. Instr. Ill. Inst. Tech., Chgo., 1950—52; sr. structural engr. Edwards Kelcey and Beck Cons. Engrs., Newark, 1952—54; ptnr. Rynar Armenakas and McCann Cons. Engrs., Newark, 1954—59; lectr. civil engring. CUNY, N.Y.C., 1954—57; assoc. prof. civil engring. Cooper Union for the Advancement Sci. and Art, N.Y.C., 1958—65; prof. engring. sci. U. Fla., Gainesville, 1965—67; prof. aerospace Poly. U., Bklyn., 1967—; Fulbright lectr. to Greece, 1972—73, 1973—74; prof., dir. Inst. Structural Analysis Nat. Tech. U., Athens, Greece, 1977—84. Vis. prof. divsn. engring. Brown U., Providence, 1964-65; cons. Vector Engring., Springfield, N.J., 1954-59; rsch. cons. Poly. Inst., Bklyn., 1962-67, Northwestern U., Evanston, Ill., 1962-65; pres. Stress-Optics, Inc., Queens, N.Y., 1970-72; bd. dirs. Greek r.r.s, 1978-80; vice-chmn. bd. dirs. Greek agy. for design and rsch. earthquake protection, 1989-92. Author: Free Vibrations of Circular Cylindrical Shells, 1969, Tensor Analysis for Engineers, 1974, Classical Structure Analysis-A Modern Approach, 1988, Modern Structural Analysis-The Matrix Method Approach, 1991, Advanced Mechanics of Materials and Applied Elasticity, 2005; patentee in field; contbr. articles to profl. jours. Chmn. bd. dirs. Poulos Philanthropic Found., Athens, Greece. Fellow ASCE, ASME. Avocation: photography. Home: 52 Clark St Brooklyn NY 11201-2402 also: Kifissou 3A Xalandri Attica 15234 Athens Greece Office: Polytechnic Univ 333 Jay St Brooklyn NY 11201-2990

ARMENTEROS, EDUARDO CARLOS, psychologist, educator; b. Havana, Cuba, Nov. 4, 1955; s. Pedro L. and Maria E. Armenteros; m. Maria A. Perez, June 26, 1982; children: Erika M., Javier E. A., Miami-Dade Coll., 1976; BS, Fla. Internat. U., 1978, MS, 1986, degree in ednl. specialist, 1995. Lic. sch. psychologist Fla., cert. profl. tchg. Fla. H.S. math. tchr. Miami-Dade County Pub. Sch., Miami, Fla., 1979—82, sch. psychologist, 1986—; h.s. tchr., counselor Christopher Columbus H.S., Miami, 1982—86; psychotherapist pvt. practice S.Miami, Fla., 1995—. Adj. prof. spl. edn. Barry U., Miami-Shores, Fla., 1997—98; adj. instr. Miami-Dade Coll., 1998—2000; adj. prof. Nova Southeastern U., Ft. Lauderdale, Fla., 2004—. Contbr. articles to profl. jours. Recipient Outstanding Tchr. award, Miami-Dade Pub. Sch., 1980, Outstanding Sch. Psychologist award, 2004. Mem.: Dade Assn. Sch. Psychologist (pres. 2002—03, Outstanding Svc. award 2003), Phi Kappa Phi, Psi Chi. Democrat. Roman Catholic. Avocations: hiking, swimming, reading, travel, coin collecting/numismatics. Office: Miami-Dade County Pub Sch Region Ctr VI 698 N Homestead Blvd Homestead FL 33033 Office Phone: 305-246-5934.

ARMENTROUT-EDWARDS, BRIDGETT A, music educator; b. Covington, Va., Nov. 19, 1959; d. Winston Kelly and Ruth Jane Armentrout; m. Matthew Edwards, Aug. 25, 1990. MusB, Western Mich. U., 1983; MA, W. Va. U., 1992. Music educator Allegheny Public Schools, Covington, Va., 1984—85; music educator and sales Music Unlimited, Inc., Lewisburg, W.Va., 1985—86; music educator Monroe County Pub. Schools, Union, W.Va., 1986—92, Augusta County Pub. Schools, Fishersville, Va., 1992—. Author: (musicals) The Century Program, 1999. Mem.: Va. Edn. Assn., Augusta County Edn. Assn., Music Educators Nat. Conf. Presbyn. Home: 219 Sherry May St Covington VA 24426 Office: Wilson Elem Sch 127 Woodrow Wilson Ave Fishersville VA 22939 Office Phone: 540-962-4585. Personal E-mail: yoshi@ntetos.net.

ARMERDING, HUDSON TAYLOR, retired college president, consultant; b. Albuquerque, June 21, 1918; s. Carl Armerding and Eva May Taylor; m. Miriam Lucile Bailey, Dec. 26, 1944; children: Carreen, Taylor, Paul, Miriam, Jonathan. AB, Wheaton Coll., 1941; AM, Clark U., 1942; PhD, U. Chgo., 1948; DD (hon.), Gordon-conwell Sem., 1972, Reformed Episcopal Sem., 1990; LLD (hon.), Houghton Coll., 1973; HumD (hon.), John Brown U., 1983; STD (hon.), Greenville Coll., 1976; LittD (hon.), Asbury Coll., 1977, Colo. Christian U., 2000. Prof. Wheaton (Ill.) Coll., 1946-48, 61-82; provost Wheaton (Ill.) U., 1963-65, pres., 1965-82; prof. Gordon Coll., Wenham, Mass., 1948-49, 50-61, dean, acting pres., 1950-61. V.p. Quarryville (Pa.) Presbyn. Retirement Cmty., 1982-99; min-at-large Officers Christian Fellowship, Englewood, Colo., 1979-2005; chmn. Site Acquisition Com., Batavia, Ill., 1975; pres. Nat. Assn. of Evangelicals, Wheaton, 1970-72; chmn. World Evangelical Fellowship, Wheaton, 1974-80. Comdr. USN, 1942-46, USNR, 1946-66. Recipient Excellence in Leadership award Officers Christian Fellowship, 2001. Mem. Am. Legion, Mil. Officer Assn., Naval Inst. Republican. Presbyterian. Avocations: travel, walking, camping, reading. Home: 527 Park Ave Quarryville PA 17566 Office: Quarryville Presbyn Retirement Cmty 625 Robert Fulton Hwy Quarryville PA 17566 Office Phone: 717-786-7321. Personal E-mail: harmerding@juno.com.

ARMES, WALTER SCOTT, retired vocational school administrator; b. Okmulgee, Okla., May 15, 1939; s. Ralph E. Armes; m. Jean Hopkins, June 5, 1965; children: Christina M., Rebecca J. BS in Edn., Ohio No. U., 1960; MS, Ind. State U., Terre Haute, 1966; postgrad., Ohio State U. Cert. supt., prin., social studies tchr., Ohio. Tchr. social studies Holmes Liberty Sch. Dist., Bucyrus, Ohio, 1960-63, Painesville Twp. Schs., 1963-64, Weathersfield Twp. Sch. Dist., Mineral Ridge, Ohio, 1964-68, Eastland Career Ctr., Groveport, Ohio, 1968-97; dir. Eastland Vocat. Sch. Dist., Groveport, 1993—97; supr. Licking County Vocat. Sch., Newark, Ohio, 1998—2002; adj. faculty Ashland (Ohio) U., 2003—. Co-founder Franklin County Tchrs. Ctr.; chmn.-elect Met. Edn. Coun. Chmn. Whitehall City Bd. Zoning and Bldg. Appeals; pres. Whitehall City Bd. Edn.; ofcl. USA Track and Field; pres.-elect Ohio Track and Field and Cross Country Ofcls Mem. Nat. Assn. Secondary Sch. Prins., Track Registry Ctrl. Ohio, Ohio Sch. Bd. Assn. (ctrl. dist. exec. bd.), Am. Sch. Bds. Assn., Phi Delta Kappa. Home: 4010 Etna St Columbus OH 43213-2317 Personal E-mail: warmes@aol.com.

ARMETTA, ELISA A., accountant; b. Bklyn., Nov. 1, 1976; d. Pasquale and Laura Armetta. BSBA in Acctg. with tax specialization, Lynn U., Boca Raton, Fla., 1997; M.Acctg., Nova Southeastern U., Ft. Lauderdale, Fla., 1998. Acctg. asst. Addison Mortgage Group, Boca Raton, 1993—94, Lease Am. Svcs., 1994—96; staff acct. David A. Katzman, P.A., 1996—98; tax acct. KPMG Peat Marwick, West Palm Beach, 1998; sr. tax acct. BDO Seidman LLP, West Palm Beach, 1998—2002; sr. acct. Vargas & Ghigliotty, LLP, Delray Beach, 2002—05; pvt. practice Armetta & Assoc. CPA's, Lake Worth, 2005—. Mem.: AICPA, Lake Worth C. of C., Am. Women's Soc. CPAs, Fla. Inst. CPAs. Roman Catholic. Avocations: dancing, exercise. Home: 22335 Palomita Dr Boca Raton FL 33428-6176 E-mail: info@cpaservices.org.

ARMEY, RICHARD KEITH (DICK ARMEY), former congressman; b. Cando, N.D., July 7, 1940; s. Glen Forest and Marion (Gutschlog) A.; m. Susan Byrd; children: Kathryn, David, Scott A., Chip, Scott Oxendine. BA, Jamestown Coll., N.D., 1963; MA, U. N.D., 1964; PhD, U. Okla., Norman, 1969. Mem. econs. faculty U. Mont., 1964-65; asst. prof. West Tex. State U., 1967-68, Austin Coll., 1968-72; assoc. prof. North Tex. State U., 1972-77, chmn. dept. econs., 1977-84; mem. U.S. Congress from 26th Tex. dist., Washington, 1985—2003; former mem. edn. and labor com.; chmn. ho. rep. conf. com., 1992-94; former mem. joint economic com.; Ho. majority leader, 1995—2003. Bd. dirs. Rent-A-Center, 2004—. Author: Price Theory, 1977, The Freedom Revolution, 1995, The Flat Tax-A Citizen's Guide to the Facts on What it Will Do For You, Your Country, and Your Pocketbook, 1996. Republican.

ARMFIELD, DIANA MAXWELL, artist, educator; b. Ringwood, Eng., June 11, 1920; d. Joseph Harold Armfield and Gertrude Mary Uttley; m. Bernard Dunstan, 1949; 3 children. Student, Slade Sch. Art, Ctrl. Sch. Arts and Crafts. Tchr. Byam Shaw Sch. Art, 1959-89. Artist-in-residence, Perth, Australia, 1985, Jackson, Wyo., 1989. One-woman shows include Browse & Darby, London, 1979-2000, 03, Royal Acad. Friends Rm. Gallery, 1995, 2004-05, Royal Cambrian Acad., 2001, Albany Gall, Cardiff, 2001, Albany Gallery, Cardiff, 2002, 05, New Acad. Gallery, 2005; author: Mitchell Beazley Pocket Guide to Painting in Oils, Mitchell Beazley Pocket Guide to Drawing, The Art of Diana Armfield (Julian Halsby); represented in pub. collections at Yale Ctr. for Brit. Art, Govt. Eng., Faringdon, Mercury Asset Mgmt., Lancaster City, Victoria and Albert Mus. Textiles. Commr. HRH Prince of Wales, Reuters, Contemporary Art Soc. Wales, Natural Trust. Mem. Royal Acad. Art, New English Art Club (hon.), Royal Cambrian Acad. (hon. ret.), Pastel Soc. (hon.), Royal Watercolor Soc. Avocations: music, gardening. Address: 10 High Park Rd Kew Richmond TW9 4BH England also: Llwynhir Parc Bala Gwynedo LL23 7YU England Office Phone: 02088766633.

ARMINANA, RUBEN, academic administrator, educator; b. Santa Clara, Cuba, May 15, 1947; came to U.S., 1961; s. Aurelio Ruben and Olga Petrona (Nart) A.; m. Marne Olson, June 6, 1954; children: Cesar A. Martino, Tuly Arminana. AA, Hill Jr. Coll., 1966; BA, U. Tex., 1968, MA, 1970; PhD, U. New Orleans, 1983; postgrad. Inst. of Applied Behavioral Scis., Nat. Tng. Labs., 1971. Nat. assoc. dir. Phi Theta Kappa, Canton, Miss., 1968-69; dir. ops. and tng. Inter-Am. Ctr. Loyola U., New Orleans, 1969-71; adminstrv. analyst City of New Orleans, 1972, adminstrv. analyst and orgnl. devel. and tng. cons., 1972-78; anchor and reporter part time STA. WWL-TV, New Orleans, 1973-81; v.p. Commerce Internat. Corp., New Orleans, 1978-83; exec. asst. to sr. v.p. Tulane U., New Orleans, 1983-85, assoc. exec. v.p., 1985-87, v.p., asst. to pres., 1987-88; v.p. fin. and devel. Calif. State Poly U., Pomona, 1988-92; pres. Sonoma State U., 1992—. TV news cons., New Orleans, 1981-88; lectr. Internat. Trade Mart, New Orleans, 1983-89, U.S. Dept. Commerce, New Orleans. Co-author: Hemisphere West-El Futuro, 1968; co-editor: Colloquium on Central America-A Time for Understanding, Background Readings, 1985. Bd. dirs. Com. on Alcoholism and Substance Abuse, 1978-79, SER, Jobs for Progress, Inc., 1974-82, Citizens United for Responsive Broadcasting, Latin Am. Festival Com.; dir. bd. advisors Sta. WDSU-TV, 1974-77; mem. Bus. Govt. Rsch., 1987-88, Coun. Advancement of Support to Edn.; mem. League of United Latin Am. Citizens, Mayor's Latin Am. Adv. Com., Citizens to Preserve the Charter, Met. Area Com., Mayor's Com. on Crime. Kiwanis scholar, 1966, Books scholar, 1966. Mem. Assn. U. Related Rsch. Prks., L.A. Higher Edn. Roundtable, Soc. Coll. and U. Planning, Nat. Assn. Coll. and U. Bus. Officers Coun., Am. Econ. Assn., Assn. of Evolutionary Econs., Am. Polit. Sci. Assn., AAUP, Western Coll. Assn. (pres. 1994-95), Latin Am. C. of C. (founding dir. New Orleans and River Region 1976-83), Cuban Profl. Club, Phi Theta Kappa, Omicron Delta Epsilon, Sigma Delta Pi, Delta Sigma Pi. Democrat. Roman Catholic. Avocation: mask collecting. Office: Sonoma State U 1801 E Cotati Ave Rohnert Park CA 94928-3609 Office Phone: 707-664-2156. Business E-Mail: ruben.arminana@sonoma.edu.

ARMINAS, SCOTT ARNOLD, chemist, poet, writer; b. S.I., N.Y., Feb. 12, 1960; s. Henry Arnold and Josephine Antoinette Arminas; m. Mariá Basora-Ruiz, Sept. 12, 1987. At, Rutgers U., 1978—79, at, 1997. Chemist Revlon Rsch. Ctr., Edison, NJ, 1987—2001. Author: Sojourn on Eternity's Edge, 2003, Campfire Tales, 1990; co-author: Tales from the Gallery, 1995. Vol. firefighter Middletown Twp. Fire Dept., Port Monmouth, NJ, 1983—86. Nominee Emily Dickenson award, The Amherst Soc., 1991; recipient Golden Poet award, World of Poetry, Sacramento, 1990, 1991. Mem.: Soc. Cosmetic Chemists, Nat. Rifle Assn., KC (3d degree, charter mem.). Roman Catholic. Achievements include patents in field. Avocations: scuba diving, music, gymnastics, pen collecting. Home: 67 Citadel Dr Jackson NJ 08527 E-mail: spartaboy@optonline.net.

ARMISTEAD, (IVOR) CARY, III, lawyer; b. Columbus, Ohio, Jan. 22, 1946; BA, Mich. State Univ., 1967; JD cum laude, Columbia Univ., 1970. Bar: D.C. 1970, Mass. 1979, US Dist. Ct. (D.C., Mass.), US Ct. Appeals (D.C., 1st cir.), US Supreme Ct. Trial atty. Antitrust Div., U.S. Dept. Justice; v.p. & asst. gen. counsel Digital Equipment Corp.; ptnr. corp. dept. Ropes & Gray, Boston, 1996—, vice chmn. corp. dept. & co-head internat. practice group. Mem. London Ct. Internat. Arbitration, England. Harlan Fiske Stone scholar. Mem.: ABA, Boston Bar Assn., New England Antitrust Planning Com. Office: Ropes & Gray 1 International Pl Boston MA 02110-2624 Office Phone: 617-951-7832. Office Fax: 617-951-7050. Business E-Mail: cary.armistead@ropesgray.com.

ARMISTEAD, KATHERINE KELLY (MRS. THOMAS B. ARMISTEAD III), interior designer, travel consultant, civic worker; b. Apr. 14, 1926; d. Joseph Anthony and Katherine Arnold (Manning) Kelly; m. Thomas Boyd Armistead III, Nov. 29, 1952. Grad., Finch Jr. Coll., 1946. Cert. travel cons. Editor news Sta. WOR, N.Y.C., 1946—51; with Dumont TV, 1951—52; editor Social Svc. Rev., L.A., 1956—57; interior designer L.A., 1963—; travel cons. Gilner Internat. Travels, Beverly Hills, Calif., 1980—. Mem. editl. bd. Previews Mag., 1984—87. Pres. Jrs. Social Svc., L.A., 1962—64; nat. chpt. chmn. Assoc. Alumnae of Sacred Heart, 1960—66; pres. Las Floristas, 1967—68; coord. Jr. Mannequin Assisteens, Assistance League So. Calif., 1971—72; pres. docent coun. L.A. County Mus. Art, 1976—77, pres. decorative arts coun., 1977—80, chmn. Am. Antiques Conf., 1979—81, mem. costume coun., mem. past pres.' coun., 1981—, mem. capital gifts campaign com.; pres. L.A. Orphanage Guild, 1969—70, bd. dirs., 1970—.

Recipient Eve award, Assistance League So. Calif. Mem.: Inst. Cert. Travel Agts., Am. Soc. Travel Agts., Lady Grand Cross Equestrian Order of the Holy Sepulchre of Jerusalem, Bel Air Garden Club, Birnam Wood Golf Club. Republican. Roman Catholic.

ARMISTEAD, WILLIAM COLE, JR., marketing professional; b. Campbell, Ala., May 29, 1944; s. William C. and Emma Belle (Overstreet) A.; m. Emily Golson, Apr. 6, 1968; children: Allyson Michelle, William C. III. BS, Samford U., 1966. Dist. mgr. Saunders Leasing System Inc., Birmingham, Ala., 1967-73, v.p., regional mgr., 1973-80, sr. v.p., 1980-83; v.p., gen. mgr. McDonnell Douglas, Phila., 1983-86; v.p., sales & mktg. Fontaine Internat., Birmingham, 1986-88; spl. asst. to the gov. State of Ala., Montgomery, 1988-92; v.p. mktg. Hanna Steel Corp., Montgomery, Ala., 1993-95; v.p. bus. devel. SBS Corp/Netzee Inc., 1996-2001; exec. v.p. Marketing Solutions, Inc., 2001—. Bd. dirs. Kings Ranch, Birmingham, 1990—. Vice chmn. Ala. Rep. Party; bd. dirs. Children's Trust Fund, 1996-2000; Dept. Youth Svcs., 1998. Republican. Avocation: family. Home: 6 Brush Creek Farm Columbiana AL 35051-9517

ARMISTEAD, WILLIS WILLIAM, academic administrator, veterinarian; b. Detroit, Oct. 28, 1916; s. Eber Merrill and Josephine Brunell (Kindred) A.; m. Martha Sidney Clark, Sept. 17, 1938 (dec. 1964); children: Willis William, Jack Murray, Sidney Merrill; m. Mary Wallace Nelson, 1967. D.V.M., Tex. A&M Coll., 1938; M.Sc., Ohio State U., 1950; PhD, U. Minn., 1955. Diplomate: hon. diplomate; Am. Coll. Veterinary Surgeons, Am. Coll. Veterinary Preventive Medicine. Pvt. practice veterinary medicine, 1938—40; instr. Sch. Veterinary Medicine Tex. A&M U., 1940—42, asst. prof. to prof. Sch. Veterinary Medicine, 1946—53, dean Sch. Veterinary Medicine, 1953—57; dean Coll. Veterinary Medicine Mich. State U., East Lansing, 1957—74; dean Coll. Veterinary Medicine, U. Tenn., Knoxville, 1974—79, chmn. strategic planning adv. com., 1988—89; v.p. agr. U. Tenn. System, 1979—87. Collaborator animal diseases and parasite rsch. divsn. Dept. Agr., 1954-65; cons., adviser commn. veterinary edn. of South So. Regional Edn. Bd., 1953-56; mem. gov.'s sci. adv. bd., 1958-60; nat. cons. to Air Force Surgeon Gen., 1960-62; mem. adv. coun. Inst. Lab. Animal Resources, NRC, 1962-66; pres. Assn. Am. Veterinary Med. Colls., 1964-65, 73-74, Spl. award, 1983; veterinary med. resident investigators selection com. U.S. VA, 1967-70; veterinary medicine rev. com. Bur. Health Professions Edn. and Manpower Tng., HEW, 1967-71; mem. Nat. Bd. Veterinary Med. Examiners, 1970-74; mem. adv. panel for veterinary medicine Inst. Medicine, NAS, 1972-74; mem. bd. agr. and renewable resources NRC, 1976-77; 1st Allam lectr. Am. Coll. Veterinary Surgeons, 1972; Conti Meml. keynote lectr. Ariz.-Calif.-Nev. Veterinary Conf., 1994; mem. curriculum com. Oak Ridge Inst. Continued Learning, 1998-2001. Contbg. author: Canine Surgery, rev. edit, 1957, Canine Medicine, rev. edit, 1959; editor: The N.Am. Veterinarian, 1950-56, Jour. Veterinary Med. Edn, 1974-80; assoc. editor: Jour. Am. Animal Hosp. Assn., 1964-70; contbr. tech. articles to profl. jours. Bd. dirs. Tenn. Farm Bur. Fedn., 1979-87, Tenn. Coun. Coops., 1982-87, Tenn. 4-H Club Found., 1979-87, Tenn. Agrl. Hall of Fame, 1979-87, Tenn. Valley Fair, 2987-2004; mem. Tenn. State Soil Conservation Com., 1979-87; mem. Southwide adv. com. So. Agribus. Forum, 1979-87; mem. adv. bd. Clarence Brown Theater, U. Tenn., 2000-02. Maj. Vet. Corps AUS, 1942—46. Recipient Meritorious Svc. award Selective Svc. System, 1972; hon. alumnus Mich. State U., 1972; recipient Disting. Alumnus award Coll. Vet. Medicine, Tex. A&M U., 1980, 75th Anniversary Achievement award Tex. A&M U. Coll. Vet. Medicine, 1991; named VP Emeritus, U. Tenn., 1987—. Mem. AAAS, U.S. Animal Health Assn., Am. Vet. Med. Assn. (pres. 1957-58, award 1977), Tex. Vet. Med. Assn. (pres. 1947-48), Mich. Vet. Med. Assn. (trustee Edn. and Sci. Trust 1970-74), Fedn. Assns. Schs. of Health Professions (pres. 1975), Tenn. Vet. Med. Assn. (Lifetime Achievement award 1995), Inst. Medicine of NAS, N.Y. Acad. Scis., Rotary (pres. 1987-88), Sigma Xi, Phi Kappa Phi, Alpha Zeta, Phi Zeta, Omega Tau Sigma (nat. Gamma award Ohio State U. 1962), Phi Eta Sigma, Gamma Sigma Delta, Omicron Delta Kappa. Lodges: Rotary. Episcopalian. Home: 801 Vanosdale Rd Knoxville TN 37909 Personal E-mail: barmistead@msn.com.

ARMITAGE, JAMES O., medical educator; b. L.A., Dec. 19, 1946; m. Nancy Elaine Roker, Aug. 12, 1967; children: Amy Jolane, Gregory Olen, Anne Marie, Joel Donald. BS, U. Nebr., Lincoln, 1969; MD, U. Nebr., Omaha, 1973. Diplomate in internal medicine, med. oncology and hematology Am. Bd. Internal Medicine. Med. intern U. Nebr. Med. Ctr., Omaha, 1973-74, resident in internal medicine, 1974-75; fellow hematology/oncology U. Iowa Hosps. and Clinics, Iowa City, 1975-77; clin. asst. prof. medicine U. Nebr. Coll. Medicine, Omaha, 1977-79, assoc. prof., 1982-87, vice chmn. dept. internal medicine, 1982-90; from assoc. prof. to Joe Shapiro prof. internal medicine Epley Inst. for Rsch. in Cancer and Allied Diseases, Omaha, 1985—; chief sect. oncology/hematology U. Nebr. Coll. Medicine, Omaha, 1986-89, prof. internal medicine, 1987—, chmn. dept. internal medicine, 1990-99, dean, 2000—03; pvt. practice hematology/oncology Omaha, 1977-79. Contbr. articles to profl. jours. Recipient Sir William Osler Teaching award, 1988, Arnold Ungerman-Robert Lubin Cancer Rsch. award, 1993, Richard and Hinda Rosenthal Found. award, 1996, numerous others. Fellow ACP, Am. Assn. Cancer Rsch., Am. Soc. Blood and Marrow Transplantation, Am. Soc. Clin. Oncology, Am. Soc. Hematology, Am. Fedn. for Clin. Rsch., Assn. Profs. Medicine, Ctrl. Soc. for Clin. Rsch., European Soc. Med. Oncology, Internat. Soc. Exptl. Hematology, Nebr. Med. Assn., Met. Omaha Med. Soc., Midwest Blood Club, Royal Coll. Physicians Edinburgh, Internat. Soc. for Hematotherapy and Graft Engring., European Hematology Soc., Phi Beta Kappa, Sigma Xi, Alpha Omega Alpha, others. Office: U Nebr Med Ctr Dept Internal Medicine 987680 Nebr Med Ctr Omaha NE 68198-0001

ARMITAGE, KAROLE, dancer; b. Madison, Wis., Mar. 3, 1954; Studied, N.C. Sch. of the Arts, with Bill Evans, U. Utah, 1971-72. Dancer Geneva (Switzerland) Opera Ballet, 1973-75, Merce Cunningham Dance Co., 1976-81; choreographer, artistic dir. The Armitage Ballet (formerly Armitage Dance Co.), N.Y.C., 1981—90; dir. MaggioDanza di Firenze, Florence, Italy, 1995—98; assoc. choreographer Centre Chorégraphique Nationale- Ballet de Lorraine, Nancy, France; dir. Venice Biennale of Contemporary Dance, 2004. Choreographer of ballets including: Ne, 1978, Do We Could 1979, Veritige, 1980, Drastic-Classicism, 1981, It Happened at Club Bombay Cinema, 1981, Slaughter on MacDougal Street, 1981, Paradise, version 1, 1981, The Last Gone Dance, 1983, Paradise, version 2, 1983, A Real Gone Dance, 1983, (with Rosella Hightower) The Nutcracker, 1983, Tasmanian Devil, 1984, GV-10, 1984, The Water Duets, 1985, The Mollino Room, 1985, The Elizabethan Phrasing of the Late Albert Ayler, 1986, The Tarnished Angels, 1987, Les Stances a Sophie, 1987, Duck Dances, 1988, Kammerdisco, 1988, GoGo Ballerina, 1988, Contempt, 1989, Forty Guns, 1990, Dancing Zappa, 1990, Jack and Betty, 1990, The Marmot Quickstep, 1991, Renegade Dance Wave, 1991, Overboard, 1991, Segunda Piel, 1992, Happy Birthday Rossini, 1992, Hucksters of the Soul, 1993, I Had A Dream, 1993, Hovering at the Edge of Chaos, 1994, Tattoo and Tutu, 1994, The Dog Is Us, 1994, The Return of Rasputin, 1994, Apollo e Dafne, 1997, Time Is the Echo of an Axe Within a Wood, 2004; (dance for TV) Parafango, 1983, Ex-Romance, 1984; (arts program) The South Bank Show, 1985; (feature films) Without You, I'm Nothing, 1989, Chain of Desire, 1991, Search and Destroy, 1994; (videoclips) Love School for the Dyvinals, 1990, Vogue for Madonna, 1991, In The Closet for Michael Jackson, 1992; (world tours) Milli Vanilli, 1990, Madonna's Blonde Ambition, 1991, The Dyvinals, 1991; (videoclips for feature film) Kuffs, 1990; writer, dir., choreographer (feature film) Hall of Mirrors, 1992. Guggenheim fellow, 1986. Office: Armitage Found 9 N Moore St Ste 4 New York NY 10013-2414

ARMITAGE, KENNETH BARCLAY, retired biology professor; b. Steubenville, Ohio, Apr. 18, 1925; s. Albert Kenneth and Virginia Ethel (Barclay) A.; m. Katie Lou Hart, June 5, 1953; children: Karole, Keith, Kevin BS summa cum laude, Bethany Coll., W.Va., 1949; MS, U. Wis.-Madison, 1951; PhD, 1954. Instr. U. Wis.-Green Bay, 1954-55; instr. U. Wis.-Wausau, 1955-56; asst. prof. biology U. Kans., Lawrence, 1956-62, assoc. prof., 1962-66, prof., 1966-96, William J. Baumgartner disting. prof., 1987-96, chmn. dept. systematics & ecology, 1982-88, dir. environ. studies program, 1976-82, dir. exptl. and applied ecology program, 1974-94, prof. emeritus, 1996—. Vis. prof. U. Modena, Italy, 1989; mem. com. examiners Grad. Record Exam. Biology Test, 1986—92, chmn., 1988—92; sr. investigator Rocky Mountain Biol. Lab, Gothic, Colo., 1962—2004, trustee, 1969—86, pres. bd. trustees, 1985—86; cons. Vancouver Island Marmot Recovery Program; vis. rschr. Queen Mary Coll., London, 1972—73. Author: (lab. manual) Investigations in General Biology, (with others) Principles of Modern Biology; contbr. articles to profl. jours.; co-editor: Holarctic Marmots as a Factor of Biodiversity, 3d Internat. Marmot Conf. proceedings; mem. editl. bd.: Ethology, Ecology and Evolution, 1989—, Ibex Jour. Mountain Ecology, 1994—, Oecologia Montana, 1996—; sci. editor: Die Murmeltiere der Welt. Pres. Douglas County chpt. Zero Population Growth, 1969-71; bd. dirs. Children's Hour, Inc., Lawrence, 1969-70; v.p. Hist. Mt. Oread, Lawrence, 1998-2004, pres., 2004—. Recipient Antarctic medal NSF, 1968, Edn. Service award U. Kans., 1979, Alumni Achievement award Bethany Coll., 1989; Knapp House fellow U. Wis., Madison, 1952-53, NSF fellow, 1952-53, 58. Fellow AAAS, Animal Behavior Soc.; mem. Am. Soc. Naturalists (treas. 1984-86), Am. Inst. Biol. Scis. (mem. task force for 90s), Ecol. Soc. Am., Am. Soc. Zoologists, Am. Soc. Mammalogists (C. Hart Merriam award 1997), Orgn. Biol. Field Stations (v.p. 1986-87, pres. 1988-89), Sigma Xi, Phi Beta Kappa, Beta Beta Beta, Gamma Sigma Kappa. Avocations: stamp collecting/philately, gardening, natural history, western history. Home: 505 Ohio St Lawrence KS 66044-2245 Office: U Kans Dept Ecology & Evolutionary Biology Lawrence KS 66045-7534 Office Phone: 785-864-3236. E-mail: marmots@ku.edu.

ARMITAGE, RICHARD LEE, former federal agency administrator; b. Boston, Apr. 26, 1945; s. Leo Holmes and Ruth H. Armitage; m. Laura Alice Samford, Apr. 15, 1968; children: Beth, Lee, Jenny, Paul. BS, U.S. Naval Acad. Naval ops. coordinator Def. Attache Office, Saigon, Vietnam, 1973-75; cons. US Dept. Def., Washington, 1975-76, Iran, 1975-76; ptnr. Agt.-Export, Bangkok, 1976-78, Washington, 1976-78; adminstrv. asst. to U.S. Senator Robert Dole Washington, 1978-79; self-employed cons. Fairfax, Va., 1979-80; fgn. policy advisor Reagan for Pres. campaign, Washington, 1980; trans. advisor U.S. Govt., Washington, 1980-81; asst. sec. def. East Asia US Dept. Def., Washington, 1981-83, asst. sec. def. internat. security affairs, 1983—89; presidential spec. negotiator for Phillippines mil. bases Washington, 1989—92; US amb. to the Newly Independent States of the former Soviet Union US Dept. State, 1992—93; pres. Armitage Assoc., 1993; dep. sec. US Dept. State, Washington, 2001—05. Served to lt. USN, 1967-73, Vietnam. Mem. Assn. Asian Studies Republican. Roman Catholic.

ARMITAGE, ROBERT ALLEN, lawyer; b. Port Huron, Mich., June 16, 1948; s. George Robert and Deloris Alene (Fitz) A.; m. Deborah Ann Wismer, Dec. 29, 1973; children: Aimee Elizabeth, Emily Ann. BA with highest honors, Albion Coll., 1966-70; MS in Physics, U. Mich., 1971, JD with honors, 1973. Bar: Mich. 1974, US Ct. Appeals Fed. cir. 1983, US Supreme Ct. 1993, DC 1994. Patent atty. The Upjohn Co., Kalamazoo, 1974-78, mgr. patent law dept., 1979-83, patent counsel, exec. dir. patent law, 1983—87, v.p. corp. patents and trademarks, 1987—93, asst. sec., 1988—93; ptnr. Vinson & Elkins, LLP, Washington, 1993—99; v.p., gen. patent counsel Lilly Rsch. Labs., 1999—2003; sr. v.p. & gen. counsel Eli Lilly and Co., 2003—. Past bd. dirs. Human Genome Sciences Inc. Pres. Hospice of Kalamazoo, 1985-87. Fellow Woodrow Wilson Nat. Fellowship Found., Princeton, NJ, 1971. Mem. Mich. Bar Assn. (chair intellectual property law sect. 1986), Am. Intellectual Property Law Assn. (pres. 1994), Intellectual Property Owners Inc. (bd. dirs. 1985-93), Assn. Corp. Patent Counsel (pres. 1993), Phi Beta Kappa. Office: Eli Lilly and Co Lilly Corporate Ctr Indianapolis IN 46285

ARMOR, DAVID J., sociologist; b. Long Beach, Calif., Nov. 11, 1938; s. John Edward Armor and Marie (Huffine) White; m. Marilyn Louise Sells, Sept. 7, 1958; children: Adrienne, Daniel. BA with highest honors, U. Calif., Berkeley, 1961; PhD, Harvard U., 1966. Asst. prof. sociology Harvard U., Cambridge, Mass., 1965-70, assoc. prof., 1970-73; sr. social scientist Rand Corp., Santa Monica, Calif., 1973-82; pres. Nat. Policy Analysts Inc., Santa Monica, 1981-86; acting asst. sec. Dept. Def., Washington, 1986-89; rsch. prof. George Mason U., 1992—2000, prof. pub. policy, 2001—. Vis. prof. sociology UCLA, 1972-73, Rutgers U., 1991-92; cons. Nat. Inst. on Alcohol Abuse and Alcoholism, Washington, 1972-73, Dept. Def., Washington, 1982-83, U.S. Commn. on Civil Rights, Washington, 1984-86. Author: American School Counselor, 1968, The Data-Text Primer, 1972, Alcoholism and Treatment, 1976, Forced Justice: School Desegregation and the Law, 1995, Competition in Education, 1997, Maximizing Intelligence, 2003. Mem. L.A. Bd. Edn., 1985-86; assoc. Pepperdine U., Malibu, 1982-86; Rep. nominee for U.S. Congress 23d Calif. dist., 1982. Fellow Woodrow Wilson Found., 1961-62, Ph.D. fellow Russell Sage Found., 1963-65. Mem. Am. Sociol. Assn. Home: 17246 Pepperstock Ln Jeffersonton VA 22724 Office Phone: 703-993-2260.

ARMS, ANNELI (ANNA ELIZABETH ARMS), artist, educator; b. NYC, May 23, 1935; d. William Emil and Elizabeth Maria (Bodanzky) Muschenheim; m. John M. Arms, Sept. 1, 1956; 1 child, Thomas C. BA, U. Mich., 1958. Represented in permanent collections U.S. State Dept., NY Pub. Libr., Libr. of Congress, N.Y. Hist. Soc. Recipient Nora Mirmont award Heckscher Mus., 1984, Guild Hall Sculpture award, 1987; scholar Art Students League N.Y., 1958. Mem. Nat. Drawing Assn., Fedn. Modern Painters and Sculptors (bd. dirs. 1988-, v.p. 1996—), Manhattan Graphics Ctr. (bd. dirs. 1995—, exhbn. chmn. 2002-), Artists Alliance East Hampton (exhbns. com. 1988—), Artists Equity N.Y. Avocations: opera, movies, swimming, museums, reading. Studio: 113 Greene St New York NY 10012-3823 E-mail: aarms2001@yahoo.com.

ARMSTRONG, ROBERT G., lawyer; b. 1947; B summa cum laude in Greek, Univ. Calif., San Diego; JD, Univ. San Diego. Bar: Calif. 1976. Ptnr. Armstrong Fishcer & Tutoli PLC, La Jolla, Calif. Co-founder, prin. shareholder Am. Acad. Estate Planning Attys., San Diego, 1992—. With USN, Vietnam. Mem.: ABA, San Diego County Bar, State Bar Calif. Office: Armstrong Fisch & Tutoli PLC 9360 Towne Ctr Dr La Jolla CA 92037 also: Am Acad Estate Planning Attys Ste 850 4365 Executive Dr San Diego CA 92121 Office Phone: 858-453-0626, 858-453-2128. Office Fax: 858-535-8241. Business E-Mail: robert@aaepa.com.

ARMSTRONG, ALEXANDRA, financial planner; b. Washington, Sept. 26, 1939; d. Rhoda Elizabeth (Forbes) Armstrong; m. Jerry J. McCoy, 1994. BA in History, Newton (Mass.) Coll. Sacred Heart, 1960. Cert. fin. planner, 1977. Exec. sec. Ferris & Co., Washington, 1961—66, registered rep., 1966—77; sr. v.p. Julia Walsh & Sons, Washington, 1977—83; pres. Alexandra Armstrong Advisors Inc., Washington, 1983—91; chmn. Armstrong, Welch & MacIntyre Inc., Washington, 1991—2000, Armstrong, MacIntyre & Severns, Inc., Washington, 2001—. Bd. experts Boardroom Reports, 1987—. Author: On Your Own: A Widow's Passage To Emotional and Financial Wellbeing, 1993, 3d edit., 2000. Mem. Washington Jr. League, 1961-2003; vice chmn. Nat. Coun. Friends of Kennedy Ctr., Washington, 1987-91; pres. Nat. Capital coun. Boy Scouts Am., 1999-2000, chmn., 2000-01, bd. dirs. N.E. region, 2005—; mem. bd. visitors Sch. Bus. Georgetown U., 1988-91; v.p. programs Internat. Women's Forum, 1991-93, v.p. membership 1997-99, dir. IWF leadership found., 2001-04; bd. dirs. Reading is Fundamental, 1993—, treas. 2000-03; chmn. Found. Fin. Planning, 1999-2000, bd. dirs., 1997-2003, 2005—. Named Bus. Woman of Yr. Washington Bus. and Profl. Women's Club, 1978; recipient award of excellence for commerce Boston Coll. Alumni Assn., 1985, Woman Who Makes a Difference award Internat. Women's Forum, 1992, Silver Beaver award Boy Scouts Am., 1991, Loren Dutton award, Internat. Assn. Registered Fin. Cons., 2003, Beta Gamma Sigma chpt. honoree Georgetown U., 1992. Mem. Fin. Planning Assn. (bd. dirs. 1980-87, chmn. emeritus, pres. 1986-87), Nat. Assn. Investment Clubs (columnist monthly mag. 1978—, Disting. Svc. award 1993), Nat. Assn. Securities Dealers (bus. conduct com. dist. 10 1986-89, vice chmn. 1988-89), Nat. Assn. Women Bus. Owners (pres. Capital Area chpt. 1980-81), D.C. Estate Planning Coun., Nat. Capital Area Coun., Econ. Club (Washington), Cosmos Club (Washington), Econ. Club, (N.Y.C.), Fin. Planning Assn. (Lifetime Achievement award 2001), Nat. Capital Area Coun. Republican. Roman Catholic. Home: 3560 Winfield Ln NW Washington DC 20007-2368 Office: 1155 Connecticut Ave NW Ste 250 Washington DC 20036-4314 Office Phone: 202-887-8135.

ARMSTRONG, ANNE LEGENDRE (MRS. TOBIN ARMSTRONG), retired ambassador; b. New Orleans, Dec. 27, 1927; d. Armant and Olive (Martindale) Legendre; m. Tobin Armstrong, Apr. 12, 1950; children: John Barclay, Katharine, Sarita A. Hixon, Tobin and James L. (twins). BA in English, Vassar Coll., 1949. Co-chmn. Rep. Nat. Com., 1971-73; counsellor to U.S. Pres., 1973-74; U.S. amb. to Gt. Britain and No. Ireland London, 1976-77; chmn. adv. bd. Ctr. for Strategic and Internat. Studies (formerly affiliated with Georgetown U.), 1981-87, chmn. bd. trustees, 1987-99, chmn. exec. com., 1999—; chmn. Pres.'s Fgn. Intelligence Adv. Bd., 1981-90; dir. Promontory Interfinancial Network, LLC, 2003—. Commn. on Integrated Long Term Strategy, 1987; adv. coun. GM Corp., 1998. Bd. regents Smithsonian Instn., 1978-94, emeritus, 1994; bd. overseers Hoover Instn., 1978-97; co-chmn. Reagan-Bush Campaign, 1980; bd. regents Tex. A&M U., 1997-2003; U.S. Commn. on Nat. Security/21st Century, 1999-2001; mem. Gov.'s Coun. Sci. and Biotech. Devel., Gov.'s Task Force on Homeland Security. Recipient Gold Medal award for disting. svc. to humanity Nat. Inst. Social Scis., 1977, Rep. Woman of Yr. award, 1979, Texan of Yr. award, 1981, Presdl. Medal of Freedom award, 1987, Golden Plate award Am. Acad. Achievement, 1989; named to Tex. Women's Hall of Fame, 1986. Mem. English-Speaking Union (chmn. 1978-80), Coun. Fgn. Rels., Am. Assocs. of Royal Acad. Trust (trustee 1985-2005, vice-chmn. 1996), Alfalfa Club, Capitol Hill Club, Phi Beta Kappa. Republican.

ARMSTRONG, BILLIE BERT, retired highway contractor; b. Roswell, N.Mex., Apr. 18, 1920; s. Gayle G. and Murphy (Shannon) A.; m. Betty-Ellen Wilcox, Aug. 16, 1941; children: Billie B. Jr., Judith C., Robert G., Riley A. Student, N.Mex. Mil. Inst., 1935-39, Washington & Lee U., 1939-41. Mng. ptnr. Armstrong & Armstrong Ltd., Roswell, 1950—, G.G. Armstrong & Son, Ltd., Roswell, 1950—. Chmn. bd. dirs. Sunwest Nat. Bank of Roswell, 1967-84; pres. Assoc. Gen. Contractors Am., Washington, 1966-67, Assoc. Contractors N.Mex., Santa Fe, 1952-53, 63; bd. dirs. Southwestern Pub. Svc. Co., Sunwest Fin. Svcs., Inc. Pres. Conquistador Coun. Boy Scouts Am., Roswell, 1981-82, bd. regents N.Mex. Mil. Inst., Roswell, 1960-62. Major U.S. Army, 1942-45. Named Citizen of Yr. Realtors N.Mex., 1969, Roswell, 1968, Jaycees, 1964; recognized for svc. to mankind Sertoma, 1966. Mem. Masons, Shriners, Jesters. Methodist. Avocation: golf. Office: Armstrong & Armstrong Ltd PO Box 1873 Roswell NM 88202-1873 Home: Apt 136 2725 N Pennsylvania Ave Roswell NM 88201-0619

ARMSTRONG, BILLIE JOE, singer, musician; b. Oakland, Calif., Feb. 17, 1972; m. Adrienne Armstrong, July 2, 1994; children: Joseph Marciano, Jacob Danger. Played with bands such as Blatz, Rancid, The Lookouts, Goodbye Harry and Corrupted Morals; currently with side band Pinhead Gunpowder; co-founder, partial owner Adeline Records; co-founder, singer, musician Sweet Children (changed name to Green Day in 1989), 1988—. Singer: Look for Love; writer (first song) Why Do You Want Him, 1986, singer, musician (first EP) 1,000 Hours, (albums) 1,039/Smoothed Out Slappy Hour, 1991, Kerplunk, 1992, Dookie, 1994 (Grammy award for Best Alternative Music Performance, 1994), Insomniac, 1995, Nimrod, 1997, Warning, 2000, American Idiot, 2004 (Viewers Choice award, MTV Video Music Awards, 2005), writer (song) Church on Sunday; composer: (films) Angus, 1995, Godzilla, 1998, Varisty Blues, 1999, Austin Powers: The Spy Who Shagged Me, 1999, Freddy Got Fingered, 2001, American Pie 2, 2001; voice (films) Live Freaky Die Freaky, 2003; actor: (films) Dreamland, 2004; guest appearances Saturday Night Live, 1994, 2005, Mad TV, 2001, (voice) King of the Hill, 1997, and several others. Recipient Video of Yr., Best Group Video, Best Rock Video, Best Editing in a Video, Best Direction in a Video for Boulevard of Broken Dreams, MTV Video Music Awards, 2005.*

ARMSTRONG, BRENDA ESTELLE, pediatric cardiologist, educator; b. Rocky Mount, N.C., Jan. 19, 1949; d. Wiley Thurber and Marguerite (Carson) A.; 1 child, Bradlee Alexander Carson Armstrong. BA, Duke U., 1970; MD, St. Louis U., 1974. Diplomate Am. Bd. Pediatrics, Am. Bd. Pediatric Cardiology. Intern in pediatrics UCLA Med. Ctr., 1974-75; resident in pediatrics Duke U. Med. Ctr., Durham, N.C., 1975-76, fellow in pediatric cardiology, 1976-79, asst. prof. pediatrics, 1979-89, assoc. prof. pediatrics, 1987—, assoc. prof., 1989—, dir. admissions, 1996—. Chief clin. svcs. div. pediatric cardiology, Duke U., 1986—, chief fellowship tng., 1986—, chief of pediatric cardiac lab., 1984—; cons. to U.S. Army and USAF, 1982—. Mem. N.C. Environ. Mgmt. Commn., Raleigh, 1979-86; bd. dirs. Montessori Children's House of Durham, 1988—, Durham Striders Track and Field Club, 1984—. Recipient Golden Apple Teaching award Duke U. Med. Sch., 1981, Thomas Kinney Teaching award Duke U. Med. Sch., 1985; named YWCA Woman of Achievement, City of Durham YWCA, 1986. Mem. Assn. Black Cardiologists, Old North State Med. Soc. (Dr. of Yr. 1987), Nat. Med. Assn., N.C. Pediatric Soc., Am. Acad. Pediatrics., Links Inc. Democrat. Episcopalian. Avocations: music, reading, sports, knitting. Office: Duke U Div Pediatric Cardiology PO Box 3195 Durham NC 27715-3195

ARMSTRONG, C. MICHAEL, retired communications executive; b. Detroit, Oct. 18, 1938; s. Charles H. and Zora Jean (Brooks) A.; m. Anne Gossett, June 17, 1961; children: Linda, Julie, Kristy. BS in Bus. Econs, Miami U., Oxford, Ohio, 1961; grad., Dartmouth Inst., 1976; LLD (hon.), Pepperdine U., 1997, Loyola Marymount U., 1998; LLD (hon.), Worcester Polytechnic Inst., 2000. With IBM Corp., 1961-92, dir. systems mgmt. mktg. div., White Plains, N.Y., 1975-76, v.p. market ops. East, 1976-78, pres. data processing divsn., 1978-80, v.p., asst. group exec. plans and controls, data processing product group, 1980-83, v.p., group exec., 1983-84, sr. v.p., group exec., 1984-92, also pres. Europe, Paris, until 1988, pres., dir. gen. World Trade Europe/Middle East/Africa, 1987-89, chmn. World Trade Corp., 1989-92; chmn., CEO Hughes Aircraft Co., L.A., 1992-93, GM Hughes Electronics (now Hughes Electronics Corp.), 1993—97, AT&T, N.Y.C., 1997—2002; chmn. Comcast Corp., 2003—04. Mem. GM Pres. Coun.; bd. dirs. Travelers Corp., Hartford, Conn., The Times-Mirror-Co., L.A., Citigroup; mem. supervisory bd. Thyssen-Bornemisza Group; chmn. Pres.'s Export Coun., The White House, 1994—. Trustee Johns Hopkins U., chmn. adv. bd. Johns Hopkins Med. Sch.; mem., CEO bd. of adv. U. So. Calif. Bus. Sch.; mem. bus. adv. coun. Miami U.; mem. Coun. on Fgn. Rels., Nat. Security Telecomm. Adv. Com., Def. Policy Adv. Com. on Trade (DPACT); adv. bd. Yale Sch. Mgmt.; vice-chmn. World Affairs Coun., L.A.; chmn. Sabriya's Castle of Fun Found.; bd. trustees Carnegie Hall. Mem. Calif. Bus. Roundtable. Office: Comcast Corp 1500 Market St Philadelphia PA 19102*

ARMSTRONG, CASSANDRA, information technology executive, librarian; b. N.Y.C., Nov. 2, 1946; d. Robert Weaver Armstrong and Skippy Blair, Eleanor Armstrong (Stepmother); life ptnr. Harold Edward Dyck; children: Richard Lee Boyum, Amarantha Dyuuaxchs, Jenny Jo Dyck. BA in Linguistics, U. Calif., San Diego, 1978; MLIS, U. Calif., Berkeley, 1982. Asst. prof., tech. services libr. Calif. State Coll., Hayward, 1982—83; cataloger Calif. Spanish Lang. Database, San Francisco, 1983—84; bibliographic sys. coord. Hispanex, Oakland, Calif., 1984—85; sr. tech. cons. libr. automoation divsn. Brodart Inc., Rancho Bernardo, Calif., 1985—87; asst. prof., tech. processing coord. libr. St. Francis Coll., Loretto, Pa., 1987—91; sys. libr. Pitts. Theol. Sem., 1991—2000; assoc. prof. tech. svcs. U. La Verne, 2000—. Adj. prof. Sch. Info. Sci. U. Pitts., 1992—94. Contbr. articles, revs. to profl. publs., chpt. to book. Adult literacy tutor Glendora (Calif.) ub. Libr., Calif. Libr. Literacy Svcs.; dir. Habitat for Humanity, La Verne, 2005. Course Transformation grantee, Multicultural Inst., U. La Verne, 2002. Mem.: ACM (treas. digital libraries meeting 1997—97), Am. Theol. Libr. Assn. (chmn. automation tech. sect. 1994—95), Am. Soc. Info. Sci. and Tech. (chmn., spl. interest group on libr. automation and networks 1996—97, chmn. spl. interest group on automated lang. processing 2001—04, chmn. Pitts. chpt. 1993—96). Avocation: travel. Home: 480 Guilford Ave Claremont CA 91711 Office: U La Verne 2040 Third St La Verne CA 91750 Office Phone: 909-593-3511 4303. Personal E-mail: armstroc@ulv.edu.

ARMSTRONG, CLAY, physiology educator; BA, Rice U., 1956; MD, Washington U., 1960. Prof. physiology U. Pa., Phila. Mem editorial bd. Journal of General Physiology, Journal of Neurophysiology. Recipient Louisa Horwitz prize Columbia U., 1996, Jacob Javits Neuroscience Rsch. award, NIH, Albert Lasker award for basic med. rsch., Lasker Found., 1999. Mem.: NAS, Soc. of General Physiologists, Biophysical Soc., Am. Physiological Soc. Office: U Pa Dept Physiology C701 Richards Bldg/ 6085 Philadelphia PA 19104-6085

ARMSTRONG, DANIEL WAYNE, chemist, educator; b. Ft. Wayne, Ind., Nov. 2, 1949; s. Robert Eugene and Nila Louise (Koeneman) A.; m. Linda Marilyn Todd, June 11, 1972; children: Lincoln Thomas, Ross Alexander, Colleen Victoria. BS, Washington and Lee U., 1972; MS in Chem. Oceanography, Tex. A&M U., 1974, PhD in Chemistry, 1977. Prof. Bowdoin Coll., Brunswick, Maine, 1978-79, Georgetown U., Washington, 1980-83, Tex. Tech. U., Lubbock, 1983-87; Curators' disting. prof., head ctr. environ. sci. and tech.; head dept. analytical chemistry U. Mo., Rolla, 1987-2000; Caldwell prof. chemistry Iowa State U., 2000—. Bd dirs. Advanced Separations Techs., Whippany, NJ; Moreton lectr. Millsaps Coll., 2001, R.A. Welch lectr., 2002, Dow lectr., 2003; lectr. Columbia U., 2003. Host Univ. Forum Radio Show, Washington, 1981-83; writer, host weekly radio show We're Sci. Nat. Pub. Radio, 1993—; author film, radio shows; contbr. articles to profl. jours. Recipient Tchg. Excellence award U. Mo., 1985, 88-89, 92, 94, Faculty Excellence award U. Mo., 1988-89, Martin medal, 1991, EAS Chromatography award, 1990, Isco award, 1992, Presdl. award, 1993, Perkin Elmer award, 1994, R&D 100 award R&D Mag., 1995, Benedetti-Pichler award Am. Microchem. Soc. 1996, Helen M. Free award, 1998, CLDG Merit award, 2001, Weber medal, 2001, Kenneth A. Spencer award for agr. and food chemistry, 2002, Chirality medal, 2003, Zuffa medal for pharm;chemistry, 2004, Dal Nogre award for separation sci., 2005; named Disting. Scholar Hope Coll., 1999; grantee Rsch. Corp., 1979, Petroleum Rsch. Fund, 1979, 91, NSF, 1981; Rsch. grantee Whatman Corp., 1981, Dept. Energy, 1984, 87, 91, 94, Dow Chem., 1985-90, NIH, 1986, 91, 95, 2000, 03, 05, EPA, 1995, Shell Co., 1989-92. Fellow Am. Assn. Pharm. Scientists; mem. Am. Chem. Soc. (49th Midwest award for chemistry 1993, award in chromatography 1999), Slovak Pharm. Soc. (hon., Vladimir J. Zuffu medal 2004), Sigma Xi, Phi Lambda Upsilon. Achievements include patents in field. Office: Iowa State U Dept Chemistry Gilman Hall Ames IA 50011 Office Phone: 515-294-1394. Business E-Mail: sec4dwa@iastate.edu.

ARMSTRONG, DARNELL, professional basketball player; b. June 22, 1968; m. Deidra; children: Arkia, Mayliah. Student, Fayetteville State. Guard Orlando Magic, Fla., 1997—. Participant NBA Slam Dunk Competition, San Antonio, 1996. Active Armstrong Allies to reward area youths for good behavior. Avocations: listening to music, watching music videos. Office: Orlando Magic 8701 Maitland Summit Blvd Orlando FL 32810-5915

ARMSTRONG, DAVID G., podiatrist; m. Tania Armstrong; children: Alexandria, Natalie, Nina. DPM, Calif. Coll. Podiatric Medicine, 1993; MSc, U. Wales Coll. Medicine; PhD, U. Manchester. Chair of rsch. and asst. dean Dr. William M. Scholl Coll. of Podiatric Medicine, North Chicago, Ill., 2004—. Office Phone: 847-578-8440.

ARMSTRONG, DAVID LIGON, psychiatrist; b. Ontario, Calif., May 5, 1927; s. John Awdry and Ruth (Harrison) A.; m. Mary Meredith, Mar. 30, 1953 (dec. Feb. 1997); children: Meredith Armstrong Richey, Paul, Adelaide Armstrong Butler. BS in Plant Sci., U. Calif., Berkeley, 1949; PhD in Genetics, U. Calif., Davis, 1956; MD, Creighton U., 1972. Diplomate Am. Bd. Psychiatry and Neurology. Dir. rsch. Armstrong Nurseries, Inc., Ontario, Calif., 1953-68; resident in psychiatry U. Calif., Irvine, 1972-75; staff psychiatrist Met. State Hosp., Norwalk, Calif., 1975—. Pres. med. staff Met. State Hosp., Norwalk, 1985-88, 97—. Patentee new varieties roses and peaches. Pres. West End United Fund, Ontario, 1958-60, Chaffey Young Reps., Ontario and Upland, Calif., 1958-60, West End Coun. Cmty. Svcs., Ontario, 1960-64; chmn. Rep. Ctrl. Com., San Bernardino County, Calif., 1960-62. With USNR, 1945-46. Mem. State Employed Physicians Assn. (pres. 1984-86), Sigma Xi, Alpha Zeta. Republican. Avocations: politics, travel, gardening. Home: 2809 E Hillside Ave Orange CA 92867-8413 Office: Met State Hosp 11401 Bloomfield Ave Norwalk CA 90650-2096 Office Phone: 652-651-3230. Personal E-mail: davidarmstrong22@sbcglobal.net. Business E-Mail: darmstro@dmhmsh.state.ca.us.

ARMSTRONG, DAVID MICHAEL, biology professor; b. Louisville, July 31, 1944; s. John D. and Elizabeth Ann (Horine) A.; children: John D., Laura C. BS, Colo. State U., 1966; MA in Teaching, Harvard U., 1967; PhD, U. Kans., 1971. From asst. prof. to prof. natural sci. U. Colo., Boulder, 1971-85, prof. ecology and evolutionary biology, 1993—, assoc. chair, 1997-99; sr. scientist Rocky Mountain Biol. Lab., Gothic, Colo., 1977, 79; resident naturalist Sylvan Dale Ranch, Loveland, Colo., 1984—; acting dir. Univ. Mus., 1987-88, dir., 1989-93. Cons. in field. Author: Distribution of Mammals in Colorado, 1972, Rocky Mountain Mammals, 1975, 87, Mammals of the Canyon Country, 1982; co-author: Mammals of the Northern Great Plains, Mammals of the Plains States, Mammals of Colorado. Mem. non-game adv. council Colo. Div. Wildlife, 1972-76, Colo. Natural Areas Council, 1975-80. Mem.: Colo. Wildlife Fedn. (bd. dirs. 2000—02), The Nature Conservancy (trustee Colo. chpt. 1989—99, 2002—, chair 1996—98), Rocky Mountain Biol. Lab. (trustee 1979—83), Southwestern Assn. Naturalists (editor 1976—80), Am. Soc. Mammalogists (editor 1981—87). Avocations: draft horses, conservation activities, writing. Office: U Colo Ecology and Evolutionary Biology PO Box 334 Boulder CO 80309-0334 Personal E-mail: mauemann@aol.com. Business E-Mail: david.armstrong@colorado.edu.

ARMSTRONG, DOUGLAS, organic chemist, educator; b. New Albany, Ind., Jan. 4, 1941; s. Robert Edwin and Mabel Gladys (McIntosh) A.; m. Moonyean Devine, June 8, 1970; children: Paul, Mary. BS in Chemistry with honors, Ind. U., 1963; PhD in Organic (Medicinal) Chemistry, U. Iowa, 1968. Rsch. assoc. MIT, Cambridge, Mass., 1968-69; asst. prof. Mass. Coll. Pharmacy, Boston, 1969-74; various ednl. and indsl. positions, 1974-85; assoc. prof. Olivet Nazarene U., Kankakee, Ill., 1985-88, prof. Bourbonnais, Ill., 1988—. Participant acad.-industry polymer edn. program Tenn. Eastman Co., 1985; Smith Kline Beecham vis. rsch. fellow U. Iowa, 1987; rsch. assoc. Purdue U., 1999-2000; rsch profl. U. Chgo., 2004; book reviewer in field. Contbr. articles to Jour. Medicinal Chemistry, Jour. Pharm. Exptl. Therapeutics, Nature. Mem. Internat. Soc. Heterocyclic Chemistry, Am. Chem. Soc. (faculty travel grantee organic chemistry divsn. 1989). Nazarene. Office: Olivet Nazarene U Dept Chemistry Bourbonnais IL 60914 E-mail: darmstrg@olivet.edu.

ARMSTRONG, DOUGLAS CARR, music educator; b. Richmond, Va., Dec. 1, 1958; s. James Harrison and Doris Carr Armstrong. BA in Music, Va. Tech, 1981; MA in Music, Radford (Va.) U., 1997. Post-grad. profession tchg. lic. Va. Band dir. Shawsville (Va.) Mid. and H.S., 1981—83, Christiansburg (Va.) H.S., 1984—86, Patrick Henry H.S., Glade Spring, Va., 1987—94, Brooke Point H.S., Stafford, Va., 1995—, First Colonial H.S., Virginia Beach, Va., 1996—97. Adjudicator various concert and marching festivals, 1990—. Named Tchr. of Yr., Stafford County Pub. Schs., 2001—02, Tchr. of Quarter, Stafford County Renaissance Program, 1999, 2000, 2001, Tchr. of. Yr., Commonwealth of Va., 2003; recipient Agnes Meyer Outstanding Tchr. award, The Washington Post, 2001—02. Mem.: Nat. Band Assn., Va. Band and Orch. Directors Assn., Va. Music Educators Assn., Music Educators Nat. Conf., Internat. Tuba-Euphonium Assn., Phi Beta Mu (sec.-treas. Alpha Chi chpt.), Phi Mu Alpha Sinfonia. Office: Brooke Point HS 1700 Courthouse Rd Stafford VA 22554 Business E-Mail: darmstro@bphs.com.

ARMSTRONG, DOUGLAS DEAN, journalist; b. Wichita, Kans., Mar. 12, 1945; s. H. Glenn and Emma F. (Starkey) A.; m. Paige Prillaman, Jan. 3, 1967 (div. Sept. 1982); children: David Douglas, Christine Elizabeth; m. Mary Alyce Dooley, Mar. 8, 1987; children: Patrick Glenn, Gillian Marie. BA, U. Minn., 1967. Entertainment writer Milw. Jour. Sentinel, 1967-72, editl. writer, 1972-74, consumer writer, 1974-81, movie critic, 1981-95, bus. writer, 1995-2000, personal fin. columnist, 1995-2000. Guest lectr. U. Wis., Milw., 1982-89; movie reviewer WISN-TV, Milw., 1984-85; movie critic WKTI-FM, Milw., 1989-97; pres. Lexington Software Corp., 1996—2003. Contbr. short fiction to Ellery Queen's Mystery Mag., Alfred Hitchcock's Mystery Mag., Boys' Life. Recipient Pub. Interest award Ctr. for Pub. Representation, 1978. Mem. Mystery Writers Am., Milw. Press Club. Avocations: video, piano, golf.

ARMSTRONG, EDWARD BRADFORD, JR., oral and maxillofacial surgeon, educator, naval officer; b. Teaneck, N.J., Sept. 24, 1928; s. Edward Bradford and Ruth Elizabeth (Fippinger) A.; AB, U. Pa., 1950; DDS, N.Y.U., 1954; m. Dusanka Vladimirovna Jakovljevic, Nov. 5, 1960; children: Edward Bradford, III, James B., Hugh B. Commd. lt. j.g. U.S. Navy, 1954, advanced through grades to capt. 1971; intern oral surgery Roosevelt Hosp., N.Y.C., 1958, assoc. attending oral surgery, 1959—, attending oral surgeon outpatient dept., 1959—, chmn., moderator Oral Surgery Staff Confs., 1963-70; resident Carle Hosp., Urbana, Ill., 1959; assoc. attending oral surgeon Flower and Fifth Ave. hosps., N.Y.C., 1960-78; asst. attending oral surgeon Hackensack (N.J.) Hosp., 1963-65; adminstrv. officer Naval Res. Dental Co. 3-2, 1965-68, exec. officer, 1968-71, comdg. officer, 1971-73; comdt.'s rep. 3d Naval Dist., Naval Acad., 1972-78, 3d Naval Dist for Dentistry, 1973-75, group staff officer for dentistry and medicine, 1973-75, Ready Res. Unit 502, 1975-77, VTU 0207, 1977-79, ret., 1979; assoc. clin. prof. oral surgery N.Y. Med. Coll., 1963-93; adj. assoc. clin. prof. oral surgery Columbia U. Sch. Dentistry, 1973-89; chmn. bd. E. & R. Armstrong, Inc., Albany, N.Y., 1966-77; pres. Edward B. Armstrong, P.C., N.Y.C., 1979-90; dir. Songtime, Inc., Boston; dir., mem. exec. com. PGP Internat. Corps, Inc. Bd. dirs., trustee Christian Mission Farms of Paraguay, Inc., 1974-84; pres., trustee Central Bible Chapel, Palisades Park, N.J.; area rep., ann. giving U. Pa., 1960-68; Blue and Gold officer Naval Acad. Admissions Com.; sec. bd. dirs., trustee Boys' Club of N.Y. Health Svcs., Inc. Diplomate Am. Bd. Oral Surgery. Fellow N.Y. Acad. Dentistry (sec., dir., pres. 1979-80), Am., Internat. Colls. Dentists (life), Am. Coll. Oral and Maxillofacial Surgeons (founding), Am. Dental Soc. Anesthesiology (hon. life); mem. ADA (life, 1st dist. life), Am. Assn. Oral and Maxillofacial Surgeons (life, N.J. rep. Ho. of Dels. 1963-65), N.Y. Soc. Oral Surgeons (life, chmn. audit and budget com. 1972-79), First Dist. Dental Soc. (life), N.Y. Dental Soc., Bklyn. Dental Soc., Yokosuka Dental Soc. (hon.), Assn. Mil. Surgeons U.S., Mil. Order World Wars, Naval Res. Assn. (life), Union League (chmn. art com. 1973-76, bd. govs. 1974-77, 82-84, v.p. 1977-80, 85-88), Met. Club (bd. gov. 1992-96, 98-2002), N.Y.C., U. Pa. Club, U. Pa. Club of Met. N.J. (dir. 1982—), Acacia, Xi Psi Phi, Psi Omega (hon.), Delta Sigma Delta. Mem. Plymouth Brethren Ch. Home: 2800 S Ocean Blvd Boca Raton FL 33432

ARMSTRONG, EDWIN RICHARD, lawyer; b. Chgo., Sept. 25, 1921; BA, Knox Coll., 1942; JD, Northwestern U., 1948. Ptnr. Reimers & Armstrong, 1949-55; assoc. Friedman & Friedman, 1957-62; ptnr. Friedman, Armstrong & Donnelly, 1962-78, Armstrong & Donnelly, Chgo., 1978—. Home: 860 N Lake Shore Dr Apt 17M Chicago IL 60611-1788 Office: 77 W Washington St Ste 515 Chicago IL 60602-2802 Office Phone: 312-372-3215.

ARMSTRONG, F(REDRIC) MICHAEL, retired insurance company executive, consultant; b. Wichita, Kans., Dec. 20, 1942; s. Frederick Dale and Virginia Pauline A.; m. Patricia R. Latif, Dec. 13, 1976 (div. 1996). BSEE, MIT, 1964; MBA, Stanford U., 1966. Mgr. capital appropriations Trans World Airlines, N.Y.C., 1966-69; corp. planner Transam. Corp., San Francisco, 1969-70; v.p. Transam. Film Svc., Salt Lake City, 1970-73, also bd. dirs.; v.p. fin. Europe Transam. Airlines, Madrid, Spain, 1973-75, v.p. planning and info. svcs. Oakland, Calif., 1975-77; exec. v.p. fin. Budget Rent a Car Corp., Chgo., 1977-83, also bd. dirs.; exec. v.p., chief adminstrv. officer Transam. Ins. Group, L.A., 1983-93, also bd. dirs.; pres. Century Indemnity Co., Century Reinsurance Co., L.A., 1995-96, also bd. dirs. Bd. dirs. Melia Internat. Hotels, Panama, The Canadian Surety Co., Ins. Value Added Network Service, River Thames Ins. Co., London, Fairmont Fin. Inc., Mason-McDuffie Ins. Svc., Inc., The Completion Bond Co. Mem. adv. coun. Pierce Coll. E-mail: marmstrong@alum.mit.edu.

ARMSTRONG, GENE LEE, systems engineer, consultant, retired aerospace transportation executive; b. Clinton, Ill., Mar. 9, 1922; s. George Dewey and Ruby Imald (Dickerson) A. m. Lael Jeanne Baker, Apr. 3, 1946; children: Susan Lael, Roberta Lynn, Gene Lee. BS with high honors, U. Ill., 1948, MS, 1951. Registered profl. engr., Calif. With Boeing Aircraft, 1948—50, 1951—52; chief engr. astronautics divsn., corp. dir. Gen. Dynamics, 1954—65; chief engr. Def. Sys. Group TRW, Redondo Beach, Calif., 1956—86, pvt. cons. sys. engring., 1986; pres., CEO Armstrong Sys. Engring. Co, Westminster, Calif., 1986—. Mem. NASA Rsch. Adv. Com. on Control, Guidance & Navigation, 1959-62 Contbr. chpts. to books, articles to profl. publs. 1st lt. USAAF, 1942-45 Decorated Air medal; recipient alumni awards U. Ill., 1965, 77 Mem. Am. Math. Soc.; AIAA, Nat. Mgmt. Assn., Am. Def. Preparedness Assn., Masons. Home: 5242 Bryant Cir Westminster CA 92683-1713 Office: Armstrong Sys Engring Co 5242 Bryant Cir Westminster CA 92683

ARMSTRONG, GREG L., oil company executive; BS, Southeastern Okla. State U., 1980. CPA. Formerly with Price Waterhouse; corp. sec. Plains Resources, Inc., 1981—88, treas., 1984—87, v.p., CFO, 1984—91, sr. v.p., CFO, 1991—92, exec. v.p., CFO, 1992, pres., COO, 1992, pres., CEO, dir., 1992—2001; chmn., CEO Plains All Am. Pipeline, LP, Houston, 2001—. Bd. dirs. Petroleum Club of Houston, IPAA Tex. Southeast Regional Bd. of Trustees, Varco Internat., 2004—. Office: Plains All Am Pipeline LP 333 Clay St Ste 1600 Houston TX 77002*

ARMSTRONG, HENRY CONNER, former Canadian government official, consultant; b. Winnipeg, Man., Can., June 16, 1925; s. William Arthur Laird and Archena May (Conner) A.; m. Barbara Fay Jackson, May 20, 1950; children: Barbara E., Nancy M., Scott J. B.Sc. in Metall. Engring., Queen's U., Kingston, Ont., 1949; MBA (Kresge fellow), U. Toronto, 1954; diploma in indsl. adminstrn. (Alcan fellow), Internat. Mgmt. Inst., Geneva, Switzerland, 1958. Various sales and marketing positions Aluminum Co. of Can., Ltd., 1954-64; commodity officer Dept. Trade and Commerce, Ottawa, Ont., 1964-66; comml. counsellor Canadian Embassy, Washington, 1966-74; chief research and planning div., resource industries and constrn. br. Dept. Industry, Trade and Commerce, Ottawa, Ont., Can., 1974-75; dir. minerals and metals div. Dept. Energy, Mines and Resources, Ottawa, Ont., 1975-81, exec. dir. internat. minerals, 1981-82, mgr. spl. projects, 1982-83; counsellor (metals, minerals and energy) Can. High Commn., Canberra, Australia, 1983-86; counsellor (commercial) Can. Embassy, Washington, 1986-89; pvt. practice cons. Ottawa, 1989—. Served with RCAF and Royal Navy Fleet Air Arm, 1944-45. Mem. Assn. Profl. Engrs. Ont., Canadian Inst. Mining and Metallurgy, Am. Soc. for Materials. Mem. United Ch. of Can. Home and Office: 2159 Delmar Dr Ottawa ON Canada K1H 5P6

ARMSTRONG, HENRY JERE, retired judge; b. Dothan, Ala., Mar. 5, 1941; s. Henry Jordan and Lillian (Taylor) Armstrong; m. Jeanne Bachmann, June 3, 1963; children: April Heather, Ashley Brooke. BA, U. Ala., Tuscaloosa, 1964, JD, 1966; postgrad., JAGs Sch., Charlottesville, Va., 1972-73; grad., Armed Forces Staff Coll., 1978. Bar: Ala. 1966, U.S. Ct. Mil. Appeals 1967, U.S. Supreme Ct. 1972, DC 1974, Va. 1984. Commd. 2d lt. U.S. Army, 1964, advanced through grades to col., 1983; def. counsel, prosecutor Ft. Ord., Calif., 1967-68; chief criminal law, chief civil law, mil. judge Ft. Shafter, Hawaii, 1968-72; chief legis. br. criminal law divsn. Dept. Army, Washington, 1973-75, exec. asst. to JAG, 1975-77; staff judge adv. 2d inf. divsn. Republic of Korea, 1978-79; exec. officer U.S. Army Trial Def. Svc., Falls Church, Va., 1979-82; exec. officer litigation divsn. Dept. Army, Washington, 1982-84; counsel to chief Immigration Judge U.S., 1984-86; judge, asst. chief immigration judge U.S. Dept. Justice, 1986-97, dep. chief immigration judge, 1997—2003; ret., 2003. Profl. responsibility adv. com. Dept. Army; guest lectr. ethics and def. advocacy U.S. Army Europe Continuing Legal Edn. seminars; faculty Nat. Jud. Coll., Reno; adv. bd. Nat. Fgn. Lang. Ctr. Johns Hopkins U. Contbr. articles to profl. jours. Elder Grace Presbyn. Ch., Springfield, Va. Decorated Legion of Merit, Meritorious Svc. medal with 2 oak leaf clusters U.S. Army, Commendation medal; named Hon. Ky. Col., 1982; fellow, Inst. Ct. Mgmt., Nat. Ctr. State Cts., Williamsburg, Va. Mem.: ATLA, Judge Advs. Assn. (bd. dirs.), Fed. Bar Assn., Va. State Bar Assn., DC Bar Assn., Ala. State Bar Assn., Phi Alpha Delta, Kappa Sigma Alumni Assn. Home: 8208 Little River Tpke Annandale VA 22003-2305

ARMSTRONG, J. HORD, III, pharmaceutical company executive; Chmn. bd., CEO D&K Healthcare Resources, Inc., Saint Louis, 1993—. Office: D&K Healthcare Resources Inc PO Box 16989 Saint Louis MO 63105-1389

ARMSTRONG, (ARTHUR) JAMES, minister, educator, consultant, writer; b. Marion, Ind., Sept. 17, 1924; s. Arthur J. and Frances (Green) A.; m. Sharon Owen, Apr. 8, 2000; children from previous marriages: Eve Stoughton, Allison, James, Teresa, John, Rebecca Putens, Leslye Armstrong Hope. AB, Fla. So. Coll., 1948; BD, Candler Sch. Theology, Emory U., 1952; DD, Fla. So. U., 1960, DePauw U., 1965; LHD, Ill. Wesleyan U., 1970, Dakota Wesleyan U., 1970, Westmar Coll., 1971, Ind. Ctrl. U., 1982, Emory U., 1982. Ordained to ministry Meth. Ch., 1948. Minister in Fla., 1945-58; sr. minister Broadway Meth. Ch., Indpls., 1958-68; bishop United Meth. Ch., Dakotas area, 1968-80, Ind. area, Indpls., 1980-83; exec. v.p. conflict resolution firm, Washington, 1984-87; vis. prof. preaching and social ministries Iliff Sch. Theology, Denver, 1985-91; sr. min. 1st Congl. Ch., Winter Park, Fla., 1991-99; exec. dir. Ctr. on Dialogue and Devel., Denver, 1984-96. Adj. prof. Rollins Col., 1992—, Fla. Ctr. Theol. Studies, 1999—; instr. Christian Theol. Sem., Indpls., 1961-68; del. 4th Gen. Assembly, World Coun. Chs., 1968, 6th Gen. Assembly, 1983; pres. Nat. Coun. Chs., 1982-83; pres. bd. ch. and soc. United Meth. Ch., 1972-76, chmn. com. for peace and self devel. of peoples, 1972-76, pres. Commn. on Religion and Race, 1976-83; exec. v.p. Pagan Internat., 1982-87. Author: Gentlemen, Start Your Engines, 1967, The Journey That Men Make, 1969, The Urgent Now, 1970, Mission: Middle America, 1971, The Pastor and the Public Servant, 1972, United Methodist Primer, 1973, 77, Wilderness Voices, 1974, The Nation Yet To Be, 1975, Telling Truth: The Foolishness of Preaching in a Real World, 1977, From the Underside, 1981, Feet of Clay, on Solid Ground, 2002; contbg. author: The Pulpit Speaks on Race, 1966, War Crimes and the American Conscience, 1970, Rethinking Evangelism, 1971, What's a Nice Church Like You Doing in a Place Like This?, 1972, The Miracle of Easter, 1980, Preaching on Peace, 1982, Ethics and the Multi-National Enterprise, 1986, The Best of the Circuit Rider, 1987, Prayerfully Pro-Choice, 1999. Vice-chmn. Hoosiers for Peace, 1968; mem. Ind. State Platform Com. Democratic Party, 1968, Nat. Coalition for a Responsible Congress, 1970. With USNR, 1942. Recipient Disting. Svc. award, Indpls. Jr. C. of C., 1959. Mem. Fla. Coun. Chs. (pres. 1996-97), Ctrl. Fla. Interfaith Alliance (co-chair 1994-96). Methodist. Office Phone: 407-678-0840. Personal E-mail: jarmstrongjsa@aol.com.

ARMSTRONG, JAMES FRANCIS, III, language educator, writer; b. Penn Yan, NY, Mar. 17, 1945; s. James Francis Armstrong Jr. and Frances (Grady) Armstrong-Barden. BA in Eglish Edn. cum laude, Hobart-William Smith, 1983; cert., Kellogg Inst., 1989. Cert. English tchr.; cert. devel. educator. English tchr. Penn Yan Jr. High Sch., 1984-85; learning specialist Community Coll. of Finger Lakes, Geneva, N.Y., 1986-87, dir. learning ctr. and libr., 1987—. Film maker Kodak, 1970; G.E.D. instr. Bd. Coop. Ednl. Svcs., Stanley, NY, 1986—87. Performer: Feels Like Spyders, 1975; author: The Asexuals, 2001, Subsect, 2002, Rock Hard, 2005; contbr. articles to profl. jours. Avocation: musician. Office: PO Box 14 Keuka Park NY 14478 E-mail: armstrjf@bluefrognet.net.

ARMSTRONG, JEFFREY LEE, oceanographer; b. Twenty-Nine Palms, Calif., Apr. 18, 1959; s. Alden David and Josephine Frances Armstrong; m. Dawn Lee Embree, July 12, 1979; children: Cassandra Jean, Shannon Elizabeth. BS in Marine Biology, Calif. State U., Long Beach, 1993, MS in Biology, 1997; PhD in Biol. Oceanography, City U. L.A., 2001. Marine biologist, consultant Orange County Sanitation Dist., Fountain Valley, Calif., 1996—97, prin. environ. specialist, 1997—2000, scientist, 2000—04, sr. scientist, 2004—; marine ecol. cons., owner Coastal Environ. Consulting, Dana Point, 1996—98, rep on nat. monitoring network design com., 2005—. Regional rep. Fish and Invertebrate Com. So. Calif. Coastal Water Rsch. Project Regional Monitoring, Westminster, 1997—, regional rep. Toxicity Com., 1997—, regional rep. Benthic Infauna Com., 2003—; mem. nat. monitoring network design com. U.S. Geol. Survey, 2005—. Contbr. text book. Mem.: So. Calif. Acad. Scis., So. Calif. Assn. Marine Invertebrate Taxonomists, Am. Fisheries Soc., Soc. of Environ. Toxicology and Chemistry (govt. rep. So. Calif. chpt. 2001—03, historian 2003—), Alpha Gamma Sigma. Avocations: baseball, sailing, science mentoring for high school students. Office: Orange County Sanitation Dist 10844 Ellis Ave Fountain Valley CA 92708-7018 Office Phone: 714-593-7455. Business E-Mail: jarmstrong@ocsd.com.

ARMSTRONG, JOHN WILLIAM, JR., retired librarian; b. Portsmouth, NH, July 24, 1920; s. John William and Candace Margie (Garvin) A.; m. Hariot Baker, Apr. 1946 (div. 1951). SB, Harvard Coll., 1942; MSLS, Simmons Coll., 1949. Libr., founder Indsl. Rels. Libr. Grad. Sch. Pub. Adminstrn. Harvard U., Cambridge, Mass., 1946-51; libr., chief acquisitions Air Force Cambridge Rsch. Ctr. USAF, 1951-94; ret. Home: 8 Peacock Farm Rd Lexington MA 02421-6317

ARMSTRONG, LANCE, professional cyclist; b. Plano, Tex., Sept. 18, 1971; s. Linda Armstrong Kelly; m. Kristin Richard, May 8, 1998 (div. Dec. 2003); 3 children. Profl. cyclist Motorola Team, 1992—96, Cofidis, 1997, United States Postal Service Cycling Team, 1998—2004, Discovery Channel Pro Cycling Team, 2005—. Author (with Sally Jenkins): (book) It's Not About the Bike: My Journey Back to Life, 2001, Every Second Counts, 2003. Founder Lance Armstrong Foundation for Cancer, 1996—. World Road-Racing Champion, 1993; U.S. Profl. Champion, 1993; Triathlete Rookie of the Year, 1988; winner Tour DuPont, 1995, 1996; Bronze medal Olympics, Sydney, Australia, 2000; Sports Illustrated Man of the Yr., 2002; Associated Press Male Athlete of the Yr., 2002, 2003, 2004; overall winner, Tour de France, 1999-2005, Espy Award for Best Comeback Athlete, ESPN, 2000, Espy Award for Best Male Athlete, 2003, 2004. Achievements include being a former swimmer and triathlete; mem. U.S. Olympic team, 1992, 1996, 2000; recovered from cancer to become only man in history to win 7 Tour de France championships. Mailing: Lance Armstrong Found PO Box 161150 Austin TX 78716-1150*

ARMSTRONG, LLOYD, JR., academic administrator, physics professor; b. Austin, Tex., May 19, 1940; s. Lloyd and Beatrice (Jackson) A.; m. Judith Glantz, July 9, 1965; 1 son, Wade Matthew. BS in Physics, MIT, 1962; PhD in Physics, U. Calif., Berkeley, 1966. Postdoctoral physicist Lawrence Berkeley (Calif.) Lab., 1965-66, cons., 1976; sr. physicist Westinghouse Rsch. Labs., Pitts., 1967-68, cons., 1968-70; rsch. assoc. Johns Hopkins U., Balt., 1968-69, asst. prof. physics, 1969-73, assoc. prof., 1973-77, prof., 1977-93, chmn. dept. physics and astronomy, 1985-87, dean Sch. Arts and Scis., 1987-93; provost, sr. v.p. for acad. affairs U. So. Calif., LA, 1993—2005, prof. physics, 1993—2005, prof. edn., 2005—, Univ. prof., 2005—. Assoc. rsch. scientist Nat. Ctr. Sci. Rsch. (CNRS), Orsay, France, 1972—73; vis. fellow Joint Inst. Lab. Astrophysics, Boulder, Colo., 1978—79; program officer NSF, 1981—83, mem. adv. com. for physics, 1985—87, mem. visitors com. physics divsn., 1991; chmn. com. atomic and molecular scis. NAS/NRC, 1985—88, mem. bd. physics and astronomy, 1989—96; mem. adv. bd. Inst. for Theoretical Physics, Santa Barbara, Calif., 1992—96, chmn., 1994—95, Inst. Theoretical Atomic and Molecular Physics, Cambridge, Mass., 1994—97, Rochester Theory Ctr. for Optical Sci. and Engring., 1996—98. Author: Theory of Hyperfine Structure of Free Atoms, 1971; contbr. articles to profl. jours. Bd. dirs. So. Calif. Econ. Partnership, 1994—2000, Calif. Coun. Sci. and Tech., 1994—2005. NSF grantee, 1972-90; Dept. Energy grantee, 1975-82. Fellow Am. Phys. Soc., Coun. on Fgn.

Rels., Pacific Coun. on Internat. Policy (bd. dirs. 1996-05). Office: U So Calif Office Provost University Park Los Angeles CA 90089-0001 Office Phone: 213-740-2101. Business E-Mail: lloydarm@usc.edu.

ARMSTRONG, MARIAN LOUISE, secondary school educator; b. Bedford, Ind., June 24, 1929; d. John Frank and Maude C. (Pafford) A. BS in Edn., Ind. U., 1952, MA in Libr. Sci., 1958. Libr. Edison Sch., Gary, Ind., 1952-56, Paris Am. Sch., 1956-57; libr., instr. Ind. U., Bloomington, 1958-69, prof., 1969-93, prof. emeritus, 1993—. Pres. Monroe County Pub. Libr., Bloomington, 1989, sec., 1992.

ARMSTRONG, MARY OGDEN, artist, graphics designer; b. Homeworth, Ohio, Sept. 30, 1933; d. Clarence George and Elsie Augusta (Kraun) Ogden; m. John Herbert Armstrong, June 7, 1958; children: Michael David, Jennifer H. Armstrong Park. BFA, Akron Art Inst., 1955; student, Cleve. Inst. Art, 1966, 69, Lakeland C.C., Kirtland, Ohio, 1989. Artist Cmty. Graphics, Cleve., 1955-57, Wyse Advt., Cleve., 1957-58, Epstein Design, Cleve., 1959-61, Epstein & Szilagyi Design, Cleve., 1963-64, 69-70; freelance artist Cleve., 1962—. Part-time artist Mktg. Comm., Willoughby, Ohio, 1977-84, Coyle & Assocs., Hudson, Ohio, 1978-91; part-time graphic artist, design Fine Arts Assn., Willoughby, 1975-2001; Equine art, 2001-05. Illustrator: Going Home, 1979, So You Are Going to Have an Operation, 1985, Loves Goes on Forever, 1990, revised, 1993, So You Are Going to Have a Heart Operation, 1993, Tooty, 1995, Santa's Helper, 1995, Baby Animals, 1995, Gray Bow, 1996. Vol. Coun. Human Rels., Cleve., 1980-89, Lake Farmpark, Lake County Met. Parks, Kirtland, Ohio, 1991-93, Kirtland Area Vets., 2003-2004, art participant Fieldstone Farm, theraputic riding ctr., 2004. Recipient Merit award Cleve. Mus. Art, 1956, Advt. Excellence award Art Dirs. Club, 1957, Artistic Excellence award JCC, 1968-69, 75. Mem. Lake County Profl. Communicators (art judge 1993-94). Avocations: travel, gardening, music, sewing, hiking. Home: 7451 Euclid Chardon Rd Kirtland OH 44094-8722 E-mail: mjjarm@core.com.

ARMSTRONG, NEAL EARL, academic administrator; b. Dallas, Jan. 29, 1941; m. Nancy L. Weinerth; 5 children. BA in Zoology, U. Tex., 1962, MA in Zoology, 1965, PhD in Zoology, 1968. Lic. Tex. Research engr. Engring. Sci., Inc., 1967—71; asst. office mgr., cons. san. engring., 1968-70; mgr. Washington Research and Devel. Lab., 1970-71; assoc. prof. civil engring. U. Tex., Austin, 1971-79, prof., 1979—, assoc. chmn. dept., 1989-96, assoc. dean acad. affairs Coll. Engring., 1996—2003, vice provost faculty affairs, 2004—. Mem. ASCE, Water Environ. Fedn. (bd. dir., 1999-2003, Svc. award 1976, 84, 96, 2003), Am. Acad. Environ. Engrs. (diplomate, trustee), Internat. Water Assn., Estuarine Rsch. Fedn. (v.p. 1975-77), Am. Soc. Engring. Edn. Office: U Tex Provists Office MAI 201 Austin TX 78712 Office Phone: 512-232-3305. Business E-Mail: neal_armstrong@mail.utexas.edu.

ARMSTRONG, NEIL A., former astronaut; b. Wapakoneta, Ohio, Aug. 5, 1930; s. Stephen A.; children: Eric, Mark. BS In Aero. Engring., Purdue U., 1955; MS in Aero. Engring., U. So. Calif. With Lewis Flight Propulsion Lab., NACA, 1955; then aero. research pilot for NACA (later NASA, High Speed Flight Sta.), Edwards, Calif.; astronaut Manned Spacecraft Center, NASA, Houston, 1962-70; command pilot Gemini 8; comdr. Apollo 11; dep. assoc. adminstr. for aeros. Office Advanced Research and Tech., Hdqrs. NASA, Washington, 1970-71; prof. aerospace engring. U. Cin., 1971-79; chmn. AIL Sys., Inc., 1989-2000, EDO Corp., 2000—02. Mem. Pres.'s Commn. on Space Shuttle, 1986, Nat. Commn. on Space, 1985-86. Served as naval aviator USN, 1949-52, Korea. Recipient numerous awards, including Octave Chanute award Inst. Aero. Scis., 1962, Presdl. Medal for Freedom, 1969, Exceptional Service medal NASA, Hubbard Gold medal Nat. Geog. Soc., 1970, Kitty Hawk Meml. award, 1969, Pere Marquette medal, 1969, Arthur S. Fleming award, 1970, Congl. Space Medal of Honor, Explorers Club medal. Fellow AIAA (hon., Astronautics award 1966), Internat. Astronautical Fedn. (hon.), Soc. Exptl. Test Pilots; mem. Nat. Acad. Engring. Achievements include being the first man to walk on the Moon, July 20, 1969. Office: EDO Corp 60 E 42nd St Ste 5010 New York NY 10165*

ARMSTRONG, NELSON WILLIAM, JR., wholesale distribution executive; b. Port Huron, Mich., Mar. 5, 1941; s. Nelson William and Kathryn J. (Clarke) A.; m. Judith A. Roth, Sept. 5, 1964; children: Nelson William III, Tad John. BA, Mich. State U., 1964—64. Acct. Gen. Motors Corp., Warren, Mich., 1964—66; in acctg. and fin. Consumers Power Co., Jackson, Mich., 1966—73; dir acctg. Ramada Inns, Inc., Phoenix, 1973—77, asst. contr., 1977—79, v.p. audit svcs., 1979—82, corp. contr., 1982—85, v.p. adminstrn., 1985—, v.p. audit and adminstrv. svcs., 1985—, v.p. corp. contr., 1987—90; v.p. adminstrn., sec. Aztar Corp., Phoenix, 1990. Office: Aztar Corp 2390 E Camelback Rd Phoenix AZ 85016-3448

ARMSTRONG, PHILLIP DALE, lawyer; b. Waukegan, Ill., Mar. 27, 1943; s. James Leonard and Bernice Frances (Nader) A.; m. Leila Robson; children: Leonard Hart, Theodore Nader, Leila VIII. BS in Chem. Engring., U. Mo., 1966; JD, Gonzaga U., 1978; LLM, U. Mo., Kansas City, 1979. Bar: N.D. 1979, U.S. Dist. Ct. N.D. 1979, U.S. Dist. Ct. Ariz. 1991, U.S. Tax Ct. 1980, U.S. Ct. Appeals 1983, U.S. Supreme Ct. 1984. Mktg. trainee Dow Chem. Co., Midland, Mich., 1966-68; chem. engr. Clark Oil and Refining, Hartford, Ill., 1968-70; life guard, pool attendant, pool mgr. various hotels and condominiums, Miami Beach, Fla., 1970-75; assoc. McCutcheon Law Firm, Minot, N.D., 1979-81; sole practice Minot, 1981—, Mandan, N.D., 1995—; founder, pres. Producers Oil & Gas Corp., 1992—. Trustee in bankruptcy for chpts. 7, 12, and 13, N.W. and S.W. divs. Dist. of N.D., 1980-95; founder Armstrong Oilwell Ops., 1996. Mem. ABA, N.D. Bar Assn., Nat. Assn. Bankruptcy Trustees, Am. Bankruptcy Inst., Exch. Club (Minot), Phi Kappa Psi (pres. 1965). Republican. Episcopalian. Home: 1006 Valley View Dr Minot ND 58703-1642 Office: Armstrong Law Firm 12 Main St S Minot ND 58701-3871

ARMSTRONG, RICHARD, museum director, curator; b. Kansas City, Mo., May 1, 1949; s. John E.H. and Lucy McHangue A. BA, Lake Forest Coll., 1971. Curator La Jolla Mus. Contemporary Art, Calif., 1975-1979; adj. curator, assoc. curator, curator Whitney Mus. Am. Art, NYC, 1981—92; curator Carnegie Mus. Art, Pitts., 1992, Henry J. Heinz II dir. Bd. dirs. BOMB mag. Mem. Artists Space (bd. dirs. 1984—), White Columns (bd. dirs. 1985—). Office: Carnegie Mus Art 4400 Forbes Ave Pittsburgh PA 15213-4080*

ARMSTRONG, RICHARD STOLL, minister, educator, poet; b. Balt., Mar. 29, 1924; s. Herbert Eustace and Elsie Davis (Stoll) A.; m. Margaret Childs, Jan. 31, 1948; children: Ellen, Richard, Andrew, William, Elsie. BA, Princeton U., 1947; MDiv, Princeton Theol. Sem., 1958; DMin, Christian Theol. Sem.-Indpls., 1978; doctoral, Temple U., 1962-68. Ordained to ministry Presbyn. Ch., 1958. Pastor Oak Lane Presbyn. Ch., Phila., 1958-68; dir. devel. Princeton (N.J.) Theol. Sem., 1968-71, v.p. devel., 1971-74, prof. ministry and evangelism, 1980-90, prof. emeritus, 1990—; pastor 2d Presbyn. Ch., Indpls., 1974-80. Life trustee Fellowship Christian Athletes, Inc., Kansas City, Mo., 1979—; mem. ch. mins. adv. bd. Christian Theol. Sem., 1975-80; bd. dirs. Nat. Conf. Christians and Jews, Ind., 1975-80, Ind. Inter-Religious Commn. on Human Equality, 1975-80. Author: The Oak Lane Story, 1971, Service Evangelism, 1979, The Pastor as Evangelist, 1984, The Pastor-Evangelist in Worship, 1986, Faithful Witnesses, 1987, The Pastor-Evangelist in the Parish, 1990, Enough, Already!, 1993, Now, That's A Miracle!, 1996, Faithful Witnesses MiniCourse, 1997, If I Do Say So Myself, 1997, Are you Really Free?, 2002, Help! I'm a Pastor, 2005; contbg. composer Carmina Princetonia, 1968; contbg. author: Westminster Dictionary of Christian Theology, 1983, The New Dictionary of Pastoral Studies, 2002. Bd. dirs. Indpls. Symphony Orch., 1978-80; trustee Am. Boychoir Sch., 1980—; trustee McDonogh Sch., Md., 1980-90; mem. adv. com., ctr. for contextual ministry Pretoria U., South Africa; mem. Nat. Coun. Presbyn. Men, 1995-98; Lt. (j.g.) USN, 1942-46. Recipient Disting. Svc. award Fellowship of Christian Athletes, 1965, Branch Rickey Meml. award, 1974, Alumni Svc. award Princeton Theol. Sem., 1974, Outstanding Svc. award Nat. Conf. Christians and Jews, 1980, Robert L. Peters award Princeton U., 1990; named Man of Week, Princeton Town Topics, 1957, 68. Mem. Presbytery of New Brunswick (v.p.), Acad. for Evangelism Theol. Edn. (pres. 1989-91, Jour. editor 1991-97, Charles Grandison Finney award 1997), Presbyn. Writers' Guild, Poetry Soc. Am., Gallup Internat. Inst., Phila. A's Hist. Soc. Presbyterian. Home: 2118 Windrow Dr Princeton NJ 08540 Office: Princeton Theol Sem PO Box 821 Princeton NJ 08542-0803 Personal E-mail: rsarm@comcast.net. Business E-Mail: richard.armstrong@ptsem.edu.

ARMSTRONG, RICHARD WILLIAM, bank executive, management consultant; b. Phila., June 18, 1932; s. Richard Mervyn and Elvina (Burns) A.; m. Barbara Robbins, Sept. 5, 1959; children: Richard W. Jr., James M. AB cum laude, Harvard U., 1954; MA, Johns Hopkins U., 1959. Disarmament specialist AEC, Washington, 1960—62; fin. mgr. NASA and OEO, Washington, 1962—67; Nat. Inst. Pub. Affairs fellow Princeton U., 1967—68; dep. mgr. Head Start, Washington, 1969-70; corp. budget dir. Chase Manhattan Bank, N.Y.C., 1970-78, fin. and adminstrv. officer real estate fin. bus., 1978-84, fin. and adminstrv. officer comml. sector, 1984-89, fin. and adminstrv. officer real estate fin. sector, 1989-91; mgmt. cons. N.Y.C., 1992—. Prin. Coun. for Excellence in Govt., 1992—. Mem. audit com. Madison (N.J.) Presbyn. Ch., 1981, mem. fin. com., 2005—; trustee, fin. officer Bethesda (Md.) Congl. Ch., 1965-67; active NJ Harvard Schs. and Scholarship Com., 1983-88; bd. dirs. Family Svc. of Morris County, NJ, 1998. Lt. USN, 1954-57 Avocations: genealogy, sailing, swimming, travel. Home and Office: 10 Pomeroy Rd Madison NJ 07940-2619

ARMSTRONG, ROBERT BEALL, physiologist, educator; b. Hastings, Nebr., Nov. 13, 1940; s. Edwin Ollis and Elena (Beall) A.; m. Ingrid Elizabeth Vaiciulenas, Apr. 9, 1966; children: Edwin John, Andrew Niel, Sarah Elizabeth. BA, Hastings Coll., 1962; MS, Wash. State U., 1970, PhD, 1973. Asst. prof. biology Boston U., 1973—78; assoc. prof. physiology Oral Roberts U., Tulsa, Okla., 1978—81, prof. physiology, 1981—85; prof. U. Ga., Athens, 1985—90, rsch. prof., 1990—92; Omar Smith prof. health and kinesiology Tex. A&M U., College Station, 1992—, Omar Smith chair, 1995—, disting. prof., 1995—, dept. head, 1992—97, 2000—02. Assoc. zoology Harvard U., Cambridge, Mass., 1977-87; external examiner Nat. U. Singapore, 1984-85; rsch. com. Am. Heart Assn., Athens, 1987-89, Assoc. editor Med. Sci. Sports Exercise, Indpls., 1985-87; contbr. articles to Jour. Applied Physiology, Am. Jour. Physiology. NSF fellow, 1970-73; grantee NIH, 1975-97, Am. Heart Assn., 1981-89, NASA, 1997-2000. Fellow Am. Coll. Sports Medicine (trustee 1986-88); mem. Am. Physiol. Soc. Office: Tex A & M U Dept Health & Kinesiology College Station TX 77843-0001 Office Phone: 979-862-2912. Business E-Mail: rb-armstrong@hlkn.tamu.edu.

ARMSTRONG, ROBIN LOUIS, physics professor, physicist; b. Galt, Ont., Can., May 14, 1935; s. Robert Dockstader and Beatrice Jenny (Grill) S.; m. Karen Elisabeth Feilberg Hansen, July 8, 1960; children: Keir Grill, Christopher Drew. BA, U. Toronto, Ont., 1958, MSc, 1959, PhD, 1961; DSc (hon.), U. N.B., Can., 2001. Rutherford Meml. fellow Oxford (Eng.) U., 1961-62; mem. faculty U. Toronto, 1962, prof. physics, 1971-90, adj. prof. physics, 1990-98, prof. emeritus, 1998—, chmn. dept., 1974-82, dean Faculty of Arts and Sci., 1982-90; pres. U. N.B., Fredericton, St. John, 1990-96, prof. physics, 1990-96, rsch. prof. physics, 1996-2001, Wilfrid Laurier U. spl. advisor to the pres., 1997-2000. Pres. Can. Inst. Neutron Scattering, 1986-89; founding dir. Can. Inst. Advanced Rsch., 1981-82, mem. rsch. coun., 1982-2000; mem. coun. Nat. Sci. and Engring. Rsch. Coun., 1991-97 mem. exec., 1992-97, v.p., 1994-97; mem. Atomic Energy Can. Ltd. R&D Adv. Com., 1999—, vice chair, 2004—; chair bd. dirs. Can. Arthritis Network, 2003—. Co-author: Mechanics, Waves and Thermal Physics, 1970, Electromagnetic Interaction, 1973; contbr. articles to profl. jours. Recipient Commemorative medal for 125th Anniversary of Can. Confedn., 1992, Designated Visitante Distinguido, U. Cordoba, Argentina, 1987. Fellow Royal Soc. Can.; mem. Can. Assn. Physicists (v.p. 1989-90, pres. 1990-91, Herzberg medal 1973, medal for achievement 1990), Can. Assn. Physics, Internat. Soc. Magnetic Resonance Medicine. Home: Ste 707 95 Prince Arthur Ave Toronto ON M5R 3P6 Canada E-mail: robinl.armstrong@sympatico.ca.

ARMSTRONG, RODNEY, librarian; b. Atlanta, Mar. 5, 1923; s. Harold Rodney and Mary Blair (Armstrong) A.; m. Katharine Price Cortesi, June 14, 1969; children: Louise Spencer Barton, Robert Knowlton. BA, Williams Coll., 1948; MS, Columbia U., 1950; HHD (hon.), U. Liberia, 2000. Libr. Phillips Exeter Acad., NH, 1950—73; dir., libr. Boston Athenaeum, 1973—97, dir., libr. emeritus, 1997—. N.E. assoc. Sotheby's. Pres. Trustees Edn. Liberia, 1974—. Decorated Purple Heart; Benjamin Franklin fellow Royal Soc. Arts, 1974 Fellow Am. Acad. Arts Scis., Soc. Antiquaries, Pilgrim Soc.; mem. ALA (life), NH Libr. Assn. (past officer, bd. dirs.), Am. Antiquarian Soc., Colonial Soc. Mass., Mass. Hist. Soc., Manuscript Soc. (bd. dirs., past pres.), New Eng. Hist. Geneal. Soc. (pres. 1977-82), Century Assn. (NYC), Grolier Club (NYC), Odd Volumes Club (pres. 1979-83). Home: Penthouse F 65 E India Row Boston MA 02110-3311 Office: Sothebys 67 1/2 Chestnut St Boston MA 02108-1121

ARMSTRONG, SONYA M., mathematics professor, researcher; children: Janelle M., Ricardo. BA in Math., CUNY, 1976; MS in Numerical Sci., Johns Hopkins U., 1980; MA in Stats., U. Rochester, 1993, PhD, 1997. Secondary math tchr. Balt. City Pub. Sch., 1976—81; aerospace engr. Westinghouse, Balti., 1981—85; assoc. prof. W.Va. State U., Institute, 1999—. Sr. warden Episcopal Ch., Charleston, W.Va., 2003—05. Named to Hall of Fame, Compeer Program, Rochester, 1995; recipient Excellence in Tchg. award, Clark Atlant U., 2004; fellow, NASA, 2003. Mem.: ACLU (v.p. mem. 2000), Nat. Coun. Tchrs. Math., Gen. Fedn. Women's Club (grants writer), Alpha Kappa Mu (faculty advisor 2002), Zeta Phi Beta (state treas. 2001). D-Conservative. Episcopalian. Avocations: travel, sewing, reading. Home: PO Box 283 Teays WV 25569 Office: WVa State Univ PO Box 1000 Institute WV 25112 Office Phone: 304-766-3390. Office Fax: 304-766-4272. Personal E-mail: calcgrmn@earthlink.net. E-mail: armstrso@wvstateu.edu.

ARMSTRONG, THEODORE MORELOCK, corporate financial executive; b. St. Louis, July 22, 1939; s. Theodore Roosevelt and Vassar Fambrough (Morelock) A.; m. Carol Mercer Robert, Sept. 7, 1963; children: Evelyn Anne, Robert Theodore. BA, Yale U., 1961; LLB, Duke U., 1964. Bar: Mo. 1964. With Miss. River Transmission Corp. and affiliated cos., 1964-85; corp. sec. Mo. Pacific Corp., 1971-75, River Cement Co., 1968-75; asst. v.p. Miss. River Transmission Corp., 1974-75, v.p. gas supply, 1975-79, exec. v.p., 1979-83, pres., chief exec. officer, 1983-85; exec. v.p. Natural Gas Pipeline of Am., 1985; sr. v.p. fin. and adminstrn., chief fin. officer Angelica Corp., St. Louis, 1986—2004, St. Louis, 2004; pvt. practice fin. cons., 2004—. Bd. dirs. UMB Fin. Corp., Custom Cuts, Inc., Cabela's, Inc. Bd. dirs., past pres. Boys and Girls Town Mo.; past pres. Tenn. Soc. St. Louis; mem. St. Louis County Boundary Commn.; former alderman, mem. bd. adjustment City of Frontenac; bd. dirs., past pres. Ctrl. Inst. for Deaf. Mem. Mo. Bar Assn., Bellerive Country Club, Saint Louis Club (pres. bd. dirs.), Yale Club (St. Louis, N.Y.C.), Phi Alpha Delta. Republican. Presbyterian. Home: 43 Countryside Ln Saint Louis MO 63131-3310 Office: 7730 Carondelet Ste 103 Saint Louis MO 63105 Office Phone: 314-862-4224. Personal E-mail: tmarmstrong@sbcglobal.net.

ARMSTRONG, THOMAS NEWTON, III, curator, consultant; b. Portsmouth, Virginia, July 30, 1932; s. Thomas Newton, Jr. and Mary Saunders (Tabb) A.; m. Virginia Whitney Brewster, May 18, 1963; children: Thomas Newton IV, Whitney, Eliot, Amory. Attended, Cornell U., 1950-54, Art Students League, summer 1953, Inst. Fine Arts, NYU, 1965-67. Pers. coord., asst. to chmn. bd. Stone & Webster, Inc., N.Y.C., 1957-65; curator, assoc. dir. Colonial Williamsburg, Abby Aldrich Rockefeller Folk Art Collection, Williamsburg, Va., 1967-71; dir. Pa. Acad. Fine Arts, Phila., 1971-73, Whitney Mus. Am. Art, 1974-90, dir. emeritus, 1990—; dir. Andy Warhol Mus., Pitts., 1993-95. Vice chmn. The Garden Conservancy; mem. scholars selection com. Henry Luce Found., Inc.; cons. Sotheby's. Adv. com. Mt. Vernon; trustee Nat. Bldg. Mus.; garden com. Winterthur; trustee N.Y. Sch. Interior Design, Greenwood Gardens, Short Hills, NJ.

ARMSTRONG-LAW, MARGARET, school administrator; b. Fargo, ND, Jan. 21, 1931; d. Theron L. and Besse Ross Armstrong; m. Robert Harold Law, Sept. 6, 1952 (div. Oct. 1964); children: William Robert, Anne Elizabeth Law Buckingham, Amy Catherine Law Barnum. BS in English, N.D. State U., 1952, MS Secondary Sch. Adminstrn., 1974; postgrad., UCLA, Moorhead State U., 1984, Mich. State U., 1985; Cert., Harvard Prin.'s Sch., London, 1986. Cert. tchr., ednl. adminstr. Tchr. Agassiz Jr. High, 1963—66, Ben Franklin Jr. High, 1969—71, North HS, Fargo, ND, 1971—74, asst. prin., 1974—78; secondary head Taipei Am. Sch., Taiwan, 1978-87, Vienna Internat. Sch., Austria, 1987-90; dir. Internat. Sch. Amsterdam, The Netherlands, 1990-97; internat. ednl. cons., 1998—. Prof. devel. com. European Coun. Internat. Schs., London, chmn. bd., 1994-96; mem. No. European Coun. Internat. Schs., head coun., 1990-97; spkr. in field. Author: (booklet, film) Future: The Quality of Life, 1975; contbr. articles to profl. jours. Adv. bd. Coll. Arts, Humanities and Social Scis., N.D. State U., 1998—2004; pres. Fargo-Moorhead Opera Bd., 1999—2001; chmn. bd. Christian edn. Plymouth Congl. Ch., Fargo, 1998—99, mem. coun., 1988—99, vice chair women's fellowship bd., 1999; chair pres. adv. bd. Minn. State U., Moorhead, 2003; bd. dirs. Trollwood Performing Arts Sch., 2002. Recipient Bd. Dirs. award for Extraordinary Svcs. European Coun. Internat. Schs., Promotion of Internat. Edn. award, 1996; named hon. mem. for disting. svcs., European Coun. Internat. Schs., 1997; scholarship named in her honor by bd. govs. Internat. Sch. Amsterdam, 1997—. Fellow: ASCD; mem.: LWV, AAUW, UN Assn. USA, De Amsterdamschekring Club, World Peace Com. (The Hague, Netherlands), World Future Soc., Rotary (bd. dirs. 1993—94, program chair 1993—94, v.p. 1994—96, pres. 1995—96, Amsterdam), Am. C. of C., Am. Women's Club/Amsterdam, Am. Assn. Sch. Adminstrs., Assn. Advancement Internat. Edn., Phi Kappa Phi. Democrat. Congregationalist. Avocations: chinese brush painting, music, reading, tennis, interior decorating.

ARMSTRONG SQUALL, PAULA ESTELLE, executive secretary; b. N.Y.C., Apr. 12, 1946; d. John Calvin and Irene (Shomo) A.; 1 child, Tonia Patricia Armstrong Fripp. Equivalency diploma, Malcolm King Coll., N.Y., 1988. Sec. Police Athletic League, N.Y.C., 1980-84, Harlem World Disco, N.Y.C., 1985-89, Nat. Black Theatre, N.Y.C., 1990-93, Manhattan Psychiat. Ctr., N.Y.C., 1994-95, Westside Bulletin Issues in Mental Health, 1996-97. Disc jockey (as Lady Pea). Avocations: art, poetry, ping pong/table tennis, music disc jockey, crochet.

ARN, SUSAN KYLE, mathematician, educator; d. Arn Clayton and Arn Kathlyn. BS, The Ohio State U., 1973. Cert. tchr. Okla., 1998, Nat. Bd. Profl. Tchg. Standards, 1998. Tchr. phys. edn., health Allen H.S., Asheville, NC, 1973—74; tchr. math, sci. Boggs Acad., Keysville, Ga., 1974—76; tchr. phys. edn., coach Caruthersville (Mo.) Elem., 1977—78; tchr. math., coach Capitol Hill H.S., Oklahoma City, 1978—97, S.E. H.S., Oklahoma City, 1997—99; tchr. pre-engring., math Metro Tech. Ctrs., Oklahoma City, 1999—. Coach basketball, softball, track and field, swimming, tennis, cross country Capitol Hill H.S., 1978—97; coach softball S.E. H.S., 1997—99. Co-author: Empowering the Beginning Teacher of Mathematics: High School, Middle School, Elementary School. Vol. Meals on Wheels, Norman, Okla., 1999—2005. Recipient Presdl. Excellence in Math and Sci. Tchg. award, NSF, 1998, Outstanding Alumni award, The Ohio State U., 1998. Mem.: ACTE, NCTM. Office: 4901 S Bryant Oklahoma City OK 73129 Office Phone: 405-605-2202. Personal E-mail: susanarn2000@yahoo.com.

ARNALL, ROBERT ESRIC, physician, health facility administrator; b. Griffin, Ga., Feb. 14, 1931; s. Paul Esric and Dolly (Henderson) A.; m. Sarah Maxwell, Jan. 18, 1933; children: Dana Kathryn, Robert Maxwell. BA, Emory U., 1953, MD, 1957. Diplomate Am. Bd. Pediatrics, Am. Bd. Med. Mgmt. Intern Atlanta VA Hosp., 1957-58; resident in pediat. Grady Meml. Hosp., Atlanta, 1958-60; chief resident Eggleston Hosp. for Children, Atlanta, 1960; med. dir. The Children's Hospital of S.W. FL, 2001—; med. dir., sys. v.p. Lee Meml. Health Sys., Ft. Myers, 1983-99; pvt. practice pediatrics Atlanta, 1960-64; pvt. practice Ft. Myers, 1964-84; ret., 2000. Instr. pediat. Emory U., Atlanta, 1960-64; attending physician Eggleston Hosp. for Children, 1960-64, Grady Hosp., 1960-64; dir. continuing med. edn. Lee Meml. Hosp., Ft. Myers, 1987-99, pres. med. staff, Ft. Myers, 1973-74, sys. v.p. physician integration, 1995-99; med. dir. Children's Hosp. S.W. Fla., Ft. Myers, 2001—; adv. bd. Lee Meml. Children's Hosp. Bd. dirs. Health Start, Ft. Myers, 1990-96, Goodwill Industries, Ft. Myers, 1989—, Edison-Ford Estates, 1991-99, Healthy Start Dist. 8 Coalition, Children's Hosp. Found., 2000—; past bd. dirs. Edison Pageant of Light, pres.; past bd. dirs. Edison Festival of Light, Children's Home Soc., United Way of Lee County, Lee County Assn. Retarded Citizens, Easter Seal Soc., Nat. Found. March of Dimes, Cmty. Coord. Coun.; co-chmn. Healthy Start Regional Perinatal Network; mem. Childrens Hosp. Devel. Bd. With U.S. Army Res., 1960-68. Recipient Disting. Svc. awards Ft. Myers H.S., 1980, Lee County Sch. Bd., 1983, Fla. H.S. Athletic Assn., 1991; named to Ft. Myers H.S. Hall of Fame Emerald Club, 2000. Fellow Am. Acad. Pediat. (subsect. adolescent medicine, past chmn. sch. health com. Fla. chpt.); mem. AMA (del. to hosp. med. staff sect. 1991-96, chmn. Southeastern Caucus 1994-96), Vol. Hosps. of Am. (task force on alternative delivery systems, task force on quality initiative, physician adv. bd., coun. med. dirs.), Fla. Med. Assn. (del. 1987-95, dist. rep. Coun. on Hosp. Med. Staffs 1989-93, vice chmn. 1991-93, chmn. 1993-95, chmn. governing coun. Organized Med. Staff sect. 1995-96, PRO com. 1991-95, long range planning com. 1995-96), Fla. Hosp. Assn. (quality assurance com.), Lee County Med. Soc. (chmn. sch. health adv. com. to Lee County sch. bd., chmn. sports medicine com. 1980-93, 99-2000), Emerald Club, Rotary (past bd. dirs.), Alpha Omega Alpha. Republican. Methodist. Avocation: golf. Home: 1324 Longwood Dr Fort Myers FL 33919-1821 Office: Children's Hosp SW Fla Health Pk Fla PO Box 2231 Fort Myers FL 33902 E-mail: arnalll324@aol.com.

ARNDT, CARMEN GLORIA, secondary school educator; b. N.Y.C., Mar. 29, 1942; d. Charles Joseph and Pura María (Rios) A. BA in Spanish, Pace U., 1968; MA in Spanish, NYU, 1970; profl. diploma, Fordham U., 1975. Lic. asst. prin., prin. Simultaneous translator UN, N.Y.C., 1968; instr. Marymount Manhattan Coll., N.Y.C., 1968-70; tchr. Bd. Edn., N.Y.C., 1970—, dir. Bilingual Comprehensive H.S., 1975-78; chmn. sch. based mgmt./shared decision com. L.D. Brandeis H.S., N.Y.C., 1990—, asst. prin., 1984, interim acting asst. prin., 1994, coord. coop. tech./trades, 1993-96, ESL and fgn. lang. dept., 1994-96, bilingual grade advisor, 1998; ret. Chmn. restructuring com. Bd. Edn., N.Y.C., 1990—; bd. dirs. 1st N.Y.C. Comprehensive Bilingual Program, 1975-79; mem. adj. faculty Fordham U., N.Y.C., 1972-75, CCNY, 1985—; coord. ESL and fgn. lang. dept. Author: Conversational Spanish, 1975, Native Language Art K-8, 1975; contbr. articles to profl. jours.; featured in Dominicanos en New York (book). Electioneer, Dem. Party, N.Y.C. Mem. P.R. Edn. Assn. (chairperson-mentor 1988, del.), United Fedn. Tchr. (del. 1985-88), State Assn. Bilingual Edn., Am. Assn. Tchrs. of Spanish and Portuguese, Assn. Suprs. Curriculum Devel., Phi Beta Kappa. Roman Catholic. Avocations: crochet, reading, walking, writing. Home: Apt 3G 50 W 97th St New York NY 10025-6005

ARNDT, CYNTHIA, educational administrator; b. NYC, Sept. 27, 1947; d. Charles Joseph and Pura Maria (Rios) A. BA, Hunter Coll., 1971, MA, 1975; profl. diploma in adminstrn., Fordham U., 1981. Adminstrv. asst. to asst. registrar Hunter Coll., N.Y.C., 1968-69; cataloguer asst. Finch. Coll. Libr., N.Y.C., 1974; tchr. N.Y. Bd. Edn., N.Y.C., 1974-82; bilingual coord. Jr. High Sch. 143, 1982-89; asst. prin. IS 164, 1989-93; project dir. Elem. Schs. in Restructuring Bilingual Sci., 1993-96; supr.-in-charge IS 136, 1996-97; asst. prin. Mott Hall, 1997—2004, prin., 2005—. Reviewer Booklist, 1981. Mem. Am. Artist Soc., Hispanic Am. Hist. Soc., Nat. Council Social Studies, N.Y. State Assn. Curriculum Devel., Puerto Rican Edn. Assn., N.Y. State Assn. Bilingual Edn., Assn. Curriculum Devel., Kappa Delta Pi, Phi Delta Kappa. Democrat. Roman Catholic. Home: 110 W 90th St Apt 4C New York NY 10024-1209 Business E-Mail: carndt@nycboe.net.

ARNDT, JANET S., former state legislator, educator; b. Providence, May 23, 1947; m. Kenneth G. Arndt; 4 children. AB, Gordon Coll., 1968; MEd, Boston U., 1970; student, U. Mass., 1998—, CAGS, 2002; EdD, U. Mass.

Amherst, 2003; cert., Advanced Grad. Study. Specialist, counselor Early Childhood, 1987—2005; N.H. state rep. Dist. 27, Rockingham, 1992—2002; mem. children, youth and juvenile justice com. N.H. Ho. of Reps., mem. constn. and statutory rev. com., chmn. election law com., 1997—2002; prin. Perley Sch., Georgetown, Mass., 2005—. Asst. prof. Gordon Coll., 1995, N.H. Tech. Coll., 1997—2001, adj. prof., 2001—, chair early childhood, elem. and spl. edn. dept., 2002—. Mem. Friends of the Libr. of Windham, chmn., 1991-92; active Girl Scouts Am., publicity chairperson; scholarship chmn. Nat. Order of Women Legislators; exec. bd. Rockingham County; events chairperson Nesmith Libr.; mem. edn. task force ALEC, mem. ch. early childhood task force; mem. nat. coun. of state legislators Coun. of State Govt.; chair Rockingham County Register of Deeds, 1996-02; mem. early childhood mental health coun., 2003-; mem. bd. N.H. Kids Coll., 2003. Recipient M. Carter award for Outstanding Libr. Svc., 1995; named Leader of Yr. Windham Girl Scouts, 1995. Mem. N.H. Order Women Legislators, Gordon Coll. Alumni Coun. Address: 8 Crestwood Rd Windham NH 03087-1429 Office Phone: 978-867-4814. Business E-Mail: jarndt@gordon.edu.

ARNDT, RICHARD TALLMADGE, writer, consultant, cultural administrator; b. Phila., Oct. 28, 1928; s. Howard Wilcox Arndt and Eleanor (Shaw) Branigan; m. Edith Robichon (div. 1964); children: Skyler Arndt-Briggs, Matthew Wilcox; m. Dorothy Serlin (div. 1973); children: Daniel Serlin, Sarah L. Piazza; m. Lois W. Roth (dec. 1986). AB, Princeton U., 1949, postgrad., 1971—72; PhD, Columbia U., 1959. Instr., asst. prof. French Columbia U., N.Y.C., 1953-61; cultural attaché U.S. embassies, Beirut, 1961-63, Colombo, 1963-66, Tehran, 1966-71, Rome, 1974-78, Paris, 1978-80; dir. policy and plans Bur. Ednl. and Cultural Affairs, U.S. Info. Agy., 1980-83; cultural coord. Near East/So. Asia, USIA, Washington, 1983-85, Dept. State, Washington, dep. dir. L.Am., dir. youth and student programs Bur. Ednl. and Cultural Affairs, 1972-74. Adj. prof. George Washington U., 1993—95; diplomat-in-residence, dir. mid-career study dept. govt. U. Va., Charlottesville, 1986—89; faculty div. psychopolitics Ctr. Mind and Human Interaction, U. Va., 1997—. Author: The First Resort of Kings: American Cultural Diplomacy in the 20th Century, 2005; co-author: The First Resort of Kings: American Cultural Diplomacy in the Twentieth Century, 2005; prin. editor: The Fulbright Difference, 1948-92, Transaction, 1993; contbr. articles to profl. jours. Pres. Internat. Soc. for Edn. Cultural and Sc. Interchange, 1986—89; mem. Coun. Internat. Programs, 1986—95, v.p., 1991—95, adv. coun., 2002—; adv. bd. Toda inst., Hawaii, 1997—; chmn. US Com. to Save Ancient Tyre, 1999—; mem. Am. for UNESCO, 1992—, pres., 2002—; bd. Nat. Peace Found., chmn., 1992—95, chmn. adv. bd., 1995—2002; adv. bd. Am. Iranian Coun.; chmn. bd. Lois W. Roth Endowment, Washington, 1986—; bd. Fulbright Assn., Washington, 1986—92, pres., 1989—91. Fulbright fellow U. Dijon, France, 1949-50, USIA mid-career fellow, 1971-72; recipient USIA Merit awards, 1963, 66, 71, Peacebuilder award, Nat. Peace Found., 2002. Mem.: Cosmos. Avocations: music, cultural diplomacy, political culture, theater, history. Home: 1870 Wyoming Ave NW Washington DC 20009-1883

ARNELL, RICHARD ANTHONY, radiologist; b. Chgo., Aug. 21, 1938; s. Tony Frank and Mary Martha (Oberman) Yaki; m. Paula Ann Youngberg, June 28, 1964; children: Carla Ann, Paula Marie, Paul Anthony. BA, Grinnell Coll., 1960; MD, U. Iowa, 1964. Diplomate Am. Bd. Radiology, Am. Bd. Nuc. Medicine. With Innc., 1968—, v.p., 1970-78, sec., 1978-90, pres., 1990—93, trustee pension profit plan, 1979-2000; pres. Moline Radiology Assocs., S.C., 1990-93, Advanced Radiology, S.C., 1993-2001, Radiology Assocs., LLC, 2000—01, Advanced Radiology Diagnostic Ctrs., LLC, 2000—01; with Moline Radiology SC. Mem. staff Luth. Hosp., Moline, 1968-88, dir. continuing mem. edn. prog. for physicians, 1979-83, bd. dirs., 1977-83; mem. staff Moline Pub. Hosp., 1968-88, Hammond Henry Dist. Ill., Geneseo, Ill.; mem. staff United Med. Ctr., 1989-92, chmn. radiology dept., 1992-94, med. dir. radiology dept., 1992-99; pres. Moline Radiology Assocs., Inc., 1990-93; mem. med. staff Mercer County Hosp., 1994-2003, Ill. Hosp., 1995-2003, Trinity Med. Ctr., 1992-2003, ret., 2003; trustee Midstate Found. for Med. Care, 1975-79, mem. exec. com., 1976-79; v.p. Quad City HMO Health Plan, 1979; clin. lectr. U. Iowa. Pres. Moline Mgmt. Assocs., Inc., 1990—; chmn. mng. com. Metro MRI Ctr., Ltd. Partnership, 1990--; supt. Sunday Ch. Sch. St. John's Ch., Rock Island, Ill., 1974-79, mem. ch. cabinet, 1975-76; del. Chs. United of Scott and Rock Island counties, Ill., 1977; mem. nat. exec. com. Augustana Coll., Rock Island, 1977-81; assoc. chmn. profl. div. United Way, 1985; bd. dirs. Luth. Hosp. Found., 1981-84, pres., 1982-84; bd. dirs. Quad Cities Health Care Resources, Inc., 1984-88; chmn. Luth. Health Care Found., 1984-88, United Health Care Found., 1989-91. Recipient David Theophilus trophy for outstanding athlete Grinnell Coll., 1960, Dr. of Distinction award Rock Island Med. Soc. Alliance, 1998. Mem. Am. Coll. Radiology, Ill. Radiol. Soc., Am. Coll. Nuc. Medicine, Soc. Nuc. Medicine, AMA, Ill. Med. Soc. (ho. of dels., 1974-79), Rock Island County Med. Soc. (exec. com. 1974-79, peer rev. com. 1975-79), Iowa-Ill. Ctrl. Med. Soc. (pres. 1978), Ctrl. Ill. Med. Assn. (v.p. 1977, pres. 1978), Ind. Physicians Assn. Western Ill. (dir. 1984-86, v.p. 1985, pres. 1986), World Med. Assn., Am. Coll. Med. Imaging, Short Hills Country Club. Office: 615 Valley View Dr Ste 101 Moline IL 61265 E-mail: rarny@aol.com.

ARNELL, WALTER JAMES WILLIAM, engineering educator, consultant; b. Farnborough, Eng., Jan. 9, 1924; arrived in U.S., 1953, naturalized, 1960; s. James Albert and Daisy (Payne) Arnell; m. Patricia Catherine Cannon, Nov. 12, 1955; children: Sean Paul, Victoria Clare, Sarah Michele. Aero. Engr., Royal Aircraft Establishment, 1946; BSc, U. London, 1953, PhD, 1967; MA, Occidental Coll., L.A., 1956; MS, U. So. Calif., 1958. Lectr. Poly. and Northampton Coll. Advance Tech., London, 1948-53; instr. U. So. Calif., L.A., 1954-59; asst. prof. mech. engring. Calif. State U., Long Beach, 1959-62, assoc. prof., 1962-66, prof., 1966-71, chmn. dept. mech. engring., 1964-65, acting chmn. divsn. engring., 1964-66, dean engring., 1967-69, rschr.; affiliate faculty dept. ocean engring. U. Hawaii, 1970-74; adj. prof. systems and insdl. engring. U. Ariz., 1981—91; pres. Lenra Assocs. Ltd., 1973—; chmn., project mgr. Hawaii Environ. Simulation Lab., 1971-72. Contbr. articles to profl. jours. Trustee Rehab. Hosp. of the Pacific, 1975—78. Fellow: Ergonomics Soc.; mem.: AAUP, AIAA, IEEE Sys. Man and Cybernetics Soc., Human Factors and Ergonomics Soc., Soc. Engring. Psychology sect., Am. Psychol. Assn. Soc., Royal Aero. Soc., Pi Tau Sigma, Phi Kappa Phi, Tau Beta Pi, Alpha Pi Mu, Psi Chi. Home: 4491 E Fort Lowell Rd Tucson AZ 85712-1106

ARNESON, ERIC E., director; s. Kenneth Lester Arneson and Kaye M. Morel; m. Tenaye Arneson, Sept. 13, 2003. BS in Polit. Sci., U. Wis., LaCrosse, 1990; MA in Coll. Student Pers., Bowling Green State U., 1992. Residence coord. Fla. State U., Tallahassee, 1992—96; area coord. U. Ill., Champaign, 1996—2001; asst. dir. residence life Western Ill. U., Macomb, 2001—04; assoc. dir. residence halls U. Miami, Coral Gables, Fla., 2004—. Advisor Ctrl. Black Student Union, Champaign, 1999—2001, Sigma Nu Frat., Champaign, 1999—2001. Aids group counselor Big Bend Cares, Tallahassee, 1995—96; vol. coach YMCA, Champaign, 1998—2000. Named Named Seminole Torchbearer, Fla. State U.; recipient GLACUHO Region Svc. award. Mem.: Fla. Housing Officers (assoc.), Internat. Assn. Coll. and Univ. Housing Officers (assoc.), Nat. Assn. Student Pers. Adminstrs. (assoc.), Am. Coll. Pers. Assn. (assoc.). Democrat. Avocations: football, basketball, reading. Office: U Miami 1211 Dickinson Dr Coral Gables FL 33146 Office Phone: 305-284-4505. Office Fax: 305-284-4956. Business E-Mail: e.arneson@miami.edu.

ARNETT, CARROLL D., chemistry educator; b. Rowlesburg, W.Va., Aug. 22, 1946; s. Jerome C. and V. Maye (Fike) A.; m. Susan P. Crafton, June 20, 1970; children: Christopher S., Lindsay S. AB in Chemistry, Duke U., 1968; postgrad., Med. Coll. Va., 1968-69; PhD in Medicinal Chemistry, U. Md., 1976; postgrad., Duke U., 1976-79. Teaching asst. Med. Coll. Va., Richmond, 1968-69; chemistry assoc. Johns Hopkins Hosp., Balt., 1969-71; grad. asst. U. Md., Balt., 1971-75; rsch. assoc. Duke U. Med. Ctr., Durham, N.C., 1976-79; chemist Brookhaven Nat. Lab., Upton, N.Y., 1979-87; assoc. prof. psychiatry and behavioral scis. U. Wash., Seattle, 1988-91, adj. assoc. prof. radiology, 1988-91; assoc. prof. dept. radiology U. Minn., Mpls., 1991—. Cons. in field. Contbr. articles to profl. jours.; patentee in field. Biomed. Research Support grantee, U. Wash., 1988. Mem.: Soc. Nuclear Medicine, Soc. Neurosci., Am. Chem. Soc., Rho Chi, Sigma Xi. Home: 351 Maple Island Rd Burnsville MN 55306-5523 Office: U Minn Dept Radiology PO Box 292 Minneapolis MN 55440-0292 E-mail: c-arnett@worldnet.att.net.

ARNETT, EDWARD MCCOLLIN, chemistry educator, researcher; b. Phila., Sept. 25, 1922; s. John Hancock and Katherine Williams (McCollin) A.; m. Sylvia Gettmann, Dec. 10, 1970; children: Eric, Brian; stepchildren: Elden, Byron, Colin Gatwood. BS, U. Pa., 1943, MS, 1946, PhD, 1949. Rsch. dir. Max Levy & Co., Phila., 1949-53; asst. prof. Western Md. Coll., Westminster, 1953-54, 1954-55; assoc. prof. chemistry U. Pitts., 1957-61, assoc. prof., 1961-64, prof., 1964-80; R.J. Reynolds prof. Duke U., Durham, NC, 1980-92, prof. emeritus, 1992—. Vis. lectr. U. Ill., 1963; vis. prof. U. Kent, Canterbury, Eng., 1970; dir. Pitts. Chem. Info. Ctr., 1967-70; mem. adv. bd. Petroleum Rsch. Fund, 1968-71; mem. com. on chem. info. NRC, 1969-71. Contbr. 200 articles to sci. jours. DuPont fellow, 1948-49, rsch. fellow Harvard U., Cambridge, Mass., 1955-57, Guggenheim fellow, 1968-69, Mellon Inst. adj. sr. fellow, 1964-80, Inst. Hydrocarbon Chemistry sr. fellow, 1980. Fellow AAAS; mem. Am. Chem. Soc. (James Flack Norris award 1977, Pitts. award Pitts. chpt. 1976, Petroleum Chemistry award 1985), NAS, The Chem. Soc., Sigma Xi, Phi Lambda Upsilon. Office Phone: 919-489-4133. Personal E-mail: edward.arnett@duke.edu.

ARNETT, WILLIAM GROVER, lawyer; b. Paintsville, Ky., Jan. 28, 1962; s. William O. and Easter (Howard) A.; m. Sabrina Roark, July 15, 1995; 1 chld, Katelynn Aydreanna. BA, Alice Lloyd Coll., 1985; JD, Chase Coll. Law, 1988. Assoc. Weinberg & Campbell, Hindman, Ky., 1988-90; asst. commonwealth atty. Ky. Prosecutorial Coun., Frankfort, 1989-90, Magoffin county atty., 1994-99; assoc. Perry & Preston, Paintsville, 1990-91; sole practice Salyersville, Ky., 1991—. Mem. Magoffin County Dem. Party, 1993—, A.B. Chandler Found., 1996—. Named to Outstanding Young Men of Am., 1985. Mem. ABA, DAR, Assn. Trial Attys. Am., Ky. Bar Assn., Ky. Acad. Trial Attys., Kiwanis Club. Office: PO Box 489 Salyersville KY 41465-0489 Business E-Mail: groverarnett@groverarnett.com.

ARNEZ, NANCY LEVI, educational leadership educator; b. Balt., July 6, 1928; d. Milton Emerson Levi and Ida Barbour (Rusk) Levi Washington. AB, Morgan State Coll., 1949; MA, Columbia U., 1954, EdD, 1958. Tchr. English Druid Jr. H.S., Balt., 1949-52, Houston Jr. H.S., Balt., 1952-57; asst. to admissions officer Tchrs. Coll., Columbia U., N.Y.C., 1957-58, grad. asst., 1957; head dept. English Cherry Hill Jr. H.S., Balt., 1958-62; assoc. prof., dir. student teaching Morgan State Coll., Balt., 1962-66; co-founder Cultural Linguistic Early Childhood Follow Through Approach; prof., asst. dir./dir. Ctr. for Inner City Studies, Northeastern Ill. U., Chgo., 1966-74; prof., assoc. dean, acting dean Sch. Edn. Howard U., Washington, 1974-80, chmn. dept. ednl. leadership, 1980-86, prof., 1980-93, prof. emeriti, 1993—. Author: Partners in Urban Education: Teaching the Inner City Child, 1973, The Struggle for Equality of Educational Opportunity, 1975, Administrative Issues in the Implementation of the Response to Educational Needs Project, 1979, The Besieged School Superintendent, 1981, School Based Administrator Training, 1982; mem. editorial bd.: Phi Delta Kappan, 1975-80, Jour. Negro Edn., 1975-80, Black Child Jour., 1980—; contbr. articles to profl. jours. State treas., mem. exec. com. Md. State council UN Children's Fund, 1965; founder Operation Champ, Balt, 1965; mem. adv. bd. Better Boys Found., Chgo., 1966-74, Mus. African-Am. History, 1969; state chmn. Right to Read, Washington, 1973-80; treas. Com. to Elect Douglass Moore to City Council, 1982. Grantee, African Am. Inst., 1974, Spencer Found., 1976, AAUW, 1977. Mem. Am. Assn. Sch. Adminstrs. (editorial bd. 1982), Assn. for Study of Afro-Am. Life and History, African Am. Heritage Assn., African Am. Writers Guild, Nat. Alliance Black Sch. Educators, D.C. Alliance Black Sch. Educators (pres. 1986-88), Phi Delta Kappa. Presbyterian. Home: 3122 Cherry Rd NE Washington DC 20018-1612

ARNHEIM, DANIEL LESLIE, psychologist; b. Pitts., Mar. 6, 1948; s. Richard Herman and Edith Libby (Levenson) A.; m. Barbara Ann Nuttridge, Dec. 6, 1969; children: Steven Paul, Michelle Ann. BS, U. Pitts., 1970; MS, Fla. State U., 1972, PhD, 1974. Lic. psychologist, Md. Clin. psychologist Fla. State Hosp., Chattahoochee, 1971; with Vocat. Rehab., Tallahassee, 1971-73; staff Regional Rehab. Ctr. Fla. State U., 1972-73; staff psychologist Spring Grove Hosp. Ctr., Balt., 1973—; prof. Loyola Coll., 1974-75, Anne Arundel C.C., 1975-79, C.C. Balt., 1976—, Catonsville C.C., 1976—, Essex C.C., 1981—; pvt. practice psychodiagnostics and therapy Balt., 1975—. Presenter workshops Fla. State U., scholar, 1970-73; cons. in field. Editor Polaris, 1969-70; contbr. articles to profl. jours. Mem. APA, Profl. Psychology Assn. Spring Grove Hosp. (pres. 1978-80), Ea. Psychol. Assn., Balt. Psychol. Assn. (sec. 1984-85), Phi Kappa Phi. Home: 10305 John Eager Ct Ellicott City MD 21042-1600 also: Ste 201 1101 N Calvert St Baltimore MD 21202-3866 Office Phone: 410-313-8137. Business E-Mail: arnheim@gl.umbc.edu.

ARNHOLD, HENRY H., investment banker; b. 1921; Served U.S. Army, 1943; with Arnholdt & Bleichroeder Inc., 1947—, chmn. Fellow: Am. Acad. Arts and Scis. Office: Arnhold & S Bleichroeder Inc 45 Broadway Fl 27 New York NY 10006-3007

ARNICK, JOHN STEPHEN, lawyer, legislative staff member, legislator; b. Balt., Nov. 27, 1933; s. John and Josephine (Gaillardo) A. BS, U. Balt., 1956; LLD, U. Balt. Law Sch., 1961. Bar Assn. U.S. Marine Corps., 1956-59; magistrate Balt. County, 1966-67; del. Md. Gen. Assembly, Annapolis, 1967-79, 87-94, 1994—; atty. pvt. practice, Balt., Md., 1962—; del. Md. Gen. Assembly, Annapolis, 1983—. Mem. Twin Dist. Dem. Club, Battle Grove Dem. Club, Sons of Italy. Mem. Ea. Balt. C. of C., Moose Lodge, New 7th Dem. Club, South East Dem. Club. Democratic. Roman Catholic. Home: 7918 Diehlwood Rd Baltimore MD 21222-3316 Office: 6914 Holabird Ave Baltimore MD 21222-6914 Office Phone: 410-288-2900.

ARNIS, EFSTATHIOS CONSTANTINOS, mechanical engineer, space naval designer; b. Thernon, Hellas, Apr. 14, 1931; s. Constantinos Efstathios and Joanna Andrew (Pachnis) A. Student, U. Athens, Hellas, 1950-51, 61-70; cert. in mech. engring. design, Technol. Sch. Benos-Palmer, Athens, 1972. Pvt. practice designer in mech. engring., 1952-94; ret., 1994. Specialist in sci. field of energization of isolated phys. sys. Contbr. articles to profl. jours.; patentee in field of centrifugal space navigation; determination of the absolute motion; distinction between inertial and gravitational mass. Mem. AIAA, AAAS, Hellenic Astron. Soc. (expert sec. 1992—), Planetary Soc., N.Y. Acad. Scis. (theoretician physicist). Avocations: astronomical obersvations, ufo investigator, alpine climbing. Home: 10 Gortynos St Hellas 112 54 Athens Greece Office: Hellenic Astron Soc 14 Voulis St Hellas 105 63 Athens Greece

ARNIZAUT-VILELLA, ANA BEATRIZ, veterinarian; b. Rio de Janeiro, Oct. 6, 1959; came to U.S., 1984; d. Fabio F. and Emilia Arnizaut de Maltos; m. Francisco J. Vilella, Sept. 24, 1988; 1 child, Isabela Beatriz. DVM, U. Fed. Rural do Rio de Janeiro, Brazil, 1982; MSc, La. State U., 1988; PhD, Miss. State U., 2002. Rsch asst. dept. virology and immunology EMBRAPA, Rio de Janeiro, 1982-84; rsch. assoc. dept. vet. microbiology and parasitology La. State U., 1988-89; natural resources specialist Dept. of Natural Resources, San Juan, P.R., 1990-92; aviary coord. Puerto Rican Parrot project Dept. of Interior-U.S. Fish and Wildlife Svc., Luquillo, P.R., 1992-93; vet. cons. P.R. Parrot Project Dept. Interior-U.S. Fish and Wildlife Svc., Luquillo, 1993-94; wildlife vet. cons. Miss. State U., 1995, grad. rsch. asst. Coll. Vet. Medicine, 1996—2002, postdoc. asst., dept. basic scis. Coll. Vet. Medicine, 2002—. Contbr. articles to profl. jours. Fellowship Brazilian Govt., 1984. Mem. Assn. Avian Vets., Wildlife Disease Assn., Soc. Tropical Vet. Medicine, Regional Coun. Vet. Medicine of Rio de Janeiro, Am. Assn. Zoo Vets., Internat. Assn. Aquatic Animal Medicine, Am. Fisheries Soc., Sigma Xi. Democrat. Roman Catholic. Office: Miss State U PO Box 6100 Mississippi State MS 39762-6100 Office Phone: 662-325-0784. E-mail: anarkizo88@yahoo.com.

ARNOLD, ALBERT JAMES, foreign language educator; b. Ballston Spa, N.Y., Nov. 8, 1939; s. Albert J. and Florence Emily (Cleveland) A.; m. Josephine Diane Valenza, June 8, 1963; 1 child, Elizabeth. AB, Hamilton Coll., 1961; MA, U Wis. Madison, 1964, PhD, 1968; cert French lang., lit., U. Paris, 1960. Instr. romance langs. Hamilton Coll., Clinton, N.Y., 1961-62; from asst. to prof. French U. Va., 1966—, chair com. comparative lit., 1974-79, 1986-89, co-chair comparative programs in literature and culture, 1989-95; dir. New World Studies, 1991-92, Caribbean Lit. Archive, 2003—. Vis. exch. prof. U. de Paris III, 1981; external examiner Queensland U., Australia, 1986, U. West Indies, 1991—, NYU, 1991, Yale U., 1994, U. West Australia, 2003; external assessor French dept. U. West Indies, 1995, 2002-03; coord. com. on comp. lit. hist. Internat. Comp. Lit. Assoc., 1992-2001; mem. internat. adv. bd. New West Indian Guide, 1992—; mem. adv. bd. Review Lit. & Arts Americas, 2003-; spkr., cons. in field. Author: Paul Valéry, 1970, Sartre, 1973, Césaire, 1981, 90, Camus, 1983; gen. editor Caraf Books, 1987-93; editor New World Studies, 1992—, Plantation Soc. in the Ams., 1999—; contbr. articles to profl. jours. ACLS fellow, 1975-76; NEH fellow Nat. Humanities Ctr., 1989-90; Fulbright fellow, 1995-96; grantee NEH, 1977, 88, 89-90, 2004; grantee U. Va., 1969, 70, 72, 75-76, 78, 80, 81-82, 86, 95-96, 2001-02, Camargo Found., 1981-82, 86, 2001, Va. Found. Humanities, 1992, 94, 2004; Queensland U. fellow, Australia, 1995, Rock Found. Bellagio Conf. Ctr., 2004. Mem. Phi Beta Kappa. Democrat. Avocations: gardening, photography, birding. Home: 310 E Beverley St Staunton VA 24401-4327 Office: U Va Dept French PO Box 400770 Charlottesville VA 22904-4770 Business E-Mail: aja@virginia.edu.

ARNOLD, ANN, artist, illustrator; b. Newcastle-upon-Tyne, 1936; d. Edmund Tefler; m. Graham Arnold, July 29, 1961. Illustrator (books) Fanny at Chez Panisse, 1992, Stop Smelling My Rose, 1997, The Children's Kitchen Garden: A Book of Gardening, Cooking, and Learning, 1997, illustrator, co-author Firehouse Max, 1997; co-author (with John Clare, Brian Patten and Eric Robinson): (books) Clare's Countryside, 1981; author: Gamblers & Gangsters: Fort Worth's Jacksboro Highway in the 1940s and 1950s, 1998, History of the Fort Worth Legal Community, 2000, History of the Fort Worth Medical Community, 2002, The Adventurous Chef: Alexis Soyer, 2002; Represented in permanent collections North Point Gallery, San Francisco, numerous exhibitions in London and the U.S. Mem.: Assn. Art Therapists (founding mem.). Address: c/o Pippin Properties Inc 155 E 38th St Ste 2H New York NY 10016*

ARNOLD, ARTHUR JOSEPH, writer, journalist; b. Kings Park, N.Y., Feb. 16, 1918; s. Gustave Arnold and Ellen Kenny; m. Margaret Dumas (div.); children: Joan, Conrad; m. Wilhelmina Staninger Arnold, Aug. 15, 1957 (dec.). Grad., Mt. Assumption Inst. H.S., Plattsburgh, N.Y. Former adjudicator VA, Newark; former jr. coll. instr. Cocoa, Fla.; former newspaper columnist, reporter, writer Plattsburgh Daily Rep. Author: Behold My Brother, 1963, A White Spring, 2000 (Book Fair award, 2000). Served with USN, 1942—45, PTO. Mem.: DAV. Democrat. Avocations: reading, writing, walking. Home: 1209 Harrison St Titusville FL 32780-3448

ARNOLD, BARBARA COOK, school librarian; b. Willimantic, Conn., June 24, 1933; d. Wendell Burnham and Frances (Waymire) Cook; m. Edmund Randolph Arnold, June 4, 1955; children: Steven E., Quin L., Lianne C. Peterson, Craig A., Kristin N. BS, U. Conn., 1955; postgrad. U. Iowa, 1974-75; MEd, East Mont. Coll., 1987. Cert. tchr., librarian. Asst. librarian U. Conn., Storrs, 1955-56; media technician Billings Sch. Dist. (Mont.), 1976-80; librarian Lockwood Sch. Dist., Billings, 1980— . Sec. LWV, Mt. Vernon, Iowa, 1974-75; bd. dirs. HACAP Tutor Program, Mt. Vernon, 1974; leader Blue Birds, Camp Fire and Cub Scouts, Potsdam, N.Y. and Mt. Vernon, 1963-73; dir. costume design for Community Theatre, Potsdam, 1964-65. Mem. ALA, Am. Assn. Sch. Librarians, Mont. Library Assn., Pacific Northwest Library Assn. (registration com. 1984). Home: 125 Kipling Ct Roseville CA 95747-5831

ARNOLD, BARBARA EILEEN, state legislator; b. North Adams, Mass., Aug. 3, 1924; d. Lester Flemming and Sarah (Van Hagen) Smith; m. William E. Arnold, Dec. 5, 1946; children: Wynn, Jefffrey, Gayle, Christopher. BA in Psychology, U. Mass.; postgrad., Keene State Coll. Spl. edn. tchr. Easter Seal Rehab. Ctr., Manchester, NH, 1967-74; state legislator NH, 1982-95; Rep. floor leader Ho. of Reps., 1989-95; mem. N.H. Coun. Vocat. Tech. Edn., 1986-95, State and Fed. Rels. Commn.; chmn. Manchester Rep. Del.; vice chmn. Ways and Means, 1992—95. Sec. N.E. State Coun. Vocat. Edn.; adv. bd. edn. N.H. Dept. Corrections; mem. adv. coun. adult rehab. Easter Seal Soc., NH, 1990—; state adv. com. Vocat. Child Care Programs, 1993—95; mem. com. for children, families, social svcs. Nat. Conf. of State Legislatures; bd. registration City of Manchester, 1999—; Manchester chmn. Dole for Pres. campaign, 1995, Gov. Judd Gregg for U.S. Senate, 1992, 2004; chair Manchester Rep. Com., 1993—95, George W. Bush for Pres., Manchester, 1999, 2004; chmn. Manchester Rep. Com., 1992—95; chmn. Manchester Senator John E. Sununu Campaign, 2002; past mem. vestry, registered lay leader, mem. diocesan commn., del. gen. conv. Episcopal Ch.; bd. dirs. ARC, 1975—96, chmn. bd. dirs., 1977—80. Mem. Nat. Order Women Legislators, Nat. Fedn. Rep. Women, Greater Manchester Federated Rep. Women's Club, N.H. Kappa Kappa Gamma Alumni Assn. (pres. 1990-91). Address: 374 Pickering St Manchester NH 03104-2744

ARNOLD, BARRY RAYNOR, philosophy educator; b. Mooresville, N.C., Sept. 29, 1951; s. Adrian Leicester and Cleo Agnes (Fisher) A.; m. Margaret Elizabeth Morelock, Aug. 15, 1984. AB cum laude, Davidson Coll., 1973; MDiv magna cum laude, Emory U., 1976, PhD, 1986. Ordained to ministry Presbyn. Ch.; cert. Christian clin. counselor Am. Counseling Assn.; lic. mental health counselor, Ind. Min. various parishes, Ga., Fla., 1976—; instr. religion, assoc. chaplain The Lovett Sch., 1980-82; prof. Andrew Coll., Cuthbert, Ga., 1983-84; asst. prof. to prof. and honors prof. U. West Fla., Pensacola, 1986—2002; pvt. practice clin. counseling, Pace, Fla., 1996—; acting chmn. dept. philosophy/religion U. West Fla., Pensacola, 1997—, chmn. dept. interdisciplinary humanities, philosophy, relig., 2000—, exec. dir. Univ. Office for Applied Ethics, 2000—, joint prof. biology and philosophy divsn. life and health scis., 2003—; prof. Bioethics and Philosophy, dir. Ctr. for Health Care Ethics U. West Fla./Sacred Heart Hosp., Pensacola, 2003—, dir. Ctr. for Health Care Ethics, 2003—; supr. interns in palliative care and bio-ethics Sacred Heart Hosp., 2004—. Counselor Pace Counseling Ctr., 1996-97; spkr. in field. Author: The Pursuit of Virtue, 1989; editor: Essays in American Ethics, 1992; gen. editor (11 vols.) The Reshaping of Psychoanalysis, 1992-2002; assoc. editor Explorations: Jour. Adventurous Thought, 1999—; contbr. articles to profl. jours. Bd. dirs. Sacred Heart Hosp., Pensacola, Bapt. Hosp.; pres., bd. dirs. Assn. for Retarded Citizens, Albany, Ga., 1978—79; bioethicist, bd. dirs. West Fla. Regional Med. Ctr., Pensacola, 1990—2003, Bapt. Hosp., 2003—, Sacred Heart Hosp., 2003—. Recipient Disting. Tchg. award UWF and Fla. State Legislature, 1988, 90, 95; Award for Disting. Contbn., Honors Program UWF, 2002; fellow Rice U., 1973-75, Emory U., 1975-76, 79-82, U. Glasgow, 1976. Fellow: Am. Coll. Counselors (cert. Christian clin. counselor, chair examiners for cert.), Am. Assn. Integrative Medicine (diplomate, nat. bd. dirs., chair nat. bd. 2002—03), Am. Bd. Child Mental Health Providers; mem.: ACA, Assn. for Cognitive Behavioral Therapists (cert. cognitive forensic therapist, cert. anxiety disorders specialist), So. Soc. Philosophy and Psychology, Am. Acad. Religion, Internat. Thomas Merton Soc., Rotary (sgt.-at-arms 1982—83), Phi Beta Kappa, A£D (hon.), Alpha Epsilon Delta, Phi Kappa Phi (sec. 1988). Democrat. Avocations: antique cards, antique cars, birdwatching. Home: 5820 Kirkland Dr Milton FL 32570-8251 Office: Univ West Fla 11000 University Pkwy Pensacola FL 32514-5750 Business E-Mail: barnold@uwf.edu.

ARNOLD, BRENT LEE, science educator, athletic trainer; b. Anderson, Ind., July 11, 1963; s. Teddy Norman and Janice Elaine Arnold; m. Hollyn T. Mangione, Sept. 13, 1963. PhD, U. of Va., 1994. Cert. athletic trainer Nat. Athletic Trainers' Assn. Bd. Certification Inc., lic. Bd. of Medicine, Commonwealth of Va. Asst. prof. U. Va., Charlottesville, 1995—2001; assoc. prof. Va. Commonwealth U., Richmond, 2001—. Athletic trainer Princeton (N.J.) U., 1988—91; scholarly presenter Return to Fitness, Glasgow, Scotland,

2004; rsch. presenter Internat. Ankle Symposium. Mem.: Nat. Athletic Trainers' Assn. (pronouncements com. chair 1997—2002, rsch. presenter), Va. Athletic Trainers' Assn. (pres. 1998—2000), Mid-Atlantic Athletic Trainers' Assn. (exec. coun. 1998—2000), Am. Coll. Sports Medicine. Office: Va Commonwealth Univ PO Box 842037 Richmond VA 23284 Office Phone: 804-828-1948.

ARNOLD, CAROLYN GAY, retired secondary school educator; b. Oakdale, La., Nov. 28, 1939; d.Samuel Sentinel and Mary Violet (Iles) Hudson; m. Paul Richard Arnold, April 16, 1960; children: Jeffrey Richard, Susan Kathleen, Jay Samuel. BS, Mcneese St. U., 1960, MEd, 1981, postgrad., 1989. Cert. high sch. tchr., La.; cert. gifted edn. and supervision, La. Tchr. piano, Lake Charles, La., 1974-77; tchr. math. Barbe High Sch., Lake Charles, La., 1978-92; instr. math. McNeese St. U., Lake Charles, La., 1988; supr. gifted and talented Calcasieu Parish, 1992—2003; ret., 2003; cons. in gifted edn., 2004—. Presenter La. Tchrs. Math., Baton Rouge, 1988, 89, Nat. Assn. Gifted Students, Little Rock, 1990, La. Assn. Gifted and Talented Students, Baton Rouge, 1987, 91; coache Acad. Team. Barbe High Sch., 1989—. Writer: math. units Am. Coll. Test, 1986-88. Recipient Woodrow Wilson Fellowship, NSF, 1986, Presdl. Award Math. Tchr., NSF, 1987. Mem. Nat. Coun. Tchrs. Math., La. Assn. Computer User Educators, Nat. Sch. Bd. Assn., Assn. Gifted and Talented Students (pres. 1975-77, Excellence in Edn. award 1996, AGTS award 2002), La. Tchrs. Math. (bd. dirs., 1987-88), United Methodist Women (pres., v.p., treas.), Delta Kappa Gamma. Republican. Methodist. Avocations: piano, gardening, sewing. Office: Gifted Edn 2423 Sixth St Lake Charles LA 70601-4819

ARNOLD, CATHERINE I., psychology educator, health educator; b. Detroit, Oct. 7, 1948; d. Walter Neilson and Catherine Goodwryn Sharp; m. Dart Murray Arnold, Nov. 27, 1990; children: Gregory Goodall, Dovin, Dart Jr., Shannon. BS, Mich. State U., 1970, MA, 1971. Tchr. Yale Pub. Sch., Yale, Mich., 1971—2005. Mem. Yale Lions Club, Yale, Mich., 1995—2004. Avocations: golf, bowling, archery, Nascar Races.

ARNOLD, CHARLES BURLE, JR., psychiatrist, writer; b. Seattle, Aug. 13, 1934; s. Charles Burle and Ruth Helene (Hadley) A.; m. Sarah J. Slagle, Dec. 16, 1972; children: Geoffrey, Christopher, Jonathan. BS cum laude, U. Puget Sound, 1956; MD, CM, McGill U., 1960; MPH, U. N.C., 1965. Diplomate: Am. Bd. Preventive Medicine. Intern U. Wash. Hosp., Seattle, 1960-61, resident, 1961; physician Peace Corps, Bolivia, Washington, 1961-64; asst. prof. health adminstrn., asso. Carolina Population Center, U. N.C., Chapel Hill, 1965-69; asst. prof. Albert Einstein Coll. Medicine, Bronx, N.Y., 1969-72; prof. public adminstrn. and clin. assoc. prof. preventive medicine NYU, N.Y.C., 1972-83, adj. prof. pub. adminstrn., 1983—; med. dir., med. rels. Met. Life Ins. Co., 1983-91, v.p. med. rels., 1991-93; psychiat. resident North Shore Univ. Hosp., Manhasset, N.Y., 1993-96, chief resident, 1995-96; pvt. practice of psychiatry, 1996-99; attending psychiatrist Augusta (Maine) Mental Health Inst., 1999—2002. Lectr. cmty. health Mt. Sinai Med. Sch., N.Y.C.; lectr. preventive medicine Downstate Med. Soc., SUNY, 1986-92; dir. Mahoney Inst. Health Maintenance, Am. Health Found., 1975-83, v.p. rsch., 1978-83, cons., 1983-86; chair Hitchcock Weekday Sch. Bd., 1986-92; chmn. Worksite Smoking subcom. N.Y. State Commn. on Smoking or Health, 1991-93; psychiatrist Drop-In Ctr., Ctr. Urban Cmty. Svcs., West Harlem, 1996-98; asst. attending psychiatrist N.Y. Presbyn. Hosp. Westchester Divsn.; dir. Open Arms Clinic; asst. clin. prof. psychiatry Cornell Med. Coll., 1998-2000. Editor, mem. exec. coun.: Transactions of Am. Acad. Ins. Medicine, 1988-93; assoc. editor Preventive Medicine Jour., 1975-83, sr. assoc. editor, 1983-85; editor Advances in Disease Prevention, 1981-83; editor-in-chief Statis. Bull., 1983-93; contbr. articles to profl. jours. Milbank Faculty fellow, 1967-74; OEO grantee, 1968-74; Population Council grantee, 1971-75; Health Research Council N.Y.C. grantee, 1972-75; Nat. Cancer Inst. grantee, 1975-83; Nat. Heart, Lung and Blood Inst. grantee, 1977-83; HEW Office Health Promotion grantee, 1978-80 Fellow Am. Coll. Preventive Medicine (pres. 1977-78); mem. N.Y. Acad. Medicine (com. on pub. health 1988—, vice chmn. 1992, chmn. 1993), Health Ins. Assn. Am. (chair com. on prevention and pub. health policy 1989-92). Home: PO Box 479 Topsham ME 04086-0479 E-mail: carnold1@suscom-maine.net.

ARNOLD, DAVID JOHN, finance educator, consultant; b. Hornchurch, Essex, Eng., Dec. 26, 1955; came to U.S., 1992; s. Albert Edward and Margaret Ann Arnold; m. Megan Eileen Brown, Sept. 9, 1978; children: Katherine, Thomas. BA, U. London, 1978; MBA, City U., London, 1988; DBA, Harvard U., 1996. Editor, mktg. mgr. Mitchell Beazley, London, 1978-83; program dir. Ashridge Mgmt. Coll., Berkhamsted, Eng., 1983-92; prof. mktg. Harvard Bus. Sch., Boston, 1996—. Author: The Handbook of Brand Management, 1992. E-mail: darnold@hbs.edu.

ARNOLD, DENNIS B., lawyer; b. Apr. 25, 1950; BA magna cum laude, SUNY Buffalo, 1972; JD, Yale U., 1975. Bar: Calif. 1976. Asst.-in-instrn. Yale Law Sch., New Haven, Conn., 1974-75; law clk. to Hon. Murray M. Schwartz U.S. Dist. Ct., Del., 1975-76; ptnr. Irell & Manella, 1980-88, Gibson, Dunn & Crutcher LLP, L.A., 1988—. Adj. assoc. prof. law Southwestern U. Sch. Law, 1980-82; advisor Restatement of Law, 2d edit., Suretyship and Guaranty, Am. Law Inst., 1989-95. Contbr. articles to profl. jours. Mem.: ABA, Am. Coll. Real Estate Lawyers, Fin. Lawyers Conf. (bd. govs. 1986—89, 1992—95, 1996—99, pres. 1999—2000), L.A. County Bar Assn. (exec. com. commercial law and bankruptcy sect. 1987—90, exec. com. real property sect. 1987—92, steering com. real estate fin. subsect. 1987—, exec. com. commercial law and bankruptcy sect. 1996—99), State Bar Calif. (real property and bus. law sect. 1978—, standing joint com. anti-deficiency laws 1985—89), Am. Law Inst. Office: Gibson Dunn & Crutcher LLP 333 South Grand Ave Los Angeles CA 90071-3197

ARNOLD, DOUGLAS P., music educator; b. Muphysboro, Ill., Feb. 12, 1970; s. Richard I. and Cecilia Arnold. Pvt. music tchr., Paducah, Ky., 1998—; music dir. St. Francis de Sales Ch., Paducah, Ky., 1998—. Profl. musician, Paducah, Ky., 1988—. Musician United Way, Paducah, 2000. Mem.: KC. Roman Catholic. Avocations: pocket billiards, travel, writing music, magic card tricks. Home: 1410 Mayfield-Metropolis Rd Paducah KY 42001

ARNOLD, EDDY, singer; b. Henderson, Tenn., May 15, 1918; m. Sally Arnold, Nov. 28, 1941; children: Dick, Jo Ann (Mrs. Pollard). Appeared on WSM Radio, Nashville, with Pee Wee King's western band Golden West Cowboys, 1940-43; co-host Grand Ole Opry radio program, 1943-48; guest appearances on numerous radio shows, including Western Theatre, RCA Victor Show, We the People, Spike Jones Show, Luncheon at Sardi's, Paul Whiteman Show, Breakfast Club; own radio show Checkerboard Square, 1947-55; made first TV appearance on Milton Berle Show, 1949; appeared in motion pictures Feudin Rhythm, 1949, Hoedown, 1950; N.Y.C. debut at Carnegie Hall, 1966, debut at Coconut Grove nightclub, Los Angeles, 1967, TV appearances include shows hosted by Ed Sullivan, Perry Como, Danny Kaye, Dinah Shore, Danny Thomas, Mike Douglas, Jackie Gleason, Johnny Carson, Les Crane, Dean Martin and Red Skelton; featured on TV spls. Profile from the Land, 1968, Kraft Music Hall Spls, 1967, 68, 69, 70, 71; appeared with symphony orchs. of Hartford, Memphis, Nashville, 1967-68; recs. include Mommy, Please Stay Home With Me, 1945, That's How Much I Love You, Bouquet of Roses (on chart longer than any other country music single), Anytime, I'll Hold You In My Heart, Don't Rob Another Man's Castle, What's He Doing in My World?, Make the World Go Away, The Last Word in Lonesome is Me, If It's a Sin, Turn the World Around, Tip of My Fingers, I Really Don't Want to Know, Tennessee Stud, Here Comes Heaven, (new albums) Hand Holdin' Songs, 1990, You Don't Miss a Thing, 1991, Last of the Love Song Singers:Then and Now, 1993, Memories Are Made of This, 1995, Greatest Songs, 1995, Eddy's Songs, 1996, The Essential Series, 1996; author: It's a Long Way from Chester County, 1969; host TNN Nashville Now, 1992—. Named to Country Music Hall of Fame, 1966; Entertainer of Year, 1967; recipient Pioneer award Acad. Country Music, 1984; Pres.'s award Songwriter's Guild, 1987; subject of TNN Spl. The Stars Come Out to Salute Eddy Arnold, A Celebration of Eddy Arnold, 1992, Nat. Medal of Arts, 2000. Address: RCA Records 1400 18th Ave S Nashville TN 37212-2809

ARNOLD, EDWARD (EDDY ARNOLD), research scientist, educator; m. Gail Ferstandig Arnold, 1981; children: Lizzie, Emmie. PhD, Cornell U., 1982. Prof., chemistry and chemical biology Rutgers U., Piscataway, NJ, adj. prof., molecular genetics and microbiology; co-established Rutgers U., Ctr. of Advanced Biotechnology and Medicine, Piscataway, NJ, 1987—, resident faculty mem., researcher, 1987—. Mem.: Cancer Inst. NJ. Established laboratory (with wife Gail Ferstandig Arnold) at Rutgers University, Center of Advanced Biotechnology and Medicine in 1987, which includes a 30 member research team that partners with Janssen Pharmaceutica (including the late Paul Janssen) and Tibotec-Virco NV (both subsidiaries of Johnson & Johnson) and a team of scientists from Gilead Sciences, NIH, Nat. Cancer Inst. (Stephen H. Hughes), and Rutgers Chemistry Department (Roger A. Jones). The team is working to develop and apply structure-based drug and vaccine designs for the treatment and prevention of serious human diseases (developed a trio of drugs that are believed to destroy HIV, the virus that causes AIDS, tenifovir, or the DAPY(diarylpyrimidine)). Office: Rutgers U Chemistry & Chemical Biology Ctr Advanced Biotechnology and Medicine 679 Hoes Ln Room 016 Piscataway NJ 08854 Office Phone: 732-235-5323. Office Fax: 732-235-5788. Business E-Mail: arnold@cabm.rutgers.edu.*

ARNOLD, ERIC DANIELL, financial analyst, security firm executive; b. Raleigh, N.C., Sept. 12, 1970; s. Earl Marvin Dunston and Mary Ann Arnold-Dunston; 1 child, Aarica. BA, N.C. Ctrl. U., Durham, 1993; MPA, N.C. Ctrl. U., 1998. Sr. materials/receiving clk. OMG Ams., Inc., Research Triangle Park, N.C., 1993-99; budget analyst Office Mgmt. and Budget City Hall, Kansas City, Mo., 1999—; security supr. mid-Atlantic region Guardsmark Security, 2002—. Vol. David Price for Congress campaign, Cary, N.C., 1998; vol. intern Register of Deeds, Durham, 1991-92. Grad. Students Assn. scholar, 1998. Mem. Am. Soc. Pub. Adminstrn., Nat. Contract Mgmt. Assn. (scholar 1998), Internat. City/County Mgmt. Assn., Doric Lodge #28, Kappa Alpha Psi, Phi Alpha Alpha. Democrat. Baptist. Avocations: singing, basketball, running, bowling, mentoring. Office: Sprint c/o Guardsmark Security 14111 Capital Blvd Wake Forest NC 27587 E-mail: earnold47@hotmail.com.

ARNOLD, FRANCES HAMILTON, chemistry educator; b. Pitts., July 25, 1956; d. William Howard and Josephine Inman (Routheau) A.; m. Andrew Evan Lange, Mar. 4, 1994; children: James Howard, William Andrew. BS magna cum laude, Princeton U., 1979; PhD in Chem. Engring., U. Calif., Berkeley, 1985. Asst. chem. engring. Calif. Inst. Tech., Pasadena, 1987-92, assoc. prof., 1992—, prof. chem. engring & biochemistry. Vis. assoc. chemistry U. Calif., Berkeley, 1986—87; ann. lectr. Advanced Ctr. Biochemical Engring. Univ. Coll., London, 1994; William Rauscher Lectr. in Chemistry Rensselaer Polytechnic Inst., 1996; Purves Lectr. in Chemistry McGill U., 1998; Lindsay Disting. Lectr. Tex. A&M, 2003; Merck-Frosst Invited Lectr. Biochemistry U. Alberta, 2003; Sir Robert Price Lectr. CSIRO, Melbourne, 2003. Contbr. articles to profl. jours. Recipient Office Naval Rsch. Young Investigator award, 1988, NSF Presdl. Young Investigator award, 1989, Van Ness Award, Rensselaer Polytechnic Inst., 1994, Profl. Progress Award, AIChE, 2000, David Perlman Lectr. Award, ACS, Biochemical Tech., 2003, Carothers Award, ACS Del. Div., 2003, Francis P. Garvan-John M. Olin Medal, ACS, 2005; grantee David and Lucile Packard fellow, 1989. Mem.: NAE, AAAS (Sci. Innovation Topical Lectr.), NAE, Inst. Medicine, Santa Fe Inst. (Sci. Bd.), Am. Inst. Medical and Biological Engring., Am. Soc. Microbiology, Protein Soc., Am. Inst. Chem. Engrs., Am. Chem. Soc., Tau Beta Pi, Phi Beta Kappa. Office: Calif Inst Tech Div of Chem & Chem Engring # 210-41 Pasadena CA 91125-0001

ARNOLD, FRED ENGLISH, lawyer; b. Mexico, Mo., May 10, 1938; s. Charles P. and Mary E. (Blackman) A.; m. Dorothy P. Offutt, Dec. 31, 1966 (div. Aug. 2002); children: Jane E., Charles P. III, Susan J., m. Jo Ann Harmon, Apr. 10, 2004. AB, Harvard U., 1960, LLB, 1963. Bar: Mo. 1963, U.S. Dist. Ct. (ea. dist.) Mo. 1964, U.S. Supreme Ct. 1966. Assoc. Thompson Coburn LLP, St. Louis, 1964-70, ptnr., 1971—. Trustee KETC/Channel 9, 2002—. Trustee Mary Inst., St. Louis, 1981-87, v.p., 1985-86; bd. dirs. Repertory Theatre of St. Louis, 1982-88; bd. dirs. Whitfield Sch., St. Louis, 1990-96, pres., 1991-93, Arts & Edn. Coun. Greater St. Louis, 1991-97, vice chmn., 1996-97; adv. com. Jordan Charitable Found., St. Louis, 1975—; bd. curators Ctrl. Meth. U., Fayette, Mo., 1997—. Mem. ABA, Am. Coll. Real Estate Lawyers, Noonday Club, (bd. govs. 2003—, pres. 2005—), The Racquet Club. Democrat. Methodist. Office: Thompson Coburn LLP One US Bank Plz Saint Louis MO 63101-1693 Home: 921 Cella Rd Saint Louis MO 63124 Business E-Mail: farnold@thompsoncoburn.com.

ARNOLD, G. DEWEY, JR., accountant; b. Montgomery, Ala., Jan. 30, 1925; s. G. Dewey and Janie Esther (Terry) A.; m. Dorothy Louise Wenger, Dec. 4, 1954; children: Susan O., G. Dewey III. BA in Econs, U. of South, 1949; postgrad. in acct., U. Tenn. C.P.A., Pa., D.C., Md. With Aladdin Industries, Inc., Nashville, 1949-50; with Price Waterhouse, 1950—, ptnr., 1961—; ptnr. in charge Washington office Price Waterhouse & Co., 1965-76, mem. policy com., 1975-80, regional mng. ptnr., 1976-85; exec. dir. Nat. Commn. on Fin. Fraud, 1985-87; sr. v.p. Audit-Intelsat., 1987—. Instr. acctg. Robert Morris Sch. Acctg., 1952-53; lectr., course dir. mgmt. acctg. Inst. Mexicano de Administracion de Negocias, A.C., 1958-64; bd. dirs. Washington Bd. Trade, 1973-75; mem. audit adv. com. Sec. Navy, 1972-75 Bd. dirs. Jr. C. of C., 1954-55; trustee Fed. City Coun., 1966—; bd. dirs. Greater Washington Ednl. TV Assn., Inc., 1970-82, Minority Contractors Ctr., 1972-74, Redskins Found., 1973—; D. C. Mcpl. Rsch. Bur., 1974-76, Wolf Trap Found., 1975-90; chmn. bd. trustees Landon Sch., 1974-79; vice chmn. D.C. Bicentennial Commn., 1971-75. Served with USNR, 1943-45. Mem. AICPA, D.C. Inst. CPAs, Nat. Assn. Accts., Md. Inst. CPAs, Am. Arbitration Assn., Chevy Chase Club, Burning Tree Club, Pine Valley Golf Club, Rolling Rock Club, John's Island Club. Office: Intelsat Global Svcs Corp Box 1B 3400 International Dr NW Washington DC 20008-3006 Home: 2700 Calvert St NW 415 Washington DC 20008-2621 Business E-Mail: dewey.arnold@intelsat.com.

ARNOLD, GARY HOWARD, film critic; b. Princeton, Ind., Aug. 22, 1942; s. Charles Howard and Ferris (Smith) A.; m. Sue Datz, Dec. 29, 1967; children— Pauline, Jane, Esther. Student, NYU, 1959-60, U. Calif., Berkeley, 1960-63. Film critic Diplomat mag., 1966; film critic, reporter Ind. Film Jour., 1968-69; film critic Washington Post, 1969-84; co-host weekly TV commentary show The Moviegoing Family, 1985-90; arts critic The Connection, Reston, Va., 1987-89; movie critic The Washington Times, Washington, 1989—. Home: 5133 1st St N Arlington VA 22203-1207 Office: The Washington Times 3600 New York Ave NE Washington DC 20002-1996 Personal E-mail: gsarnold@verizon.net.

ARNOLD, GEORGE LAWRENCE, retired advertising company executive; b. Kansas City, Mo., Sept. 30, 1942; s. James Robert and Mary Virginia (Ellington) A.; m. Mary Antoinette Turrin, Dec. 31, 1964; children: Margery, Matthew, Molly, Sara. BJ magna cum laude, U. Tex., 1965, MA cum laude, 1966. Advt. and pub. relations trainee Gen. Electric Co., Phila., 1966; advt. asst. Dallas Power & Light Co., 1967-70; dir. comm. Continuum Co. Inc., Austin, Tex., 1970-73; pres. Evans/Dallas Inc., Dallas, 1977-99; ret., 1999. Bd. dirs. Evans Group, Inc., Salt Lake City, operating com. Salt Lake City. Bd. dirs. United Way Met. Dallas, 1978, Lone Star council Camp Fire, Dallas, 1978-84. Recipient Silver Anvil award Pub. Relations Soc. Am., 1980, Gold Effie award Am. Mktg. Assn., 1981. Mem. Tex. Pub. Rels. Assn. (bd. dirs. 1978-80, 92-97, pres. 1998, Silver Spur award 1979, 85, 2003), Dallas Advt. League (pres. 1981). Democrat. Roman Catholic. Home: 912 Kneese Rd Fredericksburg TX 78624-7057

ARNOLD, HENRI, cartoonist; b. Bethlehem, Pa. s. Samuel Max and Dora (Schnur) A.; m. Harriet Chefetz, Feb. 14, 1980; children by previous marriage— Nora Sally, Ned Michael. Student, Cooper Union, 1946. Editorial/sports cartoonist Bridgeport (Conn.) Sun. Herald; cartoonist weekly humor page Chgo. Tribune, 1955-65; art dir. Chgo. Tribune-N.Y. News Syndicate, Inc., N.Y.C., 1957-77. Lectr. in field. Creator: This Man's Army, N.Y. Sun. News, 1954-64, Meet Mr. Luckey, N.Y. Daily News, 1991—; writer, cartoonist for Ching Chow, 1977—; producer Jumble, That Scrambled Word Game, 1960—; illustrator: The ABCs of Golf (by Tommy Armour), 63 vols. of Jumble, That Scrambled Word Game, 1962—, Super Jumble Puzzle Book, 1991, Jumble for Kids Book, 1992. Mem. Nat. Cartoonists Soc., Palm-Aire Country Club.

ARNOLD, J. KELLEY, United States magistrate judge; b. Lewiston, Idaho, Oct. 3, 1937; m. Diane Louise Jenkins. Student, Wash. State U., 1955-58; LLB, U. Idaho, 1961. Bar: Wash. 1961. Dep. pros. atty. Pierce County, 1963-64; atty., 1965-82; judge Wash. Superior Ct. Pierce County, Tacoma, 1982-94; magistrate judge for western Wash., U.S. Dist. Ct., Tacoma, 1994—. With U.S. Army, 1961-63. Office: US Dist Ct 1717 Pacific Ave Rm 3409 Tacoma WA 98402-3234 Business E-Mail: kelley_arnold@wawd.uscourts.gov.

ARNOLD, JAMES AUSTIN, music educator, band director, administrator; b. Ruleville, Miss., July 15, 1952; s. James Lloyd and Dorothy Jewel (Mullen) A.; m. Betsy Jean Black, Dec. 24, 1990; children: Matthew L. Hopper, Daniel L. Hopper. B of Music Edn., U. Miss., 1974, M of Music Edn., 1977; EdD, U. Ala., 1993. Cert. tchr., Ga. Dir. of bands Lamar County, Vernon, Ala., 1974-90, Columbus (Ga.) H.S. Bands, 1990-96; asst. prin. Shaw H.S., 1996—2001; dir. Bob Barr/Columbus Cmty. Band, 1997-2000; prin. Shaw H.S., 2001. Presenter U. Ala. Rsch. Workshop, Tuscaloosa, 1992-93, Ga. Music Edn. Assn., Savannah, 1994, Music Educators Nat. Conf., Winston-Salem, N.C., 1994; mem. Leadership Acad., Columbus, Ga., 1994—. Contbr. articles to jours. in field. Named Disting. Bandmaster, First Chair of Am., 1981; recipient Classroom Rsch. award Phi Delta Kappa, 1992. Mem. Music Educators Nat. Conf., Ga. Music Educators Assn. (dist. v.p. 1994), Phi Kappa Phi, 1992. Avocations: reading, golf. Home: 4824 Spring Ridge Ct Columbus GA 31909-2063 Office: Shaw HS 7601 Schomburg Rd Columbus GA 31909

ARNOLD, J(AMES) BARTO, III, marine archaeologist; b. San Antonio, Jan. 9, 1950; s. J. Barto Jr. and Wilnora (Barton) A.; children: Kathryn, Julia, Jessica; m. Jeanne Alice Bullard, 2003. BA cum laude, U. Tex., 1971, MA, 1973. Rsch. asst. Tex. Archeol. Rsch. Lab. U. Tex., Austin, 1970-72; asst. state marine archaeologist Tex. Antiquities Com., Austin, 1972-75; state marine archaeologist Tex. Hist. Com., Austin, 1975-97; dir. Tex. ops. Inst. of Nautical Archaeology, Tex. A&M U., College Station, 1997—. Cons. NOAA, 1977-91, Nat. Trust Hist. Preservation, Washington, 1979-90, Congl. Office Tech. Assessment, Washington, 1986; mem. Md. Gov.'s Adv. Com. on Marine Archaeology, Annapolis, 1987-90; mem. history area com. nat. park sys. adv. bd. U.S. Dept. Interior, 1994-95; dir. La Salle Shipwreck Project, 1995-96, Confederate Blockade-Runner Denbigh Shipwreck Project, 1997—. Co-author: Nautical Archaeology of Padre Island, 1978, Documentary Sources for the Wreck of the New Spain Fleet of 1554, 1979 (Presidio La Bahaia 1979), others; Plenum series editor Underwater Archaeology, 1995—; contbr. articles to profl. jours. Recipient Achievement award for Hist. Preservation Dept. Interior, 1980. Mem. Soc. Profl. Archaeologists (cert.; sec.-treas. 1987-89, Spl. Achievement award 1990), Soc. Hist. Archaeology (pres. 1993), Tex. Archeol. Soc., Archaeol. Inst. Am., Explorers Club, Phi Beta Kappa. Methodist. Avocations: stamp collecting/philately, science fiction. Office: Tex A&M U Inst Nautical Archaeology PO Drawer HG College Station TX 77841-5137 E-mail: barnold@tamu.edu.

ARNOLD, JAMES PHILLIP, theology studies educator, historian; b. Greenville, S.C. s. David Lee and Vera Irene (Wilson) A. MA in Am. History, U. Houston, 1979; MA in Religious Studies, Rice U., 1984, PhD in Religious Studies, 1991. Instr. Am. History U. Houston, 1972-76; instr. religion Rice U., Houston, 1976-81; instr. ch. history, biblical studies, homiletics Houston Grad. Sch. Theology, 1984-86; instr. religion and history, exec. dir. The Reunion Inst., Houston, 1986—. Pres. Living History Studies, Inc., Houston, 1993—; counselor families divided by religious cult issues; advisor to FBI on Branch Davidian crisis, Waco, Tex., 1993, Freeman crisis, 1996. Dir. Fine Arts Found., Houston, 1987—; founder Religion-Crisis Task Force, 1994. Rice U. fellow, 1980-91, U. Houston fellow, 1972-76; Tex. Com. for Humanities grantee, 1979. Mem. Am. Acad. Religion, Soc. Biblical Lit. Avocations: air-hockey, archaeology. Office: Reunion Inst 5508 Chaucer Dr Houston TX 77005-2632 Office Phone: 713-523-1861. Personal E-mail: reunion@sbcglobal.net.

ARNOLD, JAMES RICHARD, chemist, educator; b. New Brunswick, N.J., May 5, 1923; s. Abraham Samuel and Julia (Jacobs) A.; m. Louise Clark, Oct. 11, 1952; children: Robert C., Theodore J., Kenneth C. AB, Princeton U., 1943, MA, 1945, PhD, 1946. Fellow Inst. Nuclear Studies, U. Chgo., 1946-47, faculty, 1948-55; NRC fellow Harvard U., 1947-48; faculty chemistry Princeton U., 1955-58; assoc. prof. chemistry U. Calif., San Diego, 1958-60, prof., 1960-92, Harold C. Urey prof., 1983-92, chmn. dept. chemistry, 1960-63. Assoc. Manhattan Project, 1943-46; dir. Calif. Space Inst., 1980-89, interim dir., 1996-97; prin. investigator Calif. Space Grant Consortium, 1989—; mem. various bds. NASA, 1959—; space sci. bd. NAS, 1970-74, com. on sci. and pub. policy, 1970-77. Mem. editl. bd. Ann. Rev. Nuclear Chemistry, 1972, Revs. Geophysics and Space Physics, 1972-75, Moon, 1972—; contbr. articles to profl. jours. Pres. Torrey Pines Elem. Sch. PTA, 1964-65; pres. La Jolla Democratic Club, 1965-66; nat. council World Federalists-U.S.A., 1970-72. Recipient E.O. Lawrence medal AEC, 1968, Leonard medal Meteoritical Soc., 1976, Kuiper award Am. Astron. Soc., 1993; asteroid 2143 named Jimarnold in his honor, 1980; Guggenheim fellow, India, 1972-73. Mem. Nat. Acad. Sci., Am. Acad. Arts and Scis., Internat. Acad. Astronautics, Am. Chem. Soc., AAAS, Fedn. Am. Scientists, Citizens for Global Solutions. Office: U Calif San Diego Dept Chemistry Code 0524 La Jolla CA 92093 Business E-Mail: jarnold@ucsd.edu.

ARNOLD, JANET NINA, healthcare consultant; b. Poughkeepsie, NY, Apr. 23, 1933; d. Paul Dudley and Pauline Katherine (Board) Bartram; m. Robert William Arnold, Dec. 19, 1954; children: Paul Dudley, Janet Elizabeth. AB cum laude, Vassar Coll., 1955; postgrad. Sch. Med. Tech., Albany Med. Coll., 1955-56; MS in Microbiology cum laude, Vassar Coll., 1963; MHSM, Webster Coll., 1981. Rsch. asst., med. technologist H. Aird Boswell, M.D., Troy, NY, 1956-59; tchg. supr., adminstrv. cons. Vassar Bros. Hosp., Poughkeepsie, 1959-69; adv. to med. lab., lectr. med. mycology Vassar Coll., Poughkeepsie, 1961-66; asst. adminstr., lab. mgr. Boulder (Colo.) Meml. Hosp., 1975-80; cons. hosp. planning Mercy Med. Ctr., Denver, 1981-82; clin. lab. dir./adminstr. Humana, Denver, 1982-85, cons. health care mgmt., 1982-85, MRI, 1985—. Ptnr., 1988; cons. health care mgmt. Humana, Inc., 1982-96, Columbia/HCA Health Sys., 1992-96; pres. Arnold and Assocs., 1988—; ptnr. InterExec (divsn. MRI), 1994—; acad./adminstrv. cons. U. Guam, Vassar Coll., Boulder Cmty. Hosp., Humana Int., 1990-97, others; adj. faculty Vassar Coll.; sec., bd. dirs. Sanitas Fed. Credit Union, 1977-78, pres., 1979-82; teaching fellow Vassar Coll., 1961-63, unrestricted fund chmn., 1989-96, co-chair major gifts, 2002—. Assoc. editor Am. Jour. Med. Tech., 1980-88; contbr. articles to profl. jours. Contbr. NMC, 1988-92. NSF rsch. fellow, 1960-62. Mem. Am. Acad. Microbiology, Soc. for Gen. Microbiology, Am. Soc. Med. Technologists, Colo. Pub. Health Assn., Soc. Women Environ. Profls., Med. Mycological Soc. of the Ams. Republican. Episcopalian. Home: 421 Wynwood Dr Willow Street PA 17584 Office Phone: 303-543-7965. E-mail: r-j-arnold-assoc@att.net.

ARNOLD, JEFFREY L., emergency physician, researcher; s. Warren L Arnold; m. Monica Arnold; 1 child, Andrew. MD, Stanford U., Calif., 1988. Diplomate Am. Bd. Emergency Physicians. Asst. prof. of emergency medicine Tufts U. Sch. of Medicine, Springfield, Mass., 2001—03; med. dir. Yale-New Haven Ctr. for Emergency Preparedness and Disaster Response, New Haven, 2003—. Recipient Award of Appreciation, Dept. Emergency Medicine, Kangdong Sacred Heart Hosp., Hallym U., Seoul, South Korea, 1998, Emergency Internat., Balt., 1998, Disting. Alumni award, Sonoma State U., 1999, Academic Achievement awards, Baystate Med. Edn. and Rsch.

Found., 2002—03. Fellow: Am. Coll. of Emergency Physicians. Achievements include research in Evidence-based disaster medicine research. Office: Yale University School of Medicine 1 Church St 5th Fl New Haven CT 06460 Office Phone: 203-688-3224. Office Fax: 203-688-4618. Personal E-mail: arnoldmdcs@cs.com. E-mail: jeffrey.arnold@ynhh.org.

ARNOLD, JEROME GILBERT, lawyer; s. Edward F. and Annastacia (Thielen) A.; m. Judith Lindor, Dec. 18, 1971; children: Thomas, Mark, John, Jason, Maria. BS, U. Minn., 1964; LLB, U. N.D., 1967. Bar: Minn. 1967, S.D. 1967, U.S. Dist. Ct. S.D. 1967, U.S. Dist. Ct. Minn. 1973, U.S. Ct. Appeals (8th cir.) 1986. Law clk. U.S. Dist. Ct., Aberdeen, S.D., 1967-68; asst. city atty. City of Duluth, Minn., 1968-69; asst. county atty. St. Louis County, Duluth, 1969-70, chief criminal prosecutor, 1970-71; spl. asst. to county atty. County of Carlton, Minn., 1971; ptnr. Hunt & Arnold, Duluth, Minn., 1971—86; U.S. atty. U.S. Dist. Ct. Minn., Mpls., 1986—91; ptnr. Larson, Husby, Brodin & Arnold, Duluth, 1992—93; compensation judge State of Minn., Duluth, 1993—2004, 2005—; mem. Falsani, Balmer, Peterson, Quinn and Beyer, Duluth, Minn., 2004—05; compensation judge State of Minn., 2005—. Mem. adv. com. Supreme Ct. Appointments, St. Paul, 1980; chmn. selection com. 6th Jud. Dist., Duluth, 1978-83. Chmn. St. Louis City (Minn.) Bd. Adjustment, 1978-82; Rep. nominee 8th Congl. Dist, Minn., 1974; mem. state steering com. Reagan for Pres., 1976, 80, 84. Mem. Fed. Bar Assn. (bd. dirs. 1986-91), Minn. Bar Assn., Minn. Trial Lawyers Assn. Roman Catholic. Avocations: fishing, hunting. Office Phone: 218-723-1990. Office Fax: 218-723-1931.

ARNOLD, JESSE CHARLES, retired statistician; b. Bowie, Tex., Sept. 28, 1937; s. Jesse Connally and Lillie Christine Arnold; m. Peggy Lou Peveto; children: Christa Louise, Jesse Charles Arnold, Jr. BS, Southeastern State U., 1960; MS, Fla. State U., 1961, PhD, 1967. Statistician Communicable Disease Ctr., Atlanta, 1961—63; prof. stats. Va. Tech U., Blacksburg, Va., 1968—2002, head Dept. Stats., 1973—82, ret., 2002. Contbr. articles to profl. jours. Sr. asst. health svc. officer USPHS, 1961—63. Fellow, NSF, 1963—67. Fellow: Internat. Statis. Inst., Am. Statis. Assn. (chmn. stat. edn. sect. 1975—76); mem.: Biometric Soc. (pres. 1976—77). Methodist. Achievements include research in sampling, quality control, nutrition. Avocations: tennis, woodwork, writing, consulting. Home: 2011 Northside Drive Blacksburg VA 24060 Office: Virginia Tech University-Retired Hutcheson Hall Blacksburg VA 24061 Personal E-mail: jca@vt.edu.

ARNOLD, JOHN DAVID, management counselor; b. Boston, May 14, 1933; s. I. I. and Edith (Gordon) A.; children by previous marriage: Derek, Keith, Craig; m. Diane Summers, Sept. 1994. BA in Social Rels. cum laude, Harvard U., 1955. Prodn. supr., dealer svc. mgr. Arnold Stretch Mates Corp., Boston, 1957-59; asst. dir. manpower and orgn. devel. Polaroid Corp., Waltham, Mass., 1959-63; dir. internat. ops. Kepner-Tregoe & Assocs., Princeton, NJ, 1963-68; pres. John Arnold ExecuTrak Sys. Inc. and Corp. Breakthroughs! Inc., Boston, 1968—. Merger integration catalyst, conflict resolution/prevention counselor, conf. leader numerous firms; spkr. in field; bd. dirs. World Music, Orange County Philharm. Soc. Author: Make Up Your Mind, 1978, The Art of Decision Making, 1978, Shooting the Executive Rapids, 1981, How To Make the Right Decisions, 1982, Trading Up-A Career Guide: How To Get Ahead without Getting Out, 1984, How To Protect Yourself Against a Takeover, 1986, The Complete Problem Solver! A Total System of Competitive Decision Making, 1992, When the Sparks Fly: Resolving Conflict in Your Organization, 1993; contbr. articles to popular mags. Bd. dirs., v.p. programming, exec. com. Orange County Philharm. Soc., 2001-04. 1st lt. U.S. Army, 1955-57. Mem.: Orange County Philharm. Soc. (bd. dirs.). Office: John Arnold ExecuTrak Sys and Corp Breakthroughs! Inc 32031 Point Pl Laguna Beach CA 92651-6862 Office Phone: 949-499-5400. Office Fax: 949-499-7608. Personal E-mail: chimo7@cox.net.

ARNOLD, JOHN FOX, lawyer; b. St. Louis, Sept. 17, 1937; s. John Anderson and Mildred Chapin (Fox) Arnold; m. Martha Ann Freeman, June 29, 1963 (div. Oct. 1993); children: Lisa A. Galena, Laura Wray, Lynne A. Binder, Lesli Johnston; m. Ann Ruwitch, Mar. 3, 2003. AB, U. Mo., 1959, LLB, 1961. Bar: Mo. 1961, U.S. Dist. Ct. (ea. dist.) Mo. 1961, U.S. Ct. Appeals (8th cir.) 1961, U.S. Supreme Ct. 1971. Ptnr. Green, Hennings, Henry & Arnold, St. Louis, 1963-70; mem. Lashly & Baer, P.C., St. Louis, 1970—, chmn., 1987—. Active St. Louis County Charter Revision Com., 1968, Mo. State Governance Rev. Com., 2005; chmn. St. Louis County Bd. Election Commrs., 1981—86; chmn. bd. dirs. Downtown St. Louis Inc., 1996—98, Downtown St. Louis Partnership, Inc., 1997—99; chmn. bd. overseers Lindenwood U., 1992—93, bd. dirs., 1993—95. Lt. USAR, 1961—63. Named to Best Lawyers in Am.; recipient citation of merit U. Mo. Law Sch., Columbia, 1984. Fellow Am. Bar Found.; mem. ABA (mem. house of dels. 1986-90), Bar Assn. Met. St. Louis (pres. 1975-76), Mo. Bar (pres. 1984-85), Nat. Conf. Commrs. on Uniform State Laws (life, drafting com. Securities Act, Partnership Act, article 2 sales, 2A leases and 8 investment securities of Uniform Comml. Code), Am. Law Inst. (life). Republican. Office: Lashly & Baer 714 Locust St Saint Louis MO 63101-1699 Office Phone: 314-621-2939. Business E-Mail: jfarnold@lashlybaer.com.

ARNOLD, LEE, library director, archivist; b. Waukegan, Ill., Oct. 18, 1959; s. Louis Douglas and Verona Christina (Lemke) A. BA cum laude, Edgewood Coll., Madison, Wis., 1982; M of Libr. and Info. Sci., U. Wis., Milw., 1987; M of Liberal Arts, Temple U., 2000. Sales support mgr. Marshall Field and Co., Milw., Wis., 1982-88; asst. univ. libr. for adminstrv. svcs. Princeton (N.J.) U., 1988-92; tchr. English., Berlitz Schs. Lang., Princeton, 1990-92; dir. of libr. Hist. Soc. of Pa., Phila., 1992—. Contbr. articles to profl. jours.; numerous book reviews and presentations in field. Mem. Delta Epsilon Sigma. Democrat. Roman Catholic. Avocations: reading, travel, outdoors. Office: Hist Soc PA 1300 Locust St Philadelphia PA 19107-5661 Office Phone: 215-732-6200 ext 237.

ARNOLD, MARGARET MORELOCK, music educator, soprano; b. Craig AFB, Ala., May 12, 1959; d. William Daniel Morelock and Margaret Haynie Morelock Stapleton; m. Barry Raynor Arnold, Aug. 15, 1984. B of Music Edn., U. Montevallo, 1981; MEd in Music, U. South Ala., 1996. Cert. tchr. Fla., Ala. Tchr. music Staley Mid. Sch., Americus, Ga., 1981-82, Eastview Elem. Sch., Americus, Ga., 1982-84; tchr. music/mass prep. St. Thomas More Schs., Pensacola, Fla., 1984-85; tchr. music W.H. Rhodes Elem., Milton, Fla., 1985—; realtor Century 21, Richardson, Fla. Pvt. voice instr., Americus, 1981-84, Milton, 1989—; guest condr. Santa Rosa All-County Chorus, Milton, 1989, 95, Santa Rosa Celebrates the Arts, 1986-2003 Asst. dir.: arts festivals, 1993—; singer (soprano, soloist): Gulf Coast Chorale, Singfest, Inc., The Choral Soc. Pensacola, Change of Command, 2003. Dir. elem. chorus performing for Santa Rosa Convalescent Ctr., Milton, 1985—, Whiting Field, 2003, Live at the Capital, Tallahassee, 1986, Santa Rosa Celebrates the Arts, 1986-, Ptnrs. in Edn.-K-Mart and City of Milton and WEAR-TV, 1990—. Computer Software grant Santa Rosa Ednl. Found., 1994; recipient Young Artist Competition S.E. Regional award Nat. Assn. Tchrs. Singing, S.E. region, 1993; winner State of Ala. Young Artist competition, 1993; named Tchr. of Yr., W.H. Rhodes Elem., 2002 Mem. NEA, Music Tchrs. Nat. Assn., Nat. Assn. Realtors, Fla. Assn. Realtors, Santa Rosa Profl. Educators, Music Educators Nat. Conf., Pensacola (Fla.) Music Tchrs. Assn., Delta Kappa Gamma (music chair 1988-94), Kappa Delta Pi, Phi Kappa Phi. Presbyterian. Avocations: walking, gardening, volunteer for nursing home. Home: 5820 Kirkland Dr Milton FL 32570-8251 Office: WH Rhodes Elem 5563 Byrom St Milton FL 32570-3822 Business E-Mail: arnoldm@santarosa.k12.fl.us.

ARNOLD, MORRIS SHEPPARD, federal judge; b. Texarkana, Tex., Oct. 8, 1941; BSEE, U. Ark., 1965, LLB, 1968; LLM, Harvard U., 1969, SJD, 1971; MA (hon.), U. Pa., 1977, JD (hon.), 1986; LLD (hon.), U. Ark., Little Rock, 1968, U. Pa., 1985. Tchg. fellow law Harvard U., 1969-70; from asst. prof. to prof. Ind. U. Law Sch., 1971-76, prof., 1976-77, dean, 1985; prof. law, history U. Pa., 1977-81; Ben J. Altheimer disting. prof. law U. Ark., Little Rock, 1981-84; judge U.S. dist. Ct. (we. dist.) Ark., Ft. Smith, 1985-92, U.S. Cir. Ct. (8th cir.), 1992—. Vis.fellow commoner Trinity Coll., Cambridge U., 1978; v.p., dir. office of the pres. U. Pa., 1980—81; vis. prof. Stanford (Calif.) U. Law Sch., 1985. Author: Old Tenures and Natura Brevium, 1974, Yearbook 2 Richard II, 1378-79, 1975, On the Laws and Customs of England, 1980, Unequal Laws Unto a Savage Race, 1985, Select Cases of Trespass from the King's Courts, 1307-1399, 2 vols., 1985, 1987, Arkansas Colonials, 1986, Colonial Arkansas 1686-1804: A Social and Cultural History, 1991, The Rumble of a Distant Drum: Quapaws and Old World Newcomers, 1673-1804, 2000, Arkansas: A Narrative History, 2002. Chmn., Rep. party State of Ark., 1983; gen. counsel, Rep. party Ark., 1982, chmn., 1983; bd. dirs. Nature Conservancy of Ark., 1982—87, Ark. Arts Ctr., 1981—84. Decorated chevalier Ordre Palmes Acad., France; recipient Porter Literary prize, 2001, Worthen Literary prize, 2001, Ragsdale prize, 2002; Frank Knox fellow, Harvard U./U. London, 1970—71, Mus. Sci. Natural History fellow, 1986. Fellow: Am. Soc. Legal History (hon.; pres. 1981—85), Country Club of Little Rock; mem.: Am. Antiquarian Soc., Grolier Club, Union League Club of Phila., Athenaeum Club London. Office: US Cir Judge 600 W Capital Ave Rm 208 Little Rock AR 72203-2060*

ARNOLD, P. A., special education educator; b. Toledo; d. Mattie Spear; m. Earl E. Arnold. BA, BS, David Lipscomb Coll., 1960; MA, Wayne State U., 1962; MS, Nova U., 1986. Cert. spl. edn., psychology, speech, mental retardation, emotional disturbance, Bible, Fla. Tchr. dactylogy, interpreter for deaf, 1960—; tchr. Hobbs (N.Mex.) Mcpl. Schs., 1981-82; tchr. spl. edn. City Systems, Rockford and Warren, Mich., 1960-67; dir. Four-County Ctr. Handicapped, Ark., 1977-81. Dir. model project ACTION; Project TREE Tech. Resources in Exceptional Edn.; conf. presenter in fields. Author: Instructor, Light for Deaf, 1992, Ol' Time Preacher Man, 1995, Little Red Schoolhouse, 1998, Trapezoid of Children, 1999. Bd. dirs., deaf advisor Hearing Soc. Volusia County; mem. project TREE-Tech. Resources in Exceptional Edn.-Tech. Exceptional Edn.-SY 2000, Dept. Edn., Fla. State U. Ctr. Ednl. Tech. Grantee Pub. Welfare, Nat. Gardening Assn., FUTURES, Newspapers in Edn. Mem. NEA, ARC, ASCD, Volusia Ednl. Assn., Fla. Edn. Assn., Coun. for Exceptional Children, Am. Assn. on Mental Deficiency, Nat. Assn. Deaf.

ARNOLD, PAUL T., biologist, educator; s. George H. Arnold and Lillian B. Hitzeman; m. Louise M. Davidson, Oct. 25, 1986; children: Allison G., Nathaniel G. AA in Biotech., Huntington Coll., Ind., 1982; BS in Sci. of Biology, Huntington Coll., 1982; PhD in Botany, Miami U., Oxford, Ohio, 1987. Prof. of biol. sci. Young Harris Coll., Young Harris, Ga., 1987—. Co-founder & co-dir. Young Harris Coll./U. of Ga. Beekeeping Inst., Young Harris, Ga., 1991—. Contbr. articles to profl. jours. Bd. dirs. Towns-Union Fed. Educators Credit Union, Young Harris, Ga., 1991—. Recipient Outstanding Faculty award, Young Harris Alumni Found., Inc., 2003; grantee Earthwatch scholar, Raymond S. Cash Found., 2001. Mem.: Ga. Acad. of Sci., Assn. of Southeastern Biologists, Am. Inst. of Biol. Sci. Independent. Methodist. Avocations: hockey, choral singing, drawing, instrumentalist, songwriting, sailing. Office: Young Harris College 1 College St PO Box 68 Young Harris GA 30582 Office Phone: 706-379-3111 5131.

ARNOLD, PERI ETHAN, political scientist; b. Chgo., Sept. 21, 1942; s. Joseph Evon and Eve (Jacobs) A.; m. Beverly Ann Kessler, Aug. 22, 1965; children: Emma, Rachel. BA, Roosevelt U., Chgo., 1964; MA, U. Chgo., 1967, PhD, 1972. Lectr. Roosevelt U., Chgo., 1966-68; instr. polit. sci. Western Mich. U., Kalamazoo, 1970-71; asst. prof. polit. sci. U. Notre Dame, Ind., 1971-76, assoc. prof. govt., 1976-86, prof. of govt. and internat. studies, 1986; chair dept. govt., 1986-92. Compton vis. prof. of world politics Miller Ctr., U. Va., 1993-94; dir. Hesburgh Program in Pub. Svc., 1995-2001; dir. Notre Dame Semester in Washington, 1997-2001. Author: Making the Managerial Presidency, 1986 (Louis Brownlow Book award 1987), 2nd rev. ed., 1998; mem. editl. bd. Am. Jour. Polit. Sci., 1991-94, Polity, 1995—2004, Presdl. Studies Quar., 1997—; co-editor Jour. of Policy History, 1987-88; mem. editl. adv. bd. Hughes Leadership Series, Tex. A&M U. Press, 1999—; contbr. articles to profl. jours. and edited vols. Bd. dirs. South Bend Hebrew Day Sch., Mishawaka, Ind., 1985—88; chair Cmty. Rels. Coun. of Jewish Fedn. of St. Joseph Valley, South Bend, Ind., 1990—94; mem. acquisitions com. Snite Mus. Art, Notre Dame, Ind., 1994—99; trustee Congregation Beth El, South Bend, 1994—2000, sec., exec. com., 2000—02; bd. dirs. Jewish Fedn. of St. Joseph Valley, 1999—2002, v.p., 2001—03. Recipient Spl. Presdl. award U. Notre Dame, 1993, Marshall Dimock award Am. Soc. Pub. Adminstrn., 1996; grantee Am. Coun. Learned Socs., 1974; rsch. grantee Herbert Hoover Libr. Assn., 1993-94; Ford Found. fellow, 1978-81. Mem. Am. Polit. Sci. Assn. (program chmn., exec. com. presidency sect.), Midwest Polit. Sci. Assn., The Cliff Dwellers Club (Chgo.). Democrat. Jewish. Avocations: literature, music, drama. Home: 1419 E Colfax Ave South Bend IN 46617-3307 Office: U Notre Dame Dept Polit Sci Notre Dame IN 46556 Business E-Mail: peri.e.arnold.1@nd.edu.

ARNOLD, ROBERT MORRIS, banker; b. Seattle, June 6, 1928; s. Lawrence Moss and Grace Elizabeth (Heffernan) A.; children: Grace Allen Arnold, Lauren McLellan Gorter. BA in Fin. and Bus. Adminstrn., Yale U., 1951; grad., Pacific Coast Sch. Banking, 1963. With Seattle-1st Nat. Bank, 1951, 1955—, v.p., 1965-73, mgr. nat. accounts dept., 1969-73, sr. v.p., mgr. corp. bus. devel., 1973-99, also bd. dirs. Bd. dirs. Seafirst Corp. Bank of Am. Bd. dirs. Centrum Found., Fred C. Hutchinson Cancer Rsch.; trustee Poncho; bd. dirs., exec. com., fin. com. Seattle Art Mus., also mem., joint founder its Contemporary Art Coun. Officer USNR, 1951-55. Mem. Am. Inst. Banking, Mcpl. League Seattle, Yale Assn. Western Wash., Newcomen Soc. (treas. Pacific N.W. com.), Seattle Golf Club, Seattle Tennis Club, Seattle Yacht Club, University Club (Seattle), Bohemian Club (San Francisco), Thunderbird Golf Club (Palm Springs, Calif.), O'Donnell Golf Club (Palm Springs), Mission Hills Country Club (Palm Springs). Home: 1535 Parkside Dr E Seattle WA 98112-3719 Office: 1001 4th Ave Ste 4710 Seattle WA 98154-1198 also: 50 Hilton Head Dr Rancho Mirage CA 92270-1607

ARNOLD, ROLAND R., dental educator, researcher; b. Denver, Dec. 18, 1946; BS, La. State U., 1972, PhD in Microbiology, 1975. Assoc. dean dental rsch. Emory U., 1988-91; mem. study sect. NIH, 1983-91; prof. periodontics and diagnostic scis. U. NC, Chapel Hill, 1991—, dir. Dental Rsch. Ctr., 1991-96. Mem. Am. Assn. Immunologists, Am. Assn. Dental Rsch., Am. Soc. for Microbiologists, Omicron Kappa Upsilon. Office: Univ NC Dental Rsch Ctr PO Box 7455 Chapel Hill NC 27599-0001 Address: Sch of Dentistry U NC at Chapel Hill Manning Dr and Columbia St CB #7450 Chapel Hill NC 27599-7450

ARNOLD, RONALD HENRI, nonprofit organization executive, consultant; b. Houston, Aug. 8, 1937; s. John Andrew and Carrie Virginia (Henri) A.; m. Phoebe Anne Trogdon, Oct. 12, 1963 (dec. Feb. 1974); 1 child, Andrea; m. Janet Ann Parkhurst, Aug. 8, 1974; stepchildren: Andrea Wright, Rosalyn Wright. Tech. publ. Boeing Co., Seattle, 1961-71; cons. Northwoods Studio, Bellevue, Wash., 1971—; exec. v.p. Ctr. for Def. of Free Enterprise, Bellevue, 1984—. Advisor Nat. Fed. Lands Conf., 1988-92. Author: James Watt and the Environment, 1981, Ecology Wars, 1987, The Grand Prairie Years, 1987; author: (with Alan Gottlieb) Trashing the Economy, 1993; author: Politically Correct Environment, 1996, Ecoterror, 1997, Battered Communities, 1998, Undue Influence, Power to Hurt, 2000, Trust Us, 2002; editor: Stealing theNational Parks, 1987; contbg. editor: Logging Mgmt. mag., 1978—81, We. Conservation Jour., 1974—81. Recipient Editorial Achievement award Am. Bus. Press, 1981. Mem. AFTRA, Forest History Soc. Republican. Avocation: music. Home: 12605 NE 2nd St Bellevue WA 98005-3206 Office Phone: 425-455-5038. E-mail: rarnold@cdfe.org, rarnold@eskimo.com.

ARNOLD, RUTH SOUTHGATE, librarian; b. Cin., Oct. 2, 1950; d. Roger Frederick Arnold and Harriet Hendershot Wolf Arnold; m. Louis Dolive; children: Caroline Elizabeth Dolive, William Arnold Dolive. BA, Eckerd Coll., 1972; MSLS, Simmons Coll., 1977. Cert. libr. Va. Info. specialist Warner-Eddison Assocs., Inc., Cambridge, Mass., 1977—79; asst. dir. Augusta County Libr., Fishersville, Va., 1979—81; tech. svcs. libr. Staunton (Va.) Pub. Libr., 1987—91, dir., 1991—. Mem. ednl. com. Woodrow Wilson Birthplace, Staunton, 1998—2002; v.p. Staunton (Va.) Downtown Devel. Assn., 2003—04, bd. mem., 2001—04. Named Woman of the Yr., Staunton Bus. & Profl. Women's Orgn., 1997; fellow Paul Harris, Rotary, 1995. Mem.: ALA, Va. Pub. Libr. Dirs. Assn. (sec., regional rep. 1997—2002), Va. Libr. Assn. (2d v.p. 2000—01), Staunton Rotary Club (pres. 1998—99). Presbyterian. Avocations: choral singing, contra dancing. Office: Staunton Pub Libr 1 Churchville Ave Staunton VA 24401 Office Phone: (540) 332-3902. Office Fax: (540) 332-3906. Business E-Mail: arnoldrs@ci.staunton.va.us.

ARNOLD, STANLEY NORMAN, management consultant, educator; b. Cleve., May 26, 1915; s. Morris L. and Mildred (Stearn) A.; m. Barbara Anne Laing, Aug. 31, 1946; 1 child, Jennifer Laing BS in Econs., U. Pa., 1937. Co-founder, exec. v.p. Pick-N-Pay Supermarkets, Cleve., 1937-51; exec. v.p., dir. Cottage Creamery Co., Cleve., 1937-51; dir. sales promotion div. Young & Rubicam, N.Y.C., 1952-58; founder, pres. Stanley Arnold & Assocs., Inc., N.Y.C., 1958—. Cons. Ford Motor Co., United Airlines, Gen. Electric, Nat. Cash Register, IBM, Philip Morris, Am. Express, Bank of America, DuPont, Goodyear, Quaker Oats, Readers Digest, Continental Can, Hunt Foods, Moet-Hennessy, Seagram, Pan Am, Chrysler Corp., Pillsbury, Coca Cola, Gen. Mills, Lever Bros., Exxon, Arco, Hallmark, others; mem. adv. bd. Bank of Palm Springs div. Bank of Calif. subs. Mitsubishi Corp., 1989—; vis. exec. prof. Freeman Sch. Bus., Tulane U., 1998—. Author: Tale of the Blue Horse, 1968; Magic Power of Putting Yourself Over with People, 1961; I Ran Against Jimmy Carter, 1977. Syndicated daily columnist, 1943-48. Architect of plan to install new office of v.p. in White House. Contbr. articles to profl. jours. Pres. Ind. Sch. Fund of N.Y.C., 1960-66; mem. fund raising com. U.S. Olympic Team, 1984. Founding mem. Nat. Businessmen for Humphrey, 1968, Nat. Citizens for Humphrey, 1968; candidate for Dem. nomination for v.p. U.S., 1972; chmn. White House Libr. Fund Raising Com., 1961-63; corp. sponsor for The Rose as Nat. Flower, 1983-86; nat. chmn. Golf's Tribute to Ike, 1980; mem. Clinton adv. com., 1991-92; mem. Bush For Pres. Com., 2000, 04; mem. Rep. Nat. Com., 2000—. Recipient Sales Exec. award Sales Exec. Club N.Y., 1965; Wisdom award of Honor Wisdom Soc., 1979 Mem.: Outrigger Canoe Club, La Quinta Fishing Club, Desert Riders Club, Seven Lakes Country Club, Les Amis D'Escoffier, Doubles Dutch Club (N.Y.C.). Home: 162 Desert Lakes Dr Palm Springs CA 92264-5521 also: 2895 Kalakaua Ave Honolulu HI 96815-4003 also: 375 Park Ave New York NY 10152-0002 Office: 162 Desert Lakes Dr Palm Springs CA 92264-5521

ARNOLD, SUE, music educator; b. Raleigh, N.C., Apr. 20, 1946; d. Johnsey P. and Virginia Dare Arnold. B in music, Campbell U., 1969; M in music, U. Ill., 1971. Assoc. prof. Tex. Tech. U., 1971—; music dir. Christ the King Cathedral, Lubbock, Tex., 1981—; voice faculty Am. Inst. of Musical Studies, Graz, Austria, 1997. Dir. of evening programs Camp Seafarer Y.W.C.A., 1969, 72, 73, 74; mem. cast and choir Lost Colony Outdoor Drama, Manteo, NC, 1964—67. Mem.: Nat. Assn. of Tchrs. of Singing, Pi Kappa Lambda Hon. Music Soc. Democrat. Catholic. Avocation: golf. Home: 4314 45th St Lubbock TX 79413

ARNOLD, SUSAN E., consumer products company executive; b. Pitts. BA, U. Pa., 1976; MBA, U. Pitts., 1980. Joined Procter and Gamble, Cin., 1980, dir. cosmetics and fragrances, v.p. P&G Fabric Care, v.p. global personal beauty care and global feminine care, 1999—2000, pres. global personal beauty care and global feminine care, 2000—02, pres. personal beauty and feminine care, 2002—, also bd. dirs. Bd. mem. Reflect.com, Cin. Zoo, Goodyear Tire & Rubber Co. Named Top Marketer and One of the 21 to Watch in the 21st Century, Advt. Age, Career Woman of Achievement, YWCA, 2000; named one of 50 Most Powerful Women in Bus., Fortune mag., 2002, most powerful women, Forbes mag., 2005; recipient Best Boss award, Cosmetic Exec. Women, 2003. Office: Procter & Gamble Plaza Cincinnati OH 45202

ARNOLD, THOMAS IVAN, JR., former state legislator; b. Paterson, N.J. s. Thomas Ivan and Marjorie Lewis (Eccles) A.; m. Barbara Jane Phinney, July 25, 1953 (dec. June 1985); children: Thomas I., Barbara J., Edward H., Patricia J., Peter S., Dennis L., Nancy L., Richard B., Susan D., Charles P. ME, Stevens Inst. Tech., Hoboken, N.J., 1950, MS, 1954; PhD, U. Wexford, 1986. Registered profl engr., N.H. Asst. to quality mgr. Curtiss-Wright Corp., Wood Ridge, NJ, 1950-58; mgr. corp. quality control ops. Sanders Assocs., Inc., Nashua, NH, 1958-67; mgr. quality assurance RCA Corp., Burlington, Mass., 1967-72; mgr. product assurance and quality control Compugraphic Corp., Wilmington, Mass., 1972-81; mgr. quality assurance GE, Burlington, 1981-91; mem. N.H. Gen. Ct., 1992—2004, vice chair com. on election laws, 1997-98, mem. com. on sci. tech. and energy, 1999—2004, mem. com. on children and family law, 1999—2004. Moderator Sch. Dist., Brookline, 1960—2004, Town of Brookline, 1976—2004, selectman, 1968-69; chmn. Zoning Bd. Adjustment, Brookline, 1970-82; chmn. Rep. town com.; mem. N.H. State Rep. Com., 1999—2004; mem. EMT Brookline Vol. Ambulance, 1976-86; mem. N.H. Indsl. Heritage Commn., 1995-96; mem. Commn. to Study Child Support and Related Child Custody Issues, 2003-04. With USAAF, 1946-47. Mem.: NRA, Am. Soc. for Quality (sect. chmn. 1964), GO N.H., Mensa, Order of Daedalians. Republican. Episcopalian. Avocations: fixing things, wood working. Home: 10 Milford St Brookline NH 03033-2446 E-mail: TIArnold@yahoo.com.

ARNOLD, TOM, actor, comedian, producer; b. Ottumwa, Iowa, Mar. 6, 1959; s. Jack and Ruth (stepmother) A.; m. Roseanne, Jan. 1990 (div. 1994); m. Julie Champnella, 1995 (div. 1999); m. Shelby Roos, 2002. Actor, co-exec. prodr. The Jackie Thomas Show, 1992-93, HBO Tom Arnold the Naked Truth I, II, III; dir. HBO's Roseanne Live from Minn.; exec. prodr. (TV series) Tom, 1994; actor, exec.prodr. (TV series) The Tom Show, 1997-89, Roseanne, 1988-97; actor (TV films) Backfield in Motion, 1991, Body Bags, 1993, (voice) Hercules, 1998, Jackie's Back!, 1999, Arnold Schwarzenegger: Hollywood Hero, 1999, Bar Hopping, 2000, Romantic Comedy 101, 2001, (voice) Dennis the Menace in Cruise Control, 2002; (films) Hero, 1992, Undercover Blues, 1993, True Lies, 1994, Nine Months, 1995, Big Bully, 1995, The Stupids, 1996, Carpool, 1996, (also co-prodr.) McHale's Navy, 1997, Touch, 1997, Austin Powers: International Man of Mystery, 1997, Hacks, 1997, (voice) Buster and Chauncey's Silent Night, 1998, Golf Punks, 1998, Blue Ridge Fall, 1999, Animal Factory, 2000, We Married Margo, 2000, Civility, 2000, Just Sue Me, 2000, Exit Wounds, 2001, Lloyd, 2001, Fever Pitch, 2001, Ablaze, 2001, Hansel & Gretel, 2002, Children on Their Birthdays, 2002, Cradle 2 the Grave, 2003, After School Special, 2003, (voice) Goose!, 2004, Soul Plane, 2004, Happy Endings, 2005, others. Office: William Morris Agency care Michael Gruber 151 S El Camino Dr Beverly Hills CA 90212-2775*

ARNOLD, WILLIAM EDWIN, health advocate, consultant; b. Charleston, SC, Aug. 13, 1938; s. Edwin Gustaf and Sara Louise (Hitchcock) A. BA, Yale U., 1960. Pres. Dixon & Rippel, Inc., Saugerties, NY, 1965-70; v.p. Taj Enterprises Ltd., 1965-67, Bellern Rsch. Corp.; pres. Dixon & Rippel divsn., Saugerties, 1970-75; v.p. H & G Industries, Inc.; pres. World Brushworks, Inc., 1982-84; v.p. CFO Optimax III, Inc., NYC, 1983-84; mng. dir. Brush Trading, Ltd., 1983-87; pres. Chestnut Holdings Ltd., 1985-91; part-time mng. dir. Cassi Properties, 1984—; pres. Computerworx, Inc., Washington, 1999—. Pres. Swan Holding Ltd., 1985-88. Bd. dirs. ARCS, 1991-92; chair Dutchess County AIDS Consortium, 1989-95; chmn. Dutchess County HIV Health Svcs. Planning Coun., 1995-96; bd. dirs. ARCS Cmty. Educator, 1989-91; pres. Hudson AIDS Cmty. Progress, Inc., 1992-94; exec. dir. Title II Nat. AIDS Coalition, 1994-95; CEO Title II Cmty. AIDS Nat. Network, Washington, 1995—; chair ADAP Working Group, Washington, 1995—; sec.-treas. AIDS Empowerment and Treatment Internat., Washington, 2002—. 1st lt. U.S. Army, 1961-63. Mem.: Res. Officers Assn., Yale Club (Washington). Home: 1755 Seaton Pl NW Washington DC 20009-2625 Office: 1775 T St NW Washington DC 20009-7124 Office Phone: 202-588-1775. E-mail: weaids@aol.com.

ARNOLD, WILLIAM PARSONS, JR., retired internist; b. Waterbury, Conn., May 10, 1922; s. William Parsons and Dorothy Amanda (Granniss) A.; m. Mildred Opal Beleu, Oct. 27, 1948; children: Susan Emerson Arnold Brainerd, Jane Elizabeth Arnold Pittari. BS, Yale U., 1943; MD, Columbia U.,

1946. Diplomate Am. Bd. Med. Examiners. Intern St. Luke's Hosp., N.Y.C., 1946-47, resident in medicine, 1949-51, chief resident in medicine, 1951-52; pvt. practice Middlebury, Conn., 1952-89; ret., 1989. Attending physician medicine Waterbury (Conn.) Hosp., 1952-89; assoc. attending physician St. Mary's Hosp., Waterbury, 1952-89; dir. health Middlebury (Conn.) Dept. Health, 1954—; sch. physician Region 15 Elem. Schs., Middlebury, 1955-92; asst. med. examiner Conn. State M-E Office, Middlebury, 1956-84; surgeon Middlebury Vol. Fire Dept. and Middlebury Police Dept., 1964—. Capt. U.S. Army Med. Corps, 1947-49, ETO. Recipient John N. Lewis Founders award Waterbury Vis. Nurse Assn., 1988. Mem. AMA, ACP, Conn. State Med. Soc., New Haven County Med. Assn., Waterbury Med. Assn. Republican. Congregationalist. Avocations: western riding, rodeos. Home: 142 White Deer Rock Rd Middlebury CT 06762-1314

ARNOLD, WILLIAM THOMAS, software developer, chemist; b. N.Y.C., Oct. 6, 1948; s. Herbert S. and Miriam Arnold. BS in Chemistry, Carnegie-Mellon U., 1970; MS in Chemistry, Fla. State U., 1976; postgrad. in enology, U. Calif., Davis, 1977-78. Winemaker Smothers Winery, Santa Cruz, Calif., 1978-85; consulting enologist Stag's Leap Wine Cellars, Napa, Calif., 1985-87; winemaker, gen. mgr. Domaine Laurier Vineyard, Forestville, Calif., 1987-88; sr. chemist U.S. Treasury Dept., San Francisco, 1990-97; prin. William Arnold Consulting, Walnut Creek, Calif., 1997—. Lectr., U. Calif., Santa Cruz, 1998; instr., Fed. Law Enforcement Tng. Ctr., Glynco, Ga., 1992-93; extension instr. computer sci. U. Calif., Berkeley, 2000—. Author: (computer programs) Standard Curve Pro & Chemical Databases, 1997—, Technicell 80 Stock-Market Program, 1999; contbr. articles to profl. jours. Sgt., USAF, 1971-74, Washington. Recipient Gold medal for comml. cabernet sauvignon, Sonoma (Calif.) Harvest Fair, 1982, Gold medal for comml. gewurztraminer, L.A. County Fair, 1981. Mem. Assn. Ofcl. Analytical Chemists Internat. (pres. Pacific region 1997-98), Am. Soc. Enology and Viticulture (mem. tech. projects com. 1992-97). Office: W Arnold Consulting 1240 Walker Ave Apt 209 Walnut Creek CA 94596-4829

ARNOLD, WINNIE JO, retired mental health nurse; b. Cromwell, Okla., May 21, 1929; d. Robb Henry and Luella (Odom) Boatman; widowed; children: Linda, Cherie. BSEd, Okla. U., 1962; ADN, Amarillo Coll., 1974; BSN, St. Joseph's Coll., 1977. RN, Tex. Charge nurse Northwest Tex. Hosp., Amarillo; staff nurse, team leader High Plains Bapt. Hosp., Amarillo; adminstr. Healthcare Svcs., Amarillo; dir. nurses Tex. Dept. Corrections, Amarillo, 1989—97; ret., 1997. Vol. ARC. Recipient Vol. award ARC, 1989, Pilot Club, 1989. Mem. Am. Kidney Found., Women's Bus. Assn. (Bus. Woman of Yr. 1989). Home: 216 Ramada Trl Amarillo TX 79108-1128 E-mail: wjatexan@msn.com.

ARNOLD-OLSON, HELEN B., not-for-profit consultant; b. Cedar Rapids, Iowa, Sept. 22, 1948; d. Duane Arnold Sr. and Henrietta Dows; m. Edward R. Krieger Jr., May 23, 1970 (div. Aug. 1974); m. Reuben I. Olson, July 2, 1982; 1 child, Andrew R. Olson. B in Music cum laude, Cornell Coll., 1970. Office mgr. Irving R. Zimmerman Co., Chgo., 1973-75; loan officer comml. and residential Banco Mortgage Co., Chgo., 1975-77, 79-82; asst. v.p., mgr., mortgage lending Olympic Savings & Loan Assn., Berwyn, Ill., 1977-79; underwriter, cons. Fed. Housing Adminstrn., Chgo., 1976-83; co-owner, pres. and exec. chef Hawkeye Nut Co., Cedar Rapids, 1983-87; pres. Dows Farms, Inc., Cedar Rapids, 1987-96; dir. devel. YWCA of Cedar Rapids and Linn County, 1996—2000; pres. Green Light, LLC, Arnold-Olson Assocs., Hel's Kitchen, 2000—; nonprofit cons. Bd. dirs. The Dows Cos., Cedar Rapids, Cedar Rapids Airport Commn. Bd. dirs., co-chair capital campaign endorsement The History Ctr., Cedar Rapids, 1996—; v.p., bd. dirs. Friends of the Zoo, Cedar Rapids, 1997—; bd. dirs. Kingston Hill Home for Aged Women, Cedar Rapids, 1998—. Recipient Leadership for Five Seasons award Cedar Rapids Area C. of C., 1996. Mem. AAUW, Assn. Fund Raising Profls., Iowa Women's Found., Variety Club of Iowa (bd. dirs., past chair, Sunshine award 1999), Rotary. Presbyterian. Avocations: cooking, travel. Home and Office: Arnold-Olson Assocs 3840 Bever Ave SE Cedar Rapids IA 52403 E-mail: HBAO48@aol.com.

ARNOLD QUINN, HELEN RHODA, physicist; b. Melbourne, Victoria, Australia, May 19, 1943; came to U.S. 1961; d. Ted Adamson and Helen Ruth (Down) Arnold; m. Daniel James Quinn, Oct. 8, 1966; children: Elizabeth Helen, James Arnold. BS in Physics, Stanford U., 1963, MS in Physics, 1964, PhD in Physics, 1967; DSc (hon.), Notre Dame U., 2002, U. Melbourne, 2005. Rsch. assoc. Stanford Linear Accelerator Ctr., 1967—68, 1978—79, mem. permanent sci. staff, 1979—2003, edn. coord., 1988—93, asst. to dir. edn. and pub. outreach, 1998—2003, prof. physics, 2003—; hon. rsch. fellow Harvard U., 1971, rsch. fellow, 1971—72, asst. prof. physics, 1972—76, assoc. prof. physics, 1976—77. Guest scientist (non German postdoctoral rschr.) Deutsches Elektronen Sychrotron, Hamburg, 1968—70; vis. assoc. prof. Stanford U., 1976—78; vis. scientist Stanford Linear Accelerator Ctr., 1977—78. Contbr. articles to profl. jours. Pres. Contemporary Physics Edn. Project, Portola Valley, Calif., 1989-95; vol., chair Town of Portola Valley Trails Com., 1988-98; pres. Am. Phys. Soc., 2004. Decorated Hon. officer Order of Australia, 2005; recipient DIRAC medal Internat. Ctr. Theoretical Physics, Trieste, Italy, 2000; fellow Alfred Sloan Found., 1975-79. Fellow AAAS, Am. Phys. Soc. (pres. 2004); mem. Nat. Acad. Sci. Avocations: hiking, native plants. Business E-Mail: quinn@slac.stanford.edu.

ARNON, STEPHEN SOULÉ, physician, research scientist; b. Oakland, Calif., Oct. 14, 1946; s. Daniel I. and Lucile S. Arnon; m. Joyce M. Meissinger, Aug. 24, 1985; children: Eric, Christina. AB, Harvard U., 1968, MPH, 1972, MD, 1973. Lic. physician Calif. Resident physician U. Colo. Hosps., Denver, 1973—75; med. epidemiologist Ctrs. for Disease Control, Atlanta, 1975—76, Berkeley, Calif., 1976—77; founder, chief infant botulism treatment and prevention program Calif. Dept. Health Svcs., Berkeley and Richmond, 1977—. Contbr. articles and book chpts. to profl. publs. Bd. dirs. Orinda (Calif.) Pks. and Recreation Found., Orinda, 1992—. Lt. comdr. USPHS, 1975—77. Recipient Jens Aubrey Westengard and John Houghton Taylor scholarships, Harvard Med. Sch., 1968—73, Wiley medal, U.S. Pub. Health Svc., 1998, Tharapeutic Achievement award, Nat. Org. for Rare Disorders, 2004. Fellow: Am. Coll. Epidemiology, Infectious Disease Soc. Am. Achievements include creation and development of pub. svc. orphan drug Botulism Immune Globulin Intravenous (Human) BabyBIG (registered) for treatment of infant botulism; research in orphan drug development; medical and public health management of botulinum toxin if used as bioweapon. Office: Calif Dept Health Svcs 850 Marina Bay Pkwy Richmond CA 94804 Office Phone: 510-231-7600.

ARNOT, BOB (ROBERT BURNS ARNOT), physician, medical correspondent, writer; b. Boston; s. Robert E. and Mary A.; m. Courtney; children: Bobby, Hayden. B in Med. sci. and Islamic studies, Dartmouth Coll., 1972; MD, McGill Univ., Montreal, 1974. Founder Lake Placid Sports Med. Ctr., 1978; med. dir. Nat. Emergency Svc., 1980—84; med. correspondent CBS News; med. columnist Good Housekeeping, 1994—; spl. fgn. correspondent NBC News, 1996—2001, MSNBC, 2001—04. Physician, US Ski Team Olympics, 1977—80; physician XXIII Winter Olympics, Lake Placid, NY, 1980; bd. dir. US Ski Team, Save the Children, UN High Commn. for Refugees. Author: (cookbooks) Breast Cancer Prevention Diet, 1998, (self-help books) The Best Medicine: How to Choose the Top Doctors, the Top Hospitals, and the Top Treatments, 1992, Dr. Bob Arnot's Guide to Turning Back the Clock, 1995, Revolutionary Weight Control, 1997, Prostate Cancer Protection Plan, 2000, Biology of Success, 2001, Wear and Tear: Stop the Pain and Put the Spring Back in Your Body, 2003, Seven Steps to a Healthy Heart, 2005. Recipient Dupont award for report 48 Hours on Crack Street, award for team coverage of floods in Mozambique, Overseas Press Club. Fluent in Arabic; more than 6,000 hours as pilot.

ARNOTT, HOWARD JOSEPH, biology professor, dean; b. Los Angeles, Mar. 9, 1928; s. Andrew Hugh and Evelyn Leonore (Donnelly) A.; m. Wanda Jean Cross, Jan. 28, 1950; children: John Joseph, Catherine Jean Arnott-Thornton, Susan Leonore Arnott Garrett, Virginia Anne Arnott Scott. AB, U. So. Calif., 1952, MS, 1953; PhD, U. Calif., Berkeley, 1958. Asst. prof. biology Northwestern U., Evanston, Ill., 1958-64; assoc. prof. dept. botany U. Tex., Austin, 1965-68, prof., 1968-72, acting chmn. dept., 1970-71; prof., chmn. dept. biology U. So. Fla., Tampa, 1972-74; dean Coll. Sci. U. Tex., Arlington, 1974-90, prof. biology, 1974-91, Ashbel Smith prof. biology, 1991-96, dir. Ctr. for Electron Microscopy Coll. Sci., 1984—, Jenkins Garrett prof., 1996—. Vis. mem. dept. biology Tex. A&M U., 1971-75; cons. Ency. Brit. Films, NASA, Alcon Labs., Frito-Lay; bd. dirs. Ft. Worth Nature Ctr., 1985-91; chmn. 2nd Gordon Conf. Calcium Oxalate, 1989, main spkr. 4th Conf., 1993; vis. prof. Purdue U., 1990-91; Bessey lectr. Iowa State U., 1993. Advisory editor: Protoplasma; Contbr. articles, abstracts to sci. jours., chpts. to books. With USN, 1946-48. Recipient award for disting. and continued research U. Tex. at Arlington, 1984; postdoctoral fellow U. Tex., NIH, 1964-65; NSF grantee, 1963-65, NIH grantee, 1989. Mem. Am. Soc. Plant Physiology, Bot. Soc. Am., Mycol. Soc. Am., Microscopy Soc. Am., Tex. Soc. Microscopy (hon., pres. 1988-89), Sigma Xi (bd. dirs. S.W. region 1984-91), Phi Sigma. Business E-Mail: arnott@uta.edu.

ARNOTT, ROBERT DOUGLAS, investment company executive; b. Chgo., June 29, 1954; s. Robert James Arnott and Catherine (Bonnell) Cameron; children: Robert Lindsay, Sydney Allison, Richard James. BA, U. Calif., Santa Barbara, 1977. V.p. Boston Co., 1977—84; pres., chief exec. officer TSA Capital Mgmt., L.A., 1984—87; v.p., strategist Salomon Bros. Inc., N.Y.C., 1987—88; mng. ptnr. First Quadrant Corp., Morristown, N.J., Pasadena, Calif., and London, 1988—96, First Quadrant, LP, Pasadena, London, Boston, 1996—2002, chmn., 2002—04; chmn., CEO Rsch. Affiliates, LLC, 2002—. Mem. chmn.'s adv. coun. Chgo. Bd. Options Exch., 1989-94; bd. dirs. Internat. Faculty in Fin.; mem. product adv. bd. Chgo. Mercantile Exch., 1990-96; vis. prof. UCLA, 2001-03. Editor: Asset Allocation, 1988, Active Asset Allocation, 1992, Handbook of Equity Style Management, 1997, Fin. Analysts Jour., 2003—; mem. editorial bd. Jour. of Investing, 1990—, Jour. Portfolio Mgmt., 1984-2002, Jour. Wealth Mgmt., 1997—; contbr. articles to profl. jours. and chpts. to books. Mem. Inst. Internat. Rsch. (adv. bd. 1990—), Assn. for Investment Mgmt. and Rsch., Inst. Quantitative Rsch. in Fin., Toronto Stock and Futures Exch. (adv. coun. 1992—). Avocations: motorcycling, astrophotography, billiards, sommelier, travel. Office: 1st Quadrant LP 800 E Colorado Blvd Ste 900 Pasadena CA 91101-2141 Office Phone: 626-584-2101. E-mail: arnott@rallc.com.

ARNOULD, RICHARD JULIUS, economist, educator, consultant, dean; b. Rochelle, Ill., Nov. 18, 1941; s. Elliott and Blanch (Colwell) A.; m. Carol Foster, Aug. 27, 1960; children: Debra, Laura. BS, Iowa State U., 1963, MS, 1965, PhD, 1968. Instr. Iowa State U., Ames, 1963-65; asst. prof. econs. and bus. adminstrn. U. Ill., Champaign, 1967-72, assoc. prof., 1973-82, prof., 1982—2003, prof. emeritus, 2003—, dir. Coll. Rsch. Office, 1995-96, assoc. dean for acad. affairs, Coll. Commerce and Bus. Adminstrn., 1979-87, prof. econs., Coll. Medicine, 1984—, adj. prof. Inst. of Govt. and Pub. Affairs, 1987—, dir. Program in Health Econs., Mgmt. & Policy, 1989—, head dept. econs., 1996—2003; exec. dir. Am. Soc. Health Economists, 2003—. Acting dir. Exec. Devel. Ctr., part-time 1982, 84, mem. Med. Scholars Steering Com., active numerous other univ., coll. and dept. coms.; rsch. economist pricing and competition grp., USDA, 1965-67; vice chmn. Dept. Econs., U. Ill., 1970-73; vis. economist Econ. Policy Office, U.S. Justice Dept., 1973-74; regional economist U.S. Comptroller of Currency, 1976-79; vis. rsch. prof. Duke U., 1977-78; vis. rsch. scholar York (Eng.) U.; cons. Carle Found., chmn. bd., 1989-91; mem. Gov.'s Task Force on Health Care Reform, 1992-95; cons. Auditor Gen. State of Ill., GAO, Health Care Financing Adminstrn., Anti-trust div. U.S. Justice Dept., ABA, AMA, Prepaid Legal Svcs. Inst., others; bd. dirs. First Busey Trust & Investment Co.; expert witness numerous law firms; speaker profl. meetings. Author: Extra Territorial Application and Effects of Certain U.S. and Canadian Laws, 1978, (monograph) Blue Shield Fee Setting in the Physicians' Service Market: A Theoretical and Empirical Analysis, (pamphlets) Diversification and Profitability Among Large Food Processing Firms, USDA, 1970, (with R. Resek) A Comparative Cost Study of Staff Panel and Participating Attorney Panel Prepaid Legal Servcie Plans, ABA, 1982; editor spl. issue Quar. Rev. of Econs. and Bus., 1990, also book chpts. and revs.; co-editor: (with R. Rich and W. White) Competitive Approaches to Health Care Reform, 1993; contbr. numerous articles to profl. jours. Bd. dirs. City Bank Champaign, First Basey Trust and Investment Co.; trustee Carle Found., 1981-93, chmn. fin. com., 1982-86, chmn. bd., 1989-91; elder 1st Presbyn. Ch., Champaign; mem. Gov.'s Task Force on Health Care Reform; mem. U.S. Govt. Study of Econ. Underpinning of Vaccine Markets. Brookings Inst. Econ. Policy fellow, 1973; recipient Outstanding Service award, U.S. Justice Dept., 1974; grantee Internat. Bur. Edn., 1979, Carle Found., 1982-83, Grad. Research Bd., 1983-86; named Outstanding Tchr. U. Ill. various yrs. Mem. Am. Econ. Assn., So. Econ. Assn., Internat. Health Econs. Assn., Midwest Econ. Assn. Avocation: golf. Office: U Ill 1206 S 6th St Champaign IL 61820-6978 Business E-Mail: rarnould@uiuc.edu.

ARNOULT, J. TIM, bank executive; b. Beaumont, Tex. BA in Psychology, U. Tex., Austin, 1971, MBA, 1976. Pres., ctrl. region consumer and comml. banking group Bank of Am., 1990—2000, tech. & opers. exec., 2000—04, pres. global treasury svcs., 2004—. Past mem. Fin. Svcs. Roundtable; mem. BITS Adv. Coun., IBM, Info. Sys. Customer Adv. Coun. Chmn. Alexis de Tocqueville Soc. for the United Way of Ctrl. Carolinas. Recipient Outstanding Young Alumni award, U. Tex. Office: Bank of America Corp 100 N Tryon St Charlotte NC 28255

ARNOVE, ROBERT FREDERICK, education educator; b. Chgo. s. Isadore and Julie (Zeplowitz) A.; m. Toby Strout; 1 child, Anthony Keats BA, U. Mich., 1969; MA, Tufts U., 1961; PhD, Stanford U., 1969. Vol. tchr. Peace Corps, Venezuela, 1962-64; Ford Found. edn. advisor Bogota, Colombia, 1969-71; prof. comparative edn. Ind. U., Bloomington, 1969—, Ind. U.-Hangzhou, People's Rep. China, 1983; vis. prof. Stanford U., McGill U. Edn. cons. to Latin Am. ministries and agys.; dir. Overseas Study Program of Ind., Purdue, and Wis. univs. in Madrid, 1989—; USIA Exch. scholar, Ryazan, Russia, 1996, Yaounde, Cameroon, 1997, Salamanca, Spain, 2001; UNESCO-chair vis. scholar U. Palermo, Buenos Aires, 1997-2002; adv. prof. Hong Kong Inst. Edn. Author, editor, co-editor: Student Alienation, Educational Television, Education and American Culture Comparative Education, Philanthropy and Cultural Imperialism, Education and Revolution in Nicaragua, National Literacy Campaign: Historical and Comparative Perspectives, Emergent Issues in Education: Comparative Perspectives, Education as Contested Terrain: Nicaragua 1979-93, 1994, Comparative education: The Dialectic of the Global and the Local, 1999, 2003, Civil Society or Shadow State: State NGO Education Relations, 2004; prodr. (documentary) Alternative Public Schools, 1978, Asi Fue: Election Time Nicaragua, 1984; contbr. articles to profl. jours. Citizens Party candidate for U.S. Congress, 8th dist. Ind., 1982 Fulbright grantee, India, 1982; Fulbright lectr. Fed. U. Bahai, Brazil, 1995; Fulbright sr. scholar U. Iberoamericana, Dominican Republic, 2003. Mem. Comparative and Internat. Edn. Soc. (pres. 2001, hon. fellow), Latin Am. Studies Assn., Am. Ednl. Rsch. Assn. Phi Delta Kappa. Office: Ind U Sch Edn Bloomington IN 47405 Office Phone: 812-856-8374. Business E-Mail: arnove@indiana.edu.

ARNOVITZ, BENTON MAYER, editor; b. Butler, Pa., July 21, 1942; s. Paul and Miriam (Shapiro) A. AB, Cornell U., 1964; MA, NYU, 1969; grad., U.S. Army Command and Gen. Staff Coll., 1982; grad. Nat. Security Mgmt. Program, Nat. Def. U., 1986. Editor Macmillan Pub. Co., N.Y.C., 1966-73; sr. trade editor Chilton Book Co., Radnor, Pa., 1973-76; exec. editor Stein and Day Pubs., Briarcliff Manor, NY, 1976-85, v.p., 1984-85; ind. edit. svcs., 1985-89, 91-93; editl. dir. Scarborough House Pubs. divsn. BookCrafters, Peekskill, NY, 1989-91; dir. acad. pubs. U.S. Holocaust Meml. Mus., Washington, 1994—. Contbr. articles to scholarly jour. and newspapers. Trustee Field Libr. Inc., 1985-94, Westchester Libr. Sys., 1992-94; mem. Spirit of Raoul Wallenberg Humanitarian award selection com. Am. Swedish Hist. Mus. Capt. U.S. Army, 1964-66, 70; lt. col. USAR. Mem. Alpha Phi Delta. Home: 13439 Overbrook Ln Bowie MD 20715-1159 Office: 100 Raoul Wallenberg Pl SW Washington DC 20024-2126

ARNOWITT, RICHARD LEWIS, retired physics professor; b. N.Y.C., May 3, 1928; s. Leon and Belle (Feinberg) A.; m. Young In Rhee, Apr. 21, 1961; children: Michael Paul, Myron Philip. BS, MS, Rensselaer Poly. Inst., 1948; PhD, Harvard U., 1953. Rsch. assoc. Radiation Lab. U. Calif., Berkeley, 1952-54; mem. Inst. Advanced Study, Princeton, N.J., 1954-56; asst. prof. Syracuse (N.Y.) U., 1956-59, assoc. prof., 1959-62; prof. Northeastern U., Boston, 1962-86, Tex. A&M U., College Station, 1986-88, disting. prof. physics, 1988—2004, disting. prof. emeritus, 2004—, dir. Ctr. Theoretical Physics, 1986-95, head dept. physics, 1987-93; disting. prof. emeritus, 2004—. Contbr. over 200 articles to profl. jours. Fellow Guggenheim Found., 1975-76. Fellow Am. Phys. Soc. (Dannie N. Heineman prize 1994, Burgess chair high energy physics 1997—). Office: Texas A & M U Dept Physics College Station TX 77843-4242 Office Phone: 979-845-7741. Business E-Mail: arnowitt@physics.tamu.edu.

ARNSTEIN, WALTER LEONARD, retired historian; b. Stuttgart, Germany, May 14, 1930; arrived in U.S., 1939, naturalized, 1944; s. Richard and Charlotte (Heymann) Arnstein; m. Charlotte Culver Sutphen, June 8, 1952; children: Sylvia, Peter. BSS., CCNY, 1951; MA, Columbia U., 1954; PhD, Northwestern U., 1961; postgrad., U. London, Eng., 1956-57. Asst. prof. history Roosevelt U., Chgo., 1957-62, assoc. prof., 1962-66, prof., acting dean grad. divsn., 1966-67; prof. history U. Ill., Urbana, 1968-98, LAS Jubilee prof. history, 1989-98, prof. history and LAS Jubilee prof. history emeritus, 1998—, chmn. dept., 1974-78, assoc. Ctr. for Advanced Study, 1972-73. Vis. assoc. prof. history Northwestern U., 1963—64; vis. fellow Clare Hall, Cambridge U., 1982; hon. fellow U. Edinburgh, 1989. Author: The Bradlaugh Case: A Study in Late Victorian Opinion and Politics, 1965, 2d edit., 1984, Britain Yesterday and Today, 1966, 8th edit., 2001, Protestant Versus Catholic in Mid-Victorian England, 1982, (with William B. Willcox) The Age of Aristocracy, 3d edit., 1976, 8th edit., 2001, Queen Victoria, 2003; editor: The Past Speaks: Sources and Problems in British History Since 1688, 1981, 2d edit. 1993; editor: Recent Historians of Great Britain, 1990; bd. editors The Historian, 1976-2000, Am. Hist. Rev., 1982-85, Albion, 1988-93; mem. bd. advisers: Victorian Studies, 1966-75; contbr. articles profl. jours. Vice chmn. Ill. Humanities Coun., 1983-84. Served with AUS, 1951-53, Korea. Fulbright scholar, 1956-57; fellow Am. Coun. Learned Socs., 1967-68. Fellow Royal Hist. Soc.; mem. Am. Hist. Assn., Brit. Hist. Assn., N.Am. Conf. Brit. Studies (exec. com. 1971-76, v.p. 1993-95, pres. 1995-97), Midwest Conf. on Brit. Studies (pres. 1980-82), Midwest Victorian Studies Assn. (pres. 1977-80, annual Walter L. Arnstein Dissertation prize awarded in his name 1992—), Phi Beta Kappa, Phi Alpha Theta. Home: 804 W Green St Champaign IL 61820-5017 Office: U Ill Dept History 309 Gregory Hall 810 S Wright St Urbana IL 61801-3644 E-mail: warnstei@uiuc.edu.

ARNTSON, PETER ANDREW, lawyer; b. Washington, May 23, 1938; s. Paul Lee and Mary Ellen (Garrigan) A.; m. Colette Rousseau, July 11, 1962; 1 child, Eric Paul. BA, U. Va., 1960, JD, 1965; LLM in Taxation, Georgetown U., 1971; postgrad., U.S. Army War Coll., 1982. Bar: Va. 1965, U.S. Supreme Ct. 1973. Assoc., then ptnr. Phillips, Kendrick, Gearheart & Aylor, Arlington, Va., 1965-75; ptnr. McCandlish, Lilliard, Church & Best, Fairfax, Va., 1975-84, Miles & Stockbridge, Fairfax, 1984-95, McCandlish & Lillard, Fairfax, 1995—. Chmn. com. on taxation Va. State Bar, 1978; dep. commr. accts. County of Fairfax, 1994—. Chmn. bd. dirs. No. Va. Am. Heart Assn., 1978; bd. dirs. Benedictine Sch. Exceptional Children, Ridgely, Md., 1985—, Arlington Cmty. Found., 1992-96, No. Va. Cmty. Found., 1991—; mem. exec. coun. Nat. Capital Area coun. Boy Scouts Am., 1993—; founder, pres. Wakefield Ednl. Found., 1986—; trustee Claude Moore Charitable Found. 1st lt. U.S. Army, 1960-62, col. AUS, ret. Mem. ABA, Va. Bar Assn., Fairfax Bar Assn., Assn. U.S. Army, Rotary. Methodist. Home: 4047 27th Rd N Arlington VA 22207-5237 Office: McCandlish & Lillard 11350 Random Hills Rd Ste 500 Fairfax VA 22030-6044

ARO, EDWIN PACKARD, lawyer; b. Colorado Springs, Colo., July 20, 1964; s. Harold William and Margaret (Packard) A. BA, Denver U., 1986; JD magna cum laude, Boston U., 1989. Bar: Colo. 1989, U.S. Dist. Ct. Colo. 1990, U.S. Ct. Appeals (10th cir.) 1990. Law clk. Hon. Richard P. Matsch, U.S. Dist. Ct. for Colo., Denver, 1989-90; ptnr. Holme, Roberts & Owen LLP, Denver, 1990—. Hogan & Hartson LLP, Denver, dir. labor & employment practice group. Adj. prof. U. Denver Coll. of Law, 1994—; mem. Boston U. Law Rev., 1987-89. Mem. Boston U. Law Rev., 1987-89. Mem. ABA, Colo. Bar Assn., Denver Bar Assn., Faculty of Fed. Advocates. Office: Hogan & Hartson LLP One Tabor Ctr 1200 17th St Ste 1500 Denver CO 80202 Office Phone: 303-899-7389. Business E-Mail: eparo@hhlaw.com.

ARON, ALAN MILFORD, pediatric neurology educator; b. White Plains, N.Y., Oct. 15, 1933; s. Henri Jordan and Rosalind (Weinstein) A.; m. Sarah Deborah Bornstein, Dec. 29, 1963; children: Alexandra, Abigail, Adam. BS, Tufts U., 1954; MD, Columbia U., 1958. Diplomate Am. Bd. Pediatrics, Am. Bd. Psychiatry and Neurology with spl. competence in child neurology. Intern Grace New Haven Hosp. and Yale Med. Ctr., 1958-59; resident in pediatrics Babies Hosp. Columbia Presbyn. Med. Ctr., N.Y.C., 1959-61; Fellow Columbia Presbyn. Med. Ctr. and Neurologic Inst., N.Y.C., 1961—; pediatric neurologist Mt. Sinai Hosp., N.Y.C., 1961-64; dir. child neurology Mt. Sinai Sch. Medicine, N.Y.C., 1975—, prof. pediatrics and neurology, 1982—. Pres. N.Y. Pediatric Soc., N.Y.C., 1980-81. Contbr. articles to profl. jours. Recipient Lucy Moses award Clin. Research Neurologic Inst., N.Y.C., 1964. Mem. AMA, Am. Acad. Pediatrics, Am. Acad. Neurology, Child Neurology Soc., Tri-State Child Neurology Soc. (pres. 1990-91), Profs. Child Neurology, Phi Beta Kappa. Democrat. Jewish. Avocations: music, piano, opera, antiques, art. Office: Mt Sinai Sch Medicine 5 E 98th St New York NY 10029-6501 Office Phone: 212-831-4393.

ARONESENO, ELIZABETH M., special education educator; d. John A. Errington, Sr.; m. Gerald (Jerry) A. Aroneseno, Jr., June 23, 1984; children: Nicholas L., Dominic J. AA, Hilbert Coll., 1979; BA, Buffalo (N.Y.) State Coll., 1981, MA, 1984. Cert. tchr. nursery, K-6 N.Y., 1985, tchr. spl. edn. N.Y., 1985. Tchr. spl. edn. elem. sch. Hilary Pk. Acad. 27, Buffalo, 1981—84; tchr. spl. edn. Pinehurst Elem. Sch. Frontier Ctrl. Sch. Dist., Hamburg, NY, 1984—89, tchr. Blasdell Elem. Sch., 1989—94, tchr. Frontier H.S., 1994—. Chmn. Dept. Spl. Edn. Frontier Ctrl. Sch. Dist., 1998—. Assoc. leader Girl Scouts Am., Buffalo, 1981—2005. Mem.: Girl Scouts of Am. (assoc. leader 1981—2005, 25 Yr. Svc. Membership Recognition award 1990, 40 Yr. Svc. Membership Recognition award 2005), Make - A - Wish Found. (assoc.; participant in fund raising 2005), Phi Delta Kappa (membership com. 1992—2005, 5 Yr. Mem. award 1998, 10 Yr. Mem. award 2002). Avocations: quilting, skiing, reading, camping, travel. Home: 4362 Mc Kinley Pkwy Hamburg NY 14075 Office: Frontier Central School District 4432 Bay View Rd Hamburg NY 14075 Office Phone: 716-926-1720 2242. E-mail: baroneseno@frontier.wnyric.org.

ARONIN, LEWIS RICHARD, metallurgical engineer; b. Norwood, Mass., Aug. 4, 1919; s. Samuel and Celia (Acoff) A.; B.S., M.I.T., 1940; m. Natalie Eleanor Wolfson, June 19, 1947; children— Marlene Aronin Sigel, Terry Aronin Dubow. Asst. to research dir. Waltham Watch Co. (Mass.), 1940-48; staff mem. M.I.T. Metall. Project, Cambridge, 1949-54; mgr. research and devel. dept. Nuclear Metals, Inc., Concord, Mass., 1954-65; cons. Kennecott Copper Corp., Lexington, Mass., 1966-67; materials engr. Army Materials Tech. Lab., Watertown, Mass., 1967-90; pvt. cons. advanced materials devel., 1990—. Registered profl. engr., Mass. Mem. AIME, Am. Soc. Metals, AIAA, Soc. Advancement Materials and Process Engring. (treas. Boston chpt. 1976-89), Engring. Socs. New Eng. (dir. 1984-87), Sigma Xi. Lodges: Lions, Masons. Research and publs. on nuclear materials, radiation effects, beryllium, refractory materials, and advanced structural composites; patentee in field. Home and Office: 20 Ingleside Rd Lexington MA 02420-2522

ARONOFF, CRAIG ELLIS, business educator, consultant; b. Atlanta, May 18, 1951; s. Marvin Charles and Patricia (Sabin) Aronoff; m. Jane G. Miller; children: Lara Dorfman, Emily Rose, Alexander Samuel Miller. BS in Journalism, Northwestern U., 1971; MA, U. Pa., 1974; PhD, U. Tex., 1975. Asst. prof. mgmt. Ga. State U., Atlanta, 1975-79, assoc. prof., 1979-83; prof.

mgmt. Kennesaw State U., Marietta, Ga., 1983—2005, Dinos disting. chair pvt. enterprise, 1983—2005, chmn. dept. mgmt., 1984-86, eminent scholar, 1999—2005, prof. emeritus, 2005—. Founder Cox Family Enterprise Ctr., dir., 1987—2001; chmn. Cobb Transit Adv. Bd., Marietta, 1988—90; exec. dir. Bus. Owner Resources, Marietta, 1989—2000; CEO Family Bus. Comm., Inc., 1989—2002; co-founder, prin. Family Bus. Cons. Group, Inc., 1994—; bd. dirs. Whitacre Oil Co., Nioxin Rsch. Labs. Author, co-author, editor: other books, 1979—; co-editor: The Future of Private Enterprise, 3 vols., 1982—84; co-author: Family Business Leadership Series, 18 vols., 1992—, Public Relations: The Profession and the Practice, 4th edit., 1996; contbg. editor, columnist: Family Bus. Planning, Nation's Bus. mag., 1990—99; mem. editl. bd. Jour. Pvt. Enterprise Edn., 1986—, Family Bus. Rev., 1992—; exec. editor: Family Bus. Advisor, 1991—. Mem. Leadership Cobb, 1986—87; co-pres. West Side Elem. Sch. PTA, 1992—93; bd. dirs. Southeastern Legal Found., 1990—97; commr. Marietta Bd. Zoning and Planning, 1987—90; bd. dirs. Temple Kol Emeth, Marietta, 1989—92. Named Craig E. Aronoff Professorship in family bus. in his honor, Kennesaw State U., 2004; recipient Leavey award, Freedom Found., 1987, Outstanding Educator award, Nat. Fedn. Ind. Bus. Found., 1989, Disting. Leadership award, Leadership Cobb, 1988. Mem.: Ga. Coun. Econ. Edn. (trustee 1983—2004), Family Firm Inst. (bd. dirs. 1989—94, sec., treas. 1990—92, pres. 1992—94, Richard Beckhard award 1997), Family Bus. Forum (founder, bd. dirs. 1987—), Assn. Pvt. Enterprise Educators (bd. dirs. 1977—91, pres. 1978—79, Kent-Aronoff award 1988), Cobb C. of C. (vice chmn. 1986, 1991—93), Progressive Club (pres. 1976—77), Kiwanis (Outstanding Kiwanian award 1989). Home: 2061 E Side Dr NE Marietta GA 30062-6426 Office: Family Bus Consulting Group Inc 1220-B Kennestone Cir Marietta GA 30066 Office Phone: 678-277-9865. E-mail: aronoff@efamilybusiness.com.

ARONOFF, GEORGE RODGER, medicine and pharmacology educator; b. Peoria, Ill., Mar. 6, 1950; BA in Chemistry with distinction, Ind. U., 1972; MD with honors, Ind. U., Indpls., 1975, MS in Pharmacology, 1984. Diplomate Am. Bd. Internal Medicine; diplomate Am. Bd. Internal Medicine Nephrology. Intern in internal medicine Ind. U., Indpls., 1975-76, resident, 1976-77, clin. fellow div. nephrology, 1977-78, chief resident in internal medicine Wishard Meml. Hosp., 1978-79, rsch. fellow div. nephrology, 1979-80, instr. phys. diagnosis, 1977-78, instr. medicine, 1978-79, from asst. prof. to assoc. prof. medicine, 1980-87, assoc. prof. pharmacology, 1985-87; prof. medicine, prof. pharmacology U. Louisville, 1987—; mem. staff Univ. Louisville (Ky.) Hosp., 1987—. Fellow in clin. pharmacology Eli Lilly & Co., Indpls., 1979-80. Contbr. numerous articles and abstracts to profl. jours. Mem. Nat. Kidney Found. Ind., 1979-87, bd. dirs., 1985-87, mem. exec. com., 1985-87, bd. dirs. cen. Ind. chpt., 1985-87, chmn. fundraising, 1985-87; exec. com. Nat. Kidney Found. Ky., 1988-95, pres. med. and sci. adv. bd., 1989-95. Fellow ACP; mem. AAAS, Am. Fedn. Clin. Rsch., Am. Soc. Clin. Pharmacology and Therapeutics, Am. Soc. Nephrology, Cen. Soc. Clin. Rsch., Ky. State Med. Assn., Inter-Am. Soc. Chemotherapy (chmn. div. medicinal chemistry and pharmacology 1982-87), Jefferson County Med. Soc. (editorial bd. Louisville Medicine 1989-92, editor 1990), (bd. of dirs.) Renal Physicians Assn., Nat. Kidney Found. (exec. coun. nat. med. adv. bd. 1998-2000), Ky. Organ Donor Affiliates (bd. dirs. 1987-2000), Phi Eta Sigma, Phi Lambda Upsilon, Phi Beta Kappa, Alpha Omega Alpha, Sigma Xi. Office: U Louisville Kidney Disease Program 615 S Preston St Louisville KY 40202-1715

ARONOVITZ, TOD, lawyer; b. Miami, Fla., Feb. 26, 1950; AB, U. Ga., 1971; JD, U. Miami, 1974. Bar: Fla. 1974, U.S. Dist. Ct. (so. dist.) Fla. 1975, U.S. Ct. Appeals (11th cir.) 1977. Sr. ptnr. Aronovitz Trial Lawyers, Miami, Fla. Mem. Nat. Conf. Bar Presidents, So. Conf. Bar Presidents. Mem.: ABA, Dade County Bar Assn. (bd. dirs. 1976—79, 1986), Acad. Fla. Trial Lawyers, Assn. Trial lawyers Am., Am. Bd. Trial Advs., Fla. Bar (bd. govs. 1996—2001, pres.-elect 2001—02, pres. 2002—03), Soc. Bar and Gavel, Phi Delta Phi (pres. 1973). Office: Aronovitz Trial Lawyers Ste 2700 Museum Tower 150 W Flagler St Miami FL 33130-1536

ARONOW, EDWARD, psychologist, educator; b. Dec. 22, 1945; s. Hyman and Gertrude (Bakst) A.; m. Anna Aronow; children: David, Rebecca. BA in Psychology, CUNY, 1967; MA in Psychology, Fordham U., 1969, PhD in Clin. Psychology, 1973. Psychology trainee VA, NYC, 1968-72; prof. psychology Montclair (NJ) State U., 1972—; sr. clin. psychologist St. Vincent's Hosp., NYC, 1972-79; clin. psychologist Verona, NJ, 1974—. Author: Rorschach Content Interpretation, 1976, A Rorschach Introduction: Content and perceptual Approaches, 1982, The Rorschach Technique, 1994, A Practical Guide to the TAT, 2001. Fellow Am. Bd. of Assessment Psychology; mem. APA, NJ Psychol. Assn., Soc. Personality Assessment. Office: 69 Forest Ave Verona NJ 07044-1217 Personal E-mail: ed78p@yahoo.com.

ARONOW, SAUL, radiological physicist, consultant; b. N.Y.C., Oct. 4, 1917; s. Abraham and Minnie (Mirel) Aronow; m. Alice Pearlman, Feb. 12, 1942; children: Victor A, Frederick D, David B, Nathan J, Louise G, Jessie P Kravette. BEE, Cooper Union, 1939; PhD, Harvard U., 1953. Registered profl engr, Mass, cert. radiological physicist. Engr. Harvey Radio Labs., Cambridge, Mass., 1946-49; med. physicist Mass. Gen. Hosp., Boston, 1953-81; clin. engr. Project Hope, Jamaica, W.I., 1981-83; chmn. bd. Tech. in Medicine, Inc., Holliston, Mass., 1972—. Adj prof Northeastern Univ, Boston, 1975—95; instr MIT, Cambridge, 1969—83. Editor: (book) The Fallen Sky, 1963. Mem. Newton Dem. City Com. Served to 1st lt Signal Corps U.S. Army, 1942—46. Recipient Gano Dunn medal, Cooper Union Inst .Tech., 1981; NSF fellow, Harvard U., 1950, Fulbright fellow, Danmarks Tekniske Hojskole, 1969. Fellow: IEEE; mem.: Harvard Musical Assn., Soc. Nuc. Medicine, Nat. Fire Protection Assn. (mem. stds. coun. 1983—89), Assn. Advancement Med. Instrumentation (bd. dirs. 1979—82), Am. Assn. Physicists in Medicine, Folk Song Soc. Greater Boston. Jewish. Avocations: hiking, folk music. Home and Office: 86 Crofton Rd Newton MA 02468-2115 Office Phone: 617-969-9417.

ARONOW, WILBERT SOLOMON, physician, educator; b. N.Y.C., N.Y., Oct. 30, 1931; s. Simon and Bella (Safrin) A.; m. Ina Gloria Brody, Sept. 20, 1958; children: Michael Steven, Janice Susan. BS, Queens Coll., 1953; MD, Harvard U., 1957. Diplomate Am. Bd. Internal Medicine. Intern Michael Reese Hosp. and Med. Ctr., Chgo., 1957-58, resident, 1958-61; practice medicine specializing in internal medicine and cardiology; cardiologist, chief Noninvasive Cardiovascular Lab., Long Beach (Calif.) VA Hosp., 1964-72, chief cardiovascular diseases, 1973-82, asst. chief medicine for rsch., 1975-80; asso. prof. medicine U. Calif., Irvine, 1972-75, prof. medicine, 1975-82, prof. cmty. and environ. medicine, 1975-82, prof. pharmacology and therapeutics, 1976-82, vice chief cardiovascular divsn., chief cardiovascular rsch., 1974-82; prof. medicine, chief cardiovascular rsch. Creighton U., Omaha, 1982-84; chief Cardiology Clnic Westchester Med. Ctr./N.Y. Med. Coll., Valhalla, N.Y., 2001—. Vis. prof. U. Tex. Southwestern Med. Sch., Dallas, 1976, U. Man., 1979, U. Toronto, 1979, Tex. Tech U. Sch. Medicine, Lubbock, 1983, U. Medicine and Dentistry of N.J.-Rutgers Med. Sch., 1983; vis. prof. geriat. U. Rochester Sch. Medicine, 1999; cons. cardiology Orange County Med. Ctr., 1968—82; staff cardiology svc. St. Joseph Hosp., Omaha, 1982—84; cons. FDA, 1970—77, mem. ad hoc sci. ad. coms., 1970—72, mem. cardiovascular and renal adv. com., 1973—76; chmn. spl. rev. com. Nat. Cancer Inst., 1980; mem. subcom. on smoking Am. Heart Assn., 1980—83; med. dir. Hebrew Hosp. Home, 1984—2001; adj. prof. geriat. and adult devel. Mt. Sinai Sch. Medicine, 1992—; clin. prof. medicine N.Y. Med. Coll., 2001—; chief cardiology clinic Westchester Med. Ctr./N.Y. Med. Coll., 2001—, sr. assoc. program dir., rsch. mentor fellowship programs Dept. Medicine, 2003—05; cons. in field. Contbr. to rsch. publs. Served to capt., M.C. AUS, 1961-63. Fellow: ACP, Soc. Geriatric Cardiology (chmn. program com. 1993—2003, bd. dirs. 1994—2000), Coun. Clin. Cardiology of Am. Heart Assn., Gerontol. Soc. Am., Am. Geriatrics Soc., Am. Coll. Cardiology, Am. Coll. Chest Physicians (gov. So. Calif. 1977—83, vice chmn. coronary disease sect. 1978—79, chmn. coronary disease sect. 1979—81, mem. exec. coun. 1979—81, chmn. forum on cardiovasc. disease 1980—81, sec. coun. on govs. 1981—82, vice chmn. gov.'s coun.); mem.: Orange County Heart Assn. (dir. 1979—81), Long Beach Heart Assn. (dir. 1972—75), Assn. VA Cardiologists (pres. 1975—77), Am. Fedn. Med. Rsch., Am. Soc. Clin. Pharmacology and Therapeutics (chmn. cardiovasc. and pulmonary diseases sect. 1973—74, 1975—77), Phi Beta Kappa. Jewish. Home: 23 Pebbleway Rd New Rochelle NY 10804-3914 Office: Westchester Med Ctr/NY Med Coll Cardiology Divsn Macy Pavilion Rm 138 Valhalla NY 10595 Office Phone: 914-493-5311. Personal E-mail: wsaronow@aol.com. *Concern for the public health as well as for individual patient care has been the motivating force behind my medical research, teaching, and patient care. Performing work in a very careful, scientific fashion, being honest, being helpful and supportive to others, working very hard and efficiently, and being true to my principles of conduct has contributed to my success.*

ARONOWITZ, DAVID M., lawyer, chemicals executive; BA, Haverford Coll.; JD, Yale U. Assoc. Skadden, Arps, Slate, Meagher and Flom; v.p., gen. counsel, sec. Grimes Aerospace Co., Columbus, Ohio; asst. gen. counsel Taylor Pub. Co., Insilco Corp., Dublin; v.p., asst. gen. counsel The Scotts Co., Marysville, 1998—2000, sr. v.p., asst. gen. counsel, asst. sec., 2000—01, exec. v.p., gen. counsel, sec., 2001—. Office: The Scotts Co 14111 Scottslawn Rd Marysville OH 43041 Office Phone: 937-644-0011.

ARONOWITZ, JOEL ALAN, plastic and reconstructive surgeon; b. Memphis, Dec. 5, 1956; MD, Baylor Coll. Medicine, 1982. Intern in gen. surgery Baylor Coll. Medicine, 1982-83, resident in plastic surgery, 1983-87; attending plastic surgeon Cedars Sinai Med. Ctr., 1987—, vice chmn. plastic surgery divsn., 1997—2005, chmn. plastic surgery divsn., 2005—. Office: 8635 W 3rd St Ste 1090 Los Angeles CA 90048-6104 Office Phone: 310-659-0705.

ARONOWITZ, JULIAN, management consultant; b. N.Y.C., June 27, 1949; s. George and Sophie (Bailin) A. Cert. in Computer Programming, NYU, 1980; BBA, CUNY, 1989. Data analyst Bunker Ramo, N.Y.C., 1974—76; mktg. rep. Ctrl. Hosiery Sales Co., Inc., N.Y.C., 1977—87; project asst. dept. mgmt. Baruch Coll./CUNY, 1988; project asst. dept. mgr. Baruch Coll/CUNY, 1990; computer instr. adult edn. program Norwood Triangle, Bronx, NY, 1989—92; computer profl. Bob Malmet Enterprises, Bronx, 1985—96; bus. advisor N.Y.C., 1991—97; Beta tester Expansion Sys., Fremont, Calif., 1992—2001; project leader Jay Miner Soc., Inc., N.Y.C., 1998—99. Resource for Software Mag., N.Y.C., 1991—; instr. Amiga Users' Group of N.Y., 1995—; demonstrator Users' groups and other orgns., N.Y.C.; adj. lectr. Lehman Coll. CUNY, Bronx, 1998—. Columnist: BUG News; author: (tutorials) File for BBS's, Files for Disk Libraries. Exec. trustee U.S. Assn. Evening Students, N.Y.C., 1983-86; exec. v.p. Com. for Equality in Edn., N.Y.C., 1988. Regents scholar N.Y. State Dept. Edn., 1967, others. Mem. IEEE Computer Soc., Assn. Computing Machinery, Amiga Users' Group of N.Y., Bronx Users' Group (v.p. 1991—), Westchester Amiga Users' Group, Knights of Pythias (past dep. grand chancellor), Royal-Hartman Lodge (knight, Man of Yr. 1993, 97). Jewish. Avocations: swimming, drawing, billiards, walking. Home: 3390 Wayne Ave Apt G52 Bronx NY 10467-2454 Business E-Mail: jaronowitz@acm.org.

ARONS, BERNARD S., psychiatrist, educator, health services administrator; Grad., Oberlin Coll.; MD, Case Western Res. U. Psychiatrist, adminstr., instr. psychiat. residents St. Elizabeths Hosp. NIMH, Washington, dir. Dixon implementation office, 1980, chief clin. advisor, dir. med. nursing, psych. social work; assoc. dir. mental health fin. NIMH; legis. asst. to chair Health Subcom. Ways and Means Com., Washington; dir. Ctr. Mental Health Svcs. U.S. Dept. Health and Human Svcs., Washington, 1993—2003, sr. science advisor to the dir., Ctr. Mental Health Svcs., 2003—. Advisor to Mrs. Tipper Gore Office of V.P. U.S.; instr. Ctr. Mental Health Inc., Washington; clin. prof. psychiatry Georgetown U. Office: NIH/NIMH 6001 Executive Blvd Rm 8218 MSC 9669 Bethesda MD 20892-9669

ARONSON, ARTHUR LAWRENCE, retired veterinarian, toxicologist, educator, pharmacologist; b. Mpls., Aug. 24, 1933; s. Arthur Theodore and Thorene (Elfstrand) A.; m. Marilyn Ann Lundeen, Sept. 15, 1956; children: Brenda Louise, Mark Theodore, Luann Marie. BS, U. Minn., 1955, DVM, 1957, PhD, 1963; MS, Cornell U., 1959. Asst. prof. pharmacology Cornell U., 1964-67, assoc. prof., 1967-71, prof., 1971-80; prof., head dept. anatomy, physiol. sci., and radiology Coll. Vet. Medicine, N.C. State U., Raleigh, 1980-99; prof. emeritus, 1999—. Mem. com. biologic effects atmospheric pollutants NRC; mem. vet. medicine adv. com. FDA.; mem. U.S. Pharmacopeia Adv. Panel Vet. Medicine; chmn. com. recognition of pain and distress in lab. animals, Inst. Lab. Animal Resources, NAS, 1988. Co-editor Jour. Vet. Pharmacology and Therapeutics, 1992-99. Mem. Friends of Scandinavia, Carl Larsson Vasa Lodge; pres. Wake County Literacy Coun., 1997-99; vol. mentor Communities in Sch. of Wake County, 1999—; dir. N.C. State U. Women's Club English conversation classes, 2000—. Mem. AVMA (chmn. coun. on biologic and therapeutic agts. 1986-87), Am. Soc. Pharmacology and Exptl. Therapeutics, Soc. Toxicology (animals in rsch. com.), N.C. Soc. Toxicology (pres. 1985-86), Am. Acad. Vet. Pharmacology and Therapeutics (pres. 1987-89), Am. Coll. Vet. Clin. Pharmacology (pres. 1993-95), Wake County Literacy Coun. (bd. dirs. 1991-2003, pres. 1997-99), Sigma Xi, Phi Zeta. Lutheran. Home: 1213 Glendale Dr Raleigh NC 27612-4772

ARONSON, BENJAMIN, artist; b. Boston, Oct. 4, 1958; s. David and Georgianna (Nyman) A.; m. Margaret Ray Combs, Nov. 5, 1983; children: Jesse Benjamin, Alexander Raymond. BFA in Painting, Boston U., 1980, MFA in Painting, 1982. Tchg. asst. Boston U. Sch. Fine Art, 1980-82; tchr. Beaver Country Day Sch., Chestnut Hill, Mass., 1983-90; mem. U.S. Supreme Ct. Portrait Painting Team, 1989-97; guest lectr. Boston U. Summer Art Inst., 1985, Deerfield Acad., Old Deerfield, Mass., 1986, Salve Regina Coll., Newport, R.I., 1987, Mass. Coll. Art, Boston, 1987, Worcester Craft Ctr., Boston Globe Scholastic Art Awards, 1988, Boston U. Sch. Art Edn., 1988, art dept. Southeastern Middlesex U., 1988, Gordon Coll., Wenham, Mass., 1989, painting dept. Boston U. Sch. Visual Art, 1989, R.I. Sch. Design, 1990, Charrette Corp., 1991, Harvard Grad. Sch. Design, 1995, 96, 97, 98, 99; artist in residence Beaver Country Day Sch., Chestnut Hill, Mass., 1985-88. One-man shows include Nancy Lincoln Gallery, Chestnut Hill, Mass., 1983, 89, Lane Gallery, Gordon Coll., Wenham, Mass., 1986, Julia-Saul Gallery, Sudbury, Mass., 1987, Louis Newman Galleries, Beverly Hills, Calif., 1994, Jerry Solomon Gallery, Hollywood, Calif., 1996, Horwitch Newman Gallery, Scottsdale, Ariz., 1996, M B Modern, N.Y.C., 1997, 99, Sydne Bernard Fine Arts, Hollywood, 1998; exhibited in group shows at Boston U. Art Gallery, 1980, 82, Dana Hall Gallery, Wellesley, Mass., 1984, Quadrum Gallery, Chestnut Hill, 1984, DeCordova Mus., Lincoln, Mass., 1988, Copley Soc., Boston, 1990, Nat. Acad. Design, N.Y.C., 1990, 92, Urban Ctr. Mcpl. Art Soc., N.Y.C., 1991, Mickelson Gallery, Washington, 1992, Security Pacific Gallery, Seattle, 1992, Gwenda Jay Gallery, Chgo., 1992, Louis Newman Galleries, Beverly Hills, 1993, 94, Koplin Gallery, Santa Monica, Calif., 1995, Horwitch Newman Gallery, Scottsdale, 1995, 96, Jerry Solomon Gallery, Hollywood, 1996, 97, Sydne Bernard Fine Arts, Hollywood, 1997, 98, Pepper Gallery, Boston, 1997, M B Modern, N.Y.C., 1997, 98, Mangel Gallery, Phila., 1998, Soma Gallery, la Jolla, Calif., 1998, Alpha Gallery, Boston, 1999; represented in permanent collections at Reading (Pa.) Pub. Fine Art Mus., MIT, Woodshole Oceanographic Inst., Mass.; also corp. and pvt. collections; contbr. articles to profl. jours. Recipient Blanche E. Colman award for painting, 1986, 88, 1st prize in drawing Sudbury Art Assn., 1987, Mass. Lottery grant for painting, 1987, St. Botolph Club Found. grant for painting, 1988, R.I. State Coun. for Arts grant, 1989, William P. and Gertrude Schweitzer painting prize, Nat. Acad. of Design, 1990, Thomas Fisher award Am. Soc. Archtl. Perspectivists, N.Y.C., 1991, Ogden M. Pleissner painting award Nat. Acad. Design, N.Y.C., 1992. Home: 33 Wayside Inn Rd Framingham MA 01701-3021

ARONSON, CARL EDWARD, pharmacology and toxicology educator; b. Providence, Mar. 14, 1936; s. Carl Ivar and Ruth (Workman) A.; m. Marjorie Peck Boutelle, Dec. 17, 1960; children— Linda J., Kristen L. AB, Brown U., Providence, 1958; PhD, U. Vt., Burlington, 1966; MA, U. Pa., Phila., 1973. Asst. prof. pharmacology U. Pa. Sch. Medicine, Phila., 1971-75, assoc. prof. pharmacology, 1975-92; asst. prof. pharmacology and toxicology dept. animal biology U. Pa. Sch. Vet. Medicine, Phila., 1971-73, head labs. of pharmacology and toxicology, 1972-86, assoc. prof. pharmacology and toxicology, 1973-96; retired to emeritus status, 1996; instrument specialist, dept. chemistry Haverford (Pa.) Coll., 1996—. Editor Veterinary Pharmaceuticals and Biologicals, 1978-79, 80-81, 82-83, 85-86; contbr. chpts. to books, articles to profl. jours. Active local sch. dist. coms. and other civic assns. Served to 1st lt. USAFR, 1958-65. Recipient Norden award for disting. tchg. U. Pa. Sch. Vet. Medicine, 1982, Legion of Honor, Chapel of the Four Chaplains, 1984. Fellow: Am. Acad. Vet. and Comparative Toxicology, Am. Acad. Vet. Pharmacology and Therapeutics (newsletter editor 1982—2001, pres. 1983—85, Svc. award 1994, L.E. Davis Career Achievement award 2001); mem.: AAUP, Am. Soc. Pharmacology and Exptl. Therapeutics, Bay Region Mariners Sailing Assn. (treas. 1981—83, vice commodore 1986, commodore 1987), The Haven Yacht Club (charter), Masons, Sigma Xi. Lutheran. Avocations: sailing, photography, woodworking. Office: Haverford Coll Dept Chemistry 370 Lancaster Ave Haverford PA 19041-1392

ARONSON, CLIFFORD HANK, lawyer; b. Phila., Mar. 7, 1955; s. George Leonard and Gloria Harriet (Mort) A.; m. Amy Roberta Benenson, Sept. 21, 1986; children: Chloe Annette, Carter Asher, Fiona Skye BS in Econ., U. Pa., 1977; JD, Georgetown U., 1980. Bar: DC 1980, NY 1985. Assoc. Meagher & Flom, NYC, 1980-88; spl. counsel Skadden, Arps, Slate, Meagler & Flom, NYC, 1988, ptnr. antitrusts, 1989—, ptnr.-in-charge, summer associate program. Instr. Wharton Sch., U. Pa.; regular spkr. on mergers and acquisitions at Wharton's Executive Education Program. Co-editor: Mergers and Acquisitions - Understanding the Antitrust Laws. Mem. ABA (antitrust sect. 7 com.), Century Country Club, American Yacht Club Democrat. Jewish. Avocations: skiing, road biking, sailing. Home: 560 Polly Park Rd Rye NY 10580-1929 Office: Skadden Arps Slate Meagher & Flom 4 Times Sq New York NY 10036 Office Phone: 212-735-2644. Office Fax: 917-777-2644. Business E-Mail: caronson@skadden.com.

ARONSON, DAVID, artist, retired art educator; b. Shilova, Lithuania, Oct. 28, 1923; came to U.S., 1929, naturalized, 1931; s. Peisach Leib and Gertrude (Shapiro) A.; m. Georgianna B. Nyman, June 10, 1956; children: Judith, Benjamin, Abigail. Certificate, Boston Mus. Sch., 1946; LHD (hon.), Hebrew Coll., 1993; DFA (hon.), Boston U., 2005. Instr. painting Boston Mus. Sch., 1943-54; prof. art Boston U., 1962-89, founder art dept., chmn. div., 1954-62, chmn. painting dept., 1962-89, prof. emeritus, 1989—. Author David Aronson: Paintings, Drawings, Sculpture, 2005; contbr. articles to profl. jours.; one man shows include Niveau Gallery, N.Y.C., 1945, 56, Mus. Modern Art, N.Y.C., 1946, Boris Mirski Gallery, Boston, 1951, 59, 64, 69, Downtown Gallery, N.Y.C., 1953, Nordness Gallery, N.Y.C., 1960, 63, 69, Rex Evans Gallery, L.A., 1961, Long Beach (Calif.) Mus., 1961, Westhampton (N.Y.) Gallery, 1961, J. Thomas Gallery, Provincetown, Mass., 1964, Zora Gallery, LA, 1965, Hunter Gallery, Chattanooga, 1965, Kovler Gallery, Chgo., 1966, Bernard Danenberg Galleries, N.Y.C., 1969, 72, Pucker Gallery, Boston, 1976, 78, 86, 90, 94, 99, 2005, Phila. Mus. Judaica, 1990, Louis Newman Gallery, L.A., 1977, 81, 84, 86, 89, 92, Sadye Bronfman Art Ctr., Montreal, Que., Can., 1982, Horwitch Newman Gallery, Scottsdale, Ariz., 1995, 96, MB Modern Gallery, N.Y., 1997, Alter & Gil Gallery, L.A., 1999, Sp. Galerie Yoram GIL, L.A., 2002, 04; group shows include N.Y. World's Fair, 1964-65, Bridgestone Gallery, Tokyo, Royal Acad. London, Mus. Modern Art, Paris, Palazzo Venezia, Rome, Congresse Halle, Berlin, Charlottenborg, Copenhagen, Palais Des Beaux Arts, Brussels, Smithsonian Instn., 1965, retrospective exhbns. include Rose Mus., Brandeis U., Waltham, Mass., 1978, Jewish Mus., N.Y.C., 1979, Nat. Mus. Am. Jewish History, Phila., 1979, So. Middlesex U., South Dartmouth, Mass., 1983, Mickelson Gallery, Washington, 1985, Boston U., 2005; represented in permanent collections Art Inst. Chgo., Va. Mus. Fine Arts, Richmond, Bryn Mawr Coll., Brandeis U., Tupperware Mus., Orlando, Fla., Decordova Mus., Lincoln, Mass., Mus. Modern Art, Atlanta U., Atlanta Art Assn., U. Nebr., Krannert Art Mus. U. Ill., Whitney Mus. Am. Art, Colby Coll., U. N.H., Portland Mus. Art, Maine, Corcoran Gallery Art, Washington, Munson Williams Proctor Art Inst., Ithaca, N.Y., Boston Mus. Fine Arts, Smithsonian Instn., Washington, Milw. Art Inst., Pa. Acad. Fine Arts, Johnson Found., Racine, Wis., Worcester (Mass.) Art Mus., Brockton (Mass.) Mus. Art, Longy Sch. Music, Cambridge, Mass., Boston U., Jewish Community Ctr., Boston, Nat. Acad. Design, N.Y., Joseph Hirschhorn Collection, Hebrew Coll., Newton, Mass., David and Alfred Smart Mus., U. Ill., Chgo., Two-Ten Found., Boston, Pa. State U. Mus. Art, Syracuse (N.Y.) U., Beth Israel Hosp., Boston Mass. Guilford Coll. U. N.C., Greensboro Campus, U. Judaism, L.A., Fine Arts Ctr., Cheekville, Tenn., Skirball Mus., L.A., Herbert F. Johnson Mus. Art, Cornell U., Museo Sefardi, Toledo, Spain, others; sculpture commns. Container Corp. Am., 1963, 65, Reform Jewish Appeal, 1980, Combined Jewish Philanthropies, 1981, Temple Beth Elohim, Wellesley, Mass., 1982, Brandeis U. Libr., Waltham, Mass., 1983, Brandeis U. Berlin Chapel, 1996. Recipient 1st Judges prize Inst. Modern Art, Boston, 1944, 1st Popular prize, 1944; Choice Friends of Art Art Inst. Chgo., 1946; Purchase prize Va. Mus. Fine Arts, 1946; Travelling fellow Boston Mus. Sch., 1946; Grand prize Boston Arts Festival, 1952, 54; 2d prize, 1953; 1st prize Tupperware Art Fund, 1954, cert. of merit for sculpture NAD, 1990; grantee in art Nat. Inst. Arts and Letters, 1958; Purchase prize, 1961, 62, 63; purchase prize Pa. Acad. Fine Arts, also other purchase prizes; Samuel F.B. Morse Gold medal NAD, 1973; Isaac N. Maynard prize NAD, 1975; Joseph S. Isidor gold medal NAD, 1976; Guggenheim fellow, 1960; Adolph and Clara Obrig prize NAD, 1968, Academician NAD, 1970. Home: 137 Brimstone Ln Sudbury MA 01776-3200

ARONSON, DAVID WOLF, artist, educator; b. Phila., 1963; s. Joseph and Penny Aronson; m. Terri Conway (div.); children: Diana, Joshua; m. Bernadette McNulty (div.). Cert., Hussain Sch. Art, 1986; student, Pa. Acad. Fine Art, 1986—87, Temple U., 1987—88. Cert. hypnotist Am. Bd. Hypnotherapy. Freelance illustrator, Phila., 1988—; prin., owner Painter's Nest, Southampton, Pa., 1999—2001. Tchr. art Phila. (Pa.) C.C., 1995—98, Bridges at St. Gabriel, Phila., 2001—02, U. City Arts League, Phila., 2001—03, Del. County C.C., Devon, Pa., 2001—04, Wissahickon Art Ctr., Phila., 2001—04; cons. in field. Prin. works include We Love Country, Bridgeport, Pa.; creator: (films) Amerika The Brutal, 2003; Ariel's Kaddish, 2004; author (illustrator): Dreams of A Young Artist, 2004; contbr. poems to mags. Vol. Aldersgate Family Ctr., Willowgrove, Pa., 1988, Phila. (Pa.) Com. Homeless, 1989, Phila. (Pa.) Cares, 2004. Recipient Illustration award, Art Dirs. Club, 1986. Mem.: Internat. Assn. Counselors and Therapists, Nat. Guild Hypnotists, Family of Shame Artists Collective. Democrat. Home and Office: 3330 Dogwood Dr Willow Grove PA 19090

ARONSON, DONALD ERIC, management consultant, tax consultant; b. Boston, Feb. 24, 1934; s. Harry and Nathalie A.; m. Margery Roth, Sept. 27, 1955 (dec. 1981); children: Nancy, Helaine; m. Joan Gelman, Jan. 12, 1986 AB, Dartmouth Coll., 1955; MBA, Columbia U., 1959. CPA, N.Y., N.J. Mem. audit and tax staff Arthur Young & Co., N.Y.C., 1959-63, tax mgr., 1963-68, tax ptnr., 1968-72, office mng. ptnr. Saddle Brook, N.J., 1972-80; dir. mktg. Arthur Young, N.Y.C., 1980-89; dir. tax mktg. Ernst & Young, N.Y.C., 1989-92; prin., profl. svcs. firms cons. Aronson/Heintz Assocs. LLC, N.Y.C., 1995—; value added tax recovery advisor, cons. and prin. VATAmerica, L.P., N.Y.C. and Princeton, NJ, 1993—. Asst. prof. acctg. Upsala Coll., East Orange, N.J., 1963-65; asst. prof. Columbia U. Grad. Sch. Bus., N.Y.C., 1966-67; acctg. adv. bd. Columbia U. Grad. Sch. of Bus., N.Y.C., 1981-89; assoc. prof. bus. NYU, 1992-97; cons. and lectr. in field. Contbr. articles to bus. and profl. jours. Served to 1st lt. USAF, 1955-57 Recipient Montgomery prize Columbia U. Grad. Sch. Bus., 1959; award N.Y. Soc. C.P.A.s, 1959 Mem. AICPA, N.Y. State Soc. CPAs, N.J. Soc. CPAs (trustee 1975-78). Democrat. Jewish. Avocations: tennis, skiing, boating. Office: Ste 6D 2 W 67st New York NY 10023 Office Phone: 212-874-4181.

ARONSON, EDGAR DAVID, venture capitalist; b. N.Y.C., June 17, 1934; s. Aaron Solomon and Ida Claire (Minevitch) A.; m. Nancy Carol Pforzheimer, Dec. 23, 1956; children: Edgar David Jr., Alison C., Edith S., Peter Borrah. AB, Harvard U., 1956, MBA, 1962. Successively trainee, asst. cashier, v.p. 1st Nat. Bank of Chgo., 1962-67; v.p. Republic Nat. Bank of

N.Y., 1968; trainee Salomon Bros., N.Y.C., 1968-69, ltd. partner, 1970, v.p., 1971-72, gen. partner, 1972-79; mng. dir. Salomon Bros. Internat. Ltd., London, 1971-76; chmn. bd. Dillon, Read Internat., 1979-81; pres. EDACO, Inc., 1981—2002. Bd. dirs. APL N.V., Curacao, Petrogas Ltd., Hong Kong, MidAmEnergy Holdings Pte., Inc., Omaha, H.L. Oakes & Co., Inc., Panama, Hertford Internat., N.V., Curacao, Avatech Solutions, Inc., Owings Mills, Md. Author (with others): New Old World, 1962, Response to Change, 1963. Trustee Lesley Coll., Cambridge, Mass., 1981-84, South St. Seaport Mus., N.Y., 1996-2002, Marine Mil. Acad., Harlingen, Tex.; bd. dirs. Carl and Lily Pforzheimer Found., N.Y.C.; founder Nat. Mus. U.S. Marine Corps. 1st lt. USMCR, 1956-60, maj. FMF ret. res. Mem. Marine Corps Res. Officers Assn., 1st Marine Divsn. Assn., The Cruising Assn. (U.K.), Mensa, N.Y. Yacht Club, Bass Harbor Yacht Club (Maine), Harvard Club N.Y.C., Royal Cork Yacht Club (Eire), Royal Nova Scotia Yacht Squadron (Halifax), The Brook (N.Y.C.), Annabel's (London). Office: 551 Fifth Ave Rm 512 New York NY 10176-0599

ARONSON, HOWARD ISAAC, linguist, educator; b. Chgo., Mar. 5, 1936; s. Abe and Jean A. BA, U. Ill., 1956; MA, Ind. U., 1958, PhD, 1961. Asst. prof. Slavic langs. and lit. U. Wis., Madison, 1961-62; asst. prof. Slavic linguistics U. Chgo., 1962-65, asso. prof. depts. slavic langs. and lit. and linguistics, 1965-73, prof., 1973—2002, chmn. dept. linguistics, 1972-80, prof. emeritus, 2002—, chmn. dept. Slavic langs. and lits., 1983-91, 2000-01. Editor: Annual of the Society for the Study of Caucasia, 1989—. Mem. Am. Assn. Advancement Slavic Studies. Jewish. Home: 415 W Aldine Ave Apt 7B Chicago IL 60657-3601 Office: U Chgo Dept Slavic Langs and Lit Chicago IL 60637 Personal E-mail: hia5@rcn.com. Business E-Mail: hia5@uchicago.edu.

ARONSON, JASON, publisher; b. Minn., Jan. 25, 1928; s. Louis and Mollie (Weiner) A.; div.; 1 child, Jane; m. Joyce Kraus. BA, U. Minn., 1949, MD, 1953. Resident in psychiatry U. Minn. Hosps., 1954-57; asst. psychiatrist Harvard Med. Sch. and Mass. Gen. Hosp., 1959-64; editor-in-chief Internat. Jour. Psychiatry, 1962-70; pres. Jason Aronson Pubs. Inc., Northvale, N.J., 1964—. Capt. U.S. Army, 1957-59. Fellow Am. Psychiat. Assn.

ARONSON, JAY RICHARD, economics professor, researcher, academic administrator; b. N.Y.C., Aug. 26, 1937; s. Lester and Rose (Hacken) A.; m. Judith Libby Klein, Sept. 13, 1959; children: Sarah, Miriam, Anne. AB, Clark U., 1959, PhD, 1964; MA, Stanford U., 1961. Asst. prof. econs. Worcester Poly. Inst. (Mass.), 1961-65, Lehigh U., Bethlehem, Pa., 1965-68, assoc. prof., 1968-72, prof., 1972—, dir. Martindale Ctr. for Study Pvt. Enterprise, 1980—, William L. Clayton prof. bus. and econs., 1984—. Vis. scholar U. York (Eng.), 1973, hon. prof., 1996-; cons. Internat. City Mgmt. Assn.; commr. Pa. Pension Fund Study Commn. Author: books including (with J. Hilley) Financing State and Local Governments, Public Finance; editor: books including (with E. Schwartz) Management Policies in Local Government Finance, 1975, 3d edit., 1987; contbr. articles to profl. publs. Recipient Lindback award Lehigh U., 1968; recipient Stabler award Lindback award, 1974; Rockefeller fellow, 1959-61; named hon. fellow Clark U., 1962; grantee Ford Found., 1971-72, 76-77, HEW, 1978-79, Scaife Found., 1982; Fulbright research scholar, 1991, 96. Mem.: Roya Econ. Soc., Am. Fin. Assn., Nat. Tax Assn., Am. Econ. Assn. Democrat. Jewish. Home: 1804 Jennings St Bethlehem PA 18017-5235 Office: Lehigh U Dept Economy Bethlehem PA 18015

ARONSON, LOUIS VINCENT, II, manufacturing executive; b. Newark, Jan. 18, 1923; s. Alexander H. and Leona L. (Lazarus) A.; m. Joan Barbara Fisch, Nov. 2, 1945; children: James Richard, Robert A., Kathryn Ann, Diane Barbara. BS, U.S. Naval Acad., 1945. Methods engr. Ronson Corp., Newark, 1947-48, supr. prodn. control, 1948-50, v.p. charge material procurement, 1950-52, v.p. charge ops., 1952-53, pres., 1952—, also bd. dirs. Bd. dirs. NCCJ. Served as ensign USN, 1945-47. Mem. U.S. Naval Acad. Athletic Assn Home: PO Box 9 Oldwick NJ 08858-0009 Office: Ronson Corp PO Box 6707 Somerset NJ 08875-6707

ARONSON, MARC, artist; b. Seattle, June 26, 1948; s. Leonard and Marian (August) A.; m. Sue Elizabeth Steiner, June 28, 1971; 1 child, Elliot. BA, Western Wash. U., Bellingham, 1971; MA, NYU, 1989, postgrad., 1989—. Represented by nextmonet.com. One-man shows Warren Benedek Gallery, N.Y.C., 1974, Synagogue for the Arts, N.Y.C., 2002; exhibited in group shows Seattle Art Mus. Pavilion, 1971, U. Denver Sch. Art, 1975, Orgn. Ind. Artists Fed. Courthouse, Bklyn., 1977, Aldrich Mus. Contemporary Art, Ridgefield, Conn., 1978, Foster White Gallery, Seattle, 1980, Renssellaer Poly. Inst., Troy, N.Y., 1980, Sci. Mus. Tokyo, 1985, Embellishment of Statue of Liberty Barneys N.Y., 1986, Island Introductions Galveston (Tex.) Arts Ctr., 1990, Art of N.E. USA Silvermine Guild Arts Ctr., New Canaan, Conn., 1991, Nat. Midyear Exhbn. Butler Inst. Am. Art, Youngstown, Ohio, 1991, Am. 500 Centro Cultural Recoleta, Buenos Aires, 1992, The Emerging Collector, N.Y.C., 1992, Art of Northeast USA Silvermine Guild Arts Ctr., New Canaan, Conn., 1993, Butler Inst. Am. Art, Youngstown, Ohio, 1994, Washington Sq. East Galleries, N.Y.C., 1995, Art of Northeast USA Silvermine Guild Arts Ctr., New Canaan, Conn., 1996, Nat. Competition Finalists' Exhibition Provincetown, Art Assn. and Museum, 1998, S.I. (N.Y.) Biennial Juried Art Exhibition, 1998, 2001, Art of N.E. Silvermine Guild Arts Ctr., New Canaan, Conn., 1999, 2001, Provincetown (Mass.) Art Assn. and Mus., 2000, represented in permanent collection Time Warner Inc.; featured in New American Paintings, 1997. Nat. Endowment for Arts fellow, 1976, N.Y. Found. Arts fellow, 1980. Mem. Kappa Delta Pi. Jewish. Avocation: racquetball. E-mail: Durango7@earthlink.net.

ARONSON, MARK BERNE, retired lawyer, advocate; b. Pitts., Aug. 24, 1941; s. Richard J and Jean (DeRoy) Aronson; children: Robert M., Andrew A., Michael D. BS in Econs., U. Pa., 1962; JD, U. Pitts., 1965. Pvt. practice law, Pitts., 1965-90; sr. ptnr. Behrend & Aronson Law Firm, Pitts., 1967-80, Behrend, Aronson & Morrow Law Firm, Pitts., 1980-83; pres. Current Concepts Corp., Pitts., 1992-2000; ret., 2000. Real estate broker, 1972—94; cons. to attys., 1991—2002; pvt. consumer adv., 1991—2002. Trustee Pitts. Child Guidance Found., 1987—90; mem. Pitts. Coun. Edn., 1986—89; pres. Cmty. Day Sch., Pitts., 1982—84, Rodef Shalom Jr. Congregation, 1970—71; trustee Rodef Shalom Congregation, Pitts., 1979—87, Rodef Shalom Jr. Congregation, 1967—71, Brotherhood, 1990—92, 2000—01. Mem.: Am Arbitration Assn. (mem nat panel arbitrators), Tau Epsilon Rho (chancellor Eta chpt 1964—65). Republican. Jewish. Address: Ste 506-507 Churchill Mansions 2525 Greensburg Pike Pittsburgh PA 15221-3691 Personal E-mail: sue4spam@aol.com.

ARONSON, MICHAEL ANDREW, editor; b. Bklyn., Apr. 27, 1939; s. Jesse Besthoff and Marcia (Sacks) A. BA, Johns Hopkins, 1960. Asst. dir. Ind. U. Press, Bloomington, 1966-69; London editor U. Chgo. Press, 1970, sci. editor, 1971-73; editor-in-chief Johns Hopkins U. Press, Balt., 1973-78; sr. editor social scis. Harvard U. Press, Cambridge, Mass., 1978—. Office: Harvard U Press 79 Garden St Cambridge MA 02138-1447

ARONSON, MORTON JEROME, psychiatrist; b. Phila., Aug. 14, 1923; m. Margaret Rupp; children: Eris, Frederick, Scott. BA, Temple U., 1944, MD, 1947; Grad., Columbia U., 1957. Diplomate Am. Bd. Psychiatry and Neurology. Internship U.S. Naval Hosp., St. Albans, N.Y., 1947-48, residency in psychiatry Bethesda, Md., 1948-49, St. Albans, 1952-53; instr. in psychiatry Columbia U. Coll. Physicians and Surgeons, N.Y.C., 1958-75, assoc. clin. psychiatrist, 1975-76; lectr. in psychiatry Columbia U. Sch. of Social Work, N.Y.C., 1965-76; asst. clin. prof. psychiatry Columbia U. Coll. Physicians and Surgeons, N.Y.C., 1976-92; faculty Psychoanalytic Ctr. for Tng. and Rsch. Columbia U., N.Y.C., 1973—, tng. and supervising analyst, 1977—; assoc. clin. prof. psychiatry Columbia U. Coll. Physicians and Surgeons, N.Y.C., 1993—. Vis. lectr. North Shore U. Hosp., 1977-92; lectr. in field; profl. practice in psychiatry and psychoanalysis, 1953—; psychiat. cons. Manhattan Kidney Ctr., 1975-87; asst. psychiatrist Presbyn. Hosp., 1960-75, assoc. psychiatrist, 1975-76, asst. attending psychiatrist, 1976-92, assoc. attending psychiatrist, 1993-94; invited discussant and panelist in field. Co-editor: (with others) Psychotherapy: The Analytic Approach, 1992; contbr. chpts. to books including Between Analyst and Patient, 1986; contbr. articles to profl. jours. Lt. USN, 1947-53. Recipient George Goldman Disting. Tchr. award Psychoanalytic Ctr. for Tng. and Rsch., Columbia U., 1994. Fellow Am. Psychiat. Assn.; mem. Am. Psychoanalytic Assn., Assn. for Psychoanalytic Medicine, L.I. Psychoanalytic Soc. (sec. 1971-72, v.p. 1972-73, pres. 1973-74, 89-91), Nat. Nephrology Found. (v.p. 1972-92). Home: Windsor Gate Great Neck NY 11020 Office: 250 E 87th St New York NY 10128-3115 Office Phone: 212-534-5735.

ARONSON, NEIL H., lawyer; b. 1957; BA summa cum laude, with distinction, Boston U., 1979; JD, Cornell U., 1982. Bar: Mass. 1982, US Ct. Appeals (1st Cir.) 1983. Ptnr. Mintz, Levin, Cohn, Ferris, Glovsky & Popeo PC, Boston, chmn., Bus. & Fin. Sect. Contbr. articles to profl. jour.; lectr. in field. Mem.: Boston Estate Planning Coun., Nat. Assn. Corp. Dirs., MIT Enterprise Forum, Boston Chief Exec. Officers Club (former pres.), Boston Bar Assn., Mass. Bar Assn., ABA, Phi Beta Kappa. Office: Mintz Levin Cohn Ferris Glovsky & Popeo PC One Financial Center Boston MA 02111 Office Phone: 617-348-1809. Office Fax: 617-542-2241. Business E-Mail: naronson@mintz.com.

ARONSON, NORMAN LEONARD, publishing executive, consultant; b. Washington, June 7, 1924; s. Herman and Bertha Martha (Miller) A.; m. Marcia Ross Rosey, Mar. 29, 1952 (dec. Nov., 1989); children: Susan Elizabeth Aronson Baratta, John Michael. BS in Bus. and Pub. Adminstrn., Georgetown U., 1947, JD, 1949. V.p. Esquire Mag., N.Y.C., 1951-75; publisher Univ. Comms., Rahway, N.J., 1975-76; advt. dir. Signature Mag., N.Y.C., 1976-82; pres. Best Publs. Inc., N.Y.C., 1982-86; CEO Musculoskeletal Transplant Found., Little Silver, N.J., 1986-88; editor, publisher "Q" Physicians Guide to Quality, Princeton, N.J., 1988—. Entrepreneur, investor founder, pres. The Kings Ct. Restaurants, Princeton, N.J., Charlottesville, Va., Bostons Restaurant, Trenton, N.J., 1977-80; pres. The Svc. News Stands, Pentagon Bldg., Washington, 1965-75; cons. Universal Press Syndicate, Kansas City, Mo., 1988-89, Target Mktg., Kansas City, 1988—; ptnr. Medcom Ptnrs., 2001—. Publisher The Book of Bests, 1983-84. Lt. j.g. US Navy, 1942-46 PTO. Recipient Lone Sailor award, U.S. Navy, Washington, 1990. Mem. The Nassau Club (Princeton, N.J.), Univ. Club (N.Y.). Avocations: wine, cooking.

ARONSON, PETER SAMUEL, physiologist, researcher; b. Bklyn., Feb. 3, 1947; s. Harry and Sydelle Aronson; m. Marie Louise Landry, Sept. 25, 1977; children: Paul L., William L. AB, U. Rochester, 1967; MD, NYU, 1970; MA (hon.), Yale U., 1987. Diplomate Nat. Bd. Med. Examiners; diplomate in internal medicine and nephrology Am. Bd. Internal Medicine. Intern and resident in internal medicine U. N.C. Sch. Medicine, Chapel Hill, 1970-72; clin. assoc. Gerontology Rsch. Ctr., NIH, Balt., 1972-74; fellow in nephrology Yale U. Sch. Medicine, New Haven, 1974-77, asst. prof. medicine and physiology, 1977-81, assoc. prof. medicine and physiology, 1981-87, prof. medicine and cellular and molecular physiology, 1987—, C.N.H. Long prof. internal medicine, 1995—. Chief sect. nephrology Yale U. Sch. Medicine, New Haven, 1987-2002; established investigator Am. Heart Assn., 1981-86. Mem. editl. bd. Am. Jour. Physiology, 1982-86, 87-90, 96-2000, Kidney Internat., 1990-94, Jour. Biol. Chemistry, 1995-2000; cons. editor Jour. Clin. Investigation, 1993-98; contbr. rsch. articles to profl. jours. With USPHS, 1972-74. Recipient Solomon Berson Med. Alumni Achievement award NYU, 1996; co-recipient Charles W. Bohmfalk Tchg. prize in basic sci., Yale U., 2005. Fellow: AAAS; mem.: Soc. Gen. Physiologists, Internat. Soc. Nephrology, Am. Heart Assn. (exec. com. coun. on the kidney 1986—90), Am. Soc. Nephrology (Young Investigator award 1985, Homer Smith award 1994, councillor 2002—), Am. Soc. Clin. Investigation (councillor 1986—88, editl. com. 1993—98), Am. Physiol. Soc., Am. Fedn. Med. Rsch., Am. Assn. Physicians (editl. bd. procs. 1997—99), Salt and Water Club (sec. 1985—87), Alpha Omega Alpha, Phi Beta Kappa. Office: Yale Sch Medicine Dept Medicine/Nephrology PO Box 208029 New Haven CT 06520-8029

ARONSON, SETH, lawyer; b. NYC, 1955; BBA, Ohio U., 1978; JD, Loyola U., 1981. Bar: Calif. 1981, US Dist. Ct. (Ctrl. Dist. Calif.) 1983, US Dist. Ct. (So. and No. Dist. Calif.) 1985, US Ct. Appeals (9th Cir.) 1985, US Supreme Ct. 1987, US Ct. Appeals (8th Cir.) 1989. Ptnr., office head O'Melveny & Myers, LLP, LA. Bd. overseer Loyola Law Sch., 2000—, bd. vistors, 2001—; lectr. and panelist on various litig. topics at programs by the ABA, LA County Bar Assn., Assn. Bus. Trial Lawyers, Practising Law Inst., Directors Roundtable, Nat. Bus. Inst., FBA, and UCLA Law Sch. Contbr. articles in profl. jours. Bd. advisors UCLA Sch. Pub. Policy and Social Rsch., 2001—; bd. dir. Ninth Cir. Historical Soc., 2000—, Legal Aid Found., LA, 1993—2000, pres., 1998—99; bd. dir. LA C. of C., 2003—. Mem.: Assn. Bus. Trial Lawyers (bd. gov. 1992—2002, pres. 2001—02), LA County Bar Assn. (chair: complex courts com. 2000—, mem. exec. com., litig. sect. 1999—2003). Office: O'Melveny & Myers LLP 400 S Hope St Los Angeles CA 90071-2899 Office Phone: 213-430-7486. Office Fax: 213-430-6407. Business E-Mail: saronson@omm.com.

ARONSON, STANLEY MAYNARD, physician, educator; b. NYC, May 28, 1922; s. Eliuh and Lena (Hassner) A.; m. Betty Ellis, June 3, 1947; children: Susan, Lisa, Sarah; m. Gale Matheson Holmes, Oct. 12, 2003. BS, CCNY, 1943; MD, NYU, 1947; MA, Brown U., 1971; MPH, Harvard U. Sch. Pub. Health, 1981; DSc (hon.), Tougaloo Coll., 2005. Diplomate Am. Bd. Pathology, Am. Bd. Neuropathology. Resident Bellevue Hosp., Sydenham Hosp., Meml. Sloan-Kettering Ctr. for Cancer, VA Med. Ctr., NYC, 1946-51; fellow Mt. Sinai Hosp., NYC, 1951-54; faculty Armed Forces Inst. Pathology Columbia Coll. Physicians and Surgeons, 1951-54; prof. pathology, asst. dean SUNY, Bklyn., 1954-70; prof. med. sci., dean medicine Brown U., 1970-81, Univ. prof. med. sci., 1981-87, dean medicine emeritus, 1987—. Dir. labs. Kings County Hosp. Ctr., Bklyn., 1965-70; pathologist-in-chief Miriam Hosp., Providence, 1970-75; vis. prof. cmty. medicine Dartmouth Coll. Med. Sch., 1982-; lectr. Yale Sch. Medicine, 1964-65; lectr. pathology Tufts U. Sch. Medicine, 1978-; profl. lectr. Bklyn. Health Ctr., SUNY, 1970—; cons. physician neuropathology Jewish Chronic Disease Hosp., Bklyn., 1951-, NIH, 1962-, RI Hosp., Roger Williams Hosp., Meml. Hosp., Miriam Hosp., Providence VA Hosp., Butler Hosp., Providence, RI Med. Ctr., Luth. Med. Ctr., NYC. Author: (with B.W. Volk) Cerebral Sphingolipidoses, 1962, Inborn Disorders of Sphingolipid Metabolism, 1966, Sphingolipids, Sphingolipidoses and Allied Disorders, 1972, (with A. Sahs and E Hartman) Guidelines for Stroke Care, 1976; (with Adachi and Hirano) The Pathology of the Myelinated Axon, 1985, Tapestry of Medicine, 1999, Worms, Germs and Wayward Physicians, 2000, Smallpox in Colonial America, 2002, (with R. Shield), Aging in Today's World, 2003; also numerous articles; mem. editl. bd. Jour. Submicroscopic Cytology, Jour. Neuropathology and Exptl. Neurology; editl. bd., editor-in-chief RI Med. Jour.; weekly columnist Providence Jour.-Bull. Commr. US Commn. Control of Huntington's Disease, 1976-79; chmn. Legis. Commn. Dementia Related to Aging; vice chmn. RI Bd. of Med. Licensure and Discipline, 1993-2003; pres. Hospice RI, 1989—, Interfaith Health Care Ministries, 1989-91; mem. Nat. Adv. Commn. on Multiple Sclerosis, 1973-74, NIH Perinatal Rsch. Commn., Joint Commn. on Stroke Facilities, med. adv. bd. Nat. Multiple Sclerosis Soc., Dysautonomia Found., Nat. Tay-Sachs Assn., Nat. Fund for Med. Edn.; trustee Finch Univ. Health Sci., Chgo.; cons. for internat. epidemiology programs The Rockefeller Found., 1990—; chmn. bd. trustees Jewish Home for Aged, RI, 1993-94; pres. Shalom Housing for Elderly, 1993-94. With U.S. Army, 1942-46. Named to R.I. Hall of Fame, 1997. Mem. AMA, Am. Neurol. Assn., Am. Assn. Neuropathology (pres. 1971-72), NY Acad. Medicine, Am. Acad. Neurology, Am. Assn. Pathologists and Bacteriologists, Internat. Soc. Neuropathology, Assn. Am. Med. Coll., NY Neurol. Soc., APHA, Am. Osler Soc., Am. Coll. Epidemiology, NAS (com. on nutrition in med. edn. 1983-85, com. on dietary guidelines implementation 1988-90). Achievements include research on genetics, epidemiology, pathology and diagnostic features of cerebral degenerative diseases, population dynamics, pathology and epidemiology of cerebral vascular disease and organic dementia. Home: 530 Blackstone Blvd Providence RI 02906 Office: Brown U Office Med Affairs Providence RI 02912-0001 Personal E-mail: smamd@cox.net.

ARONSON, VIRGINIA L., lawyer; b. Bremerton, Wash., June 4, 1947; m. Simon Aronson. BA, U. Chgo., 1969, MA, 1973, JD, 1975. Bar: Ill. 1975. Ptnr. Sidley Austin Brown & Wood LLP, Chgo. Staff mem. U. Chgo. Law Review, 1974—75; mem. exec. & mgmt. com. Sidley Austin Brown & Wood. Contbr. articles to profl. jours. Mem. leadership coun. Chgo. Pub. Edn. Fund; mem. bd. dirs. Chgo. Ctrl. Area Com. Mem. Am. Coll. Real Estate Lawyers, Chgo. Mortgage Attys. Assn., Chgo. Fin. Exch., The Chgo. Network. Office: Sidley Austin Brown & Wood LLP Bank One Plz 10 South Dearborn St Chicago IL 60603 Office Phone: 312-853-7741. Office Fax: 312-853-7036. Business E-Mail: varonson@sidley.com.

ARONSON-FRIEDMAN, AMY ILENE, education educator; b. Shreveport, La., Oct. 5, 1963; d. Irwin Leon and Barbara Sue (Ginsburg) Aronson; m. Ido Friedman, Dec. 22, 1990. BA, George Washington U., 1985; MA, Middlebury Coll., 1986, Ga. So. U., 1992; PhD, Temple U., 2000. Cert. tchr. Pa. Instr. Ga. So. U., Statesboro, 1982—91; tchg. asst. Temple U., Phila., 1994—99; asst. prof. No. Ga. Coll. & State U., Dahlonega, 1999—2000, Valdosta State U., 2002—. Adv. bd. So. Conf. on Lang. Tchg., Atlanta, 2002—. Scholar, Fulbright, Chile, Argentina; Travel grant, Valdosta State U., 2002—03. Avocations: horseback riding, travel, yoga. Home: 124 Brandywine Rd Savannah GA 31405 Office: Valdosta State Univ Dept Modern & Classical Lang Valdosta GA

ARONZON, PAUL S., lawyer; b. L.A., 1954; BA cum laude, Calif. State U., Northridge, 1976; JD, Southwestern U., 1979. Bar: Calif. 1979, D.C. 1995, N.Y. 1996. Ptnr. & co-chmn. Fin. Restructuring Group Milbank, Tweed, Hadley & McCloy, L.A. Fellow, Am. Col. Bankruptcy; mem. ABA (antitrust law, comml. law, bankruptcy sects.), State Bar Calif. (uniform comml. code com., bus. law sect. 1984-88, co-chair article 2A subcom. 1987-88), L.A. County Bar Assn. (uniform comml. code com. 1985—), Am. Bankruptcy Inst., Fin. Lawyers Conf., Bankruptcy Study Group. Office: Milbank Tweed Hadley & McCloy 601 S Figueroa St Los Angeles CA 90017-5704 Office Phone: 213-892-4417. Office Fax: 213-629-5063. Business E-Mail: paranzon@milbank.com.

ARORA, ASHISH, economics professor; PhD, Stanford U., Calif., 1991. Vis. assoc. prof. of econ Stanford U., Stanford, Calif., 2000—00; asst. prof. Carnegie Mellon, Pitts., 1991—97, assoc. prof., 1998—2004, prof., 2004—. Office Phone: 412-268-2191. Office Fax: 412-268-5161. Business E-Mail: ashish@andrew.cmu.edu.

ARORA, MANUBIR, lawyer; b. Jodhpur, India; m. Cathi Arora. B of Nuc. Engrng., Ga. Inst. Tech., 1991; JD, Ga. State U., 1994. Bar: Ga. 1994, USAF Ct. Appeals 1994, US Dist. Ct. Ga. No. Dist. 2001, US Dist. Ct. Ga. Mid. Dist. 2002. Judge adv. USAF, Charleston, SC, 1994—98; asst. dist. atty. Fulton County Dist. Attorneys Office, Atlanta, 1998—2000; sr. assoc. Garland, Samuel & Loeb, P.C., Atlanta, 2000—; judge adv. USAFR, Marietta, Ga., 1998—. Bd. mem. Sikh Am. Soc. of Ga., Ga., 2003—04, Indus Bar Assn., Atlanta, 2002—04. Capt. USAF, 1994—98, Charleston AFB, SC. Decorated Meritorious Svc. medal USAF. Mem.: ABA, Nat. Assn. Criminal Def. Lawyers. Office: Garland Samuel & Loeb PC 3151 Maple Dr NE Atlanta GA 30305 Office Phone: 404-262-2225. Office Fax: 404-365-5041. Business E-Mail: msa@gsllaw.com.

AROUH, JEFFREY ALAN, lawyer; b. NYC, May 2, 1945; s. Isaac E. and Jean J. (Halfon) A.; m. Karen Ann Wieder, Feb. 1, 1969; children: Russell Andrew, Ilonne A. BA, U. Mich., 1966; JD cum laude, NYU, 1969. Bar: NY 1970; sr. cert. relocation profl. Assoc. Gilbert, Segall and Young, NYC, 1969-74, ptnr., 1975-2001, Holland & Knight LLP, NYC, 2001—. Spkr. field. Editor NYU Law Rev., 1969; contbr. articles to legal publs. Recipient Founders Day award NYU. Mem. ABA (bus. law sect. com. corp. compliance), NY State Bar Assn., Assn. Bar City NY, Employee Relocation Coun. (pub. policy com.), Order Coif, Hampshire Country Club, Ibis Golf Country Club. Office: 195 Broadway Fl 24 New York NY 10007 Home: 8637 Falcon Green Dr West Palm Beach FL 33412 Office Phone: 212-513-3460. Business E-Mail: jeffrey.arouh@hklaw.com.

ARPEY, GERARD J., air transportation executive; b. July 26, 1958; m. Lisa Arpey; 3 children BA, U. Tex., 1980, MBA, 1982. FAA multi-engine pilots license. Fin. analyst Am. Airlines, 1982, mng. dir. airline profitability analysis, mng. dir. fin. analysis and fleet planning, mng. dir. fin. planning, v.p. fin. planning and analysis, 1989-92, sr. v.p. planning, 1992-95, sr. v.p. fin. and planning, 1995—99; CFO AMR Corp. and Am. Airlines, exec. v.p. ops., 2000—02, pres., COO, 2002—03, pres., CEO, 2003—, Chmn., 2004—. Bd. dirs. Am. Bracom Advisors, Inc. Avocation: private pilot. Office: AMR Corp Maildrop 5621 PO Box 619616 Dallas TX 75261-9616

ARPINO, GERALD PETER, performing company executive; b. Staten Island, NY, Jan. 14, 1928; s. Luigi and Anna (Santanastasio) A. Student, Wagner Coll., PhD (hon.), 1980; student ballet under Mary Ann Wells, student modern dance under May O'Donnell and Gertrude Shurr. Dancer Ballet Russe, 1951-52; co-founder Joffrey Ballet, 1956, dancer, to 1962, former assoc. artistic dir., now artistic dir. Chgo., resident choreographer, until 1990; with faculty Joffrey Ballet Sch., NYC, from 1953, now artistic dir., 1988—, assoc. dir., 1988—, prin. choreographer, 1988—. Bd. dirs. Dance Notation Bur., Dancers in Transition; mem. adv. coun. to dept. dance Calif. State U., Long Beach, also mem. Disting. Artists Forum. Choreographer ballets including Incubus, 1962, Viva Vivaldi!, 1965, Olympics, Nightwings, both 1966, Cello Concerto, Arcs and Angels, Elegy, all 1967, Secret Places, The Clowns, Fanfarita, A Light Fantastic, 1968, Animus, The Poppet, 1969, Confetti, Solarwind, Trinity, all 1970, Reflections, Valentine, Kettentanz, all 1971, Chabriesque, Sacred Grove on Mount Talmalpais, both 1972, Jackpot, 1973, The Relativity of Icarus, 1974, Drums, Dreams on Banjos, 1975, Orpheus Times Light 2, 1976, Touch Me, 1977, Choura, L'Air d 'Esprit, Suite Saint-Saens, all 1978, Epode, 1979, Celebration, 1980, Ropes, Partita for Four, Sea Shadow, Diverdissement, 1980, Light Rain, 1981, Round of Angels, 1982, Italian Suite, Quarter-Tones, 1983, Jamboree (commd. by City of San Antonio) Adv. Sportsmedicine Edn. & Rsch. Found., L.A.; mem. adv. com. N.Y. Internat. Festival of the Arts; mem. nat. adv. coun. ITI/USA Internat. Ballet Competition; mem. hon. com. The Yard Benefit-Vineyard Celebration, 1989; mng. dir., bd. dirs. Found. for Joffrey Balllet, Inc. Served with USCG, 1945-48. Recipient Dancemagazine award, 1974, Bravo award San Antonio Performing Arts Assn., 1984, Disting. Achievement award Nat. Orgn. Italian-Am. Women, 1987, Tiffany award Internat. Soc. Performing Arts Adminstrs., 1989, Outstanding Artistic Achievement award Staten Island Coun. on Arts, 1990, Ammy award Am. Express Corp. Office: Joffrey Ballet Chgo 70 E Lake St Fl 1300 Chicago IL 60601-5917

ARQUETTE, PATRICIA, actress; b. Chgo., Apr. 8, 1968; d. Lewis and Mardi Arquette; m. Nicolas Cage, Apr. 8, 1995 (div. May 18, 2001); 1 son (with Paul Rossi), Enzo; 1 daughter (with Thomas Jane), Harlow. Actress: (films) Pretty Smart, 1986, A Nightmare on Elm Street 3: Dream Warriors, 1987, Time Out, 1988, Far North, 1988, The Indian Runner, 1991, Prayer of the Rollerboys, 1991, Especially on Sunday, 1991, Inside Monkey Zetterland, 1992, Trouble Bound, 1993, Ethan Frome, 1993, True Romance, 1993, Holy Matrimony, 1994, Ed Wood, 1994, Beyond Rangoon, 1995, Flirting with Disaster, 1996, The Secret Agent, 1996, Infinity, 1996, Lost Highway, 1997, Nightwatch, 1997, Goodbye Lover, 1998, The Hi-Lo Country, 1998, Toby's Story, 1998, Stigmata, 1999, Bringing Out the Dead, 1999, Little Nicky, 2000, Human Nature, 2001, The Badge, 2002, Deeper Than Deep, 2003, Holes, 2003, Tiptoes, 2003; (TV movies) Daddy, 1987, The Girl with the Crazy Brother, 1990, Dillinger, 1991, Wildflower, 1991 (CableACE award, 1991),

Betrayed by Love, 1994; (TV series) Medium, 2005-; (TV appearances) thirtysomething, 1990, Tales From the Crypt, 1990. Spokesperson Lee Nat. Denim Day, 1999. Office: UTA 9560 Wilshire Blvd Fl 5 Beverly Hills CA 90212-2401

ARQUIT, KEVIN JAMES, lawyer; b. Ithaca, N.Y., Sept. 11, 1954; s. Gordon James and Nora (Harris) A. BA cum laude, St. Lawrence U., 1975; JD cum laude, Cornell U., 1978. Bar: Ohio 1978, N.Y. 1980, U.S. Dist. Ct. (so. and ea. dists.) N.Y. 1980, U.S. Dist. Ct. (we. dist.) N.Y. 1983, U.S. Dist. Ct. (no. dist.) Calif. 1983, U.S. Ct. Appeals (3d cir.) 1983, U.S. Dist. Ct. (no. dist.) N.Y. 1985, U.S. Ct. Appeals(2d cir.) 1985, U.S. Supreme Ct. 1989. Assoc. Arter & Hadden, Cleve., 1978, Fish & Neave, N.Y.C., 1978-83, Harris, Beach & Wilcox, Rochester, N.Y., 1983-86; atty. advisor to chmn. FTC, Washington, 1986-87, chief staff, 1987-88, gen. counsel, 1988-89; dir. Bur. Competition, Washington, 1989-92; ptnr., dep. chmn., head Clifford Chance US LLP Antitrust Practice Group, N.Y.C., 1992—2002; ptnr. STB, 2003—. Republican. Roman Catholic. Office: Simpson Thacher & Bartlett 425 Lexington Ave New York NY 10017-3954 Business E-Mail: karquit@stblaw.com.

ARQUIT, NORA HARRIS, retired music educator, writer; b. Brushton, N.Y., June 30, 1923; d. Samuel Elton George and Esther Cecelia (Gillen) Harris; m. Gordon James Arquit, Nov. 12, 1948; children: Christine Elaine Arquit, Kevin James Arquit, Candace Susan Arquit-Martel. BS in Music Edn., Ithaca Coll., 1945, MS, 1962; postgrad., St. Lawrence U., 1946-47, 74, Cornell U., 1970-71, N.Y. State Coll., Potsdam, 1973. Cert. aerospace edn. with techicians rating. Music dir., band dir., tchr. N.Y. and N.J. State Schs., 1945—80. Guest conductor U.S. Air Force Band, Washington, Dutch and Am. band students, Schiedam, Holland, opening Am.-Can. Seaway, Massena, N.Y., 1975; U.S. Navy Band, Washington, various massed bands in U.S.A., Canada, Europe; dir. bands Worlds Fair, 1964, 65; 1st woman guest conductor Tri-State Honors Band Phillips U., Enid, Okla.; dir., coord. St. Lawrence County ann. H.S. Band Day, 1973-2002; past supvr. coll. student practice tchrs., N.Y.; mem. Mid-States Commn. Secondary Schs. and Colls. Evaluations. Author: Before My Own Time and Since, 1978, From Hamlet to Cold Harbor, 1989, Our Lyon Line, 1993, The History of the New York State, Society of the National Society of the Daughters of the American Colonists, 1994. Past adjudicator h.s. and coll. band contests; past dir., coord. ann. St. Lawrence County Band Day; past capt. aux. USAF Civil Air Patrol; past John Philip Sousa bd. dirs. rep. to Hall of Fame enshrinement of Sousa. Named Dist. Band Master Am., First Chair Am.; recipient Letter of Commendation for People to People Diplomacy for work with student band groups, Embassy at the Hague, Europe, honored for 39 yrs. of svc. on Band Day, St. Lawrence County, 2002. Mem.: AAUW (past divsn. meeting rep.), Women Band Dirs. Nat. Assn. (past nat. pres., Silver Baton), N.Y. State Ret. Tchrs. Assn., N.Am. Band Dirs. Coordinating Coun. (pres. 1978, past nat. v.p.), Am. School Band Dirs. Assn. (emeritus mem. 1980, N.Y. state chmn. 2003—, past chmn. internat. band com., past nat. and state ofcr., honored nat. covention 2003), Internat. Assn. U. Women, Colonial Daughters of the XVIIC (chpt. councillor 1988-91, past. mem. coms.), Soverign Colonial Soc., Soc. New England Women, De Schilpen Soc. (Holland), Kings County Hist. Soc. Nova Scotia, Daughters of Union Vets., N.Y. Ct. Assts. of Nat. Soc. Women Descendents of Ancient and Honorable Artillery Co. (past state officer, corr. sec., com. chmn.), Denison Soc., Daughters Am. Colonists (N.Y. state regent 1991—94, hon. state regent, life 1994), Soc. Colonial Dames of Seventeenth Century (past state officer, past state pres, registrar), Colonial Daughters Seventeenth Century (Atlantic Coast chmn. 2000—, nat. com. chmn. 2000—, past pres.), Daus. Colonial Wars, DAR (life; hon. regent Cayuga chpt., past state com. chmn., genealogical chmn.), Soc. Magna Charta Dames and Barons, Plantagenet Soc., Colonial Order of The Crown (Charlemagne), Soc. Sons and Daus. of the Pilgrims, Soc. U.S. Daughters 1812 (past pres., past Onondaga chpt. pres., past state ofcr.), Soc. Daughters of Founders & Patriots of Am. (past pres., past state pres., registrar), Soc. Sons and Daughters of Colonial Wars, Soc. New England Women, De Schilpen Mus. Soc. Netherlands, Daughters of Am. Colonists (nat. com chmn. 1994—97, Atlantic sect.chmn genealogy 2003—), Summit N.J. Club (spl. panel), Nat. Fedn. Music Club (past editl.com.), State Officers Club DAR, Ithaca Music Club (past pres.), Delta Omicron. Avocations: writing, photography, research. Home: 130 Christopher Cir Ithaca NY 14850-1702

ARREOLA, JOHN BRADLEY, financial planner; b. San Fernando, La Union, Philippines, Mar. 20, 1935; came to U.S., 1950; naturalized, 1960; s. Juanito Antonio and Catalina (Bacalzo) A.; m. Judith Anne Hughes, June 26, 1965; children: Bradley, Christopher. Student, Hartnell Coll., 1950—52; BA, San Jose State Coll., 1955. Cert. real estate appraiser; cert. internat. financier; CFP. Statistician O'Connor Hosp., San Jose, Calif., 1955—60; tax cons. Arreola-Comita & Assocs., San Jose, 1960—63; cost acct. Granger & Assocs., Palo Alto, Calif., 1963—64; mgr. cost acctg. Gen. Micro-Electronics, Santa Clara, Calif., 1964—65; chief acct. Kaiser Engrs., Calif. and Venezuela, 1965—67; comptr. Aluminio del Caroni, S.A. (Reynolds Alumnium subs.), Caracas, Venezuela, 1967—78; bus. cons. Venezuela, 1978—83; pres. Arreola, Hughes & Co. Inc., Sarasota, Fla., 1983—; CEO, pres. MAP Fin. Group of Cos., Inc., Sarasota, 1985—92; pres. J&J Enterprises, Sarasota, 1992—2001; sr. v.p. High Mark Fin. Svcs., 2002—. Mem.: Fin. Planning Assn., Internat. Assn. Fin. Planning (pres. Sarasota chpt. 1988—89), Sarasota Ski Club, Tournament Players Club PGA at Prestancia. Republican. Roman Catholic. Avocations: golf, skiing, photography, football, baseball. Home: 3900 Torrey Pines Blvd Sarasota FL 34238-2833

ARRIAGA, VICENTE, manufacturing executive; b. Tenexcontitlan, Guerrero, Mex., Sept. 11, 1967; arrived in US, 1989, naturalized, 2001; s. Eleuterio and Maria Ana (Ramirez) Arriaga; m. Cindy Lynn Marie Parisi, Oct. 16, 1995; children: Mariana, Sarah, Abigail. Cert. in Computer Numeric Control, BIR Coll., 2001. Part-time supr. Dow Jones/Wall St. Jour., Chgo., 1991—; supr. MPC Products Corp., Niles, Ill., 2001—. Roman Catholic. Home: 2841 N Springfield Ave Chicago IL 60618

ARRICALE, FRANK, psychologist, writer; b. NYC, July 31, 1955; s. Frank Clemente and Helen Veronica (Shea) Arricale; m. Linda Lee Titus, Aug. 15, 1975. BA in English and Music, La Salle U., Phila., 1977; MA in Counseling, Rider U., Lawrenceville, NJ, 1994; EdD in Counseling Psychology, Rutgers U., New Brunswick, NJ, 2001. Lic. Psychologist Pa. Counselor Rider U., Lawrenceville, 1993—94; counselor, case mgr. Self Discovery, Wayne, Pa., 1994—96; counselor Cook Coll., New Brunswick, 1998—99, Douglass Coll., New Brunswick, 1999—2000; counseling psychologist Villanova U., Pa., 2001—, Pvt. Practice, Bensalem, Pa., 2003—. Author: (fiction) Evolution, or, The Sayonara Song, Obviously Not Clairvoyant; songwriter/recording artist (CDs) Down ... but not out, Ordinary Man. Mem.: APA, Pa. Psychol. Assn. Independent. Achievements include contributed to the creation of The Center, an LLC providing psychological services in King of Prussia, PA, owned and operated by Dr. Kristine Karl Boward. Avocations: songwriting and recording, music.

ARRINGTON, CAROLYN RUTH, school system administrator, consultant; b. May 20, 1942; d. Robert Ray and Grace Dotson; m. Wayne Vernon Arrington; children: Kevin Ray, Kemp Gray, Korey shay, Wayne, Kimberly. AA, Ohio Valley Coll., 1962; BA, Fairmont State Coll., 1964; MA, W.Va. U., 1966, EdD, 1994. Cert. pub. sch. adminstr., 1993. Tchr. Greenbrier Bd. Edn., Lewisburg, W.Va., 1964-68; supr. Mason County Bd. Edn., Point Pleasant, W.Va., 1968-70; media specialist Kanawha County Bd. Edn., Charleston, W.Va., 1970-71; asst. dir., dir., asst. divsn. chief W.Va. Dept. Edn., Charleston, 1971-89, asst. state supt. schs., 1989-98; v.p. Arrington Assocs., Inc., 1998—. Edn. and bus. cons.; inspirational motivational spkr. Author numerous poems and children's stories; developer workshop materials. Bd. dirs. YWCA, Charleston, 1988—91. Recipient medal of merit Edn. Ohio Valley Coll.; SEA fellow U.S. Dept. Edn., 1984. Mem. Assn. Ednl. Comm. and Tech. (pres. 1979-80, Edgar Dale award 1975, Spl. Svc. award 1982), Wva. Ednl. Media Assn. (pres. 1975-76). Office: Arrington Assocs Inc Charleston WV

ARRINGTON, HEATHER SPELL, academic administrator; b. Durham, N.C., Apr. 20, 1979; d. Arnold Ray and Diane Huntley Spell; m. Troy Wesley Arrington, Dec. 20, 2003. BA, Meredith Coll., 2001; MA, Appalachian State U., 2003. Asst. dir. student leadership East Carolina U., Greenville, NC, 2004—05, specialist profl. staff devel. and leadership tng., 2005—. Mem.: Am. Coll. Personnel Assn. (state leader 2004—05), N.C. Coll. Personnel Assn. (pres. 2005—), Omicron Delta Kappa. Democrat. Baptist. Home: East Carolina State Univ Ste 100 Jones Hall Greenville NC 27858 Office: East Carolina State Univ 8A Mendenhall Student Ctr Greenville NC 27858

ARRINGTON, JOHN LESLIE, JR., lawyer; b. Pawhuska, Okla., Oct. 15, 1931; s. John Leslie and Grace Louise (Moore) A.; m. Elizabeth Anne Waddington, 1956 (div.); children: Elizabeth Anne, John Leslie III, Winifred L., Katherine M.; m. Linda Vance, 1972. Grad., Lawrenceville Sch., 1949; AB, Princeton U., 1953; JD, Harvard U., 1956, LLM, 1957. Bar: Okla. 1956, U.S. Supreme Ct. 1960. Assoc. Arrington, Kihle, Gaberino & Dunn and predecessor firms, Tulsa, 1957-61, ptnr., 1961-93, chmn., CEO, 1994-96; gen. counsel ONEOK, Inc., 1997-98; of counsel Gable & Gotwals, Tulsa, 1998—. Chmn. bd. dirs. Woodland Bank of Tulsa, 1979-94. Prin. draftsman Okla. Supreme Ct. rules governing disciplinary proceedings, 1980-81; bd. dirs. Tulsa County Legal Aid Soc., 1965-70, pres. 1967-70; bd. dirs. Tulsa Family Mental Health Ctr., 1982-89. Named Outstanding Young Man, Tulsa Jaycees, 1963 Mem. ABA, Tulsa County Bar Assn. (Young Lawyer award 1962, pres. 1970, Pres.'s award 1984, Professionalism award 1993), Okla. Bar Assn. (mem. profl. responsiblity commn. 1977-84, vice chmn. 1983-84, Disting. svc. award 1984, Golden Gavel award 1985, Pres.'s award 1991, Masonic award for ethics 1995), So. Hills Country Club (Tulsa), Princeton Club (N.Y.C.). Republican. Episcopalian. Home: 2300 Riverside Dr Unit 3E Tulsa OK 74114-2402 Office: 100 W 5th St Ste 1000 Tulsa OK 74103-4293

ARRINGTON, LAVARR, professional football player; b. June 20, 1978; 1 child, Keeno Lamoni. Attended, Penn State Coll. Profl. football player Washington Redskins, 2000—. With Washington Redskins Leadership Coucil's Fields for Tomorrow program. Named to NFL Pro-Bowl, 2001—03; recipient Pigskin Club Oxley award, 2002, Chuck Bednarik award, 1999, Dick Butkus award, 1999. Office: 21300 Redskin Park Dr Ashburn VA 20147 Personal E-mail: 703-478-8900.

ARRINGTON, MICHAEL BROWNE, foundation administrator; b. Chgo., Mar. 24, 1943; s. W. Russell and Ruth Marian (Browne) A.; m. DeEtta Jane Watson, Dec. 15, 1966 (div. 1969); m. Trudi Jeanne Robertson, Dec. 4, 1971 (div. 1992); children: Jennifer Lorraine, Patrick Browne. AA, Kendall Coll., Evanston, Ill.; BA in Polit. Sci., U. Ill. Adminstrv. asst. to Senate Majority Leader State of Ill., Springfield, 1966-67; dir. pub. affairs Union League Club of Chgo., 1967-68; exec. dir. South Loop Improvement Orgn., Chgo., 1968-69; pres., chief exec. officer The Arrington Found., Chgo., 1979—, Arrington Travel Ctr., Inc., Chgo., 1969-99, Recon Mgmt Svcs., Evanston, Ill., 1999—. Mem. Nat. White House Conf. Travel and Tourism, Disting. Entrepreneurship Bd., U. Ill., Chgo. Bd. dirs. Robert R. McCormick Chgo. Boys & Girls Club, 1982—, Friends of Prentice Hosp., Chgo., 1986—; mem. chancellor's adv. bd. U. Ill., Chgo. Cpl. USMC, 1962-64. Named finalist Entrepreneur of Yr., 1989, 1990, Man of Yr., Ill. Vietnam Vets Leadership Program, 1993; named to Hall of Fame, Nat. Assn. Trade and Tech. Schs., 1988, Entrepreneurship Hall of Fame, 1994; recipient Excellence in Phys. Fitness award, USMC, 1962, Significant Contbn. to Dental Health award, Ill. Dental Health Soc., 1967, Alumni Achievement award, U. Ill., 2001. Mem. World Pres.'s Orgn., Econ. Club of Chgo., Chgo. Club, Westmoreland Country Club, 100 Club Cook County, Chief Execs. Orgn. Republican. Episcopalian. Avocations: golf, boating, skiing, scuba diving. Office: Recon Mgmt Svcs Inc 929 Edgemere Ct Evanston IL 60202-1428 Office Phone: 312-726-1800. E-mail: arringtonusa@ameritech.net.

ARRINGTON, MICHAEL W., lawyer, consultant; b. Lower Merion Township, Pa., June 30, 1957; s. Wayne and Marie Arrington; m. Barbara S. Szczerba, Dec. 21, 1991; 1 child, Marc-Andrew. BS in Biology, St. Joseph's Coll., 1978; MS in Secondary Ednl. Adminstrn., Villanova U., 1980; JD, Widener U., 1997. Bar: Del. 1997, DC 1999, US Dist. Ct. Del. 1998, US Ct. Appeals Md. 1998, US Bankruptcy Ct. 2002. Dir. activities Salesianum Sch., Wilmington, Del., 1978—93; prin. Associated Concert Artists, 1985—90; dir. spl. ct. services Family Ct., 1992—2000; mng. ptnr. Parkowski, Guerke & Swayze, PA, 2000—. Chmn. Del. Juvenile Justice Adv. Group, 2004—; bd. dirs. MINCAVA, Minn. Contbr. chapters to books. Del. rep. Fed. Adv. Com. Juvenile Justice, Washington, 2004; treas. Windsor Hills Cmty. Assn., 1999—2004; pack advancement chair Boy Scouts Am., 2002—04; pres., bd. rustees First and Ctrl. Presbyn. Ch., 2003; bd. dirs. Wilmington Music Sch., 2004. Mem.: Del. State Bar Assn. (chmn. pro se litig. com. 2004), Rotary. Office: Parkowski Guerke & Swayze PA 800 King St Ste 203 Wilmington DE 19801 Office Phone: 302-654-3300. Business E-Mail: marrington@pgslegal.com.

ARROSSA, MOLLY, middle school educator; b. Boise, Idaho, Oct. 30, 1950; d. John P. and Eileen (Killoran) Molitor; m. George P. Arrossa, Oct. 21, 1972; children: Tracy, Rich. BA in English Edn., Idaho State U., 1972. Tchr. Kimberly (Idaho) H.S., 1973-77, Robert Stuart Jr. H.S., Twin Falls, Idaho, 1988—, dept. chair for lang. arts, 1991—2003. Mem. lang. arts curriculum bd. Twin Falls Sch. Dist., 1995—; TRIBES character edn. trainer. Mem. Booster Club-Athletics, Kimberly H.S., 1990—. Mem. Nat. Coun. Tchrs. English, Reader's Guild (pres. 1973-74), Delta Kappa Gamma. Avocations: reading, golf, tennis, travel. Office: Robert Stuart Jr HS 644 Caswell Ave W Twin Falls ID 83301-3707

ARROTT, ELIZABETH, journalist; b. Detroit, Oct. 1, 1960; d. Anthony Schuyler and Patricia Graham Arrott; m. Rafael Alexeevich Ekimyan, Sept. 16, 1995; children: Alexei Rafaelevich Ekimyan, Elizabeth Rafaelevna Ekimyan, Catherine Rafaelevna Ekimyan. AB, Harvard U., 1983. Moscow corr. Voice of Am., Moscow, 1993-97; anchor NewsNow Voice of Am., Washington, 1998—. Mem. Ch. LDS. Home: 5026 Reno Rd NW Washington DC 20008-2951 Office: Voice of Am 330 Independence Ave SW Washington DC 20547-0003

ARROTT, PATRICIA GRAHAM, artist, educator; b. Pitts., July 27, 1931; d. George Patterson and Helen (Gilleland) Graham; m. Anthony Schuyler Arrott, June 6, 1953; children: Anthony Patterson, Helen Graham, Matthew Ramsey, Elizabeth. BFA in Painting and Design, Carnegie-Mellon Univ., 1954; postgrad., Nat. Acad. Design, N.Y.C., 1985-87, Art Students League, 1980-91. Cert. tchr. art, Pa. Instr. children's ceramics Handcraft House, Vancouver, B.C., Can., 1970-72; courtroom artist Vancouver, B.C., Can., 1972-73; pvt. portrait artist Vancouver, N.Y.C., 1975—; instr. Art Students League, N.Y.C., 1993-99. Group shows include Nat. Acad. Design, 1990, 92, 94, Cork Gallery, Lincoln Ctr., N.Y.C., 1991, Pen & Brush Club, N.Y.C., 1988-98, Silver Point Etc., 1992-93; represented by Eleanor Ettinger Gallery, N.Y.C., 1997—. Recipient Helen M. Loggie Prize, 1990, and cert. of merit, 1994, Nat. Acad. Design; recipient Emily Nicholas Hatch award Pen & Brush Club, 1989-91, Elizabeth Morse Genius award, 1988, 90, 93, 95, others. Mem. Art Student's League (life; mem. bd. 1989-92, women's v.p. 1991-92), Am. Fine Arts Soc. (mem. bd. 1991-92), Mayflower Soc. (life), Kappa Kappa Gamma (life). United Presbyterian.

ARROW, KENNETH JOSEPH, economist, educator; b. NYC, Aug. 23, 1921; s. Harry I. and Lillian (Greenberg) Arrow; m. Selma Schweitzer, Aug. 31, 1947; children: David Michael, Andrew. BS in Social Sci., CCNY, 1940; MA, Columbia U., 1941, PhD, 1951, DSc (hon.), 1973; LLD (hon.), U. Chgo., 1967, CUNY, 1972, Hebrew U. Jerusalem, 1975, U. Pa., 1976, Washington U., St. Louis, 1989; D. Social and Econ. Scis. (hon.), U. Vienna, Austria, 1971; LLD (hon.), Ben-Gurion U. of the Negev, 1992; D in Social Scis. (hon.), Yale U., 1974; D (hon.), Université René Descartes, Paris, 1974, U. Aix-Marseille III, 1985, U. Cattolica del Sacro Cuore, Milan, Italy, 1994, U. Uppsala, 1995, U. Buenos Aires, 1999, U. Cyprus, 2000; Dr.Pol., U. Helsinki, 1976; MA (hon.), Harvard U., 1968; DLitt, Cambridge U., Eng., 1985; LLD (hon.), Harvard U., 1999; PhD (hon.), Tel Aviv U., 2001; LLD (hon.), Hitotsubashi U., 2004. Rsch. assoc. Cowles Commn. for Research in Econs., 1947—49; asst. prof. econs. U. Chgo., 1948—49; acting asst. prof. econs. and stats. Stanford, 1949—50, assoc. prof., 1950—53, prof. econs., stats. and ops. rsch., 1953—68; prof. econs. Harvard, 1968—74, James Bryant Conant univ. prof., 1974—79; exec. head dept. econs. Stanford U., 1954—56, acting exec. head dept., 1962—63, Joan Kenney prof. econs. and prof. ops. rsch., 1979—91, prof. emeritus, 1991—. Economist Coun. Econ. Advisers, U.S. Govt., 1962; cons. RAND Corp.; Fulbright prof. U. Siena, 1995; vis. fellow All Souls Coll., Oxford, 1996; overseas rsch. fellow Churchill Coll., Cambridge, 1963—64, Cambridge, 1970, 73, 86. Author: Social Choice and Individual Values, 1951, Essays in the Theory of Risk Bearing, 1971, The Limits of Organization, 1974, Collected Papers, Vols. I-VI, 1983—85; co-author: Mathematical Studies in Inventory and Production, 1958, Studies in Linear and Nonlinear Programming, 1958, Time Series Analysis of Inter-industry Demands, 1959, Public Investment, The Rate of Return and Optimal Fiscal Policy, 1971, General Competitive Analysis, 1971, Studies in Resource Allocation Processes, 1977, Social Choice and Multicriterion Decision Making, 1985. Capt. U.S. Army, 1942—46. Recipient Alfred Nobel Meml. prize in econ. scis., Swedish Acad. Scis., 1972, Kempé de Feriet medal, 1998, medal, U. Paris, 1998; fellow Social Sci. Rsch. fellow, 1952, Ctr. for Advanced Study in the Behavioral Scis., 1956—57, Guggenheim, 1972—73. Fellow: NAS (mem. coun. 1990—93), AAAS (chmn. sect. K 1983), Am. Fin. Assn., Internat. Soc. Inventory Rsch. (pres. 1983—90), Am. Econ. Assn. (exec. com. 1967—69, pres. 1973, John Bates Clark medal 1957), Inst. Math. Stats., Am. Acad. Arts and Scis. (v.p. 1979—81, 1991—93), Econometric Soc. (v.p. 1955, pres. 1956), Am. Statis. Assn.; mem.: NAS/Inst. of Medicine, Game Theory Soc., Brit. Acad. (corr.), Pontifical Acad. Social Scis., Soc. Social Choice and Welfare (pres. 1991—93), Western Econ. Assn. (pres. 1980—81), Finnish Acad. Scis. (fgn. hon.), Inst. Ops. Rsch. and Mgmt. Sci. (pres. 1963, chmn. coun. 1964, Von Neumann prize 1986, Fellows' award), Am. Philos. Soc., Internat. Econs. Assn. (pres. 1983—86). Office: Stanford U Dept Econs Stanford CA 94305-6072 Fax: 650-725-5702. Office Phone: 650-723-9165. Business E-Mail: arrow@stanford.edu.

ARROWOOD, CATHARINE BIGGS, lawyer; b. Lumberton, N.C., Nov. 27, 1951; d. Isley Murchison and Janis (Bolton) Biggs; m. Joseph S. Arrowood, Aug. 9, 1975; 1 child, Catharine Jeannette. BA cum laude, Wake Forest U., 1973, JD cum laude, 1976. Bar: N.C. 1973. Assoc. atty. gen. antitrust sect. Dept. Justice, Raleigh, N.C., 1976-77; ptnr., litig. Parker Poe Adams & Bernstein LLP, Raleigh, NC, 1977—, mem. mgmt. com., 1990—2001. Mem. panel of comml. arbitrators, Am. Arbitration Assn.; chair, Fed. Bar Adv. Council, 1995-96, Civil Justice Reform Act Com., ea. dist NC, 1997; mem. Gov.'s Adminstrv. Rules Review Commn., Raleigh, 1983-90. Editor (assoc.): Wake Forest Law Rev. Chair bd. vis., Wake Forest Univ. Law Sch., 2001-02. Fellow Am. Coll. Trial Lawyers; mem. ABA, N.C. Bar Assn., Nat. Health Lawyers Assn., N.C. Assn. Health Lawyers (bd. dirs. 1984), Phi Beta Kappa. Democrat. Baptist. Office Phone: 919-890-4142. Office Fax: 919-834-4564. Business E-Mail: cbarrowood@parkerpoe.com.

ARROWSMITH, MARIAN CAMPBELL, secondary education educator; b. St. Louis, Nov. 12, 1943; d. William Rankin and Elizabeth (Mitchell) Arrowsmith; m. William Earl Schroyer, July 23, 1983; stepchildren: Carey Jo, Amy Lynn. BS, La. State U., 1961; MEd, Southeastern La. U., 1978. Lic. tchr., La.; cert. practicum supr. Inst. for Reality Therapy. Tchr. 1st grade McDonough #26, Jefferson Parish Sch. Bd., Gretna, La., 1966; 2nd grade tchr. Woodlawn High Sch., Baton Rouge, 1966-67; kindergarten tchr. Univ. Terrace Elem. Sch., Baton Rouge, summer 1967; 1st grade tchr. Westminster Elem. Sch., Baton Rouge, 1967-72, Elm Grove Elem. Sch., Harvey, La., 1972-73; kindergarten tchr. Westminster Elem. Sch., Baton Rouge, summers 1968, 69, 70, 71, Elm Grove Elem. Sch., summer 1973; 1st grade tchr. St. Andrews Episcopal Sch., New Orleans, 1973-74; kindergarten tchr. St. Tammany Parish Sch. Bd., Folsom, La., 1974-77; early childhood specialist St. Tammany Parish Sch. Bd., Covington, La., 1977-87; prin. Woodlake Elementary Sch., 1987-99, supr. of instrn., St. Tammany Parish, 1999-; off-campus coordinating asst. St. Tammany Parish for Dept. Continuing Edn., Southeastern La. U., 1985-87; condr. workshops in field; selected ofcl. pres. Sunbelt Region of Reality Therapists, 1983; regional dir. La. and Miss. Reality Therapists, Sunbelt Bd. of Reality Therapists, 1983. Author: Helping Your Child at Home, 1982-83; Handbook for Early Childhood Tutorial Program, 1983-84. Mem. Ctr. Learning Devel. and Learning, Regina Coedn. Child Devel. Ctr. (HeadStart), Jr. League. Mem. ASCD, La. Assn. Sch. Execs., Nat. Assn. Tchrs. Math., La. Assn. Tchrs. Math., Pontchartrain Yacht Club, Delta Kappa Gamma (v.p. 1986), Alpha Delta Kappa, Kappa Alpha Theta, Phi Delta Kappa. Democrat. Methodist. Avocations: horticulture, reading, fishing, dancing. Home: 1000 Montgomery St Mandeville LA 70448-5517 Office Phone: 985-892-2276. E-mail: marianarrowsmith@charter.net.

ARROYO, F. THADDEUS, telecommunications industry executive; b. San Francisco; m. Alyssa Arroyo; 1 child. BS in Math., U. Tex., Arlington, 1986; MBA, So. Methodist U. Info. tech. Southwestern Bell; mgr., dir., v.p. Sabre Corp., sr. v.p., info. tech. svcs., sr. v.p., product mktg. and devel.; chief info. officer Cingular Wireless, Atlanta, 2001—. Recipient Disting. Alumna award, U. Tex., Arlington, 2001, Ga. Global Chief Info. Officer of Yr., 2002. Mem.: Nat. Soc. of Hispanic MBAs, N. Fulton County C. of C. Office: Cingular Wireless Glenridge Highlands Two 5655 Glenridge Connector Atlanta GA 30342

ARROYO, MARTINA, soprano; b. N.Y.C. d. Demetrio and Lucille (Washington) A. Studied successively with Marinka Gurevich, Joseph Turnau and Rose Landver; student, Kathryn Long Course Met. Opera.; BA, Hunter Coll. CUNY, 1954, DHL (hon.), 1987. Disting. prof. Ind. U., Bloomington. Debut, Carnegie Hall, 1958, leading soprano, Met. Opera, N.Y.C.; in roles including: Trovatore, Rida, Ballo, Forza, Chenier; performed opening night Met. season, 1970-71, 71-72, 73-74, performed at La Scala, Milan, Munich Staatsoper, Berlin Deutsche Oper, Rome Opera, Vienna State Opera, Covent Garden, Teatro Colon, Buenos Aires, San Francisco, Chgo., and all maj. opera houses; soloist, N.Y., Vienna, Berlin, Royal (London), Paris philharmonics, San Francisco, Pitts., Phila., Chgo., Cleve. symphonies, Concertgebouw, other maj. orchs.; frequent performer Saratoga, Ravinia, Tanglewood festivals and festivals Vienna, Berlin, Edinburgh, Helsinki; oratorios include Judas Maccabaeus; recorded for Columbia, London, Angel, DGG, Philips, EMI, RCA. Former mem. Nat. Endowment of Arts, Washington; trustee Carnegie Hall, N.Y.C. Named Outstanding Alumna Hunter Coll., N.Y.C. Office: Ludwig Branner Mgmt 165 W 66th ST New York NY 10023 E-mail: lbmgmt@aol.com.

ARSENEAU, JAMES CHARLES, physician; b. Syracuse, N.Y., Aug. 29, 1942; s. James Howard and Glenna Carolyn (Worth) A.; m. Jane Macy, July 2, 1966; children: Marc, David. AB, Syracuse U., 1964; MD, Albany Med. Coll., 1968. Intern and resident in medicine Strong Meml. Hosp., Rochester, N.Y., 1968-70, fellow in med. oncology, 1973-74; clin. assoc. med. br. Nat. Cancer Inst., Bethesda, Md., 1970-73; asst. prof. medicine U. Rochester, 1974-80, assoc. prof. medicine, 1980-83; head med. oncology unit Rochester Gen. Hosp., 1974-83; clin. assoc. prof. medicine Albany Med. Coll., 1985—; ptnr. Albany Regional Cancer Ctr., 1983—. Pres. med. staff St. Peter's Hosp., Albany, N.Y., 1993-95, bd. dirs., 1997—. Author numerous chpts. in textbooks; contbr. articles to profl. jours. Sr. Asst. Surgeon USPHS, 1970-73. Mem. Am. Soc. Clin. Oncology, Albany County Med. Soc. (exec. com. 1993—), Am Radium Soc., Upstate N.Y. Soc. Med. Oncology/Hematology (pres. 1994—), Gynecologic Oncology Group (chmn. devel. therapeutic com. 1980—), Wolfert's Roost Country Club, Zeta Psi, Alpha Omega Alpha (pres. 1966-67). Avocations: reading, chess, tennis, golf, skiing. Home: 205 Graffunder Dr Albany NY 12204-1301 Office: Albany Regional Cancer Ctr 317 S Manning Blvd Ste 330 Albany NY 12208-1774 Office Phone: 518-489-2607. Business E-Mail: james.arseneau@usoncology.com.

ARSHT, ADRIENNE, lawyer, broadcast executive, bank executive; b. Wilmington, Del., Feb. 4, 1942; d. Samuel and Roxana (Cannon) Arsht; m. Myer Feldman, Sept. 28, 1980. BA, Mt. Holyoke Coll., 1963; JD, Villanova U., 1966. Bar: Del. 1966. Assoc. Morris, Nichols, Arsht and Tunnell, Wilmington, 1966-69, Bregman, Abel and Kay, Washington, 1979-84; dir. govt. affairs TWA, N.Y.C., 1969-79; pres., chmn. bd. Land Title & Escrow Corp., Washington, 1981-86; v.p. Ardman Broadcasting Corp., Washington, 1984—, also bd. dirs.; chmn. bd. TotalBank Corp. Fla., Miami, 1986—; also bd. dirs. Totalbank Corp. Fla., Miami; chmn. Eve Stillman Corp., N.Y.C., 1989-99, also bd. dirs. Bd. dirs. Ardman, Inc., Washington, Capital Broadcasting, Inc., Kansas City, Mo., Trade Nat. Bank, Miami. Bd. dirs. Washington Opera Co., 1982-84, Am. Ballet Theatre, N.Y.C., 1984-90; founder, chmn. Van Guard Found., Washington, 1987-94, Fit and Fabulous, Washington, 1992-93; mem. exec. com. Lombardi Cancer Ctr., Washington, 1988-92; mem. Com. of 200, Coun. on Fgn. Rels.; chmn. bd. dirs. Kennedy Ctr. Prodns., inc., 1982—; U.S. adv. bd. women's internat. forum Dare to Dream Found.; exec. com., sec. Performing Arts Found., Miami. Named Woman of Yr., Am. Ballet Theatre, 1989. Mem. Del. Bar Assn., Women's Internat. Forum, Miami C. of C., Rana Soc. (founder). Office: Total Bank 2720 Coral Way Miami FL 33145-3271 Office Phone: 305-476-6258. *By giving more than you receive, you receive more than you give.*

ARSHT, EDWIN DAVID, physician; b. Phila., Oct. 6, 1929; BA in Zoology, Swarthmore Coll., 1951; MD, Jefferson Med. Coll., 1955. Diplomate Am. Bd. Family Practice; cert. med. dir./long term care. Intern Frankford Hosp., Phila., 1956; resident in gen. practice Mountainside Hosp., Montclair, N.J., 1959; pvt. practice Springfield, Pa., 1959-94; dir. med. edn. Delaware County Meml. Hosp., Drexel Hill, Pa., 1960-90, chief allergy, 1970-2000, chmn. dept. family practice, 1976-86, Riddle Meml. Hosp., Media, Pa., 1993-95; med. dir. HM Nursing Home, Springfield, 1965—. Author: Psychological Approaches to Family Practice, 1979. Chmn. commn. on med. edn. Pa. Acad. Family Practice, 1970—82. Capt. U.S. Army, 1956—58. Fellow Am. Acad. Family Physicians; mem. Delaware County Acad. Family Practice (pres. 1960-85). Home and Office: 611 W Woodland Ave Springfield PA 19064-1633 Office: Harlee Manor Nursing Home 463 W Sproul Rd Springfield PA 19064-2198

ARTEAGA, AGUSTIN, museum director, architect; b. Tierra Blanca, Mex., Feb. 14, 1958; s. Ramón and Balbína (Domínguez) Arteaga. Student, U. Metropolitana, Mexico City; M in Art History, U. Autónoma, M in Art History, postgrad., U. Autónoma, Mex. Prof. U. Autónoma, Mexico, 1983—89; dep. dir., curator Mus. Modern Art, Mexico City, 1990—94; prof. U. Nuevo Mundo, Mexico, 1993—96; nat. dir. Vis. Arts Inst. Nat. Bellas Artes, Mexico, 1994—98; dir., chief curator Mus. Palacio Belles Artes, Mexico City, 1994—99; founding dir., ch. curator Malba-Constantini Collection, Argentina, 2000—02; curator Gallery Nat. Jeu du Pauma, Paris, 2002—04, Bienal de Mercosur, Porto Alegre, Brazil, 2002—04, Mus Nat. Art, Mexico City, 2002—04; CEO, exec. dir. Mus. Art Ponce, PR, 2004—. Author: Cuerpos Terrenales, 2003. Juror Bienal Monterrey, Mexico, 2003, Found. Nat. Art Min. Culture, Mexico, 2003, Contacto Cultural Rockefeller Found., Mexico, 2003—04. Decorated Chevalier ordre des Arts Letres Republic of France. Roman Catholic. Office: Mus Art Ponce 2325 Ave Las Americas Ponce PR 00717

ARTEAGA, CARLOS L., medical researcher, director; MD with honors, U. Guayaquil, 1980; trained in internal medicine and med. oncology, Emory U., U. Tex. Health-Scis. Ctr. Cert. internal medicine Am. Bd. Internal Medicine, med. oncology Am. Bd. Internal Medicine. Faculty mem. Vanderbilt U., 1988—, prof. medicine and cancer biology, Ingram prof. cancer rsch., mem. divsn. hematology, dir. breast cancer rsch. program, dir. breast cancer specialized programs for rsch. excellence, Vanderbilt-Ingram Comprehensive Cancer Ctr. Co-chair devel. therapeutics com. Eastern Cooperative Oncology Group; mem. bd. sci. advisors Nat. Cancer Inst., 1999—2004; chmn. spl. conf. com. Am. Assn. Cancer Rsch., 2002—, bd. dirs., 2004—; mem. parent com. for review of cancer ctrs. NIH, 2004—. Assoc. editor, mem. editl. bd. Jour. Mammary Gland Biology & Neoplasia, Clin. Cancer Therapeutics, Jour. Clin. Oncology, Clin. Proteomics, Cancer Biology and Therapy; contbr. articles to profl. jours. Recipient Richard and Hinda Rosenthal Found. award, Am. Assn. Cancer Rsch., 2003. Achievements include research in the role of polypeptide growth factors and receptor tyosine kinases in mammary devel./transformation and breast cancer progression; development of molecular therapeutics in breast cancer. Office: Vanderbilt U Med Ctr 682 Preston Rsch Bldg MRB 11 Nashville TN 37232-6307 also: Vanderbilt U Med Ctr 2220 Piece Ave 777 Preston Rsch Bldg Nashville TN 37232-6307 Office Phone: 615-936-1919. Business E-Mail: carlos.arteaga@vanderbilt.edu.

ARTEMOV, VLADIMIR NIKOLAEVICH, gymnastics coach; b. Vladimir City, Russia, Dec. 7, 1964; came to U.S., 1990; s. Nikolai Filippovich and Maria vasilievna (Mileshnikova) A.; m. Susan Ann Wallace, July 28, 1991; children: Glenn Vladimirovich, Alexander Vladimirovich. Phys. conditioning instr. USSR Mil., 1987-88; staff mem. South Tex. Gymnastics Acad., 1991-92, Team USA Gynmastics Camp, 1991; head coach Kips Gymnastics, 1993—; coach Pan Am. Tng. Camp, 1994; mem. U.S.A. Nat. Coaching staff, 1990—; cons. Elios Gynmastic Tng. Ctr., Mexico, 1995—. Spkr. in field; head coach, dir. Brown's Gymnastics, San Antonio, 2005—. Contbr. articles to profl. jours. Recipient Master of Sport Internat. Class, 1981, 83, 88. Winner 4 gold medals, 1 silver medal Olympics, Seoul, South Korea, 1988, 1 gold, 1 silver medal World Championships, 1983, 1 gold, 1 silver medal, 1985, 2 gold, 1 silver, 1 bronze medal, 1987, 3 gold, 1 silver, 1 bronze medal, 1989, 1 bronze medal World Cup, 1986, 2 gold, 2 silver medals Univ. Games, 1983. Office: Brown's Gymnastics 21750 Hardy Oak Blvd San Antonio TX 78258 E-mail: artemov@mail.ev1.net.

ARTERBERRY, PATRICIA, retired elementary school educator; b. Huntingburg, Ind., Apr. 11, 1947; d. Otis T. Barnett and Fanny Delores Wessel; m. Ronnie G. Arterberry, Oct. 15, 1994; children: Eric Alan, Randall Gene, Tony Gene. BS, U. Evansville (Ind.), 1970, MA, 1973. Tchr. grade 3 Tell City (Ind.) Troy Twp. Schs., tchr. primary grades; ret., 2005. Active Boy Scouts Am.; mem. United Meth. Ch. Recipient Dist. award of Merit, Boy Scouts Am., Coun. Silver Beaver award for outstanding svc. Mem. NEA, Ind. Tchrs. Assn., TCTTCTA, Order Ea. Star, Delta Kappa Gamma. Home: 9575 Sweetwater Rd Tell City IN 47586-9707

ARTERIAN, HANNAH R., dean, law educator; b. 1949; BS, Elmira Coll., 1970; JD, U. Iowa, 1973. Bar: NY 1974. Assoc. Dewey, Ballantine, Bushby, Palmer & Wood, NYC, 1973—78; vis. assoc. prof. law U. Iowa, 1977, assoc. prof., 1978, Ariz. State U., 1979—82, prof., 1982—2002, assoc. dean, 1992—2001; dean, prof. law Syracuse U. Coll. Law, 2002—. Vis. prof. U. Houston, 1983—84. Mem.: Phi Beta Kappa, Order of the Coif. Office: Syracuse U Coll Law Ste 340 Syracuse NY 13244-1962 Office Phone: 315-443-2524. E-mail: arterian@law.syr.edu.*

ARTERTON, JANET BOND, federal judge; b. Philadelphia, Feb. 8, 1944; m. F. Christopher Arterton; two children. BA, Mt. Holyoke Coll., 1966; JD, Northeastern U., 1977. Law clk. to Hon. Herbert J. Stern U.S. Dist. Ct. N.J., 1977-78; ptnr. Garrison & Arterton, 1978-95; judge U.S. Dist. Ct. Conn., New Haven, 1995—. Fellow Am. Bar Found., Conn. Bar Found.; mem. ATLA, Nat. Employment Lawyers Assn., Conn. Employment Lawyers Assn., Conn. State Trial Lawyers Assn. (bd. govs. 1990-95), Conn. Bar Assn. (mem. adv. com. state ct. rules 1992, mem. fed. jud. selection com. 1991-93, mem. exec. com. women and the law sect. 1990-93, chairperson fed. practice sect. 1993-95. Office: US Dist Ct Conn 141 Church St New Haven CT 06510-2030

ARTEST, RON (RONALD WILLIAM ARTEST JR.), professional basketball player; b. Queensbridge, NY, Nov. 13, 1979; m. Kimsha Artest; 4 children. Student in mathematics, St. John's, 1998—99. Profl. basketball player Chicago Bulls, 1999—2002, Indiana Pacers, 2002—. Founder, CEO TruWarier Records, Stamford, Conn.; founder clothing line TruWarier Wear. Named NBA's 2003-04 Defensive Player of the Year; named to All Star Team, 2004. Achievements include selection by the Chicago Bulls in the first round (16th overall) of the 1999 NBA Draft; league leader with an average of 3.29 steals for every 48 minutes played in 2002-03. Office: Indiana Pacers Market St Arena 300 E Market St Fl 1 Indianapolis IN 46204-2603 also: TruWarier Records 500 Newfield Ave Suite 1 Stamford CT 06905

ARTHER, RICHARD OBERLIN, polygraphist, educator; b. Pitts., May 20, 1928; s. William Churchill Sr. and Florence Lind (Oberlin) A.; m. Mary-Esther Wuensch, Sept. 12, 1951; children: Catherine, Linda, William III. BS, Mich. State U., 1951; MA, Columbia U., 1960. Chief assoc. John E. Reid and Assocs., Chgo., 1951-53, dir. N.Y.C., 1953-58; pres. Sci. Lie Detection, Inc., N.Y.C., 1958—2003, chmn., 2003—; pres. Nat. Tng. Ctr. Polygraph Sci., N.Y.C., 1958—. Author: Interrogation for Investigators, 1958, The Scientific Investigator, 1964, 7th edit., Arther Polygraph Reference Guide, 1964-, 8th edit.; editor Jour. Polygraph Sci., 1966-. Fellow Acad. Cert. Polygraphists (exec. dir. 1962—), Am. Polygraph Assn. (founding mem.), Am. Assn. Police Polygraphists (founding mem., Polygraphist of Yr. 1980), N.Y. State Polygraphists (founder), N.J. Polygraphists (founder). Office: Sci Lie Detection Inc 200 W 57th St Ste 1400 New York NY 10019-3211

ARTHO, VIRGINIA LOU, writer, publications designer; b. Hereford, Tex., Feb. 18, 1956; d. David Daniel and Laura Belle (Willie) Downey; m. Edward Mike Artho, June 9, 1973; children: Jeremy, Jared, Matthew, Sarah. H.S. grad., Hereford, Tex. Asst. dir., dir. publs. Nat. Cowgirl Hall of Fame and Western Heritage Ctr., Hereford, Tex., 1991-95; adminstr. and co-editor Promised Land Network (non-profit sustainable agrl. orgn.), Hereford, 1995-96; freelance writer, designer Hereford, 1996—. Editor newsletter, mags., other publs., designer publs., Nat. Cowgirl Hall of Fame and Western Heritage Ctr., Hereford, Tex., 1991-95; newsletter editor, organizer, producer of ednl. events, Promised Land Network, Hereford, 1990-96. Author, designer, editor: (book) Isora DeRacy Young: Calf Roping Queen, 1993; co-author, editor: (book) Cowgirl Legends, 1995; editor, designer (mag.) Sidesaddle, 1991-94; designer, author: (newsletter) Big West, 1991-94; editor, designer, author The Promised Land, 1993-96; contbg. writer The Hereford Brand Newspaper, 1998—; portrait painter. Mentor Big Sch.-Big Bros., 2000—02, Big Sisters, 2001—; mem. citizen watch group Power, Stand, and Peace Farm, Hereford, Amarillo, Tex., 1982—97; mem. citizens response to legis. Nat. Campaign. for Sustainable Agr., 1994—97; lay preacher Cath. Diocese of Amarillo, 1987—; founder, pres. Hereford (Tex.) Youth Ministerial Alliance, 1989—90; organizer Hereford Fiestas Patrias Com., 1990—91; lector coord. St. Anthony's Ch., 2001—02, leader Life Teen Core, 2001—, facilitator young adult Bible study, 2003. Named (family) Hereford Family of the Yr., LDS ch. of Hereford, 1985; recipient Editor's Choice award, Nat. Libr. Poetry, 1996, 97, Outstanding Poet of 1998. Mem. Internat. Soc. Poets (Disting. Mem. 1995-96), Famous Poets Soc. (Famous Poet for 1996, 98, 99), Golden Spread Aggie Mom's Club (1st v.p., 1997-99, historian-reporter 1998-2000). Roman Catholic. Avocations: writing, art, needlecrafts, gardening, reading. Home: 223 Greenwood St Hereford TX 79045-3846

ARTHUR, GARY L., JR., energy executive; BBA, U. Ky.; MBA, Morehead State U. Various pos., to v.p. bus. ops. Ashland Petroleum; v.p. supply and distbn. Colonial Group; v.p. mktg., supply and transp. Valero Energy Corp., San Antonio, 2000, sr. v.p., mktg., 2000—. Office: Valero Corp Hdqrs One Valero Pl San Antonio TX 78212-3186*

ARTHUR, GREER MARTIN, maritime container leasing firm executive; b. Champaign, Ill., Feb. 15, 1935; s. Greer Martin and Olive Loretta (Simard) A.; m. Veronica Lattman, Nov. 30, 1968; children: Alexandra, Vincent, Tanya, Greer III. BA, Lafayette Coll., 1956; JD, Columbia U., 1961. Bar: N.Y. 1961. Acct. exec. tng. program Young & Rubicam, 1957-58; assoc. Havens, Wandless, Stitt & Tighe, N.Y.C., 1961—62; mgmt. cons. McKinsey & Co., 1962-67; asst. to v.p. internat. Scovill Mfg. Co., Waterbury, Conn.; internat. market mgr. Scovill France, Paris; market mgr. Hamilton Beach div. Scovill, Waterbury, 1967-69; pres., CEO SSI Container Corp., subs. Itel Corp., San Francisco, 1969-73; founder, chmn., pres., CEO, dir. Trans Ocean Ltd., San Bruno, Calif., 1973-96. Founder, dir., bd. dirs. Inst. Internat. Container Lessors, 1970—73, dir., 1977—96, pres., 1989—90, 1994—95; chmn. bd. dirs. Trans Ocean Distbn., Ltd., Southampton, England. Treas., trustee Phillips Brooks Sch., Menlo Park, Calif., 1980-83; bd. dirs. Nat. Alzheimer's Assn., 1994-2002, San Francisco Opera, 1999—; with Lafayette Coll. Nat. Coun., 1991-93. Mem.: World Pres. Orgn. (No. Calif. chpt. chmn. 1991—92, bd. dirs. 1994—99), Chief Exec. Orgn. (bd. dirs. 1990—91), Sharon Heights Golf Club, Lahontan Golf Club (Lake Tahoe), Lake Tahoe Yacht Club, Bankers Club, Family Club. Office: Trans Ocean Distribution 2105 Woodside Rd Woodside CA 94062

ARTHUR, HUGH THOMAS (H. THOMAS ARTHUR II), lawyer; b. 1945; BA, Wofford Coll., 1967; PhD in economics, U. SC, 1971; JD, Mercer U., Macon, Ga., 1982. Bar: SC 1982. Economics tchr., 1971—79; atty. regulatory affairs SC Electric & Gas Co., 1982—87; v.p., gen. counsel SC Pipeline Corp., 1987—96; v.p., gen. counsel, asst. sec. SCANA Corp., Columbia, SC, 1996—98, sr. v.p., gen. counsel, asst. sec., 1998—. Mem. St. David's Episcopal Ch. Mem.: Energy Bar Assn., Ga. Bar Assn., SC Bar Assn., ABA. Office: SCANA Corp 1426 Main St Columbia SC 29201-2845*

ARTHUR, JETT CLINTON, retired chemist; b. Hemphill, Tex., May 31, 1918; s. Jett Clinton Arthur and Anna Alice Smith; m. LaVerne Pitts Arthur, June 2, 1941 (dec. Nov. 30, 1997); children: Martha Stitsinger, Clinton Arthur, Laura Porter. BA in Chemistry, S.F. Austin State U., Nacogdoches, Tex., 1939; MA in Chemistry, U. Tex., 1946. Registered profl. engr., La. Sci. tchr. Appleby Pub. Sch., Tex., 1940—41; rsch. chemist USDA So. Regional Rsch. Ctr., New Orleans, 1941—43, 1946—49, rsch. chemist in charge, 1949—66, chief rsch. chemist, 1966—79. Cons., Metairie, La., 1979—; organizer numerous nat. and internat. meetings. Contbr. articles to profl. jours.:, editor 6 books. Worked with youth Boy Scouts Am., local and nat. parent-tchr. orgns. Lt. comdr. USNR, 1943—46, WWII. Named Eagle Scout; recipient award, Alpha Chi, grants in field. Fellow: AIChE (com. chmn. 1969—, award New Orleans sect.); mem.: ACS (emeritus mem. bd. cell divsn. 1994—, divsn. chmn., vol. 1946—96, abstractor founding sect. editor adv. bds., Herty medal Ga. sect., So. Chemist award, S.W. Regional award, Anselme Payen Cellulose award, chem. modification of cotton medal 2004), Chem. Heritage Found., Am. Acad. Environ. Engring., Sigma Xi. Democrat. Methodist. Achievements include patents in field; research in nuclear radiation, free radical and graft copolymerization reactions of cotton fibers to increase textile values; natural product research: cellulose, protein, enzyme. Avocations: chess, outdoor activities, sports, theology. Home and Office: 3013 Ridgeway Dr Metairie LA 70002

ARTHUR, JOHN MORRISON, retired utilities executive; b. Pitts., Aug. 17, 1922; s. Hugh Morrison and Anna Matilda (Crowe) A.; m. Sylvia Ann Martin, June 19, 1948; children: William Robert, John Martin, Andrew Scott. BEE, U. Pitts., 1944, MEE, 1947. With Duquesne Light Co., Pitts., 1944-87, asst. to chmn. bd. and pres., 1966-67, pres., 1967-68, chmn. bd., chief exec. officer, 1968-83, chmn. bd., pres., 1983-85, chmn. bd., 1986-87, ret., 1987. Trustee emeritus U. Pitts. With AUS, 1942-43. Mem. Duquesne Club, Montour Heights Country Club, Rolling Rock Club. Office Phone: 412-264-8224. E-mail: jmaama@earthlink.net.

ARTHUR, LINDSAY GRIER, retired judge, editor, writer; b. Mpls., July 30, 1917; s. Hugh and Alice (Grier) A.; m. Jean Johansen, Sept. 19, 1940; children: Lindsay G., Hugh Emil, Mollie K., Julie A. AB, Princeton U., 1939; postgrad., Harvard U., 1939-40; LLB, JD, U. Minn., 1946. Bar: Minn. 1946, U.S. Dist. Ct. Minn. 1948, U.S. Supreme Ct. 1964. Lawyer Nieman, Bosard & Arthur, Mpls., 1946-54; alderman Mpls. City Coun., 1951-54; judge Mcpl. Ct., Mpls., 1954-61; chief judge juvenile divsn. Dist. Ct., Mpls., 1961-79, 87-93, judge felony, civil divsn., 1979-83, chief judge mental health divsn., 1983-87; mediator, 1987—. Arbitrator civil and family cts., 1991—. Author: Minnesota Practice, 1974, Juvenile Case Law, 1980, Twin Cities Uncovered, 1996, A Manual for Mediators, 1995; editor Digest of Juvenile and Family Law, 1983-93; contbr. over 40 articles to profl. jours. Bd. dirs. Nat. Ctr. State Cts., Williamsburg, 1974-77, Metro YMCA, Mpls. area, 1981-85; chmn. trustees Bethlehem Luth. Ch., 1979-80. Lt. USNR, 1942-45, PTO. Mem. Nat. Coun. Juvenile Ct. Judges (pres. 1972-73, Jud. scholar 1985-2005), ABA (disabilities com. 1984-89), Am. Law Inst. (advisor divorce law 1989-93). Avocation: writing. Home: Apt 232 8505 Flying Cloud Dr Eden Prairie MN 55344-3956 E-mail: lgasr@earthlink.net.

ARTHUR, MICHAEL DEAN, music director; b. Richmond, Ky., Oct. 5, 1976; s. Billy Dean and Sharon Graham Arthur; m. Joely Lynn Choat, June 16, 2001; 1 child, Madison Grace. MusB in Edn., Morehead State U., 1999; MusM in Edn., U. Ky., 2005. Orch. dir. SE Christian Ch., Louisville, 2002—04; mem. adv. bd. Ky. Pagentry Arts Assn., Louisville, 2004—. Mem.: Music Educators Nat. Conf., Ky. Music Educator Assn., Middletown Optimist Club. Conservative. Christian. Avocations: saxophone, clarinet. Office: Eastern High Sch 12400 Old Shelbyville Rd Middletown KY 40243 Office Phone: 502-485-8383. Home Fax: 522-485-3883; Office Fax: 502-485-3883. E-mail: marthur2@jefferson.k12.ky.us.

ARTHUR, MICHAEL ELBERT, lawyer, investment advisor; b. Seattle, Oct. 9, 1952; s. Theodore E. and Gladys L. (Jones) A.; m. Claire C. Meeker, Dec. 23, 1974; children: Christine, Conor, Austin. BA, U. Calif., Santa Barbara, 1974; JD, Stanford U., 1977. Ptnr. Miller Nash LLP, Portland, Oreg., 1977—2001; fin. advisor UBS Fin. Svcs., Portland, 2001—. Trustee Chiles Found. Home: 13535 NW Lariat Ct Portland OR 97229-7001 Office: UBS Financial Svcs 805 SW Broadway Ste 2600 Portland OR 97205-3365 Office Phone: 503-225-9211. Business E-Mail: mike.arthur@ubs.com.

ARTHUR, PAUL KEITH, retired engineer; b. Kansas City, Mo., Jan. 14, 1931; s. Walter B. and Frieda J. (Burckhardt) A.; m. Joy N. Lim, Apr. 26, 1958; children: Gregory V., Lia F. Student, Ohio No. U., 1947, Taylor U., Upland, Ind., 1948-49; BSEE, Purdue U., 1956; postgrad., N.Mex. State U., 1957-78. Registered profl. engr., N.Mex.; cert. army acquisition profl.; cert. Naval engring. duty officer, Navy material profl. With White Sands Missile Range, N.Mex., 1956—2004; electronic engr. field engring. group, missile flight surveillance office, 1956-60; chief field engring group, 1960-62; project engr. Pershing Weapon Sys. Army Missile Test and Evaluation Directorate, 1962-74; chief high altitude air def. projects br., 1974-82; chief air def. materiel test divsn., 1982-91; dep dir. Materiel Test Directorate, 1991-95; dir., 1995-98; exec. dir. Nat. Range, 1998-99; dep. comdr. White Sands Test Ctr., 1999—2001, comdr., 2001—03; dep. to comdg. gen./tech. dir. White Sands Missile Range, 2003—04; ret., 2004. Mem. N.Mex. Spaceport Commn., 1994-95, Southwest Regional Space Task Force, Metro Planning Orgn.; past pres. missile range pioneer group; bd. dirs. Dagupan Electric Corp. of the Philippines. Author numerous plans and reports on weapon systems test and evaluation and topics in naval engring. Chmn. adminstrv. bd. Meth. Ch., 1992-95. Served with USN, 1949-53, USNR, 1954-87, rear adm. and sr. engring. duty officer, 1984-87. Decorated Legion of Merit, Meritorious Svc. medal, Navy Achievement medal, Navy Expeditionary medal, Mil. Order St. Barbara, Meritorious Civilian Svc., Army Decoration for Exceptional Civilian Svc.; named to White Sands Missile Range Hall of Famel, 2005; recipient ITEA Lifetime Achievement award, others. Mem. AIAA (past vice chmn.), Internat. Test and Evaluation Assn., Am. Def. Preparedness Assn. (past pres.), Assn. Old Crows, Naval Res. Assn., Res. Officers Assn. (pres. 1983-85), United Vets. Coun. (chmn. 1984-85), Am. Soc. Naval Engrs., Naval Inst., Navy League, Surface Navy Assn., Assn. U.S. Army, Purdue U. Alumni Assn. (past pres.), N.Mex. State U. Alumni Assn., Mesilla Valley Track Club, Bujutsukan Acad. Martial Arts. Home: 2050 San Acacio St Las Cruces NM 88001-1570 Personal E-mail: paul.k.arthur@comcast.net.

ARTHUR, RAY, retail executive; Degree, William Paterson Coll. CPA. With Am. Home Products; with Lederle Labs. Divsn. Am. Cyanamid; with KPMG Peat Marwick; v.p., corp. controller Gen. Signal Corp., Stamford, Conn., corp. controller; from v.p., controller to sr. v.p. pres., toysrus.com Toys R Us, Inc., Wayne, NJ, 2000—02, pres., toysrus.com, 2002—04, CFO, 2004—. Chmn. bd. William Paterson Univ. Found. Office: Toys R Us Inc 1 Geoffrey Way Wayne NJ 07470-2030

ARTHUR, RAYMOND L., retail toy and game company executive; Grad., William Paterson Coll. Plant controller Lederle Labs., Am. Cyanamid Co., 1986—89; mgr. fin. reporting Am. Cyanamid Co., 1989—94; asst. controller, asst. v.p., dir. compliance Am. Home Products Corp., Madison, NJ, 1994—97; v.p., corp. controller Gen. Signal Corp., Stamford, Conn., 1997—99, Toys "R" Us Inc., 1999—2000, Toysrus.com, 2000, v.p. fin. and adminstrn., 2000, sr. v.p., CFO, 2000—02, pres., 2002—04; CFO Toys "R" Us Inc., 2004—. Chmn. bd. William Paterson U. Found. Office: Toys R Us Inc 1 Geoffrey Way Wayne NJ 07470-2030

ARTHUR, THOMAS CARLTON, former dean, law educator; b. July 11, 1946; s. Charles Ralph and Mary Ruth (Parker) Arthur; m. Carolyn Scott Fisher, June 15, 1968; children: John, David. BA, Duke U., 1968; JD, Yale U., 1971. Bar: DC 1972, Va. 1972, U.S. Ct. Appeals (D.C. cir.) 1972, U.S. Supreme Ct. 1979. Assoc. Kirkland & Ellis, Washington, DC, 1971—77, ptnr., 1978—82; assoc. prof. Sch. Law Emory U., Atlanta, 1982—, sr. faculty mem. Law and Econs. Ctr., 1983—, interim vice provost internat. affairs, dean, 2002—05; dean of counsel Trotter Smith & Jacobs, Atlanta, 1984—92. Contbr. articles to Law Rev. Pres. Falls Ch. Cmty. Service Coun., 1974—75. Mem.: ABA, Phi Beta Kappa. Methodist. Office: Emory U Sch Law 1301 Clifton Rd Atlanta GA 30322 Office Phone: 404-712-8815. Office Fax: 404-727-0866.*

ARTHUR, WILLIAM LYNN, environmental and political program director; b. Spokane, Wash., May 22, 1954; s. Robert Cyril and Mabel Mildred (Collison) A.; m. Debora Lee Donovan, Feb. 2, 1975; children: Kathleen, Jonathan. BA in Econs., Wash. State U., 1976, postgrad., 1982-83. Rsch. asst. Wash. State U., 1976-77; project mgr. Ctr. Environ. Understanding, Cheney, Wash., 1977-78; program dir. Wash. Energy Extension Svc., Spokane, 1978-79; econs. instr. Spokane Falls CC, 1977—81; economist, cons. Biosystems Analysis Inc., Spokane, 1983; assoc. N.W. rep. Sierra Club, Seattle, 1983-87, N.W. rep., 1987-91, N.W./Alaska regional dir., 1992—2003, nat. wildlands campaign com., 2000—04, dep. nat. field dir., 2004—. Chmn. bd. N.W. Conservation Act Coalition, Seattle, 1982-83; adv. com. N.W. Renewable Resources Ctr., Seattle, 1987-91; cons. energy workshops N.W. Regional Found., Spokane, 1982; mem. exec. com. Save Our Wild Salmon Coalition, 1991-95; mem. adv. com. Inland Empire Pub. Lands Coun., 1990-2000; mem. steering com. Campaign for the Northwest, 1998-2000. Chmn., mem. city commn. Environ. Quality Commn., Pullman, Wash., 1976-77; bd. dir. Ryegrass Sch., Spokane, 1978-81; conservation rep. Internat. Mountain Caribou Tech. Com., 1978-81; bd. dirs. Wash. Citizens for Recycling, Seattle, 1980-82; chair Wash. State Environmentalists for Clinton/Gore Com., 1992, 96; environ. rep. N.W. Forest Conf. convened and chaired by Pres. Clinton, Apr. 2, 1993; mem. steering com. on No Initiative 164 Coalition, 1995; mem. Wash. State Steering Com. to Re-elect Clinton/Gore, 1996; mem Wash. State steering com. Gore for Pres., 1999-2000; chair Wash. State Environmentalists for Gore Com., 2000; mem. exec. com. Alaska Def. Initiative, 2001-2003; founding mem. WildPAC, 2000. Recipient Michael McCloskey award, Sierra Club, 2003, Spl. Achievement award, 2005. Avocations: hiking, rafting, fishing, playing guitar. Office: Sierra Club NW Office Ste 202 180 Nickerson St Seattle WA 98109-1631

ARTHURS, HARRY WILLIAM, lawyer, educator, academic administrator; b. Toronto, Ont., Can., May 9, 1935; s. Leon and Ellen (Dworkin) A.; m. Penny Milnes, June 22, 1974. BA, U. Toronto, 1955, LLB, 1958; LLM, Harvard U., 1959; LLD (hon.), Sherbrooke, Brock Law Soc. Upper Can., McGill U., U. Montreal, U. Toronto; D.Litt. (hon.), Lethbridge U.; DCL (hon.), U. Windsor. Prof. Osgoode Hall Law Sch., York U., Toronto, Ont., 1961-95, dean, 1972-77, pres., 1985—92; prof. York U., Toronto, 1995—2005. Chief adjudicator Pub. Svc. of Can., 1967-68; assoc. Can. Inst. Advanced Rsch., 1995-98; arbitrator, mediator. Author various books and articles on labor law, legal history, adminstrv. law and legal edn. to profl.

jours. V.p. Can. Civil Liberties Assn., 1964-76, pres., 1976-77; mem. U.A.W. Pub. Rev. Bd., 1967-77; vice chmn. Ont. Ednl. Rels. Commn., 1976-77; chmn. S.S.H.R.C. Study on Legal Resch. and Edn. in Can., 1980-83; bencher Law Soc. Upper Can., 1979-83; mem. Econ. Coun. Can., 1978-81; bd. dirs. Rights and Democracy, 1999-2003; commr. to Rev. Part III of Can. Labour Code, 2004—. Decorated officer Order of Can., Order of Ont. Fellow: Royal Soc. Can. (Killam Prize in the Soc. Scis. 2002), Brit. Acad. (corr.). Home: 11 Hillcrest Pk Toronto ON Canada M4X 1E8 Office: York Univ Osgoode Hall Law Sch 4700 Keele St Toronto ON Canada M3J 1P3 Office Phone: 416-736-5407. Business E-Mail: harthurs@osgoode.yorku.ca.

ARTHURS, MADELEINE HOPE, artist; b. Summit, N.J., July 4, 1966; d. Edward and Alberta (Bean) A. AB, Smith Coll., 1989; BFA with honors, Sch. of Visual Arts, N.Y.C., 1996, MFA, 1998. Intern Exit Art/The 1st World, N.Y.C., 1993-94; animation artist Magnet Pictures, Inc., N.Y.C., 1995; illustrator N.Y. Art Studios, Inc., N.Y.C., 1995; digital camera photographer Sonicnet, N.Y.C., 1995; digital programer Dia Ctr. for the Arts, N.Y.C., 1995-96; animation artist Curious Pictures, N.Y.C., 1995-96; animation Bill Plympton Studio, N.Y.C., 1996-97; archivist and studio asst. Alice Aycock/Fine Artist, N.Y.C., 1997—; animation cel painter MTV, N.Y.C., 1998-99. Painter Jeff Koons Studio, N.Y.C., 1999-00; guest artist Tchrs. and Writer PS76, Queens, N.Y., 1999, Project Read, 1999; asst. art tchr. Studio in a Sch., 2000; freelance illustrator Wall St. Jour., 2000—. One-woman shows include Smith Coll., 1988, 1st Ann. Premiere World Internat. Fine Arts Competition, 1998—99, Soho Photo Gallery, 2003, exhibited in group shows at Mus. Competition/Exhbn., Va., 1996, Soho Internat. Art Contest, N.Y.C., 1997, Sch. of Visual Arts Gallery, 1997, Exhbn./Chgo., 1997, Sch. of Visual Arts Gallery, 1998, Premiere World Internat. On-Line Fine Arts Competition, 1998, Competition/Exhbn./RSVP's Dream Competition, 1998, Catherine Lorillard Wolfe Art Club 102d ann. competition at Nat. Art Club, 1998, Best of Best Exhbn. SVA Visual Arts Mus., 2000, The Drawing Ctr. Slide Registry, 2000—, The Warehouse Exit Art/The 1st World Warehouse, 2000—, Momenta Art Gallery Benefit Exhbn., 2001, White Columns, 2002, Exit Art, N.Y.C., Represented in permanent collections Libr. of Congress, The Mag. Rack SVA Visual Arts Mus., exhibited in group shows at others; contbg. photographer (book, nat. and internat. exhbns.) Here is New York: A Democracy of Photographs, 2001—02, photographer (photographs published) Sunday Telegraph Mag., 2002. Recipient Paula Rhodes Meml. award, 1998, Merit Scholarship award Sch. of Visual Arts, 1997-98, Steuben award, New Canaan, 1997, Rhodes Family award for Outstanding Achievement/Sch. Visual Arts, 1996, Gilbert Stone scholarship, 1995, Silas H. Rhodes scholarship, 1994-96, Martha Keilig prize for Best Still Life/Landscape in Oils, Smith Coll., Northampton, Mass., 1988, Art Residency Hall Farm Ctr., Vt., 2001, others.

ARTLEY, NATHAN MONROE, music educator; b. Burlington, N.C., June 27, 1959; s. Malvin Newton and Joan (Brown) A. BS, Elon Coll., 1981; MA, Ohio State U., 1988. Dir. of orch. Salisbury (N.C.) City Schs., 1981-86; dir. of orchs. Cumberland County Schs., Fayetteville, N.C., 1988—. Adj. faculty of music Pfeiffer U., Misenheimer, N.C., 1982-84, Elon (N.C.) Coll., 1984-85. Mem. NEA, N.C. Music Educators Assn. (chair N.C. orch. divsn. 1992-94, chair Ea. N.C. orch. contest 1993-96, chair N.C. honors orch. 1990-92, chair Ea. N.C. String Solo and Ensemble Fest. 1993—), Nat. Sch. Orch. Assn. (pres. N.C. nat. sch. orch., 1991-93, creator N.C. orch. retreat 1992-93, nat. recording sec. 1997-98), Am. Strings Tchr. Assn. with Nat. Sch. Orch. Assn. (mem. staff Nat. H.S. Honors Orch., mem. nat. com. sch. orchs.), Am. Viola Soc., Omicron Delta Kappa. Avocations: travel, woodworking, reading. Home: 150 Homeplace Dr Fayetteville NC 28311-0209

ARTNER, ALAN GUSTAV, art critic, journalist; b. Chgo., May 14, 1947; s. Gustav and Katherine Rose (Lucas) A. BA, Northwestern U., 1968, MA, 1969. Apprentice music critic Chgo. Tribune, 1972-73, art critic, 1973—; contbg. editor The Art Gallery Mag., 1975-76; corr. Artnews Mag., 1977-80. Contbr. to Playbill, 1994—. Decorated Chevalier de l'ordre des Arts et des Lettres; Rockefeller Found. grantee, 1971-72 Office: Chgo Tribune Co 435 N Michigan Ave Chicago IL 60611-4066*

ARTZ, JOHN CURTIS, lawyer; b. Columbus, Ohio, Mar. 4, 1946; s. Curtis Price and Kathryn Lucille (Risley) A.; m. Nancy Eileen Jones, Apr. 5, 1969; children: John Curtis Jr., Alexander Hardie, Kathryn Cullen. BA disting. mil. grad., Allegheny Coll., 1968; JD magna cum laude, U. S.C., 1976. Bar: Pa. 1976, U.S. Dist. Ct. (we. dist.) Pa. 1976, U.S. Ct. Appeals (3d and 6th cirs.) 1996, U.S. Supreme Ct. 1980. From assoc. to ptnr. Eckert Seamans Cherin & Mellott, Pitts., 1976-94; shareholder, dir. Polito & Smock, P.C., Pitts., 1994—. Adj. asst. prof. Grad. Sch. Pub. Health U. Pitts., 1988-92; instr./lectr. Robert Morris U., Pitts., 1998—; presenter Nat. Safety Coun., Western Pa. Safety Coun., Assn. of Iron and Steel Engrs., Pa. Bar Inst., Allegheny County Bar Assn., Pitts. Human Resources Assn., Butler Human Resources Assn., Westmoreland Human Resources Assn., SMC Bus. Couns., Constrn. Fin. Mgmt. Assn., Pa. Inst. CPAs, Western Pa. Cmty. Accts., YWCA Mid-Atlantic Regional Coun. Notes editor U. S.C. Law Rev., 1975-76; contbr. articles to profl. jours. Dir. Jr. Achievement S.W. Pa., Pitts., 1994-2005, vice-chair adminstrn., 1998-2005. Capt. USAF, 1968-73. Recipient Silver and Bronze Leadership award Jr. Achievement S.W. Pa., 1993, Am. Jursiprudence award; named Pa. Super Lawyer, Law & Politics and the Pub. of Phila. Mag., 2004, 05. Fellow Allegheny County Bar Found.; mem. ABA (com. on occupl. safety and health law 1981—), Soc. for Human Resource Mgmt., Pa. Bar Assn. (com. on legal ethics and profl. responsibility 1987-94), Pitts. Human Resources Assn. (treas. 1997, sr. profl. human resources 1998—), Order of Wig and Robe, Omicron Delta Kappa. Office: Polito & Smock PC 444 Liberty Ave Ste 400 Pittsburgh PA 15222-1237 Office Phone: 412-394-3342. E-mail: jartz@politolaw.com.

ARTZT, RUSSELL M., electronics executive; b. 1947; BS, Queens Coll., 1968; MS, NY U., 1975. With Riverside Rsch. Corp., N.Y.C., 1968-72; with Standard Data Corp., 1972-76; with Computer Assocs. Internat. Inc., 1976—; v.p. Computer Assocs. Internat. Inc., 1978-83, sr. v.p. devel., from 1983, exec. v.p., rsch & devel, 1987—2002, exec. v.p., alliances & eTrust solutions, 2002—05, exec. v.p., products, 2005—, bd. dir., 1980—. Mem. Bd. Trustees Queens Coll. Found. Office: Computer Assocs Internat Inc 1 Computer Associates Plz Islandia NY 11749-7000

ARUM, ROBERT, lawyer, sports events promoter; b. N.Y.C., Dec. 8, 1931; s. Samuel and Celia (Baumgarten) Arum; m. Barbara Mandelbaum, July 2, 1960 (div. 1977); children: John, Richard, Elizabeth; m. Sybil Ann Hamada, Dec. 18, 1977 (div. 1991); m. Lovee Hazan Du Boef, Sept. 14, 1991. BA, NYU, 1953; JD cum laude, Harvard U., 1956. Bar: NY 1956. Atty. firm Root, Barrett, Cohen, Knapp & Smith, N.Y.C., 1956—61; asst. U.S. atty., chief tax sect. U.S. Atty.'s Office, So. Dist. N.Y., 1961—64; ptnr. firm Phillips, Nizer, Benjamin, Krim & Ballon, N.Y.C., 1964—72, Arum & Katz, N.Y.C., 1972—79; chmn. Top Rank, Inc.; Promoter Ali-Frazier Super Fight II, 1974, Evel Knievel Snake River Canyon Jump, 1974, Ali-Norton World Heavyweight Championship, 1976, Monzon-Valdez World Middleweight Championships, 1976, 1977, Ali-Spinks Championships, 1978, Leonard-Duran Championships, 1980, 1989, Top Rank/ESPN Boxing Series, 1980—, Arguello-Pryor Championship, 1983, Moore-Duran Championship, 1983, Hagler-Duran Championship, 1983, Hagler-Hearns Championship, 1985, Hagler-Leonard Superfight Championship, 1987, Leonard-Hearns "The War" Championship, 1989—91, Holyfield-Foreman World Heavyweight Championship, 1991, Holyfield-Holmes World Heavyweight Championship, 1992, Foreman/Morrison Heavyweight Championship, 1993, De la Hoya/Whitaker, 1997, De la Hoya/Chavez, 1996, 1998, De la Hoya/Quartey, 1999, De la Hoya/Trinidad, 1999, De la Hoya/Mosely, 2000, Morales/Barrera, 2002, De la Hoya/Vargas, 2002. Named to Boxing Hall of Fame, 1999. Mem.: Friars Club. Home: 36 Gulf Stream Ct Las Vegas NV 89113-1354 Office: 3980 Howard Hughes Pkwy Las Vegas NV 89109-0992 E-mail: erroa@aol.com.*

ARUNASALAM, VICKRAMASINGAM (WILLIE), retired physicist; b. Mathagal, Jaffna, Sri Lanka, Aug. 26, 1935; arrived in U.S., 1958, naturalized, 1973; s. Sithamparapillai and Sithamparam Vickramasingam; m. Saradamani Sivagnanasundaram, Mar. 23, 1968 (dec. Dec. 21, 1997); 1 child, Sharmila. BS, U. Ceylon, Colombo, 1957; MS, U. Mass., 1960; PhD, MIT, 1964. Asst. lectr. U. Ceylon, Colombo, Sri Lanka, 1957—58; instr. U. Mass., Amherst, 1960; from rsch. assoc. to prin. rsch. physicist Princeton (N.J.) U., 1964—80, prin. rsch. physicist, 1980—96; vis. prof. William Paterson U., Wayne, NJ, 1997—97; adj. prof. Rider U., Lawrenceville, NJ, 1999—99; assoc. editor Physics Essays, Ottawa, Canada, 1992—. Contbr. 105 articles to profl. jours. Recipient Lifetime Achievement award, Ilankai Tamil Sangam USA, 2003, Skanthavarodya Coll. Old Students Assn. of Can., 2003, Tamils Info. and Rsch. Ctr. of Toronto, 2005, World Tamil Movement of Can., 2005, Congratulatory Cert. of Greetings, Can. Govt., 2005; fellow, Am. Phys. Soc., 1979. Fellow: Am. Phys. Soc. (sr.); mem.: Sigma Xi. Achievements include research in Plasma Physics and Controlled Thermonuc. Fusion, Quantum Theory, Quantum Electrodynamics, Cosmology, Foundations of Physics, Particle Physics, Condensed Matter Theory, and Quantum Statis. mechanics; invited spkr. for approximately 25 one-hour talks in many US universities and internat. conferences or workshops; works cited as fundamental contributions in many physics books; appearing in many nat. and internat. biographical dictionaries. Home: 50 Windsor Drive Princeton Junction NJ 08550-1641 Office: Plasma Physics Lab Princeton University Princeton NJ 08543 Personal E-mail: williearunasalam@hotmail.com. E-mail: arunasalam@mail.com.

ARUNDEL, JOHN HOWARD, journalist, publisher; b. Washington, June 4, 1965; s. Arthur W. and Margaret C. (McElroy) A.; married; 1 child. BA in Polit. Sci., Duke U., 1988; MA in Internat. Econs., Johns Hopkins U., 1995. Registered fin. cons. Reporter, trainee The New York Times, N.Y.C., 1988-90; bur. chief States News Svc., Washington, 1991-92; corr. The Washington Post, Kuwait City, Kuwait, 1991; v.p. Smith Barney Citigroup, Washington, 1996—; journalist, publisher The Alexandria Times, Alexandria, Va., 2004—. Bd. mem. Va. Film Found.; bd. dirs. The Kennedy Ctr. Camelot Circle, Washington, 1995—. Author: The Student Guide to Duke, 1988, While America Slept, 2003; contbr. articles to profl. jours. Mem. Nat. Press Club. Democrat. Episcopalian. Home: 6034 Woodmont Rd Alexandria VA 22307-1158 Office: 201 King St Ste 202 Alexandria VA 22314 Office Phone: 703-739-0001. Personal E-mail: jonarundel@aol.com.

ARVAY, NANCY JOAN, lawyer; b. Pitts., Aug. 27, 1952; d. William John and Cornelia (Prince) A. BA in History, Duke U., 1974; postgrad., Columbia U., 1974-75; JD, U. S.C., 1999. Polit. and internat. comm. specialist U.S. Senate Fgn. Rels. Com., Washington, 1975-77; broadcast media rels. rep. Am. Petroleum Inst., Washington, 1977-79, Chevron U.S.A., San Francisco, 1979-82, coord. electronic news media rels., 1982-85; sr. media rels. rep. Chevron Corp., San Francisco, 1985-87; dir. pub. rels. Fireman's Fund Corp., Novato, Calif., 1987-89; v.p., ptnr. The Resource Group, San Francisco, 1989-91; pres. Arvay, Moore & Buchanan, Washington, 1991-95, Columbia, SC, 1996—99; pvt. practice law, 1999—. Pub. affairs advisor to C. Everett Koop, M.D.; lectr. Dept. Interior-Park Service, Beckley, W.Va., 1983; chmn. pub. rels. Internat. Oil Spill Conf., Washington, 1984-85. Author, coordinator: Research Studies in Business and the Media, 1980-83; contbg. author This Is Public Relations, 1985. Founding mem. San Francisco chpt. Overseas Edn. Group; mem. pub. relations com. World Affairs Council San Francisco. Mem. Pub. Rels. Soc., Radio/TV News Dirs. Assn. (assoc.), San Francisco Women in Bus. Office: 8000 Farrow Rd Columbia SC 29203-3244

ARVESON, WILLIAM BARNES, mathematics professor; b. Oakland, Calif., Nov. 22, 1934; s. Ronald Magnus and Audrey Mary (Hichens) A.; m. Lee A. Kaskutas. BS in Math, Calif. Inst. Tech., 1960; MA, UCLA, 1963, PhD, 1964. Benjamin Peirce instr. Harvard U., 1965-68; lectr. dept. math. U. Calif., Berkeley, 1968-69, assoc. prof., 1969-74, prof., 1974—, Miller rsch. prof., 1985—86, 1999—2000. Author: An Invitation to C*-algebras, 1976, A Short Course in Spectral Theory, 2001; assoc. editor: Duke Math. Jour, 1975-86, Jour. of Operator Theory, 1977-87, editor, 1987—; contbr. articles to math. jours. Served with U.S. Navy, 1952-55. John Simon Guggenheim fellow, 1976-77 Mem. Am. Math. Soc. (assoc. editor bulletin 1988-91), Edinburgh Math. Soc. (assoc. editor proceedings 1989—). Office: U Calif Dept Math Berkeley CA 94720-0001

ARVIN, ANN MARGARET, microbiology and immunology educator, researcher; Degree, Brown U.; M in Philosophy, Brandeis U.; MD, U. Pa., 1972. Resident U. Calif. San Francisco Med. Ctr., 1975; fellow Stanford (Calif.) Hosp. and Clinics, 1978; mem. faculty Stanford U. Sch. Medicine, 1978—, Lucille Packard Prof. Pediat., prof. microbiology and immunology, assoc. dean rsch., 2001—. Co-chair rsch. team investigating possible uses of flu virus in bio-terrorism Stanford U., 2003—. Trustee Am. Herpes Found.; mem. exec. com. VZV Rsch. Found. Recipient E. Mead Johnson award for rsch. in pediat., 1992. Mem.: Inst. Medicine, 2004. Office: Stanford U Sch Medicine 300 Pasteur Dr Rm G312 Stanford CA 94305 Business E-Mail: aarvin@stanford.edu.

ARVYSTAS, MICHAEL GECIAUSKAS, orthodontist, educator; b. Vilnius, Lithuania, Dec. 18, 1942; arrived in U.S., 1949, naturalized, 1961; s. Mykolas and Antanina (Kleiza) Arvystas; m. Jane Grannis, 1969 (div. 1978); m. Mary Ruth Buchness, Nov. 2, 1992. BA, Colgate U., 1965; DMD, Tufts U., 1969. Cert. Columbia U., 1973, diplomate Am. Bd. Orthodontics. Chief orthodontic sect. Morrisania City Hosp., Bronx, NY, 1973—76; dir. orthodontics ctr. for craniofacial disorders and cleft palate ctr. Montefiore Hosp. and Med. Ctr., 1973—; chief orthodontic sect. North Ctrl. Bronx Hosp., 1976—83; clin. prof. N.J. Dental Sch., Newark, 1974—, dir., lectr. undergrad. and postgrad. students, 1974—. Vis. prof. Albert Einstein Coll. Medicine, Bronx; lectr. in field. Author: Orthodonic Management of Agenesis and Other Complexitues: An Interdisciplinary Approach to Functional Aesthetics, 2003; contbr. articles to profl. jours., chpts. to books. Capt. Dental Corps USAF, 1969—71. Mem.: ADA, Am. Acad. Esthetic Dentistry (orgn. com. Greater N.Y. Dental Meeting), N.Y. Acad. Dentistry, Northeastern Soc. Orthodontists, Am. Assn. Orthodontists, Dental Soc. N.Y.C., N.Y. County Dental Soc. (bd. dirs.), Sigma Xi, Colgate U. Alumni Assn., Orthodontic Alumni Soc. Columbia U., Tufts U. Dental Alumni Assn. Office: 24 Washington Sq N New York NY 10011-9168 Office Phone: 212-777-9977. Personal E-mail: marvystas@optonline.net.

ARWADY, GEORGE E., publishing executive; b. Bklyn. 4 children. BA, Hope Coll., Holland, Mich., 1969; MA in Journalism, Columbia U., N.Y.C., 1970. Editorial writer Kalamazoo Gazette, 1970—75, pub., 1988—2004; met. editor Muskegon Chronicle, Mich., 1975—76, editor, pub., 1980—88; editor Saginaw News, Mich., 1976—80, The Star-Ledger, Newark, 2004—. Bd. dirs. Mich. Colls. Found. Recipient Disting. Alumni award, Hope Coll., 1984. Office: The Star-Ledger One Star Ledger Plaza Newark NJ 07102-1200 Office Phone: 973-392-4161.

ARYA, VIKRAM, research scientist; BS with distinction, Birla Inst. of Tech., India, 1993—97; PhD, U. Fla., 1998—2003. Rsch. trainee Ranbaxy Rsch. Lab., New Delhi, 1995, Aventis Pharm., Bridgewater, NJ, 2001; clin. pharm. reviewer Ctr. for Drug Evaluation and Rsch, Food and Drug Adminstrn., Rockville, Md., 2003—. Mem. selection com. Doctoral Dissertation Adv.,Mentioning Awards, 2002; pres. Grad. Student Coun., Coll. of Pharmacy, 2000; dept. rep. Grad. Student Coun., U. Fla. Manuscript reviewer for rsch. jours.; contbr. articles to profl. jours. Mem.: Am. Coll. of Clin. Pharmacology (student abstract award 2002, new mem. abstract award 2002), Am. Assn. Pharm. Scientists.

ARYANFAR, FARSHID, electrical engineer, electronics engineer; m. Haleh Hazer. BSc in Elec. Engring, U. Tehran, 1994, MSc in Elec. Engring, 1998; PhD, U. Mich., 2004. Rsch. asst. U. Mich., Ann Arbor, Mich., 2000—04; sr. rsch. engr. EMAG Technologies Inc., Ann Arbor, 2003—. Contbr. articles to profl. jours. Grantee, Missile Def. Agy., 2004. Mem.: IEEE. Achievements include design of miniaturized mm-wave transceivers; development of a novel scaled measurement system for wireless channel characterization; a full 3D physics-based wave propagation simulator; research in through wall imaging technique; design of miniaturized planar filters. Office: University of Michigan 1301 Beal Ave Ann Arbor MI 48109 Personal E-mail: aryanfar@yahoo.com. Business E-Mail: faryanfa@umich.edu.

ARZOUMAN, DAVID, artist, composer; b. Glendale, Calif., Mar. 28, 1955; s. Harry H. and Mary Arzouman. AA, Pasadena (Calif.) City Coll., 1982. Apprentice Norman Zammitt Studio, Pasadena, 1977—79; guest composer Bklyn. Coll., 1985—92, seminar instr., 1987—90; program designer, dir. Sophia Art Sch., Tokyo, 1999—2005. Composer: Untitled No. 1, 1986, Allegory, 1987; author: Fundamentals of Painting, 1999; composer: Precipitation, 1991. Recipient 2d prize, Internat. Inst. Electroacoustic Music, Bourges, France, 1991. Mem.: ASCAP (Std. awards 1995—97). Achievements include original work on the analogies between visual art and music, including applications of algorithmic composition, fractal geometry, and visual art principles to music. Office: 5 ITU Bldg 2d Fl 1-13-8 EBISU SHIBUYA-KU Tokyo 150-0013 Japan Personal E-mail: djartz@hotmail.com.

ARZOUMANIDIS, GREGORY G., chemist; b. Thessaloniki, Greece, Aug. 16, 1936; arrived in U.S., 1964, naturalized, 1976; s. Gerasimos and Sophia Arzoumanidis; m. Anastasia Anastasopoulos, Jan. 2, 1966; children: Sophia, Alexis. BS in Chemistry, MS in Chemistry, U. Thessaloniki, 1959; PhD in Inorganic Chemistry, U. Stuttgart, Germany, 1964; MBA, U. Conn., 1979. Research assoc. MIT, 1964-66; research chemist Monsanto, Everett, Mass., 1966-69; sr. research chemist Am. Cyanamid Co., Stamford, Conn., 1969-72, Stauffer Chem. Co., Dobbs Ferry, NY, 1972-79; research assoc. Amoco Chem. Co., Naperville, Ill., 1979-94, Argonne (Ill.) Nat. Lab., 1995-96; with Oakwood Cons., 1996—. Contbr. articles to profl. jours. Served to 2d lt. Greek Army, 1959—61. Recipient Acad. award, Govt. of West Germany, 1963, Presdl. award, Amoco Chem. Co., 1990. Mem.: AAAS, Am. Chem. Soc., Sigma Xi. Greek Orthodox. Achievements include invention of commercial catalysts for polypropylene plastics, new processes; patents in field; principal co-inventor Amoco supported polypropylene catalyst. Home: 7 S 610 Carriage Way Naperville IL 60540 Personal E-mail: arzo@sbcglobal.net.

ASAI, DAVID JOHN, biologist, educator; BS, Stanford U., Calif., 1971—75, MS, 1974—75; PhD, Calif. Inst. Tech., Pasadena, 1975—79. Prof., biol. scis. Purdue U., West Lafayette, Ind., 1985—2003, head, biol. scis., 2000—03; Stuart Mudd prof., chair, dept. biology Harvey Mudd Coll, Claremont, Calif., 2003—. Grantee, NSF, 1986—. Mem.: AAAS, Soc. Protozoologists, Biophysical Soc., Am. Soc. Microbiology, Amer. Soc. Biochemistry Molecular Biology, Am. Soc. for Cell Biology. Office: Harvey Mudd Coll Dept Biology 301 Platt Blvd Claremont CA 91711-5990 Office Phone: 909-607-2257.

ASAKAWA, TAKAKO, dancer, educator, choreographer, director; b. Toyko, Feb. 23, 1939; came to U.S., 1962; d. Kamenosuke and Chiaki Asakawa. Student, Tokyo schs., 1962-91. Prin. dancer Martha Graham Dance Co., N.Y.C., 1962-76, 81—; dancer Alvin Ailey, 1968-69, Pearl Lang, 1967, Lar Lubovitch, 1974-80. Guest tchr. at numerous schs. and univs. throughout world, including Moscow Culture Exch. Program, Martha Graham Sch., Juilliard Sch.; co.-founder Asakawalker Dance Co.; dir. Paris Opera Ballet Co., Am. Ballet Theater, Het Nationale Ballet in Amsterdam and various univs. throughout world. Performed all major roles in GRaham reperatory throughout world, including Paris Opera House, Covent Garden; Broadway and TV performances include Eliza in The King and I, Bell Tel. Hour. Named Legendary Woman of Am., St. Vincent's Hosp. Mem. Am. Guild Musical Artists Home and Office: 20 W 64th St Apt 29-E/F New York NY 10023-7180

ASANBE, COMFORT BOLA, psychologist, educator; d. David Atte and Martha Abon Odeyemi; m. Joseph Adebola Asanbe, Feb. 27, 1982 (dec. Aug. 19, 1996); children: Olaniran Omoniyi, Opeyemi Ajike. BA, U. Ilorin, Nigeria, 1983; MA in Edn., Austin Peay State U., 1989; PhD, Tenn. State U., Nashville, 1996. Lic. psychologist/health svcs. provider Tenn. Bd. of Examiners in Psychology, 2003. Tchr. Ilorin Grammar Sch., Ilorin, Nigeria, 1980—83; instr. Austin Peay State U., Clarksville, Tenn., 1997—2001; psychologist Metro-Davidson County Sch. Sys., Nashville, 2001—02; asst. prof. Tenn. Technol. U., Cookeville, Tenn., 2002—. Psychology intern U. Tenn. Med. Ctr., Memphis, 2000—01; presenter in field. Workshop presenter Stephen's Ctr. for Child Abuse Prevention, Livingston, Tenn., 2003; exec. mem. Children Internat. Edn. Coun. (CIEC) Program, Clarksville, Tenn., 1992—98. Faculty Rsch. grantee, Tenn. Technol. U., 2004. Mem.: APA, Tenn. Psychol. Assn., Southeastern Psychol. Assn., Phi Kappa Phi, Psi Chi. Avocations: travel, cooking, sewing. Office: Tenn Technol U 1000 N Dixie Ave Cookeville TN 38505-001 Office Phone: 931-372-3217. Home Fax: 931-372-3400.

ASANI, ALI S., foreign language and religious studies educator; b. Nairobi, Kenya, Oct. 28, 1954; came to U.S., 1973; s. Sultaan Ali and Shirinkhanu (Velji) A. BA summa cum laude, Harvard Coll., 1977; MA, Harvard U., 1981, PhD, 1984. From instr. to assoc. prof. Indo-Muslim culture Harvard U., Cambridge, Mass., 1983-92, prof. practice of Indo-Muslim lang. and culture, 1992—. Vis. prof. Inst. Ismaili Studies, London, 1992—; dir., co-dir. Al-Ummah Summer Program for Muslim Youth, 1984—. Author: The Bujh Niranjan: An Ismaili Mystical Poem, 1991, The Harvard Collection of Ismaili Literature in Indic Literature, 1992, Celebrating Muhammad, 1995, Ecstasy and Enlightenment: Ismaili Devotional Literature of South Asia, 2002; editor Jour. Inst. Muslim Minority Affairs. Recipient Harvard Found. medal, 2002; rsch. fellow NEH, 1986; rsch. grantee Inst. Ismaili Studies, London, 1995, Consortium for Lang. Tchg. and Learning, 1993-94, 95-96, 99-2000; Aga Khan scholar Harvard U., 1973-84. Mem. Am. Acad. Religion, Assn. for Asian Studies, Phi Beta Kappa. Moslem. Avocation: travel. Home: 203 Pemberton St Apt 3 Cambridge MA 02140-2543 Office: Harvard Univ Study of Religion NELC Cambridge MA 02138 Business E-Mail: aliasani@fas.harvard.edu.

ASARI, EIKICHI, information sciences educator, researcher; b. Fonto, Karafuto, Japan, Feb. 10, 1929; s. Shoukichi and Kiku (Kotaki) A.; m. Satsuko Yamada, June 13, 1959; 1 child, Kimie Grad., Military Scis. and Tech. Acad. Imperial Army of Japan, 1945; 1st class radio engr. (hon.), Ministry Telecom. of Japan, 1952; attended sci.: math. and computer sci., Hokkaido U., Sapporo, Japan, 1959-61, Polytech. Nippon Telegraph and Pub. Corp., Tokyo, 1964. Radio engr. Nippon Telegraph and Tel. Pub. Corp., Sapporo, 1951-64, mem. mgmt. staff, 1964-69; assoc. prof. Tokai U., Sapporo, 1969-88, Hokkaido Tokai U., Sapporo, 1988-92; prof. info. scis. Hokkaido Coll. Arts and Scis., Ebets, 1993-97. Part-time lectr. info. scis. Nat. Otaru U. Commerce, 1970-97, Sapporo Polytech. of Nippon Telegraph and Telephone Pub. Corp., Hokkaido, 1970-85, Rakuno Gakuen U., Ebets, 1997-99. Editor, author: Encyclopedia of Operations Research, 1974-75, Encyclopedia of hokkaido,1979-81; contbr. articles to profl. publs.; inventor complete solution and applications of renewal theory, 1967, microwave propagation in precipitation, 1974, theory of countermeasures for cold damage of rice cultivation in subpolar climate dists., 1973-77, weather forecast method by meteorological noises, 1989, ski resort radiosys., 1989-90 (govt. prize 1992). Commr. com. distbn. in Hokkaido, Ministry Transp., 1975-76; chmn. com. optimatization of rice cultivation in Hokkaido, Hokkaido Govt., 1977-78; chmn. com. establish planning Hokkaido teleport Hokkaido Inst. Future Advancement, 1985-86; chmn. com. ski resort radio systems Ministry Post and Telecom., 1989-90, detection of clear air turbulences, 1999. Technical corp. telecom. Imperial Army Japan, 1945-46. Recipient award of merit of cold dist. devel. Civil Assns. Dist. Devel., Hokkaido, 1991, award of merit for radio sci. devel. Hokkaido br. Ministry Post and Telecom., 1992, fellow Operations Rsch. Soc. of Japan, 1995. Mem. IEEE, UNESCO, N.Y. Acad. Scis., Hokkauido/Mass. Soc., The Planetary Soc., Ops. Rsch. Soc. Japan (councilor 1970-92), Inst. Electronics and Communication Engrs. Japan, Cold Dists. Agrl. Sci. Soc. Ministry Agriculture, Forest and Fishery of Japan. Avocations: travel, photography, mysteries and science fiction, history of wars research. Home and Office: Shinkawa 2-Jo 2-chome Kita-ku Sapporo 001-0922 Japan Office Phone: +81117618856. Office Fax: +81117618865. Personal E-mail: asarie@d2.dion.ne.jp.

ASARNOW, JOAN ROSENBAUM, psychologist, educator; d. Gerald and Ruth Spiro Rosenbaum; m. Robert Franklin Asarnow; children: David Michael, Lauren Debra. PhD, U. Waterloo, Can., 1980. Lic. Psychologist Calif. Bd. of Psychology, 1982. Asst. prof. of psychiatry & biobehavioral scis. U. Calif., LA, 1981—89, assoc. prof. of psychiatry & biobehavioral scis., 1989—95, prof. of psychiatry & biobehavioral scis., 1995—. Rsch. grant, Agy. for Healthcare Rsch. and Quality, 1998—2003, NIMH, 1990—2005, Centers for Disease Control and Prevention, 2002—05, John D. and Catherine T. MacArthur Found., 1985—89, Post-doctoral Rsch. fellow, NIMH, 1980—81, Pre-doctoral Tng. fellow, Can. Coun., 1975—78. Achievements include research in mental health treatment and servies for youth, depression, suicidality in youth and childhood-onset schizophrenia. Office: UCLA Neuropsychiatric Inst 760 Westwood Plaza Los Angeles CA 90024

ASARO, ROBERT J., engineering educator; b. Bklyn., Aug. 29, 1945; BS, Stanford U., 1967, MS, 1969, PhD material sci., 1972. Asst. prof. Brown U., 1975-79, assoc. prof., 1979-82, prof., 1982-89, U. Calif., San Diego, 1989—. Recipient Champion H. Mathewson Gold medal Minerals, Metals and Materials Soc., 1991. Mem. Am. Soc. Mining and Metall Engrs. Office: Univ Calif Eng Sci 0310 9500 Gilman Dr La Jolla CA 92093-5004

ASBILL, RICHARD M., lawyer; b. Wilmington, Del., Nov. 9, 1943; s. Mac Jr. and Jane (Winchester) A.; m. Jane Cherry (div. 1974); children: R. Brandon, Christopher L.; m. Evelyn M. Judd, May 1, 1976; children: Judd W., Carter M. BA, Princeton U., 1965; JD, U. N.C., 1968. Bar: Ga. 1968. Assoc. Jones, Bird & Howell (name changed to Alston & Bird), Atlanta, 1968-73; ptnr. Harman, Asbill, Roach & Nellis (name changed to Asbill, Porter, Churchill & Nellis), Atlanta, 1973-86, Paul, Hastings, Janofsky & Walker, Atlanta, 1986—, co-chmn. trade regulation & proprietary rights practice group, co-chmn. resort, restaurant & recreation practice group. Co-author: Franchising Law: Practice and Forms, 1992; co-author, co-editor: Fundamentals of International Franchising, 2001. Trustee, mem. exec. com., Schenck Sch., Atlanta, 1990-2000, mem. adv. bd., 2000—. Mem. ABA (governing com. Forum on Franchising 1995-2001, chair 1997-99, immediate past chair 1999-2001), Internat. Bar Assn. (vice chair Com. X 1994-98, chair 1998-2002), Capital City Club, Orchard Golf & Country Club. Avocations: golf, skiing, travel. Office: Paul Hastings Janofsky & Walker 600 Peachtree St NE Ste 2400 Atlanta GA 30308-3624 Office Phone: 404-815-2236. Office Fax: 404-685-5236. Business E-Mail: rickasbill@paulhastings.com.

ASBURY, ARTHUR KNIGHT, neurologist, educator; b. Cin., Nov. 22, 1928; s. Eslie and Mary (Knight) Asbury; m. Carolyn Holstein, May 17, 1980; children from previous marriage: Dana, Patricia Knight, William Francis. Grad., Phillips Acad., Andover, Mass., 1946; student, Stanford, 1947—48; BS, U. Ky., 1951; MD, U. Cin., 1958; MA (hon.), U. Pa., 1974. Diplomate FRCP, London, 2002. Intern in medicine Mass. Gen. Hosp., Boston, 1958—59, resident, 1959—63, fellow, 1963—65, staff neurologist, 1965—69; chief neurology San Francisco VA Hosp., 1969—74; prof. dept. neurology U. Pa., Phila., 1974—, chmn. dept. neurology, 1974—82, Van Meter prof. neurology, 1983—97; acting dean, exec. v.p. U. Pa. Sch. Medicine, 1988—89, vice dean for rsch., 1990—93, vice dean for faculty affairs, 1993—97, interim dean, 2000—01; tchg. fellow Harvard Med. Sch., 1958—65, instr., 1965—68, assoc., 1968—69; assoc. prof. neurology U. Calif. at San Francisco, 1969—73, vice-chmn., 1969—74, prof., 1973—74. Mem. nat. adv. neurol. disease & stroke coun. NIH, 1990—93; hon. prof. med. scis. Hebei Med. Coll., China, 1995. Sr. editor: Blue Books of Practical Neurology, 1980—2004, assoc. editor: Archives of Neurology, 1975—76, Annals of Neurology, 1976—81, chief editor:, 1985—93, mem. editl. bd.: Muscle and Nerve, 1977—89, Neurology, 1981—85, Jour. Neuropathology and Exptl. Neurology, 1981—83, Jour. Neurol. Scis., 1989—2001; contbr. chpts. to med. textbooks, articles to med. jours. V.p., bd. dirs. Forest Retreat Farms Inc., Carlisle, Ky., 1970—92. With U.S. Army, 1951—53. Recipient Daniel Drake medal, U. Cin., 1988, IS Ravdin Master Clinician award, U. Pa., 1999, Lindback Tchg. award, 2000; grantee, UPHS, 1967—93, Muscular Dystrophy Assn., 1974—82. Fellow: AAAS, Royal Coll. Physicians London, Am. Acad. Neurology (v.p. 1977—79, hon. 2003); mem.: Coll. Physicians of Phila. (pres. 2004—), World Fedn. Neurology (v.p. 1989—93, chair rsch. group on neuromuscular diseases 2001—05, Lifetime Achievement award for work in neuromuscular diseases 2002), Assn. Univ. Profs. Neurology (pres. 1980—82), Assn. Brit. Neurologists (hon.), European Neurol. Soc. (hon.), Soc. Neurosci., Am. Assn. Neuropathologists (v.p. 1983—84), Am. Neurol. Assn. (councillor 1976—81, pres. 1982—83, hon. 1995), Inst. Medicine. Achievements include Arthur K. Asbury Ann. award for faculty mentoring established at University Pennsylvania School of Medicine in 2004. Home: 408 S Van Pelt St Philadelphia PA 19146-1233 Office: U Pa Hosp Dept Neurology 3400 Spruce St Philadelphia PA 19104-4283 Office Phone: 215-662-2629. Business E-Mail: arthur.asbury@uphs.upenn.edu.

ASBURY, JEFFREY M., medical educator; s. E. Michael and Donnie S. Asbury; m. Sunny Pak, Dec. 4, 1999; children: Hunter Michael, Lauren. BS, Okla. Bapt. U., 1988; MS in Biochemistry, U. Okla., 1992, MD, 1998. Diplomate Am. Bd. Internal Medicine. Clin. instr. U. Okla. HSC, 2004—. Mem. bd. dirs., corp. officer, treas. Asbury Pharmacy, Inc., Oklahoma City, 2000—; dir. heart, lung and vascular clinic OU Physicians, 2004—; med. dir. OU Med. Ctr. Heart Sta., 2004—. Mem.: ACP (assoc.), Am. Heart Assn. (assoc.), Am. Coll. Cardiology (assoc.). Home: 2900 Regency Ct Oklahoma City OK 73120 Office: U Okla HSC 940 Stanton L Young Blvd Oklahoma City OK 73104 Office Phone: 405-271-7001. Home Fax: 405-848-3591. Personal E-mail: drasbury@yahoo.com. Business E-Mail: jeffrey-asbury@ouhsc.edu.

ASCENSÃO, JOÃO LUIS AFONSO, physician, researcher; b. Maputo, Mozambique, July 6, 1948; arrived in U.S., 1974; s. João F. A. and Maria (Almeida) A.; m. Vivian Pereyra, June 27, 1993; children: João André, Vítor Luís. MD, U. Lisbon Sch. Medicine, 1972, PhD, 1989. Resident U. Hosp. St. Mary, Lisbon, Portugal, 1972-74; immunology fellow Meml. Sloan-Kettering Cancer Ctr., N.Y.C., 1974-76; internal medicine resident U. Minn. Hosps., Mpls., 1977-78, hematology oncology fellow, 1979-81, instr., 1981-82, asst. prof., 1982-84; assoc. prof., assoc. dir. BMT program N.Y. Med. Coll., Valhalla, 1984-89; assoc. prof., dir. BMT program U. Conn. Health Sci. Ctr., Farmington, 1989-92; prof. medicine, pathology, microbiology and immunology U. Nev. Sch. Medicine, Reno, 1992—2002; prof. medicine George Washington U. Sch. Medicine, Washington, 2002—. Adv. bd. mem. Calif. Cancer Ctr., Modesto, 1992—; bd. mem. Nev. Am. Cancer Soc., Reno, 1992—. Editor: Regulation of Erythropoiesis, 1987, Molecular Biology of Hemopoiesis, 1988, Molecular Biology of Erythropoiesis, 1989. Portugal Sci. Found. fellow Ministry of Edn., 1974-75, Charles H. Revson Found. fellow, 1984-86; recipient Young Investigator award NIH, 1991-94. Fellow: ACP; mem.: Am. Assn. Immunology, Clin. Immunology Soc., European Soc. Med. Oncology, Internat. Soc. Exptl. Hematology (councillor), Am. Assn. Cancer Rsch., Am. Soc. Clin. Oncology, Am. Soc. Hematology. Avocations: photography, cooking, reading, collecting corkscrews. Office: George Washington Univ Divsn Hematology/Oncology 2150 Penn Ave NW 3-428 Washington DC 20002 Address: VA Med Ctr Divsn Hematology 151G 50 Irving St NW Washington DC 20422 E-mail: jascensao@mfa.gwu.edu, joao.ascensao@med.va.gov.

ASCENZO, CARL, information technology executive; BS in Bus. Adminstrn., Western New England Coll. V.p. ops. & chief info. officer Aetna Health Plans; ptner., sys. integration practice Pricewaterhouse Coopers LLP, Hartford, Conn.; sr. v.p. & chief info. officer Blue Cross Blue Shield of Mass. Mem. Soc. for Info. Mgmt. Executives, Healthcare Info. and Mgmt. Systems Soc., Mass. Health Data Consortium (bd. dir.). Office: SVP & CIO Blue Cross Blue Shield of Mass 401 Park Dr Boston MA 02215

ASCH, SUSAN MCCLELLAN, pediatrician; b. Cleve., Dec. 31, 1945; d. William Alton and Alice Lonore (Heide) McClellan; m. Marc Asch, Sept. 10, 1966; children: Marc William, Sarah Susan, Rebecca Janney. AB, Oberlin (Ohio) Coll., 1967; MA, Mich. State U., 1968, PhD, 1975; MD, Case Western Res., 1977. Diplomate Nat. Bd. Med. Examiners, Am. Bd. Pediatrics, Am. Bd. Emergency Pediatrics. Instr. sociology Mich. State U., East Lansing, 1971-73; resident in pediatrics Children's Nat. Med. Ctr., Washington, 1977-80, chief resident in ambulatory and emergency pediatrics, 1979-80; asst. to dir. Office for Med. Applications of Rsch. NIH, Bethesda, 1980-81; pvt. practice in pediatrics Millinocket (Maine) Regional Hosp., 1981-84; assoc. dir. emergency Akron (Ohio) Children's Hosp., 1984-87; asst. prof. pediatrics Northeastern Ohio U. Coll. Medicine, 1984-87; dir. emergency St. Paul Children's Hosp., 1987-91; asst. prof. pediatrics U. Minn., 1987-93, clin. asst. prof., 1993—; pvt. practice pediatrics Stillwater, Minn., 1992—; sec. Lakeview Meml. Hosp., 1999—2001, vice chief of staff, 2001—03, chief of staff, 2003—05. Nat. faculty PALS Am. Heart Assn., Mpls., Dallas, 1987-94; mem. task force, sub-bd. emergency pediatrics Am. Bd. Pediatrics, 1987-91, mem. sub-bd. emergency pediat., 1991-93. Assoc. editor Pediatric Emergency Medicine, 1992, contbr., 1992, 96; author various publs., 1970—. State bd. dirs., nat. and affiliate faculty PALS Minn. affiliate Am. Heart Assn., 1988—; chmn. SIDS task force, Minn. Dept. Maternal and Child Health, St. Paul, 1990-92. Mem. Am. Acad. Pediatrics (nat. faculty advanced pediatric life support 1989—, exec. com. sect. on emergency pediatrics 1988-90, chair Minn. emergency pediatric com. 1989-91, nat. svc. commendation 1991), Minn. Med. Assn. (emergency svcs. com. 1990, ho. of dels. 1994), Alpha Omega Alpha. Democrat. Mem. Soc. Of Friends. Avocations: travel, quarter horses. Home: 34 N Oaks Rd North Oaks MN 55127-6325 Office: Stillwater Med Group 921 Greeley St S Stillwater MN 55082-5935 Office Phone: 651-439-1234. Business E-Mail: Susan@asch.org.

ASCHAUER, CHARLES JOSEPH, JR., retired health products executive; b. Decatur, Ill., July 23, 1928; s. Charles Joseph and Beulah Diehl (Kniple) A.; m. Elizabeth Claire Meagher, Apr. 28, 1962; children: Karen A. Vorwald, Thomas Arthur, Susan A. Baisley, Karl Andrew. BBA, Northwestern U., 1950; certificate internat. bus. adminstr., Centre d'Etudes Industrielles, Geneva, Switzerland, 1951. Prin. McKinsey & Co., Chgo., 1955-62; v.p. mktg. Mead Johnson Labs. div. Mead Johnson & Co., Evansville, Ind., 1962-67; v.p., pres. automotive group Maremont Corp., Chgo., 1967-70; v.p., group exec. Whittaker Corp., Los Angeles, 1970-71; v.p., pres. hosp. products div. Abbott Labs., North Chicago, Ill., 1971-76, v.p., group exec., 1976-79, exec. v.p., dir., 1979-89, ret., 1989. Lt. Supply Corps, USNR, 1951-55. Mem.: Shadow Wood Country Club, Sunset Ridge Country Club, Econs. Club Chgo., Univ. Club Chgo.

ASCHBACHER, JAMES CARL, artist, consultant; b. Evanston, Ill., Oct. 9, 1951; s. Frederick Edward and Helen Jane A.; m. Lisa Jensen, Sept. 17, 1978. Grad. h.s., Winnetka, Ill., 1969. Founder Artist for Books, Santa Cruz, Calif., 1993; co-founder SoHo Beach Art Group, Santa Cruz, 1993-94; chmn. art com. Chaminade Conf. Ctr., Santa Cruz, 1993-94, mem. open studios com. Santa Cruz Cultural Coun., 1995—. Executed mural Santa Cruz, 1998, 2001; poster art Nat. Libr. Week, 1999, Nat. Dance Week, 2000; art donor wall Freedom Libr., Calif., 2000, Hestwood County Park, Santa Cruz, Calif., 2002, Highlands County Park, Ben Lomond, Calif., 2002, mural Freedom Libr., Calif., 2003; ceramic mural, Santa Cruz H.S. Aquatics Ctr., Calif, 2005. Cmty. adv. bd. KVSP Radio, Santa Cruz, Calif., 2005. Recipient Gail Rich award, Santa Cruz, Calif., 2005. Home and Office: 1345 Dougmar Dr Santa Cruz CA 95062 E-mail: james@aschbacherart.com.

ASCHBRENNER, SHERRY IRENE, elementary school educator; b. Des Moines, Iowa, Feb. 3, 1950; d. Ort Meinecke and Eleanor Irene Molle Meinecke; m. David Frederick Aschbrenner, July 19, 1975; children: Brian David, Jill Renae. BS, Iowa State U., 1971; MA, U. Iowa, 1992. Elem. tchr. North Linn Cmty. Schs., Coggon, Iowa, 1971—75, Mentor (Ohio) Pub. Schs., 1976, Monticello (Iowa) Cmty. Schs., 1976—. Mem.: NEA, Monticello Edn. Assn., Iowa State Edn. Assn., Am. Legion Aux., Iowa State Alumni Assn. (life), Iowa State Letterwinners Club, Kappa Delta Pi, Pi Lambda Theta, Psi Chi, Chi Omega (life). Lutheran. Avocations: reading, golf. Home: 23231 Jay Rd Monticello IA 52310 Office: Shannon Elem 321 W South St Monticello IA 52310 Office Phone: 319-465-5425. E-mail: saschbrenner@monticello.k12.ia.us.

ASCHER, JAMES JOHN, pharmaceutical executive; b. Kansas City, Mo., Oct. 2, 1928; s. Bordner Fredrick and Helen (Barron) A.; m. Mary Ellen Robitsch, Feb. 27, 1954; children: Jill Denise, James John, Christopher Bordner Student, Bergen Jr. Coll., 1947—48, U. Kans., 1946—47, student, 1949—51. Rep. B.F. Ascher & Co., Inc., Memphis, 1954-55, asst. to pres. Kansas City, Mo., 1956-57, v.p., 1958-64, pres., 1965—2001, chmn. bd., 2001—. Bd. dirs. Childrens Cardiac Ctr., 1964-70, pres., 1968-70; mem. cen. governing bd. Children's Mercy Hosp., 1968-80; bd. dirs. Jr. Achievement of Middle Am., 1970-90, pres., 1973-76, chmn., 1979-81; edn. chmn. Young Pres.'s Orgn. 6th Internat. Univ. for Pres., Athens, 1975. 1st. lt. inf., U.S. Army, 1951-53, Korea Decorated Bronze Star, Combat Infantryman's Badge Mem.: VFW, Consumer Health Care Products Assn., Am. Mgmt. Assn. (pres.'s assn.), Chief Execs. Orgn., World Pres.'s Orgn., Lenexa City C. of C., Indian Hills Country Club, Kansas City Club, Lotos Club, N.Y. Athletic Club, Mercury Club, Delta Chi. Home: 6706 Glenwood St Shawnee Mission KS 66204-1451 Office: 15501 W 109th St Lenexa KS 66219-1307

ASCHER, MARK LOUIS, legal educator; b. Junction City, Kans., Sept. 23, 1953; s. Martin Louis and Bertha May (Clark) A.; m. Kerry Elizabeth Muldowney, Feb. 6, 1982. BA, Marquette U., 1975; MA, Kans. State U., 1977; JD, Harvard U., 1978; LLM in Taxation, NYU, 1981. Bar: N.Y. 1979, Fla. 1980, Ariz. 1982. Assoc. White & Case, N.Y.C., 1978-82; assoc. prof. U. Ariz., Tucson, 1982-86, prof., 1986-2000; Sylvan Lang Prof. in Law of Trusts U. Tex., Austin, 2000—. Vis. prof. U. Tex., Austin, 1986, NYU, 1988, U. Colo., Boulder, 1989, Cornell U., 1990, U. Miami, 1995, U. Mo., 1997, U. San Diego, 1999. Author: Federal Income Taxation of Trusts and Estates, 1988, 2d edit., 1996; co-author: (with Ferguson and Freeland) Federal Income Taxation of Estates, Trusts and Beneficiaries, 2d edit., 1993, 3d edit., 1998, (with Clark, Lusky, Murphy and McCouch) Gratuitous Transfers, 4th edit., 1999; editor: Scott on Trusts, 1992—; contbr. articles to profl. jours. Served with USAF, 1971-73. Fellow Am. Coll. Trust and Estate Counsel (acad.); mem. Am. Law Inst. (adviser Restatement (3d) of Trusts). Office: U Tex Sch Law 727 E Dean Keeton St Austin TX 78705-3224 Office Phone: 512-232-6019. E-mail: mascher@mail.law.utexas.edu.

ASCHER, ROBERT, anthropologist, educator, archaeologist, film producer; b. N.Y.C., Apr. 28, 1931; s. Alfred and Claire (Eliscue) A.; m. Marcia Alper, Mar. 10, 1956 PhD, UCLA, 1960. Prof. dept. anthropology Cornell U., Ithaca, NY, 1960—2002, emeritus prof. anthropology, 2003—, prof. dept. theatre, film and dance Grad. Sch., 1960—. Fieldwork in Turkey, Mex., Eng., Peru, U.S., Israel, 1960—. Co-author: Mathematics of the Incas, 1997; contbr. articles to Anthropology and Humanism Quar., Sci., History of Sci., Visual Anthropology, other profl. jours.; filmmaker: Cycle: An Australian Myth, 1984-86, Bar Yohai: In Celebration of a Visionary, 1987-88, Blue: A Tlingit Odyssey, 1989-91, The Golem, 1992-95. Office: Cornell Univ Dept Anthropology 726 University Ave Ithaca NY 14850-3914 Business E-Mail: ra27@cornell.edu.

ASCHER, WILLIAM, program and policy educator; b. Detroit, Jan. 3, 1947; s. Meyer S. and Beckie (Berger) A.; m. Barbara Ann Hirschfelder, Dec. 21, 1968; children: Diana, Julia, David. BA, U. Mich., 1968; MPhil, Yale U., 1970, PhD, 1975. Lectr. U. Pa., Phila., 1972-73; from asst. prof. to assoc. prof. Johns Hopkins U., Balt., 1973-84; prof. Duke U., Durham, N.C., 1984—. Dir. Sanford Inst. Pub. Policy, Duke U. Ctr. Internat. Devel. Rsch., Latin Am. Studies program; bd. dirs. Policy Scis. Ctr. Author: Forecasting, 1978, Scheming for the Poor, 1984, Strategic Planning and Forecasting, 1983, Natural Resource Policymaking in Developing Countries, 1990, Communities and Sustainable Forestry in Developing Countries, 1994. Recipient Disting. Teaching award Howard Johnson Found., 1988. Jewish.

ASCHHEIM, EVE MICHELE, artist, educator; b. NYC, Aug. 30, 1958; d. Emil and Lydie Aschheim. BA, U. Calif., Berkeley, 1983; MFA, U. Calif., Davis, 1987. Asst. prof. Occidental Coll., L.A., 1990, Sarah Lawrence Coll., Bronxville, N.Y., 1994-97. Vis. critic Md. Inst. Coll. Art, Balt., 1998-2000; lectr. Princeton (N.J.) U., 1991, 93, 98, 2000, sr. lectr., 2001—, dir. visual arts program, 2003—. One-woman shows include Stefan Stux Gallery, 1997, Galerie Rainer Borgemeister, Berlin, 1999, 2001, Galleri Magnus Åklundh, Lund, Sweden, 1999, Galerie Benden and Klimczak, Cologne, Germany, 1999, U. Mass. Gallery, Amherst, 2003, Larry Becker Contemporary Art, Phila., 2004, Eve Aschheim Guy Coirriero, Patrick Verelst Gallery, Antwerp, 2004; group exhbns. include Sackler Mus., Cambridge, Mass., 1997, Kunstmuseum Winterthur, Switzerland, 1998, Acad. der Künste, Berlin, 1998, Fonds régional d'art contemporain de Picardie and Mus. de Picardie Amiens, 1997, Parrish Mus., L.I., NY, 1999, Stark Gallery, NYC, 1999, U. Calif., San Diego, 1999, Landesgalerie Oberösterreich, Linz, Austria, 1999, Pratt Gallery, NYC, 1999, So. Meth. U., 2000, NY Studio Sch., 2000, Hunter Coll. Leubsdorf Gallery, NYC, 2000, Maier Mus., Lynchburg, Va., 2000, Tucson Art Mus., 2000, Mus. Contemporary Art, Miami, 2001, D.A.A.D. Galerie, Berlin, U. Art Mus. Calif. State U., Long Beach, 2001, Colby Coll., 2002, NY Hist. Soc., 2002, O.S.P. Gallery, Boston, 2002, Black and White Gallery, Bklyn., 2003, U. Mass., Amherst, 2003, Bill Maynes Gallery, NYC, 2003, Tang Mus., Saratoga, NY, 2004, Larry Becker Contemporary Art, Phila., 2004, Lohin-Geduld Gallery, NY, 2005, The Am. Acad. Arts and Letters NY, Lori Bookstein Gallery, NYC, 2005; represented in permanent collections at Fogg Mus., Nat. Gallery, Washington, NY Hist. Soc., Hamburger Bahnhof, Berlin, M.O.C.A., Miami, Met. Mus. Art, N.Y.C., Yale U. Art Gallery, Bonn Kunstmus., Mus. Modern Art, NY; artist (catalogs) Eve Aschheim Paintings and Drawings, 1999, Eve Aschheim Drawings, 2003, Eve Aschheim Recent Work, 2005. Recipient Rosenthal award Am. Acad. Arts and Letters, 1997; fellow NEA, 1989, Pollock-Krasner Found., 1990, 2001, NY Found. for Arts, 1991; grantee Elizabeth Found., 1997. Mem. Am. Abstract Artists. E-mail: easchh@aol.com.

ASCHHEIM, JOSEPH, economist, educator; b. Hanover, Germany, May 28, 1930; s. Max and Sarah (Pfeffer) A.; married; 1 child. AB with highest honors, U. Calif. at Berkeley, 1951; A.M. (Charles H. Smith scholar), Harvard U., 1953, PhD (Thayer scholar, Willard scholar), 1954. Mem. faculty Johns Hopkins U., 1956-63; mem. faculty George Washington U., Washington, 1963-2001, prof. emeritus, 2001. Dir. rsch., econ. advisor to gov. Ctrl. Bank Kenya, 1971-72; faculty advisor D.C. univs. consortium U.S. Naval Res. Officers Tng. Corps Unit, 1984-2001; affiliated scholar Ctr. for Study of Ctrl. Banks, NYU Sch. of Law, 1995—. Author books and numerous articles in profl. jours.; editorial bd. So. Econ. Jour, 1960-63, Atlantic Econ. Jour, 1973—2005; Disting. Assoc., Internat. Atlantic Econ. Soc., 2003-. Served with AUS, 1954-56. Ford Found. Faculty Research fellow. Mem. Am. Econ. Assn., Atlantic Econ. Soc. (v.p. 1973-76), Royal Econ. Soc., Phi Beta Kappa. Jewish. Office: Georgetown Sta PO Box 3758 Washington DC 20027

ASCHOFF, LAWRENCE MICHAEL (MICK ASCHOFF), computer information scientist; b. N.Y.C., Feb. 14, 1950; s. Edward William and Marie Louise (Marshall) A. BA in Art History, U. Fla., 1971; MBA in Fin., NYU, 1984, advanced profl. cert. in computer applications and info. systems, 1988. Sales rep. VIP Fabrics, N.Y.C., 1978-81; asst. to v.p. mktg. RAM Data, N.Y.C., 1981-82; sales agt. Equitable Life Assurance Soc., N.Y.C., 1982; programmer/analyst Drexel Burnham Lambert, N.Y.C., 1984-86, sr. programmer/analyst, 1986-88, project leader, 1988-89, project mgr., asst. v.p., 1989-90; officer, project mgr. retail banking systems Manufacurer's Hanover Trust, N.Y.C., 1990-92; asst. v.p. retail banking Chem. Bank (merger with Mfr. Hanover Trust), N.Y.C., 1992-95; v.p. project mgmt. competency ctr. retail banking systems Nat. Consumer Svcs. Chase Manhattan Bank (merger with Chem.), N.Y.C., 1996-2000; dir. GITSSO Program Mgmt. Office AXA Global I.T. Org., N.Y.C., 2000—01; dir. program mgmt. office AXA Technology Svcs., 2002—. Treas. Saunders Owners of Queens, Ltd., 1989-91, 2002-, pres., 1991-2000. Clin. assoc. Suicide and Crisis Prevention Ctr., Gainesville, Fla., 1972; mem. pres.'s coun. U. Fla., 1992—. Mem. Mensa, Phi Beta Kappa (sec. L.I. Alumni Assn. 1985-87, pres. 1987-93), Alpha Lambda Delta. Democrat. Avocations: travel, exercise, history, amusement parks, arts & sciences. Office: AXA Technology Svcs 1290 AV Americas 13th Fl New York NY 10104

ASCOLESE, MICHAEL J(OHN), public relations executive; b. Bayonne, N.J., July 25, 1946; s. Michael J. and Rose (Rinaldi) A. AB, St. Peter's Coll., Jersey City, 1968. Vol. U.S. Peace Corps, Swaziland, 1968-71; reporter The Star-Ledger, Newark, 1972-77, editor, 1977-81, fin. editor, 1981-83; press rep. Allied-Signal Inc., Morristown, N.J., 1983-86, mgr. media relations, 1986-88, dir. pub. relations, 1988-94; dir. pub. rels. Price Waterhouse LLP, N.Y.C., 1994—. Dir. Vol. Action Ctr. Morris County, Morristown, 1985-89, N.J. affiliate Am. Diabetes Assn., Bridgewater, 1985-88; bd. dirs. Morris Ctr. YMCA. Mem. N.Y. Fin. Writers Assn., Pub. Relations Soc. Am. Avocation: athletics. Office: Price Waterhouse LLP 101 Hudson St Jersey City NJ 07302 E-mail: mike.ascolesc@us.pwc.com.

ASCUENA, VIKKI PEPPER, secondary school educator; b. Jerome, Idaho, Oct. 13, 1953; d. Rex and Oneita P.; 1 child, Whitney. BA, Boise State U., 1975, MA, 1980. Tchr. Meridian (Idaho) Jr. H.S., 1975-87, Meridian (Idaho) H.S., 1987—, chairperson English dept., 1993—. Curriculum writer Meridian Schs., 1980—; mem. adj. faculty Boise State U., 1988-90; developer Micron project, 1994—; developer ISAT; presenter in field. Grantee NEH Victorian Seminar, 1987; named Meridian Jr. H.S. Tchr. of Yr., 1987, Meridian H.S. Tchr. of Yr., 1994, Meridian Dist. Tchr. of Yr., 1994; recipient Excellence in Edn. award Brigham Young U., 1997. Mem. NEA, Idaho Edn. Assn., Meridian Edn. Assn., Idaho Coun. Tchrs. English (treas. 1988-91, v.p. 1991-92, pres. 1992-93, past pres. 1993-94), Support for Learning and Tchg. English (newsletter editor 1993-94). Avocations: reading, golf, Basque dance. Office: Meridian HS 1900 W Pine Ave Meridian ID 83642-1961 Office Phone: 208-888-4905. E-mail: ascuenav@meridianschools.org.

ASCUNCE, GIL, physician; b. Santa Clara, Cuba, Mar. 18, 1946; came to U.S., 1961; s. Gil and Hilda (Gonzalez) A.; m. Consuelo C. Ascunce, Sept. 30, 1972; children: Aranzazu, Gil I., Gabriel. BA, Cath. U., 1967; MD, U. Salamanca, 1973. Resident Georgetown-D.C. Gen. Svc., 1973-76; pvt. practice Arlington, Va., 1978—; clin. instr. medicine Georgetown U., Washington, 1979—. Chief clin. nutrition Arlington Hosp., 1980—. Fellow Am. Coll. Gastroenterology. Office: 1715 N George Mason Dr Ste 410 Arlington VA 22205-3666

ASENSI, GUSTAVO, advertising executive, cinematographer; b. Vitoria, Spain; came to the U.S., 1992; s. Gustavo Asensi. Student, Sch. Dramatic Arts, Madrid, 1983, Sch. Cinematography, 1983. Copywriter Delvico Bates, Madrid, 1985-86, J. Walter Thompson, Madrid, 1986-87; creative dir. HDM, Madrid, 1987-89; exec. creative dir., v.p. Publinsa, Madrid, 1989-92; sr. v.p., exec. creative dir. Font & Vaamonde Advt., N.Y.C., 1993-94, mng. ptnr., CCO, 1994—. Recipient Bronze medal Festival San Sebastian, 1990, Silver medal, 1991, Gold medal Houston Internat. Film Festival, 1995, 96, Bronze medal, 1995, Gold medal Charleston Internat. Film Festival, 1995, Grand award, 1995, Gold Clio award, 1995.

ASH, FREDERICK MELVIN, retired manufacturing company executive; b. Columbus, Ohio, June 15, 1941; s. Melvin Edward and Ida Belle (Berry) A.; m. Karen Persichetti, Apr. 7, 1979; children: Jason, Carrie. Student, U. Cin., 1959-61; BS, BA, Ohio State U., 1963; MBA in Mgmt., Rutgers U., 1982. Staff acct. chem. plastics divsn. Gen. Tire & Rubber Co., Akron, Ohio, 1963-65; office mgr., 1965-67; acctg. mgr. Lawrence, Mass., 1968; controller Newcomerstown, Ohio, 1968-70; Lawrence, 1971-73; plant mgr., 1974-76; v.p. film Jeannette, Pa., 1977; pres. Gen Tire & Rubber Plastic Film Co., Jeannette, 1977-78; bus. dir. plastics Tenneco Chems., Inc., Piscataway, 1978-80; gen. mgr. plastics, 1980-82; v.p., gen. mgr. plastics Nuodex, Inc., Edison, N.J., 1982-84; v.p. mkgt. and sales Am. Maize Products, 1985-89; v.p. ops., 1990-92; pres. ingredients divsn., 1993-95; pres., comml. dir. Cerestar USA, Inc., 1995-99. Adv. Jr. Achievement, Akron, 1965; mem. budget com. Merrimack Valley United Fund, Lawrence, 1973-74, budget com. chmn., 1975, campaign chmn., 1976, dir., 1975-76; bd. dirs. Tradewinds Rehab Ctr., Lakeshore Devel. Coun., United Way of Westmoreland County, 1977-78,

Lake Area United Way, NW Ind. Fourm, Olympia Fields/Flossmoor United Way, 1985, pres., 1986-87. U.S. Rubber scholar, 1961-63; recipient Pace Setter award Ohio State U., 1963. Mem. Nat. Assn. Accts., Soc. Plastics Industry (vice chmn. film gorup), Ind. Mfrs. Assn. (mem. bd. dirs.), Corn Refiners Assn. (bd. dirs.), Westmoreland County C. of C., Ohio State U. Alumni Assn., Rutgers U. Alumni Assn., Village 2 Homeowners Assn. (v.p.), Sea Chase Condominium Assn. (bd. dirs.), Masons, Scottish Rite, Sigma Chi, Beta Gamma Sigma. Republican. Home: 95136 Captains Way Fernandina Beach FL 32034-4386

ASH, J. MARSHALL, mathematician, educator; b. N.Y.C., Feb. 18, 1940; s. Barney and Rosalyn (Hain) A.; m. Alison Igo, Nov. 24, 1977; children: Michael A., Garrett A., Andrew A. SB, U. Chgo., 1961, SM, 1963, PhD, 1966. Joseph Fels Ritt instr. Columbia U., N.Y.C., 1966-69; asst. prof. math. DePaul U., Chgo., 1970-72, assoc. prof., 1972-74, prof., 1974—. Vis. prof. Stanford U., 1977. Author: Studies in Harmonic Analysis, 1976; contbr. articles to profl. jours. George Westinghouse fellow, 1961, NSF fellow, 1962-66. Mem. AAUP, Am. Math. Soc., Math. Assn. Am., Sigma Xi. Home: 662 Maple St Winnetka IL 60093-2312 Office: De Paul U Math Dept Chicago IL 60614 Office Phone: 773-325-4216. Business E-Mail: mash@math.depaul.edu.

ASH, JENNIFER GERTRUDE, writer, editor; b. Jan. 16, 1963; d. Clarke and Agnes Ash; m. D.A. Joseph Rudick, Apr. 7, 1990; children: Clark Albert, Amelia, Eleanor. BA, Kenyon Coll., 1985; postgrad., New Sch. Social Rsch. Assoc. editor Women's Wear Daily, 1986-87; editor Town and Country, N.Y.C., 1992—95, writer, 1995—. Author: Private Palm Beach, 1992, The Expectant Father: Facts, Tips, and Advice for Dads-to-Be, 1995, revised edit., 2001. Fellow Frick Collection. Democrat. Roman Catholic.

ASH, KAREN ARTZ, lawyer; b. Bklyn., Dec. 23, 1955; d. Bernard and Helen Artz; m. David Charles Ash, June 11, 1977; 2 children. AB in Econs. with honors, Georgetown U., 1976; JD magna cum laude, N.Y. Law Sch., 1980. Bar: N.Y. 1981, U.S. Dist. Ct. (so. and ea. dists.) N.Y. 1981. Assoc. Kaye, Scholer, Fierman, Hays & Handler, NYC, 1980-83, Amster, Rothstein & Ebenstein, NYC, 1983-88, ptnr., 1988; ptnr., co-chair Intellectual Property Practice Katten Muchin Zavis Rosenman, NYC. Lectr. in field. Author: Grey Goods and What Does It Mean to You, Trademark Licensing Do's and Don'ts, Rule 60(b)(4) F.R.C.P.; research editor N.Y. Law Rev., 1980 (cert. of merit 1980); contbr. articles to profl. jours. Fundraiser Assn. for Help Retarded Children, N.Y.C., 1978—. Mem. ABA (chairperson trademark com. 1982—), Women's Bar Assn., N.Y. State Bar Assn., U.S. Trademark Assn., NOW, N.Y. Humane Soc. Democrat. Office: Katten Muchin Zavis Rosenman 575 Madison Ave New York NY 10022 Office Phone: 212-940-8554. Office Fax: 212-940-8776. E-mail: karen.ash@kmzr.com.

ASH, MAJOR MCKINLEY, JR., dentist, educator; b. Bellaire, Mich., Apr. 7, 1921; s. Major McKinley Sr. and Helen Marguerite (Early) A.; m. Fayola Foltz, Sept. 2, 1947; children: George McKinley, Carolyn Marguerite, Jeffrey LeRoy, Thomas Edward. BS, Mich. State U., 1947; DDS, Emory U., 1951; MS, U. Mich., 1954; Doctoris Medicine Honoris Causa, U. Bern, 1975. Instr. sch. dentistry Emory U., Atlanta, 1952—53; instr. U. Mich., Ann Arbor, 1953—56, asst. prof., 1956—59, assoc. prof., 1959—62, prof., 1962—, chmn. dept. occlusion, sch. dentistry, 1962—89, dir. stomatognathic physiology lab., sch. dentistry, 1969—89, dir. TMJ/oral facial pain clinic, sch. dentistry, 1983—89, Marcus L. Ward prof. dentistry, 1984—89, prof. emeritus, rsch. scientist emeritus, 1989—; cons. N.E. Regional Dental Bd., 1988—92. Vis. prof. U. Bern, 1989, U. Tex., San Antonio, 1990-98; pres. Basic Sci. Bd., State of Mich., 1962-74; cons. over the counter drugs FDA, Washington, 1985-89. Author, co-author 70 textbooks, 1958—; editor 4 books; contbr. over 190 articles to profl. jours. Served to tech. sgt. Signal Corps, U.S. Army, 1942-45, ETO. Grantee, Nat. Inst. Dental Rsch., 1962—85. Fellow Am. Coll. Dentists, Internat. Coll. Dentists, European Soc. Craniomandibular Disorders, European Soc. Oral Physiology; mem. AAAS, ADA (cons. coun. on dental therapeutics 1982—, cons. coun. sci. affairs 1995—), N.Y. Acad. Scis., Washtenaw Dist. Dental Soc. (pres. 1963-64), Phi Kappa Phi. Presbyterian. Avocations: photography, birdwatching. Office: U Mich Sch Dentistry Ann Arbor MI 48109 Business E-Mail: mmash@umich.edu.

ASH, ROY LAWRENCE, former federal official; b. Los Angeles, Oct. 20, 1918; s. Charles K. and Fay E. (Dickinson) A.; m. Lila M. Hornbek., Nov. 13, 1943; children— Loretta Ash Danko, James, Marilyn Ash Hanna, Robert, Charles. MBA, Harvard, 1947. Chief fin. officer Hughes Aircraft Co., 1949-53; co-founder Litton Industries, Inc., Beverly Hills, Calif., 1953-72, dir., 1953-72, pres., 1961-72; chmn. Pres.'s Adv. Coun. on Exec. Orgn., 1969-71; asst. to Pres. U.S.; dir. Office Mgmt. and Budget, Washington, 1973-75; chmn. bd., chief exec. officer AM Internat., 1976-81. Co-chmn. Japan-Calif. Assn., 1965-72, 80-81; mem. vis. com. Harvard U. Kennedy Sch. Govt., 1992—; mem. Bus. Roundtable, 1977-81. Vice chmn. Los Angeles Olympic Organizing Com., 1980-85, chmn. fin. com.; trustee Calif. Inst. Tech., 1967-72, Com. for Econ. Devel., 1970-72, 75—; dir. Los Angeles World Affairs Council, 1968-72, 78—, pres., 1970-72; chmn. adv. council on gen. govt. Rep. Nat. Com., 1977-80; chmn. L.A. Music Ctr. Opera Assn., 1988-93. From pvt. to capt. Army Air Corps, 1942-46. Mem. C. of C. U.S. (bd. dirs. 1979-85, chmn. internat. policy com. 1979-85), Calif. Club, Harvard Club. Office: Ste 1600 1900 Avenue Of The Stars Los Angeles CA 90067-4407

ASH, THOMAS PHILLIP, superintendent of schools; b. East Liverpool, Ohio, June 4, 1949; s. Bobby and Elizabeth Ann (Ludwig) A.; m. Nancy Elizabeth Gauron, June 8, 1951; children: Megan Elizabeth, John Gauron. BS in Edn., Bowling Green (Ohio) State U., 1971; MS in Edn., Youngstown (Ohio) State U., 1974. Tchr. East Liverpool City Schs., 1971-73, project coord., 1973-78, asst. supt., 1978-84, supt., 1984-99, Mid-Ohio Ednl. Svc. Ctr., 2000—. Bd. dir. CF Bank, Columbiana County Mental Health Assn.; chmn. Lincoln Way Spl. Edn. Resource Ctr., 1988-89, 93-94; treas. Richland County Youth and Family Coun., 2000—. Mem. exec. coun. Columbiana County Boy Scouts Am., 1989-91, Morrow County Workforce Investment Bd., 2000—, state adv. panel for Exceptional Children 2002-; pres. East Liverpool Area United Way, 1990-92; mem. State Supt. Adv. Commn. for Spl. Edn., 1993-95. Recipient Disting. Alumni award East Liverpool High Sch. Alumni Assn., 1987, Ohio Adminstr. of Yr. award Ohio Ednl. Libr. and Media Assn., 1990. Mem. Am. Assn. Sch. Adminstrs., Buckeye Assn. Sch. Adminstrs. (pres. 1999-2000), East Liverpool Area C. of C. (bd. dirs. 1985-2000, Outstanding Educator award 1982, Disting. Svc. award 1982). Office: Mid-Ohio Educational Svs Center 1495 W Longview Ave Ste 202 Mansfield OH 44906

ASHANTI, BARON JAMES, poet, educator; b. N.Y.C., Sept. 5, 1950; s. Gladys Carroll Foxhall, David Lancaster Foxhall; life ptnr. Mary Beithe Chow, May 31, 1999; m. Brenda Cummings, Sept. 8, 1979; children: Marcus, Nova. Grad., Evander Childes H.S., Bronx, N.Y., 1964. Exec. asst. Marie Brown Assoc., N.Y.C., 1987—90; tchr., adminstr. Frederick Douglass Creative Arts Ctr., N.Y.C., 1988—98; founder, pres. The Brilliance Factory, N.Y.C., 1990—. Tchr. Tchrs. & Writers Collaborative, N.Y.C., NY, 1994—99. Author: Nubiana, vol. I, 1977, Nova, 1990, numerous poems (Killeen prize, 1982). Polit. organizer Afrikan Peoples Party, Phila., 1969—80. Sgt. USMC, 1967—71, Viet Nam. Grantee, Pen Writers, 1985. Mem.: Renaissance Writers Guild (co-founder), Black Writers Union (co-founder), Acad. Am. Poets. Avocations: archery, drawing, shaolin gung-fu, travel, photography. Home: 274 W 140th St New York NY 10030 Personal E-mail: briliancefactory@aol.com.

ASHANTI, (ASHANTI S. DOUGLAS), vocalist; b. Glen Cove, N.Y., Oct. 13, 1980; Singer: (albums) Ashanti, 2002 (Grammy award, 2002), Foolish/Unfoolish: Reflections on Love, 2002, Ashanti: The 7 Series, 2003 (nominated 2 Grammy awards, 2003), Chapter II, 2003, Ashanti's Christmas, 2003; actor: (films) Bride & Prejudice, 2004, Coach Carter, 2005; (TV films) The Muppets' Wonderful Wizard of Oz, 2005. Office: Murder Inc 825 8th Ave 20th Floor New York NY 10019

ASHAR, HANSRAJ G., structural engineer, nuclear regulator; s. Girdharlal R. and Diwaliben G. Ashar; m. Kusum H. Sampat, July 16, 1961; 1 child, Bimal H. B in Civil Engring., Lukhdhirji Engring. Coll., Morvi, India, 1955; MSCE, U. Mich., 1958. Registered profl. engr., Ohio, Md. Bridge design engr. Rackoff Assocs., Columbus, Ohio, 1958—61; diploma engr. Julius Berger A.G., Wiesbaden, Germany, 1962—63; sr. engr. various cos., 1963—68; sr. design engr. Burns & Roe, Oradell, NJ, 1969—74; sr. structural engr. U.S. Nuc. Regulatory Commn., Rockville, Md., 1974—. Tech. judge Montgomery Sci. Fair, Gaithersburg, Md., 1996—2001. Fellow: ASCE (award for significant contbn. to profession 1992), Am. Concrete Inst.; mem.: Am. Inst. Steel Constrn. (nuc. spec. com. 1996—, chair 2005). Office: US Nuc Regulatory Commn 11555 Rockville Pike Rockville MD 20852 Office Phone: 301-415-2851. Business E-Mail: hga@nrc.gov.

ASHBACH, DAVID LAURENCE, internist, nephrologist; b. Chgo., Nov. 17, 1942; s. Sol Henry and Lila Mae A.; AB, Knox Coll., 1964; MS, Case Western Reserve U., 1969, MD, 1970; Diplomate Am. Bd. Internal Medicine; m. Arlene Rosenthal Nov. 28, 1963; children: Barbara, Deborah, Robert. Intern, Presbyterian-St. Luke's Hosp., Chgo., 1970-71, resident, 1971-73, fellow in nephrology, 1973-75; practice medicine specializing in nephrology, Hammond, Ind., 1975—; pres. Nephrology Specialists P.C.; mem. staffs St. Margaret's Hosp., Hammond, Ind., Meth. Hosp., Gary, Ind., St. Anthony's Hosp., Crown Point, Ind.; asst. clin. prof. medicine Ind. U.; asst. prof. health sci. Purdue U; pres.- elect, 1995, bd. dirs; past pres. Meth. Hosp., Gary; pres. Nat. Kidney Found. Ind. affiliate, Comprehensive Renal Care Inc.; bd. dirs. Regional Organ Bd. Ill. Mem. Nat. Kidney Found. Ind., A.C.P., Am. Internat. Socs. Nephrology, Ind. Hosp. & Health Assn. (bd. dirs.), R.O.B.I. (bd. dirs.). Jewish. Home: 20457 Ithaca Rd Olympia Fields IL 60461-1341 Office: 222 Hohman Ave Hammond IN 46320-1965 also: 4802 Broadway Gary IN 46408-4509

ASHBAUGH, NANCY GOULD, writer, performing arts educator; b. Charlotte, N.Y., June 9, 1952; d. William Edward Gould and Daisy Artelli Hartley. Student, So. Oreg., 1972-74, Oreg. State U., 1975, U. Nev., 1976. Part-time instr. creative writing U. Nev.; dance instr. Author: (novels) Notorious among the People, 1978, Turn Left or Be Killed, 1980, Juno. 1987. (radio play series) Story of Bill Abrams, 1979, also short stories. Nat. Endowment Arts grantee. Home: 3667 Twain Cir Las Vegas NV 89121

ASHBERY, JOHN LAWRENCE, language educator, poet, playwright, art critic; b. Rochester, N.Y., July 28, 1927; s. Chester Frederick and Helen Ashbery. Grad., Deerfield Acad., 1945; BA, Harvard U., 1949; MA, Columbia U., 1951; postgrad., NYU, 1957—58; DLitt (hon.), Southampton Coll. of L.I.U., 1979, U. Rochester, Harvard U., Pace Univ. Copywriter Oxford U. Press, N.Y.C., 1951—54, McGraw Hill Book Co., N.Y.C., 1954—55; art critic European edit. N.Y. Herald Tribune, Paris, 1960—65; Paris corr. Art News, 1964—65, exec. editor N.Y.C., 1965—72; prof. English Bklyn. Coll., 1974—90, Disting. prof., 1980—90, Disting. emeritus prof., 1990; Charles P. Stevenson Jr. prof. langs. and lit. Bard Coll., 1990—; editor quar. rev. Art and Lit., Paris, 1964—67; art critic Art Internat., Lugano, Switzerland, 1961—62; editor Locus Solus, Lans-en-Vercors, France, 1960-62; poetry editor Partisan Rev., 1976—80; art critic New York Mag., 1978—80, Newsweek, 1980—85; Charles Eliot Norton prof. poetry Harvard U., 1989—90; conducted spl. rsch. on life and work of Raymond Roussel. Author: Turandot and Other Poems, 1953, Some Trees, 1956, The Poems, 1960, The Tennis Court Oath, 1962, Rivers and Mountains, 1966, Selected Poems, 1967, Three Madrigals, 1968, Sunrise in Suburbia, 1968, Fragment, 1969, The Double Dream of Spring, 1970, The New Spirit, 1970, Three Poems, 1972, The Vermont Notebook, 1975, Self-Portrait in a Convex Mirror, 1975, Houseboat Days, 1977, As We Know, 1979, Shadow Train, 1981, A Wave, 1984, Selected Poems, 1985, April Galleons, 1987, Flow Chart, 1991, Hotel Lautréamont, 1992, And the Stars Were Shining, 1994, Can You Hear, Bird, 1995, Wakefulness, 1998, (plays) The Heroes, 1952, The Comprimise, 1955, The Philosopher, 1963, Three Plays, 1978, (poetry) Girls on the Run, 1999, Your Name Here, 2000, As Umbrellas Follow Rain, 2001, Chinese Whispers, 2002; author: (with James Schuyler) (novels) A Nest of Ninnies, 1969, represented in numerous anthologies; contbr. articles to periodicles;, author verse set to music. Named Lit. Lion, N.Y. Pub. Libr., 1984, Poet of Yr., Pasadena City Coll., 1984; recipient Yale Series of Younger Poets prize, 1955, Harriet Monroe Poetry award, Poetry Mag., 1963, Civic and Arts Found. prize, Union League, 1966, award, Nat. Inst. Arts and Letters, 1969, Shelley award, Poetry Soc. Am., 1973, Pulitzer prize, 1976, Nat. Book award, 1976, Nat. Book Critics Circle award, 1976, Jerome J. Shestack Poetry award, Am. Poetry Rev., 1983, Bollingen prize in poetry, Yale U. Libr., 1985, Lenore Marshall poetry prize, The Nation, 1985, Common Wealth award in lit., MLA, 1986, Creative Arts award, Brandeis U., 1989, Ruth Lilly Poetry prize, Poetry Mag. and Modern Poetry Assn. and Am. Coun. for Arts, 1992, Robert Frost medal, Poetry Soc. Am., 1995, Grand prize, Biennales Internat. Poetry, Belgium, 1996, Bingham Poetry prize, Boston Rev. Books, 1998, Walt Whitman Citation of Merit, State of N.Y., N.Y. State Writer's Inst., 2000, Medal for Achievement in the Arts, Signet Soc. Harvard U., 2001, Phi Beta Kappa Poet award, Harvard U., 1979; grantee, Poet's Found., 1960, 1964, Ingram Merrill Found., 1962, 1972; scholar Fulbright scholar, U. Montpellier, France, 1955—56, Rennes, France, 1956—57; Guggenheim fellow, 1967, 1973, Rockefeller Found. fellow, 1979—80, Wallace Stevens fellow, Yale U., 1985, McArthur Found. fellow, 1985—90. Fellow: Acad. Am. Poets (chancellor 1988—99, Wallace Stevens award 2001); mem.: Am. Acad. Arts and Scis., Am. Acad. Arts and Letters (Gold medal 1997). Address: Dept Langs and Lit Bard Coll PO Box 5000 Annandale On Hudson NY 12504-5000*

ASHBURN, ROY, state senator; b. Bakersfield, Calif., Mar. 21, 1954; children: Shelley, Shannon, Stacey, Suzy. BA in Pub. Adminstrn., Calif. State Univ., Bakersfield, 1983; postgrad., Coll. Sequoias. Owner Roy Ashburn Signs, 1969—72; field rep. Supr. LeRoy Jackson, 1972—77; dist. rep. Congressman William Thomas, 1979—83; supr. Kern County, 1984—; mem. Calif. State Assembly, Sacramento, 1996—2002; mem. dist. 18 Calif. State Senate, Sacramento, 2002—. Mem. rules com. Calif. State Assembly, mem. appropriations com., mem. govt. modernization com., mem. transp. and housing com., vice chmn. pub. employees and ret. com., chmn. senate select com. def. and aerospace industry. Republican. Roman Catholic. Mailing: State Capitol Rm 5094 Sacramento CA 95814 Office: 5001 California Ave Rm 105 Bakersfield CA 93309

ASHBURN, THOMAS, information technology executive; BS, Calif. State U., Long Beach. Mgmt. Hewlett-Packard, 1967—2001, former v.p., gen. mgr. svcs.; advisor Worldwide Svcs. Orgn. BEA Systems, Inc., San Jose, Calif., 2001—02, pres. Worldwide Field Orgn., 2002—04, exec. v.p. Worldwide Field Ops., 2004—. Office: BEA Systems Inc 2315 N First St San Jose CA 95131 Office Phone: 408-570-8000. Office Fax: 800-817-4BEA, 408-570-8901.

ASHBY, DENISE STEWART, speech educator, communication consultant; b. Charleston, W.Va., Aug. 15, 1941; d. Dennison Elmer and Marie Juanita (Queripel) Ellis; m. Rudolph Krutzner III, Dec. 6, 1958 (div. 1961); m. Garth Rodney Ashby, Feb. 15, 1976; children: Kevin Krutzner, Kevin Ashby, Lisa Ashby, Scott Ashby. AA with highest honors, Diablo Valley Coll., Pleasant Hill, Calif., 1981; BA in Speech summa cum laude, Calif. State U., Hayward, 1982; MA in Speech and Communication summa cum laude, Calif. State U., 1983. Lic. beautician N.J. Bd. Cosmetology. Owner Salon 105, Somerville, NJ, 1964-66; pres. Second Hand Rose, New Providence, 1966-76, The Place Beauty Salon, 1966-76, The Place Boutique, 1966-76; mgr. LaTortuga Boutique, 1977-81; tenured instr. Diablo Valley Coll., Pleasant Hill, Calif., 1982—2005, ret., 2005; instr. Los Positas Coll., Livermore, 1985—2005; pres. Ashby & Assocs., Danville; founder, facilitator The San Ramon Valley Fibro, CPS, RSD and Chronic Pain Support. AAUW liaison Ctr. for Higher Edn., San Ramon, 1988-90. Vice pres. Danville United Presbyn. Women, 1978-79; founder/facilatator San Ramon Valley Fibromyalga Chronic Fatigue and Chronic Pain Support Group, Danville, Calif., 2000— Recipient Pres.'s award, Calif. State U., 1983. Mem. AAUW (bd. dirs. 1988-90), NAFE, Speech Comm. Assn., Pi Lambda Theta, Pi Kappa Delta (pres. 1982). Home: 82 Cumberland Ct Danville CA 94526-1819 Office: Diablo Valley Coll Golf Club Rd Pleasant Hill CA 94523 Office Phone: 925-837-0510. Personal E-mail: dsashby@msn.com.

ASHBY, EUGENE CHRISTOPHER, chemistry educator; b. New Orleans, Oct. 25, 1930; s. Anthony and Ida (Bruno) A.; m. Carolyn Turner, Sept. 13, 1952; children: Chris, Steven, Terry, Marie, Angela, Julie, Rachel. BS in Chemistry, Loyola U., New Orleans, 1951; MS in Chemistry, Auburn U., 1953; PhD in Chemistry, U. Notre Dame, 1956. Rsch. chemist Ethyl Corp., Baton Rouge, 1956-59, rsch. assoc., 1959-63; asst. prof. Ga. Inst. Tech., Atlanta, 1963-65, assoc. prof., 1965-69, prof., 1969-73, Regents prof., 1973-93, Regents prof. emeritus, 1993—. Cons. Ethyl Corp., 1980-91, Conoco, Ponca City, Okla., 1972-76, U.S. Dept. Energy, 1990-98, Ga. Dept. Edn., 1994-97, Pfizer Pharm., 1996. Contbr. over 270 articles to profl. jours. Recipient Lavoisier medal French Chem. Soc., 1971, Sigma Xi rsch. award, 1968, 75, Herty medal Am. Chem. Soc., 1983, Disting. Prof. award Ga. Inst. Tech., 1988. Avocations: tennis, cattle farming. Home: 2516 Flair Knoll Dr NE Atlanta GA 30345-1316 Office: Sch Chemistry Ga Inst Tech Atlanta GA 30332-0001

ASHBY, FRANKLIN CHARLES, JR., corporate financial executive, educator; b. Rockville Centre, N.Y., Feb. 20, 1954; s. Franklin Charles and Janet Mary (Rauscher) Ashby; m. Rita Sandra Birzkalns, June 26, 1993; 1 child, Daniel Matthew Ashby. BA, Hofstra U., 1976; MBA, N.Y. Inst. Tech., 1984; MA, Columbia U., 1987; Grad. Cert., Columbia Bus. Sch. Exec. Prog., 1987; PhD, American U., UK, 1994. V.p. & chief ed. officer Dale Carnegie & Assocs., Inc., NY, 1984—98, corporate spokesperson, 1996—98; pres. Manchester Training, Inc., 1998—2000; exec. v.p. Manchester Ptrns. Internat., Inc., 1998—2000; head Modis U., 1999—2000; incoming pres. The Chubb Inst., 2000; pres. The Leadership Capital Group LLC, 2000—. Dep. U.S. Marshal (WAE), 1975—80; radio talk show host, Career Clinic, 1986—87; doctoral dissertation advisor Columbia U., N.Y.C., 2000—01, U. Southern Miss., 2002—05, U. Mo., 2002—. Author: Contemporary Approaches to Organizational Development and the Improving of Productivity, 1994, World Class, 1995, Revitalize Your Corporate Culture, 1999; author: (foreword) The Complete Idiot's Guide to Team Building, 1999, The Complete Idiot's Guide to Human Resource Management, 2002, The Complete Idiot's Guide to Managing People, 2003; co-author: Embracing Excellence, 2001, Back on Track, 2005; author/editor Effective Leadership Programs, 1999. Chmn. PONSI Bus. Adv. Bd., Am. Coun. on Educ., 1990-93; Commn. on Educ. Credit and Credentials, 1993-98; co-chmn. Comn. on Corporate Development, 1997; designated world's #1 Dale Carnegie instructor, 1984-1998; executive producer, Carnegie Refresher Series, 1986-1997; acting pres., Columbia U. Alumni Asn. (L.I. Region), 1992; chmn. Long Island Colls. & Univs. Comt., 1984-86; Bd. Dirs. Manchester Partners Internat., Inc., 1998-2000, bd. dirs. Chubb Computer Svcs., 2000; Performance Resources Organization, Inc., 1998-99, Coalition for Fair Broadcasting, Inc., 1987-92, Advancement for Commerce & Industry, Inc., 1986-92, North Shore Montessori Sch., 2002-2003; tryout, New York Mets, Shea Stadium, 1976; mem. adv. coun.U. So. Miss. Workplace Learning and Performance Inst., 2004—. Lutheran. E-mail: fashby1@optonline.net.

ASHBY, GARMON J.N., music educator, director; b. St. Marks, Cape, S.Africa, Dec. 27, 1958; s. Godfrey William and Sally Ashby. RULM, Rhodes U., S.Africa, 1980, MusB, 1981; LRSM; MusM, Yale U., 2002, diploma in art, 2003. Dir. music Diocesan Coll., Cape Town, South Africa, 1987—2000; dir. Yale U. Chapel Choir, New Haven, 2001—03; dir. music St. Philips' in the Hills Episcopal Ch., Tuscon, Ariz., 2003—. Choral dir. Cape Town Symphony Chorus, South Africa, 1993—98; chmn. Royal Sch. Ch. Music, Cape Town, 1998—2000; bd. dirs. Royal Sch. Ch. Music Am., 2005—. 1st lt. infantry, 1982—83, S.Africa. Recipient Vocat. Svc. award, Rotary, Newlands, South Africa, 2000; scholar, Inst. Sacred Music, Yale U., 2000; E. Stanley Seder scholar, 2001. Mem.: Am. Guild Organists, Am. Assn. Anglican Musicians, Am. Choral Dir. Assn., Royal Sch. Church Music. Episcopalian. Avocations: travel, cooking, hiking, reading, theater. Home: 1312 N Honeyrose Ave Tucson AZ 85745 Office: St Philip's in the Hills Episcopal Ch 4440 N Campbell Ave Tucson AZ 85718

ASHBY, JEFFREY S., astronaut; BS in Mech. Engring., U. Idaho, 1976; MS in Aviation Systems, U. Tenn., 1993; grad., Naval Test Pilot Sch., Naval Fighter Weapons Sch. Commd. ensign USN, advanced through grades to capt.; ret.; commdg. officer Strike Fighter Squadron 94; astronaut NASA, Houston, 1999; now on spl. assignment Air Force Space Command Hdqrs., Colorado Springs, Colo. Decorated DFC, 4 Navy Air medals, 2 Navy Commendation medals, Navy Achievement medal. Achievements include logged over 7,000 flight hours; 1,000 aircraft carrier landings; logged over 660 hours in space; pilot STS-100 Endeavour (2001); logged over 11 million miles, flown 436 orbits around the Earth; pilot STS-93 Columbia; commander STS-112 Atlantis. Avocations: skiing, soaring, backpacking, fly fishing. Office: Astronaut Office/CB NASA Johnson Space Ctr Houston TX 77058

ASHBY, N. BRUCE, air transportation executive; married; 3 children. BA in Econ., MS in Ops. and Rsch., Stanford U. Various mgmt. positions United Airlines, v.p. fin. planning and analysis, v.p., treas.; v.p. mktg. and devel. Delta Air Lines; from v.p. fin. planning and analysis to sr. v.p. US Airways Group, Inc., 1996—2002, sr. v.p. alliances, 2002—, pres. U.S. Airways Express, 2002—. Office: US Airways Group Inc 2345 Crystal Dr Arlington VA 22227-0001

ASHBY, RICHARD JAMES, JR., bank executive, lawyer; b. Lancaster, Pa., Aug. 18, 1944; s. Richard James and Gloria Marie (Mayer) A.; m. Claire Lundberg, July 1, 1967; children: Douglas R., Elizabeth, Brian J. AB, Wittenberg U., 1966; JD, Ohio State U., 1969. Bar: Pa. 1969, Ohio 1969. Assoc. Arnold Bricker Beyer & Barnes, Lancaster, 1969-71; trust officer First Nat. Bank Strasburg (Pa.), 1971-73, v.p., 1973-78, Fulton Bank, Lancaster, 1978-80, sr. v.p., 1980-86, exec. v.p., 1986-91; chmn., pres., CEO Lafayette Bank, Easton, Pa., 1991-98; chmn, pres., CEO Fulton Bank, Lancaster, Pa., 1999—. Vice chmn. Lehigh Valley Econ. Devel. Corp., 1995-98. Author: Profitability in Community Bank Trust Department, 1977. Mem. adv. bd. Pa. Joint State Govt. Commn., Harrisburg, 1984—; mus. dir. Lancaster Red Rose Chorus, 1976—91; pres. Parish Resource Ctr., Lancaster, 1984—2002, Northampton C.C. Found., 1991—98, 1994—96, State Theatre, Easton, 1991—98, 1993—94, Easton Hosp., 1991—98; dir. Valley Health Found., 1992—99, Northampton County Devel. Corp., 1994—99, LeHigh Valley Partnership, 1993—98; commr. Manheim Twp., Lancaster County, 1988—92; bd. dirs. United Way of Lancaster County, 2002—, Fulton Opera House, 2002—, Lancaster C. of C., 1999—2002; bd. dirs., vice chmn. Two Rivers C. of C., 1993—99. Staff sgt. U.S. Army, 1970—76. Recipient George Beneman Meml. award Ohio State U. Coll. Law, Columbus, 1969, Am. Spirit Honor medal Army & Navy Vets Aux., Ft. Ord, Calif., 1970 Mem.: Pa. Bankers Assn., Am. Bankers Assn., Lancaster Bar Assn., Pa. Bar Assn., Lancaster Country Club, Hamilton Club. Republican. Lutheran. Avocations: barbershop quartet singing, golf, fishing. Office: 1 Penn Sq Lancaster PA 17602-2853

ASHBY, SCOTT THOMAS, music educator, entrepreneur; b. Tillsonburg, ON, Canada, July 13, 1979; s. Eldon Garth and Joyce Elaine Ashby; m. Leah Patrice Rogers, July 19, 2003. Degree, Royal Conservatory of Music; BS, Bob Jones U., 2001, MusM. Dir. bands Bethel Bapt. Christian Sch., Simcoe, Canada, 2001—02; radio announcer, asst. music libr. WMUU, Inc., Greenville, SC, 2002—04; mem. faculty music Bob Jones U., Greenville, 2004—; dir. concert winds Bob Jones Jr. H.S., Greenville, 2004—. Prin., owner Ashby Musical Enterprises. Dir.: Andrea Chenier, Elixir of Love; musician: (albums) Ivory Dreams. Mem.: Am. Choral Dirs. Assn., Music Educators Nat. Conf.

ASHCRAFT, CHARLES OLIN, business educator; b. Kiowa, Kans., June 22, 1936; s. Olin N. and Esther Pauline (Young) A.; m. Letha May Bray, June 2, 1963; children: Farrah Elaine, Kyle Bray. BBA, Phillips U., 1958, MEd, 1965; postgrad., Air War Coll., 1977; diploma, Command & Gen. Staff Coll., 1975. Cert. tchr., Alaska, residential specialist. Tchr. Anchorage High Sch., 1958-61, East Anchorage (Alaska) High Sch., 1961-65; sch. adminstr. Ursa Maj. Elem. Sch., Ft. Richardson, Alaska, 1965-68, Arcturus Jr. High Sch., Ft. Richardson, 1965-73; instr. Anchorage Community Coll., 1959-73, Bartlett High Sch., Anchorage, 1973-90, rifle coach, 1980-90. Mem. adj. faculty Command & Gen. Staff Coll., Ft. Leavenworth, Kans., 1990—. Mem. Rep. Dist. 16, Anchorage, 1986-90; scoutmaster Western Alaska coun. Boy Scouts Am., 1976-80; post advisor Explorer Scout Post, Anchorage, 1980-91. Col. USAR, 1958-91. Recipient Silver Beaver award Western Alaska Boy Scouts Am., 1984; named to U.S. Army Inf. Officer Candidate Sch. Hall of Fame, 1991. Mem. NEA (life), NRA (life), Nat. Guard Assn. of U.S. (life), Res. Officers Assn. (life), Mil. Order of World Wars (life), F&AM Glacier Lodge (PM96), Pioneers for Ala. Igloo #15, Al Aska Shrine Temple, Royal Ct. Jesters Polarcourt, Scottish Rite, Orient of Alaska, Red Cross Constantine, Masons, Anchorage Yorkrite Coll. (past gov.), Prudential Jack White Real Estate. Republican. Methodist. Avocations: skiing, competition shooting and coaching. Home and Office: 11521 Brayton Dr #D1 Anchorage AK 99516-1388 E-mail: cashcraft@alaskalife.net.

ASHCROFT, JOHN DAVID, former United States attorney general, law educator; b. Chgo., May 9, 1942; s. James Robert and Grace Pauline (Larson) Ashcroft; m. Janet Elise Roede, 1967; children: Martha, Jay, Andrew. B cum laude, Yale U., 1964; JD, U. Chgo., 1967. Bar: Mo., U.S. Supreme Ct. Asst. prof. S.W. Mo. State U., Springfield, 1967—71; assoc. prof., 1971—73; pvt. practice Springfield, 1967-73; state auditor State of Mo., 1973-75, asst. atty. gen., 1975-77, atty. gen., 1977-84, gov., 1985-92; atty. Suelthaus and Kaplan P.C., 1993-94; U.S. senator from Mo., 1995-2001; atty. gen. U.S. Dept. Justice, 2001—05; disting. prof., law and govt. Regent Univ., Virginia Beach, Va., 2005—. Mem. commerce, sci. and transp. coms., aviation subcom., comm. subcom., chmn. consumer affairs, fgn. commerce & tourism subcom., mfg. and competitiveness subcom., mem. fgn. rels. com., European affairs subcom., Near Ea. & South Asian affairs subcom., Western Hemisphere Peace Corps subcom., mem. jud. com., chmn. constitution, fedn. and property rights subcom.; mem. Presdl. Adv. Coun. Intergovtl. Affairs, The Pres.'s Export Coun.; nat. chmn. Edn. Commn. States, 1987-88, Jud. Com., Subcom., chmn. constn.; chmn. Nat. Govs. Assn. Task Force on Coll. Quality, 1985, Nat. Govs. Assn. Task Force on Adult Literacy; co-chair Renewal Alliance. Gospel singer: records include In the Spirit of Life and Liberty, The Gospel According to John; author: Lessons from a Father to a Son, 1998, (with wife) College Law for Business, 7th, 8th, 9th, 10, 11th edits., It's the Law, 1979-91; contbr. articles to profl. jours. Chmn. Task Force on Adult Literacy, Task Force on College Quality Nat. Gov.'s Assn., 1991; chmn. Rep. Gov.'s Assn., 1990; co-chmn. Rep. Platform Com., 1992. Recipient Nat. Sheriffs Assn. award, 1996; named Christian Statesman of Yr., 1996. Mem. ABA (ho. of dels.), Mo. Bar Assn., Cole County Bar Assn., Nat. Assn. Attys. Gen. (pres. 1980-81, chmn. budget com., exec. com., Wyman award 1983), Nat. Govs. Assn. (vice chmn. 1990, chmn. 1991-92, chmn. Pres.'s Commn. on Urban Families 1992). Republican. Mem. Assembly Of God Ch.*

ASHCROFT, NEIL WILLIAM, physics educator, researcher; b. London, Nov. 27, 1938; m., 1961; 2 children BSc, U. New Zealand, 1958, MSc with honors, 1960; PhD, U. Cambridge, 1964; DSc (hon.), Victoria U., Wellington, New Zealand. Sci. rsch. coun. sr. fellow Cavendish Lab. U. Cambridge, Eng., 1973-74, vis. fellow Clare Hall, 1973-74; assoc. theoretical physics Cornell U., Ithaca, N.Y., 1965-66, from asst. prof. to assoc. prof., 1966-75, prof. physics, 1975—, Horace White Chair of Physics, 1990, various adminstrv. and acad. coms., dir. Lab. of Atomic and Solid State Physics, 1979-84; dep. dir. Cornell High Energy Synchrotron Source, Ithaca, N.Y., 1978-97; dir. Cornell Ctr. for Materials Rsch., Ithaca, 1997-2000. Chaire municipale Joseph Fourier U., Grenoble, France, 1989-93, 2000—; sci. cons. Los Alamos Nat. Lab., 1976-94; adv. com. High Flux Beam Reactor, Brookhaven, 1984-90; sci. cons. Lawrence Livermore Nat. Lab., 1985—; chmn. Gordon Rsch. Conf. on Rsch. at High Pressure, 1986—, trustee 1988-92, chmn. bd. trustees, 1991—; liasion rep. Nat. Rsch. Coun. Rev. Panel on Materials, Am. Phys. Soc. div. of Condensed Matter Physics Physics; vis. com. Brookhaven Nat. Lab., 1986—; Gordon Godfrey vis. prof. U. New South Wales, Australia, 1988; mem. rsch. briefing panel on high temperature superconductivity NAS, adv. panel solid state div. Oak Ridge Nat. Lab.; Erskine fellow Canterbury U., New Zealand, 1990, Ehrenfest lectr. U. Leiden, The Netherlands, 1991; Faraday bicentennial lectr. Electrochem. Soc., 1991; mem. solid state scis. com. NRC, 1993-96. Co-author: Solid State Physics, 1975; mem. editl. bd. Jour. of Physics, 1988-94, The Phys. Rev., 1996—, Australian Jour. of Physics, 1997—; contbr. numerous articles to profl. jours. Fellow Royal Soc. guest fellow, 1984—85, overseas fellow, Churchill Coll., Cambridge U., 1984—85, 2001—, Erskine fellow, Canterbury U., 1990; Guggenheim fellow, 1984—85. Fellow AAAS, Am. Phys. Soc., Royal Soc. New Zealand (hon.); mem. Assn. Internat. pour L'Avancement de la Recherche et de la Technologie Aux Hautes Pressions (exec. com. 1995-99, Bridgman prize 2003), Nat. Acad. of Sci. Office: Cornell U Clark Hall Ithaca NY 14853-2501 Office Phone: 607-255-8613. Business E-Mail: mwa@ccmr.cornell.edu.

ASHDOWN, FRANKLIN DONALD, physician, composer; b. Logan, Utah, May 2, 1942; s. Donald and Theresa Marie (Hill) A. BA, Tex. Tech. U., 1963; MD, U. Tex., 1967. Chief of med. Holloman Air Force Base, New Mexico, 1971-73; chief of staff Gerald Champion Mem. Hosp., Alamogordo, N.M., 1976, 91, 92; pvt. practice Alamogordo, 1973—; pres. Otero County Concerts Assn., Alamogordo, 1985-94, Otero County Med. Soc., Alamogordo, 1986. Cons. N.Mex. Sch. for Visually Handicapped, Alamogordo, 1973—76. Composer of more than 80 published and recorded works. Bd. dirs. Otero County Mental Health Assn., Alamogordo, 1973-77, Flickinger Found. for Performing Arts, 1995; bd. trustees Gerald Champion Meml. Hosp., 1992. Mem. Gerald Champion Mem. Hosp., N.M. Med. Soc., Am. Soc. Internal Med., ASCAP (Standard Panel award 2000, 01, 02). Republican. Office: 1301 Cuba Ave Alamogordo NM 88310-5727 Office Phone: 505-437-4586. E-mail: fashdown@wayvarer1.com.

ASHDOWN, MARIE MATRANGA (MRS. CECIL SPANTON ASHDOWN JR.), writer, educator, cultural organization administrator; b. Mobile, Ala. d. Dominic and Ave (Mallon) Matranga; m. Cecil Spanton Ashdown Jr., Feb. 8, 1958; children: Cecil Spanton III, Charles Coster; children by previous marriage: John Stephen Gartman, Vivian Marie Gartman. Degree, Maryville Coll. Sacred Heart, Springhill Coll. Feature artist, women's program dir. daily program Sta. WALA, WALA-TV, Mobile; v.p., dir. Met. Opera Guild, N.Y.C., opera instr. in-svc. program, 1970-80, Marymont Coll., N.Y.C., 1979-85; exec. dir. Musicians Emergency Fund, Inc., N.Y.C., 1985—. Internat. adv. coun. Van Cliburn Found., 1998—; cons. No. Ill. U. Coll. Visual and Performing Arts, 1985—; lectr. in field. Author: Opera Collectables, 1979, contbr. articles to profl. jours. Recipient Extraordinary Svc. award March of Dimes, Medal of Appreciation award Harvard Bus. Sch. Club NYC, Cert. Appreciation, Kiwanis Internat., Arts Excellence award NJ State Opera, Ciparío award, Albanese-Puccini award Lincoln Ctr., 2002. Mem. AAUW, Nat. Inst. Social Scis., Com. for U.S.-China Rels. Avocations: collecting art, antique ceramics and porcelains, bookbinding. Home: 25 Sutton Pl S Apt 16K New York NY 10022-2456 Office: Musicians Emergency Fund Inc PO Box 1256 New York NY 10150-1256 Personal E-mail: dmat807@aol.com.

ASHE, AARON MATTHEW, sales professional; b. Miami, Fla., Sept. 13, 1971; s. Leslie Drue and Cheryl King Ashe; m. Lisa Rainey, July 10, 1999; 1 child, Austin James. BA in Comm., George Mason U., 1993. Account exec. Cable Networks Inc., McLean, Va., 1994-99; sales mgr. Nat. Cable Comm., Chevy Chase, Md., 1999—. Office: Nat Cable Comm 5454 Wisconsin Ave # 625 Chevy Chase MD 20815 Fax: 301-951-2650. E-mail: aaron_ashe@spotcable.com.

ASHE, ARTHUR JAMES, III, chemistry professor; b. N.Y.C., Aug. 5, 1940; s. Arthur James and Helen Louise (Hawelka) A.; m. Penelope Guerard Vaughan, Aug. 25, 1962; children: Arthur J., Christopher V. BA, Yale U., 1962, MS, 1965, PhD, 1966; postgrad., Cambridge U., 1962-63. Asst. prof. chemistry U. Mich., Ann Arbor, 1966-71, assoc. prof., 1971-76, prof., 1976—, chmn. dept., 1983-86, prof. macromolecular sci. and engring., 2000—. Vis. scientist Phys. Chemistry Inst., U. Basle, Switzerland, 1974 Mem. editorial avd. bds. profl. jours, 1984—. Alfred P. Sloan fellow, 1972-76 Mem. Am. Chem. Soc. Office: U Mich Dept Chemistry Ann Arbor MI 48109 Business E-Mail: ajashe@umich.edu.

ASHE, BERNARD FLEMMING, arbitrator, educator, lawyer; b. Balt., Mar. 8, 1936; s. Victor Joseph Ashe and Frances Cecelia (Johnson) Flemming; m. Grace Nannette Pegram, Mar. 23, 1963; children: Walter Joseph, David Bernard. BA, Howard U., 1956, JD, 1961. Bar: Va. 1961, D.C. 1963, Mich. 1964, N.Y. 1971. Tchr. Balt. Pub. Schs., 1956-58; atty. NLRB, Washington, 1961-63; asst. gen. counsel Internat. Union United Auto Workers, Detroit, 1963-71; gen. counsel N.Y. State United Tchrs., Albany, 1971-96, arbitrator, 1996—. Mem. adj. faculty Cornell Sch. Indsl. and Labor Rels., Albany div., 1981, 87, Fordham U. Law Sch., 1996-00, Roger Williams U. Law Sch., 1996-98. Contbr. articles on labor and constnl. law to profl. jours. Bd. dirs. Urban League Albany, 1979—85, 1st v.p., 1981—85; trustee N.Y. Lawyers Fund for Client Protection, 1981—, Adelphi U., Garden City, NY, 1997—2005. Recipient Nat Weinberg award, Wayne State U., Detroit, Mich., 2001. Fellow Am. Bar Found. (life), Coll. Labor and Employment Lawyers (emeritus); mem. NAACP (Thurgood Marshall Justice award 2000), ABA (chmn. sect. labor and employment law sect. 1982-83, consortium on legal svcs. and the pub. 1979-84, commn. on pub. understanding about the law 1987-91, mem. standing com. on group and prepaid legal svcs. 1996-97, ho. of dels. 1985-96, 97-2003, nominating com. 1988-91, chair drafting com., 1998-2000, bd. govs. 1991-94, exec. com. 1993-94, accreditation com. sect. legal edn. and admission to the bar 1994-98, chmn. standing com. on group and prepaid legal svcs. 1996-97, sr. lawyers divsn. coun. 1994-2000, standing com. on client protection 1998-2001, advisor commn. on judiciary in 21st century 2002-03, jour. editl. bd. 2003—), Am. Law Inst., Nat. Bar Assn., Am. Arbitration Assn. (bd. dirs. 1982-98, Whitney North Seymour Sr. medal 1989), N.Y. State Bar Assn., Albany County Bar Assn. E-mail: bfashe@csi.com.

ASHE, KATHY RAE, special education educator; b. Bismarck, N.D., Oct. 24, 1950; d. Raymond Charles and Virginia Ann (Mason) Lynch; m. Barth Eugene Olson, Aug. 11, 1973; 1 child, William Raymond; m. Fredrick A. Ashe, Aug. 5, 1994. BS, U. N.D., 1972, MS in Spl. Edn., 1987. Cert. elem. tchr. with spl. edn. credential, N.D. Instr. Grafton State Sch., N.D., 1972-74; tchr. spl. edn. Grand Forks Sch. Dist., N.D., 1974—. Bd. dirs. Agassiz Enterprises; mem. RAD com. Valley Jr. High; mem. transition governing bd., Region IV. Mem. spl. needs recreation program Grand Forks Park Bd., 1973—76; mem. Spl. Olympics Area Mgmt. Team, 1984—90; mem. region IV Low Incident Behavior Grant Com.; co-chair, vol. coord. Greater Grand Forks Soccer Club Tournament, 2000, 2001; bldg. rep. Grand Forks Edn. Assn., 2000—; bd. dirs. Assn. Retarded Citizens, Devel. Homes, Inc., N.D. Sch. Blind Found., pres., 1997—2003. Named N.D. Tchr. of Yr., Coun. Chief State Sch. Officers, 1981. Mem. AAUW (pres. 1998-2000, N.D. co-pres. 2004—), Delta Kappa Gamma (sec. 1984-86, pres. 1990-94), Alpha Phi (alumni pres. 1984-86, 90-91, alumni treas. 1995—), Phi Delta Kappa. Republican. Roman Catholic. Avocations: sporting events, civic work, cross stitch, bowling, golf. Home: 3208 Walnut St Grand Forks ND 58201-7665 E-mail: ashekathy@hotmail.com.

ASHEGHIAN, PARVIZ, economics educator; b. Tehran, Iran, Sept. 17, 1943; came to U.S., 1971; s. Davood and Toorya (Levy) A.; m. Dorothy Thurman, Mar. 24, 1977; children: Daniel, Laila. BA in Acctg., Iranian Inst. Advanced Acctg., Tehran, 1971; MBA in Internat. Bus., U. Detroit, 1973; MA in Econs., U. Fla., 1976; PhD in Econs., Ga. State U., 1980. Asst. test analyst State Orgn. for Adminstrn. and Employment Affairs, Tehran, 1966-70; auditor Ministry of Water and Power Iran, Tehran, 1970-71; instr. econs. SUNY, Potsdam, 1979-80, asst. prof., 1980-81, St. Lawrence U., Canton, N.Y., 1981-85, assoc. prof., 1985-91; prof., chmn. dept. econs. Calif. State U., San Bernardino, 1991—. Referee Jour. Econ. Devel., 1982—, Eastern Econ. Jour., 1985-91. Author: (with B. Ebrahimi) International Business, 1990, also instr.'s manual, 1990, Internat. Economics, 4th ed., 2004, Economic Develpment: A Global Perspective, 2003, The Mutinational Corporation, 1998, 3d edit, 2005, The Internal Environment and Global Business, 2004, The External Environment of Global Business, 2002, Technology Transfer in The Global Economy, 2003; referee Midwestern Jour. Bus. and Econs., 1986—, mem. editorial rev. bd., 1989—; mem. editorial rev. bd. Global Devel. Report, Jour. Devel. and Cooperation, Jour. Third World Devel., Tech. and Devel., 1987—; contbr. articles to profl. jours. Mem. Am. Econ. Assn., Acad. Internat. Bus., Fin. Mgmt. Assn., World Acad. Devel. and Cooperation, Ea. Econ. Assn., Western Econ. Assn., Atlantic Econ. Soc. Avocations: playing violin and piano, jogging, hiking. Office: Calif State U Dept Econs San Bernardino CA 92407

ASHER, AARON, retired editor, publisher; s. Samuel and Henny (Meyer) A.; m. Linda Wofsey, Oct. 11, 1956; children— Rachel, Abigail. BA with honors, U. Chgo., 1949, MA, 1952. Mem. editorial staff Alfred A. Knopf, Inc., N.Y.C., 1956-58; exec. editor Meridian Books, Inc., N.Y.C., 1958-64; sr. editor Viking Press, Inc., N.Y.C., 1964-69; dir. gen. book dept. Holt, Rinehart and Winston, Inc., N.Y.C., 1969-74; editor in chief Macmillan Pub. Co., Inc., N.Y.C., 1974; editor in chief, v.p. Farrar, Straus and Giroux, Inc., N.Y.C., 1975-81; exec. editor Harper & Row, N.Y.C., 1981-86; pub. Grove Press, N.Y.C., 1986-89, Grove Weidenfeld, N.Y.C., 1989-90, Aaron Asher Books, Harper Collins, N.Y.C., 1990-93; pub. cons., editor, translator, 1993—2005. Served with AUS, 1953-55. Home and Office: 201 W 86th St New York NY 10024-3349

ASHER, BETTY TURNER, academic administrator; b. Booneville, Ky., Oct. 19, 1944; BA, Ea. Ky. U.; MA, Western Ky. U.; EdD, U. Cin. Sr. assoc. vice provost U. Cin., 1978-80; assoc. vice chancellor acad. affairs Minn. State U. System, 1981-82; v.p. student affairs Ariz. State U., Tempe, 1982-89; pres. U. S.D., Vermillion, 1989-1996, Bus., Industry Tng., Destin, Fla., 1997—. Office: Bus & Industry Trng Serv INC 225 Main St Ste 7J Destin FL 32541-2550 E-mail: bettyasher@cox.net.

ASHER, J. WILLIAM, education educator, psychology professor; b. Gary, Ind., Apr. 12, 1927; s. Floyd Gaylord and Ruth Ann (Williams) A.; m. Katherine Collyer, Apr. 10, 1955 (dec. July 1995); children: William Collyer, Ruth Ann Asher-Lynch, James Conover, Christopher Harrigan; m. Dorothy Davidson, Nov. 7, 1998. BA, DePauw U., 1950; MS in Psychology, Purdue U., 1951, PhD, 1955; postgrad., Harvard U., 1964—65. Cert. psychologist, Ind. Rsch. coord. U.S. Office Edn., Washington, 1956—60; prof. ednl. rsch. U. Pitts., 1960—66; prof. ednl. studies and psychol. scis. Purdue U., West Lafayette, Ind., 1966—2003. Pvt. practice psychology, West Lafayette; mem. com. NRC. Author: Educational Research and Evaluation Methods, 1976; co-author: Composition Research: Empirical Designs, 1988, Educational Research, 1995; also over 100 articles. Postdoctoral fellow, 1964-65. Fellow AAAS, APA (pres. divsn. ednl. psychology); mem. Am. Ednl. Rsch. Assn., Nat. Assn. Gifted Children, Sigma Xi, Phi Delta Kappa. Office: Purdue U Ednl Studies BRNG West Lafayette IN 47907 Business E-Mail: asher@purdue.ede.

ASHER, JERRY L., retired federal agency administrator; b. Houston, Nov. 28, 1941; s. Wayne B. and Norma Faye (Morgan) M.; m. Beverly E. Herrin, Dec. 19, 1969 Idec. Dec. 1986); children: Debra Elizabeth, David Everett. BA in Polit. Sci., Georgetown U., 1963; MA in Pub. Adminstrn., U. Utah, 1965. Cert. tchr. Fiscal liaison dir. U.S.-U.K. Harrier Aircraft Project, London, 1977-80; fgn. mil. sales analyst Office of Sec. of Def., Washington, 1980-85; budget examiner U.s. Office Mgmt. and Budget, Washington, 1985-97; ret., 1997. Project budget and adminstrv. officer U.s. Naval Material Command Hdqrs., Washington, 1968-77. Author, editor: King Cotton's Lords and Ladies: A Dream Remembered, 1989. Mem. passenger rels. adv. bd. Met. Transit Authority of Houston, 1997—. Mem. English Speaking Union, Houston Forum. Episcopalian. Avocations: travel, reading, religious education. Home: 2401 Lazy Hollow Dr Apt 113 A Houston TX 77063-2570 Office Phone: 713-702-5407.

ASHER, RIKKI, artist, art educator; b. Manhattan, N.Y. d. Arthur Asher and Evelyn Lehrman; m. Royce Jeffrey Froehlich, Feb. 14, 1994. BA, CUNY, Lehman Coll., N.Y., 1976, MFA, 1981; EdD, Columbia Univ. at Tchrs. Coll., N.Y., 1991. Cert. tchr. art K-12 N.Y. Adj. prof. SCh. of Visual Arts, N.Y., NY, 1992—93, CUNY Hunter Coll., N.Y., 1993—95; asst. prof. SUNY New Paltz, New Paltz, NY, 1994—96, dir. London art, 1995—97; dir. art edn. CUNY @ Queens Coll., Queens, NY, 1996—. Bd. mem. N.Y. C. Tchrs. Assn., N.Y., 2003—; higher edn. collaboration liaison Lincoln Ctr. Inst., N.Y., 1996—98. One-woman shows include High Rothschild Found., El Salvador, Calif., 2004, exhibitions include Bronx Boroughs Pres. office, N.Y., 2003; contbr. chapters to books, articles pub. to profl. jour. Muralist Tree of Life Yoga Ctr., 2003; designer Cmty. Supported Agrl., Forest Hills, NY, 2004. Grantee Cmty. Arts Grant, Coun. on the Arts Queens, N.Y., 2002, Presdl. Grant for Multicultural, Queens Coll., 2001. Mem.: Internat. Soc. for Edn., Coll. Art Assn., Nat. Art Edn. Assn. Avocations: yoga, meditation, Buddist lecturer. Office: City Univ NY Queens Coll 65-30 Kissena Blvd Flushing NY 11367-1592

ASHER, SANFORD ABRAHAM, chemist, educator; b. Landesburgh, Federal Republic of Germany, June 18, 1947; came to the US, 1949; s. Leo Dow and Pearl (Lon) A.; m. Trina Asher, 1966 (div. 1974); children: James David, Dianne Louise; m. Nancy Lee Day, June 27, 1976; 1 child, Rachel Marie. BA, U. Mo., 1971; PhD, U. Calif., Berkeley, 1977. Rsch. asst. Petrotile Corp., St. Louis, 1967-71; rsch. fellow Harvard U., Cambridge, Mass., 1977-80; prof. U. Pitts., Pitts., 1980—, dir. Materials Rsch. Ctr.; sci. founder Glucose Sensing Tech. LLC. Cons. EG&G Princeton Applied Rsch., 1986-88, Am. Cyanamid, Stamford, Conn., 1988-90, Bristol-Myers-Squibb, Princeton, NJ, 1990—, Mine Safety Applicances Co., 1992—; McElvain lectr. U. Wis., 1989; established investigator Am. Heart Assn., 1984-89. Contbr. numerous articles to profl. jours. Recipient Spectrochemical Analysis award, Am. Heart Assn., 1996, Bowen Michelson award, 2000, Lippencott award, 2002, Pitts. award, Am. Chem. Soc., 2002, Alumni award, U. Mo. Mem. AAAS, Am. Chem. Soc., Spectroscopy Soc. Pitts. (chmn. aide to edn. 1990), Coblentz Soc. (bd. dir. 1990—). Jewish. Achievements include patents for colloidal crystalline Bragg diffraction devices and photonic crystals. Office: U Pitts Dept Chemistry Pittsburgh PA 15260 Office Phone: 412-624-8570. E-mail: asher@pitt.edu.

ASHHURST, ANNA WAYNE, foreign language educator; b. Phila., Jan. 5, 1933; d. Astley Paston Cooper and Anne Pauline (Campbell) Ashhurst; m. Ronald G. Gerber, July 22, 1978. AB, Vassar Coll., 1954; MA, Middlebury Coll., 1956; PhD, U. Pitts., 1967. English tchr. Internat. Inst. Spain, Madrid, 1954-56; asst. prof. Juniata Coll., Huntingdon, Pa., 1961-63; asst. prof. Spanish dept. Franklin and Marshall Coll., Lancaster, Pa., 1968-74, acting chmn. Spanish dept., 1972, convenor, fgn. lang. council, 1972-74; assoc. prof. dept. modern fgn. langs. U. Mo., St. Louis, 1974-78. Author: La Literatura Hispano-Americana en la Crítica Española, 1980. Mem. Welcome Wagon of Lancaster, Pa., 1968-70, 71-74 Fulbright-Hays grantee, Colombia, S.Am., summer 1963; Ford Humanities fellow, summer 1970; Mellon fellow, 1970-71 Mem. AAUW (pres. Ferguson-Florissant br. 1989-91, 95-98, chmn. St. Louis area interbranch coun. 1992-94, chair environ. task force Mo. 1992-95, local arrangements chair for Mo. state conv. 1997, Woman of Distiction award 1998), Internat. Inst. in Spain, Instituto Internacional de Literatura Iberoamericana, Am. Assn. Tchrs. Spanish and Portuguese. Home: 2105 Barcelona Dr Florissant MO 63033-2805

ASHKENAZY, VLADIMIR DAVIDOVICH, concert pianist, conductor; b. Gorky, Russia, July 6, 1937; s. David and Evstolia (Plotnova) A.; m. Thorunn Johannsdottir, Feb. 25, 1961; children— Vladimir Stefan, Nadia Liza, Dimitri Thor, Sonia Edda, Alexandra Inga. Student, Cen. Music Sch., Moscow, Moscow Conservatory; studies with, Sumbatyan, Lev Oborin. Condr., music dir. Royal Philharm. Orch., London, 1987-95; prin. guest conductor Cleve. Orch., 1987-94; music dir. Deutsches Symphonie Orchester (formerly Radio Symphony Orch.), Berlin, 1989-99, Czech Philharm. Orch., 1998—2003, European Union Youth Orch., 2001—, NHK Symphony Orch., Tokyo, 2004. London debut, London Symphony Orch. under George Hurst, later solo recital, Festival Hall, 1963, recs., concerts throughout world. Music dir. Czech Philharm. Orch., Prague, 1998-2003, European Union Youth Orch., 2002, NHK Symphony Orch., Tokyo, 2004-. Co-recipient Tchaikovsky Piano Competition award, Moscow, 1962; recipient 2d prize, Internat. Chopin Competition, Warsaw, 1955, Gold medal, Queen Elizabeth Internat. Piano Competition, Brussels, 1956, Grammy awards, 1973, 1978, 1981, 1985, 1987, 1999. Office: care Harrison/Parrott Ltd 12 Penzance Pl London W11 4PA England Office Phone: 44207 229 9166. Business E-Mail: jasper.parrott@harrisonparrott.co.uk.

ASHKIN, RONALD EVAN, international executive; b. New Rochelle, N.Y., Apr. 5, 1957; s. Abraham and Arleen (Wollins) A.; m. Rajasperi Maliapen, Nov. 25, 1984; 1 child, Jacqueline Ariel. AB magna cum laude, Harvard U., 1977; MBA, Wharton Sch., U. Pa., 1982; postgrad., Harvard U., 1993, 96. Cert. fin. planner. V.p. Continental Chem. Corp., Terre Haute, Ind., 1978-83, pres., 1983-86, New Concepts Inc., Terre Haute, 1987-90, Excelsior Corp., Terre Haute, 1990-92; dir. internat. sales Gold Eagle Co., Chgo., 1992-95, v.p. internat., 1995-97; dir. cons. The Recovery Group, Boston, 1998—, USAID Bus. Cons., Sarajevo, Bosnia, 1998-99, World Bank Pvt. Sector Adjustment Loan Program, Bucharest, Romania, 2000-01; chief of party U.S. AID Kosovo Bus. Support, Pristina, Yugoslavia, 2001—. Adj. faculty Sch. Bus., Ind. State U., 1991-92. Moderator TV show, Terre Haute, 1985-86; author weekly econs. editl. column Kahoditore newspaper, Cristina, 2001-02. Mem. Terre Haute sch. adv. com., 1984-86; bd. dirs. Glenn Civic Ctr., Terre Haute, 1985-88; mem. mktg. edn. curriculum study com. Ind. Dept. Edn. Group study exch. grantee Rotary Found., Sri Lanka and India, 1985-86; Harvard U. scholar, 1973-76; recipient Ill. Gov.'s Export award, 1995, 96. Mem. Leadership Terre Haute Alumni Assn. (chmn. 1986), Am. Prodn. and Inventory Control Soc. (local v.p. 1982-84, 86, local pres. 1985), Overseas Automotive coun., Automotive Exporters Coun. (v.p. 1994—, pres. 1995-98), Jr. Achievement (vol. cons.), Toastmasters (local v.p. 1981-82), Phi Beta Kappa. Avocations: music, outdoor recreation, travel. Home: 2529 Springville Way Henderson NV 89052 Office: c/o Pragma Corp 116 E Broad St Falls Church VA 22046

ASHLER, PHILIP FREDERIC, financial consultant; b. N.Y.C., Oct. 15, 1914; s. Philip and Charlotte (Barth) A.; m. Jane Porter, Mar. 4, 1942 (dec. 1968); children: Philip Frederic, Robert Porter, Richard Harrison; m. Elise Barrett Duvall, June 21, 1969; stepchildren: Richard Edward Duvall, Jeffries Harding Duvall. BBA cum laude, St. Johns Coll., 1935; MBA, Harvard U., 1937; grad., Indsl. Coll. Armed Forces, 1956; ScD, Fla. Inst. Tech., 1969; LLD (hon.), U. West Fla., 1969; postgrad., U. Oxford, Eng., 1988, 89, 91. Enlisted USMCR, 1932; commd. ensign USN, 1938, advanced through grades to rear adm., 1959; served in D-Day at Normandy invasion of France, Iwo Jima landings and Korea; dir. Office Small Bus., Dept. Def., Washington, 1948-49; mem. joint staff Joint Chiefs Staff, 1957-59; ret., 1959; dir. devel. Pensacola Jr. Coll., 1960-68; vice chancellor adminstrn. State Univ. System Fla., 1968-70, exec. vice chancellor, 1970-75; treas., ins. commr., fire marshal State of Fla., 1975-76, sec. of commerce, 1977-79; pres. Philip F. Ashler & Assos., Tallahassee, 1979—; chmn. bd. Cambridge Community Care, Inc., Tallahassee, 1981-86, Circle Seven Internat., Tampa, 1988-91. Past dir. Fidelity Guaranty Life Ins. Co., Balt., U.S. Fidelity & Guaranty Co., 1st Fla. Bank N.A., Tallahassee; sec., dir. Fringe Benefits Mgmt. Co., Tallahassee, 1987—; mem. Fla. Edn. Coun., 1967-68; commr. from Fla. Edn. Commn. States, 1967-68; mem. U.S. Dept. Commerce Dist. Export Coun., 1978-92; chmn. bd., dir. Fla. Internat. Vol. Corps., 1988-90, dir. emeritus, 2004—; mem. legis. adv. coun. So. Regional Edn. Bd., 1966-68; mem. Fla. Bd. Ind. Colls. and Univs., 1971-75, mem. adv. coun. for mil. edn., 1980-85; bd.

advisors Ctr. Profl. Devel., Fla. State U., 1988-96; chmn. Fla. Civil Def. Adv. Coun., 1966-69; mem. Fla. Coun. Internat. Devel., 1973-92, vice chmn., 1979-80, chmn., 1980-82, chmn. emeritus, 1990—; mem. Select Coun. on Post High Sch. Edn., 1967-68; chmn. Fla. Med. Liability Ins. Commn., 1975-76, Fla. Task Force on Auto and Workers Compensation, 1975-76; mem. Yugoslavia Adv. Coun., 1976-87, InterAm. Congress on Psychology, Bogota, Colombia, 1974, NATO Advanced Sci. Inst., W.Ger., 1973; guest lectr. U. Belgrade, Yugoslavia, 1973; adviser econ. devel. to gov. Fla., 1977-78; mission leader Japan/S.E. U.S. Assn., Tokyo, 1977; trustee Fla. Coun. on Econ. Edn., 1979-81; mem. svcs. policy adv. com. Office of U.S. Trade Rep., Exec. Office of Pres., Washington, 1980-85; mem. Republic of China/U.S.A. Econ. Coun., 1979-92. Mem. Fla. Ho. of Reps., 1963-68; chmn. bd. dirs. Fla. Heart Assn., 1969-71; bd. dirs., treas. Internat. Cardiology Found.; bd. dirs. Tallahassee Meml. Hosp., Easter Seal Soc., 1963-68; bd. dirs., mem. exec. com. Am. Heart Assn., 1971-77, Internat. Cardiology Fedn., Geneva, 1975-77; founding chmn. Tallahassee Symphony Orch., 1981-82; trustee So. Ctr. Internat. Studies, Atlanta, 1988-91; mem. adv. bd. Fla./China Inst., Miami, Fla./Japan Inst., Tampa, Fla./Brazil Inst. Decorated Bronze Star with Combat V, Korean Presdl. citation; recipient Internat. Disting. Svc. award Kiwanis Internat., 1965, Legis. award St. Petersburg Times, 1967, Disting. Svc. award Am. Heart Assn., 1965, 71, Disting. Achievement award, 1975, Disting. Floridian award for life achievement, 2005. Mem. Fla. Med. Malpractice Joint Underwriting Assn. (chmn. bd. govs. 1975-76), Nat. Assn. Ins. Commrs. (vice chmn. exec. com. 1976), Internat. C. of C. (U.S. coun. 1979-87), U.S. S.E./Japan Assn. (chmn. 1981-83), S.E. U.S./Korea Econ. Coop. Coun. (bd. dirs.), Capital Tiger Bay Club (chmn. bd. dirs.), Govs. Club (bd. govs. 1989-93, v.p. for fin. 1992-93, bd. govs. 1994-96, treas. 1996), Econ. Club Fla. (chmn. 1987-90, chmn. emeritus 1991—), Masons (32 degree), Shriners, Rotary, Kappa Delta. Episcopalian (lic. lay eucharistic minister). Home: 2115 E Randolph Cir Tallahassee FL 32308 also: 11 Riad Sultan Kasbah Tangier Morocco Office: Fringe Benefits Mgmt Co PO Box 1878 Tallahassee FL 32302-1878 E-mail: ashler@worldnet.att.net.

ASHLEY, CARL PHILIP, choral director; b. Cleve., Nov. 7, 1968; s. Shade Hall and Norma Jean Ashley; m. Marie Theresa Botto, Oct. 10, 1970. MusB in Music Edn., U. Fla., 1991; MusM, Westminster Choir Coll., 1994; D in Musical Arts, U. Miami, 2002. Music tchr. Wilbraham (Mass.) & Monson Acad., 1994—96; dir. music and worship arts Trinity United Meth. Ch., Palm Beach Gardens, Fla., 1996—98; min. music Westside Bapt. Ch., Boynton Beach, Fla., 1998—2003; dir. choral music St. Andrew's Sch., Boca Raton, Fla., 2003—; dir. choral activities Lynn U., Boca Raton, 2003—; opera chorus singer Palm Beach Opera, West Palm Beach, Fla., 1997—. Composer: (choral music) May the Lord Bless You. Choir dir. Lake Osborne Presbyn. Ch., Lake Worth, Fla., 2003—05. Named one of Outstanding Young Men of Am., 1991; named to Coll. of Fine Arts Hall of Fame, U. Fla., 1991; recipient Young Composers prize, Westminster Choir Coll., 1992; scholar, Riviera Beach (Fla.) Kiwanis Club, 1988—91; Full Friends of Music scholar, U. Fla., 1987—91, Choir scholar, First Presbyn. Ch., Gainesville, 1988—90, Murphy Choir Robes scholar, Westminster Choir Coll., 1992, 1993, Bedford scholar, 1993. Mem.: ASCAP, Fla. Music Educators Assn., Fla. Vocal Assn., Music Educators Nat. Conf., Am. Choral Directors Assn. (dist. webmaster 2004—05), Internat. Fedn. for Choral Music, Pi Kappa Lambda, Golden Key, Alpha Lambda Delta. Independent. Presbyterian. Office Phone: 561-210-2522.

ASHLEY, DARLENE JOY, psychologist; b. N.Y.C., Oct. 29, 1945; d. George Geiger and Ann Debra (Bernstein) Munzer; m. Joseph Michael O'Brien, Sept. 23, 1974 (div. June 1981); 1 child, Sundara Amber; m. Roy William Fagan, Aug. 16, 1991. BA with honors, Antioch Coll., 1966; MA, NYU, 1973; PhD, Calif. Grad. Sch., San Rafael, 1987. Lic. clin. psychologist, Hawaii, Calif.; diplomate Am. Bd. Med. Psychotherapists; lic. marriage, family and child counselor, Calif.; Biofeedback Cert. Inst. of Am. Psychology instr. Coll. of the Redwoods, 1977-82; instr. psychology North Am. Coll., San Rafael, 1980; cons., psychol. examiner Hawaii Bd. Edn., Hilo, 1982; lectr. U. Hawaii, Hilo, Manoa, 1982—; predoctoral clin. psychology intern Redwood Ctr., Berkeley, Calif., 1983-85; pvt. practice San Rafael, Berkeley, 1985-87, Darlene Ashley, PhD and Assocs., Kailua Kona, Hawaii, 1988—. Presenter in field; instr. psychology Coll. of Redwoods, Ft. Bragg, Calif., 1978-82; presenter AM-FM Sta. KMPO, Caspar, Calif., AM-FM Sta. KKON, Kealakekua, Hawaii. Author: Voluntary Controls Training Handbook, 1982; author: (cassette) Deep Relaxation, 1983. Bd. dirs. Friends of Child Advocacy Ctr., 1995-99, Island Crisis Help, 1996-99; mem. Task Force on Worker's Compensation Reform for Hawaii, 1994-95; proponent Hawaii bill pertaining to psychologists, 1988; mem. com. Rep. Virginia Isbell's Fundraiser, Kailua-Kona, 1988—. Rsch. grantee NSF, Mus. Natural History, N.Y.C., 1965, NIMH, NYU, 1968-70, fellowship NIMH, 1969, Outstanding Rsch. award Biofeedback Soc. Calif., 1987. Mem. APA, Hawaii Psychol. Assn.(bd. dir. 2003, 04), Hawaii Island Psychologists Assn. (pres.-elect 1997). Avocations: tennis, running, travel. Office: 75-5744 Alii Dr Ste 237 Kailua Kona HI 96740-1740

ASHLEY, DWAYNE, not-for-profit fundraiser; BA cum laude, Wiley Coll.; MA gov. admin., Univ. Penn.; Doctorate (hon.), Univ. D.C. Nat. exec. dir., CEO 100 Black Men of America, Inc.; devel. dir. United Negro College Fund; campaign mgr. United Way; pres., CEO Thurgood Marshall Scholarship Fund. Co-author (with Juan Williams): I'll Find a Way or Make One. Office: Thurgood Marsall Scholarship Fund Ste 1203 90 Willam St New York NY 10038 Office Phone: 212-573-8888. Office Fax: 212-573-8497.*

ASHLEY, HOLT, aerospace scientist, educator; b. San Francisco, Jan. 10, 1923; s. Harold Harrison and Anne (Oates) A.; m. Frances M. Day, Feb. 1, 1947 (wid.). Student, Calif. Inst. Tech., 1940-43; BS, U. Chgo., 1944; MS, MIT, 1948, ScD, 1951. Mem. faculty MIT, 1946-67, prof. aero., 1960-67; prof. aeros. and astronautics Stanford U., Palo Alto, Calif., 1967-89, prof. emeritus, 1989—. Spl. rsch. aeroelasticity, aerodynamics; cons. govt. agys., rsch. orgns., indsl. corps.; dir. office of exploratory rsch. and problem assessment and div. advanced tech. applications NSF, 1972-74; mem. sci. adv. bd. USAF, 1958-80, rsch. adv. com. structural dynamics NASA, 1952-60, rsch. adv. com. on aircraft structures, 1962-70, chmn. rsch. adv. com. on materials and structures, 1974-77; mem. Kanpur Indo-American program Indian Inst. Tech., 1964-65, governing bd. Nat. Rsch. Coun., 1988-91; AIAA Wright Bros. lectr., 1981; dir. Rann Inc. Co-author: Aeroelasticity, 1955, Principles of Aeroelasticity, 1962, Aerodynamics of Wings and Bodies, 1969, Engineering Analysis of Flight Vehicles, 1974. Recipient Goodwin medal M.I.T., 1952; Exceptional Civilian Service award U.S. Air Force, 1972, 80; Public Service award NASA, 1981; named one of 10 outstanding young men of year Boston Jr. C. of C., 1956; recipient Ludwig-Prandtl Ring, West German DGLR, 1987, Spirit of St. Louis Medal, ASME, 1992. Fellow AIAA (hon., assoc. editor jour., v.p. tech. 1971, pres. 1973, Structures, Structural Dynamics and Materials award 1969), Am. Acad. Arts and Scis. (Daniel Guggenheim medal 2004), Royal Aero. Soc. (hon.); mem. AAAS, NAE (aeros. and space engring. bd. 1977-79, mem. coun. 1985-91), Am. Meterol. Soc. (profl., 50th Ann. medal 1971), Phi Beta Kappa, Sigma Xi, Tau Beta Pi. Home: 475 Woodside Dr Woodside CA 94062-2375 Business E-Mail: ashley@sun-valley.stanford.edu.

ASHLEY, JEFFREY L., academic administrator; b. Danville, Ill., Nov. 17, 1967; s. Lawrence Francis and Martha Kathleen Ashley; m. Holly Michelle Ashley, Aug. 8, 1992; children: Elizabeth, Clair. BA, U. Ky., 1989; MA, Webster U., 1994. Exec. dir. Trinity H.S. Found., Louisville, 1991-96; dir. major gifts U. Louisville, 1996-97; v.p. for univ. advancement Spalding U., 1997—. Dir. B.A. Beach Properties, Inc., Louisville, 1999—; bd. dirs. Trinity H.S. Found., Louisville, 1998—, Meredith Dunn Sch., Louisville, 2000—. Avocation: baseball. Office: Spalding U 851 S 4th St Louisville KY 40203 E-mail: jeffashley3@yahoo.com.

ASHLEY, KATHLEEN LABONIS, music educator; d. Edward Francis and Modesta Bubnis Labonis; m. Richard Raymond Ashley, Nov. 24, 1984; children: Christopher, Lisa. B in music edn., Immaculata Coll., 1979; M in edn., Temple U., 1984. Cert. instrnl. II Pa. Secondary tchr. St. Basil Acad., Jenkintown, Pa., 1979—88; elem. tchr. St. Martin of Tours Dept. of Performing Arts, Phila., 1980—82; pre-sch. tchr. The Curiosity Shoppe, Doylestown, Pa., 1990—96; elem. tchr. Our Lady of Mt. Carmel, Doylestown, 1995—2000, St. Jude Sch., Chalfont, Pa., 1997—. Performing arts camp tchr. Brown Bag Arts Festival, Doylestown, Pa., 1991—96; ch. musician, performer St. Jude, Chalfont, Pa., 1997—. Composer: (songs) St. Jude School Song, 1997; arranger: instrumental music, 1979—; co-author: Pre-sch. and Elem. Sch. shows, 1990—2003. Steering com. for mid. states evaluation St. Basil Acad., Jenkintown, Pa., 1985; tchr. St. Jude Sch., Chalfont, Pa., 1994—. Scholar, Immaculata U., 1975—79. Mem.: Pa. Music Educators Assn., Nat. Cath. Educators Assn., Music Educators Nat. Conf. Avocations: drawing, painting, gardening, writing. Office: St Jude Sch 323 W Butler Ave Chalfont PA 18914 Office Phone: 215-822-9225.

ASHLEY, LOIS A., retired university reference librarian; b. Detroit, Aug. 1, 1942; d. S. Elbert and Gertrude B. Hobson; m. Melvin Allen Ashley, June 27, 1964 (dec. Nov. 1996); children: Scott E., Paul D., Craig R. AA, William Tyndale Coll., Farmington Hills, Mich., 1989, BA in Humanities, 1991; MS in LS, Wayne State U., 1993. Spl. corr. Mich. Blue Shield, Detroit, 1963-68; reservation agt. United Airlines, Dearborn, Mich., 1968-70; asst. Office of Records and Registration William Tyndale Coll., 1989-91; grad. rsch. asst. Wayne State U., Detroit, 1992-93; reference libr. U. Detroit Mercy, 1993-99; adj. Oakland C.C., 2000—. Organist Gracious Savior Luth. Ch., 2000—; mem. Friends of the Detroit Pub. Libr.; founding chair ret. mem. roundtable Mich. Libr. Assn., 2001. Recipient scholarships. Mem. ALA (Black Caucus), AAUW, Assn. Coll. and Rsch. Librs., Mich. Libr. Assn., Nat. Coun. Negro Women, Am. Guild Organists, Founders Soc. Detroit Inst. Arts, Women of the Evang. Luth. Ch. in Am., Beta Phi Mu, Delta Epsilon Chi. Mem. Evang. Luth. Ch. in Am. Home: 19934 Mark Twain St Detroit MI 48235-1607

ASHLEY, OLIVIA SILBER, public health researcher; b. Anderson, SC, Mar. 2, 1966; m. Mark Stephen Ashley, Oct. 7, 2000; 1 child, Benjamin Reeves. PhD, U. NC, Chapel Hill, 2000. Presenter in field. Author: (book) The Toddler Years: Parenting Your 1- to 3-Year-Old; contbr. articles to profl. jours. Mem.: APHA. Office: RTI Internat 3040 Cornwallis Rd Research Triangle Park NC 27709 Office Phone: 919-541-6427. Office Fax: 919-485-5555.

ASHLEY, PHILLIP SAXON, music specialist; s. John B. and Virginia Saxon Ashley. MusB, Mars Hill Coll., NC, 1976; MEd, Edn. Specialist, Clemson U., SC, 1980. Music specialist Anderson Co. Sch. Dist. 2, Honea Path, SC, 1976—2005. Deacon Honea Path Presbyn. Ch., 2002—05. Mem.: NEA (bd. dirs. 2002—), SC Music Edn. Assn., Music Edn. NC, SC Edn. Assn. (bd. dirs. 2002—). Avocations: reading, travel. Office Phone: 864-369-7612.

ASHLEY, STEPHEN B., finance company executive; b. Mar. 1940; m. Janice Ashley; 3 children. BS, Cornell U., 1962, MBA, 1964. Chmn., CEO Sibley Mortgage Corp. (formerly Sibley Corp.), Rochester, NY, 1975—95, The Ashley Group, Rochester, NY, 1997—; non-exec. chmn. Fannie Mae, Washington, 2004—. Mem. bd. dirs. The Genesee Corp., 1987—, Fannie Mae, 1995—, Exeter Fund, Inc. Mem.: Mortgage Bankers Assn. Am. (pres. elect 1992—93, pres. 1993—94). Achievements include established with wife Janice, the Stephen B. & Janice Ashley Grad. Fellowship in the Coll of Agrl. & Life Sciences, 1991. Office: The Ashley Group 600 Powers Bldg 16 W Main St Rochester NY 14614 also: Fannie Mae 3900 Wisconsin Ave NW Washington DC 20016

ASHLEY, WILLARD WALDEN C., SR., minister; b. N.Y.C., Nov. 16, 1953; s. Will and Clara (Peterkin) Ashley; m. Veronica Lamb, June 1975 (div. Sept. 1976); 1 child, Willard W.C. Ashley Jr.; m. Diane Theresa Manning, Sept. 29, 1979 (div. June 21, 2001). AAS in Fashion Buying and Mktg., Fashion Inst. Tech., 1974; BA, Montclair State Coll., 1981; MDiv, Andover Newton Sch. Theol., 1984, D of Ministry in Leadership Devel., 1992; cert. in Marriage and Family Therapy, cert. in Psychotherapy, Blanton Peale Grad. Inst., 2000. Ordained to ministry Am. Bapt. Ch., 1982. Seminarian First Bapt. Ch., Tewksbury, Mass., 1981—82; pastor New Hope Bapt. Ch., Portsmouth, NH, 1982—84; asst. dean students, dir. recruitment Andover Newton Theol. Sch., Newton, Mass., 1984—86; pastor Monumental Bapt. Ch., Jersey City, 1986—96; founder Abundant Joy Bapt. Ch., Jersey City, 1996—; resident pastoral psychotherapy Blanton-Peale Counseling Ctr., N.Y.C., 1996—2000; chmn. Abundant Joy Cmty. Devel. Corp., 1999—; COO Norwood Securities Cons., Columbia, Md., 2001—04; cons., 2005—. Mem. Am. Bapt. Statement of Concerns Com., 1988—90; co-chmn. Interfaith Cmty. Orgn., Jersey City, 2004—, mem. strategy team, 1988—95; strategy team Indsl. Areas Found., Nat. Leaders Team, 1991—92; assoc. prof. N.Y. Theol. Sem., 1992—2001, prof. Blanton Peale pastoral studies program, 1999—2001; assoc. prof. Drew Theol. Sem., 1995—98, Auburn Sem., 1998—99; dir. exec. svcs. Haris & Rothenberg Internat., 1999—2002; coord. pastoral care Barnert Hosp., Paterson, NJ, 1994—97; psychotherapist Montclair Counseling Ctr., Upper Montclair, NJ, 1998—2002; staff psychotherapist Riverside Ch., N.Y.C., 2000—; program dir. care for the care giver interfaith project Coun. Churches of City of N.Y., 2002—; lectr. U. Amsterdam, 2003. Preacher weekly radio program Sta. WNJR, Hillside, NJ., 1987-92; contbr. Men of Color Study Bible, 2002. Bd. dirs. Vis. Homemakers of Hudson, Jersey City, 1988-93, YMCA of Jersey City, 1989-93; bd. regents St. Peter's Coll., 1995-99; chmn. N.J. Convocation, Christian Disciples of Christ, 2004—. Recipient Montclair State Coll. award, 1981, H. Otherman Smith Preaching award, 1984, Citation, Phi Delta Kappa, 1989, Appreciation award, Alpha Kappa Alpha, 1990, Humanitarian award, NCCJ, Matthew Turner award for Environ. Justice, Jersey City Branch NAACP, 2004. Mem. Am. Assn. Pastoral Counselors, Am. Group Psychotherapists Assn., Am. Assn. Marriage and Family Therapists, Clin. Pastoral Edn., Ministers Coun. Am. Bapt. Ch., Blanton Peale Alumni Assn. (pres. 2002-04), North NJ Missionary Bapt. Assn., Black Psychiatrists of Greater NY, Anti-Racism Alliance of Greater NY. Mem.Disciples Of Christ Ch. Home: 7000 Boulevard E # 48F Guttenberg NJ 07093 Office: Abundant Joy Bapt Ch 137 Bowers St Jersey City NJ 07307 also: 475 Riverside Dr Ste 727 New York NY 10115 Office Phone: 201-795-0200. E-mail: wwca@aol.com.

ASHMAN, MARTIN C., federal judge; b. 1931; m. Betty Ashman; two children. JD, DePaul U., 1953. Bar: Ill. 1953, U.S. Supreme Ct. 1959. Atty. Ashman & Jaffe, 1954-70, Martin C. Ashman, Ltd., 1970-87; commr. Ill. Ct. Claims, 1974-87; corp. counsel Village of Morton Grove, Ill., 1977-87; cir. judge domestic rels. divsn., law divsn. State of Ill., 1987-95; magistrate judge U.S. Dist. Ct. (no. dist.) Ill., 1995—. Vol. Legal Svcs. Found., Chgo. Recipient Spl. Tribute award Ill. Coun. Against Handgun Violence; Outstanding Svc. to Legal Profession award, DePaul U. Law Sch., 2001. Mem. ABA, Fed. Bar Assn., Fed. Magistrate Judges Assn., Ill. State Bar Assn., Decalogue Soc. Lawyers, Chgo. Bar Assn. (Cert. of Appreciation). Office: US Dist Ct 1366 Dirksen Bldg 219 S Dearborn St Chicago IL 60604-1800 Office Phone: 312-435-5624. Business E-Mail: martin_ashman@uscourts.gov.

ASHMORE, CHARLES WATSON, performing arts educator; b. Washington, Ga., Aug. 18, 1973; s. Patty Jean and William Odell Hunt (Stepfather); m. Nicole Suzanne Johnson, May 26, 1976. MusB in Edn., U. SC., 1997. Band dir. Lugoff Elgin Mid. Sch., SC, 1997—2002, Leslie M. Stover Mid. Sch., Elgin, SC, 2002—. Page SC Ho. of Reps., Columbia, SC, 1994—96; music instr. U. of SC Summer Music Camp, Columbia, 1995—97, Parkwood H.S., Monroe, NC, 1994—97, Laing Mid. Sch., Mount Pleasant, SC. Dir.: (band performance) Southern Star Music Festival (Gold Medalist, 2004), Fiesta-val Music Festival (Toronto, Canada) (First Pl. - Jr. Divsn., 1999), Carowinds Band and Orchestra Festival (Charlotte, NC) (First Pl. - Jr. Divsn., 2001). Recipient Outstanding Performance award, SC. Band Dirs. Assn., 1998, 1999, 2000, 2001, 2002, 2003, 2004, 2005, Concert Festival - Straight Superior Ratings, 1998, 1999, 2000, 2001, 2002, 2003, 2004, 2005. Mem.: MENC (assoc.), SC Band Dirs. (assoc.; solo & ensemble festival com. 2001—03), Phi Mu Alpha Sinfonia (life; sec. 1996—97). Baptist. Avocations: travel, golf, music, basketball. Office: Leslie M Stover Mid Sch 1649 Smyrna Rd Elgin SC 29045 Office Phone: 803-438-7414.

ASHMUS, KEITH ALLEN, lawyer; b. Cleve., Aug. 19, 1949; s. Richard A. and Rita (Petti) A.; m. Marie Sachiko Matsuoka, Dec. 15, 1973; children: Emmy Marie, Christopher Todd. BA in Policy Sci., Mich. State U., 1971, MA in Econs., 1972; JD, Yale U., 1974. Bar: Ohio 1974, Calif. 1991, U.S. Dist. Ct. (no. dist.) Ohio 1975, U.S. Dist. Ct. (no., so. and cen. dists.) Calif. 1991, U.S. Dist. Ct. (so. dist.) Ohio 2000, U.S. Ct. Appeals (6th cir.) 1975, U.S. Supreme Ct. 1980. Assoc. Thompson Hine & Flory LLP, Cleve., 1974-82, ptnr., 1982—2000, ptnr.-in-charge Cleve. office, 1996-99, dept. chmn., 1999-2000; founding ptnr. Frantz Ward LLP, Cleve., 2000—. Mediator/arbitrator Am. Arbitration Assn. Comml. Employment Panels, 1995—. Co-author: Public Sector Collective Bargaining: The Ohio System, 1984. Trustee cmty. arts Baycrafters, Bay Village, Ohio, 1981-84, Hospice Coun. No. Ohio, 1982-84, Inst. for Personal Health Skills, Cleve. 1985-90; trustee Coun. Smaller Enterprises, 1990-96, 98—, 1st vice chmn., 2000-2001, chmn., 2001-03; trustee Village Found., 1997—, Vocat. Guidance Svcs. 1999-2002, Youth Opportunities Unltd., 2000—04, Cleve. Saves, 2001—, Greater Cleve. Partnership, 2004—; sec. George W. Codrington Charitable Found., 1994-2000; chmn. job placement for older persons Skills Available, Cleve., 1980-87; gov.'s appointee to Health Care Quality Adv. Coun., 1996; mem. adv. bd. Greater Cleve. Salvation Army, 1997—, treas., 2000-01, vice chmn., 2001-04, chmn. 2004—. Named one of Outstanding Vols. award Nat. Hospice Orgn., 1982, Vol. of Yr. Vocat. Guidance and Rehab. Services, 1985, 86. Fellow ABA, Ohio State Bar found. (bd. dir. 2002—); mem. State Bar Calif., Ohio State Bar Assn. (coun. dels. 1995—, bd. govs. 1998-2001, pres. 2003-04), Cleve. Bar Assn. (trustee 1985-88, 98-2001, chmn. labor law sect. 1983-84), AMA (ho. delegates 2004-); Def. Rsch. Inst., Pub. Sector Labor Rels. Assn. (exec. com. 1989-93), Am. Arbitration Assn. (chmn. comml. adv. panel 2004—), Yale Law Alumni Assn. (mem. exec. coun. 2003—). Avocations: golf, fishing. Office: Frantz Ward LLP 2500 Key Ctr Cleveland OH 44114 Office Phone: 216-515-1660. Business E-Mail: kashmus@frantzward.com.

ASHRAF, AMBIKA P., pediatrician, researcher, endocrinologist; MD, DCH, MBBS, U. Calicutta, 1996; FAAP (hon.), U. Ala., 2003. Resident Children's Hosp., Birmingham, 2002—03, fellow, instr., 2003—. Bd. mem. Camp Seale Harris for Diabetic Children, Birmingham, 2004—05. Grantee, Eli Lilly, 2004; scholar, Aventis, 2005. Fellow: Am. Acad. Pediatrics (hon.). Achievements include research in VEGF levels in diabetic children. Office: Children's Hos/UAB ACC 608 1600 7th Ave S Birmingham AL 35233 Office Phone: 205-939-9107. Office Fax: 205-939-9821. Personal E-mail: aashraf1002@yahoo.com. E-mail: aashraf@peds.uab.edu.

ASHRAFI, ASHKAN, electrical engineer; b. Tehran, Iran, Oct. 4, 1969; s. Morteza Ashrafi and Farangis Fattahi; m. Parisa Kaveh. BS in Engring., K.N.Toosi U. of Tech., Tehran, 1992; MS in Engring., K.N.Toosi U. of Tech., 1995, U. Ala., Huntsville, 2005. Instr. Islamic Azad U., Tehran, 1997—2001; part time sr. design engr. Moudje Niroo Co., Tehran, 1999—2001, Niroo Rsch. Inst., Tehran, 2000—01; grad. tchg. asst. dept. ECE U. Ala., Huntsville, 2001—. Recipient Iliana Martin Chittur Outstanding Grad. Student award, U. Ala., Huntsville, 2005, Coll. of Engring. Nat. Engrs.'s Week Outstanding Grad. Student award, 2005. Mem.: IEEE (assoc.), Eta Kappa Nu (life), Phi Kappa Phi (life). Office: U Ala Huntsville 242F Engineering Bldg Huntsville AL 35899 Office Phone: 256-824-3486. Personal E-mail: ashkan@ieee.org. E-mail: ashrafa@eng.uah.edu.

ASHTON, ADAM KELLER, psychiatrist, educator; BA, Cornell U., 1982; MS, SUNY, Buffalo, 1983, MD, 1987. Pvt. practice Buffalo Med. Group, 1995—; clin. prof. psychiatry SUNY, Buffalo, 2002—. Fellow: Am. Psychiat. Assn. (disting.). Office: Buffalo Med Group 6245 Sheridan Dr # 316 Williamsville NY 14221 Office Phone: 716-630-1202.

ASHTON, BETSY FINLEY, broadcast journalist, author, lecturer; b. Wilkes-Barre, Pa., May 13, 1944; d. Charles Leonard Hancock Jones and Margaretta Betty (Hart) Jones Layton; m. Arthur Benner Ashton, Nov. 5, 1966 (div. 1972); m. Robert Clarke Freed, May 18, 1974 (div. 1981); m. Jacob B. Underhill III, Oct. 17, 1987. BA, Am. U., 1966; postgrad., Corcoran Sch. Art, 1968; postgrad. in fine arts, Am. U., 1969-71; student in painting, Corcoran Sch. Art, 1968. Tchr. art Fairfax County Pub. Schs., Va., 1967—70; reporter, anchor Sta. WWDC, Washington, 1972—73, Sta. WMAL-AM-FM, Washington, 1973—75; corr. Sta. WTTG-TV, Washington, 1975—76, Sta. WJLA-TV, Washington, 1976—82; consumer corr. CBS News and Sta. WCBS-TV, NYC, 1982—86; sr. corr. Today's Bus., 1986—87; contbr. personal fin. CBS Morning Program, 1967, Lifetime Cable TV, 1988—; anchor FNN Money Talk, 1989; exec. editor, producer Great Giving, 2000—. Bd. dirs. Lowell E. Mellett Fund Free Responsible Press, Washington, 1979-82; courtroom artist numerous trials, Washington, 1978-81; trustee The Kenyon Rev., 2004—. Reporter TV news report Caffeine, 1981 (AAUW award 1982); reporter spot news 6 P.M. News, 1979 (Emmy award); author: Betsy Ashton's Guide to Living on Your Own, 1988. Concert master ceremonies Beethoven Soc., Washington, 1979-82; trustee Kenyon Rev., 2004—. Recipient Laurel award Columbia Journalism Rev., 1984, Outstanding Alumna award Am. U., 1985, Outstanding Media award Am. U., 1986, Best Consumer Journalism citation Nat. Press Club, 1983. Mem. AFTRA, NATAS, Author's Guild, Newswomen's Club NY, Soc. Profl. Journalists (pres. NY chpt. 1994, 2000, Washington chpt. 1980-81, bd. dirs. NY chpt., co-chair 2004 nat. conv.), Friends of Thirteen (bd. dirs.), Sigma Delta Chi Found. (bd. dirs., v.p. bd. 2004—), Alpha Chi Omega (v.p. chpt. 1964-66). Avocations: painting, drawing, golf.

ASHTON, DORE, writer, educator; b. Newark; d. Ralph N. and Sylvia (Ashton) Shapiro; m. Adja Yunkers, July 8, 1952 (dec. 1983); children—Alexandra Louise, Marina Svietlana; m. Matti Megged, 1985 (dec. 2003). BA, U. Wis., 1949; MA, Harvard U., 1950; PhD (hon.), Moore Coll., 1975, Hamline U., 1982, Minn. Coll. of Art, 2002. Asso. editor Art Digest, 1951-54; asso. critic N.Y. Times, 1955-60; lectr. Pratt Inst., 1962-63; head humanities dept. (Sch. Visual Arts), 1965-68; prof. Cooper Union, 1968—. Art critic, lectr., dir. exhbns. in arts; mem. adv. bd. John Simon Guggenheim Found, Dedalus Found. Author: Abstract Art Before Columbus, 1957, Poets and the Past, 1959, Philip Guston, 1960, The Unknown Shore, 1962, Rauschenberg's Dante, 1964, Modern American Sculpture, 1968, Richard Lindner, 1969, A Reading of Modern Art, 1970, Pol Bury, 1971, Cultural Guide for New York, 1972, Picasso on Art, 1972, The New York School: A Cultural Reckoning, 1973, A Joseph Cornell Album, 1974, Yes, But, A Critical Biography of Philip Guston, 1976, A Fable of Modern Art, 1980, American Art Since 1945, 1982, About Rothko, 1983, Jacobo Borges, 1984, 20th Century Artists on Art, 1985, Out of the Whirlwind, 1987, Fragonard in the Universe of Painting, 1988, Terence La Noue, 1992, Noguchi East and West, 1992, Ursula van Rydingsvard, 1995, Gunther Gerzso, 1995, The Delicate Thread: Teshigahara's Life in Art, 1997, À Rebours: La Rebellión Informalista, 1999, The Black Rainbow: The Work of Fernando de Szyszlo, 2003, The Walls of the Heart: The Work of David Rankin, 2001, William Tucker, 2001, also monographs; co-author (with Denise Browne Hare): Rosa Bonheur, A Life and Legend, 1981; co-editor: Redon, Moreau, Bresdin, 1961; NY contbg. editor Studio Internat., 1961—74, Opus Internat., 1968—74, XXième Siècle, 1955—70, The Brooklyn Rail, 2004—, assoc. editor Arts, 1974—92, contbr. to Vision and Value series (Gyorgy Kepes), 1966, The New Art Anthology (Gregory Battcock), 1966. Adv. bd. Guggenheim Found. Recipient Mather award for art criticism Coll. Art Assn., 1963, Art Criticism prize St. Louis Art Mus., 1988; Guggenheim fellow, 1964; Graham fellow, 1963; Ford Found. fellow, 1960; Nat. Endowment for Humanities grantee, 1980 Mem. Internat. Assn. Art Critics, Phi Beta Kappa. Home: 217 E 11th St New York NY 10003-7302 Office: Cooper Union Advancement Sci and Art 41 Cooper Sq New York NY 10003-7136 Office Phone: 212-363-5100.

ASHTON, HARRIS JOHN, lawyer; b. Elizabeth, NJ, June 21, 1932; s. Earle S. and Dorothy (Black) A.; m. Angela Murphy, Oct. 20, 1962; children: Kelly Elizabeth, Victoria Catherine. BA, Yale U., 1954; LLB, Columbia U., 1959. Bar: NY 1960. Assoc. Breed, Abbott & Morgan, 1959-62, Lovejoy, Wasson, Lundgren & Huppuch, 1962-64; partner Lovejoy, Wasson, Lundgren & Ashton, 1964-75, of counsel, 1975-81; pres., chief adminstrv. officer Gen. Host Corp., 1967-69, chmn., pres., chief exec. officer, 1970-97. Bd. dir. Bar-S

Foods Co., of 43 Franklin Templeton Group of Funds. Emeritus mem., former bd. dir. Madison Square Boys and Girls Club; trustee Greenwich Acad., 1977-81, Miss Porter's Sch., 1981-85; emeritus mem., trustee United Cerebral Palsy Rsch. and Ednl. Found., Inc.; emeritus mem., mem. bd. visitors Columbia U. Sch. Law, 1982—2003, Yale New Haven Hosp., 1990-95; bd. overseers Inst. for Civil Justice, 1999, 2002. Mem. Yale Club (NYC), Blind Brook Club, Cypress Point Club, Bohemian Club.

ASHTON, NATHAN, music educator, sound recording engineer; b. Columbia, Mo., May 29, 1973; s. Romney and Ruth Ann Ashton; m. Lydia Augustsson, July 7, 1975; children: Mikaela, Karl. BS in Biology, Purdue U., 1995; MBM in Human Resource Mgmt., Oral Roberts U., 2005. Cert. recording engr. Rec. Workshop, Ohio, 2002. Pres. Imaginative Art Ministries, Elkhart, Ind., 1996—; music tech. coord. Oral Roberts U. Music, Tulsa, Okla., 1998—, adj. music prof., 2000—. Studio mgr. Bach's Ho., Tulsa, Okla., 1999—. Cell group leader, Tulsa, Okla., 2002—04; vol. various film commns., Okla., 2001—04. Achievements include curriculum development for BA in music technology. Avocations: international travel, reading and writing fiction. Office: Oral Roberts U Music 7777 S Lewis Ave Tulsa OK 74171 Office Phone: 918-495-7619. Personal E-mail: ashtonn@sbcglobal.net. E-mail: nashton@oru.edu.

ASHTON, RICK JAMES, librarian; b. Middletown, Ohio, Sept. 18, 1945; s. Ralph James and Lydia Marie (Thornbery) A.; m. Marcia K. Zuroweste, Dec. 23, 1966; children: Jonathan Paul, David Andrew. AB, Harvard U., 1967; MA, Northwestern U., 1969, PhD, 1973; MA, U. Chgo., 1976. Instr., asst. prof. history Northwestern U., Evanston, Ill., 1972-74; curator local and family history Newberry Libr., Chgo., 1974-77; asst. dir. Allen County Pub. Libr., Ft. Wayne, Ind., 1977-80, dir., 1980-85; city libr. Denver Pub. Libr., 1985—. Mem. Ind. Coop Libr. Svcs. Authority, 1980-85, pres., 1984-85; cons. NEH, Nat. Ctr. Edn. Stats., Northwestern U. Office Estate Planning, Snowbird Leadership Inst., Houston Pub. Libr. Author: The Life of Henry Ruiter, 1742-1819, 1974, The Genealogy Beginner's Manual: A New Edition, 1977, Stuntz, Fuller, Kennard and Cheadle Ancestors, 1987 (with others) Trends in Urban Library Management, 1989, Intelligent Library Buildings, 1999. Bd. dirs. Cmty. Coordinated Child Care, Evanston, 1972-74, Three Rivers Montessori Sch., Ft. Wayne, 1977-80; bd. dirs., sec. Allen County-Ft. Wayne Hist. Soc., 1977-83; trustee Iliff Sch. Theology, 2000—; conscientious objector. Recipient Old City Hall Hist. Svc. award, 1985, Phil Milstein award Denver AIA, 1998; NDEA fellow, 1967-69, Downtown Denver award, 1996, 97, Bonfils-Stanton Found. award in arts and humanities, 2003; Woodrow Wilson fellow, 1971-72. Mem. ALA, Colo. Libr. Assn. (Libr. of Yr. 2000), Colo. Alliance Rsch. Librs. (pres. 1987-88, sec. 1993-95, chmn. 1995-2000), Urban Librs. Coun., Cactus Club. Home: 217 S Jackson St Unit A Denver CO 80209-3132 Office: Denver Pub Libr 10 W 14th Avenue Pkwy Denver CO 80204-2731 Office Phone: 720-865-2105. Business E-Mail: rashton@denver.lib.co.us.

ASHTON, THOMAS WALSH, investment banker; b. Rochester, N.Y., May 11, 1929; s. Charles Edward and Marie Margaret (Walsh) A.; m. Frances E. Hickey, May 16, 1953 (div. 1977); children: Lucy M. Van Atta, Mary B. Ashton Anders, Monica H., William T; m. Mary K Joy, Dec. 20, 1978 (dec. 1997); m. Carolyn B. Richardson, Jan. 26, 2002. BS, U.S. Mil. Acad., 1952; MBA, Harvard U., 1957. Assoc. corp. fin. Eastman Dillon Union Securities, N.Y.C, 1957-61, gen. ptnr., 1967-69; asst. v.p. Harris Upham & Co., N.Y.C., 1961-67; v.p. duPont Glore Forgan, Inc., N.Y.C., 1971-73; sr. v.p. ABD Securities Corp., N.Y.C., 1973-75; fin. cons. Am. Cancer Soc. of N.Y.C., East West Group Inc. Chmn. Peninsular Investments, Treasure Island, Fla., 1977-87; cons. Dept. Commerce, 1971; chmn. Ashton Investments, Inc., 1987—. Chmn. parents's coun. Smith Coll., 1974-76. With AUS, 1946-48, 52-55. Mem. Soc. Harvard Engrs. and Scientists (gov. 1974-75), West Point Soc. N.Y. (dir. 1971-75), Army and Navy Club (Washington), Ponte Vedra Inn and Club. Republican. E-mail: tashton749@aol.com.

ASHVO-MUÑOZ, ALIRA, language educator; arrived in U.S., 1962; d. Fernando de los Santos Muñoz Venereo and Enriqueta Díaz; m. Juan Carlos Lira-Melzi, Jan. 15, 1983 (div. June 1986). BA in Archaeology, U. Tex., 1982, MA in Anthropology, 1989, MA in Spanish, 1992, PhD, 1999. Rschr. U. Tex., Austin, 1990—92, lang. instr., 1992—98; asst. prof. Coll. of N.J., Ewing, 1999—2000, Villanova (Pa.) U., 2000, Temple U., Phila., 2001—, Gale Group scholar, 2001. Avocations: art, early music, textiles. Office: Temple U Anderson Hall Philadelphia PA 19122 E-mail: aashvomu@temple.edu.

ASHWELL, RACHEL, entrepreneur, interior designer; b. Eng. children: Lily, Jake. Founder Shabby Chic by Rachel Ashwell Label, L.A., 1989—. Author: Shabby Chic, 1996, Rachel Ashwell's Shabby Chic Treasure Hunting and Decorating Guide, 1998, The Shabby Chic Home, 2000, The Shabby Chic Gift of Giving, 2001. Office: Rachel Ashwell Shabby Chic 6330 Arizona Cir Los Angeles CA 90045

ASHWORTH, BRENT FERRIN, lawyer; b. Albany, Calif., Jan. 8, 1949; s. Dell Shepherd and Bette Jean (Brailsford) Ashworth; m. Charlene Mills, Dec. 16, 1970; children: Amy, John, Matthew, Samuel(dec.), Adam, David, Emily, Luke, Benjamin. BA, Brigham Young U., 1972; JD, U. Utah, 1975. Bar: Utah 1977. Asst. county atty. Carbon County, Price, Utah, 1975-76; assoc. atty. Frandsen & Keller, Price, Utah, 1976-77; v.p. legal affairs, sec., gen. counsel Nature's Sunshine Products, Provo, Utah, 1977—2003; chief corp. counsel Neways Internat., Springville, Utah, 2003—04; pvt. practice, 2004—. Bd. dirs., gen. counsel Carbon County Nursing Home, Price, 1976—77; mem. Provo Landmarks Commn., 1997—2002, chmn., 2002—, co-chair sesquicentennial com., 1998—99; active Provo Libr. Bd., 2000—, chmn., 2003—04, Utah County Cancer Crusade Com., 1981—83, Provo LCOC Arts subcom., 1998—99; pres. Desert Village Spani Fork, Utah, 1988—90; gen. counsel Brigham Young Acad. Found., 1995—2001; founder, chmn. George E. Freestone Boy Scout Mus., Provo, 2000—; exec. bd. Utah Nat. Pk. coun. Boy Scouts Am., 2000—; city councilman, planning commn. Payson City, Utah, 1980—82, mayor pro tem, 1982; bd. dirs. ARC, Utah County chpt., 1988—94, Springville Mus. Art, 1998—2001, Celebration Health Found., 1999—, Provo Sch. Dist. Found., 2001—03; bd. mem. Am. Heritage Sch., Am. Fork, Utah, 2002—. Mem.: ATLA, SAR (pres. Utah County chpt. 1989—90, state chpts. 1st v.p. 1990—91, state soc. pres. 1991—92, chancellor 1992—94), ABA, Am. Corp. Counsel Assn. (sec. intermountain chpt. 1990—91), Utah State Bar Assn., Southeastern Utah Bar Assn. (sec. 1977), Sons Utah Pioneers, Emily Dickinson Soc. Utah (pres. 1995—97), Kiwanis Club (v.p. 1995—96, pres. 1997—98, lt. gov. Utah Idaho dist. 2001—02), Phi Eta Sigma, Phi Kappa Phi. Home: 1377 Cambridge Ct Provo UT 84604-4178 Office: Neways Internat 2089 Neways Dr Springville UT 84663 Office Phone: 801-368-6001. E-mail: hashworths@hotmail.com.

ASHWORTH, D. NEIL, business educator; b. Richmond, Va., Dec. 29, 1947; s. Durwood O. and Lillian T. Ashworth; m. Marlene Stearns, July 8, 1972; children: Jared Logan, Jessica Nicole. BBA, U. Ky., 1970; M in Commerce, U. Richmond, 1976; MBA, PhD in Bus. Adminstrn., U. S.C., 1979. Asst. prof. mgmt. U. Miss., Oxford, 1980—81; from asst. prof. to assoc. prof. mgmt. sys. U. Richmond, 1981—90, prof., 1990—, assoc. dean Robins Sch. Bus., 1990—93, interim dean, 1993—94, chair dept., 2000—. Author: Cases in Management, 1985. Bd. dirs. Children's Home Soc. Va., Richmond, 1995—, chmn. bd. dirs., 2003—05; bd. dirs. Tuckahoe Little League, 2000—04. Master: Beta Gamma Sigma; mem.: Acad. Mgmt., Omicron Delta Epsilon. Home: 12208 McIntyre Way Richmond VA 23233 Office: U Richmond Robins Sch Bus Richmond VA 23173 Office Phone: 804-289-8673. Office Fax: 804-289-8878. Business E-Mail: nashwort@richmond.edu.

ASHWORTH, JULIE, elementary school educator; Tchr. Hawthorne Elem. Sch., Sioux Falls, S.D., 1990—. Participant Internat. Space Camp, Huntsville, Ala., 1993; S.D. tchr. participant Goals 2000 Forum, U.S. Dept. Edn., Washington, 1993; mem. S.D. Gov.'s Adv. Coun. on Cert. for Tchrs., 1994—; mem. exceptional needs standards com. Nat. Bd. for Profl. Tchg. Stds., Washington, 1994—; initiator, organizer S.D. Tchrs. Forum, 1994. Named S.D. Tchr. of Yr., Sioux Falls Sch. Dist., 1992, S.D. Elem. Tchr. of Yr., 1993. Home: 2015 Pendar Ln Sioux Falls SD 57105-3022 Office: Hawthorne Elem Sch 601 N Spring Ave Sioux Falls SD 57104-2721

ASHWORTH, KENNETH HAYDEN, public information officer; b. Abilene, Tex., Feb. 24, 1932; s. Harold Laverne and Mae Beatrice (Grote) A.; m. Emily Yaung; children: Rodney Brian, Karen Grace. BA, U. Tex., 1958, PhD, 1969; M. Pub. Adminstrn., Syracuse U., 1959. Asst. commr. Tex. Higher Edn. Coordinating Bd., Austin, 1965-69, commr. higher edn., 1976-97; vice chancellor for acad. affairs U. Tex. System, Austin, 1969-73; exec. v.p. U. Tex. at San Antonio, 1973-76. Vis. prof. govt. and pub. affairs U. Tex., Austin, 1997—, Tex. A &M U., College Sta., 1997—. Author: Scholars and Statesmen, 1972, American Higher Education in Decline, 1979, (with Norman Hackerman) Conversations on the Uses of Science and Technology, 1996, Caught Between the Dog and the Fireplug or How to Survive Public Service, 2001. Served with USN, 1951-55. Mem. Philos. Soc. Tex., Phi Beta Kappa, Phi Delta Kappa, Phi Kappa Phi, Pi Sigma Alpha. Clubs: Town and Gown. Democrat. Unitarian Universalist. Home: 7616 Rustling Rd Austin TX 78731-1365 Office: U Tex LBJ Sch Pub Affairs PO Box Y Austin TX 78713-8925 also: Tex A&M U Bush Sch Govt And Pub Svc College Station TX 77843-0001 Office Phone: 512-232-4019.

ASHWORTH, RONALD BROUGHTON, health facility executive, accountant; b. San Francisco, Apr. 19, 1945; s. Robert William and Tracy Marie (Parks) A.; m. Carol Lynn Heaps, Oct. 2, 1970; 1 dau., Christina Ann. B.B.A., U. Mo.-Columbia, 1967, M.A., 1968. C.P.A., Mo., N.C., Ill., La. With Peat Marwick Mitchell & Co., 1968-91, ptnr., 1975-91, in charge St. Louis Office health care practice, 1975-77, nat. dir. health care practice, 1978-91, Chgo., 1979-91, exec. v.p., COO, Sisters of Mercy Health System, 1991-99, pres., CEO, 1999-. Bd. dirs. Chgo. Lung Assn., Mid-Am. chpt. ARC. Recipient Haskins and Sells award, 1967; Fin. Execs. Inst. award, 1967; Alpha Kappa Psi scholar, 1967. Mem. Healthcare Fin. Mgmt. Assn., Am. Inst. C.P.A.s, Fedn. Am. Hosps., Am. Hosp. Assn., Ill. Soc. C.P.A.s. Clubs: Tavern, Medinah Country, Country Club of Mo. Office: Sisters of Mercy Health System 14528 S Outer Forty Chesterfield MO 63017

ASHWORTH, TERESA KAY, music educator; b. Fergus Falls, Minn., June 29, 1957; d. Raymond Edward and Janice Kay Beal; married, 1981; children: Braden, Taylor. BFA, U. S.D., 1979; MEd, N.D. State U., 1999, postgrad. Music educator Sioux Falls (SD) Pub. Schs., 1979—81, St. Alphonsus Schs., Chgo., 1981—82, N.W. Chgo. Elem. Sch., West Chgo., Ill., 1982—86, Naperville (Ill.) South Sch., 1986, Fergus Falls Pub. Sch., 1987—97; dir. music Minn. State Cmty. and Tech. Coll., 1997—. Mem.: Minn. Music Educators Assn. (regional chair 1998—2000), Am. Choral Dirs. Assn. (repertoire and stds. chair 2005, dist. chair 1996—98). Home: 20651 Hillcrest Rd Fergus Falls MN 56537 Office: Minn State Cmty & Tech Coll 1414 College Way Fergus Falls MN 56537 Office Phone: 218-736-1609. E-mail: teresa.ashworth@minnesota.edu.

ASIMOV, JANET JEPPSON, writer, psychiatrist; b. Ashland, Pa., Aug. 6, 1926; d. John Rufus and Rae Evelyn (Knudson) Jeppson; m. Isaac Asimov, Nov. 30, 1973. BA, Stanford U., 1948; D of Medicine, NYU, 1952; cert. in psychoanalysis, William Alanson White Inst., 1960. Diplomate Am. Bd. Psychiatry. Intern Phila. Gen. Hosp., 1952-53; resident in psychiat. medicine Bellevue Hosp., N.Y.C., 1953-56; staff psychiatrist Manhattan VA Hosp., N.Y.C., 1956-58; fellow Roosevelt Hosp., N.Y.C., 1958-60; tng. and supervising analyst William Alanson White Inst., N.Y.C., 1969—, dir. tng., 1974-83, fellow, 1974-96. Author: Mind Transfer, 1988, The Package in Hyperspace, 1988, two previous novels (as J.O. Jeppson), Murder at the Cadalic Writers' Society, 1995; co-author: (with Isaac Asimov) How to Enjoy Writing, 1987 (11 juvenile sci. fiction novels) The Norby Series, 1983—, Frontiers II, 1993; editor It Has Been A Good Life; author numerous short stories; contbr. articles to profl. publs. Mem. Am. Psychiat. Assn., Am. Acad. Psychoanalysis, Sci. Fiction Writers of Am., William Alanson White Soc., Phi Beta Kappa. Democrat. Office: 10 W 66th St New York NY 10023-6206

ASKANAS, MARK S., lawyer; b. 1960; m. Aynah V. Askanas. BA, U. Calif., Berkeley, 1982; JD, U. Calif., Davis, 1985. Bar: Calif. 1986. Assoc. Jackson, Lewis, Schnitzler & Krupman, San Francisco, 1988—93, ptnr., 1993—2001; sr. v.p. human resources, gen. counsel Ross Stores Inc., Pleasanton, Calif., 2001—. Office: Ross Stores Inc 4440 Rosewood Dr Bldg 4 Pleasanton CA 94588-3050

ASKENASE, PHILIP WILLIAM, medicine and pathology educator; b. Bklyn., June 7, 1939; s. Irving and Hilda Askenase; m. Marjorie Dopkin, June 21, 1967; children: Hilary, Isabel. BA in Physics magna cum laude, Brown U., 1961; MD cum laude, Yale U., 1965. Diplomate Am. Bd. Internal Medicine, Am. Bd. Allergy and Immunology. Intern, asst. resident in medicine Boston City Hosp., 1965-67; clin. assoc. arthritis and rheumatism sect. Nat. Inst. Arthritis and Metabolic Disease, NIH, 1957-59; Brit. Am. Heart fellow of Am. Heart Assn., London Hosp. Med. Coll., 1969-70; postdoctoral trainee in inflammatory diseases Yale U. Sch. Medicine, New Haven, 1970-71, asst. prof. medicine, 1971-75, assoc. prof., 1975-82, assoc. prof. pathology, 1981-82, prof. medicine and pathology, 1982—, chief sect. clin. immunology dept. medicine, 1985—. Attending physician Yale-New Haven Hosp., 1971—, West Haven (Conn.) VA Hosp., 1971—; vis. scientist immunoparasitology div. Nat. Inst. Med. Rsch., London, 1977-78; lectr. biology Yale U., 1981—, vis. prof. molecular immunology unit, 1991; hon. rsch. fellow tumor immunology unit dept. zoology Univ. Coll., London, 1984-85; mem. Yale Comprehensive Cancer Ctr., 1987—; ad hoc reviewer numerous med. jours; vis. prof., Woods Hole, Mass., 1980-84; mem. U.S.-Israel Binat. Sci. Found., 1982—, Med. Rsch. Coun. Can., NSF, Netherlands Cancer Found., Wellcome Truste, London, Med. Rsch. Coun., London, Can. Med. Rsch. Coun.; mem. adv. bd. spl. program in tropical diseases WHO; mem. pathology-A/study sect. NIH, 1976, mem. immunol. scis. study sect., 1983-87, ad hoc mem. allergy and immunology study sect. NIH, 1987-89 Mem. editl. bd. Jour. Clin. Immunology, 1983-88, Jour. Allergy and Clin. Immunology, 1980-85, Clin. and Diagnostic Lab. Immunology, 1983—; assoc. editor Jour. Immunology, 1976082; mem. editl. adv. bd. Jour. Molecular and Cellular Immunology, 1983—; contbr. over 200 articles, abstracts and revs. to med. jours., chpts. to books. Laurens Hammond grantee for cancer rsch., 1975-77, grantee NIH, 1987—. Fellow Am. Acad. Allergy; mem. AAAS, Am. Assn. Immunologists (membership com. 1978-82), Am. Assn. Physicians, Am. Fedn. Clin. Rsch., Am. Rheumatism Assn., Am. Soc. Clin. Investigation, Am. Soc. Tropical Medicine and Hygiene, Am. Thoracic Soc., Brit. Soc. Immunology, Clin. Immunology Soc., Collegium Internat. Allergogium, Conn. Allergy Soc., Histamine Rsch. Soc. N.Am., Reticuloendothelial Soc., Serotonin Soc., Skin. Pharmacology Soc., Soc. Investigative Dermatology, Interurban Clin. Club, Polish Acad. Arts and Scis. (fgn. corr.), Phi Beta Kappa, Alpha Omega Alpha. Office: Yale Univ Sch Medicine PO Box 208013 333 Cedar St New Haven CT 06520-8013

ASKER, JAMES ROBERT, magazine editor; b. Louisville, 1952; BA, Rice U., 1974. Reporter, columnist Houston Post, 1974—88; freelance reporter, 1988—89; mng. editor Electronic Bus., 1989—95; space tech. editor Aviation Week & Space Tech., Washington, 1989—95, Washington bur. chief, 1995—, mng. editor, 2003—. Recipient Knight Sci. Journalism fellow, MIT, Cambridge, 1987—88. Office: Aviation Week & Space Tech 1200 G St NW Ste 900 Washington DC 20005-3814 Office Phone: 202-383-2300. Business E-Mail: asker@aviationweek.com. E-mail: jim_asker@yahoo.com.

ASKEW, JAMES ALBERT, lawyer; b. Oklahoma City, Oct. 10, 1949; s. James Albert and Verlia Mae (Harlin) A. BA in History, U. Calif., Davis, 1971; JD, U. Calif.-Berkeley, 1974. Bar: Calif. 1974, various fed. dist. cts., U.S. Dist. Ct. (ea. dist.) Prin., mng. prin. in litigation Neumiller & Beardslee, Stockton, Calif., Askew & Archbold, 1995; bd. arbitrators San Joaquin County Superior Ct., San Joaquin Mcpl. Ct.; resolutions com. Calif. State Bar, 1980-81; assoc. ed. Calif. Law Review 1972-74; author A New Approach to the Intrastate Exemption: Rule 147 v3 (a)(11) Securities Law Review, 1974. Mem. San Joaquin County Bar Assn. (pres. 1979-80, bd. govs. 1977-79, 1979-94, mng. dir. 1990-94), ABA, State Bar Calif., Assn. Trial Lawyers Am., Calif. Trial Lawyers Assn., Def. Research Inst., Lawyer Rep. Delegation, Ninth Cir. Judicial Conf.(coord. com., 1993-94) Club: Yosemite (Stockton). Office: 2155 W March Lane Ste 1-D Stockton CA 95207

ASKEW, KIM JUANITA, lawyer; b. Savannah, Ga., Nov. 14, 1957; BS summa cum laude, Knoxville Coll., 1979; JD, Georgetown U., 1983. Bar: U.S. Supreme Ct., DC 1983, Tex. 1984, U.S. Ct. Appeals (5th, 4th, and 8th cir.), U.S. Dist. Ct. (No. and ea. dist. Tex.). Law clk. U.S. Dist Ct. (No. Dist. Tex.); ptnr. Hughes & Luce, LLP, Dallas. Contbr. articles to profl. publs. Mem. bd. regents Georgetown U.; bd. dirs. Victims Outreach; dir., treas. Dallas Mus. Art; former dir. Greater Dallas C. of C.; former trustee Paul Quinn Coll.; former dir. Jr. League Dallas. Named Tex. SuperLawyer, Law & Politics Mag., 2003; named an Best Lawyers in Dallas, D Mag., 2005; named one of Best Lawyers in Am., Corporate Counsel, 2003; recipient Louise Raggio award, Dallas Women Lawyers Assn., 2003, Trailblazer award, J.L. Turner Legal Assn., 2003. Mem.: ABA (mem. com. commn. on women in profession 1993—97, mem. com. on meetings and travel 1997—2000, mem. continuing legal edn. com. 2000—03, sec. litigation sect. 2002—04, chair-elect litigation sect. 2005—, mem. ho. of dels., mem. membership com., mem. coun. fund for justice and edn.), Tex. Women Lawyers, Dallas Bar Assn. (former co-chair judiciary com.), State Bar Tex. (chair continuing legal edn. com. 1997—2000, chair litigation sect. 2001—02, chair bd. dirs. 2003—04, former chair evidentiary panel dist. 6A grievance com., bd. dirs., Presdl. Citation 2000, Gene Cavin award 1999), Am. Law Inst. (chair com. on size, fed. judiciary com.). Office: Hughes & Luce LLP 117 Main St Ste 2800 Dallas TX 75201 Office Phone: 214-939-5579. Office Fax: 214-939-5849. Business E-Mail: askewk@hughesluce.com.

ASKEW, THOMAS RENDALL, physics educator, researcher, consultant; b. Geneva, Ill., June 11, 1955; s. Thomas Addelbert and Jean Mary (Somerville) A.; m. Mary Louise Kazmaier, July 15, 1978; 1 child, Steven Thomas. MS, U. Ill., 1982, PhD, 1984. Mem. tech. staff DuPont Rsch., Wilmington, Del., 1984—91; from assoc. prof. to prof. physics Kalamazoo (Mich.) Coll., 1991—. Vis. scientist Argonne (Ill.) Nat. Lab., 1992—; cons. to U.S. corps. Contbr. articles to profl. jours. Recipient Ball Meml. scholarship Gordon Coll., 1977, Mac Arthur scholarship John D. and Catherine T. Mac Arthur Found., 1991-93. Mem. Am. Phys. Soc., Material Rsch. Soc. Achievements include patents in superconductivity. Office: Kalamazoo Coll Physics Dept Kalamazoo MI 49006

ASKEW, WILLIAM EARL, chemist, educator; b. Maysville, N.C., Aug. 31, 1943; s. Carl Lee and Sally Chinese (Pope) A. BA in Chemistry, U. N.C., 1965; MA in Biology, East Carolina U., 1968; PhD in Biophys. Sci., U. Houston, 1973. Rsch. assoc. Baylor Coll. Medicine, Houston, 1973-77, Vets.' Hosp., Houston, 1973-77; instr. chemistry Houston C.C. Sys. N.W., 1977—, chair phys. scis. dept., 2000—. With U.S. Army, 1968-70. Mem. Am. Chem. Soc., Am. Acad. Sci., Tex. Jr. Coll. Tchrs. Assn., 2-Yr. Chemistry Soc. Office: Town and Country Ctr 1010 W Sam Houston N Houston TX 77043-5008

ASKEY, RICHARD ALLEN, mathematician, educator; b. St. Louis, June 4, 1933; s. Philip Edwin and Bessie May (Yates) Askey; m. Elizabeth Ann Hill, June 14, 1958; children: James, Suzanne. BA, Washington U., St. Louis, 1955; MA, Harvard U., 1956; PhD, Princeton U., 1961. Instr. in math. Washington U., St. Louis, 1958-61; instr. U. Chgo., Chgo., 1961-63; asst. prof. U. Wis., Madison, 1963-65, asso. prof., 1965-68, prof., 1968-86, Gabor Szego prof., 1986-95, John Bascom prof., 1995—2003, prof. emeritus, 2003—. Author: (book) Orthogonal Polynomials and Special Functions, 1975; author: (with G. E. Andrews and R. Roy) Special Functions, 1999; editor: Theory and Application of Special Functions, 1975, Collected Papers of Gabor Szego, 1982. Fellow Guggenheim, 1969—70. Fellow: AAAS, Am. Acad. Arts and Scis., Indian Acad. Sci. (hon.); mem.: Soc. Indsl. and Applied Math., Math. Assn. Am., Nat. Acad. Sci., Am. Math. Soc. Home: 2105 Regent St Madison WI 53726-3941 Office: U Wis Van Vleck Hall Madison WI 53706

ASKEY, THELMA J., federal agency administrator; b. Lakehurst, N.J. BA, Tenn. Tech. U., 1970; postgrad., George Washington U., Am. U. Press asst. Rep. John Duncan, 1972-74; editor Nat. Rsch. Coun. Marine Bd., 1974-76; asst. minority trade counsel Ho. Com. Ways and Means, 1976-79, minority trade counsel, 1979-94; staff dir. subcommittee trade Ho. Com. on Ways and Means, 1995-98; commr. U.S. Internat. Trade Commn., Washington, 1998—2000; dir. U.S. Trade and Devel. Agy., Arlington, Va., 2001—. Office: US Trade and Devel Agy Office Dir 1000 Wilson Blvd Ste 1600 Arlington VA 22209-3901 Office Phone: 703-875-4357.

ASKEY, WILLIAM HARTMAN, Magistrate judge, lawyer; b. Williamsport, Pa., June 21, 1919; s. Charles Fisher and Marguerite Kirlin (Hartman) A.; m. Betty Arlene Moore, July 3, 1942; 1 dau., Elizabeth Powell. BA, Bucknell U., 1941; JD, U. Pitts., 1951. Bar: Lycoming County Cts., 1951, Pa. 1952, U.S. Dist. Ct. (mid. dist.) Pa. 1952, U.S. Supreme Ct. 1960. U.S. commr. U.S. Dist. Ct. (mid. dist.) Pa., 1964-71; part-time U.S. magistrate judge, 1971—. With AAA, North Penn. Bd. dirs. Appalachia Ednl. Lab., Charleston, W.Va., 1967-85. Served to maj. USAAF, 1941-46. Mem. Lycoming Law Assn. (pres. 1968-69), Pa. Bar Assn., ABA, Fed. Bar Assn. (hon.), Fed. Magistrate Judges Assn., Charles F Greevy Jr. Inn of Ct., Masons, Ross Club (Williamsport). Office Phone: 570-323-9881.

ASKIN, FRANK, law educator; b. Balt., Jan. 8, 1932; s. Abraham and Rose (Mervis) A.; m. Marilyn Klein, Aug. 6, 1960; children: Andrea Marcy, Jonathan Michael, Daniel Simon; 1 son from previous marriage, Steven. BA, CCNY, 1966; JD, Rutgers U., 1966. Bar: N.J. 1966, N.Y. 1983, U.S. Dist. Ct. (ea. dist.) N.Y., U.S. Ct. Appeals (2d, 3d cirs.), U.S. Supreme Ct. 1971. Journalist N.Y. Post, Bergen Record, Newark Star-Ledger; disting. prof. law Rutgers Law Sch., Newark, 1975—. Vis. prof. U. Hawaii Law Sch., 1975; spl. counsel edn. and labor com. U.S. Ho. of Reps., 1976-77, cons. govt. ops. com., 1989-92; gen. counsel ACLU, 1976—. Author: Defending Rights: A Life in Law and Politics, 1997; co-editor: Enforcing Fair Housing Laws, 1970; contbr. articles to profl. jours. Nat. bd. dirs. ACLU, 1968—, sec., 1971-75, gen. counsel, 1976—; del. Dem. Nat. Conv., 1980, 88; Dem. candidate 11th dist. U.S. Ho. of Reps., N.J., 1986—. Named one of Best Lawyers in America, Woodward & White. Mem. Soc. Am. Law Tchrs. (treas. 1974-75). Office: Rutgers Law Sch 123 Washington St Newark NJ 07102-3192 Business E-Mail: faskin@kinoy.rutgers.edu.

ASKIN, WALTER MILLER, artist, educator; b. Pasadena, Calif., Sept. 12, 1929; s. Paul Henry and Dorothy Margaret (Miller) A.; child from previous marriage, Nancy Carol Oudegeest; m. Elise Anne Doyle, Apr. 17, 1993. BA, U. Calif., Berkeley, 1951, MA, 1952; postgrad., Ruskin Sch. Drawing and Fine Art, Oxford. Asst. curator edn. Legion of Honor Mus., San Francisco, 1953-54; prof. art Calif. State U., L.A., 1956-92; pub. Nose Press, Pasadena, 1984—; vis. artist Pasadena Art Mus., 1962-63, U. N.Mex., 1972, Calif. State U., Long Beach, 1974-75, Cranbrook Acad. Art, Mich., 1978, Ariz. State U., Tempe, 1979, Art Ctr. Athens Sch. Fine Arts, Mykonos, Greece, 1973, Kelpra Studio, London, 1969, 73. Chief reader Advanced Placement Program, Ednl. Testing Svc., 1982—85; chmn. visual arts panel Art Recognition and Talent Search Nat. Found. Advancement in Arts-Commn. on Presdl. Scholars; mem. advanced placement studio art exam. com. Coll. Bd., 1985—96, chmn., 1992—96, mem. Commn. of Future of Advanced Placement Program, 1999—2001, mem. acad. coun., 1989—94, chair arts adv. com., 1987—93; bd. dirs. Internat. Assn. for Humor Studies, 1989; adj. prof. Ariz. State U., 1988—90; artist-in-residence Ragdale Found., Lake Forest, Ill., 1986, John Michael Kohler Art Ctr., Sheboygan, Wis., 1987, Hambidge (Ga.) Ctr. for Arts & Sci., 1991, Vt. Studio Colony, 1988, U. Dallas, 2001; co-dir. 1st Internat. Conf. on Humor in Art, Chateau de la Bretsche, Brittany, France, 1989, 92; spkr., juror nat. travel show So. Graphics Coun. Conf., Ohio U., Athens, 1998; vis. prof. Ariz. State U., Tempe, 2001; invited artist 12 lithos Hullaballoo in Winter in collaboration with Wayne Kimball, Brigham Young U., 2001; historian art alumni group U. Calif., Berkeley, 2001—; curator "Jest for Fun"

Channel Islands Art Ctr., 2004; juror Ariz. State Ann. Exhbn., Calif. State Fair, Hawaiian Printmakers Assn. Ann., Laguna Mus. Art Ann., L.A. Printmaking Soc. Show, Nat. Watercolor Soc. Ann. Exhbn. Numerous exhbns. including one-man shows, Kunstlerhaus, Vienna, Austria, 1981, Santa Barbara Mus. Art, 1966, Hellenic-Am. Union, Athens, Greece, 1973, Hank Baum Gallery, San Francisco, 1970, 74, 76, Ericson Gallery, N.Y.C., 1978, Abraxas Gallery, Calif., 1979, 80, 81, Fla. State U., Tallahassee, 1988, Lizardi/Harp Gallery, Pasadena, 1988, 91, 95, L.A. Valley Coll., 1989, U. Dallas, 2001, Brigham Young U., 2002, Calif. State U., Channel Islands, 2002, Pasadena Playhouse Gallery, 2003, Floating Rock Gallery, Pasadena, 2004, Village Sq. Gallery, Montrose, 2005; one-man traveling show USIA, Yugoslavia, 1985-86, 15th Internat. Biennale of Prints and Drawings, Taipei Mus. Art, 1998; Pasadena's choice exhbn., Armory Ctr. for Arts, 1991, Contemporary Art in Pasadena, 1960-74, Norton Simon Mus., 1999, Taipei Fine Arts Mus., 1999, Gertrude Herbert Art Inst., Ga., 1999, Schafler Gallery, Pratt Inst., Bklyn., 1999, Kittredge Gallery, U. Puget Sound, Tacoma, 1999, Cmty. Visual Art Assn., Jackson Hole, Wyo., 1999, Wayland Bapt. U., Plainview, Tex., 1999, From Paris to Pasadena exhbn. Norton Simon Mus., 2000, Artists Do Opera exhbn. Brand Libr., Glendale, Calif., 2001, print and drawing exhbn. Bradley U., Peoria, Ill., 2000; artist L.A. Met. Transit Authority, 2003, Gallery LeLong, N.Y.C., 2003, 64th ann. exhbn. N.W. Watercolor Soc., Art Inst. Seattle, 2004, The Art of Humor Studio Channel Islands Art Ctr., 2004, others; author: A Briefer History of the Greeks, 1983, Another Art Book to Cross Off Your List, 1984, Modern Manifesto Match Game, 1998, Hidedous Headlines, 1998, Womsters and Foozlers, 1998, On Becoming an Artist, 1999, (calendar) Man, Dog, Bone Artists' Calendar; represented in permanent collections Norton Simon Mus., Pasadena, Getty Ctr. for the Arts, L.A., Mus. Modern Art, N.Y.C., Whitney Mus. Art, N.Y.C., San Francisco Mus. Contemporary Art, Albright Knox Mus., Buffalo, L.A. County Mus. Art, others; contbr. articles to profl. jours. and mags. Trustee Pasadena Art Mus., 1963-68; bd. dirs. L.A. Inst. Contemporary Art., 1978-81, Pasadena Gallery Contemporary Arts; bd. govs. Baxter Art Gallery, Calif. Inst. Tech., 1980-86; bd. dirs. The Calif. Artist, Book Program, 1985-2000; dir. The Visual Humor Project, 1989—. Recipient Outstanding Prof. award Calif. State U., 1973, Artists award Pasadena Arts Coun., 1970, award 61st ann. exhbn. N.W. Watercolor Soc., 2001, Past Pres.' award 80th ann. exhbn. Nat. Watercolor Soc., 2000, Purchase prize 3d nat. print biennial Frederick R. Weisman Mus., Mpls., 2001; named Disting. Alumnus, Pasadena City Coll.; Ruth G. Jansen Edn. Meml. grantee, grantee Pasadena Arts Commn., 1990; also over 50 awards in competitive exhbns. art. Mem.: Kavai Soc. Artists, So. Graphics Coun., L.A. Printmaking Soc. (pres. 2002—04, founding mem.), Nat. Watercolor Soc. (1st v.p. 1960), Coll. Art Assn. Am. Home and Office: PO Box D South Pasadena CA 91031-0120 *What can we do today that has any kind of meaning and value? We can search for a means to escape from conventions, from ordinariness, and from the limitations of everyday existence. We can help create the emergent fiction that is the world we live in. We can regenerate the key myths and archetypes so that life doesn't seem worth living unless one is on the side of the liberating and transformative. We can learn to play again - to not know what we are looking for, to break through the ice of habit, to know what it means to be truly alive and to experience the specialness of even the most ordinary things. We can find the god within, inspiration, magic, once again be visionaries, bring peace. The real joy is in making a better, more calm, more serene, more alive, more playful, more energized, more focused, more directed, more life filled existence for the time we're here.*

ASKINS, ARTHUR JAMES, accountant, diversified financial services company executive; b. Dec. 2, 1944; s. William J. and Rita M. (O'Brien) A.; m. Nancy E. Paulsen, Apr. 28, 1979. BS, LaSalle U., 1967; MA, Rider Coll., 1971. Cert. of specialization hospitality acctg. and mgmt. Am. Hotel and Motel Assn.; CPA, Pa., NJ; cert. fraud examiner, hotel adminstr. Tchr. Cardinal Dougherty H.S., Phila., 1967-70; pvt. practice acctg., 1967—. Recipient cert. of Commendation Twp. of Abington, Pa., 1967, Disting. Svc. award Cmty. Accts., Phila., 1982, Superstar award Resorts Internat. Casino-Hotel, 1982, Brotherhood award NCCJ, Atlantic City, 1983, Mgmt. award Resorts Internat. Casino Hotel, 1986, 1st Mgrs. award Resort Internat. Casino-Hotel, 1986, Outstanding Vol. Svc. award Big Bros./Big Sisters, 1987. Mem. AICPA, Nat. Assn. Accts. (nat. bd. dirs. 1983-85, pres. South Jersey Shore chpt. 1979-81, Cmty. Affairs award Suburban N.E. Phila. 1978), Inst. Internal Auditors (bd. dirs. 1984-89, audit com. 1979-83), NJ Soc. CPAs, Pa. Inst. CPAs, Greater Mainland C. of C., Nat. Assn. Cert. Internat. Fraud Examiners, Internat. Assn. Hosp. Accts. Republican. Roman Catholic. Office: Seneca Nation of Indians Seneca Gaming Authority PO Box 425 Niagara Falls NY 14302 Home: PO Box 428 Youngstown NY 14174-0428 Personal E-mail: ajacpa@adelphia.net.

ASKINS, JARI, lawyer, department chairman, state representative; b. Duncan, Okla., Apr. 27, 1953; d. Ollie M. and Jarita Askins. BA in Journalism, U. Okla., 1975, JD, 1980. Bar: Okla. V.p. closing office Stephens County Abstract Co., Duncan, Okla.; spl. dist. judge Stephens County, Okla., 1982—90; chmn. Okla. Pardon and Parole Bd., Okla. City, 1991—92; dep. gen. counsel Gov.'s Office, 1992—94; rep. Ho. of Reps., State of Okla., Okla. City, 1995—. Dep. majority fl. leader Okla. Ho. Reps., Okla. City, 2001—; mem. Okla. Judicial Conf., Okla. City. Mem Leadership Okla.; bd. trustees Cottey Jr. Coll., Nevada, Mo. Named to Okla. Woman's Hall of Fame, 2001. Mem.: ABA, Duncan C. of C. (Woman of Yr. 1995), Stephen's County Bar Assn., Okla. Bar Assn., Lions Club. Democrat. Office: 2300 N Lincoln Blvd Rm 301B Oklahoma City OK 73105 Home and Office: PO Box 391 Duncan OK 73534 E-mail: askinsja@lsb.state.ok.us.

ASKINS, NANCY ELLEN PAULSEN, training services executive; b. St. Paul, Nov. 2, 1948; d. Charles A. and Stasia (Sawicki) Paulsen; m. Arthur J. Askins, Apr. 28, 1979. BS in Home Econ., U. Cin., 1970, BS in Edn., 1971, MEd, 1972; postgrad., SUNY-Buffalo, 1974—76, Temple U., 1976, Walden U., 1988—92, Inst. Fin. Edn., 1982—85, Capella U., 2002. Cert. gaming supr. Edn. Inst. Am. Hotel and Motel Assn.; cert. strategic planning facilitator; cert. quality mgr. Asst. aquatic supr. Cin. Recreation Commn., 1969—72; adminstr. student affairs U. Cin., 1970—72; mem. faculty student affairs adminstrn, Tex. Luth. Coll., 1972—73; mem. faculty, student affairs adminstr. SUNY-Geneseo, 1974—76; student affairs adminstr. Temple U., Phila., 1976—78; tchr. drug awareness coord. Adams Sch. Harlandale Sch. Dist., San Antonio, 1973—74; career life ins. agt., fin. planning cons. Phoenix Mut. Life Ins. Co., Phila., 1978—81; registered rep., securities agt. Phoenix Equity Planning Corp., Phila., 1980—81; owner Paulsen-Askins Fin. Svcs., Somers Point, NJ, 1980—81; mem. women's task force Phoenix Cos., 1980—81; coord. tng. svcs. Collective Fed. Savs. & Loan Assn., Egg Harbor City, NJ, 1981—82, asst. v.p., tng. dir., 1982—84; mgr. tng. Shore Meml. Hosp., Somers Point, 1984—85, instr. wellness, 1984—88, dir. ednl. devel., 1986—89; dir edn. svcs. Holy Cross Hosp., Ft. Lauderdale, Fla., 1990—91, dir. cmty. and vol. svcs., 1991—94, part-time instr. wellness program, 1991—94; v.p. tng. and assoc. devel. Grand Casino, Biloxi, 1994—96; coord. tng. svcs. Gulf Coast Bus. Svcs., Gulfport, Miss., 1996—98; dir. quality Hollywood Casino Resort/Tunica, Robinsonville, Miss., 1998—2001; adj. prof. Webster U., Memphis, 2003. Adj. prof. bus. and social scis. Atlantic C.C. Coll., Mays Landing, N.J., 1986-89; facilitator Assertiveness Tng. Group, Interpersonal Comms. Group, orgnl. and leadership devel. seminars and cons.; owner, exec. corp. cons. Askins Tng. and Cons., 1981—; mem. bd. examiners Malcolm Baldrige Nat. Quality Award, 2001,02, 03, Pres.'s Quality Award, 2000, Tenn. Quality Award, 2000, Miss. Quality Award, 1999, 2000 (judge 2002); instr. Inst. Fin. Edn., 1982-85, Ednl. Inst., Am. Hotel ad Motel Assn., 1999-2001; nat. seminar leader, Fred Pryor / Career Track, 2000-; workshop presenter and spkr. in field; items writer Cert. Quality Improvement Assoc. Agy. chmn. United Way Campaign, Phila., 1979, 80; bd. dir. South Jersey Regional Theater, 1983-86, chmn., 1983-84; active ann. Muscular Dystrophy Telethon, Phila.; active Girl Scouts U.S., 1956-74, 84—; mem. Parish coun., parish enrichment com., 1984-88, cantor St. Joseph Roman Cath. Ch., Somers Point, 1979-89; mem., lector Christ the King Cath. Ch., Southaven, Miss., 1998-2003, St. Peter Cath. Ch., 2003—; chmn. com. Women's Club St. Luke's Cath. Ch., Coconut Creek, Fla., 1992-94, parish coun., 1993-94; bd. dir. Holly Shores Coun. Girl Scouts U.S., 1984-85; host fgn. exch. students Am. Scandinavian Student Exch. Program, 1985-87; mem. Somers Point Bd. Edn., 1986; mem. Libr. Adv. Bd. City of Margate, Fla., 1991-94, fundraising chmn., vice chmn., chmn. Recipient Brotherhood-Sisterhood Achievers award NCCJ, 1985, Rising Star award, 1997, Gold Dir. award, 1998 Carlson Learning Co., Inscape Publishing, Minn.; named Biloxi Career Woman Bus. Profl. Women/Lighthouse of Biloxi, 1995, Women of Achievement Woman of Yr. Bus. Profl. Women Clarksdale, Coahoma County, Miss., 1999. Mem. ASTD (treas. South Jersey chpt., nat. dir. savs. and lending industry group 1983-84, hosps. and healthcare industry group 1984-86, nat. conf. spkr. 1984-86, sec. Greater Broward/Ft. Lauderdale chpt. 1991, pres.-elect 1992, pres.1993, nat. dir.-elect 1990-91. dir. 1991-92, Interfaith Trainers Cons. Network), Internat. Cons. Assn., Am. Hotel & Motel Assn. (No. Miss. chpt. charter pres. 1999), Bus. and Profl. Women Buffalo (co-chair 2004-05), Women Robinsonville, Miss. (charter pres. 1999-2000), Bus. and Profl. Women Clarksdale (legis. com. chair, 1998-2000), Bus. and Profl. Women Lighthouse of Biloxi (v.p. membership, newsletter editor, chair 1997 Nat. Bus. Women's Week), Bus. and Profl. Women Miss. (state 2d v.p., state membership chair, 1996-97, state legis. chair, 1999-2000, nat. leadership chair, state pres.-elect 2002-03, state pres. 2003-04, nat. leadership chair 2004-05, individual devel. prgram co-chair Buffalo chpt., 2004-2005), Greater Camden Assn. Life Underwriters (state pres. 2003-04, chmn. Life Ins. Week for South Jersey 1978-79, bd. dir. 1979-81, pub. rels. chmn. 1979-81, chmn. state edn. 1981), Am. Soc. for Quality (features editor Competitive Advantage quality divsn. 2000-03), Am. Hosp. Assn., Am. Soc. Health Edn. and Tng., Am. Mgmt. Assn., Fla. Soc. Healthcare Edn. and Tng., Greater Mainland C. of C. (v.p., treas., membership coord. 1979-89, Pres. award 1983), Internat. Assn. Facilitators, U. Cin. Alumni of Greater Phila. Area (pres. 1980-89), Greater Ft. Lauderdale C. of C. (diplomat 1992-93, edn. com. 1993-94), Alliance/The Women's Network (bd. dir. 1983-84), Rotary Internat., Rotary of Gulfport, Rotary of Robinsonville, (sect. 1999, newsletter editor 1998-99, pres.-elect 1999-2000, pres. 2000-2001), Rotary (chairperson, long range planning com. 1999-2001, group study exch. com. 1999-2000, youth study exch. com. 1999-2000, chmn. matching grants com. 2001-2002). Democrat. Home: 444 Lockport St PO Box 428 Youngstown NY 14174-0428

ASKINS, WALLACE BOYD, manufacturing executive; b. Chgo., June 2, 1930; s. Wallace Fay and Evelyn Mae (Baker) A.; m. Trieste M. Olivieri, May 20, 1954 (div. Sept. 23, 1994); 1 child, Justin Wallace. BA, Lake Forest (Ill.) Coll., 1952; JD with honors, John Marshall Law Sch., Chgo., 1961. Bar: Ill. 1961; CPA, Ill. Sr. accountant Ernst & Young (CPAs), Chgo., 1952-55; controller, house counsel Nat. Lock Co., Rockford, Ill., 1955-65; asst. corp. controller Xerox Corp., Stamford, Conn., 1965-77; exec. v.p., chief fin. officer White Motor Corp., Cleve., 1977-81, chmn. bd., chief exec. officer, 1981-84; exec. v.p., chief fin. officer Armco Inc., Parsippany, N.J., 1984-92, also bd. dirs. Bd. dirs. Trump Hotel and Casino Resorts, Inc., Trump Entertainment Resorts, Inc. Mem. ABA, AICPA, Ill. Soc. CPA's, N.Y. Soc. CPA's, Ill. Bar Assn. Home: 153 Indian Dr Greentown PA 18426-9021 Fax: (570) 887-0693. Office Phone: 570-857-0692. E-mail: walgator@aol.com.

ASK-NANKO, LORRAINE CHARLOTTE, music educator; b. Bronx, NY, Sept. 13, 1939; d. Charles Bernt Ask and Loretta Hilda Merkel; m. Joseph Nanko, Aug. 18, 1968 (dec.). MusB, Manhattan Sch.Music, 1962, MusM, 1964. Music faculty Notre Dame H.S., NYC, 1969—72, Cardinal Hayes H.S., Bronx, NY, 1969—. fine arts chmn., 1994—. Adv. bd. City Is. Players, Bronx, 1996—. Dir. music First Presbyn. Ch. of Throggs Neck, 1979—. Recipient Outstanding H.S. Choral Conductor, 1980, Distinguished Faculty award, Cardinal Hayes H.S., 2004. Mem.: Presbyn. Assn. Musicians, Am. Guild Organists, Am. Choral Dir. Assn. Republican. Presbyn. Avocations: reading, crafts. Office: Cardinal Hayes HS 650 Grand Concourse Bronx NY 10451 Office Phone: 718-292-6100. Business E-Mail: lnanko@cardinalhayes.org.

ASKOV, EUNICE MAY, adult education educator; b. St. Louis, Nov. 20, 1940; d. David Hull and Marjorie Jane (Gutgsell) Nicholson; m. Warren Hopkins Askov, Jan. 22, 1967; children: David, Karen. BA in English, Denison U., 1962; MA in English, U. Wis., 1966, PhD in Curriculum and Instrn., 1969. English and reading tchr. Rich Twp. High Sch., Park Forest, Ill., 1962-64; reading svc. reading specialist U. Wis., Madison, 1965-66, project asst. Wis. R & D Ctr. for Cognitive Learning, 1966-67, rsch. assoc., 1969-72, lectr. dept. curriculum and instrn., 1968-69; coord. adult basic edn. programs U. Wis. Extension, 1966-67; remedial reading specialist Lincoln Jr. High Sch., Madison, 1966; adult basic edn. tchr. Madison Vocat., Tech. and Adult Schs., 1967-68; asst. prof. elem. edn. Minn. State U., Bemidji, 1972-74; assoc. prof. Pa. State U., University Park, 1974-79, prof. edn., 1980—2001, disting. prof., 2001—. Presenter seminars on adult edn., Germany, 1986, 93; cons., speaker in field; mem. editorial bd. Jour. Ednl. Rsch., Adult Edn. Quarterly, Adult Basic Edn., Am. Reading Forum Yearbook; mem. steering com. Adult Literacy and Tech.; mem. panel nat. work group on cancer and literacy Nat. Cancer Inst.; organizer, coord. Pa. State Coalition for Adult Literacy; mem. adv. coun. Nat. Coalition for Literacy. Contbr. articles to profl. publs. Fulbright sr. scholar, 1983; Literacy Leader fellow Nat. Inst. for Literacy, 1994-95; recipient Alumni Achievement award U. Wis.-Madison Sch. Edn., 1994, Career Achievement award Pa. State Coll. Edn.; Disting. fellow Flinders U. Inst. Internat. Edn., Australia, 1998; named to Reading Hall of Fame, 2005 Mem. Am. Assn. Adult and Continuing Edn. (chair, mem. various coms., bd. dir.),Commn. Profs. of Adult Edn., Am. Edn. Rsch. Assn., Am. Reading Forum, Internat. Reading Assn. (chair, mem. various coms.), Keystone State Reading Assn., Mid-State Literacy Coun. (bd. dir., pers. com., long range planning com.), Mid-State Reading Coun. (pres.), Pa. Assn. Adult and Continuing Edn., Phi Beta Kappa, Phi Delta Kappa. Democrat. Methodist. Avocations: travel, aerobics, hiking, reading. Office: Pa State U Inst for Study Adult Lit 200 Rackley Bldg University Park PA 16802-3202 Business E-Mail: ena1@psu.edu.

ASKREN, STAN A., manufacturing executive; BA Business Administration, U. of Northern Iowa; MBA, Washington U. Group v.p. The HON Co., 1998—99; Pres. Allsteel Inc., 1999—2003; exec. v.p. HNI Corp., 2001—03, Pres., bd. dir, 2003—, chmn., 2004—. Office: c/o HNI Corp 414 E Third St Muscatine IA 52761*

ASLAM, AHMED FARAZ, cardiologist, researcher; b. Lahore, Punjab, Pakistan, Dec. 15, 1974; s. Muhammad and Maqbool Aslam (Stepfather). MB, BS, MD, King Edward Med. Coll., Lahore, Pakistan, 1998. Cert. Ednl. Commn. for Fgn. Med. Grads., 2001. House staff Mayo Hosp., Lahore, Pakistan, 1998—99; med. officer Tariq Hosp., Lahore, Pakistan, 1999—2002; med. resident L.I. Coll. Hosp., Bklyn., 2002—, 2002—. Rsch. asst. Harlem Hosp., N.Y.C., 1999—2002; rsch. scholar/extern U. Of Ark. For Med. Sciences, Little Rock, 2003—03. Contbr. hematology (BEST CASE REPORT, 2003), cardiology & pulmonology (BEST CASE REPORT, 2004). Mem. quality assurance com. L.I. Coll. Hosp., Bklyn., 2002—04, mem. CPR rev. com., 2002—03, mem. disaster response team, 2002—03, asst. chief resident, 2003—. Mem.: ACP (assoc.), AMA (assoc.), Am. Soc. of Internal Medicine (assoc.), So. Med. Assn. (assoc.). Achievements include research in Determination of Ascorbic Acid (Vitamin C) Levels in Urine of Cancer Patients; Staphylococcus aureus infective endocarditis and septic pulmonary embolism after septic abortion- A Case report; QT prolongation in Diphenhydramine toxicity-A Case report; Fatal splenic sequestration crisis with multi-organ failure in an adult female with sickle cell-beta+ thalassemia; Thrombotic microangiopathic syndrome as initial presentation of HIV-Case report; Sever hypothermia associated with severe anemia: ECG findings of Osborn J waves, prolonged; Primary Lymphedema Tarda in an 88 Year Old African American male-Case report and review of literature; Diagnosing Hepatopulmonary Syndrome in patients with Interstitial Lung Disease- Use of Contrast Echocardiogram and Macroaggregated Albumin (MAA) scan-Review of Literature; Selective Proteasome Inhibitor: Bortezomib (PS 341; Velcade); Determination of Corticosteroid Levels in Herbal Products; Spectrophotometric determination of Carbamazepine in Pure and Pharmaceutical Products; Estimation of Lead in Human Blood Due to Environmental Pollution; Troponin Levels in patients with Sickle Cell Crisis- Review Article"; EKG changes in Right sided chest leads in pulmonary embolism; Prognostic value of false positive pharmacological stress test in patients with angiographically normal coronary arteries"- Retrospective cohort study; Left Ventricular Diastolic Dysfunction in patients with Adult age onset Bronchial asthma; Hyperkalemia induced failure of atrial and ventricular pacemaker capture-A Case. Home: 210 Caton Ave Apt # 3-F Brooklyn NY 11218 Office: LI Coll Hosp 339 Hicks St Mail Box No 25 Brooklyn NY 11201 Office Phone: 718-780-1881. Home Fax: 718-484-7258; Office Fax: 718-780-1300. Personal E-mail: ahmedfaslam@yahoo.com.

ASLAN, MADALYN, writer, educator; d. George Vincent Shea and Donna Marie Todd. BA with honors, U. London, 1984; BA, Cornell U., 1987; MFA, Sarah Lawrence Coll., 1991. Lectr. Coll. Psychic Studies, London, 2001—. Author: What's Your Sign? A Cosmic Guide for Young Astrologers, 2002, Madalyn Aslan's Jupiter Signs, 2003; actor: (TV series) The Martian Chronicles, 1980; (films) D.H. Lawrence. Mem.: Nat. Coun. Geo-Cosmic Rsch., Nat. Campaign for Tolerance (life; founder), Am. Fedn. Astrologers (life). Home: PO Box 717 Provincetown MA 02657 Office Phone: 212-631-5844. E-mail: madalyn@madalynaslan.com.

ÅSLUND, ANDERS, economist; b. Karlskoga, Sweden, Feb. 17, 1952; s. Ivan and Ingrid (Åblad) Å. BA, U. Stockholm, Sweden, 1976; MSc, Stockholm Sch. Econs., 1976; PhD, U. Oxford, England, 1982. Second sec. Swedish Embassy, Kuwait, 1977-78; first sec. Swedish Permanent Delegation, Geneva, 1982-84, Swedish Embassy, Moscow, 1984-87; rsch. scholar Kennan Inst. Advanced Russian Studies, Washington, 1987-88; prof., dir. Stockholm Inst. E. European Econs., Stockholm Sch. Econs., 1989-94; sr. assoc. Carnegie Endowment for Internat. Peace, Washington, 1994—, dir. Russian and Eurasian program, 2003—. Fellow World Econ. Forum, Geneva, 1991—; adj. prof. Georgetown U., Washington, 2002—. Author: Private Enterprise in Eastern Europe, 1985, Gorbachev's Struggle for Economic Reform, 1989, 91, Post-Communist Economic Revolutions: How Big a Bang?, 1992, How Russia Became a Market Economy, 1995, Building Capitalism: The Transformation of the Former Soviet Bloc, 2002; co-author: Getting It Wrong; editor 10 books on Soviet, post-Soviet and Russian econ. affairs. Sr. econ. advisor to Russian Govt., 1991—94, Ukrainian Govt., 1994—97; pres. Akaev Kyrgyz Republic, 1998—2004. Mem. Cosmos Club (Washington). Office: Carnegie Endowment Internat Peace 1779 Massachusetts Ave Washington DC 20036 E-mail: aaslund@ceip.org.

ASMA, EVREN, medical researcher; b. Ankara, Turkey, Aug. 5, 1978; s. Tahir and Muzeyeen Asma. BSc, Bilen U., 1999; MSc, U. Southern Calif., 2000, PhD, 2004. Rsch. asst. U. Southern Calif., 1999—2004, postdoctoral rsch. assoc., 2004—. Recipient Outstanding Acad. achievement, U. Southern Calif., 2001, 2003, Student Travel award, IEEE, 2001, Rsch. assistantship, U. Southern Calif., 1999—2004. Mem.: IEEE. Avocation: swimming. Office: U So Calif 2250 Alcazar St Decatur GA 30033

ASMA, LAWRENCE FRANCIS, priest; b. Waukegan, Ill., Oct. 21, 1947; s. Francis Victor and Isabelle Amelia (Recktenwald) A. BA in English, U. Wis., Whitewater, 1969; MA in English, Ill. State U., 1974; MA in Scripture magna cum laude, De Andreis Sem., 1982, MDiv, 1983. Ordained priest Roman Cath. Chr., 1983. Dir. spritual formation Cardinal Glennon Coll., St. Louis, 1983-85, instr. theology dept., 1983-85; chaplain St. Vincent's Div. DePaul Health Ctr., St. Louis, 1985—. Bd. dirs. Rosati Stabilization Ctr., St. Louis, 1988-94; vice chmn. Rosati Stabilization Ctr., 1990-94; advisor Explorers, 1991-92. Local religious superior Congregation of the Mission, 1994-99; chaplain Knights Columbus, 1996—. With USNR, 1970-72, Vietnam. Mem. Assn. Profl. Chaplains (bd. cert.), Cath. Biblical Assn., Congregation of Mission, Sigma Tau Delta. Avocations: ornithology, photography, drawing. Office: DePaul Health Center 12303 De Paul Dr Bridgeton MO 63044-2588 Office Phone: 314-344-7080. E-mail: fr_larry_asma@ssmhc.com.

ASMUS, EDWARD PAUL, music educator; b. Jan. 25, 1948; B of Music Edn., Ohio State U., 1972; M of Music Edn., U. Kans., 1976, DPhil, 1979. Prof. music SUNY, Buffalo, 1979-86, U. Utah, Salt Lake City, 1986-2000, U. Miami, Frost Sch. of Music, Coral Gables, Fla., 2000—. Office: U Miami Frost Sch Music PO Box 248165 Coral Gables FL 33124-8165 Office Phone: 305-284-2241. Business E-Mail: ed.asmus@miami.edu.

ASMUS, JOHN FREDRICH, physicist; b. Pasadena, Calif., Jan. 20, 1937; s. William F. and Eleanor E. (Kocher) A.; m. Barbara Ann Flaherty, Feb. 23, 1963; children— Joanne M., Rosemary H. BSEE, Calif. Inst. Tech., 1958, MSEE, 1959, PhDEE and Physics, 1965. Head optical systems dept. Aero Geo Astro Corp., Alexandria, Va., 1960-64; head laser dept. Gulf Gen. Atomic, San Diego, 1964-69; research staff Inst. Def. Analyses, Arlington, Va., 1969-71; v.p., bd. mem. Sci. Applications, Inc., Albuquerque, 1971-73; lectr. U. Calif., Davis, 1974, research physicist, co-founder art and sci. center San Diego, 1973—. Co-dir. JASON nat. laser program study Office of Pres. of U.S., 1971; cons. in field; mem. adv. group on electron devices Smithsonian Assocs.; featured cable, PBS TV documentaries, 1975—; conf. lectr. U. Calif. San Diego, 1999; lectr. Inst. for Human Nutrition, Setia, Crete, 2004. Contbr. sci. articles to profl. jours.; patentee metallic vapor laser, embedded pinch laser, plasma pinch annealing system, chemical decontamination with ultraviolet; introduced laser, ultrasonic and computer image enhancement techniques to art conservation, introduced laser cleaning to the field of paleontology, and revealed new features (necklace and mountain pentimenti, 1978)of da Vinci's Mona Lisa; restored Cremona Cathedral, Calif. State Capital, White House mural, Washington, Arches Nat. Pk. Pictograph, Venice Ducal Palace Sculpture, office of Galileo in U. Padova using laser radiation; devel. of laser-robotic technique for the decontamination of the Hanford nuclear weapons facility of the U.S. Dept. Energy; laser, flashlamp and pinchlamp systems for depainting stealth aircraft and decontaminating the JET TOKAMAK thermonuclear fusion reactor, Culham Lab., U.K.; laser system for branding bowhead whales at a distance. Recipient Rolex Laureate for Enterprise award for restoration Xian terra cotta warriors Montres Rolex SA, Geneva, 1990, Best Scholarly Article award Soc. for Tech. Com., 1988; named George Eastman lectr. Optical Soc. Am., 1994, Rank Prize mentor, 2004; winner IBM Supercomputing Competition for Image Enhancement of Mona Lisa, 1989; Schlumberger fellow, 1959-60, Tektronix fellow, 1960-61, Getty fellow, 1989, Oberlin Coll. fellow, 1990, Explorers Club fellow, 1997; decorated knight of Holy Sepulchre of Jerusalem, 1993. Mem.: Soc. Photo-Optical Instrumentation Engrs., Venice Soc., Nat. Trust Hist. Preservation, Am. Inst. Conservation, IEEE, Internat. Inst. Conservation of Hist. and Artistic Works, Lasers for the Conservation of Artworks (sci. bd. mem., hon. pres.), Bay Area Art Conservation Guild, Tau Beta Pi, Sigma Xi. Home: 8239 Sugarman Dr La Jolla CA 92037-2222 Office: IPAPS 0360 U Calif San Diego 9500 Gilman Dr La Jolla CA 92093-5004 Business E-Mail: jfasmus@ucsd.edu. *The lessons and adventures that pervade our stories are manifestations of God's grace.*

ASNER, EDWARD, actor; b. Kansas City, Kans., Nov. 15, 1929; s. Morris David and Lizzie (Seliger) A.; m. Nancy Lou Sykes, Mar. 23, 1957 (div., 1988), m. Cindy Gilmore, Aug. 2, 1998; children: Matthew and Liza (twins), Kathryn, Charles. Student, U. Chgo., 1947-49. Debut at Playwrights Theatre, Chgo., 1953; appeared on TV, in Off-Broadway and Broadway shows, N.Y.C., 1955-61; appeared in numerous motion pictures and TV shows, Los Angeles, 1961—; appeared in TV miniseries Rich Man, Poor Man, 1976, Roots, 1977; appeared on Slattery's People, CBS-TV, 1964-65, Mary Tyler Moore Show, CBS-TV, 1970-77, Lou Grant Show, CBS-TV, 1977-82, Off The Rack, ABC-TV, 1985, This Side of Eden, The Bronx Zoo, 1987-88, The Trials of Rosie O'Neil, 1991, Fish Police (voice) 1991, Hearts Afire, 1992-93, Thunder Alley 1994-95, Center of the Universe, 2004-; narrator TV film Narco; appeared in cable and TV films The Doomsday Flight, 1966, Doug Selby, D.A., 1969, House on Greenapple Road, 1969, Daughter of the Mind, 1970, The Old Man Who Cried Wolf, 1970, The Last Child, 1971, The Haunts of The Very Rich, 1971, Hey, I'm Alive, 1975, Life and Assassination of the Kingfish, 1977, The Gathering, 1977, The Family Man, 1979, A Small Killing, 1981, A Case of Libel, 1983, Anatomy of an Illness, 1984, Tender Is The Night, 1985, Vital Signs, 1986, The Christmas Star, 1986, Cracked up, 1987, Friendship in Vienna, 1988, Not a Penny More, Not a Penny Less, 1990, Switched at Birth, 1991, Yes, Virginia, There Is a Santa Claus, 1991,

Silent Motive, 1991, Cruel Doubt, 1992, Gypsy, 1993, Christmas Vacation 2: Cousin Eddie's Island Adventure, 2003; appeared in motion pictures The Murder Men, 1961, Kid Gallahad, 1962, The Slender Thread, 1965, The Satan Bug, 1965, The Venetian Affair, 1967, Peter Gunn, 1967, Change of Habit, 1969, Halls of Anger, 1970, They Call Me Mister Tibbs, 1970, Skin Game, 1971, Gus, 1976, Fort Apache, The Bronx, 1980, O'Hara's Wife, 1982, Daniel, 1983, Moon Over Parador, 1988, JFK, 1991, (voice) Happily Ever After, 1993, Down on the Watefront, 1993, The Animal, 2001, The Kid (voice), 2001, Elf, 2003; Higher Education (TV); Gargoyles: The Heroes Awaken (voice), 1994; Gargoyles (TV series, voice), 1994; Spider-Man (TV series, voice), 1995 & 2003; Freakazoid (TV series, voice), 1995; The Story of Santa Claus (TV), 1996; Gargoyles: The Goliath Chronicles (TV series, voice), 1996; Bruno the Kid (TV series, voice), 1996; Prep, 1997; Dog's Best Friend (TV), 1997; 187 Documented, 1997; Batman: Gotham Knights (TV series, voice), 1997, Superman (TV, voice), 1998; Payback (TV)(also prodr.), 1997; The Long Way Home (voice), 1997; Ask Harriet (tv series), 1998; Hard Rain (aka The Flood), 1998; The Closer (TV series), 1998; More Tales of the City (aka Armistead Maupin's More Tales of the City, TV series), 1998; X-Men Legends (video, voice), 2004; guest appearances on: The Untouchables, 1962 & 1963, Dr. Kildare, 1963, Gunsmoke 1964 & 1966, F.B.I., 1966, 1968, 1969, Mission Impossible, 1969, Police Story, 1974 & 1976, Rhoda, 1974, Hawaii Five-O, 1975, Highway to Heaven, 1986, Mad About You, 1996, 1997, 1998, Roseanne, 1996, The Practice, 1997 & 2004, The X-Files, 1998, The Simpsons (voice), 1999 & 2002, Buzz Lightyear of Star Command (voice), 2000, King of Hill (voice), 2001, The Wild Thornberrys (voice), 2000, Dharma & Greg, 2001, The Family Guy (voice), 2001, The Ellen Show, 2001, ER, 2003, Justice League, 2004 and numerous others. Served with Signal Corps U.S. Army, 1951-53. Recipient 5 Golden Globe Awards, 7 Emmy Awards, Flame of Truth Award, Fund for Higher Education, 1981; inducted into TV Acad. Hall of Fame, 1996. Mem. Screen Actors Guild (pres. 1981-85) Office: William Morris Agency care Brian Dubin 1325 Avenue Of The Americas New York NY 10019-6026

ASNIS, GREGORY MARK, psychiatrist; b. NYC, Oct. 6, 1946; s. Ruth Asnis; m. Lauren Chorney; 1 child, Jeremy. MD, Hahnemann Sch. of Medicine, 1968—72. Diplomate Am. Bd. of Psychiatry and Neurology, 1976. Dir., anxiety and depression program Montefiore Med. Ctr., Bronx, NY, 1981—; prof. of psychiatry Albert Einstein Sch. of Medicine, Bronx, 1981—. Contbr. articles to profl. jours. Mem.: Psychiat. Assn. (assoc.). Democrat. Office: Montefiore Med Ctr 111 East 210 St Bronx NY 10570 Office Phone: 718-920-4287. Office Fax: 718-882-4735. E-mail: asnisarts@aol.com.

ASO, KAJI, artist; b. Tokyo; BFA in Painting, Tokyo U., 1960, MFA in Printmaking, 1962. Prof. art Sch. Mus. Fine Arts, Boston, 1967—2000; founder Kaji Aso Studio, Inc., Boston, 1972—. Lectr. in field. Author: Proteus, 1977; exhibitions include Pola Art Mus., Tokyo, 2003; singer (tenor): Nat. Opera House, 2004. Recipient Honor medal, Mayor of Lisbon, Portugal, 1997. Office: Kaji Aso Studio Inc 40 St Stephen St Boston MA 02115 Office Phone: 617-247-1719.

ASOMOZA, MIGUEL A., researcher, educator; b. Medero, Mex., Sept. 14, 1935; arrived in U.S., 1982; s. Miguel and Consuelo (Bosque) Asomoza; m. Martha A. Zozaya, Apr. 22, 1960 (div. July 1971); children: Miguel A., Martha; m. Hylda A. Asomoza, Dec. 30, 1976; 1 child, Paulo E. MD, Uamaulipas Autonomous U., Tampico, Mex., 1959; degree in indsl. security systems, Nat. Autonomous U. Mex., Mexico City, 1962; DSa, Nat. Poly. Inst., Mexico City, 1974, DSc, 1980. CEO PEMEX, Petroleos Mexicanos, Mexico City, 1959—79; prof., rschr. Nat. Poly. Inst., Mexico City, 1980—82, dir. administrv. rsch. ctr., 1982—84; med. mgr. PEMEX, Mexico City, 1985—86; rschr. U. Tex. Pan-Am., Edinburg, 1987—88; rschr., cons. Technol. Inst. Reynosa, Mexico, 1995—. Contbr. articles to profl. jours. Fellow: Masons; mem.: Am. Tolerance Assn., ACLU. Republican. Central Christian Church. Achievements include introduction of new variables in labor model design and industrial production in a non-linear model. Home: 4908 N 9th St Mcallen TX 78504 Office: Technol Inst Ave Tecnologico s/u Reynosa Mexico E-mail: masamoza@rgv.rr.com.

ASONGU, JANUARIUS JINGWA, information technology executive; arrived in US, 1997; s. Nicholas Jingwa Asongu and Monique Nkeng; m. Christine Nkwayep Ngangsic, Dec. 1, 2000; children: Maria Yorkzah Ngangsic-Asongu children: Jude Jingwa Ngangsic-Asongu. PhB, Pontifical Urban U., Rome, 1993; cert. in mass. comm., U. Lagos, Nigeria, 1995; diploma in Latin, diploma in Greek, St. Thomas Aquinas Maj. Sem., Bambui, The Southern Cameroons, 1992; PhD, Pacific Western U., Hawaii, 1998; MS in Info. Tech., cert. CIO officer, U. Md., Adelphi, 2002; cert., Fed. CIO U., Washington, 2002. CEO Global Thrust Comm., Inc., Hyattsville, Md., 1999—; exec. dir. US-So. Cameroons Found., Inc., Hyattsville, 1999—; journalist various publs., Houston, 1997—99. Author: The Problem of National Unity in Cameroon, 1993, The Media & Nationalism: The Case of the Southern Cameroons (Nuffield Press Fellowship, 1998), Challenging Tyranny, 2003; editor: Houston Chronicle (AFPF, 1997), (mag.) Telecom Bus. (Telecom Profl. of the Yr., 1999), (online mag.) Global Tech. Trends; contbr. articles to profl. publs. Comm. commr. So. Cameroons Provisional Adminstrn., Washington, 2001—02. Named Best African Journalist in the US, Assn. of African Publishers, 1998; fellow, Alfred Friendly Press, 1997, Nuffield Press fellowship, Wolfson Coll., Cambridge U., 1998. Achievements include research in Southern Cameroons. Home: 6200 Brightlea Dr Lanham MD 20706 Office: Global Thrust Comm Inc 6475 New Hampshire Ave #620 Hyattsville MD 20783 Personal E-mail: asongu@yahoo.com.

ASP, WILLIAM GEORGE, librarian; b. Hutchinson, Minn., July 4, 1943; s. George William and Blanche Irene (Mattson) A. BA, U. Minn., 1966, MA, 1970; postgrad., U. Iowa, 1972-75. Dir. East Cen. Regional Libr., Cambridge, Minn., 1967-70; asst. prof. Sch. Libr. Sci. U. Iowa, 1970-75; dir. Minn. Office Libr. Devel. and Svcs., St. Paul, 1975-96, Dakota County Libr., Eagan, Minn., 1996—2003. Mem. Nat. Coun. Quality Continuing Edn. for Info., Libr. and Media Pers., 1979-85; bd. dirs. Bakken Libr. Electricity and Life, Mpls.; vice chmn. White House Conf. on Libr. and Info. Svcs. Task Force, 1980-81, chmn., 1982, mem. adv. com., 1989-91; pres. Continuing Libr. Edn. Network and Exch., 1986-87. Mem. Minn. Regional Network Bd., 1992-96. Mem. ALA (mem. coun. 1985-88, 00-02), Minn. Libr. Assn., Chief Officers State Libr. Agys. (chmn. 1979-80), Minn. Ednl. Media Orgn., Minn. Assn. Continuing and Adult Edn., Assn. Specialized and Coop. Libr. Agys. (pres. 1989-90), Am. Field Svc. Home: 4137 42nd Ave S Minneapolis MN 55406-3530

ASPERGER, JAMES, lawyer; b. Fresno, Calif., 1953; BA with highest honors, U. Calif., Davis, 1975; JD, U. Calif., LA, 1978. Bar: Calif. 1978, DC 1980. Law clerk to Hon. Stanley Mosk Supreme Ct. Calif., 1978—79; law clerk to Hon. William H. Rehnquist US Supreme Ct., 1979—80; asst. US atty. Central Dist. Calif., 1983—93; dep. chief, major frauds sect. LA US Attorney's Office, 1987—90, chief, major frauds sect., 1990—93; ptnr. O'Melveny & Myers LLP, LA, mem. policy com., chair global enforcement and criminal defense group. Lectr. continuing legal education courses on criminal law, civil enforcement actions, and the RICO statute; bd. dir. Western Ctr. on Law and Poverty, 1997—, Office of Pub. Counsel, 1998—. Assoc. editor UCLA Law Review, 1976—77, editor-in-chief, 1977—78; contbr. articles to profl. jours. Named one of Top Trial Lawyers in So. Calif., LA Bus. Jour., 1999; recipient Alumni award for Academic Distinction, U. Calif., LA. Fellow: Am. Coll. of Trial Lawyers; mem.: Fed. Bar Assn. (bd. dir., LA Chpt. 1997—), ABA (former chair, West Coast White Collar Crime Com. 1998—2000, vice-chair, Nat. White Collar Crime Com. 2000—02), Assn. Trial Lawyers of Am., Order of Coif, Phi Beta Kappa. Office: O'Melveny & Myers LLP 400 S Hope St Los Angeles CA 90071-2899 Office Phone: 213-430-6491. Office Fax: 213-430-6407. Business E-mail: jasperger@omm.com.

ASPERO, BENEDICT VINCENT, lawyer; b. Newton, N.J., Sept. 3, 1940; s. Umberto S. and Rose (Cerreta) A.; m. Sally Hennen, June 26, 1971; children: Benedict Vincent, Alexander Morgan. AB, U. Notre Dame, 1962, JD, 1966. Bar: N.J. 1970, N.Y. 1982, D.C. 1983, U.S. Dist. Ct. N.J. 1970, U.S. Supreme Ct. 1981. Assoc., then ptnr. Meyers, Lesser & Aspero, Sparta, N.J., 1971-76; atty. Benedict V. Aspero, Sparta and Morristown, N.J., 1976-82; ptnr. Broderick, Newmark, Grather & Aspero, Morristown, 1982-89, Courter, Kobert, Laufer, Purcell & Cohen, 1989-91; prin. Benedict V. Aspero, Esq., P.C., 1992—. Mem. adv. bd. First Morris Bank. Trustee Harding Twp. Civic Assn., Loyola Retreat House, 1992—99, Craig Sch., 1985—, pres. bd., 1992—2002. Mem. ABA, N.J. Bar Assn., Morris County Bar Assn., Sussex County Bar Assn., Sorin Soc. (bd. govs., sec.), Morristown Club, Essex Hunt Club. Republican. Roman Catholic. Office: 222 Ridgedale Ave PO Box 1573 Morristown NJ 07962-1573 E-mail: bvatty@GTI.net.

ASPEY, FREDERICK MORRIS (FRITZ ASPEY), lawyer; b. Phoenix, Jan. 12, 1947; s. Frederick Morris and Madge (Gieszl) Aspey; children: Tyler Jordan, Matthew Logan. BS. No. Ariz. U., 1969; JD, Ariz. State U., 1972. Bar: Ariz. 1972, U.S. Dist. Ct. Ariz. 1973, U.S. Ct. Appeals (9th cir.) 1974, U.S. Supreme Ct. 1978. Assoc. Law Office J. R. Babbitt, Flagstaff, Ariz., 1972—75; ptnr. Aspey, Watkins & Diesel, Flagstaff, 1975—. Mem. Big Bros., Flagstaff, 1974—; mem. bd. visitors Ariz. State U. Coll. Law, Tempe, 1980—; cert. holder Flagstaff Med. Ctr., 1984—. Mem.: ATLA, ABA, Ariz. Trial Lawyers Assn., Coconino County Bar Assn. (pres. 1980), Ariz. Bar Assn. (mem. adminstrn. com. 1978—82, bd. govs. 1982—92, pres. 1991—92). Democrat. Methodist. Office: Aspey Watkins and Diesel PLLC 123 N San Francisco St Flagstaff AZ 86001-5231

ASPINWALL, DAVID CHARLES, lawyer, insurance company executive; b. Denver, Apr. 15, 1955; s. Darrell David and Gwendolyn Beth (Skeels) Aspinwall; m. Inez Bussey Merritt, Dec. 5, 1981; children: Courney Merritt, Johnathan Westbrook. BA, Denver U., 1977, JD, 1980. Bar: Colo. 1980, U.S. Ct. Appeals (10th cir.), U.S. Supreme Ct. Assoc. Dunn, Crane & Burg, Denver, 1980—81, Michael S. Burg, P.C., Denver, 1981—83, Burg & Aspinwall, P.C., Denver, 1983—88; v.p. counsel, chief compliance officer Gt. West Life & Annuity Ins. Co., Greenwood Village, Colo., 1988—2003; with Legal Adv. Group AHIP, 2003—. Mem. class action working group ACLI, 1995—2000; faculty, life ins. litig. ALIABA; legal adv. com. Employment Retirement Income Security Act, 1998—2001; adv. work group AAHP, 2001—03; instr. in field; legal adv. group Am. Health Ins. Plans, 2003—, adv. group, 2003—. Mem. auction underwriting com. St. Anne's Episc. Sch., 1988—89; pre-marital facilitator Christ Episc. Ch., 1988—94; pres. Sundance Pride, 1987—90. Mem.: Ethics Officers Assn., Internat. Assn. Def. Counsel, Internat. Claims Assn. (law com. 1990—93, panel law com. presentation ann. conv. 1992), Colo. Bar Assn., Def. Rsch. Inst., Arapahoe County Bar Assn., Phi Beta Kappa. Republican. Office: Great West Life & Annuity Ins Co 8525 E Orchard Rd Ste 200 Greenwood Village CO 80111-5097 E-mail: david.aspinwall@gwl.com.

ASPLIN, EDWARD WILLIAM, retired packaging company executive; b. Mpls., June 25, 1922; s. John E. and Alma (Carlbom) A.; m. Eleanor Young Rodgers, Oct. 20, 1951; children— Sarah L., William R., Lynn E. BBA, U. Minn., 1943; postgrad., U. Mich., 1947-48, Wayne State, 1949-50, Rutgers U. Sch. Banking, 1957-59. Cost accountant Nat. Bank Detroit, 1947-50; asst. v.p. adminstrn. Northwest Bancorp., Mpls., 1950-59; v.p. mktg. Northwestern Nat. Bank, Mpls., 1959-67; chmn. Bemis Co., Inc., Mpls., 1967-88. Advisor Opportunity Ptnrs., Inc.; hon. bd. dirs. Mpls. YMCA, Minn. Hist. Soc.; adv. bd. dirs. U. Minn. Cancer Adv. Bd. Mem. Woodhill County Club, Mpls. Club.

ASPNES, DAVID ERIK, physicist, researcher; b. Madison, Wis., May 1, 1939; s. Erik A. and Anita L. (Knabe) A.; m. Edna Joyce Hall, Jan. 27, 1964 (dec. 1996); children: James D., Gary E., Ann K.; m. Cynthia Jean Ball, July 26, 1997. BSEE, U. Wis., 1960, MSEE, 1961; PhD, U. Ill., 1965. Postdoctoral rsch. assoc. U. Ill., Urbana, 1965-66, Brown U., Providence, 1966-67; mem. tech. staff Bell Labs., Murray Hill, N.J., 1967-83; sr. scientist Max-Planck-Inst., Stuttgart, Fed. Republic Germany, 1976-77; dist. mgr. Bellcore, Red Bank, N.J., 1983-92; prof. physics dept. N.C. State U., 1992-99, Disting. Univ. prof. physics, 1999—, Alumni Disting. Grad. prof., 2005. Bd. dirs. Therma-Wave, Inc. Contbr. more than 400 articles to Phys. Rev., Applied Optics, Thin Solid Films and other jours.; U.S. editor Applied Surface Sci., 1996-2001. Recipient Sr. Scientist award Alexander von Humboldt Found., 1976-77, John Yarwood medal Brit. Vacuum Coun., 1993, Max Planck Rsch. Award for Internat. Coop., 1997, Outstanding Rsch. award N.C. State U. Alumni Assn., 1997. Fellow AAAS, Am. Phys. Soc. (councillor divsn. condensed matter physics 1996-99, exec. coun. 1998-99, Frank Isakson prize 1996), Optical Soc. Am. (Wood prize 1987), Am. Vacuum Soc. (chmn. electronic materials and processing divsn. 1982-83, chmn. electronics materials and processing divsn. Internat. Union Vacuum Sci., Techniques and Applications 1986-89, bd. dirs. 1991-92, trustee 2001—03, pres. 2005, Medard W. Welch award 1998), Soc. Photo-Optical Instrumentation Engrs., World Innovation Found.; mem. IEEE, Nat. Acad. Scis., Materials Rsch. Soc., Alexander von Humboldt Assn. Am., Sigma Xi. Mem. Lds Ch. Achievements include discovery and development of reflectance-difference spectroscopy and low-field electroreflectance; development of spectroscopic ellipsometry with applications to process control; contributions to solid-state physics including 3rd derivative interpretation of low-field electroreflectance, ordering of the lower conduction bands of GaAs, elucidation of the kinetics of crystal growth by organometallic chemical vapor deposition, virtual-interface theory, simplified bond-hyperpolarization model of nonlinear optics. Office: NC State U Physics Dept Raleigh NC 27695-8202 Business E-Mail: aspnes@unity.ncsu.edu.

ASRYAN, LEVON V., physicist, electrical engineer, materials scientist; m. Anna V. Sharonova. MSc in Radiophysics and Electronics, Yerevan (Armenia) State U., 1985; PhD in Physics and Math., Ioffe Physico-Technical Inst., St. Petersburg, Russia, 1988, DSc in Phys. and Math. Scis., 2002. Rschr. Physics of Semiconductor Materials and Devices Lab. dept. radiophysics Yerevan State U., 1989—91; sr. rschr. Ioffe Physico-Technical Inst., 1992—2005; rsch. assoc. prof. dept. elec. and computer engring. SUNY, Stony Brook, 2000—04; assoc. prof. dept. materials sci. and engring. Va. Inst. Tech., Blacksburg, 2004—. Reviewer IEEE jours., Piscataway, NJ, 1998—; mem. program com. summer topical workshop on nanostructures and quantum dots IEEE LEOS, San Diego, 1999; presenter in field. Contbr. articles, series of papers to profl. publs. Recipient Best Paper award, IEEE Jour. Quantum Electronics, 2001, State Prize in Sci. and Tech. (with Zhores Alferov), Russia, 2001. Achievements include patents pending for semiconductor laser with reduced temperature sensitivity; first to theory of threshold characteristics of quantum dot lasers. Office: Va Tech Dept MSE 204 Holden Hall MC 0237 Blacksburg VA 24061 Office Phone: 540-231-7033. E-mail: asryan@mse.vt.edu.

ASSAEL, HENRY, marketing educator; b. Sofia, Bulgaria, Sept. 12, 1935; s. Stanley Isaac and Anna (Behar) A.; m. Alyce Friedman, Aug. 19, 1961; children: Shaun Eric, Brenda Erica. BA cum laude, Harvard U., 1957; MBA, U. Pa., 1959; PhD, Columbia U., 1965. Asst. prof. mktg. Sch. Bus. St. John's U., Jamaica, NY, 1962-65; asst. prof. mktg. Hofstra U., Hempstead, NY, 1965-66; prof. mktg. Stern Sch. Bus. NYU, 1966—, chmn. dept., 1979-91. Cons. AT&T, N.Y. Stock Exch., Nestle Co., Inc., CBS. Author: Educational Preparations for Positions in Advertising Management, 1966, The Politics of Distributive Trade Associations: A Study in Conflict Resolution, 1967, Consumer Behavior and Marketing Action, 1981, 6th edit. 1998, Marketing Management: Strategy and Action, 1985, Marketing: Principles and Strategy, 1990, 2d edit., 1993, Marketing: Core Concepts, 1998, Consumer Behavior: A Strategic Approach, 2004; editor: A Century of Marketing, 33 vols., 1978, Early Development and Conceptualization of the Field of Marketing, 1978, History of Advertising, 40 vols., 1985; contbr. numerous articles to profl. jours. Mem. Am. Mktg. Assn., Assn. Consumer Rsch. Office: 44 W 4th St New York NY 10012-1106 Office Phone: 212-998-0514. E-mail: hassael@stern.nyu.edu.

ASSAEL, MICHAEL, lawyer, accountant; b. N.Y.C., July 20, 1949; s. Albert and Helen (Hope) A.; m. Eiko Sato. BA, George Washington U., 1971; MBA., Columbia U. Grad. Sch. Bus., 1973; JD, St. John's Law Sch., 1977. Bar: N.Y. 1978, U.S. Dist. Ct. (so. and ea. dists.) N.Y. 1980, U.S. Supreme Ct. 1982; CPA, N.Y. Tax sr. Price Waterhouse & Co., N.Y.C. and Tokyo, 1977-78; pvt. practice law, N.Y.C., 1978—; pvt. practice acctg., N.Y.C., 1978— . Author: Money Smarts, 1982. Pres. bd. dirs. 200 Block East 74th Street Assn., 1982; bd. dirs. 200 E 74 Owners Corp., 1981—, treas., 1983-84, pres., 1984-85; mem. Yorkville Civic Council, tenant adv. com. Lenox Hill Neighborhood Assn., 1981-82. Recipient N.Y. Habitat/Citibank mgmt. achievement award, 1985. Mem. ABA, N.Y. State Bar Assn., N.Y. County Lawyers Assn., Am. Inst. CPA's, Am. Assn. Atty. CPA's, Inc., Nat. Assn. Accts., N.Y. State Soc. CPA's, Aircraft Owners and Pilots Assn. Clubs: N.Y. Road Runners, Columbia Bus. Sch. (N.Y.).

ASSAF, EUGENE F., lawyer; BA, Dickinson Coll., 1984; MA, U.Essex, U.K., 1987; JD, U. Notre Dame, 1989. Bar: Pa. 1989, D.C. 1992. Law clk. U.S. Ct. Appeals Third Cir., 1989—91; ptnr., mem. firm recruiting com. Kirkland & Ellis LLP, Washington. Office: Kirkland & Ellis LLP 655 Fifteenth St NW Washington DC 20005-5793 Office Phone: 202-879-5196. Office Fax: 202-879-5200. Business E-Mail: eassaf@kirkland.com.

AS-SALEK, JUNAID AMIN, coastal engineer, researcher; arrived in U.S., 2000, permanent resident; s. Akm Aminul and Sitara Haque; m. Syeda Asma Amin Hossain, Nov. 4, 1968; children: Jafina As-Salek, Ahnaf. PhD, Gifu (Japan) U., 1997; BSCE, Bangladesh U. Engring. and Tech., 1988. Registered profl. engr., Tex. Apprentice engr. SARM Associates Ltd., Dhaka, Bangladesh, 1988; asst. engr. Nirman Internat. Ltd., Dhaka, Bangladesh, 1988—89; water resources engr. Hifab Internat. AB, Dhaka, 1989—90; lab-in-charge & modeler Danish Hydraulic Inst., Dhaka, Bangladesh, 1990—91; rsch. scholar Gifu (Japan) U., 1991—97; postdoctoral rschr. Japan Soc. Promotion of Sci., Gifu, 1997—99; postdoctoral rsch. Inoue Found., Gifu, Japan, 1999—2000; poctdoctoral fellow The U.S. Nat. Academies, Ann Arbor, Mich., 2000—01; rsch. assoc. NOAA/ GLERL, Ann Arbor, Mich., 2001—02; postdoctoral fellow Fla. State U., Tallahassee, 2002—03; coastal engr. Fla. Dept. Environ. Protection, Tallahassee, 2003—. Contbr. articles to profl. jours. Recipient Gold medal, Bangladesh Acad. Sci., 2002; fellow, Japan Soc. Promotion of Sci., 1997—98, Inoue Found. Sci., 1999, U.S. Nat. Academies, 2000; scholar, Dhaka Edn. Bd., 1980—82, 1982—88, Japan Ministry Edn. and Culture, 1991—97. Fellow: Engineers Instn. Bangladesh. Avocations: badminton, travel, japanese language & culture, etiquette. Home: 2325 West Pensacola St Apt 162 Tallahassee FL 32304 Office: Department of Environmental Protection 5050 W Tennessee Bldg B Tallahassee FL 32304 Office Phone: 850-413-7820. E-mail: junaid.as-salek@dep.state.fl.us.

ASSELIN, JOHN THOMAS, lawyer; b. Manchester, Conn., May 13, 1951; s. Oliver Joseph and MaryRose Mildred (Dondero) A.; children: Jessica Lynn, Kristina Anne. BA, U. Conn., 1973, JD, 1976. Bar: Conn. 1976, U.S. Dist. Ct. Conn. 1976. Pvt. practice, New London, Conn., 1976—. Lectr. Practicing Law Inst. N.Y., Profl. Edn. Systems Inc. Author: Connecticut Workers' Compensation Practice Manual, The Trial Handbook for Connecticut Lawyers; contbr. articles to profl. jours. Served Conn. gov. Thomas J. Meskill, U.S. Rep. Robert Steele. Grantee Deerfield Found. Mem. ABA (lectr.), Conn. Bar Assn. (exec. com. civil justice sect.), Assn. Trial Lawyers Am., Conn. Trial Lawyers Assn. (bd. govs. 1981—), Phi Beta Kappa, Phi Kappa Phi, Pi Sigma Alpha. Roman Catholic. Avocations: horses, team penning. Office: 190 Governor Winthrop Blvd New London CT 06320-6633 Address: 38 Granite St New London CT 06320

ASSENSOH, AKWASI BRETUO, historian, educator; b. Dunkwa-on-Offin, Ghana, Apr. 1, 1946; s. Opanin Kwabena Assensoh and Abena Amoatemaah; m. Yvette Marie Alex, May 7, 1994; children: Gloria, Philip, Sam, Kwadwo, Livingston Alex; m. Irenita Benbow, 1980 (div. 1993); children: Rose-Abena, Akwasi Bretuo Jr. Diploma in Journalism, advanced diploma in Mass Comm. and Journalism, Sch. Journalism and TV, Frilsham, Eng., 1967; BA in History and Polit. Sci., Dillard U., 1981; MA in History, NYU, 1982, PhD in History, 1984. Sub-editor The Pioneer, Kumasi, Ghana, 1969—70, Monrovia, Liberia, 1970—72; editor-in-chief Daily Listener, Saturday Chronicle, Sunday Digest, 1969—70; mng. editor Internat. Observer Mag., New Orleans, 1980—81; assoc. editor African Commentary Jour., Amherst, Mass., 1990; vis. asst. prof. history Stanford U., Palo Alto, Calif., 1988—89; assoc. editor, dir. rsch. King Papers Project, Stanford U., Palo Alto, Calif., 1989—90; vis. scholar Emory U., Atlanta, 1989—90; assoc. prof. history So. U., Baton Rouge, Ind. U., Bloomington, 1995—2000; contbg. editor West Africa Mag., London, 2003—; prof. history Ind. U., Bloomington, 2002—, dir. grad. studies, 2004—06. Invited lectr. in field; editl. bd. Internat. Abraham Lincoln Jour., 2000—, Jour. 3d World Studies, 1988—, Africa and the World, London, 1987—88. Author: African Military History and Politics: Coups and Ideological Incursions, 1900-Present, 2001, African Political Leadership: A Comparative Study of Jomo Kenyatta, Julius K. Nyerere, and Kwame Nkrumah, 1998, Rev. Dr. Martin Luther King, Jr., and America's Quest for Racial Integration, 1986, Kwame Nkrumah of Africa: His Formative Years and the Shaping of his Nationalism and Pan-Africanism, 1935-1948, 1990, Essays on Contemporary International Topics, 1986, Africa in Retrospect, 1985, An Overview of Political Risk Reporting in Africa: The Liberian Example, 1985, Polygamy in the Ashanti Tribe of Ghana; a Histo-Political Overview, 1984, (historical novel) Black Woman, An African Story, 1980, (3-act play) Campus Life, 1986, Kwame Nkrumah: Six Years in Exile, 1966-1972, 1978; contbr. chapters to books, albums and revs. to profl. jours., mags. and newspapers; participant numerous TV and radio programs, various countries, 1978—99. Assoc. min. 2d Bapt. Ch., Bedford, Ind., 1998—, acting pastor, 1999—; bd. trustees Bethel AME Ch., 1996—97; sec./treas. Rev. Livingston Alex Partnership Found. Fellow NEH, 2000, others; grantee Spencer Found. rsch. conf., 2000; Fulbright-Hays faculty fellow, Asia, 1986. Mem.: PEN, Assn. Third-World Studies (pres. U.S. chpt. 2003—04), Royal African Soc. Gt. Britain and Commonwealth, Internat. Fedn. Journalists, Am.-Scandinavian Found. N.Y., African Studies Assn., Nat. Geographic Soc. Am., So. Hist. Assn., Am. Hist. Assn., Smithsonian Instn. (assoc.), NYU Alumni Assn., Dillard U. Nat. Alumni Assn. (life), Press Club of New Orleans, Rosicrucians, Masons, Alpha Phi Alpha. Baptist. Office: Indiana U Box 1933 Bloomington IN 47402 Business E-Mail: aassenso@indiana.edu.

ASSETTO, HENRY JOHN, secondary school educator; b. Coatesville, Pa., Nov. 2, 1946; s. Anthony and Elena Sarah (Catanese) A.; m. Angelina Carmela Mariniello, June 15, 1974; children: Lena Maria, Anthony Vincent, Rita Ann, Philip Henry, Michael Joseph. BA in Comprehensive Social Scis., West Chester (Pa.) U., 1968; MA in History, Pa. State U., 1975. Cert. comprehensive social scis. tchr., Pa. Tchr. world geography Harrisburg (Pa.) City Sch. Dist., 1968-69; tchr. Am. history Coatesville Area Sch. Dist., 1969—, coord. K-12 social studies, 1989—. Bd. dirs. Pa. Coun. Social Studies. Mem. Coatesville Civil Svc. Commn., 1985. Mem. NEA, Nat. Coun. Social Studies Suprs. Assn. (mem. instrn. com. 1994-97), Pa. Edn. Assn., Coatesville Area Edn. Assn., Holy Name Soc., Sons Italy in Am., Malvern Laymans Retreat League (recruiter), KC (4th degree, sec.). Republican. Roman Catholic. Avocations: reading, travel, gardening, cooking. Home: 4 Red Oak Dr Coatesville PA 19320-1260 Office: Gordon Mid Sch 351 Kersey St Coatesville PA 19320-3469

ASSINK, NELLIE GRACE, agricultural executive; b. Yakima, Wash., July 5, 1920; d. Martin Gilde and Grace Byl; m. George H. Assink, July 9, 1943 (dec. Nov. 1982); children: Macile Assink Zais, Jon Martin. BA, tchr.'s diploma in music and piano, Whitman Coll./Conserv. Music, 1942; postgrad., U. Wash. and Cen. Coll., 1944, 59. Gen. cert., Wash.; cert. supr. music. English tchr., libr. Mabton (Wash.) H.S., 1943-45; libr. Wide Hollow Sch., Yakima, 1948-49; English tchr., libr. Lower Naches (Wash.) Sch., 1960-80; pres. Assink Acres, Inc., Naches, 1982—. Ch. organist Meml. Bible Ch., Yakima, 1946-82; chmn. Christian Edn. Bd., 1981-82; bd. dirs., sec. Yakima County Farm Bur., 1985-99; libr. Meml. Bible Ch., Yakima, 1960—. Mem. Naches Union Irrigation Dist. (sec. 1993—), Yakima County Farm Bur. (past sec. 1997), Lower Naches Women's Club (pres. 1984-86, 2000-02), Yakima Music Club, Ch. Librs.-N.W. (past pres.). Republican. Avocations: genealogy, photography, classical piano. Home: 681 N Gleed Rd Naches WA 98937 Office: Assink Acres Inc 681 N Gleed Rd Naches WA 98937

ASSOUSA, GEORGE ELIAS, information technology executive, physicist, corporate executive; b. Jerusalem, Mar. 15, 1936; emigrated to U.S., 1953, naturalized, 1965; s. Elias Theodore and Virginia George (Saboura) A.; divorced; children: Mark Andrew, Virginia Noel. BA, Earlham Coll., 1957; postgrad. (Rockefeller Bros. fellow), Union Theol. Sem., 1957-58; MA, Columbia U., 1960; PhD (Nuclear Sci. fellow, Grad. fellow), Fla. State U., 1968. Mem. faculty Earlham Coll., Richmond, Ind., 1960-63; research asst., instr. nuclear physics Fla. State U., Tallahassee, 1963-68; fellow Carnegie Instn. of Washington, 1968-70, research prof., mem. sci. staff, 1970-80, sr. fellow, 1980-81; chief sci. and tech. advisor Coats Viyella, PLC, London, 1987—; chmn. Coats Viyella Techs., Ltd., London, 1987—, Mulit-Techs. Group, London, 2005—. Sci. and ednl. affairs v.p. Ideas, Inc., Washington, 1974-75; cons. Princeton U. Obs., 1971-72; cons. on Mid-East sci. Nat. Acad. Scis., 1975; advisor sci. and tech. policy to Crown Prince Hassan of Jordan, 1976-78; cons. N.J. Marine Scis. Consortium, 1980-87; Presdl. fellow, fellow program in sci., tech. and humanism Aspen Inst. for Humanistic Studies, 1978-80 Contbr.: articles in field to Phys. Rev.; co-discoverer supernova induced star formation, 1977. Co-founder, pres. Found. for Arab-Israeli Reconciliation, Washington, 1974-77, co-chmn. bd., 1977-78; founder, dir. Salzburg Internat. Affairs Seminar, 1979—; dir.-gen. Trust for Internat. Devel. and Edn., London, 1980—; pres. Partnership for Internat. Devel., Inc., Washington, 1981-86; vice chmn. Internat. Scholars for Environ. Studies Inc., 1987—; pres. Gryphon Tech. Investors, 1987-88. Mem. Internat. Astron. Union, Am. Astron. Soc., AAUP, Am. Phys. Soc., Council Fgn. Relations, Royal Inst. Internat. Affairs (assoc.), Sigma Xi. Clubs: Cosmos (Washington); Athenaeum (London). Office: Multi Techs Group 15 Straton St Mayfair London W1J 8LQ England Office Phone: 44 20 7659 6269. Office Fax: 44 20 7659 0430.

AST, BRUNO, architecture educator; b. Yugoslavia, 1949; arrived in came to the U.S., 1955; MArch, U. Ill. Faculty mem. U. Chgo., 1969; co-owner Ast and Dagdelen Archs., Chgo.; assoc. dean, assoc. prof. Sch. Arch. U. Ill., Chgo. Office: Ast & Dagdelen 1756 N Sedgwick St Chicago IL 60614 also: Univ Ill Chgo Sch Arch Dept Code 2-2405 306B JH MC 033 845 W Harrison Chicago IL 60607-7024

ASTE, MARIO ANDREA, foreign language educator; b. Carloforte, Italy, Jan. 11, 1943; came to U.S., 1966; s. Stefano and Francesca A.; m. Dorothy Elaine Balbirer, June 6, 1970; children: Stephen Robert, Marie Francesca, Kristina Elizabeth. BSEE, Tech. Inst., Cagliar, Italy, 1963; BA in Philosophy, Philos. Inst., Torino, Italy, 1966; MA in Italian, Cath. U. Am., 1969, PhD, 1971, MA in Spanish, 1978. Prof., chmn. langs. U. Mass., Lowell, 1971—2003. Bd. dirs. Internat. Inst., Lowell, pres., 1980—99. Author: La Narrativa Di Luigi Pirandello, 1979, Two Novels of Pirandello: An Essay, 1979, Grazia Deledda: Ethnic Novelist, 1989, They Came in Hope, 1995; editor: Technology Industry Labor and the Italian American Communities, 1997, Greece and Italy: Ancient Roots New Beginnings, 2003. Housing rev. bd. City of Lowell, 1981-84; pastoral fin. coun. St. Michael Parish, Lowell, 1987—. Teaching fellow Cath. U. Am., Washington, 1967; NEH grantee Stanford U., 1979, Princeton U., 1983, Cath. U., 1988. Mem. MLA (chair exec. com. 20th century Italian lit. divsn. 1996-97), Am. Assn. Tchrs. Italian (exec. bd. 2000—), Am. Assn. Italian Studies (jour. editor 1989-98, mng. editor 1998-2001), Am. Italian Hist. Assn. (exec. bd. 1992—, treas. 1997-99, pres. 2000-02), Mass. Soc. Prof. (pres. 1988-2003), N.E. Modern Lang. Assn. (exec. bd. 1998—2002, exec. bd. for Italian and Spanish 2000—), K.C. Democrat. Roman Catholic. Avocations: Lowell folk life festivals, soccer, scouting. Home: 115 Reservoir St Lowell MA 01850-2244 Office: U Mass 1 University Ave Lowell MA 01854-5009

ASTER, RICHARD (RICK) F., JR., diversified financial services company executive; b. Calif., 1949; BS with hons. in Econs., MS with hons. in Econs., U. Calif., Santa Barbara, Calif. Analyst West Coast Newburger, Loeb & Co., 1970—72; analyst Robertson, Colman, Siebel & Weisel, 1972—77; founder Aster Investment Mgmt. Inc., Larkspur, Calif., 1977—. Office: Aster Investment Management Inc 60 East Sir Francis Drake Blvd Ste 306 Larkspur CA 94939

ASTIGARRAGA, JOSE I(GNACIO), lawyer; b. Havana, Cuba, July 20, 1953; came to U.S., 1960, naturalized 1974; AA with honors, Miami Dade Community Coll., 1973; BBA summa cum laude, U. Miami, 1975; JD magna cum laude, 1978. Bar: Fla. 1978, U.S. Dist. Ct. (so. dist.) Fla. 1979, U.S. Dist. Ct. (mid. dist.) 1988, U.S. Ct. Appeals (5th and 11th cir.) 1981, U.S. Supreme Ct. 1990. Chief bailiff Dade County Juvenile and Family Ct., Miami, Fla., 1972-74; law clk.-bailiff 11th Jud. Cir., Miami, 1974-77; with firm Steel, Hector & Davis, Miami, 1978-84, ptnr., 1984—; adj. faculty U. Miami Sch. Law, Coral Gables, Fla., 1980-81; cons. World Bank; mem. U.S. del. Org. Am. States 6th Conf. on pvt. internat. law; Little Havana Activities and Nutrition Ctrs. of Dade County, Inc., 1987-94, NAFTA adv. comm. on the resolution of private commercial disputes, 1994-96; mem. panel arbitrators Comml. Arbitration and Mediation Ctr. for Ams., 1996; founder Latin Am. users coun. London Ct. Internat. Arbitration. Co-author: Secured Lenders Beware: Particular Issues Affecting Secured Lenders, 1993; adminstrv. hearing officer Dade County Sch. Bd., Miami, 1982-90; bd. dirs. Miami Children's Hosp., 1985-88, also chmn. quality assurance com., mem. fin. com.; bd. dirs. Miami Children's Hosp. Rsch. Inst., Inc., 1986-87, chmn. nominating com.; bd. dirs. Dade County Beacon Coun. Inc., 1985-95, Miami Coalition, Inc., 1988-94; mem. exec. com., chmn. schs. task force, 1988-90; trustee Fla. Internat. U. Found., 1988—. Named Harvey T. Reid scholar U. Miami Sch. Law, 1975-78, Leonard T. Abess scholar, U. Miami, 1974-75; recipient Up and Comers Law award Price Waterhouse and South Fla. Bus. Jour., 1988. Mem. ABA (com. on comml. fin. svcs., Uniform Comml. Code com., com. bus. bankruptcy 1990—, Internat. Bar Assn. (com. arbitration, insolvency), Am. Arbitration Assn. (panel on commercial fin. disputes 1994—), Am. Law Inst. (adv. transnat. insolvency project 1997), Fla. Bar Assn. (bus. law sect., sec. civil procedure rules com. 1979-84, bankruptcy UCC com. 1992—, lectr. bankruptcy seminar 1993, 94), Dade County Bar Assn. (commr. jud. campaign practices commn. 1986-87), Cuban-Am. Bar Assn., Bankruptcy Bar Assn. (v.p. 1992-94), U. Miami Sch. Law Alumni Assn. (bd. dirs. 1981-88), Greater Miami C. of C. (bd. govs. 1985-86, group chmn. econ. devel. sect. 1986-87). Office: Astigarraga Davis 16th Fl 701 Brickell Ave Miami FL 33131

ASTIN, SEAN PATRICK, actor, film director, film producer, writer; b. Santa Monica, Calif, Feb. 25, 1971; s. Michael Tell and Patty Duke, John Astin; m. Christine Louise Astin, July 11, 1992; children: Alexandra Louise, Elizabeth Louise, Isabella Louise. BA in History and English with honors, UCLA. Actor: (films) The Goonies, 1985 (Young Artist award, 1986), White Water Summer, 1987, Like Father, Like Son, 1987, Staying Together, 1989 (Young Artist award, 1990), The War of the Roses, 1989, Memphis Belle, 1990, Toy Soldiers, 1991, The Willies, 1991, Encino Man, 1992, Where the Day Takes You, 1992, Rudy, 1993, Safe Passage, 1994, The Low Life, 1995 (Pres. award Ft. Lauderdale Internat. Film Festival, 1995), Courage Under Fire, 1996, Bulworth, 1998, Boy Meets Girl, 1998, Kimberly, 1999, Deterrance, 1999, Icebreaker, 1999, The Last Producer, 2000, Dish Dogs, 2000, The Sky is Falling, 2000, The Lord of the Rings: The Fellowship of the Ring, 2001, The Lord of the Rings: The Two Towers, 2002 (Visual Effects Soc. award, 2003), The Lord of the Rings: Return of the Kings, 2003 (Best Supporting Actor award, Seattle Film Critics Soc., Best Supporting Actor award, Las Vegas Film Critics Soc.), 50 First Dates, 2004, Elvis Has Left the Building, 2004, (voice only) Balto III: Wings of Change, 2004, Smile, 2004, Slipstream, 2004, Bigger Than the Sky, 2004, Marilyn Hotchkiss' Ballroom Dancing and Charm School, 2005; (TV films) Please Don't Hit Me Mom, 1981, The Rules of Marriage, 1982, The B.R.A.T. Patrol, 1986, Harrison Bergeron, 1995; (TV series) Jeremiah, 2003—, (voice) Party Wagon, 2004,: (TV miniseries) Hercules, 2005, Into the West, 2005; dir.(producer): (short films) On My Honor, 1988; co-dir.(producer): Kangaroo Court, 1994 (nominated Acad. award Best Live Action Short, 1995); dir.(producer, writer): The Long and Short of It, 2003,: (TV films) Perversions of Science, 1997, Nickelodeon's 100 Good Deeds for Eddie McDowd; (TV series) Angel, Jeremiah; author (with Joe Layden): There and Back Again: An Actor's Tale, 2004. Active Pres.'s Coun. Svc. and Civic Participation. Mem.: Am. Fedn. Television and Radio Artists, Screen Actors Guild, Dirs. Guild Am.*

ASTLEY, AMY, editor-in-chief; married; 2 children. BA, Mich. State U., 1989. Editl. asst. House and Garden mag., asst. editor, assoc. editor; beauty assoc. Vogue mag., 1993—94, beauty dir., 1994—2005; editor-in-chief Teen Vogue, 2005—. Office: Teen Vogue 4 Times Sq New York NY 10036*

ASTMAN, BARBARA ANN, artist, educator; b. Rochester, NY, July 12, 1950; d. George William and Bertha Dinah (Meisel) A.; m. Noel Robert Harding, Feb. 23, 1977 (div. 1983); m. Joseph Anthony Baker, Aug. 29, 1984; children: Amy Astman Baker, Laura Astman Baker. A degree, RIT, 1970; grad., Ont. Coll. Art, Toronto, 1973. Prof photography dept. Ont. Coll. Art and Design (formerly Ont. Coll. Art), Toronto, 1975—; faculty York U., Toronto, 1978-80, 86. Lectr. in field. One-woman shows include Baldwin St. Gallery Photography, Toronto, 1973, Ryerson Photo Gallery, Toronto, 1974, Nat. Film Bd. Can., Ottawa, 1975, S.A.W. Gallery Inc., 1976, Sable-Castelli Gallery Ltd., Toronto, 1977, 79-84, 86, 88, 90, Jean Marie Antone Gallery, Annapolis, Md., 1979, Whitewater Gallery, North Bay, Ont., Bruce Art Gallery, Canton, NY, 1980, Mendel Art Gallery, Saskatoon, Sask., 1981, So. Alta. Art Gallery, Edmonton, 1981, Art Gallery Peterborough, Ont., 1982, Galerie du Musee, Musee du Quebec, 1986, Ctr. d'Animation et de Diffusion de la Photographie, Quebec, 1986, Thunder Bay Art Gallery, Ont., 1992, Robert McLaughlin Gallery, Oshawa, Ont., 1993, McIntosh Gallery, London, Ont., 1994, Gallery Stratford, Ont., 1994, Art Gallery of Hamilton, 1995, Edmonton Art Gallery, Kamloops Art Gallery, B.C., 1996-2005, Jane Corkin Gallery (now Corkin Shopland Gallery), 1997, 99, 2001, 03, 05, Art Gallery of Windsor, 2004, Yukon Art Ctr., Whitehorse, Yukon, 2005; group exhbns. include Lamkin Camerawork Gallery, San Francisco, 1975, Art Gallery Ont., Toronto, 1975, 80, 84, 93, Rochester (NY) Meml. Art Gallery, Montreal Mus. Fine Arts, 1975, Harbourfront Art Gallery, Toronto, 1977, 80, Sable-Castelli Gallery Ltd., 77, 81, Anna Leonowens Gallery, Halifax, N.S., 1977, London (Ont.) Regional Art Gallery, 1978, 83, Edmonton (Ont.) Art Gallery, 1978, Winnipeg Art Gallery, 1979, Everson Mus., Syracuse, NY, 1979, Galerie Luca Polazzoli, Milan, 1979, H.F. Johnson Mus. Art, Ithaca, NY, 1979, George Eastman House, Rochester, 1979, Hamilton Art Gallery, La Galerie Powerhouse, Montreal, 1981, YYZ Gallery Toronto, 1982, Forum des Halles, Paris, 1985, Graves Art Gallery, Sheffield, U.K., 1985, San Diego Art Ctr., 1986, Hallwalls Gallery, Buffalo, 1986, La Galerie des Arts Lavalin, Montreal, 1988, Pro Mus. Contemporary Art, Finland, 1988, Kamloops Art Gallery, 1989, Koffler Gallery, Toronto, 1990, Art Gallery of Peterborough, Ont., 1992, Art Gallery of Hamilton, 1993, So. Alta. Art Gallery, Lethbridge, 1994; Art Gallery Hamilton, Gallerie Arts Tech., Montreal, Basel Art Fair, Switzerland, 1998-2003, Basel Art, Miami, 2002-03, Chgo. Art Fair, 1999, Nat. Gallery Can., Ottawa, 2000, Can. Mus. Contemporary Art, North York, Ont., 2000, Can. Mus. Contemporary Photography, Ottawa, 2000-01, Nat. Gallery Can., Ottawa, Art Gallery Hamilton, 2001, Kitchener-Waterloo Art Gallery, Ont., 2001, Art Basel, 2002-2005, Basel Art Fair, 2002-2005, Toronto Photgraphers Workshop, 2002, Confedn. Art Ctr. Art Gallery, Prince Edward Island, 2003, Art Gallery of Bishop's U., Que., 2003, McMichael Gallery, Kleinburg, Ont, 2004; public collections include Agnes Etherington Art Ctr., Kingston, Ont., Art Gallery Hamilton, Art Gallery Ont., Toronto, Bibliotheque Nationale, Paris, Gallery/Stratford, Nickle Arts Mus., Calgary, Alta., Robert McLaughlin Gallery, Oshawa, Winnipeg Art Gallery, Victoria and Albert Mus., London Coord. Colour Xerox Artists' Program, Visual Arts Ont., Toronto, 1977-83; bd. dirs. Art Gallery at Harbourfront, Toronto, 1983-85; apptd. mem. City of Toronto Pub. Art Commn., 1986-89; mem. curatorial team WaterWorks Exhbn., Toronto, 1988; chmn. Toronto Arts Awards, Visual Arts Jury, 1988; bd. dirs. Arts Found. of Greater Toronto, 1989-92. Mem.: Royal Can. Acad. Arts. Office: 23 Alcina Ave Toronto ON Canada M6G 2E7 Address: Corkin/Shopland Gallery 55 Mill St Bldg 61 Toronto ON Canada M5A 3C4 E-mail: astmanba@aol.com.

ASTON, SHERRELL JERONE, plastic surgeon, educator; b. Nansemono County, Va., July 14, 1942; s. Walter Mathew, Jr. and Mary Louise (Bracy) A.; B.A., U. Va., 1964, M.D., 1968; m. Michelle Sykes, Nov. 24, 1967 (dec. July 1995); children: Walter Mathew III, Sherrell Jerone, Bradford Sykes; m. Miriam (Muffie) Isabelle Potter, Dec. 27, 1996. Intern, UCLA, 1968-69, resident, chief resident in surgery, 1969-73; Halsted fellow Johns Hopkins Hosp., 1971; resident, chief resident in plastic surgery NYU, 1973-75; chief plastic surgery service Manhattan VA Hosp., 1975-79; assoc. prof. plastic surgery NYU Med. Center, 1977-93, prof. surgery, 1993—; attending surgeon Inst. Reconstructive Plastic Surgery, NYU Med. Center; chmn. dept. plastic surgery, chmn. plastic surgery dept. Manhattan Eye, Ear and Throat Hosp., Bellevue Hosp. Diplomate Am. Bd. Surgery, Am. Bd. Plastic Surgery. Fellow ACS, N.Y. Acad. Medicine, Am. Soc. Plastic and Reconstructive Surgery; mem. N.Y. State, N.Y. County med. socs., Soc. Academic Surgeons, Pan Am. Med. Assn., Brazilian Plastic Surgery Soc., Am. Soc. for Aesthetic Plastic Surgery (pres. 1993-94), Am. Assn. for Accreditation Ambulatory Plastic Surgery Facilities (founding mem., dir. 1980), Am. Assn. Plastic Surgeons. Author numerous surg. publs. Office: 728 Park Ave New York NY 10021-4945

ASTOR, BROOKE, foundation administrator, philanthropist, writer; b. Portsmouth, N.H. d. John Henry and Mabel (Howard) Russell; m. Vincent Astor. LLD (hon.), Columbia U., 1971, Brown U., 1980; LHD (hon.), Fordham U., 1980, NYU, 1986; PhD in Biomed. Sci. (honoris causa), Rockefeller U., 1986. Pres., trustee Astor Home for Children; trustee Hist. Hudson Valley, Marconi Internat. Fellowship; trustee and hon. chmn., mem. devel. com., mem. exec. com. N.Y. Pub. Libr., N.Y.C.; life trustee, mem. conservation com. N.Y. Zool. Soc.; trustee emeritus, mem. coun. of fellows Pierpont Morgan Libr. Trustee emeritus, chmn. vis. com. dept. Asian art, mem. acquisitions com., exec. com. ex officio Met. Mus. Art, N.Y.C.; life trustee Rockefeller U. Author: Patchwork Child, 1962, rev. edit., 1993, The Bluebird Is at Home, 1965, Footprints, 1980, The Last Blossom on the Plum Tree, 1986; feature editor: House and Garden, 1946-56, cons. editor, 1956-93. Mem. N.Y. State Pk. Commn., 1967-69. Decorated dame Venerable Order of St. John of Jerusalem; recipient Anniversary medal Astor, Lenox and Tilden Founds. of N.Y. Pub. Libr., 1961, award Sisters of Good Shepherd and Children of Madonna Heights Sch. for Girls, 1963, Client Award cert. N.Y. State Assn. Architects, 1964, award Pk. Assn. N.Y.C. Inc., 1965, Honor award HUD, 1966, cert. of appreciation City of N.Y., 1967, Albert S. Bard Merit award City Club N.Y., 1967, Award of Honor, Women's Aux. N.Y. chpt. AIA, 1968, Rector's award St. Phillip's Ch., 1968, Michael Friedsam medal Archtl. League N.Y., 1968, award Brotherhood-In-Action, Inc., 1968, Outstanding Contbn. award Am. Soc. Landscape Architects, 1968, Spirit of Achievement award Albert Einstein Coll. Medicine, Yeshiva U., 1969, Good Samaritan award P. Ballentine & Sons, 1969, Good Samaritan award Prospect Block Civic Assn., 1969, Disting. Svc. award N.Y. region Rotary, 1970, YWCA honor, 1970, Housing award N.Y. Met. chpt. Nat. Assn. Housing and Redevel. Officials, 1971, $24 award Mus. City of N.Y., award N.Y. Pub. Libr., 1972, Albert Gallatin medal NYU, 1972, spl. citation AIA, 1973, Medal of Merit award Lotos Club, 1973, commendation Neighborhood Com. for the Asphalt Green, 1975, commendation ARCS Found., 1976, Pres.'s medal Mcpl. Art Soc. N.Y., 1976, Gold Medal award N.Y. Zool. Soc., 1978, Elizabeth Seton Humanitarian award N.Y. Foundling Hosp., 1978, Little Apple award Met. Mus. Art, Little Apple award Morgan Library, Little Apple award N.Y. Public Library, Little Apple award N.Y. Zool. Soc., Little Apple award Rockefeller U., Little Apple award South St. Seaport and Sta. WNET-TV/Channel 13, 1978, New Yorker for N.Y. award Citizens Com. for N.Y.C., 1980, 1st Myer Myers Cultural award City of N.Y., award Citizens Housing and Planning Coun., 1980, Bishop's Cross, Diocese of N.Y., 1980, Forsythia award Bklyn. Bot. Garden, 1981, award Pks. Coun., 1981, Woman of Conscience award Appeal of Conscience Found., 1981, commendation Lower Manhattan Cultural Coun., 1984, Disting. New Yorkers award Bowery Savs. Bank, 1984, Gov.'s Arts award State of N.Y., 1985, Am. Acad. and Inst. Arts and Letters award, 1986, Marconi Internat. Fellowship Coun. award, 1986, landmark plaque and medallion N.Y. Landmarks Preservation Found., 1987, Gold medal St. Nicholas Soc., N.Y.C., 1987, Fashion Industry award Coun. of Fashion Designers Am., 1988, Presdl. Citizen's medal Pres. Reagan, 1988, Nat. Medal of Arts, Nat. Endowment for the Arts, 1988, World Monuments Fund The Hadrian award, 1991, annual humanitarian award ARC of Greater N.Y., 1993, Eleanor Roosevelt medallion City of N.Y., 1993, 8th Annual Town & Country Most Generous American award, The Hearst Corp. and Hearst Mags., 1993, The Mayor's award of Honor and Culture, City of N.Y., 1993, 10th Annual Humanitarian award N.Y., 1993, Richard Rodgers award for Disting. Svc., Profl. Children's Sch., 1994, Scroll of Honor, N.Y. coun. Navy League of U.S., 1994; Brooke Astor Day proclaimed by Mayor of N.Y.C., March 5, 1992. Fellow Am. Acad. Arts and Scis.; mem. Mcpl. Art Soc. N.Y., Pilgrims U.S., Venerable Order St. John of Jerusalem (dame), The Century Assn., Colony Club, Knickerbocker Club, N.Y. Yacht Club, Sleepy Hollow Country Club.

ASTOR, DAVID WARREN, journalist; b. Bronx, Mar. 29, 1954; s. Harold Milton and Thelma (Oppenberg) A.; m. Laurel Cummins, May 15, 2004; 1 child from previous marriage, Maggie Elizabeth. BA in English, Rutgers U., 1976; MS in Journalism, Northwestern U., 1978. Rutgers corres. New York Times, N.Y.C., 1974-76; reporter Red Bank Register, Shrewsbury, N.J., 1976-77, Passaic (N.J.) Herald-News, 1978; assoc. editor, sr. editor Mktg. Communications Mag., N.Y.C., 1978-83; sr. editor Editor & Pub. Mag., N.Y.C., 1983—; freelance humor columnist Montclair (N.J.) Times, 2003—. Avocations: reading, guitar-playing, bicycling, cartooning. Office: Editor and Publisher 770 Broadway New York NY 10003-9595 E-mail: dastor@editorandpublisher.com.

ASTORGA, ALICIA MARGARITA, retired librarian; b. Havana, Cuba, Feb. 22, 1947; d. Rene Andres and Alicia C. Albacete; m. Maurice Astorga, June 24, 1967; children: Leslie Ann, Maurice Michael. BA, Corpus Christi State U., 1976; MLS, Drexel U., Phila., 1980; cert. webmaster, U. Del., 1998. Sch. libr. Pa., Del., Tex. Libr. Internat. Reading Assn., Newark, Del., 1981-82; head libr. Incarnate Word Acad., Corpus Christi, Tex., 1983-86; dir. librs. Ursuline Acad., Wilmington, Del., 1987—98; head libr. Unionville HS, Kenneth Square, Pa., 1998—2000; ret., 2000; owner Miramar Web Design and Cons., 1998—. DuPont Co. grantee, 1991. Mem.: ALA, Beta Phi Mu.

ASTRE, PATRICK PAUL, financial planner, writer; b. Audenge, France, Nov. 26, 1945; arrived in U.S., 1955; s. Jacques and Yvette Astre; m. Marilyn E. Astrauscas, May 28, 1964; children: Paul L., Michelle L. Heil. B, U.S. Armed Forces Inst., 1967. CFP, registered fin. cons. Prin. Astre Planning Inc., Shoreham, NY, 1984—. Author: Four Seasons of Money, 2000, (novels) Sylvans, 2002, The Last Operation, 2003, The Artifact, 2004 (Salvo Press award). Sgt. U.S. Army, 1964—67. Mem.: Nat. Spkrs. Assn., Toastmasters Internat. Roman Catholic. Avocations: writing, running, public speaking. Home: 27 Wading River Hollow Rd Ridge NY 11961 Office: Astre Planning Inc Box 480 Shoreham Plz Shoreham NY 11786 Office Phone: 631-744-9100. Fax: 631-209-0066. E-mail: patrick_ast@msn.com.

ASTRIAB, STEVEN MICHAEL, military officer; b. Pitts., Mar. 10, 1952; s. Steven Leonard and Anna (Popivchak) Astriab; m. BettyLou Elaine Gimmi, Dec. 27, 1975. BA in Psychology, Washington and Jefferson Coll., 1974; MSW in Manpower Planning, W.Va. U., 1976; grad., Commd. & Gen. Staff Coll., 1985. Commd. 2d lt. U.S. Army, 1974, advanced through grades to lt. col., 1992; div. social work officer 1st Cav. Div., Ft. Hood, Tex., 1976-77, med. platoon leader, then med. co. comdr. 15th med. bn., 1977-79; med. ops. officer 1st Cav. Div. Hdqs., Ft. Hood, Tex., 1979-81; chief M.C. procurement Office Army Surgeon Gen., Washington, 1982-85; chief combat medicine Office Project Mgr. Saudi Arabian Nat. Guard, Riyadh, 1985-88; pers. officer 62 Med. Group, Ft. Lewis, Wash., 1988-90; asst. chief staff for med. civil and mil. ops. 3d U.S. Army (Army Cen. Command), Riyadh, 1990-91; med. ops. officer Hdqrs. I Corps, Ft. Lewis, 1991-93; chief med. plans for S.W. Asia Hdqs. 3d U.S. Army, Atlanta, 1993-95, chief coalition integration for S.W. Asia, 1995-96; chief med. plans and intelligence S.W. Asia Hdqrs. 3d U.S. Army, 1996; sr. med. and fgn. mil. sales advisor U.S. Mil. Tng. Mission for Saudi Arabia, Riyadh, 1996-98; chief of ops. Divsn., exec. officer Pacific Regional Med. Command, 1998-2000; dep. surgeon U.S. Army Pacific, 2000—01, ret., 2001; project mgr. Eagle Group Internat. Ltd., Kosovo, 2001—03; proposal coord., mgr. Eagle Group Internat., Inc., Atlanta, 2003, tech. writer 9/11 project, 2003—; project mgr. emergency exercise program Ga. DPH, 2003. Assoc. faculty Ctr. Excellence Disaster Mgmt. and Humanitarian Assistance, 1999—. Author: Vendetta: Military Med. Peace Operations in Kosovo, 2003. Decorated Legion of Merit, Bronze Star, Def. Meritorious Svc. medal, Meritorious Svc. medal (7), Army Commendation medal (2), Joint Meritorious Unit award, Nat. Def. Svc. medal (2), S.W. Asia Campaign medal (3), Armed Forces Expeditionary medal, Liberation of Kuwait medal Army Ranger, Parachutist, Saudi Arabia, Kuwait. Mem.: Order Mil. Med. Merit. Republican. Baptist. Avocations: running, weight training, computer applications, Islamism research. Personal E-mail: sastriab@comcast.net.

ASTRUP, JENS LEO, retired civil engineer; b. Plentywood, Mont., Sept. 21, 1934; s. Jens Legend and Dagmar (Jensen) Astrup; m. Susanne Elizabeth Laime, Nov. 25, 1967 (div. Nov. 1985); children: Moriah Ann, Jens Aaron. BS, N.D. State U., 1956; MBA, Keller Grad. Sch. Mgmt., 1983. Registered profl. engr., Ill.; patent agt. Civil engr. City of Chgo. Dept. Urban Renewal, 1964—65, Harza Engring. Co., 1965—69; city engr. City of Williston, ND, 1969—70; civil and resident engr. Bauer Engring., Inc., Chgo., 1970—71; civil and structural sr. engr. Brown and Root, Inc., 1971—82; project engr. Lester B. Knight & Assocs., 1983—85, Comstock Engring., Inc., Oak Brook, 1985—86; sr. civil engr. Allen Engring. Co., Villa Park, 1986—88; project engr. Globetrotters Engring. Corp., Chgo., 1988—92; sr. civil engr. Clark Dietz, Inc., 1993—94. Mem.: ASCE, Am. Pub. Works Assn. N.D. (past state sec. 1969—70), Ill. Soc. Profl. Engrs. (state v.p. 1979—80, chmn. state activities com. 1976—77, chpt. pres. 1977—78). Lutheran. Home: 1117 Briarbrook Dr Wheaton IL 60187-8657 Personal E-mail: leoa2@juno.com.

ASTUCCIO, SHEILA MARGARET, educational administrator; b. Biddeford, Maine, Apr. 24, 1943; d. James T. III and Margaret H. (Cameron) Rollinson; m. Joseph Kevin Astuccio, Aug. 22, 1976 (dec. Apr. 1992); children: James M., Sheila E. BS in Edn., Salem (Mass.) State Coll., 1968, MEd, 1975; cert. advanced grad. studies, Lesley Coll., Cambridge, Mass., 1983. Cert. elem. tchr. and prin., supr., dir., Mass.; cert. instrnl. tech. grades K-12. Elem. educator Hood Elem. Sch., Lynn, Mass., 1968-79; tchr. grades 3 and 4 Lynn (Mass.) Pub. Schs., comp. coord., facilitator, 1981-84, tchr. academically talented, 1979-81, 84-85, computer program specialist, 1986-87, computer implementation team leader, MIS dir., 1987-98; adminstr. IS/MIS, 1998—; owner operator Pilot Imaging Computer Imaging, Lynn, Mass., 1991-92. Tchr. adult edn. North Shore C.C., 1982-87; part-time real estate broker, 1979—; part-time mktg. cons. IDN, 1993-95; presenter Beijing Dist. Edn. Bur., 2001; presenter in field. Mem. Chpt. II adv. coun., 1979-83; nat. grad. alumni rep. Lesley Coll., 1984-85; chair Mayor's Computer Adv. Com., 1985-86; participant Educators in Industry GE/Salem State Coll., 1983; People to People Amb. to China, 2000, 2001; sec.-gen. United Cultural Convention, 2001—. Recipient Educators in Industry cert., 1983, Novell Netware Adminstr. and Sys. Installation/Configuration certs., 1994-95, Letters of Commendation Mass. Dept. Edn., 2000, 2001. Mem. ASCD, AAUW, NAFE, NSBA, DECUS, PEI Nat. Users Group, New Eng. Pentamation Users Group, Boston Computer Soc. Office: Data Ctr LVTI 80 Neptune Blvd Lynn MA 01902-4570 Office Phone: 781-595-5794. Personal E-mail: astuccio@comcast.net. Business E-Mail: astuccios@lynnschools.org.

ASTUDILLO-PATINO, MARIBEL, recording industry executive, singer; b. New York, July 24, 1979; d. Julieta and Edgar Calderon (Stepfather), Carmen Elvira Patino and Mario Astudillo; life ptnr. Geovani R. Marichal. Pres. Ind. Label, New York, NY, 2001—; prodr. Porcelana Prodn., New York, NY, 2001—. Author (contributing poet): Silence (Internat. Soc. of Poets, 1995), Pictures (Editor's Choice Award, 1996); musical, Sounds Have Written Songs (Ind. Single featuring Dream and Contemplating, 2002), A Taste of

Queens (Ind. Album, 2003). Office: Porcelana Productions 80-50 Baxter Ave 109 Elmhurst NY 11373 Office Phone: 917-505-4574. Personal E-mail: www.porcelana.bz, poetuvgod@netscape.net. E-mail: www.porcelana.bz, porcelanagp@netscape.net.

ASTUTO, PHILIP LOUIS, retired language educator; b. N.Y.C., Jan. 5, 1923; s. Salvatore and Anna (Insalaco) A.; m. Natella M. Digia, July 4, 1953; children: Philip, Anne Marie. BA, St. John's U., 1943; MA, Columbia, 1947; PhD, Columbia U., 1956. Mem. faculty St. John's U., 1947-89, prof. Spanish, 1958-89, prof. emeritus, 1991—, dir. Latin Am. studies, 1957-60, chmn. dept. modern fgn. langs., 1961-65. Participant Prof.-Student Summer Seminar, sponsored State Dept., 1950; OAS research fellow, Quito, Bogota, 1973-74 Contbr. articles to profl. jours. Mem. coll. coun. SUNY, Farmingdale, 1988-98. 1st lt., inf. AUS, 1943-46, ETO. Recipient Pietas medal St. John's U., 1977, Faculty Outstanding Achievement medal, 1986 Mem. Am. Assn. Tchrs. Spanish and Portuguese, Am. Hist. Assn., Assn. Latin Am. Studies, MLA, Nat. Acad. History of Ecuador (fgn. corr.) Home: 11 Steuben Dr Jericho NY 11753-1414

ASUNDI, JAI, engineering educator; PhD, Carnegie Mellon U., Pitts., 2001. Vis. scientist Software Engring. Inst., Pitts., 2001—02; asst. prof. U. Tex. Dallas, Richardson, 2002—. Mem.: IEEE. Office Phone: 1-972-883-4776.

ATAEVA, AKSOLTAN, diplomat; b. Ashgabat, Nov. 6, 1944; m. Tchary Pirmoukhamedov, Apr. 25, 1969; children: Ainabat, Azat. Dipl. medicine, Turkmen State Med. Inst., 1968; DS (hon.), Soviet Union Sci. Rsch. Inst., 1989; A (hon.), Internat. Acad. Computer Scis., Kiev, Ukraine, 1993. Staff, asst. to chief doctor Hosp. No. 1, Ashgabat, Turkmenistan, 1968-80; vice dir. Regional Health Dept., Ashgabat, 1980-85; vice min., min. Health of Turkmenistan, Ashgabat, 1985-94; min. Social Security of Turkmenistan, Ashgabat, 1994-95; now permanent rep. Turkmenistan UN, N.Y.C., 1995—. Contbr. numerous articles to profl. jours. Mem. Supreme People's Coun. Turkmenistan, 1993—. Mem. Dem. Party of Turkmenistan. Avocations: art, reading, sports. Office: Presidental Palace 22 K Marx St Ashkhabad 744014 Turkmenistan also: Permanent Mission Turkmenistan UN 866 United Nations Plz Rm 424 New York NY 10017-1822

ATAL, BISHNU SAROOP, retired speech research executive; b. Kanpur, Uttar Pradesh, India, May 10, 1933; came to U.S., 1961; s. Jagannath Prasad and Lakshmi Devi (Lakshmi) A.; m. Kamla Atal, July 3, 1959; children: Alka, Namita. BS with honors, U. Lucknow, India, 1952; elec. engring. degree, Indian Inst. Sci., Bangalore, 1955; PhD in Elec. Engring., Poly. Inst. Bklyn., 1968. Sr. rsch. asst. Indian Inst. Sci., Bangalore, 1955-56, lectr., 1957-60; sr. rsch. fellow Cen. Elec. Engring. Rsch. Inst., Pilani, Rajasthan, India, 1960-61; mem. tech. staff AT&T Bell Labs., Murray Hill, N.J., 1961-85, head acoustics rsch., 1985-90, head speech rsch., 1990-97; tech. dir. AT&T Labs., Florham Park, NJ, 1997—2002. Contbr. articles to various publs. Fellow Acoustical Soc. Am., IEEE (Acoustics, Speech and Signal Processing Sr. Tech. Achievement award 1975, ASSP Sr. award 1980, Centennial medal 1984, Morris N. Liebman Meml. Field award 1986); mem. NAE, NAS (Franklin medal, 2003. Home: 6226 95th Pl SW Mukilteo WA 98275-3533 E-mail: batal@bishnu.net.

ATALA, ANTHONY JOHN, surgeon; b. July 14, 1958; m. Katherine Atala, May 13, 1985. BA, U. Miami, 1981; MD, U. Louisville, 1985, postgrad. in urology, 1990; postgrad. in pediatric urology, Harvard Med. Sch., Boston, 1992. Intern in surgery U. Louisville Sch. of Medicine, 1985-86, resident in surgery, 1986-87, resident in urology, 1987-89, chief resident in urology, 1989-90; rsch. fellow dept. surgery Children's Hosp., Harvard Med. Sch., Boston, 1990-91, clin. fellow dept. surgery, 1991-92, instr., 1992-93, asst. prof., 1993—, dir. lab. for tissue engring., 1993—, mem. investigations rev. bd., 1994—. Mem. med. adv. bd. Reprogenesis, Dallas, 1993—, Urosurge, Iowa City, 1993—, Surgijet, Boston, 1995—, Nat. Kidney Found., Boston, 1994; mem. study sect. NIH, 1996. Editor Tissue Engring., 1995—; cons. Jour. Urology, 1993—, Lancet, 1994, (book) Current Concepts in Tissue Engineering, 1995; contbr. articles to profl. jours. Bd. dirs. Nat. Kidney Found., Boston, 1996—; mem. investigations rev. bd. Harvard Med. Sch., Boston, 1994. Rsch. award ACS, 1990, Am. Acad. Pediat., 1993, 94, 96, Am. Soc. Plastic Surgery, 1994. Mem. AMA, AAAS, Am. Urol. Assn. (program com. 1995), Soc. for Basic Urol. Rsch. (program com. 1995). Achievements include patents in field, inventions in area of tissue engineering and medicine. Office: Wake Forest Univ Sch Medicine Medical Ctr Blvd Winston Salem NC 27157 Business E-Mail: cmontgom@wfubmc.edu.

ATCHER, ROBERT WHITEHILL, chemist, educator; b. Chgo., June 12, 1951; s. Robert O. and Marguerite (Whitehill) A.; m. Lisa Laidlaw, 1990 (div. 1995); 1 child, Robert Andrew Laidlaw Atcher; m. Sharon Ciessau, 1998. BA, Washington U., St. Louis, 1972; MS, U. Rochester (N.Y.), 1974, PhD, 1980; MA, U. Mo., 1976; MBA, U. N.Mex., 2004. Rsch. fellow Harvard Med. Sch., 1979-82, Peter Bent Brigham Hosp., 1979-82; rsch. affiliate nuclear engring. MIT, 1979-82; rsch. assoc. radiology Harvard Med. Sch., 1982-83, Brigham & Women's Hosp., 1982-83; rsch. affiliate Nuclear Reactor Lab. MIT, 1982-83; cancer expert, radiation oncology br. div. cancer treatment Nat. Cancer Inst., NIH, Bethesda, Md., 1983-86; adj. prof. dept. chemistry U. Md., College Park, 1984-86; group leader nuclear medicine rsch. chemistry div. Argonne (Ill.) Nat. Lab., 1986-93; radiochemist Michael Reese/U. Chgo. Ctr. Radiation Therapy, 1986-94; asst. prof. radiation oncology dept. U. Chgo., 1986-94; assoc. prof. medicine, assoc. prof. radiation oncology U. Ala., Birmingham, 1994-97; tech. staff mem. Los Alamos (N.Mex.) Nat. Lab., 1997-99; group leader Los Alamos (N.Mex.) Nat. Lab Bioscience Divsn., 1999—2003, mgr. HHS Programs, 2003—. Teaching asst. dept. chemistry U. Rochester, 1972-74; teaching asst. Sch. Journalism, U. Mo., 1974-75; advisor lab. grad. participant program Argonne Nat. Lab., 1986-93, advisor undergrad. student rsch. program, 1986-93; cons. Cytogen Corp., Princeton, N.J., 1986-90, NeoRx Corp., Seattle, 1987—, Sterling Drug, 1989-93; mem. task force Isotope Prodn./Distbn., U.S. Dept. Energy, Washington, 1990—; prof. Coll. Pharmacy U. N.Mex., Albuquerque, N.Mex., 1997— Bd. reviewers Jour. Nuclear Medicine, 1989—; editorial bd. Bioconjugate Chemistry, 1989-93. Fellow Am. Inst. Chemists; mem. AAAS, Radiation Rsch. Soc., Soc. Nuclear Medicine (pres. radiopharm. sci. coun.), Am. Chem. Soc., Fedn. Am. Scientists, N.Y. Acad. Scis., Sigma Xi, Beta Gamma Sigma. Roman Catholic. Office: Biosci Divsn MS G758 Los Alamos NM 87545-0001 E-mail: ratcher@lanl.gov.

ATCHESON, SUE HART, business educator; b. Dubuque, Iowa, Apr. 12; d. Oscar Raymond and Anna (Cook) Hart; m. Walter Clark Atcheson (div.); children: Christine A. Hischar, Moffet Zoe, Claye Williams. BBA, Mich. State U.; MBA, Calif. State Poly. U., Pomona, 1973. Cert. tchr. and adminstr. Instr. Mt. San Antonio Coll., Walnut, Calif., 1968-90. Bd. dirs. faculty assn. Mt. San Antonio Coll., mem. acad. senate, originator vol. income tax assistance; spkr. in field; lectr. in bus. mgmt. Calif. State Poly. U., Pomona, 1973—75; cons., trainer Joint Venture between Mt. San Antonio Coll. and County of Los Angeles Dept. Pub. Social Svcs., summer, 2001. Author: Fractions and Equations on Your Own, 1975. Charter mem. Internat. Commn. on Monetary and Econ. Reform; panelist infrastructure funding reform, Freeport, Ill., 1989. Mem. Cmty. Concert Assn. Inland Empire (bd. dirs.), Scripps Coll. Fine Arts Found., Recyclers Club (pres. 1996).

ATCHISON, JOSEPH EDWARD, pulp and paper industry consultant; b. Barnum, W.Va., Dec. 25, 1914; s. Edward Washington and Frederica Catherine (Kerns) A.; m. Frances Julia Winebrinier, July 3, 1951 (dec. Apr. 1965); m. Betty Jeanne Pugh, May 30, 1968; children: Leah, Robert, Scott (dec.), Kevin (dec.). BSCE, La. State U., 1938; MS in Pulp & Paper Tech., Inst. Paper Chem., 1940, PhD in Pulp & Paper Tech., 1942. Tech. dir. John Strange Paper Co., Menasha, Wis., 1946-48; chief pulp & paper br. Marshall Plan, Washington, Paris, 1948-52; mill mgr., project dir. Portarican Paper Products, Inc., San Juan, P.R., 1952-53; v.p., sr. v.p. Parsons & Whittemore, Inc., N.Y.C., 1953-67; pres., owner Joseph E. Atchison Cons., Inc., N.Y.C., 1968-97, Atchison Cons., Inc., Sarasota, Fla., 1997—. Spkr. internat. confs. *Dr. Atchison has specialized in the utilization of all types of non-wood plant fibers for the manufacture of pulp and paper and of all types, including newsprint. These fibers include sugar cane bagasse, wheat straw, rice straw, reeds, grasses, bamboo, cotton linters, He has developed appropriate processes for utilizing these raw materials and assisted many companies, in the developing countries, who do not have adequate wood, to design and build pulp and paper mills, based on whatever raw materials they had available. He has provided technical services in some 50 different countries. Enabling many countries to establish pulp and paper industries, based on using these raw materials, especially in wood-poor countries.* Author: Waste Paper Recycling, 1972, Kenaf for Paper Pulp, 1976; contbr. more than 150 articles to profl. jouors. Lt. col. U.S. Army, 1942—46. Decorated DSM Bronze Star with oak leaf cluster; named to Paper Industry Internat. Hall of Fame, 1997; named Man of Quarter, In Paper Internat., 1999. Mem. TAPPI (Gunnar Nicholson Gold medal 1996), Internat. Soc. Sugar Cane Technologists. Presbyterian. Avocations: tennis, exercise, dance, travel, theater. Office Phone: 941-377-3922. E-mail: atchconsul@comcast.net.

ATCHISON, RICHARD CALVIN, trade association director; b. Altadena, Calif., Aug. 4, 1932; s. Floyd and Clara (Warwick) A.; m. Mildred Platt, Jan. 24, 1957; children: Tracey, Hayley. BS, UCLA, 1958. Salesman, product mgr. Lever Bros., N.Y.C., 1958-61; group product mgr., then regional sales mgr. Purex Corp.; pres. Van Camp Seafood Co. div. Ralston Purina Co., 1965-81; pres. Mitsubishi Foods (USA) Inc., 1981-91; exec. dir. Am. Tuna Boat Assn., San Diego, 1991-93; pres. Internat. Bus. Cons., 1993—. With USAF, 1952-56. E-mail: richmil@adelphia.net.

ATCHLEY, CURTIS LEON, mechanical engineer; b. Lexington, Okla., June 3, 1940; s. Curtis Marvin and Hazel (Franks) A.; m. Barbara Ann Bryant, Feb. 14, 1976; children: Jeffrey Allen, Eric Andrew. BSME, U. Okla., 1970. Engr. Halliburton Oil Svc. Co., Enid, Okla., 1970-71, Tinker AFB, Midwest City, Okla., 1971-79; supervisory gen. engr. Lajes AFB, Azores, Portugal, 1979-80; gen. engr. Hdqrs. USAFE, Ramstein AFB, Fed. Republic Germany, 1980-82, Hdqrs. Air-Edn. and Tng. Command, Randolph AFB, 1985-99; ret., 1999; mem. staff Air Force Civilian Pers. Ctr., Randolph AFB, Universal City, Tex., 1983-85; engr. Davis-Monthan AFB, Tucsan, Ariz. U.S. and fgn. patentee in solar tech., U.S. patentee for light intensifying device for cameras and telescopes. Mem. Dem. Nat. Com., 1996-2005. Sgt. USAF, 1964-68 Mem. Amnesty Internat. (freedom writer), Internat. Soc. Poets (life, charter), Nashville Song Writers Assn., Broadcast Music Inc. Avocations: golf, skiing, camping, backpacking, swimming. Home: 7531 Oriental Trl San Antonio TX 78244-2400

ATCITTY, FANNIE L., elementary school educator, education educator; b. Shiprock, NM, Dec. 4, 1952; d. John and Betty Martin Lowe; m. Eugene Ronald Atcitty, Apr. 22, 1972 (dec. May 10, 2000); children: Antoinette, Ronald. BEd, Ea. N.Mex. U., 1978; M in Curriculum and Instrn., Doane Coll., 1997; M in Ednl. Leadership, Doane Coll., 2002. Elem. tchr. Central Consolidated Sch. Dist. 22, Shiprock, N.Mex., 1979—. Adj. instr. early childhood edn. program N.Mex. Highland U., Las Vegas, 1997—2002; adj. instr. edn. and tchr. prep. program Diné Coll., Shiprock, N.Mex., 1997—2002; profl. standards commn. mem. N.Mex. State Dept. Edn., Santa Fe, 2000—, tchr. assessment rev. panel, 1993—99, nat. coun. for accreditation of tchr. edn., 1997—. Contbr. poetry to lit. publs. Edn. chairperson Shiprock (N.Mex.) Cmty. Planning Commn., 1994—96; vice chair San Juan County Dem. Party, Farmington, 1998—2001; chairperson Cmty. Gov. Planning Bd., Shiprock, N.Mex., 1995—98; U.S Presdl. elector N.Mex., 1996. Recipient Golden Apple Found. award, Golden Apple Found. N.Mex., 2001. Mem.: Internat. Reading Assn., Am. Assn. Sch. Adminstrs., Las Amigas Women's Club. Democrat. Avocations: reading, walker, community events, gardening. Home: PO Box 3320 Shiprock NM 87420 Office: Mesa Elementary Sch PO Box 1803 Shiprock NM 87420

ATHAS, GUS JAMES, lawyer; b. Chgo., Aug. 6, 1936; s. James G. and Pauline (Parhas) A.; m. Marilyn Carres, July 12, 1964; children: Paula C. Vlahakos, James G., Christopher G. BS, U. Ill., 1958; JD cum laude, Loyola U., Chgo., 1965. Bar: Ill. 1965, U.S. Dist. Ct. (no. dist.) Ill. 1965, U.S. Ct. Appeals (7th cir.) 1970. With Isham, Lincoln & Beale, Chgo., 1965-69; group gen. counsel, asst. sec. ITT, Skokie, Ill., 1969-87; assoc. gen. counsel Itel Corp., Chgo., 1987; sr. v.p., gen. counsel, sec. Eagle Industries, Inc., Chgo., 1987-97; exec. v.p. adminstrn., gen. counsel, sec. Falcon Bldg. Products, Inc., Chgo., 1994-99; sr. v.p., gen. counsel Great Am. Mgmt. and Investment, Inc., Chgo., 1995-97; ptnr. Stamos & Trucco, Chgo., 2000—. Contbr. articles to profl. jours. 1st lt. U.S. Army, 1958-62. Mem. ABA, Ill. Bar Assn., Chgo. Bar Assn. Greek Orthodox. Home: 1240 Hawthorne Ln Downers Grove IL 60515-4503 Office: Stamos & Trucco 30 W Monroe Ste 1600 Chicago IL 60603 Office Phone: 312-630-7979. Business E-Mail: gathas@stamostrucco.com.

ATHERLY, ADAM JAMES, economist, educator; b. Eugene, Oreg., Nov. 20, 1966; s. Darst Barnard Atherly and Helen Hwa; m. Patricia Jean Alexander, Aug. 18, 1990; children: Rachel Alexandra, Ethan James Darst. BA, U. Ariz., 1989; MA, U. Wash., 1991; PhD, U. Minn., 1998. Asst. prof. Tulane U., New Orleans, 1998—99; assoc. prof. Emory U., Atlanta, 1999—. Contbr. articles to profl. jours. Mem.: Am. Pub. Health Assn., Internat. Soc. Pharmacoeconomics and Outcomes Rsch., Acad. Health, Delta Omega. Office: Emory University 1518 Clifton Rd NE Atlanta GA 30322 Office Phone: 404-727-1175. Office Fax: 404-727-9198. Personal E-mail: aatherl@sph.emory.edu.

ATHERTON, CHARLES HENRY, federal commission administrator; b. Kingston, Pa., June 24, 1932; s. Thomas Henry and Mary A.; m. Mary Bringhurst Davis, Dec. 15, 1967; children: Sarah Scott, Thomas Henry, Charles Henry. BA summa cum laude, Princeton U., 1954, MFA, 1957. Registered architect, D.C. Asst. sec. Fine Arts Commn., Washington, 1960-64, sec., adminstrv. officer, 1964—2004; ret., 2004. Trustee Nat. Child Rsch. Ctr., 1975-79; v.p. Washington Hist. Soc.; bd. dir. Hist. Am. Bldg. Survey Found. (elected fellow 2003), Navy Art Found.; mem. Citizens Commemorative Coin Adv. Com., 1994-2003; bd. dirs. Heurich House Found., 2003—. Lt. (j.g.) USNR, 1957—60. Recipient Martin Luther King Leadership award D.C. Pub. Libr. Sys., 1992, Centennial medal Washington chpt. AIA, 1993, Lifetime Achievement award Comm. of 100 on the Federal City, Mayor's award lifetime achievement in hist. preervation, 2004, Thomas Jefferson award for pub. architecture AIA, 2005; inductee Washington D.C. Hall of Fame, 2004. Mem. Potomac Boat Club, Cosmos Club. Home: 3127 Newark St NW Washington DC 20008-3344 E-mail: charleshatherton@yahoo.com.

ATHERTON, PETER L., music educator, singer; b. Louisville, Nov. 4, 1951; s. Sam M. and Carolynn Carpenter Atherton; m. Julie Whittaker Atherton, Aug. 16, 1998; 1 child, Emma Rose. MusB, The Julliard Sch., 1975; MusM, U. So. Calif., 1979; diploma, Internat. Acad. Soloisten, Hannover, Germany, 1980; MusD, U. Calif., L.A., Calif., 2000. Asst. prof. U. So. Calif., L.A., 1999—2001, Chapman U., Orange, Calif., 2001—, dir. operatic studies, 2001—. Asst. prof. U. Calif., L.A., 2004; mem. faculty Operafestival di Roma, Rome, 2002—05. Singer: (Operas) Seattle (Wash.) Opera, 1984—87, L.A. (Calif.) Opera, 1989—91, Operafestival of Rome, 2002—05, Balt. (Md.) Opera, Wolf Trap Opera, San Francisco (Calif.) Opera, (Broadway plays) (and other cities) Phantom of the Opera, 1992—94; musician: L.A. (Calif.) Philharmonic, San Diego (Calif.) Symphony, Orch. de la Suisse Romande, Basel Chamber Orch. Finalist, San Francisco (Calif.) Opera, 1978; named Singer of Yr., Nat. Arts Club, 1984. Mem.: Screen Actors Guild, Actors Equity Assn., Nat. Assn. Tchrs. Singing. Episc. Home: 12822 Browning Ave Santa Ana CA 92705 Office: Chapman Univ One University Dr Orange CA 92866

ATHEY, CLIFFORD L., JR., (CLAY ATHEY), lawyer, state legislator; b. Front Royal, Va., Sept. 1, 1960; m. Stacey Lynne Knox. AA, Lord Fairfax C.C., 1978; BA, Va. Commonwealth U., 1990; JD, U. Dayton, 1993. Pvt. pratice, Front Royal; coun. mem. Front Royal Town Coun., 1996—2000; mayor City of Front Royal, 2000—02; state del. dist. 18 Va. House of Dels., Va., 2002—. Mem.: Front Royal C. of C., Elks, Rotary. Republican. Methodist. Office: Gen Assembly Bldg PO Box 406 Richmond VA 23218 Address: Dist Office 35 N Royal Ave Front Royal VA 22630 E-mail: Del_Athey@house.state.va.us.

ATILGAN, TIMUR FAIK, retired structural engineer; b. Adana, Turkey, July 15, 1943; arrived in U.S., 1972; s. Faik Ahmet and Sacide (Togman) Atilgan; m. Gulsum Z. Kuzuoglu, Dec. 7, 1977 (div. 1980); m. Mirat Gurol, July 20, 1992 (div. 2002). BS in Civil Engring., Aegean U., Izmir, Turkey, 1967; MS in Structural Engring., U. Md., 1979. Registered profl. engr., Va. Civil engr. NATO/Infrastructure Dept., Ankara, Turkey, 1970-72; structural engr. Bendix Field Engring., Columbia, Md., 1977-79; sr. design engr. Northrop Svcs. Inc., NASA, GSFC, Greenbelt, Md., 1979-82; sr. antenna engr. COMSAT Gen. Corp., Washington, 1982-83; sr. structural engr. OAO Corp., Greenbelt, 1983-84; engring. specialist PRC-Kentron, Inc., Hampton, Va., 1984-86; prin. engr. Fairchild Space Co., Greenbelt, 1986-91; sr. engr. Def. Systems, Inc., McLean, Va., 1991-94; sr. staff engr. Astro Space divsn. Lockheed Martin, Valley Forge, Pa., 1995-98; sr. prin. engr. Canada-France-Hawaii Telescope Corp., Kamuela, Hawaii, 1999-2000; sr. staff engr. Lockheed Martin Corp., Moorestown, NJ, 2001—05; ret., 2005. Mem.: AIAA (sr.). Avocations: music, reading, swimming, cinema. E-mail: tatilgan@netzero.net.

ATIYAH, SIR MICHAEL FRANCIS, mathematician; b. London, Eng., Apr. 22, 1929; s. Edward Selim and Jean (Levens) A.; m. Lily J. Brown, July 30, 1955; children: John (dec.), David, Robin. BA, Trinity Coll., Cambridge, 1952, PhD, 1955; DSc (hon.), Bonn, 1968, U. Durham, 1977, Trinity Coll., Dublin, 1983, U. Chgo., 1983, Cambridge (Eng.) U., 1984; others. Fellow Trinity Coll., Cambridge, 1954-58, 97—, hon. fellow, 1976-97, master, 1990-97; hon. prof. sch. math. U. Edinburgh, Scotland, 1997—; lectr., fellow Pembroke Coll., Cambridge, 1958-61, hon. fellow, 1983. Commonwealth Fund fellow Princeton, 1955-56, prof. Inst. Advanced Study, 1969-72; reader Oxford U., 1961-63, Savilian prof. geometry, fellow New Coll., 1963-69, hon. fellow, 2000; Royal Soc. rsch. prof., fellow St. Catherine's Coll., 1973-90, hon. fellow, 1991; dir. Isaac Newton Inst. for Math. Scis., Cambridge, Eng., 1990-96; chancellor Leicester U., 1995-05; pres. Pugwash Confs. Sci. and World Affairs, 1997-02. Author: K-Theory, 1966, Commutative Algebra, 1969; contbr. articles to math. jours., also collected works, 1987, 2004. Decorated knight; recipient Fields medal Internat. Congress Mathematicians, Moscow, 1966, DeMorgan medal London Math. Soc., 1980, Feltrinelli prize Accademia Nazionale dei Lincei, 1982, King Faisal Found. Internat. prize for sci., Saudi Arabia, 1987, Order of Merit, 1993, Abel prize Norwegian Acad. Sci. and Letters, 2004. Fellow Royal Soc. (pres. 1990-95, Royal medal 1969, Copley medal 1988), Royal Soc. Edinburgh (hon., pres. 2005-, Royal medal 2003), Royal Instn. (hon.), Royal Acad. Engring. (hon.), Acad. Med. Scis. (hon.), Faculty Actuaries (hon.), Internat. Math. Union (exec co 1966-74), Math. Assn. (pres. 1981), London Math. Soc. (pres. 1975-77); mem. Nat. Acad. Scis. U.S.A. (fgn.), Leopoldina Acad. (fgn.), Am. Acad. Arts and Scis. (fgn.), Swedish Royal Acad. (fgn.), Academie des Scis. (fgn.), Royal Irish Acad. (fgn.), Am. Philos. Soc. (fgn., Benjamin Franklin medal 1993), Third World Acad. Scis., Indian Nat. Sci. Acad. (fgn.), Chinese Acad. Sci. (hon. prof.), Ukrainian Acad. Scis. (fgn.), Venezuelan Acad. Sci., Australian Acad. Sci., Russian Acad. Sci., Georgian Acad. Sci., Accademia Nazionale dei Lincei, Royal Norwegian Soc. Sci. and Letters, Spanish Royal Acad. of Sci., Order Andres Bello Venezuela, Order Cedars of Lebanon, Order of Merit Lebanon (first class). Office: U Edinburgh Sch Math James Clerk Maxwell Bldg Mayfield Rd Edinburgh EH9 3JZ Scotland Office Phone: +44-131-650-4883. Business E-Mail: m.atiyah@ed.ac.uk.

ATKIN, FLORA BLUMENTHAL, theater director; b. Balt., May 15, 1919; Dir., choreographer, musical cons. Adventure Theatre, Glen Echo Park, Md., 1953—69; founder, dir., playwright In-Sch. Players of Adventure Theatre, Glen Echo Park, 1969—82; guest adjudicator Children's Theatre Fest., 1991; presenter Sarah Spencer Award 501th Anniversary, 1999; dir. Recreational Arts Dept., Jewish Cmty. Ctr., Wash., DC, 1941—45; dance instr. Howard U., Wash., DC, 1942—43; music instr. Maret and Peter Pan Schs.; music therapist Walter Reed Hosp.; sec. Wash. DC Music Tchrs. Assn., 1941—43; state jr. counselor DC Federation of Music, 1941—43; pvt. music studio, 1950—60. Lectr. San Francisco State U., Hebrew U., Jerusalem, Colombo U., Sri Lanka, U. Md., U. Conn. Playwright: Tarradiddle Tales, 1971; Tarradiddle Travels, 1971; Golliwhoppers!, 1973; Skupper Duppers, 1975; Grampo/Scampo, 1977; Dig 'N Tel, 1978; Hold That Tiger, 1986; Tales From the Rebbe's Table, 1994. Mem. awards com. Md. Arts Coun., Montgomery County Arts Coun. Mem.: ASSITEJ, South Eastern State Theatre Conf., Am. Alliance for Theatre and Edn. Home: 5507 Uppingham St Chevy Chase MD 20815 E-mail: matkin1@comcast.net.

ATKIN, J MYRON, science educator; b. Bklyn., Apr. 6, 1927; s. Charles Z. and Esther (Jaffe) A.; m. Ann Spiegel, Dec. 25, 1947; children— David, Ruth, Jonathan. BS, CCNY, 1947; MA, NYU, 1948, PhD, 1956. Tchr. sci. Ramaz High Sch., N.Y.C., 1948-50; tchr. elem. sch. sci. Great Neck (N.Y.) pub. schs., 1950-55; prof. sci. edn. Coll. Edn., U. Ill., Urbana, 1955-79, assoc. dean, 1966-70, dean, 1970-79; prof. Sch. Edn., Stanford (Calif.) U., 1979—2004, prof. emeritus, 2004—, dean, 1979-86. Cons. OECD, Paris, Nat. Inst. Edn.; mem. edn. adv. bd. NSF, 1973-76, 84-86, vice-chmn., 1984-85, sr. advisor, 1986-87; mem. Ill. Tchr. Certification Bd., 1973-76; Sir John Adams lectr. U. London Inst. Edn., 1980, vis. scholar com. scholarly commn. Nat. Acad. Scis., People's Republic China, 1987; math. sci. edn. bd. NRC, 1985-89, nat. com. sci. edn. standards and assessment, 1992-96, com. on sci. edn. K-12, 1996-2002, vice chair, 1998, chair, 1999-2002; invited lectr. Nat. Sci. Coun., Taiwan, 1989—; resident Rockefeller Found., Bellagio Ctr., 1999; nat. assoc., Nat. Acads. of Sci., 2001-. Author children's sci. textbooks. Served with USNR, 1945-46. Fellow: AAAS (v.p. sect. Q 73 1974); mem.: NAS (assoc.), Am. Ednl. Rsch. Assn. (exec. bd. 1972—75, chmn. govt. and profl. liaison com.), Coun. Elem. Sci. Internat. (pres. 1969—70), Sigma Xi (chmn. com. on sci., math. and engring. edn.). Office Phone: 650-723-4385. Business E-Mail: atkin@stanford.edu.

ATKIN, LOUIS PHILLIP, recycling business executive; b. Rochester, NY, Apr. 18, 1951; s. Morris and Etta (Korpeck) A.; m. Jodi Rosenshein. Student, Am. Coll. Paris, 1970-71; BA, George Washington U., 1973; MA, U. So. Calif., 1977. Asst. editor Alan Landsburg Prodns., L.A., 1977-78; pres. Louis Phillip Holdings, Inc., Rochester, 1991—, Genesee Scrap & Tin Baling Corp., Inc. Pres. Atkin's Waste Materials, Inc., Rochester, 1990—, Pathways of Rochester, Inc., 1993—, Personal Pathways Inc., 1999—. Producer (with others), Jewish Community Fedn., documentary, 1982, Flights of Fancy, 1980; producer stage play Paradoxical Effects, 1987; writer, producer (play aired on Cable TV): Paradoxical Effects; writer, dir. Ceremony of Carols, 1974; scriptwriter, photographer, Posters of the First World War, 1983, exhibitor of posters, 1983. Interviewer Holocaust Com., Rochester, 1984; mem. Rochester Mus. and Sci. Ctr., 1985—, Meml. Art Gallery, 1985, Landmark Hist. Soc., Rochester, 1985—, Nat. Trust for Hist. Preservation; mem. citizens' adv. com. Solid Waste for Monroe County; bd. dirs., exec. com. Jewish Home of Rochester. NEH grantee, 1979, LIFT grantee N.Y. State Coun. Arts, 1987. Mem. Dramtists Guild (assoc.), World Pres.' Orgn., George Eastman Ho., U. So. Calif. Cinema Alumni Assn. Avocations: collecting World War I posters and political cartoon art, photography, writing. Office: 80 Steel St Rochester NY 14606-2112

ATKINS, CLAYTON H., family physician, epidemiologist, educator; b. Beech Grove, Ind., Nov. 12, 1944; s. Amos H. Atkins and Edythe E. (Dale) Heneghan; m. Carole A. Kirlin, Aug. 2, 1974; children: Brenda M. Spencer, Craig N., Angela C. AB in Chemistry, Ind. U., Bloomington, 1965, MAT in Chemistry, 1967; MD, Ind. U., Indpls., 1969; BS in Math. summa cum laude with highest honors, Butler U., 1980. Diplomate Am. Bd. Family Practice. Rotating intern Meth. Hosp. Ind. Inc., Indpls., 1969-70; pvt. practice Greenwood, Ind., 1970-94; mem. active staff family practice dept. St. Francis Hosp. and Health Ctrs., 1970—, hosp. epidemiologist, 1989—2002, with med. exec. com. Beech Grove and Indpls., Ind., 1993-96, pres. med. staff, 1995, mem. exec. mgmt. com., 1995-96; pvt. practice associated with St.

Francis Med. Group, Indpls. and Beech Grove, Ind., 1995—. Mem. courtesy med. staff family practice dept. Cmty. Hosp. South, Indpls., 1970—; instr. NSF math. for high sch. tchrs. Ind. U., Bloomington, 1966-67; instr. microbiology Ind. Ctrl. Coll. (now U. Indpls.), 1968; adj. asst. prof. Butler U. Coll. Pharmacy, Indpls., 1991-95; mem. Ops. Coun. St. Francis Med. Group, 1998-99, Mgmt. Coun. 1999-2000. Lt. col. M.C., USAFR, 1971-77, 91—. Fellow Am. Acad. Family Physicians; mem. AMA, Ind. State Med. Assn., Inpls. Med. Soc., Assn. for Practitioners in Infection Control and Epidemiology, Soc. for Hosp. Epidemiology in Am., Math. Assn. Am., Sigma Xi, Phi Kappa Phi, Phi Delta Kappa, Alpha Epsilon Delta, Phi Lambda Upsilon, Phi Eta Sigma, Mu Alpha Theta. Avocations: astronomy, cosmology, mathematics, gardening, mountain hiking. Home: 7610 W Banta Woods Dr Bargersville IN 46106-8740 Office: 8778 Madison Ave Ste 200 Indianapolis IN 46227-7202

ATKINS, DALE MORRELL, retired physician; b. Somerset, Colo., Jan. 20, 1922; s. James Perry and Lura May (Morrell) A.; m. Loretta Ilene Davidson, June 20, 1943 (dec.); children— Loretta, Linda, Peter, John. BA, U. Colo., 1943, MD, 1945, MS, 1953. Intern Mass. Meml. Hosp., 1945-46; resident medicine Colo. U. Sch. Medicine, 1948-50, resident urology, 1950-53; pvt. practice genitourinary surgery Denver, 1953-96. Mem. bd. regents U. Colo., 1963-74 Served to capt., M.C. AUS, 1946-48. Mem. Phi Beta Kappa. Home: 3860 S Dahlia St Denver CO 80237-1004

ATKINS, DENISE BETH, elementary school educator; d. Stanley and Phoebe Reed; m. Keith Scott Atkins, June 25, 1993; children: Cody, Clayton. BS in Early Edn., James Madison U., 1989; MA in Edn., Curriculum and Instrn., Ea. Mennonite U., 2005. Lic. profl. educator Va., 2001. Tchr. Grove Hill Elem. Sch., Shenandoah, Va., 1989—. Methodist. Avocation: travel. Home: 1630 Strole Farm Road Shenandoah VA 22849 Office: Grove Hill Elementary 7979 US Hwy 340 Shenandoah VA 22849 Office Phone: 540-652-8544. Business E-Mail: datkins@pagecounty.k12.va.us.

ATKINS, JOHN, concert pianist, voice educator, model; b. Kilmichael, Miss., Dec. 4, 1938; s. Luther O'Neil and Carolyn Holmes (Applewhite) A. MusB, Chgo. Mus. Coll., 1960; pvt. studies, Julliard Sch. Music and Chgo. Mus. Coll.; grad. gemology, Gemological Inst. Am., 1990. Ind. concert pianist, worldwide, 1956—; model Wilhelmina Creative, NYC. V.p. Valhalla Prodns., Inc., NYC, 1979—; cons. Warner Bros., LA, NYC, 1985-86, Goldcrest Films, London, 1985-86. Profl. solo debut New Orleans Philharm. Symphony Orch., 1956, NYC solo debut Philharm. Hall, 1965; touring concert pianist worldwide; TV appearances include The Tonight Show, Dick Cavett, Good Morning America; premiered new works numerous composers including Krenek, Puccini, Dallapiccola; collaborations numerous singers including Jan Peerce, Renata Scotto; recs. Angel, Columbia, CRI, Mercury labels; internat. voice tchr. pupils numerous major opera houses including Met. Opera, Bolshoi; editor: (chamber music) Sonata for Violin and Piano, 1966. Recipient 1st prize Music Festival South Competition, 1956, Brit. Film Inst. award, 1986. Mem. Bohemians, Acad. Internat. House of Intellectuals. Episcopalian. Avocations: bodybuilding, collecting modern Asian art. Office: Wilhelmina Creative 300 Park Ave S New York NY 10010

ATKINS, JOHN L., III, architect; b. Durham, NC, Dec. 16, 1943; s. J. Leeslie Jr. and Delores (Camp) A.; m. Sandra Kelly; children: Margaret Kelly, Ashley Jane. BArch, N.C. State U., 1966; M of Regional Planning, U. N.C., 1970. Registered architect, N.C., N.J., Va., N.Y.; cert. NCARB. Architect John D. Latimer & Assocs., Durham, NC, 1970-75; pres., CEO O'Brien/Arkins Assocs., Research Triangle Park, NC, 1975—. Founding mem., chmn. bd. visitors N.C. State U., Raleigh, 1992—; mem. exec. U. N.C. State U. Design Found., Raleigh, 1991—, also past pres.; mem., past pres. N.C. Bd. Architecture, Raleigh, 1977-87; bd. dirs., chmn. Wachovia Bank and Trust Co., 1987—. Founding mem., bd. dirs., former chmn. Research Triangle Regional Partnership, Research Triangle Park, 1989—; founding mem., chmn. exec. com. Greater Triangle Regional Coun., Research Triangle Park, 1993—; bd. dirs. Durham Ambulatory Surg. Ctr., 1996—. With U.S. Army, 1966-68. Named to NC Bd. Architecture, 1978, emeritus mem., 1988; recipient Civic Honor award, Durham C. of C., 1994. Mem.: AIA (Coll. Fellows 1991—, F. Carter Williams Gold Medal 2005). Office: O'Brien Atkins Assocs PA PO Box 12037 Research Triangle Park NC 27709-2037*

ATKINS, JOSEPH EUGENE, lawyer, mayor; b. South St. Paul, Minn., Oct. 6, 1965; s. M. Eugene and Andrienne Marion (Polta) A.; m. Julia Marie McLean Atkins, Apr. 4, 1992; children: John, Thomas, Catherine. BA in Polit. Sci., U. Minn., 1988; JD magna cum laude, William Mitchell Coll. Law, 1991. Bar: Minn. 1991, U.S. Dist. Ct. Minn. 1992. Assoc. Pritzker & Meyer, P.A., Mpls., 1991-96; ptnr. Thuet, Pugh, Rogosheske & Atkins, South St. Paul, 1996—. Adj. faculty Inver Hills Coll., Inver Grove Heights, Minn., 1991—. Editor Minn. Trial Lawyers Mag., 1995-2002. Sch. bd. mem. Ind. Sch. Dist. #199, Inver Grove Heights, 1987-90; mayor City of Inver Grove Heights, 1992-2002; Minn. State Rep., 2002—. Named one of Minn. 10 Super Lawyers, Minn. Jour. Law and Politics, 1995, one of 10 Outstanding Young Minnesotans, Minn. Jaycees, 1998, one of 10 Outstanding Young Ams., U.S. Jaycees, 2000. Mem. Minn. State Bar Assn., Minn. Trial Lawyers Assn. (bd. govs. 1993-2002), Inver Grove Heights Better Educated Students Today Found. (treas. 1993-94, pres. 1994-95). Democrat. Roman Catholic. Home: 2463 78th St E Inver Grove MN 55076-2821 Office: Thuet Pugh Rogosheske & Atkins 222 Grand Ave W Ste 100 South Saint Paul MN 55075-4000 Office Phone: 651-451-6411.

ATKINS, KENNETH EARL, retired chemist; b. Kimberly, W.Va., Feb. 20, 1939; s. Murl Earl and Mildred Irene (Williams) A.; m. Virginia Ellen Williams, July 22, 1960; children: Brian, Glenn. BS in Chemistry, W.Va. Inst. Tech., 1960; MS in Chemistry, W.Va. U., 1965. Chemist Union Carbide, South Charleston, W.Va., 1960-67, project scientist, 1967-72, devel. scientist, 1972-82, sr. devel. scientist, 1982-87, corp. rsch. fellow, 1987—. Co-author: (chpts.) Polymer Blends, 1978, SMC - Science and Technology, 1993; contbr. articles to profl. jours. Recipient Thomas Midgely medal Am. Chem. Soc., 1989. Mem. Soc. Automotive Engrs. Achievements include developed commercial process for ethylidene norbornene, the chief termonomer for EPPM rubber; discovered and developed commercial use for the most widely used shrinkage control agents for fiber reinforced thermoset composites. Home: 1311 Martha Rd South Charleston WV 25303-2915 E-mail: KVATK@aol.com.

ATKINS, PETER ALLAN, lawyer; b. N.Y.C., June 29, 1943; m. Lorraine Marilyn Feuerstadt, Apr. 3, 1966; children: Aileen Debra, Karen Jennifer. BA magna cum laude, CUNY, 1965; LLB cum laude, Harvard U., 1968. Bar: N.Y. 1969. Assoc. Skadden, Arps, Slate, Meagher & Flom LLP, N.Y.C., 1968—74, ptnr., 1975—. Mem. dean's adv. bd. Harvard Law Sch.; bd. dirs. A Better Chance, Inc. Contbr. articles to profl. jours. Mem.: ABA, Assn. of Bar of City of N.Y., N.Y. State Bar Assn. Office: Skadden Arps Slate Meagher & Flom LLP 4 Times Sq Fl 46 New York NY 10036-6595 Office Phone: 212-735-3700. Business E-Mail: patkins@skadden.com.

ATKINS, RICHARD BART, film, television producer; b. Paterson, NJ, May 11, 1951; s. S. Stephen and Alice B. (Stein) A.; m. Joanna Pang; 1 child, David. AB in Polit. Sci., Princeton U., 1973. With Cadence Industries, N.Y.C., 1973-74; mgr. TV program devel. Benton & Bowles, N.Y.C., 1977-79, mgr. daytime programming, 1980; v.p. prodn. Telecom Entertainment, N.Y.C., 1981-83; pres. Atkins Pictures Inc./A-Films, Florham Park, N.J., 1984—. Programming and prodn. cons. Hearst Entertainment, Whittle Communications, D'Arcy Masius Benton & Bowles, King World Prodns., 1989-91, Quartier Latin, Paris, 1992, TeleVest, 1997-98. Prodr. (TV films) Shocktrauma, 1982, Murder in Coweta County, 1983, The Gift of Love: A Christmas Story, 1983, Trapped in Silence, 1986; exec. in charge prodn. About Sarah, 1998, Christmas in America, 1990; prodr., writer (videocassette) Knowing Childbirth, 1985; prodr., writer (feature film) Forced March, 1989; producer: (feature film) Asunder, 2000; dir. (documentary) Mongolia, 1995; author: Method to the Madness: Hollywood Explained, 1975, (musical plays) Getting to Know You, 1994, 97, In the Mirror, 1995, 98, Independence, 1996. Mem. Friar's Club, Princeton Club. Jewish. Avocations: golf, computers. Home and Office: A-Films 105 Barringer Ct West Orange NJ 07052 E-mail: datk@aol.com, afilms@aol.com.

ATKINS, ROBERT, art critic, art educator, art historian, journalist, editor; BA High Honors, U. Calif., Riverside, 1972; student, U. London, 1971-72; MA in Art History, U. Calif., Berkeley, 1976. Staff columnist The Village Voice, N.Y.C., 1987—94; founder, editor TalkBack! A Forum for Critical Discourse, 1995—97; editor-in-chief The Arts Technology Entertainment Network, 1996—98; co-dir. McBride Ctr. for Arts Criticism & History, 1999—; media art editor The Media Channel, 1999—2001; rsch. fellow, STUDIO for Creative Inquiry Carnegie-Mellon U., 1999—2000; editor, prodr. Artery: The AIDS-Art Forum, 2000—02; instr. Rhodes Island Sch. Design, 2001. Lectr. in field; cons. in field; teaching assoc. Mills Coll., Oakland, 1976; tchr. Vista C.C., Berkeley, 1979-82, Coll. of the Redwoods, Ft. Bragg, Calif., 1980-81, Md. Inst. Coll. Art, 1984-87, Assn. Ind. Colls. Art, 1985, Moore Coll. Art, Phila., 1986-87, San Francisco Art Inst., 1986 & 88, San Francisco State U., 1983-1998, RI Sch. Design, 2001; vis. assoc. prof. art history, San Francisco State U.; Roman J. Witt vis. prof., U. Mich., 2002; mem. Independent Curators, Inc., Exhbn. Com., 1992-2000. Author: ArtSpeak: A Guide to Contemporary Ideas, Movements, and Buzzwords,1945-Present, 1990, ArtSpoke: A Guide to Modern Ideas, Movements, and Buzzwords, 1848-1944, 1993; co-author (exhbn. catalog and book for travelling mus. exhbn.): From Media to Metaphor: Art About AIDS, 1991, (catalog) "Critic's Choice," Eaton/Shoen Gallery, San Francisco, 1981(also curator), "Apologia," Union Gallery, San Jose State U., 1981(also curator), "About TV," Just Above Midtown, NY, 1983(also curator), "Introduction: Alan Shepp," Stephen Wirtz Gallery, San Francisco, 1982, "Currents: David Ireland," New Mus. of Contemporary Art, NY, 1984 (also curator), "San Francisco/Science Fiction," San Francisco Art Commn. Gallery, Otis-Parsons Gallery (LA), Clocktower Gallery, NY, 1984 (also curator), "Between Science and Fiction," for the 18th Sao Paulo Bienal, Brazil, 1985 (also curator), "What's Happening: Contemporary Art from Calif., Washington, and Oregon," Alternative Mus., NY, 1984, "Art Against AIDS: Washington, DC," American Found. for AIDS Rsch., NY, 1990, "Of Luminosity, Accident and Power Sanders," (for the exhbn. Stephen Hannock), James Graham & Sons, NY, 1996, "Rinaldo Hopf: Golden Queers," (for the exhbn. of the same name), Wessel + O'Connor Gallery, NY, 1998, "Interactivity and Intervention: Peter d'Agostino's Art of Ideas," (for the exhbn., Peter d'Agostino: Interactivity and Intervention, 1978-99), Lehman Coll. Art Gallery, Bronx, NY, 1999, "Fusion! Artists in a Research Setting," (for the exhbn. of the same name), Carnegie Mellon U., Pitts., 2001 (also curator), and several others; contbr. articles to Advocate, Aperture, Arena (Spain), art + architecture, Art + Text (Australia), Art and Auction, Art Aurea (Germany), Art in America, Art Journal (College Art Association), Art Paper, ArtByte, Artery: The AIDS-Arts Forum (online), Artforum, ArtLook (CD-Rom), ArtNews, ARTS BT (Japan), Cahier/Witte de With (Netherlands), California, California Monthly, Contemporanea, Elle, Esquire (Japan), Flash Art (Italy), Glass Art Journal, High Performance, Images & Issues, Le Millenium (Japan), Live LA Inst. of Contemporary Art Journal, The Media Channel (online), New Art Examiner, Newsday, New West, NY Mag., NY Times, Poz, Print News, San Francisco Bay Guardian, 7 Days, Studio International, TalkBack! A Forum for Critical Discourse (online), Vogue, Wired (Japan), Wolkenkrazer (Germany), World Art; curator N.O. Show, South of Market Cultural Center (San Francisco), Fashion Moda (the Bronx), 1982, Positive Actions: The Visual AIDS Competition, Clocktower Gallery, DC 37 Union Headquarters, Longwood Gallery (all New York), 1990, From Media to Metaphor: Art About AIDS, (with Thomas Sokolowski), Independent Curators, NY, 1991-1994 (9 mus. tour), Decoding Gender, Sch. 33 Art Ctr., Balt., 1992, Peter D'Agostino: Interactivity and Intervention, 1978-99, Lehman Coll. Art Gallery, Bronx, NY, 1999. Founder Visual AIDS, 1988 (originators of Day Without Art and Red Ribbon), (11--The September 11 Project: Cultural Intervention in Civic Society; co-founder Artists' Survival Workshop, 1986; mem. exec. com. Ctr. for Long Distance Art & Culture, CUNY, 1995-. NEA fellow, 1981; HEH Summer Seminar for Coll. Tchrs., U. Hawaii, 1981; recipient Mfrs. Hanover Art/World award for Disting. Newspaper Art Criticism, 1985, Penny McCall Found. award in the Visual Arts, for an independent writer/curator, 2001. Mem. Coll. Art Assn., Internat. Assn. Art Critics (bd. mem.), Phi Beta Kappa. Home: 603 W 111th St Apt 6W New York NY 10025-1805 Address: 2600 S Palm Canyon Dr #37 Palm Springs CA 92264*

ATKINS, RONALD RAYMOND, lawyer; b. Kingston, N.Y., Mar. 8, 1933; s. A. Raymond and Charlotte S. A.; m. Mary-Elizabeth Empringham, June 23, 1956; children: Peter Herrick, Timothy Barnard, Suzanne Elizabeth. BS in Econs., U. Pa., 1954; JD, Columbia U., 1959. Bar: N.Y. 1959. Assoc. Pell, Butler, Curtis & LeViness, N.Y.C., 1959-61, ptnr., 1962-67; ptnr. Bisset & Atkins, N.Y.C., 1967—, also Greenwich, Conn., 1982—; also of counsel Davidson, Dawson & Clark, LLP, N.Y.C.; mem. vis. com. Dept. Medieval Art and Cloisters, Met. Mus. Art.; mem. Coun. of Friends, NYU Inst. Fine Arts; trustee Mianus Gorge Preserve, Inc., chmn., 1984-94,trustee Yale Libr. Assoc. 2004-; Westmoreland Sancutary. 1st lt. U.S. Army, 1954-56. Fellow Frick Collection, Pierpont Morgan Libr.; mem. ABA, N.Y. State Bar Assn., Assn. Bar City N.Y., Medieval Acad. Am., Coll. Art Assn., Assn. Art History, Internat. Ctr. Medieval Art chmn. fin. com. 2005-. Republican. Episcopalian. Club: University (N.Y.C.), Grolier Club (N.Y.C.), Field Club (Greenwich, Conn.), Penn Club (N.Y.C.), Greenwich (Conn.) Croquet Club, St. Nicholas Soc. City of N.Y. also: 777 North St Greenwich CT 06831-3105 Office Phone: 203-661-8100.

ATKINS, ROSEMARY, civic worker; b. Hutchison, Kans., Apr. 11, 1936; d. Spencer Blankenship and Isabelle (Rowell) Moyer; m. John D. Atkins, Dec. 25, 1957; children: John Mark, James Robert. BS, Okla. Bapt. U., 1958; postgrad., U. Mo., Kansas City, 1967-68. R.N. Mem. faculty Met. Jr. Coll., Kansas City, Mo., 1965-68; nursing supr. Truman Med. Ctr. East, Jackson County, Mo., 1979-83. Dir. coll. dept., Sunday sch., Birchwood Bapt. Ch., Independence, Mo., 1963-68; chair Suburban Y, YWCA, Raytown, Mo., 1978, 79; coord. family ministries, Broadway Bapt. Ch., Kansas City, Mo., 1982-90; vol. for Blue-River-Kansas City Bapt. Assn. in area of family ministries; mem. funds rsch. and neighborhood comts. Raytown Reaching for Tomorrow, 2002-04, Continuing Progress, 2005—; mem. Continue Progress in Raytown. Mem. Sigma Theta Tau. Republican. Avocations: family, china painting, investing, travel, photography. Home: 9111 E 57th St Raytown MO 64133-3230

ATKINS, VICKI ALVINDA, realtor; b. South Bend, Ind., Nov. 16, 1945; d. Alvin Lee Atkins and Mildred Josephine Taylor-Atkins; children: Marvin L., Becky L. Student, Ind. U., South Bend, 1977—80. Property mgmt. various cos., Atlanta; realtor Remax Greater Atlanta, 2001—. Bd. sec. Learn To Grow, Inc., Atlanta. Fellow: Nat. Assn. Realtors, Atlanta Bd. Realtors (Mktg. Specialist of Yr. award 1999). Avocations: golf, travel. Home: 2431 Weatherstone Cir SE Conyers GA 30094 Office: Remax Greater Atlanta 1585 Holcomb Bridge Rd Roswell GA 30076 E-mail: vickiatkins@bellsouth.net.

ATKINS, VICTOR KENNICOTT, JR., investment banker; b. Seattle, Feb. 8, 1945; s. Victor Kennicott and Elizabeth (Tanner) A. AB, Harvard U., 1967, MBA, 1972. Assoc. Blyth Eastman Dillon & Co., N.Y.C., 1972-75, v.p., 1976-78, 1st v.p., 1978-79, E.F. Hutton & Co., N.Y.C., 1979-81, sr. v.p., 1981-84; pres. Covington Ptnrs., 1984-85, Equity Income Ptnrs. Capital Corp., Southampton, 1987-94, also bd. dirs.; chmn. Polaris Industries Capital Corp., Southampton, 1987-94, also dir.; pres., dir. Am. Nat. Security Inc., Omaha, 1992-95. Internat. adv. bd. Laidlaw Holdings, Inc., N.Y.C., 1995-96. Lt. USNR, 1967-70, Vietnam. Decorated Bronze Star, Cross of Gallantry Republic of Vietnam. Mem. The Brook Club (N.Y.C.), Southampton Club, Nat. Golf Links, Pacific Union Club (San Francisco), Bohemian Club (San Francisco), Meadow Club of Southampton, The Valley Club (Montecito), Birnam Wood Golf Club (Montecito), Santa Barbara Yacht Club.

ATKINS, WILLIAM AUSTIN, SR., (BILL ATKINS), former state legislator; b. Tate, Ga., Aug. 16, 1933; s. Austin and Gladys Atkins; m. Jennifer Lee Atkins; children: Chip, Paige; stepchildren: Stacy, Justin. BS in Pharmacy, Mercer U., 1954. Former owner Atkins Pharmacy, Smyrna, Ga.; mem. Ga. Ho. of Reps., 1982-94, mem. appropriations, regulated beverages and industry coms.; dir. Drugs and Narcotics Agy. State of Ga., 1994—. Past chair Cobb County Joint House and Senate Legis. Delegation; past chmn. Ga. State Bd. Pharmacy. Leader, vocalist Bill Atkins Band. Adminstrv. bd. 1st United Meth. Ch., 1998-2003; bd. dirs. Mercer U. Sch. Pharmacy; governing bd. Brawner Hosp., 1993-96; long-range planning bd. Smyrna Hosp., 1993-96. With U.S. Army, 1955—57. Recipient Appreciation plaque Ga. div. Am. Cancer Soc., 1991, Legislator of Yr. Friendship award Personal Care Homes of Ga., 1991, Liberty Bell award Cobb County Bar Assn., 1991, Pharmacist of Yr. in Ga. award, Phi Delta Chi, 1978, One of a Kind award Cobb Clean Commn., 1992, Meritorious Svc. award Mercer U., So. Sch. Pharmacy, 1992, others. Mem. Ga. Pharm. Assn. (award for dedication and svc. to profession of pharmacy 1986, Cmty. Svc. award 1997, Bowl of Hygiea award 1997), Ga. Pharmacists Assn. (past bd. dirs.), Ga. Assn. Chiefs of Police, 7th Dist. Pharmacists Assn. (past pres.), Atlanta Metropol, Cobb C. of C., Moose (named Mr. Cobb County 1993), Nat. Sheriff's Assn. Home: 4719 Windsor Dr SW Smyrna GA 30082-4465 Office Phone: 404-656-5100. Business E-Mail: batkins@gdna.ga.gov.

ATKINS, WILLIAM PAUL, lawyer; b. Balt., Mar. 17, 1962; s. Raymond Melvin and Julia Anne (Lacey) A.; m. Lesley Moira Brand, Jan. 22, 1994. BS in Phys. Scis., U. Md., 1986; MBA, JD, U. Balt., 1992; LLM in Intellectual Property, George Washington U., 1996. Bar: Md. 1992, D.C. 1993, Va. 2001; U.S. Patent and Trademark Office, 1995; US Dist. Ct. (Md., DC, ea., we. Va.), US Ct. Appeals (4th, DC, Fed. cir.), US Supreme Ct. Assoc. Cushman Darby & Cushman I.P. group Pillsbury Madison Sutro, Washington, 1992—96; ptnr. Pillsbury Winthrop LLP, McLean, Va., 1996—2005; ptnr. & co-chair, intellectual property section, mem. mng. bd. Pillsbury Winthrop Shaw Pittman LLP, McLean, Va., 2005—. Editor in chief U. Balt. Law Forum, 1991-92. Mem. ABA, Am. Intellectual Property Law Assn., Md. Bar Assn., D.C. Bar Assn., Bar Assn. of DC (pres.-elect 2004) Avocation: collecting egg-beaters. Office: Pillsbury Winthrop Shaw Pittman LLP 1600 Tysons Blvd Mc Lean VA 22102 Office Phone: 703-905-2007. Office Fax: 703-905-2500. Business E-Mail: william.atkins@pillsburylaw.com.

ATKINSON, A. KELLEY, insurance company executive; b. Tulsa, Okla., July 7, 1947; s. Milton A. Atkinson and Helen G. Brower; m. Patricia L. Morton, June 28, 1969 (dec. 1991); children: Gregory, Brent; m. Pamela A. Bender, Feb. 14, 1993. BS, Tex. Christian U., 1969; MBA, Ariz. State U., 1972. Sales rep. Mallinckrodt, Inc., Saint Louis, 1972-73, assoc. product mgr., 1973-74, regional sales mgr., 1974-76, mgr. market rsch. & data systems, 1976-77; mgr. product mktg. Intermedics, Inc., Freeport, Tex., 1977-79, dir. mktg., 1979-82, v.p. mktg., 1982-83; pres., COO Neuro Systems, Inc., Garland, Tex., 1983; pres. BoMed Mfg., Irvine, Calif., 1984; pres., CEO Physicians Health Plan Utah, Salt Lake City, 1984-87, United Health Care Ga., Atlanta, 1987-98, v.p. asst. projects, 1998—. Pres. Ga. Assn. HMOs, Atlanta, 1989, 94-96; adj. prof. Mercer U., Atlanta, 1990-92. Treas. Windward Cmty. Svcs. Assn., Alpharetta, Ga., 1995-96. Avocations: computer science, fly fishing. Office: United Healthcare 3720 Davinci Ct Norcross GA 30092-7627

ATKINSON, ANN LENNETTE, funeral director; b. Washington, Dec. 9, 1949; d. Samuel and Alma (Zimmerman) Williams; m. Oct. 6, 1968 (div. 1980); children: Lois, Jonathan, Crystal, Thomas; m. Melvin Atkinson, Feb. 4, 1985. AA in Mortuary Sci., Fayetteville Community Coll., N.C., 1982; BA in Elementary Edn., U. D.C., 1990; MA in Psychology, Cambridge U., 1998; PhD in Metaphysics and Sci., 2002. Lic. mortician, N.C. Mortician Colvin Funeral Home, Fayetteville, NC, 1979—82; tchr. Forsyth Cen. Coll., Winston-Salem, 1982-83; autopsy asst. Vets. Hosp., Washington, 1984—2000; receptionist Temporary Resources, Washington, 1986-87; micro-photographer Library of Congress, Washington, 1987-88; tchr. D.C. Pub. Schs., 1988-89; pres., coordinator Restorative Svcs., Suitland, Md., 1988—; tchr. phys. sci. Wilson County Sch. Sys., NC. Author: Unlock the Myths about the Funeral Industry, 1988; contbr. articles to profl. jours. Vol. tax asst. IRS, 1988; mem. Missionary Soc., N.C. Club First Bapt. Ch. With U.S. Army, 1974-75. Recipient Golden Poet award. Mem. Nat. Funeral Dirs. Assn., Am. Legion, Nat. Poetry Soc., Darden Alumna Assn., Sigma Phi Sigma. Democrat. Baptist. Avocations: tennis, reading, writing, poetry, french cooking. Home: 704 Cemetery St Wilson NC 27893

ATKINSON, ARTHUR JOHN, JR., pharmacologist, educator; b. Chgo., Mar. 22, 1938; s. Arthur John and Inez (Hill) Atkinson; m. Mary Jo Yunker, May 12, 1984. AB in Chemistry, Harvard U., 1959; MD, Cornell U., 1963. Intern, asst. resident medicine Mass. Gen. Hosp., Boston, 1963-65; chief resident, Howard Carroll fellow medicine Passavant Meml. Hosp., Chgo., 1967-68; fellow clin. pharmacology U. Cin., 1968-69, asst. prof. pharmacology, 1969; vis. scientist dept. toxicology Karolinska Inst., Stockholm, 1970; from asst. prof. to assoc. prof. medicine and pharmacology Northwestern U., Chgo., 1970—76, prof., 1976-94; corp. v.p. clin. devel. and med. affairs Upjohn Co., 1994-95; v.p. clin. R & D and worldwide clin. pharmacology Pharmacia & Upjohn, Inc., 1995-96; adj. prof. pharmacology Ctr. for Drug Devel. Sci., Georgetown U., 1996—2005. With NIH, USPHS, 1965—67; sr. advisor clin. pharmacology to dir. clin. ctr. NIH, 1998—2005; vice chair safe medication use expert com. U.S. Pharmacopeia, 2000—05. Recipient Faculty Devel. award in clin. pharmacology, Pharm. Mfrs. Assn., 1970—72, award of excellence in clin. pharmacology, 2002; scholar Burroughs Wellcome, 1972—77. Master: ACP; mem.: Assn. Am. Physicians, Am. Soc. Clin. Pharmacology and Therapeutics (pres. 1995—96, Rawls Palmer award 1983, Henry W. Elliott award 2004, Oscar B. Hunter award 2005), Am. Soc. Pharmacology and Exptl. Therapeutics (Harry Gold award 1989), Gibson Island Club, Chgo. Yacht Club, Alpha Omega Alpha. Home: 6176 Hidden Lake Cir Richland MI 49083 Personal E-mail: art_atkinson@msn.com. Business E-Mail: aatkinson@cc.nih.gov.

ATKINSON, BARBARA F., dean, medical educator, executive vice chancellor; b. Mpls., Oct. 19, 1942; MD, Jefferson Med. Coll., Thomas Jefferson Univ., 1974. Diplomate Am. Bd. Anatomic and Clin. Pathology, Am. Bd. Cytopathology. Intern Hosp. U. Pa., Phila., 1974—75, resident in pathology, 1975—78; mem. faculty U. Kans., Kansas City; dir. resident program U. Kans. Med. Ctr., Kansas City, exec. vice chancellor. Assoc. scientist Wistar Inst. Anatomy and Biology, 1983—87; mem. staff dept. pathology Hosp. of U. Pa., 1978—87, dir. cytopathology, 1978—87, med. program dir. Sch. Cytotech., 1978—86; chmn. dept. pathology and lab. medicine Med. Coll. Pa., 1987—94; dir. Delaware Valley Regional Lab. Svcs., Med. Coll. Hosps. and St. Christopher's Hosp. for Children, 1991—96; chmn. dept. pathology and lab. medicine Med. Coll. Pa. and Hahnemann U., 1994—96; trustee Am. Bd. Pathology, 1992—95, pres., 1998—. Mem. editl. bd. Lab. Investigation, 1988—94, Modern Pathology, 1990—94, Human Pathology, 1992—94, manuscript reviewer Cancer, Diagnostic Cytopathology, Modern Pathology, 1988—94, abstract rev. bd. U.S. and Can. Acad. Pathology, 1989—92, rev. panel Am. Soc. Clin. Pathology Abstract, 1991—96; contbr. articles to profl. jours., chapters to books. Bd. dirs., treas. Laennec Soc. Phila., 1979—81; bd. dirs. Thyroid Soc. Phila., 1982—84; exec. com., bd. dirs. Med. Coll. Pa., 1994—96; bd. trustees Hahnemann U., 1994—96. Recipient Golden Apple Tchg. award for excellent sci. tchg., 1994; grantee, NIH, 1985—88, Takeda-Abbott R&D, 1989—94, NIA, 1991—94. Fellow: ASIM, Coll. Am. Pathologists; mem.: NAS (mem. Inst. Medicine), U.S. and Can. Acad. Pathology, Am. Soc. Clin. Pathology (Janet M. Glasgow Meml. scholarship 1974), Am. Soc. Cytopathology. Office: U Kans Med Ctr Mail Stop 2015 3901 Rainbow Blvd Kansas City KS 66160 Office Phone: 913-588-1440. Business E-Mail: batkinson@kumc.edu.

ATKINSON, DAVID NEAL, law educator; b. Leon, Iowa, Feb. 12, 1940; s. Cecil L. and Lena M. (Enarson) A. BA, U. Iowa, 1962, JD, 1965, MA, 1966, PhD, 1969. Bar: Iowa 1965, U.S. Supreme Ct. 1971. Asst. prof. polit. sci. U. Mo., Kansas City, 1967-71, assoc. prof. polit. sci., 1971-75, prof. polit. sci.

and law, 1986—, chmn. dept. polit. sci., 1979-81, 89-91, Curators' Distinguished Tchg. Prof., 1999—. Author: Leaving the Bench: Supreme Court Justices at the End, 1999; mem. editl. bd. The Am. Rev. of Politics, 1990-93; contbr. articles to profl. jours. Recipient Shelby Storck award for outstanding undergrad. teaching U. Mo.-Kansas City, 1976, Alumni Reunion Tchg. award, 1995. Mem. Am. Polit. Sci. Assn. (Outstanding Tchg. award 1999), Supreme Ct. Hist. Assn. Home: 6502 W 49th St Mission KS 66202-1715 Office: Univ of Mo Dept Polit Sci 213 Haag Hall 5100 Rockhill Rd Kansas City MO 64110-3143 Office Phone: 816-235-2793. Business E-Mail: atkinsond@umkc.edu.

ATKINSON, DENESE STEPHENS, academic administrator; d. Kennith Joe and Melba Steele Stephens; m. Mitchell J. Atkinson, Dec. 2, 1988; 1 child, Pryce Gentry. BBA, Pikeville (Ky.) Coll., 1988. Dir. fin. aid Big Sandy Cmty. and Tech. Coll., Prestonsburg, Ky., 1999—2004, bus. affairs, 2004—. Mem.: KHEAA (mem.adv. com. student aid), Ky. Assn. Student Fin. Aid Administrs., Ky. Col. Office Phone: 606-886-7372.

ATKINSON, GEORGE H., federal agency administrator, chemistry professor; BS, Eckerd Coll., 1967; PhD, Ind. U., 1971; postdoctoral fellow, Nat. Bureau of Standards, Washington, DC, 1971—73. Prof. chemistry & optical sci. U. Ariz.; sr. fellow sci., tech., & diplomacy U.S. Dept. State, 2001, sr. advisor for sci & tech., 2002—03; sci. & tech. advisor Office of U.S. Sec. of State, 2002—. Vis. prof. disting. Univ. and rsch. insts., Japan, Great Britain, Germany, Israel, and France. Recipient Sr. Alexander von Humboldt Award, 1989, 1995, 1999, Sr. Fullbright Award, Lady Davis Professorship, SERC Award. Achievements include development of program (Jefferson Sci. Fellows program) that creates a new relationship between the Am. scientific and engring. academic communties and the U.S. Dept. State. Office: US Dept State 2201 C St NW Washington DC 20520

ATKINSON, GORDON, chemistry educator; b. Bklyn., Aug. 29, 1930; s. John and Margaret (Barrie) A.; m. Betty Lou Dilmore, Apr. 1, 1976; children: Alan Gordon, Gwyneth, Valerie. BS in Chemistry, Lehigh U., 1952; PhD in Phys. Chemistry, Iowa State U., 1956. Instr chemistry U. Mich., Ann Arbor, 1957-61; asst. prof. U. Md., College Park, 1961-64, assoc. prof., 1964-67, prof., 1967-71; prof. chemistry U. Okla., Norman, 1971—, chmn. dept. chemistry, 1971-74; dean Grad. Coll., 1974-79, vice provost for research adminstrn., 1974-79. Cons. in field.; Fulbright prof. Copenhagen U., 1967-68 Author: Reactions and Reason, 1973; Contbr. articles to profl. jours. Recipient Excellence in Teaching award U. Md., 1963, Regent's award for research U. Okla., 1983 Fellow N.Y. Acad. Sci., Am. Inst. Chemists; mem. Am. Chem. Soc., AAAS, AAUP, Sigma Xi, Phi Beta Kappa, Tau Beta Pi, Phi Kappa Phi, Phi Lambda Upsilon, Kappa Sigma. Democrat. Unitarian-Universalist. Home: 1419 Greenbriar Dr Norman OK 73072-6858 Office: Okla U Dept Chemistry 620 Parrington Oval Norman OK 73019-3050

ATKINSON, GORDON C., lawyer; b. Kansas City, Mo., May 16, 1955; BA cum laude, Harvard Univ., 1977; JD, Univ. Chgo., 1981. Bar: NY 1982, Calif. 1986, US Dist. Ct. (so., ea. dist. NY, so., ea., no., ctrl. dist. Calif.). Assoc. Rogers & Wells, NYC, 1981—85; ptnr., litigation Cooley Godward, San Francisco, 1985—, vice chmn. litigation dept. Founder & past pres. Chgo. Law Found.; adj. prof. Univ. Calif., Hastings. Trustee San Francisco Day Sch.; past pres. & mem. exec. com. Sunny Hills Children's Garden. Mem.: ABA, Bar Assn. San Francisco, Calif. State Bar, NY State Bar Assn., Santa Clara County Bar Assn. Office: Cooley Godward LLP 20th Fl 1 Maritime Plz San Francisco CA 94111-3580 Office Phone: 415-693-2088. Office Fax: 415-951-3699. Business E-Mail: atkinsongc@cooley.com.

ATKINSON, HAROLD WITHERSPOON, utilities executive, consultant, real estate broker; b. Lake City, S.C., June 12, 1914; s. Leland G. and Kathleen (Dunlap) A.; m. Pickett Rancke, Oct. 6, 1946; children: Henry Leland, Harold Witherspoon. BSEE, Duke U., 1934; MS in Engring., Harvard U., 1935. Registered profl. engr., Mass. Various postitions in sales, engring. Cambridge Electric Light Co., Mass., 1935-39, 46-73, asst. mgr. power sales dept., 1946-49, gen. mgr., 1957-73, dir., 1959-84, exec. v.p., 1972-73. Mgr. Pee Dee Electric Membership Corp., Wadesboro, N.C., 1939-46; gen. mgr. Cambridge Steam Corp., 1951-73, v.p., 1959-73, dir. 1955-84. Chmn. Cambridge traffic bd., 1962-73; pres. Cambridge Ctr. Adult Edn., 1962-64; v.p. Cambridge Mental Health Assn.; chmn. allocations com. Greater Boston United Cmty. Svcs., 1971-72; chmn. Cambridge Commn. Svcs., 1955-56; adv. bd. Cambridge Coun. Boy Scouts Am.; mem. corp. chmn. camping com. Cambridge YMCA, 1964-71; chmn. Cambridge chpt. ARC, 1969-71; trustee of trust funds Town of Harrisville, N.H., 1976-83; treas. North Myrtle Beach Citizens Assn., 1982-84. Served from pvt. to capt. AUS, 1942-45. Mem. IEEE (sr.), Mass. Soc. Profl. Engrs., Elec. Inst. (pres. 1971), Harvard Engring. Soc., Cambridge C. of C. (pres. 1957-58), Newcomen Soc. N.Am., Cambridge Boat (treas. 1962-65), Cambridge Club (pres. 1972-73), Bay Tree Golf Club, Plantation Club, Civitan (pres. Wadesboro 1940-41), Rotary (pres. Cambridge club 1959-60, former v.p. North Myrtle Beach, S.C. club), Phi Beta Kappa, Tau Beta Pi, Pi Mu Epsilon. Home: Covenant Towers Apt 409W 5001 Little River Rd Myrtle Beach SC 29577 Personal E-mail: HaroldHALW@aol.com.

ATKINSON, HOLLY GAIL, physician, journalist, business executive, author, lecturer, human rights activist; b. Detroit, Oct. 20, 1952; d. John S. and Patricia Atkinson; m. Galen Jay Guengerich, Nov. 18, 2000. BA in Biology magna cum laude, Colgate U., 1974; MD, U. Rochester, 1978; MS in Journalism, Columbia U., 1981. Diplomate Nat. Med. Bds. Intern in internal medicine Strong Meml. Hosp., Rochester, N.Y., 1978-79; rschr. Walter Cronkite's Universe show CBS News, N.Y.C., 1981-82; med. reporter CBS Morning News, N.Y.C., 1982-83; on-air co-host Bodywatch health show PBS, 1983-88; contbg. editor and health columnist New Woman mag., 1983-88; on-air corr., med. editor, sr. v.p. programming/med. affairs Lifetime Med. TV, 1985-93; assoc. editor Journal Watch, 1986-90; med. corr. Today Show NBC News, N.Y.C., 1991-94; editor HealthNews, 1994—; exec. v.p. Reuters Health, N.Y.C., 1994-98, pres., CEO, 1998-2000; CEO New Media Health Answers Inc., 2000; pres. allHealth.com (iVillage health), 2000—. Lectr. Dept. Pub. Health Cornell U. Med. Coll., 1997—. Author: Women and Fatigue, 1986. Vol. nat. and local level Am. Heart Assn., 1984-91, bd. dirs., chmn. nat. comms. com. Am. Heart Assn., 1987-91; bd. dirs. Phys. Human Rights, 1994— (pres. 2002-), NOW Legal Def. and Edn. Fund, 1996—, Soc. Advancement Women's Health Rsch., 1997-99, Am. Lyme Disease Found, 1997-98. Recipient Young Achievers award Nat. Coun. Women, 1986, Achievement award Soc. Advancement Women's Health Rsch., 1995. Mem. Phi Beta Kappa.

ATKINSON, JAMES BLAKELY, writer, editor; b. Honolulu, Nov. 24, 1934; s. Edward Clay and Gertrude (Blakely) A.; m. Starr Koester, Sept. 10, 1960 (dec. Oct. 1978); 1 child, Andreas Edward; m. Gretchen A. Holm, June 28, 1980; stepchildren: Nils, Katrina. AB in History, Swarthmore Coll., 1956; MA in Am. Lit. with honors, Columbia U., 1961, PhD in Comparative Lit. with distinction, 1968. Tchr. English Coll. Benjamin Franklin, Orléans, France, 1958-59; thcr. French, English and Am. history St. David's Sch., N.Y.C., 1960-62; asst. prof. English Dartmouth Coll., Hanover, N.H., 1966-73, Earlham Coll., Richmond, Ind., 1973-78; mem. core faculty Capital U., Dayton, Ohio, 1978-79; asst. prof. English Rutgers U., Camden, N.J., 1979-87; vis. scholar dept. Romance langs. U. Pa., 1987-89; ind. scholar, 1989—. Author: Machiavelli: The Prince, 1976; co-author: Machiavelli, The Complete Comedies, 1985, Machiavelli and His Friends: Their Personal Correspondence, 1996, Footprints of the Past, 1996, The Sweetness of Power: Machiavelli, Discourses on Livy and Guicciardini, Considerations of Discourses, 2002, Massacre at Oradour, 2004, New Hampshire's Cornish Colony, 2005; contbr. articles to profl. jours.; translator Pres. Cornish (N.H.) Hist. Soc., 1992—. With inf. U.S. Army, 1956-58. Mem. AAUP, MLA, Renaissance Soc. Am. Democrat. Mem. Soc. Of Friends. Avocations: hiking, gardening, art and antiques. Home: 117 Town House Rd Cornish NH 03745-4639 Personal E-mail: atholm@valley.net.

ATKINSON, JEFF JOHN FREDERICK, lawyer, educator, writer; b. Mpls., Nov. 12, 1948; S. Frederick Melville Atkinson and Patricia Atkinson Farnes; m. Janis Pressendo, Dec. 22, 1982; children: Tara, Abigail, Grant, Kelsey. BS, Northwestern U., 1974; JD summa cum laude, DePaul U., 1977. Bar: Ill. 1977, U.S. Ct. Appeals (7th cir.) 1977, U.S. Dist. Ct. (no. dist.) Ill. 1978, U.S. Supreme Ct 1982. Editor, reporter various Chgo. area newspapers and radio stas., 1967-71; assoc. Jenner & Block, Chgo., 1977-80; pvt. practice Evanston, Wilmette and Chgo., 1980—. Vis. prof., instr. Loyola U. Law Sch., Chgo., 1982-91; adj. prof. DePaul U. Coll. Law, Chgo., 1991—; spl. govt. employee and pvt. sector advisor U.S. State Dept., 1997—; prof.-reporter Ill. Jud. Conf., 1989—. Author: Modern Child Custody Practice (2 vols.) 1986, 2d edit., 2000, Am. Bar Assn. Guide to Family Law; contbr. articles on criminal, family, constl. law, health law and ethics to various publs. Elected bd. v.p. Avoca Sch., 1999-2001, sec., 2002—. Mem. ABA (chmn. child custody com. 1983-84, 86-87, 89-92, mem. editl. bd. Family Advocate 1988-96, mem. publs. devel. bd. 1984-89, mem. task force on needs of children 1983-85, chmn. rsch. com. 1987-88, advisor to Nat. Conf. Commrs. on Uniform State Laws 1994—, Merit awards 1984, 86-94, 2000), ACLU (bd. dirs. Ill. div. 1972-74), Ill. Bar Assn., Am. Health Lawyers Assn., Northwestern U. Coll. Alumni Assn. (v.p. 1987-89). Home: 3514 Riverside Dr Wilmette IL 60091-1050 E-mail: jatkin747@aol.com.

ATKINSON, LAWRENCE RUSH, IV, (RICK ATKINSON), journalist; b. Munich, Nov. 16, 1952; s. Larry Rush and Margaret Jean (Howe) A.; m. Jane Ann Chestnut, May 12, 1979; children: Rush, Sarah. BA, East Carolina U., 1974; MA, U. Chgo., 1975. Reporter Pittsburg (Kans.) Morning Sun, 1976-77, The Kansas City (Mo.) Times, 1977-83, The Washington Post, 1983—85, dep. nat. editor, 1985—87, investigative reporter, 1989—91, Berlin corr., 1993—95, asst. mng. editor, 1996—. Author: The Long Gray Line, 1989, Crusade, 1993, An Army At Dawn, 2002 (Pulitzer Prize, 2002). Recipient Pulitzer prize, 1982, Livingston Award for internat. reporting, 1983, John Hancock Award for Excellence, 1989, George Polk Award for nat. reporting, 1990, PEN special citation for non-fiction, 1990, Pulitzer prize, 1999, numerous other journalism awards. Office: Washington Post 1150 15th St NW Washington DC 20071-0002

ATKINSON, MICHAEL PEARCE, lawyer; b. Ft. Worth, Feb. 19, 1946; s. Charles Pearce and Nancy Lou (Thompson) A.; m. Melissa Jan Potter, July 17, 1976; children: Charles Travis, Kellen Elizabeth. BA, U. Okla., 1968, JD, 1972; MS, U. Tex., 1975. Bar: Okla. 1972, U.S. Dist. Ct. (we. and ea. dists.) Okla. 1972, U.S. Dist. Ct. (no. dist.) Okla. 1975, U.S. Ct. Appeals (10th cir.) 1981. Ptnr. Jones, Atkinson, Williams, Bane & Klingenberg, Enid, Okla., 1972, Best Sharp Thomas Glass & Atkinson, Tulsa, 1980—87, Thomas Glass Atkinson Haskins Nellis & Boudreaux, Tulsa, 1980—83, Atkinson Haskins Nellis Holeman Phipps Brittingham & Gladd, Tulsa, 1994—2004, Atkinson Haskins & Nellis Brittngham Gladd & Carwile, 2005—; asst. pub. defender Office of Oklahoma County Pub. Defender, Oklahoma City, 1973; asst. dist. atty. Office of Okla. County Dist. Atty., Oklahoma City, 1974. Asst. adj. prof. Coll. Law U. Tulsa, 1976-77. With USAR, 1970-72. Master Am. Inns of Ct. (emeritus); fellow Internat. Acad. Trial Lawyers, Am. Coll. Trial Lawyers; mem. Internat. Assn. Def. Counsel (faculty trial acad. 1986), Am. Bd. Trial Advocates (pres. Okla. chpt. 1995, diplomate). Presbyterian. Avocations: hunting, fishing, running. Home: 2440 E 28th St Tulsa OK 74114-5611 Office: Atkinson Haskins Nellis Brittngham Gladd & Carwile 525 S Main St Tulsa OK 74103-4509 E-mail: matkinson@ahn-law.com.

ATKINSON, NOLAN N., JR., lawyer; b. Norristown, Pa., Jan. 14, 1943; AB, Boston U., 1964; LLB, Howard U., 1967; LLM in Internat. Law, U. Pa., 1969. Bar: Pa. 1969, US Ct. Appeals 3rd Cir., US Dist. Ct. Ea. Dist. Pa. Ptnr. Zack, Myers & Atkinson, Phila., 1972—75, Atkinson & Archie, P.C., Phila., 1975—91, Duane Morris LLP, Phila., 1991—, mem. firm bd. partners, 1998—2000, head Phila. comml. litig. practice group, chmn. diversity com. Instr. legal method U. Pa., 1969—70; instr. trial advocacy Temple U., 1974—90; chair Philadelphia Diversity Law Group, Inc., 2001—. Recipient Rainbowmaker Award, Minority Corp. Counsel Assn., 2004. Mem.: ABA (sect. litig.), Phila. Bar Assn. Office: Duane Morris LLP 1 Liberty Pl Philadelphia PA 19103-7396 Office Phone: 215-979-1920. Office Fax: 215-979-1020. Business E-Mail: nnatkinson@duanemorris.com.

ATKINSON, RICHARD CHATHAM, academic administrator, cognitive scientist; b. Oak Park, Ill., Mar. 19, 1929; s. Herbert and Margaret Atkinson; m. Rita Loyd, Aug. 20, 1952; 1 dau., Lynn Loyd. Ph.B., U. Chgo., 1948; PhD, Ind. U., 1955. Lectr. applied math. and stats. Stanford (Calif.) U., 1956—57, assoc. prof. psychology, 1961—64, prof. psychology, 1964—80; asst. prof. psychology UCLA, 1957—61; dep. dir. NSF, 1975—76, acting dir., 1976, dir., 1976—80; chancellor, prof. cognitive sci. and psychology U. Calif., San Diego, 1980—95; pres. U. Calif. Sys., 1995—2003, pres. emeritus, 2003—. Author: (with others) Introduction to Psychology, 14th edit., 2003, Computer Assisted Instruction, 1969, An Introduction to Mathematical Learning Theory, 1965, Contemporary Developments in Mathematical Psychology, 1974, Mind and Behavior, 1980, Stevens' Handbook of Experimental Psychology, 1988. Served with AUS, 1954—56. Guggenheim fellow, 1967; fellow Ctr. for Advanced Study in Behavioral Scis., 1963; recipient Disting. Rsch. award Social Sci. Rsch. Coun., 1962, Vannevar Bush award, 2003. Fellow APA (Disting. Sci. Contbn. award 1977, Thorndike award 1980), AAAS (pres. 1989-90), Am. Psychol. Soc. (William James fellow 1985), Am. Acad. Arts and Scis.; mem. NAS, Soc. Exptl. Psychologists, Am. Philos. Soc., Nat. Acad. Edn., Inst. of Medicine, Cosmos Club (Washington), Explorers Club (N.Y.C.). Home: 6845 La Jolla Scenic Dr S La Jolla CA 92037-5738 Office: U Calif San Diego Rm 5212 McGill Hall La Jolla CA 92093-0109 Business E-Mail: RCA@ucsd.edu.

ATKINSON, RICHARD LEE, JR., internal medicine educator; b. Petersburg, Va., May 15, 1942; s. Richard Lee and Ruth (Scarborough) A.; m. Susan Stayner Hume, Aug. 13, 1966; children: Catherine Crane, Barbara Hill, Deborah Gildea. BA, VA Mil. Inst., 1964; MD, Med. Coll. Va., 1968. Liaison endocrinologist Vanderbilt U., Nashville, 1973-74; adj. asst. prof. UCLA, 1975-77; asst. prof. internal medicine U. Va. Sch. Medicine, Charlottesville, 1977-83; assoc. prof. internal medicine U. Calif., Davis, 1983-87; prof. internal medicine Ea. Va. Med. Sch., Norfolk, 1987-93; assoc. chief staff for rsch. VA Med. Ctr., Hampton, Va., 1987-93; prof. medicine and nutritional scis., dir. Beers-Murphy Clin. Nutrition Ctr. U. Wis., Madison, 1993—2002; emeritus prof. medicine and nutritional scis. U. Wis., Madison, 2002—; dir. Obesity Inst. Medstar Rsch. Inst., Washington, 2002—04; pres. Obetech, LLC, Richmond, Va., 2004—, dir. Obesity Rsch. Ctr., 2004—. Mem. nutrition study sect. NIH, 1991-95, chair, 1993-95; chair subcom. on obesity in the mil. NAS, 1999-2003. Contbr. articles to profl. jours. Maj. U.S. Army, 1970—74. Mem. N.Am. Assn. Study Obesity (pres. 1990-91), Am. Soc. Clin. Nutrition (pres. 1994-95), Am. Obesity Assn. (pres. 1995-). Home: 6077 Barkers Mill Rd Mechanicsville VA 23111 Office: Obetech LLC Va Biotech Rsch Pk 800 E Leigh St Richmond VA 23219 Office Phone: 804-344-5360.

ATKINSON, VALERIE J., writer, webmaster; b. Austin, Tex., Mar. 3, 1959; d. Vernon T. and Mildred K. (Heaton) A. *Father, Vernon Thurman Atkinson, grew up picking cotton and strawberries in Pasadena, Texas. Son of Delbert Atkinson and Josephine Thurman Atkinson, Pasadena settlers, Vern worked his way out of poverty. Eventually, Vern graduated from Rice University, with a degree in chemical engineering, and also from Annapolis Naval Academy. He served as city councilman in Pasadena where his brother had served as mayor. Atkinson Elementary bears the family name in remembrance of the Atkinson legacy in Pasadena.* BA, U. Tex., 1981; postgrad., U. Salamanca, Spain, 1983, City U., London, 1987. Assoc. exec. State Bar of Tex./Mead Data, Austin, 1988-93; sys. adminstr. First Tex. Lawyer's Bull. Bd. Svc., Austin, 1993—; dir. Paralegal Svcs. Internat., 1993—; tech. analyst Sprint Paranet, 1998; tech. solutions cons. Sprint Enterprise Network Svcs., 1999. Spkr. in field; booth facilitator Profl. Games' League/Advanced Micro Devices; web rsch. splst. Cybercity program KTSA, San Antonio, summer, 1998, tech. analyst Sprint Paranet Inc., 1998—; charter del. UK high tech mision Invest Britain Bur., 2000. Author: Paralegal Guide to Intellectual Property, 1994; editor newsletter Legal Asst. News, 1989-90; writer Tex. Pocket Part to Accompany The Law of Real Property, 1993, Legal Research Via Internet International Thomson, 1998; commentator, interviewer: (radio program) Inside the Internet, KOOP 91.7, Austin, 1996-98; web coord. AMD Global Mktg. programs; web developer Latin Am. Website for AMD, 1998. Named Geek of the Week, Internet Week Mag., 1998; grantee fellowship, Am. Coun. on Germany, 2004. Mem. Acad. Am. Poets, Soc. Authors U.K., Brit. Writers Guild, Austin Bilingual Toastmasters (v.p. profl. devel.), Nat. Writers Union. Avocation: calligraphy. Office: Paralegal Svcs Internat PO Box 1539 Kyle TX 78640 Office Phone: 512-791-1585.

ATKINSON, WILLIAM JAMES, JR., retired cardiologist; b. Mobile, Ala., July 4, 1917; s. William J. and Gertrude (Smith) A.; m. Glenda E. Street, Oct. 29, 1949; children: Glenda Street, Regina Creswell, William James III. BA cum laude, Amherst Coll., 1939; MD, U. Pa., 1943; MS in Internal Medicine, St. Louis U., 1949. Diplomate Am. Bd. Internal Medicine, Am. Bd. Cardiovasc. Disease. Intern Phila. Gen. Hosp., 1943—44; resident in medicine St. Louis City Hosp., 1946—48; resident in cardiology St. Louis U., 1948—49; pvt. practice specializing in internal medicine/cardiology Mobile, Ala., 1949—. Chief cardiac clinic Mobile City Hosp., 1950-60; electrocardiographer Mobile Infirmary, 1949-92, Providence Hosp., 1949-75; cardiologist Diagnostic and Med. Clinic, 1949-92; mem. staff U. South Ala. Med. Ctr. Hosp., Mobile Infirmary, Providence Hosp.; chmn. bd. Diagnostic and Med. Clinic P.A., 1973-92; clin. assoc. prof. medicine U. Ala., 1964-89; clin. assoc. prof. medicine U. South Ala., 1973-92; ret.; life counselor Med. Assn. State of Ala. Capt. M.C., AUS, 1944-46. Decorated Bronze Star; recipient 4 Battle Stars, Combat Med. medal. Fellow ACP, Am. Coll. Cardiology, Am. Coll. Chest Physicians; mem. AMA, Am. Heart Assn., Ala. Heart Assn. (pres. 1955, chmn. bd. 1956), Am. Soc. Clin. Pharmacology and Therapeutics, Rotary, Mobile Country Club, Mobile Yacht Club. Republican. Episcopalian. Home: 3965 Byronell Ct Mobile AL 36693-5502

ATLAS, CRAIG MITCHELL, lawyer; b. Buffalo, Apr. 22, 1959; s. Irving and Gloria Atlas; m. Karen Geller. BA, Mich. State U., 1980, M in Labor and Indsl. Rels., 1981; JD, SUNY, Buffalo, 1986. Bar: N.Y. 1987, U.S. Dist. Ct. (no. dist.) N.Y. 1987, U.S. Dist. Ct. (we. dist.) N.Y. 1991, U.S. Ct. Appeals (2d cir.) 1991. Tchg. asst. Law Sch. SUNY, Buffalo, 1984-85; law clk. N.Y. State Pub. Employment Rels. Bd., Buffalo, 1985-86; assoc. O'Hara & O'Connell, P.C., Syracuse, N.Y., 1986-93, Scolaro, Shulman, Cohen, Lawler, Burstein & Ferrara, P.C., Syracuse, N.Y., 1993-94, Ferrara, Fiorenza, Larrison, Barrett & Reitz, P.C., Syracuse, N.Y., 1994-97, ptnr., 1998—. Mem. ABA, N.Y. Bar Assn., Onondaga County Bar Assn., Indsl. Relations Research Assn. Home: 517 Scott Ave Syracuse NY 13224-1909 Office: Ferrara Fiorenza Larrison Barrett & Reitz PC 5010 Campuswood Dr East Syracuse NY 13057-1229 Office Phone: 315-437-7600. E-mail: cmatlas@ferrarafirm.com. *Notable cases include: Bd. Edn. Watertown City Sch. Dist. vs. Watertown Edn. Assn., 93 N.Y. 2d. 132, 1999; Grogan vs. Hoiland Patent Ctrl. Sch. Dist., 262 A.D. 2d 1009.*

ATLAS, DAVID, meteorologist, research scientist; b. Bklyn., May 25, 1924; s. Isadore and Rose (Jaffee) A.; m. Lucille Rosen, Sept. 26, 1948; children: Joan Linda, Robert Fred. BSc, NYU, 1946; MSc, MIT, 1951, DSc in Meteorology, 1955. Chief weather radar br. Air Force Cambridge Research Labs., Bedford, Mass., 1948-66; prof. meteorology U. Chgo., 1966-72; dir. atmospheric tech. div. Nat. Center for Atmospheric Research, Boulder, Colo., 1972-73, dir. nat. hail research expt., 1974-75; dir. lab. for atmospheric sci. Nasa Goddard Space Flight Ctr., Greenbelt, Md., 1977-84, disting. vis. scientist, 1988—; sr. research assoc. dept. meteorology U. Md., 1985-87; disting. vis. scientist Jet Propulsion Lab. Calif. Inst. Tech., 1984-92. Chmn. panel on remote atmospheric probing, also mem. com. on atmospheric scis., NAS, 1975-82, mem. on modernization of the Nat. Weather Svc., 1996-99—; mem. weather radar beyond NEXRAD, 2001-02; vis. scientist Coop. Inst. for Marine and Atmospheric Scis., U. Miami, 1988-99. 1st lt. USAAF, 1943—46. Recipient Loeser award Air Force Cambridge Rsch. Labs., 1957, O'Day award, 1964; Robert M. Losey award AIAA, 1966; NASA Outstanding Leadership medal, 1982; Presdl. Meritorious Sr. Exec. award, 1983; NSF sr. postdoctoral fellow Imperial Coll., London, 1959-60 Fellow Am. Meteorol. Soc. (councilor 1961-64, 72-74, Meisinger award 1957, assoc. editor publs. 1957-74, pres. 1975, Cleveland Abbè award 1983, Remote Sensing award 1991, Carl Gustav Rossby medal 1996, hon. 2001), Am. Geophys. Union, Am. Astron. Soc., Royal Meteorol. Soc. (Symons Meml. medal 1989), AAAS (chmn. atmospheric and hydrospheric scis. sect. 1986); mem. NAE, IEEE (Dennis J. Picard medal for radar techs. and applications 2004), Internat. Radio Sci. Union (pres. inter-union commn. on radio meteorology 1969-72). Achievements include invention of weather radar devices. Personal E-mail: davnlu@comcast.net. Business E-Mail: datlas@alum.mit.edu.

ATLAS, JAMES ROBERT, editor, writer; b. Chgo., Mar. 22, 1949; s. Donald and Nora (Glassenberg) Atlas; m. Anna O'Conor Sloane Fels, Aug. 2, 1975; children: Amelia Eyre, William Easton. BA, Harvard U., 1971; postgrad. (Rhodes scholar), Oxford (Eng.) U., 1971-73. Staff writer Time, NYC, 1977-78; asst. editor book rev. NY Times, 1978-81; assoc. editor Atlantic Monthly, 1981-85; contbg. editor Vanity Fair, NYC, 1985-87; asst. editor NY Times Mag., 1987-97; staff writer The New Yorker, 1997-99. Founding editor Penguin Lives. Author: Delmore Schwartz: The Life of an American Poet, 1977, The Great Pretender, 1986, Battle of the Books, 1992, Bellow: A Biography, 2000, My Life in the Middle Ages: A Survivor's Tale, 2005; contbr. articles to nat. mags. Office: Atlas Books 10 E 53d St 36th Fl New York NY 10022

ATLAS, JAY DAVID, philosopher, consultant, linguist, educator; b. Houston, Feb. 1, 1945; s. Jacob Henry and Babette Fancile (Friedman) A. AB summa cum laude, Amherst (Mass.) Coll., 1966; PhD, Princeton (N.J.) U., 1976. Mem. common rm. Wolfson Coll., Oxford, England, 1978, 1980; vis. fellow Princeton U., 1979; rsch. assoc. Inst. for Advanced Study, Princeton, 1982-84; vis. lectr. U. Hong Kong, 1986; prof. Pomona Coll., Claremont, Calif., 1989—, chair dept. linguistics and cognitive sci., 2001—03, Peter W. Stanley Prof. linguistics philosophy, 2003—. Sr. assoc. Jurecon, Inc., L.A.; lectr. 2d European Summer Sch. in Logic, Lang. and Info., 1990; examiner U. Edinburgh, Scotland, 1993, U. Groningen, Netherlands, 1991, 93-97, vis. rsch. prof., 1995, 2005; vis. prof. UCLA, 1988-95, Max Planck Inst. for Psycholinguistics, Nijmegen, Netherlands, 1997, 2005; vis. fellow Amherst Coll., 2004. Author: Philosophy Without Ambiguity, 1989, Logic, Meaning, and Conversation, 2005; contbr. to PC Laptop Computer Mag., 1994, articles to profl. jours. Mem. Am. Philos. Assn., Linguistic Soc. Am. Office: Pomona Coll 550 N Harvard Ave Claremont CA 91711-4410 Office Phone: 909-621-8947. E-mail: jatlas@alumni.princeton.edu.

ATLAS, LIANE WIENER, writer; b. N.Y.C. d. Louis and Frances (Ferne) Wiener; m. Martin Atlas, Mar. 5, 1944 (dec. Mar. 1997); children: Stephen Terry, Jeffrey L. AB, Vassar Coll., 1943; postgrad., Johns Hopkins U., 1953-55. Cert. fin. planner. Fgn. affairs officer Dept. State, Washington, 1962-68; sr. economist U.S. Commerce Dept., Washington, 1968-75, U.S. Treasury Dept., Washington, 1975-79, Riggs Nat. Bank, Washington, 1980-82; v.p. Fintapes Inc., Washington, 1984-87, pres., 1987-95; freelance writer Washington, 1995—. Mem. U.S. delegation UN Econ. Orgns., N.Y.C., Geneva, 1963, 64, 68, 79. Author: Middle East Financial Institutions, 1977, (audio cassettes) What Every Wife Should Know, 1986, rev., 1992, Financial Planning for Divorce, rev. edit. 1992; freelance writer Changing Times and other mags., 1982-87. Treas. Entertaining People/Washington Home, 1986—90, Smithsonian Craft Show, 1993—95, Smithsonian Women's Com., 1996—97; mem. Kennedy Ctr. Cirs. Bd., 1999—; info. specialist Nat. Gallery Art, 2004—; treas. NCC-OWL, 2005—. Fellow in econs. Johns Hopkins U., Balt., 1954-55; recipient Cert. of Appreciation U.S. Treasury Dept., Washington, 1977. Mem.: OWL (treas. D.C. chpt. 2005—), Washington Ind. Writers, Inst. CFPs, Smithsonian Women's Com., Washington Print Club, Vassar Club of Washington. Avocations: print collecting, travel. Home: 2254 48th St NW Washington DC 20007-1035

ATLAS, NANCY FRIEDMAN, judge; b. N.Y.C., May 20, 1949; BS, Tufts U., 1971; JD, NYU, 1974. Bar: N.Y. 1975, U.S. Dist. Ct. (so. and ea. dists.) N.Y. 1975, U.S. Ct. Appeals (2nd cir.) 1975, U.S. Dist. Ct. (so. dist.) Tex. 1982, U.S. Ct. Appeals (5th cir.) 1982, U.S. Dist. Ct. (no. dist.) Tex. 1989. Law clk. to Hon. Dudley B. Bonsal U.S. Dist Ct. (so. dist.) N.Y., 1974-76; assoc. Webster & Sheffield, 1977-78; asst. U.S. atty. So. Dist. N.Y., 1979-82; shareholder Sheinfeld, Maley & Kay, P.C., Houston, 1982-95, also bd. dirs.; judge U.S. Dist. Ct. Tex., Houston, 1995—. Lectr. numerous programs CLE. Mng. editor NYU Ann. Survey Am. Law, 1973-74; contbr. numerous articles to profl. jours. Chair Tex. Higher Edn. coord. Bd., 1992-95; mem. Tex. Coun. Workforce and Econ. Competitiveness, 1993-95. Fellow: ABA Found., Houston Bar Assn., State Bar Tex.; mem.: FBA, ABA (co-divsn. dir. litigation sect. 1996—98, co-chair ADR com. 1994—95, mem. coun. 1998—2001, bus. and litigation joint task force on bankruptcy practice 1994—98), Am. Law Inst., Houston Bar Found. (trustee), Phi Beta Kappa. Office: US Courthouse 515 Rusk St Ste 9015 Houston TX 77002-2605

ATLAS, SCOTT J., lawyer; b. Austin, Tex., Jan. 15, 1950; s. Morris and Rita Jean (Willner) A.; m. Nancy Ellen Friedman, Mar. 26, 1983; 2 children. BA magna cum laude, Yale U., 1971; JD with honors, U. Tex., 1975. Bar: Tex. 1975, U.S. Dist. Ct. (so. dist.) Tex. 1976, U.S. Ct. Appeals (5th cir.) 1976, U.S. Supreme Ct. 1979, U.S. Ct. Appeals (11th cir.) 1981, U.S. Dist. Ct. (we, no. and ea. dists). Law clk. to judge U.S. Ct. Appeals (5th cir.), Austin, 1975—76; assoc. Vinson & Elkins, Houston, 1976—82, ptnr., 1982—. Mem. bd. visitors U. Tex. Law Sch., 1982-90; mem. Chancellors Coun. U. Tex., exec. com., 2001-; mem. Com. of 125, U. Tex., Austin, 2003--; lectr. numerous law schs. and legal orgns. Chancellor, Coif, editor-in-chief Tex. Law Rev.; contbr. numerous articles to profl. jours. Founding pres. Houston Shakespeare Festival, 1980-82; v.p., co-founder Tex. Lyceum Assn. Inc., 1983-85; exec. com. Alley Theatre, Houston, 1983—, ex-officio, 1989—; bd. dirs. ADL S.W. Region, 1998—, exec. com., 1999-, v.p., 2001—; past bd. dirs. Tex. Opera Theatre, Cultural Arts Coun. of Houston, Young Audiences Houston, others; county coord. U.S. Sen. Lloyd M. Bentsen, 1987-92; mem. adv. com. Law Firm Project of the Pro Bono Inst., 1991-, chmn., 1997-2001. Named one of Outstanding Young Houstonians, Jaycees, 1984-85, Outstanding Young Lawyer in Houston, Houston Young Lawyers Assn., 1984, Outstanding Young Tex. Exes, Tex. Ex-Students Assn., 1989, Tex. Monthly's Tex. Super Lawyers in Bus. Litigation, 2003, 04, 05, EEOC's 40th Ann. Civil Rights All Stars, 2005; named Lawyer of the Yr., Mex.- Am. Bar Assn. Tex., 1996, Disting. Alumnus for Cmty. Svc., U. Tex. Law Alumni Assn., 2000; recipient Azteca Civil Rights award, LULAC Dist. XVIII, 1993, spl. recognition for contbns. to cross-border relationships Tex.-Mex. Bar Assn., 1997, Pub. Interest award Tex. Law Fellowship, 1998, ADL Karen Susman Jurisprudence award, 2002. Fellow Houston Bar Found. (founder, life), Tex. Bar Found. (life), Am. Bar Found. (life); mem. ABA (chmn. litig. sect. 2002-03, chmn. appellate practice com. litigation sect. 1985-89, coun. mem. litigation sect. 1989-92, exec. com. 1992-96, standing com. on pro bono and pub. svc. 1995-98, co-chair strategic planning implementation task force litigation sect. 1996-97, dir. divns. litigation sect. 1997-98, co-chair fed. practice task force litigation sect. 1998-2000, liaison to civil adv. com. jud. conf. on rules of practice and procedure 1998-2000, planning com. mem. London 2000 meeting 1996-2000, working group on UCITA 2001-2002, task force on advocacy for the assn. and profession 2002-2003, Pro Bono Publico award 1986), State Bar Tex. (jud. selection funding com. 1985-87, liaison with law schs. 1988-90, legal aid to indigent com. 1986, numerous coms. 1986-87), Alliance for Jud. Funding (bd. dirs. 1992-95, 2003—), Tex. Law Rev. Assn. (past pres., bd. dirs. 1977-95, ex officio, bd. dirs. 1995— Leon Green award 1997), U. Tex. Ex-Students Assn. (exec. coun. 1992-98), Houston Bar Assn. (vol. lawyers program bd. 1998-2000), Houston U. Tex. Ex-Students Assn. (bd. dirs. 1991-92), Yale U. Alumni Club (class sec. 1991-96, coun. 1986-87, local dir. 1982-89, 90-91). Avocations: golf, books. Office: Vinson & Elkins LLP 1001 Fannin St Ste 2300 Houston TX 77002-6760 Business E-Mail: satlas@velaw.com.

ATLAS, SETH J., lawyer; b. N.Y.C., 1958; s. Anthony H. and Elena A.; m. Clare F. Russo; 1 child, Emily BS in Chemistry cum laude, Yale Coll., 1980; JD, Columbia U., 1983. Bar: N.Y. 1984, U.S. Dist. Ct. (so. and ea. dists.) N.Y. 1984, U.S. Patent Office 1986, U.S. Ct. Appeals (fed. cir.) 1987. Assoc. Stroock and Stroock and Lavan, N.Y.C., 1983-86, Morgan and Finnegan, N.Y.C., 1986-95, ptnr., 1996—. Mng. editor Columbia U. Jour. Environ. Law, 1982-83. Named Harlan Fiske Stone scholar, 1981, 83. Mem. ABA, N.Y. Bar Assn., N.Y. County Lawyers Assn., N.Y. Intellectual Property Law Assn., Am. Intellectual Propr. Law Assn. Office: Morgan & Finnegan LLP 3 World Financial Ctr New York NY 10281-2101 Business E-Mail: sjatlas@morganfinnegan.com.

ATLAS, TERRY, journalist; b. Washington, 1952; BA in Econs. and Polit. Sci., U. Rochester, 1974. Energy reporter Chgo. Tribune, Washington, 1978—83, Washington corr., 1983—86, chief diplomatic corr., Washington bur., 1986—97, Washington news editor, 1997—99; asst. mng. editor (nation and world) U.S. News & World Report, Washington, 1999—. Named Bagehot fellow, Columbia U., 1976—77. Office: US News and World Report 1050 Thomas Jefferson St NW Washington DC 20007-3837

ATLEE, DEBBIE GAYLE, sales consultant, medical educator; b. Oklahoma City, Jan. 8, 1955; d. Harold Phillip and Ella Ruth (Birks) A. BS in Nursing, U. Okla., 1977. RN, Okla.; cert. diabetes educator. Team leader ob-gyn Bapt. Med. Ctr. of Okla., Oklahoma City, 1977-80, asst. clin. supr. urology, 1980-81, nursing educator, diabetes educator, 1981-84; sales specialist Boehringer Mannheim Diagnostics, Inc., Indpls., 1984-99; diabetes educator Dept. Endocrinology U. Okla. Coll. Medicine, 1999-2000; bus. sales mgr. NovoNordisk Pharms., Inc., Princeton, NJ, 2000—02; diabetes case mgr. Ediba Diabetes Ctr. Excellence Integris Bapt. Med. Ctr., Okla. City, 2002—. Mem. regional piloting adv. group Nat. Diabetes Adv. Bd., Oklahoma City, 1984-85. Named Outstanding Bus. Woman, Bus. and Profl. Women, Capitol Hill chpt., 1981, Salesperson of Yr. 1987; recipient Outstanding Sales Achievement award, 1985, 87, 90, 91. Mem. Am. Diabetes Assn. (exec. bd. Met. chpt. 1985—, pres. 1987), Am. Assn. Diabetes Educators, Western Okla. Diabetes Educators (pres. 1984, 2005, Outstanding Svc. and Dedication award 1984, chpt. svc. award 1985, chpt. edn. award 1984), Nat. Bd. Cert. Diabetes Educator, U.S. Power Squadron (bd. dirs. Oklahoma City 1984, 87), U. Okla. Alumni Assn. (life). Republican. Roman Catholic. Avocations: sailing, photography, gardening, music. E-mail: debbie.atlee@hotmail.com.

ATLEE, JOHN LIGHT, physician, consultant; b. Lancaster, Pa., Feb. 22, 1941; s. John Light Jr. and Ann (Stevens) A.; m. Barbara Sheaffer, June 20, 1964 (dec. Apr. 14, 1967); m. Barbara Sanford, Feb. 3, 1968; children: Sarah Sanford, John Light. BA, Franklin and Marshall Coll., 1963; MD, Temple U., 1967, MS in Pharmacology, 1971. Diplomate Am. Bd. Anesthesiology. Intern Germantown Hosp., Phila., 1967-68; resident in anesthesiology Temple U. Hosp., Phila., 1968-70; postdoctoral rsch. fellow pharmacology Temple U. Grad. Sch. Medicine, 1970-71; staff anesthesiologist U.S. Naval Hosp, Bethesda, Md., 1971-73; asst. prof. anesthesiology U. Wis., Madison, 1973-78; assoc. prof. anesthesiology, 1978-85, prof. anesthesiology, 1985-88, Med. Coll. Wis., Milw., 1988—. Mem. editl. bd., referee, cons. peer rev. jours. Anesthesia & Analgesia, Am. Heart Jour., Am. Jour. of Physiology, Anesthesiology, Med. and Biol. Engring. and Computing, Jour. of Cardiothoracic and Vascular Anesthesia; chmn., CEO Cardiac Control Techs.; cons. Medtronic Inc., Sr. Devices, Inc., 1995-98, CardioCommand Inc., ESP Pharma. Author: Perioperative Cardiac Arrhythmias, 1985, 2d edit., 1990, Arrhythmias and Pacemakers, 1996; editor: Perioperative Management of Pacemaker Patients, 1992, Complications in Anesthesia, 1999, Critical Care Cardiology in the Perioperative Period, 2001, Complicanze in Anestesia (Italian), 2001; contbr. articles to profl. jours. Lt. comdr. USN, 1971—73. Grantee, NIH, 1978—96. Fellow: Am. Heart Assn., Am. Coll. Cardiology and Anesthesiology; mem.: Am. Soc. Exptl. Pharmacology and Therapeutics, Soc. Register Assn., Heart Rhythm Soc., Assn. Univ. Anesthesiologists, Am. Soc. Anesthesiologists, Sigma Xi. Republican. Episcopalian. Achievements include development of non-invasive, esophageal-based patient monitoring and therapy (oximetry, electrocardiography, pacing, etc.); first respond ER(TM); patents in field. Home: W 309 N 6698 Caddy Court Hartland WI 53029-9249 Office Phone: 414-805-6100. Personal E-mail: jatlee@wi.rr.com.

ATOR, GREGORY A., otolaryngologist, consultant; BSEE, Tex. A&M U., 1981; MD, Baylor Coll., 1985. Diplomate Am. Bd. Otolaryngology, 1992. Resident UCLA, 1991—92; fellow in otologyneurotology Baylor Coll. Medicine, 1991—92; asst. prof. U. Kans. Med. Ctr., Kansas City, 1992—97, assoc. prof., 1997—. Bd. dirs. Kans. Commn. for Deaf and Hard of Hearing, Topeka. Fellow, Baylor Coll. Med. Otology-Neurotology, 1991—92; grantee, NIH, Nat. Inst. Deafness and Communicable Disorders. Achievements include research in Sudden hearing loss, Medical informatics. Office: Dept Otolaryngology Univ KS 3901 Rainbow Mailstop 3010 Kansas City KS 66160 Office Phone: 913-588-6731. E-mail: gator@kumc.edu.

ATRAK, TAISSER M., pediatrician, director; b. Lebanon, Beirut, Jan. 10, 1959; m. Amani Noor Hashisho, Jan. 5, 1971. Cert. neonatal-perinatal medicine Am. Bd. Pediat., 1997. Attending neonatologist St Mary's Hosp., Grand Rapids, Mich., 1990—91, St Mary's Hosp./Columbia Hosp., West Palm Beach, Fla., 1991—96; cons. neonatologist Aramco Oil Co., Dharhan, Saudi Arabia, 1996—2002; attending neonatologist West Boca Med. Ctr., Boca Raton, Fla., 2002—04; dir. neonatology Lake Norman Med. Ctr., Moorsville, NC, 2004—. Dir. neonatal ICU Lake Norman Med. Ctr. Fellow, U. Mo. Columbia Sch. Medicine, 1990. Office: Lake Norman Regional Med Ctr 171 Fairview Rd Moorsville NC 28078 Office Phone: 704-660-4390.

ATREYA, SUSHIL KUMAR, planetary-space science educator, astrophysicist; b. Apr. 15, 1946; came to U.S., 1966, naturalized, 1975; s. Harvansh Lal and Kailash Vati (Sharma) A.; 1 child, Chloë E. ScB, U. Rajasthan, India, 1963, MSc, 1965; MS, Yale U., 1968; PhD, U. Mich., 1973. Rsch. assoc. physics U. Pitts., 1973-74; asst., then assoc. rsch. scientist U. Mich., Ann Arbor, 1974-78, asst. prof., 1978-81, assoc. prof. atmospheric sci., 1981-87, prof. atmospheric and space sci., 1987—, dir. planetary sci. lab. Assoc. prof. U. Paris, 1984-85, vis. prof., 2000, 01; vis. sr. rsch. scientist Imperial Coll., London, 1984; mem. sci. expt. and investigation team Mars Sci. Lab., sample analysis Mars Ste., Juno-Jupiter Polar Orbiter, Cassini-Huygens Probe to Saturn-Titan, Galileo Jupiter Probe, Nozomi, Mars Express and Venus Express Missions, Russian Mars '96 and Soviet Phobos projects, Voyager spacecraft missions to the giant planets, Comet Rendezvous/Asteroid Flyby, 1986-92, Japanese Mars Mission, 1999-2004, and SpaceLab I; guest observer/investigator on Spitzer Telescope, Hubble Space Telescope, Internat. Ultraviolet Spectrometer and Copernicus Orbiting Astron. Obs.; mem. sci. working groups, adv. coms. NASA, Jet Propulsion Lab., European Space Agy. Author: Atmospheres and Ionospheres of the Outer Planets and their Satellites, 1986; editor: Planetary Aeronomy and Astronomy, 1981, Outer Planets, 1989, Cometary Environments, 1989, Origin and Evolution of Planetary and Satellite Atmospheres, 1989; contbr. numerous articles to books and profl. jours. Recipient NASA award for exceptional sci. contbns. Voyager Project, 1981, NASA Group Achievement award for Voyager Ultraviolet Spectrometer Investigations, 1981, 86, 90, NASA Group Achievement awards for Galileo Probe Mass Spectrometer experiment, and for Significant Outstanding Contbns. to the Galileo Probe and Orbiter to Jupiter, Excellence in Rsch. award U. Mich. Coll. Engring., 1995. Mem. AAAS, Internat. Assn. Meteorology and Atmospheric Scis. (pres. commn. planetary atmospheres and their evolution 1987-95, sec. 1983-87), Am. Geophys. Union (assoc. editor Geophys. Rsch. Letters jour. 1986-89), Internat. Astron. Union, Am. Astron. Soc., Internat. Acad. Astronautics (academician 1993—). Office: Space Rsch Bldg Univ Mich Ann Arbor MI 48109-2143

ATTAALLAH, AHMED FIKRY, physician, anesthesiologist; b. Giza, Giza, Egypt, Aug. 22, 1971; MD, Cairo U. Sch. Medicine, 1994, MSc, 1999, PhD, 2005. ECFMG USA, 2000. Intern Kasr El-Aini Hosp., Cairo U., Egypt, 1995—96, anesthesiology resident, 1996—99, anesthesiology asst. lectr., 1999—; intern Police Authority Hosp., Egypt, 1996—96; cardiac anesthesiologist / intensives care unit Dar Al-Fouad Hosp., Egypt, 1999—2000; anesthesiology rsch. fellow W.Va. U., Morgantown, W.Va., 2000—01, anesthesiology resident, 2001—05. Mem.: AMA, Internat. Anesthesia Rsch. Soc. (IARS), The Am. Soc. of Regional Anesthesia and Pain medicine (RAMP), Soc. Neuroscience (SFN), Soc. Neurosurgical Anesthesia and Critical Care (SNACC), Am. Soc. Anesthesiologists (ASA), W.Va. Soc. Anesthesiologist, The Ctrl. Soc. Egyptian Anesthesiologists, Am. Pain Soc., Cairo Doctors' syndicate. Office: Dept Anesthesiology WVU 3618 Health Sci Ctr Morgantown WV 26505 Office Phone: 304-598-4122. Office Fax: 304-598-4037. E-mail: fikrya@rcbhsc.wvu.edu.

ATTAL, GENE (FRED EUGENE ATTAL), hospital executive; b. Oct. 6, 1947; s. Sam Arthur and Olga (Johns) A.; m. Marsha Ablah, July 26, 1970; children: Christopher, Allison, Anne. BJ with spl. honors, U. Tex., 1970; MS, Columbia U., 1972. Pub. rels. exec. Westinghouse Electric Corp.; sr. v.p. fund devel. Seton Healthcare Network, 1975—; pres. Seton Fund, Austin, 1975—. Mem. faculty U. Tex. Recipient Telstar Excellence in Comm. award, annually, 1978-81, Arthur W. Page award U. Tex., 1986; NDEA fellow in langs. U. Tex., 1968-69, Internat. fellow Columbia U., 1972; recipient Sy Seymour award, Assn. for Healthcare Philanthropy, 2003, Beverly Sheffield award, Austin County Fedn., 2005. Mem. Am. Soc. Hosp. Pub. Rels. (regional dir.), Assn. Healthcare Philanthropy (internat. bd. dirs., chair bd. dirs. 2000-01), Tex. Soc. Hosp. Pub. Rels. (pres. 1981), Barton Creek Country Club. Greek Orthodox. Home: 1201 Constant Springs Dr Austin TX 78746-6615 Office: 1201 W 38th St Austin TX 78705-1006 Office Phone: 512-324-1990.

ATTANASI, EMIL DONALD, economist, municipal official; b. Newark, July 5, 1947; s. Dominick Joseph and Katherine (Cavitch) Attanasi; m. Diana Elizabeth Frank, Aug. 29, 1969; children: Jennifer, Katherine, Marie. BA in Math., magna cum laude, Evangel. Coll., 1969; MA in Econs., U. Mo., 1971, PhD, 1972; MS in Statis. Sci., George Mason U., 2003. Economist U.S. Geol. Survey, Reston, Va., 1972—. Mem. faculty George Mason U., Fairfax, Ala., 1979—80; commr. Vienna Town Planning Commn., 1983, vice chmn., 1989—90, 2001, chmn., 1991—92; lectr. U.S. Congl. Fellows, Washington, 1982. Contbr. articles to profl. jours.; co-editor: Spl. Jour. Issues of Procs. of Mineral Econs. Symposium, 1980—83. Trustee Fairfax Assembly of God, 1980—84; trustee, bd. dirs. Key to Life Assembly of God, McLean, Va., 1977—78. Recipient Cmty. Builders award, Masonic Lodge, 1993, Meritorious Svc. award, U.S. Dept. Interior, 1994; U. Mo. fellow, 1969—72. Mem.: Am. Inst. Mining Engrs. (sec. local minerals econs. subsect. 1985—86), Am. Econ. Assn., So. Econ. Assn. (jour. referee), Omicron Delta Epsilon (treas. 1971—73).

ATTANASIO, JOHN BAPTIST, dean, law educator; b. Jersey City, N.J., Oct. 19, 1954; s. Gaetano and Madeline (Germinario) A.; m. Kathleen Mary Spartana, Aug. 20, 1977; children: Thomas, Michael. BA, U. Va., 1976; JD, NYU, 1979; diploma in law, Oxford U., 1982; LLM, Yale U., 1985. Bar: Md. 1979, U.S. Dist. Ct. Md. 1980, U.S. Ct. Appeals (4th cir.) 1980, U.S. Supreme Ct. 1983. Pvt. practice, Balt., 1979-81; vis. asst. prof. law U. Pitts., 1982-84; assoc. prof. law U. Notre Dame, Ind., 1985-88, prof. law, 1988-92; Regan dir. Kroc Inst. for Internat. Peace Studies, 1991-92; dean Sch. of Law St. Louis U., 1992-98; dean, William Hawley Atwell chair constnl. law So. Meth. U. Sch. Law, Dallas, 1998—. Co-author: Constitutional Law, 1989, Understanding Constitutional Law, 1993. Chair adv. bd. Ctr. for Civil and Human Rights, 1990-92; mem. Fulbright awards area com., 1994-96; bd. dirs. Legal Svcs. Ea. Mo., 1996-98; bd. dirs. Ctr. for Internat. Recipient Legal Teaching award Sch. of Law, NYU, 1994. Mem. Ctrl. States Law Sch. Assn. (v.p. 1992-94), Phi Beta Kappa, Alpha Sigma Nu. Roman Catholic. Office: So Meth U Dedman Sch Law PO Box 750116 3315 Daniel Ave Dallas TX 75205-0116 Business E-Mail: jba@smu.edu.

ATTAWAY, JOHN A., JR., lawyer; b. Charleston, W.Va., July 17, 1958; BA in mgmt. sciences, Duke U., 1980; JD, Stetson U., 1982; LLM in taxation, U. Fla., 1984. Bar: Fla. 1983. Assoc. atty. Raymond, Rupp & Wienberg, Boca Raton, Fla., 1984—86; ptnr. Lane Trohn Bertrand & Vreeland, Lakeland, Fla.; corp. counsel Publix Super Markets Inc., Lakeland, Fla., 1997—2000, gen. counsel, sec., 2000—04, sr. v.p., gen. counsel, 2005—. Chmn. United Way of Ctrl. Fla., 1997—98. Office: Publix Super Markets Inc 3300 Airport Rd Lakeland FL 33811

ATTEBERY, LOUIE WAYNE, language educator; b. Weiser, Idaho, Aug. 14, 1927; s. John Thomas Attebery and Tressie Mae (Blevins) Attebery Miller; m. Barbara Phyllis Olson, Dec. 31, 1947; children: Bobby Lou, Brian Leonard. BA, Albertson Coll. of Idaho, 1950; MA, U. Mont., 1951; PhD, U. Denver, 1961. Tchr. Middleton (Idaho) H.S., 1949-50, Payette (Idaho) H.S., 1951-52, Nyssa (Oreg.) H.S., 1952-55, East H.S., Denver, 1955-61; prof. English Albertson Coll. Idaho, Caldwell, 1961-99, holder Eyck-Berringer chair English, 1987-98, acting acad. v.p., 1983-84; pres. West Shore Press, 1998—. Vis. fellow Harvard U., Cambridge, Mass., 1993-94. Author: The College of Idaho, 1981-91, A Centennial History, 1991, Sheep May Safely Graze: A Personal Essay on Tradition and A Contemporary Sheep Ranch, 1993, The Most of What We Spend, 1998, Albertson College of Idaho: The Second Hundred Years, 1999, J.R. Simplot: A Billion the Hard Way, 2000; editor: Idaho Folklife: Homesteads to Headstones, 1985; editor Northwest Folklore, 1985-91; gen. editor U. Idaho Northwest Folklife series, 1991-2004. Trustee Idaho Hist. Soc., 1984-91, Albertson Coll. Idaho, 2003—. With USN, 1945-46. Bruern fellow, U. Leeds, Eng., 1971—72. Mem. Western Lit. Assn. (exec coun. 1964-65), Assn. Lit. Scholars and Critics, 1995-. Methodist. E-mail: lattebery@albertson.edu.

ATTENBOROUGH, BARON RICHARD SAMUEL, actor, producer, director, goodwill ambassador; b. Cambridge, England, Aug. 29, 1923; s. Frederick Attenborough; m. Sheila Beryl Grant Sim, 1945; 3 children. Leverhulme scholar to Royal Acad. Dramatic Art, 1941 (Bancroft Medal); DLitt (hon.), U. Leicester, 1970, U. Kent, 1981, U. Sussex, 1987; DCL (hon.), U. Newcastle, 1974; LLD (hon.), Dickinson Coll., 1983; DLit (hon.), Am. Internat. U., 1994; DLitt (hon.), Cape Town, 2000. Fleming Meml. lectr. R.T.S., 1989; Cameron Mackintosh vis. prof. of theatre Oxford U., 1996; pro-chancellor U. Sussex, 1970-98, chancellor 1998—. First stage appearance as Richard Miller in Ah, Wilderness, Intimate Theatre, Palmers Green, 1941; Ralph Berger in Awake and Sing, Arts (West End debut), 1942; The Little Foxes, Piccadilly, 1942; Brighton Rock, Garrick, 1943. Joined RAF 1943; seconded to RAF Film Unit for Journey Together, 1944; demobilized, 1946. Returned to stage in The Way Back (Home of the Brave), Westminster, 1949; To Dorothy a Son, Savoy, 1950, Garrick, 1951; Sweet Madness, Vaudeville, 1952; The Mousetrap, Ambassadors, 1952-54; Double Image, Savoy, 1956-57, St. James's, 1957; The Rape of the Belt, Piccadilly, 1957-58; film appearances: In Which We Serve (screen debut), 1942, Schweik's New Adventure, 1943, The Hundred Pound Window, 1944, A Matter of Life and Death, 1946, School for Secrets, 1946, The Man Within, 1947, Dancing With Crime, 1947, Brighton Rock, 1947, London Belongs to Me, 1948, The Guinea Pig, 1948, The Lost People, 1949, Boys in Brown, 1949, Morning Departure, 1950, Hell is Sold Out, 1951, The Magic Box, 1951, Gift Horse, 1952, Father's Doing Fine, 1952, Eight O'Clock Walk, 1952, The Ship That Died of Shame, 1955, Private's Progress, 1956, The Baby and the Battleship, 1956, Brothers in Law, 1957, The Scamp, 1957, Dunkirk, 1958, The Man Upstairs, 1958, Sea of Sand, 1958, Danger Within, 1959, I'm All Right Jack, 1959, Jet Storm, 1959, SOS Pacific, 1959, The League of Gentlemen, 1959, The Angry Silence (also co-prod.), 1960, All Night Long, 1961, Only Two Can Play, 1962, The Dock Brief, 1962, The Great Escape, 1963, Seance On a Wet Afternoon (also prod., Best Actor, San Sebastian Film Festival and Brit. Film Acad.), 1964, The Third Secret, 1964, Guns at Batasi (Best Actor, Brit. Film Acad.), 1964, The Flight of the Phoenix, 1965, The Sand Pebbles (Hollywood Golden Globe), 1966, Dr. Dolittle (Hollywood Golden Globe), 1967, The Bliss of Mrs. Blossom, 1968; Only When I Larf, 1968, The Magic Christian, 1969, Loot, 1970, The Last Grenade, 1970, A Severed Head, 1970, 10 Rillington Place, 1971, (voice) Cup Glory, 1972, And Then There Were None, 1974, Rosebud, 1975, Brannigan, 1975, Conduct Unbecoming, 1975, The Chess Players, 1977, The Human Factor, 1979, Jurassic Park, 1993, Miracle on 34th St., 1994, E=mc2, 1996, Hamlet, 1996, The Lost World: Jurassic Park, 1997, Elizabeth, 1998, Puckoon, 2002 (also writer, dir.); (video-voice) The Trespasser, 1998; (video) Joseph and the Amazing Technicolor Dreamcoat, 1999; (TV series-voice) Tom and Vicky, 1999; (TV) David Copperfield, 1969, The Railway Children, 2000, Jack and the Beanstalk: The Real Story, 2001; producer: Whistle Down the Wind, 1961; The L-Shaped Room, 1962; producer, dir. Oh! What a Lovely War (16 Internat. Awards including Hollywood Golden Globe and BAFTA UN Award), 1968, Young Winston (Hollywood Golden Globe), 1972, Gandhi (8 Oscars, 5 Brit. Acad. TV and Film Artists Awards, 5 Hollywood Golden Globes, Dirs.' Guild of Am. Award for Outstanding Directorial Achievement), 1980-81, Cry Freedom (Berlinale Kamera, BFI award tech. achievement), 1987, Chaplin, 1992, Shadowlands, 1992 (Alexander Korda award for outstanding Brit. film of yr., BAFTA), In Love and War, 1997, Grey Owl, 1998; dir. A Bridge Too Far (Evening News Best Drama Award), 1976, Magic, 1978, A Chorus Line, 1985; publications: In Search of Gandhi, 1982, Richard Attenborough's A Chorus Line (with Diana Carter), 1986, Cry Freedom, A Pictorial Record, 1987; actor: Light Keeps Me Company (Europe), 2000, The Railway Children, 2000 (TV), Joseph and the Amazing Technicolor Dreamcoat, 2000. Goodwill amb. UNICEF, 1987—; mem. Brit. Actors' Equity Assoc. Council, 1949-73, Cinematograph Films Council, 1967-73, Arts Council of Great Britain, 1970-73; formed Beaver Films with Bryan Forbes, 1959, Allied Film Makers, 1960; dir. Chelsea Football Club, 1969-82, life v.p., 1993—; dir. Young Vic, 1974-84; chmn. The Actor's Charitable Trust, 1956-88, pres., 1988—; chmn. European Script Fund, 1988-96, hon. pres., 1996—, Combined Theatrical Charities Appeals Council, 1964-88, pres., 1988—; chmn. Brit. Acad. Film and TV Artists (v.p. from 1971-94, chmn. trustees, 1970-, pres. 2002-), 1969-70, Royal Acad. Dramatic Art, mem. council 1963—, chmn., 1972—, Capital Radio, 1972-92, life pres., 1992—, Help a London Child, 1975—; trustee King George V Fund for Actors and Actresses, 1973—; chmn. U.K. Trustees Waterford-Kamhlaba Sch., Swaziland (gov. 1987—), 1976—, Duke of York's Theatre, 1979-92, Brit. Film Inst., 1981-92, Goldcrest Films & TV, 1982-87, Com. of Inquiry into the Arts and Disabled People, 1983-85, Channel Four TV (dep. chmn. 1980-86), 1987-92, Brit. Screen Adv. Council, 1987—; Gov. Nat. Film Sch., 1970-81, 96, hon. pres. 96; pres. Muscular Dystrophy Group of Great Britain (v.p. 1962-71), 1971-96, hon. pres. 1996—; pres. The Gandhi Found., 1983—, Brighton Festival, 1984-95, Brit. Film Yr., 1984-86; trustee Tate Gallery, 1976-82, 94-96, Tate Found., 1986—, Found. Sport and Arts, 1991—; pres. Arts for Health, 1989—, Gardner Centre Arts, Sussex U., 1990—; gov. Motability, 1977—; patron Kingsley Hall Community Ctr., 1982—; R.A. Centre Disability & Arts, Leicester, 1990-; life v.p. Chelsea Football Club. Decorated Commander Brit. Empire, 1967, Knighted 1976; recipient Evening Std. Film award, 40 yrs. svc. to Brit. Cinema, 1983, Praemium Imperiale award, 1998, Martin Luther King Jr. Peace Prize, 1983, Padma Bhushan, India, 1983, award of merit for humanitarianism in film making, European Film awards, 1988, Shakespeare prize Outstanding Contbn. European culture, 1992, Patricia Rothermere award for lifelong service to theatre, London Evening Standard Theatre award, 2003; named Commandeur, Ordre des Arts et des Lettres, France, 1985; Chevalier, Order de la Legion d'Honneur, France, 1988; named Freeman of City of Leicester, 1990; named fellow Kings Coll. London, 1993; named Baron, Life Peer of Long Borough of Richmond upon Thames, 1993; recipient hon. fellowship U. Wales, Bangor, 1997, Manchester Poly., 1994, Kings Coll., 1993. Fellow BAFTA, Brit. Film Inst.; mem. Garrick Club, Beefsteak Club. Avocations: collecting paintings and sculpture, listening to music, watching football. Home: Old Friars Richmond Green Surrey England Office: Richard Attenborough Prodns Twickenham Studio Saint Margaret's Middlesex TW1 2AW England*

ATTOLE, MARY BERTHA, writer; b. Lafayette, La., Dec. 12, 1958; d. Antoine and Elia Guillory Attole. Student, So. U., Baton Rouge, La., 1976—80. Tchr.'s aide Glendale Elem., Eunice, La., 1980—82; mem. staff Fred's Dept. Store, Eunice, 1983—85, John's IGA Grocery Store, Eunice, 1985—88. Author: My Brother's Keeper, 2001. Vol. So. Poverty Law Ctr.'s Civil Rights Meml. Visitors Ctr. Wall of Tolerance; active Creole Heritage

Found., Northwestern State U., 2005—; vol. St. Matilda Cth. Ch., Eunice, 1991—. Mem.: Alpha Mu Gamma. Democrat. Roman Catholic. Avocations: reading, genealogy, comedy, classic television, pets. Home: 310 N Martin Luther King Dr Eunice LA 70535

ATTRIDGE, DANIEL F., lawyer; b. Washington, Oct. 4, 1954; s. Patrick and Teresa A.; m. Anne Asbill, Aug. 23, 1980; children: James, William, and Thomas. BA magna cum laude, U. Pa., 1976; JD cum laude, Georgetown U., 1979. Bar: D.C. 1980, U.S. Dist. Ct. D.C. 1980, U.S. Ct. Appeals (D.C. cir.) 1980, U.S. Supreme Ct. 1983, U.S. Dist. Ct. Md. 1985, U.S. Ct. Appeals (fed. cir.) 1985, U.S. Ct. Appeals (2d.cir.) 1987, U.S. Ct. Claims 1988, U.S. Ct. Appeals (4th and 6th cirs.) 1990, U.S. Ct. Appeals (8th cir.) 1997, U.S. Ct. Appeals (1st cir.) 2000, U.S. Ct. Appeals (11th cir.) 2003, U.S. Ct. Appeals (9th cir.) 2004. Law clk. to judge Oliver Gasch U.S. Dist. Ct. D.C., Washington, 1979-80; assoc. Kirkland & Ellis LLP, Washington, 1980-85, ptnr., 1985—. Faculty Nat. Inst. Trial Advocacy, 1991—. Exec. editor Georgetown U. Law Jour., 1978-79. Trustee Fed. City Coun., 2003—. Fellow Am. Bar Found.; mem. ABA (vice chmn. antitrust sect. Sherman Act sect. 2 com. 1999-2002), D.C. Bar Assn. (bd. govs. 1996-99, co-chair litigation sect. 1993-96). Roman Catholic. Home: 1249 Cherry Tree Ln Annapolis MD 21403-5023 Office: Kirkland & Ellis LLP 655 15th St NW Fl 12 Washington DC 20005-5793 Business E-Mail: dattridge@kirkland.com.

ATTRIDGE, RICHARD BYRON, lawyer; b. Atlanta, Oct. 14, 1933; s. Archibald Angus and Katherine Elizabeth (Babb) A.; m. Florence Law, Dec. 14, 1963; children: Anne Habersham, Elizabeth Barnes, R. Byron Jr. BA, Princeton U., 1955; LLB, Emory U., 1961. Bar: Ga. 1960. Ptnr. King & Spalding, Atlanta, 1960—. Chmn. State Bd. of Bar Examiners, Ga., 1978-83. Vice chmn. Cmty. Rels. Com., Atlanta, 1968-73; various local charities; vestry Episc. Ch. 1st lt. U.S. Army, 1956-57. Fellow Am. Coll. Trial Lawyers; mem. ABA, State Bar Ga. (bd. govs. 1974-83), Atlanta Bar Assn. (pres. 1971-72), Lawyers Club Atlanta, Capital City Club (bd. dirs. 1989—), Piedmont Driving Club. Avocations: hunting, fishing, tennis. Home: 2820 Habersham Rd NW Atlanta GA 30305-2959 Office: King & Spalding 191 Peachtree St NE Ste 40 Atlanta GA 30303-1740 Office Phone: 404-572-4787. E-mail: battridge@kslaw.com.

ATTWOOD, DAVID THOMAS, physicist, researcher; b. N.Y.C., Aug. 15, 1941; s. David Thomas and Josephine (Banks) A.; divorced; children: Timothy David, Courtney Catherine, Kevin Richard; m. Linda Jean Geniesse, Aug. 3, 1991. BS, Hofstra U., 1963; MS, Northwestern U., 1964; D Engring. Sci., NYU, 1972. Physicist Lawrence Livermore Nat. Lab., Livermore, Calif., 1972-83, Lawrence Berkeley Nat. Lab., Berkeley, Calif., 1983—; sci. dir. Advanced Light Source, 1985—88; prof. in residence dept. elec. engring. and computer sci. U. Calif., Berkeley, 1989—, founding chair applied sci. and tech. PhD program. Founder Ctr. for X-Ray Optics, Lawrence Berkeley Lab., 1983; assoc. dir. NSF EUV Sci. Tech. Ctr., 2003—. Author: Soft X-Rays and Extreme Ultraviolet Radiation: Principles and Applications, 2000; editor: (with B.L. Henke) X-Ray Diagnostics, (with J. Bokor) Short Wavelength Coherent Radiation, (with F. Zernike) Extreme Ultraviolet Lithography, (with W. Meyer-Ilse and T. Warwick) X-Ray Microscopy; reviewer numerous sci. jours.; contbr. numerous articles to profl. publs. Fellow: Optical Soc. Am.; mem.: AAAS, Am. Phys. Soc. Achievements include research on x-ray optics and microscopy, extreme ultraviolet lithography, synchrotron radiation, partially coherent x-rays, and laser-plasma interactions. Office: Lawrence Berkeley Nat Lab Ctr X-ray Optics Berkeley CA 94720

ATTWOOD, JAMES ALBERT, JR., investment company executive; b. Lake Forest, Ill., Apr. 20, 1958; s. James Albert and Pauline Veryl (Ellwood) A.; m. Leslie Kim Williams. BA in Applied Math., summa cum laude, MA in Stats., Yale U., 1980; MBA, JD, Harvard U., 1985. Bar: Mass., N.Y., D.C. Assoc. Hewitt Assocs., Rowayton, Conn., 1980-81; v.p. Goldman, Sachs & Co., N.Y.C., 1985-96; exec. v.p. strategic devel. and planning GTE Corp., Irving, Tex., 1996-2000; exec. v.p. strategy, devel. and planning Verizon Comm., N.Y.C., 2000; mng. dir. The Carlyle Group, N.Y.C., 2000—. Co-chmn. Dex Media, Englewood, Colo., 2002—. Democrat. Presbyterian. Office: The Carlyle Group 520 Madison Ave New York NY 10022

ATWATER, BRIAN F., geologist; BS, Stanford U., 1973, MS, 1974; PhD, U. Del., 1980. Geologist US Geol. Survey, mem. Pacific N.W. Earthquake Hazards Team; affiliate prof. dept. earth and spaces sciences & quaternary rsch. ctr. U. Washington, Seattle, assoc. editor Quaternary Rsch. jour., 1994—2001. Guest rschr. U. Tokyo, Geol. Survey of Japan. Named one of 100 Most Influential People of 2005, Time mag. Office: U Washington Dept Earth & Space Sciences 710 Condon Hall Box 351310 Seattle WA 98195 Office Phone: 206-553-2927. Office Fax: 206-553-8350. Business E-Mail: atwater@ess.washington.edu.*

ATWATER, PHYLLIS Y., municipal official; b. Memphis, Nov. 4, 1947; d. Jeff D. and Thelda E. A.; m. John R. Ernst, Dec. 28, 1972. BA, Vassar Coll., 1968; MA, Boston U., 1970; postgrad., New Sch. Soc. Rsch., N.Y.C., 1974-82. Lectr. math. Tufts U., Medford, Mass., 1970-72; instr. math. higher edn. program Boston Model Cities Adminstrn., 1970-74, coord. program, 1971; instr. econs. SUNY, Old Westbury, 1977-82; dep. dir. adminstrn. and fin. Divsn. Solid Waste Mgmt., Commonwealth of Mass., 1984-88; pres. and chief operating officer Recoverable Resources/R2B2, Inc., Bronx, NY, 1989-91; dir. divsn. solid waste N.Y. State Dept. Environ. Conservation, 1992-93, regional dir. N.Y.C., 1993-95; pvt. practice computer svcs. cons., 1995-99; computer specialist N.Y.C. Dept. Employment, 1999—2002, assoc. commr. for info. tech. and adminstrn., 2002—03; admin. staff analyst N.Y.C. Dept. Small Bus. Svcs., 2003—. Assoc. Recycling Adv. Coun., EPA, Washington, 1990-93; vice chair Manhattan Solid Waste Adv. Bd., N.Y.C., 1991-92. Mem. founding bd. advisors N.Y. Feminist Art Inst., N.Y.C., 1979—81; bd. advisors The Labor Inst., N.Y.C., 1985—97, West Harlem Environ. Action Inc., N.Y.C., 1996—99; founder, pres., bd. dirs. Inst. for Labor and the Cmty., N.Y.C., 1997—; sec. bd. dirs. O.R.E., Inc., N.Y.C., 1998—; bd. dirs. Scenic Hudson, Inc., Poughkeepsie, NY, 2001—. Ford Found. fellow Nat. Fellowship Fund, 1975-78, Danforth Found., 1980-82.

ATWATER, TONY, university president; b. Nashville, Mar. 11, 1952; s. Herman and Lonnie May A.; m. Beverly Laverne Roberts, Dec. 20, 1980. AAS in Radio and TV Prodn., Va. Western Cmty. Coll., 1972; BA in Mass Media Arts, Hampton U., 1973; PhD in Comm., Mich. State U., 1983. Prof. journalism Mich. State U., East Lansing, 1983-91; dept. chmn. Rutgers U., New Brunswick, N.J., 1991-95; assoc. v.p. Univ. Toledo, Ohio, 1995-99; dean profl. studies Northern Ky. U., Highland Heights, 1999-2001; provost Youngstown (Ohio) State U., 2001—05; pres. Ind. U. Pa., Ind., Pa., 2005—. Asst. dir. Mich. State U. Honors Coll., East Lansing, 1988-91; bd. trustee Northwest Ohio Pub. TV Found., Toledo, 1997-99; bd. dirs. Covington (Ky.) Ednl. Found., 2000-01. Mem. editl. bd. Jour. of Broadcasting and Electronic Media, 1996-2000. Expert panel mem. Gov.'s Taskforce Youth and Substance Abuse, Lexington, Ky., 2000-01; mem. Leadership Cin., 2000-01. Mich. State U. doctoral fellow 1979, Tchg. fellow The Poynter Inst., 1990, Univ. Adminstrn. fellow Univ. Conn., Storrs, 1994, postdoctoral fellow Ford Found., U. Mich., 1988; rsch. grantee NSF, Toledo, 1988-89. Mem. Internatl Comm. Assn., Assn. Edn. Journalism and Mass Comm. (pres. 1992-93), Broadcast Edn. Assn., Soc. Profl. Journalists, Phi Kappa Phi Avocations: international travel, theater, public speaking. Office: Ind U Pa Sutton Hall Rm 201 1011 S Dr Indiana PA 15705 Office Phone: 724-357-2200. E-mail: tatwater@ysu.edu, tatwater@iup.edu.

ATWATER, VERNE STAFFORD, finance educator; b. Pitts., Aug. 22, 1920; s. Verne L. and Priscilla (Brodeur) Atwater; m. Evelyn Lowe, May 29, 1943; children: Lynda Mary Atwater Pyfrin, Louise Christine Atwater Cross. BA, Heidelberg Coll., 1942; MBA, Harvard U., 1943; PhD, NYU, 1961; LHD, Heidelberg Coll., 1989. Asst. prof. bus. adminstrn. Syracuse U., 1946-50; asst. to chmn. bd. N.J. Bank, Paterson, 1950-56; dir. adminstrn. Ford Found., 1956-61; rep. Argentina/Chile, 1961-63; dir. Latin Am. and Caribbean Program, 1963-64, v.p., 1964-68; pres. Westinghouse Learning Corp., N.Y.C., 1968-71; chmn., chief exec. officer Central Savs. Bank, N.Y., 1971-81; prof. fin. Lubin Grad. Sch. Bus., Pace U., N.Y.C., 1981-90, vice dean, 1984-86, prof. emeritus in residence, 1990-2001; lead ind. dir., 2003—04. Bd. dirs. Hudson City Bancorp., 1981—2005; mem. Nat. Commn. Electric Fund Transfers, 1975—77, Pres.'s Task Career Devel., 1967—68, N.J. Housing Fin. Agy., 1966—70. Chmn. Woodlawn Cemetery, 1994—98, James T. Lee Found.; chmn. bd. trustees Heidelberg Coll., 1982—89. Lt. USNR, 1943—46. Mem.: Univ. Club (N.Y.C.), Arcola Country Club (dir. Paramus, N.J.). Home: PO Box 1176 232 Boston Post Rd Amherst NH 03031-1176 Office Phone: 603-673-8026. Personal E-mail: singndo@aol.com.

ATWELL, NEDRA WHEELER, education educator, consultant; b. Louisville, Ky., Sept. 24, 1950; d. James Riley and Elsie Parsley Skaggs; m. Charles William Atwell, Aug. 10, 2000; children: Donald Wheeler, Jonathan Wheeler. BA in hist. and psychology, Western Ky. U., 1972, MA in exceptional child edn., 1988; EdD in ednl. leadership, Vanderbilt U., 1995. Cert. dir.special edn. U. Ky., Lexington, 1989, Ky. Standard Cert. for Tchrs. of Exceptional Children. LBD tchr. New Providence Sch., Clarksville, Tenn., 1972—75; prin. and ednl. therapist Rivendell America, Bowling Green, 1986—88; area program cons. Ky. Dept. Edn., Frankfort, 1988—90; dir. profl. devel. consortia Ky. Valley Ednl. Consortia, Hazard, 1990—97; special edn. faculty Alice Lloyd Coll., Pippa Passes, Ky., 1994—97; adj. grad. faculty Morehead State U., Ky., 1996—97; dir. tchr. edn., assoc. prof. Va. Intermont Coll., Bristol, 1997—2000; assoc. prof., personnel preparation grant coord. Radford U., Va., 2000—02; assoc. prof. special instrnl. programs, exceptional edn. Western Ky. U., Bowling Green, 2002—. Co-editor Tchr. Educators Jour. ATE-VA; copy editor Southeast Regional Assn. Tchr. Educators Jour., editl. bd. Author: (book) KVEC Principal Institute 1, 1992, KVEC Principal Institute 2, 1993, Affective Data Interpretation, 1993, Beans, Buses, and Basketball, 1993, Building School Communities for All, 1994, Change Process, 1995, The Instructional Leader's Primer in Systems Thinking, 1995, SMART: Science and Math Appalachian Regional Teachers Instructional Manual, 1996, Implementing School Centered Decision-Making, 1996, HEART: Humanities Education Appalachian Regional Teachers Integrated Curriculum Guide, 1996, Kentucky and Missouri School Improvement Models, 1997, Lighting Strikes Twice, 1997, Troubled Students and School, 1999. Mem.: Ky. Inst. Women Sch. Adminstrn. (mentor), Southeast Regional Assn. Tchr. Educators, Am. Assn. Tchr. Educators, Va. Assn. Tchr. Educators (exec. bd., editl. bd.), Nat. Staff Devel. Coun., Am. Coun. Rural Special Edn., Coun. Exceptional Children, VA Declaration (editor), Coun. Children Behavioral Disorders, VA Fedn. (past pres.), Coun. Exceptional Children, VA Fedn. (past pres.), Ky. Reading Assn., Internat. Reading Assn., Am. Ednl. Rsch. Assn., Am. Assn. U. Women, Appalachian Studies Assn., Phi Delta Kappa (v.p. membership, Radford U. chpt.). Office: Western Ky U 1 Big Red Way Bowling Green KY 42101 Office Phone: 270-745-4647. E-mail: nedra.atwell@wku.edu.

ATWELL, ROBERT HERRON, academic administrator; b. Washington, Pa., Jan. 26, 1931; s. R. Boice and Elsie (Herron) A.; m. Suzanne Fogg, Apr. 22, 1989; children by previous marriages: Mary, Robert, John, Nancy, Carl, Catherine, Cynthia. BA, Coll. Wooster, 1953; MA in Pub. Adminstrn., U. Minn., 1957. Budget examiner U.S. Bur. Budget, Washington, 1957-60; fiscal economist, loan officer U.S. Devel. Loan Fund, Dept. State, 1960; budget examiner, program analyst for higher edn. and med. research programs U.S. Bur. Budget, 1961-62; program planning officer, asst. chief Cmty. Mental Health Ctrs. br. NIMH, HEW, 1962-65; vice chancellor for adminstrn. U. Wis., Madison, 1965-70; pres. Pitzer Coll., Claremont, Calif., 1970-78; v.p. Am. Coun. Edn., 1978-84, pres., 1984-96, pres. emeritus, 1996—. Chmn. coun. Claremont Coll., 1971—72; pres. Ind. Colls. So. Calif., 1974—75; trustee Eckerd Coll., Edn. Mgmt. Corp., Argosy U., Western State U. Coll. Law; mem. adv. bd. Inside Track Learning; bd. dirs. Nat. Ctr. for Pub. Policy and Higher Edn. With AUS, 1953-55. Home: 447 Bird Key Dr Sarasota FL 34236-1805

ATWOOD, CHARLES L., recreational facility executive; MBA in Fin., Tulane U. CPA. From acct. to sr. v.p., CFO Harrah's Entertainment Inc., Las Vegas, 1979—2001, sr. v.p., 2001—, CFO, 2001—. Bd. dir. Equity Residential Trust. Mem.: AICPA. Office: Harrahs Entertainment Inc One Harrahs Ct Las Vegas NV 89119

ATWOOD, COLLEEN, costume designer; b. Ellensburg, Wash. Degree, Cornish Sch. Fine Arts, Seattle. Films include: Firstborn, 1984, (TV movie) Out of the Darkness, 1985, Bring on the Night, 1985, Manhunter, 1986, Critical Condition, 1987, Someone to Watch Over Me, 1987, The Pick-Up Artist, 1987, Torch Song Trilogy, 1988, Married to the Mob, 1988, Fresh Horses, 1988, For Keeps, 1988, Hider in the House, 1989, The Handmaid's Tale, 1989, Joe Versus the Volcano, 1990, Edward Scissorhands, 1990, Silence of the Lambs, 1991, Rush, 1991, Lorenzo's Oil, 1992, Love Field, 1992, Philadelphia, 1993, Born Yesterday, 1993, Cabin Boy, 1994, Wyatt Earp, 1994, Ed Wood, 1994, Little Women, 1994 (Acad. award nominee, best costume design 1994), Mars Attacks!, 1996, That Thing You Do, 1996, Beloved, 1998, Mumford, 1998, Sleepy Hollow, 1999, Golden Dreams, 2001, The Mexican, 2001, Planet of the Apes, 2001, The Tick, 2001, CinéMagique, 2002, Chicago, 2002 (Academy award, best costume design, 2003), Big Fish, 2003, Lemony Snicket's A Series of Unfortunate Events, 2004, Memoirs of a Geisha, 2005.*

ATWOOD, EDWARD CHARLES, economist, educator; b. N.Y.C., Dec. 2, 1922; s. Edward Charles and Bertha Margaret (Moloney) A.; m. June Matilda Ruschmeyer, Mar. 30, 1946; children— Edward Terrell, Jeffrey Terrell. AB, Princeton U., 1946, MA, 1950, PhD in Econs, 1959. Teaching fellow U. Buffalo, 1946-47; part-time instr. Princeton U., 1948-50; instr. Denison U., 1950-52; from asst. to assoc. prof. Washington and Lee U., 1952-60, dean students, 1961-69, dean Sch. Commerce, 1969-86, Lewis W. Adams Prof. of Econs., 1986-93, prof. econs. emeritus, 1993—. Econ. cons. Bankers Trust Co., N.Y.C., 1956; economist Gen. Electric Co., 1960-61; tchr. courses Am. Inst. Banking, Va. Sch. Banking, 1957-59; co-chmn. Va. Council Higher Edn. Bus. Adminstrn. Task Force, 1985-86; dir. United Va. Bankshares/Rockbridge, Lexington; vis. prof. Tamkang U., Taiwan, Fall, 1986; vis. fellow U. Coll., Oxford U., Spring, 1987. Pres. Rockbridge Area Housing Corp., 1974-75; trustee Lawrenceville Fathers Assn; mem. Southbury-Middlebury Scholarship Fund, 2000-2001; mem. Waterbury Found., 2001—; deacon United Ch. Christ, Southbury, 2001—. Served with USNR, 1942-46. Mem. Am. Assembly Collegiate Schs. Bus. (initial accreditation com., continuing accreditation com. 1969-86), Am., So. econ. assns., Am. Bankers Assn (selection com. 1973-74), Beta Gamma Sigma, Omicron Delta Kappa, Omicron Delta Epsilon. Congregationalist. Home: 389B Heritage Vlg Southbury CT 06488-1717

ATWOOD, FREIDA GARLAND, small business owner, computer consultant; b. Lowell, Mass., Apr. 22, 1945; d. Franklin ALberto and Rhoda Lucy (Richardson) G.; m. Frank Warren Atwood, July 22, 1967 (div. July 1979); 1 child, Zac. BEd in Elem. Edn., Keene (N.H.) State Coll., 1967; MEd in Learning Disabilities, Rivier Coll., Nashua, N.H., 1979. Cert. ednl. leadership, Fl., N.H.; cert. Montessori, Fla., N.H.; cert. in elem. learning disabilities, Fla., N.H. Learning disabilities specialist, N.C., N.H., 1967-90, Orlando, Fla., 1967-90; elem. tchr. N.C., N.H., Orlando; tchr. learning disabilities Glenridge Mid.-Sch., 1990-92; tchr. presch. Montessori Acad., Winter Park, 1992-93; tchr. math. and biology Oviedo (Fla.) H.S., 1995-96; computer cons., CEO, FreeJu Prodn. Studio, Winter Park, Fla., 1995—; pres. Garland Inst., Titusville, Fla., 2004—. Algebra and reading tchr. internat. schs., Colombia, Germany, Bahamas; intensive reading tchr. Titusville (Fla.) H.S. Author computer software, newspaper column, 1997-2000, newsletter, Magoo-Members Helping Members, 1997-2000. Pres. Bay Pointe Condo Assn., 1999—2000. Tech. grantee pvt. com., Frankfurt, Germany, 1983-86. Mem.: AAUW, Brevard Reading Coun., World Class Schs., Winter Park C. of C. (mem. edn. com. 1997—). Avocations: tennis, golf, photography, scuba diving, reading. Office: Garland Inst 43 E Broad St Titusville FL 32796 Office Phone: 321-403-7038. Personal E-mail: Garland@cfl.rr.com. Business E-Mail: freeju@cfl.rr.com.

ATWOOD, HOLLYE STOLZ, lawyer; b. St. Louis, Dec. 25, 1945; d. Robert George and Elise (Sauselle) Stolz; m. Frederick Howard Atwood III, Aug. 12, 1978 (div.); children: Katherine Stolz, Jonathan Robert. BA, Washington U., St. Louis, 1968; JD, Washington U., 1973. Bar: Mo. 1973. Jr. ptnr. Bryan Cave, St. Louis, 1973-82, ptnr., 1983—2001, mem. exec. com., 1995-2000, of counsel, 2002—. Bd. dirs. St. Louis coun. Girl Scouts U.S., 1976-86; trustee John Burroughs Sch., St. Louis, 1983-86. Mem. ABA, Met. St. Louis Bar Assn., Washington U. Law Sch. Alumni Assn. (pres. 1983-84), Noonday (St. Louis) (bd. govs. 1983-86). Office: Bryan Cave One Metropolitan Sq 211 N Broadway Saint Louis MO 63102-2733 E-mail: hsatwood@bryancave.com.

ATWOOD, JAMES R., lawyer; b. White Plains, NY, Feb. 21, 1944; s. Bernard D. and Joyce Rose Atwood; m. Wendy Fisler, Aug. 22, 1981 (div.); children: Christopher Charles, Carl Fisler; m. Nancy A. Udell, Oct. 6, 2001. BA in Economics & Polit. Sci., magna cum laude, Yale U., 1966; JD Valedictorian, summa cum laude, Stanford U., 1969. Bar: Calif. 1969, DC 1970. Law clk. to Judge Shirley Hufstedler US Ct. Appeals (9th cir.), L.A., 1969-70; law clk. to Chief Justice Warren Burger US Supreme Ct., 1970-71; dep. asst. sec. Econ. & Bus. Affairs US Dept. of State, Washington, 1978—79, sr. dep. legal adv., 1979—80; mem. Covington & Burling, Washington, 1971-78, ptnr., 1977-78, 81—, chmn. Antitrust & Consumer Protection Practice Group. Acting prof. law Stanford U., 1980. Co-author (with Kingman Brewster): Antitrust & Am. Bus. Abroad, 1981. Bd. visitors Stanford U. Sch. Law, 1995—97. Mem.: DC Bar Assn., Am. Soc. Internat. Law, ABA. Office: Covington & Burling 1201 Pennsylvania Ave NW Washington DC 20004-2401 Office Phone: 202-662-5298. Office Fax: 202-662-6291. Business E-Mail: jatwood@cov.com.*

ATWOOD, JOHN BRIAN, dean; b. Wareham, Mass., July 25, 1942; s. Ellsworth Savary and Bernice Anita (Perkins) A.; m. Susan Johnson, Aug. 3, 1991; children: John, Deborah, Michelle. BA, Boston U., 1964; postgrad., Am. U., 1970, LLD (hon.), 1995. Mgmt. intern Nat. Security Agy., Washington, 1964-66; fgn. svc. officer U.S. Dept. State, Washington, 1966-71; legis. asst. to Senator Thomas F. Eagleton, 1971-77; dep. asst. sec. for congl. rels. U.S. Dept. State, Washington, 1977-79, asst. sec., 1979-81; dean, profl. studies and acad. affairs Fgn. Svc. Inst., Washington, 1981-82; v.p. Internat. Reporting and Info. Systems, Washington, 1982—; exec. dir. Dem. Senatorial Campaign Com., Washington, 1982-84; pres. Nat. Dem. Inst. for Internat. Affairs, Washington, 1985-93; adminstr. U.S. AID, Washington, 1993-99; pres. Citizens Internat., Boston, 1999—2002; prof. Harvard U., Cambridge, Mass., 1999—; dean Hubert H. Humphrey Inst. Pub. Affairs U. Minn., Mpls., 2002—. Mem. Coun. Fgn. Rels., UN Assn. Bd. dirs. Nat. Dem. Inst., Freedom House, World Peace Found., Acad. Ednl. Devel. Recipient Harvard Prize Book award, 1959. Mem. Boston U. Alumni Assn. Office: Hubert H Humphrey Inst for Public Affairs 300 Humphrey Ctr 301 19th Ave Minneapolis MN 55455 Office Phone: 612-625-0669. E-mail: jbatwood@hhh.umn.edu.

ATWOOD, MARGARET ELEANOR, writer; b. Ottawa, Ont., Can., Nov. 18, 1939; d. Carl Edmund and Margaret Dorothy (Killam) A. BA, U. Toronto, 1961; AM, Radcliffe Coll., 1962; postgrad., Harvard U., 1962-63, 65-67; LittD (hon.), Trent U., 1973, Concordia U., 1980, Smith Coll., Northampton, Mass., 1982, U. Toronto, 1983, U. Waterloo, 1985, U. Guelph, 1985, Mt. Holyoke Coll., 1985, Victoria Coll., 1987, Univ. de Montréal, 1991, McMaster U., 1996; LLD (hon.), Queen's U., 1974. Lectr. in English U. B.C., 1964-65, Sir George Williams U., 1967-68, U. Alta., 1969-70; asst. prof. English York U., Toronto, 1971-72; writer-in-residence U. Toronto, 1972-73, U. Ala., Tuscaloosa, 1985. Berg Chair NYU, 1986; writer-in-residence Macquarie U., Australia, 1987, Trinity U., San Antonio, 1989. Author: (poetry) Double Persephone, 1961, The Circle Game, 1967, The Animals in That Country, 1968, The Journals of Susanna Moodie, 1970, Procedures for Underground, 1970, Power Politics, 1971, Poems for Voices, 1970, You Are Happy, 1975, Selected Poems, 1976 (Am. edit. 1978), Selected Poems, 1966-84, 1990, Margaret Atwood Poems, 1965-75, 1991, Two-Headed Poems, 1978, True Stories, 1981, Interlunar, 1984, Selected Poems II: Poems Selected and New, 1976-1986, 1986, Morning in the Burned House, 1995; (novels) The Edible Woman, 1969 (Am. edit. 1970), Surfacing, 1972, (Am. edit. 1973), Lady Oracle, 1976, Life Before Man, 1979, Bodily Harm, 1981, The Handmaid's Tale, 1985, Cat's Eye, 1988 (City Toronto Book award 1989, Coles Book of the Yr. 1989, Can. Booksellers Assn. Author of the Yr., 1989, Book of the Yr. award Found. for Advancement of Can. Letters, Periodical Marketers Can., 1989, Torgi Talking Book award 1989), The Robber Bride, 1993 (award for Fiction Can. Authors Assn., 1993, Trillium award for Excellence in Ont. Writing 1993, Regional Commonwealth Lit. award), Alias Grace, 1996 (Giller Prize 1996, Medal of Honor for Literature, Nat. Arts Club 1997), The Blind Assassin, 2000 (The Booker Prize 2000, nominee for Internat. IMPAC Dublin Literary award, Dashiell Hammett Prize, Internat. Assn. of Crime Writers, 2001), Oryx and Crake, 2003 (Booker prize shortlist, 2003), Writing With Intent: Essays, Reviews, Personal Prose: 1983-2005, 2005; (short stories) Dancing Girls, 1977, Bluebeard's Egg, 1983, Murder in the Dark, 1983, Wilderness Tips, 1991 (Trillium award 1992, Book of the Yr. award Periodical Marketers of Can., 1992), Good Bones, 1992; (juvenile) Up in the Tree, 1978, Anna'a Pet, 1980, For the Birds, 1990, Princess Prunella & the Purple Peanut, 1995; (non-fiction) Survival: A Thematic Guide to Canadian Literature, 1972, Second Words: Selected Critical Prose, 1982, Strange Things: The Malevolent North in Canadian Literature, 1995, Negotiating with the Dead, 2002, Curious Pursuits, 2005. Recipient E.J. Pratt medal, 1961, Pres.'s medal U. Western Ont., 1965, YWCA Women of Distinction award, Gov. Gen.'s award, 1966, 1st pl. Centennial Commn. Poetry Competition, 1967, Union Poetry prize Chicago, 1969, Bess Hoskins prize of Poetry Chicago, 1974, City of Toronto Book award, 1977, Can. Booksellers Assn. award, 1977, award for short fiction Periodical Distbr. Can., 1977, St. Lawrence award for Fiction, 1978, Radcliffe Grad. medal, 1980, Molson award, 1981, Internat. Writer's prize Welsh Arts Council, 1982, Book of Yr. award Periodical Distbrs. of Can. and Found. for Advancement Can. Letters, 1983, Los Angeles Times Fiction award, 1986, Gov. Gen.'s Lit. award, 1986, Ida Nudel Humanitarian award, 1986, Toronto Arts award, 1986, Arthur C. Clarke award for Best Sci. Fiction, 1987, shortlisted for Ritz Hemingway prize, Paris, 1987, Commonwealth Lit. Prize regional award, 1987, 94, Silver medal for Best Article of Yr. Council for Advancement and Support of Edn., 1987, Nat. Mag. award 1st prize, 1988, Sunday Times award for literary excellence, YWCA Women of Distinction award 1988, Centennial medal Harvard U., 1990, John Hughes prize Welsh Devel. Bd., 1992, Commemorative medal 125th Anniversary of Can. Confedn., 1992, Trillium award for excellence in Ont. writing, 1995; Guggenheim fellow, 1981; decorated companion Order of Can., 1981, Order of Ont., 1990; named Woman of Yr. Ms. Mag., 1986, Humanist of Yr., 1987, Chevalier de l'Ordre des Arts et des Lettres, 1994. Fellow Royal Soc. of Can., Am. Acad. Arts and Scis. (fgn. hon. lit. mem. 1988). Office: c/o Carrol & Graf Avalon Publishing NY Divsn 245 W 17th St New York NY 10011-5300*

ATWOOD, WILLIAM HENRY, II, musician; b. Hartford, Conn., Aug. 16, 1979; s. Albert William and Carol Ann Atwood. MusB, U. Hartford, 2001; MusM, Rider U., 2003. Dir. music Immaculate Conception Ch., Terryville, Conn., 1996—2001, Somerville, NJ, 2003—, St. Paul the Apostle Ch., Highland Park, NJ, 2001—03; organist Diocese Metuchen, NJ, 2004—. Mem.: Am. Choral Dirs. Assn., Am. Guild Organists (dean student chpt. 2002—03), Nat. Pastoral Musicians Assn. (asst. dir. 2003—). Roman Catholic. Office Phone: 908-526-3016. Personal E-mail: gotmusic79@aol.com.

ATWOOD PINARDI, BRENDA, artist, educator; b. Hyannis, Mass., Mar. 14, 1941; d. John Adolph and Alice Maria (Cahoon) Atwood; m. Enrico Vittorio Pinardi, Aug. 6, 1966. BSE, Mass. Coll. Art, 1963; postgrad., L'Accademia di Belle Arte, Rome, 1963-64; MFA, R.I. Sch. Design, 1967.

Prof. art U. Mass., Lowell, 1967—2003, prof. emeritus, 2003—. Group exhbns. include: DeCordova Mus., Lincoln, Mass., Fuller Mus. of Art, Brockton, Mass., Newport (R.I.) Art Mus., Laguna Gloria Mus., Austin, Tex.; represented by Vorpal Gallery, N.Y.C. and San Francisco, other pvt. mus. and corp. collections.

ATZ, SARAH J., music educator; b. Hillsdale, MI, Oct. 20, 1957; BA, Judson Coll., Elgin, Ill., 1980; MA cum laude, U. Louisville. Cert. tchr. Ky. Music tchr. Oswego (Ill.) Sch. Dist., 1981; band tchr. Dundee (Ill.) Sch. Dist., 1982; tchr., music/chorus Jefferson County Pub. Schs., Louisville, 1988—93; handbell dir. First Bapt. Ch., Elgin, Ill., 1980—82, Peter's Creek Bapt. Ch., Library, Pa., 1984—87, St. Paul's Episc. Ch., Louisville, 1988—89. Office: Carrithers Middle Sch 4320 Billtown Rd Louisville KY 40299

AUBE, RANDY ALAN, accountant; b. Alpena, Mich., Sept. 27, 1957; s. Robert E. Aube and Marsha L. (Jacobs) Wise. Grad., Tiffin U., 1982. CPA, Ohio, Fla. Staff acct. Arthur Young & Co., Toledo, 1982-87, mgr., 1987-88; v.p. fin. GB Mfg. Co., Delta, Ohio, 1988-94; contr. Marine Air Systems, Inc., Pompano Beach, Fla., 1995-96, Huizenga Holdings, Inc., Ft. Lauderdale, Fla., 1997—. Mem. AICPA, Ohio Soc. CPAs, Fla. Soc. CPAs. Office: Huizenga Holdings Inc 450 E Las Olas Blvd Ste 1500 Fort Lauderdale FL 33301-4212

AUBELE, TAMI MARISCO, corporate communications specialist; b. Pitts., Sept. 18, 1976; d. Donald Joseph and Diana Jean Marsico; m. Michael Thomas Aubele, Dec. 11, 2004. B, Ind. U. of Pa., 1999; M, Point Pk. U., 2004. Cert. yogafit levels 1 & 2, cpr, first aid. News clerk Valley News Dispatch, Tarentum, Pa., 1999—2000; admin. sec. UPMC Health Sys., Pitts., 2000—04; media relations extern UPMC News Bureau, Pitts., 2004; comm. coord. Am. Red Cross, Pitts., 2004—. Mem.: Ind. U. Pa. Alumni Assn. Avocations: yoga, crafts, reading, writing. Office Phone: 412-263-3118. E-mail: tmarsico@comcast.net.

AUBERGER, MARCIA A., lawyer; b. Rochester, NY, Nov. 8, 1963; BA, SUNY, Buffalo, 1985; JD, South Tex. Coll. of Law, 1989. Bar: Tex. 1989, DC 1998. Ptnr. Trademark Venable LLP, Washington, DC. Lectr. in field. Contbr. articles top profl. jours. Mem.: ABA (mem. Intellectual Property Sect.), Intellectual Property Owners Assn. (mem. US Trademark Law Com.), Women's Bar Assn. of DC, DC Bar (mem. Intellectual Property Sect.), Assn. for Protection of Intellectual Property, Am. Intellectual Property Law Assn., Internat. Trademark Assn., State Bar Tex. Office: Venable LLP 575 7th St NW Washington DC 20004 Office Phone: 202-344-4969. Office Fax: 202-344-8300. E-mail: maauberger@venable.com.

AUBERTIN, MADELINE KATHERINE, retired nursing educator, medical/surgical nurse, mental health services professional; b. Detroit, May 16, 1930; Grad., Providence Hosp. Sch. Nursing, 1951; BS in Nursing Edn., Mercy Coll., 1959; MEd, Wayne State Coll., 1995. RN, Mich. Staff nurse Vets. Hosp., Dearborn, Mich., 1951-58; staff nurse, nursing educator St. John's Hosp., St. Louis, 1960-64; staff nurse U. Mich., Ann Arbor, 1965-66; instr., staff nurse Harper Hosp., Detroit; insvc. dir., nursing instr. Holy Cross Hosp., Detroit, 1966-68; insvc. instr., dir. Grace Hosp., Detroit, 1968-72; nursing instr. Wayne County Community Coll., Detroit, 1972-96; ret., 1996. Mem. ARC, Detroit, 1962-92, Am. Heart Assn., Southfield, Mich., 1962-92, Assn. for Learning Disabilities, Farmington, Mich., 1972-92, Nat. League of Nursing, Detroit, 1962-92. Democrat. Roman Catholic. Avocations: singing, church choir, sewing, reading. Home: 9576 Winston Redford MI 48239-1660

AUBERY, STEPHEN ROYSTON EDMUND, film producer; b. Kingston Upon Hull, Yorkshire, Eng., July 4, 1951; came to U.S., 1964; s. Gerald Royston and Doreen (Stevens) A.; m. Rose Marie Marks, Feb. 23, 1973 (div. Dec. 1991); children: Suzanne Marie, Julia Dawn, Wendy Lynn, Katrina Rose; m. Tamara Phizacklea, Oct. 4, 1994 (div. May 2000); m. Cheryl Curran, Dec. 28, 2002. Student, U. Utah, 1968—70, Brigham Young U., 1974—75; BA in Mktg., Stafford U., London, 2004. Sound dept. mgr. Brigham Young U. Motion Picture Studio, Provo, Utah, 1972-76; film prodr., ptnr. Linton Prodns., Salt Lake City, 1976-79; prodr., gen. ptnr. Seven Star Pictures, Salt Lake City, 1979-82; news editor KUTV Inc., Salt Lake City, 1982-84; film prodr., mgr. LDS Audiovisual, Salt Lake City, 1984-94; film prodr. Challenger Schs., Salt Lake City, 1994—95; film prodr., owner Encore Prodns., Salt Lake City, 1995-96; film prodr. Mountain Prodns., Inc., Draper, Utah, 1997-99, Mark Phillips Philms & Telephision, L.A., 1999-2000; film prodr., owner flixnpix.com, L.A., 2000—01; sr. dir. mktg., video prodr. ACS Workforce Svcs., Austin, Tex., 2001—. Film dept. instr. U. Utah, Salt Lake City, Brigham Young U., Provo; mgr., lead singer, guitarist Tapestry top 40 soft rock dance band, 1980-98 Co-author, prodr., cinematographer (screenplay, book, film) Knocking at Heaven's Door, 1980; prodr. (film) Temple Open House, 1992 (Telly award 1993); prodr., dir. (film) Phonics Fun, 1993 (two Telly awards 1994), From Thoughts to Things, 1997 (Telly & Communicator award 1997); prodr., dir., dir. photography, editor, Undercover Stings, Learning Channel, 1999, The Jer-Z Games, Disney Channel, 2000, K-9 Cops-The Learning Channel, 2000, Bridges to Freedom, 2000, First Impressions, 2000 (Videographer Excellence award and Communicator award and Cindy Award 2001), A Unique Alternative Education Experience, 2003 (Communicator award 2003, Videographer award 2004, MCA-I award 2004); author, contbg. editor Super 8 Filmaker Mag., 1975-80. Bd. dirs. World Firefighters Assistance League, Salt Lake City. Mem. Internat. TV Assn., Soc. Motion Picture and TV Engrs. (presenter tech. paper L.A. conv. 1974-80, cert. presentation 1995), Media Comm. Internat. Avocations: vocal performing, playing guitar, computers. Mailing: 2011 Campfield Pwy Austin TX 78745-6347 Office Phone: 512-344-4014. Business E-Mail: stephen.aubery@acs-inc.com.

AUBIN, BARBARA JEAN, artist; b. Chgo., Jan. 12, 1928; d. Philip Theodore and Dorothy May (Chapman) A. BA, Carleton Coll., 1949; B Art Edn., Sch. Art Inst. Chgo., 1954, M Art Edn., 1955. Lectr. Centre D'Art & Haitian Am. Inst., Port-Au-Prince, Haiti, 1958-60; asst. prof. Sch. Art Inst. Chgo., 1960-67, Loyola U., 1968-71; lectr. Calumet Coll., Hammond, Ind., 1971-75; prof. art Chgo. State U., 1971-91; ret., 1991. Vis. prof., artist Wayne State U., Detroit, Mich., 1965; vis. artist St. Louis C.C., Forest Park, Mo., 1980-81, U. Wis., Green Bay, 1981; co-curator Art for the Next Millennium Kimo Theatre Gallery, Albuquerque, 1997; spkr. and exhibiting artist, Womens's Caucus For Art Regional Conf./Exhibition, 1999. One-woman shows include Countryside Arts Ctr., Arlington Heights, Ill., 1954, 87, Avant Arts Gallery, Chgo., 1954, Riccardo's Restaurant and Gallery, Chgo., 1956, Evanston (Ill.) Twp. H.S., 1958, Centre d'Art, Port-au-Prince, Haiti, 1960, Chgo. Pub. Libr., 1960, Chgo. Acad. Fine Arts, 1965, Oxbow Summer Sch. Fine Arts, 1965, Lewis Towers Gallery, Loyola U., Chgo., 1970, Chgo. State U., 1971, 74, 85, North River Cmty. Gallery, Northeastern Ill. U., Chgo., 1974, Ill. Arts Coun., Chgo., Crossroads-Jr. Mus., Art Inst. Chgo., 1976, Fairweather Hardin Gallery, Chgo., 1978, 80, 85, 90, U. Wis., 1981, Illini Union Gallery, U. Ill., Urbana, 1986, Artemisia Gallery, Chgo., Katerina's, Chgo., 2002; exhibited in group shows at Art Inst. Chgo., 1960, 78, 80, 85, 89, Vanderpoel Art Assn., Beverly Art Ctr., Chgo., 1992, Ancient Echoes, Chgo., 1992, Renaissance Ct., Chgo. Cultural Ctr., 1993, 2001, 2002, Artemisia Gallery, Chgo., 1994, Art Place Gallery, Chgo, 1994, Chgo. State U., 1994, Chgo. Women's Caucus for Art, 1994, 98, 2000, Eastern Ill. U., Charleston, 1991, 1993-2001, ARC Gallery, Chgo., 1995, 97, 2004, N.Mex. Art League, Albuquerque, 1996, Mirage Gallery, Albuquerque, Barrington Arts Coun., 1997, Meridian Ctr., Washington, 1997, Chgo. Women's Caucus for Art No. Ill. U., 1998, Springfield Art Mus., Mo., 1999, (Patron Purchase award), Beacon St. Gallery, Chgo., 1999, DeKalb (Ill.) Area Women's Ctr., 1999, Mini-Millennium Women's Caucus For Art Nat. Gallery, 2000, Eastern Ill. U., Charleston, Ill., 2000-01, Chgo. Cultural Ctr., 2001-02; represented in permanent collections at Art Inst. Chgo., Ill. State Mus., Ball State Mus., Calumet Coll., Hammond, Ind., Shimer Coll., Waukegon, Ill., Kemper Group Collection, Long Grove, Ill., State of Ill. Bldg., Chgo., Seyfarth, Shaw, Fairweather & Geraldson, Washington, Ernst & Ernst, Chgo., Foote, Cone & Belding, Chgo., U.S. League of Savs. and Loans, Chgo., Northside Industries, Chgo., Keck, Cushman, Mahin & Cate, Chgo., Gould, Inc., Rolling Meadows, Ill., First Nat. Bank Chgo., Internat. Mineral and Chem., Skokie, Ill.; reporter Women Artists News, 1977, 80, 83-86. V.p. Midwest region Womens Caucus for Art, Chgo., 1982-88; founding mem. local chpt. Chgo. Women's Caucus for Art, 1973, bd. dirs., 2002-05; bd. dirs. Chgo. Artists' Coalition, 1992-94 Recipient George D. Brown Fgn. Travel fellow Sch. Art Inst. Chgo., 1955-56; Art grant Fulbright fellow, 1958-60, Huntington Hartford Fedn. grant, 1963, Project Completion grant Ill. Arts Coun., 1978-79, Chgo. Cultural Ctr., 2002, CAAPS grant, 2002. Mem. Arts Club Chgo., Chgo. Artists' Coalition, Chgo. Womens Caucus for Art. Home: The Hallmark 2960 N Lake Shore Dr #405 Chicago IL 60657-5645 Personal E-mail: dittofeline@aol.com.

AUBREY, BRYAN, literature educator, writer; b. Beckenham, Kent, Eng., Sept. 6, 1949; came to U.S., 1981; s. Ronald Edmund and Mignon Estelle (Clifford) A. BA in Religious Studies, U. Lancaster, Eng., 1977; PhD in English Lit., U. Durham, Eng., 1982. Asst. prof. lit. Maharishi Internat. U., Fairfield, Iowa, 1981-84, assoc. prof. lit., 1985-86, adj. assoc. prof. lit., 1987—; editor, writer Fast Times Mag., San Marcos, Calif., 1988—. Author: Watchmen of Eternity, 1986, English Romantic Poetry, 1991; contbr. articles to Studies in Mystical Lit., Studia Mystica, Aligarh Critical Miscellany. Avocations: opera, current affairs, meditation and spirituality. Home: 1100 E Madison Ave Fairfield IA 52556-3737 E-mail: wotan@kdsi.net.

AUBRIOT, ERIC, chef; m. Stephanie Aubriot. Chef Trio, Evanston, Ill., Carlos', Highland Park, Ill.; owner, chef Aubriot, Chgo. Named One of Six Hot Chgo. Chefs, Chgo. Social, 1998, Best New Restaurant, Esquire mag., 1998, Chgo. mag., 1998.

AUCH, WALTER EDWARD, security firm executive; b. Detroit, Apr. 12, 1921; s. Fred J. and Beatrice H. (Higgins) A.; m. Patricia H.; children: Walter Edward, Timothy R., Terrance H. Student, Albion Coll., also U. Detroit, 1939-42, Cornell U., 1959. Stockbroker William C. Roney & Co., Detroit, 1946-55; sr. partner Bache & Co., N.Y.C., 1955-64, Paine, Webber, Jackson & Curtis, N.Y.C., 1964-70; pres. Nat. Securities & Research Corp., N.Y.C., 1970-72; exec. v.p. duPont, Glore, Forgan, Inc., N.Y.C., 1972-73; pres. duPont Walston, Inc., 1973-74; COO Paine, Webber, N.Y.C., 1974-79; chmn., chief exec. officer Chgo. Bd. Options Exchange, 1979-86, cons., 1987—. Bd. dirs. Smith Barney Trak Fund, Legg Mason Allocation Series Funds, Multiple Discipline Trust, Nicholas/Applegate Funds, UBS Funds, U.S. Bancorp Advisors Funds. Trustee Albion Coll., 1981-1990, Hillsdale Coll., 1991-. With USAAF, 1942-45. Mem. Bond Club N.Y., Bond Club Chgo., Chgo. Club, Greenwich Country Club, Paradise Valley Country Club (Scottsdale), Crystal Downs Country Club (Crystal Lake, Mich.), Sigma Chi. Home (Summer): 2700 Crystal Dr Crystal Lake Beulah MI 49617 Address: 6001 N 62nd Pl Paradise Valley AZ 85253 *When I was a boy, my grandfather advised me to "live every day in such a way that the line behind the hearse gets longer." I've tried hard to follow that advice.*

AUCHINCLOSS, LOUIS STANTON, writer; b. Lawrence, NY, Sept. 27, 1917; s. Joseph Howland and Priscilla (Stanton) A.; m. Adele Lawrence, Sept. 1957; children: John, Blake, Andrew. Student, Yale U., 1939; LLB, U. Va., 1941; LittD, NYU, 1974, Pace U., 1979, U. of the South, 1986. Bar: NY 1941. Assoc. Sullivan & Cromwell, 1941-51, Hawkins, Delafield & Wood, N.Y.C., 1954-58, ptnr., 1958-86. Author: The Indifferent Children, 1947, The Injustice Collectors, 1950, Sybil, 1952, A Law for the Lion, 1953, The Romantic Egoists, 1954, The Great World and Timothy Colt, 1956, Venus in Sparta, 1958, Pursuit of the Prodigal, 1959, The House of Five Talents, 1960, Reflections of a Jacobite, 1961, Portrait in Brownstone, 1962, Powers of Attorney, 1963, The Rector of Justin, 1964, Pioneers and Caretakers, 1965, The Embezzler, 1966, Tales of Manhattan, 1967, A World of Profit, 1968, Motiveless Malignity, 1969, Second Chance, 1970, Edith Wharton, 1971, I Came As a Thief, Richelieu, 1972, The Partners, A Writer's Capital, 1974, Reading Henry James, 1975, The Winthrop Covenant, 1976, The Dark Lady, 1977, The Country Cousin, 1978, Persons of Consequence, 1979, Life, Law and Letters, 1979, The House of the Prophet, 1980, The Cat and the King, 1981, Watchfires, 1982, Exit Lady Masham, 1983, The Book Class, 1984, Honorable Men, 1985, Diary of a Yuppie, 1986, Skinny Island, 1987, The Golden Calves, 1988, Fellow Passengers, 1989, The Vanderbilt Era, 1989, The Lady of Situations, 1991, False Gods, 1992, Three Lives, 1993, Tales of Yesteryear, 1994, The Style's The Man, 1994, Collected Stories, 1994, The Education of Oscar Fairfax, 1995, The Man Behind the Book, 1996, LA Gloire, 1996, The Atonement, 1997, The Anniversary, 1999, Her Infinite Variety, 2000, Woodrow Wilson, 2000, Theodore Roosevelt, 2002, Manhattan Monologues, 2002, Writers and Personality, 2005. Trustee emeritus Josiah Macy, Jr., Found.; chmn. Mus. City of N.Y. Lt. USNR, 1941-45. Mem. AAAL (pres. emeritus), Assn. Bar City N.Y., Century Assn. Episcopalian.*

AUCHINLECK, RICHARD H., exploration company executive; b. Vancouver; married; 1 child. B.Applied Sci. in Chem. Engring., U. B.C., 1976. With Gulf Canada Resources Ltd., Calgary, Alta, 1976—, gas utilization engr., supt. heavy oil ops., joint interest coord., mgr. engring., mgr. fin. (major projects group), gen. mgr. north bus. unit, 1991-93, v.p., 1993-95, sr. v.p. internat. and exploration, 1995-97, COO, 1997-98, pres., CEO, 1998—; CEO Gulf Indonesia Resources, 1997-98. Bd. dirs. Gulf Indonesia Resources, Canadian Energy Rsch. Inst. Mem. Assn. Profl. Engrs., Geologists and Geophysicists of Alta., Canadian Heavy Oil Assn. (life, hon. dir.). Avocations: restoring and driving vintage sports cars, skiing, music.

AUCHLY, CHRISTOPHER M, music educator; s. William J. and M. Dione Auchly. B in Music Edn., Ctrl. Meth. Coll., Fayette, Mo., 1991. Pcii DESE, 1991. Dir. of bands Tipton H.S., Tipton, Mo., 1991—94; asst. dir. of bands Lee's Summit H.S., Mo., 1994—95; dir. of bands Lee's Summit North H.S., Mo., 1995—98, Festus H.S., Mo., 1999—. Distr. band v.p. Kansas City (Mo.) Metro Dist., 1996—98, East Ctrl. Dist., Festus, Mo., 2004—. Mem.: Nat. Band Assn., Mo. Music Educators, Mo. Bandmasters, Phi Beta Mu, Phi Mu Alpha. Independent. Roman Catholic. Avocations: biking, walking, photography, travelilng. Office: Festus High School 501 Westwind Drive Festus MO 63028 Office Phone: 636-937-5410.

AUCHTER, JOHN RICHARD, retired lawyer; b. Springfield, Mass., May 1, 1922; s. Frank and Alfaretta (Thurston) A.; m. Norma Jean Ledger Wood; children: Susan Adrienne (dec.), Richard Hagen, Ellen Laura, John Lovejoy, Sarah Jean. BA, Amherst Coll., 1947; JD, Northeastern U., 1950. Bar: U.S. Supreme Ct. 1964, U.S. Dist. Ct. Mass. 1965. Agt. and title atty. Commonwealth Land Title Ins. Co., First Am. Title Ins. Co.; title atty. Lawyers Title Ins. Co.; ptnr. Auchter, Bozenhard, Socha & Ely and predecessor firms, Springfield and Palmer, Mass., 1959-85; counsel Bozenhard, Socha, Ely & Kolber, West Springfield, Mass., 1985—94; pvt. practice Palmer, 1985-94; ptnr. Auchter & Thompson, Palmer, 1995—98; ret., 1999. Instr. real estate law Western New Eng. Coll., Springfield, Mass., 1966—69; land ct. examiner, 1956—; justice of peace, 1974—2000. Contbr. articles to profl. jours. Bd. dirs. Goodwill Industries of Springfield/Hartford Area, Inc., 1952-, pres. 1961-67, 73, chmn bd. 1974-75; bd. dirs. Alcoholism Services of Greater Springfield, 1973-75, Palmer Ambulance Service, 1984-97; chmn. bd. dirs. Western Mass. chpt. Kidney Found. Mass., 1971-75. Cpl. CAC, AUS, 1943-46. Mem. ABA, Mass. Bar Assn., Hampden County Bar Assn., Am. Judicature Soc., Mass. Conveyancers Assn., Estate Planning Coun. Hampden County, Quaboag Valley C. of C., Inc. (bd. dirs. 1978—, pres. 1978-81, chmn. legis. com. 1981—), Exch. Club (co-founder Suburban Springfield 1985—), Meadowbrook Green Condominium Assn. (bd. dirs. 1999-, pres. 1999-2001), Home Builders Assn. Greater Springfield (bd. dirs. 1956-58, counsel), VFW (chmn. voice of democracy com. 1969-72), Theta Delta Chi. Clubs: Exchange (Springfield)(pres. 1959-60, bd. dirs. New Eng. dist. 1982-85). Home: 39 Meadowbrook Ln Palmer MA 01069-1134 Office: 39 Meadowbrook Ln Palmer MA 01069-1134 Office Phone: 413-283-6860.

AUCUTT, RONALD DAVID, lawyer; b. St. Paul, Dec. 28, 1945; s. Howard Lewis and Eleanor May (Malcolm) A.; m. Grace Diane Kok, Apr. 3, 1976; children: David Gerard, James Andrew. BA, U. Minn., 1967, JD, 1975. Bar: Minn. 1975, D.C. 1976, Va. 1978, Tex. 1999, U.S. Supreme Ct. 1978, U.S. Tax Ct. 1980, U.S. Dist. Ct. D.C. 1980, U.S. Ct. Appeals (D.C. cir.) 1980, U.S. Ct. of Claims 1980, U.S. Claims Ct. 1982, U.S. Ct. Appeals (fed. cir.) 1982, U.S. Dist. Ct. (ea. dist.) Va. 1986, U.S. Ct. Appeals (4th cir.) 1986. Assoc. Miller & Chevalier, Chartered, Washington, 1975-81, ptnr., 1982-98, McGuireWoods LLP, McLean, Va., 1998—. Mem. bd. advisors IRS Practice Alert, N.Y.C., 1987—93; adj. prof. Sch. Law U. Va., 1998—2003; mem. adv. com. Philip E. Heckerling Inst. on Estate Planning U. Miami, 1999—. Mem. bd. advisors Jour. Taxation Exempt Orgns., 1989-2000, Bus. Entities, N.Y.C., 1999—; mem. editl. bd. Estate Planning, N.Y.C., 1993—, mem. adv. bd. Tax Mgmt. Estates, Gifts, and Trusts Jour., 1999—; editl. adv. bd. Bus. Valuation Update, Portland, Oreg., 1999—; contbr. articles to profl. publs. Orgn. Security and Coop. in Europe internat. observer Bulgarian Parliamentary Election, 1997; sec.-treas. Miller and Chevalier Charitable Found., Washington, 1980—82, pres., 1993—97; bd. dirs. Coun. for Ct. Excellence, Washington, 1993—99, Advocates Internat., Fairfax, Va., 1997—2000, vice chmn., 1999—2000; mem. adv. bd. Trinity Law Sch., Santa Ana, Calif., 1998—2001; bd. visitors U. Minn. Law Sch., 1998—2004; bd. regents Trinity Internat. U., Deerfield, Ill., 2000—; bd. dirs. Evang. Free Ch. Am., Mpls., 1986—92, vice moderator, chmn. bd. dirs., 1993—95, moderator, 1995—97. Lt. USN, 1970—73. Fellow: Am. Coll. Trust and Estate Counsel (bd. regents 1996—, chmn. bus. planning com. 1997—2000, sec. 1999—2000, treas. 2000—01, v.p. 2001—02, pres.-elect 2002—03, pres. 2003—04), Am. Coll. Tax Counsel, Am. Bar Found.; mem.: ABA (chair taxation sect., com. on estate and gift taxes 1986—88, vice chmn. com. on govt. submissions 1989—91, liaison to sect. real property, probate and trust law 1990—, chmn. com. on govt. submissions 1991—93, coun. 1993—97, vice chair com. ops. 1998—2000), Christian Legal Soc., Internat. Acad. Estate and Trust Law (exec. coun. 2000—04, academician), U. Minn. Law Alumni Assn. (bd. dirs. 1998—2004), Met. Club Washington. Home: 3417 Silver Maple Pl Falls Church VA 22042-3545 Office: McGuireWoods LLP 1750 Tysons Blvd Ste 1800 Mc Lean VA 22102-4215 Office Phone: 703-712-5497. Business E-Mail: raucutt@mcguirewoods.com.

AUDET, PAUL ANDRE, retired newspaper executive; b. Quebec, Can., Mar. 14, 1923; s. Sylvio and Rose Aimee (Cloutier) A.; m. Michele Richard, Sept. 13, 1947; children: Francine, Andre, Marc. D. Honoris Causa (hon.), U. Québec, 1985. Newspaper reporter L'Evenement Jour., 1942-44; staff writer The Canadian Press, 1944, asst. mng. editor, 1945-48, sales and sales mgr. printing dept., 1948-54; advt. dir. Le Soleil Quebec, 1955-74; pres., gen. mgr., 1974-88. Past pres. Edimedia, Inc., Que. Opera Co. Named hon. col. Les Voltigeurs de Que. Regt. Mem. Ordre des Chevaliers de Meduse, Garrison Club, Order of Can. Roman Catholic. *Whatever you do or you are, try to be the best. Somehow, some day, someone is bound to find out and you will be rewarded accordingly.*

AUDET, PAUL L., diversified financial services company executive; BA with hons. in Acct. and Econs., Rutgers U. Sr. acct. Price Waterhouse & Co.; mgr. fin. reportingand analysis Paine Webber Inc.; sr. v.p. corp. fin. First Fidelity BankCorp; CFO, sr. v.p. PNC, 1991—98; mng. dir. BlackRock Inc., N.Y., 1998—, CFO, 1998—. Office: BlackRock Inc 40 East 52nd St New York NY 10022

AUDIA, CHRISTINA, librarian; b. Carolina, W.Va., July 6, 1941; d. John and Roze (Horvath) A. BS in Edn., Wayne State U., 1967, MS in L.S., 1969. Cert. librarian, Mich. Chief libr. original cataloging dept. Detroit Pub. Libr., 1980-89, bibliographic database mgr., 1989—. Specialist for monograph cataloging Mich. Libr. Consortium, 1987-89; mem. Dalnet Database Standards Com., 1989—. Mem. ALA. Avocations: gardening, travel, metal detecting. Office: Detroit Pub Libr Database Mgmt Dept 5201 Woodward Ave Detroit MI 48202-4093

AUER, MATTHEW ROBERT, science educator; s. Peter Louis and Rheta Ethel Auer; m. Anne Kristen Dowling; children: Emma Marie, John Dowling. AB, Harvard U., Cambridge, Mass., 1984—88; MALD, Tufts U., Medford, Mass., 1988—90; MS, MPhil, Yale U., New Haven, Conn., 1991—94, PhD, 1991—96. Profl. forester Soc. Am. Foresters, 2004. Asst. prof. Ind. U., Bloomington, 1996—2002, assoc. prof., 2002—. Team leader U.S. AID, Washington, 1998; adviser Sci. Applications Internat. Corp., McLean, Va., 1998—2003; exec. coun. mem. Soc. for the Policy Scis., New Haven, 1998—2004; editor-in-chief Policy Scis., New Haven, 2005—; sr. adviser U.S. Forest Svc., Washington, 2001—; team leader Alliance to Save Energy, Washington, 2003. Author: (book) Restoring Cursed Earth: Appraising Environmental Policy Reforms in Central and Eastern Europe and Russia; contbr. articles to profl. jours. Adv. bd. mem. U.S. Marine Mammal Commn., Washington, 1997—2000, Dushkin/McGraw Hill, Guilford, Conn., 1998—2005; adviser U.S. AID, Washington, 2000; acting asst. dir. policy, internat. programs U.S. Forest Svc., Washington, 2002, internat. negotiator, 2001—05; program evaluator NSF, Washington, 2003—04. Named Outstanding Instr., Ind. U., 1998, 2000, 2004; recipient Award of Excellence, Sasakawa Peace Found., 1995, Tchg. Excellence Recognition award, Ind. U., 1997—98, Trustee Tchg. award, 2001—02, 2005, Faculty Colloquium on Excellence in Tchg., 2002, Pres.'s award, 2005, Myres S. McDougal prize, Soc. for the Policy Scis., 2001; grantee, Smith Richardson Found., 1993, U.S. Dept. Agr., 1993—94, NRC, 1998—99, U.S. Forest Svc., 2001—05, Open Soc., Budapest, 2003; Sasawkawa Young Leader, Sasakawa Peace Found., 1989—90, Global Change fellow, U.S. Dept. Energy, 1992—95. Mem.: Soc. Am. Foresters, Soc. for the Policy Scis. (exec. coun. 1998—2004). Office Phone: 812-855-4944.

AUERBACH, ALAN JEFFREY, economist, educator; b. NYC, Sept. 27, 1951; s. William and Tess (Kasper) A.; m. Gay Cameron Quimby, June 25, 1978; children: Ethan, Andrew. BA, Yale U., 1974; PhD, Harvard U., 1978. Asst. prof. dept. econs. Harvard U., Cambridge, Mass., 1978-82, assoc. prof., 1982-83; assoc. prof. dept. econs. U. Pa., Phila., 1983-85, prof., 1985-94, chmn. dept., 1988-90, prof. Sch. Law, 1990-94; Robert D. Burch prof. of tax policy and pub. fin. U. Calif., Berkeley, 1994—, chmn. dept., 2001—02. Author: The Taxation of Capital Income, 1983 (David A. Wells prize); co-author: Dynamic Fiscal Policy, 1987, Macroeconomics: An Integrated Approach, 1995, Generational Accounting Around the World, 1999; editor: Corporate Takeovers, 1988, Mergers and Acquisitions, 1988, Fiscal Policy: Lessons from Economic Research, 1997; co-editor: Handbook of Public Economics, Vol. I, 1985, Vol. II, 1987, Vol. III, 2002, Vol. IV, 2002, Demographic Change and Fiscal Policy, 2001, Ageing, Financial Markets, and Monetary Policy, 2002, Toward Fundamental Tax Reform, 2005; editor jour. Econ. Perspectives, 1995-96. Fellow Am. Acad. Arts and Scis., Econometric Soc.; mem. Am. Econ. Assn. (exec. com. 1992-94, v.p. 1999), Phi Beta Kappa. Home: 110 El Camino Real Berkeley CA 94705-2823 Office: U Calif Berkeley Dept Econs 549 Evans Hall Berkeley CA 94720-3880 Business E-Mail: auerbach@econ.berkeley.edu.

AUERBACH, ANITA L., clinical psychologist; b. Flushing, N.Y., Dec. 23, 1946; d. Ben and Gussie (Zuckerman) Weiss; m. Steven Miles Auerbach, May 25, 1969. BA cum laude, SUNY, Buffalo, 1968, MA, 1970; PhD (N.Y. State Regents fellow 1970-72), George Washington U., 1977. Diplomate Am. Bd. Med. Psychotherapists, Internat. Acad. Behavioral Medicine. Chief rsch. Youth Crime Control Project D.C. Dept. Corrections, 1970-74; intern clin. psychology No. Va. Tng. Ctr., Fairfax, 1974-75, staff psychologist, then chief psychol. svcs., 1975-79; pvt. practice clin. psychology Commonwealth Psychol. Assocs. PLC, McLean, Va., 1979—; founder,dir. Commonwealth Psychol. Assocs., 1979—, pres., 1979—. Lectr. Washington Tech. Inst., 1972-74, George Mason U., 1978—82; asst. clin. prof. psychology George Washington U., 2003—; cons. in field. Contbr. articles to profl. jours. Mem. adv. bd. World Children's Chor, 2000—02; mem. family edn. project Joseph P. Kennedy Jr. Found., 1977—79; mem. regional appeals bd. No. Va. Pub. Sch. Sys., 1977—79; mem. adv. bd. Value Options Behavioral Health, 2001—. Recipient N.Y. State Scholar Incentive award, 1969. Mem. APA, Am. Soc. Clin. Hypnosis (approved cons.), Va. Acad. Clin. Psychologists, Va. Psychol. Assn., No. Va. Soc. Clin. Psychologists, Washington Soc. Study Clin. Hypnosis, Psi Chi, Alpha Lambda Delta. Office: 1479 Chain Bridge Rd Mc Lean VA 22101-5730 Office Phone: 203-734-0787.

AUERBACH, BOB SHIPLEY, librarian; b. N.Y.C., Dec. 14, 1919; s. Leo and Gertrude Anne (Shipley) A.; m. Mary Carson, July 13, 1954 (div. Mar. 1976); children: Hopi, Jennine. BA, NYU, 1948; MA in Libr. Sci., Vanderbilt U., 1956. Asst. libr. Shepherd Coll., Shepherdstown, W.Va., 1956-57, Coll. Steubenville (Ohio), 1957-58; libr. Tecumseh High Sch, New Carlisle, Ohio, 1958-59, Urbana (Ohio) Coll., 1959-61; dir. Capital Libr. Svc., Greenbelt, Md., 1961-72; reference libr. U. D.C., Washington, 1972-87; libr. World Hunger Edn. Svc., Washington, 1988-91; retired, 1991—. Chair Peoples Party Md., 1972-73, Md. Green Party, 1998-2001; mem. Green coun. Green Nat. Com., Lawrence, Mass., 1995-97; chair Greenbelt Greens, 1990-2001, Socialist Discussion Group, Washington, 1975—; mem. Nat. Com. Socialist Party, 1991-95, alt. mem. nat. com., 1995-97, nat. com. mem., 1997-99; mem. state com. Md. Green Party, 2001—, candidate for Congress, 5th Dist., Md., 2002, 04. Mem. ALA, AAUP, Am. Polit. Sci. Assn., Washington Independent Writers Assn. Avocations: stamp collecting/philately, button collecting. Home: 14 X Ridge Rd Greenbelt MD 20770 Personal E-mail: bauerbach1@aol.com.

AUERBACH, ERNEST SIGMUND, lawyer, insurance company executive, writer; b. Berlin, Dec. 22, 1936; arrived in U.S., 1938; s. Frank L. and Gertrude Auerbach; m. Jeannette Taylor; 1 child, Hans Kevin. AB, George Washington U., 1958, JD, 1961; postgrad., U.S. Army Gen. Staff Coll., 1975. Bar: D.C. 1962, Pa. 1978. Atty. So. Ry. Co., Washington, 1961-62; commd 1st lt. U.S. Army, 1962, advanced through grades to col.; served in Germany, Vietnam, Pentagon; div. counsel Xerox Corp., Stamford, Conn., 1970-75; mng. atty. NL Industries, Inc., N.Y.C., 1975-77; from asst. to assoc. gen. counsel, staff v.p. INA Corp., Phila., 1977-79; sr. v.p. INA Svc. Co., 1979-82; sr. v.p., chief of staff INA Internat., 1982-83; pres. internat. life and group ops. CIGNA Worldwide Corp. div. CIGNA Corp., 1984-89; mng. dir. Crusader Life Ins. PLC, Reigate, Eng., 1984-86, chmn., 1986-89; pres., COO N.Y. Life Worldwide Holding, Inc., N.Y.C., 1989-90; pres., CEO Paperless Claims, Inc., N.Y.C., 1991-92; dir. to gen. Seguros Azteca Ins. Co., Mexico City, 1992-93; sr. cons. Anderson Consulting, Mexico City, 1993-95; sr. v.p. United Ins. Cos., Inc., Irving, Tex., 1995-97, also pres., CEO student ins. divsn., 1996-97, pres., CEO ins. group, 1997; pres., COO Software Testing Assurance Corp., N.Y.C., 1998; pres., CEO Tesia Corp., N.Y.C., 1998—2001, chmn., bd. dirs., 2002; sr. v.p. Strickland Group, N.Y.C., 2001—03; v.p. ALICO divsn. AIG Corp., 2003—04; regional v.p. AIA divsn. AIG Corp., Hong Kong, 2004—. Mem. adv. bd. revbox.com, 1998—2001. Author: Joining the Inner Circle: How To Make It As A Senior Executive, 1990; contbg. author: The Wall St. Jour. on Mng., 1990; contbr. articles to legal, fin., news, and def. jours. Mem. Am. Coun. on Germany, 1980-2000; computer sys. tech. adv. com. Dept. Commerce, 1974-76; mem. bd. adv. dirs. Salvation Army, Mexico City, 1993-94; commr. bd. adjustment City of Coppell, Tex., 1996-97. Ret. col. USAR, 1985. Decorated Legion of Merit with oak leaf cluster, Bronze Star. Mem.: Westchester-Fairfield Corp. Counsel Assn. (founding officer 1973—78), Ret. Army Judge Advocate Assn., Audubon Soc. (pres., bd. dirs. Greenwich chpt. 1999—2002, bd. dirs. Conn. chpt. 2002—04), Spl. Forces Assn., Army and Navy Club (Washington chpt.), Nat. Arts Club (N.Y.C.), Univ. Club (N.Y.C.). Home: 150 Southwoods Terr Southbury CT 06488 Office Phone: 852-283-6396. Personal E-mail: colauerbach@earthlink.net.

AUERBACH, JEFFREY IRA, lawyer; b. N.Y.C., Mar. 21, 1953; s. Robert Frank and Jo Ann (Kitt) A.; m. Terry Harriet Tretter, June 17, 1984; children: Andrew Daniel, Michael Harrison. BS, Cornell U., 1975; MPhil, Yale U., 1977, PhD, 1981; JD, George Washington U., 1989. Bar: D.C. 1989, U.S. Dist. Ct. D.C. 1989, Md. 1990, U.S. Ct. Appeals (fed. cir.) 1990, U.S. Ct. Appeals (D.C. cir.) 1990. Postdoctoral fellow Nat. Cancer Inst., Bethesda, Md., 1981—82; assoc. sr. investigator SmithKline & French Lab., Phila., 1982—84; rsch. geneticist W.R. Grace & Co., Columbia, Md., 1984—86; patent examiner U.S. Patent & Trademark Office, Washington, 1986; law clk. to assoc. Saidman, Sterne et al., Washington, 1986—90; ptnr. Myers, Rose & Liniak, Bethesda, 1990—91; assoc. Weil, Gotshal & Manges, Washington, 1991—93; ptnr. Howrey & Simon, Washington, 1993—2000, Liniak, Berenato et al, Bethesda, 2000—. Pres., founder Replicon, Inc., 1995-2003, DC Assoc., LLC, 2003-; sci. advisor Trade Logistics and Strategies, LLC, Bethesda, 2000—; lectr. Johns Hopkins U., 2000—; bd. Am. Com. for Weizmann Inst. for Sci., Washington, 2002—. Inventor externalization of products of bacteria, methods for the isothermal amplification of nucleic acid molecules, in vitro amplification of DNA via circular replicons tech. used for the sequencing of human genome. Postdoctoral fellow Am. Cancer Soc., 1981. Mem. ABA, Am. Intellectual Property Law Assn., Md. State Bar Assn., Fed. Cir. Bar Assn, Montgomery County Md. Bar Assn. (chair IP sect.). Republican. Avocations: stained glass, bicycling, skiing, scuba diving. Home: 13109 Jasmine Hill Ter Rockville MD 20850-3662 Office: Liniak Berenato et al 6550 Rock Spring Dr Bethesda MD 20817-1132 Office Phone: 301-896-0600.

AUERBACH, JEROLD S., academic administrator, educator; b. Phila., May 7, 1936; s. Morry M. and Sophie (Soloff) A.; m. Susan H. Levin, May 16, 1982; children: Shira, Rebecca; children from previous marriage Jeffrey, Pamela. BA, Oberlin Coll., 1957; MA, Columbia U., 1959, PhD, 1965. Lectr. Queens Coll. CUNY, 1964-65; asst. prof. Brandeis U., Waltham, Mass., 1965-71, Wellesley (Mass.) Coll., 1971-72, assoc. prof., 1972-77, prof., 1977—. Vis. scholar Harvard Law Sch.; Fulbright lectr. Tel Aviv U., 1974-75. Author: Labor and Liberty, 1966, Unequal Justice, 1976, Justice Without Law?, 1983, Rabbis and Lawyers, 1990, Jacob's Voices, 1996, Are We One?, 2001. Guggenheim Meml. Found. fellow, 1974-75; fellow NSF, 1979-80, NEH, 1986-87, 91-92. Office: Wellesley Coll 106 Central St Wellesley MA 02481-8268 Personal E-mail: jsauerbach@comcast.net.

AUERBACH, JOHN M., city health department administrator; With Uhpham's Corner Health Ctr., Dorchester, Mass.; dir., AIDS bur. Mass. Dept. Pub. Health; exec. dir. Boston Pub. Health Commn., 1998—. Office: Boston Pub Health Commn 1010 Massachusetts Ave Boston MA 02118

AUERBACH, JOSEPH, former lawyer, law educator; b. Franklin, N.H., Dec. 3, 1916; s. Jacob and Besse Mae (Reamer) A.; m. Judith Evans, Nov. 10, 1941; children: Jonathan L., Hope B. Pym. AB, Harvard U., 1938, LLB, 1941. Bar: N.H. 1941, Mass. 1952, U.S. Ct. Appeals (1st, 2d, 3d, 5th, 7th and D.C. cirs.), U.S. Supreme Ct. 1948. Atty. SEC, Washington and Phila., 1941—43, prin. atty., 1946—49; fgn. svc. staff officer U.S. Dept. State, Dusseldorf, Germany, 1950—52; ptnr. Sullivan & Worcester, Boston, 1952—82, counsel, 1982—; lectr. Boston U. Law Sch., 1975—76, Harvard Bus. Sch., Boston, 1980—82, prof., 1982—83, Class of 1957 prof., 1983—87, prof. emeritus, 1987—; prof. Harvard Ext. Sch., 1988, Harvard Ext. Sch., 1991—95. Bd. dirs. Nat. Benefit Life Ins. Co., N.Y.C. Author: (with S.L. Hayes, III), Investment Banking and Diligence, 1986, Underwriting Regulation and Shelf Registration Phenomenon in Wall Street and Regulation, 1987, also chpt. to book, papers and articles in field. Trustee Mass. Eye and Ear Infirmary, Boston, 1981—, chmn. devel. com., 1985-88, chmn. nominating com., 1993-94; mem. adv. bd., former chmn. devel. com. Am. Repertory Theatre, Cambridge, Mass., 1985—; bd. dirs., past pres. Friends of Boston U. Librs., 1972—; past v.p., bd. dirs. Shakespeare Globe Ctr., N.A., 1983-90; overseer New Eng. Conservatory of Music, 1992-98, mem. fin. com.; bd. dirs. English Speaking Union, Boston, 1995-98; chair 1938 Harvard Pres. Assn.; active Harvard Coll. Fund, Harvard Law Sch. Fund. Decorated Army Commendation medal; recipient Disting. Svc. award Harvard Bus. Sch., 1996, Disting. Teaching award 1993, Exemplary Svc. award Harvard Extension Sch., 1995. Mem. ABA, Mass. Bar Assn., Boston Bar Assn., Harvard Mus. Assn., St. Botolph Club, Harvard Club N.Y.C., Shop Club, Downtown Club. Home: 300 Boylston St Apt 512 Boston MA 02116-3923 Office: Sullivan & Worcester 1 Post Office Sq Ste 2300 Boston MA 02109-2129 also: Harvard Bus Sch Cumnock Hall Rm 300 Boston MA 02163

AUERBACH, JUDITH DIANE, public health service officer; b. San Francisco, Aug. 14, 1956; d. Harold B. and Dorothy A. (Greenfeld) A. BA in Sociology, U. Calif., Berkeley, 1974, MA in Sociology, 1981, PhD in Sociology, 1986. Asst. prof. Widener U., Chester, Pa., 1986—87; Congl. sci. fellow Rep. Pat Schroeder's Office, Washington, 1988—89; dir. Inst. for Study Women and Men U. So. Calif., L.A., 1989—90; assoc. dir. govt. affairs Consortium Soc. Sci. Assocs., Washington, 1990—92; sr. program officer Inst. Medicine Nat. Acad. Sci., Washington, 1992—95; coord. chair behavioral and social scis. Office AIDS Rsch., NIH, Bethesda, Md., 1995; dir. behavioral and social sci. program and HIV prevention sci.; v.p. pub. policy Am. Found. for AIDS Rsch., Washington, 2003—. Vis. prof. UCLA, 1987-88; cons. in field; presenter in field Author: In the Business of Child Care, 1988; (with others) Family Day Care: Current Research, 1992, Children at Risk in America, 1993; co-editor: AIDS and Behavior: An Integrated Approach, 1994; contbr. articles to profl. jours. Recipient Best Policy Paper/Poster award Soc. Psychol. Study Soc. Issues, 1992; NEH fellow, 1987, Soc. Rsch. in Child Devel. fellow, 1988-89. Mem. Am. Sociol. Assn., Sociologists for Women in Soc., Assn. Pub. Policy Analysis and Mgmt. Democrat. Jewish. Office: AmFAR #802 1828 L St NW Washington DC 20036-5104

AUERBACH, MARSHALL JAY, lawyer; b. Chgo., Sept. 5, 1932; s. Samuel M. and Sadie (Miller) A.; m. Carole Landsberg, July 3, 1960; children: Keith Alan, Michael Ward Student, U. Ill.; JD, John Marshall Law Sch., 1955. Bar: Ill. 1955. Sole practice, Evanston, Ill., 1955-72; ptnr. in charge matrimonial law sect. Jenner & Block, Chgo., 1972-80; mem. firm Marshall J. Auerbach & Assocs., Ltd., Chgo., 1980—. Mem. faculty Ill. Inst. Continuing Legal Edn. Author: Illinois Marriage and Dissolution of Marriage Act, enacted into law, 1977; Historical and Practice Notes to Illinois Marriage and Dissolution of Marriage Act, 1980-88; contbr. chpts. to Family Law, Vol. 2 Fellow Am. Acad. Matrimonial Lawyers; mem. Ill. State Bar Assn. (chmn. family law sect. 1971-72), ABA (vice-chmn. family law sect. com. for liaison with tax sect. 1974-76) Home and Office: Marshall J Auerbach & Assoc Ltd 30 N La Salle St Ste 3400 Chicago IL 60602 Office Phone: 312-853-3300.

AUERBACH, PAUL IRA, lawyer; b. N.Y.C., Dec. 30, 1932; s. Joseph and Fannie (Steingard) Auerbach; children: Stuart Andrew, Beth Royce. LLB, Bklyn. Law Sch., 1954; CLU, Am. Coll., 1980, ChFC, 1982. Bar: N.Y. 1955, Fla. 1991, U.S. Dist. Ct. (so. and ea. dists.) N.Y., U.S. Dist Ct. (so. dist.) Fla. 1991. Trial counsel Cosmopolitan Mutual Ins. Corp., N.Y.C., 1955-57, Hertz Corp., N.Y.C., 1957-59; ptnr. Brent, Phillips, Auerbach & Dranoff, Rockland, N.Y., 1959-63; prin. Paul I. Auerbach, Atty. at Law, N.Y.C. and Bronx, 1963-97, Palm Beach Gardens, Fla., 1990—. Founder Young Dem. Com., Bronx, 1955-60; committeeman Rep. Com., South Orangeton, N.Y., 1970-76. Mem.: KP, Rotary (chmn. drug prevention com. 1970—74), ABA, South Palm Beach County Bar Assn. (chmn. elder law commn.), Nat. Acad. Elder Law Attys., Internat. Assn. Fin. Planners, Planned Giving Coun. of Palm Beach County (v.p.), Tax Inst. of Palm Beach County, Fla. Bar Assn., Palm Beach County Bar Assn., North Palm Beach County Bar Assn. (pres. 1999—2000), Bronx Bar Assn. (chmn. criminal law com. 1990—91), N.Y. State Bar Assn., Masons. Avocations: tennis, gourmet food, golf. Home: 11215 Curry Dr Palm Beach Gardens FL 33418 Office Phone: 561-775-2734. Personal E-mail: piaesq@yahoo.com.

AUERBACH, SEYMOUR, architect; b. N.Y.C., May 28, 1929; s. Nathan and Jennie (Norman) A.; m. Alyce Kelly, Oct. 21, 1963 (div. 1977); children: Kalin Marie Hyman, Alison Kelly; m. Patricia Sullivan, July 31, 1985 (div. 1991). B.Arch., Yale U., 1951. Assoc. firm Satterlee & Smith (Archs.), Washington, 1955-59; ptnr. Cooper & Auerbach (Archs.), Washington, 1960-69, Walton, Madden, Cooper & Auerbach (Archs.), Washington, 1970-71; pvt. practice Washington, 1971—. Pres. Kamak Enterprises, Inc., sole propr. for patent commercialization; developer, architect Battery Subdiv., Washington, Buck's Knoll Farm, Yellow Spring, W.Va.; prof. architecture Cath. U. Am., 1960-99; cons. construction failures, 1982—. Prin. works include Nat. Visitor Ctr., Washington, campus plan and dormitories, Georgetown U., Olam Tikvah Synagogue, Fairfax, Va., Brith Sholom Synagogue, Bethlehem, Pa., resort cmtys., Rehoboth Beach, Del., campus for Bowling Brook prep; patentee in unrelated fields. Bd. mgrs. Chevy Chase Village, Md., 1973-77, vice chmn. bd., 1976-77; mem. archtl. adv. panel Union of Am. Hebrew Congregations. With C.E. U.S. Army, 1951-54. Decorated knight honor and merit Imperial Russian Order St. John of Jerusalem; recipient award excellence in architecture Met. Washington Bd. Trade, 1964, Papal Benemerenti medal, 1994, Rsch. Ctr. award Georgetown U., 1964; winner award competition for design of Copley Plaza, Boston, 1967, award for excellence in arch. Washington Bd. Trade, 1964, Potomac Valley award, 1964; William Wirt Winchester fellow, 1951. Fellow AIA; mem. AAUP, Soc. Archtl. Historians, Guild Religious Architecture, Cosmos Club Washington, Yale Club Washington. Republican. Jewish. Home and Office: 115 Hesketh St Chevy Chase MD 20815-4222 Business E-Mail: syauer@comcast.net. *I consider it to be of the highest calling to be involved in the improvement of man's physical environment: not only his shelter, but also his public environment and the implements he uses. In this context I have held architecture to be an Applied, rather than a Fine, Art. I consider it to be a higher calling to be a designer than to be an architect and I find the greatest of personal pleasure in solving individual problems of design for man, by myself, without regard to "style", and without regard to political or other irrelevant considerations.*

AUERFELD, JAY HOWARD, elementary school educator; b. Bklyn., Apr. 7, 1964; s. Arthur Ira and Barbara Susan Auerfeld; m. Edna Rose Auerfeld, July 10, 1994; children: Maylynne, Julia, Caroline. BA in Edn., Queens Coll., 1990; MA in Edn., Brockport U., 1995. Tchr. NYC Bd. Edn., Queens, NY, 1990—93, Hilton (NY) Central Schs., Hilton, 1993—99, Ramapa Central Sch., Suffern, NY, 2000—.

AUFDERHEIDE, ARTHUR CARL, pathologist; b. New Ulm, Minn., Sept. 9, 1922; s. Herman John and Esther (Sannwald) A.; m. Mary Lillian Buryk, Jan. 26, 1946; children: Patricia Ann, Tom Paul, Walter Herman. MD, U. Minn., 1946; DSc (hon.), Coll. of St. Scholastica, 1983. Chief dept. pathology Mpls. VA Hosp., 1952-53, St. Mary's Hosp., Duluth, Minn., 1953-57; chief dept. pathology Sch. Medicine U. Minn., Duluth, 1970-87, dean Sch. Medicine, 1974-75, dir. paleobiology lab. Sch. Medicine, 1977—. Mem. Plaisted Polar Expdn., 1968; rsch. cons. anthropology lab. U. Colombia, Bogota, 1989—, Pigorini Mus., Rome, 1988, Archeol. Mus. of Tenerife, Canary Islands, 1989-90; chmn. sci. com. Cronos Rsch Project, Santa Cruz, Tenerife, 1991—. Author: Cambridge Ency. Author: Scientific Study of Mummies 2002 Human Paleopathology, 1998; co-editor: Paleopathology, 1991; author: (documentary film) Copper Eskimo, 1970; contbr. numerous articles to profl. publs. Chmn. civil com. to devel. a degree-granting med. sch., Duluth, 1988. Capt. U.S. Army, 1947-49. Fellow AAAS; mem. Paleopathology Assn., N.Y. Acad. Scis. Democrat. Lutheran. Achievements include research in soft tissue paleopathology. Home: 4711 Colorado St Duluth MN 55804-1512 Office: U Minn 10 University Dr Duluth MN 55812-2403 Office Phone: 218-726-7911. E-mail: aaufderh@d.umn.edu.

AUFHAUSER, DAVID D., lawyer, former federal agency administrator; b. N.Y.C., Nov. 19, 1950; married; 3 children. A.B., Wesleyan U., 1972; MBA, Harvard U., 1974; JD, U. Pa., 1977. Bar: Pa. 1977, D.C. 1978. Lawyer Williams and Connolly LLP, Washington, 1977—2001, counsel, 2003—04; gen. counsel U.S. Dept. Treasury, Washington, 2001—03; global gen. counsel, gen. counsel for the Americas UBS Investment Bank, 2004—. Mem. steering com. Civil Justice Reform Task Force, 1992; gen. counsel credentials com. Rep. Convention, 1992; mem. legal adv. group Rep. House Leadership Conf., 1993—94; counsel President's Group on Financial Markets, 2001—03; chmn. Nat. Security Coun. Policy Coordinating Com. on Terrorist Financing, 2001—03; Treasury Rep. U.S. Dept. Justice, Corp. Fraud Task Force, 2002—03; sr. fellow Ctr. for Strategic & Internat. Studies, 2004—. Recipient The U.S. Treasury Dept. Alexander Hamilton award for Disting. Service, 2003, CIA Disting. Svc. award and seal, 2003, FBI Disting. Svc. and Leadership Citation, 2003, U.S. Secret Svc. Dir.'s Honor award, 2003. Mem.: bd., Fed. Financing Bank, 2001-03, Civil Justice Reform Task Force, 1992, Edward Bennett Williams Inns of Ct., 2002-03, Bush-Cheney Election Contest Legal Representation Team, 2000-01, Phi Beta Kappa. Republican. Office: UBS Investment Bank 1 Finsbury Ave EC2M 2PP England E-mail: daufhauser@wc.com.

AUFILL, BENNETT BRANTLEY, III, lawyer; b. Hillsboro, Tex., Feb. 15, 1943; s. Bennett Brantley II and Lucille (Pinkerton) A.; m. Mary Ella Keeter; children: Bennett Brantley IV, Benjamin Arthur. BA in Chemistry, Tex. Christian U., 1965; MS in Mech. Engring., U. N.Mex., 1971; JD, South Tex. Coll. Law, Houston, 1974; MBA, So. Meth. U., 1987. Bar: Tex. 1975. Registered profl. engr. Tex. 1975. Physicist USAF Weapons Lab., Albuquerque, 1967-71; prin. engr. Houston Lighting & Power, 1971-76; environ. coord. Exxon (Carter Mining Co.), Gillette, Wyo., 1977-80; atty. Ctrl. & Southwest, Dallas, 1980-90; assoc. Burleson Pate & Gibson, Dallas, 1991-93; pvt. practice Dallas and Hillsboro, 1993—. Adj. prof. Cox Sch. of Bus., So. Meth. U., 1990-94; tchr. Southeastern Paralegal Inst., Dallas, 1988— Spkr. 20th annual Tex. Oil & Gas Inst., 1994. Mem. Am. Legion (past comdr. Hillsboro Post 4, 1995-97), panel of arbitrators N. Y. Stock Exch., 1993—. Capt. USAF, 1967-71. Recipient E.E. Townes award South Tex. Coll. Law, 1975. Mem. Tex. Supr.'s Assn., S.W. adv. com. Am. Arbitration Assn. Meth. Avocation: ranching. Office: PO Box 731 Hillsboro TX 76645-0731 Office Phone: 254-582-9725. E-mail: aufill@hillsboro.com.

AUFSES, ARTHUR HAROLD, JR., surgeon, medical educator; b. N.Y.C., Feb. 8, 1926; s. Arthur Harold and Beatrice (Hauser) A.; m. Harriet Whitman, Dec. 28, 1947; children: Arthur Harold III, Carolyn Aufses Blashek. Student, Columbia U., 1942-43; BS, Union Coll., 1944; MD, Columbia U. Coll. Physicians and Surgeons, 1948. Diplomate Am. Bd. Surgery. Intern Presbyn. Hosp., N.Y.C., 1948-49, resident in surgery, 1950-51, 53-54, Mt. Sinai Hosp., N.Y.C., 1954-56; practice medicine specializing in surgery N.Y.C., 1956-97; prof. Mt. Sinai Med. Ctr., N.Y.C., 1974—; chmn. dept. surgery Mt. Sinai Sch. Medicine, N.Y.C., 1974-96, L.I. Jewish Med. Ctr., 1971-74; prof. surgery SUNY-Stony Brook, 1971-74; surgeon-in-chief Mt. Sinai Hosp., N.Y.C., 1974-96. Contbr. articles to med. jours. Bd. dirs. 92d St. YMHA, 1974—. 1st lt. U.S. Army, 1951-53. Recipient Jacobi medallion Mt. Sinai Med. Ctr., 1979; recipient Gold Headed Cane award Mt. Sinai Med. Ctr., 1982 Fellow ACS (2nd v.p. 1996-97), Am. Surg. Assn. (2nd v.p. 1995-96), Am. Coll. Gastroenterology (pres. 1986-87), Assn. of Program Dirs. Surgery (pres. 1989-91), N.Y. Acad. Medicine; mem. Soc. Surg. Oncology, Am. Gastroent. Assn., N.Y. Surg. Soc. (pres. 1979-80), Soc. Surgery Alimentary Tract, Brazilian Coll. Surgeons, Chilean Congress Surgeons, Portuguese Soc. Gastroenterology. Jewish. Home: 1185 Park Ave New York NY 10128-1308 Office: Mt Sinai Sch Medicine Box 1077 1 Gustave L Levy Pl New York NY 10029-6500 Office Phone: 212-659-9560. Business E-Mail: arthur.aufses@mssm.edu.

AUGELLI, JOHN PAT, geographer, educator, writer, consultant, rancher; b. Celenza, Italy, Jan. 30, 1921; s. Pat John and M. Antoinette (Iacaruso) A.; divorced; children: John, Robert. BA, Clark U., 1943; MA, Harvard U., 1949, PhD, 1951. Teaching fellow Harvard U., Cambridge, Mass., 1948—49; from asst. to assoc. prof. geography U. P.R., Rio Piedras, 1949—51; assoc. prof. U. Md., College Park, 1952—61; prof. U. Kans., Lawrence, 1961—70, 1971—91; prof. geography, dir. Ctr. Latin Am. Studies U. Ill., Champaign-Urbana, 1970—71. Lectr., travel cons. Mediterranean and Latin Am. cruises, 1991-95; mem. Bd. Fgn. Scholarships, Washington, 1967-70; cons. Nat. Geographic Soc., Washington, 1984-87; del. U.S. Acad. Scis., New Delhi, 1968; sec. Coun. of Inter-Am. Affairs, Washington, 1959-60. Author: Caribbean Lands, 1965, Puerto Rico, 1973, Middle America, 3d edit., 1989; cons.; (atlas) World & North America, 1984; contbr. 76 articles to profl. jours. Served to lst lt. U.S. Army, 1943-46, PTO, Res., 1949-51. Recipient Fulbright research grant, 1982. Fellow Am. Geog. Soc.; mem. Assn. Am. Geographers (sec. 1966-69), Latin Am. Studies Assn. (pres. 1969), Nat. Council Geographic Edn. (master tchr. 1979), Conf. of Latin Americanist Geographers (outstanding contbn. to research and teaching award 1982). Democrat. Roman Catholic. Avocations: travel, fishing. Address: 35 Mediterranean Blvd E Port Saint Lucie FL 34952-8557 Office Phone: 772-343-9673.

AUGELLO, WILLIAM JOSEPH, lawyer; b. Bklyn., Apr. 5, 1926; s. William J. and Catherine (Ehalt) A.; m. Elizabeth Deasy, July 1, 1950; children: Thomas, Charles, Patricia, William, Peggy Ann, James. LLB, Fordham U., 1950; BA, Dartmouth Coll., 1946. Bar: N.Y. 1951. Individual practice law, N.Y.C., 1953-71; mem. firm Augello, Deegan & Pezold, Huntington, N.Y., 1971-78; sr. mem. firm Augello, Pezold & Hirschmann, Huntington, 1978—98. Treas., dir. Transp. Arbitration Bd., Inc., 1978-96; chmn. accreditation com. Certified Claims Profl. Accreditation Council, Inc., Washington, 1981-96; exec. dir. Transp. Consumer Protection Coun. Inc., Huntington, 1974-2003; exec. dir., gen. counsel Freight Transp. Cons. Assoc.; adv. com. pvt. internat. law study group maritime matters Dept. State; co-chmn. uniform liability regime working group Ctr. Inter-Am. Trade; adj. prof. U. Ariz.; faculty U. Denver Intermodal Transportation Inst., bd. dirs. Inst. Logistical Mgmt.; lectr. in field. Author: Freight Claims in Plain English, 1979, 3d edit., 1995, Transportation Insurance in Plain English, 1985, Defending and Avoiding Undercharge Claims and Suits, 1991, Doing Business Under the New Transportational Law: The Negotiated Rates Act of 1993, 94, How to Read Tariffs to Avoid Surprises, 1994, Shippers Domestic Truck Bill of Loding, 1996, A Guide to Transportation After the I.C.C., 1996, Protecting Shippers Interests, 1997, Corporate Procedures for Shipping and Receiving, 1998, Transportation, Logistics and the Law, 2001, 04; co-author: Freight Claim Prevention in Plain English, 1985, Transportation Contracts in Plain English, 1991, Q & A in Plain English, 1999. Served with USN, 1944-46. Recipient Harry E. Salzberg Medallion award Syracuse U., 1994, Transp. Educator of Yr. award Operation Stimulus, 1996; named Nat. Transp. Man of Yr., Delta Nu Alpha, 1979-80. Mem. Maritime Law Assn., Transp. Lawyers Assn. (Disting. Svc. award 1988), Suffolk County Bar Assn., Assn. Transp. Law, Logistics and Policy, El Con Conquistador Country Club (Tucson), Delta Nu Alpha. Republican. Roman Catholic. Mailing: 2198 E Amaranth St Tucson AZ 85737-7205 Office Phone: 520-825-3997. E-mail: williamaugello@comcast.net. *Few things in life are more gratifying than helping others reach their full potential or just providing them with a means to advance up the corporate ladder with their heads higher than before.*

AUGENSTEIN, BRUNO W., research scientist, researcher; b. Germany, Mar. 16, 1923; came to U.S., 1927, naturalized, 1935; s. Wilhelm C. and Emma (Mina) A.; m. Kathleen Greenlaw, May 27, 1950; children: Karen, Eric, Christopher. Sc.B. in Physics and Math, Brown U., 1943; MS in Aero, Calif. Inst. Tech., 1945. Supr. N.Am. Aviation Co., 1946-48; asst. prof. Purdue U., 1948-49; Navaho project leader, 1948; sr. scientist Rand Corp., 1949-58; ICBM project leader, 1952-56; chief scientist satellite programs; dir. planning Lockheed Missiles & Space Co., 1958-61; spl. asst. for reconnaisance and intelligence, dep. dir. intelligence activities Office Sec. Def., 1961-65; now cons.; rsch. adviser Inst. Def. Analyses, 1965-67; v.p. research Rand Corp., Santa Monica, Calif., 1967-71, chief scientist, 1971-72, resident cons., 1972—, sr. scientist, 1976—, emeritus scientist, 1995—, corp. scholar emeritus, 2001—. Cons., NAS, Bur. Budget, 1965—, Nat. Bur. Standards, 1971—, Xerad, Inc., 1972—, Dept. Navy, NSF, NASA, 1973—, Dept. Def., 1978—, Hi Tech Investment Mgmt., Inc., 1983; chmn. naval health systems rev. com. Office Sci. Tech. Policy, 1975—, cons., 1978—; v.p. rsch., bd. dirs. Spectravision, Inc.; bd. regents, asst. chmn. Nat. Libr. Medicine, HEW, 1967-73; mem. NAS computer sci. com. Nat. Bur. Standards, 1971-79, chmn., 1973-76; chmn., editor, Internat. Conf. on Antiproton Sci. and Tech., 1987; initiated Dept. Def. program on micro air vehicles, 1992. Guest contbr., editor Chaos, Solitons and Fractals Jour., 1995, 99. Recipient Distinguished Pub. Service award for reconnaisance and intelligence direction Dept. Def., 1965 Mem. Am. Inst. Physics, AIAA, AAAS, IEEE, Math. Assn. Am., Am. Nuclear Soc., Philosophy of Sci. Assn., N.Y. Acad. Scis., Beta Theta Pi. Home: 1144 Tellem Dr Pacific Palisades CA 90272-2244 Office: 1700 Main St Santa Monica CA 90401-3208

AUGSBURGER, AARON DONALD, clergyman; b. Elida, Ohio, Dec. 21, 1925; s. C.A. and Estella R. (Shenk) A.; m. Martha L. Kling, June 5, 1948; children: Phyllis Augsburger Ressler, Patricia Augsburger, Don Richard. BA, Mennonite Coll., 1949; MRE, Ea. Bapt. Sem., Phila., 1956; DEd, Temple U., 1963. Ordained to ministry Mennonite Ch., 1951. Mem. pers. and student svcs. coms. Mennonite Bd. Missions and Charities, 1954-70; pastor students, tchr. Christian edn. Ea. Mennonite Coll., Harrisonburg, Va., 1958-64; asst. dean Goshen (Ind.) Sem., 1964-65; pastor, bishop North Goshen (Ind.)

Mennonite Ch., 1965-70; tchr. psychology Goshen (Ind.) Coll., 1965-66; pastor Park View Mennonite Ch., Harrisonburg, 1974-80; prof. Ea. Mennonite Sem., 1980-89; pastor Bahia Vista Mennonite Ch., Sarasota, Fla., 1989-96; dir. pastoral care Mennonite Home, Lancaster, Pa., 1996—. Author: Creating Christian Personality, 1966, A Pattern for Living, 1993; editor: Marriages That Work, 1984, Reshaping Your Marriage, 1996. Guidance counselor Bethany Christian High Sch., Goshen, 1966-68, supr., 1968-70; moderator Gen. Assembly of Mennonite Chs., 1971-73. Home: 151 Miller Rd Chambersburg PA 17201-9230

AUGSPURGER, JOSEPH DALE, chemist, researcher; b. Bloomington, Ill., June 14, 1959; s. Delmar Guy and Thelma Katherine (Streid) A.; m. Laura Beth Glynn, June 22, 1985; children: Carolyn Pearl, Michele Elizabeth. BS in Chem. Engring., U. Ill., 1981, PhD in Chemistry, 1990. Buyer Campus Crusade for Christ, San Bernardino, Calif., 1981-85, fin. adminstr. Laguna Niguel, Calif., 1985-86; teaching and rsch. asst. U. Ill., Urbana, 1986-90; asst. rsch. scientist Ind. U.-Purdue U., Indpls., 1990-93; postdoctoral assoc. Cornell U., Ithaca, N.Y., 1993—. Contbr. articles to Jour. of Computational Chemistry, Jour. of the Am. Chem. Soc., Jour. of Chem. Physics. Eastman Kodak scholar, 1978-81; Leukemia Soc. of Am. spl. fellow, 1994—. Mem. Am. Chem. Soc., Am. Physical Soc., Tau Beta Pi. Office: Cornell U Baker Lab Ithaca NY 14853

AUGUR, MARILYN HUSSMAN, distribution executive; b. Texarkana, Ark., Aug. 23, 1938; d. Walter E. and Betty (Palmer) H.; m. James M. Augur, Dec. 29, 1962; children: Margaret M. Hancock, Elizabeth H. Taylor, Ann Louise Hardaway. BA, U. N.C., 1960; MBA, So. Meth. U., 1989. Pres. North Tex. Mountain Valley Water, Dallas, 1989—. Bd. dirs. Camden News Pub. Co., Little Rock, Living Waters, Dallas, 2005—; mem. vestry St. Michael and His Angels Ch., 2003— Trustee Hussman Found., Little Rock, 1991—, U. Tex. Southwestern Med. Found., 1993—, Nat. Jewish Hosp., 1993—2000, Marilyn Augur Family Found., Dallas, 1991—; bd. dirs. Baylor Health Sys. Found., 1992—, chmn., 1995; bd. dirs. Tate Lectr. Series, 1994—2000; mem. adv. bd., Salvation Army, 1996-, chmn. William Booth Soc., 1999-2000; mem. Tex. Bus. Hall Fame, 1992—98, exec. com., 1994—95; mem. Dallas Citizens Coun., 1994—2004; bd. dirs. Dallas County C.C. Dist. Found., 1995—; bd. mem. Dallas Helps, 1995—99, Charter 100, 1998—, Baylor Oral Health Found. Bd., 1998—2001; mem. exec. bd. So. Meth. U. Dedman Law Sch. & Cox. Bus. Sch., 1998—; bd. dirs. Children's Health Care Sys. Found., 1998—. Mem. Dallas Country Club, Crescent Club, Dallas Women's Club, Beta Gamma Sigma. Episcopalian. Avocations: travel, skiing, trekking. Office: North Tex Mountain Valley Water 4209 McKinney Ave Ste 202B Dallas TX 75205-5439 Personal E-mail: ntmvw1@aol.com.

AUGUST, DAVID ALLEN, surgeon; b. N.Y.C., Apr. 16, 1955; s. Robert Irwin and Rhoda (Greene) A.; m. Barbara Ann Peck; children: Sandy, Harry, Eitan. BS in Life Scis., MIT, 1976; MD, Yale U. Sch. Medicine, 1980. Diplomate Am. Bd. Surgery. Resident in surgery Yale - New Haven Hosp., 1980-86; fellow in surg. oncology Nat. Cancer Inst., Bethesda, Md., 1982-84; surgeon RW Johnson Med. Sch. - U. Hosp., New Brunswick, N.J.; educator UMDNJ. Bd. dirs. N.J. Am. Cancer Soc., 1996—. Mem. Soc. Univ. Surgeons, Assn. Acad. Surgery, Am. Coll. Surgeons, Am. Soc. Parenteral and Enteral Nutrition. Office: Cancer Inst NJ 195 Little Albany St New Brunswick NJ 08901-1914 Office Phone: 732-235-7701.

AUGUST, ROBERT OLIN, retired journalist; b. Ashtabula, Ohio, Oct. 6, 1921; s. Frank and Lillian (Olin) A.; m. Marilynn Eccles, Sept. 23, 1943; 1 dau., Alison. BA, Coll. Wooster, 1943. With Cleve. Press, 1946-82, staff sports dept., 1950—, covered profl. football, 1953-58, exec. sports editor, 1957-58, sports editor, 1958-64, sports columnist, 1964-67, sports columnist, sports editor, 1967-79, gen. columnist, asst. to editor, 1979-81, assoc. editor, 1981-82; sports editor Lake County News-Herald, 1982-89. Sports columnist 4 Ingersoll newspapers, 1982—2003; nationally syndicated columnist Wiser Side of 60 Universal Press Syndicate, 1982-86. Author: Fun and Games, 2001, And The Wiser Side of 60, 2002. Served from ensign to lt. (j.g.) USNR, 1943-46. Recipient Cleve. Newspaper Guild awards, 1958, 61, 81, 82, 83; inducted into Cleve. Journalism Hall of Fame, 1988. Mem. Sigma Delta Chi (Disting. Svc. award 1981). Home: 1140 Hedgecliff Dr Wooster OH 44691-3088 Personal E-mail: raugust106@aol.com.

AUGUSTA, JUDITH WOOD, librarian; b. Apr. 29, 1940; BA, Wellesley Coll., 1962; MLS, So. Conn. State U., 1994. Adminstrv. asst. Joint Ctr. for Urban Studies of Harvard and MIT, Cambridge, Mass., 1966-72; indexer Rsch. Publs. Inc., Woodbridge, Conn., 1980-90; head libr. Derby (Conn.) Neck Libr., 1994—. Sec. Valley Arts Coun., 2001—04. Co-chair Healthy Valley/Valley Coun. for Health and Human Svcs., 2002—; mem. citizen's adv. bd. Shelton, Conn., 2000—. Recipient Healthy Valley Vol. award 1999, Conn. Post Woman of Substance award, 2000. Mem.: Derby Hist. Soc. (bd. dirs.). Office: 307 Hawthorne Ave Derby CT 06418-1122 Office Phone: 203-734-1492. Business E-Mail: jaugusta@biblio.org. E-mail: laughter@ix.netcom.com.

AUGUST-DEWILDE, KATHERINE, banker; b. Bridgeport, Conn., Feb. 13, 1948; d. Edward G. and Benita Ruth (Miller) Burstein; m. David deWilde, Dec. 30, 1984; children: Nicholas Alexander, Lucas Barrymore. AB, Goucher Coll., 1969; MBA, Stanford U., 1975. Cons. McKinsey & Co., San Francisco, 1975-78; dir. fin. Itel Corp., San Francisco, 1978-79; sr. v.p., CFO PMI Group, San Francisco, 1979-85, pres., CFO, 1988-91; CEO, pres. First Republic Thrift & Loan of San Diego, 1988-96; exec. v.p. First Republic Bank, San Francisco, 1987—, sr. v.p., chief fin. officer, 1985-87, COO, 1996—. Mem. policy adv. bd. Ctr. for Real Estate and Urban Econs., U. Calif., Berkeley, 1987—2000; bd. dirs. First Republic Bank, Trainer, Wortham & Co., Inc. Bd. dirs. San Francisco Zool. Soc., 1993-2001, vice-chair, 1995-2000; trustee Carnegie Found., 1999-2004, Town Sch. for Boys, San Francisco, 1999-2004, vice chmn., 2004-; mem. adv. coun. Stanford U. Grad. Sch. Bus., 2003-; trustee Mills Coll., 2004-. Mem. Women's Forum (bd. dirs.), Bankers Club, Belvedere Tennis Club, Villa Taverna. Home: 2650 Green St San Francisco CA 94123-4607 Office: First Republic Bank 111 Pine St San Francisco CA 94111-5602 Office Phone: 415-296-3707. Business E-Mail: kaugust@firstrepublic.com.

AUGUSTINE, HILTON H., JR., computer company executive; Degree in elec. engring., U. Wis. Salesman IBM; founder Global Mgmt. Sys. Inc., 1988—, chmn., CEO Bethesda, Md., 1996—. Office: Global Mgmt Sys Inc GMSI 2201 Wisconsin Ave NW Ste 300 Washington DC 20007-4105 Office Phone: 202-471-4674. Office Fax: 202-625-9016. E-mail: Hilton.Augustine@gmsi.com.

AUGUSTINE, JEROME SAMUEL, merchant banker; b. Racine, Wis., May 7, 1928; s. Lester Samuel and Pearl (Hilker) A.; m. Camilla Sewell, Feb. 7, 1953; children: Theodore Samuel Purnell, Julia Sewell Augustine Marshall, Elizabeth Stroebel Augustine Burgoyne. AB cum laude, Harvard U., MBA, 1952. Cons. Scudder, Stevens & Clark, Boston, 1952-56; founder, treas., dir. Vencap, Inc., Boston, 1956-58; treas., dir. Consumer Products, Inc., Boston, 1956-58; founder, treas., dir. Microsonics, Inc., Hingham, Mass., 1956-58; treas., dir. Capitol Mgmt. Corp., Boston, 1956-58; cons. Kidder, Peabody & Co., Boston, 1958-64; pres. Cosmos Am. Corp., N.Y.C., 1964-66; founder, pres., dir. Cosmos Securities Corp., 1965-70, Cosmos (Bahamian) Ltd., Nassau, 1964-70; mng. dir. J. Samuel Augustine & Co., Ltd., Toronto, Ont., Can., 1966—. 1st v.p. Van Alstyne, Noel & Co., N.Y.C., 1973-74; v.p. Wright Investors' Svc., Bridgeport, 1974-87, sr. v.p., 1987-92; pres. Kredietbank (Belgium) Global Asset Mgmt., Stamford, 1992-94. Trustee Low-Heywood Sch.; trustee The Augustine Family Charitable Trust; chmn. bd. The Hannaford St. Silver Band. Named to Washington Hall of Fame, 1986. Mem. Boston Fin. Rsch. Assocs. (gov. 1960-64, v.p. 1963-64), New Eng. Amateur Rowing Assn. (past pres.), Union Boat Club, Harvard Club, Noroton Yacht Club, Royal Canadian Yacht Club, Ox Ridge Hunt Club, Centaur Polo Club, Royal Ascot Polo Club, East India Club (London). Anglican. Office: 3219 Yonge St Ste 119 Toronto ON Canada M4N 3S1 Fax: 416-250-0811. Office Phone: 416-250-7762. Personal E-mail: augustco@hotmail.com.

AUGUSTINE, KATHY MARIE, controller, state legislator, secondary school educator; b. L.A., May 29, 1956; d. Philip Blase and Katherine Alice (Thompson) A.; 1 child, Dallas; m. Chaz Higgs, Sept. 12, 2003. AB, Occidental Coll., 1977; MPA, Calif. State U., Long Beach, 1983. Flight attendant Continental Airlines, Houston, 1978-83; crew scheduler Delta Airlines, L.A., 1983-88; tchr. Diocese of Reno/Las Vegas, 1990-96; mem. Nev. Assembly, 1992-94, Nev. Senate, 1994-98. Mem. Nev. State Bd. Fin. Mem. Rep. Women's Club, Las Vegas, Nev., 1992—; former coun. of State Govts. West, chair elec. restructuring. Recipient Achievement award Bank of Am., Calif., 1974, Achievement Medallion Am. Legion, 1974, Congressional Internship grantee, Washington, 1975, Disting. Alumni award Calif. State U. Long Beach, 1997, Cmty. Appreciation award Frontier Girl Scout Coun., 1996, Svc. Excellence award Rep. Legis. of Yr., 1998; named Italian Am. of Yr., Augustus Soc. of So. Nev., 2003. Mem.: AAUW, Dept. Transp. Exec. Br. Audit Com. (bd. dirs.), Nat. Assn. State Auditors, Comptrollers and Treasurers, Jr. League of Las Vegas. Republican. Roman Catholic. Home: 9673 Otter Way Reno NV 89521-8513 Office Phone: 775-684-5632. Business E-Mail: kaugust@govmail.state.nv.us.

AUGUSTINE, NORMAN RALPH, not-for-profit developer, educator, government agency administrator; b. Denver, July 27, 1935; s. Ralph Harvey and Freda Irene (Immenga) A.; m. Margareta Engman, Jan. 20, 1962; children: Gregory Eugen, René Irene. BSE magna cum laude, Princeton U., 1957, MSE, 1959; DEng (hon.), Rensselaer Poly. Inst., 1988; DSc (hon.), U. Colo., 1989; ED (hon.), McDaniel Coll., 1990; DEng (hon.), U. Md., 1992; D Aerospace Mgmt. (hon.), Embry Riddle U., 1992; DEng (hon.), Stevens Inst., 1993; HHD (hon.), Wheeling Jesuit Coll., 1994; DSc (hon.), SUNY, 1994; DEng (hon.), U. Ctrl. Fla., 1995, Worcester Polytech., 1996; LHD (hon.), U. Denver, 1996, Georgetown U., 1997, Trinity Coll., 1997; DEng (hon.), U. Ariz., 1997; LLD (hon.), Duke U., 1997; DEng (hon.), Milw. Sch. Engring., 1998; D of Engring. (hon.), Colo. Sch. Mines; DSc (hon.), Arcadia U., 1998. Rsch. asst. Princeton U., 1957-58; program mgr., chief engr. Douglas Aircraft Co., Inc., Santa Monica, Calif., 1958-65; asst. dir. def. rsch. and engring. U.S. Govt., Office of Sec. Def., Washington, 1965-70; v.p. advanced systems Missiles and Space Co., LTV Aerospace Corp., Dallas, 1970-73; asst. sec. army The Pentagon, Washington, 1973-75, undersec. army, 1975-77; v.p. ops. Martin Marietta Aerospace Corp., Bethesda, Md., 1977-82; pres. Martin Marietta Denver Aerospace Co., 1982-85, sr. v.p. info. systems, 1985, from pres., COO to chmn., CEO, 1986-95, also bd. dirs.; pres. Lockheed Martin Corp., Bethesda, 1995-96, pres., CEO, 1996-97; lectr. (rank of prof.) Princeton U., 1997—; former chair. American Red Cross, Washington. Chmn. exec. com. Lockheed Martin Corp., Bethesda, Md., 1998—; bd. dirs. Phillips Petroleum Co., Procter & Gamble Co., New Am. Schs. Devel. Corp.; cons. office Sec. of Def., 1971—, Exec. Office Pres., 1971-73, Dept. Army, Dept. Air Force, Dept. Navy, FAA, Dept. Energy, Dept. Transp.; mem. USAF Sci. Adv. Bd.; chmn. Def. Sci. Bd., Exel Comm., 1997—; mem. NATO Group Experts on Air Def., 1966-70, NASA Rsch. and Tech. Adv. Coun., 1973-75, chmn. Space Sys. and Tech. Adv. Bd., 1985-89; mem. Chief of Naval Ops. Exec. Bd., 1989-92; chmn. def. policy adv. com. on trade, 1988-91, 93—; lectr. Princeton U., 1997—. Author: Augustine's Laws; co-author: The Defense Revolution, 1990, Augustine's Travels, 1997; mem. adv. bd. Jour. Def. Rsch., 1970—; assoc. editor Def. Systems Mgmt. Rev., 1977-82; mem. editorial bd. Astronautics and Aerospace. Trustee Johns Hopkins U., Princeton U., MIT; mem. bd. govs. Colonial Williamsburg, 1996—; chmn. White House/NASA Adv. Com. on Future of U.S. Space Program, 1991, Nat. Security Telecomm. Adv. Com., U.S. Antarctic Program Rev. Com., 1996-97; nat. program evaluation com., coun. v.p. Boy Scouts Am., pres., 1993—; chmn. ARC; mem. Pres.'s Com. of Advisors on Sci. and Tech. Recipient Meritorious Svc. medal Dept. Def., 1979, 5 Disting. Civilian Svc. medals Dept. Def., Nat. Engring. award Am. Assn. Engring. Socs., 1991, Am. Acad. Achievement Golden Plate award, 1995, James Madison medal Princeton U., 1995, Blumenthal award Johns Hopkins U. Sch. Engring., 1996, Gold Eagle award Soc. Am. Mil. Engrs. Acad. of Fellows, 1996, Ralph Coates Roe medal ASME, 1996, M. Eugene Merchant Mfg. medal, 1997, Nat. Medal of Technology, 1997; named Personality of Yr., Flight Internat. Aerospace, 1996. Fellow IEEE (Founders' award 1996), AIAA (hon., bd. dirs. 1978-85, pres. 1983-84, Goddard medal 1988), Am. Astron. Soc., Am. Helicopter Soc. (dir. 1974-75), Royal Aero. Soc.; mem. NAE (chmn. 1994—, Arthur M. Bueche award 1991), Am. Acad. Arts and Scis., Internat. Acad. Astronautics, Assn. U.S. Army (pres. 1980-84, chmn. 1990—, George C. Marshall medal), Nat. Security Indsl. Assn. (Forrestal medal 1988), Indsl. Coll. Armed Forces (Eisenhower award 1990), Armed Forces Comm. and Electronics Assn. (Sarnoff medal 1990), Nat. Space Club (Goddard Trophy 1991), Rotary (Nat. Space Trophy 1992), Planetary Soc. (bd. dirs.), Phi Beta Kappa, Sigma Xi, Tau Beta Pi. Presbyterian. Office: Lockheed Martin Corp 6801 Rockledge Dr Bethesda MD 20817-1877

AUGUSTSSON, PETER, former automotive executive; b. Göteborg, Sweden, Mar. 2, 1955; MME, Chalmers U. Tech. Sr. v.p. Volvo Car Corp., 1993—94; exec. v.p. SKF Europe, 1995, Saab Automobile AB, Trollhattan, Sweden, 1998—2000, CEO, 2000—05, chmn., 2002—05; v.p. GM Europe, 2000—05.

AUGUSTYN, FREDERICK JOHN, JR., librarian; b. Stamford, Conn., Aug. 4, 1951; s. Fred John and Helen Josephine (Bienkowski) A. BA, Boston U., 1973; student, U. Wis., 1973-77; MA, MLS, U. Md., 1983, PhD, 1996. Tchg./rsch. asst. dept. history U. Md., College Park, 1979-83; libr. Libr. of Congress, Washington, 1984—. Congl. Constituent tour guide, 1992—. Book reviewer Libr. of Congress, Choice, Libr. Jour. Mem. ALA, Am. Hist. Assn., Am. Assn. State and Local History, Orgn. Am. Historians, Popular Culture Assn., Am. Econ. Assn., Phi Alpha Theta, Beta Phi Mu. Avocations: political campaign collectibles, sport history, popular culture, linguistics. Home: 7800 Hanover Pky # 301 Greenbelt MD 20770-2620 Office Phone: 202-707-3273. Business E-Mail: faug@loc.gov.

AUGUSTYNSKI, ADAM J., lawyer; b. Chgo., June 16, 1965; s. Marian Marcin and Genowefa (Jedrzejek) A.; m. Michele Honora Thorne, Sept. 28, 1991; 1 child, Alexander Thorne. AB with honors, Harvard U., 1986; JD, Northwestern U., 1990. Bar: Ill. 1990. Asst. legis. office U.S. Senator Alan Dixon, Washington, 1984; asst. office of chief of staff U.S. Senator Paul Simon, Washington, 1985; spl. asst. to pres. Polish Nat. Alliance, Chgo., 1989-94; pvt. practice Chgo., 1991—. Democrat. Roman Catholic. Avocations: sports, international politics. Office: 5850 W Bryn Mawr Ave Chicago IL 60646-6226 Home: 1215 Cleveland St Wilmette IL 60091-1324 Office Phone: 773-775-0044.

AUH, YANG JOHN, librarian, educational administrator; b. Chulla Namdo, Korea, Mar. 18, 1934; came to U.S., 1962, naturalized, 1971; s. Sam Hyuck and So Yae (Suh) A.; m. Karen Kyung-ja Kim, Mar. 11, 1969; 1 child, Alice Kim. BA, Chung-ang U., 1957; MA in LS, Western Mich. U., 1964; Cert. in Libr. Adminstrn. Devel., U. Md., 1973; Cert. in Advanced Librarianship, Columbia U., 1975; Cert. in Mgmt., Clarkson U., 1978; MBA, St. John's U., 1979; postgrad., NYU, 1996, Oxford (Eng.) U., 1997. Asst. libr. Korean Nat. Libr., Seoul, 1957; tech. svcs. libr. Korean Mil. Acad. Libr., Seoul, 1958-61; asst. libr. Branch County Libr., Coldwater, Mich., 1964; head union catalog L.I. U. Librs., Greenvale, N.Y., 1965-68; head catalog dept., tech. svcs. coord. Wagner Coll. Libr., S.I., N.Y., 1968-71, libr. dir., 1972-84, dir. Libr. and Learning Resources Ctr., 1984-2000; dir. Internat. Exch. program Wagner Coll., S.I., N.Y., 2000—; vis. prof. Chung-Ang U., Seoul, 2000—; pres. Highland Realty Mgmt., 1984—; dean internat. study & program Daebul U., Mokpo, Republic of Korea, 2001—. Evaluator, Commn. Higher Edn., Middle States Assn. Colls. and Schs., 1984; trustee Am. Friends of Chung-ang U., 1979—, vis. prof., 2000—; dean internat. study and program Daebul U., Mokpo, Korea, 2001—; life dep. gov., bd. govs. Am. Biographical Inst., Inc., Raleigh, N.C., 1998—; adv. coun. Internat. Biographical Ctr., Cambridge, Eng., 1999—. Fellow, HEW, 1973, 1978. Mem. ALA, N.Y. State Libr. Assn., Korean Libr. Assn., N.Y. Librs. Club, Omicron Delta Kappa (chpt. admintrv. mem. 1995). Office: Wagner Coll Horrmann Libr One Campus Rd Staten Island NY 10301-4428

AUKOFER, FRANK ALEXANDER, journalist; b. Milw., Apr. 6, 1935; s. Herbert Anselm and Wanda Mary (Kaminski) A.; m. D. Sharlene Talatzko, Aug. 6, 1960; children: Juliann Navarrete, Matthew P., Becky Hawryluk, Joseph J. BA in Journalism, Marquette U., 1960; Fellowship Cert., Northwestern U., 1967. With The Milw. Jour. Sentinel (merger The Milw. Jour., Sentinel), 1960-2000; with Washington Bur. The Milw. Jour. Sentinel, 1970-2000, bur. chief; ret., 2000. Writer syndicated column on automobiles DriveWays, 1985—; automobile columnist Artists & Writers Syndicate, Scripps Howard News Svc. With USAF Res., 1952-60. Recipient Byline award for lifetime achievement in journalism Marquette U., 1992, Profl. Merit award Marquette U., awards from Wis. Press. Assn., Milw. Press Club, Soc. Profl. Journalists; Vis. Profl. Freedom Forum First Amendment scholar Vanderbilt U., 1994-95. Mem. Nat. Press Club (pres. 1978, bd. dirs. bldg. corp., Corr. award), Nat. Press Found. (pres., chmn. bd. 1980-85, bd. dirs.), Soc. Profl. Journalists, Standing Com. Corr. U.S. Congress (sec. 1976), Washington Automotive Press Assn. (pres. 1987-88), Gridiron Club Washington. Roman Catholic. Home: 6325 Beachway Dr Falls Church VA 22044

AULBACH, GEORGE LOUIS, retired real estate company executive; b. York, Pa., July 9, 1925; s. George A. and Mary N. (Goulden) Aulbach; m. Gertrude Frisby, June 24, 1949 (dec. Apr. 2004); children: Jeanne, Cynthia, Patricia, Kathleen, Barbara; m. Florence Hipschman, July 9, 2005. BSCE, Villanova U., 1945. Registered profl. engr., Pa., Ga. Field engr., estimator, chief engr., project mgr., exec. v.p R.S. Noonan, Inc., York, Pa., 1946-63; pres., CEO R.S. Noonan, Inc. & Noonan Engring. Corp., York, Pa., 1963-72; pres. systems bldg. divsn. McCrory-Sumwalt, Columbia, SC, 1972-76; pres., CEO Laing Properties, Inc., Atlanta, 1976-90; ret., 1990. Adv. bd. dirs. Bank South, Atlanta; vice-chmn., dir. Cath. Continuing Care Retirement Cmtys., Inc.; adv. bd. Ga. Tech. Rsch. Inst.; dir., treas. York, Pa. Meml. Osteo. Hosp., 1966—72; pres. York ABC Corp., 1966—72. Bd. dirs. Northside Hosp. Found., Cath. Housing Initiative; trustee So. Tech. Found.; cons. non-profit corp. developing affordable housing; chmn. sch. implementation com. Cath. Archdiocese of Atlanta, chmn. fin. com.; vice chmn. Cath. Continuum Care Com. Lt. (j.g.) USN, 1943—46. Decorated Knight Comdr. St. Gregory Vatican. Roman Catholic. Business E-Mail: imdutchman@citcom.net.

AULD, FRANK, psychologist, educator; b. Denver, Aug. 9, 1923; s. Benjamin Franklin and Marion Leland (Evans) A.; m. Elinor James, June 29, 1946 (dec. June 1990); children: Mary, Robert, Margaret; m. Elinor Leah Levine, Dec. 8, 1996 (dec. Dec. 2004). AB, Drew U., 1946; MA, Yale U., 1948, PhD, 1950. Cert. psychologist, Mich., Ont. Instr. psychology Yale U., New Haven, 1950-52, asst. prof., 1952-59; asso. prof. Wayne State U., Detroit, 1959-61, prof., 1961-67, dir. clin. psychology tng. program, 1960-66; prof. U. Detroit, 1967-70, dir. psychol. clinic, 1967-69; prof. U. Windsor, Canada, 1970—91, prof. emeritus, 1992—. Cons. in field. Author: Steps in Psychotherapy, 1953, Scoring Human Motives, 1959, Resolution of Inner Conflict, 1991, 2d edit., 2005; contbr. articles to profl. jours. Chmn. Dearborn (Mich.) Community Council, 1962; mem. adv. com. on coll. work Episcopal Diocese Mich., 1962-71. Recipient Alumni Achievement award Drew U., 1965 Fellow Am. Psychol. Assn. (evaluation com. 1961-66); mem. Can. Assn. U. Tchrs., Can., Mich. psychol. assns., Ont. Psychol. Assn. (edn. and tng. bd. 1976-91, Lifetime Achievement award 1998), Conn. State Psychol. Soc. (pres. 1958), Soc. Psychotherapy Research, Phi Beta Kappa, Sigma Xi. Office: U Windsor Dept Psychology Windsor ON Canada N9B 3P4 E-mail: frankauld@aya.yale.edu.

AULD, ROBERT HENRY, JR., biomedical engineer, educator, consultant, writer; b. Akron, Ohio, Sept. 19, 1942; s. Robert Henry Sr. and Elsie Mae (Rollans) A.; children: Sheila Kay, Jason Craig; stepson: Christopher William Weiss. BSBA, Biomed. Engr., U. San Francisco, 1978. Registered profl. engr., Calif.; cert. clin. engr. Reg. svc. mgr. scientific products div. AHSC, Sunnyvale, Calif., 1963-68; founder, gen. mgr. Lab. Instrument Svc., Campbell, Calif., 1968-77; nat. mgr. Biomed. Svcs. Group Pilot Project Honeywell, Inc., Denver, 1977-79; internship Stanford U. Med. Ctr., 1976, UCSF, 1978; profl. engr. Robert Auld Enterprises, San Jose, Calif., 1979-86; dir. clin. engring. St. Louis Reg. Med. Ctr., 1987-89; engring. mgr. Robert Auld Engring.-West, Imperial, Mo., 1989—, biomedical engr. cons. Santee, Calif., 1989—; nat. svc. mgr. R.C. Network, Cleveland, OH, 1990-99; expert examiner State of Calif. Bd. Registration for Profl. Engrs., Sacramento, 1995-99. Seminar dir. ASMT, Phoenix AZ., 1968-79; instrument workshop seminar coordinator, Stanford U. Med. Ctr., 1980-84; engring. advisor St. Louis Reg. Career Access Ctr., 1987-89, U. Mo., Rolla and St. Louis. Author: The Clone Factory (A True Story About Police), 1992; contbr. articles to profl. jours. Apptd. hazardous waste com. State of Mo., 1988—90; del. at large Rep. Legion of Merit, Imperial, Mo., 1990—93; registrar of voters, pecinct inspector San Diego County, 2004. Recipient Govs. Golden Spike award, Calif., 1986. Mem. IEEE, N.Y. Acad. Scis., Am. Soc. Hosp. Engrs., NSPE, Mo. Soc. Profl. Engrs. (chmn. 1988-89, chmn. minority Math Counts pilot project 1987-89), Order Demolay (life). Republican. Achievements include development of device for equilibrating gases in a liquid or blood for measurement of gases in blood; patent pending for dual halogen colormetric light source; Innovator "Single Source Service", "Parts Banks" for Clinical Equipment for Health Care Facilities. Office: Robert Auld Engring West 943 Tenth Ave Ste 228 San Diego CA 92101 Mailing: PO Box 40541 San Diego CA 92164 E-mail: redwood2c2@aol.com.

AULETTA, KEN, columnist; b. Bklyn., 1942; married; 1 child. BA in History, SUNY, Oswego, 1963; MA in Polit. Sci., Syracuse U., 1965; LittD (hon.), SUNY, 1990. Exec. editor Manhattan Tribune; first exec. dir. NYC Off Track Betting Corp.; staff writer and weekly columnist Village Voice; contbg. editor NY Mag.; chief polit. corr. NY Post, 1974; polit. columnist Daily News, NYC, 1977—93; media critic, columnist New Yorker mag., NYC, 1993—. Nat. judge Livingston Awards; trustee, mem. exec. com., chmn. of nominating com. Pub. Theatre/NY Shakespeare Festival; mem. Columbia Journalism Sch. Task Force; juror Pulitzer Prize; trustee Nightingale-Bamford Sch. Author: Three Blind Mice: How the TV Networks Lost Their Way, Greed and Glory on Wall Street, The Highwaymen: Warriors of the Information Superhighway, others, The Streets Were Paved With Gold, Hard Feelings, The Underclass, The Art of Corporate Success, World War 3.0; Microsoft and Its Enemies, Random House, Backstory: Inside the Business of News, Penguin Press, 2003; guest editor: The Best Business Stories of the Year 2002, Random House. Named a Literary Lion, NY Pub. Libr.; recipient Nat. Mag. award, 2001, America's Premier Media Critic, Columbia Journalism Review. Office: The New Yorker 4 Times Sq New York NY 10036-6561

AULETTA, ROBERT ANTHONY, playwright, educator; b. NYC, Mar. 5, 1940; s. Anthony Andrew Auletta and Margaret Stark; m. Carol Carey, Mar. 23, 1964 (div. July 1979); children: Colleen, Deirdre; m. Jeni Ann Breen, Sept. 13, 1985. BA in English Lit., Queens Coll., N.Y.C., 1958—64; MFA in Playwriting, Yale U., 1966—69. Asst. prof., dept. theatre U. Ill., Champaign, 1969—74; playwriting instr. Yale U., New Haven, 1974—77, 1993—95, Harvard U., Cambridge, Mass., 1985—97; adj. prof. Sch. of Visual Arts, NYC, 1975—. Founder, dir. Black Reality Theater, New Haven, 1968—69; dir., plays Krannert Ctr. for the Performing Arts, Champaign, Ill., 1969—74. Author: (plays) Walk the Dog, Willie, 1983, Ajax, 1986, The Persians, 1993. Recipient Obie Award, The Village Voice, 1982, Hollywood Drama League Award, L.A. Critics, 1986. Democrat. Roman Catholic. Avocations: gardening, painting. Home: 484 W 43rd St Apt 26C New York NY 10036 Office: Sch Visual Arts 209 E 23rd St New York NY 10010 Office Phone: 212-592-2624. Personal E-mail: rauletta@sbcglobal.net.

AULL, ELIZABETH BERRYMAN, real estate development executive; b. Independence, Mo., 1951; d. Homer Hayter and Mary Elizabeth (Wulfert) A. AA, Christian Coll., 1971; BS, U. Mo., 1973; master gardener, U. Mo. ext., Columbia, 1996; grad., Econ. Devel. Inst., 1992. With Mo. Senate Staff and

Dept. Revenue, Jefferson City, 1973-74; administrv. asst. B. State Devel. Agy., St. Louis, 1974-76, Bingham Sketches, Inc., St. Louis, 1976; rate/routing analyst Mo. Pacific R.R., St. Louis, 1976-78; sr. property mgmt. specialist Burlington No. Inc., St. Louis, Springfield, Mo., 1978-87; dir., prop. mgmt. Glacier Park Co. subs. Burlington No., Inc., 1987-88; indsl. devel. mgr. Burlington No. R.R., Omaha, 1989-91, with Ft. Worth, 1991-95; indsl. and market devel. exec. Bd. dirs. Indpendence Ctr., St. Louis, 1982-83, Mental Health Assn. Greater St. Louis, 1982-83, Mental Health Assn. of Ozarks, Springfield, 1983-87; mem. Jr. League St. Louis, 1980-83, Jr. League Springfield, 1984-88, Jr. League, Omaha, 1989-92, Jr. League Ft. Worth, 1992—; chmn. bldg. subcom. Ozark Food Harvest Springfield Coun. of Chs., 1987-88; pres. Greater St. Louis Area Christian (Columbia) Coll. Alumni Assn., 1981-83; greeting card chmn. UNICEF Com. S.W. Mo., 1997. Named one of Outstanding Young Women Am., 1978, 80, 81. Mem. DAR, Dau. Am. Colonists, Colonial Dames 17th Century, Celtic Soc., German, Austrian and Swiss Soc., Friends of the Springfield Art Mus. Republican. Avocations: travel, art, herb gardening, genealogy. Home: 2391 E Wayland St Springfield MO 65804-3332

AULL, JAMES STROUD, retired bishop; b. Winnsboro, S.C., Mar. 3, 1931; s. Luther Bachman and Ruth (Bull) A.; m. Virginia Kloeppel, Aug. 9, 1958; children: Diane, James Jr. (dec.), Virginia Ruth. AB magna cum laude, Newberry Coll., 1953; MDiv cum laude, Luth. Theol. So. Sem., Columbia, S.C., 1960; M in Systematic Theology, Luth. Sch. Theology, Chgo., 1970; PhD, Duke U., 1971; DD (hon.), Newberry Coll., 1988. Ordained to ministry United Luth. Ch. in Am., 1961. Pastor St. Timothy Luth. Ch., Camden, S.C., 1961-62; instr., staff mem. Luth. Theol. So. Sem., Columbia, S.C., 1962-79; sec. S.C. Synod, Luth. Ch. in Am., Columbia, 1979-87, bishop, 1988-96; ret., 1996. Author: Obey My Voice: a Form Critical Study of Selected Prose in the Book of Jeremiah", 1971. Trustee Newberry Coll., 1972-96, sec., 1977-82; trustee Luth. Home, White Rock, S.C., 1988-96, Lutheridge/Lutherock Ministries, Inc., 1988-96; bd. dirs. divsn. for edn. Evang. Luth. Ch. Am., Chgo., 1988-91, mem. ch. coun., 1991-96, trustee, mem. bd. pensions, 1997-2003; mem. adv. bd. Lowman Home, 2003-2004. Mem. Soc. Bibl. Lit., Rotary (bd. dirs. 1987-90, pres. 1996-97). Lutheran. Home: PO Box 608 White Rock SC 29177-0608 E-mail: jimaull3@aol.com.

AULL, SUSAN, physician; b. N.Y.C. d. Eugene and Ines Aull. BA, Vassar Coll., 1981; MD, N.Y. Med. Coll., 1986. Diplomate Am. Acad. Phys. Medicine and Rehab., Am. Acad. Pain Mgmt. Intern L.I. Coll. Hosp., Bklyn., 1986-87; phys. medicine and rehab. PGY II, III Westchester County Med. Ctr., Valhalla, N.Y., 1987-89; phys. medicine and rehab. PGY IV Lincoln Hosp., Bronx, N.Y., 1989-90, Ctrl. Fla. Physicians Rehab., Orlando, 1990-91; med. dir. dept. phys. medicine and rehab. Halifax Med. Ctr., Daytona Beach, Fla., 1992-99; med. dir. 21st Century Rehab. and Wound Mgmt. Ctr., Maitland, Fla., 1992; staff dept. internal medicine Winter Park (Fla.) Meml. Hosp., 1991-96; pvt. practice WWPM&R, Winter Park and Sarasota, 1991—2002; multi-specialty group practice, dir. phys. medicine and rehab. Ctrl. Fla. Physicians Rehab., Orlando, 1990-91; physician Advanced Sports Medicine Ctr., 2002—04, S. Aull MD PA, 2002—. Electrodiagnostic cons. SEA Med. Svcs., P.A., Goldenrod, Fla., 1990-96; adj. clin. prof. U. Ctrl. Fla., Orlando, 1991-96. Author: (with others) Strength Conditioning for Preventive Medicine, 1992, ISC Control Points - New Generation of Pressure Points, 1993. Recipient Leadership award Defensive Tactics Newsletter, 1993; grantee PPCT Mgmt. Systems, Inc., 1992. Fellow Am. Acad. Phys. Medicine and Rehab.; mem. AMA, Am. Acad. Pain Mgmt., Am. Coll. Sports Medicine. Office: 1921 Waldemere St Ste 609 Sarasota FL 34239 Office Phone: 941-957-6500.

AULT, ETHYL LORITA, special education educator, consultant; b. Bklyn., May 30, 1939; d. Albert Nichols Fadden and Marion Cecil (Corrigan) Snow; (div.); children: Debra Marie Ault Butenko, Milinda Lei Jones, Timothy Scott. BS, Ga. State U., MEd, 1976, cert. in spl. edn. 6th yr., 1984. Tchr. spl. edn. Butts County Sch. System, Jackson, Ga., 1972-73, Rockdale County Sch. System, Conyers, Ga., 1973-75, lead tchr., 1975-77; cons. spl. edn. Newton County Sch. System, Covington, Ga., 1977-79; curriculum specialist spl. edn. La Grange (Ga.) Sch. System, 1979-83, dir. spl. edn., 1983-94, dir. accredited studies curriculum, 1994—, dir. student svcs., 1995—; collaboration process trainer State of Ga., 1990—, dir. student svcs./spl. program, 1996-2000; fine arts cons. Troup County Schs., 2001—. Instr. La Grange Coll., 1984-97, assoc. prof., 1997—; mem. Tchr. Competency Testing Commn., Atlanta, 1988—, Task Force Documentation and Decision Making, Atlanta, 1988—. Contbg. editor: (manual) Mainstream Modification Handbook, 1989. Chairperson Jud. Adv. Panel, LaGrange, 1988; bd. dirs. Crawford Tng. Ctr. Adv. Panel, La Grange, 1985—; pres. West Ga. Youth Coun. Bd., La Grange, 1980—; mem. State Adv. Panel for Spl. Edn.; bd. dirs. Troup County Hist. Soc., 1999—; mem. State of Ga. Task Force on Alt. Edn., 1998—. Mem. Coun. Exceptional Children, Ga. Assn. Edn. Leaders, Ga. Assn. Curriculum and Instrn. Supervision, Ga. Coun. Adminstrs. Spl. Edn. (v.p. 1988—, pres.-elect 1989, pres. 1992—, Gifted State Task Force 1994—), La Grange Women's Club (v.p. 1989—), Profl. Assn. Ga. Spl. Educators (Adminstr. of Yr. 1993), Ga. Supporters of the Gifted, Nat. Assn. for Gifted Edn., Ga. Assn. for Gifted Students (pres.-elect 2000-2001), Kiwanis (pres.-elect LaGrange chpt. 1999-2000, pres. 2000-01, gov. elect 2004-2005, lt. gov. divsn. 12 Ga. 2005—), LaGrange Women's Club (pres. 2005—), Phi Delta Kappa (pres. 2000-2001), Lafayette Soc. Arts (bd. dirs., v.p., pres. 2005—). Democrat. Episcopalian. Avocations: swimming, fishing, walking, gardening. Home: 441 Gordon Cir Lagrange GA 30240-2621 Office: LaGrange Coll Board St Lagrange GA 30240

AULT, JAMES MASE, bishop; b. Sayre, Pa., Aug. 24, 1918; s. Tracey Everett and Bessie (Mase) A.; m. Dorothy Mae Barnhart, Dec. 22, 1943; children: James Mase, Kathryn Louise, Elizabeth Ann, Christopher John (dec.). AB magna cum laude, Colgate U., 1949; BD magna cum laude, Union Theol. Sem., N.Y.C., 1952, STM, 1964; postgrad., St. Andrews U., Scotland, 1966; DD, Am. U., Washington, 1968; LLD (hon.), Albright Coll., 1973, Ohio Wesleyan U., 1973; DHL (hon.), Drew U., 1986; LHD (hon.), Allegheny Coll., 1987. Ordained to ministry Meth. Ch. as deacon, 1951, as elder, 1952. Tool engr. Ingersoll-Rand Co., 1936-42; pastor Meth. Ch., Preston, N.Y., 1946-49, Carlton Hill Meth. Ch., East Rutherford, N.J., 1951-53, Meth. Ch., Leonia, N.J., 1953-58, First Meth. Ch., Pittsfield, Mass., 1958-61; dean students, asso. prof. practical theology Union Theol. Sem., N.Y.C., 1961-64, prof. practical theology, dir. field edn., 1964-68; dean, prof. pastoral theology Theol. Sch., Drew U., Madison, N.J., 1968-72; bishop Phila. area United Meth. Ch., 1972-80, bishop Pitts. area, 1980-88, bishop Wyo. conf., 1990; prof. contemporary ministries Theol. Sch. Drew U., Madison, N.J., 1988-91, interim dean Theol. Sch., 1990-91; sec. council of bishops United Meth. Ch., 1980-84, pres. council bishops, 1986-87. Mem. governing bd. Nat. Coun. Chs. of Christ in U.S.A., 1981-84; mem. central com. World Coun. Chs., 1981-91; mem. exec. com. World Meth. Coun., 1981-88. Author: Responsible Adults for Tomorrow's World, 1962. Mem. sr. exec. ecumenical seminar Hartford Theol. Sem. and the Lilly Endowment, 1989-92; chair U.S. Bossey com. World Coun. Chs., 1994-98. Lt. U.S. Army, 1942-46. Faculty fellow Am. Assn. Theol. Schs., 1965-66. Mem. AAUP, Acad. Polit. and Social Sci., Phi Beta Kappa. Methodist. Home: 1 Amoskegan Dr Brunswick ME 04011-9524 E-mail: jmaorda@gwi.net.

AULT, MARSUE H., music educator; b. Washington, Ind., Apr. 20, 1949; d. Roscoe Earl Bissey and Allegra Moore; m. Jonas T. Ault, Aug. 16, 1970; children: Amanda Lynn, Brandon Nicholas. B in Music Edn., U. Evansville, 1970; MS in Music Edn., Ind. State U., 1980. Music educator North Knox Sch. Corp., Bicknell, Ind., 1972—77, Vincennes (Ind.) Cath. Sch., 1983—84, Linton (Ind.)-Stockton Sch. Corp., 1984—. Organist Meth. Ch., Sandborn, Ind., 1976—. Recipient Tchr. of Yr., Civitan Club, Linton, 1992. Mem.: NEA, Classroom Tchrs. Assn., Ind. State Tchrs. Assn., Ind. Music Educators Assn., Music Educators Nat. Conf. Methodist. Avocations: reading, travel. Home: 15858 N Cemetery Rd Sandborn IN 47578

AUMACK, SHIRLEY JEAN, financial planner, tax preparer; b. Newark, May 17, 1949; d. Herbert O. and Edythe V. (England) Marlatt; m. Kenneth J. Aumack, Oct. 25, 1969; children: Douglas, Steven. BA in Econs., Wilson Coll., 1971. Cert. fin. planner, enrolled agt., retirement counselor; registered investment advisor; registered rep., investment exec., accredited tax advisor Fin. Network. Account exec. N.J. Bell Telephone, Scotch Plains, 1972—76; ptnr., ind. contr. Personal Mgmt. and Planning Inc., Matawan, NJ, 1982—90; pvt. practice fin. planner tax and fin. aspects of divorce Fair Haven, 1990—; mng. supr. Employee Fin. Edn. Divsn. Fin. Network Investment Corp., 1998—. Instr. fin. planning Monmouth County Park Sys., Lincroft, NJ, 1991, Rutgers U., 1993—94, Rumson Cmty. Edn., 1995. Pres. Performing Arts Soc., Rumson Fair-Haven Regional High Sch., 1992-94. Mem.: Fin. Planning Assn., Accreditation Coun. for Accountancy and Taxation (tax advisor), Nat. Assn. Enrolled Agts., Inst. Cert. Fin. Planners, Internat. Assn. for Fin. Planning (seminar spkr. 1990). also: 2 Ethel Rd Bldg 201A Edison NJ 08817-2839 Office: 1 Bethany Rd #1-20 Hazlet NJ 07730-1663 Office Phone: 732-335-8777. E-mail: shirley@sjaumack.com.

AUMANN, R. KARL, state official, lawyer; b. Balt., May 17, 1960; s. Frederick Carl and Marjorie Patterson (Rue) A.; m. Susan Langley Mueller, Sept. 20, 1986. BA, Loyola Coll., Balt., 1982; JD, U. Balt., 1985. Bar: Md. 1986, U.S. Dist. Ct. Md. 1986. Assoc. Power and Mosner PA, Towson, Md., 1986-88, Miles & Stockbridge, Balt., 1988—91; counsel, sr. policy advisor Appalachian Regional Commn., 1991—94; chief adminstr., dist. dir. for Congressman Ehrlich, 1994—2003; Sec. of State, State of Md., Annapolis, 2003—. Mem. SAR. Roman Catholic. Office: State House Office Sec State Annapolis MD 21401

AUNE, ADONICA SCHULTZ, education educator, consultant; d. Lloyd James Schultz and Margaret Estelle Gulbranson; m. Robert Dale Aune, Jan. 1, 2001; children: Shane David Seaver, Jerod Keith Seaver, Travis Adonis Seaver. PhD, U. of N.D., 1994. Instructional Tech. U. of Minn., 2002. Lectr. Little Hoop C.C., Ft. Totten, ND, 1991; English expert Hefei U. of Tech., China, 1994; asst. prof. Christian Invention Computer Coll., Seoul, 1996; English tchg. cons. China Airlines, Taipei, Taiwan, 1997—99; adj. prof. U. of Minn., Crookston, 2000—02, U. of N.D., Grand Forks, 2002—. Dir.: (performance) Milk Dreams (Cmty. Theatre, 2003). Recipient Hatton Cmty. Theatre Hall of Fame, 2000. Mem.: Internat. Literacy and Edn. Rsch. Network (assoc.). Achievements include research in Aviation Ambiguity. Avocations: golf, bicycling, travel, swimming, writing. Home: 815 40th Ave S #K143 Grand Forks ND 58201 Office: Box 7169 U of ND Grand Forks ND 58201 Personal E-mail: adonica.schultz@und.nodak.edu.

AUNE, DEBRA BJURQUIST, lawyer; b. Rochester, Minn., June 13, 1956; d. Alton Herbert and Violet Lucille (Dutcher) Bjurquist; m. Gary ReMine, June 6, 1981 (div. June 1993); children: Jessica Bjurquist ReMine, Melissa Bjurquist ReMine; m. David Aune, Jan. 1, 1995. BA, Augsburg Coll., 1978; JD, Hamline U., 1981. Bar: Minn. 1981. Assoc. Hvistendahl & Moersch, Northfield, Minn., 1981-82; adjuster Federated Ins. Cos., Owatonna, 1982-84; advanced life markets advisor Federated Life Ins. Co., Owatonna, 1984-87; mktg. svcs. advisor Federated Ins. Cos., Owatonna, 1987-89, 2d v.p., corp. legal counsel, 1989-92, v.p. gen. counsel, 1992-95, 1st v.p., gen. counsel, 1996-99; ind. cons., 1999—. Mem. Hamline Law Rev., 1979-80. Pres. Owatonna Ins. Women, 1983-84; charter commr. City of Owatonna, 1992—. Mem. ABA, Minn. State Bar Assn., 5th Dist. Bar Assn., Steele County Bar Assn. (sec. 1986-87, v.p. 1987-88, pres. 1988-89), Assn. Life Ins. Counsel, Alliance Am. Insurers (legal com. 1989—). Lutheran. Office: Federated Ins Cos 121 E Park Sq Owatonna MN 55060-3046

AUNG, KENDRICK THAN, mechanical engineer, educator; b. Yangon, Myanmar, June 5, 1961; B in Engring., Yangon Inst. Technology, 1983; M in Engring., Asian Inst. Technology, Bangkok, Thailand, 1991; PhD, U. Mich., 1996. Instr. Yangon Inst. Technology, Myanmar, 1984-88; rsch. asst. U. Mich., Ann Arbor, 1993-96; rsch. fellow Ga. Inst. Technology, Atlanta, 1996-98; rsch. asst. prof. U. So. Calif., L.A., 1999—2001; asst. prof. Lamar U., Tex., 2001—. Mem.: ASEE, ASME, AIAA (sr.), Combustion Inst., Am. Assn. Engring. Edn. Home: 2725 Mahan Rd Beaumont TX 77707 Office: Lamar Univ PO Box 10028 Beaumont TX 77710 Office Phone: 409-880-8764. E-mail: aungkt@hal.lamar.edu.

AUNSPAUGH, ALLAN, minister; b. Grandview, Mo., Aug. 20, 1959; s. George E. and Joan F. Aunspaugh; m. Anne Baker Aunspaugh, July 27, 1985; children: Rachel A., Emily K., Alyssa G. BA, Ark. Tech U., 1982; MusM, Southwestern Bapt. Theol. Sem., Tex., 1987. Min. of music and adminstrn. Fianna Hills Bapt. Ch., Fort Smith, Ark., 1991—97; min. of music First Bapt. Ch., Rayville, La., 1999—2003, Second Bapt. Ch., Liberty, Mo., 2003—. Presenter Mo. Choral Dirs. Assn., Columbia, Mo., 2005. Mem. Kiwanis Internat., Rayville, La., 1999—2003; pres. Beard PTA, Fort Smith, Ark., 1995—97. Mem.: Am. Choral Dirs. Assn., Chorister's Guild, Youthcue. Baptist. Home: 1141 Silverleaf Ln Liberty MO 64068 Office: Second Bapt Ch 309 E Franklin Str Liberty MO 64068 Office Phone: 816-781-2824.

AUPING, MICHAEL G., curator; b. Portland, Oreg., Oct. 17, 1949; s. Jack Louis and Jane (Hammel) A.; m. Patricia Contreras, Aug. 22, 1974; children: Alicia Contreras, Jonathan Contreras. AA, Santa Ana Coll., 1969; BA, Calif. State U., Fullerton, 1971; MA, Calif. State U., Long Beach, 1975. Editor #1 Powell Libr. UCLA, 1975-77; assoc. curator Univ. Art Mus., Berkeley, Calif., 1977-80; head of curatorial, curator 20th century art Ringling Mus. Art, Sarasota, Fla., 1980-84; chief curator Albright-Knox Art Gallery, Buffalo, 1984-93, Modern Art Mus. of Ft. Worth, 1993—. Instr. art history Citrus Coll., Azusa, Calif., summer, 1977, San Francisco Art Inst., spring, 1978; adj. lectr. U. Calif., Santa Barbara, fall, 1977, U. Buffalo, 1988—89; guest curator Artist's Space, NY, 1988; panelist mus. aid program N.Y. State Coun. on Arts, 1988—89, Fed. Adv. Com. for Internat. Exhbns., NEA and Rockefeller Found., 1992—; curator Whitney Biennial, 2000; cons. commr. Am. Pavilion 1990 Venice Biennale, Italy; mem. adv. com. Intermus. Conservation Lab., CARE Pub., Art in Pub. Places, Met.-Dade area, 1984—, The Bush Found., St. Paul, 1985; cons. L.A. County Dept. Parks Cultural Arts sect., 1973; grant panelist mus. programs spl. exhbns. NEA, Washington, 1985; panelist, on-site evaluator Artists Orgn., N.Y.C., 1983; visual arts panelist Divsn. Cultural Affairs State of Fla., Tallahassee, 1980, Tallahassee, 81. Author: Francesco Clemente, 1985, Jenny Holzer, 1992, Drawing Rooms: Jonathan Borofsky, Sol LeWitt, Richard Serra, 1994, Arshile Gorky: The Breakthrough Years, 1995, Tatsuo Miyajima: Big Time, 1996, Susan Rothenberg Paintings, 1996, Georg Baselitz: Portraits of Elke, 1997, Agnes Martin/Richard Tuttle, 1998, House of Sculpture, 1999, Natural Deceits, 2000, Philip Guston Retrospective, 2003, Anselm Kiefer: Heaven and Earth, 2005; TV appearances including CBS Sunday Morning, 1988; mng. editor L.A. Inst. Contemporary Art Jour., 1976-77; contbr. articles to profl. jours.; organizer exhbns. Office: Modern Art Mus 3200 Darnell St Fort Worth TX 76107

AURAND, CHARLES HENRY, JR., music educator; b. Battle Creek, Mich., Sept. 6, 1932; s. Charles Henry and Elisabeth Dirk (Hoekstra) A.; m. Donna Mae Erb, June 19, 1954; children: Janice, Cheryl, Sandra, Charles III, William. MusB, Mich. State U., 1954, MusM, 1958; PhD, U. Mich., 1971. Cert. tchr., Mich., Ohio. Asst. prof. music Hiram Coll., Ohio, 1958-60; dean, prof. music Youngstown State U., 1960-73; dean No. Ariz. U., Flagstaff, 1973-88, prof. music, 1988-94, prof. emeritus, 1994—. Chmn. Ariz. Alliance for Arts Edn., 1974-77; solo clarinetist Flagstaff Symphony; solo, chamber music and orch. musician, 1973-86; fine arts cons. Miami U. of Ohio, 1982 Author: Selected Solos, Methods, 1963; solo clarinetist Sonora Winds, 2002—; musician: Foothills Chamber Choir, Soranan Winds. Elder Presbyn. Ch., 1965; chmn. Boy Scouts Am., Coconino dist., 1974-78; bd. dirs. Ariz. Com. Arts for the Handicapped, 1982-88, Flagstaff Symphony Orch., 1973-85, Flagstaff Festival of Arts, 1973-89, Sedona Chamber Mus. Soc., 1989-99, Sedona Med. Ctr., 1998-2002, Civic Orch. Tucson, 2003—; conf. dir. Internat. Clarinet Soc., 1991; pres. Citizens for an Alt. Route, 1995-98; mem. Ariz. Town Hall, 1996—; bd. dirs. Sedona Med. Ctr. Found., 1998-2002; mem. Foothills Chamber Music Ensemble; mem. Ariz. Town Hall, 1996-2002; solo clarinet Sonora Winds, 2002—. 1st lt. USAF,1955-57 Recipient award of merit Boy Scouts Am., 1977; cert. appreciation John F. Kennedy Ctr. Performing Arts, 1985. Mem. Am. Assn. Higher Edn., Ariz. Humanities Assn., Music Educators Nat. Conf., State Adminstrs. of Music Schs. (chmn. 1971-73), Internat. Clarinet Soc./ClariNetwork Internat. (conf. dir. 1991), No. Ariz. U. Retirees Assn. (pres. 1997-98), SAR (pres. No. Ariz. chpt. 2000-02, pres. Ariz. Soc. 2003—, state pres. 2003-04), Kiwanis (pres. 1984-85). Republican. Presbyterian. Avocations: golf, tennis, bridge. Home: 37738 S Hill Side Dr Tucson AZ 85739-2221 Personal E-mail: chaurand@earthlink.net.

AURBACH, HERBERT ALEXANDER, sociology educator; b. Cleve, Aug. 6, 1924; s. Nate and Sara (Munitz) A.; m. Rebecca Rachel Blumenfeld, Nov. 2, 1952 (dec. July 1999); children— Jacquelyn Aurbach Scheidlinger, Seth Jacob. BS, Western Res. U., 1948; PhD, U. Ky., 1960. Asst. rural sociologist Miss. State Coll., 1954-55; asst. prof. sociology and research asso. N.C. State Coll., Raleigh, 1955-57; research dir. Pitts. Commn. Human Relations, 1957-61; rsch. assoc., asst. prof. sociology U. Pitts., 1961-66; assoc. prof. edn. and sociology Pa. State U., 1966-70; prof. sociology Buffalo State Coll., 1970-93, chmn. dept. sociology, 1970-74, prof. emeritus, 1993—. Assoc. dir. Nat. Study Am. Indian Edn., 1968-69 Author: (with Estelle Fuchs) The Status of American Indian Education, 1970; Assoc. editor: Social Problems, 1966-74; Contbr. profl. jours. Bd. dirs. Citizens Commn. Criminal Justice, Buffalo and Erie County, 1972-74, Anti-Defamation League of B'nai B'rith, Buffalo, 1971-75, Coun. of Sr. Citizens Clubs of Buffalo and Erie County, 1997-01; co-chair adult edn. com. Temple Shaarey Zedek, Buffalo, 1995-2004, bd. trustees, 1998-2004, fin. sec., 2002-04; mem. sr. svcs. adv. bd. Town of Amherst, 1997-2000. Decorated Air medal with 4 clusters; recipient N.Y. State/United Univ. Professions Excellence award, 1991; fellow So. Fellowship Fund, 1956-57. Mem. Soc. Study Social Problems (sec. 1965-69, treas. 1966-74, exec. officer 1975-86, v.p. 1987-88, chair bylaws com. 1988—2002, chair youth, aging and life course divsn. 1993-94, chair Lee Founders award com. 1999-2000), Am. Assn. Ret. Persons/VOTE (27th congl. dist. coord. 1993-95), Nat. Coun. Sr. Citizens (Amherst chpt. v.p. 1997-98, pres. 1998-99). Home: 120 Meyer Rd Apt 413 Amherst NY 14226-1013

AURELIAN, LAURE, medical sciences educator; b. Bucharest, Romania, June 17, 1939; came to U.S., 1963, naturalized, 1971; d. George I. and Stella (Ben-Joseph) A.; M.S., Tel-Aviv U., 1962; Ph.D., Johns Hopkins U., 1966; m. I.I. Kessler, Nov. 24, 1970; 1 dau., Amalia D. Asst. prof. dept. lab. animal medicine and microbiology Johns Hopkins U. Sch. Medicine, Balt., 1969-74, assoc. prof. dept. biophysics and biochemistry, 1975-82, assoc. prof. dept. comparative medicine and biophysics, 1974-82, prof. div. biophysics, 1982—; prof. dept. pharmacology U. Md., 1982—, dir. virology/immunology labs., 1984—; mem. NIH study sects. internat. teaching, 1973; mem. sci. adv. com. Internat. Biomed. Inst. UNESCO, 1987—. Recipient Hon. medal Disting. Contribution to Gynecol. Oncology U. Bologna, Italy, award Premio XXIV Casalli 90 ASS, Pro Loco Bronte Edizione Speciale Medicina, Catania, K. Vephvadze Meml. award Georgian Soc. Oncologists; ACS grantee, 1970-74; NIH grantee, 1969—; WHO grantee, 1980—; others; named Disting. Young Scientist, Md. Acad. Sci., 1970. Mem. David Boyes Soc. Gynecol. Oncology, Brit. Coll. Can. (hon.) Am. Soc. Microbiology, AAAS, Am. Assn. Immunologists, Soc. Exptl. Biology and Medicine, Md. Acad. Sci., N.Y. Acad. Sci., Am. Assn. Cancer Research, Reticuloendothelial Soc. Editor Jour. Soviet Oncology, 1980-86, European Jour. Gynecol. Oncology, 1982—, Internat. Jour. Oncology, 1993—, In Vivo, 1994-2004, Clin. and Diagnostic Lab. Immunology, 2000—, Frontiers in Biosci, 1997—, Genetics Vaccine and Therapy, 2003—, Cancer Therapy, 2003—; contbr. articles to profl. jours. Home: 3404 Bancroft Rd Baltimore MD 21215-3105 Office Phone: 410-706-3895. Business E-Mail: laurelia@umaryland.edu.

AURELL, JOHN KARL, lawyer; b. Tulsa, Sept. 26, 1935; s. George E. and Maxine (Reagor) A.; m. Jane Brevard Collins, Oct. 1, 1960; 1 child, Jane B. BA, Washington and Lee U., 1956; LLB, Yale U., 1964. Bar: Fla. 1964, D.C 1971, U.S. Dist. Ct. (no., mid. and so. dists.) Fla., U.S. Ct. Appeals (5th and 11th cirs.), U.S. Supreme Ct. Gen. counsel to Gov. State of Fla., Tallahassee, 1979-80; ptnr. Ausley & McMullen, 1994—2002, sr. counsel, 2002—. Mem. Fed. Jud. Nominating Commn. Fla.; chmn. No. Dist. Fla., 1993—97. Mem. exec. com., v.p. Yale Law Sch. Assn., 1975-80; mem. Orange Bowl Com. 1st lt. U.S. Army, 1956-57. Fellow Am. Bar Found., Internat. Soc. Barristers, Am. Coll. Trial Lawyers; mem. ABA, Fla. Bar Assn. (bd. govs. young lawyers sect. 1966-71), Am. Law Inst., Exch. Club, Yale Club (N.Y.C.), Econ. Club Fla. (chmn. 1997-98), Southwood Golf Club, Havana Country Club Democrat. Home: 1225 Live Oak Plantation Rd Tallahassee FL 32312-2509 Office: Ausley & McMullen PO Box 391 Tallahassee FL 32302-0391 Office Phone: 850-425-5426. Business E-Mail: jaurell@ausley.com.

AURIANA, ANGELO, chef; b. Bergamo, Italy; Former mem. staff Antico Ristorante dell'Angelo, Bergamo, Hotel Exelsior San Marco, Bergamo; former chef Primi, Santa Monica, Calif. Instr. Let's Get Cooking, Sur La Table. Active Am. Cancer Soc., Meals on Wheels, SOS, The James Beard Found. Office: Valentino 3115 Pico Blvd Santa Monica CA 90405

AURIEMMA, GENO, women's college basketball coach; m. Kathy; children: Jenna, Alysa, Michael. BA, West Chester U., 1981. Coach boys' basketball Bishop Kenrick High Sch., 1979-81; asst. women's basketball coach U. Va., 1981-85, St. Joseph's U., Phila., 1984; head coach U. Conn., 1985—. Mem. Kodak All-Am. Selection Com., chair, 1992; voting mem. USA Today/WBCA Topo 25 Poll-In; co-head coach Nat. Sr. All-Stars; coach USA Basketball Select Team, Colorado Springs, Colo.; asst. coach USA World U. Games Women's Basketball Team, 1995; head coach West Team U,S. Olympic Festival, San Antonio, 1993; spkr. Nat. High Sch. Coaches Assn. Convention, Conn. Chair Why-Me of New Eng.; chair (hon.) AHA. Named Women's Basketball Nat. Coach of Yr., 1997, 2000, 2002; Naismith Nat. Coach of the Yr., 1995, 1997, 2000, 2002; Coach of Yr. AP, 1995, 1997, 2000, 2003; recipient Victor award Women's Basketball Coaches Assn., 1995, 1996, 2000; NCAA Division I Champion 2000, 2002, 2003, 2004. Office: U Conn 2095 Hillside Rd Storrs Mansfield CT 06269-9017

AURIEMMO, FRANK JOSEPH, JR., financial holding company executive; b. N.Y.C., Mar. 16, 1942; s. Frank Joseph and Jean (Celano) A.; m. Annette Marie Rounds, Oct. 14, 1967; children: Frank Bertram, Adam Rounds, Lucas James. BBA in Corp. Fin., Iona Coll., 1964; postgrad., NYU, 1967-69. Trust adminstr. Chase Manhattan Bank, NA, N.Y.C., 1965-67; investment analyst Paine, Webber, Jackson & Curtis, N.Y.C., 1967-69; sr. investment analyst Hayden, Stone, Inc., N.Y.C., 1970, Bache & co., N.Y.C., 1970-72, Hornblower & Weeks, Hemphill, Noyes, N.Y.C., 1972-74; with USLIFE Corp., N.Y.C., 1974-97, 2d v.p., analyst, 1979-83, 2d v.p. corp. fin., 1983-84, v.p. fin. ops., 1984, v.p., treas., 1984—, sr. v.p., treas., 1995-97; founder, pres., CEO, Kittiwake Assocs., LLC, Bronxville, N.Y., 1997—. V.p. subs. U.S. Life Ins. Co., All Am. Life Ins. Co., Old Line Life, USLIFE Credit Life, 1984-97; bd. dirs., v.p., treas. New D Corp., Iowa, 1983-97; dir. Midwest Property Mgmt. Co. With U.S. Army and N.Y. Army N.G., 1964-70. Mem. Nat. Assn. Bus. Economists, The Planning Forum, N.Y. Soc. Security Analysts, Assn. Ins. and Fin. Analysts, Fin. Analysts Fedn. Mem. Conservative Party. Avocations: hunting, fishing, target shooting, reading military history. Office: Kittiwake Assocs LLC PO Box 1093 Saratoga Springs NY 12866 Home: 2 Harvest Ln Wilton NY 12831

AURIN, ROBERT JAMES, entrepreneur; b. St. Louis; m. Kathryn L. Engel, 1998. B in Journalism, U. Mo., 1965. Copywriter Leo Burnett Co., Chgo., 1971-72, Young & Rubicam, Inc., Chgo., 1972-73; from copywriter to v.p., creative dir. Foote, Cone & Belding, Inc., Chgo., 1973-79; exec. v.p., dir. creative services Grey-North Inc., Chgo., 1979-82; pres. Robert Aurin Assocs., Chgo., 1982—; owner ROMAR Investments Co., Chgo., 1984-99. Exec. creative dir. DraftWorldwide, Inc., 1996-99. Served to lt. USN, 1965-70, Vietnam. Office Phone: 773-549-3434.

AURNER, ROBERT RAY, II, retail development executive; b. Madison, Wis., Mar. 24, 1927; s. Robert Ray and Kathryn (Dayton) A.; m. Phyllis Barrett, 1951 (div. 1966); children: Sheryl, Roxanne, Kathryn, Suzanne, Robert III; m. Deborah Marion Lucas, Jan. 31, 1976 (div. 1999); children: William Lucas, Christopher Ray. AA, Monterey Peninsula Coll., 1949; BA, Calif. State U. Fresno and Occidental Coll. Eagle Rock, 1950; postgrad., U. Calif., Berkeley, Duquesne U., Pitts. Lic. in real estate, Calif., Pa., N.Y.; registered investment advisor. Announcer Radio Sta. WSUI, Iowa City, 1946-48; featured celebrity Cowboy Bob, William Randolph Hearst Radio Sta. WISN-CBS, Milw., 1950-51; sr. sales supr. Shell Oil Co., San Francisco, 1952-60; dir. devel. ctrl. Calif. coast svc. sta. Gulf Oil Corp., 1960-67; ea. divsn. mgr. ops. Sunray DX Oil Co. (merger Sunoco), Tulsa, 1967-72; mgr. site devel. Milex Auto Diagnostic Tune-Up and Brakes, Inc., Plymouth Meeting, Pa., 1972-74; mgr. real estate store devel. Pitts. divsn. Atlantic & Pacific Tea Co. Supermarkets, 1974-77; real estate adminstr. store devel. N.E. U.S. region Steak and Ale - Bennigan's Restaurant divsn. Pillsbury Cos.; real estate mgr. N.Y. and Phila. regions Burger King Corp. restaurant divsn. Pillsbury Cos., Md., Va., NY, NJ, Pa., Del. and Conn., 1977-87; real estate mgr. Ky. Fried Chicken and Pizza Hut divsns. Pepsico, Inc., Metro SMSA, N.Y.C. and No. N.J., 1987-89; nat. dir. real estate, cons. store devel. Nathan's Famous Coney Island Hot Dog Restaurants, Inc., N.Y.C., 1989-90; ret., 1990. Founder, chmn. bd. dirs., pres., CEO Bristlecone Trading and Devel., Inc., Carmel, Calif.; pres., CEO Aurner and Assocs., Consultants, Carmel, 1987—, chmn. bd. dirs., 1990—; tower devel. cons. So. N.J. Nextel Wireless Telecom. Corp., N.J., 1994-95; founder Trader Bob Fashions Inc., Carson City, Nev., 1997; career counselor U.S. Coast Guard Acad. and Pub. Affairs. Officer and flotilla comdr. Flotilla 64 C.G. Aux., Coast Guard Sta., Monterey, Calif., 2000—04; divsn. chmn. Nat. Safe Boating Week USCG Aux., 2001—05; lt. comdr., exec. officer, treas., membership chmn. Monterey Bay Sail and Power Squadron, Unit U.S. Power Squadrons Hdqrs., Calif., 2003—; dist. safety officer San Francisco Bay region Power Squadron, 2004—, squadron comdr., 2005—. With USN, 1944—46, PTO. Named to Hon. Order Ky. Col., Gov. of Ky., Commodore in Okla. Navy Gov. Johnston Murray of Okla. Mem.: Moss Landing Harbor Safe Boating Com., Moss Landing C. of C., Navy League Monterey Peninsula, Carmel Valley (Calif.) C. of C. (bd. dirs., sec. 1999—2003), USS Yellowstone Assn. (USNR), Elkhorn Yacht Club, Rotary Club of Monterey, Buccaneer Club of N.Y. (past pres. N.Y. and Conn.), Monterey Peninsula Yacht Club, Pacheco Club of Monterey, Monterey Elks Club, Sigma Alpha Epsilon. Republican. Episcopalian. Avocation: Civil War history. Office: Aurner & Assocs Inc PO Box 222135 Carmel CA 93922-2135 also: Bristlecone Trading & Devel Carmel CA 93923 Personal E-mail: traderbob2@aol.com.

AUSENBAUM, HELEN EVELYN, social worker, psychologist; b. Chgo., May 16, 1911; d. Herbert Noel and Mayme Eva A. AB, U. Calif., Berkeley, 1938, MSW, 1956. Social worker Alameda Welfare Commn., Oakland, Calif., 1939-42; exec. dir. ARC, Richmond, Calif., 1943-51; tchr. fifth grade Castro Elem. Sch., El Cerrito, Calif., 1951-53; guidance cons. Oakland Pub. Schs., 1953-76; founder, dir. Orinda Counseling Ctr., 1959-95; program dir. Support Svcs., Walnut Creek, Calif., 1978-84. Chair Rossmoor Com. for Common Concern, 1994-96, Mental Health Task Force Contra Costa County, 1978-84; mem. Contra Costa County Adv. Coun. on Aging, 1984-97. Mem. chair nominating com. Rossmoor Dem. Club, 1996; mem. and co-chair Mental Health Profls. of Rossmoor. Mem. NASW, Rotary. Democrat. Presbyterian. Avocations: stamps, freighter travel, reading. Home: 1936 Tice Valley Blvd Walnut Creek CA 94595-2203

AUSICH, WILLIAM IRL, geology educator; b. Kewanee, Ill., Feb. 2, 1952; s. Anton and Sarah Margaret (Tubbs) A.; m. Regina Sharlene Dolk, Aug. 4, 1973; children: Elizabeth, Arlene, Mary. BS, U. Ill., 1974; MA, Ind. U., 1976, PhD, 1978. Vis. asst. prof. Wright State U., Dayton, Ohio, 1978-79, asst. prof., 1979-82, assoc. prof., 1982-84, Ohio State U., Columbus, 1984-90, prof., 1990—. Panelist Nat. Rsch. Coun. Com., Washington, 1989—. Contbr. articles to profl. jours. Advisor Worthington (Ohio) Pub. Schs., 1990—. Recipient Antarctic Svc. medal NSF, 1989; Fulbright fellow, 1992. Mem. AAAS, Geol. Soc. Am., North Cen. Geol. Soc. Am. (vice chmn. 1984), North Cen. Paleontol. Soc. (chmn. 1989-90), Paleontol. Soc. (Schuchert medal 1990), Ohio Acad. Scis., SEPM (co-program chmn. 1988, Outstanding Paper award 1979), Internat. Paleontol. Assn. Office: Ohio State U Dept Geol Scis 125 S Oval Mall 155 S Oval Mall Columbus OH 43210-1308

AUSIELLO, DENNIS ARTHUR, nephrologist; b. Chelsea, Mass., Sept. 12, 1945; s. Hugo Italo and Gilda (Santosuoosso) A.; m. Susan Johnson, May 10, 1969; children: Jeffrey, John. BA, Harvard Coll., 1967; MD, Univ. Pa., 1971. Diplomate Am. Bd. Internal Medicine, Am. Bd. Nephrology. Intern, resident in medicine Mass. Gen. Hosp., Boston, 1971-73; rsch. fellow NIH, Bethesda, Md., 1973-75, Mass. Gen. Hosp., Harvard Medical Sch., Boston, 1976-77; clinical staff medical svcs. Mass. Gen. Hosp., Boston, 1976—; instr., asst., assoc. prof. Harvard Medical Sch., Cambridge, 1976-93, prof. medicine, 1993—96; physician in chief medical svcs. Mass. Gen. Hosp., Boston, 1996—; Jackson prof. clin. medicine Harvard Medical Sch., 1996—. Recipient Dr. O.H. Perry prize Univ. Pa., 1971, NIH Merit award NIH, 1988, 1996. Fellow Molecular Medicine Soc.; mem. Am. Soc. Nephrology, Internat. Soc. Nephrology, Am. Fedn. for Clinical Rsch., Am. Soc. for Clinical Investigation, Assn. Am. Physicians, Assn. Profs. Medicine, Am. Acad. Arts and Sci. (elected mem.), Inst. Medicine. Office: Massachusetts Gen Hosp 55 Fruit St # St740 Boston MA 02114-2696

AUSLANDER, MITCHELL J., lawyer; b. NYC, July 1, 1956; BA, NYU, 1977; JD, Rutgers U., 1980. Bar: NY 1981, US Dist. Ct., So. and Ea. Dists. NY 1981, US Ct. Appeals, 2nd Cir. 1988, US Supreme Ct. Ptnr. litig. dept. Willkie Farr & Gallagher LLP, NYC. Mem.: ABA, Assn. Bar of City NY, NY County Lawyers Assn. Office: Willkie Farr & Gallagher LLP 787 Seventh Ave New York NY 10019 Office Phone: 212-728-8201. Office Fax: 212-728-9201. E-mail: mauslander@willkie.com.

AUSLIN, MICHAEL ROBERT, history professor; b. Aurora, Ill., Mar. 17, 1967; s. Donald and Myra Shulman Auslin; m. Ginko Ueyama, May 6, 1992; 1 child, Benjamin Ichiro. BS, Georgetown U., 1988; MA, Ind. U., 1991; PhD, U. Ill., 2000. Asst. prof. Yale U., New Haven, 2000—. Founding dir., project Japan-U.S. rels. Yale U., New Haven, 2004—. Author: (non-fiction book) Negotiating with Imperialism: The Unequal Treaties and the Culture of Japanese Diplomacy; contbr. television documentary, non-fiction book, encyclopedia. Recipient Dir. award, Yale Ctr. Internat. and Area Studies, 2004; fellow, U. Ill., 1999, Smith Richardson Found., 2003, Internat. and Area Studies fellow, Yale Ctr. Internat. and Area Studies, 2004—, Jr. Faculty Fellow, Whitney Humanities Ctr., 2004—; scholar, Fulbright Fgn. Scholarship Bd., 1997—98; Contemporary Soviet Affairs and Internat. Rels. fellow, Ind. U., 1990, Morse fellow, Yale U., 2003—04. Mem.: Am. Hist. Assn., Coun. Fgn. Rels. (assoc.), Fulbright Assn. (life), Assn. Asian Studies (life). Office: Dept History Yale Univ 320 York St New Haven CT 06520-8324 Office Phone: 203-432-1364. Office Fax: 203-432-7587.

AUSMAN, ROBERT K., surgeon, research and development company executive; b. Milw., Jan. 31, 1933; s. Donald Charles and Mildred (Shafrin) A.; m. Christine McCann, 1992. Ed., Kenyon Coll., 1953; MD, Marquette U., 1957. Damon Runyon cancer fellow U. Minn., 1958-61; dir. Health Research Inc. Roswell Park Meml. Inst., 1961-69; dep. dir. Fla. Regional Med. Assn., 1969-70; v.p. clin. research Baxter Travenol Labs., 1970-82, pres. advanced devel. group, 1982-90; pres. Mildon Corp., 1985—, Citation Pub. Co., 1991—. Clin. prof. surgery Med. Coll. Wis., 1972—. Named Outstanding Young Man in N.Y. Buffalo Evening News, 1966, Citizen of Year, 1967 Mem.: Am. Assn. Cancer Rsch., Am. Soc. Clin. Oncology, Masons. Home: PO Box 3538 Long Grove IL 60047 Office: Willow Valley Rd Long Grove IL 60047

AUST, JOE BRADLEY, surgeon, educator; b. Buffalo, Sept. 8, 1926; s. Joe Bradley and Edith (Derby) A.; m. Constance Ann MacMullin, June 18, 1949; children— Jay Bradley, Bonnie Jean, Barbara Ann, Linda Lee, Mary Louise, Tracey Roberta. MD, U. Buffalo, 1949; MS in Physiology, U. Minn., 1957, PhD in Surgery, 1958. Diplomate: Am. Bd. Surgery, Am. Bd. Thoracic Surgery. Intern U. Minn. Hosps., 1949-50, resident, 1950-58; scholar Am. Cancer Soc. U. Minn., 1957-62, mem. faculty, 1957-66, prof. surgery, 1964-66; prof. surgery, chmn. dept. U. Tex. Med. Sch., San Antonio, 1966-96, prof. dept. surgery, 1996—. Cons. Minn. State Prison, 1958-62, Anoka State Hosp., 1962-65, Brooke Army Med. Hosp., 1967—, Wilford Hall USAF Hosp., 1967—, Audie Murphy Meml. VA Hosp., 1973—; nat. cons. to surgeon gen. USAF, Washington, 1975-78 Served with M.C. USNR, 1950-52. Fellow ACS; mem. Am. Surg. Assn., Western Surg. Assn., So. Surg. Assn., Cen. Surg. Assn., Soc. U. Surgeons, Soc. Head and Neck Surgeons, Am. Assn. Cancer Rsch., Soc. Surg. Oncology, San Antonio Surgical Soc., Am. Assn. Cancer Edn., Halsted Soc., Soc. Clin. Oncology, Transplantation Soc., Sigma Xi, Alpha Omega Alpha, Phi Ch. Achievements include spl. research cancer immunity, regional cancer chemotherapy, shock, homotransplantation. Office: U Tex Med Sch 7703 Floyd Curl Dr San Antonio TX 78284-6200

AUST, STEVEN DOUGLAS, biochemistry, biotechnology and toxicology educator; b. South Bend, Wash., Mar. 11, 1938; s. Emil and Helen Mae (Crawford) A.; m. Nancy Lee Haworth, June 5, 1960 (dec.); children: Teresa, Brian; m. Karen Hurley, July 16, 2004. BS in Agr., Wash. State U., 1960, MS in Nutrition, 1962; PhD in Dairy Sci., U. Ill., 1965. Postdoctoral fellow dept. toxicology Karolinska Inst., Stockholm, 1966; New Zealand facial exzema sr. postdoctoral fellow Ruakura Agrl. Rsch. Ctr., Hamilton, 1975-76; mem. faculty dept. biochemistry Mich. State U., East Lansing, 1967-87, prof., 1977-87, assoc. dir. Ctr. for Environ. Toxicology, 1980-85, dir. Ctr. for the Study of Active Oxygen, 1985-87; dir. biotech. ctr. Utah State U., Logan, 1987-91, prof. chem. biochemistry, 1987—. Dir. basic rsch. and tng. program Super Fund Nat. Inst. Environ. Health Scis., 1988-96; mem. toxicology study sect. NIH, 1979-83; mem. environ. measurements com., mem. sci. adv. bd. EPA, 1980-83; mem. toxicology data bank, mem. peer rev. com. Nat. Libr. Medicine, 1983-85; mem. Mich. Toxic Substance Control Commn., 1979-82, chmn., 1981-82; pres., founder Intech One-Eighty Corp., North Logan Utah, 1993-99, pres. 1999—; mem. adv. panel for metabolic biochemistry program NSF, 1998; mem. EPA/DOE/NSF/ONR Joint Program on Bioremediation, 1998. Contbr. articles to profl. jours. Recipient Nat. Rsch. Svc. award NIH, USPHS, Dupont Sci. and Engring. award, 1988, Alumni Achievement award Wash. State U., 1998, Gov.'s medal sci. and tech., 2002, Univ. Outstanding Grad. Mentor award, 2003; named D. Wynne Thorne Rschr. of Yr., 2003; NRC facial eczema fellow Ruakura Agrl. Rsch. Ctr., Hamilton, 1975. Fellow Acad. Toxicology Scis., Oxygen Soc.; mem. Am. Soc. Biol. Chemists, Am. Soc. Pharmacology and Exptl. Therapeutics, Soc. Toxicology, Am. Chem. Soc. (Kenneth A. Spencer award 2004), Am. Soc. Microbiology Office: Utah State U Ctr Integrated Bioo Sys Logan UT 84322-4705 Office Phone: 435-797-2730. E-mail: sdaust@cc.usu.edu.

AUSTAN, FRANK ACOSTA, clinician, educator; b. Medellin, Colombia, Apr. 29, 1951; arrived in U.S., 1959; s. Guillermo Austan and Lillian Acosta; m. Joan Robin Pliner, July 14, 1974; children: Lara Nicole, Jason Michael. AB, U. Miami, 1980; MSc, Nova Southeastern U., Ft. Lauderdale, Fla., 1983. Lic. Bd. Medicine, Fla., Pa., Nat. Bd. for Respiratory Care, 1978. Dir. respiratory care Berlin West Jersey Hosp., Berlin, NJ, 1986—99, Temple U. Hosp. and Med. Sch., Phila., 1999—. Asst. prof. Miami-Dade C.C., Miami, Fla., 1980—82; clin. instr. Respiratory Therapy Inst., Miami, 1982—83; sr. instr. dept. medicine Hahnemann Med. Coll. and Hosp., Phila., 1983—86; clin. instr. Univ. Medicine and Dentistry, Newark, 1992—. Contbr. articles to profl. jour. Mem.: Am. Coll. Chest. Physicians, Am. Thoracic Soc., Am. Assoc. Respiratory Care (Respironics Fellowships Prize 2000). Democrat. Achievements include Contrb. to med. lit. via Heart & Lung Jour., Am. J clin. hypnosis in the clin. area of ventilator weaning, treatment of asthma and chronic obstructive pulmonary disease, artery puncture pain reduction. Office: Temple Northeastern Hosp 2304 E Allegheny Ave Philadelphia PA 19134 E-mail: austanf@te.temple.edu.

AUSTEN, K(ARL) FRANK, internist, educator; b. Akron, Ohio, Mar. 14, 1928; s. Karl and Bertle (Jehle) Austen; m. Joycelyn Chapman, Apr. 11, 1959; children: Leslie Marie, Karla Ann, Timothy Frank, Jonathan Arthur. AB, Amherst Coll., 1950; MD, Harvard U., 1954. Intern in medicine Mass. Gen. Hosp., 1954—55, asst. resident, 1955—56, sr. resident, 1958—59, chief resident, 1961, asst. in medicine, 1962—63, asst. physician, 1963—66, chief pulmonary unit, 1964—66, also cons. in medicine; practice medicine, specializing in internal medicine, allergy and immunology Boston, 1962—66; USPHS postdoctoral research fellow Nat. Inst. Med. Research, Mill Hill, London, 1959—61; asst. in medicine Harvard Med. Sch., 1961, instr., 1961—62, assoc. in medicine, 1962—64, asst. prof., 1965—66, assoc. prof., 1966—68, prof., 1969—72, Theodore Bevier Bayles prof. medicine, 1972—; physician-in-chief Robert B. Brigham Hosp., Boston, 1966—80; chmn. dept. rheumatology and immunology Brigham and Women's Hosp., Boston, 1980—95, dir. lab. inflammation and allergic disease rsch. sect., 1995—. Mem. fellowship subcom. Arthritis Found., 1968—71, chmn., 1971; mem. coun. Infectious Disease Soc. Am., 1969—71; mem. arthritis tng. grants com. Nat. Inst. Arthritis and Metabolic Diseases, NIH, 1970—73; NHLB adv. coun., 1994—; mem. directing group, task force on immunology and disease Nat. Inst. Allergy and Infectious Diseases, 1972—73; bd. dirs. Arthritis Found., 1972—75, chmn. manpower study com., 1972—73, chmn. rsch. com. Multipurpose Arth. Ctr., 1972—76; chmn. rsch. com. Med. Found., Inc., 1972—76; mem. Am. Bd. Allergy and Immunology, 1973—78, Nat. Commn. on Arthritis and Related Musculoskeletal Diseases, 1975—76, Allergy and Immunology Rsch. com., NIAID, 1975—79, chmn., 1976—79; chmn. nomenclature com. Internat. Union Immunol. Socs., 1983—; mem. adv. com. to the dir. NIH, 1986—90, mem. nat. heart, lung and blood adv. com., 1966—80. Mem. editl. bd.: Arthritis and Rheumatism, 1968—81, Proc. of Transplantation Soc., 1968—82, Jour. Infectious Diseases, 1969—79, Jour. Exptl. Medicine, 1971—, Immunol. Comm., 1972—85, Clin. Immunology and Immunopathology, 1972—89, Proc. of NAS, 1978—83, Clin. and Exptl. Immunology, 1978—88, Internat. Jour. Immunopharmacology, 1984, Advances in Immunology, 1985—, Advances in Pharmacology, 1989—; contbr. articles to profl. jours. Trustee Amherst Coll., 1981—. Capt. M.C. U.S. Army, 1956—58, Walter Reed Army Inst. Rsch. Recipient Warren Alpert Found. prize, 1999. Mem.: ACP, NAS (chmn. sect. on med. microbiology and immunology 1983—86), Internat. Soc. Immunopharmacology (pres. 1994), Internat. Assn. Allergology and Clin. Immunology, Fedn. Am. Soc. Exptl. Biology, Am. Acad. Allergy and Immunology (exec. com. 1970—72, sec. 1977—80, pres. 1981), Assn. Am. Physicians (recorder 1978—84, pres. 1989—90), Am. Acad. Arts and Scis., Transplantation Soc., Am. Rheumatism Assn., Am. Soc. Clin. Investigation, Brit. Soc. Immunology, Am. Assn. Immunologists (pres. 1977—78), Am. Soc. Exptl. Pathology, Am. Soc. Pharm. and Exptl. Therapeutics, Inst. Medicine, Interurban Clin. Club. Office: BWH Dept Rhem & Allergy Smith Bldg Room 638 75 Francis St Boston MA 02115 Office Phone: 617-525-1300. Office Fax: 617-525-1310.*

AUSTEN, W(ILLIAM) GERALD, surgeon, educator; b. Akron, Ohio, Jan. 20, 1930; s. Karl and Bertl (Jehle) Austen; m. Patricia Ramsdell, Jan. 28, 1961; children: Karl Ramsdell, William Gerald Jr., Christopher Marshall, Elizabeth Patricia. BS, MIT, 1951; MD, Harvard U., 1955; HHD (hon.), U. Akron, 1980; DSc (hon.), U. Athens, 1981, U. Mass., 1985, Northeastern Ohio U. Coll. Medicine, 1996. Diplomate Am. Bd. Surgery, Am. Bd. Thoracic Surgery. Intern, then resident in surgery Mass. Gen. Hosp., Boston, 1955—61, chief surg. cardiovasc. rsch. unit, 1963—69, chief surgery, 1969—97, surgeon-in-chief, 1989—97, surgeon-in-chief emeritus, 1997—; surgeon clinic surgery Nat. Heart Inst., 1961—62; CEO, pres. Mass. Gen. Physicians Orgn., Boston, 1994—98, CEO, chmn., 1998—99, chmn., 1999—2000, hon. trustee, chmn. emeritus, 2000—. Assoc. in surgery Harvard Med. Sch., 1963—65, assoc. prof. surgery, 1965—66, prof. surgery, 1966—74, Edward D. Churchill prof. surgery, 1974—; mem. residency review com. surgery Accreditation Coun. Grad. Med. Edn., 1988—93; bd. dirs. Abiomed, Inc., The Smithers Group, Inc. Author, editor: med. textbooks; contbr. articles to profl. jours. Mem. corp. MIT 1972-2005, life mem. corp., 1982-2005, life mem. corp. emeritus, 2005—, mem. exec. com. corp., 1986-98; trustee John S. and James L. Knight Found., 1986-, vice chmn., 1991-96, chmn., 1996-; bd. dirs. Found. Biomed Rsch., 1988-2000; trustee Mass. Eye and Ear Infirmary, 1991-, Ptnrs. HealthCare System Inc., 1994-97, Mass. Gen. Hosp., 1997-99, Dana Farber/Ptnrs. Cancer Care Inc., 1999-, Mass. Taxpayers Found., 2000—, North Shore Med. Ctr., 2001—; hon. trustee Mass. Gen. Hosp., 1999—; hon. trustee Akron Art Mus., 2004— Markle scholar, 1963-68. Fellow AAAS, Royal Coll. Surgeons Eng. (hon.), Am. Acad. Arts and Scis.; mem. NAS Inst. Medicine, Am. Heart Assn. (pres. 1977-78, Gold Heart award 1980), Am. Surg. Assn. (sec. 1979-84, pres. 1985-86), Am. Assn. Thoracic Surgery (v.p. 1987-88, pres. 1988-89), Am. Bd. Surgery (mem. bd. 1969-74, sr. mem. 1974-), Am. Bd. Thoracic Surgery (bd. dirs. 1984-90), ACS (regent 1982-91, chmn. bd. regents 1989-91, pres. 1992-93), Assn. Acad. Surgery (pres. 1970), Soc. Univ. Surgeons (sec. 1967-70, pres. 1972-73), New Eng. Surg. Soc. (Disting. Svc. award 2002), New Eng. Cardiovasc. Soc. (pres. 1972-73), Mass. Heart Assn. (pres. 1972-74, Paul Dudley White Cardiac award 1981). Home: 330 Beacon St Apt C66 Boston MA 02116-1190 Office: Mass Gen Hosp BUL 3 Boston MA 02114-2696 Office Phone: 617-726-2050. E-mail: wgausten@partners.org.

AUSTER, NANCY EILEEN ROSS, economics educator; b. N.Y.C., Aug. 19, 1926; d. Norman L. and Edith Cornelia (Jacobson) Ross; m. Donald Auster, Aug. 18, 1946; children: Carol J., Ellen R. AB, Barnard Coll., 1948; MBA, Ind. U., 1954. Rsch. assoc. The Conf. Bd., N.Y.C., 1948-51; editor publs. Bur. Bus. Rsch. Ind. U., Bloomington, 1954-56; lectr. St. Lawrence U., Canton, N.Y., 1962-66; from asst. prof. to prof. Canton Coll., SUNY, 1966-82, disting. svc. prof. econs., 1982-91, disting. svc. prof. econs. emeritus, 1991—. Pres. univ. faculty senate SUNY, 1973-75; mem. chancellor's adv. com. disting. tchg. prof. SUNY, 1983-86, chair, 1986-87. Author: (with Donald Auster) Men Who Enter Nursing: A Sociological Analysis, 1970; contbr. articles to profl. jours. Chair adv. coun. St. Lawrence County CETA, Canton, 1977-82. Recipient Professions Excellence award N.Y. State/United Univ. Professions, 1991; USPHS grantee, 1966-70. Unitarian-Universalist. Avocations: running, skiing, birding, quilting. Home: 21 Craig Dr Canton NY 13617-1211

AUSTER, PAUL, writer; b. Newark, Feb. 3, 1947; s. Samuel and Queenie (Bogat) A.; m. Lydia Davis, Oct. 6, 1974 (div. 1979); 1 child, Daniel; m. Siri Hustvedt, June 16, 1981; 1 child, Sophie. BA, Columbia U., 1969, MA, 1970. Lectr. Princeton (N.J.) U., 1986-90. Author: (poetry) Unearth, 1974, Wall Writing, 1976, Fragments From Cold, 1977, Facing the Music, 1980, Disappearances: Selected Poems, 1988, Collected Poems, 2004, Collected Prose, 2005, (non-fiction) White Spaces, 1980, The Invention of Solitude, 1982, The Art of Hunger, 1982, expanded edit., 1992, Why Write?, 1996, Translations, 1997, Hand to Mouth, 1997, The Red Notebook, 2002; author: (with Sam Messer) The Story of My Typewriter, 2002; author: (fiction) City of Glass, 1985, Ghosts, 1986, The Locked Room, 1986, In the Country of Last Things, 1987, Moon Palace, 1989, The Music of Chance, 1990, Leviathan, 1992, Mr. Vertigo, 1994, Timbuktu, 1999, The Book of Illusions, 2002, Oracle Night, 2003, Auggie Wren's Christmas Story, 2004, (films) Smoke, 1995 (Ind. Spirit award, 1996), Blue in the Face, 1995, Lulu on the Bridge, 1998; editor: The Random House Book of Twentieth-Century French Poetry, 1982, I Thought My Father was God and Other True Tales from NPR's National Story Project, 2001. Decorated commandeur de l'Ordre des Arts et des lettres (France), Prix Médicis Etranger; recipient Morton Dauwen Zabel award, Am. Acad. Arts & Letters; fellow, Nat. Endowment for the Arts, 1979, 1985. Mem. PEN. Office: care Carol Mann Agy 55 5th Ave New York NY 10003-4301

AUSTILL, ALLEN, dean emeritus; b. Newton, Mass., June 22, 1927; s. William E. and Anna (Pifer) A.; m. Joan Mildred Sellery, June 4, 1950; children: Randolph Allen, Christopher Scott, Lara Anne. BA, U. Chgo., 1948, MA, 1951; LHD (hon.), New Sch. Social Rsch., 1987. Research asso. Council State Govts., Chgo., 1951-52; mem. faculty, dir. admissions and placement St. Johns Coll., 1953-55; dir. student housing U. Chgo., 1955-57; tchr., dean students SUNY-Stony Brook, 1957-61; cons. Ford Found., Middle East, Amman, Jordan, 1962; mem. faculty, asso. dean New Sch. Social Research, 1962-64, dean, 1964-79, v.p. acad. affairs and exec. dean, 1979-82, dean, 1982-87, chancellor, 1987-89. Cons. Chatham Coll., 2000, Corcoran Gallery Coll., 2003; cons. title I Higher Edn. Act, State N.Y.; mem. council academic fellows Shimer Coll., 1971-80; mem. N.Y. Regents Adv. Task Force for Adult Edn., 1972-77, chmn., 1976-77; chmn. bd. dirs. Harpers Mag. Found., 1988—; bd. dirs. Ednl. Mgmt. Network, 1985-95; chmn. vis. com. Am. Mus. Natural History, 1990. Author: (with others) Higher Education in the Forty-Eight States, 1952; Summary of State Legislation and Elections (with others), 1953. Pres. Friends of Cresskill Libr., 1969-71; mem. vis. com. continuing edn. Harvard U., 1977-83; mem. Boston Ctr. for Adult Edn., 1990—, chair bd. trustees, 1991-95. With AUS, 1945-46. Home: 103 Belmont St Somerville MA 02143 E-mail: aaustill@comcast.net.

AUSTIN, ARTHUR DONALD, II, lawyer, educator; b. Staunton, Va., Dec. 2, 1932; s. George Milnes and Mae (Eichner) A.; m. Irene Clara Wittenberg, June 12, 1960; 1 son, Brian Carl. BS in Commerce, U. Va., 1958; JD, Tulane U., 1963. Bar: Va. 1964, D.C. 1970. Asst. prof. Coll. of William and Mary, Williamsburg, Va., 1963-64, Bowling Green State U., Ohio, 1964-66; asst. prof. law Cleve. State U., 1966-68; prof. law Case Western Res. U., Cleve., 1968-70, 72-78, Edgar A. Hahn prof. jurisprudence, 1978—. Atty. Dept. Justice, Washington, 1970-71 Author: Antitrust: Law, Economics, Policy, 1976, Complex Litigation Confronts the Jury System, 1984, The Empire Strikes Back: Outsiders and the Struggle Over Legal Education, 1998; contbr. articles to law revs. Served with U.S. Army, 1952-54. Decorated Bronze Star medal with V, Purple Heart. Home: 1174 Stony Hill Rd Hinckley OH 44233-9538 Office: 11075 East Blvd Cleveland OH 44106-5409 Office Phone: 216-368-3289.

AUSTIN, BECKY SUE, medical technician; b. Olean, NY, Feb. 16, 1963; d. Wayne Phillip and Sara Jane Austin. AAS, Alfred Agrl. and Tech. Coll., 1983. Med. technologist Bradford (Pa.) Regional Med. Ctr.; prin. technologist urines/coagulation and serology Bradford Regional Med. Ctr. Office: Bradford Regional Med Ctr 116 Interstate Pkwy Bradford PA 16701

AUSTIN, CLAUDE LIDELL, retired surgeon; b. Winona, Miss., Jan. 4, 1919; s. Luther Barksdale Austin and Cora Claudine Carter; m. Elizabeth Hightower, Sept. 2, 1944 (dec. Mar. 1990); children: Larry, Richard; m. Merry Cobb Lowry, Feb. 1, 1991. BA, U. Miss., 1940, BS, 1944; MD, Jefferson Med. Sch., 1946. Pvt. practice, Hattiesburg, Miss., 1947—91; ret., 1992. Pres. med. staff Hattiesburg Hosp., 1969—80; established vol. med. office and ongoing med. care Home of Grace, 1997—. Pres. Belle Fontaine Beach Assn., Ocean Springs, Miss., 1995; bd. dirs. Rotary Club, Hattiesburg, 1947. Fellow: Internat. Coll. Surgeons; mem.: AMA, Miss. State Med. Assn. Republican. Methodist. Avocation: deep sea fishing. Home: 7601 Belle Fontaine Dr Ocean Springs MS 39564-8490 Office: Home of Grace 14200 Jericho Rd Ocean Springs MS 39565

AUSTIN, DANFORTH WHITLEY, newspaper executive; b. Hutchinson, Kans., Sept. 21, 1946; s. Whitley and Mary Frances (Danforth) Austin; m. Gail Ellen Davenport, Sept. 2, 1967; children: Stephen D., Richard D. BS, U. Kans., 1968. Staff reporter The Wall St. Jour., Dallas, Detroit, 1970—76, spl. writer N.Y.C., 1976—78, news editor, 1978, bur. chief Pitts., 1978—83, from asst. to deputy nat. editor N.Y.C., 1984—86, spl. reports editor, 1986—87; dir. corp. rels. Dow Jones and Co. Inc., N.Y.C., 1987—89; dir. circulation Wall St. Jour., Barron's, Princeton, N.J., 1989-95; v.p. circulation Wall St. Jour., 1992—95, v.p., gen. mgr., 1995—2002; v.p. Dow Jones & Co. Inc., 2002—. Vice chmn. Ottaway Newpapers Inc., Campbell Hall, NY, 2002—03, chmn., CEO, 2003—. Trustee William Allen White Found., U. Kans., Lawrence, 1996—; sr. warden St. Peter's Episcopal Ch., Brentwood, Pa., 1981; lay reader Episcopal Diocese of Pitts., 1981—83, Diocese of Newark, 2001—; vestryman St. George's Episcopal Ch., Maplewood, NJ, 1985—88; bd. dirs. Episcopal Ch. Found., N.Y.C., 2002—. Sgt. U.S. Army, 1968—70, Vietnam. Decorated Bronze Star, Air medal. Mem.: N.Y. Newspaper Pubs. Assn. (bd.

dirs. 2000—02), Soc. Profl. Journalists, Kappa Sigma. Home: 51 Joanna Way Short Hills NJ 07078-3206 Office: Ottaway Newspapers Inc 97 Rt 416 PO Box 401 Campbell Hall NY 10916 Office Phone: 845-294-8181. Business E-Mail: dan.austin@dowjones.com.

AUSTIN, DANIEL WILLIAM, lawyer; b. Springfield, Ill., Feb. 24, 1949; s. Daniel D. and Ruth A. (Ahrenkiel) A.; m. Lois Ann Austin, June 12, 1971; 1 child, Elizabeth Ann. BA, Millikin U., 1971; JD, Washington U., 1974. Bar: Ill. 1974, U.S. Dist. Ct. (cen. dist.) Ill. 1979, U.S. Ct. Appeals (7th cir.) 1980, U.S. Supreme Ct. 1980, U.S. Tax Ct. 1986. Assoc. Miley & Meyer, Taylorville, Ill., 1974-78; ptnr. Miley, Meyer & Austin, Taylorville, 1978-81; prin. Meyer, Austin & Romano P.C., Taylorville, 1981—. Pres. United Fund, Taylorville, 1980, Christian County YMCA, Taylorville, 1983-85, St. Vincent Meml. Hosp. Found., 1998—. Named one of Outstanding Young Men Am., 1985, Outstanding Citizen of City of Taylorville, 1993. Mem. ABA, Ill. Bar Assn., Christian County Bar Assn., Order of Barristers, Sangamo Club. Democrat. Presbyterian. Avocations: golf, photography. Home: 14 Westhaven Ct Taylorville IL 62568-9064 Office: Meyer Austin & Romano PC 210 S Washington St Taylorville IL 62568-2245 Office Phone: 217-824-4931.

AUSTIN, ELIZABETH RUTH, retired elementary school educator; b. Glendale, Calif., June 28, 1928; d. Lloyd Lewis Austin and Mary Elizabeth Berryman. BA, Scripps Coll., 1950; postgrad., Occidental Coll., 1950—51, UCLA, 1959, U. S.C., 1961, Orange State Coll., 1964, U. Calif., Santa Barbara, 1975. Admitting office clk. Hosp. Good Samaritan, L.A., 1976—93; elem. tchr. Alhambra, Calif., 1951—55, L.A., 1957—62, Newport Beach, Calif., 1962—65, San Marino, Calif., 1974—76; ret. Home: 1428 S Marengo Ave Alhambra CA 91803

AUSTIN, GRANT WILLIAM, real estate appraiser; b. Toronto, July 15, 1954; m. Joanne Austin; 1 child, Kelly Rae. BA summa cum laude, York U., 1983; MS, U. St. Thomas, 2003. Cert. gen. appraiser Fla. Pres. Am. Valuation, Inc., Ft. Lauderdale, Fla., 1998—. Author: Calculator Skills for the HP 19B, 1995, Property Owner's Guide to Condemnation, 1998. Mem.: Assn. Eminent Domain Profls. (v.p., dir. 1994—95), Market Rsch. Soc., Appraisal Inst. (chair pub. rels. com. 1995—97), Lambda Alpha Internat. (pres. 1997—99). Avocations: golf, tennis. Office Phone: 954-349-9725. Personal E-mail: amervalu@bellsouth.net.

AUSTIN, H(ARRY) GREGORY, lawyer; b. N.Y.C., Mar. 18, 1936; s. Harry Gregory and Pauline (Moore) Austin; m. Deanna Ruth Anderson, Nov. 28, 1970; children: Sabrina Elizabeth, Harry Gregory III, Anne Catherine. BE, Yale U., 1957, postgrad., 1958; JD, U. Mich., 1961; LLD (hon.), Lincoln U., 1976. Bar: Colo. 1961, U.S. Supreme Ct. 1974. Assoc. Holland & Hart, Denver, 1962—73, ptnr., 1977—2001, of counsel, 2002—; gen. counsel SBA, Washington, 1973—75; solicitor, gen. counsel U.S. Dept. Interior, Washington, 1975—77; dir. Rocky Mountain Pub. Broadcasting Network, 1994—. Bd. dirs. Rocky Mountain Pub. Broadcasting Sys., Inc. Trustee Colo. Legal Aid Found., Denver, 1984—91, chmn., 1988—91; mem. adv. com. Colo. Sec. of State, 1996—; bd. dirs. Children's Hosp., Denver, 1985—97, Rocky Mountain PBS, 2004—, Denver Police Found., 2004—. 1st lt. USAR, 1957—64. Fellow: Am. Bar Found.; mem.: Denver Bar Assn., Colo. Bar Assn. (chmn. bus. entities subsect. bus. law sect. 1987—89, vice chmn. bus. law sect. 1989—91, chmn. 1991—93, chmn. partnership laws com. 1993—), Am. Law Inst., Metro Denver C. of C. (bd. dirs., sec. 1995—97). Republican. Office: Holland & Hart LLP 555 17th St Ste 3200 Denver CO 80202-3979 Business E-Mail: gaustin@hollandhart.com.

AUSTIN, HARRY GUIDEN, engineering and construction company executive; b. Belton, Tex., Dec. 10, 1917; s. Harry Guiden and Emma Lena (Brown) A.; m. Elizabeth Ann Heard, Aug. 31, 1940; children— Lucy Ann, Elizabeth Austin Page, Catherine Austin Wyatt. BS in Elec. Engring, Tex. A&M Coll., 1938; MBA, Harvard U., 1940; H.H.D., Wiley Coll. Registered profl. engr., Tex. With Pan Am. Airways, Miami, Fla., 1940-41; elec. engr. Brown Shipbldg. Co., Houston, 1941-45; with Brown & Root, Inc., Houston, 1945—, v.p., 1960-65, sr. v.p., 1965-68, sr. group v.p., 1968-70, exec. v.p. engring. and constrn., 1970-78; also dir.; pres. Hael, Inc., Houston, 1978—. Mem. Tex. A&M Geosci. Coun. Bd. dirs. Retina Rsch. Found. Mem. NSPE, IEEE, Mus. Fine Arts, Petroleum Club, Houston Country Club, Rive rhill Country Club (Kerrville, Tex.). Methodist. Home: 267 Pine Hollow Ln Houston TX 77056-1501 Office: Hael Inc 267 Pine Hollow Houston TX 77056-1501

AUSTIN, JACOB (JACK AUSTIN), Canadian government official; b. Calgary, Alta., Can., Mar. 2, 1932; s. Morris and Clara Edith (Chetner) A.; m. Natalie Veiner Freeman, Apr. 2, 1978; children: Edith Clare, Sharon Jill, Barbara Joan. BA, LLB, U. B.C.; LLM, Harvard U.; postgrad., U. Calif., Berkeley; ScD in Social Sci., U. East Asia. Bar: B.C. 1958, Yukon 1966. Chief of staff to prime min., 1974-75; dep. min. energy, mines and resources, 1970-74; mem. Senate, 1975—; leader of the govt. in the Senate, 2003—; min. of state, 1981-82; min. of state for social devel., 1982-84. Mem. Vancouver Club, Rideau Club. Liberal. Jewish. Office: The Senate 275 S CB Ottawa ON Canada K1A 0A4

AUSTIN, JEANNETTE HOLLAND, genealogist, writer; b. Atlanta, July 28, 1936; d. Laurel Benjamin Holland and Marguerite Elizabeth Evans; m. Jerry Franklin Austin, May 13, 1977 (dec. Mar. 1993); 1 child, Christopher Lewis (dec.); 1 child from previous marriage, Suzanne Teri Stucki. Legal sec. Smith, Field, Doremus & Ringel, Atlanta, 1954—63; profl. genealogist Atlanta, 1964—; owner www.genealoty-books.com, www.georgiapioneers.com. With Family History Ctr. Ch. LDS, Jonesboro, Ga., 1988—99. Author: The Georgians, 1984, Holland 1000-1988, 1988, Abstracts of Georgia Wills, DeKalb County Probate Records, etc., The Georgia Frontier, 3 vols., 2005. Recipient cert., Atlanta Ga. Temple, 2001. Republican. Mem. Lds Ch. Avocations: drawing, singing, painting, drama, biking. Home: 3010 Sherwood Dr Saint Simons Island GA 31520 Personal E-mail: jha@georgiapioneers.com.

AUSTIN, JESSE HINNANT, III, lawyer; b. Jacksonville, N.C., Feb. 12, 1954; s. Jesse Hinnant and Helen (Canady) A.; m. Deborah Pitman, Oct. 16, 1982; children: Emily Katherine, Anne Elizabeth. BS, U. N.C., 1976; JD with distinction, MBA, Emory U., 1980. Bar: Ga. 1980, U.S. Dist. Ct. (no. dist.) Ga. 1980, U.S. Dist. Ct. (mid. dist.) Ga. 1983, U.S. Ct. Appeals (4th, 5th and 11th cirs.) 1983, U.S. Dist. Ct. (no. dist.) Tex. 1989. Ptnr. Powell, Goldstein, Frazer & Murphy, Atlanta, 1980—, Paul, Hastings, Janofsky & Walker LLP, Atlanta, vice chmn. corp. dept., co-chmn. fin. svc. & creditors' rights practice group. Mem. ABA (litigation and business law sect., bankruptcy com., subcom. second creditors and chpt. 11), Am. Bankruptcy Inst., Ga. State Bar Assn. (litigation and bankruptcy sect.), Order of Coif, Order of Barristers, Phi Beta Kappa, Phi Eta Sigma, Beta Gamma Sigma, Beta Alpha Psi. Office: Paul Hastings Janofsky & Walker LLP 600 Peachtree St NE Ste 2400 Atlanta GA 30308-2222 Office Phone: 404-815-2208. Office Fax: 404-815-2424. Business E-Mail: jessaustin@paulhastings.com.

AUSTIN, JIM E., secondary school educator; b. Glasgow, Ky., Sept. 13, 1950; s. James E. and Avo S. (Blankenship) A.; m. Marlene D. Robison, Aug. 21, 1971; 1 child, Mishael. BA, Eastern Ky. U., Richmond, 1972; MRE, Southwestern Bapt. Theol. Sem., Ft. Worth, 1975; MA, Eastern Ky. U., Richmond, 1980; postgrad., Spalding U., 1980. Minister music/youth First Bapt. Ch., London, Ky., 1976-77; tchr. Model Lab. Sch., Richmond, Ky., 1979-80, Univ. Breckinridge Sch., Morehead, Ky., 1980-81, Bethlehem High Sch., Bardstown, Ky., 1981-85, Moore High Sch., Louisville, 1985-92, tech. edn. trainer, 1986—, chmn. first participatory mgmt. steering com., 1990-92; tchr. DuPont Manual High Sch., Louisville, 1992—2002; math. cons. Ky. Dept. Edn., 2002—. Curriculum writer, in-svc. leader Jefferson County Pub. Schs., Louisville, 1988—; presenter in field. Named Tchr. of the Yr., Highview Optimists, 1990. Mem. NEA, Nat. Coun. Tchrs. Math., Internat. Soc. Tech. in Edn., Assn. Supervision and Curriculum Devel., Ky. Edn. Assn., Ky. Coun. Tchrs. Math., Jefferson County Tchrs. Assn., Greater Louisville Coun. Tchrs. Math. (outstanding teaching award 1992), Sch. Sci. and Math. Assn. Baptist. Avocations: reading, golf, tennis, basketball. Home: 3815 Iron Horse Way Louisville KY 40272-2914 Office: Ky Dept Edn 500 Mero St 18th Flr CPT Frankfort KY 40601 Office Phone: 502-564-2106. Business E-Mail: jaustin@kde.state.ky.us.

AUSTIN, JOHN D., corporate financial executive; CPA. Acct. Deloitte & Touche LLP; asst. controller Gen. Med. Corp., 1991—95; corp. controller Performance Food Group, 1995—98, corp. treas., 1998—2001, sec., 2000—01, v.p., 2001—03, cheif fin. officer, sr. v.p., 2003—. Office: Performance Food Group PO Box 29269 Richmond VA 23242-0269

AUSTIN, JOHN DAVID, retired finance company executive; b. Memphis, Jan. 16, 1936; s. Thomas L. and Vela M. (Davis) Austin; m. Dorothy Clemans, Dec. 31, 1959 (div.); children: Laura Jan, David John; m. Marilyn C. Brewster, Nov. 2, 1985; 1 child, Christopher Brewster. BBA, Ga. State U., 1961. Acct. Price Waterhouse & Co., Atlanta, 1961—64, sr. tax acct. Miami, 1964—67; audit mgr. N.C. Nat. Bank Corp., Greensboro, 1968, v.p., gen. auditor Charlotte, 1969—73; sr. v.p., dir. corp. planning 1st Nat. Bank Mobile, Ala., 1973—74; sr. v.p. Southeast Nat. Bank. Pa., Malvern, 1974—75, exec. v.p., 1975—83, acting pres., CEO, 1978—80; sr. v.p. Va. Fed. Savs. and Loan, Richmond, 1984, exec. v.p., 1985, pres., also bd. dirs., 1986—88; exec. v.p. and CEO, also bd. dirs. Citizens Fed. Savs. & Loan, Salisbury, NC, 1988—90; self employed Marietta, Ga., 1990—91; v.p., CFO Atlanta Cutlery Corp, Conyers, Ga., 1991—96, COO, 1993—96, ret. Former pres. United Arts Coun. of Rowan; former bd. dirs. Chester County Mental Health/Mental Retardation Bd., The Chester Group, Del. County Econ. Devel. Com., Del. County Cmty. Coll. Found., St. John's Hosp. With U.S. Army, 1957—59. Home: 1303 Spring Gate Cir Woodstock GA 30189-5489

AUSTIN, JOHN DELONG, retired judge; b. Cambridge, N.Y., May 31, 1935; s. John DeLong and Mabel Cowles (Bascom) A.; m. Marcia Kay Behan, Aug. 15, 1969 (dec.); children: John DeLong, Susan Behan. AB, Dartmouth Coll., 1957; postgrad., u. Minn., 1959; JD, Albany Law Sch., 1969. Bar: N.Y. 1970. Editl. dir. Glens Falls (N.Y.) Times, 1960-66; sole practice Glens Falls, 1970-79; law asst. Warren County Judge and Surrogate, 1975-79, N.Y. State Supreme Ct., 1980-84; judge Warren County Family Ct., NY, 1984-99, Warren County Ct. and Surrogate's Ct., 1999—2003; ret. Instr. Adirondack Comm. Coll., Glens Falls. Editor New Eng. Hist. and Geneal. Register, 1970-73; contbr. hist. and geneal. articles to various periodicals. Councilman Town of Queensbury, N.Y., 1969-71, supr., 1972-74; budget officer Warren County, N.Y., 1974; mem. N.Y. State Local Govt. Records Adv. Coun. With U.S. Army, 1958-60. Recipient Adminstrv. Law prize Albany Law Sch., 1969. Fellow Am. Soc. Genealogists; mem. N.Y. State Bar Assn., Warren County Bar Assn., Mohican Grange, Elks. Republican.

AUSTIN, JOHN H., health care administrator; Dir. Coventry Health Care, 1988-99, chmn. bd., 1995-99, CEO; chmn., CEO Arcadian Mgmt. Svcs., 1997—; pres. profl. svcs. divsn. Unihealth, 1997—; health care cons., 1992-94; dir. QuadraMed Corp., 1995-98. Exec. vice-pres. Health Plan Am., Calif. Fax: 801-493-0752.*

AUSTIN, JOHN H.M., radiologist; b. Boston, Mass., 1939; MD, Yale U., 1965. Cert. Diagnostic Radiology. Prof., radiology Columbia U. Coll. Physicians and Surgeons, 1973—; resident, radiology UCSF Med. Ctr., San Francisco, 1966—68, fellowship, radiology, 1968—70; radiologist N.Y.-Presbyn. Hosp., Columbia U. Med. Ctr., N.Y.C., 1973—. Former pres. Fleischner Soc. Office: NY Presbyn Hosp Dept Radiology 622 W 168th St MHB 3-202C New York NY 10032-3784

AUSTIN, JOHN NORMAN, classics educator; b. Anshun, Kweichow, China, May 20, 1937; s. John Alfred and Lillian Maud (Reeks) A. BA, U. Toronto, 1958; MA, U. Calif.-Berkeley, 1959, PhD, 1965. Vis. lectr. Yale U., New Haven, 1971; asst. prof., then assoc. prof. UCLA, 1966-76; Aurelio prof. Greek Boston U., 1976-78; prof., chmn. dept. classics U. Mass., Amherst, 1978-80; prof. classics U. Ariz., Tucson, 1980—, acting dean humanities, 1987-88, head dept. classics, 1995—2000, prof. emeritus, 2000—. Vis. prof. Leeds U., 1999. Author: Archery at the Dark of the Moon, 1975, Meaning and Being in Myth, 1990, Helen of Troy and Her Shameless Phantom, 1994; editor: (with others) The Works of John Dryden, vol. III; sr. editor Calif. Studies Classical Antiquity, vols. VI and VII. Jr. fellow Ctr. for Hellenic Studies, 1968-69, J.S. Guggenheim Found. fellow, 1974-75 Episcopalian. Home: 3200 NE 36th St #1216 Fort Lauderdale FL 33308 Office Phone: 954-566-4883. Personal E-mail: normana764@aol.com.

AUSTIN, KAREN, retail executive; b. Delphos, Ohio; BS in Computer Sci., Tri-State U. Various positions Kmart Corp., 1984—2002, sr. v.p., chief info. officer Troy, Mich., 2002—. Office: Kmart Corp 3100 W Big Beaver Rd Troy MI 48084

AUSTIN, KAREN LISA, psychologist; b. St. Louis, Fla., Mar. 13, 1975; s. Henry M. and Nancy M. Fendrich; m. Steven McLean Austin, Feb. 21, 2004. BS, Fla. State U., 1997; MS, Edn. Specialist, U. South Fla., 2000. Cert. profl. educaor Fla. Dept. Edn. Sch. psychologist Pasco County Sch., Zepyrhills, Fla., 2000—01, Hillsborough County Sch., Tampa, Fla., 2001—05. Mem.: Fla. Assn. Sch. Psychologists, Nat. Assn. Sch. Psychologists, Pi Kappa Phi.

AUSTIN, LINDA S., psychiatrist; b. 1951; m. Marshall Austin (div.); children: Stephanie, Matt. At, Stanford U.; BA, Duke U., 1973; MD, Duke U. Sch. of Medicine, 1976. Resident in psychiatry Duke U.; clin. instr. psychiatry Georgetown U., Washington; pvt. practice Chevy Chase, Md.; staff Med. U. S.C., 1986—89, asst. prof. psychiatry, 1989—99, assoc. dean pub. edn., 1996, prof. psychiatry, 1999—2000; staff Ea. Maine Med. Ctr. Heritage Psychiat. Assn., Bangor, Maine, 2000—. Dir. Obsessive-Compulsive Disorder program Med. U. S.C., 1989, mem. Hurricane Hugo response team, 89; featured in Depression: The Storm Within Am. Psychiat. Soc., 1990; host What's on Your Mind Nat. Pub. Radio, 1990—; TV appearances. Author: (books) What's Holding You Back? Eight Critical Choices for Women's Success, 1999, Heart of the Matter: How to Find Love. How to Make it Work., 2003; editor: Responding to Disaster: A Mental Health Clinician's Guide, 1989. Fellow child psychiatry, Georgetown U. Address: Heritage Psychiatric Assn Ste 403 15 Columbia St Bangor ME 04401

AUSTIN, LOLA HOUSTON, psychologist; b. San Antonio, Dec. 27, 1939; d. Albert and Sarah Leola Houston; m. Craig L. Austin, July 4, 1972; children: Madie Grabda, Polly Toro, Julia Austin Bingamon, Carrie Austin Young. BA in Edn., North Tex. State U., 1966; MA in Edn., U. Incarnate Word, 1973; PhD in Clin. Psychology, Fielding Inst., 1987; postgrad. study in neuropsychol. evaluation, Santa Barbara, Calif., 2000. Elem. sch. tchr. Edgewood Ind. Sch. Dist., San Antonio Ind. Sch. Dist., Northside Ind. Sch. Dist., San Antonio, 1960—75; reading specialist Northside Ind. Sch. Dist., San Antonio, 1971—76; owner, dir. D & R Reading Clinic, San Antonio, 1976; psychologist San Antonio, 1997; neuropsychol. evaluator, 2000. Cons. Psychol. Corp., San Antonio, PAR; evaluator Child Protective Svcs., San Antonio. Co-chmn. fair King William Hist. Orgn., San Antonio, co-chair food booths. Mem.: APA, Nat. Acad. Neuropsychology, Delta Kappa Gamma (charter mem. Iota Beta chpt.). Office: McCullough Ctr for Mental Health Ste 101 2515 McCullough San Antonio TX 78212

AUSTIN, MARILYN CLAIRE, academic administrator; b. Richmond, Ind., Nov. 10, 1935; d. Alfred W. and Esther Mae Austin; m. David A. Baldwin, Aug. 10, 1957 (div. Aug. 19, 1990); children: Sarah Lynn Baldwin, Rebecca Ann Baldwin, Emily Elizabeth Baldwin. BS with Distinction, Ind. U., 1957; PhD, Rutgers U., 1963. Lectr. Augusta Coll., Ga.; asst. provost Dartmouth Coll., Hanover, NH, 1971—72, asst. v. p. student affairs, assoc. dean, vice provost, 1984—87; program officer higher edn. Charles A. Dana Found., N.Y.C., 1987—91; dir. spl. edn. Sunapee H.S., NH, 1991—99, Fair Haven Union H.S., Vt., 1999—2002. Adj. prof. English Dartmouth Coll., 1966—87, v.p. Rassias Found., 1984—87; bd. trustees U. Sys. N.H., Durham, 1980—84, Colby-Sawyer Coll., New London, 1974—80, The Spence Sch., N.Y.C., 1988—93. Editor: My Mark Twain; contbr. articles to profl. jours. State coord. Am. Coun. on Edn., Nat. Identification Program Advancement Women Higher Edn. Adminstrn., Hanover, 1978—80; founder, chair Com. Concerns Women New Eng. Colls. and Univs., 1973—87; chair United Devel. Svcs., Hanover, 1982—97. Liberal. Mem. Lds Ch. Avocation: backpacking. Home: 2 Ridge Rd Hanover NH 03755 Personal E-mail: austinnelson@valley.net.

AUSTIN, PHILIP, research scientist; b. Pitts., Jan. 5, 1957; s. Martin and Jacqueline Austin; children: Jade, Rachel. BA in History, BS in Math., Widener U., 1977; MS in Astronomy, MS in Physics, U. Tex., 2002, postgrad., 2003—; hon. degree, Oxford (Eng.) U., 1973, Seria (Italy) Coll., 1976. With Zayre Corp., 1977—89, Sams Stores/Walmart Corp., 1989—94; scientist Fla., 2002—; prof. astronomy U. Fla. Pres., CEO Austin Finl. Group. Writer: Am. Scientist, 1993—2001; co-author: Astron. Jour., 2000. Recipient Rice medal honors, NYC. Mem.: ACLU, Am. Scientists, Union League, Widener Alumni Club, Space Telescope Team, Univ. Club, Mensa Soc., Sigma Xi. Democrat. Jewish. Avocations: collecting rare old books, collecting and restoring old cars. Mailing: 3829 Nimblewill Ct Port Saint Lucie FL 34952-3151

AUSTIN, PHILIP EDWARD, academic administrator; b. Fargo, N.D., 1942; s. William and Angelyn A.; children: Patrick William, Philip James. BS, N.D. State U., 1964, MS, 1966; MA, Mich. State U., 1968, PhD, 1969; hon. doctorate, Autonomous U. Guadalajara, Mexico, N.D. State U., U. Ala. Economist U.S. Office of Mgmt. and Budget, Washington, 1971-74; dep. asst. sec. HEW, Washington, 1974-77, acting asst. sec., 1977; dir. doctoral program in edn. policy George Washington U., Washington, 1977-78; v.p. for acad. affairs, prof. econs. and fin. Bernard Baruch Coll., N.Y.C., 1978-84; pres., prof. econs. Colo. State U., Fort Collins, 1984-89; chancellor U. Ala. System, Tuscaloosa, 1989-96; pres. U. Conn., Storrs, 1996—. Served with U.S. Army, 1969-71. Decorated Bronze Star. Office: U Conn Office of the Pres Storrs Mansfield CT 06269-2048 Office Phone: 860-486-2337. Business E-Mail: philip.austin@uconn.edu.

AUSTIN, REGINA, law educator; BA, U. Rochester, 1970; JD cum laude, U. Pa., 1973. Law clk to Judge Edmund B. Spaeth Superior Ct of Pa., 1973—74; assoc. Schnader, Harrison, Segal & Lewis, Phila, 1974—77; asst. prof. U. Pa. Law Sch., Phila, 1977—83, assoc. prof., 1983—90, prof., 1990—96, William A. Schnader prof., 1996—. Vis. prof. Stanford Law Sch., 1991, Brooklyn Law Sch., 1998, Columbia Law Sch., 2000; vis. assoc. prof. Harvard Law Sch., 1989—90. Contbr. articles to law jours. Office: U Pa Law Sch 3400 Chestnut St Philadelphia PA 19104 Office Phone: 215-898-5185. Office Fax: 215-573-2025. E-mail: raustin@law.upenn.edu.

AUSTIN, ROBERT CLARKE, naval officer; b. Cleve., Sept. 5, 1931; s. Clarke Albert and Margaret Jane (Richardson) A.; m. Joyce Ann Bisese, Apr. 22, 1957; children— Susan Lynn, James Holden, Robert Clarke, Cecelia Ann. BS, U.S. Naval Acad., 1954; MS in Physics, Naval Postgrad. Sch., 1963. Enlisted U.S. Navy, 1948, commd. ensign, 1954, advanced through grades to rear adm., 1980; commdg. officer USS Finback, 1968-72; comdr. Submarine Devel. Group Two, 1974-76; commdg. officer Naval Submarine Sch., 1976-78; chief of staff submarine force U.S. Atlantic Fleet, 1979-80; dep. dir. for internat. negotiations for Plans and Policy Directorate, Joint Chiefs of Staff, Pentagon, Washington, 1981-82; chief naval tech. tng., 1982-86; supt. Naval Postgrad. Sch., 1986-89; ret. USN, 1989; pres. Austin Assocs., Inc., Alexandria, Va., 1989-97. Decorated Def. Superior Service Medal, Legion of Merit with 4 gold stars, Meritorious Service medal, others. Mem. Sigma Xi. Episcopalian. E-mail: rcaustinva@aol.com.

AUSTIN, ROBERT EUGENE, JR., lawyer; b. Jacksonville, Fla., Oct. 10, 1937; s. Robert Eugene and Leta Fitch A.; children: Robert Eugene, George Harry Talley; m. Carolyn Rhea Songer. BA, Davidson Coll., 1959; JD, U. Fla., 1964. Bar: Fla. 1965, D.C. 1983, U.S. Supreme Ct. 1970; cert. in civil trial law Nat. Bd. Trial Advocacy. Pvt. practice law, 1965—. Asst. state atty., 1972; mem. Jud. Nominating Commn. and Grievance Com. 5th Dist. Fla.; gov. Fla. Bar, 1983; trustee U. Fla. Law Ctr.; mem. com. on std. jury instns. Fla. Supreme Ct. Chmn. Lake Dist. Boy Scouts Am.; asst. dean Leesburg Deanery Diocese Cen. Fla.; trustee Fla. House, Washington, U. Fla. Law Ctr., 1983—, chmn., 1988-90. Named one of The Best Lawyers in Am., Leading Fla. Lawyers. Mem. Am. Law Inst., Lake County Bar Assn., Roscoe Pound Am. Trial Found., Kappa Alpha, Phi Delta Phi Democrat. Episcopalian. Home: PO Box 490200 Leesburg FL 34749-0200 Office: 1330 Citizens Blvd Ste 401 Leesburg FL 34748-3942 Office Phone: 352-782-1020. E-mail: reajr@robertaustinlaw.com.

AUSTIN, ROBERTA JONES, elementary school educator; b. Clearwater, Fla., July 28, 1930; d. Wallace Theodore and Eloise (Knight) Jones; m. Ned Payne Austin, Oct. 18, 1952; children: David, Robin, Samuel, Frances, Genevieve, Laura. BS in Pub. Sch. Music, Queens Coll., Charlotte, N.C., 1952; postgrad. Sch. Edn., U. Colo., 1962-64; MA in Adminstrn. and Supervision, Appalachian State U., 1981. Cert. elem. and music tchr., sch. adminstr., N.C. Tchr. music grades 7 and 8 Denver Pub. Schs., 1961-62, tchr. grade 6, 1970-71; tchr. music grades 1 through 6 Adams County Sch. Dist. 12, Northglenn, Colo., 1962-63, elem. tchr., 1963-70; tchr. Playhouse Presch., L.A., 1972; elem. tchr. Watauga County Schs., Boone, N.C., 1973-97; retired, 1997; home sch. dir., tchr., 1998-99. Chairperson curriculum com. Adams County Sch. Dist. 12, 1965-70; chairperson/liaison calendar com. Watauga County Schs., 1975-80, instr. writing workshop for tchrs., 1982, 86, 90, 92; dir. after-sch. program and cmty. sch. Hardin Pk. Sch., Boone, 1980-85. Editor: (compilation of children's writings) Out of Our Children's Minds, 1967, (compilation of tchr.'s writings) In The Shadow of Howard's Knob, 1990. Com. woman Dem. Precinct, Denver, 1968-71, pres., Boone, N.C., 1999—; vol. coord. Summer Youth Employment Program, Denver, 1969; active Boone chpt. N.C. Ctr. for Internat. Understanding, 1993—, Blue Ridge Cmty. Theatre, 1979—; tutor, coord. ESL program High Country Amigos, Boone, 2000-2004; treas. Boone Unitarian Universalist Fellowship, 2000-2002, v.p., 2002-2003, pres., 2003-2004, choir dir., 2000—; pres. Parents, Family, and Friends of Lesbians and Gays of Boone, 2001-2005. Recipient trip to Russia, named N.C. Tchr. of the World, Children's Mus. About the World, Raleigh, N.C., 1993. Mem. NEA, N.C. Edn. Assn. (faculty rep. 1973—), Internat. Friendship Link. Avocations: music, drama, reading, writing. Home: 1561 Winklers Creek Rd Boone NC 28607-8904

AUSTIN, SAM M., physicist, educator; b. Columbus, Wis., June 6, 1933; s. A. Wright and Mildred G. (Reinhard) A.; m. Mary E. Herb, Aug. 15, 1959; children: Laura Gail, Sara Kay. BS in Physics, U. Wis., 1955, MS, 1957, PhD, 1960. Rsch. assoc. U. Wis., Madison, 1960; NSF postdoctoral fellow Oxford U., Eng., 1960-61; asst. prof. Stanford U., Calif., 1961-65; assoc. prof. physics Mich. State U., East Lansing, 1965-69, prof., 1969-90, univ. disting. prof., 1990-2000, univ. disting. prof. emeritus, 2000—, chmn. dept., 1980-83, acting dean Coll. Natural Sci., 1994, assoc. dir. Cyclotron Lab., 1976-79, rsch. dir., 1983-85, co-dir., 1985-89, dir., 1989-92. Guest Niels Bohr Inst., 1970; guest prof. U. Munich, 1972-73; sci. collaborator Saclay and Lab. Rene Bernas, 1979-80; vis. scientist Triumf-U. B.C., 1993-94; invited prof. U. Paris, Orsay, 1996; mem. grant selection com. for sub-atomic physics, NSERC (Can.), 1996-99; mem. com. on nuc. physics NRC, 1996-99; mem. steering com. Nuc. Physics Summer Sch.; mem. internat. adv. com. and exec. com. NSF Joint Inst. for Nuc. Astrophysics, 2003—. Author, editor: The Two Body Force in Nuclei, 1972, The (p,n) Reaction and Nucleon-Nucleon Force, 1980; editor Phys. Rev. C, 1988-2002, Virtual Jour. Nuclear Astrophysics; assoc. editor Atomic Data and Nuc. Data Tables, 1990—. Fellow NSF, 1960-61, Alfred P. Sloan Found., 1963-66; recipient Mich. Assn. of Governing Bds. Disting. Prof., 1992. Fellow AAAS (chair nominating com.), Am. Phys. Soc. (vice chmn. nuc. physics divsn. 1981-82, chmn. 1982-83, exec. com. 1983-84, 86-89, coun. 1986-89, coun. exec. com. 1987-88, panel on pub. affairs 1996-98); mem. APS, Sigma Xi (Sr. rsch. award 1977). Achievements include research in nuclear physics, nuclear astrophysics and nitrogen fixation. Home: 1201 Woodwind Trl Haslett MI 48840-8994 Office: Mich State U Nat Supercondr Cyclotron Lab East Lansing MI 48824 Business E-Mail: austin@nscl.msu.edu.

AUSTIN, SANDRA IKENBERRY, nursing educator, consultant; b. Lexington, Va., Dec. 22, 1941; d. William Peters and June Virginia (Blackwell) Ikenberry; m. Joseph M. Austin, Apr. 10, 1965; children: Joseph M. Jr., Susan C., Christopher M. BSN, U. Va., 1963; MSN, U. Calif., L.A., 1967; EdD, U. Mass., 1997. RN, Mass. Pub. health nurse Dept. Health, Waynesboro, Va., 1963-64; instr. U. Va., Charlottesville, 1964-65; staff nurse Santa Monica (Calif.) Hosp., 1965-66; faculty nursing Boston U., 1968-69, Quinsigamond C.C., Worcester, Mass., 1969-70, Fitchburg (Mass.) State Coll., 1973-96; assoc. prof. nursing Framingham (Mass.) State Coll., 1997—; project dir., sr. health edn. cons. HealthCo Consulting Inc., Shrewsbury, Mass., 1996—. Mem. Shrewsbury Town Meeting, 1992—95; chair steering com. Framingham State Coll. Nursing Honor Soc., 1998, faculty counselor/advisor, 1999—, pres., 1999—; people to people ambassador program delegate China Healthcare Info., 2004. HBO and Co. Nurse scholar, 1995. Mem.: Assn. Critical Care Nurses, Nat. League Nursing (awards com. 1999—2001), Assn. Women's Health, Obstet. and Neonatal Nurses, Am. Ednl. Rsch. ASsn., Sigma Theta Tau (Epsilon Beta edn. chair 1993—95, Rho Phi chpt. pres. 2002—, rsch. grant 1996), Pi Lambda Theta. Republican. Congregationalist. Avocations: computer multimedia production, reading, walking. Home: 100 Harrington Farms Way Shrewsbury MA 01545-4081 Office: Framingham State Coll Nursing Dept Framingham MA 01701 Office Phone: 508-626-4715.

AUSTIN, SANDRA JENELLE, school librarian, language educator; b. Ashdown, Ark., Mar. 31, 1958; d. Farce Desoto and Vester Alice Christopher; m. Glen Thomas Austin, July 26, 1986; children: Alicia Laverne, Glen Thomas Jr. EdB summa cum laude, U. Ark., 1980, MA, 1982; MLS, Tex. Women's U., 2000. Cert. tchr. Tex. Tchr. French, libr. Ark. HS, Texarkana, 1982—92; libr. Tex. HS, Texarkana, 1992—2002, tchr. French, libr., 2002—. Mem. tech. task force Texarkana Ind. Sch., Tex., 2000—. Mem. literacy coun. Miller County, Ark., 2001, Bowie County, Tex., 2001; sec. bd. dirs. Texarkana Mus. Sys., Tex., 2003—. Mem.: ALA (staff reporter Chgo. 2001—, sec. distance learning interest group Chgo. 2002—), Tex. Libr. Assn., Libr. and Info. Tech. Assn., Kappa Delta Pi, Beta Phi Mu. Avocation: gardening. Office: Texarkana Ind Sch Dist 4241 Summerhill Rd Texarkana TX 75503

AUSTIN, STEPHEN, music educator, musician; m. Johanna Austin; 1 child, Julianna. MusB in Edn., U. Ky., 1992; MusM, McNeese State U., Lake Charles, La., 1994. Band dir. Elkhorn Mid. Sch., Frankfort, Ky., 1993—96; jazz band dir., asst. band dir. Franklin County H.S., Frankfort, Ky., 1993—96; band dir. East Ramapo Sch. Dist., Spring Valley, NY, 1996—97; dir. of bands Middletown (N.Y.) H.S., 1997—. Mem.: N.Y. State Band Dirs. Assn., N.Y. State Sch. Music Assn., Orange County Music Educators Assn. (exec. bd. mem. 2000, exec. adminstr. Summer Music Inst. 2004, auditions coord. 2001—05, pres. 2005—), Internat. Trumpet Guild. Office: Middletown HS 20 Gardner Ave Ext Middletown NY 10940 Office Phone: 845-341-5950.

AUSTIN, TERRI JO, state representative; b. Elwood, Ind., May 17, 1955; m. Michael Austin; 2 children. B in Elem. Edn., B in Elem. Edn., M in Spl. Edn., Ball State U.; degree in Ednl. Adminstrn. and Supervision, Butler U. Classroom tchr., dist. adminstr. Anderson Cmty. Sch. Corp., 1983—; nat. cons. U.S. Dept. Edn.; dir. Madison County Cmty. Alliances to Promote Edn.; state rep. dist. 36 Ind. Ho. of Reps., Indpls., 2002—, vice chair, commerce and econ. devel. com., mem. ways and means, pub. policy, ethics and vets. affairs, and tech. R & D coms. Asst. prof. Anderson U.; vice chair econ. trade and cultural affairs NCSL; pub. policy and vets. affairs RMM. Candidate Ind. Ho. of Reps., 2000; mem. alumni bd. Ball State Tchrs. Coll. Mem.: United Way of Madison County, AAUW, LWV, Anderson Area C. of C., Anderson Rotary Club. Democrat. Episcopalian. Office: Ind Ho of Reps 200 W Washington St Indianapolis IN 46204-2786 Office Phone: 800-382-9842. E-mail: h36@in.gov.

AUSTIN, WANDA MURRY, systems engineer; b. N.Y.C., Sept. 08; d. Murry Pompey and Helen Lewis; m. Wade Austin Jr.; children: Wade, Wendell. MS in Sys. Engring., U. Pitts., 1977; PhD in Sys. Engring., U. So. Calif., 1988. Engr. Rockwell Internat., Anaheim, Calif., 1977-79, Aerospace Corp., El Segundo, Calif., 1979—. Contbr. chpt. to book: Quantitative Simulation, 1991. Recipient Outstanding Achievement award Women in Aerospace, 1996, King Spirit of the Dream award Space and Missile Sys. Ctr., 1999. Fellow AIAA; mem. Soc. Women Engrs. (sr., award 1996). Office: Aerospace Corp 15049 Conference Ctr Dr Chantilly VA 20151

AUSTIN-GARRISON, MARTHA A., education educator, researcher; d. Buck and Martha (Smallcanyon) Austin; m. Edward R Garrison, May 27, 1978; children: Nanibaa' A. Garrison, Bijiibaa' K. Garrison, Edward Austin Garrison II. MA in Edn., Ariz. State U., 2002. Faculty Dine Coll., Shiprock, N.Mex., 1990—; sec. Kayenta (Ariz.) Rsch. Assocs., Inc., 1980—. Rsch. project dir. Navajo Ethno-Medical Ency. Project, Kayenta, Ariz., 1975—80. Mem. Ariz. State Wide Health Cordinating Coun. Edward Sapir sscholar, Summer Linguistics Inst. at U. N.Mex., 1995. Home: P O Box 1950 Kayenta AZ 86033 Office: Dine College P O Box 580 Shiprock NM 87420 Office Phone: 505-368-3571. Personal E-mail: maustin@dinecollege.edu.

AUSTON, DAVID HENRY, former academic administrator, electrical engineer, educator; b. Toronto, Ont., Can., Nov. 14, 1940; arrived in U.S., 1963; BS, U. Toronto, 1962, MS, 1963; PhD, U. Calif., Berkeley, 1969. Rsch. physicist GM, Santa Barbara, Calif., 1963—66; tech. staff AT&T Bell Labs., Murray Hill, NJ, 1969—82, head dept., 1982—87; former prof. Columbia U., N.Y.C., chmn. elec. engring. dept., 1990, dean sch. engring. and applied sci., 1991—94; provost Rice U., Houston, 1994—99; pres. Case Western Res. U., Cleve., 1999—2002, Kavli Found. and The Kavli Inst., Oxnard, Calif. Author 1 book; contbr. scientific papers. Fellow: IEEE (Quantum Elecs. award 1990, Morris E. Leeds award 1991), Am. Phys. Soc., Am. Acad. Arts and Scis., Optical Soc. Am. (R.W. Wood prize 1985); mem.: NAE, Nat. Acad. Scis. Achievements include patents in field of 7. Office: The Kavli Inst 1801 Solar Dr Ste 250 Oxnard CA 93030

AUSTRIACO, NICANOR PIER GIORGIO, clergy member, researcher; b. Manila, The Phillipines, Nov. 1, 1968; s. Nicanor Camacho and Lilia Robles A. BSE in Bioengring. summa cum laude, U. Pa., 1989; PhD in Biology, MIT, 1996. Joined Order Preachers (Dominicans). Fellow Ludwig Inst. for Cancer Rsch. U. Coll. London, 1996-97; seminarian Dominican House of Studies, Washington, 1997—. Contbr. articles to profl. jours. Fellow Internat. Human Frontier Sci. Program, 1996-97, Howard Hughes Med. Inst., Bethesda, 1990-95; recipient Best Article award Nat. Assn. Engring. Coll. Mags., 1997. Roman Catholic. Home and Office: Dominican House of Studies 487 Michigan Ave NE Washington DC 20017-1584

AUSTRIAN, ROBERT, internist, medical educator, department chairman; b. Balt., Apr. 12, 1916; s. Charles Robert and Florence (Hochschild) Austrian; m. Babette Friedmann Bernstein, Dec. 29, 1963; stepchildren: Jill Bernstein, Toni Bernstein. AB, Johns Hopkins U., 1937, MD, 1941; DSc (hon.), Hahnemann Med. Coll., 1980, Phila. Coll. Pharmacy and Sci., 1981, U. Pa., 1987; DSc (hon.), SUNY, 1996. Diplomate Am. Bd. Internal Medicine. House officer Johns Hopkins Hosp., 1941—50, asst. dir. med. out-patient dept., 1951—52; assoc. prof. medicine, then prof. medicine SUNY Coll. Medicine, 1952—62; John Herr Musser prof., chmn. rsch. medicine U. Pa. Sch. Medicine, 1962—86, prof. emeritus, chmn. emeritus, 1986—. Attending physician Hosp. U. Pa.; Tyndale vis. lectr. and prof. Coll. Medicine U. Utah, 1964; spl. rsch. on infectious diseases, bacterial genetics; mem. Meningococcal Infections Commn., 1964—72, Commn. on Acute Respiratory Disease, 1965—72, Commn. Streptococcal and Staphylococcal Diseases, 1970—72, Armed Forces Epidemiol. Bd.; cons. surgeon gen. U.S. Army R&D Command, 1966—69; mem. subcom. streptococcus and pneumococcus Internat. Com. Bacteriol. Nomenclature; mem. allergy and immunology study sect. Nat. Inst. Allergy and Infectious Diseases, 1965—69, mem. bd. sci. counselors, 1967—70, chmn., 1969—70; mem. WHO Expert Adv. Panel Acute Bacterial Diseases, 1979—2001. Mem. editl. bd.: Jour. Bacteriology, 1964—69, Am. Rev. Respiratory Diseases, 1963—66, Bacteriol. Rev., 1967—71, Jour. Infectious Diseases, 1969—74, Antimicrobial Agents and Chemotherapy, 1972—86, Infection and Immunity, 1973—81, Revs. of Infectious Diseases, 1979—89, Vaccine, 1983—, guest editor: Drugs and Aging, 1999. Trustee Johns Hopkins U., 1963—69. Capt. M.C. U.S. Army, 1943—46. Recipient U.S. Typhus Commn. medal, 1947, Albert Lasker Clin. Med. Rsch. award, 1978, Phila. award, 1979, Willard O. Thompson award, Am. Geriatric Soc., 1981, Lifetime Sci. award, Inst. Advanced Studies in Immunology and Aging, 1997, Pasteur Merieux MSD award, 1st Internat. Symposium on Pneumococci and Pneumococcal Diseases, 1998, Maxwell Finland award, Nat. Found. for Infectious Diseases, 2001. Master: ACP (James D. Bruce Meml. award 1979); fellow: AAAS (chmn. sect. on med. scis. 1975), Am. Acad. Microbiology, N.Y. Acad. Scis.; mem.: NAS, Johns Hopkins Soc. Scholars, Infectious Disease Soc. Am. (pres. 1971, Maxwell Finland lecture award 1974, Bristol award 1986), Interurban Clin. Club (pres. 1970), Coll. Physicians Phila. (pres.-elect 1986, pres. 1988—89, Meritorious Svc. award 1980, Disting. Svc. medal 1997), Philadelphia County Med. Soc. (Strittmatter award 1979), N.Y. Acad. Medicine (sec. sect. microbiology 1961—62), Am. Assn. Immunologists, Balt. Med. Soc., Inst. Medicine, Am. Fedn. Clin. Rsch., Harvey Soc., Soc. Exptl. Biology and Medicine, Am. Philos. Soc., Am. Soc. Microbiology (v.p. N.Y. br. 1961—62), Am. Clin. and Climatol. Assn. (pres. 1984), Am. Soc. Clin. Investigation, Assn. Am. Physicians, 14 W. Hamilton St. Club, Omicron Delta Kappa, Alpha Omega Alpha, Sigma Xi, Phi Beta Kappa. Office: U Pa Sch Medicine Dept Rsch Medicine 522 Johnson Pavilion Philadelphia PA 19104-6088 Office Phone: 215-662-3186.

AUTELITANO, PHILIP M., marketing professional, consultant, writer; b. Schenectady, NY, Jan. 23, 1973; s. Philip Sr. M and Patricia M Autelitano; m. Tamara Leigh Robinson, Feb. 9, 1999; children: Ezekiel, Bruno. Cert. Guerrilla Mktg. Coach Guerrilla Mktg. Internat., 2004. Pres. P. M. Autelitano & Associates, Inc., Delray Beach, Fla., 1992—; ceo Mojo Beverage Co., Boca Raton, Fla., 1999—2001; pub./editor-in-chief Beachcomber Mag., Delray Beach, Fla., 2001—. Author: (book) 250 Ways to Save Money, Increase Sales and Maximize Your Profits!, Simplified Marketing Management, (e-book) 36 Ways to Promote Your Book Online.for Free!. Philanthropic and fundraising activities Mr. Holland's Opus Found., Caring Ho. Project, et al, Delray Beach, Fla., 2001—; pro bono mktg. and mgmt. consulting to minority entrepreneurs and start-ups Delray Beach, Fla., 2001—; philanthropic and fundraising activities Make-A-Wish Found., Albany, NY, 1995—96, Ronald McDonald Ho., 1995—96. Democrat-Npl. Roman Catholic. Achievements include Health & Fitness, 1998-1999, Credited with developing and introducing the first branded electrolyte-enhanced bottled water to the world. Avocations: writing, reading, classical guitar, travel. Office: P M Autelitano & Assoc Inc PO Box 7203 Delray Beach FL 33482-7203 Office Phone: 561-276-0931. E-mail: phil@urguru.com.

AUTEN, ARTHUR HERBERT, history professor; b. Cleve., Dec. 25, 1936; s. Herbert and Gladys Perry (Sessions) A.; m. Patricia Ann Kichak, June 5, 1971; children: David Arthur, Daniel Joseph. AB magna cum laude, Case Western Res. U., 1959, MA, 1960, PhD, 1965; cert. ednl. mgmt., Harvard U., 1972, CAS, 1977. Instr., asst. prof. history Westminster Coll., New Wilmington, Pa., 1963—66; asst. prof. history Colo. State U., Ft. Collins, 1966—69; v.p. planning, devel. and evaluation, dean Arts & Scis., U. Guam, Agana, 1970—76; pres. Alliance Coll., Cambridge Springs, Pa., 1977-81; acad. dean Coll. Basic Studies, U. Hartford, West Hartford, Conn., 1981-87, prof. history, 1987—2002. Sec. Pa. region 9/10 HIgher Edn. Planning Coun., 1979—80; vis. scholar Grad. Sch. Edn., Harvard U., 1988, prof. emeritus, 2002. Author: Critical Thinking Exercises for Western Civilization Courses, 1993, Readings in the History of Western Civilization: From the Dawn of Civilization to Columbus, From Columbus to Napoleon, From Napoleon to the Space Age, 1996; adv. editor Ann. Edits.: Am. History, 12th edit., 1993, 13th edit., 1995, 14th edit., 1997, 15th edit., 1999, 16th edit., 2001, 17th edit., 2002, Ann. Edits.: Western Civilization, 6th edit., 1991, 7th edit., 1993, 8th edit., 1995, 9th edit., 1997, 10th edit., 1999, 11th edit., 2001, 12th edit., 2002, World Civilization: A Brief History, 2d edit., 1993, 3d edit., 1998, A History of Civilization, 9th edit., 1995, Discovering the Western Past, 3d edit., 1995, Sources of the West, 3d edit., 1996. Cmty. devel. assistance com. City/Colls./Bus. Partnership, Meadville, Pa., 1980; mem. ednl. svcs. for cmty. devel., Guam Terr., 1972-76; spkr., events planner Kiwanis, Cambridge Springs, Pa., 1978-81; mem. Nat. Trust for Hist. Preservation. Recipient Hon. Membership pin, Polish Nat. Alliance, 1980, Cmty. Svc. citation, Mayor of Meadville, 1980, Ann. Svc. award, Gov. of Guam, 1976, Hon. Jagiellonian U. pin, Internat. Student Exch., 1979, Outstanding Educators Am. award, 1972, Tchg. Excellence designation, 1969; scholar U. Hartford scholar in humanities, 1997. Fellow: Phi Beta Kappa; mem.: New Eng. Hist. Assn., Am. Hist. Assn., Nat. Coun. Social Studies, Nat. Assn. Devel. Edn. (presenter, chair nat. conf. 1987, 1989—91, chmn. profl. interest group 1989—94, presenter, chair nat. conf. 1993, 1997, Dean's Recognition award 1986, cert. appreciation 1990, 1991, 1992), Orgn. Am. Historians (life Recognition award 1992), Mystic Seaport Mus. Am. and the Sea, Colonial Williamsburg Found., Phi Delta Kappa, Chi Omicron Gamma. Avocations: travel, theater, chess, model railroading, reading. Home: 17 Peddler Dr Windsor CT 06095-1748

AUTEN, DAVID CHARLES, lawyer; b. Phila., Apr. 4, 1938; s. Charles Raymond and Emily Lillian (Dickel) A.; m. Suzanne Crozier Plowman, Feb. 1, 1969; children: Anne Crozier, Meredith Smedley. BA, U. Pa., 1960, JD, 1963. Bar: Pa. 1963. Ptnr. Reed Smith LLP (and predecessors), Phila., 1963—. Author articles in field. V.p. N.E. Cmty. Mental Health Ctr., 1971-72; vice chmn. alumni ann. giving U. Pa., 1975-77, 81-82, chmn., 1982-84, trustee, 1977-80, 83-88; pres. Gen. Alumni Soc., 1977-80; chmn. Benjamin Franklin Assocs., 1975-77, 81-82, bd. overseers Sch. Arts and Scis., 1983-96; trustee U. Pa. Health Sys., 1995—, Pa. Medicine, 2002-, Springside Sch., 1985-88, v.p., 1987-88; pres. Soc. of Coll., 1975-77; v.p. Assn. Reps. for Educated Action, 1971-79; bd. mgrs. Presbyn.-U. Pa. Med. Ctr., 1980—, vice chmn., 1983-85, 88-95, chmn., 2002—; trustee Presbyn. Found. for Phila., 1986—, vice chm., 1996-98, chmn., 1998—; bd. mgrs. Phila. City Inst., 1981—, treas., 1990-99; bd. dirs. Kearsley Home, 1974-2002, treas., 1990-96, chmn., 1996-2002; bd. mgrs. St. Peter's Sch., 1975-88, pres., 1978-79; bd. dirs. Greater Phila. Internat. Network, 1989-94, Com. of Seventy, 1990-2003, Courtland Found., Del Pres Health Care Inc., New Courtland Elder Svs., chmn., 1998—; mem. econ. devel. com. Greater Phila. First Corp.; rector's warden Christ Ch., Phila., 1996-2001. Mem. ABA, Pa. Bar Assn. (vice chmn. real property sect. 1985-87, chmn. 1987-88), Am. Land Title Assn., Phila. Bar Assn. (vice chmn. young lawyers sect. 1971-72), Juristic Soc. (pres.), Am. Coll. Real Estate Lawyers, Interfrat. Alumni Coun. U. Pa. (pres. 1970-74), French Am. C. of C. (bd. dirs. 1989—), Phi Beta Kappa, Theta Xi (pres. 1974-76, chmn. found. 1977-86), Rittenhouse Club (pres. 1979-82), Union League (bd. dirs., v.p., pres. 1993-94, chmn. Lincoln Found. 1996-2002), Fourth St. Club (bd. dirs. 1998-2000), Phila. Club. Episcopalian (vestryman). Home: 120 Delancey St Philadelphia PA 19106-4303 Office: Reed Smith LLP 2500 One Liberty Pl Philadelphia PA 19103

AUTEN, DONALD R., lawyer; b. Phila., July 27, 1946; BA cum laude, U. Pa., 1968, JD cum laude, 1971. Bar: Pa. 1972, Mass. 1998, US Tax Ct., US Dist. Ct. Ea. Dist. Pa., Supreme Ct. Pa., Supreme Ct. Mass. Judicial clk. to Hon. Thomas A. Masterson US Dist. Ct. Ea. Dist. Pa., 1971—72; assoc. Duane Morris LLP, Phila., 1972—77, ptnr., 1978—, chair firm tax dept., 1994—99, co-chair firm health law dept., 1999—, mem. partners bd. Fellow Am. Coll. Tax Counsel; mem. ABA (chair affiliated and related corporations com. 1983-85, mem. taxation sect.), Pa. Bar Assn. (mem. tax law sect.), Phila. Bar Assn. (bd. governors 1995-96, mem. tax sect., vice chair 1993-94, chair 1995-96, mem. bus. law sect. healthcare subcom.), Am. Health Lawyers Assn., Pa. Soc. Healthcare Attorneys. Office: Duane Morris LLP One Liberty Pl Philadelphia PA 19103-7396 Office Phone: 215-979-1969. Office Fax: 215-979-1020. Business E-Mail: auten@duanemorris.com.

AUTHELET, KEITH A., information technology executive; Sr. dir., bus. process and tech. mgmt. Lotus Services Group; v.p. & chief info. officer Gilbane Bldg. Co., Providence. Bd. dir. WhyData. Named one of top 10 CIOs, Info. Week mag., 2001, one of top tech. innovators, 2004. Office: VP & CIO Gilbane Bldg Co Seven Jackson Walkway Providence RI 02903 Business E-Mail: kauthelet@gilbaneco.com.

AUTHEMENT, PATTY LYNN, music educator; d. Claymile, Sr. and Linda Leonard LeCompte; m. Troy Joseph Authement, June 16, 1995; children: Courtney Lynn, Ryan Joseph. B of Music Edn., Nicholls State U., Thibodaux, La., 1995. Cert. tchr. La., 1996. Band dir. H.L. Bourgeois H.S., Gray, La., 1995—98, Grand Caillou Mid. Sch., Houma, La., 1998—. Named Tchr. of the Yr., Grand Caillou Mid. Sch., 2004—05; recipient Outstanding Student Tchr. award, Nicholls State U., Coll. of Edn., 1995; grantee, Terrebonne Found. for Acad. Excellence grantee, 2001—02. Mem.: Music Educator's Nat. Conf. (assoc.), La. Bandmasters Assn. (assoc.), Dist. VII Band Dirs. Assn. (assoc.). Independent. Roman Catholic. Avocations: reading, music, movies, Nascar. Office Phone: 985-879-3001.

AUTHEMENT, RAY P., college president; b. Chauvin, La., Nov. 19, 1928; s. Elias Lawrence and Elphia (Duplantis) A.; m. Barbara B. Braud, June 1, 1950; children: Kathleen Elizabeth, Julie Ann. BS, U. Southwestern La., 1950; MS, La. State U., 1952; PhD, 1956. Instr. La. State U., Baton Rouge, 1952-56; asso. prof. McNeese State Coll., Lake Charles, La., 1956-57, U. Southwestern La., 1957-59, prof. math., from, 1959, acad. v.p., 1966-73, pres., 1973—. Vis. prof. U. N.C., Chapel Hill, 1962-63 Mem. Downtown Devel. Com. Lafayette, 1972—; commr., mem. exec. com. Lafayette Econ. Devel. Authority, 1988—; mem. La. Bicentennial Commn., 1973, Lafayette Bicentennial Commn., 1973, Econ. Devel. Com., Lafayette, 1973, Sch. Bd. Fatima Parish, Lafayette, 1963-65; bd. dirs. United Way, 1973, U. Southwestern La. Found., 1967, Gulf South Rsch. Inst., 1985-91; trustee Lafayette Gen. Hosp., 1981—; mem. bd. advisers John Gray Inst., 1982-91, St. Joseph Sem., 1967; mem. Commn. Colleges So. Assn. Colls., 1981-83; active Cajundome Commn., 1988—; bd. dirs. Lafayette Health Ventures, Inc., 1989—, Enterprise Ctr. of La., Inc., 1990—, Affiliated Blind of La., Inc., 1991—, La. Partnership for Tech. and Innovation, 1989—, chmn., 1993; chmn. Acadiana Navigation Channel Task Force, 1990—; bd. dirs. Coun. for a Better La., 1992—, La. chpt. Leukemia and Lymphoma Soc., 2005. Named Outstanding Citizen of Acadiana Internat. Rels. Assn. Acadiana, 1991; recipient Lafayette Civic Cup award, 1991. Mem. AAAS, Lafayette C. of C. (dir. 1983—), Blue Key, Phi Kappa Phi, Kappa Mu Epsilon, Sigma Pi Sigma, Phi Kappa Theta. Roman Catholic. Home: PO Drawer 41008 Lafayette LA 70504 Office: U La at Lafayette PO Drawer 41008 Lafayette LA 70504

AUTIN, ERNEST ANTHONY, II, chemistry professor, consultant; b. Thibodaux, La., Sept. 18, 1957; s. Ernest Anthony Autin and Louella Theresa (Foret) Matherne; m. Debra Anne Breaux; children: Daniel Joseph, Theresa Renee, Beau-Thomas Bryan. BS, Nicholls State U., 1979; MS, U. So. Miss., 1982; postgrad., Tulane U., 1986-87. Cert. master practitioner neuro-linguistic programming. Sr. rsch. chemist DAP, Inc., Dayton, Ohio, 1982-83; head chemistry dept. South Coast Sugars, Raceland, La., 1983-84; asst. prof. chemistry Nicholls State U., Thibodaux, 1984-90; dir. tng., internal orgnl. planning and devel. cons. Fina Oil & Chem. Co., Port Arthur, Tex., 1990-92, process/quality engr. La Porte, Tex., 1992-93; internal Orgnl. Planning and Devel. cons. Entergy Svcs., Inc., Beaumont, Tex., 1993-95; mgr., performance improvement and change mgmt. Ernst & Young, Houston, 1995-96; exec.-in-residence info. svcs. and info. techs. Temple-Inland, Inc., Diboll, Tex., 1995—97; mgmt. cons., owner E.A. Autin & Co., 1997—. Faculty advisor Nicholls State U. Scis. Soc., 1984—90; sci. coord. COGNIS program Upward bound, Thibodaux, 1984—90; cons. La. sugar cane industry, 1984—90; cons. heavy metal analysis, 1984—90; spkr., 1985—; sr. lead project mgr. Engring. Tech. Support Fossil Energy Bus. Support, Beaumont, 1994—95. Author: Reach to the Wounded Healer, 2004, Of the Oaks, 2005; contbr. articles to various publs. Music min. St. Thomas Aquinas Cath. Student Ctr., Thibodaux, 1984—90; bd. dirs. Port Arthur (Tex.) YMCA, 1990—92, sustaining campaign chairperson, 1991—92; bd. dirs. fed. credit union Nicholls State U., 1984—86. Recipient Grand Prytanis Key Leader award, 1993—94, T.K.E. Grand Prytanis award, 1995. Mem.: ASTD (cert. HRD prol. U. Okla. 1992), Am. Chem. Soc., Am. Soc. Sugar Cane Technologists, Soc. Plastic Engrs., Am. Inst. Chemists, Tau Kappa Epsilon, Tau Kappa Epsilon (grantee advisor 1980—90, chpt. advisor 1981—82, Top Alumni award 1982, 1990), Phi Kappa Phi (sec. 1985—86). Avocations: jogging, tennis, salt water fishing, weightlifting.

AUTRY, ALAN, mayor, actor, former professional football player, film company executive; b. Shreveport, La., 1952; m. Kimberlee Autry; children: Lauren, Heather, Austin. Attended, U. of the Pacific. Quarterback Green Bay Packers; founder & pres. Dirt Road Prodns.; mayor City of Fresno, Calif., 2001—. Office: 2600 Fresno St 2nd Fl Fresno CA 93721-3600 E-mail: mayor@fresno.gov.*

AUTRY, CAROLYN, artist, art history educator; b. Dubuque, Iowa, Dec. 12, 1940; d. William Tilden and Vela (Laseman) A.; m. Peter Elloian, May 27, 1966; 1 dau., Cybele Justine. BA, U. Iowa, 1963, MFA, 1965. Instr. art, art history Baldwin-Wallace Coll., Berea, Ohio, 1965-66; adj. assoc. prof. art history dept. art Ctr. for Visual Arts U. Toledo, 1966-2001. Artist-in-residence Sch. Arts in France, Lacoste, 1984, Lacoste, 87, adj. instr. in printmaking, 87. Exhbns. include San Francisco Mus. Art, 1973, Oakland Mus., 1975, Santa Barbara Mus., 1975, U. Mo., 1975, Ljubljana Internat. Biennial, 1975, 81, 87, Internationale Grafik Biennale, Frechen, W. Ger., 1976, Biella, Italy, 1976, Genoa, Italy, 1976, Leverkusen, Fed. Republic Germany, 1977, Phila. Mus. Art, 1980, 97, Visual Arts Ctr., Anchorage, Alaska, 1980, U. Louisville, 1981, U. Dallas, 1981, Grunwald Ctr. Graphic Arts, UCLA, 1981, Ohio State U., 1982, Belle Arts & Graphic Inc., Nyack, N.Y., 1982, Mus. Arts and Sci., Macon, Ga., 1983, U. Tenn., Knoxville, 1983, Pratt Graphics Ctr., NYC, 1983, Calif. State Coll. San Bernardino, 1983, Am. Embassy Cultural Ctr., Belgrade, Yugoslavia, 1983, Taipei Fine Arts Mus., 1983, 85, 87, 89, 91, 95, Museo Arte Contemporaneo, Ibiza, Spain, 1984, Drake U., 1985, Fla. State U., 1985, Irvine (Calif.) Fine Arts Ctr., 1986, Inter-graphic Internat., East Berlin, 1984, 87, Met. Mus. Art Ctr., Coral Gables, Fla., 1987, Fifth Internat. Graphic Exhbn., Catania, Italy, 1988, Korean Cultural Svc. Gallery, L.A., Walker Hill Gallery, Seoul, Korea, and Korean Embassy Cultural Ctr., Paris, 1989, Barbican Art Centre, London, Salford (Gt. Britain) Mus., Mead Gallery, U. Warwick, Coventry, Gt. Britain, Brighton and Poly. Gallery, Brighton, Gt. Britain, 1989, Internat. Exhbn. Prints, Kanagawa, Japan, 1989, 90, 95, 97, Gallery Fine Arts Ctr. Seoul, 1989, Nat. Exhbn. Prints, Ringling Sch. Art and Design, Sarasota, Fla., 1990, Internat. Impact Art Festival, Kyoto City Mus., Japan, 1990, 91, 92, 93, 94, Ohio Drawing and Printmaking Invitational, Upper Arlington, 1991, Fondation Mona Bismarck, Paris, 1991, Fine Arts Assn. Gallery, Hanoi, Republic of Vietnam, 1991, Prints Internat., 1992, Silvermine Guild Arts Ctr., New Caanan, Conn., 1993, Taejon (Korea) Expo Graphic Art, 1993, Soc. Am. Graphic Artists 65th Nat., N.Y.C., 1993, Architecture in Contemporary Printmaking, Boston Archtl. Ctr., 1994, Am. Inst. Architecture, Washington, 1994, U. N.H., 1995, Midwest Select, South Bend Regional Mus. of Art, Ind., 1994, Triton Mus., Santa Clara, Calif., 1995, Mansfield (Ohio) Art Ctr., 1995, 20th Harper Nat. Exhbn., Macomb, Ill., 1996, Hunterdon Art Ctr., Clinton, N.J., 1996, Soc. Am. Graphic Artists 66th Nat. Print Exhbn., Hanover, N.J., 1997, Internat. Print Triennial, Cracow, Poland, 1997, Fla. Printmakers Ann. Nat. Print Exhbn., Jacksonville, 1997, 2000, Institut Franco-Américain, Rennes, France, 1997, Prized Impressions, Internat. Exhbn. of Prints, Phila. Mus. of Art, 1997, Nat. Print Exhbn., Calif. State Univ. Chico, 1997, 22d nat. Print Biennial Silvermine Guild Arts Ctr., Conn., 1998, Counterpoint Exhbn. Hill Country Arts Found., Tex., 1998, 99, 2000, Printmakers 98, Pittsburgh Ctr. for the Arts, Penn., 1998, U. Hawaii, Hilo, 2000, 13th Ann. McNeese Nat. Works on Paper Exhbn., McNeese State U., Lake Charles, La., Baton Rouge (La.) Gallery, 2000, Printwork 2K, 2000, The 7th Ann. Nat. Juried Exhbn., Barrett Art Ctr., Poughkeepsie, N.Y.C., 2000, 1st Biennial Nat. Print Competition, No. Ariz. U., Flagstaff, 2002, Internat. Print exhbn. invitational, Minsk, Belarus, 2002, Soc. Am. Graphic Artists 69th Nat. Exhbn. Arts Student League, NY, 2002, Interior/Exterior

Landscapes, U. Wyo., Laramie and U. Dallas, Irving, Tex., 2002, 23d Nat. Print Exhbn., Art Link Contemporary Art Gallery, Ft. Wayne, Ind., 2003, L.S. Printmakers Soc. Juried Membership Exhbn., Brand Libr. Art Galleries, Glendale, Calif., 2003, Boston Printmakers Juried N.Am. Print Exhbn., 1971-81, 86-87, 2003, Soc. Am. Graphic Artists, Susan Teller Gallery, N.Y.C., 2004, Calif. State U., Chico, 2004, Calif. Soc. Printmakers 90th Ann. Exhbn., Works Gallery, San Jose, 2004, Artlink 24th Ann. Nat. Print Exhbn., Fort Wayne, Ind., 2004, 25th Ann. Nat. Print Exhbn., 2005, Calif. Soc. Printmakers 91st Ann. Exhbn., San Francisco Bay Model Visitor Ctr., Sausalito, 2005, Soc. Am. Graphic Artists, Art Students League of NY, 2005, Print Clubo f Albany Artist Mem. Show, Cooperstown (NY) Art Assn. Gallery, 2005, others; represented in permanent collections Libr. of Congress, Phila. Mus. Art, Worcester Art Mus., MountHolyoke Coll., U. Colo.,Bradley U., Calif. State U., San Diego, Ga. State U., U. S.D., U.N.D., U. Louisville, St. Lawrence U., U.Dallas, Hunterdon Art Ctr., Clinton, N.J., Fitchburg (Mass.) Mus., Duxbury (Mass.) Art Complex, Elvehjem Mus. Art U. Wis.-Madison, Inst. per la Cultura E L'Arte, Catania, Italy, Lakeview Mus. Arts and Scis., Peoria, Ill., Nat. Mus. Fine Arts, Hanoi. Recipient Boston Printmakers N.Am. Print Exhbn. award 1971, 79, 80, 81, 87, Pennell award Libr. Congress, 1971, 75, Phila. Print Club awards, 1972, 75, 79, Wesleyan Coll. Internat. award of merit, 1980, Anne Steele Marsh award Hunterdon Art Ctr., Clinton, N.J., 1991, Bradley U. Nat. award, 1991, Friends of the Janet Turner Gallery Nat. Exhbn. award Chico State U., Calif., 1995, Exhbn. award 16th Nat. Print Exhbn., Artlink, 1996, Exhbn. award 17th Nat. Print Exhbn., 1997, Counterpoint, 2000, Nat. Exhbn. award The Hill Country Arts Found., 2000, Exhbn. award 5th Nat. Print Exhbn., Calif. State U., Chico, 2004; Ford Found. grantee, 1961-63, Ohio Arts Coun. grantee, 1979, 90, Yale-Norfolk Summer Sch. Art and Music scholar, 1962. Mem.: The Print Club of Albany (Ledyard Logswell Jr. Meml. prize 1995), Coll. Art Assn. Am., Calif. Soc. Printmakers, Soc. Am. Graphic Artists (Jo Miller award 1985, Phillip Monteith award 1986, George Sharmon Purchase prize 2005), LA Printmakers Soc., Boston Printmakers (Louis Black award 1971), Phi Beta Kappa. Address: 26114 W River Rd Perrysburg OH 43551-9128 Office Phone: 419-872-9558. Personal E-mail: autello@aol.com.

AUTRY, CHERYL RENEE, special education educator; b. Houston, Jan. 14, 1949; d. Joe and Susie Autry; children: Ajani Mazi, Kimani Khary. *Until the age of three, I lived in numerous foster homes. As miracles occur, I was adopted by my aunt and uncle, Susie and Joe Autry. I grew up on their 65-acre farm in Kohrville, a suburb of Houston, Texas. My school was five miles from the farm and at times I had to walk to school. I wore clothing made from feed sacks. My shoes were never too large: if they were too big, I stuffed them with paper; if they were too small, the toes were cut out. In spite of hardship, I pursued a college education; knowledge is priceless and cannot be taken away.* AA, Skyline Coll., 1978; BA, U. Calif.-Berkeley, 1981. Tchr. spl. edn. Spring Ind. Sch. Dist., Houston, 1996—. Author: (books) Harvest Time, Our World, short stories, poems. Founder, mem. Women History Mus., Washington, 1996, Friends of Pres. Clinton, Little Rock, 2004; leadership coun. So. Poverty Law Ctr., Montgomery, Ala., 2002. Mem.: Am. Fedn. Tchrs. Avocations: writing, gardening, walking. Home: 2238 Laurel Oaks Houston TX 77014

AUWERS, STANLEY JOHN, motor carrier executive; b. Grand Rapids, Mich., Mar. 22, 1923; s. Joseph T. and Cornelia (Moelhoek) A.; m. Elizabeth Kruis, Apr. 6, 1946; children— Ellen (Mrs. William Northway), Stanley John, Thomas. Student, Calvin Coll., 1940-41; BBA, U. Mich., 1943. C.P.A., Mich. With Ernst & Ernst, Detroit, 1943-51; controller Interstate Motor Freight System, Grand Rapids, Mich., 1951-61, v.p., controller, 1961-65, v.p. finance, 1965-69, exec. v.p., 1969-72; also dir.; pres. Transam. Freight Lines, Detroit, 1973—. Chmn. cost com. Mich. Trucking Adv. Bd. to Mich. Pub. Service Commn., 1958-63; mem. citizens com. to study Mich. tax structure advisory Mich. Ho. Reps., 1958 Mem. Am. Motor Carriers Central Freight Assn. (gov. regular common carrier conf.), Mich. Motor Carriers Central Freight Assn. (v.p., gov.), Tax Execs. Inst., Am. Inst. C.P.A.s, Trucking Employers. Presbyterian. Home: 3099 Lakeshore Dr Douglas MI 49406 Office: 3684 28th St SE Grand Rapids MI 49512-1606 E-mail: sauwers@umich.edu.

AVADHUT, HITENDRANANDAACARYA, spiritual counselor, yoga instructor; b. Raigarh, India, Jan. 24, 1968; s. Shouki Lal and Shanti Devi Gupta. BA, Guru Ghasidas U., Bilaspur, India, 1988. Sec. Renaissance Universal Anada Marga, Dallas, 1992—. Avocations: music, poetry. Home: 3157 CR 1670 Willow Springs MO 65793 Office: Renaissance Universal 2355 Trellis Pl Richardson TX 75081 E-mail: hitendrananda@hotmail.com.

AVAKIAN, GAYANE, pianist, organist; b. Baku, USSR, Apr. 25, 1956; arrived in US, 1992; d. Albert Avakov and Janeta Avakova. BA, Spl. Music Sch., Baku, Azerbaijan, 1974; MusM, State Conservatory, Yerevan, Armenia, 1979, DMA, 1984; piano performance studies, Julliard, NYC, 2002—04. Prof. piano Komitas State Conservatory, Yerevan, 1984—92; faculty NY Conservatory, Queens, NY, 1993—95, LI Sch. Music, Albertson, 1995—2004; pianist Holy Martyrs Armenian Day Sch., Bayside, NYC, 1998—2004. Sub. organist Armenian Ch. Holy Martyrs, Bayside, NY, 1993—2004, St. Sarkis Armenian Ch., Douglaston, NY, 1992—2004; organist First Ch. Christ Scientist, Flushing, NY, 1992—2004. Musician: (solo and chamber recitals) Julliard Sch., Weil Recital Hall at Carnegie, NY, Staller Ctr. for the Arts, Stony Brook, NY, Harry Chapin Lakeside Theatre, NY, St. Bartholomew Ch., NY. Pianist HMAD Sch. benefit, 2004; concert, fundraiser musician St. Illuminator Sch., Woodside, NY, 2004, Armenian Aged Home, Fair Lawn, NJ, 2004; music dir. Flintridge Montessory Sch., 2005—; organist 1st Ch. Christ, Sciedntist, Altadena, Calif., 2005—. Recipient Third Prize, 1st Trans-Caucasian Chamber Music Competition, USSR, 1982, Best Accompanist Diploma, Internat. Competition, Germany, 1987, Spl. Prize of Press, Music Competition, Trapani, Italy, 1989, Second Prize, Internat. Chamber, Trapani, 1989. Mem.: Music Tchr. Assn. Calif., Am. Guild Organists. Home: 3635 Third Ave Glendale CA 91214 E-mail: gapiano@cs.com.

AVAKOFF, JOSEPH CARNEGIE, medical consultant, law consultant; b. Fairbanks, Alaska, July 15, 1936; s. Harry B. and Margaret (Adams) Avakoff; m. Teddy I. Law, May 7, 1966; children: Caroline, Joe E., John. AA, U. Calif., Berkeley, 1956, AB, 1957; MD, U. Calif., San Francisco, 1961; JD, Santa Clara U., 1985. Bar: Calif. 1987; diplomate Am. Bd. Surgery, Am. Bd. Plastic Surgery. Physicist U.S. Naval Radiol. Def. Lab., San Francisco, 1957, 59; intern So. Pacific Gen. Hosp., San Francisco, 1961-62; resident in surgery Kaiser Found. Hosp., San Francisco, 1962-66; resident in plastic surgery U. Tex. Sch. Medicine, San Antonio, 1970-72; pvt. practice specializing in surgery Sacramento, 1966-70; pvt. practice specializing in plastic surgery Los Gatos and San Jose, Calif., 1972-94; cons. to med. and legal professions, 1994—. Clin. instr. Sch. Medicine U. Calif., Davis, 1967—70; chief dept. surgery Mission Oaks Hosp., Los Gatos, 1988—90; chief divsn. plastic surgery Good Samaritan Hosp., San Jose, 1988—91; expert med. reviewer Med. Bd. Calif., 1995—2001; spl. cons. Calif. Dept. Corps., 1997—2002; presenter numerous med. orgns. Contbr. articles to profl. jours. Mem. San Jose Adv. Commn. Health, 1975—82; bd. govs. San Jose YMCA, 1977—80. Mem.: AMA, Union Am. Physicians and Dentists, Santa Clara County Med. Assn., Santa Clara County Bar Assn., Calif. Med. Assn., Phi Beta Kappa, Phi Eta Sigma. Republican. Presbyterian. Avocations: music, photography, computer programming. Home: 6832 Rockview Ct San Jose CA 95120-5607

AVALLE-ARCE, JUAN BAUTISTA, Spanish language educator; b. Buenos Aires, May 13, 1927; came to U.S., 1948; s. Juan B. and Maria Martina Avalle-Arce; m. Constance Marginot, Aug. 20, 1953 (dec. 1969); children: Juan Bautista, Maria Martina, Alejandro Alcantara; m. Diane Janet Pamp, Aug. 30, 1969 (div.); children: Maria la Real Alejandra, Fadrique Martín Manuel. AB, Harvard U., 1951, MA, 1952, PhD, 1955; LittD (hon.), U. Castilla-La Mancha, Spain. Tutor, Harvard U., 1953-55; asst. prof., then assoc. prof. Spanish, Ohio State U., 1955-62; prof. Spanish, Smith Coll., Northampton, Mass., 1962-66, Sophia Smith prof. Hispanic studies, 1966-69; William Rand Kenan, Jr. prof. Spanish, U. N.C., Chapel Hill, 1969-85; prof. Spanish U. Calif., Santa Barbara, 1985—, chmn. dept. Spanish and Portuguese, 1991-95, dir. Summer Inst. Hispanic Langs. and Culture, 1991—, José Miguel de Barandiarán prof. Basque studies, 1993—. Vis. scholar Univ. Ctr. Ga., 1972, lectr., 1961—, Univ. Ctr. Va., 1976; vis. prof. U. Salamanca, 1982, 84, 86, 88, U. Málagà, 1987, 90, 91, U. della Tuscia (Italy), 1988, Sophia U. (Japan), 1988, Kyoto U. Fgn. Affairs, 1988, U. Cuyo, U. Buenos Aires, 1989, Alcalá de Henares, 1995; vis. Hillyer Prof. Humanities U. Nev., Reno, 1996; Eccles scholar State U. Utah, 2003, Garner vis. scholar, 2003; PhD program evaluator N.Y. State Bd. Regents; cons. Coun. Grad. Schs. in U.s.; reader Nat. Humanities Ctr., Govt. Found. for 5th Centennial of Discovery of Am., Spain; cultural corr. Radio Nacional de España; ofcl. guest Euskadiko Erradio, Spain, 1988-89. Author: Conocimiento y vida en Cervantes, 1959, La novela pastoril española, 1959, 2d enlarged edit., 1974, La Galatea de Cervantes, 2 vols., 1961, 2d rev. edit., 1987, Gonzalo Fernández de Oviedo, 1962, 2d edit., 1989, El Inca Garcilaso en sus Comentarios, 1961, Deslindes cervantinos, 1961, Three Exemplary Novels, 1964, Bernal Francès y su Romance, 1966, El Persiles de Cervantes, 1969, Los entremeses de Cervantes, 1969, Don Juan Valera y Morsamor, 1970, El cronista Pedro de Escavias Una vida del Siglo XV, 1972, Suma cervantina, 1973, Narradores hispanoamericanos de hoy, 1973, Las Memorias de Gonzalo Fernández de Oviedo, 2 vols., 1974, El Peregrino en su patria de Lope de Vega, 1973, Nuevos deslindes cervantinos, 1974, Temas hispánicos medievales, 1975, Don Quijote como forma de vida, 1976, Dintorno de una època dorada, 1978, Cervantes, Don Quixote, annotated critical edit., 2 vols., 1978, rev. and enlarged edit., 1995, Cervantes, Novelas ejemplares, annotated edit., 3 vols., 1982, Lope de Vega, Las hazañas del Segundo David, 1984; La Galatea de Cervantes: 400 Años Despuès, 1985, Garci Rodriguez de Montalvo: Amadís de Gaula, 2 vols., 1985, Amadís de Gaula: El primitivo y el de Montalvo, 1991, Lecturas, 1987, Gonzalo Fernández de Oviedo, Batallas y quinquagenas, 1989, Garci Rodriguez de Montalvo Amadis de Gaula, 2 vols., 1991, Cancionero del Almirante don Fadrique Euriquez, 1993, Enciclopedia Cervantina, 1995, Poesía completa de Jorge de Montemayor, 1996, La épica colonial, 2000, Una obra olviera de Gonzalo Fernandez de Ovideo, 2003. Trustee Teutonic Order of the Levant, Marqués de la Lealtad. Recipient Bonsoms medal Spain, 1961; Guggenheim fellow, 1961; grantee Am. Coun. Learned Socs., 1965, 68; grantee NEH, 1968, 1978-80; grantee Am. Philos. Soc., 1961, 67; recipient Susan Anthony Potter Lit. prize, 1951; Centro Gallego Lit. prize, 1947; Diploma of Merit, Università delle Arti, Italy; named Grand Companion, Societé Internationale de la Noblesse Héréditaire. Sr. fellow Southeastern Inst. Medieval and Renaissance Studies; hon. fellow Soc. Spanish and Spanish Am. Studies; fellow Colegio Mayor Arzobispo D. Alonso de Fonseca of U. Salamanca; mem. MLA, Acad. Lit. Studies, Am. Acad. Rsch. Historians Medieval Spain, Academia Argentina de Letras, Anglo Am. Basque Studies Soc., Cervantes Soc. Am. (pres. 1979—), Ctr. for Medieval and Renaissance Studies, UCLA (assoc.), Soc. de Bibliofilos Espanoles, Modern Humanities Rsch. Assn., South Atlantic MLA, Asociación de Cervantistas (bd. mem.), Assn. Internac. de Hispanistas, Renaissance Soc. Am. (nat. del. to exec. coun. 1971), Real Sociedad Vascongada de Amigos del Pais, Centro de Estudios Jacobeos, Inst. d'Etudes Medievales, Inst. de Lit. Iberoamericana, Hispanic Soc. Am., Acad. Lit. Studies (charter), Mediaeval Acad. Am., Real Academia de Buenas Letras de Barcelona, Instituto Internacional de Literatura Iberoamericana, Sovereign Mil. Teutonic Order of the Levant (bailiff, knight grand cross, Grand Prior, Grand Priory of the U.S.), Harvard Club. Clubs: Triangle Hunt (Durham) (gentleman Whipper-in); U. N.C. Polo, Combined Training Events Assn. Office: U Calif 4323 Phelps Hall Santa Barbara CA 93106

AVALOS, HECTOR IGNACIO, language educator; b. Nogales, Sonora, Mexico, Oct. 8, 1958; s. Magdalena Avalos Bernal and Ignacio Arizmendi; m. Cynthia Dee Schultz, May 8, 2000. PhD, Harvard U., 1991. Carolina minority postdoctoral fellow U. N.C., Chapel Hill, 1991—93; assoc. prof. Iowa State U., Ames, 1993—. Dir. U.S. Latino studies program Iowa State U., Ames. Author: (book) Illness and Health Care in the Ancient Near East: The Role of the Temple in Greece, Mesopotamia, and Israel. Exec. dir. sci. exam. of religion com. Coun. for Secular Humanism, Amherst, NY, 1997. Independent. Avocations: travel, music, debate. Home: 3604 Grand Ave Ames IA 50010 Office: Iowa State Univ 402 Catt Hall Ames IA Office Phone: 515-294-0051. Office Fax: 515-294-0780. E-mail: havalos@iastate.edu.

A'VANT, ELIZABETH ROSE, school psychologist, educator; d. Avelino José Rose and Alice; m. John Peter A'Vant, Feb. 26; children: Alexander Rose, Johnathan, Derrek. BS in Early Childhood Edn., Wheelock Coll., Boston, 1980; MA in Edn. Psychology, RI Coll., Providence, 1984, cert. of advanced grad. studies, 1987. Cert. life profl. sch. psychologist State of RI and Mass., life profl. tch. elem. edn. State of RI and Mass. Tchr. Bishop McVinney Elem. Sch., Providence, 1981—84, Cmty. Prep. Sch., Providence, 1984—87; sch. psychologist Newport Regional Spl. Edn. Program, Portsmouth, RI, 1987—88; ednl. cons. Jostens Learning Corp., Orlando, Fla., 1988—89, New Haven, 1989—90; outpatient supervisor Map Alcohol and Drug Rehab., Providence, 1990; sch. psychologist Providence Sch. Dept., 1990—; field examiner Psychol. Corp., San Antonio, 2002—. Cons. Ctr. Individualized Tng. and Edn., Providence, 2003—. Scholarship chairwoman Cape Verdean Profl. Ctr., 2001—. Mem.: Nat. Assn. Sch. Psychologists, RI Sch. Psychologist Assn. (Profl. Svc. award 1996), Down Syndrome Soc. RI (scholarship chairwoman 1998—). Roman Catholic. Avocations: reading, photography, baking, travel. Home: 29 Mark Dr Lincoln RI 02865 Office: Providence Sch Dist 797 Westminster St Providence RI 02907

AVANT, GAYLE, political scientist, educator; b. Mercedes, Tex., Aug. 23, 1940; s. George Clarence and Winnie Lela (Bagley) Avant; m. Patricia Kay Coalson, Sept. 1, 1970; children: Samantha, Celia. BA, U. Tex., 1962; MA, U. N.C., 1965, PhD, 1969. Devel. officer AID/State Dept., Washington, 1966—68; asst. prof. Miami U., Oxford, Ohio, 1968—70; assoc. prof. polit. sci. Baylor U., Waco, Tex., 1970—. Vis. prof. polit. sci., sr. lectr. U. Ballarat, Australia, 1996—97. Editor: Foundations of Citizenship, 1990. State dir. Fellowship of Baptist Educators, 2005; dir. Baylor Washington Program, 1985—92; treas. Am.-Thai Found. Bd., 1993—; sec. treas. Coins for Tchrs., 2001—. Mem.: Internat. Assn. Christian Higher Edn., Am. Polit. Sci. Assn. Baptist, Tex. Coun. Social Studies, Nat. Coun. Social Studies, S.W. Social Sci. Assn. Office Phone: 254-710-6052. Business E-Mail: Gayle_Avant@Baylor.edu.

AVANT, ROBERT FRANK, physician, educator; b. Chisholm, Minn., 1937; m. Betty Jensen, Dec. 28, 1962; children: Paul, Gregory, Todd. MD, U. Minn., 1963. Intern San Bernardino, Calif. County Hosp., 1963-64; chief of family practice Glenwood Hills Hosp., 1970-71, chief of staff, 1972; dir. family practice residency North Meml. Hosp., Mpls., 1973-77; asst. prof. dept. family practice and cmty. health U. Minn., 1973-77; chmn. dept. family medicine Mayo Clinic, Rochester, Minn., 1977-91, assoc. prof. family medicine, 1977-84; prof. family medicine Mayo Med. Sch., Rochester, 1984-93; Sanders prof. primary care Mayo Clinic, Rochester, 1986-93; chmn. dept. family medicine Mayo Clinic Jacksonville, 1991-93; dep. exec. dir. Am. Bd. Family Practice, Lexington, Ky., 1991-97, exec. dir., 1998—2002, sr. exec., 2003—. Capt. MC, USAF, 1964-66. Office: Am Bd Family Practice 2228 Young Dr Lexington KY 40505-4219

AVARD, JOSEPH L., mathematician, educator; b. Carleton, Okla. s. Joseph Samuel and Ada Irene Avard; children: Steven, Samuel, Nathan, Alan, Jamie. BS, Southeastern State Coll., 1961; MS, Okla. State U., 1965, EdD, 1967. Statis. analysis specialist Standard Oil of Jersey Rsch. Prodn. Lab., Tulsa, 1957—58; space flight rschr. Douglas Aircraft Corp., El Segundo, Calif., 1958—60; programming studies/rschr. Sys. Devel. Corp., Santa Monica, Calif., 1960—61; rschr. NASA, Boston, 1967—70; math. prof. N.E. La. U., Monroe, 1967—89; prof. math. So. Ark. U., Magnolia, 1989—, chmn. math. dept., 1989—93. Mem.: Soc. Indsl. and Applied Math. Avocation: flying airplanes. Home: 6003 Pleasant Ln Texarkana TX 75503 Office: So Ark U SAU Box 9357 Magnolia AR 71753

AVARD, MARGARET MARIE, environmental science educator; d. Stephen Lewis and Bonnie Jean Avard; m. Bryon Keith Clark, Mar. 18, 2000; 1 child, Gerald Clark. BS in Geology, Centenary Coll., Shreveport, La., 1983; MS in Geoscis., U. Tex., Dallas, 1991; PhD in Environ. Sci., U. Okla., 1998. Assoc. prof. Southea. Okla. State U., Durant, 1989—. Cons. Pathcro Environ., Sherman, Tex., 1994—2000. Contbr. articles to profl. jours. Cons., negotiator Luella Landfill Opposition Assn., Sherman, 2003—05. Grantee Okla. Ctr. for Advancement of Sci. and Tech., NASA Opportunities for Visionary Academics, Dwight D. Eisenhower Math. and Sci. Program, NSF. Mem.: NSTA, N.Am. Lake Mgmt. Soc., Nat. Earth Sci. Tchrs. Assn., Nat. Assn. Geology Teachers, Geol. Soc. Am., Ocean Conservancy, Narural Resources Def. Coun., Okla. Clean Lakes Assn. Democrat. Avocations: travel, environmental issues, outdoor activities. Office: Southea Okla State U 1405 N 4th Ave PMB 4200 Durant OK 74701 Office Phone: 580-745-2664. E-mail: mavard@sosu.edu.

AVARY, ROGER ROBERTS (FRANK BRAUNER), film director, producer, writer; b. Flin Flon, Manitoba, Canada, Aug. 23, 1965; s. Edwin Roberts and Brigitte (Bruninghaus) A. Student, Art Ctr., Pasadena, Calif., 1985-88. Writer D'Arcy, Masius, Benton & Bowles, L.A., 1989-90, J. Walter Thompson, L.A., 1990—. Writer: (film) 99 Days, 1991, (with Mario Puzo) The Lorch Team, 1992; writer, dir. (film): Killing Zoe, 1994 (Yubari Internat. Film Festival Best Film award, 1994, Mystfest Best Film award, 1994, Mystfest Critics prize, 1994, Cannes Prix Tres Spl. Best Film award, 1994), True Romance, 1993; exec. prodr. (film): The Last Man, 1999; writer, prodr., dir. (film): The Worm Turns, 1993, The Rules of Attraction (screenplay), 2002; co-exec. prodr. (film): Boogie Boy, 1997; co-writer (film): Pulp Fiction, 1994 (L.A. Film Critics Assn. Best Screenplay award, 1995, N.Y. Film Critics Cir. Best Screenplay award, 1995, Boston Soc. Film Critics Best Screenplay award, 1995, Nat. Soc. Film Critics Best Screenplay award, 1995, Chgo. Soc. Film Critics Best Screenplay award, 1995, BAFTA Best Screenplay award, 1995, Acad. award best screenplay 1995), Hatchetman, 1995, (children's book) Marshall's Dreams, 1991, (music video) for the group The Go Go's song The Whole World Lost Its Head, 1994; writer, dir., prodr. (TV movie) Mr. Stitch, 1995, Odd Jobs, 1997; actor: Phantasm IV: Oblivion, 1998 Office: Creative Artists Agy Care Rob Paris 9830 Wilshire Blvd Beverly Hills CA 90212-1804*

AVEDON, MARCIA J., pharmaceutical executive; BA summa cum laude in Psychology, U. N.C., 1983; MS in Indsl. and Orgnl. Psychology, George Washington U., 1987, PhD with hons. in Indsl. and Orgnl. Psychology, 1989; MS in Exec. Program, Rutgers U. Intern U.S. Army Civilian Ctr., 1984; assoc. cons., sr. cons., cons. Booz-Allen & Hamilton, Inc., 1985—90; program mgr. Anheuser-Busch Cos., Inc., 1990—92, sr. cons., 1992—93, mgr. corp. succession planning, 1993—94, dir. mgmt. and orgn. devel. Campbell Taggart Inc., 1994—95; dir. orgn. and leadership devel. Honeywell Internat., 1995—97, v.p. human resources and comms. Performance Polymers, 1997—2000, v.p. human resources and comms. Performance Polymers and Chems., 2000—01, v.p. corp. human resources, 2001—02; v.p. talent mgmt. and orgn. effectiveness Merck & Co., Inc., Whitehouse Station, NJ, 2002, sr. v.p. human resources, 2003—. Advr. bd. Human ResourcesOfficer's Acad., mem. corp. leadership coun. Bd. dirs. Jersey Battered Women's Svcs., 2000—; mem. adv. bd. Masters in Human Resources U. S.C., 1998—; corp. sponsor Cornell Ctr. for Advanced Human Resource Studies, 2001—. Mem.: Pharm. Human Resources Assn., Healthcare Businesswomen's Assn., Am. Psychol. Assn., Human Resources Policy Assn. (mem. personnel roundtable), Soc. for Human Resources Mgmt., Soc. for Indsl. and Orgnl. Psychology. Office: Merck & Co Inc PO Box 100 1 Merck Dr Whitehouse Station NJ 08889-0100

AVELLA, JOHN THOMAS, educational administrator; b. Passaic, N.J., June 23, 1957; s. John T. and Margaret Louise (Watson) Avella; m. Patricia Ann Gianotti; children: Katelyn Mary, Shaylyn Clare. BS in Spl. Edn., Trenton State Coll., 1981; MA in Ednl. Adminstrn., Georgian Ct. Coll., 1986; EdD, Nova Southeastern U., 1999. Tchr. Lacey Twp. (N.J.) Bd. Edn., 1982-88; supr. Union City Edn. Svcs. Commn., Westfield, N.J., 1988-89; prin., asst. supt. Monmouth Ocean Edn. Svcs. Commn., Freehold, N.J., 1989—. Mem. Nat. Assn. Sch. Adminstrs. Avocations: sports, music. Office: 100 Tornillo Way Ste 1 Asbury Park NJ 07712-7520

AVELLA, JOSEPH RALPH, business professor; b. N.Y.C., Nov. 13, 1942; s. Salvatore Ralph and Bianca (Artoni) A.; m. Elizabeth Theresa Eberhardt, Aug. 12, 1967 (div. May 1991); children: Edward Jay, James Joseph. BS in Chemistry, Rensselaer Poly. Inst., 1964; MA, Cath. U. Am., 1992, PhD, 1995; MBA, Capella U., 2001. Mgr. Md. ops. The Great Atlantic and Pacific Tea Co., Inc., 1978-83; program mgr. Honeywell Fed. Sys., Inc., McLean, Va., 1984-86, mgr. integration svcs., 1987-89; dep. dir. mobilization Office of Sec. Def., Washington, 1990-92, dir. internat. programs, 1992-93; sr. fellow global strategy program Potomac Found., McLean, 1995-98; prof. and acad. dean Am. Mil. U., Manassas, Va., 1995-98; exec. v.p. Capella U., 1998—2001, prof. bus., 2001—; mem. faculty Touro U., 2004—. Cons. Masi Rsch. Cons., Inc., Washington, 1995-97; exec. sec. NATO Forces Comm., Brussels, Belgium, 1992-94; seminar moderator U.S. Naval War Coll., Newport, R.I., 1989-91; pres. Delphic Consulting Inc., 1998. Contbr. articles to profl. jours. With USNR, 1970-95. Recipient Achievement award No. Va. Navy League, 1989, Cert. of Appreciation Sec. of Navy, 1986, 88, Award of Appreciation U.S. Naval Sea Cadet Corps, 1986. Mem. Am. Polit. Sci. Assn., Ctr. for Study of Presidency (contbg. author), U.S. Strategic Inst., Assn. Naval Aviation (past chpt. sec.), Navy League of U.S. (former mem. bd. dirs.), U.S. Naval Inst. (contbg. author), Pi Sigma Alpha. Office: Capella Univ 222 S 9th St 20th Fl Minneapolis MN 55402 Home: 313 Pine Glen Way Englewood FL 34223 Office Phone: 941-223-4880. E-mail: javella@aol.com.

AVENI, BEVERLY A., executive aide; b. Stamford, Conn., Sept. 2, 1959; d. Lucille F. (Ferretti) A.; m. Steven Munson. BA in Polit. Sci., U. Conn., 1981. Legal asst. Cummings and Lockwood, Stamford, 1981-86; family law paralegal Piazza, Melmed and Ackerly, P.C., Stamford, 1986-88; litigation paralegal Abate and Fox, Stamford, 1988-95; exec. aide to mayor City of Stamford, 1995—. Pres. Conn. Assn. Paralegals, 1989-91; mem. seminar faculty, co-author seminar skills book for paralegal Conn. Discovery Skills, 1995. Vol. counselor Rape and Sexual Abuse Crisis Ctr., Stamford, 1983-87; dist. rep. Dem. City Com., Stamford, 1992-96, sec., 1994-96; local coord. Sen. Christopher Dodd's 1992 Reelection Campaign, 1994-96; mem. congl. dist. adv. coun. Conn. Permanent Commn. on Status of Women, 1996; mem. commn. City of Stamford's XV Charter Revision Commn., 1994-95; mem. Mayor's cabinet; Mayor's rep. on various civic coms. and bds.; bd. dirs. Women's Bus. Devel. Ctr., 1999—. Avocation: exercise. Office: City of Stamford 888 Washington Blvd Stamford CT 06901-2902 Home: # B 71 Dora St Stamford CT 06902-5414 Office Phone: 203-977-4150.

AVENT, CHARLES KIRK, medical educator; b. Memphis, Oct. 27, 1939; s. C. Harold and Emily Schoolfield (Wallace) A.; m. Rosalie Phillips Adams, Aug. 16, 1962 (div. Mar. 1981); children: Emily Wallace, Mary Adams Avent Mezera; m. Nancee Ruth Neel, Dec. 17, 1983; 1 child, Clayton Burns Neel. BA magna cum laude, Vanderbilt U., 1961; MD, Harvard Med. Sch., 1965. Diplomate Am. Bd. Internal Medicine. Resident in medicine Univ. Hosp., Birmingham, 1965-68; fellow in infectious disease U. Washington, Seattle, 1968-70; from instr. medicine to prof. U. Ala. Sch. Medicine, Birmingham, 1970—2002, prof. medicine emeritus, 2002—; med. dir. of disease control Jefferson County Dept. of Health, Birmingham, Ala., 2003—. Dir. med. clerkships U. Ala. Sch. Medicine, Birmingham, 1981-2002, title IX coord., 1976-78. Author: Medicine for Mountaineering, 1992. Mem. Am. Coll. Physicians, Infectious Disease Soc. Am., Phi Beta Kappa, Alpha Omega Alpha. Office: Jefferson Co Dept Health Box 2648 Birmingham AL 35202-2648

AVENT, SHARON L. HOFFMAN, manufacturing company executive; b. St. Paul, Feb. 7, 1946; d. Ebba and Harold Hoffman; m. Terry Avent; 2 children. Student, Hamline U., St. Paul. With Smead Mfg. Co., Hastings, Minn., 1965—, pres., CEO, 1998—; acquired The Atlanta Group (now Smead-Europe), Hoogezand, Netherlands, 1998—. Bd. dirs. Hastings Public Sch. Found. Named Minn. World Trader of the Year, World Trade Week, Inc., 2002; recipient Spirit of Life honoree, City of Hope, 2003. Office: Smead Mfg Co 600 Smead Blvd Hastings MN 55033-2219

AVERA, STEPHEN R., lawyer, food products executive; b. Tallahassee, Fla., Oct. 19, 1956; BA magna cum laude, U. Ala., 1978, JD, 1981. Bar: Ala. 1981, Army Ct. Mil. Rev. 1981, U.S. Ct. Mil. Appeals 1982, Fla. 1987, Ga. 1988. Assoc. gen. counsel labor rels. Flowers Foods Inc. (formerly Flower Industries), Thomasville, Ga., 1986—92, gen. counsel, 1992—, sec., gen. counsel, 2002—. Capt. U.S. Army JAGC, 1981-86. Mem. ABA, Fla. Bar Assn., Ala. State Bar, State Bar Ga. Office: Flowers Foods Inc 1925 Flowers Cir Thomasville GA 31757-1137

AVERBOOK, BERYL DAVID, retired surgeon; b. Superior, Wis., Aug. 17, 1920; s. Abraham B. and Clara (Zeichig) A.; m. Gloria Sloane, Apr. 2, 1955; children: Bruce Jeffrey, Allan Wayne. Student, Superior State Tchrs. Coll., 1938-39; BS, U. Wis., 1942, MD, 1945; postgrad., U. Colo., 1948-50. Diplomate in gen. surgery and gen. vascular surgery Am. Bd. Surgery. Intern. Akron (Ohio) City Hosp., 1945-46; resident VA Hosp., Denver, 1948-50, Rochester (N.Y.) Gen. Hosp., 1950-51, VA Hosp., L.A., 1951-54; practice medicine specializing in gen. surgery, Torrance, Calif., 1948—2004; ret., 2004. Instr. surgery UCLA-Harbor Gen. Hosp., 1954-58; practice tumor and vascular surgery, Torrance, 1961—; asst. prof. surgery UCLA Med. Ctr., 1958-61, asst. clin. prof. surgery, 1961-64; chief surg. services Los Angeles County Harbor Gen. Hosp., Torrance, 1954-61. Contbr. articles to profl. jours. Served to capt. M.C., AUS, also res. Fellow ACS; mem. AMA, LA County Med. Assn., NY Acad. Scis., LA Acad. Medicine, Am. Geriatric Soc., Am. Assn. Med. Colls., Am. Assn. Vascular Surgery, Am. Assn. Head and Neck Surgery, Soc. for Vascular Surgery, Soc. Clin. Vascular Surgeons, Long Beach Surg. Soc., Am. Soc. Gen. Surgery, So. Calif. Vascular Surg. Soc., Internat. Soc. Vascular Surgery, Phi Beta Kappa, Phi Delta Epsilon Chem. Soc., Rho Chi Pharm. Soc. Home: 6519 Springpark Ave Los Angeles CA 90056-2223 Personal E-mail: baverbook@aol.com.

AVERCH, HARVEY ALLAN, economist, educator, academic administrator; b. Denver, Dec. 18, 1935; s. Louis and Gussie (Weiner) A.; m. Barbara Ann Duvall, July 5, 1962; children: Elizabeth, Caroline. AB. summa cum laude (Univ. scholar), U.Colo., 1957; PhD (Univ. fellow, Ford Found. fellow), U. N.C., 1962. Sr. staff economist Rand Corp., Santa Monica, Calif., 1961-71; dir. Div. Social Systems and Human Resources, Research Applications Directorate, NSF, Washington, 1971-74, dep. asst. dir. for analysis and planning, 1974-75, acting asst. dir. for sci. edn., 1975-76, asst. dir. for sci. edn., 1976-77, asst. dir. sci., technol. and internat. affairs, 1977-82, sr. staff assoc. Office of Dir., 1985-89; prof. pub. adminstrn., acting dir. Fla. Internat. U., 1989-90, prof., dir., 1990-94, prof., 1994—. Mem. faculty UCLA, 1963-64, Calif. Inst. Tech., 1967, Rand Grad. Inst., 1970-71; vis. prof. policy scis. and econs. U. Md.-Baltimore County, 1982-85, adj. prof. policy scis. and econs., 1985— . Author: Behavior of the Firm Subject to Regulatory Constraint, 1962, Asymmetry and Arms Control: Some Basic Considerations, 1963, (with M. Lavin) Simulation of Decision-Making in Crisis: Three Manual Gaming Experiments, 1964, (with F. Denton and J. Koehler) A. Crisis of Ambiguity: Political and Economic Development in the Philippines, 1970, The Matrix of Policy in the Philippines, 1971, (with others) How Effective is Schooling: A Critical Review and Synthesis of Research Findings, 1972, How Effective is Schooling: A Critical Review of Research, 1974, A Strategic Analysis of Science and Technology Policy, 1985, Applied Social Science, Policy Science, and The Federal Government, 1987, Measuring The Cost-Efficiency of Basic Research Investments, 1987, Exploring the Cost-Efficiency of Basic Research Funding in Chemistry, 1989, Policy Research for the University Research System, 1989, Private Markets and Public Interventions, 1990, The Political Economy of R&D Taxonomies, 1991, Practice of Research Evaluation in the United States, 1991, Evaluation of Projects and Portfolios, 1992, Systematic Use of Expert Judgment, 1994, Evaluation of Urban Model, 1997, The Rhetoric of War: Language, Argument and Policy During the Vietnam War, 2002; chief co-editor Policy Studies Rev., 1990—; contbr. articles to profl. jours. Chmn. U.S./Israel Binat. Sci. Found., 1979. Recipient Meritorious Service award NSF, 1973, Disting. Service award, 1977 Mem. Phi Beta Kappa. Office: Fla Internat U Sch Policy & Mgmt PCA 362C Miami FL 33199 E-mail: averchh@fiu.edu, averchh@bellsouth.net.

AVERILL, BRUCE ALAN, chemistry professor; b. Bucyrus, Ohio, May 19, 1948; s. Kenneth L. Averill and Mildred (Reid) Krug; m. Patricia Ann Eldredge, Aug. 23, 1986; children: Lindsay Patricia, Alan Eldredge, Ryan Eldredge. BS, Mich. State U., 1969; PhD, MIT, 1973. Asst. prof. chemistry Mich. State U., East Lansing, 1976-81, assoc. prof. chemistry, 1981-82, U. Va., Charlottesville, 1982-88, prof. chemistry, 1988-94; prof. biochemistry U. of Amsterdam, 1994-2001; disting. univ. prof. chemistry U. Toledo, 2001—; Jefferson Sci. fellow U.S. Dept. State, 2004—. Mem. biophysics adv. panel NSF, Washington, 1985-88; mem. faculty forum for sci. rsch. U. Va., Charlottesville, 1984-88; group leader protein rsch. and coord. chemistry working parties Dutch Found. Chem. Rsch., 1995-2001, mem. exec. com. protein rsch. working party, 1996-99. Acquisitions editor ChemTracts-Inorganic Chemistry, 2002—; contbr. more than 140 articles to sci. jours. A.P. Sloan fellow, 1981-83; recipient creativity award NSF, 1991. Mem. AAAS, Am. Soc. Biochemistry and Molecular Biology, Am. Chem. Soc., Royal Soc. Chemistry, Soc. Biol. Inorganic Chemistry, Sigma Xi. Office: U Toledo Dept Chemistry 2801 W Bancroft Rd Toledo OH 43606-3390 Business E-Mail: baa@utoledo.edu.

AVERILL, ELLEN CORBETT, secondary education science educator, administrator; b. Milledgeville, Ga. d. Felton Conrad and Vivian Iris (Brookins) Corbett; m. George Edmund Averill, July 31, 1971; 1 child, John Conrad. BS, U. Ga., 1966, MS, 1971; teaching cert., Columbus Coll., 1979, EdS, 1994. Grad. teaching asst. U. Ga., Athens, 1966-68; tchr. sci. Decatur (Ga.) City Schs., 1971-72; tchr. sci., chair dept. Kendrick High Sch., Columbus, Ga., 1980—. Rsch. asst. Caretta Rsch. Project, Savannah (Ga.) Sci. Mus., 1985, NEWMAST, Kennedy Space Ctr., 1986; rsch. assoc. Inhalation Toxicology Rsch. Inst., Albuquerque, summer, 1990; instr. sci. Gov.'s Honor Program Valdosta State Coll., summer, 1991, Woodrow Wilson Biotechnology Inst., Princeton, N.J., 1993. Contbr. articles to newspapers, jours.; inventor The Wrap-All, 1992. Mem. Nat. Sci. Tchrs. Assn. (program com., regional conf. 1993), Nat. Assn. Biology Tchrs. (Outstanding Biology Tchr. 1990-91), Ga. Sci. Tchrs. Assn. (dist. VI rep. 1988-90, secondary rep. 1990-91, pres.-elect 1991-92, pres. 1992-93, conf. coord. ann. conf. 1992, Dist. VI Sci. Tchr. of Yr. 1995), Coalition for Excellence in Sci. Edn. (orgnl. com. 1992-93), Ga. Sci. Tchrs. Edn. Found. (chair 1994-98), Valley Area Sch. Tchrs. (charter, pres.-elect 1996-97, pres. 1997-98), Muscogee Area Literacy Assn. (treas. 1992-93), Phi Delta Kappa (PDK Tchr. of Yr. 1992, v.p. 2002-), Delta Kappa Gamma Edn. Soc. Unitarian-Universalist. Avocations: procelain art, gardening, amateur radio operator. Home: 126 Waterway Dr Cataula GA 31804-4407 Office: Kendrick High Sch 6015 Georgetown Dr Columbus GA 31907-4698 E-mail: eaverill@ldl.net.

AVERILL, JAMES REED, psychology professor; b. San Francisco, Nov. 29, 1935; s. Dupree Reed and Rosalie Averill. BA, San Jose U., 1959; PhD, UCLA, 1966. Psychologist U. Calif.-Berkeley, 1966-71; mem. faculty U. Mass., Amherst, 1971—, prof. psychology, 1976—. Served with U.S. Army, 1954-57. Fulbright fellow W. Germany, 1959-60 Mem. APA, Am. Psychol. Soc., Internat. Soc. for Rsch. on Emotion. Office: U Mass Dept Psychology Amherst MA 01003 Business E-Mail: averill@psych.umass.edu.

AVERSA, DOLORES SEJDA, educational administrator; b. Phila., Mar. 26, 1932; d. Martin Benjamin and Mary Elizabeth (Esposito) Sejda; m. Zefferino A. Aversa Jr., May 3, 1958; children: Dolores Elizabeth, Jeffrey Martin, Linda Maria. BA, Chestnut Hill Coll., 1953. Owner Personal Rep. & Pub. Rels., Phila., 1965-68; ednl. cons. Franklin Sch. Sci. and Arts, Phila., 1968-72; pres., owner, dir. Martin Sch. Bus., Inc., Phila., 1972—. File reader, cons. for ct. reporting and travel tng. Southwestern Pub. Co., 1990; mem. ednl. planning com. Ravenhill Acad., Phila., 1975-76. Active Phila. Mus. ARt, Phila. Drama Guild; mem. Met. Opera Guild, 2002; sec. Rep. Exec. Com., Phila.; mem. 8th Ward Rep. Exec. Com. Mem.: Lower Bucks County C. of C., Am. Soc. Travel Agts. (PAC chmn. 1997—, sch. divsn., nat. educators com., sec. Del. chpt., edn. chmn.), Hist. Soc. Pa., World Affairs Coun. Phila., Phila. Hist. Soc., Pa. Sch. Counselors Assn., Am. Bus. Law Assn., Pa. Bus. Edn. Assn., Nat. Bus. Edn. Assn., Andrea Doria Survivor Assn., Chestnut Hill Coll. Alumnae Assn. (sec. class '53), Phila. Orch., Am.-Italy Soc., Met. Opera Guild, Stone Harbor Golf Club (Rep. exec. com. 8th ward Phila.). Roman Catholic. Home: 2111 Locust St Philadelphia PA 19103-4802 Office: 2417 Welsh Rd Philadelphia PA 19114-2213 Personal E-mail: msb-aversa@erols.com.

AVERY, A. NELSON, physician, medical educator; b. Austin, Tex., June 1, 1947; s. Charles N. Jr. and Lucille S. Avery; 1 child, Mary. BA, U. Tex., 1969; MD, U. Tex., Galveston, 1973. Diplomate Am. Bd. Internal Medicine, Am. Bd. Preventive Medicine, Occupational Medicine and Med. Toxicology. Resident in internal medicine U. Tex. Med. Br., Galveston, 1973-76; ptnr. Capital Med. Clinic, Austin, Tex., 1976-93; dir. Ctr. for Occupl. and Corp. Health, Austin, Tex., 1993-96; assoc. prof., dir. environ. health U. Tex. Med. Br., Galveston, 1996—, dir. occupl. med. residency, 1998—. Sr. occupl. med. cons. Motorola Semiconductor Products Sector, 1992—; sr. med. cons. Tex. Workers Compensation Ins. Fund, Austin, 1994—. Pres. Old Enfield Homeowners Assn., Austin, 1984-88. Recipient Ashbel Smith Dist. Alumni award, U. Tex. Med. Br. Mem. AMA, APHA, Am. Coll. Occupl. and Environ. Medicine, Soc. for Occupl. and Environ. Health, Semiconductor Safety Assn., Tex. Med. Assn., U. Tex. Med. Br. Alumni Assn. (pres. 1993-94, chmn. devel. bd. dirs. 1995-97), Alpha Omega Alpha. Avocation: scuba diving. Office: U Tex Med Br 301 University Blvd Galveston TX 77555-5302 E-mail: navery@utmb.edu.

AVERY, DONALD HILLS, metallurgist, educator; b. Hartford, Conn., May 7, 1937; s. Charles Raymond and Loma Ellinor (Mulholland) A.; m. Marianna Pinchot, Dec. 3, 1994; children: Jon Weymouth, Nathaniel Caleb, Jessica van Voast. Student, Loomis Inst., 1951-55; BS, MIT, 1959, ScD, 1962; MA, Brown U., 1969. Lic. profl. engr.; lic. pvt. dectective. Pres. Strathmore Research Co., Cambridge, Mass., 1961-69; dir. research Armor Flite Group, Rangely, Maine, 1973-83; pres. A.T.S. Cons. Engrs., 1980—; dir. A.P.C. Engrs., East Providence, R.I., 1977-82; asst. prof. M.I.T., 1962-66, Brown U., 1966-69, asso. prof., 1969-74, prof. engring., 1974-97, prof. emeritus, 1997—. Vis. scholar, prof. U. Capetown, 1974, 76, 79, 82, 83; vis. fellow Yale U. Sch. Forestry, New Haven, 1995; vis. prof. Wharton Sch. U. Pa., 1999-01. Contbr. articles to profl. jours.; patentee in field. NSF fellow, 1959-62; Ford fellow, 1965; rsch. scholar Tanzania, 1976, 79; rsch. scholar Malawi, 1982, 83 Mem. AIME (Metall. Soc.), AAAS, AAU, AAW, WCS (MW chpt. chair), Am. Soc. Metals (past chmn. R.I., Howe medal 1965), Soc. Plastics Engrs., Soc. Automotive Engrs., Hist. Metall. Soc., History Sci. Soc., Soc. History Tech., Hope Club, Explorers Club, Athenaeum, Barrington Yacht Club, Kasungu Farmers. Home: 142 Toandos Rd Quilcene WA 98376-9687 Office: Brown U Div Engring Providence RI 02912-0001

AVERY, ELIZABETH FUSELER, librarian; b. Phila., June 15, 1947; d. Demitry John and Adah (Mench) Pollock. AB, Coll. William and Mary, 1968; MS, Drexel U., 1972, cert. advanced study, 1993. Head biology libr. U. Pa., Phila., 1969-73; head cataloger Marine Biol. Lab., Woods Hole, Mass., 1973-74; libr. Nat. Marine Fisheries, Woods Hole, 1974-75; libr. dir. Tex. A & M U., Galveston, 1975-81, U.S. Merchant Marine Acad., Kings Point, N.Y., 1981-83; rsch. mgr. ISI, Phila., 1986-89; head scis. and tech. Colo. State U. Librs., Ft. Collins, 1989-95; dir. Lamar U. Libr., Beaumont, Tex., 1995—. Recipient Blackwell award ALA, 1994. Mem. Internat. Assn. Aquatic and Marine Sci. Librs. and Info. Ctrs. (pres. 1979-80, pres./pres.-elect 1991-94, editor proceedings, 1990-92, newsletter editor 1997—). Avocations: reading, photography.

AVERY, GORDON BENNETT, medical educator, neonatologist; b. Beirut, Dec. 10, 1931; s. Bennett Franklin and Margaret Anne (Scales) A.; m. Ruth Elizabeth Butler, June 12, 1954 (div.); children: Melody Anne, Wendy Jean, Heidi Elizabeth; m. Penny Glass, Nov. 4, 1989; children: Alexander, Andrew, Anthony. AB, Harvard U., 1953; MD, U. Pa., 1958, PhD, 1959. Dir. div. neonatology Children's Hosp. Nat. Med. Ctr., Washington, 1963-90, physician-in-chief, chief acad. officer, 1990-98; prof. dept. pediats. George Washington U., Washington, 1971-98, prof., chmn. dept. pediatrics, Sch. Med. and Health Scis., 1990-98; prof. pediats. emeritus, 1998—; chief oper. officer Children's Rsch. Inst., Washington, 1990-98. Adv. com. FDA, Washington, 1979-83, 88-91; cons. Nat. Inst. Child Health and Human Devel., 1978—, Bethesda Naval Hosp., 1980—, Walter Reed Army Hosp., 1981—; mem. Mayor's adv. bd. on maternal and infant health, 1986-90. Editor: Neonatology, Pathophysiology and Management of the Newborn, 1975, 3d edit., 1987, 4th edit., 1994, 6th edit., 2005; co-editor: Atlas of Neonatal Procedures, 1983; edtl. bd. Pediat. Jour., 1980-86. Bd. dirs. Pathfinder, Boston, 1975-86, Children's Rsch. Inst., Washington, Children's Hosp., Children's Nat. Med. Ctr. Lt. Med. Svc. Corps., USN, 1958-63. Mem. Soc. for Pediatric Research, Am. Pediatric Soc., Am. Acad. Pediatrics (chmn. fetus and newborn com. 1977-90), National Capital Med. Found. (chmn. perinatal mortality com. 1979-82), Peruvian Pediatric and Surg. Socs. (hon.), Nat. Perinatal Assn. (legis. com.). Avocations: cello, tennis. Home: 4655 36th St S # 2B Arlington VA 22206-1748 Office: Children's Nat Med Ctr 111 Michigan Ave NW Washington DC 20010-2916

AVERY, KAY BETH, secondary school educator; b. Pueblo, Colo., Apr. 11, 1950; d. John S. and Juanita M. (Burrus) Faris; m. Charles W. Avery, May 21, 1971; children: Cassie Louise, Carrie Leigh. BA in Speech and English, Ft. Hays (Kans.) State U., 1982; MS in Edn. Media tech., U. Miami, 1984, EdD in Instrnl. Leadership, 1986. Cert. tchr. speech, English, media, supervision and adminstrn. Tchr. English Unified Sch. Dist. 211, Norton, Kans., 1973-74; tchr. English, speech Dededo (Guam) Mid. Sch., 1974-78; tchr. English Bur. Indian Affairs, Ft. Wingate, N.Mex., 1979-80, Gallup (N.Mex.) H.S., 1980-83; media specialist Oak Ridge H.S., Orlando, Fla., 1986-90; curriculum resource tchr. Osceola H.S., Kissimmee, Fla., 1990-93; tchr. English Poinciana H.S., Kissimmee, 1993-99; curriculum resource tchr., English tchr. Tech. Edn. Ctr. of Osceola, Kissimmee, 1999—. Facilitator of new methods, such as CRISS reading strategies and coop. learning. Contbr. articles to profl. jours. Co-chairperson sch. renewal com. Poinciana in Osceola Sch. Dist. Grantee Osceola County, 1991, 94, 95, 96, Found. for Osceola Edn., 1994, 96, Fla. Dept. Edn., 1990, Orange County, 1989, 90. Mem. NEA, ASCD, Internat. Reading Assn., Fla. Reading Assn., Nat. Coun. Tchrs. English, Fla. Coun. Tchrs. English, Phi Delta Kappa. Home: 219 Iowa Woods Cir W Orlando FL 32824-8638

AVERY, MARY ELLEN, pediatrician, educator; b. Camden, NJ, May 6, 1927; d. William Clarence and Mary (Miller) Avery. AB, Wheaton Coll., Norton, Mass., 1948, DSc (hon.), 1974, Trinity Coll., 1976, U. Mich., 1975, Med. Coll. Pa., 1976, Albany Med. Coll., 1977, Med. Coll. Wis., 1978, Radcliffe Coll., 1978; DSc, U. So. Calif., 2003; DSc (hon.), Harvard U., 2005, MA (hon.), 1974; MD, Johns Hopkins U., 1952; LHD (hon.), Emmanuel Coll., 1979, Northeastern U., 1981, Russell Sage Coll., 1983, Meml. U., Newfoundland, 1993; DHL, Johns Hopkins U., 1999; LLD, Queen's U., Kingston, Ont., 2000, U. So. Calif., 2003. Intern Johns Hopkins Hosp., 1953—54, resident, 1954—57; rsch. fellow in pediat. Boston, 1957—59, Balt., 1959—69; assoc. prof. pediat. Johns Hopkins U., 1964—69; prof., chmn. dept. pediat. McGill U. Med. Sch., 1969—74; physician-in-chief Montreal Children's Hosp., 1969—74; Thomas Morgan Rotch prof. pediat. Harvard U. Med. Sch., Boston, 1974—97; physician-in-chief Children's Hosp. Med. Ctr., Boston, 1974—85; prof. emerita Harvard U. Med. Sch., Boston, 1997—. Mem. Med. Rsch. Coun. Can.; mem. study sect. NIH, 1968—71, 1984—88. Author: The Lung and Its Disorders in the Newborn Infant, 4th edit., 1981; author: (with A. Schaffer) Avery's Diseases of the Newborn, 8th edit., 2004; author: (with G. Litwack) Born Early, 1984, editor (with H.W. Taeusch and R. Ballard); author, editor: (with L. First) Pediatric Medicine, 1988, 2d edit., 1994, also articles:, mem. editl. bd.: Pediatrics, 1965—71, Am. Rev. Respitory Diseases, 1969—73, Am. Jour. Physiology, 1967—73, Jour. Pediatrics, 1974—84, Medicine, 1985, Johns Hopkins Med. Jour., 1978—82, Clin. and Investigative Critical Care Medicine, 1990—96, New Eng. Jour. Medicine, 1990—95. Trustee Wheaton (Mass.) Coll., 1965—85, Radcliffe Coll., Johns Hopkins U., 1982—88. Recipient Mead Johnson award in pediatric rsch., 1968, Trudeau medal, Am. Thoracic Soc., 1984, Nat. Medal of Sci., NSF, 1991, Marta Philipson award, Karolinska Inst., Stockholm, 1998; Markle scholar in med. scis., 1961—66. Fellow: NAS (mem. coun. 1997—), AAAS (dir. 1989, pres. 2004—05), Royal Coll. Physicians of Edinburgh, Am. Acad. Arts and Scis., Am. Acad. Pediat., Internat. Pediatric Assn. (standing com. 1986—89); mem.: Am. Pediatric Soc. (pres. 1990, John Howland award 2005), Royal Coll. Pediat. and Child Health (hon.), Inst. Medicine (coun. 1987, Walsh McDermott award 2000), Soc. Pediatric Rsch. (pres. 1972—73), Am. Physiol. Soc., Can. Pediatric Soc., Alpha Omega Alpha, Phi Beta Kappa. Home and Office: Children's Hosp 300 Longwood Ave # HU432 Boston MA 02115-5737 Office Phone: 617-355-8330. Business E-Mail: mary.avery@tch.harvard.edu.

AVERY, ROBERT DEAN, lawyer; b. Youngstown, Ohio, Apr. 23, 1944; s. Donald Carson and Alta Belle (Simon) Avery; m. Ann Mitchell Lashen, May 16, 1993; 1 child from previous marriage, Benjamin Robert. BA, Northwestern U., 1966; JD, Columbia U., 1969. Bar: Ohio 1971, Calif. 1973, Ill. 2001. Law clk. to Hon. Robert P. Anderson U.S. Ct. Appeals 2d Cir., N.Y.C., 1969-70; assoc. lawyer Jones Day, Cleve., 1970-74, L.A., 1974-76, ptnr., 1977-98, adminstrv. ptnr., 1990-92, ptnr. Chgo., 1999—. Editor: Columbia Law Rev., 1968—69. Dir. Wilshire YMCA, L.A., 1981—88; mem. bd. govs. Northwestern U. Libr., 2004—. Harlan Fiske Stone scholar. Home: 45 E Division St Chicago IL 60610-2316 Office: Jones Day 77 W Wacker Dr Chicago IL 60601-1662 Office Phone: 312-269-4103. Business E-Mail: rdavery@jonesday.com.

AVERY, ROBERT NEWELL, sculptor; b. May 22, 1940; s. Robert Newell and Margaret (Andrews) A.; m. Karen Lissol, Aug. 27, 1963 (div. 1978); 1 child, Robert Walter; m. Amanda Fair Jones, May 5, 1979; 1 child, Melinda Hopkins. BFA, Calif. Coll. Arts and Crafts, Oakland, 1962; postgrad., Coll. of San Mateo, Calif., 1969-70, Coll. of Redwoods, 1975-76. Freelance comml. artist, Mendocino, Calif., 1971-75; exec. dir. Mendocino Art Ctr., Inc., 1975-79; proprietor Missing Link Prodns., Mendocino, 1979-93; mng. dir. Mezzanine Gallery at Daly's, Ft. Bragg, Calif., 1986-87, 91-93; exec. dir. Staunton/Augusta Art Ctr., Staunton, Va., 1995-96; proprietor Avery Studio Gallery, Staunton, 1996—. Art dir. The Mendocino Rev., 1983-91; judge Sonoma County Fair, Santa Rosa, Calif., 1977; auctioneer many arts/ednl./polit. events; art dir. The Mendocino Rev. #3, 1975; disc jockey Radio Sta. KMFB-FM, Mendocino, 1971-73, KJAZ-FM, Berkeley, Calif., 1960-61; lead player (play) The Great American Desert, 1975, Candida, 1977, Mousetrap, 1978, Rain, 1979, The Real Inspector Hound, 1984; prodr.: Twin Peaks (stage play), 1985; host interviewer: Art View, 1987-89, The Now and Then Show, 1985-91; prodr., programmer radio show: Odd Bob Comedy Show, KZYX-FM, 1989-90. Contbr. articles, photographs, illustrations to profl. jours.; columnist The Mendocino Daily Planet, 1972-73, The Mendocino Beacon, 1975-79, The New Settler Interview, 1986, Mendocino Grapevine, 1977-82; illustrator: The House that Jack Built; one man shows include Winona Gallery, Mendocino, 1990, Stock Exch. Deli, Waynesboro, Va., 1995, Augusta County Libr., Fishersville, Va., 1996; group shows include Mendocino Art Ctr., 1986, 1990, 91-93, Mayhew Wildlife Gallery, Mendocino, 1986-93, Mezzanine Gallery, Ft. Bragg, 1986-88, Caspar Studios Gallery, 1990, Shenandoah Valley Art Ctr., Waynesboro, Va., 1994-95, Beverley St. Studio Sch., Staunton, Va., 1995, Jordan Gallery, Charlottesville, Va., 1995, Lynchburg Fine Arts Ctr., 1995, Augusta Art Ctr., 1997, others Master of ceremonies 4th of July Parade, Mendocino, 1976-93; judge Bodega Bay Fisherman's Festival Ann. Arts Show, 1976; chmn. art acquisition com. Augusta Hosp. Corp., 1997; mem. founding bd. Mendocino Performing Arts Co., Inc.; past pres. Mendocino Cmty. Land Trust, Inc.; trustee Mendocino Unified Sch. Dist., 1973-77, pres., 1977; past dir. Mendocino Bus. and Profl. Coun.; mem. citizen's adv. coun. Coll. of the Redwoods, 1979-80; mem. exec. com. Calif. Arts Coun., Rural Arts Svcs., 1978-79; trustee Mendocino Art Ctr., Inc., 1980-85, chmn. citizen's adv. com., 1991, hon. life mem. Recipient numerous sculpture awards various art assns. Mem. Assn. of Sci. Fiction Artists, Internat. Sculpture Commn. Home and Office: 4855 Morris Mill Rd Swoope VA 24479-2323 E-mail: avery@ntelos.net.

AVERY, STEPHEN G. BRODIE, marketing professional, consultant, sales executive; b. Bklyn., Apr. 22, 1938; s. Charles Leslie and Virginia (Cox) A.; m. Frona Sinexon (div. 1980); children: Heather Brodie, Wyckham Christie; m. Ellen Lowe, 1993. Student, Cornell U., 1962-64. Dir. food svc. Rutgers U., Camden, N.J., 1962-66, Franklin Pierce Coll., Rindge, N.H., 1967; advt. mgr. Keen (N.H.) Sentinel, 1967-68; advt. sales mgr. Yankee Pub. Co., Dublin, N.H., 1968-91; exec. commr. N.H. Highland Games, 1992-98. Bd. dirs., New Eng. Travel and Tourism Rsch. Assn.; mem. N.H. Can. Trade Coun., 2001—; mem. scholarship com. N.H. N.G., 2001—. Producer, dir. N.H. Internat. Mil. Tattoo, 1997—. Mem. N.H. Ho. of Reps., Concord, 1988—, chmn. state and fed. rels. com., commerce com.; del. White House Conf. Tourism, 1995; mem. Gov.'s task Force Travel & Tourism; vice chmn. N.H. Commn. Smithsonian Festival, 1997; lay eucharistic min. Episcopal Ch.; mem. N.G. Scholarship Com.; town moderator, 2000--. Fellow Soc. Antiquaries (Scotland); mem. Vt. Lodging and Restaurant Assn. (bd. dirs. 1982-88), Yankee Festival and Event Assn. (chmn. 1997), N.H. Gathering of Scottish Clans (bd. dirs. 1985-91), St. Andrews Soc. (chief convenor 1999—), Scottish Club of Twin States, Am. Scottish Found. Republican. Episcopalian. E-mail: nhscot@monad.net.

AVERY, STEPHEN NEAL, playwright, writer; b. Hot Springs, Ark., Mar. 20, 1955; s. Leo A. Avery and Dedette Carol (Miles) Andree; m. Kathleen Annette Twin, Sept. 7, 1979. Free-lance reporter Hot Springs Sentinel-Record and New Era, 1970-73. Author: (plays) Hungry: 3 Plays, 1991, Because, 1991, Insidious, 1992, Burning Bridges, 1999. Leadership coun. So. Poverty Law Ctr.; founding mem. The Nat. Campaign for Tolerance; founders cir. Ark. State U./Mountain Home Cultural Arts Ctr.; active US Holocaust Meml. Mus., Simon Wiesenthal Ctr., Beil Hashoah Mus. of Tolerance; mem. scholarship com. Am. Indian Edn. Found.; active Nat. Rep. Congl. Com., World Jewish Congress, pres. coun.; active Am. Jewish Com. With USN, 1973—77. Mem.: Drama League, Theatre Comms. Group, Authors League Am., Dramatists Guild Inc., Save Ellis Island (charter), Carter Ctr., Nat. Trust Hist. Preservation, Nat. Campaign Tolerance, Habitat for Humanity Internat., Nat. Mus. Women in Arts, Nat. D-Day Mus. (charter), Nat. Mus. Am. Indian (charter), Rep. Senatorial Inner Cir., Rep. Nat. Com. Pres. Club. Avocation: museum and gallery exhbns.

AVERY, WILLIAM JOSEPH, packaging manufacturing company executive; b. Chgo., June 20, 1940; s. Floyd Joseph and Margaret Mildred (Musard) A.; m. Sharon Bajorek, Sept. 5, 1959; children: Michelle, Martin, Sheryl. Grad. in Indsl. Mgmt., U. Chgo., 1968. With Crown Cork & Seal Co. Inc., Phila., 1959—, v.p. sales, 1974-79, sr. v.p. mfg. and sales, 1979-80, exec. v.p., 1980-81, pres., 1981-96, chmn., CEO, 1990—. Roman Catholic. Office: Crown Cork & Seal Co Inc 1 Crown Way Philadelphia PA 19154-4599

AVERYT, GAYLE OWEN, retired insurance executive; b. Montgomery, Ala., Oct. 13, 1933; s. Edwin Franklin and Asenath Pratt (Murfee) A.; m. Margaret Rosborough Finlay, June 15, 1963; children: Caroline Averyt Lord, Margaret McQueen, Elinor Finlay. BS cum laude, Davidson Coll., 1955; MBA, Harvard U., 1958; D Pub. Svc. (hon.), U. S.C., 1989. Chmn. bd. Colonial Cos., Inc., Columbia, S.C., 1970-93. Bd. dirs. UNUM Cor., 1993-99; bd. dirs., treas. Palmetto Bus. Forum, 1977-94;. mem. S.C. Ins. Commn., 1976-84, S.C. State Ports Authority, 1994-99. Trustee Davidson Coll., N.C., 1980-84; pres. S.C. Orch. Assn., 1986-88. Recipient Order of Palmetto State of S.C., 1994, Disting. Alumnus award Davidson Coll., 1997—; named Business Man of Yr. S.C. C. of C., 1989, Man of the Decade Columbia Met. Mag., Humanitarian of Yr. Palmetto Soc. of United Way of Midlands, 2004; inducted into S.C. Bus. Hall of Fame, 1998. Mem. Phi Beta Kappa. Home: 1717 Greene St Columbia SC 29201-4014 Office: Colonial Cos Inc 1200 W Colonial Life Blvd Columbia SC 29210-7646

AVESING, SUSAN LYNN, quality assurance professional; b. Muscatine, Iowa, Feb. 15, 1963; d. Kenneth DeWayne and Dorothy Jean Phelps; children: Kristen Marie, Joshua Thomas. BS in Chemistry, BS in Biology, Marycrest Internat. U. Cert. ASQ quality auditor Am. Soc. Quality, 2001.

Quality control lab technician Grain Processing Corp., Muscatine, Iowa, 1984—92, quality control lab supr., 1992—96, quality assurance supr., 1996—2000, assoc. quality assurance specialist, 2001—. Mem.: Am. Soc. Quality. Office: Grain Processing Corporation 1600 Oregon St Muscatine IA 52761-1475 Office Phone: 563-264-4683. Office Fax: 563-264-4617. Business E-Mail: susan_avesing@grainprocessing.com.

AVESON, MARTHA CARALYN, pharmaceutical company executive; m. Russell Edward Aveson, Sept. 19, 1981. AS, Essex County Coll., 1974; BA, Rutgers U., 1976; MA, Montclair State U., 1983. Lab. technician Airwick Products, Teterboro, N.J., 1977-79; chemist SmithKlineBeecham, Parsippany, N.J., 1979-84; chemist II Shulton Toiletries, Inc., Clifton, N.J., 1984, Church and Dwight, Inc., Princeton, N.J., 1985-86; rsch. scientist Whitehall-Robins, Inc., Hammonton, N.J., 1986-92; sr. rsch. scientist/sr. clin. supplies assoc. Bayer Corp., Morristown, N.J., 1992-99. Patentee in field. Mem. Internat. Soc. Pharm. Engrs., Am. Chem. Soc. Avocations: skiing, hiking. Home: 5193 E Baseline Rd Belgrade MT 59714 E-mail: MTAveson@aol.com.

AVI, (AVI WORTIS), author; b. N.Y.C., Dec. 23, 1937; s. Joseph and Helen (Zunser) Wortis; children: Shaun Wortis, Kevin Wortis; m. Linda Wright; stepchildren: Katie Spina, Robert Spina, Jack Spina. BA, U. Wis., 1959, MA, 1962; MS in Libr. Sci., Columbia U., 1964. Staff mem. Lincoln Ctr. Libr. of Performing Arts, N.Y.C., 1962-70, Lambeth Pub. Lib., London, 1968; asst. prof., humanities libr. Trenton (N.J.) State Coll., 1970-86; writer, 1968—. Dir. workshop Young People's Fiction, Ill. Wesleyan U. Writers Conf., 1983, course in children's lit., 1986; tchr. course in writing for Children, UCLA Extension, 1987, course in aesthetics and ideology of children's lit., Simmons Coll., Boston, 1987, course in history of children's lit. Simmons Coll., 1988, course The Writers's Achievement, Simmons Coll., spring 1990; condr. more than 2000 workshops and seminars with children, parents and educators in U.S. and abroad. Author: Things That Sometimes Happen, 1970, Snail Tale, 1972 (One of Best Books of Yr. Brit. Book Coun. 1973), No More Magic, 1975 (Spl. award Mystery Writers Am. 1975), Captain Grey, 1977, Emily Upham's Revenge, 1978 (Spl. award Mystery Writers Am. 1979, Book of Month PCRRT, 1978), Encounter at Easton, 1980 (Christopher award 1980), The History of Helpless Harry, 1980 (Book of the Month PCRRT 1980), Man from the Sky, 1980 (IRA Children's Choice 1980), A Place Called Ugly, 1981, Who Stole the Wizard of Oz, 1981, Sometimes I Think I Hear My Name, 1982, Shadrach's Crossing, 1983 (Spl. award Mystery Writers Am. 1983), Devil's Race, 1984 (ALA Best Books Hi-Lo 1984), The Fighting Ground, 1984 (O'Dell award 1984, ALA Notable Book, One of Best Books for Young Adults 1984, Notable Children's Trade Books in Social Studies 1984, Jefferson Cup award Honor Book Va. Libr. Assn. 1985, Book of the Month PCRRT 1984), Wolf Rider, 1986 (named One of Best Books for Young Adults, ALA 1986, N.Y. Pub. Libr. 1986, One of Best Books of the 80s, Booklist 1989, Recommended Book for Reluctant Readers 1986, Va. Young Readers award 1990), Romeo and Juliet—Together (and Alive!)—at Last, 1987 (LA/YASD Recommended Book for Reluctant Readers, 1988, IRA Children's Choice 1988, named One of Best Books of Yr., Bank St. Coll. Children's Book Com., Wis. Children's Book Ctr. 1988), Something Upstairs, 1988 (Rhode Island award 1991, named One of Best Books of Yr. Libr. Congress 1989), The Man Who Was Poe, 1989, (named One of Best Books of Yr., N.Y. Pub. Libr. 1989, Notable Children's Book, NCTE 1990, One of Best Books of Yr., Libr. Congress 1990), The True Confessions of Charlotte Doyle (IRA Children's Choice award 1990, Lopez Meml. Found. award 1990, Golden Kite award Soc. Children's Book Authors 1991, named One of Best Books of Yr., Child Study Assn. 1990, Notable Childrn's Trade Book in the Lang. Arts 1990, N.Y. Pub. Lib. Best Books for Teens 1990, Editors' Choice, Booklist 1990, ALA Notable Book, 1990, YASD Best Books for Young Adults 1991, Newbery Honor Book 1991), Nothing But the Truth, 1991, (Newbery Honor Book, 1992, Horn Book-Boston Globe award Honor Book, 1992, ALA Notable Book, 1992, named One of Best Books of Yr.-Hornbook, SLJ, 1991, YASD Best Books for Young Adults, 1992, Pub. Weekly Best Books of 1991, Am. Booksellers Children's Choice List, 1992, Best Books for Teens, N.Y. Pub. Libr., 1992, Notable Nat. Coun. Social Studies/Children's Book Council, 1991, Blue Ribbon Book Bulletin of Ctr. Children's Books), Windcatcher, 1991, Who Was that Masked Man, Anyway?, 1992, Blue Heron, 1992, City of Light, City of Dark, 1993, The Bird, The Frog and the Light, 1994, The Barn, 1994, Tom, Babette & Simon, 1995, Poppy, 1995, Beyond the Western Sea, 1996, Crispin: The Cross of Lead, (Newbery Medal Winner 2003); contbr. articles to jours. in field. Mem.: Authors Guild. Avocation: photography. Home: 859 S York St Denver CO 80209-4646

AVIL, RICHARD DANIEL, JR., lawyer; b. Phila., Nov. 28, 1948; s. Richard Daniel and Elizabeth (McGinley) A.; m. Karen Mudry, May 27, 1972; children: Sierra Soo, Brier Sung, Winston Richard. BEE, Villanova U., 1970; JD, Cornell U., 1974. Law clk. US Dist. Ct. Northern Dist. NY, 1974-75, 75-76, US Ct. Appeals Second Cir., NYC, 1976-77; assoc. Jones Day, Cleve., 1977-83, ptnr., 1984-91, ptnr., chair energy Washington, 1991—. Spkr. in field. Mem.: Energy Bar Assn. Office: Jones Day 51 Louisiana Ave NW Washington DC 20001-2113 E-mail: rdavil@jonesday.com.

AVILA, CARLOS ALBERTO, physics researcher, inventor; b. Arecibo, P.R., May 7, 1950; s. Manuel Antonio Avila and Natalia Rivera; children: Carlos Jr., Rolando, Elias, David; m. Shelia Diana Avila. BEd in Chemistry, NYU, 1976, BA, 1978, MEd in Sci. Edn., 1986; BAW in Chemistry and Gen. Sci., Inter Am. U., P.R., 1988; MA in Sci. Edn., NYU, 1992; DSc Astrophysics of Particles, Postdoctoral degree in Quantum Physics and Artificial Intelligence, U. Oxford, Eng. Tchr. of sci. Dept. Edn., P.R., 1976-86, tchr. chemistry lab., 1992-93; rschr. physics dept. U. P.R., 1993—; pres., owner EBINC-CINCE, Inc. Spanish cmty. svcs. staff Dept. Edn., Penns Grove, N.J., 1982-83; substitute tchr. Dept. Edn., Meml. H.S., 1983-84; owner, pres. CINCE; with Mission to Planet Earth and Earth Observing System programs, NASA. Songwriter: Men Should Understand, others; author: Space is Not Empty - It is the 5th State of the Matter, Beyond Einstein Equation & Modifying Einstein Equation: E=Mc2 singularity was modified to Up=ME.C, Universe Not Expanding; contbr. scientific papers. Special elite U.S. Army, 1971—75, with U.S. Army, 1991—92. Nominee Nobel Prize in Physics, Internat. Peace prize; named Internat. Outstanding Scientist of Yr., 2005—06. Mem. Nat. Sci. Assn., IP&R Inventors and Pub./Rsch. Corp. (recipient Internat. Personality of Yr., Cambridge, Eng., others), Am. Fedn. Tchrs., Puerto Rico Fedn. Tchrs., Am. Legion. Achievements include invention of Thermoelectric battery and power plant using the same; development of Avila's Singunification Theory; new technology in antigravity to put anybody in orbit with no need of chemical polluted fuels, theory called antigravitational equilibrium; technology to restore ozone holes in the atmospheric layer statosphere both South and North Poles; used the pendulum pacemaker to build up a sismograph that will be robotized and used to detect earthquakes up to 5 minutes before destructive waves reach populated cities; development of Thermoelectric Generator in orbit to capture sun radiations (solar wind) and transform it into electricity to light up the internat. space sta. in orbit. Avocations: reading science and technology books and magazines, music. Home and Office: PO Box 14 Angeles PR 00611-0014 also: 40150 Friar Tuck Trl Zephyrhills FL 33540-7702 Office Phone: 787-894-7702. Personal E-mail: praf@ostnet.com. E-mail: ivanhoe@caribe.net.

AVILES, ALICE ALERS, psychologist; b. N.Y.C; d. Jose Oscar and Pauline (Irizarry) Alers; m. Jose A. Aviles, Aug. 13, 1954 (div. Oct. 1981); children: Jeffrey (dec.), Brian, Gregory; m. Clifford M. Goldman, June 29, 1997. BS magna cum laude, SUNY, Oswego, 1955; MA, Queens Coll., 1978; PhD, Yeshiva U., 1984; postdoctoral diploma in psychoanalysis and psychotherapy, Adelphi U., 1991. Lic. psychologist, N.Y. Tchr. elem. schs., Spring Valley, NY, 1955, Erlangen Am. Sch., Germany, 1955—56, Uniondale, NY, 1956, Freeport, NY, 1957—58, Island Park, NY, 1973—75; psychology clk. Fifth Ave. Ctr. for Counseling and Psychotherapy, N.Y.C., 1978—80; psychology intern St. Vincent's Hosp. and Med. Ctr., N.Y.C., 1980—81; psychologist Kingsboro Psychiat. Ctr., Bklyn., 1981—84; psychologist to assoc. psychologist South Beach Psychiat. Ctr., Bklyn., 1984—86; pvt. practice Valley Stream, NY, 1985—. From staff psychologist to sr. psychologist Luth. Med. Ctr., Bklyn., 1986-95; cons. Beach Terrace Care Ctr., Long Beach, N.Y., 1995-97; mem. adv. com. Hispanic Counseling Ctr. of Family Svc. Assn. of Nassau County, Hempstead, N.Y., 1978-80; cons. Nassau County Extended Care Ctr., Hempstead, 1997-99, Resort Nursing Home, Far Rockaway, N.Y., 1998-2000, Woodmere (N.Y.) Rehab. and Health Care Ctr., 1999-2000. Ford found. grad. fellow, 1978-81. Mem. APA, N.Y. State Psychol. Assn., Nassau County Psychol. Assn. (mem. pvt. practice com. 1992-93), Adelphi Soc. Psychoanalysis and Psychotherapy. Office Phone: 516-791-8326.

AVILES, CARLOS E., geriatrics nurse; b. Quito, Ecuador; arrived in U.S., 1963; s. Enrique Aviles and Celeste Serrano; 1 child, Tony. Degree in Nursing, Columbus (Ohio) C.C., 1975; cert. in Pulmonary Function, Cin. (Ohio) U., 1986; cert. in Audiometry, Ohio State U., 1989. RN Ohio, 1975. Nurse, head Dept. Children's Hosp., Columbus, 1968—79; asst. adminstr. Hosp. Voz Andes, Shell, Ecuador, 1980—81, dir., 1979—80; emergency staff Children's Hosp., 1981—86; health svcs. staff Buttelle Meml. Inst., Columbus, 1986—91; home health care nurse Ptnrs. Olsten, Columbus, 1991—99; prin., owner CEARN Home Health, Westerville, Ohio, 1999—. Author: 50 Years of Poetry, 2005. With U.S. Army, 1964—66. Recipient Ctrl. Svc. award, Ind. State U., 1976. Mem.: Am. Assn. Poetry. Independent. Achievements include patents pending for. Avocations: swimming, poetry, painting, antiques, coin collecting/numismatics. Home and Office: 3733 Paris Blvd E Westerville OH 43081-4156 Office Phone: 614-895-7262.

AVILES, DIONEL M., civilian military employee, former federal agency administrator; b. Bryan, Tex. BS in Mech. Engring., U.S. Naval Acad., 1983; MBA, George Washington U., 1993. Program engr. Naval Air Systems Command; asst. to dir. nat. security divsn. Office Mgmt. and Budget The White House, Washington, 1991—95; profl. staff mem. U.S. Ho. Rels. Com. on Armed Svcs., Washington, 1995—2001; asst. sec. (fin. mgmt. & comptr.) Dept. Navy, US Dept. Def., Washington, 2001—04, under sec., 2004—. Served in USN, 1983—88. Office: USN 1000 Pentagon Washington DC 20350

AVINS, STYRA, musician, writer; b. Bronx, NY; d. William and Suzanne Avins; m. Josef Eisinger, June 24, 1963; children: Alison, Simon. BA, CCNY, 1959; postgrad., Juilliard Sch., 1958-59; MM, Manhattan Sch. Music, 1963. Solo cellist Seoul Symphony, 1959-60; cellist Am. Symphony, N.Y.C., 1966-68, N.Y. City Opera Orch., N.Y.C., 1967-68, Young Audiences, Wyndham Ensemble, N.Y.C. and N.J., 1970-85, Cameo Trio, N.Y.C., 1982-86, Queens Symphony, N.Y., 1981—. Artistic exec. dir. Cmty. Chamber Concerts, N.Y. and N.J., 1982-88; adj. prof. music history Drew U., Madison, N.J., 1995—; guest faculty Chamber Music Conf. of the East, 1999—. Author: Johannes Brahms: Life and Letters, 1997 (Royal Philharm. Soc. award 1998); contbg. author Performing Brahms, 2003 (Best Rsch. book on Music award, 2005); contbr. articles to profl. jours. Trustee Hunterdon Land Trust Alliance, Frenchtown, N.J., 1998—; at-large officer Musconetcong Mountain Conservancy, Hampton, N.J., 2002--; mem. adv. sch. bd. com. Bethlehem Township Sch. Bd., N.J., 1998-99; agrl. liaison to county agrl. bd. Bethlehem Township Gov. Body, 1997—. Recipient Excellence award, Assn. Record Sound Collections, 2004. Mem. Am. Musicol. Soc. (conf. del.), Am. Brahms Soc. (bd. dirs.), Assoc. Fedn. Musicians (Local 802), The Bohemians, Violoncello Soc. N.Y., Violoncello Soc. London, Phi Beta Kappa. Jewish. Avocation: open space preservation activities. Office: 197 W Houston St New York NY 10014 Office Phone: 212-929-7273.

AVIS, WARREN EDWARD, JR., lawyer; b. Detroit, June 25, 1950; s. Warren Edward Avis and Suzanne (Packer) Bauman; m. Deborah Kah, Nov. 16, 1985; children: Warren E. III, William E. BA, Brown U., 1972; JD, U. Detroit, 1978. Bar: Mich. 1979, U.S. Dist. Ct. (ea. dist.) Mich. 1979, Fla. 1980, U.S. Ct. Appeals (11th cir.) 1981, U.S. Dist. Ct. (mid. and so. dists.) Fla. 1981, U.S. Dist. Ct. (so. dist.) Fla. 1987. Assoc. Montgomery, Lytal, Reiter, Denny & Searcy, P.A., Searcy, Pa., 1981-84; sr. assoc. Smathers & Thompson, West Palm Beach, Fla., 1984-88; founder, ptnr. Avis & Avis, P.A., Palm Beach, 1989—. Founder, dir. Palm Beach Precision Molding Co., Riviera Beach, Fla., 1994-97, Avis-Rummery Internat. Real Estate Inc. Mem. Palm Beach Civic Assn., Preservation Found. Palm Beach, 1997—; analyst Small Bus. Devel. Ctr., North Palm Beach, 1990. Mem. The Fla. Bar, Palm Beach County Bar Assn., North Palm Beach C. of C. (dir. 1996—), Soc. of Four Arts Palm Beach. Republican. Episcopalian. Avocations: sailing, flying. Home: 217 La Puerta Way Palm Beach FL 33480-3223 Office: Avis & Avis PA 125 Worth Ave Ste 221 Palm Beach FL 33480-4430

AVISE, JOHN CHARLES, geneticist, educator; b. Grand Rapids, Mich., Sept. 19, 1948; s. Reginald Dean and Edith Dorothy (Johnson) A.; m. Joan Marie Yanov, Dec. 24, 1979; 1 child, Jennifer Ann. BS, U. Mich., 1970; MA, U. Tex., 1971; PhD, U. Calif., Davis, 1975. Asst. prof. U. Ga., Athens, 1975-79, assoc prof., 1980-84, prof., 1985—. Author: Molecular Markers, Natural History and Evolution, 1994, 2d edit., 2004, The Genetic Gods: Evolution and Belief in Human Affairs, 1998, Phylogeography: The History and Formation of Species, 2000, Captivating Life: A Naturalist in the Age of Genetics, 2001, Genetics in the Wild, 2002, The Hope, Hype and Reality of Genetic Engineering, 2004; contbr. articles to profl. jours. Recipient William Brewster Meml. award Am. Ornithologists' Union, 1997 Mem. AAAS, NAS. Avocations: nature study, sports. Office: Univ of Ga Dept of Genetics Athens GA 30602 Business E-Mail: avise@uga.edu.

AVIV, JONATHAN ENOCH, otolaryngologist, educator; b. NYC, Aug. 24, 1960; s. David Gordon and Rena (Rod) A.; children: Caleigh Kiam, Nikki Claire, Blake Victor. BA, Columbia U., 1981, MD, 1985. Diplomate Am. Bd. Otolaryngology, Nat. Bd. Med. Examiners. Resident dept. surgery Mount Sinai Med. Ctr., N.Y.C., 1985-87, resident dept. otolaryngology, 1987-90, fellow microvascular surgery, 1990-91; prof., dir. divsn. laryngology, med. dir. voice and swallowing ctr. Coll. Physicians and Surgeons, Columbia U., N.Y.C., 1991—. Co-founder AP Healthcare, L.L.C., Surgery 411. Author: FEESST: Flexible Endoscopic Evaluation of Swallowing with Sensory Testing, 2005; contbr. chapters to books, articles to profl. jours. Fellow Am. Soc. Head and Neck Surgery; mem. AMA, ACS (faculty), Am. Acad. Otolaryngology, Am. Acad. Facial, Plastic and Reconstructive Surgery, Am. Broncho-Esophagological Assn. (v.p. 2001-03, pres. 2005), Am. Laryngological Assn., N.Am. Skull Base Soc., NY Head and Neck Soc., NY Laryngological Soc. (past pres.), Triological Soc. Achievements include development of and a patent for method and device to endoscopically measure sensory discrimination in throat and voice box. Office: Columbia-Presbyn Med Ctr Dept Otolaryngology 630 W 168th St New York NY 10032-3702 Office Phone: 212-326-8475, 212-305-1602. Personal E-mail: javivmd@aol.com. Business E-Mail: jea10@columbia.edu.

AVOSEH, MEJAI BOLA MIKE, literature and language professor, researcher; PhD, U. Ibadan, 1991. Tchr. NYC Pub. Sch., Bklyn., 2002—04; asst. prof. U. S.D., Vermillion, 2004—. Sr. lectr. U. Namibia, Windhoek, 1989—2001. Contbr. articles to profl. jours. Recipient Internat. award Literacy Rsch.-Spl. Mention, UNESCO, 1992; fellow, Can. Internat. Devel. Assn., 1999, Commonwealth Learning, 1999, German Adult Edn. Assn., 2000; grantee, U. S.D., 2004. Mem.: AAUP, Mo. Valley Adult Edn. Assn., Assn. World Edn. Denmark (Danish Min. Fgn. Affairs Travel fellow 2001), Am. Assn. Adult and Continuing Edn. Democrat. Avocation: travel. Office: U SD Sch Edn Vermillion SD 57069 Office Fax: 605-677-5438. E-mail: mavoseh@usd.edu.

AVOURIS, PHAEDON, chemical physicist; b. Athens, Greece, June 16, 1945; came to U.S., 1970. s. Dionisios and Ourania (Nomikos) A.; m. Alice Laura Dearden, Oct. 7, 1976; 1 child, Ann. BS, Aristotle U., Thessaloniki, greece, 1968; PhD, Mich. State U., 1974. Postdoctoral fellow U. Calif., L.A., 1975-77; rsch. assoc. AT&T Bell Labs., Murray Hill, N.J., 1978; rsch. staff IBM Watson Rsch. Ctr., Yorktown Heights, N.Y., 1978-84, mgr. chem. physics, 1984—, now mgr. nanoscale sci. & tech. group. Panel for chem. sci. Nat. Rsch. Coun., Washington, 1990—. Editor: (book) Atomic and Nanoscale Modifications of Materials; contbr. articles to profl. jours. including Phys. Rev., Sci., Jour. Chem. Physics. Recipient Medard W. Welch award in vacuum sci. Am. Vacuum Soc., 1997. Fellow Am. Phys. Soc.; mem. Am. Chem. Soc. (adv. editl. bd. 1990—). Achievements include pioneering the study of surface chemistry on atomic scale with scanning tunneling microscopy, the manipulation of individual atoms; contbutions to understanding of electronically excited states at surfaces. Office: IBM Watson Rsch Ctr PO Box 218 Yorktown Heights NY 10598

AVRAM, HENRIETTE DAVIDSON, librarian, government official; b. N.Y.C., Oct. 7, 1919; d. Joseph and Rhea (Olsho) Davidson; m. Herbert Mois Avram, Aug. 23, 1941; children: Lloyd, Marcie, Jay. Student, Hunter Coll., N.Y.C., George Washington U.; ScD (hon.), So. Ill. U., 1977; DLitt (hon.), Rochester Inst. Tech., 1991; DSc (hon.), U. Ill., 1993. Systems analyst, methods analyst, programmer Nat. Security Agy., 1952-59; systems analyst Am. Rsch. Bur., 1959-61, Datatrol Corp., 1961-65; supervisory info. systems specialist Libr. of Congress, Washington, 1965-67, asst. coord. info. systems, 1967-70, chief MARC Devel. Office, 1970-76, dir. Network Devel. Office, 1976-80, dir. processing systems, network and automation planning, 1980-83, asst. libr. for processing svcs., 1983-89, assoc. libr. Collection Svcs., 1989-92; ret. Libr. Congress, 1992; chmn. network adv. com. Libr. of Congress, Washington, 1981-92, chmn. emerita network adv. com., 1992—. Chair subcom. 2 sectional com. Z39 Am. Nat. Standards Inst., 1966-80, RECON Working Task F, 1968-73, Internat. Rels. Round Table, 1986-87, subcom. 4 working group 1 on character sets Internat. Orgn. for Standardization, 1971-80; lectr. sch. of info. and libr. sci. Cath. U. Am., Washington, 1973-80, com. mem. strategies for 80's, 1980-81; bd. visitors libr. and learning resources com., 1980; mem. internat. standards coord. com. Info. Sys. Standards Bd., 1983-86; del. to U.S. nat. com. UNESCO/Gen. Info. Program, 1983; chair internat. rels. com. Nat. Info. Standards Orgn., 1983-92. Bd. editors: Jour. Library Automation, 1970-72; contbr. articles to profl. jours. Recipient Superior Svc. award Libr. of Congress, 1968, Margaret Mann citation, 1971, Fed. Woman's award, 1974, Achievement award ALA/Libr. Info. Tech. Assn., 1980, Meritorious Svc. award ANSI, 1992, Disting. Exec. Svc. award Fed. Govt., 1990; co-recipient Rsch. Libr. of Yr. award Assn. Coll. and Rsch. Libr. Acad., 1979. Fellow Internat. Fedn. Libr. Assns. and Instns. (chair working group on content designators 1972-77, chair profl. bd. 1979-81, mem. program mgmt. com. 1983-90, mem. exec. bd. 1983-87, 1st v.p. 1985-87); mem. ALA (bd. dirs., past pres. info sci. and automation div., John Ames Humphrey Forest Press award 1990, Melvil Dewey award 1981, Lippincott award 1988, Hon. Membership award 1997), Am. Soc. Info. Sci. (spl. interest group on libr. automation and networks 1965), Spl. Librs. Assn. (Recognition award 1990), Assn. Libr. and Info. Sci. Edn. (Libr. of Congress disting. svc. award 1992), Assn. Bibliog. Agys. Gt. Britain, Australia, Can. and U.S. (del. 1977—). Home: 44041 Fieldstone Way California MD 20619-2097 E-mail: havram@erols.com.

AVRAM, MORRELL M., nephrologist, educator, consultant; b. N.Y.C., Nov. 11, 1929; m. Maria G. Kunzle; children: Rella Marie, Marc Robert, Eric Michael, Mathew Mendel, David Keith. BS, L.I. U., 1951, DS (hon.), 1988; MD, U. Geneva, 1959. Intern L.I. Coll. Hosp., Bklyn., 1959-60, chief resident, 1962-63, fellow in nephrology, 1963-64, chief hemodialysis lab., 1964—, first dir. renal clinic, 1966—, first chief div. nephrology, 1970—, chief renal clin. rsch. lab., 1987—; clin. prof. SUNY, Bklyn., 1979—; cons. in field. Cons. Southampton Hosp., Univ. Hosp., SUNY, Cath. Med. Ctr.—Bklyn./Queens; vis. physician Kings County Med. Ctr., N.Y.C., 1964—; founder, dir. The Bklyn. Kidney Ctr., 1971—; vis. prof. numerous univs. including U. Conn., U. Ariz., SUNY, Johns Hopkins U., Harvard U., UCLA, univs. in Beijing, Rio de Janeiro, Tel Aviv, Cairo; speaker in field. Author: Parathyroid Hormone in Kidney Disease, 1980, Prevention of Kidney Disease and Long-Term Survival, 1982, Protenuria, 1985; (with C. Giordano) Ambulatory Peritoneal Dialysis, 1990; contbg. author numerous books; mem. editorial bd. Nephron, 1978—, Clin. Nephrology, 1981—, Dialysis and Transplantation, 1980—, Jour. Geriatric Nephrology and Urology, 1990—, Internat. Jour. Artificial Organs, 1978—, Internat. Jour. Pediatric Nephrology, 1980, Jour. Diabetic Complications, 1987, Hypertension, 1975-77, Urology Times, 1974-84; reviewer various publs.; contbr. numerous articles to profl. jours. Chmn. med. adv. bd. Nat. Kidney Found. N.Y./N.J., Inc., 1982-87, med. adv. bd. mem. 1999; founding mem. Am. Soc. Hypertension, 1986—; bd. dirs., exec. com. World Affairs Coun., 1989—; bd. mem. St. Luke's Roosevelt Hosp. Ctr., L.I. Coll. Hosp., Pianofest; co-chmn. bd. dirs. World Affairs Coun., Southampton, N.Y.; active numerous community and svc. orgns. With U.S. Army, 1951-53, Korea. Clin. rsch. tng. fellow L.I. Coll. Hosp., 1968—, Nat. Kidney Found. fellow L.I. Coll. Hosp., 1969—; recipient Lester Hoenig award Nat. Kidney Found., 1984. Fellow ACP; mem. AMA, AAAS, Am. Soc. Nephrology, Am. Soc. for Internal Organs (editor Transactions XXXIII 1987), Internat. Soc. Nephrology, Internat. Soc. Artificial Internal Organs, Bklyn. Acad. Medicine, Am. Anthropol. Soc., N.Y. Acad. Scis., N.Y. Soc. Nephrology (pres. 1977-78), Renal Network N.Y. (pres. 1978-79). Home: 115 Remsen St Brooklyn NY 11201-4212 Office: LI Coll Hosp Div Nephrology Atlantic Ave Brooklyn NY 11201-5526

AVRESKI, DIMITER RANGUELOV, computer scientist, educator; b. Konare, Bulgaria, June 22, 1944; s. Rangel Dimitrov and Slavka Ivanova Avreski; m. Veneta Kirilova Koleva; children: Antoaneta Dimitrova, Alex Dimitrov. MS in Elec. and Telecommunication Engring., Tech. U., Sofia, Bulgaria, 1962—67; PhD, Acad. Scis. and Moscow Inst. Transport, 1970—73. Assoc. prof. Tech. U., Sofia, Bulgaria, 1973—91; rschr. CNRS, LAAS, Toulouse, France, 1991—92; rsch. prof., computer sci. dept. Tex. A&M U., College Station, 1992—96; assoc. prof. Boston U., 1996—2000; prof. Northeastern U., Boston, 2000—. Contbr. articles to profl. jours. Grantee, Compaq/Hewlett Packard, 1995—2002, NSF, 1996—2005. Mem.: IEEE (program chair, confs.). Achievements include first to invent a method for formal verification of software, protocols and embedded systems; research in a method for optimizing the performance of system area network (SAN); a method for tolerating muliple node and link failures in irregular topologies for wired and mobile networks; the original method for congestion management in high-speed networks (SAN).

AVRIT, RICHARD CALVIN, defense consultant, career officer; b. Tillamook, Oreg., Feb. 18, 1932; s. Roy Calvin and Mary Louise (Morgan) A.; m. Alice Jane Tamminga, July 10, 1959; 1 dau., Tamra Jane. BS in Engring, U.S. Naval Acad., 1953; MS in Engring. Electronics, U.S. Naval Postgrad. Sch., 1960; postgrad., U.S. Naval War Coll., 1971-72. Commd. ensign U.S. Navy, 1953, advanced through grades to rear adm., 1979; served weapons dept. U.S.S. George K. Mackenzie, 1953-54; ops. dept. U.S.S. Willis A. Lee, 1954-57; comdg. officer U.S.S. Sumner County, 1960-63; project officer, staff of comdr. Operational Test and Evaluation Force, Key West, Fla., 1963-66; exec. officer U.S.S. Berkeley, 1966-68; ops. officer, AAW project officer Comdr. Cruiser Destroyer Florilla Nine, 1968-70; comdg. officer U.S.S. Sellers, 1970-71; mil. asst. for surface guns and missiles to asst. dir. Ocean Control Directorate, Def. Research and Engring., Office Sec. of Def., 1972-76; comdg. officer U.S.S. Harry E. Yarnell, 1976-78; chief of staff, comdr. Naval Surface Force U.S. Atlantic Fleet, 1978-79; project mgr. for Saudi Naval Expansion Program, Naval Material Command, Washington, 1979-82; dir. navy logistics plans Office Chief of Naval Ops., Washington, 1982-84; cons. Info. Spectrum, Inc., 1984-88; pres. Mil. Data Corp., Arlington, Va., 1989-91; small bus. cons., 1992—. Decorated D.S.M., Legion of Merit (3), Bronze Star with Combat V, Meritorious Service Medal (2). Mem. Naval Inst., IEEE. Methodist. Home: 4839 Keswick Ct Dumfries VA 22025-1084 Personal E-mail: dick-a-keswick@att.net, dick.avrit@verizon.net.

AVRUNIN, GEORGE SAM'L, mathematician, computer scientist, educator; b. Detroit, Mar. 2, 1952; s. Daniel and Louise (Rosengard) A.; m. Jill Melanie Spitz, Aug. 31, 1981; 1 child, Eleanor. BS, U. Mich., 1972, MA, 1974, PhD, 1976. Asst. prof. math. U. Mass., Amherst, 1976-82, assoc. prof. math., 1982-91, prof. Amherst, 1991—. Vis. asst. prof. U. Va., Charlottesville, 1980; adj. prof. computer sci. U. Mass., Amherst, 1992—. Author: The Structure of Conflict, 1988; contbr. articles to jours. Mem. IEEE Computer Soc., Am. Math. Soc., Assn. Computing Machinery (assoc. editor Transactions on Software Engring. and Methodology 2005—), Assn. Women in Math., Math Assn. Am. Achievements include co-development of stratification theorem for module varieties; of inequality necessary conditions method for analysis of concurrent computer systems; of models of preference and conflict. Office: U Mass Dept Math Amherst MA 01003 E-mail: avrunin@math.umass.edu.

AVSHARIAN, ROUPEN, prosecutor, academic administrator; b. Beirut, Oct. 29, 1962; s. Minas Avsharian and Angele Torossian; m. Jacqueline Markarian, May 17, 1992; children: Sareen Tina, Lara Cathy. BS in Law, We. State U. Coll. Law, 1994, JD, 1995; MA in Nat. Security Studies, Am. Mil. U., 2004. Mediation and negotiation: Straus Inst. Dispute Resolution, Pepperdine U. Sch. 2003; prins. conduct peace support ops. UN Inst. Tng. and Rsch., 2002. Adminstrv. asst./rschr. City Of Pasadena, 1985—86; real estate salesperson Town and Ranch Realty, Inc., La Canada-Flintridge, Calif., 1987—91; asst. clk. La Superior Ct., L.A., 1991—96; pvt. practice Northridge, Calif., 1996—; dept. chair, lectr. Mashdots Coll., Glendale, Calif., 2001—. Mediator La Superior Ct., L.A., 2003—. Recipient St. Mesrob Mashdots Disting. Svc. award, Mashdots Coll., 2002; scholar Armenian Studies scholarship, Armenian Gen. Benevolent Union, 1994. Master: Glendale Masonic Lodge (worshipful master 1994—95); mem.: Armenian Coun. Am. (chmn. 2001—04), State Bar Calif. (probation monitor 1993—96), Calif. Assn. Realtors (licentiate; mem.), Nat. Assn. Realtors (licentiate; mem.), San Fernando Valley Bar Assn. (licentiate), Am.-Arab Bar Assn. (licentiate), Calif. Bar Assn. (licentiate; mem.), ABA (licentiate; mem.), Acad. Polit. Sci. (assoc.), So. Calif. Mediation Assn. (assoc.), Townhall L.A. (assoc.), L.A. World Affairs Coun. (assoc.), Mid. East Studies Assn. (assoc.). R-Consevative. Avocations: travel, reading. Office: Law Offices Roupen Avsharian 18531 Roscoe Blvd Ste 213 Northridge CA 91324 Home Fax: 818-349-7801. Personal E-mail: ravsharian@aol.com.

AVULA, XAVIER J., engineering educator, researcher; arrived in U.S., 1962; s. Ezekiel and Navamani Avula; m. Sulochana Avula, Aug. 17, 1960; children: Priya Batchu, Sylvia Laudon. BSc, Andhra Christian Coll., Guntur, India, 1955; BTech with honors, Indian Inst. Tech., Kharagpur, India, 1960; MS, Mich. State U., East Lansing, 1964; PhD, Iowa State U., Ames, 1968. Sect. office mech. Neyveli Lignite Corp., Neyveli, India, 1960—61; vis. scientist Inst. Fundamental Rsch., Braunschweig, Germany, 1961—62; grad. rsch. asst. Mich. State U., East Lansing, 1962—66, Iowa State U., Ames, 1966—67; asst. prof. U. Mo., Rolla, 1967—73, assoc. prof., 1973—77, prof., 1979—2002; vis. scientist Air Force Rsch. Lab., Dayton, Ohio, 1999—2001; rsch. prof. Washington U., St. Louis, 2003—. Cons. U. Dayton, Ohio, 1978—85, Air Force Rsch. Lab., Wright Patterson AFB, 1983—88; vis. scientist Air Force Office Scientific Rsch., Washington, 1986—88; editor-in-chief Math. and Computational Modelling jour., 1979—90, Math. and Computer Modelling Program Press, 1979—99, Math. Modelling and Scientific Computing jour., 1993—, Math. Modelling and Scientific Computing Principia Scientia, 1999—. Sr. Postgrad. fellow, NRC, 1974—76, NAS, 1998—2000. Mem.: Internat. Assn. Math. Modelling (pres. 1979—), Assn. Computing Machinery, Am. Soc. Mech. Engrs. Avocations: tennis, reading. Office: Washington U Campus Box 1185 One Brookings Dr Saint Louis MO 63130

AWAIS, GEORGE MUSA, obstetrician, gynecologist; b. Ajloun, Jordan, Dec. 15, 1929; arrived in U.S., 1951; s. Musa and Meha (Koury) A.; m. Nabila Rizk, June 24, 1970 AB, Hope Coll., 1955; MD, U. Toronto, 1960. Diplomate Am. Bd. Obstetrics and Gynecology. Intern U. Toronto Hosps., Canada, 1960—61, resident in ob-gyn, 1961—64, chief resident, 1965, Harlem Hosp., Columbia U., N.Y.C., 1966; asst. ob-gyn Cleve. Met. Gen. Hosp., 1967, assoc. ob-gyn, 1969; instr. ob-gyn Case We. Res. U., Cleve., 1967—70, asst. ob-gyn MacDonald House, 1970, asst. prof., 1970, asst. clin. prof. dept. reproductive biology, 1971, asst. ob-gyn Univ. Hosps., 1971; mem. staff, dept. gynecology Cleve. Clinic Found., 1971—91. Chmn. dept. ob-gyn. King Faisal Specialist Hosp. and Rsch. Ctr., Riyadh, 1975-76; cons. panel mem. Internat. Corr. Soc. Obstetricians and Gynecologists, 1971; emeritus staff Cleve. Clinic Found., 1991; pres. Task Force on Humanitarian Aid and Relief Inc., 1997. Contbr. articles to publs. in field, papers, reports to confs., TV appearances, Saudi Arabia Named Grand Officer of Order of Independence His Majesty King Hussein of Jordan, 1992. Fellow ACS, Am. Coll. Obstetricians and Gynecologists, Royal Coll. Surgeons Can.; mem. AMA, AAAS, Am. Infertility Soc., Arab Am. Med. Assn. (pres. 1991—, chmn. humanities relief 1996), Acad. Medicine of Cleve. Office: Cleve Clinic Found Emeritus Office EE/40 9500 Euclid Ave Cleveland OH 44195-0001 Office Phone: 216-444-6814. Business E-Mail: emeritus@ccf.org.

AWAKUNI, GENE I., academic administrator, psychologist; BA, MA, Univ. Hawaii, Manoa; PhD in psychol., Harvard Univ. Dir. counseling & psychol. svc. Univ. Calif., Irvine, asst. vice chancellor Santa Barbara; v.p. student affairs Calif. Poly., Pomona; vice provost, student affairs Stanford Univ.; chancellor Univ. Hawaii, West Oahu, 2005—. Co-author: Resistance to Multiculturalism: Issues and Interventions. Mem.: Asian Pacific Americans in Higher Edn. (past pres.). Office: Univ of Hawaii West Oahu 96-129 Ala'Ike Pearl City HI 96782*

AWAZU, YUKIKA, corporate financial executive; MBA, MA in Econs., U. Ill., Chgo., 2002. Founder YA Rsch. & Solutions; rsch. fellow Inst. for Engaged Bus. Rsch., Chgo., 2004; co-founder, v.p. Engaged Enterprise, Chgo., 2004—. Author: Engaged Knowledge Management; contbr. articles to profl. jours. Recipient H.B. Earhart student fellowship of Hoover Instn., Stanford U., 1997—98, 1998—99. Office: Engaged Enterprise Tower # 3705 555 W Madison St Chicago IL 60661

AXEL, RICHARD, pathology and biochemistry educator; b. NYC, July 2, 1946; AB magna cum laude, Columbia U., 1967; MD, Johns Hopkins U., 1970. Intern dept. pathology Columbia U. Coll. Physicians and Surgeons, N.Y.C., 1970-71; fellow Inst. Cancer Research, 1971-72; vis. fellow dept. pathology Columbia U., 1971-72; research assoc. USPHS, NIH, 1972-74; asst. prof. dept. pathology Inst. Cancer Research, Columbia U., 1974-78, prof. depts. pathology and biochemistry, 1978—. Mem. molecular biology study sect. NIH, 1981-, Ctr. for Neurobiology and Behavior; Univ. lectr. Columbia U., 1983; investigator, Howard Hughes Med. Inst. Assoc. editor: Cell, 1976-; contbr. articles to profl. jours. Recipient Irma T. Hirschl Career Scientist award, 1976, Young Scientist award Passano Found., 1979, Alan T. Waterman award, 1982, Eli Lilly award, 1983, Scientific Award, Moet Hennessy, Louis Vuitton, 1992, Disting. Scholar award, Kappa Chpt., Columbia, Sigma Xi Scientific Rsch. Soc., 1998, Mayor's award (NY)for Excellence in Science and Tech., 1998, Bristol Myers Squibb award for disting. achievement in neuroscience rsch., 1998, Perl/Univ. of NC Neuroscience prize, 2003, Internat. Gairdner award, 2003, co-recipient Nobel Prize in Medicine, 2004. Mem. NAS (Richard Lounsbery award 1989), Am. Acad. Arts and Scis., Phi Beta Kappa, GM Adv. Council, Cancer Rsch. Found., Am. Philosophical Soc. Achievements include discovery of (with Linda Buck) the odorant receptors and the organization of the olfactory system. Office: Howard Hughes Med Inst Columbia U Hammer Health Scis Ctr 701 W 168th St Room 1014 New York NY 10032-2704 Office Phone: 212-305-6915. Office Fax: 212-923-7249. E-mail: ra27@columbia.edu.

AXELROD, CHARLES PAUL, lawyer; b. N.Y.C., Oct. 23, 1941; s. Abraham and Lillian Rose (Neidetch) A.; m. Susan J. Schiender; children: Seth Jordan, Tracy Brooke. BS, NYU, 1963; JD, Bklyn. Law Sch., 1966. Bar: N.Y. 1966, U.S. Ct. Appeals (2d cir.) 1967, U.S. Dist. Ct. (so. dist.) N.Y. 1970, U.S. Supreme Ct. 1974, U.S. Dist. Ct. (ea. dist.) N.Y. 1975, U.S. Ct. Appeals D.C. 1979. Ptnr. Goldstein & Axelrod, N.Y.C., 1980-94, Camhy, Karlinsky & Stein LLP, N.Y.C., 1994-99, Greenberg Traurig LLP, 1999—. Chmn. legis. sub-com. study of securities laws N.Y. State Assembly, 1972; adj. prof. law Pace U., Pleasantville, N.Y., 1976-77. Vol. atty. City of N.Y. Com. on Human Rights, 1972. Mem. ABA (com on corp governance, com. on fed. reg. of securities, sub-com. on civil lit. and SEC enforcement matters, sub-com. on NASD corp. fin. rules), N.Y. State Trial Lawyers Assn., N.Y. County Lawyers Assn., N.Y. State Bar Assn., Nat. Assn. Securities Dealers (bd. arbitrators), Com. on Securities and Exchs. (N.Y.C.). Democrat. Jewish. Office: Greenberg Traurig LLP 200 Park Ave New York NY 10016 Office Phone: 212-801-9200. Business E-Mail: axelrodc@gtlaw.com.

AXELROD, EVAN M., psychologist, educator; s. David and Carrie Axelrod; m. Michelle Axelrod; children: Sam children: J. T. BA in Psychology, U. Puget Sound; D of Psychology, U. Denver. Bd. cert. traumatic stress expert Am. Acad. Experts Traumatic Stress, 2004. Clin. police psychologist Nicoletti-Flater Assocs., Lakewood, Colo., 2000—. Adj. prof. U. Denver Grad. Sch. Profl. Psychology. Contbr. text book. Grantee, U. Puget Sound, 1996—97. Mem.: APA, Colo. Psychol. Assn., Soc. Police and Criminal Psychology, Am. Acad. Experts Traumatic Stress, Internat. Assn. Chiefs of Police, Colo. Assn. Peer Support (hon.), Psi Chi. Achievements include research in Interpersonal Violence on the Internet and Cyber-Terrorism; Impact of Divorce on the Adjustment of College Students. Office: Nicolettii-Flater Assocs 3900 S Wadsworth Blvd Denver CO 80235 Office Phone: 303-989-1617. Personal E-mail: e2axe@aol.com.

AXELROD, GLEN SCOTT, publishing company executive, pet product company executive; b. Newark, Nov. 4, 1953; s. Alan Robert and Janet Lee Axelrod; m. Jennifer Anderson, June 24, 1979; children: Jason Aaron, Daniel Jay. BA in Biology, Rutgers U., 1975; MSc in Zoology/Ichthyology, Rhodes U., Grahamstown, South Africa, 1978. Rschr. in phylogenetics Rhodes U. and Mus. Comparative Zoology, Harvard U., 1978-79; asst. to pres., sr. editor TFH Pubs., Inc., Neptune City, N.J., 1979-81; asst. to prin. Six Star Cablevision Group, Englewood, N.J., 1981-82; exec. v.p. Breckenridge Devel. Corp., Wayne, NJ, 1985-92; pres., CEO Design Svcs., Riverdale, NJ, 1992-95; pres. GJA Prodn. Corp., Colts Neck, NJ, 1982—; exec. v.p. TFH Pubs., Inc., Neptune City, 1996-97, pres., CEO, 1997—. Bd. dir. TFH Pubs., Inc. Exec. editor Tropical Fish Hobbyist mag., 1998—; contbr. articles to profl. jours. Trustee, treas. Deerhaven Assn., Mahwah, 1990—97. Recipient Best New Dog and Cat Product award, Pet Industry Distbrs. Assn., 1999, 2000, Best New Product award, PETCO, 2001, Spirit Recognition award, 2003, Best New Gift-Gen. Merchandise Product award, Am. Pet Products Mfrs. Assn., 2002, Best New Product-Dog and Cat, 2003. Fellow The Zool. Soc. London (sci.), Masons. Achievements include patents in field; research in taxonomic description of new Pisces species. Avocations: skiing, diving, hiking, aquarium hobbyist, writing. Office: TFH Publications Inc One TFH Plz 3d & Union Neptune City NJ 07753

AXELROD, JONATHAN GANS, lawyer; b. N.Y.C., Oct. 23, 1946; s. Arthur and Rosalind (Gans) Axelrod; m. Carol Jean Zachary, Jan. 16, 1983; children: Zachary Arthur, Tristan Gans. AB, Dartmouth Coll., 1968; JD, Columbia U., 1971; LLM in Labor Law, George Washington U., 1975. Bar: N.Y. 1971, D.C. 1975. Trial atty. App. Ct. Br. NLRB, 1971-74; asst. gen. csl Ea. Conf. Teamsters, 1974-80; ptnr. Beins, Axelrod, Osborne, Mooney & Green, Washington, 1980-96, Beins, Axelrod, Kraft, Gleason & Gibson, P.C., Washington, 1996—. Contbr. articles to profl. jours. Mem. ABA, D.C. Bar Assn. (co-chmn. sect. on labor law 1985-89, steering com. 1990-91). Office: Beins Axelrod Kraft Gleason & Gibson PC 1717 Massachusetts Ave NW Washington DC 20036-2001 Office Phone: 202-328-7222. Business E-Mail: jaxelrod@bakgg.com.

AXELROD, LEONARD, management consultant; b. Oct. 27, 1950; s. Morris and Doris S. A. BA, Ind. U., 1972; MPA, U. So. Calif., 1974; JD, Hamline U., 1982. Asst. dir. Ind. Jud. Ctr. Ind. U. Sch. Law, Indpls., 1974-76; cons. Booz, Allen & Hamilton, Washington, 1976-77; staff assoc. Nat. Ctr. State Cts., St. Paul, 1977-82; ptnr. Ct. Mgmt. Cons., Mpls., Va., 1982-87, Friedman, Farrar & Axelrod, Mpls., 1984-86; prin. Ct. Mgmt. Cons., Mpls., 1987-94; v.p. CMC Justice Svcs., Inc., Mpls., 1994—; project mgr. Legal Rsch. Ctr., Mpls., 1996-97; ct. adminstr. U.S. Bankruptcy Ct., Mpls., 1997—2004; adj. prof. Coll. Mgmt. Met. State U., 1998—. Cons. Ctr. Jury Studies, Vienna, Va., 1979-82, Calif. Atty. Gen., 1972-73, Control Data Bus. Advisers, Mpls., 1982-88; arbitrator BBB, 2002—. Author: North Dakota Bench Book, 1982; contbr. articles to profl. jours.; assoc. editor Law Rev. Digest, 1982. Mem. presdl. search com. Hamline U., 1980-81; reporter Minn. Citizen Conf. on Cts., 1980; appointed to The Petrofund Bd., 1994. Samuel Miller scholar, 1981. Mem. ABA, ASPA, So. Calif. Soc. Pub. Adminstrn., Booz, Allen & Hamilton Alumni (pres. Minn. 1980), The Brandeis Soc. (exec. dir. Mpls. 1980), U. so. Calif. Midwest Alumni (exec. bd. Chgo. 1974), Phi Alpha Alpha, Phi Alpha Delta. Office: PO Box 11967 Saint Paul MN 55111-0967 Office Phone: 612-398-7345. E-mail: cmc@justice.com.

AXELROD, LLOYD, endocrinologist, educator; b. Bklyn., July 29, 1942; s. Louis E. and Sadie Rachel (Katz) A.; 1 child, Catherine Louise. AB, Princeton U., 1963; MD, Harvard U., 1967. Diplomate in endocrinology, diabetes and metabolism Am. Bd. Internal Medicine. Intern in medicine Peter Bent Brigham Hosp., Boston, 1967-68, jr. resident in medicine, 1968-69, rsch. fellow endocrinology, 1969-70, asst. in medicine, 1970-72; resident in medicine Mass. Gen. Hosp., Boston, 1970-71, clin. and rsch. fellow in medicine, 1971-72, chief resident in medicine, 1973, asst. in medicine, 1974-78, asst. physician, 1979-80, assoc. physician, 1981-89, physician, 1989—, chief James Howard Means firm, 1989—; chief med. unit Mass. Eye and Ear Infirmary, Boston, 1977-85. Instr. medicine Harvard Med. Sch., 1973-76, asst. prof. medicine, 1976-83, assoc. prof. medicine, 1983—; chmn. spl. rev. group Nat. Inst. Arthritis, Diabetes and Digestive and Kidney Diseases NIH, 1984-85; staff com. on ethics and stds. practice Mass. Gen. Hosp., 1989-94, ad hoc com. on informed consent, 1989-95, pharmacy com. 1985-90, tng. program com., med. svcs., 1989—, tchg. and tng. coun., med. svcs., 1997-, com. mem., instr. primary care program, 1974-88; chief's com. Mass. Eye and Ear Infirmary, 1977-85, patient care com., 1977-85, planning com., 1977-85, other coms.; standing com. on alumni fellowships Harvard Med. Sch., 1980-97; chmn. Harvard Med. Sch. bicentennial com. Mass. Eye and Ear Infirmary, 1981-83; preceptor New Pathway Project in Gen. Med. Edn. Harvard Med. Sch., 1986-88; cons. U.S. Atty., Dept. Justice, 1999, 2003, State of Calif. Dept. of Justice, 2001; lectr. in field. Co-author: (with others) Pineal Tumors, 1977, Human Health and Disease, 1977, Handbook of Drug Therapy, 1979, Textbook of Rheumatology, 1981, 4th rev. edit., 1993; Reviews on Endocrine Related Cancer, 1981, Conn's Current Therapy, 36th edit., 1984, Pathophysiology The Biological Principles of Disease, 2d edit., 1985, Anti-inflammatory Steroid Action: Basic and Clinical Aspects, 1989, Principles and Practice of Endocrinology and Metabolism, 1990, 3d rev. edit., 2001, Joslin's Diabetes Mellitus, 13th edit., 1994, Endocrinology, 4th edit., 2001, Endocrinology Mebabolism Clin. N.Am., 2003; editor Endocrinology Rounds, 2002—; mem. editl. bd. Diabetes, 1988-90; contbr. articles to profl. jours. Mem. U.S. Del. to China, 1975; mem. Mass. Gen. Hosp. Del. to China, 1979; mem. Guangdong com. of Mass. fgn. bus. coun. Commonwealth of Mass., 1981-82; adv. coun. Gov. Michael S. Dukakis on Mass.-Guangdong Friendship Agreement, 1984-88; diabetes guidelines work group Diabetes Control Program, Dept. Pub. Health Commonwealth of Mass., 2001, 03. Daland fellow for rsch. in Clin. Medicine Am. Philos. Soc., 1974-77. Fellow ACP; mem. Am. Diabetes Assn., Am. Fedn. Med. Rsch., NY Acad. Scis., Endocrine Soc., AAAS, Fuller Albright Soc. Harvard Med. Sch., Phi Beta Kappa, Alpha Omega Alpha. Achievements include discovery prostacyclin prodn. by adipose tissue, regulation of lipolysis by prostaglandins in adipose tissue and role of prostacyclin in pathogenesis of hemodynamic complications of diabetic ketoacidosis; description of insulin-like growth factor II(IGF-II) in pathogenesis of tumor-induced hypoglycemia and scholarly contributions on glucocorticoid therapy. Office: Mass Gen Hosp Diabetes Unit Fruit St Boston MA 02114-2620

AXELROD, NORMAN, retail company executive; BS, Lehigh U.; MBA, NYU. CEO, pres. Jaclyn, Inc. Linens 'n Things, Inc., Clifton, N.J., 1988—, also bd. dirs., chmn. bd. dirs., 2000—. Office: 6 Brighton Rd Clifton NJ 07012-1647

AXELROD, NORMAN N. (NORMAN NATHAN AXELROD), optical technical planning and technology application consultant; b. N.Y.C., Aug. 26, 1934; s. Louis E. and Sadie (Katz) A.; m. Victoria Ann Grant, Mar. 21, 1975; children: Lauren Grant, Brian George. AB, Cornell U., 1954; postgrad., U. Paris, France, 1958; PhD in Optics and Physics, U. Rochester, 1959. Aerospace scientist NASA, Goddard Space Flight Ctr., Washington, 1959-60; rsch. fellow U. London, 1960-61; asst. prof. U. Del., 1961-65; mem. tech. staff Bell Labs., Murray Hill, N.J., 1965-72; prin. Axelrod Assocs., N.Y.C., 1972—. Bd. dir. World Resources Devel. Corp., Input-Output Tech., Inc.; mem. adv. bd. Del. Dept. Edn., 1963-64; participant vis. scientist program Am. Inst. Physics, 1963-64; advisor to White House, 1969-70, French Ministry Nat. Def. and War, 1971, Am. Consumer Products, Inc., Baker-Botts, Bausch & Lomb, Calor plc, Compuscan, Corning, CPC, Delco, Finnegan, Henderson et al, GE, Gen Probe, Honeywell, IBM, ITT, Internat. FiberCom, Gen-Probe, Konishiroku, Johnson & Johnson, Labatt, Lear Siegler, Lockheed Martin, Medtronic, Recognition Equipment Inc., Perkin-Elmer, Sharp, Procter & Gamble, Samsung, Sensar, Teradyne, Timken Co., Unilever Rsch., Wall St. Jour., Wheatland Tube, Woodgrain Millwork; guest cons. Marine Biol. Lab., Woods Hole, Mass., 1993—; pro bono Met. Mus. Art, 1969-72, CUNY Grad. Vision Rsch. Biology, 2001—, Georgetown Med. Sch., 2005—. Editor: Optical Properties of Dielectric Films, 1968; book reviewer, cons. John Wiley & Sons, 1965-68, Rheinhold-Van Nostrand, 1968-70, Pergamon Press, 1969-70; contbr. articles to profl. jours. Patentee in field. Boldt scholar; recipient Fortune 500 Corp. award for tech. contbn., 1990; grantee NATO, NSF, Office of Naval Rsch. Fellow AAAS; mem. IEEE, Am. Phys. Soc., Am. Optical Soc., Soc. Mfg. Engrs. (cert. by stature as CMfgE in machine vision), Del. Acad. Sci., N.Y. Acad. Sci., Electrochem. Soc., Sigma Xi, Sigma Pi Sigma, Pi Mu Epsilon. Home: 445 E 86th St New York NY 10028-6433 Office: Norman Axelrod Assocs 121 W 27th St Ste 601 New York NY 10001-6207 Office Phone: 212-741-6302. E-mail: naxelrod@axelrodassociates.com.

AXELSON, CHARLES FREDERIC, retired accounting educator, food products executive; b. Chgo., Apr. 24, 1917; m. Dorothy L. Jepson, July 23, 1940 (dec. Oct. 1994); children: Linda Axelson Masters, Fred, Lorraine Axelson Gresty; m. Marion I. Murray, Mar. 11, 1995. AB, MBA, U. Chgo., 1937. Staff acct. Lybrand, Ross Bros. & Montgomery, Chgo., 1938-41; with U.S. Gypsum Co., Chgo., 1941-70, asst. controller, 1946-52, controller, 1952-60, controller, asst. treas., 1960-70; v.p. controller Libby, McNeill & Libby, Chgo., 1970-78; v.p., chief fin. officer Lawry's Foods, Inc., Los Angeles, 1978-82; prof. acctg. U. So. Calif., Los Angeles, 1982-85; vis. lectr. Darling Downs Inst. Advanced Edn., Toowoomba, Queensland, Australia, 1985; lectr. acctg. Calif. State Poly. U., Pomona, 1985-92; lectr. emeritus, 1992—95. Lectr. acctg. Northwestern U., 1946-53; bd. dirs. Air Conditioning Co., 1982-96; bd. dirs. Goodwill Industries So. Calif., 1982—. Trustee emeritus Nat. Louis U.; bd. dirs. Ability First (formerly Crippled Children's Soc. So. Calif.), chmn., 1986-89, vice-chmn., 1990-99. Named to Calif. Poly. Acctg. Hall of Fame, 1996; named Lipton Vol. of Yr., 1997. Mem. AICPA, Fin. Execs. Internat. (past dir. L.A. chpt., past pres. Chgo. chpt., past nat. dir., past v.p. Midwestern area), Phi Delta Theta. Clubs: Town Hall (Los Angeles). Presbyterian. Home: 888 S Orange Grove Blvd # 2-w Pasadena CA 91105-1790 *Whatever successes I've had - business and personal - can be traced to self-discipline, a good education, a reputation for integrity, much reading, good health, outside interests to offset business pressures and lots of advance planning.*

AXELSON, JOSEPH ALLEN, professional sports team executive, publishing executive; b. Peoria, Dec. 25, 1927; s. Joseph Victor Axelson and Florence (Ealen) Massey; m. Malcolm Rae Smith, Oct. 7, 1950 (dec.); children: David Allen, Mark Stephen, Linda Rae. BS, Northwestern U., 1949. Cert. judge Kansas City Barbeque Soc. Sports info. dir. Ga. So. U., Statesboro, 1957-60, Nat. Assn. Intercollegiate Athletics, Kansas City, Mo., 1961-62; tournament dir. Bowling Proprs. Assn. Am., Park Ridge, Ill., 1963-64; asst. exec. sec. Nat. Assn. Intercollegiate Athletics, Kansas City, Mo., 1964-68; exec. v.p., gen. mgr. Cin. Royals Profl. Basketball Team, Cin., 1969-72; mgr. Cin. Gardens, 1970-72; pres., gen. mgr. Kansas City Kings Profl. Basketball Team, Kansas City, Mo., 1972-79, 82-85; lectr. Fred Pryor Seminars, Overland Park, Kans., 1978—83; pres., gen. mgr. Sacramento Kings Profl. Basketball Team, 1985-88, exec. v.p., 1988-90; pres. Arco Arena, Sacramento, 1985-88; exec. v.p. Sacramento Sports Assn., Arco Sports Complex, 1988-90, Profl. Team Publs., Inc., Stamford, Conn., 1991-92; pub. Between The Vines Newsletter, 1993—. Exec. v.p. ops. NBA, N.Y.C., 1979-82, chmn. competition and rules com., 1975-79; trustee Naismith Basketball Hall of Fame; co-host The Sports Page, Sta. KFMB-AM, San Diego, 1994-97. Author: Basketball Basics, 1987. Mem. Emil Verban Meml. Soc., Washington. Capt. Signal Corps. AUS, 1949-54. Named Nat. Basketball Exec. of Yr. The Sporting News, St. Louis, 1973, Sportsman of Yr., Rockne Club, Kansas City, 1975; recipient Annual Dirs. award Downtown, Inc., Kansas City, Mo., 1979, Nat. Assn. Intercollegiate Athletics Frank Cramer Nat. Svc. award, 1983, Man of Yr. award Sacramento (Calif.) C. of C., 1986, Sacramento Bus. Cmty. award, 1986; named to Ga. So. U. Sports Hall of Fame, 1990. Mem. Am. Philatelic Soc., Soc. for Am. Baseball Rsch., Phi Kappa Psi, Morse Telegraph Club, Inc. Republican. Presbyterian. Home and Office: 230 B Ave Coronado CA 92118-1970

AXELSON, LINDA RAE, event planning specialist; b. Statesboro, Ga., May 22, 1959; d. Joseph Allen and Malcolm Rae (Smith) Axelson; m. Aug. 29, 1981 (div. Feb. 1989). BA in Spanish, Baker U., 1981. Acct. Lois A. Brozey, CPA, San Diego, 1981-82; bus. mgr. San Diego Chicken, Inc., 1983; discount brokerage mgr. Union Bank and Trust, Bartlesville, Okla., 1984; bus. mgr. ARCO Arena, Sacramento, 1985-86, box office mgr., 1987-91, San Diego Sports Arena, 1991-92, Arrowhead Pond of Anaheim, Calif., 1993-96; asst. contr. Stamford Ctr. for the Arts, 1997-98, box office mgr., 1999—2000; events mgr. Allied Domecq Spirits and Wine N.Am., 2001—03; acct. supr. Relay Event Mktg., NYC, 2004—. Cons. Don Chargin Boxing Prodns., L.A., 1987—. Recipient scholarship Baker Univ., 1981. Mem. Alpha Chi Omega (sch. com. chmn. 1981), Sigma Delta Pi, Alpha Mu Gamma. Republican. Presbyterian. Avocation: collector of mystery novels and miniatures. Home: 67 River St New Canaan CT 06840 E-mail: axelson932@optonline.net.

AXEN, GARY JAMES, geology educator; b. Tucson, Jan. 6, 1957; s. Duane George and Neva Jane (Hermann) A. BS, MS, MIT, 1980; PhD, Harvard U., 1991. Vis. instr. Idaho State U., Pocatello, 1981-82; instr. No. Ariz. U., Flagstaff, 1982-85, rsch. fellow, 1985-87; vis. lectr. (part-time) MIT, Cambridge, Mass., fall 1991, Harvard U., Cambridge, spring 1992, postdoctoral fellow (part-time), 1991-92; investigador titular CICESE, Baja California, Mexico, 1992-95; asst. prof. UCLA, 1995—. Cons. Hydro Geo Chem, Inc., Tucson, 1980-81. Contbr. articles to profl. jours. Recipient McDermott scholarship MIT, 1975-78, NSF Grad. fellowship Harvard, 1987-90. Fellow Geol. Soc. Am.; mem. AAAS, Am. Geophysical Union, Union Geofisica Mexicana, Sigma Xi. Achievements include research in extensional tectonics--documentation of existence, geometric/kinematic evolution of large-slip low angle normal faults, and the mechanics of their movement. Office: UCLA Dept Earth And Space Scis Los Angeles CA 90095-0001

AXFORD, ROY ARTHUR, nuclear engineering educator; b. Detroit, Aug. 26, 1928; s. Morgan and Charlotte (Donaldson) A.; m. Anne-Sofie Langfeldt Rasmussen, Apr. 1, 1954; children: Roy Arthur, Elizabeth Carole, Trevor Craig Charles. BA, Williams Coll., 1952; BS, MIT, 1952, MS, 1955, DSc, 1958. Supr. theoretical physics group Atomics Internat., Canoga Park, Calif., 1958-60; assoc. prof. nuc. engring. Tex. A&M U., 1960-62, prof., 1962-63; assoc. prof. nuc. engring. Northwestern U., 1963-66; assoc. prof. U. Ill., Urbana, 1966-68, prof., 1968—. Cons. Los Alamos (N.Mex.) Nat. Lab., 1963— Vice-chmn. MIT Alumni Fund Drive, 1970-72, chmn., 1973-75; sustaining fellow MIT, 1984. Mem. ASME, Am. Nuc. Soc. (Excellence in Undergrad. Tchg. award 1990, 95, 97, 99, 2002, 04, disting. faculty Alpha Nu Sigma 1991), SAR (sec.-treas. Piankeshaw chpt. 1975-81, v.p. chpt. 1982-83, pres. chpt. 1984-86), Kiwanis (charter life patron fellow 1992), Sigma Xi, Tau Beta Pi, Phi Kappa Phi. Home: 2017 S Cottage Grove Ave Urbana IL 61801-6353

AXILROD, STEPHEN HARVEY, global economic consultant, economist; b. N.Y.C., June 21, 1926; s. Jacob James and Pearl (Feltenstein) A.; m. Katherine Podolsky, July 1, 1950; children: Peter, Emily Axilrod Hildner,

Richard. Student, So. Meth. U., 1943-44; AB magna cum laude, Harvard U., 1948; MA, U. Chgo., 1950, postgrad., 1951-52. Assoc. dir. div. research and statistics Fed. Res. Bd., Washington, 1970-73, advisor to bd. govs., 1973-76, staff dir. for monetary and fin. policy, 1976-86; economist domestic fin. Fed. Open Market Com., Washington, 1974-78, economist, 1978-81; staff dir., sec. Fed. Open Market Commn., Washington, 1981-86; vice chmn. Nikko Securities Internat., N.Y.C., 1986-94; cons. internat. orgns. and ctrl. banks on policy ops., 1994—; cons. global econs. and markets pvt. practice, 1994—. Advisor Brookings Panel on Econ. Activity, Washington, 1986-89; mem. investment com. Japan Soc., 1987-2003; mem. adv. coun. Ctrl. Bank of Oman, 1993-99. Contbr. articles on monetary policy, credit and securities markets, transformation of policy ops. and markets in emerging countries and related matters to books, newspapers, mags. and profl. jours. Bd. mem. Fin. Svcs. Vol. Corp., 2005—. With USN, 1944—46. Mem. Phi Beta Kappa. Avocations: flute, tennis, reading, hiking, squash. E-mail: staxil@aol.com.

AXINN, GEORGE HAROLD, rural sociology educator; b. Jamaica, N.Y., Feb. 1, 1926; s. Hyman and Celia (Schneider) A.; m. Nancy Kathryn Wigsten, Feb. 17, 1945; children: Catherine, Paul, Martha, William. BS, Cornell U., 1947; MS, U. Wis., 1952, PhD, 1958. Editorial asst. Cornell U. Geneva, N.Y., 1947; bull. editor U. Md., College Park, 1949; chmn. dept. rural communication U. Del., Newark, 1950; mem. faculty Mich. State U., East Lansing, 1953—, assoc. dir. coop. extension service, 1955-60; coordinator U. Nigeria program, 1961-65, prof. agrl. econs., 1970-85, prof. resource devel., 1985-95, prof. emeritus, 1996—, asst. dean internat. studies and programs, 1964-85; pres., exec. dir. Midwest Univs. Consortium for Internat. Activities, Inc., 1969-76, 1969-76. FAO rep. to Nepal, 1983-85, India and Bhutan, 1989-91; cons. World Bank, 1973-74, Ford Found., 1968, UNICEF, 1978, FAO, 1974, 87, 89, Govt. of India, 1988-90; vis. prof. Cornell U., Ithaca, N.Y., 1958-60, U. Ill., Urbana, 1969-70 Author: Modernizing World Agriculture: A Comparative Study of Agricultural Extension Education Systems, 1972, New Strategies for Rural Development, Rural Life Associates, 1978, FAO Guide Alternative Approaches to Agricultural Extension, 1988, Collaboration in International Rural Development - A Practitioner's Handbook (with Nancy W. Axinn), 1997; contbr. articles to various publs. Served with USNR, 1944-46. Recipient Outstanding Alumni award Cornell U. Coll. Agrl. and Life Sci., 1993; W.K. Kellogg Found. fellow, 1956-57. Home: 280 E Morning Sun Ct Tucson AZ 85704-6945 Personal E-mail: axinn@msu.edu.

AXINN, STEPHEN MARK, lawyer; b. NYC, Oct. 21, 1938; s. Mack N. and Lili H. (Tannenbaum) A.; m. Stephanie Chertok, May 12, 1963; children: Audrey, David, Jill. BS, Syracuse U., 1959; LLB, Columbia U., 1962. Bar: N.Y. 1962, U.S. Supreme Ct. 1962. Assoc. Cahill & Gordon, N.Y.C., 1963-64, Malcolm A. Hoffman, N.Y.C., 1964-66, Skadden, Arps, Slate, Meagher & Flom, N.Y.C., 1966-69, ptnr., 1970-97, Axinn, Veltrop & Harkrider LLP, N.Y.C., 1997—. Lead counsel WorldCom-Spring major investigation and litigation antitrust divsn. U.S. Dept. Justice, 1999-2000; adj. prof. Law Sch. NYU, 1981-83, Law Sch. Columbia U., 1983-85; counsel Bellsouth and Cingulgar in acquisition of AT&T Wireless. Author: Acquisitions Under H-S-R, 1980; contbr. articles to profl. jours. Chmn. lawyers div. United Jewish Appeal, N.Y.C., 1985-87; mem. exec. com., treas. Jewish Theol. Sem. Am., 1984-96; mem. bd. visitors Columbia Law Sch., 1993-98; mem. adv. panel on environ. crimes by orngs. U.S. Sentencing Commn., 1992-94. Capt. U.S. Army, 1965-68. Mem. ABA (council antitrust sect. 1983-85), N.Y. State Bar Assn. (chmn. antitrust sect. 1982-83). Office: Axinn Veltrop & Harkrider LLP 1370 Ave of the Americas New York NY 10019-6708 also: 1801 K St NW Washington DC 20006 Business E-Mail: sma@avhlaw.com.

AXLEY, FREDERICK WILLIAM, lawyer; b. Chgo., June 23, 1941; s. Frederick R. and Elena (Hoffman-Pinther) A.; m. Cinda Jane Russell, Mar. 29, 1969; children: Sarah Elizabeth, Elizabeth Jane. BA, Holy Cross Coll., 1963; MA, U. Wis., 1966; JD, U. Chgo., 1969. Bar: Ill. 1969, U.S. Dist. Ct. (no. dist.) Ill. 1969, U.S. Ct. Appeals (7th cir.) 1970. Assoc. McDermott, Will & Emery, Chgo., 1969-74, jr. ptnr., 1974-80, sr. ptnr., 1980—. Trustee Wilmette Elem. Sch. Dist. #39, Ill., 1976-81, Ill. chpt. Nature Conservancy, 1983-91; bd. dirs. Bus. and Profl. People for the Pub. Interest, Chgo., 1984—; bd. dirs. Friends of the Chgo. River, 1994—, pres., 1998—; bd. dirs. Shore Line Place, 1994—, pres. 2001—, Interfaith Housing Devel. Corp., 1997—, 1st. v.p., 2000—. Served to lt. USN, 1963-65. Mem. Mich. Shores Club (Wilmette). Democrat. Roman Catholic. Office: McDermott Will & Emery 227 W Monroe St Ste 3100 Chicago IL 60606-5096 E-mail: faxley@msn.com.

AXLEY, HARTMAN, retired real estate planner, underwriter; b. Madison, Wis., Apr. 17, 1931; s. Ralph Emerson and Katharine Nella (Hartman) A.; m. Marguerite Ann Thessin, Sept. 4, 1954; children: Colleen Lynn Axley Patrick, Timothy Hartman Axley. BA, U. Wis., 1952, JD, 1956; MSFS, Am. Coll., Bryn Mawr, Pa., 1983. CLU, cert. fin. planner, accredited estate planner; chartered fin. cons.; registered health underwriter. Assoc. atty. Holland & Hart, Denver, 1956-58; life underwriter Colo. Assocs. of Allmerica Fin. (formerly State Mut. Cos.), Denver, 1958—2003. Mem. bd. editl. advisors Fin. Svc. Advisors (formerly Life and Health Insurance Sales), Lexington, Ky.; mem. Colo. Ethics in Bus. Alliance Bd., 1995—, v.p., 2001-; mem. Denver Estate Planning Coun., pres., 1968-69; founding mem. Boulder County Estate Planning Coun., 1976—. Author: National Ski Patrol Ski Lift Evacuation Manual, 1975, National Ski Patrol Awards Manual, 1980. Bd. dir. Met. Denver YMCA, 1978-81; bd. dirs. S.W. Denver Family YMCA, 1973—, chmn. bd. dir., 1978-81; mem. First Aider Mile High chpt. ARC, Denver, 1956-86; bd. dir., officer Community Concert Assn. Denver, 1962-65; bd. dir. Colo. Ski Mus., 1994—, vice chair, 2003-; chair Colo. Ski Hall of Fame, 1996-99; mem. Nat. Ski Patrol System, 1948—, asst. nat. dir., 1969-76, Rocky Mountain div. dir., 1963-69 (Minnie Dole award 1988, Schobinger Outstanding Adminstr. award 1973); mem. Olympic Ski Patrol, Squaw Valley, Calif., 1960; mem., patroller Arapahoe Basin Ski Patrol, 1956-85, front range dir., 1961-63; coord. badminton Rocky Mountain Sr. Games, 1987—. Capt. USAF (JAG), 1952-60. Named to Roll of Honor, Mile High ARC, 1974, to Denver YMCA Hall of Fame, Met. Denver YMCA, 1987, to Colo. Ski Hall of Fame, 1993; recipient Award of Merit (Lifesaving) ARC, 1959, J. Stanley Edwards award Colo. and Denver Assn. Life Underwriters, 1980, Badminton medal Rocky Mountain Sr. Games, 1987—, U.S. Badminton Assn. Sr. Championship, 1988, 92, U.S. Nat. Sr. Games, 1991, 93, 95, 97, 99, 2001, 2003, 2005. Mem. ABA (real property, probate and trust sect.), Nat. Assn. Estate Planners and Couns. (bd. dirs. 1970-76, pres. 1974-75, dir. emeritus 1989—, patron chair 1975—, accreditation com. 1991—, Hartmark Axley award for outstanding svc. and achievement 2004), Nat. Assn. Estate Planners (founding mem. bd. dirs. 1987), Soc. of Fin. Svcs. Profls. (bd. dirs. 1992-95, western region v.p. 1994-95, nat. pub. rels. com. 1990-94, vice chair 1992, chair baby boomer rsch. project 1990, Colo.-Wyo. liaison 1992-97), Estate Law Specialists Bd. Inc. (founding mem., bd. dirs. 1996—), Am. Soc. CLU and ChFC (Rocky Mountain chpt. bd. dirs. 1985-91, pres. 1989-90), Assn. Advanced Life Underwriters (Colo. liaison, 1996-2000), Nat. Assoc. of Ins. and Fin. Advisors (Wesley Whitney award 1995, qualifying and life mem., Million Dollar Round Table 1970-85), Colo. Ins. Commr.'s Adv. Coun. (chmn. 1990—), Colo. Assn. Commerce and Industry (Health Care Task Force 1990-94), Nat. and Colo. Assoc. of Ins. and Fin . Advisors (Nat. Quality award, Nat. Sales Achievement award), Life Underwriter Charities, Inc. (founding mem. bd. dirs. 1989-92), Metro Denver Assn. Health Underwriters (founding mem. bd. dirs. 1990-92, legis. chair 1990-92), Colo. State Assn. Health Underwriters (charter 1986—, founding mem. bd. dirs. 1986-92, legis. chair 1986-92), Nat. Assn. Health Underwriters (leading producers roundtable 1981-89), U.S. Badminton Assn. (staff vol. Olympic Games Atlanta 1996), U. Wis. Alumni Assn. (bd. dirs. 1970-89, Spark Plug award 1977), Wis. Bar Assn., Blade Mil. R.O.T.C. and Provist Corps, Denver Athletic Club (bd. dirs. 1984-87, Sr. Athlete of Yr. 1997, Legend 2003), Phi Delta Phi (life mem.), Phi Mu Alpha. Congregationalist. Avocations: skiing, badminton, deltiophile, singing, travel. Home and Office: 1845 S Jay Way Lakewood CO 80232-7095 Office Phone: 720-941-9703.

AXON, DONALD CARLTON, architect; b. Haddonfield, NJ, Feb. 27, 1931; s. William Russell Sr. and Gertrude L. (Ellis) A.; m. Rosemary Smith, Sept. 1952 (div. Oct. 1967); children: Donald R., James K., Marianne Axon Flannery, Darren H., William R. II; m. Janice Jacobs, Mar. 16, 1968; stepchildren: Jonathan Lee, Elise Marie. BArch, Pratt Inst., 1954; MS in Arch., Columbia U., 1966. Registered architect, NY, Pa., Calif. Designer, drafter Keith Hibner, Assoc., Hicksville, NY, 1954-56; designer Charles Wood, Riverhead, NY, 1956-59; architect, prin Donald C. Axon, Assoc., Wantaugh, NY, 1959; ptnr. Bailey-Axon & Assoc., Long Beach, NY, 1960-66; project mgr. Caudill Rowlett Scott, Houston, 1966-69; in-house arch. Kaiser Permanente Hosp., LA, 1969-75; dir. med. facilities Daniel Mann Johnson Mendenhall, LA, 1975-78, Lyon Assoc., LA, 1979-80; pres. Donald C. Axon, FAIA, Inc., LA, 1980—. Tchr. bldg. sci. program U. So. Calif., 1978-82; lectr. in field; profl. advisor dept. architecture U. Tex., 1968-69; advisor to chmn. Sch. Architecture Rice U., Houston, 1968-69; profl. dir. Future Architect Am., 1965-66. Mem. Crestwood Hills Assn., bd. dir. 1971-75, pres., 1973-75, archtl. rev. com., 1987—; bd. dir. Brentwood Community Fedn., 1973-75, v.p., 1974-75. Recipient LA Beautiful award KPH Norwalk Hosp. Fellow AIA, Royal Soc. Health, Health Facilities Inst., Am. Coll. Healthcare Arch. (founding fellow),(Calif. regional bd. dir. 1987-89, mem. various subcoms., chair steering com. 1980, liaison 1991—, bd. dir. L.A. chpt. 1983-84, pres. 1986, chair com. on architecture for health 1974, chair health facilities com. Calif. coun. 1975, Disting. Svc. citation 1992), mem. Am. Soc. Healthcare Engr., Archtl. Found. LA (founding, v.p. 1985-89, pres. 1989-90), Internat. Conf. Bldg. Ofcl., Am. Hosp. Assn., Forum for Health Care Planning (bd. dir. 1982—, pres. 1993-94). Office: 24302 Carlton Ct Laguna Niguel CA 92677-3718 Fax: 949-360-8114. E-mail: donaxon@aol.com.

AXTELL, CLAYTON MORGAN, JR., lawyer; b. Deposit, N.Y., Aug. 4, 1916; s. Clayton Morgan and Olive Aurora (Vosburgh) A.; m. Margaret Williamson Ritchie, Apr. 24, 1943 (dec.); children: Margaret R. Axtell Stevenson, Clayton Morgan III, Karen R. Axtell Arnold, Susan R. Axtell. AB, Cornell U., 1937, JD, 1940. Bar: N.Y. 1940, U.S. Dist. Ct. (no. dist.) N.Y. 1941, U.S. Supreme Ct. 1964. Assoc. Hinman, Howard & Kattell, Binghamton, N.Y., 1940-48, ptnr., 1948—. Former mem. adv. bd. First-City Nat. Bank, Binghamton; bd. dirs. Farmers Nat. Bank, Deposit, N.Y., First City Nat. Bank, Binghamton. Pres. N.Y. State Sch. Bd. Attys., Albany, 1962-63, Broome County Bar Assn., Binghamton, 1967-68, Conrad and Virginia Klee Found., 1977-2003; mem. N.Y. State Rep. Com., Binghamton, 1988-93. 1st lt. US Army, 1942-46 ETO. Decorated Bronze Star U.S. Army, 1945, Croix de Guerre, Govt. of France, 1945; recipient Disting Svc. award U.S. Jr. C. of C., 1942; named Young Man of Yr. Binghamton Jr. C. of C., 1949. Mem. ABA, N.Y. State Bar Assn., Hillcrest -Port Dick Kiwanis (past pres.), Binghamton Club. Republican. Lutheran. Home: 1338 Chenango St Binghamton NY 13901-1539 Office: Hinman Howard & Kattell 80 Exchange St Binghamton NY 13901-3490

AXTELL, JAMES LEWIS, history professor; b. Endicott, NY, Dec. 20, 1941; s. Arthur James Axtell and Laura (England) Levinsky; m. Susan Carol Hallas, Aug. 31, 1963; children: Nathaniel Harsen, Jeremy England. BA, Yale U., 1963; PhD, U. Cambridge, Eng., 1967. Asst. prof. Yale U., New Haven, 1966-72; assoc. prof. Sarah Lawrence Coll., Bronxville, N.Y., 1972-75; vis. prof. Northwestern U., Evanston, Ill., 1977-78; prof. Coll. of William and Mary, Williamsburg, Va., 1978—; William R. Kenan Jr. prof. of humanities Coll. William and Mary, Williamsburg, Va., 1986—. Author: The Educational Writings of John Locke, 1968, The School Upon a Hill, 1974, The European and the Indian, 1981, The Invasion Within, 1985 (prize, 1985, 2 prizes, 1986), After Columbus, 1988, Beyond 1492, 1992, The Indians' New South, 1997, The Pleasures of Academe, 1998, Natives and Newcomers, 2001; editor: The Indian Peoples of Eastern America, 1981; contbr. articles to profl. jours. in field. Recipient Outstanding Faculty award Va. State Coun. Higher Edn., 1988; NEH fellow, 1975-77, 86, 92, J.S. Guggenheim Meml. Found. fellow, 1981-82, Am. Coun. Learned Socs. fellow, 1987. Fellow Am. Acad. Arts and Scis.; mem. Soc. Am. Historians, Am. Soc. for Ethnohistory (pres. 1988-89), The Champlain Soc., Am. Hist. Assn., Orgn. Am. Historians, Colonial Soc. Mass., Pilgrim Soc, Mass. Hist. Soc. Democrat. Avocation: book collecting. Home: 109 Walnut Hills Dr Williamsburg VA 23185-3426 Office: Coll of William & Mary Dept History Williamsburg VA 23187-8795 Office Phone: 757-221-3730. E-mail: jlaxte@wm.edu.

AXTHELM, NANCY, advertising executive; V.p./prodn. group head Grey Worldwide (formerly Grey Advt. Inc.), sr. v.p., dep. dir. broadcast prodn., 1990—92, sr. v.p., dir. broadcast prodn., 1992—93, exec. v.p., dir. broadcast prodn., 1993—. Office: Grey Worldwide 777 3rd Ave Fl 10 New York NY 10017-1302

AYABE, SIDNEY K., lawyer; b. Honolulu, June 15, 1945; s. Yoshio and Betty S. Ayabe; m. Gloria Doo, June 7, 1977; children: Lisa, Sara, Marie. BA, Lawrence U., Appleton, Wis., 1967; JD, U. Iowa, 1970. Dep. atty. gen. State Atty. Gen.'s Office, Honolulu, 1970-72; ptnr. Ayabe Chong Nishimoto Sia & Nakamura, Honolulu, 1972—. Dir. Mediation Ctr. of the Pacific, Honolulu, 1997—; mem. Jud. Selection com., 2001—, chair, 2003—. Recipient Cert. of Appreciation for contbn. in real estate Hawaii Real Estate Commn., 1987, Spl. Bd. Recognition award Neighborhood Justice Ctr., 1998. Fellow Am. Coll. Trial Lawyers (state chair 2002-03, Appreciation for Outstanding Leadership as chair of Hawaii state com. 1995); mem. ABA, Am. Bd. Trial Advocates (assoc.), Hawaii State Bar Assn. (pres. 1995), Internat. Assn. Def. Counsel, Hawaii Def. Lawyers Assn. (v.p. 1989). Home: 1745 Nalulu Pl Honolulu HI 96821-1338 Office: Ayabe Chong Nishimoto et al #2500 Pauahi 1001 Bishop St Ste 2500 Honolulu HI 96813-3590

AYAD, JOSEPH MAGDY, retired psychologist; b. Cairo, May 21, 1926; arrived in U.S., 1949, naturalized, 1961; s. Fahim Gayed and Victoria Gabour (El-Masri) Ayad; m. Widad Fareed Bishai, May 29, 1954; children: Fareed Merritt, Victor Maher, Michael Joseph, Mona Elaine. BA in Social Scis., Am. U., Cairo, 1946; MA in Clin. Psychology, Stanford U., 1952; PhD in Clin. Psychology, U. Denver, 1956. Trans. Hoover Inst. War and Peace Stanford U., 1950—51; asst. to chief psychologist Colo. Psychopathic Hosp., 1952—54; cons. Child Guidance Clinic State Dept. Pub. Welfare, Denver, 1953—56; cons. psychologist Dept. Pub. Welfare State of Tex., 1957—72; cons. psychologist Dept. Insts. Social and Rehab. Svc. State of Okla., 1960—72; cons. psychologist N.Mex. Dept. Pub. Welfare, 1960—72; lectr. Fitzsimmons Army Hosp., Denver, 1953—54; vis. psychologist Child Guidance Clinic State Dept. Pub. Welfare, Pueblo, Colo., 1953—54; staff psychologist Cons. Psychol. Svc., Denver, 1956—57, High Plains Neurol. Ctr., Amarillo, Tex., 1973—2002; pres. JMA Cattle Co., Amarillo, 1973—2002; v.p., treas. Filigon Inc., Amarillo, 1962—75, pres., 1976—2002, ret., 2002. Mem. profl. adv. bd. Amarillo Mental Health Assn., 1968—69. Contbr. articles to profl. jours. Mem. Amarillo Child Welfare Bd., 1961—63; area chmn. U. Denver Fund Raising Campaign, 1963; mem. profl. adv. bd. St. Paul's Meth. Ch. Sch. for Children with Learning Disabilities, Amarillo, 1969—70. Recipient Grad. Sr. award in philosophy, Am. U. at Cairo, 1946. Mem.: APA, Calif. Psychol. Assn., Tex. Psychol. Assn., Potter-Randall County (Tex.) Psychol. Soc. (pres. 1974), Am. Assn. Marriage and Family Therapists, Internat. Assn. Applied Psychology, Am. Psychol. Soc., Amarillo Country Club. Presbyterian. Home: 4239 Erik Ave Amarillo TX 79106-6008 Office Phone: 806-352-8840.

AYAFOR, MARTIN CHUNGONG, ambassador; b. Awing, Bamenda, Cameroon, Mar. 15, 1947; arrived in US, 1980; s. Joseph Chungong and Regina Ngwing; m. Justina Melo Chinda, Dec. 26, 1973; children: Akwesey Ngwenyi, Ayafor Temengye, Ngwingmba Azisch, Apiseh Ayakeh, Aziwoh Afeseh, Nchinda Sehlakwe. BA wih honors in hist., U. Cameroon, Cameroon, 1972; MPhil in polit. sci., Internat. Rel.; doctorate in internat. rels., Inst. of Cameroon, Cameroon, 1974; MBA in pub. mgmt., Higher Inst. of Pub. Mgmt. of Cameroon, 1985. Cert. Pub. Svc. Diplomat Pub. Svc. Bd. Exams., Cameroon, 1980. Head UN divsn. Min. of Fgn. Affairs, Yaounde, Cameroon, 1977—80; second counselor Cameroon Mission to UN, N.Y.C., 1981—83; head diplomatic affairs' divsn. Presidency of the Republic, Yaounde, 1983—89; permanent sec. Min. of Livestock, Fisheries and Animal Ind., Yaounde, 1989—90, Min. of External Rels., Yaounde, 1990—92; min., dir. Cabinet of the Prime Min., Head of Govt., Yaounde, 1992—96; ambassador, dep. permanent rep. Cameroon to the UN, N.Y.C., 2002—. Mem. UN Sec.-Gens. Adv. Bd. on Security and Disarmament Matters, N.Y.C., 1992—96; chmn. Panel of Experts on Sierra Leone, UN, N.Y.C., 2000—01, Panel of Experts on Liberia, UN, 2001—02; dir. publication Peace and Security Studies, Yaounde Internat. Inst., 1992. Contbr. articles various profl. jours. Mem. Cameroon Nat. Scholarships Commn., 1977—79; examiner, mem. Cameroon Gen. Cert. of Edn. Jury, 1977—79; mem. bd. dirs. Trans-Cameroon Railway Corp., 1984—89, Cameroon Nat. Water Corp., 1985—90; chmn. bd. dirs. Nat. Fin. Credit Corp., 2000—03. Recipient Knight Order of Valor, Govt. of Cameroon, 1986, Officer Order of Valor, 1989, Comdr. Order of Valor, 2002. Mem.: Cameroon Assn. of Diplomats (permanent sec. 1980—), Club '58 Social Club, Pub. Works Social Club (v.p. 1978—80). Avocations: reading, soccer, basketball, music, hunting. Home: 184-15 Avon Rd Jamaica NY 11432 Office: Cameroon Mission To The UN 22 E 73rd St New York NY 10021 Office Phone: 212-794-2295. Office Fax: 212-249-0533. Business E-Mail: tataayafor@aol.com.

AYALA, FRANCISCO JOSÉ, geneticist, educator; b. Madrid, Mar. 12, 1934; came to U.S., 1961, naturalized, 1971; s. Francisco and Soledad (Pereda) A.; m. Hana Lostakova, Mar. 8, 1985; children by previous marriage: Francisco José, Carlos Alberto. BS, Universidad de Madrid, 1954, D. honoris causa, 1986; MA, Columbia U., 1963, PhD, 1964; D. honoris causa, Universidad de León (Spain), 1982, Universidad de Barcelona, Spain, 1986, U. Athens, Greece, 1991, U. Vigo, Spain, 1996, U. Islas, Baleares, Spain, 1998, U. Valencia, Spain, 1999, U. Bologna, Italy, 2001, U. Vladivostok, Russia, 2002; D., Masaryk U., Czech. Rep., 2003. Research assoc. Rockefeller U., 1964-65; asst. prof. Providence Coll., 1965-67, Rockefeller U., 1967-71; assoc. prof. to prof. genetics U. Calif., Davis, 1971-87, disting. prof. biology Irvine, 1987-89, Donald Bren prof. of Biol. scis., 1989—, univ. prof., 2003—. Bd. dirs. basic biology NRC, 1982-91, chmn., 1984-91, mem. commn. on life scis., 1982-91; mem. nat. adv. coun. Nat. Inst. Gen. Med. Scis.; mem. exec. com. EPA, 1979-80; mem. adv. com. directorate sci. and engring. edn. NSF, 1989-91; mem. nat. adv. coun. for human genome rsch. NIH, 1990-93; mem. Pres. com. advisors sci. and tech., 1994-2001. Author: Population and Evolutionary Genetics, 1982, Modern Genetics, 1980, 2d edit., 1984, Evolving: the Theory and Processes of Organic Evolution, 1979, Evolution, 1977, Molecular Evolution, 1976, Studies in the Philosophy of Biology, 1974. Recipient medal Coll. de France, 1979, Mendel medal Czech Republic Acad. Scis., 1994, Hon. Gold medal Acad. Nat. dei Lincei, Rome, 2000, U.S. Nat. Medal of Sci. award 2001, gold medal Stazione Zoological Naples, 2003; Guggenheim fellow, Fulbright fellow. Fellow AAAS (Sci. Freedom and Responsibility award 1987, bd. dirs. 1989-93, pres.-elect 1993-94, pres. 1994-95, chmn. of bd. 1995-96, chmn. com. on health of sci. enterprise 1991—, mem. nat. coun. for sci. and edn. for phase II, project 2061 1990—); mem. NAS (sect. population biology evolution and ecology chmn. 1983-86, councillor 1986-89, bd. dirs. Nat. Acad. Corp. 1990—), Am. Acad. Arts and Scis., Am. Soc. Naturalists (sec. 1973-76), Genetics Soc. Am., Am. Genetic Assn. (hon. life, Wilhelmine E. Key award), Ecology Soc. Am., Am. Philos. Soc., Soc. Study Evolution (pres. 1979-80), Royal Acad. Scis. Spain (fgn. mem.), Russian Acad. Natural Scis. (fgn. mem.), Mex. Acad. Scis. (fgn. mem.), Acad. Nat. dei Lincei (Rome) (fgn.), Serbian Acad. Scis. & Arts (fgn. mem.), Sigma Xi (William Procter prize 2000, pres. 2003—). Home: 2 Locke Ct Irvine CA 92617-4034 Office: U Calif Dept Ecology & Evolution Irvine CA 92697-0001 Office Phone: 949-824-8293. Business E-Mail: fjayala@uci.edu.

AYALA, JOHN L., librarian, dean; b. Long Beach, Calif., Aug. 28, 1943; s. Francisco and Angelina (Rodriguez) Ayala; m. Patricia Marie Dozier, July 11, 1987 (dec. Jan. 19, 2001); children: Juan, Sara; m. Gloria Ann Aulwes, Dec. 28, 2002. BA in History, Calif. State U., Long Beach, 1970, MPA, 1981; MLS, Immaculate Heart Coll., L.A., 1971. Libr. paraprofl. Long Beach Pub. Lib., 1963-70; libr. L.A. County Pub. Libr., 1971-72, Long Beach City Coll., 1972-90, assoc. prof., 1972-90, pres. acad. senate, 1985-87; dean, Learning Resources Fullerton (Calif.) Coll., 1990—, evening/weekend supr., 1997—99, adminstr. study abroad program, 2000—. Chmn. Los Angeles County Com. to Recruit Mexican-Am. Librs., 1971-74; mem. acad. senate Calif. Cmty. Colls., 1985-90; pres. Latino Faculty/Staff Assn., NOCCD, 1993-2000. Editor: Calif. Librarian, 1971. Served with USAF, 1966-68, Vietnam. U.S. Office Edn. fellow for libr. sci., 1970-71. Mem. ALA (com. mem. 1971—, Melvil Dewey award com. 1998—), Calif. Libr. Assn., REFORMA Nat. Assn. to Promote Spanish Speaking Libr. Svc. (founding mem., v.p., pres. 1973-76), Arnulfo Trejo Libr. of the Yr. Award 2001, from Reforma), Calif. State U.-Long Beach Alumni Assn. (treas. 2003—). Democrat. Roman Catholic. Office: Fullerton College Library 321 E Chapman Ave Fullerton CA 92832-2011 Home: 607 E Las Palmas Dr Fullerton CA 92835-1617 Office Phone: 714-992-7061.

AYALA, ORLANDO, information technology executive; b. Bogota, Colombia; married; 4 children. BA in Mgmt. Info. Sys. With NCR Corp., Dayton, Ohio, 1981—91, product & sales mgr., 1985—88; sr. dir. Latin Am. region Microsoft Corp., Miami, 1991—95, sr. v.p., intercontinental region Redmond, Wash., 1995—98, sr. v.p., South Pacific & Amer. region, 1998—2000, group v.p., worldwide sales, mktg. & svc. group, 2000—03, sr. v.p., small & midmarket solutions & ptnr. group, 2003—. Office: Microsoft Corp One Microsoft Way Redmond WA 98052-6399

AYALON, DANIEL, ambassador; b. Tel Aviv, 1955; m. Anne Ayalon; 2 children. B in Econ., Tel Aviv U.; MBA, Bowling Green U., Ohio. Sr. fin. exec. internat. trading co., Israel; dep. chief of mission Panama, 1991—92; dir. Bur. of Israel Amb. to UN, NY, 1993—97; dep. fgn. policy adv. to prime min., 1997—2001; chief fgn. policy adv. to prime min., 2001—02; amb. to U.S., 2002—. Capt. (ret.) Armored Corps Israel Def. Forces. Office: Embassy of Israel 3514 International Dr NW Washington DC 20008

AYARS, PATTI, human resources specialist, health products executive; B in Bus. Adminstrn. with highest distinction, U. Neb. Various internat. and domestic human resources positions Monsanto Corp./Pharmacia, 1981—2001; v.p. human resources Roche Diagnostic Corp., Indpls., 2001—. Co-author: (book) Mastering Momentum: A Practical and Powerful Approach for Successful Change. Office: Roche Diagnostics Corp 9115 Hague Rd Indianapolis IN 46256-1025 Office Phone: 317-521-2000. Office Fax: 317-845-2221. E-mail: payars@creatingloyalty.com.*

AYASO, MANUEL, artist; b. Coruna, Galicia, Spain, Jan. 1, 1934; came to U.S., 1947, naturalized, 1955; s. Jose and Dolores (Dios) A.; m. Lucia Rivas, May 2, 1959; children: Monica, Jose Luciano. Student, Newark Sch. Fine and Indsl. Art, N.J., 1953-56. One-man shows include Cober Gallery, N.Y.C., 1961—68, Forum Gallery, 1970—74, Ft. Worth Art Ctr., 1964, SUNY-Oswego, 1965, Witt meml. Mus., San Antonio, 1967, Casa de Galicia, Madrid, Spain, 1994, N.Y. Armory, 1995, Casa da Parra, Santiago de Compostela, Spain, 1997, exhibited in group shows at 22d Biennial Internat. Watercolor Exhbn., Bklyn. Mus., 1963, U. Mex., Mexico City, 1963, Exhibit Contemporary Am. Artists, Nat. inst. Arts and letters, 1962—71, Whitney Mus. Am., 1963, Vatican Exhibit Contemporary Am. Spiritual Art, Rome, 1976, The Fine Line: Drawing with Silver in Am., 1985—86, Objects and Drawings from the Sanford M. and Diane Besser Collection, 1992—93, Casa da Cultura, Riveira La Coruna, Museo Valleinclan Puebla del Caraminal, La Coruna, 2001, retrospective exhbn., Fundacion Museo del Grabado, Artes, Riviera, Spain, 2002—03. Served with U.S. Army, 1956-58. Recipient St. Paul Gallery and Sch. Art Purchase award, 1961; Tiffany Found. Award, 1962; Ford Found. grantee, 1964; recipient Nat. Inst. Arts and Letters Childe Hassam Purchase award, 1971, hon. mention 2d Ann. Int. Exhibit of Miniature Art, Del Bello Gal, Toronto, Can., 1987. Mem. Nat. Geog. Soc., Smithsonian Instn., Whitney Mus. Am. Art, N.J. State Mus. Roman Catholic. Address: 12 Vincent Pl Verona NJ 07044-3022

AYBAR, ROMEO, architect; b. Buenos Aires, Feb. 8, 1930; came to U.S., 1960, naturalized, 1965; s. Aristobulo Romeo and Maria Sara (Figoli) A.; m. Rose Delia Caceres, Oct. 18, 1954; children: Patricia Monica Aybar Waler, Viviana Sylvia Aybar Pugaczewski, Cynthia Jenny Aybar Giordano. B.Arch., U. Buenos Aires, 1954. Lic. architect, N.J., Pa., Del., Md., Vt., Va.; registered planner, N.J.; cert. Dept. Def. fall-out shelter analyst. Pvt. practice architecture, Buenos Aires, 1955-60; sr. draftsman Widersum Assocs., N.Y.C., 1960-61; job capt. Mahony Troast, Clifton, N.J., 1961-63; project mgr. R. Cadien Architect, Cliffside Park, N.J., 1963-67; ptnr. Cadien & Aybar, Cliffside Park, N.J., 1968-69; sr. ptnr. The Aybar Partnership-Architects and Planners, Ridgefield, N.J., 1969—; organizer, dir. First Fed. Bank, Clifton, N.J. Mem. adv. bd. archtl. drafting course The Plaza Sch., Paramus, N.J., 1971—; lectr. Ft. Lee High Sch., Ridgefield High Sch., N.J. Sch. Architecture, N.J. Inst. Tech., others; mem. adj. faculty Montclair State Coll., 1971-74 Mem. Indsl. Safety Council N.J., 1973-78; mem. Ridgefield Zoning Bd. Adjustments, 1969-71, chmn., 1972-73; mem. Hudson Riverfront Planning Commn. State of N.J., 1979-81; acting bldg. insp. City of Ridgefield, 1968; mem. planning commn. Ellis Island & Statue of Liberty Restoration Master Plan, 1979-80. 1st lt., pilot N.J. wing CAP, 1978. Recipient Dir.'s award Architects League N.J., 1971, 84, 86, Vegliante Meml. award Architects League N.J., 1973, Outstanding Excellence in Design award N.J. Soc. Architects, 1971, 73, citation for Outstanding Svcs. Am. Concrete Assn., 1979; named Jerseyan of Week Star Ledger Publs., 1979. Fellow AIA (N.J. regional dir. 1981-83, 125th Anniversary Presdl. citation 1982, Presdl. citation 1982, citation Dedicated Svcs. 1983); mem. Archtl. League No. N.J. (pres. 1975), N.J. Soc. Architects (dir. 1971, established Romeo Aybar Scholarship 1973, treas. 1974-75, pres. 1979, award of Honor 20 Yrs. Meritorious Accomplishments 1988, regional dir. 1983), Aircraft Owners and Pilots Assn., Nat. Pilots Assn. Clubs: Ridgefield Exchange (pres.) (1972-73); Ridgefield Exchange (dir. N.J. dist.) (1973-74). Republican. Home: 2150 Center Ave Fort Lee NJ 07024-5806 Office: Aybar Partnership 605 Broad Ave Ridgefield NJ 07657-1697 Office Phone: 201-568-0229. E-mail: rafaia@aol.com.

AYCOCK, JOSEPH WILLIAM, music educator, auto racing official; b. Charlotte, NC, Sept. 6, 1979; s. Joseph William and Patricia Dale Aycock. MusB in Music Edn., Appalachian State U., Boone, NC, 2002. Orch. dir. Charlotte-Mecklenburg Schools, 2002—; race ofcl. Lowe's Motor Speedway, Concord, NC, 2003—; dir. of music Meml. United Meth. Ch., Charlotte, 2004—05. Adjudicator Fla. Fedn. of Judge's Assn., Frostproof, 2005—; vol. Bands of Am., Indpls., 2001—; prin. percussionist Winthrop U. Olde English Wind Ensemble, Rock Hill, SC, 2004—. Contest dir. Carolina Winter Ensemble Assn., Charlotte, 2004—05. Mem.: Am. Guild of English Handbell Ringers, Fla. Fedn. of Judge's Assn., Music Educators Nat. Conf., Phi Mu Alpha Sinfonia (sec. 2001—02). Reform. Methodist. Avocations: golf, travel, cooking. Home: 2061 University Heights Ln Charlotte NC 28213 Office Phone: 980-343-5750. Personal E-mail: joey@joeyaycock.com.

AYDELOTTE, MYRTLE KITCHELL, retired nursing administrator; b. Van Meter, Iowa, May 31, 1917; d. John J. and Larava Josephine (Gutshall) Kitchell; m. William O. Aydelotte, June 22, 1956; children: Marie Elizabeth, Jeannette Farley. BS, U. Minn., 1939, MA, 1947, PhD, 1955; postgrad., Columbia U. Tchrs. Coll., 1948. Head nurse Charles T. Miller Hosp., St. Paul, 1939—41; surg. tchg. St. Mary's Hosp. Sch. Nursing, Mpls., 1941—42; instr. U. Minn., 1945—49; dir., dean State U. Iowa Coll. Nursing, 1949—57, prof., 1957—62; assoc. chief nurse VA Hosp. Rsch. for Nursing, Iowa City, 1963—64, chief nursing rsch., 1964—65; prof. U. Iowa Coll. Nursing, 1964—76, 1982—88; exec. dir. ANA, 1977—81; ret., 1988. Dir. nursing U. Iowa Hosps. and Clinics, 1968—76; mem. sci. adv. bd. Ctr. Health Rsch. Wayne State U., 1972—76, Inst. Medicine, 1973—; cons. U. Minn., 1970, 82, 90, U. Rochester, 1971, U. Mich., 1970, 73, U. Colo., 1970—71, U. Hawaii, 1972—73, Ariz. State U., 1972, U. Nebr., 1972—73. Mem. editl. bd.: Nursing Forum, 1969—72, Jour. Nursing Adminstrn., 1971; contbr. articles to profl. jours. Mem., v.p. Iowa City Libr. Bd., 1961—67; mem. Johnson County Bd. Health, 1967—70; mem. adv. com. family living courses Iowa City Bd. Edn., 1970—72. Served with Nurse Corps. U.S. Army, 1942—46. Mem.: ANA, Am. Acad. Nursing, Inst. Medicine, Sigma Theta Tau (rsch. com. 1968—72). Home: 1570 East Ave Apt 202 Rochester NY 14610

AYELE, KASSAHUN, ambassador; b. Bale Goba, Ethiopia, June 17, 1949; married; 2 children. BSc. in Mech. Engring., Haile Sellasie U., Addis Ababa; MSc in Machine Design, Leeds U., England, 1988. Shift engr. to factory chief engr. Metahara Sugar Factory, Metahara, Ethiopia, 1973—83; sr. project engr. Indsl. Projects Svc., 1982—92; tech. expert Ethio-Libyan Joint Sugar Co., 1983—84; acting gen. mgr. Devel. Projects Study Authority, Addis Ababa, Ethiopia, 1992—93; head of Productive and Support Svcs. Bur. Office of Prime Min., Ethiopia, 1993—95; Min. of Trade and Industry Ethiopia, 1995—2001; Ethiopian amb. to the U.S., Washington, 2001—. Office: Embassy of Ethiopia 3506 International Dr NW Washington DC 20008

AYER, CAROL ANNE, librarian; b. Olympia, Wash., Sept. 6, 1953; d. Harold Stevens and Leoni (Bleston) A. BS, Portland State U., 1975; M of Librarianship, U. Wash., 1977. Libr. USDA Forest Svc., Juneau, Alaska, 1980—87, Washington, 1987, libr. dir. Ogden, Utah, 1987—. Bd. dirs. Pinto Horse Assn. Am., Bethany, Okla., 1990—. Mem. Am. Libr. Assn., Spl. Librs. Assn., Utah Libr. Assn. (sec. spl. libr. sect. 1990-94, bd. dirs. 1997-2002). Democrat. Unitarian-Universalist. Avocations: horses, travel, reading. Office: USDA Forest Svc Rocky Mountain Rsch Sta 324 25th St Ogden UT 84401-2310 Business E-Mail: cayer@fs.fed.us.

AYER, DONALD BELTON, lawyer; b. San Mateo, Calif., Apr. 30, 1949; m. Anne Norton; children: Christopher, Alison BA in History with great distinction and honors, Stanford U., 1971; MA in History, Harvard U., 1973, JD cum laude, 1975. Bar: Calif. 1975, D.C. 1978. Law clk. to Judge Malcolm R. Wilkey U.S. Ct. Appeals D.C. Cir., 1975-76; law clk. to Justice William H. Rehnquist, U.S. Supreme Ct., Washington, 1976-77; asst. U.S. atty. criminal div. No. Dist. Calif., San Francisco, 1977-79, in charge San Jose office, 1978-79; assoc. Gibson Dunn & Crutcher, San Jose, Calif., 1979-81; U.S. atty. Eastern Dist. Calif., Sacramento, 1982-86; prin. dep. solicitor gen. Dept. Justice, 1986-88; ptnr. JonesDay, Washington, 1988—; dep. atty. gen. U.S. Dept. Justice, Washington, 1989-90; adminstrv. ptnr. Jones, Day, Reavis & Pogue, Washington, 1991-93, chair gov. disputes sect., 1993-96, office chair pro bono com., 2003—, firm-wide chair pro bono com., 2004—, chmn., gov. regulatory practice, 2005—. Mem. Calif. State Bar Fed. Cts. Commn., 1983-86; mem. exec. com. 9th Cir. Jud. Conf., 1983-85; mem. Atty. Gen.'s Adv. Com. of U.S. Attys., 1986; publs. com. U.S. Supreme Ct. Hist. Soc., 1991—. Articles editor Harvard U. Law Rev., 1974-75; contbr. articles to legal jours. Pres. Stanford Young Reps., 1970-71; mem. vestry St. Mary's Episc. Ch., 1987-90; bd. dirs. Langley Non-Profit Housing Corp., 1990-98; mem. Fed. City Coun., 1991-93; mem. adv. com. State and Local Legal Ctr., 1992—; trustee Potomac Sch., McLean, Va., 1994-2000; bd. dirs. Am. Rivers, Inc., 1997—, treas., 1998-2004; bd. advisors Supreme Ct. Inst. of Georgetown U., 1999—. Fellow Am. Bar Found. (life); mem. ABA (litigation sect., task force on internat. criminal ct. 1991-94), Am. Bar Found., Am. Acad. Appellate Lawyers (mem. com. 1997-2002), Am. Law Inst., D.C. Bar Found. (adv. bd. 1992—), Calif. State Bar, D.C. Bar Assn. (ct. funding com. 2000-01), NYU Inst. Jud. Adminstrn. (bd. dirs. 2000—), Edward Coke Am. Inn of Ct. (master). Office: Jones Day Reavis & Pogue 51 Louisiana Ave NW Washington DC 20001 Office Phone: 202-879-4689. Personal E-mail: dbatrout@aol.com.

AYER, KRISTIN VANDER MEER, accountant; b. Natick, Mass., Nov. 25, 1951; d. John William and Jeanne (Dunton) Vander Meer; m. Richard Woodman Ayer II, July 1, 1972; children: Richard III, Matthew, Gregory, Amanda. BS in Bus. Acctg., U. Coll. Northeastern U., Boston, 1979. Cert. color analyst; enrolled agt. IRS. Comml. casualty underwriter Comml. Union Ins., Boston, 1971-80; v.p. living color div. Ayer Enterprises, Natick, 1981-91; founder ACCU Books, Uxbridge, Mass., 1991—. Treas. Brown Sch. PTA, Natick, 1987-88; co-pres. Whitinsville Christian Sch. Mothers' Club, Uxbridge, 1991—. Mem. Am. Inst. of Profl. Bookkeepers, Sigma Epsilon Rho. Republican. Avocations: skating, needlecraft. E-mail: kaofaccubooks@yahoo.com.

AYER, RAMANI, insurance company executive; BS, Indian Inst. Tech., Bombay; MS in Chem. Engring., D in Chem. Engring., Drexel U. With The Hartford, Hartford, Conn., 1973—, asst. sec., staff asst. to chmn. and chief exec., 1979-83; v.p. HartRe, 1983-86; pres. Hartford Specialty Co., 1986-89; sr. v.p. The Hartford, 1989-90, exec. v.p., 1990-91; pres., COO property-casualty ops. Hartford Fire Ins. Co., 1991-97; chmn., CEO, pres. The Hartford Fin. Svcs. Group, Inc., 1997—. Past chmn. Ins. Svcs. Office; bd. dirs. Ins. Info. Inst. Trustee Mark Twain House, Hartford, Conn.; chmn. Metro Hartford Regional Econ. Alliance; bd. dirs. Hartford Hosp.; trustee Drexel U.; mem. Bus. Roundtable. Mem. Am. Ins. Assn. (bd. dirs., past chmn. task force catastrophic issues, past vice chmn. spl. bd. com. workers compensation), Am. Inst. Property and Liability Underwriters (trustee), Ins. Inst. Am. (trustee). Office: Hartford Plz 60 Asylum Ave Hartford CT 06105-3840

AYER, WILLIAM S., air transportation executive; m. Pam Ayer; 1 child. Degree, Stanford U.; MBA, U. Wash. From v.p. strategy and route planning to sr. v.p. ops. Horizen Air Industries, 1985—95, sr. v.p. ops., 1995; from v.p. mktg. and planning to pres. Alaska Air Group, Inc., Seattle, 1995—2003, pres., 2003—, chmn., CEO, 2003—. Office: Alaska Air Group Inc 19300 Pacific Hwy South Seattle WA 98188

AYERS, ANNE LOUISE, small business owner, consultant, counselor; b. Albuquerque, Oct. 22, 1948; d. F. Ernest and Gladys Marguerite (Miles) A. BA, Kans. U., 1970; MEd, Seattle Pacific U., 1971. Staff cons. in student devel. Cen. Wash. State U., Ellensburg, 1971-72; dir. Aerospace Def. Command Resident Edn. Ctrs. for N.D. and Mont. Chapman U., Orange, Calif., 1972-74; instr. psychology Hampton (Va.) U., 1973-75; edn. svc. specialist Gen. Ednl. Devel. Ctr., Fort Monroe, Va., 1975-77; edn. specialist U.S. Army Transp. Sch., Ft. Eustis, Va., 1977-79, Nat. Mine Health and Safety Acad., Beckley, W.Va., 1979-89; edn. svcs. specialist NASA Hdqrs., Washington, 1989-96; ret., 1996. Pres. Appalachian Love Arts, Martinsburg, W.Va., 1983—; tchr. undergrad. and grad. evening classes in psychology, 1972-74; program mgr. NASA Tchr. Resource Ctr. Network Program; sub. counselor Berkley County, W.Va. Inventor decorative pen/thermometer holder/corsage, psychedelic jewelry process. Mem. Nat. Soc. Inventors, Nat. Assn. Women Deans Adminstrn. and Counselors, Internat. Soc. Photographers, Alumnus of Growing Vision (Century in Edn. award), Mayflower Soc. Methodist. Avocations: travel, collecting gems and shells, coin collecting/numismatics, rock and fossil collecting, oboe and clarinet. Home and Office: 480 Tanbridge Dr Martinsburg WV 25401-4695

AYERS, CHRISTOPHER JAMES, special education educator; b. Pequannock Township, NJ, Apr. 17, 1979; s. James Loring and Judith Eileen Ayers; m. Jessica Kathleen McLelland, Dec. 28, 2003; 1 child, Samantha Marion. BS in Telecom. Mgmt., DeVry U., 2001; BA in tchr. of handicapped summa cum laude, Kean U., 2004. Cert. handicapped tchr. Kean U., NJ, 2004. Spl. edn. tchr. Perth Amboy Bd. Edn., 2002—. Asst. varsity football coach Perth Amboy H.S., 2002; supplemental instr. Perth Amboy Bd. Edn., 2002—; club leader 21st Century, Perth Amboy, NJ, 2004—. Vol. Edison Youth Svc. Corps, 2001—05. Mem.: Coun. Exceptional Children. Home: 22 Paul St Fords NJ 08863 Personal E-mail: yellowstonenp44@aol.com.

AYERS, EDWARD, dean; BA, U. Tenn., 1974; PhD, Yale U., 1980. Hugh P. Kelly prof. history U. Va., Charlottesville, Va., dean Coll. and Grad. Sch. Arts and Scis. Author: Vengeance and Justice: Crime and Punishment in the Nineteenth-Century American South, 1984, The Edge of the South: Life in Nineteenth Century Virginia, 1991, The Promise of the New South: Life after Reconstruction, 1992 (James Rawley prize Orgn. Am. Historians, 92), The Strange Career of Thomas Jefferson: Race, Slavery, and American Memory, 1943-1993, 1993 (Frank L. and Harriet C. Owsley award So. Hist. Assn., 93), All Over the Map: Rethinking American Regions, 1996, The Oxford Book fo the American South: Testimony, Memory, and Fiction, 1997, American Passages: A History of the United States, 2000, The Valley of the Shadow: Two Communities in the American Civil War--The Eve of War, 2000, In the Presence of Mine Enemies: War in the Heart of America, 1859-1863, 2003 (Bancroft prize, 2004), What Caused the Civil War: Reflections on the South and Southern History, 2005. Named Univ. Prof. of Yr., Carnegie Found., 2003; recipient James Willard Hurst prize, Law andSoc. Assn., 1986. Mem.: Am. Assn. Arts and Scis. Office: Univ Virginia PO Box 400772 419 Cabell Hall Charlottesville VA 22903*

AYERS, HARRY BRANDT, editor, publisher, columnist; b. Anniston, Ala., Apr. 8, 1935; s. Harry Mell and Edel Olga (Ytterboe) A.; m. Josephine Ehringhaus, Dec. 9; 1 child, Margaret. BA in History, U. Ala., Tuscaloosa, 1959; LHD (hon.), U. Ala., Birmingham, 1994, U. Ala., 1994. Polit. writer The Raleigh (N.C.) Times, 1959-61; corr. Bascom Timmons Bur., Washington, 1961-63; mng. editor The Anniston Star, 1963-69, editor, pub., 1969—. Chair Consolidated Publ. Co., 1998—; commentator Pub. Radio, NPR "Morning Edition." Mem. adv. bd. Inside Story, Pub. Broadcasting System, N.Y.C., 1981-85; co-editor: You Can't Eat Magnolias, 1972; co-author: A Bicentennial Portrait of the American People, U.S. News Books, 1976, Inaugural Book President Carter, 1977, Dixie Dateline, 1983; frequent contbr. to internat. and nat. newspapers. Trustee Talladega (Ala.) Coll., 1972-89, Wooster Sch., Danbury, Conn., 1989-90, Century Found., 1985—, Ctr. for Excellence in Govt., 1985-88, Am. Com., Internat. Press Inst., Vienna, 1985—; bd. dirs. So. Ctr. for Internat. Studies, Atlanta, 1979—, Bd. Fgn. Scholarships, Washington, 1981-84; mem. adv. bd. Am. Ditchley Found., London; mem. Coun. Fgn. Rels., N.Y.C., 1983—; bd. dirs. Inter-Am. Press Assn., Miami, 1992-93, 2003—; chmn. UN Day Ala., 2000. Named Disting. Journalism Grad., U. Ala., 1967; recipient Human Rels. award Am. Jewish Com., 1977, Green Eyeshade award Soc. Profl. Journalists, 1985, Editl. Leadership award, Soc. Newspaper Editors, 2003; named to Ala. Acad. Honor, 1991; fellow Nieman Found., Harvard U., 1968, sr. fellow Gannett Ctr., Columbia U., 1989; inductee Hall of Fame, U. Ala. Sch. Comm., 2000, Tutwiler dist. svc. award, 2002, Lifetime achievement award, Ala. Press Assn., 2003 Mem. Ala. Press Journalism Found. (founding pres. 1969), Am. Soc. Newspaper Editors (Editl. Leadership award 2003), So. Newspaper Pubs. Assn. (dir. 1981-84), Century Assn. N.Y.C., Met. Club Washington, The Summit Club Birmingham. Democrat. Episcopalian. Home: 1 Booger Holw Anniston AL 36207-6805 Office: Anniston Star PO Box 189 Anniston AL 36202-0189

AYERS, HOWARD T., lawyer; b. St. Louis, 1944; BA in Econ. & Bus. Adminstrn., Rice U., 1966; JD with honors, U. Houston, 1969. Bar: Tex. 1969. Ptnr., Real Estate Andrews Kurth LLP, Houston, mng. ptnr. of firm, 1997—, chmn. mgmt. com., 2001—. Bd. dir. U. Houston Law Found.; adv. bd. Tex. State Bank. Mem.: Tex. Coll. Real Estate Attys., ABA, State Bar Tex., Houston Real Estate Lawyers Coun., Houston Bar Assn., Order of Barons, Phi Kappa Phi, Phi Alpha Delta. Office: Andrews Kurth LLP 600 Travis St Ste 4200 Houston TX 77002-3090 Office Phone: 713-220-4044. Office Fax: 713-238-7151. Business E-Mail: hayers@andrewskurth.com.

AYERS, JEFFREY DAVID, lawyer; b. Grant, Nebr., Nov. 30, 1960; s. William D. and Lela R. (Gilmore) A.; m. Shelly Jo Dodds, June 11, 1988; children: Sydney Elizabeth, Bailey Anne. BS, Graceland U., 1982; MBA, JD, U. Iowa, 1985. Bar: Mo. 1985. Assoc. Stinson, Mag & Fizzell, Kansas City, Mo., 1985—88, Bryan, Cave, McPheeters & McRoberts, Kansas City, 1989—92; ptnr. Blackwell Sanders Peper Martin LLP, Kansas City, Mo., 1992—95, mng. ptnr. London, 1996—99; sr. v.p., gen. counsel and corp. sec. Aquila Mcht. Svcs., Inc., Kansas City, 1999—2002; v.p., assoc. gen. counsel GE Ins. Solutions, Kansas City, 2003—05; sr. v.p., gen. counsel, corp. sec. NovaStar Fin., Inc., 2005—. Mayor City of Lake Tapawingo, Mo., 1993-96. Trustee Little Blue Valley Sewer Dist., 1994-95. Democrat. Mem. Cmtys. of Christ. Office: Nova Star Fin Inc 8140 Ward Pky ste 380 Kansas City MO 64114 Personal E-mail: jayers@kc.rr.com.

AYERS, KATHY VENITA MOORE, librarian; b. Amherst, Tex., Jan. 15, 1946; d. Charles Edward and Jean (Willman) Moore; children: Suzanne Flanary, Charles Flanary. BA, U. Ill., 1972, MLS, 1974. Cert. profl. libr., N.Mex.; cert. tchr., N.Mex. Dir. children's libr. Hayner Pub. Libr., Alton, Ill., 1974-76; dir. Ruidoso (N.Mex.) Pub. Libr., 1978-80; libr. media specialist Horgan Libr., N.Mex. Mil. Inst., Roswell, 1985-93; libr. N.Mex. Sch. Visually Handicapped, Alamogordo, 1993—. Workshop presenter Lewis & Clark Regional Libr. Systems, Ill., 1975; outreach programer Hayner Pub. Libr., 1974-76; del. Pre-White Ho. Conf., State of N.Mex., 1991. Contbr. articles to newspapers and profl. jours. Bd. dirs. Alton Symphony, 1975; mem. Altrusa, Ruidoso, 1979-84, Friend of Roswell Pub. Libr.; sec. Ruidoso Summer Festival, 1979; bd. dirs. Supts. Adv. Bd., Roswell, N.Mex., 1987-89; pres. Friends of Libr., Ruidoso, 1980-83, Parent Advocacy for Gifted Edn., 1990-92; v.p. Sunset PTA; bd. dirs. N.Mex. Libr. Found., 1992—; mem. State Task Force on Sch. Librs., 1999. Recipient Svc. award, Altrusa, 1979, Sunset PTA, 1989. Mem. N.Mex. Libr. Assn. (libr. devel. com., ednl. tech. roundtable vice chair 1991, chair elect 1992, co-chair state conv. local arrangements 1990-91, 2d v.p. 1993-94, 1st v.p. 1994-95, pres. 1995-96, Libr. Leadership award 2001), N.Mex. Acad. and Rsch. Librs. (vice chair 1992, pres. 1993), N.Mex. Taskforce for Sch. Librs., Kiwanis (bd. dirs. 1990-92). Avocations: travel, stained glass, music, hiking. Office: Bovina ISD PO Box 70 Bovina TX 79009

AYERS, RICHARD WAYNE, electric power industry executive, writer, journalist; b. Atlanta, Aug. 23, 1945; s. Harold Richard and Martha Elizabeth Ayers; m. Nancy Katherine Martin, Aug. 9, 1969. BBA, Ga. State Coll., 1967; MBA, Ind. U., 1969. Specialist mktg. comm. rsch. GE, Schenectady, NY, 1969—70, copywriter lamp divsn. Cleve., 1970—73, supr. distbr. advt. & sales promotion, 1973—75, supr. comml. & indsl. promotional programs Lighting Bus. Group, 1975—79, mgr. comml. & indsl. market distbr. and promotional programs, 1979—87, mgr. comml. & indsl. comm., 1987—91, mgr. mktg. comms., 1992—2000; reporter, feature writer Tampa Bay newspapers, 2000—. Lectr. in field. Author: Winning Through Promotion, 1987, 1996, Cleveland and the Western Reserve, 2000, 2004, Ohio's Lake Erie Vacationland, 2000, St. Petersburg: The Sunshine City, 2001, Tampa Bay's Gulf Beaches: The Fabulous 1950's and 1960's, 2004. Bd. dirs. Indian Rocks Beach Hist. Mus.; mem. Belleair Beach Parks Bd., 2003—; dir.-at-large Ga. Young Reps., 1966—67. Recipient Best Indsl. Promotion award, Advt. Age, 1974, Incentive Showcase award, Nat. Premium Sales Exec. Assn., 1975, 1976, 1987, 1991, Golden Communicators award, Factory mag., 1976, Leader award, Direct Mktg. Assn., 1983, Top prize, Am. Lighting Assn., 1990—92, 1995—98, Addy award, Am. Advt. Assn., 1992, Gold Tower award, Bus. Mktg. Assn., 1998, ProComm award, 1998, Best Original Writing award, Cmty. Papers Fla., 2003. Mem.: Eflun Soc., Blue Key, Beta Gamma Sigma, Delta Sigma Pi. Home: 2900 Gulf Blvd #304 Belleair Beach FL 33786 Office Phone: 727-593-2686.

AYI, BERTHA SERWA, infectious disease specialist, internist; b. Akim Oda, Eastern Region, Ghana, Feb. 1, 1971; d. Samuel Kwaku and Hannah Akua Gyamerah; m. Richard Sowah Ayi, May 22, 1999; children: Michael Okpoti, Henry- Josiah Ako, Richmond- Joshua Anyiteye. MB. ChB, U. Ghana Med. Sch., 1997; Internal Medicine Residency Tng., Good Samaritan Hosp. of Md. Inc. Affiliated with Johns Hopkins Univ, Baltimore, Maryland. USA, 1999—2002; Infectious Disease Fellowship Tng., Creighton U. Med. Ctr. and Univ of Nebr. Med. Ctr., Omaha VA Med. Ctr., Omaha, Nebraska. USA, 2002—04. Diplomate Am. Bd. Internal Med., Am. Bd. Internal Med. subspecialty Bd. Infectious Disease, 2004. House staff pediat., gen. surgery, urology, orthops., trauma Korlebu Tchg. Hosp., Accra, Ghana, 1997—98; intern, jr. and sr. resident Good Samaritan Hosp., Balt., 1999—2002; infectious disease fellow tng. Creighton U. Med. Ctr., U. Nebr. Med. Ctr., Omaha, 2002—04; jr. faculty fellow Creighton U. Med. Ctr., Omaha, 2002—04; adj. asst. prof. internal medicine Nebr. Med. Ctr., Omaha, 2004—; assoc. med. dir. Mercy Infectious Disease and Epidemiology Ctr. Reviewer Clin. Infectious Diseases Jour., 2003—, Chest jour. Co-author: Blastomycosis. In Conn's Current Therapy 2005, 2005, Infections of Leisure; contbr. articles to profl. jours. Motivational spkr. and spkr. on reproductive health issues Planned Parenthood Assn. of Ghana, Accra, Ghana, 1995—97; spkr. marriage, counselling Internat. Ctrl. Gospel Ch., Accra, Ghana, 1997—98. Recipient Opthalmology Award for Graduating Med. Students, Alcon-Paracelsus pharmacy, 1997, Deans Award for Academic Excellence, U. of Ghana Med. Sch., 1995, Honors in Surgery, Pathology, Microbiology, Biochemistry, 1994-1997. Mem.: Infectious Disease Soc. Am., Am. Coll. Physicians. Avocations: sewing, baking. Office: Mercy Infectious Disease and Epidemiology Ctr 801 5th St Sioux City IA 51101

AYINE, GABRIEL BONG-BAANE, mathematics professor; m. Gabriella Alebna; 1 child, Sydney Kabobre. PhD, Howard U., 2002. Nat. svc. U. of Cape Coast, Ghana, 1981—82; sr. supt. Ghana Edn. Svc., 1982—85; assoc. prof. Howard C.C., Columbia, Md., 1995—. Preparing Future Faculty Tchg. Assoc. fellow, Howard U., 1994—96. Mem.: Am. Math. Assn. Roman Catholic. Office: Howard C C 10901 Little Patuxent Pky Columbia MD 21044 Office Phone: 410-772-4483. Office Fax: 410-772-4401. Personal E-mail: gayine@bwwonline.com. E-mail: gayine@howardcc.edu.

AYKROYD, DANIEL EDWARD, actor, writer; b. Ottawa, Ont., Can., July 1, 1952; came to U.S., 1975; s. Peter Hugh and Lorraine G. (Gougeon) A.; m. Maureen Lewis May 10, 1974 (div.); m. Donna Dixon, April 29, 1983; children: Danielle, Belle, Stella. Attended, Carleton U., 1969, Doctorate (hon.), 1994. Mem. Toronto Co. of Second City Theater; star in CBS TV series Coming Up Rosie; writer, actor: NBC's Saturday Night Live, 1975-79; motion picture appearances include (actor) Love at First Sight, 1974, 1941, 1979, Mr. Mike's Mondo Video, 1979, Neighbors, 1981, Doctor Detroit, 1983, Trading Places, 1983, Twilight Zone, 1983, Nothing Lasts Forever, 1984, Into the Night, 1985, Caddyshack II, 1988, The Great Outdoors, 1988, My Stepmother is an Alien, 1988, Driving Miss Daisy, 1989, My Girl, 1991, Sneakers, 1992, Chaplin, 1992, My Girl 2, 1994, Exit to Eden, 1994, (voice) Antz, 1998, 50 First Dates, 2004, Christmas with the Kranks, 2004; (actor, co-screenwriter) The Blues Brothers, 1980, Ghostbusters, 1984, Spies Like Us, 1985, Dragnet, 1987, Ghostbusters II, 1989, Coneheads, 1993, Canadian Bacon, 1994, Tommy Boy, 1995, Rainbow, 1995, Casper, 1995, Sgt. Bilko, 1996, My Fellow Americans, 1996, getting Away With Murder, 1996, Feeling Minnesota, 1996, Celtic Pride, 1996, Grosse Pointe Blank, 1997, Blues Brothers 2000, 1997, The Arrow, 1997, Susan's Plan, 1998, Diamonds, 1999 (actor, dir., screenwriter) Nothing But Trouble, 1991, (exec. prodr.) One More Saturday Night, 1986; performed (with John Belushi) as the Blues Brothers; albums include: Briefcase Full of Blues, Made in America, The Blues Brothers (motion-picture soundtrack), Best of the Blues Brothers, The Essential Blues Brothers; guest-columnist for Premiere magazine, 1992; TV guest appearances include All You Need is Cash, Steve Martin's Best Show Ever, Tales From the Crypt, HBO, 1992, Soul Man, 1997, The Nanny, 1993, 94, Home Improvement, 1997, According to Jim, 2002, 03. Recipient Emmy award 1976-77. Mem. Writers Guild Am. West, AFTRA. Office: Creative Artists Agy care Fred Specktor 9830 Wilshire Blvd Beverly Hills CA 90212-1804

AYLESWORTH, OWEN ROY, retired firefighter, genealogist, philanthropist; b. Appleton, Wisc., Jan. 21, 1926; s. Frederick Donovan and Adeline Louise Minnie (Hauert) A.; m. Mary Hildred Horton, Aug. 23, 1946 (div. Sept. 1949); children: Sheldon Roy, Earl Lynn; m. Mary Corrine Patti Gray, Dec. 26, 55 (div. Nov. 1964); 1 child, Nancy Denise. AA, Santa Barbara City Coll., 1973. Fireman City of Santa Barbara, Calif., 1950-56, alarm operator, 1956, fire engr., 1956-62, fire capt., 1962-69, 76-79, fire tng. officer, 1969-76, acting fire battalion chief, 1976. Webmaster, Aylesworth.net; dir. v.p., pres. City Employee's Assn., 1961-69; coord. fire sci. Santa Barbara City Coll., 1969-74, instr. 1972-74. Author, editor: Caleb Sheldon Aylesworth His Descendents, 1963, 82, Hauert Family Genealogy, 1965, 73, Baron/Bertino Family, 2003. Instr. advanced first aid and emergency care ARC; cardiopulmonary resustation instr. Am. Heart Assn.; life mem. Santa Barbara Fireman's Relief Assn., 1952-64, v.p. 1964-66. With U.S. Navy, 1944-47. Mem. Calif. State Fire Tng. Officers Assn. (life), Calif. Firefighters Assn. (life, state conf. del. 1955-61), Santa Barbara High Sch. Alumni Assn. (life, bd. dirs. 1974-76, treas. 1976-94, sec. 1994-96, exec. sec. 2000—, dir. membership 1996—, Disting. Alumnus award 1993). Avocations: genealogy, research, woodworking, aestheometry, metal sculpture. Home: 621 W Arrellaga St Santa Barbara CA 93101 E-mail: olenug@aol.com.

AYLING, COREY JOHN, lawyer; b. N.Y.C., Sept. 5, 1957; s. Henry F. and Julia C. Ayling; m. Teresa J. Schwarzenbart, Mar. 20, 1984 (div. Oct. 1991); children: John, Lindsay; m. Robin E. Johnson, Oct. 10, 1992; children: Blake, Claire, Alex. AB, Cornell U., 1979; MA, NYU, 1981; JD, U. Wis., 1984. Bar: Wis. 1984, Minn. 1984, U.S. Dist. Ct. (we. dist.) Wis. 1984, U.S. Dist. Ct. Minn. 1985, U.S. Dist. Ct. Ariz. 1994, U.S. Ct. Appeals (8th cir.) 1985, U.S. Ct. Appeals (9th cir.) 1996, U.S. Ct. Appeals (D.C. cir.) 1989, U.S. Supreme Ct. 1995. Law clk. U.S. Ct. Appeals-7th Cir., Chgo., 1984-85; assoc. O'Connor & Hannan, Mpls., 1985-88, ltd. ptnr., 1989-90; assoc. McGrann, Shea et al, Mpls., 1990-91, shareholder, 1992—. Mem. Fed. Pub. Defender Panel, Mpls., 1986—. Articles editor Wis. Law Rev., 1983-84; contbr. articles to profl. jours. Vol. atty. Minn. Civil Workers Union, Mpls., 1987—. Office: McGrann Shea et al 800 Nicollet Mall 2600 US Bancorp Ctr Minneapolis MN 55402 Office Phone: 612-338-2525. Business E-Mail: cja@mcgrannshea.com.

AYLING, HENRY FAITHFUL, editor, consultant, journalist, poet; b. Bklyn., Dec. 30, 1931; s. Albert Edward John and Mina Campbell McCurdy (Lindsay) A.; m. Julia Corinne Gornto, 1954; children: Campbell, Eben, Corey, Harry, Faith. BA, Grinnell Coll., 1953; MA, Columbia U., Calif. State U., Carson, 1984; 2 grad. teaching certs., Calif. State U., Carson, 1985. Asst to registrar Columbia U., N.Y.C., 1958-59; supr. crew scheduling Pan Am World Airways, Jamaica, N.Y., 1959-62, supr. payload control, 1963-65; mgr. crew scheduling Seabd. World Airlines, Jamaica, 1962-63, 65-68, mgr. system control, 1968-80; mgr. ops. control Flying Tiger Line, 1980-84; instr. English, ESL Long Beach (Calif.) City Coll., 1984-85; mng. editor IEEE Expert, IEEE Computing Futures IEEE Computer Soc., Los Alamitos, Calif., 1985-90, editorial dir. Computer Soc. Press, 1990-93; writer, editor, cons., 1993—. Mem. editorial bd. Expert Mag., 1986-90, CamAm Programming Inc., 1987-88; columnist Mag. Design and Prodn. mag., 1988-89; contbr. articles to profl. mags. and tech. books; contbr. poetry to various mags. and anthologies. Bd. dirs. Playa Serena Home Owners Assn., Playa Del Rey, Calif., 1983-85. Recipient Maggie awards Western Publs. Assn., 1988-89, IEEE Computer Soc. Golden Core award, 1997. Avocations: music, fine arts. Home and Office: 78291 Allegro Dr Palm Desert CA 92211-1894 Personal E-mail: jcayling@msn.com.

AYLOR, JAMES HIRAM, engineering educator; b. Charlottesville, Va., May 30, 1946; s. Melvin Winfrey and Mary Yager (Payne) A.; m. Sherry Lynn Kendall, Oct. 20, 1973; children: Jennifer K., David A. BSEE, U. Va., 1968, MSEE, 1971, PhD in elec. engring., 1977. Mem. faculty elec. engring. U. Va., Charlottesville, 1978—, chair dept. elec. engring., 1996—2003, assoc. dean. academic programs Sch. Engring. and Applied Sciences, 2003—, interim dean. Sch. Engring. and Applied Sciences, 2004—, Louis T. Rader Prof. Author: Performance and Fault Modeling with VHDL, 1991, Codesign of Embedded Systems: A Unified Hardware/Software Representation, 1996. Recipient Outstanding Svc. award Va. Engring. Found., Charlottesville, 1991. Fellow: IEEE (pres. computer soc. 1993, editor-in-chief IEEE Computer). Methodist. Office: U Va Sch Engring and Applied Sciences Box 400246 Charlottesville VA 22904-4246

AYLWARD, J. PATRICK, lawyer; b. Walla Walla, Wash., Aug. 20, 1951; s. James F. and Mary Jane (Little) A.; m. Peggy D. Deobald, Feb. 13, 1982; children: Alana Nicole, Sean Patrick. BA, Stanford U., 1973; JD, U. Wash., 1976. Bar: Wash. 1976, U.S. Dist. Ct. (ea. dist.) Wash. 1980, U.S. Tax Ct. 1984, U.S. Ct. Appeals (9th cir.) 1984, U.S. Dist. Ct. (we. dist.) 1987. Assoc. Hughes, Jeffers and Danielson, Wenatchee, Wash., 1976-81; prin. Jeffers, Danielson, Sonn and Aylward, P.S., Wenatchee, 1981—. Mem. Ltd. Practice Bd., Olympia, Wash., 1985-90; tchr., panel mem. Continuing Edn. Seminars for Attys. and Ltd. Practice Officers, 1981—; mem. Pacific Real Estate Inst., 1997—. Vol. Wash. State Centennial Games, Wenatchee, 1989. Mem. ABA (real property, probate and trust sect.), Am. Coll. Real Estate Lawyers, Wash. State Bar Assn. (exec. com. real property, probate and trust sect. 1991-93, legis. com. 1988—, chair legis. com. 1994-95, Pres. award 1996), Chelan-Couglas County Bar Assn. (pres. 1990-91, v.p. 1988-90, past sec., participant legal aid and edn. programs 1976—), Aircraft Owners and Pilots Assn., Exch. Club. Avocations: flying, skiing, hunting, golf, sports car racing. Office: Jeffers Danielson Sonn & Aylward PS 2600 Chester Kimm Rd Wenatchee WA 98801-2005 Office Phone: 509-662-3685. E-mail: pata@jdsalaw.com.

AYLWARD, MARCIA EILEEN, artist, educator; b. Kansas City, Mo., Jan. 27, 1956; d. Charles Livingston and Rosemary Anita (Hughes) Aylward; m. John Davis Carroll, Oct. 9, 1993. BFA, Kansas City Art Inst., 1988; MFA, Parsons Sch. Design, 1991. Art instr. Kansas City Art Inst., Maplewood Woods C.C., Kansas City, Mo., Kansas City Acad.; asst. prof. Avila U., 1996—. Exhibitions include Cambridge Art Assn., 1999 (Nat. Prize show, 1999), 2000 (Nat. Prize show, 2000), Thornhill Gallery, 2001, Framing Girl Gallery, 2001. Home: 6010 Oak St Kansas City MO 64113-2217

AYLWARD, RONALD LEE, lawyer; b. St. Louis, May 30, 1930; s. John Thomas and Edna (Ketcherside) A.; m. Margaret Cecilia Hellweg, Aug. 10, 1963; children: Susan Marie Jotte, Stephen Ronald, Carolyn Ann Dolan. AB, Washington U., St. Louis, 1952, JD, 1954; student, U. Va., 1955. Bar: Mo. 1954, Ill. 1961, U.S. Supreme Ct. 1968. Assoc. Heneghan, Roberts & Cole, St. Louis, 1958-59; asst. counsel Olin Corp., East Alton, Ill., 1960-64; asst. gen. counsel INTERCO, Inc., St. Louis, 1964-66, assoc. gen. counsel, mgr. law dept., 1966-69, asst. sec., 1966-74, gen. counsel, 1969-81, mem. oper. bd., 1970-92, v.p., 1971-81, mem. exec. com., dir., 1975-92, exec. v.p., 1981-85, vice chmn. bd. dirs., 1985-92; chmn., pres. Aylward & Assocs., Inc., St. Louis, 1992—. Mem. dist. export coun. U.S. Dept. Commerce, 1974-77; dir., mem. exec. com. Boatmen's Nat. Bank St. Louis, 1982-91, trust estates com., 1982-85, chmn. audit com., 1986-91; bd. dirs. Boatmen's Bancshares, Inc., mem. audit com., 1984-91, mem. compensation com., 1986-91; trustee Maryville U., 1989-92, chmn. bd., 1991-92. Trustee St. Louis Coun. World Affairs, sec., 1977—84; chmn. lay bd. DePaul Health Ctr., 1979—81; mem. exec. com. lay bd., 1981—89; mem. lay adv. bd. Chaminade Coll. Prep. Sch., 1980—84, chmn. bd. trustees, 1981—84; mem. lay bd. Acad. of the Visitation, 1981—85; bd. dirs. Cath. Charities of St. Louis, 1994—2001, vice chmn., 1995—97, chmn., 1997—99; mem. coun. Archdiocesan Devel. Appeal, 1994—97, chmn., 1996—97, vice chmn., 1995—97, mem. exec. com., 1995—97, chmn. rev./planning com., 1995—96, chmn., 1996—, hon. life mem.; mem. fin. coun. Archdiocese of St. Louis, 1995—98, mem. investment com., 1995—97; bd. dirs. St. Louis chpt. Nat. Found. March of Dimes, 1974—84, sec., 1976—78, chmn., 1979—82; bd. dirs. Cardinal Ritter Inst., 1975—90, chmn. pers. com., 1986—90; bd. dirs. St. Louis chpt. ARC, 1977—82, Linda Vista Montessori Sch., 1975—77, BBB Greater St. Louis, 1978—81, YMCA Greater St. Louis, 1981—2001, adv. dir., 2001—, NCCJ, 1992—93; bd. dirs. Carindal Glennon Children's Hosp., 1991—96, mem. exec. com., 1992—96, bd. dirs. Found., 1996—2001, dir.emeritus, 2001—; bd. dirs., fin. United Way Greater St. Louis, 1986—2001; mem. investment com. St. Louis Cmty. Found., 1993—95. With U.S. Army, 1955—58. Recipient of Order of St. Louis's King, Archdiocese of St. Louis. Mem.: NAM (taxation com. 1970—76, pub. affairs com. 1973—76, govt. ops./expenditures com. 1973—78), St. Louis Bar Assn., Mo. Bar Assn. (sr. counselor), Serra Internat., Am. Soc. Corp. Secs. (pres. St. Louis regional group 1972—73), Am. Apparel Mfrs. Assn. (bd. dirs. 1983—85), Am. Footwear Industries Assn. (nat. affairs vice chmn. 1970, chmn. 1971—75), Assoc. Industries Mo. (bd. dirs. 1973—80, 2d v.p. 1974—76, exec. com. 1974—80, pres. 1976—78), St. Louis C. of C. (legis. and tax com. 1966—74, vice-chmn. 1970—71), Creve Grove Racquet Club, Serra Club (trustee 2004—05), Bellerive Country Club (bd. dirs. 1981—84), Rotary (bd. dirs. St. Louis Club 1976—79), Mo. Athletic Club, Bellerive Country Club, Old Kinderhood Golf Club, Order of St. Louis King, Knights of Malta, Knights of Holy Sepulcher, Delta Theta Phi (pres. St. Louis Alumni 1963, dist. chancellor Mo. 1970—79). Home: 55 Muirfield Saint Louis MO 63141-7372 Office: Aylward and Assoc Inc 55 Muirfield Ct Saint Louis MO 63141 Office Phone: 314-434-5585. *Having something to achieve is the essence of my career. Continuing to set higher goals throughout life has made it both interesting and rewarding.*

AYNALEM, GETAHUN M., epidemiologist, researcher; b. Quorem, Wollo, Ethiopia, Mar. 21, 1954; s. Aynalem Mekonnen and Ennanu Belay. MD, U. Sarajevo, 1980; MPH, U. N.C., 1992. Lic. Ednl. Commn. Fgn. Med. Grads., 1995. Gen. duty med. officer, dir. med. svcs. Assab Hosp., Ethiopia, 1981—84; resident Med. Faculty Addis Ababa U., 1984—88; physician, asst. prof. ob-gyn. Tikur Anbessa Hosp., 1988—90; program coord., health educator San Joaquin County Dept. Pub. Health, Stockton, Calif., 1993—95; rsch. coord., cmty. health specialist Mass. Prevention Ctr., Worcester, 1995—98; epidemiologist Mass. Dept. Pub. Health, Boston, 1998—2000, L.A. County Dept. Pub. Health, 2000—. Dir. pediat. HIV/AIDS surveillance L.A. County Dept. Health Svcs., 2000—; dir. Assab Hosp., 1981—84. Recipient Haile Selassie First prize, Ethiopian Govt., 1972, Marshall Bronze Tito Honorrary award, Yugoslave Govt., 1979; fellow, Rockefeller Found., Internat. Clin. Epidemiology Network, 1990, U. N.C., Chapel Hill, 1990—91; scholar, Yugoslave Govt., 1974. Home: 11455 Chandler Blvd North Hollywood CA 91601 Office: LA County Dept Health 2615 S Grand Ave #500 Los Angeles CA 90007 Office Phone: 213-744-5966. Home Fax: 213-749-9606; Office Fax: 213-749-9606. Personal E-mail: gaynalem@dhs.co.la.ca.us.

AYOTTE, KELLY A., state attorney general; b. Nashua, NH, 1968; BA, Pa State U.; JD, Villanova U. Law clerk for Hon. Sherman Horton, NH Supreme Ct., 1993—94; litigator, McLane, Graf, Raulerson and Middleton, Nashua, NH, 1994—98; asst. atty. gen., homicide unit State of NH, 1998—2000, sr. asst. atty. gen., chief, homicide unit, 2000—02, legal counsel to gov., 2003, dep. atty. gen., 2003—04, atty. gen., 2004—. Named among 11 Remarkable Women in NH, NH Mag.; recipient Kirby award, Bar Found., 2004. Office: Off of Atty Gen 33 Capitol St Concord NH 03301-6397

AYOUB, NAKHLÉ MICHEL, dermatologist, researcher; b. Beirut, Feb. 27, 1973; s. Michel Nakhlé Ayoub and Dunia Deeb Rizkalla. BS, Notre Dame de Jamhour, 1990; MD, St. Joseph U., 1997, dermatologist, 2003. Resident Etranger des Hosp. de Paris, 2002; dermatologist Hôtel-Dieu de France Hosp., Beirut, 2003—. Author: (clin. rsch.) Protein Z deficiency in Sneddon's syndrome (Best clin. rsch., 48th congress of the French Soc. of Internal Medicine, 2003), (clin. study) Circumcision in a multiethnic social setting (Best original communication, 7th panarab congress of dermato-venereology, 2000); contbr. articles to profl. jours. Raising funds for cath. schools scholarships Lebanus, Beirut, Lebanon, 2000—01. Fellow Pitié Salpêtrière Hosp., Collège de Médecine des hôpitaux de Paris, 2001—02; Clin. rsch. grant, Société Française de Dermatologie, 2001—02. Mem.: League of French speaking dermatologists, Lebanese Order Physicians. Roman Catholic. Home: 925 Canterbury Rd Apt 735 CO Dr Rouphael Alanta GA 30324 Office: Hôtel-Dieu de France hospital Achrafieh Beirut 16-6830 Lebanon Office Phone: 00961-3662900. Office Fax: 00961-1616160. E-mail: nakhleayoub@yahoo.com.

AYRAL-CLAUSE, ODILE, language educator, writer; arrived in U.S., 1965; m. Gary Dwyer, May 21, 2004; 1 child, Celia. BA, U. Wy., 1968; PhD, U. Colo., 1975. Prof. Calif. Poly. State U., San Luis Obispo, 1975—. Author: Camille Claudel: A Life, 2002; editor: Sabine Sicaud: Le Rêve Inachevé, 1996; contbr. articles to profl. jours. Coord. Amnesty Internat., San Luis Obispo, 1993—96; cmty. antiwar activist, 2003—05. Mem.: Calif. Faculty Assn., Am. Assn. Tchrs. of French. Avocations: painting, drawing, hiking. Office: Calif Poly State Univ Modern Langs Dept San Luis Obispo CA 93407 Business E-Mail: oayral@calpoly.edu.

AYRAULT, EVELYN WEST, psychologist, writer; b. Mar. 3, 1922; d. John and Evelyn (West) A. BS, Fla. State Coll. for Women, 1945; MA, U. Chgo., 1947. Chief psychologist, asst. prin. Crippled Children's Sch., Jamestown, N.D., 1947-48; psychologist, tchr. spl. edn. dept. Sharon (Pa.) Pub. Schs., 1948-50; chief psychologist, instr. Med. Coll. Va., Richmond, 1950-52; pvt. practice psychology N.Y.C., 1952-68; clin. psychologist Erie, Pa., 1968—. Dir. psychol. svcs. United Cerebral Palsy Assn., Miami, Fla., 1952-54, Erie County (Pa.) Crippled Children's Soc., 1968-78; mem. med. staff Health-South Great Lakes Rehab. Hosp., Erie, Pa., 1986—; psychol. cons. Shriners Hosp. for Crippled Children, Erie. Author: Take Step, 1963, You Can Raise Your Handicapped Child, 1964, Helping the Handicapped Teenager Mature, 1971, Growing Up Handicapped, 1978, Sex, Love, and the Physically Handicapped, 1981, Beyond a Physical Disability: The Person Within, 2001. Mem. APA, CEC, Pa. Psychol. Assn., Psi Chi. Home: 5436 E Lake Rd Apt 818 Erie PA 16511-1449 Home Fax: 814-897-0341. Personal E-mail: evfscw@att.net.

AYRES, CAROLE BRIGGS, nurse, consultant; d. Charles Wesley Briggs and Shirley Mae Roewert; m. Carter Morgan Ayres, Nov. 21, 1977; children: Christopher Charles, Andrew Morgan. BA, U. of Wis., 1973; MBA, U. Wis., 1981; BSN, Edgewood Coll., 1996. RN Bd. of Nursing, Wis., 1997. Nurse intern U. of Wis. Hosp. and Clinics, Madison, Wis., 1997; staff nurse Meriter Hosp., 1997—2000; nurse cons. REM Wisconsin, 1997—. Bd. of dirs. Wis. Family Ties, Madison, 1992—96. Author: (biography for children) At the Controls: Women in Aviation, (science book for children) Research Balloons, (children's biography) Women in Space, (children's thrill sports book) Ballooning, (thrill sports for children) Sport Diving, (children's sports) Skin Diving is for Me. Member, adv. West YMCA, Madison, 2003—; parent mem. Wis. Family Ties, 1992—. Scholar Sheenberger scholar, Wis. Assn. on Mental Retardation, 1996. Mem.: Madison Knitters Guild (corr.). Unitarian. Avocations: knitting, swimming, travel, reading, aerobics. Office: REM Wis 1317 Applegate Rd Madison WI 53705 Personal E-mail: cayres3@hotmail.com. E-mail: Carole.Ayres@TheMentorNetwork.com.

AYRES, GLENN ALEX, scriptwriter, film producer; s. John Underwood and Alice Hutchinson Ayres; m. Janine Patrice Cooper, Aug. 16, 2003; m. Pamela Jean Williams, Mar. 23, 1979 (div. Mar. 1994); 1 child, Ariel Lee. BA, Harvard U., 1976; MA, George Mason U., 1983; MFA, UCLA, 1991. Editor Harvard Lampoon Mag., Cambridge, Mass., 1972—75; sr. editor Running Times Mag., Woodbridge, Va., 1977—91, L.A., 1977—91; rsch. writer Army Rsch. Inst., Alexandria, Va., 1983—85; editor, author Penguin U.S.A., N.Y.C., 1989—98; screenwriter CBS Prodns., L.A., 1992—94, 20th Century Fox, Paramount, 1995—, London, 1995—; exec. prodr. Supernova Prodns., L.A., 2002—03. Script cons., L.A., 1997—, London, 1997—; writing coach, L.A., 1994—98. Author: (screenplays) Marlowe, Search for Grace, 1994; editor: The Wit & Wisdom of Mark Twain, 1987. Bd. dirs. Cabin Owners Assn., 2002—. Mem.: Pen USA, Authors Guild, Writers Guild Am. Avocation: running. Home: 35115 Bouquet Canyon Rd Santa Clarita CA 91390

AYRES, IAN, law educator; b. Kansas City, Mo., Feb. 27, 1959; s. Marion Jordon and Karen (Koester) A. BA, Yale U., 1981, JD, 1986; PhD in Econs., MIT, 1988. Bar: Ill. 1987. Law clk. to Hon. James K. Logan US Ct. Appeals, 1986—87; rsch. fellow Amer. Bar Assoc., 1987—91; asst. prof. Northwestern U., Chgo., 1987-90, assoc. prof., 1990—91; vis. prof. Yale U., New Haven, 1991, U. Ill, 1997—98; guest scholar Brookings Inst., Washington, 1990-91; prof. Stanford (Calif.) Law Sch., 1992-94; William K. Townsend prof. Yale U. Law School, New Haven, 1994—. Vis. prof. U. Va., Charlottesville, 1989-90. Editor Law & Social Inquiry, 1990. Democrat. Office: Yale U Law Sch PO Box 208215 New Haven CT 06520-8215 E-mail: ian.ayres@yale.edu.*

AYRES, JANICE RUTH, social services administrator; b. Idaho Falls, Idaho, Jan. 23, 1930; d. Low Ray and Frances Mae (Salem) Mason; m. Thomas Woodrow Ayres, Nov. 27, 1953 (dec. 1966); 1 child, Thomas Woodrow Jr. (dec.). MBA, U. So. Calif., 1952, M in Mass Comms., 1953. Asst. mktg. dir. Disneyland, Inc., Anaheim, Calif., 1954-59; gen. mgr. Tamasha Town & Country Club, Anaheim, Calif., 1959-65; dir. mktg. Am. Heart Assn., Santa Ana, Calif., 1966-69; state exec. dir. Nev. Assn. Mental Health, Las Vegas, 1969-71; exec. dir. Clark Co. Easter Seal Treatment Ctr., Las Vegas, 1971-73; mktg. dir., fin devel. officer So. Nev. Drug Abuse Coun., Las Vegas, 1973-74; exec. dir. Nev. Assn. Retarded Citizens, Las Vegas, 1974-75; assoc., cons. Don Luke & Assocs., Phoenix, 1976-77; program dir. Inter-Tribal Coun. Nev., Reno, 1977-79; exec. dir. Ret. Sr. Vol. Program, Carson City, Nev., 1979—. Chair sr. citizen summit State of Nev., 1996; apptd. by Gov. Guinn, Nev. Commn. Aging, 2001; presenter in field; apptd. del. by Gov. of Nev. White House Conf. on Aging, 2005. Del. White Ho. Conf., 2005; bd. suprs. Carson City, Nev., 1992—; obligation bond com., legis. chair; commr. Carson City Parks and Recreation, 1993—; bd. dirs. Nev. Dept. Transp., 1993; active No. Corp. for Nat. and Cmty. Svc. by Gov., 1994, V&TRR Commn., 1993, re-appointed by Gov., 2005—, chair, 1995, vice-chair, chair pub. rels. com., bd. dirs. Hist. V&TRR Bd.; chair PR Cmty./V&RR Commn. Nev. Home Health Assn.; appointed liaison Carson City Sr. Citizens Bd., 1995; chair summit Rural Nev. Sr. Citizens, Carson City; pres. No. Nev. R.R. Found., 1996—; chair Tri-Co-R.R. Commn., 1995, Gov.'s Nev. Commn. for Corp. in Nat. and Comty. Svc., 1997—, pres., 1998, Carson City Pub. Transp. Commn., 1998—; Carson City Commn. for Clean Groundwater Act, 1998—; chairperson Celebrate Svc. Conf. Americore, 2000; appointed by Gov. of Nev. Commn. on Aging, 2001—; appointed by Nev. Gov. New Nev. Commn. to Restructure the Historic V&T R.R., 2002—; mem. Nev. Commn. on Aging, 2001—; apptd. rep. of gov. to Nev. Commn. Recruitment V&T RR, 2002; apptd. by Nev. Treas. Brian Krolicki Women's Commn. Fin., 2003—; re-appointed to commn. by Gov. Nev. Commn. for Nat. and Cmty. Svc., 2005—; apptd. del. to White House Conf. on Aging Nev. Gov., 2005. Named Woman of Distinction, Soroptimist Club, 1988, Outstanding Dir. of Excellence, Gov. State of Nev., 1989, Outstanding Nev. Women's Role Model, Nev. A.G., 1996, Woman of Distinction, Carson Valley Optimist, 2002, Nev.'s Outstanding Older Worker for Experience-Works, 2002, Oldest CEO in Nev., 2002, Outstanding Nev. Pvt. Citizen, Nev. Gov. Kenny Guinn, 2003, Outstanding Dir., Vol. Action Ctr., J.C. Penney Co., invitee to White Ho. for outstanding contbns. to Am.; recipient Gold award, Western Fairs Assn., 2000, Woman of Distinction award, Soroptimist, 2003, Carson City Optimist, 2003, Nat. Optimist Conv., Reno, Nev., 2003, Outstanding Svc. to Seniors Blue Star award, Sanford Ctr. on Aging, 2004, Outstanding Contbn. to Success of Women in Bus., Carson Valley Sorpotomists. Mem.: AAUW, Nat. Assn. Ret. and Sr. Vol. Dirs., Inc. (pres. 2003, nat. pres. 2003—), Internat. Assn. Bus. Commentators, No. Nev. Railroad Found. (pres. 1996—, 2005—08), Am. Soc. Assn. Execs., Nev. Assn. Transit Svcs. (bd. dirs., legis. chmn.), Nev. Fair and Rodeo Assn. (pres.), Nat. Soc. Fund Raising Execs., Women in Radio and TV, Pub. Rels. Soc. Am. (chpt. pres., Outstanding 25 Yr. Svc. award 2004), Internat. Platform Assn., Am. Mktg. Assn. (bd. dirs. 1999—), Am. Mgmt. Assn. (bd. dirs.), Nat. Women's Polit. Caucus, Nev. Women's Polit. Caucus. Home: 1762 Montelena Ct Carson City NV 89703-8376 Office: Ret Sr Vol Program 501 E Caroline St Carson City NV 89701-4054 Office Phone: 775-687-4680 ext. 2. Business E-Mail: branded@rsvp.carson-city.nv.us.

AYRES, JEFFREY PEABODY, lawyer; b. Waltham, Mass., Sept. 23, 1952; s. John Cecil and Dora Hoxie A.; m. Janet Diehl, May 31, 1980; children: Brendan Peabody, Caroline Bradfield, Gordon Pettit. BA cum laude, Harvard U., 1974; JD magna cum laude, George Washington U., 1977. Bar: D.C. 1977, Md. 1978, U.S. Ct. Appeals (3d, 4th and D.C. cirs.), U.S. Dist. Ct. Md., U.S. Dist. Ct. D.C., U.S. Supreme Ct. 1985. Assoc. Arent, Fox, Kintner, Plotkin & Kahn, Washington, 1977-78, Venable, Baetjer & Howard, Balt., 1978-85, ptnr., 1986; ptnr., chair Ethics Com. Venable LLP, Towson, Md. Contbr. articles to profl. jours. Alt., del. and parliamentarian Episcopal Diocesan Conv.; sr. warden Ch. of the Redeemer, 2002—. Mem. ABA, Md. Bar Assn., Balt. Bar Assn. (chair labor and employment sect. 1998-2000), Md. Atty. Grievance Commn. Peer Review Com., Harvard Club Md. (pres. 1989-94, v.p. 1994-2002), Harvard Alumni Assn. (regional dir. 1995-98). Democrat. Episcopalian. Avocations: running, bicycling. Home: 7120 Sheffield Rd Baltimore MD 21212-1629 Office: Venable LLP 210 Allegheny Ave PO Box 5517 Towson MD 21204 Office Phone: 410-494-6282. Office Fax: 410-821-0147. E-mail: jpayres@venable.com.*

AYRES, JOHN E., JR., hotel executive; Gen. mgr. trainee Hilton Hotels Corp., Chgo.; owner Fulton's Folley Restaurant, Harrington Park, NJ; gen. mgr. Marriott Hotels and Resorts; sr. mem. exec. team The Breakers, Paom Beach, Fla.; owner, mgr. Coral Beach Hotels and Resorts, Naples, Fla.; chmn., CEO Coral Beach Hotels & Clubs, Naples, Fla. Mailing: 9180 Galleria Ct Ste 600 Naples FL 34109-4385

AYRES, MARY ELLEN, federal official; b. Spokane, Wash., June 23, 1924; d. Frank H. and Marion (Kellogg) A. Student, U. Wash., 1942-43; BA, Stanford U., 1946; postgrad., Am. U., 1960. With Henry von Morpurgo, Advt., 1946-47; reporter Wenatchee Daily World, Wash., 1947-50, Washington Post, 1951-52; with U.S. Fgn. Service, Dept. State, 1950-51; mem. editorial staff Changing Times, 1952-61; editor Family Guide, Kiplinger Washington Editors, 1958-61, Bur. Labor Stats., Manpower Adminstrn., U.S. Dept. Labor, 1962-67; pub. info. specialist Bur. Indian Affairs, U.S. Dept. Interior, 1967-75; writer-editor Bur. Labor Stats., 1975—. Tchr. newsletter class Dept. Agriculture Grad. Sch., 1975-89, editing style and technique class, 1987-89; past treas. Govt. Info. Orgn. Mem. publicity com. Nat. Capitol YWCA, 1982-83; dir. Wenatchee High Sch. Scholarship Found., 1988-95. Mem. Nat. Assn. Govt. Communicators (founding treas., dir. 1975-80, 89-91, chmn. Blue Pencil Contest 1987, nat. capital chpt. treas. 1989), Nat. Press Club (Washington), Washington Athletic Club (Seattle), Am. News Women's Club, Stanford U. Alumnae Assn., Kappa Kappa Gamma. Episcopalian. Home: 2400 Virginia Ave NW Apt C802 Washington DC 20037-2657 Office: Bur Labor Stats 2 Massachusetts Ave NE Washington DC 20212-0022 Fax: 202-691-7890. Office Phone: 202-691-5856. E-mail: ayres_m@bls.gov.

AYRES, ROBERT MOSS, JR., retired university president; b. San Antonio, Sept. 1, 1926; s. Robert Moss and Florence (Collett) A.; m. Patricia Ann Shield, Sept. 10, 1955; children: Robert Atlee, Vera Patricia. Student, Tex. Mil. Inst., 1944; BA, U. of the South, 1949, DCL, 1974; postgrad., Oxford (Eng.) U., 1949; MBA, U. Pa., 1952. With Kidder, Peabody & Co., Phila., N.Y.C., 1950-52; with Dittmar & Co., San Antonio, 1952-53; pres., dir. Russ & Co., Inc., San Antonio, 1953-73; sr. v.p., dir. Rotan Mosle Inc., San Antonio, 1973-77; pres. U. South, Sewanee, Tenn., 1977-88, pres. emeritus, 1988—; past pres. So. Univ. Conf.; chmn. So. Coll. and Univ. Union. Former allied mem. N.Y. Stock Exch., Am. Stock Exch.; bd. dirs. Rail Tex. Corp., Howell Corp., James Avery Craftsman. Past pres. Assn. Alumni U. of South; past pres. bd. dirs. Bexar County chpt. ARC; past pres. bd. trustees Tex. Mil. Inst.; trustee, past chmn. bd. regents U. of South; trustee Brother's Bro. Found.; mem. exec. coun. Episcopal Ch., 1976-82, also mem. nat. and world mission com., dir., past pres. St. Mary's Episcopal Ctr.; mem. Commn. on Ministry Com. Diocese of Tex.; past bd. dirs. Inst. European Studies, Presiding Bishop's Fund World Relief, Alfalit, Internat.; vol. exec. dir. Vol. in Mission, 1976; bd. dirs. Inst. of Servant Leadership, Soc. Promotion of Christian Knowledge/U.S.A., Salvation Army, Episcopal Hist. Soc. With USN, 1944-46; lt. Res. 1949-60. Mem. San Antonio Soc. Fin. Analysts (past pres.), Securities Industries Assn. (past mem. governing coun.), Investment Bankers Assn. Am. (past chmn. Tex. group), Nat. Assn. Securities Dealers (past mem. dist. com.) Young Pres. Orgn., Order of Alamo, Tex. Cavaliers, Argyle, Am. Soc. Order of St. John, Sigma Alpha Epsilon. Episcopalian (mem. exec. bd. diocese W. Tex.; vestryman). Clubs: San Antonio German, San Antonio Country. Home: 5705 Scout Island Cv Austin TX 78731-3386

AYRES, STEPHEN MCCLINTOCK, physician, educator; b. Elizabeth, N.J., Oct. 29, 1929; s. Malcolm B. and Florence M. A.; m. Dolores Kobrick, June 11, 1955; children: Stephen (dec.), Elizabeth, Margaret. BA, Gettysburg Coll., 1951; MD, Cornell U., 1955. Intern N.Y. Hosp., N.Y.C., 1955, resident, 1958-61; dir. cardio-pulmonary lab. St. Michael's Hosp., Newark, 1961-63, St. Vincent's Hosp. and Med. Ctr., N.Y.C., 1963-73; physician-in-chief St. Vincent Hosp., Worcester, Mass., 1973-75; prof., chmn. dept. internal medicine St. Louis U. Med. Ctr., 1975-85; dean Med. Coll. Va., Richmond, 1985-93; dean emeritus, dir. office internat. health program Med. Coll. Va./Va. Commonwealth U., Richmond, 1993—. Author: Care of the Critically Ill, 3d edit., 1988; co-author: Textbook of Critical Care, 1988, Nutritional Support of the Critically Ill, 1988; editor: Major Issues in Critical Care Medicine, 1984; contbr. articles to profl. jours. Chmn. bd. Found. for Critical Care, 1985—. Served with M.C., U.S. Army, 1956-58. Fellow ACP, Am. Coll. Cardiology, Am. Coll. Chest Physicians; mem. Soc. Critical Care Medicine (pres.

1979-80), Am. Lung Assn., Assn. Am. Physicians, Am. Soc. Clin. Investigation. Home: 5103 Cary Street Rd Richmond VA 23226-1644 Office: Med Coll Va PO Box 565 Richmond VA 23218-0565

AYRES, TED DEAN, lawyer; b. Hamilton, Mo., July 14, 1947; m. Marcia Sue Busselle; children: John Corbett, Jackson Frazer, Joseph Dean. BSBA, Ctrl. Mo. State Coll., 1969; JD, U. Mo., 1972. Bar: Mo. 1972, U.S. Dist. Ct. (we. dist.) Mo. 1972, U.S. Ct. Appeals (8th cir.) 1977, U.S. Supreme Ct. 1977, Colo. 1984, U.S. Dist. Ct. Colo. 1984, U.S. Ct. Appeals (10th cir.) 1984, Kans. 1987. Law clk. to presiding justice Mo. Supreme Ct., Jefferson City, 1972-73; ptnr. Stubbs & Ayres, Chillicothe, Mo., 1973-74; atty. Southwestern Bell Tel. Co., St. Louis, 1974-76; counsel U. Mo., Columbia, 1976-84; gen. counsel U. Colo., Boulder, 1984-86, Kans. Bd. Regents, Topeka, 1986-92, gen. counsel, dir. govtl. rels., 1992-96; acting pres. Pitts. State U., 1995; gen. counsel, assoc. to pres. Wichita (Kans.) State U., 1996—2002, interim dir. Edwin A. Ulrich Mus. Art, 1999-2000, v.p., gen. counsel, 2002—, dir. equal employment opportunity, 2003—. Adj. asst. prof. coll. bus. adminstrn. U. Colo., Denver, 1984-85, adj. assoc. prof., 1985-86; spl. asst. atty. gen. State of Colo., 1984-86, State of Kans., 1986—; presenter region II conf. Assn. Coll. Unions Internat., U. Mo., Rolla, 1983; spkr. Soc. Colo. Archivists, U. Colo., Boulder, 1985; adj. prof. Washburn U., Topeka, 1989; adj. prof. kinesiology and sport studies Wichita State U., 1999—; spl. cons. to pres. Southwestern Coll., Winfield, Kans., 2003-. Contbr. articles to profl. jours. Adv. com. Boone County (Mo.) Cmty. Svcs.; com. social concerns Mo. United Meth. Ch., 1979-81, supervisory com. Mothers' Morning Out program, 1980-84; adminstv. bd., com. on fin. and stewardship 1st United Meth. Ch., Topeka, 1989-91, family life coun., 1994-95; trustee Mid-Mo. chpt. Nat. Multiple Sclerosis Soc., 1981-84; bd. mgrs. Topeka YMCA-Downtown Br., 1991-96, fedn. coun. Indian Guides program, 1988-91; pack treas. Boy Scouts Am., 1990-95; bd. dirs. Innovative Tech. Enterprise Corp., 1991-94, S.W. Youth Athletic Assn., Inc., 1994-96, Friends of Topeka Zoo, 1995-2000, Wichita Tech. Corp., 1997-, Wichita State U. Hist. Preservation Commn., 1998-; parents coun. Truman State U., 1997-99. Curator scholar, 1969-70, Omar E. Robinson scholar, 1970-71, John M. Dalton Ednl. Trust scholar 1971-72. Mem. Mo. Bar Assn., Nat. Assn. Coll. and Univ. Attys. (chairperson Southwestern region 1979-81, bd. dirs. 1985-88, com. mem. 1996-97), del. and presenter numerous CLE workshops), U. Mo. Alumni Assn. (life; bd. dirs. Wichita chpt., 2004-). Home: 2820 Tallgrass St Wichita KS 67226-1815 Office: Wichita State Univ 203 Morrison Hall Wichita KS 67260-0001 Office Phone: 316-978-3001. Business E-Mail: ted.ayres@wichita.edu.

AYSCUE, EDWIN OSBORNE, JR., lawyer; b. May 21, 1933; s. Edwin Osborne and Grace Elizabeth A.; m. Emily Mizell Urquhart, Aug. 17, 1957; children: Grace, E. Osborne, Emily Hassel, Margaret Certain. Grad. cum laude, Phillips Acad., Andover, Mass., 1951; AB in Polit. Sci., U. N.C., Chapel Hill, 1954; LLB with honors, U. N.C., 1960. Bar: N.C. 1960, U.S. Supreme Ct. 1979. Of counsel Helms Mulliss & Wicker, PLLC (and predecessor firms), Charlotte, 1960—. Mem. Civil Justice Reform Act Com., Western Dist. N.C., 1991—95. Editor-in-chief: N.C. Law Rev., 1959-60; contbr. articles to profl. jours. Bd. dirs. Legal Svcs. of So. Piedmont, 1983-85, Am. Judicature Soc., 1985-89, Legal Svcs. of N.C., 1984-85, 88-94, Am. Judicature Soc., 1985-89, U.S. Supreme Ct. Hist. Soc., 1999-2003; bd. vis. U. N.C. Chapel Hill, 2000-04; trustee St. Mary's Sch., Raleigh, N.C., 2000-2004; sr. warden Christ Episcopal Ch., 1990-91. Lt. USNR, 1955-57. Fellow: Am. Coll. Trial Lawyers (pres. 1998—99), Am. Bar Found. (life); mem.: ABA (ho. of dels. 1991—95, standing com. fed. judiciary 2001—04), People's Republic of Cuba Legal Exch. (chair 2001), People's Republic of China Legal Exch. (chair 1987), Anglo-Am. Legal Exch. (co-chair 1999—2000), Mecklenburg County Bar (pres. 1980—81), N.C. State Bar, N.C. Bar Assn. (pres. 1984—85, Gen. Practice Hall of Fame), 4th Cir. Jud. Conf., Nat. Conf. Bar Pres., U. N.C. Chapel Hill Law Alumni Assn. (pres. 1999—2000), Order of Coif, Order Golden Fleece, Charlotte Country Club, Phi Beta Kappa. Democrat. Episcopalian. Office: Helms Mulliss & Wicker PLLC PO Box 31247 Charlotte NC 28231-1247 Office Phone: 704-343-2058. Business E-Mail: ozzie.ayscue@hmw.com.

AYUB, YACUB, financial consultant; b. Bombay, May 14, 1944; s. Ayub and Aziza Abbas; children: Murtaza, Marzia. MBA, U. Karachi, Pakistan, 1966. CPC, CEP. Rep. officer United Bank of Pakistan, Tehran, 1966-73; calling officer Bank Credit and Commerce Internat. (Iran Arab Bank), Tehran, 1974-78; audit officer Bank Credit and Commerce Internat., London, 1978-79, mgr. br. ops. Panama City, Panama, 1979-83, mgr. mktg. and bus. devel. N.Y.C., 1983-88; fin. cons. Investment & Mgmt. Cons. Inc., Holmdel, 1988—2002; morgage cons. Residential & Comml., 2002—. Fellow Life Underwriters Tng. Coun. Republican. Home: 1001 Plaza Dr Woodbridge NJ 07095-1116 E-mail: ayubm@aol.com. *Perseverance, hard work, faith and hope are the true ingredients to success. Add to it honesty and trust which leads to great achievements in business and life.*

AYUS, JUAN CARLOS, nephrologist; b. Buenos Aires, Feb. 25, 1941; arrived in U.S., 1973; s. Jose and Matilde A.; m. Linda Maria Giudici; children: Sebastian, Mariana. BS, Nat. Coll., 1959; MD, U. Buenos Aires, 1967. Diplomate Am. Bd. Internal Medicine, Am. Bd. Nephrology. Resident in internal medicine U. Buenos Aires, 1968-71, fellow in nephrology, 1971-72; resident in internal medicine U. Mass., Worcester, 1973-74, U. Minn., Mpls., 1974-75; fellow in nephrology U. Calif., San Francisco, 1975-77; chief renal svc. Ben-Taub Regional hosp., Houston, 1977-84; from assoc. prof. to prof. medicine Baylor Coll. Medicine, Houston, 1984—2001; prof. medicine U. Tex. Health Sci. Ctr., San Antonio, 2001—. Recipient Gold Insignia, Spanish Soc. Nephrology, 1999. Fellow ACP; mem. L.Am. Soc. Nephrology (sec.-treas. 1993-96, v.p. 1996-99), Argentine Soc. Critical Care (founder). Home: 2412 Westgate Houston TX 77019 Office Phone: 713-795-9333. Business E-Mail: ayus@uthscsa.edu. E-mail: carlosayus@yahoo.com.

AYYALA, RAMESH S., ophthalmologist, educator; b. Hyderabad, India, Feb. 12, 1962; s. Shastry Ayyala; m. Deepthi Murthy, Dec. 13, 1989; children: Divya, Ram. BS, Osmania U., Hyderabad, 1979; MD, Gandhi Med. Coll./Osmania U., 1985. Diplomate Am. Bd. Ophthalmology. Tng. in glaucoma and cornea Osmania U., 1988; internal medicine intern Danbury C.C., Yale U., Conn., 1993—94; glaucoma fellow Mass. Eye and Ear Infirmary, Boston, 1994—95; corna/external diseases fellow Univ. Eye Assocs., Boston U. Med. Ctr., 1995—96; resident in ophthalmology U. South Fla., Tampa, 1996—99; asst. prof. ophthalmology Tulane U., 1999—, assoc. prof. ophthalmology, 2004—; chief ophthalmology sect. Med. Ctr. La., Charity Campus, New Orleans, 1999—2001, dir. glaucoma svcs., 1999—; dir. residency program dept. ophthalmology Tulane U. Health Scis. Ctr., 2004—. Author: (jour. article) Archives of Ophthalmology, Survey of Ophthalmology, (jour. letter) Ophthalmology, (book) Anterior Segment Disease: A Diagnostic Color Atlas; co-author: (jour. article) Eye, Ophthalmic Surgery and Lasers, Cornea, Ophthalmology, Am. Jour. of Ophthalmology, (book contribution) Corneal Disorders: Clin. Diagnosis and Mgmt.; contbr. book Ophthalmology, e-medicine. Organizer/participant Rural Eye Camps, India, 1986—88; participant Prevent Blindness Mass., Boston, 1995—96; presenter AARP, New Orleans, 2003. Scholar Nat. Merit Scholarship, Govt. of India, 1977—85. Fellow: Royal Coll. Ophthalmology, Royal Coll. Surgeons; mem.: AMA, Chandler-Grant Glaucoma Soc., Indian Assn. Ophthalmology, Am. Glaucoma Soc., New Orleans Acad. Ophthalmology, Am. Acad. Ophthalmology, Assn. for Rsch. in Vision and Ophthalmology. Achievements include patents pending for Ocular Slow-Release Antifibrotic-Agent Delivery Sys; development of bldg. glaucoma drainage device based on Starling Resistor device with advantages over existing models. Avocations: travel, movies, cooking, gardening. Office: Tulane Univ Health Scis Ctr 1430 Tulane Ave SL-69 New Orleans LA 70112-2699 E-mail: rayyala@tulane.edu.

AYYUB, BILAL M., engineer, educator, engineering executive, researcher; b. Shweikeh, Tulkaram, Palestine, Jan. 5, 1958; came to U.S., 1980; s. Mohammed S. and Thuraya Ayyub; m. Deena L. Ziadeh, June 27, 1987; children: Omar, Rami, Samar, Ziad. BSCE, U. Kuwait, 1980; MSCE, Ga. Inst. Tech., 1981, PhD, 1983. Registered profl. engr., Md. Asst. prof. dept. civil engring. U. Md., College Park, 1983-88, assoc. prof., 1988-93, prof., 1993—, gen. dir. Ctr. for Tech. and Sys. Mgmt.; pres. BMA Engring. Inc., Md., 1988—; CEO Decide-Now.com, Inc., 2000—03. Cons. prof. Carderock divsn. of Naval Surface Warfare Ctr., USN; cons. USCG, Groton, Conn., 1987-90, USN, Crystal City, Va., 1990—, ASME, Washington, 1990—, Internat. Monetary Fund, Washington, 1993, Chevron Rsch. and Tech. Corp., Richmond, Calif., 1992-94, U.S. Army Corps. of Engrs., Washington, 1994—; mem. adv. bd. to internat. jours. and Naval Engrs. Jour., 1989-2005; gen. chmn. Internat. Symposium on Uncertainty Modeling and Analysis, 1990, 93, 95, 2003; dir. Ctr. for Tech. and Sys. Mgmt. Editor: Analysis and Management of Uncertainty, 1992, Uncertainty Modeling and Analysis, 1995, Uncertainty Modeling in Finite Element, Fatigue and Stability of Systems, 1997, Uncertainty Modeling in Vibration, Control and Fuzzy Analysis in Structural Systems, 1997, Uncertainty Modeling and Analysis in Civil Engineering, 1998, Uncertainty Modeling and Analysis in Engineering and the Sciences, 1997; editor: (textbooks) Numerical Methods for Engineers1995, Elicitation of Expert Opinions for Uncertainty and Risks, 2001, Probability, Statistics and Reliability for Engineers, 2d edit., 2003, Risk Analysis in Engineering and Economics, 2003; contbr. articles to profl. jours. Recipient Cert. of Appreciation, U.S. Army C.E., 1995; grantee, NSF, 1985—92, Md. State Hwy. Adminstrn., 1986—90, USN, 1990—95, U.S. Army C.E., 1994—95. Fellow ASCE (Outstanding Rsch. Oriented Paper award 1988, Edmund Friedman award 1989, Walter L. Huber Civil Engring. Rsch. award 1997, chmn. reliability of offshore structures com. 1993-96, assoc. editor Jour. Structural Engring., mem. com. on fatugue and fracture reliability, mem. tech. adminstrv. com. on structural safety and reliability 1993-96), Soc. Naval Archs. and Marine Engrs. (chmn. panel on design procedure and philosophy of the hull structures com., Jour. Ship Rsch. com.), ASME (polit. action com. 1990—, risk-based tech. rsch. com.); mem. IEEE (sr.), NRC (working groups of marine bd.), Am. Soc. Naval Engrs. (life, Jimmie Hamilton award 1986, 93, 2000, 02, chmn. naval engrs. jour. com.), Am. Concrete Inst., Am. Acad. Mechanics, N.Am. Fuzzy Info. Processing Soc. (K.S. Fu award 1995, gen. chmn. ann. conf. 1995), Computer Soc. Achievements include risk and uncertainty analysis in engineering, homeland security and protection of critical infrastructure and key assets, design guidelines for posttensioned composite bridges, general guidelines for risk-based inspection, structural reliability assessment using variance reduction techniques, uncertainty modeling and analysis in engineering, fuzzy logic in civil engineering, reliability-based design of marine structures, reliability assessment and reliability-based design of navigation structures. Office: U Md Dept Civil & Environ Engr College Park MD 20742-0001 Business E-Mail: ayyub@umail.umd.edu.

AZAD, SUSAN S., lawyer; BS, Oreg. State U., 1984; JD, UCLA, 1989. Bar: Calif. 1989. With Latham & Watkins, L.A., 1989—, ptnr., 1997—. Mem. assocs. com. Latham & Watkins, L.A., 1992—94, fin. com., 1995—97, ethics com., 2001—. Mem.: ABA, L.A. County Bar Assn. (litigation sect., former mem. jud. election evaluations com., former mem. Calif. and state bar ct. rules com.), Calif. Women Lawyers. Office: Latham and Watkins LLP 633 W Fifth St Ste 4000 Los Angeles CA 90071 Office Phone: 213-485-1234.

AZADIAN, HARRY Y., physician; b. Somerville, Mass., Dec. 21, 1934; s. Vahan and Grace B. (Emanatian) A.; m. Carol Ann Fitzpatrick, June 24, 1956; children: Jeffrey, Todd. BS, Tufts U., 1956; MD, Harvard Med. Sch., 1960. Intern U. Calif. Hosps., San Francisco, 1960-61; resident in surgery Boston City Hosp. Harvard Surg. Svc., 1964-68, Harvard Svc., Boston, 1964-68; pvt. practice Cambridge, Mass., 1969-89; occupational physician Raytheon Co., Lexington, Mass., 1989—2001, corp. med. dir. Fellow Am. Coll. Surgeons, Am. Coll. Occupational Medicine. Republican. Avocations: scuba diving, skiing. Office Phone: 617-710-4565. E-mail: cazadian@aol.com.

AZADZOI, KAZEM M., urologist, educator; b. Feb. 10, 1957; s. Nasim and Amena Azadzoi; m. Jamila Azadzoi; children: Naweed Azad, Roya Azad, Michelle Azad. MD, Kabul (Afghanistan) U., 1983; MA, Boston U., 1990. Prof., pathology and urology Boston U. Med. Sch., 2002—; dir., urology rsch. VA Boston Healthcare Sys., 2002—. Mem. adv. bd. European Urol. Soc. Ann. Meeting, Istanbul, Turkey, 2000; ad hoc cons. NIH, Veterans Affairs Ctrl. Office. Contbr. articles to profl. jours., chpts. to books; mem. editl. bd. Brit. Jour. Urology Internat. Recipient prize in med. rsch., Jean-Francois Ginestie, 1990, 1996, Endourology Soc., 1993, Jack Lapides, 1998, AVA/Circon, 2000; grantee, NIH, 1987—88, 1992—97, 2000—05, Veterans Affairs Ctrl. Office, 1991—94, 1998—2001, 2001—05, Gentronics Inc., 1998—99, Pfizer Pharmaceuticals, 2000, 2001, 2002, 2003, POM Wonderful Inc., 2003—05, Ely-Lilly Pharmaceuticals, 2004, Yamanouchi Pharmaceuticals, 2005. Mem.: N.E. Smooth Muscle Soc., Nat. Bladder Found., Internat. Soc. for Impotence Rsch., Internat. Continence Soc., Am. Urol. Assn. Achievements include development of the first experimental model of pelvic ischemia. Office: VA Boston Healthcare Sys 150 S Huntington Ave Boston MA 02130 Office Phone: 617-232-9500 5602. E-mail: kazadzoi@bu.edu.

AZANK, ROBERTO, artist; b. Buenos Aires, Nov. 3, 1955; came to U.S., 1979; s. Neazi and Dora Margarita (Estevez) A.; m. Monika Schifler, Oct. 20, 1990; 1 child, Rudi Vinicius. Student, U. Arch., Buenos Aires, 1975-78. One-man shows include Marcos J. Alegria Sch. Fine Arts, P.R., 1991, Consulate Gen. of Argentina, N.Y.C., 1997, Lizan Tops Gallery, East Hampton, N.Y., 1998, Albers Fine Arts, Memphis, 1998, Albert White Gallery, Toronto, 1998, Hooks-Epstein Galleries, Houston, 1998, Brewster Arts Ltd., N.Y.C., 1999, Addison-Ripley Fine Art, Washington, 1999, 2003, Byron Cohen Gallery, Kansas City, Mo., 2000, Albert Einstein U., N.Y.C., 1999, Eleonore Austerer Gallery, San Francisco, 2001, 02, 03, 04, Palm Springs, Calif., 2003, Gomez Gallery, Balt., 2001, Bachelier-Cardonsky Gallery, Kent, Conn., 2001, 03, Austerer-Crider Gallery, Palm Springs, 2002, Ctr. of Earth Gallery, Charlotte, N.C., 2003, Eleonore Austerer Gallery, Palm Desert, Calif., 2003, 05, Simmons Gallery, San Francisco, 2004, 05, Patricia Rovzar Gallery, Kirkland, Wash., 2004; group exhbns. include Olympia and York Gallery, N.Y., 1991, Galaxy Gallery, Miami Beach, Fla., 1990, SUNY, Albany, 1993, Ramis Barquet Gallery, Miami, 1997, N.Y. Arts Mag. 2d City-wide Biennial, 1997, Mulligan Shanoski Gallery, San Francisco, 1998, Elite Fine Art, Miami, 1998, Art Miami, '98, 1998, Lyons Wier Gallery, Chgo., 1998, Artspace/Va. Miller Gallery, Miami, 1998, Meredith Kelly Fine Arts, Santa Fe, 1998, 2000, 02, 03, Kougeas Gallery, Boston, 1999, William Havu Gallery, Denver, 1999, Art Miami, 2000, 01, Palm Springs Art Fair, 2000, 01, Eleonore Austerer Gallery, 2000, Ctr. of Earth Gallery, Charlotte, N.C., 2002; represented by Robert Miller Gallery, N.Y., Addison-Ripley Gallery, Washington, Artspace/Virginia Miller Gallery, Miami, Eleonore Austerer Gallery, San Francisco and Palm Springs; works featured in publs. including N.Y. Arts Mag., New Am. Painting, Waterfront Week, Kansas City Star, The Washington Post, Miami Herald, Palm Springs Life; included in pub. collections at Washington Conv. Ctr., Am. Express Fin. Advisors, Spring Telecomms., also pvt. collections. Avocations: classical music, astronomy, chess. Office: Roberto Azank Studio 8 Watch Hill Rd New Paltz NY 12561-2705 Office Phone: 845-255-3525. E-mail: RobertoAzank@mac.com.

AZAR, ALEX MICHAEL, II, federal agency administrator, lawyer; AB, Dartmouth U., 1988; JD, Yale U., 1991. Bar: U.S. Dist. Ct. Md. 1994, U.S. Dist. Ct. D.C. 1999, U.S. Ct. Appeals Md. 1993, U.S. Ct. Appeals (D.C. cir.) 1994, U.S. Ct. Appeals (4th cir.) 1994, U.S. Ct. Appeals D.C. 1995, U.S. Supreme Ct. 1999. Law clk. to Hon. J. Michael Luttig U.S. Ct. Appeals (4th cir.), 1991—92; law clk. to Justice Antonin Scalia US Supreme Ct., 1992—93; assoc. Kirkland & Ellis, Washington, 1993—94; assoc. ind. counsel Whitewater Investigation, 1994—96; ptnr. Wiley, Rein & Fielding, Washington, 1996—2001; gen. counsel US Dept. Health & Human Services., Washington, 2001—05, dep. sec., 2005—. Office: US Dept Health & Human Services 200 Independence Ave SW Rm 614G Washington DC 20201 Office Phone: 202-690-7741, 202-690-6133. Office Fax: 202-690-7998, 202-690-7755.

AZAR, FRED S., biomedical engineer, researcher; BEE, McGill U., 1993; MS in BioEngring., Ecole Centrale Paris, 1994; PhD, U. Pa., 2001. Med. imaging R&D Royal Victoria Hosp., Montreal, 1993, GE Med. Sys., Buc, 1994; rsch. scientist Montreal Neurol. Inst., 1994—95; breast cancer imaging rschr. U. Pa., Phila., 1995—2001; biomed. engring. cons. Sarnoff Corp., Princeton, 2002; biomed. engring. scientist Siemens Corp., Princeton, NJ, 2002—. Contbr. articles to profl. publs. Fellow Dean's fellow, U. of Pa., 1995—96, Bus. Towne fellow, U. Pa., 1996—2000, Academic fellow, U. of Pa., 1998. Mem.: IEEE (life bioengring. paper award 2000), Engring. Medicine Biology Soc., IEEE Computer Soc., Am. Soc. Therapeutic Radiology Oncology (assoc.). Achievements include research in deformable 3D model of the breast for predicting mechanical deformations during interventional medical procedures; development of the OMIRAD platform, the optical and multimedal imaging platform for research assessment and diagnosis in the network for translational research in optical imaging. Personal E-mail: fredazar@alumni.upenn.edu.

AZAR, HENRY AMIN, retired medical educator; b. Egypt, Dec. 21, 1927; s. Amin Antonios and Agnes Garabed (Nazaretian) A.; m. Rose Theresa Connell, Apr. 19, 1960; children: Henry Amin Jr., Philip John. BA, Am. U., Beirut, 1948, MD, 1952; PhD in History, U. N.C., 1998. Diplomate Am. Bd. Pathology. Intern N.Y.C. Hosp., 1952-53; resident Columbia-Presbyn. Hosp. Med. Ctr., N.Y.C., 1955-56, N.Y.-Cornell, Med. Ctr., N.Y.C., 1956-57, Mass. Meml. Hosp., Boston, 1957-58; asst. prof. pathology Am. U., Beirut, 1958-60; asst. prof. and assoc. prof. pathology Coll. Physicians and Surgeons, Columbia U., 1960-70; dir. surg. pathology, prof. U. Kans., 1970-72; chief lab. service James A. Haley Vets. Hosp., Tampa, Fla., 1972-83, chief anatomic pathology, 1983-92; prof. U. South Fla., 1973-92, prof. emeritus, 1992. Rsch. prof. pathology U. N.C., 1998—. Author: Multiple Myeloma and Related Disorders, 1973, Diagnostic Electron Microscopy: The Hemopoietic System, 1979, Pathology of Human Neoplasms, 1988, Ibn Zuhr (Avenzoar): The Translation of His Work into Latin and His Image in Medieval Europe, 1998; contbr. articles to profl. jours. Fellow Coll. Am. Pathologists; mem. Assn. Vet. Chiefs Lab. Svc. (pres. 1981-83), Arthur Purdy Stout Soc. (sec. 1983-87, pres. 1990-91), Pathology Alumni Found. (emeritus trustee) Harvey Soc., Internat. Acad. Pathology (emeritus), Hematopathology Soc., Am. Assn. for History of Medicine, Soc. Internat. History of Sci. and Philosophy Arab Islam, Am. U. Beirut Alumni Assn. (pres. Tampa Bay chpt. 1985-87), History of Pathology Soc. (pres. 1996-97). Syrian Orthodox. Home: 1700 Old Oxford Rd Chapel Hill NC 27514-2132

AZAR, J. J., engineering educator; b. Tripoli, Lebanon, Sept. 19, 1937; arrived in U.S., 1957; s. Joseph and Sarah Azar; m. Zaetta Jean Bradshaw, Dec. 23, 1961; children: Scott J., Steven Zay. BS, U. Okla., 1960, MS, 1961; PhD, U. Okla., Norman, 1965. Lic. profl. engr., Okla. Asst. prof. U. Tulsa, Okla., 1965—69, assoc. prof., 1969—75, prof., 1975—96, McMen Chair prof., 1996—2002, prof. emeritus, 2002—. Dir. U. Tulsa Drilling Rsch. Projects, 1975—96; chmn. award com. AIME, N.Y.C., 1997. Author: Matrix Structural Analysis, 1972, Aircraft Structures, 1982, Drilling Fluids, 1986; contbr. articles to profl. jours. Mem.: Nat. Acad. Engring., Soc. Petroleum Engrs. (chmn. award com. 1994—, Disting. Achievement Prof. in Petroleum Engring. 1997, Drilling Engring. award 1998, Disting. Mem. award 2004). Republican. Presbyn. Avocations: tennis, golf, skiing. Home: 4130 72nd St Tulsa OK 74136 Office: U Tulsa 600 S College Tulsa OK 74104 Personal E-mail: adc.training@sbcglobal.net.

AZARA, NANCY JEAN, sculptor, book artist, educator; b. NYC, Oct. 13, 1939; d. Joseph Frank and Nancy Ann (Como) A.; 1 child: Nana Olivas. AAS, Finch Coll., 1959; postgrad., Lester Polokav Studio, 1960-62, Art Students League N.Y., 1964-67; BS, Empire State Coll., 1974. Theatrical costume designer, 1959-66; tchr. visual arts Jewish Guild for the Blind, N.Y.C., 1966-67; tchr. art Community Edn. program N.Y.C. Bd. Edn., 1967-68; art cons., 1969-70; tchr. fine arts, summer session, 1970; mem. faculty Bklyn. Coll., 1973-75, 75, 76; ind. studies instr. Empire State Coll., 1975; mem. faculty Bklyn. Mus. Art Sch., 1975-77, Coll. New Rochelle, 1979-81, 81-82. Exec. dir., founding mem. Women's Ctr. for Learning N.Y. Feminist Art Inst., 1979-80, also mem. faculty; guest lectr. in field; mem. adv. bd., A.I.R. Gallery, 2000-. One-woman shows include: Fourteen Sculptors Gallery, N.Y.C., 1976, WARM Gallery, Mpls., 1986, Bard Coll., N.Y.C., 1977, Soho 20 Gallery, N.Y.C., 1984, 87, John Jay Coll., N.Y.C., 1984, Artemisia Gallery, Chgo., 1985, A.I.R. Gallery, N.Y.C., 1992, Lannon Gallery, Chgo., 1990, E.M. Donahue and AIR Galleries, N.Y.C., 1994, Tweed Mus. Art, Duluth, Minn., 1995, Art Space, Jersey City State Coll., 1996, Gertrude Herbert Inst. Art., Augusta, Ga., 1997, Rudolph E. Lee Gallery, Coll. Architecture, Arts and Humanities, Clemson (S.C.) U., 1997, Donahue/Sosinski Art, N.Y.C., 1997, Gwinnett Fine Arts Ctr., Duluth, Ga., 1998; exhibited in group shows at Picola Formata Galleria Numero, Florence, Italy, 1968, Queens Coll., N.Y.C., 1975, Gallery 10 Ltd., Washington, 1978, Sculpture Ctr., N.Y.C., 1980, Landmark Gallery, N.Y.C., 1980, Franklin Furnace, N.Y.C., 1980, Tweed Gallery, Plainfield, N.J., 1982, William Paterson Coll., N.J., 1982, Kathryn Markel Gallery, N.Y.C., 1982, Jack Tilton Gallery, N.Y.C., 1983, Ceres Gallery, N.Y.C., 1984, Rotunda Gallery, N.Y.C., 1984, 80 Washington Sq. East Gallery, N.Y.C., 1984, Hand in Hand Gallery, N.Y.C., 1985, Janco Dada Mus., Israel, 1985, Del. Ctr. Contemporary Arts, Wilmington, 1991, The Arch. Grand Army Pla., Bklyn., 1991, Muse Gallery, Phila., 1991, Rempire Gallery, N.Y.C., 1991, Images of Destruction and Regeneration, Tenn., Visual Narratives, Conn., Layering, N.Mex., 1993, Snug Harbor Cultural Ctr., Staten Island, N.Y., 1994, 96, Sweetbriar (Va.) Coll, 1994, Bolinas (Calif.) Mus., 1994, 96, Paterson (N.J.) Mus., U. Mus., LaCrosse, Wis., 1994, Open Ctr., N.Y.C., 1994, Berkshire Artisans Gallery, Pittsfield, Mass., 1995, Sun Cities Art Mus., Sun City Ariz., 1995, Wall Gallery, John Jay Coll., N.Y.C., 1995, Esperanza Peace Ctr., San Antonio, 1995, Tribeca 148 Gallery, N.Y.C., 1995, AIR Gallery, N.Y.C., 1995-97, Artemesia Gallery, Chgo., 1996, CRCA Gallery, U. Tex., Arlington, 1996, SoHo 20, N.Y.C., 1996, Luise Ross Gallery, N.Y.C., 1997, Coll. Art Assn., N.Y.C., 1997, Wood Street Gallery, Chgo., 1997, Manoa Art Gallery, U. Hawaii, Honolulu, 1997, Cleve. State U., 1997, Kingsborough C.C., 1998, Coll. Art and Design, Toronto, Can., 1998, Katherine Weems Ctr., Sch. Mus. Fine Arts, Boston, 1998, Saci Gallery, 1999, Donahue/Sosinski gallery, NYC, 2000, Froelick Gallery, Portland, Oreg., 2001, 04, Western Wyo. C.C., 2002, Interchurch Ctr., NYC, 2002, The Inquiring Mind, Saugerties, N.Y., 2003, U. Vt., Burlington, 2003, Froelick Gallery, Portland, Oreg., 2004, The Firehouse Art Gallery, Nassau C.C., 2004, Nassau County CC, L.O., 2004, Aubura Seminary, N.Y.C., 2005, others; group shows include: Brydcliffe Woodstock (N.Y.) Guild, 2003, Susquehanna Art Mus., Harrisburg, Pa., 2003, Brick Bottom Gallery, Somerville, Mass., 2003, Froelick Gallery, Portland, Oreg., 2004, We. Wyo. C.C., Rock Spring, Wyo., 2004, Auburn Sem., N.Y.C., N.Y., 2005, Samuel Dorsky Mus. Art SUNY, New Paltz, N.Y., 2005; artist (permanent collections) Robert Wood Johnson U. Hosp., Hamilton, N.J.; works in pvt. collections; author: Spirit Taking Form, 2002. Recipient Elan Lifetime Achievement award, Women's Studio Ctr., N.Y.C., 2004. Mem. Women's Caucus for Art (adv. bd. 1980-83), Coll. Art Assn. Home: 91 Franklin St New York NY 10013-3408 Office Phone: 212-925-5777. Personal E-mail: nancy@nancyazara.com.

AZARIA, HANK, actor; b. NYC, Apr. 25, 1964; m. Helen Hunt, 1995, div. 2000. BA, Tufts U., 1987. Motion picture and T.V. actor. Actor: (films) Cool Blue, 1988, Pretty Woman, 1990, Quiz Show, 1994, Now and Then, 1995, Heat, 1995, The Birdcage, 1996, Grosse Pointe Blank, 1997, Godzilla, 1998, Great Expectations, 1998, Homegrown, 1998, Celebrity, 1998, The Cradle Will Rock, 1999, Alligatropolis, 1999, Mystery Men, 1999, Mystery Alaska, 1999, Tuesdays With Morrie (Emmy award, 2000), 1999, C-Scam, 2000, America's Sweethearts, 2001, Bark, 2002, Along Came Polly, 2004, Dodgeball: A True Underdog Story, 2004; (TV movies) Frank Nitti: The Enforcer, 1988, Tuesdays with Morrie, 1999, Fail Safe, 2000, Uprising, 2001; (TV guest appearances) Family Ties, 1988, Growing Pains, 1985, The Fresh Prince of Bel-Air, 1990, Babes, 1990, Herman's Head, 1991, Friends, 1994, 2001, 2002, 2003, Tales From the Crypt, 1995, If Not for You, 1995, Mad About You, 1996-97; voice characterizations The Simpsons (voice of Apu, Chief Wiggum, Moe Syzlak, and others), 1989— (Emmy award for animation voice-over, 1998, 2001, 2003), Beethoven, 1994, Spider-Man, 1995, Anastasia, 1997, Stressed Eric (also prodr.), 1998, Futurama, 1999, Bartok the Magnificent (also co-prod.), 1999, CyberWorld, 2000; actor, prodr., dir., writer: (film) Nobody's Perfect, 2004; exec. prodr.: (TV series) Imagine That,

2002; actor, prodr.: Huff, 2004-; broadway: Monty Python's Spamalot, 2005 (Theatre World award, 2005). Recipient: Light on the Hill award, Tufts U., 1999. Office: Endeavor 9701 Wilshire Blvd 10th Floor Beverly Hills CA 90212*

AZARIAN, MARY, illustrator; b. Washington, D.C., Dec. 8, 1940; d. L. G. and Eleanor Schneider; m. Tomas Azarian, July 24, 1962; 3 children. BA, Smith Coll., 1963. Elementary sch. teacher, Walden, Vt., 1963—67; freelance printmaker and illustrator, 1967—; founder Farmhouse Press, 1969—. One-woman shows include Lyndon State Coll., U. Conn., Chandler Gallery, Northfield, Vt., Beaver Coll. in the Schlesinger Libr., Radcliffe Inst. Advanced Study, Harvard U., Brown U., Lyman Allyn Art Gallery, Conn., Brattleboro Mus., Vt., Helen Day Art Ctr., Snowflake Bentley, 1999 (Caldecott award, 1999), The Wild Flavor, 1973, The Art of Living and Other Stories, 1981, The Caprilands Kitchen Book, 1981, The Magic Dulcimer, 1983, The Man Who Lived Alone, 1984, The Wildman: A Short Fable, 1985, Country Kitchens Remembered, 1986, Stubbornness, 1986, Talk Less and Say More, 1986, Gridley Firing, 1987, Caring for Your Own Dead, 1987, As Sweet as Apple Cider, 1988, Sea Gifts, 1989, Not By Bread Alone, 1990, Salty Wisdom, 1990, Barley Break, 1992, Where the Deer Were, 1994, A Symphony for the Sheep, 1996, Barn Cat: A Counting Book, 1998, Faraway Summer, 1998, The Four Seasons of Mary Azerian, 2000, Visits with the Amish, 2000, The Race of the Birkebeiners: A True Story, 2001, When the Moon Is Full, 2001, Louisa May and Mr. Thoreau's Flute, 2002, From Dawn till Dusk, 2002, A Christmas Like Helen's, 2004; author, illustrator: Farmer's Alphabet, 1981, From Barley to Beer: A Traditional English Ballad, 1982 (Parent's Choice award for illustration, 1983), A Gardener's Alphabet, 2000.

AZARNOFF, DANIEL LESTER, pharmaceutical company consultant; s. Samuel J. and Kate (Asarnow) A.; m. Joanne Stokes, Dec. 26, 1951; children: Rachel, Richard, Martin. BS, Rutgers U., 1947, MS, 1948. Asst. instr. anatomy U. Kans. Med. Sch., 1949—50, rsch. fellow, 1950—52, intern, 1955—56, resident, Nat. Heart Inst. research fellow, 1956—58, asst. prof. medicine, 1962—64, assoc. prof., 1964—68, dir. clin. pharmacology study unit, 1964—68, assoc. prof. pharmacology, 1965—68, prof. medicine and pharmacology, 1968, dir. Clin. Pharmacology-Toxicology Ctr., 1967—78, Disting. prof., 1973—78, also prof. medicine, 1965—67, pres. Sigma Xi Club, 1968—69, clin. prof. medicine, 1982—96, prof. medicine, 1997—; Nat. Inst. Neurol. Diseases and Blindness spl. trainee Washington U. Sch. Medicine, St. Louis, 1958—60; asst. prof. medicine St. Louis U. Sch. Medicine, 1960—62; sr. v.p. worldwide R&D, G.D. Searle & Co., Skokie, 1978; pres. Searle R&D, Skokie, 1979—85, Azarnoff Assocs., Inc., Evanston, Ill., 1986—87, D.L. Azarnoff Assocs., So. San Francisco, Calif., 1987—; prof. pathology, clin. prof. pharmacology Northwestern U. Med. Sch., 1978—85; sr. v.p. clin. regulatory affairs Cellegy Pharms., San Francisco, 1998—2003; commr. Nat. Commn. on Orphan Diseases, 1985—87; chmn. bd. dirs. Alpha RX Corp., South San Francisco, Calif., 1992—94; clin. prof. med. Stanford U. Sch. Med., 1998—2002. Professorial lectr. U. Chgo., 1978-86; dir. Second Workshop on Prins. Drug Evaluation in Man, 1970; chmn. com. on problems of drug safety NRC-NAS, 1972-76; chmn. bd. dirs. Oread, Inc., Lawrence, Kans., 1998-99; CEO Cibus Pharms., Burlingame, Calif., 1996-97; cons. numerous govt. agys.; chmn. bd. dirs. Cibus Pharm., Inc., 1996-97; CEO, chmn. bd. dirs. Vitalsensor, Inc., 2004—. Editor: Devel. of Drug Interactions, 1974-77, Yearbook of Drug Therapy, 1977-79; series editor: Monographs in Clin. Pharmacology, 1977-84; mem. editl. bd. Drug Investigation, Brit. Jour. Clin. Pharmacology, Clin. Pharmacol. Therapy, Clin. Pharmacokinetics, Clin. Drug Investigation, 1989—, others. Served with U.S. Army, 1945-46. Recipient Ginsburg award in phys. diagnosis U. Kanas. Med. Ctr., 1953, Outstanding Intern award, 1956, Ciba award for gerontol. rsch., 1958, Rectors medal U. Helsinki, 1968, Nathanial T. Kwit Meml. Disting. Svc. award Am. Coll. Clin. Pharmacology, 2002; named Disting. Med. Alumnus, U. Kans. Coll. Health Sci., 1995; John and Mary R. Markle scholar, 1964, William N. Creasy vis. prof. clin. pharmacology Med. Coll. Va., 1975; Bruce Hall Meml. lectr. St. Vincents Hosp., Sydney, 1976, 7th Sir Henry Hallett Dale lectr. Johns Hopkins U. Med. Sch., 1978; Fulbright scholar Karolinska Inst., Stockholm, 1968. Fellow ACP, N.Y. Acad. Scis., Am. Assn. Pharm. Scientists (Rsch. Achievement award in clin. scis. 1995), AAAS (chmn. elect pharm. sect. 2001, chmn. pharm. divsn. 2002-03); mem. AMA (vice chmn. coun. on drugs 1971-72, editl. bd. jours.), Am. Soc. Clin. Nutrition, Am. Nutrition Instn., Am. Soc. Pharmacology and Exptl. Therapeutics (chmn. clin. pharmacology divsn. 1969-71, mem. exec. com. 1966-73, 78-81, del. 1975-78, bd. publ. trustees), Am. Soc. Clin. Pharmacology and Therapeutics (Oscar B. Hunter Meml. award 1995), Am. Fedn. Clin. Rsch., Brit. Pharmacol. Soc., Ctrl. Soc. Clin. Rsch., Royal Soc. for Promotion Health, Inst. Medicine of Nat. Acad. Scis., Soc. Exptl. Biology and Medicine (councillor 1976-80), Internat. Union Pharmacologists (sec. clin. pharmacology sect. 1975-81, internat. adv. com. Paris Congress 1978), GPIA (blue ribbon com. on generic medicine 1990), Sigma Xi. Office: D.L. Azarnoff Assoc 433 Airport Blvd Ste 225 Burlingame CA 94010-2011 Office Phone: 650-343-9222. Business E-Mail: dan@azarnoffassociates.com.

AZAROFF, LEONID VLADIMIROVITCH, physics professor; b. Moscow, June 19, 1926; came to U.S., 1939, naturalized, 1945; s. Vladimir Ivanovitch and Maria Yulievna (Odlen) A.; m. Carmen Wade, Mar. 9, 1946 (div. July 1968); m. Beth Sulzer, Mar. 4, 1972; children: David, Richard, Lenore. BS cum laude, Tufts Coll., 1948; PhD, MIT, 1954. Research physicist Armour Research Found., Chgo., 1953-54, sr. scientist, 1954-57; asso. prof. metall. engring. Ill. Inst. Tech., Chgo., 1957-61, prof., 1961-66; prof. physics, dir. Inst. Material Sci., U. Conn., Storrs, 1966-92. Guest physicist Brookhaven Nat. Lab., 1961, 62, 64; vis. prof. U. Mass., 1978—79, 1985—86; cons. Owens-Ill., Philips Electronics, Hilger-Watts, Inc.; U.S. del. Internat. Union Crystallography, tchg. commn., 1963—69; bd. dirs. Conn. Product Devel. Corp.; pres. Conn. Acad. Sci. and Engring., Hartford, 1976—82; transl. editor Am. Inst. Physics, N.Y.C., 1958—99. Author 8 books, including X-Ray Diffraction and X-Ray Spectroscopy, 1973, Physics Over Easy, 1996; also articles. With AUS, 1944-46. Recipient ofcl. citation Conn. Gen Assembly, 1982, 91. Fellow Am. Phys. Soc. (cons. editor), Mineral. Soc. Am.; mem. AAAS (dir.), IEEE (sr.), Am. Soc. Engring. Edn., Conn. Acad. Sci. and Engring. (pres. 1976-82), Am. Crystallographic Assn., Am. Inst. Mining Engrs., Am. Inst. Electronic Engrs., Internat. Union Physics, Internat. Union Crystal Growth, Sigma Xi, Phi Kappa Phi (pres. Medford Mass. chpt. 1947-48), Sigma Pi Sigma. Republican. Russian Orthodox. Office: U Conn Inst Materials Sci PO Box 136 Storrs Mansfield CT 06268-0136 E-mail: leeazaroff@cs.com. *I have always adhered to the principle that anything worth doing at all is worth doing as well as possible. Therefore, I select very carefully the tasks to undertake.*

AZCUENAGA, MARY LAURIE, government official; b. Council, Idaho, July 25, 1945; AB, Stanford U., 1967; JD, U. Chgo., 1973. Bar: Dist. of Columbia, Calif., U.S. Supreme Ct. Atty. FTC, Washington, 1973-75, asst. to gen. counsel, 1975-76; staff atty. San Francisco regional office, 1977-80, asst. regional dir., 1980-81, asst. to exec. dir., 1981-82; litigation atty. Office of Gen. Counsel, 1982, asst. gen. counsel for legal counsel, 1983-84, commr. Washington, 1984-98; atty., shareholder Heller, Ehrman, White, & McAuliffe LLP, 1998—. Mem. Adminstrv. Conf. of the U.S., 1990-95. Trustee Food and Drug Law Inst., 1990-97, Advisory Bd. FDLI, 1997-98, Natl. Advertising Review Bd., 1998—, ERA Review Bd., 1998—. Office: 166 K St NW Ste 300 Washington DC 20006-1228

AZER, NIGEL MERRIETT, orthopedic surgeon, medical researcher; b. Anniston, Ala., Aug. 21, 1970; s. Rida and Valerie Azer; m. Elizabeth Ann Frye, Dec. 15, 1970; 1 child, Josefine. MD, U. Va., Charlottesville, 1996. Lic. physician Va., Md., DC, Mass., 2003. Residency U. Va., Charlottesville, 1996—2002; fellowship Harvard Med. Sch., Boston, 2002—03; surgeon-in-chief Wash. Orthop. Ctr., Washington, 2003—. Arthroplasty and biol. reconstruction fellow Brigham and Woman's Hosp., Boston, 2002—03. Author: (textbook chapters) Painful Total Knee Arthroplasty. Mem.: Royal Soc. Medicine U.K., Med. Soc. Va., Aerospace Med. Assn. Achievements include research in Cell Based Gene Therapy enhances bone repair. Avocations: tennis, motorsports, physical fitness, music, travel. Office: Washington Orthop Ctr 2112 F St NW Ste 804 Washington DC 20037

AZER, SAMY AZIZ, gastroenterologist, educator, medical educator; b. Cairo, Mar. 28, 1953; s. Aziz Azer and Sania Sedrak; m. Mary Azer; children: Sarah, Diana. B in Medicine and Surgery, Ain Shams U., Cairo, 1977, M in Medicine, 1983; MEd, U. New South Wales, 1993; PhD, U. Sydney, 1995; postgrad. in Pub. Health, U. NSW, 1997. Resident in internal medicine Govt. of Health, Egypt, 1979-80, cons. in medicine, 1983-84, 1984-89; vis. med. officer Ain Shams U. Hosps., 1980-83; postdoctoral fellow U. Kans. Med. Ctr., 1994; sr. lectr. in med. edn. U. Melbourne, Australia, 1999—, dir. problem-based learning tng. program faculty medicine, dentistry and health scis., 2001—, chair semesters 1 - 5, faculty medicine, dentistry and health scis., 2002—, chair faculty excellence in tchg. awards comm., faculty of medicine, dentistry, and health scis., 2003—04, anti-discrimination advisor, 2004—. Cons. NIHS, Australia, 1995; lectr. spkrs. bur. ACG, Australia, 1996; instr. pathology and grad. med. program, faculty medicine U. Sydney, 1997, sr. lectr. in med. edn., 1998—99. Co-author: Our Children, 1987; writer med. column El-Telegraph, Australia, 1996-97; contbr. chpts. to books, articles to profl. jours. Mem. ch. coun. Fairfield Anglican Chs., Australia, 1994, 95; elder Presbyn. Ch. of Australia, South Yarra, Victoria, 2002. Scholar Ministry of Edn., Egypt, 1968-71, undergrad. scholar, 1972-77, postgrad. scholar U. Sydney, 1993-94. Fellow Am. Coll. Gastroenterology, Royal Soc. of Health; mem. U. New South Wales Union (life), Gastroenterol. Soc. Australia, Am. Assn. for Study Liver Disease, Am. Coll. Gastroenterology. Presbyterian. Avocations: painting, soccer, history of medicine. Office: FEU Faculty Medicine U Melbourne Dentistry & Health Scis Parkville VIC 3010 Australia Business E-Mail: azer2000@ophisnet.com.au.

AZIEL, BARBIE-DAE, writer, artist, poet; b. Dansville, NY, Apr. 4, 1948; d. Augustus Oran and Jean Elis (Nease) Lawrence; children: Nina-dae, Donald Lee. Student, Elim Bible Inst., Lima, N.Y., 1967—69. V.p. Donald Furniture Showroom, N.Y.C., 1974—79, Furniture Plus, Inc., Houston, 1979—84; pres. Furniture & Merchandise, Naples, Fla., 1986—91; realtor Watson Realty, Longwood, Fla., 2002—03; v.p. Richer Originals, Inc., Altamonte Springs, Fla., 2003—. Author: Death Hath No Grave, 2003, Writing with Mighty Paucity, 2000, Literary Style Trademark, 2003, Mighty Paucity's Passage, 2004. Mem. Partnering for Violence Free Homes, Fla. Coalition Against Violence, Orlando, 2002, Rep. Party Roundtable, Washington, 1990. Named Poet of Merit, Internat. Soc. Poets, 2002; recipient Best in Show award, Golden Gate Women's Club, Naples, 1997. Mem.: Women's Caucus for the ARts (Merit award 2002), First Friday-Rollins Coll. Avocations: painting, sculpting, singing, writing. Office Phone: 828-349-7405.

AZIZ, KHALID, petroleum engineering educator; b. Bahawalpur, Pakistan, Sept. 29, 1936; arrived in US, 1952, naturalized; s. Aziz Ul and Rshida (Atamohammed) Hassan; m. Mussarrat Rizwani, Nov. 12, 1962; children: Natasha, Imraan. BS in Mech. Engring., U. Mich., 1955; BSc in Petroleum Engring., U. Alta., 1958, MSc in Petroleum Engring., 1961; PhD in Chem. Engring., Rice U., 1966. Jr. design engr. Massey-Ferguson, 1955-56; various position to asst. prof. petroleum engring. U. Alta., 1960-62; various positions, chmn. bd. Neotech. Cons. Ltd., 1972-85; mgr., dir. Computer Modelling Group, Calgary, Alta., 1977-82; various positions to chief engr. Karachi (Pakistan) Gas Co., 1958-59, 62-63; various positions to prof. chem. and petroleum engring. U. Calgary, 1965-82; hon. prof., 1994—2001; prof. petroleum engring. dept. Stanford (Calif.) U., 1982—, assoc. dean rsch. Sch. Earth Scis., 1983-86, chmn. petroleum engring. dept., 1986-91, 94-95, Otto N. Miller prof. in earth scis., 1989—. Co-author: Flow of Complex Mixtures in Pipes, 1972, Petroleum Reservoir Simulation, 1979; contbr. articles to profl. jours. Recipient Diploma of Honor, Pi Epsilon Tau, 1991; Chem. Inst. Can. fellow, 1974, Killam Resident fellow U. Calgary, 1977, Blaise Pascal Earth Scis. medal 2005 Mem. AIME (hon.), European Assn. Geoscientists and Engrs., European Acad. Scis., Soc. Petroleum Engrs. (disting. mem., Ferguson award 1979, Reservoir Engring. award 1987, Lester C. Uren award 1988, Disting. Achievement award for Petroleum Engring. Faculty 1990, hon. mem. 1996), Nat. Acad. Engring., Russian Acad. Natural Scis. (fgn.), European Acad. of Sci. (Blaise Pascal medal in Earth Scis., 2005). Moslem. Achievements include rsch. in multiphase flow of oil/gas mixtures & steam in pipes & wells, multiphase flow in porous media, reservoir simulation (black-oil, compositional, thermal, geothermal), natural gas engring., hydrocarbon fluid phase behavior. Office: Stanford U Dept Petroleum Engring Stanford CA 94305-2220

AZMAN, ROSIANA LYNNE, psychologist, educator; d. Ben Kamarudin and Aziza Belle Azman. PhD, U. Hawaii, 2003. Sr. sales assoc. The Sharper Image, Kahului, Hawaii, 1997—99; lectr. U. Hawaii, Honolulu, 2000—02, Kapiolani C.C., 2002—02; asst. adminstr. West Maui Healthcare Ctr., Lahaina, 1993—2003; instr. psychology Kapiolani C.C., 2003—. Manoa connections learning cmty. faculty U. Hawaii, Honolulu, 2000—01. Author: Instructor's Manual: Self-Directed Behavior, Instructor's Manual: Learning Skills for College and Life; contbr. chapters to books. Chairperson Vote Azman Com., Lahaina, Hawaii, 2002—02. Mem.: NEA, APA, Am. Psychol. Soc., Am. Ednl. Rsch. Assn., Psi Chi, Golden Key. Achievements include development of Scale of Educational Attitudes.

AZNAR, JOSÉ MARIA, former prime minister of Spain, political organization official; b. Madrid, Feb. 25, 1953; Student, U. Complutense, Madrid; JD, U. Madrid. Former tax inspector; joined Rioja br. Alianza Popular, 1978; dep. sec.-gen., mem. Cortes, 1982; premier Castilla y León Autonomous Region, 1987; pres. Partido Popular (formerly Alianza Popular), 1990—; oposition leader Govt. of Spain, Madrid, 1990-96, prime min., 1996—2004, pres., 1996—2004; disting. scholar in the practice of global leadership Georgetown U., Washington, 2004—. Author: Libertad y Solidaridad, 1991, La Segunda Transición, 1994, La España en la que Yo Creo, 1995. Office: Georgetown U 37th & O St NW Washington DC 20057

AZODO, ADA UZOAMAKA, French language educator, African women's studies educator, writer; d. Bertram Enuma and Bessie Chineze; m. Michael Valentine Udennaka Azodo, Mar. 6, 1976; children: Uchendu I.C., Queen-Ijeoma A., Chijioke U., Okechukwu A. Dipl III degré, U. Dakar, Senegal, 1974; BA in French with honors, U. Ife, Nigeria, 1975; MA in French, U. Lagos, Nigeria, 1983, PhD in French/African Lit., 1990. French tutor Police Coll., Ikeja, Lagos, Nigeria, 1975-76; lectr. II Ministry of Edn., Lagos, 1976-77, 82-84; translator French/Portuguese French/Portuguese Festac (Black Festival of Art & Culture), Lagos, 1977; grad. asst. U. Lagos, 1984, 85, lectr., 1986; asst. mgr. pers. Nigerian Telecomm., Lagos, 1986-88; adj. asst. prof. St. John Fisher Coll., Rochester, N.Y., 1991-94, dir. internat. studies, 1993-94. Adj. asst. prof. SUNY, Geneseo, 1992-93, 95—. Author: L'Imaginaire Dans Les Romans de Camara Laye, 1993, Emerging Perspectives Ama Ata Aidoo, 1999, Emerging Perspectives on Mariama Bâ, 2003. Vol. Jewish Home of Rochester, 1988-92, Sunday Sch. Edn. Immaculate Conception Ch., Rochester, 1990—. Nat. award and Open scholar U. Ife, 1972; Rsch. grant SUNY, Geneseo, 1992; named Disting. Dau. Ngene Village, Amawbia/Nigeria, 1992; recipient Friends of the Rochester Pub. Libr. recognition, 1994. Mem. MLA, Alliance Francaise Rochester, Assn. Depts. Fgn. Langs., African Lit. Assn., Rochester Assn. for UN (bd. dirs. 1994—), Upstate N.Y. African Assn. (exec. mem. 1994—). Roman Catholic. Avocations: walking, swimming, sewing. Office Phone: 219-980-6629. Business E-Mail: aazodo@iun.edu.

AZOPARDI, KORITA MARIE, retired secondary school educator; b. Galveston, Tex., Jan. 30, 1941; d. John and Cecil Marie (Kierbow) Hamilton; m. Benny Lee Azopardi, May 27, 1960; children: Connie, B. Lee Jr. BS in Edn. and Math., S.W. Tex. State U., 1961; MA in Math., St. Louis U., 1970. Tchr. Navarro Pub. Schs., Geronimo, Tex., 1961-62, Victoria (Tex.) Ind. Sch. Dist., 1962-65, St. Louis Ind. Sch. Dist., 1965-67, Normandy Ind. Sch. Dist., St. Louis, 1967-69, Mary Inst., St. Louis, 1969-71, Corpus Christi (Tex.) Ind. Sch. Dist., 1979-84, Calallen Ind. Sch. Dist., Corpus Christi, 1984-99; ret., 1999. Mem. NEA, Nat. Coun. Tchrs. of Math., Math. Assn. Am., Tex. Coun. Tchrs. of Math., Tex. State Tchrs. Assn., Tex. Computer Edn. Assn. Republican. Baptist. Avocation: ranching. Home: 6630 County Road 434 Stockdale TX 78160-6156 E-mail: azopardi@gvec.net.

AZRIN, NATHAN HAROLD, psychologist, educator; b. Boston, Nov. 26, 1930; s. Harry and Esther (Alper) A.; m. Victoria Behar Besalel, Jan. 25, 1953; children— Rachel, Michael, David, Richard. BA cum laude, Boston U., 1951, MA, 1952; PhD, Harvard U., 1956. Mem. faculty So. Ill. U., Carbondale, 1958-80, prof. rehab., 1959-80; rsch. dir. Anna (Ill.) Mental Health Ctr., 1958-80; prof. Nova Psychol. Clinic, Nova U., Ft. Lauderdale, Fla., 1980-87, Nova Southeastern U., Ft. Lauderdale, 1980—. Author: Token Economy, 1968, Toilet Training in Less than a Day, 1974, Toilet Training the Retarded, 1973, Habit Control, 1977, Job Club, 1980, Finding a Job, 1982. Editor psychol. jours. Served with AUS, 1956-58. Mem. Am. Psychol. Assn. (pres. div. 25 1963, ann. award applications in psychology 1975), Fla. Assn. Behavior Analysis (pres.), Midwestern Psychol. Assn. (pres.), Assn. Advancement Behavior Therapy (pres., Lifetime Achievement award 1997), Midwestern Analysis of Behavior Assn. (pres.) Home: 5151 Bayview Dr Fort Lauderdale FL 33308-3433 Office: Nova Southeastern U 3301 College Ave Fort Lauderdale FL 33314-7796 Office Phone: 954-262-5704. Business E-Mail: azrin@nova.edu.

AZUA, JON IMANOL (JON IMANOL AZUA MENDIA), consultant, former Basque vice president; First v.p., econ. affairs, minister, industry & energy Basque Govt., Spain; mng. ptnr. BearingPoint, Inc., Bilboa, Spain; dir., bus. consulting Arthur Andersen, Spain, ptnr., dir., strategy group. Author: Alianza Coopetitiva Para la Nueva Economia, 2000. Bd. trustee Solomon R. Guggenheim Mus., NYC. Mailing: SR Guggenheim Mus Bd Trustees 1071 Fifth Ave New York NY 10128-0173

AZZI, JENNIFER L., professional basketball player; b. Oak Ridge, Tenn., Aug. 31, 1968; d. James and Donna Azzi. Diploma, Stanford U., 1990. Basketball player Arvika Basket, Sweden, 1995—96, Viterbo, Italy, Orchies, France, San Jose Lasers, 1996—99, Salt Lake City Starzz, 1999—2002, San Antonio Stars, 2003—. Mem. Nat. Women's Basketball Team. Named Al-Pac 10 1st team, 1988, 1989, 1990, MVP, NCAA Final Four, 1990, NCAA West Region, 1990, Naismith Nat. Player Yr., 1990; recipient gold medal, Goodwill Games, 1994, World Championship Qualifying team, 1993, U.S. Olympic Festival West Team, 1987, 2 gold medals, World Championship and Goodwill Games, 1990, bronze medal, Pan Am. Games, 1991, World Championship team, 1994, Wade Trophy, 1990, Kodak All-Am. 1st team, 1989, 1990, gold medal, U.S. Olympic Team, 1996. Office: San Antonio Silver Stars One SBC Ctr San Antonio TX 78219

AZZOLI, VAL, music company executive; b. Toronto, Canada, 1955; Grad. in bus. admin., Seneca Coll., Ontario, Canada, 1977. Sr. vp., gen. mgr. Atlantic Recording Corp., N.Y.C., 1991—93, exec. v.p., gen. mgr., 1993—95, co-chmn., co-CEO, 1995—. Office: Atlantic Group 1290 Avenue Of The Americas New York NY 10104-0101

BAAB, CARLTON, advertising executive; BSEE with honors, U. So. Calif.; MBA, Harvard Grad. Sch. Bus. Adminstrn. V.p., gen. mgr. Levolor Corp.; co-founder, pres. MobileSoft Corp.; CFO CKS Group, Cupertino, Calif., 1994—98, COO, 1995—96, exec. v.p., sect., 1995—98; COO & CFO RemarQ Communities, Inc., San Jose, Calif., 1999—2000; v.p. fin., CFO Certive, Inc., Redwood City, Calif., 2000—01; mng. prin. Astoria Capital Mgmt., 2001; pres., CEO Raining Data Corp., Irvine, Calif., 2001—. Bd. dir. PeopleSoft, 1999—, Momentum Bus. Applications, Inc. Bd. councilors U. So. Cailf., Sch. Engring. Office: Raining Data Corp 17500 Cartwright Rd Irvine CA 92614-5846 Office Phone: 949-442-4400. Office Fax: 949-250-8187. E-mail: carltonbaab@rainingdata.com.

BAACK, PAULA D., music educator; b. Omaha, Nebr., June 13, 1949; d. Paul and Wilma I. Teigeler; m. Robert A. Morris, May 10, 1969 (div. Oct. 1979); m. L. Thomas Baack, July 26, 1980; 1 child, Paul R. BS, U. Nebr., 1971, MusM, 1973. Cert. tchr. Nebr., Cmty. Coll. Tchr. Ariz. Dir. choral Lincoln Pub. Schs., Nebr., 1971—97; dir. choral, voice coach Scottsdale C.C., Ariz., 1998—; dir. scarlet and cream singers, 1995—97. Asst. prof. U. Nebr., Lincoln, 1995—97. Named Nat. Anthem Singer for Phoenix Coyotes Hockey Game. Mem.: Nat. Assn. Tchrs. Singing, Ariz. Music Educators Assn., Music Educators Nat. Conf., Nebr. Choral Dirs. Assn. (exec. bd. 1995—97), Nebr. Music Educators Assn. (exec. bd. 1993—95). Republican. Avocations: bicycling, singing, dance. Home: 11083 E Oberlin Way Scottsdale AZ 85262 Office: Scottsdale Cmty Coll 9000 E Chaparral Rd Scottsdale AZ 85256 Office Phone: 480-423-6750. Business E-Mail: paula.baack@sccmail.maricopa.edu.

BAAS, JACQUELYNN, museum director, art historian; b. Grand Rapids, Mich., Feb. 14, 1948; BA in History of Art, Mich. State U.; PhD in History of Art, U. Mich. Registrar U. Mich. Mus. Art, Ann Arbor, 1974-78, asst. dir., 1978-82; editor Bull. Museums of Art and Archaeology, U. Mich., 1976-82; chief curator Hood Mus. Art, Dartmouth Coll., Hanover, N.H., 1982-84, dir., 1985-89, U. Calif. Berkeley Art Mus. and Pacific Film Archive, Calif., 1989-99, emeritus dir., 1999—; program dir. Awake: Art and Buddhism, 1999—2004. Cons. in field; organizer exhbns.; ind. art historian; lectr. in field. Author: Smile of the Buddha: Eastern Philosophy and Western Art, 2005; contbr. articles and essays to jours. and books. Mem. Coll. Art Assn. Am., Am. Assn. Mus. Address: PO Box 162 The Sea Ranch CA 95497-0162 Office Phone: 510-406-4455. Business E-Mail: jbaas@mcn.org.

BAASAN, RAGCHAA, diplomat; b. Ulaanbaatar, Mongolia, Nov. 19, 1943; d. Tumer and Demberel (Tsendsuren) Ragchaa; m. Jamsran Gendendaram, Sept. 1967; children: Enhbat, Enhtsetseg, Enhtuvshin. Diploma, Moscow Inst. Fgn. Langs. Asst. officer Ministry of External Rels., Ulaanbaatar, 1967-69; diplomat Mongolian Embassy in India, New Delhi, 1969-74; attache Ministry of External Rels./Asian Dept., Ulaanbaatar, 1974-78, 2d sec., 1981-83, Mongolian Embassy, Kabul, Afghanistan, 1978-81, Embassy Mongolia, New Delhi, 1983-88; 1st sec., counsellor Ministry External Rels., Ulaanbaatar, 1988-97; 1st sec., polit. Embassy Mongolia, Washington, 1997—. Decorated Polar Star Order (Mongolia); recipient Honor of Svc. award Govt. of Mongolia, 1991/ Buddhist. Avocations: reading, analysing, knitting, cooking. Home: XI Region SA Apt 26 Ulaanbaatar Mongolia Office: Embassy of Mongolia 2833 M St NW Washington DC 20007-3712 E-mail: Baasan@aol.com.

BABA, ISAMU, construction company executive; b. Oita, Japan, June 13, 1923; s. Gunroku and Kimiko Baba; m. Fumiko Takita, Nov. 3, 1948; children: Shiro, Kyoko Kojima. B in Engring., Osaka (Japan) U., 1945; PhD, Waseda U., Japan, 1990. Cert. architect, cons. engr., value specialist. Mgr. R & D Fujita Corp., Tokyo, 1965-75, dir., 1975-85, exec. v.p., 1985-90, sr. exec. v.p., 1990-94, exec. adviser, 1994—. Author: The Method of Value Engineering in the Construction Industry, 1975, Basics of Construction Value Engineering, 1983, Application of Construction Value Engineering, 1983, Illustration of the Method of Keeping Costs Down in the Construction Industry, 1984, The Study of Development and Application of Value Engineering For Construction Site Management, 1990, Terminos Practicos de Ingenieria Civil y Arquitectura, 1993. Chmn. bd. trustees Tottori Women's Coll., Japan, 1991—, exec. adviser, 1999—. Recipient Presdl. Citation Soc. Am. Value Engrs., 1981, Soc. award Associated Gen. Contractors of Japan, 1985, Presdl. Citation Archtl. Inst. Japan, 1992, 4th Order of Merit with the Rising Sun, 1998. Mem. Internat. Coun. Bldg. Rsch., Studies and Documentation, Soc. Japanese Value Engrs. (trustee, Best Paper prize 1973, Promotional Achievment award 1984, Presdl. Citation 1990), Soc. Korean Value Engrs. (adviser), Archtl. Inst. Japan, Japanese Value Engring. (Soc. award 1990), Soc. Japanese Value Specialis (pres.). Avocation: noh (japanese classic art). Home: 2-29-21 Irima-cho Chofu Tokyo 182 Japan Office: Fujita Corp 4-6-15 Sendagaya, Shibuya-ku Tokyo 151 Japan

BABA, MARIETTA LYNN, business anthropologist, university administrator; b. Flint, Mich., Nov. 9, 1949; d. David and Lillian (Joseph) Baba; m. David Smokler, Feb. 14, 1977 (div. 1982); 1 child, Alexia Nicole Baba Smokler. BA with highest distinction, Wayne State U., 1971, MA in Anthropology, 1973, PhD in Phys. Anthropology, 1975; MBA, Mich. State U., 1994. Asst. prof. sci. and tech. Wayne State U., Detroit, 1975-80, assoc. prof. anthropology, 1980-88, prof., 1988—, spl. asst. to pres., 1980-82, econ. devel. officer, 1982-83, asst. provost, 1983-85, assoc. provost, 1985-89, dir. internat. programs, interim assoc. dean Grad. Sch., 1988-89, assoc. dean Grad. Sch., 1989-90, acting chair dept. anthropology, 1990-92, chair dept. anthropology, 1996-2001; dean, prof. anthropology Mich. State U. Coll. Social Sci., East Lansing, 2001—. Program dir. transformations to quality orgns., dir. social, behav., and econ. scis. NSF, 1994—96; evolution rschr. Wayne State U., 1975—82; cons. GM Rsch. Labs., 1988—92, Electronic Data Sys., 1990—93, McKinsey Global Inst., 1991; rsch. contractor GM/EDS, 1990—94; vis. scholar IBM Almaden Svcs. Rsch. Inst., 2005; lectr. in field. Adv. for editor orgnl. anthropology: American Anthropologist, 1990-93; issued letters patent for method to map joint ventures and maps produced thereby; contbr. articles to profl. jours.; patentee in field. Mem. State Rsch. Fund Feasibility Rev. Panel, 1982—84; mem. adv. panel on tech. innovation and U.S. trade U.S. Congl. Office Tech. Assessment, 1990—91, mem. panel on electronic enterprise, 1993—94; active Leadership Detroit Class IV, 1982—83; dir. Mich. Tech. Coun. (S.E. divsn.), 1984—85. With USAF, 1992—94. Job Partnership Tng. Act grantee, 1981-90, NSF grantee, 1982, 84-85, 99-01. Fellow Am. Anthrop. Assn. (bd. dirs. 1986-88, exec. com. 1986-88, del. to Internat. Union Anthrop. and Ethnol. Sci. 1990-94, chair global commn. anthropology 1993-98), Nat. Assn. Practice Anthropology (pres. 1986-88), Soc. Applied Anthropology, Phi Beta Kappa, Sigma Xi (Morton Fried award 1991), Beta Gamma Sigma. Office Phone: 517-355-6675.

BABAO, DONNA MARIE, retired community health and psychiatric nurse, educator; b. St. Louis, May 6, 1945; d. Wilbert C. and Cecelia (Hogan) Bremer; widowed; 1 child, Tonya J. Diploma, Henry Ford Hosp. Sch. Nursing, Detroit, 1966; BSN, Calif. State U., Sacramento, 1978, MS in Nursing, 1990; MA in Edn., Calif. State U., Chico, 1985. Cert. pub. health nurse; master tchr. cert.; cert. clin. use of interactive guided imagery. Staff nurse U. Calif. Med. Ctr., San Francisco, 1968-72; staff and charge CCU nurse Children's Hosp. of San Francisco, 1972-78; pub. health nurse Sutter-Yuba Health Dept., Yuba City, Calif., 1979-81; prof. nursing Yuba Coll., Marysville, Calif., 1981-2000; psychiat. charge nurse Sunridge Hosp., Yuba City, 1994-96; RN case mgr. Home Health Care Mgmt. Inc., Chico, Calif., 2004—05; office nurse, case mgr. Oregon House Cmty. Clinic, Calif., 2005—. Mem. exam. item writing panel NCLEX-RN, 1998. Writer health column, 1986-90; chpt. to textbooks; reviewer nursing textbooks and jour. articles; contbr. articles to profl. jours. 1st lt. Nurse Corps, U.S. Army, 1966-68. Mem. Vietnam Vets. Am., Imagery Internat., Henry Ford Hosp. Alumni Assn. Nursing. Office Phone: 800-400-0727. Personal E-mail: dbabao@hotmail.com.

BABAOGLU, REHIM, lawyer; b. Milan, Apr. 16, 1946; came to U.S., 1951; s. Rehim and Tarlan (Nadir) B.; m. Lydia Amelia Zajcew, Nov. 30, 1968; children: Laura, R. Christopher. BA, Rutgers U., Newark, 1969; JD, U. Memphis, 1974. Bar: Tenn. 1974, U.S. Ct. Appeals (6th cir. 1983 and 8th cir. 1980), U.S. Ct. Internat. Trade, U.S. Supreme Ct. 1979. Probation officer Essex County Probation Dept., Newark, 1969-71; ptnr. Crislip, Clausel & Babaoglu, Memphis, 1974-78; assoc. prof. Law Sch. U. Memphis, 1978-80; assoc. Farris, Hancock, Gilman & Hellen, Memphis, 1980-82; ptnr. Byrd, Cobb, Norwood, Lait & Babaoglu, Memphis, 1982-90, Byrd & Cobb, Memphis, 1990-96; propr. Law Offices of Rehim Babaoglu, Memphis, 1996-2000; divorce proctor Shelby County Cir. Ct., 1999—; ptnr. Thomason, Hendrix, Harvey, Johnson & Mitchell, 2000—. Bd. dirs. Memphis Area Legal Svcs. Inc., 1984—, chmn., 1994-97. V.p. Memphis Ballet Co., 1979; treas. Transitional Ctr. for Women, Memphis, 1980-88. Staff sgt. USAR, 1968-75. Mem. ABA, Memphis Bar Assn. (fee dispute com. 1984-88, chmn. lawyer referral svc. com., CLE com., bd. dirs. 1990-92, 95-97), Am. Immigration Lawyers Assn., Amnesty Internat. Republican. Roman Catholic. Avocations: art collecting, russian studies, strength aerobics. Home: 1741 N Parkway Memphis TN 38112-5016 E-mail: babaoglur@thomason.law.com.

BABAUTA, JUAN NEKAI, governor; b. Saipan, No. Mariana Islands, Sept. 7, 1953; s. Santiago Miyasaki and Carmen (Nekai) B. BS, MA, Ea. N.Mex. U., 1976; MS, U. Cin., 1979. Health planner TTPI Dept. Health Services, Saipan, 1977; dep. exec. dir. State Health Planning and Devel. Agy., Saipan, 1979; exec. dir. Saipan, 1980-86; senator No. Marianas Commonwealth Legislature, Saipan, 1986—90; resident rep. to U.S. Commonwealth of No. Mariana Islands, 1990—2002, gov., 2002—. Co-chmn. 902 Covenant Negotiation team; instr. No. Marianas Coll., Saipan, 1986. Chmn. bd. regents No. Marianas Coll., 1982-83, 84-86; chmn. Bd. Edn., Saipan, 1982-83, 84-86; mem. Med. Profession Licensing Bd., Saipan, 1983-86, Nat. State Bd. Edn., Saipan, 1982-86. Mem. Phi Kappa Phi. Republican. Roman Catholic. Avocation: reading. Office: Office of the Governor PO Box 501004 Saipan MP 96950 Office Phone: 670-664-2280.

BABAYI, ROBERT S., lawyer; b. Tehran, Iran, Jan. 18, 1959; BSEE, Fla. Internat. U., 1981; JD, U. Miami, 1992. Bar: Fla. 1992, DC 2000, US Patent and Trademark Office. Of counsel Patent Prosecution and Intellectual Property Litig. Depts. Venable LLP, Washington, DC. Contbr. articles to profl. jours. Mem. Washington DC Cmty. for Family Life Svcs., Coalition for Homeless. Mem.: ABA, Am. Intellectual Property Law Assn. Office: Venable LLP 575 7th St, NW Washington DC 20004 Office Phone: 202-344-4045. Office Fax: 202-344-8300. E-mail: rsbabayi@venable.com.

BABB, ALBERT LESLIE, biomedical engineer, educator; b. Vancouver, B.C., Can., Nov. 7, 1925; came to U.S., 1948, naturalized, 1954; s. Clarence Stanley and Mildred (Gutteridge) B.; m. Marion A. McDougall; children—Eugene Matthew, Philip Leslie, Christine Louise. BASc., U. B.C., 1948; MS, U. Ill., 1949, PhD, 1951; student Internat. Sch. Nuclear Sci. and Engring., Argonne Nat. Lab., 1956, 57. Chem. engr. Nat. Research Council Can., 1948; research engr. Rayonier, Inc., 1951-52; faculty U. Wash., Seattle, 1952—, chmn. nuclear engring. group, 1957-65, prof. chem. engring., 1960—, acting chmn. dept. chem. engring., 1985, dir. nuclear reactor labs., 1962-72, prof. nuclear engring., 1965-91, prof. emeritus nuclear engring. and chem. engring., 1991—, chmn. dept. nuclear engring., 1965-81, acting chmn. dept. nuclear engring., 1984-86, adj. prof. bioengring., 1985-91; v.p. rsch. Meridian Med. Corp., Seattle, 1991—. Del. Japan-U.S. Seminar on Nuclear Engring. Edn., 1974; lectr. hemodialysis engring. USSR Ministry of Health, Moscow, 1976; lectr. biomed. engring. Norwegian Nephrological Soc., Oslo, 1980; lectr. hemodialysis engring. Kuratorium für Hemodialyse, Münster, Germany, 1980, Clinique Iser, Munich, Germany, 1980, Mcpl. Hosp., Hvidovre, Denmark, 1980, State Hosp., Copenhagen, 1980; mem. Assembly Engring., NRC, Com. Transp. Plutonium by Air; cons. med. engring., 1952— Contbr. chpts. to books, profl. jours. Trustee Pacific Sci. Center Found., mem. exec. com., 1973-80. Named Engr. of Yr., Wash. State Profl. Engrs. Assn., 1989; recipient citation, Wash. Joint Legis. Com. Nuc. Energy, 1968, Pioneer award, Am. Kidney Found., 1982, Sigma Xi award, 1982, Am. Engr. Specifying award for excellence in design artificial kidney systems, 1970, Disting. Tchg. award, Coll. Engring. U. Wash., 1987, Clyde Shields Disting. Svc. award, N.W. Kidney Found., 1992, Alumni Achievement award, U. Ill., 1993, Tchg. Excellence award, Aspen Tech. Inc., 1999, 2000, Lifetime Achievement award, Nat. Dialysis Conf., Seattle, 2003, Internat. Soc. Hemodialysis, 2003. Fellow Am. Inst. Chemists, Am. Inst. Chem. Engrs. (Engr. Distinction award), Am. Nuclear Soc. (v.p. 1982-83, chmn. 1983-84), Am. Inst. Med. and Biol. Engring.; mem. NAS (chmn. com. on future devel. nuclear power 1990, mem. Inst. Medicine), NAE (memberships com.), Engrs. Joint Coun., Am. Soc. Engring. Edn. (chmn. nuclear engring. divsn. 1965-66), Internat. Soc. Artificial Organs, Am. Soc. Artificial Internal Organs, European Dialysis and Transplantation Assn., Inst. Medicine, Biomed. Engring. Soc., Sigma Xi, Tau Beta Pi, Pi Mu Epsilon, Alpha Chi Sigma. Clubs: U. Wash. Pres.', Wash. Athletic. Presbyterian. Achievements include co-inventing continous central artificial kidney system for low cost treatment in centers, also co-inventor automatic artificial kidney system for overnight unattended hemodialysis of patients in homes, and techniques for early diagnosis of cystic fibrosis in children using a nuclear reactor; formulated dialysis index for prescribing minimum adequate treatment for patients undergoing hemodialysis; co-inventor, dir. design and devel. extracorporeal system for treatment of sickle cell anemia; co-developer computerized wearable insulin pump for diabetics; patentee systems for stblzn. of structures in permafrost, also field of artificial kidney, artificial pancreas, and respiratory diagnostics. Home: 3237 Lakewood Ave S Seattle WA 98144-7229

BABB, DOUGLAS J., lawyer; V.p., gen. counsel Burlington No. Railroad Co., Ft. Worth, 1990—2000; exec. v.p., sec., gen. counsel Beverly Enterprises Inc., Fort Smith, Ark., 2000—04, exec. v.p., chief admin. & legal officer, 2004—. Office: Beverly Enterprises Inc 1000 Beverly Wy Fort Smith AR 72919

BABB, FRANK EDWARD, lawyer; b. Maryville, Mo., Dec. 22, 1932; s. Dale Victor and Esther (Hull) B. BS, Northwest Mo. State U., Maryville, 1954; LL.B., Harvard U., 1959. Ptnr. McDermott, Will & Emery, Chgo., 1959-90, of counsel, 1991—. With CIC U.S. Army, 1954-56. Mem. Univ. Club Chgo., Am. Alpine Club.

BABB, HAROLD, psychologist, educator; b. Mosheim, Tenn., Sept. 4, 1926; s. Ray Edward and Mary Louise (Brown) B.; m. Marjorie Craig Leask (Sept. 27, 1947); children: Patricia Craig, Barbara Lou, David Edward. BA, Wayne State U., 1950; MA, Ohio State U., 1951, PhD, 1953. Asst. prof., assoc. prof., chmn. dept. psychology Coe Coll., 1953-58; prof., chmn. dept. psychology Hobart and William Smith Colls., 1958-63; NIH, NIMH exec. sec., grants specialist, 1963-64; prof., chmn. dept. psychology U. Mont., Missoula, 1964-71; prof. psychology SUNY-Binghamton, 1971-95, prof. emeritus, 1995—, chmn. dept., 1971-74. Contbr. articles on psychology to profl. jours. Served with USNR, 1944-46. NIMH research grantee, 1960-62; NSF research grantee, 1968-69 Fellow Am. Psychol. Assn., Am. Psychol. Soc.; mem. AAAS, AAUP, Ea. Psychol. Assn., Midwestern Psychol. Assn., Psychonomic Soc., Sigma Xi Home: RR 1 Box 1957 Stanley Lake Rd Friendsville PA 18818 E-mail: hbabb@epix.net.

BABB, JOSEPH DOLBY, physician; b. Columbus, Ohio, Apr. 16, 1939; s. Joe A. and Dorothe (Dolby) B.; m. Anne Tanner Hammerlund, Sept. 2, 1969 (div. Apr. 1985); children: Elizabeth Anne, Peter Dolby; m. Margo Tregenza, Oct. 10, 1990. BA magna cum laude, Kenyon Coll., Gambier, Ohio, 1961; MD, Johns Hopkins U., 1966. Diplomate in internal medicine and cardiovascular diseases Am. Bd. Internal Medicine; cert. physician, Pa., Conn., N.C. Intern Mass. Gen. Hosp., Boston, 1966-67, resident in internal medicine, 1967-68, clin. and rsch. fellow, 1970-72; teaching fellow Harvard Med. Sch., Boston, 1970-72; asst. prof. med. cardiology Pa. State U. Sch. Medicine, Hershey, 1972-76, assoc. prof., 1976-80; chief of cardiology Bridgeport (Conn.) Hosp., 1980-95; clin. assoc. prof. medicine (cardiology) Yale U., New Haven, 1980-95; prof. medicine (cardiology) East Carolina U. Sch. Medicine, Greenville, 1995—. Bd. dirs., pres. Alcohol and Drug Dependency Coun., Westport, Conn., 1987-95. Maj. U.S. Army, 1968-70, Vietnam. Fulbright fellow, Utrecht, Netherlands, 1961-62. Fellow Am. Coll. Cardiology (gov. 1987-90, 2002—), Am. Heart Assn. (coun. clin. cardiology), Soc. Cardiac Angiography and Intervention (trustee 1993-99, pres. 2001-02), Coalition of Cardiovasc. Orgns. (pres. 2004-05) Avocations: fishing, hiking. Office: East Carolina U Sch Med PCMH Teaching Annex Rm 352 Greenville NC 27858-4354 Business E-Mail: babbj@mail.ecu.edu.

BABB, JUDITH ANN, communications educator, journalist; b. Dallas, Sept. 13, 1949; d. Henry Leon and Yvonne Marie (Bailey) Killen; children: Emily Rebecca, Drew Bailey. BA in Journalism, N. Tex. State U., 1971, MA in Journalism, 1980. Cert. journalism educator; master journalism educator. Tchr., newspaper advisor Lincoln High Sch., Dallas Ind. Sch. Dist., 1972-76; tchr. yearbook and newspaper advisor Skyline High Sch., Dallas Ind. Sch. Dist., 1976-87; tchr., yearbook advisor Highland Park High Sch., Dallas, 1987—98; photographer, instr. Hillcrest HS, Dallas Ind. Sch. Dist., 1998—; prof. journalism, yearbook and newspaper advisor So. Meth. U., 1999—2004; with Lifetouch Publishing Co., Inc., 2004—. Instr. workshop Interscholastic League Press Conf., Austin, Tex., 1984—, Dallas County Schs. Publs. Workshop, 1986—; dir. workshop Taylor Pub. Co. Denton, Dallas, 1988-89; workshop leader Wash. Journalism Educators Assn., Evergreen, 1988; instr. yearbook workshop Stanford (Calif.) U., 1990-93, Tex. Women's U., Denton, 1991-92; co-founder The Redesign Inst., St. Louis, Portland, Oreg., 1993, St. Louis, Dallas, Portland, 1994. Adviser The Origin-Just Your Type, 1986 (Gold Crown 1987), The Origin-You of All People, 1987 (Gold Crown 1988), The Origin-Balancing the Books, 1985 (Silver Crown 1986), The Highlander-For a Limited Time Only, 1988 (State Champion 1989), The Highlander, 1989, At Face Value, 1989 (Silver Crown 1990), Word of Mouth, 1991 (State Champion 1992, Silver Crown 1992), Call It What You Want, 1992 (State Champion 1993, Silver Crown 1993); adviser Issue mag. (4th pl. Best of Show Nat. Scholastic Press 1993). Recipient Edith Fox King award Interscholastic League Press Conf., 1980, NSPA Pioneer award, 1997, CSPA Gold Key award, 1998.; named Tex. HS Journalism Tchr. of Yr., 1996. Mem. Dallas County Schs. Journalism Com., Nat. Scholastic Press Assn. (Pioneer award 1999), Columbia Scholastic Press Assn., Journalism Edn. Assn. (sec. 1990-94, newswire editor 1990-94, Medal of Merit 1993, Disting. Yearbook adviser 1998), Coll. Media Advisors (chair ethics com. 2001—), Golden Key. Republican. Episcopalian. Avocations: photography, water sports, guitar, reading, skiing, motorcycling. Office: So Meth U 3140 Dyer St Ste 314 Dallas TX 75275

BABB, PAMELA DAWN, family and consumer science educator; b. St. Cloud, Minn., Apr. 27, 1962; d. Ronald Paul and Janice Elaine Haselhuhn; m. Mark Alan Babb, Sept. 29, 1984 (div. Feb. 9, 1991); children: Eric Lloyd, Taylor Paul. Grad. in Vocation Home Econs. Edn., Emporia State U., 1984. Tchr. family and consumer sci. Olathe South H.S., Kans., 1985—90, Emporia H.S., Kans., 1994—96, Garden City H.S., Kans., 1997—. Mem.: Kans. Assn. of Career and Tech. Educators (assoc.). Home: 302 E Olive Garden City KS 67846 Office: Garden City HS 1412 N Main Garden City KS 67846 Office Phone: 620-276-5170. Personal E-mail: mzbabb@hotmail.com. Business E-Mail: pbabb@gckschools.com.

BABB, RALPH W., JR., banker; b. Sherman, Tex., Feb. 4, 1949; s. Ralph Wheeler and Billie Margaret (Odneal) B.; m. Barbara Louise Alexander, Aug. 30, 1970; children: Dana P., Derek R. BS in Acctg., U. Mo., Columbia, 1971. CPA, Mo. Audit mgr. Peat, Marwick, Mitchell & Co., CPA's, St. Louis, 1971-78; contr., sr. v.p. Mercantile Bancorp. Inc., St. Louis, 1978-83, treas., sr. v.p., 1979-83, CFO, exec. v.p., 1983-94, vice chmn., 1987-95; EVP, CFO Comerica Bank, Comercia Inc., Detroit, 1995—99, vice chmn., CFO, 1999—2001, CFO, 2002, chmn., pres., CEO, dir., 2002—. Mem. Fin. Execs. Inst. (pres. St. Louis chpt. 1986-87). Methodist. Office: Comerica Inc PO Box 75000 Detroit MI 48275-0001

BABBEL, DAVID FREDERICK, finance and insurance educator; b. Salt Lake City, Apr. 12, 1949; s. Frederick William and June (Andrew) Babbel; m. Mary Jane Benson, Aug. 27, 1975; children: Tara Nicole, Elise Kiera, Karisa Rose, Tyson Frederick. BA, Brigham Young U., 1973; MBA, U. Fla., 1975, PhD, 1978; MA (hon.), U. Pa., 1986. Prof. fin. U. Calif., Berkeley, 1978—85; prof. fin. and ins. Wharton Sch., U. Pa., Phila., 1985—. V.p. Goldman, Sachs & Co, New York, NY, 1987, cons.; pres. A/L Technology, Bryn Mawr, Pa.; cons. IBM, Chase, MMC, World Bank, Verizon, Morrison-Knudson, Aetna, GE Capital, Met Life, 1978—. Author: 6 books on fins and ins; contbr. articles to profl jours. Pres. Brasilia, Brazil Mission of L.D.S. Ch., 2002—. Fellow Fulbright, 1976—77. Republican. Office: Wharton Sch U Pa 304 Colonial Penn Ctr Philadelphia PA 19104 E-mail: babbel@wharton.upenn.edu. *Any idea, without at least some element of absurdity, is probably not worth further consideration.*

BABBIN, JED LLOYD, lawyer; b. N.Y.C., Mar. 16, 1950; s. Harold H. and Pearl (Bander) B.; m. Frances Kloker, June 22, 1975 (div. 1990); children: Jacob Harold, Norman Tyler; m. Sharon Cohen. BE, Stevens Inst. Tech., Hoboken, N.J., 1970; JD, Samford U., 1973; LLM, Georgetown U., 1978. Bar: Ala. 1973, D.C. 1978. Assoc. McKenna, Connor & Cuneo, Washington, 1977-81; v.p., gen. counsel Shipbuilders Coun., Washington, 1977-81; dir. contract policy Lockheed Corp., Washington, 1985-90; dep. under sec. of def. acquisition planning Office Sec. of Def., Washington, 1990-91; ptnr. McGuire, Woods, Battle & Boothe, Washington, 1991-94, Tighe, Patton, Tabackman & Babbin, Washington, 1994-2000, O'Connor & Hannan, LLP, Washington, 2000—. Columnist Am. Spectator Online, Nat. Rev. Online. Contbg. editor: The American Spectator Mag.; author: Legacy of Valor, 2000, Inside the Asylum: Why the United Nations and Old Europe are Worse Than You Think, 2004. Bd. dirs. Columbia Lighthouse for the Blind, 2002—. Capt. USAF, 1973—77. Republican. Jewish. Avocations: fishing, bird hunting. Office Phone: 202-887-1400. Business E-Mail: jbabbin@oconnorhannan.com.

BABBIO, LAWRENCE T., telecommunications industry executive; BEE, Stevens Inst. Tech.; MBA, NYU. Various engring. positions N.J. Bell Tel., 1966-85; v.p. tech. applications Bell Comm. Rsch., 1985-87; v.p. ops. and engring. Bell Atlantic Network Svcs., 1987-91; exec. v.p., COO Bell Atlantic Corp., 1991-95, vice chmn., 1995-99, pres., COO, 1999—2000; pres., vice chmn. Verizon Comm. (formed when Bell Atlantic and GTE merged), 2000—. Chmn. Grupo Iusacell; chmn. bd. trustees, Stevens Inst. of Tech.; bd. dirs. Hewlett-Packard Co., ARAMARK Corp., formerly bd. dir.Compaq Computer Corp. Office: Verizon Ste 2407B 1095 Avenue Of The Americas New York NY 10036-6704

BABBITT, SAMUEL FISHER, retired university official; b. New Haven, Feb. 22, 1929; s. Theodore and Margaret (Fisher) B.; m. Natalie Zane Moore, June 28, 1954; children: Christopher Converse, Thomas Collier, Lucy Cullyford. BA, Yale U., 1953, MA, 1957, PhD, 1965; LLD (hon.), Hamilton Coll., Clinton, N.Y., 1968. Asst. dean Yale Coll. Grad. Sch., New Haven, 1953-57, 63-66; dean of men Vanderbilt U., Nashville, 1957-62; chief coll. and univ. liaison Office Pub. Affairs, U.S. Peace Corps, Washington, 1962-63; pres. Kirkland Coll., Clinton, N.Y., 1966-78; v.p. program planning and resources Meml. Sloan-Kettering Cancer Ctr., N.Y.C., 1979-83; v.p. devel. Brown U., Providence, 1982-90, sr. v.p. The Campaign, 1990-93, sr. advisor to pres. for Far Eastern Affairs, 1993-96. Mem. N.Y. State Commn. on Civil Rights, 1968-76. Author: The 49th Magician, 1966; producer: (film) The Eyes of the Amaryllis, 1981. Bd. dirs. Sandra Feinstein-Gamm Theatre. With inf. U.S. Army, 1948-51, Korea. Decorated Silver Star. Mem. Century Assn. (N.Y.C.). Democrat. E-mail: sambabb1@cox.net.

BABBY, ELLEN REISMAN, educational association administrator; b. Montreal, Que., Can., Oct. 21, 1950; came to U.S., 1973; d. Mark Reisman and Rose Gutwillig (Reisman); m. Lon Scott Babby, June 17, 1973; children— Kenneth Robert, Heather Lynn. Student, McGill U., 1968-70; BA, Beaver Coll., 1972; MA, Lehigh U., 1973, Yale U., 1976, M.Phil., 1977, PhD, 1980. Tchr. elem. schs. to coll. levels; instr. resident assoc. program Smithsonian Instn., Washington, 1980-82; exec. dir. Assn. for Can. Studies in U.S., Washington, 1982—91; with Nat. Fgn. Lang. Ctr. Johns Hopkins U., Washington, 1992-94; sr. dir. planning and devel. Nat. Assn. Fgn. Student Affairs Assn. Internat. Educators, Washington, 1995—99; v.p. Am. Coun. On Edn., Washington, 1999—. Author: Play of Language and Spectacle: A Structural Reading of Selected Texts by Gabrielle Roy, 1986. Contbr. articles on Quebec lit. to profl. jours. Mem. Am. Soc. Assn. Execs., Assn. Fund Raising Profls., Yale Alumni (del. 1989-92). Office: Am Coun On Edn One Dupont Cir #800 Washington DC 20036 Business E-Mail: ellen_babby@ace.nche.edu. E-mail: ellen@babby.com.

BABBY, LON S., lawyer; b. Bklyn., Feb. 21, 1951; BA, Lehigh U., 1973; JD, Yale U., 1976. Bar: Conn. 1976, D.C. 1977, U.S. Supreme Ct. 1981, U.S. Claims Ct., 1986; cert. agt. Nat. Basketball Players Assn., Nat. Football League Players Assn., Maj. League Baseball Assn. Law clk. to Hon. M. Joseph Blumenfeld Dist. Conn., 1976-77; mem. Williams & Connolly, Washington, 1977—. Adj. faculty George Washington U. Law Sch., 1991-92. Editor Yale Law Jour., 1974-76; contbr. articles to profl. jours. Trustee Naismith Meml. Basketball Hall of Fame, 2002—. Mem. ABA, D.C. Bar, Conn. Bar Assn., Phi Beta Kappa, Omicron Delta Kappa. Office: Williams & Connolly 725 12th St NW Washington DC 20005-5901 Office Phone: 202-434-5561. Business E-Mail: lbabby@wc.com.

BABCOCK, BARBARA ALLEN, lawyer, educator; b. Washington, July 6, 1938; d. Henry Allen and Doris Lenore (Moses) Babcock; m. Thomas C. Grey, Aug. 19, 1979. BA, U. Pa., 1960; LLB, Yale U., 1963; LLD (hon.), U. San Diego, 1983, U Puget Sound, 1988. Bar: Md. 1963, DC 1964. Law clk. US Ct. Appeals, DC, 1963; assoc. Edward Bennett Williams, 1964—66; staff atty. Legal Aid Agy., Washington, 1966—68; dir. Pub. Defender Svc. (formerly Legal Aid Agy.), 1968—72; asst. atty. gen. US Dept. Justice, 1977—79; assoc. prof. Stanford U., 1972—77, prof., 1977—, Ernest W. McFarland Prof. Law, 1986—97, Judge John Crown prof. law, 1997—2004, Judge John Crown prof. emerita, 2004—. Author (with others): Sex Discrimination and The Law: History, Theory and Practice, 1996; co-author (with Massaro): Civil Procedure: Problems and Cases, 2001; contbr. articles profl. jour. Recipient John Bingham Hurlbut Award for Excellence in Tchg., Stanford U., 1981, 1986, 1998, 2004, Margaret Brent Women Lawyers of Achievement Award, ABA, 1999. Democrat. Office: Stanford U Sch Law Stanford CA 94305

BABCOCK, CATHERINE EVANS, artist, educator; b. Rydal, Pa., Feb. 23, 1924; d. William Wayne and Marion (Waters) Babcock; m. Douglas Paul Torre, May 28, 1977; 2 stepchildren. Diploma, Sarah Lawrence Coll., 1942; BFA, Temple U., 1944, MFA, 1948. Tchr. Rudolf Steiner Sch., 1949; tchr. jr. high sch. Stratford, Conn., 1959-63; tchr. elem. art Locust Valley Primary and Elem. Sch., 1963-68; instr. Darien Cmty. Ctr., 1975-81; art tchr. Rowayton Arts Ctr., Conn., 1979—, also bd. mem. Rec. sec. Portrait painter; artist to Sea Svc. (USCG and USN); equestrian artist Fairfield Hunt Club Show's Benefit Horse Show, 1993; watercolor tchr. Darien Cmty. Assn., 1993-94. Illustrator: Atheneum, 1968 (Libr. award), Cutaneous Cryosurgery (Douglas Torre), 1978, rev., 1979; translator: Undertow (Finn Havrevold), 1968; painter, mural for Babcock Surg. Wards, Temple U. Hosp., Phila., 1944; designer display Cryosurgery of Skin Cancer, Dallas, 1979 (Gold award); art work appeared Carriage Barn Arts Ctr. Waveny Park, New Canaan, Conn., 2004; author: Biography in American References, 1989, Vikings Habitat, River of Dreams, 1994, Poetic Voices of America, 1995, Best Pastels, 1996, Chips and Chirps of Verses, 1998, Theatre of the Mind; exhbns. include internat. miniature shows Fine Arts Club, Washington, 1984, New Canaan Soc. for the Arts, 1988, 93, Grand Nat. Salmagundi Club, St. Petersburg Mus., Fla., Degas Pastel Soc., New Orleans, 1990-95, Mus. of Art, New Orleans, 1990, (portrait of husband) NY Hosp., Amb. Ernst Jaakson Mus. in Tallin, Estonia, 2001, Portrait of Sr. Ambassador of UN 1997, now in mus. in Estonia, 2001; Cert. of Excellence from Miniature Spc. of Washington for portrait of a firefighter, 2002; author numerous poems. Recipient awards including 10 USCG awards, Am. Acad. Dermatology Art Shows, 2 award, Rowayton Arts Ctr., 1993—94, Best Poems award, Nat. Libr. Poetry, 1996, Amherst Soc. award, Sparrowgrass Soc. award, cert. appreciation, USCG, 1971—82, Naval Sta. of N.Y., 1981, 1st prize, Rowayton Art Ctr., 2000, USCG award, Alexander Hamilton Custom House, 2000, Mdal of Honor, IBC Internat. Pro. Ctr., Cambridge, Eng., 2004, Internat. medal Honor, Cambridge, 2003, Albert Schweitzer Sci. and Peace medal, Spain, 2004. Mem. Internat. Soc. Poets (lifetime, Merit award 1997, medal 1997, 2 Silver cups 2003, 2004), Met. Portrait Inst., Conn. Pastel Soc., Pastel Soc. Am. (cert. of merit), USCG Art Program (ofcl. artist), COGAP Artist. Congregationalist. Home and Office: 122 Rowayton Ave Norwalk CT 06853-1409 Office Phone: 203-838-8082.

BABCOCK, CHARLES LUTHER, classics educator; b. Whittier, Calif., May 26, 1924; s. Robert Louis and Margarette Estelle (Fuller) B.; m. Mary Ayer Taylor, Aug. 6, 1955; children: Robert Sherburne, Jennie Rownd

Chapman, Jonathan Taylor. AB in Latin, U. Calif., Berkeley, 1948, MA in Latin, 1949, PhD in Classics, 1953. Asst. in classics U. Utah, Salt Lake City, 1949-50; instr. classics Cornell U., Ithaca, N.Y., 1955-57; acting. instr. Stanford U., Calif., summer 1956; asst. prof. classical studies U. Pa., Phila., 1957-62, assoc. prof., 1962-66, asst. dean, vice dean of coll., 1960-62, 62-64, acting dean, spring 1964; prof. classics Ohio State U., Columbus, 1966-92, prof. emeritus, 1992—, chmn. dept., 1966-68, 80-88, dean Coll. of Humanities, 1968-70. Prof.-in-charge summer sch. Am. Acad. in Rome, 1966, resident in classical studies, 1986, acting Mellon prof.-in-charge sch. classical studies, 1988-89, chmn. adv. coun. sch. classical studies, 1992-94; Latin exam. com. Advanced Placement Program, 1967-74, chmn., 1972-74; prof.-in-charge Intercollegiate Ctr. Classical Studies, Rome, 1974, chair mng. com., 1975-82; scholar in residence Hope Coll., 1993. Co-author: Aspects of Roman Civilization, 1980; contbr. articles on Latin lit. (especially Horace), Latin epigraphy, Roman civilization. Served to capt. inf. U.S. Army, 1943—47, ETO. Univ. fellow in classics U. Calif., Berkeley, 1951-53; Fulbright scholar in classics, Rome, 1953-55. Fellow Am. Acad. in Rome (trustee 1981-83, trustee emeritus 1994—); mem. Am. Philol. Assn. (bd. dirs. 1968-72), Classical Assn. of Mid. West and South (Ovatio award 1982, pres. 1977-78), Vergilian Soc. Am. (pres. 1975-76), Assn. Depts. Fgn. Langs. (pres. 1986), Archeol. Inst. Am., Ohio Classical Conf., Phi Beta Kappa (pres. Epsilon of Ohio 1969-70), Phi Kappa Phi, Phi Sigma Kappa (former pres. U. Calif., regional dep. 1949-51), Scabbard and Blade Club (Pa., hon.), Philomathean Soc. (Pa. hon.), Greater Columbus Latin Club. Home: 973 Lynbrook Rd Columbus OH 43235-3307 Office: Ohio State U Dept Greek & Latin 230 N Oval Mall Columbus OH 43210-1319 Office Phone: 614-292-2744. E-mail: babcock.2@osu.edu.

BABCOCK, CHARLES LYNDE, IV, lawyer; b. Bklyn., June 23, 1949; s. Charles Lynde III and Dorothy (Yates) B.; children: Katherine Kester, Barbara Yates. AB, Brown U., 1971; JD, Boston U., 1976. Bar: Tex. 1977, U.S. Dist. Ct. (no. dist.) Tex. 1977, U.S. Dist. Ct. (so. dist.) Tex. 1979, U.S. Ct. Appeals (5th and 11th cirs.) 1979, U.S. Supreme Ct. 1980, U.S. Dist. Ct. (we. dist.) Tex. 1981, U.S. Ct. Appeals (9th and 10th cirs.) 1982, U.S. Dist. Ct. (ea. dist.) Tex. 1982. Sportswriter Phila. Inquirer, 1971-73; law clk. to presiding justice U.S. Dist. Ct. (no. dist.) Tex., Dallas, 1976-78; assoc. Jackson, Walker, Winstead, Cantwell & Miller, Dallas, 1978-83, ptnr., 1983—, now Jackson Walker LLP, Dallas. Author: Business Law for Executives, 1977, Texas Media Law handbook, 1984; contbr. articles to legal jours. Bd. dirs. Freedom of Info. Found. Tex., 1995—. Recipient Disting. Pro Bono Svc. award North Tex. Legal Svcs. Found., 1986. Fellow Tex. Bar Found., Am. Coll. Trial Lawyers; mem. ABA, Tex. Bar Assn. Mem. Soc. Of Friends. Avocation: sports. Office: Jackson & Walker LLP Ste 6000 901 Main St Dallas TX 75202-3797

BABCOCK, CHARLES WITTEN, JR., lawyer; b. Kansas City, Mo., Dec. 6, 1941; s. Charles W. and Esther L. (Marcy) B.; m. Sharon K. Chamberlain, June 26, 1976; children: David, William, Susan, Stephen. BA with honors, U. Mo., 1963; JD, Harvard U., 1966. Bar: Mo. 1966, Mich. 1971. Judge advocate USMC, various locations, 1966-69; assoc. Blackwell, Sanders, Kansas City, 1969-71; staff atty. Gen. Motors Corp., Detroit, 1971—. Contbr. articles to profl. jours. Bd. dirs. Mothers Against Drunk Driving, 1992-99, nat. chmn., 1996-98. Avocation: amateur radio. Home: 917 Grand Marais St Grosse Pointe MI 48230-1867

BABCOCK, JO, artist, educator; b. St. Louis, Feb. 24, 1954; s. Boyd Leon and Shirley Lynn (Hamm) B.; m. Kitty Costello, May 25, 2003. Student, UCLA, 1975; BFA, San Francisco Art Inst., 1976, MFA, 1979. Color printer Rolling Stone mag., San Francisco, 1976, Outside mag., San Francisco, 1977; cameraman 1st Calif. Press, San Francisco, 1977-80; electrician Bros. Electric, San Francisco, 1984-89; assoc. prof. San Francisco Art Inst., 1989-93; exhibit designer Levi Strauss & Co., 1989—. One-man shows include Zwinger Gallery, Berlin, 1987, Marcuse Pfeiffer Gallery, N.Y.C., 1988, Artspace, San Francisco, 1989, Visual Studies Workshop, Rochester, N.Y., 1990, Ctr. for the Arts, San Francisco, 1995, Oakland (Calif.) Mus., 1997, Kyle Roberts Gallery, San Francisco, 1992, Addison Gallery Am. Art, Andover, Mass., 1997, Chgo. Art Inst., 1982, CEPA, Buffalo, 1988, others; exhibited in group shows at Friends of Photography Gallery, Carmel, 1976, Sao Paulo (Brazil) Bienal, San Francisco Mus. of Modern Art, 1989, Rena Bransten Gallery, San Francisco, 1991, Oliver Art Ctr., CCAC, 1991, Lieberman & Saul, N.Y., 1991, Tampa Mus. Art, 1992, San Jose Mus. Art, 1992, Palm Springs Desert Mus., 1993, 100 Years of Landscape Art in the Bay Area, M.H. de Young Mus., San Francisco, 1995, Bay Area Landscapes, 1995, The Alternative Mus., N.Y., 1981, Wooster St. Gallery, N.Y., 1981, Living Mus., Rejkjavik, Iceland, 1983, 10 on 8, N.Y., 1983, Windows on White, N.Y., 1984, Public Image, N.Y., 1984, Otis Parsons Gallery, L.A., 1985, Hotel Project, Oakland, Calif., 1986, Roanoke (Va.) Mus. Fine Art, 1988, Ctr. for contemporary Arts, Santa Fe, 1988, Artists at the Rock, Alcatraz, Calif., 1988, others; represented in permanent collections at San Francisco Mus. Modern Art, Bklyn. Mus., Newport Harbor Art Mus., Lightwork, Syracuse, N.Y., La Biblioteque, Avignon, France, San Francisco Pub. Libr., San Francisco Arts Commn., George Eastman House, Rochester, N.Y., Nat. Collection, Smithsonian Instn., others. Grantee City of Oakland, 1985, N.Y. State Coun. on Arts, 1988, Nat. Endowment for Arts, 1990. Mem. Primitive Hunting Soc. Avocation: building pinhole cameras. Studio: 378 San Jose Ave Apt B San Francisco CA 94110-3700 Personal E-mail: jobabcock@jobabcock.com.

BABCOCK, LYNDON ROSS, JR., environmental engineer, educator; b. Detroit, Apr. 8, 1934; s. Lyndon Ross and Lucille Kathryn (Miller) B.; m. Betty Irene Immonen, June 21, 1957; children: Lyndon Ross III, Sheron Lucille Babcock Fruehauf, Susan Elizabeth Babcock Williams, Andrew Dag BSChemE, Mich. Tech. U., 1956; MSChemE, U. Washington, 1958, PhD in Environ. Engring., 1970. Chem. engr. polymers Shell Chem. Co., Calif., N.J., N.Y., 1958-67; assoc. prof. environ. engring., geography, pub. health U. Ill., Chgo., 1970-75, prof. environ. engring., geography, pub. health, 1975-90, prof. emeritus, 1990—, dir. environ. health scis. program Sch. Pub. Health, 1978-79, dir. environ. and occupational health scis. program Sch. Pub. Health, 1979-84, assoc. dean Sch. Pub. Health, 1984-85. Cons. WHO, 1985, Interam. Devel. Bank, 1990-91, Environ. Secretariat Fed. Dist., Mexico City, 1995-97; USA coord. air quality project for Gestión de la Calidad del Aire, Mexico City, 1986-92; environ. cons./lectr. Tech. Instns., Mexican Secretariat of Pub. Edn., 1993-95; vis. prof. El Colegio de Mexico, Mexico City, 1996-2000. Mem. editorial bd. The Environ. Profl., 1979-90; contbr. environ. articles to profl jours.; patentee plastics composition and processing. Bd. dirs. Chgo. Lung Assn., 1981-92. Fulbright lectr., Turkey and India, 1975-76, Mexico, 1986-87, 1992-93; fed. and state environ. research and edn. grantee Mem. Air and Waste Mgmt. Assn. (chmn. Lake Michigan sect. 1977-78), League Am. Bicyclists, Chicagoland Bicycle Fedn. (v.p. 1985-86). Office: U Ill Sch Pub Health EOHS MC922 2121 W Taylor St Chicago IL 60612-7260 Office Phone: 517-579-3232. E-mail: lyndonrb@comcast.net.

BABCOCK, MARGUERITE LOCKWOOD, addictions treatment therapist, educator, writer; b. Jacksonville, Fla., Jan. 1, 1944; d. Allen Seaman and Emilie (Lockwood) B. BA in Art History, Am. U., 1965; M Counselor Edn., U. Pitts., 1982. Lic. profl. counselor, Pa.; cert. addictions counselor Pa., nat. cert. counselor, master's addiction counselor (nat.). Addictions therapist South Hills Health Sys., Pitts., 1979—81; addiction therapist, clin. supr., clin. dir. Alternatives Turtle Creek Mental Health/Mental Retardation/D&A Ctr., Pitts., 1981—86; addictions therapist, coord. Ligonier Valley Treatment Ctr., Stahlstown, Pa., 1986—88; addictions clin. supr., unit dir. Ctr. for Substance Abuse Mon-Yough, McKeesport, Pa., 1988—96; quality assurance Mon-Yough, McKeesport, 1996—97; clin. supr. Sojourner House, Pitts., 1997—2000; co-founder, addictions cons. consortium Outcomes Builders, 2000—. Adj. instr. in addictions courses Seton Hill Coll., Greensburg, Pa., 1989-91, C.C. Allegheny County, West Mifflin, Pa., 1989-91, Pa. State U., McKeesport, 1993-97; pvt. trainer, writer, Acme, Pa., 1985—; ind. info. profl. in addictions, 2003—. Co-author, co-editor: Challenging Codependency: Feminist Critiques, 1995; mem. editl. bd. Jour. Tchg. in Addictions, 2000—; contbr. articles to profl. jours. Fellow Andrew Mellon Found., 1966-68, NSF, 1967. Mem.: Alpha Lambda Delta, Phi Kappa Phi. Avocation: website designer. Home and Office: 3533 Rt 130 Acme PA 15610-9712 Office Phone: 724-593-7139. E-mail: allele@lhtc.net.

BABCOCK, MICHAEL WARD, economics professor; b. Bloomington, Ill., Dec. 10, 1944; s. Bruce W. and Virginia (Neeson) B.; m. Virginia Lee Brooks, Aug. 4, 1973; children: John, Karen. BSBA, Drake U., 1967; MA in Econs., U. Ill., 1971, PhD in Econs., 1973. Tchg. asst. U. Ill., Urbana, 1968, 71, rsch. asst., 1972; prof. econs. Kans. State U., Manhattan, 1972—, Cons. Santa Fe, Burlington No., and Union Pacific R.R., Brotherhood of Maintenence Way, United Transp. Union, Kans. Dept. Transp., Kans. Dept. Agr., U.S. Dept. Agr., Kans. Dept. Commerce. Gen. editor Jour. Transp. Rsch. Forum; contbr. articles to profl. jours., newspapers, mags. Apptd. to Kans. Govs. R.R. Working Group to Evaluate Class I R.R. Mergers, 1995, 96, 2000. With U.S. Army, 1969-71. Recipient A.T. Kearney award Transp. Rsch. Forum, 1987, 89, UPS Found. award, 1990, Outstanding Rsch. in Agrl. Transp. award Burlington No. R.R., 1994, Rail-Tex. Corp. award Transp. Rsch. Forum, 1997; grantee U.S. Army C.E., 1978-79, USDA, 1978-80-82, 84-85, 96-97, 2000, Kans. Dept. Agr., 1987, Kans. Wheat Commn., 1989, 92, 93, Midwest Transp. Ctr., 1989, 92-93, Kans. Dept. Transp., 1991—, Mid-Am. Transp. Ctr., 1995-96, Herbert O. Whitten Svc. award Transportation Rsch. Forum, 2005 Mem. Am. Assn. Agrl. Economists, Missouri Valley Econ. Assn., Mid-Continent Regional Sci. Assn., So. Regional Sci. Assn., Transp. Rsch. Forum (gen. editor Jour., Herbert O. Whitten Svc. award 2005), Transp. Rsch. Bd., Coun. Logistics Mgmt., So. Econs. Assn., We. Econs. Assn., Beta Gamma Sigma, Omicron Delta Epsilon. Home: 720 Harris Ave Manhattan KS 66502-3614 Office: Kans State U Dept Econs Manhattan KS 66506 Office Phone: 785-532-4571. Business E-Mail: mwb@ksu.edu.

BABCOCK-LUMISH, TERRY LYNNE, researcher; b. Miami, Fla., Mar. 30, 1976; d. Robert Malcolm and Saundra Ellen Lumish; m. Brian Christopher Babcock, June 20, 2001. BS, Carnegie Mellon U., Pitts., 1997; MPA, Ind. U. Sch. Pub. & Environ. Affairs, 1999; DPhil in Econ. Geography, U. Oxford, Eng., 2004. Lilly cmty. assistance fellow Gov. Frank O'Bannon's Children's Environ. Initiative, Inpls., 1997—99; presdl. mgmt. fellow Coun. of Econ. Advisers, US Dept. of Treasury, Washington, 1999—2001; rschr. To V.P. Al Gore, Alexandria, Va., 2001—02; assoc. fellow Rothermere Am. Inst., Oxford, 2002—; pres. Islay Consulting LLC, Sierra Vista, Ariz., 2005—. Dir. Truman Scholars Assn., Washington, 2002—05. Recipient Sr. Leadership award, Carnegie Mellon U., 1997, Stephen Omer Lee award for Outstanding Engring. & Pub. Policy Project, 1996; fellow Presdl. Mgmt. fellow, United State Office of Pers. Mgmt., 1999—2001; scholar, Harry S. Truman Scholarship Found., 1996; Clarendon scholar, U. of Oxford, Oxford U. Press, 2002—05. Mem.: Am. Assn. of Geographers, Rotary Internat., Pi Alpha Alpha, Phi Kappa Phi, Phi Beta Kappa. Avocations: travel, hiking, gourmet cooking. Office Phone: 520-803-0801.

BABER, BOB, dean; b. Utica; BA in Pub. Rels. and Journalism, Utica Coll.; M in News/Editl. Journalism, Ball State U. Instr. journalism Utica Coll., Syracuse U., Syracuse, NY; dir. pub. relations SUNY Inst. Tech., Utica/Rome; dir. comm. & devel. Pratt at Munson-Williams-Proctor Arts Inst., Utica, NY, 1999—2002, dir. comm. & interim Dean Sch. Art, 2002—03, Dean Sch. Art, 2003—. Co-author (with Joe Chilberg): N.Y. Wine Country, 1980. Former pres. Downtown Utica Devel. Assn., Utica, NY; sec. bd. Oneida County Conv. & Visitors Bur.; bd. dirs. GroWest Inc.; former pres. Utica Kiwanis Club, SUNY Coun. U. Advancement & Devel. Office: Office of the Dean Pratt MWP Arts Inst 310 Genesee St Utica NY 13502

BABIC, MICHAEL WALTER, lawyer; b. McKeesport, Pa., Nov. 4, 1951; s. Walter V. and Elizabeth J. B.; m. Virginia L. Metzger. BS magna cum laude, Pa. State U., 1973; postgrad., Johns Hopkins U., 1976; JD, Franklin Pierce Law Ctr., 1980. High sch. tchr. Harford County Bd. Edn., Bel Air, Md., 1973-77; ptnr. Hartman Underhill & Brubaker, Lancaster, Pa., 1980—. Bd. dirs. Lancaster Guidance Ctr. 1988-95. Mem. Pa. Bar Assn., Lancaster County Bar Assn., Hamilton Club. Republican. Roman Catholic. Avocations: baseball, tennis, golf, squash. Home: 813 Westminster Dr Lancaster PA 17601-1452 Office: Hartman Underhill & Brubaker 221 E Chestnut St Lancaster PA 17602-2705 Office Phone: 717-299-7254.

BABIK, DENNIS ALLEN, social worker, consultant; b. Johnstown, Pa., Sept. 6, 1943; s. Stephen Edward and Bernice Ann (Britz) B.; m. Esther Rebecca Rosenbaum, Jan. 18, 1992 (div. Feb. 1996). BS, U. Pitts., 1967; MSW, Marywood U., 1972; PhD, NYU, 1991. Cert. expert in traumatic stress Am. Acad. Experts in Traumatic Stress; lic. social worker Pa., N.Y., Tex., R.I.; cert. Article 81 court evaluator. Med. caseworker John Kane Hosp., Pitts., 1967, 70; psychiat. social worker Dutchess County Dept. Mental Hygiene, Poughkeepsie, N.Y., 1972-83; clin. dir. Veterans Coalition, Beacon, N.Y., 1986-93; pvt. practice social work Rhinebeck and Newburgh, N.Y., 1981-96; clin. supr. Riceland Reg. Mental Health Authority, Rosenberg, Tex., 1997-98; behavior specialist Alternative Cmty. Resource Program, Johnstown, Pa., 2000—; pvt. practice specializing in victims of trauma, 2000—. Program cons. N.Y. State Dept. Correctional Svcs., Albany, 1985-93; mem. nat. adv. coun. U.S. Jaycees, Tulsa, 1976-78; adj. instr. Dutchess County Cmty. Coll., Poughkeepsie, 1972-82; presenter, facilitator workshops, 1975-90. Contbr. to book: Incoming, 1998; contbr. articles to newspapers, profl. jours. With U.S. Army, 1967-69. Decorated Bronze Star; named Outstanding Young Man Am., U.S. Jaycees; recipient Disting. Svc. Cross, 1968, Outstanding Achievement award, U.S. Jaycees. Fellow: N.Y. State Soc. Clin. Social Workers; mem.: APA, Am. Acad. Experts in Traumatic Stress, Internat. Soc. Traumatic Stress Studies, The Menninger Soc., Nat. Assn. Social Workers, Mid-Hudson Valley Multiple Sclerosis Soc. (adv. bd. 1980—83, Red Cross nat. disaster team 2001), Ft. Bend County C. of C., Vietnam Vets. of Am. Roman Catholic. Achievements include development of and direction of a therapeutic program to assess and treat traumatized incarcerated veterans within N.Y. State correctional system. Avocations: reading, music, hiking, jogging, outdoor sports. Home: 1202 Virginia Ave Johnstown PA 15906

BABIN, CLAUDE HUNTER, history professor; b. Baton Rouge, Feb. 6, 1924; s. Ventress Victor and Essie (Bond) B.; m. Barbara Ann Murphy, Dec. 29, 1947; 1 son, Claude Hunter. BA, La. State U., 1945; MA, U. Wis., 1946; PhD, Tulane U., 1954; LLD, Hendrix Coll., 1965. Instr. history U. Miami, Fla., 1946-49; grad. fellow Tulane U., 1949-54; asst. prof., asso. prof., then prof. history Ark. A. and M. Coll., Monticello, 1954-60, acad. dean, 1960-62, pres., 1962-71; chancellor U. Ark. at Monticello, 1971-77, prof. history, 1977-92, chancellor, prof. emeritus, 1992—. Ford fellow, 1951-52 Mem. Am. Hist. Assn., Ark. Hist. Assn., Ark. Farm Bur. Fedn., Drew County Hist. Soc., Kappa Sigma, Phi Alpha Theta, Pi Sigma Alpha. Democrat. Methodist. Home: 135 Ross Ave Monticello AR 71655-4249

BABIN, STEVEN MICHAEL, atmospheric scientist, researcher; b. Lawton, Okla., Sept. 6, 1954; s. Cleveland Victor Jr. and Delys Lilian (Lowry) B.; m. Pamela Gail Nee, June 23, 1990; 1 child, Heather Rebecca. BS in Engring. Physics spl. distinction, U. Okla., 1976; MD, U. Okla., Oklahoma City, 1980; MSEE, U. Pa., 1983; MS in Meteorology, U. Md., 1994, PhD in Meteorology, 1996. Diplomate Am. Bd. Med. Examiners. Assoc. instr. pathology and lab. medicine U. Pa. Hosp., Phila., 1980-82; sr. engr. Applied Physics Lab. Johns Hopkins U., Laurel, Md., 1983—. Presenter in field. Contbr. articles to profl. jours. Engring. scholar Frontiers Sci. Found., 1972, Spl. scholar Nat. Merit Found., 1972. Mem. IEEE (sr.), Am. Meteorol. Soc., Am. Geophysics Union (life), Am. Mensa (life), Union Radio-Sci. Internat., Sigma Xi, Tau Beta Pi, Alpha Epsilon Delta, Phi Eta Sigma. Achievements include discovery of hurricane effects on open ocean phytoplankton blooms; investigation of meteorological effects on microwave propagation in the marine boundary layer; design and development of data acquisition and analysis software in use on helicopters, rocketsondes, buoys, etc.; development of optical waveguide pH sensor; design and creation of working proportional counter for exo-electron research. Office: Johns Hopkins U Applied Physics Lab Johns Hopkins Rd Laurel MD 20723-6099

BABITZKE, THERESA ANGELINE, health facility administrator; b. Madison, Ill., Dec. 19, 1925; d. Victor Joseph and Angela (Ziolkowski) Sobolewski; m. Douglas Christ Babitzke, May 2, 1953; children: Charlotte, Mary Ann, Rose Marie, Helen. Student, Quincy Coll., 1943; diploma, St. John's Sch. Nursing Edn., Springfield, Ill., 1949; student, U. Ill., Chgo., 1970; BA, St. Francis Coll., 1973; MA in Gerontology summa cum laude, Sangamon State U., 1982. Co-founder, admin. dir. Mayslake Village, Oakbrook, Ill., 1962, St. Paschal's Infirmary, Oakbrook, 1962; night supr. Godair Home, Hinsdale, Ill., 1958-72; DON King Bruwaert House, Hinsdale, 1973-76; head nurse Mt. Sinai Hosp., Chgo., 1976-82; DON Rosary Hill Home, Justice, Ill., 1989—. Election judge Rep. Com. DuPage County, 1953-98, 2003; mem. adv. bd. Gower Grade Sch., 1973-76; mem. adv. com. Burr Ridge Marriot Brighton Gardens Assisted Living, 1996—. Named Ill. Nurse of Yr. of the Midwest, 1981, Catholic Woman of Yr. 1962, St. Mary's Ch., Joliet, Ill. Mem. Downers Grove and Suburban Nurses Club (pres. Downers Grove chpt.), U. of Ill. Gerontology, Forty and Eight, Premier Nurse Ill., Am. Legion Aux., Sigma Phi Omega (Eta chpt. U. Ill.). Roman Catholic. Avocations: travel, bicycling, doll collecting, reading.

BABIUK, LORNE ALAN, virologist, immunologist, researcher; b. Canora, Sask., Can., Jan. 25, 1946; s. Paul and Mary (Mayden) Babiuk; m. Betty Lou Carol Wagar, Sept. 29, 1973; children: Shawn, Kimberley. BSA, U. Sask., Saskatoon, 1967, MSc, 1969, DSc, 1987; PhD, U. B.C., Vancouver, 1972. Postdoctoral fellow U. Toronto, Ont., Can., 1972-73; asst. prof. We. Coll. Vet. Medicine, Saskatoon, Sask., 1973-75, assoc. prof., 1975-79, prof., 1979—; assoc. dir. rsch. Vet. Infectious Disease Orgn., Saskatoon, 1984-93, dir., 1993—. Cons. Molecular Genetics, Mpls., 1980—84, Genentech, San Francisco, 1981—84, Ciba Geigy, Basel, Switzerland, 1984—91; Can. rsch. chair in vaccinology. Contbr. chapters to books, articles to profl. jours. Recipient award, Can. Soc. Microbiology, 1990, Am. Vet. Immunology, 1992, Xerox-Can. Forum, 1993, Emerging Sci. and Tech. award for innovation, 1995, Pfizer award in animal health, 1998, Nat. Merit award, 1998, Bill Snowden Meml. award, 2000, Saskatchewan Order of Merit, 2004, Saskatchewan Centennial medal, 2005. Fellow: Royal Soc. Can., Infectious Disease Soc. Am. (Can. Rsch. chair in vaccinology 2001); mem.: Internat. Soc. Antiviral Rsch., Soc. Gen. Microbiology, Can. Soc. Microbiology, Am. Soc. Virology, Am. Soc. Microbiology, Internat. Soc. Interferon Rsch. Achievements include 22 patents in field. Home: 245 East Pl Saskatoon SK Canada S7J 2Y1 Office: Vaccine & Infectious Disease Orgn Univ Saskatchewan 120 Veterinary Rd Saskatoon SK S7N 5E3 Canada S7N 5E3 Office Phone: 306-966-7465. Business E-Mail: babiuk@sask.usask.ca.

BABLER, WAYNE E., lawyer, retired utilities executive; b. Orangeville, Ill., Dec. 8, 1915; s. Oscar E. and Mary (Bender) B.; m. Mary Blome, Dec. 27, 1940; children: Wayne Elroy Jr., Marilyn Anne Monson, Sally Jane Sperry. BA, Ind. Cen. Coll., 1935; JD, U. Mich., 1938; LLD, Ind. Cen. U., 1966. Bar: Mich. 1938, N.Y. 1949, Mo. 1955, Wis. 1963, U.S. Supreme Ct. 1963. Assoc. Bishop & Bishop, Detroit, 1938-42, ptnr., 1945-48; atty. AT&T, 1948-55; gen. solicitor Southwestern Bell Tel. Co., St. Louis, 1955-63, v.p., gen. counsel, sec., 1965-80, ret., 1980; v.p., gen. counsel Wis. Tel. Co., Milw., 1963-65. Bd. dirs., chmn. St. Louis Soc. Crippled Children; bd. dirs. St. Louis Symphony Soc. Mem. ABA (chmn. pub. utility sect. 1978-79), Fed. Comms. Bar Assn., Mo. Bar. Assn. Home: Apt 345 1 McKnight Pl Saint Louis MO 63124-1985

BABLER, WAYNE E., JR., lawyer; b. Detroit, Apr. 29, 1942; s. Wayne E. and Mary E. (Blome) B.; m. Patricia A. Ward, Feb. 5, 1972; children: Dean W., Anne E. BA, Wittenberg U., 1964; JD, U. Wis., 1967. Bar: Wis. 1967, U.S. Ct. Appeals (7th cir.) 1971, U.S. Supreme Ct. 1980, U.S. Dist. Ct. (ea. and we. dists.) Wis., 1967, U.S. Dist. Ct. (ctrl. and no. dists.) Ill. 1987, U.S. Dist. Ct. (ea. and we. dists.) Mich. 1990; U.S. Ct. Appeals (9th and 10th cirs.) 1981, U.S. Ct. Appeals (D.C. cir.), 1983. Assoc. Quarles, Herriott, Clemons, Teschner & Noelke, Milw., 1971-74, Quarles & Brady, Milw., 1974-76, ptnr., 1976—. Rep. of chief justice Wis. Supreme Ct. to Wis. Jud. Compensation Com., 1983—84. Author: (with others) Business and Commercial Litigation in Federal Court, 1998; Rsch. editor Wis. Law Rev., 1966-67, Antitrust, Federal Civil Litigation, State Civil Litigation. Mem. U. Wis. Benchers Soc.; campaign cabinet United Performing Arts Fund, Inc., Milw., 1977-78; bd. dirs. Milw. Bar Found., 1976-79, treas., 1977-78; bd. dirs. Wis. Bar Found., 1983-2000, pres., 1985-87; bd. dirs. Legal Aid Soc. Milw., 1997—. With JAGC, USN, 1967-71. Fellow: Wis. Law Found., Am. Coll. Trial Lawyers (state chair 2002—04), Am. Bar Found.; mem.: ABA (ho. of dels. 1984—96), Bar Assn. 7th Fed. Cir., State Bar Wis. (bd. govs. 1983—87), Milw. Bar Assn. (bd. dirs. 1976—83, pres. 1981—82), Tripoli Country Club, Univ. Club, Order of Coif. Home: 1475 E Fairy Chasm Rd Milwaukee WI 53217-1433 Office: Quarles & Brady 411 E Wisconsin Ave Milwaukee WI 53202-4497 Office Phone: 414-277-5529. Business E-Mail: web@quarles.com.

BABLIN, MARK EDWARD, security administrator, mortgage consultant; b. Amsterdam, N.Y., Oct. 30, 1949; s. Edward and Diane B.; m. Mediatrix Ferrer, Aug. 8, 1983 (div. May 1989); children: Francis, Michael, Alex. BS, Siena Coll., 1971; student, Albany State U., 1972. Real estate mgr. Kasow Estates, Phila., 1972-76; credit mgr. Pub. Fin. and Assoc. Fin., Montclair, N.J., 1976-84; security cons. Arboc Security, Reading, Pa., 1984-87; with chem. sales dept. HyTest Industry, Springfield, N.J., 1988-90; dir. corp. security Benjamin Moore/Ingersoll Rand, Woodcliff Lake, N.J., 1990—; mortgage sales cons. Mercury Mortgage, Fairfield, N.J., 1998—; corp. security dir. N.Y. Life Investment, Parsippany, NJ, 2005—. Mem. N.J. Rep. State Com., Trenton, 1988—. Mem. N.J. Rep. Heritage Coun. (nat. vice chair 2000-, Ethnic Leader of Yr. 1989). Roman Catholic. Avocations: photography, travel, history, sports, literature. Home: 53 Linden St Millburn NJ 07041-2132 Office: 169 Luckawanna Ave Parsippany NJ 07054

BABLITCH, WILLIAM A., lawyer, retired state supreme court justice; b. Stevens Point, Wis., Mar. 1, 1941; BS, U. Wis., Madison, 1963, JD, 1968; MA, U. of Virginia, 1987. Bar: Wis. 1968. Pvt. practice law, Stevens Point, Wis.; dist. atty. Portage County, Wis., 1969-72; mem. Wis. Senate, 1972-85, senate majority leader, 1976-82; justice Wis. Supreme Ct., Madison, 1983—2003; atty. Michael Best & Friedrich, Madison, 2003—. Volunteer US Peace Corp., Liberia, 1963—65. Mem.: Nat. Conf. State Legislators (exec. com. 1979). Office: Michael Best & Friedrich One S Pinckney St Ste 700 Madison WI 53703 Office Phone: 608-283-0100. Office Fax: 608-283-2275. E-mail: wabablitch@michaelbest.com.

BABROWSKI, CLAIRE HARBECK, retail executive; b. Ottawa, Ill., July 25, 1957; d. John Clayton Harbeck and Corrine Ann (Lavender) French; m. David Lee Babrowski, July 3, 1982; 2 stepdaughters. Student, U. Ill., 1975-77; MBA, U. N.C., 1995. Dental asst., Ottawa, 1975-76; crew person McDonald's Corp., Ottawa, 1974-76, mem. restaurant mgmt. Champaign, Ill., 1976-80, ops. and tng. cons. St. Louis, 1980-84, ops. mgr., 1984-86, dir. nat. ops. Oak Brook, Ill., 1986-88, dir. ops. Phila., 1988-89, sr. regional mgr. Raleigh, NC, 1989—92, regional v.p., 1992—95, corp. v.p. ops., 1995—97, sr. v.p. ops., 1997—98, exec. v.p. U.S. Restaurant Sys., 1998—99, exec. v.p. Worldwide Restaurant Sys., 1999—2001, pres. McDonald's Asia/Pacific/the Middle East and Africa, 2001—03, chief restaurant ops. officer, 2003—04; exec. v.p., COO RadioShack Corp., Fort Worth, Tex., 2005—. Chmn. N.C. Ronald McDonald's Children's Charities, Raleigh, 1989-95; relationship ptnr. Donatos Pizza, Pret A Manger, Chipotle Mexican Grill, chmn. bd. dirs. Author: (manual) Training Consultants Development Program, 1987. Mem. N.C. Restaurant Assn. (bd. dirs. 1992-95). Republican. Roman Catholic. Avocations: tennis, gardening. Office: 300 RadioShack Cir Fort Worth TX 76102 Office Phone: 817-415-3011. Office Fax: 817-415-2647.*

BABSKY, ANDRIY M., biologist, researcher; b. Sokal, Ukraine, Mar. 18, 1957; arrived in U.S., 1995; s. Myroslav M. Babsky and Hanna A. Babska; m. Uliana Babska; children: Yaromyr, Ostap. BS, Lviv State U., Lviv, Ukraine, 1979, PhD, 1985. Rschr. Inst. of Biol. Physics, Pushcino, Russia, 1983—86; rschr., head of the lab. Lviv State U., Lviv, Ukraine, 1986—95; vice-dean Lviv State U., Sch. of Biology, Lviv, Ukraine, 1994—95; post-doctoral rschr. U. Pa., Biochemistry/Biophysics, Phila., 1995—2001; rsch. assoc. Ind. U., Radiology, Indpls., 2002—. Lectr. Lviv State U., Lviv, Ukraine, 1990—95.

Editor: (editing) The Galician Herald; contbr. scientific papers over 130 pub. worldwide to profl. jour. Recipient Diploma for Winner of the All-Ukrainian Competition for Bachelor's Projects, 1979. Mem.: Ukrainian Physiol. Soc., Internat. Soc. for Magnetic Resonance in Medicine. Achievements include patents for #MBL 00769036 Succinic Acid as an Adrenomimetic Compound (Ukraine). Avocations: bicycling, soccer, sports, painting, photography. Office: Ind Univ 950 W Walnut St R2 E124 Indianapolis IN 04602 Office Phone: 317-278-9681. Business E-Mail: ababsky@iupui.edu.

BABSON, IRVING K., publishing company executive; b. Tel Aviv, Apr. 15, 1936; came to U.S., 1940; s. Matthew and Miriam B.; m. Laurie Sher; children: Stacey B., Mia L., Christopher. BBA, CCNY, 1957; postgrad. NATD seminars, Harvard U., 1965. Dir. Tribune/Fox Cos., 1987-90; chmn. BMT Publs., Inc., Tulsa, 1989-91, Convenience Store News, U.S. Distbn. Jour., Gaming Bus. Mag., Smokeshop Mag., N.Y.C., Jour. Petroleum Mktg., N.Y.C.; mng. ptnr. Babson Capital Ventures, J.V., 1995—, Holdsworth Investments Inc., Belize, 1995—. Ptnr. Mag. Devel. Fund, Babson Family Investment, J.V., N.Y.C., Babson Capital, 1988. With AUS, 1956-57. Mem. Nat. Assn. Corp. Dirs. Clubs: Friars. Home: 19707 Turnberry Way Aventura FL 33180-2566

BABSON, JANE FRANCES, artist, writer; b. Leitchfield, Ky., Aug. 17, 1925; d. William Winstead McCall and Matilda Caroline Hahn; m. David Frederick Babson, Aug. 7, 1954; children: David Winstead, Leila Jane. BA, Mt. Holyoke Coll., 1947; MFA in Art and Art History, U. Ill., 1949. Registrar The Corcoran Gallery of Art, Washington, 1952—54, curator of prints, 1953—54. Author: The Epsteins: A Family Album, 1984, The Search for the Indian, 2001, 3 children's books; contbr. woodcut prints to collection of Nat. Air and Space Mus. Founder Stamford (Conn.) Art Assn., 1970. Named hon. citizen, City of Wakayama, Japan, 1984. Mem.: Nat. Trust for Historic Preservation, Am. Crafts Coun., Soc. Archtl. Historians, Greater N.Y. Ind. Pubs. Assn. (bd. dirs. 2002—). Avocations: swimming, travel, clothing design. Home and Office: The Winstead Press Ltd 202 Slice Dr Stamford CT 06907 Office Phone: 203-322-4941. Office Fax: 203-629-2545. Personal E-mail: winstead.press@verizon.net.

BABUL, NAJIB, pharmaceutical executive; BSc in Pharm., U. BC, 1987; PharmD, SUNY, 1987. Dir., clin. rsch. Purdue Pharma, Toronto, Canada, 1989—97; v.p., global clin. drug devel. & therapeutic leader, analgesia & rheumatology Scirex Corp., Phil., 1997—2000; ceo TheraQuest Bioscis., Phil., 2001—. Author clincal drug development 100 peer rev. sci. pubs. accute and chronic pain Neurology, Pain, Cancer, Lancet, Anesthesiology, Clinical Pharmacology & Therapeutics & Journal of Rheumatology. Mem. Met. Toronto Epilepsy Assn., 1985—87. Fellow Med. Rsch. Coun. Can.; scholar, Columbia Coll., 1997-98; Dr. Pernarowski Meml. Scholarship pharm. chemistry, U. BC, 1980. Mem.: Am. Assn. Pharm. Scientists, Osteoarthritis Rsch. Soc. Internat., Internat. Assn. Study of Pain, Internat. Anesthesia Rsch. Soc., Am. Soc. Clin. Pharmacology and Therapeutics, Am. Coll. Clin. Pharmacology, Am. Acad. Neurology, Am. Coll. Rheumatology, Ea. Pain Assn., Am. Pain Soc. Achievements include first group to demonstrate the efficacy of opioids in neuropathic pain; first to demonstrate the efficacy of narcotics in osteoarthritis using contemprorary research methodology; first to characterize the pharmacokinetics of the opioid, hydromorphone, in children and the accumulation of its principal metabolite in renal failure; first to demonstrate the route specificity of oral and rectal morphine pharmacokinetics in healthy subjects and cancer patients; first to demonstrate the clinical equivalence of rectal and subcutaneous morphine in patients with cancer pain; first to first to demonstrate the efficacy of oral opioids in children with pain of sickle cell crisis; patents pending for methods of treating pain and compositions. Office Phone: 610-272-2071.

BABULA, WILLIAM, university dean; b. Stamford, Conn., May 19, 1943; s. Benny F. and Lottie (Zajkowski) B.; m. Karen L. Gemi, June 19, 1965; children: Jared, Joelle. BA, Rutgers U., 1965; MA, U. Calif., Berkeley, 1967, PhD, 1969. Asst. prof. English U. Miami, Coral Gables, Fla., 1969-75, assoc. prof., 1975-77, prof., 1977-81, chmn. dept. Eng., 1976-81; dean of arts and humanities Sonoma State U., Rohnert Park, Calif., 1981—. Author: Shakespeare and the Tragicomic Archetype, 1975, Shakespeare in Production, 1935-79, 1981; (short stories) Motorcycle, 1982, Quarterback Sneak, 1983, The First Edsel, 1983, Ransom, 1983, The Last Jogger in Virginia, 1983, The Orthodontist and the Rock Star, 1984, Greenearth, 1984, Football and Other Seasons, The Great American Basketball Shoot, 1984, Ms. Skywriter, Inc., 1987; (plays) The Fragging of Lt. Jones (1st prize Gualala Arts Competition, 1983), Creatures (1st prize Jacksonville U. competition 1987), The Winter of Mrs. Levy (Odyssey Stage Co., New Play Series 1988), Nat. Playwright's Showcase, 1988, Theatre Americana, 1990 (James Ellis award), Basketball Jones, Black Rep of Berkeley, 1988, West Coast Ensemble, Festival of One Acts, 1992, Mark Twain Masquers, 9th Ann. Festival One Act Plays, 1994 (2d Place award), The Last Roundup, 1991 (Odyssey Stage Co.); (novels) The Bombing of Berkeley and Other Pranks (1st prize 24th Ann. Deep South Writers' Conf. 1984), St. John's Baptism, 1988, According to St. John, 1989, St. John and the Seven Veils, 1991, St. John's Bestiary, 1994, St. John's Bread, 1999; contbr. articles to profl. pubs. and short stories to lit. mags. Mem. Shakespeare Assn. of Am., Dramatists Guild, Assoc. Writing Programs, Mystery Writers Am., Phi Beta Kappa. Office: Sonoma State U Sch Arts and Humanities Rohnert Park CA 94928 Business E-Mail: william.babula@sonoma.edu.

BACA, JIM, mayor; BSBA, U. N.Mex. Mayor City of Albuquerque, 1997—. Former dir. alcohol and beverage control State of N.Mex., press sec. to gov., commr. pub. lands; past asst. to mayor, gen. mgr. Rio Grande Conservancy Dist.; former dir. Fed. Bur. Land Mgmt.; nat. cons. pub. land and conservation issues. Served with USAF.*

BACA, JOE, congressman; b. NM, Jan. 23, 1947; m. Barbara Baca; children: Joe Jr., Jeremy, Natalie, Jennifer. BS in Sociology, Calif. State U., L.A., 1971. Ptnr. Interstate World Travel, San Bernardino, Calif.; formerly with cmty. rels. divsn. GTE; spkr. pro tempore Calif. State Assembly, Sacramento, 1992-97, asst. spkr. pro tempore, spkr.'s fed. govt. liaison, mem. rules com., 1997-98; mem. rules com., vet. affairs com., pub. employment and ret. com., energy, utilities and comm. com., local govt. com., govtl. orgn. com. Calif. State Senate, 1998-99; mem. U.S. Congress from 42nd Calif. Dist., Washington, 1999—; mem. agriculture and sci. coms. U.S. Ho. Reps. Trustee San Bernardino Valley Coll. Dist., 1979—. With U.S. Army, 1966-68, Vietnam. Named Citizen of Distinction San Bernardino Area LWV, Kiwanian of Yr. Greater San Bernardino Kiwanis Club, Disting. Citizen Inland Empire Dist. Boy Scouts Am., Outstanding Legislator Calif. Rifle and Pistol Assn., VFW, 1994-95, Legislator of Yr. Am. Legion, Dept. Calif.; recipient Minority Male of Yr. award Greater Riverside Area Urban League. Democrat. Office: US Ho Reps 328 Cannon Ho Office Bldg Washington DC 20515-0543 also: 201 N E St Ste 102 San Bernardino CA 92401-1520*

BACA, JOSEPH FRANCIS, retired judge; b. Albuquerque, Oct. 1, 1936; s. Amado and Inez (Pino) Baca; m. Dorothy Lee Burrow, June 28, 1969; children: Jolynn, Andrea, Anna Marie. BA in Edn., U. N.Mex., 1960; JD, George Washington U., 1964; LLM, U. Va., 1992. Asst. dist. atty. 1st Jud. Dist., Santa Fe, 1965-66; pvt. practice Albuquerque, 1966-72; dist. judge 2d Jud. Dist., Albuquerque, 1972-88; justice N.Mex Supreme Ct., Santa Fe, 1989—2002, chief justice, 1995-97; ret., 2002. Spl. asst. to atty. gen. Office of N.Mex Atty. Gen., Albuquerque, 1966—71. Bd. dirs. State Justice Inst., 1994—, vice chmn., 1999—; Dem. precinct chmn. Albuquerque, 1968; del. N.Mex Constl. Conv., Santa Fe, 1969. Named one of 100 Most Influential Hispanics, Hispanic Bus. Mag., 1997, 1998; recipient Judge of the Yr. award, People's Commn. Criminal Justice, 1989, Quincentennial Commemoration Achievement award, La Hispanidad Com., 1992, Luchando pro la Justicia award, Mex. Am. Law Students Assn. U. N.Mex Law Sch., 1993, J. William Fulbright Disting. Pub. Svc. award, George Washington U. Alumni Assn., 1994, Recognition and Achievement award, Commn. Opportunities for Minorities in the Profession, 1992, others. Mem.: ABA, N.Mex Hispanic Bar Assn. (Outstanding Hispanic Atty. award 2000), Santa Fe Bar Assn., Albuquerque Bar Assn., Am. Jud. Soc. (bd. dirs. 1999—), Scribes (bd. dirs. 1998—), Am. Law Inst., N.Mex Bar Assn. (Outstanding Jud. Svc. award 1998, Disting. Jud. Svc. award 2002), Hispanic Nat. Bar Assn. (Lincoln-Juarez award 2000), Alumni Assn. (pres. 1980—81), KC, Kiwanis (pres. Albuquerque chpt. 1984—85, dep. grand knight 1968). Roman Catholic. Avocation: reading history. Office Phone: 505-821-6881. E-mail: jbaca01@msn.com.

BACA, SHERRY ANN, secondary school educator; b. Huron, S.D., Jan. 11, 1950; d. Myron Marion Moberg and Emily Ann (Matkovich) Baxter; m. Ed R. Baca, Oct. 14, 1972; children: Jamie Marie, Jennifer Lea. BS in Edn., No. Ariz. U., 1971, MAT in Math., 1972. Cert. secondary sch. math. tchr., secondary sch. prin., supr. Tchr. math. Prescott Jr. High, Ariz., 1972—75; adj. tchr. math. Yavapai Coll., Prescott, 1975—84; tchr. math. grades 7-9, dept. chmn. Granite Mt. Jr. High, Prescott, 1976—88; math. coord. Prescott Unified Schs., 1979—; tchr. math. grades 9-12 Prescott H.S., 1988—. Adj. math. instr. Prescott Coll., 1980—, No. Ariz. U., 1988—; dir. math. sci. N. Ctrl. Ariz. Consortium, 1992—; presenter and lectr. at many ednl. workshops and confs.; mem. Math. Scis. Edn. Bd., Washington, 1997-2000. Editor (monthly sci./math. newsletter) Prescott Unified Schs., 1979—; contbr. articles to profl. pubs. Recipient Quality Edn. Program award, Ariz. Dept. Edn., 1981, Gov.'s citation for excellence in math. tchg., 1984, Presdl. award for excellence in math. tchg., 1984, Disting. Alumni award No. Ariz. U., 1989, State Farm Good Neighbor award, 1992, Outstanding Women in Edn. award, Delta Kappa Gamma, 1992, 93, Toyota's Investment in Math. Excellence award, 1997; featured in mags. and on TV; named U.S. West Tchr. of Yr. for Ariz., 1993; recipient Tandy Tech. Scholar award for excellence in math. tchg., 1995; runner up Yavapai County H.S. Tchr. Yr., 2003 Mem. Nat. Coun. Tchrs. of Math., Nat. Coun. Suprs. of Math., Coun. Presdl. Awardees in Math. (co-historian 1989—), Ariz. Assn. Tchrs. of Math. (sec. 1984-87, v.p. 1989-91, newsletter editor 1991-95, 99—, pres. 1995-97), Ariz. Sci. Tchrs. Assn., Ariz. Alliance for Math. Sci. and Tech. Edn. (bd. dirs. 1986-88, adv. bd. 1988—, continued svc. award 1991), Ariz. Math. Coalition (adv. bd. 1990—), Ariz. Math. Network (regional dir. 1989-91), Sch. Sci. and Math. Assn., Phi Delta Kappa (many offices), Alpha Delta Kappa Avocations: clog dancing, piano. Office: Prescott High Sch 1050 Ruth St Prescott AZ 86301-1790 E-mail: sherry.baca@prescottschools.com.

BACA, STACEY, newscaster; married. BA in Broadcast News, U. Colo., Boulder, 1991. Staff writer Brighton Std.-Blade, Colo., 1991—92, Denver Post, 1992—96; anchor weekend am news WTKR-TV, Norfolk, Va., 1996—98, KNSD-TV, San Diego, 1999—2002, reporter, 1999—2002; co-anchor Sunday Morning News and reporter WLS-TV, Chgo., 2002—. Mem.: Nat. Assn. of Hispanic Journalists. Office: WLS-TV 190 N State St Chicago IL 60601

BACALL, LAUREN (BETTY JOAN PERSKE), actress; b. NYC, Sept. 16, 1924; m. Humphrey Bogart, May 21, 1945 (dec. 1957); children: Stephen, Leslie; m. Jason Robards, July, 1961 (div.); 1 son, Sam. Student pub. schs., Am. Acad. Dramatic Art. Actress in Broadway plays Franklin Street, 1942, Goodbye Charlie, 1959; motion picture actress, 1944—, film appearances include To Have and Have Not, 1944, Confidential Agent, 1945, The Big Sleep, 1946, Dark Passage, 1947, Key Largo, 1948, Young Man With a Horn, 1949, Bright Leaf, 1950, How To Marry a Millionaire, 1953, Woman's World, 1954, The Cobweb, 1955, Blood Alley, 1955, Written on the Wind, 1956, Designing Woman, 1957, The Gift of Love, 1958, Flame Over India, 1959, Shock Treatment, 1964, Sex and the Single Girl, 1965, Harper, 1966, Murder on the Orient Express, 1974, The Shootist, 1976, Health, 1980, The Fan, 1981, Tree of Hands, 1987, Appointment With Death, 1987, Mr. North, 1988, Misery, 1990, A Star for Two, 1991, All I Want for Christmas, 1991, Ready to Wear (Prêt-à-Porter), 1994, My Fellow Americans, 1996, The Mirror Has Two Faces, 1996 (Golden Globe award, 1997, SAG award, 1997), The Line King: Al Hirschfield, 1996, Le Jour et la Nuit, 1997, Diamonds, 1999, Dogville, 2003, The Limit, 2003, Birth, 2004, (voice) Howl's Moving Castle, 2004; appeared in Broadway play Cactus Flower, 1966-68, Applause, 1969-71 (Sarah Siddons award 1975); also road co., 1971-72, London co., 1972-73 (Tony award for best actress in a musical 1970); Broadway play Woman of the Year, 1981 (Tony award for best actress in a musical 1981, Sarah Siddons award 1983), Sweet Bird of Youth, 1983 (London, 1985, Australia, 1986, L.A., 1987; TV spl. The Paris Collections, 1968, Applause, 1973, A Commercial Break (Happy Endings), 1975; TV movies: Perfect Gentlemen, 1978, Dinner at Eight, 1989, The Portrait, 1992, A Foreign Field, 1993, From the Mixed Up Files of Mrs. Basil E. Frankweiler, 1995, Too Rich: The Secret Life of Doris Duke, 1999; author: Lauren Bacall: By Myself, 1978, Now, 1994, By Myself and Then Some, 2005; guest appearances include: "What's My Line?", 1953 & 1965, The Rockford Files, 1979, Chicago Hope, 1998, "So Graham Norton", 2000; (voice): (TV)The Man Who Had Everything, 1998, Madeline: Lost in Paris, 1999. Recipient Am. Acad. Dramatic Arts award for achievement, 1963, Standard award London Evening, 1973, Nat. Book award, 1980; decorated comdr. Order of Arts and Letters (France), 1995; named 50 Most Beautiful People in the World, People, 1997. Office: care Johnnie Planco William Morris Agy 1325 Avenue of the Americas New York NY 10019-6026

BACANI, NICANOR-GUGLIELMO VILA, civil and structural engineer, consultant; b. Dagupan City, Pangasinan, Philippines, Jan. 10, 1947; s. Jose Montero and Felisa (Vila) B.; m. Julie Bacani, June 24, 1972; children: Julinor, Jazmin, Joymita, Normina, Nicky, Noel. BSCE, U. Philippines, 1968, M in Engring. Stuctures, 1973. Registered profl. engr., Philippines. Structural engr. FR Estuar, PhD. Assocs., Quezon City, Philippines, 1970-72; civil structural engr. BestPhil Cons., Dagupan City, 1972-73; engring. mgr. Supreme Structural Products, Inc., Manila, 1974; chief engr. Tecphil Cons., Quezon City, 1974-76; v.p. Erectors, Inc., Makati, Philippines, 1977-81; pres. NGV Bacani & Assocs., various locations, 1981—. Advisor, cons. Met. Manila Office of Commr. Planning, 1980-85; profl. lectr. U. Manila Grad. Sch., 1982-83; resource person Nat. Engring. Ctr. U.P., Quezon City, 1983—; cons. Geo. J. Fosdyke Assocs., L.A., 1985-86, Victor Constrn. & Devel., 1986-87, Stanley Assocs. Internat., 1988, H.A. Simons Internat., 1988-90, Azlon Devel. Corp., 1990—; pres. Mgmt. Design & Investment Co., 1987—; sr. structural cons. Seismic Engring. Ltd., 1990—; sr. cons. Davey Gibson Cons., 1991-92; pres. Bestphil Can., 1992—, Seismic Cons., 1993—; cons. Chemetics Internat., 1994—; sr. cons. Sturdy Engring. Corp., Wash., 1997—; pres. Bestphil Enterprises Internat., 2000—. Author: A Reference for Engineers and Builders, 1983. Mem. Internat. Assn. Bridge and Structural Engrs. Switzerland, Assn. Structural Engrs. Philippines (life, bd. dirs. 4 terms), U. Philippines Alumni Engrs. Assn. (life), Nat. Geog. Soc., Nature Conservancy. Avocations: guitar playing, choir, dance. Home: 1119 Chase Park Dr Bacliff TX 77518-2486

BACARELLA, FLAVIA, artist, educator; b. Bklyn. d. Salvatore John and Angeline Mary B. MA, New Sch. for Social Rsch., N.Y.C., 1975; MFA, Bklyn. Coll./CUNY, 1983; student, N.Y. Studio Sch., 1980. Asst. prof. Herbert H. Lehman Coll., Bronx, 1995—. Grantee N.Y. Found. Arts, 1986. Mem. Coll. Art Assn. Office: Herbert H Lehman Coll Bedford Park Blvd W Bronx NY 10468 Office Phone: 718-960-8259. Business E-Mail: flavia.bacarella@lehman.cuny.edu.

BACAS, ANDREW R., data processing executive; BA, Yale U.; MS, NYU; MBA, Wharton Sch. V.p. Simmons & Co. Internat.; vice chmn., CEO ImageMAX Inc., Fort Washington, Pa.; with Key Prin. Ptnrs., San Francsico. Vis. faculty Assn. Corp. Growth. Former flight officer USN. Office: Key Prin Ptnrs LLC Three Embarcadero Ctr Suite 2900 San Francisco CA 94111 Office Phone: 415-733-2494. Office Fax: 415-733-2466. E-mail: abacas@kppinvest.com.*

BACCIGALUPPI, ROGER JOHN, agricultural products executive; b. N.Y.C., Mar. 17, 1934; s. Harry and Ethel (Hutcheon) B.; m. Patricia Marie Wier, Feb. 6, 1960 (div. 1978); children: John, Elisabeth, Andrea; m. Iris Christine Walfridson, Feb. 3, 1979; 1 child, Jason. BS, U. Calif., Berkeley, 1956; MS, Columbia U., 1957. Asst. sales promotion mgr. Maco Mag. Corp., N.Y.C., 1956-57; merchandising asst. Honig, Cooper & Harrington, San Francisco and L.A., 1957-58, 1958-60, asst. dir. merchandising, 1960-61; sales rep. Blue Diamond Growers (formerly Calif. Almond Growers Exch.), Sacramento, 1961-64, mgr. advt. and sales promotion, 1964-70, v.p. mktg., 1970-73, sr. v.p. mktg., 1973-74, exec. v.p., 1974-75, pres., 1975-91; founder RB Internat., Sacramento, 1992—. Vice chmn., bd. dirs. Agrl. Coun. Calif., 1975-91; mem. consumer-prodr. com., adminstrn. com.; mem. U.S. adv. com. Trade Policy and Negotiations, 1983-2002; mem. U.S. adv. bd. Rabobank Nederlands, 1988-91; mem. Calif. World Trade Commn., 1993-2001; mem. adv. coun. Nat. Ctr. for Food and Agr. Policy Resources for Future, 1990-99. Vice chmn. Calif. State R.R. Mus. Found.; chmn. Cmty. Colls. Found.; vice chmn. Grad. Inst. Cooperative Leadership, 1986-87, chair, 1987-89; bd. dirs. Valley Vision, Inc., 1995-2003. With AUS, 1957. Mem. Calif. C. of C. (chmn. internat. trade com. 1988-94, bd. dirs. 1988—, vice chmn. bd. 1992-94, chmn. bd. 1995, Sacramento Host Com. (chmn. 1997, 98), Calif. for Higher Edn., Grad. Inst. Coop. Leadership (chmn., trustee), Grocery Mfrs. Am., Inc. (bd. dirs. 1988-91), Sutter Club. Office: RB Internat 777 Campus Commons Rd Ste 200 Sacramento CA 95825-8343

BACCUS, R. EILEEN TURNER, academic administrator; b. Oxford, N.C., Aug. 8, 1944; d. Nathaniel Benjamin and Gloria Constance (Davis) Turner; B.A., Fisk U., 1964; M.B.A., U. Conn., 1975, Ph.D., 1978; 1 son, Christopher Lloyd. Programmer, systems analyst IBM, N.Y., Mo., 1964-66; substitute tchr., Lakenheath AFB, Eng., 1967-69; asst. dir. fin. aid U. Conn., Storrs, 1970-74, asst. to dean Sch. Edn., 1974-77, dir. personnel services div., 1977-81; adminstr. treasury ops. Aetna Life & Casualty Co., Hartford, Conn., 1981-82, ops. mgr. discretionary asset mgmt., 1982-86; pres. Thames Valley State Tech. Coll., Norwich, Conn., 1986-92; pres. Northwestern Conn. Community Tech. Coll., Winsted, 1992-2004, ret.; cons. Ford Found., 1976, Tchr. Corps, 1977, Meriden (Conn.) Schs., 1979—; dir. Conn. Savs. & Loan Assn. Mem. planning com. Conn. Legis. Black Caucus, 1980; mem. mgmt. team Ujima, Inc., Hartford, 1978-80; co-chmn. bd. Hartford Scholarship Found., 1971-75; treas. bd. Cmty. Coun. Capitol Region, 1982-86; mem. community adv. bd. Jr. League Hartford, Inc., 1982—84. Mem. Am. Ednl. Rsch. Assn., Internat. Platform Assn., Links, Inc., Rotary Internat., Phi Delta Kappa, Pi Lambda Theta, Delta Sigma Theta. Democrat. Episcopalian. Home: 87 Woodland Ave Bloomfield CT 06002-1806

BACEVICIUS, JOHN ANTHONY, V, (JOHN BACE), research executive; b. Chgo., Mar. 8, 1953; s. John Anthony IV and Mary Ann (Slazas) B.; m. Irene Joyce Rooney, Oct. 16, 1976; 1 child, John Anthony VI. BS in Psychology, Polit. Sci., Rockford Coll., 1975; MS in Journalism, Northwestern U., 1982; postgrad., Union Inst., John Marshall Law Sch. Accredited pub. rels. profl. Reporter, editor United Press Internat., Chgo., 1974-79; managing editor WCFL-AM, Mutual Broadcasting, Chgo., 1979-80; writer, editor WIND. Group W Westinghouse, Chgo., 1980-81; reporter, writer WBBM-AM, CBS News, Chgo., 1981-82; comms. advisor IBM Corp., Chgo., 1982—91; pres. J.A. Bace Comms., Inc., 1991—; dir. mktg., rsch. and industry rels. Technology Solutions Co., Chgo., 1995-97; v.p., dir. rsch. and knowledge assets Gartner, Inc., Chgo., 1997—. Asst. prof. Northwestern U., Evanston, Ill., 1988-92; mgr. media rels. Zenith Data Systems, 1992-93. Nat. Sea Explorer Boy Scouts Am. Com., Irving, Tex., 1986-95, recipient Quartermaster award, 1972, Silver Beaver award, 1990; Vigil honor, 1971. Gannett fellow, Northwestern U., 1981. Mem. NATAS, Pub. Rels. Soc. Am., Internat. Assn. Bus. Comms., U.S. Naval Inst., Publicity Club of Chgo., Soc. Profl. Journalists, Radio-TV News Dirs. Assn., U.S. Navy League (life). Roman Catholic. Avocations: backpacking, hiking, sailing, photography. Home: 252 W Washington Ave Lake Bluff IL 60044-2036 Office: Gartner Inc Sears Tower 233 S Wacker Dr Ste 1810 Chicago IL 60606 Office Phone: 312-612-6548. E-mail: john.bace@gartner.com.

BACH, CHARLES L., JR., lawyer; b. N.Y.C., Aug. 28, 1952; s. Charles L. and Carolyn Ann (Sidoti) B.; m. Robin Dolsky; children: Alison Rose, Christina Anne. BA magna cum laude, St. John's U., 1974; JD, Albany Law Sch., 1977. Bar: N.Y. 1978, U.S. Dist. Ct. (so. dist.) N.Y. 1978, (ea. dist.) N.Y. 1979, U.S. Ct. Appeals (2d cir.) 1979. Asst. dist. atty. Office of Dist. Atty., Bronx (N.Y.) County, 1977-81; assoc. Heidell, Pittoni & Moran, P.C., N.Y.C., 1981-85; ptnr. Heidell, Pittoni, Murphy & Bach, P.C., N.Y.C., 1985—. Mem. Def. Rsch. Inst., N.Y. County Lawyers Assn., N.Y. State Def. Lawyers Assn., Assn. for Hosp. Risk Mgmt. Roman Catholic. Office: Heidell Pittoni Murphy & Bach LLP 99 Park Ave Fl 7 New York NY 10016-1506 Office Phone: 212-286-8585. Business E-Mail: cbach@hpmb.com.

BACH, FRANCES CAMILLE, educational consultant; b. Duncan, Miss., July 8, 1950; d. Dong Jung Gong and Kwock Ying So; m. Charles Edward Bach, Feb. 18, 1989; children: Gary Dwayne Malec, Kevin Lee Malec. BME, Miss. U. Women, 1971; MS, Tex. A&M U., 1991. Substitute tchr. Johnstown Pub. Sch., Pa., 1978—85; music tchr. Jackson Pub. Schs., Miss., 1985—86; choir tchr. San Antonio Ind. Sch. Dist., 1986—92, fine arts adminstr., 1992—. Tex. fine arts cadre Tex. Edn. Agy. Fine Arts, Austin, 2000—. Recipient Salute to Quality in Edn., 1995. Mem.: ASCD, Tex. Art Educator Assn. (conf. co chair 2001—02, Outstanding Tex. Art Adminstr. 2002), Tex. Music Educators Conf. (mem. at large 2004—), Tex. Music Adminstr. Conf. (pres., v.p., sec 1996—2002, Tex. Music Adminstrs. Conf. 2005). Achievements include Ambassador to Germany with Mariachi group; By invitation only mariachi group in Guadalajara. Home: 14215 Woodlark San Antonio TX 78231 Office: San Antonio Ind Sch Dist 237 W Travis St San Antonio TX 78205 Office Phone: 210-354-9907. Office Fax: 210-227-3611. Personal E-mail: fcbach@swbell.net. E-mail: cbach@saisd.net.

BACH, JAN MORRIS, composer, educator; b. Forrest, Ill., Dec. 11, 1937; s. John Nicholas and Anne (Morris) B.; m. Dalia Zakaras; children: Dawn, Eva. MusB, U. Ill., 1959, MusM, 1961, MusD, 1971; postgrad., U. Va., Arlington, 1963-65, Yale U., summer 1960, Berkshire Music Ctr., summer 1961. Instr. music U. Tampa, Fla., 1965-66; prof. music No. Ill. U., DeKalb, 1966—2002, Presdl. Rsch. prof. Dekalb, 1982-86, Disting. Rsch. prof., 1986—; composer-in-residence Institut de Hautes Etudes Musicales, Montreux, Switzerland, 1976; editor for brass compositions M.M. Cole, Chgo., 1969-72. Mem. Ill. Arts Coun., 1986-89, Ind. Arts Coun., 1992. Composer: Skizzen, 1967, Woodwork, 1970, Eisteddfod, 1972, Turkish Music, 1968, Four Two-Bit Contraptions, 1971, The System, 1973, Dirge for a Minstrel, 1974, Three Choral Dances, 1975, Laudes, 1975, Piano Concerto, 1975, Three Bagatelles, 1978, Hair Today, 1978, The Happy Prince, 1978, My Wilderness, 1979, Student from Salamanca, 1979, Rounds and Dances, 1980, Horn Concerto, 1982, Helix, 1984, Escapade, 1984, Dompes & Jompes, 1986, Harp Concerto, 1986, Trumpet Concerto, 1987, A Solemn Music, 1987, Triptych, 1989, Euphonium Concerto, 1990, With Trumpet and Drum, 1991, Anachronisms String Quartet, 1991, People of Note, 1993, Concerto for Steelpan and Orchestra, 1994, The Last Flower, 1995, Foliations, 1995, Bassoon Concertino, 1996, Pilgrimage, 1997, Variations on a Theme of Brahms, 1997, Kimberly's Song, 1998, Dear God, 1998, NIU MIUSIC, 1999, In the Hands of the Tongue, 1999, The Duel, 1999, Songs of the Streetwise, 2000, Music for a Low Budget Epic, 2001, If Music be the Food of Love, 2001, Tuba Concerto, 2003, Choral Fanfare, 2003, The Haunted Palace, 2004, Penny Poems, 2004, A Prayer of Intercession, 2004, A Little Knight Music, 2005, (CDs) The Happy Prince, 1980, Laudes: The NY Brass Quintet, 1980, Rounds and Dances: Premieres, 1984, Four Two-Bit Contraptions: Is This the Way to Carnegie Hall?, 1986, Introducing the Bowie Brass Quintet, 1989, Skizzen: American Wind Music, 1990, Eisteddfod: Chamber Music for Flute, Harp, and Strings, 1990, Meridian Arts Ensemble, 1991, Heavy Metal, 1993, 20th Century Wind Chamber Music, 1994, Clockworks, 1995, Concert Variations: Eu-Fish, 1995, Fanfare and Fugue: Contrasts for Trumpets, 1995, In the Shadow of a Miracle, 1996, Triptych: Premier, 1996, Praetorius Suiet: Jubilee, 1997, Garten von Freuden und Traurigkeit, 2000, The Duel: Spring Flowers, 2000, Obsessions, 2002, Steelpan Concerto: Paul Freeman Introduces Exotic Concertos, 2002, My Very First Solo: My Very First Solo, 2003. Served with U.S. Army, 1962—65. Recipient BMI student composers 1st prize, 1957, Koussevitsky composition award, 1961, Harvey Gaul composition award, 1973, Mannes Opera award, 1973, Pulitzer prize nomination, 1973, 81, 82, 84, 92, SAI composition award, 1974, Excellence in Tchg.

award No. Ill. U., 1978, choral composition award Brown U., 1978, Nebr. Sinfonia Chamber Orch. contest, 1979, N.Y.C. Opera contest, 1980; commns. include Tuba Brotherhood, 1977, Internat. Trumpet Guild, 1978, 86, Internat. Brass Congress, 1980, Greenwich Philharmonia, 1981, Orch. of Ill., 1982, NACWPI, 1982, Minot Symphony, 1984, Am. Brass Quintet-Chamber Music Am., 1988, Sacramento Symphony-N.C. Symphony, 1989, Camarata Singers, 1991, WFMT-Vermeer Quartet, 1991, Woodstock Chimes Fund, 1994, Ronen Chamber Ensemble, 1994, Stockholm Chamber Brass, 1994, Eileen Gress-N.C. Symphony, 1995, Elmhurst Symphony, 1996, Ramon Parcells, 1996, Palos Park Cmty. Chorale, 1997, Cantori of Hobart and William Smith Colls., 1998, Northern Ill. Children's Chorus, 1999, So. Bend Chamber Singers, 1999, Robert Sims, 1999, Regina H. Helcher, 2000, Jeff Nesseth, 2001, Jay Hunsberger-Fla. West Coast Symphony,2002, Gloria Musicae, 2003, Diane Ragains, 2004, Fox Valley Arts Hall of Fame, 2004, Kaneland Cmty. Schs., 2005, Zephyr Brass Trio, 2005, Walker Bowman, 2005. Mem. Coll. Mus. Soc., Broadcast Music, Phi Eta Sigma, Phi Mu Alpha, Phi Kappa Phi, Pi Kappa Lambda., Omicron Delta Kappa Office Phone: 815-753-7003. Personal E-mail: janbach@janbach.com.

BACH, ROBERT J., information technology executive; BA in Econ., U. N.C.; MBA, Stanford U. Fin. analyst Morgan Stanley & Co.; with Microsoft Corp., 1988—, bus. ops. mgr., Microsoft Europe, 1990—92, v.p. mktg., desktop applications div., v.p., learning, entertainment, & productivity div., 1996—98, sr. v.p. games divsn., chief Xbox officer, 1998—. Office: Microsoft Corp One Microsoft Way Redmond WA 98052-6399

BACH, THOMAS HANDFORD, lawyer, investor; b. Vineland, N.J., Dec. 25, 1928; s. Albert Ludwig and Edith May (Handford) B. AB, Rutgers U., 1950; LLB, Harvard U., 1956. Bar: N.Y. State bar 1957. Assoc. firm Hawkins, Delafield & Wood, N.Y.C., 1956—61, Reed, Hoyt, Washburn & McCarthy, N.Y.C., 1961—62; ptnr. Bach & Condren, N.Y.C., 1963—71, Bach & McAuliffe, N.Y.C., 1971—79, Stroock & Stroock & Lavan, N.Y.C., 1979—88, Sullivan & Donovan, N.Y.C., 1989—2000, of counsel, 2000—02, Sullivan, Donovan & Gentile, N.Y.C., 2002—03, Gentile & Turpen, N.Y.C., 2003—; arbitrator Nat. Assn. of Securities Dealers Reg., N.Y.C., 2000—. Co-counsel N.Y. State Senate Housing and Urban Devel. Com., 1971; fiscal cons. N.Y.C. Fin. Adminstrn., 1967-70; asst. counsel State Fin. Com., N.Y. State Constl. Conv. of, 1967; del. U.S./Japan Bilateral Session, 1988, Moscow Conf. on Law and Bilateral Econ. Rels., 1990; spkr. Practicing Law Inst., Mcpl. Bond Workshop, N.Y., 1995-97. Contbr. articles to profl. jours.; co-author: A Guide to Certificates of Participation, 1991, the Handbook of Municipal Bonds, 1994. Mem. N.Y. State Commn. to Study Constl. Tax Limitations, 1974-75; chmn. subcom. Pub. Securities Assn., 1990-91. Served with U.S. Army, 1951-53, 1st lt. U.S. Army, 1952-53, Japan. Mem. ABA (state and local govt., dispute resolution and internat. law. sects.), N.Y. State Bar Assn., Assn. of Bar of City of N.Y., N.J. Bar Assn., N.Y. Mcpl. Analysts Group (chmn. 1973-74), Mcpl. Forum of N.Y., Market Technicians Assn. (affiliate), Internat. Fin. Svcs. Vol. Corps. Episcopalian. Home: 4 E 89th St New York NY 10128-0636 also: 615 W Oak Rd Vineland NJ 08360-2262 Office: Gentile and Turpen 20th Flr 40 Exchange Pl New York NY 10005 Office Phone: 212-747-0130.

BACHAND, ALICE JEANNE, school library media specialist; b. Sayre, Pa., Sept. 21, 1957; d. Charles Edward and Donna Jeanne (Osborne) Merrick; m. James Joseph Bachand, July 17, 1982; children: Janelle Alison, Jodi Nicole. Student, Paul Valéry U., Montpellier, France, 1977-78; BA, Wartburg Coll., 1979; MLS, Emporia State U., 1985. French tchr. Dunlap (Iowa) H.S., 1979, Clifton-Clyde H.S., Clyde, Kans., 1980-85; sch. libr. media specialist Hillcrest H.S., Cuba, Kans., 1984-86, Linn (Kans.) H.S., 1986-92, Clay Center (Kans.) Cmty. Middle Sch., 1992—. V.p. WELCA, Concordia, Kans., 1989-91; sec. of edn., ALCW, Concordia, 1982-84; brownie helper Girl Scouts of Am., Clyde, 1995-96; ch. librarian, Concordia Lutheran Ch., 1984—. Mem. NEA (Kans. chpt. pres. 1991-92), DAR, Kans. Reading Assn., Kans. Assn. Sch. Librarians (nominating com. 1992), Thunderbird Reading Coun. Lutheran. Avocations: reading, sewing, crafts. Home: 1626 N 270 Rd Clyde KS 66938 Office: Clay Ctr Cmty Middle School 935 Prospect St Clay Center KS 67432-1849

BACHARACH, MELVIN LEWIS, venture capitalist; b. Oakland, Calif., May 14, 1924; s. Max and Ellen Mildred (LeValley) B.; m. Vera Patricia Mortimer, Aug. 20, 1950; children: Kimberly Bacharach Arnone, Craig Ronald. BSBA, U. Calif., Berkeley, 1948. With Levi Strauss & Co., 1948-79, v.p., then exec. v.p., 1973-79, pres. U.S. group, 1975-79, also bd. dirs., mem. exec. com.; pres., CEO Internat. Bus. Sponsors, Inc., 1979-86, also bd. dirs.; pres., CEO VMB, Inc., San Francisco, 1986—; mng. ptnr. Diamond View LP, San Francisco, 1973—. Bd. dirs. Internat. Bus. Sponsors, Inc., Above the Belt, Inc. Patentee in field. Served as pilot USNR, 1942-46, 51-53. Decorated Air medal. Mem. U. Calif. Bus. Adminstrn. Alumni Assn., Beta Gamma Sigma, Pi Lambda Phi. Clubs: Marine Meml., Mira Vista Country, Concordia Argonaut, Palm Valley Country, Avondale Golf Club.

BACHE, ROBERT JAMES, physician, medical educator; MD, Harvard U. Diplomate Am. Bd. Internal Medicine, Am. Bd. Cardiovasc. Disease. Resident in internal medicine Duke U., Durham, N.C., assoc. prof. medicine; prof. medicine U. Minn., Mpls. Contbr. articles to profl. jours. Fellow Am. Coll. Cardiology; mem. Am. Soc. for Clin. Investigation, Assn. of Am. Physicians, Assn. Univ. Cardiologists, Am. Heart Assn. Office: U Minn Med Sch Med Box 508 Mayo 420 Delaware St SE Minneapolis MN 55455-0374 Office Phone: 612-624-8970. Business E-Mail: bache001@umn.edu.

BACHELDER, BEVERLY BRANDT, secondary school educator, assistant principal; b. Fort Dodge, Iowa, June 24, 1954; d. Olaf Ottesen and Eleanor Berg Brandt; m. Robert Stephen Bachelder, Sept. 17, 1977; children: Stephen Edward, Elizabeth Margrethe. BA, Luther Coll., 1976; MusM, Yale U., 1978; MA in Modern English Lit., U. Kent, 1979. Lic. Educator (kindergarten through twelfth grade vocal music and seventh through twelfth grade English) Mass. Dept. Edn., 1980. Vocal music tchr. Douglas Sch. Sys., Mass., 1980—81; English lang. arts tchr. Douglas Jr., Sr. HS, 1982—2004, co-founder and advisor of nat. jr. honor soc. - Roberta Wagner chpt., 1990—2003; co-chair of accreditation steering com. Douglas HS, 2002—, co-chair of New England Assn., English dept. chair, 2003—04, acting asst. prin., 2004—05, asst. prin., 2005—; dir. of music Zion Luth. Ch., Worcester, Mass., 1980—97, First Congl. Ch., Auburn, Mass., 1997—2000. Dir. music First Congl. Ch., Auburn, Mass., 1997—2000; organist, choir dir. Christ Episcopal Ch., Rochdale, Mass., 2000—, choir dir., 2000—. Mem. First Congl. Ch., Oxford, Mass., 1984. Finalist Mass. Tchr. of Yr. award, Mass. Dept. Edn., 1986; recipient Internat. Understanding award, Rotary Found., 1978-79, Douglas Tchr. of Yr. award, Douglas Jr./Sr. HS, 1986, Horace Mann Tchr. award, Douglas Jr., Sr. HS, 1986-87. Mem.: Am. Guild of Organists, Assn. Supr. and Curriculum Devel., Mass. Secondary Schs. Adminstrs.' Assn. Home: PO Box 67 North Oxford MA 01537 Office: Douglas HS 33 Davis St Douglas MA 01516

BACHELDER, CHERYL ANNE, marketing professional; b. Columbus, Ohio, May 4, 1956; d. Max Edwin and Margaret Anne Stanton; m. Christopher Frank Bachelder, June 13, 1981; 2 children. BS, Ind. U., 1977, MBA, 1978. Asst. product mgr. Procter & Gamble Co., Cin., 1978-81; product mgr. The Gillette Co., Boston, 1981-84; sr. product mgr. R.J.R. Nabisco, Planters Life Savers Co., Parsippany, N.J., 1984, group product mgr., 1985-87; dir. mktg. Winston-Salem, N.C., 1987; v.p. mktg. R.J.R. Nabisco, Planters Life Savers Co., Winston-Salem, N.C., 1988-91; v.p., gen. mgr. Life Savers Div., Nabisco Foods Group, 1991-92; pres. Bachelder & Assoc., 1992-95; v.p. mktg. and product devel. Domino's Pizza Inc., Ann Arbor, Mich., 1995—2001; pres. KFC, 2002—. Named one of 100 best and brightest women in advt. Advt. Age mag., Chgo., 1988; featured in Fortune Mag. People to Watch column, 1990.*

BACHELDER, JOSEPH ELMER, III, lawyer; b. Fulton, Mo., Nov. 13, 1932; s. Joseph Elmer and Frances Evelyn (Gray) B.; m. Louise Este Mason, June 12, 1955; children: Louise Stewart Bachelder Alcock, Christina Cathryn Bachelder Dufresne, Hilary Houston. BA magna cum laude, Yale U., 1955; LLB, Harvard U., 1958. Bar: N.Y. 1959. Assoc. Mudge, Rose, Guthrie & Alexander, N.Y.C., 1958-67, McKinsey and Co., Inc., N.Y.C., 1967-69; ptnr. Satterlee and Stephens, N.Y.C., 1969-72, Leboeuf, Lamb, Lieby & MacRae, N.Y.C., 1972-80; founder, sr. ptnr. Law Offices Joseph E. Bachelder, N.Y.C., 1980—; chmn. The Bachelder Group, Inc., 1989—. Lectr. NYU Ann. Inst. on Fed. Taxation, 1972-74, Practicing Law Inst., 1977-80, 2000, Am. Law Inst., 1980, 97, 98, The Conf. Bd., 1986. Co-author, editor: Employee Stock Ownership Plans, 1979; columnist N.Y. Law Jour. 1977—; speaker Academia Symposia Stanford Law Sch., 1999, 2000, Northwestern U., Kellogg Sch. Bus., 1999, U. Del., 2000. Mem. Princeton Twp. (N.J.) Zoning Bd., 1981-82; trustee Concord (Mass.) Acad., 1986-92. Fellow Am. Coll. Tax Counsel; mem. ABA, N.Y. State Bar Assn., Assn. of Bar of N.Y.C. Clubs: The Down Town Assn. (N.Y.), Yale Club N.Y.; Bedens Brook (Princeton), Nassau (Princeton); Siasconset Casino (Nantucket, Mass.). Republican. Congregationalist. Home: 226 Constitution Dr Princeton NJ 08540-6712 Office: 780 3rd Ave New York NY 10017-2024

BACHELDER, ROBERT STEPHEN, minister; b. Middletown, NY, Nov. 2, 1951; s. Stephen and Dorothy Esther (Gunderson) B.; m. Beverly June Brandt, Sept. 17, 1977; children: Stephen, Elizabeth. AB, Dartmouth Coll., 1973; MDiv, Yale U., 1978. Ordained to ministry United Ch. of Christ, 1978. Money markets trader RI Hosp. Trust Nat. Bank, Providence, 1973-75; pastor United Ref. Ch., Pangbourne, England, 1978-79; min. 1st Congl. Ch., Shrewsbury, Mass., 1980-84; min. for mission and svc. Worcester (Mass.) Area Mission Soc., 1984—. Advisor to religious congregations for charitable giving. Author: Mystery and Miracle, 1983, Between Dying and Birth, 1983; contbr. chpts. to books, articles to profl. jours. Vice chmn. Housing for All, 2003—; bd. dirs. Mass. Coun. of Chs., 1991—93, Worcester Interfaith, 1992—94, Worcester County Ecumenical Coun., 1992—96, Mass. Conv. Congl. Mins., 1983—85, Ctrl. Assn. Mass. Conf., United Ch. of Christ, 1983—, Worcester Coop. Coun., 1985—89, Accord: The Ctr. for Human Rels., 1991—93, Corx, Inc., 1993—, WCHR Securities, Inc., 1993—, Mass. Congl. Fund, 1999—, New Am. Cmty. Forum, 1995—97, Pakachoag Cmty. Music Sch., 1996—98, Congl. Christian Hist. Soc., 1997—, Worcester Pastoral Counseling Ctr., 1998—2000, Greater Worcester Cmty. Found. Exec. Com., 1998—, Colony Retirement Homes, 1998—, Worcester Area Campus Ministry, 1998—, Jeremiah's Hospice, 2000—, Accion Worcester, 2002—, United Way of Ctrl. Mass., 2000—; chair Bus. Advisory Coun Martin Luther King Jr. Bus. Empowerment Ctr., 1999—, bd. dirs., 1993—99; chair Capital Devel., 1996—2001; mem. City Mgr.'s Housing Task Force, 1990—92; distbn. com. mem. Fed. Emergency Mgmt. Agy., Ctrl. Mass., 1984—86, Housing Ind. Fund, 1989—92, Greater Worcester Cmty. Found., 1994—2000, chair, 1998—2000; bd. dirs. Higgins Armory Mus., 1993—2002, pres., 1997—99; v.p. Worcester Housing Partnership, 1991—93; pres. Habitat Worcester, 1984—86, Worcester Cmty. Loan Fund, 1986—90, Worcester Com. on Homelessness and Housing, 1988—91, Worcester Cmty. Housing Resources, 1993—95. Recipient award Pernet Family Svc., 1993, Outstanding Charitable Svc. award United Ch. of Christ, 1995, Nipmuc Women's Health Coalition award, 1999, Spirit in Art award, 2002, Exemplary Leadership award Nat. Conf. on Cmty. and Justice, 2002. Mem.: Worcester Com. on Fgn. Rels., United Ch. of Christ Ministers' Fellowship (pres. 1982—83), St. Wulstan Soc., Dartmouth Club of Ctrl. Mass. (pres. 1991—93). Home: PO Box 67 North Oxford MA 01537-0067 Office: Worcester Area Mission Soc 128 Central St Auburn MA 01501-2820 Personal E-mail: wamsucc@bigplanet.com.

BACHER, SUSAN LORRAINE, nursing educator; b. Norfolk, Va., Oct. 6, 1953; d. Temp and Edith Lorraine Tullos; m. Raymond Fred Bacher, Aug. 24, 2002; children: Linda, Nicole;children from previous marriage: Charles Hawks, Kevin Hawks, Justin Hawks. RN, Bapt. Meml. Hosp. Sch. Nursing, Memphis, 1974; BSN magna cum laude, Memphis State U., 1990. RN Ohio, Tenn., Ky., cert. periperative nurse, RN 1st asst. RN staff nurse, pvt. duty, office nurse, home health nurse, Memphis, 1974—80; oper. rm. staff nurse, RN 1st asst. Meth. North Hosp., Memphis, 1980—92; quality improvement, staff devel. coord. Baptist Tipton County Hosp., Covington, Tenn., 1992; staff RN, RN 1st asst. Good Samaritan Hosp/Mercy Anderson Hosp., Cin., 1992—96; instr., adj. faculty cons. Cin. State Tech. and C.C., 1993—99, instr., full-time faculty, 2001—; perioperative educator Tri Health (Bethesda and Good Samaritan Hosps.), Cin., 1996—2001. Author: (videotape/study guide) Safely Positioning the Surgical Patient, 1996. Pres. Lucy Elem. Sch. PTA, Memphis, 1986. Recipient Nat. Def. medal, 1990, 2003, Navy Achievement medal, 1994, Navy and Marine Corps Achievement medal, 1998. Mem.: Assn. Surg. Technologists, Assn. Mil. Surgeons of the U.S., Assn. periOperative Registered Nurses (v.p. local chpt. 1991—92, nat. continuing edn. approval com. 1993—94, bd. dirs. 1993—95, nat. audiovisual com. 1994—96, pres.-elect 1995—96, pres. 1996—97, nat. com. on edn. 1996—98, bd. dirs. 1997, 1998, 1999, nat. membership com. Ky. rep. 2000—02, v.p. 2000—02, sec. 2002—04, v.p. 2004—), Naval Res. Assn., Sigma Theta Tau. Mem. Disciples Of Christ. Avocations: dance, camping, singing, sports. Office: Cin State Tech and CC 3520 Central Pky Cincinnati OH 45223 Office Phone: 513-569-1231. Office Fax: 513-569-1659. Business E-Mail: susan.bacher@cincinnatistate.edu.

BACHICHA, JOSEPH ALFRED, physician, educator; b. Rock Springs, Wyo. s. Alfred and Helen B. BA, Stanford U., 1977; MD, Boston U., 1982. Diplomate Am. Bd. of Ob-Gyn. Intern St. Luke's-Roosevelt Hosp., N.Y.C., 1982-83; resident in ob-gyn. Stanford U. Hosp., Palo Alto, Calif., 1983-86; pvt. practice Chgo., 1986-95; asst. prof. ob-gyn. U. Calif., San Francisco, 1996-97, assoc. prof., 1997-99; med. dir. Pacific Occupl. Health Med. Assocs., South San Francisco, 1999—2003; assoc. physician Kaiser Permanente, 2000—, chief, patient edn. and health promotion Hayward, Calif., 2004—. Cons. WHO, UN Family Planning Assn.; asst. prof. Northwestern U., Chgo., 1986-95; Gen. Hosp., 1996-99, dir. student edn. dept. ob-gyn., San Francisco, 1995-99, dir. obstetrics, 1998-99; dir. Excelsior Group Health Care for Women and Children, San Francisco, 1995-99; dir. low-risk obstetrics, coord. undergrad. med. edn. Prentice Women's Hosp., Chgo., 1990-95; mem. Liaison Com. on Med. Edn.; physician, educator Carnegie Found., Ghana, 1989, Project Hope, Nicaragua, 1992. Contbr. articles to profl. jours. Mem. Chgo. Coun. Fgn. Rels. Grad. fellow Rotary Found., 1980; mem. Harvard Macy Scholars Inst., 1995. Fellow ACOG, Assn. Profs. Gynecology and Obstetrics, Internat. Coll. Surgeons, Royal Soc. Medicine; mem. AMA, APHA, Nat. Bd. Med. Examiners, Am. Assn. Maternal and Neonatal Health, Am. Fertility Soc., Chgo. Gynecol. Soc., San Mateo County Med. Soc., Stanford U. Alumni Assn., Boston U. Sch. Medicine Alumni Assn., Commonwealth Club Calif. Roman Catholic. Avocations: mystery books, cross country skiing, weight training, running, aerobics. Office: 27400 Hesperian Blvd Hayward CA 94545 Business E-Mail: joseph.bachicha@kp.org.

BACHMAN, ARTHUR, lawyer; b. Phila., Nov. 18, 1947; s. Stanley Bachman and Ann (Rosen) Flashner; m. Linda Kay Moss, June 8, 1969 (div.); children: Helene, Allison. BBA, Temple U., 1969, JD, 1972, postgrad., 1980. Bar: Pa. 1972. Atty., advisor legis./regulations divsn. Office Chief Coun. IRS, Washington, 1972-76; assoc. Fox, Rothschild, O'Brien & Frankel, 1976-79; ptnr. Blank Rome L.L.P., Phila., 1979—. Instr. Am. Coll., 1986, 88, Temple U., 1988; lectr. Estate Planning Coun. Lehigh Valley, 1983, C. of C. of Cherry Hill, N.J., 1985, Nat. Conf. CPA Practitioners, 1988, Am. Soc. Pension Actuaries, 1988, Internat. Soc. Employee Benefit Specialists, 1991; guest spkr. Harry S. Gross radio program Sta. WCAU, 1987, 88, 89. Co-author: (booklets) The REA's Joint and Survivor Annuity Rules--Coping with the Regulations, 1986, How to Defer Income with IRA's and Sec. 401(k) Plans, 1987, Evaluation of Probable Impact of Proposed Nondiscrimination Regs: An Interview with 8 Pension Experts, 1990, An Evaluation of the Proposed Regulations on Separate Lines of Business, 1991, ERISA: A Comprehensive Guide, 1991-97, A Second Look at Final Regulations on FICA and FUTA Tax on Non-Qualified Deferred Compensation; contbr. articles to jours., chpts. to books. Mem. Pa. Bar Assn. (lectr. 2001), Phila. Bar Assn., Am. Soc. Pension Actuaries Benefits Coun. Del. Valley (bd. dirs. 1997-2005, lectr. 2001, 04), Phi Alpha Delta, Alpha Epsilon Pi, Beta Gamma Sigma. Office: Blank Rome LLP Fls 10-13 One Logan Square Philadelphia PA 19103-2521 Office Phone: 215-569-5715. E-mail: Bachman@BlankRome.com.

BACHMAN, DAVID CHRISTIAN, orthopedic surgeon; b. Peoria, Ill., Apr. 11, 1934; s. Leland Alvin and Elsie May (Springer) B.; m. Betty June Foster, Sept. 9, 1956; children: Lynne Allison, Laura Ailene. BA, Goshen Coll., 1958; MD, Northwestern U., 1962. Intern Cook County Hosp., Chgo., 1962-63; resident in orthopaedic surgery Northwestern U. Med. Sch., 1963-67; practice medicine specializing in orthopaedic surgery Chgo., 1967-80; practice specializing in ski injuries, 1980-93; with Mountain Med. Services, Telluride, Colo., 1982-87, Ouray Mountain Rescue Team, Inc., Ouray Med. Ctr., Ouray, Colo.; coroner Ouray County, Colo., 1982-93; mem. staffs Northwestern Meml. Hosp., Children's Meml. Hosp., Grant hosp., (all Chgo.), 1967-80, Montrose Meml. Hosp., Colo., 1984-93; med. cons. Western Area U.S. Postal Svc. Dir. Ctr. for Sports Medicine, Northwestern U. Med. Sch., 1978-80; team physician Chgo. Bulls, Nat. Basketball Assn., 1967-80; asst. prof. dept. orthop. surgery Northwestern U. Med. Sch., 1967-80; syndicated columnist on sports medicine Dr. Jock, 1976-90; cons. Western area U.S. Postal Svc., 1996-97; sr. area med. dir. Western Area U.S. Postal Svc., 1997-2002, Pacific Arae U.S. Postal Svc., 2002—. Author: (with Marilyn Preston) Dear Doctor Jock ...The Peoples Guide to Sports and Fitness, 1980, (with others) The Diet That Lets You Cheat, 1983, (with Tod Bacigalupi) The Way it Was, 1990, (with Robert Pickering) The Use of Forensic Anthropology, 1996. Elder Presbyn. Ch., 1965—; rsch. assoc. anthropology dept. Denver Mus. Natural History, 1994-99. Mem. ACS, Am. Acad. Orthop. Surgery, Am. Orthop. Soc. for Sports Medicine, Phi Rho Sigma. Presbyterian. Home: 552 Shorebird Cir # 1101 Redwood City CA 94065 Office: 390 Main St San Francisco CA 94105 Office Phone: 415-536-6420. Business E-Mail: david.c.bachman@usps.gov.

BACHMAN, HENRY LEE, electrical engineer, engineering company executive; b. Bklyn., Apr. 29, 1930; s. Solomon and Frances (Cortese) B.; m. Doris Engelhardt, Dec. 8, 1951; children: Steven, Diane, Lorraine. BEE, Poly. U., N.Y., 1951, MSEE, 1954; postgrad. Advanced Mgmt. Program, Harvard U., 1972. Engr., mgr. Wheeler Labs., Great Neck, NY, 1951-55, exec. v.p., dir., 1967-68, pres., dir., 1968-70; product line dir. BAE Sys. Comms., Nav., Identification and REconnaissance, Green Lawn, NY, 1970-72; v.p. quality assurance and logistics Marconi Aerospace Systems, Green Lawn, 1973-75, v.p. quality assurance and customer svc., 1975-78, v.p. ops., 1978-84, v.p. engring., 1985-90, v.p. market planning, 1991, v.p. spl. projects, 1992-95, ret. v.p., 1996, dir. tech. mktg., 1996—. Chmn. L.I. Forum for Tech., 1985—86; cons. Rsch. Found. of State Univ. of N.Y., 2001—. Contbr. articles to profl. jours. Pres., bd. dirs. Friends of L.I. Mus. Sci. and Tech., 1994-96; bd dirs. Huntington Arts Coun., 1994-96; mem. Pres.'s Adv. Com. on Indsl. Innovation, 1979. Named Fellow and Disting. Alumnus Poly. Inst., N.Y., 1986; recipient Engring. Mgr. of Yr. award IEEE/Engring. Mgmt. Soc., 1985. Fellow AAAS, IEEE (life fellow, Centennial medal 1984, Haradem Pratt award 1995, exec. v.p. 1984, treas. 1985, pres. 1987, pres. IEEE Found. 1994-99, v.p. projects 2000-02, dir. 1986-2002, pres. emeritus 2003, fellow com. 2004—, 3d Millennium medal 2000), Sigma Xi, Tau Beta Pi, Eta Kappa Nu (eminment mem.). Avocations: sailing, opera, piano. Home: 5 Brandy Rd Cold Spring Harbor NY 11724-2401 Office: BAE Systems Mail Sta 1-30 Greenlawn NY 11740 E-mail: h.bachman@ieee.org.

BACHMAN, JERALD GRAYBILL, psychologist, researcher; b. Harrisburg, Pa., Oct. 20, 1936; s. Jacob Clarence and Harriet Mathias Bachman; m. Virginia Ludy, Nov. 28, 1957; children: Terri Lynne Dyer, Steven Jerald, Jon Andrew. AB, Lebanon Valley Coll., 1958; MA, U. Pa., 1961, PhD, 1962. Rsch. asst. U. Pa., Phila., 1958-59, asst. instr., 1959-62; study dir. U. Mich., Survey Rsch. Ctr., Inst. for Social Rsch., Ann Arbor, 1962-67, sr. study dir., 1967-72, program dir., sr. rsch. scientist, 1972-98, disting. rsch. scientist, 1998—, rsch. prof., 2003—. Mem. nat. adv. panel Nat. Ctr. for Ednl. Stats., Washington, 1982—; mem. com. on mil. performance NAS, Washington, 1983-89, mem. com. on youth population and mil. recruitment, 1999-2003. Author: (book series) Youth in Transition, 1967-78, The All-Volunteer Force, 1977, Smoking, Drinking, and Drug Use in Young Adulthood, 1997, The Decline of Substance Use in Young Adulthood, 2002; cons. editor Am. Jour. Sociology, 1983-85; contbr. chpts. to books and articles to profl. jours. NSF fellow, Washington, 1959, 60, 62. Mem. Am. Assn. for Pub. Opinion Rsch., Soc. for Psychol. Study Social Issues, Inter-Univ. Seminar on Armed Forces and Soc. Avocations: sailing, cross country skiing, house renovation, hiking, travel. Office: Inst for Social Rsch Univ Mich 426 Thompson St Ann Arbor MI 48104-2321 E-mail: jbachman@umich.edu.

BACHMAN, JOHN GILBERT, electrical engineer, writer; b. Wheeling, W.Va., Sept. 20, 1942; s. Carl William Bachman and Angela Marie (Bonaventura) Willis; m. Marilyn Jean Messier, July 30, 1991; m. Kathryn Elizabeth Sauvageot (div.); children: Pamela Sue, James; m. Marilyn J. Cofsne. BSEE, W.Va. U., 1965. Design engr. Westinghouse Electric, Balt., 1965—69; supr. engr. Sanders Assocs., Inc., Nashua, NH, 1969—76; sr. engr. Harris Corp., Nashua, 1976—81; sr. mgr. Wang Labs., Inc., Lowell, Mass., 1981—87; CEO Analog Tech. Ctr., Amherst, NH, 1987—91, AnaTek Corp., Amherst, 1991—. Contbr. columns in newspapers. Chief Amherst (N.H.) Fire Dept., 1992—95. Mem.: IEEE, Am. Soc. Advancement Sci. Achievements include patents in field. Home: 100 Merrimack Rd Amherst NH 03031

BACHMAN, KATHARINE ELIZABETH, lawyer; b. Harrisburg, Pa., Oct. 28, 1953; d. Neal D. and Helen (Alexander) B. BA summa cum laude, Dickinson Coll., 1975; JD, NYU, 1978. Bar: Mass. 1978. Sr. ptnr., hiring ptnr. Hale & Dorr, Boston, 1978—2004; ptnr., vice chmn. Real Estate dept. Wilmer Cutler Pickering Hale & Dorr, Boston, 2004—. Bd. dirs. Greater Boston Legal Services. Editor (articles): Annual Survey of Am. Law. Mem. single family adv. com. Mass. Housing Fin. Agy., Boston, 1985—; trustee Dickinson Coll., Carlisle, Pa., 1987—; mem. New Eng. Adv. Com. Trust for Pub. Land; past chmn. Develop. & Fin. Task Force Boston 2000; mem. exec. com. Mass. chpt. Nat Assn. Indsl. & Office Properties. Named a Mass. Super Lawyer, Boston Mag., 2004; named one of Top 50 Female Mass. Lawyers, 2004; Root Tilden scholar. Mem. Am. Coll. Real Estate Lawyers, Mass. Bar Assn., Boston Bar Assn., New Eng. Women in Real Estate (past pres.), Phi Beta Kappa. Avocation: housing rehabilitation. Office: Wilmer Cutler Pickering Hale & Dorr 60 State St Boston MA 02109-1816 Office Phone: 617-526-6216. Office Fax: 617-526-5000. Business E-Mail: katherine.bachman@wilmerhale.com.

BACHMAN, KENNETH LEROY, JR., lawyer; b. Washington, Aug. 24, 1943; s. Kenneth Leroy and Audrey Teresa (Torrence) B.; m. Sharon Abel, June 18, 1966; children— Laura Ann, Eric Kenneth. A.B. summa cum laude, Ohio U., 1965; J.D. cum laude, Harvard U., 1968. Bar: D.C. 1968, U.S. Ct. Appeals (D.C. cir.) 1971, U.S. Supreme Ct. 1981. Law clk. to judge U.S. Dist. Ct. So. Dist. N.Y., 1968-70; assoc. Cleary, Gottlieb, Steen & Hamilton, Washington, 1970-76, ptnr., 1976— . Mem. ABA. Contbg. editor Oil and Gas Price Regulation Analyst, 1978-83, Natural Gas Journal, 1983-85; contbr. articles to profl. jours. Home: 5332 Falmouth Rd Bethesda MD 20816-2915 Office: 1752 N St NW Washington DC 20036-2904

BACHMANN, BILL, photographer; b. Pa., Mar. 4, 1946; s. Ernest Edward and Helen May (Himler) B. BS, Roberts Wesleyan Coll., Rochester, N.Y., 1967; MBA, NYU, 1971; postgrad., U. London, U. Calif., Berkeley, Rochester Inst. Tech., U. Pitts., Ft. Lauderdale Art Inst. Freelance comml. and advt. photographer, Miami, N.Y.C., Orlando, 1972—. Worked in over 150 countries worldwide; instr. photography Triangle Inst., 1992, S.E. Ctr. for Creative Arts, Daytona, 1990—; vis. instr. photography at several colls. and univs.; guest numerous TV programs, 1978—; lectr. in field. Prin. works include Miami Herald, 1978-80, Fla. Tourism, 1982—, Sheraton Hotels, 1982—, Gen. Mills Restaurants, 1983—, Olive Garden, 1986—, Marriott Hotels, 1992—, Bahamas Tourism, 1984-, Radisson Hotels, 1986—, Grosvenor Hotels, 1988—, Revlon, 1991—, Harris Corp., 1993—, Sea Escape Cruises, 1988—, Century Club, 2000—, Regent China Tours, 1999—, Burger

King, 1988—, Caribbean Travel & Life, 1990—, Fuji, 1990—, Far & Wide, 2000—, Nickelodeon, 1989—, Merv Griffin's Paradise Island, Bahamas, 1990—, Kodak Films, 1976—, McDonalds, 1987—, Stern Mag., 1987—, AAA, 1985—, Regal Boats, 1990—, Renaissance Cruises, 1996—, Universal Studios, 1990—, General Tours, 2002—, Citibank VISA, 1990—, Delta Airlines, 1991—, Am. Showcase, 1991—, Ed McMahon, 2004—, Creative Black Book, 1994—, PepsiCo, 1994—, Hilton Hotels Internat., 1992—, NuSkin, 1995—, Pizza Hut, 1996—, Grey Poupon, 1995—, Atlantis Resort, 1996—, Arnold Palmer, 1996—, Home Depot, 1996—, Whale Cay, 1997—, Sandals Resorts, 1997—, People Mag., 1998—, Grand Circle Tours, 1999—, Pitcom, 1999, Saga Holidays, 1999-2001, Regent China Tours, 1999—, Backstreet Boys, 2000, Cooper Tires, 2000—, Brendan Tours, 2001—, SIKA, 2002—, Condor Adventures, 2004—, Sony, 2003—, Venus Williams, 2003—, Reebok, 2003—, Sony, 2003—, Vantage Tours, 2004, Kodak World Calendar, 2004, United Way, 2004, Continental Air, 2004Ed McMahon, 2004, Condor Adventures, 2005; dir. TV commls. and videos, 1987—; author: Clicking the Shutter is the Easy Part, 1988, Introspective World, 1996, Welcome Back Berlin, 1990, Bali-Paradise in Indonesia, 1994, Shooting Figure Studies, 1990, Kathmandu, A Jewel Discovered, 1996, One Dream Too Many, 1989, Images of Women, 1997, Treasures of the Caribbean, 1992, China's Greatest Resource, It's Diverse People, 1997, Orlando-The City Beautiful, 1998, Traveling After Terrorism, 2002, Travel Hints for Photographers, 2003, Images of Woman, 2004, Send Me Anywhere, 2005; photographer 295-Day Kodak World Photo Tour, 1992-95, Photo Pro Mag., 1991—; photgraphed over 900 mag. covers; contbr. articles to profl. jours Bd. dirs. Big Bros.; active Vols. in Action, 1989—. Named Photographer of Yr. Fla. Peoples Choice Awards, 1987, Photographer of Yr. Asia, 1993; recipient Addy awards, 1976—. Mem. One Club (bd. dirs. 1988—), Sales and Mktg. Execs. (bd. dirs., officer), Am. Soc. Media Photographers N.Y., Orlando C. of C. (pres.' club 1983—), Cen. Fla. Photographers Assn. (v.p., bd. dirs. 1983—), Fla. Motion Pictures and TV Guild, Heathrow Club (social dir. 1986—), Rotary. Republican. Methodist. Avocations: skiing, tennis, golf, writing. Home and Office: PO Box 950833 Lake Mary FL 32795-0833 Office Phone: 407-333-9988. Personal E-mail: bill@billbachmann.com.

BACHMANN, GLORIA ANN, obstetrician, gynecologist, educator; b. Newark, N.J., Nov. 4, 1949; d. Paul Bachmann and Rose Detrolio; 1 child, Michael. BA, Rutgers U., 1970, MMS, 1972; MD, U. Pa., 1974. Diplomate Am. Bd. Ob-Gyn., Am. Bd. Med. Examiners. Resident in ob-gyn. Hosp. of the U. of Pa., 1974-78; instr. U. Medicine & Dentistry N.J./Robert Wood Johnson Med. Sch., New Brunswick, N.J., 1978-81; asst. prof. Robert Wood Johnson U. Hosp., New Brunswick, N.J., 1981-86, assoc. prof., 1986-92, prof., 1992—. Chief ob-gyn. Robert Wood Johnson U. Hosp., 1992—; dir. Women's Health Inst. Editl. bd. Maturitas, 1989—, Med. Crossfire, 1998, Managing Menopause, 1998—, Jour. of Reproductive Medicine, 1999—, Med. Aspects of Human Sexuality, 1989-92, OBG Mgmt., 1994—, Menopaul Mgmt., 1991-93, Obstetric Gynecology, 1990-94; contbr. chpts. to books and articles to profl. jours. Dir. Women's Wellness and Health Care Connection, New Brunswick, N.J., 1998—. Recipient Recognition award March of Dimes, 1982, 83, Planned Parenthood, 1987, 88, Award for Women's Health Edn. YMCA, 1984, Judge Advocate Gen. award Tri-State Metro, 1984, Lifetime Achievement award Middlesex County Commn. on the Status of Women, 1995, Women of Achievement award Del. Valley Girl Scouts, 1996. Fellow Am. Coll. Ob-Gyn. (Issue of the Yr. award 1988); mem. Am. Fertility Soc., Internat. Menopause Soc., Am. Med. Women's Assn. (Gender Equity Recognition 1994), N.J. Obs.-Gyn. Soc., N.Am. Menopause Soc., Acad. of Medicine of N.J., Phi Beta Kappa. Office: Robert Wood Johnson Med Sch Women's Health Inst 125 Paterson St Rm 2104 New Brunswick NJ 08901-1962 E-mail: gloria.bachmann@umdnj.edu.

BACHMANN, JOHN WILLIAM, security firm executive; b. Centralia, Ill., Nov. 16, 1938; s. George Adam and Helen (Johnston) B.; m. Katharine I. Butler; children: John C., Kristene Ellen Bachmann Wright. AB, Wabash Coll., 1960; MBA, Northwestern U., 1962; LLD (hon.), Wabash Coll., 1990. Rschr. Edward Jones, St. Louis, 1962-63, investment rep., 1963-70, gen. ptnr., 1970-80, mng. ptnr., 1980—2003, sr. ptnr., 2004—. Bd. dirs. Am. Airlines, Inc., NASD, The Monsanto Co. Trustee Wabash Coll., Crawfordsville, Ind., 1980—; chmn. bd. visitors Drucker Ctr. Claremont (Calif.) Grad. Sch., 1987—; past chmn., bd. dirs. Arts and Edn. Coun. Greater St. Louis; commr. St. Louis Art Mus.; past chmn. St. Louis Symphony Soc.; past chmn. St. Louis Regional Chamber and Growth Assn.; chmn. US C. of C., 2004-05, chmn. exec. com. 2005-. Mem. Nat. Assn. Securities Dealers (past dist. chmn.), Securities Industry Assn. (bd. dirs., chmn. 1976-79), Securities Industry Found. for Econ. Edn. (chmn. trustees 1988-92), St. Louis Club, Bogey Club. Office: Edward Jones 12555 Manchester Rd Saint Louis MO 63131 Office Phone: 314-515-2626.

BACHMANN, KURT T., astronomer, educator; b. Louisville, Ky., July 2, 1960; s. Thomas H. and Dorris E. (Dietrich) B. BS, Calif. Inst. Tech., 1982; MA, Columbia U., 1984, MPh, 1985, PhD, 1988. Asst. prof. physics Widener U., Chester, Pa., 1988-91; vis. scientist Nat. Ctr. for Atmospheric Rsch., Boulder, Colo., 1991-93; jr. scientist Nat. Solar Observatory, Tucson, 1993-95; asst. prof. physics Birmingham-So. Coll., 1995. Contbr. articles to profl. jours including Astrophys. Jour., Solar Physics, The Phys. Rev., Nuclear Instrumentation and Methods, Am. Jour. Physics. Fellow Tau Beta Pi; mem. Am. Astron. Soc. (com. on employment 1995-98), Am. Assn. Physics Tchrs., Coun. Undergrad. Rsch., Project Kaleidoscope Faculty for the 21st Century. Achievements include: measured frequencies of high degree solar p-mode and f-mode oscillations; showed that indices of solar activity exhibit hysteresis patterns. Office: Birmingham So Coll PO Box A22 Birmingham AL 35254-0001

BACHMANN, RICHARD ARTHUR, retired oil industry executive; b. Green Bay, Wis., Dec. 6, 1944; s. Richard Arthur and Anita Sidonia (Dohmeyer) B.; children: Richard A., Joseph E., Christina J.; m. Toni Van Zandt, July, 24, 2004. BBA, Wis. State U., 1967; MBA, U. Wis., 1968. Mgr. fgn. fin. Exxon Corp., N.Y.C., 1968-78; v.p., treas. Itel Corp., San Francisco, 1978-81; sr. v.p. fin. and adminstrn., CFO La. Land and Exploration Co., New Orleans, 1981-85, exec. v.p. fin. and adminstrn., CFO, 1985—95, also bd. dirs.; pres., COO, 1995-97; pres., CEO, chmn. bd. Energy Ptnrs., Ltd., New Orleans, 1997—. Bd. dirs. Audubon Inst., 1987-91, Aquarium of Americas, 1989-91; bd. dirs., governing com. Univ. Health Care Sys. Gov. Com., 1995; bd. dirs. Penn Va. Corp., 1997-2002, Superior Energy Svcs. Inc., 1999-2004. Bd. dirs., exec. coun., pres., trustee Boy Scouts Am., 1988—, nat. coun., chmn. supply com., 1990-95; bd. dirs., found. mem. Young Aspirations/Young Artists, Inc., 1988-95; bd. dirs., chmn. fin. oversight com., 1989-91; bd. dirs., chmn., mentor/coach Covenant House, 1990-95; bd. govs., adv. bd. mem. Isadore Newman Sch., 1990-; found. prin., bd. dirs., chmn. emeritus, Summerbridge, 1990-; role model Young Leadership Coun.; bd. dirs. Tulane U. Hosp. & Clinic, 1995-, Xavier U. La., 2004-, Trico Marine Svcs., Inc., 2005-. Office: Energy Partners Ltd 201 Saint Charles Ave Ste 3400 New Orleans LA 70170-1026 Office Phone: 504-799-1944.

BACHMANN, RICHARD H., lawyer; b. Ft. McClellan, Ala., 1953; BA, Southwestern U., 1974; JD, U. Houston, 1977. Bar: Tex. 1977. Ptnr. Butler & Binion, Houston, 1988—93, Snell & Smith P.C., 1993—98; exec. v.p., chief legal officer, sec. Enterprise Products Ptnrs. LP, Houston, 1999—. Fellow Tex. Bar Found., Houston Bar Found.; mem. ABA, State Bar Tex., Houston Bar Assn., Order Barons, Phi Delta Phi. Office: Enterprise Products Ptnrs LP PO Box 4324 2727 N Loop West Houston TX 77210 Business E-Mail: rbachmann@eprod.com.

BACHMANN, WILLIAM THOMPSON, dermatologist; b. Orange, N.J., Mar. 21, 1940; s. George Kirsten and Agnes Mary (Cunningham) B.; m. Carolyn Emily Loeber, Dec. 28, 1961 (div. June 1971); children: John Kirsten, William Thompson; m. Judith Richmond, June 20, 1981; 1 stepchild, Julia Garriga. AB, Williams Coll., 1962; MD, Boston U., 1966. Diplomat Am. Bd. Internal Medicine, Am. Bd. Dermatology. Intern St. Francis Hosp., Hartford, Conn., 1966-67, resident, 1967-68, Yale New Haven (Conn.) Hosp., 1971-72, 72-74; dermatologist Westerly (R.I.) Hosp. Lt. comdr. USN, 1969-71. Fellow Am. Coll. Physicians, Am. Acad. Dermatology; mem. New England Dermatological Soc., R.I. Med. Soc., Yale Soc. Attendings in Dermatology (sr. attending mem.), Alpha Omega Alpha. Avocations: boating, photography. Office: 39 East Ave Westerly RI 02891-3113

BACHNER, JOHN PHILIP, business consultant; b. Boston, Nov. 8, 1944; s. Barnard and Bertha (Bellar) B.; m. Patricia B. Gartenhaus, June 14, 1997. AB, Harvard U., 1966. Screenplay writer Screen Presentations Inc., Washington, 1967-68; account exec. Hoffman Assocs. Inc., Silver Spring, Md., 1968-71; pres. Bachner Communications Inc., Silver Spring, 1971—. Pres. Bachner Mgmt. Systems, 1973—; exec. v.p. Cons. Engrs. Coun. of Met. Washington, Silver Spring, 1971-96, Property Mgmt. Assn., Silver Spring, 1973-96, Washington Area Coun. Engring. Labs., Silver Spring, 1975-93; exec. v.p. ASFE, 1973—; pres., chmn. bd. Constrn. Industry Tech. Inc., Silver Spring, 1973—; pres. Most for the Lease, 1982—; v.p. Bachner R.E., 1985-97; exec. v.p. Mid-Atlantic Coun. of Shopping Ctr. Mgrs., 1986-93; exec. v.p. Inst. Profl. Practice, Silver Spring, 1988-94, Coll. Property Mgmt. Found., Silver Spring, 1988-96; pres. Cons. Engrs., Ednl. Found. Inc., 1990-99; exec. dir. Profl. Liability Agts. Network Inc., 1991-98, Mid-Atlantic Cancer Rsch. Found., Silver Spring, 1992-95, Internat. Found. Advancement of Thrombosis and Hematosis Rsch. Inc., Silver Spring, 1992-98, Design and Constrn. Quality Inst., 1992-95, Calif. R.E. Inspection Assn., 1993-98, Metro Washington Heat Pump Assn., 1994-99, Intelligence Builders Inst., 1994; pres. Bus. Art and Graphics, 1993-97. Author: Marketing and Promotion for Design Professionals, 1977, Guide to Practical Property Management, 1991, Practice Management for Design Professionals, 1991, ASFE Contract Reference Guide, 3d edit., 1996, 3.1 edit., 1998, ECS Contract Reference Guide, 1997, 2nd edit., 1999, RA&MCO Contract Reference Guide, 1997, 2d edit., 2002, Derailed by Dispute, 2003; writer 25 motion picture screenplays; contbr. over 1500 articles to profl. publs., popular mags.; columnist, author contract reference guides, 1996-2000. Pres. Engrs.' Leadership Found., 1999—2003; bd. govs. Found. for Profl. Practice, 2001—. Home: 9206 Sterling Montague Dr Great Falls VA 22066-4002 E-mail: john@bachner.com.

BACHOP, WILLIAM EARL, JR., retired anatomist, zoologist; b. Youngstown, Ohio, Aug. 31, 1926; s. William Earl Sr. and Mary Agnes (Murray) B.; m. Annabelle Adams, Dec. 27, 1958 (dec. 2001); children: Alice Mary, Margaret Anne. BA, Western Res. U., 1950; MS, Ohio State U., 1958, PhD, 1963. Asst. prof. biology U. Omaha, 1963-65; postdoctoral fellow U. Wash., Seattle, 1965-69; asst. prof. zoology Clemson (S.C.) U., 1969-73; gross anatomy studentship Bowman Gray Med. Sch., Winston-Salem, N.C., 1973-74; asst. prof. anatomy Nat. Coll. Chiropractic, Lombard, Ill., 1974-77, assoc. prof. anatomy, 1977-81, prof. anatomy, 1981-96, prof. emeritus, 1996—, also acting chmn. dept. anatomy, 1974-76, chmn. dept. anatomy, 1976-86; ret., 1996. Vis. scientist NSF, Omaha, 1963-65, Inst. Marine Scis., Morehead City, N.C., summer 1972; gen. anatomy examiner Bd. Chiropractic Examiners, Boulder, Colo., 1975-76; summer fellowship NSF, Columbia U., N.Y.C., 1960. Author: (chpt.) Early Embryology of Fish, 1974, Development of the Spine and Spinal Cord, 1995; contbr. articles to profl. jours. Served to cpl. U.S. Army, 1951-53. Recipient Nebr. Coop. grant NSF, 1964, Rsch. associateship U. Mich., 1964, Tuition scholarship NIH, 1973. Mem. Am. Assn. Anatomists, Am. Assn. Clin. Anatomists, Ill. State Acad. Scis. Achievements include research establishing that giant nuclei in yolk sac syncytium of oviparous teleostean embryos contains polyploid amounts of DNA; establishing that respiratory deficient strains of bakers yeast lacked elementary particles in their mitochondria. Home: 1133 S Finley Rd Apt 410 Lombard IL 60148-3872

BACHRACH, CHARLES LEWIS, advertising agency executive; b. NYC, Feb. 22, 1946; s. Herbert and Lilla Clare (Blumberg) B.; m. Lois Susan Davis, Sept. 12, 1968; 1 dau., Jennifer Leigh. BS, Ithaca (N.Y.) Coll., 1968. Assoc. producer MPO Sports Co., N.Y.C., 1968-69; unit mgr. NBC, N.Y.C., 1969; with Ogilvy & Mather, Inc., N.Y.C., 1969—, sr. v.p. broadcast, 1978-83, dir. Network and Programming Dept; sr. v.p. network and programming Western Internat. Media, 1983-89, exec. v.p., 1989—; pres. Western Internat. Syndication, 1983—; sr. v.p., dir. network and program purchasing Rubin Postaer & Assocs., L.A., 1990-92, exec. v.p., dir. media and resources and programming, 1992—. Vis. prof. Ithaca Coll. Sch. Communications; vis. lectr. New Sch.; guest lectr. UCLA, Calif. State, L.A., Marymount Coll.; guest commentator NPR, CNN, NBC. Contbr. articles to profl. publs. Judge Internat. Emmy Awards.; Lobbyist N.Y. State pvt. colls.; bd. dirs. Caption Ctr., 1992. Recipient Disting. Alumni award Ithaca Coll., 1980, Aid to Advt. Edn. award Am. Advt. Fedn., 1986, Media Maven award Advt. Age, 1996; named One of Top 100 Young People in Advt., 1985. Mem. AAAA (com. broadcast network and programming), TV Acad. Arts and Scis., L.A. Advt. Club (bd. dirs. 1989). Office: Rubin Postaer and Assocs 1333 2d St Santa Monica CA 90401-1100 Home: 317 N Palm Dr Apt 3E Beverly Hills CA 90210-4106

BACHRACH, HOWARD L., biochemist; b. Faribault, Minn., May 21, 1920; s. Harry and Elizabeth (Panovitz) Bachrach; m. Shirley F. Lichterman, June 13, 1943; children: Eve E., Harrison J. BA in Chemistry, U. Minn., 1942, PhD in Biochemistry, 1949. Research chemist synthetic rubber Jos. E. Seagram & Co., 1942; Research asst. explosives research lab. Nat. Def. Research Com. project Carnegie Inst. Tech., Pitts., 1942—45; research asst. U. Minn., Mpls., 1945—49; biochemist, foot-and-mouth disease mission USDA, Denmark, 1949—50; research biochemist virus lab. U. Calif-Berkeley, 1950—53; chief scientist, head biochem. and phys. investigation Plum Island Animal Disease Ctr., Greenport, NY, 1953—80, research chemist, advisor to dir., 1981—89, sci. collaborator, 1989—95. Charter mem. Sr. Exec. Svc. U.S. Govt., 1979; mem. viral and rickettsial grants subcom. Walter Reed Army Inst. Tsch., 1982—85; cons. Pan Am. Health Orgn., Brazil, 1981, Coop. State Res. Svcs. USDA, 1982—83; cons. Office Sec. Assessment U.S. Congress, 1984—85, cons, 1988—89, Nat. Cancer Inst., 1984—87, Tex. A&M U. Inst. Bioscis. and Techs., 1987—89; Theobald Smith lectr. Am. Soc. Microbiology, 1981. Contbr. 20 chpts. to books, more than 150 original articles to sci. publs. Named to USDA Agr. Sci. Hall of Fame, 1987; recipient Naval Ordnance Devel. award, 1945, Cert. of Merit, USDA, 1960, Disting. Svc. award, 1982, U.S. Presdl. citation, 1965, U.S. Sr. Exec. Svc. award, 1980, Newcomb Cleveland prize, AAAS, 1982, Nat. Award for Agrl. Excellence, 1983, Alexander von Humboldt award, 1983, Nat. Medal Sci., Pres. Ronald Reagan, 1983, ISI Citation Classics Publ., 1986. Fellow: N.Y. Acad. Sci.; mem.: Am. Soc. Virology, Am. Chem. Soc. (Kenneth A. Spencer medal 1983, 50 yr. mem. 1997), Am. Coll. Veterinary Microbiologists (hon.), Nat. Acad. Scis. U.S. (Nominated to Wisdom Hall of Fame 2000), Phi Lambda Upsilon, Gamma Alpha, Sigma Xi. Achievements include development of first purification and electron microscopic visualization of polio and foot-and-mouth disease viruses; subunit vaccines--protection of swine with a protein isolated from foot-and-mouth disease virus; reported first effective recombinant DNA cloned viral protein vaccine for use in animals or humans; described comparative molecular pathways of replication for all classes of animal and human viruses. Home: 10220 Andover Coach Cir Apt G2 Lake Worth FL 33467-8137 Personal E-mail: howshy@aol.com.

BACHRACH, LAURA KEYES, medical educator; b. Boston, Dec. 11, 1947; d. Bradford Keyser and Rosamond Esselen Bachrach; m. Charles Grant Prober, Sept. 13, 1949; children: Meghan Keyes Prober, Andrew Bradford Prober. BA, Harvard U., 1970; MD, Tufts U. Med. Sch., 1976. Asst. prof. of pediat. Stanford U. Sch. of Medicine, Stanford, Calif., 1988—92, assoc. prof. of pediat., 1993—2000, prof. of pediat., 2000—. Office: Stanford U Sch of Medicine 300 Pasteur Dr Stanford CA 94305-5208 Office Phone: 650-723-5791.

BACHRACH, NANCY, advertising executive; b. Providence, Jan. 29, 1948; d. David and Maida Horovitz. BA magna cum laude, Conn. Coll. for Women, 1969; MA with honors, Brandeis U., 1973, PhD, 1975. Assoc. dir. Grey France, Paris, 1980—84; sr. v.p., account mgmt. Grey Advt., N.Y.C., 1985—91, exec. v.p., 1992—2001, chief mktg. officer, 2001—. Author: The Irrefutability of Skepticism, 1975. Named one of 100 Best and Brightest Women, Advt. Age, 1988; named to Acad. Women Achievers, 1992. Office: Grey Advt Inc 777 3rd Ave New York NY 10017-1401

BACHUS, SPENCER T., III, congressman, lawyer; b. Birmingham, Ala., Dec. 28, 1947; m. Linda; children: Warren, Stuart, Elliott, Candance, Lisa. BA, Auburn U., 1969; JD, U. Ala., 1972. Atty., 1972—; mem. Ala. State Senate, 1982-83, Ala. Ho. of Reps., 46th dist., 1984—86; repr. 6th dist. Ala. State Bd. of Ed., 1987—91; sr. ptnr. Bachus, Dempsey, Carson, & Steed; mem. U.S. Congress from 6th Ala. dist., 1993—, mem. banking and fin. svcs. com., transp. and infrastructure com., vets. affairs com. & jud. com. Vice chmn. Jefferson County Legis. Del. Mgr. Guy Hunt's Gubernatorial campaign, 1986; del. Rep. Nat. Conv., 1988; mem. Ala. Bd. Edn.; chmn. Ala. State Rep. Exec. Com., 1991. Served in USAR, 1969—71. Recipient Commr's. merit award as Outstanding Rep. Ala. Dept. Human Resources, 1986, Henry M. Somerville award U. Ala. Republican. Office: US Ho of Reps 442 Cannon Bldg Washington DC 20515-0106 also: Dist Off 1900 Internat Park Dr Birmingham AL 35243*

BACHUS, WALTER OTIS, retired military officer, retired professional society administrator; b. Grand Saline, Tex., Oct. 27, 1926; s. Walter Harry and Gladys Marie Bachus; m. Helen Singer, Dec. 12, 1946; children: Bruce, Leslie. BSCE, Tex. A&M U., 1950; M in Indsl. Engring., NYU, 1957; grad., Army War Coll., 1968; grad. Advanced Mgmt. Program, Harvard U., 1973. Registered profl. engr., Tex., Wash., D.C. Officer Corps Engrs. U.S. Army, 1950, advanced through grades to brig. gen.; ret., 1978; exec. dir. Soc. Am. Mil. Engrs., Alexandria, Va., 1978-93, ret., 1993. Decorated D.S.M., Legion of Merit, Bronze Star, Army Commendation medal; recipient Sec. of Def. Pub. Svc. medal. Christian Scientist. Home: 3808 Great Neck Ct Alexandria VA 22309-2634 E-mail: bachusw@cox.net.

BACHYNSKI, MORREL PAUL, physicist; b. Bienfait, Sask., Can., July 19, 1930; s. Nick and Karolina (Bachynski) B.; m. Slava Krkovic, May 1959; children: Caroline Dawn, Jane Diane. B.Eng., U. Sask., 1952, M.Sc., 1953; PhD, McGill U., 1955; LLD (hon.), U. Waterloo, 1993; DSc (hon.), McGill U., 1994; LLD (hon.), Concordia U., 1997. Mem. sci. staff RCA Ltd., Montreal, Que., 1955-58, dir. microwave physics lab., 1958-65, dir. research, 1965-72, dir. research and devel. labs., 1972-75, v.p. research and devel., 1975-76; pres. MPB Technologies Inc., Pointe Claire, Que., 1976—; Scitec, 1974-75. Author: (with Johnston and Shkarofsky) The Particle Kinetics of Plasmas, 1968; contbr. Recipient David Sarnoff Gold medal, 1963, Prix Scientifique du Quebec, 1973, Can. Enterprise Devel. award, 1977, Prix PME Que., 1984, Medal of Achievement Can. Rsch. Mgmt. Assn., 1988, Can. awards for Business Excellence-Entrepreneurship, 1989, 90, Prix award Assn. Que. Dirs. Indsl. Rsch., 1991, Prix Lionel Boulet, 2001. Fellow: IEEE, Can. Acad. Engring. (pres. 2003—04), Can. Aero. and Space Inst., Royal Soc. Can. (Thomas W. Eadie medal 2003), Am. Phys. Soc.; mem.: Sci. Coun. Can., Can. Assn. Physicists (pres. 1968, medal of achievement 1984, Applied Physics medal 1995), Engring. Inst. Can. (hon.). Home: 78 Thurlow Rd Montreal PQ Canada H3X 3G9 Office: MPB Techs Inc 151 Hymus Blvd Pointe-Claire PQ Canada H9R 1E9 Office Phone: 514-694-8751. Personal E-mail: m.p.bachynski@mpbc.ca. E-mail: m.p.bachynski@mpb-technologies.ca.

BACIGALUPI, DON, museum director; BA summa cum laude, U. Houston; MA, PhD, U. Tex., Austin. Dir., chief curator Art Mus. at U. Houston; curator contemporary art San Antonio Mus. Art; exec. dir. San Diego Mus. Art, 1999—2003; dir. Toledo Mus. Art, 2004—. Named one of 50 People to Watch, San Diego Mag., 2000. Office: Toledo Museum Art PO Box 1013 Toledo OH 43697

BACK, ROBERT WYATT, investment company executive, pharmaceutical executive, consultant; b. Omaha, Dec. 22, 1936; s. Albert Edward, Jr. and Edith (Elliott) Back; m. Linaya Gail Hahn, Aug. 30, 1964; children: Christopher Frederick, Gregory Franklin. BA, Trinity Coll., 1958; postgrad., London Sch. Econs. and Polit., 1959-60, Harvard U., 1960-61; MA, Yale U., 1960. CLU; CFA, ChFC. Head trader, reinsurance rep., security analyst Lincoln Nat. Life Ins. Co., Fort Wayne, Ind., 1964-69; sr. investment analyst Allstate Ins. Co., Northbrook, Ill., 1969-72; investment adv. acct. mgr. Brown Bros. Harriman & Co., Chgo., 1972-74; asst. v.p., investment analyst Harris Trust & Savs. Bank, 1974-82; v.p. instnl. rsch. Prescott Ball & Turben, 1982-83, Blunt, Ellis & Loewi, Inc., 1983-84; v.p. instnl. equity sales Rodman & Renshaw, Inc., 1984-87; v.p. instnl. rsch. ins. Legg, Mason, Wood & Walker, Inc., 1987-89; mng. dir. instnl. dept. J.E. Liss & Co., 1989-92; sr. v.p., sales mgr. SNC Capital Mgmt., 1991—; CEO IPOSITE.COM Inc. Mng. dir. investor pub. rels. CCR Assocs.; sr. advisor Ivy Coll. Privileges; mng. dir. Ivy Coll. Privileges Ltd. Liability Cos., Revenyouniverse; arbitrator N.Y. Stock Exchange, 2002—04; expert witness Nat. Assn. of Security Dealers, 2004; exec. chmn. Skull and Bones Coll. Presenters; mng. dir. Sarbanes-Oxley Nat. Pub. Awareness Forum; lectr. in field. Co-author: Yale in the Modern World: The Yale Presidential Succession, Yale in the Modern World: Bush/Clinton/Bush, Big Money and the Presidential Elections, Adult Authors: Big Money Hurting Yale's Future; contbr. articles to profl. jours. Active founding coun. Nat. Edn. Access Fund, 1992; pres. Buffalo Grove Police Pension Fund, 1973—90; mem. long-range planning com. Adlai Stevenson HS, Prairie View, Ill., 1980—82; chmn. investments Ill. Police Pension Fund Assn., Chgo., 1985—87; fund mgr. AIDS/HIV Select Fund, 1992—; mem. corp. Scholarships for Ill. Residents; vice chmn. Wheaton Media Commn., 1996—; deacon Presbyn. Ch. Capt. USAFR, 1961—64. Woodrow Wilson fellow, Yale U., 1958, English-Speaking Union fellow, London Sch. Econs., 1959, Russian Rsch. fellow, Harvard U., 1960—61. Fellow: Fin. Analysts Fedn. (internat. del. 1974—); mem.: Am. Coll. CLUs and ChFCs (bd. dirs. 1986—87), Inst. CFAs (sec., bd. dirs. Chgo. chpt. 1980—84, lectr.), Am. Assn. Individual Investors (life), Soc. First Divsn. (life), Harvard Club Chgo. (schs. com.), Yale Club Chgo. (bd. dirs. alumni assn. del. 1972—, coord. grad. and profl. alumni), Trinity Club (mem. exec. com. Chgo. chpt. 1987—90, mem. scholarship Ill. residents divsn. 1973—, fin. com.), Rotary (ch.n. leadership confs., Paul Harris fellow 1995), Phi Beta Kappa (jr.), Pi Gamma Mu. Republican. Avocations: skiing, travel, homeland security. Home and Office: Ivy College Privileges Ltd Liability Cos 225 N Dorchester Ave Wheaton IL 60187-4707 Office Phone: 630-668-3277. Personal E-mail: backfocus_bob2002@yahoo.com.

BACKE, IONE ELIZABETH, retired elementary school educator; b. Crawfordsville, Ind., July 28, 1919; d. Jesse Caster and Ione Tribbett; m. Donald F. Backe, Nov. 2, 1985; m. McCarthy, Jr. Lawrence James (div.); children: James L. McCarthy III, Alberta Ruth McCarthy Adams, Charles R. McCarthy, William F. McCarthy, Richard M. McCarthy, Martin K. McCarthy, Brian C. McCarthy. BA in Speech/Comm., U. Mich., 1941; postgrad., Ind. State U., Terre Haute. Tchr. St. Bernard's Sch., Crawfordsville, Ind., 1966—70, Newmarket Elem. Sch., Ind., 1070—1985; substitute tchr. Montgomery County Schs., Ind., 1985—90. Spl. needs tutor/counselor, Crawfordsville, Ind., 2000—03. Vol. Mar. of Dimes Mothers Mar., Crawfordsville, Ind.; tour leader Ln. Pl., Crawfordsville, Ind.; chairwoman Candlelight Christmas Tour, Montgomery County Hist. Soc., Crawfordsville, Ind., 1951—2004; den mother Cub Scouts, Crawfordsville, Ind., 1963—68; parish dir. Meals on Wheels, Crawfordsville, Ind., 1997—2004; mem. St. Bernard's Parish, Crawfordsville, Ind., 1942—2004; dir. Elizabeth Ministry, Crawfordsville, Ind., 1989—2004; bd. dirs. Montgomery County Hist. Soc., Crawfordsville, Ind., 1949—2003; class reunion com. U. Mich. Class of 1941, Ann Arbor, 1942—2004. Named Sagamore of Wabash, Gov. of Ind., 2004; recipient Cert. of Merit, St. Bernard's Parish, Crawfordsville, Ind., 1997, Fifty Yr. Spl. Svc. award, Montgomery County Hist. Soc., 1999, Citizen of the Yr., Montgomery County C. of C., 2001. Mem.: AAUW, Am. Legion Aux. (pres. 1955—56, Past Pres.'s Parlay 1956—2004), Psi Iota Xi (life; Gamma Xi chpt. v.p. 1956—57, chairwoman cards and flowers com., patrons com., geranium com., vol. speech and hearing clinics, Person of Yr. 2001, Nat. award 2001). Roman Catholic. Avocations: travel, avid Wolverine supporter (U. Mich.). Home: 703 E Main St Crawfordsville IN 47933

BACKER, RONALD GEORGE, lawyer; b. Pitts., Apr. 27, 1951; s. Philip Ralph and Eleanor (Wintner) B.; m. Leslie Wershbale, Oct. 13, 1985; children: Emma, Seth. BS, Univ. Pitts., 1973, JD, 1976. Bar: Pa. 1976, U.S. Dist. Ct. (we. dist.) Pa. 1976, U.S. Ct. Appeals (3d cir.) 1980, U.S. Ct. Appeals (fed. cir.) 1992, U.S. Ct. Appeals (4th cir.) 1992. Law clk. to Judge Maurice Louis Ct. of Common Pleas of Allegheny County, Pitts., 1976-78; atty. Messer and Shilobod, Pitts., 1978; atty., ptnr. Rothman, Gordon, Foreman and Groudine, Pitts., 1978—. Contbr. articles to profl. jours. Bd. dirs. Adat Shalom Synagogue, Fox Chapel, Pa., 1994—; coach youth sports, 1984—. Avocations: biking, golf, reading. Office: Rothman Gordon Foreman & Groudine Grant Building Fl 3 Pittsburgh PA 15219-2203

BACKER, WILLIAM EARNEST, food products executive; b. Fulton, Mo., Dec. 3, 1922; s. William Earnest and Ida Lorraine (Smith) B.; m. Marjorie Jean Keller, Dec. 25, 1943; children: W. Dale, Vicki Lynn McDaniel, Carolyn Sue Cave. BA in Chemistry, Westminster Coll., 1943; postgrad., Wayne U., 1954. Chemistry lab. technician Delco Remy, Muncie, Ind., 1943—44; gen. mgr. Backer Potato Chip Co., Fulton, Mo., 1946—50, pres., CEO, 1957—88, chmn. of bd., 1988—; regional sales exec. A.P. Green Refractories, Mexico, Mo., 1950—51, salesman Detroit, 1951—53; test engr. Ford Motor Co., Dearborn, Mich., 1953—57. Patentee M39-20mm Cannon components, package machine components, socket holder, socket wrench sorter having Braille for the blind. Pres. Fulton C. of C., 1977, also bd. dirs., chmn. planning and zoning; v.p. adminstrn./product sales Great Rivers coun. Boy Scouts Am., Columbia, Mo., 1980-92, also current trustee; chmn. bldg. and grounds Westminster Coll., Fulton, 1990-91; chmn. nominating com. Children's Hosp., Columbia; established Fulton Visitor Ctr./Collector Vehicle Mus., 1996; founding bd. dirs. The Carpenter's Kids, 1999. Recipient Resolution, donation for bldg., Callaway County Commrs., Fulton, 1989, Disting. Eagle Scout award Nat. Eagle Scout Assn., 1995, Disting. Eagle Scout award Mo. Ho. of Reps., 1996, Excellence in Cmty. Svc. award Daughters of the Am. Revolution, 2000; named Disting. Indsl. Developer, Fulton Rotary, 1994. Mem. Kiwanis Internat. (lt. gov. Mo./Ark. divsns 1987-88), Fulton Kiwanis (pres. 1968, Kiwanian of Yr. 1984, 94), Kingdom of Callaway (pres.-elect 2003). Republican. Presbyterian. Avocation: collector of vintage automobiles. Home: PO Box 128 Fulton MO 65251-0128 Office: Backer Potato Chip Co One Industrial Rd Fulton MO 65251 Office Phone: 573-642-5344. E-mail: w.e.backer@sbcglobal.net.

BACKLAR, BYRON, lawyer; b. St. Louis, May 5, 1925; s. Joseph and Rosemary Backlar; m. Marilyn Willner, May 28, 1961 (dec. Mar. 6, 1970); children: Roger, Fredric; m. Patricia Harris, May 20, 1977. AB, Washington U., St. Louis, 1948; MS, U. Chgo., 1950; JD, Washington U., 1955. Bar: Mo. 1956, U.S. Dist. Ct. (ea. dist.) Mo. 1956. Atty. Lyng, McLeod, Abells, and Lyng, 1953—56; atty., corp. adminstr. various indsl. cos., Los Angeles County, Calif., 1955—65; instr. ext. UCLA, 1961—67, mgr. life and health scis. office extramural support, 1965—67, asst. dir. office extramural support, 1967—70, dir. office extramural support, 1970—71, asst. dean for adminstrn. sch. medicine, 1971—84; cons. Nat. Inst. Allergy and Infectious Diseases/NIH, Rockville, Md., 1993; assoc. dean for adminstrn., assoc. prof. sch. medicine Oreg. Health Sci. U., Portland, 1984—97, assoc. dean emeritus and assoc. prof., 1997—. Mem. exec. bd. and Oreg. Health and Sci. U. rep. Puget Sound Fed. Health Coun., 1994—96; chmn. joint com. Bd. Med. Quality Assurance and Calif. Med. Schs., 1975—84; commr. Commn. on Higher Edn.'s Role in Influencing the Devel. of Fed. Rsch., Edn. and Tng. Policy of the Nat. Coun. Univ. Rsch. Adminstrs., 1971; exec. com. bd. dirs. Assoc. Western Univs., 1969—71. Chmn. adv. com. of mentally gifted minor program Santa Monica-Malibu Sch. Dist., Calif., 1976—77; chair Health Ptnrs. Coun. of Vol. Health Agencies in L.A. County, United Way, 1983—84; pres. L.A. Coastal Cities unit Am. Cancer Soc., 1979—80, pres. Oreg. divsn., 1990—92; mem. coord. com. Oregon Partnership for Cancer Control, 2002—; bd. dirs. Venice (Calif.) Family Clinic, 1979—84; bd. dirs. Calif. divsn. Am. Cancer Soc., 1981—84, bd. dirs. Metro unit, 1999—2002, bd. dirs. N.W. divsn. Alaska, Mont., Oreg., Wash., 2001—; bd. dirs. Cascadia Behavioral Healthcare, Inc., Multnomah County, Oreg., 2001—, bd. sec., 2003—; mem. bd. dirs. Oregan Adv. Ctr., 2005—. With USN, 1943—45, PTO. Decorated two battle stars; named Vol. of the Yr., L.A. Coastal Cities unit Am. Cancer Soc., 1982, Vol. of Yr., Am. Cancer Soc.; recipient Disting. Svc. award, Faculty and Profl. Staff Assn. of Harbor Gen. Hosp., 1976, Meritorious Svc. award, Rsch. and Edn. Inst., Inc. of Harbor-UCLA Med. Ctr., 1983, Leadership medal Oreg. divsn., Am. Cancer Soc., 1992. Fellow: Nat. Contract Mgmt. Assn. (Lifetime Cert. of Profl. Contract Mgmt.); mem.: Assn. of Am. Med. Colls. (mem. group on faculty practice U.S. and Can. 1987—88, chair group on bus. affairs western region 1996, chair group on bus. affairs U.S. and Can. 1995—96), Portland Yacht Club, Cabrillo Beach Yacht Club, Sigma Xi, Phi Delta Phi. Avocations: sailing, reading, woodworking, photography. Home: 4160 SW Greenleaf Dr Portland OR 97221

BACKLIN, JIM, legislative staff member; b. Mpls., July 4, 1942; Grad., West Point Mil. Acad., 1966. With mfg. dept. Procter & Gamble; plant mgr. Potlatch Corp., Scranton, Pa.; with Nat. Life Vt.; v.p. Anderson Products Inc.; chmn. Minn. 5th Congl. dist. Ronald Reagan Presdl. Campaign; with office intergovtl. affairs Sec. VA; chief of staff U.S. Rep. Roscoe G. Bartlett. Founder, organizer Cheboygan Mich. Hockey Assn.; active Harvest Christian Fellowship, Frederick, Md. Office: US Rep Roscoe G Bartlett 2412 Rayburn Ho Office Bldg Washington DC 20515-0001

BACKLIN, WILLIAM WAYNE, music educator, composer; b. Mason City, Iowa, Apr. 24, 1957; s. Rodney Joseph and Shirley Ruth Backlin; m. Jolene Kay Thompson, Mar. 20, 1958; children: Aaron Scott, Jeffrey Thomas. A, North Iowa Area C.C., 1977; MusB in Edn., Drake U., 1979; MusM, U. No. Iowa, 2003. Cert. ministerial Iowa, 1995; tchg. Iowa, 2001. Vocal music instr. Nora Springs-Rock Falls Cmty. Schools, Iowa, 1977—86; choral music instr. Mason City H.S., 1986—92; piano, music theory and history educator North Iowa Area C.C., Mason City, 1995—. Bd. dirs. Ter. Hill Piano Scholarship, Des Moines, 1986—90; project scholar team leader North Iowa Area Edn. Agy., Iowa, 1986; headline spkr. Iowa Choral Dir.'s Assn., Mason City, 1989; edn. evaluator North Ctrl. Accreditation Team, Sioux City, Iowa, 1991, Ames, Iowa, 91. Composer: (songs) We Who Live in America, Civil War Chronicles, Psalm 145, Nicea, Agnus Dei, Little Bird (Holocaust Memoires), Spirit of the Lord, (commissioned choral work) U. Northern Iowa, Waldorf Coll., Iowa Choral Dirs. Assn. (Choral Composition Commissioning Competition, 2005), North Iowa Area C.C. Named Outstanding Educator, Mason City Cmty. Sch. Dist., 1991, winner composition competition, Iowa Choral Dirs. Assn./Iowa Composers Forum, 2005. Mem.: Nat. Fedn. H.S. (assoc.). Home: 6 Hampshire CT Mason City IA 50401 Office: North Iowa Area Community College 500 College Dr Mason City IA 50401

BACKMAN, GERALD STEPHEN, retired lawyer; b. N.Y.C., Apr. 16, 1938; s. Morris and Marion (London) B.; m. Susan Pergament, Sept. 3, 1961 (dec. May 1978); children: Jonathan A., Kenneth S.; m. Barbara Fried Kaynes, Nov. 3, 1979 (dec. Jan. 2003); children: Jonathan J. Kaynes, Adam R. Kaynes. BA, U. Pa., 1959; LLBcum laude, Harvard U., 1962. Assoc. Weil, Gotshal & Manges LLP, N.Y.C., 1962-70, ptnr., 1970—2004; ret., 2004. House counsel The Associated Merchandising Corp., N.Y.C., 1965-68; lectr. N.Y.U., 1973, Irving Trust Co., N.Y.C., 1981-88; adj. prof. law Fordham U. Sch. Law, N.Y.C., 2000—, Miami U. Sch. Law, 2004—; mem. Tri-Bar Opinion Com., 2000—. Bd. dirs. Hewlett-East Rockaway (N.Y.) Jewish Ctr., 1976-97, chmn. legal com., 1974-85, sec., 1980-82; bd. dirs. 25 E. 86th St. Corp., N.Y.C., 1996-99. Mem.: ABA, Assn. Bar N.Y.C., N.Y. State Bar Assn. (trustee bus. law sect. 2000—03, chmn. securities regulation com. 2000—03), Am. Arbitration Assn. (arbitrator), Nat. Assn. Corporate Dirs. (former chmn., pres. N.Y. chpt., mem. blue ribbon commn. on audit coms.), Masons. Republican. Jewish. Avocations: golf, skiing, tennis, fishing. Office: Weil Gotshal & Manges LLP 767 5th Ave New York NY 10153-0119 Home: 10 Pink Creek Ave #301W Fairfield CT 06824 also: 3400 SW 27th Ave Apt 903 Miami FL 33133 Personal E-mail: gback@aol.com. Business E-Mail: Gerald.Backman@Weil.com.

BACKMAN, VADIM, biomedical engineer, educator; b. St. Petersburg, Russia, May 7, 1973; arrived in U.S., 1996, naturalized, 2002; s. Yuri and Galina Backman. MS, St. Petersburg Technical U., 1996, MIT, 1998; PhD, Harvard U., 2001. Rsch. asst. Ioffe Phys. Tech. Inst. Russian Acad. Sci., St. Petersburg, 1993—96; rsch. asst. MIT, Cambridge, Mass., 1996—2000, rsch. assoc., 2000—01; asst. prof., dir. biomed. optical imaging & spectroscopy lab. Northwestern U., Evanston, Ill., 2001—. Cons. MIT, Cambridge, 2001—. Author: Handbook of Optical Biomedical Diagnostics, 2002, Biomedical Optical Engineering, 2002; contbr. articles to profl. jours. Recipient Best Paper award in New Techs. in Biomedical Optics and Med. Imaging, Nat. Sci. Found., 2002, Nat. Sci. Found. Career award, 2003; fellow, George Soros Internat. Sci. Found., 1995, Lester Wolfe fellow, 1999, Poitras fellow, 2000; scholar, GM Cancer Rsch. Found., 2002. Mem.: Am. Physical Soc., Optical Soc. Am. Achievements include invention of light scattering spectroscopy; tri-modal spectroscopy of tissue. Office: BME Dept Northwestern Univ 2145 Sheridan Rd Evanston IL 60208 Office Phone: 847 491-3536. Office Fax: 847 491-4928. Business E-Mail: v-backman@northwestern.edu.

BACKMAN, WALLY, professional baseball coach, retired professional baseball player; b. Hillsboro, Oregon, Mar. 22, 1959; Player New York Mets, 1980—88, Minnesota Twins, 1989, Pittsburgh Pirates, 1990, Philadelphia Phillies, 1991—92, Seattle Mariners, 1993; manager Class A, Chicago White Sox, Winston-Salem, 2001, Double-A, Chicago White Sox, Birmingham, 2002—03, Class A, Arizona Diamondbacks, Lancaster, 2004, Arizona Diamondbacks, 2004. Achievements include mem. World Series Champion New York Mets, 1986.

BACKSTROM, C. STEPHEN, communications executive; Degree, Drexel U. CPA. Accountant Touche Ross & Co. (now Deloitte & Touche LLP), Phila.; from founder Tax Dept. to v.p. Comcast Corp., Phila., 1981—86, v.p., taxation, 1986—. Bd. dir. Comcast Found, Comcast Capital Corp. Bd. trustees Medford (N.J.) United Meth. Ch., chmn. fin. com. With U.S. Army. Mem.: Media Industry Tax Group, Coun. of State Taxation, Inst. for Professionals in Taxation, Tax Exec. Inst., Broadband Tax Inst. (bd. dir., past pres.), Little Mill Country Club, Men's Golf Assn. (mem. greens com., officer). Office: Comcast Corp 1500 Market St Philadelphia PA 19102

BACKUS, GEORGE EDWARD, theoretical geophysicist; b. Chgo., May 24, 1930; s. Milo Morlan and Dora Etta (Dare) B.; m. Elizabeth Evelyn Allen, Nov. 15, 1961 (div. 1971); children: Benjamin, Brian, Emily; m. Varda Esther Peller, Jan. 8, 1977 PhB, U. Chgo., 1947, BS in Math., 1948, MS in Math. and Physics, 1950, 53, PhD in Physics, 1956; D honoris causa, Inst. de Physique de Globe, Paris, 1995. Jr. mathematician Inst. for Air Weapons, Chgo., 1951-53; physicist Project Matterhorn, Princeton, N.J., 1957-58; asst. prof. math. MIT, Cambridge, 1958-60; assoc. prof. geophysics U. Calif. San Diego, La Jolla, 1960-62, prof. geophysics, 1962-94, rsch. prof. geophysics, 1994-99, prof. geophys. emeritus, 1999—. Mem. vist. com. Institut de Physique du Globe de Paris, 1987; co-chmn. Internat. Working Group on Magnetic Field Satellites, 1983-90; chair acad. senate U. Calif., San Diego, 1992-93. Contbr. articles to profl. jours. Guggenheim Found. fellow, 1963, 71; Royal Soc. Arts fellow, London, 1970— Fellow Royal Astron. Soc. (Gold medal 1986), Am. Geophys. Union (John Adam Fleming medal 1986); mem. NAS (com. on grants and fellowships Day Fund 1974-79, com. on sci. and pub. policy 1971-74), Académie des Sciences (France), Am. Phys. Soc., Am. Math. Soc., Math. Assn. Am., Soc. for Indsl. and Applied Math., Am. Geophys. Union. Avocations: skiing, swimming, bicycling, hiking, history. Office: IGPP U Calif San Diego La Jolla CA 92093-0225 E-mail: gbackus@ucsd.edu.

BACKUS, JOHN, computer scientist; b. Phila., Dec. 3, 1924; m. Una Stannard, 1968; children: Karen, Paula. BS, Columbia U., 1949, AM, 1950; D.Univ. (hon.), U. York, Eng., 1985; ScD (hon.), U. Ariz., 1988; D honoris causa, Université de Nancy 1, France, 1989; ScD (hon.), Ind. U., 1992. Programmer IBM, N.Y.C., 1950—53, mgr. programming rsch., 1954—59; staff mem. IBM T.J. Watson Rsch. Ctr., Yorktown Heights, NY, 1959—63; IBM fellow IBM Rsch., Yorktown Heights and San Jose, Calif., 1963—91; mgr. functional programming IBM Almaden Rsch. Ctr., San Jose, 1980—91; cons., 1991—. Mgr. Incest Info. Bay Area, 1992—2003. With U.S. Army, 1943—46. Recipient W. Wallace McDowell award, IEEE, 1967, Nat. Medal of Sci., 1975, Harold Pender award, Moore Sch. Elec. Engring., U. Pa., 1983, Achievement award, Indsl. Rsch. Inst., Inc., 1983. Fellow: Am. Acad. Arts and Scis.; mem.: NAE (Charles Stark Draper prize 1993), NAS, Assn. Computing Machinery (Turing award 1977). Achievements include system design of IBM 704, Fortran programming lang., Backus-Naur Form lang., function level programming; mem. design group ALGOL 60 lang. Home: 970 Garden Way Ashland OR 97520

BACKUS, JOHN KING, former chemical company research administrator; b. Buffalo, May 22, 1925; s. Arthur Osgood and Lois V. (King) B.; m. Marjorie North, June 18, 1950; children: David King, Lois Victoria, Laura North Scott, Ruth Ellen Grillo. BA in Chemistry and Math., Hamilton Coll., 1947; MS in Phys. Chemistry, Cornell U., 1950, PhD, 1952. Rsch. chemist Procter & Gamble Co., Cin., 1952-53; rsch. chemist, supr. Gen. Mills, Inc., Tonawanda, N.Y., 1953-61; rsch. specialist Mobay Corp. (now Bayer Corp.), Pitts., 1962-64, group leader, 1964-67, mgr. applications rsch., 1967-68, mgr. rsch. svcs., 1968-90; ret., 1990. Participant profl. confs. Patentee in field (3); contbr. articles to tech. jours. Chmn. bd. dirs. Bach Choir Pitts., 1969-70; bd. dirs. Western Pa. Safety Coun., 1975-90, mem. exec. com., 1983-90, chair safety and health conf., 1980; mem. Pitts. Concert Chorale, 1989-2000; mem. coun. First Luth. Ch., Pitts., 1978-80, 84-87, 92-93, pres., 1979; mem. coun. southwestern Pa. synod Evang. Luth. Ch. in Am., 1992-97, 2002-05; co-pres. chpt. AFS Internat. Scholarships, 1972-75, host parent, 1969-70, 79; pres. H.S. Parent-Faculty Assn., 1970-71; advisor Explorer Post, 1967-68; chair corp. sect. United Way Western Pa., 1981-82; organizer, dir. Bayer Choir, 1978-90. With U.S. Army, 1944-46. Mem. Am. Chem. Soc. (environ. improvement com. 1990-95, chmn. elect Pitts. sect. 1992, chmn. 1993, dir. 1995-2003, chmn. elect chemists club group 2000, chmn. 2001-03), N.Y. Acad. Scis., AAAS, Soc. Plastics Industry (chair tech. conf. of urethane divsn. 1977), Sigma Xi. Republican. Avocations: music, gardening, swimming. Home: 9441 Katherine Dr Allison Park PA 15101-2020 E-mail: mjbackus@worldnet.att.net.

BACKUS, MARCIA ELLEN, lawyer; b. Melrose, Mass., Sept. 8, 1954; d. Milo Morlan and Barbara (Cairns) B.; m. Robert M. Roach Jr., June 14, 1986. BA, U. Tex., 1976, JD, 1983. Bar: Tex. 1983. Assoc. Vinson & Elkins, Houston, 1983-90, ptnr., 1991—. Mem. ABA, State Bar Tex., Houston Bar Assn. Office: Vinson & Elkins 1101 Fannin St Ste 2300 Houston TX 77002-6910 E-mail: mbackus@velaw.com.

BACON, A. SMOKI, television host; b. Brookline, Mass., Jan. 29, 1928; d. Alfred Leon and Ruth Dorothy (Burns) Ginepra; m. Edwin Conant Bacon, May 11, 1957 (dec. July 1974); children: Brooks Conant, Hilary Conant; m. Richard Francis Concannon, Oct. 13, 1979. Student, Art Inst. Boston, 1947; grad., Jackson Von Ladau Sch. Design, Boston, 1951. Pub. rels. cons., Boston, 1968—; pres. Bacon-Concannon Assocs., Boston, 1979—95; dir. craftsmobiles Summerthing Program, Boston, 1966—73; dir. exhibits Citifair, Boston, 1974; dir. Victorian exhibits Bicentennial Boston 200, 1975, dir. spl. events, 1976; cons. spl. events. Inst. Contemporary Art, 1977—78; cons. spl. events Boston Tea Party Ship, 1976—79; fundraiser Mass. Assn. Mental Health, 1979; dir. promotions Met. Ctr., 1979; coord. grand finale celebration Boston Jubilee 350, 1979—80; coord. Elliot Norton Awards, 1983; pub. rels. Dyansen Gallery, Boston, 1987—88, French Speaking League, 1987; cons. spl. events Jordan Marsh, 1987; fundraiser, pub. rels. Boston Philharm., 1988; coord. 30th anniversary celebration Charles Playhouse, 1988; fundraiser Elliot Norton Awards, 1989; coord. benefit New Eng. Premiere of film Glory Afro-Am. Mus., 1990; pub. rels. cons. Boston Chamber Music Soc., 1990; pub. rels. Paul Sorota Gallery Fine Arts, 1990—91; fundraising cons. Internat. Inst., 1991; pub. rels., fundraiser Brookline H.S. Sesquicentennial Celebration, 1992—93; co-host radio show Celebrity Time, 1980—; co-host TV show On the Town. Guest lectr. Boston U. Sch. Pub. Rels., 1979, publicity club Boston ARC, 1987, Radcliffe Coll. 4 O'Clock Forums, 1989, YMCA, Mass Polit. Women's Conf., Women's Italian Club, Brookline Rotary, Harvard Coll. Rotary Club; contbg. editor Design Times Mag. Social calendar editor Boston Tab Newspaper, 1987-90; contbg. editor Design Times Mag.; columnist BeaconHill News. Candidate Dem. State Rep., Mass., 1980; Bastille Day chmn. French Libr. Boston, 1994—; local adv. com. Nat. Trust for Historic Preservation; bd. dirs. Boston Lit. Hour; host parents com. Harvard Coll.; bd. dirs. Mugar Libr., Spl. Collections, 1994—; vis. com. Mus. Fine Arts, Eqyptian Dept., 1994—; bd. trustees Boston Arts Festival, 1960-63; bd. dirs., treas. Samaritans, Boston, 1974-84; art auction chairperson WGBH-Pub. Radio-TV, Boston, 1969-70; bd. dirs. Urban League Ea. Mass., Boston, 1975-85, Elders Living at Home Program, Boston City Hosp. Kids Fund; former mem. numerous civic coms. Recipient Woman of Great Achievement award Cambridge Young Women's Assn., 1991, appreciation award The Samaritans, 1991, Leadership award Friends of Pub. Garden, 1975; named One of Boston's 100 Female Leaders, Boston Mag., 1980, One of Boston Area Schs. Notable Grad. List, 1994, Appreciation award Samaritans, 1991, Honors on 70th birthday Gov. Argeo Paul Cellucci, Pres. of Senate Thomas Birmingham, Spkr. Ho. of Reps. Thomas Finnerman and Mayor of Boston Thomas Menino, 1998; Guest of Honor, Womens' City Club Ann. Dinner Dance, 1979; honored Those Who Help Keep Boston's Non-Profit Agencies Alive Horizons for Youth, 1972, Charitable and Civic Endeavors Boston Italian Women's Club, 1995; named to Women of Great Achievement, Cambridge Young Women's Assn., 1991; donated personal ofcl. documents Women's Time Capsule Schlesinger Libr. Radcliffe Coll., 1981; honoree Gibon House Mus., 2003. Mem. AAUW, Harvard Club Boston, Women's City Club. Democrat. Avocation: artistics graphics. Home: 94 Beacon St Ste 1 Boston MA 02108-3329 Office: Bacon Concannon Assocs 94 Beacon St Boston MA 02108-3329 Office Phone: 617-536-1188. Office Fax: 617-523-1998. Personal E-mail: SmokBacon@aol.com.

BACON, BRETT KERMIT, lawyer; b. Perry, Iowa, Aug. 8, 1947; s. Royden S. and Aldeen A. (Zuker) B.; m. Bonnie Jeanne Hall; children: Jeffrey Brett, Scott Michael. BA, U. Dubuque, 1969; JD, Northwestern U., 1972. Bar: Ohio 1972, U.S. Ct. Appeals (6th cir.) 1972, U.S. Supreme Ct. 1980. Assoc. Thompson, Hine & Flory, Cleve., 1972-80, ptnr., 1980-2000; founding ptnr. Frantz Ward, Cleve., 2000—. Spkr. in field. Author: Computer Law, 1982, 84. V.p. profl. sect. United Way, Cleve., 1982-86; pres. Shaker Heights Youth Ctr., Inc., Ohio, 1984-86; elder Ch. of Western Res., 1996—. Mem. Fedn. Ins. and Corp. Counsel, Bar Assn. Greater Cleve., Cleve. Play House Club (officer 1986-94, pres. 1991-93, pres. mem's com. 1993-96), Pepper Pike Civic League (trustee and treas. 1994-97). Home: 8190 Devon Ct Chagrin Falls OH 44023 Office: Frantz Ward LLP Key Ctr Ste 2500 127 Public Sq Cleveland OH 44114 Business E-Mail: bbacon@frantzward.com.

BACON, BRUCE RAYMOND, physician; b. Amherst, Ohio, Nov. 7, 1949; s. Raymond Clifford and Cathryn E. (Fowell) B.; children: Jeffrey Dale, Laurie Katherine. BA in chem., Coll. Wooster, 1971; MD, Case Western Reserve U., 1975. Diplomate Am. Bd. Internal Medicine and Gastroenterology. Asst. prof. medicine Case Western Reserve U., Cleve., 1982-87, assoc. prof. medicine, 1987-88; assoc. prof. medicine, chief gastroenterology sect. La. State U., Shreveport, 1988-90; prof. internal medicine, dir. gastroenterology divsn. St. Louis U. Sch. Medicine, St.Louis, 1990—. Chair subsplty. bd. gasteroenterology Am. Bd. Internal Medicine, 1999-2003. Co-author: Essentials of Clinical Hepatology, 1993; co-editor: Liver Disease: Diagnosis and Management, 2000; contbr. numerous articles to profl. jours. Fellow ACP, Am. Coll. Gastroenterology, Am. Soc. Clin. Investigation; mem. Am. Assn. Study Liver Disease (pres. 2004). Presbyterian. Avocation: photography. Office: St Louis U Health Sci Ctr 3635 Vista Ave PO Box 15250 Saint Louis MO 63110-0250 Office Phone: 314-577-8764.

BACON, CAROLINE SHARFMAN, investor, consultant; b. Ann Arbor, Mich., Aug. 27, 1942; d. Mahlon Samuel and Mary Patricia (Potter) Sharp; m. William Lee Sharfman, Sept. 5, 1964 (div. 1985); m. James Edmund Bacon, Nov. 4, 1989. BA with distinction, U. Mich., 1964; MBA, Columbia U., 1975; M.A.R., Yale U., 2004. Assoc. Goldman, Sachs & Co., N.Y.C., 1975-80, v.p., 1980-83, Goldman Sachs Money Markets Inc., N.Y.C., 1983-90; sr. cons. investor rels. Burson-Marsteller, 1991; mng. dir. Johnnie D. Johnson & Co. Investor Rels., N.Y.C., 1992-95. Mem. Phi Beta Kappa, Phi Sigma Iota, Beta Gamma Sigma. Episcopalian.

BACON, CHARLES, chemistry professor, physics professor; b. Cadillac, Mich., May 23, 1953; s. Robert Bruce and Barbara Lou Bacon; m. Mary Kamela Bacon, Dec. 21, 1985. BS, Mich. State U., 1975; MS, Mont. State U., 1977; PhD, Mich. Tech. U., 1990. Prof. physics and chemistry Ferris State U., Big Rapids, Mich. Exec. dir. Sylvan Learning Ctr., Cadillac, Mich.; bd. dirs. Mich. Ctr. Learning, Paris; cons. Analyze and Apply, East Lansing, Mich. Author: Science and Crime: Active Learning, 2000, Physics I: An Active Learning Inquiry, 2001, Do Something: A Guide to..., 2004. County chmn. Wexford Rep. Party, Cadillac, 1983—88. Fellow, Mich. Polymer Consortium, 1988—90, Whirlpool, 1989. Mem.: Phi Lambda Upsilon. Avocations: golf, gardening. Home: 22570 21 Mile Rd Paris MI 49338 Office: Ferris State U 805 Campus Dr Big Rapids MI 49307

BACON, DIANA HOLFORD, hydrologist, researcher; b. Fairfax, Va., Aug. 4, 1961; d. Donald Lloyd Holford and Eunice (Stunkard) Smith; m. John Anthony Bacon, May 22, 1993; 1 child, Evan Jeffrey. BS in Geology, George Mason U., 1983; MS in Hydrology, N.Mex. Inst. of Mining/Tech., 1986; PhD in Geology, Wash. State U., 1997. Cert. Lic. Hydrogeologist Wash. Sr. rsch. scientist Pacific N.W. Nat. Lab., Richland, Wash., 1986—. Contbr. articles to profl. jours. including Water Resources Rsch., Environ. Sci. and Tech., Global Biogeochem. Cycles, and Jour. Geophys. Rsch, Computers and Geosciences. Mem. Am. Geophys. Union, Geol. Soc. of Am., Materials Rsch. Soc. Office: Pacific NW Nat Lab 3200 Q Ave Richland WA 99352 E-mail: diana.bacon@pnl.gov.

BACON, DONALD CONRAD, writer, editor; b. Jacksonville, Fla., Jan. 15, 1935; s. Francis Herbert and Myrtis Ann (Gunter) B.; m. Barbara Lee Barnwell, June 22, 1957; children— Elizabeth, Jennifer (dec.). BS in Journalism, U. Fla., 1957. Staff writer Wall St. Jour., 1957-61; Congl. fellow, 1961-62; staff writer Washington Star, 1962-63; successively Congl. corr., White House corr., sr. corr. and columnist Newhouse News Service, 1963-75; asso. editor U.S. News & World Report mag., Washington, 1975-79, sr. editor, 1979-81, asst. mng. editor, 1981-88; sr. editor Nation's Business, 1988-89; project dir. Ency. of U.S. Congress, Washington, 1989-95; pres. Fund for the Study of Congress, 1989—. Author: Congress and You, 1969; co-author: The New Millionaires, 1961, Rayburn-A Biography, 1987 (Best Biography award Tex. Hist. Commn. 1987, Best Book award Washingtonian mag. 1987); co-editor: Encyclopedia of the United States Congress, 1995 (Best Reference Source Libr. Jour., 1995). Recipient (with others) Loeb award U. Conn., 1961; award for excellence in journalism Lincoln U., Jefferson City, Mo., 1977, Disting. Alumnus award, U. Fla. Coll. Journalism, 2001. Home: 3809 E West Hwy Chevy Chase MD 20815-5918 Personal E-mail: donbacon@erols.com.

BACON, EDMUND NORWOOD, city planner; b. Phila., May 2, 1910; s. Ellis W. and Helen (Comly) B.; m. Ruth Holmes, Sept. 16, 1938 (dec. May 1991); children: Karin Ellis, Elinor Ruth, Hilda Holmes, Michael Comly, Kira, Kevin Norwood. B.Arch., Cornell U., 1932. Archtl. designer, Shanghai, China, 1934; with W. Pope Barney, architect, Phila., 1935; supr. city planning Inst. Research and Planning, Flint, Mich., 1937-39; mng. dir. Phila. Housing Assn., 1940-43; co-designer Better Phila. Exbn.; also sr. land planner Phila. City Planning Commn., 1946-49, exec. dir., 1949-70, also devel. coordinator, 1968-70; v.p. design devel. Mondev Internat. Ltd., 1972-87. Prof. adviser in Franklin D. Roosevelt Meml. Competition, 1959; adj. prof. U. Pa., 1950-87 Author: Design of Cities, 1967, rev. edit., 1974; prod.: Understanding Cities film series Rome: Impact of an Idea, Paris: Living Space, John Nash and London, The American Urban Experience, The City of the Future, 1983. Mem. Pres.'s Citizen's Adv. Com. Recreation and Natural Beauty, 1966-69; Trustee Am. Acad. in Rome, 1965-76. Recipient Art Alliance Phila. medal achievement, 1961, Man of Yr. award City Bus. Club Phila., 1962, Brown medal award Franklin Inst., 1962, R.S. Reynolds award for community architecture, 1976, Fairmount Park Art Assn. medal of honor, 1976, Gold medal Royal Instn. Chartered Surveyors, 1974, Chgo. Archtl. award, 1989, Sir Patrick Abercrombie prize Internat. Union Architects, 1990, Planning Pioneer award Am. Inst. Cert. Planners, 1993; Ford Found. travel fellow, 1959; Rockefeller fellow, 1963; Nat. Endowment for the Arts Disting. Designer fellow, 1987, emeritus fellow Urban Land Inst., 1989, Plym disting. professorship in architecture U. Ill. Fellow AIA (medal 1976), Am. Inst. Planners (Distinguished Service award 1971, Phila. award 1983, Penn Club award 1984) Address: 2117 Locust St Philadelphia PA 19103-4802

BACON, GEORGE EDGAR, pediatrician; b. N.Y.C., Apr. 13, 1932; s. Edgar and Margaret Priscilla (Anderson) B.; m. Grace Elizabeth Graham, June 30, 1956; children: Nancy, George, John BA, Wesleyan U., 1953; MD, Duke U., 1957; MS in Pharmacology, U. Mich., 1967. Diplomate Am. Bd. Pediatrics, subsplty. Bd. Pediatric Endocrinology. Intern in pediatrics Duke Hosp., Durham, N.C., 1957-58; resident in pediatrics Columbia-Presbyn. Med. Ctr., N.Y.C., 1961-63; from instr. to prof. emeritus U. Mich., Ann Arbor, 1963—86, prof. emeritus, 1986—, chief pediatric endocrinology svc., dept. pediatrics, 1970-83, dir. house officer programs, dept. pediatrics, 1981-86, assoc. chmn. dept. pediatrics, 1983-86, mem. senate assembly, 1978-80; vice chmn. dir.'s adv. coun. Univ. Hosp., Ann Arbor, 1981-82; prof. pediatrics Tex. Tech U., Lubbock, 1986—90, chmn. dept., 1986—90, chmn. med. practice income plan, 1989; chief staff pediatrics Lubbock Gen. Hosp., 1986—90; dir. med. edn. and rsch. Butterworth Hosp., Grand Rapids, Mich., 1990-91, med. dir. dept. pediatrics, 1991—95; prof. pediatrics Mich. State U., East Lansing, 1990—95; pediatric endocrinologist Univ. Mich. Hosp., Ann Arbor, 1995—, Detroit Med. Ctr., Southfield, Mich., 1996—2001. Coord. prof. svc. C.S. Mott Children's Hosp., 1973-83, mem. exec. com. for clin. affairs, 1975-76, 77-79, assoc. vice chmn. med. staff, 1978-79; chmn. exec. com. Women's Hosp., Holden Hosp., Ann Arbor, 1973-82. Author: A Practical Approach to Pediatric Endocrinology, 1975, 3d edit., 1990; contbr. articles to profl. jours. Capt. U.S. Army, 1958-61. Fellow Am. Acad. Pediatrics (treas. Mich. chpt. 1983-86, alt.-at-large 1995-2001, coun. Tex. chpt. 1986-89, Pediatrician of Yr. Mich. chpt. 2002); mem. Am. Pediatric Soc., Pediatric Endocrine Soc. Home: 3911 Waldenwood Dr Ann Arbor MI 48105-3008 Office: U MIch Med Ctr Dept Pediatrics PO Box 718 Ann Arbor MI 48109-0718 Office Phone: 734-764-5175. E-mail: gbacon4999@aol.com.

BACON, GEORGE HUGHES, JR., retired systems analyst; b. Phila., Mar. 4, 1935; s. George Hughes Sr. and Alice Olive (Campbell); divorced; children: Christopher Scott, Melissa Anne Hinkle. BA in English Lit. and Music, Temple U., 1957; MS in Ednl. Adminstrn., U. Pa., 1968. Computer programmer 1st Pa. Bank, Phila., 1960-62; tchr. Bucks County, Pa., 1962-72; assoc. dir. Kranzley and Co., Cherry Hill, N.J., 1973-74; computer programmer Phila. Nat. Bank, 1975-77; cons. Sci. and Computer Tech. Inc., Malvern, Pa., 1978-79; lead systems analyst Ednl. Testing Svc., Princeton, N.J., 1979-86; cons. in field, 1986. Cons., lectr. computer literacy and software Abington (Pa.) Pub. Libr., 1983-84, Jenkintown (Pa.) Music Sch., 1984, Fudan U., Shanghai, China, 1985 Vol. aide Mercer County Geriatric Unit, Lawrenceville, N.J., 1986, Holy Redeemer Hosp., Meadowbrook, Pa., 1988-98, Rydal Park Retirement Home, 1989—; cons. Abington Sch. Bd., 1989-98; tutor Abington Pub. Libr. Literacy Project, 1988; mem. headmaster's coun. Am. Boychoir, Princeton, 1987, Abington Presbyn. Ch. Mem. Temple U. Coll. Arts and Scis. Alumni Assn., U. Pa. Grad. Sch. Edn. Alumni Assn., Phila. Orch. Assn., Friends of Princeton U. Avocations: films, public television and radio, classical music, reading. Home: 1515 The Fairway Rydal PA 19046-1435

BACON, JAMES M., information scientist; m. Robin Praker, May 9, 1998; children: Dylan, Camryn, Bailey. Cert.: Tex. (public law enforcement officer) 1996. Mgr. info. tech. and human resources ops. Buchanan Assocs., Houston, 2000—03; health programs analyst U. Tex. Med. Br., Galveston, 2004—. Dep. sheriff Galveston County Sheriff's Office, Tex., 1996—98; asst. imaging systems adminstr. Galveston County Clk.'s Office, Tex., 1996—2000. Amb. Galveston C. of C., Tex., 1998—2004. With USN, 1989—93. Decorated Desert Storm award USN, United Arab Emirates. Mem.: Elks (officer 1997—98). Achievements include development of Developed a business unit from the ground up, in which my corporation gave recognition across the US that my unit was to be set a presidence as a Model setup for new operations that occur in the US.

BACON, KEVIN, actor; b. Phila., July 8, 1958; s. Edmund and Ruth Bacon; m. Kyra Sedgwick, Sept. 3, 1988; 2 children: Travis and Sosie Ruth. Actor: (off-Broadway debut) Getting Out, Marymount Manhattan Theatre, 1978, (Broadway debut) Slab Boys, Playhouse Theatre, 1983, other stage prodns. include Glad Tidyings, 1979-80, Mary Barnes, 1980, Album, 1980, Forty-Deuce, 1981, Flux, 1982, Poor Little Lambs, 1982, Men Without Dates, 1985, Loot, 1986, (feature films) National Lampoon's Animal House, 1978, Starting Over, 1979, Hero at Large, 1980, Friday the 13th, 1980, Only When I Laugh, 1981, Diner, 1982, Footloose, 1984, Quicksilver, 1985, White Water Summer, 1987, Planes, Trains and Automobiles, End of the Line, 1988, She's Having a Baby, 1988, Criminal Law, 1989, The Big Picture, 1989, Tremors, 1990, Flatliners, 1990, Queens Logic, 1991, He Said/She Said, 1991, Pyrates, 1991, JFK, 1992, A Few Good Men, 1992, The Air Up There, 1994, The River Wild, 1994, Murder in the First, 1995, Apollo 13, 1995, Balto (voice only), 1995, Sleepers, 1996, Destination Anywhere, 1997, Telling Lies in America, 1997, Picture Perfect, 1997, Digging to China, 1997, My Dog Skip, 1999, Stir of Echoes, 1999, Hollow Man, 2000, Novocaine, 2001, Trapped, 2002, Mystic River, 2003, In the Cut, 2003, Cavedweller, 2004; actor, exec. prodr. Wild Things, 1998, The Woodsman, 2004; actor, prodr. Loverboy, 2004; (TV movies) The Gift, 1979, Enormous Changes at the Last Minute, 1982, The Demon Murder Case, 1983, Mister Roberts, 1984, The Little Sister, 1984, Lemon Sky, 1988; actor, dir. Losing Chase, 1996; (TV series) Search for Tomorrow, 1979; (TV appearances) Frasier (voice only), 1994, Mad About You, 1996, Will & Grace, 2002; musician (albums with The Bacon Brothers) Forosoco, 1997, Getting There, 1997, Can't Complain, 2001. Office: William Morris Agy 151 S El Camino Dr Beverly Hills CA 90212-2775

BACON, LOUIS ALBERT, retired consulting civil engineer; b. Champaign, Ill., Apr. 10, 1921; s. Harrison Waxler and Mabel Mae (Watson) B.; m. Clara Elizabeth Manny, Aug. 28, 1943; children: Robert Louis, David Kenneth, William Harrison. BSCE, U. Ill., 1943. Registered profl. engr., Ga., Ill.; registered structural engr., Ill. Wing designer Douglas Aircraft Co., El Segundo, Calif., 1943-44; structural designer C.A. Metz Engring. Co., Chgo., 1946-47; chief structural engr. Shaw, Metz & Dolio, architects-engrs., Chgo., 1947-53; chief structural engr., assoc. ptnr. Shaw, Metz & Assocs., Chgo., 1953-66; pres. P&W Engrs., Inc., cons., Chgo., 1966-74; v.p., head Atlanta div. Stanley Cons., Inc., 1974-76; v.p., dir. engring. div. Heery Internat., Inc., Atlanta, 1976-84, dir. mktg. to fed. govt., 1984-89; ret. Mem. planning com. City of Brookfield, Ill., 1951-54, mem. bd. local improvements, village trustee, 1954-59; mem. Glen Ellyn (Ill.) Environ. Protection Commn., 1971-74; pres. Ridgeview Neighborhood Civic Assn., Atlanta, 1980-82, sec.-treas. 1991—2003; chmn. Fulton County Developers Adv. Com., 1981; bd. dirs. Literacy Vols. Am.-Met. Atlanta, 1992-95, 1996-2002, pres., 1993-94; commr. Housing Authority Fulton County, 1995—2003, vice chmn., 1998-99, chmn., 1999-2003; vol. Habitat for Humanity, Atlanta, 1994-96; bd. dirs. Cancer Network St. Joseph's Hosp. Atlanta, 1995-99, 2003-04; founder, chmn., Ga. Prostate Cancer Coalition, 1998—. With USNR, 1944-46. Recipient Outstanding Achievement award Engrs. of Met. Atlanta, 1980, medal of honor Ga. Engring. Found., 2003; named Engr. of Yr., Engrs. of Met. Atlanta, 1984 Fellow ASCE, Soc. Am. Mil. Engrs. (v.p. 1988-89), NSPE (life, dir. 1966-69, v.p. 1969-71, pres.-elect 1982-83, pres. 1983-84, divsn. chmn. profl. engrs. in pvt. practice 1971-72, Chmn.'s award profl. engrs. in pvt. practice 1972, PEPP award 1976, Disting. Svc. award 1993); mem. Ill. Soc. Profl. Engrs. (hon. mem., pres. 1964-65, Ill. award 1968), Ga. Soc. Profl. Engrs. (Pres.'s award Sandy Springs chpt. 1980, Engr. of Yr. award 1982), Engrs. Greater Atlanta (Engr. of Yr. 1984), U. Ill. Civil Engring. Alumni Assn. (pres. 1980-82, Disting. Alumnus award 1985), U. Ill. Alumni Assn. (Loyalty award 1985, Constituent award 1988), Chi Epsilon. Methodist. Home: 1431 Parkview Blvd Stone Mountain GA 30087-6722

BACON, MELVIN LEON, secondary school educator; b. Denver; s. Joe Melvin and Francis Miriam (Baughman) B.; m. Deborah Ann Booz, Oct. 12, 1974; children: Sarah Elizabeth, Joseph Melvin. BA in History and Earth Sci., Met. State Coll., Denver, 1973; MA in Ednl. Media, U. No. Colo., 1983. Cert. secondary history tchr., Colo. Tchr. Edn. Dept. of Western Australia, Perth, 1975-77; social studies tchr., chair dept. Brighton (Colo.) Dist. 27J, 1977—. Mem. N. Ctrl. Evaluation Teams, Greeley, Colo., 1980; presenter in field. Co-author: Bent's Fort Crossroads of Culture on the Santa Fe Trail, 1995; contbr. poems, story, articles to profl. publs. Named Outstanding Am. History Tchr. for Colo., DAR, 1992, Hon. Mention Outstanding Am. History Tchr. Am. History, Nat. DAR, 1992, Outstanding Am. History Tchr., Colo. Daus. Colonial Wars, 1993. Mem. Colo. Coun. for Social Studies (Outstanding Social Studies Educator award 1990), Nat. Coun. Social Studies, Denver Antique Auto Club, Rocky Mountain Packard Club, Kaiser-Fanzor Club. Republican. Baptist. Avocations: travel, stamps, coins, study of American West, american paper. Home: 379 Weld CR 29 Brighton CO 80603 Office: Brighton HS 270 S 8th Ave Brighton CO 80601-2132 Office Phone: 303-655-4160. E-mail: mbacon@brightonps.k12.co.us, commodore1949@netzero.net.

BACON, PHILLIP, geographer, author, consultant; b. Cleve., July 10, 1922; s. Hollis Phillip and Emma (Schneider) B.; m. Dorothy Willey, 1951 (div. 1980); children: Laura Bacon Fraser, Phillip Everett; m. Jane Lowrie, 1980 (dec. 1991); m. Sandra Sullivan, 1995. Cadet, The Citadel, 1940-42; AB, U. Miami, 1946; MA, George Peabody Coll. for Tchrs. (now Vanderbilt U.), 1951, EdD, 1955. Tchr. social studies, tactical officer Castle Heights Mil. Acad., Lebanon, Tenn., 1946-47; tchr. social studies, tactical officer Army and Navy Acad., Carlsbad, Calif., 1948-53; grad. asst. geography George Peabody Coll. for Tchrs. (now Vanderbilt U.), 1953-55; dean Grad. Sch., 1963-64; acting dir. Library Sch., 1964; asst. prof. geography U. Pitts., 1955-57; vis. asst. prof. geography Columbia U. Tchrs. Coll., 1956-57, assoc. prof., 1957-60, prof., 1960-63, 64-66; prof. geography and social studies edn. U. Wash., Seattle, 1966-71, co-dir. tri-univ. project in elementary edn., 1967-71; prof. geography U. Houston, 1971-85, chmn. dept., 1973-78, prof. geography and anthropology emeritus, 1985—. Instr. history George Peabody Coll. for Tchrs., 1951; vis. prof. geography U. Colo., 1961, U. Wash., 1965, 79; Jennings lectr., 1963; vis. scholar N.C. Central U., 1966; vis. lectr. geography U. Tex., 1966, NSF vis. scientist, 1970-72; Disting. vis. prof. social studies edn. and geography Seattle Pacific U., 1977-79, vis. prof., geographer-in-residence, Coll. Edn., U. N.Mex., 1993-95; co-coord. N.Mex. Geog. Alliance, 1993-97; mem. editl. adv. bd. World Book Ency., 1965-84; bd. cons. World Book Atlas, 1965-70; cons. editor Golden Press, 1958-61; ednl. dir. Golden Book Inst. Knowledge, 1960-61; cons. book divsn. Time, Inc., 1960-69; cons. social sci. project Ednl. Rsch. Coun. Am., 1962-70; steering com. HS Geography Project, 1965-70; cons. U.S. Office Edn., 1964-71; mem. Wash. State Social Studies Adv. Commn., 1968-71; dir. Follett Social Studies Program, 1980-83, Allyn and Bacon elem. social studies program, 1983-85, dir. Summer Geography Inst., N.Mex. Geographic Alliance, 1993-97; social scis. cons. Harcourt Brace, 1985-2002, Holt, Rinehart and Winston, 1989-97; prof. geography grad. faculty U. Colo., Boulder, 1999-2000; geography cons. Harcourt Brace Elem. Social Studies Program Stories in Time, 1997, 2000, SWAP Project, Colo. Dept. Edn., 1998, Social Studies Texan, 2003-; cons. in field. Author: Australia, Oceania, and the Polar Lands, 1961, North America, 1961, Children's Picture Atlas of the World, 1966, (with Norman Carls and Frank E. Sorenson) Knowing Our Neighbors in the United States and Canada, 1966, Regions Around the World, 1970, (with R.R. Boyce) Towns and Cities, 1970, (with others) The United States and Canada, 1970, (with P.V. Greco) The Story of Latin America, 1970, (with others) America: In Space and Time, 1976, Exploring Our World, 1982, (with Donald C. Fairweather) World Regions, 1983, (with James B. Kracht) Our World Today, 1983, (with M. Evelyn Swartz) Our State: California, 1983, World Geography, The Earth and Its People, 1989; editor: Focus on Geography, Key Concepts and Teaching Strategies, 1970; co-editor (with Lorrin G. Kennamer) Foundations of World Regional Geography Series, 1970; cons. editor: (with others) Life Pictorial Atlas of the World, 1961; mem. adv. bd.: (with others) Jour. of Geography, 1967-70, Social Edn., 1975-78; editl. dir.: (with others) Field Social Studies Program, 1972-73; co-dir.: (with others) Addison-Wesley Elementary Social Studies Program, 1973-80; ednl. cons. The American Nation, Reconstruction to the Present, 1986, The American Nation, Beginnings Through Reconstruction, 1986, Triumph of the American Nation, 1986, World History: People and Nations, 1990, The Story of America, 1994; sr. editl. advisor HBJ Social Studies, K-7, Landmark edits., 1988; contbr. articles to profl. jours., chpts. to books. Mem. adv. bd. Grad. Sch., U. Colo., 1987-93. With USNR, 1942-45. Recipient Teaching Excellence award U. Houston, 1975, 79, 80 Mem. NEA (life), Assn. Am. Geographers (coun. 1976-79, chmn. publs. com. 1976-78), Nat. Coun. for Geog. Edn. (life, pres. 1966, disting. svc. award 1974), Alaska Geog. Soc., Nat., Tex., N.Mex. (exec. bd. 1992-95), Social Studies Couns. (exec. bd. 1992-95), Vanderbilt U. Alumni Assn. (dir. 1979-83), Peabody Coll. Alumni Assn. (pres. 1981-83, Disting. Alumnus award 1986, alumni bd. 1994-95), Peabody Coll. Roundtable, Sigma Xi, Sigma Alpha Epsilon, Phi Delta Kappa, Kappa Delta Pi, Kappa Phi Kappa (life), Omicron Delta Kappa, Gamma Theta Upsilon, Pi Gamma Mu. Presbyterian. Home: 2718 Caribbean Dr Grand Junction CO 81506-1712 Personal E-mail: sanphil@aol.com.

BACON, SHERRI LEAH, elementary school educator; b. Tipton, Mo., Jan. 24, 1968; d. Robert Lee and Sharon Regina (Schreck) Fulton. BS in Edn., Ctrl. Mo. State U., 1990; MS in Edn., Troy State U., 1996. 6-8th grade tchr. Moniteau R-V, Latham, Mo., 1990-92; 6th grade tchr. N.W. Middle Sch., Clarksville, Tenn., 1992-93; 1st grade tchr. Norman Smith Elem., 1993-94; early childhood ctr. tchr. Dawning Point, Enterprise, Ala., 1994-96; tchr. 3d grade Sacred Heart Sch., 1998-99, tchr. 1st grade Robbinsdale, Minn., 1999-2000; tchr. 3d grade Columbia Cath. Sch., Mo., 2000—. Mem. Gamma Sigma Sigma (pres., 1st v.p., sec., Outstanding Mem. award 1990), Kappa Delta Pi. Avocation: reading. Home: 11298 Campbell Bridge Dr Prairie Home MO 65068

BACON, SUSAN M., language educator, educator; children: Alexis, Camille. BA, U.S. Fla., 1968; MA, Ind. U., 1970; PhD, Ohio State U., 1985. Instr. Coll. of Wooster, Ohio, 1970-83; asst. prof. U. Cin., 1985-92, assoc. prof., 1992—. Contbr. to profl jours. Recipient Pimsleur award, 1994; grantee NEH, 1994-96. Mem. Am. Assn. Univ. Suprs. and Coords. (Spanish section head), Am. Coun. Tchrs. Fgn. Language, Am. Assn. Tchrs. Spanish and Portuguese, Am. Ednl. Rsch. Assn., Spl. Interest Group Second Language (treas., program chmn., chair). Office: U Cin Ml 377 Dept Of Rll # 377 Cincinnati OH 45221-0001

BACON, SYLVIA, judge, law educator; b. Watertown, SD, July 9, 1931; d. Julius Franklin and Anne Rae (Hyde) B. AB, Vassar Coll., Poughkeepsie, N.Y., 1952; cert., London Sch. Econs., 1953; LLB, Harvard U. Law Sch., 1956; LLM, Georgetown Law Ctr., Washington, 1959. Bar: D.C. 1956, U.S. Supreme Ct. 1963. Law clk. to fed. judge, 1956-57; asst. U.S. Atty. Washington, 1957-65; assoc. dir. Pres. Commn. on Crime in D.C., 1965-67; trial atty. spl. projects U.S. Dept. Justice, 1967-69; exec. asst. U.S. atty. Washington, 1969-70; judge D.C. Superior Ct., Washington, 1970-92; judge-in-residence Columbus Sch. Law Cath. U. Am., Washington, 1993-95, lectr., 1995—2002, disting. lectr., 2002—; adjudicator Office of Compliance, U.S. Legis. Br., Washington, 1996—. Adj. prof. Georgetown Law Ctr., 1960-70, 72-74; faculty Nat. Inst. Trial Advocacy, 1973-75, 91—, fed. and local jud. confs., 1970-90; bd. dirs. DC Law Students in Ct., 2002-; lectr. Nat. Coll. Criminal Def., 1975-82; faculty Nat. Jud. Coll., 1974-79; lectr. Am. Acad. Jud. Edn., 1972-82. Bd. dirs. Nat Home Libr. Found., 1968-70. Fellow ABA (gov. 1988-91); mem. AAUW, D.C. Bar Assn. (bd. dirs. 1965-67), DC Women's Bar Assn., Am. Inns of Ct., Exec. Women in Govt., Bus. and Profl. Women's Assn., Nat. Assn. Women Judges, Supreme Ct. Hist. Soc., Phi Beta Kappa. Home: 2500 Q St NW Washington DC 20007-4373 Office: Cath U Am Columbus Sch Law 3600 McCormack Dr NE Washington DC 20064-0001 Office Phone: 202-319-6618. Business E-Mail: bacon@law.edu.

BACON, VICKY LEE, lighting services executive; b. Oregon City, Oreg., Mar. 25, 1950; d. Herbert Kenneth and Lorean Betty (Boltz) Rushford; m. Dennis M. Bacon, Aug. 7, 1971; 1 child, Randene Tess. Student, Portland Community Coll., 1974-75, Mt. Hood Community Coll., 1976, Portland State Coll., 1979. With All Electric Constrn., Milwaukie, Oreg., 1968-70, Lighting Maintenance Co., Portland, Oreg., 1970-78; svc. mgr. GTE Sylvania Lighting Svcs., Portland, 1978-80, br. mgr., 1980-83; div. mgr. Christenson Electric Co. Inc., Portland, 1983-90, v.p. mktg. and lighting svcs., 1990-91, v.p. svc. ops. and mktg., 1991—2000; CEO, owner Dryer Electric, Inc., 2002—. Chmn. Oreg. Ltd. Energy Com., 1993—; vice chmn. to labor commr. Oreg. State Apprenticeship Coun., 1996—. Mem. Energy Contractors Assn., Illuminating Engring. Soc., Nat. Elec. Contractors Assn. (bd. dirs. Oreg. Columbia chpt. 1997—), Nat. Assn. Lighting Maintenance Contractors, Elec. Contractors Assn., Office: Dryer Electric Inc PO Box 3514 Portland OR 97208-3514

BACOW, LAWRENCE SELDON, academic administrator, environmental scientist, educator; b. Detroit, Aug. 24, 1951; s. Mitchell Leon and Ruth Wertheim Bacow; m. Adele Fleet, June 1, 1975; children: Jay, Kenneth. SB, MIT, 1972; JD, M in Pub. Policy, Harvard U., 1976, PhD, 1978. Bar: Mass. 1978. Asst. prof. law and environ. policy MIT, Cambridge, 1977-84, assoc. prof. law and environ. policy, 1984-90, dir. Ctr. for Real Estate, 1990-92, prof. law and environ. policy, 1992-97, Lee and Geraldine Martin prof. environ. studies, 1997—2001, chmn. faculty, 1995-97, chancellor, 1998—2001; pres. Tufts Univ., 2002—. Vis. assoc. prof. law Hebrew U., Jerusalem, 1981-82; rsch. assoc. Harvard Law Sch., Cambridge, 1982-88; vis. prof. Politecnico di Torino, Italy, 1990, U. Bari, Italy, 1991, Gabriela Mistral U., Santiago, Chile, 1992, 93, 94, 95, 97, Faculty Econs.-U. Amsterdam, The Netherlands, 1993-94; rsch. fellow The Tinbergen Inst., Amsterdam, 1993-94. Author: Bargaining for Job Safety and Health, 1980; co-author: (with M. O'Hare and D. Sanderson) Facility Siting and Public Opposition, 1982, (with L. Susskind and M. Wheeler) Resolving Environmental Regulatory Disputes, 1983, (with M. Wheeler) Environmental Dispute Resolution, 1984. Mem. presdl. transition team Occupl. Safety and Health Adminstrn., 1977; mem. socio-econ. subcom. NAS Com. on Surface Mining and Reclamation, 1978-79; advisor Mass. Spl. Legis. Commn. on Hazardous Water, 1980; gubernatorial appointee Mass. Hazardous Waste Facility Site Safety Coun., 1980-83; Town Meeting mem., Arlington, Mass., 1981-83; advisor Israel Environ. Protection Svc., 1981-83; chair citizens adv. com. Mass. Water Resources Authority, 1989; exec. com. One Thousand Friends Mass., 1989-95; advisor Cross Israel Hwy. Commn., 1994-95; dir. MIT Hillel, Cambridge, 1995-98, Jewish Cmty. Housing for the Elderly, Brighton, Mass., 1995—; trustee Hebrew Coll., Brookline, Mass., 1999—, Wheaton Coll., Norton, Mass., 1999—, dir. Am. Coun. on Edn., 2003—. Recipient William S. Ballard award Am. Soc. Real Estate, 1991; adminstrn. fellow Harvard U., 1972-76, post-doctoral fellow Ford Found., 1977; Legal scholar Ctr. for Pub. Resources, 1985. Mem. Am. Acad. Arts and Scis., Mass. Bar Assn., Phi Beta Kappa. Jewish. Avocations: sailing, skiing, running. Office: Tufts University President's Office Ballou Hall Medford MA 02155 E-mail: bacow@tufts.edu.*

BADAL, DANIEL WALTER, psychiatrist, educator; b. Lowellville, Ohio, Aug. 22, 1912; s. Samuel S. and Angelina (Jessen) Badal; m. Julia Lovina Cover, June 1939 (dec. May 1968); children: Petrina Badal Gardner, Julia Badal Graf, Peter C.; m. Eleanor Bosworth Spitler, Sept. 5, 1969 (dec. Feb. 1994). AB, Case Western Res. U., 1934, MD, 1937. Resident in medicine, neurology and psychiatry Peter Bent Brigham Hosp., Mass. Gen. Hosp., Boston City Hosp., 1937-41; fellow in psychiatry and neurology Harvard U., Boston, 1941-45; asst. prof. psychiatry Washington U., St. Louis, 1945; mem. faculty Sch. Medicine Case Western Res. U., Cleve., 1946—, assoc. clin. prof. emeritus psychiatry, 1983—; practice medicine specializing in psychiatry and psychoanalysis Cleve., 1955—2002; ret., 2002. Mem. faculty Cleve. Psychoanalytic Inst., 1975—. Author: Treatment of Depression and Related Moods, 1988, 2005, Treatment of Chronic Depression, 2003, Treating Chronic Depression--Psychotherapy and Medication, 2003; contbr. articles to profl. jours. Fellow NRC Office Sci. R&D, 1941—45. Fellow: Am. Psychiat. Assn. (cert. Excellence Tchg. 1999), Internat. Psychoanlytic Assn. (life); mem.: AMA, Cleve. Psychoanalytic Soc. (pres. 1963), Phila. Assn. Psychoanalysis, Am. Psychoanalytic Soc., Acad. Medicine Cleve., Cleve. Psychiat. Soc., Ohio Med. Assn. Office: Judson Pk Apt 312 2181 Ambleside Rd Cleveland OH 44106

BADALAMENT, ROBERT ANTHONY, urologist, oncologist; b. Detroit, Mar. 20, 1954; s. Louis F. and Grace D. (Costello) B.; m. Providence F. Vitale, Nov. 9, 1980; children: Louis F., Peter P., Grace F. BS in Biology, So. Meth. U., 1976; MD, Emory U., 1980. Diplomate Am. Bd. Urology. Surg. intern Henry Ford Hosp., Detroit, 1980-81, surg. resident, 1981-82, urologic resident, 1982-85; fellow in urologic oncology Meml. Sloan Kettering Cancer Ctr., N.Y.C., 1985-87; asst. prof. Ohio State U., Columbus, 1987-92, assoc. prof., 1992-95, prof. Sch. Pub. Health, 1995—; mem. attending staff Arthur James Cancer Ctr., Columbus, 1990-95, Crittenton Hosp., Rochester Hills, Mich., 1995—. Contbr. chpt. to book, articles to profl. jours. Fellow ACS; mem. AMA, Soc. Urologic Oncology. Office: Rochester Urology PC 1135 W University Dr Ste 420 Rochester Hills MI 48307-1893

BADALAMENTI, ANTHONY, financial planner; b. St. Louis, Apr. 1, 1940; s. Sebastino and Grace (Orlando) B.; 1 child, Annette Marie. BS in Acctg., Washington U., 1970. CPA, Mo.; registered investment advisor. Staff acct. Fischer & Fischer, CPAs, St. Louis, 1959-63; acct. McDonnell Aircraft Corp., St. Louis, 1963-65; asst. chief acct. Dempsey Tegler, Inc., St. Louis, 1965-66; contr. Cummins Mo. Diesel, Inc., St. Louis, 1966-67; sr. acct. Elmer Fox & Co., CPAs, St. Louis, 1967-71; pvt. practice St. Louis, 1972-94; fin. planner Asset Builders Fin. Planners, St. Louis, 1995—. Tchr. Meramec C.C., St. Louis, 1973—. Mem. Mo. Soc. CPAs, Crestwood-Sunset Hills C. of C. (pres. 1980-81, Bus. Profl. Month award 1986, 91), Rotary (pres. Crestwood-Sunset Hills chpt. 1982-83). Republican. Roman Catholic. Avocations: basketball, softball, dance. Home: 1865 Locks Mill Dr Fenton MO 63026-2662 Office: 4901 S Lindbergh Blvd Saint Louis MO 63126 E-mail: abtp@sbcglobal.net.

BADALAMENTI, ANTHONY FRANCIS, mathematician, researcher; b. Bronx, N.Y., Feb. 2, 1943; s. Charles Salvator and Carmella-Maria (D'Ambrosio) Badalamenti; m. Karolina V. Kungl, Nov. 30, 1968 (div.); 1 child, Paul Anthony. BS, Manhattan Coll., 1964; MS, Stevens Inst. Tech., 1967; PHD equivalent, Bell Tel. Labs., 1967; PhD, Poly. Inst. Bklyn., 1970. Mem. tech. staff Bell Telephone Labs., 1964-70; asst. prof. Fairleigh Dickinson U., 1970-72; mem. tech. staff Gen. Rsch. Corp., 1972-74; dir. revenue modeling and reporting Western Union Telegraph Co., 1974; rsch. scientist Rockland Rsch. Inst. (now Nathan Kline Inst. Psychiat. Rsch.), Orangeburg, N.Y., 1975—. Vis. scientist Nathan Kline Inst., 1993—; cons. in field. Contbr. articles to profl. jours. Italian Charities Am. scholar, Bklyn. Poly. Inst. scholar. Mem.: Soc. Psychoanalytic Psychotherapy, Am. Soc. Cybernetics, N.Y. Acad. Scis., Soc. Gen. Sys. Rsch., Soc. Indsl. and Applied Math., Am. Math. Soc., Assn. Computing Machinery, Am. Stats. Assn., Bergen County Alumni Soc. Manhattan Coll. (v.p.). Home: 19 Crest St Apt 3B Westwood NJ 07675-3128 Office Phone: 201-358-8754. E-mail: afjb@ix.netcom.com.

BADALAMENTI, FRED LEOPOLDO, artist, educator; b. Long Island City, NY, June 25, 1935; s. Leopoldo and Concetta (Vitale) B.; m. Barbara J. Frankenfield, June 14, 1959; children: Katherine, Alexander, Frederick. Student, Pratt Inst., 1953-55, U. Alaska, 1957-58; BS, SUNY, New Paltz, 1961; MFA, Bklyn. Coll., 1967. Art tchr. Newburgh (NY) Pub. Schs., 1960-63, Deer Park (NY) High Sch., 1963-65; prof. emeritus Bklyn. Coll., 1967-92. Vis. prof. art, lectr. SUNY, Stony Brook, 1977-78, 80, 81, 83; dep. chmn. studio art Bklyn. Coll., 1990-92, dep. chmn. grad. art, 1972-89; dir. First St. Gallery, NYC, 1978; adj. faculty art dept. Bklyn. Coll., 1992-93, Stony Brook U., 1993-99. One man shows include Suffolk Community Coll., 1971, First Street Gallery, 1973, 76, 80, 89, Nassau County Mus. Fine Arts, 1987, St. Joseph's Coll., 1987, Alfred Van Loen Gallery, South Huntington, NY, 1998; exhibited paintings, drawings representational art in NYC, LI,

1967—. With USAF, 1955-59. Bklyn. Coll. grad. fellow, 1965-67. Mem. Coll. Art Assn., AAUP. Avocations: travel, tennis, gardening. Home: 182 Lower Sheep Pasture Rd East Setauket NY 11733-1826 E-mail: pasture@optonline.net.

BADASH, LAWRENCE, science history educator; b. Bklyn., May 8, 1934; s. Joseph and Dorothy (Langa) B.; children: Lisa, Bruce. BS in Physics, Rensselaer Poly. Inst., 1956; PhD in History of Sci., Yale U., 1964. Instr. Yale. U., New Haven, 1964—65, research assoc., 1965-66; from asst. to assoc. prof. U. Calif., Santa Barbara, 1966-79, prof. history of sci., 1979—2002, prof. emeritus, 2002—. Dir. summer seminar on global security and arms control U. Calif., 1983, 86, energy rsch. group, 1992, pacific rim program mem., 1993-95; cons. Nuclear Age Peace Found., Santa Barbara, 1984-90. Author: Radioactivity in Am., 1979, Kapitza, Rutherford, and the Kremlin, 1985, Scientists and the Development of Nuclear Weapons, 1995; editor: Rutherford and Boltwood, Letters on Radioactivity, 1969; Reminiscences of Los Alamos, 1943-45, 1980. Bd. dirs. Santa Barbara chpt. ACLU, 1971-86, 96—, pres., 1982-84, 96-98; nat. bd. dirs. Com. for a Sane Nuclear Policy, Washington, 1972-81; mem. Los Padres Search and Rescue Team, Santa Barbara, 1981-94. Lt. (j.g.) USN, 1956-59. Grantee, NSF, Cambridge, Eng., 1965-66, 69-72, 90-92, Am. Philos. Soc., New Zealand, 1979-80, Inst. on Global Conflict and Cooperation, Univ. Calif., 1983-87; J.S. Guggenheim fellow, 1984-85. Fellow AAAS (sect. mem. at large 1988-92), Am. Phys. Soc. (chmn. divsn. of history of physics 1988-89, exec. com. forum on physics and society 1991-93); mem. History of Sci. Soc. (founder West Coast chpt., chpt. bd. dirs. 1971-73, nat. coun. 1975-78). Democrat. Jewish. Avocation: backpacking. Office: Univ Calif Dept History Santa Barbara CA 93106-9410

BADDING, JOHN VICTOR, chemistry professor; b. Buffalo, May 6, 1962; s. Victor George and Nancy (Clark) B.; m. Mizue Abe, Dec. 28, 1993. BS, Manhattan Coll., N.Y.C., 1984; PhD, U. Calif., Berkeley, 1989. Asst. prof. chemistry Pa. State U., University Park, 1991-97, assoc. prof. chemistry, 1997—. Contbr. articles to profl. jours. Packard fellow, 1993; NSF Young Investigator awardee, 1993. Office: Pa State U Dept Chemistry University Park PA 16802 E-mail: jbadding@chem.psu.edu.

BADDOUR, ANNE BRIDGE, pilot; b. Royal Oak, Mich. d. William George and Esther Rose (Pfiester) Bridge; m. Raymond F. Baddour, Sept. 25, 1954; children: Cynthia Anne, Frederick Raymond, Jean Bridge. Student, Detroit Bus. Sch., 1948—50; BA, Pine Manor Coll. Stewardess Ea. Airlines, Boston, 1952—54; instr. aero. Powers Sch., Boston, 1958; co-pilot, flight attendant Raytheon Co., Bedford, Mass., 1958—63; flight dispatcher, ferry Pilot Comerford Flight Sch., Bedford, 1974—76; adminstrv. asst., ferry pilot Jenney Beachcraft, Bedford, 1976; mgr., pilot Balt. Airways, Inc., Bedford, 1976—77; rsch. test pilot Lincoln Lab. Flight Test Facility MIT, Lexington, 1977—97. Aviation cons., corp. pilot Energy Resources, Inc., Cambridge, Mass., 1974-84; holder World Class speed records for single-engine aircraft; Boston to Goose Bay, Labrador, 1985, Boston to Reykjavik, Iceland, 1985, Portland, Maine to Goose Bay, 1985, Portland to Reykjavik, 1985, Goose Bay to Reykjavik, 1985; records for twin-engine aircraft: Sept Isles to Goose Bay, 1988, Mont Joll to Goose Bay, 1988, Presque Isle to Goose Bay, 1988, Millinocket to Goose Bay, 1988, Bedford to Goose Bay, 1988, Goose Bay to Narssassrag, Greenland, 1988, Narssassrag to Klevelevic, Iceland, 1988, Narssassrag to Reykjavik, 1988, Bedford to Narssassrag, 1988, Millinochet to Narssassrag, 1988, Presque Isle to Narssassrag, 1988, Bedford to St. John, 1991, Bedford to Charlottetown, 1991, Charlottetown to Kennebunk, 1991, Charlottetown to Portsmouth, 1991, Muncton to Bedford, 1991, St. John, to Kennebunk, 1991, St. John to Bedford, 1991, World Class Speed Records Single-Engine Aircraft, 1991, Bedford, Mass. to Sydney, Nova Scotia, Bedford, Mass. to Sydney, Nova Scotia to Beford, Mass., Portsmouth, New Hampshire to Sydney Nova Scotia to Portsmouth, Brunswick to Sydney Nova Scotia to Brunswick. Mem. campaign coun. Mus. Transp., Boston; mem. coun. assocs. French Libr. in Boston; commr. Commonwealth of Mass., Mass. Aero. Commn., 1979—83; trustee bd. adminstrn. Amelia Earhart Birthplace Mus., 1992—93; trustee Daniel Webster Coll., Nashua, NH, 1995—; v.p., trustee Friends of the Libr. Spl. Collections Boston U., 1997—; trustee Viscaya Mus., 2002—; bd. dirs. Smithsonian Nat. Air & Space Mus., 1998—, Cambridge Opera, 1977—79, Miami-Dade Maritime Mus., 2004—. Named Pilot of Yr., New Eng. sect. Internat. Women Pilots Orgn./The Ninety-Nines Inc., 1992; named to Internat. Aviation Forest of Friendship, Atchison, Kans., 1991, Women in Aviation Internat. Pioneer Hall of Fame, 2005; recipient trophy, Phila. Transcontinental Air Race, 1954, New Eng. Air Race, 1957, Clifford B. Harmon trophy, Internat. Aviatrix, 1988, recipient Spl. Recognition award, FAA, 1990. Mem.: DAR, Women in Aviation Internat. (Pioneer Hall of Fame award 2005), Friends of Switzerland, Bostonian Soc., Nat. Pilots Assn., U.S. Sea Plane Pilots Assn., Assn. Women Transcontinental Air Race, Soc. Exptl. Test Pilots, Aircraft Owners Pilots Assn., Fedn. Aeronautique Internat., Nat. Aero. Assn., Ninety-Nines (New Eng. Safety trophy 1986), Beach Colony Club, Fairchild Tropical Garden Club, Harvard Travellers Club, Boston Women's Travel Club, Chilton Club, Belmont Hill Club, Aero Club New Eng. (v.p. 1978—80, dir. 1978—2002).

BADDOUR, STEVEN A., lawyer, state legislator; BA, U. Mass.; JD, Mass. Sch. Law. Atty.; state rep. Mass. House, 2002—. Mem. Holy Family Men's Guild, Son's of Italy, Methuen Historical Soc. Democrat. Office: Rm 520 State House Boston MA 02133

BADDOURA, RASHID JOSEPH, emergency medicine physician; b. Beirut, Aug. 4, 1947; came to U.S., 1974; s. Joseph and Renée Baddoura; m. Rola Tohme, July 15, 1989; children: Joseph, Philip, Karen. BS, Am. U. Beirut, 1970, MD, 1974. Diplomate Am. Bd. Emergency Medicine (examiner 1984-89), Am. Bd. Internal Medicine, Am. Bd. Pulmonary Diseases. Intern Am. U. Med. Ctr., Beirut; resident in internal medicine St. Joseph's Hosp. & Med. Ctr., Paterson, N.J., 1974-76; fellow in pulmonary and critical care Duke U., 1976-79; dir. emergency dept. Meml. Hosp., Danville, Va., 1981-84; corp. med. officer, mem. med. adv. bd. Coastal Healthcare Group, Durham, N.C., 1981-86; assoc. dir. emergency dept. Valley Hosp., Ridgewood, NJ, 1986-90, dir. emergency dept., 1990—2000; ptnr., bd. dirs. Valley Emergency Assocs., 1986—, Valley Regional Emergency Group, 1999—; pres. Valley Emergency Assocs., 2002—; ptnr., bd. dirs. Bergen Regional Emergency Group, 1998—2003. Mem. bd. Coastal Found. for Med. Edn., Durham, 1984-89; clin. asst. prof. emergency medicine Georgetown U., Washington, 1986-89. Fellow Am. Coll. Emergency Physicians, Am. Coll. Chest Physicians; mem. Am. Coll. Physician Execs. Avocations: hunting, fishing, philosophy, classical music. Office: Valley Hosp Dept Emergency Medicine Ridgewood NJ 07451 Office Phone: 201-447-8318.

BADEER, HENRY SARKIS, physiology educator; b. Mersine, Turkey, Jan. 31, 1915; arrived in US, 1965, naturalized, 1971; s. Sarkis and Persape Hagop (Koundakjian) B.; m. Mariam Mihran Kassarjian, July 12, 1948; children: Gilbert H., Daniel H. MD, Am. U., Beirut, Lebanon, 1938. Gen. practice medicine, Beirut, 1940—51; asst. instr. Am. U. Sch. Medicine, Beirut, 1938—45, adj. prof., 1945—51, assoc. prof., 1951—62, prof. physiology, 1962—65, acting chmn. dept., 1951—56, chmn., 1956—65; rsch. fellow Harvard U. Med. Sch., Boston, 1948—49; prof. physiology Creighton U. Med. Sch., Omaha, 1967—91, emeritus prof., 1991—, acting chmn. dept., 1971—72. Vis. prof. U. Iowa, Iowa City, 1957-58, Downstate Med. Center, Bklyn., 1965-67; mem. med. com. Azounieh Sanatorium, Beirut, 1961-65; mem. research com. Nebr. Heart Assn., 1967-70, 85-88. Author textbook Spanish translation; contbr. chpts. to books, articles to profl. jours. Recipient Golden Apple award Students of AMA, 1975, Disting. Prof. award, 1992; Rockefeller fellow., 1948-49; grantee med. research com. Am. U. Beirut, 1956-65 Mem. Internat. Soc. Heart Rsch., Am. Physiol. Soc., Internat. Soc. for Adaptive Medicine (founding mem.). Home: 2808 S 99th Ave Omaha NE 68124-2603 Office: Creighton U Med Sch 2500 California Plz Omaha NE 68178-0001 *My success seems to be related to having set a goal and persevering in achieving it; satisfaction in or enjoyment of the performance of my daily task no matter how mundane; and eagerness to learn from personal experience or the experience of others.*

BADEL, JULIE, lawyer; b. Chgo., Sept. 14, 1946; d. Charles and Saima (Hrykas) Badel. Student, Knox Coll., 1963—65; BA, Columbia Coll., Chgo., 1967; JD, DePaul U., 1977. Bar: Ill. 1977, U.S. Dist. Ct. (no. dist.) Ill. 1977, U.S. Dist. Ct. (ea. dist.) Mich. 1989, U.S. Dist. Ct. (no. dist.) Ind. 2002, U.S. Ct. Appeals (7th and D.C. cirs.) 1981, U.S. Supreme Ct. 1985. Hearings referee State of Ill., Chgo., 1974-78; assoc. Cohn, Lambert, Ryan & Schneider, Chgo., 1978-80, McDermott, Will & Emery, Chgo., 1980-84, ptnr., 1985-2001, Epstein, Becker & Green, PC, Chgo., 2001—. Legal counsel, mem. adv. bd. Health Evaluation Referral Svc. Chgo., 1980-89; bd. dirs. Alternatives, Inc., Chgo. chpt. Asthma and Allergy Found., 1993-94, Glenwood Sch. Author: Hospital Restructuring: Employment Law Pitfalls, 1985; editor DePaul U. Law Rev., 1976-77. Mem. ABA, Chgo. Bar Assn., Labor & Employment Alliance for Women, Columbia Coll. Alumni Assn. (1st v.p., bd. dirs. 1981-86), Pi Gamma Mu. Office: Epstein Becker & Green 150 N Michigan Ave Ste 420 Chicago IL 60601-7553 Business E-Mail: jbadel@ebglaw.com.

BADEN, MICHAEL M., pathologist, educator; b. Bronx, July 27, 1934; s. Harry and Fannie (Linn) B.; m. Judianne Densen-Gerber June 14, 1958 (div. 1997, dec. 2003), 3 children; m. Linda Kenney. BS, CCNY, 1955; MD, NYU, 1959. Diplomate Am. Bd. Pathology. Intern, first med. div. Bellevue Hosp., NYC, 1959-60, resident, 1960-61, resident in pathology, 1961-63, chief resident in pathology, 1963-64, fellow in pathology, 1964-65; pvt. practice in pathology NYC, 1965—; asst. med. examiner City of NY, 1961-65, jr. med. examiner, 1965-66, assoc. med. examiner, 1966-70, dep. chief med. examiner, 1970-78, 79-81, 83-86, chief med. examiner, 1978-79; dep. chief med. examiner, dir. labs. Suffolk County, NY, 1981-83; dep. chief med. examiner NYC, 1983-86; dir. forensic scis. unit NY State Police, 1986—; instr. in pathology NYU, NYC, 1964-65, asst. prof. pathology, 1966-70, assoc. prof. forensic medicine, 1970-89. Adj. prof. law NY Law Sch., NYC, 1975-88, John Jay Coll. Criminal Justice, NYC, 1989-90, 93; vis. prof. pathology Albert Einstein Sch. Medicine, NYC, 1975—; lectr. pathology Coll. Physicians and Surgeons, Columbia U., NYC, 1975—, adj. prof. pathology and lab. medicine, 1993—; asst. vis. pathologist Bellevue Hosp., NYC, 1965-75; adj. prof. pathology and lab. medicine Albany (NY) Med. Sch.; lectr. Drug Enforcement Adminstrn., Dept. Justice, 1973—; vis. lectr. Fairleigh Dickinson Dentistry, Hackensack, NJ, 1968-70; spl. forensic pathology cons. NY State Organized Crime Task Force, 1971-75; chmn. forensic pathology panel US Ho. of Reps. select coms. on assassinations of Pres. John F. Kennedy and Dr. Martin Luther King, Jr., 1977-79; mem. med. adv. bd. Andrew Menchell Infant Survival Found., 1969-74; mem. cert. bd. Addiction Svcs. Agy., NYC, 1966-69; preceptor health research tng. program NYC Dept. Health, 1968-79; v.p. Coun. for Interdisciplinary Communication in Medicine, 1967-69; forensic pathology cons. NY State Police, 1985—. Author: Alcohol, Other Drugs and Violent Death, 1978, Unnatural Death, 1989 (with Marion Roach) Dead Reckoning: New Science of Catching Killers, 2001, (novels with Linda Kenney) Remains Silent, 2005; contbr. articles on forensic medicine to profl. jours.; mem. editorial bd. Am. Jour. Drug and Alcohol Abuse, 1973—, Internat. Microfilm Jour. Legal Medicine, 1969-73, Contemporary Drug Problems, 1971; host, HBO series, Autopsy, 1995-2000. Active NY adv. bd. Odyssey House, Inc., 1966-76; bd. dirs. NY Coun. on Alcoholism, sec., 1969-79; bd. dirs. Belco Scholarship Found., Inc., 1971-87. Recipient Great Tchr. award NYU, 1980 Fellow Coll. Am. Pathologists (chmn. toxicology subcom. 1972-74), Am. Soc. Clin. Pathologists (mem. drug abuse task force 1973—), Am. Acad. Forensic Scis. (program chmn. 1971-72, sec. sect. pathology and biology 1970-71, exec. com. 1971-74, v.p. 1982-83); mem. Med. Soc. County NY (mem. pub. health com. 1966-76), Soc. Med. Jurisprudence (corr. sec. 1971-78, v.p. 1979-81, pres. 1981-85, chmn. bd. 1985—), Nat. Assn. Med. Examiners, NY Path. Soc., NY State Med. Soc., AMA, Internat. Royal Coll. Health Office: 142 E End Ave New York NY 10028-7503*

BADER, ALFRED ROBERT, chemist; b. Vienna, Apr. 28, 1924; came to U.S., 1947, naturalized, 1964; s. Alfred and Elizabeth Maria (Serenyi) B.; m. Isabel Overton, Jan. 26, 1982; children from previous marriage: David, Daniel. BS in Engring. Chemistry, Queens U., Can., 1945, BA in History, 1946, MS in Organic Chemistry, 1947, LLD (hon.), 1986; MA, Harvard U., 1949, PhD, 1950; DS (hon.), U. Wis.-Milw., 1980, Purdue U., 1984, U. Wis.-Madison, 1984, Northwestern U., 1990; D.Univ. (hon.), U. Sussex, Eng., 1989; DSc, U. Edinburgh, 1998, Glasgow U., 1999, Masaryk U., 2000. Rsch. chemist PPG Co., Milw., 1950-53, group leader, 1953-54; chief chemist Aldrich Chem. Co., Milw., 1954-55, pres., 1955-81, chmn., 1981-91; pres. Sigma-Aldrich Corp., 1975-80, chmn., 1980-91, chmn. emeritus, 1991-92; pres. Alfred Bader Fine Arts, Milw., 1991—. Author: Adventures of a Chemist Collector, 1995; patentee in field. Guest curator Milw. Art Mus., 1976, 89. Recipient Winthrop-Sears medal Chem. Industry Assn., 1980, J.E. Purkyne medal Acad. Scis., Czech Republic, 1994, Gold medal Am. Inst. Chemists, 1997, Boron USA award, 1997; named Entrepreneur of Year Research Dirs. Assn., 1980, Hon. Citizen, U. Vienna, 1995, Comdr. of the Brit. Empire, 1998. Fellow: Royal Soc. Arts, Royal Soc. Chemistry (hon.); mem.: Appraisers Assn. Am., Am. Chem. Soc. (award Milw. sect. 1971, Parsons' award 1995, named one of the top 75 disting. contbrs. to the chem. enterprise in the last 75 years 1998), Univ. Club (Milw.). Jewish. Office: Alfred Bader Fine Arts 924 E Juneau Ave Ste 622 Milwaukee WI 53202-2748 Fax: 414-277-0709. Office Phone: 414-277-0730. E-mail: baderfa@execpc.com.

BADER, DIEDRICH, actor; b. Alexandria, Va., Dec. 24, 1966; s. William and Gretta Bader; m. Duley Rodgers, 1998. Actor in feature film debut in dual role as twins Jethro and Jethrine in remake of TV series: The Beverly Hillbillies; actor (film): Teresa's Tattoo, 1994, Office Space, 1999, The Assassination File, Certain Guy, 1999, Couple Days...A Period Place, 2000, Jay & Silent Bob Strike Back, 2001, Kim Possible, 2002, Evil Alien Conquerors, 2002, (voices in films) Baby Blues, 2000, The Zeta Project, 2001, Lloyd in Space, 2001, Recess: School's Out, 2001, Ice Age, 2002, The Country Bears, 2002, Dead and Breakfast, 2004, (voice) Dinotopia: Curse of the Ruby Sunstone, 2004, Napoleon Dynamite, 2004, Eurotrip, 2004, Miss Congeniality: Armed and Fabulous, 2005; (TV movies) Preppie Murder, 1989; (tv series): Danger Theatre, 1993, The Drew Carey Show, 1995—2004, (voice) Hercules, 1998-99, Center of the Universe, 2004-05; tv guest appearances include: 21 Jump Street, 1987, Fresh Prince of Bel-Air, 1990, Star Trek: The Next Generation, 1987, Cheers, 1982, Quantum Leap, 1989, Broken Badges, 1990, Flying Blind, 1992, Diagnosis Murder, 1993, Frasier, 1993, Gargoyles, 1994, Murphy Brown, 1988, Happy Hour, 1999, (voice) King of the Hill, 1999, (voice) The Simpsons, 2000, The Norm Show, 2001; exec. prodr. Jimmy Scott: If You Only Knew, 2002.*

BADER, GERALD LOUIS, JR., lawyer; b. St. Louis, Mar. 15, 1934; s. Gerald L. and Mabel A. (Stephens) B.; (div.); children: Gerald L. III, Stephanie, Cynthia, Carlie, Deborah; m. Barbara Anne Lien, June 2, 1979; children: Matthew Stephen, Mary Rachel. BA, Washington U., 1956; LLB, U. Mich., 1959. Bar: Colo. 1960, Mo. 1960, N.Y. 1961, U.S. Supreme Ct. 1972. Assoc. White & Case, N.Y.C., 1960-62, 64-65, Hodges, Silverstein & Harrington, Denver, 1965-68; pres. Bader and Assocs. P.C., Denver, 1969—. Sec. Denver Rep. Ctrl. Com., 1969-73; pres. Rocky Mountain Child Devel. Fedn., Denver, 1982-90; dir. Ctrl. City Opera House Assocs., Denver, 1984-2002, The Legal Ctr., Denver, 1992-98. 1st lt. U.S. Army, 1962-64. Mem.: Phi Beta Kappa. Republican. Roman Catholic. Avocations: golf, skiing. Office: Bader and Assocs LLC 14426 E Evans Denver CO 80014 Office Phone: 303-534-1700. Business E-Mail: gbader@baderassociates.com.

BADER, IAN, architectural firm executive; b. Johannesburg, Mar. 4, 1954; naturalized, 1991; BArch, U. Witwatersrand, Johannesburg, 1977, MArch, 1981. Registered N.Y., N.J. With Christelis & Victor, Johannesburg, 1975, I.M. Pei & Ptnrs., 1981—89, Pei Cobb Freed & Ptnrs., 1989—99, ptnr. N.Y.C., 1999—. Lectr. U. Witwatersrand, Johannesburg, 1978, U. Detroit, 1979, Parsons Sch. Design, N.Y.C., 1984—86. Exhibitions include Battery Park, N.Y., 1983, Fashion Inst. Tech., 1984, Artist's Space, N.Y., 1987. Named one of 40 Under 40, Interiors Mag., 1986; recipient Wits U. Sr. bursary, Human Scis. Rsch. Coun., 1978. Office: Pei Freed & Ptnrs LLP 88 Pine St New York NY 10005

BADER, IZAAK WALTON, lawyer; b. N.Y.C., June 20, 1922; s. Maximillian Bader and Ida (Sussman) R.; m. Betty Sands Bader, Mar. 26, 1972. AB in Chemistry, NYU, 1942, JD, 1968. Bar: N.Y., D.C., U.S. Supreme Ct. Atty., FTC, Washington, 1948-50; asst. counsel N.Y. State Rent Com., N.Y.C., 1950-54; patent counsel Swingline Inc., 1954-72; sr. ptnr. Bader & Bader, White Plains, N.Y., 1972—; counsel Heart Disease Found., 1970-76, Ind. Investment Protective League, N.Y.C., 1972—; spl. counsel La. State Employees' Retirement System, Tchrs.' Retirement System of La., State Bd. Adminstrn. Fla., Lindner Fund, Inc., Shriners Hosps. for Children. Mem. ABA, N.Y. State Bar Assn., Westchester County Bar Assn. Democrat. Home: 2980 Riverside Dr Coral Springs FL 33065-1008 Office: PO Box 770787 Coral Springs FL 33077-0787

BADER, JOHN MERWIN, lawyer; b. Wilmington, Del., June 29, 1919; s. Merwin Oldrin and Escalyn (Connell) Bader; m. Constance Wulffaert, Dec. 27, 1944 (div. Oct. 1965); children: Andrew M., Mary Donley, Eileen Williams, Matthew J.; m. Anne S. Shane, Jan. 15, 1973 (dec. Jan. 5, 2003). BA, Villanova U., 1941; LLB, U. Pa., 1948. Bar: Del. 1948, U.S. Supreme Ct. 1956. Pvt. practice, Wilmington, 1948-56, 66-70; ptnr. Balick and Bader, Wilmington, 1956-59, Bader and Biggs, Wilmington, 1959-66, Bader, Dorsey & Kreshtool, Wilmington, 1970-81; pvt. practice Wilmington, 1981—88; of counsel Tomar, O'Brien, Kaplan, Jacoby & Graziano, Wilmington, 1988—2001. Counsel Rep. State Com., Wilmington, 1975-85; mem. Ethics Commn., City of Wilmington, 1998-2001. 1st lt. U.S. Army, 1941-45. Mem. Del. Bar Assn. (v.p. 1969-71), ATLA (bd. govs. 1969-73, 75-80), Del. Trial Lawyers Assn. (pres. 1977-80), Elks, Kiwanis, Univ. and Whist Club (Wilmington). Home: Apt 4316 4830 Kennett Pike Wilmington DE 19807 E-mail: baderj@aol.com.

BADER, KATHLEEN M., chemicals executive; B in Liberal Arts, Notre Dame; MBA, U. Calif., Berkeley. Joined Dow Chem. Co., Chgo., 1973—, corp. v.p. Quality and Business Excellence, 1999, pres. bus. group styrenics and engineered products Zurich, Switzerland, 2000—04; chmn., pres., CEO Dow Cargill, Minnetonka, Minn., 2004—. Chair dept. pvt. sector sr. advisory com. Homeland Security; adv. coun. US Homeland Security, 2002—; bd. dirs. Textron Inc., Providence, 2004—. Internat. bd. dir. Habitat for Humanity; dean's coun. Harvard Sch. Govt. Named One of 50 Most Powerful Women in Internat. Bus., Fortune Mag., 2001—03. Office: Dow Cargill 15305 Minnetonka Blvd Minnetonka MN 55345 Office Phone: 877-423-7659.

BADER, ROBERT SMITH, biology and zoology educator, researcher; b. Falls City, Nebr., June 18, 1925; s. Ray Jay and Grace (Smith) B.; m. Joan Larson; children: Douglas, Jonathan, Eric, Joel. BS, Kans. State U., 1949; PhD, U. Chgo., 1954. From instr. to asst. prof. biology U. Fla., 1952-56; from asst. prof. to prof. zoology U. Ill., Urbana, 1956-68; prof. biology, dean Coll. Arts and Scis., U. Mo., St. Louis, 1968-83, rsch. prof., 1983-85; rsch. assoc. dept. history U. Kans., 1985-91. Adj. prof. history Kans. State U., 1986-91. With USNR, 1943-45. Achievements include research on Kansas history, prohibition history, Biblical theology. Home: 2165 Squirrel Rd Neosho Falls KS 66758-7122 E-mail: jlbader@terraworld.net.

BADER, ROCHELLE LINDA (SHELLEY BADER), educational administrator; BA in Speech Arts, BA in Edn., Hofstra U., 1970; MLS, U. Md., 1973; EdD, George Washington U., 1993. Mgmt. intern Office Civil Pers., Dept. of the Army, Pentagon, Washington, 1971; circulation libr. George Washington U. Med. Libr., Washington, 1971-73; head reference libr. Himmelfarb Health Scis. Libr./George Washington U. Med. Ctr., Washington, 1973-75, head Audio Visual Study Ctr., 1975-78, chief Access and Facilities Svcs. Divsn., 1978-79, chief Reader Svcs. Divsn., 1979-80, assoc. dir., 1980, dir., 1980-90; dir. ednl. resources George Washington U. Med. Ctr., Washington, 1990—, assoc. v.p. ednl. resources, 1998—. Audio visual cons. Regional Med. Libr. Program, D.C. Metro area, 1977-79; mem. nat. adv. com. U. Iowa, 1984-85; mem. Med. Ctr. Faculty Senate Com. on Health Scis. Programs, George Washington U., Washington, 1989, chmn. Health Scis. Programs Ednl. Evaluation Com., 1993—, many other coms.; adv. com. Found. for Health Svcs. Rsch., 1992-93; presenter in field. Consulting editor: Biomedical Comms., 1983-84; mem. editorial rev. bd.: The Jour. of Biocommunication, 1988-92, Annual Statistics of Medical School Libraries in the United States and Canada, 12th, 13th and 14th edits., 1989-93; contbr. articles to profl. jours. Grantee Coun. on Libr. Resource, 1989-90, Nat. Libr. Medicine, 1991, NSF, 1993-94; recipient Disting. Svc. award Health Scis. Comms. Assn., 1986. Mem. Am. Med. Informatics Assn. (exec. com. edn. workshop group 1991—, MLA rep. to adv. coun. 1992—), Assn. Am. Med. Colls. (group on med. edn., coun. on acad. scos. 1991—), Assn. Acad. Health Scis. Libr. Dirs. (pres. 1986-87, chmn. fin. com. 1987-88), Assn. Biomedical Comms. Dirs. (membership com. 1989-91, program com. 1991), Health Scis. Comms. Assn. (coord. interactive media festival 1990-91, chmn. awards com. 1992, pres. 1984-85), Med. Libr. Assn. (bd. dirs. 1995—), Beta Phi Mu. Home: 12225 Seline Way Potomac MD 20854-2872 Office: George Washington U Med Ctr 2300 I St NW Washington DC 20037-2336

BADER, WILLIAM BANKS, historian, former corporate executive, foundation executive; b. Atlantic City, Sept. 8, 1931; s. Edward L. and Celeste Bader (Burkard) B.; m. Gretta Lange, Dec. 19, 1953; children: Christopher, Katharine, John, Diedrich. BA, Pomona Coll., 1953; MA, Princeton U., 1960, PhD, 1964. With Libr. of Congress, 1954—55; with Office Nat. Estimates, 1962—64; lectr. history Princeton U., 1964—65; with Dept. State, 1965—66, U.S. Senate Fgn. Rels. Com., 1966—69; program officer, then European rep. Ford Found., 1969—73; program officer Office European and Internat. Affairs, 1973—74; fellow Woodrow Wilson Internat. Ctr. Scholars, 1974—75; dir. fgn. intelligence task force U.S. Senate, 1975—76; asst. dep. under sec. for policy Dept. Def., 1976—78; dir. staff U.S. Senate Fgn. Rels. Com., 1978—81; v.p. SRI Internat.-Washington, Arlington, 1981—87; sr. v.p. SRI Internat., Menlo Park, Calif., 1988—92; pres. Eurasia Found., Washington, 1992—96; with World Bank Group, Washington, 1996—97, Ctr. Strategic and Internat. Studies, 1997—98; asst. sec. of state ednl. and cultural affairs Dept. State, 1998—2001; with World Bank Group, Washington, 2001—02; v.p. Nat. Def. U., 2000—04, Internat. Fin. Corp., 2005—. Adj. prof. Georgetown U. Author: Austria Between East and West: 1945-1955, 1966, The U.S. and the Spread of Nuclear Weapons, 1968, The Taiwan Relations Act: A Decade of Implementation, 1989; also articles. Bd. dirs. Samuel H. Kress Found. Served as officer USNR, 1955-58, capt. Res. ret. Recipient Meritorious Svc. medal Dept. State, 1966, Sec. Def. medal for outstanding pub. svc., 1979, Osterreichische Ehrenkreuz fur Wissenschaft und Kunst 1. Klasse (officer's cross) Republic of Austria, 1991. Mem. Coun. Fgn. Rels., Internat. Inst. Strategic Studies, Cosmos Club Washington Roman Catholic. Office: Internat Fin Corp 2121 Pennsylvania Ave NW Washington DC 20433

BADER, W(ILLIAM) REECE, lawyer; b. Portland, Oreg., Oct. 31, 1941; s. William Lange and Phyllis Harriet (Cole) B.; m. Jean McCarty, Aug. 3, 1963 (div. 1993); children: Lawson R., Cole R.; m. Alicia Spatafore, June 14, 1998. BA, Williams Coll., 1963; JD, Duke U., 1966. Bar: D.C. 1967, Calif. 1969, U.S. Dist. Ct. D.C., U.S. Dist. Ct. (no., ctrl., ea. and so. dists.) Calif., U.S. Ct. Appeals (D.C., 2d, 3d, 7th, 9th and fed. cirs.), U.S. Tax Ct., U.S. Claims Ct., U.S. Supreme Ct. Law clk. to judge U.S. Ct. Appeals (D.C. cir.), Washington, 1966-68; assoc. Orrick, Herrington & Sutcliffe LLP, San Francisco, 1968-74, ptnr., 1974—. Mem. legal adv. bd. Hastings Law Ctr. Found., 1981-87; mem. securities disputes resolution com. Ctr. for Pub. Resources, 1990—; mem. nat. arbitration and med. com. NASDR, 1994-98; mem. ad hoc com. on ct. facilities and design U.S. Jud. Conf., 1969-72, mem. adv. com. on civil rules, 1982-87, mem. standing com. on rules of practice and procedure, 1987-90; lectr., panelist Practicing Law Inst., ABA Am. Law Inst., Internat. Franchise Assn., Calif. Electronic Assn., many others; arbitrator, mediator Nat. Assn. Securities Dealers Regulation Inc., 1979—, Am. Arbitration Assn., 1979—, N.Y. Stock Exch., 1984—, Nat. Futures Assn., 1985—, Pvt. Adjudication

Found., 1987-96. Mem. editl. bd. Alternatives, 1991—; editor: Securities News, 1993-94, Securities Arbitration, 1999--, Private Securities Litigation Reform Act Reporter, 1996—; contbr. article to profl. jours. Trustee North Park Coll. and Theol. Sem., Chgo., 1984-89, sec., 1985-86, chmn., 1986-89. Fellow Am. Bar Found., Environ. Law Inst.; mem. ABA (litig., bus., natural resources, dispute resolution sects.), State Bar Calif. (litig., bus., environ. sects.), Securities Industry Assn. (compliance and legal divsn.), Futures Industry Assn. (compliance and legal divsn.), Bar Assn. San Francisco, D.C. Bar Assn. Avocations: collecting toy trains, squash, reading, travel. Home: 62 Lloyden Dr Atherton CA 94027-3834 Office: Orrick Herrington Sutcliffe LLP 1020 Marsh Rd Menlo Park CA 94025-1021 Office Phone: 650-614-7440. E-mail: wrbader@orrick.com.

BADERTSCHER, DAVID GLEN, law librarian, consultant; b. Morrow, Ohio, Jan. 31, 1935; s. Glen C. and Blanche (Cluff) Badertscher; m. Betty Jo Shafer, June 25, 1965. BS, Ind. State U., 1957, MS, 1962, Rosary Coll., 1967. Tchr. Rockville HS, Ind., 1957-59, Medinah Elem. Sch., Ill., 1961-63; libr. Elgin Acad., Ill., 1963-64; tchr. Beachwood HS, Ohio, 1964-65; libr. Chgo. Pub. Libr., 1965-66; circulation, asst. reference libr. U. Chgo. Law Sch., 1966-70; libr. Schiff Hardin Waite Dorschel & Britton, Chgo., 1970-73; exec. libr. Georgetown U. Law Ctr., Washington, 1973-78; dir. libr. Milbank, Tweed, Hadley & McCloy, N.Y.C, 1978-80; prin. law libr. N.Y. Supreme Ct., N.Y.C., 1980—. Cons. Urban Rsch. Corp., Chgo., 1970—73, Herner & Co., 1977—, R. R. Bowker & Co., 1981—91, Nat. Ctr. State Cts., 1992—96; advisor Computer Law Svc., 1972—82, EIS, 1978—; adj. prof. Baruch Coll., 1982—2002; bd. dirs. N.Y. Met. Reference and Rsch. Libr. Agy., chmn. bd. pers. com., 1989—93; mem. judges com. automation and tech. State of N.Y. Unified Ct. Sys., 1994—96. Contbr. articles to profl. jours. Mem. corp. adv. bd. Tech. Forum Internat., 1997—. With U.S. Army, 1959—61. Mem.: ABA (assoc.; mem. com. sci. and tech. criminal justice sect. 2000—), Assn. Info. Mgrs., Am. Soc. Info. Sci. (editor SIG/Law Newsletter 1975—79), Chgo. Assn. Law Librs. (pres., conf. chmn. 1970—72, mem. com. automation and tech. judges N.Y. 1994—96), Am. Assn. Law Librs. (chmn. com. automation, sci. devel. 1970—72, chmn. state, city, and county law librs. sect. 1989—90, mem. adv. com. law libr. jour. 1989—91, conv. grantee 1970), Medinah Tchrs. Assn. (pres. 1962—63). Home: 257 Orchard St Apt 8 Westfield NJ 07090-3130 Office: NY Supreme Ct 100 Centre St New York NY 10013-4308

BADESCU, MIRCEA, mechanical engineer; arrived in US, 1997; s. Stelian and Constantina Badescu; m. Carmen Silvia Slavov, June 28, 1997; 1 child, Stephan Anthony. Diploma in Engring., Tech. Mil. Acad., Bucharest, Romania, 1992; PhD, Rutgers U., 2003. Rsch. engr. Diving Ctr., Constanta, Romania, 1992—97; tchg. asst. Rutgers U., New Brunswick, NJ, 1999—2003, instr., 2003—03, post-doctoral assoc., 2003—04; caltech post-doctoral scholar Calif. Inst. Tech., Pasadena, Calif., 2004—05; engring. staff Calif. Inst. Tech., Jet Propulsion Lab, Pasadena, 2005—. Cons. Northeastern U., Boston, 2004—04; intern GM R&D Ctr., Warren, Mich., 2001. Reviewer: Jour. of Mech. Design, 2003—05; contbr. articles to profl. jours. Mem.: ASME (chmn., organizer session of congress and exposition 2003). Achievements include patents for active quick connecting / disconnecting connector; method and apparatus for push-button control; semiautomatic pistol for underwater bolt welding; research in reconfigurable robots using parallel platforms as modules; workspace analysis of nanoscale viral protein linear motors. Office: Jet Propulsion Laboratory 4800 Oak Grove Drive MS 67-119 Pasadena CA 91109 Office Phone: 818-393-5700. Office Fax: 818-393-4057. Personal E-mail: mircea.badescu@jpl.nasa.gov.

BADGER, DAVID HARRY, lawyer; b. Indpls., June 16, 1931; s. David Henry and Mayme Pearl (Wright) B.; m. Donna Lee Bailey, June 24, 1954; children: David Mark, Lee Ann, Steven Michael. BEE, Rose Poly. Inst., 1953; JD, Ind. U., 1964. Bar: Ind. 1964, U.S. Dist. Ct. (so and no. dists.) Ind. 1964, U.S. Patent Office 1964, U.S. Ct. Customs and Patent Appeals 1971, U.S. Ct. Appeals (fed. cir.) 1982. Engr. GE, 1953-56, Ransburg Corp., Indpls., 1956-62; chief elec. engr. Rex Metal Craft, Inc., Indpls., 1963-64; patent counsel, corp. sec. Ransburg Corp., Indpls., 1964—76; legal counsel Ball Corp., Muncie, Ind., 1976-77; ptnr. Jenkins, Coffey, Hyland, Badger & Conard, Indpls., 1977-82; mng. ptnr. Brinks, Hofer, Gilson & Lione, Indpls., 1982-98. Contbr. articles to profl. jours.; patentee in U.S. and fgn. countries. With USN, 1953-55, lt. comdr. USNR. Named Hon. Alumnus Rose Hulman Inst. Tech., 1987. Mem. ABA (various coms.), IEEE, Ind. Bar Assn. (various coms.), Am. Intellectual Property Law Assn. (various coms.), Licensing Execs. Soc. (various coms.), Indpls. Bar Assn., Internat. Assn. Intellectual Property Law, Indpls. Jazz Club (bd. dirs. 1983-85, 95-97), Junto of Indpls. (bd. dirs. 1997-99). Office: Brinks Hofer Gilson & Lione 1 Indiana Sq Ste 1600 Indianapolis IN 46204-2045 Personal E-mail: badger938@aol.com.

BADGER, DOUG, federal agency administrator; BA, U. Del.; MDiv, Westminster Theol. Sem. Various policy positions HHS and Social Security Adminstrn., Washington, 1985—89; asst. staff dir., staff dir. Senate Rep. Policy Com., chief of staff to asst. majority leader Sen. Don Nickles U.S. Senate, Washington, 1989—99; ptnr. Ernst & Young, Washington, 1999—2002; Spl. Asst. to Pres. for Econ. Policy Washington, 2002—. Office: Nat Econ Coun 1600 Pennsylvania Ave NW Washington DC 20500

BADGER, PHILLIP CHARLES, agricultural engineer; b. Lodi, Ohio, Jan. 7, 1948; s. Clifford Russell and Helen Pauline (Fair) B.; m. Cheryl Lynn Baker, Aug. 14, 1971 (div. Feb. 1999); children: Brian, Scott, Mark; m. Bonnie Watkins, Aug. 14, 1999. BS in Agrl. Engring., Ohio State U., 1971, MS in Agrl. Engring., 1973; MBA, Vanderbilt U., 1993. Registered profl. engr., Ohio, Ala. Design engr. Ideanamics, Columbus, Ohio, 1972—74; rsch. assoc., project engr. Ohio State U. and Ohio Agrl. R & D Ctr., Wooster, 1975—78, ext. specialist, rsch. assoc., 1978—79; mgr. waste heat utilization project TVA, Muscle Shoals, Ala., 1979—80, mgr. small scale fuel ethanol project, 1980—82, mgr. fuel ethanol from non-woody cellulose program, 1982—84; mgr. Regional Biomass Energy program Dept. Energy, Muscle Shoals, 1984—, leader TVA biomass applications group, 1994—, leader mgr. regional biomass energy program, 1994—99; pres. Gen. Bioenergy, Inc., Florence, Ala., 1999—; pres., chief mgr. Renewable Oil Internat., Florence, 2000—, ROI Ala. Ops. LLC, Florence, ROI Mass. Ops. LLC, Springfield. Mem. biomass and waste energy com. Electric Power Rsch. Inst., Palo Alto, Calif., 1990—; mem. Renewable Energy and Efficiency Inst. Quality Control Bd., 1996—. Author: Conserving Energy in Ohio Greenhouses, 1979 (Am. Soc. Agr. Engrs. blue ribbon award 1979); mem. editl. bd. CIGR Electronic Jour.; contbr. articles to profl. jours. Bd. dirs. New Uses Coun., 1997—. Recipient Tech. Achievement award Dept. Energy, 1985, 96, 98, Outstanding Tech. Presentation award WATTec '89, 1989, Cert. of Environ. Achievement, Nat. Awards Coun. for Environ. Sustainability, 1994-99, Industry Leader award Fiber Fuels Inst., 1993. Mem. Am. Soc. Agrl. Engrs. (v.p. energy com. 1990-91, pres. 1991-92), Am. Solar Energy Soc., Am. Assn. Indsl. Crops, Internat. Solar Energy Soc., Nat. Mgmt. Assn., Am. Assn. Indsl. Crops, Biomass Energy Rsch. Assn. (bd. dirs. 1987—), New Uses Coun. (bd. dirs. 1997—), Coun. of Forest Engring., Coun. for Agrl. Sci. and Tech., Florence Exch. Club (bd. dirs. 1985-86). Office: Gen Bioenergy Inc Renewable Oil Internat LLC and ROI Ala Ops PO Box 26 Florence AL 35631-0026

BADGER, RONALD KAY, lawyer; b. Horton, Kans., Aug. 24, 1933; s. Clarence E. and Josephine L. (Rick) Badger; m. Janet L. Horner, Feb. 16, 1963; children: Hellen L. Badger Haag, Ronald K. Jr., Laura J. Badger Davis. BS in Bus., U. Kans., 1958, BS in Law, 1961, JD, 1968. Bar: Kans. 1961, U.S. Dist. Ct. Kans. 1961, U.S. Ct. Appeals (10th cir.) 1973, U.S. Supreme Ct. 1982, U.S. Ct. Claims 1990. Law clk. to Hon. Arthur J. Stanley Jr., U.S. Dist. Ct. Kans., Kansas City, 1961—62; spl. asst. to U.S. atty. for dist. of Kans., Dept. Justice, Topeka, 1962—64; assoc. Foulston & Siefkin, Wichita, Kans., 1964—66; atty. in contract adminstrn. Boeing Co., Wichita, 1966—68; pvt. practice Wichita, 1968—. Bd. dirs. Envision, 2002—. Mem. bd. edtiors Kans. Bar Jour., 1966—82; contbr. articles to profl. jours. Bd. dirs. Wichita Symphony Soc., 1970—2003. Mem.: FBA (pres. Kans. chpt. 1978—80), Internat. Assn. Lions Clubs, Christian Legal Soc. (pres. Wichita Downtown Club 2001—03), Wichita Estate Planning Coun. (sec. 1996—97, pres. 1997—98), Wichita Bar Assn., Kans. Bar Assn., Lions (pres. Wichita Downtown Club 1984—85). Republican. Office: 330 N Main St Wichita KS 67202 Office Phone: 316-263-8762.

BADGER, THOMAS MARK, pediatrics educator, researcher; b. Modesto, Calif., Mar. 21, 1945; s. Robert Albert and Valeria (Eaves) B.; m. Cheryl Ann Jordan, Aug. 26, 1967; 1 child, Mark Jordan. BS in Biology and Chemistry, Calif. State U., Fresno, 1968; MS in Audiology, U. Mo., 1970, PhD in Nutritional Biochemistry, 1973. Rsch. assoc. in biochemistry U. Mo., Columbia, 1973-74; instr. psychiatry and neuropharmacology Washington U., St. Louis, 1974-77; asst. prof. reproductive neuroendocrinology Harvard Med. Sch., Boston, 1977-82, assoc. prof., 1982-86; prof. pediatrics U. Ark. Med. Scis., 1986—; asst. in biochemistry Mass. Gen. Hosp., Boston, 1977-82, assoc. in biochemistry, 1982-86, dir. basic rsch. Vincent reproductive endocrine unit, 1979-86, dir. pediatric rsch. U. Ark. for Med. Scis., 1986-95; dir. rsch. Ark. Children's Hosp., 1986—; dir. Ark. Children's Hosp. Rsch. Inst., 1993—; assoc. dean Coll. Medicine U. Ark. for Med. Scis., 1993—; dir. Ark. USDA Human Nutrition Ctr., 1995—. spl. cons. Rsch. Ctr. Nat. Inst. for Drug Abuse, 1978—, Nat. Inst. Alcohol and Alcohol Abuse, 1990—. NIH fellow, 1975-77. Mem. Soc. for Exptl. Biology and Medicine, Endocrine Soc., Soc. Neurosci., Soc. Pediatric Rsch., Am. Inst. Nutrition, Soc. Pediatric Rsch. Soc. Neuroendocrinology, Soc. Reproductive Endocrinology, Rsch. Soc. of Alcoholism, Coll. Problems of Drug Dependence, Internat. Brain Rsch. Orgn., Internat. Soc. Neuroscience, Sigma Xi, Phi Lambda Upsilon, Gamma Sigma Delta. Contbr. articles on endocrinology and nutrition to sci. jours.; research on nutrition, growth, development and reproduction, mechanisms of hormone and drug actions, effects of alcohol and drugs of abuse on brain function and development, physiology of hypothalamus and pituitary gland. Home: 13404 Ridgehaven Rd Little Rock AR 72211-2220

BADGETT, STEVEN, artist; b. Ill., 1962; Co-founder & mem. SIMPARCH, 1996—; lectr. Weber State U., Ogden, Utah, 1997; resident Brandenburgischer Kunstverein, Potsdam, Germany, 1998; lectr. U. Utah, Salt Lake City, 1999; resident Ctr. Land Use Interpretation, LA, 1999, 2003; lectr. Columbus Coll. Art & Design, Ohio, 2001, Documenta XI, Kassel, Germany, 2002. Exhibitions include Highwayscape, Weber State U., Ogden, Utah, 1997, An Investigation of Trans-Architecture in Western Am., 1997, Rise Overrun, Plan B Evolving Arts, Santa Fe, 1997, L'Arche, Ecole Nationale d'Art, Cergy, France, 1998, SIMPARCH, Bemis Ctr. Contemporary Arts, Omaha, 1998, Ship from the Desert, Maschinenhalle, Potsdam, Germany, 1998, Moorings Project, 1998, The Unit, Ctr. Land Use Interpretation, Wendover, Utah, 1999, Free Basin, Hyde Pk. Arts Ctr., Chgo., 2000, Spec, Renaissance Soc., U. Chgo., 2001, Mood River, Wexner Ctr. Arts, Columbus, Ohio, 2002, Documenta XI, Kassel, Germany, 2002, Session the Bowl, Deitch Projects, NY, 2002, Whitney Biennial, Whitney Mus. Am. Art, NY, 2004, InSITE, San Diego, 2005. N. Mex. Arts Coun. Grant, 1997, Creative Capital Grant, 2002. E-mail: spedread@hotmail.com.*

BADGLEY, JOHN ROY, architect; b. Huntington, W.Va., July 10, 1922; s. Roy Joseph and Fannie Myrtle (Limbaugh) B.; m. Janice Atwell, July 10, 1975; 1 child, Adam; children by previous marriage: Dan, Lisa, Holly, Marcus, Michael. AB, Occidental Coll., 1943; MArch, Harvard U., 1949; postgrad., Internat. Ctr., Vincenza, Italy, 1959. Lic. Calif. Pvt. practice, San Luis Obispo, Calif., 1952—65; chief arch., planner Crocker Land Co., San Francisco, 1965—80; v.p. Cushman & Wakefield Inc., San Francisco, 1980—84; pvt. practice San Rafael, Calif., 1984—2001. Prof. Calif. State U., San Luis Obispo, 1952—65. Bd. dirs. Ft. Mason Ctr., Angel Island Assn. With USCGR, 1942-54. Mem. AIA (emeritus), Am. Arbitration Assn., Golden Gate Wine Soc. Home and Office: Unit C 403 Avenida Castilla Laguna Woods CA 92637 Office Phone: 949-855-6637. E-mail: jrbadgley@1world.net.

BADGLEY, MARK, fashion designer; b. East St. Louis, Ill., 1961; Grad., Parsons Sch. Design, NY. Apprenticeship with Donna Karan; founder, ptnr. Badgley Mischka, NYC, 1985—; ptnr. Badgley Mischka Dress. Recipient Mouton Cadet Young Designer award, 1989, Dallas Internat. Apparel Rising Star award, 1992; named Top 10 American Designers, Vogue. Office: 525 7th Ave Fl 18 New York NY 10018-4901

BADGLEY, THEODORE MCBRIDE, retired psychiatrist, neurologist; b. Salem, Ala., June 27, 1925; s. Roy Joseph and Fannie (Limbaugh) B.; m. Mary Bennett Wells, Dec. 30, 1945; children: Justice O'Neil, Jan Badgley, Mona Jean Covey, Jason Wells, James John, Mary Rose Bleier. Student, Occidental Coll., 1942-44; MD, U. So. Calif., 1949. Diplomate: Am. Bd. Psychiatry and Neurology. Intern Letterman Gen. Hosp., San Francisco, 1949-50, resident in psychiatry, 1950-53; commd. capt. M.C. U.S. Army, 1950, advanced through grades to lt. col., 1967; chief mental hygiene cons. service Ft. Gordon, Ga.; and asso. clin. prof. psychiatry and neurology Med. Coll. Ga., 1954-55; resident in neurology Walter Reed Gen. Hosp., Washington, 1955-57, asst. chief psychiatry service, 1957-59, chief psychiatry service, 1959-62, asst. chief psychiatry and neurology, 1962-63, dir. edn. and tng. psychiatry, 1957-63; chief dept. psychiatry and neurology U.S. Army Gen. Hosp., Landstuhl, Germany, 1963-66; chief psychiatry outpatient dept. Letterman Gen. Hosp., 1966-67; ret., 1967; dir. Kern View Mental Health Center, Bakersfield, Calif., 1967-69; pvt. practice medicine specializing in med. and forensic neuropsychiatry Bakersfield, 1967-93; pres. Sans Doloroso Inst., Bakersfield, 1969-93. Lectr. community health service orgns., profl. confs., seminars. Contbr. articles to profl. jours. Fellow Am. Psychiat. Assn. (disting. life); mem. Kern County Psychiat. Soc. (pres. 1972-93), Kern County Med. Soc. (pres. 1981).

BADHAM, JOHN MACDONALD, motion picture director; b. Luton, Eng., Aug. 25, 1939; came to U.S., 1945; s. Henry Lee and Mary Iola (Hewitt) B.; 1 child, Kelly MacDonald; m. Julia Laughlin, 1992. BA, Yale U., 1961, MFA, 1963. Assoc. producer Universal Studios, 1969-70; pres. Gt. Am. Picture Show; chmn. bd. JMB Films, Inc. Pres. Badham Co.; guest lectr. UCLA, Yale U., U. So. Calif., Amherst Coll. Assoc. producer TV movies Night Gallery, 1969, Neon Ceiling, 1970; assoc. producer, dir. TV movies The Senator, 1970 (Emmy award nomination 1971); dir. numerous episodes of The Bold Ones, others; motion pictures for TV include The Law (Emmy nomination 1974), 1974 (ARD reihe 'das film festival award 1975), Isn't It Shocking, 1973, Reflections of Murder, 1973, The Impatient Heart (Christopher award 1971), The Gun, (So. Calif. Motion Picture Council award 1974), The Godchild, 1974, Sorrow Floats, 1998; theatrical motion pictures include The Bingo Long Travelling All Stars and Motor Kings (NAACP image award nomination 1976), Saturday Night Fever, 1977, Dracula, 1979 (Grand prize 9th Internat. Sci. Fiction Festival of Paris, Best Horror Film award and, 1st George Pal Meml. award, both Acad. of Sci. Fiction Fantasy and Horror Films), Whose Life Is It Anyway, 1981, Blue Thunder, 1983, War Games (Best Dir., Acad. of Sci. Fiction Fantasy and Horror Films), 1983, American Flyers, 1985, Short Circuit, 1986, Stakeout, 1987, Bird on a Wire, 1989, The Hard Way, 1990, Point of No Return, 1993, Another Stakeout, 1993, Drop Zone, 1994, Nick of Time, 1995, Incognito, 1998, Floating Away, 1998, (TV) The Jack Bull, 1999, The Last Debate, 2000, My Brother's Keeper, 2002, Obsessed, 2002, Footsteps, 2003; exec. prodr. motion picture Rebound, 1996. Bd. dirs. Indian Spring Sch. Served with U.S. Army, 1963-64. Mem. Dirs. Guild Am., Am. Film Inst., Acad. Motion Picture Arts and Scis., Yale Drama Alumni Fund (chmn.). Office: c/o Jeff Berg, Nick Reed ICM 8942 Wilshire Blvd Beverly Hills CA 90211

BADLANI, GOPAL, medical educator; Degree in internal sci., Bombay U., 1968; MD, T.N. Med. Coll. Bombay U., 1972. Resident L.I. Jewish Med. Ctr., NY, 1975, St. Agnes Hosp., Balt., 1976, L.I. Jewish Med. Ctr., 1980; fellow Baylor U. Sch. Medicine, Houston, 1983; clin. asst. Queen Mary Hosp., Sidcup, England, 1975; pvt. practice East Nassau Med. Group, NY, 1980—83; attending physician L.I. Jewish Med. Ctr., 1983—; attending physician dept. urology Queens Hosp. Ctr., Jamaica, NY, 1983—, chief dept. urology, 1983—96; chief neurology and prosthetics, dept. urology L.I. Jewish Med. Ctr., New Hyde Park, NY, 1990—; assoc. prof. dept. urology Albert Einstein Coll. Medicine, Bronx, 1992—96, prof. dept. urology, 1996—; program dir., assoc. chmn. dept. urology North Shore L.I. Jewish Med. Ctr. Contbr. articles various profl. jours. Recipient Essay Contest award, Urological Soc., 1979, 1st prize Movie, Am. Urology Assn., 1990. Mem.: Queens Urol. Soc., Bklyn. Urol. Soc., N.Y. Acad. Medicine (chmn. 1995—96), Soc. for Minimally Invasive Therapy, L.I. Urol. Soc. (pres. 1990—92), Urodynamic Soc., Assn. Indian Urologists in N.Am., Endourology Soc. (treas.), N.Y. State Med. Soc., Nassau County Med. Soc., Am. Urol. Assn. Achievements include patents for vesico-vaginal ambulatory monitor, 1992. Office: Long Island Jewish Med Ctr Dept Urology 270-05 75th Ave New Hyde Park NY 11042 Office Phone: 718-470-7225. E-mail: gbadlani@lij.edu.

BADLER, NORMAN IRA, computer and information science educator; b. L.A., May 3, 1948; s. Bernard and Lillian Lorraine Badler; m. Virginia Renke, June 14, 1968; children: Jeremy, David. BA in Creative Studies, U. Calif., Santa Barbara, 1970; MS in Computer Sci., U. Toronto, Toronto, 1971, PhD in Computer Sci., 1975. Lectr. U. Toronto, 1973-74; asst. prof. computer and info. sci. U. Pa., Phila., 1974-79, assoc. prof., 1979-86, prof., 1986—, Cecilia Fitler Moore prof., 1990-94, dir. Ctr. for Human Modeling and Simulation, 1994—, assoc. dean Sch. Engring. and Applied Sci., 2001—. Mem., chmn. program coms. numerous confs. and workshops. Co-author: Simulating Humans, 1993; co-editor: Making Them Move, 1990; contbr. numerous articles to profl. jours. Grantee Advanced Rsch. Projects Agy., NASA, NSF, U.S. Army, USAF. Mem. IEEE Computer Soc., Assn. for Computing Machinery (vice chmn. spl. interest group on graphics 1979-81, mem. spl. interest group on artificial intelligence), Cognitive Sci. Soc., Am. Assn. for Artificial Intelligence, Phi Beta Kappa. Democrat. Jewish. Avocations: home renovation, cooking. Office: U Pa Computer & Info Sci Dept Philadelphia PA 19104-6389 Office Phone: 215-898-5862. E-mail: badler@seas.upenn.edu.

BADLISHAH, ABDUL HALIM MU'ADZAM SHAH, Sultan of Kedah; b. Alor Star, Kedah, Malaysia, Nov. 28, 1927; s. Sultan Badlishah of Kadeh; m. Tunku Hajjah Bahiyah, Mar. 1956; 3 children. Grad., Sultan Abdul Hamid Coll., Alor, 1949; diploma social sci. and pub. adminstrn., Oxford (Eng.) U., 1955; D. Polit. Sci. (hon.), Thammasat U., Bangkok, Thailand. With Dist. Office, then Treasury Alor State, 1955—; raja muda of Kedah, 1949-57; regent, 1957-58; sultan State of Kedah, 1958—. Dep. king, then king Conf. of Rulers, 1965-75; col.-in-chief Royal Malay Regt., 1975. Decorated D.K., 1964, D.K.M., 1971, D.M.N., 1959, D.U.K., 1958, S.P.M.K., 1964, D.K., 1969, D.K. (Pehang), 1970, 1st class Order Rising Sun (Japan), 1970, Bintang Maha Putera, Klas Satu (Indonesia), 1970, hon. knight grad cross Order Bath (U.K.), 1972, assoc. knight Order St. John, 1972, Order Ramnata (Thailand), 1973. Avocations: gold, billiards, photography, tennis. Office: c/o Press Attache Malaysian Embassy 3516 International Ct NW Washington DC 20008-2851

BADMAN, JOHN, III, real estate developer, architect; b. Kansas City, Mo., July 11, 1944; s. John II and Barbara (Smith) B.; m. Katherine Ballantine, May 12, 1984; children: Lindsay Cathryn, Barbara Smith, John IV. BA, Yale U., 1966, MArch, 1969, postgrad., 1969-70, M in Environmental Design, 1971. Registered architect, Conn.; real estate broker, Conn. Gen. mgr. S.J. Willy, Architects, New Haven, Conn., 1971-73; v.p. Schumacher & Forelle, Great Neck, N.Y., 1973-77, exec. v.p., 1986-87; dir. planning and devel. Dravo Engrs., N.Y.C., 1977-81; sr. v.p. Parsons, Brinckerhoff, Quade & Douglas, N.Y.C., 1981-86, also bd. dirs.; chmn., chief exec. officer Ballantine and Badman, Inc., Real Estate Developers, Greenwich, Conn., 1986—; sr. v.p. H.W. Lochner, Planners and Engrs., 1991—. Chmn. Conf. of Patriotic and Hist. Socs., N.Y.C., 1993—. Mem. Lacrosse all-Am. Team U.S. Intercollegiate Lacrosse Assn., 1966. Mem. AIA, Soc. Colonial Wars (coun. 1987—, chmn. exec. com. 1996—, gov. 1996—), The Pilgrims of the U.S., Colonial Order of the Acorn (chancellor 1997—), Baronial Order of the Magna Charta, Jamestown Soc., Nat. Coun. Archtl. Registration Bds. (cert.), New Eng. Soc. N.Y., Round Hill Assn., Mayflower Soc., Plymouth Com., Yale Club (N.Y.C.), Greenwich Country Club, Greenwich Polo Players Club, Adirondack League Club (Old Forge, N.Y.). Republican. Episcopalian. Home: 20 Mackenzie Gln Greenwich CT 06830-3421

BADRA, ROBERT GEORGE, theology studies educator, humanities educator; b. Lansing, Mich., Dec. 8, 1933; s. Razouk Anthony and Anna (Paul) Badra; m. Maria Theresa Beer, Oct. 25, 1968 (div. 1973); m. Kristen Lillie Stuckey, Dec. 30, 1977 (div. 2001); children: Rachal Jennifer, Danielle Elizabeth Jane. BA, Sacred Heart Sem., 1957; MA, Western Mich. U., 1968; MDiv, St. John's Provincial Sem., 1985. Ordained priest Roman Cath. Ch., 1961. Mem. faculty Kalamazoo Valley CC, 1968—, prof. philosophy, religion and humanities, 1968—. Adj. prof. Nazareth Coll., 1985—91, Siena Heights U., 1993—; mem. faculty ministry formation Cath. Diocese Kalamazoo, 1999—. Bd. dirs. Kalamazoo Coun. Humanities, 1983—86, Van Buren Youth Camp, 1993—95, v.p. bd. dirs., 2002—. Recipient Edn. award, Exxon, 1996; grantee NEH, 1991—. Mem.: Assn. Religion and Intellectual Life. Office: Kalamazoo Valley CC PO Box 4070 Kalamazoo MI 49003-4070 Personal E-mail: bbadra1579@aol.com.

BADU, ERYKAH, singer, songwriter; b. Dallas, Feb. 26, 1971; children: Puma, Seven. Student, Dallas Sch. Arts. Singer, songwriter: single On and On, 1997 (Grammy award for best female vocal performance, 1998), Baduizm, 1997 (Grammy award for best R&B album, 1997), Live!, 1997, Mama's Gun, 2000, Worldwide Underground, 2003; actor: (films) Cider House Rules, 1999, Blues Brothers, 2000, House of D, 2004. Recipient Favorite New Soul/R&B Artist award, Am. Music Awards, 1998, Grammy award for Best Rap Performance by a duo or group for You Got Me, 1999. Office: Motown Records 6th Fl 1755 Broadway New York NY 10019-3743*

BAE, FRANK S.H., law librarian, educator; b. Chung King, Szechuan, China, Dec. 19, 1941; came to U.S., 1967; s. Tse H. and Yu F. (Wang) B.; m. Anne Rita Donavan, March 15, 1975; children: Stephen, David, Marie, Elizabeth. LLB, Nat. Taipei U., 1965; MCL, U. Miami, Fla., 1968; MS, U. Wis., 1970; JurD (hon.), New England Sch. Law, Boston, 1977. Dir. law libr. New England Sch. Law, 1970—, asst. prof. law, 1970-73, assoc. prof. law, 1973-74, prof. law, 1974—. Co-author: Searching the Law, 3d edit., 2005, Surety's (Secondary Obligor's) Rights under the Restatement of the Law. Mem. New England Law Libr. Consortium (bd. dirs.). Office: New Eng Sch Law Libr 154 Stuart St Boston MA 02116-5616 Business E-Mail: fbae@faculty.nesl.edu.

BAE, SEONGTAE, electrical engineer; b. Seoul, Republic of Korea, Apr. 10, 1968; s. Young-Sik Bae and Jum-Hong Kwon. PhD, U. Minn., 2002. Rsch. scientist Korea Inst. Sci. and Tech., Seoul, Republic of Korea, 1993—96; rschr. U. Minn. Ctr. Micromagnetics and Info. Tech., Mpls., 1998—2002. Contbr. numerous articles to profl. jours. Math. tchr. Buk-Boo Teenager Sch., Seoul, Republic of Korea, 1989—92. Recipient Excellent prize, Republic of Korea, 1991, Student Travel award, Internat. Conf., Japan, 2000, Young Rschr. award, 2000. Mem.: IEEE, Am. Physics Soc. Home: 1150 Cushing Cir #204 Saint Paul MN 55108 E-mail: sbae@ece.umn.edu.

BAE, SUE HYUN, psychologist, educator; b. Seoul, Kyung-Gee, Republic of Korea, Aug. 3, 1969; d. Jong Hoa Bae and Jeeyoung Kim. BA, U. Calif., Berkeley, 1991; MEd, MA, Columbia U., 1994; PhD, U. Chgo., 2001. Psychotherapist Cancer Treatment Ctr. of Am., Gurnee, Ill., 1998—99; clin. adminstr. Heartland Alliance, Chgo., 1999—2001; asst. prof. Ill. Sch. Profl. Psychology Chgo., Argosy U., 2001—. Adj. faculty Ill. Inst. Art, Chgo., 2001; diversity tng. cons. Anixter Ctr., Chgo., 2003; child psychologist Anxiety Clinic M. Mark McKee, PsyD and Assocs., 2004—. Author: (book) The Psychotherapist's Perspective, 2003; contbr. articles to profl. jours. Recipient Faculty Rsch. award, Ill. Sch. Profl. Psychology, 2001. Mem.: APA, Soc. for Psychotherapy Rsch. Achievements include research in international psychology; cross-cultural studies, cross-cultural/multicultural psychotherapy; diversity training and teaching. Avocations: travel, golf, music. Office: Argosy U Ill Sch Profl Psychology 350 N Orleans Chicago IL 60605 Office Phone: 312-279-3944.

BAECHLER, CONSTANCE ELAINE, writer, educator; b. Long Branch, NJ, Nov. 29, 1971; d. Virginia Bruell and James William Burch; life ptnr. Rajesh Gopal. BA in Lit., Valdosta State U., Ga., 1990—92; MA in Lit., Valdosta State U., Atlanta, 1992—94; MFA in Poetry, Ga. State U., Atlanta, 1994—97, PhD, 1998—2004. Freelance writer, Atlanta, 1990—; instr. Ga. State U., Atlanta, 1994—. Tutor, writing ctr. Ga. State U., Atlanta, 1994—2002. Author: (novels) American Sita, Coconut Milk, (poetry collection) From Tongue to Toes: Hunger Poetry. Mem.: Zona Rosa, Women's Wordslingers Guild, Internat. Women's Writing Guild, Ga. Writers, Inc. Avocations: painting, reading, travel. Office: Ga State Univ Univ Plaza Atlanta GA 30303 Personal E-mail: fififou@mindspring.com.

BAECKER, DAVID ALAN, humanities educator; s. Charles Harvey and Charlotte Wray Baecker. BA, Wash. U., St. Louis, 1991—95; MFA, Fla. State U., Asolo Conservatory, 1997—2000. Tchr., programs creator Perry-Mansfield Performing Arts Sch., Steamboat Springs, Colo., 1999—; Harder-Mcclellan vis. disting. prof. humanities Russell Sage Coll., Troy, NY, 2002—. Asst. to prodr. Timothy Childs Theatrical, NYC, 2000—01. Actor: (various plays and musicals). Dir. Lysistrata Project, Troy, 2002—03. Mem.: Actors Equity Assn. (life). Avocations: travel, theater, dogs. Office: Russell Sage Coll 45 Ferry St Troy NY 12180 Office Phone: 518-244-2263. Office Fax: 518-244-4545. E-mail: baeckd@sage.edu.

BAECKLER, VIRGINIA VAN WYNEN, librarian, writer; b. Englewood, N.J., June 18, 1942; d. Kenneth Gregg and Esther Grace (Thompson) Van Wynen; m. William W. Baeckler, Apr. 9, 1971; children— Gregg William, Sarah Angela. B.A., Cornell U., 1964, M.A., 1967; postgrad. Moscow State U. (USSR), 1967-69; M.L.S., Rutgers U., 1972. Head Slavic acquisitions Princeton U. Library, 1969-71; head Mercer County Library, Ewing, N.J., 1972-75; dir. Sources, Hopewell, N.J., 1975—; dir. Plainsboro (N.J.) Pub. Libr., 1991— . Author: Go, Pep and Pop!, 1976, PR for Pennies, 1978, Sparkle!, 1980, Storytime Science, 1986. Vol., tchr. YWCA of Princeton, N.J., 1979— . Mem. Nat. Sci. Tchrs. Assn., Alliance for Arts and Edu.,ALA, Ednl. Media Assn. (lobbyist). Democrat. Home: 26 Hart Ave Hopewell NJ 08525-1425

BAEHNMAN, GRETA MAE, music educator; b. Plum City, Wis., Aug. 1, 1951; d. Rudolph C. and Lucille Helen (Hoffman) Swanson; m. Steven Charles Baehnman, June 16, 1979. B of Music Edn., U. Wis., 1974. K-12 vocal music Weyauwege (Wis.) Fremont Schs., 1974-77, elem. music tchr., 1974—2002, choral dir 6-12, 2002—. Bd. dirs. Ctrl. Wis. Uniservice Coun., Wausau. Active children's ch. choir S.S. Peter and Paul Ch., Weyauwega, 1983-85. Mem. NEA, Weyauwega-Fremont and Edn. Assn. (v.p. 1991-93), Wis. Edn. Assn., Wis. Music Edn. Assn., Music Edn. Nat. Conf. Roman Catholic. Office: Weyauwega-Fremont Schs PO Box 580 Weyauwega WI 54983-0580 Office Phone: 920-867-2148 319.

BAEHR, THEODORE, religious organization administrator, writer, communications executive; b. NYC, May 31, 1946; m. Liliana Milani, 1975; children: Theodore Peirce, James Stuart Castiglioni, Robert Gallatin, Evelyn Noelle. Student in French lit., U. Bordeaux and Toulouse, France, 1967; student in English lit., Cambridge (Eng.) U., 1967; student in German lit., U. Munich, 1968; BA in Comparative Lit., Dartmouth Coll., 1969; JD, NYU, 1972; postgrad. Inst. Theology, Cathedral St. John the Divine, 1978—80. Rsch. engr. Precision Sci. Co., Chgo., 1964-65; legal cons. firm Dandeub, Fleissig & Assocs., NYC, 1970-71; law student asst. US Atty.'s Office, so. Dist. NY, 1971-72; pres. Agape Prodns., NYC, 1972-79, chmn. bd., 1979-82; exec. dir. Good News Comm., Inc., NYC, 1978-80, chmn. bd., 1980—; pres. Episc. Radio-TV Found., Inc., Atlanta, 1981-82, Trinity Concepts, 1982; cons. media; dir. TV Ctr. CUNY at Bklyn. Coll., 1979-80, 82—; pub. Movieguide Mag., 1985—. Episc. Communicators, 1981-84; exec. prodr. Ch.'s Presence at World's Fair, Knoxville, Tenn., 1982; dir. Am. Theater Actors, Episc. Comm. Author: Faith in God and Generals, 2003, What Can We Watch Tonight, 2003, Frodo and Harry, 2003, So You Want To Be In Pictures, 2004, Narnia Beckons, 2004, Getting the Word Out, 1986, Narnia Beckons: C.S. Lewis' The Lion, The Witch and The Wardrobe and Beyond; editor (commentator): NYU Law Sch. newspaper, 1969—72, Contemporary Drug Problems, 1971—72, Atlanta Area Christian News; creator, coord. Communicate Workshops, 1979, creator, writer, editor Episc. Ch. Video Resource Guide and Episcopal Video/TV Newsletter, 1979; prodr.(dir., writer): (various TV and radio programs including) Movieguide®, Joy of Music, Perspectives, PBS, 1981—82, Religionwise on WGST, CBS, 1981— (Religion in Media award), Hollywood's Reel of Fortune, 1991, The Media-Wise Family, 1998; dir.: Runaways (Chgo. Intercom Gold plaque and Religion in Media award, 1989); prodr.: In Their Own Words, Was It Love (Religion in Media award). V.p. Ctr. for TV in Humanities, 1982; chmn. bd. Christian Film & TV Commn., 1978—; bd. dirs. Nat. Religious Broadcasters, Celebrate Life, Religious Heritage of Am., Dorsey Theatre, Nat. Think Tank, Mission Am., Nehemiah Inst., Coalition on Revival; mem. steering com. Theol. Summit Conf.; bd. dirs. Am. Theatre of Actors, Nat. Coun. on Bible Curriculum in Pub. Schs., United Srs. Assn., Campus Renewal Ministries Nat. Broadcast Day of Prayer; bd. dirs., nat. adv. bd. United Srs. Assn. Recipient Pres.'s award, LifeNET, 1998, Eagle award, Nat. Religious Broadcasters, 2001. Mem. Mission Am., Bishop in Ind. Christian Chs. Internat., Nat. Press Club. Fax: 805-383-4089. Office Phone: 805-383-2000. E-mail: movieguide@compuserve.com, Ted@TedBaehr.com.

BAEHREN, JAMES W., lawyer; b. Toledo, June 11, 1950; BS, Ohio State U., 1972, MBA, 1974; JD, U. Toledo, 1978. Assoc. Fuller & Henry, 1978—85, ptnr., 1985—92; dir. fin. Owens-Illinois Inc., Toledo, sr. v.p., gen. counsel, corp. sec. Mem.: Toledo Bar Assn., OH State Bar Assn. 1978, ABA. Home: 4656 Dovewood Ln Sylvania OH 43560 Office: Owens-Illinois One Seagate Toledo OH 43666 Office Phone: 419-247-5000. Office Fax: 419-247-7107.

BAEK, EUN-OK, instructional technology educator; d. Jae-Heum Baek and Gyong-Ja Kim. BEd, Chinju Nat. U. of Edn., South Korea, 1987; MEd, Korea Nat. U. of Edn., South Korea, 1993, Ind. U., Bloomington, IN, 2001; PhD, Ind. U., Bloomington, 2002. Tchr. NamJung Elem. Sch., ChangWon, Republic of Korea, 1987—94, TaeBang Elem. Sch., ChangWon, Republic of Korea, 1994—96; instrnl. designer St. Meinrad Sch. of Theology, St. Meinrad, Ind., 1998—2000; grad. tchg. asst. DePauw U., Greencastle, Ind., 2000—02; grad. rsch. asst. Ind. U., Bloomington, 2001—02; asst. prof. Calif. State U. San Bernardino, 2002—. Online cmty. coord. Preparing Tomorrow's Tchrs. to Use Tech. grant U.S. Dept. Edn., Calif. State U., San Bernardino, Calif., 2002—05; adv. bd. com. mem. Fund for the Improvement of Post Secondary Edn., U.S. Dept. Edn., U. Calif., Riverside, 2002—; rev. bd. mem. for techtrends Assn. for Ednl. Comm. and Tech., Bloomington, Ind., 2005—. Contbr. articles to profl. jours., chapters to books. Recipient Scholarship of Tchg. and Learning, Tchg. Resource Ctr., Calif. State U. San Bernardino, 2004, Tchg. Skills Study award, 2003—04; fellow Summer Rsch. fellow, Faculty Profl. Devel. Coordinating Com., Calif. State U. San Bernardino, 2003; grantee Rsch. grantee, Ind. U., 2001; Mini grantee, Faculty Profl. Devel. Coordinating Com., Calif. State U. San Bernardino, 2003—05. Mem.: Assn. for the Advancement of Computing in Edn., Assn. for Ednl. Comm. and Tech., Am. Ednl. Rsch. Assn., Phi Beta Delta. Office: California State University 5500 University Pkwy San Bernardino CA 92407 Office Phone: 909-537-5454. Office Fax: 909-537-7522. Business E-Mail: ebaek@csusb.edu.

BAEK, SEUNG JOON, engineering educator; s. NamHae Baek and HaeJa Lee; m. Haeseon Baek, Apr. 1, 1970; children: Grace Jihae, Eunice Jiseung. PhD, U. Md., 1998. Asst. prof. U. Tenn., Knoxville, Tenn., 2003—. Office: Univ Tenn 2407 River Dr Knoxville TN 37996 Office Phone: 865-974-8216.

BAENA, MARISA, professional golfer; b. Pereira, Colombia, June 1, 1977; Bachelor, Univ. Ariz. Achievements include Winner: HSBC Women's World Championship. Office: Ladies Professional Golf Assn 100 International Golf Drive Daytona Beach FL 32124-1092*

BAER, HAROLD, JR., retired federal judge; b. N.Y.C., Feb. 16, 1933; s. Harold and Edna (Jacobus) B.; m. Suzanne Harris, Aug. 18, 1957; children: Elizabeth Jane, Linda Gail. Grad. magna cum laude, Hobart Coll., 1954; LLB, Yale U., 1957. Bar: N.Y. 1959, U.S. Dist. Ct. (so. dist.) N.Y. 1961, U.S. Ct. Appeals (2d cir.) 1961, U.S. Supreme Ct. 1964. Asst. U.S. atty., chief organized crime unit, U.S. Atty.'s Office for So. Dist. N.Y., N.Y.C., 1961-66, 1st asst. U.S. atty., chief criminal divsn., 1970-71; exec. dir. civilian complaint rev. bd. N.Y.C. Police Dept., 1966-67; ptnr. Guggenheimer & Untermyer, N.Y.C., 1968-70, 72-82; justice N.Y. State Supreme Ct., 1982-92; exec. jud. officer Jud. Arbitration and Mediation Svcs./Endispute, 1992-94; judge U.S. Dist. Ct. (so. dist.) N.Y., N.Y.C., 1994—2005. Mem. N.Y.C. mayoral com. alleged police corruption, 1993, 94. Contbr. articles to law jours. Mem. N.Y. State Bar Assn. (ho. of dels. 1977-89, 93-96), N.Y. County Lawyers Assn. (pres. 1979-81, bd. dirs., mem. exec. com.), Assn. Bar City N.Y. (criminal justice coun. 1980-82, judiciary com. 1993-94), Network Bar Leaders (founder, chmn. 1981-83), Assn. Justices N.Y.C. and N.Y. State (officer). Office Phone: 212-805-0184.

BAER, JOHN METZ, entrepreneur; b. Md., June 30, 1908; s. Adam Daniel and Leah Bertie (Metz) B.; m. Joan Cushwa, Oct. 16, 1976; children: John Metz, Deborah Ann. BS, Goshen Coll., 1932. Food distgn. cons.; pres. Profl. Arts Assocs. Inc., Greencastle (Pa.) Ice and Cold Storage Inc., Baer Packing Corp., Greencastle. Nat. Frozen Foods Assn. ofcl. rep. to 1st Internat. Foods Conf., Paris, 1950; participant numerous internat. food confs. Pres. Washington County Hosp., Hagerstown, 1958-60, Washington County Bd. Edn., 1962-68; bd. dirs. Am. Heart Assn. of Md.; trustee Hagerstown Jr. Coll.; chmn. United Way of Washington County; hon. mem. Greater Hagerstown Club; chmn. Hagerstown Parking Authority; bd. dirs. Md. Symphony Orch. Mem. Produce Mktg. Assn. (past pres.), Fountainhead Country Club, Hagerstown C. of C. (pres.), Assembly of Hagerstown, Rotary. Republican. Methodist. Home: 13217 Hillandale Rd Hagerstown MD 21742-2647 Office: 5 Public Sq Hagerstown MD 21740-5528 Fax: 301-739-0171. E-mail: ppoarts5211@juno.com.

BAER, JOHN RICHARD FREDERICK, lawyer; b. Melrose Park, Ill., Jan. 9, 1941; s. John Richard and Zena Edith (Ostreyko) B.; m. Linda Gail Chapman, Aug. 31, 1963; children: Brett Scott, Deborah Jill. BA, U. Ill., Champaign, 1963, JD, 1966. Bar: Ill. 1966, U.S. Dist. Ct. (no. dist.) Ill. 1967, U.S. Ct. Appeals (7th cir.) 1969, U.S. Ct. Appeals (DC cir.) 1975, U.S. Ct. Appeals (9th cir.) 1979, U.S. Supreme Ct. 1975. Assoc. Keck, Mahin & Cate, Chgo., 1966-73, ptnr., 1974-97; of counsel Sonnenschein Nath & Rosenthal LLP, Chgo., 1997-99, ptnr., 2000—. Mem. Ill. Atty. Gen.'s Franchise adv. bd., 1992-94, 96—, chair 1996—. Editor Commerce Clearing House Sales Representative Law Guide, 1998—; mem editl. bd. U. Ill. Law Forum, 1964-65, asst. editor, 1965-66; contbg. editor: Commercial Liability Risk Management and Insurance, 1978. Mem. Plan Commn., Village of Deerfield (Ill.), 1976-79, chmn., 1978-79, mem. Home Rule Study Commn., 1974-75, mem. home rule implementation com., 1975-76. Mem. ABA (topics and articles editor Franchise Law jour. 1995-96, assoc. editor 1996-99, editor-in-chief The Franchise Lawyer 1999-2002, governing com. Forum on Franchising 2003—), Internat. Franchise Assn. (legal/legis. com. 1990—), Inter-Pacific Bar Assn., Ill. State Bar Assn. (competition dir. region 8 nat. moot ct. 1974, profl. ethics com. 1977-84, chmn. 1982-83, spl. com. on individual lawyers advt. 1981-83, profl. responsibility com. 1983-84, standing com. on liaison with atty. registration and disciplinary commn. 1989-93, ISBA/CBA com. on ethics 2000 1999—), Internat. Bar Assn. Office: Sonnenschein Nath & Rosenthal LLP 8000 Sears Tower 233 S Wacker Dr Chicago IL 60606-6491 Office Phone: 312-876-2604. Business E-Mail: jbaer@sonnenschein.com.

BAER, MAX, state supreme court justice; b. Pittsburgh, Pa., Dec. 24, 1947; s. Henry and Helen Baer; m. Beth Love Hartman; 2 children. BA, U. Pittsburgh, 1971; JD, Duquesne U., 1975; Ms of Tax Program, Robert Morris Coll., 1985—86. Dep. atty. gen. State of Pa., 1975—79; atty. priv. practice, 1980—89; judge Allegheny County Ct. of Common Pleas, 1989—93, Allegheny County Ct. of Common Pleas Family Div., 1993—99; justice Pa. Supreme Ct., 2003—. Former chair Domestic Relations Procedural Rules Com.; ex officio rep. Juvenile Ct. Judges Commn.; former mem. Joint State Govt. Commn. on Adoption Law & Services to Children; former chair Pa. Conference Trial Judges Family Law Section. Named Adoption Advocate of Yr., Pa. Dept. Public Welfare, 1997, Most Valuable Peacemaker, Pa. Council of Mediators, 2004; recipient Adoption 2002 Excellence award for Jud. Innovation, Fed. Dept. Hlth. & Human Services, 1998, Robert S. Steward award for disting. service to Pa. families, 1998, Child Advocacy award for legal contributions advancing welfare of children, 1999, Jud. Achievement award for advancing pro bono activities, 1999, Champion of Children award, Homeless Children's Ed. Fund, 2003. Mem.: Pa. Bar Assn. (Named Child Advocate of Yr. 2000). Office: Pa Supreme Ct 1515 Market St Philadelphia PA 19102

BAER, MICHAEL ALAN, political scientist, educator; b. Atlanta, Feb. 4, 1943; s. Kurt Arthur and Beulah (Mendelson) Baer; m. CHarlotte Glazer, Aug. 16, 1964; children: Daniel Noach, Naomi Aviva. BA, Emory U., 1964; MA, U. Oreg., 1966, PhD, 1968. Rsch. asst. Ctr. Advanced Study Ednl. Adminstrn., U. Oreg., 1964-68; faculty U. Ky., Lexington, 1968-90, prof. polit. sci. and pub. adminstrn., 1980-90, chmn. dept. polit. sci., 1977-81, dean Coll. Arts and Scis., 1981-90; polit. analyst WAVE-TV, Louisville; prof. polit. sci. Northeastern U., Boston, 1990-2000, provost, sr. v.p. acad. affairs, 1990-98; sr. v.p. for programs and analysis Am. Coun. on Edn., Washington, 1998—; dir. Ctr. for Policy Analysis, Washington, 1998-2000. Co-author: (book) Lobbying: Influence and Interaction in American State Legislatures, 1969; co-editor: Political Science in America, 1991; mem. editl. bd.: State and Local Govt. Rev., 1977—81; contbr. articles to profl. jours. Bd. dirs. Coun. Colls. Arts and Scis., 1983—89, pres., 1988; rec. sec. Bluegrass chpt. Ky. Assn. Gifted Edn., 1983—85; mem. Mayor's com. to establish Lexington Children's Mus., 1988—90, bd. dirs., 1990; mem. coun. Inter Univ. Consortium for Polit. and Social Rsch., U. Mich., 1988—94, chmn., 1990—92; bd. dirs. Congregation Ohavay Zion, Lexington, 1976—78, Ctrl. Ky. Jewish Assn., 1970—74, pres., 1973—74; bd. dirs. Ctrl. Ky. Civil LIberties Union, 1973—77, Bluegrass chpt. NCCJ, 1980—81, Jamaica Pond Assn., 1992—97. Fellow Leverhulme, 1974—75. Mem.: Nat. Capitol Area Polit. Sci. Assn. (bd. mem. 2001—06, pres. 2004—05), Nat. Assn. Univ. and Land Grant Colls. (commn. on arts and scis. 1986—90, chmn. 1990), Ky. Conf. Polit. Sci., So. Polit. Sci. Assn. (chmn. nominating com. 1993—94, 1996), Brit. Politics Group (exec. coun. 1978—80), Midwest Polit. Sci. Assn. (exec. coun. 1980—83), Am. Polit. Sci. Assn. (endowed programs com. 1993—94, 1995—98, centennial celebration com. 2002—03, com. on tchg. and learning 2004—05, tchg. and learning com. 2004—). Home: 4103 38th St NW Washington DC 20016-2217 Office: Am Coun on Edn 1 Dupont Cir NW Washington DC 20036-1110 Office Phone: 202-939-9551. E-mail: michael_baer@ace.nche.edu.

BAER, RALPH AUGUST, physician; b. Paterson, N.J., July 15, 1933; s. Ralph August and Anna Marie (Lyle) B.; A.B., Princeton U., 1955; M.D., Cornell U., 1959; m. Shirley E. Nicholls, Mar. 31, 1990; 1 child from a previous marriage: Diane Elizabeth. Intern, Bellevue Hosp., N.Y.C., 1959-60, asst. resident, 1960-62, chief resident, 1962-63; Nat. Heart Inst. fellow in cardiology N.Y. Hosp.-Cornell Med. Center, 1963-64; asst. attending physician N.Y. Hosp.-Cornell Med. Center, 1965-79, asso. attending physician, 1979—; instr. Cornell U. Med. Coll., 1965-72, clin. asst. prof. medicine, 1972-79, clin. assoc. prof., 1979—; v.p., med. dir. U.S. Trust Co. of N.Y., N.Y.C., 1970-81, sr. v.p., med. dir., 1981— . Bd. elders United Presbyn. Ch. Served to lt. col. M.C., U.S. Army, 1968-70. Diplomate Am. Bd. Internal Medicine, Nat. Bd. Med. Examiners. Mem. Am. Soc. Internal Medicine, N.Y. State Soc. Internal Medicine (dir. 1979-84, treas. 1984-86, v.p. 1986, pres. 1987-88, immediate past pres., 1980-89, chmn. task force on occupational health 181-83) N.Y. County Soc. Internal Medicine (dir. treas. 1978-80, pres.-elect 1980-82, pres. 1982-84), AMA, Med. Soc. State N.Y., N.Y. County Med. Soc. (chmn. subcom. on prescription abuse 1985-93, chmn. med. econs. com. 1993—, bd. dirs. 1993—), Westside Clin. Soc., Soc. Alumni Bellevue Hosp., N.Y. Acad. Medicine, Am. Heart Assn., Republican. Presbyterian. Clubs: Princeton Club of N.Y., Griffis Faculty Club. Office: US Trust Co NY 114 W 47th St New York NY 10036-1510

BAER, RICHARD N. (RICH BAER), lawyer; b. Glen Cove, N.Y., Mar. 30, 1957; married; 2 children. BA, Columbia U., 1979; JD, Duke U., 1983. Chmn., litigation dept. Sherman & Howard Law, Denver; spl. legal counsel to chmn. and CEO Richard C. Notebaert Qwest Comms. Internat. Inc., Denver, 2001—02, exec. v.p., gen. counsel, 2002—. Office: Qwest Comms Internat Inc Legal Dept 1801 California St Denver CO 80202

BAER, SUSAN M., airport executive; married; 1 child. BA in urban studies and anthropology, Barnard Coll.; MBA, NYU. Mgmt. analyst Port Authority of NY and NJ, mgr. pub. svcs. divsn. Tunnels, Bridges and Terminals Dept., mgr. Lincoln Tunnel, 1985—86, mgr. Port Authority Bus Terminal Manhattan N.Y.C., 1986—88, gen. mgr. Aviation Customer and Mktg. Svcs., 1988—94, gen. mgr. LaGuardia Airport Flushing, NY, 1994-98, gen. mgr. Newark Internat. Airport NJ, 1998—. Office: Newark Int & Teterboro Airports Conrad Rd, Bldg 1 Newark NJ 07114

BAER, WALTER S., think-tank executive; b. Chgo., July 27, 1937; s. Walter S., Jr. and Margaret S. (Mayer) B.; m. Miriam R. Schenker, June 18, 1959 (div. 1987); children: David W., Alan B.; m. Jeri Weiss, Oct. 23, 1988. BS, Calif. Inst. Tech., 1959; PhD (NSF fellow), U. Wis., 1964. Rsch. physicist Bell Telephone Labs., Murray Hill, N.J., 1964-66; White House fellow Washington, 1966-67; White House sci. adv. staff, 1967-69; cons. and sr. scientist RAND Corp., Santa Monica, Calif., 1970-81, dir. energy policy program, 1978-81; dir. advanced tech. Times Mirror Co., Los Angeles, 1981-89; deputy v.p. domestic rsch. RAND Corp., Santa Monica, Calif., 1990—. Cons. UN, maj. U.S. corps, 1970—; dir. Aspen (Colo.) Cable TV Workshop, 1972-73, L.A. Ednl. Partnership; pres. KCRW Found., Santa Monica, Calif.; adv. bd. Columbia U. Inst. Tele-Info., U.S. Com. for Internat. Inst. Applied Systems Analysis; dir. Am. Tng. Internat.; mem. gov. coun. on info. tech. State of Calif. Author: Interactive Television, 1971, Cable Television: A Handbook for Decisionmaking, 1973, also articles; editor: The Electronic Box Office, 1974, w/ RAND Cable Television Series, 1974; editorial bd.: Telecommunications Policy, 1976—, Internat. Ency. Communications. Mem. European Community Visitor, 1978. Recipient U. Wis. award for excellence in teaching, 1960; Preceptor award Broadcast Industry Conf., 1974— Fellow AAAS (chmn. Indsl. Sci. Sec. 1992-93); mem. IEEE (mem. com. on comm. and info. policy 1994—), Am. Phys. Soc., Internat. Inst. Communications, Sigma Xi. Office: RAND 1700 Main St Santa Monica CA 90401-3297 Business E-Mail: baer@rand.org.

BAER, WERNER, economist, educator; b. Offenbach, Germany, Dec. 14, 1931; came to U.S., 1945, naturalized, 1952; s. Richard and Grete (Herz) B. 58776, CUNY, N.Y.C., 1953; MA, Harvard U., 1955, PhD, 1958; D honoris causa, Fed. U. Pernambuco, Brazil, 1988, New U. Lisbon, Portugal, 2000; D honoris causa (hon.), Fed. U. Ceara, Brazil, 1993. Instr. Harvard U., 1958-61; asst. prof. Yale U., New Haven, 1961-65; asso. prof. Vanderbilt U., Nashville, 1965-69, prof., 1969-74; prof. econs. U. Ill., Urbana, 1974—. Vis. prof. U. São Paulo, Brazil, 1966-68, Vargas Found., Brazil, 1966-68; Rhodes fellow St. Antony's Coll., Oxford (Eng.) U., 1975 Author: The Brazilian Economy: Growth and Development, 5th edit., 2001, Privatization in Latin America, vol. 17, 1994, The Changing Role of International Capital in Latin America, 1998; co-author: (with P. Elosegui and A. Gallo) The Achievements and Failures of Argentina's Neo-Liberal Policies, 2002, (with J. Bang) Privatization and Equity in Brazil and Russia, 2002, (with E. Amann) Anchors Away: The Costs and Benefits of Brazil's Devaluation, 2003; co-editor: Latin America-Privatization, Property Rights and Deregulation, 1993, (with W. Maloney) Neo-Liberalism and Income Distribution in Latin America, 1997, (with W. Miles, A. Moran) The End of the Asian Myth, 1999, The State and Industry in the Development Process, 1999 (with E. Amann) Neoliberalism and it's Consequences in Brazil, 2002; contbr. articles to profl. jours. Decorated Order So. Cross (Brazil). Mem. Am. Econ. Assn., Latin Am. Studies Assn. Home: 1703 Devonshire Dr Champaign IL 61821-5901 Office: U Ill 1407 W Gregory Dr Urbana IL 61801-3606 Office Phone: 217-333-8388. Business E-Mail: wbaer@uiuc.edu.

BAER, WILLIAM J., lawyer; b. May 31, 1950; s. Joseph and Roses B.; m. Nancy Hendry; children: Michael Hendry, Andrew Hendry. BA, Lawrence U., 1972; JD, Stanford U., 1975. Bar: Wis., 1975, D.C., 1981, U.S. Ct. Appeals D.C., 1989, U.S. Supreme Ct. 1999. Trial atty. divsn. nat. advertising FTC, Washington, 1975-76, asst. to dir. bureau consumer protection, 1976-77, atty. advisor to chmn., 1977-78, asst. gen. counsel for legis., 1978-80; assoc. Arnold & Porter, Washington, 1980-83, ptnr., 1984-95; dir. Bur. of Competition FTC, Washington, 1995-99; ptnr., head antitrust practice group Arnold & Porter, Washington, 2000—. Contbr. articles to profl. jours. Trustee Lawrence U. Mem.: ABA. Democrat. Avocations: tennis, golf. Office: Arnold & Porter LLP 555 12th St NW Ste 810 Washington DC 20004-1200 Office Phone: 202-942-5936. Office Fax: 202-942-5999. Business E-Mail: william.baer@aporter.com.

BAERG, RICHARD HENRY, podiatrist, surgeon; b. L.A., Jan. 19, 1937; s. Henry Francis and Ruth Elizabeth (Loven) B.; children from previous marriage: Carol Elizabeth, William Richard, Michael David, Brie Ann, Niccolo, Monica, Deven, Arianna, Mia. AA, Reedley Coll., 1956; BS, Samuel Merritt U., Sch. Podiatric Medicine, 1965, DPM, 1968, MSc in Foot Surgery, 1970; MPH in Med. Adminstrn., U. Calif., Berkeley, 1971; ScD (hon.), N.Y. Coll. Podiatric Medicine, 1980; LittD (hon.), Ohio Coll. Podiatric Medicine, 1984; postgrad. Sch. Edn. and Pub. Health, U. Mich., 1973—74; postgrad. Sch. of Bus. and Sch. of Edn., Harvard U., 1975. Diplomate Am. Bd. Podiatric Surgery (foot and ankle surgery), Am. Bd. Podiatric Orthopedics and Primary Podiatric Medicine (exec. dir. 1980-90), Am. Bd. podiatric Pub. Health (bd. dirs. 1980-89). Intern Highland Alameda County Gen. Hosp., Oakland, Calif., 1969; resident in surgery Pacific Coast Hosp., San Francisco, 1970; acad. dean N.Y. Coll. Podiatric Medicine, N.Y.C., 1971-74; v.p., dean Samuel Merritt U., Sch. Podiatric Medicine, Oakland, Calif., 1974-76; chief podiatric medicine Los Angeles County-U. So. Calif. Med. Ctr., 1976-78; dir. So. Calif. Podiatric Med. Ctr., 1976-78; pvt. practice Beverly Hills, Calif., 1976-78; dean Roseland Franklin U. Coll. Podiatric Medicine, Chgo., 1978-79; mem. spl. med. adv. group to sec. Dept. Vets. Affairs, Washington, 1976-79, dir. podiatric service, dept. medicine and surgery, 1979-84, acting dir., 1984-86; health resources adminstrn. cons. Dept. Health and Human Svcs., Washington, 1974-88; chief podiatry VA Med. Ctr., Loma Linda, Calif., 1984-89; dir. residency tng. Loma Linda Foot Clinic, 1990; exec. v.p., med. dir. Dr. Footcare Corp., Montclair, Calif., 1988-90; faculty podiatry U. N.C. Hosps., Chapel Hill, 1992—; clin. prof. Sch. of Podiatric Medicine Barry U., Miami, Fla., 1993—; clin. prof. Med. Sch., U. N.C., 1992—; staff podiatrist Morehead Hosp., Eden, N.C., 1997-2000. Mem. podiatric staff Chapel Hill Surg. Ctr., 1993—; chief of podiatry Umstead Hosp., Butner, N.C., 1997-2000, VA Med. Ctr., Huntington, W.Va., dir. residency tng. chief podiatry sect., 2000-02; assoc. clin. prof. Stanford U. Med. Sch., 1974-76; clin. prof. Temple U. Coll. Podiatric Medicine, 1979-86, Des Moines U. Medicine and Health Sci., 1984-, U. NC Sch. Medicine, 1980-90; prof. dept. surgery Marshall U. Sch. Medicine, Huntington, W.Va., clin. prof. podiatric medicine and surgery Pikeville Coll. Sch. Osteopathic Medicine; pres. Baerg & Assocs.; cons. foot surgery, Las Vegas, 2002—; mem. podiatry adv. panel NAS Inst. Medicine, 1974; mem. bd. podiatric medicine Calif. Dept. Consumer Affairs, 1989-90, chmn. residency, edn. and hosp. inspection com. Contbg. author: (text) Podiatric Medicine and Public Health, 1987; mem. editl. bd. Jour. Podiatric Edn., Yearbook of Podiatric Medicine and Surgery, Mil. Medicine Jour.; contbr. over 30 articles to profl. jours., 3 chpts. to textbooks. With M.C. U.S. Army and USN, 1958-64. Mead-Johnson fellow, 1968-69. Fellow USPHS, Am. Podiatric Med. Assn. (com. on pub. health 1971-84, coun. podiatric edn. 1975-84, chmn. profl. edn. com. 1977-78, com. on hosp. 1980-85, Kenison award 1984, cert. appreciation 1990, com. on pub. health and preventive medicine), Am. Coll. Foot and Ankle Surgeons, Am. Coll. Foot & Ankle Orthopedics and Medicine (exec. dir. 1980-90), Acad. Ambulatory Foot Surgery; mem. APHA (governing coun. 1977-80, chmn.

podiatric health sect. 1991-94, chmn. nominating com. 1994-96), Am. Acad. Podiatric Adminstrs. (exec. dir. 1990-91), Nat. Bd. Podiatric Med. Examiners (bd. dirs.), Assn. Podiatrists in Fed. Svc., Am. Assn. Colls. Podiatric Medicine (exec. com. 1973, pres. 1980-81), Assn. Mil. Surgeons U.S., Nat. Acads. of Practice (podiatric medicine 1985), N.C. Foot and Ankle Soc. (bd. dirs. ins. com. 1994-97, cons. 1997-2000, chmn. zone III 1994-97, rep. N.C. Health Care Reform Com. 1994-97), Coun. Med. Sch. Affiliated Podiatrists (bd. dirs., dir. region 10), N.C. Symphony Assn., Palm Mortuaries (Las Vegas), Mason (Scottish Rite, 32 degree), Sigma Pi Epsilon, Pi Delta. Republican. Office Phone: 702-241-9006. Personal E-mail: rhbaerg@aol.com.

BAERGA, CARLOS OBED ORTIZ, professional baseball player; b. San Juan, P.R., Nov. 4, 1968; Player Cleve. Indians, 1989-96, N.Y. Mets, 1996—98, San Diego Padres, 1999, Cleve. Indians, 1999, Boston Red Sox, 2002, Arizona Diamondbacks, 2003—04, Washington Nationals, 2005—. Mem. Am. League All-Star Team, 1992-93. Named. to Am. League Silver Slugger Team, 1993-94. Office: 2400 East Capitol St SE Washington DC 20003

BAERMANN, DONNA LEE ROTH, real estate property executive, retired insurance analyst; b. Carroll, Iowa, Apr. 28, 1939; d. Omer H. and Mae Lavina (Larson) Real; m. Edwin Ralph Baermann, Jr., July 8, 1961 (dec. Aug. 1997); children: Beth, Bryan, Cynthia. BS, Mt. Mercy Coll., Ames, 1973; student, Iowa State U.-Ames, 1957-61. Cert. profl. ins. woman; fellow Life Mgmt. Inst. ins. agt. Luthern Mut. Ins. Co., Cedar Rapids, Iowa, 1973; home economist Iowa-Ill. Gas & Electric Co., Cedar Rapids, Iowa, 1973-77; supr. premium collection Life Investors Ins. Co. (now Aegon USA), Cedar Rapids, Iowa, 1978-83, methods and procedures analyst, 1987-94; pres., CEO Baermann Apts. Inc., 1992-94, owner, pres., 1992—. Mem. telecom. study group com. 1982-83, mem. productivity task force, 1984-94, TAB cert. facilitator, 2001—. Vol. Mercy Med. Ctr., Cedar Rapids, Iowa, 2002—; apptd. by Mayor and City Coun. Housing Bd. Appeals, Cedar Rapids, 2003. Mem. Internat. Platform Assn., Citizens Com. for Person with Disabilities, Nat. Assn. Ins. Women, Nat. Mgmt. Assn. (bd. dirs. Cedar Rapids chpt.), DAR, Knights of Malta (named Damsel of Ancient Order of St. John, N.Y.C.), Chi Omega. Republican. Presbyterian. Home: 361 Willshire Ct NE Cedar Rapids IA 52402-6922 Personal E-mail: dlrbaer@worldnet.att.net.

BAERNSTEIN, ALBERT, II, mathematician, educator; b. Birmingham, Ala., Apr. 25, 1941; s. Albert and Kathryn (Wiesel) B.; m. Judith Haynes, June 14, 1962; children— P. Renée, Amy. Student, U. Ala., 1958-59; AB, Cornell U., 1962; MA, U. Wis., 1964, PhD, 1968. Instr. math. U. Wis., Whitewater, 1966-68; asst. prof. math. Syracuse U., N.Y., 1968-72; assoc. prof. math. Washington U., St. Louis, 1972-74, prof. math., 1974—. Fulbright sr. research scholar Imperial Coll., London, 1976-77 Mem. Am. Math. Soc., Math. Assn. Am. Office: Washington U Dept Math Saint Louis MO 63130

BAERWALD, SUSAN GRAD, television broadcasting company executive producer; b. Long Branch, N.J., June 18, 1944; d. Bernard John and Marian Grad; m. Paul Baerwald, July 1, 1969; children: Joshua, Samuel. Degre des Arts and Lettres, Sorbonne, Paris, 1965; BA, Sarah Lawrence Coll., 1966. Script analyst United Artists, L.A., 1978-80; v.p. devel. Gordon/Eisner Prodns., L.A., 1980-81; mgr. mini-series and novels for TV, NBC, Burbank, Calif., 1981-82, dir. mini-series and novels for TV, 1982, v.p. mini-series and novels for TV, 1982-89; exec. producer NBC Prodns., 1989-95, Savoy Pictures TV, 1995-96, Citadel Entertainment, 1996-97; sr. lectr. Am. Film Inst., 1999. Producer (TV movies) Blind Faith, 1990, One Spl. Victory, 1991, Cruel Doubt, 1992, A Time to Heal, 1994, Inflammable, 1995 (TV miniseries) Lucky/Chances, 1990. Bd. dirs. The Paper Bag Players, N.Y.C., 1974—, Women in Film Found., 2000, Non-Profit Alliance W.O.M.E.N., Inc., 1998; vol. L.A. Children's Mus., 1978-80; mem. awards com. Scott Newman Found., 1982-84; bd. dirs. L.A. Goal, 1996—. Recipient Vol. Incentive award NBC, 1983. Mem. ATAS (bd. govs. 1993-97, nat. awards chmn. 1997-98), Am. Film Inst., Hollywood Radio and TV Soc.

BAESEL, DAVID LEE, music educator; b. Fairmont, W.Va., Mar. 13, 1948; s. Edgar George and Nancy Lee Baesel; m. Brenda Joan Maxey, June 24, 1972; children: Mark David, Paul George-Edgar, Amy Nicole. MusM in edn., Ariz. State U., 1966—72. Bandsman US Marine Band, Washington, 1976—96; adj. prof. of music Barry U., Miami Shores, Fla., 1999—2002, Gulf Coast C.C., Panama City, Fla., 1998—. Performing, tchg. Gulf Coast C.C., Panama City, Fla., 1998—. Musician (orchestral arranger): (church related) He's Alive/Other Praise Background Arranging. Steering com. Orch. of St. Andrew Bay, Panama City, Fla., 1998—2005. Gunnery sgt. USMC, 1976—96, Marine Barracks 8th and I Sts, SE Washington, DC. Mem.: Piano Technician's Guild (assoc.). Avocations: swimming, poetry, stamp collecting/philately. Home: 100 Camelot Circle Panama City FL 32405 Office: Sgt Pepper Music 100 Camelot Circle Panama City FL 32405 Office Phone: 850-774-2868. Personal E-mail: sgtpepper48@hotmail.com. E-mail: peppersax48@hotmail.com.

BAESEL, STUART OLIVER, architect; b. Charlotte, N.C., Feb. 5, 1925; s. Edward Franklin and Rose (Engel) B.; m. Betsey London Cordon, Nov. 23, 1949; children— Stuart Oliver, Betsey London, Cordon Telfair Student, U. N.C., 1940-42, Ecole des Beaux Arts, Fountainbleau, France, 1948; B.Arch., N.C. State U., 1950; M.Arch., Cranbrook Acad. Art, 1951. Architect A.G. Odell, Jr. & Assocs., Charlotte, 1951-55; architect-designer Skidmore, Owings, Merrill, N.Y.C., 1955-59, LBC & W Assocs., Columbia, S.C., 1959-65; dir. design J.N. Pease Assocs., Charlotte, 1965-72; mem. faculty Architecture Sch. Calif. State U., Pomona, 1972-74; prin. Stuart Baesel, Architect, Design Group, La Jolla, Calif., 1972—. Dir., sec. treas. Design World, Inc., Charlotte, 1968-72; dir., pres. Space Planning Assocs., Charlotte, 1966-72 Editor: Rev. Architecture, Columbia, S.C., 1962-65 Cons. Charlotte Planning Bd., 1954. Served with USAAF, 1943-46, PTO Recipient various profl. awards, including Honor award S.C. chpt. AIA, 1964, 65, 66, N.C. chpt. AIA, 1956, 66, 68, 69, 70, 72 Fellow AIA (bd. dirs. N.C.); mem. N.Y. Archtl. League, Phi Delta Theta Clubs: La Jolla Beach and Tennis. Episcopalian. Home: 303 Coast Blvd Unit 1 La Jolla CA 92037-4635 Office: PO Box 1237 La Jolla CA 92038-1237 also: Les Flots Bleus 06230 Villefranche Sur Mer France

BAESLACK, WILLIAM, III, (BUD BAESLACK), engineering educator; b. Cleve. s. William Baeslack Jr.; 3 children. B in welding engring., Ohio State U., 1973, M in welding engring., 1974; PhD in materials engring., Rensselaer Poly. Inst., 1978. Asst. prof. Ohio State U. Coll. Engring., 1982—85, assoc. prof., 1985—89, prof., 1989—99, chair dept. welding engring., 1991—94, assoc. dean rsch. and coll. devel., 1994—98, dean, 2004—; interim v.p. rsch. Ohio State U., 1998—99; pres. Ohio State U. Rsch. Found., 1998—99; prof., dean Rensselaer Poly. Inst. Sch. Engring., 1999—2004. Am. Soc. Engring. Edn. faculty rsch. fellow David Taylor Naval Ship Rsch. and Devel. Ctr., Annapolis, 1985; vis. scientist The Welding Inst., Cambridge, 1989—90. Lt. USAF, 1978—82, Air Force Materials Lab, lt. col. USAFR, 1983—. Fellow: Am. Soc. Metals Internat., Welding Inst., Am. Welding Soc. (Comfort A. Adams Lecture Award); mem.: Nat. Soc. Profl. Engineers, Am. Soc. Engring. Edn., AAAS. Office: Coll Engring The Ohio State U 142 Hitchcock Hall 2070 Neil Ave Columbus OH 43210-1278

BAETZ, TRACY L., museum director; m. Frederic Baetz. BA in History and Govt., Coll. William and Mary, 1992; MA in Am. Studies, Fla. State U., 1993. Asst. collections mgr. John Q. Adams Ctr. for the History of Otolaryngology, Am. Acad. Otolaryngology, Alexandria, Va., 1994—95; project specialist Smithsonian Instn.-Nat. Air and Space Mus. and Am. Festival Japan '94 project, Washington, 1994—95; curatorial specialist and edn. outreach coord. Smithsonian Instn.-America's Smithsonian Exhbn. Team, Washington, 1995—97; program and bus. affairs mgr. Smithsonian Instn.-Smithsonian Affiliations, Washington, 1997—2003; exec. dir. The Brick Store Mus., Kennebunk, Maine, 2003—. Contbr. exhibition catalogue; author: (article/review) Curator: The Museum Journal; editor: (newsletter) The Affiliate. Office: The Brick Store Museum 117 Main St Kennebunk ME 04043 Office Phone: 207-985-4802. Office Fax: 207-985-6887.

BAETZHOLD, HOWARD GEORGE, language educator; b. Buffalo, Jan. 1, 1923; s. Howard Kuster and Harriet Laura (Hofheins) B.; m. Nancy Millard Cheesman, Aug. 5, 1950; children: Howard King, Barbara Millard. Student, Brown U., 1940-43, MIT, 1943-44; AB magna cum laude, Brown U., 1944, A.M., 1948; PhD, U. Wis., 1953. Asst. dir. Vets. Coll., Brown U., Providence, 1947-48, dir., 1948-49, admissions officer, 1948-50; teaching asst. U. Wis.-Madison, 1950-51; asst. to assoc. dean Coll. Letters and Sci., 1951-53; asst. prof. English Butler U., Indpls., 1953-57, assoc. prof., 1957-67, prof. English, 1967-88, Rebecca Clifton Reade prof., 1981-88, Rebecca Clifton Reade prof. emeritus, 1988—, head dept., 1981-85. Vis. prof. U. Del., summer 1963. Author: Mark Twain and John Bull: The British Connection, 1970; co-editor: The Bible According to Mark Twain: Writings on Heaven, Eden and the Flood, 1995, paperback edit., 1996, Three Decades of Odes, 1997; contbr. articles to profl. jours., Dictionary Lit. Biography, Mark Twain Ency. Mem. OASIS (Older Adult Svcs. and Info. Sys.) adv. coun., 1996-2002, Indpls. Art Ctr., Indpls. Mus. Art. Served to lt. A.C., AUS, 1943—46. Recipient Butler Svc. medal, 2004; named Sagamore of the Wabash, 1988; faculty fellow Butler U., 1957-58, 69-70, Butler U. fellow, 1986, 87, John S. Tuckey meml. rsch. fellow Elmira Coll. Ctr. for Mark Twain Studies at Quarry Farm, 1990—, Henry Nash Smith fellow, 2001—; grantee Am. Philos. Soc., 1967, Am. Coun. Learned Socs., 1958. Mem. AAUP (v.p. state conf. 1955), MLA, Ind. Coll. English Assn. (exec. bd. 1983-85), Am. Lit. Assn., Mark Twain Cir. Am. (exec. com. 1987-88, hon. life mem. 1995), Am. Philatelic Soc., Greater Ind. Masters Swimming Assn., Indpls. Lit. Club (2d v.p. 1985-86, 1st v.p. 1987-88, 92-93, pres. 1993-94), Butler U. Odd Topics Soc., Ovid Butler Soc. (exec. com. 1998—), Delta Upsilon. Home: 6723 Riverview Dr Indianapolis IN 46220-1628

BAEZ, JOAN CHANDOS, vocalist; b. S.I., NY, Jan. 9, 1941; d. Albert V. and Joan (Bridge) B.; m. David Victor Harris, Mar. 1968 (div. 1973); 1 son, Gabriel Earl. Appeared in coffeehouses, Gate of Horn, Chgo., 1958, Ballad Room, Club 47, 1958-68, Newport (R.I.) Folk Festival, 1959-69, 85, 87, 90, 92, 93, 95, extended tours to colls. and concert halls, 1960s, appeared Town Hall and Carnegie Hall, 1962, 67, 68, U.S. tours, 1970—, concert tours in Japan, 1966, 82, Europe, 1970-73, 80, 83-84, 87-90, 93—, Australia, 1985; rec. artist for Vanguard Records, 1960-72, A&M, 1973-76, Portrait Records, 1977-80, Gold Castle Records, 1986-89, Virgin Records, 1990-93, Grapevine Label Records (UK), 1995-97, Guardian Records, 1995-97, European record albums, 1981, 83, award 8 gold albums, 1 gold single; albums include Gone From Danger, 1997, Rare, Live & Classic (box set), 1993, Dark Chords on a Big Guitar, 2003, Bowery Songs, 2005; author: Joan Baez Songbook, 1964, (biography) Daybreak, 1968, (with David Harris) Coming Out, 1971, And a Voice to Sing With, 1987, (songbook) An Then I Wrote, 1979. Extensive TV appearances and speaking tours U.S. and Can. for anti-militarism, 1967-68; visit to Dem. Republic of Vietnam, 1972, visit to war torn Bosnia-Herzegovina, 1993; founder, v.p. Inst. for Study Nonviolence (now Resource Ctr. for Nonviolence, Santa Cruz, Calif.), Palo Alto, Calif., 1965; mem. nat. adv. coun. Amnesty Internat., 1974-92; founder, pres. Humanitas/Internat. Human Rights Com., 1979-92; condr. fact-finding mission to refugee camps, S.E. Asia, Oct. 1979; began refusing payment of war taxes, 1964; arrested for civil disobedience opposing draft, Oct., Dec., 1967. Office: Diamonds & Rust Prodns PO Box 1026 Menlo Park CA 94026-1026 Office Phone: 650-328-0266.

BAEZ-TORRES, AXEL ALBERTO, anatomist, pathologist; b. Ponce, PR, Sept. 13, 1963; s. Jose Wigberto Baez-Torres and Osdila Torres-Lugo; m. Raquel Lugo-Diaz, May 20, 1989; children: Axel Manuel, Frances Marie. BS, U. PR, 1985; MD, U. PR Sch. Medicine, 1990; degree in anatomic and clin. pathology, U. Dist. Hosp., Rio Piedras, 1995. Diplomate Am. Bd. Pathology, Nat. Bd. Med. Examiners. Chief resident U. Dist. Hosp., Rio Piedras, 1994; staff pathologist San Pablo Pathology Group, Bayamon, PR, 1996; med. dir. So. Pathology Svc., Ponce, 1996—2000; dir. pathology dept. Hosp. La Conception, San German, PR, 2000—. Asst. clin. prof. Ponce Sch. Medicine, 1996—, senator-acad. senate, 1997—2003; dep. commr. for PR Coll. Am. Pathologists, 1997—. Contbr. articles to profl. jours. Fellow: Am. Soc. Clin. Pathologists, Coll. Am. Pathologists; mem.: Internat. Acad. Pathology, PR Coll. Physicians. Roman Catholic. Avocation: reading. Home: Mansion Real 232 Isabel St Coto Laurel PR 00780 Office: Hosp La Conception Pathology Dept Highway #2 KM 173.4 San German PR 00683

BAGAN, GRANT ALAN, lawyer; b. Chgo., Dec. 27, 1953; s. Seymour Jack and Joyce (Klass) B. m. Laurie Beth Weiss, Aug. 19, 1978; children: Stacy, Michelle, Ashley. BA cum laude, Tulane U., 1976; JD magna cum laude, U. Ill., 1979. Bar: Ill. 1979. Assoc. McDermott, Will & Emery, Chgo., 1979-85, ptnr., mem. firm exec. mgmt. com., chmn. corp. dept., 1985—. ABA. Office: McDermott Will & Emery LLP 111 W Monroe St Chicago IL 60603-4096 Office Phone: 312-984-7567. Office Fax: 312-984-7700. Business E-Mail: gbagan@mwe.com.

BAGAN, MERWYN, neurological surgeon; b. Phila., Jan. 25, 1936; s. Frank and Shirley (Lindenbaum) B.; m. Carol Augusta Joseph, Nov. 14, 1964; children: Eric, Seth, Karin. AB, Dartmouth Coll., 1957; MD, Boston U., 1962, MPH, 1995. Diplomate Am. Bd. Neurol. Surgery. Neurol. surgeon Surg. Neurology Profl. Assn., Concord, N.H., 1970-93; chmn. Healthsource, Inc., Hooksett, 1985-97. Chmn., pres. Healthsource N.H., Concord, 1985-93; adj. asst. prof. clin. surgery (neurosurgery) Dartmouth Med. Sch., 1981-88; vis. prof. dept. surgery Tribhuvan U. Inst. Medicine, Kathmandu, Nepal, 1997-2000. Lt. comdr. USPHS, 1963-65. Recipient Disting. Alumnus award Boston U. Sch. Medicine, 1993, alumni award Boston U., 1999, Suprabal Gorkha Dakshina Bahu award, 2000. Fellow ACS; mem. AMA, Am. Assn. Neurol. Surgeons (pres. 1992-93, humanitarian award 2000), N.H. Med. Soc. (pres. 1983), Congress of Neurol. Surgeons (Disting. Svc. award 1990), Found. Internat. Edn. Neurol. Surgery (chmn.), Alpha Omega Alpha. Home: 173 School St Concord NH 03301-2568

BAGATELLE, WARREN DENIS, investment banker; b. Mt. Vernon, N.Y., Aug. 19, 1938; s. S. Jerry and Rose (Firestone) B.; m. Hedy Schwartz, Nov. 22, 1962; children: David S., Tracy L., Adrien G. BA in Econs., Union Coll., 1960; MBA in Fin., Rutgers U., 1961. CPA N.Y. Audit mgr. Arthur Andersen & Co., N.Y.C., 1962-69; v.p. fin. & adminstrn. Ilex Optical Co., Inc., Rochester, N.Y., 1969-73; CEO Meson Electronics Inc., Rochester, N.Y., 1973-74; v.p. fin. Cross River Products, Inc., Rochester, N.Y., 1974-77; exec. v.p. Univ. Soc., Inc., Mahwah, N.J., 1977-81; v.p. corp. fin. Josephthal Lyon & Ross Inc., N.Y.C., 1981-84, chmn. chief exec. officer, 1984-87; mng. dir. Loeb Ptnrs. Corp., N.Y.C., 1987—. Bd. dirs. Fuel Cell Energy, Inc., Danbury, Conn., Electro Energy, Inc., Danbury, Matrix Ascent Ptnr., LLC, NYC, Matric Ascent Ptnrs.; chmn. bd. dirs. Virtual Scripics LLC, Rochester, NY, 2002—; ptnr. HSB Capital, 1984—. With USCG, 1961-62. Mem.: AICPAs, Antique and Classic Boat Soc. (dir. 1993—97, treas. 1997—2002), Am. Legion. Avocation: antique & classic boats. Office: Loeb Ptnrs Corp 61 Broadway New York NY 10006-2701 Office Phone: 212-483-7000.

BAGBY, JOSEPH RIGSBY, financial investor; b. Banner Elk, N.C., Aug. 23, 1935; s. Wesley Marion and Ila Paunee (Rigsby) B.; m. Martha Green, Jan. 1, 1965; 1 child, Meredith Elaine. Student, Fla. State U., 1955; BBA, U. Miami, 1959; MCR, Inst. Corp. Real Estate, West Palm Beach, Fla., 1977. Employee and supr. Miami Herald Pub. Co., 1953-63; rsch. and sales asst. Oscar Dolly Assocs., Miami, 1961-63; sales, appraising and property mgr. Jack Thomas Realty, Miami, 1963-65; dir. corp. real estate Burger King Corp., Miami, 1965-70; founder, pres. Internat. Assn. Corp. Real Estate Execs., Coral Gables, Fla., 1969-88; chmn. bd. trustees Nat. Assn. Corp. Real Estate Execs., Coral Gables, Fla., 1973-88, bd. dirs., 1971—; pres., founder Property Resources Corp. and 20 other investment cos., Miami and Palm Beach, 1970—. Founder merger and acquisition investment co., 1997; mem. businessman's adv. com. U.S. Postal Svc., Washington, 1984-88. Author: Real Estate Financing Desk Book, 1975, rev. edits. 1977, 81, Real Estate Directory, 1975. Pres. interfraternity coun. U. Miami (co-editor campus newspaper); mem., chmn. fin. com. St. Edward's Cath. Ch., Palm Beach, Fla., 1985-93. With U.S. Army, 1959-61. Named to Hall of Fame, Nat. Assn. Corp. Real Estate Execs., 1991. Mem. Nat. Assn. Location Analysts and Negotiators (founder), Internat. Corp. Real Estate Execs. Assn. (life hon. mem., bd. dirs. Corenet Global), Progress Club of Miami (co-founder), Optimist (founding mem. Miami Downtown club), Rotary (Harris fellow), Interfaith Cotillian (co-founder), Sigma Chi (pres. 1958), Alpha Kappa Psi. Democrat. Avocations: swimming, tennis. Home: 125 Brazilian Ave Palm Beach FL 33480-4221 Office: Property Resources Corp PO Box 3149 Palm Beach FL 33480-1349

BAGBY, MARTHA L. GREEN, real estate holding company executive, writer, publishing executive; b. West Palm Beach, Fla., June 17, 1937; d. Hampton and Louise (Lambert) Green; m. Joseph R. Bagby, 1966; 1 child, Meredith E. AA, Palm Beach Jr. Coll., 1957; AB, U. Miami, 1959; MA, Pa. State U., 1964. Tchr. journalism, english Palm Beach County, 1959—62; instr. journalism Pa. State U., 1962—63; city editor, writer Palm Beach News and Life, 1963—64; editor Alfred Hitchcock Mag., Riviera Beach, Fla., 1964; editor, supr. editl. svc., pub. rels. employee newspaper Nat. Airlines, Inc., Miami, Fla., 1965—73; corp. sec., chmn. bd. Property Resources Co., Palm Beach, Fla., 1971—. Life dir. CareNet Global, 2002—; Ill. franchisee Burger King Corp.; founder Internat. Health Awareness Assn.; lectr. journalism Dade, Palm Beach counties; instr. Barry Coll., Miami; pub. The Bagbys Health Digest, 1985—. Author: Stranglehold, 1977, The Complete Real Estate Dictionary, 1992, The Real Estate Financing Deskbook, 1979-90; author: (with others) The Complete Real Estate Book. Mem. exec. bd. Childbirth and Parent Edn. Assn., Miami. Mem.: Internat. Assn. Corp. Real Estate Execs. (founder, trustee, exec. editor, dir. life), Women in Comm. (pres.), Air Transport Assn. Am., Airline Editors Conf. (chmn.), S. Fla. Indsl. Chmn. Internat. Council Indsl. Editors, Fla. Pub. Relations Assn. Office: 125 Brazilian Ave Palm Beach FL 33480-4221

BAGDIKIAN, BEN HAIG, journalist, educator; b. Marash, Turkey, Jan. 30, 1920; came to U.S., 1920, naturalized, 1926; s. Aram Theodore and Daisy (Uvezian) B.; m. Elizabeth Ogasapian, Oct. 2, 1942 (div. 1972); children: Christopher Ben, Frederick Haig; m. Betty L. Medsger, 1973 (div.); m. Marlene Griffith, 1983 AB, Clark U., 1941, LittD, 1963; LHD, Brown U., 1961, U. R.I., 1992. Reporter Springfield (Mass.) Morning Union, 1941-42; assoc. editor Periodical House, Inc., N.Y.C., 1946; successively reporter, fgn. corr., chief Washington corr. Providence Jour., 1947-62; contbg. editor Saturday Evening Post, 1963-67; project dir. study of future U.S. news media Rand Corp., 1967-69; asst. mng. editor for nat. news Washington Post, 1970-71, asst. mng. editor, ombudsman, 1971-72; nat. corr. Columbia Journalism Review, 1972-74; prof. Grad. Sch. Journalism U. Calif., Berkeley, 1976-90, dean, Grad. Sch. Journalism, 1985-88, prof. emeritus, Grad. Sch. Journalism, 1990—. Keynote spkr. Coun. Europe Ministerial Conf. on Mass Media Policy, Kiev, Ukraine, 2005. Author: In the Midst of Plenty: The poor in America, 1964, The Information Machines: Their Impact on Men and the Media, 1971, The Shame of the Prisons, 1972, The Effete Conspiracy, 1972, Caged: Eight Prisoners and Their Keepers, 1976, The Media Monopoly, 1983, 6th edit., 2000, Double Vision: Reflections on My Heritage, Life and Profession, 1995, The New Media Monopoly, 2004; also pamphlets; contbr.: The Kennedy Circle, 1961; editor: Man's Contracting World in an Expanding Universe, 1959; bd. editors Jour. Investigative Reporters and Editors, 1980-88. Mem. steering com. Nat. Prison Project, 1974-82; trustee Clark U., 1964-76; bd. dirs. Nat. Capital Area Civil Liberties Union, 1964-66, Com. to Protect Journalists, 1981-88, Data Ctr., Oakland, Calif., 1990-97; pres. Lowell Mellett Fund for Free an Responsible Press, 1965-76; acad. adv. bd. Nat. Citizens Com. for Broadcasting, 1978—; judge Ten Most Censored Stories, 1976-98. Recipient George Foster Peabody award, 1951, Sidney Hillman Found. award, 1956, Most Perceptive Critic citation Am. Soc. Journalism Adminstrs., 1978, Career Achievement award Soc. Profl. Journalists, John and Catherine Zenger award, 1996, James Madison award ALA, 1998, Wayne Danielson award, U. Tex., 2005; named to R.I. Journalism Hall of Fame, 1992; fellow Ogden Reid Found., 1956, Guggenheim fellow, 1961-62. Mem. ACLU. Home: 25 Stonewall Rd Berkeley CA 94705-1414 Personal E-mail: benmar@uclink4.berkeley.edu. *Personal philosophy: The most compelling principles in my life have been, in private life the pervasive need of love and trust in human relations, in public life dignity of the individual combined with devotion to the common good, in intellectual life a distrust of detachment from the human condition, and in journalism honesty and clarity.*

BAGGER, RICHARD HARTVIG, pharmaceutical executive; b. Plainfield, N.J., Mar. 27, 1960; s. Donald Hartvig and Elizabeth Claire (Broback) B.; m. Barbara Jane Laird, May 14, 1988; Katherine Bianca, Jennifer Anne, Meredith Skye. AB, Princeton U., 1982; JD, Rutgers U., 1986. Bar: N.J. 1986, U.S. Dist. Ct. N.J. 1986. Legis. aide N.J. Gen. Assembly, Trenton, 1979-82; mem. profl. staff Select Com. on Aging U.S. Ho. Reps., Washington, 1982-83; assoc. McCarter & English, Newark, 1986-91; asst. gen. counsel Blue Cross and Blue Shield of N.J., Inc., Newark, 1991-93; mgr. civic affairs Pfizer, Inc., N.Y.C., 1993-96, dir., state corp. affairs, 1996-99, nat. dir. state govt. rels., 1999—2002, v.p. govt. rels., 2002—03, sr. v.p. govt. rels., pub. affairs and policy, 2003—. Trustee N.J. Hist. Trust, Trenton, 1986-89, Westfield Found., 1995-2001, Westfield United Way, 2003-, Overlook Found., 2001-04, Pub. Policy Ctr. of N.J., 2003-, Citizens Budget Commn. of N.Y., 2003-, Healthcare Inst., NJ, 2004-, NJN Found., 2005-; bd. govs. N.J. Hist. Soc., 1989-98. Editor, author Rutgers Law Rev., 1985-86. Active Westfield Planning Bd., 1987—92; councilman Town of Westfield, NJ, 1984—90, mayor, 1991—92; mem. N. J. Gen. Assembly, 1992—2002, N.J. Senate, 2002—03; dist committeeman Union County Reps., Westfield, NJ, 1980—83, 1987. Episcopalian. Office: Pfizer Inc 235 E 42nd St New York NY 10017-5755 Office Phone: 212-573-7646. E-mail: rich.bagger@pfizer.com.

BAGGETT, DONNIS GENE, journalist, editor; b. Livingston, Tex., July 16, 1952; s. Sam Jr. and Mavis Baggett; m. Beverly Brown; children: Valerie Shaddix, David Shaddix. BA, Stephen F. Austin State U., 1973. Reporter, photographer East Tex. Eye, Livingston, Tex., 1973-74, co-editor, 1974; reporter Longview (Tex.) Morning Jour., 1974-75, East Tex. editor, 1975-76; reporter The Dallas Morning News, 1976, asst. night city editor, 1977, asst. state editor, 1977-82, state editor, 1982-94, asst. mng. editor, 1994-95; pub., editor The Eagle, Bryan-College Station, Tex., 1996—. Chmn. Tex. Agrl. Summit Exec. Com., 1997—98; bd. dirs. Brazos Valley Mus. Natural History, Am. Heart Assn.; bd. dirs., campaign chair Brazos Valley United Way, 2000; mem. adv. bd. Washington-on-theBrazos State Park Assn. Mem.: Soc. Profl. Journalists, Tex. Press Assn. (dir.), Tex. Daily Newspaper Assn. (dir., chair assn. legis. adv. com.), Press Club of Dallas (sec. 1990—91, treas. 1991—92, pres. 1992—94). Methodist. Avocation: ranching.

BAGGETT, FRED W., lawyer; b. Stuttgart, Ark., May 15, 1945; BA, Univ. Fla., 1967; JD, Fla. State Univ., 1970. Bar: Fla. 1970. Exec. asst. to Chief Justice Supreme Ct. Fla., 1970—72; shareholder, chair, nat. govt. affairs practice Greenberg Traurig, Tallahassee. Adj. prof. law Fla. State Univ. Chmn. Tallahassee/Leon County Planning Agy., Capital Cultural Center, Tallahassee; sec. Florida Judicial Coun., Ounce of Prevention Fund of Fla. Fellow: Am. Bar Found.; mem.: Internat. Bar Assn., Tallahassee Bar Assn. Office: Greenberg Traurig 101 E College Ave PO Drawer 1838 Tallahassee FL 32302 Office Phone: 850-222-6891. Office Fax: 850-681-0207. Business E-Mail: baggettf@gtlaw.com.

BAGGETT, STEVEN RAY, lawyer; b. Fayetteville, Ark., July 3, 1963; s. Harold Ray and Norma June (King) B.; m. Amy Lynn Griggs, Jan. 2, 1999; c. Lauren Michelle, Brooke Lindsey. BA, U. Ark., 1985; JD, So. Meth. U., 1988. Bar: Tex. 1988, U.S. Dist. Ct. (no. dist.) Tex. 1988, U.S. Ct. Appeals (5th cir.) 1992, U.S. Dist. Ct (so. and ea. dists.) Tex., 2005. Assoc. Thompson & Knight, Dallas, 1988-95, shareholder, ptnr., 1996—. Recipient Am. Jurisprudence awards Bancroft-Whitney Co., 1985-86. Fellow Dallas Bar Found.; mem. Tex. Bar Assn., Dallas Bar Assn. (spkrs. com. 1997-2004, media rels. com. 2004—, state fair trial by jury com. 1998-2001, jud. com. 1999-2001, 2004—, cmty. involvement com. 1999-2001, law in schs. and cmtys. com. 1999), Ark. U. Alumni Assn., So. Meth. U. Law Sch. Alumni Assn., Phi Beta Kappa. Avocations: weight training, running, ice skating, music. Office: Thompson & Knight 1700 Pacific Ave Ste 3300 Dallas TX 75201-4693 Office Phone: 214-969-1700. E-mail: baggetts@tklaw.com.

BAGGETT, W. MIKE, lawyer; b. Waco, Tex., Nov. 8, 1946; s. Bill R. and Jenna (Robertson) B.; m. Jo Kilpatrick, May 28, 1968; children: Carl, Cary. BBA, Tex. A&M U., 1968; JD cum laude, Baylor U., 1973. Bar: Tex. 1973. Law clk. Tex. Supreme Ct., Austin, 1973—74; assoc. Winstead, Sechrest & Minick, Dallas, 1974-79, shareholder, 1979—, chmn. and chief exec. officer, 1992—. Chair reverse mortgage rules com., chair home equity loan foreclosures rules com. Tex. Supreme Ct. Author: Texas Foreclosure: Law & Practice, 1983, Texas Practice Series West, 2nd edit., 2001, Real Estate Litigation, Texas Practice Guide West, 2002; co-author: Lender Liability Law and Litigation, 1989. Trustee Tex. A&M Found., 1989-98, chmn., 1992-93; mem. Joint Select Com. on Judiciary, 1988; bd. dirs. Tex. Higher Edn. Coordinating Bd., 1989-95, North Tex. Commn., Dallas Citizens Coun., State Fair of Tex., Southwestern Bell-SMU Athletic Forum; chmn. Dallas Ft. Worth Regional Sports Commn.; chmn., CEO, Cotton Bowl Athletic Assn. 1st lt. U.S. Army, 1968-71, Vietnam. Decorated Bronze Star; named Tex. Aggie Lawyer of Yr., 2004; named among Top 10 Bus. Litigators in Dallas/Ft. Worth, Dallas Bus. Jour., Best Lawyer, D Mag., Super Laywer, Top 100 in Dallas/Ft. Worth, Tex. Monthly. Master: Patrick E. Higginbotham Am. Inn Ct.; fellow: Am. Bd. Trial Advocates, The Ctr. for Am. and Internat. Law, Dallas Bar Found. (chmn. and trustee), Tex. Bar Found., Am. Bar Found.; mem.: Dallas Bar Assn. (pres. chmn., bd. dirs.), Tex. Bar Assn. (bd. cert. civil trial com. 1983, bd. dirs., adminstrn. justice com., exec. com.), Greater Dallas C. of C. (bd. dirs.), Baylor Law Sch. Alumni Assn. (pres., bd. dirs.), Assn. Former Students Tex. A&M U. (pres. 1988, Outstanding Alumni Coll. Bus. 1996, Disting. Alumni 1998), Ctrl. Dallas Assn. (chmn.), City Club, Royal Oaks Club. Methodist. Office: Winstead Sechrest & Minick 5400 Renaissance Tower 1201 Elm St Ste 5400 Dallas TX 75270-2199 Office Phone: 214-745-5303.

BAGGOTT, THOMAS MCCANN, lawyer; b. Dayton, Ohio, Feb. 10, 1943; s. Horace Worman and Dorothy F.; m. Mary Louise Ricker, Dec. 20, 1969; children: Roland W., Porscha M. BA, Ohio State U., 1967; JD, Ohio No. U., 1971. Bar: Ohio 1971, U.S. Dist. Ct. (so. dist.) Ohio 1971, U.S. Supreme Ct. 1997. Referee Montgomery County Probate Ct., Dayton, 1971-73; prosecuting atty. City of Vandalia, Ohio, 1974; assoc. Baggott Logan & Gianuglou, Dayton, 1975-80; ptnr. Baggott Law Offices Co., Dayton, 1980-87; prin. Thomas M. Baggott Co., Dayton, 1987-91; ptnr. Altick & Corwin, Dayton, 1991-2000; magistrate Montgomery County Probate Ct., 2000—. Mem. Assn. Trial Lawyers Am., Ohio State Bar Assn., Ohio Acad. Trial Lawyers (trustee 1977-84), Ohio Magistrates Assn. (chmn. probate com., trustee 2000—), Dayton Bar Assn. (treas. 1985-86, chmn.), Miami Valley Trial Lawyers Assn. Office: 41 N Perry St Dayton OH 45402-1431

BAGHAEI-RAD, NANCY JANE BEBB, elementary school educator; b. Amsterdam, N.Y., Apr. 8, 1963; d. Warren D. Bebb and Joan Pipito (Ruck) B. BS, SUNY, Oswego, 1986; MEd, Lesley Coll., 1989; AAS, Cazenovia Coll., 1983; post grad., Columbia U. Cert. tchr., N.Y., N.J. Program dir. Adirondack Camp for Boys and Girls, Glenburnie, N.Y.; tchr. kindergarten Perth Cen. Sch., Amsterdam, N.Y.; tchr. St. Mary's Inst., Amsterdam; literacy evaluator Boston Plan for Excellence/Trotter Sch., Roxbury, Mass.; 1st grade tchr. Doane Stuart Sch., Albany, N.Y.; tchr. Mildred E. Strang Mid. Sch., Yorktown Heights, N.Y.; coord. gifted and talented, primary computer tchr. Highland Avenue Sch., Midland Park, N.J. Coord. elem. gifted and talented Scotia-Glenville Sch. Dist., NY; academic head Lower Sch. Brown Sch., Schenectady, NY. Named Tchr. of Yr. Gov. of N.J., 1994. Mem. ASCD.

BAGIAN, JAMES PHILIP, former astronaut, public health service officer, medical educator; b. Phila., Feb. 22, 1952; s. Philip and Rose Barbara (Mollick) G.; m. Tandi Marie Benson, June 1, 1984; children: Krista, Kimberly, Brian. BSME, Drexel U., 1973, LLD (hon.), 1988; MD, Jefferson Med. Coll., 1977. Diplomate Nat. Bd. Med. Examiners, Am. Coll. Preventive Medicine; cert. aerospace medicine; registered, cert. profl. engr., Pa. Process engr. 3M Co., Bristol, Pa., 1973; gen. surgery resident Geisinger Med. Ctr., Danville, Pa., 1977—78; flight surgeon NASA, Houston, 1978—79, astronaut, 1980—95; anesthesia resident U. Pa., Phila., 1979—80; dir. Nat. Ctr. for Patient Safety, Vets. Health Adminstrn., Ann Arbor, Mich., 1998—. Adj. asst. prof. mil. and emergency medicine Uniformed Svcs. U. Health Scis.; clin. asst. prof. preventive medicine and cmty. health U. Tex. Med. Br. Patentee in field. Bd. dirs. City of Seabrook (Tex.) Parks Bd., 1986-89. Col. USAF, 1989—. Recipient Sikorsky Helicopter Rescue award Sikorsky Helicopters, 1990, Spaceflight award Internat. Aeronautical Fedn., 1990. Mem. NAE, Aerospace Med. Assn., Am. Human Factor Soc., Inst. Medicine, 2004. Office: National Center for Patient Safety PO Box 486 Ann Arbor MI 48106-0486

BAGINSKI, MAUREEN A., federal agency administrator; b. Feb. 3, 1955; married. BA in Russian and Spanish, MA in Slavic lang., SUNY, Albany; at, Moriz Torez Fgn. Lang. Inst., Moscow. Russian lang. instr. Nat. Security Agy./Ctrl. Security Svc., 1979, sr. ops. officer, nat. ops. ctr., signals intelligence nat. intelligence officer Russia, exec. asst. to the dir., dep. chief global access program, chief, directorate of ops., consumer products and svcs., asst. dep. dir. tech. and sys., chief, officer of the dir., dir. signals intelligence, 2001—03; exec. asst. dir. office of intelligence FBI, Washington, 2003—. Recipient Sustained Exec. Leadership award, Dir. Ctrl. Intelligence. Avocations: gardening, kayaking. Office: Fed Bur Investigation J Edgar Hoover Bldg 935 Penn Ave NW Washington DC 20535-0001

BAGLEY, CATHY LORRAINE, obstetrician, gynecologist; b. Bklyn., Apr. 17, 1961; BA, Dartmouth Coll., 1978-82; MD, Brown U., 1986. Diplomate Am. Bd. Ob-Gyn. Resident Cook County Hosp., Chgo., 1986-90; ob-gyn. Dept. HHS, Chgo., 1990-92; mem. staff The Hammond Clinic, Munster, Ind., 1992-93, St. Lawrence Hosp., Lansing, Mich., 1993-94; ob-gyn. Ctrl. City Ob/Gyn. Assocs., Inc., Macon, Ga., 1994—, pres., 1998—. Fellow Am. Coll. Ob-Gyn.; mem. AMA (Physicians Recognition award 1997). Avocations: tennis, jazz appreciation and promotion. Office: Ctrl City Women's Specialists PC 556-B 3d St Macon GA 31201-

BAGLEY, CHARLES FRANK, III, lawyer; b. Dec. 3, 1944; m. Kirsten L., Aug. 19, 1967; children: Charles F. IV, Gordon T. BA, Rhodes Coll., 1966; JD, Washington & Lee U., 1969. Judge advocates gen. ct. lt. U.S. Navy, 1969-74; ptnr. Campbell, Woods, Bagley, Emerson, McNeer & Herndon, 1974—. Pres. bd. dirs. tri state coun. Boy Scouts of Am., 1982-85; bd. dirs. Contact Huntington, Hospice Huntington, chmn. 1987-89; active Huntington Area C. of C., Enslow Park Presbyn. Ch. Fellow Internat. Soc. Barristers, West Va. Bar Found.; mem. ABA, Va. Bar Assn., W.Va. State Bar Assn. (bd. govs. 1986-93, pres. 1991-92), W.Va. Bar Assn. (exec. coun. 1986-95, pres. 1993-94), Def. Trial Coun. W.Va. (bd. govs. 1985-90), Cabell County Bar Assn. (pres. 1985-86), Internat. Assn. Ins. Coun., Def. Rsch. Inst., Inc. (state chmn. 1985-90). Address: 1123 12th Ave Huntington WV 25701-3423

BAGLEY, CONSTANCE ELIZABETH, lawyer, educator; b. Tucson, Dec. 18, 1952; d. Robert Porter Smith and Joanne Snow-Willstadter. AB in Polit. Sci. with distinction, with honors, Stanford U., 1974; JD magna cum laude, Harvard U., 1977. Bar: Calif. 1978, N.Y. 1978. Tchg. fellow Harvard U., 1975-77; assoc. Webster & Sheffield, N.Y.C., 1977-78, Heller, Ehrman, White & McAuliffe, San Francisco, 1978-79, Bingham McCutchen, San Francisco, 1979—84, ptnr., 1984-90; lectr. bus. law Stanford (Calif.) U., 1988-90, lectr. mgmt., 1990-91, lectr. law and mgmt., 1991-95, sr. lectr. law and mgmt., 1995-2000, GSB Trust faculty fellow, 1997-98, lectr. Stanford Exec. Program; lectr. Stanford Mktg. Mgmt. Exec. Program; sr. lectr. bus. adminstrn. Harvard Bus. Sch., Boston, 1999-2000, assoc. prof., 2000—. Bd. dirs. Alegre Enterprises, Inc., Latina Publ. LLC, 1995-2000; corp. practice series adv. bd. Bur. Nat. Affairs, 1984—; faculty adv. bd. Stanford Jour. Law, Bus. and Fin., 1994—; lectr., planning com. Calif. Continuing Edn. Bar, L.A., San Francisco, 1983, 85-87; lectr. So. Area Conf., Silverado, 1988; mem. faculty Young Pres. Orgn. for Pres., Hong Kong, 1988, Praque, Czech Republic, 2002; mem. nat. adj. coun. Nat. Assn. of Securities, 2005—. Author: Mergers, Acquisitions and Tender Offers, 1983, Managers and the Legal Environment: Strategies for the 21st Century, 1991, 4th edit., 2002, Winning Legally: How to Create Value, Marshal Resources and Manage Risk, 2005; co-author: Negotiated Acquisitions, 1992, Cutting Edge Cases in the Legal Environment of Business, 1993, 2d edit. 1998, Proxy Contests and Corporate Control: Strategic Considerations, 1997, Proxy Contests and Corporate Control: Conducting the Proxy Campaign, 1997, The Entrepreneur's Guide to Business Law, 1998, 2d edit., 2003; contbg. editor: Calif. Bus. Law Reporter, 1984-95; mem. editl. bd. Jour. Internet Law, 1997-99, 2001—; staff editor Am. Bus. Law Jour., 2000-. Vestry mem. Trinity Episcopal Ch., San Francisco, 1984-85; vol. Moffit Hosp. U. Calif., San Francisco, 1983-84; bd. dirs. Youth and Family Assistance, Redwood City, Calif., 1996-99. Mem. ABA, Nat. Assn. Securities Dealers (nat. adjudicatory coun. 2005—), Acad. Mgmt., Acad. Legal Studies in Bus., Harvard Faculty Club, Cap and Gown Soc., Phi Beta Kappa. Republican. Office: Harvard Bus Sch Soldiers Field Boston MA 02163-1317 Office Phone: 617-495-6963. Business E-Mail: cbagley@hbs.edu.

BAGLEY, GRANT P., federal official, physician; b. Salt Lake City, Apr. 20, 1941; s. Ben G. and Marie P. Bagley; m. Margaret Holther, June 8, 1961; children: Susan, David Grant, John Paul. BS in Genetics, U. Utah, 1961, JD, 1989; MD, George Washington U., 1965; postgrad., U. Md., 1969-70. Diplomate Am. Bd. Obstetrics and Gynecology, Am. Bd. Legal Medicine; lic. physician, Utah, D.C., Colo., Md., Idaho, Calif.; bar: Utah 1989, Colo. 1991, U.S. Dist. Ct. Utah. Intern LDS Hosp., Salt Lake City, 1965-66; resident Washington Hosp. Ctr., 1968-70, chief resident, 1970-71, resident obstetrics/gynecology, 1968-72; asst. prof. dept. ob-gyn. U. Utah, Salt Lake City, 1972-74; law clk. Hansen & Anderson, Salt Lake City, 1987-88; med. dir., CEO Utah Women's Health Ctr., Salt Lake City, 1974-89; fellow health policy planning and analysis The Rand Corp., Santa Monica, Calif., 1989-90; asst. atty. gen. Utah State Atty. Gen., Salt Lake City, 1990-91; med. officer U.S. FDA, Rockville, Md., 1991-93, USPHS Indian Health Svc., Chinle, Ariz., 1993-94, Health Care Fin. Adminstrn. Bur. Policy Devel., Balt., 1994—. Mem. courtesy staff Lakeview Hosp., Bountiful, Utah, 1974-91, Valley West Hosp., Granger, Utah, 1971—, LDS Hosp., Salt Lake City, 1971-82; mem. active staff Holy Cross Hosp., Salt Lake City, 1971-91, St. Mark's Hosp., Salt Lake City, 1974-91; mem. clin. staff U. Utah, Salt Lake City, 1971-91; vice-chmn. dept. ob-gyn. Holy Cross Hosp., Salt Lake City, 1987-89; clin. instr. Coll. Nursing, U. Utah, 1983-90; assoc. clin. prof. dept. ob-gyn. U. Utah Sch. Medicine, 1985-90. Contbr. articles to profl. jours. Treas., bd. dirs. Nat. Abortion Fedn., 1982-88; del. Episcopal Diocese Conv., Utah. Maj. USAF, 1966-68. NIH fellow, 1971, Pew Found. fellow, 1989, William H. Leary scholar U. Utah Law Sch.; recipient Commrs. Spl. Citation FDA, 1992. Fellow Am. Coll. Obstetricians and Gynecologists, Am. Coll. Legal Medicine; mem. AMA (Physicians Recognition award 1972, 77, 80, 83, 86, 89), ABA, Utah State Med. Assn. (del. 1986-90), Salt Lake County Med. Soc. (exec. com., sec. 1988-89), Assn. Planned Parenthood Profls., Nat. Health Lawyers Assn., Med. Group Mgmt. Assn., Soc. Office Based Surgery, Masons (3d degree), Shriners. Democrat. Episcopalian. Avocations: amateur radio, private pilot, scuba diving, collection of early 20th century authors. Home: 1101 Francis Ave Baltimore MD 21227-4204 Office: 5600 Fishers Ln Rockville MD 20852-1750

BAGLEY, JAMES ROBERT, freelance writer; b. Valdosta, Ga., Dec. 7, 1946; s. Rayford Virdoe Bagley and Frances Cowart; m. Carol Ann Blackman, Dec. 17, 1972; children: James Brennan, Kimberly Ann. BS, Valdosta State U., 1975. Numerous positions including dep. sheriff, probation officer, 1975-85; clerical specialist Fla. Hwy. Safety Dept., Tallahassee, 1985-86; freelance writer, Tallahassee, 1986-89; security officer Mus. Fla. History, Tallahassee, 1989-93; cons. State Bd. Adminstrn., Tallahassee, 1994-95; freelance writer. Author: (poetry) The Star, 1977, The Alchemist, 1980, Soul-Speak from the Matrix, 1985, I Am No River Like Yesterday, 1995, (novels) Lustmords of Bithinsinia, 1995, Tetrarcha, 2000, The World is...Cube, 2004. With U.S. Army, 1966-69, Vietnam. Recipient cert. of appreciation Lions Club, Valdosta, 1977. Mem. Author's Guild, Acad. Am. Poets, 22nd Infantry Regiment Soc., Charlie Co. Assn. Home and Office: 2317 Limerick Dr Tallahassee FL 32309-3508 Office Phone: 850-668-1840. E-mail: bodea7@comcast.net.

BAGLEY, PHILIP JOSEPH, III, lawyer; b. Richmond, Va., Nov. 24, 1941; s. Philip Joseph Jr. and Louise (Bourne) B.; m. Sally Ann Twedell, Aug. 18, 1967; children: Elizabeth Bourne Faulkner, Anne Tunstall Twedell. BA, U. Richmond, 1963; LLB, U. Va., 1966. Bar: Va. 1966, U.S. Supreme Ct. 1972. Assoc. Troutman Sanders LLP, Richmond, 1970—74, ptnr., 1974—, and practice group leader, comml. develop. and real estate investments group; v.p. Richmond Real Estate Group, 2002—03, pres., 2003—04. Chmn. state adv. coun. Nat. Legal Svcs. Corp., Richmond, 1977-79; bd. dirs. Legal Svc. Corp. Va., 1978-86. Legal advisor Jr. League Richmond, 1977—; bd. dirs. Richmond Symphony, 1986-96, pres. 1992-94; bd. dirs. Richmond Eye and Ear Hosp., 1988—, pres. 1991-96; trustee Benedictine H.S., 1994-2002, pres., 1996-2002; bd. dirs. Carpenter Ctr. Performing Arts, 1995—, mem. exec. com., 1998—; bd. dirs., mem. exec. com. Va. Performing Arts Found., 2001—; bd. dirs. Richmond Renaissance, 2002—. Fellow Am. Law Found., Va. Bar Found.; mem. ABA (lectr. real estate financing com. 1984, title ins. com. 1987, leasing 1992, coun. real property, probate and trust law sect. 1993-98, sec. 1998-2000, vice-chair real property divsn. 2000-02, chair-elect 2002-03, chair 2003—), Am. Coll. Real Estate Lawyers (bd. govs. 1988-97, treas. 1991-93, v.p. 1993-94, pres. 1995-96), Anglo-Am. Real Property Inst. (bd. govs. 1995—), Coun. for Am.'s 1st Freedom (bd. govs. 1994-2000, pres. 1996-2000), Internat. Coun. Shopping Ctrs. (co-chair law conf. com. 1996-98), Va. Bar Assn., Richmond Bar Assn., Country Club Va., Commonwealth Club, Order of Coif, Phi Beta Kappa, Omnicron Delta Kappa, Raven Soc., Phi Alpha Delta. Roman Catholic. Office: Troutman Sanders Bldg 1001 Haxall Point Richmond VA 23218-1122 Office Phone: 804-697-1444. Office Fax: 804-698-5199. Business E-Mail: phil.bagley@troutmansanders.com.

BAGLEY, TERRENCE M., lawyer; b. Richmond, Va., 1955; BA, Va. Commonwealth U., Richmond, 1977; JD, Campbell U., Buies Creek, NC, 1982. Bar: Va. 1982, Pa. 1991, US Ct. Appeals 4th Cir. 1982, US Cir. Ct. We. & Ea. Districts Va. Ptnr. McGuireWoods LLP, Richmond, Va., 1993—, chair firm complex products liability & mass tort litig. dept., 2004—. Mem.: Def. Rsch. Inst., Pa. Bar Assn. Office: McGuireWoods LLP One James Ctr 901 E Cary St Richmond VA 23219 Office Phone: 804-775-4371. Office Fax: 804-698-2008. Business E-Mail: tbagley@mcguirewoods.com.

BAGLEY, WILLIAM THOMPSON, lawyer; b. San Francisco, June 29, 1928; s. Nino J. and Rita V. (Thompson) Baglietto; m. Diane Lenore Oldham, June 20, 1965; children: Lynn Lorene, William Thompson, Walter William, Shana Angela, Tracy Elizabeth. AB, U. Calif., Berkeley, 1949, JD, 1952. Bar: Calif. 1953, U.S. Supreme Ct. 1967. Atty. Pacific Gas & Electric Co., 1952-56; assoc. Gardiner, Riede & Elliott, San Rafael, Calif., 1956-60; ptnr. Bagley Bernt & Bianchi, San Rafael, 1961-74; mem. Calif. Legis., 1961-74; chmn. Commodity Futures Trading Commn., Washington, 1975-79; ptnr. Nossaman, Guthner, Knox and Elliott, San Francisco, 1980—. Mem. Calif. Pub. Utilities Commn., 1983-86; mem. Calif. Transp. Commn., 1983-89, chmn., 1987-88. Bd. editors Calif. Law Rev., 1951-52. Bd. regents U. Calif., 1989-2002; trustee Marin Cmty. Found., 2004—; bd. dirs. Nat. Futures Assn., Calif. Coun. Environ. and Econ. Balance, Edmund G. Brown Inst. Govtl. Affairs, L.A.; chmn. bd. Calif. Rep. League, 1980-82. Recipient Freedom of Info. award Sigma Delta Chi, 1970, Golden Bear award Calif. Pk. Commn., 1973; named Most Effective Assemblyman, Capitol Press Corps, 1969, Legislator of Yr., Calif. Trial Lawyers Assn., 1970, Alumnus of Yr., U. Calif. Alumni Assn., 2002. Mem. ABA, Calif. State Bar Assn., World Trade Club, Elks Club (life), Phi Beta Kappa, Alpha Tau Omega. Presbyterian. Office Phone: 415-398-3600. Personal E-mail: diane_bagley@comcast.net.

BAGLIO, VINCENT PAUL, aerospace transportation executive; b. Patchogue, NY, Feb. 18, 1960; s. Lorenzo and Nancy (Morello) B.; m. Katerina Barnova, Apr. 3, 2002. BS, Princeton U., 1982; MS, Poly. U., Bklyn., l986; MBA, Hofstra U., 1993. Product mgr. integrated sys. and aerostructures sector Northrop Grumman Corp., Bethpage, N.Y., 1982-99; mgmt. cons. Beacon Cons. Svcs. Inc., 1999-2000; sr. mgr. bus. devel. Cubic Transp. Sys., Inc., N.Y.C., 2000—02; dir. engring. and program mgmt. Smiths Aerospace-Electronic Sys., L.I., NY, 2002—04; v.p., gen. mgr. Farmingdale ops. Herley Industries, NY, 2004; program mgr. advanced capabilities devel. Northrop Grumman Corp., Bethpage, NY, 2004—. Contbr. articles to profl. jours. Alumni schs. com. Princeton (N.J.) U.; chmn. Princeton Alumni Assn. of L.I. Mem. AIAA (tech. com. 1995-97), Soc. Automotive Engrs. (indsl. lectr. 1990-91), Internat. Coun. Aero. Scis. (program com. 1989-93), Friends Princeton Football. Avocations: golf, running. Office: Northrop Grumman Corp Mail Stop X04 14 925 S Oyster Bay Rd Bethpage NY 11714 Office Phone: 516-704-3870. Business E-Mail: vincent.baglio@ngc.com.

BAGNALL, LINDSAY LOMAX, not-for-profit fundraiser; d. Victor William and Jacqueline (Bryant) Lomax; m. Kent Alan Bagnall, May 4, 1985; 2 children. BA, U. Mo., Rolla, 1976. Co-owner, v.p. human resources Kent Jewelry and Fine Gifts, Rolla, 1985—; exec. v.p. Mo. Sch. Mines U. Mo. - Rolla, 2002—. Advisor juggling club U. Mo., Rolla, 2001—, advisor Panhellenic, 2003—. Vol. Ozark Actors Theater, Rolla, 1985—, Pub. Radio Sta. KUMR, Rolla, Mo., 1985—; mem. Arts Rolla!, 1990—, Friends of Rolla Pub. Libr., 1990—; vol. Mark Twain Elem. PTO, Rolla, Mo., 1995—2002; mem. Champions Rolla Edn., 1995—; vol. parent adv. com. Mark Twain Elem. Sch., Rolla, 2003—. Mem.: Coun. Advancement and Support Edn., Rolla Area C. of C., U. Mo. Rolla, Mo. Sch. Mines Alumni Assn. (exec. dir.), P.E.O. Internat. (rec. sec. 1997—99, chair publicity 1999—2003, chair auditing 2000—, initiation corr. sec. 2001—04), Duston-Dustin Family Assn. (life), Coterie U. Mo.-Rolla, Phelps County Alumnae Panhellenic (treas. 1990—91, tel. chair 1990—91, chair scholarship com. 2000—01, co-chair cotillion 2000—02). Avocations: theater, art collecting, travel, reading. Home: 16541 State Route F Rolla MO 65401 Office: MSM-UMR Alumni Association Castleman Hall 1870 Miner Circle Rolla MO 65409-0650 Office Phone: 573-341-6327. Personal E-mail: bagnall@socket.net. Business E-Mail: lindsayb@umr.edu.

BAGNALL, ROGER SHALER, history professor; b. Seattle, Aug. 19, 1947; m. 1969; 2 children BA, Yale U., 1968; MA, U. Toronto, Ont., Can., 1969; PhD in Classical Studies, U. Toronto, 1972. Asst. prof. classics Fla. State U., 1972-74; asst. prof. Greek and Latin Columbia U., N.Y.C., 1974-79, assoc. prof. classics and history, 1979-83, prof., 1983—, dean Grad. Sch. Arts and Scis., 1989-93. Pres. Egyptological Sem. of N.Y., 1981-83; vis. prof. U. Florence, Italy, 1981, 89, Bar-Ilan U., Israel, 1986, U. Warsaw, Poland, 1989, U. Helsinki, Finland, 1994, Am. U. Cairo, 2004; Hamilton vis. rsch. fellow Christ Ch., Oxford, 1995-96; prof. U. Calif.-Berkeley, 2005. Author: The Administration of the Ptolemaic Possessions, 1976, Ostraka in Amsterdam Collections, 1976, The Florida Ostraka: Documents from the Roman Army in Upper Egypt, 1976, Bullion Purchases and Landholding in the 4th Century, 1977, Egypt in Late Antiquity, 1993, Reading Papyri, Writing Ancient History, 1995; co-author: Ostraka in the Royal Ontario Museum, 2 vols., 1971-76, The Chronological Systems of Byzantine Egypt, 1978, 2d edit., 2004, Columbia Papyri VII, VIII, 1978, 90, Consuls of the Later Roman Empire, 1987, Demography of Roman Egypt, 1994, Reading Papyri, Writing Ancient History, 1995. Am. Coun. Learned Soc. grantee, 1975, fellow, 1976-77; Am. Philos Soc. grantee, 1984, 84; NEH fellow, 1984-85, Guggenheim fellow, 1990-91, Fowler Hamilton Vis. Rsch. fellow Christ Church, Oxford, England, 1995—. Fellow Am. Numismatic Soc., Am. Acad. Arts and Scis.; mem. Am. Philol. Assn. (sec.-treas. 1979-85, bd. dirs. 1988-91), Am. Philos. Soc., Am. Soc. Papyrologists (pres. 1993-96), Acad. Royale de Belgique. Office: Columbia U 606 Hamilton Hall New York NY 10027

BAGRATUNI, SUREN, musician, educator; arrived in US, 1990; 1 child, Marta. MusD, Moscow (Russia) Conservatory, 1989; diploma in Art, New Eng. Conservatory, 1993. Prof. cello U. Ill., Urbana, Ill., 1995—2000, Mich. State U., East Lansing, Mich., 2000—. Artistic dir. Cello Plus. Music Festival, East Lansing, 2000—. Musician: (albums) Crumb, Khudoyan, 1994, Prokofiev, Shostakovich, 1996, Beethoven, Brahms, 1997, Tchaikovsky, Rachmaninov, 1997, Arensky, 1997, Rachmaninov, Stravinsky, 2002, Music of Bach, 2004 (Multiple U. awards). Office Phone: 517-432-9793.

BAGSHAW, JOSEPH CHARLES, molecular biologist, educator; b. Niagara Falls, N.Y., Sept. 2, 1943; s. Joseph Stanley and Nancy Jo (Pannabaker) Pash; children: Joseph Scott, Alan David. BA, Johns Hopkins U., 1965; PhD, U. Tenn., Oak Ridge, 1969. Research fellow Mass. Gen. Hosp., Boston, 1970-71; asst. prof. molecular biology Wayne State U., Detroit, 1971-77, assoc. prof., 1977-84; prof. biology and biotech. Worcester (Mass.) Poly. Inst., 1984—. Dir Worcester Consortium PhD Program Biomedical Sci, 1985—. Editor (with others): Cell and Molecular Biology of Artemia Development, 1989. Predoctoral fellow, NSF, rsch. grantee, NIH, USDA. Mem.: AAAS, Am. Soc. Cell Biology, Am. Soc. Biochemistry and Molecular Biology. Office: Worcester Poly Inst Dept Biology/Biotech Worcester MA 01609-2280 Office Phone: 508-831-5930. E-mail: jbagshaw@wpi.edu.

BAGSHAW, MALCOLM A., radiation oncologist, educator; b. Adrian, Mich., 1925; BA, Wesleyan U., 1946; MD, Yale U., 1950. Diplomate Am. Bd. Radiology. Surg. intern Grace-New Haven Hosp., 1950-51, resident in surg. pathology, 1951-52; resident in radiology U. Mich., 1953-56, clin. instr. radiology, 1955-56; instr. Stanford U., Palo Alto, Calif., 1956-59, asst. prof., 1959-62, assoc. prof., 1962-69, prof., 1969-92, Henry S. Kaplan-Harry Lebeson prof. emeritus, 1992—, dir. div. radiation therapy, 1960-92, chmn. radiology dept., 1972-86, chmn. radiation oncology dept., 1986-92. Resident etranger Inst. Gustave-Roussy, France, 1962-63; cons. radiation therapy VA Hosp., Palo Alto, Calif., 1960-92. Recipient Medal of Honor, Am. Cancer Soc., 1984, Gold medal Nihon U. Sch. Medicine, Japan, 1984, Gold Medal award Am. Soc. for Therapeutic Radiology and Oncology, 1985, Disting. Alumnus award Wesleyan U., 1996, Charles P. Kettering Gold medal Gen. Motors Co., 1996, Cancer Fighter of Yr. Beckstrand Cancer Found., 2003. Mem. AMA, Radiol. Soc. N.Am. (Gold medal 1999), Am. Coll. Radiology (Gold medal 2002). Office: 300 Pasteur Dr Palo Alto CA 94304-2203

BAGUISI, ALEXANDER, embryologist; b. Quezon City, Metro Manila, Philippines, Feb. 6, 1959; s. Federico and Purificacion Baguisi; m. Stella Marie Samaniego, Apr. 29, 1958; children: Kathrine Marie, Rosalyn Marie, Michael Alexander. MS, U. Coll. Dublin, Ireland, 1999. Rsch. embryologist TranXenoGen Inc., Shrewsbury, Mass. Contbr. articles to profl. jours., chpts. to books. Recipient Spl. Achievement award, UP Vanguard Inc., 1979, Gold Medal for target shooting, Armed Forces of the Philippines, 1978; scholar, UP Vanguard Inc., 1977—80. Achievements include invention of methods of cloning animals using the Induced Enucleation and the Telophase- II techniques to produce cloned mice and transgenic goats respectively; method for targeted germline production of birds using primordial germ cells. Method useful for avian transgenesis and conservation programs; research in avian embr germ cells, can be transferred into the embryonic vasculature and contribute to somatic lineage formation of the different organs in syngeneic and allogeneic transplant recipients; hypothermic preservation and cryopreservation of animal embryos can be enhanced using antifreeze proteins and glycoproteins from polar dwelling fish; developed a triple fluorescent staining method to vitally identify live, necrotic and apoptotic cells simultaneously; first to clone the worlds first transgenic goats using somatic cell nuclear transfer. The first to have cloned two different species of animals using two novel techniques. Avocations: tennis, reading, travel, soccer. Office: TranXenoGen Inc 800 Boston Turnpike Shrewsbury MA 01545 E-mail: abaguisi@tranxenogen.com.

BAGWILL, JOHN WILLIAMS, retired pension fund administrator; b. Seattle, Aug. 9, 1930; s. John Williams and Amy (Munday) B.; m. Emily Bend Sedgwick, Dec. 28, 1953; children: John Williams III, David Sedgwick, Elizabeth Bagwill Komjathy. BA, Hamilton Coll., 1952; MBA, Harvard U., 1958. CFP. Asst. to pres. George O. Muir, Inc., N.Y.C., 1961-64; v.p. Fin. Instns. Retirement Fund, White Plains, N.Y., 1964-85, exec. v.p., 1985-87, pres., 1987-94; ret., 1994. Gov. Newport (R.I.) Health Care Corp., 1997; cons. long-term care issues, 1999—. Bd. dirs. Town Club New Castle, Chappaqua, N.Y., 1975-79, pres., 1978-79; alumni coun. Hamilton Coll., 1977-82, pres., 1980-82; trustee, treas. Newport Art Mus., 1997—. Mem. Newport Reading Rm., Quindecim Club Episcopalian. Personal E-mail: jbagwilljr@aol.com.

BAGYI, JOHN MARTIN, lawyer; b. Albany, N.Y., Apr. 7, 1971; s. John Alexander and Barbara Bagyi; m. Dania Alyse Benmosche, Oct. 1, 2004. BA, SUNY, Albany, 1993; JD, Union U., 1996. Cert. sr. profl. in human resources Human Resources Certification Inst., 1999. Intern to Hon. Ralph W. Wmith, Jr., U.S. Dist. Ct. (no. dist.) N.Y., Albany, 1995; assoc. atty. Bond, Schoeneck & King, PLLC, Albany, NY, 1996—2003, ptnr., 2004—. Bd. dirs. Capital Region Human Resources Assn., Albany, NY. Columnist (bi-monthly articles) Profl. Ins. Agents Mag; contbr. articles to profl. jours. Exec. com., bd. dirs. Albany Law Sch. Nat. Alumni Assn., NY, 1999; co-chair capital leadership steering com. Albany Colonie Regional C. of C., NY, 2001—04. Recipient James Unger Meml. prize, Rockefeller Coll., 1993, 40 Under Forty award, Capital Dist. Bus. Rev., 2004, Assoc. Mem. of the Yr., N.Y State Assn. of Health Care Providers, 2003. Mem.: ABA, N.Y. State Law Assn., N.Y. State Bar Assn. (labor and employment sect., liaison Young Lawyers sect. 2002—03), Nat. Eagle Scout Assn. Office: Bond Schoeneck & King PLLC 111 Washington Ave Albany NY 12206 Office Phone: 518-533-3229. Office Fax: 518-533-3299. Business E-Mail: jbagyi@bsk.com.

BAHADUR, BIRENDRA, operations research specialist; b. Gorakhpur, India, July 1, 1949; came to Can., 1981; s. Bijai Bahadur and Shakuntala Srivastva; m. Urmila Bahadur, May 29, 1970; children: Shivendra, Shachindra. BS in Physics, Chemistry and Math., Gorakhpur U., 1967, MS in Physics, 1969, PhD, 1976. Rsch. scholar physics dept. Gorakhpur U., 1969-76, asst. prof. physics dept., 1976-77; sr. sci. officer Nat. Phys. Lab. India, New Delhi, 1977-81; v.p. R&D Data Images, Ottawa, Ont., Can., 1981-85; mgr. R&D Litton Data Images, Ottawa, 1985-91; engr. mgr. liquid crystal display material and process Litton Systems, Can., Toronto, 1988-97; prin. engr. Display Ctr. Rockwell Collins Inc., 1997—. Adj. prof. dept. computers and elec. enging. Waterloo (Can.) U., 1995; active various Internat. Confs. on Liquid Crystals; participant numerous profl. meetings; mem. liquid crystal tech. com. SID, 1993—. Author: Liquid Crystal Displays, 1984; editor: Liquid Crystals--Applications and Uses, vol. I, 1990, vol. II, 1991, vol. III, 1992; mem. editoral bd. Displays, 1993—, Liquid Crystal Today, 1995—; mem. abstracting panel Liquid Crystal Abstracts, 1978-80; author more than 75 articles. V.p. nat. capitol region India Can. Assn., 1989-90, pres., 1990-91. Grantee Indsl. Rsch. Assistance Program, NRC Can., 1982-85, 84-87, 88-91, Wright Patterson AFB, 1991-94. Mem. Internat. Liquid Crystal Soc., Soc. Info. Displays (dir. Upper Midwest chpt. 2003--, Spl. Recognition award 1993, LC tech. com. 1993—, chmn. 1997), Inst. Physics, Soc. de Chimie Physique. Achievements include patent for Process for Production of Printed Electrode Pattern for Use in Electro-Optical Display Devices (India); co-development of technology of various liquid crystal displays; patent for wide viewing angle dye doped TN LCDs with retardation sheets. Home: 935 71st St NE Cedar Rapids IA 52402-7295 Office: Rockwell Collins Inc Mail Sta 106-191 400 Collins Rd Cedar Rapids IA 52498-0001 Office Phone: 319-295-9251. E-mail: bbahadur@rockwellcollins.com.

BAHADURSINGH, ANIL M., surgeon, educator; s. Chet and Eva Bahadursingh; m. Lauren Tran; children: Sophie, Elizabeth. MB BCh, Royal Coll. Surgeons, 1987. Asst. prof. St. Louis U., 2002—. Fellow: Am. Coll. Surgeons; mem.: Am. Coll. Colon and Rectal Surgeons. Office: St Louis U 3635 Vista Ave Saint Louis MO 63110

BAHAL, VISHAL, cardiologist; b. Ghaziabad, India, July 28, 1967; s. Prem Nath and Lata Bahal. BS in Biology with honors, Ursinus Coll., 1989; DO, Phila. Coll. Osteo. Medicine, 1993. Diplomate Am. Bd. Internal Medicine, Am. Osteo. Bd. Internal Medicine. House physician Nazareth Hosp., Mercy Haverford Hosp., 1995-97, Holy Redeemer Hosp., Meadowbrook, Pa., 1995-97, 99—; rotary internship U. Med. and Dentistry of N.J., Stratford, 1993-94; intern and resident in internal medicine Med. Coll. Pa.-Hahnemann U. Hosp., Phila., 1994-97; hospitalist ICU Vencor Hosp., Chgo., 1998-99; hospitalist CCU and postsurg. cardiac unit St. Francis Hosp., Evanston, Ill., 1997-99; cardiology fellow Deborah Heart and Lung Ctr., Browns Mills, NJ, 1999—2002; staff ICU/CCU phys. Hamilton Hosp., 2000—01; invasive cardiologist Chester County Hosp., West Chester, Pa., 2002—. Ho. physician Holy Redeemer Hosp., 1995—97, med. housestaff coord.; officer com. on interns and residents U. Medicine and Dentistry of N.J., 1993—94; med. technologist Temple U. Hosp., Phila., 1991—93. Active Social Vision of Mankind, 1994—. Mem.: ACP, AMA, N.J. Assn. Osteo Physicians and Surgeons, Am. Coll. Osteo. Internists, Am. Osteo. Assn., Am. Coll. Cardiology, Beta Beta Beta. Avocations: weightlifting, sports, boating, video movie production, flying. Home: 311 Belmont Ct Mullica Hill NJ 08062-3638

BAHASH, ROBERT J., publishing executive; b. New Brunswick, NJ, 1945; BS in Acctg., Mt. St. Mary's Coll., 1966; MBA in Fin., NYU, 1972. CPA. Joined as mgr. fin. auditing McGraw-Hill, Inc., N.Y.C., 1974, various finance-related positions, 1974—83, exec. v.p., fin., McGraw-Hill Book Co., 1983; sr. v.p. corp. fin. operation The McGraw-Hill Companies, N.Y.C., 1985, exec. v.p. & CFO, 1988—. Am. Inst. of CPAs. Office: McGraw-Hill Inc Ste 383 1221 Avenue Of The Americas New York NY 10020-1095

BAHL, ROY WINFORD, economist, educator, consultant; b. Miami, Fla., June 28, 1939; s. Roy Winford and Vista Lee (Becks) B.; m. Marilyn Seifried, Dec. 22, 1963; children: Renee, Alexandra, Martin, Ashley. BA, Greenville (Ill.) Coll., 1961; MA, U. Ky., 1963, PhD in Econs., 1965. Asst. prof. econs. W.Va. U., Morgantown, 1965-67; economist IMF, Washington, 1967-71; prof. econs. Syracuse (N.Y.) U., 1971-88, Maxwell prof. polit. economy, 1985-88; prof. econs. Ga. State U., Atlanta, 1988-96, dir. Policy Rsch. Ctr., 1988-96, dean Andrew Young sch. policy studies, 1996—. Bd. dirs. N.Y. State Energy Authority, Albany, 1979-87, Lincoln Found., Phoenix, 1986-93; mem. So. Growth Policies Bd., 1997—; cons. World Bank, Washington, 1971—. Author: Urban Public Finance in LDCs, 1992, Economic Growth and Fiscal Plan, 1992, Fiscal Policy in China, 1999; editor: The Jamaican Tax Reform, 1991, Restructuring Local Government Finance, 2003. Recipient Fiscal medal Govt. of Philippines, 1986, Disting. Economist award State of Ky., 1989. Mem. Nat. Tax Assn. (pres. 1986), Am. Econs. Assn., So. Econs. Assn. (v.p. 1993). Democrat. Office: Ga State U Andrew Young Sch Policy Studies 35 Broad St Ste 602 Atlanta GA 30303-2302

BAHL, TRACY L., healthcare executive; Studied in law, Whittier Coll. Sch. of Law; undergrad. degree in bus. and health, Gustavus Adolphus Coll.; diplomat, Am. Coll. Healthcare Exec. With UniHealth Am., Calif., Maxicare Healthplans, Calif.; dir, provider relations CIGNA HealthCare Calif., Calif.; v.p., exec. dir. CIGNA HealthCare New York; pres., gen. mgr. CIGNA HealthCare Mid-Atlantic; pres., strategic bus. svcs. United HealthCare Corp., Hartford, Conn., 1998; pres. Unipirse Strategic Solutions, 1998—2002; sr. v.p., comml. health plan CIGNA HealthCare; sr. v.p., chief mktg. officer UnitedHealth Group, Minnetonka, Minn., 2002—. Office: United Health Group Ctr 9900 Bren Rd East Minnetonka MN 55343

BAHLKE, CONRAD GEORGE, lawyer; b. Phila., Sept. 17, 1958; m. Roxane Orgill; children: Charlotte, Nolan. BA, Oberlin Coll., 1980; MBA, JD, U. Chgo., 1984. Bar: Mass. 1985, N.Y. 1988. Atty. Fed. Res. Bd., Washington, 1984-87; assoc. White & Case, N.Y.C., 1987-94; assoc., spl. counsel Schulte Roth & Zabel LLP, N.Y.C., 1994-2000; ptnr. Weil, Gotshal & Manges LLP, N.Y.C., 2000—. Contbr. articles to profl. publs. Trustee Oberlin (Ohio) Coll., 1980—83. Mem.: ABA (mem. com. futures and derivative investments, chmn. subcom. 2000—), Assn. Bar City of N.Y. (mem. com. futures regulation 1992—95, 1996—99, 2000—), Phi Beta Kappa. Episcopalian. Avocations: art, music, travel, sports. Office: Weil Gotshal & Manges LLP 767 5th Ave New York NY 10153 Office Phone: 212-310-8630. Business E-Mail: conrad.bahlke@weil.com.

BAHLMAN, WILLIAM THORNE, JR., retired lawyer; b. Cin., Jan. 9, 1920; s. William Thorne and Janet (Rhodes) B.; m. Nancy W. DeCamp, Mar. 21, 1953; children: Charles R., William Ward, Baker D. BA, Yale U., 1941, LL.B., 1947. Bar: Ohio 1947. Prin. Paxton & Seasongood, L.P.A., Cin., 1947-67, 73-88; ptnr. Paxton & Seasongood, Cin., 1954-67, Thompson Hine, LLP, Cin., 1989-94; prof. law U. Cin. Coll. Law, 1967-73, lectr., 1965-67, 73-77; ret., 1994. Served with USAAF, 1942-46. Mem. Am. Law Inst., ABA, Ohio State Bar Assn., Cin. Bar Assn. Office: Thompson Hine LLP 312 Walnut St Fl 14 Cincinnati OH 45202-4024 Office Phone: 513-352-6716. E-mail: WilliamBahlman@ThompsonHine.com.

BAHL-MOORE, ELIZABETH ANN, art educator, artist; b. Sayre, Pa., Dec. 29, 1978; d. John Anthony Bahl and Margaret Marie Hildebrandt; m. William Andrew Moore, June 13, 1998. BFA magna cum laude, Longwood U., 2002. Cert. tchr. Va. Instr. art Longwood Ctr. Visual Arts, Farmville, Va., 2003; tchr. art Culpeper (Va.) County Pub. Schs., 2003—. Instr. art summer enrichment Culpeper (Va.) County Pub. Schs., 2004; founder After Sch. Art Club Program Culpeper, 2004. Exhibitions include Heart Va. Art and Craft Outdoor Festival, 2003, 2004. Vol. Prince Edward Elem., Farmville, 2003; vol., founder afterschool art club program, Culpeper, Va.; bd. dirs. Voices of Blue Ridge, Culpeper, 2004—. Mem.: Va. Art Edn. Assn., Nat. Art Edn. Assn., Nat. Mus. Women in Arts, Phi Kappa Phi. Office: Culpeper Middle Sch 14300 Achievement Dr Culpeper VA 22701

BAHLS, STEVEN CARL, academic administrator, educator; b. Des Moines, Sept. 4, 1954; s. Carl Robert and Dorothy Rose (Jensen) B.; m. Jane Emily Easter, June 18, 1977; children: Daniel David, Timothy Carl, Angela Emily. BBA, U. Iowa, 1976; JD, Northwestern U., Chgo., 1979. Bar: Wis. 1979, Mont. 1989; CPA, Iowa. Assoc. Frisch, Dudek & Slattery, Milw., 1979-84, dir., 1985; assoc. dean and prof. U. Mont. Sch. of Law, Missoula, 1985-94; dean., prof. law sch. Capital U. Law Sch., Columbus, Ohio, 1994—2003; pres. Augustana Coll., Rock Island, Ill., 2003—. Coordinating exec. editor Northwestern U. Law Rev., 1979. Pres.-elect Illowa coun. Boy Scouts Am.; bd. dirs. Quad Cities United Way, Ill. Quad Cities C. of C., Quad Cities Symphony Orch., Putnam Mus. Mem. ABA, Am. Agrl. Law Assn. (past pres.), Wis. Bar Assn., Mont. Bar Assn., Order of Coif. Avocations: photography, travel, hiking. Home: 1100 35th St Rock Island IL 61201 Office: Augustana College 639 38th Street Rock Island IL 61201-2296

BAHN, GILBERT SCHUYLER, retired mechanical engineer, researcher, novelist; b. Syracuse, N.Y., Apr. 25, 1922; s. Chester Bert and Irene Eliza (Schuyler) B.; m. Iris Cummings Birch, Sept. 14, 1957 (dec.); 1 child, Gilbert Kennedy. BS, Columbia U., 1943; MSME, Rensselaer Poly. Inst., 1965; PhD in Engring., Columbia Pacific U., 1979. Registered profl. engr., N.Y., Calif. Chem. engr. GE Co., Pittsfield, Mass., 1946-48, devel. engr. Schenectady, 1948-53; sr. thermodynamics engr. Marquardt Co., Van Nuys, Calif., 1953-54, rsch. scientist, 1954-64, rsch. cons., 1964-70; engring. specialist LTV Aerospace Corp., Hampton, Va., 1970-88, ret., 1988. Freelance rschr. FDR at Nadir, 1988—2000, Am. hist. demography, 2000—; mem. JANNAF Performance Standardization Working Group, 1966—73, Thermochemistry Working Group, 1967—72; propr. Schuyler Tech. Libr., 1952—. Author: Reaction Rate Compilation for the H-O-N System, 1968, Blue and White and Evergreen: William Byron Mowery and His Novels, 1981, Oliver Norton Worden's Family, 1982, Studies in American Historical Demography to 1850, Vol. 1, 1987, Overall Population Trends, Age Profiles, and Settlement, Vol. 2, 1987, The Wordens, Representative of the Native Northern Population, Vol. 3, 1994, Computerized Treatment and Statistical Evaluation of the 1790 Federal Census for the Northern Half of the State of New York, Vol. 4, 1999, Computerized Treatment and Statistical Evaluation of the 1790 Federal Census for the Southern Half of the State of New York, Vol. 5, 1999, Surname Counts and Given Name Counts in the 1790 Federal Census of New York, The Ancient Worden Family in America: A Story of Growth and Migration, 1988, FDR at Nadir: 1937 & 1938, 1993, Senator Alva B. Adams of Colorado, 1993, Senator Bennett Champ Clark of Missouri, 1993, Senator Walter F. George of Georgia, 1993, Senator Guy Mark Gillette of Iowa, 1993, Senator Augustine Lonergan of Connecticut, 1993, Senator Frederick Van Nuys of Indiana, 1993, Senator Patrick Anthony McCarran of Nevada, 1994, Senator Ellison D. Smith of South Carolina, 1995, Senator Millard E. Tydings of Maryland, 1996, Franklin D. Roosevelt's Appointments and Itineraries for the New Deal Years in Alphabetical Fashion, 1996, Infestation of Yankees: Reference Guide to Union Troops in Confederate Territory, 1998, American Place Names of Long Ago, 1998, One Man's Platform, 1998, Slaves and Nonwhite Free Persons in the 1790 Federal Census of New York, 2000, Franklin D. Roosevelt's Appointments and Itineraries for the War Years in Alphabetical Fashion, 2000, Worden Surname Census, 1640-1850, As of 2000, 2000, Four Novels: We Were All Men of Honor, Paul Adams, Hero?, "Need to Know", 2001, Vicky in Time: Alternative History of the Princess Royal, Victoria Adelaide Mary Louisa, 2002, The Worden Surname from Peter Worden of Yarmouth to 1850, 2002, The Long Life of Enos Warren, 2003, Collected Novels: Other Men's Dreams, Mother Was a Faro Dealer, All the Winter of Our Sins, Red Red One, Plastic Cookies, Bottled Tea, Job Never Had It So Good, Certain Rules, Jasmine, Ambition, Christy and Joey and Five Long Years, 1940-1945, 2003, Novels of 2003: Some Roads Lead to Happiness, Too Old for the Home Guard, Triplets, Tension, Broken Premises, The BJ99 Survivors, A Quite Uncommon Woman, Shortcut to Motherhood, 2003, Seeking Immirants: Finding Patriots, A and B Surnames, 2004, Meeting Needs, "Maggie in Sunshine", 2004, Consort of the Mill Owner's Daughter, 2004, Naked Amnesia, 2004, Assignment to Brinley, 2004, The Weekly Diary of Bridget (Brij) Forest, 2004, Allie, Not Allura, 2004, A Gentle Hug, Then Love and Faith Forever, 2004, Delayed Vengeance, 2004, Rest Stop Rescue, 2004, Two Studies of Character, 2004, Orphan Princess of the Emirate, 2004, Blood Ties One by One, 2004, Twenty Minutes to a Lifetime, 2004, Mints and John and Mr. Wilson, 2004, It Started with a Business Card, 2004, Meting Needs, 2004, Maggie Is Sunshine, 2004, many others; founding editor Pyrodynamics, 1963—69, procs. editor Kinetics, Equilibria and Performance of High Temperature Systems, 1960, 1963, 1967; contbr. articles to profl. jours. Air raid warden, 1941-43; active Boy Scouts Am., 1958-78. Capt. USAAF, 1943-46. Recipient Silver Beaver award Boy Scouts Am., 1970. Mem. ASME, Combustion Inst. (sec. western states sect. 1957-71), Soc. for Preservation Book of Common Prayer. Democrat. Episcopalian (Vestryman 1968-70). Achievements include discovery of free radical chemical species diboron monoxide, 1966. Home: 4519 N Ashtree St Moorpark CA 93021-2156

BAHNER, SUE (FLORENCE SUZANNA BAHNER), broadcast executive; d. William and Florence (Quinlivan) McElwee; m. David S. Bahner; children: Suzanna Elizabeth, Caryl Aileen. Grad., Columbia Bus. Coll., 1950. Various exec. sec. positions, 1954-74; office mgr. Sta. WYRD, Syracuse, N.Y., 1974, gen. mgr., 1974-80, Sta. WWWG-AM, Rochester, N.Y., 1980-93, WDCW, Syracuse, 1993-98; pres. The Cornerstone Group, 1986—90, Crossway Cons., 1997—. Bd. dirs. Rescue Mission, Syracuse, ENRB, 2005—; active Eastern Hills Bible Ch. Mem. Greater Syracuse Assn. Evangelicals (treas. 1993-97), N.Y. State Assn. Evangelicals (sec. 1998-2000), Nat. Religious Broadcasters (pres. ea. chpt. 1984-98, bd. dirs. 1983—, 2d v.p. 1998-2000, mem. exec. com. 1992—). Office: Natl Religious Broadcasters 7839 Ashton Ave Manassas VA 20109-2883

BAHNER, THOMAS MAXFIELD, lawyer; b. Little Rock, 1933; m. Sara M. Bahner; 3 children. BS, Carson-Newman Coll., 1954; JD, U. Va., 1960. Bar: Tenn. 1960, Va. 1960, U.S. Dist. Ct. (ea. dist.) Tenn. 1961, U.S. Supreme Ct. 1970, U.S. Ct. Appeals (6th cir.) 1971, U.S. Ct. Appeals (8th cir.) 1971, U.S. Ct. Appeals (4th cir.) 1975, U.S. Ct. Appeals (3d cir.) 1988, U.S. Ct. Appeals (fed. cir.) 1991, U.S. Ct. Appeals (9th cir.) 1999, U.S. Ct. Appeals (11th cir.) 1999, U.S. Dist. Ct. (we. dist.) Tenn. 2002. Assoc. Kefauver, Duggan and McDonald, Chattanooga, 1960—62; ptnr. Duggan, McDonald & Bahner, Chattanooga, 1962—64, Chambliss, Bahner, Crutchfield, Gaston and Irvine (name changed to Chambliss, Bahner & Stophel), Chattanooga, 1964—. Chmn. adv. commn. civil rules Tenn. Supreme Ct., 1982—89, chair adv. com. drafting Tenn. rules of evidence, 1983—89, mem. bd. profl. responsibility, 1982—85, chmn. fin. com., 1984—85; bd. commrs. Hamilton County Law Libr. Contbr. chapters to books. Bd. dirs. Orange Grove Ctr., Chattanooga, 1962—99, pres., 1974—75, chmn., 1976—77; mem. bd. trustees, sec. BOTA Found., 1985—; mem. bd. trustees Carson-Newman Coll., Jefferson City, Tenn., 1975—2002, chmn. bd. trustees, 1983—87, 1990—92, mem. pres. search com., 1977, 1999—2000; mem., dir., organizer Ea. Dist. Tenn. U.S. Dist. Hist. Soc., v.p. Ea. Dist. Tenn., 1993—; mem., organizer, bd. dirs. Tenn. Supreme Ct. Hist. Soc., pres., 1997; active Hamilton County Sch. Bd., 1970—75; bd. dirs. Chattanooga Symphony, 1980—83, Chattanooga United Way, 1990—96, chmn. fund drive profl. divsn., 1992; mem. merit selection panel for Bankruptcy Judges U.S. Dist. Ct., 1993—94; mem. award com. Liberty Bell. Recipient Disting. Alumni award, Carson-Newman Coll., 1984. Fellow: Va. State Bar, Chattanooga Bar Found. (life; founder), Am. Bar Found. (life), Tenn. Bar Found. (life; founder); mem.: ABA (Tenn. Bar del. 1984—90, nominating com. 1990—99, bd. govs. 1999—2002, exec. com. 2001—02, state del., chmn. standing com. on law and litigation), Chattanooga Trial Lawyers Assn., Chattanooga Bar Assn. (pres. 1969—70, med.-legal com., pres.'s award 1995, Ralph H. Kelley Humanitarian award), Tenn. Def. Lawyers Assn., Tenn. Bar Assn. (bd. govs. 1975—82, pres. 1980—81), Conf. So. Bar Pres. (chmn. 1980—81), 6th Cir. Jud. Conf. (life), Am. Bd. Trial Advs., Estate Planning Coun. (bd. dirs. 1971—72), Am. Coll. Trial Lawyers (state com. 1995—99, profl. com. 1998—), Am. Judicature Soc., Internat. Assn. Def. Counsel, Chattanooga Rotary Club (sec. 1989—91, 1st v.p. 1997—98, pres. 2001—02), Signal Mountain Golf and Country Club, Mountain City Club, Am. Inns Ct. (master), Delta Theta Phi. Baptist. Home: 718 Parsons Ln Signal Mountain TN 37377-2704 Office: Chambliss Bahner & Stophel PC 1000 Tallan Bldg 2 Union Sq Ste 1000 Chattanooga TN 37402-2500 Office Phone: 423-756-3000. Business E-Mail: mbahner@cbslawfirm.com.

BAHR, ALICE HARRISON, librarian; b. N.Y.C., July 24, 1946; d. Arthur and Charlotte (Waterstradt) Harrison; m. Robert A. Bahr, Feb. 14, 1971; children: Aimee Marie Malone, Keith Lenert Bahr. BA, Temple U., 1968; MLS, Drexel U., 1972; MA, Lehigh U., 1975, PhD, 1980. Asst. reference libr. Lehigh U., Bethlehem, Pa., 1971-74, teaching asst., English Dept., 1974-80; instr. part-time Cedar Crest Coll., Allentown, Pa., 1980-82; project libr., govt. publs. Cedar Crest, Muhlenberg Coll. Librs., Allentown, 1980-84, project libr., online systems, 1985-88; dir. Spring Hill Coll. Libr., Mobile, Ala., 1988—. Author monographs on libr. subjects.; editor: Coll. and Undergraduate Librs.; contbr. articles profl. jours. Recipient Lawrence Henry Gipson award for 18th Century Studies, Lehigh U., 1979. Mem. Am. Libr. Assn., Ala. Libr. Assn., Network Ala. Acad. Librs. (exec. coun., publications com., chmn.). Avocation: scuba diving. Office: Spring Hill Coll Libr 4000 Dauphin St Mobile AL 36608-1780

BAHR, CARMAN BLOEDOW, internist; b. Middletown, Ohio, Mar. 24, 1931; d. Edwin Louis and Berneice Mae (Bacon) Bloedow; m. Walter Julien Bahr, Aug. 28, 1968 (dec. Sept. 1971). BA cum laude, Miami U., Oxford, Ohio, 1952; MD, Ohio State U., 1956; MS, U. Okla., 1996. Cert. diabetes educator, 1986, 92. Intern St. Luke's Hosp., Chgo., 1956-57; resident U. Okla. Health Sci. Ctr., 1957-60; assoc. prof. medicine Okla. Health Sci. Ctr., 1971-93, prof. emeritus, 1993. Fellow: ACP (Joslin 50 Yr. medal 2001); mem.: AMA (Physician's Recognition award 1976, 1979, 1982, 1985, 1988, 1991, 1994, 1998), Okla. Med. Assn., Am. Med. Women's Assn., Western Okla. Diabetes Educators, Am. Assn. Diabetes Educators, Am. Diabetes Assn. (chpt. pres. 1989, Robert Endress award 1985), Phi Beta Kappa. Home: 5609 N Everest Ave Oklahoma City OK 73111-6729 Office: VA Med Ctr 921 NE 13th St Oklahoma City OK 73104-5007 Personal E-mail: cbb2@cox.net.

BAHR, DONALD WALTER, retired chemical engineer; b. Chgo., Dec. 13, 1927; s. Walter James and Justine Antonia (Schwegler) Bahr; m. Mary Estelle Zieverink, Oct. 15, 1960; children: Donald Walter Jr., Susan Mary. BS ChemE, U. Ill., 1949; MSChemE, MS in Gas Tech., Ill. Inst. Tech., 1951. Registered Profl. Engr., Ohio. Aero rsch. scientist Lewis Flight Propulsion Lab. NASA, Cleve., 1951—54; chem. engr. GE Co., Cin., 1956—62, engring. mgr. Phila., 1962—68, GE Aircraft Engines, Phila., 1968—94. Vice chmn. jet engine fuels panel NASA Lewis Rsch. Ctr., Cleve., 1973—76. Contbr. articles to profl. jours. 1st lt. USAF, 1954—56. Named to Propulsion Hall of Fame for GE, 1995; recipient Outstanding Engring. Achievement award, GE Co., 1982. Fellow: ASME (combustion and fuels com. 1975—, vice chmn. combustion and fuels com. 1985—87, chmn.combustion and fuels com. 1987—89, Tom Sawyer award 1998, Aircraft Engine Tech. award 2003), AIAA (Air Breathing Propulsion award 1983); mem.: NAE, Coordinating Rsch. Coun. (aviation fuel, lubricant and other equpment com.), Gen. Aviation Mfrs. Assn. (environ. com.), Aerospace Industries Assn. (chmn. aircraft engine emissions com. 1971—95), Combustion Inst. (bd. advisors ctrl. states sect. 1986—, chmn. bd. advisors 1993—95, chmn. ctrl. states sect. 1995—97). Republican. Roman Catholic. Home: 12195 Pickwick Pl Cincinnati OH 45241-1791

BAHR, EHRHARD, Germanic languages and literature educator; b. Kiel, Germany, Aug. 21, 1932; came to U.S., 1956; s. Klaus and Gisela (Badenhausen) B.; m. Diana Meyers, Nov. 21, 1973; stepchildren: Gary, Timothy, Christopher. Student, U. Heidelberg, Germany, 1952-53, U. Freiburg, 1953-56; MS Ed. (Fulbright scholar), U. Kans., 1956-58; postgrad., U. Cologne, 1959-61; PhD, U. Calif., Berkeley, 1968. Asst. prof. German UCLA, 1968-70, assoc. prof., 1970-72, prof., 1972—2003, prof. emeritus, 2003—, chmn. dept. Germanic langs., 1981-84, 93-98, chair grad. council, 1988-89. Author: Irony in the Late Works of Goethe, 1972, Georg Lukacs, 1970, Ernst Bloch, 1974, Nelly Sachs, 1980; editor: Kant, What is Enlightenment?, 1974, Goethe, Wilhelm, Meister's Apprenticeship, 1982, Goethe, Wilhelm, Meister's Journeyman Years, 1982, History of German Literature, 3 vols., 1987—88, 2nd edit., 1998—99, The Novel as Archive: The Genesis, Reception and Criticism of Goethe's Wilhelm Meisters Wanderjahre, 1988; co-editor: The Internalized Revolution: German Reactions to the French Revolution, 1789-1989, 1992; commentary Thomas Mann: Death in Venice, 1991, reprint, 2005, Goethe: Wilhelm Meisner's Apprenticeship, 1982; contbr. articles to profl. jour. Recipient Disting. Teaching award UCLA, 1970, Humanities Inst. award, 1972, summer stipend NEH, 1978 Mem. MLA, Am. Soc. 18th Century Studies, Am. Assn. Tchrs. German, Western Soc. 18th Century Studies, German Studies Assn. (pres. 1987-88), Pacific Ancient & Modern Lang. Assn., Lessing Soc., Goethe Soc. N.Am. (exec. sec. 1979-89, pres. 1995-97). Office: UCLA Dept Germanic Langs Los Angeles CA 90095-1539 Business E-Mail: bahr@humnet.ucla.edu.

BAHR, ELAINE S., history instructor; d. Robert and Janice Bahr. AA, Ellsworth C.C., 1997; BA in History, U. No. Iowa, 1999; MA, Iowa State U., 2003. Vista vol., Fort Dodge, Iowa, 1999—2000; grad. tchg. asst. Iowa State U., Ames, Iowa, 2000—03; rsch. intern Anacostia Mus. African-Am. History and Culture, Anacostia, 2003; casual carrier US Postal Svc., Iowa Falls, Iowa, 2003—04; adj. history instr. Ellsworth C.C., Iowa Falls, 2004—. Grad. rep. Alluniv. Jud. Bd., 2001—03. Judge Nat. History Day, College Park, Md., 2003—04, spl. awards coord. Des Moines, 2003—04. Mem.: Iowa Falls Hist. Assn. (assoc.), Am. Hist. Assn. (assoc.). Avocations: genealogy, scrapbooking, travel.

BAHR, JANE MARIE, writer, retired language educator; BS in English, U. Wis., River Falls, 1971; MST in English, U. Wis., Whitewater, 1978. English tchr. Whitewater (Wis.) H.S., 1973—82, Eau Claire (Wis.) Meml. H.S., 1985, Glenwood City H.S., summers 1990-91; freelance writer Wis. Fellowship of Poets, 1981—, Wis. Regional Writers' Assn., 1985—, Wis. Arts Bd. Grant, 1998. Author poems in numerous publs. including Wis. Poets' Calendars, Poetry Out of Wis. V, Free Verse, Poetry Motel, Wallpaper Broadside Series, Poesy and others WRWA Soar scholar Sch. of Arts, U. Wis., Madison, 1999.

BAHR, LAUREN S., publishing executive; b. New Brunswick, NJ, July 3, 1944; d. Simon A. and Rosalind J. Bahr. Student, U. Grenoble, France, 1964; BA (Branstrom scholar), MA, U. Mich., 1966. Asst. editor New Horizons Pubs., Inc., Chgo., 1967, Scholastic Mags., Inc., N.Y.C., 1968-71; supervising editor Houghton Mifflin Co., Boston, 1971; product devel. editor Appleton-Century-Crofts, N.Y.C., 1972-74; sponsoring editor McGraw-Hill, Inc., N.Y.C., 1974-75; editor Today's Sec. mag., 1975-77; sr. editor Media Systems Corp., N.Y.C., 1978; sr. editor coll. dept. CBS Coll. Pub., N.Y.C., 1978-82, mktg. mgr. fgn. langs., dir. mktg. adminstrn., 1982-83; from dir. devel. coll. divsn. to pub. cons. Harper & Row, N.Y.C., 1983-91; v.p., editl. dir. Atlas

Edits., Inc., N.Y.C., 1991-98; dir. publs. Bank St. Coll. Edn., N.Y.C., 1999—2000; mng. editor Inkwell Pub., N.Y.C., 2000—02; editl. dir. 4 Lakes Colorgraphics, 2002—. Democrat. Jewish. Home: 444 E 82nd St New York NY 10028-5903

BAHRANI, ZAINAB, education educator; BA, Ind. U., 1981; MA, N.Y.U. Inst. of Fine Arts, 1984, PhD, 1989. Assoc. prof. of art history and archaeology Columbia U., 2002—; prof. U. Vienna, SUNY Stonybrook. Curator Met. Mus. Art. Grantee, Am. Schools of Oriental Rsch., The Met. Mus. of Art, Getty Found., Guggenheim. Office: 1190 Amsterdam Ave New York NY 10027

BAHRE, JEANNETTE, language educator, librarian; b. Darby, Pa., Dec. 28, 1948; d. Paul Florent and Jeanne S. Gibson; m. Stephen Alan Bahre, May 14, 1974; children: Kimberly, Christian, Rachael. BA, Merrimack Coll., 1970; MEd, U. Ariz., 1979. Cert. experienced tchr., NH; English tchr., tutor, libr., Mass. Tchr. English and social studies, Mass., 1970—; libr. St. Augustine Sch., Andover, Mass., 1980-83, Beverly Sch. for Deaf, Mass., 1988-89; instr. No. Essex C.C., Haverhill, Mass., 1982-84, libr. evening svc., 1986-88; tchr., advisor Linton Hall Sch., Bristow, Va., 1985-86; lectr. George Mason U., Fairfax, Va., 1985-86; tchr., tutor Even Start: Family Lit. Project, Amesbury, Mass., 1990-93; Chpt. I tutor Seabrook Elem. Sch., NH, 1994-95; libr. So. Hampton Pub. Libr., NH, 1994—99. Summer seminar for tchr. Univ. N.H., N.H. Humanities Found., 1997; tchr. Family Scrapbooks program New England Found. Humanities, Lawrence, Mass., 1997; participant summer seminar for tchr. U. NH NHH Found., 1997, 2001; tutor, 1970—. Editor Four Winds, adult student Lit. Jour., 1992-96. Grantee NEH, 1988.

BAHRIM, CRISTIAN, physicist, educator; b. Bucharest, Romania, June 8, 1967; arrived in US, 1998; s. Corneliu and Elena Bahrim; m. Bogdana Mioara, June 28, 1967. BS, H.S. Math & Physics, Bucharest, 1985; MS, U. Bucharest, 1991; PhD, U. Paris XI, 1997. Rsch. asst. Nat. Inst. Lasers, Plasma and Radiation, Bucharest, 1991-97, prin. sci. rschr., 1998-99; rsch. assoc. J. R. MacDonald Lab. Kans. State U., Manhattan, 1998—2001; asst. prof. dept. chemistry and physics Lamar U., Beaumont, Tex., 2001—, asst. prof. dept. elec. engring., 2005—. Contbr. articles to profl. jours. Scholar French Govt., 1992-96. Mem. Romanian Phys. Soc., French Optical Soc., Am. Phys. Soc., Am. Assn. Advancement Sci. Romanian Orthodox. Avocations: history, astronomy, biology, sports. Office: Lamar U Dept of Chem and Physics Beaumont TX 77710 Office Phone: bahrimcx@hal.lamar.edu, 409-880-8290.

BAI, QIANSHEN, art historian, educator; BA, Peking U., 1982; MA in Polit. Sci., Rutgers U., 1990; MA in Hist. Art, Yale U., 1992, MPhil in Hist. Art, 1993, PhD in Hist. Art, 1996. Instr. Asian art hist. Western Mich. U., Dept. Art, 1995, asst. prof. Asian art hist., 1996—97, Boston U., 1997—. Vis. asst. prof. Harvard U., Dept. of Hist. of Art and Architecture, 2002. Fellow Guggenheim Meml. Found., 2004. Mem.: Calligraphy Overview (mem. adv. bd. 1987—), Canglang Calligraphy Soc. (founding mem. 1982—92). Office: Boston U Art Hist Dept 725 Commonwealth Ave, Rm 302 Boston MA 02215 Office Phone: 617-353-2520.*

BAICA, MALVINA FLORICA, mathematician, educator, researcher; b. Oravita, Banat, Romania, Nov. 3, 1942; came to U.S., 1968, naturalized, 1973; d. Adam and Cornelia (Stefan) Bunghiu; m. Adrian Baica, Sept. 14, 1963. BS in Math. and Physics, U. Timisoara, Romania, 1964, MS in Math., 1965, Ill. Inst. Tech., 1974; PhD in Math., U. Houston, 1980. Asst. prof. Western Ill. U., Macomb, 1978-80, Marquette U., Milw., 1980-81, Marshall U., Huntington, W.Va., 1981-83, Valparaiso (Ind.) U., 1983-84, U. Wis., Whitewater, 1984—89, assoc. prof., 1989—92, prof., 1992—. Contbr. articles to profl. jour.s on algebraic number theory and number theory. Recipient U. Wis. Excellence in Rsch. award, 1988. Mem. N.Y. Acad. Scis., Pi Mu Epsilon. Achievements include development of an algorithm in a complex field which turned out to be the Generalized Euclidean Algorithm and The Euler System of the Algebraic Number Theory used to approach unsolved problems in algebraic number theory and number theory including Fermat's Last Theorem in Euclidean; discovery of Baica's trigonometric identities; research in algebraic number theory and number theory. Office Phone: 262-472-1716. Business E-Mail: baicam@uww.edu.

BAIER, BRET, news correspondent; Bachelor's Degree in Polit. Sci. and English, DePauw Univ., Greencastle, Ind. Production asst. CNN; anchor, reporter WJWJ-TV, Beaufort, SC; polit. reporter, substitute anchor WRAL-TV (CBS), Raleigh, NC; weekend anchor WREX-TV (NBC), Rockford, Ill.; reporter FOX News Channel, Atlanta, 1998, nat. security corr. Recipient SC Associated Press award for Superior TV Journalism. Office: FOX News Channel 1211 Avenue of the Americas New York NY 10036*

BAIER, EDWARD JOHN, retired public health service officer, industrial hygiene engineer, consultant; b. Pitts., Apr. 1, 1925; s. Edward O. and Lucy M. Baier; m. Grace Cecelia McDonald, Jan. 15, 1947; children: Edward Michael, Grace Cecelia. BS, U. Pitts., 1946, MPH (fellow), 1955. Lic. indsl. hygienist Ill., cert. internat. hazard control mgmt. Hazard Control Mgr. Cert. Bd., hazardous materials mgmt. Inst. Hazardous Materials Mgmt., safety profl. Bd. Cert. Safety Profls. Chief indsl. hygiene sect. Dept. Health State of Pa., 1956-68, dir. divsn. occupl. health, 1968-71, Dept. Environ. Resources, 1971; dir. Bur. Mines and Occupl. Health and Safety, 1971-72; dep. dir. Nat. Inst. for Occupl. Safety and Health, HEW, Rockville, Md., 1972-78; corp. dir. indsl. hygiene and toxicology Diamond Shamrock Corp., Cleve., Dallas, 1978-82; dir. tech. support OSHA, Dept. Labor, 1982-89; cons. in occupl. and environ. health and safety, 1989—. Lectr. in field. Contbr. articles to profl. jours. Chmn. West Shore coun. Boy Scouts Am., 1970-71; sec. Upper Allen Twp. (Pa.) Sewer Authority, 1970-72. Fellow Am. Indsl. Hygiene Assn. (pres. 1975-76, Cummings Meml. award 1982, Edward J. Baier Tech. Achievement award 1984); mem. Am. Conf. Govt. Indsl. Hygienists (chmn. 1968-69), Am. Acad. Indsl. Hygiene (founder, pres. 1987-88), Indsl. Hygiene Roundtable (steward 1975-76), Inst. Hazardous Materials Mgmt. (cert. hazardous materials mgrs. bd. examiners 1991—, bd. dirs., vice chmn. 1993-2001, Disting. Diplomate award 2001), Nat. Am. Indian Safety Coun., N.Y. Acad. Scis., Pa. Soc. Profl. Engrs., Am. Bd. Indsl. Hygiene (bd. dirs. 1970-76). Roman Catholic. Office Phone: 703-743-5186.

BAIER, JOYCE F., science educator, department chairman; d. J Frank and Maryanna A Baier. BA, Ursuline Coll., 1964—67; MA, Wesleyan U., 1970—73. Permanent High School Standard Ohio Dept. of Edn., 1978. Sci. and math tchr. St. John H.S., Ashtabula, Ohio, 1967—70, Villa Maria H.S., Pa., 1970—74; sci. tchr. Magnificat H.S., Rocky River, Ohio, 1974—83, Ctrl. Cath. H.S., Canton, 1983—87, St. Vincent-St. Mary H.S., Akron, 1987—89; math. tchr. Cleve. Mcpl. Schools, 1989—91; sci. and math tchr. Bklyn. City Schools, Ohio, 1991—. Copresenter, physics modeling workshop U. of Akron, Ohio, 2001. Fin. decisions Bklyn Sch. Employees Credit Union, 1997—2005. Recipient Jennings Scholar, Martha Holden Jennings Found., 2000; Summer Study grant, Wake Forest U. NSF, 1968, U. of SI: NSF, 1985, U. of Akron (OH), 2000, Wesleyan U.: NSF, 1970, 1971, 1972. Mem.: Nat. Coun. of Teachers of Math., Nat. Assn. of Secondary Sch. Principals, Assn. of Supervision and Curriculum Devel., NSTA, Am. Assn. of Physics Teachers. Avocations: gardening, yoga, puzzles, reading. Office: Bklyn City Sch Dist 9200 Biddulph Rd Brooklyn OH 44144 Office Phone: 216-485-8191. E-mail: joyce.baier@lnoca.org.

BAIER, LUCINDA, corporate financial executive; BS in acctg., MS in acctg., Ill. State U. Self employed, 1984—87; experienced tax staff Arthur Andersen, 1987—89, experienced tax sr., 1989—90, tax mgr., 1990—93; corp. dir., taxes Gen. Dynamics, 1993—97; tax dir. ICI Americas, 1997, v.p. taxation, 1998, v.p. fin., 1998—99; sr. v.p. fin., tax and treas. US Office Products, 1999, sr. v.p. merchandising, 1999—2000; v.p., taxes Sears, Roebuck and Co., 2000—01, v.p. fin. credit services and fin. products, 2001—03, sr. v.p., gen. mgr., credit and fin. products, 2003—. Mem.: Executives Club of Chgo.

BAIER, ROBERT EDWARD, chemist, educator; b. Buffalo, Oct. 31, 1939; s. Harry Edward Baier and Florence Elizabeth (Manno) Militello; m. Corinne May Bongiovanni, Sept. 9, 1961; children: Valerie Ann, Anne Marie. BS in Engring. and Physics, Cleve. State U., 1962; PhD in Biophysics, SUNY, Buffalo, 1966. Registered profl. engr., Ohio, N.Y. Postdoctoral fellow NAS-NRC, Washington, 1966-68; rsch. physicist Cornell Aero. Lab., Buffalo, 1968-72; staff scientist Calspan Advanced Tech. Ctr., Buffalo, 1972-84; rsch. prof. biophys. scis. SUNY, Buffalo, 1983—, exec. dir. NSF Industry/U. Coop. Rsch. Ctr., 1988—; exec. dir. Ctr. for Advanced Tech. in Healthcare, Buffalo, 1985-89; prof., dir. biomaterials grad. program SUNY, 1998—. Mem. Soc. Biomaterials (mem. coun., sec.-treas., pres. 1974—). Home: 37 Rosedale Blvd Buffalo NY 14226-3347 Office: SUNY 110 Parker Hall Buffalo NY 14214-3007 Office Phone: 716-829-3560. Business E-Mail: baier@buffalo.edu.

BAIER, ROSA, public health service officer; BA, Wellesley Coll., Mass., 2000; MPH, Brown U., Providence, 2004. Rsch. asst. Policy Analysis, Inc., Brookline, Mass., 2001—02; project coord. Quality Partners of RI, Providence, 2002—. Scholar, Brown U., 2002—04. Mem.: RI Pub. Health Assn. Achievements include research in nursing home quality of care. Office: Quality Partners of Rhode Island 235 Promenade Street Suite 500 Box 18 Providence RI 02906 Office Phone: 401-528-3205. E-mail: rbaier@riqio.sdps.org.

BAIER, SUSAN LOVEJOY, music educator; b. Canandaigua, N.Y., Jan. 30, 1953; m. Michael Francis Baier, July 17, 1976; children: Michael Franklin, Kimberly Lovejoy. MusB magna cum laude, Grove City Coll., 1975; EdM, Converse Coll., 1994. Cert. tchr. S.C. String tchr. Akron (Ohio) Pub. Schs., 1975—76; Suzuki violin tchr. Jewish Cmty. Ctr., Pitts., 1976—78, Carnegie Mellon U. Pre-Coll., Pitts., 1976—78; string tchr. Spartanburg (S.C.) County Dist. 7, 1979—94, Spartanburg (S.C.) County Dist. 6, 1994—2002, dist. orch. coord., 2002—. Violinst Greater Spartanburg Philharm., 1995—; mem. string quintet, violin soloist Nazareth Presbyn. Ch., Moore, SC, 1995—. Named Outstanding Tchr., Tchg. Music mag., 2000. Mem.: S.C. Music Educators Assn. (orch. divsn., festival chmn., all-state chmn., treas., pres.-elect, pres.), Am. String Tchrs. with Nat. Sch. Orch. Assn., Music Educators Nat. Conf. Office: Dorman HS 1050 Cavalier Way Roebuck SC 29376 Office Phone: 864-342-8943. E-mail: baierl@spartanburg6.k12.sc.us.

BAIGIS, JUDITH ANN, nursing educator, academic administrator; b. Washington, Pa., July 26, 1941; d. Andrew J. and Mary Margaret (Mitchell) Baigis; m. Robert Wachbroit, June 26, 1989. Diploma, Geisinger Hosp. Sch. Nursing, Danville, Pa., 1962; BS, NYU, 1968, PhD, 1979. RN, Md., D.C. Instr. nursing NYU, N.Y.C., 1970-73, CUNY Lehman Coll., Bronx, N.Y., 1973-79; dir. community health nursing program U. Pa. Sch. Nursing, Phila., 1979-87; dir. long-term care Johns Hopkins U. Sch. Nursing, Balt., 1987-92; assoc. dean for rsch. Georgetown U. Sch. Nursing, Washington, 1992—, interim dean, 1998-99, prof., 1992—. Contbr. articles to nursing jours. Nat. Inst. Nursing Rsch. grantee, 1988-96. Mem. ANA, APHA, Am. Acad. Nursing, Assn. Community Health Nursing Educators. Office: Georgetown U Sch Nursing Box 571107 3700 Reservoir Rd NW Washington DC 20007-2111 Office Phone: 202-687-5127. Business E-Mail: baigisj@georgetown.edu.

BAIK-HAN, WON H., pediatrician, educator, consultant; b. Seoul, Jong Ro Gu, Republic of Korea, July 22, 1956; arrived in U.S., 1983; d. Hong In Baik and Ok Hee Chang; m. Muyol Han, Nov. 15, 1986; children: Jeffrey J. Han, Steven J. Han. MD, Ewha Woman's U., Seoul, 1981. Diplomate Am. Bd. Pediat. Intern Soon Chun Hyang U. Hosp., Seoul, Republic of Korea, 1981—82, resident in pediat., 1982—83; pediat. externship St. Elizabeth Hosp. Ctr., Youngstown, Ohio, 1983—84; vol. pediat. physician Flushing (N.Y.) Hosp. Med. Ctr., 1984—86, resident in pediat., 1986—89; fellow in allergy and clin. immunology St. Luke's/Roosevelt Hosp. Ctr., N.Y.C., 1989—91; clin. fellow in allergy & immunology and medicine Columbia U., N.Y.C., 1989—91; dir. pediat. allergy and immunology Flushing (N.Y.) Hosp. Med. Ctr., 1991—, dir. pediat. allergy and asthma clinic, 1991—, consulting physician medicine and pediat., 1991—, com. mem. pharmacy therapeutic com., 1999—. Dir. pediat. allergy Wyckoff Heights Med. Ctr., Bklyn., 1995—99; consulting physician pediat., allergy and immunology N.Y. Hosp. Queens, Flushing, 1997—2000; dir. pediat. allergy clinic Jamaica (N.Y.) Hosp. Med. Ctr., 2000—; asst. prof. pediat. Albert Einstein Coll. Medicine, Bronx, 1994—96, asst. clin. prof. pediat., 1999—; clin. asst. prof. pediat. Cornell U. Med. Coll., N.Y.C., 1997—99; regional spkr. allergy immunology Schering Plough Pharm. Co., NJ, 2001—. Author (with D.M. Rubin): Pediatric Emergency Medicine-Self Assessment and Review, 1994; author: (with A. Stock) Allergic & Immunologic Disease: Pediatric Emergency Medicine-Self Assessment and Review, 2nd edit., 1998. Consulting physician The Korean Am. Nail Assn. N.Y., Inc., Flushing, 1998—, The Korean Sr. Citizen Ctr., Corona, NY, 1999—. Recipient Presentation award for allergy and asthma, Soon Chun Hyang U. Hosp., Seoul, 1992, Physicians Recognition award, AMA, 1999—, Contbn. award for Korean Health Fair, Korean-Am. Nail Assn. N.Y., Inc., Flushing, 1999. Fellow: Am. Acad. Pediat.; mem.: Coalition for Asian Am. Children and Families (com. mem.), N.Y. Allergy, Asthma and Immunology Soc., Am. Acad. Allergy, Asthma and Immunology (Travel Grand award for rsch. project 1991), Hunter Coll. H.S. Korean-Am. Parents Assn. (pres. 2002—). Avocations: drawing and painting, playing pingpong and tennis, singing, collecting coins, stamps and collectibles, collecting antiques. Office: 1st Fl 143-20 Sanford Ave Flushing NY 11355 Office Phone: 718-460-3943.

BAILAR, BARBARA ANN, retired statistician; b. Monroe, Mich., Nov. 24, 1935; d. Malcolm Laurie and Clara Florence (Parent) Dezendorf; m. John Francis Powell (div. 1966); 1 child, Pamela; m. John Christian Bailar; 1 child, Melissa. BA, SUNY, 1956; MS, Va. Poly. Inst., 1965; PhD, Am. U., 1972. With Bur. of Census, Washington, 1958-88, chief Ctr. Rsch. Measurement Methods, 1973-79, assoc. dir. for statis. standards and methodology, 1979-88; exec. dir. Am. Statis. Assn., Alexandria, Va., 1988-95; sr. v.p. for survey rsch. Nat. Opinion Rsch. Ctr., Chgo., 1995—2001. Instr. George Washington U., 1984-85; head dept. math. and stats. USDA Grad. Sch., Washington, 1972-87. Contbr. articles, book chpts. to profl. publs. Pres. bd. dirs. Harbour Sq. Coop., Washington, 1988-89. Recipient Silver medal U.S. Dept. Commerce, 1980. Fellow Am. Statis. Assn. (pres. 1987); mem. AAAS (chair sect. stats. 1984-85), Internat. Assn. Survey Statisticians (pres. 1989-91), Internat. Statis. Inst. (Pres.'s invited speaker 1983, v.p. 1993-95), Cosmos Club. Personal E-mail: babailar@aol.com.

BAILAR, GREGOR S., finance company executive; BSEE, Dartmouth Coll. Various positions Perot Sys. Corp., Next Computer, Inc., and Hewlett Packard Co.; mng. dir. and v.p. for advanced devel. for global corp. banking Citicorp, 1994—98; chief info. officer & exec. v.p. ops. and tech. NASD, 1997—2001; exec. v.p. & chief info. officer Capital One Fin., Va., 2001—. Bd. dir. Digitas, Inc. Named one of top tech. innovators, Info. Week mag., 2004. Office: EVP & CIO Capital One Fin 1680 Capital One Dr Mc Lean VA 22102

BAILE, CLIFTON A., biologist, researcher; b. Warrensburg, Mo., Feb. 8, 1940; s. Harold F. and Salome (Mohler) B.; m. Beth Lucile Hoover, Aug. 21, 1960; children: Christopher A., Marisa B. BS in Agr., Bus., Cen. Mo. State U., 1962; PhD in Nutrition, U. Mo., 1965; MA (hon.), U. Pa., 1979. NIH rsch. fellow Sch. Pub. Health Harvard U., Boston, 1964-66, from. instr. to asst. prof. Sch. Pub. Health, 1966-71; mgr. neurobiol. rsch. SmithKline Animal Health, Phila., 1971-75; from assoc. prof. to prof. Sch. Vet. Medicine U. Pa., Phila., 1975-82; disting. fellow, dir. R & D Monsanto Agrl. Co., St. Louis, 1982-95; adj. prof. nutrition Sch. Medicine Washington U., St. Louis, 1982-95; adj. prof. dept. animal sci. U. Mo., 1982-95; dist. prof. animal sci. and food and nutrition U. Ga., Athens, 1995—; Ga. Rsch. Alliance Eminent scholar Agrl. Biotech., Athens, 1996—; CEO, ProLinia, Inc., 1999—. Presenter in field. Contbr. over 300 articles to sci. publs. Rsch. fellow Ralston Purina, 1962-64, spl. postdoctoral fellow NIH, 1969; recipient Georgia Lamar Dodd award, 2002. Mem. Am. Soc. Animal Sci. (bd. dirs. 1990-93, animal growth and devel. award 1989), Am. Physiol. Soc., Am. Inst. Nutrition, Am. Dairy Sci. Assn. (Am. Feed Mgmt. award 1979), Soc. Neurosci., Endocrine Soc. Achievements include 17 patents in field; research in control and feed intake and regulation of energy balance. Office: U Ga 444 ADS Complex Athens GA 30602-2771 Office Phone: 706-542-4094. Business E-Mail: cbaile@uga.edu.

BAILEY, ADAM SEAN, management consultant; b. Rome, Ga., Apr. 5, 1974; s. Adam Bailey and Brenda Hall-Bailey. BA in Psychology, Morehouse Coll., 1998; MPA, Ga. State U., 2001. Tech. and ops. officer Bank of Am., Atlanta, 1995—2000; mgmt. analyst Nat. Cancer Inst., Rockville, Md., 2001—. Active Habitat for Humanity, Atlanta, 1999—2001. Mem.: Am. Soc. for Pub. Adminstrs., Kappa Alpha Psi. Avocation: tennis, reading, racquet ball. Office: Nat Cancer Inst 6116 Executive Blvd Ste 603 Rockville MD 20852 Home: 1232 46th St SE Washington DC 20019

BAILEY, AMOS PURNELL, clergyman, journalist, writer; b. Grotons, Va., May 2, 1918; s. Louis William and Evelyn (Charnock) B.; m. Ruth Martin Hill, Aug. 22, 1942 (dec. 1992); children: Eleanor Carol Bailey Harriman, Anne Ruth Bailey Page, Joyce Elizabeth Bailey Richardson, Jeanne Bailey Dodge-Allen; m. Betty Lou Sheffield, Mar. 5, 1994. BA, Randolph-Macon Coll., 1942, DD, 1956; BD, Duke U., 1948; ThM, Union Theol. Sem., 1957; postgrad., Ecumenical Inst., Jerusalem, 1977. Ordained to ministry United Meth. Ch., 1942; pastor Emporia, Va., 1938, Beulah UMC Ch., Richmond, Va., 1938-43, New Kent circuit, 1943-44, Oak Grove United Meth. Ch., Norfolk, Va., 1948-50, Grace United Meth. Ch., Newport News, 1950-54, Centenary Ch., Richmond, 1954-61; supt. Richmond dist. United Meth. Ch., 1961-67; sr. minister Reveille Ch., Richmond, 1967-70; assoc. gen. sec., div. chaplains Bd. Higher Edn. and Ministry United Meth. Ch., Washington, 1970-79; v.p. Nat. Meth. Found., 1979-82; interim minister Herndon Ch., 1985-86; pres., CEO Nat. Temple Ministries, Inc., Fredericksburg, Va., 1982—. Pres. S.E.J. and S.C.U. Comms., 1968-76; dir. Reeves-Parvin Co., 1978-85; v.p. Va. Conf. Bd. Missions, 1955-61, Meth. Commn. Town and Country Work, 1956-67; mem. Meth. Commn. on Higher Edn., 1960-70, Meth. Interbd. Coun., 1960-70; del. Southeastern Jurisdictional Conf., 1964, 68, Gen. Conf., 1964, 66, 68, 70, World Meth. Conf., London, 1966, Denver, 1970, Dublin, 1976, Rio de Janeiro, 1996; exec. com. Congress, 1987-88; fin. com. Nat. Ch. Growth Rsch. Ctr., 1986-89; frequent chaplain U.S. Senate, U.S. Ho. of Reps., Va. Gen. Assembly; mem. coun., exec. com., pres. comms. com. Southeastern Jurisdiction, 1968-76; pres. Joint Comms. Com., 1968-76; vice chmn. Ministry to Svc. Pers. in East Asia, 1972-79; mem. Commn. on Interpretation, Va. Conf. Bd. Ordained Ministry, 1974-82; participant Ednl. Study Mission to Eng., 1988. Author: Daily Bread, 1997, Daily Bread, The Second Slice, 1999; syndicated columnist Daily Bread, 1945— (50th Anniversary award 1995), syndicated radio devotional, 1945-69; condr. weekly radio counseling program The Night Pastor, 1955-69, Sunshine and Shadows, 1967-70; contbr. articles to profl. jours. Mem. exec. com. Va. Conf. Bd. Edn., 1968-72; mem. World Meth. Coun., Va. Commn. Aging; pres. adv. bd. Richmond Welfare Dept., 1956-68, Va. Conf. Bd. Ministry, Richmond Pub. Assistance Com., Richmond Coun. Alcoholism, Citizen Adv. Bd. Duke U. Comprehensive Cancer Ctr., 1995-01; group chmn. industry divsn. Richmond United Givers Fund, 1961; chmn. chaplains adv. coun. VA, Washington; bd. mgrs. Richmond YMCA, 1961-69; bd. dirs. Va. Meth. Advisers; trustee Randolph-Macon Coll., 1960-82, trustee emeritus, 1986; bd. visitors Duke Div. Sch., 1964-70; trustee So. Sem., 1961-76. With Chaplains Corps AUS, 1945-47. Recipient Disting. Alumni award, Duke Div. Sch., 2001; scholar A. Purnell Bailey Preministerial, Randolph-Macon Coll., 2002; Two Million Dollar scholar fund, 2002. Mem.: DAV (life), Duke Div. Alumni Assn. (pres.), Meth. Hist. Soc., Kiwanis, Kiwanis Club. Home: Apt 1312 12100 Chancellors Village Ln Fredericksburg VA 22407-6595 Office: PO Box 41296 Fredericksburg VA 22404-1296 Personal E-mail: b17815@verizon.net. *Life for me is rich and meaningful in a Christian commitment which allows a free and unfettered search for truth. Discipline of time and resources, the love of persons in my sphere of activity, a devoted family — all are part of the life I cherish daily.*

BAILEY, AUDRA JO, music educator; b. Davenport, Iowa, Apr. 24, 1981; d. Allen Ray and Kristi Lyn Bailey. B Music Edn., St. Ambrose U., Davenport, Iowa, 2003. Cert. Tchr.Music Iowa. Band dir. Calmers-Wheaton Sch., Iowa, 2003—04, Pleasant Valley Conf. Schs., Iowa, 2004—. Mem. Quad Cities Wind Ensemble, 2001—; head labor-mgmt. com. Pleasant Valley Sch. Conf., Iowa, 2004—. Mem.: Music Educators Nat. Conf., S.E. Iowa Bandmasters Assn., Iowa Bandmasters Assn. Avocations: running, wind instruments. Home: 2338 W 40th St Davenport IA 52806 Office: Pleasant Valley Jr HS PO Box332 Pleasant Valley IA 52767 E-mail: audrabailey@hamptonroads.net.

BAILEY, BARRY STONE, sculptor, educator; b. High Point, N.C., Oct. 21, 1952; s. Richard Junior and Dorothy (Harris) B. MFA, East Carolina U., 1978. Sculptor, New Orleans, 1980—; curator, visual arts coord. Contemporary Arts Ctr., New Orleans, 1980-82; curator La. World Expo., New Orleans, 1984; instr. La. State U., Baton Rouge, 1985; prof. U. Ga., Cortona, Italy, 1992, 96, 2002; asst. prof. Tulane U., New Orleans, 1989-93, assoc. prof., 1993—. Grantee: Sculpture grant for Italy, Ford Found., Cortona, Italy, 1977, NEA/So. Arts Found., 1987. Office: Tulane U Newcomb Art Dept - Sculpture New Orleans LA 70118 Business E-Mail: bailey@tulane.edu.

BAILEY, BEATRICE NAFF, language educator, researcher; b. Roanoke, Va., July 7, 1957; d. Wesley W. Jr. and Angelia (Hunt) Naff; m. William Glenn Bailey, Nov. 5, 1994. BA in English, Longwood Coll., 1979; MA in Theology, Bethany Theol. Sem., 1981; EdD, Va Tech., 1987. Prof. Clemson (S.C.) U., 1991—, dir. Clemson Writing Project, 1993—. Author: Our Upcountry: Teachers and Students Write About Place, 2000, Literacy Clubs for At Risk Girls, 1988, (with others) Religious Schools and America, 1988, Planning Models Matter in English Education, 1989. Recipient A.L. Burruss Rsch. and Svc. award, 1991, Good Apple award SCCTE, 1998, Career Woman of Yr. award Easley Bus. and Profl. Women, 1998. Mem. Nat. Coun. Tchrs. English (Promising Researcher award 1988, Richard Meade rsch. award 1990), Nat. Conf. Rsch. English, Phi Delta Kappa (Rsch. award 1988). Avocations: golf, tennis, collecting nativity scenes. Office: Clemson U 401 Tillman Hl # B Clemson SC 29634-0001

BAILEY, BLAKE, writer; b. Sept. 12, 1946; BBA, Tex. Christian U., 1970; JD, Baylor U., 1973. Coop. atty. United Auto Workers; pres. East Tex. Trial Lawyers Assn., 1996—97. Author: Zapatista, 2001, The Edge of the Cave, 2001, A Tragic Honesty: The Life and Work of Richard Yates, 2003. Mem.: ABA, ATLA, Am. Bd. Trial Advs. (diplomate), Tex. Bar Assn.

BAILEY, BURCK, lawyer; b. Vinita, Okla., Aug. 22, 1934; s. Frank and Frances (Burckhalter) B.; m. Sandra Barnett, Apr. 17, 1981. BA, Westminster Coll., 1958; LLB, NYU, 1961. Bar: Mo. 1961, Okla. 1963, U.S. Supreme Ct. 1969. Assoc. Morrison, Hecker, Cozad & Morrison, Kansas City, Mo., 1961-63; asst. atty. gen. State of Okla., Oklahoma City, 1963-66; ptnr. Duval, Head, McKinney & Bailey, Oklahoma City, 1966-67, Fellers, Snider, Blankenship, Bailey & Tippens, Oklahoma City, 1967—. Fellow Am. Coll. Trial Lawyers (state chmn. 1993), Internat. Acad. Trial Lawyers, Am. Bar Found.; mem. ABA (ho. dels. 1987-88), Am. Acad. Appellate Lawyers, Okla. Bar Assn. (pres. 1988), Okla. County Bar Assn. (pres. 1983-84, mem. Okla. Jud. nominating commn. 1997-2003). Office: Fellers Snider Blankenship Bailey & Tippens 100 N Broadway Ste 1700 Oklahoma City OK 73102 Office Phone: 405-232-0621.

BAILEY, CARRIE E., music educator; b. Reading, Pa., Feb. 1, 1977; d. Richard Carl and Sharon Elizabeth Francis. MusB, West Chester (Pa.) U., 1999. Tchr. Carrie Francis Flute Studio, Hamburg, Pa., 1993, St. James Cathedral Sch., Orlando, Fla., St. James Conservatory of Performing Arts, Orlando, Fla. Mem.: Music Tchr. Nat. Assn., Pi Kappa Lambda. Home: 5231 Albert Dr Winter Park FL 32792

BAILEY, CECIL DEWITT, aerospace engineer, educator; b. Zama, Miss., Oct. 25, 1921; s. James Dewitt and Matha Eugenia (Roberts) B.; m. Myrtis Irene Taylor, Sept. 8, 1942; children: Marilyn, Beverly. BS, Miss. State U., 1951; MS, Purdue U., 1954, PhD, 1962. Commd. 2d lt. USAF, 1944, advanced through grades to lt. col., 1965, pilot, 1944-56, sr. pilot, 1956-60, command pilot, 1960-67, asst. prof. Air Force Inst. Tech., 1954-58, assoc. prof., 1965-67, ret., 1967; assoc. prof. aero. and astronautical engring. Ohio State U., Columbus, 1967-69, prof., 1970-85, prof. emeritus, 1985—. Dir. USAF-Am. Soc. Engring. Edn. summer faculty rsch. program, Wright-Patterson AFB, Ohio, 1976—78. Contbr. articles to profl. jours., scientific papers. Mem. Soc. Exptl. Stress Analysis, Am. Soc. Engring. Edn., Am. Acad. Mechanics, Res. Officers (life), Ret. Officers Assn. (life), Ohio State U. Retirees Assn. (life), Am. Legion (life), USAF Officers Club, Sigma Xi, Sigma Gamma Tau Achievements include research in direct analytical solution to both conservative and non-conservative sys; first to successfully demonstrate algebraic equations of motion for non-stationary, time dependent sys. which bypass the differential equations of motion completely. Home and Office: 4176 Ashmore Rd Columbus OH 43220-4683 also: Dept Aerospace Engring Appl Mech Ohio State U Columbus OH 43210 Personal E-mail: cecildbailey@aol.com.

BAILEY, CHAMP, professional football player; b. June 22, 1978; m. Hanady Bailey; 1 child. Student, U. GA. Defensive back Washington Redskins, 1999—2003, Denver Broncos, 2004—. Named NCAA All-American, 1998; named to NFC Pro-Bowl Team, 2000, 2002—04; recipient Bronko Nagurski Award, 1998. Office: c/o Denver Broncos 13655 Broncos Pkwy Englewood CO 80112*

BAILEY, CHARLES WALDO, II, journalist, writer; b. Boston, Apr. 28, 1929; s. David Washburn and Catherine Ruth (Smith) B.; m. Ann Card Bushnell, Sept. 9, 1950; children: Victoria Britton, Sarah Tilden. Grad., Phillips Exeter Acad., 1946; AB magna cum laude, Harvard U., 1950. Reporter, Mpls. Tribune, 1950-54; reporter, corr. Washington bur. Mpls. Tribune, Des Moines Register, Look mag., 1954-67; chief Washington bur. Mpls. Tribune, 1968-72, editor, 1972-82, Mpls. Star and Tribune, 1982; Washington editor Nat. Pub. Radio, 1984-87. Mem. Standing Com. Corr., Washington, 1962-63; pres. White Ho. Corr. Assn., 1969-70. Author: Conflicts of Interest: A Matter of Journalistic Ethics, 1984, The Land Was Ours, 1991; co-author: (with Fletcher Knebel) No High Ground, 1960, Seven Days in May, 1962, Convention, 1964; contbr. to Candidates 1960, 1959, Exeter Remembered, 1965, The President's Trip to China, 1972, The Media and Foreign Policy, 1990. Trustee Carnegie Endowment for Internat. Peace, Henry L. Stimson Ctr. Mem. Coun. on Fgn. Rels., Gridiron Club, Cosmos Club. Home: 3001 Albemarle St NW Washington DC 20008-2102

BAILEY, CHARLES-JAMES NICE, linguistics educator; b. Middlesborough, Ky., May 2, 1926; s. Charles Wise and Mary Elizabeth (Nice) B. AB in Classical Philology with highest honors, Harvard U., 1950, MTh, 1955; DMin, Vanderbilt U., 1963; AM, U. Chgo., 1966, PhD, 1969. Faculty dept. linguistics U. Hawaii, Manoa, 1968-71, Georgetown U., 1971-73; prof. Technische U. Berlin, 1974-91, prof. emeritus, 1991—. Vis. prof. U. Mich., Ann Arbor, 1973, U. Witwatersrand, Johannesburg, 1976, U. Brunei, Darussalam, 1990; Forcheimer prof. U. Jerusalem, 1986; propr. Orchid Land Publs.; hon. col. Staff Gov. of Ky. Fellow: Internat. Soc. Phonetic Scis. (life), Netherlands Inst. Advanced Study (life); mem.: N.Y. Acad. Scis., European Acad. Scis., Arts and Letters (corr.), Am. Dialect Soc. (life), Linguistic Soc. Am. (life), AAAS (life). E-mail: o1p@orlapubs.com.

BAILEY, CINDY ANN, elementary school educator; b. Red Cloud, Nebr., Apr. 6, 1952; d. Bruce Richard and Bernice June (Fielder) Corrick; BS in elem. edn., Fort Hays State U., 1975. Tchr. Beloit Elem., Beloit, Kans., 1975—85, Lincoln Elem., Augusta, Kans., 1987—2005. Avocations: reading, gardening, crafts, sewing, antiques. Office: USD 402 1801 Dearborn Augusta KS 67010

BAILEY, CLAUDIA JEAN, retired librarian, artist; b. Akron, Ohio, July 2, 1936; d. Lloyd Carl Lowe and Vergie P. Hively; m. Richard E. Bailey; children: Laurel Lynn Bailey-Wallace, Robert E. BA, Asbury Coll., 1960; MALS., U. Mich., 1966; MA, Ohio State U., 1970; BFA, U. R.I., 1992. Ref. libr. Columbus Pub. Libr., Columbus, Ohio, 1966—68; head journalism, acting head social work libr. Ohio State U., Columbus, Ohio, 1969—70; head fine arts libr. Bridgeport Pub. Libr., Bridgeport, Conn., 1970—72; head providence campus libr. CC of R.I., Providence, 1972—76, head Lincoln campus libr. Lincoln, RI, 1976—82, coord. ref./collection devel., 1982—87, ref. libr. Warwick, RI, 1987—97. Co-sponsored libr. concerts and art exhibits Bridgeport Pub. Libr., Bridgeport, Conn., 1971—72; chairperson, faculty sabbatical com. CC of R.I., Warwick, RI, 1979—80. Author: A Guide To Reference And Bibliography For Theatre Research, 1971, A Guide To Reference And Bibliography For Theatre Research., 2d edit., 1983. Scholar Grad. Libr. Sci., State Of Ohio, 1965-66, Scholar Grad., London Theatre Libraries, 1968. Mem.: NEA, Ariz. Edn. Assn., Westbrook Fine Arts Assn., Ariz. Art Alliance. Liberal. Avocations: art collages, drawing, painting, singing, opera, theater. Home: 19483 N 90th Ln Peoria AZ 85382-8560 Personal E-mail: cjbailey20@cox.net.

BAILEY, COLIN BARRY, curator; b. London, Oct. 20, 1955; arrived in U.S., 1985, arrived in Can., 1995, arrived in U.S., 2000; s. Max and Hilda (Feldman) B.; life ptnr. Alan P. Wintermute. BA, Brasenose Coll., Oxford, Eng., 1978; diploma in history of art, U. Paris IV, Sorbonne, 1982-83; MA, Oxford U., 1982, PhD, 1985. Asst. curator European painting and sculpture The Phila. Mus. Art, 1985-89; curator European painting and sculpture Kimbell Art Mus., Ft. Worth, 1989-90, sr. curator, 1990-94; chief curator Nat. Gallery Can., Ottawa, Ont., 1995-98, dep. dir., chief curator, 1999-2000; chief curator The Frick Collection, N.Y.C., 2000—. Vis. prof. U. Pa., 1988; vis. prof. dept. art Bryn Mawr Coll., 1989; vis. prof. dept. art history Columbia U, 2005. Author: The First Painters of the King, 1985, The Loves of the Gods: Mythological Painting from Watteau to David, 1992, Renoir's Portraits, 1997, Jean-Baptiste Greuze, The Laundress, 2000, Patriotic Taste: Collecting Modern Art in Prerevolutionary Paris, 2002; co-author: Masterpieces of Impressionism & Post-Impressionism, 1989; gen. editor: Gustav Klimt, Modernism in the Making, 2001;co-author, gen. editor: The Age of Watteau, Chardin and Fragonard: Masterpieces of French Genre Painting, 2003; mem. editl. bd. The Oxford Art Jour., 1982-84. Decorated chevalier de l'Order des Arts et des Letters (France), 1994; Clark fellow Sterling and Francine Clark Art Inst., Williamstown, 1999; recipient Mitchell prize, 2002-03; Paul Mellon sr. vis. fellow Ctr. Advanced Studies Visual Arts, Nat. Gallery Art, Washington, 1994 Mem.: Assn. Art Mus. Curators (trustee 2003—). Avocations: running, tennis, piano, opera. Home: 419 E 57th St New York NY 10022-3060 Office: The Frick Collection 1 E 70th St New York NY 10021 E-mail: Bailey@frick.org.

BAILEY, DANIEL ALLEN, lawyer; b. Pitts., Aug. 31, 1953; s. Richard A. and Virginia (Henry) B.; m. Janice Abraham, Oct. 10, 1981; children: Jeffrey, Megan. BBA, Bowling Green State U., 1975; JD, Ohio State U., 1978. Bar: Ohio 1978, U.S. Dist. Ct. (so. dist.) Ohio 1978, U.S. Tax Ct. 1979. Ptnr. Arter & Hadden, Columbus, Ohio, 1978—2003, chair exec. com., 2000—03; mem. Baily Cavalieri LLC, Columbus, 2003—, chair bd. mgrs., 2003—. Co-author: Handbook for Corporate Directors, 1985, Liability of Corporate Officers and Directors, 7th edit., 2002. Bd. dirs. Columbus Met. Community Action Orgn., 1979-80, Franklin County Head Start, Columbus, 1979-80, Faith Luth. Ch., Whitehall, Ohio, 1985-90, Luth. Social Svcs. Cen. Ohio, 1991-2000, Concorde Counseling Svcs., 2000—. Mem. ABA, Ohio Bar Assn., Columbus Bar Assn., Phi Kappa Phi, Beta Gamma Sigma, Omicron Delta Kappa. Office: Bailey Cavalieri LLC 10 W Broad St Ste 2100 Columbus OH 43215-3422 Office Phone: 614-229-3213.

BAILEY, DANIEL B., lawyer, entrepreneur; b. Topeka, Kans., Sept. 13, 1959; s. Daniel J. Bailey and Paula R. Upton; m. Mary Michele Hand, July 16, 1988 (div.); children: Catherine Clare, Colin Daniel. BBA, Washburn U., Topeka, 1981; JD, Washburn U., 1987. Bar: Kans. 1987, U.S. Dist. Ct. Kans. 1987, Wyo. 1993, U.S. Dist. Ct. Wyo. 1993, U.S. Ct. Appeals (10th cir.) 1993, U.S. Supreme Ct. 2004. Pres. Lubnau, Bailey & Dumbrill, P.C., Gillette, Wyo., 1992—. Mem. Moonshiner Devel., LLC, Gillette, 1999—, The Jealous Mistress, LLC, Gillette, 1991—; pres. Simplify, Inc. d/b/a Sir Speedy, 2004—. Mem.: Gillette Energy Rotary Club (pres. 1998—99, asst. dist. gove. dist. 5440 1999—2000). Republican. Roman Catholic. Home: 6000 Stone Place Ave Gillette WY 82718 Office: Lubnau Bailey & Dumbrill PC PO Box 1028 300 S Gillette Ave #2000 Gillette WY 82716 Office Phone: 307-682-1313. E-mail: dan@etseq.com, sirspeedy@vcn.com.

BAILEY, DANIEL CARL, higher education administrator; b. Manchester, Conn., June 10, 1967; s. Donald James Bailey and Mary Ann Reilly. BA, Antioch Coll., 1989; MSW, Wash. U., St. Louis, 1993. Rsch. asst. St. Louis Regional Med. Ctr., 1992—93; rsch. assoc. Bklyn. Acad. Music, 1993—94; devel. rschr. U. Mass., Amherst, 1994—95, asst. mgr. devel. rsch., 1995—97; asst. dir. corp./found. prospect mgmt. sys. Wash. U., St. Louis, 1997—99; dir. corp. and found. rels. Kennedy Krieger Inst., Balt., 1999—2001, U. Del., Newark, 2001—. Mem. Pa./NJ/Del. Regional Corp. and Found. Rels. Roundtable, Phila., 2001—; founder, chmn. Balt. region Assn. Fundraising Profls. Corp. and Found. Rels. Roundtable, 2000—01; bd. dirs. Mo.-Kans. chpt. Am. Prospect Rsch. Assn., St. Louis, 1992—93; mem. cmty. adv. com., cmty. partnership initiative Rohm & Haas Electronic Materials CMP, Inc., Newark, 2002—; mem. Stine-Haskell Rsch. Ctr. Newark cmty. adv. panel E.I. du Pont de Nemours and Co., Newark, 2003—. Mem.alumni bd. devel. and admissions coms. Antioch Coll., Yellow Springs, Ohio, 2000—01; mem. devel. com. Kristol Ctr. for Jewish Life, U. Del.; chmn. cemetery com., bd. dirs. Chestertown (Md.) Havurah, 2002—04; mem. Yellow Springs Havurah, 1989—90; co-pres., mem. St. Louis Lesbian and Gay Havurah, 1991—93; mem. Gay and Lesbian Havurah, Balt., 1999—2003; Jewish educator Jewish Cmty. Amherst, Mass., 1994—96; prin. Congregation Ahavis Achim, Keene, NH, 1996—97; mem. Ctrl. Reform Congregation, St. Louis, 1997—98, Brith Sholom Knesseth Israel Congregation, Richmond Heights, Mo., 1998—99, Jewish Cmty. HS, St. Louis, 1998—99; bd. dirs. Skinker-DeBaliviere Cmty. Coun., St. Louis, 1998—99, Hotline for Help Inc., Brattleboro, Vt., 1995—97. Nominee Harold Grinspoon award for Excellence in Jewish Edn., Springfield, Mass., 1995; Julia Lathrop fellow, Wash. U., 1991—93. Democrat. Jewish. Office: U Del George Evans House 5 W Main St Newark DE 19716 Business E-Mail: dbailey@udel.edu.

BAILEY, DARLYNE, social worker, educator; b. N.Y.C., July 21, 1952; d. Arthur and Iris B. AB in Psychology and Secondary Edn., Lafayette Coll., 1974; MSc in Psychiatric Social Work, Columbia U., N.Y.C., 1976; PhD Orgn. Behavior, Case Western Reserve U., 1988. Lic. ind. social worker, Ohio. Coord. specialized treatment Essex County Guidance Ctr., East Orange, N.J., 1976-82; dir. emergency access svcs. Cmty. Mental Health Orgn., Englewood, N.J., 1980-83; field instr. NYU Sch. Social Work, 1981-82; instr. Weatherhead Sch. Mgmt., Case Western Reserve U., Cleve., 1986-87; asst. prof. Mandel Sch. Applied Social Sci., Case Western Reserve U., Cleve., 1988-94, dean and assoc. prof., 1994-99, dean and prof., 1998—2001; dean and v.p. acad. affairs Tchrs. Coll., Columbia U., N.Y.C., 2002—, acting pres., 2003. Cons. to numerous profl. groups; orgnl. devel. specialist Mid-Atlantic Regional Med. Edn. Ctr. VA, Brecksville, Ohio, 1985-88, Shaker Heights (Ohio) Sch. Dist., 1988-90, Cuyahoga Plan, Cleve., 1989-90; trainer 9-to-5 Nat. Assn. Working Women, Cleve., Family Children and Adult Svcs., Columbus, 1988, Exec. Tng. Inst., 1988-90, The Free Med. Clinic of Greater Cleve., Cuyhoga County Dept. Human Svcs., Sr. and Adult Svcs., Luth. Chaplaincy Svc., Cleve., 1993, KPMG Peat Marwick project, Chgo., 1990-91, Ghana Assn. Pvt. Vol. Orgns. in Devel., Accra, 1992-94, Old Stone Ch. Project, Cleve., 1994, Cleve. Rape Crisis Ctr. Project, 1995 Co-author: (book) Strategic Alliances Among Health and Human Services Organizations: From Affiliations to Consolidations, 2000, Managing Human Resources in the Human Services, 2001; contbr. articles to profl. jours., chapters to books and book reviews. Mem. exec. com. bd. trustees Heights Youth Ctr., Inc., Cleveland Heights, Ohio, 1983-95; mem. Human Resources Devel. Com., Neighborhood Ctrs. Assn., Cleve., chair mgmt. and governance task force, 1988-90; bd. trustees Neighborhood Ctrs., Cleve., 1991-94, Tiffin U., 1992-95, Fedn. for Cmty. Planning, Cleve., 1995, Nat. Coun., Cleve., 1995; mem. book rev. com. NASW Press, Washington, 1992-95; cons. editor Social Work, 1996; mem. philantropy and volunteerism adv. com. Kellogg Found., Battle Creek, Mich., 1992; chairwoman Mandel Ctr. Nonprofit Orgn. Named Nat. Group XIII fellow, W.K. Kellogg Nat. Leadership Program; recipient George Washington Kidd award, Lafayette Coll., Easton, Pa., 1994, Crain's Cleveland Bus. Women Influence award, 1997; fellow, Salzburg Seminar, Austria, 1997. Fellow: Nat. Assn. Social Workers, Am. Othopysciatric Assn.; mem.: Coun. Social Work Edn. (bd. dirs.), Nat. Bd. Organizational Behavior Tchg. Soc. (past co-chair), Leadership Cleveland Class. Office: Tchrs Coll Columbia U 525 W 120th St New York NY 10027

BAILEY, DAVID MICHAEL, physician, internist; b. Aberdeen, S.D., Oct. 18, 1951; s. Timothy Clement and Mary Bernadine (Artz) B.; m. Janis Lynn Cazzell. BS, Cen. Mo., 1974; MD, U. Okla., 1981. Diplomate Am. Bd. Internal Medicine, added qualifications in geriatric medicine. Intern in internal medicine U. Okla. Teaching Hosps., Oklahoma City, 1981-82, resident in internal medicine, 1982-84; staff physician St. Anthony Hosp., Oklahoma City, 1984—, vice chmn. dept. of medicine, 1988-91; pvt. practice Assocs. in Internal Medicine, Oklahoma City, 1984-91; staff physician Pinnacle Rehab. Hosp., 1988—, sec. med. staff, 1988—98, pres. med. staff, 1999—2000; staff physician Okla. Neurosurg. Inst. Spine Ctr., Oklahoma City, 1991-96, Presbyn. Sr. Health, Oklahoma City, 1996-99, Presbyn. Hosp., Oklahoma City, 1996—; physician Capstone Internal Medicine, Oklahoma City, 1999-2000, Innovative Med. Assocs., Oklahoma City, 2000—. Mem. AMA, ACP, ASIM, Okla. State Med. Assn., Oklahoma County Med. Soc., Am. Geriatrics Soc. Office: 721 NW 6th St Ste A Oklahoma City OK 73102

BAILEY, DAVID NELSON, pathology educator, dean, academic administrator; b. Anderson, Ind., June 21, 1945; s. Omer Nelson and Louise Genevieve (Hurst) B. BS with high distinction, Ind. U., 1967; MD, Yale U., 1973. Diplomate Nat. Bd. Med. Examiners, Am. Bd. Pathology (Clin. and Chem. Pathology). Clin. fellow dept. lab. medicine Yale U., 1973-75; asst. resident specializing in clin. pathology Yale-New Haven Hosp., 1975-76, chief resident specializing in clin. pathology, 1976-77; asst. prof. pathology U. Calif., San Diego, 1977-81, assoc. prof. pathology, 1981-86, prof. pathology, 1986—, head div. lab. medicine, 1983-89, 94-98, acting chmn., 1986-88, chmn. dept. pathology, 1988—99, 2000—01; dir. toxicology lab. U. Calif. Med. Ctr., San Diego, 1977—, dir. clin. labs., 1982-99, interim vice chancellor for health scis., dean, 1999-2000, dep. vice chancellor for health scis., 2001—, dean for faculty/student matters, 2003—. Mem. editorial bd. Jour. Analytical Toxicology, 1979—, Clin. Chemistry Jour., 1983-93, Am. Jour. Clin. Pathology, 1991—; contbr. articles to profl. jours. Recipient Gerald T. Evans award Acad. Clin. Lab. Physicians and Scientists, 1993; Merit scholar Ind. U., 1963-65, Arthur R. Metz scholar, 1965-67. Mem. Calif. Assn. Toxicologists (pres. 1981-82), Acad. Clin. Lab. Physicians and Scientists (pres. 1988-89), Am. Assn. Clin. Chemistry, Am. Chem. Soc., Assn. Pathology Chmn. (sec.-treas. 1996-99), Phi Lambda Upsilon, Alpha Omega Alpha. Office: U Calif San Diego Sch Medicine 9500 Gilman Dr La Jolla CA 92093-0602 Office Phone: 858-822-5577. Business E-Mail: dnbailey@ucsd.edu.

BAILEY, DAVID ROY SHACKLETON, classics educator; b. Lancaster, Eng., Dec. 10, 1917; came to U.S., 1968; s. John Henry Shackleton and Rosamund Maud (Giles) B.; m. Kristine Zvirbulis, 1994. BA, Gonville and Caius Coll., Cambridge, Eng., 1939, MA, 1943, LittD, 1958; LittD (hon.), U. Dublin, 1984. Fellow Gonville and Caius Coll., 1944-55, praelector, 1954-55, dep. bursar, 1964, sr. bursar, 1965-68, Univ. lectr. Tibetan, 1948-68; fellow, dir. studies in classics Jesus Coll., Cambridge, 1955-64; vis. lectr. classics Harvard U., 1963, prof. Greek and Latin, 1975-82, Pope prof. Latin lang. and lit., 1982-88, prof. emeritus, 1988—; prof. Latin U. Mich., Ann Arbor, 1968-75, adj. prof., 1989—. Vis. Andrew V.V. Raymond prof. classics SUNY, Buffalo, 1973-74; vis. fellow Peterhouse, Cambridge, 1980-81, Inst. For Advanced Study, Princeton U., 1986. Author: The Satapancasatka of Matreeta, 1951, Propertiana, 1956, Cicero's Letters, 10 vols., 1965-81, Cicero, 1971, Profile of Horace, 1982, Anthologia Latina I, 1982, Horatius, 1985, Cicero's Philippics, 1986, An Onomasticon to Cicero's Speeches, 1988, Ciceronis Epistulae, 4 vols., 1987-88, Lucanus, 1988, Quintilianus, Declamationes Minores, 1990, Martialis, 1990, Martial, 3 vols., 1993, Back From Exile, 1994, Homoeoteleuton in Latin dactylic poetry, 1994, Onomasticon to Cicero's Letters, 1995, Onomasticon to Cicero's Treatises, 1996, Selected Classical Papers, 1997, Cicero Letters To Atticus, 4 vols., 1999, Valerius Maxinus, 2 vols., 2000, Cicero, Letters to Friends, 3 vols., 2001, Cicero, Letters to Quintus and Brutus, 2002, Statius, Silvae, 2003, Statius Thebaid, 2 vols., 2004, others; contbr. articles on Oriental and classical subjects to profl. jours.; editor Harvard Studies in Classical Philology, 1978-84. Recipient Charles J. Goodwin award of merit, 1978; Nat. Endowment for Humanities fellow, 1980-81; Kenyon medal, Brit. Acad., 1985; hon. fellow Gonville and Caius Coll. Fellow Brit. Acad., Am. Acad. Arts and Scis.; mem. Am. Philos. Soc., Soc. for Promotion of Roman Studies (hon.).

BAILEY, DAWN MARIE, fund raising systems consultant; b. L.A., June 23, 1972; d. Dayton Dana and Pamela Jean Bailey. BS, U. So. Calif., 1994. Supr. Am. Tours Internat., L.A., 1993—96; donor recruiter ARC, L.A., 1996—98, devel. rep. nat. hdqrs. Washington, 1998—99; sr. cons. Blackbaud Inc., Chgo., 1999—. Mentor Am. Tours Internat., 1994-95. Vol. Rep. Party, L.A., 1992-96; grad. Riordan Vol. Leadership Devel. Program, L.A., 1995-96. Mem. Nat. Soc. Fund Raising Execs. Office: Blackbaud 2000 Daniel Island Dr Charleston SC 29492 E-mail: Dawn.Bailey@blackbaud.com.

BAILEY, DOROTHY JEAN, secondary school educator, consultant; b. Clarksdale, Miss., Jan. 24, 1948; d. A.D. and Nancy (Morbley) Bailey; 1 child, Miko Dawn Montgomery. AA Sociology, Compton Coll., 1969; BA Sociology, Cal State Univ. Long Beach, 1972; MA Pub. Adminstrn., Pepperdine Univ., 1977; MS Sch. Counseling, Univ. La Verne, 2001. Lic. real estate Calif., 1988, pupil personnel svcs. credential Calif., 2002. Social sci. analyst Libr. of Congress/Congressional Rsch. Svc., Washington, 1979—86; realtor Century 21 Sparrow, Long Beach, Calif., 1988—92; program coord. Martin Luther King Jr./Charles R. Drew Univ. of Medicine and Sci., L.A., Calif., 1989—90; case mgr./ early intervention network coord. Cal State Univ. Long Beach Found., Calif., 1992—94; cons. So. Calif. Alcohol & Drug Programs, Inc., Downey, Calif., 1994, Miller Children's Hosp. of Long Beach, Calif., 1994—95; program coord. Minority AIDS Program, L.A., Calif., 1995—97; tchr. advisor L.A. Unfied Sch. Dist/Harbor Occupl. Ctr., San Pedro, Calif., 1999—2001, tchr., 1997—. Mem.: Women Educators, Calif. Coun. for Adult Edn. (sec. 1999—2002, pres. 2002—03, State Excellence in Tchg. 2003). Avocations: collecting seashells, mentoring, reading, walking, art. Office: LA Unified Sch Dist/Harbor Occpul Ctr 740 N Pacific Ave San Pedro CA 90731

BAILEY, ERIC JON, medical anthropologist, health scientist administrator; b. Springfield, Ohio, Aug. 24, 1958; s. Jean Ethel and Roger William Bailey; m. Gloria Jean Harden, May 27, 1989; children: Ebony Lynne, Darrien Douglass, Marcus Marcelus. BA, Miami U., 1980, MA, 1983; MPH, Emory U., 1995; PhD, Wayne State U., 1988. Asst. prof. U. Houston, 1988—90; assoc. prof. Ind. U. Purdue U. at Indpls., 1990—98; health scientist adminstr., NIH, Bethesda, Md., 1999—2004, Charles R. Drew U. Medicine and Sci., 2004—. Health cons. Ind. State Health Dept., 1993—96. Author: (books) Medical Anthropology and African American Health, Urban African American Health Care, African American Alternative Medicine. Fellow Nat. Inst. of Health Postdoctoral Fellowship Award, NIH, 1993-1995. Mem.: APHA. Democrat-Npl. Avocations: weightlifting, jogging, exercise. Office: Dept Health & Human Svs 6707 Democracy Blvd Bethesda MD 20892 Personal E-mail: ebailey8@aol.com. E-mail: baileye@od.nih.gov.

BAILEY, EXINE MARGARET ANDERSON, soprano, educator; b. Cottonwood, Minn., Jan. 4, 1922; d. Joseph Leonard and Exine Pearl (Robertson) Anderson; m. Arthur Albert Bailey, May 5, 1956. BS, U. Minn., 1944; MA, Columbia U., 1945; profl. diploma, 1951. Instr. Columbia U., 1947-51; faculty U. Oreg., Eugene, 1951—, prof. voice, 1966-87, coordinator voice instrn., 1969-87, prof. emeritus, 1987—; faculty dir. Salzburg, Austria, summer 1968, Europe, summer 1976. Vis. prof., head vocal instrn. Columbia U., summers 1952, 59; condr. master classes for singers, developer summer program study for h.s. solo singers, U. Oreg. Sch. Music, 1988—, mem. planning com. 1998-99 MTNA Nat. Convention. Profl. singer, N.Y.C.; appearances with NBC, ABC symphonies; solo artist appearing with Portland and Eugene (Oreg.) Symphonies, other groups in Wash., Calif., Mont., Idaho, also in concert; contbr. articles, book revs. to various mags. Del. fine arts program to Ea. Europe, People to People Internat. Mission to Russia for 1990. Recipient Young Artist award N.Y.C. Singing Tchrs., 1945, Music Fedn. Club (N.Y.C.) hon. award, 1951; Kathryn Long scholar Met. Opera, 1945 Mem. Nat. Assn. Tchrs. Singing (lt. gov. 1968-72), Oreg. Music Tchrs. Assn (pres. 1974-76), Music Tchrs. Nat. Assn. (nat. voice chmn. high sch. activities 1970-74, nat. chmn. voice 1973-75, 81-85, NW chmn. collegiate activities and artists competition 1978-80, editorial com. Am. Music Tchr. jour. 1987-89), AAUP, Internat. Platform Assn., Kappa Delta Pi, Sigma Alpha Iota; Pi Kappa Lambda. Home: 17 Westbrook Way Eugene OR 97405-2074 Office: U Oreg Sch Music Eugene OR 97403 Office Phone: 541-343-5206. *My chief goal in life is to realize my potentials through perfecting my innate talents and capabilities.*

BAILEY, F. LEE (FRANCIS LEE BAILEY), lawyer; b. Waltham, Mass., June 10, 1933; m. Florence Gott (div. 1961); m. Froma Portney (div. 1972); m. Lynda Hart, Aug. 26, 1972 (div. 1980); m. Patricia Shiers, June 10, 1985. Student, Harvard U., 1950—52, student, 1957; LLB, Boston U., 1960. Bar: U.S. Dist. Ct. Mass. 1961, U.S. Ct. Appeals (1st cir.) 1963, U.S. Tax Ct. 1964, U.S. Ct. Appeals (6th cir.) 1964, U.S. Supreme Ct. 1964, U.S. Ct. Appeals (2d cir.) 1967, U.S. Ct. Appeals (10th cir.) 1968, U.S. Ct. Appeals (3d cir.) 1969, U.S. Ct. Appeals (9th cir.) 1970, U.S. Ct. Appeals (4th and 7th cirs.) 1971, U.S. Dist. Ct. (we. and no. dists.) Tex. 1980, U.S. Ct. Mil. Appeals 1981, U.S. Ct. Appeals (8th and 11th cirs.) 1984, U.S. Ct. Appeals (5th cir.) 1985, U.S. Dist. Ct. (ea. dist.) Wis. 1991. Prin. Law Offices of F. Lee Bailey, West Palm Beach, Fla. Author (with Harvey Aronson): The Defense Never Rests, 1971; author: Cleared for the Approach, 1977; author: (with John Greenya) For the Defense, 1976; author: Novel Secrets, 1979, How to Protect Yourself Against Cops In California and Other Strange Places, 1982, To Be a Trial Lawyer, 1983; author: (with Henry Rothblatt) numerous works in field of criminal law. Lt. USMC, 1952—56. Mem.: ATLA, ABA.*

BAILEY, FRED ARTHUR, history professor; b. Dumas, Ark., Mar. 28, 1947; s. Fred L. and Dorothy M. B.; m. Bonnie Mignon Pitt, Aug. 22, 1968; children: Amber McClendon, Alex, Stan. BA, Harding U., 1970; MA, U. Tenn., 1972, PhD, 1979. Assoc. prof. history Freed-Hardeman Coll., Henderson, Tenn., 1973-84; T.K. Ann prof. Am. history Johns Hopkins U./Nanjing U. Ctr. Chinese/Am. Studies, Nanjing, China, 1993-94; prof., chair dept. history Abilene (Tex.) Christian U., 1984—. Author: Class and Tennessee's Confederate Generation, 1987 (Book award 1988), William Edward Dodd: The South's Yeoman Scholar, 1997; contbr. articles to profl. jours. Mem. Orgn. of Am. Historians, So. Hist. Assn. Mem. Chs. of Christ. Home: 1400 Compere Blvd Abilene TX 79601 Fax: 915-674-2369. E-mail: baileyf@acu.edu.

BAILEY, FRED COOLIDGE, retired engineering consulting company executive; b. Claremont, N.H., Oct. 5, 1925; s. Howard Perry and Helen Gare (Coolidge) B.; m. Mary Beecroft Cunningham, June 26, 1948; children: Susan Bailey Hunter (dec.), Stephen Coolidge, Elizabeth Bailey George. BS, MIT, 1948, MS, 1949. Registered profl. engr., Mass. Research engr. Caterpillar Tractor Co., Peoria, Ill., 1949-51; asst. tech. dir. com. ship structural design Nat. Acad. Scis., Washington, 1952-55; engr. Lessells & Assocs., Inc., Boston, 1955—65; pres. Teledyne Engring. Services, Waltham, Mass., 1965—86, chmn., 1986-87; group exec. Teledyne Inc., Waltham, Mass., 1983-87, cons., 1987-90, ret., 1990. Chmn. exec. com. Lexington Savs. Bank, 1989-94, chmn. bd. dirs., 1994-97; dir. Affiliated Cmty. Bancorp, 1995-98. Chmn. bd. Fire Commrs., Lexington, Mass., 1964—69; mem. Bd. Selectmen,

1969—78; trustee Cary Meml. Libr., Lexington, 1971—78, pres., 1972—77; trustee Symmes Hosp., Arlington, Mass., 1969—2001, mem. exec. com., 1977—89, v.p., 1978—80, pres., 1980—81; trustee Brookhaven at Lexington, 1986—, chmn. pres., 1994—96; chmn. Choates-Symmes Health Svcs., 1981—83; v.p. Charles River Mus. Industry, 1983—86, trustee, 1984—, pres., 1986—89. With USNR, 1944—46. Fellow Soc. for Exptl. Mechanics (pres. 1968-69, recipient Tatnall award 1974, hon. mem. 1992); mem. Soc. Naval Architects and Marine Engrs. (recipient Linnard prize 1972), ASME, Am. Welding Soc. Home: 48 Coolidge Ave Lexington MA 02420-1838

BAILEY, GORDON FREEBORN, JR., lawyer; b. July 24, 1944; s. Gordon F. and Carridelle G. B.; m. Anne Paulk, Mar. 18, 1967; children: Gordon F. III, Clark, Allison BA, Birmingham So. Coll., 1966; JD, U. Ala., 1969. Bar: Ala. 1969, D.C. 1973. Pub. defender program, Mobile, Ala., 1969; ptnr. Isom, Jackson & Bailey, Anniston, Ala., 1973-99. Spl. asst. atty. gen. State Ala., 1981— . Mem. alumni bd. dirs. Birmingham So. Coll., mem. State Child Support Enforcement Com., 1980—; pres. bd. dirs. Vol. Action Ctr., 1980-81; mem. recreation adv. commn. City of Anniston, 1979—. Served to capt. JAGC, U.S. Army, 1969-73. Recipient Pres.'s Child Support Cmty. Svc. award Nat. Child Support Enforcement Assn., 1999. Mem. ABA, D.C. Bar Assn., Eastern Regional Child Support Enforcement Assn. (life) (pres. 1986), Ala. bar Assn., Ala. State bar (family law sect. pres. 1997-98), Calhoun/Cleburne County Bar Assn. (pres. 1981-82), Ala. Jud. Coll. Faculty Assn. (hon.). Methodist. Club: Kiwanis (pres. 1981-82) (Anniston, Ala.). Office: PO Box 1930 1001 Noble St Ste 230 Anniston AL 36202

BAILEY, HAROLD RANDOLPH, surgeon; b. Palestine, Tex., Jan. 20, 1943; m. Kelly Curry Bailey. BA in Biology summa cum laude, Rice U., 1964; MD, U. Tex., Dallas, 1968. Diplomate Am. Bd. Surgery, Am. Bd. Colon and Rectal Surgery. Intern straight surg. Parkland Hosp., Dallas, 1968-69; resident gen. surgery U. Tex. Med. Sch./Hermann Hosp., Houston, 1969-73; fellow colon and rectal surgery Ferguson-Droste-Ferguson Hosp., Grand Rapids, Mich., 1973-74; clin. faculty U. Tex. Med. Sch., Houston, 1974—, dir. residency tng. program colon and rectal surgery, 1984—, clin. prof. surgery, 1986—; clin. faculty Baylor Coll. Medicine, 1986—, clin. prof. surgery, 1999—. Assoc. examiner Am. Bd. Colon and Rectal Surgery, 1985—89, bd. dirs., 1989—97, chmn. exam. com., 1995—97, pres., 1996—97, sr. examiner, 1997—; chief staff Park Plaza Hosp., Houston, 1988—90. Bd. dirs. Am. Cancer Soc., Greater Houston unit, 1989-93, v.p., 1991-93, pres., 1993-95; mem. vestry Palmer Meml. Episcopal Ch., Houston, 1979-83, 84-86, chmn. fin. com., 1984-86; mem. fund coun. Rice U., Houston, 1993-95, class fund drive chmn. 1993-95). Recipient George Waldron award Hermann Hosp., 1970, Violet Keller award, 1973; named to Good Housekeeping mag. 400 Best Doctors in U.S., 1991, Good Housekeeping mag. Best Cancer Doctors in U.S., 1993; named Disting. Alumnus, Rice U., 2000. Fellow ACS (chmn. adv. coun. colon and rectal surgery 1996-2001, bd. govs. 2002-04, bd. regents 2003—), Internat. Soc. Univ. Colon and Rectal Surgeons (program com. 1986), Am. Soc. Colon and Rectal Surgeons (treas., exec. coun. 1993-99, pres. 1999-2000), Tex. Surg. Soc.; mem. AMA, Tex. Soc. Colon and Rectal Surgeons (pres. 1981, exec. sec. 1982-88), Tex. Med. Assn., Tex. Soc. Gastrointestinal Endoscopy, Harris County Med. Soc., Houston Surg. Soc., Phi Beta Kappa, Alpha Omega Alpha. Office: Colon & Rectal Clinic 6550 Fannin St Ste 2307 Houston TX 77030-2723 Office Phone: 713-790-9250. Business E-Mail: h.r.bailey@uth.tmc.edu.

BAILEY, HELEN MCSHANE, historian, consultant; b. Gardner, Kans., Oct. 17, 1916; d. Harry Cramer and Maude Ethel (Kramer) McShane; m. James Edwin Bailey, Feb. 23, 1946; children: James Edwin, Barbara Ann Bailey Crawford. BA, Bethany Nazarene Coll., 1938. Adminstrv. asst. Office Chief of Staff, U.S. Army, Washington, 1941-48; historian U.S. Army ofcl. history of World War II, U.S. Army, Washington, 1948-58; research asst. George C. Marshall Research Found., Washington, 1958-59; historian Orgn. Joint Chiefs of Staff, Dept. Def., Pentagon, Washington, 1968-87; cons., 1987—. Mem.: Am. Hist. Assn., Soc. Historians Am. Fgn. Rels., World War Two Studies Assn., Soc. History in Fed. Govt. Republican. Lutheran. Home: 9451 Lee Hwy Apt 415 Fairfax VA 22031-1812

BAILEY, HENRY JOHN, III, retired lawyer; b. Pitts., Apr. 4, 1916; s. Henry J. and Lenore Powell Bailey Cahoon; m. Marjorie Jane Ebner, May 30, 1949 (dec. July 1998); children: George W., Christopher G., Barbara W., Timothy P. Student, U.S. Naval Acad., 1934-36; BA, Pa. State U., 1939; JD, Yale U., 1947. Bar: N.Y. 1948, Mass. 1963, Oreg. 1974. Ins. investigator Liberty Mut. Ins. Co., N.Y.C., 1941-42; atty. Fed. Res. Bank of N.Y., N.Y.C., 1947-55; asst. v.p. Empire Trust Co., N.Y.C., 1955-56; atty., legal dept. Am. Bankers Assn., N.Y.C., 1956-62; editor Banking Law Jour., Boston, 1962-65; asso. prof. law Willamette U., Salem, Oreg., 1965-69, prof., 1969-81, prof. emeritus, 1981—, adj. prof., 1981-83, scholar in residence, 1987; counsel firm Churchill, Leonard, Brown & Donaldson, Salem, 1981-85; vis. prof. sch. law U. Akron, 1983-84; vis. prof. coll. of law Fla. State U., 1984-85; vis. prof. sch. law Rutgers U., Camden, N.J., 1985-87. Cons., lectr. to bar and banking groups; lectr. Banking Sch. of South, Baton Rouge, 1972, 73, 75. Author: Brady on Bank Checks (The Law of Bank Checks), 1960, 3d edit., 1962, 4th edit., 1969, 5th edit., 1979, 6th edit., 1987 and periodic supplements, 7th edit. (with Richard B. Hagedorn), 1992, (with Richard B. Hagedorn) rev. edit. 2 vols., 1997, periodic supplements, Uniform Commercial Code Forms, 1963, (with Clarke and Young) Bank Deposits and Collections, 1972, UCC Deskbook: A Short Course in Commercial Paper, 1973, (with Robert D. Hursh) The American Law of Products Liability, 2d edit, 1984, (with William D. Hawkland) The Sum and Substance of Commercial Paper, 1976, 80, 88, Secured Transactions in a Nutshell, 1976, 2d edit., 1981, 3d edit. (with Richard B. Hagedorn), 1988, (with Richard B. Hagedorn) 4th edit., 2000, Oregon Uniform Commercial Code, 3 vols., 1983, 84, 86, 88, 2d edit. 3 vols., 1990, New 1990 Uniform Commercial Code: Article 3, and 4, periodic supplements; contbr. articles on sales, products liability, comml. paper and secured transactions to legal jours. 1st lt. USAAF, 1942-45; lt. col. Res.; ret. Mem. Am. Bar Assn. (chmn. subcom. on comml. paper 1965-66, 79-81), Am. Law Inst. (mem. editorial bd. The Practical Lawyer 1981-93, emeritus mem. editorial bd. 1993—, 50 Yr Commemorative medal, 2004), Oreg. State Bar, Lambda Chi Alpha. Republican. Roman Catholic. Office: Coll Law Willamette U Salem OR 97301

BAILEY, HERBERT SMITH, JR., retired publisher; b. N.Y.C., July 12, 1921; s. Herbert Smith and Viola (Howe) B.; m. Elizabeth M. Brown, June 26, 1943; children: John R., James C., Robin E., George W. AB, Princeton U., 1942, LLD (hon.), 1986; LHD (hon.), Yale U., 1976. Sci. editor Princeton U. Press, 1946-52, editor, 1952-54, dir., 1954-86; ret., 1986. Past bd. dirs. Nat. Enquiry into Scholarly Publ., Franklin Book Programs, Princeton Bank; past mem. adv. com. on tech. publs. AEC; bd. govs. Wesleyan U. Press; past mem. bd. visitors Duke U. Press; past chmn. sci. info. coun. NSF; vis. fellow Nat. Humanities Ctr., 1984; R.R. Bowker lectr., 1977; mem. publs. com. Am. Scientist. Author: The Art and Science of Book Publishing, 1970; contbr. articles to profl. jours. Past mem. Princeton Regional Bd. Edn.; past mem. and chmn. long range planning Princetown Twp. Bd. of Edn.; past commr. Commn. on Preservation and Access; bd. dirs. Triangle Opera. Lt. USNR, 1942-45. Mem. Am. Book Pubs. Coun. (past bd. dirs.), Assn. Am. Pubs. (past bd. dirs., Curtis Benajmin award for creative pub. 1987), Assn. Am. Univ. Presses (past bd. dirs. and pres.), Am. Philos. Soc. (mem. publs. and program coms.), Sigma Xi. Home: 6 Carolina Meadows Apt 302 Chapel Hill NC 27517-8525

BAILEY, HIGGINS D., health products executive; BA in Biology, Eastern Wash. U.; MS in Program Planning and Pers., EdD in Adminstrn. and Mgmt., U. Calif., Berkeley. Bud. mgr. Thomas T. Anderson Law Firm, Indio, Calif., 1991—; pres., CEO Pharm. Ednl. and Devel. Found. at Med. U. S.C., Charleston, SC, 1995—96; officer, dir. Entropin, Inc., Indio, Calif., 1992—, now chmn. bd. dirs. Office: Entropin Inc 45926 Oasis St #810 Indio CA 92211*

BAILEY, HUGH COLEMAN, university president; b. Berry, Ala., July 2, 1929; s. Coleman Costello and Susie (Jenkins) B.; m. Ahleida Joan Seever, Nov. 17, 1962; children: Debra Jane, Laura Joan. AB with honors, Samford U., 1950; MA, U. Ala., 1951, PhD, 1954. Instr. history and polit. sci. Samford U., 1953-54, asst. prof., 1954-56, assoc. prof., 1956-59, prof., 1959-75, chmn. dept., head div. social scis., 1967-70; dean Howard Coll. Arts and Scis., 1970-75; v.p. for acad. affairs Francis Marion U., Florence, S.C., 1975-78; pres. Valdosta (Ga.) State Univ., 1978—2002, pres. emeritus, 2002—. Mem. commn. colls. So. Assn. Colls. and Schs., 1974-75; v.p. Ala. Acad. Sci., 1968-69; pres. Ala. Writers Conclave, 1971-73 Author: John Williams Walker, 1964, 2003, Hinton Rowan Helper: Abolitionist-Racist, 1965, 2003, Edgar Gardner Murphy: Gentle Progressive, 1968, 2003, Liberalism in the New South, Southern Social Reformers and the Progressive Movement, 1969, America: The Framing of a Nation, 2 vols, 1975; Editorial bd.: Social Sci. Vice pres. Homewood City Bd. Edn., 1972-75; pres. Valdosta chpt. ARC, 2001-03; bd. dirs. Salvation Army; chmn. Valdosta Habitat's Jimmy Carter Work Project, 2002-03, Partnership for Health, 2004-05. Guggenheim fellow, 1963-64; Am. Council Learned Socs. fellow, 1965-66; recipient award merit Am. Assn. State and Local History, 1967 Fellow Royal Soc. Arts; mem. Valdosta C. of C., Pi Gamma Mu (trustee, nat. trustee-at-large 1969-71, nat. 1st v.p. 1978-84, pres. 1984-90), Kiwanis. Episcopalian. Home: 3224 Wildwood Plantation Circle Valdosta GA 31605-1031 Office: Valdosta State Univ 1500 N Patterson St Valdosta GA 31698-0001

BAILEY, JAKE SCHULTZ, volunteer, retired electrical engineer; b. Middlesboro, Ky., Dec. 29, 1927; s. Charles Wise and Mary Elizabeth (Nice) Bailey; m. Barbare Jean McClelland, Sept. 11, 1947; children: Linda Heguy, Mary Marjorie, Alan Curtis. BSEE, U. Ala., 1949; postgrad., U. Minn., 1958. Registered profl. engr., 7 ea. states. Engr. Memphis Light Gas & Water Divsn., 1949—52, Boeing Airplane Co., Wichita, Kans., 1952—54; part-time engr. Carl Green, Elec. Cons., Wichita, 1953—54; evaluation engr. design evaluation dept. aero divsn. Honeywell, Mpls., 1954—56, design engr. F-100 autopilot design group aero divsn. chmn. edn. com. Honeywell exec. forum, 1956—58; sr. electronics engr. Link divsn. Gen. Precision Inc., Binghamton, NY, 1958—59; systems exptl. engr. systems exptl. engring. missile and space dept. GE Co., Phila., 1960—61, mgr. exptl. methods and tech. spacecraft dept. King of Prussia, Pa., 1961—62, project systems engr. systems engring. spacecraft dept., 1962, sr. engr. Nimbus operational systems spacecraft dept., 1962—64, project systems engr., operational systems engring., 1964—65, systems engr. advanced simulation requirements re-entry systems dept., 1965—66, cons. engr. simulation engring. lab. re-entry systems dept., chmn. G.E. math. simulation workshop, 1966—70; pres. B&G Corp., Valley Forge, Pa., 1969—74; chief elec. engr. Zenith Engrs., Inc., Ardmore, Pa., 1974—75; sole proprieto Jake S. Bailey, P.E., Phoenixville, Pa., 1975—81; mgr. Elec. Engring. Archtl. Design Cons. Internat., Milan, 1981—82; chief elec. engr. Haines Lundberg Waehler, N.Y.C., 1982—83; elec. design engr. John D. Hollingsworth, Greenville, SC, 1984—87; design engr. on contract Michelin Tire, Greenville, 1987—92; ret., 1992. Author: (book) Relationships Without Entanglements, 1997; contbr. articles to profl. jours. Dale Carnegie instr. and cons., 1959—72; vol. fireman Vestal Fire Co., Vestal, NY, 1958—60; vol. S.C. Dept. Probation, Anderson, SC, 2000—02; vol. Bible tchr. Mariner Nursing Care, Seneca, 1992—. Lt. USNR, 1949—69. Named Vol. of the Yr., Mariner Health Care, S.C. Dept. Probation, Parole and Pardon Svcs. Mem.: IEEE (sr.), Loyal Order of Ky. Cols. Avocation: private flying. Home: 1403 Leeward Rd Anderson SC 29625-5927 E-mail: cookieborie@bellsouth.net.

BAILEY, JAMES STEPHEN, scientist; b. Paris, Tex. s. Hal Lee and Minnie Yvonne (Swint) Bailey. BSEE, U. Tex., Arlington, 1965, MSEE, 1968, PhD in Elec. Engring. and Physics, 1971; MS in Physics, So. Meth. U., Dallas, 1982. Registered profl. engr., Tex. Analog computer engr. Gen. Dynamics Corp., Ft. Worth, 1964—66, project engr., 1985—91; microwave rsch. engr. Collins Radio Co., Dallas, 1966—68; engring. specialist assigned to Gen. Dynamics Vought Corp., Dallas, 1973—76, engring. specialist, 1976—78, pvt. cons. Ft. Worth, 1983—85; scientist Rockwell-Collins Inc., Dallas, 1978—80; pvt. cons. Ft. Worth, 1982—83, 1989—. Fund raising, vol. tchr. local univs. Lt. col. USMC, 1971—94. Mem.: Sigma Xi, Sigma Pi Sigma, Eta Kappa Nu, Tau Beta Pi. Baptist. Achievements include research in baseband adaptive signal generation electronics, flight control design and simulation, communications; electronic warfare, antennas, weapons systesm. Avocations: hiking, scuba diving, flying, amateur radio. Home and Office: 4401 Bellaire Dr Ste 226 Fort Worth TX 76109-5180

BAILEY, JANET DEE, publishing company executive; b. Newark, Aug. 23, 1946; d. Richard and Mary Louise (Dee) Shapiro; m. John Frederick Bailey, May 9, 1971; children: Jason David, Juliana Dee. BA, U. Del., 1968; MBA, Pace U., 1981. Prodn. editor Prentice-Hall, Inc., Englewood Cliffs, N.J., 1968-70; dir. publs. Spl. Libraries Assn., N.Y.C., 1970-76; dir. mktg. services Knowledge Industry Publs., White Plains, N.Y., 1978-81, v.p., 1984-85; dir. inventory and contracts Macmillan Book Clubs, N.Y.C., 1981-84; group pub. Elsevier Sci. Pub. Co., N.Y.C., 1985-95, v.p. global mktg., 1996-99; v.p. STM books John Wiley & Sons, 1999—. Mem. Assn. Am. Publishers (chmn. jours. com., PSP exec. coun.), Soc. for Scholarly Publishing. Office: John Wiley & Sons Inc 605 Third Ave New York NY 10158

BAILEY, JERRY, jockey; b. Dallas, Aug. 29, 1957; Prof. jockey, 1974—. Recipient George Woolf Award, Jockey's Guild, 1992, Mike Venezia Award, New York Racing Assoc., 1993. Achievements include inducted into Racing Hall of Fame, 1995; winner: Kentuky Derby with Sea Hero, 1993, with Grindstone, 1997, Preakness Stakes with Hansel, 1991, with Red Bullet, 2000, Belmont Stakes with Hansel, 1991, with Empire Maker, 2003. Office: care Jockeys Guild 250 W Main St Lexington KY 40507-1714*

BAILEY, JOHN P., lawyer; b. Wheeling, W.Va., May 2, 1951; BA, Dartmouth Coll., 1973; JD, W.Va. U., 1976. Bar: W.Va. 1976, Ohio 1981, U.S. Dist. Ct. (no. and so. dists.) W.Va. 1976, U.S. Dist. Ct. (so. dist.) Ohio 2000, U.S. Ct. Appeals (4th cir.) 1977, U.S. Supreme Ct. 1981. Law clk. to Hon. Charles H. Haden, II, U.S. Dist. Judge (no. and so. dists.) W.Va., 1976—78; asst. pros. atty., 1985—86; atty. Bailey, Riley, Buch & Harman, LC, Wheeling, W.Va. Chmn. Workers' Compensation Appeal Bd., 1985—91. Mem.: ABA, Nat. Assn. Criminal Def. Lawyers, W.Va. Trial Lawyers, W.Va. State Bar (bd. govs. 1992—95, 1998—2001, pres. 2003—04, 2003), Ohio County Bar Assn., W.Va. Bar Assn. (exec. coun. 1988—94, pres. 1992—93), Order of Coif, Phi Delta Phi. Office: Bailey Riley Buch and Harman PO Box 631 Riley Bldg 53 Fourteenth St Ste 900 Wheeling WV 26003-0081 Office Phone: 304-232-6675. E-mail: jbailey@brbhlaw.com.

BAILEY, JUDITH IRENE, academic administrator, consultant; b. Winston-Salem, N.C., Aug. 24, 1946; d. William Edward Hege Jr. and Julia (Hedrick) Hege; m. Brendon Stinson Bailey, Jr, June 8, 1968. BA, Coker Coll., 1968; MEd, Va. Tech., 1973, EdD, 1976; postgrad., Harvard U., 1994, 1994—95. Tchr. Chariho Regional H.S., Wood River Junction, RI, 1969—70, Prince William County Pub. Schs., Woodbridge, Va., 1968—72; asst. prin. Osbourn H.S., Manassas, Va., 1973; secondary sch. coord. Stafford (Va.) County Schs., 1973—74; middle sch. coord. Stafford County Schs., 1975—76; human rels. coord. Coop. Extension Svc. U. Md., College Park, 1976—79; dep. dir. Coop. Extension Svc. U. D.C., Washington, 1980-88; asst. v.p., dir. Coop. Extension U. Maine, Orono, 1988—92, interim v.p. for rsch. and pub. svc., 1992—93, v.p. rsch. and pub. svc., 1993—95, v.p. acad. affairs, provost, 1995—97; pres. No. Mich. U., Marquette, 1997—2003, Western Mich. U., Kalamazoo, 2003—. Adj. prof. George Mason U., Fairfax, Va., 1978; grad. student adv. U. Md., 1979—80; spkr. and cons. in field; trustee Bronson Healthcare Group, Kalamazoo, 2003—; mem. steering com. Mich. Tri-Tech. Corridor, 2003—; mem. governing bd. Bioscis. Rsch. and Commercialization Ctr., 2003—; pres. Western Mich. U. Rsch. Found. Co-author: Contingency Planning for a Unitary School System; contbr. articles to profl. jours. Co-vice chmn. Lake Superior Cmty. Partnership, 1997—2003; bd. trustees Marquette (Mich.) Gen. Health Sys., 1998—2003; mem. Mich. Humanities Coun., 1999—2002, sec., treas., 2002; mem. adv. bd. Huntington Bank, 2003—; apptd. by gov. to Mich. Quarter Commn., 2004; mem. Am. Coun. Edn. Commn. on Women, 2004; trustee Southwest Mich. First; active Greater Kalamazoo United Way, mem.; bd. dirs. Pine Tree State 4-H Found., 1988—97, Maine Toxicology Inst., 1992—95, Bangor (Maine) Symphony Orch, 1991—97, Shorebank, 1997—2003, Gilmore Keyboard Festival, 2003—. Recipient Disting. Alumni Achievement award, Coker Coll., 1998, Northwoods Woman Educator of Yr. award, 1999, Case V Chief Exec. Leadership award, 2002; fellow Susan Coker Watson fellow, 1967. Mem.: AAUW, Greater Kalamazoo (Mich.) United Way, Grand Rapids Econ. Club, Econ. Club Marquette County (bd. dirs. 1997—2003), Rotary (Paul Harris fellow 2004), Epsilon Sigma Phi (sec. Mu chpt. 1987, v.p. 1988, State Disting. Svc. award), Phi Kappa Phi, Phi Delta Kappa. Republican. Avocations: cooking, hiking. Home: 1201 Short Rd Kalamazoo MI 49008 Office: Western Mich U Office of the President 1903 W MIchigan Kalamazoo MI 49008-5202 Business E-Mail: judi.bailey@wmich.edu.

BAILEY, JUDY LONG, outreach and education specialist, social worker; d. John H. and Sibyl K. Long; m. Charles A. Bailey, Jan. 1, 2001. BA, West Ga. U., Carrollton, 1969. Social caseworker Coweta Dept. of Family Svcs., Newnan, Ga., 1971—72, Lexington (SC) Dept. of Family Svcs., 1972—74; social work supr. Prince William Dept. Social Svcs., Manassas, Va., 1974—76; program specialist U.S. Dept. Agr., Washington, 1976—80; program analyst U.S. EPA, Washington, 1980—. Vol. Animal Welfare League of Arlington, Va., 1979—97, Fairfax County Pk. Authority, Alexandria, Va., 1990—2000. Mem.: Nat. Audubon Soc., Best Friends Animal Soc., Nature Conservancy. Avocations: gardening, animal welfare, reading. Home: 5004 Grimm Drive Alexandria VA 22304 Office: US EPA 4502T 1200 Pennsylvania Ave NW Washington DC 20460 Personal E-mail: dixicat22@msn.com.

BAILEY, K. RONALD, lawyer; b. Sandusky, Ohio, July 30, 1947; s. Kenneth White and Virginia McClung (Sheddan) B.; m. Sara Ann Geary Bressler, Mar. 14, 1969 (div. June 1973); 1 child, Matthew Scott; m. Lynn Darlene Kammer, Aug. 31, 1973; children: Thomas Keith, Kenneth Richard. B in Liberal Studies summa cum laude, Bowling Green State U., 1979; JD, Cleveland-Marshall Law Sch., 1982; grad., Gerry Spence's Trial Lawyers Coll., 1994. Bar: Ohio 1983, U.S. Dist. Ct. (no. dist.) Ohio 1983, U.S. Dist. Ct. (D.C. cir.) 2000, U.S. Ct. Appeals (6th cir.) 1985, U.S. Supreme Ct. 1992. Tool, diemaker Gen. Motors, Sandusky, 1968-84; sole practice Huron, Ohio, 1983-87; sr. trial atty. K. Ronald Bailey & Assocs. Co., Legal Profl. Assn., Sandusky, 1987—. Chmn. Charter Rev. Com. of Huron, 1984. Mem. adv. bd. Salvation Army, 2004—. Mem. ABA (criminal justice sect., white collar crimes com.), Nat. Assn. Criminal Def. Lawyers, Ohio Bar Assn. (coun. dels. 1998—, criminal justice sect., white collar crimes com., criminal law com.), Erie County Bar Assn., Ohio Assn. Criminal Def. Lawyers (bd. dirs., v.p. publs. 1991-93, 97-98, treas. 1994, pres. 1995-96, chmn. capital litigation 1997—, Pres.'s award 1989-95, 97-98, v.p. CLE, 1997-98). Democrat. Pentecostal. Avocations: reading, photography, painting, swimming, drag racing. Home: 121 Sycamore Dr Norwalk OH 44857-1914 Office: K Ronald Bailey & Assocs Co Legal Profl Assn 220 W Market St Sandusky OH 44870-2515 Office Phone: 416-625-6740. Business E-Mail: krbailey@baileyandassoc.com.

BAILEY, KAY WOOD, management consultant; b. Wilmington, Del. m. Richard H. Bailey. Adminstr. prison arts program Del. Dept. Correction, Dover, 1986—2002; pres., founder A.B.C. Consulting, Smyrna, Del., 2002—. Founder, pub., editor Wyoming (Del.) Gazette, Internat. Correctional Arts Network Jour.; career adv. bd. Wesley Coll., Dover, Del., 2004—. Friend of the libr. bd. Del. State U., Dover, 2004—; corres. sec. Underground Railroad Coalition Del., Wilmington, 2004—; past bd. dirs. Del. Symphony, Grand Opera House. Named Del. Trailblazer of the Yr., Agenda of Del. Women, 1991, hon. African Am., Star Hill A.M.E. Ch., 1995, Del. Mother of the Yr., Del. Chpt. Am. Mothers, 1997, Del. Art Educator of the Yr., Art Educators Del., 2000, Del. Communicator of Achievement, Del. Press Assn., 2002; recipient She Knows Where She's Going award, Girls Inc., 1993, Nat. Communicator of Achievement, Nat. Fedn. Press Women, 2002—03. Mem.: Sons of Civil War Union Vets. (v.p. Mary Torbert aux.). Home: 105 Front St Camden Wyoming DE 19934-1123

BAILEY, KEITH E., petroleum pipeline company executive; b. 1942; married. BS, Mo. Sch. Mines, 1964. With Continental Pipe Line, 1964—66; with Yellowstone Pipeline, 1966, Continental Pipeline, 1966—73, William Pipe Line Co. Inc., Tulsa, 1973—83, past pres.; pres., chief oper. officer N.W. Ctrl. Pipeline Corp., Tulsa; past exec. v.p. fin. and adminstrn. The Williams Cos., Tulsa, pres., 1992; former chmn., pres., CEO The Williams Cos., Inc., Tulsa. Dir. APCO Argentina Inc.*

BAILEY, KELLY FRANK, occupational health company executive; b. Havre, Mont., June 7, 1949; s. George William and Valeria Lucille (Novak) B.; m. Rebecca Vance, June 21, 1969 (div. Mar. 1976); 1 child, Jonathan Noel; m. Teresa Brewer, June 12, 1992; 1 child, Destin Mariah. BS in Chemistry and Human Biology, Lamar U., Beaumont, Tex., 1973. Cert. indsl. hygienist. Chief chemist Olin Corp., Beaumont, 1973-74; environ. chemist Celanese Chem. Co., Bay City, Tex., 1974-77; wastewater ind. cons. Bay City, 1975-78; tech. rep. Hercules Inc., Houston, 1978; plant indsl. hygienist Celanese Chem. Co., Houston, 1978-79; chem. divsn. indsl. hygienist Vulcan Chems. Co., Birmingham, Ala., 1979-84; corp. mgr. occupational health Vulcan Materials Co., Birmingham, 1984—. Chmn. safety and health com. Nat. Stone Assn., Washington, 1997-99; chmn., pres. Indsl. Health Coun., Birmingham, 1997-2002; apptd. Nat. Mine Safety and Health Rsch. Adv. Com., 2002—. Contbg. author: Occupational Health Programs in Mining, 1997, Health and Safety Management in Mining. Named Safety and Health Profls. of Yr., Nat. Stone Assn., Washington, 1993. Mem. Am. Indsl. Hygiene Assn., Am. Acad. Indsl. Hygiene, Ala. Am. Indsl. Hygiene Assn. (pres. 1982-83, apptd. mine safety and health rsch. adv. com.). Avocations: guitar, camping, canoing, fly fishing. Office: Vulcan Materials Co 1200 Urban Center Dr Birmingham AL 35242-2545 E-mail: bailey@vmcmail.com.

BAILEY, LEONARD LEE, surgeon; b. Takoma Park, Md., Aug. 28, 1942; s. Nelson Hulburt and Catherine Effie (Long) B.; m. Nancy Ann Schroeder, Aug. 21, 1966; children: Jonathan Brooks, Charles Connor. BS, Columbia Union Coll., 1964; postgrad., NIH, 1965; MD, Loma Linda (Calif.) U., 1969. Diplomate Am. Bd. Surgery, Am. Bd. Thoracic Surgery. Intern Loma Linda U. Med. Ctr., 1969-70, resident in surgery, 1970-73, resident in thoracic and cardiovasc. surgery, 1973-74; resident in pediatric cardiovasc. surgery Hosp. for Sick Children, Toronto, Canada, 1974-75; resident in thoracic and cardiovasc. surgery Loma Linda U. Med. Sch., 1975-76, asst. prof. surgery, 1976-86, prof. surgery, 1986—, prof. pediatric cardiac surgery, 1976—, chief divsn. cardiothoracic surgery, 1988-92, chair dept. surgery, 1992—. Mem. ACS, Am. Assn. Thoracic Surgery, Am. Surg. Assn., Am. Coll. Cardiology, Western Thoracic Surg. Assn., Soc. Thoracic Surgery, Western Soc. Pediatric Rsch., Internat. Soc. for Heart Transplantation, Am. Heart Assn., Internat. Assn. for Cardiac Biol. Implants, Am. Soc. for Artificial Internal Organs, Pacific Coast Surg. Assn., Western Assn. Transplant Surgeons, Internat. Soc. for Cardiovasc. Surgery, United Network for Organ Sharing, The Transplant Soc. Democrat. Adventist. Office: Loma Linda U Med Ctr and Children's Hosp 11175 Campus St Ste 21120 Loma Linda CA 92350-1700 Office Phone: 909-558-8744. Business E-Mail: lbailey@som.llu.edu.

BAILEY, MARY BEATRICE, retired health science association administrator; b. Pitts., Dec. 24, 1933; d. Harry Chantler and Beatrice Iseli (Koenig) B. Diploma in Nursing, Allegheny Gen. Hosp., Pitts., 1956; BSNE, Chatham Coll., Pitts., 1956; MSN, Duke U., Durham, 1967. Cert. nursing adminstr., advanced. Staff nurse, head nurse, nursing supr. Allegheny Gen. Hosp., Pittsburgh, 1956-60; nursing instr. pediatrics Duke U. Sch. Nursing, Durham, N.C., 1960-61; nursing instr. med. surg Rex Hosp. Sch. Nursing, Raleigh, N.C., 1962-63; nursing supr. Rex Hosp., Raleigh, 1964-71, patient care coord., 1972-86, clin. dir., 1987, dir. nursing info. system, 1987-95. Author: The Role of the Mother with her Hospitalized Child, 1966. Vol. Rn open door clinic, Raleigh, 1987-88, Meals on Wheels, Wake Co., 1996—, Raleigh Little Theatre, 1993—; mem. N.C. Coalition for Choice; elected N.C. Bd. of Nursing, 1991-93, 94-96. Named to The Great 100 N.C. Nurses, 1992. Mem. NOW, N.C. Coun. Women's Orgns., N.C. League for Nursing, N.C. Nurses

Assn. (life, treas. 1977-79), Great 100 (charter treas. 1989), Zonta Club of Raleigh (charter treas.). Democrat. Episcopalian. Avocations: reading, theater, music, sports. Home: 311 Furches St Raleigh NC 27607-4015

BAILEY, MICHAEL DAVID, history professor; b. Cleve., June 22, 1971; s. Murray and Bernadette Bailey. BA, Duke U., Durham, N.C., 1993; PhD, Northwestern U., Evanston, Ill., 1998. Asst. prof. of history Iowa State U., Ames, 2003—. Author: (book) Battling Demons: Witchcraft, Heresy, and Reform in the Late Middle Ages, Historical Dictionary of Witchcraft; contbr. encyclopedia. Fellow Fulbright fellow, US Fulbright Com., 1996—97, DAAD fellow, German Academic Exch. Svc., 1997—98, Mellon fellow in the humanities, U. of Pa. Humanities Forum, 2003—04. Mem.: Medieval Acad. of Am., Am. Soc. of Ch. History, Renaissance Soc. of Am., Am. Hist. Assn., Phi Beta Kappa. Office: Iowa State University Dept of History 603 Ross Hall Ames IA 50011 Office Phone: 515-294-1284.

BAILEY, NAN HUTCHINS, mathematician, educator; b. Tyler, Tex., July 2, 1952; d. Lemuel Conner and Martha (Hawes) Hutchins; m. Blake Henry Bailey, Nov. 1, 1984 (div. May 1998); children: Laura Elizabeth, Katherine Conner. Premier deg., Sorbonne U., 1972; BA in Math and French, Hollins U., 1974; MS in Math., George Mason U., 1977. Tchr. Math. London County Ind. Sch. Dist., Sterling Park, Va., 1974—75; tchr. h.s. Dept. Def., Okinawa, Japan, 1977—78; tchr. Math., French Carlsbad Ind. Sch. Dist., Carlsbad, Calif., 1979—81; tchr. Math. Crooked Oak Ind. Sch. Dist., Oklahoma City, 1981—83; instr. Math. U. Tex. Tyler, 1984—85, Tyler Jr. Coll., Tyler, 1987—94; tchr. Math. Tyler Ind. Sch. Dist., Tyler, 1997—. Bd. regents Tex. Women's U., Denton, 1992—98. Named Educator of Distinction, Coca Cola Found., 2002, Secondary Tchr. of Yr., Tyler Ind. Sch. Dist., 2002. Democrat. Presbyterian. Avocations: hiking, reading, pen and ink drawing, philosophy. Home: 800 Fox Cove Tyler TX 75703 Office: John Tyler High Sch 1120 NNW Loop 323 Tyler TX 75704

BAILEY, NETTIE WHITNEY, retired educator; b. Chgo., Dec. 26, 1932; d. Greene Raspberry and Gertrude Ellen Whitney; m. Clifford James Bailey, May 24, 1952 (dec. 1996); children: Judith Venay (dec.), Clifford James, Debra Ellen. BA, Chgo. State U., 1965; MA, Northwestern U., 1971. Kindergarten, elem. sch. tchr., libr. Beidler Elem. Sch., asst. prin. Chgo. Bd. Edn., Chgo., 1965-88; ret., 1988. Tutor, 1999-2002; local sch. cmty. rep. Beidler Elem. Sch., 1997-2002, edn. cons., 2000-02; ednl. cons. DePaul U., 1999-2002. Author: Learning Without Books: Grades 4-6, 1998, (poems) Peace in the Midst of the Storm, 1998, Correcting Deficiencies in the Basic Skills, 2002. Sunday sch. supt., supt. children's dept. St. Stephen AME Ch., Chgo.; bd. dirs. Garfield Pk. Conservatory Alliance, 1999—. Featured on program Someone You Should Know, Sta. WLS-TV (Channel 7) Chgo., 1999, 2002. Avocations: collecting elephants, crossword puzzles, playing scrabble. Home: 3443 W Fulton Blvd Chicago IL 60624-1913

BAILEY, PRESTON EDWARD, music educator; b. Hollywood, Calif., Mar. 27, 1950; s. Lemuel Conner and Myradelle Peck Bailey; children: Celeste Michelle, Crystal Danielle. BA in Music Edn., Sonoma State U., 1992. Customer svc. Betnun Music & Stein on Vine, Hollywood, Calif., 1977—81; various prodn. positions Las Palmas Prodns., 1979—83; musician Music Americana, L.A., 1976—83; ind. tchr. music varius schs., Sonoma, 1988—92, Marin, 1988—92; dir. elem. music Petaluma City Schs., 1992—2000; dir. music Petaluma Jr. High Sch., 2000—. Recipient Hon. Svc. award, McKinley Sch. PTA, Petaluma, 1994. Mem.: Music Educators Nat. Conf. Home: 114 Post St Petaluma CA 94952 Office: Petaluma Jr High Sch 700 Bantam Way Petaluma CA 94952

BAILEY, REEVE MACLAREN, museum curator; b. Fairmont, W.Va., May 2, 1911; s. Joseph Randall and Elizabeth Weston (Maclaren) B.; m. Marian Alvinette Kregel, Aug. 13, 1939; children— Douglas M., David R., Thomas G., Susan Helen. Student, Toledo U., 1929-30; AB, U. Mich., 1933, PhD, 1938. Instr. zoology Iowa State Coll. (now univ.), 1938-42, asst. prof., 1942-44; asst. prof. zoology U. Mich., 1944-50, asso. prof., 1950-59, prof., 1959-81, prof. emeritus, 1981—. Assoc. curator Mus. Zoology, 1944-48, curator, 1948—; rsch. assoc. Am. Mus. Nat. History, 1964—. Contbr. over 160 articles, bulls., revs. to profl. jours. on ichthyology and herpetology. Fellow Iowa Acad. Sci.; mem. Am. Soc. Ichthyologists and Herpetologists (editl. bd., v.p. 1954, pres. 1959, Robert H. Gibbs Jr. Meml. award 1995), Am. Fisheries Soc. (pres. 1974, hon. mem. 1979—, recipient Award of Excellence 1980, Meritorious Svc. award 1989, Justin W. Leonard award of excellence Mich. chpt. 1985), Am. Inst. Fisheries Rsch. Biologists (Outstanding Achievement award 1996), AAAS (coun. 1968-72), Ecol. Soc. Am., Soc. Study Evolution, Soc. Systematic Biologists, Soc. Limnology and Oceanography, Mich. Acad. Sci., Arts and Letters. Avocation: ichthyology expeditions in US, Bermuda, Bolivia, Guatemala, Paraguay, and Zambia. Home: 4001 Glacier Hills Dr Apt 325 Ann Arbor MI 48105-3652 Office: Univ Mich Museum Zoology Ann Arbor MI 48109 E-mail: reevemarian@yahoo.com.

BAILEY, RICHARD BRIGGS, investment company executive; b. Weston, Mass., Sept. 14, 1926; s. George William and Alice Gertrude (Cooper) B.; m. Rebecca C. Bradford, June 20, 1950 (div. Dec. 1974); children: Ann, Elizabeth, Richard, Rebecca; m. Anita S. Lawrence, Sept. 12, 1980 (div. 1990); 1 child, Alexandra. BA, Harvard, 1948, MA, 1951; postgrad., Grad. Sch. Bus. Adminstrn., 1966. Prodn. engr. C. Brewer & Co., Honolulu, 1951-53; prodn. engr. Raytheon Co., Waltham, Mass., 1953-54; security analyst Keystone Custodian Funds, Boston, 1955-59; industry specialist Mass. Investors Trust, 1959-69; v.p. Mass. Fin. Svcs., Co., Boston, 1969-77, pres., 1978-82, chmn., dir., 1982-91, ret., 1991. Chmn. Lincoln (Mass.) Fin. Com., 1966-68. Trustee Plimoth Plantation, Inc., Plymouth, Mass., Phillips Exeter Acad., Exeter, N.H., 1978-82, Handel and Haydn Soc. 2d lt. Signal Corps, AUS, 1944-46. Decorated Letter of Commendation. Republican. Episcopalian. Address: c/o William F Kehoe Taylor Ganson & Perrin 160 Federal St Boston MA 02110

BAILEY, RITA MARIA, investment advisor, psychologist; b. Germany; d. Ludwig and Getrude Fleischmann; m. William W. Bailey; children: Anne Christine, Cynthia Patricia. BS in Psychology, Austin Peay U., 1975, MA in Psychology, 1977, postgrad., 1977—79. Cert. counselor Tenn. Editor U.S. Army Spl. Warfare Inst., Ft. Bragg, NC, 1970—74, edn. officer, 1979-82, Augsburg (Germany) Cmty. Ctr., 1982-85; pvt. practice counseling Leavenworth, Kans., 1985-90; pvt. practice investments, 1990—. Author: Extroversion and Introversion, 1978, Special Warfare Training Plan, 1981; author, editor: tng. manual Foreign Small Arms, 1982. Dir. Energy Conservation Campaign, Clarksville, 1976; founder, dir. Women's Support Ctr., Leavenworth, 1986. Mem.: Nat. Assn. Investors, Alpha Mu Gamma. Roman Catholic. Avocations: long distance swimming, gardening, German poetry.

BAILEY, ROBERT, JR., advertising executive; b. Kansas City, Kans., Apr. 27, 1945; s. Robert and Sarah (Morgan) B.; m. Rita Carol Burdinie, June 26, 1971; children: Rebecca, Sarah. AB, U. Kans., 1967; MA, Northwestern U., 1968, PhD, 1972, MBA, 1979. Research supr. BBDO Chgo., 1973-78, v.p. research dir., 1978-82, sr. v.p., mktg. services dir., 1982-85, exec. v.p., rsch. dir. Author: Radicals In Urban Politics, 1974; contbr. articles to profl. jours. Mem. Am. Mktg. Assn. Office: BBDO Chgo 410 N Michigan Ave Ste 8 Chicago IL 60611-4273 Business E-Mail: bob.bailey@bbdoch.com.

BAILEY, ROBERT C., opera company executive; b. Metropolis, Ill., Dec. 28, 1936; m. Sally McDermott, July 13, 1958. BA in Speech, U. Ill., 1958, MA in English, 1960; BM in Applied Voice, Eastman Sch. Music, 1965; MM in Applied Voice, New Eng. Conservatory Music, 1969. Music prodr. Nat. Pub. Radio, Washington, 1971-73, dir. cultural programming, 1973-75; mgr. Western Opera Theatre, San Francisco, 1975-79; instr. arts mgmt. Golden Gate U., San Francisco, 1977-82; cons. arts mgmt. San Francisco, 1980-82; gen. dir. Portland Opera Assn., Oreg., 1982—; dir. Opera Am., 1995—2001. Cons. On-Site Program Nat. Endowment Arts, Washington, 1982—; judge Met. Opera Auditions, 1977—. Recipient Chevalier in the Order of Arts and Letters French Govt., 1999. Mem. Bohemian Club (San Francisco), City Club (Portland), Arlington Club, Rotary Club. Office: Portland Opera Broadway In Portland 211 SE Caruthers St Portland OR 97214-4549

BAILEY, ROBERT ELLIOTT, finance company executive; b. Logansport, Ind., Mar. 29, 1932; s. Edwin William and Elizabeth Carolyn (Elliott) B.; m. Geraldine E. Hershberger, Jan. 31, 1954; children: Susan Elaine, Kathryn Jane. BS in Acctg., Ind. U., 1954; LLB, South Tex. Coll. Law, 1962. CPA, N.Y. Ptnr. Arthur Andersen & Co., Chgo., 1958-72; exec. v.p., dir., CFO Damson Oil Corp., N.Y.C., 1972-82; exec. v.p., CFO ENI Cos., Seattle and Houston, 1982-85; exec. v.p., CFO, dir. Gearhart Industries, Inc., Ft. Worth, Tex., 1985-88; corp. fin. cons., 1988-91; chmn. fin. The Turner Corp., N.Y.C., 1991-93; sr. v.p., CFO Rotondo Cos., Avon, Conn., 1993-94; dir. fin. UCAR, Danbury, Conn., 1995-96, Tauck Tours, Inc., Westport, Conn., 1996-98. Bd. dirs. Berlin Steel Constrn. Co., Kensington, Conn. Capt. USAFR, 1958. Mem. AICPA, Tex. Bar Assn., N.Y. CPA Soc., Fla. CPA Soc. Home: #209 988 Boulevard of the Arts Sarasota FL 34236-4833

BAILEY, ROBERT SHORT, lawyer; b. Bklyn., Oct. 17, 1931; s. Cecil Graham and Mildred (Short) B.; m. Doris Furlow, Aug. 29, 1953 (dec. 2001); children: Elizabeth Jane Goldentyer, Robert F., Barbara A. Jongbloed. AB, Wesleyan U., Middletown, Conn., 1953; JD, U. Chgo., 1956. Bar: Ill. 1965, U.S. Dist. Ct. D.C. 1956, U.S. Supreme Ct. 1960. Atty. criminal divsn. U.S. Dept. Justice, 1956-61, asst. U.S. atty. No. dist. Ill., 1961-65; ptnr. LeFevour & Bailey, Oak Park, Ill., 1965-68; pvt. practice, Chgo., 1968—. Panel atty. Fed. Defender Program, 1965—. Mem. NACDL (faculty 1976-78, legis. chmn. 1976-78). Home: 17 Timber Trail Streamwood IL 60107-1353 Office: Ste 860 53 W Jackson Blvd Chicago IL 60604-3607 Office Phone: 312-427-6050. E-mail: bobsbailey@comcast.net.

BAILEY, ROBIN BUNCH WOODS, conductor; b. Madison, W.Va., July 8, 1958; d. Robert Garland and Orpha VanHoose Bunch; m. Kevin E. Bailey, Aug. 19, 2000; m. William L. Woods, July 7, 1984 (div.). B of Music Edn., W.Va. Wesleyan Coll., 1981; MA in Music Theatre, Conducting, Marshall U., 1994. Tchr. gen. music, band Boone County Schs., Madison, W.Va., 1981—86; band dir. Chapmanville Jr. High Sch., 1987—91; youth devel. 4-H agt. Boone County Ext. Svc., 1996—98; band, choral dir. Madison Mid. Sch., 1998—. Adj. faculty Shawnee State U., Portsmouth, Ohio, 1991—96, So. W.Va. C.C., Logan, 1991—96; adj. faculty, staff Marshall U., Huntington, 1991—96; staff asst. Huntington Chamber Orch., 1999; 4-H camping asst. W.Va. U. Ext. Svc., Morgantown, 1979—81. Secondary polit. advisor W.Va. Jr. Chamber, 2000—, state pres., 1998—2000; v.p. C.R.E.A.T.E., Madison, W.Va., 2002—. Mem.: Madison-Danville Jaycees (pres., v.p., program mgr., bd. dirs.). Methodist. Avocations: musical theatre, Star Trek. Home: 262 Osborne Ave Madison WV 25130

BAILEY, STEPHANIE B.C., city health department administrator; BS, Clark U., Worchester, Mass.; MS in health svcs. adminstrn., Coll. of St. Francis; MD, Meharry Med. Coll., Nashville. Dir., health Metro Pub. Health Dept. of Nashville/Davidson Co., 1995—. Bd. dirs. Centerstone Cmty. Health Ctrs. Inc., 2002—. Mem. Nat. Adv. Com. on Rural Health, Nat. Adv. Com. for Elimination of Tuberculosis, Nat. Adv. Com. to CDC Dir. Recipient Excellence in Pub. Health award, ASTHO, 1999. Mem.: Nat. Assn. of County and City Health Officials (bd. mem.). Office: Metro Pub Health Dept 311 23rd Ave N Nashville TN 37203

BAILEY, STEPHEN FAIRCHILD, retired museum director, ornithologist; b. Stamford, Conn., Feb. 7, 1948; s. Edwin Montgomery and Frances (Sherman) B.; m. Karen Lynn Burtness, Aug. 18, 1971 (div. July 1987). BA in Biology magna cum laude, Beloit Coll., 1971; PhD in Zoology, U. Calif., Berkeley, 1978. Mus. dir. Pacific Grove (Calif.) Mus. of Natural Hist., 1992—2004; ret., 2004. Collections mgr. for ornithology and mammalogy Calif. Acad. Scis., San Francisco, 1984-92; biol. cons., 1979-92; adj. prof. biology San Francisco State U., 1986—; tchr. Albany Adult Sch., Calif., 1979-85. Co-author Atlas of the Breeding Birds of Monterey County, 1993; co-author, photographer Audubon Society Master Guide to Birding 3 vols., 1983; regional editor Am. Birds, 1985-98; contbr. articles to profl. jours. Rsch. fellowship Christensen Rsch. Inst., Papua New Guinea, 1989. Mem. Am. Birding Assn. (elected), Ecol. Soc. Am. (life), Am. Ornithologists Union, Cooper Ornithol. Soc. (life), Pacific Seabird Group, Phi Eta Sigma, Phi Beta Kappa. Avocations: birding, travel, nature study, military history. Home: 4564 Valley West Blvd Apt C Arcata CA 95521 E-mail: sfbailey@reninet.com.

BAILEY, SUSAN RUDD, physician; BS, Tex. A&M U., 1979, MD, 1981; postgrad., Mayo Grad. Sch. Medicine, 1981-84, 84-86. Diplomate Am. Bd. Pediatrics, Am. Bd. Allergy and Immunology; lic. Tex. Assoc. cons. dept. pediatrics Mayo Clinic, Rochester, Minn., 1987; pvt. practice, allergy and clin. immunology Fort Worth (Tex.) Allergy and Asthma Assocs., 1988—. Instr. in pediatrics Mayo Med. Sch., 1986-87; bd. dirs. Accreditation Coun. on Continuing Med. Edn., 2004—; presenter in field. Mem. editl. bd. Annals Allergy, Asthma and Immunology, 1997—2003; contbr. articles to profl. jours. Bd. visitors Scott and White Clinic, 1994—; adv. bd. M.D. Anderson Physicians, 1992-94; bd. regents Tex. A&M U. Sys., 1999-2005; mem. AMA Coun. Med. Edn. Exec. Com., 2005- Recipient Residents' award Northwest Pediatric Soc., 1984, Leon Unger award Am. Coll. Allergists, 1985, Geigy fellow, 1987, travel grantsee, dist. fellow Am. Coll. Allergy, Asthma & Immunology, 1998. Mem. AMA (chmn. med. student sect. 1980-81, chmn. com. on women in medicine 1987-89, coun. med. edn. 2004-), Mayo Assn. of Fellows (treas. 1984-85), Mayo Alumni Assn. (exec. com. 1983-87, 1995-2002), The Mayo Alumnus (adv. bd. 1983-87), Tarrant County Med. Soc. (bd. dirs. 1990—, v.p. 1994-95, pres.-elect 1995-96, pres. 1996-97, trustee 1998—2001), Minn. Med. Assn. (trustee 1984-85), Tex. Med. Assn. (vice spkr. 1997-2001, spkr. 2001—05, various coms.), Am. Acad. Pediats., Am. Coll. Allergy and Immunology (bd. regents 1994-97, chair publs. com. 2003—), Alpha Omega Alpha, Alpha Zeta, others. Office: 5929 Lovell Ave Fort Worth TX 76107-5029

BAILEY, SUZANNE LYNNE, nursing educator; d. Leroy Nelson and Lloyd Victoria McCoy; m. Garry Ray Bailey, July 18, 1982; children: Christopher, Andrew. BS, U. Evansville, 1982; MS, Ind. U., 1997. RN Ind. Nurse Welborn Hosp., Evansville, 1982—87, Evansville Surgery Ctr., 1987—2003; clin. nurse specialist St. Mary's Med. Ctr., Evansville, 1998—2003; asst. prof. U. Evansville, 2000—. Vol. Pub. Edn. Found., Evansville, 2003—05. Recipient Deans Tchg. award, U. Evansville, 2002. Mem.: Midwest Bus. and Health Adminstrn. Assn. (bd. dirs. 2004—05), Sigma Theta Tau (counselor 2002—05).

BAILEY, T. WAYNE, political science professor; BA in polit. sci. with honors, U. Fla.; MA in polit. sci. and history, Peabody Coll., Vanderbilt U.; PhD in polit. sci., U. Fla. Prof. polit. sci. Stetson U., DeLand, Fla., 1983—. Chair Govt. Rels. Com.; cons. in field. Vol. Am. Lung Assn., Fla., pres., 1994—95; mentor to students in govt. careers; vol. Dem. Party; past del. Dem. Nat. Convention. Named J. Ollie Edmunds chair, 1984—85; recipient Will Ross medal, Am. Lung Assn., Hubert H. Humphrey Outstanding Statesman award, Fla. Dem. Party, 1983, Ed Dunn Leadership award, Tiger Bay Club, Volusia County, Discovery Health Channel Med. Honors, 2004. Achievements include urged the Am. Lung Assn. of Fla. to shift its focus from small ednl. programs to lobbying for stronger legis. The 1985 Fla. Clean Indoor Air Act has improved the health of Fla. residents lungs. Office: Stetson Univ 421 N Woodland Blvd Deland FL 32720

BAILEY, THERESA L., director, consultant; d. George and Fammie Barnes Bailey, Albert, Sr. Evans; 1 child, Natasha N. BS, Alcorn State U., Miss., 1979, MS, 1994; PhD, Fla. State U., 2002—. Sec. Dept. of Fine Arts, Alcorn State U., Lorman, Miss., 1979—82; home health Adams County Health Dept., Natchez, Miss., 1982—83; gen. acct. The Piney Woods Country Life Sch., Miss., 1983—90; asst. to the v.p. for instl. advancement Tougaloo Coll., Miss., 1990—92, program adminstr., 1992—93; grants coord. Tuskegee U., Ala., 1993—95; assoc. in grants devel. Divsn. of Sponsored Rsch., Fla. A&M U., Tallahassee, 1995—2002, acting assoc. dir. sponsored rsch., 2002—. Pres., CEO TLB & Assocs.; cons. U. of Ark., Pine Bluff, 1997; instr., cons. Minority Health Professions Found., Atlanta, 1999; cons. Johnson C. Smith U., Charlotte, 1998, Miss. Valley State U., Itta Bena, Fla., 2000. Mem. Tallahassee Mus., 2003, Tallahassee Urban League, 2003; polit. campaign supporter, worker Charles Sheppard Campaign for State Govt., Lorman, Miss.; mem. Alcorn State U. Nat. Alumni Assn., Lorman, Miss. Mem.: AREA, Sisters of the Acad., Phi Delta Kappa, Nat. Coun. of Univs. Rsch. Administrs., Soc. of Rsch. Administrators (SRA) (mem. external rels. com. 1996—2000), Nat. Sponsored Programs Administrs. Alliance (chairperson membership com. 1997—2001). Democrat. Avocations: travel, reading, music, art, real estate. Office: Florida A&M U 400 Foote Hilyer Administrn Ctr Tallahassee FL 32307 Personal E-mail: tlbassociate@earthlink.net. E-mail: theresa.bailey@famu.edu.

BAILEY, THOMAS ANTHONY, lawyer; b. Milw., Nov. 20, 1942; s. Lawrence C. and Phyllis E. (Croasdaile) B.; m. Barbara Mary Dobbin, June 10, 1967; children: Mary Elizabeth, Kathleen, Erin, Brian, Sean, Bridget, Kevin, Michael. BS in Fin., Marquette U., 1964, JD, 1967; postgrad., U. Va. Law Sch., 1968-70. Bar: Wis. 1967, U.S. Supreme Ct. 1977. Asst. dist. atty. Milw. County, Milw., 1967-68; ptnr. Fricker & Bailey, Milw., 1972-92, Bailey Law Offices, Whitefish Bay, Wis., 1992—. Supr. Milw. County Bd., 1979—. Capt., U.S. Army, 1968-72. Fellow Am. Acad. Matrimonial Lawyers; mem. Milw. Bar Assn. (pres. 1984-85, chmn. family law sect.), Wis. Bar Assn., Wis. Acad. Trial Lawyers, St. Thomas More Lawyers Soc. (pres. 1980-81). Home and Office: Bailey Law Offices 130 W Silver Spring Dr Milwaukee WI 53217-4707

BAILEY, VICKY A., lobbyist; b. Indpls. BS, Purdue U.; postgrad., Ind. U., Indpls. Promotions dir. Glass Container divsn. Owens-Ill., Inc., Alton; asst. admissions officer Ind. U. Sch. Medicine; commr. Fed. Energy Regulatory Commn., 1993—2000; pres. PSI Energy, Inc., Ind., 2000—01; asst. secy. int. affairs and domestic policy U.S. Dept. Energy, Washington, 2001—04; ptnr. Johnston & Associates, LLC, Washington. Rep. to bd. trustees N.AM. Electric Reliability Coun.; mem. exec. com. Gt. Lakes conv. Mid-Am. Regulatory Commrs. Conf.; mem. Keystone Ctr. Energy Bd.; mem. Harvard Electricity Policy Group. Mem. Ind. Coun. for Econ. Edn.; active Boys and Girls Club of Indpls.; past pres. Indpls. Pub. Schs. Edn. Found., Ind. Humanities Coun., Nat. Coalition of 100 Black Women. Recipient Ind. Sagamore of the Wabash award. Mem. Nat. Assn. Regulatory Utility Commrs. (exec. and electricity coms.). Republican. Office: Johnston & Assocs 2099 Pennsylvania Ave NW Ste 1000 Washington DC 20006 Office Phone: 202-659-8400. Office Fax: 202-659-1340.*

BAILEY, WILLIAM HARRISON, artist, educator; b. Council Bluffs, Iowa, Nov. 17, 1930; s. Willard Kendall and Marjorie Esther (Cheyney) Bailey; m. Sandra Stone, May 28, 1958; children: Ford Hamilton, Alix Brook. Student, U. Kans., 1948-51; BFA, Yale U., 1955, MFA, 1957; HHD (hon.), U. Utah, 1987; DFA (hon.), Adelphi U., Pa. Acad. Fine Arts, 2004. Instr. art Yale U., New Haven, 1957-61, asst. prof., 1961-62, adj. prof., 1969-73, prof., 1973-79, Kingman Brewster prof., 1979-95, Kingman Brewster prof. emeritus, 1995—, dean Sch. Art, 1974-75; asst. prof., assoc. prof. Ind. U., 1962—68, prof., 1968-69. Mem. Nat. Coun. Arts, 1992—97. Exhibitions include Robert Schoelkopf Gallery, NYC, 1968, 1971, 1974, 1979, 1982, 1986, Galleria Il Gabbiano, Rome, 1985, 1989, 1993, Glleria Il Gabbiano, 1997, John Berggruen Gallery, San Francisco, 1988, Robert Schoelkopf Gallery, NYC, 1990—91, Andre Emmerich Gallery, 1992, 1994—95, Alpha Gallery, Boston, 1998, Robert Miller Gallery, NYC, 1999, 2003, Palace of the Legion of Honor, San Francisco, 2003, Betty Cuningham Gallery, NYC, 2005, Represented in permanent collections Mus. Modern Art, Whitney Mus., Hirshorn Mus., St. Louis Art Mus., Neu Galerie Der Stadt Aachen, Germany, Pa. Acad., Yale Art Gallery. With U.S. Army, 1951—53. Alice Kimball English Travelling fellow, 1955, Guggenheim fellow, 1965, Ingram Merrill fellow, 1975. Mem.: Conn. Acad. Arts and Scis., Nat. Coun. Arts, Academia di Belli Arti, Perugia, Acad. San Luca, Rome, Am. Acad. Arts and Letters, Nat. Acad. Design, Smithsonian Archives Am. Art (trustee), Tiffany Found. (bd. dirs.), Yaddo (mem. corp.). Office: Yale U Sch Art Dept Painting Printmaking New Haven CT 06520

BAILEY, WILLIAM HENRY, real estate appraiser; b. Kingsport, Tenn., Jan. 28, 1949; s. Fred M. and Ora Juanita (Barton) B.; m. Sharon Shanks, Nov. 17, 1973 (div.); 1 child, Allison Michelle; m. Penny S. Shoemaker, Dec. 26, 1983; children: Alexandra Amanda, William Henry. BS in Real Estate, East Tenn. State U., 1972. Salesman, auctioneer, appraiser C. Worley Richardson, Real Estate & Auction, Church Hill, Tenn., 1971-76; salesman, appraiser The Property Shop, Mt. Carmel, Tenn., 1976-78; broker, auctioneer, appraiser, owner Preferred Properties Realty & Auction, Mt. Carmel, 1978-81; appraiser, pres. W. Henry Bailey Appraisers, Mt. Carmel, 1981—; adj. prof. East Tenn. State U., 2002—, bd. dirs., dept. econs. and fin., 2005—. Rep. pub. rels. com. Appraisal Inst., State of Tenn., 1990-92, chmn., 1997-99, mem. representing ETN, 2000—; del. Holston Meth. Conf., Lake Junaluska, N.C., 1991; mem. curriculum com., dept. fin. and econs. East Tenn. State U. Pres., sec., treas. Church Hill (Tenn.) Housing Devel. Corp., 1973—; mem. Planning Comm., City of Church Hill, 1975-77, alderman, 1975-77; pres. Carter's Valley Elem. Sch. PTSO, Church Hill, 1982; gov. appointed commr. Tenn. Real Estate Appraisal Commn., 1994-97; alderman City of Mt. Carmel, 1998—; mem., appraisal mem. Ea. Tenn./S.W. Va. Appraisal Com.; mem. Mt. Carmel Regional Planning Commn., 2002--; mem. adv. bd. econs. and fin. East Tenn. State U., 2002--. Named Ky. Col., Commonwealth of Ky., Frankfort, 1973. Mem. Soc. Real Estate Appraisers (pres. Tenneva chpt. 1986-87, co-chmn. legis. com. 1987-91, candidate guidance com. chmn. 1987-91, Appraiser of Yr. 1989, Gideon Internat. Jaycees (external v.p. Church Hill, Tenn. chpt. 1973-74), Masons, Shriners, Upper East Tenn. Appraiser Coalition (chpt. pres. S.W. Va. 1994, chmn. Tenn., Va. regional MLS appraisal com. 1994). Methodist. Avocations: teaching real estate, lay speaker in church, farming. Office: W Henry Bailey Appraisers 117 Commerce St Kingsport TN 37660-4348 Home: PO Box 2288 Kingsport TN 37662-2288 Office Phone: 423-723-2233. E-mail: hbailey@preferred.com.

BAILEY, WILLIAM WADDELL, writer, communications executive; s. George W. and Phyllis K. Bailey; m. Rita Maria Fleischmann. BA in Psychology, U. Miss., 1973; MA in Internat. Rels., U. So. Calif., 1985; disting. grad., Command and Gen. Staff Coll., 1987. Cert. software engr. Commd. 2d lt. U.S. Army, 1973, advanced through grades to lt. col., officer Ft. Bragg, N.C., 1973-82; software mgr. U.S. Govt., Augsburg, Germany, 1982-85, modernization mgr. Leavenworth, Kans., 1985-90, divsn. chief Arlington, Va., 1990-92, spl. exec., 1992-93; sr. advisor to pvt. orgns. Washington, 1993-97; pres. Writer's Ink, Fayetteville, N.C., 1997—; resident artist Urban Arts Prgm., 1998, Arts and Tech., 1999. Cons. Sierra Cybernetics, Yorba Linda, Calif., 1993—. Author, editor: 2004 Future Architecture, 1987, Modernization Plan, 1989; author: Desert Storm Lessons Learned, 1991; contbr. articles, stories and poems to mags. and jours. Mem. fundraising com. Hist. Mus., Fayetteville, 1981; mem. Arts Coun., 1996—. Decorated Legion of Merit. Avocations: astronomy, fencing.

BAILEY-WELLS, DEBORAH, lawyer; BA with honors, Mills Coll., 1980; JD, Univ. San Francisco, 1984. Bar: Calif. 1984, US Dist. Ct. (no., ctrl., so. & ea. Calif.), US Ct. Appeals (9th & Fed. cir.), US Supreme Ct. Adminstrv. ptnr. & mem. mgmt. com. Kirkpatrick & Lockhart Nicholson Graham LLP, San Francisco. Contbr. articles to profl. jours. Mem.: ABA, Am. Intellectual Property Bar Assn., Internat. Trademark Assn., San Francisco Intellectual Property Law Assn., Silicon Valley Intellectual Property Assn. Office: Kirkpatrick & Lockhart Nicholson Graham LLP 10th Fl 4 Embarcadero Ctr San Francisco CA 94111-4121 Office Phone: 415-249-1065. Office Fax: 415-249-1001. Business E-Mail: dbaileywells@klng.com.

BAILIN, MICHAEL TRAHERN, physician; BS in biology, Mass. Inst. Tech., 1976—80; MD, Harvard Med. Sch., Boston, 1980—84. Bd. cert. anesthesiologist Am. Bd. Anesthesiology, 1988. Pres. Narragansett Bay Anesthesia, Providence, 2004—; chief, dept. anesthesiology The Miriam

Hosp., Providence, 2004—; resident and chief resident in anesthesiology Mass. Gen. Hosp., 1985—88, anesthesiologist, 1988—2003; chief, anesthesiologist St. Vincent Hosp., Worcester, Mass., 2003—04.

BAILLIE, JAMES LEONARD, lawyer; b. Mpls., Aug. 27, 1942; s. Leonard Thompson and Sylvia Alfreda (Fundberg) B.; m. Jacqueline McGlamery; children: Jennifer, Craig, John. AB in History, 1964; JD, U. Chgo., 1967. Bar: Minn. 1967, U.S. Dist. Ct. Minn. 1968, U.S. Ct. Appeals (8th cir.) 1969, U.S. Ct. Appeals (5th cir.) 1980. Law clk. to presiding justice U.S. Dist. Ct., Mpls., 1967-68; assoc. Fredrikson & Byron, P.A., Mpls., 1968-73, shareholder, 1973—. Mem. ABA (litigation sect. co-editor Bankruptcy Litigation 1998, bus. law sect. editl. bd. Bus. Law Today 1993-98, bus. sect. chair pro bono com. 1999-2003, section coun 2003—, standing com. on lawyer pub. svc. responsibility 1991-96, chmn. 1993-96, nat. pro bono award 1984, John Minor Wisdom award 1999), Minn. State Bar Assn. (chmn. bankruptcy sect. 1985-88, sec. 2000-01, treas. 2001-02, pres. elect., 2003-03, pres. 2003-04), Hennepin County Bar Assn. (sec. 1992-93, treas. 1993-95, pres. elect., 1995-96, pres. 1996-97). Office: Fredrikson & Byron PA 200 S 6th St # 4000 Minneapolis MN 55402 Office Phone: 612-492-7013. Business E-Mail: jbaillie@fredlaw.com.

BAILLIE, JOAN M., chemicals executive, biology educator; b. Manchester, N.H., Mar. 11, 1950; d. Robert Eugene and Doris Theresa (Dube) Nippert; m. Richard Douglas Baillie, Oct. 4, 1986. BA in Sci., Mt. St. Mary Coll., Hooksett, N.H., 1971; MA in Biology, East Carolina U., 1974. Microbiology technologist Becton Dickinson, Research Triangle Park, NC, 1974—76; mgr. quality control Bio Data Corp., Willow Grove, Pa., 1976—78; various positions to nat. accounts mgr. E.I. Du Pont, Wilmington, Del., 1978—89, DuPont cons. Ptnrs. in Sci. program Deepwater, NJ, 1993—. Program mgr. Straight at You WJIC, Salem, NJ, 1990—99; instr. biology Salem C.C., Carneys Point, NJ, 1997—2000, instr., dept. chair, 2001—; dir. Ctr. for Cmty. Edn. and Recreation, 1991—92; bd. dirs. Salem CC. Found., 1990—, chmn., 1993—98; bd. trustees Salem C.C., 1995—97. Bd. dirs. Salem County chpt. Am. Heart Assn., 1993-97, pres., 1993-95; founding mem. Friends of Pennsville Pub. Libr., 1991, trustee, 1995-97, pres., 1992-94; vol. coord. Salem County Health Heart Program, 1990-97; mem. panel for K-12 edn. Salem County Profl. Devel. Bd., 2000—; founding mem., mem. exec. com. Salem County 2000 Edn. Coun., 1991—; mem. exec. com. Goals 2000, Salem County, 1991—. Recipient Excellence award, N.J. Cmty. County Colls., 1992. Mem. Delta Kappa Gamma. Avocations: reading, paper crafts, travel, teaching art classes for children. Home: 2 Lenape Dr Pennsville NJ 08070 Office: E I DuPont Co Chambers Works Deepwater NJ 08023 E-mail: jbaillie@snip.net.

BAILLIE, RICHARD THOMAS, economist, educator; b. London, Feb. 14, 1948; arrived in US, 1979; s. Thomas Edward Baillie and Muriel Hervét Podmore; m. Anne Rosalind Waller, Nov. 2, 1974. BS, Middlesex U., London, 1970; MS, U. Kent, Canterbury, Eng., 1972; PhD, London Sch. Econs., 1978. Prof. Mich. State U., East Lansing, 1988-92, 93-98, A. J. Pasant prof., 1998—; prof. Georgetown U., Washington, 1992-93. Cons. Fed. Res. Bank Cleve., 1994-98; vis. scholar Fed. Res. Bank St. Louis, 1994; part-time prof. Queen Mary U., London, 1999—. Grantee NSF, 1992, 93, 99; fellow Jour. Econometrics, 1997. Fellow Am. Statis. Assn.; mem. Econometric Soc., Am. Fin. Assn., Am. Econ. Assn. Avocations: travel, tennis, wine, film, cricket. Home: 1090 Whittier Dr East Lansing MI 48823 Office: Mich State U Dept Econ East Lansing MI 48824 Office Phone: 517-355-1864. Business E-Mail: baillie@msu.edu.

BAILLIEUL, JOHN BROUARD, aerospace engineering and applied mathematics educator; b. Boise, Idaho, May 13, 1945; s. Paul Brouard and Geneva (Gillam) B.; m. Patricia Pfeiffer; children: Emily, Charlotte, John Paul. BA, U. Mass., Amherst, 1967; M in Math., U. Waterloo, Waterloo, Can., 1969; MS, Harvard U., 1973, PhD in Applied Math., 1975. Asst. prof. math. Georgetown U., Washington, 1975-79; sr. mathematician Sci. Systems, Inc., Cambridge, Mass., 1979-83; Vinton Hayes vis. scientist Harvard U., Cambridge, 1983-85; prof. aerospace and mech. engring. Boston U., 1985—, prof. mfg. engring., 1988—, prof. elec. and computer engring., 2001—, dir. div. engring. and applied sci., 1990-93, assoc. dean Coll. Engring., 1993—96, chmn. dept. mfg. engring., 1994-99, chmn. dept. aerospace/mech. engring., 1999—. Cons. Sci. Systems, Inc., Cambridge, 1985-87, AMD Corp., Stratford, Conn., 1986, Computational Engring., Inc., Laurel, Md., 1988-89; vis. sr. scientist Lab. for Info. and Decision Systems, MIT, 1991; chmn. dept aerospace/mech. engring., 1992-93. Author: Mathematical Control Theory, 1998; assoc. editor IEEE Transactions on Automatic Control, 1984—85, 1989—92, editor-in-chief, 1992—98; assoc. editor: IEEE Robotics and Automation Soc. newsletter, Bifurcation and Chaos in Applied Scis. and Engring.; mem. editl. bd. Procs. IEEE, Comm. in Info. and Systems, Robotics and Computer Integrated Mfg.; contbr. articles to profl. jours. U.S. Dept. Energy grantee, USAF Office Sci. Rsch. grantee Boston U., 1985—, NSF grantee; frequent grantee for study nonlinear control theory and mechanics Fellow IEEE (mem. publs. bd., 3D Millennium medal 2000). Home: 105 Longmeadow Rd Belmont MA 02478-1709 Office: Boston U Aero Mech Engring 110 Cummington St Boston MA 02215-2407

BAILON, GILBERT, newspaper executive; From mem. staff to v.p., exec. editor Dallas (Tex.) Morning News, 1986—97, exec. editor, 1997—2004, v.p., 1997—2004; pres., editor Al Dia (Spanish language newspaper of Dallas Morning News), 2002—04, pub., editor, 2004—. Mem.: Am. Soc. Newspaper Editors (bd. dir.), Nat. Assn. Hispanic Journalists (past pres.). Office: The Dallas Morning News PO Box 655237 508 Young St Dallas TX 75202-4828*

BAILYN, BERNARD, historian, educator; b. Hartford, Conn., Sept. 10, 1922; s. Charles Manuel and Esther (Schloss) Bailyn; m. Lotte Lazarsfeld, June 18, 1952; children: Charles David, John Frederick. AB, Williams Coll., 1945, LittD (hon.); MA, Harvard U., 1947, PhD, 1953, LLD (hon.), 1999; LHD (hon.), Lawrence U., Bard Coll., Clark U., Yale U., Grinnell Coll., Trinity Coll., Manhattanvill Coll., Dartmouth Coll., U. Chgo., Coll. of William and Mary, Pa. State U.; LittD (hon.), Rutgers U., Fordham U., La Trobe U., Australia, Washington U., St. Louis. Mem. faculty Harvard U., Cambridge, Mass., 1953—, editor in chief John Harvard Libr., 1962—70, Winthrop prof. history, 1966—81, Adams U. prof., 1981—93, emeritus, 1993—, dir. Charles Warren Ctr. for Studies in Am. History, 1983—94. Sr. fellow Soc. Fellows Harvard U., 1982—2005; Trevelyan lectr. Cambridge U., 1971; mem. inst. advanced study Princeton (N.J.) U., 1980—81, trustee, 1989—94; Pitt prof. Cambridge U., 1986—87; dir. Internat. Seminar on Atlantic History Harvard U., 1995—. Co-author (with Lotte Bailyn): Mass. Shipping 1697-1714, A Statis. Study, 1959; author: New Eng. Merchants in the 17th Century, 1955, Edn. in the Forming of Am. Society, 1960, The Ideological Origins of the Am. Revolution, 1967 (Pulitzer prize, 1968, Bancroft prize, 1968), The Origins of Am. Politics, 1968, The Ordeal of Thomas Hutchinson, 1974 (Nat. Book award, 1975), The Peopling of Br. North Am.: An Intro., 1986, Voyagers to the West, 1986 (Pulitzer prize, Saloutos award Immigration History soc., Triennial Book award Soc. of the Cin.), Faces of Revolution, 1990, On The Tchg. and Writing of History, 1994, To Begin the World Anew, 2003, American History: Concept and Contours, 2005; co-author: The Gt. Republic, 1977; editor: Pamphlets of the Am. Revolution 1750-1776, 1965, The Apologia of Robert Keayne, 1965, The Debate on the Constitution, 2 vols., 1993; co-editor: The Intellectual Migration, Europe and Am., 1930-1960, 1969, Law in Am. History, 1972, Perspectives in Am. History, 1967—77, 1984—86, The Press and The Am. Revolution, 1980, Strangers Within the Realm, 1990. With AUS, 1943—46. Recipient Robert H. Lord award, Emmanuel Coll., 1967, medal, Fgn. Policy Assn., 1998, Catton prize for lifetime achievement in writing of history, Soc. Am. Historians, 2000, Centennial medal, Harvard Grad. Sch. Arts and Scis., 2001; hon. fellow, Christ Coll., Cambridge U., Jefferson lectr., NEH, 1998, First Millenium lectr., White House, 1998. Fellow: Royal Hist. Soc. (corr.); mem.: Academia Europaea, Russian Acad. Scis., Mex. Acad. History and Geography, Brit. Acad., Mass. Hist. Soc. (Kennedy medal 2004), Am. Philos. Soc. (Thomas Jefferson medal 1993, Henry Allen Moe prize 1994), Nat. Acad. Edn., Am. Acad. Arts and Scis., Am. Hist. Assn. (pres. 1981). Home: 170 Clifton St Belmont MA 02478-2604 Office: Harvard U History Dept Cambridge MA 02138

BAILYN, LOTTE, psychologist, educator; b. Vienna, July 17, 1930; came to U.S., 1937; d. Paul Felix Lazarsfeld and Marie (Jahoda) Albu; m. Bernard Bailyn, June 18, 1952; children: Charles, John. BA in Math. with high honors, Swarthmore Coll., 1951; MA in Social Psychology, Harvard U., 1953, PhD in Social Psychology, 1956; PhD (hon.), U. Piraeus, Greece, 2000. Rsch. assoc. Grad. Sch. Edn., Harvard U., Cambridge, Mass., 1956-57, rsch. assoc. dept. social rels., 1958-64, lectr., 1963-67; instr. dept. econs. and social sci. MIT, Cambridge, 1957-58, rsch. assoc. Sloan Sch. Mgmt., 1969-70, lectr., 1970-71, from sr. lectr. to prof., 1971-91, T Wilson prof. mgmt., 1991—2005, prof. mgmt., 2005—, chair MIT faculty, 1997-99; acad. visitor Imperial Coll. Sci., Tech. and Medicine, London, 1991, 1995, 2000; disting. vis. prof. Radcliffe Coll., 1995-97. Trustee Cambridge Savs. Bank, 1975-98; mem. adv. coun. Suffolk U. Mgmt. Sch., Boston, 1983-86; mem. sr. coun. Leadership Devel. Inst., Rutgers U., 1986-89; panel mem. NAS, NRC, Washington, 1988-90; mem. task force in career devel. and maintenance IEEE, Washington, 1982-90; vis. scholar Imperial Coll. Sci. and Tech., London, 1982, New Hall, Cambridge (Eng.) U., 1986-87; scholar-in-residence Rockefeller Found. Study and Conf. Ctr., Bellagio, Italy, 1983; vis. fellow U. Auckland, N.Z., 1984. Author: Mass Media and Children, 1959, Living with Technology, 1980, Breaking the Mold: Women, Men, and Time in the New Corporate World, 1993; co-author: Working with Careers, 1984, Relinking Life and Work: Toward a Better Future, 1996, Beyond Work-Family Balance: Advancing Gender Equity and Workplace Performance, 2002; mem. editl. bd. Jour. Engring. and Tech. Mgmt., Cmty., Work and Family; contbr. chpts. to books and articles to profl. jours. Trustee Radcliffe Coll., 1974-79, Cambridge Fin. Group, Inc., 1998-2005; bd. dirs. Families and Work Inst., 1995—, Cambridge Savings Bank, 1998-2005; adv. group, Creating Options: Models for Flexible Faculty Career Pathways, Office of Women in Higher Edn., Am. Coun. Edn., 2003-; com. Women in Sci. and Engring., Nat. Acad. Sci., 2004-. Recipient Grad. Soc. medal Radcliffe Coll., 1998, Everett Cherrington Hughes award for careers scholarship Acad. of Mgmt., 2003, Work Life Legacy award, Families and Work Inst., 2005. Fellow APA; mem. Acad. Mgmt., Am. Sociol. Assn. Home: 170 Clifton St Belmont MA 02478-2604 Office: MIT Sloan Sch Mgmt 50 Memorial Dr Cambridge MA 02142-1347 Business E-Mail: lbailyn@mit.edu.

BAIM, ERIC M., lawyer; b. Pitts., Jan. 23, 1972; BA in Psychology with highest honors, U. NC, Chapel Hill, 1994; MA in Clin. Psychology, U. Cin., 1998; MA in Pub. Policy, JD, Duke U., 2001. Bar: Va. 2001, DC 2002, US Ct. Appeals 4th Cir. Assoc. Shaw Pittman LLP, Sonnenschein Nath & Rosenthal LLP, Washington, 2003—. Mem.: ABA (mem. health law sect.), Va. Bar Assn., DC Bar Assn. (mem. health law sect.), Am. Health Lawyers Assn. Office: Sonnenschein Nath & Rosenthal LLP Ste 600, E Tower 1301 K St NW Washington DC 20005 Office Phone: 202-408-9160. Office Fax: 202-408-6399. Business E-Mail: ebaim@sonnenschein.com.

BAIMA, JULIE MARTIN, special education educator; b. Lincolnton, N.C., July 26, 1969; d. Thomas Luther Martin and Grace Turbyfill Caudle; m. Charles Joseph Baima, Nov. 21, 1992; children: Madison Lyndsey, Ronald Thomas. BS, Ga. Coll., 1991, EdM, 1996; specialist in edn., Ga. Coll. and State U., 2000. Cert. early childhood edn. tchr., specific learning disabilities tchr., mental retardation specialist. Spl. edn. tchr. Washington County Bd. Edn., Sandersville, Ga., 1992—93, Bibb County Bd. Edn., Macon, Ga., 1993—2002, Monroe County Bd. Edn., Forsyth, Ga., 2002—. Mem.: NEA, Ga. Edn. Assn., Macon Jr. Woman's Club (1st v.p. 2000—02, pres. 2002—). Republican. Episcopalian. Avocations: walking, reading, scrapbooks. Home: 230 Northridge Dr Macon GA 31220

BAIMEEDI, PRAVEEN REDDY, neurosurgeon; b. Hyderabad, India, May 11, 1974; s. Venkat Reddy and Jamuna Reddy Baimeedi; m. Kiranmai Reddy Dwaram. MBBS, Osmania Med. Coll., Hyderabad, 1997. Ho. staff Nizams Inst. Med. Scis., Hyderabad, 1998—2003; fellow Beth Israel Med. Ctr., NYC, 2004—. Pres. Resident Doctors Assn., Hyderabad, India, 1998—2003. Mem.: Andra Pradesh Neuroscientists Assn. (assoc.), Neurol. Soc. India (assoc. Golden Jubilee award). Achievements include research in role of MRI CSF flow studies in management of chiari malformation. Home: 353 E 17 Th St Apt 6 A New York NY 10003 Office: Beth Israel Med Ctr 16th St First Ave New York NY 10003 Office Phone: 212-844-6896. E-mail: pbaimeed@chpnet.org.

BAIN, C. RANDALL, lawyer; b. Greeley, Colo., Feb. 1, 1934; s. Walter Lockwood and Harriet Lucille (Stewart) B.; m. Joanne Berg, Aug. 4, 1956 (div.); children: Jennifer Harriet, Charles Alvin; m. Lois Jean Frazier, Feb. 1, 1973 (dec.); 1 child, Frazier; m. Anna Scalise, Dec. 16, 2000. BA, Yale U., 1955, LLB, 1960. Bar: Ariz. 1961, U.S. Dist. Ct. Ariz. 1961, U.S. Ct. Appeals (9th cir.) 1963, U.S. Supreme Ct. 1968, U.S. Ct. Appeals (fed. cir.) 1992. Ptnr. Brown & Bain, Phoenix, 1961—2003, pres., 1972—87, exec. v.p., 1987—96, of counsel, 2003—04, Perkins, Coie, Brown & Bain, 2004—. Adj. prof. law Ariz. State U. Sch. Law, 2000-01. Trustee Phoenix Country Day Sch., 1983-94; chmn. bd. dirs. Ariz. Audubon, 2003—. Fellow Am. Bar Found.; mem. ABA, Ariz. Bar Assn. (chmn. fee arbitration com. 1982-86), Am. Law Inst., Yale U. Law Sch. Alumni Assn. (exec. com. 1982-85, 93-97), Audubon Ariz. (chmn. bd. dirs. 2003-). Office: Perkins Coie Brown & Bain PA 2901 N Central Ave Ste 2000 Phoenix AZ 85012-2788

BAIN, CONRAD STAFFORD, actor; b. Lethbridge, Alta., Can., Feb. 4, 1923; came to U.S., 1946, naturalized, 1946; s. Stafford Harrison and Jean Agnes (Young) B.; m. Monica Marjorie Sloan, Sept. 4, 1945; children: Kent Stafford, Mark Alexander, Jennifer Jean. Grad., Am. Acad. Dramatic Art, 1948. Founder Actors Fed. Credit Union, 1962 Broadway appearances include Candide, 1957, Lost in the Stars, 1958, Hot Spot, 1963, Advise and Consent, 1961, Twigs, 1971, Uncle Vanya, 1973, On Borrowed Time, 1991; off-Broadway appearances include The Iceman Cometh, 1957, Hogan's Goat, 1966, Scuba Duba, 1967, The Kitchen, 1968, Steambath, 1969, The Dining Room, Pasadena Playhouse, 1991, On Borrowed Time, 1992, Ancestral Voices, 1999; film appearances A Lovely Way to Die, 1967, Who Killed Mary Whats er Name, 1968, Up the Sand Box, 1970, C.H.O.M.P.S, 1979, Child Bride of Short Creek, 1982, Postcards from the Edge, 1990; Pasadena Playhouse The Dining Room, 1991; co-star: (TV) Maude, 1971-78; star: (TV) Diff'rent Strokes, 1978-86, Mr. President, 1987—. Served with Canadian Army, World War II. Mem. Actors Equity Assn. (councilor 1962-76), ANTA West (dir. since 1977) Clubs: Players (N.Y.C.). Office: 1230 Chicory Ln Los Angeles CA 90049-1403 *I have come to realize that each job no matter how small must be an end in itself, and that each day of whatever character must be lived for that day, in all its fullness. Yesterday is gone, regret is a waste, and tomorrow is unknown.*

BAIN, DONALD KNIGHT, lawyer; b. Denver, Jan. 28, 1935; s. Francis Marion and Jean (Knight) B.; divorced; children: Stephen A., Andrew K., William B. AB, Yale U., 1957; LLB, Harvard U., 1961. Bar: Colo. 1961. Assoc. Holme Roberts & Owen, Denver, 1961—67, ptnr., 1967—2004, chmn. exec. com., 1988-90, counsel, 2005—; chmn. Colo. Rep. Com., 1993-97. Bd. dirs. Fairmount Cemetery Co.; mem. grievance com. Colo. Supreme Ct., 1975-80, chmn., 1980. Trustee Denver Pub. Libr. Friends Found., 1978—96, Denver Found., 1989—95, chmn., 1993—95; trustee Berger Found., 1994—96; trustee, chmn. Colo. Coun. on Arts, 1999—2005; trustee Human Svcs., Inc., 1970—81, chmn., 1979—80; trustee Colo. Humanities Program, 1975—78; mem. Denver Pub. Libr. Commn., 1983—91; active Rep. Nat. Com., Washington, 1993—97; candidate for mayor City of Denver, 1987, 1991; bd. dirs. Rocky Mountain Corp. Pub. Broadcasting, 1975—83, Downtown Denver, Inc., 1977—2004, Denver Metro C. of C., 1998—, BigHornAction.org, 1999—2003, Auraria Found., 1986—, Legal Aid Found., Colo., 1999—2005, Auraria Higher Edn. Ctr., 1978—89, chmn., 1986—89. Fellow Royal Geog. Soc., Am. Coll. Trial Lawyers, Explorers Club; mem. ABA, Colo. Bar Assn., Denver Bar Assn., Colo. Yale Assn. (pres. 1974-76), Assn. Yale Alumni (bd. govs. 1982-85), Selden Soc., Am. Antiquarian Soc., Internat. Wine and Food Soc., Confrerie des Chevaliers du Tastevin, Western Stock Show Assn., Cactus Club, Denver Country Club, Mile High Club, Denver Law Club, Grolier Club, Yale Club, Colo. Mountain Club, Capitol Hill CLub, Univ. Club (Denver). Republican. Avocation: antiquarian book collecting. Home: 1201 Williams # 13C Denver CO 80218 Office: Holme Roberts & Owen LLP 1700 Lincoln St Ste 4100 Denver CO 80203-4541 Office Phone: 303-861-7000. Business E-Mail: don.bain@hro.com.

BAIN, DOUGLAS G., lawyer, air transportation executive; b. Charlottesville, Va., Mar. 12, 1949; BA, U. Va., 1971, JD, 1974. Bar: Calif. 1974, Wash. 1982, Ill. 2005. Atty. U.S. Air Force, Pillsbury, Madison & Sutro; various positions in legal dept. including sr. counsel & assist. gen. counsel Boeing Co., Chgo., 1982—96, v.p. legal, contracts, ethics and govt. rels. comml. airplanes group, 1996—99, v.p., gen. counsel, 1999—2000, sr. v.p., gen. counsel, 2000—. Office: Boeing Co MC 5003-1001 100 N Riverside Chicago IL 60606-1596

BAIN, ELAINE RUGIENIUS, elementary school educator; b. Pottsville, Pa., Aug. 17, 1944; d. Adolph Andrew and Helen Eleanor (Bluis) Rugienius; m. Donald Bruce Bain Jr., Dec. 2, 1966; children: Elizabeth Rebecca, Donald Bruce III, Alexander McKay. Cert., Temple U., 1971; BA, Pa. State U., 1966; MA, Ea. Mich. U., 1989; postgrad., Madonna U., 1992-94. Cert. tchr. Pa., Va., Mass., Mich. Tchr. York (Pa.) City Schs., 1966, Alexandria (Va.) City Schs., 1967, Shikellamy Schs., Sunbury, Pa., 1967-68, Groton (Mass.) Sch. Dist., 1968-69, Phila. City Schs., 1969, Plymouth (Mich.) Canton Cmty. Schs., 1990—. Adj. instr. Schoolcraft Coll., Livonia, Mich., 1988—. Pres. Plymouth Cmty. Arts Coun., 1988-90; mem. EMU Circle Excellence. Mem. AAUW (edn. found. projects chair), Nat. Coun. Tchrs. English, Mich. Reading Assn., Pa. State Alumni Assn., Am. Assn. of Univ. Women, Wayne County Reading Assn. (technology chair), Theta Phi Alpha, Phi Kappa Phi. Episcopalian. Avocations: reading, children's theatre productions, alumni association activities, community volunteer activities. Office: East Mid Sch 1042 South Mill St Plymouth MI 48170

BAIN, JAMES ARTHUR, pharmacologist, educator; b. Langdon, N.D., May 22, 1918; s. James Hamilton and Mabel (Aldritt) B.; m. Eleanor Theo Hohaus, Dec. 5, 1947; children: Andrew J., Peter T. AA, Wayland Jr. Coll., 1938; BS, U. Wis., 1940, PhD, 1944. Research asst. McArdle Meml. Lab., U. Wis., 1940-44, Rockefeller fellow, 1946-47; research asso. U. Ill., 1947-50, asst. prof., then asso. prof., 1952-54; mem. faculty dept. pharmacology Emory U., 1954—, prof., 1954-89, chmn. dept., 1957-62, dir. div. basic health scis., 1960-76; exec. asso. dean Emory U. (Sch. Medicine), 1976-88, prof. emeritus, 1988—, cons. to dean, v.p., 1989-93. Cons. to govt., nat. agys., industry, 1954— Contbr. articles profl. jours. Mem. Am. Chem. Soc., Am. Soc. Pharmacology and Exptl. Therapeutics, AAAS. Home: 1800 Clairmont Lake # 518 Decatur GA 30033-4040

BAIN, JAMES WILLIAM, lawyer; b. Suffern, NY, Dec. 19, 1949; s. William James and Agnes (Hoey) B.; m. Colleen K., Mar. 23, 1974; children: Rebecca, Meghan. BA, U. Conn., 1972; JD, U. Fla., 1976. Bar: Fla. 1977, U.S. Dist. Ct. (ea. dist.) Tenn. 1980, Tenn. 1984, U.S. Ct. Appeals (11th cir.) 1984, U.S. Ct. Appeals (D.C. cir.) 1984, Colo. 1986, U.S. Dist. Ct. Colo 1986, U.S. Ct. Appeals (10th cir.) 1988, U.S. Supreme Ct. 1998. Counsel TVA, Knoxville, 1977—85; dir. Roath & Brega, P.C., Denver, 1985—89, Brega & Winters, P.C., Denver, 1989—2003; ptnr. Benjamin, Bain & Howard LLC, Greenwood Village, Colo., 2003—. Instr. U. Fla., Gainesville, 1976, U. Colo., Boulder, 1987-90; seminar chmn. Inst. for Advanced Legal Study, Denver, 1987. Contbr. articles to profl. jours.; editor constrn. law column Colo. Lawyer. Recipient Civil Litigation Writing award for 1986-87, Denver Colo. Bar Assn., 1987. Mem. ATLA, Colo. Bar Assn., Fla. Bar Assn., Am. Judicature Soc., Am. Arbitration Assn. (arbitrator 1986). Avocations: soccer, skiing, biking, basketball. Office: Benjamin Bain & Howard LLC 7315 E Orchard Rd Ste E400 Greenwood Village CO 80111 Office Phone: 303-290-6600. Business E-Mail: JamesBain@BBHLegal.com.

BAIN, LINDA L., academic administrator; BS in Phys. Edn. summa cum laude, Ill. State U., 1962, MS in Phys. Edn., 1968; PhD in Phys. Edn. and Learning Theory, U. Wis., 1974. Instr. Lowell Elem. Sch., Wheaton, Ill., 1962-64, East Peoria (Ill.) H.S., 1964-68, U. Mich., Ann Arbor, 1968-69; asst. prof. U. Ill., Chgo., 1969-75, U. Houston, 1975-78, assoc. prof., 1978-83, prof., 1983-88, chmn. dept. health, phys. edn. and recreation, 1980-82, assoc. dean rsch. Coll. Edn., 1982-88; prof. Calif. State U., Northridge, 1988-95, dean Sch. Comm., Health and Human Svcs., 1988-95, interim provost, v.p. academic affairs, 2003—; prof. San Jose (Calif.) State U., 1995—2000, provost, v.p. academic affairs, 1995—2000. Alderson lectr. U. Tex., 1982; Amy Morris Homans lectr. Nat. Assn. Phys. Edn. in Higher Edn., 1989; Ethel Martus Lawther lectr. U. N.C., Greensboro, 1992; Scholar lectr. Ill. State U., 1993; presenter in field. Co-author: Transition to Teaching: A Guide for the Beginning Teacher, 1983, The Curriculum Process in Physical Education, 1985, 2d edit., 1995; reviewer Rsch. Quar. for Exercise and Sport, 1977-95, Jour. Phys. Edn., Recreation and Dance, 1976-88; mem. editl. adv. bd. Youth and Soc., 1984-95, Jour. Phys. Edn., Recreation and Dance, 1984-87; editl. bd. Jour. Tchg. in Phys. Edn., 1985-95, Quest, 1991-94; book rev. editor Rsch. Quar. for Exercise and Sport, 1991-94; contbr. articles to profl. jours., chpts. to books. Bd. dirs. Am. Cancer Soc., San Fernando Valley, Calif., 1993-95; mem. health project policy bd. Calif. Phys. Edn., 1994-95; mem. met. bd. YMCA of Santa Clara Valley, 1998—; bd. dirs. Met. San Jose Collaborative for Acad. Excellence, 1998—; mem. hon. com. No. Exposure: New Art from Japan, San Jose Inst. Contemporary Art, 1999. Marie L. Carns fellow, 1972-73, Fellow AAHPERD, 1980, Am. Leadership Forum Silicon Valley, 1999; recipient Rsch. award So. Assn. Phys. Edn. of Coll. Women, 1983, Honor award AAHPERD, 1990, Jose Maria Cagigal Scholar lectr. Assn. Internat. Ecoles Superieures d'Edn. Physique, 1990, Disting. Adminstrn. award Nat. Assn. Phys. Edn. in Higher Edn., 1993, Alumni Achievement award Ill. State U., 1995, U. Wis. Sch. Edn., 1997, Tribute to Women in Industry award YWCA, Santa Clara Valley, 1999. Fellow Am. Acad. Kinesiology and Phys. Edn.

BAIN, SCOTT E., lawyer; b. Windom, Minnesota, Apr. 12, 1971; BSEE summa cum laude, Univ. of Minn., 1994; JD, Boalt Hall School of Law, Univ. of CA. Berkeley, 1997. Bar: D.C., Minnesota, U.S. Supreme Ct., U.S. Ct. of Appeals Fourth, Ninth Fed. Circuits, U.S. Dist. Ct., Minn., U.S. Patent and Trademark Office. Mng. editor Berkeley Tech. Law Jour.; law clk. to the Hon. Randall R. Rader U.S. Ct. Appeals (Fed. cir.), 1998—99; partner Wiley Rein & Fielding LLP, 2005—. Mem.: Am. Intellectual Property Law Assoc., Am. Bar Assoc. Office: Wiley Rein & Fielding 1776 K Street NW Washington DC 20006 E-mail: sbain@wrf.com.*

BAIN, TRAVIS WHITSETT, II, manufacturing and retail executive; b. San Antonio, Mar. 4, 1934; s. Travis Whitsett and Zelma Gladys (Middleton) B.; m. Karlen Jo Bruner, May 30, 1957; children: Travis W. III, James Henry III. B in Chem. Engring., U. Tex., 1956; MBA, Harvard U., 1958. Mfg. supt. Tex. Instruments, Dallas, 1958-61; sr. assoc. McKinsey and Co., L.A. and Chgo., 1961-65; exec. v.p., COO Trend Line Corp., Jackson, Miss., 1965-81; pres., CEO W.E. Walker Stores, Inc., Jackson, 1981-86; CEO Sunbelt Nursery Group, Inc., Ft. Worth, 1986-87; investor, cons. Bain Assocs., Ft. Worth, 1987-88; pres. Jarman Shoe Co. div. Genesco Inc., Nashville, 1988-92, Bain Enterprises, Inc. dba Sandler Pools, Plano, Tex., 1993-99; chmn. Tex. Custom Pools, Inc., Plano, 1999—. Bd. dirs. Atmos Energy Corp., Dallas, 1988—, Tex. Commerce Bank, Ft. Worth, 1986-88, Delta Industries, Inc., Jackson, 1984—; chmn. bd. dirs. Master Pools Guild, 1997-99. Bd. dirs. New Stage Theatre, Jackson, 1980-86, Boy Scouts Am., Ft. Worth, 1986-88, Miss. Ballet Internat., Jackson, 1984-86; bd. dirs., exec. com. Nashville Ballet, 1989-92; mem. placement coun. Owen Sch. Mgmt. Vanderbilt U., Nashville, 1984-92; mem. adv. bd. CBA Found. U. Tex., Austin, 1987—. Mem. Dallas Exec. Assn. (pres. 1998-99). Republican. Presbyterian. Avocations: gardening, tennis, jogging, travel, scuba diving. Office: Tex Custom Pools Inc 4016 W Plano Pkwy Plano TX 75093-5696 Fax: 972-596-9460. Office Phone: 972-596-7393. E-mail: travkar@mail.airmail.net, tbain@texascustompools.com.

BAIN, WILLIAM DAVID, electronics engineer, writer; b. Flint, Mich., Sept. 3, 1958; s. William David and Frances Geraldine B. Student, Jordan Coll., 1984-85. Theater mgr. asst. Northwest Theater, Flint, 1975-81, Commonwealth Theater, Denver, 1981-82; theater mgr., promotions asst. Towne Cinemas, Flushing, Mich., 1987-91; pvt. practice Flint, 1991—. Author: Oasis, 1995, Inspirational Collection, 1997, Tear Drops Fall Like Rain, 1997, Romantic Collection, 1997, Verses From The Heart, 1999. Mem. Comms. com. Democratic Party, 1994-98; delegate Democratic Party, 1996-98; elected exec. bd. trustees UAW, 1999—2002. Mem.: United Automobile, Aerospace, Agrl. Implement Workers, Jerry B. Jenkins Christian Writers Guild, Poetry Soc. Am., The Acad. Poets. Avocations: writing, nature photography, gardening, cookouts, political advocate for people. Home and Office: PO Box 70 Flushing MI 48433 E-mail: Author58@yahoo.com.

BAIN, WILLIAM DONALD, JR., lawyer, chemicals executive; b. Rochelle, Ill., July 1, 1925; s. William Donald and Gretchen (Kittler) B.; m. Pauline Thomas, Jan. 14, 1950 (dec. Nov. 1991); children: Elizabeth Kittler Zibart, Anne Alexander, Nancy Hemenway Cotè; m. Barrie Feighner, Mar. 30, 1996. BS in Econs, U. Pa., 1947; JD, Washington and Lee U., 1949. Bar: S.C. 1952. Mortgage loan field rep. Travelers Ins. Co., Hartford, Conn., Cleve.; Orlando, Fla., 1949-51; with Moreland-McKesson Chem. Co., Spartanburg, S.C., 1951-83, pres., 1965-83, also dir.; v.p., gen. mgr. McKesson Chem. Corp., San Francisco, 1982-84. Bd. dirs. Cote Color & Chem. Co., Inc., Spartan Comms. Corp., Tietex Corp.; co-founder, bd. dirs. Affiliated Chem. Group, Bermuda; ptnr. Triple B Ptnrs. Mem. Spartanburg Sch. Bd., 1958—72, chmn., 1963—72; trustee Converse Coll., 1968—92, chmn. bd., 1985—92; chmn. alumni bd. Washington and Lee U., 1979—82; trustee Hollins (Va.) Coll., 1992—98; bd. dirs. Mary Black Meml. Hosp., 1975—96, chmn., 1980—82; trustee Mary Black Found., 1996—2002; trustee, former chmn. Spartanburg County Found.; bd. dirs. Spartanburg Animal Shelter, 2002—; mng. dir. Bain Found. With USAAC, 1943—45. Mem. S.C. Bar Assn., Rotary. Republican. Presbyterian.

BAIN, WILLIAM JAMES, JR., architect; b. Seattle, June 26, 1930; s. William James and Mildred Worline (Clark) B.; m. Nancy Sanford Hill, Sept. 21, 1957; children: David Hunter, Stephen Fraser (dec.), Mark Sanford, John Worthington. BArch, Cornell U., 1953. Lic. 1st class architect, Japan, lic. architect in 18 states, Can., Guam, U.K. Consulting ptnr. NBBJ (formerly Naramore, Bain, Brady & Johanson), Seattle. Mem. affiliate program steering com. Coll. Architecture and Urban Planning, 1969-71; organizer founding bd. dirs. Pacific N.W. Bank; lectr. Wash. State U., NYU, Cornell, Tech. Transfer Inst. Japan. Prin. works include U. Wash. South Campus, U.S. Pavilion at Expo '74 Worlds Fair, Honolulu Mcpl. Bldg., Two Union Square High-Rise Office Bldg., Four Seasons Olympic Hotel and Sun Mountain Lodge, U.S. Courthouse, Seattle, Bagley Wright Theater and Paramount Theater renovation, Saitama Prefecture Demonstration Housing, Japan, Pacific Place Retail Complex, others. Bd. dirs. Arts Fund, 1989—, Arboretum Found., 1971-; bd. dirs. Downtown Seattle Assn., 1980—, 1st vice-chmn., 1990-91, chmn., 1991-92; bd. dirs. Seattle Symphony Orch., 1974-87, pres., 1977-79; mem. adv. coun. Coll. Architecture, Art & Planning, Cornell U., 1987-91, 94—, vis. com. U. Washington, 1999—; archl. adv. to bd. dirs. Seattle Pub. Libr. Citizen's Adv. Bd., 1997. With C.E., U.S. Army, 1953-55. Recipient Cert. of Achievement Port of Whittier, Alaska, 1955, Disting. Alumnus award Lakeside Sch., 1985; named to Hall Fame, Nat. Assn. Indsl. Pks., 2004 Fellow AIA (pres. Seattle chpt. 1969, chmn. N.W. regional student profl. fund 1971, pres. Wash. coun. 1974, co-commn. Seattle centennial yr., Seattle medal 1997, Hall of Fame, 2004), N.W. Regional Archtl. Found. (pres. 1975); mem. Royal Inst. Brit. Architects, Japan Inst. Architects, Seattle C. of C. (bd. dirs. 1980-83), Urban Land Inst., Pacific Real Estate Inst., N.W. Forum, Am. Arbitration Assn. (comml. panel 1975—), L'Ogive Soc., Seattle Athletic Club, Seattle Tennis Club, Town Hall (bd. dirs. 2002—), Rotary (bd. dirs. 1970-72, svc. found. bd. 1976-80), Lambda Alpha Internat. (Robert Filly award 2003), Phi Delta Theta. Clubs: Rainier, Wash. Athletic, Tennis (Seattle); University. Episcopalian. Home: 2033 1st Ave Seattle WA 98121-2132 Office: NBBJ 111 S Jackson St Seattle WA 98104-2881 Business E-Mail: bbain@nbbj.com.

BAINBRIDGE, FREDERICK FREEMAN, III, architect; b. Charlottesville, Va., Sept. 15, 1927; s. Frederick Freeman and Cornelia Winston (Burnley) B.; m. Binki Baker, Jan. 6, 1948 (div. Nov. 1972); children—Burnley, Susan Winifred, Meriwether, Robin; m. Anna Bacon, Jan. 1976; 1 son, Nicholas Gordon. B.Arch., U. Va., 1950; M. Indsl. Design, Kansas City Art Inst., 1952. Asst. prof. Sch. Architecture Clemson (S.C.) U., 1952-55; asso. firm Toombs, Amisano & Wells (Architects), Atlanta, 1955-62; prin. firm Martin & Bainbridge, Atlanta, 1962-70, Bainbridge & Assos., 1970—. Southeastern project architect U. Ky. civil defense research project, 1964; vis. critic Ga. Inst. Tech., 1964-67 Chmn. archtl. rev. com. Atlanta Civic Design Commn., 1967— . Served with USNR, 1944-46. Recipient honor awards S. Atlantic Region AIA, 1964, 66, 68, 70; honor award prestressed Concrete Inst., 1967 Mem. AIA. Clubs: Fairington Golf and Tennis, Amelia Island Plantation; Farmington Country (Charlottesville, Va.). Home: Oldham Farm PO Box 317 Ivy VA 22945-0317 Office: 6795 Brandon Mill Rd NW Atlanta GA 30328-2028

BAINBRIDGE, JOHN SEAMAN, retired lawyer, retired academic administrator; b. NYC, Nov. 1, 1915; s. William Seaman and June Ellen (Wheeler) Bainbridge; m. Matharine Barker Garrett, Feb. 3, 1943 (div. July 24, 1968); 1 child, John Seaman; m. Elizabeth Kung-Ji Liu Bainbridge, May 13, 1978. BS, Harvard U., 1938; LLB, JD, Columbia U., 1941. Bar: NY 1941, Md 1946, US Dist. Ct./Md. 1946, US Supreme Ct. 1946, US Dist. Ct. (so. dist.)/NY 1948. Gen. practice law, Md., 1945—56, 1945—56; asst. dean Columbia U. Law Sch., 1956—65; assoc. dir. Internat. Fellows Program, 1960—62; asst. to pres. Columbia U., 1965—66; dir. Project on Staffing of African Instns. of Legal Edn. and Rsch., 1962—72; assoc. dir. Ctr. Adminstrn. of Justice, Wayne State U., Detroit, 1972—74; dir. planning Sch. Law, Pace U., Westchester County, NY, 1974—76; assoc. dean, dean, prof. law No. Ill. U. Coll. Law, Glen Ellyn, 1976—81; vis. prof., assoc. dean Del. Law Sch., Wilmington, 1981—82; dean, prof. law Touro coll. Sch. Law, Huntington, NY, 1982—85. Cons. Edward John Noble Found., 1959—61, Inst. Internat. Edn., 1962—67. Author: The Study and Teaching of Law in Africa, 1972. Lt. comdr. USNR, 1940—46. Mem.: ABA, African Law Assn. in Am., Inc., Peace Corps Lawyers Project, Sons of Revolution, Harvard (NYC). Sr Presbyn. Home: 102 Crosslands Dr Kennett Square PA 19348

BAINES, HENRY T., SR., supermarkets executive; Founder Super Thrift supermarket, 1978; CEO Baines Mgmt., Balt.; operates 10 inner-city supermakets Balt. Office: Baines Mgmt 200 S Arlington Ave Ste 300 Baltimore MD 21223-2672

BAINES, KEVIN HAYS, astronomer, research scientist; b. Norwalk, Conn., Feb. 11, 1954; s. Elliot A. and Martha Ellen (Ashcroft) B.; m. Jenine Bsharah, June 4, 1982; children: Emily Ansara, Christopher Lewis. BA, Amherst Coll., 1976; MA, Washington U., St. Louis, 1978, PhD, 1982. Resident rsch. assoc. NRC-JPL, Pasadena, Calif., 1982-84; rsch. scientist Jet Propulsion Lab. Calif. Tech. Inst., Pasadena, 1984—2003, prin. scientist, Jet Propulsion Lab., 2003—. Co-investigator Galileo Near-Infrared Mapping Spectrometer and Cassini Visual-Infrared Mapping Spectrometer expts. Contbr. articles to profl. jours. Flight dir. Aero Assn. Calif. Tech. Inst., 1986, 99--, treas., 1987-99. Virgil I. Grissom Astronaut fellow Washington U., 1976-79. Mem. AAAS (planetary scis. divsn.). Republican. Achievements include research in determination of vertical cloud/haze structures of Uranus and Neptune; role of asteroid-impact generated sulfuric gases on dinosaur extinctions; first to detect the spectrally-identifiable discrete ammonia ice clouds in Jupiter; determination of methane and ortho/para hydrogen above solar averages in Uranus and Neptune; near-infrared spectral imagery and analysis of the atmospheric cloud and compositional structures of Jupiter, Saturn and Titan from the Galileo and Cassini spacecraft; near-infrared imagery and spectroscopy of Venus surface; near-infrared photometry of rings and satellites of Uranus and Saturn. Avocations: flight instructing, scuba diving. Home: 778 Forest Green Dr La Canada Flintridge CA 91011 Business E-Mail: kbaines@aloha.jpl.nasa.gov.

BAINES, MICKEY, academic administrator; s. Michael W. Baines and Katherine A. Faines; m. Andrea S. Baines, June 12, 2004. BS in Theatre, Speech and Dance, U. S.C., 1997. Asst. dir. resident life Elizabethtown (Pa.) Coll., 1998—2000; cons. Franklin Covey, Providence, 2000; dir. h.s. life N.C. Sch. of Arts, Winston-Salem, NC, 2001—02; asst. dir. accelerated programs Albright Coll., Reading, Pa., 2002—04, co-dir. accelerated programs, 2004—. Cons., dir. drama troupe, Millersville, Pa., 1998—99. Mem.: Assn. Continuing Higher Edn., Am. Coll. Personnel Assn. Methodist. Avocation: basketball. Office: Albright Coll PO Box 15234 13th & Bern St Reading PA 19612

BAINS, HARRISON MACKELLAR, JR., retired finance company executive; b. Pasadena, Calif., July 8, 1943; s. Harrison MacKellar and Celeste Adele (Callahan) B.; m. Leslie E. Tawney, Mar. 7, 1970; children: Harrison MacKellar, III, Tawney Elizabeth. BA, U. Redlands, 1964; MBA, U. Calif., Berkeley, 1966. Asst. v.p. Citibank N.A., 1968-72; asst. treas. Richardson-Merrell Inc., 1972-76; v.p. treas. Nabisco Inc., East Hanover, N.J., 1976-81; sr. v.p., treas. Nabisco Brands, Inc., East Hanover, N.J., 1981-85; v.p., treas. RJR Nabisco, Inc., Winston-Salem, N.C., 1985-87; sr. v.p. Chase Manhattan Bank, N.Y.C., 1987-88; v.p., treas. Bristol-Myers Squibb Co., N.Y.C., 1988—2002, acting CFO, 2002, v.p., treas., 2002—04; ret. Mem. Fin. Execs. Inst., Food Safety Council (treas. 1980—)

BAINS, LESLIE ELIZABETH, banker; b. Glen Ridge, N.J., July 28, 1943; d. Pliny Otto and Dorothy Ethel (Keeley) Tawney; m. Harrison Mackellar Bains Jr.; Harrison III, Tawney Elizabeth. BA, Am. U., 1965. Asst. treas. Citicorp, N.Y.C., 1965-73; v.p. Mfrs. Hanover, N.Y.C., 1973-80; v.p., divsn. exec. Chase Manhattan Bank, N.Y.C., 1980-86, v.p., group exec., 1986-87, sr. v.p. group exec., 1987-91; mng. dir. Global Pvt. Banking Group Citibank, N.Y.C., 1991-93; exec. v.p. Republic Nat. Bank, N.Y.C., 1993-2000; sr. exec. v.p. HSBC Bank USA, N.Y.C., 2000—, mem. sr. mgmt. com. Bd. dirs., chair fin. com. Interplast, 1991. Chmn. Edni. Cable Consortium, Summit, NJ, 1987—91; bd. dirs., chair fin. com. Interplast Found.; bd. dirs. Junior Achievement of N.Y.; mem. exec. com., bd. dirs., chair devel. com. Roundabout Theater; bd. trustees Am. U., 1994—, vice chair bd. trustees, 2001—; bd. dirs. Jr. Achievement, N.Y.C., 1996—, chair investment com.; bd. visitors Terry Sanford Inst. Pub. Policy Duke U., Duke U. Med. Sch. Named Achiever of Yr. YWCA, 1985, One of Top 100 Women in Corp. Am., Bus. Month., 1989. Fellow Fgn. Policy Assn; mem. Am. Bankers Assn. (bd. dirs. pvt. banking coun.), Fin. Women Internat. (vice chmn. Edn. Found. 1980-81, treas. 1981-83, v.p. 1983-84, pres. 1984-85), Fin. Women's Assn., Women and Founds., Coun. Fgn. Rels., The Econ. Club of N.Y. Office: HSBC Bank USA 452 5th Ave New York NY 10018-2706

BAINTON, DONALD J., diversified manufacturing company executive; b. N.Y.C., May 3, 1931; s. William Lewis and Mildred J. (Dunne) B.; m. Aileen M. Demoulins, July 10, 1954; children: Kathryn C., Stephen L., Elizabeth A., William D. BA, Columbia U., 1952, postgrad., 1960. With Continental Group, Inc., 1954—67, gen. mgr. prodn. planning, 1967—68, gen. mgr. mfg. Ea. divsn., 1968—73, gen. mgr. Pacific divsn., 1973—74, gen. mgr. Ea. divsn., 1974—75; v.p., gen. mgr. ops. U.S. Metal, 1975—76; exec. v.p., gen. mgr. CCC-USA, 1976—78, corp. exec. v.p., pres. diversified ops., 1978—79; pres. Continental Can Co., 1979—81, Continental Packaging, 1981—83, exec. v.p., operating officer parent co., bd. dirs., 1979—83; chmn., CEO, dir. Viatech Inc., Syosset, NY, 1983—92; chmn., CEO Continental Can Co., Inc., Boca Raton, Fla., 1992—99; chmn., CEO, dir. Continental Can Co., Sunrise, Fla., 1999—. Bd. dirs. Viatech Inds., LLC. Bd. dirs. Columbia Coll. With USN, 1952-54, Korea. Mem. Inst. Applied Econs. (dir.), Milbrook Country Club (Greenwich, Conn.), Winged Foot Club (Mamaroneck, N.Y.), Union League Club (N.Y.C.), Royal Palm Yacht and Country Club (Boca Raton, Fla.). Republican. Roman Catholic. Office: Continental Can Co 5001 N Hiatus Rd Sunrise FL 33351-8018 Office Phone: 954-578-1447. E-mail: dbainton@viatechind.com.

BAINTON, DOROTHY FORD, pathology educator, researcher; b. Magnolia, Miss., June 18, 1933; d. Aubrey Ratcliff and Leta (Brumfield) Ford; m. Cedric R. Bainton, Nov. 28, 1959; children: Roland J., Bruce G., James H. BS, Millsaps Coll., 1955; MD, Tulane U. Sch. of Medicine, 1958; MS, U. Calif., San Francisco, 1966. Postdoctoral rsch. fellow U. Calif., San Francisco, 1963-66, postdoctoral rsch. pathologist, 1966-69, asst. prof. pathology, 1969-75, assoc. prof., 1975-81, prof. pathology, 1981—, chair pathology, 1987-94, vice chancellor acad. affairs, 1994—2004; ret. Mem. Inst. of Medicine, NAS, 1990—. NIH grant, 1978-98. Fellow AAAS, Am. Acad. Arts & Scis.; mem. FASEB (bd. dirs.), Am. Soc. for Cell Biology, Am. Soc. Hematology, Am. Soc. Histochemists and Cytochemists, Am. Assn. of Pathologists. Democrat. Address: 50 Ventura Ave San Francisco CA 94116 E-mail: dbainton@mac.com.

BAINTON, J(OHN) JOSEPH, lawyer; b. Long Branch, N.J., May 21, 1947; s. Robert L. and Elizabeth (Dowling) B.; 1 child, John Joseph Jr. BA, Kenyon Coll., 1969; JD, Rutgers U., Newark, 1973. Bar: N.Y. 1973. Assoc. Burke & Burke, N.Y.C., 1972-76; ptnr. Reboul, MacMurray, Hewitt, Maynard & Kristol, N.Y.C., 1976-89, Shea & Gould, N.Y.C., 1989-90, Whitman & Ransom, N.Y.C., 1991-92, Ross & Hardies, N.Y.C., 1993-98, Bainton McCarthy LLC, N.Y.C., 1998—. Contbr. articles to legal jours. Mediator Mandatory Mediation Program So. Dist. N.Y. Mem.: Nat. Inst. Trial Advocacy (faculty), Products Liability Adv. Coun., Internat. Anticounterfeiting Coalition (bd. dirs. 1986—92), Internat. Trademark Assn. (editor The Trademark Reporter 1976). Avocation: yacht racing. Office: Bainton McCarthy LLC 26 Broadway New York NY 10004 also: Bainton McCarthy LLC 3 Stamford Landing 46 Southfield Ave Stamford CT 06902 also: Bainton McCarthy LLC 320 Carleton Ave Central Islip NY 11722-4502 also: Bainton McCarthy LLC 774 Broad St Newark NJ Office Phone: 212-480-3500. E-mail: bainton@baintonlaw.com.

BAINUM, PETER MONTGOMERY, aerospace engineer, consultant; b. St. Petersburg, Fla., Feb. 4, 1938; s. Charles J. Bainum and Mildred (Trincher) Salyer; m. Carmen Cecilia Perez, Sept. 7, 1968; 1 child, David P. BS, Tex. A&M U., 1959; SM, MIT, 1960; PhD, Cath. U., 1967. Asst. engr. Naval Supersonic Lab. MIT, Cambridge, 1959—60; sr. engr. Martin Co., Orlando, Fla., 1960—62; staff engr. Fed. Sys. divsn. IBM, Bethesda, Md., 1962—65; sr. staff, aerospace engr., cons. Applied Physics Lab. Johns Hopkins U., Laurel, Md., 1965—69, 1969—72; assoc. prof. Howard U., Washington, 1969—73, prof., 1973—90, disting. prof., 1990—2002, disting. prof. emeritus, 2003—. V.p. rsch., cons. WHF & Assocs., Bethesda, 1977-86; mem. NASA/PSN Tether Applications Simulation Working Group, 1987; lectr. various internat. univs., rsch. ctrs. and confs.; hon. vis. prof. Universidad Francisco Marroquin, Guatemala, 1991. Editor, co-editor 20 books, 1981-2004; contbr. articles to profl. jours. Judge, D.C. Sci. Fair, Washington, 1973. Recipient Ralph R. Teetor award Soc. Automotive Engrs., 1971. Fellow: AAAS, AIAA (capital sect. cmty. action com. 1975—76, space transp. com. 1989—93, astrodynamics com. 3 terms, Sustained Svc. award 2005), Brit. Interplanetary Soc., Am. Astronautical Soc. (v.p. internat. 1986—96, bd. dirs., Brouwer award 1990, Spark M. Matsunaga Meml. award 2001); mem.: Internat. Astronautical Fedn. (materials and structures com. 1992—), Japanese Rocket Soc. (hon.), Internat. Acad. Astronautics, Sigma Xi. Office: Howard Univ Dept Of Mechanical Engr Washington DC 20059-0001 Office Phone: 202-806-6612. Business E-Mail: pbainum@howard.edu. *With a doctoral degree comes significant responsibilities: to search out truth scientifically, to safeguard it, and to apply it to the shaping of both private and public life.*

BAIO, JAMES R., diversified financial services company executive; Former sr. mgr., acct. Ernst & Young; risk mgr. Franklin Templeton Investments, 1989—93; former treas. Templeton funds, 1993—96; past treas. Templeton mut. fund series; sr. v.p., CFO Franklin Resources, San Mateo, Calif., 2003—. Office: Franklin Resources 1 Franklin Pky bldg 970 1st Fl San Mateo CA 94403

BAIO, JOSEPH T., lawyer; b. NYC, July 24, 1953; BA, Columbia U., 1975; JD cum laude, NYU, 1978. Bar: NY 1979. Ptnr., litig. dept. Willkie Farr & Gallagher LLP, NYC, chair Mktg. Com. Lectr. Columbia U.; dir. inMotion, 1998—. Mem.: Assn. Bar of City NY. Office: Willkie Farr & Gallagher LLP 787 Seventh Ave New York NY 10019 Office Phone: 212-728-8203. E-mail: jbaio@willkie.com.

BAIR, BRUCE BLYTHE, lawyer; b. St. Paul, May 26, 1928; s. Bruce B. and Emma N. (Stone) B.; m. Jane Lawler, July 19, 1952; children: Mary Jane, Thomas, Susan, Barbara, Patricia, James, Joan, Bruce, Jeffrey. BS, U. N.D., 1950, JD, 1952. Bar: N.D. 1952, U.S. Dist. Ct. N.D. 1955, U.S. Ct. Appeals (8th cir.) 1971, U.S. Supreme Ct. 1974. Assoc. Lord and Ulmer, Mandan, ND, 1955-57; ptnr. Bair, Bair, and Garrity, Mandan, 1957—2001, of counsel, 2002—. Spl. asst. atty. gen. N.D. Milk Mktg. Bd., 1967—; chmn. bd. Bank of Tioga, 1984-2003, also bd. dirs.; Rep. precinct committeeman, 1956-70, chmn. Morton County Rep. Com., 1958-62, mem. N.D. Rep. State Cen. Com., 1962-67; pres. sch. bd. St. Joseph's Cath. Ch., 1967-68; bd. dirs. Mandan Pub. Sch. Dist. #1, 1971-77; exec. com. Internat. Assn. Milk Control Agys., 1970-2000; bd. regents U. Mary, Bismarck, N.D., 1984—. 1st lt. JAG Corps USAF, 1952-55. Mem.: ABA, N.D. Bar Assn., Am. Coll. Barristers (sr. counsel), Am. Legion, Elks, Rotary. Roman Catholic. Home: 901 3rd St NW Mandan ND 58554-2537 Office: 210 1st St NW Mandan ND 58554-3115

BAIR, EDWARD JAY, chemistry educator; b. Ft. Collins, Colo., June 30, 1922; s. Jay Albert and Edith Hectos (Pegg) B.; m. Dorothy Helen Bimson, June 29, 1958. BS, Colo. State U., 1943; PhD, Brown U., 1949. Chemist Tenn. Eastman Corp., Oak Ridge, 1943-46; research assoc. U. Wash., 1949-54; mem. faculty Ind. U., 1954-90, prof. chemistry, 1965-90, prof. chemistry emeritus, 1990—. Mem. Am. Chem. Soc. Home: 609 Bell Trace Ct Bloomington IN 47408-4410 Office Phone: 812-855-5437. Business E-Mail: bair@indiana.edu.

BAIR, GERALD D., state government official; BS in Bus. Adminstrn., Morningside Coll., 1965. From corp. auditor to dir. revenue and finance Department of Revenue, Des Moines, 1965-75, dir. revenue and finance, 1975—. Mem. Fedn. Tax Adminstrs. (exec. bd.), Legislative Interstate Coop. com., Ankeny Rotary (internat. bd.), Drake U. adv. council. Office: Iowa Revenue and Finance Dept Hoover State Office Bldg Des Moines IA 50319-0001

BAIR, JEFFREY HOWARD, sociologist, educator; s. Howard Vernon and Violette Marie Bair; m. Karen Willcockson, Aug. 13, 1966; 1 child, Kendra Eve. PhD, U. Kans., Lawrence, 1971. Prof. Emporia State U., Kans., 1973—2004. Col. USAR, 1970—96. Home: 2110 Morningside Dr Emporia KS 66801

BAIR, ROYDEN STANLEY, retired architect; b. New Rochelle, N.Y., Jan. 21, 1924; s. Roy S. and Ruth Irene (Farmer) B.; m. Margaret Davis Powell, Sept. 7, 1946 (dec. July 1972); children: Katherine, David, Laurence (dec. 1990), Andrew, Matthew; m. Martha Ann Cooper, July 7, 1973. BS in Civil Engring., Purdue U., 1947; BArch, MIT, 1950. Registered architect, Tex, Fla.; registered profl. engr., Tex. Construction adminstrn. Skidmore, Owings & Merrill, Chgo., 1950—51; draftsman J.N. MacCammon, Dallas, 1953-56; sr. assoc. Harrell & Hamilton, Dallas, 1956-67; sr. architect Lloyd Morgan Jones, Houston, 1967-68; owner R.S. Bair, Architects, Houston, 1969-95; ptnr. Turner & Bair Architects, Houston, 1996—2002. Capt. U.S. Army, 1942-46, 51-53. Mem. AIA (fellowship 1988, pres. Houston chpt. 1982), Construction Specifications Inst. (nat. pres. 1979, fellowship 1972), Construction Scis. Rsch. Found. (v.p. 1980-87), Tex. Soc. Architects. Home: 9573 Doliver Dr Houston TX 77063-1010 E-mail: stanandmartha@houston.rr.com.

BAIR, SHEILA COLLEEN, federal agency administrator; b. Wichita, Kans., Apr. 3, 1954; d. Albert E. and Clara F. (Brenneman) B.; m. Scott Cooper; 1 child, Preston Carlos. BA in Philosophy, U. Kans., 1975, JD, 1978. Bar: Kans. 1979. Teaching fellow Sch. Law, U. Ark., Fayetteville, 1978-79; atty.-advisor HEW, Kansas City, Mo., 1979-81; legal and policy advisor Office of Senator Bob Dole, Washington, 1981-86; of counsel Kutak, Rock & Campbell, Washington, 1986-87; dir. rsch. Bob Dole for Pres., Kans., 1987-88; legis. counsel N.Y. Stock Exch., Washington, 1988-91; commr. Commodity Futures Trading Commn., Washington, 1991—, acting chmn., 1993; Asst Secy Financial Inst Dept Treasury, Washington, 2001—. Candidate U.S. Ho. of Reps. from 5th Kans. dist., 1990; mem. bd. govs. Sch. Law, U. Kans., 1990-93; bd. dirs. Women's Campaign Fund, 1991—. Mem. ABA. Democrat. Office: Univ Mass Amherst 121 Presidents Dr #320 Amherst MA 01003

BAIR, TOM, publishing executive; Ad dir. Fairchild Sports Group, 1992—93; territory mgr., New England Men's Health, NY, 1993—95, advertising mgr., 1995—97, advertising dir., 1997—2000, assoc. pub., 2000—01, Golf Digest Cos., 2001—04, v.p., publisher, 2004—. Office: Golf Digest Co 20 Westport Rd PO Box 850 Wilton CT 06897 Office Phone: 212-286-2888.*

BAIR, WILLIAM ALOIS, engineer; b. Bklyn., Aug. 13, 1931; s. Henry Auchu and Anna Margaret (Zidar) B.; m. Patricia Anne Doyle, July 23, 1955; children: William A. Jr., Joseph M. Student, Pa. State U., 1949-51; BS in Engring., U.S. Naval Acad., 1955; BS in Civil Engring., Rensselaer Poly. Inst., 1958; MS in Nuclear Engring., U. Calif., 1966; grad. advanced mgmt. program, Wharton Sch., 1987. Registered profl. engr., N.Y., N.J., Pa., Conn., Md., Del., Va., S.C., Ga., D.C. Commd. ensign USN, 1955, advanced through grades to comdr., 1969; with USN Civil Engr. Corps, 1957—77; ret. USN, 1977; project mgr. Ebasco Svc. Inc., Princeton, NY, 1977—85, Raytheon Engrs. & Constrn., N.Y.C., 1988—96; dir. program planning and devel. Ebasco Svcs. Inc., N.Y.C., 1985—88; pres. Bair Engring. Cons., 1996—. Appointed mem. spl. 3 man NATO tech. com. to evaluate effectiveness of European Airfield Phys. Protection Program to counter damage from attack by Warsaw Pact Nations, 1972-75. Author: Helium 3 Neutron Spectrometer, 1966; contbr. articles to profl. jours. Scoutmaster Boy Scouts Am., Rockville, Md., 1969-70; coun. mem. European br., Casteau, Belgium, 1971-75. Decorated Legion of Merit, Bronze Star with V, Joint Svc. Commendation medal, Vietnamese Cross of Gallantry, Vietnamese Medal of Honor 1st class. Fellow ASCE; mem. Am. Nuclear Soc., Soc. Am. Mil. Engrs., Am. Legion, VFW. Republican. Roman Catholic. Achievements include research and development of innovative processes/procedures for decontamination and demolition of radioactive contaminated structures. Home and Office: Bair Engring Cons 21 Lorrie Ln Princeton Junction NJ 08550-5112

BAIR, WILLIAM J., retired radiobiologist; b. Jackson, Mich., July 14, 1924; s. William J. and Mona J. (Gamble) B.; m. Barbara Joan Sites, Feb. 16, 1952; children: William J., Michael Braden, Andrew Emil. BA in Chemistry, Ohio Wesleyan U., 1949; PhD in Radiation Biology, U. Rochester, 1954. NRC-AEC fellow U. Rochester, 1949-50, rsch. assoc. radiation biology, 1950-54; biol. scientist Hanford Labs. of GE, Richland, Wash., 1954-56, mgr. inhalation toxicology sect., biology dept., 1956-65, Battelle Meml. Inst., 1965-68; mgr. biology dept. Pacific Northwest Nat. Labs., Richland, 1968-74, dir. life scis. program, 1973-75, mgr. biomed. and environ. rsch. program, 1975-76, mgr. environ. health and safety rsch. program, 1976-86, mgr. life scis. ctr., 1986-93, sr. advisor health protection rsch., 1993—2002; ret., 2002. Demonstrated toxicology of plutonium and carcinogenesis of radioactive particles in lung; lectr. radiation biology Joint Ctr. Grad. Study, Richland, 1955-75; cons. to adv. com. on reactor safeguards Nuc. Regulatory Commn., 1971-87; mem. com. on plutonium toxicology; subcom. inhalation hazards, com. pathologic effects atomic radiation NAS, 1957-64, ad hoc com. on hot particles of subcom. biol. effects ionizing radiation NAS-NRC, 1974-76, vice-chmn. com. on biol. effects of ionizing radiation, BEIR IV Alpha radiation, 1985-88, battlefield radiation exposure com., 1997-99; chmn. task force on biol. effects of inhaled particles Internat. Commn. on Radiol. Protection, 1970-79, com. 2 on permissible dose for internal radiation, 1973-93, chmn. task group on respiratory tract models, 1984-93; mem. Nat. Coun. on Radiation Protection and Measurements, 1974-92, hon. mem., 1992-, com. on maximum permissible concentration of radionuclides for occupl. and nonoccupl. exposure, 1970-74, com. basic radiation protection criteria, 1975-93, chmn. ad hoc com. on hot particles, 1974, chmn. ad hoc com. internal emitter activities, 1976-77, com. on internal emitter stds., 1977-92, chmn. com. mgmt. of persons contaminated with radionuclides, 2004—, Lauriston S. Taylor lectr., 1997; radiation adv. com. and sci. adv. bd. EPA, 1993-99; founder, pres. Herbert M. Parker Found., 1987-94, bd. trustees, 1994-; cons. in field, 2002-. Author 200 books, articles, reports, chpts. in books. With U.S. Army, 1943—46. Decorated Bronze Star; recipient Combat Infantry Badge US Army, E.O. Lawrence Meml. award AEC, 1970, cert. of appreciation AEC, 1975, Alumni Disting. Achievement citation Ohio Wesleyan U. Fellow AAAS (life), Health Physics Soc. (life, bd. dirs. 1970-73, 83-86, pres. elect 1983-84, pres. 1984-85, Disting. Sci. Achievement award 1991, Herbert H. Parker award Columbia chpt. 1998, J.N. Stannard lectr. No. Calif. chpt. and Sierra Nev. chpt. 2004); mem. Internat. Commn. Radiological Protection, Radiation Rsch. Soc., Soc. Exptl. Biology and Medicine (vice chmn. N.W. chpt. 1967-70, 74-75), Sigma Xi. Avocations: wildlife photography, woodcarving, fly fishing, orchids, wood turning. Home: 578 Clermont Dr Richland WA 99352-1966

BAIRD, BRIAN N., congressman; b. Chama, N.Mex., Mar. 7, 1956; m. Rachel Nugent. BS, U. Utah, 1977; MS, U. Wyo., 1980, PhD, 1984. Mem. faculty dept. psychology Pacific Luth. U., 1986—97; mem. U.S. Congress from 3d Wash. dist., 1999—; mem. transp. and infrastructure, sci., and budget. Cons. clin. psychologist St. Charles Med. Ctr., 1994-96. Author: The Internship Practicum Handbook, Are We Having Fun Yet?. Mem.: Wash. State Psychol. Assn., APA. Democrat. Office: US Ho of Reps 1421 Longworth Ho Office Bldg Washington DC 20515-0001*

BAIRD, BRUCE ALLEN, lawyer; b. Cin., Mar. 26, 1948; s. William Wendell and Audrey (Geignetter) B.; m. Erica Borden, July 27, 1975 (div. 1993); 1 child, Jessica; m. Nicolette Adair Heidepriem, Sept. 17, 1993; 1 child, William. BA, Cornell U., 1970; JD, NYU, 1975. Spl. asst. to dep. atty. gen. U.S. Dept. Justice, Washington, 1975-76; law clk. to presiding judge U.S. Ct. Appeals (2d cir.), Brattleboro, Vt. and N.Y.C., 1976-77; assoc. Davis, Polk & Wardwell, N.Y.C., 1977-80; asst. U.S. atty. U.S. Attys. Office (so. dist.) N.Y., N.Y.C., 1980-86, dep. chief criminal div., 1986-87, chief narcotics unit, 1987, chief securities and commodities frauds unit, 1987-89; of counsel Covington & Burling, Washington, 1989-91, ptnr., 1991—. Editor in chief NYU Law Rev., 1974-75. Mem. ABA (co-chair securities and commodities fraud subcom. of white collar crime com. of criminal justice sect. 1994—), N.Y. State Bar Assn. (profl. jud. ethics com. 1982-89), Assn. of Bar of City of N.Y. (profl. jud. ethics com. 1979-82, 86-89), Fed. Bar Council, D.C. Bar Assn. Republican. Presbyterian. Home: 5404 Edgemoor Ln Bethesda MD 20814-1326 Office Phone: 202-662-5122. E-mail: bbaird@cov.com.

BAIRD, CHARLES BRUCE, lawyer, consultant; b. DeLand, Fla., Apr. 18, 1935; s. James Turner and Ethelyn Isabelle (Williams) B.; m. Barbara Ann Fabian, June 6, 1959 (div. Dec. 1979); children: C. Bruce Jr., Robert Arthur, Bryan James; m. Byung-Ran Cho, May 23, 1982; children: Merah-Iris, Haerah Violet. BSME, U. Miami, 1958; postgrad., UCLA, 1962-64; MBA, Calif. State U., 1966; JD, Am. U., 1971. Bar: Va. 1971, U.S. Dist. Ct. (ea. dist.) Va. 1971, D.C. 1973, U.S. Dist. Ct. D.C. 1973, U.S. Ct. Appeals (4th cir.) 1974, U.S. Supreme Ct. 1975. Rsch. engr. Naval Ordnance Lab., Corona, Calif., 1961-67; aerospace engr. Naval Air Systems Command, Washington, 1967-69; cons. engr. Bird Engring. Rsch. Assts., Vienna, Va., 1969-71; prof. Def. Systems Mgmt. Coll., Ft. Belvoir, Va., 1982; spl. asst. for policy compliance USIA Voice of Am., Washington, 1983-84. Cons. Booz, Allen & Hamilton, Inc., Bethesda, 1975-82, IBM, Bethesda, Md., 1984, Logistics Mgmt. Inst., McLean, Va., 1986-98, 2002—, TelcoExchange.com, 1998-2000, 2001; adj. prof. Fla. Inst. Tech., 1988. Contbr. articles to profl. jours.; inventor computer-based comm. systems for the gravely handicapped. Bd. govs. Sch. Engring. U. Miami, 1957; trustee Galilee United Meth. Ch., Arlington, Va., 1983-87. Mem. Va. Trial Lawyers Assn., Assoc. Trial Lawyers Am., Internet. Soc., Fed. Comm. Bar Assn., ACLU, NRA, Sigma Alpha Epsilon. Home and Office: 5396 Gainsborough Dr Fairfax VA 22032-2744 Office Phone: 703-239-9492.

BAIRD, DOUGLAS GORDON, law educator, dean; b. Phila., July 10, 1953; s. Henry Welles and Eleanora (Gordon) B. BA in English, summa cum laude, Yale U., 1975; JD, Stanford U., 1979; LLD (hon.), U. Rochester, 1994. Law clk. to Hon. Shirley M. Hufstedler US Ct. Appeals 9th Cir., 1979, law clk. to Hon. Dorothy W. Nelson, 1980; asst. prof. law U. Chgo. Law Sch., 1980-83, prof., 1984—87, Harry A. Bigelow prof. law, 1988—96, Harry A. Bigelow disting. svc. prof. law, 1996—, assoc. dean, 1984-87, dean, 1994-99. Vis. prof. law Stanford U., 1987—88, Yale U., 2000; Robert Braucher vis. prof. law Harvard U., 1993. Author: The Elements of Bankruptcy, 1992; co-author: (with T. Jackson) Cases, Problems, and Materials on Security Interests in Personal Property, 1984, Cases, Problems, and Materials on Bankruptcy, 1985, (with Gertner & and Picker) Game Theory and the Law, 1994. Fellow: Am. Coll. Bankruptcy, Am. Acad. Arts & Sciences. Office: U Chgo Sch Law 1111 E 60th St Chicago IL 60637-2776 Office Phone: 773-702-9571. E-mail: dbaird@uchicago.edu.

BAIRD, DOUGLAS JAMES, investment banker; b. Rochester, N.Y., Feb. 3, 1962; s. James David and Carol Agatha (Pascale) B.; m. Sarah Lee Stevenson, Dec. 12, 1987; children: David Harrington, Henry Stevenson, Roxanna Margaret. Diploma, Deerfield (Mass.) Acad., 1980; AB Dartmouth Coll., 1984; MBA, Amos Tuck Sch., Hanover, N.H., 1989. Fin. analyst pub. fin. group Merrill Lynch Capital Markets, N.Y.C., 1984-85, jr. assoc. internat. fin. group, 1985-86; assoc. equity transactions group Merrill Lynch Europe Ltd., London, 1986-87; assoc. mergers and acquisitions Merrill Lynch Capital Markets, N.Y.C., 1988, Alex. Brown & Sons, Balt., 1989-91, v.p. corp. fin. environ. svcs., 1991-93, mng. dir. equity capital markets, 1993-99; head U.S. equity capital mkts. Deutsche Bank Securities, NYC, 2000—. Mem. adv. bd. applied corp. fin. program U. Wis., Madison; mem. bd. advisors Ind. Securities Rsch., LLC; trustee Boys' Latin Sch. of Md.; bd. dirs. PACT: Helping Children with Spl. Needs; intern, White House Office of Media Relations and Planning, 1983. Mem. Yale Club of N.Y.C., Maryland Club, Webhannet Country Club, Balt. Country Club, Univ. Club, Downtown Assn. Republican. Episcopalian. Office: Deutsche Bank Securities 60 Wall St New York NY 10005 Home: 55 East 72nd St New York NY 10021

BAIRD, DUGALD EUAN, automotive executive; b. Aberdeen, Scotland, Sept. 16, 1937; came to U.S., 1979; s. Dugald and Matilda Deans (Tennant) B.; m. Angelica Hartz, May 24, 1961; children: Camilla N., Maiken E. MA in Geophysics, Cambridge U., 1960; LLD, Aberdeen U., 1995, Dundee U., 1998; DSc, Heriot-Watt U., 1999. Joined Schlumberger, 1960, various field assignments worldwide, 1979—86, chmn., CEO, 1986—2003; ret., 2003; chmn. Rolls-Royce Plc, 2003—. Mem. Prime Min. Com. Nat. de la Sci., France, 1998—2002, Prime Mins. Coun. Sci. and Tech, England, 2000—, adv. com. Banque de France, 2001—; mem. bd. ScottishPower. Trustee Carnegie Instn., Washington, 1998—. Office: Rolls-Royce plc 65 Buckingham Gate London SW1E 6AT England

BAIRD, EDWARD ROUZIE, JR., retired lawyer; b. Norfolk, Va., Aug. 29, 1936; s. Edward Rouzie and Eleanor Gray (Perry) B.; m. Nell McGlaughon, Oct. 8, 1967 (dec. Oct. 1973); 1 child, Eleanor Gray; m. Abby St. John Starke, Feb. 5, 1977; children: Abby St. John, Edward Rouzie V. BA, U. Va., 1960, LLB, 1967. Assoc. Baird, Creshaw & Ware, Norfolk, 1967—68; asst. dist. counsel U.S. Army C.E., Norfolk, 1968—73; asst. U.S. Atty. U.S. Atty.'s Office, Norfolk, 1973—77; sole practice Norfolk, 1977—82, 1999—2004; ptnr. Willcox & Baird, Norfolk, 1982—99. Served to lt. (j.g.) USN, 1960-63. Mem. Soc. Cincinnati, Va. Club (Norfolk). Home: 1711 Cloncurry Rd Norfolk VA 23505-1717

BAIRD, JAMES, lawyer; b. Ann Arbor, Mich., Oct. 23, 1943; BA, Mich. State Univ., 1965; JD, Univ. Wis., 1968; LLM highest honors, George Washington Univ., 1970. Bar: Wis. 1968, Ill. 1972. Articles editor Wis. Bar Jour., 1967-68; atty. to bd. mem. NLRB, 1968-70; asst. dir. Labor Mgt. Rels. Svc., Washington, 1970—72; ptnr. Seyfarth, Shaw, Fairweather & Geraldson, Chgo., 1978—. Chmn. Ill. State C. of C. Labor Rels. Comm., 1978—80. Mem. ABA (mgmt. chmn. com. state labor law devels. 1975-76, com. state and local govt. bargaining 1976-79, sect. labor rels. law, chmn. com. pub. employee bargaining, sect. urban, state and local govt. law 1981-84, mem. gov. coun. sect. urban, state and local govt. law 1991-92, sect. chair, urban, state and local govt. law 1994-95, ho. del. 1994-, bd. gov. 2004-), Fed. Bar Assn. (mem. state and local govt. reaction panel 1972—). Address: Seyfarth Shaw Fairweather & Geraldson 55 E Monroe St Ste 4200 Chicago IL 60603-5863

BAIRD, JAMES ABINGTON, retired judge; b. Kirksville, Mo., Jan. 28, 1926; s. James Abington and Dorothy (LaGest) Baird; m. Georgia Jane Suliburk, Mar. 29, 1948 (dec. Dec. 1999); children: James Abington III, Mary J.; m. Alice K. Barter, Dec. 2, 2000. BS, U. Mich., 1949; JD, U. Toledo, 1957. Bar: Ohio 1957. Sales rep. Fruehauf Trailer Co., Chgo., 1949-50, Warren-Teed Products Co., Toledo, 1951-52, Dictaphone Corp., Toledo, 1952-53; pres. Kaiser-Frazer dealership, Caro, Mich., 1950-51; claims adjuster Nationwide Ins. Co., Toledo, 1953-57; pvt. practice Toledo; judge Sylvania Ohio Mcpl. Ct., 1970-82; ret., 1982. Chmn. Sch. Levy campaigns Sylvania Pub. Sch. Sys., 1968—69, candidate sch. bd., 1969. With USNR, 1944—46. Mem.: Toledo Bar Assn., U. Toledo Alumni Assn., U. Mich. Alumni Assn., Bowling Green Country Club, Phi Delta Theta. Home: 85 Nottingham Cross Bowling Green OH 43402-9384 E-mail: baird@wcnet.org.

BAIRD, JOHN ABSALOM, JR., retired academic administrator; b. Honolulu, Sept. 13, 1918; s. John Absalom and Helen (Bates) Baird; m. Virginia Walton, Mar. 8, 1941 (dec. 1983); m. Clare A. Emmons, May 12, 1984 (dec. 1998). AB, Princeton U., 1940; postgrad., Johns Hopkins U., 1941. Asst. supt. Charles S. Walton Co., 1942-47, asst. sec. and dir., 1947-52, v.p., 1952-72; asst. pres. Ea. Bapt. Theol. Sem., Phila., Ea. Coll., St. Davids, Pa., 1952-61, v.p., 1961-88, advisor to pres., 1988—2002; ret., 2002. Author: A Leap of Faith, 1972, The Whole Gospel for the Whole World, 1975, All Things are Thine, 1976, Profile of a Hero, 1977, The Shining Fire, 1979, Horn of Plenty, 1982, Great House, 1984, Promises to Keep, 1989, More Than Knowledge, 1992, Power of One, 1997, Inheritance of Value, 1999; contbr. articles to profl. jours. Trustee, v.p. Pa. Lupus Found.; trustee Ludington Libr., Bryn Mawr, Ralston House, Phila., Vol. Svcs. for the Blind, Phila., 1971—85; vice chmn. Main Line br. YMCA Greater Phila., 1947—63; Phila. Main Line dist. chmn. Valley Forge coun. Boy Scouts Am., 1952—54, dist. commr., 1954—56; mem. adv. bd. Phila. Inglis House, 1963—2003; bd. dirs. Am. Ednl. Film and Video Ctr., 1964—2002; chmn. bd. trustees Shipley Sch., Bryn Mawr, Pa., 1972—78; v.p. Pa. chpt. Lupus Found. Am., 1973—95; trustee 4th Bapt. Mission Found., 1976—80, Seaman's Ch. Inst., Phila., 1998—2003; bd. dirs. Pa. United Theol. Sem. Found., Pitts.; v.p., bd. dirs. Am. Sunday Sch. Union, Phila., 1957—69; mem. adv. bd. Phila. Inglis House, 1963—2003; bd. dirs. Watchman Examiner Corp., N.Y.C., 1958—70, Athenaeum, Phila., Beaumont Retirement Cmty.; bd. corporators, bd. dirs. Covenant Life Ins. Co., 1968—92; mem. Union League. Recipient Honor medal, Freedom Founds., 1973. Mem.: Geneal. Soc. Pa. (dir. 1988—2003), Am. Coll. Pub. Rels. Assn., Hist. Soc. Pa. (dir. 1992—2001), Pa. Acad. Fine Arts, U.S. Naval Found., Am. Alumni Coun., Am. Bapt. Pub. Rels. Assn., U.S. Naval Inst., Am. Assn. Sem. Staff Officers (pres. 1966—68), Am. Philatelic Soc., Am. Rose Soc., Merion Cricket Club (Haverford, Pa.), Right Angle Club, Penn Club, Soc. Colonial Wars (gov. 1994—97), English-Speaking Union, S.R., Order Fgn. Wars, Colonial Soc. Pa. (gov. 1994—97), Soc. of Cin. (pres. Del. 1972—75, sec. gen. 1977—83), Loyal Legion. Republican. Presbyterian. Home: 74 Pasture Ln # 116 Bryn Mawr PA 19010-1766

BAIRD, JULIAN THOMPSON, JR., art dealer; b. Harlingen, Tex., Jan. 28, 1938; s. Julian Thompson and Faye Devilbiss Baird; m. Carol Friedell Baird (div. 1985); m. Elaine Fraser Baird, Jan. 9, 1986. AB magna cum laude, Harvard U., 1960, PhD, 1968; BA, Oxford (Eng.) U., 1962, MA, 1967. Assoc. prof. Boston U., 1967-80; pres. Baird Enterprises d/b/a Tree's Place, Orleans, Mass., 1981—. Lectr. Cape Mus. Fine Art, Old Lyme Acad. Art, St. Botolph Club, Boston, others; keynote spkr., organizer Nat. Conf. on Representational Painting, 2004. Contbr. articles to profl. jours. Mem. Orleans Charter Commn., 1989-90; pres. Orleans Bd. of Trade, 1983-84, Orleans Taxpayers Assn., 1985-87; fine wine charity auctioneer Cape Mus. Fine Arts, 1994-96. Recipient Spl. Distinction award Boston U. Alumni Assn., 1990; named one of 400 People Who Brighten Our LIves, Cape Cod Life mag., 2005. Mem. St. Botolph Club, Oxford and Cambridge Soc. Avocations: collecting art, wine and books, boating, gardening, computers, investing. Home: 4 Mayflower Cir PO Box 666 Orleans MA 02653-0666 Office: Tree's Place 62 Route 6A Orleans MA 02653-2411 Office Phone: 508-255-1330. E-mail: jbaird@pobox.com.

BAIRD, KATHLEEN MARY, lawyer; b. Milw., Dec. 15, 1949; d. Paul Jerold Block and Eileen Louise Dreger; m. Brian D. Baird, Dec. 19, 1971 (div. Aug. 15, 1995); children: Brian, Stephen, Kristine. BA in Polit. Sci., U. Wis., 1972, JD. Bar: Wis. 1976, U.S. Dist. Ct. (ea. and we. dists.) Wis. 1976. Hearing examiner Dept. Industry, Labor and Human Rels., Milw., 1976—77; asst. corp. counsel Milwaukee County, Milw., 1977—83, prin. asst. corp. counsel, 1977—83, asst. family ct. commr., 1983—84; pvt. practice Milw., 1992—. Mem. Wauwatosa Sch. Bd., chair sch. referendum com.; trustee Wauwatosa (Wis.) Pub. Libr., chair bd. trustees. Mem.: Milw. Bar Assn. (chair law practice mgmt. com.), Assn. Conflict Resolution, Internat. Acad. Collaborative Profls., Collaborative Family Law Coun. Wis. (bd. dirs.), Wis. Assn. Mediators, Soc. Family Lawyers, Assn. Women Lawyers. Office: 2300 N Mayfair Rd Ste 9070 Wauwatosa WI 53226 Business E-Mail: kathbair@execpc.com.

BAIRD, LEONARD LYNN, social scientist, educator, researcher, editor; s. Russel Thomas and Edith Isabel Baird; m. Rosanne Clark Baird, Oct. 19, 1962; children: William Russell, Diana Ragan. BA, U. Calif., LA, 1962, MA, 1965, EdD, 1966. Rsch. psychologist Am. Coll. Testing Program, Iowa City, 1966—69; sr. rsch. psychologist Ednl. Testing Svc., Princeton, NJ, 1969—83; prof. U. Ky., Lexington, 1983—94, Ohio State U., Columbus, 1994—; editor Jour. of Higher Edn., Columbus, 1994—. Editl. bd. Rsch. in Higher Edn., 1987—96. *The Journal of Higher Education, founded in 1930, is the oldest, largest, and most cited journal in the world, devoted exclusively to research and scholarship about higher education.* Author: (books) The Elite Schools, 1977; author: (and editor) Understanding Student and Faculty Life, 1980, Increasing Grad. Student Retention, 1993; contbr. chapters to books, articles to profl. jours. Recipient Sydney Suslow award for outstanding rsch., Assn. for Instl. Rsch., 1991, Sr. Scholar award, Am. Coll. Pers. Assn., 2003. Office: Ohio State Univ 301 Ramseyer Columbus OH 43210 Business E-Mail: baird.62@osu.edu.

BAIRD, MARIANNE SAUNORUS, critical care clinical nurse specialist, administrator; b. Chgo., Dec. 15, 1953; d. John and Irene Saunorus; m. Thomas W. Baird, Sept. 10, 1983; 1 child, Rachel. BSN, Loyola U., Chgo., 1975; MSN, Emory U., 1982. Critical care RN, cert. advanced cardiac life support instr., Ga. Supr. surg. nursing Rush-Presbyn. St. Lukes Med. Ctr., Chgo., 1978—80; from staff nurse, clin. mgr. intensive care unit to case mgr. St. Joseph's Hosp., Atlanta, 1982—96, case mgr. depts. pulmonary and nephrology, 1996—2001; clin. assoc. faculty Emory U., Atlanta, 1990—; clin. nurse specialist for critical care and med.-surg. nursing St. Joseph's Hosp., Atlanta, 2001—. RN preceptor, ednl. staff Genentech, Inc., 1995-2002. Author several nursing textbooks; contbr. articles to profl. jours. Mem. med. supply com. Atlanta Com. for Olympic Games, 1994-96. Recipient Fed. traineeship Emory U., 1980-81; named one of Outstanding Young Women of Am., 1991. Mem. AACN (bd. dirs. Atlanta chpt. 1984-86), Soc. Critical Care Medicine, Am. Holistic Nurses Assn., Blue Key, Kappa Gamma Pi, Sigma Theta Tau. Office: 5665 Peachtree Dunwoody Rd NE Atlanta GA 30342-1701 Business E-Mail: mbaird@sjha.org.

BAIRD, PATRICIA ANN, physician, educator; b. Rochdale, Eng. arrived in Can., 1955; d. Harold and Winifred (Cainen) Holt; m. Robert Merrifield Baird, Feb. 22, 1964; children: Jennifer Ellen, Brian Merrifield, Bruce Andrew BSc in Biol. Sci. with honors, McGill U., 1959, MD, CM, 1963; DSc (hon.), McMaster U., 1991; D (hon.), U. Ottawa, 1991; LLD (hon.), Wilfrid Laurier U., 2000. Intern Royal Victoria Hosp., Montreal, Que., Can., 1963-64; resident, fellow in pediat. Vancouver Gen. Hosp., B.C., Can., 1964-67; instr. pediat. U. B.C., Vancouver, 1968-72, from asst. prof. to prof., 1972-94, Univ. Killam Disting. prof., 1994—; head dept. med. genetics Grace Hosp., Vancouver, 1981-89, Children's Hosp., Vancouver, 1981-89, Health Scis. Centre Hosp., 1986-89. Med. cons. B.C. Health Surveillance Registry, 1977-90; chmn. genetics grants com. Med. Rsch. Coun., Ottawa, Ont., Can., 1982-87, mem. coun., 1987-90; mem. Nat. Adv. Bd. on Sci. and Tech. to Fed. Govt., 1987-91; mem. genetic predisposition study steering com. Sci. Coun. Can., 1987-90; chair Royal Commn. on New Reproductive Technologies, 1989-93, Plemer's Coun. on Aging Sr. Issues, 2005—; co-chair Nat. Forum Sci. and Tech. Couns., 1991; v.p. Can. Inst. for Advanced Rsch., 1991-2002, vice chmn. bd., 2002--; bd. dirs. Biomed. Rsch. Centre, 1986-89; bd. govs. U. B.C., 1984-90; temporary cons. WHO, 1999, 2000, 01, mem. human genetics ELSI planning group, 2000-02, mem. expert adv. panel on human genetics, 2002—. Contbr. articles to med. jours. Decorated officer Order of Can., 2000, Order of B.C., 1992; recipient Commemorative medal for Confedn. of Can., 1992, Queen's Golden Jubilee medal, 2002. Fellow RCP Can., Royal Soc. Can., Can. Coll. Med. Geneticists (v.p. 1984-86); mem. Am. Soc. Human Genetics (chair nominating com. 1987-89), B.C. Med. Assn., Can. Med. Assn., Genetics Soc. Can., Genetic Epidemiology (adv. bd. 1991-94), Internat. Fedn. of Gyn. and Obs. (mem. ethics com. 1997-99). Avocations: skiing, bicycling, music. Office: U BC Dept Med Genetics Vancouver BC Canada V6T 1Z3 Business E-Mail: pbaird@interchange.ubc.ca.

BAIRD, PENNY DRUE, interior designer; b. N.Y.C., July 19, 1951; d. Philip Robert and Terri Baird; m. Fred Deutsch, Dec. 31, 1991; children: Alexander Baird Deutsch, Benjamin Baird Deutsch, Philip Baird Deutsch; 1 child, Adam Baird Alpert. BA, U. Rochester, 1973; PsychD, Yeshiva U., 1991; attended, NY School of Interior Design. Pres. Dessins LLC, N.Y.C., 1982—. Archtl. Digest, 1997, 1998, 2000. Pres. City Meals on Wheels, N.Y.C., 1985—90; mem. women's com. N.Y. Hosp., N.Y.C., 1994—; mem. women's bd. Albert Einstein Coll. Medicine, N.Y.C., 1990—. Mem.: Phi Beta Kappa. Office: Dessins LLC 787 Madison Ave New York NY 10021

BAIRD, RICHARD, human resources specialist; m. Linda Baird; children: Ben, Jessica, Blythe. Grad., Albion Coll., 1978. Dir. fin. and human resources Coopers & Lybrand, Detroit, various positions including ops. ptnr. U.S. bus. assurance practice; pres., CEO LAI Compass; global ops. leader assurance and bus. adv. svcs. Pricewaterhouse Coopers, LLP, 1999—. Head INSEAD-Pricewaterhouse Coopers rsch. initiative for high performance orgns.; bd. dirs. Albion Coll., chmn. bd. trustees, chmn. Liberal Arts at Work. Office: PricewaterhouseCoopers LLP 300 Madison Ave 24th Fl New York NY 10017*

BAIRD, ROBERT DAHLEN, retired theology studies educator; b. Phila., June 29, 1933; s. Jesse Dahlen and Clara (Sonntag) Baird; m. Patty Jo Lutz, Dec. 18, 1954; children: Linda Sue, Stephen Robert, David Bryan, Janna Ann. BA, Houghton Coll., 1954; BD, Fuller Theol. Sem., 1957; STM, So. Meth. U., 1959; PhD, U. Iowa, 1964. Instr. philosophy and religion U. Omaha, 1962-65; fellow Asian religions Soc. Religion in Higher Edn., 1965-66; asst. prof. religion U. Iowa, Iowa City, 1966-69, assoc. prof., 1969-74, prof., 1974-2001, prof. emeritus, 2001—, acting dir. Sch. Religion, 1985, dir., Sch. Religion, 1995—2000; Leonard S. Florsheim Sr. Eminent Scholar's chair New Coll., U. South Fla., Sarasota, 1988-89. Vis. prof. Grinnell Coll., 1983; Goodwin-Philpot Eminent chair in religion Auburn U., 2001—03; adj. prof. Ripon (Wis.) Coll., 2005—. Author: Category Formation and the History of Religions, 1971, 2d paperback edit., 1991; author: (with W. R. Comstock et al) Religion and Man: An Introduction, 1971, Indian and Far Eastern Religious Traditions, 1972; editor: Methodological Issues in Religious Studies, 1975, Religion in Modern India, 1981, 4th edit., 2001, Essays in History of Religions, 1991, Religion and Law in Independent India, 1993, 2d edit., 2005; book rev. editor: Jour. Am. Acad. Religion, 1979—84; contbr. articles to profl. jours. Ford Found. fellow, 1965—66, Sr. fellow, Am. Inst. Indian Studies, 1972, 1992, Faculty Devel. grantee, U. Iowa, 1979, 1986, 1992. Mem.: N.Am. Assn. Study Religion, Assn. Asian Studies, Am. Acad. Religion. Democrat. Presbyterian. Office: 113 Glenn Dr Cottage Grove WI 53527 E-mail: robert-baird@uiowa.edu.

BAIRD, SUSAN ELIZABETH, secondary education educator, writer; b. L.A., May 7, 1954; d. Thomas Alva Baird and Sarah Ann (Mott) Durand; m. David Patrick Hogan, Apr. 5, 1980; 1 child, Adam Michael Hogan. BA in Secondary Edn./English Media Endorsement, So. Oreg. State Coll., 1982, MA in Humanities, 1989. Cert. Oreg. std. tchr. secondary edn. media endorsement. Tchr. English Ashland (Oreg.) Mid. Sch., 1983—. Advisor Speech and Theatre Clubs, Ashland Mid. Sch., 1989—, Teen Poetry Readings, 1990—; lectr. human rights Ashland Sch. Dist., 1988—. Contbr. articles to mags. Spkr. Common Ground Conf., Ashland, 1991; adminstr. Rogue Valley Coalition Cultural Diversity Conf., Ashland, 1992, Nat. Coalition Bldg. Inst., Ashland, 1994; people to people citizen amb. del. to So. Africa, 1998. Miss. Project grantee So. Oreg. R&D, 1988, Mark Twain Prodn. grantee, 1989. Mem. NEA, NAACP, Nat. Coun. Tchrs. English, So. Poverty Law Ctr., N.W. Coalition Human Dignity. Avocations: theater, travel, gardening. Office: Ashland Mid Sch 100 Walker Ave Ashland OR 97520-1399 E-mail: susan.baird@ashland.k12.or.us.

BAIRD, THOMAS BRYAN, JR., retired lawyer; b. Newport News, Va., June 21, 1931; s. Thomas Bryan and Mary Florence (Rieker) B.; m. Mildred Katherine Clark, June 23, 1956; children: Sarah, Thomas Bryan III, William, Laura. BA, U. Va., 1952; LLB, U. Tenn., 1960. Bar: Tenn. 1964, Va. 1969, U.S. Dist. Ct. (we. dist.) 1970. With Stat Farm Ins., Knoxville, Tenn., 1960-68; asst. commonwealth atty. Wytheville, Va., 1969-71; commonwealth atty. Wythe County, 1972-98; prin. Thomas B. Baird, Jr. Trustee Simmerman Home for the Aged, 1972-83. Served with U.S. Army, 1953-55. Democrat. Presbyterian.

BAIRD, WILLIAM DAVID, retired anesthesiologist; b. Dallas, Feb. 17, 1922; s. John B. and Sue S. B.; m. Virginia Claye Sanders, June 27, 1948; children: Linda B. Moore, Cynthia B. Matthews, C. Sanders Baird, Ginger B. Stark, J. Davies Baird. BA, Rice Inst., Houston, 1949; MD, U. Tex., 1953. Diplomate Am. Bd. Anesthesiologists. Intern U. Tex. Med. Br. Hosps., Galveston, 1953-54, resident in anesthesiology, 1954-56, fellow, instr. anesthesiology, 1956-57; pvt. practice anesthesiology Garland, Tex., 1957-80; med. cons. Garland Cmty. Hosp., 1980-81, Branson & Misko, 1981-93. Clin. instr. U. Tex. SW Br., 1963-80; chief anesthesiology Garland Clinic and Hosp., 1957-75, Garland Meml. Hosp., 1975-78; exec. staff com. Meml. Hosp. Garland, 1975-78; adv. bd. Presbyn. Hosp. Dallas, 1969. Author: Some Descendants of John Baird, A Genealogy, 1997; editor, pub.: The 17th Sortie Newsletter of the 17th Bomb Group/Wing Reunion Assn. Precinct chmn. Rep. party, Garland, 1969-74; bd. dirs. Garland YMCA, 1972-74. Fellow Am. Coll. Anesthesiologists; mem. AMA, Am. Soc. Anesthesiologists, Tex. Med. Assn., Dallas County Med. Soc., Tex. Soc. Anesthesiologists, Dallas County Anesthesiology Soc., Dallas County Hist. Soc., Dallas County Pioneer Assn., Marauder Men of Metroplex, B-26 Marauder Hist. Soc. Republican. Avocations: genealogy, 17th bomb group history, farming, hunting, fishing. E-mail: wdbaird@aol.com.

BAIRD, WILLIAM MCKENZIE, chemical carcinogenesis researcher, biochemistry professor; b. Phila., Mar. 23, 1944; s. William Henry Jr. and Edna (McKenzie) Baird; m. Elizabeth A. Myers, June 21, 1969; children: Heather Jean, Elizabeth Joanne, Scott William. BS in Chem., Lehigh U., 1966; PhD in Oncology, U. Wis., 1971. Postdoctoral fellow Inst. Cancer Rsch., London, 1971—73; from asst. to assoc. prof. biochemistry Wistar Inst., Phila., 1973—80; assoc. prof. medicinal chem. Purdue U., West Lafayette, Ind., 1980—82, prof., 1982—97, Glenn L. Jenkins prof. medicinal chem., 1989—97, dir. Cancer Ctr., 1986—97, faculty participant, biochemistry program Cancer Ctr., 1980—97; dir. environ. Health Sci. Ctr. Oreg. State U., Corvallis, 1997—2000, prof., dept. environ. and molecular toxicology, 1997—, prof. dept. biochemistry and biophysics, 1997—. Adv. com. on biochemistry and chem. carcinogenesis Am. Cancer Soc., 1983—86; mem. chem. pathology study sect. NIH, 1986—90. Assoc. editor: Cancer Rsch., 1986—98; contbr. articles to profl. jours. Grantee NCI. Mem.: AAAS, Soc. Toxicology, Environ. Mutagen Soc., Am. Soc. Biochemistry and Molecular Biology, Am. Chem. Soc., Am. Assn. Cancer Rsch., Internat. Soc. for Study of Xenobiotics. Office: Oreg State U Environ and Molecular Toxicology 1007 ALS Bldg Corvallis OR 97331-7301 Office Phone: 541-737-1886. Business E-Mail: william.baird@orst.edu.

BAIRD, ZOË, foundation president, lawyer; b. Bklyn., June 20, 1952; d. Ralph Louis and Naomi (Allen) B.; m. Paul Gewirtz, June 8, 1986; 2 children. AB, U. Calif., Berkeley, 1974, JD, 1977. Bar: Washington, 1979, Calif. 1977, Conn. 1989. Law clk. Hon. Albert Wollenberg, San Francisco, 1977-78; atty., advisor Office Legal Counsel U.S. Dept. Justice, Washington, 1979-80; assoc. counsel to Pres., The White House, Washington, 1980-81; assoc., then ptnr. O'Melveny & Myers, Washington, 1981-86; counsellor, staff exec. GE, Fairfield, Conn., 1986-90; v.p., gen. counsel Aetna Life & Casualty, Hartford, 1990-93, sr. v.p., gen. counsel, 1993-96; pres. Markle Found., N.Y.C., 1998—. Bd. dirs. Chubb Corp. Bd. dirs. James A. Baker III Inst. for Pub. Policy, Lawyers for Children Am., Brookings Inst., Save the Children. Mem. Am. Law Inst., Coun. on Fgn. Rels., Convergys Corp. Office: Markle Found 10 Rockefeller Plaza 16th Fl New York NY 10020-1903 E-mail: info@markle.org.

BAIRSTOW, FRANCES KANEVSKY, arbitrator, mediator, educator; b. Racine, Wis., Feb. 19, 1920; d. William and Minnie (DuBow) Kanevsky; m. Irving P. Kaufman, Nov. 14, 1942 (div. 1949); m. David Steele Bairstow, Dec. 17, 1954; children: Dale Owen, David Anthony. Student, U. Wis., 1937-42; BS, U. Louisville, 1949; student, Oxford U., England, 1953-54; postgrad., McGill U., Montreal, Que., Can., 1958-59. Rsch. economist U.S. Senate Labor-Mgmt. Subcom., Washington, 1950-51; labor edn. specialist U. P.R., San Juan, 1951-52; chief wage data unit WSB, Washington, 1952-53; labor rsch. economist Can. Pacific Ry. Co., Montreal, Canada, 1956-58; asst. dir. indsl. rels. ctr. McGill U., 1960-66, assoc. dir., 1966-71, dir., 1971-85, lectr., indsl. rels. dept. econs., 1960-72, from asst. prof. to assoc. prof. faculty mgmt., 1972—83, prof., 1983-85; lectr. Stetson Law Sch., Fla.; spl. master Fla. Pub. Employees Rels. Commn., 1985-97. Cons. Nat. Film Bd. Can., 1965—69; arbitrator Que. Consultative Coun. Panel Arbitrators, 1968—83, Ministry Labour and Manpower, 1971—83, United Air Lines and Assn. Flight Attendants, 1990—95, Am. Airlines and Transport Workers Union, 1997—98, State U. Sys. Fla., 1990—2003, FDA, 1996—98, Social Security Adminstrn., 1996—2003, Am. Airlines, 1997—, Tampa Gen. Hosp., 1996—, Cargo Internat. Airlines, 2001, Govt. of Fla. and Fla. State Police, 2002—, Bell South and Comm. Workers Am., 2003—, USAF at Warner Robins and AFGE, 2003—; mediator Can. Pub. Svc. Staff Rels. Bd., 1973—85, So. Bell Tel., 1985—, AT&T and Comm. Workers Am., 1986—; cons. on collective bargaining arbitration OECD, Paris, 1979. Contbg. columnist: Montreal Star, 1971—85. Chmn. Nat. Inquiry Commn. Wider-Based Collective Bargaining, 1978; dep. commr. essential svcs. Province of Que., 1976—81. Recipient Sefton award, U. Toronto, 2005; Fulbright fellow, 1953—54. Mem.: Ctrl. Fla. Indsl. Rels. Rsch. Assn. (pres. 1999), Nat. Acad. Arbitrators (bd. govs. 1977—80, program chmn. 1982—83, v.p. 1986—88, nat. coord. 1987—90), Indsl. Rels. Rsch. Assn. Am. (mem. exec. bd. 1965—68, chmn. nominating com. 1977), Can. Indsl. Rels. Rsch. Inst. (mem. exec. bd. 1965—68). Home and Office: 4650 54th Ave S # 511 Saint Petersburg FL 33711

BAISDEN, ELEANOR MARGUERITE, retired airline compensation executive, consultant; b. Bklyn., Nov. 7, 1935; d. Vernon McKee and Ethel Mildred (Cockle) Baisden. BA, Hofstra U., 1970. Clk. Trans World Airlines, N.Y.C., 1953-55, sec., 1955-64, compensation analyst, 1964-75, compensation mgr., 1975-85, dir. compensation and orgn. planning, 1985-88, dir. compensation and adminstrn., 1988-97; ret., 1997; owner, mgr. Embassy Estates Rental Properties, 1997—. Bd. dirs., treas. Weatherby Lake Improvement Co., 1997-2001. Mem. Airline Pers. Dirs. Conf. (pers. com. 1984-86), Airline Tariff Pub. Co. (pers. com. 1978-86), Nat. Fgn. Trade Coun. (compensation com. 1980-84), Internat. Pers. Assn. (co. rep. 1980-84), Mensa, Weatherby Lake Yacht Club (Mo.), BIG Investment Club (treas. 1998-2001), DAR, Kansas City Lyric Opera Guild (bd. dirs. 2005—), Kansas City Symphony Guild (dir. 2005—), Red Hat Soc. (chpt. pres. 2003-05), Alpha Sigma Lambda (scholar 1965-66). Republican. Methodist. Avocations: boating, swimming, piano, travel. Home: 7818 NW Scenic Dr Kansas City MO 64152-1643

BAISLEY, JAMES MAHONEY, retired lawyer; b. Dec. 21, 1932; s. Charles Thomas and Katherine (Mahoney) B.; m. Barbara Brosnan, Sept. 7, 1960; children— Mary Elizabeth, Katherine, Barbara, Paul, Genevieve, Charles, James BS, Fordham U., 1954, LLB, 1961. Bar: N.Y. 1961, Ill. 1969. Assoc. Naylon, Aronson, Huber & Magill, N.Y.C., 1961-66; asst. counsel GTE Corp, 1966-69; v.p., gen. counsel GTE Automatic Electric Inc., Northlake, Ill., 1969-81; gen. counsel, v.p. W. W. Grainger Inc., Skokie, Ill., 1981-92, corp. sec., 1991-2000, ret., 2000. Bd. dirs. EAC, Inc. Served with USMC, 1954-57 Mem. ABA, Chgo. Bar Assn., Union League Club Chgo., North Shore Country Club. Republican. Roman Catholic. Home: 530 Longwood Ave Glencoe IL 60022-1737 Office: W W Grainger Inc 100 Grainger Pkwy Lake Forest IL 60045-5201

BAISLEY, ROBERT WILLIAM, music educator; b. New Haven, Apr. 5, 1923; s. Joseph V. and Mary (Bergin) B.; m. Jean Shanley, July 30, 1955; children: Joan Ann, Susan Jean, Elizabeth Veronica. Mus.B., Yale U., 1949; MA, Columbia U., 1950. Tchr. Cherry Lawn Sch., Darien, Conn., 1950-51; dir. Neighborhood Music Sch., New Haven, 1951-56; asst. prof. piano, exec. officer Sch. Music Yale U., New Haven, 1956-65; prof. music Pa. State U., University Park, 1965-87, chmn. dept. music, 1965-79. Concert pianist in various concerts, recitals, radio and TV. Vol. United Fund, New Haven, 1951-65; rep. to Coun. of Social Agys., 1951-60; mem. adv. coun. Salvation Army, 1963-65; bd. dirs. Ctrl. Pa. Festival of Arts (pres. 1969-71). Served with AUS, 1942-45. Recipient cert. of merit Yale U., 1979 Mem. Coll. Music Soc., Yale U. Sch. Music Alumni Assn. (pres. 1979-82, 89-94, exec. com. 1977-97). Home: 454 Park Ln State College PA 16803-3207 Office: Pa State U Music Dept University Park PA 16802

BAITY, JOHN COOLEY, lawyer; b. South Bend, Ind., June 22, 1933; s. Roscoe Flake and Gladys Paula (Kline) B.; m. Patricia Ann Bowen, Nov. 9, 1985; children: Keith F., John C. Jr., Cheryl R., Michael P., Philip J., Mark A. AB with highest honors, U. Mich., 1955, JD summa cum laude, 1958. Bar: Ill. 1958, N.Y. 1961, Calif. 1977, D.C. 1979. Assoc. Cravath, Swaine & Moore, N.Y.C., 1960-62, Donovan Leisure Newton & Irvine, N.Y.C., 1962-65, ptnr., 1966-83, Hunton & Williams, N.Y.C., 1983-84, Baity & Joseph, L.A., 1984-86, Milbank, Tweed, Hadley & McCloy LLP, N.Y.C., 1986—. Gen. counsel U.S. Golf Assn., Far Hills, NJ, 1980—85. Chmn. fin. com., coun. and exec. com. Union Internat. Contre le Cancer, 1995—; trustee Am. Cancer Soc. Found., 2003—, treas., 2004—; trustee Nat. Hypertension Assn., N.Y.C., 1981—91; bd. dirs. Am. Cancer Soc., Atlanta, 1983—87, 1990—2002, treas., 1994—98, vice chmn., 1998—99, chmn.-elect, 1999—2000, chmn., 2000—01. Mem. N.Y. State Bar. Assn., Calif. Bar Assn., Order of Coif, Phi Beta Kappa, Phi Kappa Phi. Office: Milbank Tweed Hadley & McCloy LLP 1 Chase Manhattan Plz Fl 46 New York NY 10005-1413 Office Phone: 212-530-5168. Office Fax: 212-530-5219. Business E-Mail: jbaity@milbank.com.

BAITZ, JON ROBIN, playwright; b. LA, 1961; Playwright-in-residence N.Y. Stage and Film Co., N.Y.C. Author: The Film Society, 1987, Dutch Landscape, 1989, The Substance of Fire, 1991, The End of the Day, 1992, Three Hotels, 1993, People I Know, 2002, The Paris Letter, 2005. Playwrights Horizon Revson fellow; recipient Playwright USA award Theatre Comm. Group, 1987, Academy award in Lit. Am. Acad. of Arts and Letters, 1994. Mailing: Roundabout Theatre 231 W 39th St Ste 1200 New York NY 10018*

BAIUL, OKSANA, clothing designer, former figure skater; b. Dnepropetrovsk, Ukraine, Nov. 16, 1977; d. Marina Baiul. Clothing designer Oksana Baiul Collection. Skating tours include Champions on Ice, 1993, 94, 95, 96, 97, 98, The Great Skate II: Charity Event, 1995, Great Skate III, 1997, Nutcracker on Ice, 1995, CBS Spl.: Too Hot to Skate, 1995, 96, Sergei Grinkov: Celebration of a Life, 1996, CBS Spl.: Wizard of Oz on Ice, 1996, An Evening with Champions: Charity Benefit, 1997, 98, Fire on Ice: Charity Event, 1998, 75 Yrs. of Disney Magic, 1998, FTD Champions on Ice, 1999. Recipient 2d Pl. award women's figure skating European Championships, 1993, 1st Pl. award women's figure skating World Figure Skating Championships, 1993, Gold medal women's figure skating Olympic Games, 1994, 2d Pl. Nikon Championship, 1994, 4th Pl. Am. Skating Invitational, 1994, 2d Pl. Ice Wars Overall Team Results, 1995, 98, 2d Pl. Gold Championships, 1995, 2d Pl. Rock'n' Roll Championships, 1996, 1st Pl. Ice Wars Overall Team Results, 1997, 3d Pl. Skate TV Championships, 1998, among others. Office: Oksana Baiul Collection GO Enterprises 177 Main Street 395 Fort Lee NJ 07024

BAIZA, MARY PESINA, development management consultant; b. Mission, Tex., May 28, 1944; d. Patricio and Maria Cuevas (Gutierrez) Pesina; m. Eusebio Molina Baiza, Jan. 8, 1966; children: Julie Suzanne, Elizabeth. Cert. in Nursing, South Plains Coll., 1966; BS, Tex. Tech. U., 1984. Cons. Eastfield Coll., Mesquite, Tex., 1972-76; coord. Heath Sci. Ctr. Tex. Tech U., Lubbock, 1977-83; interior designer J.C. Penney, Lubbock, 1984-85; dir. Guadalupe Econ. Svc. Inc., Lubbock, 1985-87; coord. Cmty. Resource Group, Inc., Lubbock, 1988-99; mem. nat. drinking water adv. coun. EPA, 1999—. Dir. South Plains Assn. Govts., Lubbock, 1992; v.p. Christ the King Sch. Bd., 1981-83; mem. health edn. bd. St. Mary's of the Plains Hosp., 1988. Recipient Marble plaque City of Roaring Spring, 1990, Leadership Tex. Found. for Women award, 1992. Mem. Am. Mktg. Assn. (sec. 1983-90). Democrat. Roman Catholic. Avocations: jogging, choir.

BAJA, LAURO LIBOON, JR., diplomat; m. Norma Baja; children: Maria Elizabeth Baja Facundo, Lauro III. B of Laws, BS in Jurisprudence, U. of Philippines; Fgn. Svc. course, Oxford U. Legal officer Office of Legal Affairs, Dept. of Fgn. Affairs, 1962—63, Office of Adminstrn., Dept. of Fgn. Affairs, 1964; chief Treaties Divsn., Dept of Fgn. Affairs, 1965—66; third sec., then second sec. Philippine Embassy, London, 1967—72; first sec., then career min. Philippine Mission to UN, NYC, 1973—76; exec. dir. Office of UN and other Internat. Orgns., NYC, 1977—79; chief coord. and spl. asst. to sec. of fgn. affairs Dept. of Fgn. Affairs, 1980—95; asst. sec. for Asian and Pacific Affairs, 1993—97; Philippine amb. to Brazil, 1986—93, to Italy, 1997—98; sr. undersecretary of fgn. affairs, 1998—2003; permanent rep. of Philippines to UN, NYC, 2003—. Recipient Outstanding Amb. of Yr., Brazil, 1991, Carlos Gomes Gold medal, Sao Paolo, Brazil, 1992, Ordem de Gran Cruz de Rio Branco, Brazil, 1993, Ufficiale nell Ordine, Italy, 1998. Office: Philippine Ctr Bldg 556 5th Ave New York NY 10036

BAJAD SUNIL, UTTAMRAO, pharmacologist, researcher; b. Shendla, Maharashtra, India, Feb. 20, 1972; s. U.N. and Radha Bajad. M.Pharm., Ph.D., U. Inst. Pharm. Scis., Panjab U., Chandigarh, India, 2002. Sr. project fellow Regional Rsch. Lab (CSIR), Jammu, India, 1996—97, sr. rsch. fellow, 1997—2000, rsch. officer, 2000, rsch. assoc., 2000—02; rsch. assoc. dept. med. sci. Sch. Vet. Medicine U. Wis., Madison, 2002—. Recipient Khatib Gold Medal, Medley pharm. Ltd., 1994, U. Gold Medal, Amaravati U., G.P.Nair Award, Indian Drug Manufacturers Assn., Indian Pharm. Assn. Medal, Indian Pharm. Assn., Maharashtra Br.; fellow Sr. Rsch. Fellowship, Coun. of Sci. and Indsl. Rsch., India, Rsch. Associateship; scholar Jr. Rsch. Fellowship, U. Grants commn., India. Mem.: Internat. Soc. Study of Xenobiotics. Achievements include 6 international research papers and one patent. Home: 209 Eagle Heights Apt # F Madison WI 53705 Personal E-mail: sbajad@yahoo.com. E-mail: bajads@svm.vetmed.wisc.edu.

BAJAJ, MANDEEP, medical researcher, educator; s. Jasbir and Avninder Bajaj; m. Kavita Bajaj, Feb. 11, 1997; 1 child, Kabir. MD, All India Inst. of Med. Scis., 1989. Diplomate Am. Bd. of Internal Medicine, 1994, Am. Bd. of Endocrinology, Diabetes and Metabolism, 1997. Fellow dept. of medicine Harvard Med. Sch., Boston, 1994—97; asst. prof. of medicine U. Tex. Health Sci. Ctr., San Antonio, 2000—04; assoc. prof. of medicine U. Tex. Med. Br., Galveston, 2004—. Dir. diabetes rsch. unit U. Tex. Health Sci. Ctr., San Antonio, 2000—04; dir. diabetes edn. U. Tex. Med. Br., Galveston, 2004—. Nat. task force on intensive insulin treatment Am. Coll. Of Endocrinology, Fla., 2004. Recipient Leo Davidoff award, Albert Einstein Coll. Medicine, 1994. Fellow: ACP, Am. Coll. Endocrinology. Achievements include Original Contributions To The Understanding Of The Pathophysiology Of Type 2 Diabetes And The Role Of Free Fatty Acids In The Causation Of Insulin Resistance And Type 2 Diabetes; Original Contributions To The Understanding Of The Role Of Adipocytokines In The Pathogenesis Of Insulin Resistance And Type 2 Diabetes.

BAJCSY, RUZENA, computer engineer; MSEE, Slovak Tech. U., 1957, PhD, 1967; PhD in Artificial Intelligence, Stanford U., 1972. Asst. prof. dept. computer and info. sci. U. Pa., 1972—77, assoc. prof., 1977—84, prof., 1984—, chmn. dept. computer and info. sci., 1985—90, head GRASP Lab.; asst. dir. Directorate for Computer and Info. Sci. and Engring. NSF; prof., dir. Ctr. for Info. Tech. Rsch. in the Interest of Society, U. Calif., Berkeley, 2003—. Mem. rev. bd. computer sci. dept. Stanford U., 1997. Contbr. articles to profl. publs. Fellow: AAAI, IEEE; mem.: NAE, Computer Rsch. Assn. Women, Nat. Inst. Medicine. Office: Ctr for Info Tech Rsch in Interest of Society 284 Hearst Meml Mining Bldg MC 1764 Berkeley CA 94720-1764 Business E-Mail: bajcsy@eecs.berkeley.edu.

BAJURA, RICHARD ALBERT, academic administrator, mechanical engineer, educator; b. Duquesne, Pa., Feb. 2, 1941; BSME, Notre Dame, 1962, MSME, 1964, PhD, 1967. Energy rsch. dir. W.Va. U., Morgantown, 1984-90; rsch. engr. Babcok & Wolcox R&D Ctr., Alliance, Ohio, 1967-68; postdoctoral rschr. Johns Hopkins U., Balt., 1968-69; prof. mech. engring. W.Va. U., Morgantown, 1969—, assoc. provost, 1990-94; dir. Nat. Rsch. Ctr. for Coal and Energy, 1994—. Editor: Polyphase Flow Transport Technology, 1980. Mem. ASME (v.p. basic engring. 1998-2001), Am. Soc. Am. Engring., Washington Coal Club (pres. 1999). Office: WVa U Nat Rsch Ctr for Coal & Energy PO Box 6064 Morgantown WV 26506-6064 Office Phone: 304-293-2867. Business E-Mail: Richard.Bajira@mail.wvu.edu.

BAJURA, RITA A., research scientist; B in Chem., Mercyhurst Coll., Erie, Pa.; M in Engring., West Va. Univ. With Dept. of Energy, 1980—, dir., Nat. Energy Tech. Lab., 1996—. Appointed to West Va. State's Energy Task Force, 2001. Named to Acad. of Disting. Alumni of Mech. Engring and Mech., West Va. Univ., 2000; recipient Achievement award for contributions to coal industry, Washington Coal Club, 2001, Pitt award, annual award for innovation in coal conversion, Univ. Pitts. Sch. Engring., 2002. Office: Dir NETL-DOE 3610 Collins Ferry Rd PO Box 880 Morgantown WV 26507-0880 Business E-Mail: Rita.Bajura@netl.doe.gov.

BAKALAR, JOHN STEPHEN, printing company executive, publishing executive; b. Lynn, Mass., Feb. 10, 1948; s. Leo and Ann Beatrice (Lepie) B.; m. Christine Lake Heilman, Sept. 24, 1972; children: Brooke Heilman, Jessica Heilman, Luke Heilman. BA, U. Pa., 1970; MBA, Stanford U., 1973. Investment mgr. First Chgo. Corp., Chgo., 1973-76; treas. Rand McNally & Co., Skokie, Ill., 1976-78, v.p. fin., treas., 1978-86, exec. v.p., 1986-93, pres., chief oper. officer, 1993-98. Dir. Racing Champions. Adv. bd., dir. Broader Urban Involvement and Leadership Devel., Chgo., 1976—; dir. Friends for Health; fellow Leadership Greater Chgo., 1987-88; trustee North Shore Country Day Sch. Found., Winnetka, Ill., 1997—. Mem. Econ. Club Chgo., Northmoor Country Club (Highland Park, Ill.), Country Club of the Rockies (Edwards, Colo.), Eagle Springs Country Club (Wolcott, Colo.). Home: 1760 Dale Ave Highland Park IL 60035-3303

BAKALOV, BOJKO NENTCHEV, mathematician; b. Karlovo, Bulgaria, May 9, 1973; arrived in U.S.A., 1996; s. Nencho Bakalov and Maria Bakalova; m. Vesselina Rousseva. PhD, MIT, 2000. Liftoff mathematician Clay Math. Inst., Cambridge, Mass., 2000; Miller rsch. fellow U. Calif., Berkeley, 2000—03; asst. prof. dept. math. NC State U., Raleigh, NC, 2003—. Contbr. articles to profl. jours. (Charles W. and Jennifer C. Johnson prize, 2000); author: (monograph) Lectures on Tensor Categories and Modular Functors. Recipient Miller Rsch. fellowship, Miller Inst. for Basic Rsch. in Sci., 2000—03. Mem.: Am. Math. Soc. Office: NC State Univ Dept Math Raleigh NC 27695 Business E-Mail: bojko_bakalov@ncsu.edu.

BAKALY, CHARLES GEORGE, JR., lawyer, mediator; b. Long Beach, Calif., Nov. 15, 1927; s. Charles G. Sr. and Doris (Carpenter) B.; m. Patricia Murphey, Oct. 25, 1952; children: Charles G. III, John W., Thomas B. AB, Stanford U., 1949; JD, U. S.C., 1952. Assoc. O'Melveny & Myers, L.A., 1956-63, ptnr., 1963-94; mem. JAMS, L.A., 2000—. Mem. Commn. on Calif. State Govt. Orgn. and Economy, 1991-94, President's Nat. Commn. on Employment Policy, 1992-94; mem. 9th Cir. Jud. Conf. Lawyer Del. Ch., 1984-87, mem. indigent def. panel, 1992-94; chmn. Calif. Dispute Resolution Adv. Coun., 1987-88; pres. Dispute Resolution Svcs. Bd. Dirs., Calif. Dispute Resolution Coun. Author: (with Joel M. Grossman) Modern Law of Employment Relationships, 1983, 2d edit. 1989; contbr. chpts. to books. Capt. JAG, U.S. Army, 1952-56. Named one of Top 50 Mediators in Calif., LA Daily Jour., 2004. Fellow Am. Coll. Trial Lawyers, Coll. Labor and Employment Lawyers, Internat. Acad. Mediators; mem. ABA (chmn. sect. labor and employment law 1981-82, sect. dispute resolution), L.A. County Bar Assn. (trustee, chmn. labor law sect. 1976-77, dispute resolution sect.), Lincoln Club (pres. 1989-91), Chancery Club, Valley Hunt Club (Pasadena, Calif.), Calif. Club (L.A.), Bohemian Club (San Francisco). Office: JAMS 707 Wilshire Blvd Ste 4600 Los Angeles CA 90017 Office Phone: 213-253-9758. Business E-Mail: cbakaly@jamsdale.com.

BAKANOWSKY, LOUIS JOSEPH, artist, educator, architect; b. Conn., Oct. 8, 1930; s. Louis Joseph Bakanowsky and Alice (Sullivan) Derda; m. Marie A. Golas, Jan. 27, 1951; 1 child, Louis J., III. BFA, Syracuse U., 1957; MArch, Harvard U., 1961. Registered architect. Asst. prof. architecture Cornell U., Ithaca, N.Y., 1961; assoc. prof. Harvard U., Cambridge, Mass., 1963-71, prof. architecture, 1972—, prof. visual arts., 1975-97, Osgood Hooker prof. visual studies emeritus, 1997—, chmn. dept. visual and environ. studies, 1976-86. Dir. Carpenter Ctr. for Visual Arts, 1984-90; prin. Cambridge Seven. Assocs., 1962—99; prin. Rosebud Environ. Design Group, 2000—. Prin. works include U.S. Pavillion for Expo '67, Montreal, Can., Henry DuPont Libr., Pomfret Sch., Conn., Columbia Sch., Rochester, N.Y., Rostropovich residence; (sculpture) Carl Siembab Gallery, Boston, 1958; represented in various pub. an pvt. collection. With USAF, 1951-53. Grantee Nat. Endowment Arts, 1979, 83, Graham Found. for Advanced Studies in Fine Arts, 1983. Fellow AIA (design awards 1967, 70). Office: Harvard U Carpenter Ctr for Visual Arts 24 Quincy St Cambridge MA 02138-3804

BAKARICH, MICHAEL N., retired military officer, retired nuclear energy industry executive, museum director; b. Chgo., May 6, 1928; s. Michael Nicholas Bakarich and Sarah Grace McCool; m. Carolyn Cross, Dec. 31, 1952; children: Victoria, Janis, Ann, Stephanie, Ashley, John, Michael, Kimberley, Caroline, Elizebeth. Bachelors, U. Okla., 1951; Masters, Pa. State U., 1974; diploma, U.S. Army War Coll., 1974. Sgt. U.S. Army, Ft. Bragg, NC, 1946—48, advanced through ranks to brig. gen., 1951—80, ret., 1980; mgr. adminstrv. svcs. Bechtel, Ann Arbor, Mich., 1980—84; mgr. materials, purchasing and contracts Grand Gulf nuc. sta. Entergy, Port Gibson, Miss., 1984—95, St. Francisville, La., 1995—2000, mgr. emergency preparedness Riverbend nuc. sta., 2000—03; dir. Yesterday's Children Antique Doll and Toy Mus., Vicksburg, Miss., 2003—. Mem.: Vicksburg Main St. Program, Vicksburg C. of C. Republican. Avocations: marksmanship, exercise, gardening, hunting, fishing. Home: 4855 Fisher Ferry Rd Vicksburg MS 39180 Office: Yesterday's Children Antique Doll & Toy Mus 1104 Washington St Vicksburg MS 39183 Office Phone: 601-638-0650. E-mail: mbakarich@aol.com.

BAKAY, ROY ARPAD EARLE, neurosurgeon, educator; b. Chgo., Mar. 5, 1949; s. Archie Joseph and Marjory (Jordahl) B.; m. Joann P. Feiertag; children: Mark, Scott, Candace, Jacqueline. BS, Beloit Coll., 1971; MD, Northwestern U., 1975. Diplomate Am. Bd. Med. Examiners, Am. Bd. Neurol. Surgeons. Intern U. Mich., Ann Arbor, 1975-76; resident in neurosurgery U. Wash., Seattle, 1976-82; acting instr., asst. in neurosurgery U. Wash. Med. Sch., Seattle, 1980-82, NIH fellow, 1981-82; asst. prof. sect. neurol. surgery Emory U. Med. Sch., Atlanta, 1982-88, dir. neurol. surgery resident rsch., 1984-2000, assoc. prof., 1988-93, prof., 1993-2000; mem. R & D Com. VA Med. Ctr., Decatur, Ga., 1982-86, sect. chief neurol. surgery, 1982-95; affiliate scientist neurobiology Yerkes Regional Primate Rsch. Ctr., Atlanta, 1982—, vice chmn. dept. neurol. surgery, 1995-2000; prof., vice chmn. Rush-Presbyn.-St. Luke's Med. Ctr., Chgo., 2000—, dir. Movement Disorder Surg. Ctr., 2000—; with Chgo. Inst. Neurosurgery and Neurorsch., 2000—. Author: (with others) Yearbook of Science and Technology, 1989; abstractor Jour. Surg. Gynecology and Obstetrics, 1978-86; mem. editorial bd. Jour. Contemporary Neurosurgery, 1987-93; mem. editorial rev. bd. Neurosurgery, 1994—; contbr. articles to profl. jours., chpts. to books. Chmn. profl. adv. bd. Ga. chpt. Epilepsy Found. Am., 1987-88; mem. adv. panel U.S. Congl. Office Tech. Assessment, Washington, 1988-90; profl. rep. Am. Cancer Soc., Atlanta, 1987-90. Recipient Resident Rsch. award Western Neurosurgery Soc., 1979, No. Pacific Soc.Neurology and Psychiatry, 1979, Soc. Neurology Anesthesists and Neurology Supportive Care, 1981; named one of Outstanding Athletes of Am., 1971, Am. Best Doctor, 1994—. Mem. AAAS, Soc. Neurosci., Am. Stereotactic and Functional Neurosurgeons (v.p. 1988-91, pres. 1991-93), Am. Assn. Neurol. Surgeons (chmn. GRAFT Registry Com. 1987-95), Congress Neurol. Surgeons (v.p. joint com. 1988-91, pres. 1991-93), Am. Soc. Neural Transplantation and Repair (founding 1992, counsilor, 1992-99, pres.-elect 1999, pres. 2000). Presbyterian. Avocations: hiking, camping, skiing, fishing, team sports. Office: Rush Presbyn St Lukes Med Ctr 1725 W Harrison St Chicago IL 60612

BAKEMAN, CAROL ANN, travel writer, singer; b. San Francisco; d. Lars Hartvig and Gwendolyne Beatrice (Zimmer) Bergh; m. Delbert Clifton Bakeman; children: Laurie Ann, Deborah Ann. Student, UCLA, 1954-62. Singer Roger Wagner Chorale, L.A. Master Chorale, 1964-86, The Wagner Ensemble, 1991—; libr. Hughes Aircraft Co., Culver City, Calif.; head econs. libr. Planning Rsch. Corp., L.A., 1961-63; corp. libr. Econ. Cons., Inc., L.A., 1963-68; head econs. libr. Daniel, Mann, Johnson & Mendenhall, archs. and engrs., L.A., 1969-71, corp. libr., 1971-77, mgr. info. svcs., 1978-81, mgr. info. and office svcs., 1981-83, mgr. adminstrv. svcs., 1983-96, sr. assoc., 1996-98, assoc. v.p., 1998—; travel mgr. AECOM Tech. Corp., 1996—2004. Assoc. v.p. Corp. Consol. Svcs., Inc., (divsn. AECOM), 1997-2004; pres., Creative Libr. Sys., L.A., 1974-83; libr. cons. ArchiSystems (divsn. SUMMA Corp.), L.A., 1972-81; contbr. Business Travel Executive, 2005— Contbr. articles to profl. jours. Mem. Assistance League, So. Calif., 1956-86, nat. auxilaries com., 1968-72, 75-78, nat. by-laws com., 1970-75, assoc. bd. dirs., 1966-76. Mem. AFTRA, SAG, Am. Guild Musical Artists, Adminstrv. Mgmt. Soc. (v.p. L.A. chpt. 1984-86, pres. 1986-88, internat. conf. chmn. 1988-89, internat. bd. dirs. 1988-90, internat. v.p. mgmt. edn. 1990-92), L.A. Master Chorale Assn. (bd. dirs. 1978-83), Wagner Ensemble (bd. dirs.), L.A. Bus. Travel Assn. (hon., bd. dirs. 1995, sec. 1997, v.p. 1998, pres. 1999, past pres. 2000, bd advisor 2001-2002), Nat. Bus. Travel Assn. (nat. conv. seminar com. 1994-95, conv. vol. chmn. 1994, 2000, nat. conv. panelist 2001, 03, profl. svc. award 2001).

BAKER, ADRIENNE MARIE, lawyer; b. Bklyn., Sept. 29, 1959; d. Pat Adrian and Marie Frances (Patti) Catanese. SB in Physics, MIT, 1981; JD magna cum laude, Boston U., 1985, LLM in Taxation, 1991. Bar: Mass. 1985, U.S. Ct. Claims 1986, U.S. Patent and Trademark Office 1986, N.Y. 1988, U.S. Dist. Ct. Mass. 1990. Assoc. Gaston & Snow, Boston, 1985-87, Coudert Bros., N.Y.C., 1987-88, Dechert Price & Rhoads, Boston, 1988-93; ptnr. Dechert LLP (Dechert Price & Rhoads), Boston, 1993—. Contbr. articles to profl. jours. Justinian Law Soc. scholar, 1985. Mem. ABA, Boston Bar Assn. Roman Catholic. Avocations: cooking, tennis, squash, sailing, travel. Office: Dechert LLP 200 Clarendon St 27th Fl Boston MA 02116 E-mail: adrienne.baker@dechert.com.*

BAKER, ALTON FLETCHER, III, editor, publishing executive; b. Eugene, Oreg., May 2, 1950; s. Alton Fletcher Jr. and Genevieve B.; m. Wendy, Jan. 27, 1979; children: Benjamin A., Lindsay A. BA in Comms., Washington State U., 1972. Reporter Associated Press, 1972-79; asst. city editor The Register-Guard, Eugene, 1979-80, city editor, 1980-82, mng. editor, 1982-86, editor, 1986-87, editor, publisher, 1987—; pres. Guard Publishing Co., Eugene, 1987—. Pres. Cmty. Newspapers, Inc., Portland. Pres. YMCA, Eugene, 1989, United Way of Lane County, Eugene, 1985-01, Eugene Festival Musical Theatre, 1990-94. Mem.: Oreg. Newspaper Pubs. Assn. (pres. 1999), Eugene Country Club (pres. 1999). Avocation: golf. Office: Guard Publishing Co 3500 Chad Dr Eugene OR 97408-7348 Office Phone: 541-338-2318.

BAKER, ANITA, singer; b. Toledo, Jan. 26, 1958; m. Walter Bridgeforth, Jr., Dec. 24, 1988; 1 child, Walter Baker Bridgeforth. Mem. funk band Chapter 8, Detroit, 1978-80; receptionist Quin & Budajh, Detroit, 1980-82; ind. singer, songwriter, 1982—. Rec. artist: (with Chapter 8) I Just Wanna Be Your Girl, 1980, (solo albums) The Songstress, 1983, Rapture, 1986 (Grammy award for best rhythm and blues vocal performance 1987), Giving You the Best That I Got, 1988 (Grammy awards for best rhythm and blues song, 1988, best rhythm and blues performance, female, single, 1988, best album, 1989), Compositions, 1990 (Grammy award for best rhythm and blues performance, 1990), Rhythm of Love, 1994 (Grammy award nominee for best album 1995, best female vocal 1995, best song 1995); songs include No More Tears, Angel, Caught Up in the Rapture, Sweet Love (Grammy award best rhythm and blues song 1987), Same Ol' Love, You Bring Me Joy, Been So Long, No One in the World. Recipient Grammy award gospel, soul, best performance, duo, group, choir or chorus, 1987, NAACP Image award, best female vocalist and best album of yr. also: 8216 Tivoli Cove Dr Las Vegas NV 89128-7446

BAKER, ANITA DIANE, lawyer; b. Atlanta, Sept. 4, 1955; d. Byron Garnett and Anita (Swanson) B.; m. Thomas Johnstone Robison III, Sept. 26, 1995. BA summa cum laude, Oglethorpe U., 1977; JD with distinction, Emory U., 1980. Bar: Ga. 1980. Assoc. Hansell & Post, Atlanta, 1980—88, Kitchens, Kelley, Gaynes, Huprich & Shmerling, 1989—90; asst. gen. counsel Nations-Bank Corp., 1991—97; v.p., gen. counsel Adaris Corp., 1997—99; pvt. practice Atlanta, 1999—2004, Baker Law Group, LLC, Roswell, Ga., 2005—. Trustee Oglethorpe Univ. Mem.: North Fulton Bar Assn., Stormy Petrel Bar Assn., Ga. Assn. Women Lawyers, Atlanta Bar Assn., Ga. Bar Assn., Oglethorpe U. Nat. Alumni Assn. (pres.), Atlanta Hist. Soc., Pace Acad. Alumni Assn., Ga. Alliance of Private Clubs, Concourse Athletic Club, Omicron Delta Kappa, Alpha Chi, Phi Alpha Theta, Phi Alpha Delta, Order of Coif. Office: 555 Sun Valley Dr Ste N4 Roswell GA 30076

BAKER, ANN LONG, language educator; b. Shelbyville, Ind., Sept. 2, 1954; d. Martin Meredith Cherry and Lois Jayne Slaton; m. Scott Elliott Baker, Aug. 23, 1975; children: Kyle Martin, Holly Alison. BA with distinction in Spanish Edn., Purdue U., 1976; MA Edn., U. Evansville, 1982. Lectr. in Spanish U. Evansville, Ind., 1984—2000, asst. prof. Spanish, 2000—, chair dept. fgn. langs., 2003—. Interpreter Pan Am. Games, Indpls., 1987. Active Castle H.S. PTO, Castle H.S. Band Boosters Orgn. Mem.: MLA, Ind. Fgn. Lang. Tchrs. Assn., Soc. Hispanic Am. (past pres., treas.), Am. Coun. Tchg. of Fgn. Langs., Am. Assn. Tchrs. of Spanish and Portuguese, Kappa Delta Pi, Alpha Lambda Delta, Phi Sigma Iota, Sigma Delta Pi, Phi Beta Kappa, Phi Kappa Phi. Home: 7277 Nottingham Dr Newburgh IN 47630 Office: U Evansville 1800 Lincoln Ave Evansville IN 47722 Office Phone: 812-479-2196. Business E-Mail: ab39@evansville.edu.

BAKER, ARLENE ANN, speech pathology/audiology services professional, consultant; d. John E. and Julia A. Machnik; children: Natasha, Ethan. BA, Regis Coll., 1972; MS, U. Ariz., 1974. Cert. clin. competence Am. Speech Lang. Hearing Assn., 1974. Speech lang. pathologist Spurwink Sch., Portland, Maine, 1979—90, Portland (Maine) Pub. Sch., 1990—93; clin. dir. Sundance Rehab., Portland, 1993—97; speech lang. pathologist Portland (Maine) Pub. Schs., 1997—99, Sundance Rehab., 1999—2004, Goodall Hosp., Sanford, 2004—. Candidate State Legis., South Portland, Maine, 2002. Mem.: Maine Speech Lang. Hearing Assn. (pres. 1982), Am. Speech Lang. Hearing Assn., Appolacian Mountain Club. Republican. Roman Cath. Home and Office: 735 Highland Ave South Portland ME 04106 Office Phone: 207-490-7439.

BAKER, BETTY LOUISE, retired secondary school educator; b. Chgo., Oct. 17, 1937; d. Russell James and Lucille Juanita (Timmons) B. BE, Chgo. State U., 1961, MA, 1964; PhD, Northwestern U., 1971. Cert. tchr. secondary and elem. grades 3-8 math., Ill. Tchr. math. Harper H.S., Chgo., 1961-70, Hubbard H.S., Chgo., 1970-94, also chmn. dept.; ret., 1994. Instr. Moraine Valley C.C., 1982-86, 94—; reader AP calculus exams. Ednl. Testing Svc. Contbr. articles to profl. jours. Cultural arts chmn. Hubbard Parents-Tchrs.-Students Assn., 1974-76, 1st v.p., program chmn., 1977-79, 82-84, pres. 1979-81; organist Hope Luth Ch., 1964-95, accompanist S.W. Luth. Chorus, 1987—; organist and choir dir. Faith Luth. Ch., Oak Lawn, 1995—. Univ. fellow, 1969-70. Mem. Nat. Coun. Tchrs. Math., Ill. Coun. Tchrs. Math., Chgo. Tchrs. Union, Nat. Coun. Parents and Tchrs. (life), Sch. Sci. and Math. Assn., Am. Guild of Organists, Luth. Collegiate Assn., Walther League Hiking Club, Met. Math. Club Chgo., Kappa Mu Epsilon, Rho Sigma Tau, Mu Alpha Theta (sponsors), Kappa Delta Pi, Pi Lambda Theta, Phi Delta Kappa. Home: 6330 Pine Ridge Dr Apt 1D Tinley Park IL 60477-4928 Personal E-mail: bakermus@sbcglobal.net.

BAKER, BRINDA ELIZABETH GARRISON, community health nurse; b. Groveland, Ga., May 9, 1946; d. Archie and Nora Lee (Haynes) Garrison; m. Jerome Baker, Feb. 1970 (div. 1972); children: Katrina Lenyse Adams, Kelbert Lenard Adams. Student, Savannah (Ga.) State Coll., 1964-68; LPN, Savannah Tech. Sch., 1968; ADN, Armstrong State Coll., 1984, BSN, 1990; postgrad., Armstrong Atlantic State U. RN, Ga.; cert. provider BLS, Am. Heart Assn. LPN Candler Gen. Hosp., Savannah, 1968-72, staff nurse Cross Country Traveling Corps, 1990; LPN Ga. Regional Hosp., Savannah, 1972-74, sr. staff nurse, 1989-92; LPN St. Joseph Hosp., Savannah, 1974-84, staff nurse, 1984-90; sr. nurse, clinic supr. Chatham County Health Ctr., Savannah, 1992-95, clinic supr., 1995—. Part-time clin. instr. Armstrong State Coll., Savannah, 1991—. Mem. ANA, Ga. Nurses Assn., Assn. Nurses in AIDS Care. Democrat. Roman Catholic. Avocations: bowling, reading, gardening, music, sports. Home: 1307 E 71st St Savannah GA 31404-5735 Office: Chatham County Health Dept 2 Wheeler St Savannah GA 31405

BAKER, BRUCE EDWARD, orthopedic surgeon, consultant; b. Oswego, N.Y., Mar. 22, 1937; s. Elbert J. and Reatha (Hartranft) B.; m. Patricia Therese Gormel, Aug. 19, 1961; children: Brett, Clayton, Sean, Reatha. BSME, Syracuse U., 1959; MD, SUNY-Syracuse, 1965. Intern State U. Iowa, Iowa City, 1965-66, asst. resident, 1966-67; resident orthopaedics SUNY-Upstate Med. Ctr., Syracuse, 1969-72, NIH orthopaedic rsch. fellow, 1972-73, asst. prof. orthopaedic surgery, 1973-79, assoc. prof., 1979-86, prof., 1986-89. Dir. univ. sports medicine svc. divsn. dept. orthopaedic surgery 1980-89; team physician, dir. sports medicine athletic dept., Syracuse U., 1973-93, orthopaedic cons. Student Health Ctr., 1973-93, staff SUNY Hosp., Syracuse, 1973-89, Syracuse VA Hosp., 1973-89, A.C. Silverman Pub. Health Hosp., 1973-77, Crouse-Irving Meml. Hosp., 1973—; cons. in field. Contbr. numerous articles to profl. jours. Capt. USAF, 1967-69. Recipient AMA Physicians Recognition award, 1978, Bronze medal award Am. Roentgen Ray Soc., 1980, Gold medal award Sound Slide Prodn. Conditioning, 1977; Syracuse U. scholar, 1955; N.Y. State Regents scholar, 1955-59; USPHS grantee, 1973-74; Hendricks Research fund grantee, 1973-75; NIH grantee, 1974-76, 76-77. Fellow ACS, Am. Acad. Orthop. Surgeons; mem. AMA, Med. Soc. State N.Y., Onondaga County Med. Soc., Orthop. Rsch. Soc., Am. Coll. Sports Medicine, N.Y. Soc. Orthop. Surgeons, Royal Soc. Medicine, Internat. Soc. Arthroscopy, Knee Surgery and Orthop. Sports Medicine, Am. Orthop. Soc. Sports Medicine, European Soc. Sports Trauma, Knee Surgery and Arthroscopy, Arthroscopy Assn. N. Am. Office: 600 E Genesee St Ste 117 Syracuse NY 13202-3108 Office Phone: 315-476-2670.

BAKER, BRUCE JAY, lawyer; b. Chgo., June 18, 1954; s. Kenneth and Beverly (Gould) B. Student, U. Leeds, Eng., 1974-75; BS, U. Ill., 1976; JD, Washington U., 1979. Bar: Ill. 1979, U.S. Dist. Ct. (no. dist.) Ill. 1984. Asst. atty. gen. antitrust divsn. State of Ill., Chgo., 1979-83; assoc. Mass, Miller & Josephson Ltd., Chgo., 1983-86; sr. counsel Discover Card Services Inc., Riverwoods, Ill., 1986-89; sr. legis. counsel Dean Witter Fin. Svcs. Group, Riverwoods, 1989-91; gen. counsel Ill. Commr. Banks and Trust Cos., Chgo., 1991-94; ptnr. Schiff Hardin & Waite, Chgo., 1994-99, of counsel, 1999-2001, Barak, Ferrazzano, Kirschbaum, Perlman & Nagelberg, Chgo., 2001—; exec. v.p., gen. counsel Ill. Bankers Assn., 1999—. Gen. editor Advising Illinois Financial Institutions, 2002; contbr. articles to profl. jours. Registered lobbyist Ill. Legislature, Springfield, 1985-91, 94—. Named Ill. State scholar, 1972. Mem. ABA (antitrust com., banking com., chmn. state banking law devels. task force 1998—), Ill. State Bar Assn. (comml. banking and bankruptcy sect.), Chgo. Bar Assn. (fin. insts. com.), Ill. Bankers Assn. (legis. counsel 1985-86, gen. counsel 1994—, Disting. Bank Counsel award 1991, 97). Office: Ill Bankers Assn 10 S LaSalle St ste 950 Chicago IL 60603-3502 also: Barack Ferrazzano Et Al 333 W Wacker Dr Ste 2700 Chicago IL 60606 E-mail: bbaker@ilbanker.com.

BAKER, BRUCE LEE, psychology educator, consultant; b. Cambridge, Mass., July 23, 1940; s. Karl Watson and Elizabeth Cole (Bland) B.; m. Patricia McNeal, Feb. 24, 1966 (div. Oct. 1978); children: Kristen, Jason; m. Jan Blacher, Jan. 27, 1985; children: Alexander, Spencer. BA in Psychology, Brown U., 1962; PhD in Clin. Psychology, Yale U., 1966. Lic. psychologist, Calif. Asst. prof. psychology and social rels. Harvard U., Cambridge, 1966-69; assoc. prof. edn., lectr. social rels., 1969-75; assoc. prof. psychology UCLA, 1975-77, prof., 1977—2005, chmn. clin. psychology, dir. tng. program clin. psychology, 1985-91; pvt. practice psychology L.A., 1979—2003; disting. prof. UCLA, 2004—, psychology dept. sr. vice chair, 2004—. Vis. prof. Harvard U. Med. Sch., Boston, 1982-83; mem. profl. adv. bd. May Inst., 1987-98, Melmark New Eng., 1998—; bd. trustees Bancroft Neurohealth, N.J., 1988—. Co-author: Abnormal Psychology, 1980, 2nd rev. edit., 1986, Readings in Abnormal Psychology, 1981, As Close As Possible, 1977, Steps to Independence, 1975-83, rev. 2nd edit., 1988, 3rd edit., 1996, 4th edit., 2003; mem. editl. bd. Jour. Behavior Therapy and Exptl. Psychology, 1975-98, Am. Jour. Mental Retardation, 1981-83, 85-87, 93—, Family Process, 1979-85, Jour. Intellectual and Devel. Disability, 1989, Mental Retardation, 1997—, Family Relations, 2002. Founder, dir. Camp Freedom, Ossipee, N.H., 1969-75. Grantee Dept. Edn., 1984-90, Nat. Inst. Child Health and Human Devel., 1971-75, 77-83, 98—, Social and Rehab Svcs. Adminstrn., 1970-75. Fellow Am. Assn. Mental Retardation (pres. psychology divsn. 1993-95, bd. dirs. 1994-95, chair publs. com. 1996-98, Rsch. award region II 1986); mem. APA (pres. divsn. 33, 2005—, Young Psychologist award 1969), Western Psychol. Assn. Democrat. Avocation: travel, swimming, tennis, family. Home: 144 S Plymouth Blvd Los Angeles CA 90004-3836 Office: Dept Psychology UCLA Los Angeles CA 90024 E-mail: baker@psych.ucla.edu.

BAKER, BRUCE ROY, artist, illustrator; b. Syracuse, N.Y., July 18, 1937; s. Morse Roy and Gladys Irene (Hilton) B.; m. Helen Louise Butler, Apr. 16, 1965; children: Paul, Suzanne, Diana, Amy. BS in Art Edn., New Paltz Coll., 1959; MS in Art Edn., Syracuse U., 1966. Cert. tchr. N.Y. Tchr. art Catskill (N.Y.) Pub. Schs., 1959-62, Cortland (N.Y.) City Schs., 1964-66, Marcellus (N.Y.) Ctrl. Schs., 1966-92; pvt. practice artist, illustrator Marcellus, 1992—. Tchr. art Mex. (N.Y.) Acad., 1975-76. Works exhibited in group shows Artists of Ctrl. N.Y.-Munson-Williams-Procter Inst., Utica, 1969, N.Y. State Fair, Syracuse, 1973, 74, 75, Cooperstown (N.Y.) Ann., 1974; contbg. painter Leopold F. Landsberger, N.Y.C., 1979-86; contbg. illustrator Firestone Pub. Corp., Miami Lakes, Fla., 1982-2001, Spartacus/Centurian, Reno, 1983—, Quadriga Art, Inc., N.Y.C., 1993—; illustrator (book) Erotic Art of Bruce Baker, 1995; contbr. articles to profl. jours. With U.S. Army, 1962-64. Recipient Hon. Mention (sculpture) N.Y. State Fair, 1975, 2004, 1st prize (graphics), 2004 Avocations: reading, golf. Home: 11 1st St Marcellus NY 13108-1114

BAKER, C. EDWIN, law educator; b. 1947; BA, Stanford U., 1969; JD, Yale U., 1972. Asst. prof. U. Toledo, 1972-75, U. Oreg., Eugene, 1975-79, assoc. prof., 1979-81, prof., 1981-82, U. Pa., Phila., 1982—86, Nicholas F. Gallichio prof. law, 1986—. Fellow, vis. prof. Kennedy Sch. Govt., U. Tex., 1980, Harvard U., 1992-93, Cornell U., 1993; attny. ACLU, 1977-78. Author: Human Liberty and Freedom of Expression, 1989, Advertising and a Democratic Press, 1994; contbr. articles to law jours. Fellow Harvard U., Cambridge, Mass., 1974-75. Office: U Pa Law Sch 3400 Chestnut St Philadelphia PA 19104-6204 Office Phone: 215-898-7419. Office Fax: 215-573-2025. E-mail: ebaker@law.upenn.edu.

BAKER, C. MARK, lawyer; BA summa cum laude, Yale Univ., 1981; JD with highest honors, Duke Univ., 1984. Bar: Tex. 1984. Law clk. Hon. John R. Brown US Ct. of Appeals (5th cir.), 1984—85; ptnr., co-head firmwide internat. dept. and arbitration dept. Fulbright & Jaworski, Houston. Arbitrator and mediator World Intellectual Property Assn.; bd. dirs., arbitrator London Ct. Internat. Arbitration. Contbr. articles to profl. journals; lectr. in field. Fellow: Tex. Bar Found., Houston Bar Found., Chartered Inst. of Arbitrators, London, England; mem.: ICC Commn., Am. Arbitration Assn. (bd. dir, internat. panel, nat. sports resolution panel), Ct. of Arbitration for Sport, Lausanne, Switzerland, Internat. Bar Assn., Coll. of the Bar of Tex., State Bar Tex. Avocations: fishing, hunting, tennis, opera. Office: Fulbright & Jaworski Ste 5100 1301 McKinney Houston TX 77010-3095 Office Fax: 713-651-5151, 713-651-5246. Business E-Mail: mbaker@fulbright.com.

BAKER, CARL GWIN, science administrator; b. Louisville, Nov. 27, 1920; s. Edward Forrest and Naomi (Taylor) B.; m. Lois Eleane Oxsen, Mar. 24, 1949 (div. May 1975); children: Cathryn, Jeannette; m. Catherine Valerie Smith, May 23, 1975. AB in Zoology, U. Louisville, 1942, MD, 1944, DSc (hon.), 1980; MA in Biochemistry, U. Calif., Berkeley, 1949. Lic. med. practice, Ky., Calif. Rsch. investigator Biochemistry Lab. Nat. Cancer Inst., NIH, Bethesda, Md., 1949-52, 53-55, staff grants and fellowships br., 1952-53, asst. to NIH assoc. dir., 1956-57, asst. dir., acting sci. dir., 1958-61, assoc. dir. program, 1961-67, sci. dir. etiology, 1967-69; dir. Nat. Cancer Inst., Bethesda, 1969-72; dir. program policy staff Health & Human Svcs. Adminstr., Rockville, Md., 1975-76; med. dir. Ludwig Inst. Cancer Rsch., Zurich, Switzerland, 1977-85, ret., 1985; adj. instr. U. Md., College Park, 1989—. Mem. gov. coun. Internat. Agy. for Cancer Rsch., Lyon, France, 1969-72. Assoc. editor Jour. of the Nat. Cancer Inst., 1954-55; mem. editl. adv. bd. Cancer Jour., 1965-73; contbr. articles to jours. Biochemistry, Oncology, Mgmt. Sci. Del. State Bd. Edn., Annapolis, Md., 1957; mem. exec. com. adv. panel on health Am. Revolution Bicentenial Commn., Washington, 1970-72; v.p. 10th Internat. Cancer Congress, Houston, 1970. Asst. surgeon gen. USPHS, 1970—. Decorated PHS Meritorious Svc. medal; Jane Coffin Childs Fund fellow, 1946-48, Spl. fellow Nat. Cancer Inst., NIH, 1949. Mem. Am. Assn. Cancer Rsch. (bd. dirs. 1972-76), Am. Chem. Soc. (divsn. biol. chemistry, sec. 1955-57, councillor 1958-61), Am. Soc. Biochemistry and Molecular Biology, Soc. Exptl. Biology and Medicine, Cosmos Club, Sigma Xi, Alpha Omega Alpha, Phi Kappa Phi. Achievements include research in application of systems analysis and planning to strategic planning in medical research and laying the foundations for development of national cancer plan. Home: 19408 Charline Manor Rd Olney MD 20832-1044 Personal E-mail: baker1934@comcast.net.

BAKER, CARLETON HAROLD, physiology educator; b. Utica, NY, Aug. 2, 1930; s. Harold George and Loretta (Darling) B.; m. Sara Frances Johnson, July 20, 1963; children: Elizabeth Ann, Janet Lee. BA, Utica Coll. of Syracuse U., 1952; MA, Princeton U., 1954, PhD, 1955. Asst. instr. Princeton (N.J.) U., 1952-54, asst. in research, 1954-55; asst. prof. Med. Coll. Ga., Augusta, 1955-61, assoc prof., 1961-67, prof., 1967; prof. physiology and biophysics U. Louisville Health Scis. Ctr., 1967-71; prof., founding chmn. dept. physiology and biophysics U. South Fla. Coll. of Medicine, Tampa, 1971—92, dep. dean for research and grad. studies, 1980-82, prof surgery, physiology and biophysics, dir. surg. rsch., 1992-95; prof. emeritus U. South Fla., 1995—; rsch. prof. physiology U. S.C. Coll. Medicine, Columbia, 1994-2001. Rsch. com. mem. Am. Heart Assn., Louisville, 1969-71; rsch. com., bd. dirs. Am. Heart Assn. of Fla., Tampa, 1971-85; NIH program project site visit team, 1982-84, mem. LCME Accreditation Survey Team, 1980-81; cons. U. Louisville Grad. Sch., East Carolina U. Grad. Program. Editor: Microcirculatory Technology, 1986; mem. numerous editorial bds.; contbr. numerous articles in field. Pres. Augusta Choral Soc., 1963; v.p. Blount Rd. Homeowners Assn., Lutz, Fla., 1986-93; bd. dirs. Friends of Augusta. Grantee NIH, 1960-92, Am. Heart Assn., 1968-97; recipient Svc. awards Am. Heart Assn. Fla., 1974, 77, Disting. Scientist award U. South Fla. Coll. Medicine, 1981, Outstanding Artist/Scholar award Phi Kappa Phi, 1991, Dean's Citation U. So. Fla. Coll. Medicine, 1991, Founder award, 1992. Fellow: Am. Physiol. Soc. (fellow cardiovasc. sect. mem. com. 1982—85); mem.: Shock Soc. (mem. program coms.), European Microcirculatory Soc., Microcirculatory Soc., Torch Club Internat. Republican. Avocations: golf, fishing. Home: 4039 Old Waynesboro Rd Augusta GA 30906-9254 Personal E-mail: microves@bellsouth.net.

BAKER, CAROLYN SIMMONS, library director, consultant, researcher; MLS, NC Ctrl. U., 1998. Instr. Wake Tech. CC, Raleigh, NC, 1988—98; dir. archives Shaw U., Raleigh, 1999—. Libr. III North A&T State U., Greensboro, NC, 1999.

BAKER, CATHLEEN ANN, publishing executive; b. Grand Rapids, Mich., Mar. 12, 1945; BA in Art History, U. Mich., 1967; MA in Art History, Syracuse U., 1986; PhD in Mass Comm., U. Ala., 2004; MFA in Book Arts, U. of Ala., Tuscaloosa, AL, 2000. Assoc. prof. Buffalo State Coll., 1978—93; ind. scholar, 1993—; pub. Legacy Press, Tuscaloosa, Ala., 1997—; adj. instr. U. Ala., Tuscaloosa, 2001—03. Author: By His Own Labor: The Biography of Dard Hunter, 2000, Endgrain Designs & Repetitions: The Pattern Papers of John DePol, 2000. Editor, designer Discovering Ala., Tuscaloosa, 1997—. Fellow Jacob K. Javits fellow, U.S. Dept. Edn., 1998—2002; grantee, NEH, 1989. Fellow: Internat. Inst. Conservation, Am. Inst. Conservation (bd. dirs.); mem.: Hand Papermaking, Inc. (bd. dirs., bd. advisors), Friends of Dard Hunter, Inc. (hon.), Kappa Tau Alpha. Office Phone: 734-761-1543. E-mail: info@legacy-press.com.

BAKER, CHARLES D., health insurance company executive; Former founder, co-dir. The Pioneer Inst.; former sec. health and human svcs., sec. adminstrn. and finance to former Gov. Mass. William Weld, 1991—98; pres., CEO Harvard Vanguard Med. Assocs., 1998, Harvard Pilgrim Health Care, Quincy, Mass., 1999—. Office: Harvard Pilgrim Healthcare 90 Worcester St Wellesley MA 02481

BAKER, CHARLES DUANE, business administration educator; b. Newburyport, Mass., June 21, 1928; s. Charles Duane and Eleanor (Little) B.; m. Alice Elizabeth Ghormley, 1955; children: Charles D., Jonathan G., Alexander K. AB, Harvard, 1951, MBA, 1955. With Westinghouse Electric Corp., Elmira, N.Y., 1955-57, Jersey City, 1957-61; v.p., treas. United Research, Inc., Cambridge, Mass., 1961-65; various positions through chmn., chief exec. Harbridge House, Inc., Boston, 1965-69, 72-83; prof. bus. adminstrn. Northeastern U., Boston, 1985—. Dep. under sec. U.S. Dept. Transp., Washington, 1969-70, asst. sec. policy and internat. affairs, 1970-71; under sec. U.S. Dept. HHS, Washington, 1984-85; presiding dir. Millipore Corp., 1986-87; adv. bd. dept. health policy Harvard Med. Sch.; chmn. McLean Heath Svcs. Inc. Author various studies dealing with mgmt. transp., health care, pub. policy. Mem. vis. com. Harvard U.; bd. dirs. Pioneer Inst. for Pub. Policy, Millipore Corp., Am. Med. Response, Inc.; trustee, chmn. McLean Hosp.; pres. Hall-Mercer Hosps.; trustee Harvard Med. Ctr., 1996-99; mem. Group Ins. Commn. Lt. (j.g.) USNR, 1946-48, 51-53. Recipient Award for Outstanding Achievement U.S. Govt., 1971 Mem. Pi Eta, Beta Gamma Sigma (Hon.). Clubs: Essex County; Harvard, Comml., Clover (Boston); E. India (London); Metropolitan (Washington). Republican. Congregationalist. Home: 81 Marmion Way Rockport MA 01966-1928 Office: Northeastern U 319 Hayden Hall 360 Huntington Ave Boston MA 02115-5000

BAKER, CHARLES E., lawyer; b. Dallas, June 1, 1957; BA in econ., U. Cambridge, U.K., 1978; JD, U. Toronto, 1981; MBA, U. Denver, 2001. Assoc. Fraser & Beatty, 1983—88, ptnr., 1988—93; dir. bus. devel. Ball Corp., Broomfield, Colo., 1993—95, dir. corp. compliance, 1994—97, sr. dir. bus. devel., 1995—99, assoc. gen. counsel, 1999—2004, gen. counsel, asst. corp. sec., 2004—. Mem.: Colo. Bar Assn., Law Soc. Upper Can. Office: Ball Corp 10 Longs Peak Dr Broomfield CO 80021-2510 Home: 2459 S St Paul St Denver CO 80210-5516 Office Phone: 303-460-2586. Office Fax: 303-460-2691. Business E-Mail: cbaker@ball.com.

BAKER, CHARLES STEPHEN, music educator; b. Cleve., July 25, 1942; s. LeRoy Williams and Nellie Angela (Burskey) B. BMus, Oberlin Coll. Conservatory, 1964; MA, Case Western Reserve U., 1967. Cert. music educator, Ohio. Tchr. music Madison Local Schs., Mansfield, Ohio, 1964-65, Wickliffe (Ohio) City Schs., 1967-96; pvt. clarinet instr., freelance clarinet performer Sch. of Fine Arts, Willoughby, Ohio, 1969—. Prin. clarinet, assoc. condr. Lakeland Civic Orch., Mentor, Ohio, 1972—. Named to Hall of Fame, City of Wickliffe, Ohi0, 2005; recipient Disting. Svc. award, Sch. of Fine Arts, 1992. Mem. NEA, Ohio Music Edn. Assn. (gen. music com. mem. 1972-99, 25 Yr. Svc. award 1991), Music Educators Nat. Conf. (N.E. region chair 1986-92, 94-98, all-state orch. chair 1990-92), Lake County Music Educators (sec. v.p., pres.), Ohio Edn. Assn., Am. Fedn. Musicians, U.S. Figure Skating Assn. Roman Catholic. Avocations: figure skating, photography, gardening, travel. Home: 5476 A Wildwood Ct Willoughby OH 44094-3261 Personal E-mail: cbakermus@aol.com.

BAKER, CONSTANCE H., lawyer; b. Washington, Sept. 2, 1948; AB summa cum laude, Vassar Coll., 1969; JD, Cath. U. Am., 1975. Bar: Md. 1975, DC 1998. Asst. atty gen. State Md., 1979-81; ptnr. Health Care Group, Venable LLP, Balt. State prosecutor Md. Bd. Physicians; guest lectr. managed care liability Johns Hopkins U. Sch. Medicine and Sch. of Profl. Studies and Bus. Edn., 1997—. Editl. bd. mem. Physician Orgns. and Med. Staff, 1997; contbr. articles to profl. jours. Bd. dirs. HopeWell Cancer Support. Mem. ABA (forum com. on health care law and health care litigation), AMA (mem. Doctors Adv. Svc. 1993-), Md. State Bar Assn. (section on health care law), Nat. Health Lawyers Assn. (bd. dir. 1977-88), Am. Acad. Hosp. Attys. (Md. rep.), Am. Med. Assn. (Doctors Adv. Network), Wranglers Law Club. Office: Venable LLP 1800 Mercantile Bank & Trust Bldg 2 Hopkins Plz Ste 2100 Baltimore MD 21201-2982 also: 575 7th St NW Washington DC 20004 Office Phone: 410-244-7535, 202-344-8102. Office Fax: 410-244-7742, 202-344-8300. E-mail: chbaker@venable.com.

BAKER, CORNELIA DRAVES, artist; b. Woodbury, N.J., Mar. 2, 1929; d. Carl Zeno and Cornelia (Powell) Draves.; m. Philip Douglas Baker, July 16, 1955; children: Brinton, Todd, Claudia, Samuel. Student, Ohio Wesleyan U., 1947-50, Goethe U., Frankfurt, Germany, 1950-52. Travel dir. Am. Youth Hostels, Inc., N.Y.C., 1953-57. Artist Cornelia Gallery, Kumamoto, Japan, 1990—; gallery dir. Presbyn. Ch., Franklin Lakes, N.J., 1988-97, Marcella Geltman Gallery, New Milford, N.J., 1993-96; bd. dirs. Bergen Mus. Art and Sci., N.J., 1996-2000, corr. sec., mem. exec. com., 1999-2000. One-woman shows include Ramapo Coll., 1986, Shimada Mus., Kumamoto, 1990, Sekaikan Gallery, Tokyo, 1990, Am. Ctr., Fukuoka, 1990, Bergen Mus. Art and Sci., 1993, L'Atelier Inc. Gallery, 1994, N.Y. Theol. Sem., N.Y.C., 1996, The Gallery, Franklin Lakes, 1997, 2003, Office Congressman S.R. Rothman, Hackensack, N.J., 1997, Lee Hecht Harrison, Paramus, N.J., 1998, Willows Cafe, Ramsey, N.J., 2000. The Gallery, Franklin Lakes, 2003; represented in permanent collections Bergen Mus. Art and Sci., Paramus, Beekley Internat. Skiing Fine Art and Graphics. Chair social problems com. Borough of Franklin Lakes Coun., 1973-76. Recipient Best of Show award Ringwood Manor Assn. of the Arts, 1987, Bergen Mus. Art and Sci., 1989, Emeriti award for excellence N.J. Ctr. for Visual Arts, 1989, Excellence cert. Internat. Art Competition, 1988, Women Making History in Arts award Bergen County, N.J., 1993, Crabbie award Art Calendar, 1994, Gold prize RISO Edn. Found., Japan, 1997, Artist Showcase award Manhattan Art Internat., 2000, merit award Salute to Women in Arts. 2000. Mem. Nat. Assn. Women Artists (printmaking jury chmn. 1992-94), Salute to Women in the Arts (pres. 1988-90), Mastodon Artists Soc. (life), Altrusa Club of Bergen County, N.J. Republican. Presbyterian. Avocation: travel. Home: 293 Green Ridge Rd Franklin Lakes NJ 07417-2011 Personal E-mail: cdbaker@optonline.net.

BAKER, D. JAMES, marine administrator, environmental scientist; b. Long Beach, Calif., Mar. 23, 1937; s. Donald James and Lillian Mae (Pund); m. Emily Lind Delman, Sept. 7, 1968. BS in Physics, Stanford U., 1958; PhD in Exptl. Physics, Cornell U., 1962; LHD (hon.), Nova U., 1993. Rsch. assoc. in phys. oceanography U. R.I., Kingston, 1962-63; NIH postdoctoral fellow in chem. biodynamics U. Calif., Berkeley, 1963-64, Harvard U., Cambridge, Mass., 1964-66, asst. prof. oceanography, 1966-70, assoc. prof., 1970-73; group leader deep-sea physics Pacific Marine Environ. Lab. Nat. Oceanog. and Atmospheric Adminstrn., Seattle, 1977-79; rsch. assoc. prof. dept. oceanography U. Wash., Seattle, 1973-75, rsch. prof. dept. oceanography, 1975-79, sr. oceanographer Applied Physics Lab., 1973-86, adj. prof. dept. atmospheric scis., prof. Sch. Oceanography, 1979-86, chmn. dept. oceanography, 1979-81, dean Coll. Ocean and Fishery Scis., 1981-83; disting. vis. scientist Jet Propulsion Lab., Calif. Inst. Tech., Pasadena, 1982-93; pres. bd. govs. Joint Oceanog. Instns. Inc., Washington, 1983-93; under sec. commerce oceans and atmosphere Nat. Oceanic and Atmospheric Adminstrn., Washington, 1993—2001; pres. & CEO Acad. Natural Scis., Phila., 2002—. Guest investigator Woods Hole Oceanographic Instn., 1968-69, vis. scholar, 1970; mem. adv. com. NAS, Nat. Oceanic and Atmospheric Adminstrn. and other internat. bodies; co-chair environ. and natural resources com. Nat. Sci. and Tech. Coun., 1993-2001; ex-officio mem. Pres.'s Coun. on Sustainable Devel., 1993-2001; chair Fed. Com. for Meteorol. Svcs. and Supporting Rsch., 1993-2001; mem. Govt.-Univ.-Industry Rsch. Roundtable Coun., NAS/NRC, 1993-2001. Author: Planet Earth-The View from Space, 1990; co-editor-in-chief Geophys. Fluid Dynamics 1975-79; mem. editl. bd. Dynamics of Atmospheres and Oceans, 1979-88, Marine Tech. Soc. Journ., 1986-89, Oceanus Mag., 1992-93, Jour. Environ. Sci. Policy, 2001-; contbr. articles to profl. jours. Recipient COSPAR Vikram Sarabhai award, 1998; spkr., Whitehouse/Smithsonian Inst. Millennium celebration, 2000. Fellow: AAAS, Am. Meteorol. Soc. (coun. 1982—88, pub. awareness com. 1991—93); mem.: Am. Soc. Limnology and Oceanography, Meteorol. and Oceanog. Soc., Challenger Soc. Marine Sci. Can., Marine Tech. Soc., Oceanography Soc. (climate change com. 1977—80, interim pres. 1988—89, pres. 1989—92, past pres. 1992—93), Am. Geophys. Union, Am. Philos. Soc., Sigma Xi. Achievements include patent for deep-sea pressure gauge with two colleagues. Avocations: piano, banjo, guitar. Office: Acad Natural Scis 1900 Benjamin Franklin Pkwy Philadelphia PA 19103 Office Phone: 215-299-1016.

BAKER, DANIEL C., plastic surgeon, educator; b. N.Y.C., 1942; m. Nina Griscom. MD, Columbia Coll., 1968. Bd. cert. Med. Examiners, bd. cert. plastic surgery. Resident surgery UCLA, 1969—70, NYU Med.; clin. fellow Columbia Presbyn. Med. Ctr., 1977—78; assoc. prof. plastic surgery N.Y. Med. Ctr. Sch. Medicine, N.Y.C., NY; pvt. practice.

BAKER, DANIEL RICHARD, computer company executive, consultant; b. Copenhagen, Mar. 19, 1932; came to U.S., 1936; s. Arthur and Molly (Needman) B.; m. June Ellin Nebenzahl, Oct. 2, 1960; children: David Charles, Jill Alison. Student, Tufts Coll., 1949—51; BA, Bklyn. Coll., 1957; postgrad., Fairleigh Dickinson U., 1961—64, Am. U., 1968—69; grad. Realtors Inst., U. Va., 1972. Math tchr. N.Y.C. Pub. Schs., 1958—59; computer programmer Sys. Devel. Corp., Paramus, NJ, 1959—61; programmer analyst ITT, Paramus, 1961—64; sr. mathematician Melpar Corp., Falls Church, Va., 1964—65; sys. analyst Wolf R & D Corp., Bladensburg, Md., 1965—66, Aries Corp., McLean, Va., 1966—68; sr. sys. analyst N. Am. Rockwell Corp., Roslyn, Va., 1968—70; pres. Data Assocs., Fairfax Station, Va., 1970—. Real estate broker. Group leader Dale Carnegie Sales Courses; vol. Ann. Fund Campaign Tufts Coll., 1976—. With AUS, 1954-55, vet. Korean War. Mem.: No. Va. Assn. Realtors Pioneer Club, Va. Assn. Realtors (dir. 1977—80, 1983—97, Lifetime award 1992, 1994—2005), Nat. Assn. Realtors (No. Va. chpt. multilist com., edn. com., pub. rels. com., 5-yr. Million Dollar Sales Club award), Charles Tufts Soc., Silvanus Packard Soc., Washington Tufts Club (v.p. 1975). Office: Data Assocs 5622-G Ox Rd Fairfax VA 22039-1018 Personal E-mail: would_i_kid_you@yahoo.com. E-mail: ridem_cowboy@usa.com.

BAKER, DAVID A., obstetrician, gynecologist, educator; s. Milton and Sonia Baker; m. Judy Marshel, May 26, 2001; children: Dara A., Dawn G., Erica J. BS, Bklyn Coll., 1967; MS, U. Rochester, 1969; MD, SUNY, Bklyn., 1973. Diplomate Am. Bd. Ob-Gyn, 1979. Instr. ob-gyn U. Vt. Med. Ctr., Burlington, 1977—79; asst. prof. ob-gyn SUNY, Stony Brook, 1979—85; assoc. prof. dept. ob-gyn. SUNY Health Sci. Ctr., Stony Brook, 1985—98, prof. dept. ob-gyn., 1998—; assoc. prof. SUNY Dental Sch., Stony Brook, 1985—. Contbr. articles to profl. jours. Cons. LI HELP group, Beth Page, NY. Grantee Westat, NIAID, 1992—2003. Fellow: ACOG. Achievements include research in management and treament of Herpes virus infections. Avocation: gardening. Office: Dept Ob-gyn Health Scis Ctr SUNY Stony Brook NY 11794-8091 E-mail: dbaker@notes.cc.sunysb.edu.

BAKER, DAVID ARTHUR, retired small business owner, manufacturing executive; b. Cranston, RI, Jan. 5, 1941; s. Andrew Harris and Phyllis Evelyn (Partridge) B.; m. Anne Marie Perron, July 14, 1959; children: Susan Marie, Pamela Phyllis. Diploma, Brit. Inst. Homeopathy, Middlesex, Eng., 1995, DHM, 1996. With Supreme Coat Co., Worcester, Mass., 1960-74; owner D.A. Baker Mfg. Co., Auburn, Mass., 1975—2000, Eagle's Nest Video Prodns., Auburn, 1985; operator NORFED Currency Redemption Ctr., Leicester, Mass.; ret. Treas. Tax Law Rsch. Group, 2005. *Although retired in principal, spends much time studying law and researching the tax code, monetary policy, and Social Security system of the United States. Very active in the tax honestly movement, and also in reform of our monetary, legal, and Social Security systems. Goal is to present some of the evidence collected before a Congressional or Senate committee.* Prodr. (video) Popular Amazons, 1986, Macaws, 1987, Cockatoos, 1988, Parrot Keeping, 1989, others; author: Beliefs. Bd. dirs. Royal Arts Found. Belcourt Castle, Newport, RI; res. dep. sheriff Worcester County; active Madison Found., U.S. Navy War Coll. Found., We the People Congress Recipient Cert. of Merit, Les Comités des Vins de France, 1982; Decorated knight Order of St. John. Fellow Brit. Inst. Homeopathy; mem. NRA (Nat. Patriots medal), Am. Coll. Heraldry, Homeopathic Acad. Naturopathic Physicians, Internat. Platform Soc., Internat. Soc. Food and Wine, Nat. Trust Hist. Preservation, Fully Informed Jury Assn., Tax Law Rsch. Group, Am. Jury Assn., Tax Law Rsc. Group, Save-A-Patriot Fellowship, Boston Soc. Aviculture (treas. 1983-85, Outstanding Svc. award 1984), Preservation Soc. Newport County, Exotic Cage Bird Soc. (co-founder, bd. dirs. 1986-88, Outstanding Svc. award 1985), Friends of Ballroom Dancing, Friends of the Royal Arts Found. (v.p.), Freedom Found., Rolls Royce Owners Club (life), Daimler and Lanchester Club, Club Maxine's, Health Scis. Inst., Leicester Bus. Assn. (v.p.), Knight Cottage Assn. (pres.), St. Andrew Soc. R.I., Higgins Armory, Frohsinn Club, Save A Patriot Fellowship. Avocations: art, antiques, shooting, boating, aviculture. Office: Eagles Nest Villa 196 Leicester St Auburn MA 01501-1406

BAKER, DAVID HIRAM, nutritionist, educator; b. DeKalb, Ill., Feb. 26, 1939; s. Vernon T. and Lucille M. (Severson) B.; m. Norraine A. Baker; children: Barbara G., Michael D., Susan G., Debora A., Luann C., Beth A. BS, U. Ill., 1961, MS, 1963, PhD, 1965. Sr. scientist Eli Lilly & Co., Greenfield, Ind., 1965-67; mem. faculty U. Ill., Champaign-Urbana, 1967—, prof. nutrition, dept. animal sci., nutritional biochemist, 1974—, dept. head, 1988-90. Author: Sulfur in Nonruminant Nutrition, 1977, Bioavailability of Nutrients for Animals, 1995; mem. editorial bd. Jour. Animal Sci., 1969-73, Jour. Nutrition, 1975-79, 89-99, Poultry Sci., 1978-84, Nutrition Revs., 1983-92; contbr. numerous articles to sci. jours. Chmn. bd. Champaign-Urbana Teen Challenge Drug Rehab. Program, 1977-80. Recipient Disting. Svc. award USDA, 1987; Univ. Scholar award, 1986; Nutrition Rsch. award, 1986; Am. Feed Mfrs., 1973; Merck award, 1977; Paul A. Funk award, 1977; H. H. Mitchell Tchg. award, 1979, 85; Broiler Rsch. award, 1983. Mem. NAS, Am. Soc. Animal Sci. (Young Scientist award 1971, Gustaf Bohstedt award 1985, Hoffman LaRoche award 1985, Morrison award 1994), Poultry Sci. Assn., Am. Soc. Nutritional Sci. (Borden award 1986, Dannon award 2003), Fedn. Am. Socs. Exptl. Biology, Sigma Xi, Phi Kappa Phi, Alpha Zeta, Gamma Sigma Delta. Home: 2609 Wadsworth Ln Urbana IL 61802-9403 Office: U Ill Nutrition Dept Urbana IL 61801 Office Phone: 217-333-0243. E-mail: dhbaker@uiuc.edu.

BAKER, DAVID REMEMBER, lawyer; b. Durham, NC, Jan. 17, 1932; s. Roger Denio and Eleanor Elizabeth (Ussher) B.; m. Myra Augusta Mullins, Nov. 2, 1955 PhB, U. Chgo., 1949; BA, Birmingham-So. Coll., 1951; JD, Harvard U., 1954. Bar: Ala. 1954, NY 1963, U.S. Supreme Ct. 1972. Assoc. Cabaniss & Johnston, Birmingham, Ala., 1957-62, Chadbourne, Parke, Whiteside & Wolff, N.Y.C., 1962-66, ptnr., 1967-86, Jones, Day, Reavis & Pogue, N.Y.C., 1986-93, Afridi, Angell & Baker, N.Y.C., 1993-96, Gersen, Baker & Wood LLP, N.Y.C., 1997-98, Baker, Johnston & Wilson LLP, Birmingham and N.Y.C., 1998—2003; of counsel Haskell Slaughter Young & Rediker, LLC, Birmingham and N.Y.C., 2003—. Gen. counsel Econ. Club N.Y., 1977—; dir. HIEnergy Techs., Inc. Co-editor Due Diligence, Disclosures and Warranties in the Corporate Acquisition Practice, 1988, 2d edit., 1992; author articles and book chpts. Pres. N.Y. Legis. Svc., N.Y.C., 1975-98, chmn., 1998—; mem. adv. com. Ctr. for N.Y.C. Law, 2000—; sec., dir. Jr. Achievement of N.Y., 1973-99; dir. Jr. Achievement of Greater Birmingham, 1999—; trustee Birmingham-So. Coll., 1985—. With U.S. Army, 1954-57. Mem.: Ala. Law Inst., Musica Viva N.Y. (pres. 1994—96), NY State Bar Assn. (exec. com. bus. law sect. 1987—89, exec. com. internat. law and practice sect. 1991—92, chmn. internat. investment and devel. com. 1991—92), Assn. Lloyd's Mems. (N.Am. adv. bd.), Internat. Bar Assn. (vice chmn. bus. orgn. com. 1986—90, rep. to U.S. mems. N.Y. area 1988—2000, chmn. com. on trusts for bus. 1990—94, prin. rep. to UN in N.Y. 1993—), Birmingham Bar Assn. (chmn. history and archives com. 2002), Ala. Bar Assn., Assn. Bar City N.Y. (chmn. com. on state legis. 1968—70), Am. Law Inst., Am. Arbitration Assn. (nat. panel), ABA (liaison com. fin. acctg. stds. bd.), Met. Club NYC, Harvard Club NYC, Birmingham Athletic Club. Democrat. Unitarian Universalist. Avocation: bridge. Home: 1200 Beacon Pkwy E Apt 500 Birmingham AL 35209-1041 Office: Haskell Slaughter Young & Rediker LLC 1400 Park Pl Tower 2001 Park Pl N Birmingham AL 35203-2700 also: Fl 30 515 Madison Ave New York NY 10022 Office Phone: 205-251-1000. Business E-Mail: drb@hsy.com.

BAKER, DAVID WARREN, earth scientist; b. Great Falls, Mont., Nov. 9, 1939; s. Roy Earnest Baker and Thora Leona Martin; m. Evelyn Elizabeth Herbstrith, 1962 (div. 1978); children: Erik Conrad, Andrew Craig, Paula Alicia. PhD, UCLA, 1969; MS in Natural sci., Swiss Fed. Inst. Tech., 1964; BS, MIT, 1961. Consulting earth scientist, owner Little Belt Consulting Svcs., Monarch, Mont., 1984—; rsch. geologist Gulf R & D Corp., Pitts., 1976—83; asst. prof. U. Ill., Chgo., 1970—76. Cons. Export Bd. of Zambia, Lusaka, 1995—95, World Bank, Lusaka, 1995. Scoutmaster Boy Scouts Am., Oak Park, Ill., 1970—76, New Alexandria, Pa., 1976—82. Mem.: Tobacco Root Geol. Soc., Mont. Geol. Soc., Nat. Ctr. Sci. Edn., Geol. Soc. Am., Am. Geophys. Union. Unitarian. Achievements include first to Reconstructed plate tectonic history of Montana; research in Determined plate tectonic origin of Yogo Sapphire Deposit in Montana; first to Developed technique to analyze extremely deformed rock (mylonite) using X-rays and spherical harmonic analysis; Conducted field courses for Montana teachers on plate tectonic history of Montana. Home and Office: Little Belt Consulting Svcs PO Box 906 Monarch MT 59463 E-mail: dbaker@3rivers.net.

BAKER, DEBORAH, editor, writer; b. Charlottesville, Va., Mar. 28, 1959; d. Jeffrey John Wheeler and Barbara Ann Baker; m. Amitav Ghosh, Feb. 15, 1990; children: Lila, Nayan. Affiliated degree, Cambridge (Eng.) U., 1980; BA, U. Va., 1981. Editl. dir. Overlook, N.Y.C., 1986-88; assoc. pub. Sheep Meadow, The Bronx, 1993-95; exec. editor Kodansha, N.Y.C., 1995-99; sr. editor Little Brown, N.Y.C., 2000—. Author: In Extremis: The Life of Laura Riding, 1993 (finalist for Pulitzer prize), Making a Farm: The Life of Robert Bly, 1982. Office: care Georges Borchardt Inc 136 E 57th St New York NY 10022-2707

BAKER, DEXTER FARRINGTON, manufacturing executive, director; b. Worcester, Mass., Apr. 16, 1927; s. Leland Dyer and Edith (Quimby) B.; m. Dorothy Ellen Hess, June 23, 1951; children: Ellen L., Susan A., Leslie A., Carolyn J. BS, Lehigh U., 1950, MBA, 1957. Sales engr. Air Products & Chem., Inc., Allentown, Pa., 1952-56, gen. sales mgr., 1956-57, mng. dir., 1957-64, chief exec. ops. in Europe, bd. dir., 1964-67, exec. v.p., 1967-78, pres., 1978-86, 90-91, chmn., pres., 1990-91, chmn., chief exec. officer, 1986-92, chmn. exec. com. bd. dir., 1992-98. Former chmn. investment policy US Trade Rep. Bd. assocs. Muhlenberg Coll.; trustee Harry C. and Mary M. Trexler Found. Served with USNR, 1945-46; with U.S. Army, 1950-52. Mem. AIChE, Am. Mgmt. Assn., Nat. Assn. Mfrs. (former chmn.), Theta Chi. Presbyterian (elder). Office: Air Products and Chems Inc 7201 Hamilton Blvd Allentown PA 18195-1501

BAKER, DIANE R.H., dermatologist; b. Toledo, Nov. 17, 1945; BS, Ohio State U., 1967, MD cum laude, 1971. Diplomate Am. Bd. Dermatology. Intern U. Wis. Hosp., Madison, 1971-72, resident in dermatology, 1972-74, Oreg. Health Sci. Ctr., Portland, 1974-76; pvt. practce, Portland, 1976—. Clin. prof. dermatology Oreg. Health Sci. U., 1986—; mem. med. staff Meridian Park Hosp., Tualatin, Oreg., 1981—; dir. Am. Bd. Dermatology, 1995—, v.p., 2001. Mem.: AMA (del. 1995—), Oreg. Dermatol. Soc., Am. Dermatol. Assn. (v.p. 2001), Am. Acad. Dermatology (v.p. 1990), Alpha Omega Alpha. Office: 1706 NW Glisan St Ste 2 Portland OR 97209-2225

BAKER, DON L., band director; b. Dover, N.J., Jan. 18, 1967; s. Donald B. and Elaine Baker. MusB, Rutgers U., 1993. Cert. music tchr. Dept. of Edn., N.J. Dir. of bands Lincoln H.S., Jersey City, 1993—95, Rutherford H.S., NJ, 1995—. Drill instr. Columbia H.S., Maplewood, NJ, 1985—96. Mem.: Internat. Assn. of Jazz Educators, Music Educators Nat. Conf., Porsche Club of Am. (Enthusiast of the Yr. 1993). Home: 30-L Garden Terr North Arlington NJ 07031 Office: Rutherford H S 56 Elliott Pl Rutherford NJ 07070 E-mail: leadtrupet@aol.com.

BAKER, DONALD, lawyer, director; b. Chgo., May 28, 1929; s. Russell and Elizabeth B.; m. Gisela S. Carli, Oct. 6, 1960; children: Caryna, Andrew, Russell. Student, Deep Springs Coll., Calif., 1947-49; JDS., U. Chgo., 1954. Bar: Ill. 1955, N.Y. 1964. Ptnr. Baker & McKenzie, Chgo., 1955-94, ret., 1994; sec., gen. counsel, bd. dirs. Air South, Inc., Columbia, S.C., 1994-95. Bd. dirs. Trimedyne, Inc., Cardiomedics, Inc. Bd. dirs. exec. com. Mid-Am. Com., Chgo., 1980-94. Mem. ABA. Clubs: Michigan Shores (Wilmette, Ill.). E-mail: dbaker5727@aol.com.

BAKER, DONALD GENE, social sciences educator; b. Elgin, Ill., Feb. 16, 1932; s. Glenn O. and Helen K. Baker; m. Barbara L. Sands; 1 child, Catherine K. BA in Polit. Sci., Denver U., 1953; MA in Polit. Sci., Syracuse U., 1957, PhD in Social Scis., 1961. Asst. prof., dir. dept. Am. studies Skidmore Coll., Saratoga Springs, N.Y., 1959-64; assoc. prof., then prof. Southampton (N.Y.) Coll. of L.I. U., 1964—2005, dir. social scis. divsn., 1964-70; prof. C.W. Post Coll. L.I. U., NY, 2005—. Cons. Peace Corps, Washington, 1964-67, N.Y. State Dept. Edn., Albany, 1964-66, AID, Washington, 1977-79; dir. Grad. Legis. Intern Program, Albany, 1962-67. Author: Politics of Race, 1975, Race, Ethnicity and Power, 1983. Cpl. U.S. Army, 1954-56. Rsch. fellow U. Rhodesia, 1976-78, U. Zimbabwe, 1981, Victoria U., New Zealand, 1993; assoc. rsch. fellow Yale U., 1992-93; rsch. grantee St. Antony's Coll., Oxford U., Eng., 1980-81, 86. Democrat. Avocations: travel, writing. Home: PO Box 701 Hampton Bays NY 11946-0607 E-mail: donald.baker@liu.edu.

BAKER, DONALD P., lawyer; b. L.A., Oct. 27, 1947; s. Albert G. and Janet C. Baker; m. Caroline E. BA magna cum laude, U. Redlands, 1970; JD, UCLA, 1973. Bar: Calif. 1973. Ptnr. Latham & Watkins, L.A., chair transp. practice group, 1991—. Dir. UCLA Pub. Interest Law Found., 1982-84, UCLA Alumni Assn., 1984-86, Japan Am. Symphony Assn. L.A., 1992-95; dir. Western Justice Ctr. Found., 1988—, pres., 1995—; trustee Claremont Grad. U., 2002—. Fellow ABA (numerous coms. and offices), Nat. Assn. Colls. and Univ. Attys., Star Bar Calif. (com. jud. nominees evaluation 1981-82), Internat. Bar Assn., L.A. County Bar Assn. (pres. 1986-87, numerous coms. and offices, Shothuck-Price Meml. award 1999), Barristers L.A. County Bar Assn. (pres. 1979-80, numerous coms. and offices), L.A. County Bar Found. (sec. 1983-84), Japan Am. Soc. So. Calif. (bd. dirs., v.p. 1992—)Chancery Club, Order of the Coif. Office: Latham & Watkins 633 W 5th St Ste 4000 Los Angeles CA 90071-2005

BAKER, DOUGLAS M., JR., service industry executive; Previously in various mktg. and mgmt. positions Proctor & Gamble Co.; with Ecolab, St. Paul, 1989, sr. v.p. inst. sector, 2001—02, pres., COO, 2002—04, pres., CEO, bd. dir., 2004—. Office: Ecolab 370 Wabasha St N Saint Paul MN 55102*

BAKER, DUSTY (JOHNNIE B. BAKER JR.), professional baseball team manager; b. Riverside, Calif., June 15, 1949; Student, Am. River Coll. Player Atlanta Braves, 1968-75, L.A. Dodgers, 1976-83, San Francisco Giants, 1984, Oakland A's, 1985-86; coach San Francisco Giants, 1988-92, mgr., 1993—2002, Chgo. Cubs, 2002—. Mem. Nat. League All-Star Team, 1981-82. Recipient Silver Slugger award, 1980-81, Gold Glove, 1981; named to Sporting News All-Star Team, 1980. Office: Chgo Cubs Wrigley Field 1060 W Addison Chicago IL 60613-4397*

BAKER, EDWARD KEVIN, retail executive; b. Chester, Ill., Nov. 25, 1948; s. Edward Louis and Betty Lou (Huch) B.; m. Janet Lynn Verbal, Oct. 26, 1967 (div. 1973); l child, Shawn Allen; m. Doris Mary Kubala, June 12, 1975; stepchildren: Jimmy Lee, Jennifer Lou Godard. Mgr. F.W. Woolworth Co., St. Louis, then Dallas, 1968-74; pres. Baker Mktg. Co., Dallas, 1974-76; mgr. E.B. Mott Co., Dallas, 1976-83; mkt. mgr. Michaels Stores Inc., San Antonio, 1983-86, dir. merchandising Irving, Tex., 1986-88, dir. mgmt. devel., 1988-89, v.p. ops., 1989-91; sr. v.p. ops., distbn. mktg. Silk Greenhouse Inc., Tampa, 1990-91; dir. ops. mdse. Crafts & More div. Ames Dept. Stores, Rocky Hill, Conn., 1991-92; pres. E.K. Baker Group, Inc., Treasure House Stores, Inc., Seattle, 1993—, chief oper. officer, bd. dirs. Author The Edge 1988; producer (video) Framing Technique 1989; editor (video) Art Materials 1989. Mem. Southwest Craft & Hobby Assn. (bd. dirs. 1987-93), Am. Soc. Tng. Dirs., Art Materials Trade Assn., Am. Soc. Decorative Painters, Profl. Picture Framers Assn. Lutheran. Avocation: restoring antique furniture. Personal E-mail: ekdbaker@sbcglobal.net.

BAKER, EDWARD L., JR., physician, science facility executive; b. Chattanooga, Nov. 18, 1946; s. Edward Lamar and Sue B. Baker; m. Pamela Taylor, June 21, 1969; children: Justin, Ryan, Lindsay. BA, Vanderbilt U., 1968; MD, Baylor U., 1972; MPH, Harvard U., 1979, MS, 1980. Diplomate Am. Bd. Internal Medicine, Am. Bd. Occupational Medicine. Commd. USPHS, 1974—, advanced through grades to rear adm., 1995, asst. surgeon gen.; asst. prof. Harvard U. Sch. Pub. Health, Boston, 1980-82, assoc. prof., 1982-85; asst. dir. Nat. Inst Occupl. Safety and Health Ctr. Disease Control, Atlanta, 1985-88, dep. dir. Nat. Inst. Occupl. Safety and Health, 1988-90, asst. surgeon gen., dir. Pub. Health Practice Program Office, 1990—. Bd. dirs. Internat. Commn. on Occupl. Health, 1986-92. Author, editor 100 sci. articles and book chpts. Fellow Am. Coll. Epidemiology; mem. APHA, Am. Coll. Occupl. and Environ. Medicine (authorship award 1988), Soc. Occupl. and Environ. Health, Royal Soc. Medicine (London, vis. fellow). Home: 755 Kirk Rd Decatur GA 30030-4529

BAKER, EDWARD MARTIN, engineering and industrial psychologist; b. Bklyn., Mar. 13, 1941; s. Harold H. and Paula B.; m. Shige Jajiki; 1 son, Evan Keith. BA, CCNY, 1962, MBA, 1964; PhD (Research fellow), Bowling Green State U., 1972. Human factors research engr. environ. and safety engrng. staff Ford Motor Co., Dearborn, Mich., 1972-77, tech. tng. assoc. mgmt. and tech. tng. dept. Detroit, 1977-79, orgn. devel. cons., personnel and orgn. staff, 1979-81, statis. assoc., ops. support product quality office, 1981-83, statis methods mgr. Asia-Pacific and Latin-Am. automotive ops., 1983-87, dir. total quality planning, cons. and statis. methods corp. quality office, 1987—, dir. quality strategy and ops. support, 1990-92; sr. fellow Aspen Inst., Wye, Md., 1992-95. Deming scholars MBA program adv. bd. Fordham U., 1992—, adj. faculty MBA program, 1994—; cons. in field. Author: Scoring a Whole in One, 1999; contbr. articles to profl. jours.; editorial referee: Jour. Quality Tech. 1974-75, 77-81. Trustee W. Edwards Deming Inst., Washington, 1993-2003. Fellow Am. Soc. Quality (Brumbaugh award 1975, Craig award 1976, 79, 86, 88, Ishikawa medal 1995, Deming medal 1997). Home and Office: PO Box 5797 Scottsdale AZ 85261-5797 E-mail: lifemap@ix.netcom.com.

BAKER, ELIZABETH CALHOUN, magazine editor; b. Boston; d. John Calhoun and Elizabeth Marshall Evans B. BA cum laude, Bryn Mawr Coll.; MA, Radcliffe Coll. Fulbright scholar Inst. d'Art et d'Archeologie and Ecole du Louvre, Paris; Instr. art history Boston U., Wheaton Coll., Norton, Mass.; assoc. editor Art News, N.Y.C., 1963-65, mng. editor, 1965-73; editor Art in Am. mag., N.Y.C., 1973—. Instr. art history Sch. Visual Arts, N.Y.C., 1968-74; freelance art criticism. Recipient Lifetime Achievement award Coll. Art Assn., 1992; Nat. Endowment for Arts grantee, 1972 Office: Art in America Brant Publications 575 Broadway Fl 5 New York NY 10012-3230

BAKER, ELLEN SHULMAN, astronaut, physician; b. Fayetteville, N.C., Apr. 27, 1953; d. Melvin Shulman; m. Kenneth J. Baker; 2 daughters. BA in Geology, SUNY, Buffalo, 1974; MD, Cornell U., 1978; grad. Air Force Aerospace Medicine Course, Brooks AFB, San Antonio, Tex., 1981; MS in Public Health, U. Tex., 1994. Diplomate Am. Bd. Internal Medicine. Resident U. Tex. Health Sci. Ctr., San Antonio; med. officer NASA Lyndon B. Johnson Space Ctr., Houston, 1981-84, astronaut candidate, 1984-85, astronaut, 1985—, mission specialist Shuttle Orbiter Atlantis flight STS-34, 1989, mission specialist Shuttle Columbia flight STS-50, 1992, mission specialist Shuttle Atlantis flight STS-71, 1995, lead astronaut for med. issues; astronaut rep. Edn. Working Group at Johnson Space Ctr. Achievements include having logged more than 686 hours in space. Avocations: skiing, swimming, running, movies, music, reading. Address: NASA Johnson Space Ctr Astronaut Ofc Houston TX 77058

BAKER, FLOYD WILMER, surgeon, retired military officer; b. Leavenworth, Kans., May 25, 1927; s. Floyd Winfield and Lolita Clare (Somers) B.; m. Darlene Marie Fulk, Apr. 10, 1949; children: Linda Marie, Diane Louise, Barbara Jayne. BA, U. Kans., 1950, MD, 1953; grad., Army Command and Gen. Staff Coll., 1964, Indsl. Coll. Armed Forces, 1967. Diplomate: Am. Bd. Surgery. Commd. 1st lt. U.S. Army, 1953, advanced through grades to maj. gen., 1980; intern Madigan Gen. Hosp., Tacoma, 1953-54; resident in gen. surgery Fitzsimons Army Hosp., Denver, 1955-59; dir. personnel and tng. Office of Surgeon Gen., 1970-71; comdg. gen. Brooke Army Med. Center, Ft. Sam Houston, Tex., 1974-78; Letterman Army Med Center, Presidio of San Francisco, 1978-81; chief surgeon U.S. Army, Europe; comdg. gen. U.S. Army 7th Med. Command, 1981-83, U.S. Army Health Services Command, Ft. Sam Houston, 1983-86; retired U.S. Army, 1986. Served with USNR, 1945-46. Decorated Legion of Merit (2), Meritorious Service medal, Army Commendation medal (3), Air medal (2), Disting. Service medal. Fellow Am. Coll. Physician Execs.; mem. AMA, Soc. U.S. Army Flight Surgeons. Republican. Baptist. Home and Office: 1413 Wiltshire Ave San Antonio TX 78209-6050 E-mail: fbaker1@satx.rr.com.

BAKER, FREDERICK MILTON, JR., lawyer; b. Flint, Mich., Nov. 2, 1949; s. Frederick Milton Baker and Mary Jean (Hallitt) Rarig; m. Irene Taylor; children: Jessica, Jordan. BA, U. Mich., 1971; JD, Washington U., St. Louis, 1975. Bar: Mich. 1975, U.S. Dist. Ct. (we. dist.) Mich. 1980, U.S. Dist. Ct. (ea. dist.) Mich. 1981, U.S. Ct. Appeals (6th cir.) 1983, U.S. Supreme Ct. 1986. Instr. law Wayne State U., Detroit, 1975-76; rsch. atty. Mich. Ct. Appeals, Lansing, 1976-77, law clk. to chief judge, 1977; asst. prof. T.M. Cooley Law Sch., Lansing, 1978-80; ptnr. Willingham & Cote, Lansing, 1980-86, Honigman, Miller, Schwartz & Cohn, Lansing, 1986—2004; commr. Mich. Supreme Ct., 2005—. Adj. prof. T.M. Cooley Law Sch., 1980—86, 1995—96, Detroit Coll. Law Mich. State U., East Lansing, 2001—. Author: Michigan Bar Appeal Manual, 1982; editor Mich. Bar Jour., 1984—; contbr. articles to profl. jours. Founder, pres. Sixty Plus Law Ctr., Lansing, 1978-87, bd. dirs., 1987—; mem. cmty. adv. bd. Lansing Jr. League, 1983-90; co-founder, dir., sec.-treas. John D. Voelker Found., 1989—; bd. dirs. Greater Lansing chpt., ACLU 1997-2004; treas. Kehillat Israel, 1996-98; trustee Thoman Found., 2000-, Lansing Area Cmty. Trust, 2003—; pres. Gerald Beckwith Fund, 2002-04. Recipient Disting. Brief award T.M. Cooley Law Rev., 1988, 99. Fellow Mich. State Bar Found.; mem. ABA (Outstanding Single Project award 1980), Mich. Bar Assn. (vice chmn. jour. adv. bd. 1984-87, chmn. jour. adv. bd. 1987—, young lawyers sect. coun. 1980-84, grievance com. 1982-84, John W. Cummiskey award 1984), Ingham County Bar Assn. (Disting. Vol. award 2000), Big Oak Club (Baldwin, Mich.). Unitarian Universalist. Avocations: photography, fishing, running, frisbee, writing. Home: 5127 Barton Rd Williamston MI 48895-9304 Office: Mich Supreme Ct PO Box 30104 Lansing MI 48909 Office Phone: 517-373-0260. E-mail: bakerf@courts.mi.gov.

BAKER, GEORGE CHISHOLM, engineering executive, consultant; b. Dartmouth, N.S., Can., Oct. 29, 1918; s. Clifford Lyall and Edith (Chisholm) B.; m. Ethel Marie Suzanne Humbert, Jan. 2, 1942; children: Alison Marie, Catherine Ann. Diploma, Royal Mil. Coll. Can., 1939, D Engring. (hon.), 1988; BA in Sci., Toronto U., 1946; D Engring. (hon.), Tech. Coll. N.S., 1987; DCL, Acadia U., 1993. Registered profl engr., Can. Pres. Kentville (N.S.) Pub. Co. Ltd., 1948-77; engr. Kentville Electric Commn., 1960-81; exec. v.p. Tidal Power Corp., Halifax, N.S., 1971-89; pres. G.C. Baker Engring. Ltd., Kentville, 1977—. Chmn. Cam Pubs. Ltd., New Glasgow, N.S., 1978-2002. Contbr. numerous articles to profl. pubs. Chmn. Acadia U. Inst., Wolfville, N.S., 1968-70; gov. Acadia U., Wolfville, 1979-92. Maj. Signal Corps Royal Can. Army, 1939-46. Decorated Order of Brit. Empire, Order of Can. Fellow Engring. Inst. Can., Can. Acad. Engring.; mem. IEEE (Centennial Gold medal). Office: G C Baker Engring Ltd 536 Main St Kentville NS Canada B4N 1L3

BAKER, GEORGE HAROLD, III, physicist; b. Cheverly, Md., Mar. 23, 1949; s. George Harold Jr. and Betty (Fost) B.; m. Donna Prillaman, Jun 21, 1975; children: Matthew C., Jeffrey P., Virginia E. BA, Western Md. Coll., 1971; MS, U. Va., 1974; PhD, USAF Inst. Tech., Dayton, Ohio, 1987. Teaching asst. U. Va., Charlottesville, 1971-73; physicist Harry Diamond Labs., Adelphi, Md., 1973-77, Def. Nuclear Agy., Alexandria, 1977-87, group leader, 1987-89, asst. for program devel., 1989-94; chief innovative concepts divsn., 1994-96; Def. Threat Reduction Agy. dir. Springfield (Va.) Rsch. Facility, 1996-99; sr. scientist Northrop-Grumman, Alexandria, Va., 1999—2000; assoc. prof. James Madison U., 1999—, dir. Inst. for Infrastructure and Info. Assurance, 2002—03; mem. Congl. EMP Commn. staff, 2002—04. Mem. exec. bd. Nat. Def. Indsl. Assn. Homeland Security, 2005—; cons. in field. Contbr. articles to profl. jours. Tchr. Agape Christian Fellowship, Chantilly, Va., 1974-94, elder, 1994-2000; music and youth leader New Life Fellowship, Annandale, Va., 1979-83; canvasser Citizens for Sensible County Planning, Fairfax County, Va., 1989-2000. Fellow: Nuc. Electromagnetic Soc. (chmn. program com. 1984, co-chair non-proliferation and arms control underground focus group 1996—99, session chair 1998, chmn. nat. HPM conf. steering group 1999, session chair 2002, mem. nat. com. 2001—); mem.: IEEE (session chmn. 1987, 1992), Forum for Mil. Application of Directed Energy, Directed Energy Profl. Soc. (charter), Assn. Old Crows, Phi Delta Theta. Achievements include patent for optically coupled differential voltage sensor, 1976; co-developer sea-going nuclear EMP simulator concept, 1979; initiated Def. Nuclear Agy. EMP underground test program, 1983, High Power Microwave program, 1984, space nuclear power, 1994. Office: Coll Integrated Sci and Tech James Madison U MSC 4102 Harrisonburg VA 22807 Business E-Mail: bakergh@jmu.edu.

BAKER, GEORGE S., federal official; b. Green's Harbour, Nfld., Can., Sept. 4, 1942; 4 children. Student, polit. sci. and econs., Meml. U. of Newfoundland, U. New Brunswick. Chief clk. Nfld. Ho. Assembly, 1967—68, editor Hansard; sec. Commonwealth Parliamentary Assn., 1967—68; elected mem. Ho. of Commons, Gander-Grand Falls, 1974—2002, chmn. standing com. on fisheries and oceans, mem. fin. com., trade and econs. affairs com., fisheries and forestry com., environment com.; parliamentary sec. Min. Transport, 1975—76, Min. Fisheries, Transp., Environment and Nat. Revenue, 1975—76, Min. Nat. Revenue, 1976; party critic Atlantic Develop., 1989; assoc. party critic Treasury Bd., 1990; min. vets. affairs, sec. state Atlantic Can. Opportunities Agy., 1999—2000; appointed mem. Senate of Can., 2002—. Past chmn. Atlantic Caucus; past mem. Exec. Caucus. Office: Senate Canada Ottawa ON Canada K1A 0A4 Office Phone: 613-947-2517.

BAKER, GLORIA MARIE, artist; b. Petersburg, Ind. m. James Daniel Baker; children: David, Christopher. Pvt. practice, Evansville, Ind., 1976—. Artist (painting) Aztec Village, 1994 (Grumbacher Gold Medallion and The Excellence Gold award, 1994), The Dedicated, 1991 (Brown and Williamson Tobacco Corp. award, 1991, Dr. Martin Hydrus award Ga. Watercolor Soc., 03), The Domes, 1997 (2d pl.), Ascent to the Cathedral, 1998 (St. Cuthbert's Mill award, 1998, Grumbacner Bronze award), Double Ascent, 1999 (Winsor & Newton award, Document Framing Svc. award, 1999, 1st pl. Evansville Art Guild, Peabody Coal Co. award), Past, Present & Future, 1997, The Ascent (Houston B. Adams award, Evansville Mus. Arts & Sci.), Cathedral of Light, 2000 (2d pl., Dir.'s Choice award, 2000), The Dedicated, 1993, (included in books) Best of Watercolor, Best of Watercolor 2, Landscape Inspirations, The Complete Best of Watercolor, Vol.s 1 & 2, Chgo. Art Rev., 4th edit., Evansville Mus. of Arts and Sci. GiftShop, 2003; solo exhbn., Mus. Arts and Sci., Evansville, Ind., 2003, Evansville Mus. of Arts & Sci., 2003. Chmn. Celia Sprue Assn., Evansville, 1995—. Nominee Internat. Visual Artist of the Yr., Internat. Biog. Ctr./Cambridge, England, 2004. Mem.: Niagara Frontier Watercolor Soc., Watercolor Soc. Ala. (signature mem.), Ga. Watercolor Soc. (winner Nat. Exhibit 2003, Dr. Martin Hydrus award 2003), Pa. Watercolor Soc., Ky. Watercolor Soc., Petroleum Wives Club (v.p. 2003). Avocations: golf, gardening, reading, ballroom dancing. Home: 2711 Knob Hill Dr Evansville IN 47711 Personal E-mail: james_18510@msn.com.

BAKER, GRANT CODY, civil engineering educator; b. Eugene, Oreg., May 16, 1956; s. Irwin Gerald and Louise (Powell) B.; m. Tina Louise Denton, Apr. 9, 1988; children: Jessica, Calvin, Benjamin. BSChemE, U. Wash., 1978; MS in Mining Engring., U. Alaska, 1983, PhD in Geophysics, 1987. Chem. engr. UOP, Chgo., 1978-79; comml. fisherman F/V Patricia Sue, Anchorage, 1979-80; asst. prof. mech. engring. U. Alaska, Fairbanks, 1988-94, asst. prof. civil engring. Anchorage, 1994—2002, assoc. prof. civil engring., 2002—. Author, pub. Edutech, Anchorage, 1992—. Author: Bridge to Engineering, 1993, FORTRAN Reference Programs, 1995, ANSI C Reference Programs, 1996, BASIC Reference Programs, 1996, ANSI C++ Reference Programs, 1998. Named Engring. Prof. of Yr., 1993, 94, 96, 97, U. Alaska student chpt. ASME, ASCE. Republican. Baptist. Avocation: walking with family. Home: PO Box 240986 Anchorage AK 99524-0986 Office: U Alaska 3211 Providence Dr Anchorage AK 99508-4614 E-mail: baker@alaska.net.

BAKER, HARRISON SCOTT, application developer, consultant; b. Marion, Ohio, Mar. 12, 1950; s. Stanley Wallace and Starling (Dixon) Baker. BA, BS, Fla. State U., 1972, 80; MBA, Embry-Riddle Aeronaut. U., 1986. MCSE, cert. computing tech. Computing Tech. Industry Assn., network assoc. Cisco Sys., Inc., 2003, A+, Network+, Security +, Server +, iNet + Comptia; lic. radiotelephone with radar endorsement FCC. Mgr. Vincent Auto Parts, Inc., Marathon, Fla., 1972-78; maintenance supr. Eastern Air Lines, Inc., Miami, 1980-92; computer cons. Upper Sandusky, Ohio, 1992—. Author: Index to the Muster Rolls of PA in War of 1812, 1995, Early Settlers of Wyandot County, 1995, 1890 Veterans Census For Wyandot County, Ohio, 2004; indexer Obituaries in Upper Sandusky newspapers 1868-1911, 1994, Obituaries in Upper Sandusky newspapers 1912-1937, 1996, Obituaries in Upper Sandusky newspapers 1938-1958, 1997, Obituaries in Upper Sandusky newspapers 1959-1979, 1997, Journal of William Kennedy Beall, 1999, Civil War Soldiers Buried in Wyandot County, Ohio, 2000, Civil War Veterans Buried at the Ohio Veterans Home, 2001, American Prisoners of War Held at Halifax During the War of 1812, 2004. Trustee Wyandot County Geneal. Soc., 1995—2001. Mem.: SAR (pres. Hancock chpt. 1995—96), Assn. Computing Machinery, IEEE Computer Soc., Sons of Vets. Res. (capt., pub. info. officer 2000—03), Sons of Union Vets. (camp sec. 1994—98, Dept. of Ohio signals officer 1999—2000, nat. chief of staff 2002—03), Soc. War of 1812 (Ohio pres. 1996—99). Avocations: electronics, genealogy. Home: 353 Hilltop Dr Upper Sandusky OH 43351-9241 Business E-Mail: hsbaker@udata.com.

BAKER, HENRY S., JR., retired bank executive; b. Balt., June 10, 1926; s. Henry S. and Frances (Robinson) B.; m. Marian Stockton Towsend, June 12, 1948; children— Frances, Sandra, Stockton. BA, Johns Hopkins U., 1950; grad. with honors, Grad. Sch. Banking, Rutgers U., 1957. With Md. Nat. Bank, Balt., 1950-86, sr. exec. v.p., 1973-86. Chmn. Redwood Capital Mgmt. Co., AAA Md., Ins. Agy. Inc., 1983-90, Ind. Coll. Fund Md., 1984-89; v.p., bd. dirs. Manab Properties. Chmn. Md. chpt. Nature Conservancy, 1984-90; chmn. investment com. Kennedy Inst. for Handicapped Children, 1985-88, Episcopal Diocese Md., 1974-80; trustee, treas. Garrison Forest Sch., 1962-88, St. Paul's Sch. for Girls, 1968-77; pres. Jr. Achievement Met. Balt., 1971, Florence Crittenden Home, 1964-66; bd. dirs. Keswick, Home for Incurables, 1965, 1991, 1979; gen. campaign chmn. United Way Cen. Md., 1979. With USNR, 1944-46. Mem. Assn. Res. City Bankers, Md. Bankers Assn. (pres.), Md. State C. of C. (treas., dir.) Republican.

BAKER, HERMAN, medical educator, writer; b. N.Y.C., Jan. 22, 1926; s. Harry and Fannie Baker; m. Shirley Levitz, Nov. 15, 1952; children: Elliott Robert, Joel Martin. BS, CCNY, 1946; MS, Emory U., 1948; PhD, NYU, 1956. Cert. specialist human nutrition Am. Bd. Nutrition. Research asst. Columbia U., N.Y.C., 1949-50; research assoc. Mt. Sinai Hosp., N.Y.C., 1950-60; assoc. prof. medicine N.J. Med. Sch., Jersey City, 1960-70, prof. medicine and preventive medicine Newark, 1970—. Author: Clinical Vitaminology: Methods and Interpretation, 1968; contbr. articles to profl. jours. Fellow: Am. Coll. Nutrition. Avocation: music. Home: 27 Wilk Rd Edison NJ 08837-2726 Office: NJ Med Sch ADMC 1618A 30 Bergen St Newark NJ 07107-3001 Office Phone: 973-972-4664. E-mail: bakerhe@umdnj.edu.

BAKER, HOLLIE L., lawyer; b. 1953; BA, Baylor Univ., 1975; JD, Univ. Denver, 1982. Bar: Colo. 1982, DC 1987, Mass. 1997, US Ct. Appeals (Fed cir.), US Patent & Trademark Office. Ptnr., vice chmn. Intellectual Property dept. Wilmer Cutler Pickering Hale & Dorr, Boston. Contbr. articles to profl. jours. Mem.: ABA (council mem., Intellectual Property Law sect.), Am. Intellectual Property Law Assn., Boston Patent Law Assoc., Licensing Exec. Soc., Patent & Trademark Office Soc. Office: Wilmer Cutler Pickering Hale & Dorr 60 State St Boston MA 02109 Office Phone: 617-526-6110. Office Fax: 617-526-5000. Business E-Mail: hollie.baker@wilmerhale.com.

BAKER, HOLLIS MACLURE, furniture manufacturing company executive; b. Allegan, Mich., Apr. 27, 1916; s. Hollis Siebe and Ruth (MacClure) B.; m. Betty Jane Brown, Aug. 2, 1947; children: Tomelyn Ann, Susan MacClure; m. Elsie Margarite Leigh, Aug. 27, 2003. Student, U. Va., 1935-37. With Baker Furniture, Inc., Holland, Mich., 1938-40, 45-73, v.p., treas., 1959-61, pres., 1961-70, chmn. bd., 1970-73; v.p., gen. mgr. Grand Rapids Chair Co., Mich., 1959-61, pres., 1961-70. V.p., dir. Manor House, Inc., N.Y.C., 1958-70; pres. Boyne City R.R. Co., Mich., 400 Bldg. Corp., Palm Beach, Fla.; dir. Mich. Nat. Bank, Lansing, 1968-83, Am. Seating Co., Grand Rapids, 1973-83, Mich. Nat. Bank, Grand Rapids, 1959-84, Norton Gallery, Palm Beach, 1984-91. Author: A Brief History of Schloss Branzoll, 1975, A History of the Chateau de Caussade, 1980, A History of the Chateau de la Roque, 1985, Five Castles Are Enough, 1989. Bd. dirs. USCG Found., 1981-91. Lt. (s.g.) USNR, 1941-45. Mem. Nat. Assn. Furniture Mfrs. (dir.), Furniture Mfrs. Assn. Grand Rapids (dir., past pres 1970-84), Zeta Psi. Clubs: Brook (N.Y.C.), River (N.Y.C.), New York Yacht (N.Y.C.), Leash (N.Y.C.); Kent Country (Grand Rapids), University (Grand Rapids), Indian (Grand Rapids), Peninsular (Grand Rapids); Everglades (Palm Beach), Bath and Tennis (Palm Beach); Buck's (London). Episcopalian. Home: 301 Chapel Hill Rd Palm Beach FL 33480-4124 Office: 2220 Wealthy St Grand Rapids MI 49506

BAKER, HOWARD HENRY, JR., lawyer, former ambassador, former senator; b. Huntsville, Tenn., Nov. 15, 1925; s. Howard Henry and Dora (Ladd) B.; m. Joy Dirksen, Dec. 22, 1951 (dec. 1993); children: Darek Dirksen, Cynthia; m. Nancy Landon Kassebaum, Dec. 7, 1996. Student, U. of South, Tulane U.; LLB, U. Tenn., 1949; diploma (hon.), Yale U., Dartmouth Coll., Georgetown U., Bradley U., Pepperdine U., Centre Coll. U.S. senator from, Tenn., 1967-85; minority leader, 1977-81; majority leader, 1981-85; ptnr. Vinson & Elkins, Washington, 1985-87; chief of staff Office of the Pres. U.S., Washington, 1987-88; ptnr. Baker, Worthington, Crossley, Stansberry & Woolf, Knoxville, Tenn., 1985-87, 88-95, Baker, Donelson, Bearman & Caldwell, Washington, 1995—2000; U.S. amb. to Japan U.S. Dept. State, Tokyo, 2001—05; sr. counsel Baker, Donelson, Bearman, Caldwell & Berkowitz, Washington, 2005—. Bd. dirs. Pennzoil Co., Forum Internat. Policy; chmn. bd. dirs. Cherokee Aviations; mem. internat. adv. bd. Barrick Gold Corp; vice chmn. Senate Watergate Com.; mem. President's Fgn. Intelligence Bd., 1985-90; mem. Coun. Fgn. Rels., Wash. Inst. Fgn. Affairs; internat. councilllor Ctr. Strategic and Internat. Studies. Author: (books) No Margin for Error, 1980, Howard Baker's Washington, 1982, Big South Fork Country, 1983, Scott's Gulf, 2000. Bd. regents Smithsonian Instn. With USN. Named to Hall of Fame, Photo Mktg. Assn., 1994; recipient Jefferson award for Greatest Pub. Svc. performed by elected or apptd. ofcl., 1982, Presdl. Medal of Freedom, 1984, Internat. award, Am. Soc. Photographers, 1993. Office: Baker Donelson Bearman Caldwell & Berkowitz Lincoln Sq 555 Eleventh St NW 6th Fl Washington DC 20004

BAKÉR, J. A., II, executive management advisor and consultant, architect, financial engineer; b. N.Y.C., Dec. 12, 1944; s. Leonard Ernest and Miriam Violet (Roché) B. Postgrad. in fin. svcs. mgmt., The Am. Coll., 1994—. ChFC, CLU, fin. planning advisor, property/casualty/liability field underwriter, comml. and personal lines, life broker; cert. instr.; cert. in advanced mgmt. Cons. mgr. Life Ins., N.Y.C., 1964—79; supr. Physician's Planning Group, Atty.'s Planning Svc., Bus. Planning Svcs., Profl. Svc. Corp., N.Y.C., 1979—81; chief satisfaction officer J A L B Enterprises, East Garden City, NY, 1980—91, emeritus, 1991—. Monitor N.Y. State continuing edn. program, 1996-, instr. continuing profl. edn. program, 1996-99, licensing courses, 1996-99. Bd. dirs. Medic Alert, Nassau County, N.Y., 1985-87; rep. The Living Bank, Houston; nominated mem.: Citizen Ambassador Program Internat. Recipient Cert. of Appreciation, VFW D.C., 2002. Fellow Life Underwriters Coun.; mem. Nat. Assn. Life Underwriters, Falls Church, Va. (emeritus, pres. Cortland N.Y. chpt. 1974-75, legis. chair 1972-74, v.p. pub. info. Nassau County 1980-87, instr. Bklyn. 1987-90, Queens 1991-92), Am. Automobile Assn., Wash. State, Am. Coun. Ind. Life Underwriters, Soc. Fin. Svc. Profls., N.Y.C. Life Underwriters Assn., Fraternal Order of Police, N.Y.C. Civil Svc. Ret. Employee Assn., Gen. Agts. Mgrs. Assn. Internat. (Falls Church, Va., charter), United Assn. Entrepreneurs N.Y.C., Ithaca (N.Y.) Jaycees (past dir.), Sovereign Mil. Order of Malta N.Y.C. (pilgrim 1999), Am. Assn. N.Y.C., Nat. Orgn. for Men, Smithsonian Inst. Assn. (Washington nat. assoc.), The Srs. Coalition. Office Phone: 646-405-0303.

BAKER, J. DENNIS, surgeon; b. Flint, Mich., 1938; MD, Columbia U., 1966. Diplomate Am. Bd. Surgery, Am. Bd. Gen. Vascular Surgery. Intern Bellevue Hosp. Ctr., N.Y.C., 1966-67; resident in surgery Tufts U.-New Eng. Med. Ctr., Boston, 1969-73; resident in vascular surgery Henry Ford Hosp., Detroit, 1973-74; fellow in surgery Tufts U., Boston, 1972-73; chief sect. vascular surgery VA Med. Ctr., Sepulveda, Calif., 1974-94; attending surgeon UCLA Med. Ctr., L.A., 1974—; staff surgeon West L.A. VA Med. Ctr., 1994—; acad. faculty UCLA Sch. Medicine, 1974—. Fellow ACS; mem. Am. Heart Assn., Am. Surg. Assn., Soc. Clin. Vascular Surgery, Soc. Vascular Surgery, Western Vascular Surgery. Office: UCLA Gonda Vascular Ctr 200 Medical Plz Ste 510 Los Angeles CA 90095-6908 Office Phone: 310-825-3684. E-mail: jbaker@mednet.ucla.edu.

BAKER, JACK SHERMAN, architect, educator; b. Champaign, Ill., Aug. 8, 1920; s. Clyde Lee and Jane Cecilia (Walker) B. BA with honors, U Ill., 1943, MS, 1949; cert., N.Y. Beaux Art Inst. Design, 1943. Aero engr., designer Boeing Aircraft, Seattle, 1943-44; assoc. Atkins, Barrow & Lasswith, Urbana, 1947-50; pvt. practice architecture Champaign, 1947—; mem. faculty U. Ill. Sch. Architecture, Urbana, 1947—, prof. architecture, 1950-90, acting prof. emeritus, 1990—97, Disting. prof. emeritus, 1997—, former mem. exec. com. Hon. bd. dirs. Gerhart Music Festival, Guntersville, Ala., Stravinsky awards, Champaign, Conservatory of Cen. Ill.; hon. bd. dirs. Ruth Hindman Found., Huntsville, Ala.; dir., performer personal performance loft space for Interaction of the Arts and Architecture, 1960—; participant U. Ill. Exploring the Arts course (Act-NCEA award), 1970—, campus honors program, 1995—; former mem. Chancellor's com. on graphic design and art acquisition and installation, former mem. adv. bd., designer of exhbn., Krannert Mus., U. Ill., engr. basic, Ft. Leonard Wood, Mo., topog. engr., Ft. Blevoir, Va. Exhibitions include watercolors, archtl. drawings and photography, Monograph and Retrospective Arch. Exhibit: "I" Space Gallery, Chgo., 1997, U. Ill. Temple Buell Arch. Gallery, 1998, Temple Buell Hall Gallery, 2000, Japanese House Drawings Exhibit, Krannert Art Mus., U. Ill., 1998; contbr. articles to numerous jours. and confs. Mem. U. Ill. Pres.'s Coun., U. Ill. Bronze Cir., 1986; mem. mus. bd. and affiliate World Heritage Mus.; former mem. adv. bd. Krannert Ctr. for Performing Arts, Assembly Hall U. Ill.; exhbn. designer World Heritage Mus., U. Ill. Served with U.S. Army, AFH, 1945-46, Caserta, Italy, ETO. Recipient "prix d'Emulation Societe des Architectes Diplomes par le Gouvernment" Beaux-Arts medal, 1942, cert. for dedicated and disting. svc., Nat. AIA Com. on Environ. and Design, 1955, Decade of Achievement award, World Heritage Mus., 1992, Art and Humanities award, 1981, 1982, Honor award for advancing profession architecture, CIC/AIA, 1983, Excellence in Edn. award and medal, IC/AIA, 1989, Heritage award, PACA, 1997, numerous other honors and design excellence awards in field, Recognition award, U. Ill. Found., 2001. Fellow: AIA (medal 1977), Nat. Coun. Archtl. Registration Bds. (cert.); mem.: Soc. Archtl. Historians, Ill. Coun./AIA, The Nature Conservancy, Nat. Resources Def. Coun., Gargoyle, Scarab, Cliff Dwellers Club (Chgo.), Alpha Rho Chi. Home: 71 1/2 E Chester St Champaign IL 61820-4149 Office: U Ill 117 Temple Hoyne Buell Hall 611 Taft Dr MC-621 Champaign IL 61820-6922 Office Phone: 217-333-1330.

BAKER, JACK THOMAS, design engineer; b. Nov. 7, 1924; s. George J. and Oneta L. Baker; m. Sylvia E. Tofte, July 1, 1971; children: Frances, Robert, Catherine, Cynthia, Christine, Jason, Justin. BS, U.S. Maritime Acad., 1945; ME, Stevens Inst. Tech., 1949. Cons. design engr. Sebco Mfg. Co., Greenwich, NY, 1964—74; v.p. gen. mgr. Universal Convection Corp., 1975—91; cons. All Phase Corp., 1992—98; design engr. Miller Mechanical Svcs. Corp., Greenwich, 1998—. V.p., gen. mgr. Universal Convection Corp., pres., chief exec. officer; cons. in field. Author articles on waste energy recovery. Achievements include patents for energy recovery and the environment.

BAKER, JAMES ADDISON, III, ambassador, lawyer, former secretary of state; b. Houston, Apr. 28, 1930; s. James A. and Bonner (Means) B.; m. Susan Garrett, Aug. 6, 1973; 8 children. BA, Princeton U., 1952; LL.B., U. Tex., 1957. Bar: Tex. 1957. Assoc. Andrews Kurth Campbell & Jones, Houston, 1957-81; undersec. US Dept. Commerce, Washington, 1975-76; deputy chmn. del. ops. Pres. Ford Com., Washington, 1976; campaign chmn. George Bush, 1979-80; sr. adviser Reagan-Bush Com., 1980-81; mem. Reagan Transition Team, Washington, 1980-81; chief of staff The White House, Washington, 1981-85; sec. US Dept. Treasury, 1985-88; campaign chmn. George Bush's Presdl. campaign, 1988; sec. US Dept. State, Washington, 1989-92; chief of staff, sr. counselor to Pres. The White House, Washington, 1992-93; sr. ptnr. Baker & Botts, L.L.P., Washington and Houston, 1993—; spl. envoy to Iraqi for debt reduction, 2003—. Hon. chmn. James A. Baker III Inst. for Public Policy Rice U., 1993—; sr. counselor, The Carlyle Group, 1993-. Trustee Woodrow Wilson Internat. Ctr. for Scholars, Smithsonian Inst., 1977—; bd. dirs. Rice U., hon. chmn. James A. Baker III Inst. for Pub. Policy, 1993—. Recipient Presdl. Freedom medal Pres. Bush, 1991, Woodrow Wilson award Princeton U., Jefferson award The Am. Inst. for Pub. Svcs., John F. Kennedy Sch. Govt. award Harvard U., The Hans J. Morganthau award, The George F. Kennan award, Alexander Hamilton award Dept. Treasury, Disting. Svc. award Dept. State. Mem. ABA, Tex. Bar Assn., Houston Bar Assn., Am. Judicature Soc., Phi Delta Phi, bd. dirs, Electronic Data Corp., 1996-2003. Avocations: hunting, fishing, tennis, golf. Office: Baker & Botts LLP 1 Shell Plz 910 Louisiana Houston TX 77002 also: The Carlyle Group 1001 Pennsylvania Ave NW Ste 220 S Washington DC 20004-2505*

BAKER, JAMES BARNES, architect; b. N.Y.C., Feb. 18, 1933; s. William Edgar and Violet (Twachtman) B.; children: Mary Morgan, James Edgar, Catriona Griswold, Frederick Alden; m. Rosemary Burgis, June 14, 1997 (dec. 2001). AB, Princeton U., 1954; M.Arch., Yale U., 1960. With firms Blake & Neski, N.Y.C., 1960-62, George Lewis, N.Y.C., 1962-63, Kahn & Jacobs, N.Y.C., 1963-64; ptnr. firm Baker & Blake, N.Y.C., 1964-72, Baker/Grinnell, N.Y.C., 1972-74; cons., 1974-77; dir. Llewelyn Davies Assocs., N.Y.C., 1976-78; pres. Tower Devel. Group Inc., Ohio, 1978-83, Park-Tower Devel. Co., Ltd., Bermuda, 1978-83, Springland Assocs, Inc., 1983-90; prin. Baker & Baker, Architects, N.Y.C., 1990—; pres. Tech. Panel Systems, 1992-93; mng. dir. William McDonough Archs., 1993-94, Forge Co., N.Y.C., 2002; chief exec. Forge Llewellyn, London, 1994—2004, The Forge Co. LTD, 2004—. Vis. prof. Sch. Architecture, CUNY, 1964-89. Trustee Darrow Sch., Mt. Lebanon Shaker Village. Recipient design awards HUD, others. Fellow AIA (bd. dirs., design awards, pres., 2005—); mem. Am. Arbitration Assn., Holland Soc., St. Nicholas Soc., Squadron A. also: Worchippuc Co of Chartered Arch Crossways House Mayfield Sussex TN20 GAB England

BAKER, JAMES EDGAR, federal judge, law educator; BA, Yale, 1982; JD, Yale, 1990. Attorney adviser Law Enforcement and Intelligence, U.S. Dept. of State, 1990—93; atty. advisor Oceans and Internat. Environ. & Scientific Affairs US Dept. of State, 1993; deputy legal adviser NSC, Washington, 1994—97; special asst., legal adviser to Pres. The White House, Washington, 1997—2000; judge US Ct. Appeals for the Armed Forces, Washington,

2000—. Vis. lecturer Yale Law Sch. Co-author (with W.M. Reisman): (non-fiction) Regulating Covert Action, 1992. Office: US Ct Appeals Armed Forces 450 E St NW Washington DC 20442 also: Yale Law Sch PO Box 208215 New Haven CT 06520 E-mail: james.baker@yale.edu.

BAKER, JAMES EDWARD, city planner; b. San Antonio, Tex., Aug. 4, 1961; s. Jim and Dora Pitts B. BA, BBA, BFA, So. Meth. U., 1983; MS, Trinity U., San Antonio, Tex., 1995, U. Tex., 1997; student, U. Phoenix Online, 2001—. Tech. writer II JANA, Inc., San Antonio, 1985-86; adminstrv. asst. United Svcs. Automobile Assn., San Antonio, 1987-89; Brackenridge fellow Trinity U., San Antonio, 1993-95; HUD fellow U. Tex., Austin, 1995-97; city planner City of New Braunfels, Tex., 1997-2000; devel. planner City of Georgetown, Tex., 2000; sr. planner City of Dallas, Tex., 2001—05; diversity fellow Tex. A&M U., Coll. Sta., Tex., 2005—. Presenter in polit. sci. Mem. emerging leaders program Nat. Congress Cmty. Econ. Devel., 2001. With U.S. Army, 1989—93, with USAR, 1993—2004, with USAFR, 2004—. Decorated 3 Army Commendation medals, 3 Army Achievement medals, Kuwait Liberation medal, Joint Svc. Achievement medal, Joint Meritorious Unit award, Good Conduct medal, Army Reserve Component Achievement medal, Nat. Def. Svc. medal, Armed Forces Expeditionary medal, S.W. Asia Svc. medal, Global War on Terrorism Expeditionary medal, Armed Forces Svc. medal, Army Res. Components Overseas Tng. Ribbon, Army Forces Res. medal with 2 M Devices, Army Non-commn. Officer Profl. Devel. ribbon, Small Arms Expert Marksmanship Rifle ribbon, Army Svc. ribbon, NATO medal, Kuwait Liberation medal Kingdom Saudi Arabia, Govt. Kuwait, AF outstanding Unit award; recipient Global War on Terrorism Svc. medal. Mem. Air Force Sgts. Assn., VFW, Am. Inst. Cert. Planners, Kiwanis, Prince Hall Freemasons, Delta Sigma Phi (pres. Lambda chpt. 1981-82). Avocations: outdoor photography, wing chun, weight tng.

BAKER, JAMES EDWARD SPROUL, retired lawyer; b. Evanston, Ill., May 23, 1912; s. John Clark and Hester (Sproul) B.; m. Eleanor Lee Dodgson, Oct. 2, 1937 (dec. Sept. 1972); children: John Lee, Edward Graham (dec. Aug. 1988). AB, Northwestern U., 1933, JD, 1936. Bar: Ill. 1936, U.S. Supreme Ct. 1957. Practice in, Chgo., 1936—; assoc. Sidley & Austin, and predecessors, 1936—48, ptnr., 1948—81; of counsel Sidley Austin Brown and Wood, 1981—93. Lectr. Northwestern U. Law Sch., 1951-52; nat. chmn. Stanford U. Parents Com., 1970-75; mem. vis. com. Stanford Law Sch., 1976-79, 82-84, Northwestern U. Law Sch., 1980-89, DePaul U. Law Sch., 1982-87. Served to comdr. USNR, 1941-46. Fellow: Am. Coll. Trial Lawyers (regent 1974—81, sec. 1977—79, pres. 1979—80); mem.: ABA, Soc. Trial Lawyers Ill., Chgo. Bar Assn., Ill. State Bar Assn., Bar Assn. 7th Fed. Cir., Northwestern U. Law Alumni Assn. (past pres.), Pauma Valley Country Club (Calif.), Lawyers Club (Chgo.), Univ. Club (Chgo.), John Evans Club (chmn. 1982—85, Northwestern U.), John Henry Wigmore Club (past pres.), Law Club (pres. 1983—85, Chgo.), Westmoreland Country Club (Wilmette, Ill.), Sigma Nu, Phi Lambda Upsilon, Order of Coif. Republican. Methodist. Office: Sidley Austin Brown & Wood Bank One Plz 10 S Dearborn St Chicago IL 60603

BAKER, JAMES L., JR., plastic surgeon; b. Somerville, N.J., 1936; MD, U. Amsterdam, 1964. Cert. in Plastic Surgery 1973. Intern Monmouth Med. Ctr., Long Branch, NJ, 1964—65, resident, gen. surgery, 1965—69; resident, plastic surgery Orlando Regional Med. Ctr., Fla., 1969—71; fellow, hand surgery U. Louisville, 1971; clin. prof., surgery, divsn. plastic surgery U. S. Fla., 1991—; pvt. practice. Mem.: Am. Soc. for Aesthetic Plastic Surgery (co-chair, breast surgery com.). Office: 400 W Morse Blvd Ste 203 Winter Park FL 32789-4280

BAKER, JAMES P., lawyer; b. Washington, 1952; m. Elizabeth Baker. BA, U. Santa Clara, Calif., 1975, JD, 1980; LLM, Georgetown U., 1982. Bar: Calif. 1980. Ptnr. Brobeck, Phleger & Harrison, San Francisco, 1999—2003, Orrick, Herrington & Sutcliffe LLP, San Francisco, 2003—05, Jones Day, San Francisco, 2005—. Office: Jones Day 555 California St Fl 26 San Francisco CA 94104-1500 Office Phone: 415-626-3939. Business E-Mail: jbaker@jonesday.com.

BAKER, JANE E., secondary school educator; b. Birmingham, Ala., Sept. 13, 1956; d. John R. and Betty (Cockrell) B. BS, Auburn U., 1978; MA, U. Montevello, 1991. Tchr. Minor Jr. High Sch., Edgewater Jr. High Sch., Birmingham; instr. spl. studies U. Ala., Birmingham; tchr. Warrior (Ala.) Middle Sch.; second mile tchr. Jefco Bd. Edn., Birmingham, 1990; tchr. Bottenfield Jr. High Sch.; asst. prin. Shades Valley high Sch./Jefferson County Internat. Baccalaureate Sch.; prin. Minor Jr. High Sch., Gresham Mid. Sch., Shades Valley High Sch. Mem. Am. Heart Assn., Middle Sch. Study, Am. Cancer Soc., Nat. Mid. Sch. Assn., Nat. Assn. Secondary Sch. Prins., Ala. Assn. Secondary Sch. Prins.

BAKER, JEAN HARVEY, history professor; b. Balt., Feb. 9, 1933; d. F. Barton and Rose (Lindsay) Hopkins Harvey; m. R. Robinson Baker, Sept. 12, 1953; children— Susan Dixon, Robinson Scott, Robert W., Jean Harvey. AB, Goucher Coll., Towson, Md., 1961; MA, Johns Hopkins U., Balt., 1965, PhD, 1971. Lectr., instr. history Notre Dame Coll., Balt., 1967-69; instr. history Goucher Coll., Balt., 1969, asst. prof. history, 1969-75, assoc. prof. history, 1975-78, prof. history, 1979-82, Elizabeth Todd prof. history, 1981—. Author: The Politics of Continuity, 1973, Ambivalent Americans, 1976, Affairs of Party, 1983, Maryland: A History, Mary Todd Lincoln: A Biography, 1986, The Stevensons: A Family Biography, 1995, Sisters: The lives of American Suffragists, 2005; co-author: Civil War and Reconstruction, 2002; editor: Md. Hist. Mag., 1979, Votes for Women: The Suffrage Battle Revisited, 2001, James Buchanan, 2004. Am. Coun. Learned Socs. fellow, 1976, NEH fellow, 1982, Newberry Libr. fellow, 1991, Rockefeller Found. fellow, 1998; recipient Faculty Teaching prize Goucher Coll., 1979, Willie Lee Rose prize in Southern history, 1989. Mem.: Am. Hist. Assn., Orgn. Am. Historians, Berkshire Conf. Women Historians, Phi Beta Kappa. Democrat. Office: Goucher Coll History Dept 1021 Dulaney Valley Towson MD 21204 Office Phone: 410-337-6267. Business E-Mail: jbaker@goucher.edu.

BAKER, JEAN MORRISON, writer; b. Mustang, Colo., Dec. 31, 1923; d. Henry Star Morrison and Mary Elton Morrison Chamblin; m. Claude William Baker (dec.); children: Rodney Lee, Claudia Jean. BA, U. Mo., Kansas City, 1985. Ednl. sec. Kansas City (Mo.) Sch. Dist., 1960-85; writer, 1985—. Pres., sec. assoc. Kansas City (Mo.) Sch. Dist., 1976, 83. Author: (book) Old Spoons, 1996 (Thornton Menn award runner-up 1996); contbr. poetry to anthologies. Vol. Peace Corps, Ghana, Africa, 1973-74. Mem. Internat. Rels. Coun., Nat. League Am. PEN Women, Inc., Returned Peace Corps Vols. Democrat. Avocations: reading, writing, hiking, theater, travel, family. Home: 2600 NW Vesper St Blue Springs MO 64015-3357

BAKER, JIMMY H., former state finance administrator; BA, Troy State U.; Master degree, Auburn U. Asst. state supt. Dept. Edn., Montgomery, Ala., dep. supt. edn. adminstrv. and fin. svcs.; dir. fin. State of Ala., Montgomery. Office: 105 N State Capitol 600 Dexter Ave Montgomery AL 36104-3734

BAKER, JOANNE EVELYN, retired government agency administrator; b. Crucible, Pa., Dec. 1, 1933; d. George Joseph and Anna Leona (Kagle) Cormack; m. Warren Clair Baker, July 7, 1956 (dec. May 1968); m. James Lewis Wilson, June 2, 1970; (div. Sept. 1984); former stepchildren: James Lloyd, John Thomas, Charles Edward, Debra Ruth, Jeff Lee Wilson Cert. applied music, Waynesburg Coll., 1951. Various clerical positions including Exec. Offices Pres., Washington, 1951-66; supr. USN, Washington, 1966-71; pres., treas. Little Round Top Farm, Inc., Gettysburg, Pa., 1971-86; logistician USN-U.S. Army, Gettysburg, Pa., 1974—90, ret., 1990. Program mgr. electronic comm. end items and for Ship Alterations (SHIPALT), 1974-77, Ship Parts Control Ctr. (SPCC), Mechanicsburg, Pa., Army Stock Fund program mgr., 1977-80, 84-90, chief consolidated property account (CPA), 1980-81, U.S. Army Garrison (USAG), Ft. Ritchie, Md.; insp. Office of Insp. Gen. 7th Signal Command, U.S. Army, Ft. Ritchie, Md., 1981-84; chief supply and svcs. divsn., 1984-89, chief plans and resources mgmt. divsn., 1989-90; logistics directorate USAG, Ft. Detrick, Frederick, Md.; mgmt. cons., 1991-. Author: Reflections, 1974 Bd. dirs. Adams County Mental Health Assn., Gettysburg, 1982-87 Recipient Sustained Superior Achievement award Dept. Navy, 1975, Dept. of Army 1986; named Outstanding Woman of Yr. Ft. Detrick, 1986, recipient Comdr.'s award, 1990. Mem. World Inst. of Achievement (life). Roman Catholic. Avocations: handwriting analysis, writing children's stories, ceramics, piano, studying self-improvement and psychology. Home: 5605 Shookstown Rd Frederick MD 21702-2704

BAKER, JOHN EDWARD, cardiac biochemist, educator; b. London, Eng., Dec. 12, 1954; arrived in U.S., 1984; s. Edward D. and Florence I. (Dobson) Baker; m. Mary E. Zurawski, Oct. 29, 1988; children: David J., Elizabeth A. BSc, Poly. Wolverhampton, Eng., 1977; PhD, St. Thomas' Med. Sch., London, 1984. Sr. biochemist Cen. Pathology Labs., London, 1977-78; rsch. asst. St. Thomas' Hosp. Med. Sch., London, 1978-84; rsch. fellow Med. Coll. Wis., Milw., 1984-86, vis. prof., 1986-87, asst. prof. cardiothoracic surgery, 1987-92, assoc. prof., 1992-99, assoc. prof. pediat. surgery, biochemistry, pharmacology, 1999-2001, prof., 2001—. Mem. peer rev. rsch. com. NIH, 2002—. Mem. editl. bd.: Am. Jour. Physiology, Heart and Circulatory Physiology, Jour. Molecular and Cellular Cardiology; contbr. articles to profl. jours. Founder Heart Sci. Found., Ltd.; bd. dirs., v.p. Adelaide Banaszynski Sch. Piano Studies. Grantee, NIH, 1989, 1990, 1993, 1997, 2000, 2001, Culpeper Found., 1987, Ronald McDonald Children's Charities, 1989, 1991, Children's Hosp. Found., 1995. Mem.: Am. Heart Assn. (mem. peer rev. rsch. com. Wis. affiliate 1989—93, mem. peer rev. rsch. com. Northland affiliate 1999—2001, mem. coun. basic. sci., mem. Nat. Inst. of Health Study Sections 2002—). Methodist. Achievements include patents for method for sealing blood vessel puncture sites and method for coating intraluminal stents. Avocations: walking, music. Office: Med Coll Wis 8701 W Watertown Plank Rd Milwaukee WI 53226-3548 Office Phone: 414-456-8706. Business E-Mail: jbaker@mcw.edu.

BAKER, JOHN GREGORY, psychologist, educator; b. Buffalo; BA, Canisius Coll.; MA, SUNY, Buffalo, 1983, PhD, 1988. Bd. cert. in clin. health psychology. Rsch. asoc., adj. asst. prof. Calif. State U., Long Beach, 1989-90; staff psychologist Rancho Los Amigos Med. Ctr., Downey, Calif., 1990-94; clin. asst. prof. SUNY Buffalo Sch. Medicine, 1994—. Contbr. chpt. to book, articles to profl. jours. Recipient Mary E. Switzer Disting. Rsch. award Nat. Inst. on Disability and Rehab. Rsch., 1996; NIH fellow in med. rehab. rsch., 1994, fellow in outcomes rsch. Kessler Inst. for Rehab., U. Medicine and Dentistry of N.J., 1997. Fellow Am. Acad. Clin. Health Psychology; mem. APA. Office: SUNY Buffalo ECMC Rehab Medicine 462 Grider St Buffalo NY 14215-3021

BAKER, JOHN MILNES, architect; b. Port Jefferson, NY, Oct. 15, 1932; s. Alan Griffin and Lucy Hayden (Milnes) B.; m. Virginia Lea Busser (div. 1969); children: Ian Archbald, Jennifer Lea (Mrs. Christopher Warren); m. Elizabeth Jennings Morrison, Jan. 17, 1970; children: James Morrison, Hayden Sheffield. BA, Middlebury Coll., 1955; March, Columbia U., 1960. Designer, draftsman Sir Basil Spence, London, 1960-61; project mgr., later project architect Rogers & Butler, N.Y.C., 1962-64; project architect John A. Pruyn, AIA, N.Y.C., 1965-66; pvt. practice architecture N.Y.C., 1967-68, 75-79; ptnr. Manice & Baker, N.Y.C., 1968-74; pvt. practice architecture specializing in residential design Katonah, N.Y., 1979—. Pres. J.M. Baker Houses Inc.; lectr. New Sch. for Social Rsch., N.Y.C. Author: How to Build a House with an Architect, 1977, rev. edit., 1988, The Baker Family and the Edgar Family of Rahway, N.J. and New York City, 1972, American House Styles: A Concise Guide, 1994. Past trustee N.Y. Revels Inc.; past trustee Bedford Free Libr.; mem. Katonah Hist. Dist. Adv. Commn., Town of Bedford, Historic Buildings Preservation Commn. Home designs included among Better Homes and Garden Top Ten Homes Plans, 1982; 3 designs selected by USIA for Design U.S.A., a traveling exhibit in USSR, 1989-90. Mem. AIA, Nat. Coun. Archtl. Registration Bds., Am. Arbitration Assn. (panel mem.), Soc. Archtl. Hists., St. Nicholas Soc. (past pres.), Holland Soc. N.Y. (past trustee), St. Andrews Soc., Colonial Lords of Manors in Am. (v.p.), New Eng. Soc., Order Founders and Patriots, Soc. Colonial Wars, Pilgrims, Corinthians, Coffee House, Squadron A, Century Assn. (N.Y.C.), Bellport Bay Yacht (Club past trustee), Bedford Golf and Tennis Club, Norwalk Yacht Club. Home: Rivendell Girdle Ridge Rd Katonah NY 10536 Office: 85 Girdle Ridge Rd Katonah NY 10536-3814 E-mail: jmbaker@bestweb.net.

BAKER, JOHN RUSSELL, utilities executive; b. Lexington, Mo., July 21, 1926; s. William Frederick and Flora Anne (Dunford) B.; m. Elizabeth Jane Torrence, June 16, 1948; children— John Russell, Burton T. BS, U. Mo., 1948, MBA, 1962. With Mo. Public Service Co., Kansas City, 1948—, treas., 1966-68, v.p. fin., 1968-71, sr. v.p., 1971-73, exec. v.p., 1973—, also dir. Lectr. fin. U. Mo.; vice-chmn. Aquila Inc., 1991—. Vice-pres. Mid-Continent coun. Girl Scouts U.S., 1981; mem. adv. coun. Sch. Acctg., U. Mo., Columbia. Recipient Outstanding alumnus award Sch. Adminstrn. U. Mo., Kansas City, 1965; citation of merit U. Mo., 1995. Mem. Tax Execs. Inst. (pres. Kansas City 1968), U. Mo. Sch. Adminstrn. Alumni Assn. (pres. 1965). Clubs: Kansas City. Republican. Methodist. Home: 205 NW Oxford Ln Lees Summit MO 64063-2118 Office: Aquila Inc 20 W 9th St Kansas City MO 64105-1704

BAKER, JOHN STEVENSON (MICHAEL DYREGROV), writer; b. Mpls., June 18, 1931; s. Everette Barrette and Ione May (Kadletz) B. BA cum laude, Pomona Coll., Claremont Colls., 1953; MD, U. Calif. at Berkeley and San Francisco, 1957. Writer, 1958—; book cataloger Walker Art Center, Mpls., 1958-59; editor, writer neurol. rsch. articles Lewis E. Phillips Psychobiol. Rsch. Fund, Mpls., 1960—61. Contbr. articles and poetry to various publs. in Eng. and U.S.; author 65 pub. poems, 21 short essays and 10 sets of aphorisms. Donor numerous species of native plants and seeds to Minn. Landscape Arboretum, U.S. Nat. Arboretum and Arnold Arboretum, Harvard U., papers of LeRoi Jones and Hart Crane to Yale U., Brahms recs. to Bennington Coll., several others; pres. Mission Lakes Assn., Merrifield, Minn., 1989-90. Recipient Disting. Service award Minn. State Hort. Soc., 1976; Cert. of Appreciation U.S. Nat. Arboretum, 1978; property registered as a Minn. Natural Area Minn. chpt. Nature Conservancy, 1990. Mem. Ctr. for Plant Conservation, Nat. Audubon Soc., Nature Conservancy, Nat. Mus. Am. Indian, Nat. Trust for Hist. Preservation, Met. Opera Guild, Phi Chi, Nu Sigma Nu. Office: PO Box 16007 Minneapolis MN 55416-9998

BAKER, JONATHAN RAMON, mathematics educator; b. Atlanta, Ga., July 3, 1974; s. Johnny and Joyce Baker; m. Courtney Anne Marks, Mar. 21, 1998; 1 child, Sophia. BA, Northwestern U., Evanston, Ill., 1994; MA, post grad., Ohio State U., Columbus, 1996—. Tchg. asst. Ohio State U., Columbus, 1994—96; instr. math. Columbus State C.C., 1996—. Advisor Campus Outreach, Columbus, 2001—. Vol. Big Brothers Big Sisters, 2001—; ministry leader S.E. Columbus Columbus Ch. of Christ, 1998—, mem. bd. dir., 2001—. Finalist Disting. Tchr. award, Columbus State C.C., 1999. Mem.: Am. Statis. Assn., Alpha Phi Alpha. Avocations: basketball, reading, family activities. Home: 1816 Rock Creek Dr Grove City OH 43123-1584 Office: Columbus State CC Davidson Hall #416 550 E Spring St Columbus OH 43215 E-mail: jbaker03@cscc.edu.

BAKER, JOSEPH RODERICK, III, aviculturist; b. Middletown, Ohio, Sept. 26, 1947; s. Joseph Roderick and Lois Patricia (Barnhart) B. BS in Math., Rensselaer Poly. Tech., 1969. Systems rep. Burroughs Corp., Honolulu, 1973-80; mgr. data processing Kenault Inc., Honolulu, 1980-81; v.p. Software Solutions Inc., Honolulu, 1982-83; br. mgr. DataPhase Corp., Honolulu, 1983-88; pres. Birds of Paradise, Kurtistown, Hawaii, 1987—. Lt. (j.g.) USN, 1969-73. Mem. Am. Fedn. Aviculture, Nat. Cockatoo Soc., Macaw Soc. Am., Eclectus Soc. (bd. dirs.), Am. Contract Bridge League, Pionus Breeders Assn., Amazona Soc., Pyrrhura Breeders Assn., Pionus Parrot Rsch. Found., Inc., Aviculture Microbiology Found., Inc. Avocation: bridge. Office Phone: 808-966-6966. E-mail: bopahi@aol.com.

BAKER, JUDITH ANN, retired computer technician; b. Junction City, Kans., Mar. 2, 1947; d. David Daniel and Mildred Elaine Bates; m. Jimmy Ray Baker, Oct. 8, 1972; 1 child, Jimmy Ray Jr. Student, East Ctrl. U., 1993—98; postgrad., Tulsa C.C., 1999—. Cert. travel and tourism Draughon Coll., 1988. ADA support group leader; newsletter editor Multiple Sclerosis Assn. Am., Okla., 1995—. Leader support group Multiple Sclerosis Soc. Am., Ada, Okla., 2000—. Recipient Best Support Group Leader award S.E. region and 10 state area, Multiple Sclerosis Soc. Am., 2004. Mem.: Ada Writing Club. Avocations: writing, painting, crafts, decorating. Home: 3816 US Hwy 377 Ada OK 74820 Office Phone: 580-310-0181. E-mail: paradise@adacomp.net.

BAKER, KATHY WHITTON, actress; b. Midland, Tex., June 8, 1950; Appearances include (theatre) Fool for Love, 1983 (Obie award 1983, Theatre World award 1984), Desire Under the Elms, 1984, Aunt Dan and Lemon, 1986, (films) The Right Stuff, 1983, Street Smart, 1987 (Nat. Soc. Film Critics Best Supporting Actress award 1987), Permanent Record, 1988, A Killing Affair, 1988, Clean and Sober, 1988, Jacknife, 1989, Dad, 1989, Mr. Frost, 1989, Edward Scissorhands, 1990, Article 99, 1992, Jennifer 8, 1992, Mad Dog and Glory, 1993, To Gillian on Her 37th Birthday, 1996, Inventing the Abbotts, 1997, The Cider House Rules, 1999, Things You Can Tell Just By Looking at Her, 2000, The Glass House, 2001, Ten Tiny Love Stories, 2001, Assassination Tango, 2002, Cold Mountain, 2003 (TV movies) Nobody's Child, 1986, The Image, 1990, One Special Victory, 1991, Weapons of Mass Distraction, 1997, Oklahoma City: A Survivor's Story, 1998, Lush Life, 1993, Not in This Town, 1997, ATF, 1998, A Season of Miracles, 1999, Sanctuary, 2001, Door to Door, 2002, Too Young to Be a Dad, 2002 (TV series) Picket Fences, 1992-1996 (Emmy award Outstanding Lead Actress in a Drama Series, 1993, 1995, Golden Globe award, Best Actress in a TV Drama Series, 1994), Boston Public, 2001-2002, Murphy's Dozen, 2003. Office: ICM Rep Corey Weissman 8942 Wilshire Blvd Beverly Hills CA 90211-1934

BAKER, KEITH MICHAEL, history professor; b. Swindon, England, Aug. 7, 1938; arrived in US, 1964; s. Raymond Eric and Winifred Evelyn (Shepherd) B.; m. Therese Louise Elzas, Oct. 25, 1961 (div. 1999); children— Julian, Felix. BA, Cambridge U., 1960, MA, 1963; postgrad., Cornell U., 1960-61; PhD, U. London, 1964. Instr. history and humanities Reed Coll., 1964-65; asst. prof. European history U. Chgo., 1965-71, assoc. prof., 1971-76, prof., 1977-89, master collegiate div. social scis., 1975-78, assoc. dean coll., 1975-78, assoc. dean div. social scis., 1975-78, chmn. commn. grad. edn., 1980-82; chmn. Council Advanced Studies in Humanities and Social Scis., 1982-86; prof. European history Stanford U., 1989—, J.E. Wallace Sterling prof. in humanities, 1992—, chair dept. history, 1994-95; Anthony P. Meier family prof. humanities, dir. Stanford Humanities Ctr., 1995-2000, cognizant dean humanities, 2000—03; dir. France-Stanford Ctr. for Interdisciplinary Studies, 2002—. Vis. assoc. prof. history Yale U., 1974; mem. Inst. Advanced Study, Princeton (N.J.), 1979-80; vis. prof., dir. studies Ecole des Hautes Etudes en Scis. Sociales, Paris, 1982, 84, 91; fellow Ctr. for Advanced Study in Behavioral Scis., Stanford (Calif.) U., 1986-87; vis. prof. UCLA, 1989; vis. fellow Clare Hall, Cambridge (Eng.) U., 1994; chair scholars com. Am. Com. on the French Revolution, 1989. Author: Condorcet: From Natural Philosophy to Social Mathematics, 1975, Inventing the French Revolution, 1990; prin. author: Report Commission on Graduate Education, U. Chgo., 1982; editor: Condorcet: Selected Writings, 1977, The Political Culture of the Old Regime: The Old Regime and the French Revolution, 1987, The Terror, 1994; co-editor Jour. Modern History, 1980-89, What's Left of Enlightenment?, 2001. Decorated chevalier Ordre des Palmes Académiques; fellow, NEH, 1967—68; ACLS study fellow, 1972—73, Guggenheim fellow, 1979. Fellow AAAS, Am. Philos. Soc.; mem. Am. Hist. Assn. (com. on coms. 1991-94), Soc. French History Studies (co-pres. 2005), Am. Soc. for 18th Century Studies (v.p. 1999, pres. 2000-01). Office: Stanford Univ Dept History Stanford CA 94305-2024 Office Phone: 650-723-2651. Business E-Mail: kbaker@stanford.edu.

BAKER, KENDALL L., academic administrator; b. Clearwater, Fla., Nov. 1, 1942; s. Robert B. and Anne E. Baker; m. Tobin Ratliff McGough, Apr. 12, 1981; children: Kraig, Kris, John, Shannon, Brian. BA with honors, U. Md., 1963; MA, Georgetown U., 1967, PhD, 1969. Instr., Dept. Polit. Sci. U. Wyo., Laramie, 1967-69, asst. prof., 1969-73, assoc. prof., 1973-77, prof., 1977-82, chmn., 1979-82, asst. v.p. for Acad. Affairs, 1976-77; dean, Coll. Arts & Scis., Bowling Green State U., Ohio, 1982-87; v.p., provost No. Ill. U., DeKalb, 1987-92; pres. U. N. D., 1992-99, Ohio Northern U, 1999—. Cons. on survey research to various agys. and polit. candidates, 1967—; panel chmn. Rocky Mt. Social Sci. Conv. 1973, We. Social Sci. Conv., 1975, Council Colls. Arts and Scis., 1983, 86; guest participant study trip to Fed. Republic of Germany, 1977; election observer Fed. Republic of Germany, 1980. Author: The Wyoming Legislature: Lawmakers, the Public, and the Press, 1973; (with R. Dalton and K. Hildebrandt) Germany Transformed: Political Culture and the New Politics, 1981; contbr. articles on polit. sci. to profl. jours. Coach Laramie Soccer Assn., 1978-81. Mem. Am. Polit. Sci. Assn. (chmn. panel ann. conv. 1983), Midwest Polit. Sci. Assn. (chmn. panel ann. conv. 1985, 86), Conf. Group on German Politcs (exec. com. 1984-87, co-editor newsletter 1985-91), Phi Kappa Phi, Omicron Delta Kappa, Pi Sigma Alpha. Home: 920 West Lima Ada OH 45810 Office: President's Office 525 S Main St Ada OH 45810-1599 Office Phone: 419-772-2030. Business E-Mail: k.baker@onu.edu.

BAKER, KENT ALFRED, broadcasting executive, publishing company executive; b. Sioux City, Iowa, Mar. 22, 1948; s. Carl Edmund Baker and Miriam M. (Hawthorn) Baker Nye. Student, Iowa State U., 1966-70. Editor Iowa State Daily, 1969-70; mem. U.S. Peace Corps., 1971-72; editor The Glidden (Iowa) Graphic, 1973-75; bur. chief The Waterloo (Iowa) Courier, Iowa, 1975; state editor The Des Moines Register, 1976-77; news dir. Sta. WQAD-TV, Moline, Ill., 1978; Sunday editor The Des Moines Sunday Register, 1979; news dir. Sta. KHON-TV, Honolulu, 1980-95; v.p., gen. mgr. KHON-TV, Honolulu, 1996-2000; pres. Baker Newspapers, 2000—. Pub. The Moville Record, 2000—. Mem. Hoover Libr. Assn., Iowa State U. Alumni Assn., Iowa Newspaper Assn., Iowa Hist. Soc. Office: The Moville Record 12 South Second St Moville IA 51039 Home: PO Box Moville IA 51039 E-mail: record@netins.net.

BAKER, KERRY ALLEN, management consultant; b. Selmer, Tenn., Sept. 21, 1949; s. Austin Clark and Betty Ann (Brooks) B.; m. Ellen Fleming. BIE, Ga. Inst. Tech., 1971; MBA, Ga. State U., 1973; JD, Memphis State U., 1987. With dept. law State of Ga., 1971—73; engr. N.W. Ga. divsn. Gold Kist Inc., Ellijay, 1977—80; sr. mfg. engr. Plough, Inc., Memphis, 1980—82, mgr. indsl. engring., 1983—86, supr. mfg. engr., 1986—90; mgr. plant bus. Clorox Co., Dyersburg, Tenn., 1990—95; mgr. ops. Huish Detergents, Inc., Dyersburg, 1995; exec. dir. Mgmt. Recruiters of Dyersburg, 1996—97; mgr. adminstrn. Gabriel Ride Products, Pulaski, Tenn., 1998—99; pres. Rock Ridge Ventures, Inc., Dyersburg, 1997—; contr. Mahle Motorsports, Inc., Fletcher, NC, 2000—. Decorated Order of St. Barbara. Mem. Inst. Indsl. Engrs., Am. Prodn. and Inventory Control Soc., Scabbard and Blade, Masons, Phi Delta Phi. Methodist. Home: PO Box 87 Arden NC 28704-0087 Business E-Mail: kerry.baker@us.mahle.com. E-mail: kbaker151@earthlink.net.

BAKER, LEE EDWARD, biomedical engineering educator; b. Springfield, Mo., Aug. 31, 1924; s. Edward Fielding and Oneita Geneva (Patton) B.; m. Jeanne Carolyn Ferbrache, June 20, 1948; children: Carson Phillips, Carolyn Patton. BEE, U. Kans., 1945; MEE, Rice U., 1960; PhD in Physiology, Baylor U., 1965. Registered profl. engr., Tex. Asst. prof. electrical engring. Rice U., Houston, 1960-64; asst. prof. physiology Baylor U. Coll. Medicine, Houston, 1965-69, assoc. prof., 1969-75; prof. biomed. engring. U. Tex., 1975-82, Robert L. Parker Sr. Centennial Prof. Engring. Austin, 1982-2000, prof. emeritus, 2000—. Co-author: Principles of Applied Biomedical Engineering, 1968, 3d edit., 1989; author, co-author scientific papers. Served to lt. USN, 1943-46, PTO, 1951-53. Spl. research fellow NIH, 1964-65. Fellow Am. Inst. Med. and Biol. Engring., Royal Soc. Medicine; mem. IEEE (sr.), Biomed. Engring. Soc. (sr.), Am. Physiol. Soc. Avocation: gardening. Office: Univ Tex ENS 610 Biomed Engring Program Austin TX 78712

BAKER, LEONARD MORTON, manufacturing executive; b. Medford, Mass., Oct. 2, 1934; s. Abraham and Sarah B.; m. Ruth Lee Edelstein, June 15, 1958; children: Charles Harold, Andrew Mark, Douglas Jon. BS in Chemistry, Harvard U., 1956; PhD in Phys.-Organic Chemistry, MIT, 1960. With Union Carbide Corp., 1959-92, assoc. dir., then dir. rsch. and devel., 1969-77, v.p. rsch. and devel. N.Y.C., 1977-80, v.p., gen. mgr. coatings materials div., 1980-82, v.p. splty. chems. div., 1982-84, corporate dir. tech., 1984-86, v.p. splty. and services Bus. Group., 1986, corp. v.p. tech., 1986; sr. v.p. tech., chief tech. officer Praxair, Inc., Danbury, Conn., 1992—2002; cons. Tech. Planning and Assesment, 2003—. Bd. dirs. Rogers (Conn.) Corp. Exec. bd. Cornell Inst. Biotech.; mem. sci. adv. com. MIT; mem. materials sci. adv. bd., vis. com. U. Conn.; industry rep. Nat. Acad.-Industry Program, NRC; industry adv. panel NSF; mem. industry adv. bd. Presdl. Sci. Adv. Commn.; mem. sci. adv. bd. Conn. Coll.; active Nat. Industry Coun. for Sci. Edn., adv. bd. Coun. for Competitiveness Rsch. Devel. MIT fellow, 1956-57; NSF fellow, 1957-58; Sun Oil Corp. fellow, 1958-59 Mem. AICE, N.Y. Acad. Scis. (sci. policy com.), Am. Chem. Soc., Indsl. Rsch. Inst. (fed. sci. and tech. com. pre-coll. edn. com., rsch. com.), Council Chem. Rsch. (gov. bd., univ./industry liaison com.), Soc. Chem. Industry, Dirs. Indsl. Rsch., Am. Mgmt. Assn. (rsch. and devel. council), Conn. Acad. Sci. and Engring., Sigma Xi. Home: 60 Lyons Plains Rd Westport CT 06880-1305 Office: Praxair Inc Old Ridgebury Rd Danbury CT 06817-0001 Personal E-mail: lenmbaker@aol.com.

BAKER, LUCINDA, writer; b. Atlanta, Ill., July 10, 1916; d. Hazle Howard and Adah Rebecca (Mason) B.; m. Willard Alan Greiner, June 27, 1946. Student, Ariz. State Coll., 1934-38. Author: Place of Devils, 1976, Walk the Night Unseen, 1977, Memoirs of First Baroness, 1978, The Painted Lady, 1998; contbr. short stories to mags. Mem. Author's Guild, Mystery Writers Am., Romance Writers Am.

BAKER, LUCY, artist; b. Wellesley, Mass., Feb. 24, 1955; m. Kenworth William Moffett, Apr. 15, 1983 (div. 1990); 1 child; 1 stepdaughter. BFA, Goddard Coll., 1975; cert. welding, Platt Tech., 1977. Represented by Galerie Gerald Piltzer, Paris. Lectr. Fed. Res. Bank, Boston, Cambridge Sch. Weston, 1997. Contbr. to book New, New, Painting, 1992; one woman exhbns. include Waltham (Mass.) Studios, 1981-84, Babson Coll., Wellesley, Mass, 1983, Shippee Gallery, N.Y.C., 1987, Fine art 2000, Stamford, Conn., 1996; group exhbns. include Grand Palais, Paris, 1993, Chgo. Art Fair, 1993, 94, Musee des Beaux-Arts, Charleroi, Belgium, 1993, The Nice (France) Mus., 1993, Stadtische Galerie Goppingen, Ger., 1993, F.I.A.C. French Art Fair, Paris, 1993, N.Y. Art Fair, 1994, Espace Tour Eiffel, Paris, 1994, Salander-O'Reilly Gallery, N.Y.C., 1994 Gallery Galleryism, Seoul, South Korea, 1995, Robert Vanderleelei, Alberta, Can., 1996, Galerie Piltzer, Paris, 1996, Fine Art 2000, 1996, York Coll. CUNY, N.Y.C., 1997, Stamford Ctr. for the Arts, 1997, Palm Beach (Fla.) Mus. Contemporary Art, 1997, Griffis Art Ctr., New London, Conn., 1997, Miami Art Fair, 1997; mem. New New Painters abstract art movement; mem. adv. bd. Woman Mag., 1997-98. Mem. Boston Painters and Sculptors (pres.). Home: 2 Mission St Baltic CT 06330-1213

BAKER, LYNN DALE, lawyer, educator; b. Miles City, Mont., Jan. 11, 1946; s. Robert Franklin and June D. (Babcock) B.; m. Imogene D. Baker, Oct. 8, 1967 (div. 1987); children: Channing Treavor, Chanelle Tete, Cory Justin. BA, U. Mont., 1968, JD, 1986; MA, U. of the Ams., 1970. Bar: Mont. 1986, U.S. Dist. Ct. (fed. dist.) 1986, U.S. Ct. Appeals (9th cir.) 1987. H.s. tchr. The Glenham (S.D.) Sch., 1970-71; linguist, title VII Rocky Boy (Mont.) Schs., 1971-74; prof. edn. U. Alberta, Edmonton, 1974-78; paralegal Hartelius & Ferguson, Great Falls, Mont., 1979-83, atty., 1986-87; ptnr. Hartelius, Ferguson & Baker, Great Falls, 1987-95, Hartelius, Howard, Crosswhite & Baker, LLP, Lakeside, Mont., 1995—. Adj. prof. Coll. of Great Falls, 1991—; cons. bilingual edn. N.W. Regional Ednl. Lab., Portland, Oreg., 1972-74; dir. Far North Ednl. Lab., Edmonton, 1974-79. Nat. Indian Bilingual Edn. Conf., Billings, Mont., 1974; mem. Province of Alberta Cross Cultural Edn. Com., 1974-78; paralegal program adv. com. May Coll., Great Falls, Mont., 1994—. State bd. mem. MS Soc. of Great Falls, 1993—; com. mem. Am. Cancer Soc. Jail-A-Thon, Great Falls, 1987-92; vol. atty. Am. Radio Relay League, Newington, Conn., 1990—; mem. Cascade County Dem. Com., 1992—. Mem. ABA (com. on women and minorities 1992—), Mont. Bar Assn., Am. Trial Lawyers Assn., Mont. Trial Lawyers Assn., Cascade County Bar Assn. Democrat. Avocations: amateur radio (k7luh), paragliding, fishing, teaching, auto racing. Office: Hartelius Ferguson Baker & Kazda 600 Central Ave Great Falls MT 59401-3179

BAKER, LYNNE RUDDER, philosophy educator; b. Atlanta, Feb. 14, 1944; d. James Maclin and Virginia (Bennett) Rudder; m. Thomas B. Baker III, Feb. 1, 1969. BA, Vanderbilt U., 1966, MA, 1971, PhD, 1972; student, Johns Hopkins U., 1967-68. Asst. prof. philosophy Mary Baldwin Coll., Staunton, Va., 1972-76, Middlebury (Vt.) Coll., 1976-79, assoc. prof., 1979-84, prof., 1984-94, acting dean arts and humanities, 1982, chairperson humanities divsn., 1982-85, acting chairperson philosophy, 1986-87; prof. U. Mass., Amherst, 1989—, dir. philosophy grad. program, 1994—. Mem. panel to select summer seminars NEH, Washington, 1982, mem. panel to select fellows, 1989—90; Gifford lectr. U. Glasgow, Scotland, 2001. Author: Saving Belief: A Critique of Physicalism, 1988, Explaining Attitudes: A Practical Approach to the Mind, 1995, Persons and Bodies: A Constitution View, 2000; contbr. scholarly articles to profl. jours. Trustee Vanderbilt U., Nashville, 1969-70, mem. alumni bd. dirs., 1985-89. Mellon fellow, 1974, NEH fellow, 1983-84, Nat. Humanities Ctr. fellow, 1982-83, Woodrow Wilson Internat. Ctr. for Scholars fellow, 1988-89. Mem. Am. Philos. Assn. (program com. 1983, exec. com. 1992-95), Soc. for Philosophy and Psychology, Soc. Christian Philosophers (exec. com. 1992-95), Soc. Women in Philosophy, Phi Beta Kappa. Democrat. Episcopalian. Office: U Mass Dept Philosophy Amherst MA 01003

BAKER, MARIA LUISE, retired secondary school educator; b. Bad Reichenhall, Germany, Oct. 18, 1947; came to U.S., 1948; d. William and Maria Eleanore (Bauer) McStay; m. Clyde Norman Baker, July 29, 1969 (div. Jan. 1975). BA in Spl. Edn., Social Studies, U. No. Colo., 1969. Cert. tchr. secondary social studies/spl. edn. K-12. Tchr. spl. edn. Adams City H.S., Commerce City, Colo., 1969-76, 79-89, tchr. social studies, 1989—; tchr. spl. edn. Adams City Mid. Sch., Commerce City, 1976-79, mentor coord., 2002—03. Performance assistance team, mem. mentor program Adams County Sch. Dist. #14, 1990—; presenter insvcs. in field. Mem. Denver Mus. of Natural History, Denver Art Mus. Recipient Disting. Tchr. award/Colo., 1991-92, A-Plus Tchr. - Channel 4 (NBC), 1994; Title II mini-grantee, Title I grantee. Mem.: Am. Fedn. Tchrs. (v.p. 1979—82, pres. 1993—2001), Nat. Coun. for the Social Studies, Colo. Hist. Soc., Colo. Wildlife Fedn. Avocations: gardening, needlecrafts. Office: Adams City High School 4625 E 68th Ave Commerce City CO 80022-2381 Business E-Mail: mbaker@acsd14.k12.co.us.

BAKER, MARK ALLEN, writer, art historian; b. Binghamton, N.Y., Mar. 27, 1957; s. Ford William and Marilyn A. (Allen) B.; divorced; children: Aaron Anthony, Elizabeth Margaret, Rebecca Jeanne. BA, SUNY, Oswego, 1979. Computer operator Gen. Electric Corp., Liverpool, N.Y., 1980-81, tng. specialist, 1981-82; art dir. Genigraphics Corp., Liverpool, 1982-83, mgr. market rsch., 1983-85, exec. asst. to pres. and CEO, 1985-86, corp. bus. planner, 1986-90. Pvt. rschr., 1986—; historian Internat. Boxing Hall Fame; appeared in numerous pubs. such as USA Today and also on TV, including VH-1. Author: Baseball Autograph Handbook, I and II, 1990, Team Baseballs, All Sport Autograph Guide, 1994, Complete Guide to Boxing Collectibles, 1995, Auto Racing, 1995, Collector's Guide to Celebrity Autographs, 1996, Rock and Roll Memorabilia, 1997, The Standard Guide to Collecting Autographs, 1999, Advanced Autograph Collecting, 1999, Collector's Guide to Celebrity Autographs, 2000, Sports Collectibles, 2001; contbr. articles to profl. jours. Lifetime donor mem. Baseball Hall Fame, Historian Internat. Boxing Hall of Fame. Mem. Am. Mgmt. Assn. (pres. 1985—), Assn. Computer Mfrs. (pres. 1985—), Assn. Med. Illustrators (corp. rep., pres. 1986—), Am. Assn. Individual Investors (pres. 1987—), Siggraph (pres. 1985—), Manuscript Soc. Avocations: forensic document analysis, literature, finance. Address: 7322 Dartmoor Xing Fayetteville NY 13066-2476

BAKER, MARK BRUCE, lawyer, educator; b. Bridgeport, Conn., Dec. 27, 1946; s. Phillip and Lillian (Islovitz) Bader; m. Sandra Fay Wolf, June 9, 1968 (div. 1982); 1 dau. Rachel Barrett Bader; m. Nora Kay Mandell, Dec. 30, 1984; 1 dau. Lisa Anne Baker. BBA, U. Miami, Coral Gables, Fla., 1968; JD, So. Meth. U., 1974. Bar: Tex. 1974. Assoc. firm Herndon, Girand and Dooley, Dallas, 1974-76; ptnr. firm Pailet and Bader, Dallas, 1976-80; prof. internat. law U. Tex., Austin, 1980—; of counsel Bard and Groves, Houston, 1981—83, Goodall and Davison, Austin, 1991—; gen. counsel Embree Constrn. Group, Inc., Austin, Tex., 1987—2000; corp. counsel Kinnect, Inc., A Lloyds of London Co., 2005—. Chmn. bd. Embree Health Care Group, Inc. Contbr. articles to legal publs. Bd. dirs. Jewish Cmty. Coun. Austin, 1983-86, Big Bros./Big Sisters Program, 1999—, Vol. Svcs. of Children's Hosp. of Austin, 2003—. Recipient Outstanding Asst. Prof. award U. Tex., 1982, Outstanding Class Lectr. award, 1984, Tex. Excellence Tchg. award U. Tex. Alumni Assn., 1983. Mem. ABA, Union Internat. des Avocats, Am. Friends Wilton Park (sec.-treas. 1982-84), Tex. Bar Assn. (internat. law sect.), Austin Fgn. Trade Coun., Am. Bus. Law Assn. (internat. law sect., pres. 1990-91). Home: 406 Brookhaven Trl Austin TX 78746-5413 Office: Bldg 3 Ste 601 1250 Capital of Tx Hwy S Austin TX 78746 Office Phone: 512-422-3003. Business E-Mail: m.baker@mail.utexas.edu.

BAKER, MARY ALICE, communications educator, consultant; b. Stuart, Okla., Sept. 9, 1937; d. James Roy and Emma M. (Bird) B. BS, U. Okla., 1959, MA in Speech, 1966; PhD in Comm., Purdue U., 1983. Speech and debate tchr. SE High Sch., Oklahoma City, 1959-65; instr. Ea. Ill. U., Charleston, 1966-69; prof. Lamar U., Beaumont, Tex., 1966-75, 78—, dir. forensics, 1969-75, Regents' Merit prof., 1984, pres. faculty senate, 1986-88. Contbr. articles to profl. jours. Trustee Edn. Com. for Nat. Coun. for Tchr. Retirement Sys., 2003—05; mem. R & D com. Nat. Coun. Tchr. Retirement Sys., 2003; trustee Tchrs. Retirement Sys. Tex., 1999—, chair ethcis com., vice chmn. bd., 2003—04. David Ross fellow, 1977. Mem. Tex. Speech Comm. Assn. (regional rep. 1978-88), Nat. Comm. Assn. Am., Tex. Assn. Coll. Tchrs. (regional v.p. 1985-88, pres.-elect 1988-89, state pres. 1989-90, state bd. legis. liason 1997-99), Tex. Forensics Assn. (pres. 1974), Internat. Comm. Assn., Zeta Phi Eta, Alpha Delta Pi. Democrat. Episcopalian. Avocations: reading, politics, travel. Office: Lamar U Dept Communication Beaumont TX 77710

BAKER, MARYCAROL GERMAINE, physical therapist, educator; b. Elgin, Ill., Dec. 10, 1954; d. Donald Joseph Mock and Helen Marie Braun Mock; m. Larry D. Baker, Dec. 22, 1984; children: Matthew C., Michelle C. BS in Biology, Ill. Benedictine U., 1976; MS in Phys. Therapy, U. Ill., 1979. Lic. phys. therapist Ill., Idaho, Mo., Ind., Wash., cert. tchr. Mo. Phys. therapist U. Ill. Hosp., Chgo., 1979—81, DuPage-West Cook Spl. Svcs., Honsdale, Ill., 1981—84, Adult Child Devel. Ctr., Lewiston, Idaho, 1984—86, Asotin Spl. Svcs., Clarkston, Wash., 1985—91, Raker Home Health, Richmond, Ind., 1992—94; pvt. instr. Baker Sch., Mapaville, Mo., 1994—; phys. therapist Jefferson Meml. Hosp., Crystal City, Mo., 2004—. Asst. instr. Premiers TKD, Hillsboro, Mo., 1999—; instr. piano MC Studios, Mapaville, 1999—; instr. U. Ill., Chgo., 1982—84; cons. in field. Vol. Mastedon Art Svc. Regional Fair, Hillsboro, Mo., 1995—, Internat. Sci. and Environ. Fair, Portland, Oreg., 2004. Recipient Outstanding Sci. Tchr. award, Mastodon Art Sci. Regional Fair, 2004, 2005. Mem.: Nat. Guild Piano Tchrs., Am. Phys. Therapy Assn., Amateur Athletic Union Taekwondo (referee, coach 1996—2005). Avocation: dance. Home: 3698 Plass Rd Festus MO 63028 E-mail: LBkr6412@hotmail.com.

BAKER, MELVIN, pharmacist; b. Cleve., Sept. 6, 1931; s. Barnet and Florence (Kleinman) B. BA In Biol. Scis., Ohio State U., 1954; BSc in Pharmacy, U. Toledo, 1959. Registered pharmacist, Ohio. Dir. pharmacy svcs. Richmond Heights (Ohio) Gen. Hosp., 1964-86; chief pharmacy svcs. City of Cleve. Dept. Pub. Health, 1999—. Cons. Greater Cleve. Hosp. Assn., 1966-86, A.K.A. Ctr. for Health Affairs. Recipient Cert. of Recognition, Greater Cleve. Hosp. Assn., 1976, 80, Cert. of Commendation, Legislature of State of Ohio, 1984. Mem. AMA (affiliate), Am. Pharm. Assn., Am. Soc. Health Sys. Pharmacists, Ohio Soc. Health Sys. Pharmacists, Cleve. Soc. Health Sys. Pharmacists (bd. dirs. 1980-86), No. Ohio Acad. Pharmacy (bd. dirs. 1978—), Masons, Scottish Rite, Shriners, Alpha Zeta Omega (pres. 1991-92, 98-99). Avocations: humor, storytelling, lecturing, comedy. Home: PO Box 24937 Cleveland OH 44124-0937

BAKER, MERL, engineering educator; b. Cadiz, Ky., July 11, 1924; s. Jesse F. and Argie (Coyle) B.; m. Emily Wilson, Sept. 14, 1946; children: Merl Wilson, Marilyn Ruth. BS in Mech. Engring., U. Ky., 1945; MS, Purdue U., 1948, PhD, 1952. Grad. asst. Purdue U., 1946-48; mem. faculty U. Ky., 1948-63, prof. mech. engring., 1955-63; exec. dir. Ky. Research Found., 1953-63; coordinator, dir. U. Ky. coop. programs with AID, 1956-63, exec. dir. research and relations with industry, 1957-63; dean U. Mo. Sch. Mines and Metallurgy, 1963; chancellor U. Mo., Rolla, 1964-73, spl. asst. to pres. statewide system, 1973-77; coordinator energy conservation program Oak Ridge Nat. Lab., 1977-79, energy mgmt. specialist, 1979-82; provost U. Tenn.-Chattanooga, 1982-85, prof. engring., 1985-97, dir. Ctr. for Career Enhancement, 1985-97; engring. cons. Lexington, Ky., 1997—. Recipient Disting. Alumnus award U. Ky., 1965, Disting. Engring. Alumnus award Purdue U., 1968; named Outstanding Mech. Engr., 1991; named to U. Ky. Engring. Hall of Distinction, 2003. Fellow Am. Soc. Engring. Mgmt. (bd. dirs.), Am. Soc. Engring. Edn.; mem. ASHRAE (award of merit tchg. 1959, chmn. edn. com. 1960-61, Disting. Svc. award 1971), NSPE (pres. Tenn. Soc. 1995-96), UMR Acad. Engring. Mgmt., Ky. Acad. Sci., Newcomen Soc. N.Am., Cosmos Club (Washington), Blue Key, Scabbard and Blade, Sigma Xi, Phi Kappa Phi, Phi Eta Sigma, Tau Beta Pi, Pi Tau Sigma, Sigma Pi Sigma, Omicron Delta Kappa, Chi Epsilon, Rotary Club of Lexington. Home and Office: 1973 Blairmore Rd Lexington KY 40502-2432 Office Phone: 859-268-6190.

BAKER, MITCHELL, computer software development foundation administrator; AB in Asian Studies, JD, U. Calif., Berkeley. Former assoc. gen. counsel Netscape Comm. Corp.; joined mozilla.org, 1998, gen. mgr., 1999—; pres. Mozilla Found., 2003—. Bd. dirs. Open Source Applications Found.; adv. bd. SpikeSource. Named one of 100 Most Influential People of 2005, Time mag. Office: Mozilla Found Ste C 1350 Villa St Mountain View CA 94041-1126*

BAKER, NADINE DIANE, writer; b. Jilo, W.Va., Sept. 3, 1948; d. Douglas and Bertha Evelyn (Adams) Dial; m. Ernest Wilson Holmes Jr., Sept. 3, 1964 (div. 1979); children: Deana Kay McGlamory, Ernest Wilson Holmes; m. Stone Dwayne Baker (dec. 1996). Cert. nursing asst., S.W. C.C., Richlands, Va., 1992. Cosmetologist Am. Hair Stylest Assn., 1977—80; nursing asst. NC, Va. and W.Va., 1989—97; freelance writer, poet W.Va. Poetry Soc., 2001—. Author: (poems) Mind and Spirit Unity I, 2002, Cooking in the Spirit, 2003; contbr. poems to lit. publs. Recipient cert. of recognition, Famous Poets Soc., 2000, hon. mention, W.Va. Poetry Soc., 2001. Baptist. Home: 45 Riverside Dr Apt 704 Welch WV 24801

BAKER, NADINE LOIS, cardiovascular technician; b. Balt., Apr. 16, 1955; d. David and Elizabeth Baker. Sr. cardiology technician U. Md. Med. Sys., Balt., 1989-95; cardiovasc. technician Md. Gen. Hosp., Balt., 1997—; assisted living care provider, 1999—. Sabbath sch. supt. Sharon Seventh-Day Adventist Ch., Balt., 1996. Home: PO Box 5364 Baltimore MD 21209-0364

BAKER, P. JEAN, lawyer, mediator; b. June 28, 1948; BS summa cum laude, Wright State U., Dayton, Ohio, 1973; MBA, Northeastern U., Boston, 1989; JD, Calif. Western U., San Diego, 1993. Bar: Calif. 1993; cert. mediator. With GenRad Inc., Boston, 1974-82; mktg./sales staff GE Co., Boston, 1982-84; major accounts mgr. Fluke Mfg. Co., Boston, 1984-89; pub. rels. mgr. Racal Dana, Irvine, Calif., 1989-90; legal intern Pub. Defenders Dependancy, San Diego, 1992; law clk. Civil divsn. U.S. Atty., San Diego, 1992; personal injury atty. L.H. Parker, Long Beach, Calif., 1993; mediator/atty. Baker & Assocs., San Diego, 1993-94; dir. Orange County region Am. Arbitration Assn., Irvine, 1994-97, v.p. Washington, 1997—. Mediator San Diego Mediation Ctr., 1993-97; trainer mediation skills Am. Arbitration Assn., 1994-97; adj. prof. Western State U., Irvine, 1995-96; MCLE presenter San Diego County Bar, 1994, State Bar of Calif., 1996, ABA, 1997-2003; mediator Superior Ct., San Diego, 1994-97, U.S. Bankruptcy Ct. (cen. dist.) Calif., 1995-97; adj. prof. Columbus Sch. of Law, Washington, 1997-2001, Georgetown Law Sch., 2005-; coach Georgetown Law Sch. Mediation Advocacy Team, 2003. Bd. dirs. Legal Aid Soc., San Diego, 1994, T. Homann Law Assn., San Diego, 1994, Counsel for Ct. Excellence, 2003-04. Recipient Am. Jurisprudence awards, 1992. Mem. ABA, D.C. Bar Assn., State Bar of Calif., Energy Bar Assn., Va. Bar Assn., Md. Bar Assn., Women's Bar Assn. Avocations: tennis, golf. Office: American Arbitration Assn 1776 Eye St NW Ste 850 Washington DC 20006 Office Phone: 202-223-7093. E-mail: BakerJ@adr.org.

BAKER, PAMELA, lawyer; b. Detroit, Apr. 6, 1951; d. William D. and Lois (Tukey) Baker; m. Jay R. Franke, June 10, 1972; children: Baker Eugene, Alexandra Britell. AB, Smith Coll., 1972; JD, U. Wis. Madison, 1976. Bar: Ill. 1976, Wis. 1976. Ptnr. Sonnenschein, Nath & Rosenthal, Chgo., also co-mng. ptnr. Chgo. office, vice chair nat. employee benefits and exec. compensation practice group. Contbr. articles to profl. jour. Fellow Am. Coll. Employee Benefits Counsel (charter), Am. Bar Found.; mem. ABA (mem. employee benefits com. 1984—, chair-elect 1998-99, chair 1999-2000, mem. plan mergers and acquisitions com. 1985— mem. fed. regulation of securities com. 1989—, chair 1989-95), Ill. State Bar Assn. (sec. employee benefits sect. coun. 1989-90, vice chair 1990-91, chair 1991-92), Chgo. Bar Assn. (employee benefits com. 1978—, sec. 1984-85, vice chair 1985-86, chair 1986-87, fed. taxation com. 1980—, exec. coun. 1982-85). Office: Sonnenschein Nath & Rosenthal Sears Tower 233 S Wacker Dr Ste 8000 Chicago IL 60606-6491

BAKER, PATRICIA ANN, publishing executive; b. Englewood, N.J., Apr. 3, 1939; BA, St. Mary's Coll., 1961. Prodn. designer Little, Brown Pubs., 1961-63; mktg. & promotion dir. Sunset Books, 1963-68; design & prodn. mgr. Hoover Instn. Press, Stanford, Calif., 1981-89, exec. editor, 1989—. Office: Hoover Instn Press Stanford U Stanford CA 94305-6010

BAKER, PAUL RAYMOND, historian, educator; b. Everett, Wash., Sept. 28, 1927; s. Loren Robbins and Alma Irene (Ball) B.; m. Elizabeth O. Kemp, Feb. 11, 1972; 1 dau., Alice Elizabeth. AB, Stanford U., 1949; MA, Columbia U., 1951; PhD, Harvard U., 1960. Staff editor Ency. Americana, N.Y.C., 1952-55; instr., asst. prof. Calif. Inst. Tech., Pasadena, 1960-63; lectr. U. Calif.-Riverside, 1963-64, U. Oreg., Eugene, 1964-65; assoc. prof., then prof. history NYU, N.Y.C., 1965-99, emeritus prof., 1999—, dir. Am. civilization program, 1972-92. Mem. media panel NEH, 1978; vis. schlar Am. Acad. in Rome, 1959. Editor: Views of Society and Manners in America, 1963; gen. editor: American Problem Studies series, 40 vols., 1968—; author: The Fortunate Pilgrims, 1964, Richard Morris Hunt, 1980, Stanny: the Gilded Life of Stanford White, 1989; compiler: The Atomic Bomb, 1968, The Atomic Bomb, rev. edit., 1976; co-author: The American Experience, 5 vols., 1976, 79, (Spanish translation) Nueva Historia de los Estados Unidos, 1986; (with others) Master Builders, 1985, The Architecture of Richard Morris Hunt, 1986, (French translation) Richard Morris Hunt Architecte, The Italian Presence in American Art, 1860-1920, 1992, Henry Adams and His World, 1993, La Virtù e la Libertà, 1995. Mem. Glen Ridge Hist. Preservation Commn., 1994-96. Kennedy travel fellow Harvard U., 1958-59, NEH fellow, 1982. Mem. Am. Studies Assn. (pres. met. N.Y. chpt. 1968-69, Mary C. Turpie prize for outstanding contbns. to tchg. advisement and program devel. 1994), Orgn. Am. Historians, Victorian Soc. in Am., Phi Beta Kappa (v.p., pres. Beta of N.Y. 1966-70). Home: 90 Hillside Ave Glen Ridge NJ 07028-2212 Office: NYU Dept History 53 Washington Square South New York NY 10012-1098

BAKER, PAUL THORNELL, anthropology educator; b. Burlington, Iowa, Feb. 28, 1927; s. Palmer Ward Baker and Viola Isabelle (Thornell) Loughlin; m. Thelma Marion Shoher, Feb. 21, 1949; children: Deborah C., Amy L., Joshua S., Felicia B. Student, U. Miami, 1947—49; BA, U. N.Mex., 1951; PhD, Harvard U., 1956. Rschr. U.S. Army Q.M., Natick, Mass., 1952—57; asst. prof. anthropology Pa. State U., University Park, 1957—61, assoc. prof., 1961—65, prof., 1965—81, Evan Pugh prof. anthropology, 1981—87, Evan Pugh prof. emeritus, 1987—, head dept., 1980—85. Sci. advisor Wenner-Gren Found., N.Y.C., 1980—83; mem. U.S. Commn. for UNESCO, 1982—84, exec. commn., 1983—84. Editor: Biology of Human Adaptability, 1966, Man in the Andes, 1976, Biology of High Altitude Peoples, 1978, The Changing Samoans, 1986; co-author (with G.A. Harrison, J.M. Tanner, D.R. Pilbeam): Human Biology, 1988. With U.S. Army, 1945—47. Decorated Yugoslavian Order of the Golden Star with Necklace; recipient Huxley medal, Royal Anthrop. Inst. Gt. Brit., 1982; fellow, Guggenheim Found., 1974—75; scholar Fulbright rsch. scholar, 1962. Fellow: Am. Anthrop. Assn. (assoc. editor jour. 1973—76); mem.: NAS, Internat. Union Anthropol. and Ethnol. Scis. (hon. life, v.p. 1988—93, sr. v.p. 1993—98), Internat. Assn. Human Biologists (pres. 1980—89, Franz Boas Disting. Achievement award), Human Biology Coun. (pres. 1974—77), Am. Assn. Phys. Anthropologists (pres. 1969—71, Charles R. Darwin Lifetime Achievement award 1993). Address: 603 Village Crossing DR Chapel Hill NC 27517-7563

BAKER, PETER MITCHELL, laser scientist, educator; b. London, July 18, 1939; arrived in U.S., 1966; s. George Edward and Clarice Baker; m. Sunny Baker, Oct. 15, 1988; 1 child, Scott George. BSc in Physics with honors, London U., 1963. Sr. physicist Itek Corp., Lexington, Mass., 1966-69; sr. v.p. Micronetic Sys., Burlington, Mass., 1969-74; tchr. physics Hillcrest Sch., Nairobi, Kenya, 1975-77; pres. Quantrad Corp., Torrance, Calif., 1977-84, Ebtec Calif., Huntington Beach, 1985-88; exec. dir. Laser Inst. Am., Orlando, Fla., 1988—. Lectr. lasers UCLA Ext., 1986—88. Contbr. articles to profl. jours. Recipient CEO award for Outstanding Small Bus., 1982. Fellow: Laser Inst. Am. (pres. 1987); mem.: Bd. Laser Safety Inc. (chmn. 2003), Coun. of Engring. and Sci. Soc. Execs. (pres. 2004—05). Avocations: walking, tennis. Office: Laser Inst Am 13501 Ingenuity Dr Ste 128 Orlando FL 32826-3009
My guiding principle is "Do What You Say".

BAKER, PHILIP STEVEN, dentist, educator; m. Jacqulyn Bennett Bennett, June 25, 1995. DDS, Loyola U., 1978; BS in Biology, Regis Coll., 1974. Diplomate Am. Bd. Prosthodontics, 2005. From clin. instr. to asst. prof. Sch. Dentistry Loyola U., Chgo., 1978—85; from asst. prof. to assoc. prof. Coll. Dentistry U. Fla., Gainesville, Fla., 1987—98; assoc. prof. Sch. Dentistry Med. Coll. Ga., Augusta, Ga., 1998—. Named Outstanding Tchr. of Yr., U. Fla. Coll. Dentistry, 1989. Mem.: Am. Coll. Prosthodontists (pres. Ga. sect. 2003—04). Office: MCG School of Dentistry 1459 Laney Walker Boulevard Augusta GA 30912 Office Phone: 706-721-2881.

BAKER, R. ROBINSON, surgeon; b. Balt., Dec. 30, 1928; s. Henry Scott and Frances (Robinson) B.; m. Jean Harvey, Sept. 12, 1953; children: Susan, Scott, Robert, Jean. AB, Johns Hopkins U., 1950, MD, 1954. Diplomate Am. Bd. Surgery, Bd. Thoracic Surgery. Intern Johns Hopkins U., 1954-55; sr. asst. surgeon Nat. Heart Inst., 1955-57; asst. resident Johns Hopkins Hosp., 1957-58, resident, 1958-61, chief surg. resident, 1961-62; surgeon-in-charge Johns Hopkins Hosp. (Breast Clinic), 1970—, Johns Hopkins Hosp. (Oncology Center), 1976; prof. surgery Johns Hopkins U., 1967—, prof. oncology, 1975—, Warfield M. Firor porf. surgery, 1991—; mem. (Coop. Lung Cancer Detection Group), 1971—. Recipient grants Am. Cancer Soc., 1966-71, grants John A. Hartford Found., 1968-73, grants Upjohn Co., 1973, grants Sterling-Winthrop Rsch. Inst., 1975—; named hon. fellow Royal Coll. Surgeons of Ireland. Fellow ACS, Royal Coll. Surgeons (hon.); mem. Soc. Univ. Surgeons, Am. Assn. Thoracic Surgery, So. Thoracic Surg. Assn., Soc. Head and Neck Surgeons, AMA, Am., So. Surg. Assns., Elkridge (Balt.) Club,

Fishers Island (N.Y.) Club, Hay Harbor Club (Fishers Island). Home: 8717 Mcdonogh Rd Baltimore MD 21208-1021 Office: 600 N Wolfe St Baltimore MD 21287-0005 Business E-Mail: rrbaker@jhmi.edu.

BAKER, REBECCA LOUISE, musician, music educator, consultant; b. Covina, Calif., Apr. 12, 1951; d. Allan Herman and Hazel Margaret (Maki) Flaten; m. Jerry Wayne Baker, Dec. 22, 1972; children: Jared Wesley, Rachelle LaDawn, Shannon Faith. Grad. high sch., Park River, N.D.; student, Trinity Bible Inst., 1968-69. Sec. Agrl. Stblzn. & Conservation Svc. Office, Park River, N.D., 1969; pianist, singer Paul Clark Singers & Vic Coburn Evangelistic Assn., Portland, Oreg., 1969-72; musician, singer Restoration Ministries Evangelistic Assn., Richland, Wash., 1972-80; musician, pvt. instr. Calvary Temple Ch., Shawnee, Okla., 1980-81; organist, choirmaster St. Francis Episcopal Ch., Tyler, 1984-87; co-founder, owner Psalmist Sch. of Music & Recording Studio, Whitehouse, 1983—; pianist/entertainer Willowbrook Country Club, Tyler, Tex., 1991—; pianist, vocalist Mario's Italian Restaurant, Tyler, 1994—. Pianist Garner Ted Armstrong, Tyler, 1986—; pianist, dir. Children's Choir, Calvary Bapt. Ch., Tyler, 1987—; pianist, entertainer Ramada Hotel, Tyler, 1988-90; pianist Whitehouse (Tex.) Sch. Dist. choirs, 1988—; accompanist Tyler Area Children's Chorale, 1988-90, Univ. Interscholastic League; pvt. instr. keyboard and vocal. Composer: Religious Songs (12 on albums), 1979; pianist, arranger, prodr., rec. artist 6 albums; editor, arranger: Texas Women's Aglow Songbook, 1987; editor Shekinah Glory mag., 1989—; developer improvisational piano course; star, prodr. weekly, nationally syndicated mus. religious programs for TV, 1995, 96, Proclaim His Glory, 1997—; played for receptions honoring Gov. George Bush, Tex. Senator Phil Gramm and Congressman John Bryant. Performer, spkr. many charitable, civic and religious orgns., Tex. and U.S. including AAUW, Kiwanis Clubs; co-founder Psalmist Mins. Internat., 1988—; founder, pres. Christian Music Tchr.'s Assn., 1991; worship leader Mayor's Prayer Breakfast, Tyler, 1994. Mem. Women's Aglow Fellowship (music dir., spkr., performer at retreats and tng. seminars). Republican. Full Gospel. Avocations: travel, reading, interior decorating, collecting. Home and Office: Psalmist Music & Recording PO Box 4126 Tyler TX 75712 Office Phone: 903-581-5461. E-mail: sweetpsalmisi@netzero.com.

BAKER, RICHARD GRAVES, geologist, educator, palynologist; b. Merrill, Wis., June 12, 1938; s. Dillon James and Miriam Baker; m. Debby J.Z. Baker; children: Kristina Kae, James Dillon, Charity Ann. BA, U. Wis., 1960; MS, U. Minn., 1964; PhD, U. Colo., 1969. Asst. prof. geology U. Iowa, Iowa City, 1970-75, assoc. prof., 1975-81, prof., 1981—, chmn. dept., 1992-95, prof. botany, 1988-92, prof. biol. scis., 1992-2000, prof. emeritus, 2000—. Contbr. articles to profl. jours., chapters to books. Chmn. Iowa chpt. Nature Conservancy, Des Moines, 1981-82. Grantee NSF, 1984-86, 88-90, 94-97, NOAA, 1992-93; recipient Disting. Scientist award Iowa Acad. Sci., 2001. Fellow Geol. Soc. Am., Iowa Acad. Sci.; mem. Am. Quaternary Assn., Ecol. Soc. Am. Office: Univ Iowa 121 Trowbridge Hall Dept Geosci Iowa City IA 52242-1319 Business E-Mail: dick-baker@uiowa.edu.

BAKER, RICHARD HUGH, congressman; b. New Orleans, May 22, 1948; m. Karen Carpenter; children: Brandon, Julie. BA, La. State U., 1971. State rep. La. Dist. 64, former chmn. com. on transp., hwys. and pub. works, 1981-82, state rep.; mem. La. Ho. of Reps., 1972—86, 100th-106th Congresses from 6th La. Dist., 1987—; mem. transp. and infrastructure com. and vets. affs. com.; chmn. Banking & Fin. Svcs. subcom. on Capital Mkts., Securities and Govt. Sponsored Enterprises; also real estate broker. Republican. Methodist. Office: US Ho of Reps 341 Cannon House Offc Bldg Washington DC 20515-1806*

BAKER, RICHARD SOUTHWORTH, lawyer; b. Lansing, Mich., Dec. 18, 1929; s. Paul Julius and Florence (Schmid) B.; m. Kathleen E. Yull, 1956 (dec. 1964); m. Marina J. Vidoli, 1965 (div. 1989); children: Garrick Richard, Lydia Joy; m. Barbara J. Walker, 1997. Student, DePauw U., 1947—49; AB cum laude, Harvard, 1951; JD, U. Mich., 1954. Bar: Ohio 1957, U.S. Dist. Ct. (no. dist.) Ohio 1958, U.S. Tax Ct. 1960, U.S. Supreme Ct. 1971, U.S. Ct. Appeals (6th cir.) 1972. Mem. firm Fuller & Henry, and predecessors, 1956-91; pvt. practice Toledo, 1991—. Chmn. nat. com. region IV Mich. Law Sch. Fund, 1967-69, mem.-at-large, 1970-85. Bd. dirs. Assn. Harvard Alumni, 1970-73. Served with AUS, 1954-56. Fellow Am. Coll. Trial Lawyers; mem. ABA, Ohio Bar Assn., Toledo Bar Assn., Toledo Club, Harvard Club (pres. Toledo chpt. 1968-77), Capital Club, Phi Delta Theta, Phi Delta Phi. Office: 2819 Falmouth Rd Toledo OH 43615-2215

BAKER, RICK, make-up artist; b. Binghamton, N.Y., Dec. 8, 1950; s. Ralph B. and Doris (Hamlin) Baker; m. Elaine Parkyn (div. 1984); m. Silvia Abascal, Nov. 10, 1987. Spl. effects makeup artist on the following films Octaman, 1971, The Thing With Two Heads, 1972, Pirahna, 1972, Bone, 1972, The Exorcist, 1973, Schlock, 1973, Live and Let Die, 1973, Hell Up in Harlem, 1973, It's Alive, 1974, Death Race 2000, 1975, Black Caesar, 1975, Squirm, 1976, Food of the Gods, 1976, King Kong, 1976, Track of the Moonbest, 1976, Zebra Force, 1976, Kentucky Fried Movie, 1977, Star Wars, 1977, The Incredible Melting Man, 1978, It's Alive 2, 1978, The Fury, 1978, Tanya's Island, 1980, The Funhouse, 1980, The Incredible Shrinking Woman, 1981, An American Werewolf in London, 1981 (Acad. award Best Makeup), Videodrome, 1983, Greystoke: The Legend of Tarzan, Lord of the Apes, 1984, Starman, 1984, My Science Project, 1985, Cocoon, 1985, Ratboy, 1986, Captain Eo, 1986, Harry and the Hendersons, 1987 (Acad. award Best Makeup), Summer School, 1987, Missing Link, 1988, Coming to America, 1988, Gorillas in the Mist, 1988; co-prodr.: Gorillas in the Mist, 1988; Spl. effects makeup artist on the following films Gremlins 2; The New Batch, 1990; co-prodr.: Gremlins 2; The New Batch, 1990; Spl. effects makeup artist on the following films The Rocketeer, 1991, Ed Wood, 1994 (Acad. award Best Makeup), Wolf, 1994, Batman Forever, 1995, The Amazing Panda Adventure, 1995, Just Cause, 1995, The Nutty Professor, 1996 (Acad. awd. Best Makeup), The Frighteners, 1996, Escape from L.A., 1996, Men in Black, 1997 (Acad. awd. Best Makeup, 1997), Mighty Joe Young, 1998, Life, 1999, TV work includes (movies) The Autobiography of Miss Jane Pittman, 1974 (Emmy award Best Makeup), An American Christmas Carol, 1979, Something Is Out There, 1988, Body Bags, 1993, TV work includes (series) Davey and Goliath, 1960—65, Werewolf, 1987—88, Beauty and the Beas, 1987—90, designed spl. makeup effects for Michael Jackson's Thriller, 1983, The Klumps, How the Grinch Stole Christmas (Acad. awd. Best Makeup), Planet of the Apes., Men in Black II, 2002, The Ring, 2002, Haunted Mansion, 2003, Hell Boy, 2003, Cursed, 2005, The Ring II, 2005. Office: IATSE Local 706 828 N Hollywood Way Burbank CA 91505-2831*

BAKER, ROBERT EDWARD, lawyer, retired finance company executive; b. Albion, Mich., May 6, 1930; s. Robert Charles and Loretto A. (Barrett) B.; m. Mary Anne Mulcahy, Feb. 20, 1965. BBA, U. Mich., 1952, LLB, 1955. Bar: Mich. 1956. Atty. legal dept. Chrysler Corp., Detroit, 1955-64; with Chrysler Fin. Corp., Troy, Mich., 1964-90, also bd. dirs., v.p. corp. fin., 1970-80, v.p. fin., gen. counsel, 1980-85, vice chmn. bd., 1985-90; regional dir. Mich. Nat. Bank, 1978-90. Trustee Independence One Mut. Funds, Farmington Hills, Mich., 1990-2002. Trustee Comprehensive Health Svcs., Inc., 1972-99, chmn. bd., 1977-99; trustee, sec. Rose Hill Ctr., Inc., Holly, Mich., 1989—; trustee Sacred Heart Major Sem., Detroit, 1996—, chmn. fin. com., 2000—. With CIC, AUS, 1955-57. Recipient Disting. Service award Am. Fin. Services Assn., 1981 Mem. ABA, State Bar of Mich., Am. Assn. Sovereign Mil. Order of Malta, Orchard Lake Country Club, Dutch Settlers Soc. Albany. Roman Catholic.

BAKER, ROBERT ERNEST, JR., retired foundation executive; b. Tuscaloosa, Ala., Oct. 17, 1916; s. Robert Ernest and Faye (Whitson) B.; m. Billye Louise Driskell, June 25, 1947; 1 son, Brent Driskell. BS in Indsl. Engring, U. Ala., 1939. Registered profl. engr., Tex. Indsl. engring., mgmt. and fin. cons., 1939-62; exec. adminstr., sec. Moody Found., Galveston, Tex., 1962-97; ret., 1997. Mem.: Arty. (Galveston). Presbyterian. Home: 6 Adler Cir Galveston TX 77551-5828

BAKER, ROBERT FRANK, molecular biologist, educator; b. Weiser, Idaho, Apr. 9, 1936; s. Robert Clarence and Beulah (Hulet) B.; m. Mary Margaret Murphy, May 29, 1965; children: Allison Leslie, Steven Mark. BS, Stanford U., 1959; PhD, Brown U., 1966. Postdoctoral rsch. assoc. Stanford (Calif.) U., 1966-68; asst. prof. dept. biol. scis. U. So. Calif., L.A., 1968-72, assoc. prof., 1972-83, prof., 1983—, dir. molecular biology div., 1978-80, mem. Comprehensive Cancer Ctr., 1984—. Vis. assoc. prof. Harvard U. Med. Sch., Boston 1975-76; mem. genetic study sect. NIH, Bethesda, Md., 1977-79, 82 Contbr. articles to profl. jours. Grantee NIH, NSF, 1968—. Mem. Am. Soc. Zoologists, Am. Soc. Microbiology, Sigma Xi. Avocations: amateur radio, electronics. Home: 607 Almar Ave Pacific Palisades CA 90272-4208 Office: U So Calif Dept Molecular Biology Mc 1340 Los Angeles CA 90089-1340 Office Phone: 213-740-5565. Business E-Mail: baker@molbio.usc.edu.

BAKER, ROBERT I., manufacturing executive; b. Bridgeport, Conn., Sept. 28, 1940; s. Irwin Henry and Anna (Keane) B.; m. Patricia Turoczi, Nov. 28, 1968; children: Scott Allen, Christopher Keane. BA, U. Conn., 1962; postgrad., Syracuse U., 1975, U. Pa., 1978. With U.S. Electric Motors div. Emerson, Milford, Conn., 1963-66; with Henry G. Thompson div. Vt. Am., Branford, Conn., 1966-75, pres., gen. mgr. Magna div. Elizabethtown, Ky., 1977-84, corp. v.p., 1982-84, pres., CEO, Louisville, 1984-91; pres., owner Distbrs. Source, Portsmouth, N.H., 1991-92; CEO The Chamberlain Group, Inc., Elmhurst, Ill., 1992-96, The Chamberlain Group, Elmhurst, 1996—2000; ret., 2000. Cons. in field; bd. dirs. Chamberlain, Durasol, Brinkmann. Mem. Medinah Country Club, Abenaqui Country Club. Avocations: skiing, golf, woodworking. Home: 56 Old Bay Rd PO Box 2164 New Castle NH 03854

BAKER, ROBERT KERRY, college administrator, author, editor; b. Glendale, Calif., Nov. 24, 1948; m. Linda Jean Voorhees, Jan. 14, 1972 (div. 1978). BA in French, Calif. State U., Northridge, 1971; MA in French, UCLA, 1973, MLS, 1976; EdD in Ednl. Leadership, No. Ariz. U., 1996. Cert. life libr., Wash., cmty. coll. instr., Calif. Asst. catalog libr. Gonzaga U., Spokane, Wash., 1976-77; pub. svcs. libr. Spokane C.C. Coll., 1977-80, tech. svcs. libr., 1980-83; libr. dir. Lower Columbia Coll., Longview, Wash., 1983-90; coll. adminstr. Pima C.C., 1990-97, libr., 1998—. Author: Introduction to Library Research in French Literature, 1978; Doing Library Research, 1981; editor Westview Guides to Library Research, Boulder, Colo., 1979; contbr. articles to publs. in field. Marjorie Sether Mardellis fellow, UCLA, 1975. Mem. ALA, Am. Assn. Higher Edn., Ariz. State Libr. Assn., Assn. Coll. and Rsch. Librs., Phi Kappa Phi. Office: Pima CC 401 N Bonita Ave Tucson AZ 85709-5060 Office Phone: 520-206-6485. Business E-Mail: Robert.Baker@pima.edu.

BAKER, ROBERT LEON, military officer; b. Oak, Nebr., Feb. 7, 1925; s. Oscar E. and Ada Veru (Davis) B.; m. Rebecca Chandler, Dec. 12, 1956; children: Rebecca Ann, Jay Milton, Betsy Jean, Robert Leon, Bruce Chandler, Brenda Carole. BS in Liberal Arts, La. Poly. Inst., 1945; BS in Medicine, MD with highest honors, U. Ark., 1949; grad. program health systems mgmt., Harvard U. Grad. Sch. Bus., 1972. Diplomate: Am. Bd. Obstetrics and Gynecology. Apprentice seaman U.S. Navy, 1943, commd. lt. (j.g.), M.C., 1949, advanced through grades to rear adm., 1973; rotating intern Tripler Gen. Hosp., Honolulu, 1949-50; resident in obstetrics and gynecology U.S. Naval Hosp., Oakland, Calif., 1954; assigned U.S. and overseas as obstetrician-gynecologist; chmn. dept. obstetrics and gynecology Naval Hosp., Portsmouth, Va., 1969-72; med. aide Office Comdr. in chief, NATO, 1970-72; dir. grad. tng. and chmn. dept. ob-gyn. Naval Regional Med. Center, Oakland, 1973-75, comdg. officer Phila., 1975-77, Naval Aerospace and Regional Med. Center, Pensacola, Fla., 1977-79; chief ob-gyn. service Baxter Gen. Hosp., Mountain Home, Ark., 1980-82. Clin. prof. Va. Commonwealth U. Med. Sch., 1971—72; med. dir. Hospice of Ozarks, 1984—96. Contbr. articles to med. jours. Bd. dirs. Phila. YWCA, 1975-77, USO, Phila., 1976-77, Pensacola, Fla., 1978-80, Baxter County Regional Hosp., 1985-87, also various bds. tng. insts., 1980—; bd. dirs. Ctrl. Ark. Radiation Therapy Inst., 1990-96, 98—, chmn. adv. bd. Mountain Home, 1990—; pres. Baxter County chpt. Am. Cancer Soc., 1995-96; founding mem. Internat. Coll. Hospice/Palliative Care, 1995; mem. Make A Wish Found.; bd. dirs. Internat. Hospice Inst. and Coll., 1996-99. Decorated Legion of Merit, Meritorious Service medal, Navy Commendation medal; recipient Letters of Commendation Comdr. in Chief NATO, Sec. Navy; recipient Wish Team award for Ark., Make A Wish Found., 1996. Fellow: ACOG (chmn. armed forces dist. Navy sect. 1967—69, vice chmn. armed forces dist. 1971—74, asst. sec. 1977—79); mem.: AMA (del. 1976—77), Acad. Hospice Physicians (founding mem.), Ark. Med. Soc. (del. 1982—2002), Baxter County Med. Soc. (v.p. 1982—84), Assn. Mil. Surgeons U.S. (chpt. pres. 1973—74), Union League (Phila.), Phi Chi, Alpha Omega Alpha. Mem. Christian Ch. (Disciples Of Christ). Home: PO Box 44 Mountain Home AR 72654-0044 Office: 3763 Highway 5 S Mountain Home AR 72653-5944 E-mail: admbak@mtnhome.com. *Time is critical for top management. It is divided into People time and Paper time. People time, almost invariably, must take precedence at any moment, but paper time still demands and must be accomplished. People time demonstrates concern. This perception by people of concern by management is the essential element of true leadership, and the essence of morale. One who can follow this precept while, at the same time completing paper work, is a top manager. This takes time.*

BAKER, ROBERT M.L., JR., academic administrator, research scientist; b. L.A., Sept. 1, 1930; s. Robert M.L. and Martha (Harlan) Baker; m. Bonnie Sue Vold, Nov. 14, 1964; children: Robert Randall, Robert M.L. III, Robin Michelle Leslie. BA summa cum laude, UCLA, 1954, MA, 1956, PhD, 1958. Cons. Douglas Aircraft Co., Santa Monica, Calif., 1954—57; sr. scientist Aeronutronic, Newport Beach, 1957—60; head Lockheed Aircraft Rsch. Ctr., West L.A., 1961—64; assoc. mgr. math. analysis Computer Scis. Corp., El Segundo, 1964—80; pres. West Coast U., L.A., 1980—. Faculty UCLA, 1958—72; dir. Internat. Info. Systems Corp., Pasadena, Transp. Scis. Corp., L.A.; appointee Nat. Accreditation Adv. Com. U.S. Dept. Edn., 1987—90. Author: An Introduction to Astrodynamics, 1960, 2d edit., 1967, Astrodynamics-Advanced and Applied Topics, 1967, 1987; editor: Jour. Astron. Scis., 1961—76, SCL. To maj. USAF, 1960—61. Named Outstanding Young Man of Yr., 1965; recipient Dirk Brouwer award, 1976. Fellow: AAAS, AAIA (assoc.), Brit. Astro. Soc., Meteoritical Soc., Am. Astro. Soc.; mem.: Am. Phys. Soc., Sigma Pi Sigma, Sigma Xi, Phi Beta Kappa. Achievements include patents in field. E-mail: bakerjr@attbi.com.

BAKER, ROBERT THOMAS, interior designer; b. Kansas City, Mo., Mar. 23, 1932; s. Robert Blume and Justina (Early) B. BA in Art, U. Mo., Columbia, 1954, MA in Interior Design, 1962; cert., Parsons Sch. Design, N.Y.C., 1958. Interior designer Edward Keith, Inc., Kansas City, Mo., 1958-60, 63-71, Nereoux Interiors, New Iberia, La., 1960-61, Bloomingdales, N.Y.C., 1962-63, Thomas Price Interiors, Kansas City, Mo., 1971-78; owner Robert Baker Interiors Inc., Kansas City, 1978-89; chmn. interior design dept. Au Marché, Inc., Kansas City, 1989; pres. Baker Design, Inc., Kansas City, 1989—. Mem. guidance com. Found. Interior Designer Edn. Research, 1972-82 Bd. visitors Found. Interior Design Edn. Research, 1984-90. Mem. adv. bd. Toy & Miniature Mus. Kansas City, 1985—; bd. govs., chmn. adv. bd. Hand-in-Hand, 1995—. With USAAF, 1954-57. Award of merit Mo.W./Kans. chpt., 1971 Fellow Am. Soc. Interior Designers (pres. Mo.W./Kans. chpt. 1966-72, 73-74, regional v.p. 1969-71, nat. gov. 1969-74) Presbyterian. Home and Office: 12801 Cherry St Kansas City MO 64145-1308 Office Phone: 816-942-8699. *As strange as it may sound in this day and age, I have always tried my best to treat my clients, my suppliers, my peers, and whomever I come in contact with, in the same manner that I hope they would treat me. Professionally, I have always tried to project my clients personality and interests so that the completed job reflects them and not me. To me, an interior is not a success if it winds up looking like the designer rather than the person, or persons, for whom it was designed.*

BAKER, ROBERT W., lawyer; b. Wilmington, Del., Sept. 7, 1956; B in bus., economics, and acctg., U. Del.; JD, U. Tex., Austin. Bar: Tex. 1981, La. 1986. Joined Tenneco Energy, 1983, named v.p., assoc gen. counsel, 1995, sr. v.p., assoc. gen. counsel; (Tenneco Energy merged with El Paso Corp., 1996); named sr. v.p., assoc. gen. counsel El Paso Corp., Houston, 1996, sr. v.p., dep. gen. counsel, 2002—03, exec. v.p., 2003—, pres. El Paso Merchant Energy subsid., 2003, gen. counsel, 2004—. Office: El Paso Corp 1001 Louisiana St PO Box 2511 Houston TX 77002-2511

BAKER, ROLAND JERALD, finance educator; b. Pendleton, Oreg., Feb. 27, 1938; s. Roland E. and Theresa Helen (Forest) B.; m. Judy Lynn Murphy, Nov. 24, 1973; children: Kristen L., Kurt F., Brian H. BA, Western Wash. U., 1961; MBA, U. Mich., 1968. Cert. purchasing mgr., profl. contract mgr. Asst. dir. purchasing and stores U. Wash., Seattle, 1970-75; mgr. purchasing and material control Foss Launch & Tug Co., Seattle, 1975-79; faculty Shoreline C.C., 1972-79, 98—, Pacific Luth. U., 1977-79, Edmonds C.C., 1974-79; chmn. educators group Nat. Assn. Purchasing Mgmt., Tempe, Ariz., 1976-79, exec. v.p., 1979-98; pres. Nat. Assn. Purchasing Mgmt. Svcs., Tempe, Ariz., 1989-95. Faculty Ariz. State U., Tempe, 1988-91; world bus. adv. Coun. Am. Grad. Sch. of Internat. Mgmt., Glendale, Ariz., 1994-98; adv. bd. blockbuy-.com, Inc., 1999-01, Perfect.com., Inc., 2000—; exec. v.p. MyGroupbuy Inc., 2000-03, also bd. dirs.; mem. faculty Shoreline C.C., Seattle, 1998—. Author: Purchasing Factomatic, 1977, Inventory System Factomatic, 1978, Policies and Procedures for Purchasing and Material Control, 1980, rev. edit., 1992. With USN, 1961-70, comdr. Res., 1969-91. Recipient Disting. Achievement award Ariz. State U. Coll. Bus., 1997; U.S. Navy postgrad. fellow, 1967. Mem. Purchasing Mgmt. Assn. Wash. (pres. 1978-79), Nat. Minority Supplier Devel. Coun. (bd. dirs.), Am. Prodn. and Inventory Control Soc., Nat. Assn. Purchasing Mgmt. (exec. v.p. 1979-97), Nat. Contract Mgmt. Assn., Internat. Fedn. Purchasing and Materials Mgmt. (exec. com. 1984-87, exec. adv. com. 1991-98). Office: Shoreline CC 16101 Greenwood Ave N Seattle WA 98133-5667 Business E-Mail: jbaker@shoreline.edu.

BAKER, RONALD JAMES, language educator, academic administrator; b. London, Aug. 24, 1924; s. James Herbert Walter and Ethel Frances (Miller) B.; m. Helen Gillespie Elder, Sept. 3, 1949; children: Ann, Lynn, Ian, Sarah, Katherine; m. Frances Marilyn Frazer; 1 son, Ralph Edward. BA, U. B.C., Can., 1951, MA, 1953; LLD (hon.), U. N.B., Can., 1970, Mt. Allison U., 1977, U. P.E.I., 1989, Simon Fraser U., 1990. Lectr. U. B.C., 1951-53, instr., 1953-54, 56-57, asst. prof., 1957-62, sec. Senate Com. Acad. Orgn., 1961-62, assoc. prof., 1962-63; prof. English Simon Fraser U., 1964-69, dir. acad. planning, 1964-65, head dept. English, 1964-68; first pres. U. P.E.I., Charlottetown, Can., 1969-78, univ. prof., 1979-91. Dir. Inst. Dept. Leadership, U. P.E.I., David MacDonald Stewart prof. Can. studies, 1988-91; disting. vis. prof. U. New Eng., Australia, 1984; mem. Acad. Bd. B.C., 1963-69, Joint Bd. Tchr. Edn. B.C., 1964-66; mem., chmn. various selection coms. including Can. Coun., 1971-77, Nat. Def. Dept., 1981-98, Can. Radio-TV and Telecomm. Commn., 1982-87; bd. govs. N.S. Tech. Coll., Holland Coll., 1968-78, Killam Prize Com., 1984-87, Molson Prize Com., 1987-88; chair mil. and strategic studies com. Nat. Def. Can., 1989-98. Editor: The Faculty Handbook, 1960; author (with W. G. Hardwick): North Shore Regional College Study, 1965, Regional College Study: Delta, Langley, Richmond, Surrey, 1966; contbr. articles to profl. jours. Mem. interim coun. U. No. B.C., 1989-90; presiding officer Can. Citizen Ct., 1990-; vol. advisor First Nations Bands, Can. Exec. Svc. Orgn., 1984-. Served with RAF, 1943-47. Decorated Officer Order of Can., 1978; recipient Can. Centennial medal, 1967, Jubilee medal, 1977, Disting. Mem. award Can. Soc. Study of H.E., 1988, Can. 125 medal, 1992, Golden Jubilee medal, 2002; Humanities Rsch. Coun. Can. fellow, 1954, 55, grantee, 1968; Royal Soc. Can. fellow, 1954-56; Can. Coun. rsch. grantee, 1969. Mem. Assn. Univs. and Colls. Can. (dir. 1972-78), Assn. Atlantic Univs. (pres. 1976-78), Can. Soc. for Study Higher Edn. (v.p. 1974, pres. 1975-76, named Disting. Mem. 1988), Assn. Can. Univ. Tchrs. English (pres. 1967-68), Can. Linguistic Assn. (exec. 1966-67). Office Phone: 604-591-2562. Personal E-mail: rjfbaker@hotmail.com.

BAKER, RONALD LEE, folklore educator; b. Indpls., June 30, 1937; m. Catherine Anne Neal, Oct. 21, 1960; children: Susannah Jill, Jonathan Kemp. BS, Ind. State U., Terre Haute, 1960; MA, Ind. State U., 1961; postgrad., U. Ill., 1963-65; PhD, Ind U., 1969. Instr. English U. Ill., Urbana, 1963-65; teaching assoc. Ind. U., Ft. Wayne, 1965-66; prof. English Ind State U., Terre Haute, 1966—, chmn. dept., 1980—; vis. lectr. U. Ill., 1972-73; vis. assoc. prof. Ind. U., Bloomington, 1975, vis. prof., 1978, 84. Author: Folklore in the Writings of Rowland E. Robinson, 1973, Hoosier Folk Legends, 1982, Jokelore, 1986, French Folklife in Old Vincennes, 1989, The Study of Place Names, 1991, From Needmore to Prosperity: Hoosier Place Names in Folklore and History, 1995, Homeless, Friendless, and Penniless: The WPA Interviews with Former Slaves Living in Indiana, 2000; (with others) Indiana Place Names, 1975. Fellow Am. Folklore Soc.; mem. MLA, Am. Name Soc. (v.p. 1981-82), Hoosier Folklore Soc. (pres. 1970-79, exec. sec.-treas. 1988-2000). Home: 3688 N Randall St Terre Haute IN 47805-9736 Office: Indiana State University Terre Haute IN 47809-9989 Office Phone: 812-237-3163. E-mail: ronbaker@indstate.edu.

BAKER, RONALD PHILLIP, service company executive; b. Kansas City, Mo., Feb. 15, 1942; s. Harry and Ruth Sarah (Bornstein) B.; m. Marilyn Gitterman, Dec. 27, 1964 (div. Dec. 1993); children: Kevin, Corey; m. Kendra F.; m. Dierdre Christensen, May 8, 1994. Student, U. Okla., 1960—63; BA in Sociology and Govt., postgrad., U. Mo. Kansas City, 1965. Acct. rep. Am. House and Window Cleaning Co., Kansas City, 1965—69; dist. mgr. ops. Am. Bldg. Svcs., Kansas City, 1969—72; pres. BG Maintenance Mgmt., Kansas City, 1972—86; chmn. bd. dirs. BGM Industries, Kansas City, 1987—. Bd. dirs. Flo Harris Supporting Found. V.p. Jewish Cmty. Ctr., Kansas City, 1985—88, pres., 1989—90, Jewish Vocat. Svcs., Kansas City, 1985—88; v.p. Jewish Fedn. Greater Kansas City, 1992—93; bd. dirs. Village Shalom, 1998—2003, chmn., CEO search com., 2002, chmn. bd. dirs., 2003—; bd. dirs. Jewish Cmty. Campus of Greater Kansas City, 2004, Beth Shalom Synagogue, Kans. City, 1985—89, Jewish Cmty. Rels. Bur.; exec. com. Jewish Cmty. Campus, 2005; bd. dirs. Flo Harris Supporting Found., Jewish Cmty. Ctrs. Assn., 1989—93, mem. exec. com., 1990—91; bd. dirs. Jewish Fedn. Greater Kansas City, 1986—92, Jewish Cmty. Found. Greater Kansas City, 1991—94, mem. strategic planning com., 1997; bd. dirs. Village Shalom, chmn. of bd. dirs., 2004, 2005. Mem. Bldg. Svc. Contractors Assn. Internat. (bd. dirs., chmn. seminars, conv. spkr., pres. club 1981-93, edn. com. 1981-90, chmn. edn. com. 1989—, info. ctrl. com. 1985-93, chmn. ann. conv. 1988, exec. com. 1988—, treas. 1989, v.p. 1990-92, pres. 1994, chmn. fin. com. 1990, exec. com., chair strategic planning task force 1989-90, chmn., CEO seminar com. 1997-99, strategic planning com. 1996—, govt. affairs com. 1996—), Bldg. Owners and Mgrs. Assn. Kansas City, Jewish Fedn. Kansas City (v.p. 1986-87, 91-93, co-chmn. fin. resources planning com., Young Leadership award 1981), Menninger Found. (pres. Topeka chpt. 1986—), Hallbrook Country Club, Sigma Alpha Mu, Delta Sigma Pi. Republican. Avocations: water sports, boating, skiing, running, reading. Office: BGM Industries 1225 E 18th St Kansas City MO 64108-1605 Office Phone: 816-421-8088. Personal E-mail: rbaker@bgserve.com.

BAKER, ROSALYN HESTER, state senator; b. El Campo, Tex., Sept. 20, 1946; BA, Southwest Tex. State U., 1968; grad., U. Southwestern La., 1969. Lobbyist, asst. dir. Govt. Rels. Nat. Edn. Assn., Washington, 1969-80; owner, retail sporting goods store Maui, Hawaii, 1980-87; legis. aide to Hon. Karen Honita Hawaii Ho. of Reps., Honolulu, 1987, mem., 1989-93, house majority leader, 1993, state senator Hawaii, 1993-98, majority leader, 1995-96; dir. office econ. devel. County of Maui, Hawaii, 1999—2002, chair health com., 2003—. Co-chair ways and means com., 1998; co-chair rules com. Hawaii State Dem. Conv., 1990, chair health com. 2003, resolutions com. 1994; mem. energy environ. com., trans., mil. affairs, govt. ops. com.; vice chmn. consumer protection and housing com. Del.-at-large Dem. Nat. Conv., 1984, 92, 96; mem. exec. com. Maui County Dem. Com., 1986-88; mem. Workforce Investment Bd., Lahaina Town Action Com.; former vice chmn. Maui Svc. Area Bd. om Mental Health and Substance Abuse; former unit pres. Am. Cancer Soc., bd. dirs., Hawaii-Pacific; bd. dirs. Maui Econ. Devel. Bd.; mem. Am. Cancer Soc. Mem.: Maalaea Cmty. Assn., Kihei Cmty. Assn., West Maui

Taxpayers Assn. Democrat. Home: PO Box 10394 Lahaina HI 96761-0394 Office: State Capitol Rm 220 Honolulu HI 96813 Office Phone: 808-586-6070. Business E-Mail: senbaker@capitol.hawaii.gov.

BAKER, RUSSELL WAYNE, columnist, writer; b. Loudoun County, Va., Aug. 14, 1925; s. Benjamin Rex and Lucy Elizabeth (Robinson) B.; m. Miriam Emily Nash, Mar. 11, 1950; children: Kathleen Leland, Allen Nash, Michael Lee. BA, Johns Hopkins U., 1947, L.H.D., Hamilton Coll., Franklin Pierce Coll., Princeton U., Yale U., Long Island U., Conn. Coll.; LL.D., Union Coll.; D.Litt., Wake Forest U., U. Miami, Rutgers U., Columbia U.; H.H.D., Hood Coll. With Balt. Sun, 1947-54; mem. Washington bur. N.Y. Times, 1954-62; columnist editorial page N.Y. Times, 1962—; column Observer nationally syndicated N.Y. Times News Svc. Author: City on the Potomac, 1958, American in Washington, 1961, No Cause for Panic, 1964, All Things Considered, 1965, Our Next President, 1968, Poor Russell's Almanac, 1972, The Upside Down Man, 1977, So This Is Depravity, 1980, (with others) Home Again, Home Again, 1979, Growing Up, 1982, The Rescue of Miss Yaskell and Other Pipe Dreams, 1983, The Good Times, 1989, There's a Country in My Cellar, 1990; editor The Norton Book of Light Verse, 1986, Russell Baker's Book of American Humor, 1993. Served with USNR, 1943-45. Recipient Frank Sullivan Meml. award, 1976, George Polk award for commentary, 1979, Pulitzer prize for disting. commentary, 1979, Pulitzer prize for biography, 1983, Elmer Holmes Bobst prize for nonfiction, 1983, Howland Meml. prize Yale U., 1989, Fourth Estate award Nat. Press Club, 1989. Mem. Am. Acad. and Inst. Arts and Letters (elected 1984), Am. Acad. Arts and Scis. (fellow 1993). Office: NY Times 229 W 43rd St New York NY 10036-3959*

BAKER, SAUL PHILLIP, geriatrician, cardiologist, internist; b. Cleve., Dec. 7, 1924; s. Barnet and Florence (Kleinman) B. BS in Physics, Case Inst. Tech., 1945; postgrad., Western Res. U., 1946-47; M.Sc. in Physiology, Ohio State U., 1949, MD, 1953, PhD in Physiology, 1957; JD, Case Western Res. U., 1981. Intern Cleve. Met. Gen. Hosp., 1953-54; sr. asst. surgeon Gerontology Br. Nat. Heart Inst, NIH, now Gerontology Research Ctr., Nat. Inst. Aging, 1954-56; asst. vis. staff physician dept. medicine Balt. City Hosps. (now Francis Scott Key Hosp.) and Johns Hopkins Hosp., 1954-56; sr. asst. resident in internal medicine U. Chgo. Hosps., 1956-57; asst. prof. internal medicine Chgo. Med. Sch., 1957-62; assoc. prof. internal medicine Cook County Hosp. Grad. Sch. Medicine, Chgo., 1958-62; assoc. attending physician Cook County Hosp., 1957-62; practice medicine specializing in geriatrics, cardiology, internal medicine Cleve., 1962-70, 72-93; cons., 1993—. Head dept. geriatrics St. Vincent Charity Hosp., Cleve., 1964-67; cons. internal medicine and cardiology Bur. Disability Determination, Old-Age and Survivors Ins., Social Security Adminstrn., 1963—; cons. internal medicine City of Cleve., 1964—; medicare med. cons. Gen. Am. Life Ins. Co., St. Louis, 1970-71; cons. internal medicine and cardiology Ohio Bur. Worker's Compensation, 1964—; cons. cardiovascular disease FAA, 1973—; cons. internal medicine and cardiology State of Ohio, 1974—. Contbr. articles to profl. and sci. jours. Mem. sci. coun. Northeastern Ohio affiliate Am. Heart Assn.; former mem. adv. com. Sr. Adult div. Jewish Community Ctr. Cleve.; mem. vis. com. colls. Case Western Res. U.; former mem. com. older people Fedn. Community Planning Cleve. Fellow AAAS (life), Am. Coll. Cardiology, Gerontol. Soc. Am. (former Ohio regent), Am. Geriatrics Soc., Cleve. Med. Libr. Assn. (life); mem. Am. Physiol. Soc., AMA, Ohio Med. Assn., N.Y. Acad. Scis. (life), Chgo. Soc. Internal Medicine, Am. Fedn. Clin. Rsch., Soc. Exptl. Biology and Medicine, Am. Diabetes Assn., Diabetes Assn. Greater Cleve. (profl. sect.), Am. Heart Assn. (fellow council arteriosclerosis), Nat. Assn. Disability Examiners, Nat. Rehab. Assn., Am. Pub. Health Assn., Acad. Medicine Cleve., Internat. Soc. Cardiology (coun. epidemiology and prevention), Am. Soc. Law and Medicine, Cleve. Clinic Club(past sec.), Lake County Med. Soc. (hon,) Masons (32 degree), Shriners, Sigma Xi, Phi Delta Epsilon, Sigma Alpha Mu (past pres. Cleve. alumni club). Home: PO Box 24246 Cleveland OH 44124-0246 Office Phone: 440-461-6716.

BAKER, SHIRLEY KISTLER, university administrator; b. Lehighton, Pa., Mar. 16, 1943; d. Harvey Daniel and Miriam Grace (Osenbach) Kistler; m. Richard Christopher Baker, Oct. 22, 1966; children: Nicholas Christopher, India Jane. BA, Muhlenberg Coll., 1965; MA, MALS, U. Chgo., 1974. Undergrad. libr. Northwestern U., Evanston, Ill., 1974-76; access libr. Johns Hopkins U., Balt., 1976-82; assoc. dir. librs. MIT, Cambridge, 1982-89; dean univ. librs. Washington U., St. Louis, 1989-95, vice chancellor for info. tech., dean univ. librs., 1995—. Contbr. articles to profl. jours. Mem. ALA, Nat. Info. Standards Orgn. (bd. dirs. 1990-94), Assn. Rsch. Librs. (bd. dirs. 1996-2002, pres. 2000-01), Coalition for Networked Info. (steering com. 1999—), Mo. Libr. Network Corp. (bd. dirs. 1990-00). Democrat. Avocations: reading, travel. Home: 6310 Alexander Dr Saint Louis MO 63105-2223 Office: Washington U Campus Box 1061 1 Brookings Dr Saint Louis MO 63130-4899 E-mail: baker@wustl.edu.

BAKER, STANLEY BECKWITH, education educator; b. Mpls., Sept. 3, 1935; s. Stanley Forrest and Dorothy Ruth (Beckwith) Baker; m. Barbara Ann Laufenburger, Aug. 17, 1957 (dec.); children: Susan Elizabeth, David Alan; m. Mary Esther Clark Martin, June 10, 2000. BA, Augsburg Coll., 1957; MA, U. Minn., 1963; PhD, SUNY, Buffalo, 1971. Lic. profl. counselor N.C., nat. cert. counselor. Tchr. social studies Spring Valley (Wis.) HS, 1957-63; tchr. history Janesville (Wis.) HS, 1963-66, sch. counselor, 1964-67, Parker HS, Janesville, 1967-69; from asst. prof. to assoc. prof. edn. Pa. State U., University Park, 1971—84, prof., 1984—94, N.C. State U., Raleigh, 1994—, head dept., 1994—2001. Office: NC State U PO Box 7801 Raleigh NC 27695-7801 Office Phone: 919-515-6360. Business E-Mail: stanley-baker@ncsu.edu.

BAKER, STEPHEN C., lawyer; b. Harvey, Ill., 1953; AB, Duke Univ., 1975; JD, Villanova Univ., 1980. Bar: Pa. 1980. Ptnr. Stradley Ronon Stevens & Young, Phila., 1981—2001; ptnr., chair insurance practice group Drinker Biddle & Reath LLP, Phila., 2001—. Dir. Royer-Greaves Sch. for the Blind. Mem.: ABA, Pa. Bar Assn. Office: Drinker Biddle & Reath LLP One Logan Sq' 18th & Cherry Sts Philadelphia PA 19103-6996 Office Phone: 215-988-2769. Office Fax: 215-988-2757. Business E-Mail: stephen.baker@dbr.com.

BAKER, STEPHEN DENIO, physics professor; b. Durham, N.C., Nov. 30, 1936; s. Roger Denio and Eleanor Elizabeth (Ussher) B.; m. Paula Eisenstein, June 24, 1962; children: Hannah Hitzhusen, Sarah Topper. BS, Duke U., 1957; MS, Yale U., 1959, PhD, 1963. Lectr. physics Rice U., Houston, 1963-66, asst. prof., 1966-69, assoc. prof., 1969-73, prof., 1973—2004, prof. emeritus, 2004—. Office: Rice Univ Dept Physics-MS 61 6100 Main St Houston TX 77005-1892

BAKER, STEPHEN R., physician; b. Bklyn., Mar. 22, 1942; s. Louis and Edith Helen (Kalm) B.; m. Marjorie Gilman, Sept. 18, 1971; children: Amelia, Elizabeth, Catherine, Nina. BA, Wesleyan U., Middletown, Conn., 1964; MD, Albert Einstein Sch. Medicine, 1968; MPhil, Columbia U., 1980. Staff radiologist Albert Einstein Coll. Medicine, Bronx, N.Y., 1972-73, 75-76; pvt. practice radiology Perth Amboy, N.J., 1976-78; staff radiologist Cabrini Hosp., N.Y.C., 1978-79; ast. dir. radiology Albert Einstein Coll. Medicine, 1980-86, acting chmn. radiology, 1986-90; chmn. radiology N.J. Med. Sch., Newark, 1990—, assoc. dean grad. med. edn., 2000—. Mem. exec. bd. Radiology Outreach Found., San Francisco, 1994-2002; bd.dirs. Children of Chernobyl, N.J., 1996-99. Author: 10 books; editor-in-chief Emergency Radiology, 2000—, asst. editor Am. Jour. Radiology, 1999—. Maj. U.S. Army, 1973-75. Named Disting. Alumnus, Wesleyan U., 2004. Mem. Am. Soc. Emergency Radiology (pres. 1994-95), Soc. Chairmen Acad. Tech. Depts (pres.-elect). Avocations: geography, history, softball, classical piano. Office: UMDNJ-NJ Med Sch Dept Radiology 150 Bergen St Newark NJ 07103-2406 E-mail: bakersr@umdnj.ed.

BAKER, STUART DAVID, lawyer; b. N.Y.C., July 2, 1935; s. Stuart and Edith (Kennelly) B.; m. Alixandra Fitzwilliam-Tate Collins, June 16, 1980; children from previous marriage— Stuart Richard, David Michael, Elisabeth Kendall BA, Hamilton Coll., 1957; LLB, Columbia U. Bar: N.Y. 1960. Assoc. Chadbourne, Parke, Whiteside & Wolff, N.Y.C., 1960-69, ptnr., 1969-85, Chadbourne & Parke, N.Y.C., 1985—, mem. mgmt. com., 1985-95, 96—. Exec. v.p. Purdue Frederick Co., Purdue Pharma L.P.; dir. Napp Pharm. Group Ltd. (UK), Mundipharma Labs. GmbH, Mundipharma AG (Switzerland); mem. supervisory bd. Mundipharma GmbH, Germany, 1994—. Vestryman St. Mary's Ch., Scarborough-on-Hudson, N.Y., 1967-76, sr. warden, 1974-76; chmn. zoning bd. appeals Town of Ossining, N.Y., 1968-78; mem. Coun. of Diocese of N.Y., 1974-79; bd. dirs. Legal Aid Soc., 1993-99; bd. trustees St. Peters Sch., 1975-99. Mem. N.Y. State Bar Assn., Conn. Bar Assn., Westchester County Bar Assn., Assn. Bar City of N.Y., Suffolk County Bar Assn., Internat. Bar Assn. (rapporteur), Inter-Am. Bar Assn., Union Internat. des Avocats, Swiss Am. C. of C., SAR, Sleepy Hollow Country Club, River Club (N.Y.C.), Netherlands Club (N.Y.C.), Water Mill Beach (N.Y.) Club (pres. 1991-96). Episcopalian. Avocations: fly fishing, tennis, golf, windsurfing. Home: 16 Sutton Pl New York NY 10022-3057 Office: Chadbourne & Parke LLP 30 Rockefeller Plz Fl 31 New York NY 10112-0129

BAKER, SYLVA SARA, librarian; b. Phila., Jan. 6, 1932; d. Benjamin and Irene (Borteck) Cann; m. David Baker, June 13, 1954; children— Cynthia, Joseph, Julia, Theodore. B.A., U. Pa., 1952, M.A. in History, 1953; M.L.S., Drexel U., 1973. Librarian Delaware County Planning Commn., Media, Pa., 1972-77; exec. sec. Tri-State Coll. Library Coop., Rosemont, Pa., 1977-79; v.p. Acad. Natural Scis., Phila., 1980—; cons. Carnegie Mus. Natural History, Pitts., 1984; trustee Pa. Library Network, 1985— . Contbr. to Museum Librarianship, 1985. Mem. Spl. Libraries Assn. (v.p. Phila. chpt. 1985-86, pres. 1986-87), Assn. Coll. and Research Libraries (sec. Delaware Valley chpt. 1981-83), Soc. for History of Natural History, Pa. Hort. Soc. (long range planning com. 1985). Avocations: gardening; microcomputers; birding. Office: Acad of Natural Scis 19th and Pkwy Philadelphia PA 19103

BAKER, TANIA ANN, biology professor, researcher; BS in BioChemistry, U. Wisconsin, 1983; PhD, Stanford U., 1988. Postdoctoral fellow Stanford U., NIH; asst. prof. biology MIT, 1992—97; investigator Howard Hughes Medical Inst., 1994—; assoc. prof. biology MIT, 1997—99, prof. biology, 1999—2002, Whitehead prof. biology, 2002—. Asst. molecular biologist Mass. Gen. Hospital, Boston. Recipient Young Investigator award, NSF, Harold E. Edgerton award, Eli Lilly award, Am. Soc. of Microbiology. Fellow: Am. Acad. Arts & Sciences; mem.: Am. Soc. for Biochemistry & Molecular Biology (Schering-Plough Scientific Achievement award 1998). Office: MIT Biology Dept 31 Ames St Room 68-132 Cambridge MA 02139 also: Howard Hughes Medical Inst 400 Jones Bridge Rd Chevy Chase MD 20815-6789

BAKER, THOMAS EUGENE, law educator; b. Youngstown, Ohio, Feb. 25, 1953; s. John M. and Helen Marie (Kish) B.; m. Jane Marie Schussler, June 15, 1974; 1 child, Thomas Athanasius. BS cum laude, Fla. State U., 1974; JD with high honors, U. Fla., 1977. Bars: Fla. 1979, U.S. Dist. Ct. (no. dist.) Tex. 1979, U.S. Supreme Ct. 1982, U.S. Ct. Appeals (5th cir.) 1979, U.S. Ct. Appeals (11th cir.) 1981. Law clk. to presiding judge U.S. Ct. Appeals (5th cir.) Ga., Atlanta, 1977—79; prof. law Tex. Tech. U., Lubbock, 1979—98, Alvin R. Allison prof., 1992—98; jud. fellow U.S. Supreme Ct., Washington, 1985—86, acting adminstrv. asst. to chief justice, 1986—87; James Madison chair constnl. law, dir. constnl. law ctr. Drake U. Law Sch., Des Moines, 1998—2002; mem. founding faculty Coll. of Law, Fla. Internat. U., Miami, 2002—. Mem. adv. bd. Am. Criminal Law Rev., Washington, 1981-85; standing com. rules and procedures U.S. Jud. Conf., 1990-95; vis. prof. U. Fla., 1994; Fulbright prof. U. Athens, Greece, 1993; bd. editors Preview U.S. Supreme Ct. Cases, 1991—. Author: Rationing Justice on Appeal: The Problems of the U.S. Court of Appeals, 1994, The Most Wonderful Work: Our Constitution Interpreted, 1996, Federal Court Practice and Procedure: A Third Branch Bibliography, 2001; author: (with T. Floyd) Can a Good Christian Be a Good Lawyer?, 1998; author: (with J. Williams) Constitutional Analysis in a Nutshell, 2d edit., 2003; author: (with R. Jarvis and A. McClurg) Amicus Humoriae: An Anthology of Legal Humor, 2004; author: (with J. Stack) At War with Civil Rights and Civil Liberties, 2005; mem. editl. bd. Jour. Supreme Ct. History, 1991—93; contbr. articles to profl. jours. Recipient Faculty Rsch. award Tex. Tech U., 1996, 94, 83, Outstanding Law Prof. award, 1988, 89, Spencer A. Wells U. Tchg. award, SBA Pres.'s award Drake Law Sch., 2002, Pioneer award Fla. Internat. U. Coll. Law, 2003; Justice Tom C. Clark fellow Jud. Fellows, 1986. Mem. ABA (various sects. and coms.), Am. Law Inst. (elected), Am. Judicature Soc. (bd. dirs. 2000-02), Order of Coif. Byzantine Catholic. Avocations: pottery, racquetball. Office: Fla Internat U Coll Law University Park GL 496 Miami FL 33199 Office Phone: 305-348-8342. Business E-Mail: thomas.baker@fiu.edu.

BAKER, THOMAS LINDSAY, history professor, museum director, consultant; s. Garnell A. and Mary Lois (Miller) Baker; m. Julie Ann Philips, July 6, 1990; stepchildren: Adam K. Shaw, Jason C. Shaw. BA, Tex. Tech. U., Lubbock, 1969, MA, 1972, PhD, 1977. Program mgr. history of engring. program Tex. Tech. U., Lubbock, 1970—75, 1977—79; Fulbright lectr. Tech. U. of Wroclaw, Poland, 1975—77; curator agr. and tech. Panhandle-Plains Hist. Mus., Canyon, Tex., 1978—87; curator history Ft. Worth Mus. Sci. and History, 1987—89; asst. prof. mus. studies Baylor U., Waco, 1989—97; dir. Tex. Heritage Mus. Hill Coll., Hillsboro, 1997—2002; W.K. Gordon endowed chair Tarleton State U., Stephenville, 2002—. Cons. Tex. Ednl. Devel. Lab., Austin, Tex., 1974—75, Inst. Texan Cultures, San Antonio, 1978—79, Kans. State Hist. Soc., Topeka, 1986—87; coun. mem. Internat. Molinological Soc., Netherlands, 1993—2000. Author: Field Guide to American Windmills, 1985, Adobe Walls: History and Archeology, 1986, More Ghost Towns of Texas, 2003; editor: Windmillers' Gazette. Pres. Rotary Club of Hillsboro, Tex., 2001—02. Recipient Father Leopold Moczygemba award, Polish-Am. Priests Assn., 1990, cert. of Commendation, Am. Assn. State and Local History, 1993, Glenda Morgan award, Tex. Hist. Commn., 1999. Fellow: Tex. State Hist. Assn.; mem.: Western History Assn., Tex. Assn. of Museums. Avocations: photography, antique automobiles, backpacking. Office: Tarleton State U Box T 0190 Stephenville TX 76402

BAKER, THOMAS WILLIAM, lawyer; b. Buffalo, Mar. 29, 1950; s. David Clayton Jr. and Marjorie Lois (Hagen) B. AB, Syracuse U., 1972; MBA, Ga. State U., 1978; JD, Vanderbilt U., 1981. Assoc. Smith, Cohen, Ringel, Kohler & Martin, Atlanta, 1981-84, Harkleroad Hardy, Atlanta, 1984-85, Fortson & White, Atlanta, 1985-86; spl. asst. to gen. mgr. Pitts. Pirates Baseball Club, 1986; ptnr., corp. securities practice group Troutman Sanders LLP, Atlanta, 1998—. Mem. ABA, Atlanta Bar Assn. Clubs: Atlanta Renegades Rugby (pres. 1984—). Lutheran. Office: Troutman Sanders LLP 600 Peachtree St NE Atlanta GA 30308-2216 Office Phone: 404-885-3198. Office Fax: 404-962-6505. Business E-Mail: tom.baker@troutmansanders.com.

BAKER, THURBERT E., state attorney general; b. Rocky Mount, N.C., Dec. 16, 1952; m. Catherine Baker; children: Jocelyn, Chelsea. BA in Polit. Sci., U. NC, Chapel Hill, 1975; JD, Emory U., 1979. With US Environ. Protection Agy.; private pratice; mem. Ga. Ho. of Reps., 1988—90, asst. adminstrn. fl. leader, 1990—93, adminstrn. fl. leader, 1993—97; atty. gen. State of Ga., 1997—. Mem. Coun. on Fgn. Rels. Trustee Statewide Ga. Diabetes Bd., Ebenezer Bapt. Ch., Atlanta; bd. dir. DeKalb Coll. Found.; mem. DeKalb County Libr. Bd.; bd. dir. Nat. Med. Soc., Emory U. Named one of America's Top Black Lawyers, Black Enterprise Mag., 2003. Mem.: State Bar Ga. (bd. governor, mem., jud. nominating commn.), Nat. Assn. of Atty. Gen. (v.p., vice-chair, Homeland Security Com., rep., ABA House of Delegates), Nat. Med. Soc.-Emory U., DeKalb County C. of C. (bd. dirs.). Democrat. Office: Atty Gen Dept Law 40 Capitol Sq SW Atlanta GA 30334-9003

BAKER, TIMOTHY DANFORTH, physician, educator; b. Balt., July 4, 1925; s. Frank and Alice Elizabeth (Chandler) B.; m. Susan Lowell Pardee, June 23, 1951; children: Timothy, David, Susan. BA, Johns Hopkins U., 1948, MPH, 1954; MD, U. Md., 1952. Intern U. Md. Hosp., Balt., 1952-53; resident pub. health N.Y. State Dept. Pub. Health, N.Y.C., 1953-56; health officer Syracuse, NY, 1958-59; asst. and acting chief health USAID, India, 1956-58; assoc. prof. Johns Hopkins U. Sch. Pub. Health, Balt., 1959-67, asst. dean, 1959-77, prof. internat. health, health svcs. adminstrn., and environ. health, 1967—, pres. faculty gen. assembly, 1987—, dir. Hubert H. Humphrey scholars program, 1987—. V.p., dir. Univ. Assocs., 1973-77; vis. prof. epidemiology U. Minn., 1976; dir. Intermed., 1982—; external examiner U. Singapore; vis. prof. Am. U., Armenia, 1999; mem. Surgeon Gen.'s Com. on Global Health, 2004; mem. Md. Gov.'s Commn. on Minority Health, Md. Gov.'s Task Force on Violence; cons. in field. Author: Health Manpower in a Developing Economy, Assessment of Health Status and Needs, International Health Perspectives; contbr. articles to profl. publs. First vice chmn. Balt. com. Rep. Party; del., nominating com. Rep. party; bd. dirs., treas. Pan Am. Health Edn. Found. Served with USAF, 1943-45; USPHS, 1956-58. Recipient Disting. Grad. award, Balt. Poly Inst., Heritage award, Johns Hopkins U. Fellow: AAAS; mem.: APHA (chmn. epidemiology sect., internat. health sect., Lifetime Achievement award 1994), Balt. Med. Soc. (chmn. med. care com.), Md. Pub. Health Assn. (pres.), Md. Med. Soc. (chmn. health manpower com., ho. of dels.), Delta Omega, Omicron Delta Kappa. Republican. Home: 4705 Keswick Rd Baltimore MD 21210-2322 Office: Johns Hopkins U Sch Hygiene 615 N Wolfe St Baltimore MD 21205-2103 Office Phone: 410-614-3819. Business E-Mail: tbaker@jhsph.edu.

BAKER, VERNON G., II, lawyer; BA, Dartmouth Coll.; JD, Am. U. Assoc. Schnader, Harrison, Segal & Lewis, 1978—80; counsel Scott Paper Co.; assoc. gen. counsel Advanced Material Group; v.p., gen. counsel, Corp. Rsch. Tech. Hoechst Celanese Corp; sr. v.p., gen. counsel, sect. Meritor, 1999—2000; sr. v.p., gen. counsel ArvinMeritor, 1999—. Named Trailblazer Award, Minority Corp. Counsel Assn. Office: Arvin Meritor Inc 2135 W Maple Inc Troy MI 48084

BAKER, VICTOR RICHARD, geologist, hydrologist, researcher, research scientist, educator; b. Waterbury, Conn., Feb. 19, 1945; s. Victor A. Baker and Doris Elizabeth (Day) MacGregor; m. Pauline Marie Heaton, June 10, 1967; children: Trent Heaton, Theodore William. BS, Rensselaer Poly. Inst., 1967; PhD, U. Colo., 1971. Geophysicist U.S. Geol. Survey, Denver, 1967-71; asst. prof. geology U. Tex., Austin, 1971-76, assoc. prof., 1976-81; prof. U. Ariz., Tucson, 1981—, Regents' prof., 1988—, head dept. hydrology and water resources, 1996—2004. Cons. Lunar and Planetary Inst., Houston, 1983—86, Salt River Project, Phoenix, 1984—87, Argonne (Ill.) Nat. Lab., 1983—93, Sandia (N.Mex) Nat. Labs., 1991—92, U.S. Bur. Reclamation, 1994—2000; com. mem. NRC, Washington, 1978—, NASA, 1978—; vis. fellow Nat. Inst. Hydrology, Roorkee, India, 1987—88, Deccan Coll., Pune, India, 1987—88, U. Adelaide, Australia, 1988, Udall Ctr. Studies Pub. Policy, Tucson, 1994—95. Co-editor: The Channeled Scabland, 1978, Flood Geomorphology, 1988, Global Continental Paleohydrology, 1995, Palaeohydrology and Environmental Change, 1998, Ancient Floods, Modern Hazards, 2002; co-author: Surficial Geology, 1981; editor: Catastrophic Flooding, 1981; author: The Channels of Mars, 1982. Capt. U.S. Army, 1971—72. Recipient David Linton award, Brit. Geomorphological Rsch. Group, 1995; Rsch. grantee, NASA, 1975—, NSF, 1977—, Fulbright Sr. Rsch. fellow, 1979—80, Vis. fellow, Australian Nat. U., Canberra, 1979—80. Fellow: AAAS (chmn. geol., geography sect. 1992—93, councilor 1992—93), Am. Geophys. Union, Geol. Soc. Am. (chmn. planetary geology divsn. 1986, Quaternary geology and geomorphology divsn. 1987, councilor 1990—93, v.p. 1996—97, pres. 1997—98, Easterbrook Disting. Scientist award 2004), European Union Geoscis. (hon.); mem.: Polish Acad. Scis. (fgn. mem.), History Earth Scis. Soc., Nat. Assn. Geology Tchrs., Internat. Union Quaternary Rsch. (pres. commn. global paleohydrology 1995—99), Am. Quaternary Assn., Internat. Assn. Geomorphologists (treas. 1993—97), Sigma Xi. Office: U Ariz Dept Hydrology & Water Resources Tucson AZ 85721-0011 Office Phone: 520-621-7875. E-mail: baker@hwr.arizona.edu.

BAKER, VINCENT LAMONT, professional basketball player; b. Lake Wales, Fla., Nov. 23, 1971; 3 children. BA in Comm., Hartford U., 1993. Player Milw. Bucks NBA, 1993—97; forward Seattle Supersonics NBA, 1997—2002, Boston Celtics NBA, 2002—04, NY Knicks NBA, 2003—05, Houston Rockets NBA, 2005—. Cameo appearence (films) He Got Game. Founder The Stand Tall Found.; volunteer, In The Bag Milw. MACC Fund. Named NBA All Star, 1995—97; named one of 99 Good Guys in Sports, The Sporting News, 1999; named to NBA All-Rookie First Team, 1994, All-NBA Third Team, 1996—97, All-NBA Second Team, 1997—98. Avocations: singing, cooking, pool. Mailing: Houston Rockets 1510 Polk St Houston TX 77002*

BAKER, W. RANDOLPH, brewery executive; Joined Anheuser-Busch Cos. Inc., St. Louis, 1970, various positions to chief exec. and chmn., Busch Entertainment Corp., 1983—96, v.p., CFO, 1996—. Bd. dirs. St. Louis Chapter of the Asthma and Allergy Found. of America. Office: Anheuser-Busch Cos Inc One Busch Pl Saint Louis MO 63118

BAKER, WADE FRANKLIN, retired state bar executive; b. Jackson County, Ill., Dec. 30, 1919; s. Robert David Jr. and Lillian May (Damron) B.; m. Mary Eleanor LaClair, June 29, 1947; 1 child, Denise Ann. BEd, So. Ill. U., 1941; LLB, Lincoln Coll. Law, Springfield, Ill., 1950. Bar: Ill. 1950, Mo. 1957. Asst. sec., counsel Ill. Bar Assn., 1946-57; exec. dir., sec. The Mo. Bar, Jefferson City, 1957-84; pres. B.P. & G. Adv. Svcs., Inc., Jefferson City, 1985-91; ret. Former sec. Mo. Bar Found.; former sec.-treas. Mo. Bar Research, Inc., Mo. Legal Aid Soc.; former treas., asst. sec. Mo. Press Bar Commn. Chmn. adminstrv. bd. 1st United Meth. Ch., 1981—82; dir. for life Meml. Hosp. With anti-aircraft arty. U.S. Army, 1942—46, ETO, with anti-aircraft arty. U.S. Army, 1951—52. Decorated Bronze Star; recipient Bicentennial award Mo. Bar, 1976, Fred Bolton award Nat. Assn. Bar Execs., 1978, Non-Alumni award U. Mo., 1975. Mem. Mo. Bar Assn., Jefferson City Rotary (pres. 1966-67), Jefferson City YMCA (co-founder, former bd. mem.). Home: 2505 Orchard Ln Jefferson City MO 65109-0607

BAKER, WALTER ARNOLD, lawyer; b. Columbia, Ky., Feb. 20, 1937; s. Herschel T. and Mattie B. (Barger) B.; m. Jane Stark Helm, Apr. 24, 1965; children: Thomas Herschel, Ann Tate. AB magna cum laude, Harvard U., 1958, LLB, 1961. Assoc. Brown, Ardery, Todd & Dudley, Louisville, 1961-63; ptnr. Wilson, Baker, Herbert and Garmon, Glasgow, Ky., 1963-67; pvt. practice Glasgow, 1967-81, 83—; asst. gen. counsel Office Sec. Def., Washington, 1981-83; justice Supreme Ct. of Ky., Frankfort, 1996. Rep. Ky. Ho. of Reps., 1968-71, senator State of Ky., 1972-81, 89-96; active Ky. Coun. on Postsecondary Edn., 1997—; pres. Ky. Hist. Soc., 2001-03. Lt. col. USAFR. Mem. Ky. Bar Assn., Barren County Bar Assn., Glasgow Rotary, Glasgow Golf and Country Club, Phi Beta Kappa. Republican. Episcopalian. Address: 917 S Green St Glasgow KY 42141-2086 Office: 213 S Green St Glasgow KY 42141-2694 Office Phone: 270-651-3715. Business E-Mail: wbaker@glasgow.com.

BAKER, WARREN J(OSEPH), university president; b. Fitchburg, Mass., Sept. 5, 1938; s. Preston A. and Grace F. (Jarvis) B.; m. Carol Ann Fitzsimons, Apr. 28, 1962; children: Carrie Ann, Kristin Robin, Christopher, Brian. BS, U. Notre Dame, 1960, MS, 1962; PhD, U. N.Mex., 1966. Rsch. assoc., lectr. E. H. Wang Civil Engring. Rsch. Facility, U. N.Mex., 1962-66; assoc. prof. civil engring. U. Detroit, 1966-71, prof., 1972-79, Chrysler prof., dean engring., 1973-78, acad. v.p., 1976-79; NSF faculty fellow MIT, Cambridge, 1971-72; pres. Calif. Poly. State U., San Luis Obispo, 1979—. Mem. Bd. Internat. Food and Agrl. Devel., USAID, 1983-85; mem. Nat. Sci. Bd., 1985-94, Calif. Bus. Higher Edn. Forum, 1993-98; founding mem. Calif. Coun. on Sci. and Tech., 1989—; trustee Amigos of E.A.R.T.H. Coll., 1991-96; bd. dirs. John Wiley & Sons, Inc., 1993—; bd. regents The Am. Archtl. Found., 1995-97; co-chair Joint Policy Coun. on Agr. and Higher Edn., 1995—; mem. Bus.-Higher Edn. Forum, 2001—; bd. dirs. Westport Innovations, Inc., 2002-. Contbr. articles to profl. jours. Mem. Detroit Mayor's Mgmt. Adv. Com., 1975-76; mem. engring. adv. bd. U. Calif., Berkeley, 1984-96; bd. dirs. Calif. Coun. for Environ. and Econ. Balance, 1980-85, Soc. Mfg. Engrs. Edn. Found., 2001-, bd. dirs., 2002-04; trustee Nat. Coop. Edn. Assn.; chmn. bd. dirs. Civil Engring. Rsch. Found., 1989-91, bd. dirs., 1991-94. Fellow Engring. Soc.

Detroit, ASCE (chmn. geotech. divsn. com. on reliability 1976-78, civil engring. edn. and rsch. policy com. 1985-89); mem. NSPE (pres. Detroit chpt. 1976-77), Am. Soc. Engring. Edn., Am. Assn. State Colls. and Univs. (bd. dirs. 1982-84), Nat. Assn. State Univ. and Land-Grant Coll. (commn. on info. tech. 1995-, chair 2003-, bd. dirs. 2003-). Office: Calif Poly State U Office of Pres 1 Grand Ave San Luis Obispo CA 93407-1000 Office Phone: 805-756-6000. Business E-Mail: presidentsoffice@calpoly.edu.

BAKER, WILLIAM DUNLAP, lawyer; b. St. Louis, June 17, 1932; s. Harold Griffith and Bernice (Kraft) B.; m. Kay Stokes, May 23, 1955; children: Mark William, Kathryn X., Beth Kristie, Frederick Martin. AB, Colgate U., 1954; JD, U. Calif., Berkeley, 1960. Bar: Calif. 1961, Ariz. 1961, U.S. Supreme Ct. 1969. Practice in, Coolidge, 1961, Florence, 1961-63, Phoenix, 1963—; law clk. Stokes & Moring, 1960; spl. investigator Office Pinal County Atty., 1960-61, dep. county atty., 1961-63; partner McBryde, Vincent, Brumage & Baker, 1961-63; assoc. atty. Rawlins, Ellis, Burrus & Kiewit, 1963-65, partner, 1965-81; pres., atty. Ellis & Baker, P.C., 1981-84, Ellis, Baker, Lynch, Clark & Porter P.C., 1984-86, Ellis, Baker, Clark & Porter, P.C., 1986-89, Ellis, Baker & Porter, P.C., 1989-92, Ellis Baker & Porter Ltd., Phoenix, 1992-95, Ellis, Baker & Porter, P.C., Phoenix, 1995-99, Ellis & Baker, P.C., 1999—. Referee Juvenile Ct. Maricopa County Superior Ct., 1966-85 Contbr. articles to profl. jours. Mem. Gov.'s Adv. Coun., Phoenix, 1969-71, Ariz. Environ. Planning Commn., 1974-75; bd. dirs. Agri-Bus. Coun., 1978—, sec., 1978-82; pub. mem. State Bd. Accountancy, 1995-03, sec., 1998-99, treas., 1999-00, pres., 2000-02, law com., 2004-; mem. Nat. Assn. Bds. Accountancy, litig. com., 2001-03, nominating com., 2002-04; legal counsel Ariz. Com. Rep. Party, 1965-69, mem. exec. com., 1972-78; vice-chmn. Maricopa County Rep. Com., 1968-69, chmn., 1969-71; bd. dirs. San Pablo Home for Youth, 1964-72, pres., 1971; bd. dirs. Maricopa County chpt. Nat. Found. March of Dimes, 1966-71, campaign chmn., 1970; trustee St. Luke's Hosp., 1976-85, sec., 1978-82, chmn., 1982-85; bd. dirs. Luke's Men, 1971-80, pres., 1976-77; bd. dirs. Combined Health Resources, 1982-85, St. Luke's Health Sys., 1977-95, chmn., 1985-89; bd. dirs. St. Luke's Health Initiatives, 1995—, vice chair, 2000-02, treas., 2005—; bd. dirs., v.p. Ariz. Anglican Cursillo Movement, 1982-86; Western dist. layman rep. Nat. Episcopal Cursillo Com., 1996-98; regional v.p. Colgate Alumni Corp., 1977-82; vice chancellor Episcopal Diocese Ariz., 1970-96, ch. atty, 1996-03; sr. warden Christ Ch. of Ascension, 1983-86, 2001-03, chancellor, 2004-; bd. dirs. Ariz. Anglican Coun., Ltd., 2003-. Served to 1st lt. USAF, 1954-57. Mem. ABA, Nat. Water Resources Assn. (life, co-chmn. task force on reclamation law 1990-97, resolutions com. 1990-93, chmn. state caucus 1993—, mem. fed affairs com 2000-, chair water supply task force 2000—, Pres.'s award 1991), Ariz. Soc. CPAs (hon.), Ariz. Bar Assn., Calif. Bar Assn., State C. of C. (bd. dirs. 1988-92), Maricopa County Bar Assn., Flagstaff Golf Assn. (bd. dirs. 1992-93, 94-96, pres. 1994-95), Phoenix Country Club, Sigma Chi, Phi Delta Phi. Episcopalian. Home: 1627 E Cactus Wren Dr Phoenix AZ 85020-5550 Office: Ste 320 7310 N 16th St Phoenix AZ 85020 Office Phone: 602-956-8878. E-mail: wdb@ellisbaker.com.

BAKER, WILLIAM FRANKLIN, public broadcasting company executive; b. Cleve., Sept. 20, 1942; s. William Franklin and Rita Marie (Huebner) Baker; m. Jeannemarie Gelin, June 22, 1968; children: Christiane, Angela. BA in Comms. and Organizational Behavior, Case Western Res. U., 1965, MA, 1968, PhD, 1972; DSc St. John's U. (hon.), N.Y., 1981; LLD (hon.), St. Elizabeth Coll., 1995; DHL (hon.), L.I. U., 2000; PhD (hon.), New Sch. Univ., 2002, Seton Hall U., 2003. Exec. prodr. Sta. WEWS-TV, Cleve., 1971—75, asst gen. mgr., 1975—77; v.p., gen. mgr. Sta. WJZ-TV, Balt., 1977—78; pres. Group W. Prodns., Hollywood, Calif., 1978—79, Group W-TV, N.Y.C., 1979—81; chmn. Group W-TV Satellite Comm., N.Y.C., 1981—87; pres., CEO Sta. WNET, N.Y.C., 1987—. Bd. dirs. Playhouse Pictures Internat., PBS, Leitch Video Ltd., The Consumers Union, Rodale Press; owner Rudder Mag., Schneider Vineyards, Grey Island Sys., Freedom Comm., Pub. Broadcasting Sys. (PBS). Author: Down the Tube: An Insider's View of American Television, 1998, Lighthouse Island, Our Family Retreat, 2004; exec. prodr.: (films) The Face: Jesus in Art, 2001. Bd. trustees St. Elizabeth Coll., Intrepid Air-Space Mus.; vice chmn. N.Y. Arts, 1997; bd. dirs. Lowell Obs., Liberty Sci. Ctr., Lamont-Doherty Earth Obs., Mus. Bibl. Art. Named to Broadcasting and Cable Hall of Fame, 2004, N.Y. State Broadcasting Hall of Fame, 2005; recipient 8 Emmy awards, 2 Twyla M. Conway awards, Dupont Columbia Journalism award (2), Triscort award (2), 1991, Modern Lang. award, Iona Coll., 1991, Silver Cir. award, N.Y. TV Acad., Humanitarian award, So. Manhattan Arts Coun., 1999, Frank Knox Media medal, U.S. Navy League, 1999, Comm. honor, U. San Diego, Sarnoff citation, Radio Club Am., 2002, medal, St. Nicholas Soc., 2004. Fellow: Am. Acad. Arts & Scis., Explorers Club (South Pole expdn. 1974, North Pole expedn. 1983, South Pole expdn. 1984, 1988, 1996); mem.: NATAS (past pres. N.Y. chpt., Gabriel award for outstanding broadcaster 1998, trustees' award), Nat. Lighthouse Mus. (bd. dirs.), N.Y. Yacht Club. Roman Catholic. Home: 2 Highgate Rd Riverside CT 06878-2611 Office: 450 W 33rd St New York NY 10001-2603 Business E-Mail: baker@thirteen.org.

BAKER, WILLIAM OLIVER, retired research chemist; b. Chestertown, Md., July 15, 1915; s. Harold May and Helen (Stokes) Baker; m. Frances Burrill, Nov. 15, 1941; 1 child, Joseph Burrill. BS, Washington Coll., 1935, ScD (hon.), 1957; PhD, Princeton U., 1938; ScD (hon.), Georgetown U., 1962, U. Pitts., 1963, Seton Hall U., 1965, U. Akron, 1968, U. Mich., 1970, St. Peter's Coll., 1972, Poly. Inst. N.Y., 1973, Trinity Coll., Dublin, Ireland, 1975, Northwestern U., 1976, U. Notre Dame, 1978, Tufts U., 1981, N.J. U. Medicine and Dentistry, 1981, Clark U., 1983, Fairleigh Dickinson U., 1983, Rockefeller U., 1990; DEng. (hon.), Stevens Inst. Tech., 1962, N.J. Inst. Tech., 1978; LLD (hon.), U. Glasgow, 1965, U. Pa., 1974, Kean Coll., N.J., 1976, Lehigh U., 1980, Drew U., 1981, Monmouth Coll., 1973, Clarkson Coll. Tech., 1974, Princeton U., 1993, Rutgers U., 1995. With AT&T Bell Labs., 1939—80, in charge polymer research and devel., 1948—51, asst. dir. chem. and metall. research, 1951—54, dir. research, phys. scis., 1954—55, v.p. research, 1955—73, pres., 1973—79, chmn. bd., 1979—80; retired. Bd. dirs. Gen. Am. Investors, Inc.; dir. Health Effects Inst., 1980—95; vis. lectr. Northwestern U., Princeton U., Duke U.; Schmitt lectr. U. Notre Dame, 1968; Harrelson lectr. N.c. State U., 1971; Herbert Spencer lectr. U. Pa., 1974; Charles M. Schwab Meml. lectr. Am. Iron and Steel Inst., 1976; NIH lectr., 58; Metall. Soc. Am. Inst. Mining Engrs./Am. Soc. Metals disting. lectr., 76; Miles Conrad Meml. lectr. Nat. Fedn. Abstracting and Indexing Svcs., 1977; Wulff lectr. MIT, 1979; Mayo Found. lectr., 80; Logue lectr., 81; Whitehead lectr. U. Ga., 1985; Lazerow lectr. U. Pitts., 1984; Taylor lectr. Pa. State U., 1984; other lectureships; cons. Office Sci. and Tech., 1977—81; mem. Princeton Grad. Coun., 1956—64; bd. visitors Tulane U., 1963—82; mem. commn. sociotech. systems NRC, 1974—78, also chmn. adv. bd. on mil. pers. supplies, 1964—78, mem. com. oh phys. chemistry of divsn. chemistry and chem. tech., 1963—70; also steering com. Pres.'s Food and Nutrition Study Commn. Internat. Rels. NAS-NRC, 1975; mem. panel on phys. chemistry Office Naval Rsch., 1948—51; past mem. Pres.'s Sci. Adv. Com., 1957—60; nat. sci. bd. NSF, 1960—66; past chmn. Nat. Sci. Info. Coun., 1959—61; mem. sci. adv. bd. NSA, 1959—76, cons., 1976—, Dept. Def., 1958—71; cons. to spl. asst. Pres. for sci. and tech., 1963—73; cons. Panel of Ops. Evaluation Group USN, 1960—62; mem. N.J. Bd. Higher Edn., 1967—94, exec. com., 1970—94, vice chmn., 1970—72, 1982—84; mem. liaison com. for sci. and tech. Libr. Congress, 1963—73; mem. Pres.'s Fgn. Intelligence Adv. Bd., 1959—77, 1981—90; chmn. diplomatic telecommunication systems policy bd. Dept. State, 1984—; chmn. Pres.'s Adv. Group Anticipated Advances in Sci. and Tech., 1975—76; vice chmn. Pres.'s Com. Sci. and Tech., 1976—77; bd. regents Nat. Libr. Medicine, 1969—73; bd. visitors Air Force Systems Command, 1962—73; mem. mgmt. adv. coun. Oak Ridge Nat. Lab., 1970—78; mem. Nat. Commn. on Librs. and Info. Scis., 1971—75, Commn. on Critical Choices for Ams., 1973—75, Nat. Cancer Adv. Bd., 1974—80, Nat. Commn. on Excellence in Edn., 1981—83, Nat. Commn. on Jobs and Small Bus., 1985—87, Nat. Commn. on Role and Future State Colls. and Univs., 1985—87; mem., vice chmn. Commn. on Sci. and Tech. N.J., 1985—; mem. Carnegie Forum on Edn. Sci. Tech. and The Economy, 1985—; co-chmn., nat. coun. on sci. and tech. edn. AAAS, 1985—; mem. adv. panel Inst. Materials Rsch. Nat. Bur. Stds., 1966—69; mem. Coun. Trends and Perspectives U.S. C. of C., 1966—74; chmn. tech. panels adv. to Nat. Bur. Standards NAS-NRC, 1969—78; mem. Nat. Coun. Ednl. Rsch., 1973—75; mem. energy R & Dadv. coun. Energy Policy Office, 1973—75; mem. Project Independence adv. com. Fed. Energy Adminstrn., 1974—75; mem. Gov.'s Com. to Evaluate Capital Needs N.J., 1974—75; mem. governing bd. Nat. Enquiry into Scholarly Communication, 1975—79; mem. adv. coun. N.J. Regional Med. Libr., 1975—; mem. Spl. Libr. Assn., 1985—, Fed. Emergency Mgmt. Adv. Bd., 1980—93, Gas Rsch. Inst. Adv. Bd., 1978—85; mem. adv. bd. N.J. Sci./Tech. Ctr., 1980—86; mem. sci. adv. bd. Robert A. Welch Found., 1968—; mem. vis. com. for chemistry Harvard U., 1959—72; mem. coun. Marconi Fellowships, 1978—; vis. com., divsn. chemistry and chem. engring. Calif. Inst. Tech., 1969—72; vis. com. on scis. and math. Drew U., 1969—; assoc. in univ. seminar on tech. and social change Columbia U., 1969—80; vis. com., dept. materials sci. and engring. MIT, 1973—76; bd. overseers Coll. Engring. and Ap1plied Sci. U. Pa., 1975—; bd. dirs. Coun. on Libr. Resources, 1970—, Clin. Scholar Program Robert Wood Johnson Found., 1973—76, Third Century Corp., 1973—76, EDUCOM, 1985—92; organizer labs. for numerous cos.; originator nat. tech. means of satellite survey Nat. Security Coun. Orgn. Fed. Telecommunications System; co-sponsor Nat. Cancer Plan, Nat. Materials Program; co-founder Aerospace Corp., 1961, Health Effects Inst., 1980—95, N.J. Commn. on Sci. and Tech., 1985—. Contbr. High Polymers, 1945, Symposium on Basic Research AAAS, 1959, Rheology vol. III, 1960, Technology and Social Change, 1964, Science: The Achievement and the Promise, 1968, Annual Review of Materials Science, 1976, Advancing Materials Research, 1987, various other books; editl. adv. bd. Jour. Info. Sci., past mem. adv. editl. bd. Chem. and Engring. News, hon. editl. adv. bd. Carbon, contbr. numerous articles to tech. jours. Trustee Urban Studies, Inc., 1960—78, Aerospace Corp., 1961—76, Carnegie-Mellon U., 1967—87; now trustee emeritus Princeton U., 1964—86, Fund N.J., 1974—, Harry Frank Guggenheim Found., 1976—, GM Cancer Rsch. Found., 1978—, Charles Babbage Inst., 1978—, Newark Mus., 1979—89; trustee Rockefeller U., 1960—90, chmn. emeritus, 1990—; trustee Andrew W. Mellon Found., 1965—90, chmn., 1975—90, chmn. emeritus, 1990—; chmn. Rockefeller U., 1980—90. Co-recipient Nat. medal Tech., 1985, Thomas Alva Edison Sci. medal, State of N.J., 1987, Nat. Materials Advancement award, Fedn. Materials Socs., 1987, Nat. medal of Sci., 1988; named one of 10 top scientists in U.S. industry, 1954; recipient Perkin medal, 1963, Honor scroll, Am. Inst. Chemists, 1962, award to execs., ASTM, 1967, Edgar Marburg award, 1967, Indsl. Rsch. Inst. medal, 1970, Frederik Philips award, IEEE, 1972, Indsl. Rsch. Man of Yr. award, 1973, Procter prize, Sigma Xi, 1973, James Madison medal, Princeton U., 1975, Mellon Inst. award, 1975, Soc. Rsch. Adminstrs. award for disting. contbns., 1976, von Hippel award, Materials Rsch. Soc., 1978, Fahrney medal, Franklin Inst., 1977, N.J. Sci./Tech. medal, 1980, Jefferson medal, N.J. Patent Law Assn., 1981, David Sarnoff prize, AFCEA, 1981, Vannevar Bush prize, Nat. Sci. Bd., 1981, Pres.'s Nat. Security medal, 1983, Baker medal, Security Affairs Support Assn., 1984, Disting. Svc. award, Nat. Assn. Gov. Bd., 1993, Philip Hauge Abelson prize, AAAS, 1995, Lifetime Achievement award, Marconi Fellows, 2003; fellow Harvard U., 1937—38, Procter, 1938—39. Fellow: Am. Acad. Arts and Scis., Franklin Inst., Am. Inst. Chemists (Gold medal 1975), Am. Phys. Soc.; mem.: NAE (Bueche prize 1986), NAS, Indsl. Rsch. Inst. (medal 1970), Inst. Medicine, Am. Philos. Soc., Am. Chem. Soc. (Priestly medal 1966, Parsons award 1976, Willard Gibbs award 1978, Madison Marshall award 1980), Dirs. of Indsl. Rsch., Princeton Club of Northwestern N.J., Chemists Club of N.Y. (hon.), Cosmos Club, Sigma Xi, Omicron Delta Kappa, Phi Lambda Upsilon. Achievements include patents for (13); research in semiconducting polymers; solid state structure of linear polymers-polyamides and polyester; influence of microstructure on mechanical and engineering properties of rubbers and plastics; development of polyethylene for cable sheathing and microwave dielectric; synthesis and properties of polymer carbon-pattents as resistor; microphonic and composite (fibrous) material; dynamic mechanics of polymers; relaxation times of dilute macromolecules. Office: c/o Rockefeller Univ 1230 York Ave New York NY 10021-6307

BAKER, WILLIAM THOMPSON, JR., lawyer; b. N.Y.C., Jan. 19, 1944; s. William Thompson and Elizabeth (Baird) B.; children: Alice Whetherly, Richard Cass, Heather Thompson. BA cum laude, Yale U., 1965; JD, U. Va., 1968. Bar: N.Y. 1968, U.S. Dist. Ct. (so. and ea. dists.) N.Y. 1969, U.S. Supreme Ct. 1990, U.S. Ct. Appeals (D.C. cir.), 1992. Assoc. Thelen, Reid & Priest (formerly known as Reid & Priest), N.Y.C., 1968-74, ptnr, 1975—, mng. ptnr., 1986-87, mem. exec. com., 1980-82, 86-91, chmn. exec. com., 1990-91. Chmn. or co-chmn. Utility/Energy Svcs. Group Dept., 1991—2002; chmn. legal com. Edison Electric Inst., 1997-99; chmn. Electric Policy and Regulatory Group, 2003-. Trustee Episcopal Sch. in City of N.Y., 1969-71, Chase Wildlife Found., 2003—, sec./treas., 2005—. Mem. ABA (chmn. subcom. pub. utility holding company act 1990—, vice chmn. subcom. pub. utility sect. 2004—), New York County Lawyers Assn., Assn. Bar City N.Y., Hotchkiss Sch. Alumni Assn. (bd. govs. 2003—, sec., treas. 2005—), Union Club N.Y.C., Yale Club N.Y.C., N.Y. Anglers Club Republican. Episcopalian. Avocations: fishing, fly tying, rod building, wood working.

BAKER, WILLIAM W., nonprofit company executive; b. Jamaica, N.Y., Nov. 29, 1963; s. William and Rosa; m. Robin Lisa Baker, Sept. 7, 1991. Student, Cornell U., 1981-87. Dir. rhetorical scholarship labs. Cornell U., Ithaca, N.Y., 1987-88; dir. debate Columbia U., N.Y.C., 1988-91, stragetic comms. officer, 1992-94; chief mgmt. officer Unitarian Universalist UN Office, N.Y.C., 1992-95; N.Am. coord. Internat. Assn. for Religious Freedom, N.Y.C., 1995-99; exec. dir., CEO Impact Coalition, N.Y.C., 1999—. Pres. Baker Cons. Svc., N.Y.C., 1993—; corp. adv. bd. Lakeside Faily and Children's Svcs., N.Y.C., 1992-97. Sr. editor periodical Window on the world, 1995-96; editor mag. Survey of Activities of Religious Non-Govtl. Ops, 1998, 2000. Assembly dist. leader Dem. Party, Queens, N.Y., 1992; mem. focus group on religion Hague Appeal for Peace, N.Y.C., 1999. Recipient Will Baker Limited Prep. award in his honor Binghamton U., 1990, Don Brownlee award Cross Exam. Debate Assn., 1999, Glen Pelham award for nat. svc., 2001. Mem. Internat. Assn. for Religous Freedom (UN rep. 1996—, layout editor IARF World 1998, Svc. award 1999), N.Am. Interfaith Network (bd. dirs. 1997—), Nat. Soc. Fundraising Execs., Assn. for Fundraising Profls., Cornell Forensics Alumni Assn., Delta Sigma Rho. Democrat. Methodist. Avocations: bridge, chess, racquetball. Office: IMPACT Coalition 330 W 42d St Ste 2420 New York NY 10036

BAKER, ZACHARY MOSHE, librarian; b. Mpls., June 8, 1950; s. Michael Harry and Margaret Esther (Zanger) B. BA, U. Chgo., 1972; MA, Brandeis U., 1974; MA in LS, U. Minn., 1975. Head tech. svcs. Jewish Pub. Libr., Montreal, Que., Can., 1981-87; asst. libr. Yivo Inst. for Jewish Rsch., N.Y.C., 1976-80, assoc. libr., 1980-81, head libr., 1987-99; Reinhard family curator Judaica & Hebraica collections Stanford U. Librs., 1999—. Hist. cons. Que. Inst. Rsch. on Culture, Montreal, 1983; libr. cons. U.S. Holocaust Meml. Coun., Washington, 1984-85, Fla. Atlantic U., Boca Raton, 1994, Ariz. State U., Tempe, 1998. Contbg. author: From a Ruined Garden, 1983, 98; author, contbg. editor Toledot, 1978-82, Judaica Librarianship, 1983—; editor: Yiddish Catalog and Authority File of the Yivo Library, 1990, Judaica in the Slavic Realm, 2003, Ira Nowinski, Photographer as Witness, 2004. Crown fellow Brandeis U., 1973-74; travel and rsch. grantee Andrew W. Mellon Found., 1997, Lucius N. Littauer Found., 1990, 94, 96, 98/ Mem. ALA, Assn. Jewish Librs. (pres. 1994-96), Assn. for Jewish Studies, Coun. Archives and Rsch. Libr. in Jewish Studies (pres. 1998-02), Phi Beta Kappa, Beta Phi Mu. Avocations: map and atlas collecting, current events, travel. Office Phone: 650-725-1054. Business E-Mail: zbaker@stanford.edu.

BAKER-FROILAND, MARY LOU, elementary school educator; b. Rochester, Minn., Mar. 5, 1960; d. Alfred W. and Phyllis (Virock) F.; m. Brian E. Baker, 1994. BS in Elementary Edn., U. Minn., 1983; ESL degree, Pan Am. U., 1989; M of Ednl. Adminstrn., Tex. A&M U., 1997. 2nd grade tchr. Brownsville (Tex.) Ind. Sch. Dist./Villa Nueva Sch., 1984-86; 6th, 3rd grade tchr. Gonzalez Elementary Sch., Brownsville, 1986-88; 4th grade tchr. Windcrest Elementary Sch., San Antonio, 1988-90; tchr. Nimitz Mid. Sch., San Antonio, 1990—92; tchr. 6th grade social studies, 6th & 7th grade English as 2d lang. John Nance Garner Mid. Sch., 1992—2000; asst. prin. Eisenhower Mid. Sch., 2000—. Mem. Internat. Reading Assn., Am. Fedn. Tchrs., U. Minn. Alumni Assn., Delta Kappa Gamma, Alpha Delta Pi. Home: 506 Balfour Dr Windcrest TX 78239-2523

BAKER-KINCAID, BRIDGET, publishing executive; b. Eugene, Oreg., Sept. 14, 1955; d. Edwin Moody and Patricia Baker; m. Guy Dominique Wood, June 30, 1977 (div. Oct. 1981); m. Rayburn Keith Kincaid, June 27, 1987; stepchildren: Benjamin Kincaid, Jacob Kincaid. BA in English, French and Theatre, Lewis and Clark Coll., 1977; MA in Journalism, U. Oreg., 1985. Circulation dist. supr. Register-Guard, Eugene, 1978—80, pub. rels. coord., 1980—83, promotion dir., 1983—86, mktg. dir., 1986—88, corp. pub. rels. dir., 1989—. Bd. dirs. Lane Met. Partnership, treas., 2005—, Guard Pub. Co., 1987—, bd. dirs. Bd. dirs. Art Found. Western Oreg., chmn., 1997—99; pres. Baker Family Found., 1998—; bd. dirs. Wilani Coun. Camp Fire, 1982—88, pres. bd. dirs., 1986—88; bd. dirs. Lane County United Way, 1982—88, cmty. info. com. chairperson, 1982—84, chair planning com., 1987—88; bd. dirs. Eugene Opera, 1988—91, pres. bd. dirs., 1990—91; bd. dirs. Lane C.C. Found., 1995—97, Lane Metro Partnership, 2003—, treas., 2005—, Round Table of Eugene, 2005—, sec., 2004—, bd. dirs. Named Woman of the Yr., Lane County Coun. Orgns., 1994; recipient 1st pl. advt. award, Editor and Pub. Mag., 1984, 1st pl. TV promotion, 1st pl. newspaper rsch. award, 1988, Best Mktg. Idea/Campaign award, Oreg. Newspaper Pub. Assn., 1984, 1985. Mem.: Pub. Rels. Soc. Am. (pres. greater Oreg. chpt. 1995—96, Spotlight award 1986), Internat. Mktg. Assn. (bd. dirs. western region 1986—88, internat. bd. dirs. 1995—2001, 1st pl. Best in the West awards 1983—91), Round Table of Eugene (treas. 2005, sec. 2005—), Eugene C. of C. (bd. dirs. 1989—92), U. Oreg. Alumni Assn. (bd. dirs. 1990—93), Eugene Yacht Club, Downtown Athletic Club, Town Club (bd. dirs. 1995—97), Zonta Internat. (pres. Eugene Club 1994—96, area dir. 1997—98, lt. gov. Dist. 8 1998—2000, gov. 2000—02, internat. pub. rels. chair 2002—04, Woman of the Yr. 2002). Republican. Avocations: sailing, bird hunting, performing arts. Office: Guard Pub Co PO Box 10188 Eugene OR 97440-2188

BAKER KNOLL, CATHERINE, lieutenant governor; b. Pitts. d. Nicholas James and Theresa Mary (May) Baker; m. Charles A. Knoll Sr. (dec.); children: Charles A. Jr., Mina B., Albert B., Kim Eric. BS in Edn., Duquesne U., 1952, MS in Edn., 1973. Dir. western Pa. region Safety Adminstrn. Dept. Transp., Pitts., 1971-79; exec. dir. community svc. Dept. of Adminstrn., Allegheny County, Pa., 1980-88; treas. Pa. Treasury Dept., Harrisburg, 1988—2003; lt. gov State of Pa., 2003—. Owner, operator pvt. bus. firm, Pitts., 1952-70. Mem. Pa. Dem. State Com., Pa. Fedn. Dem. Women, YMCA Bd., Pitts., Harrisburg, Duquesne U. Alumni Bd., Mom's House, Zontas Inc. Bd. Mem. Nat. Assn. State Treas,, Women Execs. in State Gov., Coun. State Gov. (exec. com. ea. region). Democrat. Roman Catholic. Office: Governor Office 225 Main Capitol Bldg Harrisburg PA 17120

BAKER PRICE, MARJORIE JANET, small business owner, mental health nurse; d. Leonard and Ruth Baker; children: Anna Price, Elizabeth Price, David Price, Sarah Rossiter. BSN, BS in English and Theater, SUNY, Brockport, 1974. RN N.Y., 1974; cert. hypnotherapy Hypnodyne Inst., 1999, Reiki Master USUI ISch. Reiki, 1996. Cons./trainer/owner Centering Tools, Rochester, NY, 1987—; cons./trainer NY State Nurses Assn. Author/editor Centering Tools, Rochester, NY, 1987—. Author: (book) Merinda and the Magic Mirror, (31 tapes for self-empowerment) Releasing the Past; co-author: (CD and book) Power Intuition; featured columnist: Natures Widsom. Finalist Ebusiness of the Yr. Exec., Rochester Ebusiness Assn., 2004; recipient Florence R. Halloren Outstanding Psychiat. Nurse award, Livingstone County Health Dept., 1985, Nurse Presenter award, Am. Imagery Conf., 1987. Mem.: Hypnotherapy Inst., Nurse Healers, Genesee Valley Nurses Assn. (assoc.), Livingstone County Nurse Practioner (assoc.; pres. 1975—76). Office: Centering Tools PO Box 68015 Rochester NY 14618 Office Phone: 585-244-6210. Office Fax: 585-244-6210*51. Personal E-mail: marjorie@centeringtools.com.

BAKER-TEMPLETON, ANGIE AUBURN, elementary school educator; b. Winchester, Tenn., June 29, 1968; d. Auburn Wayne and Evelyn Grammer Baker; m. Shields Wilson Templeton, Jr., June 26, 1999. BS in Elem. Edn., Mid. Tenn. State U., Mufreesboro, 1990; MEd in Adminstrn. and Supervision, Mid. Tenn. State U., 1994; Ednl. Specialist, Mid. Tenn. State University, 1996. Lic. tchr. Tenn. Dept. of Edn., 1991, cert. ednl. supr. and adminstr. Tenn. Dept. of Edn., 1994. Tchr. Franklin County Sch. Sys., Winchester, Tenn., 1991—95, Rutherford County Bd. of Edn., Murfreesboro, Tenn., 1995—. Adj. faculty mem. Mid. Tenn. State U. Dept. of Elem. Edn., Murfreesboro, 2001—. Mem. Amb. for Mid. Tenn. Med. Ctr., Murfreesboro, LWV, Murfreesboro, Tenn., 2005. Named Best Mannered Tchr., Nat. League of Jr. Cotillions, 2004, Outstanding Tchr. of the Yr., Homer Pittard Campus Sch., 2005; recipient Outstanding First Yr. Tchr. - Sallie Mae Tchg. award, Franklin County Bd. of Edn., 1992; grantee, Bus. Edn. Partnership - Nissan grantee, 2003—05. Mem.: NEA, Tenn. Assn. Math. Tchrs., Nat. Coun. Tchrs. Math., Rutherford County Edn. Assn., Franklin County Edn. Assn., Tenn. Edn. Assn., Mary Tom Berry Reading Coun. (treas. 2003—), Internat. Reading Assn., Delta Kappa Gamma. Democrat. Ch. Of Christ. Avocations: gardening, travel. Home: 133 Winsford Ct Murfreesboro, TN TN 37130 Office: Homer Pittard Campus School PO Box 4 MTSU Mufreesboro, TN 37132 Office Phone: 615-895-1030. Personal E-mail: templetona@rcs.k12.tn.us. E-mail: atemplet@mtsu.edu.

BAKHT, BAIDAR, civil engineer, researcher, educator; b. Delhi, India, Sept. 4, 1940; arrived in Can., 1973; s. Mukhtar and Anwar Jehan Chishti; m. Anita Das, Sept. 11, 1968; children: Natasha, Sacha. BSc in Engring. Aligarh (India) U., 1962; MSc, Imperial Coll., London, 1972; DSc, London U., 1990. Registered profl. engr., Ont., Can. Asst. engr. Heavy Engring. Corp., Ranchi, India, 1962-66; engr. Dept. Environ., London, 1967-73; prin. rsch. engr. Ministry Transp. Ont., 1974-97; pres. JMBT Stuctures Rsch., Inc., Toronto, Ont., 1997—. Adj. prof. civil engring. U. Toronto, U. Man., 2000—. Co-author: Bridge Analysis Simplified, 1985, Bridge Analysis by Microcomputer, 1988, Soil-steel Bridges: Design and Construction, 1993, Bridge Engineering, Recent Innovations, 1994; Bridge Superstructures, New Developments, 1996; translator 17 books of Urdu poetry to English, 1985—; contbr. over 190 articles to profl. jours.; co-inventor unique deck slab of bridges, inventor of stressed-log bridge. Recipient Moisseif award ASCE, 1982, President's medal Road and Transp. Assn. Can., 1985, Profl. Engrs. Ont. Engring. medal, 1997. Fellow: Profl. Engrs. Ont. (Engring. medal 1996), Engring. Inst. Can. (Gzowski medal 1983), Can. Soc. for Civil Engring. (Pratley award 1988, 1994, Vance award 1996, award for outstanding contbn. to bridge engring. 2002, A.B. Sanderson award 2004), Instn. Engrs. (India) (cert. of merit 1990). Avocation: translating urdu poetry into english. E-mail: bbakht@rogers.com.

BAKIC, PREDRAG R., radiology research scientist; b. Belgrade, Yugoslavia, Apr. 5, 1967; s. Radomir R. Bakic and Vera M. Djukic-Bakic; m. Teodora Gajic-Bakic, Sept. 18, 2004. PhD in Elec. and Computer Engring., Lehigh U., 2000. Postdoctoral fellow in radiology Thomas Jefferson U., Phila., 2001—03; rsch. assoc. in radiology U. Pa., Phila., 2003—. Contbr. articles to profl. jours. Bd. mem. Serbian Ea. Orthodox Ch. of St. Nicholas, Phila., 2001—04, pres., 2004. Rsch. Seed grant, Radiol. Soc. of NAm., 2003-2005. Mem.: IEEE. Office: Univ Pa 3400 Spruce St Philadelphia PA 19104 Office Phone: 215-746-8758.

BAKI-HASHEMI, SAEID, education educator, department chairman; b. Tehran, Iran, May 12, 1957; arrived in U.S., 1973; s. Mossa Baki-Hashemi and Ziba Zoroofi; m. Sherry Baki-Hashemi, 1986; children: Kaivon Baki, Kaveh Baki, Sarah Baki. BA, Univ. Louisville, Louisville, Ky., 1980, MS, 1983. Instr. Somerset C.C., Somerset, Ky., 1983—84; lab supr. Ind. Univ., Kokomo, Ind., 1984—86; assoc. prof. head math and sci. dept. Ancilla Coll., Donaldson, Ind., 1986—96; dept. chair., assoc. prof. Shelby State C.C.,

Memphis, 1996—2000, Southwest Tenn. C.C., Memphis, 2000—. Recipient NIH Bridge Program, Washington, 2000. Mem.: Am. Biology Tchrs., Anatomy and Physiology Soc. Avocations: water sports, swimming, boating, scuba diving.

BAKITAS, MARIE ANNE, adult nurse practitioner, researcher; b. Bridgeport, Conn., June 27, 1957; d. Thomas Henry Bakitas and Helen Terpak; life ptnr. Melvin Lawrence LaClair; children: James Christopher Whedon, Ryan Eugene Whedon. AD, BSN, U. Bridgeport, 1980; MS, Boston U., 1983; postgrad. in Nursing Sci., Yale U., 2001—. Cert. advanced oncology nurse, 1995, adult nurse practitioner, 1999. Staff RN, Norwalk Hosp., Conn., 1977—80; primary nurse Dana Farber Cancer Inst., Boston, 1982—83; hematology/oncology clin. nurse specialist Dartmouth Hitchcock Med. Ctr., Lebanon, NH, 1983—98, nurse practitioner, palliative care, 1998—; rsch. asst. prof. Dartmouth Med. Sch., Hanover, NH, 1998—. Author: (text book) Bone Marrow Transplantation: Principles, Practice and Nursing Insights, 2d edit. (Am. Jour. of Nursing Book of the Yr., 1997). Recipient Best Ethics Article award, Dimensions in Critical Care Nursing, 1991, Excellence in Clin. Practice Writing award, Oncology Nursing Forum, 1992, N.H. Nurse of Yr. award, N.H.Nurses Assn., 2001, Trish Greene Quality of Life lectureship, Oncology Nursing Soc., 2001, Cert. Hospice and Palliative Nurse of Yr. award, Hospice and Palliative Nurses Assn., 2003, Doctoral Tng. award, Dept. of Def., Breast Cancer Program, 2003-2006; Doctoral scholarship, Am. Cancer Soc., 2005-2006. Mem.: Am. Acad. of Nursing, Sigma Theta Tau. Office: Dartmouth Hitchcock Med Ctr 1 Medical Center Dr Lebanon NH 03756 Office Phone: 603-653-3524.

BAKKE, DENNIS W., energy company executive; m. Eileen Bakke. MBA, Harvard U. With Fed. Energy Agy.; with Energy Productivity Ctr., Carnegie Mellon U.; co-founder The AES Corp., Arlington, Va., 1981, pres. & CEO, 1994—2002; now pres., CEO Imagine Schools. Co-author: Creating Abundance-America's Least Cost Energy Strategy, 1984, author: Joy at Work: A Revolutionary Approach to Fun on the Job, 2005. Pres. Mustard Seed Found. Mem. Am. Gass Assn. (past dir.). Address: PVG Press PO Box 70525 Seattle WA 98127 Office: Imagine Schools Ste 610 1005 N Glebe Rd Arlington VA 22201 Fax: 703-528-4510.*

BAKKEN, ERIC ALLEN, lawyer; b. June 22, 1967; BS, St. Mary's U.; JD, William Mitchell Coll. Law. Bar: 1994. With Regis Corp., Edina, Minn., 1994—, v.p. law, 1998—2004, v.p., gen. counsel, sec., 2004—. Mem.: ABA, Minn. Bar Assn., Hennepin County Bar Assn. Office: Regis Corp 7201 Metro Blvd Edina MN 55439 Office Phone: 952-947-7777.

BAKKENSEN, JOHN RESER, lawyer; b. Pendleton, Oreg., Oct. 4, 1943; s. Manley John and Helen (Reser) B.; m. Ann Marie Dahlen, Sept. 30, 1978; children: Michael, Dana, Laura. AB magna cum laude, Harvard U., 1965; JD, Stanford U., 1968. Bar: Oreg. 1969, Calif. 1969, U.S. Dist. Ct. Oreg. 1969. Ptnr. Miller, Nash, Wiener, Hager & Carlsen, Portland, Oreg., 1968-99; pvt. practice lawyer, arbitrator, mediator and trustee. Lawyer del. 9th Cir. Jud. Conf., San Francisco, 1980-82. Author: (with others) Advising Oregon Businesses, 1979, Arbitration and Mediation, supplement, 2000. Past bd. dirs. Assn. for Retarded Citizens, Portland; advisor Portland Youth Shelter House; mem. and counsel to bd. dirs. Friends of Pine Mountain Observatory, Portland. Mem. ABA (forum on constrn. industry), Am. Arbitration Assn., Oreg. State Bar, Oreg. Assoc. Gen. Contractors (legal com. 1991, counsel to bd. dirs. 1992), Arbitration Svc. Portland, Inc. (arbitrator), Multnomah Athletic Club. Avocation: astronomy. Office Phone: 503-245-0385.

BAKKER, THOMAS GORDON, lawyer; b. San Gabriel, Calif., Aug. 18, 1947; s. Gordon and Eva Marie (Hoekstra) B.; m. Charlotte Anne Kamstra, Aug. 1, 1969; children: Sarah, Jonathan. AB in History, Calvin Coll., Grand Rapids, Mich., 1969; JD, U. Mich., 1973. Bar: Ariz. 1973, U.S. Dist. Ct. Ariz. 1973, U.S. Ct. Appeals (9th cir.) 1973. Staff reporter Ariz. Criminal Code Revision Com., Phoenix, 1973-75; asst. atty. gen. State of Ariz., Phoenix, 1975-77; staff atty. div. 1 Ariz. Ct. Appeals, Phoenix, 1977-79; assoc. Burch, Cracchiolo et al, Phoenix, 1979-80; from assoc. to ptnr. Olson, Jantsch, Bakker, Phoenix, 1980—. Vice chmn. tort and ins. practice sect. Appellate Advocacy Commn., 1982-83; judge pro tem div. 1 Ariz. Ct. Appeals, 1985, 92. Served with U.S. Army, 1969-71. Fellow Ariz. Bar Found. (founding fellow); mem. Ariz. Bar Assn., Maricopa County Bar Assn., Am. Health Lawyers Assn., Def. Rsch. Inst., Ariz. Assn. Def. Counsel 163. Mem. Christian Reformed Ch. Avocations: reading, golf, aerobics, fishing. Office: Olson Jantsch Bakker 7243 N 16th St Phoenix AZ 85020-5203 Office Phone: 602-861-2705. E-mail: tgb@ojbb.com.

BAKKO, ORVILLE EDWIN, retired health facility administrator; b. Kenyon, Minn., Oct. 10, 1919; s. Marcus and Caroline (Leding) B.; m. Norma Evelyn Cronquist, Sept. 25, 1951; children: Sandra Karen, Kristi Camille. BA, St. Olaf Coll., Northfield, Minn., 1941; M. in Hosp. Adminstrn., Northwestern U., 1948. Adminstrv. intern, resident U. Iowa Hosps., 1947-49; adminstrv. asst. Kadlec Hosp., Richland, Wash., 1949-50, asst. adminstr., then adminstr., 1950-56; asst. supt. Arroyo Del Valle Sanatorium, Livermore, Calif., 1956-60, Highland Hosp., Oakland, Calif., 1958-60; adminstr. Fairmont Hosp., San Leandro, Calif., 1960-82. Vis. scholar Agder Coll., Kristiansand, Norway, 1983-84. Author: The Administrative Internship-What Can the Field Contribute to the Program?, 1948, Administration of Group Clinics, 1949, Employee Safety Program, 1970, Survey of Medical Rehabilitation in Norway, 1984. Mem. Alameda County Work Safety Com., 1959-72; mem. med. svcs. adv. com. Chabot Coll., San Leandro, 1962-72; mem. dis. svcs. adv. com. area 1 Regional Med. Program, 1970-72; mem. Emmanuel Faith Comm. Ch., prayer chmn. King's Followers Class; 2d v.p., bd. dirs. Wash. State Hosp. Assn., 1954-55; pres. S.E. Wash. Hosp. Coun., 1953-54; chmn. Tri-City Hosp. Coun., 1954-56; trustee Commn. on Accreditation Rehab. Facilities, 1974-76; mem. Internat. Hosp. Fedn., 1982-88. Capt. Med. Adminstrv. Corps, AUS, 1942-46, NATOUSA. Decorated officer Ordre du Nichan-Iftikhar (Tunisia). Fellow Am. Coll. Healthcare Execs. (life); mem. Am. Hosp. Assn. (life, governing coun. rehab. and chronic disease hosp. sect. 1972-77, chmn. 1976), Calif. Hosp. Assn. (mem. com. on continuing care and rehab. 1967-70), Assn. Western Hosps., Health Care Execs. No. Calif., East Bay Hosp. Conf. (exec. com. 1971-72), Richland Toastmasters Club (officer 1949-56), Los Rios Homeowners Assn. (bd. dirs., chmn. landscape com. 1994-96), Rotary (charter). Mem. Emmanuel Faith Comm. Ch. Home: 11887 Caminito Corriente San Diego CA 92128-4552

BAKLANOFF, ERIC NICHOLAS, economist, educator; b. Graz, Austria, Dec. 9, 1925; came to U.S., 1937, naturalized, 1943; s. Nicolas W. and Lucille (King) B.; m. H. Christina Janes, June 17, 1956 (div. June 1973); children: Nicholas, Tanya, Ana-Maria; m. Joy Driskell, June 6, 1982. Student, Antioch Coll., 1943-44; AB, Ohio State U., 1949, MA, 1950, PhD, 1958; postgrad. (Fulbright scholar), U. Chile, 1957, Harvard Grad. Sch. Bus. Adminstrn., 1959; postgrad. (NDEA postdoctoral fellow), U. Tex., summer 1963. Instr. econs. Ohio State U., 1957-58; asst. prof. La. State U., 1958-61, assoc. prof., 1961-62; prof. econs., dir. Latin Am. Studies Inst., 1965-68; assoc. prof. econs., dir. Grad. Center for Latin Am. Studies, Vanderbilt U., 1962-65; prof. econs., dean for internat. studies and programs U. Ala., 1969-73, bd. visitors rsch. prof. econs., 1974-92, rsch. prof. econs. emeritus, 1992—. Disting. vis. prof. Luther Coll. summer 1965; cons. Am. Council on Edn., USAF Inst., Pres.'s Southeastern Council on Latin Am. Studies, 1963-64, U.S. Dept. Edn., Centro de Estudios y Communicacion Economica, Am. Enterprise Inst. Pub. Policy Rsch., Fed. Rsch. divsn., Hispanic divsn. Libr. of Congress. Author: Expropriation of U.S. Investments in Cuba, Mexico and Chile, 1975, The Economic Transformation of Spain and Portugal, 1978, La Transformation Economica de Espana y Portugal: La economia del Fanquismo y del Salazarismo, 1980; author: (with Jeffrey Brannon) Agrarian Reform and Public Enterprise in Mexico: The Political Economy of Yucatan's Henequen Industry, 1987; author: (with Edward H. Moseley) Competing for Latin American Markets: A Business Perspective on the Spanish-American War Centennial, 1999; author: (with others) Revolutionary Change in Cuba, 1971, Modern Brazil: New Patterns and Development, 1971, Background to Revolution: The Development of Modern Cuba, 1979, Yucatan: A World Apart, 1980, The Iberian-Latin America Connection: Implications for U.S. Foreign Policy, 1986, State Shrinking: A Comparative Analysis of Privatization, 1987, The Alabama Economy: Issues for the 1990s, 1990, Portugal: Ancient Country, Young Democracy, 1990, Portugal: A Country Study, 1994, Cuba in Transition, 2001; contbg. author: others, editor, contbg. author: The Shaping of Modern Brazil, 1969, New Perspectives of Brazil, 1966, Mediterranean Europe and the Common Market, 1976, Competing for Latin American Markets: A Business Perspective on the Spanish American War Centennial, 1999, The Handbook of Portuguese Studies, 1999, El Triángulo Económico: España-USA-America Latina, 2002; contbr. articles to profl. jours. Active Boy Scouts Am. Served with USNR, 1944-46, PTO. Decorated Knight of Grace, Hospitaler and Mil. Order St. Lazarus of Jerusalem, Malta obedience; named Outstanding Scholar U. Ala., 1980-81; fellow Ctr. Advanced Study Behavioral Scis., 1964-65; grantee U.S. Dept. State, Spain, 1974; rsch. fellow Andrew W. Mellon Found., 1987. Mem. Delta Chi, Beta Gamma Sigma, Sigma Delta Pi, Omicron Delta Epsilon, Phi Beta Delta. Eastern Orthodox. Office: U Ala PO Box 870224 Tuscaloosa AL 35487-0154 Office Phone: 205-348-7842. Business E-Mail: Ebaklano@cba.ua.edu.

BAKRI, YOUNES NOAMAN, surgeon, oncologist, gynecologist; b. Amman, Jordan, Dec. 29, 1950; s. Noaman Ibrahim and Sadia Karim Bakri; children: Noaman, Nadine, Linda, Dina. PhD, U. of Alexandria, Alexandria, 1975. Board Certified Gynecologic Oncology Hussein Coll., Jordan, 1964, Board Certified Obstetrics/Gynecology Hussein Coll., Jordan, 1964. Prof. gynecology and dir. U. of SD, Sioux Falls, SD, 1994—97; educator Va. Med. Sch., Norfolk, Va., 1982, Thomas Jefferson U., Philadelphia, Pa., 1980. Dir. gynecologic oncology King Faisal Specialist Rsch. Ctr., Riyadh, Saudi Arabia, 1999. Recipient Photography Contest award, Wash. Post, 1993. Achievements include invention of Temponade Balloon For Treatment Of Obstetrical Hemorrhage. Office: Geisinger Health System 100 North Academy Danville PA 17822

BAKRIS, GEORGE, nephrologist, educator; b. Athens, June 15, 1952; arrived in U.S., 1952; s. Louis George Bakris and Athena Petros Marolias; m. Demetria Mary Arges, Nov. 26, 1983; children: Athena, Louis. BA in Biology/Psychology, Ind. U., 1974; MA in Human Devel., U. Chgo., 1975, MD in Medicine, 1981. Diplomate Am. Bd. Internal Medicine, Am. Bd. Nephrology, bd. cert. specialist in clin. hypertension Am. Soc. Hypertension. Staff nephrologist, dir. renal rsch. Ochsner Clinic, New Orleans, 1988-91; asst. prof. medicine, dir. nephrology fellowship program U. Tex. Health Sci. Ctr., San Antonio, 1991-93; assoc. prof. preventive medicine and internal medicine Rush U. Med. Ctr., Chgo., 1993-98, prof., vice chmn. dept. preventive med., prof. internal med., 1998—, dir. Hypertension Clinic Rsch. Ctr., 1998—. Adj. asst. prof. medicine Tulane U. Sch. Medicine, New Orleans, 1988—91; cons. cardiorenal divsn. FDA, Rockville, Md., 1993—2003; chmn. hypertension exec. coun. Nat. Kidney Found., N.Y.C., 1998—2000. Editor: (book) Hypertension: A Clinician's Guide to Diagnosis and Treatment, 2d edit., 2000, The Kidney in Hypertension, 2004; co-editor: International Handbook of Hypertension, 2004; jour. guest editor: Jour. Mineral and Electrolyte Metabolism, 1998; contbr. articles to profl. jours.; editor: Am. Jour. Nephrology, 2002. Grantee, Nat. Inst. Diabetes and Digestive Diseases, 1994—2001, 2002—, heart, lung and blood divsn. NIH, 1996—2001, Clin. Rsch. Tng., prin. investigator, 1999—. Fellow: ACP, Am. Heat Assn. Coun., Am. Heart Assn. (coun. high blood pressure rsch. 1992—), Am. Coll. Clin. Pharmacology (pres. 2000—02). Greek Orthodox. Avocations: writing music, guitar, golf, bowling. Office: Rush Univ Med Ctr Dept Preventive Medicine 1700 W Van Buren St Ste 470 Chicago IL 60612-3228 Office Phone: 312-563-2195. Office Fax: 312-942-8119. Business E-Mail: George_Bakris@rush.edu. E-mail: gbakris@earthlink.net.

BAKROW, WILLIAM JOHN, college president emeritus; b. Parson, Kans., Apr. 22, 1924; s. Leonard A. and Edith B.; m. Maree Bakrow (dec.); children: Bruce Wrigley, Caren Edith, Lance. BA, Brown U., 1948; MS, Ind. U., 1958, EdD, 1960; LLD (hon.), St. Mary Coll., Omaha, St. Ambrose U. Reporter Providence Jour., 1948-51; legis. corr. U.P., Albany, N.Y., 1951-56; dir. devel. U. Buffalo, 1956-59, Canisius (N.Y.) Coll., 1961-66; pres. Motorola Exec. Inst., Oracle, Ariz., 1966-73, St. Ambrose U., Davenport, Iowa, 1973—87, Montserrat Coll. Art, Beverly, Mass., 1988-89; ptnr. B & F Assocs., Rockport, Mass. Dir. Southeast Nat. Bank Moline, Ill., Sears Mfg. Co., Davenport., Mercy Hosp., Davenport, Handicapped Devel. Ctr., Davenport; Mem. Scott County Govtl. Study Commn., 1974— Mem. Illowa Council exec. bd. Boy Scouts Am., 1975—; trustee Palmer Jr. Coll., Davenport, St. Katherine's-St. Mark's Sch., Bettendorf, Iowa, dir. Endicott Coll., Beverly, Mass., pres. Montserrat Coll. of Art, Beverly; mem. Rockport fin. com., Rockport planning bd., supt. schs. selection com.; bd. dirs. Iowa Handicapped Devel. Served with USNR, 1942-46. Home and Office: Unit 218 201 Brooksby Villiage DR Peabody MA 01960-1489

BAKTIR, SELCUK, electrical engineer, researcher, computer engineer, researcher; b. Kayseri, Turkey, Feb. 14, 1978; s. Ayse and Mehmet Baktir. BSc, Bilkent U., 2001; MSc, Worcester Poly. Inst., 2003. Tchg. asst. Elec. and Computer Engring. Dept. Worcester Poly. Inst., Mass., 2001—02, rsch. asst. Cryptography and Info. Security Lab. Elec. and Computer Engring. Dept., 2001—. Contbr. articles to profl. jours. Bd. of Trustees Scholarship, Bilkent U., Ankara, Turkey, 1997—2001. Mem.: Internat. Assn. Cryptologic Rsch., IEEE Info. Theory Soc., IEEE Computer Soc., IEEE. Achievements include invention of new finite field representation called Optimal Tower Fields. In this representation inversion, the slowest of all finite field operations, can be performed as fast as multiplication. Personal E-mail: selcukbaktir@hotmail.com.

BAKUN, ANDREW, marine science professor; b. Tacoma, Apr. 20, 1939; s. Andrew and Jeanette Cecelia Bakun; children: Joelle Marjorie Bakon Spinose, Matthew Francis Bakon. BS, U. Wash., 1962, MS, 1968; PhD, Oreg. State U., 1987. Staff scientist U.S. Program Biology, Internat. Indian Ocean Expedition - Rsch. Vessel Anton Broon, 1962—65; oceanographer U.S. Nat. Oceanis and Atmosphere Adminstr., 1968—83; dir. Pacific Fisheries Environ. Group, Monterey, Calif., 1983—92; sr. fisheries resources officer Food and Agrl. ORgn. UN, Rome, 1992—99; dir. rsch. IRD, Sete, France, 1999—2001; prof. U. Miami, 2002—. Vis. sr. scientist Interant. Rsch. Inst. Climate Prediction, NYC, 2001—02; chmn. scientific guiding Intergovtl. Oceanographic, 1984—94; mem. group program ocean sci. Commn. Food and Agrl. Orgn. of UN. Author: Patterns in the Ocean, 1996. With U.S. Army, 1957. Mem.: ACLU. Avocation: scuba diving.

BAKWIN, EDWARD MORRIS, banker; b. N.Y.C., May 13, 1928; s. Harry and Ruth (Morris) B. BA, Hamilton Coll., 1950; MBA, U. Chgo., 1961. With Nat. Stock Yards Nat. Bank, National City, Ill., 1953-55; with Mid-City Nat. Bank Chgo., 1955—2001, pres., 1962-72, chmn. bd., CEO, 1967—2001, Mid-City Fin. Corp., 1982—2001, Darling-Del. Corp., Chgo., 1972-86, Nat. Stock Yards Co., 1985-93; chmn. bd. MBFI, Chgo., 2001—. Mem. Chgo. Crime Commn. Adv. bd. U. Chgo., 1967—; bd. dirs. Duncan-Med. YMCA, 1963-72, Northwestern Meml. Hosp., 1980-88; bd. dirs. West Ctrl. Assn., 1962-67, pres., 1962-65; trustee Am. Mus. Fly Fishing, 1990—. With AUS, 1951-52. Mem. Am. Bankers Assn., Ill. Bankers Assn. (bd. govs. 1966-69), Explorers Club, Adventurers Club (Chgo.), Chgo. Yacht Club, Mid-Am. Club, N.Y. Yacht Club. Home: Apt 8207 175 E Delaware Pl Chicago IL 60611-1756 Office: MBFI Ste 612 801 W Madison St Chicago IL 60607

BALA, SAM G., surgeon; b. Cavite, The Philippines, Dec. 1, 1942; came to U.S., 1973, naturalized, 1982; m. Rosario C. Bala; children: Jennifer, Christine. BS in Pre-Medicine, Far Ea. U., Manila, 1965, MD, 1969. Resident in surgery Mary Johnston Hosp., Manila, 1969-72, chief resident, 1972-73; resident in gen. surgery L.I. Jewish Med. Ctr., 1973-75, SUNY, Stony Brook, 1975-79, chief resident, 1979-80, asst. clin. instr., 1979-80; pvt. practice, Dade City, Fla., 1981—. Mem. staff Dade City Hosp. (now Pasco Cmty. Hosp.), 1981—, chief hyperalimentaton, 1981-85, chmn. continuing med. edn., 1983-86, trustee, 1998—; chief surgery East Pasco Med. Ctr., Zephyrhills, Fla., 1988, now mem. staff. Exec. dir. troup 402, Boy Scouts Am., 1985—, also life mem.; bd. dirs. Pasco Hernando Coll. Found., 1990—, Cath. Charities Diocese of St. Petersburg, Tampa and Pasco, 1997—, Dade Co. C. of C., 1995-97, East Pasco Habitat for Humanity, 2000—; bd. trustees Pasco Regional Med. Ctr., 1999—; mem. First United Meth. Ch., fin. bd. Paul Harris fellow Dade City Rotary Club, 1989. Fellow Am. Soc. Abdominal Surgeons; mem. AMA, So. Med. Soc., Soc. Laparoendoscopic Surgeons, Dade City C. of C. (bd. dirs. 1995-97), Rotary (life)(bequest soc., benefactor, pres. Dade City chpt. 1988-89, Paul Harris fellow). Home: 37931 E Palm Ave Dade City FL 33525 Office: Pasco Cmty Hosp 13100 Ft King Rd Dade City FL 33525

BALABAN, ALEXANDRU T., chemistry professor, researcher; b. Timisoara, Romania, Apr. 2, 1931; s. Teodor and Florica Balaban; m. Cornelia Florea, Dec. 3, 1955; children: Teodor-Silviu, Irina-Alexandra Buhimschi. Chem. Engr., Poly. U., Bucharest, 1953, PhD in Organic Chemistry, 1959, DrHabil, 1974; Dr. honoris causa, U. Timisoara, 1997. Radiochemist Inst. Atomic Physics, Bucharest, Romania, 1957, head lab., 1957-75; sr. rsch. officer Internat. Atomic Energy Agy., Vienna, 1967-69; asst. prof. chemistry Poly. U., Bucharest, 1957-65, assoc. prof., 1965-70, prof., 1970—99, Tex. A & M U., Galveston, 1993—95, 2000—. Author: Steric Fit in Quantitative Structure-Activity Relations, 1980, Pyrylium Salts, 1982, Olefin Metathesis and Ring-Opening Polymerization of Cyclo-Olefins, 1985, Annulenes, Benzo-, Hetero-, Homo-Derivatives and Their Valence Isomers, 1986, Labelled Compounds and Radipharmaceuticals Applied in Nuclear Medicine, 1986, Modeling of Cancer Genesis and Prevention, 1990; editor: Chemical Applications of Graph Theory, 1976, From Chemical Topology to the Three-Dimensional Geometry, 1997, Topological Indices and Related Molecular Descriptors in QSAR/QSPR, 1999; mem. editl. bd. Revue Roumaine de Chimie, Match, Polycyclic Aromatic Compounds and others Fellow World Acad. Theoretical Organic Chemists, European Acad. Arts and Sci.; mem. Acad. of Romania (v.p. 1995, N. Teclu prize 1962), Hung Acad. Sci. (hon. 2001), Am. Chem. Soc. (H. Skolnik award 1994), Royal Soc. Chemistry, Internat. Acad. Math Home: Apt C4 3220 69th St Galveston TX 77551 Office: Tex A & M U Galveston 5007 Ave Galveston TX 77551 Office Phone: 409-741-4313. Business E-Mail: balabana@tamug.edu.

BALABAN, BOB, actor, director; b. Chgo., Aug. 16, 1945; s. Elmer and Elenore (Pottasch) B.; m. Lynn Grossman, Apr. 1, 1977; children: Mariah, Hazel. BA, NYU; studied with Uta Hagen, Viola Spolin. Studied with Second City comedy troupe, Chgo.; theatrical appearences include (off-Broadway) You're a Good Man Charlie Brown, 1967, Up Eden, 1968, The Basic Training of Pavlo Hummel, 1971, The Children, 1972, Marie and Bruce, 1980, The Three Sisters, 1982, Some Americans Abroad, 1991, (Broadway) Plaza Suite, 1968, The White House Murder Case, 1970, Some of My Best Friends, 1977, The Inspector General, 1978 (Best Featured Actor in Play Tony award nominee 1979), Speed the Plow, 1991, (regional theatre) The Boys Next Door, 1986, Who Wants to be The Lone Ranger?, 1971; dir. play: Girls, Girls, Girls, 1980; film debut in Midnight Cowboy, 1969; film appearences include Me Natalie, 1969, The Strawberry Statement, 1970, Catch-22, 1970, Making It, 1971, Bank Shot, 1974, Report to the Commissioner, 1975, Close Encounters of the Third Kind, 1977, Girlfriends 1978, Altered States, 1980, Absense of Malice, 1981, Prince of the City, 1981, Whose Life Is It Anyway?, 1981, 2010, 1984, In Our Hands, 1984, End of the Line, 1987, Dead Bang, 1989, Alice, 1990, Little Man Tate, 1991, Bob Roberts, 1992, Greedy, 1994, City Slickers Two, 1994, Waiting for Guffman, 1996, Deconstructing Harry, 1996, Clockwatchers, 1997, Jakob the Liar, 1999, Three to Tango, 1999, Tex, the Passive Aggressive Gunslinger, 2000, Natural Selection, 2000, Ghost World, 2000, The Mexican, 2001, The Majestic, 2001, A Mighty Wind, 2003, Marie and Bruce, 2004, Scene Stealers, 2004, Trust the Man, 2005; dir. films: Parents, 1989, My Boyfriend's Back, 1993, The Last Good Time, 1996, Subway Stories, 1997; TV debut in The Mod Squad; TV appearences include (film) Marriage: Year One, 1971, The Face of Fear, 1990, Giving up the Ghost, 1998, Swing Vote, 1999 (series episodes) Seinfeld, 1993; dir. TV series: Legend, 1995, Strangers with Candy, 1999, Now and Again, 1999-2000, Deadline, 2000-01, Dead Last, 2001, Twilight Zone, 2002-03; dir. TV films: The Brass Ring, 1983, No Joking, 2004, The Exonerated, 2005; actor, dir. TV series: Hopless Pictures, 2005; writer, prodr films: The Last Good Time, 1994; exec. prodr. films: The Definite Maybe, 1997; actor, prodr. films: Godsford Park, 2001 Mem. AEA, SAG, AFTRA, Astoria Found. (bd. dirs.).*

BALABAN, VIVIAN, librarian, elementary school educator; b. Mount Vernon, N.Y., July 23, 1933; d. William and Claire Eisenberg Balaban. BS in Edn., CCNY, 1955; MS in Libr. Svc., Columbia U., 1960. Cert. elem. sch. tchr. grades K-6 N.Y., 1955, libr. N.Y., 1960. 2nd grade elem. sch. tchr. Brentwood (N.Y.) Pub. Schs., 1955—56; libr. trainee N.Y. Pub. Libr., N.Y.C., 1957—59, Mount Vernon (N.Y.) Pub. Libr., 1960—61; reference libr. CUNY Hunter Coll. Libr., N.Y.C., 1961—95. Vol. Headstart Day Care-Ednl. Alliance, N.Y.C., 1995—2003. Mem.: Chelsea For Peace. Democrat. Jewish. Avocations: travel, movies, theater, music, reading. Home: 350 W 24th St Apt 10C New York NY 10011-2228

BALADI, NAOUM ABBOUD, surgeon; b. Aleppo, Syria, May 26, 1956; came to U.S., 1979; s. Abboud and Nadia Baladi; m. Houda Leon, Sept. 19, 1979; children: Carine, Christina, Stephanie. BA, Coll. Champagnat, Aleppo, Syria, 1973; MD, Aleppo U., 1979. Diplomate Am. Bd. Gen. Surgery, Am. Bd. Thoracic Surgery. Surgeon in tng. U. Mass., Worcester, 1980-85; cardiac surgeon in tng. U. N.Mex., Albuquerque, 1985-87; fellow heart and lung transplantation U. Pitts., 1987-88; cardiac surgeon St. Mary's Hosp., San Francisco, 1988—; pres. Pacific Cardiovasc. Surgeons, Daly City, Calif., 1993—; med. dir. Cardio Med. Solutions, Fountain Valley, Calif., 1996—. Fellow ACS, Internat. Soc. Heart and lung Transplantation, Soc. Thoracic Surgeons. Avocations: painting, soccer, swimming, travel. Office: Pacific Cardiovasc Surgeons 1500 Southgate Ave Ste 209 Daly City CA 94015-2231 E-mail: nbaladimd@home.com.

BALAGURU, PERUMALSAMY, civil engineering educator; b. Tamil Nadu, India, Mar. 26, 1947; s. Perumal and Kengammal (Perumal) Ramasamy; m. Suryaprabha Venkatesalu, June 6, 1974; children: Balasoundhari, Balamuralee. BS with honors, U. Madras, Coimbatore, India, 1968; MS with distinction, Indian Inst. Sci., Bangalore, 1970; PhD, U. Ill., 1977. Assoc. lectr. U. Madras, 1970-73; asst. prof. Rutgers State U. N.J., Piscataway, 1977-82, assoc. prof., 1982-88, prof., 1988—2002, dist. prof., 2002—; program dir. Nat. Sci. Found., 2002—04. Presenter in field. Author: Fiber Reinforced Cement Composites, 1992; editor books; contbr. more than 250 articles to profl. jours. Named Outstanding Alumni, U. Ill.-Chgo., Tchr. of Yr., Rutgers U., 1985; recipient Long Standing Contbrn. award, Internat. Ferrocement Soc., Tchr. of Yr., Rutgers U., 1992. Fellow Am. Concrete Inst.; mem. ASCE. Office: Rutgers U 623 Bowser Rd Piscataway NJ 08854 Office Phone: 732-445-3537. Business E-Mail: balaguru@rci.rutgers.edu.

BALAJI, K.C., urologist, researcher; s. K.C. and Vijaya Krishnaswamy; m. Shoba Charavarthy Mani, Apr. 4, 1991; children: Navin Charavarthy, Nandita Charavarthy. MB BS, Madras Med. Coll., India, 1986. Cert. med. dr. Indian Med. Coun., Am. Bd. Urology. Resident in urology U. Mass. Med. Ctr., Worcester, 1993—97; fellow in urol. oncology Meml. Sloan Kettering Cancer Ctr., N.Y.C., 1997—99; asst. prof., dir. urol. oncology So. Ill. U. Sch. Medicine, Springfield, 1999—2000; assoc. prof., dir. urol. oncology rsch. U. Nebr. Med. Ctr., Omaha, 2000—. Urol. oncologist U. Nebr. Med. Ctr., Omaha, 2000—. Actor, writer Tamil Plays - Amateur. Vol. Indian Assn. Nebr., Omaha. Fellow: Royal Coll. Surgeons Edinburgh; mem.: Am. Urol. Assn. Achievements include research in prostate cancer; robotic urological surgery. Office: U Nebr Med Ctr 982360 Omaha NE 68198-2360 E-mail: kcbalaji@unmc.edu.

BALANDRAN, STELLA VARONA, interpreter, lyricist, composer, writer; b. NYC, May 16, 1932; d. Rafael Patricio Garcia and Stella Ginorio; m. Ricardo Balandran; m. Emilio Varona; children: Charles Varona, Henry Varona, Emil Varona. Student, Middlesex C.C., Middletown, Conn., 1966—68, New Haven U., 1970—72, U. Davis, 1990—92; cert. paralegal, Napa Valley Coll., 1993. Cert. mediator Conflict Resolution and Rsch. Inst. Interpreter Meriden (Conn.) Police Dept. Ct., 1961—72; elderly specialist

City of Meriden, 1972—74; mgr. Am. Cancer Soc., Vallejo, Calif., 1982—87; paralegal Solano County Legal Assistance, Vallejo, 1987—94; dir. Spanish Translations Lake County, Umatilla, Fla., 1997—; interpreter LanguageLine, Monterey, Calif., 2000—02. Composer: (Album) De Amantes A Extraños, 1987, (Album) Dare to Dream, 1991; author: (poetry) Am. Poetry Assn., World of Poetry, Nat. Libr. Poetry. Pres. Friends of the Libr., Umatilla, 1999—2000; bd. mem. Commn. on Aging, Meriden, 1972—74, Bd. Suprs. Affirmative Action Com., Solano County, Calif., 1992—93; pres. P.R. Rep. Club, Meriden, 1964—67; del. Dem. State Conv., Orlando. Named Disting. Poet, 1996; named to, Internat. Poetry Hall of Fame, 1996; recipient various awards, San Francisco Festival de la Cancion, 1986, 1987, 1988, 1989, 1990, 1992, 1998. Mem.: ASCAP, NARAS, Am. Soc. Composers, Authors, Pubs., Latin Assn. Rec. Arts and Scis. Roman Catholic. Avocation: volunteer English as Second Language Teacher . Office: Spanish Translations of Lake County 95 S Trowell Ave Umatilla FL 32784 Business E-Mail: EstelaBMus@CS.Com.

BALANIS, CONSTANTINE APOSTLE, electrical engineering educator; b. Trikala, Thessaly, Greece, Oct. 29, 1938; came to U.S., 1955; s. Apostolos G. and Erini (Vlahocostas) B.; m. Helen Jovaras, May 21, 1972; children: Erini, Stephanie. BSEE, Va. Poly. Inst., 1964; MEE, U. Va., 1966; PhDEE, Ohio State U., 1969; Doctorate (hon.), Aristotle U. Thessaloniki, Greece, 2004. Electronics engr. NASA, Hampton, Va., 1964-70; asst. professorial lectr. George Washington U. Extension, Hampton, 1968-70; vis. assoc. prof. dept. elec. engring. W.Va. U., Morgantown, 1970-72, assoc. prof., 1972-76, prof., 1976-83; prof. dept. elec. engring. Ariz. State U., Tempe, 1983-91, Regents' prof., 1991—, dir. Telecommunications Rsch. Ctr., 1988-99. Cons. Motorola Inc., Scottsdale, Ariz., 1984-94, Loral Def. Systems, Litchfield Park, Ariz., 1986-88, Gen. Dynamics, Pomona, Calif., 1986-87, Naval Air Warfare Ctr., Patuxent River, Md., 1977-90, Naval Surface Warfare Ctr., Dahlgren, Va., 1985-86, Nat. Radio Astronomy Observatory, Green Bank, W.Va., 1972-74; Boeing, Seattle, 1996, Rockwell Internat., Cedar Rapids, Iowa, 1997. Author: Antenna Theory: Analysis and Design, 1982, 3d edit., 2005, Advanced Engineering Electromagnetics, 1989; patentee in field. Recipient Halliburton Best Researcher award W.Va. U., 1983, Russ award for Rsch., Ohio U., 1984, Teaching Excellence award Ariz. State U., 1988, also Outstanding Grad. Mentor award, 1996-97; grantee and contracts NASA, Army Rsch. Office, NSF, Office Naval Rsch., Dept. of Energy, Dept. of Transp., Naval Air Warfare Ctr., Naval Surface Warfare Ctr., Motorola Inc., Gen. Dynamics, Boeing Helicopter Sys., Sikorsky Aircraft, Rockwell Internat., Boeing Helicopters, IBM, 1972—. Fellow (life) IEEE (Individual Achievement award region 6, 1989, Spl. Engring. Professionalism award Phoenix sect. 1992, Third Millennium award 2000, AP Soc. Chen-To Tai Disting. Educator award 2005); mem. Sigma Xi, Phi Kappa Phi, Eta Kappa Nu, Tau Beta Pi. Avocations: golf, jogging, tennis, bowling. Home: 3154 E Encanto St Mesa AZ 85213-6110 Office: Ariz State U Dept Elec Engring Tempe AZ 85287-7206 Business E-Mail: balanis@asu.edu.

BALANOFF, CLEM, county election director; b. Chgo., Apr. 14, 1953; m. Virginia Balanoff; 2 children. Student, Ripon Coll., 1971-73. Mem. Ill. House, 1989-95; Dem. candidate U.S. House, 1994, 96. Home: 5606 S Blackstone #3 Chicago IL 60637 Office: Cook County Clerk 69 W Washington 5th flr Chicago IL 60602 Office Phone: 312-603-0925. Business E-Mail: clem2@balanoff.com.

BALAS, EGON, applied mathematician, educator; b. Cluj, Romania, June 7, 1922; came to U.S., 1967, naturalized, 1973; s. Ignat and Boriska B.; m. Edith Lovi, 1948; children: Anna, Vera. Diploma licenciae, Bolyai U., Cluj, 1949; D.Sc.Ec. summa cum laude, U. Brussels; D.U. in Math., U. Paris; PhD (hon.), U. Miguel Hernandez, Spain, 2002; Doctorate in Math. (hon.), U. Waterloo, 2005. Asso. prof. econs. Inst. Econ. Sci., Bucharest, 1949-58; analyst Designing Inst. Forestry and Timber Industry, Bucharest, 1959-64; head math. programming sector Center Math. Stats. of Romanian Acad., 1964-66; research mathematician Internat. Computation Centre, Rome, 1966; vis. prof. ops. research U. Toronto, 1967, Stanford U., 1967; Ford disting. research prof. Carnegie Mellon U., 1967-68; prof. indsl. adminstrn. and applied math. Carnegie-Mellon U., 1968—, univ. prof., 1990—, holder GSIA alumni chair, 1980—; Thomas Lord Prof. Ops. Rsch., 1997—. Vis. ops. rsch. analyst Fed. Energy Adminstrn., 1976; cons. NSF grantee, 1972—; vis. prof. Maths. Inst. Köln, 1980-81. Author: Will to Freedom: A Perilous Journey Through Fascism and Communism, 2000 (transl. into Hungarian, Italian, Romanian and French); assoc. editor: Ops. Rsch., 1967-96, Zeitschrift für Ops. Rsch.; adv. editor: Discrete Applied Math., Jour. Combinatorial Optimization, Naval Rsch. Logistics; mem. editl. bd. Computational Optimization and Applications, Discrete Optimization, Revue Française d'Automatique et Rsch. Operationelle, Annals of Operations Rsch., European Jour. Operational Rsch.; contbr. articles to profl. jours. INFORMS fellow, 2002; recipient Alexander von Humboldt Sr. U.S. Scientist award, 1980-81, John von Neumann Theory award, 1995, Euro Gold medal, 2001, Citation Classic, Current Contents, 1982. Mem. SIAM, Math. Programming Soc. (coun. 1989-92), Inst. Mgmt. Scis. (coun. 1972-75), Oper. Rsch. Soc., Inst. Operatives Rsch. and Mgmt. Scis., Hungarian Acad. Sci. Achievements include research in math. programming, integer and disjunctive programming, combinatorial optimization, graphs, networks, crew scheduling, machine sequencing, energy models; devel. of scheduling system for steel rolling. Home: 136 Beechwood Ln Pittsburgh PA 15206-4526 Office: Tepper School Business Carnegie Mellon Univ Pittsburgh PA 15213 Office Phone: 412-268-2285. Business E-Mail: eb17@andrew.cmu.edu.

BALASH, JEFFREY LINKE, investment banker; b. NYC, Nov. 2, 1948; s. George Everett and Jeanne Marie (Linke) B. BA in Econs. summa cum laude, Princeton, 1970; MBA, JD cum laude, Harvard U., 1974. Bar: N.Y. 1974. Asst. to chmn. Louis-Dreyfus Corp., N.Y.C., 1974-76; dir. Avon Products, N.Y.C., 1976-79; mng. dir. Lehman Bros., N.Y.C., 1979-85, Drexel Burnham Lambert, Beverly Hills, Calif., 1985-90; founding ptnr. Anthem Ptnrs., L.A. and N.Y.C., 1991-92; chmn. Comstock Ptnrs., L.L.C., Beverly Hills, Calif., 1992—. JL Furnishings, L.L.C., Gardena, 1997—2002; CFO, chief strategic officer Telephony at Work, 1999—2002; co-founder Comstock Captial Ptnrs. LLC, 2002—. Bd. dirs. Joffrey Ballet, NYC, and LA, 1986-89; alumni coun. Harvard U. Bus. Sch., Boston, 1989-92; major gifts com. Family Club, Princeton U. Class 1970; founder Sons of Bacchus Baker scholar Harvard U. Sch. Bus. Adminstrn., 1974. Mem. Harvard Bus. Sch. Assn. So. Calif. (bd. dirs. 1999-2003), Phi Beta Kappa. Republican. Roman Catholic. Avocations: travel, wine, jazz, art, films. Home: 9430 Readcrest Dr Beverly Hills CA 90210-2552 Office Phone: 310-278-6444. Business E-Mail: jdalash@alumni.princeton.edu. E-mail: jbcash@comstockpartners.com.

BALASI, MARK GEOFFREY, architect; b. Chgo., Feb. 29, 1952; s. Alfred Victor and Betty Lou (Biggs) B.; m. Barbara Jane Ritt, May 25, 1985; children: Geoffrey Adam, Maria Elizabeth. Student, Ecole-des-Beaux-Arts, Versailles, France, 1974—75; BS in Archtl. Studies, U. Ill., 1975; postgrad., U. Wis., 1986, postgrad., 1989, postgrad., 1992. Lic. arch., Ill., Mich., Ohio. Arch. Davy McKee, Chgo., 1976-80, Perkins & Will, Chgo., 1980-82; prin. Hansen Lind Meyer Inc., Chgo., 1982-95; v.p. Phillips Swager Assocs., Naperville, Ill., 1995—2003, HDR Architecture, Inc., Chgo., 2003—. Lectr. Italian Nat. Ctr. Hosp. Bldg. and Technique. Editor: Balasi Archives, U. Iowa Librs. Spl. Collections; author: Sgt. Balasic WWI Album-Austro-Hungarian Army, 1996, Balasic Family Vaudeville Album, 1994; contbr.: (with Paul F. Stevens) Low Level Liberators in World War II, 1998; contbr. articles to profl. jours.; prin. works include Villa Schaefer, Mattoon, Ill., Nunamaker House, Mattoon, Mary Brown Stephenson Radiation Oncology Ctr., Zion, Ill. Active Hist. Preservation Comm., McHenry County, Ill. Mem. AIA (Nat. Coun. Archtl. Registration Bds. cert.), Am. Soc. Hosp. Engring., Acad. Architecture for Health, Health Facility Inst., PB4Y Assn., U. Ill. Alumni Assn. Avocations: genealogy, entomology, travel. Office: HDR Architecture Inc 8550 W Bryn Mawr Ave Ste 900 Chicago IL 60631-3223 Office Phone: 773-380-7900. Business E-Mail: mark.balasi@hdrinc.com.

BALAS-WHITFIELD, SUSAN, artist; b. NJ; m. Marshall Whitfield. B.A., Rutgers U., Newark, 1964, N.Y. U., N.Y., 1961—64, Douglass Coll., New Brunswick, 1960—61. Tchr. WM. R. Satz. Sch., Holmdel, NJ, 1976—89; artist, 1976—. Author: (novels) Into The Triangle, A Teacher's Trot, 1989. Pres. Ranch Property Owners Assoc., Durango, Colo., 2000—03. Recipient Full Signature Mem., Pastel Society of Am., 2001, Artist of the Yr., Durango Co. Chamber of Commerce. Mem.: Pastel Soc. of Am., Salmagundi Club. Avocations: motorcycling, skiing, running, hiking. Home: 308 CottonWood Creek Rd Durango CO 81301 Studio: 22521 E Rowland Dr Aurora CO 80016 Office Phone: 970-259-0774. E-mail: susan@balasart.com.

BALAY, ROBERT ELMORE, editor, librarian; b. Wichita, Kans., Oct. 6, 1930; s. Loren Elmore and Gladys Lois (Crites) B.; m. Harriette Shirley Anderson, Dec. 23, 1961; children— Christopher Loren, Anne Gladys, Jean Mary BA, Macalester Coll., 1952; MA, U. Minn., 1954; MS in Libr. Sci., Columbia U., 1959. Tech. writer Beech Aircraft Corp., Wichita, 1956-58; asst. librarian Grumman Aircraft Corp., Bethpage, N.Y., 1959-62, Gen. Precision, Little Falls, N.J., 1962-64; asst. sci. librarian Wayne State U., Detroit, 1964-68, adj. instr. library sci., 1966-67; head reference dept. Yale U. Library, New Haven, 1968-86; reference editor Choice mag., Middletown, Conn., 1986—. Author: Early Periodical Indexes, 2000; editor: Guide to Reference Books, 11th edit., 1996; contbr. articles to profl. jours. Served with U.S. Army, 1954-56 Recipient Isadore Gilbert Mudge-R.R. Bowker award for reference svc., ALA, 2004. Democrat. Home: 97 Livingston St New Haven CT 06511-2411 Office: Choice Mag 100 Riverview Ctr Middletown CT 06457-3445

BALBACH, HAROLD EDWARD, environmental scientist; b. Chgo., Sept. 26, 1936; s. Harold Edward and Lillian Mildred (Best) B.; m. Margaret Ann Kain, Sept. 2, 1961. BE, Chgo. State U., 1959; MS, U. Ill., 1961, PhD, 1965. Cert. profl. agronomist, 1982; cert. sr. ecologist, 2002. Prof. Ea. Ill. U., Charleston, 1966-72; environ. scientist rsch. lab. U.S. Army C.E., Champaign, Ill., 1972-90; sr. rsch. fellow Army Environ. Policy Inst., Champaign, 1990-92; mgr. rsch. program U.S. Army C.E., Champaign, 1992-95, sr. rsch. scientist, 1995-96, 1999—, divsn. chief land mgmt. lab., 1996-99. Co-author: Environmental Assessment, 1993, 2001. Bd. trustees Champaign County Hist. Mus., 1995—, pres., 1996—. Fellow Soc. Am. Mil. Engrs. (life, pres. Illini Post 1990-92, 96-97, nat. bd. dirs. 1999-2002); mem. Am. Soc. Agronomy (bd. dirs. 1985-89, 99-2002, chair biosecurity com. 2003—), Am. Soc. Hort. Sci., Ecol. Soc. of Am., Internat. Soc. Hort. Sci., Soc. for Am. Archeology, Nat. Trust for Hist. Preservation, Ill. Hist. Soc., Assn. for Southeastern Biology (gopher tortoise coun.). Avocations: historic preservation, prairie restoration. Office: US Army Engr Rsch and Devel Lab PO Box 9005 Champaign IL 61826-9005

BALBACH, STANLEY BYRON, lawyer; b. Normal, Ill., Dec. 26, 1919; s. Nyle Jacob and Gertrude (Cory) B.; m. Sarah Troutt Witherspoon, May 22, 1944; children: Stanley Byron Jr., Nancy Ann Fehr, Barbara Haines, Edith. BS, U. Ill., 1940, LLD, 1942. Bar: Ill. 1942, Fla. 1980, U.S. Ct. Appeals (7th cir.) 1961, U.S. Supreme Ct. 1950. Ptnr. Couchman & Balbach, Hoopeston, Ill., 1945-48, Webber & Balbach, Urbana, 1948-81, Balbach & Fehr, Urbana, 1981—. Nat. chmn. Jr. Bar Conf., 1955. Author: Reverse Mortgages, 1997, The Lawyers Guide to Retirement: Serving a New Clientele in a Second Career in Real Estate, 1998. Capt. USAAF, 1942-45 (pilot). Mem. ABA (ho. of dels. 1956, lawyer title guaranty fund com., past mem. coun. law office practice and real property, probate and trust law sects.), LWV, Ill. State Bar Assn. (elder law com., Laureate of the Acad. Ill. Lawyers 2002), Am. Judicature Soc., Masons, Rotary, Phi Delta Phi, Alpha Kappa Lambda. Home: 1009 S Douglas Ave PO Box 217 Urbana IL 61803 Office: Balbach & Fehr Box 301 102 E Broadway Ave Urbana IL 61801-2705 Office Phone: 217-367-1011.

BALBEKOV, VALERI I., physicist, researcher; b. Poushkin, Leningrad Region, Russia, Sept. 6, 1939; arrived in U.S., 1997, permanent resident, 2001; s. Ivan I. Balbekov and Olga I. Balbekova; m. Tatiana I. Mishenkova; 1 child, Olga. Master Degree in Physics, Moscow State U., Moscow, Russia, 1956—62; PhD in Physics, Phys. Inst. of USSR Acad. of Sci., Moscow, 1965. From jr. scientist to sr. scientist II Inst. for High Energy Physics, Protvino, Russia, 1965—2000; scientist II Fermi Nat. Accelerator Lab., Batavia, Ill., 2001—. Sr. lectr. Moscow State U., Russia, 1980—86; assoc. prof. Moscow Phy.-Tech. Inst., 1986—92; guest scientist Superconducting Supercollider Lab., Dallas, 1993—94, Fermi Nat. Accelerator Lab., Batavia, ILL., 1997—2001. Home: 742 Graham Rd North Aurora IL 60542 Office: Fermilab MS 231 PO Box 500 Batavia IL 60510 Personal E-mail: balbekov@aol.com. Business E-Mail: balbekov@fnal.gov.

BALBI, KENNETH EMILIO, environmental specialist, researcher; b. NYC, Apr. 13, 1963; s. George Emilio and Blanca Amelia (Fonseca) B.; m. Julie Ann Lopez, Feb. 19, 1989; children: Danielle Elizabeth, Joshua Emilio. MD, U. Ctrl. del Este, Dominican Republic, 1985; BS, SUNY, Albany, 1989. Rsch. assoc. Montefiore Med. Ctr., NY, 1988-94; govtl. and instnl. cons. SCITEC Corp., Kennewick, Wash., 1994-95; dir. tng. and profl. svcs. U.S. Lead, Oyster Bay, NY, 1995-97; v.p., co-founder ANDO Internat., Bklyn., 1995—2002; dir. franchise ops. PRO-TECT Franchising Inc., Oyster Bay, NY, 1996-97; v.p. rsch. & design AIA Environ. Corp., Astoria, NY, 1997-99; pres., founder "E" The Solution, Inc., Douglaston, NY, 2002—. Contbr. articles to profl. jours. Mem. St. Michael's Hispanic Assn., Flushing, N.Y., 1991—, Cuban-Am. Assocs., Flushing, 1988—, Alliance to End Childhood Lead Poisoning, Washington, 1992—. Mem.: ASTM, AAAS, Nat. Environ. Health Assn., Am. Indsl. Hygiene Assn., United Internat. Med. Grads., NY Acad. Scis., InterAm. Coll. Physicians and Surgeons, Nat. Assn. for Search and Rescue. Roman Catholic. Home: 24015B Oak Park Dr Douglaston NY 11362 Office: "E" The Solution Inc PO Box 620790 Douglaston NY 11362 Office Phone: 718-229-8859. Personal E-mail: kbalbi@aol.com.

BALBOA, MARCELO, professional soccer player; b. Cerritos, Calif., Aug. 8, 1967; s. Luis Balboa; m. Cindy Balboa. Grad., San Diego State U., 1988. Player U.S. Nat. Team, 1988—, San Diego Nomads, APSL, 1989, San Francisco Blackhawks, APSL, 1990—91, Colo. Foxes, APSL, 1992, Leon, Mex. 1st Divsn., 1995—96, Colo. Rapids, 1996—. Mem. U.S. World Cup Team, 1994—. Named MVP Cup, 1994, Colo. Rapids, 1997. also: US Soccer Fedn 1801 S Prairie Ave # 1811 Chicago IL 60616-1319 Office: 1000 Chopper CIR Denver CO 80204-5805

BALCER, CHARLES LOUIS, college president emeritus, educator; b. McGregor, Iowa, May 23, 1921; s. Ludwig Frank and Iva (Vaughan) B.; m. Martha Elizabeth Belgum, Jan. 6, 1944; children— Mary Elizabeth, Mark Lewis, Beth Louise, Brian Charles. BS, Winona (Minn.) State Tchrs. Coll., 1942; MA, State U. Iowa, 1949, PhD, 1954; DHL (hon.), Augustana Coll., 2003. Tchr. Minn. and Iowa high schs., 1942-43, 46-47; instr. State U. Iowa, 1947-50; high sch. prin. Detroit Lakes, Minn., 1950-54; assoc. prof. speech St. Cloud (Minn.) State Coll., 1954-56, prof., acad. dean, 1958-64; prof. speech SUNY-Oswego, 1956-57; pres. Augustana Coll., Sioux Falls, S.D., 1965-80, pres. emeritus, 1980—, Disting. Service prof., 1980-95, interim chair edn. dept., 1999-00. Interim pres., CEO Good Samaritan Soc., 1997-98. Author: (with H. F. Seabury) Teaching Speech. Mem., bd. dirs. Evang. Luth. Good Samaritan Soc.; mem. Marquette Bank of S.D., Sioux Falls Symphony Assn. Served with AUS, 1943-46. Decorated knight 1st class Royal Order St. Olav (Norway); named to S.D. Hall of Fame, 2003. Mem. Speech Communication Assn. Am., Central States Speech Assn. (pres. 1954), NEA, Assn. Higher Edn., Delta Sigma Rho, Kappa Delta Pi, Phi Delta Kappa. Democrat. Home: 111 W 17th St # 115 Sioux Falls SD 57104-4901 Personal E-mail: clbalcer@aol.com. *I have learned that the purpose of this earthly life is not happiness. It is to be useful, to be honorable, to be compassionate. It is to matter— to have it made some difference that you lived at all.*

BALCERZAK, STANLEY PAUL, hematologist, oncologist, director, retired medical educator; b. Pitts., Apr. 27, 1930; BS, U. Pitts., 1953; MD, U. Md., 1955. Diplomate Am. Bd. Internal Medicine, Am. Bd. Hematology, Am. Bd. Oncology. Instr. medicine U Chgo., 1959-60, U. Pitts., 1962-64, asst. prof., 1964-67; assoc. prof. medicine Ohio State U., Columbus, 1967-71, prof., 1971-99, prof. emeritus, 1999—, dir. div. hematology and oncology, 1969-94, dep. dir. Ohio State U. Comprehensive Cancer Ctr., 1984-97, assoc. chmn. dept. medicine, 1984-98, dir. Hemophilia Ctr., 1975-79, 1981-99. Mem. clin. rev. com. Am. Cancer Soc., N.Y.C., 1976-82 Contbr. chpts. to books, numerous articles to profl. jours. Served to capt. U.S. Army, 1960-62 Recipient numerous grants Fellow ACP; mem. Central Soc. for Clin. Research (chmn. subsplty. council in hematology 1980-81, councillor 1980-83), Am. Soc. for Clin. Oncology, Am. Assn. for Cancer Research, Am. Soc. Hematology, Phi Beta Kappa, Alpha Omega Alpha Home: 3113 N 3 Bs And K Rd Sunbury OH 43074-9582 Office: Ohio State U Divsn Hematology Oncology 320 W 10th Ave Columbus OH 43210-1240 Office Phone: 614-293-8729. Business E-Mail: balcerzak.1@osu.edu.

BALCH, CHARLES M., surgeon, educator; b. Milford, Del., Aug. 24, 1942; m. Carol Mitchell; 4 children. BS cum laude, U. Toledo, 1963; MD, Columbia U., 1967. Diplomate Am. Bd. Surgery (bd. dirs. 1986-1992). Intern in surgery Duke U. Med. Ctr., Durham, N.C., 1967-68; resident in gen. surgery U. Ala., Birmingham, 1970-71, 73-75, asst. prof. to assoc. prof. dept. surgery, 1975-81, prof, 1981-85, chief sect. surg. oncology, 1979-85, asst. to assoc. prof. dept. microbiology, 1975-82, prof., 1982-85; assoc. scientist to sr. scientist, sr. investigator cellular immunobiology unit Comprehensive Cancer Ctr., U. Ala., 1975-85, assoc. dir for clin. studies, 1979-85, acting dir., 1982-83; head div. surgery and anesthesiology U. Tex.-M.D. Anderson Cancer Ctr., Houston, 1985-94, v.p. hosp. and clinics, 1993-94, chmn. dept. surgical oncology, 1985-94, prof. surgery, 1993-96, exec. v.p. health affairs, 1994-96; pres., CEO City of Hope, 1996—98; exec. v.p. Am. Soc. Clinical Oncology, Alexandria, Va. Assoc. chmn. dept. surgery U. Tex., 1985-94; staff surgeon, chief oncology rsch. VA Hosp., Birmingham, 1975-85; vis. prof., Eleanor Roosevelt internat. fellow U. Sydney, Australia, 1983; chmn. nat. intergroup melanoma com., Nat. Cancer Inst., NIH, 1981—, mem. subcom. bd. sci. counselors, 1980-86, mem. bd. sci. counselors, 1987-1991, other coms., 1978—; mem. Kettering selection com. GM Cancer Rsch. Found., Inc., 1986, vice chmn., 1987-88, mem. awards assembly, 1988—; prof. surgery & oncology, Johns Hopkins Med. Institutions, 2000-. Author: (with G.W. Milton) Cutaneous Melanoma: Clinical Management and Treatment Results Worldwide, 1985; author, editor: Surgical Approaches to Cutaneous Melanoma, 1985; author over 100 book chpts. including Hardy's Textbook of Surgery, 1988, The Physiologic Basis of Modern Surgical Care, 1988, Textbook on Clinical Oncology, 1991, Advances in Surgery, 1991, Cancer: Principles and Practice of Oncology, 1989, Current Surgical Therapy, 3d edit., 1989; author over 280 jour. articles, abstracts; mem. editorial bds. Practical Rev. in Cancer Mgmt., 1979-85, Ala. Jour. Med. Scis., 1979-81, Jour. Biol. Response Modifiers, 1981—, Am. Jour. Clin. Oncology, 1981-84, Jour. Surg. Rsch., 1982-88, Jour. Immunology, 1982-85, Cancer Treatment Reports, 1984— (also adv. bd.), Jour. Clin. Oncology, 1986—, Archives Surgery, 1986—, Surgery, 1986—, European Jour. Cancer, 1989—, Melanoma Rsch., 1990—, Postgrad. Gen. Surgery, 1991—, many others; editor The Melanoma Letter, 1986-93, Breast Diseases: A Year Book Quarterly, 1990—, Annals of Surgical Oncology, 1993—; assoc. editor Advances in Surgery, 1986—, Cancer Rsch., 1989—. Program specialist USPHS, 1968-70. Immunology fellow Lab. Dr. J. Feldman, La Jolla, Calif., 1971-73; NIH grantee, 1980-84, 83-85, 84-87, 84-86,87-1993, VA, 1981-84, 84-89, CEP grantee, 1990-92, NCI grantee, 1987-94. Fellow ACS (various coms. on commn. on cancer, 1980—, chmn. edn. com. 1981-84, chmn. cancer mgmt. course con. 1981-83, assoc. Internat. Fedn. Surg. Colls. 1988—, mem. surg. forum 1985-91, grantee 1984-88, 85-91); mem. AMA, Am. Cancer Soc. (bd. dirs. Ala. divsn. 1983-85, exec. bd. Bay Area chpt. Houston 1986—, clin. fellowship nat. divsn. 1985-87, mem. profl. edn. subcom. clin. fellowship 1988), Am. Radium Soc. (chmn. publs. com. 1982-84), Am. Soc. Clin. Oncology (sci. and publs. coml 1987-90, bd. dirs.), Assn. Acad. Surgery (sec.-treas. 1981-83, pres.-elect 1983-84, pres. 1984-85, exec. coun. 1982-86), Assn. Surg. Edn., Conjoint Coun. Surg. Edn. (cancer com. 1985—), Soc. Biol. Therapy, Soc. Surg. Oncology (sec. 1986-88, v.p. 1989-90, chmn. membership com. 1986-89, clin. rsch. and govt. rels. com. 1983-85, pres. elect 1990-91, pres. 1991-92), Soc. Univ. Surgeons (councilman 1982-85), Southeastern Cancer Study Group (chmn. surg. com. 1978-85, exec. com. 1979-85, chmn. melanoma/sarcoma com. 1983-85), Am. Soc. Clin. Investigation, Am. Assn. Cancer Edn., Am. Assn. Cancer Rsch., Am. Assn. Immunologists, Am. Assn. Transplant Surgeons, Am. Surg. Assn., European Soc. Surg. Oncology, Harris county Med. Soc., Houston Surg. Soc., Jefferson County Med. Soc., John Kirklin Soc., Pan-Pacific Surg. Assn., Reticuloendothelial Soc., Soc. Internat. de Chirurgie, Soc. Surg. Chmn., Tex. Surg. Soc., WHO Melanoma Group, others. Office: Am Soc Clinical Oncology 1900 Duke St #200 Alexandria VA 22314

BALCH, GLENN MCCLAIN, JR., academic administrator, minister, writer; b. Shattuck, Okla., Nov. 1, 1937; s. Glenn McClain and Marjorie (Daily) Balch; m. Diana Gale Seeley, Oct. 15, 1970; children: Bryan, Gayle, Wesley, John. Student, Panhandle State U., 1958-60, So. Meth. U., summers 1962-64; BS, S.W. State U., Okla., 1962; BD, Phillips U., 1965; JD, L.A. Coll. Law, 1969; MA, Chapman U., 1973, MA in Edn., MA in Psychology, Chapman U., 1975, MA in Sch. Counseling; PhD, Alliant Internat. U., 1978; postgrad., Claremont Grad. Sch., 1978-70, U. Okla., 1965-66. Ordained to ministry Meth. Ch., 1962. Sr. min. First Meth. Ch., Eakly, Okla., 1960-63, Calumet, Okla., 1963-65, Goodrich Meml. Ch., Norman, Okla., 1965-66, First Meth. Ch., Barstow, Calif., 1966-70, Brea (Calif.) United Meth. Ch., 1978-89; asst. dean Chapman U., Orange, Calif., 1970-76; v.p. Hope Internat. U., Fullerton, Calif., 1976-79; pres., CEO So. Calif. Inst., Fullerton, Calif., 1988-95; pres. Westmar U., Le Mars, Iowa, 1995-96; exec. v.p. Advance Cons. Network (name now Synergistics, Inc.), Rochester, NY, 1996—; pres. Synergistics Tng., LLC, Churchville, NY, 2003—. Mental health cons. U.S. Army, 1969; edn. cons. USAF, 1974—75. Bd. dirs. Found. Internat. Cmty. Assistance, 1988—96. With USMC, 1956—57. Named Man of the Yr., Jr. C. of C., Bartow, 1969; recipient Eastern Star Religious Tng. award, 1963, 1964; Broadhurst fellow, 1963—65. Mem.: Nat. Assn. Sports Psychologists (diplomate), Calif. Assn. Family Therapists, Elks, Shriners, Masons, Rotary (pres. 1969—70, 1983—84, 1999—2000, dist. gov. 1987—88, 1988—89). Home and Office: Synergistics Tng LLC 39 Bowen Rd Churchville NY 14428-9737 Office Phone: 585-889-1822. E-mail: glenn@synergisticstraining.com.

BALCH, NELDA CAROLINE KURTZ, humanities educator; b. Kelley's Island, Ohio, July 13, 1916; d. Robert John and Lydia Amelia (Schnittker) K.; m. Donald Arthur Balch, Aug. 8, 1948 (dec. 1969). BA, Albion (Mich.) Coll., 1937; MA, U. Minn., 1938; student, Yale U., 1941, Northwestern U., 1946, U. Mich., Mich. State U., U. Oregon. Asst. prof. Simpson Coll., Indianola, Iowa, 1939-43, West Liberty (W.Va.) State Coll., 1946, Linfield Coll., McMinnville, Oreg., 1946-52; prof., chair Kalamazoo (Mich.) Coll., 1954-81, prof. non-traditional classes, 1981-85, dir., reader Faculty Readers, 1960-92, dir., reader Noontime Tales, 1985—, emeritus prof., 1981—. Author: The Kalamazoo College Festival Playhouse; contbr. articles to Notable Women in American Theatre, 1989; dir., playwright Noel Coward, 1989, Camille and Rodin, Gertrude Stein, Paula M. Becker, Mabeland; actress; featured in Emancipated Spirits, 1983. Founder, mng. dir. Festival Playhouse, Kalamazoo, 1964-81; active Friends of Art Ctr., Venice, Fla., 1990—, Kalamazoo Arts Coun., 1987-94; Aero Club dir. ARC, Eng. and France, 1943-45; dir. Readers' Theatre, Venice Pub. Libr., 1996—, ann. readers benefit program, 1995—. Recipient Cmty. Arts. Medal, Kalamazoo Arts Coun., 1985; tchg. fellow U. Minn., 1938-39; Nelda K. Balch Playhouse dedicated in her honor, 1981. Mem. Am. Assn. Univ. Women (former v.p.), Kalamazoo Art Inst., Phi Beta Kappa. Democrat. Methodist. Avocations: painting, walking, swimming, writing, volunteerism. Home: 1780 B Lake Pl Venice FL 34293-1942

BALCH, SAMUEL EASON, lawyer; b. Madison, Ala., Sept. 5, 1919; s. Joseph Austin and Clara Irene (Vaughn) B.; m. Elizabeth Gordon Brock, Apr. 17, 1943; children: Samuel Eason Jr., Elizabeth Gordon Balch Lanier, Gene Austin Balch Limbaugh, Ann Warwick Balch Miano. BS in Commerce and Bus. Adminstrn, U. Ala., 1940; LLB, U. Va., 1948, JD, 1970. Bar: Va. 1947, Ala. 1948, U.S. Supreme Ct. 1960, U.S. Ct. Appeals (11th cir.) 1981, U.S. Ct.

Appeals (5th cir.) 1965. Assoc. Martin, Turner & McWhorter, 1948; sr. ptnr. Balch & Bingham (and predecessor firms), 1962-89, of counsel, 1990—. Bd. dirs. Ala. Power Co., 1970-90; chmn. legal com. Edison Electric Inst., 1979-81, chmn. econs., pub. policy and strategic planning, exec. adv. com., 1986-88. Served to major AUS, 1941-46, ETO, PTO. Life fellow Am. Bar Found.; mem. ABA (mem. coun. pub. utility law, telecomms. and transp. sect.), Fed. Energy Bar Assn., Ala. Bar Assn., Birmingham Bar Assn., Newcomen Soc., Am. Judicature Soc., Farrah Law Soc., Mountain Brook Club, The Summit Club, The Club (Birmingham, Ala.), Kappa Sigma. Episcopalian. Home: 4227 Old Leeds Rd Birmingham AL 35213-3211 Office: PO Box 306 1710 6th Ave N Birmingham AL 35203-2015 Office Phone: 205-226-3400. Business E-Mail: ebalch@balch.com.

BALCOM, ORVILLE, engineer; b. Inglewood, Calif., Apr. 20, 1937; s. Orville R. and Rose Mae (Argo) B.; children: Cynthia, Steven. BS in Math., Calif. State U., Long Beach, 1958, postgrad., 1958-59, UCLA, 1959-62. Engr. AiResearch Mfg. Co., 1959-62, 64-65; chief engr. Meditron, El Monte, Calif., 1962-64, Astro Metrics, Burbank, Calif., 1965-67; chief engr., gen. mgr. Varadyne Power Systems, Van Nuys, Calif., 1968-71; owner, chief engr. Brown Dog Engring., Lomita, Calif., 1971—. Patentee in field. Mem. IEEE Computer Group, Independent Computer Cons. Assn., Torrance Athletic Club. Home: 24521 Walnut St Lomita CA 90717-1260 Office: PO Box 427 Lomita CA 90717-0427

BALCOMB, MARY NELSON, design studio owner; b. Mich., Apr. 29, 1928; d. Andrew and Selma (Martin) Nelson; m. Robert S. Balcomb, July 3, 1948; children: Stuart V., Amis. AA, Am. Acad. Art, 1948; BFA cum laude, U. N.Mex., 1968; MFA, U. Wash., 1971. Advt. mgr. Broome Furniture Co., Albuquerque, 1949-55; designer Custom Interiors, Albuquerque, 1956-66; art tchr. Sandia Girls' Sch., Albuquerque, 1966-68; co-owner Woolcot, Inc., Bellevue, Wash., 1975-80; owner Balcomb Design Studio, Silverdale, Wash., 1981—. Author: Nicolai Fechin, Russian-American Artist, 1975 (Rounce and Coffin award), Les Perhacs, Sculptor, 1975, William F. Reese, American Artist, 1984 (Rounce and Coffin award), Robin-Robin/A Journal, 1995, Sergei Bongart, Russian-American Artist, 2002; contbr. articles to periodic jours. Creator Children's Art Ctr. Found., Seattle, 1972, bd. dirs., 1972-80. Recipient Painting award Frye Art Mus., 1994, Honorarium Prix de West Nat. Cowboy Hall of Fame and We. Heritage Mus., 1995. Mem. Author's Guild, Phi Kappa Phi, Lambda Rho. Home: PO Box 1922 Silverdale WA 98383-1922

BALD, GARY M., federal agency administrator; With lab. divsn. FBI, Wash., 1977—81, with Albany divsn., 1981—84, with. Phila. divsn., 1984—89, with office profl. responsibility inspection divsn., 1989—91, supr. organized crime and drug matters Newark divsn., 1991—95, with inspection divsn., 1995—96, chief policy planning and analysis unit criminal investigative divsn., 1996, asst. spl. agent in charge Atlanta divsn., 1996—99; from criminal to inspection divsn. FBI Hdqs., 1999—2002; spl. agent in charge Balt. divsn. FBI, 2002—03, dep. asst. dir. counterterrorism ops., 2003—04, asst. dir. counterterrorism divsn., 2004, exec. asst. dir. counterterrorism and counterintelligence, 2004—05, dir. Nat. Security Svc., 2005—. Office: FBI J Edgar Hoover Bldg 935 Pennsylvania Ave NW Washington DC 20535-0001

BALD, RONALD JAMES, military officer; b. Dover, NJ, Mar. 6, 1965; s. Ronald Alan Bald and Jeanette Ann Carlstedt; m. Wanda Hope Yates; children: Matthew children: William. BS Civil Engring., USCG Acad., New London, Conn., 1987; MA Pub. Mgmt., U. Houston, 1995; JD, Tulane U., 2003. Deck watch officer/ops. officer U.S. Coast Guard Cutter Buttonwood, Galveston, Tex., 1987—89; adminstrv. officer/aids to nav. officer U.S. Coast Guard Group Galveston, Galveston, Tex., 1989—93; ops. officer USCG Vessel Traffic Svc. Houston/Galveston, Galena Park, Tex., 1993—96; supply officer U.S. Coast Guard Cutter Boutwell, Alameda, Calif., 1996—98; cmdg. officer U.S. Coast Guard Cutter Cushing, San Juan, PR, 1998—2000; asst. legal officer USCG Acad., New London, Conn., 2003—. Lt. comdr. (O-4) USCG, 1987. Recipient Coast Guard Commendation Medal, Seventh Coast Guard Dist., 1998—2000, Coast Guard Pacific Area, 1996—98, Eighth Coast Guard Dist., 1993—96, Coast Guard Achievement Medal, 1993, 1990—93, 1990—91, Commandant's Letter of Commendation, Coast Guard Group Galveston, 1993, James A. Wysocki Trial Advocacy award, Tulane U. Sch. Law, 2003, Cicero C. Sessions Trial Advocacy award, 2003, Trial Advocacy award, N.Y.C. Bar Assn., 2003; Stiles scholar for maritime law, Tulane Maritime Ctr., Tulane U. Sch. Law, 2002—03. Mem.: ABA, ASPA, Miss. Bar Assn. Avocation: coaching youth athletics. Office: US Coast Guard Acad 15 Mohegan Ave New London CT 06320-8100 Home: 8 Bittersweet Dr Gales Ferry CT 06335-1003 Office Phone: 860-444-8254. Personal E-mail: rhwmbald@comcast.net.

BALDACCI, DAVID, writer; b. Va., 1960; married. BA Polit. Sci., Va. Commonwealth Univ.; JD, Univ. Va. Former trial, corp. atty, Washington. Nat. amb. Nat. Multiple Sclerosis Soc.; co-founder Wish You Well Found. Author: (novels) Absolute Power, 1996 (WH Smith's Thumping Good Read award for fiction, Britain, 1997, Gold Medal for Best Mystery/Thriller, Southern Writers Guild, 1996), Total Control, 1996 (Gold Medal for Best Mystery/Thriller, Southern Writers Guild, 1997), The Winner's, 1997, The Simple Truth, 1998, Saving Faith, 1999 (NY Times bestseller, Publisher's Weekly bestseller), Wish You Well, 2000 (selected inaugural book for All America Reads nat. reading program), Last Man Standing, 2001 (No. 1 on NY Times bestseller list), The Christmas Train, 2002, Split Second, 2003 (NY Times bestseller), Hour Game, 2004, (children's books) Fries Alive!, 2005; author: (seven) screenplays. Mailing: c/o Author Mail Warner Books 1271 Ave of Americas New York NY 10020*

BALDACCI, JOHN ELIAS, governor, former congressman; b. Bangor, Maine, Jan. 30, 1955; m. Karen Weston; 1 child, Jack. BA in History, U. Maine, 1986. With Momma Baldacci's Restaurant, Bangor; mem. Bangor City Coun., 1978-81, Maine State Senate, 1982-94, 104th-106th Congress from 2d dist., 1994—2002; Governor, 2003—. Mem. agr. com. Maine State Senate, transp. com., regional whip North East. Democrat. Office: Office of the Governor #1 State House Station Augusta ME 04333-0001

BALDAIA, PETER, curator; b. Sept. 12, 1953; BA, R.I. Coll., 1978; postgrad., Brown U., 1979; MA, Boston U., 1982. Curator Fuller Mus. Art, Brockton, Mass., 1986—91; curator exhibits and collections Rockford Art Mus., 1992—94; chief curator Huntsville (Ala.) Mus. Art, 1994—2004, dir. curatorial affairs, 2004—. Office: Huntsville Mus Art 300 Church St South Huntsville AL 35801 Office Phone: 256-535-4350 ext. 218. Business E-Mail: pbaldaia@hsvmuseum.org.

BALDANZA, B. BEN, air transportation executive; BA in Econs., Syracuse U.; MA in Pub. Affairs, Princeton U. Fin. analyst, mgr. yield mgmt. and fin. depts. Am. Airlines, 1985—91; dir. fin. analysis N.W. Airlines, 1991—93, mng. dir. yield mgmt.; mgr. UPS, 1993—94; joined Continental Airlines, 1994—97, exec. v.p.; mng. dir., COO Grupo Taca, 1997—99; sr. v.p. mktg. and planning US Airways, Inc., Arlington, Va., 1999—. Office: US Airways 2345 Crystal Dr Arlington VA 22227

BALDASSANO, CORINNE LESLIE, radio executive; b. N.Y.C., May 16, 1950; d. Nicholas and Olga Baldassano. BA cum laude, Queens Coll., CUNY, 1970; MA in Theatre, Hunter Coll., CUNY, 1975; MBA in Fin., NYU, 1986. Program dir., ops. mgr. Sta. KAUM-FM, Houston, 1977-79; dir. programming Sta. WSAI-FM, Cin., 1979-81, ABC Contemporary and FM Radio Networks, N.Y.C., 1981-84; regional mgr. affiliate rels. United Stas. Radio Networks, N.Y.C., 1985-87; dir. ABC Entertainment Radio Networks, 1987-90; v.p. programming ABC Radio Networks, 1990-94, Unistar Radio Networks, L.A., 1994, SW Networks, N.Y.C., 1994-95, sr. v.p. programming, 1995; gen. mgr. radio divsn. AP, 1997-99; v.p. broadcast programming soundsbig.com, 1999—. Guest lectr. Wharton Sch. Bus., Phila., 1983, St. John's U., N.Y.C., 1983-84; bd. dirs. Country Radio Broadcasters, Inc., Nashville, 1990—, chmn. agenda com., 1990. Alumni mem. Govs. Com. Scholastic Achievement, N.Y.C., 1984-85. Named among 20 Most Influential Women in Radio, Radio Ink Mag., 1999. Mem. NYU Bus. Forum (bd. dirs. 1988-91, v.p., treas. 1990-91), Internat. Radio and TV Soc. (planning com., faculty/industry seminar 1986, 87, chmn. Summer Fellowship Program 1988), Nat. Music Found. (N.Y. bd. 1992-93, 94-96). Democrat. Roman Catholic. Avocations: travel, theater, dance, running, music.

BALDECCHI, BRUCE HUGO, physician, anesthesiologist; b. Feb. 21, 1947; BS, U. So. Calif., 1970; MD, U. Colo., 1974. Intern San Bernardino County Med. Ctr., 1974-75; resident UCLA Hosp., 1975-77; med. dir. Carson Ambulatory Surgery Ctr., Carson City, Nev., 1986—2005; attending anesthesiologist Carson-Tahoe Hosp., Carson City, Nev., 1977—; med. dir. Sierra Surgery and Imaging, 2005—. Office: Sierra Surgery and Imaging 1400 Medical Pkwy Carson City NV 89703

BALDESSARI, JOHN ANTHONY, artist; b. National City, Calif., June 17, 1931; s. Anton and Hedvig B.; divorced; children: Annamarie, Antonio. BA, San Diego State U., 1953, MA, 1957; postgrad., Otis Art Inst., Chouinard Art Inst., L.A., 1957-59. Asst. prof. U. Calif., San Diego, 1968-70; mem. faculty Calif. Inst. Arts, Valencia, 1970-85; prof. art U. Calif., L.A. One-man shows include La Jolla Mus. Art, Calif., 1960, 66, Southwestern Coll., Chula Vista, Calif., 1962, 64, 75, Molly Barnes Gallery, Los Angeles, 1968, Richard Feigen Gallery, N.Y.C., 1970, Eugenia Butler Gallery, Los Angeles, 1970, Galerie Konrad Fischer, Dusseldorf, Fed. Republic Germany, 1971, 73, Art and Project, Amsterdam, The Netherlands, 1971, 72, Galerie MTL, Brussels, 1972, 75, Antwerp, Belgium, 1974, Galeria Franco Toselli, Milan, Italy, 1972, 74, Jack Wendler Gallery, London, 1972, 74, Sonnabend Gallery, N.Y.C., 1973, 75, 78, 79, 80, 81, 84, 86, 87, 90, 92, Galerie Sonnabend, Paris, 1973, 75, Inst. Modern Art, Brisbane, Australia, 1976, Inst. Contemporary Art, Sydney, Australia, 1976, Ohio State U., Columbus, 1976, Portland Ctr. for Visual Arts, Oreg., 1978, Whitney Mus. Am. Art., N.Y.C., 1978, Inst. Contemporary Art, Boston, 1978, Mcpl. Van Abbemuseum, Eindhoven, The Netherlands, 1980, 81, Mus. Folkwang, Essen, Fed. Republic Germany, 1981, Rudiger Schötte Gallery, Munich, 1981, Albright-Knox Gallery, Buffalo, 1981, Contemporary Art Ctr., Cin., 1982, Contemporary Arts Mus., Houston, 1982, Samangallery, Genoa, Italy, 1975, 81, Margo Leavin Gallery, L.A., 1984, 86, 88-89, 92, Douglas Drake Gallery, Kansas City, Mo., 1983, Marianne Deson Gallery, Chgo., 1983, Swain Sch. Design, New Bedford, Mass., 1983, Contemporary Arts Mus., Houston, Anderson Gallery, Richmond, Va., 1982, Galerie Peter Pakesch, Vienna, 1984, 86, Galerie-Laage Salomon, Paris, 1984, 88, Univ. Art Mus. U. Calif., Berkeley, 1986, Santa Barbara (Calif.) Mus. Art, 1986, Multiples Inc., N.Y.C., 1986-87, Cen. Nat. D'Art Contemporain de Grenoble, 1987, Dart Gallery, Chgo., 1987, Lisson Gallery, London, 1988, Primo Piano, Rome, 1988, Palais des Beaux-Arts, Brussels,1988, Hanover, Kastner-Gesellschaft, 1989, Cirrus, L.A., 1989, Centro de Arte Regina Sofia, Madrid, 1989, Cape Musée d'Art Contemporain, Bordeaux, Instituto Valenciano de Arte Moderno, Centro Julio Gonzàlez, Valencia, Spain, Lawrence Oliver Gallery, Phila., 1989, Galerie Meert Rihoux, Brussels, 1989, 92, Mus. Contemporary Art, L.A., 1990, Galerie Crousel Robelin, BAMA, Paris, 1991, Galerie Weber, Alexander Y Cobo, Madrid, 1991, traveling to San Francisco Mus. Modern Art, Hirshorn Mus. and Sculpture Garden, Walker Art Ctr., Whitney Mus. Am. Ar, Musée d'art Contemporain de Montréal; various others; group shows include Richard Feigen Gallery, N.Y.C., 1968, U. Calif. San Diego Art Gallery, 1968, Dwan Gallery, N.Y.C., 1969, Eugenia Butler Gallery, Los Angeles, 1969, Hayward Gallery, London, 1969, 80, Jewish Mus., N.Y.C., 1970, Moore Coll. Art, Phila., 1970, Sonnabend Gallery, N.Y.C., 1972, 73, 74, 78, 80-81, 84, 86-87, 90, Contemporary Arts Mus., Houston, 1972, 78, San Francisco Art Inst., 1972, Galerie Sonnabend, Paris, 1973, Kennedy Ctr., Washington, 1974, Paula Cooper Gallery, N.Y.C., 1975, 81, 89, Los Angeles County Mus. Art, 1973, 74, 81, 87, Sch. Visual Arts, N.Y.C., 1977, Mus. Fine Arts, Houston, 1977, Inst. Contemporary Arts, Boston, 1978, High Mus. Art, Atlanta, 1980, Westkunst, Cologne, Fed. Republic Germany, 1981, 5th Internat. Biennale, Vienna, Austria, 1981, Stedelijk Mus., Amsterdam, The Netherlands, 1974, 81, Kestner-Gesellschaft, Hanover, Fed. Republic Germany, 1982, Albright-Knox Gallery, Buffalo, 1982, Multiples Inc., 1982, Donald Young Gallery, Chgo., 1990, Whitney Mus. Am. Art, N.Y., 1969, 72, 76, 77, 78, 79, 83, Marianne Deson Gallery, 1983, 87, Douglas Drake Gallery, N.Y.C., 1987, Mus. Modern Art, N.Y.C., 1970, 71, 72, 75, 77, Art Inst. Chgo., 1979, 85, Mus. Contemporary Art, Chgo., 1969, 77, 79, Mus. Contemporary Art, Los Angeles, 1986-88, Holly Solomon Gallery, N.Y.C., 1986-87, Hoffman Borman Gallery, Santa Monica, Calif., 1987, Mus. Modern Art, Toyama, Japan, 1987, Newport Harbor Art Mus., Newport Beach, 1969, 74, 87, 89, Barbara Krakow Gallery, 1987, Bank of Boston Art Gallery, 1987, Phoenix Art Mus., 1987, Los Angeles Mcpl. Art Gallery, 1987, Castello Di Rivoli, Torino, 1987, Bess Cutler Gallery, N.Y.C., 1987, Marian Goodman Gallery, N.Y.C., 1987, 88, 89, 90, LACE, Los Angeles, 1987, Museums Ludwig in den Rheinhallen der Kolner Messe, Cologne, Fed. Republic of Germany, 1989, Centre Georges Pompidou, Grande Halle-La Villette, Paris, 1989, Met. Mus. Art, N.Y.C., 1989, Mus. Modern Art, N.Y.C., 1989, various others; represented in permanent collections, Mus. Modern Art, N.Y.C., Stedelijk Mus., Amsterdam, Holland, Kunstmuseum, Basel, Switzerland, Australian Nat. Gallery, Mus. Contemporary Art, L.A. and Chgo., Whitney Mus. Am. Art, N.Y.C., Met. Mus. Art, N.Y.C., Houston Mus. Fine Art; contbr. articles to profl. jours., photographic reproductions to books; subject of numerous articles. Nat. Endowment for Arts grantee, 1973, 74, 75. Fellow: Am. Acad. Arts and Scis. Office: Sonnabend Gallery 536 W 22nd St New York NY 10011-1108 also: Margo Leavin Gallery 812 N Robertson Blvd Los Angeles CA 90069-4929 Office: U Calif Dept Art 1100 Kinross Ave Ste 245 PO Box 951615 Los Angeles CA 90095

BALDIGA, JOSEPH HILDING, lawyer; b. Woonsocket, R.I., Dec. 18, 1962; s. Robert S. and Lois E. (Wickstrom) B.; m. Mary P. Baldiga, June 9, 1990; children: Lucy Porter, Robert Kenneth. BA, Boston Coll., 1984, JD, 1987. Bar: Mass. 1987, U.S. Dist. Ct. Mass. 1988. Assoc. Peabody & Brown, Boston, 1987-88, Goodwin Procter & Hoar, Boston, 1988-94; ptnr. Mirick O'Connell, Worcester, Mass., 1994—. Trustee Dynamy, Worcester, 1997—. Chestnut St. Mktg. House Assn., Millville, Mass,. 1992—. Mem. Mass. Bar Assn., Boston Bar Assn. (co-chair bankruptcy sect. 2000—), Worcester Bar Assn., Am. Bankruptcy Inst., Comml. Law League, Turnaround Mgmt. Assn. Office: Mirick O'Connell 100 Front St Worcester MA 01608-1425 Fax: 508-791-8502. E-mail: jhbaldiga@modl.com.

BALDOCK, BRIAN F., corporate financial executive; Bd. dirs., mem. remuneration and audit com. Sygen Internat. plc., Berkeley, Calif., 1993—, chmn. bd., 1999—. Sr. ind. dir. Marks and Spencer, 1996—, non- exec. chmn., 1999—2000. Mem.: Chartered Inst. Mktg. (fellow), British Inst. Mgmt. (companion), Royal Society of Arts (fellow). Office: 3033 Nashville Rd Franklin KY 42134-6975

BALDRIDGE, J. DOUGLAS, lawyer; b. 1962; BA magna cum laude, Fla. State U., 1984; JD cum laude, George Washington U., 1987. Bar: Fla., Supreme Ct. Fla., Va., Va. Supreme Ct., Md., Md. Ct. Appeals, DC, US Bankruptcy Ct., DC, US Bankruptcy Ct., Md., US Bankruptcy Ct. (ea. dist.) Va., US Ct. Appeals (1st, 3rd, 4th and 11th cirs.), US Ct. Appeals, DC, US Ct. Appeals, Fed. Cir., US Ct. Fed. Claims, US Dist. Ct., DC, US Dist. Ct., Colo., US Dist. Ct., Md., US Dist. Ct. (ea. dist.) Va., US Dist. Ct. (middle dist.) Fla., US Supreme Ct. Ptnr. Comml. Litig. Dept. Venable LLP, Washington, DC. Recipient Justice for All, Voting Rights Project Award, AAPD, 2004. Mem.: Mortar Bd., Phi Delta Phi, Omicron Delta Kappa, Phi Beta Kappa. Office: Vanable LLP 575 7th St NW Washington DC 20004 Office Phone: 202-344-4703. Office Fax: 202-344-8300. E-mail: jbaldridge@venable.com.

BALDRIDGE, STEVEN KENT, law educator; b. Laramie, Wyo., Apr. 25, 1964; s. Robert Charles and Sherie Williams Baldridge; m. Miyoko Odawara Baldridge, Oct. 5, 1992; children: Leila Odawara, Zachary Eugene, Maia Elizabeth. BA, Washington & Lee U., 1989; JD, Brigham Young U., 1992, PhD, 1996. Bar: Calif. 1995, Va. 2005. Mem. program faculty Brigham Young U., Provo, Utah, 1996; asst. prof. Barry U., Miami Shores, Fla., 1996—98, So. Va. U., Buena Vista, 1998—2004, registrar, 1998—2000, asst. dean students, 2000—04, assoc. prof., 2004—. Cons. in field. Adult leader Boy Scouts Am., Buena Vista, 2001—; missionary LDS Ch., Colombia, 1983—85. Mem.: Va. Polit. Sci. Assn., Ednl. Law Assn., Am. Ednl. Rsch. Assn. Republican. Mem. Lds Ch. Avocations: Japanese gardening, cooking. Home: 164 Larch Ave Buena Vista VA 24416 Office: So Va U 1 Univ Hill Dr Buena Vista VA 24416 Office Phone: 540-261-8417.

BALDRIGE, LETITIA, writer, management consultant; b. Miami Beach, Fla. d. Howard Malcolm and Regina (Connell) B.; m. Robert Hollensteiner; children: Clare, Malcolm. BA, Vassar Coll., 1946; postgrad., U. Geneva, 1946-48; DHL (hon.), Creighton U., 1979, Mt. St. Mary's Coll., 1980, Bryant Coll., 1987, Kenyon Coll., 1990. Personal-social sec. to amb. Am. Embassy, Paris, 1948-51; intelligence officer Washington, 1951-53; asst. to amb. Am. Embassy, Rome, 1953-56; dir. pub. rels. Tiffany & Co., 1956-60; social sec. The White House, 1961-63; pres. Letitia Baldrige Enterprises, Chgo., 1964-69; dir. consumer affairs Burlington Industries, 1969-71; pres. Letitia Baldrige Enterprises, Inc., Washington, 1972—. Author: Roman Candle, 1956, Tiffany Table Settings, 1958, Of Diamonds and Diplomats, 1968, Home, 1972, Juggling, 1976, Amy Vanderbilt's Complete Book of Etiquette, 1978, Amy Vanderbilt's Everyday Etiquette, 1979, The Entertainers, 1981, Letitia Baldrige's Complete Guide to Executive Manners, 1985, Letitia Baldrige's Complete Guide to a Great Social Life, 1987, Complete Guide to the New Manners for the '90s, 1990, New Complete Guide to Executive Manners, 1993, (novel) Public Affairs Private Relations, 1990, More Than Manners! Raising Today's Kids to Have Kind Manners and Good Hearts, 1997, In the Kennedy Style, 1998, Legendary Brides, 2000, A Lady, First, 2001, New Manners fr New Times, 2003. Mem. adv. bd. Woodrow Wilson House, Washington, Malcolm Baldrige Nat. Quality Awards, Woodrow Wilson Nat. Fellowship Found. Republican. Personal E-mail: lbaldrige@aol.com.

BALDUCCINI, MARCELLO, computer scientist, researcher; MS in Computer Sci., U. Statale di Milano, Milan, Italy, 1998. Rsch. asst. Tex. Tech U., Lubbock, Tex., 2001—. Office: CS Dept Texas Tech University 8th and Boston Lubbock TX 79409 Office Phone: 806-742-1191. E-mail: marcello.balduccini@ttu.edu.

BALDUINO, MICHAEL J., paper company executive; BA summa cum laude in econ., St. Peter's Coll., 1972; MBA in corp. fin., NYU Grad. Sch. of Bus., 1975. V.p., mktg. Internat. Paper Co., Imperial Bondware Corp., Stamford, Conn., 1992—94; v.p.-converted, products divsn. Federal Paper Board Co., Inc., 1994; v.p., mktg., comml. products James River Corp.; v.p., gen. mgr., food svc. Internat. Paper Co., Imperial Bondware Corp., Stamford, Conn., sr. v.p., mktg. and sales, 2000—. Office: Internat Paper Co 400 Atlantic St Stamford CT 06921

BALDWIN, ALEC (ALEXANDER RAE BALDWIN III), actor; b. Massapequa, N.Y., Apr. 3, 1958; s. Alexander Rae Jr. and Carol (Martineau) B.; m. Kim Basinger, August 19, 1993 (div. Feb. 2002), daughter Ireland Eliesse. Student, George Washington U., 1976-79; BFA, NYU, 1979-80, 93; studies with Marcia Haufrecht, Lee Strasberg Theater Inst., N.Y.C., 1979-80; studies with Mira Rostova, N.Y.C., 1982, 87, studies with Elaine Aiken. Ind. actor, 1980—. Actor: (films) Forever Lulu, 1987, She's Having a Baby, 1987, Beetlejuice, 1988, Married to the Mob, 1988, Great Balls of Fire, 1989, Talk Radio, 1988, Working Girl, 1988, The Hunt for Red October, 1990, Miami Blues, 1990, Alice, 1990, The Marrying Man, 1991, Prelude to a Kiss, 1992, Glengarry Glen Ross, 1992, Malice, 1993, The Getaway, 1994, The Shadow, 1994, Looking For Richard, 1996, The Juror, 1996, Heaven's Prisoners, 1996, Ghosts of Mississippi, 1996, Bookworm, 1997, The Edge, 1997, Thick as Thieves, 1998, Outside Providence, 1998, Mercury Rising, 1998, (also prodr.) The Confession, 1999, Notting Hill, 1999, Thomas and the Magic Railroad, 2000, State and Main (also exec. prodr.), 2000, Pearl Harbor, 2001, Cats & Dogs (voice), 2001, Final Fantasy: The Spirits Within (voice), 2001, The Royal Tenenbaums (voice), 2001, The Devil and Daniel Webster (also prodr.), 2001, The Cooler, 2003 (Acad. Award nomination for best supporting actor, 2004, Golden Globe nomination for best supporting actor, 2004, Screen Actors Guild Award nomination for best supportinga actor, 2004), The Cat in the Hat, 2003, Along Came Polly, 2004, The Last Shot, 2004, The Spongebob Squarepants Movie (voice), 2004, The Aviator, 2004; (TV series) Cutter to Houston, 1982, The Doctors, 1980-82, Knot's Landing, 1984-85; (TV movies) Love on The Run, 1985, A Streetcar Named Desire, 1995, Dress Gray (miniseries), 1986, The Alamo: 13 Days to Glory, 1986, Sweet Revenge, 1990, Nuremberg (also prodr.), 2000, Path to War, 2002(on Broadway) Loot (Theatre world award 1986), 1986, Serious Money, 1988, Prelude to a Kiss (Obie Award), 1990, A Streetcar Named Desire, 1992, South Pacific, 2005; guest appearances include The Simpsons (voice), Larry Sanders Show, Inside the Actors Studio, Will & Grace, 2005. Recipient Theater World award Theater World Pubs., 1986, Linda McCartney Meml. Award, People for the Ethical Treatment of Animals, 2005; named Outstanding New Talent on Broadway. Mem. SAG, AFTRA, Actors Equity Assn. Democrat. Roman Catholic.

BALDWIN, ALLEN ADAIL, lawyer, writer; b. St. Augustine, Fla., July 15, 1939; s. Larrie Paul and Bertha Mae (Capallia) B. BA, Brigham Young U., 1969; JD, So. U., Baton Rouge, 1975. Bar: Fla. 1975. Tchr. Putnam County Sch. Bd., Palatka, Fla., 1969-71; pvt. practice Palatka, 1975—. Author: Tricks to Make the Angels Weep, 1986, Call It Not Heaven, 1991, Redeem Us From Virtue, 1992. Mem. Lds Ch. Avocations: reading, swimming, hiking. Office: 308 St Johns Ave Palatka FL 32177-4723 Office Phone: 386-325-7549.

BALDWIN, BRUCE GREGG, botany educator, researcher; b. San Luis Obispo, Calif., Oct. 24, 1957; s. Robert Lee and Sally Louise (Elrod) B. BA in Biol. Scis. with honors, U. Calif., Santa Barbara, 1981; MS in Botany, U. Calif., Davis, 1985, PhD in Botany, 1989. NSF postdoctoral fellow U. Ariz., Tucson, 1990-92; asst. prof. dept. botany Duke U., 1992-94; curator Jepson Herbarium U. Calif., Berkeley, 1994—, asst. prof. in residence dept. integrative biology, 1994-98, assoc. prof. in residence dept. integrative biology, 1998-2000, assoc. prof. dept. integrative biology, 2000—. Mellon vis. scholar Rancho Santa Ana Bot. Garden, 1994. Contbr. articles to profl. jours. and books, reviewer; chief editor Jepson Flora project, 1994—. Recipient NSF Nat. Young Investigator award, 1994; Calif. Acad. Scis. fellow, 1999—. Mem. Am. Soc. Plant Taxonomists (publicity com. 1993—, coun. 2002—), Calif. Bot. Soc. (pres. 2000—), Soc. Systematic Biology (coun. 2004—). Achievements include research in plant systematics, phylogenetics, plant cytogenetics and chromosome evolution, plant speciation, California floristics, phytogeography, insular evolution. Home: 2408 Parker St Berkeley CA 94704-2812 Office: U Calif Berkeley Jepson Herbarium Dept Integrative Biology 1001 Valley Life Scis Bldg 2465 Berkeley CA 94720-2465 E-mail: bbaldwin@berkeley.edu.

BALDWIN, C. STEPHEN, human resources specialist; b. Washington, Dec. 10, 1938; s. Charles Franklin and Helen Rosenbaum Baldwin; m. Barbara Radloff, Apr. 12, 1980; children: Matthew Charles, Timothy Stephen, Alexandra Virginia Helen; m. Sandra Walls Baldwin, July 31, 1965 (div. 1976); children: Heather Anne, Jennifer Nancy Pye. BA, Amherst Coll., Mass., 1960; JD, Yale U. Law Sch., New Haven, 1965; MEd, Hunter Coll., N.Y.C., 2003. Bar: D.C. 1965; cert. demography Princeton U. Office of Population Rsch., 1972, registered French Language Speaker UN, 1982, lic. tchr. NY State, 2003. Asst. to rep. The Ford Found., Kuala Lumpur, Malaysia, 1965—67, staff assoc. N.Y.C, 1967—69, asst. rep. Dhaka, Pakistan, 1969—71; staff assoc. The Population Coun., N.Y.C., 1972—77; specialist in population affairs UN, 1978—99; sr. ptnr. Prefix Pre-Dispute Solutions, 1999—; N.Y.C. tchg. fellow, tchr. 3rd grade N.Y.C. Bd. of Edn., 2001—03; exec. dir. Learning Disabilities Assn. of N.Y.C., 2003—. Vice-chmn. bd. dir. World Edn., N.Y.C., NY, 1978—86. Author: Age at Marriage: A Comparative Study in Tunisia, Sri Lanka, and Malaysia, 1977. Founding bd. dirs. South Bronx Classical Charter Sch., 2005—; bd. mem. Learning Disabilities Assn. of NY State, Albany, NY, 2003—. With U.S. Army, 1960—62. Fellow, Ford Found./Population Coun., 1971—72. Mem.: Internat. Union for the Sci.

Study of Population. Home: Apt 12-F 110 Riverside Dr New York NY 10024 Office: Learning Disabilities Assn of NYC Ste 303 27 West 20th St New York NY 10024 Office Phone: 212-645-6730. Office Fax: 212-924-8896. Personal E-mail: csbldanyc@verizon.net.

BALDWIN, CALVIN BENHAM, JR., retired science administrator; b. Radford, Va., Dec. 22, 1925; s. Calvin Benham and Louise (Delp) B.; m. Elizabeth Buell, Mar. 10, 1951; children: Susan B., Sally C., Ann H. AB, U. N.C., 1949, postgrad., 1949—51; MPA, Harvard U., 1961. Rsch. asst. Inst. Rsch. Social Scis., Chapel Hill, NC, 1949-50; methods examiner NIH, Bethesda, Md., 1953-55, budget examiner, 1955-57, adminstrv. officer, 1957-58, adminstrv. officer divsn. gen. med. sci., 1958-61; exec. officer Divsn. Gen. Med. Scis., Bethesda, 1961-62, Nat. Inst. Child Health, Bethesda, 1963-70, Nat. Cancer Inst., Bethesda, 1970-80; assoc. dir. adminstrn. NIH, Bethesda, 1980-86. Mem. Montgomery County Econ. Coun., Rockville, Md., 1982—85, Bethany Beach (Del.) Town Coun., 1991—92, 1994—96; pres. Bethany Beach Landowners Assn., 1998—2002; mem. Bethany Beach Planning Commn., 1998—2004. Recipient W.A. Jump meritorious award HEW, 1960; recipient Superior Svc. award HEW, 1973 Mem. NIH Alumni Assn. (pres. 1995-97), Phi Beta Kappa. Democrat. Unitarian Universalist. Home: 10705 Weymouth St Garrett Park MD 20896-0017 E-mail: cbbaldwin@aol.com.

BALDWIN, CAROLYN WHITMORE, lawyer; b. Newton, Mass., July 9, 1932; d. Henry Jr. and Grace M. (Chase) W.; m. Peter Arthur Baldwin, Sept. 3, 1955; children: Sarah M., Robert H., Judith H. Student, U. Coll. of Southwest, Exeter, Eng., 1952-53; BA cum laude, Middlebury Coll., 1954; MA in Library Sci., U. Chgo., 1971; JD, Franklin Pierce Coll., Concord, N.H., 1977. Bar: N.H., 1977, U.S. Dist. Ct. N.H. 1977. Exhibits dir. U. Chgo. Library, 1970-73; manuscripts librarian N.H. Hist. Soc., Concord, 1973-74; library cataloger Franklin Pierce Law Ctr., Concord, 1973-77, dir. environ. law clinic, 1978-82; assoc. Murphy and McLaughlin, Laconia, N.H., 1977-78; sole practice Concord, 1983-90; ptnr. Baldwin & de Seve, Concord, 1991-97; of counsel Baldwin & Callen, 1997—. Supervising editor: Historic Districts in New Hampshire, a Handbook for Establishing and Administering Historic Districts, 1980; contbr. articles to profl. and other jours. Mem. Lakes Region Planning Commn., Meredith, N.H., 1977-90, chmn., 1982-83, 86-87; chmn. N.H. Natural Resources forum, Concord, 1983-86, Water Resources Action Project, 1985, Gilmanton (N.H.) Conservation Commn., 1974-80; mem. N.H. Commn. for Humanities, Concord, 1977-80; mem. Gilmanton Planning Bd., 1982-94, chmn., 1986-92; selectman Town of Gilmanton, 1995-98; pres. Gilmanton Hist. Soc., 2002-03; mem. Zoning Bd. of Adjustment, Gilmanton, 1998—; bd. dirs. Granite State Pub. Radio, 1980-83, N.H. Main St. Ctr., 1998—, vice chair, 2003—; exec. dir. Environ. Law Coun., N.H., 1978-82; vice chmn. N.H. Hist. Preservation Task Force, 1983-84. Recipient Pres.'s medal NH Planners Assn., 1985, Environ. Leadership award N.E. Environ. Network, 1989, Ayers award Lakes Region Planning Commn., 2004, Bd. Mem. of Yr. award NH Main St. Ctr., 2005. Mem. N.H. Bar Assn. (mcpl., govt. law sect., mem. environ. law sect.), N.H. Assn. Regional Planning Commns. (chmn. legis. com. 1984-86), Franklin Pierce Law Ctr. Alumni Assn. (pres. 1979-80). Democrat. Mem. Unitarian Universalist Ch. Avocations: skiing, family, gardening. Office: 101 N State St Concord NH 03301-4334 Office Phone: 603-225-2585. Business E-Mail: cbaldwin@nhlandlaw.com.

BALDWIN, CHRISTOPHER, operations manager, writer, editor; b. Passaic, NJ, May 31, 1949; s. George Henry and Elinore Dawn Baldwin; m. Elaine Lois Baldwin (div.); 1 child, Kristen Elizabeth; m. Janet Mary Meres, Oct. 17, 1998. BA, William Patterson U., 1974, MA, 1975. Ops. mgr. Schering Plough Corp., Carteret, NJ, 1980—85; dir. ea. ops. Ricoh Corp., Fairfield, NJ, 1985—96; gen. mgr. CGI Industries, Lodi, NJ, 1996—2002; writer, editor Arbor Books, NYC, 2002—. Editor, author: book rev. sect. Combat Mag., 2004—; author: (novels) Night of the Barbarian, 1981, The Butcher and the Calf, 1995. Writer Am. Conservative Union, DC, 1988. Recipient Victims of 9/11 Svc. Aid award, Praxair Corp., Bethlehem, Pa., 2002. Republican. Roman Catholic. Avocations: history, politics, bridge, photography. Home: 100 Hillside Ave Allendale NJ 07401 Office: 100 Hillside Ave Allendale NJ 07401

BALDWIN, DAVID ALLEN, political science professor; b. Indpls., July 28, 1936; s. James Howell and Pearl Mabel (Fisher) B.; m. Marilyn Claire Austin, Aug. 10, 1957 (div. Sept. 1990); children: Sarah, Rebecca, Emily; m. Helen Virginia Milner, May 24, 1991. AB, Ind. U., 1958; MA, Princeton U., 1961, PhD, 1965; MA (hon.), Dartmouth Coll., 1978. Asst. prof. govt. Dartmouth Coll., Hanover, N.H., 1965-70, assoc. prof. govt., 1970-75, John S. Dickey Prof., 1975-80, prof. govt., 1980-85; prof. polit. sci. Columbia U., N.Y.C., 1985-89, Ira Wallach prof., 1989—2004, Ira Wallach prof. emeritus, 2005—. Dir. Inst. of War and Peace Studies, Columbia U., 1987-94. Author: Foreign Aid, 1966, Economic Statecraft, 1985 (Kammerer award 1986), Paradoxes of Power, 1989, Economic Development and Foreign Policy, 1966; editl. bd. Internat. Orgn., 1984-97, Polit. Sci. quar., N.Y.C., 1989-94, Jour. Internat. Affairs, 1988—. Mem. Coun. on Fgn. Rels., N.Y.C., 1986—. 1st lt. U.S. Army, 1962-63. Recipient Moffat Econs. prize Ind. U., Bloomington, 1958, fellowships German Marshall Fund, Washington, 1982-83, Brookings Instn., Washington, 1964-65, Danforth Found., St. Louis, 1958-64. Mem. Am. Polit. Sci. Assn. (recipient Kammerer award 1986), Internat. Polit. Sci. Assn., Internat. Studies Assn., British Internat. Studies Assn., Acad. Polit. Sci., Phi Beta Kappa. Home: 450 Riverside Dr New York NY 10027-6801 Office: Inst of War & Peace Studies Columbia University 420 W 118th St New York NY 10027-7213

BALDWIN, DAVID SHEPARD, physician; b. Rochester, N.Y., Sept. 5, 1921; s. Jacob and Anna B.; m. Halee Morris, June 24, 1945; children: Neil, Andrew, Daniel, James. BA, U. Rochester, 1943, MD, 1945. Intern Barnes Hosp., St. Louis, 1945-46; resident in medicine Bellevue Hosp., N.Y.C., 1946-48; renal fellow in medicine and physiology NYU Sch. Medicine, 1948-50, mem. faculty, 1950—, prof. medicine, nephrology, 1972—2004, prof. emeritus, 2004—. Attending physician Bellevue Hosp.; hon. attending physician NYU Hosp.; mem. coun. high blood pressure rsch. AHA. Author papers in med. jours., chpts. in books. Served as officer M.C. AUS, 1953-55. Mem. AHA, Harvey Soc., Am. Soc. Nephrology, Am. Soc. Clin. Investigation, Internat. Soc. Nephrology, N.Y. Soc. Nephrology (pres. 1974-75), N.Y. Heart Assn. Home: 333 E 69th St New York NY 10021-5560 Office: NYU Sch Medicine 550 1st Ave OBV CD679 New York NY 10016-6402 Office Phone: 212-263-5635. Business E-Mail: david.baldwin@med.nyu.edu.

BALDWIN, DEWITT CLAIR, JR., pediatrician, educator; b. Bangor, Maine, July 19, 1922; s. DeWitt Clair and Edna Frances (Aikin) B.; m. Michele Albre, Dec. 27, 1957; children: Lisa Anne, Mireille Diane. BA, Swarthmore Coll., 1943; postgrad. Div. Sch., Yale U., 1943-45, MD, 1949; ScD (hon.), Northeastern Ohio U. Coll. Medicine, 2003. Diplomate Am. Bd. Med. Examiners, Am. Bd. Pediatrics, Am. Bd. Family Practice. Intern, then resident in pediatrics U. Minn. Hosps., Mpls., 1949-51; rsch. fellow Yale Child Study Ctr., New Haven, 1951-52; instr., asst. prof. pediatrics U. Washington Sch. Medicine, Seattle, 1952-57; resident in psychiatry Met. State Hosp., Waltham, Mass., 1957-58; chief resident in psychiatry Mass. Meml. Hosps., Boston, 1958-59; fellow in child psychiatry Boston City Hosp., 1959-61; asst. prof. pediatrics Harvard Med. Sch., Boston, 1961-67; prof., chmn. behavioral scis. and community health U. Conn. Health Ctr., Farmington, 1967-71; prof. chmn. behavioral scis. U. Nev. Sch. Medicine, Reno, 1971-73, dir. health scis. program, 1971-81, prof. psychiatry and behavioral scis., 1971-83, asst. dean rural health, 1977-83, prof. emeritus psychiatry and behavioral scis., 1983—; pres. Earlham Coll. and Earlham Sch. Religion, Richmond, Ind., 1983-84, Connor Prairie Pioneer Settlement Mus., Noblesville, Ind., 1983-84; dir. office edn. rsch. AMA, Chgo., 1985-88, dir. divsn. med. edn., rsch., info., 1988-91, scholar-in-residence, 1991—2002, sr. assoc. Inst. Ethics, 1991—2002, scholar-in-residence Accreditation Coun. for Grad. Med. Edn., 2002—; adj. prof. psychiatry and behavioral scis. Northwestern U. Med. Sch., Chgo., 1986—; adj. prof. med. edn. U. Ill. Coll. Medicine, Chgo., 1988-93; pres. Med. Edn. and Rsch. Assocs., Inc., Chgo., 1992—. Trustee Friends World Coll., Huntington, N.Y., 1980-83; bd. dirs. Nat. League Nursing, N.Y.C., 1981-83, Gt. Lakes Colls. Assn., 1983-84, Am. Rural Health Assn., 1985-87; mem. Nat. Bd. Med. Examiners, 1979-88, Nat. Adv. Coun. Nursing Tng., 1978-82; mem. coun. acad. socs. AAMC, Washington, 1987-94. Author: (with others) Behavioral Sciences and Medical Education, 1983, other books; author, editor: (with others) Interdisciplinary Health Care Teams in Teaching and Practice, 1981, Interdisciplinary Health Team Training, 1978; contbr. over 150 articles to scholarly publs. Recipient Rsch. Career Devel. award USPHS, 1961-67, Louis Gorin award in rural health, 1991, John P. McGovern award Health Scis., 1997; Commonwealth Fund fellow, 1951-52, Milbank Fund fellow, 1968, Rural Health fellow WHO, 1976. Mem. Assn. Behavioral Scis. and Med. Edn. (pres. 1978-79, 90-91), Nev. Bd. Oriental Medicine (pres. 1976-83). Democrat. Mem. Soc. Of Friends. Home: 1550 N Lake Shore Dr Chicago IL 60610 Office: Ste 2000 515 State St Chicago IL 60610 Business E-Mail: dbaldwin@acgme.org.

BALDWIN, EDWIN STEEDMAN, lawyer; b. St. Louis, May 5, 1932; s. Richard and Almira (Steedman) B.; m. Margaret Kirkham, July 1, 1958; children: Margaret B. Dozler, Edwin S. Jr., Harold K. AB, Princeton U., 1954; LLM, Harvard U., 1957. Bar: Mo. 1957, U.S. Dist. Ct. (ea. dist.) Mo. 1957. Assoc. Teasdale, Kramer & Vaughan, St. Louis, 1957-64; ptnr. Armstrong Teasdale, LLP, St. Louis, 1965-97, of counsel, 1998—. Fellow Am. Coll. Trust and Estate Counsel, St. Louis Country Club, Noonday Club. Republican. Episcopalian. Avocations: golf, hunting, sailing. Office: Armstrong Teasdale LLP 1 Metropolitan Sq Ste 2600 Saint Louis MO 63102-2740 Office Phone: 314-342-8055. Business E-Mail: tbaldwin@armstrongteasdale.com.

BALDWIN, FRANK BRUCE, III, lawyer; b. Phila., Oct. 18, 1939; s. Frank Bruce and Eleanor Elizabeth (Dutton) B.; m. Joan L. Crowell, June 23, 1962; children: Elisa Rose, Bruce Andrew, Christopher Dutton. AB cum laude, Harvard U., 1961; LLB magna cum laude, U. Pa., 1964; LLM, U. London, 1965. Bar: Pa. 1966, Calif. 1967, U.S. Ct. Appeals (3d cir.) 1982. Vis. asst. prof. law U. Pa., 1965-66; acting assoc. prof. law U. Calif.-Davis, 1966-69; assoc. Morgan, Lewis & Bockius, Phila., 1969-72, 73-74; v.p., gen. counsel A.V.C. Corp., Phila., 1972-73; asst. gen. counsel IU Internat. Corp., Phila., 1974-82; ptnr. Saul, Ewing, Remick & Saul, Phila., 1982-83, Ehmann & Baldwin, 1983-85, Obermayer, Rebmann, Maxwell & Hippel, 1985-90; shareholder, dir. Baldwin Renner Clark & Buckwalter, PC, 1990-99; shareholder Monteverde, McAlee & Hurd, P.C., 1999—; stated clk. Presbytery of Phila. Gowen fellow, 1964-65. Mem. ABA, Pa. Bar Assn., Phila. Bar Assn., State Bar Calif., Order of Coif, Rittenhouse Club. Democrat. Presbyterian. Reporter Del. Criminal Code, Proposed Ofcl. Draft, 1967. Office: Monteverde McAlee & Hurd 1617 Jfk Blvd Ste 1500 Philadelphia PA 19103-1815 Office Phone: 215-557-2900. E-mail: fbaldwin@monteverde.com.

BALDWIN, GEORGE CURRIDEN, physicist, researcher; b. Denver, May 5, 1917; s. Harry Lewis and Elizabeth (Watson) B.; m. Winifred M. Gould, Apr. 27, 1952; children— George T., John E., Celia M. BA, Kalamazoo Coll., 1939; MA, U. Ill., 1941, PhD, 1943. Instr. physics U. Ill., Urbana, 1943-44; rsch. assoc. GE, Schenectady, N.Y., 1944-55, nuclear engr. Cin., 1955-57; reactor mgr. Argonne (Ill.) Nat. Lab., 1957-58; physicist Gen. Engring. Lab. GE, Schenectady, 1958-67; adj. prof. nuclear engring. and sci. Rensselaer Poly. Inst., Troy, N.Y., 1964-67, prof., 1967-77, prof. emeritus, 1977—; staff mem. Los Alamos (N.Mex.) Nat. Lab., 1975-87; vis. scientist, 1987-99; ret., 1987. Author: An Introduction to Nonlinear Optics, 1969; contbr. articles on nuclear and radiation physics to sci. publs. Councilman, Niskayuna, N.Y., 1965-69; mem. Zoning Bd., 1969-77. Recipient Disting. Alumnus award Kalamazoo Coll., 1987. Fellow Am. Phys. Soc.; mem. AAAS, Phi Beta Kappa, Sigma Xi, Phi Kappa Phi, Gamma Alpha. Achievements include discovery of nuclear giant dipole resonance; research on gamma-ray lasers; discovery of 1776 Escalante inscription. Business E-Mail: geoc142857@covad.net.

BALDWIN, GEORGE KOEHLER, retired retail executive; b. Cedar Rapids, Iowa, Nov. 17, 1919; s. Nathan and Ada Lillian (Koehler) B. BBA, State U. Iowa, 1942. From office mgr. to mgr. Wapsie Valley Creamery, Cedar Rapids, Iowa, 1946-60; treas., head payroll, accounts payable, sales audit dept. Armstrong's Inc., Cedar Rapids, 1960-87; also bd. dirs., treas. Armstrong's of Dubuque, Iowa, 1982-87; ret., 1987. Mem. adv. coun. Firstar Club, Firstar Bank, Cedar Rapids; theatre organist, 1961—. Composed and copyrighted for band Kinnick Stadium band march, 1992. Mem. Cedar Rapids Performing Arts Commn.; bd. dirs., pres. Cedar Rapids Cmty. Concert Assn., 1993-2005; pres. State U. of Iowa Concert Band, 1941-42; sec., treas., asst. conductor El Kahir Shrine Band of Cedar Rapids; bd. dirs. Cedar Rapids Stamp Club, 1997-2000; chmn. adminstrv. bd. Trinity United Meth. Ch., 1987-92, head usher and staff parish rels. com. chmn.; apptd. by mayor to Cedar Rapids Mcpl. Band Commn., 1994, vice chmn. 1998—; organist Paramount and Iowa theaters, Cedar Rapids, 1961—. With U.S. Army, 1942-46, ETO. Decorated Bronze Star medal; named hon. Ky. Col.; George K. Baldwin day proclamation in his honor, Mayor of Cedar Rapids, Apr. 16, 1987. Mem. VFW, Cedar Rapids Consumer Credit Assn. (pres. 1968-69), Am. Theatre Organ Soc. (bd. dirs., treas. Cedar Rapids chpt.), Am. Legion, Rotary, Masons, Shriners (past pres. uniformed units), Rotary Svc. Club (chmn. fellowship com., sgt. of arms), State U. Iowa Pres.'s Club and Alumni Assn. Methodist. Home: 1017 F Ave NW Cedar Rapids IA 52405-2724 E-mail: baldwingeo@aol.com.

BALDWIN, GORDON BREWSTER, retired law educator; b. Binghamton, N.Y., Sept. 3, 1929; s. Schuyler Forbes and Doris Ambeline (Hawkins) B.; m. Helen Louise Hochgraf, Feb., 1958; children: Schuyler, Mary Page. LLB, Cornell U., 1953; BA, Haverford Coll., 1950. Bar: N.Y. 1953, Wis. 1965. Pvt. practice, Rochester and Rome, N.Y., 1953-57; prof. law U. Wis., Madison, 1957-99, Evjue-Bascom prof. law, 1991-99, emeritus prof., 1999—, assoc. dean law, 1968-70, dir. officer edn., 1972-99; of counsel Murphy & Desmond, S.C., Madison, Wis., 1986-95. Chmn. internat. law U.S. Naval War Coll., 1963-64; Fulbright prof., Cairo, 1966-67, Tehran, Iran, 1970-71; lectr. State Dept., Cyprus, 1967, 1969, 1971; counselor internat. law U.S. Dept. State, Washington, 1975-76, cons., 1976-77; vis. prof. Chuo U., Tokyo, 1984, Giessen U., Fed. Republic Germany, 1987, 92, Thommasat U., Thailand, 1997; cons. U.S. Naval War Coll., 1961-65; chmn. screening com. on law Fulbright Program, 1974; mem. constl. law com. Multi-State Bar Exam, 1972-82; chmn. State Pub. Def. Bd., 1980-83, Wis. Elections Bd., 1991-96; cons., rep. Marshall Island Constn. Conv., 1990. Mem. Wis. Bd. Elections, 1991-95, Wis. Land Coun., 1998-2002, Wis. State Ethics Bd., 2000-2003. Ford Found. fellow, 1962-63 Fellow Am. Bar Found.; mem. AAUP (nat. coun. 1975-78, pres. Wis. conf. 1986-87), Bar Assn. (vice chmn. sect. on individual rights 1973-75), Fulbright Alumni Assn. (dir. 1979-82), Am. Law Inst., Order of Coif, Madison Lit. Club (pres. 1985-86, 2000-03), Univ. Club, Rotary (pres. Madison 1980, dist. gov. 1999-00), Phi Beta Kappa. Home: 3958 Plymouth Cir Madison WI 53705-5212 Office: U Wis 975 Bascom Mall Sch Law Madison WI 53706-1399 E-mail: gbaldwin@wisc.edu.

BALDWIN, HAROLD SCOTT, pediatrician, educator; b. Honolulu, Dec. 22, 1954; MD, U. Va. Sch. Medicine, 1981. Diplomate Am. Bd. Pediat. Intern U. Rochester/Strong Meml. Hosp., NY, 1982—86, resident in pediat.; assoc. prof. Children's Hosp., Phila.; fellow in pediatric cardiology U. Iowa Coll. Med., Iowa City, 1986—90; prof. pediatrics, cell and devel. biology, prof. pediat. Vanderbilt U. Med. Ctr., Nashville; vice chmn. lab. scis. pediat., chief divsn. pediatric cardiology Vanderbilt Children's Hosp., Nashville. Recipient Established Investigator award, Am. Heart Assn., 1995. Office: Vanderbilt U Med Ctr D2220 Med Ctr N 1161 21st Ave S Nashville TN 37232 E-mail: scott.baldwin@vanderbilt.edu.

BALDWIN, HENRY FURLONG, banker; b. Balt., Jan. 15, 1932; s. Henry du Pont and Margaret (Taylor) B.; div.; children: Mary Stevenson, Severn Eyre. AB, Princeton U., 1954. With Merc.-Safe Deposit & Trust Co., Balt., 1956—2001; pres. Merc. Bankshares Corp. and Merc.-Safe Deposit & Trust Co., Balt., 1970-76, chmn., CEO, 1976-2001; chmn. Merc. Bankshares Corp., Balt., 2001—03. Bd. dirs. W.R. Grace & Co., Wills Group, Inc., dir., chmn. bd. NASDAQ; dir. Platinum Underwriters Holdings, Alleghany Energy. Trustee Johns Hopkins Medicine, 1989-94; trustee emeritus Johns Hopkins U., Marine Corps Heritage Found., Va. Hist. Soc. With USMC, 1954-56. Office: 2 Village Sq Ste 258 Baltimore MD 21210 Office Phone: 410-237-5251. E-mail: hfbaldwin@merctrust.com.

BALDWIN, IRENE S., corporate executive, real estate investor; b. Dodge City, Kans., Sept. 8, 1939; d. Albert A. McMichael and Eleanor L. (Johnson) McMichael McGrath; m. Miles Edward Baldwin, June 30, 1961. BS, Friends U., 1961. Dress designer, Wichita, 1959-61; social worker Sedgwick County, Kans., 1963-65; owner motel chain Kans., 1965—; comml. and agrl. real estate investor, 1971—. Owner motel chain, Kans., 1965—; comml. and agrl. real estate investor, 1971—; corp. sec.-treas. Baldwin, Inc., Kans., 1970—, fin. advisor, 1970—; pvt. practice fin. cons., Colby, Kans., 1975—; founder, advisor Charitable Found., Kans., 1980—; fundraiser various charitable orgns., 1982—; pvt. placement of homeless animals, Kans. and Nebr., 1965—; helped develop 1st artificial front leg for canines, 1985. Contbr. articles to profl. jours.; author: (short stories) My Pal Chopper, 2002. Fundraiser various charitable orgns., 1982—; pvt. placement of homeless animals, Kans. and Nebr., 1965—. Avocations: horseback riding, hiking, travel, sewing, drawing. Address: 2320 S Range Ave Colby KS 67701-9056

BALDWIN, JEFFREY KENTON, lawyer, educator; b. Palestine, Ill., Aug. 8, 1954; s. Howard Keith and Annabelle Lee (Kirts) B.; m. Patricia Ann Mathews, Aug. 23, 1975; children: Matthew, Katy, Timothy, Philip R. BS summa cum laude, Ball State U., 1976; JD cum laude, Ind. U., 1979. Bar: Ind. 1979, U.S. Dist. Ct. (so. dist.) Ind. 1979, U.S. Ct. Appeals (7th cir.) 1979, U.S. Dist. Ct. (no. dist.) Ind. 1984. Majority leader's staff Ind. Senate, Indpls., 1976; instr. Beer Sch. Real Estate, Indpls., 1977-78, Am. Inst. Paralegal Studies, Indpls., 1987—; dep. Office Atty. Gen., Indpls., 1979-81; mng. ptnr. Baldwin & Baldwin, Danville, Ind., 1979—. Agt. Nat. Attys. Title Assurance Fund, Vevay, Ind., 1983—; officer, bd. dirs. Baldwin Realty, Inc., Danville; conf. participant White House Conf. on Small Bus. (Ind. meeting 1994), congl. appointee, 1995; bd. dirs. Small Bus. Coun. Bd. dirs. Hendricks Civic Theatre, Inc.; organizer, Hendricks County Young Republicans, 1972; sec. Hendricks County Rep. Com., 1978-84; bd. dirs. Hendricks County Assn. for Retarded Citizens, Danville, 1982-86; cons. Hendricks County Right for Life, Brownsburg, Ind., 1984—; mem. philanthropy adv. com. Ball State U., Muncie, Ind., 1987—; judge Hendricks County unit Am. Cancer Soc., 1987; coordinator region 2 Young Leaders for Mutz, Indpls., 1987-88; cubmaster WaPaPh dist. Boy Scouts Am., 1988, S.M.E. chmn., 1988-89; steering com. Ind. Lawyers Bush/Quayle; founder, chmn. Christians for Positive Reform; candidate for Congress 7th Congl. Dist. of Ind.; del. to Annual Conf. South Ind. Conf. of United Meth. Ch., 1993, 95-98, 2000; host com. Midwest Rep. Leadership Conf., 1997; dist. coord. Hoosier Famiies for John Price for U.S. Senate; advisor John Price for Gov., 1999-2000; v.p. Danville Little League Baseball, 1998—. Recipient Presdl. award of honor Danville Jaycees, 1980; named hon. sec. State Ind., 1980. Mem. ABA, Ind. Bar Assn., Hendricks County Bar Assn., Indpls. Bar Assn., Internat. Platform Assn., Nat. Assn. Realtors, Ind. Assn. Realtors, Met. Indpls. Bd. Realtors (Hendricks County div.), Federalist Soc., Ind. Farm Bur., Nat. Fedn. Ind. Bus., Ind. C. of C., Danville C. of C. (sec. 1986), Moot Ct. Soc., Blue Key, Phi Soc. Methodist. Home: PO Box 63 Danville IN 46122-0063 Personal E-mail: jbbfc@aol.com.

BALDWIN, JEFFREY NATHAN, pharmacy educator; b. Sidney, NY, Dec. 20, 1947; s. Reverdy Ernest and Helen Elizabeth (Humphrey) B.; m. Suzanne Marie Smith, Dec. 27, 1969; children: Paul Kevin, Gregory Michael. AS, Jamestown C.C., 1967; BS in Pharmacy summa cum laude, SUNY, Buffalo, 1970; DPharm, U. Ky., 1973. Lic. pharmacist Ky., Nebr. Resident in pharmacy U. Ky.-A.B. Chandler Med. Ctr., Lexington, 1970-73; pharmacy faculty U. Nebr. Med. Ctr., Coll. Pharmacy, Omaha, 1973—; med. faculty U. Nebr. Med. Ctr., Coll. Medicine, Omaha, 1977—. Pres., co-founder Nebr. Coun. for Continuing Pharm. Edn., Inc., Omaha, 1980-82. Contbg. author: Points of Light: A Guide for Assisting Chemically Dependent Health Professional Students, 1996, sect. editor: Applied Therapeutics: The Clinical Use of Drugs, 1995, 2001; contbr. over 25 chpts. to books, over 30 articles to profl. jours. Chmn. Nebr. Pharmacist Recovery Network, Lincoln, Nebr., 1988—; scout leader Mid Am. Coun. Boy Scouts Am., Omaha, 1983—, chair tng. com., 1997—98, trustee, 2000—, exec. com., 2001—; counselor Camp CoHoLo, Gretna, Nebr., 1985—98, 2000, 2002, 2004, bd. dirs., 2003—. Recipient Leadership award, McKesson, 1995. Fellow Am. Pharm. Assn. (Merit award 1995), Am. Soc. Health-Sys. Pharmacists (chair pediatric pharmacy spl. interest group 1977-78), Am. Assn. Colls. Pharmacy (chair substance abuse spl. interest group 1988-97, chair pharmacy practice sect. 1998-99), Nebr. Pharmacists Assn. (pres.-elect 1994-95, pres. 1995-96, chmn. bd. 1996-97, NARD Leadership award 1995, Cora Mae Briggs award, 2002, Bowl of Hygeia award 2005) Avocations: travel, camping. Office: 982135 Nebr Med Ctr Omaha NE 68198-2135 Business E-Mail: jbaldwin@unmc.edu.

BALDWIN, JOHN, legal association administrator, lawyer; b. Salt Lake City, Feb. 9, 1954; BA, U. Utah., 1977, JD, 1980. Bar: Utah 1980, U.S. Dist. Ct. Utah 1980, U.S. Ct. Appeals (10th cir.) 1984. Assoc. Jardine, Linebaugh, Brown & Dunn, Salt Lake City, 1980-82; asst. atty. gen. Utah Atty. Gen.'s Office, Salt Lake City, 1982-85; dir. Utah Divsn. Securities, Salt Lake City, 1985-90; exec. dir. Utah State Bar, Salt Lake City, 1990—. Adj. assoc. prof. mgmt. Eccles Sch. Bus., U. Utah. Mem. N.Am. Securities Adminstrs. Assn. (bd. dirs. 1987-90, pres. 1988-89), U. Utah Young Alumni Assn. (bd. dirs. 1987-90), U. Utah Beehive Honor Soc. (bd. dirs. 1993-97), U. Utah Alumni Assn. (bd. dirs. 1995-97). Office: Utah State Bar 645 S 200 E # 310 Salt Lake City UT 84111-3837

BALDWIN, JOHN CHARLES, surgeon, researcher; b. Ft. Worth; BA summa cum laude, Harvard U., 1971; MD, Stanford U., 1975; MA Privatim (hon.), Yale U., 1989. Diplomate Am. Bd. Internal Medicine, Am. Bd. Surgery, Am. Bd. Thoracic Surgery. Fellow in medicine Harvard Med. Sch., Boston, 1975-77; fellow in surgery, resident in surgery Mass. Gen. Hosp., 1977-81; resident in cardiothoracic surgery Stanford (Calif.) U., 1981-82, chief resident cardiothoracic surgery, 1983, asst. prof., 1984-87; dir. heart-lung transplantation transplant rsch. lab. Stanford U., 1986-87; prof. surgery and chief cardiothoracic surgery Yale U., New Haven, 1988-94; cardiothoracic-surgeon-in chief Yale-New Haven Hosp.; DeBakey/Bard prof., chmn. Baylor Coll. Medicine, Houston, 1994-98; sr. attending physician, chief surg. svcs. Meth. Hosp., Houston, 1994-98; sr. attending physician, surgeon in chief Ben Taub Gen. Hosp., Houston, 1994; dean med. sch., v.p. health affairs Dartmouth Coll., 1998—2004; pres., CEO CBR Inst. Biomed. Rsch., Boston, 2005—. Bd. dirs. United Network Organ Sharing, 1984-87; mem. clin. rsch. com. ad hoc rsch. grant rev. Cystic Fibrosis Found.; trustee New Eng. Organ Bank, 1988; mem. solid organ transplant com. Blue Cross & Blue Shield of Conn., 1990-94; mem. sci. adv. bd. Alexion Pharms., Inc., 1991-94; bd. dirs. Baylor Coll. Medicine Healthcare, Inc.; mem. adv. bd. Donate Life Found.; mem. exec. faculty Baylor Coll. of Medicine, pres.'s coun.; bd. dirs. New England chpt. Transplant Recipients Internat. Orgn., 1992-94. Co-editor: Thoracic Surgery, Oxford Textbook of Surgery, 1989—; assoc. editor Jour. Applied Cardiology, 1985-92; editorial bd. Jour. Thoracic and Cardiovascular Surgery, 1990-97, Transplantation, 1990—, Transplantation Sci., 1992-95, Andromeda Interactive Ltd., The Cardiovasc. System Interactive Teaching Program, 1993—; contbr. numerous articles and book chpts. in field. Mem. Harvard Club Schs. Com., Harvard Coll. Fund, Harvard U. Undergrad. Admissions Interview Com.; fellow Timothy Dwight Coll. Yale U., Yale U. Art Gallery Assocs.; mem. appointments and promotions com. Sch. Medicine, Yale U., 1991-94, bd. dirs. Neighborhood Music Sch. New Haven., 1989-92; bd. overseers Harvard U., 1995—; bd. permanent officers Yale U., 1988-94. John Harvard scholar, 1969, 70, Wendell scholar Harvard U., 1969, Rhodes scholar Oxford U., 1971, Alumni scholar Stanford Sch. Medicine, 1974; medalist Gothenburg (Sweden) Thoracic Soc., 1985; recipient Medaille de la Ville de Bordeaux French Thoracic Soc., 1987, travelling lectureship, 1988, Master Tchr. award Cardiovascular Revs. & Reports, 1990; travelling fellow Australia and New Zealand chpt., ACS, 1989; traveling lectureship, 1989. Fellow ACP, ACS, Royal Coll. Surgeons (Eng., traveling lectr. 1989), Am. Coll. Angiology, Am. Coll. Cardiology (mem.

transplantation com. 1991-94, chmn. task force cardiac donor procurement Bethesda Conf. 1992), Am. Coll. Surgeons (bd. govs. 1993-97), Am. Coll. Chest Physicians, Mass. Med. Soc.; mem. AMA, AAAS, Am. Assn. Thoracic Surgery (mem. com. grad. edn. thoracic surgery 1992-97, chmn. Evarts A. Graham Meml. Traveling Fellowship com. 1993-99), Am. Soc. Transplant Surgeons (com. on heart transplantation 1986-89, adv. com. in issues 1989—, chmn. subcom. on heart transplantation, physician payment reform commn. 1989-92), Nat. Heart, Lung and Blood Inst. (cons. divsn. extramural affairs rev. br. 1990—), Assn. Acad. Surgery, Am. Physiol. Soc., Am. Heart Assn. (mem. rsch. grant peer rev. subcom 1984-87, coun. circulation, cert. of appreciation for outstanding svc. 1986), Am. Surg. Assn., Am. Thoracic Soc., Am. Soc. Artificial Internal Organs, Am. Soc. Extracorporeal Tech., Am. Assn. Lab. Animal Sci., Am. Organ Transplant Assn., Am. Venous Forum, Internat. Soc. Heart and Lung Transplantation (chmn. program com. 1988), Internat. Assn. Cardiac Biol. Implants, Internat. Fedn. Surg. Colls., Internat. Soc. Cardiovasc. Surgery, Internat. Soc. Cardio-Thoracic Surgeons (pres. 1999), Internat. Soc. for Heart Rsch. (mem. Am. sect.), Internat. Soc. for Artificial Organs, Mediterranean Assn. for Cardiology and Cardiac Surgery, New Century Soc., Thoracic Surgery Found. for Rsch. and Edn., Norman E. Shumway Surg. Soc., New Eng. Surg. Soc., Pan Am. Med. Assn. (coun. on organ transplantation), North Am. Soc. Pacing and Electrophysiology, Societe Internat. de Chirurgie, Royal Soc. Medicine, Soc. Univ. Surgeons, Thoracic Surgery Dirs. Assn. (chmn. curriculum com. transplantation 1993-94), Transplantation Soc., Assn. Alumni of Magdalen Coll. Oxford U., Assn. Rhodes Scholars, Acad. Surg. Rsch., Assn. Surg. Edn., Assn. Program Dirs. in Surgery, Conn. Thoracic Soc., Harris County Med. Soc., Calif. Med. Assn., Calif. Thoracic Soc., Calif. Thoracic Soc. Respiratory Care Assembly, No. Calif. Cystic Fibrosis Found., So. Calif. Transplant Soc., Conn. Med. Soc., Conn. Soc. Am. Bd. Surgeons, Mass. Med. Soc., N.Y. Soc. Thoracic Surgery, Harvard Med. Alumni Assn. (assoc.), Soc. Crit. Care Medicine, Soc. Thoracic Surgeons, Southeastern Surg. Congress, Southern Surg. Assn., Southwestern Surg. Congress, Tex. Surg. Soc., Halsted Soc., Houston Surg. Soc. Soc. for Organ Sharing, San Francisco Surg. Soc., Santa Clara Med. Soc., Stanford Med. Alumni Assn., Stanford Club Conn., Harvard Clubs San Francisco, Peninsula, N.Y.C., So. Conn., Houston, Boston, Mory's Assn., New Haven Lawn Club, Inner Quad Stanford U., The Hasty Pudding Club - Inst. 1770, Quinnipiack Club, Forum World Affairs, Ambs. Roundtable, Oxford Soc., Phi Beta Kappa, others. Office: The CBR Inst Biomeducal Rsch 200 Longwood Ave Boston MA 02115 Office Phone: 617-278-3000. Business E-Mail: baldwin@cbr.med.harvard.edu.

BALDWIN, JOHN EDWIN, chemistry professor; b. Berwyn, Ill., Sept. 10, 1937; s. Francis Miller and Irville (Miller) B.; m. Anne Kruesi Nordlander, Sept. 23, 1961; children— Claire Miller, John Nordlander, Wesley Hale. AB summa cum laude, Dartmouth Coll., 1959; PhD, Calif. Inst. Tech., 1963. Mem. chemistry faculty U. Ill., 1962-68; prof. chemistry U. Oreg., Eugene, 1968-84; dean Coll. Arts and Scis., 1975-80; prof. chemistry Syracuse U., N.Y., 1984-2000, disting. prof., 2000—, Wm. R. Kenan, Jr. prof. sci., 2005—. Cons. Stauffer Chem. Co., Office Sci. and Tech., NIH; 150th anniversary vis. prof. Chalmers U., 1990. Author: Experimental Organic Chemistry, 1965, also articles.; Adv. bd.: Organic Reactions. Guggenheim fellow, 1967; Sloan fellow, 1966-68; recipient Sr. U.S. Scientist award Alexander von Humboldt Found., 1974-75, Syracuse Sect. award Am. Chem. Soc., 1997. Home: 5 Brattle Rd Syracuse NY 13203-2803

BALDWIN, JOHN WESLEY, history professor; b. Chgo., July 13, 1929; s. Edward N. and H. Gladys (McDaniel) B.; m. Jenny Jochens, Dec. 24, 1954; children: Peter, Ian, Birgit (dec.), Christopher. BA, Wheaton Coll., 1950; MA, Pa. State U., 1951; PhD, Johns Hopkins, 1956. Instr., then asst. prof. U. Mich., Ann Arbor, 1956-61; mem. faculty Johns Hopkins U., Balt., 1961—, prof. history, 1966—, Charles Homer Haskins prof. history, 1986—, prof. emeritus, 2001—; prof. e'tranger Coll. de France, 1984, 95. Author: The Medieval Theories of the Just Price, 1959, Masters, Princes and Merchants, 2 vols, 1970, The Scholastic Culture of the Middle Ages, 1971, City on the Seine: Paris under Louis IX, 1226-1270, 1975, The Government of Philip Augustus, 1986 (French transl. 1991), Les Registres de Philippe Auguste, 1992, The Language of Sex: Five Voices from Northern France Around 1200, 1994, (French translation) Les Languages de l'amour, 1997, Aristocratic Life in Medieval France: The Romances of Jean Renart and Gerbert de Montreuil, 1190-1230, 2000, Le Livre de Terres et de Revenues de Pierre du Thillay, 2002; editor (with Richard Goldthwaite) Universities in Politics: Case Studies from the Late Middle Ages and Early Modern Period, 1972. Decorated Chevalier de la légion d'honneur (France), Chevalier Ordre des Arts et des Lettres (France); Prix Litteraire Etats-Unis-France, 1992; Guggenheim fellow, 1960-61, 83-84, Howard fellow, 1960-61, Fulbright fellow, 1953-55, 65-66, Sr. fellow NEH, 1972-73, 90-91; grantee Am. Coun. Learned Socs., 1965-66. Fellow Medieval Acad. Am. (v.p. 1994, pres. 1996-97, Charles Homer Haskins medal 1990), Am. Acad. Arts and Scis., Am. Philos. Soc., Brit. Acad. (corr.); mem. Soc. for French Hist. Studies, Royal Danish Acad. Scis. and Letters (fgn.), Am. Hist. Assn., Commn. Internat. de Diplomatique (hon.), Acad. Inscriptions et Belles Lettres (France) (assoc. fgn.), Société Nationale des Antiquaires de France (assoc. corr. fgn.), Institut de France. Office: Johns Hopkins U Dept History Baltimore MD 21218 also: 18 rue de Bièvre 75005 Paris France

BALDWIN, LIONEL VERNON, retired university president; b. Beaumont, Tex., May 30, 1932; s. Eugene B. and Wanda (Wiley) B.; m. Kathleen Flanagan, Sept. 3, 1955; children: Brian, Michael, Diane, Daniel. BS, U. Notre Dame, 1954; SM, MIT, 1955; PhD, Case Inst. Tech., 1959. Rsch. engr. Nat. Adv. Com. Aerosci., Ohio, 1957-59; unit head NASA, 1959-61; assoc. prof. engring. Colo. State U., 1961-64, acting dean Coll. of Engring., 1964-65, dean and prof. Coll. of Engring., 1966-84; pres. Nat. Tech. U., Ft. Collins, Colo., 1984—2000; ret., 2000. Served to capt. USAF, 1955-57. Recipient award for plasma rsch. NASA, 1964, Kenneth Andrew Roe award Am. Assn. Engring. Soc., 1996. Fellow Am. Soc. Engring. Edn. (chmn. engring. deans coun.); mem. ASME, IEEE, NSPE, Sigma Xi, Tau Beta Pi, Sigma Pi Sigma. Achievements include patentee apparatus for increasing ion engine beam density. Home: 1900 Sequoia St Fort Collins CO 80525-1540 Personal E-mail: lionelvbld@comcast.net.

BALDWIN, MARIE HUNSUCKER, retired secondary school educator; b. Dallas, Dec. 22, 1923; d. Clyde Augustus and Charlotte (Moore) Hunsucker; m. Brewster Baldwin, Aug. 20, 1946 (dec. July 1992); children: Jean Baldwin McLevedge, David, Stephen, Christopher. BS in Edn., Tex. Tech. U., 1944; MFA in Writing, Norwich U., 1988. Tchr. Pub. Sch., Corpus Christi, Tex., 1944-45, Presbyn. Day Sch., Corpus Christi, 1945-46, Pub. Sch., Moriah, N.Y., 1964-66; field dir. Vt. Girl Scout Coun., Burlington, 1966-78; ret. Vice chair Vt. State Dem. Com., Montpelier, 1976-80; apptd. mem. Gov.'s Adult Edn. Coun., 1985-89; founder, pres. Vt. Caths. for Free Choice, 1989—; elected Justice of the Peace, Middlebury, Vt., 1989—. Mem. ACLU (bd. 1984-90), AAUW, LWV (founder, pres. 1952-56), Cath. Daus. Am., Bus. and Profl. Women. Avocations: creative writing, walking, reading.

BALDWIN, MARK PHILLIP, atmospheric scientist; b. Schenectady, N.Y., Mar. 4, 1958; s. Robert Earl and Helen May (Rudowski) B.; m. Rebecca Helen Tuttle, Sept. 11, 1962; 1 child, Ryan Tuttle. BS, SUNY, Albany, 1980, MS, 1981, U. Wash., 1984, PhD, 1987. Cert. cons. meteorologist. Postdoctoral rsch. assoc. N.W. Rsch. Assocs., Inc., Bellevue, Wash., 1987-89, rsch. scientist, 1989—. Referee profl. jours. Contbr. articles to profl. publs. Mem. Am. Meteorol. Soc., Adirondack 46ers, Sigma Pi Sigma. Achievements include discovery of upper stratospheric tropical-extratropical quasi-biennial oscillation in atmospheric observations; research on documentation of stochastic nature of freezing process; use of statistical arguments in solar-QBO-atmospheric observations. Home: 2360 Squak Mountain Loop SW Issaquah WA 98027-4418 Office: NW Rsch Assocs Inc PO Box 3027 Bellevue WA 98009-3027

BALDWIN, PATRICIA ANN, lawyer; b. Detroit, May 3, 1955; d. Frank Thomas and Margaret Elyne Mathews; m. Jeffrey Kenton Baldwin, Aug. 23, 1975; children: Matthew, Katherine, Timothy, Philip. BA summa cum laude, Ball State U., 1976; JD, Ind. U., 1979. Bar: Ind. 1979, U.S. Dist. Ct. (so. dist.) Ind. 1979. Ptnr. Baldwin & Baldwin, Danville, Ind., 1979-94; dep. pros. atty. Hendricks County, Danville, 1980-90, pros. atty., 1995—; dep. pros. atty. Boone County, Ind., 1990-94. Sec.-treas., dir. T.F.W., Inc., Danville, 1983—90. Active Girl Scouts U.S., 1964—2000; vol. Boy Scouts Am., 1986—; mem. Hendricks County Rep. Women, 1976—, pres., 2001—03; mem. parish coun. Mary Queen of Peace Cath. Ch., 1976—80, 1981—83; bd. dirs. Cath. Social Svcs., Archdiocese of Indpls., sec. bd. dirs., 1986—92; bd. dirs. Cummins Mental Health Ctr., 1982—86, Youth as Resources Hendricks County, 1995—2001. Mem.: Hendricks County Bar Assn., Ind. Pros. Attys. Assn., Nat. Dist. Attys. Assn., Danville Conservation Club. Office: One Courthouse Sq #105 Danville IN 46122 Office Phone: 317-745-9283.

BALDWIN, PETER ARTHUR, psychology professor, writer, minister; b. Andover, Mass., Apr. 7, 1932; s. Alfred Graham and Katherine (Ashworth) B.; m. Carolyn Whitmore, Sept. 3, 1955; children: Sarah MacDonald Baldwin-Welcome, Judith Helen Baldwin-Gleason, Robert Henry. BA, Middlebury Coll., 1955; S.T.B., Boston U., 1959, PhD, 1964; student, New Coll., U. London, 1957-58. Lic. psychologist, N.H.; approved cons. in clin. hypnosis, Am. Soc. Clin. Hypnosis. Ordained to ministry Unitarian-Universalist Ch., 1959; pastor 2d Ch., Boston, 1955-57, in Dighton, Mass., 1958-62; religious counselor M.I.T., 1959-63; exec. dir. Liberal Religious Youth, Unitarian Universalist Assn., 1963-66; asst. prof. Crane Theol. Sch., Tufts U., 1965-67, Meadville Theol. Sch., U. Chgo., 1967-73; pastor All Souls 1st Universalist Soc., Chgo., 1971-73; assoc. prof. psychology New Eng. Coll., Henniker, N.H., 1973-74; vis. assoc. prof. psychology Colby-Sawyer Coll., New London, N.H., 1974-76; assoc. prof. dept. clin. psychology Antioch-New Eng. Grad. Sch., Keene, N.H., 1976—; pvt. practice, 1976—. Dir. Sr. High and Family Insts., Rowe, Mass., 1967-74; Nat. Edn. Conf. lectr. Williston Acad., 1967; Judy lectr., Omaha, 1970; invited speaker 5th Internat. Congress on Gestalt Therapy, Valencia, Spain, 1993. Recipient; Disting. Svc. Antioch New Eng. Grad. Sch., 1994, New Hampshire Psychological Assn., Margaret M. Riggs Disting. Contribution award, 1995. Fellow: ISDF, N.H. Psychol. Assn. (pres. 1980—81, 1988—90); mem.: APA, Unitarian- Universalists Mins. Assn., Liberal Religious Youth (life). Democrat. Home: 113 Pancake Hill Rd Gilmanton NH 03237 Office: Univ Assocs in Psychology 222 West St Keene NH 03431-2455

BALDWIN, RALPH BELKNAP, retired manufacturing executive, astronomer; b. Grand Rapids, Mich., June 6, 1912; s. Melvin D. and Julie (Belknap) B.; m. Lois Virginia Johnston, Aug. 3, 1940; children: Melvin Dana II, Pamela, Bruce Belknap. BS, U. Mich., 1934, MS, 1935, PhD, 1937, LLD (hon.), 1975; ScD (hon.), Grand Valley State U., 1989, Aquinas Coll., 1999. Asst. dept. astronomy U. Mich., 1935-36, U. Pa., 1937-38; instr. dept. astronomy Northwestern U., 1938-42; lectr. Adler Planetarium, Chgo., 1940-42; sr. physicist Applied Physics Lab. Johns Hopkins, Silver Spring, Md., 1942-46, cons. East Grand Rapids, Mich., 1946-47; acting supt. schs. East Grand Rapids, 1947; prodn. mgr. Oliver Machinery Co., Grand Rapids, 1947-56, dir., 1948-87, successively personnel dir., prodn. mgr., sec., 1949-56, v.p., 1956-70, pres., 1970-84, chmn. bd., 1984-87. Chmn. bd. Internat. Woodworking Machinery and Furniture Supply Fair-U.S.A., 1969-70, 77-78 Author: The Face of the Moon, 1949, The Measure of the Moon, 1963, The Moon— A Fundamental Survey, 1966, The Deadly Fuze: Secret Weapon of World War II, 1980, They Never Knew What Hit Them, 1999; contbr. articles to profl. jours. Recipient Presdl. Cert. of Merit, 1947, U.S. Naval Bur. Ordnance award, 1945, U.S. Army Chief of Ordnance award, 1945, Disting. Alumnus award U. Mich., 1967, Woodworking and Furniture Digest award Forest Products Rsch. Soc., 1973, J. Lawrence Smith medal Nat. Acad. Scis., 1979, G.K. Gilbert award Geol. Soc. Am., 1986, Disting. Alumni award Ctrl. HS, Grand Rapids, 1997 Fellow AAAS, Am. Geophys. Union, Meteoritical Soc. (Leonard medal 1986, Barringer medal 2000), Am. Acad. Arts and Scis.; mem. Am. Astron. Soc., Royal Astron. Soc. Can. (hon.), Grand Rapids Mus. Assn., NAM (dir. 1963-64), Employers Assn. Grand Rapids (pres. 1960-64), Woodworking Machinery Mfrs. Assn. (pres. 1964-68). Home: 4780 Aston Gardens Way Naples FL 34109 Personal E-mail: drrbb5898@yahoo.com.

BALDWIN, RICHARD EDWARD, III, military training official; b. Phila., Mar. 4, 1979; s. Richard E. Baldwin and Heather C. Firth; m. Athena P. Cartwright, Jan. 18, 2000; 1 child, Richard E. IV. Security Forces Tech. Tng., Security Forces Acad., 1999. Installation entry controller 14 Security Forces Squadron, Columbus, Miss., 1999—2000, installation armorer, 1999—2000, installation patrolman, 2000—02, installation desk sgt., 2001—02; narcotics investigator Airforce Office Spl. Tng., 2003—04; tng. mgr. 14 Security Forces Squadron, 2003—. Ednl. counselor 14 Securtity Forces Squadron, Columbus, Miss., 2003—04. Mem. Golden Triangle Crimestoppers, West Point, Mo., 1989—2004, Miss. Film Commn., Columbus, Miss., 2002—. Sgt. USAF, 1999—, Mo. Mem.: Peacekeepers Assn. (pres. 2003—04, treas. 2002—03). Cath. Avocations: art, films, cooking, acting, prop design. Home and Office: 400 Forrest Blvd Apt 13 Columbus MS 39702

BALDWIN, ROBERT FREDERICK, JR., lawyer; b. Syracuse, N.Y., Sept. 20, 1939; s. Robert Frederick and Marjorie Elizabeth (Thompson) Baldwin; m. Jeanella M. Mastrobattisto, Apr. 26, 1980; m. Margaret Melissa Richards, Aug. 19, 1962 (div.); children: Robert Frederick, Melissa Brooke. BSBA, Syracuse U., 1962, LLB, 1964. Bar: N.Y. 1964, U.S. Dist. Ct. (no. dist.) N.Y. 1980, Fla. 1982, U.S. Ct. Mil. Appeals 1965, U.S. Tax Ct. 1968, U.S. Ct. of Claims 1980, U.S. Supreme Ct. 1968. Assoc. Hancock, Estabrook, Ryan, Shove & Hust, Syracuse, NY, 1968—73; ptnr. Hancock, Estabrook Ryan, Shove & Hust, Syracuse, NY, 1974—84; prin. Green & Seifter, Attys, P.C., Syracuse, NY, 1984—96; ptnr. Baldwin & Sutphen, LLP, Syracuse, 1996—. Atty. Village Fayetteville, Fayetteville, 1974—94; adj. prof. law Syracuse U. Coll. Law, 1977—2004. Contbr. articles to profl. jours. Mem., deferred gifts com. ARC, CNY chpt., Syracuse, 1980—84; vice-chair Onondaga County Indsl. Devel. Agy., Syracuse, 1996—2002, chmn., 2004—, DestiNY USA Benefits Maximization Com., Syracuse, 2002; bd. mem. Planned Parenthod CNY, Syracuse, 1978—84; trustee Fayetteville Cemetary Assn., 1974—80; bd. mem. UN Assn. CNY, Syracuse, 1971—74; trustee Fayetteville Libr. Assn., 1976—79; pres., mem. Onondaga Pastoral Counselling Ctr., Syracuse, 1994—2002; bd. govs. Citizens Found., Syracuse, 1973—76; mem. Assn. Retarded Citizens CNY, Syracuse, 1976—79; mem, steering com. Syracuse U. Tax Inst., 1980—2002. Comdr. USNR, 1965—85. Fellow: Am. Coll. Trust & Estate Counsel (chair, employee benefits com. 1997—2000); mem.: Estate Planning Coun. Ctrl. NY (pres. 1973—74), Nat. Assn. Estate Planning Couns. (pres. 1982—83), Onondaga County Bar Assn. (dir. 1976—79). Home: 5153 Burnside Dr Jamesville NY 13078 Office: Baldwin & Sutphen LLP 100 Clinton Sq Ste 320 Syracuse NY 13202 Office Phone: 315-477-0100. Personal E-mail: rbaldwin@baslaw.com.

BALDWIN, ROBERT LESH, biochemist, educator; b. Madison, Wis., Sept. 30, 1927; s. Ira Lawrence and Mary (Lesh) B.; m. Anne Theodora Norris, Aug. 28, 1965; children: David Norris, Eric Lawrence. BA, U. Wis., 1950; D.Phil. (Rhodes scholar), Oxford (Eng.) U., 1954. Asst. prof., then asso. prof. biochemistry U. Wis., 1955-59; mem. faculty Stanford, 1959—, prof. biochemistry, 1964-98, prof. emeritus, 1998—, chmn. dept., 1989-94. Vis. prof. Collège de France, Paris, 1972, Tsinghua U., Beijing, 2002; mem. adv. panel biochemistry and biophysics NSF, 1974—76; mem. NIH study sect. molecular and cellular biophysics, 1984—88. Assoc. editor Jour. Molecular Biology, 1964-68, 75-79; mem. editorial bd. Trends Biochem. Sci., 1977-84, Biochemistry, 1984—, Protein Sci., 1992-97. Mem. award panel Searle Scholars, 1993—96, 1997—98; mem. adv. panel in biophysics Burroughs-Wellcome, 1995—2001. Recipient Wheland award in chemistry U. Chgo., 1995; Guggenheim fellow, 1958-59. Fellow Am. Biophysics Soc. (coun. 1977-81, Founder's award 1999); mem. NAS, Am. Soc. Biol. Chemists (Merck award 1999), Am. Chem. Soc., Am. Acad. Arts and Scis., Protein Soc. (coun. 1993-95, Stein and Moore award 1992). Home: 1243 Los Trancos Rd Portola Valley CA 94028-8125 Office: Stanford Med Sch Dept Biochemistry Beckman Ctr Stanford CA 94305-5307 E-mail: bbaldwin@cmgm.stanford.edu.

BALDWIN, SHAUN MCPARLAND, lawyer; b. Chgo., Oct. 19, 1954; BS, No. Ill. U., 1976; JD with distinction, John Marshall Law Sch., 1980. Bar: Ill. 1980, U.S. Dist. Ct. (no. dist.) Ill. 1980, U.S. Ct. Appeals (7th cir.) 1981. Assoc. McKenna, Storer, Rowe, While & Farrug, Chgo., 1980-86, Tressler, Soderstrom, Maloney & Priess, Chgo., 1986-87, ptnr., 1987—. Mem. ABA, Ill. Bar Assn., Def. Rsch. Inst. (chair ins. law com. 1996-98), Ill. Assn. Def. Trial Counsel (bd. dirs. 1996, amicus com. chair 1992—98), Ill. Appellate Lawyers Assn. (bd. dirs. 1987-89), John Marshall Alumni Assn. (bd. dirs. 1982-86), Internat. Assn. Def. Trial Counsel (chair membership com. 1996-97, chair casualty ins. com. 1995-96), Profl. Liability Underwriting Soc. Office: Tressler Soderstrom Maloney & Priess 233 S Wacker Dr Ste 2200 Chicago IL 60606-6399 Office Phone: 312-627-4000, 312-627-4014. Business E-Mail: sbaldwin@tsmp.com.

BALDWIN, STANLEY F., lawyer; b. 1948; BA, JD, U. Tex. Various sr. officer and gen. counsel positions CIGNA Healthplans, Inc.; sr. v.p., sec. EQUICOR-Equitable HCA Corp., Nashville; gen. counsel EPIC Healthcare Group, Dallas, 1990—97; gen. counsel, sec. Amerigroup Corp., Va. Beach, Va., 1997—. Mem.: State Bar Tex., Tenn. Bar Assn. Office: Amerigroup Corp 4425 Corporation Ln Virginia Beach VA 23462 Office Phone: 757-490-6900. Office Fax: 757-473-2738.

BALDWIN, SUSAN OLIN, commissioner, management consultant; b. Battle Creek, Mich., Sept. 1, 1954; d. Thomas Franklin and Gloria Joan (Skidmore) Olin; m. James Patrick Baldwin, Sept. 15, 1979; children: Christopher Mark, David James. BA, Miami U., Ohio, 1976; JD, U. Cin., 1979. Bar: Ohio 1979, Mich. 1984. Assoc. editor Am. Legal Pub. Co., Cin., 1979—80; corp. atty. Hosp. Care Corp., Cin., 1980—84; legal counsel Peak Health Plan, Cin., 1984; assoc. Cook & Goetz, P.C., Bloomfield Hills, Mich., 1984—91, Pringle & Assocs., P.C., Farmington Hills, Mich., 1991—94; exec. dir. Calhoun County Econ. Devel. Forum, Battle Creek, 1994—2003; owner Am. Computer Svcs., Battle Creek, 2002—; commr. Battle Creek City, 2003—. Mem. steering com. Ctr. Workforce Excellence, 1994—96, Barriers to Employment, 1996—2003; bd. dirs. BC/Cal/Kal Inland Port Devel. Corp., Forum Greater Kalamazoo, 1995—2001, Calhoun County Health Improvement Program, 1998—99; mem. Battle Creek Cmty. Leadership Acad., 1996—97, Battle Creek Area C. of C., 1998—2003, mem. adv. bd., 1998—, S.W. Mich. Healthplan Purchasing Alliance, 1998—2000; adv. bd. Starr Commonwealth Battle Creek Child Guidance Ctr., 1998—; mem. Cmty. Devel. Block Grant Coun., 1996—99. Contbr. articles to profl. jours. Pres. Hunter's Green Homeowner's Assn., Independence, Ky., 1982—83; chairwoman Safety Town Cmty. Project, 1993—95; v.p. fin. Jr. League Battle Creek, 1996—98; key communicator Minges Brook PTA, 1993—2001, treas., 1994—96, 1998—99; bd. dirs. Vol. Ctr. Battle Creek, 1999—, sec., 2003—05; bd. dirs. Battle Creek Cmty. Found. Philanthropic Devel. Com., 1998—, Lakeview Sch. Dist. Com. Continuous Improvement, 1999—2002; chair S. Ctrl. Mich. Jr. Achievement Campaign, 1999, Calhoun County Crossroads Initiative, 1999—2002; bd. dirs. Habitat for Humanity, 2003—; mem. Mayor's Commr. Compensation Commn., 1997—2003; mem. capital campaign com.-making BC Green Leila Arboretum, 1999—2000; mem. exec. bd. Battle Creek Unltd., 2003—. Mem.: ABA, Am. Businesswomen's Assn. (v.p. 1980—81, editor 1980), Ohio State Bar, State Bar Mich., Battle Creek Area C. of C. (bd. dirs. 1998—), Birmingham Evening Newcomers Club (treas. 1986—87, pres. 1988), Phi Alpha Delta, Alpha Lambda Delta. Office: 164 W Hamilton Ln Battle Creek MI 49015-4030 Office Phone: 269-963-8124. Personal E-mail: sbaldwin4bc@aol.com.

BALDWIN, TAMMY, congresswoman, lawyer; b. Madison, Wis., Feb. 11, 1962; AB in Govt. & Math, Smith Coll., Northampton, Mass., 1984; JD, U. Wis., Madison, 1989. Mem. Madison City Council, Wis., 1986; supr. Dane County Bd. of Supervisors, 1986-1994; pvt. practice as atty., 1989-92; mem. 78th dist. Wis. State Assembly, 1993-99; mem. U.S. Congress from 2d Wis. dist., Washington, 1999—, mem. budget com., judiciary com., energy and commerce com. Mem.: Nat. Women's Polit. Caucus, Wis. State Bar Assn., Internat. Network Lesbian and Gay Officials, ACLU, NOW. Democrat. First woman to serve in the US Ho. of Reps. from Wis.; first openly gay person to be elected to Congress as a non-incumbent. Office: US Ho of Reps 1022 Longworth Ho Office Bldg Washington DC 20515 also: Dist Off 10 E Doty St Ste 405 Madison WI 53703-5103*

BALDWIN, WILLIAM, editor; b. 1951; BA in Linguistics, Harvard U., 1973. Reporter News Jour., Wilmington, Del., 1974—80; sr. editor Forbes Mag., Washington, 1974—80, asst. mng. editor, 1980—87, exec. editor, 1988—92, mng. editor, 1992—98, editor, 1999—. Office: Forbes Mag 60 5th Ave New York NY 10011

BALDWIN, WILLIAM HOWARD, retired lawyer, foundation administrator; b. Detroit, Feb. 21, 1916; s. Howard Charles and Ruth E. (Jensen) B.; m. Carol Lees, May 24, 1947; children: Susan, Jeffrey (dec.), Julie, Deborah. BA, Williams Coll., 1938; JD, U. Mich., 1941. Bar: Mich. 1941. Ptnr. Dykema Gossett, Detroit, 1970-77, of counsel, 1977—; chmn., trustee Kresge Found., Troy, Mich., 1963-87. Asst. U.S. prosecutor Nuremburg Trials, 1946. Served with USAAF, 1942-45, lt. col. (ret.). Mem. ABA, Mich. Bar Assn. Republican. Episcopalian. Home: 4620 Saint James Ave Vero Beach FL 32967-7336 E-mail: hbal@aol.com.

BALDWIN, WILLIAM RUSSELL, optometrist, foundation administrator; b. Danville, Ind., July 29, 1926; s. Edward Claire and Letha Verona (Russell) B.; m. Honey Esther Fisher, Aug. 16, 1947; children: Linda Marie Smith (dec.), Leslie Ann Baldwin Bloom. BS, Pacific U., 1949, OD, 1951, ScD (hon.), 1991; MS, Ind. U., 1956, PhD, 1964; LHD (hon.), New Eng. Coll., 1982; D.S. (hon.), SUNY, 1998; DS (hon.), Pa. Coll. Optometry, 2003. Pvt. practice, Beech Grove, Ind., 1951-54; dir. optometry clinic Ind. U., Bloomington, 1959-63; dean Coll. Optometry Pacific U., Forest Grove, Oreg., 1963-69; pres. New England Coll. Optometry, Boston, 1969-79; dean Coll. Optometry U. Houston, 1979-90; pres. River Blindness Found., 1990-96, chmn. bd. dirs., 1996—2001. Author: (with C.R. Schick) Corneal Contact Lenses, Fitting Procedures, 1962, (with others) The Refractive State of the Eye, 1969, Pediatric Optometry, 1988; editor Vision Science Symposium, Ind. U., 1988, (with others) Refractive Anomalies, 1991. Mem. exec. com. Rep. Ctrl. Com., Washington County, Oreg., 1963-69; chmn. arts, scis. divsn. Ind. Reps., 1962-63; chmn. Vellore India Hosp. Fund Drive, 1959-61; mem. men's adv. coun. Bloomington Hosp., 1959-63, bd. dirs. Am. Optometric Found., 1998-2003. Recipient Alumni Svc. award Ind. U., 1977, Pacific U., 1995, Gold Medal award Beta Sigma Kappa, 1968, Lifetime Achievement award Prevent Blindness Am., 1995, Disting. Svc. award USPHA Vision Sect., 1998, Social Justice Action award New Eng. United Meth. Conf., 1999, Disting. Svc. award World Coun. Optometry, 2000; named Man of Vision Prevent Blindness Mass., 1994; Disting. scholar Nat. Acad. Practice, 1994, Disting. Svc. award, Vis. Section Am. Pub. Health Assn., 1998. Fellow AAAS, Am. Acad. Optometry (life, chmn. sect. on edn. 1984-87); mem. working group Nat. Rsch. Coun. Com. Vision of NAS, Am. Optometric Assn. (chmn. com. on rsch. 1964-69, chmn. task force on manpower 1968, Disting. Svc. award 1992), Assn. Schs. Colls. Optometry (pres. 1974-76, chmn. internat. optometric edn.), Tex. Soc. to Prevent Blindness (v.p. 1985-90), Nat. Soc. to Prevent Blindness Am. (bd. dirs. 1988-96, chm. 1st World Conf. on Optometric Edn. 1990), Optometric Rsch. Inst. (bd. dirs. 1995-2001), Rotary, Sigma Xi, Sigma Nu, Kappa Kappa Sigma. Office Phone: 812-333-2013. Personal E-mail: bilbold@insightbb.com.

BALDYGA, LEONARD J., retired diplomat, researcher; b. Chgo., Mar. 19, 1932; s. Stanislaw J. and Frances T. (Gorzynski) B.; m. Joyce Brinkley, June 25, 1960; children: Natalya M., Sarah E. AA, J. Sterling Morton Coll., 1954; BS, So. Ill. U., 1959; M Internat. Affairs, Columbia U., 1962. City editor Marion (Ill.) Daily Rep., 1958-59; fin. writer Am. Banker, N.Y.C., 1959-61; overseas, 1963-78; dep. dir. Europe U.S. Info. Agy., Washington, 1979-81, dir., 1981-83, 92-94; minister, counselor Am. Embassy, Rome, 1983-88, New Delhi, 1988-91; sr. rsch. assoc. Washington, 1994—. Acting dir. Murrow Ctr. Tufts U. Fletcher Sch. Law and Diplomacy, Medford, Mass., 1991-92, adj. prof., 1991-92. Mem. editl. bd. Polish Ency. Britannica. Trustee St. Stephen's

Sch., Rome, 1984—88; bd. dirs. Ptnrs. for Dem. Change, Washington, Pub. Diplomacy Coun., Sabre Found., Polish Inst. Arts and Scis., N.Y.C. Decorated Polish Order of Merit Republic of Poland, 1994, Commander's Cross, 2002; recipient Presdl. Disting. Svc. award White House, 1984, Edward R. Murrow award Tufts U., 1988, Presdl. Merit award White House, 1988. Office: Internat Rsch/Exchs Bd 2121 K St NW Ste 700 Washington DC 20037 Office Phone: 202-247-9409. Personal E-mail: ljbjbb@aol.com.

BALE, CHRISTIAN, actor; b. Haverfordwest Pembrokeshire, Wales, Jan. 30, 1974; s. David Bale and Gloria Steinem (Stepmother); m. Sibi Blazic; 1 child. Actor: (TV films) Anastasia: The Mystery of Anna, 1986, Treasure Island, 1990, A Murder of Quality, 1991, Mary, Mother of Jesus, 1999; (TV miniseries) Heart of the Country, 1987; (films) The Land of Faraway, 1987, Empire of the Sun, 1987, Henry V, 1989, Newsies, 1992, Swing Kids, 1993, Royal Deceit, 1994, Little Women, 1994, (voice) Pocahontas, 1995, The Secret Agent, 1996, Portrait of a Lady, 1996, Metroland, 1997, Velvet Goldmine, 1998, All the Little Animals, 1998, A Midsummer Night's Dream, 1999, American Psycho, 2000, Shaft, 2000, Captain Corelli's Mandolin, 2001, Laurel Canyon, 2002, Reign of Fire, 2002, Equilibrium, 2002, The Machinist, 2004, Howl's Moving Castle, 2004, Batman Begins, 2005. Actively involved with various civic organizations including Happy Child Mission, Ark Trust, Redwings Sanctuary, Greenpeace, World Wildlife Found., Dian Fossey Gorilla Fund. Office: Endeavor Talent Agency LLC 9701 Wilshire Blvd 10th Fl Beverly Hills CA 90210*

BALÉE, WILLIAM L., anthropology educator; b. Ft. Lauderdale, Fla., Oct. 12, 1954; s. William Lockert Balée and Lorraine Kathryn Monahan; m. Maria da Conceição Bezerra, Mar. 9, 1987; children: Nicholas, Isabel. BA with high honors, U. Fla., 1975; MA, Columbia U., 1979, MPhil, 1980, PhD, 1984. Assoc. rschr. ecology Museu Paraense Emílio Goeldi, Belém, Brazil, 1988-91, chair ecology, 1990-91; assoc. prof. anthropology Tulane U., New Orleans, 1991-98, prof., chair dept. anthropology, 1998-2001, prof. anthropology, 1998—. Adj. prof. anthropology CUNY, 1983-84, SUNY, Purchase, 1982; adj. prof. social scis. CUNY, 1983; adj. prof. sociology and anthropology Rutgers U., 1984; vis. assoc. prof. Ctr. for L.Am. Studies, U. Fla., 1990; fieldwork with forest peoples in Amazon of Brazil and Bolivia, 1980-2003; acad. cons. Smithsonian Instn., 2000—04. Author: Footprints of the Forest: Ka'apor Ethnobotany, 1994 (award Soc. Econ. Botany, 1996); editor: Advances in Historical Ecology, 1998, Jour. Ethnobiology, 1999—2002; mem. editl. bd.:, 2002—04; co-editor: Resource Management in Amazonia: Indigenous and Folk Strategies, Advances in Economic Botany, vol. 7, 1989, Hist. Ecology Series, 1998—; contbr. articles to profl. jours., chapters to books. Decorated officer Order of the Golden Ark (Netherlands), 1993; NY Bot. Garden fellow, 1984-88, Fulbright-Hays fellow, 1980-81, Newcomb Coll. fellow, 1992-94, Conselho Nacional de Desenvolvimento Tecnológico e Científico fellow, 1988-91; grantee OAS, 1981-82, Ford Found., 1989-90, Jessie Smith Noyes Found., 1990-91, World Wildlife Fund, 1991-92, 2003, Tulane U., 1992, Wenner-Gren Found., 1993-94; apptd. to 60th and 61st Coll. Disting. Lectrs., Sigma Xi, 1997-99; recipient Outstanding Book of Yr. award Soc. Econ. Botany. Fellow Am. Anthrop. Assn.; mem. Soc. Ethnobotanists (India), Soc. Ethnobiology, Soc. Anthropology of Lowland S.Am. (pres. 2002-05), Soc. Etnobiologia e Etnoecologia, Phi Beta Kappa (pres. Alpha of La. 1997-98), Phi Kappa Phi. Office: Tulane U Dept Anthropology 1021 Audubon St New Orleans LA 70118-5238 Office Phone: 504-865-5336.

BALES, EUGENE HAMLIN, retired secondary school educator; b. Kansas City, Kans. s. Eugene Leroy Bales and Dorothy Hamlin; m. Eleanor Joan Sutton, Dec. 19, 1939; children: Ellen, Sarah. BSEd, N.W. Mo. State U., 1969, MA in History, 1975. Cert. tchr. Mo. H.S. social studies tchr. Orrick (Mo.) Sch. Dist., 1969—70; jr. H.S. social studies tchr. South Page Sch. Dist., College Springs, Iowa, 1970—77; jr. H.S. grammar and writing tchr. Savannah (Mo.) Sch. Dist., 1977—87, title I elem. remedial math. tchr., 1987—2000. Author: Rudolph Encouraged by His Therapist, 1997; contbr. short stories, poems, articles to lit. publs. Actor in theatre productions Andrew County Fair, Savannah, 1999, 2001, 2003; vol. bell ringer Salvation Army, St. Joseph, Mo., 2004; actor Andrew County Fair Theater; del. state nominating bd. Dem. Party, Des Moines, 1971. Recipient 4th Pl. short stories contest, Writers' Digest mag., 1964, prize for short story, Ozark Creative Writers, 2000, award sr. writing contest, Greyhound Bus, 2001. Mem.: Mo. Writers Guild, Iowa State Edn. Assn. (del.), Savannah Tchrs. Assn. (treas.). Democrat. Mem. Christian Ch. Avocations: reading, walking, golf, art galleries, travel. Home: 1000 W Main St Savannah MO 64485 E-mail: gjbales@centurytel.net.

BALES, FLOSSIE KATHLEEN, retired librarian, systems analyst; b. El Dorado, Kans., Sept. 4, 1938; d. Francis Justus and Flossie Mae (Smith) O'Reilly; m. Royal Eugene Bales, Apr. 16, 1960; children: David Scott, Elizabeth Laurel. B in Music Edn. magna cum laude, Wichita State U., 1960; MLS, U. Calif., Berkeley, 1968. Tchr. music Larkspur (Calif.)/Corte Madera Sch., 1961-62; libr. clk. Palo Alto (Calif.) Pub. Libr., 1962-67; cataloger Stanford (Calif.) U., 1968; children's libr. Santa Clara County, Los Altos, Calif., 1975; cataloger Santa Clara County Libr., San Jose, Calif., 1976-78; instr. cataloging U. Calif., Berkeley, 1982, 84-85; with user svcs. staff Rsch. Librs. Group, Mt. View, Calif., 1978-80, systems analyst, 1980-89, mgr. online applications, 1989-92, sr. analyst, 1993—97, QA mgr., 1997—2000; ret., 2000. Contbr. articles to profl. jours. Chairperson curriculum com. Los Lomitas Sch., Menlo Park, Calif., 1975-77; bd. dirs. El Camino Youth Symphony, Los Altos, 1983-87, co-pres., 1985-87. Mem. ALA (chairperson cataloging and classification sect. 1991-92, various appts. 1982—), Nat. Info. Standards Orgn. (chairperson standards devel. com. 1990-92). Democrat. Avocations: music, gardening, needlecrafts, theater. Home: 1225 Sherman Ave Menlo Park CA 94025-6012 E-mail: bales.r@sbcglobal.net.

BALES, GERTRUDE A., retired otolaryngologist; b. Greensboro, N.C., 1926; MD, U. Rochester, 1952. Diplomate Am. Bd. Otolaryngology. Intern Strong Meml. Hosp., Rochester, N.Y., 1952-53, resident, 1953-55; clin. assoc. prof. otolaryngology U. Rochester, 1968-96; chief of staff Canandaigua (N.Y.) VA Med. Ctr., 1993—96; ret., 1996. Fellow ACS; mem. Am. Acad. Otolaryngology/Head and Neck Surgery.

BALES, JOHN FOSTER, III, retired lawyer; b. Springfield, Mass., July 17, 1940; s. John Foster II and Jean (Torrence) Bales; m. Jane Lee Black, Sept. 11, 1965; children: Patricia, Elizabeth, Susan. BS in Engring., Princeton U., 1962; LLB, U. Va., 1965; LLM, Georgetown U., 1972. Bar: U.S. Supreme Ct. 1972. Staff atty. U.S. SEC, Washington, 1970-72; assoc. Morgan, Lewis & Bockius, Phila., 1972-76, ptnr., 1976—2001. Bd. dirs. Ind. Publs., Inc., 1986—. Trustee U.S. com. refugees, 1998—2001; vice-chmn. bd. trustees Ind. Presbyn. Med. Ctr., Phila., 1988—95, Acad. Natural Scis., Phila., 1995—; trustee Presbyn. Found., Phila., 1995—96, Immigration Refugee Svcs. Am., 1998—2001. Mem.: ABA, Colo. Bar Assn., Phila. Bar Assn., Pa. Bar Assn., Va. Bar Assn. Republican. E-mail: johnfbales@hotmail.com.

BALES, KENT ROSLYN, language educator; b. Anthony, Kans., June 19, 1936; s. Roslyn Francis and Irene E. (Brinkman) B.; m. Maria Gyorei, Aug. 25, 1958; children— Thomas Imre, Elizabeth Irene BA, Yale U., 1958; MA, San Jose State U., 1963; PhD, U. Calif., Berkeley, 1967. Instr. Menlo Sch., Menlo Park, Calif., 1958-63; acting instr. U. Calif., Berkeley, 1967; asst. prof. English U. Minn., Mpls., 1967-71, assoc. prof. English, 1971-82, prof. English, 1982—, chmn. dept. English, 1983—88, 2000—03. Vis. fellow Lit. Studies Inst., Budapest, Hungary, 1973-74, 80-81, 88-89. Contbr. chpts. to books and articles to profl. jours. Fulbright lectr., Budapest, 1980, Fulbright Rsch. fellow, Budapest, 1988-89. Mem. MLA, Midwest Modern Lang. Assn. Home: 2700 Irving Ave S Minneapolis MN 55408-1049 Office: Univ Minn Dept English 207 Church St SE Minneapolis MN 55455-0134 E-mail: bales@umn.edu.

BALES, ROYAL EUGENE, philosophy educator; b. Pratt, Kans., Sept. 23, 1934; s. Harold Thomas and Gladys (German) B.; m. Flossie Kathleen O'Reilly, Apr. 16, 1960; children— David Scott, Elizabeth Laurel B.Music Edn. cum laude, U. Wichita, 1956, MA, 1960; PhD, Stanford U., 1968. Tchr. music Kans. Pub. Schs., 1956-57, 59-60; instr. philosophy Menlo Coll., Atherton, Calif., 1962-69, prof., 1970-2000, prof. emeritus, 2000—, chmn. social scis. and humanities, 1971-74, dean liberal arts, 1974-79, provost, 1979-87, standing mem. president's adv. council, 1971-87. Vis. fellow Harris-Manchester Coll., Oxford U., 1994, 98; Wong vis. prof. Guangdong U. of Law and Bus., Guangzhou, China, 1999. Contbg. author: About Philosophy, 2006; contbr. articles to profl. jours. Pres. El Camino Youth Symphony Assn., 1985-87; bd. govs. Harris-Manchester Coll., Oxford, 1994—. Scholar and fellow U. Wichita, 1952-60, Stanford U., 1966-67; prin. investigator NSF, Menlo Coll./Stanford, 1971-72; research grantee Stanford-Warsaw Exchange, Poland, 1969-70. Mem. Am. Philos. Assn., Soc. for Bus. Ethics, Save San Francisco Bay Assn., Phi Mu Alpha Sinfonia. Democrat. Avocations: classical music, designing and constructing furniture. Home: 1255 Sherman Ave Menlo Park CA 94025-6012 Office: Menlo Coll Florence Moore Bldg 1000 El Camino Real Atherton CA 94027-4300 Personal E-mail: bales.r@sbcglobal.net. Business E-Mail: ebales@menlo.edu.

BALES, VIRGINIA SHANKLE, health administrator; BA in Chemistry, Emory U., Atlanta, 1971, MPH, 1977. Dep. dir. Nat. Ctr. Chronic Disease Prevention and Health Promotion Ctrs. for Disease Control and Prevention, 1988—98, dep. dir. program mgmt., 1998—2002, dir. adult and cmty. health divsn. Nat. Ctr. for Chronic Disease Prevention and Health Promotion, 2002—. Office: CDC DHHS Mailstop D14 1600 Clifton Rd NE Atlanta GA 30329-4018

BALEY, THOMAS RICHARD, management consultant; b. Cleveland, June 2, 1948; s. Richard Frank and Betty (Collins) B.; m. Margaret J. Keeler, Apr. 15, 1972; children: Christopher Thomas, Timothy Robert, Peter Charles. BA in Biology, Kenyon Coll., 1970; MS in Computer Sci., Rensselaer Poly. Inst., 1974. Supr. Aetna Life Ins. Co., Hartford, Conn., 1970-76; owner Tech. Cons., Avon, Conn., 1976-86; sr. mgr. Touche Ross, Atlanta, 1986-90; nat. program dir. banking Broadway & Seymour, Inc., 1990-97, group v.p. computer mgmt. sci. corp., 1997-99; sr. v.p. Computer Assn. Internat., 2000—. Contbr. numerous revs. to Computing Revs., 1972—. Dir. Avon Library Bd., 1980-85; bd. dirs. Avon chpt. United Fund, 1983-86. Mem. IEEE, Assn. Computing Machinery (chmn. bus. computers sect.), Assn. Systems Mgmt., Data Processing Mgmt. Assn. Avocations: whale conservation, scuba diving. Home: 3359 Stovehill Ct SE Marietta GA 30067-5163 Office: Tech Consulting Group 3359 Stovehill Ct SE Marietta GA 30067 Office Phone: 770-425-8777. E-mail: tbaley@tccww.com.

BALFE, ROBERT CRAMER, III, prosecutor; b. West Palm Beach, Fla., 1968; m. Jennifer Balfe; children: Ryan, Luke. BS, Ark. State Univ.; JD, Univ. Ark., 1994. Bar: Ark. 1995. Dep. pros. atty. Benton County, Ark., 1995—2001, pros. atty., 2001—04; U.S. atty. (we. dist.) Ark. U.S. Dept. Justice, 2004—. Office: US Atty 414 Parker St Fort Smith AR 72901

BALFOUR, HENRY HALLOWELL, JR., medical educator, researcher, physician, writer; b. Jersey City, Feb. 9, 1940; s. Henry Hallowell and Dorothy Kathryn (Dietze) B.; m. Carol Lenore Pries, Sept. 23, 1967; children: Henry Hallowell III, Anne Lenore, Caroline Dorothy. BA, Princeton U., 1962; MD, Columbia U., 1966. Diplomate Am. Bd. Pediatrics. Attending pediatrician Wright-Patterson AFB, Ohio, 1968-70; asst. prof. U. Minn., Mpls., 1972-75, assoc. prof., 1975-79, prof. lab. medicine, pathology and pediatrics, 1979—, dir. div. clin. virology, 1974—. Mem. Nat. AIDS Clin. Trials Group NIH, 1987—, chmn. virology com. Nat. AIDS Clin. Trials Group, 1989-92, mem. exec. com., 1992-94; vice chmn. ACTG exec. com., 1994; prin. investigator Internat. Ctr. for Antiviral Rsch. and Epidemiology (I CARE), 1995—. Author: (with Ralph C. Heussner) Herpes Diseases and Your Health, 1984; contbr. numerous sci. articles to profl. jours. Mem. Am. Soc. Microbiology, Soc. Pediatric Rsch., Am. Pediatric Soc., Infectious Disease Soc. Am Lutheran. Avocations: oenophile, francophile, fishing, travel. Home: Box 100 PO Box 100 Annandale MN 55302-0100 Office: U Minn Health Sci Ctr MMC 437 Mayo 420 Delaware St SE Minneapolis MN 55455-0392 Office Phone: 612-626-5670. Business E-Mail: balfo001@umn.edu.

BALIBAN, JEFFREY LEE, accountant, economist; b. Phila., Jan. 8, 1956; s. Norman and Claire (Cohen) B.; m. Dorothy Renee Dessalet, Sept. 1, 1979; children: Adam David, Rachel Elizabeth, Elliott Ian. BS in Acctg., Fairleigh Dickinson Univ., 1977; MA in Econs., U. Tex., 1995. CPA, Pa., Tex. Acct. Ernst & Whinney, N.Y.C., 1977-79, Campos & Stratis, Phila., London, Dallas, 1979-99, ptnr., 1985, exec. com., 1989-96; ptnr. KPMG, LLP, 1999—, ptnr.-in-charge forensic & litigation svcs. western region, 2000—. Contract instr. Ctr. Prof. Edn. Inc.; spkr., presenter in field. Contbr. articles to profl. jours. Tchr., youth dir. Unity Group, Dallas, 1993-94, mem. fin. com., 1994. Mem. AICPA, Am. Soc. Appraisers, Am. Arbitration Assn., Nat. Assn. Cert. Fraud Examiners, Inst. Dirs. London, Pa. Inst. CPAs, Tex. Soc. CPAs (mem. mgmt. svcs. com. Dallas chpt.). Home: 32 Washington Ave Westport CT 06880-2548

BALICK, KENNETH D., management consultant; b. Albany, N.Y., Nov. 27, 1960; s. Sidney M. and Carole (Kaufmann) B. BS in Indsl. and Labor Rels., Cornell U., 1983; MPA, Harvard U., 1986. Legis. aide to mem. Japan Parliament, Tokyo, 1983-84; dir. Asian programs Carnegie Coun. on Ethics and Internat. Affairs, N.Y.C., 1986-90; pres. Trans-Pacific Consulting Group, N.Y.C., 1990-94; asst. to CEO Nomura Securities Internat., Inc., N.Y.C., 1994-97; dir. internat. bus. devel. Capital Co. of Am., N.Y.C., 1998-99; founder, pres. RockBridge Global Advisors, 1999—. Pub. spkr. in field. Henry Luce scholar. Mem. Coun. on Fgn. Rels.

BALIGA, RAGAVENDRA RAMAKRISHNA, cardiologist, researcher; b. Mangalore, India, Mar. 17, 1960; s. Ram Krishna and Shanthi Baliga; m. Jayashree Baliga, May 1, 1990; children: Anoop, Neena. MBBS, St. John's Med. Coll., Bangalore, India, 1984; MD, Bangalore Med. Coll., 1988; MBA, U. Mich., Ann Arbor, 2004. Diplomate Nat. Bd. Medicine, New Delhi, 1988; mem. Royal Coll. Physicians, Eng., 1991. Intern, resident St. John's Med. Coll. Hosp., Victoria Hosp., Bangalore, 1983-87; sr. house officer Nat. Spinal Injuries Ctr., Stoke Mandeville, England, 1988-89; clin. rsch. fellow St. Mary's Hosp. Med. Sch., London, 1989-90; clin. tutor U. Aberdeen, Scotland, 1990-92; registrar in cardiology Hammersmith Hosp., London, 1993-95; scientist Harvard Med. Sch./Brigham & Women's Hosp., Boston, 1995-97; heart failure fellow Boston U. Med. Sch., 1997-98; heart transplant fellow U. Tex. Southwestern Med. Sch., Dallas, 1998-99; asst. prof. medicine U. Mich., Ann Arbor, 1999—2005; dir. Cardiology Sect. Ohio State U. Hosp. East, 2005—. Clin. prof. internal medicine Ohio State U., Columbus, Ohio, 2005—. Editor-in-chief St. John's Jour. Medicine, 1988; author: 200 Short Cases in Clinical Medicine, 1993, Multiple Choice Questions in Clinical Medicine, 1994, 250 Short Cases in Clinical Medicine, 3d edit., 2003; editor University of Michigan Cardiology Textbook, 2003; mem. editl. bd. Current Journal Review of American College of Cardiology, 2003. Recipient Nat. Rsch. Svc. award NIH, 1995-97, Astra Found. travel award, Eng., 1995. Fellow: Royal Coll. Physicians Edinburgh, Am. Coll. Cardiology; mem.: Soc. Authors Great Britain, Royal Coll. Surgeons and Physicians Glasgow. Avocations: photography, travel. Home: 4682 Tattersall Ct Columbus OH 43230 Office Phone: 619-257-3044.

BALIS, MOSES EARL, biochemist, educator; b. Phila., June 19, 1921; s. Harry and Frances (Spector) B.; m. Bernice M. Lamborg, Dec. 30, 1945; children— Frances Andrea, Ellen Joyce. BA, Temple U., 1943; MS, U. Pa., 1947, PhD, 1949. With Sloan-Kettering Inst., 1949-87, head nucleoprotein metabolism sect., 1957—, asso. mem., 1960-65, mem., 1965-87, chief div. cell metabolism, 1970-87; chair inst. senate, 1981-83; cons. Sloan-Kettering Inst., 1987-91; asso. prof. Med. Coll. Cornell U., 1954-66, prof. biochemistry, 1966-87, chmn. biochemistry unit, 1969-74; owner M.E. Balis, Inc., Fla. Vis. lectr. Adelphi U., 1963-64; cons. chemistry dept. Manhattan Coll., 1981-86; mem. study sects. Am. Cancer Soc., NIH.; mem. planning com. Nat. Cancer Plan; mem. rev. com. Nat. Large Bowel Cancer Program, 1977-81; pres. Med. Research Investment Fund, 1984-89. Mem. editorial bd. Cancer Rsch., 1969-73; assoc. editor, 1974-82. Served to lt. (j.g.) USNR, 1944-46. Recipient Research Career award USPHS, 1963 Mem. Am. Chem. Soc. (past sect. chmn.), AAAS, Am. Cancer Soc., Am. Soc. Biol Chemistry and Molecular Biology, Harvey Soc., Am. Assn. Cancer Rsch., Sigma Xi. Achievements include research, numerous publs. on metabolism of purines in normal and malignant tissues; determined biochem. action of anti-cancer drugs, biochemical nature of genetic defects. Home and Office: 2792 Donnelly Dr Apt 2512 Lantana FL 33462 Personal E-mail: mebalis@bellsouth.net.

BALISTRERI, WILLIAM FRANCIS, pediatric gastroenterologist; b. Geneva, NY, June 24, 1944; s. Francis William and Mary (Yannotti) B.; m. Rebecca Ann McLeod, May 31, 1969; children: Anthony, Jennifer, William Phillip. Student, St. Bonaventure U., 1962; BA, SUNY, Buffalo, 1966; MD, U. Buffalo, 1970. Diplomate Am. Bd. Pediat., Sub. Bd. Pediat. Gastroenterology. Intern Children's Hosp. Med. Ctr., Cin., 1970-71, resident, 1971-72, postdoctoral fellow, 1972-74; rsch. fellow Mayo Clinic, Rochester, Minn., 1974; pediat. instr. Sch. Medicine U. Cin., 1972-74; staff pediatrician U.S. Naval Hosp., Phila., 1974-76; asst. prof. pediat. U. Pa. Sch. Medicine, 1976-78; from assoc. prof. pediat. to prof. medicine U. Cin. Sch. Medicine, 1978-91, prof. pediat., 1983—; prof. medicine U. Cin., 1991—. Bd. dirs. Am. Bd. Pediat., 1991-97, chmn. sub-bd. of pediatric gastroenterology, 1991-93; mem. ednl. coun. Nat. Hepatology Detection and Treatment Prevention Program, 1993-98. Author, editor: Pediatric Hepatology, 1990, Pediatric Gastroenterology and Nutrition, 1990, Jour. Pediatrics, 1995—, Liver Disease in Children 2000, 2005. Lt. comdr. USN, 1974-76. Recipient Disting. Alumnus award U. Buffalo Sch. Medicine, 1993, Disting. Alumnus award, 2005. Mem. Am. Assn. for Study of Liver Disease (pres. 1999-2000), N.Am. Soc. for Pediat. Gastroenterology and Nutrition (editor-in-chief Western Hemisphere Jour. 1991-95, pres. 1985-86), Am. Gastroenterol. Assn. Roman Catholic. Avocations: skiing, hiking. Office: Children's Hosp Med Ctr 3333 Burnet Ave Cincinnati OH 45229-3026 Office Phone: 513-636-4594. Business E-Mail: william.balistreri@cchmc.org.

BALK, ALFRED WILLIAM, journalist; b. Oskaloosa, Iowa, July 24, 1930; s. Leslie William and Clara Irene (Buell) B.; m. Phyllis Lorraine Munter, June 7, 1952; children: Laraine M., Diane M. Student, Augustana Coll., Rock Island, Ill., 1948—49; BS, Northwestern U., 1952, MS, 1953. Reporter Rock Island Argus, 1946-50; newswriter, prodr. WBBM (CBS), Chgo., 1952-53; reporter Chgo. Sun-Times, 1956; mag. writer, pub. rels. J. Walter Thompson Co., Chgo., 1957-58; freelance writer nat. mags., including spl. writer Saturday Evening Post, 1958-66; feature editor Saturday Rev., 1966-68, editor at large, 1968-69; vis. scholar Russell Sage Found., 1968-69; lectr. journalism, editor Columbia Journalism Rev., 1969-73; editor World Press Rev., 1974, editor, pub., 1975-84, editl. dir., 1985-86, editl. cons., contbg. editor, 1986-94; mng. editor IEEE Spectrum, NYC, 1989-91; assoc. prof. Syracuse (NY) U., 1991-94; freelance writer, cons., 1994—. Cons., rapporteur 20th Century Fund Task Force on Nat. News Coun., 1971-72, Ford Found., Markle Found.; faculty Bread Loaf Writers Conf., Middlebury, Vt., 1971; exec. sec. NY Gov.'s Com. on Employment Minority Groups in News Media, 1968-69; adv. com. World Press Inst., 1984-96. Author: The Free List: Property Without Taxes, 1970, A Free and Responsive Press, 1973, The Myth of American Eclipse: The New Global Age, 1990, Movie Palace Masterpiece: Saving Syracuse's Loew's State/Landmark Theatre, 1998, The Rise of Radio, from Marconi through the Golden Ages, 2005; co-editor: Our Troubled Press, 1971. Bd. dir. Am. Jour. Nursing Co., 1990—93, Landmark Theatre Found., 1996—99. Mem. Am. Soc. Mag. Editors (exec. coun. 1977-83), Soc. Mag. Writers (pres. 1967), Soc. Profl. Journalists, Overseas Press Club (gov. 1978-79), Century Assn. Home: 13225 Michigan Ave Huntley IL 60142-7480

BALK, ROBERT A., medical educator; BA, U. Mo., Kansas City, 1976, MD, 1978. Resident internal medicine U. Mo., Kansas City, 1978—81; fellow pulmonary and critical care medicine U. Ark., Little Rock, 1981—83, instr. medicine, 1981—83, asst. prof. medicine, 1983—85; staff physician Little Rock VA Med. Ctr., 1983—85; asst. prof. medicine Rush-Presbyn.-St. Luke's Med. Ctr., Chgo., 1985—88, assoc. prof., 1988—95, prof. medicine, 1995—, asst. dir. sect. pulmonary medicine, 1985—90, med. dir. respiratory care svcs., 1985-93, med. dir. noninvasive respiratory care unit, 1985—87, co-dir. med. intensive care unit, 1986—88, dir. med. intensive care unit, 1988-95, assoc. dir. sect. pulmonary & crit. care medicine, 1993—97, assoc. dir. sect. critical care medicine, 1995—2002, dir. pulmonary & critical care medicine fellowship tng. program, 1994—, dir. pulmonary and critical care medicine, 2002—; J. Bailey Carter prof. med. ctr. Rush Med. Coll., Chgo., 2002. Contbr. articles to profl. jours. Recipient Dedicated Svc. & Superior Individual Effort in Patient Care Alice Sachs Meml. award, 1991, Alfred Soffer Rsch. award, Am. Coll. Chest Physicians, 1995, Take Wing award, U. Mo.-Kansas City Sch. Medicine, 1998. Office: Rush Univ Med Ctr 1653 W Congress Pkwy Chicago IL 60612-3833 E-mail: rbalk@rush.edu.

BALKA, SIGMUND RONELL, lawyer; b. Phila., Aug. 1, 1935; s. I. Edwin and Jane (Chernicoff) B.; m. Elinor Bernstein, May 29, 1966. AB, Williams Coll., 1956; JD, Harvard U., 1959. Bar: Pa. and D.C. 1961, N.Y. 1969, U.S. Supreme Ct. 1966. Sr. atty. Lilco, Mineola, N.Y., 1969-70; v.p., gen. counsel Brown Boveri Corp., North Brunswick, N.J., 1970-75; asst. gen. counsel Power Authority State N.Y., N.Y.C., 1975-80; gen. counsel Krasdale Foods, Inc., N.Y.C., 1980—. Pres. Graphic Arts Coun. N.Y., 1980—. Chmn. Hunts Point Environ. Protection Coun., N.Y.C., 1980—, Soc. for a Better Bronx, 1985—; chair fellows, mem. vis. com. Williams Coll. Mus. of Art, 1996—99; exec. com. bd. trustees Queens Mus. of Art, 2001—; chmn. law com. N.Y.C. Cmty. Bd. 6, Queens, 1980—88, chmn. econ. devel. com., 1988—99; chmn. Bronx Borough Pres.'s Adv. Com. on Resource Recovery, 1988—90; bd. dirs. Bronx Arts Coun., 1981—2003, Greater N.Y. Met. Food Coun., 1986—, Jewish Repertory Theatre, 1987—, chmn., 2001—. Fellow Am. Bar Found., N.Y. Bar Found.; mem. ABA (co-chmn. pro bono project corp. law dept. 1986-88, chmn. 1988-90, com. of corp. gen. counsel 1974—, planning chmn. 1994-96, membership chmn. 1996-98, pro bono chair 2000—), Am. Corp. Counsel Assn. (bd. dirs. Met. N.Y. chpt. 1987—, bd. dirs. Found. 1992-99), Assn. Bar City N.Y. Office: Krasdale Foods Inc 400 Food Center Dr Bronx NY 10474-7098 Office Phone: 718-378-1100 x2125.

BALKE, FRANK H., language educator, director; arrived in U.S., 1954; s. Bruno and Annemarie Balke; m. Nancy Gardner; children: Anacka, Koert. BS chemistry, Univ. Okla., Norman, Okla., 1961, MA German, 1964; PhD, Univ. Oreg., Eugene, Oreg., 1980. Instr. State Coll. Iowa, Cedar Falls, Iowa, 1964—69; asst. prof. Univ. No. Iowa, Cedar Falls, Iowa, 1969—72, Oreg. Coll. of Edn., Monmouth, Oreg., 1972—80; assoc. prof. Western Oreg. State Coll., Monmouth, Oreg., 1980—86; full prof. Western Oreg. Univ., Monmouth, Oreg., 1987—. Dir. Oreg. Summer State Bd., Monmouth, Oreg., 1975—, Internat. Studies, Monmouth, Oreg., 1987—2000, Internat. Study Abroad, Monmouth, Oreg., 2000—. Author: A Summer Study Abroad Effect of Study Abroad on Students of German, 1980. Soccer ofcl. NISOA, OISA, SSRA, Salem, Oreg., 1985—. Recipient Tchr. of the Yr., Conf. of Oreg. Language Tchr., 1979, Hon. Citizen, C. of C., Austria, 1984. Mem.: Am. Assn. Tchrs. of German. Achievements include Initiated and directed internat. study abroad at Oreg. Coll. of Edn., now Western Oreg. Univ; development of and initiated cert. for German tchg. major at OCE and the internat. studies academic program of Western Oreg. Avocations: skiing, tennis, theater, reading, stamps. Office: Western Oreg Univ Office of Study Abroad Monmouth OR 97361

BALKE, VICTOR H., bishop; b. Meppen, Ill., Sept. 29, 1931; s. Bernard H. and Elizabeth A. (Knese) B. BA in Philosophy, St. Mary of Lake Sem., Mundelein, Ill., 1954, STB in Theology, 1956, MA in Religion, 1057, STL in Theology, 1958; MA in English, St. Louis U., 1964, PhD, 1973. Priest Roman Cath. Ch., 1958. Asst. pastor, Springfield, Ill., 1958—62; chaplain St. Joseph Home Aged, Springfield, 1962—63; procurator, instr. Diocesan Sem., Springfield, 1963—70, rector, instr., 1970—76; ordained, installed 6th bishop Crookston, Minn., 1976—. Mem.: Lions, KC. Office: Chancery Office PO Box 610 Crookston MN 56716-0610*

BALKIN, JACK M., law educator; b. Kansas City, Mo., Aug. 13, 1956; AB, Harvard U., 1978, JD, 1981; PhD, Cambridge (Eng.) U., 1995. Bar: NY 1983. Law clk. US Ct. Appeals (5th cir.), Houston, 1981-82; assoc. Cravath, Swaine & Moore, N.Y.C., 1982-84; vis. asst. prof. U. Mo. Law Sch., Kansas City, 1984-85, asst. prof., 1985-88; vis. assoc. prof. U. Tex., Austin, 1988-89, prof. and Graves, Dougherty Hearon & Moody centennial faculty fellow, 1989-91, Charles Tilford McCormick prof., 1991-94; M.D. Anderson vis. prof. law Queen Mary and Westfield Coll., U. London, 1991-92; vis. prof. Yale Law Sch., New Haven, 1992-93, Lafayette S. Foster prof., 1994—98, dir. Info. Soc. Project, 1997—, Knight prof. Constl. Law and the First Amendment, 1998—. Vis. prof. Harvard U., 2000. Office: Yale Law Sch PO Box 208215 New Haven CT 06520-8215 E-mail: jack.balkin@yale.edu.*

BALKMAN, THAD, lawyer, state representative; b. Long Beach, Calif., Oct. 23, 1971; s. James and Sonya (Ward) Balkman; m. Amy Balkman; children: Adeline, Jackson, Miles. BA in Polit. sci., Brigham Young U., 1994; JD, U. Okla., 1998. Bar: Okla. Sales rep. Zee Safety, 1994—95; assoc. Stanley M. Ward Law Office, 1998—2001; rep. Ho. of Reps., State of Okla., Okla. City, 2000—. Minority whip Okla. Ho. of Reps., Okla. City, 2000—; vice chmn. mental health com. Okla. Ho. of Reps., Okla. City, 2000—, mem. econ., devel., higher edn., judiciary coms., 2000—. Various positions in leadership, programs chair Last Frontier Coun-Sooner Dist. BSA, Norman, Okla., 1999—. Mem.: Okla. Bar Assn., Cleve. County Bar Assn. Republican. Office: 2300 N Lincoln Blvd Rm 327 Oklahoma City OK 73105 Home and Office: 3403 36th Ave NE Norman OK 73026 E-mail: balkmanth@lsb.state.ok.us.

BALKOWIEC, AGNIESZKA ZOFIA, science educator, researcher; b. Sokolow Podlaski, Poland, Sept. 30, 1968; d. Anna and Jerzy Michal Balkowiec. MD, Med. U. Warsaw, Poland, 1993, PhD, 1995. Instr. physiology Med. U. Warsaw, 1993—95, asst. prof., 1995—99; rsch. assoc. Case Western Res. U., Cleve., 1997—2001, instr. neuroscis., 2001—02; asst. prof. Oreg. Health & Sci. U., Portland, 2002—. Contbr. articles to profl. jours.; ad hoc reviewer Neuroscience, Brain Rsch. Recipient Sci. award, Polish Min. Health and Social Welfare, 1994, 1996, Prime Min. of Poland, 1996; fellow, Found. Polish Sci., 1995; grantee, Am. Heart Assn., 2002—, NIH, 2004—, Nat. Heart, Lung and Blood Inst., 2004—. Mem.: Nat. Inst. Health, Am. Heart Assn. (basic cardiovas. scis. coun. 2002, grantee 2002—), Soc. Neurosci. Achievements include discovery of the role of activity of nerve cells in regulation of growth factors; invention of setup for immunodetection of growth factors released from neurons following electrical stimulation. Avocations: travel, gourmet cooking, classical music. Office: Oregon Health & Sci U 611 SW Campus Dr Portland OR 97239 Office Phone: 503-418-0190. Business E-Mail: balkowie@ohsu.edu.

BALKRISHNAN, RAJESH, education educator; s. Pv and Shanta Balkrishnan; life ptnr. George W. Simmons. BS, U. Bombay, 1995; PhD, U. N.C., Chapel Hill, N.C., 1999. Asst. prof. Wake Forest U., Winston-Salem, NC, 1999—2003; assoc. prof. U. Tex., Houston, 2003—04; merrell dow prof. Ohio State U., Columbus, Ohio, 2005—. Contbr. articles pub. to over 100 profl. jour. Recipient Brooks Scholar in Academic Medicine, Wake Forest U., 2001-2003. D-Liberal. Hindu. Avocations: movies, classical music, reading. Home: 1056 Pennsylvania Ave Columbus OH 43201 Office: Ohio State Univ 500 West 12th St Columbus OH 43210 Office Phone: 614-292-6415. Office Fax: 614-292-1335. Personal E-mail: rbgws@sbcglobal.net. Business E-Mail: balkrishnan.1@osu.edu.

BALL, ALAN, screenwriter; b. Atlanta, 1957; Student in theater, Fla. State U. Founding mem., writer, actor, dir. Alarm Dog Rep. Playwright: The M Word, 1991, Five Women Wearing the Same Dress, 1993, Made For a Woman, Bachelor Holiday, Your Mother's Butt and The Amazing Adventures of Tense Guy; Screenwriter, co-prodr. (feature film) American Beauty, 1999 (Oscar for best screenplay 1999, Golden Globe for best screenplay motion picture 2000, Satellite award for best original screenplay 2000; best screenplay BFCA award, DGA award, ALFA award, SEFCA award and WGA Screen award 2000), The M Word, 2004; screenwriter, creator, exec. prodr. (tv series) Grace Under Fire, 1993; co-exec. prodr. (tv series) Cybill, 1995; exec. prodr., creator (tv series) Oh Grow Up, 1999; screenwriter, dir., exec. prod. (tv series) Six Feet Under, 2001-2005 (Emmy for outstanding director for a drama series 2002). Office: c/o Andrew Cannava United Talent Agy 9560 Wilshire Blvd Fl 5 Beverly Hills CA 90212-2401*

BALL, AMY CATHERINE, education program manager; b. Abingdon, Va., Aug. 24, 1975; d. Willis and Darlene Crabtree Ball. BA in sci., Va. Tech. U., 1996; M, Hollins U., 1998. Sales mktg. Farm Success, Abingdon, 1996—98, Kirklands, Roanoke, Va., 1998; mktg. dir. CFC Inc., Culpeper, Va., 1999—2000; educator The Crisis Ctr., Bristol, Va., 2000—02; edn. program dir. Washington County Schs., Abingdon, 2002—. Mem. adv. bd. CAUSE, Emory, Va., 2000—, Teen Dating Violence Coalition, Charlottesville, Va., 2001—02. Chmn. Bristol Coalition, 2002. Va. Exposition grantee, 1994. Mem.: Internat. Boer Goat Assoc., Va. Forage Coun., Am. Angus Assn. Democrat. Home: 26912 Denton Valley Rd Abingdon VA 24211 Office: Damascus Neighborhood Academy 21308 Monroe Rd Abingdon VA 24236

BALL, ARMAND BAER, former association executive, consultant; b. Dubach, La., Sept. 30, 1930; s. Armand Baer and Lovera (Sanderson) B.; m. Beverly Jane Hodges, Sept. 15, 1957; children: Kathryn Lynn, Robin Armand. BA, La. Coll., 1951; MRE, Southwestern Bapt. Theol. Sem., 1953; MS, George Williams Coll., 1960. Royal Ambassador dir. Fla. Bapt. Conv., Jacksonville, 1953-57; program dir. Woodlawn Boys' Club, Chgo., 1957-58; camp/youth dir. YMCA, Nashville, 1958-62; exec. dir. YMCA Camps Widjiwagan/duNord, St. Paul YMCA, 1962-74; exec. v.p. Am. Camping Assn., Martinsville, Ind., 1974-88; cons., 1988—; assoc. Campaign Assocs., Phila., 1989—. Author: (with Beverly H. Ball) Basic Camp Management, 2004; editor: A Cost Study of Resident Camps, 1985; Internat. Camping Fellowship newsletter, 1987-97; co-editor: Business and Finance, Site and Facilities; Trendlines newsletter. Cons. Ctr. for Disease Control, St. Petersburg (Russia) Children's Camps, Malaysian Tourist Bd., Pan-Am. Inst. of Phys. Edn. (Venezuela), Heritage Conservation and Recreation Svc., Project Reach, Boy Scouts Am., United Ch. of Christ, YMCA, Episcopal Ch.; mem. Internat. Camping Fellowship; bd. dirs., pres. Sanibel-Captiva Conservation Found.; bd. mem. Cmty. Housing Resources, Inc.; chair Sanibel Parks and Recreation Com.; mem. adv. com. Seaworld and Busch Gardens Camp; mem. adv. bd. Ctr. for Environ. and Sustainability Edn., Fla. Gulf Coast U. Recipient Disting. Svc. award Am. Camping Assn., 1989, Druszba award, 2002; named Citizen Yr., Sanibel, Fla., 1999, Disting. Alumni Yr., Aurora U., 2003, Disting. Alumni award, George Williams Coll./Aurora U., 2003. Mem. Am. Soc. Assn. Execs. (cert. assoc. exec. life), World Future Soc., Audubon Soc., Canadian Camping Assn., Kiwanis (Hixon award). Home and Office: 1351 Middle Gulf Dr Apt 2A Sanibel FL 33957-4631 Office Phone: 239-472-0536. Personal E-mail: alphaball@worldnet.att.net.

BALL, BETTY JEWEL, retired social worker, consultant; b. Sherman, Tex., Aug. 9, 1933; d. Emmett Jesse and Ethel Viola (Chesnut) B. BS, Okla. Bapt. U., 1954; M.Religious Edn., Carver Sch., 1958; MSW, Smith Coll., 1964. Cert. and lic. clin. social workers, Ill. Psychiat. social worker Inst. for Juvenile Rsch., Chgo., 1964-66; dir. child devel. ctr. Infant Welfare Soc. Chgo., 1966-71; dir. day hosp. for children Madden Mental Health Ctr., Chgo., 1971-78; child and adolescent coord. Ill. Dept. Mental Health, Chgo., 1978-83; pvt. practice social work cons. Hoffman Estates, Ill., 1983-93. Home and Office: 1225 Via Rafael San Marcos CA 92069-7102

BALL, BRENDA JOYCE SIVILS, retired secondary school educator; Tchr., English, AP lit. and writing Pine Bluff High Sch., Ark. Contbr. Named Ark. State English Tchr. of Yr., 1992.

BALL, CARROLL RAYBOURNE, anatomist, researcher, medical educator; b. Leakesville, Miss., Oct. 11, 1925; s. Marvin Hugh and Elizabeth (Hillman) B.; m. Jannie Vee Brooks, Sept. 5, 1947 (dec. 1954); children: Hugh Brooks, Peter Stephen; m. Sally Ann Montgomery, Mar. 22, 1963 (div. 1976); 1 child, Lou Ellen. BA, U. Miss., 1947, MS, 1948, PhD, 1963. Grad. asst. in zoology U. Miss., Oxford, 1946-48; instr. Duke U., 1948-51; instr. anatomy Med. Sch. W.Va. U., 1951-57; asst. prof. biology U. So. Miss., 1957-60; asst. prof. U. Miss. Med. Ctr., Jackson, 1963-66, assoc. prof., 1966-71, prof., 1971-99. Contbr. numerous articles to profl. jours. Pres. Jackson Civil War Round Table, 1983-84; chmn. Hist. Coker House Restoration Project, 1984-99; v.p. Magnolia chpt. Nat. Assn. Watch and Clock Collectors, 1980-82; bd. dirs. Miss. Hist. Soc., 1976-79, 85-88, 93-96. Lt. comdr. USNR, 1944-71, PTO. NIH predoctoral trainee, 1960-63; Miss. Heart Assn. grantee, 1963-66 Mem. Am. Assn. Anatomists, Soc. Exptl. Biology and Medicine, Am. Assn. Pathology, So. Assn. Anatomy, Miss. Acad. Sci., Hattiesburg Jr. C. of C. (sec. 1959-60), Order of First Families of Miss. (Gov. Gen. 2001-2003), Sigma Xi, Alpha Epsilon Delta, Theta Nu Sigma, Beta Beta Beta (pres. 1947-48), Omicron Delta Kappa, Pi Kappa Alpha (sec. 1943-44) Methodist.

BALL, DAN H., lawyer; BA cum laude, Bradley U., 1974; JD Order of the Coif, U. Mo., 1978. Bar: Mo. 1978, Ill. 1979. Ptnr., group leader Product Liability Bryan Cave LLP, St. Louis. Fellow: Am. Coll. Trial Lawyers. Office: Bryan Cave LLP One Metropolitan Sq 211 N Broadway, Ste 3600 Saint Louis MO 63102 Office Phone: 314-259-2200. Office Fax: 314-552-8200. E-mail: dhball@bryancave.com.

BALL, DAVID TERRY, university chaplain, academic administrator; b. Cin., Aug. 15, 1960; s. John Terry and Ellen (Graham) B.; m. Kim Keethler, Mar. 15, 1997; children: Anna Marie Cooper, Vincent Terry Cooper, John Terry Ball, Lisa Alison Ball. BA, Ohio Wesleyan U., 1982; MDiv, Boston U., 1986; JD, U. Calif., Berkeley, 1991; PhD, Grad. Theol. Union, Berkeley, 1998. Bar: Calif. 1991. Assoc. Farella, Braun & Martel, San Francisco, 1991-94; pastor First United Meth., Wapakoneta, Ohio, 1995-96; dir. religious life and John W. Alford Ctr. Svc.-Learning, Denison U., Granville, Ohio, 1996—. Mem. faculty Nat. Svc. Leadership Inst., San Francisco, 1999—; adj. faculty Meth. Theol. Sch., Delaware, Ohio, 1999—; regional trainer Learn and Serve Exch., Washington, 1999—; mem. exec. com. Ohio Campus Compact, Granville, 1997-2000. Author: John Calvin and the Emergence of Judicial Review, 2001; contbr. articles to profl. jours. including The Christian Century, The Nat. Law Jour., Novum Testamentum. Founder Interfaith Legal Svcs., Columbus, Ohio, 1999; bd. dirs. Family Health Svc., Newark, Ohio, 1997—, Licking County Housing Coaltion, Newark, 1997—; mem. Granville Ministerium, 1996—. Paul Harris fellow Rotary Internat., 1983-84; grantee Denison U., 1998, 2000; Martin Luther King Jr. grantee Corp. for Nat. Svc., Washington, 1997. Mem. Nat. Assn. Coll. and Univs. Chaplains, Am. Acad. Religion, State Bar Calif. Democrat. Mem. Am. Baptist Ch. Avocation: golf. Home: 231 Broadway W Granville OH 43023-1119 Office: Denison U PO Box M Granville OH 43023-0810 E-mail: ball@denison.edu.

BALL, DEBORAH LOEWENBERG, dean, education educator; BA, Mich. State U., 1976, MA, 1982, postgrad., 1981—83, PhD, 1988. Elementary classroom teacher, 1975—88; mem. faculty Mich. State U., East Lansing, 1988—96; Arthur F. Thurnau prof. U. Mich. Sch. Edn., Ann Arbor, 2000—03, William H. Payne collegiate prof. math., 2003—, interim dean, 2005—. Lead author Stds. for Tchg. sect. Profl. Stds. for Tchg. Math., Nat. Coun. Tchrs. Math., 1989—91; mem. adv. bd. Investigations in Number, Data, Space, 1991—96; mem. Commn. on Behavioral and Social Sci. Edn. Nat. Rsch. Coun., NAS, 1996—99, mem. math. learning study, 1999—2000; chair math. study panel RAND Project: Improving the Quality of Educational Research and Devel., 1999—2000; mem. commn. on undergrad. experience U. Mich., 2000—01; co-chair tchr. edn. study Internat. Commn. on Math. Instrn., 2002—; bd. trustees Math. Scis. Rsch. Inst. U. Calif., Berkeley, 2003—. Contbr. articles to profl. jours.; mem. editl. bd.: Am. Ednl. Rsch. Jour., 1999—, Jour. Ednl. Rsch., 1990—93, Elem. Sch. Jour., 1991—. Recipient Raymond B. Cattell Early Career award for programmatic rsch., Am. Ednl. Rsch. Assn., 1997, Award for outstanding Scholarship on Tchr. Edn., Assn. Colls. and Schs. of Edn. in State Univs. and Land Grant Colls. and Affiliated Pvt. Univs., 1990. Office: U Mich 4119 Sch Edn Bldg 610 E University Ann Arbor MI 48109-1259*

BALL, DONALD L., retired language educator; b. Balt., Oct. 25, 1922; s. Ambrose Markley and Daisy Gertrude (Anderson) B.; stepmother Thelma (Bonneville) B.; m. Barbara Jean Stevens, May 3, 1950; children: Helen Ball Williams, Ann S., Allison Ball Miller, Markley Ball Rizzi. BA, U. Richmond, 1948; MA, U. Del., 1951; PhD, U. N.C., 1965. Asst. mgr. resort hotels in Md. and Fla., 1948-53; instr. English Va. Mil. Inst., Lexington, 1953-57; part-time instr. U. N.C., Chapel Hill, 1957-60; faculty Coll. William and Mary, Williamsburg, Va., 1960-89, prof., 1976-89; vis. prof. English U.S. Mil. Acad., West Point, N.Y., 1984-85. Author: Samuel Richardson's Theory of Fiction, 1971, Fighting Amphibs-The LCS(L) in World War II, 1997; contbr. articles to profl. publs. Served to lt. (j.g.) USNR, 1943-46, PTO. Research grantee Coll. William and Mary, 1978. Mem. MLA. Episcopalian. Avocations: genealogy, history, music. Home: 1 Cole Ln Williamsburg VA 23185-3313

BALL, DONALD MAURY, agronomist, consultant; b. Owensboro, Ky., Aug. 5, 1945; s. William Alonzo and Mary Ruth (Waltrip) B.; Vonda Lee Hatcher, June 3, 1967; children: Kelly Wayne, Allison Lee. BS, Western Ky. U., 1968; MS, Auburn U., 1973, PhD, 1976. Cert. profl. agronomist. Ext. agronomist Auburn (Ala.) U., 1976-88, ext. agronomist/prof., 1988-97, alumni prof., 1997—2002. Mem. nat. adv. com. Alfalfa Coun., Davis, Calif., 1983-2003; tech. advisor Oreg. Tall Fescue Commn., Salem, 1990—; tech. liaison Oreg. Clover Commn., Salem, 1994—; del. Internat. Grassland Congress, Nice, France, 1989; spkr. in field. Author: Southern Forages, 1991, Practical Forage Concepts, 1999; contbr. over 550 articles to profl. and applied jours. and trade mags. Elder First Presbyn. Ch., Auburn, 1982-85. With U.S. Army, 1968-71. Recipient Superior Svc. award USDA, Washington, 1986, Extension Excellence award Auburn Univ. Alumni Assn., 1988, Alumnus of Yr. award Western Ky. Univ. Dept. Agrl., Bowling Green, 1990, Hall of Disting. Alumni, 2000. Fellow Am. Soc. Agronomy (Crops and Soils award 1984, ext. Agronomy Edn. award 1993), Crop Sci. Soc. Am.; mem. Am. Forage and Grassland Coun. (pres. 1990-91, Merit award 1984, Medallion award 1993), So. Pasture and Forage Crop Improvement Conf. (chair 1987-88). Democrat. Office: Auburn Univ Dept Agronomy & Soils Auburn AL 36849

BALL, GORDON VICTOR, literature educator, writer, editor, filmmaker, photographer; b. Paterson, NJ, Dec. 30, 1944; s. Gordon Victor and Daisy Belle Ball; m. Kathleen Louise Zobel, Aug. 11, 1980; 1 child, Daisy Barbara. BA, Davidson Coll., 1966; MA, U. N.C., 1976, PhD, 1980. Asst. prof. Old Dominion U., Norfolk, Va., 1981—85; fulbright specialist lectr. Am. Lit. Sophia, Rikkyo, Waseda Univs., Tokyo, 1983—84; from asst. to assoc. prof. Tougaloo (Miss.) Coll., 1985—89; Am. culture specialist Adam Mickiewicz U., Poznan, Poland, 1986, 1988; from asst. prof. to prof. Va. Mil. Inst., Lexington, 1989—. Sec. Com. on Poetry, Inc., NYC, 1969—; nat. adv. bd. ALSOS, Va., 2000—04. Author: '66 Frames: A Memoir, 1999; editor (with Allen Ginsberg): Allen Verbatim: Lectures on Poetry, Politics, Consciousness, 1974 (Pulitzer nominee, 1974); contbr. photographs to books and jours. Recipient numerous ind. filmaking awards, Fulbright Specialist Lectureship, Coun. Internat. Exch. of Scholars, 1983—84. Mem.: Filmakers Coop., Canyon Cinema, Modern Lang. Assn. Avocations: photography, film making. Home: 339 Sugar Creek Rd Lexington VA 24450 Office: Va Mil Inst Lexington VA 24450 Business E-Mail: ballgv@vmi.edu.

BALL, GREGORY FRANCIS, biological psychology educator; b. Washington, May 6, 1955; s. William Howard and Angela Marie (Hosinski) B. BA, Columbia U., 1977; PhD, Rutgers U., 1983. Postdoctoral fellow Rockefeller U., N.Y.C., 1983-86, asst. prof. biol. psychology, 1986-88, Boston Coll., Chestnut Hill, Mass., 1988-91; from asst. prof. to assoc. prof. biol. psychology Johns Hopkins U., Balt., 1991—98, prof., 1998—. Contbr. numerous articles to profl. jours. Charles Revson Found. biomed. fellow, 1986-88; USPHS fellow, 1983-86. Fellow APA; mem. Am. Ornithologists Union, Soc. for Neurosci., Animal Behavior Soc., Soc. for Integrated and Comparative Biology, Am. Psychol. Soc. Office: Johns Hopkins U 230 Ames Hall 3400 N Charles St Baltimore MD 21218-2680 Office Phone: 410-516-7910. E-mail: gball@jhu.edu.

BALL, HOWARD GUY, educational association administrator, educator; b. Lancaster, Ohio, Aug. 4, 1930; s. Howard Emitt and Edith Mildred (Clark) B.; married; children: Brian, Maryla. BS, Ohio State U., 1952, MS, 1969, PhD, 1972. Edn. specialist Ohio Dept. Edn., Columbus, 1964-71; assoc. prof. N.C. State U., 1971-74; mem. faculty Ala. A&M U., Normal, 1974—; prof. emeritus Ala. A&M U. (Sch. Library Media); chmn. bd. Communicon, Inc., Huntsville, Ala. Chmn. Media Svcs., Inc.; pres. Higby Inc.; dir. So. Inst. for Black Studies, 1995-96. Mem. editorial bd. Library Scene, 1979-80, Media and Methods: Early Years, 1984-85; contbr. articles to profl. jours.; authored, directed: Training of Librarians in CATV, 1975. Mem. Ala. Council Human Relations, 1978—, Ala. Democratic Council, 1978—; sec. Orgn. Inner City Govts., 1977— . Recipient NAACP Community award, 1976, Raleigh C. of C. educator's award, 1973 Mem. ALA, Assn. Educators Communication and Tech., Assn. Ednl. Research (regional v.p. 1985-86), Phi Beta Kappa, Phi Delta Kappa, Kappa Alpha Psi. Clubs: Masons. Presbyterian. E-mail: howard2255@aol.com.

BALL, JAMES HERINGTON, retired lawyer; b. Kansas City, Mo., Sept. 20, 1942; s. James T. Jr. and Betty Sue (Herington) B.; m. Wendy Anne Wolfe, Dec. 28, 1964; children: James H. Jr., Steven Scott. AB, U. Mo., 1964; JD cum laude, St. Louis U., 1973. Bar: Mo. 1973. Asst. gen. counsel Anheuser-Busch, Inc., St. Louis, 1973-76; v.p., gen. counsel, sec. Stouffer Corp., Solon, Ohio, 1976-83; sr. v.p., gen. counsel Nestle Enterprises, Inc., Solon, 1983-91; gen. counsel, sr. v.p. Nestle USA, Inc., Glendale, Calif., 1991-99. Editor-in-chief St. Louis U. Law Jour., 1972-73. Bd. dirs. Alliance for Children's Rights, L.A., 1992-99, Am. Swiss Found., N.Y.C., 1996-99. Lt. comdr. USN, 1964-70, Vietnam. Mem. Mo. Bar Assn. E-mail: Balljimh@bellsouth.net.

BALL, JOHN FLEMING, advertising and film production executive; b. Evanston, Ill., Apr. 26, 1930; s. Edward Hyde and Kathleen (Fleming) B.; m. Anne Idabelle Firestone, Nov. 9, 1957; children— John Fleming, Jr., David Firestone, Sheila Ball Burkert. BA, Princeton, 1952. Assoc. producer, progam exec. CBS, N.Y.C., 1955-59; with J. Walter Thompson Co., N.Y.C., 1959—, v.p., 1965—, dir. programs, 1965-67, dir. broadcasting, 1967—83, pres., dir. Survival Anglia Ltd. div., 1972—; pres. Trident Anglia Inc., 1976—; chmn. John F. Ball Prodns., John F. Ball Co., 1984—. Trustee Found. Am. Dance; chmn. instructional TV, Archidiocese of N.Y.; bd. dirs. Hist. Soc. Town of Greenwich, Conn. With USN, 1952-54. Mem. Knights of Holy Sepulchre of Jerusalem Knights of Sovereign Mil. Order of Malta, Knights of Order of St. Gregory the Gt., Cap and Gown Club of Princeton U. (N.Y.C.), Links Club, Round Hill Club (Greenwich), Nassau Club (Princeton), Am. Club (London), Princeton Triangle Club (chmn. emeritus grad. bd.). Home: Deer Park Greenwich CT 06830 also: Northport Point Northport MI 49670 Office: 4 Woodside Rd Greenwich CT 06830-3819 E-mail: jfbp@aol.com.

BALL, JOHN PAUL, publishing company executive; b. N.Y.C., Dec. 15, 1946; s. William Emil and Else (Schmid) B.; m. Jayne Barbara Irwin, Jan. 30, 1970 (div. 1991); m. Eileen M. Mitchell, Oct. 25, 1997. Student, N.Y. Sch. Printing, 1964. Prodn. assoc. Macmillan Co., N.Y.C., 1964-65; asst. to pres. Frederick Fell, Inc., N.Y.C., 1965-69; v.p. William Morrow & Co., Inc., N.Y.C., 1969-86; sr. v.p. mfg. and paper purchasing Macmillan Pub. Co., N.Y.C., 1986-94; pub. and graphic arts cons., chmn. bd. Electronic Pub. Svcs. Inc., N.Y.C., 1994—; exec. v.p., sec. Hungry Minds, Inc., N.Y.C., Calif., 1996—2001; cons. in pub. N.Y.C., 2001—04; sr. v.p. fin. and ops. Dorling Kindersley USA, 2004. Recipient Comet Press award graphic arts, 1964, Columbia Scholastic Press Assn. Best Editorial Writing award, 1965. Office: Electronic Pub Svcs Inc 15 E 32d St 2d Fl New York NY 10016 Business E-Mail: jball@e-p-s.com.

BALL, JOHN ROBERT, healthcare executive; b. Opelika, Ala., July 16, 1944; s. John Cooper Jr. and Ellen Beverly (Williams) B.; m. Cornelia Anne Phillips, Aug. 13, 1966 (div. 1983); children: Kristen Anne, John Robert; m. Pamela Preston Reynolds, Jan. 9, 1988. AB, Emory U., 1966; JD, Duke U., 1971, MD, 1972. Rsch. assoc. Duke U. Sch. Medicine, Durham, NC, 1971—72, resident in medicine, 1972-74; asst. to dir. office asst. sec. for health USPHS, Rockville, Md., 1974-76; chief med. audit br. bur. quality assurance HEW, Rockville, 1976-77; sr. policy analyst Office Sci. and Tech. Policy Exec. Office of Pres., Washington, 1978-81; assoc. exec. v.p. ACP, Phila., 1981-86, exec. v.p., 1986-94, also master; sr. scholar Assn. Acad. Health Ctrs., Washington, 1994-95; exec. v.p., acting pres., CEO Pa. Hosp., Phila., 1995-96, pres., CEO, 1996-99; sr. v.p. The Lewin Group, Falls Church, Va., 2000; exec. v.p. Am. Soc. Clin. Pathology, Chgo., 2002—. Robert Wood Johnson clin. scholar George Washington U., Washington, 1977-79; bd. mgrs. Pa. Hosp., 1988-97; bd. dirs. Milbank Meml. Fund. Assoc. editor Jour. Am. Geriatrics Soc., 1984-86; mem. editorial bd. Internat. Jour. Tech. Assessment in Health Care, 1986-89, European Jour. Internal Medicine, 1988-94, Duke U. Law Jour., 1969-71; contbr. articles to profl. jours. Sr. surgeon USPHS, 1974-77. John Gordon Stipe scholar, Nat. Merit scholar, Emory U., 1962. Mem. Inst. Medicine of NAS, N.C. Bar Assn., Am. Clin. and Climatol. Assn., Soc. Med. Adminstrs. Democrat. E-mail: johnrball@hotmail.com.

BALL, KAREN EVANS, secondary school educator; b. Coeburn, Va., Nov. 6, 1947; d. James I. and Waverly (Robinette) Evans; m. R.N. Ball, Mar. 25, 1967; 1 child, Michelle. BA, U. Ctrl. Fla., Orlando, 1972; MS, Nova U., Ft. Lauderdale, Fla., 1991. Tchr., chair social studies dept. Brevard County Sch. System, Titusville, Fla., 1972—. Sponsor Model Student Senate, Brevard County, 1980-88, Mock Trial, Brevard County, 1984-89, Youth Adv. Coun., City of Titusville. Named Social Studies Tchr. of Yr., Social Studies Coun., Cocoa Beach, Fla., 1985, Tchr. of Yr., Titusville H.S., 2003, other awards. Mem. Nat. Coun. Social Studies, Am. Polit. Sci. Assn., Alpha Delta Kappa (membership chair 1992-93), Delta Kappa Gamma (world fellowship chair 1992—, chmn. membership com. 1999—, v.p. 2000—), Kappa Delta Pi. Methodist. Avocations: reading, travel. Office: Titusville High Sch 150 Terrier Trl Titusville FL 32780 E-mail: ballk@brevard.k12.fl.us.

BALL, MARCIA, vocalist; b. Orange, Tex., Mar. 20, 1949; m. Gordon Fowler. Student, La. State U., 1967. Mem. band Freda and the Firedogs, Austin, Tex., 1972-74; founder, mem. band Marcia Ball Band (formerly Marcia and the Misery Bros.), 1975. Performer (solo recording) I Want to Be a Cowboy's Sweetheart, 1975, (album) Circuit Queen, 1978, Soulful Dress, 1983, Hot Tamale Baby, 1986, Gatorhythms, 1989, Dreams Come True, 1991, Blue House, 1994, Let My Play with Your Poodle, 1997, Sing It!, 1998 (Grammy nominee for best contemporary blues album), Presumed Innocent, 2001, So Many Rivers, 2003; appeared at New Orleans Jazz and Heritage Festival, 1978-99. Recipient W.C. Handy award, 1998.

BALL, MARION JOKL, academic administrator; b. South Africa; d. Ernst and Erica Jokl. Student, Northwestern U., 1957-58; BA in Math. with distinction, U. Ky., 1961, MA in Math., 1965; EdD, Temple U., 1978. Math tchr. Bryan Station High Sch., Lexington, Ky., 1961-62; programmer, instr. dept. behavioral sci., and computer sci. U. Ky. Med. Ctr., Lexington, 1965-68; asst. dir., med. computer activity, asst. prof. Temple U., Phila., 1968-72; dir. computer systems and mgmt. group, assoc. prof. Temple U. Health Scis. Ctr., Phila., 1972-85; dir. acad. computing U. Md., Baltimore, 1985-87, assoc. v.p. info. resources, prof., 1985-91; v.p. Info. Svcs. U. Maryland, 1991—; adj. prof. sch. nursing Johns Hopkins U., Baltimore; v.p. clin. solutions divsn. Healthlink Inc., Houston, 2001—. Bd. dirs. Intellimed, CliniCom, Inc., 1986-88; panel mem. Nat. Libr. Medicine, 1985-86, 1988—; adv. bd. Systems Dimensions Ltd., 1974-75, Nat. Assn. Hosp. Admitting Mgrs., 1983-85, Sperry Corp., 1984—, MEAD Co., 1985, Office Tech. Assessment, 1987, Educom Consulting Group, 1988-89; chmn. Am. Med. Informatics Assn. Transition Task Force on Membership, 1989; chmn. Am. Med. Informatics Assn. internat. affairs com.; U.S. rep. MEDINFO, 1983—, MEDINFO scientific program com., 1989—; rsch. devel. com. Am. Med. Record Assn.,

1978-83; mem. tech. subcom. com. on improving patient records, Inst. Medicine, co chair, 1989-91; cons. in field. Author: Selecting a Computer System for the Clinical Laboratory, 1971, What is AComputer?, 1972, How to Select a Computerized Hospital Information System, 1973; author: (with S Charp) Be a Computer Lieterate!, 1978, author: (with K. Hannah)Using Computers in Nursing (nursing book yr. award 1985), 1984; author: (with others) Healthcare Information Management Systems: A Practical Guide, 1990, New Hospital Information Systems, 1988, Nursing Informatics: Where Caring and Technology Meet, 1988, Cancer Informatics: Essential Technologies for Clinical Trials, 2002. Fellow NSF, Phila. Coll. Physicians. Mem. Am. Med. Informatics Assn. (Morris F. Collen Award, 2002), Am. Assn. for Med. Systems and Informatics, Am. Hosp. Assn., Am. Med. Records Assn., Internat. Med. Informatics Assn. (pres. 1992—), Assn. for Computing Machinery, Healthcare Information and Mgmt. Systems Soc. (bd. dirs. 1989-92), Montessori Soc., Network of Women in Computer Tech., Phila. Coll. Physicians, Inst. Medicine (tech. subcom. and bd. dirs. on improving the patient record 1989—, Mortarboard Sr. Woman's Honor Soc., Delta Phi Alpha, Kappa Delta Pi, Phi Mu Eplison; fellow Am. Coll. Med. Informatics, 1984-. Home: Roland Pk N 5706 Coley Ct Baltimore MD 21210-1344 Office: U of Md Info Svcs 100 N Greene St Baltimore MD 21201-1563

BALL, MARKHAM (ROBERT BALL), lawyer, arbitrator, educator; b. Wilmington, Del., Mar. 24, 1934; s. Robert William and Helen (Slepicka) B.; m. Harriet Laura Janney, July 6, 1957; children: Laurence Markham, Richard Janney, Martha Harriet, Julia Helen. BA magna cum laude, Amherst Coll., 1956; BA with honors, Oxford (Eng.) U., 1958, MA, 1973; LLB, Harvard U., 1960. Bar: D.C. 1961, U.S. Supreme Ct. 1968. Law clk. U.S. Supreme Ct., Washington, 1960-61; assoc. Covington and Burling, Washington, 1961-64; asst. gen. counsel U.S. Office Econ. Opportunity, Washington, 1964-66; staff dir. U.S. Peace Corps, Washington, 1966-67; from assoc. to ptnr. Leva, Hawes, Symington, Martin and Oppenheimer, Washington, 1967-77; gen. counsel U.S. Agy. for Internat. Devel., Washington, 1977-79, mem. adv. com. on vol. fgn. aid, 1981-88; ptnr. Wald, Harkrader and Ross, Washington, 1980-85, Morgan, Lewis and Bockius, Washington, 1986-98, Holland and Knight, Washington, 1998—2002. Sr. fellow, dir. Alternative Dispute Resolution Ctr. Internat. Law Inst., Washington, 2002—; lectr. Law Sch. U. Va., 1991—2001; adj. prof. Law Sch. Georgetown U., 2002—. Mem. adv. bd. Brasenose Coll. Charitable Found., Oxford, 1988—. Fellow Am. Bar Found.; Rhodes scholar Phi Beta Kappa, 1956-58. Mem. ABA, Internat. Bar Assn., Am. Arbitration Assn. (mem. internat. arbitration adv. panel 2002—), Alexandria Literary Soc. (sec. 1981—). Home: 7223 Stafford Rd Alexandria VA 22307-1806 Office: Internat Law Inst 1055 Thomas Jefferson St NW Washington DC 20007-5259 Office Phone: 202-247-6006. E-mail: mball@ili.org.

BALL, MARTIN JOHN, linguist, educator; b. Tywyn, Cymru-Wales, Wales, Feb. 23, 1951; s. John Alfred Ball and Iris Mary Standley; m. Nicole Müller, July 12, 2000. BA (Hons), U. of Wales, Bangor, 1973; MA, U. of Essex, Colchester, Eng., 1976; PhD, U. of Wales, Cardiff, 1985. Sr. lectr. S Glamorgan Inst., Cardiff, Wales, 1978—86, Poly. of Wales, Pontypridd, Wales, 1987—91; prof. of phonetics and linguistics U. of Ulster, Jordanstown, Northern Ireland, 1992—2000; Hawthorne-Regents' endowed prof. U. of La. at Lafayette, 2000—. Hon. prof. U. of Wales Inst., Cardiff, 2004—; editor Clin. Linguistics and Phonetics, London, 1987—; assoc. editor Jour. of Multilingual Comm. Disorders, London, 2003—. Author (and editor): (books) over 20 monographs and edited collections; contbr. articles to profl. jours., chapters to books. Mem. Liberal Democrats, London and Cardiff, United Kingdom, 1971—2004. Fellow: Royal Coll. of Speech and Lang. Therapists (London) (hon.); mem.: Internat. Clin. Linguistics and Phonetics Assn. (pres. 2000). D-Liberal. Office Phone: 337-989-6721.

BALL, MILLIE (MILDRED PORTEOUS BALL), editor, journalist; b. New Orleans, Nov. 15, 1945; d. Harold Curtis and Mildred (Porteous) B.; m. Keith Cooper Marshall, Oct. 17, 1981. BA, Fla. State U., 1967. Editor young people's page The Times-Picayune, New Orleans, 1967-71, city desk reporter, 1971-79, staff writer Dixie Mag., 1979-82, staff writer living sect., 1982-89, travel editor, 1990—. Author: (with others) Fodor's New Orleans, 1990, Gault Millau New Orleans, 1991. Recipient various writing awards AP, La. Press Assn., Press Club New Orleans, Odyssey House, 1970-90, Lowell Thomas award Soc. Am. Travel Writers Found., 1992, Bronze Travel Journalist of Yr. award, 1994, Silver-Best Self-Illustrated Story award, 1994, Best Fgn. Story in Newspaper award, 1992, Best Newspaper Travel Sect., 1994, 95. Mem. Chi Omega. Presbyterian. Home: 530 Chartres St New Orleans LA 70130-2110 Office: The Times-Picayune 3800 Howard Ave New Orleans LA 70125-1429

BALL, NEAL, management consultant; b. Chgo., Oct. 7, 1935; s. Clyde E. and Alice Julia (Shillin) Ball. BSc, U. Ill., 1959; cert. advanced mgmt., Northwestern U., 1963. Pub. affairs asst. Am. Hosp. Supply Corp., Evanston, Ill., 1960-63, dir. pub. affairs, 1965-71; cons. N. Ball Assocs., Chgo., 1963-65; dep. press sec. The White House, Washington, 1971-73; v.p. Am. Hosp. Corp., Evanston, 1973-86; advisor Neal Ball Co., Chgo., 1986—. Dir. Nat. Med. Fellow, N.Y.C., 1984—; mem. adv. com. Johns Hopkins Sch. Pub. Health, Balt., 1990-96; chmn. vis. com. Ctr. East Asian Studies U. Chgo., 1990-96, chair hon. com.; dir. Internat. Music Found., 1984-94; mem. adv. com. Krannert Mus. Art, 1992-2000. Dir. Internat. Vistors Ctr. Chgo., 1982—; vice-chmn. com. on Africa and the Ams. Art Inst. Chgo.; founder, hon. chair Am. Refugee Comm., Mpls., 1978—; bd. govs. Internat. House U. Chgo., 1986-2000; pres. Friends of the Windows, Chgo., 1994—; mem. nat. adv. com. U.S. Comm. for UNICEF, N.Y.C., 1996-98, dir. nat. adv. com., 1998—; dir. Grifols-Lucas Found., Barcelona, 1998—. Recipient World of Children award UNICEF, 1980, Gold medallion Internat. Visitors Ctr. of Chgo., 2000. Mem. Univ. Club (Washington), The Casino (Chgo.). Home and Office: 1335 N Astor St Chicago IL 60610-2152 E-mail: nball@concentric.net.

BALL, OWEN KEITH, JR., lawyer; b. Louisville, Feb. 19, 1950; s. Owen Keith and Martha Katherine (Guntherberg) B.; m. Shirley Marie Galinski, Sept. 16, 1972. BSCE, U. Kans., 1972, JD, 1980. Bar: Mo. 1980, U.S. Dist. Ct. (we. dist.) Mo. 1980, Kans. 1988, U.S. Dist. Ct. Kans. 1988. Ptnr. Smith, Gill, Fisher & Butts P.C., Kansas City, Mo., 1980-87; pvt. practice loan broker Lawrence, 1987-88; pvt. practice, 1988-91; legal counsel Marian Merrell Dow Inc., Kansas City, Mo., 1991-92; corp. counsel Marion Merrell Dow Inc., Kansas City, Mo., 1992-95, Hoechst Marion Roussel, Inc., Kansas City, Mo., 1995-99; sr. corp. counsel Aventis Pharms., Bridgewater, NJ, 1999—2005; ret., 2005. Staff to investigate safety of the Hyatt Regency Hotel, Kansas City C. of C., 1981. Lt. USN, 1972-77. Avocation: classical music.

BALL, PATRICIA ANN, physician; b. Lockport, N.Y., Mar. 30, 1941; d. John Joseph and Katherine Elizabeth Ball; m. Robert E. Lee, May 18, 1973 (div. 2004); children: Heather Lee, Samantha Lee. BS, U. Mich., 1963; MD, Wayne State U., 1969. Diplomate Am. Bd. Internal Medicine, Am. Bd. Hematology, Am. bd. Med. Oncology. Intern, resident Detroit Gen. Hosp., 1969-71; resident Jackson Meml. Hosp., Miami, Fla., 1971-72; fellow Henry Ford Hosp., Detroit, 1972-74; staff physician VA Hosp., Allen Park, Mich., 1974-77; pvt. practice in hematology and oncology Bloomfield Hills, Mich., 1977—. Faculty dept. medicine Wayne State U. Sch. Medicine, Detroit, 1974—. Mem.: AMA, ACP, Mich. Soc. Hematology and Oncology, Oakland County Med. Soc., Mich. Med. Soc., Detroit Inst. Arts, Founders Soc., Alpha Omega Alpha. Avocations: photography, skiing. Office: 44038 Woodward Ave Ste 101 Bloomfield Hills MI 48302-5036 Office Phone: 248-360-8244. E-mail: pball@dmc.org.

BALL, REX MARTIN, urban planner, architect; b. Oklahoma City, June 14, 1934; s. Ralph Martin and Sarah Mae (Kellner) B. BArch, Okla. State U., 1956; MArch, MIT, 1958. Lic. arch. Nat. Coun. Arch. Registration Bd.; cert. planner Am. Inst. Cert. Planners. With HTB Inc. (archtl., engring., interior planning firm), Oklahoma City, 1958-94; chmn. emeritus HTB Inc., 1958-94; founder, pres. Planning Assocs. Inc., 1960—; founder, pres., chmn., CEO Mid Continent Design Group, 1968—. Presdl. appt. to U.S. Commn. of Fine Arts, 1994-97. Exhibitor U.S./USSR exhibit "The Socially Responsible Environment, 1980-90; contbr. articles to profl. jours. Chair Tulsa Preservation Com., 1997—; facilitator Internat. Coalition Art Deco Socs., 2003—; oversite com. Vision 2025, Tulsa, 2003—; bd. dirs. Price Tower Mus., 1998—; past treas. Philbrook Mus.'s Pacers. Recipient Bus. in the Arts award, 1988, 5 Who Care Corp. Humanitarian award, Gannett Found., 1988, Curt Schwartz Bus. in the Arts award, 1989, Phoenix award/Downtown Now, 1992, Cityscape award City of Oklahoma City, 1992, Disting. Alumni award Okla. State U., 1995. Fellow: AIA (emeritus, mem. nat. com. on design, past pres. ea. Okla. chpt.); mem.: Soc. Am. Mil. Engrs. (former sustaining mem.), MIT Alumni Assn. (past Okla. pres.), Nat. Trust Hist. Preservation, Am. Planning Assn., Oklahoma City C. of C. (bd. dirs. 1980—90, former v.p.), Okla. State U. Alumni Assn. (life; past bd. dirs., pres. Tulsa and Okla. counties), Tulsa C. of C. (past bd. dirs.), Tulsa Art Deco Soc. (chair), Tulsa Hist. Soc. (bd. dirs. 2000—, chair 6th World Congress on Art Deco 2001), Air Force Assn. (past pres. Gerrity chpt.), Nat. Bldg. Mus., Okla. Heritage Assn., Blue Key Club, Urban League Greater Oklahoma City (former bd. dirs.), Sigma Nu, Alpha Rho Chi. Home: 2926 E 39th St Tulsa OK 74105-3704 Fax: 918-748-9688. E-mail: ballrexm@aol.com.

BALL, ROBERT M., social security and health insurance specialist; MA, Wesleyan U. With Fed. Bur. Old Age and Survivors Ins., 1939—46; asst. dir. Social Security Adminstrn., 1949—52, acting dir., dep. dir., 1953—61, commr., 1962—73; ret., 1973; founding chair Nat. Acad. Social Ins., Washington, chair bd. dirs., 1986—96. Vis. scholar Inst. Medicine, 1973—80, Ctr. for Study of Social Policy, 1980—87; mem. Nat. Commn. on Social Security Reform, 1982—83; staff dir. Adv. Coun. on Social Security, 1948—49, chmn., 1965, mem., 1989—91, 1994—96. Author: (book) Social Security: Today and Tomorrow, 1978, Because We're All In This Together, 1989, Straight Talk About Social Security: An Analysis of the Issues in the Current Debate, 1998, Insuring the Essentials: Bob Ball on Social Security, 2000, Fixing Social Security, 2005; contbg. author: book Social Security in the 21st Century, 1997; contbr. articles to jours. Home and Office: 10450 Lottsford Rd Collington 5112 Mitchellville MD 20721-3302 Home (Summer): 321 Bear Island Lovejoy Sands Meredith NH 03253 Office Phone: 301-541-5097. Business E-Mail: rmball@nasi.org.

BALL, ROBERT M(YERS), social security, welfare and health policy specialist, writer, lecturer; b. NYC, Mar. 28, 1914; s. Archey Decatur and Laura Elizabeth (Crump) Ball; m. Doris Jacqueline McCord, June 30, 1936; children: Robert Jonathan, Jacqueline Ball Smith. AB, Wesleyan U., 1935, MA, 1936; degree (hon.), U Md., Wesleyan U., Yale U. With Bur. Old Age and Survivors Ins., Social Security Bd., 1939-46, asst. dir., 1949-52, acting dir., 1953, dep. dir., 1953-62, commr. social security, 1962-73; sr. scholar Inst. Medicine, Nat. Acad. Scis., 1973-80; writer, lectr., cons., 1980—. Asst. dir. com. edn. and social security Am. Coun. Edn., 1946—49; staff dir. adv. coun. Social Security, 1948—49, chmn., 1965, mem., 79, 91, 96; staff dir. pension study Nat. Planning Assn., 1950—52; mem. Nat. Commn. Social Security Reform, 1982—83, White Ho. Conf. Social Security, 1998. Author: Pensions in the United States, 1952, Social Security Today and Tomorrow, 1978; author: (with Thomas N. Bethell) Straight Talk about Social Security, 1998; author: Insuring the Essentials, Bob Ball on Social Security, Century Foundation, 2000; author: (with Thomas N. Bethell) Because We're All in This Together, Families USA Foundation, 1989; contbr. chapters to books, articles to profl. jours. Named to Health Care Hall of Fame, 1999; recipient Disting. Svc. award, Nat. Civil Svc. League, 1958, Rockefeller Pub. Svc. award, 1961, Arthur J. Atlmeyer award, 1968, Clarence A. Kulp award, Am. Soc. Risk and Ins., 1980, Elizur Wright award, Presdl. award, Am. Soc. Aging, 1988, Arthur S. Fleming award, 1989, Andrus award, AARP, 1990, Cruikshank award, Nat. Coun. Sr. Citizens, 1990, Nat. award, UN Internat. Yr. Older Persons, 1999, Maxwell A. Pollack award for productive living, 2000. Mem.: Nat. Acad. Social Ins. (founding chmn. bd.), Gerontol. Soc. Am. (award 1996), Nat. Coun. Aging (Ollie Randall award 1983), Nat. Acad. Pub. Adminstrn., Inst. Medicine (Lienhard award 1991, Com. to Preserve Social Security and Medicare award 2003, Franklin and Eleanor Roosevelt award for Disting. Svc. 2005), Phi Beta Kappa, Delta Kappa Epsilon. Home and Office: 10450 Lottsford Rd Collington#5112 Mitchellville MD 20721-3302 Office Phone: 301-541-5097. Business E-Mail: rmball@nasi.org.

BALL, RUSSELL ALLEN, pathologist; b. Huntington, W.Va., Aug. 25, 1962; s. Russell Lee and Freda Joyce Ball; m. Margaret Marie Ball; children: Katherine Marie, John Russell. BA in Biology, Va. Wesleyan Coll., Norfolk, 1984; MD, W.Va. U, Morgantown, 1989. Cert. anatomic pathology USN, 1994, clin. pathology USN, 1994, dermatopathology Harvard Med. Sch., 1997. Post-sophomore fellow in pathology W.Va. U. Sch. Medicine, Morgantown, W.Va., 1986—87; rsch. asst. Nat. Cancer Inst., Bethesda, Md., 1988; chmn. hosp. quality mgmt. bd. U.S. Naval Hosp., Rota, Spain, 1994—96, dept. head lab., 1994—96; med. dir. of blood bank Nat. Naval Med. Ctr., Bethesda, Md., 1997—99, dir. of surg. pathology, 1999—99; med. examiner Wake County, Raleigh, NC, 1999—2001; pathologist Rex Healthcare, Raleigh, 1999—2001; clin. asst. prof. Bowman-Gray Sch. Medicine, Winston-Salem, 2001—, U. of N.C. Sch. Medicine, Chapel-Hill, 2001—; dermatopathologist Greensboro Pathology Assoc., 2001—; chmn. pathology svc. peer rev. com. Moses Cone Health Sys., 2002—03; del. to N.C. Med. Soc. N.C. Assn. of Pathologists, Raleigh, 2003—. Sci. advisor Angiogenesis Found., Boston, 1997—; cons. Hoffman-La Roche Pharmaceuticals, Nutley, NJ, 1999—. Contbr. articles to profl. jours. Lt. comdr. USN, 1989—2000. Decorated Navy and Marine Corps Commendation medal US Navy; recipient Smith Kline French award, Faculty of W.Va. U. Med. Sch., 1989, Ishiyaku award, W.Va. U. Sch. of Medicine, 1989, Disting. Alumnus award, Va. Wesleyan Coll., 1992; scholar US Navy Health Professions, US Navy, 1985. Fellow: Am. Soc. of Dermatopathologists, Coll. of Am. Pathologists, Am. Acad. of Dermatology (assoc.); mem.: N,C, Dermatology Assn., Omicron Delta Kappa. Achievements include research in injection site reactions; melanocytic nevi and melanoma; anti-angiogenesis therapy of cutaneous cancer. Office Phone: 336-387-2500.

BALL, STEPHEN DAVID, musician, educator; b. San Diego, Sept. 3, 1954; s. William James and Elizabeth Maude (Brady) Ball; children: Nathan, Angele, Justin, Jessica, Taylor. MusB, San Diego State U., 1978, MA in Music, 1980. Calif. profl. credential in music edn. Music tchr. South Bay Union Sch. Dist., San Diego, Tierra del Sol Mid. Sch., Lakeside, Calif., Vista Acad. Visual Performing Arts, Calif.; sub. violinist San Diego Symphony, 1982—84; electric violinist Ballad Mongers, El Cajon, Calif., 1994—. Musician: (CD recs. Ballad Mongers) Door to Door, (CD recs. Rinaldi Strings) Classic Hymns, Classic Christmas. Named Hon. Mention, LDS Ch. Music Com., Salt Lake City. Mem. Lds Ch. Office: Mendoza Elem Sch 2050 Coronado Ave San Diego CA 92154 Office Phone: 619-424-0182.

BALL, TRAVIS, JR., school administrator, editor; b. Newport, Tenn., July 13, 1942; s. Travis and Ruth Annette (Duyck) Ball. BA, Carson Newman Coll., 1964; MA, Purdue U., 1966. Instr., then asst. prof. English Ill. Wesleyan U., Bloomington, 1966—69; vis. prof. English Millikin U., 1969; asst. headmaster, chmn. English Brewster Acad., Wolfeboro, NH, 1969—72; dir. admissions, asst. to headmaster Park Tudor Sch., Indpls., 1972—88; cons. Selwyn Sch., Denton, Tex., 1988—89; pres. Travis Ball & Assocs., 1980—88; dir. comm. Verde Valley Sch., Sedona, Ariz., 1988—91; editor Projects in Enrollment Mgmt., 1992—2000. Mem. commn. on curriculum and grad. requirements Ind. Dept. Pub. Instrn., 1974—76; mem. adv. coun. Ednl. Records Bur.; reviewer Nat. Stds. Project in Sci., Civics and Govt., 1994—95; ednl. cons., 1992—. Editor: Tchrs. Svc. Com. Newsletter for English Tchrs., 1977—82; dept. editor: English Jour., 1976—82, editor/pub.: Contact: Newsletter for Admissions Mgmt., 1980—88, contbg. editor: The Developing Leader, 2003—. Mem.: ASCD, Phi Delta Kappa, Pi Kappa Delta, Nat. Assn. Ind. Schs. (workshop faculty 1986, 1997), Coun. Advancement and Support Edn. (adv. com. on ind. schs.), Nat. Coun. Tchrs. English, Ind. Schs. Assn. Ctrl. States, Ind. Non-Pub. Edn. Assn. (treas., dir., vice chmn.), Sigma Tau Delta. Baptist. Office: 1739 Log Church Rd Newport TN 37821-5535 Personal E-mail: ball1739@bellsouth.net.

BALL, WILLIAM KENNETH, lawyer; b. DeQueen, Ark., Jan. 15, 1927; s. William P. and Lucille (Jeter) B.; m. Ella Hubbard Scaife, Dec. 28, 1950; children— Lucy Jane, William Ramsay, Charles Scaife. JD, U. Ark., 1953. Bar: Ark 1953, U. S. Supreme Ct., 1971. Law clk. to assoc. justice Ark. Supreme Ct., 1953-54; practice in Monticello, 1954-99; ptnr. Ball, Barton & Hoffman, 1958-99; city atty. Monticello, 1961-93; of counsel Ball, Barton & Hoffman, 1999—. Spl. justice Supreme Ct. Ark., 1975. Served with AUS, 1945-47, 50-52. Mem. Fellow Ark. Bar Found.; mem. Ark. Bar Assn., S.E. Ark. Bar Assn. (pres. 1957-58), Rotary (pres. 1962-63), Kappa Sigma, Delta Theta Phi. Presbyterian. Home: 104 Westminster Dr Monticello AR 71655-4814 Office: Ball Barton & Hoffman 106 W Oakland Ave Monticello AR 71655-4114

BALLABH, PRAVEEN, medical educator; arrived in U.S., 1996; s. Vishwa Ballabh Prasad and Radha Ballabh; m. Jaishree Kumari, Mar. 29, 1960. MD, Banaraj Hindu U., Varanasi, India, 1984. Diplomate in pediatrics and neonatology Am. Bd., 2001. Fellow neonatology N.Y. Presbyn. Hosp. Cornell U., N.Y.C., 1998—2001; asst. prof. N.Y. Med. Coll. and Westchester Med. Ctr., Valhalla, 2001—. Contbr. articles to profl. jours. Grantee, United Cerebral Palsy Rsch. Found., 2003. Mem.: AMA (assoc.). Achievements include research in neuroscience; pathogenesis of intraventricular hemorrhage; immunopathogensis of chronic lung disease of prematurity and pharmacokinetics of betamethasone in single and twin pregnanacy; intraventricular hemorrhage in premature infants and corticosteroid receptors in the developing human brain. Office: NICU Weschester Med Ctr Grassland Reservation Valhalla NY 10550 Personal E-mail: pballabh2@msn.com.

BALLAL, DILIP RAMCHANDRA, mechanical engineering educator; b. Nagpur, India, Jan. 16, 1946; came to U.S., 1979; s. Ramchandra Govind Ballal and Padma (Balwant) Zadkar; m. Shubhangi Sadashiv Ayachit, Dec. 17, 1975; children: Rahul, Deepti. BSME, Coll. Engring., Bhopal, India, 1967; PhD, Cranfield (U.K.) Inst. Tech., 1972, DSc in Engring. (hon.), 1983. Registered profl. engr., Ohio. Lectr. mech. engring. Cranfield Inst. Tech., 1972-79; sr. staff engr. GM Rsch. Labs., Warren, Mich., 1979-83; prof. mech. engring. U. Dayton (Ohio), 1983—. Cons. GMR Labs. and GE Aircraft, Warren, Cin., 1987—. Author: (with others) Combustion Measurements and Modern Development in Combustion, 1990, 91; contbr. about 130 articles on combustion, turbulence, heat transfer and pollution to profl. jours. Project leader Engrs. Club Dayton, 1986, 88, 90; judge, organizer "Odyssey of Mind" Sch. Contest, Dayton, 1985, 87, 88; vice chmn. edn. com. Miami Valley Sch., Dayton, 1988, 90. Named Outstanding Engr., Engrs. Club, Dayton, 1988. Fellow ASME (chmn. combustion and fuels com. 1995—, Best Rsch. award 1986, 92), AIAA (Energy Systems award 1993). Achievements include patents on Ignitor Plug for Jet Engine Combustor. Home: 950 Olde Sterling Way Dayton OH 45459-3100 Office: U Dayton KL 465 300 College Park Ave Dayton OH 45469-0001

BALLANFANT, KATHLEEN GAMBER, newspaper executive, public relations company executive; b. Horton, Kans., July 11, 1945; d. Ralph Hayes and Audrey Lavon (Heryford) G.; children: Andrea, Benjamin. BA, Trinity U., 1967; postgrad. NYU, 1976, Am. Mgmt. Inst., 1977, Belhaven Coll., 1985. Pub. info. dir. Tex. Dept. Community Affairs, Austin, 1972-74; pub. affairs mgr. Cameron Iron Works, Houston, 1975-77, Assoc. Builders and Contractors, Houston, 1982-84; pres. Ballanfant & Assoc., Houston, 1977-82, 84—; pres. Village Life Inc., 1985—; pres., chief exec. officer Village Life Publs.; owner Village Life newspaper, Southwest News newspaper, Houston Observer/Times newspaper, Village Life Printing & Typesetting, South Post Oak newspaper; mem. adv. council on Construction Edn., Tex. So. U., Houston, 1984—; mem. task force on ednl. excellence Houston Ind. Sch. Dist., 1983—; mem. devel. bd. Inter First Fannin Bank, 1986-88; bd. dirs. Bellaire Hosp., Westbury-Southwest Assn., Westland YMCA. Author: Something Special-You, 1972, Prevailing Wage History in Houston, 1983; editor newspaper Bellaire Texan, 1981-82, Austin Times, 1971. Vice pres. West Univ. Republic Women's Club, Houston, 1984—; fgn. vis. chmn. Internat. Inst. Edn., Houston, 1980—; docent Houston Zoo, 1982; bd. dirs. Westland YMCA. Named Tex. Woman of Achievement Tex. Womans Hosp., 1986; recipient Apollo IX Medal of Honor Gov. Preston Smith, 1970, Child Abuse Prevention award Gov. Dolph Briscoe, 1974, Friends of Bellaire Parks Pres. award, Houston Police Depts Media award, 2004; Mem. Tex. Community Newspaper Assn. (pres. 1988-89, bd. dirs. 1987-96), Bellaire C. of C. (bd. dirs. 1987-90, sec., treas. 1988), Inland Press Assn. (bd. dirs. 2001, weekly com. chmn. 2001-), Houston C. of C. (Leon Roster award),Rotary (asst. dist. gov. 2004—), Rotary Club (past pres.). Republican. Presbyterian. Avocations: traveling, racquetball, reading. Office: Village Life Inc 5160 Spruce St Bellaire TX 77401-3309 Personal E-mail: vlswnews@aol.com.

BALLANTINE, JOHN TILDEN, lawyer; b. Louisville, Feb. 26, 1931; s. Thomas Austin and Anna Marie (Pfeiffer) B.; m. Mary January Strode, May 15, 1954 (div. 1964); children: John T. Jr., William Clayton, Douglas C.; m. Beverley Jo Hackley, Dec. 8, 1967; 1 child, Susan Marie. BA with high distinction, U. Ky., 1952; JD, Harvard U., 1957. Bar: Ky. 1957, U.S. Ct. Appeals (6th cir.) 1958, U.S. Supreme Ct. 1982. Law clk. to presiding judge U.S. Dist Ct. (we. dist.) Ky., 1957-58; assoc. then ptnr. Ogden Newell & Welch PLLC, Louisville, 1958—. Mem. civil rules com. Ky. Supreme Ct., 1988—2002; jud. nominating com. Ky. Supreme Ct. and Ct. Appeals, 2005—; adj. prof. Brandeis Sch. Law U. Louisville. Bd. dirs. Family and Children Agy., Louisville, 1965-75, pres., 1971-74; bd. dirs. Our Lady of Peace Hosp., Louisville, 1968-73, 88—, chmn., 1968-69, 91-93; bd. dirs. Met. United Way, Louisville, 1975-81; mem. Hist. Landmarks and Preservation Dists. Commn., Louisville, 1976-88; bd. dirs. Ky. Derby Festival, Louisville, 1975-81, v.p., 1975. 1st lt. USAF, 1952-54. Recipient Outstanding Young Man in Field of Law award Louisville Jaycees, 1966. Fellow Am. Coll. Trial Lawyers; mem. ABA, Ky. Bar Assn. (bd. govs. 1996-2002, ho. of dels. 1985-91, chmn. 1989-90, clients' security fund 1993-96, Ky. evidence rules rev. commn. 1995-2002, ethics com. 2000, rules com. 2003—, Outstanding Lawyer award 2003), Louisville Bar Assn. (bd. dirs. 1969-71, 88, 89, 92, 93, 96-2002, pres. 1970, profl. responsibility com. 1988-93, past chmn. physician-atty. com.), U.S. 6th Cir. Ct. Appeals Jud. Conf. (life), Fed. Def. and Corp. Counsel, Ky. Def. Counsel (pres. 1981-82), Louis D. Brandeis Am. Inn of Ct., Ky. Character and Fitness Com., Pendennis Club, The Law Club, Phi Beta Kappa. Office: Ogden Newell & Welch PLLC 1700 Citizens Plaza 500 W Jefferson St Ste 1700 Louisville KY 40202-2874 Business E-Mail: jballantine@ogdenlaw.com.

BALLANTINE, MORLEY COWLES (MRS. ARTHUR ATWOOD BALLANTINE), editor; b. Des Moines, May 21, 1925; d. John and Elizabeth (Bates) Cowles; m. Arthur Atwood Ballantine, July 26, 1947 (dec. 1975); children— Richard, Elizabeth Ballantine Leavitt, William, Helen Ballantine Healy. AB, Ft. Lewis Coll., 1975; LHD (hon.), Simpson Coll., Indianola, Iowa, 1980, U. Denver, 2002. Pub. Durango (Colo.) Herald, 1952-83, editor, pub., 1975-83, editor, chmn. bd., 1983—; dir. 1st Nat. Bank, Durango, 1976—2002, Des Moines Register & Tribune, 1977-85, Cowles Media Co., 1982-86. Mem. Colo. Land Use Commn., 1975-81, Supreme Ct. Nominating Commn., 1984-90; mem. Colo. Forum, 1985—; trustee Choate/Rosemary Hall, Wallingford, Conn., 1973-81, Simpson Coll., Indianola, Iowa, 1981-2002, U. Denver, 1984-2002, Fountain Valley Sch., Colorado Springs, 1976-89, trustee emerita, 1993—; mem. exec. com. Ft. Lewis Coll. Found., 1991—. Recipient 1st place for editl. writing Nat. Fedn. Press Women, 1955, Outstanding Alumna award Rosemary Hall, Greenwich, Conn., 1969, Outstanding Journalism award U. Colo. Sch. Journalism, 1967, Disting. Svc. award Ft. Lewis Coll., Durango, 1970, Athena award Female Cmty. Leader, 1997; named to Colo. Cmty. Journalism Hall of Fame, 1987, Colo. Bus. Hall of Fame, 2002; named Citizen of Yr., Durango Area Chamber Resort Assn., 1990, Colo. Philanthropist of Yr. Colo. Assn. Found./Assn. Fundraising Profls., 2000, Bonfils-Stanton Found. award, 2002. Mem. Nat. Soc. Colonial Dames, Colo. Press Assn. (bd. dirs. 1978-79), Colo. AP Assn. (chmn. 1966-67), Federated Women's Club Durango, Mill Reef Club (Antigua, W.I.) (bd. govs. 1985-91). Episcopalian. Address: care Durango Herald PO Drawer A Durango CO 81302

BALLANTYNE, RICHARD LEE, lawyer; b. Evanston, Ill., Dec. 10, 1939; s. Frank and Grace (Bowles) B.; children: Richard L. Jr., Brant. BS in Engring., U. Conn., 1965, MBA, 1967; JD with honors, George Washington U., 1969. Bar: Mass., 1970, Fla. 1994, U.S. Dist. Ct. Mass. 1976, U.S. Patent Office 1982. Dir. corp. devel. Itek Corp., Lexington, Mass., 1969-73, assoc. counsel, 1973-75; corp. counsel, sec. Goodhope Industries, Springfield, Mass., 1975-77; gen. counsel, asst. treas., sec. Compugraphic Corp., Wilmington, Mass., 1977-82; v.p., gen. counsel, sec. Prime Computer Inc., Natick, Mass., 1982-89, Harris Corp., Melbourne, Fla., 1989—. Served with U.S. Army, 1958-61. Mem. ABA, N.E. Corp. Counsel Assn. Inc. (pres. 1984-86), Licensing Execs. Soc., Am. Soc. Corp. Secs, Computer Law Forum. Republican. Avocations: jogging, golf. Office: Harris Corp 1025 W Nasa Blvd Melbourne FL 32919-0002

BALLARD, CHARLES ALAN, investment banker; b. St. Louis; s. Fred William and Fern Ann (Markham) B. BBA, So. Meth. U., 1963. V.p. fin. Systems Capital Corp., Phila., 1967-69; exec. v.p., dir. Vanderbilt Corp., Phila., 1969-71; assoc. Dillon, Read & Co. Inc., N.Y.C., 1971-72, v.p., 1972-78, sr. v.p., 1979-80, mng. dir., 1980-90, sr. advisor, dir., 1990-99; chmn., dir. Ballard Properties Inc., Phila., 1982—; pres., dir. Ballard Marine, Inc., 1986—; sr. advisor UBS Warburg, N.Y.C., 1999—. Mem. council Nat. Municipal League, N.Y.C., 1981-85; mem. adv. bd. Nat. Entrepreneurship Found., Bloomington, Ind., 1983—, The Energy Bur., N.Y.C., 1981— . Recipient Merit award U. Wis.-La Crosse, 1975; recipient Achievement award Lions Club, Houston, 1963 Mem. N.Y. Stock Exchange (assoc.), Securities Industry Assn. (vice chmn. 1980-81, exec. com., bd. dirs. 1984-85), Investment Banking Com. (steering com. 1981—, vice chmn. 1981, 83, 86, 87, chmn. 1985). Clubs: Union League (Phila.); The Links (N.Y.C.); Merion Golf (Ardmore, Pa.); India House; Lighthouse Point (Fla.) Yacht and Racquet. Office: 299 Park Ave New York NY 10171-0002

BALLARD, DAVID EUGENE, anesthesiologist; b. Carlsbad, N.Mex., July 30, 1949; s. Samuel Lafayette and Kathleen (Krebs) B.; m. Patricia Ann Lafferty, June 11, 1972; 1 child, Leslie Christine. BA, U. Kans., 1971; MD, U. N.Mex., 1975. Diplomate Am. Bd. Anesthesiology. Intern and resident N.C. Meml. Hosp., U. N.C., Chapel Hill, 1975-78; pvt. practice Anesthesia Cons. Associated, El Paso, Tex., 1978-86; chief anesthesia sect. VA Med. Ctr., Albuquerque, 1986-88; chmn. dept. anesthesiology Lovelace Med. Ctr., Albuquerque, 1988-98; dir. anesthesiology, asst. prof. West Mesa Med. Ctr., Albuquerque, 2003—04. Asst. prof. anesthesiology, U. N.Mex., 1986-88, mem. resident selection com., 1986-88; asst. prof. anesthesiology U. N.C., Chapel Hill, 1991-96. Mem. Am. Soc. Anesthesiologists (alt. del. 1988-91, mem. com. on physician resources 1993-94), AMA, Internat. Anesthesia Rsch. Soc., Anesthesia Patient Safety Found., Soc. Ambulatory Anesthesia, Tex. Soc. Anesthesiologists (alt. del. dist. 5, 1986), Greater Albuquerque Anesthesia Soc. (pres., v.p. 1987-89), N.Mex. Med. Sch. Alumni Assn. (bd. dirs. 1984-92, exec. com. 1988-90). Avocation: golf. Office: Lovelace Med Ctr 5400 Gibson Blvd SE Albuquerque NM 87108-4763 Office Phone: 505-262-7197. Business E-Mail: david.ballard@lovelacesandia.com. E-mail: dadun2@aol.com.

BALLARD, ERNESTA, lumber company executive; BA, U. Pa.; MA, MBA, Harvard U. Regional adminstr. Pacific NW EPA, 1983—86; CEO Cape Fox Corp., 1989-94; founder, prin. Ballard & Assocs., Ketchikan, Alaska, 1994-97; commr., Dept. Environ. Conservation State of AK, Juneau, 2002—04; sr. v.p. corp. affairs Weyerhaeuser Co., Federal Way, Wash., 2004—. Mem. bd. govs. U.S. Postal Svc., Washington, 1997—2005. Bd. dirs. Alaska Forest Assn., S.E. Alaska Regional Aquaculture Assn., Ketchikan Gen. Hosp., LifeCenter NW. Office: Weyerhaeuser Co PO Box 9777 Federal Way WA 98063-9777*

BALLARD, JEFFREY LAWRENCE, surgeon, educator; b. L.A., May 26, 1960; s. James Larry and Ellen Ballard; m. Tami Lynn Haroldson, May 20, 1983; children: Lauren Nicole, Katelyn Paige. BS in Biology, Stanford U., 1982; MD, Vanderbilt U., 1986. Diplomate in vascular surgery Am. Bd. of Surgery, 2001, in general surgery Am. Bd. of Surgery, 2000. Surg. internship U. Ariz., 1986—87; urgent care physician Cigna Southwest, Tucson, 1987—88; surg. residency Maricopa Med. Ctr., Phoenix, 1988—92; vascular residency Med. Ctr. Loma Linda (Calif.) U., 1992—93, prof. surgery Sch. Medicine, 1993—2004. Fellow: Soc. Vascular Surgery (disting.); mem.: ACS (bd. govs. 2002—05), So. Calif. Vascular Surg. Soc. (pres. 2005—), Pacific Coast Surg. Assn., Western Vascular Soc. (sec., treas. 2002—05), Peripheral Vascular Surgery Soc. (pres. 2002—03). Republican. Office: 1140 W La Veta Ave Ste 850 Orange CA 92868 Office Phone: 714-560-4450. Business E-Mail: jlb@vascularspecialistsoc.com.

BALLARD, JOHN STUART, retired mayor, lawyer, educator; b. Akron, Ohio, Sept. 30, 1922; s. Irby S. and Sarah (McCormick) B.; m. Ruth Frances Holden, Oct. 22, 1949; children: Susan, Karen, John H., Mark, Ward; m. 2d, Patricia D. Whittenberger, Oct. 20, 1990. AB, U. Akron, 1943; LL.B., U. Mich., 1948. Bar: Mich. 1948, Ohio 1949. Spl. agt. FBI, 1949-52; atty. pvt. practice, Akron, Ohio, 1952—56, 1964—65; pros. atty. Summit County, 1957-64; mayor City of Akron, 1966-80; ret., 1995. Adj. assoc. prof. dept. pub. adminstrn. and urban studies U. Akron, 1980—95. Candidate for U.S. senator from Ohio, 1962. Served with inf. AUS, 1943-46. Recipient Distinguished Service award Akron Jr. C. of C., 1957 Episcopalian. Home: 171 Granger Rd Unit 144 Medina OH 44256-7312 *It is true that in giving we receive.*

BALLARD, KEITH RICHARD, music educator; b. San Diego, Jan. 17, 1963; s. Gerald Thompson and Dolores Ann Ballard; m. Jodi Lynn Ballard, July 27, 1987; children: Brian, Nicole. BS in Comm., Ariz. State U., 1986, BS in Music Edn., 1993. Cert. tchr., Ariz., Calif. Tchr. Phoenix Union H.S., 1995-96, San Diego City Schs., 1997-98, Sweetwater Union H.S. Dist., Chula Vista, Calif., 1998—. Mem. ednl. adv. bd. Congressman Bob Filner, Chula Vista, 2000; bd. dirs. Mariachi Scholarship Found., San Diego, 2000-01; fine arts scholarship evaluator Ford Ednl. Scholarship, San Diego, 2000-01. Recipient Cool Sch. award CBS Channel 8-TV, 2000; named Tchr. of the Yr. Wal-Mart, 2001, Tchr. of Yr. Fox News, 2001, Tchr. of Yr. San Diego County Edn. Dept., 2001. Mem. Music Edn. Assn. (Calif. Music Educator of the Yr. 2001). Democrat. Avocations: writing music, swimming, travel. Home: 198 G St # A Chula Vista CA 91910 Office: Montgomery HS 3250 Palm Ave San Diego CA 92154

BALLARD, KELLY ELIZABETH, music educator; b. Detroit, May 29, 1975; d. Dennis Michael and Susan Ann Cavinaw; m. Anthony Wayne Ballard, Jan. 6, 2001. B Music Edn., Emporia State U., 1998. Cert. music tchr. Kans., Orff-Schulwerk level 2. K-6 music tchr. Stafford (Kans.) Cmty. Schs., 1998—2003; K-5 music tchr. Geary County Schs., Junction City, Kans., 2003—. Mem., vol. Junction City Art Gallery, 2004. Mem.: NEA, Geary County Reading Assn., Am. Orff Schulwerk Assn., Kans. Music Educators Assn. Avocations: gardening, reading. Office Phone: 785-717-4650. E-mail: theballards2001@yahoo.com.

BALLARD, LAURA CLAY, small business owner; b. Biloxi, Miss., June 29, 1951; d. Elbert Homer Jr. and Jacqueline May (Giblin) Clay; m. Steven Anthony Register (div. Apr. 1982); 1 child, Steven Scott; m. Frank James Butscher, Aug. 20, 1982 (div. Nov. 2000); m. Raymond Michael Ballard, Oct. 7, 2001. AS in Bus. Adminstrn., Jefferson State Jr. Coll., 1986; BS Social and Behavioral Sci. cum laude, U. Ala., 1987. Teletype operator Blue Cross Blue Shield, Columbus, Ga., 1971-72, asst. supr. data control, 1972-77; mgr. data processing So. Foods, Inc., Columbus, 1977-80, Zurn Industries, Birmingham, Ala., 1980-85; pres. Maid for All Seasons, Inc., Birmingham, 1989-92; owner Visual Studio, Trussville, Ala., 1993—; realtor Century 21 and Realty South, Trussville, 1997-99; customer rels. mgr. Jay Toyota, 2000—02; dir. customer rels. The Maids, Birmingham, 2002; adminstr. customer rels. L. Kianoff & Assocs., Birmingham, 2002—04. Avocations: gardening, photography, golf, birdwatching, computers. Home: 6275 Brookstone Blvd Columbus GA 31904-2962 Personal E-mail: radiantredrunr@yahoo.com.

BALLARD, LINDA CHRISTINE, financial aid director; b. Houston, Aug. 19, 1959; d. Roosevelt Larue Sr. and Helen Ruth B.; 1 child, Alexandria Nickole Ballard-Demming. BBA, U. Houston, 1982. Data control supr. U. Houston, 1982-85, data entry supr., 1985-87, fin. aid. counselor, 1987-92, U. St. Thomas, Houston, 1992-93, dir. fin. aid, 1993—2000; dir. fin. aid and vet. affairs U. Houston at Clear Lake, Tex., 2000—01; dir. fin. aid Tex. So. U., Houston, 2001—. Chair sexual harassment com. U. Houston, 1991-93; mem. staff devel. com. U. St. Thomas, 1993-96, mem. data mgrs. com., 1995-97, 99, mem. scholar com., 1994-99, mem. enrollment mgmt. com., 1998-2000; mem. early awareness com. Tex. Assn. Fin. Aid Adminstrn., 2000—; presenter in field. Dir. youth dept. Greater True Vine Ch. Mem. Nat. Assn. Fin. Aid Adminstrs., Tex. Assn. Fin. Aid Adminstrs. (early awareness com. 2000—), Nat. Coalition Builders Inst. (train the trainer). Avocations: high school awareness programs, travel, financial aid compliance issues, workshops in field. Home: 5326 Linden Chase Ln Houston TX 77066-3218 Office: Texas Southern University 3100 Cleburne Houston TX 77004

BALLARD, LOUIS WAYNE, composer; b. Miami, Okla., July 8, 1931; s. Charles Guthrie and Leona Mae (Quapaw) B.; m. Ruth Sands, Dec. 6, 1965; children by previous marriage: Louis Anthony, Anne Marie, Charles Christopher. B.Mus. and Music Edn., U. Tulsa, 1954; M.Mus., 1962; D.Mus. (hon.), Coll. Santa Fe, 1973; D.Mus. (hon.), William Jewell Coll., 2001. Dir. vocal and instrumental music Nelagoney (Okla.) Public Sch., 1954-56; dir. vocal music Webster High Sch., Tulsa, 1956-58; pvt. music tchr., 1959-62; music dir. Inst. Am. Indian Arts, Santa Fe, 1962-65, dir. performing arts, 1965-69; nat. dir. music edn. curriculum and rev. Bur. Indian Affairs, Washington, 1969-79. Lectr., clinician, 1960—; pres. First Am. Indian Films, Inc., 1969—; disting. vis. prof. music Wm Jewell Coll., Liberty, Mo., 2000—. Composer, Santa Fe, 1979—; guest composer West German Music Festival, Saarbrü, 1986, Musik im 20 Jahrhundert, Ariz. State U., 1992, U. Ill. at Champagne, 1992, Ea. Music Festival, Greensboro, N.C., 1994, 95, 96; gala concert Carnegie Hall, 1992; full concert in Beethoven Chamber Music Hall, Bonn (first Am. composer), 1989; (ballet) Koshare, 1964, The Four Moons, 1967, Maid of the Mist and the Thunderbeings, 1991; (orchl. music) Fantasy Aborigine, Nos. I, II, III, IV, V; (chamber music) Rhapsody for Four Bassoons, Incident at Wounded Knee, Desert Trilogy, Ritmo Indio, Katcina Dances for cello-piano suite; (choral cantatas) The Gods Will Hear, Portrait of Will Rogers, Thus Spake Abraham; (oratorio) Dialogue Differentia text in Latin, Lakota-Sioux, English, Live On, Heart of My Nation (choral cantate with native Am. dialect), Manitoo, Gitche Manitoo (Am. Indian Doxology); (band works) Nighthawk Keetowa; (percussion) Cecega Ayuwipi, Music for the Earth and the Sky; (guitar) Quetzalcoatl's Coattails, 1992, The Lonely Sentinel, 1993, The Fire Moon (string quartet), A City of Silver, A City of Fire, A City of Light (piano concert pieces), numerous others.; commd. writer Lila Wallace Reader's Digest Arts Ptnrs./Meet the Composer, 1991; commd. writer (opera) Ministry Lower Saxony (Germany), 1993-94; author: The American Indian Sings, Book 1, 1970, Book 2, 1991, American Indian Chants for the Classroom, Oklahoma Indian Chants for the Classroom, 2004, also articles. Recipient 1st Marion Nevins MacDowell award chamber music, 1969, Nat. Indian Achievement award, 1972, Catlin Peace Pipe award Nat. Indian Lore Assn., 1976, ASCAP award, 1966-88, Lifetime Music Achievement award First Americans in Arts, 1997; F.B. Parriott grad. fellow, 1969; grantee Ford Found., 1970; grantee Nat. Endowment Arts, 1967, 69, 76, 79; commd. by Martha B. Rockefeller Found., 1969, Am. Composers Orch., 1982, commd. by Ministry Lower Saxony for Opera in Norden Gymnasium, West Germany, 1994; named to Okla. Music Hall of Fame, 2004. Mem. ASCAP, Music Educators Nat. Conf. (chmn. minority concerns com. for N.Mex. 1976), Am. Symphony Orch. League, Internat. Soc. for Polyaesthetic Music Edn. and Performance (lectr.), Phi Beta Kappa (alumni mem. Beta chpt. Okla. 1999). Lodges: Masons, Scottish Rite (32d degree). Office: PO Box 4552 Santa Fe NM 87502-4552 Personal E-mail: ogx88@msn.com.

BALLARD, MARION SCATTERGOOD, software development company executive; b. Montclair, N.J., Dec. 19, 1939; d. Alfred G. and Helen F. (Galey) Scattergood; m. Frederic L. Ballard Jr., Dec. 20, 1974; children: William, Robert; 1 stepchild, Anne A. Ballard. BA, Smith Coll., 1961; MA, U. Pa., 1963; MBA, American Univ., 1990. Lectr. Temple U., Phila.; mathematician UNIVAC, Blue Bell, Pa.; v.p. FINPAC Corp., Narberth, Pa.; pres. DataPlus, Inc, Washington. Former chmn. bd. Sandy Spring Friends Sch., Washington Area Women's Found.; former sec. bd. Sidwell Friends Sch.; bd. dirs. Levine Sch. Music. Mem. Nat. Assn. Women Bus. Owners, Phi Beta Kappa, Sigma Xi. E-mail: marionballard@comcast.net.

BALLARD, MARY MELINDA, corporate communications specialist, consumer products company executive; b. Sikeston, Mo., Apr. 21, 1958; d. Claude M. and Mary (Birnbach) B.; m. Emil Pena, Jan. 1, 1989 (div. July 1990); m. Ronald C. Allison, Oct. 1994; 1 child, Reese Colton Allison. BA, Monmouth U., 1976; MBA, NYU, 1980; postgrad., Columbia U. V.p. corp. comm. United Brands Co., N.Y.C., 1976—79; v.p. mktg. Oscar de la Renta Ltd., 1979—81; pres., CEO Ficom Internat., Inc., N.Y.C., 1981—89; exec. v.p. Ruder Finn Inc., N.Y.C., 1989—; dir., CEO MBP Interests Inc., 1989—; ptnr. Affinity Ins. Advisors, 2003—, Kamero Ptnrs., 1994—; pres. Policyholders of Am., 2002—; officer, dir. Tex. Interlock Corp., 1995—96; exec. v.p., CFO Millenium Tech. Transfer, Inc., 1996—; officer dir. Capital Bank, 1997—; ptnr. Affinity Ins. Advisors, LLP, 2004—. Bd. dirs. Reese Colton Enterprises, Inc., Millenium Tech. Transfer, Inc., Nat. Coun. Real Estate Investment Fiduciaries; pres. Policyholders of Am., 2002—; mem. adv. bd. Tex. Tech U., 2002—; cons., ins. adviser. Contbr. articles to profl. jours. Trustee Ballard Family Found., Children's Aid Soc.; exec. mem. Tex. Dem. Roundtable, 1994—. Recipient CLIO Ann. Report award Fin. World, 1984, 86. Mem. Internat. Assn. Bus. Communicators (Golden Quill 1984), Pub. Investor Relsa. Inst. Methodist. Avocations: collecting art, thoroughbred race horses, ranching. Home and Office: 15 Orange St Charleston SC 29401 E-mail: mballardal@aol.com.

BALLARD, MICHAEL RAY (MICKEY BALLARD), minister, music educator; b. Hammond, La., Apr. 24, 1969; s. Milton Ray Ballard and Carol Ann Carter; m. Sue Ellen Sanders, Jan. 19, 1964; 1 child, Jacob Wayne. BFA, La. Tech U., Ruston, La., 1994; MusM Voice Performance, MusM Music Edn., U. Miss., Oxford, Miss., 1996; M of Ch. Music, So. Bapt. Theol. Sem., Louisville, Ky., 2003. Vis. instr. voice and vocal jazz Ea. Ky. U., Richmond, Ky., 1997—2000; min. music First Bapt. Ch., Richmond, Ky., 2000—. Adj. Ky. Music Educators Assn., Louisville, 1997—2002, Music in the Pks., Pa., 1999—2002; clinician Stephen Collins Foster Music Camp, Richmond, Ky., 1998—2000. Singer: (musical theater) Anything Goes (Tech Tony Award: Best Supporting Actor, 1993); creator (eku vocal jazz ensemble) Musical Performances; singer: (vocal auditions) Nat. Assn. of Tchrs. of Singing (Divsn. Winner in Regional and State Competitions, 1996), (Operas) Susannah; soloist (choral symphony/requiem) Mozart Requiem. Mem./advisor Richmond C. of C., Richmond, Ky., 2000—; min. of music First Bapt. Ch., Richmond, Ky., 2000—; advisor Bapt. Student Union, Richmond, Ky., 1998—99. Recipient Undergraduate Singer of the Yr., La. Tech U., 1994; Grad. Honors Fellowship, U. Miss., 1994-1996. Mem.: Bapt. Ch. Music Conf., Nat. Assn. of Tchrs. of Singing, Am. Choral Dirs. Assn. (life). Bapt. Avocations: travel, golf, sports. Home: 113 Prewitt Dr Richmond KY 40475 Office: First Bapt Ch 425 Eastern Bypass Richmond KY 40475 Office Phone: 859-623-4028. Personal E-mail: mickey.ballard@firstbaptistnet.com.

BALLARD, MILDRED LOUISE, retired adult nurse practitioner; b. Clearfork, Okla., Sept. 14, 1930; d. Clarence Edward and Fannie Elsie VanBeber; m. Carl Adrian Brown, Jan. 24, 1948 (div. Oct. 1978); children: Stephen P. Brown, Linda June Brown-Larson; m. Jerry Denton Ballard, Nov. 5, 1978 (dec. Nov. 1996). ASN, C.C. of Denver, 1978; BSN, U. North Colo., 1983. Cert. adult nurse practitioner. Lic. practical nurse Greeley (Colo.) Med. Group, 1972-78, staff nurse, 1978-85, adult nurse practitioner, 1985-86, Kaiser Permanent, East Hartford, conn., 1985-96, ret., 1996. Pioneer nursing practitioner receiving hosp. privileges No. Colo. Med. Ctr., 1985-86; citizen amb. to exchange med. info. People to People Program, Europe and China, 1988-90. Contbr. short story to book. Mem. adv. bd. RVNA, Greeley, 1985—86; chmn. Arthritis Found., Greeley, 1983—86; vol. organizer United Way, Greeley, 1984—86; preceptor for nursing practitioner students U. Conn., East Hartford, 1988—96; mem. com. Greeley C. of C., 1985; vol. West Springfield Meals on Wheels Program, Mass.; participant Ms. Senior Ma, 2001. Named Mother of Yr., Radio Sta. KFKA, 1968. Democrat. Avocations: quilting, stained glass, writing, exercise, ballroom dance. Home: 7 Fox Hunt Cir Granby CT 06035 Personal E-mail: milquil.l@juno.com.

BALLARD, NANCER H., lawyer; b. Buffalo, N.Y., May 20, 1954; d. Robert L. and Frances H. Ballard; 1 child, Andrew. BA in Creative Writing, Ithaca U., 1975; MA in Counseling, Goddard Grad. Sch., 1977; JD, Northeastern U., 1984. Coop. intern Nat. Consumer Law Ctr., Boston, fall 1982; clk. to staff attys. office U.S. Ct. Appeals 9th Cir., spring 1983; clk. to hon. Hugh Bownes U.S. Ct. Appeals 1st Cir., 1984-85; assoc. Goodwin, Procter & Hoar, Boston, 1985-91, ptnr., 1991—. Tchg. asst. Ithaca (N.Y.) Coll., spring 1975, instr., 1975-76; dir. edn. Counseling Svcs., Inc., 1976-78, interim exec. dir., 1977; instr. Boston Ctr. for Adult Edn., 1976-78; tchg. asst. criminal law Northeastern U. Coll. Criminal Justice, Boston, 1983-84; chairperson ins. practice group Goodwin, Procter & Hoar, Boston, 1990-98, co-chair environ. dept., 1996-97; vis. rsch. scholar Wellesley (Mass.) Ctrs. for Women, 1996-98; vis. scholar Brandeis U. Women's Studies Program, Waltham, Mass., 1998—; spkr. in field. Contbr. articles to profl. jours. Mem. ABA (tort and ins. practice sect. 1989—, sect. litigation 1990—, sect. law practice mgmt. 1994—), Mass. Bar Assn., Boston Bar Assn. (co-chair task force on profl. challenges and family needs 1998-99), Women's Bar Assn. Mass. (appts. com. 1990—, 1995 Gala fundaising com., co-chair appts., endorsements and awards com. 1996—, employment issues com. 1997—, bd. dirs. 1997—). Office: Goodwin Procter & Hoar Exchange Pl Boston MA 02109-2803

BALLARD, ROBERT DUANE, marine geologist; b. Wichita, Kans., June 30, 1942; s. Chester Patrick and Harriet Nell (May) B.; m. Marjorie C. Jacobsen, July 1, 1966 (div.); children: Todd (dec.), Doug; m. Barbara Earle, Jan. 1991; children: Benjamin, Emily. BS, U. Calif., Santa Barbara, 1965; postgrad., U. Hawaii, 1965—66, U. So. Calif., 1966—67; PhD of Oceanography, U. R.I., 1974. Asst. scientist Woods Hole (Mass.) Oceanog. Instn., 1974-76, assoc. scientist, 1976-83, sr. scientist, 1983-97, scientist emeritus, 1997—; prof. oceanography Grad. Sch. Oceanography, dir. Inst. Archaeol. Oceanography U. R.I., 2001—; explorer-in-residence Nat. Geog. Soc., 1989—. Cons. dep. chief naval ops. for submarine warfare, 1983; founder, pres. Inst. for Exploration, Mystic Aquarium, Conn., 1995—; vis. scholar Stanford U., 1979-80, cons. prof., 1980-81, founder and dir. Deep Submergence Lab., 1983—; bd. dirs., founder Jason Found. for Edn.; trustee Sea Rsch. Found. Author: Exploring Our Living Planet, 1983, Discovery of the Titanic, 1989, Discovery of the Bismarck, 1990, The Wreck of the ISIS, 1990, The Lost Ships of Guadalcanal, 1993, Explorations, 1995, Exploring the Lusitania, 1995; author (with Michael Sweeney) Return to Titanic: A New Look at the World's Most Famous Lost Ship, 2004. With U.S. Army, 1965-67; with USN, 1967-70. Recipient Sci. award Underwater Soc. Am., 1976, Newcomb Cleveland prize AAAS, 1981, Cutty Sark Sci. award, 1982, Centennial award Nat. Geog. Soc., 1988, Westinghouse award AAAS, 1990, Golden Plate award Am. Acad. Achievement, 1990, U.S. Navy Robert Dexter Conrad award for Sci. Achievement, 1992, Nat. Humanities medal, 2003. Mem. Geol. Soc. Am., Marine Tech. Soc. (Compass Disting. Achievement award 1977), Am. Geophys. Union, Explorers Club (Lone Sailor award, Hubbard medal). Achievements include being the leader of the first and second expeditions to reach sunken ship Titanic, 1985, 86, discover of Bismarck, 1989, Yorktown, 1998, PT-109, 2002; pioneered the use of manned submersibles for ocean research, participating in or leading more than 110 deep-sea expeditions; invented the first photographic remotely operated vehicle, while working at Woods Hole Oceanographic Institution, Mass.; discovered chemosynthetic life-forms off the Galápagos Islands, where he was one of the first to see hydrothermal vents, aka "black smoker". Office: Inst for Exploration 55 Coogan Blvd Mystic CT 06355-1927

BALLARD, ROBERTA A., pediatrics educator; AB in Chemistry, Earlham Coll., 1061; MD, U. Chgo., 1965. Diplomate Am. Bd. Pediat., Am. Bd. Neonatal Medicine, Am. Bd. Neonatal and Perinatal Medicine (chmn. 1992-95). Intern, then resident in pediat. U. Chgo. Hosps., 1965-67; resident in pediat. Stanford (Calif.) U., 1967-68; fellow in neonatology George Washington U. Hosp., Washington, 1968-69; fellow Cardiovasc. Rsch. Inst., 1970-72; acting dir. newborn svcs., instr. pediat. George Washington U. Hosp., Washington, 1969-70; dir. newborn svcs. Mt. Zion Med. Ctr.-U. Calif., San Francisco, 1972-90, chief dept. pediat., 1975-90, asst. clin. prof. pediat., 1973-75, adj. asst. prof., 1975-87, adj. assoc. prof., 1985-88, prof., 1988-91; chief div. neonatology dept. pediat. Children's Hosp. Phila., 2004—04; dir. neonatology and newborn svcs. Hosp. of U. Pa., Phila., 1994—; prof. pediat.-ob-gyn., dir. neonatology fellowship progrram U. Pa. Sch. Medicine, 1991—2004. Mem. panel for consensus devel. infantile apnea and home monitoring NIH, 1986-87; mem. adv. bd. neonatal network Nat. Inst. Child Health and Human Devel., 1991—. Editor: Pediatric Care of the ICN Graduate, 1988, (with W. Taeusch) Schaffer and Avery's Diseases of the Newborn, 6th edit., 1991, 8th edit., 2004; reviewer Pediat., Jour. Pediat., Jour. Perinatology, Pediat. Pulmonology, Pediat. Rsch., New Eng. Jour. Medicine, Am. Jour. Ob-gyn., Archives Pediat. and Adolescent Medicine; mem. editl. bd. Contemporary Pediat.; contbr. articles to profl. jours. Grantee, NIH, 1993—. Mem. Am. Acad. Pediat., Soc. for Pediat. Rsch., Am. Pediatric Soc. Achievements include research on prevention and treatment of respiratory diseases in the newborn, antenatal steroids, chronic lung disease, inhaled nitric oxide to prevent chronic lung disease. Office: Childrens Hosp Phila 3535 Market Ste 1584 Philadelphia PA 19104-4399 E-mail: ballard@email.chop.edu.

BALLARD, SHERRY REBECCA, elementary school educator, insurance agent; b. Gastonia, NC, Apr. 17, 1951; d. William and Faye Laverne Bowlin; m. Michael Anthony Ballard, Nov. 22, 1969; children: Michael Anthony Jr.(dec.), Bryan Anthony. BA in Early Childhood Edn., Sacred Heart Coll., 1981. Sec. Bowlin Assoc., Gastonia, NC, 1967—69; asst. buyer Family Dollar Stores, Charlotte, NC, 1969—73; tchr. Gastonia County Sch., NC, 1977—; ins. agent ING, Minot, ND, 1993—; fin. planner Legacy Estates, Monroe, NC, 2000—. Fin. sec. Parent-Tchr. Orgn., Stanley, NC, 1996—. Pres. Ladies Auxilary for Stanley Vol. Fire Dept., 2003—; mem. New Life Bapt. Ch., Stanley, NC, 1974—. Named Tchr. of Year, Springfield Sch., 1996. Mem.: Alpha Delta Kappa. Republican. Baptist. Avocations: horseback riding, crafts, gardening, cooking. Personal E-mail: beckyb633@juno.com.

BALLARD, STEVEN C., academic administrator; m. Nancy Adams; children: Nathan, Laine. BA in History, U. Arizona, 1970; PhD in Political Science, Ohio State U., 1976. Post-doctoral fellow U. Okla., 1976—78, assoc. dir. sci. & policy, 1978—87, dir. sci. & policy, 1987—89; founding dir. Margaret Chase Smith Ctr. for Pub. Policy U. Maine, Orono, 1989—98; dir. State Govt. Partnership prog. U. Maine System, 1990—92; chair. dept. public admin. U. Maine, 1991—94; vice provost rsch. & dean grad. sch. Bowling Green State U., 1998—2001; provost & vice chancellor academic affairs U. Missouri, Kansas City, 2001—04; chancellor East Carolina U., 2004—. Co-author: (with Mike Devine, and others) Energy From the West: A Technology Assessment of Western Energy Resource Development, 1981, Water and Western Energy: Impacts, Issues, and Choices, 1982, (with Mike Devine, Michael Chartock, D.A. Huettner & Elizabeth Gun) Decentralized Electricity Production, 1987, (with Tom James, Mike Devine, Mark Meo, Time Adams & Lani Malysa) Innovation Through Technical and Scientific Information: Government and Industry Cooperation, 1989; co-editor: (with Thomas E. James) The Future of the Sunbelt: Issues in Managing Growth and Change, 1983. Office: E Carolina U E Fifth St Greenville NC 27858

BALLARD, SUSAN DOYON, library director; d. Alfred O. and Mary M. Doyon; m. Roger P. Ballard, June 28, 1985. BA in English Lit., U. NH, 1974; MS in Libr. and Info. Sci., Simmons Coll., 1975. Media Supervisor Dept. of Edn., NH, 1978, Computer Technology Educator Dept. of Edn., NH, 2000. Dist. libr. Londonderry (NH) Sch. Dist., 1975—78, media coord., 1978—85, dir., libr. and media svcs., 1985—95, dir., libr. media and tech. svcs., 1995—; instr. Fitchburg (Mass.) State Coll., 1984, Plymouth (NH) State Coll., 1989;

adj. faculty Rivier Coll., Nashua, NH, 2003—. Editor: (book) The Count on Reading Handbook. Mem. Thomson Gale Adv. Bd., 2004—, H.W. Wilson Libr. Adv. Panel, 2004—. Named to Hall of Fame, Londonderry H.S., 1987; recipient NH Excellence in Edn. award for Ednl. Media, NH Dept. of Edn., 1994, Commitment to Excellence in Edn., Greater Manchester Chamber of Commerce, 2001. Mem.: ASCD, NH Ednl. Media Assn. (pres. 1992—93, Outstanding Svc. award 1994, Pres.'s award 1997), NH. Libr. Assn., New Eng. Ednl. Media Assn. (pres. 1994—95), Internat. Soc. for Tech. in Edn., Assn. for Ednl. Comm. and Tech., Am. Assn. of Sch. Librarians (sec. 1993—96, Nat. Sch. Libr. Media Program of Yr. 2000), NH Soc. for Tech. in Edn., Gamma Delta Epsilon, Alpha Xi Delta. Office: Londonderry Sch Dist 268 Mammoth Rd Londonderry NH 03053 Office Phone: 603-432-6920 ext. 108. Business E-Mail: sballard@londonderry.org.

BALLARD, TERRY LEE, librarian, educator; b. Phoenix, Aug. 24, 1946; s. Sam Hugh and Florence May (Anderson) B.; m. Donna Gael Weiss, Jan. 23, 1972;1 child, Robert Daniel. BA, Ariz. State U., 1968, MEd, 1980; MLS, U. Ariz., 1989. Libr. asst. Phoenix Pub. Libr., 1969-90; systems librarian Adelphi U., Garden City, N.Y., 1990-95; libr. automation coord. NYU Law Sch., N.Y.C., 1995-97; automation librarian Quinnipiac U., Hamden, Conn., 1997—. Vis. prof. Palmer Libr. Sch., Brookville, N.Y., 1995—; adj. libr. St. Johns U., Jamaica, N.Y., 1992-95; adj. prof. So. Conn. State U., New Haven, 2000-01. Author: Innopac: A Reference Guide, 1995; co-author: Dictionary of American Biography, 1971-75, supplements, 1971-75, 76-80, Whole Library Handbook-2, 1994, Cybrarian's Manual, 1997, Scribners Encyclopedia of American Lives, 1998, 2000; columnist Info. Today, 1996-2001; contbr. articles to profl. jours. Recipient Productivity award City of Phoenix, 1983-88, Outstanding Article award Computers in Librs. mag. Mem. ALA, Nassau County Libr. Assn. (acad. & spl. librs. divsn., pres. 1995, v.p. 1994-95, bd. dirs.). Democrat. Avocations: astronomy, collecting first editions of Mark Twain. Office: Quinnipiac Univ Libr Mt Carmel Ave Hamden CT 06518 Office Phone: 203-582-8945. E-mail: terry.ballard@quinnipiac.edu.

BALLBACH, PHILIP THORNTON, political consultant, investor; b. Lansing, Mich., May 22, 1939; s. Nathan Anthony and Thelma Frances (Bowes) B. BA, Mich. State U., 1960; student, U. Mich., 1960-61; MA, Mich. State U., 1967. Social worker State of Mich., Corunna, 1961-64; legis. aide State Rep. H. James Starr, Lansing, Mich., 1964-67; exec. asst. State Atty. Gen.'s Dept., Lansing, Mich., 1967-81; county commr. Ingham County, Mason, Mich., 1980-93. Pub., Lansing This Weekend, 1963-64, The Gooseneck Tidings, 1977. Coord. Greater Lansing Assn. for Cmty. Edn., 1961-66; mem. Lansing Bd. Election Canvassers, 1965-69; dir. Cmty. Mental Health Bd., Lansing, 1977-99; treas. Zolton Ferency for Gov. Com., 1977-83; county liaison Eastside Neighborhood Orgn., Lansing, 1980-93; commr. Tri-County Regional Planning Com., Lansing, 1981-84; chairperson Ingham County Emergency Planning Com., Mason, Mich., 1988-93; campaign dir. Citizens for Pub. Recycling, Lansing, 1990; treas. People Achieving Legis. Power, 1992-95; campaign coord. Citizens for a Better Lansing, 1993-2003; bd. dirs. Peace Edn. Ctr., 1999-2005. Recipient Achievement award Nat. Assn. Counties, 1986, Dem. Party Ferency Activist Achievement award, 1998. Mem. Mich. Assn. Community Mental Health Bds. Democrat. Avocations: writing, history studies, skiing, softball. Home: 2723 E Lake Lansing Rd East Lansing MI 48823-9703 Office Phone: 517-487-3312.

BALLENGER, CASS (THOMAS CASS BALLENGER), former congressman, retired plastics company executive; b. Hickory, N.C., Dec. 6, 1926; s. Richard E. and Dorothy (Collins) B.; m. Donna Davis, June 14, 1952; children: Cindy Ballenger Brinkley, Melissa Ballenger Jordan, Dorothy Davis Weaver. Student, U. N.C., 1944-45; BA, Amherst Coll., 1948. Pres. Plastic Packaging, Hickory, 1957-86, chmn. bd., 1986—; pres. Hickory Paper Box Co., 1961-80; mem. 100th-108th Congresses from 10th N.C. dist., 1986—2005; ret.; chmn., founder Plastic Packaging, Inc., Hickory. Mem. edn. and workforce com., internat. rels. com. County commr. Catawba County, N.C., 1966-74, chmn. commn., 1970-74; mem. N.C. Ho. of Reps., Raleigh, 1974-76, N.C. Senate, Raleigh, 1976-86. Mem. Hickory C. of C. Lodges: Rotary (pres. Hickory club). Republican. Episcopalian. Avocations: golf, swimming. Office: Plastic Packaging Inc Box 2029 Hickory NC 28601

BALLENGER, HURLEY RENÉ, electrical engineer; b. Jacksonville, Ill., Nov. 26, 1946; s. Leonard Hurley and Katherine Natalie (Daniel) B.; m. Sandra Ann Rubley, Dec. 9, 1966. Student, Ill. Coll., 1964-65, 75. Technician electronics div. Hughs Aircraft, Inc., Tucson, 1973; maintenance supr. Fiatallis N.Am., Springfield, Ill., 1973-75, project engr., 1975-83, plant engr., 1983-86; tech. advisor CNC/CAM Fiatallis Europe, Lecce, Italy, 1986-87; plant engr. Illini Tech., Inc., Springfield, Ill., 1988, plant and mfg. engr., 1988-98; facilities engr. Phoenix Internat. (formerly Illini Tech., Inc.), Springfield, Ill., 1998—. Mem. career adv. bd. Lincoln Land Community Coll., Springfield, 1983-85. Served to staff sgt. USAF, 1965-72, Vietnam. Lutheran. Avocations: photography, home computing. Office: Phoenix Internat 5300 Rising Moon Rd Springfield IL 62707-6228

BALLENGER, JULIA NELL, education educator; b. Tyler, Tex., Jan. 26, 1949; d. Joe Ceafus and Mozel Marie Warren; m. Charles A. Ballenger Jr., May 1, 1971; 1 child, Chadwick. BS in Spl. Edn. Psychology, Tex. A&M U., 1970, Med in Elem. Edn., 1973; PhD in Edn. Adminstrn., U. Tex., 1996. Prin., program coord. Tyler Ind. Sch. Dist., Tex., 1989—92; exec. asst. to assoc. supt. Austin Ind. Sch. Dist., 1992—99; asst. prof. Stephen F. Austin State U., Nacogloaches, 2001—05, E.J. Campbell Disting. prof., 2005—. Mem. adv. bd. Stephen F. Austin State U., 2004—, mem. Coll. Edn. U. Ctr., 2004—. Mem.: AAUW (v.p. 2003—04), Nat. Coun. Profls. Edn. Adminstrn., Am. Assn. Ednl. Adminstrs., Phi Delta Kappa (pres. 2004). Democrat. Baptist. Avocation: reading. Home: Ridge Crest Townhouse 3230 Pearl St # 21 Nacogdoches TX 75965 Office Phone: 936-468-2908.

BALLENTINE, ALAN LANE, information technology manager, consultant; b. Anniston, Ala., Sept. 18, 1961; s. Lawrence M. and Elaine S. Ballentine; children: Christian T., Wesley J., Gabriel I. BA, Samford U., 1983; MDiv, So. Bapt. Theol. Sem., 1990. Cert. program developer Vitria Tech., Calif., 2005. Min., pastor United Ch. Christ, 1991—95; sr. cons. Software Spectrum, Inc., Chgo., 1995—97; tech. arch. InfoImage, Inc., Chgo., 1997—99; project mgr. Hot Samba, Schaumburg, Ill., 1999—2000; mgr. Vitria Tech., Sunnyvale, Calif., 2000—. Mgr. healthcare sys. project Vitria Tech., 2003—05, mgr. telecom. sys. project, 2001—04. Pres. Ralph Bermele Little League, Chgo., 1994—95; active Habitat for Humanity; pres. Cooper County Mental Health Assn., Boonville, Mo., 1992—94. 1st lt. U.S. Army, 1984—90. Named Outstanding Young Man, Outstanding Young Men of Am., 1989. Mem.: Ala. Info. Tech. Assn. Liberal. Episc. Avocations: hiking, camping, travel, reading. Office Phone: 408-212-2700.

BALLER, JAMES, lawyer; b. Berlin, Jan. 19, 1947; s. Samuel and Irene (Lusczanowska) B.; m. Marlene Berlin, May 21, 1972; children: Erica Berlin, Julia Berlin. AB, Dartmouth Coll., 1969; JD, Cornell U., 1972. Bar: U.S. Ct. Appeals (D.C. cir.) 1973, U.S. Ct. Claims 1974, U.S. Dist. Ct. D.C. 1973, U.S. Supreme Ct. 1978, U.S. Ct. Appeals (5th cir.) 1991, U.S. Ct. Appeals (fed. cir.) 1986. Assoc. Covington & Burling, Washington, 1972-79; ptnr. Baller & Downey, Washington, 1979-81; sole practice Washington, 1981-83; ptnr. Baller Hammett P.C., Washington, 1983-94; with The Baller Herbst Law Group, P.C., 1994—. Cons. in field. Contbr. articles to profl. jours. Legal counsel, bd. dirs., chmn. bd. Spl. Approaches to Juvenile Assistance, Washington, 1975-81; bd. dirs. Sun Found., 1986-93, pres., 1988-93; bd. dirs. DC Stoddert Soccer League, 1997—. Mem. ABA, Nat. Assn. Telecomm. Officers and Advisors, Dartmouth Lawyers Assn. Avocations: hockey, soccer, photography, skiing, reading. Home: 4526 30th St NW Washington DC 20008-2125 E-mail: jim@baller.com.

BALLESTEROS, PAULA MITCHELL, nurse; b. Jonesport, Maine, Oct. 18, 1950; d. Paul Frederick and Janice Madeline (Beal) Mitchell; m. Ernesto Gascon Ballesteros, Apr. 4, 1981; children: Christopher, Jonathan. BS in Profl. Arts, St. Joseph's Coll., 1984; BSN, Husson/Ea. Me. Med. Ctr. Baccalaureate Sch. Nursing, 1994; MS in Bus., Husson Coll., 2004. Cert. Nursing Administrn. Patient care mgr. Eastern Maine Med. Ctr., Bangor, 1974—, trustee, 1993-95. Chairperson adv. bd. Ea. Maine Tech. Coll., Bangor, Me., 1993-94; pres. Me. Coun. Nurse Mgrs., 1991-93, Ea. Me. Med. Ctr. auxiliary, Bangor, Me., 1993-95. Contbr. articles to profl. jours. Mem. St. Joseph Hosp. Auxiliary. Mem. Am. Orgn. Nurse Execs., Penobscot Med. Soc. Auxiliary, Me. Assn. Hosp. Auxiliaries (pres. 1994—). Democrat. Protestant. Avocations: skiing, tennis, reading. Home: 78 Packard Dr Bangor ME 04401-2531 Office: Ea Maine Med Ctr 489 State St Bangor ME 04401-6616 Office Phone: 207-973-7371. Business E-Mail: pballesteros@emh.org.

BALLESTEROS, VICTOR HUGO, dean; b. Chgo., Feb. 8, 1973; s. Jenner and Fanny Ballesteros (Stepmother); m. Myrandi Nichole Phipps; children: Brynlee Madison, Maycee Rian. BA, Dallas Bapt. U., 1991—94, MEd, 1995—97. Dean students Dallas Bapt. U., 2000—03; dean student affairs Parker Coll. of Chiropractic, Dallas, 2003—. Deacon First Bapt. Ch., Waxahachie, Tex., 2001—03. Mem.: Assn. Christians in Student Devel., Tex. Assn. Coll. and U. Student Personnel Adminstrs., Assn. Chiropractic Colls. Conservative. Avocations: mountain biking, gardening. Office: Parker Coll Chiropractic 2525 Walnut Hill Ln Dallas TX 75229 Office Phone: 214-902-2422. Office Fax: 214-902-2427. Business E-Mail: vballesteros@parkercc.edu.

BALLIETT, JOHN WILLIAM, entrepreneur, real estate executive; b. Rochester, NY, Sept. 10, 1947; s. Charles Garrison and Burnetta Elizabeth (Purtell) B.; m. Betsy Jane Van Patten, Jan. 25, 1969; 1 child, Noelle Elizabeth. BS in Physics, Grove City Coll., 1969; postgrad., U. Rochester, 1969-71. Devel. engr. Eastman Kodak Co., 1969-70; scientist Tropel Inc., 1970, mgr. applied optics, 1971-72, mktg. mgr., 1972-73; exec. v.p., dir. Quality Measurement Sys., Inc., Penfield, N.Y., 1973-77; pres. QMS Internat., Inc., Penfield, 1974-77, Balliett Assocs., Sarasota, Fla., 1978—, Shore Lane Devel. Corp. subs. (merger Sandbar Devel. Corp.), 1981—, 1990—. Pres., pub. Suncoast TV Facts, Inc., Sarasota, 1979-81; pres. Charter One, Inc., Sarasota, 1981—, Palma Sola Enterprises, Inc., 1990—; chmn., CEO Charter One Hotels & Resorts, Inc., 1989—; pres. Alacho Inc., 1992—; pres. Servus Hotel Group, Inc., N.Y.C., 1997-; mng. ptnr. Bayon Bleu, LLC, 2003; spkr. at nat. and internat. timesharing confs. Contbr. articles on timesharing to profl. publs.; patentee optical sys. Founding dir. Internat. Found. for Timesharing. Mem. Fla. Bar (citizen mem. grievance com.), U.S. C. of C., Sarasota County C. of C., Am. Land Devel. Assn., Nat. Timeshare Coun., Fla. Hotel-Motel Assn. Home: 1404 Westbrook Dr Sarasota FL 34231-3549 Office: 2032 Hillview St Sarasota FL 34239-2334

BALLIETT, WHITNEY, writer, critic; b. N.Y.C., Apr. 17, 1926; s. Fargo and Dorothy (Lyon) B.; m. Blue Hurley King, 1951; children: Julia, Elizabeth, Will; m. Nancy Kraemer, 1965; children: Whitney, Jamie. BA, Cornell U., 1951. Mem. editl. staff New Yorker mag., N.Y.C., 1951—2001, successively collator, proofreader, reporter, 1951-57, staff writer, 1957—; columnist on jazz; book, movie, theater and art reviewer, reporter. Author: The Sound of Surprise, 1959, Dinosaurs in the Morning, 1962, Such Sweet Thunder, 1966, Super-Drummer: A Profile of Buddy Rich, 1968, Ecstasy at the Onion, 1971, Alec Wilder and His Friends, 1974, New York Notes, 1976, Improvising, 1977, Night Creature, 1981, Jelly Roll, Jabbo, and Fats, 1983, American Musicians: Fifty-Six Portraits in Jazz, 1986, American Singers: Twenty-Seven Portraits in Song, 1988, Barney, Bradley and Max: Sixteen Portraits in Jazz, 1989, Goodbyes and Other Messages: A Journal of Jazz, 1981-90, 91, American Musicians II: Seventy Two Portraits in Jazz, 1996, Collected Works: A Journal of Jazz, 1954-2001, 2002; contbr. to N.Y. Rev. Books, 1998—. Recipient Acad. award in lit. Am. Acad. Arts and Letters, 1996. Mem. Century Assn.

BALLIN, WILLIAM CHRISTOPHER, international shipping, investments, and energy advisor; b. Ft. Wayne, Ind., May 3, 1927; s. Christopher T. and Katherine (Nolles) B.; m. Dolores Mary Witte-Jack, June 18, 1948; children: Stuart, Kirk, Scott, Elizabeth. BA, U. Toledo, 1950; postgrad., Colo. Coll., Am. U.; advanced degree, Imede, Lausanne, Switzerland. Pub. affairs coord. Marathon Oil Co., Findlay, Ohio, 1954-61, Washington rep., 1961-63; European mgr. govt., corp. relations Marathon Internat. Oil Co., Geneva, 1963-69; v.p. Crosby Kelly Investor and Corp. Devel., N.Y.C., 1969-70; sr. v.p. Am. Export Lines, Inc., N.Y.C., 1970-76, exec. v.p., 1976-77; chmn. Overland Trust Fin. Svcs., Geneva and N.Y.C., 1978—. Vice chmn. Contship Holdings, INT, B.M.V.; bd. dirs. Contship Asia, Pacific, Hong Kong, Valley-Kuwait Group, Kuwait, CMA-CGM Am.; advisor Atechma Cie, Paris. Mem. Pres.'s Delegation to Algeria, 1987. Office: Malagnou House-CP 424 1208 Geneva Switzerland

BALLINGER, CHARLES WILLIAM, sanitary engineer, consultant; b. Athens, Ohio, Oct. 24, 1949; s. William Pearl Ballinger and Ruth Virginia Bayless; m. Lynn Dorland Ballinger, July 12, 1996. BSCE, Ohio Univ., Athens, Ohio, 1972, MS in Sanitary and Structural Engr., 1973. Registered civil, Ariz., 1980, sanitary, Ariz., 1993, cert. civil, Calif., 1986, lic. profl., Fla., 2002, cert. Mich., 1979, lic. civil, Nev., 1994, cert. profl., New Mex., 1994, lic. N.C., 2002, Ohio, 1976, Oreg., 1996, Utah, 1994; cert. wastewater treatment 3 Ariz., 1987. Dist. engr. Ohio EPA Southeast Dist., Logan, Ohio, 1973—74; project engr. A.E. Stilson and Assoc., Columbus, Ohio, 1974—76; project mgr./project engr. Gilbert/Commonwealth Assoc., Jackson, Mich., 1976—79; asst. project mgr. Brown and Caldwell, Tucson, 1979—82; cont. supr. (in Saudi Arabia) Bechtel Inc., San Francico, 1982—83; project mgr./project engr. Moore-Knickerbocker and Assoc., Phoenix, 1984—86; resident engr. and proj. engr. Camp, Dresser, and McKee Inc., Phoenix, 1986—91; project mgr. Coe and Van Loo Cons., Inc., Phoenix, 1991—93; pres. Ballinger Cons. P.C., Scottsdale, Ariz., 1993—. Mem.: NFPA, ASCE, Water Environ. Fedn., Instrumentation, Sys., and Automation Soc., Constrn. Specifications Inst., Ariz. Water and Pollution Control Assn., Ariz. Small Utilities Assn., Am. Water Works Assn., Am. Pub. Works Assn., Am. Coun. of Engrng. Co. of Ariz., Am. Coun. of Engrng. Co. Avocations: scuba diving, snorkeling, camping, dance. Office: Ballinger Cons P C PO Box 12187 Scottsdale AZ 85267

BALLINGER, JAMES K., art museum executive; b. Kansas City, Mo., July 7, 1949; s. Robert Eugene and Yvonne (Davidson) B.; m. Nina Lundgaard, Aug. 21, 1971; children— Erin, Cameron BA, U. Kans., 1972, MA, 1974. Gallery coordinator Tucson Art Ctr., 1973; registrar U. Kans., Lawrence, 1973-74; curator collections Phoenix Art Mus., 1974-81, asst. dir., 1981, dir., 1982—. Author: (exhbn. catalogues) Beyond the Endless River, 1980, Visitors to Arizona 1846 to 1980, 1981, Peter Hurd, 1983, The Popular West, 1982, Thomas Moran, 1986, Frederick Remington, 1989. Bd. dirs. Balboa Art Conservation Ctr. Fellow Am. Assn. Mus. Dirs. (bd. dirs.), Western Assn. Art Museums; mem. Central Ariz. Mus. Assn. (v.p. 1983) Avocations: hiking, basketball, travel. Office: Phoenix Art Mus 1625 N Central Ave Phoenix AZ 85004-1685

BALLINGER, ROYCE EUGENE, academic administrator, educator; b. Burkburnett, Tex., Feb. 21, 1942; s. Royce and Luceil Evelyn (Tucker) B.; m. Ruth Ann Hamshar, May 15, 1976. BA, U. Tex., 1964; MS, Tex. Tech U., 1967; PhD, Tex. A&M U., 1971. Asst. prof. biology Angelo State U., San Angelo, Tex., 1971-74, assoc. prof., 1974-76, U. Nebr., Lincoln, 1976-82, dir. biol. scis., 1982-90, prof., 1982—, assoc. vice chancellor rsch., 1993-2000; dir. Nebr. EPSCoR, Lincoln, 1993—; asst. exec. v.p., provost U. Nebr., Lincoln, 2000—. Bd. govs. Ctr. Gt. Plains Studies U. Nebr., Lincoln, 1981-88; internat. adv. panel Chinese U. Devel. Project, World Bank, Montreal, Can., 1988; nat. adv. coun. BIOCOM, S.C., 1992-96; dir. Nebr. EPSCoR, Lincoln, 1993—. Author: How to Know Amphibians and Reptile, 1983; contbr. 125 articles to profl. jours. Governing bd. mem. Nat. EPSCoR Coalition, Washington, 1995-98, 99—, sec., 2000. Rsch. grantee NSF, 1968-80, 93—, Dept. Energy, 1993, 2000—, Dept. Def., 1993, NASA, 1993. Mem. Am. Soc. Ichthyologists & Herpetologists (bd. govs. 1985-87), Sigma Xi. Office: Nebr EPSCoR UNL Campus 203 Whittier Bldg Lincoln NE 68583-0848 E-mail: rballinger1@unl.edu.

BALLINGER, WALTER FRANCIS, surgeon, educator; b. Phila., May 16, 1925; s. Robert I. and Frances (Taylor) B.; children: Walter Francis, Christopher Bardin, David Gordon; m. Mary Randolph Gordon Dickson, Oct. 4, 1980. Student, Cornell U., 1942-44; MD, U. Pa., 1948. Intern 1st Surg. Div., Bellevue Hosp., N.Y.C., 1948-49, asst. resident surgery, 1949-50, chief resident surgery, 1955-56; asst. resident surgery Columbia-Presbyn. Med. Center, 1953-55; from instr. to assoc. prof. Jefferson Med. Coll., Phila., 1956-63; assoc. prof. surgery Johns Hopkins Sch. Medicine, 1964-67; Bixby prof., head dept. surgery Washington U. Sch. Medicine, St. Louis, 1967-78, prof. surgery, 1978-92, prof. emeritus surgery, 1992—. Med. dir. health adminstrn. program Wash. U. Sch. Medicine, 1993—99. Editor: Research Methods in Surgery, 1964, The Management of Trauma, 1968, 4th edit., 1985, (with T. Drapanas) Practice of Surgery: Current Review, 1972, 2d edit., 1974; editor-in-chief (with G. Zuidema) Surgery, 1971-97, (with J. Hepner) Best Practices and Benchmarking in Healthcare; mem. editl. bd. Brit. Jour. Surgery, 1989-94. Served to capt. U.S. Army, 1950-52. Markle scholar med. sci., 1961-66 Mem. Am. Surg. Assn., Soc. Clin. Surgery, Soc. Univ. Surgeons, A.C.S., James IV Assn., Halsted Soc. Home: 1203 Log Cabin Ln Saint Louis MO 63124-1528

BALLIRO, JOSEPH JAMES, SR., lawyer; b. Boston, May 21, 1928; s. James and Anna (DeLambo) B.; m. Amalia Barreda, Sept. 20, 1986; children by previous marriage: James, Joseph, Jullianne, Patrice, Linda. AA, Northeastern U., 1948; LLB, Boston U., 1951. Bar: Mass. 1951. Asst. counsel Vol. Def. Assn., Boston, 1951-55; sr. counsel Joseph J. Balliro, Atty.-at-Law, Boston, 1955—. Fellow Am. Coll. Trial Lawyer; mem. ABA, Mass. Trial Lawyers Assn. (pres.), Nat. Assn. Trial Defense Lawyers, Mass. Bar Assn. Named one of top Boston lawyers, Boston mag., 2004. Office: 99 Summer St Ste 1650 Boston MA 02110-1200 Office Phone: 617-737-8442.

BALL-KILBOURNE, GARY LEE, minister; b. Washington, Feb. 14, 1953; s. George J. and Ernestelle (Loffler) Kilbourne; m. Debra G. Ball, Sept. 5, 1976; children: Matthew, Zachary. BA, Western Md. Coll., 1974; MDiv, Garrett-Evang. Theol. Sem., 1978; MA, Vanderbilt U., 1983, PhD, 1988. Ordained to ministry United Meth. Ch., 1976. Pastor Harper's Ferry (W.Va.) United Meth. Parish, 1978-80, Missouri Valley Parish, Washburn, N.D., 1983-85, Center (N.D.) United Meth. Ch., 1985-87, First United Meth. Ch., Jamestown, N.D., 1987-91; editor Adult Publs. United Meth. Pub. House, Nashville, 1991—. Conf. sec. N.D. Annual Conf., 1985-91. Co-author: (study guide) In Defense of Creation, 1986; contbr. articles to profl. jours. Dempster fellow Gen. Bd. of Higher Edn. and Ministry of the United Meth. Ch., 1983; Harold Stirling Vanderbilt scholar Vanderbilt U., 1980. Mem. Am. Acad. Religion, Soc. Christian Ethics, Christian Educators Fellowship. Home: 8207 Sawyer Brown Rd H-3 Nashville TN 37221 Office: PO Box 801 Nashville TN 37202-0801

BALLMAN, DONNA MARIE, lawyer; b. Mansfield, Ohio, July 23, 1959; d. Earl J. and Florine (Hansel) B. BA, Wellesley (Mass.) Coll., 1981; JD, U. Miami, 1986. Bar: Fla. 1986, U.S. Dist. Ct. (so. and mid. dists.) Fla., U.S. Ct. Appeals (11th cir.) 1999, U.S. Ct. Appeals (fed. cir.) 2002; cert. mediator. Assoc. Hornsby & Whisenand, Miami, Fla., 1987-90; prin. Donna M. Ballman, PA, Ft. Lauderdale, Fla., 1990—. Bd. dirs. Grand Jury Assn. Fla.; councilwoman Cmty. Coun. Two Dade County, 1997-98. Paul B. Anton scholar U. Miami Sch. Law, 1985-86, Fla. Assn. Women Lawyers scholar, 1985. Mem. Assn. Trial Lawyers Am., Am. Arbitration Assn., Nat. Coun. Jewish Women (life), Nat. Assn. Women's Bus. Owner's (mem. bd. dirs., co-chair govt. affairs com. 1991-92), Fla. Bar, Fla. Assn. for Women Lawyers (mem. bd. dirs. 1992-95, chair legis. com. 1991-92, chair gender bias com. 1992-95), Grand Jury Assn. Fla. (Woman of Distinction award 1995), Dade County Bar Assn. (sr. citizens handbook com., young lawyers sect. 1988, vol. lawyers 1988-89), Downtown Bus. and Profl. Women (Woman of Yr. award 1991-92, 1st v.p. 1992-94), Million Dollar Adv. Forum, Omicron Delta Kappa. Office: Donna M Ballman PA Ste 3010 4801 S University Dr Fort Lauderdale FL 33328 Office Phone: 954-680-6669. Personal E-mail: ballmand@mindspring.com.

BALLMAN, PATRICIA KLING, lawyer; b. Cin., May 1, 1946; d. John Joseph and Margaret Elizabeth (Stacy) Kling; children: Andrew J., Cara E. BS with honors, St. Louis U., 1967; JD with honors, Marquette U., 1977. Bar: Wis. 1977, U.S. Dist. Ct. (ea. and we. dist Wis.) 1980, U.S. Ct. Appeals (7th Cir.) 1983, U.S. Ct. Appeals (8th Cir.) 1986, U.S. Supreme Ct. 1986. Ptnr. Quarles & Brady, Milw., 1977—. Officer lawyer regulation Dist. II Com. Mem. fin. divsn., chair pers. subcom. United Way, 2000—02; past chair Shorewood Bd. of Rev.; mem. Gov.'s Task Force on Ethics Reform in Govt., 2002; bd. dirs. The Benedict Ctr., 2004—, Wis. Law Found. Master: Fairchild Inns of Ct.; mem.: ABA, Am. Acad. Matrimonial Lawyers (pres. Wis. chpt. 2002—04), Wis. Bar Assn. (pres. 2002—03), Milw. Bar Assn. (pres. 1995—96). Office: Quarles & Brady 411 E Wisconsin Ave #2040 Milwaukee WI 53202-4461 Office Phone: 414-277-5000. E-mail: pkb@quarles.com.

BALLMER, STEVEN ANTHONY, computer software company executive; b. Farmington Hills, Mich., Mar. 24, 1956; s. Frederick and Beatrice (Dworkin) Ballmer; m. Connie Snyder, 1990; 3 children. BA in Applied Math. & Econ., Harvard U., 1977; postgrad., Stanford U., 1979—80. Asst. product mgr. Procter & Gamble Co., 1977—79; with Microsoft Corp., Redmond, Wash., 1980—, v.p. mktg., v.p. corp. staffs, sr. v.p. sys. software, exec. v.p. sales & support, 1992—98, pres., 1998—2001, CEO, 2000—. Bd. dirs. Microsoft Corp., 2000—, Accenture, 2001—; bd. overseers Harvard U.; adv. coun. Stanford Bus. Sch. Avocations: exercise, jogging, playing basketball. Office: Microsoft Corp 1 Microsoft Way Redmond WA 98052-8300

BALLONE, EILEEN MARIE, music educator, musician, organist; b. Hackensack, N.J., May 6, 1946; d. Frank Albert and Marie Lillian (Mancini) Caiazzo; m. Henry Frederick Ballone, May 4, 1968; children: Brian James, Marie Elena. BA in Elem. Edn., Caldwell Coll., 1986; MS in Elem. Edn., Marywood Coll., 1992; student, Fairleigh Dickinson U., 1965—66, Bergen C.C., Paramus, N.J., 1979—81. Liturgically cert. musician Archdiocese Newark; cert. elem. edn. tchr., nursery sch. tchr. N.J. Pvt. organ tchr., 1963—; with N.J. Bell Tel. Co., 1967—68, Am. Book-Stratford Press, INc., Saddle Brook, NJ, 1968—70; music tchr. Sacred Heart Sch., Rochelle Park, NJ, 1979—84, Annunciation Sch., Paramus, NJ, 1981—83, St. Anne's Sch., Fair Lawn, NJ, 1983—85, St. Philip the Apostle Sch., Saddle Brook, 1984—86; music tchr. grades K-8 St. Francis Assisi Elem. Sch., Ridgefield Park, NJ, 1986—; music tchr., chair music dept. Paramus Cath. Girls Regional H.S., 1986—90; music tchr. grades K-8 St. Leo's Elem. Sch., Elmwood Park, NJ, 1990—91, St. Philip the Apostle Elem. Sch., Saddle Brook, 1999—2000. Organist, choir dir. St. Michael's Ch., Palisades Park, NJ, 1967—77; asst. organist St. Margaret Cortona Ch., Little Ferry, NJ, 1978—84, St. Philip the Apostle Ch., Saddle Brook, 1978—84, head organist, 1984—86; dir. music, organist, choir dir. Our Lady Queen of Peace Ch., Maywood, NJ, 1987—99; dir., organist children's choir St. Francis Assisi Ch., Ridgefield Park, 1999—2003, dir. children's bell choir, 2000, dir., organist, choir dir., 2000—02; dir. music, organist, choir dir. St. Margaret Cortona Roman Cath. Ch., Little Ferry, 2002—. Den mother Cub Scouts Pack 222 St. Philip the Apostle Parish, Saddle Brook; com. mem. Brownie Troop 772 St. Philip the Apostle Parish, Saddle Brook; v.p. St. Philip the Apostle Home-Sch. Assn., Saddle Brook, 1977—79, pres., 1979—83. Mem.: Nat. Pastoral Musicians Assn. (pres. 2004—), Am. Fedn. Musicians, Nat. Assn. Pastoral Musicians (pres. music edn. divsn. 2004—, chpt. mem., dirs. music ministry divsn.), Choristers Guild, N.J. Music Edn. Assn., Music Educators Nat. Conf., Nat. Cath. Edn. Assn. Roman Catholic. Home: 23 Rochelle Pkwy Saddle Brook NJ 07663-4616 Office Phone: 201-641-9159. Personal E-mail: musicmomemb@yahoo.com.

BALLOT, MICHAEL HARVEY, business administration educator, consultant; b. N.Y.C., Jan. 8, 1940; s. Max and Claire (Bayer) B.; m. Nancy Diann Christiansen, Feb. 23, 1963; children: Michele Ann Dodge, Feb. 23, 1963; childrne: Michele Ann Dodge, David Andrew, Edward Carter. BME, Cornell U., 1962; MBA, U. Santa Clara, 1964; MA in Econs., Stanford U., 1968, PhD in Bus. and Econs., 1973. Mfg. engr. Lockheed Missiles & Space

Co., Sunnyvale, Calif., 1962-64, Beckman Instruments, Palo Alto, Calif., 1964-65; asst. prof. econs. Chico (Calif.) State Coll., 1968-71; asst. prof. bus. adminstrn. U. Pacific, Stockton, Calif., 1971-74, assoc. prof., 1974-79, prof., 1979—. Cons., spkr. in field; arbitrator, Stockton, Calif., 1975—. Author: Decision-Making Models in P/OM, 1986, Labor Management-Relations in a Changing Enviroment, 1996 (2d edit.). Cons. U.S. Dept. Transp., 1973, Stockton State Hosp., 1974, Stockton Econ. Devel. Agy., 1971, 85-86. Mem. Decision Scis. Inst., Am. Econs. Assn., Soc. Computer Simulation, Am. Acad. Polit. and Social Sci., Prodn. and Ops. Mgmt. Assn., Indsl. Rels. Rsch. Assn., Beta Gamma Sigma. Home: 5149 Gadwall Cir Stockton CA 95207-5331 Office: U of the Pacific Eberhardt Sch Bus Stockton CA 95211-0001 Office Phone: 209-946-2623.

BALLOTS, JOAN HESSDORFER, secondary school educator; b. Phila., Jan. 2, 1932; d. Harry Charles and Helen Marie (Tracy) Hessdorfer. BS in Edn., Temple U., 1953; MS in Edn., U. Bridgeport, 1969. Tchr. Sayre Jr. High Sch., Phila., 1953-55, Lincoln High Sch., Phila., 1955-58, Saxe Jr. High Sch., New Canaan, Conn., 1958—95. Mem. trustees' task force Temple U., Phila., 1987—, chmn. appropriate role of non-revenue sports com., 1987—. Sec., vice chmn. New Canaan Rep. Town Com., 1976-86, del. to state convs., 1976-86; mem, sec. New Canaan Town Coun., 1986-95; mem. athletic coun. Temple U.; bd. trustess Temple U., Phila. Pa., 1995—; mem. bd. vis. Temple U. Sch. Dentistry. Recipient F. Eugene Dixon award Temple Univ. Gen. Alumni Assn., 1989. Mem. New Canaan Country Club. Avocations: golf, fishing, watercolor painting, photography, politics.

BALLOU, JANICE DONELON, research director; b. New Brunswick, N.J., May 13, 1944; s. Peter and Kathryn (Koval) Donelon; m. Donald Thomas Ballou, Nov. 12, 1966 (div. 1984); children: Peter, David. BA, Douglas Coll., 1966; MA, Rutgers U., 1977. Tchr. Sayreville (N.J.) Jr. High Sch., 1966-71; dir. field ops. Eagleton Inst., Rutgers U., New Brunswick, NJ, 1977-80, assoc. dir., 1980-82, dir. Star-Ledger/Eagleton Poll, dir. Ctr. for Pub. Interest Polling, 1989—2001; v.p. divsn. head Louis Harris & Assocs., N.Y.C., 1982-86; v.p. group head Response Analysis, Princeton, N.J., 1986-89; v.p., dep. dir. surveys and info. svc. Mathematica Policy Rsch., Inc., Princeton, NJ, 2001—. Bd. dirs. Inst. Rsch. on Aging and Health Fin., Princeton, N.J., Essex C.C. Found. Contbg. author: Polling America. An Encyclopedia of Public Opinion, 2005. Co-founder Parents Drug and Alcohol Coun., Highland Park, N.J., 1991; bd. dirs. Rutgers Substance Abuse Task Force, New Brunswick, 1990-93, The Citizen's Com. on Biomed. Ethics, Summit, N.J., 1993-98; chair Pathways to Participation Civic Edn. Program com., New Brunswick, 1992; grad. bd. Leadership N.J., 1991-99; pres. Bd. Leadership N.J. Grad. Orgn., 1995; mayor Highland Park Econ. Devel. Com., 1999. Leadership N.J. fellow Partnership for N.J., 1990, Ford Found. fellow, 1990; named Alumnae of Yr. by Highland Park High Sch., 1992. Mem. Am. Assn. Pub. Opinion Rsch. (pubs. chair 1988-90, sec.-treas. 1991-93, standards chair 1999-2001, councillor-at-large 2002—), Nat. Network State Polls (mem. exec. coun. 1989—), Nat. Coun. Pub. Polls (mem. exec. coun. 1993—), N.J. Internat. Forum Women (sec.), N.J. Assn. for Pub. Opinion Rsch. (pres. 2002—), Douglass Soc. (Douglass Coll. assoc. alumnae). Avocations: raising christmas trees, travel, hiking, outdoor activities, reading. Office: Mathematica Policy Rsch PO Box 2393 Princeton NJ 08543-2392 Office Phone: 609-750-4049.

BALLOU, KENNETH WALTER, retired transportation executive, dean; s. Thomas Walter and Anne M. (Blanck) A.; m. Ann Dysart; children— Stephen K., Jeffrey S., Laura A., Ellen S. AB, Ed.M., Tufts U.; postgrad., Rutgers U., UCLA, Wharton Sch., U. Pa., NYU. Tchr., Verona, NJ; asst. dir. admissions Northeastern U., Boston, dir. admissions, dean univ. relations, dean Univ. Coll., dean adult edn.; pres. Wellesley Motor Coach Co., Mass., 1978-88; v.p., gen. mgr. Waters Bus. Systems., Inc., Framingham, Mass. Cons. U.S. Office of Edn., various colls.; corporator Framingham Savs. Bank, 1980-85; mem. Spl. Legis. Commn. on Sch. Transp. Safety; sr. lectr. in mngt. Northeastern U., 1979-90. Author monographs in field of adult edn. and sch. transp. Chmn. Framingham Sch. Com.; corporator Framingham Union Hosp.; corporator Northeastern U., mem. nat. coun., bd. overseers, mem. long range planning com., life mem. President's Club; bd. dirs. Mass. Osteo. Hosp.; life mem. Danforth Mus. Art, Framingham Hist. Assn.; mem. Sudbury Valley Trustees, Cahoon Mus.; past mem. bd. assessors 1st Parish, Framingham; endowed Childrens Gallery of Danforth Mus. and established the Dean Kenneth W. Ballou Family Scholarship, Northeastern U.; trustee Cotuit Pub. Libr. Mem. AAUP, Assn. Higher Edn., Am. Mgmt. Assn., Adult Edn. Assn., Am. Assn. Continuing Edn., Coun. Advancement of Edn., Am. Pers. and Guidance Asn., Mass. Audubon Soc., Ariz. Hist. Soc., Zeta Psi, Heritage Mus., Hyannis Yacht Club, Barnstable Newcomers Club (past pres.), Kings Way Golf Club. Home: 19 Roosevelt Rd Cotuit MA 02635

BALLOUN, JOSEPH EUGENE, lawyer; b. Hays, Kans., June 16, 1929; m. Patricia Balloun (div.); children: Michael, Kristen; m. Sheila Gail Wombles; 1 child, David Balloun. BS degree, U. Kans., 1951, JD, 1954. Bar: Kans. 1954, Kans. Supreme Ct., U.S. Dist. Ct. (Kans.), U.S. Ct. Appeals (10th cir.) 1963, U.S. Tax Ct. 1972, U.S. Supreme Ct. Atty. USAF, Enid, Okla., 1955-57, Ostrum & Balloun, Russell, Kans., 1957-62, Turner & Balloun, Great Bend, Kans., 1962-72, Payne & Jones, Olathe, Kans., 1972-80, Balloun & Bodinson, Olathe, Kans., 1980-84; ptnr. Shook, Hardy & Bacon, Overland Park, Kans., 1984—, vice chmn. gen. litig. div. Mem. Kans. 10th judicial dist. nominating commn.; mediator U.S. Dist. Ct. Kans. Bd. mem. Child Abuse Prevention Coalition, Johnson County, Kans., Foster Children Johnson County, Inc. Recipient Justinian award, Johnson County Bar Assn., Whittaker award, Lawyers Assn. Kans. City. Fellow Am. Coll. Trial Lawyers; mem. ABA (Pro Bono award), Kans. Bar Assn., Kans. Assn. Def. Counsel (past pres.), Am. Bd. Trial Advocates; master emeritus Kans. Inn of Ct., Order of the Coif. Office: Shook Hardy & Bacon 10801 Mastin Ste 1000 84 Corporate Woods Overland Park KS 66210-1697 Office Phone: 913-451-6060. Office Fax: 913-451-8879.

BALLOW, MARK, immunologist, educator; b. Harrisburg, Pa., Sept. 8, 1943; m. Molly Ballow, June 25, 1967; children: Sarah, Mara, Andrew. BA, Rutgers U., 1965; MD, U. Chgo., 1969. Diplomate Nat. Bd. Med. Examiners, Am. Bd. Pediatrics, Am. Bd. Allergy and Immunology, Diagnostic Lab. Immunology. Intern, resident Yale-New Haven Hosp., 1969-71; fellow U. Minn., 1971-73; chief clin./exptl. immunology U. Conn. Health Ctr., Farmington, 1975-79, assoc. prof. pediatrics, 1979-85, prof. pediatrics, 1985—; prof., chief allergy and immunology divsn. Children's Hosp. Buffalo, SUNY at Buffalo, 1988—. Dir. Am. Bd. Allergy and Immunology, 1993-99. Fellow Am. Acad. Allergy and Immunology (Carl Arbesman Meml. lectr. 1994); mem. Soc. Pediatric Rsch., Clin. Immunology Soc., Am. Pediatric Soc., Phi Beta Kappa. Avocations: skiing, tennis. Office: SUNY-Buffalo/Childrens Hosp Dept Allergy & Immunology 219 Bryant St Buffalo NY 14222-2006 Office Phone: 716-878-7105. Business E-Mail: ballow@buffalo.edu.

BALLOWE, JAMES, language educator, writer; b. Carbondale, Ill., Nov. 28, 1933; s. Frank Charles and Wilma Ruth (Maynard) B.; children: Jeffrey, Mary; m. Ruth Ganchiff. BA, Millikin U., 1954; MA, U. Ill., 1956, PhD, 1963. Tchr. pub. schs. Decatur, Ill., 1954-55; grad. asst. U. Ill., 1955-61; asst. prof. English Millikin U., 1961-63; mem. faculty dept. English Bradley U., Peoria, Ill., 1963-99, prof., chmn., 1971-74, dean Grad. Sch., 1974-86, assoc. provost, 1979-86, dean communications and fine arts, 1986-90, disting. prof. emeritus of English, 1999—; chmn. Commn. Instns. Higher Edn., North Central Assn., 1985-86. Narrator Herrin Massacre, Nat. Pub. Radio, 1997. Author: (poetry) The Coal Miners, 1979, (history) The Story of the Morton Arboretum, 2003; editor: George Santayana's America, 1967, Anglo-Welsh Poetry, 1989. Mem. Ill. Arts Coun., 1975-83, Ill. State Mus. Bd., 1976—, Ill. Humanities Coun., 1997-2002. Recipient Poetry award Ill. Arts Coun., 1975, 78, Creative Non-fiction award Ill. Arts Coun., 1993. Mem. Ill. Assn. Grad. Schs. (pres. 1979-80), Midwestern Assn. Grad. Schs. (pres. 1978-79). Home: PO Box 302 Ottawa IL 61350-0302 Personal E-mail: jcballowe@aol.com.

BALL-SARET, JAYNE ADAMS, small business owner; b. East St. Louis, Ill., Apr. 10, 1956; d. H. Jay and Faye M. (Adams) Ball; m. Mitchell I. Saret. BA, Ea. Ill. U., 1977, MA, 1983. Interior designer Carter's Furniture, Charleston, Ill., 1977-85; from customer svc. advisor to dir. client svc. Consol. Comm., Mattoon and Charleston, 1985—94; owner, designer Grand Ball Costumes, 1985—. Pres., dir. Charleston Cmty. Theatre, 1983—85. Mem.: Phi Alpha Eta. Republican. Avocations: singing, directing, acting, sewing. Office: Grand Ball Costumes 609 6th St Charleston IL 61920-2018 Office Phone: 217-345-2617.

BALLY, ALBERT W., retired petroleum geologist, geology educator; PhD, U. Zurich, Switzerland, 1953. Harry Carothers Weiss prof. geology Rice U., Houston, now prof. emeritus. Contbr. articles to profl. jours. Recipient R.J.W. Douglas Meml. medal Can. Soc. Petroleum Geologists, 1996, Signey Powers Meml. award Am. Assn. Petroleum Geologists. Achievements include research in the structure of foreland folded belts, the formation of allochthonous salt sheets in a continental slope environment, mechanical separation of crust and sediments from the underlying lithosphere, inversion of half-grabens in a major orogenic mechanism. Office: Rice U Dept Geology MS126 6100 S Main St Houston TX 77005-1892

BALMAN, STEVEN K., lawyer; b. Wichita, Kans., Nov. 2, 1956; s. Nan Poston Balman, Gail Eugene Balman; m. Kelly Sue Knopp, June 1, 1991 (div. 2002); 1 child, Elizabeth Grace. AB, Harvard U., 1978; JD, U. Tex., 1981. Bar: Okla. 1981. Assoc. Conner & Winters, Tulsa, Okla., 1981—88; ptnr. Bond & Balman, Tulsa, 1988—96; sr. ptnr. Baker & Hoster, Tulsa, Okla., 1996—97; dir. Inhofe, Jorgenson & Balman, Tulsa, 1997—99, Sneed Lang, P.C., Tulsa, 1999—. Adj. prof. law U. Tulsa, Okla., 1991—; judge temporary divsn. panel LXL Okla. Ct. of Civil Appeals, Tulsa, 1992—93; adj. settlement judge U.S. Dist. Ct., No. Dist. Okla., Tulsa, 1998—. Editor-in-chief Am. Jour. Criminal Law, 1981; contbr. articles to profl. jours. Okla. membership chair U.S. Supreme Ct. Hist. Soc., Washington, 1992—93; mem. judicial conf. U.S. Ct. of Appeals, 10th cir., 1989—. Mem.: Tulsa County Bar Assn. (bd. dirs. 1997—), Am. Inns of Ct. Hudson Hall Wheaton Chpt. (sec. 1995—96), Am. Law Inst. (emeritus), Federalist Soc. (pres. Tulsa lawyers chpt. 2000—). Methodist. Office: Sneed Lang PC 2 W 2nd St Ste 2300 Tulsa OK 74103 Office Phone: 918-583-3145. Office Fax: 918-582-0410. Business E-Mail: sbalman@sneedlang.com.

BALMER, THOMAS ANCIL, state supreme court justice; b. Longview, Wash., Jan. 31, 1952; s. Donald Gordon and Elisabeth Clare (Hill) B.; m. Mary Louise McClintock, Aug. 25, 1984; children: Rebecca Louise, Paul McClintock. AB, Oberlin Coll., 1974; JD, U. Chgo., 1977. Bar: Mass. 1977, D.C. 1981, U.S. Dist. Ct. Mass. 1977, Oreg. 1982, U.S. Dist. Ct. Oreg. 1982, U.S. Ct. Appeals (9th cir.) 1982, U.S. Ct. Appeals (D.C. cir.) 1983, U.S. Supreme Ct. 1987. Assoc. Choate, Hall & Stewart, Boston, 1977-79, Wald, Harkrader & Ross, Washington, 1980-82; trial atty. antitrust divsn. U.S. Dept. Justice, Washington, 1979-80; assoc. Lindsay, Hart, Neil & Weigler, Portland, Oreg., 1982-84, ptnr., 1985-90, Ater Wynne LLP, Portland, 1990—93, 1997—2001; dep. atty. gen. State of Oreg., Salem, 1993-97; justice Oreg. Supreme Ct., Salem, 2001—. Adj. prof. of law Northwestern Sch. Law Lewis and Clark Coll., 1983-84, 90-92. Contbr. articles to law jours. Active mission and outreach com. United Ch. of Christ, Portland, 1984-87, Met. Svc. Dist. Budget Com., Portland, 1988-90; bd. dirs. Multnomah County Legal Aid Svc., Inc., 1989-93, chair 1992-93; bd. dirs. Chamber Music Northwest, 1997-2003, Classroom Law Project, 2000—, U.S. Dist. Ct. Hist. Soc., 2003-, Oreg. Law Inst., 2005—. Mem. ABA, Oreg. Bar Assn. (chmn. antitrust sect. 1986-87, mem. fed. practice and procedure com. 1999-2001). Home: 2521 NE 24th Ave Portland OR 97212-4831 Office: Oreg Supreme Ct Supreme Ct Bldg 1163 State St Salem OR 97310 Office Phone: 503-986-5717. Business E-Mail: thomas.balmer@ojd.state.or.us.

BALMORI, DIANA, landscape designer; b. Gijon, Spain, June 4, 1936; d. Clemente and Dorothy (Ling) Hernando-Balmori. Diploma in architecture, U. Tucuman, Argentina, 1960; BA in Urban History, UCLA, 1968, PhD, 1973; student in Landscaping, Radcliffe U., 1989. Asst. prof. SUNY, Oswego, 1974-78, assoc. prof., 1978-79; assoc. Cesar Pelli & Assocs., New Haven, 1977-81, prin. for landscape and urban design, 1981-90; prin. Balmori Assocs., New Haven, 1990—; critic Yale U. Sch. Architecture, 1990—; lectr. Yale U. Sch. Forestry and Environ. Studies, 1990—; Davenport Chair of Archtl. Design Yale Sch. of Architecture, 2004. Apptd. mem. Commn. Fine Arts, 2003. Author: Beatrix Farrand, Beatrix Jones Ferrand (1872-1959) Fifty Years Of American Landscape Architecture, 1982, Beatrix Farrand's American Landscapes, 1985, Transitory Gardens, Uprooted Lives, 1993, Redesigning the American Lawn, 1993, Saarinen House and Garden: A Total Work of Art, 1995; contbr. Beatrix Farrand At Dumbarton Oaks: The Design Process of a Garden; co-author: The Land and Natural Development (LAND) Code: Guidelines for Environmentally Sustainable Land Development. Chmn. civic alliance World Trade Ctr. Meml. Com., N.Y.C.; mem. program com. N.Y. New Visions; bd. dirs. Minetta Brook Com. for Comprehensive Design Landscape Plan for White Ho. Recipient Pub. Space award Conn. chpts. AIA/Am. Soc. Landscape Architects, 1990, Judges award Harry Chapin Media Aawards, 1995; grantee Ossabaw Found., 1980, N.Y. State Coun Arts, 1987, Carolyn Found., 1990, Nat. Endowment for the Arts, 1990, 92; rsch. fellow NYU, 1982. Mem. Am. Soc. Landscape Architects, Catalog of Landscape Records (bd. dirs.), Van Alen Inst. (mem. exec. com.), Am. Hist. Assn. Office: Balmori Assocs 129 Church St Ste 304 New Haven CT 06510-2056 E-mail: diana.balmori@yale.edu.

BALMUTH, BERNARD ALLEN, retired film editor; b. Youngstown, Ohio, May 19, 1918; s. Joseph and Sadie (Stein) B.; m. Rosa June Bergman, Mar. 2, 1952; children: Mary Susan, Sharon Nancy. BA in English, UCLA, 1942. Postal clk. U.S. Postal Svc., LA, 1946-55; asst. and apprentice film editor, film editor LA, 1955-90; ret., 1990. Instr. film editing dept. of the arts UCLA Ext., 1979-99 (cert. of appreciation); film editing cons. Am. Film Inst., LA, 1982-92. Author: The Language of the Cutting Room, 1979, Introduction to Film Editing, 1989. Initiator petition STOP Save TV Original Programming and Stop Excessive Reruns, 1971-75. Adminstrn. non-commd. officer U.S. Army, 1942-45. Recipient Honor Cert. for Contbn. Acad. TV Arts and Scis., 1974, Emmy nomination Best Editing, 1982, Mimes award for acting Youngstown Coll., 1937. Mem. Am. Cinema Editors (life, bd. dirs. 1982-85, 97-99, sec. 1985-87, v.p. 1987-91, chmn. spl. awards com. 1988-99, hon. historian 1993-, Ace Heritage award, 2003), Hollywood Entertainment Labor Coun. (rep. for Editors Guild 1972-2002), Stage Soc. (bd. dirs., sec. 1949-54), TV Acad. Motion Picture Editors (mem. exec. com. peer group 1988-). Democrat. Jewish. Avocations: cinema, theater, dance, cinema books. Address: care Rosallen Publs PO Box 927 North Hollywood CA 91603-0927

BALMUTH, MICHAEL A., retail executive; With Bamberger's; exec. v.p., gen. mdse. mgr. Karen Austin Petites, 1986—88; sr. v.p., gen. mdse. mgr. Bon Marche, Seattle, 1988—89; joined Ross Stores, 1989, various positions including sr. v.p., gen. merchandise mgr., exec. v.p merchandising, 1993-96, CEO, vice chmn., 1996—, CEO, vice chmn., pres., 2005—. Office: Ross Stores Inc 4440 Rosewood Dr Pleasanton CA 94588*

BALNAVE, RICHARD D., law educator; b. NJ, 1949; BA, Coll. William and Mary, 1971; MA, SUNY, Albany, 1973; JD, Case Western Reserve U., 1977. Bar: Va. 1986. Staff atty. to mng. atty. Legal Services of Northeastern Pa., Wilkes-Barre, 1977—80; atty. pvt. practice Wilkes-Barre, 1980—84; asst. prof. U. Va. Sch. Law, 1984—90, assoc. prof., 1990—96, prof., 1997—. Dir. Va. Dispute Resolution Ctr., 1987—91; mem. commn. on needs of children Va. Bar Assn., 1990—96; mem. ct. improvement project adv. com. concerning foster care and adopting Supreme Ct. Va., 1995—. Office: U Va Sch Law 580 Massie Rd Charlottesville VA 22903-1789 Office Phone: 434-924-7582. E-mail: rdb@virginia.edu.

BALOFF, NICHOLAS, business educator, consultant; b. San Francisco, Aug. 9, 1937; s. Nicholas Boris and Emily (Ersunoff) B.; children— Steven Nicholas, Katherine Louise. BS with highest honors, U. Calif., Berkeley, 1959; SM, M.I.T., 1960; PhD, Stanford U., 1963. Registered profl. engr., Okla., Calif. Asst. prof. bus. adminstrn. U. Chgo., 1963-67; prof. U. Del Valle, Colombia, 1965; assoc. prof., div. dir. Stanford (Calif.) U., 1967-73; prof., dean Coll. Bus. Adminstrn., U. Okla., Norman, 1973-76; dean and prof., 1976-77; prof. Sch. Bus. and Pub. Admnstrn., Washington U., St. Louis, 1976—. Cons. Proctor & Gamble, Kellwood Corp., Dept. Health and Human Svcs., U. Mich. Mallinckrodt Med. Inc., Gen. Am. Life Ins., Four Seasons Nursing Ctrs., Inc., McKinsey & Co., Ford Found., Assn. Am. Med. Colls., Citicorp, Nestle Food Corp., Pet Inc., Monsanto, Levi Strauss, Kaiser, Deutsche Fin. Svcs. Contbr. articles to profl. jours. Fellow Ford Found., 1960-63, fellow MIT, 1959, U. Calif. scholar, 1957-59. Mem. Sigma Xi, Beta Gamma Sigma, Tau Beta Pi, Alpha Pi Mu. Office: Washington Univ PO Box 1133 Saint Louis MO 63188-1133 Business E-Mail: baloff@wustl.edu.

BALOG, RITA JEAN, retired librarian; b. Ashtabula, Ohio, Sept. 24, 1930; d. Frederick Carroll and Marguerite Ethel (White) Grady; m. Richard Francis Balog, Oct. 16, 1949 (dec. Feb. 1988); children: Rebecca Kay, Richard Francis Jr., Ronald Frank, Robert Henry; m. Charles R. Haapala, Oct. 24, 1999. AA, Kent State U., 1977, BA in Gen. Studies, 1978, MLS, 1980. Clk., typist Harbor Pub. Libr., Ashtabula, 1973-75, children's libr., 1975-80; libr., dir. Harbor-Topky Meml. Libr., Ashtabula, 1980-97; ret., 1997. Vol. libr. Thomas Jefferson Elem. Sch., Harbor Spl. Sch., Ashtabula, 1972-75. Sec., mem. Ashtabula Archtl. Restoration and Rev. Bd., 1975-95; vol. leader Lake River coun. Girl Scouts U.S., Niles, 1958-73, mem. nominating com., 1989-91, bd. dirs., 1991-95, child camp dir.; trustee Coun. Ashtabula County Librs., chair, 1994-96. Mem. ALA, AAUW, Ohio Libr. Assn., N.E. Ohio Libr. Assn. (regional adv. bd. 1984-86), Coun. Ashtabula County Librs. (pres. 1985-86), Ashtabula Area Mus. and Hist. Soc. (trustee 1992-98), Zonta (pres. 1987-89). Democrat. Avocations: collecting rocks, wild flowers, swimming, needlecraft.

BALOGH, ANDRAS, mathematician, educator; s. Andras and Andrasne Zsuzsanna Balogh; m. Erika Marki Marki, July 15, 1989; children: Beatrix, Andras Jr. PhD, Tex. Tech U., Lubbock, 1997. Vis. asst. prof. Idaho State U., Pocatello, 1997—98; project scientist U. of Calif., San Diego, La Jolla, Calif., 1998—2002; asst. prof. math. U. of Tex. - Pan Am., Edinburg, Tex., 2002—. Conf. editl. bd. mem. IEEE Control Systems Soc., 2004—; assoc. editor Internat. Jour. of Robust and Nonlinear Control, United Kingdom, 2004—. Grantee, Dept. of Def., Army Rsch. Office grantee, 2003—. Mem.: Am. Math. Soc. Office: The University of Texas - Pan American Department of Mathematics Edinburg TX 78541-2999 Office Phone: 956-381-2119.

BALOGH, MARY, writer; b. 1944; BA in English lang. and lit. with honors, U. Wales, 1965, diploma of edn., 1967. English tchr. Kipling HS, Saskatchewan, Canada, 1967—82, Windthorst HS, Saskatchewan, 1982—88, prin., 1982—88. Author: numerous books including most recently, A Masked Deception, 1985, The Trysting Place, 1986, Secrets of the Heart, 1988, A Gift of Daisies, 1989, A Promise of Spring, 1990, Devil's Web, 1990, Snow Angel, 1991, Christmas Beau, 1991, A Christmas Promise, 1992, Courting Julia, 1993, Tempting Harriet, 1994, Lord Carew's Bride, 1995, The Temporary Wife, 1997, The Last Waltz, 1998, One Night for Love, 1999, More Than a Mistress, 2000, No Man's Mistress, 2001, A Summer to Remember, 2002, Slightly Married, 2003, Slightly Wicked, 2003, Slightly Scandalous, 2003, Slightly Tempted, 2004, Slightly Sinful, 2004, Slightly Dangerous, 2004. Home: Box 571 Kipling SK Canada S0G 2S0 Office: c/o Random House 1745 Broadway New York NY 10019 E-mail: author@marybalogh.com.

BALOGLU, SEYHMUS, hospitality and tourism educator; b. Diyarbakir, Turkey, July 1, 1966; s. Cahide and Zulfikar Baloglu; m. Zerrin Kezban Keklik; children: Deniz Dogukan, Derin Burak. BS, Mersin Turizm Isletmecilik ve Otelcilik Y.O., 1989; MBA, Hawaii Pacific U., 1993; PhD, Va. Poly. & State U., 1996. Cert. Hospitality Educator Am. Hotel and Motel Assn., 1999. Rsch. assoc. Mersin Turizm Isletmecilik ve Otelcilik Y.O., Mersin, Turkey, 1989—91; gen. mgr. IKM Turizm Ltd., Alanya, Turkey, 1987—89; assoc. prof. U. of Nev., Las Vegas, 1996—. Cons. Asis, 1999—2002, The Edn. Found. of PCMA, 2000, Sta. Casinos, Inc., Las Vegas, 1999—2000, McCarran Internat. Airport, Las Vegas, 1999—2000, The Ednl. Inst. of Am. Hotel and Lodgry Assn., 1997—98; presenter in field various confs., including World Gaming Congress Casino Ops. CHRIE Conv. Svcs. Mktg. Conf. Symposium on Consumer Psychology. Contbr. articles and revs. to profl. jours., 2001 (Emerald Mgmt. Revs. Citation of Excellence, 2001), chapters to books. Bd. mem. Coral Edn. Corp., Reno, 1998—2002. Fellow Turkish Higher Edn. Coun., 1991—96. Mem.: Internat. Soc. Travel and Tourism Educators, Hospitality Sales and Mktg. Assn., Travel and Tourism Rsch. Assn. (awards), Internat. Coun. on Hotel, Restaurant and Instn. Edn., Am. Mktg. Assn. Office: U Nev Las Vegas 4505 Maryland Pkwy Box 456023 Las Vegas NV 89154-6023 Office Phone: 702-895-3932. Business E-Mail: baloglu@ccmail.nevada.edu.

BALOUN, JOHN CHARLES, retired wholesale distribution executive; b. Chgo., May 1, 1934; s. John Nicholas and Anne (Giera) B.; m. Lynette Anne Jehs, July 27, 1963 (dec. Apr. 1998); children: John Christopher, Michael Warren. BSc, DePaul U., 1956. CPA, Ill. Audit staff Arthur Andersen & Co., Chgo., 1956-63; contr., asst. sec. Super Food Svcs., Inc., Chgo., 1963-67, treas., 1967-68, Dog'N Suds, Inc., Champaign, Ill., 1968-69; dir. planning and control distbn. divsn. Champion Internat., Inc., Chgo., 1969-74; treas. IGA, Inc., Chgo., 1974-77, v.p., 1977-80; v.p. fin. IGA Inc., Chgo., 1986-93, contr., 1993-96; ret. IGA, Inc., 1996; v.p. fin. Allied Van Lines, Inc., Broadview, Ill., 1980-83; contr., dir. corp. devel. Altair Corp., Northbrook, Ill., 1984-86. Pres. bd. dirs. No. Ill. Food Bank, St. Charles, Ill., 1990-91, bd. dirs., 1988-93, 96-2002. 2d lt. AUS, 1957. Republican. Home: 610 Western Ave Glen Ellyn IL 60137-4058 E-mail: jbaloun919@aol.com, jbaloun@netsoupe.com.

BALOW, IRVING HENRY, retired education educator; b. Wabasha, Minn., Jan. 19, 1927; s. Laurence Christian and Katherine (Yost) B.; m. Joyce Elizabeth Binner, June 8, 1950 (dec. 1980); children: Mary, Thomas, Michael, Robert, Ann.; m. Alta Sitton, June 27, 1981. BS, U. Minn., 1951, MA, 1957, PhD, 1959. Elementary sch. tchr., Theilmam, Minn., 1951-53; tchr. elem. sch. Wabasha, 1953-54, 56-57; instr. U. Minn., 1957-59; mem. faculty U. Calif., Riverside, 1959—, prof. edn., 1968—, chmn. dept., 1963-70, assoc. dean, 1970-71, acting dean, 1971-72, dean, 1972-87, acting dean Grad. Sch. Mgmt., 1990-92; retired, 1992. Reading cons., 1959—. Contbr. articles to profl. jours. Served with USAAF, 1945-47. Home: 29410 Winding Brook Dr Menifee CA 92584 Personal E-mail: ibalow@earthlink.net.

BALOWS, ALBERT, microbiologist, educator; b. Denver, Jan. 3, 1921; s. Lazerus and Anna (Kleiner) B.; m. Patricia Ann Barker, Oct. 7, 1956; children: Eve Ellen, Daniel Scott. BA in Biology (Lowell scholar), Colo. Coll., 1942; MS in Microbiology, Syracuse U., 1948; PhD (Haggin fellow), U. Ky., 1952. Diplomate: Am. Bd. Med. Microbiology. Microbiologist St. Joseph Hosp., Lexington (Ky.) Clinic, 1952-69; dir. bacteriology div. Ctrs. Disease Control, USPHS, Atlanta, 1969-81; asst. dir. lab. sci. Ctrs. Disease Control, USPHS (Ctr. Infectious Diseases), 1981-88; dir. emeritus Ctr. Disease Control, USPHS (Ctr. Infectious Diseases), 1988. Asst. prof. medicine U. Ky. Med. Ctr., Lexington, 1960-63, assoc. prof. medicine and cell biology, 1963-69; prof. lab. medicine Emory U. Sch. Medicine, 1970-98, prof. lab. medicine emeritus, 1998; prof. biology Ga. State U., Atlanta, 1970—89; lectr. Am. Soc. Microbiology Found., 1974-76; cons. clin. microbiology VA Hosp., Good Samaritan Hosp., Lexington, 1965-69; Med. Svc. Corps Dept. Army, 1973-79; chair expert panel WHO Internat. Collaborating Ctr. for Rsch. Syphilis Serology and Immunology, 1974-82; bd. dirs. WHO Internat. Collaborating Ctr. for Rsch. and Ref. in Antibiotic Susceptibility Testing, 1975-82, WHO Internat. Collaborating Ctr. for Rsch. and Ref. in Diagnostic Methods and Materials, 1985-88; mem. expert panels bacterial diseases, biol. standardization, lab. sci. WHO, Geneva, 1977-88. Founding editor-in-chief Jour. Clin. Microbiology, 1974-79, Current Microbiology, 1982—2005; editor Applied Microbiology, 1965-74, Ann. Rev. Microbiology, 1979—, C.C. Thomas med. microbiology series, 1964-90; author, editor over 75 books on microbiology and infectious disease; mem. editorial bds. 6 sci. jours.; editor: The Prokaryotes, 1981, sr. editor: The Prokaryotes, 2d edit.,

1991; gen. editor: Topley & Wilson's Microbiology & Microbal Infections, 9th edit., 1998 (winner Advanced Edited Book category Med. Soc. London 1998); contbr. articles to profl. jours. Bd. dirs. Lexington chpt. NCCJ, 1960—64. With U.S. Army, 1943—46, with M.C. U.S. Army, 1943—46, ETO. Named Lab World Microbiologist of Yr., 1980; recipient Becton-Dickinson award in clin. microbiology, 1981, Silver medallion for outstanding contbns. to clin. microbiology Italian Soc. Microbiology, 1983, Louis T. Benezet Disting. Alumni award Colorado Coll., 1988, Abbott Labs. award for devel. of rapid lab. diagnostic techs., 1990, Disting. Profl. Recognition award, Am. bd. Med. Microbiology, 1997, bioMerieux Sonnenwirth award for exemplary leadership in clin. microbiology, 1999; named to Alumni Hall Fame, Palmer H.S., 2004 Fellow Am. Acad. Microbiology (bd. govs. 1973-77, 89-95, chmn. 1975-76), N.Y. Acad. Scis., AAAS, Am. Pub. Health Assn., Infectious Disease Soc. Am., Am. Acad. Lab. Physicians and Scientists; mem. Am. Soc. Microbiology (pres.-elect 1979-80, pres. 1980-81, council, also mem. council policy com. 1974-82, P.R. Edwards award for outstanding service furthering high profl. ideals and standards in microbiology from S.E. br. 1987, elected hon. mem. 1988), Am. Soc. Clin. Pathology, Soc. Gen. Microbiology, AAUP, Med. Mycol. Soc. Am., Soc. Applied Bacteriology, Am. Veneral Disease Assn., South Ctrl. Assn. Clin. Microbiology (hon.), Assn. State & Territorial Pub. Health Lab. Dirs. (hon.), Sci. Writers Guild, Sigma Xi, Blue Key, Omicron Delta Kappa, Tau Kappa Alpha, Zeta Beta Tau, B'nai B'rith. Home and Office: 105 Bay Colt Rd Alpharetta GA 30004-3531 Office Phone: 770-343-9271. Personal E-mail: abalows@aol.com. *Self esteem, good will and understanding are achieved by effective communication. Regrettably we fail because we do not listen. I have patterned my life after an ancient Chinese proverb: "First you must learn to listen well; then you will know that you have talked too much.".*

BALSAM, THEODORE, physician; b. N.Y.C., Apr. 11, 1931; s. Abraham and Esther (Golden) B.; m. Barbara Korn, Dec. 25, 1952; children: Hugh, Adrienne, Lisbeth. BA, NYU, 1952; MD, Chgo. Med. Sch., 1957; MPH, Johns Hopkins U., 1959. Diplomate Am. Bd. Internal Medicine. Intern Charity Hosp., New Orleans, 1957-58; fellow Johns Hopkins U., Balt., 1958-59; resident in medicine Bklyn. Hosp., 1959-61, fellow in gastroenterology, 1961-62; physician USPHS, S.I., 1964-97; pvt. practice Founders Med. Group, Chgo., 1997—. Pres. med. staff Louis A. Weiss Meml. Hosp., Chgo., 1976-78, 93-95, dir. patient hosp. orgn., 1996—. Mem. Sch. Bd., Lincolnwood, Ill., 1970-72. Fellow Am. Coll. Gastroenterology; mem. AMA, Ill. State Med. Soc., Chgo. Med. Soc. Avocation: travel. Office: Weiss Meml Hosp 4640 N Marine Dr Chicago IL 60640-5719 Office Phone: 773-564-5355.

BALSAMELLO, JASON REED, academic administrator, guidance counselor, principal; b. Hillsborough, NJ, Feb. 27, 1974; s. Elizabeth Reed and James Balsamello; m. Melissa Marley, Oct. 26, 2002. B in Spl. Edn., M in Counselor Edn., Kean U., 1999, M in Ednl. Adminstrn., 2001. Cert. sch. adminstr. NJ. Supr., tchr., elem. tchr. of handicapped, counselor Smerset County Ed. Services Commn., Somerset, NJ, 1999—2002; divsn. leader Daisy Recreation, East Brusnswick; prin. Hillcrest Acad. South Campus, Union County Edn. Svcs. Commn., Westfield, NJ. Recipient Governor's Tchr. Recognition award, Somerset County, 2001. Mem.: N.J. Prin. and Suprs. Assn., Union County Educators Assn., NJ Educators Assn. Avocation: Tae Kwon Do. Home: 24 Briar Cir Green Brook NJ 08812 Office: Union County Ed Svsc Commn Hillcrest Acad South Campus Westfield NJ 07090 Personal E-mail: mrandmrsb@verizon.net.

BALSAMELLO, MELISSA (MARLEY), elementary school educator; b. Red Bank, N.J., Aug. 5, 1975; d. Lucille (Perillo) M. BA in Psychology Douglass Coll., Rutgers U., 1997, EdM in Spl. Edn., 1998, postgrad., 1998—2001. Cert. early childhood edn., elem. edn., spl. edn., supr., psychology, dance/vocat. arts. Religious edn. tchr. St. Leo and Great, Lincroft, N.J., 1991-93; respite care provider, counselor ARC of Somerset, Manville, N.J., 1995; group leader, tchr. Happy Campers Ecology Camp, New Brunswick, 1996; tchg. asst., subsitute tchr. Douglass Child Study Ctr., New Brunswick, 1996-98; tchg. asst., field worker Douglass Devel. Disability Ctr., New Brunswick, 1995-96; store mgr. Pyramid Books, Highland Park, N.J., 1997-98; tchr., camp group leader Douglass Girl's Camp, New Brunswick, 1997-98; adminstrv. asst. to pres. United Bolt & Besel, 1998; tchr. 1st grade Franklin Park Sch., Somerset, NJ, 1998—2002, dance ensemble advisor, choreographer, 2000—02; 1st grade tchr., PTO tchr. rep., lunch supr. Woodrow Wilson Sch., Westfield, NJ, 2002—05; pre-K autism tchr. Jefferson Sch., 2005—. Mem. selection com. Douglass Alumni Soc., 1995-97; program facilitator Coll. Orientation and Recruitment Svcs., 1995-96; house chairwoman Coll. Residence Life, 1995-98; mentor Douglass Coll. Emerging Leaders Program, 1995-98; divsn. leader, specialist Daisy Recreation, East Brunswick, 1997-99; counselor Friday Night Live, East Brunswick, 1999-2000; divsn. leader/specialist Daisy Recreation Ctr., East Brunswick, 1997-98; honors rev., tutor 2-8th, Edison, N.J., 1999-2003. Pres. Am. Assn. Mental Retardation, Rutgers chpt., 1995-96; vol., asst. coach N.J. Spl. Olympics, 1996-97. Recipient Presdl. Cmty. Svc. award, Ocean Twp., Washington, 1992, scholarship North Monmouth AAUW, 1996-97. Mem. ASCD, N.J. Edn. Assn., Am. Ednl. Rsch. Assn., Franklin Twp. Edn. Assn., Am. Assn. Mental Retardation (pres. chpt. 1995-97), N.J. Assn. Edn. Young Children, Rutgers U. Student Edn. Assn., Chi Sigma (pres. 1995). Avocations: dance, singing. Home: 24 Briar Cir Green Brook NJ 08812 Office Phone: 732-424-8436. Personal E-mail: mrandmrsb@verizon.net.

BALSAMO, STEPHEN, brokerage house executive; Sr. v.p., chief credit officer First Options, Chgo.; exec. v.p., fin. LIT America, 1990, CFO, chmn. exec. com., vice chmn., 1992; spl. ltd. partner Spear Leeds & Kellogg, 1995, mng. dir., 1998, CFO N.Y.C. Office: Spear Leeds & Kellogg 30 Hudson St Jersey City NJ 07302 Office Fax: (212) 433-7254.

BALSER, ROBERT EDWARD, animation film producer, director; b. Rochester, N.Y., Mar. 25, 1927; s. Syrel Jesse and Goldie (Weisenberg) B.; m. Cima Diane Feinberg, June 25, 1950; 1 child, Trevel Morley. BA, UCLA, 1950. Dir. animation TVC, London, 1967-68, WorldWide Prodn., Barcelona, Spain, 1969-70, Halas and Batcheler, London, 1971-72; owner, dir. Pegbar Prodns., Barcelona, 1972-93; dir. TV series Cromosoma, Barcelona, 1994-95; retired cons. Barcelona, 1995; animation cons. Egypt, 1996, 1996-99. Pres. "CARTOON" (media program), 1988-2004; v.p. ASIFA Internat., 1979-94, pres. Spain, 1980-93; lectr. in field. Co-dir. The Yellow Submarine, 1967-68; supv. dir. The Jackson 5, 1971; producer numerous ednl. and TV series. V.p. Benjamin Franklin Found., Barcelona, 1986—, Am. Soc. Barcelona, 1986-90; pres. Benjamin Franklin Sch. Bd., Barcelona, 1986-95. With USN, 1945-46. Recipient EMMY award NATAS, 1980; 1st prize publicity Venice and Annecy Festivals, Italy and France, 1964, Acad. Motion Picture Arts Scis. Democrat. Jewish. Avocations: film, collecting stamps and coins.

BALSIGER, DAVID WAYNE, television director, writer, television producer, television director, researcher; b. Monroe, Wis., Dec. 14, 1945; s. Leon C. and Dorothy May (Meythaler) B.; children from previous marriages: Jennifer Anne, Lisa Atalie, Lori Faith. Student, Pepperdine U., Malibu, Calif., 1964-66, Cypress Jr. Coll., 1966, Chapman Coll. World Campus Afloat, Orange, Calif., 1967-68, Internat. Coll., Copenhagen, 1968; BA, Nat. U., San Diego, 1977; LHD (hon.), Lincoln Meml. U., Harrogate, Tenn., 1978. Chief photographer, feature writer Anaheim (Calif.) Bull., 1968-69; pub., editor Money Doctor, consumer mag., Anaheim, 1969-70; media dir. World Evangelism, San Diego, 1970-72; dir. mktg. Logos Internat. Christian Book Pubs., Plainfield, N.J., 1972-73; pres., dir. Master Media, advt. agy., Costa Mesa, Calif., 1973-75; pres. Balsiger Lit. Svc., Costa Mesa, 1973-78; v.p. communications Donald S. Smith Assocs., Anaheim, Calif., 1975-78; dir. creative devel. Sunn Classic Pictures, L.A., Salt Lake City, 1976-78; owner Writeway Lit. Assocs., Costa Mesa, 1978-92, Balsiger Enterprises, Costa Mesa, 1978-92, Bibl. News Svc., 1980-90; v.p. Donald S. Smith Assocs., Anaheim, 1982-86; owner BNS Publs., 1986-92; v.p. Am. Portrait Films Internat., Anaheim, 1990-91; chief rschr., field prodr., dir. Sun Internat. Pictures, Salt Lake City, 1992-94; exec. producer, dir. audio-video-media divsn. Group Publs., Loveland, Colo., 1994-98; sr. v.p., prodr., rights supr. Grizzly Adams Prodns., Loveland, Colo., 1998—. Vis. prof. Nat. U., San Diego, 1977—80. Author: (amazing stories books) The Satan Seller, 1972, The Back Side of Satan, 1973, Noah's Ark: I Touched It, 1974, One More Time, 1974, It's Good to Know, 1975, In Search of Noah's Ark, 1976, The Lincoln Conspiracy, 1977, Beyond Defeat, 1978, On The Other Side, 1978, 8 Mini Guide Books (travel series), 1975, (amazing coincidence books) Presidential Biblical Scorecard, 1980, 1984, 1988, Protection Scorecard, North Africa, 1987, 1988, 1989, Candidates Biblical Scorecard, 1986, Scoreboard Alert, 1989, Face in the Mirror, 1993, Ancient Secrets of the Bible, 1994, The Incredible Discovery of Noah's Ark, 1995, The Incredible Power of Prayer, 1996 (Dove Family Approved Seal, Film Adv. Bd. Excellence award, 1997, Freedom's Found. George Washington medal, 3 Telly awards, Worldfest Charleston award), The Evidence for Heaven, 2005; dir.(field producer, writer, researcher): (TV films) Operation Thanks, 1965, The Life and Times of Grizzly Adams, 1976—77, In Search of Noah's Ark, 1976, The Lincoln Conspiracy, 1977, The Bermuda Triangle, 1977, Ancient Secrets of the Bible, 1992 (9 awards including Worldfest Charleston award, 1995), Ancient Secrets of the Bible II, 1993, Mysteries of the Ancient World, 1994, Ancient Secrets of the Bible Collectors Series, 1995 (6 awards including 2 communicator awards of excellence); prodr.(6 TV shows and videos): Angels Sent on Assignment, 1996; dir.(field producer, writer, researcher): (TV films) The Incredible Power of Prayer, 4 vols., 1997; exec. prodr.: (video) Chadder's Stowaway Adventure, 1996 (Film Adv. Bd, Excellence award, 1996), (videos) Sing and Play Music Video, 1996, Sing and Play Music Jamboree, 1997, Chadder's Wild Frontier Advemture, 1997, Encounter with the Unexplained (series 52 vols.), 2002—03 (21 awards including 3 Telly awards and 1 Omni Intermedia award); prodr.: (TV series, spls.) Secrets of the Bible Code Revealed, 1998, The Bible Code: Future and Beyond, 1999 (5 awards including 1 videographer award of excellence), Millenium Fears: Fact or Fiction?, 1999, Miracle and Wonder of Prayer (series), 2000 (7 awards including 2 communicator awards of distinction); prodr.: (TV series) (spls.) The Search for Heaven, 2004, The Evidence for Heaven, 2004; prodr.: (TV series, spls.) George W. Bush: Faith in the White House, 2004, Breaking the DaVinci Code, 2005; (TV series) Xtreme Mysteries (104 vols.), 2003; chief rschr.: (TV series, and videos) many others.; author: numerous law enforcement publs. Press agt. John G. Schmitz congl. campaign, 1972, Gordon Bishop supr. campaign, Orange County, 1970; press agt. asst. Ronald Reagan for Gov., statewide, 1966; statewide campaign mgr. James E. Johnson for U.S. Senate, 1974; campaign mgr. Dave Gubler Congl. campaign, 1974; candidate Costa Mesa City Coun., 1980; Rep. candidate for Congress from 38th Dist. Calif., 1978; mem. Calif. Rep. Assembly, 1975-78, 81-84, Rep. Assocs. Orange County, 1977-79; mem. World Affairs Coun. Orange County and San Diego, 1969-70; assoc.mem. Calif. Rep. Cen. Com., 1969-70; bd. dirs. Chapman Coll. World Campus Afloat, 1967, Chrisma Ministries, Orange, Calif., 1969-73; founder Ban the Soviets Coalition, 1983-84; exec. com. Anatole Fellowship, 1983-87; founder, pres. Nat. Citizens Action Network, 1984-95; bd. dirs. Internat. Ch. Relief Fund, 1987-92. Recipient Vietnam appreciation citation Am. Soldiers in Vietnam, 1966, George Washington Honor medal Freedoms Found., 1978, 79, Religion in Media Angel trophy, 1981, 85, 87, 88, 89, 92, 93, 94, 95, 5 Telly awards for Ancient Secrets series, 1996; named Writer of Month Calif. Writer, 1967; grand winner Mercury award for Pub. Affairs, 1987, Gold Mercury award for Pub. Affairs Mag., 1987, Silver Mercury award for affairs video script, 1988, Nat. Faith and Freedom award Religious Heritage of Am., 1994; named to Lit. Hall of Fame, 1977; hon. tourism amb. Rep. of South Africa, 1991. Mem. Nat. Univ. Pres. Assocs., Coun. on Nat. Policy, Internat. Christian Visual Media Assn. (bd. mem.), Nat. Religious Broadcasters, Internat. Bible Reading Assn. (adv. bd.), Acad. TV Arts and Scis., Am. Film Mkt. Assn., Internat. Press Assn. (adv. bd.), Fellowship European Braodcasters. Address: PO Box 1987 Loveland CO 80539-1987 Personal E-mail: dwbalsiger@ultrasys.net. *I believe successful people have a God given purpose strong enough to make them form the habit of doing things they don't like to do in order to accomplish their purpose. Every single qualification for success is acquired through habit. People form habits and habits form futures.*

BALSILLIE, JIM, information technology executive; b. Seaforth, Feb. 3, 1961; married; 2 children. B of Commerce, U. Toronto, 1984; MBA, Harvard Bus. Sch., 1989. Chartered acct., Ont. With Ernst & Young, Toronto; exec. v.p., bd. dirs. Sutherland-Shultz Ltd., Kitchener; chmn., co-CEO Rsch. in Motion Ltd., Waterloo, Canada, 1992—. Founder The Centre for Internat. Governance Innovation, 2002. Named one of World's 100 Most Influential People, Time Mag., 2005. Office: Rsch in Motion Ltd 295 Phillip St Waterloo ON N2L 3W8 Canada

BALSLEY, PHILIP ELWOOD, entertainer; b. Augusta County, Va., Aug. 8, 1939; s. Henry Elwood and Marjorie Walden (Fielding) B.; m. Wilma Lee Kincaid, July 21, 1962; children— Gregory, Mark, Leah. Grad. high sch. With group Statler Bros., 1961—. Treas. Statler Bros. Prodns., 1973—. Bd. dirs. Happy Birthday U.S.A. Recipient numerous Grammy awards, Country Music Assn. awards. Presbyterian. Office: PO Box 2703 Staunton VA 24402-2703

BALSTAD, ROBERTA, social scientist; b. Mpls., June 25, 1940; d. Gerhard Oliver and Laverne K. (Anderson) Balstad; m. Gary David Lange, Nov. 26, 1959 (div. 1968); m. Floyd John Miller, June 15, 1969 (div. 2004); 1 child, Aaron Gerhard. BA, U. Minn., 1964, MA, 1970, PhD, 1973. Rsch. assoc. AIA, Washington, 1974; staff assoc. Social Sci. Rsch. Coun., Washington, 1975-81; exec. dir. Consortium Social Sci. Assns., Washington, 1981-84; divsn. dir. NSF, Washington, 1984-93; pres., CEO Consortium Internat. Earth Sci. Info. Network (CIESIN), University Center, Mich., 1993-98; adj. prof. natural resources policy behavior U. Mich., 1993-97; sr. rsch. scientist, dir. CIESIN Columbia U., NYC, 1998—. Guest scholar Woodrow Wilson Internat. Ctr. Scholars, 1994; sr. assoc. mem. St. Anthony's Coll., U. Oxford, England, 1991—92; mem. chmn. NATO adv. panel on Advanced Sci. Insts./Advanced Rsch. Workshops, Brussels, 1988—91; chmn. steering com. space applications and commercialization Nat. Rsch. Coun., 1999—2002, mem. exec. com. Space Studies Bd., 1995—2000, mem. climate rsch. com., 1997—99, mem. com. on global change rsch., 1999—2002; chmn. U.S. Nat. Com. on Sci. and Tech. Data, 2003—; mem. U.S. Nat. Com. IIASA, 1995—; chmn. adv. bd. Luxembourg Income Survey, 1987—91. Author: City and Hinterland, 1979; editor (with Harriet Zuckerman) Science Indicators: Implications for Research and Policy, 1979; contbr. articles to profl. jours.; translator poetry of Jorge Luis Borges, 1989, 90, 91, N.P. von Wyk Louw, 1998. Bd. trustees Newport Schs., Kensington, Md., 1986-91, St. Anthony's Coll. Trust, U. Oxford, 1994—, sec., 1997-2000, chair, 2000—, bd. dirs. Open GIS Consortium 2003—; adv. trustee Environ. Rsch. Inst. Mich., 1995-98. Recipient NSF Meritorious Svc. award, 1993. Fellow: AAAS (com. mem., chmn. 1987—93), NY Acad. Scis.; mem.: Coun. Fgn. Rels., Am. Lt. Translators Assn., Internat. Social Sci. Coun. (com. 1991—95, v.p. 1992—94), US Man Biosphere Program (com., chmn. 1989—91), Cosmos Club. Lutheran. Office: CIESIN Columbia U PO Box 1000 Palisades NY 10964-8000 Office Phone: 845-365-8988.

BALSTER, BARBARA ANN, elementary school educator; b. Ames, Iowa, Dec. 27, 1949; d. John Reamond and Bernadine Mary May; m. David Michael Balster, Oct. 5, 1974; children: Brian Matthew, Kevin Christopher. BA, Cornell Coll., Mt. Vernon, Iowa, 1972; MA, U. No. Colo., 1977. Cert. tchr., Iowa, reading recovery tchr., 1993, Orton Gilligham tchr., 2003. Elem. tchr. Monticello (Iowa) Community Schs., 1978—, mem. vertical team, 1992-94. Reading recovery tchr., 1993; Orton-Gillingham instr., 2003. Vol. Monticello Dem. Com., 1988-92; Sunday sch. tchr. United Meth. Ch. Monticello, 1990-91, troop treas. Boy Scouts Am.; treas. Movin' Up! Kids. Mem. NEA (chief negotiator 1997—), Iowa Edn. Assn., Monticello Edn. Assn., Beta Club (treas. 2003—, youth group leader 1994-2003). Avocations: travel, biking, reading, walking. Home: 135 Park Blvd Monticello IA 52310-1815 Office: Monticello Community Schs 321 W South St Monticello IA 52310-1942 Office Phone: 319-465-5425.

BALSTER, ROBERT LOUIS, alcohol/drug abuse services professional; b. St. Cloud, Minn., Oct. 12, 1944; s. Louis and Marion Balster; m. Sandra Kay Herwig, June 25, 1966; 1 child, Sarah Elizabeth. BS, U. Minn., 1966; PhD, U. Houston, 1970. Postdoctoral fellow in psychiatry and pharmacology U. Chgo., 1970-72; rsch. assoc. in psychiatry Duke U., Durham, N.C., 1972-73; asst. prof. pharmacology Med. Coll. Va., Richmond, 1973-78, assoc. prof., 1978-84, prof. pharmacology, 1984—2003, Luther A Butler prof. pharmacology, 2003—; dir. Inst. for Drug and Alcohol Studies, 1993—. Chmn. Drug Abuse Adv. Com., FDA, Rockville, Md., 1983-84; mem. Robert Wood Johnson Rsch. Network on Etiology of Tobacco Dependence, 1997-2005; mem. adv. bd. Partnership for Drug Free Am. Editor-in-chief Drug Alcohol Dependence, 1998—; contbr. articles to profl. jours. Recipient NIH Merit award, 1993-2004, Va. Commonwealth U. Faculty award of Excellence, 1999, Coll. on Problems of Drug Dependence Mentoring award, 2000, Faculty Tchg. Excellence award Va. Commonwealth U. Sch. Medicine, 2003. Fellow Coll. on Problems of Drug Dependence (charter fellow, pres. 1995-96), Am. Coll. Neuropsychopharmacology, Am. Psychol. Assn. (pres. psychopharmacology divsn. 1989-90, chair bd. sci. affairs 1995-96); mem. European Behavioral Pharmacology Soc. (coun. mem. 1986-94). Achievements include development of laboratory methods for studying the behavioral effects of drugs of abuse and procedures for drug abuse potential evaluation. Office: Va Commonwealth U PO Box 980310 Richmond VA 23298-0310 Business E-Mail: balster@hsc.vcu.edu.

BALTAKE, JOE, film critic; b. Camden, N.J., Sept. 16; s. Joseph John and Rose Clara (Bearint) B.; m. Susan Shapiro Hale. BA, Rutgers U., 1967. Film critic Gannett Newspapers (suburban), 1969, Phila. Daily News, 1970-85; movie editor Inside Phila., 1986—; film critic The Sacramento Bee, 1987—; syndicated movie critic Scripps Howard News Svc., 1999—. Leader criticism workshop Phila. Writer's Conf., 1977-79; film critic. Contbg. author: Encyclopedia of American Lives, Vol. 6, 2003; contbg. editor: Screen World, 1973-87; author: The Films of Jack Lemmon, 1977, updated, 1986; contbr. articles to Films in Rev., 1969-2000, broadcast criticism for Prism Cable TV, 1985; cons. Jack Lemmon: American Film Institute Life Achievement Award, 1987, Jack Lemmon: A Life in the Movies, 1990. Juror, program essayist Phila. Internat. Film Festival, 2004—05. Recipient Motion Picture Preview Group award for criticism, 1986, citation Phila. Mag., 1985, First Pl. commentary award Soc. Profl. Journalists, 1995, citation Sacramento News & Rev., 2000. Office: Sacramento Bee 2100 Q St Sacramento CA 95816-6899 Office Phone: 856-354-9048. Personal E-mail: joe.baltake@verizon.net. *Life's philosophy: "Living well is the best revenge."*

BALTAZZI, EVAN SERGE, engineering research consulting company executive; b. Izmir, Turkey, Apr. 11, 1921; came to U.S., 1959, naturalized, 1964; s. Phocion George and Agnes Zoe (Varda) B.; m. Nellie Despina (Biorlaro), July 17, 1945; children— Agnes, James, Maria D.Phys. Scis., Sorbonne U., Paris, 1949; D.Phil. in Chemistry, Oxford (Eng.) U., 1954. Rsch. dir., prof. rsch. French Nat. Rsch. Ctr., Paris, 1947-59; group leader organic chemistry rsch. Nat. Aluminate Corp., Chgo., 1959-61; mgr. organic chemistry sect. IIT Rsch. Inst., Chgo., 1961-63; dir. rsch. lab. Addressograph-Multigraph Corp., Chgo. and Cleve., 1963-77; pres. Evanel Assocs., Sagamore Hills, Ohio, 1977—. Mem. com. on U.S. currency NRC, 1985-86. Author: Basic American Self-Protection, 1972, Kickboxing, 1976, Stickfighting, 1977, Self-Protection at Close Quarters, 1981, Self-Protection Complete: The A.S.P. System, 1992, Dog Gone West: A Western for Dog Lovers, 1994, Plato and Socrates Trial, 1995, Alternative: Tai Chi Chaun, 2004-2005; patentee in field; originator Am. Self-Protection System. Mem. judo com. U.S. Olympic Com., 1967-74 Recipient Citizen of Yr. award Citizenship Coun. Met. Chgo., 1964; Outstanding Achievement award in sci. Immigrants Service League, 1965, citation, 1965; Outstanding Program award YMCA, 1967; recognition award Gordon Rsch. Confs., 1976; Ohio Spl. Olympics Gold medal volunteering award, 1999; named Outstanding Scientist of XXth Century Internat. Biog. Ctr., 2000; NRC Can. fellow, 1955, Brit. Coun. fellow, 1952-54 Fellow Am. Inst. Chemists (vice chmn. Chgo. chpt. 1970), Am. Chem. Soc. (sr.), Royal Chem. Soc. U.K., Soc. Photog. Scientists and Engrs. (pres., bd. dirs. Cleve. chpt. 1975-82), Am. Self-Protection Assn. (pres. 1965—), N.Y. Acad. Scis. Avocations: fencing, Judo, Aikido, American self-protection. Personal E-mail: ebaltazzi@aol.com.

BALTER, BERNICE, religious organization administrator; Exec. dir. Women's League for Conservative Judaism, N.Y.C., 1978. Nat. adv. bd. MAZON. Mailing: Women's League for Conservative Judaism 475 Riverside Dr New York NY 10115 Office Phone: 212-870-1260 ext. 7157. Office Fax: 212-870-1261. E-mail: bbalter@wlcj.org.

BALTER, FRANCES SUNSTEIN, civic worker; b. Pitts. d. Elias and Gertrude Susntein; m. James Stone Balter, May 15, 1948; children: Katherine (Mrs. Ross Anthony) (dec.), Julia Frances, Constance Cantor, Daniel Elias. Student, Sarah Lawrence Coll., 1939-41, New Sch. Social Rsch., 1941-43; cert. Inst. Arts Adminstrn., Harvard U., 1973. Adminstrv. asst., assoc. prodr. Ednl. TV Sta. WQED-TV, Pitts., 1963-67; prodr., mng. dir. Freedom Readers, 1964-67; co-founder, incorporator, sec. bd. dirs. Pitts. Coun. Arts, 1967-70; cultural cons. Mayor's Office Dir. Office Cultural Affairs, Pitts., 1968. Initiator Three Rivers Arts Festival 1960; co-dir. Ohio and Miss. River Valley Art Festival, 1961-62; mem. Pa. Coun. Arts, 1972-78; co-founder Pioneer Crafts Coun., Mill Run, Pa., 1972; exec. dir. Poetry on the Buses, 1974—. Author of poems. Bd. dirs. Coun. for Arts MIT, 1985-93, Palm Beach Festival, 1987-89. Named Woman of Yr. Art Post-Gazette, 1969. Mem. Nat. Soc. Arts and Letters (Pitts. chpt.).

BALTER, LESLIE MARVIN, business communications educator; b. N.Y.C., Feb. 27, 1920; s. Harry and Rose Balter; m. Frances Hughes; 1 child by previous marriage, Kenneth Robert (dec. 1979); 1 child by previous marriage, Sheila Beth. BSEE, Columbia U., 1941; postgrad., Rutgers U.; MA, NYU, 1969. Civilian radio engr. Signal Corps Devel. Lab., Ft. Monmouth, N.J., 1941-45, in ETO, 1942; chief engr. Masters Crystal Co., quartz crystal prodn., 1945-46; founder, dir. Jersey City Tech. Inst., 1947—; founder br. operation as Paterson (N.J.) Inst., 1956—; founder Sch. Bus. Machines tchg. IBM machines Plaza Sch., Paramus, N.J., 1958—; cons. test engr. Consumers Rsch., Washington, N.J. Contbr. articles to Electronic Design Mag., Bus. Edn. World, Tech. Edn. News. Mem. N.J. Vocat. Edn. Master Plan Com. Comm.; chmn. Jersey City CD Coun., 1950-53; pres. Ferncroft Park Coop. Mem. IEEE (life, participant Legacies 1994), N.J. Assn. Pvt. Career Schs. (pres. 1971), N.J. Bus. Edn. Assn., Columbia Club N.Y., Delta Pi Epsilon. Home: 41 Ferncroft Park Ramsey NJ 07446-2575 Office: Plaza Sch of Technology c/o PC Tech 2815 John F Kennedy Blvd Jersey City NJ 07306-3936 E-mail: lbalter@optonline.net.

BALTHASER, GERDA HAAS, elementary school educator; b. Syracuse, N.Y., Apr. 3, 1936; d. Max Oskar and Luise (Emmert) Haas; m. Robert George Balthaser, June 13, 1959; children: Scott, Debbie Balthaser Ziegler. BS in Elem. Edn., Elizabethtown (Pa.) Coll., 1965; MS Elem. Edn., Kutztown U., 1968; Cert. in Early Childhood Edn., Millersville U., 1988. Tchr. kindergarten Hamburg Area Sch. Dist., Pa., 1963-68; tchr. 2nd grade Cornwall-Lebanon Sch. Dist., Pa., 1968-70, tchr. kindergarten, 1970—99; ret., 1999. Class agt. for devel. office Elizabeth Coll., 1989—; pres. Ch. Women United of Lebanon County, 1993-97; pres. Women of Evangelical Lutheran Ch. of Am.(WELCA), Hill Lutheran Ch., Cleona, Pa., 2001-2005; coord. World Day of Prayer, Ch. Women United Lebanon County, 1998-2002; vol. reader Reach Out and Read, Hyman Caplan Hosp., Lebanon, Pa., 2002—; elections clerk Lebanon County, Pa., 2001—. Mem. PASR (Pa. Assn. of Sch. Retirees), AAUW (Lebanon Valley br. sec. 1990-94, Lebanon Valley br. treas. 1999-2003, Woman of Yr. 1993), LebCoPASR (Lebanon County Pa. Assn. of Sch. Retirees),Lebanon County Ednl. Honor Soc. (corr. sec. 1979-80, rec. sec. 1990-92, treas. 1996-97), Elizabethtown Coll. Alumni Coun. (pres. 1985-86), Delta Kappa Gamma (chpt. pres. 1988-90, parliamentarian 1990-92, Alpha Alpha state hist. records chmn. 1991-93, state fin. com. 1993-96, Alpha Alpha State Conv. treas. 2002-, Alpha Alpha State scholarship com., 1996-99, Alpha Alpha State Founders' scholar 1987, Golden Gift leadership/mgmt. seminar scholarship 1993). Democrat. Lutheran. Avocations: reading, travel, swimming. Home: 2005 Kline St Lebanon PA 17042-5724 E-mail: ghbalth@aol.com.

BALTHASER, LINDA IRENE, retired academic administrator; b. Kokomo, Ind., Feb. 25, 1939; d. Earl Isaac and Evelyn Pauline (Troyer) Showalter; m. Kenneth James Balthaser, June 1, 1963. BS magna cum laude, U. Ind., 1961; MS, Ind. U., 1962. Tchr. bus. edn. Southport H.S., Indpls., 1962-63; sec. administrv. sec. office of pres. Ind. U., Bloomington, 1963-66; with Ind. U.-Purdue U., Fort Wayne, 1969—, asst. to dean arts and letters, 1970—86, asst. dean arts and letters, 1986—87, asst. dean arts and scis., 1987—2002, asst. dean emerita, 2002—. Founding co-dir. Weekend Coll., 1979-80; bd. dirs. Associated Chs. Fort Wayne, 1980; mem. Ind. com. Nat. Mus. Women in Arts. Ind. Conf. N. Evang. United Brethren Ch. scholar, 1957-61. Trustee United Ch. of Christ, 1994—97, exec. coun., 2000—, asst. moderator, 2004, moderator, 2005—. Recipient Women of Achievement award, YWCA, 1990. Mem.: AAUW (trustee 1995—97, coll. & univ. rep. 2000—02, Nat. grantee Ft. Wayne br. 1995), Assn. IPFW Women (pres. 1967—68, steering com. co-chair 1998—99, steering com. sec. 1999—2003, co-chair 2003—04), Fort Wayne Zool. Soc., Fort Wayne Mus. Art, Embassy Theatre Found., Fort Wayne-Allen County Hist. Assn., Mensa, Phi Kappa Phi, Alpha Chi, Phi Alpha Epsilon, Delta Pi Epsilon. Home: 2917 Hazelwood Ave Fort Wayne IN 46805-2403 Office: 2101 E Coliseum Blvd Fort Wayne IN 46805-1445 Personal E-mail: balthase@ipfw.edu.

BALTIMORE, DAVID, academic administrator, microbiologist, educator; b. NYC, Mar. 7, 1938; s. Richard I. and Gertrude (Lipschitz) B.; m. Alice S. Huang, Oct. 5, 1968; 1 dau., Teak. BA in Chemistry with high honors, Swarthmore Coll., 1960; postgrad., MIT, 1960—61; PhD, Rockefeller U., 1964. Postdoctoral rschr. MIT, Cambridge, Mass., 1964—65; research assoc. Salk Inst. Biol. Studies, La Jolla, Calif., 1965—68; from assoc. prof. microbiology to dir. MIT, Cambridge, Mass., 1968—82, founding dir. Whitehead Inst. Biomed. Rsch., 1982—90; pres. Rockefeller U., N.Y.C., 1990—91, prof., 1990—94; pres. Calif. Inst. Tech., Pasadena, 1997—. Bd. govs. Weizmann Inst. Sci., Israel; co-chmn. Commn. on a Nat. Strategy of Aids; ad hoc program adv. com. on complex genome, AIDS rsch. adv. coun. NIH, chair vaccine adv. com., 1997—2002; bd. dirs. MedImmune, Inc., 2003—. Mem. editorial bd. Jour. Molecular Biology, 1971-73, Jour. Virology, 1969-90, Sci., 1986-98, New Eng. Jour. Medicine, 1989-94. Bd. govs. Weizmann Inst. Sci., Israel; bd. dirs. Life Sci. Rsch. Found. Recipient Gustav Stern award, 1970, Warren Triennial prize Mass. Gen. Hosp., 1971, Eli Lilly and Co. award, 1971, Nat. Acad. Scis. US Steel award, 1974, Gairdner Found. award, 1974, Nobel prize in physiology & med., 1975, Nat. medal of Sci., 1999, Warren Alpert Found. prize, 2000, Sci. Achievement award AMA, 2002. Fellow AAAS, Am. Med. Writers Assn. (hon.), Am. Acad. Microbiology; mem. NAS, Am. Acad. Arts and Scis., Inst. Medicine, Am. Philos. Soc., Pontifical Acad. Scis., Royal Soc. (Eng., fgn.), French Acad. Scis. (fgn. assoc.). Office: Calif Inst Tech 1200 E California Blvd 204 Parsons Gate Pasadena CA 91125-0001 Office Phone: 626-395-6301.

BALTIMORE, ROBERT SAMUEL, pediatrician, epidemiologist; b. N.Y.C., Nov. 3, 1942; s. Richard Irving and Gertrude (Lipshitz) B.; m. Nancy Virginia Ward, June 16, 1967 (dec. Aug. 1977); 1 child, Gwen; m. Katalin Rachel Radnay, Sept. 24, 1978; 1 child, Richard. AB, U. Chgo., 1964; MD, SUNY, Buffalo, 1968. Diplomate in pediatrics and pediatric infectious diseases Am. Bd. Pediatrics. Intern U. Chgo. Hosps. and Clinics, 1968-69, resident in pediatrics, 1969—71; postdoctoral fellow Walter Reed Army Inst. Rsch., Washington, 1971-74; postdoctoral fellow, instr. Harvard Med. Sch., 1974-76, asst. prof. pediats. and epidemiology, 1976-81; assoc. prof. pediatrics and epidemiology Yale U. Sch. Medicine, New Haven, 1981—95, prof. pediatrics, epidemiology, pub. health, 1995—. Co-editor: Topics in Critical Care Pediatrics, 1984, Pediatric Infectious Diseases: Principles and Practice, 1995, 2d edit., 2002. Asst. dir. health Town of Orange, Conn., 1990—. Maj. U.S. Army, 1971-74. Rsch. grantee NIH, 1981-84, Cystic Fibrosis Found., 1988-90, Ctrs. for Disease Control and Prevention, 1990-2005. Fellow Infectious Diseases Soc. Am., Pediatric Infectious Diseases Soc., Soc. for Pediatric Rsch., Am. Acad. Pediatrics, Am. Pediat. Soc., Soc. for Healthcare Epidemiology. Democrat. Jewish. Avocations: gardening, hiking. Home: 188 Crocker Ct Orange CT 06477-3025 Office: Yale Univ Sch Medicine 333 Cedar St New Haven CT 06520-8064 E-mail: robert.baltimore@yale.edu.

BALTUCH, GORDON HIRSH, neurosurgeon; b. Montreal, Que., Can., Apr. 24, 1960; arrived in U.S., 1978; s. Siegmar Udo Baltuch and Carol Leila Wevrick; m. Vivian Ariane Barbara Wasmuht-Perroud, Mar. 28, 1997; children: Orphee Sarah, Axel Noah. BA, Harvard U., 1981; MSc, Stanford U., 1982; MD, McGill U., Montreal, 1986, PhD, 1995. Diplomate Am. Bd. Neurol. Surgery. Neurosurgery fellow CHUV, Lausanne, Switzerland; neurosurgeon Montreal Gen. Hosp., 1995—96; assoc. prof. neurosurgery U. Pa., Phila., 1996—. Assoc. dir. PADRECC, Vets. Hosp., Phila., 2001—; dir. Ctr. Functional and Restorative Neurosurgery. Named Top Dr., Phila. Mag., 2005; recipient Mastroianni Clinical Innovator award, 2003; grantee, NIH, 1998—, VA, 2001—. Fellow: ACS, Royal Coll. Surgeons Can., Coll. Physicians of Phila.; mem.: Am. Assn. Neurol. Surgeons. Office: Hosp U Pa 5 Silverstein 3400 Spruce St Philadelphia PA 19104 Home: 268 S 3rd St Philadelphia PA 19106 Office Phone: 215-662-7788. Business E-Mail: baltuch@med.upenn.edu.

BALTZ, PATRICIA ANN (PANN BALTZ), retired elementary school educator; b. Dallas, June 20, 1949; d. Richard Parks and Ruth Eileen (Hartschuh) Langford; m. William Monroe Baltz, Sept. 6, 1969; 1 child: Kenneth Chandler. Student, U. Redlands, 1967-68; BA in English Lit. cum laude, UCLA, 1971. Cert. tchr. K-8, Calif. Tchr. 4th grade Arcadia (Calif.) Unified Sch. Dist., 1972-74, 92—, substitute tchr., 1983-85, tchr. 3dr grade, 1985-87, tchr. 6th grade, 1987-90, tchr. 4th and 5th grade multiage, 1990—2005, ret., 2005. Sci. mentor tchr. Arcadia Unified Sch. Dist., 1991-94; mentor Tech. Ctr. Silicon Valley, San Jose, Calif., 1991. Tchr. rep. PTA, Arcadia, 1980-93; mem. choir, children's sermon team, elder Arcadia Presbyn. Ch., 1980-93; chaperone, vol. Pasadena (Calif.) Youth Symphony Orch., 1988-90; vol. Am. Heart Assn., 1990-92. Recipient Outstanding Gen. Elem. Tchr. award, Outstanding Tchr. of the Yr. award Disney's Am. Tchr. Awards, 1993, Calif. Tchr. of Yr. award Calif. State Dept. Edn., 1993, Georgie award Girl Scouts of Am., 1993, The Self Esteem Task Force award L.A. County Task Force to Promote Self-Esteem & Personal & Social Responsibility, 1993, Profl. Achievement award UCLA Alumni Assn.; apptd. to Nat. Edn. Rsch. Policies & Priorities Bd., U.S. Sec. Edn. Richard Riley; Pann Baltz Mission Possible Scholar named in her honor. Mem. NEA, Nat. Sci. Tchrs. Assn., Calif. Tchr. Assn., Arcadia Tchrs. Assn. Avocations: reading, singing, calligraphy, book-making, computers. Home: 1215 S 3rd Ave Arcadia CA 91006-4205

BALTZER, REBECCA A., musicologist, researcher, consultant; b. Memphis, June 17, 1940; d. Ralph Neal and Sherard Rawles Baltzer; m. Charles Edward McCarthy, Mar. 17, 1984. AB in English magna cum laude, Randolph-Macon Woman's Coll., 1962; MA in Musicology, Boston U., 1964, PhD in Musicology, 1974. Part-time instr., lectr. in music Boston U., 1964—67; prof. musicology Sch. Music U. Tex., Austin, 1967—, assoc. dean Grad. Sch., 1982—86. Cons. Nat. Endowment for Humanities, Washington, 1979—80, Ednl. Testing Svc., Princeton, NJ, 1986—88; vis. prof. music Princeton U., 1996. Editor, transcriber: Le Magnus liber organi de Notre-Dame de Paris, 1995, co-editor, contbr.: book of essays The Divine Office in the Latin Middle Ages, 2000 (Hon. Mention in Philosophy & Religion, from the Profl. and Scholarly Pub. (PSP) br. of the Assn. of Am. Publishers, 2001); co-editor: The Union of Words and Music in Medieval Poetry, 1991; editor of the music: edition & translation of medieval poetry Guillaume de Machaut: Remede de Fortune, 1988; contbr. articles to profl. jours. Dissertation fellow, AAUW, 1966—67. Mem.: Soc. for Am. Music, Early Music Am., Coll. Music Soc., Medieval Acad. Am. (local arrangements chair ann. meeting 2000), Am. Musicological Soc. (bd. dirs. 1980—82, v.p. 1988—90, treas., mem. exec. com. 1993—2000, Alfred Einstein award 1973), Pi Kappa Lambda, Phi Beta Kappa. Episcopalian. Avocations: reading, photography, travel. Home: 68 Sundown Parkway Austin TX 78746-5258 Home Fax: 512-471-7836.

BALZ, DANIEL JOHN, newspaper editor, journalist; b. Freeport, Ill., May 5, 1946; s. Charles Edward and Phyllis Victoria (Irion) B.; m. Nancy Jean Johnson, June 14, 1969; 1 child, John Paul. BS in Journalism, U. Ill., Champaign, 1968, MS in Communications, 1972. Reporter Phila. Inquirer, 1972; reporter Nat. Jour., Washington, 1972-76, dep. editor, 1976-78; reporter, editor Washington Post, 1978-85, nat. editor, 1985-89, reporter, 1989—. Served with U.S. Army, 1968-71. Office: Washington Post 1150 15th St NW Washington DC 20071-0002

BALZARINI, STEPHEN EDWARD, historian, educator; b. Great Falls, Mont., Aug. 7, 1948; s. James and Jean Mildred (Stordock) Balzarini; m. Margaret Louise Belden, June 12, 1971; 1 child, James Benjamin Belden. BA, Mont. State U., 1970; PhD, Wash. State U., 1979. Asst. archivist Wash. State U., Pullman, 1978—83; asst. prof. Gonzaga U., Spokane, Wash., 1983—92, assoc. prof., 1992—. Adj. asst. prof. Gonzaga U., Spokane, 1978—83; acad. dir. Internat. Liberal Arts Colls. Abroad, London, 1988, London, 2002; dept. chmn. Gonzaga U., Spokane, 1993—99, Spokane, 2004—; presenter, spkr. in field. Planning commn. Colfax (Wash.) Sch. Dist., 2001, levy funding organizing com., 2002—03; spokesman Colfax HS Wrestling Club, 1997—. Mem.: N.W. Conf. on Brit. Studies, Am. Hist. Assn., Whitman County Hist. Soc. Avocations: woodworking, golf. Home: 303 E Thorn Colfax WA 99111 Office: Gonzage Univ History Dept 502 E Boone Ave Spokane WA 99258 Office Phone: 509-373-6697.

BALZEKAS, STANLEY, JR., museum director; b. Chgo., Oct. 8, 1924; s. Stanley and Emily B.; widowed; children— Stanley, III, Robert, Carole Rene. BS, DePaul U., Chgo., 1950, MA, 1951. Pres. Balzekas Mus. Lithuanian Culture, Chgo., 1966—, Balzekas Motor Sales, Chgo., 1952—; hon. consul Consulate of the Republic of Lithuania, Palm Beach, Fla. Hon. consul for Republic of Lithuania, Palm Beach, Fla. Trustee Lincoln Acad., Cath. Charities, Am.-Lithuanian Coun.; chmn. Sister Cities/Chgo.-Vilnius Friendship Com., Trade & Cultural Ctr.; mem. adv. bd. Chgo. Cultural Affairs; hon. consul Rep. of Lithuania, Palm Beach, Fla. Served with AUS, 1942-45, ETO. Decorated Bronze Star; decorated 3d degree order Grand Duke Gediminas, Pres. Lithuania; recipient Wigilia medal Polish Geneal. Soc. Am., medal DAR, Disting. Alumni award DePaul U., 1991, Zygimantas Augustas medal Vilnius, 2001, Order Lithuanian Numismatics medal, 2003. Mem. Am. Assn. Mus., Ethnic Cultural Preservation Coun. (pres. 1977—), Press Club (Chgo.), Literary Club (Chgo.), City Club (Chgo., ethnic chmn.), Exec. Club (Chgo.), Am. Legion Office: 4030 S Archer Ave Chicago IL 60632-1140 Office Phone: 773-582-6500. E-mail: president@lithuanianmuseum.org.

BALZER, ROBERT LAWRENCE, journalist; b. DesMoines, June 25, 1912; s. Albert Taylor and Selma Olivia (Peterson) Balzer; m. Emily Abel, Dec. 6, 1936 (div. Aug. 1945). BA in English cum laude, Stanford U., 1935. Buddhist monk 1956. Owner Balzer's on Larchment, L.A., 1935—59; wine columnist L.A. Times, 1964—96. Chmn. food and wine Taste of Am. Presdl. Inaugural Washington, Reagan, 1981, 85, Taste of Am. Presdl. Inaugural Reagan, 1989. Author: Beyond Conflict, 1962, Los Angeles Time Book of California Wine, 1984; wine/restaurant editor: Travel Holiday Mag., 1974—92; actor(priest): (films, with Gloria Swanson and dir. Curtis Harrington) Killer Bees, 1974, (minister); (films, with dir. John Shclesinger) Day of the Locust, 1975; anchor (radio K-MZT 105.1fm) RLB The Word on Wine, L.A., 1994—2003. Tchr. wines of Calif. Long Beach (Calif.) Parks and Recreation, 1970—2003. With USAF, 1942—43. Decorated Royal Order of Sahametrei King Norodom Sihanouk, Cambodia; recipient Cordon Bleu award, Wine and Food Soc., L.A., 1939, Golden Bacchus award, Italian Trade Commn., 1972. Home: 10551 Hillsboro Rd Santa Ana CA 92705

BALZHISER, RICHARD EARL, research and development company executive; b. Wheaton, Ill., May 27, 1932; s. Frank E. and Esther K. (Merrill Werner) B.; m. Christine Karnuth, 1951; children: Gary, Robert, Patricia, Michele. BS in Chem. Engring., U. Mich., 1955, MS in Nuclear Engring., 1956, PhD in Chem. Engring., 1961. Mem. faculty U. Mich., Ann Arbor, 1961-67; White House fellow, spl. asst. to sec. Dept. Def., Washington, 1967-68; chmn. dept. chem. engring. U. Mich., 1970-71; assoc. dir. energy, environ. and natural resources White House Office of Sci. and Tech., Washington, 1971-73; dir. fossil fuel and advanced systems Electric Power Rsch. Inst., Palo Alto, Calif., 1973-79, sr. v.p. R&D, 1979-87, exec. v.p. R&D, 1987-88, pres., chief exec. officer, 1988-96, pres. emeritus, 1996—. Bd. dirs. Reliant Energy, Electro Source, Aerospace Corp.; mem. adv. bd. Nat. Renewable Energy Lab.; mem. pres. com. on sci. and tech. energy studies I and II, Pres.'s Com. on Sci. and Tech. Energy Studies, 1997-99. Co-author: Chemical Engineering Thermodynamics, 1972, Engineering Thermodynamics, 1977. Mem. Ann Arbor City Coun., 1965-67, mayor pro tem, 1967. Named to Acad. All-Am., U. Mich. Football, 1952, Acad. All-Am. Hall of Fame, 2002. Mem. Nat. Acad. Engring. Lutheran. Office: Electric Power Rsch Inst 3412 Hillview Ave Palo Alto CA 94304-1344 Office Phone: 650-855-2141. Office Fax: 650-855-2090. Business E-Mail: rbalzhis@epri.com.

BAM, FOSTER, lawyer; b. Bridgeport, Conn., Jan. 11, 1927; s. Frederick and Alma (Foster) B.; m. Sallie A. Baldwin; children: Sylvia Carol, Sheila Catherine, Eric Foster. Grad., Loomis Sch., 1944; AB, Yale U., 1950, LLB, 1953. Bar: N.Y. 1954, Conn. 1968. Mem. faculty acctg. Yale, 1952-53; with Spence & Hotchkiss, N.Y.C., 1954-55; asst. U.S. dist. atty. So. Dist. N.Y., 1955-58; ptnr. Kramer, Levin, Naftalis & Frankel (formerly Feldman, Kramer, Bam, Nessen), N.Y.C., 1958-67, Cummings & Lockwood, 1968—. Bd. dirs. The Evergreen Funds. Trustee Phoenix Sci. Ctr.; chmn. Am. Mus. Fly Fishing, Calif. Acad. Sci.; trustee Bermuda Biol. Sta. for Rsch. Recipient Johnny Foyle Meml. award, 1969. Mem. ABA, Conn. Bar Assn., Greenwich Bar Assn., Exptl. Aircraft Assn., Phi Beta Kappa. Home: 51 Londonderry Dr Greenwich CT 06830-3508 Office: Cummings & Lockwood 2 Greenwich Plz Ste 3 Greenwich CT 06830-6353

BAMBERGER, GERALD FRANCIS, plastics marketing consultant; b. Hannover, Germany, Sept. 20, 1920; came to U.S., 1938, naturalized, 1943; m. Ursula Friede, Mar. 27, 1946; children— Gale, Richard, Annette, Peter. Comml. diploma, Ecole Supérieure de Commerce, Neuchatel, Switzerland, 1938. Pres. A. Bamberger Corp., Bklyn., 1938-54, Interplastics Corp., N.Y.C., 1955-62; prodn. mgr. plastics div. Cities Service Corp., Hicksville, N.Y., 1963-67; pres. Bamberger Polymers, Inc., New Hyde Park, N.Y., 1967-85; plastics mktg. cons., 1985—. Served with M.I. AUS, 1943-46. Decorated Bronze Star. Mem. Soc. Plastics Industry, Soc. Plastics Engrs., Plastics Pioneers Assn. Personal E-mail: gfbamberger@att.net.

BAMBERGER, LAUREN R., writer, photojournalist; b. York, Pa., July 2, 1978; d. Jeffrey Lee and Brenda Elaine Bamberger. Degree, Inst. Children's Lit., 2001. Writer, photographer The Chief of Police Mag., Miami, Fla., 2001—, 1st Responder Newspaper, Newburgh, NY, 2001—, Am. Police Beat, Cambridge, Mass., 2002; photographer 9-1-1 Mag., San Jose, 2002—; writer, photographer Law and Order Mag., Deerfield, Ill., 2003—. Contbr. stories to mags.; author: Amy's Goodbye, 2003, Morgan's Giraffe, 2004, Until They All Come Home, 2004. Mem. Little Compton Vol. Fire Dept., 2003—; key vol. U.S. Marine Corps Res., 2002—. Recipient 1st pl., Inspirational Writers Alive, Tex., 2001, Outstanding Achievement in Amateur Photography award, Internat. Soc. Photographers, 2004. Mem.: Police Writers Assn., Am. Legion (pres. Post 37 2004). Avocations: reading, writing, photography. Home and Office: 46 William Sisson Rd Little Compton RI 02837 Office Phone: 401-635-2328. E-mail: laurenrbamberger@cox.net.

BAMBERGER, MICHAEL ALBERT, lawyer; b. Berlin, Feb. 29, 1936; s. Fritz and Kate (Schwabe) B.; m. Phylis Skloot, Dec. 19, 1965; children: Kenneth A., Richard A. AB magna cum laude, Harvard U., 1957, LLB magna cum laude, 1960. Bar: NY 1960, DC 1982. Assoc. Proskauer Rose Goetz & Mendelsohn, N.Y.C., 1960-69, Finley, Kumble, Wagner, Heine, Underberg, Manley, Myerson & Casey, N.Y.C., 1970, ptnr., 1971-87, Sonnenschein Nath & Rosenthal LLP, N.Y.C., 1987—. Adj. prof. Benjamin Cardozo Sch. Law, Yeshiva U., 2001—; lectr. Boalt Hall, U. Calif., 2006-; mem. faculty various legal seminars and insts.; mem. joint editl. bd. on unincorporated orgn. accts. ABA/Nat. Conf. Commrs. on Uniform State Laws, 1994—, chair, 2003-05; chmn. bd. Transcontinental Music Publs., New Jewish Music Press. Author: Reckless Legislation: How Lawmakers Ignore the Constitution, 2000; co-editor: State Limited Partnership Laws, 7 vols. and supplements, 1987—; editor Harvard Law Rev., 1958-60; contbr. articles to profl. jours. V.p., bd. dirs. Leo Baeck Inst., Selfhelp Cmty. Svcs.; bd. dirs. Ctr. Jewish History. Mem. ABA (com. on ltd. partnerships 1980—, chair com. on tech. and intellectual property 1992-95, chair, ad hoc com. on security interests in intellectual property 1990-98), First Amendment Lawyers Assn., N.Y. State Bar Assn. (exec. com. comml. and fed. litig. sect. 1989-93), Assn. Bar City N.Y. (com. on fed. legis. 1979-82, com. on civil rights 1982-86, chmn. 1983-86), N.Y. County Lawyers Assn. (securities com. 1980-82). Jewish. Home: 172 E 93d St New York NY 10128-3711 Office: Sonnenschein Nath & Rosenthal LLP 1221 Ave of Americas New York NY 10020-1001 Office Phone: 212-768-6756.

BAMBERGER, PHYLIS SKLOOT, lawyer, educator, retired judge; b. N.Y.C., May 2, 1939; d. George Joseph and Martha (Wechselblatt) S.; m. Michael A. Bamberger, Dec. 19, 1965; children: Kenneth, Richard. BA, Bklyn. Coll., 1960; LLB, NYU, 1963. Bar: N.Y. 1963, U.S. Supreme Ct. 1967, U.S. Ct. Appeals (2d cir.) 1965, U.S. Dist. Ct. (so. dist.) N.Y. 1966, U.S. Dist. Ct. (ea. dist.) N.Y. 1979. Assoc. Legal Aid Soc., N.Y.C., 1963-67; assoc.-in-charge criminal appeals Bur. Legal Aid Soc., N.Y.C., 1967-72; atty.-in-charge, fed. def. svcs. unit/appeal Legal Aid Soc., N.Y.C., 1972-88; judge N.Y. State Ct. Claims designated to sit in the N.Y. State Supreme Ct., Bronx County, 1988—2005. Instr. N.Y. State Judicial Inst. and other venues, 1990—; mem. N.Y. State Chief Judge's Jury Project, 1993—94; mem. com. on alternatives to incarceration Office of Ct. Adminstrn., 1994—96, mem. criminal law and procedure adv. com., 1994—98, co-chair, 1998—; mem. N.Y. State Chief Judge's Commn. on the Jury, 2003—; on the Future of Indigent Def. Svcs., 2004—. Author: Criminal Appeals Handbook, 1984; editor, contbr. Practice Under the Federal Sentencing Guidelines, 1988, 90, 93, 2000 (also supplements); author, compiler Recent Developments in State Constitutional Law, 1985; contbr. numerous articles to publs. Mem. ABA, N.Y. State Bar assn. (co-chair presdl. com. on problems in criminal justice sys. 1986-88, mem. com. on the future of the profession), Assn. of Bar of City of N.Y. (mem. coun. on criminal justice 2004—, chair com. on provision of legal svcs. to persons of moderate means 1995-98, 21st century com. 1992-95, chair com. on probation 1993-94), Phi Beta Kappa.

BAMBERGER, SHEILA LISTER, retired secondary school educator; b. N.Y.C., Sept. 23, 1935; d. Louis and Rebecca (Levitan) Lister; m. Henry Bamberger, June 21, 1959; children: Judith, Miriam. BS, SUNY, Albany, 1957; postgrad., CUNY, 1957-60, SUNY, New Paltz, 1966-68, Syracuse U., 1989-91; MST, Univ. N.H., 1996. Cert. secondary math. tchr., N.Y. Tchr. Malverne (N.Y.) Pub. Schs., 1957-61, Cen. Dauphin Sch. Dist., Harrisburg, Pa., 1980-82, Utica (N.Y.) City Sch. Dist., 1982-88; bookkeeper Leitman, Siegel & Payne, P.A., Birmingham, Ala., 1977-79; tchr. math. Clinton (N.Y.) Cen. Sch., 1988—99, treas., 1999—2001; facilitar Mohawk Valley Inst. of Learning in Retirement, 1999. Co-exec. V.P. Nat. Assn. of Ret. Reform Rabbi's, 2005—. Bd. dir., officer Vassar Hosp. Assn., Poughkeepsie, N.Y., 1972-75; bd. dir. A Better Chance, Clinton, 1990—, acad. com. chmn. 1991-93; bd. mem. Charles T. Sitrin Home, 1999-, Players of Utica, 2004-, treas 2005—; mem. nat. women's com. Brandeis U., regional pres., 1976-78; donor treas. Hadassah, 1987—. Recipient Outstanding Educator award Rotary Internat., Utica, 1985, 87, 91, svc. award Hadassah, 1989, 90. Mem. Nat. Coun. Tchrs. Math., Assn. Math. Tchrs. N.Y. State (county chmn. 1987—, chmn. publs. 1990-93, chmn. hospitality com. 1992, registration com. chmn. 1993, v.p. 2001), Assn. Math. Tchrs. Oneida County (organizer, compiler Mathletics 1983), SUNY-Albany Alumni Assn. (treas. 1989-92, svc. award 1977, 87), Delta Kappa Gamma (v.p. 1988-92, pres. 1992—). Avocations: tennis, bridge, gardening, sewing. Home: 122 Proctor Blvd Utica NY 13501-6119

BAMBERG-REVIS, ETHEL M., minister, educator; d. William Henry Bamberg, Sr. and Ella Mae McCollough; 1 child, Terrence Edward Terrell Bamberg. BA in Religious Edn., No. Bapt. Sch. Religion, 1980; BA in Psychology, Coll. New Rochelle, 1984; MDiv, Hood Theol. Sem., 1996; grad. cert. in Christian ministry, N.Y. Theol. Sem., 1982, grad. cert. in Pastoral Care and Counseling, 1983. Cert. domestic violence counselor Nat. Bd. Addictions Examiners, pastoral addictions counselor Nat. Bd. Addictions Examiners. State chaplain Hagedorn Gero-Psychiat. Hosp., Glen Gardner, NJ, 1988—92; interim pastor 1st Bapt. Ch. Anderson, Port Murray, NJ, 1990—92; chaplain resident Carolinas Med. Ctr., Charlotte, NC, 1992—93; asst. dir. residence life Livingstone Coll., Salisbury, NC, 1993—96, dir. residence life, 1996—99; adult basic edn. instr. Rowan-Cabarrus C.C., Salisbury, 1994—2001, 2003; chaplain VA Med. Ctr., Salisbury, 1994—. Chaplain Salisbury Police Dept., 1999—; active New Jubilee Chorus, Salisbury, 2001—. Mem.: AAUW (chairperson internat. affairs com.), NAACP, Assn. Clin. Pastoral Educators, Assn. Profl. Chaplains (bd. cert. chaplain). African Methodist Episcopal Zion. Avocations: creative writing, horseback riding, reading, singing. Office: WG Hefner VA Med Ctr 1601 Brenner Ave Salisbury NC 28144

BAMBURG, JAMES ROBERT, biochemistry professor; b. Chgo., Aug. 20, 1943; s. Leslie H. and Rose A. (Abrahams) B.; m. Alma Y. Vigo, June 7, 1970 (div. Dec. 1984); children: Eric Gregory, Leslie Ann; m. Laurie S. Minamide, June 22, 1985. BS in Chemistry, U. Ill., 1965; PhD, U. Wis., 1969. Project assoc. U. Wis., Madison, 1968-69; postdoctoral fellow Stanford U., Palo Alto, Calif., 1969-71; from asst. to full prof. Colo. State U., Ft. Collins, 1971—, acad. coordinator cell and molecular biol. program, 1975-78, interim chmn. dept. biochemistry, 1982-85, 88-89, assoc. chmn., 1996—99, assoc. dir. neuronal growth and devel., 1986-90, dir. neuronal growth and devel., 1990—96, dir. molecular cell integrative neuroscience, 2002—. Vis. prof. MRC Molecular Biol. Lab., Cambridge, Eng., 1978-79, MRC Cell Biophysics Unit, London, 1985-86, Children's Med. Rsch. Inst., U. Sydney, Australia, 1992-93, U. Calif. San Diego, 1999-2000; mem., chmn. NIH Biomed. Scis. Study Sect., Bethesda, Md., 1980-85; ad hoc mem. Physiol. Chem. Study Sec., 1997, Molecular Devel. Cell Neurosci., 1998-99, 2001, Cell Biol. Function, 2001-03; mem. adv. bd. Macromolecular Resources, 1999—, Boulder Lab. 3D Fine STructure, 1994—, Alaska Basic Neurosci. Program, 2000—. Contbr. articles to sci. jours.; mem. editl. bd. Cell Motil Cytoskel. Fellow NSF, 1964-65, Nat. Multiple Sclerosis Soc., 1969-71, J.S. Guggenheim Found., 1978-79, Fogarty Ctr., 1985-86, 92-93, W. Evans Vis. scholar U. Otago, N.Z., 1991; recipient Disting. Svc. award Colo. State U. 1989, 2005, Outstanding Adviser award, 1996. Mem. Am. Chem. Soc., Am. Soc. Cell Biology, Am. Soc. Biochem. Mol. Biol., Internat. Neurochem. Soc., Soc. for Neurosci., Sigma Xi (pres. CSU chpt. 1989). Home: 2125 Sandstone Dr Fort Collins CO 80524-1825 Office: Colo State U Dept Biochemistry Mrb Rm 235 Fort Collins CO 80523-1870 Business E-Mail: jbamburg@lamar.colostate.edu.

BAMFORD, JOSEPH CHARLES, JR., gynecologist, obstetrician, educator, medical missionary, author; b. Paterson, NJ, Oct. 23, 1930; s. Joseph Charles and Luise (Whitehead) Bamford; m. Susan Jane Hall, Apr. 13, 1951; children: Joseph Charles III, Elizabeth Ann. BS, Rutgers U., 1952; MD, NY Med. Coll., 1956. Diplomate Am. Bd. Ob-Gyn. Intern U. Vt., 1956—57; resident in ob-gyn NY Med. Coll., N.Y.C., 1957—60, asst. clin. instr. dept. ob-gyn, 1960—64, clin. instr., 1964—65, asst. prof., 1965—70, assoc. prof., 1970—72, asst. dean, 1966—68, assoc. dean, 1968—72, acting v.p. hosp. affairs, 1971—72; sect. chief psychosomatic ob-gyn Met. Hosp. Ctr., N.Y.C., 1963—72, chief svc., 1971—72; practice medicine specializing in ob-gyn Paterson, NJ, 1962—66; practice medicien specializing in ob-gyn St. Johnsbury, Vt., 1972—76; asst. obstetrician and gynecologist Flower and Fifth Ave. hosps., N.Y.C., 1960—66, asst. attending, 1966—70, attending, 1970—72; asst. vis. obstetrician and gynecologist Met. Hosp. Ctr., N.Y.C., 1960—66, assoc., 1968—70, vis., 1970—72; vis. ob-gyn Indian Health Svc. Hosp., Ft. Defiance, Ariz., 1981; clin. asst. ob-gyn Paterson Gen. Hosp., 1962—64, assoc. attending, 1964—66, attending, 1966—67; cons., 1967; attending obstetrician and gynecologist Northeastern Vt. Regional Hosp., St. Johnsbury,

1972—76, cons., 1976—85. Vis. obstetrician and gynecologist St. Jude Missions Hosp., St. Lucia, 1986; med. officer Tumutumu Mission Hosp., Kenya, 1987—88; cons. Beatrice D. Weeks Meml. Hosp., Lancaster, NH, 1972—80; vol. program steering com. for retired physicians Vt. Med. Soc., 1996—2001; chmn. subcom. for fact finding Mayor's Com. for Hosp. Facilities Planning, Paterson, 1964—66. Contbr. articles to profl. jours. Chmn. med. adv. com. Passaic County (NJ) Com. for Planned Parenthood, 1965—67; mem. NJ Com. on Med. Edn., 1965—66; trustee Greater Paterson Gen. Hosp., 1966—2000, So. Vt. Art Ctr., 1997—2002; pres. Lyndon State Coll. Found., 1980—84, Kagando Mission Hosp. Found., 2003—. Lt. comdr. USNR, 1960—62. Fellow: ACOG (mem. com. on course coord. 1977—79); mem.: Caledonia County Med. Soc. (v.p. 1974—75), Vt. Med. Soc. (mem. jud. com. 1975—77), Ob-Gyn. Soc. NY Med. Coll. (mem. exec. com. 1963—66), No. New England Acad. Medicine. Home: Box 724 Myrickview Vlg Dorset VT 05251

BAN, JANET F., music educator; b. Cleve., Jan. 16; d. Stanley Henry and Catherine (Nowak) Florzack; children: Charlie, Hallie. BFA in Music Edn., Ohio U., 1973; MusM in Edn., Duquesne U., 1975. Music educator Pitts. Pub. Schs., 1975—82, Montour Sch. Dist., McKees Rocks, Pa., 1976—77; pvt. practice Pitts., 1985—93; music educator, choral dir. Mt. Lebanon Sch. Dist., Pitts., 1993—. Substitute tchr. Mt. Lebanon Sch. Dist., Pitts., 1991—93; adv. com. music study group Peters Twp. Sch. Dist. Active Jr. League Pitts., 1986—90; music study com. Mt. Lebanaon Sch. Dist., Pitts., 1985; v.p., bd. dirs. Mendelssohn Choir Pitts., 1993. Mem.: Am. Choral Dirs. Assn., Music Educators Nat. Conf., Mt. Lebanon Jr. Women's Club (sec. 1984—). Presbyterian. Avocations: running, golf, cooking. Home: 544 Bigham Rd Pittsburgh PA 15211 Office: Mt Lebanon Sch Dist 11 Castle Shannon Blvd Pittsburgh PA 15228

BAN, STEPHEN DENNIS, gas industry executive; b. Hammond, Ind., Dec. 16, 1940; s. Stephen and Mary Veronica (Holecsko) Ban; m. Margie Cahill, Aug. 17, 1963; children: Stephen, Mary Beth, Brian. BSME, Rose Hulman Inst. Tech., 1962; MS in Engring. Sci., Case Inst. Tech., 1964, PhD in Engring., 1967. Chief divsn. fluid and chem. processes Battelle Columbus (Ohio) Labs., 1970-72, chief divsn. emission sys., 1972-76, corp. coord. engring. scis. program, 1972-76; v.p. R & D Bituminous Materials, Inc., Terre Haute, Ind., 1976-81, Gas Rsch. Inst., Chgo., 1981—2000, sr. v.p. R & D ops., 1983-86, exec. v.p., COO, 1986-87, pres., CEO, 1987—2000; dir. Office Tech. Transfer Argonne Nat. Lab., 2002—. Mem. indsl. adv. bd. U. Ill., Chgo., 1983—93; mem. Coun. Energy Engring. Rsch., Washington, 1983—87; mem. energy rsch. adv. bd. U.S. Dept. Energy, Washington, 1987—90, mem. adv. com. renewable energy and energy efficiency joint ventures, 1992—95; mem. Natural Gas Coun., 1993—97; mem. bd. dirs. Energen Corp., Birmingham, Ala., UGI Corp., Phila. Fellow, NDEA, 1962—65, NSF, 1965—67. Mem.: U.S. Energy Assn., Sigma Xi, Tau Beta Pi. Office: 9700 S Cass Ave Argonne IL 60439-4832 Office Phone: 630-252-8111. Business E-Mail: sdban@anl.gov.

BANA, ERIC, actor; b. Melbourne, Australia, Aug. 9, 1968; m. Rebecca Gleeson, 1997; 2 children. Actor: (films) The Castle, 1997, Chopper, 2000, Black Hawk Down, 2001, The Nugget, 2002, Hulk, 2003, Troy, 2004, (voice) Finding Nemo, 2003; actor, prodr., writer: TV films Eric, 1996—97; actor: (TV series) Full Frontal, 1993—96; actor, writer: TV series The Eric Bana Show Live, 1997; actor: (TV guest appearances) All Saints, 1999, 2000. Mailing: c/o PMK Pub Rels 650 Fifth Ave 33rd Fl New York NY 10019

BANACH, ART JOHN, graphic artist; b. Chgo., May 22, 1931; s. Vincent and Anna (Zajac) B. Grad. Art. Inst. of Chgo., 1955; pupil painting studies Mrs. Melin, Chgo.; m. Loretta A. Nolan, Oct. 15, 1966; children: Heather Anne, Lynnea Joan. Owner, dir. Art J. Banach Studios, 1949—, cartoon syndicate for newspapers, house organs and advt. functions, 1954—, owner and operater advt. agy., 1954-56, feature news and picture syndicate, distbn. U.S. and fgn. countries. Dir. Speculators S Fund. Recipient award 1st Easter Seal contest Ill. Assn. Crippled, Inc., 1949. Chgo. Pub. Sch. Art Soc. Scholar. Mem. Artist's Guild Chgo., Am Mgmt. Assn., Chgo. Assn. of Commerce and Industry, Chgo. Federated Advt. Club, Am. Mktg. Assn., Internat. Platform Assn., Chgo. Advt. Club, Chgo. Soc. Communicating Arts, Am. Ctr. For Design, Chgo. Calligraphy Collective, Columbia Yacht Club, Advt. Execs. Club, Art Dirs. Club (Chgo.). Home: 1076 Leahy Cir East Des Plaines IL 60016-6050

BANAS, C(HRISTINE) LESLIE, lawyer; b. Swindon, Wiltshire, Eng., Oct. 29, 1951; arrived in U.S., 1957; d. Stanley M. and Helena Ann (Boryn) Banas; m. Dale J. Buras, May 1, 1976; children: Eric Buras, Andrea Buras. BA magna cum laude, U. Detroit, 1973; JD cum laude, Wayne State U., 1975. Bar: Mich. 1976, U.S. Supreme Ct. 1980. Atty. Hyman & Rice, Southfield, Mich., 1976-77, Hyman, Gurwin, Nachman, Friedman & Winkelman, Southfield, 1977-82, ptnr., 1982-87, Honigman Miller Schwartz and Cohn LLP, Detroit, 1987—. Mem. Mich. Land Title Stds. Com. Contbg. editor: Assisted Housing Alert; contbr. articles to profl. jours. Bd. mem. Women's Leadership Forum; bd. visitors Wayne State U. Sch. of Nursing. Mem.: ABA, Mich. Land Title Standars Com., Fed. Bar Assn., State Bar Mich. (bd. dirs. real property law sect. coun., coun. treas.), Detroit Athletic Club, Women's Econ. Club (past pres.). Roman Catholic. Avocations: gardening, photography, skiing. Office: Honigman Miller Schwartz and Cohn LLP 32270 Telegraph Rd Ste 225 Bingham Farms MI 48025-2457 Office Phone: 248-566-8406. Business E-Mail: lbanas@honigman.com.

BANAS, CONRAD MARTIN, mechanical engineer, chief scientist; b. Warren, Mass., Nov. 27, 1927; s. Martin and Caroline (Krupska) B.; m. Erna Maier, Sept. 19, 1949 (div. Nov. 1970); children: Stephen, Richard, Susan, Patricia, Pamela; m. Gene Tomaiuolo Banas, July 19, 1974; children: Jonathan, Jeremy. BSME, Worcester Poly., 1953; MSME, U. Conn., 1957, MS in Physics, 1965. Registered profl. engr., Conn. Asst. rsch. engr. United Technologies Rsch. Ctr., East Hartford, Conn., 1953-57, rsch. engr., 1957-61, sr. rsch. engr., 1961-76, mgr. indsl. laser processing, 1976-90; chief scientist United Technologies Indsl. Lasers, South Windsor, Conn., 1990-93; cons. Laser Materials Processing, 1993—. Adj. asst. prof. U. Hartford, 1957-62; lectr. U. Conn., Storrs, 1963-67. Patentee in field; contbr. articles to profl. jours. Sgt. U.S. Army, 1945-48. Recipient Adams Lecture award Am. Welding Soc., 1988, Co. Excellence awards United Technologies, 1983, 87, 89, Outstanding Achievement award Pa. State Applied Rsch. Lab., 1996. Fellow Laser Inst. of Am. (Arthur L. Schawlow award 1997); mem. Am. Welding Soc., Am. Soc. Metals, Tau Beta Pi, Sigma Xi. Avocations: skiing, softball, bicycling, sailing. Home: 56 Volpi Rd Bolton CT 06043-7547 E-mail: conniebanas@hotmail.com.

BANAS, EMIL MIKE, physicist, researcher; b. East Chicago, Ind., Dec. 5, 1921; s. John J. and Rose M. (Valcicak) B; m. Margaret Fagyas Welton, Oct. 9, 1948; children: Mary K., Barbara A. French. BA, Benedictine U., 1943; postgrad. (U.S. Rubber fellow), U. Notre Dame, 1954, PhD, 1955. Author (autobiography): For the Life of Me, 2005. Recipient medal of St. Benedict, Benedictine U., 1999. Mem. Pres. Assocs. of Benedictine U., VFW (life), Sigma Pi Sigma. Home: 425 NW Orion Dr Pullman WA 99163-3526

BANAS, SUZANNE, middle school educator; b. Miami, Fla., Mar. 28, 1959; d. Frank and Norma (Eliscu) B. BA in Sci., U. Miami, 1981, MS, 1986; PhD, Union Inst., 1994. Cert. tchr. sci. gifted LD & EH, Fla.; Nat. Bd. Cert. Tchr. early adolescence generalist Nat. Bd. Profl. Tchg. Stds. Lead tchr. Dade County Pub. Schs., Miami, 1988—; curriculum writer Gender Equity Network, Miami, 1993—97, Arise Found., Miami, 1995—97; tchr., chairperson dept. sci., team leader Cutler Ridge Mid. Sch., Miami, 1990—; adj. prof. Fla. Internat. U., Miami, 1996—. Advisor Acad. for Instrnl. Leadership, Miami, 1994-96, Annenberg Challenge Grant, Miami, 1995-96; cons. Urban Sys. Initiative, 1995-98; Internet tchr. trainer/mentor, 1998—. Recipient Fla. Explores! award Fla. State U./TDRA, 1993, Tchr. of Yr. award Cutler Ridge Mid. Sch., 1996, Sharing success award dept. of environ. edn., 2000. Mem. Miami Dade County Sci. Tchrs. Assn. (pres. 1994—), Fla. Assn. Sci. Tchrs. (bd. dirs. 1998—), Nat. Sci. Tchrs. Assn. Office: Richmond Heights Mid Sch Sci Zoo Magnet 15015 SW103 Ave Miami FL 33176

BANASIK, ROBERT CASMER, health facility administrator, educator; b. Detroit, Dec. 8, 1942; s. Casmer John and Lucille Nathalie Banasik; m. Jacqueline Mae Miller, Aug. 28, 1965 (div. 1985); children: Robert John, Marcus Alan, Jason Andrew; m. Barbara Jean Willows, Oct. 12, 1985. BSME, Wayne State U., 1965; MS in Indsl. Engring., Tex. Tech Coll., 1967; MBA, Ohio State U., 1973, PhD, 1974. Registered profl. engr., Ohio; lic. nursing home adminstr., Ohio. Mgmt. systems engr. Riverside Meth. Hosp., Columbus, Ohio, 1970, 71; owner, mgmt. systems cons. Banasik Assocs., Columbus, 1972—; dir. mgmt. systems engring. Grant Hosp., Columbus, 1973-78; owner, mgr. RMJ Investment Enterprises, Columbus, 1975-85; pres. Omnilife Systems, Inc., Columbus, 1979—, RMJ Mgmt., Inc., 1983-85, Bryant Health Ctr., Inc., Ironton, Ohio, 1983—, Equity Mgmt., 1985—; owner Omnivend, 1985—. Adminstr. Patterson Health Ctr., Columbus, 1980-99, Parkview Health Ctr., Inc., Volga, S.D., 1986—, Hamilton (Ohio) Health Ctr., Inc., 1986-97, Shelby Manor Health Ctr., Inc., Shelbyville, Ky., 1986—; corp. sec. Clintonville Family Practice, Columbus, 1987—, Samaritan Care Ctr., Inc., Medina, Ohio, 1988—, Sanctuary at Whispering Meadows, Dayton, Ohio, 1997—, The Sanctuary at Tuttle Crossing, Columbus, 1997—, Patterson Resdl. Care, 1999—; asst. prof. Capital U. Grad. Sch. Adminstrn., Columbus, 1973-79, assoc. prof., 1979-97, prof., 1997—, Squire chmn. in small bus. and entrepreneurship, 1997—; pres. Banasik & Strayer Architects and Engrs., Columbus, 1988-93; dir. Asset Data Systems, Columbus; adj. prof. Union Inst., Cin., 1992—. Editor: Topics in Hospital Material Management, 1978-84; contbr. articles to profl. jours.; participant expert witness testimony forensic statis. methods. Pres. bd. dirs. United Cerebral Palsy Franklin County, 1979-80; mem. founding bd. Support Resources, Inc., 1978-85; bd. dirs. Transp. Resources, Inc., 1979-80, Dennison Health Systems, 1988-93, bd. dirs., 1988-97; bd. advisors Seicon, 1999—; pres. indsl. adv. bd. Tex. Tech U., 1987-88, mem. deans coun. Sch. Engring., 1995—; pres. Ohio Acad. Nursing Homes, Columbus, 1986-89, bd. dirs., 1986—; mem. adv. indsl. bd. dept. mech. engring. Wayne State U., 1994; mem. adv. bd. Sch. Nursing Capital U., 1995—. Named Disting. Engr. Tex. Tech U., 2000. Mem. Am. Hosp. Assn., NSPE (dir. Franklin County chpt. 1976-77), Ohio Soc. Profl. Engrs., Am. Inst. Decision Scis., Am. Coll. Health Care Adminstrs., Airplane Owner & Pilots Assn. (lic. pilot), Tex. Tech Acad. Engrs., Sigma Xi, Beta Gamma Sigma, Alpha Pi Mu, Phi Kappa Phi, Alpha Kappa Psi. Lutheran. Office: PO Box 8309 Columbus OH 43201-0309

BANASZYNSKI, CAROL JEAN, secondary school educator; b. Hawkins, Wis., Jan. 3, 1951; BS in Biology, U. Wis., LaCrosse, 1973; MS in Profl. Devel., U. Wis., Whitewater, 1987; MS in Ednl. Leadership, Cardinal Stritch U., 2002. Tchr. Deerfield Cmty. Schs., 1973—. Coach Youth T-ball/softball; co-chairperson Adopt-A-Highway; group leader 4-H Club; counselor Boy Scout Environtl. Merit Badge program Recipient Wis. H.S. Tchr. of Yr., 1997-98, Wis. Tchr. of Yr. 1998, Award of Excellence Wis. Assn. of Sch. Bds., 1997, Wis. Dept. of Instrn., 1997, Wis. Edn. Assn. Coun., 1997, Wis. Legis. Citation for Tchg. Excellence, 1997-98; named Educator of Yr. Nat. H.S. Assn., 1998, Outstanding Tchr. Radioshack/Tandy, 1999; Kohl fellowship, 1997, Monsanto fellowship, 2000. Mem. ASCD, Nat. Biology Tchrs. Assn., Nat. Sci. Tchrs. Assn., Wis. Secondary Sci. Tchrs. (state conf. presenter), BioNet, DEA (scholarship com. chairperson), Wis. Edn. Assn. Coun.

BANCEL, MARILYN, fund raising management consultant; b. Glen Ridge, N.J., June 15, 1947; d. Paul and Joan Marie (Spangler) B.; m. Rik Myslewski, Nov. 20, 1983; children: Carolyn, Roxanne. BA in English with distinction, Ind. U., 1969. Cert. fund raising exec. Ptnr. The Sultan's Shirt Tail, Gemlik, Turkey, 1969-72; prodn. mgr. High Country Co., San Francisco, 1973-74; exec. dir. East Bay Performance, Inc., 1976—79; pub. Bay Arts Rev., Berkeley, Calif., 1976-79; dir. devel. Oakland (Calif.) Symphony Orch., 1979-81; assoc. dir. devel. Exploratorium, San Francisco, 1981-86, dir. devel., 1986-91; prin. Fund Devel. Counsel, San Francisco, 1991-93; v.p. The Oram Group, Inc., San Francisco, 1993—. Co-chmn. capital campaign com. Synergy Sch., San Francisco, 1995-2000; adj. prof. U. San Francisco, 1993—. Author: Preparing Your Capital Campaign, 2000. Mem. adv. bd. Mus. City of San Francisco, 1995—, San Francisco Bot. Gardens, 1998-99. Fellow U. Strasbourg, France, 1968. Mem. Assn. Fundraising Profls. (bd. Golden Gate chpt. 1996-98, chmn. National Philanthropy Day, 2000, Outstanding Fundraising Exec. award 2002), Am. Assn. Fund Raising Counsel, Devel. Execs. Roundtable, Phi Beta Kappa. Democrat. Avocation: gardening. Office: 328 Duncan St San Francisco CA 94131-2022 also: The Oram Group Inc 275 Madison Ave New York NY 10016 Office Phone: 415-821-2534. Business E-Mail: mbancel@oramgroup.com.

BANCROFT, ANN E., polar explorer; b. Mendota Heights, Minn., 1955; d. Dick and Debbie Bancroft Former tchr., coach, wilderness instr., St. Paul, Minn. Mem. Steger Internat. Polar Expedition, 1986 (first woman to reach the North Pole by dogsled); leader Am. Women's Antarctic Expedition, 1993 (first women's team to reach the South Pole on skis); mem. The Bancroft Arnesen Expdn. (first all women's crossing of Antarctica), 2000; founder (with Liv Anderson) yourexpedition internat. motivation co. Subject (corp. video) Vision of Teams, 1998, (documentary) Poles Apart, 1999; featured in Remarkable Women of the 20th Century, 1998. Founder Ann Bancroft Found; spokesperson Learning Disabilities Assn., Wilderness Inquiry (co-chair capital campaign), Girl Scouts U.S.A; bd. dirs. Youth Frontiers; judge Nuclear-Free awards, Nat. Women's Hall of Fame inductions. Named Ms. Mag. Woman of Yr., 1987 Glamour Mag. Woman of Yr., 2001; inductee Girls and Women in Sport Hall of Fame, 1992, Nat. Women's Hall of Fame, 1995; recipient Women First award YWCA, 1993; first woman in world to travel across the ice to North and South poles; (with Liv Anderson) first women in history to sail and ski across Antartica's landmass. Mem.: Melpomene Inst. and Medica (adv. bd.). Office: yourexpedition 119 N 4th St Ste 406 Minneapolis MN 55401-1790 Fax: 612-333-1325. E-mail: susan@yourexpedition.com.

BANCROFT, GEORGE MICHAEL, chemical physicist, educator; b. Saskatoon, Sask., Can., Apr. 3, 1942; s. Fred and Florence Jean B.; m. Joan Marion MacFarlane, Sept. 16, 1967; children: David Kenneth, Catherine Jean. B.Sc., U. Man., 1963; M.Sc., 1964; PhD, Cambridge (Eng.) U., 1967, MA, 1970, Sc.D. (E.W. Staecie fellow), 1979. Univ. demonstrator Cambridge U.; then teaching fellow Christ Coll.; mem. faculty U. Western Ont., London, now prof. dept. chemistry. Author: Mössbauer Spectroscopy, 1973; also articles in photoelectron spectroscopy, synchrotron radiation studies; revs. Mössbauer Spectroscopy. Recipient Harrison Meml. prize, 1972, Meldola medal, 1972, Rutherford Meml. medal, 1980, Alcan award, 1990, Herzberg award, 1991, Can. Inst. of Chemistry Palladium medal, 1996, Morley medal Am. Chem. Soc., 1998; Guggenheim fellow, 1982-83; named Officer of the Order of Can., 2003. Fellow Royal Soc. Can.; mem. Royal Soc. Chemistry, Can. Chem. Soc., Can. Geol. Soc., Can. Physics Soc. Mem. United Ch. Can. Clubs: Curling, Tennis (London). Office: U Western Ont Chem Dept London ON Canada N6A 5B7 Office Phone: 519-661-4117. E-mail: gmbancro@uwo.ca.

BANCROFT, JAMES RAMSEY, lawyer; b. Ponca City, Okla., Nov. 13, 1919; s. Charles Ramsey and Maude (Viersen) Bancroft; m. Jane Marguerite Oberfell, May 28, 1944. AB, U. Calif., Berkeley, 1940, MBA, 1941; JD, Hastings Coll. Law, 1949. Bar: Calif. 1950; CPA, Calif. With McLaren, Goode, West & Co., CPAs, San Francisco, 1946-50; ptnr. Bancroft, Avery & McAlister, San Francisco, 1950-86, of counsel, 1986-92; pres. Madison Properties, Inc., San Francisco, 1967-98, Adams Properties, Inc., 1969-79, Adams-Western Inc., 1969-78; chmn. bd. United Nuc. Corp., Falls Church, Va., 1972-82, UNC Resources, 1978-82, dir., 1984-85; chmn. bd. Madison Capital Inc., San Francisco, 1986-93, Adams Capital Mgmt. Co., 1987-88, pres., 1988—2004; mng. ptnr. Bancroft Investments, San Francisco, 1980—; owner, mgr. Bancroft Vineyard, 1982—; of counsel Bancroft & McAlister, San Francisco, 1986—99; dir., chmn. exec. com. Brown & Haley, Tacoma, 1999—. Former pres. Suisun Conservation Fund; former dir. Suisun Resource Conservation Dist.; former trustee Dean Witter Found., 1952-94; pres. Harvey L. Sorensen Found.; bd. dirs. Calif. Urology Found.; former dir. San Francisco Found. for Rsch. and Edn. Orthop. Surgery; trustee, former chmn. Pacific Vascular Rsch. Found. Lt. USNR, 1942-46. Mem. ABA, Confrérie des Chevaliers du Tastevin, Bohemian Club, Pacific Union Club, Order of Coif, Phi Beta Kappa. Office: 221 Main St Ste 440 San Francisco CA 94105-1913

BANCROFT, MARGARET ARMSTRONG, lawyer; b. Mpls., May 9, 1938; d. Wallace David and Mary Elizabeth (Garland) Armstrong; m. Alexander Clerihew Bancroft, Mar. 14, 1964; 1 child, Elizabeth Armstrong. BA magna cum laude, Radcliffe Coll.-Harvard U., 1960; JD cum laude, NYU, 1969. Bar: NY 1971. Reporter Mpls. Star and Tribune, 1960-61, UPI, N.Y., N.J., 1961-66; counsel Law Firm of Dechert LLP. Adj. prof. law NYU Sch. Law. Bd. dirs., exec. com. Vis. Nurse Svc. NY; chair. Vis. Nurse Svc. NY Home Care, Inc. Mem. ABA (bus. law sect.), N.Y. State Bar Assn. (securities regulation com.), Assn Bar City N.Y. (com. on investment mngmt. regulation), Am. Law Inst. Office: Law Firm of Dechert LLP 30 Rockefeller Plz Fl 22 New York NY 10112-2200 Office Phone: 212-698-5590. Business E-Mail: margaret.bancroft@dechert.com.

BANCROFT, PAUL, III, investment company executive; b. N.Y.C., Feb. 27, 1930; s. Paul and Rita (Manning) B.; m. Monica M. Devine, Jan. 2, 1977; children by previous marriage: Bradford, Kimberly, Stephen, Gregory. BA, Yale U., 1951; postgrad., Georgetown Fgn. Svc. Inst., 1952. Account exec. Merrill Lynch Pierce Fenner & Smith, N.Y.C., 1956-57; assoc. corp. fin. dept. F. Eberstadt & Co., N.Y.C., 1957-62; ptnr. Draper, Gaither & Anderson, Palo Alto, Calif., 1962-67; with Bessemer Securities Corp., N.Y.C., 1967-92; ind. venture capitalist N.Y.C., 1992—. V.p. Venture Capital Investments, 1967—74, sr. v.p. securities investments, 1974—76, pres., CEO, dir., 1976—87; cons. Bessemer Securities Corp., 1988—92; founder, past pres. and chmn. Nat. Venture Capital Assn. 1st lt. USAF 1952-56, Mem. Yale Club, Pacific Union Club, Bohemian Club. Home and Office: 1750 Taylor St San Francisco CA 94133

BANDAR, PRINCE BIN SULTAN BIN ABD AL-AZIZ AL SAUD, former ambassador; b. Taif, Saudi Arabia, Mar. 2, 1949; s. Prince Sultan ibn Abdulaziz al-Saud; m. Princess Haifa bint Faisal ibn Abdulazia al-Saud; children— Lulua, Rema, Khalid, Faisal. B.A., Brit. Royal Air Force Acad., Cranwell, Eng., 1969; Grad., Advanced Fighter and Instr. Pilot Program, USAF, 1979; M.A., Johns Hopkins U., 1980. Fighter pilot Royal Saudi Air Force, Dhahran Air Base, Khamis Mushayt Air Base, Taif Air Base, 1969-82, comdr. 7th Royal Saudi Air Force Squadron, 1976-79, comdr. Peace Hawk Project, Dhahran, 1976-79; in charge spl. AWACS Saudi Arabian Liaison Mission to U.S., 1981; mem. Saudi Arabia Mil. Mission to U.S., def. and mil. attache, 1982-83; mem. Saudi Del. to UN Gen. Assembly, 1983; Saudi Arabian ambassador to U.S., 1983-2005. Served to col. Royal Saudi Air Force. Decorated Flying Hawk medal; King Abdulaziz Sash, for work in attaining Lebanese ceasefire, King Fahd, 1983. Muslim.

BANDEEN, ROBERT ANGUS, management consultant; b. Rodney, Ont., Can., Oct. 29, 1930; s. John Robert and Jessie Marie (Thomson) Bandeen; m. Mona Helen Blair, May 31, 1958; children: Ian Blair, Mark Everett, Robert Derek, Adam Drummond. BA, U. Western Ont., 1952; PhD, Duke U., 1959; LLD (hon.), U. Western Ont., 1975, Dalhousie U., 1978, Queens U., 1982; DCL (hon.), Bishop's U., 1978. Asst. economist Can. Nat. Rys., Montreal, 1955-56, research statistician, 1956-58, staff officer planning, 1958-60, chief costs and stats., 1960, chief devel. planning, 1960-66, dir. corp. planning, 1966-68, v.p. corp. planning and fin., 1968-71, v.p. Great Lakes region, 1971-72, exec. v.p. fin. and adminstrn., 1972-74, pres., CEO, 1974-82; chmn., pres., CEO Crown Life Ins. Co., 1982-84, chmn. CEO, 1984-85; chmn., pres., CEO Cluny Corp., Toronto, 1986—. Former chancellor Bishop's U.; gov. participation Can. Olympic Trust; bd. dirs. Nat. Challenge Sys., Inc. Gov. participation Can. Olympic Trust; senator Shakesperean Festival Found.; mem. Isle Maligne Soc. Duke U. Decorated knight Order St. John, officer Order of Can.; recipient Salzberg medal, Syracuse U., 1982. Mem.: York, Cambridge Club (Toronto), Mount Royal Club (Montreal), Delta Upsilon. Home and Office: Cluny Corp 305-1166 Bay St Toronto ON Canada M5S 2X8

BANDER, EDWARD JULIUS, law librarian emeritus, lawyer; b. Boston, Aug. 10, 1923; s. Abraham and Ida (Lendman) B. BA, Boston U., 1949, LLB, 1951; MLS, Simmons Coll., 1955. Bar: Mass. 1951. Asst. reference libr. Harvard U., Cambridge, Mass., 1954-55; libr. U.S. Ct. Appeals (1st cir.), Boston, 1955-60; asst. libr., asst. prof. NYU, N.Y.C., 1960-70, assoc. prof., curator, assoc. libr., 1970-78; prof., libr. Suffolk U. Law Sch., Boston, 1978-90, libr., prof. emeritus, 1991—. Author: Mr. Dooley and the Choice of Law, 1963, Mr. Dooley and Mr. Dunne, 1981, Justice Holmes Ex Cathedra, 1966, 91, Searching the Law, 1986, Shakespeare on Lawyers and the Law, 1998, Bardell V. Pickwick: The Most Famous Fictional Trial in the English Language, 2004. Served with USN, 1942-46. Recipient Dean Frederick A. McDermott award, Suffolk U. Student Bar Ass, 1980. Mem. Assn. Am. Law Schs., New Eng. Law Libr. Democrat. Jewish. Office: 50 Church St Concord MA 01742-3050 Business E-Mail: ebander@suffolk.edu.

BANDER, MYRON, physics professor, dean; b. Belzyce, Poland, Dec. 11, 1937; came to U.S., 1949, naturalized, 1955; s. Elias and Regina (Zielonka) B.; m. Carol Heimberg, Aug. 20, 1967. BA, Columbia U., 1958, MA, 1959, PhD, 1962. Postdoctoral fellow CERN, 1962-63; research assoc. Stanford Linear Accelerator Center, 1963-66; mem. faculty U. Calif., Irvine, 1966—, prof. physics, 1974—, dean phys. scis., 1980-86; chair dept. physics, 1992-95. Sloan Found. fellow, 1967-69 Fellow Am. Phys. Soc. Office: U Calif Irvine CA 92697-0001 Office Phone: 949-824-5945. Business E-Mail: mbander@uci.edu.

BANDERAS, ANTONIO, actor; b. Malaga, Spain, Aug. 10, 1960; m. Ana Leza, 1988 (div. 1996); m. Melanie Griffith, 1996; 1 child. Launched signature women's fragrance Diavolo Donna, 1999; launched signature men's fragrance Spirit, 2004. Films include: Labyrinth of Passion, 1982, Pestanas postizas, 1982, Y del sefuro...Ilbranos señor!, 1983,El Senor Galindez, 1983, El Caso Almeria, 1983, The Stilts, 1984, La corte de Faraon, 1985, Requiem por un campesino espanol, 1985, The Puzzle, 1986, 27 Hours, 1986, Matador, 1986, Delirios de amor, 1986, The Way They Were, 1987, Law of Desire, 1987, The Pleasure of Killing, 1988, El Acto, 1987, Baton Rouge, 1988, Women on the Verge of a Nervous Breakdown, 1988, Going South Shopping, 1988, Si que dicen que cai, 1989, The White Dove, 1989, Tie Me Up! Tie Me Down!, 1990, Against the Wind, 1990, New Land, 1991, Woman in the Rain, 1991, Madonna: Truth or Dare, 1991, Borges Tales, Part I, 1991, The Mambo Kings, 1992, Shoot!, 1993, Outrage, 1993, Philadelphia, 1993, The House of the Spirits, 1993, Il Giovane Mussolini, 1993, Of Love and Shadows, 1994, Interview With the Vampire, 1994, Never Talk to Strangers, 1995, Miami Rhapsody, 1995, Four Rooms, 1995, Desperado, 1995, Assassins, 1995, Two Much, 1996, Evita, 1996, The Mask of Zorro, 1997, Crazy in Alabama, 1998, The 13th Warrior, 1999, The White River Kid, 1999, Play It to the Bone, 1999, Dancing in the Dark, 2000, The Body, 2000, Spy Kids, 2001, Original Sin, 2001, Femme Fatale, 2002, Spy Kids: Island of Lost Dreams, 2002, Frida, 2002, Ballistics: Ecks vs. Sever, 2002, Spy Kids 3-D: Game Over, 2003, Imagining Argentina, 2003, And Starring Pancho Villa as Himself, 2003 (TV), Once Upon a Time in Mexico, 2003, Shrek 2 (voice), 2004; dir. Crazy in Alabama, 1999, Malaga Burning, 2000; prodr. White River Kid, 1999, Forever Lulu, 2000. TV movies: La Otra historia de Rosendo Juarez, 1990 Office: c/o Emanuel Nunez Creative Artists Agy 9830 Wilshire Blvd Beverly Hills CA 90212-1804 also: Agents Assocs/Guy Bonnet 201 Rue du fauborg Saint Honore Paris 75008 France

BANDES, SUSAN JANE, museum director, educator; b. NYC, Oct. 18, 1951; d. Ralph and Bessie (Gordon) Bandes. BA, NYU, 1971; MA, Bryn Mawr Coll., 1973, PhD, 1978; postgrad., Mus. Mgmt. Inst., Berkeley, Calif., 1990. Asst. prof. Sweet Briar Coll., Va., 1978-83; project dir. Am. Assn. Mus., Washington, 1983-84; program officer J. Paul Getty Trust Grant Program,

L.A., 1984-86; prof., dir. Kresge Art Mus. Mich. State U., East Lansing, 1986—. Author, editor: Caring for Collections, 1984, Affordable Dreams: The Goetsch-Winckler House and Frank Lloyd Wright, 1991; author: Abraham Rattner, The Tampa Museum of Art Collection, 1997, Pursuits and Pleasures: Baroque Paintings from the Detroit Institute of Arts, 2003; editor: The Prints of John S. de Martelly, 1903-1979; author, curator: Pursuits and Pleasures: Baroque Painting from the Detroit Institute of Arts, 2003. Recipient award Am. Philos. Soc., 1981, Publ. award AIA, 1990; Samuel H. Kress fellow, 1972-73, 75-76, Whiting fellow, 1976-77; Fulbright-Hayes grant, 1974-75. Mem. Nat. Inst. for Conservation (treas. 1986-90), Mich. Alliance for Conservation (treas. 1994-95, sec. 1996-97, treas. 1997-98, pres. 1998-2000), Mich. Mus. Assn. (bd. dirs. 1987-92), Mich. Coun. for Humanities (coun. 1988-92), Midwest Art History Soc. (bd. dirs. 1997-2000). Avocation: collecting oriental rugs. Office: Mich State U Kresge Art Mus East Lansing MI 48824 Office Phone: 517-353-9834. Business E-Mail: bandes@msu.edu.

BANDI, NAGESH, research scientist; b. Visakhapatnam, Andhra, India, Oct. 15, 1974; s. Narasayya Lakshmi and Sri Lakshmi Bandi; m. Kavitha Koushik Bandi. B.Pharmacy, Andhra U., 1995, M.Pharmacy, 1998; postgrad., U. Nebr., Omaha, 1998—. Rsch. fellow Andhra U., 1996—98; grad. rsch. asst. U. Nebr., Omaha, 1998—99, grad. tchg. asst., 1999—2000, grad. fellow, 2000—. Mem. bd. studies Andhra U., 1996—; co-moderator grad. symposium Edn. Beyond Grad. Studies to Become Successful Indsl. Scientists, 2002. Contbr. numerous articles to profl. jours. Grantee Grad. fellow, U. Nebr. Med. Ctr., 2001. Mem.: Am. Assn. Pharm. Scientists. Avocations: cooking, travel, sports, music, driving. Home: 411 S 41st St Apt 2 Omaha NE 68131 Office: Glaxosmithkline 1500 Littleton Rd Parsippany NJ 07054

BANDIC, ZVONIMIR Z., physicist, researcher, electrical engineer; s. Zvonimir and Dragana Bandic; m. Snezana Bandic. BS in Elec. Engring., U.Belgrade, Yugoslavia, 1994; MS, Applied Physics, Calif. Inst. of Tech., Pasadena, 1995, PhD, Applied Physics, 1999. Rsch. staff mem. IBM Almaden Rsch., San Jose, Calif., 1999—2002, Hitachi Rsch., San Jose, Calif., 2003—. Mem.: IEEE, Materials Rsch. Soc. Achievements include patents for the field of high power Gallium Nitride electronic devices; The Field Of Magnetic Printing, Magnetic Storage And Servo; design of Gallium Nitride novel electronic devices; research in Disk Drive Servo, magnetic lithography, patterned media, nanotechnology, nanofabrication, e-beam lithography, carbon-nanotube based electronics. Office: Hitachi Rsch 650 Harry Rd San Jose CA 95120 Office Phone: 408-323-7206. Personal E-mail: Zvonimir.Bandic@hitachigst.com.

BANDLER, DONALD KEITH, diplomat; BA in Polit. Sci., Kenyon Coll.; MA, St. John's Coll.; JD, George Washington U. Various fgn. svc. assignments, 1976—2002; dir. Israel and Arab-Israeli Affairs U.S. Dept. of State, 1994-95; dep. chief of mission, charge d'affaires Am. Embassy, Paris, 1995-97; spl. asst. to pres. and sr. dir. European Affairs Nat. Security Coun., 1997-99; amb. to Cyprus, 1999—2002; sr. v.p. Monsanto Co., Washington, 2002—03; sr. dir. Kissinger McLarty Assocs., Washington, 2004—. Participant Sr. Seminar for fgn. affairs profls., 1993-94. Decorated French Legion of Honor, 1998; recipient Superior Honor awards State Dept. Home: 5624 Greentree Rd Bethesda MD 20817 Office: Kissinger McLarty Assocs 1775 Pennsylvania Ave NW Washington DC 20006

BANDLER, JOHN WILLIAM, electrical engineering educator, consultant; b. Jerusalem, Nov. 9, 1941; m. Beth; children: Lydia, Zoe. BSc, Imperial Coll. Sci. and Tech., London, 1963, PhD, 1967; DSc, U. London, 1976. With Mullard Rsch. Labs., England, 1966-67; postdoctoral fellow, sessional lectr. U. Man., Canada, 1967-69; asst. prof. McMaster U., Hamilton, Canada, 1969-71, assoc. prof., 1971-74, prof. elec. engring., 1974-2000, prof. emeritus, 2000—, chmn. dept., 1978-79, dean faculty, 1979-81, coord. group on simulation, optimization and control, 1973-83, dir. rsch. in simulation optimization systems rsch. lab., 1983—. Pres. Optimization Systems Assocs., Inc., 1983-97, Bandler Corp., Inc., 1997—. Contbr. articles to profl. jours. Recipient Automated Measurements Career award Automatic Radio Frequency Techniques Group, 1994, Microwave Application award IEEE Microwave Theory and Techniques Soc., 2004. Fellow IEEE, Inst. Elec. Engrs. U.K., Royal Soc. Can., Engring. Inst. of Can., Can. Acad. of Engring.; mem. Electromagnetics Acad., Assn. Profl. Engrs. Province of Ont. Office: McMaster U Dept Elec & Comp Engring Hamilton ON Canada L8S 4L7 *Proceeding in a direction not sanctioned by my peers has always proved tough, but the results achieved have almost always been worth the effort.*

BANDLER, MARTIN, physician; b. Vienna, Oct. 2, 1930; came to U.S., 1954; s. Sidney and Sara (Feinsinger) B.; m. Frances Feffer; children: Bruce, Gail, Ruth. MD, Dalhousie U., 1954. Diplomate Am. Bd. Internal Medicine. Intern Victoria Genl. Hosp., Halifax, N.S., Can., 1953-54; resident in medicine Jewish Hosp., Bklyn., 1954-56, fellow in gastroenterology, 1956-57; physician-in-charge divsn. gastroenterology U.S. Naval Hosp., Phila., 1957-59; pvt. practice Bklyn., 1959—; clin. instr. SUNY, 1959-70, clin. asst. prof. medicine, 1970—. With USN, 1957-59. Fellow ACP, Am. Coll. Gastroenterology; mem. AMA, Kings County Med. Soc., N.Y. Med. Soc., Am. Soc. Gastrointestinal Endoscopy, Bklyn. Gastroenterol. Soc. (v.p. 1972-73, pres. 1973-74), N.Y. Soc. for Gastrointestinal Endoscopy. Office: 954 President St Brooklyn NY 11215-1604 Office Phone: 718-783-6364. E-mail: fmbandler@aol.com.

BANDLOW, LINCOLN DEE, lawyer, law educator; b. Palm Springs, Calif., Apr. 1, 1966; s. Richard Dee Bandlow and Victoria Lynn Black; m. Natalie Christine D'Annibale, Sept. 4, 1999; children: Dean Reagan, Valentina Jacqueline. BA in Polit. Sci., UCLA, 1990; JD magna cum laude, Boston U., 1993. Bar: Calif. 1994. Assoc. Gibson, Dunn & Crutcher, L.A., 1994—97; legal affairs The Carsey-Werner Co., Studio City, Calif., 1997—98; mem. Leopold, Petrich & Smith, L.A., 1998—. Assoc. prof. U. So. Calif., L.A., 1996—. Contbr. articles to profl. jours. Mem.: L.A. Copyright Soc. (trustee, treas., sect., v.p., pres.-elect 1999—2004, pres. 2005—), L.A. County Bar Assn. Republican. Avocations: beach volleyball, surfing. Office: Leopold Petrich & Smith Ste 3110 2049 Century Park East Los Angeles CA 90067-3274 Office Phone: 310-277-3333. Office Fax: 310-277-7444. Business E-Mail: lbandlow@lpsla.com.

BANDO, PATRICIA ALICE, food service executive; b. Detroit, Apr. 4, 1953; d. Hiro Walter and Fumi Patricia (Takemoto) B. BS in Dietetics, Mich. State U., 1975; MA in Food Svc. Adminstrn., NYU, 1985. Registered dietitian. Dietetic intern The N.Y. Hosp., N.Y.C., 1975-76, clin. dietitian, sr. dietitian/adminstrv., 1981-86; food and beverage mgr. Trump Palace Hotel, Atlantic City, N.J., 1986; gen. mgr., dining dept. Cornell U., Ithaca, N.Y., 1986-89, asst. dir., dining dept., 1989-92, dir., dining dept., 1992-95, Boston Coll., Chestnut Hill, Mass., 1995—. Fundraiser One to One Mentoring, Boston, 1998. Mem. ADA, Mass. Dietetic Assn., Nat. Assn. of Coll. and Univ. Food svcs. (conf. edn. chair 1996-97), N.Y. So. Tier Dietetic Assn. (treas. 1992-95), Soc. of Foodsvc. Mgmt., Nat. Restaurant Assn., Mass. Restaurant Assn. (bd. dirs. 2003—, Employer Choice award 2003, IFMA Silver Plate award 2004), New Seabury Country Club, Omicron Nu. Episcopalian. Avocations: golf, painting, watercolor, gourmet cooking. Home: 14 Holly Way Framingham MA 01701-4857 Office: Boston Coll Dining Svcs 66 Commonwealth Ave Chestnut Hill MA 02467-3843

BANDOURIAN, HRIPSIME, investment advisor; b. Yerevan, Armenia, Sept. 30, 1977; d. Daniel Bandourian and Alla Tevosyants. MS, Brigham Young U., 2001; postgrad. in Bus., Harvard Bus. Sch., 2004—. Investment strategist Goldman Sachs, N.Y.C., 2001—04. Contbr. articles to profl. jours. Sec. Relief Soc., LDS Ch., N.Y.C., 2000—03. Recipient Office of Rsch. and Creative Activity award, Brigham Young U., 1998-1999; acad. scholarship, 1995-1999, Harvard Bus. Sch. fellowship, Harvard Bus. Sch., 2004-2006.

BANDOW, DOUGLAS LEIGHTON, editor, columnist, consultant; b. Washington, Apr. 15, 1957; s. Donald E. and Donna J. (Losh) B. AA, Okaloosa-Walton Jr. Coll., Niceville, Fla., 1974; BS in Econ., Fla. State U., 1976; JD, Stanford U., 1979. Bar: Calif. 1979 D.C. 1984. Sr. policy analyst Reagan for Pres. Com., Los Angeles, 1979-80, Arlington, Va., 1980, Office of Pres. Elect, Washington, 1980-81; spl. asst. to the Pres. for policy devel. White House, Washington, 1981-82; editor Inquiry Mag., Washington, 1982-84; sr. fellow Cato Inst., Washington, 1984—; nat. syndicated columnist Copley News Svc., San Diego, 1983—. Author: Unquestioned Allegiance, 1986, Beyond Good Intentions: A Biblical View of Politics, 1988, Human Resources and Defense Manpower, 1989, The Politics of Plunder: Misgovernment in Washington, 1990, The Politics of Envy: Statism as Theology, 1994, Tripwire: Korea and U.S. Foreign Policy in a Changed World, 1996; editor: U.S. Aid to the Developing World, 1985, Protecting the Environment, 1986; co-editor: The U.S.-South Korean Alliance, 1992, Perpetuating Poverty, 1994; contbr. articles to periodicals. Recipient Freedom Leadership award Freedoms Found., Valley Forge, Pa., 1977; recipient cert. for polit. and journalistic activities Freedoms Found., Valley Forge, Pa., 1979; named Man of Yr. N.Y. State Coll. Reps., 1982; recipient Nat. Young Am. award Boy Scouts Am., 1977. Mem. Calif. Bar Assn., ABA, D.C. Bar Assn., Washington Ind. Writers. Office: Copley News Svc PO Box 120190 San Diego CA 92112*

BANDROWSKI, PAUL, information technology executive; Former dir. advanced tech. for worldwide ops. Sara Lee Corp.; former v.p. bus. devel. SOFTBANK Svcs. Group, former chief tech. officer; vice chmn., founder Reciprocal, former pres., CEO; vice chmn. Sunhawk.com, Seattle, 2000—. Office: Sunhawk.com Corp 1463 E Republican St Seattle WA 98112-4517

BANDT, PAUL DOUGLAS, radiologist; b. Milbank, SD, June 22, 1938; s. Lester Herman and Edna Louella (Sogn) B.; m. Mary King, Aug. 26, 1962 (div. Feb. 1974); children: Douglas, Peggy; m. Inara Irene Von Rostas, Apr. 1, 1974; 1 child, Jennifer. BS in Edn. with distinction, U. Minn., 1960, BS in Medicine, D in Medicine, U. Minn., 1966. Diplomate Am. Bd. Diagnostic Radiology, Am. Bd. Nuc. Medicine. Intern USPHS, San Francisco, 1966-68, physician Las Vegas, Nev., 1968-69; resident Stanford U., Palo Alto, Calif., 1969-72; physician Desert Radiologists, Las Vegas, 1972—, pres., 1982—. Chmn. dept. radiology Desert Springs Hosp., Las Vegas, 1992—; past chief of staff U. Med. Ctr. So. Nev., Las Vegas; assoc. prof. surgery U. Nev. Sch. Medicine. Contbr. articles on diagnostic radiology to profl. jours. Recipient Nev. Physician of Yr. award, 1998. Mem. Am. Coll. Radiology, Am. Coll. Nuc. Medicine, Clark Med. Soc., Nev. State Med. Soc. Avocations: skiing, scuba diving, photography. Office: Desert Radiologists 2020 Palomino Ln Las Vegas NV 89106-4812 Office Phone: 702-384-5210. E-mail: pdb3810@yahoo.com.

BANDURA, ALBERT, psychologist, educator; b. Mundare, Alta., Can., Dec. 4, 1925; arrived in U.S., 1949, naturalized, 1956; m. Virginia Varns; 2 children. BA, U. B.C., 1949, D.Sc. (hon.), 1979; MA in Psychology, U. Iowa, 1951, PhD in Psychology, 1952. Prof. psychology Stanford U., 1953—, David Starr Jordan prof. social sci. in psychology, 1973—. Author: (with R.H. Walters) Adolescent Aggression, 1959, (with R.H. Walters) Social Learning and Personality Development, 1963, Principles of Behavior Modification, 1969, Aggression, 1973, Social Learning Theory, 1977, Social Foundations of Thought and Action: A Social Cognitive Theory, 1986; editor: Psychological Modeling: Conflicting Theories, 1971, Self-Efficacy in Changing Societies, 1995, Self-Efficacy: The Exercise of Control, 1997. Recipient Disting. Lifetime Contbn. award, Soc. for Advancement of Behavior Therapy, 2001, Disting. Achievement Alumni award, U. Iowa, 2005;, Guggenheim Found. fellow, 1972. Fellow: Ctr. Advanced Study in Behavioral Sci., Am. Acad. Arts and Scis.; mem.: APA (pres. 1974, Disting. Scientist award divsn. 12 1972, Disting. Sci. Contbn. award 1980, Outstanding Lifetime Contbn.t award 2004), Can. Psychol. Assn. (hon. pres. 1999), Internat. Soc. Rsch. on Aggression (Disting. Contbn. award 1980), Western Psychol. Assn. (pres. 1980, Lifetime Achievement award 2003), Calif. Psychol. Assn. (Disting. Scientist award 1973, Lifetime Disting. Contbr. award 1998, Healthrac award for disting. contbns. to health promotion 2002, McGovern medal for disting. contbn. to health promotion sci. 2004), Inst. Medicine NAS, Am. Psychol. Soc. (William James award 1989, James Cattell award 2003). Office: Stanford U Dept Psychology Stanford CA 94305-2130 Business E-Mail: Bandura@psych.Stanford.edu.

BANDURSKI, BRUCE LORD, retired ecologist, environmental scientist; b. Waterbury, Conn., June 28, 1940; s. Stanley Alexander Bandurski and Virginia Ann (VanRensselaer) Bandurski Hinckley. BS with honors, Mich. State U., 1962; postgrad., George Washington U., 1964-65, USDA Grad. Sch., 1965-66. Park ranger Yellowstone Nat. Pk., Nat. Pk. Svc., Wyo., 1962-63; sci. reference analyst USPHS, Washington, 1963-65; intelligence ops. specialist U.S. Army, Washington, 1965-66; analyst planner U.S. Dept. Interior, Washington, 1966-74, coord., br. chief, Nat. Environ. Policy Act officer, 1974-83; on detail as ecologist, ecomgmt. advisor Internat. Joint Commn. U.S. and Can., Washington, 1983-85, sr. ecomgmt. advisor, ecologist, 1985-2000. Dep. game warden Commonwealth Va., 1968-70; mem. faculty USDA Grad. Sch., 1968-96, subcom. Fed. Interagy. Com. on Edn., 1967-74, Internat. Joint Commn. Task Force on Indicators Implementation, 1997-2000; watch dir., dep. and acting mission dir. U.S. Man-in-Sea program, St. John, V.I., 1970; chmn. Conservation Roundtable of Washington, 1970-71; chmn. com. on definitions, spl. com. on environ. protection U.S. nat. com. World Energy Conf., Washington, 1981-85; mem. exec. com. Great Lakes Sci. Adv. Bd., 1986-92; liaison Coun. Great Lakes Rsch. Mgrs.; mem. steering com. Great Lakes-St. Lawrence Ecosys. Model Framework; mem. Steering Group on Marine Environ. Monitoring, Commn. on Engring. and Tech. Studies, NRC, 1986-87; mem. Lake Superior Biodiversity Project Adv. Com. Nat. Wildlife Fedn.; initiator multi year project Ecol. Com. Great Lakes Sci. Adv. Bd., 1990-94; mem. Internat. Joint Commn. Task Force on Indicators for Evaluation, 1994-96; mem. Lake Erie Task Force, 1994-97; co-organizer of first binational conf. on exotic species and the shipping industry; dir. Binat. Workshop on Indicators of Ecosystem Integrity/Diversity, 1998; mgr. Wildcat Mountain Natural Area The Nature Conservancy; guest lectr. No. Va. C.C., U. Wis., Bucknell U., Am. U., U. Pitts., Am. Law Inst.-ABA. Writer planning and recreation impact mgmt. series, 1967-73; author U.S. Bur. Land Mgmt. Environ. Mgmt. Procedures, 1976-84 (Achievement award 1978, 79, 84), Ecology and Economics: Partners for Productivity, 1973; co-author: The Ecosys. Approach: Theory and Ecosys. Integrity, 1993, More Recreation: Implications for the Tropical Ecosystem, 1969, Toward a Transboundary Monitoring Network, 1986. Mem. AAAS, Ecol. Soc. Am. (charter Met. Washington chpt.), Internat. Assn. for Ecology, Am. Soc. Naturalists, The Wildlife Soc., Am. Soc. Mammalogists, Fed. Profl. Assn., Washington Soc. Engrs., Outdoor Ethics Guild, Nature Conservancy, Maine Coast Heritage Trust, Island Inst., Earthwatch, Assn. Ecosystem Rsch. Ctrs., Internat. Soc. for Ecosystem Health (charter), Am. Mus. Women in the Arts (charter), Nat. Campaign Tolerance (founder), Friesian Horse Assn. N.Am., Friesian Horse Soc., Friends of Ky. Ednl. TV, Alpha Zeta, Beta Beta Beta. Achievements include origination of no action alternative in U.S. Federal Government NEPA process; development of first college level course on NEPA process and instruction of same, 1971-96; originator concept of tiered/scaled environmental impact statements; catalyzed the first strategic planning endeavor of Internat. Joint Commn., USA and Can; development of standards for recruiting and hiring first systems ecologist for Fed. Govt. Home: 355 Grover Criswell Rd Cynthiana KY 41031

BANDY, JACK D., lawyer; b. Galesburg, Ill., June 19, 1932; s. Homer O. and Gladys L. (Van Winkle) B.; m. Betty McMillan, Feb. 18, 1956; children: Jean A. Bandy Abramson, D. Michael, Jeffery K. BA, Knox Coll., 1954; LLB, U. La Verne, 1967. Bar: Calif. 1972, U.S. Supreme Ct. 2000. Safety engr. Indsl. Indemnity Co., L.A., 1960-65, sr. safety engr., 1965-69, resident safety engr., 1969-72; trial atty. Employers Ins. of Wausau, L.A., 1972-79; mng. atty. Wausau Ins. Cos., L.A., 1979-92; arbitrator, mediator L.A. Superior Mcpl. Ct., 1992—. Contbr. articles to profl. jours. Youth leader YMCA, Mission Hills, Calif., 1965-72. Served with U.S. Army, 1954-56. Mem. Calif. State Bar, Am. Soc. Safety Engrs. (cert. safety profl.). E-mail: ikwimd@yahoo.com.

BANDYOPADHYAY, AMITABHA, engineering educator; b. Calcutta, West Bengal, India, Dec. 25, 1954; arrived in U.S., 1980; s. Ashoke Kumar and Kalpana Bandyopadhyay; m. Aditi Chattopadhyay, June 19, 1988; 1 child, Anika Banerjee. BE, U. Calcutta, 1976; MS, Pa. State U., 1987, PhD, 1991. Registered profl. engr., N.J., N.Y. Structural engr. M.N. Dastur & Co., Calcutta, 1976—80; lead engr. United Engrs. and Constructors, Phila., 1980—84; instr. Pa. State U., University Park, 1984—90; disting. svc. prof. SUNY, Farmingdale, 1990—. Dept. chair SUNY, Farmingdale, NY; cons. archtl. and constrn. mgmt., Holbrook, 1984—. Contbr. articles to profl. jours. Named Engring. Educator Yr., NSPE, 2001. Mem.: Am. Soc. Engring. Edn. (chmn. Mid Atlantic sect. 2003), ASCE, Chi Epsilon. Office: SUNY Farmingdale Lupton Hall RT 110 Farmingdale NY 11735 Office Phone: 631-420-2378.

BANE, BERNARD MAURICE, publishing company executive; b. Nov. 23, 1924; s. Julius and Rhoda (Trop) B. Student, Northeastern U., 1946—48. Various sales and merchandising positions, 1949—55; with BMB Pub. Co., Boston, 1965—, pub., 1965—. Author, pub.: The Bane in Kennedy's Existence, 1967, Is President John F. Kennedy Alive... and Well?, 1973, Is President John F. Kennedy Alive... and Well?, 16th edit., 1997, On the Impact of Morality in Our Times, 1985, Vatican "One": The Fault Line of Vatican II, 1986; prodr., host: The Fringe Voice, 1989—99. Chmn. Local Miss Am. Pageant, 1961. Mem.: Am. Soc. Notaries, Nat. Notary Assn.

BANE, JAMES WALLACE, music educator; b. Youngstown, Ohio, May 22, 1943; s. William Wallace and Evelyn June Bane; m. Glenice Gail DeWald, Feb. 16, 1974; children: Shannon Marie, Jamie Suzanne. M. Music, Cleve. Inst. of Music, Cleveland, OH, 1970; BA Music, Ohio State Univ., Columbus, OH, 1965; D. Music (hon.), Nat. Conservatory, Mexico City, Mexico, 1978. Cert. provisional Tchg. OH, 1966, permanent tchg. OH, 1978. Educator Ctrl. Jr. H.S., Cleveland, Ohio, 1966—70, Cuyahoga Heights H.S., Cuyahoga Heights, 1970—74, Cleve. Heights H.S., Cleveland Heights, 1974—2001, Hiram Coll., Hiram, 2001—. Assoc. dir. All-American Youth Honor Band, Miami, Fla., 1972—75; guest dir. Cleve. Youth Wind Symphony, Cleveland, Ohio; guest lectr. Cleve. State Univ., Cleveland, Ohio. Composer: (musical compositions) wrote 6 compositions for Jazz Ensemble. Bands com. Ohio Music Edn. Assn., Cleveland, Ohio, 2002—; adv. bd. Cleve. Music Sch. Settlement, Cleveland, Ohio, 1998—2002. Recipient Key to the City of U. Heights, OH, City of Cleve. Heights, 2001, Spl. Tribute Award, Tri-C Jazz Festival, 2001, Proclamation Award, City of Cleve. Heights, OH, 2001, Outstanding Jazz Educator of the Yr., 1996, Outstanding Tchr. Award, 1994. Mem.: Chautaugua Lit. and Sci. Cir., Internat. Assn. of Jazz Educators, Music Educators Nat. Conf. Avocation: boating. Office: Hiram College PO Box 67 Hiram OH 44234 E-mail: banejw@hiram.edu.

BANERJEE, ABHIJIT VINAYAK, economics professor; b. Feb. 21, 1961; BSc, U. Calcutta, 1981; MA, Jawaharlal U., 1983; PhD, Harvard U., 1988. Asst. prof. economics Princeton U., Princeton, NJ, 1988—92, Harvard U., 1992—93; Pentti J.K. Kouri career devel. assoc. prof. economics MIT, Cambridge, Mass., 1993—94, assoc. prof. economics, 1994—96, prof. economics, 1996—2003, Ford Found. internat. prof. economics, 2003—. Vis. asst. prof. economics Harvard U., 1991; pres. Bur. Rsch. in Econ. Analysis and Devel., 2003—04; mem. jr. recruitment com. Dept. Economics MIT, 1993—94, theory sr. hiring com., 1994—95, mem. grad. admissions com., 1994—95; dir. poverty action lab MIT, 2003—. Assoc. editor: Quarterly Jour. Economics, 1993—95, mem. editl. bd.: Rev. Devel. Studies, 1996—, fgn. editor: Rev. Economic Studies, 1998—; contbr. articles to profl. jours., chapters to books. Recipient Mahalanobis Meml. Medal, 2000, Malcolm Adeshesiah award, 2001; grantee, MacArthur Found., 1996—2002; Alfred P. Sloan Rsch. Fellow, 1994—96, NSF, 1995—2000, Guggenheim Fellow, 2000. Fellow: Econometric Soc., Am. Acad. Arts and Scis. Office: MIT Dept Economics E52-243B 50 Meml Dr Cambridge MA 02142-1347 Office Phone: 617-253-8855. Office Fax: 617-253-1330. E-mail: banerjee@mit.edu.*

BANERJEE, KAUSTAV, electrical and computer engineering educator; arrived in U.S., 1991; s. Gokul Chandra and Arati Banerjee; m. Sheetal Gavankar, Dec. 22, 1994. PhD, U. Calif., Berkeley, 1999. Rsch. asst. dept. elec. engring. computer sci. U. Calif., Berkeley, 1993—99; vis. rschr. Tex. Instruments, Dallas, 1997—98; rsch. assoc. Ctr. for Integrated Systems, Stanford (Calif.) U., 1999—2002; vis. rsch. fellow Swiss Fed. Inst. of Tech., Lausanne, Switzerland, 2001; vis. faculty Microprocessor Rsch. Labs, Intel Corp., Hillsboro, Oreg., 2002; asst. prof. dept. elec. and computer engring. U. Calif., Santa Barbara, 2002—. Tech. cons. Magma Design Automation Inc., Cupertino, Calif., 2000—01; tech. cons. Fujitsu Labs of Am., Sunnyvale, 2002. Author: (paper (38th design automation conf.) Analysis of On-Chip Inductance Effects using a Novel Performance Optimization Methodology for Distributed RLC Interconnects, 2001 (Best Paper Award ACM/IEEE Design Automation Conf., 2001); contbr. more than 100 articles to profl. jours. and refereed internat. confs. Mem.: IEEE. Business E-Mail: kaustav@ece.ucsb.edu.

BANERJEE, PRASHANT, industrial engineer, educator, computer scientist; b. Calcutta, West Bengal, India, Apr. 15, 1962; came to U.S., 1986; s. Prabhat K. and Bani Banerjee; m. Madhumita Banerjee, Dec. 11, 1987; children: Jay, Ann. BSME, Indian Inst. Tech., Kanpur, India, 1984; MS in Indsl. Engring., Purdue U., 1987, PhD, 1990. Indsl. engr. Tata Steel Co., Jamshedpur, India, 1984-85; asst. prof. U. Ill., Chgo., 1990-96, assoc. prof., 1996—. Cons. Caterpillar Inc., Peoria, Ill., 1992, Motorola Inc., 1994—97, Monsanto, Inc., 1996—; tech. adv. bd. mem. Motorola Labs, 2002; chief tech. officer Indsl. Virtual Reality, Inc., 2000—. Author: Automation and Control of Manufacturing Systems, 1991, Object-oriented Technology in Manufacturing, 1992, Virtual Manufacturing, 2001; contbr. articles to profl. jours. Grantee NSF rsch., 1992, 1995, 2000, Nat. Inst. Standards and Tech. rsch., 1995. Fellow: ASME; mem.: Inst. Indsl. Engrs. Avocations: sports, current events, religious discussions. Home: 708 Kirstin Ct Westmont IL 60559 Office: Univ Ill Engring Dept Chicago IL 60607-7022

BANERJEE, SUBHASH, cardiologist; s. Bankim Behari and Smriti Banerjee; m. Pooja Banerjee, Oct. 14, 1990; children: Avantika, Rahul. MD, Minsk State Med. Inst., Russia, 1992. Diplomate Am. Bd. of Internal Medicine, 2003. Interventional cardiologist N.Mex. Cardiac Care, Las Cruces, 2004—. Fellow, U. Iowa Hosps. and Clinics, 199-2003. Mem.: AMA (life). Achievements include research in Basic Science and Cardivascular Research. Office: NMex Cardiac Care 4351 E Lohman Ave Las Cruces NM 88011 Office Phone: 505-521-3270. Office Fax: 505-521-3504.

BANERJEE, UTPAL, biology professor, research scientist; b. New Delhi; BS in chemistry, St. Stephens Coll., New Delhi; M in phys. chemistry, Indian Inst. Tech.; PhD in chemistry, post doctorate studies in biology, Calif. Inst. Tech. Asst. prof. Univ. Calif., LA, 1988—94, prof., 1994—, chair Molecular Cell & Devel. Biology Dept. Prof. Howard Hughes Med. Inst. Office: 1506D Gonda Neuroscience and Genetics Rsch Ctr 695 Charles Young Dr Los Angeles CA 90095-1761 Office Phone: 310-206-5439, 310-825-2980.

BANERJEE, (BIMAL BANERJEE), artist, educator; b. Calcutta, India, Sept. 4, 1939; naturalized, 1978; s. Dashurathee and Madhabilata B. DFA with 1st class honros, Indian Coll. Art, Calcutta, 1960; postgrad., Coll. Art, New Delhi, 1965-67, Atelier 17, Paris, 1967-69; graduate study, Ecole des Beaux-Arts, Paris, 1967-70; postgrad., Pratt Inst., N.Y.C., 1969-72, NYU, 1976; MA, Columbia U, 1980; EdM, Columbia U., 1981, EdD, 1988. Lectr. NAD, N.Y.C., 1969, Bloomfield Coll., NJ, 1980—81, Parsons Sch. Design/New Sch., N.Y.C, 1979, faculty, 1983—88; art therapist St. John's Episc. Hosp., Queens, NY, 1981—83; tchr., art cons. N.Y.C. Pub. Schs., 1984—2001; art tchr. Cath. H.S., N.Y.C., 1987; lectr. Columbia U. Tchrs. Coll., N.Y.C., 1988—2001. Guest lectr. Tchrs. Coll., Columbia U., 1984. Multi-media performance artist shows include Parsons Sch. Design/New Sch., 1986, Columbia U., 1978, 79, 84, Hofstra U., 1979, Just Above Midtown Gallery, N.Y.C., 1977, 78, Bertha Urdang Gallery, N.Y.C., 1976, Fremar Gallery, L.I., N.Y., 1974, Galerie du Haut Pave, Paris, 1968-69, Mcpl.

Galeria, Levanto, Italy, 1968, Kumar Gallery, New Delhi, 1970, Arts & Prints Gallery, Calcutta, 1963, 64, Art Heritage Gallery, New Delhi, 1990, Chitrakoot Gallery, Calcutta, 1990, Bertha Urdang Gallery, N.Y.C., 1991, Chemould Gallery, Calcutta, 1993, Cite Internationale des Arts, Paris, 1994, 99, numerous others; internat. biennials in Paris, Tokyo, Rejika, Miami, Hawaii, Bradford, Eng., Biella, Ibiza, Triennale-India, Berlin Triennale, Joan Miro Drawing prize, Barcelona, Ljubljana, others; exhibited in 38 one-man shows, U.S., Europe and India; introduced new media Fumage and Carbontransfer; represented in permanent collections Mus. Modern Art, Paris, Mus. Modern Art, Barcelona, Spain, Mus. Fine Arts, Boston, Mus. Art, Iowa City, Mus. Modern Art de la Ville de Paris, Mus. Internat. of Electrography Art, Cuenca, Spain, Ctr. National d'Art Contemporain, Paris, Ministry Cultural Affairs, France, Neil Saek Gallery, Johannesburg, South Africa, Nat. Gallery Modern Art, New Delhi, Nat. Acad. Art, New Delhi, Essex Libr., London, The Pallas Gallery, London, Bibliothèque Nat.de France, Paris, Honolulu Acad. Art, Rockefeller Bros. Found., N.Y.C., N.Y. Pub. Libr. Art Collection, N.Y.C., Bklyn. Mus., others; represented in pub. collections Mus. Modern Art, Paris, Mus. Modern Art, Barcelona, Mus. Fine Arts, Boston, Mus. Art, Iowa City, Mus. Modern Art de la Ville de Paris, Mus. Internat. Electrography Art, Cuenca, Spain, Centre National d'Art Contemporain, Paris, Min. Cultural Affairs, France, Neil Sack Gallery, Johannesburg, Nat. Gallery Modern Art, New Delhi, Nat. Acad. Art, New Delhi, Essex Libr., London, Pallas Gallery, London, Bibliotechque Nationale, Paris, Honolulu Acad. Art, Rockefeller Bros. Fund, N.Y.C., N.Y. Pub. Libr., N.Y.C., Radford U. Mus., Va., Bklyn. Mus. Inst. Arts and Scis., Radford U. Mus., Bklyn. Mus., others; contbr. articles, poetry, short stories, children's lit. to profl. jours. Founding mem. Bill Clinton Presdl. Found., Little Rock, Wall of Tolerance, Nat. Campaign for Tolerance, Montgomery, Ala. Recipient awards Hawaii Biennial, 1971, 73, 79, Arthur Kaplan award, 1978, award Painters and Sculptors Soc., 1972, Culturelle Internat. award, Paris, 1968, Nat. award Nat. Art Acad., India, 1967, 70, State Acad. award Bengal State, and Punjab State, 1967, Statue of Victory world cultural prize Nat. Ctr. Study and Rsch., Salsomiggiore, Italy, 1984, also others; grantee Govt. of India, 1965-67, Govt. of France, 1967-70, Adolph and Esther Gottlieb Found., 1989; India Govt. nat. scholar, French Govt. scholar. Mem. Mus. Modern Art, Found. for Community of Artists of N.Y.C., Coll. Art Assn. of Am., Print Club Philadelphia, World Print Council, Smithsonian Instn., Ancient Art—Paris, Wall of Tolerance (founding mem., Nat. campaign for tolerance, Montgomery, Ala. Home: Loft 2C 106 Ridge St New York NY 10002-2554 Office: Bertha Urdang Gallery 23 E 74th St New York NY 10021-2617

BANERJI, RANAN BIHARI, mathematics professor; b. Calcutta, India, May 5, 1928; came to U.S., 1961, naturalized, 1969; s. Bijan Bihari and Setabja (Chatterji) B.; m. Purnima Purkayastha, July 8, 1954; children: Anindita Banerji Spielberg, Sunandita Banerji Ogawa. BS, Patna U., 1947; MS, Calcutta U., 1949, DPhil, 1956. Rsch. scholar Calcutta U., 1950-53, lectr., 1956; vis. asst. prof. Pa. State U., 1953-55; maintenance engr. Indian Statis. Inst., 1956-58; faculty Case Western Res. U., 1958-74, prof. computer sci., 1968-74, Temple U., Phila., 1974-82; prof. math. and computer sci. St. Joseph's U., Phila., 1983-92, prof. emeritus, 1993—. Vis. prof. U. Paris, U. Vienna, U. Calcutta, Czech Tech. U.; asst. prof. engring. U. N.B., Can., 1959-61; cons. in field. Author: Theory of Problem Solving, 1969, Artificial Intelligence, 1980; (with M. Mesarovic) Non-numerical Problem Solving, 1969; (with A. Elithorn) Artificial and Human Intelligence, 1986, Formal Techniques in Artificial Intelligence, 1989;assoc. editor Elsevier Sci. Pubs., Amsterdam; reviewer computing, mathematics reviews; contbr. articles to profl. jours. Gold medalist univs. Patna and Calcutta. Fellow Am. Assn. Artificial Intelligence; mem. ACLU, Common Cause, Sci. within Consciousnes, Computer Profls. for Social Responsibility. Hindu Quaker. Home: 7 Macarthur Blvd Apt N409 Collingswood NJ 08108-3648 Office: St Joseph's U Dept Math and Computer Sci 5600 City Ave Philadelphia PA 19131-1308 Office Phone: 856-869-0021. Business E-Mail: rbanerji@sju.edu. *It is my belief that the only successful actions by men and women are those done in selfless service to God. The rest, however laudable, are risky at best.*

BANEY, RALPH RAMIUTAR, retired education educator, artist; b. San Fernando, Trinidad, Sept. 22, 1929; s. Baney and Bhagia Seecharan; m. Vera Parasram Baney, Nov. 29, 1958; 1 child, Clarence Vishnu. Cert. for art teachers, Brighton Coll. Art, 1961—62, nat. diploma in design, 1957—61; MFA, U. Md., 1971—73, PhD, 1974—80; DLitt, U. West Indies, 2004. Elem. sch. tchr. Trinidad Govt., San Fernando, 1950—57; art supr. Min. of Edn. and Culture, San Fernando, 1963—71; grad. asst. U. Md., 1972—75; prof. CCBC-Dundalk, Balt., 1976—99; freelance sculptor Ellicott City, Md. One-man shows include Georgetown U., 1974, Columbia Ctr. for the Arts, 2003, exhibitions include Nat. Mus. Trinidad, 2004. Recipient Gold medal of merit, Trinidad Govt., 1973, Award of excellence, Trinidad Assn. in Wash., 2002. Mem.: Wash. Sculptors Group, Royal Brit. Soc. Sculptors, Sculptors Guild. Avocations: gardening, photography. Home: 5203 Talbots Landing Ellicott City MD 21043 Personal E-mail: baneyrr@yahoo.com.

BANEY, RICHARD NEIL, physician, internist; b. Phila., Apr. 13, 1937; s. Robert Emmet and Mary Elizabeth (Hedges) B.; m. Carolyn Vern Kurey, Feb. 17, 1962; children: Richard N. Jr., Michael D., Marisa V., Brian E. BS, Georgetown U., 1958; MD, U. Pitts., 1963. Diplomate Am. Bd. Internal Medicine, Am. Bd. Rheumatology. Intern VA & Parkland Hosp., Dallas, 1963—64; resident U. Pitts., 1967—70; internist Jess Parrish Hosp., Titusville, Fla., 1971—76, chief med. staff, 1974—76; internist Melbourne (Fla.) Internal Med. Assocs., Holmes Regional Med Ctr., 1976—95; sr. v.p. med. affairs Holmes Regional Med. Ctr., Melbourne, Fla., 1995—96; CEO Health First Physicians, 1995—98; med. officer M.S. Endeavor, 1999—. Trustee Holmes Regional Med. Ctr., Melbourne, 1984-95; founding dir., chmn. bd. dirs. Reliance Bank Fla., Melbourne, 1985-95; founding dir., chmn. bd. Bank Brevard, 1996-2004, dir., 2004—. Trustee Fla. Inst. Tech., Melbourne, 1985—, mem. exec. com., 1987—, vice chmn. bd. trustees, 1991—2002; pres. Canaveral chpt. Am. Heart Assn., Rockledge, Fla., 1973—74; chmn. bd. trustees Sea Pines Rehab. Hosp., Melbourne, 1992—94. Fellow ACP; mem. Am. Coll. Rheumatology, Am. Coll. Physicians Execs., Brevard County Med. Soc. (pres. 1977-78), Navy League U.S., Eau Gallie Yacht Club (commodore 1985-86), Coast Club (bd. dirs. 1985-91, chmn. bd. 1989-91). Republican. Avocations: bicycling, travel, collecting antique maps, golf. Office Phone: 321-953-5593. Personal E-mail: RNBaney@aol.com.

BANFELDER, ROBERT JOSEPH, writer, literature educator; s. Kilian Banfelder and Victoria Sulka-Banfelder; life ptnr. Donna Derasmo; 1 child, Jason Robert. MA in English, Queens Coll., Flushing, New York, 1976. Adj. lectr. Queensborough C.C., Bayside, NY, 1981—92, Queens Coll., Flushing, NY, 1981—82. Cons. B & J Consulting, Bayside, NY, 1981—96; instr. SUNY, Purchase, NY, 1988, Mosholu Montefiore Cmty. Ctr., Bronx, NY, 1989; lectured Kirby Forensic Psychiat. Ctr., Ward's Island, NY, 1999. Author: No Stranger Than I (reviewed as brilliant by Towers News re Amazon), The Signing, The Triumvirate, Trace Evidence, The Author, The Teacher, Knots, The Good Samaritans; reviewer Guide to Writing, 3d edit.; contbr. articles to mags. Lance cpl. USMC, 1960—62. Fellow: Poets & Writers (hon.); mem.: N.Y. Sportfishing Fedn. (bd. dirs.), Peconic River Sportsman's Club, Ea. Flyrodders of LI, Loyal Order of Moose. Avocations: fishing, boating, hunting. Home and Office: 141 Riverside Drive Riverhead NY 11901 Personal E-mail: rjb@eclipse.net.

BANG, JENS, communications company executive; Dir. mktg. The Timberland Co., 1980-82; former sr. level mgr. various companies, including Reebok Internat., The Rockport Co.; pres., COO Cone Comms., Inc., Boston, 1999—. Office: Cone Inc 90 Canal St Boston MA 02114-2018

BANGASSER, RONALD PAUL, physician; b. Freeport, Ill., Jan. 25, 1950; s. Paul Francis and Florence (Ihm) B.; m. Susan Marie Andretta, June 19, 1971; children: Debra, Sandi. BA, Northwestern U., Chgo., 1971; MD, Chgo. Med. Sch., 1975. Physician Valley Family Med., Yucaipa, Calif., 1978-93, Beaver Med. Group, Redlands, 1993—. Med. dir. San Bernardino Found. for Med. Care, 1984-89, Redlands Med. Group, Redlands, Calif., 1986-92, Calif. Found. for Med. Care, San Francisco, 1991-94, Beaver Med., Redlands, 1997-2001; legis. com. CMA, 1991-95, 2000—, LOPAC, San Bernardino, 1992—, legis. affairs commn. Calif. Acad. Family Practice, 1994—; bd. dirs. CAL PAC. Bd. dirs. Blue Shield of Calif., 1998—. Mem. AMA (Calif. del. chair 1995-99), Calif. Med. Assn. (bd. dirs. 1995—, vice spkr. 1999-2001, exec. com. 1999—, spkr. 2001-03, pres.-elect 2002-03, pres. 2003-04). Republican. Roman Catholic. Avocations: scuba diving, skiing, swimming, hiking. Home: 12724 Valley View Ln Redlands CA 92373-7632 Office: Beaver Med Group 242 Cajon St Redlands CA 92373-5202 E-mail: rbangass@epiclp.com.

BANGEL, HERBERT K., lawyer; b. Norfolk, Va., May 29, 1928; m. Carolyn Kroskin; children: Nancy Jo, Brad J. BS in Commerce, U. Va., 1947, JD, 1950. Bar: Va. 1949, U.S. Dist. Ct. (ea. dist.) Va., U.S. Ct. Appeals (4th cir.), U.S. Tax Ct., U.S. Bd. Immigration Appeals, D.C., U.S. Supreme Ct. Ptnr. Bangel, Bangel & Bangel, Portsmouth, Va., 1950—. Bd. dirs. Portsmouth Enterprises, Inc., Dominion Bank Greater Hampton Roads, Tidewater Profl. Sports Inc.; substitute judge Portsmouth Gen. Dist. Ct., 1979-84; mem. U.S. Ct. Appeals (4th cir.) Jud. Conf. Commr. Eastern Va. Med. Authority (named changed to Med. coll of Hampton Rds.), 1983-91, vice chmn., 1987-88; pres., chmn. Portsmouth Area United Fund, 1971-73; bd. dirs. Portsmouth Indsl. Found., 1968-90, bd. dirs. Urban League Tidewater (Va.), 1978-79, Tidewater chpt. Am. Heart Assn., 1983-84, Portsmouth Community Trust Distbn. Com., 1977-87, chmn., 1985-86; bd. dirs. Maryview Hosp., 1969-87; trustee Portsmouth-Chesapeake Area Found., 1968-72, United Community Funds and Councils Va., 1970-71, others; chmn. Portsmouth Redevel. and Housing Authority, 1977-83. Named First Citizen, City of Portsmouth, 1974. Mem. ABA, Va. Bar Assn., Portsmouth Bar Assn. (pres. 1964), Norfolk Bar Assn., Tidewater Trial Lawyers Assn. (bd. dirs. 1968-73), Va. Trial Lawyers Assn. (bd. govs. 1970), Assn. Trial Lawyers Am., Suburban Country Club (pres. 1961-62), Oceans Club (bd. dirs. 1973-76), Town Point Club (bd. govs. 1983—), Portsmouth Sports Club, Moose, Elks, B'nai B'rith. Democrat. Jewish. Home: 1 Crawford Pkwy Apt 1702 Portsmouth VA 23704-2613 Office: Bangel Bangel & Bangel PO Box 760 Portsmouth VA 23705-0760

BANGERTER, KIRSTIN R., secondary school educator; d. James B. and Mary Lee Ramsey; m. Shane Bangerter, May 2, 1986; children: Austin, Paige. MEd, Ft. Hays State U., 2001. Cert. tchr. Kans., 1993. Elem. tchr. Unified Sch. Dist. 443, Dodge City, Kans., 1993—2002, tchr. english, 2002—. Adj. faculty Newman U., Dodge City, Kans., 1996—. Nominee Kans. Tchr. of Yr., Master Tchrs. of Unified Sch. Dist. 443, 2005. Mem.: Dodge City (Kans.) C. of C. (mem. 21st century leadership com. 2005), Delta Kappa Gamma (assoc.; pres. 2004—, Golden Gift Spl. Stipend award 2005). Republican. Avocations: reading, travel, watersports, decorating, writing. Office: Dodge City High School 2001 Ross Blvd Dodge City KS 67801 Office Phone: 620-227-1611.

BANGS, CATE (CATHRYN MARGARET BANGS), film production designer, interior designer; b. Tacoma, Mar. 16, 1951; d. Henry Horan and Belva Virginia (Grandstaff) B.; m. Steve Gobin, Nov. 1, 1986 (div. 2002). Student, Hammersmith Coll Art and Bldg., London, 1971; BA cum laude, Pitzer Coll., 1973; MFA, NYU, 1978. Owner Flying Pencil Design, L.A., 1981—. Prodn. designer: Lucky Day, 1990; (TV series) My So Called Life, 1994, Fudge-A-Mania, 1994; set designer: (TV series) Picket Fences, 1995-96, (film) Home Alone 3, 1997, Midnight in the Garden of Good and Evil, 1997; art dir.: (film) Volcano, 1997, (TV) Nothing Sacred, 1997-98 (Emmy and SMPTAD-ADG nomination 1998), Charmed, 1998-99, Level 9, 2000, The Huntress, 2000-01, (film) The Fighting Temptations, 2002, (TV) Threat Matrix, 2003, Desperate Housewives, 2004-05 (ADG award 2004, Emmy nomination). 1st v.p. Friends of the Highland-Camrose Bungalow Village, 1985—97; bd. dirs. Ctr. Film and TV Design, 2002—. Hollywood Heights Assn., 1985—87, Cahuenga Pass Property Owners Assn., 1990. Recipient Dramalogue Critics award, 1983. Mem. Art Dirs. Guild (cert.; exec. bd. 1997-99, 2000—, sec. 2005—), Set Designers and Model Makers (cert., exec. bd. 1980—, v.p. 1989-91, pres. 1991-99), United Scenic Artists. Democrat. Buddhist. Home: 9861 Shadow Way St Shadow Hills CA 91040-1543

BANGS, F(RANK) KENDRICK, former business educator; b. Lostant, Ill., May 17, 1914; s. Mark Howard and Mary Hay (Henning) B.; m. Elizabeth Jane Paisley, May 19, 1944; children— John Kendrick, James Paisley. B.E., Ill. State Normal U., 1936; M.P.S., U. Colo., 1946; Ed.D., Ind. U., 1952. Tchr. bus. Rosiclare (Ill.) High Sch., 1936-37, Carmi (Ill.) High Sch., 1937-42; asst. prof. bus. adminstrn. U. Colo., Boulder, 1946-58, assoc. prof., 1958-64, prof., 1964-81, chmn. gen. bus. div., 1964-79; vis. prof. Coll. Bus., Ill. State U., Normal, 1979-80, 84, U. Tex-Austin, 1982, Southwestern La U., Lafayette, 1983, 85, 86, 87, U. Colo., 1987-88. Cons. adminstrv. mgmt., small bus. Chmn. fin. stability bd. Colo. Pvt. Schs. Assn., 1977— Contbr.: articles to Jour. Bus. Edn. Served with inf. U.S. Army, 1942-46. Decorated Bronze Star; recipient Robert L. Stearns award U. Colo. Alumni, 1976; John Robert Gregg award Gregg div. McGraw-Hill Pub. Co., 1978 Mem. Mountain-Plains Bus. Edn. Assn. (pres. 1958-59, Leadership award 1967-68), Nat. Bus. Edn. Assn. (co-editor yearbook 1975, nat. pres. 1967-68), Adminstrv. Mgmt. Soc. (pres. Denver chpt. 1963-64, Diamond Merit award 1967), Colo. Bus. Edn. Assn. (pres. 1956-57), Beta Gamma Sigma, Delta Pi Epsilon (nat. pres. 1968-69, pres. Research Found. 1979—) Clubs: Rotary (Boulder). Presbyterian. Home: 4840 Thunderbird Dr Apt 188 Boulder CO 80303-3829

BANGS, NELSON A. (TONY BANGS), lawyer; BS, Trinity U., 1975; JD, So. Meth. U., 1978. Bar: Tex. 1979. Assoc. atty. Winstead, McGuire, Sechrest & Trimble, 1979-81; staff atty. Dr. Pepper Co., 1981-83, sr. staff atty., asst. sec., 1983-84; gen. counsel and sec. Dr. Pepper Co. & The Seven-Up Co., Dallas, 1986-88, from v.p. to sr. v.p., sec., gen. counsel, 1988—2001; sr. v.p., gen. counsel, sec. Neiman Marcus Group, 2001—. Mem.: ABA, U.S. Trademark Assn., Am. Soc. of Corporate Secretaries, Dallas Bar Assn. Office: Neiman Marcus One Marcus Square, 1618 Main Street, Dallas TX 75201

BANGS, SCOTT, physician; b. Blue Earth, Minn., Sept. 21, 1972; s. Keith and Marian Bangs; m. Rebecca Bulver, July 26, 1997; children: Michael, Lindsay. MD, Med. Coll. of Wis., 1995—99. Bd. Cert. Family Practice Minn., 2002. Resident physician UT Valley Family Practice Residency Program, 1999—2002; family physician Owatonna Clinic - Mayo Health Sys., Owatonna, Minn., 2002—. Contbr. articles to profl. jours. Recipient Andrew W. Mayberry Excellence In Tchg. award, UT Valley Family Practice Residency Program, 1999—2002. Fellow: ACP; mem.: Am. Acad. of Family Physicians. Lutheran. Avocations: sports, music, golf. Office: Owatonna Clinic - Mayo Health System 2200 26th St NW Owatonna MN 55060 Business E-Mail: bangs.scott@mayo.edu.

BANGS, SUSAN ELIZABETH, bilingual educator, language educator; b. Rockford, Ill., Sept. 14, 1952; d. Nesbitt Hoyt Bangs Jr. and Elizabeth (Van Wagner) Bangs; 1 child from previous marriage, Jonathan Michael Bangs. Student, Merrimack Coll., 1970-72; BA, Pa. State U., 1973; MA, West Chester U., 1977; EdD, Boston U., 1986. Cert. tchr., Mass. Asst. prof. Cath. U. P.R., Ponce, 1978-83; bilingual tchr. 2d grade Frost Sch., Lowell, Mass., 1986-90; prof., coord. English as 2d lang. program Harrisburg (Pa.) Area Community Coll., 1990—. Adj. prof. U. Lowell, 1988-90. Author: Images of Puerto Rico, 1983. Lucretia Crocker fellow Mass. Dept. Edn., 1988-89. Fellow Lucretia Crocker Tchrs.' Acad.; mem. Serra (bd. dirs. 1988-89). Roman Catholic.

BANGS, WILL JOHNSTON, lawyer; b. N.Y.C., Oct. 7, 1923; s. Lawrence Cutler and Alma Elizabeth (Johnston) B.; m. Judith Esther Lindhal, July 27, 1957; children: Marjorie Elizabeth, Martha Ellen Alice. BA, Middlebury Coll., 1948; LLB, U. Mich., 1953. Bar: Mass. 1953, U.S. Dist. Ct. (Mass. dist.) 1955, U.S. Supreme Ct. 1973. Staff atty. Liberty-Mut. Ins. Co., Boston, 1953-56; sr. ptnr. Choate, Hall & Stewart, Boston, 1956—. Mem. fin. com., Concord, Mass., 1968-70; mem. Carlisle (Mass.) Conservation Commn., 1972-78, Carlisle Town Rep. Com., 1982-89. With U.S. Army, 1943-46. Fellow Am. Coll. Trial Lawyers; mem. ABA, Boston Bar Assn., Somerset Club, Concord Country Club. Home: 119 Bingham Rd Carlisle MA 01741-1537 Office: Exchange Pl 53 State St Boston MA 02109-2804

BANHAM, SANDRA RODGERS, language educator; b. Washington, June 3, 1947; d. Philip Ray Rodgers and Mildred Elizabeth (Rodgers) Nisonger; m. Richard LeRoy Banham; children: Kassaundra, Richard LeRoy Jr., Philip Rodgers, Jeffrey Edward. BA in English/French magna cum laude, U. Utah, 1969, MA, 1973; MA in English/Sociology, S.W. Tex. State U., 1986; MA in TESOL, U. Miss., 1994, PhD in English Edn., 1995. Tchr. Jordan Sch. Dist., Salt Lake City, 1972-74; instr. Austin (Tex.) C.C., 1974-87, So. Meth. U., Dallas, 1988-89; writing cons./instr. U. Memphis, 1989-91; instr. N.W. Miss. C.C., Senatobia, 1991—. Cons. in field. Author: Resource guide to Teaching Literature, 1980; co-author: Global business Trends Procedures, 1996; editor Acctg. Sys. Jour., 1989-91, British Lit. I & II on-line; contbr. articles to profl. jours. Named Woman of the Yr., Austin C.C., 1986, Tchr. of the Yr., 1981. Mem. MLA, Two Yr. Coll. Assn. (mem. awards selection com.), Nat. Assn. Developmental English, Nat. Coun. Tchrs. English, Am. Coun. on Tchg. Fgn. Lang., Miss. Coun. Tchrs. English (presenter 1993, 99, 2003-), Two Year Coll. English Assn., Phi Kappa Phi, Phi Delta Kappa, Alpha Delta Pi. Avocation: reading. Office: Northwest Miss Cmty Coll 4975 Highway 51 N # 5504 Senatobia MS 38668-1714 Office Phone: 662-562-3202.

BANICK, CHERYL R., librarian, writer, researcher; b. St. Johnsbury, Vt., Oct. 21, 1956; d. Joseph T. and Adeline Shelley Banick. AS in Computer Sci., C.C. of R.I., Warwick, 1984; BS in Bus. Adminstrn., U. R.I., 1986, M in Libr. Info. Studies, 1993. Med. libr. VA Med. Ctr., Providence, 1989—. Mem. adv. com. U. R.I. Grad. Sch. Libr. and Info. Studies, 2002—05, chair adv. com., 2004—05; severe weather spotter Nat. Weather Svc., 2002—; chmn. adv. com. Grad. Sch. Libr. and Info. U. R.I., 2004—05, mem. libr. futures steering com., 2004—, chmn. web subcom., 2003—. Author (written for Mrs. Tipper Gore): Resources in Mental HeaLth (White House Conf. on Mental Illness), 1999; contbr. (chpt.): Scientific and Clinical Literature for theDecade of the Brain, 1993, contbr. articles to profl. jours., contbr. essay: What the OCLC Interlibrary Loan Service Means to Me, 1999, contbr. bibliography resources listing Core Pub. Health Jours. Project, 2003, book reviewer. Recipient Gold Std. Search award, Nat. Libr. of Medicine, 1998, Consumer Health award, Nat. Commn. on Librs. and Info. Sci., 2004. Mem.: Coalition Libr. Advs., R.I. Libr. Assn. (mem. futures steering com. 2004—, chair web subcom. 2005—), Spl. Librs. Assn. (R.I. chpt. chair pub. rels. 1996—99, pres. R.I. chpt. 2001—02, chair networking com. R.I. chpt. 2002—). Avocations: christian chorale singing, writing, photography, fitness walking. Home: 27 Cedar Pond Dr Apt 9 Warwick RI 02886-0854

BANIK, DOUGLAS HEIL, marketing executive; b. Camden, N.J., May 21, 1947; s. Wilmer Harry and Marie Grace (Heil) B.; m. Marcia Lynne Knotts, Jan. 31, 1981 (div. June 1986); children: Shannon Danae Vezina, Corey Jamison Vezina; m. Lauren Clark Abbe, Oct. 4, 1986; 1 child, Mark Mitchell Banik. AB, Harvard U., 1969; MA, U. Pa., 1970, PhD, 1973. Asst. prof. psychology Wellesley (Mass.) Coll., 1973-76; assoc. dir. rsch. Benton & Bowles, N.Y.C., 1976-79; v.p. rsch. Advt. Rsch. Found., N.Y.C., 1979-81; v.p., assoc. dir. rsch. Saatchi & Saatchi Compton, N.Y.C., 1981-83; v.p., dir. mktg. rsch. Ogilvy & Mather, L.A., 1983-86; sr. v.p., dir. rsch. and strategic planning D'Arcy Masius Benton & Bowles, Chgo., 1987-90, dir. strategic svcs., 1990-93, dir. strategy, 1993-94; ind. cons. mktg. strategy, 1995-96; program mgr. Worldwide Comm. Rsch. IBM Corp., 1996—. Cons. Med. Ctr., U. Calif., Davis, 1986, Columbia Pictures, Inc., Studio City, Calif., 1987; mem. Ill. Gov.'s Task Force on Telecomm., 1992. Editor: Jour. Advt. Rsch., 1979-80. Pres. Roosevelt Island Resident's Assn., N.Y.C., 1979-81; mem. com. infants, children, pregnant and lactating mothers White House Conf. on Nutrition Edn., 1979; pres. Garibaldi Sq. Homeowners Assn., Chgo., 1991. Merit scholar Harvard U., 1965-69; Nat. Sci. Found. fellow U. Pa., 1969-73. Avocations: motorcycling, sailing, photography, marine biology, cutting horses. Office: IBM Corp Rt 100 Somers NY 10589 E-mail: dbanik@us.ibm.com.

BANIK, SAMBHU NATH, psychologist; b. Joypara, India, Nov. 7, 1935; s. Padma L. and Kadambini B.; m. Promila (Roy), Nov. 16, 1968; children: Sharmila, and Kakali. BS, Calcutta U., 1956, MS, 1958; PhD, Bristol U., 1964. Staff psychologist Des Moines Child Guidance Ctr., 1965; sr. psychologist, dir. internship tng. Univ. Hosp., Saskatoon, Canada, 1965-69, dir. psychol. svcs., 1969-71; asst. chief mental health svc. Glenn Dale Hosp. and D.C. Village, 1971-81; chief South Cmty. Mental Health Ctr., Washington, 1981-84, chief child and youth svc., 1984-88; clin. adminstr. N.E. S.E. Family Ctr., Washington, 1988—. Pres. Family Diagnostic and Therapeutic Ctr., Washington, 1993—; exec. dir. President's Com. on Mental Retardation HHS, Washington, 1990-93, cons. psychologist, 1993—; pres. Banik and Assoc. Family Diagnostic and Therapeutic Ctr., 1993—; v.p. devel., chmn. Third World Found., 1993—; asst. prof. U. Sask., 1965-71; vis. prof. Bowie State Coll. Md., 1972-81, prof. psychology, 1993; vis. prof. Thakur Hariprasad Inst., India, 1994. Contbg. articles to profj. journals. Mem. nat. adv. coun. on drug abuse, 1987-90; mem. adv. bd. ARC, Washington, 1987-90; founder, pres. Prabashi, Inc., 1974-78, Assn. Indians in Am., 1980-84; pres. E.S.-Asia Found., 1995—; v.p. India Cultural Coordinating Com., 1979-80, Indian Am. Forum for Polit. Edn., 2000; sec. gen. Asian Pacific Am. Cultural Heritage Coun., 1981-82; treas. Asian Pacific Am. Heritage Coun., 1982-84; mem. spl. com. 3d Conv. Asian Indians in N.Am., 1984, chmn. Indian Am. Forum Polit. Edn., Md., 1986-88, 94—; chmn. Third World Found., 1993—; adv. bd. Ednl. India Found., Inc., 1993—, Commonwealth Assn. for the Mentally Handicapped and Developmental Dis., 1992—, Md. com. on diversity, 2000; chmn. Internat. Cooperation and Coordinating Com. 11th World Congress on Mental Retardation, 1993-94; bd. trustees Woodley House, Washington; pub. mem. Svc., Personel, Rev. Bd., Wash., 1996; commr. Commn. People with Disabilities, Montgomery County, Human Rights Commn., 2004—, State Md. Human Rels. Commn., 2005; elected Md. Bush-Cheney del. Rep. Nat. Conv., 2004. Recipient Dept. Humanitarian Svc. Award D.C., 1986; Cmty. Svc. Award U.S. Asia Found., 1995, Disting. Profl. Svc. Award Ariz. Brain Injury Assn., 1999, Mother Teresa Internat. Millennium Award, 2002, Lifetime Achievement award World Painters Forum, 2004; elected Bush del. to Rep. Nat. Conv. Mem. APA, Am. Group Psychotherapy Assn., D.C. Psychol. Assn.; Intenrat. Acad. Forensic Psychology; Nat. Health Svc. Providers in Psychology. Home: 8606 Bradmoor Dr Bethesda MD 20817-3633 Office Phone: 202-342-3832. E-mail: sbanik7539@comcast.net.

BANISTER, JUDITH, demographer, educator; b. Washington, Sept. 10, 1943; d. William Price and Helen Barbara (Myers) B.; m. Kim Woodard, Dec. 17, 1966; children: Adrian Banard, Dawn Banard. BA in History, Swarthmore Coll., 1965; PhD in Demography, Stanford U., 1978. Postdoctoral rsch. fellow East-West Population Inst., Honolulu, 1978-80; statistician/demographer U.S. Bur. of Census, Washington, 1980-82; chief China br. Ctr. for Internat. Rsch., 1982-92, chief Washington, 1992-94; chief Internat. Programs Ctr., 1994—97; part-time prof. George Washington U., Washington, 1981-92; prof. demography divsn. social sci. Hong Kong U. Sci. and Tech., 1997—2001. Sr. cons. Beijing Javelin Investment Consulting Co., 2001—; hon. prof. Social Sci. Rsch. Ctr., Hong Kong U., 2002—. Author: China's Changing Population, 1987, Vietnam Population Dynamics and Prospects, 1993; co-author: The Population of North Korea, 1992, Human Dimensions of Asian Security, 1996; contbr. articles to profl. jours. Mem.: Am. C. of C. Beijing, Assn. Asian Studies, Internat. Union for Sci. Study of Population, Population Assn. Am. Office: Beijing Javelin Investment Cons Co Guan Cheng Yuan (Citichamp Palace) Building 16 Ste 21-A Haidian District Beijing 100088 China Office Fax: (8610) 6235 5459. Personal E-mail: banister@163bj.com.

BANISTER, SUZANNE, music educator, composer; b. Hopkinsville, Ky., Feb. 24, 1951; d. John Turner and Joyce Davis Banister. B of Music Edn., Western Ky. U., 1973; MusM, U. Akron, 1985; PhD, Kent State U., 1993. Band dir. Corydon Ctrl. H.S., Ohio, 1973—75, Coventry H.S., 1975—78, Green H.S., Ohio, 1978—90; prof. Washburn U., Topeka, 1993—2000, Western Wash. U., Bellingham, 2000—. Exch. prof., South Africa, 2002.

Com. mem. Wash. State Arts Commn., Seattle, 2000—01, Profl. Edn. Adv. Bd., Seattle, 2000—02, Tchr. Edn. Advocacy Bd., Seattle, 2000—02; organist Christian Sci. Ch., Bellingham, 2000—01. Democrat. Methodist. Avocations: golf, travel. Office: Western Wash U Dept Music 516 High St Bellingham WA 98225 Home: 1856 Cascade View Dr Camano Island WA 98282-8483 Business E-Mail: suzanne.banist@wwu.edu.

BANK, BARBARA J., sociology educator; b. Chgo., Dec. 13, 1939; d. Julius Charles and Anna Catherine (Damm) Bank; m. Bruce Jesse Biddle, June 19, 1976. BS in Edn., Ill. State U., Normal, 1961; MA, U. Iowa, 1968, PhD in Sociology, 1974. Tchr. Rich Twp. H.S., Park Forest, Ill., 1961-63; from instr. to prof. emerita U. Mo., Columbia, 1969—, dir. grad. studies dept. sociology, 1978-82, chair dept. sociology, 1981-84. Vis. fellow Australian Nat. U., Canberra, 1984-85, 88, 93. Author: Contradictions in Women's Education, 2003; co-editor: Gender, Equity, and Schooling: Policy and Practice, 1997; assoc. editor Social Psychology of Edn., 1994-2000; contbr. articles to profl. jours.; presenter in field. Recipient Purple Chalk Tchg. award Coll. Arts and Scis., U. Mo., 1998; Fulbright sr. scholar, 1985; William T. Kemper fellow Excellence in Teaching, 2000. Mem. profl. orgns. Avocations: travel, reading. Home: 924 Yale Columbia MO 65203-1874 Office: U Mo Dept Sociology Columbia MO 65211-0001 Office Phone: 573-882-9174. Business E-Mail: bankb@missouri.edu.

BANK, MELISSA S., writer; BA in Am. studies, Hobart & William Smith Colleges, 1982; MFA in fiction, Cornell U., 1988. Editl. asst. Putnam Pub. Group, NYC; copywriter McCann Erickson, NYC. Author: The Girls' Guide to Hunting and Fishing, 1999, The Wonder Spot, 2005; Stories have appeared in Chgo. Tribune, Zoetrope, The North American Rev., Other Voices, Ascent. Office: Penguin Group 375 Hudson St New York NY 10014 Address: c/o Molly Friedrich Aaron Priest Literary Agy 708 Third Ave New York NY 10017*

BANKE, KATHY M., lawyer; b. Glendale, Calif., Mar. 1, 1953; married; 2 children. BA, Calif. State U., Sacramento, 1973; JD, U. Colo., Boulder, 1979. Bar: Calif. 1979, US Dist. Ct. Ea. Dist. Calif. 1979, US Dist. Ct. No. Dist. Calif. 1982, US Dist. Ct. Ctrl. Dist. Calif. 1983, US Ct. Appeals 9th Cir. 1983, US Supreme Ct. 2000, US Ct. Appeals 3rd Cir. 2004. With Crosby Heafey Roach & May (combined with Reed Smith in 2003), 1982—2003; ptnr. Reed Smith LLP, Oakland, Calif., 2003—, also practice group leader appellate group. Adj. asst. prof. law in civil appellate advocacy Hastings Coll. Law, 1990—93; practitioner-advisor in civil appellate advocacy Boalt Hall Sch. Law, 1994—98. Mem.: Calif. Acad. Appellate Lawyers, Am. Acad. Appellate Lawyers. Office: Reed Smith LLP 1999 Harrison St Ste 2400 Oakland CA 94612-3572 Office Phone: 510-466-6765. Office Fax: 510-273-8832. Business E-Mail: kbanke@reedsmith.com.

BANKERS, JAMES, military officer; BS in Psychology, ND State U., 1968; postgrad., Air Command and Staff Coll., 1982, Air War Coll. Commd. USAF, 1968, advanced through grades to maj. gen., 2001; student undergrad. pilot tng. Sheppard AFB, Tex., 1968—69; squadron pilot 604th Spl. Ops. Squadron, Bien Hoa Air Base, Vietnam, 1969—70; tng. officer 603d Spl. Ops. Squadron, Hurlburt Field, Fla., 1970—71; instr. pilot 426th Spl. Ops. Squadron, England AFB, La., 1971—72, 917th Spl. Ops. Squadron, Barksdale AFB, La., 1972—77; wing tactics officer 434th Tactical Fighter Wing, Grissom AFB, Ind., 1977—80; wing safety officer, squadron ops. officer, dir. 459th Tactical Airlift Wing, Andrews AFB, Md., 1980—84; wing dep. comdr. for ops. 459th Mil. Airlift Wing, Andrews AFB, Md., 1984—87; comdr. 910th Tactical Airlift Group, Youngstown Air Res. Base, Ohio, 1987—92, 315th Airlift Wing, Charleston AFB, SC, 1992—97, 439th Airlift Wing, Westover Air Res. Base, Mass., 1997—99; asst. vice comdr. Hdqrs. AF Res. Command, Robins AFB, Ga., 1999—2000; comdr. 22d AF AF Res. Command, Dobbins Air Res. Base, Ga., 2000—. Decorated Legion of Merit, DFC, Air medal with 9 oak leaf clusters.

BANKERT, RICHARD L., meteorologist, researcher; s. Larry I. and Beverly A. Bankert; m. Karen L. Lopez, May 24, 1997. BS Cum Laude, Pa. State U., Univ. Pk., Pa., 1983, MS, 1987. Rsch. asst. Pa. State U., Univ. Pk., Pa., 1987—90; meteorologist Naval Rsch. Lab., Monterey, Calif., 1990—. Sci. and technol. activities commn. Am. Meteorol. Soc., 1995—2001. Contbr. articles pub. to profl. jour. (Alan Berman Rsch. Publ. Award, 1994), chapters to books. Recipient Performance and Contbn. Award, Naval Rsch. Lab., 1992-2004; scholar Edwin L. Drake Meml. Scholarship, Pa. State U., 1982. Mem.: Am. Meteorol. Soc., Golden Key, Chi Epsilon Pi.

BANKHEAD, SHEILA WALSH, librarian; b. Middletown, Conn., May 23, 1934; d. Joseph William Walsh and Annamay Smith; m. Malvern Bankhead, Dec. 26, 1955; children: Jennifer Ann Pena, Henry Miller, Joseph Randolph, Benjamin Lewis. BA, Conn. Coll., 1952—56; MLS, So. Conn. State U., 1986—87. Econ. rsch. asst. Twentieth Century Fund, N.Y.C., 1960—63; br. libr. Cass County Pub. Libraries, Cassopolis, 1978—79; music & art asst. libr. Bristol Pub. Libr., 1980—82, music & art libr., 1982—83; asst. libr. Hendrix Day Sch., Jacksonville, 1985—86; head, reference & info. svcs. N.W. Regional Libr. Sys., Panama City, Fla., 1987—. Cons. various libr. vendors, 2000—03; presenter in field, Fla. Author: (presentation) Internet for Teachers, (booklet) Suggested Internet Sites. Mem. Friends of St. Andrews State Pk., Panama City, Fla., Bay County Cmty. Orgn., Panama City. Mem.: Amnesty Internat., ACLU, Fla. Libr. Assn., Omicron Delta Epsilon (life), Beta Phi Mu (life). Democrat. Avocations: writing, travel. Home: 7430 S Lagoon Dr Panama City FL 32408 Office: NW Regional Libr Sys 25 W Government St Panama City FL 32401 E-mail: bankhead@nwrls.lib.fl.us.

BANKMAN, JOSEPH, law educator; b. 1955; AB, U. Calif., Berkeley, 1977; JD, Yale Law Sch., 1980. Assoc. Tuttle & Taylor, LA, 1984—88; asst. prof. U. So. Calif. Law Ctr., 1984—88; prof. Stanford Law Sch., 1988—97, Helen L. Crocker faculty scholar, 1993—97, Ralph M. Parsons prof. law and bus., 1997—. Office: Stanford Law Sch Crown Quadrangle 559 Nathan Abbott Way Stanford CA 94305-8610 Office Phone: 650-725-3825. Office Fax: 650-725-0253. Business E-Mail: jbankman@stanford.edu.

BANKO, RUTH CAROLINE, retired library director; b. Phillipsburg, NJ, Mar. 28, 1931; d. Arthur William and Virginia Miller (Wilson) Osborn; m. Marvin Kenneth Banko (dec.); children: David, Sallie, Susan, Joseph, Elisabeth. Cert. libr. tech. asst., Northampton AreaC.C. Salesman Stanley Home Products, 1958-95; dir. Riegelsville (Pa.) Pub. Libr., 1974-97. Social ambudsman County Agy. on Aging, Doylestown, Pa.; asst. dir. Pearl Buck Found., Dublin, Pa.; mem. Riegelsville Fire Aux., 1992—; councilman, Planning Commn., Riegelsville Borough Coun., 1972-89; mem. States Legis. Com., 1972-88; mayor Borough of Riegelsville, 1990-97; disaster chmn., blood chmn., bd. mem. ARC, Doylestown, 1966-86; pres. jr. high and area coun. PTA, Easton, 1966-74; pres. Boro Coun., 1980-81; v.p., trustee Riegelsville Pub. Libr. Recipient Svc. award ARC, Doylestown, Bucks County Libr. Dist., Life Membership award PTA, 1972; named children's rm. in her honor Ragelsville Pub. Libr., 2005 Mem. Pa. Boroughs Assn. (legis. com. 1972-97), Pa. Mayors Assn., Easton Area Coun. PTAs (life). Democrat. Lutheran. Home: 449 Easton Rd Riegelsville PA 18077-0223

BANKOFF, JOSEPH R., lawyer; b. Newark, Dec. 22, 1945; BS, Purdue U., 1967; JD, U. Ill., 1971. Bar: Ill. 1971, Ga. 1972. Law clk. to Hon. Walter P. Gewin U.S. Ct. Appeals (5th cir.), 1971-72; ptnr. King & Spalding LLP, Atlanta. Asst. editor U. Ill. Law Forum, 1969-70. Mem. ABA, Ill. State Bar Assn., State Bar Ga., Atlanta Bar Assn., Nat. Inst. Trial Advocacy (trustee 1995—, chmn. 2005-), Am. Law Inst., Order of Coif, Omicron Delta Kappa. Office: King & Spalding LLP 191 Peachtree St NE Ste 4900 Atlanta GA 30303-1740 Office Phone: 404-572-4600.

BANKOS, JEAN, educational association administrator, educator; History tchr. Lafayette-Winona Mid. Sch.; pres. Va. Edn. Assn., Richmond, 2000—. Bldg. rep. Lafayette-Winona Mid. Sch.; mem. legis. com., negotiations team, lobby team, scholarship com., bd. dirs. Norfolk City Pub. Sch. Mem.: Va. Edn. Assn. (econ. benefits com., legis. com., bd. dirs., exec. and budget com.), Chesapeake Edn. Bay Assn. (sec., chair UniServ Coun.), Edn. Assn. Norfolk (pres. 1989—91). Office: Va Edn Assn 116 S Third St Richmond VA 23219

BANKS, ALLAN RICHARD, artist, art historian, researcher; b. Dearborn, Mich., Feb. 15, 1948; s. Henry Selman and Lillian Margaret (Radovic) B.; children: Christine Marie, Aaron Richard; m. Holly Hope Tumblin, Jan. 1997. Ind. pvt. study, Soc. Arts and Crafts, Detroit, 1966-69; student, Atelier Lack, Inc., Mpls., 1970-73, R.H. Ives Gammell Studio, Williamstown, Mass., 1976. Artist, with studio in, Newburg, N.Y., 1979-81, Huron, Ohio, 1981-87; portrait artist, with studio in Spring Hill, Fla., 1987-93; dir. Atelier of Plein Air, Safety Harbor, Fla., 1993—. Lectr./demonstrator Portraits South, Inc., Raleigh, N.C., 1993, Atelier LeSueur, Mpls., 1995. Exhibited in group shows Sotheby's, N.Y.C., 1997, Guild of Boston Artists, 1996, 20th Century Exhbn., Amarillo Tex.-Springville, Utah, 1982, Butler Inst. Am. Art, Vixseboxse Art Galleries, Cleve., Salmagundi Club, Amarillo (Tex.) Art Ctr., Maryhill Mus. Art, Goldendale, Wash., Historic East-West Russia Exhibit, 1996, others; represented in collections at Wadsworth Athenaeum, Newark Art Mus., Montclair (N.J.) Mus., Hamilton Fish Meml. Libr., Nat. Portrait Gallery/Smithsonian. Trustee Mus. Natural History, Safety Harbor, 1995—; mem. bd. advisors Art Renewal Ctr., N.Y.C.; mem. Downtown Bus. Assn., Inc., Safety Harbor, 1994—. Elizabeth T. Greenshields Found. fellow, Montreal, 1972, 73; John and Anna Stacey Found. grantee, N.Mex., 1979, Ohio Arts Coun. grantee. Mem. Am. Soc. Portrait Artists (vice chmn. 2000-01), Am. Soc. Classical Realism (pres. 1997—), Met. Mus. Art, Appleton Mus. Art (Ocala, Fla.), Salmagundi Club, New Am. Acad. Ard. Lutheran. Avocations: travel, museums. Home: PO Box 233 Safety Harbor FL 34695-0233

BANKS, BRITT D., lawyer; b. Ft. Collins, Colo., Aug. 21, 1961; BS cum laude, U. Denver, 1983; JD, U. Colo., 1988. Bar: Colo. 1989, US Dist. Ct. Dist. Colo. 1991, US Ct. Appeals 10th Cir. 1991. Law clerk to Hon. Oliver Seth US Ct. Appeals 10th Cir., 1988—89; atty. Holland & Hart, 1989—93; joined Newmont Mining Corp., Denver, 1993, assoc. gen. counsel, 1996—2001, sec., 2001—04, v.p., gen. counsel, 2001—. Mem.: Colo. State Bar. Office: Newmont Mining Corp 1700 Lincoln St Denver CO 80203

BANKS, CHARLES AUGUSTUS, III, manufacturing executive; b. 1940; BA in Internat. Rels., Brown U., 1962. With Cameron Brown Co., 1965-67, Ferguson Enterprises Inc., Newport News, Va., 1967—, pres., COO, 1989-93, pres., CEO, 1993—. With USN, 1962—64. Office: Ferguson Enterprises Inc 12500 Jefferson Ave Newport News VA 23602-4314

BANKS, DAVID RUSSELL, former health care executive; b. Arcadia, Wis., Feb. 15, 1937; s. J. R. and Cleone Banks; married; children: Melissa, Michael. BA, U. Ark., 1959. Vice pres. Dabbs, Sullivan, Trulock, Ark., 1963—74; chmn., chief exec. officer Leisure Lodges, Ft. Smith, Ark., 1974—77; registered rep. Stephens Inc., Little Rock, 1974—79; pres., CEO Beverly Enterprises, Ft. Smith, Ark., 1989—2001, chmn. bd., dir., 1990—2001. Dir. Nat. Coun. Health Ctrs., Pulaski Bank, Little Rock. With U.S. Army. Home: PO Box 4520 Fayetteville AR 72702-4520

BANKS, DEIRDRE MARGARET, retired church organization administrator; b. Melbourne, Australia, May 9, 1934; came to U.S., 1975; d. Haldane Stuart and Vera Avice (Fisher) B. MA, Simpson Coll., 1980. Missionary nurse Leprosy Mission, Kathmandu, Nepal, 1960-69; dean of women Melbourne Bible Inst., 1970-75; asst. to dir. Bible Study Fellowship, Oakland, Calif., 1975-79; dir. adult ministries First Covenant Ch., Oakland, 1980-87, assoc. pastor for adults, St. Paul, 1987-89; exec. dir. Covenant Women Ministries, Chgo., 1989-99; interim pastor Bowie (Md.) Ch. of the Redeemer Covenant, 2005. Spkr. in field. Chair ch. edn. bd. Pacific S.W. Conf. Evang. Ch., 1985-87, Gilead Group, Oakland, 1985-87; bd. dirs., chair Gilead Group Housing for Abused and Homeless Women and Children; bd. chmn. Barnabas Project for Abused and Homeless Women and Children, 1990-93; mem. bd. world mission Evang. Covenant Ch., 1986-89; bd. Covenant Enabling Residences Inc. for Developmentally Disabled Adults, pres., 1996-98; pastor Mission Covenant Ch., Orange, Mass., 2000-04. Mem. Evangel. Covenant Ch. Personal E-mail: dmbanks7@aol.com.

BANKS, ERIC, conductor, composer; s. Frederic and Marsha Banks; life ptnr. David Gellman. BA, Yale U., 1990; MusM, U. Wash., 1992, MA, 1996, MusD, 1995, PhD, 1998. Founding dir. The Esoterics, Seattle, 1993—; prof. music Cornish Coll. of the Arts, Seattle, 2004. Fulbright/Lois Roth scholar, 1997.

BANKS, ERIC KENDALL, lawyer; b. St. Louis, Aug. 21, 1955; s. Willie James Banks Jr. and Grace (Kendall) Palmer; children: Brittany Renee, Bryson Kendall. BSBA, U. Mo., St. Louis, 1977; JD, U. Mo., Columbia, 1980. Bar: Mo. 1980, Ill. 1988, U.S. Dist. Ct. (we. dist.) Mo. 1980, U.S. Dist. Ct. (ea. dist.) Mo. 1984, U.S. Ct. Appeals (8th cir.) 1984, U.S. Ct. Appeals (D.C. cir.) 1998, U.S. Tax Ct. 1988, U.S. Supreme Ct. 1996. Asst. gen. counsel Mo. Pub. Svc. Commn., Jefferson City, 1980-84; asst. atty. Office Circuit Atty., St. Louis, 1984-87; pvt. practice, St. Louis, 1987-91, Clayton, Mo., 1991-92; corp. counsel Siegel-Robert, St. Louis, 1992-97; city counselor City of St. Louis, 1997-99; ptnr. Thompson, Coburn, 1999—, Thompson Coburn, St. Louis, 1999—. Adj. prof. civil law St. Louis U. Law Sch., 1987—92, Washington U. Sch., 1991; sec. bd. dirs. Black Leadership Tng. Program, St. Louis, 1975—77. Sec. bd. dirs. Wesley House Assn.; bd. trustees U. Law Sch. Found.; bd. dirs. DeSailes Cmty. Housing Corp., Am. Red Cross Bi-State chpt. St. Louis Met. Leadership Program fellow, 1975-77, named 100 Leaders for the New Millenium, St. Louis Bus. Jour., 2000; Cochran Cmty. Svc. award, Young Lawyers Sect. Mo. Bar Assn., 2002. Mem. ABA (labor and employment com.), Bar Assn. Met. St. Louis, Mo. Bar Assn., Mound City Bar Assn., Bar Assn. Met. St. Louis. Clubs: Toastmasters Internat. (adminstrv. v.p. 1983, William Tellman award 1982). Lutheran. Avocations: Karate, reading, photography, public speaking, community work. Home: 2755 Russell Blvd Saint Louis MO 63104-2137 Office: Thompson Coburn One US Bank Plz Saint Louis MO 63101 Fax: (314) 552-7256. E-mail: ebanks@thompsoncoburn.com.

BANKS, FRED LEE, JR., former state supreme court presiding justice, lawyer; b. Jackson, Miss., Sept. 1, 1942; s. Fred L. and Violet (Mabry) B.; m. Taunya Lovell, June 5, 1967 (div. 1975); children: Rachel R., Jonathan L.; m. Pamela Gipson, Jan. 28, 1978; 1 child, Gabrielle G. BA, Howard U., 1965, JD cum laude, 1968. Bar: Miss. 1968, U.S. Dist. Ct. (no. and so. dists.) Miss. 1968, U.S. Ct. Appeals (5th cir.) 1968, D.C. 1969, U.S. Supreme Ct. 1971. Ptnr. Banks, Owens & Byrd and predecessor firms Anderson, Banks, Nichols & Stewart; Anderson, Banks, Nichols & Leventhal; Anderson & Banks, Jackson, 1968-85; rep. Miss. Ho. of Reps., 1975; judge Miss. 7th Cir. Ct., Hinds County and Yazoo County, 1985-91; assoc. justice Miss. Supreme Ct, Jackson, 1991—2000; presiding justice Miss. Supreme Ct., Miss., 2000—01; ptnr. Phelps Dunbar, LLP. Chair Spl. Com. on Jud. Campaign Intervention, 2002, 04; mem. Miss. Bd. Bar Admissions, 1978-81; pres. State Mut. Fed. Savs. and Loan, Jackson, 1976-89; mem. minority adv. com. U. Miss. Sch. of Law. Bd. dirs. NAACP, 1981—; mem. Nat. Adv. Com. for the Edn. of Disadvantaged Children, 1978-80; del. Dem. Nat. Conv., 1976, 1980; co-mgr. Miss. Carter-Mondale presidl. campaign, 1976; legislator Miss. Ho. of Reps., Jackson, 1976-85; bd. visitors Miss. Coll. Sch. of Law. Mem. ABA, Magnolia Bar Assn., Nat. Bar Assn., Hinds County Bar Assn., Am. Inns of Ct., Charles Clark Inn, Miss. Bar Assn., D.C. Bar Assn., Sigma Pi Phi. Roman Catholic. Home: 976 Metairie Rd Jackson MS 39209-6948 Office: 200 S Lamar St Ste 500 Jackson MS 39201

BANKS, HENRY H., orthopedist, educator, dean; b. Boston, Mar. 9, 1921; s. Isaac and Bessie B.; m. Judith Epstein, June 1945; children: Nancy (Mrs. Curt Civin), Betsy (Mrs. David Epstein), Steven. AB cum laude, Harvard U., 1942; MD, Tufts U., 1945. Diplomate Am. Bd. Orthopedic Surgery (pres. 1978-79, exec. dir. 1979-86). Surg. intern Beth Israel Hosp., Boston, 1945-46, asst. resident in surgery, 1947-49; asst. resident orthopedic lab. and pathology Children's Hosp., Boston, 1949-50, asst. resident orthopedic surgery, 1950-51, Mass. Gen. Hosp., Boston, 1951-52; chief resident orthopedic surgery Peter Bent Brigham Hosp., Boston, 1952, Children's Hosp. Med. Center, Boston, 1952-53; practice medicine, specializing in orthopedic surgery Boston, 1953—; prof. Tufts U. Sch. Medicine, 1970-90, prof. emeritus, 1990—, chmn. dept. orthopedic surgery, 1970-84, assoc. dean, 1972-82, sr. assoc. dean med. affairs, 1982, acting med. dean, then med. dean, 1983-90, dean emeritus, 1990—; dir. orthopedic surgery Boston City Hosp., 1970-74; orthopedic surgeon-in-chief New Eng. Med. Center Hosps., 1970-84. Orthopedic surgeon children's Hosp. Med. Ctr., 1953-70, Peter Bent Brigham Hosp., 1953-70, chief orthopedic surgery, 1968-70. Author: A Century of Excellence: The History of Tufts University School of Medicine, 1893-1993, 1993, Orthopaedic Surgery at Tufts University School of Medicine, 1893-1998, 1998; editor: The Pediatric Clinics of North America-Musculoskeletal Disorder I, 1967; guest editor: Clinical Orthopedics and Related Research, 1968, Orthopedic Clinics of North America, 1976, 78; contbr. articles to profl. jours. With M.C. AUS, 1945-47. Mem. AMA, ACS, Am. Orthopedic Assn. (v.p. 1986-87), Am. Acad. Orthopedic Surgeons, Am. Acad. Cerebral Palsy (pres.), Eastern Orthopedic Assn., Mass. Med. Soc., Internat. Soc. Orthopedic Surgery and Traumatology, Boston Orthopedic Club (pres.), Pediatric Orthopedic Soc., Am. Bd. Orthopedic Surgery (sec., pres. 1973-79, exec. dir. 1979-86, Univ. Club (Boston). Home: 54 Commonwealth Ave Boston MA 02116-3043 Office: 136 Harrison Ave Boston MA 02111-1817

BANKS, JAMES ALBERT, educational research director, educator, researcher; b. Marianna, Ark., Sept. 24, 1941; s. Matthew and Lula (Holt) Banks; m. Cherry Ann McGee, Feb. 15, 1969; children: Angela Marie, Patricia Ann. AA, Chgo. City Coll., 1963; BE, Chgo. State U., 1964; MA (NDEA fellow 1966-69), Mich. State U., 1967, PhD, 1969; LHD (hon.), Bank St. Coll. Edn., 1993, U. Alaska, Fairbanks, 2000, U. Wis., Parkside, 2001, DePaul U., 2003, Lewis and Clark Coll., 2004. Tchr. elementary sch. Joliet, Ill., 1965, Francis W. Parker Sch., Chgo., 1965-66; asst. prof. edn. U. Wash., Seattle, 1969-71, assoc. prof., 1971-73, prof., 1973—, Russell F. Stark univ. prof., 2001—, chmn. curriculum and instrn., 1982-87; dir. Ctr. Multicultural Edn., Seattle, 1991; fellow Ctr. Advanced Study Behavioral Scis., Stanford, Calif., 2005—. Vis. prof. edn. U. Mich., 1975, Monash U., Australia, Australia, 1985, U. Warwick, England, 1988, U. Minn., 1991; vis. lectr. U. Southampton, England, 1989; Harry F. and Alva K. Ganders disting. lectr. Syracuse U., 1989; Tyler eminent scholar chair Fla. State U., 1998; Carl and Alice Daeufer lectr. U. Hawaii, Manoa, 1999; Sachs lectr. Tchrs. Coll. Columbia U., 1996; disting. scholar lectr. Kent State U., 1978; Read disting. lectr. Kent State. U., 2005; 20th ann. faculty lectr. U. Wash., 2004—05; disting. scholar lectr. U. Ariz., 1979, Ind. U., 1983; vis. scholar Brit. Acad., 1983; com. examiners Ednl. Testing Svc., 1974—77; nat. adv. coun. on ethnic heritage studies, U.S. Office Edn., 1975—78, com. on fed. role in ednl. rsch. NAS, 1991-92, mem. com. on developing a rsch. agenda on edn. of ltd. proficient and bilingual students, 1995—97; mem. bd. on children, youth and families NRC and Inst. of Medicine/NAS, 1999—. Author: Teaching the Black Experience, 1970, Teaching Strategies for the Social Studies, 1973, 5th edit., 1999, Teaching Strategies for Ethnic Studies, 1975, 7th edit., 2003, Multiethnic Education: Practices and Promises, 1977, An Introduction to Multicultural Education, 1994, 2d edit., 1999, Educating Citizens in A Multicultural Soc., 1997; author: (with Cherry Ann Banks) March Toward Freedom: A History of Black Americans, 1970, 2d edit., 1974, rev. 2nd edit., 1978; author: Multiethnic Education: Theory and Practice, 1981, 3rd edit., 1994, 4th edit., (new title) Cultural Diversity and Education: Foundations, Curriculum, and Teaching, 2001; author: (with others) Curriculum Guidlines for Multicultural Education, 1976, rev. edit., 1992; author: We Americans: Our History and People, 2 vols., 1982; contbg. author Internat. Ency. of Edn., 1985, Handbook of Research on Teacher Education, 1990, Handbook of Research on Social Studies Teaching and Learning, 1991, Encyclopedia of Ednl. Rsch., 1992, Handbook of Research on the Education of Young Children, 1993, Review of Research in Education, vol. 19, 1993, Encyclopedia of Black Studies, 2005, Preparing Teachers for a Changing World, 2005; editor: Black Self-Concept, 1972, Teaching Ethnic Studies: Concepts and Strategies, 1973; editor: (with William W. Joyce) Teaching Social Studies to Culturally Different Children, 1971; editor: Teaching the Language Arts to Culturally Different Children, 1971, Education in the 80's: Multiethnic Education, 1981; editor: (with James Lynch) Multicultural Education in Western Societies, 1986; editor: (with C. Banks) Multicultural Education: Issues and Perspectives, 1989, 5th edit., 2004; editor: Handbook of Research on Multicultural Education, 1995, 2d edit., 2004, Multicultural Education, Transformative Knowledge, and Action, 1996, Diversity and Citizenship Education: Global Perspectives, 2004; mem. editl. bd. Jour. of Tch. Edn., 1985—89, Coun. Interracial Books for Children Bull., 1982—92, Urban Edn., 1991—96, Race, Ethnicity and Education, 1998—, Tchrs. Coll. Record, 1998—2002, Multicultural Perspectives, 2000—03; contbr. articles to profl. jours. Recipient Disting. Career Rsch. award, Nat. Coun. for the Social Studies, 2001, Outstanding Young Man award Wash. State Jaycees, 1975, Outstanding Service in Edn. award Seattle U. Black Student Union, 1985, Pres.'s award TESOL, 1998, Disting. Alumni award Coll. Edn., Mich. State U., 2004, UCLA medal, 2005; Spencer fellow Nat. Acad. Edn., 1973-76; Kellogg fellow, 1980-83; fellow Rockefeller Found., 1980, Ctr. Advanced Study in Behavioral Scis., Stanford U., 2005— Mem. ASCD (bd dirs. 1976-79, Disting. lectr. 1986, Disting. scholar, lectr. 1994, 97), Nat. Acad. Edn. (bd. dirs. 2003—), Nat. Coun. Social Studies (bd. dirs. 1973-74, 80-85, pres. 1982, Disting. Career Rsch. in Social Studies award 2001), Internat. Assn. Intercultural Edn. (editl. bd.), Social Sci. Edn. Consortium (bd. dirs. 1976-79), Am. Ednl. Rsch. Assn. (com. on role and status of minorities in edn. rsch. 1992-94, publs. com. 1995-96, pres.-elect 1996-97, pres. 1997-98, exec. bd. 1998-99, Disting. scholar/rschr. on minority edn. 1986, Rsch. Review award 1994, Disting. Career Contbn. award 1996, Social Justice in Edn. award 2004), Phi Delta Kappa, Phi Kappa Phi, Golden Key Nat. Honor Soc., Kappa Delta Pi. Office: Ctr Advanced Study Behavioral Scis 75 Alta Rd Stanford CA 94305-8090 Office Phone: 650-321-2052. Office Fax: 650-321-1192. *One of the greatest strengths of our nation is its tremendous ethnic, racial, and cultural diversity. A major goal of my career is to increase understanding and communication across different ethnic, cultural and racial groups and to make it possible for each ethnic, cultural and racial group to make its greatest contribution to the nation. My belief that educational institutions can play a major role in improving race relations in our nation has greatly influenced my life and career.*

BANKS, KAREN S., language educator; b. Mt. Holly, NJ, Nov. 24, 1956; d. David Randolph and Barbara Ann Harris; m. John I. Banks; children: John, Kenda, Jarrett, Jordan. BA, Princeton U., 1978; MA, Rutgers U., 1997. Cert. social studies tchr. N.J., English tchr. N.J., elem. edn. tchr. N.J., supr.'s cert. N.J. Tchr. Burlington County Juvenile Detention Ctr., New Lisbon, NJ, 1980—84, NJ Dept. Corrections, Trenton, 1984—86; tchr. social studies Allentown (N.J.) H.S., 1986—87, Voorhees (N.J.) Mid. Sch., 1987—88; tchr. English Cinnaminson (N.J.) H.S., 1988—91; elem. tchr. New Albany Elem. Sch., Cinnaminson, 1991—97; tchr. English Delran (N.J.) H.S., 1997—. Trainer assessors Nat. Bd. Profl. Tchg. Stds., Princeton, NJ, 2000—; adj. prof. Burlington County Coll., Pemberton, NJ, 2001—. Mem.: Assn. Supervision and Curriculum Devel., Nat. Coun. Tchrs. English. Baha'I. Avocations: reading, travel, needlecrafts. Home: 122 Millbrook Dr Willingboro NJ 08046-3108 Office: Delran HS 50 Hartford Rd Delran NJ 08075 Personal E-mail: bankar@hotmail.com. Business E-Mail: karen.banks@delran.k12.nj.us.

BANKS, MARVIN R., JR., investment company executive; BA in Acctg., U. Tex., Austin. CPA Ernst & Young; with Gables Residential Trust, Atlanta, 1987—, sr. v.p., sec., CFO, 1990—. Mem. Urban Land Inst. Office: 2859 Paces Ferry Rd SE Ste 1450 Atlanta GA 30339-5716

BANKS, MELBA LUCILLE, minister, chaplain, religious organization executive; b. Asheville, N.C., May 18, 1940; d. Jeter Hezekiah and Rhoda Annie Purdue (White) Ralph; m. David Clyde Burnette, Jan. 21, 1958 (dec.); children: Daniel Lin, Margaret Dawn (dec.); m. Ralph Junior Banks, Oct. 23, 1971. BA in Religion, Mars Hill Coll., 1982; MDiv, Southeastern Sem., 1988;

D of Ministry, Lexington Theol. Sem., 1994. Pvt. music tchr., Buncombe County, N.C., 1960-68; sec. Christmount Christian Assembly, Black Mountain, N.C., 1969-71, bus. mgr., coord., 1971-77, exec. dir., 1977-94; chaplain VAMC, Asheville, 1995, chief chaplain, 1999—. Vol. chaplain N.C. Dept. Corrections, Black Mountain, Raleigh, 1993—, St. Joseph's Hosp., Asheville, 1986-94; pres. Swannanoa Valley Med. Ctr., Black Mountain, 1988-89; chair water safety coun. ARC, Asheville area, 1987; cons. Martin Luther King Corp., Swannanoa, 1994, Black Mountain C. of C., 1986. Recipient Sam Leonard award Kiwanis Club Swannanoa Valley, 1989, Woman of Yr. award Sourwood chpt. Am. Bus. Women's Assn., 1985; Z. Smith Reynolds Found. grantee, 1993, Horizon 2000 Cmty. Based Alternative grantee, 1994. Mem. NAACP, Internat. Assn. Conf. Ctr. Adminstrs., N.C. Correctional Assn., Nat. Assn. Va. Chaplains (pres. 2001—). Mem. Christian Ch. (Disciples Of Christ). Avocations: music, needlecrafts, swimming. Home: PO Box 446T Ridgecrest NC 28770-0446

BANKS, MICHAEL C., lawyer; b. 1962; BS, St. John's U.; JD, SUNY, Buffalo. Bar: NJ 1989, NY 1990. Ptnr. Milbank, Tweed, Hadley & McCloy LLP, NYC. Exec. prodr.: Law Review, SUNY, Buffalo. Named one of Am. Top Black Atty., Black Enterprise, 2003. Office: Milbank Tweed Hadley & McCloy LLP 1 Chase Manhattan Plz New York NY 10005-1413 Office Phone: 212-530-5308. Business E-Mail: mbanks@milbank.com.

BANKS, PATRICIA ANNE, music educator, minister; d. Jethro Nichols and Rena Blanche Johnsey Banks. BS in Edn., U. of North Tex., 1966; MusM, S.W. Bapt. Theol. Sem., 1976; student, Southwestern Bapt. Theol. Sem., 1976—81, The Anglican Sch. of Theology, 2000—04. Ordination to the diaconate Episcopal Diocese of Ft. Worth, 2002; cert. in piano and theory Music Teachers' Nat. Assn., 1996. Tchg. fellow and adj. prof. of music Southwestern Bapt. Theol. Sem., Fort Worth, Tex., 1973—81; pvt. tchr. of piano, music theory, music history Banks Piano Studio, Fort Worth, Tex., 1975—92; founder and dir. of precollege music dept. Howard Payne U. Sch. of Music, Brownwood, Tex., 1991—2000; assoc. prof. of music Howard Payne U. Sch. of Music and Fine Arts, 1991—; founder and dir. of music computer lab/music tech. dept. Howard Payne U. Sch. of Music, 1992—. Workshop clinician Van Cliburn Piano Inst., Fort Worth, 1994. Vestry mem. St. John's Episcopal Ch., Brownwood, Tex., 1998—2000. Mem.: Music Tchrs. Assns. (adjucator, workshop clinician), Nat. Guild Piano Tchrs. (adjucator 1997—), Heart of Tex. Music Tchrs.' Assn. (pres., student affiliate chmn., Tchr. of Yr. award), Tex. Music Tchrs.' Assn. (v.p. for student affairs, dir., tech. chmn., Tchr. of Yr. award 1996), Tex. Fedn. of Music Clubs (dist. jr. festival chmn.), Ft. Worth Music Tchrs. Assn. (pres., student affiliate chmn., Tchr. of Yr. award), Am. Coll. of Musicians (faculty mem. 1976), Kappa Kappa Psi (hon.), Tau Beta Sigma (hon.). Episc. Avocations: reading, travel. Office: Howard Payne University School of Music and Fine Arts Brownwood TX 76801 E-mail: pbanks@hputx.edu.

BANKS, PETER MORGAN, physics professor; b. San Diego, May 21, 1937; s. George Willard and Mary Margaret (Morgan) B.; m. Mary E. Stewart, Dec. 28, 2002; children by previous marriage: Kevin, Michael, Steven, David. MS in E.E, Stanford U., 1960; PhD in Physics, Pa. State U., 1965. Postdoctoral fellow Institut d'Aeronomie Spatiale de Belgique, Brussels, 1965-66; prof. applied physics U. Calif., San Diego, 1966-76; prof. physics Utah State U., 1976-81, head dept. physics, 1976-81; vis. assoc. prof. Stanford U., 1972-73, prof. elec. engring., 1981-90, dir. space, telecommunications and radiosci. lab., 1982-90, dir. ctr. for aeronautics and space info. systems, 1983-90; prof. atmospheres, oceans, and space sci. U. Mich., 1990-95, adj. prof., 1996-2000; dean Coll. Engring., U. Mich., 1990-95; pres. Earth Data Corp., 1985-86; pres., CEO Environ. Rsch. Inst. Mich., 1995-97, ERIM Internat., Inc., 1997-99; ptnr. XR Ventures, LLC, 2000—04; CEO Akonni Biosystems, Inc., 2003; pres. Inst. for the Future, Menlo Park, Calif., 2004—. Vis. scientist Max Planck Inst. for Aeronomie, Germany, 1975; pres. La Jolla Scis., Inc., 1973—77, Upper Atmosphere Rsch. Corp., 1978—82; chmn. NASA adv. com. on sci. uses of space sta., 1985—87; prin. investigator space shuttle experiments, 1982, 85, 91; mem. Jason Group, 1983—97; bd. dirs. Tecumseh Products Corp., X-Rite Corp., Handylab, Inc., Chaos Telecomms., Inc.; chmn. bd. trustees Consortium Internat. Earth Sci. Info. Networks, 1991—94; co-chmn. NRC Commn. on Phys. Scis., Math. and Applications, 1998—2000. Author: (with G. Kockarts) Aeronomy, 1973, (with J.R. Doupnik) Introduction to Computer Science, 1976; assoc. editor: Jour. Geophys. Research, 1974-77; assoc. editor: Planetary and Space Sci, 1977-83, regional editor, 1983-86; contbr. numerous articles in field to profl. jours. Mem. space sci. adv. council NASA, 1976-80. Served with U.S. Navy, 1960-63. Recipient Appleton prize Royal Soc. London, 1978, Space Sci. award AIAA, 1981, NASA Disting. Service medal, 1986; Alumni fellow Pa. State U., 1982 Fellow Am. Geophys. Union; mem. Internat. Union Radio Sci., Nat. Acad. Engring., Cosmos Club. Episcopalian. Home: 5602 Newanga Ave Santa Rosa CA 95405 Office: Inst for the Future 124 University Ave Palo Alto CA 94313 Office Phone: 650-233-9516. E-mail: pbanks@sonic.net.

BANKS, R. RICHARD, law educator; b. 1964; BA, MA, Stanford U., 1987; JD, Harvard U., 1994. Assoc. O'Melveny & Myers, San Francisco, 1994—95; Reginald F. Lewis fellow Harvard Law Sch., Cambridge, Mass., 1996—97; jud. clk. to Hon. Barrington D. Parker, Jr. US Dist. Ct. So. Dist. NY, White Plains, 1997—98; asst. prof. Stanford Law Sch., Calif., 1998—2001, assoc. prof., 2001—04, prof. law, 2004—, Justin M. Roach, Jr. faculty scholar, 2004—. Reginald F. Lewis Fellowship, Harvard Law Sch., 1996, Mark de Wolfe Howe Fund Fellowship, 1997, Jr. Faculty Fellowship, Ctr. for Comparative Studies of Race & Ethnicity, Stanford Law Sch., 2001. Office: Stanford Law Sch Crown Quadrangle 559 Nathan Abbott Way Stanford CA 94305-8610 Office Phone: 650-723-6591. Business E-Mail: rbanks@stanford.edu.

BANKS, RELA, sculptor; b. Yaroslav, Poland, Oct. 8, 1933; came to U.S., 1947; d. Jacob and Frieda (Weintraub) Heuberg; m. Stanley Frederic Banks, Aug. 9, 1953; children: Andrew Howard, J. Monica, Gary Mitchell. Student, Mus. Modern Art, 1957, Art Students League, N.Y.C. and Woodstock, N.Y., 1958-61, Summit (N.J.) Art Ctr., 1966-75. Chmn. nat. juried exhibit Summit Art Ctr., 1976, mem. adminstrv. com., 1977-79, chmn. standing com. spl. events, trustee; mem. exec. com. Phoenix Gallery, N.Y.C., 1983; chmn. membership com. Stone Sculpture Soc. N.Y., 1980-82. One-woman shows include Robins Art Gallery, South Orange, N.J., 1973, Montclair (N.J.) Coll., 1974, Caldwell (N.J.) Coll., 1974, 83, Summit Art Ctr., 1976, Newark Acad., Livingston, N.J., 1976, Douglas Coll., New Brunswick, N.J., 1978, First Women's Bank, N.Y.C., 1979, Phoenix Gallery, 1979, 81, 83, Morris Mus. Arts and Scis., Morristown, N.J., 1983, Ann Leonard Gallery, Woodstock, 1983, NECCA Mus., Bklyn., Conn., 1985, Schiller-Wapner Galleries, N.Y.C., 1985, 87, Ann Norton Sculpture Galleries, West Palm Beach, Fla., 1987, David Gary Ltd, Millburn, N.J., 1988; exhibited in group shows at Phoenix Gallery, 1979, 83, Morris Mus. Art, 1979, 83, Invitational Woodstock Artists Assn., 1980, 84, Eilaine Benson Gallery, Bridgehampton, N.Y., 1980, Searles Art Ctr., Great Barrington, Mass., 1980, Nabisco Art Gallery, 1981, Summit Art Ctr., 1981, First Womens Bank, 1981, Fairleigh Dickinson U., Madison, N.J., 1983, NYU Grad. Sch. Bus., 1983, AT&T Gallery, Basking Ridge, N.J., 1984, Shering Plough Gallery, N.J., 1984, New Orleans Mus. Art, 1986, Gallery Contemporary Art at U. Colorado Springs, Colo., 1986, Schiller-Wapner Galleries, 1986, Lever House, N.Y.C., 1986, Aldrich Mus. Contemporary Art, Ridgefield, Conn., 1986, Okla. Art Ctr., Oklahoma City, 1987, "After Henry Moore", Emily Lowe Mus., Hofstra U., Hempstead, N.Y., 1988, group exhibition, Poland; represented in permanent collections New Orleans Mus. Art, Everson Mus., Syracuse, N.Y., Morris Mus. Sci. and Art, Okla. Art Ctr., Vassar Coll. Gallery, Poughkeepsie, N.Y., Millburn (N.J.) Pub. Library, Minn. Mus. Art, Mpls., Woodstock Hist. Soc., Fordham U., Lincoln Ctr., N.Y.C., Aldrich Mus. Contemporary Art, Warsaw Mus., Poland, various pvt. and corp. collections. Mem. Woodstock Artists Assn. Office: Rela Banks Studio 272 Yerry Hill Rd Woodstock NY 12498 Office Phone: 845-679-2798.

BANKS, RICHARD CHARLES, ornithologist; b. Steubenville, Ohio, Apr. 19, 1931; s. Clinton Seeger and Elizabeth Mae (Harter) B.; m. Gladys Sparks, July 14, 1967; children: Randall C., David R. BS, Ohio State U., 1953; MA, U. Calif., Berkeley, 1957, PhD, 1961. Curator birds and mammals San Diego Natural History Mus., San Diego, 1961-66; zoologist U.S. Fish and Wildlife Svc., Washington, 1966-93, Nat. Biol. Svc., Washington, 1993-97, U.S. Geol. Survey, Washington, 1997—2002. Rsch. assoc. Smithsonian Instn., Washington, 1966—90, 2003—; adj. prof. George Mason U., Fairfax, Va., 1985, 91. Editor: Ornithological Newsletter, 1976-92. 1st lt. U.S. Army, 1953-55, Korea. Fellow: Am. Ornithologists' Union (sec. 1968—72, v.p. 1987—88, pres.-elect 1992—94, pres. 1994—96); mem.: Washington Biologists Field Club (pres. 1990—93), Biol. Soc. Washington (pres. 1979—80, editor 2004—), Cooper Ornithol. Soc. (hon.), Wilson Ornithol. Soc. (2d and 1st v.p. 1987—91, pres. 1991—93), Am. Assn. Zool. Nomenclature (pres. 2001—03). Home: 3201 Circle Hill Rd Alexandria VA 22305-1609 Office: US Geological Survey-MRC 111 Nat Mus Natural History PO Box 37012 Washington DC 20013-7012 Office Phone: 202-633-0783. Personal E-mail: rcbalone@aol.com. Business E-Mail: banksr@si.edu.

BANKS, ROBERT KALEY, real estate executive, lawyer, food products executive; b. Nampa, Idaho, May 10, 1949; s. Charles C. and Betty F. (Piersal) B.; m. Teresa M. Banks, June 19, 1971; children: Ryan Scott, Andrea Marie. BS in Psychology, USAF Acad., 1971; MA in Psych., St. Mary's U., San Antonio, Tex., 1973, MA in Guidance and Counseling, 1975; MBA, JD cum laude, Ariz. State U., 1980. Bar: Ariz., 1980, Idaho, 1981. Commd. 2d lt. USAF, 1971, advanced through grades to maj., retired lt. col., 1977; law clk. to presiding justice Idaho Supreme Ct., Boise, 1980-81; atty. Albertson's, Inc., Boise, 1981-84, dir. property mgmt., 1984-87, reg. real estate dir., 1987, v.p., real estate, group v.p., real estate, sr. v.p., real estate, 1987—2000, exec. v.p., development, 2000—05. Supt. Sunday sch. USAF Acad., 1970; advisor Explorer post Boy Scouts Am., Phoenix, 1978; founding dir. Eagle (Idaho) Ranch Homeowner's Assn., 1988-89. Mem. A&F Credit Union (vice chmn. 1983—), Idaho Liaisons Officers (comdr. 1985—). Avocations: running, basketball, fishing, backpacking. Office Phone: 208-841-2000. Personal E-mail: bobbanks@aol.com.

BANKS, RUSSELL, financial planner, consultant; b. N.Y.C., Aug. 2, 1919; s. Thomas and Fay (Cowen) B.; m. Janice Reed, June 19, 1949; 1 son, Gordon L. BBA, CCNY, 1936-40; JD, N.Y. Law Sch., 1960. Bar: N.Y. 1961. Sr. acct. Selverne, Davis Co., N.Y.C., 1940-45; pvt. practice N.Y.C., 1945-61; exec. v.p. Met. Telecomm. Corp., Plainview, N.Y., 1961-62; pres., former CEO Grow Group, Inc. (formerly Grow Chem. Corp.), N.Y.C., 1962-95, also dir., 1962-95; pres. Russell Banks & Co. Ltd., 1995—. Cons. Imperial Chem. Industries, PLC., 1995-96; adj. prof. bus. adminstrn. Baruch Coll., 1996-98. Editor: Managing the Small Company. Recipient award of achievement Sch. of Bus. Alumni Soc. of CCNY, 1977; Winthrop-Sears medal Chem. Industry Assn., 1980 Mem. Nat. Paint and Coatings Assn. (past pres.), Am. Mgmt. Assn. (gen. mgmt. planning coun. 1966-95, former trustee, exec. com.), Met. Club, Sky Club. Home: 330 S Ocean Blvd Apt D5 Palm Beach FL 33480-4206

BANKS, THEODORE LEE, lawyer; b. Chgo., Nov. 5, 1951; s. Morris M. and Ruth Lilly (Gray) B.; m. Cheryl Deborah Steinhardt, Aug. 20, 1972; children: Miriam, Rebecca, Sarah. BA, Beloit Coll., 1972; JD, U. Denver, 1975. Bar: Colo. 1976, Ill. 1976, U.S. Dist. Ct. (no. dist.) Ill. 1976, U.S. Supreme Ct. 1981, U.S. Ct. Appeals (6th cir.) 1985. Atty. Kraft, Inc., Glenview, Ill., 1976-80, gen. atty., 1980-81; corp. counsel Dart & Kraft, Inc., Northbrook, Ill., 1981-86, sr. counsel litigation and trade regulation, 1986-88, group counsel food ingredients, 1988-89; asst. to gen. counsel Kraft Gen. Foods, Inc., Glenview, 1989-94; assoc. gen. counsel Kraft Foods, Inc., 1994—. Bd. dirs. Keep Chgo. Beautiful. Author: International Antitrust Law, 1981, Distribution Law for the Practitioner, 1989, Distribution Law Antitrust Principles, 1993, Corporate Legal Compliance Handbook, 2003; contbr. articles to profl. jours. Mem. ABA. Office: Kraft Foods Inc Three Lakes Dr Northfield IL 60093

BANKS, TYRA, model, actress; b. LA, Dec. 4, 1973; Founder Tyra Banks Scholarship, 1992, T-Zone summer camp for girls, 2000; lectr. at UCLA, Johns Hopkins, Georgetown U., others. Appeared on covers of Elle, Essence, Sports Illustrated, GQ Mag., Cosmopolitan, Shape, Harper's Bazaar, Esquire, Arena, Vogue, Victoria's Secret Catalog (contract with mag.). Featured in comml. for McDonald's, Nike, Pepsi, Nat. Milk Processor Promotion bd. Actor: (films) Higher Learning, 1995, A Woman Like That, 1997, Love Stinks, 1999, Love & Basketball, 2000, Coyote Ugly, 2000, Halloween: Resurrection, 2002, (voice) Eight Crazy Nights, 2002, Larceny, 2004; (TV films) Inferno, 1992, The Apartment Complex, 1999, Life-Size, 2000; (TV series) Fresh Prince of Bel-Air, 1993-94; (guest appearances) (TV series) include New York Undercover, Mad TV, The Oprah Winfrey Show, Just Shoot Me. Creator, writer, prodr., host, judge (TV series) America's Next Top Model, 2003-, host, exec. prodr. The Tyra Banks Show, 2005-. Achievements include being the first African American Woman on the cover of Sports Illustrated Swimsuit Issue. Office: IMG Models 304 Park Ave S Ph N New York NY 10010-5339*

BANKS, VIRGINIA ANNE (GINGER BANKS), association administrator; b. Dallas, Mar. 19, 1949; d. James Houston and Mary Virginia (Bussey) B. B of Journalism, U. Tex., 1971. Traveling cons. Alpha Omicron Pi Fraternity, Indpls., 1971-73, adminstrv. asst. Nashville, 1973-74; pub. info. officer Tex. Dept. of Community Affairs, Austin, 1974-76; asst. dir. of comm. State Bar of Tex., Austin, 1976-78, assoc. editor Tex. Bar Jour., 1977-79, mng. editor Tex. Bar Jour, 1979-91, comm. dir., 1991-99, dir. pub. svcs. divsn., 1992-99, dir. info. tech. divsn., 1999-2000, dir. mem. svcs. divsn., 2000-01; spkr. Campuspeak, Inc., 2003—05. Internat. rush chmn. Alpha Omicron Pi, Nashville, 1976-77, internat. v.p. ops., 1977-81, internat. pres., 1981-85, v.p. found., 1985-90, fraternity devel. com., 1985-89, pres. Pi Kappa Corp., 1991-95, mem. Austin Alumnae chpt., 1973—, alumnae adv. com. network specialist, 1996-98, del. nat. panhellenic Conf., 1987-93, chmn. Perry award com., 1992-98, rituals, traditions and jewelry com., 1998—, chair rituals, traditions and jewelry com., 1998—; com. to devel. relationship statement, Nat. Panhellenic Conf., 1983, del., 1987-93, area advisor coll. Panhellenics com., 1985-88, chmn. liaison com., 1987-88, Project Future collegiate concerns com., 1987-89, field cons. seminar com., 1987, chmn., 1988, resolutions com., 1988, chmn. pub. rels. com., 1991-93, ednl. devel. com., 1991-93; spkr. in field. Editor Alpha Omicron Pi Centennial History Book, 1995-97; contbr. articles to mags. Bd. dirs. Lone Star Girl Scout Coun., Austin, 1973-75, Nat. Interfraternity Found., 1986-89, M.L. Roller scholarship com., 1988-89, nominations com., 1988-89; mem. Humane Soc. Austin, 1981—; chmn. mag. adv. com. Ex-Students Assn., U. Tex., Austin, 1989-95; active Tarrytown United Meth. Ch. Recipient presdl. citation State Bar of Tex., 1981, 90, 94, presdl. citation Alpha Omicron Pi, 1988, 97. Mem. Am. Soc. Assn. Execs., Assn. Fraternity Advisors, Internat. Assn. Bus. Communicators, Nat. Assn. Bar Execs. (mem. pub. svcs. activities com. 1995-98, vice-chair pub. svc. activities com. 1996-97, chair pub. svcs. activities com. 1997-98, chair awards com. 1995-96, pub. rels. and comms. sect. 1991—, mem. sect.'s comms. audit com. 1994-95, chair sect.'s comms. audit com. 1995-98, mem. sect.'s coun., 1997-2000, sect.'s program com. 1995-98, co-chair sect.'s program com. 1996-98, sect.'s sec. 1998-2000, chair leadership award com. 2002, recipient, Wally Richter Leadership award, 2001), Women in Comms., PEO Sisterhood (chpt. R recording sec. 2002-04, treas. 2004—), Alpha Omicron Pi (Austin alumnae chpt., Rose award 1991, Adele K. Hinton award 1997). Avocations: gardening, sailing, cooking. Home: 3108 W Terrace Dr Austin TX 78757-4332

BANKSON, MARJORY ZOET, former religious association administrator; m. Peter Bankson. BA in Govt. and Econs., Radcliffe Coll., 1961; M in Am. History, U. Alaska, 1961; postgrad., Va. Episcopal Sem., 1985; LLD, Va. Theol. Sem., 1999. H.S. history and English tchr.; counselor Dartmouth Coll., 1969-70; profl. potter, 1970-80; pres. Faith at Work, Falls Church, Va., 1985-2001. Editor, contbr. Faith@Work mag.; has written for Living Pulpit, Response, The Seminary Journal. Author: Braided Streams: Esther and a Woman's Way of Growing, Seasons of Friendship: Naomi and Ruth as a Pattern, This Is My Body: Creativity, Clay, and Change, The Call of the Soul: Six Stages of Spiritual Development, 1999 (videos) The Potter and Clay, With Tongues of Fire: Five Women from the Book of Acts. Mem. Ch. of the Savior, 1976—, Seekers Ch., Washington, DC, preacher, teacher Sch. Christian Living. Office: 106-B East Broad St Falls Church VA 22046-4501 E-mail: faithatwork@aol.com.

BANKSTON, ARCHIE MOORE, lawyer; b. Memphis, Oct. 12, 1937; s. Archie M. and Elsie Bernice (Shaw) B.; m. Emma Ann Dejan, Apr. 16, 1966; children— Louis, Alice. BA, Fisk U., 1959; LLB, Washington U., St. Louis, 1962, MBA, 1964. Bar: Mo. 1963, N.Y. 1966. Asst. divsn. counsel Gen. Foods Corp., White Plains, N.Y., 1964-67, product mgr. Maxwell House divsn., 1967-69; asst. sec. and corp. counsel PepsiCo, Inc., Purchase, N.Y., 1969-72; divsn. counsel Xerox Corp., Stamford, Conn., 1973; sec. and asst. gen. counsel Consol. Edison Co. of N.Y. Inc., N.Y.C., 1974-89, sec., assoc. gen. counsel, 1989—2002. Sec. Consolidated Edison, Inc., N.Y.C., 1998—2002; exec.-in-residence Coll. New Rochelle, NY, 2002—. Mem. 100 Black Men, Inc., N.Y.C.; former trustee Beth Israel Med. Ctr.; trustee Hoff-Barthelson Music Sch., Scarsdale, NY; past mem. Westchester County African Am. Adv. Bd.; former trustee Coll. New Rochelle; former bd. dirs. Urban League of Westchester County, Associated Black Charities, Mental Health Assn. Westchester County. Recipient Black Achievers in Industry award, Harlem br. YMCA, 1971, Merit award, Black Exec. Exch. Program Nat. Urban League, 1974, Disting. Svc. Commendation awards, Mental Health Assn., 1987, 1992, Jerome H. Holland Power of Humanity Corp. award, Am. Red Cross, 2001. Mem.: ABA, Am. Soc. Corp. Secs. (mem. audit, edn. and securities industry com., chmn. budget com. and membership com., chmn. 50th anniversary nat. conf. com., bd. dirs., Disting. Svc. award 2000), N.Y. State Bar Assn., Westchester Clubmen (pres.), Alpha Phi Alpha, Sigma Pi Phi, Phi Delta Phi. Office: Consol Edison Co NY Inc 4 Irving Pl New York NY 10003-3502 also: The College of New Rochelle 29 Castle Place New Rochelle NY 10805 E-mail: bankstona@coned.com.

BANNARD, WALTER DARBY, artist, art critic; b. New Haven, Sept. 23, 1934; s. Homes and Janet (Darby) B. BA, Princeton U., 1956. Chmn. dept. art and art history U. Miami, Fla., 1989-97. Lectr. in field, 1969—; vis. prof. Princeton (N.J.) U., 1974, also other univs.; mem. grad. faculty Sch. Visual Arts, N.Y.C., 1984-89; curator Hans Hoffman Hirshorn Mus., 1976; mem. internat. exhbn. com., 1976-78; co-chmn. internat. panel for visual arts Nat. Endowment for Arts, 1979-81; founder, editor newcrit.org, 2001—. Contbr. articles and revs. on modern painting to profl. jours.; contbg. editor: Artforum, 1973-74; 75; one-man shows internat. galleries and mus. include retrospective Balt. Mus. Art, 1973, retrospective U. Tampa, 1997, retrospective Lowe Mus., 1999; numerous internat. group shows; represented in permanent collections at Mus. Modern Art, N.Y.C., Whitney Mus. Am. Art, Met. Mus. Art, N.Y.C., Guggenheim Mus., N.Y.C., others; juror numerous competitions, 1969—; sole juror Australian Bi-Centenary Art Competition, 1988; founder, editor newCrit.org. Recipient Nat. Found. Arts award, 1968-69; Francis J. Greenburger Found. award, 1986; John Simon Guggenheim Meml. Found. fellow, 1968; Richard A. Florsheim Art Fund grantee, 1991. Office: 1540 Levante Ave Miami FL 33124 Office Phone: 305-284-2493. Personal E-mail: wbannard@aol.com.

BANNEN, JOHN THOMAS, lawyer; b. LaCrosse, Wis., Oct. 29, 1951; s. James J. and Ruth J. (Frisch) Bannen; m. Carol A. Swanson, Aug. 16, 1975; children: Ryan M., Kelly A., Erin C. BA summa cum laude, Coll. St. Thomas, 1973; JD, Marquette U., 1976; LLM in Taxation, DePaul U., 1989; BA in Spanish, U. Wis., 2003. Bar: Wis. 1976, U.S. Dist. Ct. (ea. and we. dists.) Wis. 1976, U.S. Tax Ct. 1979, U.S. Claims Ct. 1983, U.S. Supreme Ct. 1984. Shareholder Charne, Clancy & Taitelman, S.C., Milw., 1976-91; ptnr. Quarles & Brady, Milw., 1991—. Bd. dirs. Guardianship Svcs. Indigents, Milw., 1983—87; mem. adv. bd. Sch. Sisters Notre Dame, 1993—98, pres., 1995—98; mem. coun. Christ the King Parish, Wauwatosa, Wis., 1989—93, trustee, 1996—98. Fellow: Am. Coll. Trust and Estate Counsel (state law coord. Wis. 1990—95, chmn. com. employee benefits 2001—05); mem.: ABA, Wis. Bar Assn. (bd. dirs. probate sect.), Assn. Advanced Life Underwriters (assoc.). Avocations: reading, gardening, Spanish language, cooking. Office: Quarles and Brady LLP Ste 2040 411 E Wisconsin Ave Milwaukee WI 53202-4497 Office Phone: 414-277-5859. E-mail: jtb@quarles.com.

BANNICK, JANICE CAROL, automotive dealerships executive; b. Clinton, Iowa, Oct. 12, 1938; d. Claus John and Irma Jeanne (Switzer) Greve; m. Robert T. Gallagher, May 21, 1958 (div. Apr. 1967); children: Angela Jeanne, Carol Ellen; m. Mearl G. Bannick, June 24, 1967 (dec. Aug. 1991). Student, Old Dominion Coll., Norfolk, Va., 1956-58, U. Wis., Milw., 1980-83, U. Tex., Arlington, 1983-86, Bradley U., 1992-94. Contr. Kimberly Chrysler-Plymouth, Inc., Davenport, Iowa, 1974-79; cons. Davenport and Milw., 1979-80; contr. Stark Oldsmobile, Inc., Menomonee Falls, Wis., 1980-83; bus. mgr., field rep. Motors Holding divsn. Gen. Motors Corp., Detroit, 1986-89; contr., CFO S&K Chevrolet Pontiac and Oldsmobile, Peoria, Ill., 1989-96; automotive cons. Peoria and Springfield, Ill., 1996-97; contr., dealer acctg. Gen. Acceptance Corp., Bloomington, Ind., 1997-98; CFO Anthony Pontiac, Gurnee, Ill., 1998-2000, Lou Bachrodt Automall & Bachrodt Pontiac, Rockford, Ill., 2000-01; team sales rep. Internat. Teamworks Inc., Vacaville, Calif., 2001—; contr. Magouirk Chevrolet-Olds, Inc., Dodge City, Kans., 2001—02; cons. MSXI, Ford Motor Co. Dealer Devel., Detroit, 2003—. Bd. dirs., treas. St. Marks Luth. Ch., Chillicothe, Ill., 1994-96, Peoria Art Gild, 1995-96. Republican. Avocations: watercolor painting, reading, running, walking, antique refinishing, gourmet cooking, golf. Home: 6318 N Ripley St Davenport IA 52806-2126 E-mail: bannick777@aol.com.

BANNICK, MATTHEW, Internet company executive; BA with hons. in Econs. and Internat. Studies, U. Washington, 1991; MBA, Harvard U., 1993. US diplomat, Germany; cons. McKinsey and Co., Europe, 1992, McKinsey and Co., US, 1993—95; with Navigation Techs., 1995—99, pres. N.Am. Divsn., 1997—99; from v.p. product and cmty. to sr. v.p. global online payments eBay Inc., San Jose, Calif., 1999—2003, sr. v.p. global online payments, 2003—. Mem.: Phi Beta Kappa. Office: eBay Inc 2145 Hamilton Ave San Jose CA 95125-5905

BANNIGAN, EUGENE F., lawyer; b. Bklyn., July 1, 1941; BA, Alfred U., 1964; JD cum laude, Bklyn. Law Sch., 1969. Bar: N.Y. 1969. Asst. U.S. atty. S Dist. N.Y., 1972-76, chief narcotics unit, 1975-76; pntr. Lord, Day & Lord, Barrett Smith, N.Y.C.; ptnr. Morgan Lewis & Bockius LLP, N.Y.C., mem. mgmt. com. & leader litig. practice group-N.Y. Office. Mem. ABA, Fed. Bar Coun., Assn. Bar City N.Y. Office: Morgan Lewis & Bockius LLP 101 Park Ave New York NY 10178 Office Phone: 212-309-6815. Office Fax: 212-309-3001. Business E-Mail: ebannigan@morganlewis.com.

BANNISTER, DAN WESLEY, retired historian; b. Erie, Pa., May 13, 1921; s. Earl Ford Bannister and Hortense Elizabeth Ashley; m. Cornelia Dennis; children: Dan W. III, Shelley Ashley, James Earl. BS, Ind. U., 1942; JD cum laude, Albany Law Sch., 1946; LLD, Lincoln Coll., 1998. Pvt. practice law, Rochester, N.Y., 1947-50; contr. Vaisey Bristol Shoe Co., Rochester, 1949-50; fin. contr. dir. Allstate Ins. Co., Skokie, 1951-61; v.p. Security Ins. Group, Springfield, Ill., 1962-75; pres. Horace Mann Ins. Group, Springfield, 1974-80; sr. v.p. Comml. Credit Co., Balt., 1974-80; pres. Gulf Ins. Group, Dallas, 1981-85. Pres. Abraham Lincoln Assn., Springfield, 1946-47, dir., 1991—, exec. com., 1994—. Mem. Chartered Property and Casualty Underwriters, Casualty Actuarial Soc., Actuarial Assn. Am. Episcopalian. Office: Abraham Lincoln Assn 1 Old State Capitol Plz Springfield IL 62701-1512 Mailing: 3224 Eagle Watch Dr Springfield IL 62704

BANNISTER, GEOFFREY, academic administrator, geographer; b. Manchester, Eng., Sept. 19, 1945; came to U.S., 1973; s. Leslie and Doris (Shankland) B.; m. Margaret Janet Sheridan, Jan. 28, 1968; children: Katherine, Janet. BA, U. Otago, New Zealand, 1967, MA with honors, 1969; PhD, U. Toronto, Can., 1974. Asst. prof. Boston U., 1973-77, acting chmn. geography, 1977-78, dean liberal arts, grad. sch., 1978-87; exec. v.p. Butler U., Indpls., 1987-89, pres., 1989—. Cons. Urban Affairs Ministry of State,

Can., 1973; legal cons. U.S. Dept. of State 1982-84; bd. dirs. Somerset Group, Ind. Nat. Bank. Co-author atlas Spatial Dynamics of Postwar County Economic Change, 1977; contbr. articles to profl. jours. Chmn. bd. trustees Cambridge (Mass.) Montessori Sch., 1979-80; mem. corp. Sea Edn. Assn., Woods Hole, Mass., 1979-87; bd. dirs. United Way of Cen. Ind., 1990—, chmn. 1992 Premeire Campaign, edn. chmn.; bd. dirs. Greater Indpls. Progress Com., 1988—; pres. Midwest Collegiate Cons; chmn. World Rowing Championship, 1994. Fellow U. Toronto, 1970-71, Can. Council, 1972. Mem. Nat. Labor/Higher Edn. Coun., Nat. Assn. Scholars, Indpls. Bus. Jour. Blue Ribbon Panel, Indpls. Commn. on African-Am. Males, C. of C., Econ. Club, English Speaking Union U.S. (Indpls. br.), Coun. Urban Coll. of Arts, Letter and Scis., Kiwanis, Phi Beta Kappa. Avocations: bicycling, golf, skiing. Home: 22 Wilder Rd Cummington MA 01026-9732

BANNISTER, MICHAEL E., corporate financial executive; BBA, Memphis State Univ. Held a number of br. and regional mgmt. oper. positions Ford Credit North Am. Region, 1973; mgr. North Atlantic Region Ford Motor Credit Co., Dearborn, Mich., 1991, mgr. Atlantic Region, 1991—93, v.p. mktg., 1993—95; exec. dir. European sales ops. Ford Motor Credit Co. Europe, 1995—97; chmn. Ford Fin. Europe, 1997—2003; pres., COO Ford Motor Credit Co., Dearborn, Mich., 2003—. Office: Ford Motor Credit Co One American Rd Mail Drop 7440 Dearborn MI 48126-2701

BANNISTER, ROBERT CORWIN, JR., historian, educator; b. Bklyn., June 4, 1935; s. Robert C. and Ruth (Allen) B.; m. Joan Turner, June 8, 1958; children: Robert Stanley, Emily E., Paul Andrew, James Peter. BA, Yale U., 1955, Oxford U., Eng., 1957, MA, 1961; PhD, Yale U., 1961. Instr. history Yale U., New Haven, 1960-62; asst. to full prof. Swarthmore Coll., Pa., 1962-98, ret., 1998. Bicentennial prof. U. Helsinki, 1977-78; Fulbright prof. U. Rome, 1985, U. Leiden, Netherlands, 1992; mem. advanced placement program Ednl. Testing Service, Princeton, N.J., 1963-79; vis. prof. U. Queensland, Australia, 1988. Author: Ray Stannard Baker, 1966, Social Darwinism: Science and Myth, 1978, Sociology and Scientism, 1987, Jessie Bernard: The Making of a Feminist, 1991; editor: American Values in Transition, 1972, On Liberty, Society and Politics: The Essential Essays of William Graham Sumner, 1992. Mem. Am. Studies Assn., Orgn. Am. Historians Democrat. Office: Swarthmore College Ave Swarthmore PA 19081-1390 E-mail: rbannis1@swarthmore.edu.

BANNON, ANTHONY LEO, museum director; b. Hanover, N.H., Dec. 6, 1942; s. Robert E. and Frances Ann (Cacioppo) B.; children: Nicholas, Brendan. BS, St. Bonaventure, 1964; MA, SUNY, Buffalo, 1974, PhD, 1996. Tchr. sci. and English Father Baker High Sch., Lackawanna, N.Y., 1964-66; critic Buffalo News, 1966-85; dir. Burchfield-Penney Art Ctr., asst. v.p. cultural affairs SUNY Coll. at Buffalo, 1985-96; dir. George Eastman House Internat. Mus. Photography and Film, Rochester, NY, 1996—. Chmn. visual arts program panel N.Y. State Coun. on Arts, N.Y.C., 1986—88; co-chmn. arts programming com. World Univ. Games, Buffalo, 1991—93; co-chmn. adv. coun. ArtsAction, NY, 1999—2002; vice chmn. Empire State Craft Alliance, Saratoga Springs, NY, 1988—93; chmn. adv. bd. Quick Fine Arts Ctr. St. Bonaventure U., 1996—2002. Author: The Photo-Pictorialists of Buffalo, 1981, The Taking of Niagara, 1983, Arcadia Revisited, 1989, Painterly Photographs: Contemporary Handworked Images, 1980, Grace Woodworth: Photographer Outside the Common Lines, 1984, ArtPark, 1989, Ansel Adams, 2003, Steve McCurry, 2005; organized major exhibits for Albright-Knox Art Gallery, Buscaglia-Castellani Art Gallery, Niagara U., N.Y., State Mus. of N.Y., Albany, Washington D.C. Project for the Arts; Burchfield-Penney Art Ctr. and Rockwell Hall Performing Arts Ctr., SUNY Coll., Buffalo, David Anderson Gallery, others. Mem. vestry Ch. Good Shepherd, Buffalo, 1986—89; bd. dirs. Greater Rochester Visitors Assn., 1996—97, Rochester Arts and Cultural Coun., 1998—2003, High Falls Film Festival, 2004—; trustee N.Y. State Alliance of Arts Orgns., 1998—2002, bd. sec., 1999—2001; bd. dirs. Rochester Sch. for the Deaf, 1998—, N.Y. State Coun. on Humanities, 1999—; mem. adv. coun. to the sec. Smithsonian Instn., 2001—; mem. adv. coun. Chautauqua Art Ctr., 1998—; bd. dirs. Santa Fe Ctr. Photography, 2002—. Recipient Excellence in Writing about Deafness award Gallaudet Coll., 1985, Merit award Am. Photog. Hist. Soc., 1982; Profl. Study Leave grantee N.Y. State/United Univ. Professions, 1993, Outstanding Arts Adminstr. award The Buffalo Partnership, 1995, Arts award, St. Bonaventure U., 2002. Mem. Am. Assn. Mus., Mus. Assn. N.Y. State (counselor 1994-2003), Gallery Assn. N.Y. State (trustee 1997-2000), Buffalo State Coll. Found. (trustee 1985-91), Soc. Photog. Edn. Assn. Art Mus. Dirs. Office: George Eastman House 900 East Ave Rochester NY 14607-2298 E-mail: tbannon@frontiernet.net, tbannon@geh.org.

BANNON, WILLIAM FARRELL, lawyer; b. Milw., Aug. 28, 1952; s. William Francis and Marquerite Patricia (Faust) B.; m. Marla Lorraine McDowell, Dec. 9, 1972 (div. Aug. 1983); children: Shawn, Aaron, Jason. BS in Justice Adminstrn., Bringham Young U., 1978; JD, U. Utah, 1982. Bar: Utah 1982, U.S. Dist. Ct. Utah 1982, U.S. Ct. Appeals (10th cir.) 1987, Minn. 1989, U.S. Dist. Ct. Minn. 1989, U.S. Ct. Appeals (8th cir.) 1994; cert. civil trial specialist. Deputy Salt Lake County Sheriff, Salt Lake City, 1977-80; atty. Strong & Hanni, Salt Lake City, 1982-85; asst. atty. gen. Utah Atty. Gen.'s OFfice, Salt Lake City, 1986-88; ptnr. Schneider, Johnson & Bannon, Willmar, Minn., 1989-94, Johnson & Bannon, Willmar, 1994—. Mem. Minn. State Bd. Legal Cert. Dirs. Western Minn. Legal Svcs., Willmar, 1990—; former mem. New London-Spicer, Minn. Sch. Bd., 1993—. Mem. ABA, ATLA, Am. Arbitration Assn., Minn. Trial Lawyers Assn. (former bd. govs.), Lions. Office: Johnson & Bannon PO Box 1334 Willmar MN 56201-1334 E-mail: advocate@tds.net.

BANOFF, SHELDON IRWIN, lawyer; b. Chgo., July 10, 1949; BSBA in Acctg., U. Ill., 1971; JD, U. Chgo., 1974. Bar: Ill. 1974, U.S. Tax Ct. 1974. Ptnr. Katten Muchin Rosenman LLP, Chgo., 1974—. Chmn. tax conf. planning com. U. Chgo. Law Sch., 1993-94. Co-editor Jour. of Taxation, 1984—; contbr. articles to profl. jours. Mem. ABA, Chgo. Bar Assn. (fed. taxation com., mem. exec. coun. 1980—, chmn. large law firm com., 1999-2000), Am. Coll. Tax Counsel. Office: Katten Muchin Rosenman LLP 525 W Monroe St Chicago IL 60661-3693 Office Phone: 312-902-5200. Business E-Mail: sheldon.banoff@kattenlaw.com.

BANOUN, RAYMOND, lawyer; b. June 1, 1945; BA, CCNY, 1965; JD with honors, George Washington U., 1968. Bar: D.C. 1968, U.S. Supreme Ct. 1980. Law clk. to Hon. Harold H. Green Superior Ct. Washington, 1968-70; asst. atty. gen. Washington, 1970-84; dep. chief and acting chief fraud divsn., 1981-83; sr. litigation counsel, 1983-84; ptnr. Arent, Fox, Kintner, Plotkin & Kahn, Washington, 1984-91; ptnr. bus. fraud practice Cadwalader, Wickersham & Taft, Washington, 1991—, mng. ptnr. Washington office. Spl. asst. U.S. atty. ctrl. dist. Calif., 1977-80. Contbr. articles to profl. jours. Fellow Am. Coll. Trial Attys.; mem. ABA (vice chmn. white collar crime com. criminal justice sect. 1985-86, chmn. 1986-88, coun. criminal justice 1988-91), Internat. Bar Assn. (vice-chmn. bus. crimes com. sect. bus. law 1988-92, chmn. 1992—). Office: Cadwalader Wickersham & Taft LLP Suite 1100 1201 F St NW Washington DC 20004-1218 Office Phone: 202-862-2426. Office Fax: 202-862-2400. Business E-Mail: ray.banoun@cwt.com.

BANS, PHIL, retired corporate security professional; b. Ft. Lewis, Wash., Feb. 28, 1962; s. Phil Sr. and Rebecca Martinez Bans; m. Esperanza Marquez, Nov. 7, 1978; 1 child, Phil III. AA in Gen. Edn., Hartnell Coll., 1995. Maintence offcl. So. Pacific RR, Salinas, Calif., 1983-86; corp. security officer Electronic Data Systems, Salinas, 1986-95. Tng. officer EDS (GM), L.A., Plano, Tex.; tng. officer Corp. Security Officer Disaster Preparedness, 1992-94. Treas. honors club Hartnell Coll., 1994-95; v.p. Salinas Youth Football, 1998; exec. v.p. Salinas Colts/Broncos Youth Football, Salinas, 1999—, bd. dirs. 1998—; sec., exec. bd. Monterey Bay Youth Football League, Salinas, 1999—; vol. Palma H.S., basketball/baseball concession chair 1998-99. Democrat. Avocations: sports memorbilla, card collecting, coca cola collector. Office: Phils Collectibles PO Box 56 Salinas CA 93902-0056 Fax: 831-771-1750. E-mail: philbans@prodigy.net.

BANSAK, STEPHEN A., JR., investment banker, financial consultant; b. Bridgeport, Conn., Sept. 19, 1939; s. Stephen A. and Genevieve Bansak; m. Susan Jean Dizon, July 20, 1984; children: Cynthia A., Thomas S., Stephen A. III, Kirk C. BS, Yale U., 1961; MBA, U. Pa., 1968. With Kidder, Peabody & Co., Inc., N.Y.C., 1968-89, v.p., 1971-75, co-mgr. dept. corpl fin., 1975-84; vice chmn. Kidder, Peabody Internat., N.Y.C., 1984—. Bd. dirs. Kidder Peabody P.R., KP Realty Advisers; sr. cons. Concord Internat. Ptnrs., 1990—, bentley Assocs., 1990-92; vice chmn. Myers, Craig, Vallone, Francois, Inc., 1992-93; sr. advisor Universal Tech. inst., 1995-97, Motay Electronics, Inc., 1993-97, Buenavenjura Filamor Echuas (Manila), 1991-94; vis. lectr. Wharton Grad. Sch., U. Pa., 1989; past bd. dirs. Filbrin, Inc., Lighthouse Ptnrs.; bd. dirs. Troy Bioscis., Inc.; bd. dirs., vice chmn. Computerized Med. Sys., Inc.; mem. adv. bd. Global Health Care Ptnrs. (DLJ Mcht. Banking 1998-2001); past adv. com. Manschot Opportunity Fund. Past trustee, v.p. Rumson (N.J.) Country Day Sch. Lt. USN, 1962-66, Vietnam. Mem. Philippine-Am. C. of C. (bd. dirs.), U.S.-Asia inst. (past bd. dirs.), India House (past pres. Broad St. Club), Yale Club N.Y.C., Troon Golf and Country Club, Securities Industry Assn. (chmn. corp. fin. com., rule 415 com.), Am. Stock Exch. (ofcl. 1988-91). Office Phone: 480-585-6670. E-mail: pennhavena@aol.com.

BANSAL, ARVIND KUMAR, computer scientist, educator; arrived in U.S., 1984; m. Rekha Gupta. Ph. D. (Computer Sci.), Case Western Res. U., Cleveland, Ohio, USA, 1984—88; M. Tech (Computer Sci.), Indian Inst. of Tech., Kanpur, UP, India, 1981—83, B. Tech (Elec. Engring.), 1974—79. Asst. exec. engr. Indian Tel. Industries, Allahabad, India, 1979—81; sys. analyst Tata Engring. and Locomotive Co., Pune, India, 1983—84; grad. rsch. asst. Case Western Res. U., Cleve., 1984—88; asst. prof. Kent (Ohio) State U., 1988—93; summer rsch. faculty Argonne (Ill.) Nat. Lab., 1994—94; visting scientist European Molecular Biology Lab., Heidelberg, Germany, 1995—95; rsch. fellow U. of Melbourne, Melbourne, Australia, 1996—96; assoc. prof. Kent (Ohio) State U., 1993—2005, prof., 2005—. Contbr. articles to profl. jours. Mem.: AAAS, IEEE (Appreciation award 2001), Internat. Soc. of Computational Biology, Assn. of Computing Machinery, N.Y. Acad. of Sci. Office: Kent State U Kent OH Office Phone: 330-672-9035. Office Fax: 330-672-7824. Business E-Mail: arvind@cs.kent.edu.

BANSAL, PREETA D., lawyer; b. Roorkee, India; d. M.K. and Prem Lata Bansal. AB magna cum laude, Harvard-Radcliffe Coll., 1986; JD magna cum laude, Harvard Law Sch., 1989. Law clerk to Chief Judge James L. Oakes US Ct. of Appeals, Second Circuit, 1989—90; law clerk to Justice John Paul Stevens US Supreme Ct., 1990—91; counsel Arnold & Porter, Washington; counselor to asst. atty. gen. Joel Klein US Dept. of Justice, Washington, 1993—96; special counsel Office of the White House Counsel, Washington, 1996; counsel Gibson, Dunn & Crutcher, NYC, 1996—99; solicitor gen. State of NY, 1999—2001; vis. prof. of constitutional law U. Nebr. Coll. of Law, 2002; counsel Skadden, Arps, Slate, Meagher & Flom, 2003—. Commentator on legal issues CNN, CSPAN & PBS news programs; vis. fellow John F. Kennedy Sch. of Govt., Harvard U., 2003; commr. & chair US Commn. Internat. Religious Freedom, 2003—; commr. NYC Mayor Bloomberg's Election Modernization Task Force, 2005—. Author: (numerous articles) Harvard Law Review, Yale Law Journal, Fordham Intellectual Property, Media & Entertainment Law Journal, Villanova Law Review. Office: Skadden, Arps, Slate, Meagher & Flom Four Times Square New York NY 10036 Office Phone: 212-735-2198. Office Fax: 212-777-2198. E-mail: pbansal@skadden.com.*

BANSIL, ARUN, research scientist; s. P. C. and L. Bansil; m. Rama Bansil; children: Nisha, Amit, Rajat. PhD, Harvard U., Cambridge, Massachusetts, 1969—73; MA, SUNY at Stonybrook, Long Island, New York, 1967—69; B.Sc. (Honors), U. of Delhi, Delhi, India, 1964—67. Prof. of physics Northeastern U., Boston, 1987—, assoc. prof. of physics, 1981—87, asst. prof. of physics, 1976—81, founding dir., advanced sci. computation ctr., 1999—; editor, jour. of physics and chemistry of solids Elsevier Sci., Oxford, United Kingdom, 1994—; founding dir., elmo lab. Northeastern U., Boston, 1998—; exec. officer Physics Dept., Northeastern U., Boston, 1998—2000; hon. prof. (docent) Tampere U. of Tech., Tampere, Finland, 1989—; sci. cons. Netherlands Energy Rsch. Found. (ECN), Petten, Netherlands, 1987—; resident assoc. Argonne Nat. Lab., Argonne, Ill., 1991—; mem., commn. on charge, spin and momentum densities Internat. Union of Crystallography, 1993—2002, prof. edn., 2002—. Guest sr. sci. Lawrence Berkeley Nat. Lab., 2002—. Author (authored or co-authored 170 publications) and 7 conference proceedings as of 2002. Recipient Robert D. Klein U. Lectr., Northeastern U., 2002, Listed in Am. Men and Women of Sci., 1991-, Mem., Phi-Beta-Delta Internat. Honor Soc., 1995-, Mem., Internat. Adv. Bd., Jour. of Advanced Materials (Algeria), 1996-, Mem., Editl. Adv. Bd., Materials Sci. Found., Trans Tech Publications, Switzerland, 1997-; fellow TOKTEN Fellow, UN Devel. Program (UNDP), 1993,1994; grantee Many grants from nat. and internat. funding agencies, 1976-. Mem.: Am. Phys. Soc. (life).

BANTA, PETER GRAY, lawyer; b. Hackensack, N.J., Jan. 24, 1935; s. Horace Ferris and Alice Edna (Evertz) B.; m. Nancy Joyce, Feb. 2, 1963 (div. Jan. 1981); children: Laurie, Eric; m. Marion Strobach, Apr. 17, 1982. AB, Williams Coll., 1957; JD, Harvard U. Law Sch., 1960. Bar: N.J. 1960, U.S. Dist. Ct. N.J. 1961, U.S. Ct. Appeals (3d cir.) 1970, U.S. Supreme Ct. 1985, N.Y. 1988. From assoc. to ptnr. Winne & Banta, Hackensack, 1960—90; sr. ptnr. Winne, Banta, Rizzi, Hetherington & Basralian, Hackensack, 1990—2000, of counsel, 2000—. Ethics com. Supreme Ct. N.J., 1974-77. Trustee Legal Svcs. N.J., 1981-85, Aviation Hall of Fame N.J., 1982-2004, Hackensack U. Med. Ctr., 1993-2002, Musconetcong Watershed Assn., 2002—. Mem. N.J. State Bar Assn. (trustee banking sect. 1981-84, chmn. media law com. 1997-99). Avocations: bicycling, adventure travel. Office: Winne Banta Hetherington Basralian and Kahn 25 Main St Hackensack NJ 07601-7015 Home: 215 Asbury West/Portal Rd Asbury NJ 08802-1151 Office Phone: 201-487-3800. E-mail: pgbanta@earthlink.net.

BANTA, VIVIAN L., insurance company executive; b. Lebanon; arrived in US, 1968; m. Robert Field; 1 child, Brandon. B in psychology, U. of Pacific, Stockton, Calif., 1972. With Bank of Am., 1972—87, Chase Manhattan Corp., 1987—97, sr. v.p. global securities svcs., 1991—93, exec. v.p. global securities svcs., 1993—95, exec. v.p. global investor svcs. (Chase Manhattan Corp. merged with Chemical Banking Corp.), 1995—97; sr. v.p., chief adminstrv. officer individual fin. svcs. Prudential Fin., 1998—2000, exec. v.p., CEO US Consumer Group, 2000—02, vice chmn. ins., 2002—. Named one of the 50 Most Powerful Women in Bus., Fortune, 2001, 2002, 2003, Most Powerful Women, Forbes mag., 2005. Office: Prudential Fin Inc 751 Broad St Newark NJ 07102-3777*

BANTEL, LINDA MAE, former museum curator, consultant; b. King City, Calif., May 30, 1943; d. Clifford Burnett and Helen Vernelle (Mallicotte) Bantel; m. David Hollenberg, June 15, 1980; 1 child, Matthew Bantel Hollenberg. MA, NYU, 1973. Rsch. cons. N.Y. Hist. Soc., N.Y.C., 1975—76; guest co-curator Art Mus. of South Tex., Corpus Christi, 1977—79; rsch. assoc. Met. Mus. Art, N.Y.C., 1978—80; curator, dir. Mus. Pa. Acad. Fine Arts, Phila., 1980—95. Co-author (with James Thomas Flexner): The Face of Liberty: Founders of the U.S., 1975; author (with Marcus Burke): Spain and New Spain: Mexican Colonial Arts in Their European Context, 1979; author: The Alice M. Kaplan Collection, 1980, William Rush, American Sculptor, 1982; contbr. American Paintings in the Metropolitan Museum of Art Vol. II: A Catalogue of Works by Artists Born Between 1816-1845, 1985, Raphaelle Peale Still Lifes, 1988, contbr. (with others) Searching Out the Best, 1988, contbr. to Antiques mag., 1989; editor (with Jacolyn A. Mott): American Sculpture in the Museum of American Art of the Pennsylvia Academy of the Fine Arts, 1997. Mem.: Am. Assn. Mus., Coll. Art Assn. Home: 703 W Phil Ellena St Philadelphia PA 19119-3513 E-mail: lindabantel@aol.com.

BANTON, JULIAN WATTS, banker; b. Gladstone, Va., Aug. 8, 1940; s. John Dorman and Elizabeth (Watts) B.; m. Donna Lea Brown, July 9, 1960; children— Courtney Blair, Stephanie Paige BS, Va. Commonwealth U., 1965; MBA, U. Richmond, 1968; grad. Advanced Mgmt. Program, Harvard U., 1977. Exec. v.p. Bank of Va., Richmond, 1965-77; pres. Bank of Va. Internat., Richmond, 1977-82; exec. v.p. SouthTrust Bank Ala., Birmingham, 1982—, pres., 1986—. Contbr. articles to profl. jours. Bd. dirs., v.p. Sci. Mus. Va.; chmn. ann. fund raiser Ala. Symphony, Birmingham; bd. dirs. Ala. Symphony, Jr. Achievement, Birmingham, Campfire, Grad. Sch. Banking, Washington, Operation New Birmingham; co-chmn. 1986 campaign United Way Central Ala., ann. fund drive; mem. U. Ala. Birmingham Leadership Council. Served with U.S. Army, 1958-61. Mem. Robert Morris Assocs. (com. chmn. 1972-82), Bank Assn. for Fgn. Trade (committeeman 1978), Am. Arbitrators Assn. Clubs: Harvard (N.Y.C.). Lodges: Rotary. Methodist. Office: SouthTrust Bank Ala NA PO Box 2554 420 20th St N Birmingham AL 35203-5200

BANTON, STEPHEN CHANDLER, lawyer; b. St. Louis; s. William Conwell and Ruth (Chandler) B. AB, Bowdoin Coll., 1969; JD, Washington U., St. Louis, 1973, MBA, 1974. Bar: Mo. 1973, U.S. Dist. Ct. (ea. and we. dists.) Mo. 1973. Asst. pros. atty. St. Louis County, 1973-75; sole practice Clayton, Mo., 1975-83; ptnr. Quinn, Ground & Banton, Manchester, Mo., 1983—. Pres. Coll. for Living, 1997-98. Exploring chmn. St. Louis coun. Midland Dist. Scouts, 1975-77; pres. Am. Youth Hostels Ozarks area, 1976-80; trustee St. Louis Art Mus., 1985-94; mem. Rockwood Sch. Bd., 1997—. Served with USMC. Recipient Leadership award Lafayette Community Assn., 1983, Service award The Meramec Palisades Community Assn., 1985, Service award Profl. Remodeling Assn., 1985, Service award St. Louis Symphony Orch., 1985. Mem. ABA, Mo. Bar Assn., St. Louis County Bar Assn., Bar Assn. Met. St. Louis, Assn. Trial Lawyers Am., St. Louis County League of C. of C. (pres. 1978), West Port C. of C. (bd. dirs. 1978-81, Service award 1983), Rotary (pres. Ballwin club 1997-98), Toastmasters (adminstrv. v.p.), Lions (pres. 1977), Kiwanis (pres. West County club 2001-02), Gideons (pres. Frontenac 1999-2002). Republican. Office: Quinn Ground & Banton 14611 Manchester Rd Ballwin MO 63011-3700 Home: 929 Saint Paul Rd Ballwin MO 63021-6061 Office Phone: 636-394-7242. Business E-Mail: scbanton@qgb-lawfirm.com.

BANTRY, BRYAN, entrepreneur, producer, director; b. Jacksonville, Fla., Oct. 12, 1956; Owner, operator dog-walking svc., 1969-73; photographer's agt. Patrick Demarchelier, 1973—; owner Bryan Bantry Hair-Makeup Agy., N.Y.C., 1973—, Bryan Bantry Celebrity Model Mgmt., N.Y.C., 1992—; chmn., chief exec. officer Royal Atlantic Airways, N.Y.C., 1987—. Co-prodr. (Broadway plays) You Can't Take it With You, 1983, Aren't We All, 1985, (off-Broadway plays) Greater Tuna, 1982, Hey Ma...Kaye Ballard, 1984; creator TV pilot Man's Best Friend, 1983; prodr. (feature documentary) The Cream Will Rise: The Sophie B. Hawkins Story, 1998; theatre prodr. (Broadway musical) Street Corner Symphony, 1997-98; prodr., co-dir. feature short film Eventual Wife, 2000. Chmn. Batoto Yetu inner-city youth program, N.Y.C., 1992-2002; bd. dirs. The Trevor Project, L.A. Mem.: League of Am. Theatres and Prodrs. E-mail: bb@waggingtail.com.

BANWART, SIDNEY C., human resources specialist; Diploma in Chem. Engring., Iowa State U.; MBA, U. Ill. Various engring. and mgmt. positions including devel. engr. Caterpillar, Inc., Peoria, Ill., 1968—86, mgr. quality control and engring., mgr. tech. svcs. Mexico, 1986—89, quality control mgr., tech. svcs. mgr., motor grade product mgr. Aurora and Decatur, 1989—95, gen. mgr. large engine ctr. Lafayette, Ind., 1995—97, v.p., head tech. svcs. divisn., 1997—2000, head component products divsn., 1998—2000, chief info. officer, head systems and processes divisn., 2000—04, v.p. human svcs. divisn. Peoria, Ill., 2004—. Bd. dirs. Carter Machinery, Salem, Va., Weitz Co., Des Moines. Recipient Ill. 4-H Alumni award, 2004. Mem.: Ill. Manufacturer's Assn., Human Resources Policy Assn. Office: Caterpillar Inc 100 NE Adams St Peoria IL 61629 Office Phone: 309-675-1000. Office Fax: 309-675-1182.*

BANZHAF, HENRY SPENCER, economist; b. Chgo., Nov. 18, 1969; s. Henry Spencer Badet and Frances Joslin Banzhaf; m. Melissa Christine Ruby, June 5, 1999; 1 child, Elizabeth Spencer. BA, Duke U., 1992, MA, 1996, PhD, 2001. Economist Rsch. Triangle Inst., Rsch. Triangle Pk., NC, 1992—94, Triangle Econ. Rsch., Durham, 1994—95; tchg. asst. Duke U., 1995—97, instr., 1998—99; fellow Resources for Future, Washington, 2001—; adj. asst. prof. Georgetown U., 2003—. Cons.-in-residence Triangle Econ. Rsch., Durham, 1995—98. Co-author: Environmental Policy Analysis with Limited Information, 1998. Fellow, Mustard Seed Found., 1998—2001; grantee, NSF, 2003—05, EPA, 2005—. Mem.: History Econs. Soc., Am. Assn. Environ. & Resource Econs., Am. Econ. Assn. Office: Resources for Future 1116 P St NW Washington DC 20036

BANZHAF, JOHN F., III, legal association administrator, law educator; b. NYC, July 2, 1940; s. John F., Jr. and Olga Banzhaf; m. Ursula Maag, 1971. BS in Elec. Engring, MIT, 1962; JD magna cum laude, Columbia U., 1965. Civilian research asst. Signal Corps Engring. Labs., 1957; research engr., cons. Lear Siegler Corp., 1959-62; editor Columbia Law Rev., 1964-65; research fellow Nat. Municipal League, 1965; law clk. to U.S. Dist. Judge Spottswood W. Robinson III, 1965-66; asso. firm Watson, Leavonworth, Kelton & Taggart, NYC, 1967; founder, exec. dir. Action on Smoking and Health, Washington, 1968—, Nat. Inst. Legal Activism, 1980—; prof. law and legal activism Nat. Law Center, George Washington U., 1968—; exec. dir. Action on Safety and Health, 1971-80, Open America, 1975-80; founder Nat. Center for Law and the Deaf, 1975—. Bd. dirs. Consumers Union, 1971 Recipient 17th ann. Sat. Rev. award distinguished TV programming in pub. interest, 1969; Advt. Age award, 1967, 68; those who made advt. news, 1967, 68; Benjamin Franklin Lit. and Med. Soc. award, 1981 Mem. Sigma Xi, Eta Kappa Nu, Tau Beta Pi, World Tech. Network. Home: 2810 N Quebec St Arlington VA 22207-5215 Office: Action on Smoking and Health 2013 H St NW Washington DC 20006-4207 E-mail: jbanzhaf@law.gwu.edu. *Despite the increasing complexity of society, and the seemingly overwhelming power of large institutions both public and private, one determined individual can still have a significant and beneficial impact on society. (I was responsible, as an individual, for over 200 million dollars worth of free radio and television time for anti-smoking commercials which led to the ban on cigarette commercials.).*

BAO, GANG, biomedical engineer, educator; s. Xicheng Bao and Yuying Sun; m. Bo Fan, Sept. 27, 1978; 1 child, Xiaoyan Robert. PhD, Lehigh U., 1987. Asst. prof. Johns Hopkins U., Balt., 1991—95, assoc. prof., 1995—99, Ga. Inst. of Tech., Atlanta, 1999—2003, prof., 2003—. Co-founder, chief sci officer Vivonetics, Atlanta, 2003—. Editor (editor-in-chief): Mechanics and Chemistry of Biosystems. Recipient Rsch. Initiation award, NSF of USA, 1992, Cutting Edge Rsch. award, Ga. Inst. of Tech., 2005, Outstanding Achievement in Rsch. Program Devel. award, Ga. Inst. Tech., 2000; Gotshall fellowship, Lehigh U., 1985-1987, Sr. Scientist fellowship, French Govt., 1998, Translational Rsch. grant, Wallace H. Coulter Found., 2001-2003. Mem.: ASME, Biomedical Engring. Soc. Achievements include patents pending for Dual FRET molecular beacons; Peptide-linked molecular beacons; Multifunctional magnetic nanoparticle probes. Office: Georgia Inst Tech 313 Ferst Dr Atlanta GA 30332 Office Phone: 404-385-0373. Business E-Mail: gang.bao@bme.gatech.edu.

BAO, KATHERINE SUNG, pediatric cardiologist; b. Soochou, Kiangsu, China, Sept. 7, 1920; came to U.S., 1953; d. Yung H. Bao and Ming King; m. William S. Ting, May 2, 1948; children: Gordon K., Albert C. MD, Nat. Ctrl. Univ. Med. Coll., Nanking, China, 1944. Diplomate Am. Bd. Pediatrics. Intern Mercer Hosp., Trenton, N.J., 1953; resident in pediats. and cardiology Children's Meml. Hosp. Northwestern U., Chgo., 1954-57; fellow in pediatric cardiology Children's Hosp. L.A., Calif., 1957-59, attending cardiologist Calif., 1960—; chief pediatric cardiology City of Hope Med. Ctr., Duarte, Calif., 1965-68; chief heart bd. L.A. Unified Sch. Dist. and PTA Splty. Health Clinics, L.A., 1968—90; attending pediatrician, cardiologist Hollywood Presbyn. Med. Ctr., L.A., 1970—, UCLA, L.A., 1973—. Vis. pediatric cardiologist to univs. in Taipei Nat. Sci. Coun., Republic of China, 1983; U.S. pres.'s appointee Pres.'s Com. on Nat. Medal of Sci., 1983-85; adv. com. on health and med. care svcs. Dept. Health Svcs., Calif., 1988-90; pres. Chinese Physicians Soc. of So. Calif., 1969; speaker in field. Active Rep. Eagle, Rep. Presdl. Task Force, Rep. Presdl. Round Table. Rsch. Fellow Cardiologist,

NIH, 1960-63; recipient Physician of Yr., Hon. Svc. award Calif. Congress of PTA, Inc., 1984, U.S. Rep. Senatorial Medal of Freedom, 1994; named Internat. Scientist of Yr., IBC, Cambridge, Eng., 2001, Woman of the Yr., ABI, 2002. Fellow Am. Acad. Pediatrics; mem. AMA, AAAS, World Med. Assn., Calif. Med. Assn., L.A. County Med. Assn., Am. Heart Assn., Internat. Cir. of L.A. World Affairs Coun., N.Y. Acad. Scis., Hollywood Acad. Medicine (pres. 1995), Scripps Clinic La Jolla (coun.). Achievements include pioneered research in cardiac arrhythmia in infants and children; research in congenital heart disease in adults. Office: PO Box 10456 Beverly Hills CA 90213-3456

BAPTIST, ALLWYN J., healthcare consultant; b. India, July 10, 1943; came to U.S., 1971; s. Peter L.G. and Trescilla (Lobo) B.; m. Anita Lobo, Sept. 8, 1973; children: Alan, Andrew, Annabel, Arthur. BCS, U. Calcutta, India, 1962; cert. mgmt., U. Chgo., 1978. CPA, Ill; chartered acct., India. Divisional acct. Rallis India Ltd., Bombay, 1967-71; mgr. Chgo. Blue Cross, 1972-79; sr. mgr. Price Waterhouse, Chgo., 1979-84; v.p., dir. Truman Esmond and Assocs., Barrington, Ill., 1984-86; ptnr. Laventhol and Horwath, Chgo., 1986-90, BDO Seidman, Chgo., 1991-2000; pres. Baptist Cons. Inc., 2000—. Mem. adv. bd. St. Mary of Nazareth Hosp., 1989—, mem. gov. bd., 1992-94, 96-98, lifetime trustee. Contbr. articles to profl. jours. Mem. fin. com. St. James Ch., Arlington Heights, Ill., 1987; mem. AICPA Health Care Com., 1991-94. Mem. Healthcare Fin. Mgmt. Assn. (dir., sec. 1983-85, pres. 1988-89, recipient William J. Follmer award 1984, Reeves award 1989, Muncie Gold award 1992, founders medal of honor 1998), India Cath. Assn. Am. (treas. 1980, 87, pres. 1988). Avocations: travel, reading, tennis, golf. Office: Bapt Cons Inc 126 E Wing St Arlington Heights IL 60004

BAPTIST, ERROL CHRISTOPHER, pediatrician, educator; b. Colombo, Sri Lanka, Feb. 24, 1945; came to U.S., 1974; s. Egerton Cuthbert and Hyacinth Margaret (Colomb) B.; m. Christine Rosemary Francke, Aug. 7, 1976; children: Lauren Marianne, Erik Christopher. MB, BS, U. Ceylon, 1969. Diplomate Am. Bd. Pediat. Intern Colombo Gen. Hosp. and Children's Hosp., 1969-70; resident house officer Dist. Hosp., Gampola, Sri Lanka, 1970-71, Base Hosp., Kegalle, Sri Lanka, 1971-74; family practitioner Marawila, Sri Lanka, 1974; resident in pediat. Coll. Medicine and Dentistry N.J., Newark, 1975-77; pvt. practice, Rockford, Ill., 1977—. Asst. prof. pediat. U. Ill. Coll. Medicine, Rockford, 1977-94, assoc. prof., 1994-2000, clin. prof. pediats., 2000—; chmn. dept. pediat. St. Anthony Med. Ctr., Rockford, 1986—. Fellow Am. Acad. Pediat.; mem. So. Med. Assn. Roman Catholic. Home: 5112 Parliament Pl Rockford IL 61107-5066 Office: Mulford Village Office Park 461 N Mulford Rd Rockford IL 61107-5190 Office Phone: 815-397-2400. Personal E-mail: harmonica7@aol.com.

BAPTISTA, ROBERT CHARLES, JR., federal official, lawyer; b. Buffalo, Sept. 14, 1948; s. Robert C. Sr. and Martha E. (Cole) B.; m. Denise C. Totemeier, June 29, 1974; children: Maria, Robert III. BA, Wheaton (Ill.) Coll., 1970; MA, No. Ill. U., 1976; JD, U. Ill., 1982. Bar: Ill. 1982. Law clk. to Hon. R. Lanier Anderson U.S. Ct. Appeals (11th cir.), Macon, Ga., 1982-83; assoc. Mayer, Brown & Platt, Chgo., 1983-89, ptnr., 1989—2002; chmn. NLRB, Washington, 2002—.

BAPTISTE, THOMAS L., career military officer; b. Calif., Mar. 4, 1951; m. Judy Cardoza; 2 children. BSBA in Fin., Calif. State U., 1973; student navigator tng., Mather AFB, Calif., 1973-74; student, MacDill AFB, Fla., 1974-75, 81-82, Williams AFB, Ariz., 1977-78, Squadron Officer Sch., 1977; student F-4 qualification tng., George AFB, Calif., 1978-79; student, Air Command and Staff Coll., 1986; MPA, Golden Gate U., 1987; student, Air War Coll., 1990, Johns Hopkins U., 1997, Syracuse U., 1997. Commd. 2d lt. USAF, 1973, advanced through grades to lt. gen., 2004; weapons sys. officer and instr. 44th Tactical Fighter Squadron, Kadena Air Base, Japan, 1975-77; aircraft comdr., standardization and evaluation officer 334th Tactical Fighter Squadron, Seymour Johnson AFB, N.C., 1979-81; stationed at MacDill AFB, Fla., 1982-84, 85-89; F-16 instr. pilot and chief, standardization/evaluation div. 8th Tactical Fighter Wing, Kunsan Air Base, S. Korea, 1984-85; asst. dir. nuc. ops. Hdqs. Def. Nuc. Agy., Alexandria, Va., 1990-92; comdr. 52d Ops. Group, Spangdahlem Air Base, Germany, 1992-94; chief weapons tech. control div. Joint Staff, Pentagon, Washington, 1994-96, asst. dep. dir. internat. negotiations, 1994-96, directorate strategic plans and policy, 1994-96; dep. comdr. Can. N. Am. Aerospace Def. Command Region, Winnipeg, Manitoba, 1996-98; comdr. Cheyenne Mountain Ops. Ctr., Cheyenne Mountain Air Sta., Colorado Springs, Colo., 1998-99; asst. chief of staff ops. HQ Allied Air Forces Southern Europe, Naples, Italy, 2000—02; asst. chief of staff ops. div. SHAPE, 2002—04; dir. ops. Joint Forge & Joint Guardian, Mons, Belgium, 2002—04; dep. chmn. mil. com. NATO, Brussels, 2004—. Decorated Def. Superior Svc. medal with two oak leaf clusters, Def. Meritorious Svc. medal, Air medal, Joint Svc. Comendation medal, Air Force Commendation medal, Combat Readiness medal with oak leaf cluster. Office: NATO Blvd Leopold III 1110 Brussels Belgium

BAQUET, CHARLES R., III, former federal agency administrator, international studies educator; b. New Orleans, Dec. 24, 1941; BA, U. Xavier, 1963; MPA, Syracuse U., 1975. With Fgn. Svc., 1968, consular officer Paris, 1969-71; gen. svcs. officer bldg. mgmt. Dept. of State, 1971, adminstrv. officer Bur. Adminstrn., 1971-75, spl. asst. to Asst. Sec. of Adminstrn., 1978-79; gen. svcs. officer U.S. Consulate Gen., Hong Kong, 1975-76; councillor adminstrv. affairs U.S. Embassy, Beirut, 1976-78; dep. Office of Ops., 1979-83; dir. regional mgmt. ctr. U.S. Embassy, Paris, 1983-87; sr. seminar Fgn. Svc. Inst., 1987-88; with U.S. Consul Gen., Cape Town, South Africa, 1988-91; U.S. amb. to Djibouti, 1991-93; dep. dir. Peace Corps, Washington, 1994—2002; dir. Ctr. for Internat. Studies, Xavier U., La., 2002—. Vol. Peace Corps, Somali Republic, 1965-67. Office Phone: 504-520-5490. Business E-Mail: crbaquet@xula.edu.

BAQUET, DEAN PAUL, newspaper editor; b. New Orleans, Sept. 21, 1956; s. Edward Joseph and Myrtle (Romano) B.; m. Dylan F. Landis, Sept. 6, 1986; 1 child, Ari Theogene Landis. Student, Columbia U., 1974. Investigative reporter The Times Picayune/The States Item, New Orleans, 1978-84, Chgo. Tribune, 1984-87, assoc. met. editor for investigations, chief investigative reporter, 1987-90; met. reporter NY Times, 1990-92, spl. projects editor bus. desk, 1992—94, spl. project editor office exec. editor, 1994—95, deputy met. editor, 1995, nat. editor, 1995—2000; mng. editor LA Times, 2000—05, editor, 2005—. Recipient Pulitzer Prize for investigative reporting, 1988. Achievements include first African-American editor to run the newsroom for the LA Times. Office: LA Times 202 W First St Los Angeles CA 90012*

BAR, ROBERT S., endocrinologist, educator; b. Gainesville, Tex., Dec. 2, 1943; s. Samuel and Emma (Kaplan) B.; m. Laurel Ellen Burns, June 23, 1970; children: Katharine June, Matthew Tomas. BS, Tufts Univ., 1964; MS in Biochemistry, MD, Ohio State U., 1970. Medicine intern Pa. Hosp., Phila., 1970-71; medicine resident Ohio State Univ., Columbus, 1971-72; asst. prof., dept. medicine Univ. Iowa, Iowa City, 1977-82, assoc. prof., dept. medicine, 1982-86, prof., dept. medicine, 1986—. Acting dir. divsn. of endocrinology and metabolism, U. Iowa, 1985-90; dir. diabetes-endocrinology rsch ctr., U. Iowa, 1986—, nat. rsch. svc. award in endocrinology, 1984—, endocrinology fellowship program, 1979—, divsn. of endocrinology and metabolism, 1990—; mem. ad hoc study sect. NIH, 1985, dir. diabetes-endocrinology rsch. ctr. 1986; mem. editorial bd. Jour. of Clin. Endocrinology and Metabolism, 1984-87; mem study sect. Nat. Veterans Adminstrn., 1984-87; v.p. rsch. Nat. Am. Diabetes Assn., 1987-88; mem. orgn. com. Endothelium and Diabetes Symposium, Melbourne, 1988; dir. VA/JDF Diabetes Rsch. Ctr., 1997; mem. study sect. numerous assns. and coms.; guest reviewer numerous jours. Editor Endocrinology, 1987-89, Advances in Endocrinology and Metabolism, 1989—. Mem. Am. Diabetes Assn., Am. Soc. for Clin. Investigation, Assn. Am. Physicians, Endocrine Soc., Ctrl. Soc. for Clin. Rsch., Sigma Xi. Office: U Iowa Hwy 6 West 3E19 VA Iowa City IA 52246

BAR, ROSELYN R., lawyer; b. 1958; BA, U. Rochester; JD, Bklyn. Law Sch. Bar: NY 1984, Fla. 1984, Calif. 1990. Atty. Skadden, Arps, Slate, Meagher, and Flom, NYC, L.A.; corp. counsel Sun Am. Inc.; asst. gen. counsel, asst. corp. sec. Martin Marietta Materials, Raleigh, NC, 1994—2001, v.p., gen. counsel, sec., 2001—. Mem.: Fla. Bar Assn., Calif. Bar Assn., NY Bar Assn. Office: Martin Marietta Materials Inc 2710 Wycliff Rd PO Box 30013 Raleigh NC 27622 Office Phone: 919-783-4603. E-mail: roselyn.bar@martinmarietta.com.

BARA, JEAN MARC, finance and communications executive, artist; b. Roubaix, France, Aug. 22, 1946; came to U.S., 1970; s. Henri and Marie Antoinette (Dousseau) B.; m. Marian Yu, May 8, 1973; 1 child, Patrick Luc. B in Engring., Fed. U. Rio Grande do Sul, Brazil, 1969; MBA, Columbia U., 1972. With Chase Manhattan Bank, 1972-88; assigned Chase's Brazilian affiliate Banco Lar Brasileiro, 1978-80, mng. dir., head corp./retail mktg., planning, product mgr. Rio de Janeiro, 1980; v.p., head Brazil/Argentina/Paraguay liaison office Chase Manhattan Bank, N.Y.C., 1980-82, v.p. corp. banking team, Latin Am. coord. mining and metals, 1983, v.p. nat. positioning group, 1984; corp. fin. exec. Chase Investment Bank, 1985-88; with Young & Rubicam, N.Y.C., 1988—, v.p., corp. treas., 1988-89, sr. v.p., corp. treas., 1989-91; exec. dir., CFO Landor Assocs., N.Y.C., 1992-94; CFO Burson Marsteller, 1997-98; pres. Ams.-Ea. Region, chief learning officer Landor Assocs., 1998—; pres. Americas, 2000—; generative artist, 2001—. Mem. Beta Gamma Sigma. Home and Office: PO Box 4446 Greenwich CT 06831-0408

BARAB, PATSY LEE, nutritionist, realtor; b. Indpls., Sept. 24, 1934; 1 child, Gregory (dec.); m. John D. Barab Jr., Apr. 8, 1995. BS, Mich. State U., 1956, MA, 1970. Asst. prof. Med. Coll. Ga., Augusta, 1972-82; nutrition cons., 1982—. Assoc. Meybohm Realty, Inc., Augusta, 1987—. Docent Morris Mus. Art, 1992—; mem. program com. Gertrude Herbert Art Inst., 1992—94; mem. promotion com. Imperial Theater, bd. dirs., 2001—03. Mem.: AARP, CRS, GRI, Nutritionists in Nursing Edn. (nat. chmn. 1983—84), Nutrition Today Soc. (charter), Soc. Nutrition Edn., Ga. Dietetic Assn., Am. Dietetic Assn., Million Dollar Club (life), Pi Beta Phi, Omicron Nu. Home and Office: 3051 Walton Way Augusta GA 30909 Personal E-mail: patsypink3@aol.com.

BARABASH, CLAIRE, lawyer, special education services professional, psychologist; b. N.Y.C., Oct. 22, 1940; d. Maurice Isaac and Sarah (Libowsky) B. BA, Bklyn. Coll., 1960; MS, CUNY, 1962; PhD, NYU, 1979; JD, Bklyn. Law Sch., 1994. Bar: N.J. 1994, N.Y. 1995, Ala. 2000; Diplomate Am. Coll. Forensic Examiners; lic. psychologist, sch. psychologist; cert. sch. dist. adminstr. Psychology intern Bklyn. Coll. Edn. Clinic, 1962-63; sch. psychologist Yonkers (N.Y.) Bd. Edn., 1963-65, N.Y.C. Bd. Edn., 1965-78, regional coord., 1978-82, dept. asst. supt., 1982-95, asst. supt. for clin. svcs., 1991-92; pvt. practice Margaretville, NY, 1996—99; forensic cons., 1999—. Adj. assoc. prof. NYU, 1979-80, L.I. U., Bklyn., 1988-93. Named Outstanding Spl. Educator of Yr. Orthodox Jewish Tchrs., 1990, Brian E. Tomlinson award for disting. contbns. in psychology, 1991. Mem. APA, ABA, N.Y. State Bar Assn., N.Y.C. Assn. Sch. Psychologists (pres. 1979-80), Adminstrv. Women in Edn. (Woman of Yr. 1989, chair mentoring com. 1989-90), Acad. for Pub. Edn. Home: 101 Clark St Brooklyn NY 11201-2746

BARACH, JEFFREY ALVAN, management educator; b. N.Y.C., Aug. 15, 1934; s. Alvan L. and Frederica P. (Barbour) B.; m. Katarina Roth (div. 1982); 1 child, Jeffrey Alvan; m. Barbara J. Howell, Dec. 26, 1997. AB cum laude, Harvard U., 1956, MBA, 1961, DBA, 1967, postgrad. individual studies program, 1977. Tech. writer Honeywell Corp., Phila., 1956-58; account exec., copywriter Renner, Inc., Phila., 1958; tech. writer Teleregister Corp., Stanford, Conn., 1959; rsch. asst. Harvard U. Bus. Sch., 1961-62; asst. prof. Tulane U. Sch. Bus., 1965-68, assoc. prof. mgmt., 1968-86, prof. mgmt., 1986—2004; mktg. and mgmt. cons. New Orleans, 1965—; prof. emeritus Tulane U. Sch. Bus., 2004—. Mem. Met. Crime Commn. of New Orleans, recipient extraordinary service award, 1978. Recipient Detur prize Harvard Coll., 1953; Wissner award Tulane U., 1979, 82; Ford Found. grantee, 1962-63. Mem. AAUP, Acad. Mgmt., Soc. for Bus. Ethics, Beta Gamma Sigma. Clubs: Krewe d'Etat, Krewe of Bacchus. Author: Individual, Business and Society, 1977; co-author: Leadership and the Job of the Executive, 1996; contbr. articles on mktg. and mgmt. to profl. jours. Author: Individual, Business and Society, 1977; co-author: Leadership and the Job of the Executive, 1996; contbr. articles on mktg. and mgmt. to profl. jours. Mem. Met. Crime Commn. of New Orleans. Recipient Extraordinary Svc. award Met. Crime Commn. of New Orleans, 1978, Detur prize Harvard Coll., 1953, Wissner award Tulane U., 1979, 82; Ford Found. grantee, 1962-63. Mem. AAUP, Krewe d'Etat, Krewe of Bacchus, New Orleans Yacht Club, Beta Gamma Sigma. Office: Tulane U AB Freeman Sch Bus New Orleans LA 70118 E-mail: jbarach@cox.net.

BARADZI, AMELIA, stained glass artist, restorationist; b. Bay Shore, New York, Mar. 26, 1947; d. Stephen A. and Frances (De Palma) Baradzi. BA, La. Tech. U., 1970. Cert. K-6 tchr., La. Tchr. St. John's Elem. Sch., Central Islip, NY, 1971—72; pres. Stained Glass Creations Ltd., Bay Shore, NY, 1972—91; sec., treas. Baradzi Glass Inc., Bay Shore, NY, 1991—92; owner, mgr. Amelia Baradzi Studio, Bay Shore, NY, 1993—, L.I. Stained Glass Restoration and Conservation Studio, Bay Shore, NY, 1995—, Stained Glass Restoration Co., Bay Shore, NY, 1998. Designer, mfr., commissions art glass Poinsettia, 1985-87, Story of Creation, 1987, Peacock, 1989; designer, mfg. leaded glass Edwardian flowercases and sconces, 1994; restoration of St. Andrews Ch. Saltaire, Fire Island, NY., 2003. Mem. Bus. Improvement Dist., Bay Shore, N.Y. 1994-95. Roman Catholic. Avocations: fishing, gardening, painting, reading. Home and Office: Amelia Baradzi Studio 50 Bay Ave Bay Shore NY 11706-8753 Office Phone: 631-665-5011. E-mail: abarad@optonline.net.

BARAGONA, MICHELLE ALISE, science educator; b. Flowood, Miss., Sept. 23, 1976; d. Thomas Charles and Lynn Ruth Baragona; m. J. Owen Sparks. BS, La. Tech U., 1999; MS, U. So. Miss., 2002. Lab. asst. U. So. Miss., Hattiesburg, 1999—2001; natural sci. instr. N.E. Miss. C.C., Booneville, 2001—. Advisor Christians on Campus, Booneville, Miss., 2001—05. Mem.: AAAS, Soc. Integrative and Comparative Biology, Miss. Assn. Sci. Church Of Christ. Office: NE Miss CC 101 Cunningham Blvd Booneville MS 38829 Office Phone: 662-720-7258. Business E-Mail: mabaragona@nemcc.edu.

BARAGWANATH, ALBERT KINGSMILL, curator, writer; b. Lima, Peru, July 20, 1917; s. John Gordon and Leila Radcliff (Morris) B.; m. Eileen Mary Flanagan, Sept. 1, 1943; children— Joan Baragwanath Shaw, Janice, John Blackburn, Patricia. Grad., Hill Sch., Pottstown, Pa., 1936; BA, Princeton, 1940; MA in Am. History, Columbia, 1952. With traffic and sales dept. Eastern Air Lines, N.Y.C., 1946-50; librarian Mus. City N.Y., 1952-58, curator prints and portraits, 1959—, sr. curator, 1963-79, sr. curator emeritus, 1980—. Mem. N.Y.C. Mayor's Task Force on Municipal Archives, 1966; mem. adv. com. Mus. Am. Folk Art, 1969— Author: More Than a Mirror to the Past: The First Fifty Years of the Museum of the City of New York, 1973, 50 Currier & Ives Favorites, 1978, 100 Currier & Ives Favorites, 1978; New York Life at the Turn of the Century in Photographs, 1985; contbr.: New York City Guide, 1964, Currier and Ives, Chronicles of America, 1968. Served from pvt. to capt. AUS, 1941-46, ETO; Served from pvt. to capt. AUS, PTO. Decorated Combat Inf. badge. Mem. Am. Hist. Print Collectors Soc. (dir.) Home: 20 Summit Ave Larchmont NY 10538-2930 Office: 1220 5th Ave New York NY 10029-5221

BARAKAT, RICHARD, oncologist, gynecological surgeon; b. Kuwait City, Kuwait, July 15, 1959; MD, SUNY, Bklyn Health Sci. Ctr., 1985. Cert. obstetrics and gynecology 1992, gynecologic oncology 1994. Intern NYU-Bellevue Med. Ctr., 1985—86, resident, obstetrics and gynecology, 1986—89; assoc. prof. obstetrics and gynecology Cornell U. Med. Ctr.; fellow, obstetrics and gynecology Meml. Sloan-Kettering Cancer Ctr., NYC, 1989—91, oncologist, gynecology, 1994—, chief, gynecology svc., dept. surgery, 2001—. Vice-chmn. Cancer Prevention Com., Gynecologic Oncology Group; examiner Am. Bd. of Obstetrics and Gynecology. Editl. bd.: Gynecologic Oncology Jour., Oncology, lead editor: MSKCC-MDACC Handbook of Gynecologic Oncology, assoc. editor: Atlas of Procedures in Gynecologic Oncology, Principles and Practice of Gynecology Oncology, 4th edit. Founder and past pres. Met. Gynecological Cancer Soc. of NY. Avocations: golf, tennis. Office: Meml Sloan-Kettering Cancer Ctr 1275 York Ave New York NY 10021-6007 Office Fax: 212-638-9245.

BARAM, MICHAEL S., lawyer, law educator; b. 1935; BS, Tufts Univ., 1957; LLB, Columbia Univ., 1960. Bar: Mass. 1962. Ptnr. Bracken & Baram, Boston; prof. Boston Univ. Sch. Law, Boston Univ. Sch. Pub. Health; dir. Ctr. Law & Tech., Boston Univ. Cons. EPA, United Nations, U.S. Congress, Chem. Mfr. Assn. Author: Environmental Law and the siting of facilities, 1976, Alternatives to Regulation: Managing Risks to Health, Safety and the Environment, 1982, Transnational Corporations and Industrial Hazards Disclosure, 1991; co-author: Managing Chemical Risks: Corporate Response to Sara Title III, 1992, Safety Management, 1998. Vol. atty. Conservation Law Found., Mass., 2002—; mem. bd. dir. Belmont Land Trust, Mass. Office: Boston University School of Law 765 Commonwealth Ave Boston MA 02215-1401

BARAMKI, THEODORE ATALLAH, gynecologist, reproductive endocrinologist; b. Jerusalem, May 6, 1931; s. Atallah T. and Cecile (Madbak) B.; m. Ingrid Ringe, Dec. 27, 1969. MD, Cairo U. Sch. Medicine, 1957. Diplomate in ob-gyn. and in reproductive endocrinology Am. Bd. Ob-Gyn. Resident in ob-gyn. Johns Hopkins Hosp., Balt., 1960—64; fellow in reproductive endocrinology Johns Hopkins U., Balt., 1964-66; head divsn. reproductive endocrinology Greater Balt. Med. Ctr., 1978-2001, dir. prenatal diagnostic ctr., 1981—2000. Assoc. prof. ob-gyn. Johns Hopkins Med. Sch., 1980—. Co-author: Medical Cytogenetics, 1967. Recipient 1st Class Independence medal, Jordan, 1974. Fellow Am. Coll. Ob-gyn.; mem. Md. Ob-gyn. Soc. (pres. 1976-77, cert.). Republican. Office: 10753 Falls Rd Ste 335 Lutherville MD 21093 Office Phone: 410-583-2761.

BARAMOVA, IRINA ANTONOVA, investment banker; b. Geneva, May 5, 1972; d. Anton Donchev and Eugenia Nedialkova B. BA in Applied Econs., BA in Bus. Adminstrn., Am. U. in Bulgaria, Bulgaria, 1995; MBA, Duke U., Durham, NC, 1999. Series 7 NASD, 1999, Series 63 NASD, 1999. Client svc. dir. Leo Burnett & Co., Sofia, Bulgaria, 1995—97; tchg. asst. Duke U., Durham, NC, 1998—99; sr. assoc. Merrill Lynch & Co., N.Y.C., 1999—2003; convertible securities analyst trainer Merrill Lynch & Co., N.Y.C., 2000—02, co-head recrutiting team to Duke U., 2001—02; assoc. v.p. HSH Nordbank, N.Y.C., 2003; dir. fin. analysis Endo Pharms., Chadds Ford, Pa., 2004—. Founder Marco Polo Global Hedge Fund, Sofia, Bulgaria, 2003—. Translator: confidential documents for the UNDP. Fuqua fellowship, Duke U., 1997, 1998, Ann. Scholarship, Am. U. in Bulgaria, 1991 - 1995. Mem.: PADI (licentiate), BalkanTourist (assoc.; ski instr. 1988—95). Greek Orthodox. Avocations: skiing, jogging, exercise, tennis, rollerblading.

BARAN, JAN WITOLD, lawyer, educator; b. Ingolstadt, Germany, May 14, 1948; came to U.S., 1951; s. Jerzy Leopold and Leonce Sidonie (Vanden Bussche) B.; m. Kathryn Kavanagh, June 16, 1979; children: Brendan Jerzy, Maria Leonce, Elise Jett, Anna Margaret. BA, Ohio Wesleyan U., 1970; JD, Vanderbilt U., 1973. Bar: Tenn. 1973, D.C. 1976, U.S. Dist. Ct. D.C. 1980, U.S. Ct. Appeals D.C. 1980, U.S. Ct. Appeals (10th cir.) 1994, U.S. Supreme Ct. 1980, U.S. Ct. Appeals (5th cir) 2001. Legal counsel Nat. Rep. Congl. Com., Washington, 1975-77; exec. asst. Fed. Election Commn., Washington, 1977-79; assoc. Baker & Hostetler, Washington, 1979-81, ptnr., 1981-85, Wiley Rein & Fielding LLP, Washington, 1985—. Gen. counsel, George Bush for Pres., Inc., 1987-88; gen. counsel, Bush-Quayle, Inc., 1988; lectr., co-chair Practicing Law Inst., Corp. Polit. Activities, Washington, 1978—. Author: The Election Law Primer for Corporations, 1984, 88, 92, 2000, 02, 04. Chmn. nat. adv. bd. Jour. of Law and Politics, 1983—; gen. counsel Am. Bicentennial Presdl. Inaugural Inc., 1989, Rep. Nat. Com., 1989-92; mem. Pres. Commn. Fed. Ethics Law Reform; amb., head U.S. del. World Adminstrv. Radio Conf. WARC, Malaga, Spain, 1992; mem. Gov.'s Commn. on Govt. Fin. Reform, Va., 2001. Patrick Wilson scholar, 1970-73. Mem. ABA (chmn. com. election law 1981-2000), D.C. Bar Assn., FBA (chmn. polit. campaign and election law com. 1981-83). Roman Catholic. Office: Wiley Rein & Fielding LLP 1776 K St NW Ste 900 Washington DC 20006-2332

BARANCO, GREGORY T., automobile dealership executive; CEO Baranco Lincoln-Mercury, Inc., Duluth, Ga., Baranco Pontiac-GMC Truck=Subaru Inc., Decatur, Ga., Acura of Tallahassee; pres., CEO Baranco Automotive Group, Decatur. Office: Baranco Body Shop 2030 Jessica Daron Ct Lilburn GA 30047-8421

BARANDES, ROBERT, lawyer; b. Bklyn., May 15, 1947; s. Max and Helen (Berger) B.; m. Joan Noveck, May 28, 1970 (div. Jan. 1981); m. Kathleen Lindsey, Aug. 22, 1982 (div. Jan. 1986). Student, U. Coll., London, 1967-68; BA magna cum laude, Union Coll., Schenectady, N.Y., 1969; JD, Harvard U., 1972. Bar: N.Y. 1973, U.S. Dist. Ct. (so. and ea. dists.) N.Y. 1976. From assoc. to ptnr. Barandes, Rabbino & Arnold, N.Y.C., 1972-81; ptnr. Roper, Barandes & Fertel, LLP, N.Y.C., 1981-99; of counsel Beckman, Millman & Sanders LLP, N.Y.C., 2000; ptnr. Beckman, Lieberman & Barandes, LLP, N.Y.C., 2001—. Prodr. (on Broadway) The News, 1986, Broadway revival of Damn Yankees, 1994-96, (on Broadway) Epic Proportions, 1999, Broadway revival of Bells Are Ringing, 2001. Assoc. producer: (Broadway Play) On The Waterfront, 1995, Lyricist Musical Etched in Stone, 1984; writer, lyricist, musical Star Crossed Lovers, 1984; bookwriter, lyricist musical Almost Eden, 1990. Mem. ABA, League Am. Theatres and Producers, Phi Beta Kappa. Jewish. Avocations: writing, skiing, golf, tennis. Office: Beckman Lieberman & Barandes LLP 116 John St Rm 1313 New York NY 10038-3303 Business E-Mail: RBarandes@BLBLLP.com.

BARANOVICH, DIANA LEA, music educator; b. New Orleans, Nov. 1, 1961; d. Walter Horace and Margaret (Rothman) B.; m. Robert Charles Shoup, June 12, 1982; children: Nadia Lea, Raymond Christopher., Tammy Tran MusB, Loyola U., 1983, MEd, 1986; Dalcroze cert., Carnegie-Mellon U., 1993; postgrad., U. Houston, 1990-93. Cert. tchr. music, dance, drama, English, h.s. counselor, Tex. Tchr. music St. Tammany Schs., Slidell, La., 1983-84, Lynn Oaks Sch., Braithwaite, La., 1984-86; choir dir. Fort Bend Pub. Sch., Houston, 1990-93; tchr., cons. music and dance New Orleans, 1996—. Prof. music edn. Normal U. Beijing, China, 1995-97; cons., trainer tchrs. music and dance Kinderland Learning Ctr., Singapore, 1996—; vol. tchr. dance, movement and Chinese studies Alice Harte Elem. Sch., New Orleans, 1996-99; pvt. tchr. piano and movement, 1996—; tchr. tap dancing and choreography New Orleans Dance Acad., 1997-99; fine arts coord. Malaysian Ministry Edn., Kuala Lumpur, 2002—. Contbr. articles to profl. jours. Sponsor St. Joseph's Indian Sch., Childreach, Food for the Poor. Mem. Music Tchrs. Nat. Assn., Music for People, Dalcroze Soc. Am. (patron). Avocations: theater, ethnic dancing, creative writing, composing children's music, piano. Home: 2531 Binz St Houston TX 77004-7565

BARANOWSKI, EDWIN MICHAEL, lawyer, writer; b. Utica, N.Y., Jan. 26, 1947; s. Edwin Joseph and Mary Jane Baranowski; m. Shelley Osmun, Dec. 27, 1969. BA, Hamilton Coll., 1968; JD, U. Va., 1971. Bar: N.Y. 1972, Ohio 1982. Assoc. Kenyon & Kenyon, N.Y.C., 1971-81; v.p. Plaskolite, Inc., Columbus, 1981-82; ptnr., chmn. intellectual property law sect. Porter Wright Morris & Arthur, Columbus, Ohio, 1981-98; mem. adv. bd. for program in law and tech. U. Dayton Sch. of Law, 1991—. Mem. Rep. Nat. Com., 1975—; spl. patent counsel City of Columbus, 1995—; founder, chmn. Tracess Cm. of Am.; adj. prof. comm. and negotiation MBA program Otterbein Coll., 1998—. Patentee of 12 patents in wheelchair accessibility devices, and wound care methods. Mem. ABA (co-author, editor Preliminary Injunctions in Patent Litigation 1981, Comparative and False Advertising Under 15 U.S.C. Section 1125(a)- A Five Year Review 1994), Assn. Bar City N.Y., Columbus

Intellectual Property Law Assn. (past pres.), Hamilton Coll. Ctrl. Ohio Alumni Assn. (pres. 1990—, alumni leadership coun. 1992—), Ohio Rails-to-Trails Conservancy (bd. dirs. 1989-95), St. Michael's Lancers (hon.), Rocky Fork Hunt and Country Club, Breakers Club, Chi Psi. Home: 75 Marrus Dr Gahanna OH 43230-2154 Office: Porter Wright Morris & Arthur 41 S High St Ste 2800 Columbus OH 43215-6194

BARANSKI, CHRISTINE, actress; b. Buffalo, N.Y., May 2, 1952; d. Lucien and Virginia (Mazerowski) B.; m. Matthew Cowles, Oct. 15, 1983. BA, Juilliard Sch., 1974. Actor: (plays) include 'Tis a Pity She's a Whore, The Real Thing (Antoinette Perry award 1984), Cat on a Hot Tin Roof, She Stoops to Conquer, Angel City, Blithe Spirit, Coming Attractions, The Undefeated Rumba Champ, Otherwise Engaged, A Midsummer Night's Dream (Obie award 1983), Rumors (Antoinette Perry award 1989), Nick and Nora, 1991, Lips Together Teeth Apart, 1992; (films) Soup for One, 1982, Lovesick, 1983, Crackers, 1984, 9 1/2 Weeks, 1986, Legal Eagles, 1986, The Pick-up Artist, 1987, Reversal of Fortune, 1990, The Night We Never Met, 1993, Life with Mikey, 1993, Addams Family Values, 1993, The War, 1994, The Ref, 1994, Getting In, 1994, New Jersey Drive, 1995, Jeffrey, 1995, The Birdcage, 1996, The Odd Couple II, 1998, Bulworth, 1998, Cruel Inventions, 1999, Bowfinger, 1999, How the Grinch Stole Christmas, 2000, The Guru, 2002, Chicago, 2002, Marci X, 2003, Welcome to Mooseport, 2004; (TV series) Another World, 1983, All My Children, 1984, Cybill, 1995-98 (Emmy award for best supporting actress in a comedy series, 1995, Am. Comedy Award for funniest supporting female performer in a TV series, 1996), Happy Family, 2003; (TV films) Playing for Time, 1980, A Midsummer Night's Dream, 1982, Big Shots in America, 1985, The House of Blue Leaves, 1987, To Dance with the White Dog, 1993, Eloise at the Plaza, 2003, Eloise at Christmastime, 2003. Actor, exec. prodr.: (TV series) Welcome to New York, 2000-01.

BARANY, JAMES WALTER, industrial engineering educator; b. South Bend, Ind., Aug. 24, 1930; s. Emery Peter and Rose Anne Barany; m. Judith Ann Flanigan, Aug. 6, 1960 (div. 1982); 1 child, Cynthia Getty. BSME, Notre Dame U., 1953; MS in Indsl. Engring., Purdue U., 1958, PhD, 1961. Prodn. worker Studebaker Corp., 1949-52; prodn. liaison engr. Bendix Aviation Corp., 1955-56; mem. faculty Sch. Indsl. Engring. Purdue U., West Lafayette, Ind., 1958—, now prof., assoc. head indsl. engring. Sch. Indsl. Engring. Cons. Taiwan Productivity Ctr., Western Electric, Gleason Gear Works, Am. Oil Co., Timken Co. Served with U.S. Army, 1954—55. Recipient Best Counselor award Purdue U., 1978, Best Engring. Tchr. award, 1983, 89, Outstanding Indsl. Engring. Tchr. award, 1983, 87, 89, Outstanding Tchr. award Purdue U., 1989, Marion Scott Faculty Exemplary Character award Purdue U., 1993, 2000, NSF and Easter Seal Found. rsch. grantee, 1961, 63, 64, 65; Purdue Tchg. Acad. founding fellow, 1997, Indiana Gov.'s Sagamore of the Wabash award, 1998; named Purdue Book Great Tchrs., 1999. Mem. Inst. Indsl. Engring. (life, Fellows award 1982, Disting. Educator award 1989, Disting. Svc. award 1992, Cert. of Svc. Appreciation 1994, Work Measurement award 2000, Young Engr. Mentoring award 2001), Soc. Mfg. Engr., Am. Soc. Engring. Edn., Methods Time Measurement Rsch. Assn., Human Factors and Ergonomics Soc., Order of Engr., Sigma Xi, Alpha Pi Mu, Tau Beta Pi (Eminent Engr. award 1982). Home: 1120 Northwestern Ave W West Lafayette IN 47906-2503 Office: Purdue U IE GRIS 315 N Grant St West Lafayette IN 47907-2023 Office Phone: 765-494-5435. Business E-Mail: jwb@ecn.purdue.edu.

BARASCH, CLARENCE SYLVAN, lawyer; b. N.Y.C., May 20, 1912; s. Morris and Bertha Lydia (Herschdorfer) B.; m. Naomi Bosniak, July 1, 1957; children: Lionel, Jonathan. AB, Columbia U., 1933, JD, 1935. Bar: N.Y. 1936, U.S. Dist. Ct. (so., ea. and no. dists.) N.Y. 1936, U.S. Ct. Appeals (2d cir.) 1936. Pvt. practice, N.Y.C., 1935—. Lectr. law of real estate brokerage at various real estate bds.; faculty of N.Y. Real Estate Bd. on courses for lic. renewals required by the Dept. of State of N.Y.; chmn. Columbia U. Law Sch. Class of 1935 Ann. Fund 1965—, Columbia Coll. Class of 1933 Ann. Fund, 1977-79; decade chmn. Columbia Coll. Ann. Fund; pres. Jewish Campus Life Fund, Inc. of Columbia U., 1970-87. Author: (with Elliot L. Biskind) The Law of Real Estate Brokers, 1969; also cumulative supplements, 1971-83; contbr. articles to profl. jours. Mem. adv. bd. to chaplain Columbia U., N.Y.C., 1950-70. Capt. Signal Corps AUS, 1942-46. Recipient cert. of appreciation Columbia U., 1981, medal for conspicuous svc. Columbia U., 1984. Mem. ABA, N.Y. State Bar Assn. (real property com.), N.Y. County Lawyers Assn. (com. on real estate brokerage matters), Real Estate Bd. N.Y. (mem. legis and law cms., 1970—, arbitration panel 1989—, rev. ann. Diary and Manual and author of summary of real estate brokerage law and related legal matters 1991—), Am. Arbitration Assn. (arbitration panel 1986—), Men's Club (bd. dirs. 1972-80), Columbia U. Law Sch. Alumni Assn. (bd. dirs. 1985-89). Jewish. Home: 1016 5th Ave New York NY 10028-0132 Office: 425 Park Ave New York NY 10022-3506 Office Phone: 212-838-0286.

BARASCH, DAVID M., lawyer, former prosecutor; BA summa cum laude, State U. of NY at Stony Brook, 1970; JD, Cornell U. Sch. of Law, 1974. Consumer advocate Commonwealth of Pa., 1983—90; special asst. to Gov. Robert P. Casey, 1990—93; U.S. atty. U.S. Dist. Ct. (mid. dist.) Pa., 1993—2001; mem. McNees Wallace & Nurick, Harrisburg, Pa. Apptd. Atty. General's Advisory Com., 1999. Mem.: Pa. Energy Develop. Authority (bd. dirs. 1983—90), Pa. Bar Assn., Nat. Assn. State Utility Consumer Advocates (v.p. 1985—87, pres. 1987—89). Office: McNees Wallace & Nurick 100 Pine St PO Box 1166 Harrisburg PA 17108-1166 Office Fax: 717-237-5300.

BARASCH, MAL LIVINGSTON, lawyer; b. NYC, May 14, 1929; s. Joseph and Ernestine (Livingston) Barasch; m. Ann Beckley, May 19, 1962; children: Amy Pitacairn, Jody Taylor. BS in Econs. with distinction, U. Pa., 1951; LLB, Yale U., 1954. Bar: NY 1957, U.S. Dist. Ct. (so. dist.) NY 1960, U.S. Tax Ct. 1960. Assoc. Mudge Rose Guthrie Alexander & Ferdon, NYC, 1957-62, Rosenman & Colin, NYC, 1962-67; ptnr. Rosenman & Colin, LLC, 1968-2000; counsel Katten Muchin Rosenman LLP and predecessor, 2000—. Mem. exec. com., 2d v.p. libr. NY Law Inst., 1979—2000. Treas., bd. dirs. Lenox Hill Neighborhood House; dist. leader, mem. exec. com. NY County Dem. Com., 1961—65; bd. dirs. Visions, Svcs. for the Blind and Visually Impaired. With U.S. Army, 1954—56. Fellow: Am. Coll. Trust and Estate Counsel, NY Bar Found.; mem.: Internat. Acad. Estate and Trust Law (acamedician, exec. com. 2000—04), Assn. Bar City of NY (chmn. com. trusts, estates and surrogates cts. 2000—03), Univ. Club (N.Y.C.), Beta Gamma Sigma. Home: 1225 Park Ave New York NY 10128-1132 E-mail: mal.barasch@kmzr.com.

BARASH, ANTHONY HARLAN, lawyer; b. Galesburg, Ill., Mar. 18, 1943; s. Burrel B. and Rosalyne J. (Silver) B.; m. Jean Anderson, May 17, 1965; children: Elizabeth, Matthew, Katherine, Andrew. AB cum laude, Harvard U., 1965; JD, U. Chgo., 1968. Bar: Calif. 1969, S.C. Assoc. Irell & Manella, L.A., 1968-71, Cox, Castle & Nicholson, L.A., 1971-74, ptnr., 1975-80, Barash & Hill, L.A., 1980-84, Wildman, Harrold, Allen, Dixon, Barash & Hill, L.A., 1984-87, Barash & Hill, L.A., 1988-93, Seyfarth, Shaw, Fairweather & Geraldson, L.A., 1993-96; sr. v.p. corp. affairs, gen. counsel Bowater, Inc., Greenville, S.C., 1996—. Bd. dirs. Deauville Restaurants, Inc. Trustee Pitzer Coll., 1981-98, vice-chmn., 1984-96; pres., bd. dirs. Beverly Hills Bar Assn. Found., 1983-96; bd. dirs. Nat. Equal Justice Libr., Urban League of the Upstate, Peace Ctr. for the Performing Arts. Fellow Am. Bar Found. (life); mem. ABA, S.C. Bar, State Bar Assn. Calif., Greenville County Bar Assn., Beverly Hills Bar Assn. (bd. govs. 1979-81, 88-94, pres. 1992-93), Harvard Club N.Y. Home: 1212 Shadow Way Greenville SC 29615-3843 Office: Bowater Inc 55 E Camperdown Way Greenville SC 29601-3597

BARASH, PAUL GEORGE, anesthesiologist, educator; b. Bklyn., Feb. 22, 1942; s. Abraham Malcolm and Rose (Shenker) B.; m. Norma Ellen Bernard, Aug. 19, 1967; children: David, Daniel, Jed BA, CCNY, 1963; MD, U. Ky., 1967; MA (hon.), Yale U., 1982. Diplomate Am. Bd. Anesthesiology. Intern SUNY Kings County Hosp., Bklyn., 1967-68; resident Yale-New Haven Hosp., 1970-72, chief resident, 1972-73; asst. prof. anesthesiology Yale U., New Haven, 1973-78, assoc. prof., 1978-82, prof., 1982—, assoc. dean clin. affairs, 1991-94. Chmn. dept. anesthesiology, Yale U., New Haven, 1983-94. Assoc. editor: Advances in Anesthesia, 1984; assoc. editor Jour. Clin. Monitoring, 1984 Surgeon USPHS, 1968-70 Fellow Am. Coll. Anesthesiology, Am. Coll. Chest Physicians; mem. Soc. Cardiovasc. Anesthesiologists (pres. 1984-86), Conn. Soc. Anesthesiologists (pres. 1982-83), Internat. Anesthesia Rsch. Soc., Am. Soc. Anesthesiologists (editor-in-chief Anesthesia Refresher Courses 1985-96). Home: 867 Robert Treat Ext Orange CT 06477-1649 Office: Yale U Sch Medicine 333 Cedar St New Haven CT 06510-3289

BARAT, SHAWN L, music educator; b. Hollywood, Fla., Mar. 24, 1972; s. Gary C and Seama M (Bass) Barat. MusB, U. Fla., Gainesville, 1995, MusM, 2000. Cert. K-12 Music Tchr. Fla., 1995. Dir. of bands Forest H.S., Ocala, Fla., 1995—98; grad. asst in bands U. of Fla., Gainesville, Fla., 1998—2000; dir. of bands Winter Haven (Fla.) H.S., 2000—. Guest condr. Highlands County Honor Band, Sebring, Fla., 2002, Lake County Honor Band, Eustis, Fla., 2002. Mem.: Nat. Band Assn. (Fla. chmn. 2002), Fla. Bandmasters Assn. (all state chmn. 2004—). Office: Winter Haven HS Band 600 6th Street SE Winter Haven FL 33880 Home: 615 Terranova Dr Winter Haven FL 33884-3429 Personal E-mail: slbarat@hotmail.com. E-mail: whhsband01@hotmail.com.

BARATIAN, CHRISTIAN A., lawyer; b. Oakland, Mich., Mar. 28, 1974; s. Vic and Kathleen Baratian; m. Jacqueline Baratian; 1 child, Taylor McLean. BS in Polit. Sci. and Philosophy, Grand Valley State U., 1996; JD, Ind. U., 1999. Bar: Va. 1999, Md. 2000. Atty. Sodexho, Gaithersburg, Md., 1999—. Mem.: ABA, Wash. Met. Assn. Corp. Counsel, Assn. Corp. Counsel, Order of Omega, Omicron Delta Kappa. Office: Sodexho Ste 1239 9801 Washingtonian Blvd Gaithersburg MD 20878 Business E-Mail: christian.baratian@sodexhousa.com.

BARAUSKY, KENNETH P., aerospace company executive; b. White Plains, N.Y., Apr. 15, 1944; m. Julie Killam; children: Paul, Mark, Amy, adam. BS in aero. Engring., U.S. Naval Acad., 1967. Commd. USN, 1967, advanced through grades to rear admiral; instr. Tng. Squadron Three; comdr. Fleet Logistics Support Squadron Forty; mission comdr., patrol plane comdr., asst. maint. officer Patrol Squadron Forty Four, 1971-73; officer Tng. and Adminstrn. of Res., Hdqr. Navy Recruiting Command, 1973; head Aviation Officer Cand. and Officer Cand. Sch.; ops. officer Patrol squadron Sixty-Four, 1977-80; adminstrv. officer Res. Anti-Submarine Warfare Tng. Ctr., 1980; ret. With USNR, 1980-97. Decorated Navy Commendation medal (3). Address: 212 W Kilbride Williamsburg VA 23188-8926

BARB, CYNTHIA MARIE, mathematics professor; b. Akron, Ohio; d. Gene and Mary Barb; m. Andrew Shkolnik, 1988. BS magna cum laude in Math., BS in Statistics, U. Akron, 1985, cert. in Secondary Edn., 1985-86, MS in Math., 1990; PhD in Curriculum and Instrn. Math. Edn., Kent State U., 1997. Cert. 7-12 tchr., Ohio. Grad. teaching asst. U. Akron, 1985-86; long term substitute Tallmadge (Ohio) City Schs., 1987-88, Stow (Ohio) City Schs., 1988-89; instr. math. U. Akron, 1989-90; asst. prof. Kent State U. Stark Regional Campus, Canton, Ohio, 1990—2002; assoc. prof. Kent State U., 2003—. Spkr. on math. edn. Contbr., referee articles to profl. jours. and book reviewer. Acad. scholar U. Akron, 1985-86, grantee NSF, 2002—. Mem. Am. Ednl. Rsch. Assn., Math. Assn. Am., Nat. Coun. Tchrs. Math., Ohio Coun. Tchrs. Math., Phi Sigma Alpha, Alpha Lambda Delta. Avocations: dance, theater. Office: Kent State U Stark Regional Campus 6000 Frank Ave NW Canton OH 44720-7599

BARBA, HARRY, writer, publisher, educator; b. Bristol, Conn., June 17, 1922; s. Michael Hovanessian and Sultone (Mnatsignanian) B.; m. Roberta Ashburn Riley, 1955 (div. 1963); 1 child, Gregory Robert; m. Marian Andrea Homelson, Oct. 29, 1965. AB, Bates Coll., 1944; MA, Harvard U., 1951; MFA, U. Iowa, 1960, PhD with honors, 1963; postgrad., NYU, 1955-56, Boston U., 1950-51, NYU, 1955-56, CCNY, 1956-57, Columbia U., 1957-58, U. Middlebury, 1945. Stringer, feature writer Bristol (Conn.) Press, 1944-45; file clk. supr. new departure GM Corp., 1944-45; instr. English and writing Wilkes Coll., 1947, U. Conn., Hartford, 1947-49; tchr. English Seward Park H.S., N.Y.C., 1955-59; instr. U. Iowa, 1959-63; asst. prof. Skidmore Coll., 1963-68; prof. English, dir. writing Marshall U., Huntington, W.Va., 1968-70, title I writing arts dir., 1969-70; comml. and pub. svcs. radio-TV interviewee, reader, lectr., 1961—; prof. English, dir. writing Marshall U., Huntington, W.Va., 1968-70; Title I Writing Arts dir. W.Va., 1969-70. Vis. prof., Fulbright grantee, vis. Am. specialist Damascus U., 1963-64; disting. vis. lectr. contemporary lit., cons. SUNY, Albany, 1977-78; reader, lectr. USIS Libr., Damascus, Syria, 1963-64; innovator, dir., devel. writers confs. for creative growth in several nat., regional and urban contexts, 1964—; pres., pub., exec. dir. Harian Creative Books, Ballston Spa, N.Y., 1967—; cons. Bantam Books, Random House, 1967, 69-70, Nat. Found. for Arts, Nat. Found. for Humanities, U.S. Dept. Edn., N.Y. State Coun. Arts, N.Y. State Edn. Dept., Poets & Writers, Inc., Harvard U., others; pres. several instns., 1963—, founding pres. and socially functional writer; founder, dir. Skidmore's Writers and Educator's Conf., 1967, Workshop Under the Sky, 1970—. Author: For the Grape Season, 1960, 3 By Harry Barba, 1967, 3 X 3, 1969, The Case for Socially Functional Education, Art and Culture, 1970—74, One of A Kind (The Many Faces and Voices of America), 1976, The Day the World Went Sane, 1979; author: (compiled and co-edited with Marian Barba) (series) What's Cooking in Congress? A Congressional Smorgasbord of Recipes, 1979, 1983; author: Gospel According to Everyman, 1981, Round Trip to Byzantium, 1985 (Pulitzer prize nominee, 1985), When the Deep Purple Falls, a Story (PEN Syndicated Fiction award, 1985); author: (co-published with Princeton U. Press) Mona Lisa Smiles, 1993; reviewer: plays Three Plays by William Saroyan; author: The Nightingale Sings. Founder, dir. Skidmore Coll. Writers and Educators Conf., 1967, Adirondack-Metroland Writers and Educators Conf., 1967—. Grad. fellow U. Iowa, 1961-62, Yaddo residence fellow, 1950, Macdowell Colony residence fellow, 1970, World's Hall of Fame in Lit., 1997—, Guggenheim fellow, 1989-90; Skidmore rsch. grantee, 1965-68, N.Y. State coun. Arts grantee, 1971, U. Benedeum grantee, 1969; established Harian Creative awards for fiction, poetry, essays, mus. compositions, photography and graphic arts, 1973; chair in his name World Acad. Letters, 2004. Mem. MLA, Coll. English Assn., Authors Guild, Writers Union PEN, Com. Small Press Editors and Pubs., Harvard Grad. Soc. Advanced Study and Rsch., Harvard Alumni Assn., Harvard Club N.Y. (dir. 1975-79). Achievements include writing and educating for the mainstreaming of Am.'s multiple ethnic, religious, and racial groups, and for increasing the authority of the UN. Home and Office: 47 Hyde Blvd Ballston Spa NY 12020-1607 Office Phone: 518-885-6699.

BARBA, JULIUS WILLIAM, lawyer; b. Arlington, N.J., May 22, 1923; s. John and Rose (Lettiere) B.; m. Susan Vartanian, Oct. 24, 1970; children: Susan Elizabeth, Christina Barba. BA, Princeton U., 1947; LLB, U. Pa., 1950. Bar: N.J. 1950, N.Y. 1981, U.S. Supreme Ct. 1959, U.S. Ct. Appeals (D.C. cir.) 1960, U.S. Dist. Ct. D.C. 1969, U.S. Ct. Appeals (2d cir.) 1973. Assoc. Young, Shanley, Foehl, Congleton & Fisher, Newark, 1950-54; asst. spl. counsel to Pres. Eisenhower, Washington, 1954-57; ptnr. Shanley & Fisher, P.C., Morristown, 1957—; bd. dirs. Selective Ins. Group, Inc., Branchville, N.J., 1983. Bd. trustees Peck Sch., Morristown, N.J., 1982, Kent Place Sch., Summit, N.J.; mem. membership corp. Morristown Meml. Hosp., 1979, trustee, 1984; chmn. N.J. State Fin. Com., 1974-76; bd. dirs. Atlantic Health Systems, Inc. Served to lt. (j.g.) USNR, 1943-46, PTO. Mem. ABA, N.J. State Bar Assn., D.C. Bar Assn., Morris County Bar Assn., Essex County Bar Assn. Republican. Roman Catholic. Clubs: Met. (Washington); Baltusrol Golf (Springfield, N.J.), Morris County Golf (Convent, N.J.); Shinnecock Hills Golf (Southampton, N.Y.). Home: Long Hill Rd New Vernon NJ 07976 Office: Shanley & Fisher PC 131 Madison Ave Morristown NJ 07960-6086

BARBADORO, PAUL JAMES, federal judge; b. Providence, June 4, 1955; s. Donald James and Elizabeth B.; m. Inez E. McDermott, Aug. 16, 1986; children: Katherine E., John James. BA cum laude, Gettysburg Coll., 1977; JD magna cum laude, Boston Coll., 1980. Bar: N.H. 1980. Asst. atty. gen. N.H. Atty. Gen., Concord, 1980-84; legal counsel U.S. Sen. Warren B. Rudman, Washington, 1984-86, Orr & Reno, Concord, 1986-87; dep. chief counsel U.S. Senate Iran-Contra Com., Washington, 1987; dir. Rath, Young, Pignatelli and Oyer, Concord, 1987-92; judge U.S. Dist. Ct., Concord, 1992—, chief judge, 1997—2004. Mem. adv. group for dist. of N.H., Civil Justice Reform Act, Concord, 1992-94; mem. long range planning com. N.H. Supreme Ct., 1989-90; mem. 1st Cir. Jud. Coun., 1994-96, 2005—, jud. conf. com. on automation and tech., 1996-2001; adj. prof. Franklin Pierce Law Ctr., 1997-98. Mem. N.H. Bar Assn. (chmn. unauthorized practice of law com. 1982-84, com. on cooperation with the cts. 1997—), U.S. Dist. Ct. N.H. Bar, 1st Cir. Ct. Appeals Bar, Order of Coif. Office: WB Rudman Courthouse 55 Pleasant St Rm 409 Concord NH 03301-3938

BARBAGALLO, JOSEPH C., small business owner; b. Lawrence, Mass., June 18, 1943; s. Joseph Mario and Katherine Barbagallo; m. Phyllis Kathleen Manzi, Feb. 22, 1969; children: Derek Shane, Joseph Thomas. BSEE, U. Mass., Lowell, 1966. Sales Manzi Dodge, Lowell, Panasonic, NJ; mfg. rep. W. B. Mktg., Woburn, Mass.; owner Belmont Provision, Lowell, Colony Foods, Lawrence, Mass. Facilitator engring. sem. U. Mass., Lowell, 1999—2003. Mem. U. Mass. Lowell Found., 2000—. Capt. USAF. Recipient Alumni award, U. Mass., Lowell, 2001. Mem.: Lawrence C. of C., Lowell Lions Club. Roman Catholic. Avocations: reading, poetry, travel. Home: 47 Belmont Ave Lowell MA 01852 Office: Colony Foods 439 Haverhill St Lawrence MA 01841

BARBAGELATA, ROBERT DOMINIC, lawyer; b. San Francisco, Jan. 9, 1925; s. Dominic Joseph and Jane Zeffra (Frugoli) B.; m. Doris V. Chatfield, June 8, 1956; children: Patricia Victoria, Robert Norman, Michael Alan. BS, U. San Francisco, 1947, JD, 1950. Bar: Calif. bar 1950, U.S. Supreme Ct. bar 1964. Pvt. practice, San Francisco, 1950—; judge pro-tem San Francisco County Superior Ct., 1992-95. Lectr. U. San Francisco Law Sch., Pacific Med. Center. Contbr. to legal jours. Served with USNR, 1943-46. Mem. Calif. State Bar, Calif. Trial Lawyers Assn. (lectr., v.p.), Am. Bd. Trial Advocates (nat. pres. 1981-82, Trial Lawyer of Yr. 1986-87, San Francisco chpt. Pres. Don E. Bailey Professionalism award 2003, Lifetime Achievement award 2004, 05), Assn. Trial Lawyers Am., San Francisco Trial Lawyers Assn. (Lifetime Achievement award 2003), Am. Coll. Trial Lawyers, Internat. Soc. Barristers, San Francisco Lawyers Club. Roman Catholic. Home: 819 Holly Rd Belmont CA 94002-2214 Office: 109 Geary St San Francisco CA 94108-5632

BARBAN, ARNOLD MELVIN, advertising executive, educator, writer; b. San Antonio, Sept. 17, 1932; s. Sam and Ida Dollie B.; m. Barbara Marie Fox, June 2, 1955; children: Polly Gwen, Pamela Florence. BBA, U. Tex., 1955, MBA, 1959, PhD, 1964. Asst. to v.p. Joske's of Tex., San Antonio, 1955-56; asst. prof. U. Houston, 1959-64; from asst. prof. to prof. in communications U. Ill., Urbana, 1964-83; prof. U. Tex., Austin, 1983-87; prof. advt. U. Ala., Tuscaloosa, 1987-2000, chmn. advt. and pub. rels. dept., 1992-97, prof. emeritus, 2000—. Rsch. prof. communications dept. U. Ill., 1972-83, head advt. dept., 1978-83; cons. Gulf Oil Corp., Houston, 1962, 64, Farm Rsch. Inst., Urbana, 1965-83, Dept. Def., Ft. Sheridan, Ill., 1984; cons. editor Grid Pub. Co., Columbus, Ohio, 1974-84. Author: Readings in Advertising and Promotion Strategy, 1968, Essentials of Media Planning, 1987, 3d edit., 1993, Advertising Media Sourcebook, 4th edit., 1997, Advertising: Its Role in Modern Marketing, 8th edit., 1994, Advertising Media: Strategy and Tactics, 1992, Advertising Campaign Strategy, 1996; editor U. Houston Bus. Rev., 1962-64; cons. editor Jour. Advt., 1979-81; mem. editl. rev. bd. Jour. Current Issues and Rsch. in Advt., 1980-2001, Jour. Advt., 1983-88, 91-94; contbr. articles to profl. jours. Cons. Democratic congl. campaign, Champaign, Ill., 1972. Sgt. U.S. Army, 1956-58. Recipient Outstanding Svc. award Houston Advt. Club, 1964, disting. svc. award Dicionary Internat. Biography, Cambridge, England; fellow U. Tex., Austin, 1960, 1962, Am. Acad. Advt., 1986. Fellow Am. Acad. Advt. (pres. 1981-82, Sandy award 1997). Home: 136 N Stallion Estates Dr Spring Branch TX 78070 Office Phone: 830-885-6878. E-mail: barban@gvtc.com.

BARBARIN, OSCAR ANTHONY, psychologist; b. New Orleans, July 25, 1945; s. Oscar Anthony and Inez M. (Molison) B. AB, St. Joseph's Sem., Washington, 1968; MA, NYU, 1971; PhD in Psychology, Rutgers U., 1975. Dir. community field sta. U. Md., College Park, 1974-79; assoc. prof. U. Mich., Ann Arbor, 1979-2000, dir. family devel. project, 1981-96, prof. psychology and social work, 1990-2000, dir. ctr. for the child and the family, 1992-94, exec. dir. South Africa Initiative, 1996-2000; Preyer disting. prof. social work, fellow Porter Graham Child Devel. Ctr., U. N.C., Chapel Hill, 2000—. Author: Childhood Cancer and the Family, 1987, Mandela's Children, 2000. Fellow APA, Am. Orthopsychiat. Assn. (bd. dirs., pres. 2001—); mem. Assn. of Black Psychologists (life). Office: Frank Porter Granan Child Devel Inst 517 South Greensboro St Carrboro NC 27510-8040

BARBAROSH, CRAIG A., lawyer; b. Bklyn., Aug. 13, 1967; BA, Univ. Calif., Santa Barbara, 1989; JD with distinction, Univ. of the Pacific, 1992. Bar: Calif. 1992, US Ct. Appeals (9th cir.). Extern law clk. Judge James N. Barr, US Bankruptcy Ct, ctrl. dist. Calif.; ptnr., co-chmn. Insolvency & Restructuring practice, office mng. ptnr. Pillsbury Winthrop Shaw Pittman, Orange County, Calif. Editor (articles): Univ. of the Pacific Law Rev. Named an Outstanding Young Bankruptcy Lawyer, Turnarounds & Workouts mag.; named one of Top 20 Lawyers Under Age 40, Daily Jour. Calif. Law Bus.; recipient CLAY Lawyer of the Year award, Calif. Lawyer mag., 2001. Mem.: Am. Bankruptcy Inst., Calif. Bankruptcy Forum, Orange County Bankruptcy Forum, Orange County Bar Assn., Order of the Coif. Office: Pillsbury Winthrop Shaw Pittman 7th Fl 650 Town Center Dr Costa Mesa CA 92626 Office Phone: 714-436-6822. Office Fax: 714-436-2800. Business E-Mail: craig.barbarosh@pillsburylaw.com.

BARBATO, ANTHONY, educational association administrator, medical educator; BA, U. Windsor; MD, Stritch Sch. Medicine, Loyola U. Chgo. Cert. bd. cert. Am. Bd. Internal Medicine, Am. Bd. Endocrinology and Metabolism. Asst. prof. Stritch Sch. Medicine, Maywood, Ill., 1976—81, assoc. prof., 1981—86, prof. of medicine, 1986—; exec. v.p., health affairs Loyola U. Health Sys., Maywood, Ill., provost, health affairs, chief admin. officer, health affairs, v.p., health affairs; dean Stritch Sch. Medicine, Maywood, Ill., exec. dean, asst. chmn., medicine for post-grad. edn., program dir., internal medicine residency; pres. Loyola U. Health Sys., 1995—; prof. medicine Stritch Sch. Medicine, 1995—. Chmn. Assoc. Academic Health Ctrs., 2000; sr. health policy adv. com. Rep. Danny Davis. Office: 2160 S First Ave Maywood IL 60153

BARBE, BETTY CATHERINE, marketing professional, retired financial analyst; b. Chgo., Dec. 24, 1930; d. Norbert Lambert and Helen Weishaar; m. Edward William, Aug. 8, 1953; children: Leonard Walter, Roger Andrew. Student, U. Toledo, 1970, 85. Acct. Gorr Printing, Allstate Ins., Muntz TV, Chgo., 1947-53; hostess Welcome Wagon Internat., Maumee, Ohio, 1965-70; v.p. sec., cost acctg. Craftmaster, Toledo, 1970-72; sec., estimator Grinnell Fire Protection, Toledo, 1972-73; exec. sec., payroll Crow, Inc. Aviation, 1973-77; asst. city clk., payroll City of Perrysburg, 1977-83, tax adminstr., 1983-98, ret., 1998; mktg. exec. Melaleuca, Inc. The Wellness Co., 2003—. Sec., vice chair Ohio Women's Policy and Rsch. Commn.; mem. adv. coun. Ohio Bicentennial Commn.; reading coach Evening St. Sch., Park Elem. Sch., Bluffsview Elem. Sch., 2001; active Big Sisters of Toledo, 1979, YWCA; vol. New Albany LPGA Golf Classic, Jamie Farr LPGA Golf Classic, Worthington Rep. Women's Club, 1999, Ptnrs. for Citizenship and Character; tutor Ohio Reads. Paul Harris fellow Dublin-Worthington Rotary, Rookie Rotarian of Yr., 1999-00; honoree Maumee Valley coun. Girl Scouts U.S., 1990; named Woman of Yr., Bus. and Profl. Women Black Swamp Region II. Mem. Internat. Inst., Nat. Notary Assn., Nat. Fedn. Bds. and Profl. Women, Key to the Sea Bus. and Profl. Womens Orgn. (pres. 1982-84), Maumee Bus. and Profl. Women (pres. 1995-97), Maumee Valley Toastmasters (pres. 1989—, area gov.), Toledo Opera Soc. Assn., Two Toledos (sec., 1st v.p.), Christ Child Soc., Maumee C. of C. (sec.), Samagama Club, Zonta II (treas.), Maumee Valley Historical Soc., Rotary (sec. Dublin-Worthington chpt.). Republican.

Roman Catholic. Avocations: football, reading, sewing, crafts, travel. Home: 806 Drummond Ct Columbus OH 43214 Office: Melaleuca Inc Wellness Co 3910 So Yellowstone Hwy Idaho Falls ID 83402-6003 Personal E-mail: babybarby4@aol.com.

BARBE, DAVID FRANKLIN, electrical engineer, educator; b. Webster Springs, W.Va., May 26, 1939; s. Damon and Mary K. (Cooper) Barbe; m. Irene Theresa Barbe; children: John David, Jane Suzanne. BSEE with high honors, W.Va. U., 1962, MSEE, 1964; PhD in Elec. Engring., Johns Hopkins U., 1969. Instr. elec. engring. W.Va. U., Morgantown, 1962-65; fellow engr. Westinghouse Advanced Tech. Lab, Balt., 1965-71; head functional devices sect. Electronics divsn. Naval Rsch. Lab., Washington, 1971-74, head microelectronics br., 1974-79, asst. electronics and phys. scis., 1979-83; dir. Submarine and ASW Programs Submarine and ASW Sys., Office Sec. of Navy, 1983-85; prof. elec. and computer engring. U. Md., College Park, 1985—, assoc. dir. Md. Tech. Enterprise Inst., 1985-87, exec. dir. Md. Tech. Enterprise Inst., 1987—, interim dir., assoc. dean engring., 1999—2001, exec. dir., 2001—. Mem. adv. group electron devices Dept. Def., 1971—79, 1987—90; mem. steering com. Internat. Conf. Charge-Coupled Devices, Edinburgh, 1974, Edinburgh, 76, San Diego, 75; lectr. 1st Internat. NATO Congress Charge-Coupled Devices U. Louvain-La Neuve, Belgium, 1975; mem. program com. Internat. Solid State Circuits Conf., 1993—; pres. Elec. Engring. Acad. W.Va. U., 1995—97; faculty dir. Hinman Campus Entrepreneurship Opportunities Program, 2000—. Contbr. articles on electronics and tech. entrepreneurship to profl. jours. Recipient Dept. Def. award, 1979, Very High Speed Integrated Circuits Pioneer award, 1987, Disting. Alumni award, Elec. and Engring. Acad., W.Va. U., 1990. Fellow: IEEE (assoc. editor Electron Devices Newsletter 1975—79, adminstrv. com. Electron Devices Soc. 1977—83, nat. lectr. 1987—88, awards bd. 1990—94); mem.: Soc. Photographic and Instrumentation Engrs., Am. Soc. Engring. Edn. (Outstanding Entrepreneurship Educator award 2003, pres. entrepreneurship divsn. 2005—), Eta Kappa Nu (charter mem.), Tau Beta Pi. Home: 6532 Burgundy Ln Clarksville MD 21029-2600 Office: U Md Md Tech Enterprise Inst Potomac Bldg College Park MD 20742-0001 Office Phone: 301-405-3902. Business E-Mail: dbarbe@umd.edu.

BARBE, WALTER BURKE, education educator; b. Miami, Fla., Oct. 30, 1926; s. Victor Elza and Edith (Burris) B.; m. Marilyn E. Wood, Feb. 7, 1967; 1 child, Frederick Walter. BS, Northwestern U., 1949, MA, 1950, PhD, 1953. Tchr. Dade County Bd. Pub. Instrn., 1947; asst. Psycho-Ednl. Clinic Northwestern U., 1949-50; instr. psychology, dir. reading clinic Baylor U., 1950; asst. prof. elementary edn. Kent State U., 1952-53, prof., head spl. edn. dept., 1960-64; adj. prof. U. Pitts., 1964-72, Ohio State U., 1972-89; pub. Modern Learning Press, 1997—; prof. Keystone Coll., 2001—. Editor Highlights for Children, 1964-92, bd. dir.; prof. edn., bd. dir. Jr. League Reading Center, U. Chattanooga, 1953-59; bd. dir. Zaner-Bloser; bd. dirs. internat. council Improvement of Reading Inst.; prof. Keystone Coll., 2001-02. Author: Reading Clinic Directory, 1955, (with Ralph Roberts) Teenage Tales, 1957, (with Dorothy Hinman) We Build Our Words, 1957, Educators Guide to Personalized Reading, 1961, Helping Children Read Better, 1970; sr. author: (with Paul Witty) Creative Growth with Handwriting Series, 1975, Personalized Reading Instruction: New Techniques that Increase Reading Skill and Comprehension, 1975, (with Jerry Abbott) Barbe Reading Skills Check Lists, 1975, (with Swassing and Milone) Teaching through Modality Strengths: Concepts and Practices, 1979; sr. editor: (with Joseph Renzulli) Psychology and Education of the Gifted: Readings, 3d edit, 1980, Basic Skills in Kindergarten, 1980, Resource Book for Kindergarten Teachers, 1980, (with Kurt Reed) The Glass Industry in Wayne County, PA, 1802 to Present, 2003; editor: Teaching of Reading; Selections, 1965, (with Edward Frierson) Educating Children with Learning Disabilities, 1967, Compass Points in Literature, Searchlights in Literature, 1969, Helping Children with Special Needs Series, 1974; author: (with Francis, Braun) Spelling: Basic Skills for Effective Communication, 1982, (with Lucas, Wasylyk) Basic Skills for Effective Communication, 1984, (with others) Handwriting: Basic Skills and Application Series, 1984, Growing Up Learning, 1985, (with Francis, Gentry, San Jose) Spelling Connections: Words Into Language, 1988, (with others) Reading and Study Skills Mastery, 1996, (with others) Vocabulary, Word Analysis and Comprehension, 1996, Some Folks Like Cats and Other Poems, 2002, I Asked a Tiger to Tea and Other Poems, 2002. Chair exec. com. bd. dirs. Dorflinger-Suydam Wildlife Sanctuary, 1992—. With AUS, 1944-46. Fellow Am. Psychol. Assn.; mem. Nat. Assn. Gifted Children (pres. 1958), Touchstone Applied Sci. Assn. (bd. dirs. 1997—), Internat. Reading Assn. (Disting. Svc. award 1992). Democrat. Presbyterian. Address: 214 9th St Honesdale PA 18431-1911 Personal E-mail: waltco@ezaccess.net.

BARBEE, ELSIE ANN, artist; b. Nashville, Dec. 5, 1932; d. Harry Amos Gardner and Nora Bell Clark; m. Claude Gene Barbee, June 8, 1951; children: C.G. Jr., Ava Leigh Thompson, Andrew Clark. Student, David Lipscomb U., 1950—51, Austin Peay U., 1970—71, U. Tenn., 1971—72; studied with, Bruce Corban, 1978—84. Bookkeeper Rick Schwartz, Nashville, 1951—52; tchr. Adairville (Ky.) H.S., 1953—63; organizer, Wedding Chapel, Springfield, Tenn., 1988—94; owner Barbee Artworks, Springfield, 1994—. Exhibited in group shows at Falls Creek Falls, 1993 (Pennyrite award, 93), South Ctrl. Art Show at the Parthanon (1st pl. awards). Mem.: Women in the Arts, Tenn. Art Works. Mem. Ch. Of Christ. Avocations: cooking, reading, flower arranging, teaching art classes. Office: Elsie Barbee's Art Works Mount Juliet TN 37122

BARBEE, MARY KEENUM, clergywoman; b. North Kansas City, Mo., June 15; d. John Carroll Keenum and Virginia E. Garton Runyon; m. David E. Barbee, Aug. 30, 1956 (div. May 1983); children: Mark, Mike, Midge, Eric. BA, U. No. Colo., 1959; MA, U. N.Mex., 1983; student, So. Meth. U. Cert. assn. exec.; ordained minister United Meth. Ch., 1992. Tchr. Roaring Fork Schs., Basalt, Colo., 1962-63; bus. owner The Peppermint Tree, Aspen, Colo., 1963-69; asst. dean students U. N.Mex., Albuquerque, 1978-88; exec. dir. Pi Lambda Theta, Bloomington, Ind., 1988-89, Nat. Interfrat. Found., Indpls., 1989—98; minister United Meth. Ch., Cody, Wyo., 1999—. Mem. Sigma Sigma Sigma (nat pres. 2001-04). Home: PO Box 788 Aspen CO 81612-0788 Office: PO Box 1416 Cody WY 82414

BARBER, BEN BERNARD ANDREW, journalist; b. Warwick, Eng., May 2, 1944; came to U.S., 1948; s. Stephen S. and Miriam (Idler) B.; m. Risa Richman (div. Apr. 1982); children: Karen Cloud, Forest; m. Nognoy Pinsanoa, Apr. 23, 1983 (div. Feb. 2000); children: Stephanie, Natalie. Cert. in French lang. and civilization, Sorbonne U., Paris, 1964; BA, Trinity Coll., Hartford, Conn., 1964; cert. in Asian studies, Gannett fellow, U. Hawaii, 1987; MJ, Boston U., 1979. Reporter Middlesex News, Framingham, Mass., 1979; free-lance reporter Miami (Fla.) Herald, Boston Globe, Balt. Sun, Toledo Blade, San Francisco Examiner, London Observer, Newsweek, Network News Svc., San Diego Union, Omni mag., MacLean's mag., L'Actualite, Atlantic mag.; Miami corr. USA Today, 1983-86; internat. desk editor United Press Internat., 1989-90; policy analyst Refugee Policy Group, 1991-92; correspondent Sunday Age, Melbourne, Australia; state dept. corr. The Washington Times, 1994—2003; sr. writer/editor U.S. AID, 2003—. Trainer journalism workshops U.S. Info. Agy., Africa; adj. prof. Sch. Fgn. Svc., Georgetown U., 1999. Contbr. articles to profl. jours. Jewish. Avocation: international travel. Office: US AID 1300 Pennsylvania Ave NW Washington DC 20523 Office Phone: 202-712-1000.

BARBER, BERNARD BRADLEY, academic administrator, lawyer; b. Fresno, Calif., June 19, 1946; s. Bernard Bode Barber and Therese Elaine Camy; m. Cynthia Jeanne Barber, Aug. 23, 1987; children: Katharine, Jeanne, Anne Marie. AB in History, U. Calif., Berkeley, 1968; JD, U. Calif., 1971. Bar: Calif. 1972. Asst. to vice-chancellor U. Calif., Berkeley, 1971-74; atty. Brobeck, Phleger, et al, San Francisco, 1974-78; dir. planned giving Tulane U., New Orleans, 1978-81; asst. chancellor U. Calif., San Francisco, 1981-83; v.p. legal U. Calif. Berkeley Found., 1984-94; asst. vice chancellor, devel. U. Calif., Berkeley, 1991-94; asst. v.p. instnl. advancement Office of Pres. U. Calif. Sys., Oakland, 1994—. Mem. U. Calif. Trust, London; trustee Los Alamos Nat. Lab. Found., Santa Fe, N.Mex. Mem. Phi Beta Kappa. Office: U Calif 1111 Franklin St Oakland CA 94607 E-mail: brad.barber@ucop.edu.

BARBER, CHARLES EDWARD, publishing executive, journalist; b. Miami, Fla., Oct. 30, 1939; s. James Plemon and Margaret Katherine (Grimes) B. m. Judith Margaret Tuck, May 28, 1960 (dec.); children: Janet Lynn Wood, Christopher Edward AA, Santa Fe Community Coll., 1971. Prodn. mgr. dept. student publs. U. Fla., Gainesville, 1966-68, ops. mgr., 1968-70, asst. dir., 1970-72, dir. div. publs., 1974; prodn. mgr. State Univ. System Press, Gainesville, 1975-76; pres., gen. mgr. Campus Communications, Inc., Gainesville, 1976—. Pres. The Herald Pub. Co., Inc., 1990—, Tuck Barber & Assocs., 1995—; pub. The High Springs Herald, 1990—; dir. Campus Press; cons. in field. Co-author: (with Judy Barber) screenplay This Small Island, 1989; adv. editor Fla. Quar., 1973-74; contbr. articles to profl. jours. Mem. citizens adv. coun. Stephen Foster Elem. Sch., Gainesville, 1976-77, Santa Fe H.S., 1991, Spring Hill Mid. Sch., 1992; mem. Friends of Five, 1975-77, Friends of Libr., 1975-77; mem. Fla. Newspaper Oral History Project, 1996—; chmn. book com. Fla. State Prison, 1973-85, 89-94; bd. dirs. Gainesville H.S. Band Boosters, 1978-79, 83-84, treas., 1984; key communicator Alachua County Sch. Bd., 1980-91, judge countywide spelling bee, 1997-2004; spl. registered dep. sheriff Alachua County Sheriff's Dept., 1979-92, Monroe County Sheriff's Dept., 1997—; mem. gifted students boosters Howard Bishop Mid. Sch., 1980-82; dir. Howard Bishop Band Boosters, 1980-82; mem. pres.'s coun. U. Fla., 1978—; mem. Leadership Gainesville, 1979, Leadership Fla., 1997—; mentor Coll. Leadership Fla., U. Fla. English Lang. Inst., 1998-2001; mem. steering com. Fla. Alliance for Better Campaigns, chair regional coalition, 1998; mem. Fla. Correct Ct. Com. for 2000 Census, 1998-2000; pack com. chmn. Cub Scouts Am., 1977-78; dir. The Prevention Partnership, 1992-94, Hippodrome State Theatre, 1992-95, bd. advisors. With USCGR, 1957-65. Recipient Nat. 1st pl. for Editl. Writing Hearst Found., 1965, Svc. award Santa Fe C.C., 1982, Cert. of Appreciation Big Bros. and Big Sisters of Gainesville, 1984, Vols. for Internat. Student Affairs, 1986, 88, 89, 90, Fla. Track Club, 1988, U. Fla. Divsn. Housing, 1990, 91, Addy award Gainesville Advt. Fedn., 1986, 87, 2003, Gold Addy, Fla. and Caribbean Dist., 2003; Recognition for Cold War Svc. U.S. Sec. Def.; named to Ind. Fla. Alligator Hall of Fame, 1996. Mem.: Disting. Order of Gator, Soc. Profl. Journalists (treas. No. Fla. chpt. 1972—75, 1986—91, pres.'s club 1994—95, Helen Thomas award for lifetime achievement in journalism 2003), First Amendment Found (trustee 1999—2001), So. Univ. Newspapers (bd. dir. 1980—89), Soc. of News Design, New Media Fedn., Newspaper Assn. Am., Nat. Newspaper Assn. (H.M. for weekly newspaper promotion 1996), Col. Media Advisers, Internat. Newspapers Mktg. Assn., Internat. Newspapers Fin. Execs., Gainesville Advt. Fedn. (bd. dir. 1979—80, Addy award 1986), U. Fla. Coll. Journalism and Comm. (journalism adv. coun. 2000—), Foresight Inst., Fla. Bus. Leadership Network, Fla. Press Found (bd. trustees 2001—, 1st pl. award for newspaper promotion 1992, award for weekly newspaper advt. 1993, 1st pl. award for editl. writing 1994, 1st pl. award for weekly newspaper advt. 1994, Best of Show award weekly newspaper advt. 1994, 1st pl. award weekly newspaper promotion 1995, 1st pl. award for weekly newspaper cmty. svc. 1995, 3rd. pl. award weekly newspaper advt. 1996, 3rd pl. weekly newspaper promotion 1997, award of appreciation,US Census 2000), Fla. Press Assn. (bd. dir. 1992—2001, chmn. continuing edn. com. 1992—2001, v.p. 1997, pres. 1998, chmn. bd. dirs. 1999—2000, Award of Appreciation 1999, Award of Appreciation for 10 years Svc. on Bd. Dirs. 2001, 1st pl. award for Creative Use of Newspaper 2001), Fla. Newspaper Advt. and Mktg. Execs. (chmn. edn. com. 1984—87), Fla. Scholastic Press Assn. (newspaper judge 1981—85, Gold Medallion for svc. 2003), Coll. Newspaper Bus. and Advt. Mgrs. (bd. dir. 1980—81), Am. Advt. Fedn., Am. Collegiate Network (adv. com. 1989—91), Leadership Gainesville Alumni Assn., U. Fla. Nat. Alumni Assn., High Springs C. of C., Alachua C. of C., Gainesville Area C. of C., Alligator Alumni Assn. (bd. dir. 1980—, named Mr. Alligator 1986), Substance Abuse Prevention Partnership (coun. 1992—95), Am. Red Cross (bd. dir., N.Ctrl. Fla. chpt.), Red Herring Club, Nat. Press Club, Rotary Internat. (sustaining, sec. 1993—94, Paul Harris fellow), Alpha Phi Gamma. Office: Campus Comm Inc PO Box 14257 Gainesville FL 32604-2257

BARBER, DONALD GENE, JR., purchasing agent; b. Wimpole Park, Eng., Apr. 7, 1959; s. Donald Gene Barber and Carmel Maxine Adkins; m. Debbie Sue Lee, July 14, 1978; children: Donald Gene III, Debra Lee. Regents degree, Fairmont State Coll., W.Va., 1984. Cert. mgr. Inst. Cert. Profl. Mgrs., 2002, adminstrv. mgr. Inst. Cert. Profl. Mgrs., 2002. With USAF, 1977—89, advanced through grades to 1st lt., inventory mgmt. specialist (munitions) Minot Air Force Base, ND, 1977—81, supr., intercontinental ballistic missile reentry systems maintenance unit Vandenberg Air Force Base, Calif., 1985—87, munitions accountable systems officer, 1987—89; stores foreman Amoco Polymers, Marietta, Ohio, 1990—95; stores supr. James River Corp., Kalamazoo, 1995—95; purchasing mgr. Bosch Braking Systems, Frankfort, Ohio, 1997—98, sr. buyer Clarksville, Tenn., 1998—99; materials mgmt. team leader Potlatch Corp., Warren, Ark., 1999—2000; dir. Indsl. Am. LLC & MROLink Corp., Reston, Va., 2000—01; dir., mem. purchasing programs Packaging Machinery Mfrs. Inst., Arlington, Va., 2001—02; divsn. purchasing mgr. Innertech, a Divsn. of Intier Automotive Interiors of Am. Inc., Nashville, Ill., 2002—. Chmn. Mid-Ohio Valley Supplier Exhbn., Nat. Assn. of Purchasing Mgmt. - Mid-Ohio Valley Inc., Parkersburg, W.Va., 1983—84. Mem.: Am. Purchasing Soc. (cert. purchasing profl. 2002), APICS-The Ednl. Soc. for Resource Mgmt., Inst. for Supply Mgmt. (accredited purchasing practitioner 1999, cert. purchasing mgr. 2003), Am. Mensa Ltd (life), Air Force Assn. (life). Office: Intier Automotive 18355 Enterprise Ave Nashville IL 62263 Home: 12888 S Cir 8 Dr Okawville IL 62271 Office Phone: 618-327-5181. Office Fax: 618-327-9441. Personal E-mail: donbarber@donbarber.net. Business E-Mail: don.barber@intier.com.

BARBER, EARL EUGENE, management consultant; b. Dayton, Ohio, Dec. 8, 1939; s. Earl Garnet and Mary Helen (Brown) Barber; m. Sandra Kay Reese, Mar. 11, 1960; children: Steven, Amy, Dana. BS, Ball State U., 1963; MDiv, Asbury Theol. Sem., Wilmore, Ky., 1977. Tchr. Muncie (Ind.) Cmty. Schs, 1963-65; exec. mem. GM, Muncie, 1965-73; pres. Barber Electric, Wilmore, 1973-77; sr. pastor Calvary Temple, Plainview, Tex., 1977-79; exec. Borg Warner Corp., Muncie, 1979-84; COO Barber Cons. Resources, Muncie, 1984—. Author: Statistical Process Control for the Worker, 1985, Statistical Process Control: The Basic Tools, 1986, Team Leader Training, 1989, Problem Solving, 1992, 1996, Understanding SPC for Short Production Runs, 1990, Total Quality Management, 1991, Team Building, 1992, Problem Solving, 1994, Time Management, 1995. Mem. Mayor's Task Force, Muncie, 1980. Mem.: Am. Soc. Quality Control (sustaining mem., Ptnrs. award for Quality 1989), Delaware County Ministerial Assn., Epsilon Pi Tau. Republican. Methodist. Avocations: writing, music, boating. Office: Barber Cons Resources Inc 4501 N Wheeling Ave Unit 9B-2 Muncie IN 47304-6028

BARBER, ELAINE T. See FUDA, SIRI NARAYAN K.K.

BARBER, GARY, motion picture company executive; Chief oper. officer Morgan Creek Prodns., L.A.; pres. Morgan Creek Internat., L.A. Exec. prodr. (films) Midnight Crossing, 1988, Communion, 1989, Young Guns II, 1990, Pacific Heights, 1990, Robin Hood: Prince of Thieves, 1991, Freejack, 1992, White Sands, 1992, Stay Tuned, 1992, The Crush, 1993, True Romance, 1993, Major League II, 1994, Ace Ventura, Pet Detective, 1994, Trial by Jury, 1994, Imaginary Crimes, 1994, Chasers, 1994, Silent Fall, 1944, Ace Ventura, When Nature Calls, 1995, Two if by Sea, 1996. Office: Morgan Creek Prodns 4000 Warner Blvd Bldg 76 Burbank CA 91522-0001

BARBER, JAMES ALDEN, navy officer, educator; b. Poplar Bluff, Mo., May 6, 1934; s. James Alden and Ellamay (Morris) B.; m. Beverly June Kingsbury, June 12, 1955; children: Judith Lynn Barber Joyce, Steven Alden, Susan Barber Blackwell. BA in Econs., U. So. Calif., 1955; MA in Econs., Vanderbilt U., 1960; MA in Internat. Rels., Stanford U., 1964, PhD in Polit. Sci., 1965. Commd. ensign USN, 1955, advanced through grades to capt., 1975; comdg. officer USS Hissem, 7th Fleet, Vietnam, 1966-68; Stephen B. Luce Prof. Naval Strategy US Naval War Coll., Newport, RI, 1968-71; comdg. officer USS Schofield, 7th Fleet, Vietnam, 1971-72; exec. asst. under sec. Navy Washington, 1975-76; comdg. officer USS Horne, 7th Fleet, 1977-79; dep. dir. Politico-Mil. Affairs, Navy Dept., Washington, 1979-82; dep. dir., sr. fellow Strategic Concepts Devel. Ctr., Washington, 1982-84; CEO, pub. US Naval Inst., Annapolis, Md., 1984-99; sr. lectr. sys. mgmt. US Naval Postgrad. Sch., Annapolis, 1998—. Author: Social Mobility and Voting Behaviour, 1970, Naval Shiphandler's Guide, 2005; co-author: Military and American Society, 1972; contbr. articles to encys. and profl. jours. Decorated Bronze Star with combat V, Legion of Merit, also others; recipient Alfred Thayer Mahan award, US Navy League, 1971, Meritorious Pub. Svc. award USCG, 1999, Dist. Pub. Svc. award Dept. Navy, 2000. Mem. Coun. Fgn. Rels., US Naval Inst., Interuniv. Seminar Armed Forces Soc., Naval Inst. Found., U.S. Naval Acad. Found., U.S. Naval Sailing Assn., NY Yacht Club. Democrat. Presbyterian. Avocations: gardening, book collecting, sailing. E-mail: jaldenb@aol.com.

BARBER, JANICE ANN, lawyer; b. Buffalo, May 30, 1947; d. Warren Richard and Betty A. (Stabler) B. BA with high distinction, U. Ky., 1969; JD cum laude, SUNY, Buffalo, 1977. Bar: N.Y. 1978, U.S. Dist. Ct. (we. dist.) N.Y. 1978, U.S. Supreme Ct., 1994. Reporter The Times-Union, Rochester, N.Y., 1969-74; assoc. Smith, Murphy & Schoepperle, Buffalo, 1977-84, ptnr., 1985-95, Brown & Tarantino, LLC, 1995—; lectr. Sch. Law SUNY, Buffalo, 2004—. Lectr., adj. faculty SUNY Buffalo Law Sch., 2004—. Warden Episcopal Ch. of the Good Shepherd, 2001-2004; bd. dir. Parkside Cmty. Assn., 1996—, v.p. 2004—, Pro-Zoo, Buffalo Zoo, 2000-01, AAUW Buffalo Br., 2005- Mem. N.Y. State Bar Assn., Erie County Bar Assn., Audubon Soc., Roycrofters (life), Buffalo Olmsted Conservancy, Preservation Coalition of Buffalo and Erie Co. (trustee 2003-05), 20th Century Club, Phi Beta Kappa Democrat. Episcopalian. Home: 139 Woodward Ave Buffalo NY 14214-2311 Office Phone: 716-849-6500. E-mail: JanBfflo@cs.com, jbarber@btattys.com.

BARBER, JERRY RANDEL, medical device company executive; b. Killarney, W.Va., Sept. 23, 1940; s. Edward Clay and Nora (Mullins) B.; m. Carrolyn Rae Acree, June 9, 1964; 1 child, Alyssa Rae. BSChemE, W.Va. U., 1962; MSChemE, Ohio State U., 1964, PhD, 1968. Rsch. engr. Union Carbide Corp., South Charleston, W.Va., 1968-73, group leader rsch., 1973-77, assoc. dir. rsch., 1977-81, dir. rsch. Tarrytown, N.Y., 1981-89, dir. new bus. and tech. devel. Danbury, Conn., 1989-93; gen. mgr. Medisyn Techs., Corp., Las Vegas, Nev., 1993-94; mng. dir. Medisyn Techs. Ltd., Arklow, Ireland, 1994-97; exec. v.p. techs. McGhan Med. Corp., Santa Barbara, Calif., 1997-98; v.p. R & D Mentor Corp., Irving, Tex., 1998-2000, Santa Barbara, Calif., 2000—. Mem. AIChE, Am. Acad. Sci., Sigma Xi. Democrat. Methodist. Home: 2785 Poli St Ventura CA 93003-1556 Office: Mentor Corp 301 Mentor Dr Santa Barbara CA 93111-2360 Office Phone: 805-879-6616. Personal E-mail: jrbarber7@aol.com.

BARBER, LLOYD INGRAM, retired university president; b. Regina, Sask., Can., Mar. 8, 1932; s. Lewis Muir and Hildred (Ingram) B.; m. Muriel Pauline MacBean, May 12, 1956; children: Muir, Brian, Kathleen, David, Susan, Patricia. BA, U. Sask., 1953, B in Comm., 1954; MBA, U. Calif., Berkeley, 1955; PhD, U. Wash., 1964; LLD (hon.), U. Alta., 1983, Concordia U., 1984; postgrad., U. Regina, 1993. Hon. chartered acct. Instr. commerce U. Sask., 1955-57, asst. prof., 1957-64, assoc. prof., 1964-65, prof., 1965-68, 74-76, dean commerce, 1965-68, v.p., 1968-74; pres. U. Regina, Sask., prof. adminstrn., 1976-90; dir. Sask. Inst. for Pub. Policy, 2003—. Indian claims commr. Govt. of Can., 1969-76, hon. lt. col.; spl. inquirer for Elder Indian Testimony, 1977-81; bd. dirs. Bank of N.S., 1976-03, The Molson Cos., Teck-Cominco, N.W. Co. Ltd., 1990-02, Can. West Global Comm. Corp., Greystone Capital Mgmt. Inc.; cons. to bus. and govt.; hon. prof. Shandong U. Trustee Inst. Rsch. on Pub. Policy, 1972-79; bd. dirs. Indian Equity Found., 1978-79, Can. Scholarship Trust Fund, Regina United Way, 1977-79; past bd. dirs. Wascana Centre Authority; bd. dirs. Nat. Mus. Nature, Inst. Sask. Enterprise, Can. Polar Commn.; bd. dirs., past trustee Can. Scheneley Football Awards; adv. com. to Rector on pub. affairs award Concordia U., 1983; past mem. Northwest Territories Legis. Coun., 1967-70, Natural Sci. and Engring. Rsch. Coun. Officer Aboriginal Order of Can.; recipient Vanier medal, 1978; named hon. Sask. Indian Chief Little Eagle. Mem. Am. Inst. Pub. Adminstrn., Nat. Stats. Coun., Assn. Univs. and Colls. Can. (past pres.), Am. Econ. Assn., Can. Econ. Assn., Order of Can. (companion), Sask. Order of Merit, Assn. Commonwealth Univs. (coun.), Assiniboia Club, Regina Beach Yacht Club, Masons. Mem. United Ch. Office: PO Box 510 Regina SK Canada S0G 4C0 Office Phone: 306-729-2336. E-mail: barberl@uregina.ca.

BARBER, MALCOLM, auction house executive; Joined Sotheby's, London, 1969, mgr. Belgravia sales office then mgr. Bond Street sales office, 1972—80, with car dept., 1975—80, mgr. car dept., 1980—88, head internat. car dept., mng. dir. ops. Amsterdam, 1988—95; group mng. dir. Brooks Auctioneers, 1995—2000; CEO Bonhams & Butterfields, 2003—; group mng. dir. Bonhams Worldwide, 2003—. Office: Bonhams & Butterfields 220 San Bruno Ave San Francisco CA 94103

BARBER, MARK EDWARD, lawyer; b. Enumclaw, Wash., Dec. 30, 1952; s. Earl Marion Barber and Delila Mae Willis Lontz; m. Pamela Johnson, Aug. 30, 1974; 1 child, Matthew Edward. BA, U. Wash., 1975; JD, Pepperdine U., 1978. Bar: Wash. 1978, U.S. Dist. Ct. Wash. 1978, U.S. Ct. Appeals (9th cir.) 1980, U.S. Supreme Ct. 1985. Atty. Heavey & Woody, Inc. P.S., Seattle, 1978—79; sole practitioner Seattle, 1979—81; atty., prin. shareholder Warren Barber & Fontes, P.S., Renton, Wash., 1981—. Bd. dirs. Justice Polit. Action Com., Tacoma, 1993-95, Sunset Valley Farms Homeowners Assn., Issaquah, Wash., 1991-92, 95-96. Mem. ATLA, Wash. State Bar Assn., King County Bar Assn., Wash. State Trial Lawyers Assn. (pres. 1995-96). Office: Warren Barber et al 100 S 2nd St Renton WA 98055-2013 Office Phone: 425-255-8678. E-mail: mebarber@seanet.com.

BARBER, MARTHA GAYLE, lawyer; b. High Point, NC, Oct. 7, 1953; BA, Duke Univ., 1975; JD, Wake Forest Univ., 1981. Bar: NC 1982. Ptnr., chair, intellectual property-trademark, copyright group Alston & Bird LLP, Charlotte, NC. Frequent author, spkr. on trademark issues. Mem.: Internat. Trademark Assn. (bd. dir. 2000—03). Office: Alston & Bird LLP Ste 4000 Bank of Am Plz 101 S Tryon St Charlotte NC 28280-4000 Office Phone: 704-444-1018. Office Fax: 704-444-1111. Business E-Mail: mbarber@alston.com.

BARBER, RUSSELL BROOKS BUTLER, television producer; b. Nov. 11, 1934; s. Russell Brooks and Verga Merrill (Lesher) Butler. BA, U. Puget Sound, 1957; AM, Stanford U., 1959; PhD, Northwestern U., 1963. Exec. prodr. Sta. WCBS-TV, N.Y.C., 1964-71; religion editor Sta. WNBC-TV, N.Y.C., 1973-90, media lectr., 1993—. Adj. prof. pub. comm. Nova Southeastern U., Ft. Lauderdale, Fla., 2002—. Author: Among First Patriots, 1976. Advisor Templeton Found., London, 1976—; dir. Coun. Chs. N.Y.C., 1979—; mem. comms. com. Am. Cancer Soc. N.Y., N.Y.C., 1978—, N.Y.C. Mission Soc., 1979—, Laymen's Nat. Bible Com., N.Y.C., 1983—, Conn. Diocese Episcopal Ch., Hartford, 1984—, media cons., prodr., host Diocese Armenian Ch. of Am., 1992—; established Barber Scholars, U. Puget Sound, Tacoma, 1978—, Nat. Lecture Tours on Media; bd. dirs. Inst. for Religion & Pub. Policy, Washington, D.C., 1998—. Recipient Faith and Freedom award Religious Heritage Am., St. Louis, 1982, Emmy awards NATAS, N.Y.C., 1984, 85, 88, U. Thant Peace award UN Peace Meditation, 1986, Gabriel award Nat. Cath. Assn. for Broadcasters and Communicators, 1987, Trisccort award Roman Cath. Ch., 1988, Nat. Cmty. Svc. award, U. Puget Sound, 2003; named Knight Comdr. Order St. John of Jerusalem, N.Y.C., 1985. Mem. NATAS, World Assn. Christian Comms. Home: Oasis Tower 434 180 Isle of Venice Dr Fort Lauderdale FL 33301 Office: Enlightenment Enterprises Inc 400 E 58th St Ste 17G New York NY 10022-3060 Office Phone: 954-895-5725. Personal E-mail: rbbb2@aol.com.

BARBER, TIKI, professional football player, sportscaster; b. Roanoke, Va. m. Ginny Barber. B in Bus., U. Va. Running back N.Y. Giants, N.Y.C., 1997—; sportscaster Sta. WCBS-TV, N.Y.C., 2000—. Fill-in host Sta. WFAN-AM-FM. Named to NFC Pro-Bowl Team, NFL, 2004. Office: CBS 524 W 57th St New York NY 10019*

BARBER, TIMOTHY G., lawyer; b. Elgin, Ill., May 26, 1955; BA, Kenyon Coll., 1977; JD cum laude, Wake Forst U., 1985. Bar: NC 1985, US Supreme Ct., US Dist. Ct. Ea., Mid., & We. Districts NC, US Ct. Appeals Fed. Cir., US Ct. Appeals 4th Cir. Mem. Womble Carlyle Sandridge & Rice PLLC, Charlotte, NC, chair recruiting com., 1993—97, chair bus. litig. practice group, 1998—. Arbitrator Am. Arbitration Assn. Mem.: ABA (litig. sect.), Mecklenburg County Bar Assn., NC Bar Assn. (litig. sect.). Office: Womble Carlyle Sandridge & Rice PLLC One Wachovia Ctr Ste 3500 301 S College St Charlotte NC 28202-6037 Office Phone: 704-331-4937. Office Fax: 704-338-7839. Business E-Mail: tbarber@wcsr.com.

BARBERA, JOSE EDUARDO, international trade professional; b. Cordoba, Argentina, Aug. 8, 1950; came to U.S., 1988; s. Antonio and Petrona (Moreno) B. Lic. Bus. Adminstrn., U. Cordoba, Argentina, 1979; MBA, U. Wis., 1984; postgrad., U. Cordoba, 1985—. CPA, Argentina. Gen. mgr. Bertolina S.A., Cordoba, 1972-82; advisor Govt. of Cordoba, 1985-87; undersec. Ministry of Fgn. Trade, Cordoba, 1987—; dir. Cordoba Trade Ctr., N.Y.C., 1989—. Prof. U. Cordoba, 1982-90, Cath. U., Cordoba, 1984-85, U. Rio IV, Argentina, 1984; U.S. rep. Banco de la Prov. de Cordoba in N.Y., 1987. Mem. Am. Soc., Argentine Am. C. of C. Avocations: hiking, tennis, camping. Office: Cordoba Trade Ctr 52 E End Ave # 7A New York NY 10028-7954 Office Phone: 914-831-0797. E-mail: jeb866@yahoo.com.

BARBERA, JOSEPH, motion picture and television producer, cartoonist; b. N.Y.C., Mar. 24, 1911; s. Vincente and Frances Barbera; m. Sheila Holden; children: (by former marriage) Lynne Meredith, Jayne Earl, Neal Francis. Grad., Am. Inst. Banking. Banking clk. Irving Trust Co., N.Y.C., 1930-32; storyboard writer, sketch artist Van Beuren Studio, N.Y.C., 1932-34; animator Terrytoons, New Rochelle, 1934-37; head animation dept. MGM, 1955-57; co-founder with William Hanna Hanna-Barbera Prodns., 1957—. Dir. with Hanna of short animated films including Puss Gets the Boot, 1940 (Academy award nomination best animated short subject 1940), The Nightmare Before Christmas, 1941 (Academy award best animated short subject 1941), Yankee Doodle Mouse, 1943 (Academy award best animated short subject 1943), Mouse Trouble, 1944 (Academy award best animated short subject 1944), Quiet, Please!, 1945 (Academy award best animated short subject 1945), The Cat Concerto, 1946 (Academy award best animated short subject 1946), Dr. Jekyll and Mr. Mouse, 1947 (Academy award nomination best animated short subject 1947), The Little Orphan, 1948 (Academy award best animated short subject 1948), Hatch Up Your Troubles, 1949 (Academy award nomination best animated short subject 1949), Jerry's Cousin, 1950 (Academy award nomination best animated short subject 1950), The Two Mouseketeers, 1951 (Academy award best animated short subject 1951), Johann Mouse, 1952 (Academy award best animated short subject 1952), Touche, Pussy Cat, 1954 (Academy award nomination best animated short subject 1954), Good Will to Men, 1955 (Academy award nomination best animated short subject 1955), One Droopy Knight, 1957 (Academy award nomination best animated short subject 1957); animated programming series with Hanna include The Ruff and Reddy Show, 1957-60, The Huckleberry Hound Show, 1958-62 (Emmy award 1960), Yogi Bear, 1958-62, The Quick Draw McGraw Show, 1959-62, The Flintstones, 1960-66 (Golden Globe award 1965), Top Cat, 1961-62, Lippy the Lion, 1962, Touche Turtle, 1962, Wally Gator, 1962, The Jetsons, 1962-67, 69-76, 79-81, 82-83, 85, The Adventures of Jonny Quest, 1964-65, 67-72, 79, 80-81, The Magilla Gorilla Show, 1964-67, The Peter Potamus Show, 1964-67, Tom and Jerry, 1965-72, 75-78, 80-82, The Atom Ant/Secret Squirrel Show, 1965-68, Sinbad, Jr., the Sailor, 1966, The Abbott and Costello Cartoon Show, 1966, Laurel and Hardy, 1966-67, Space Kiddettes, 1966-67, Space Ghost, 1966-68, Frankenstein, Jr. and the Impossibles, 1966-68, Sampson and Goliath, 1967-68, Birdman and the Galaxy Trio, 1967-68, The Herculoids, 1967-69, Moby Dick and the Mighty Mightor, 1967-69, Shazzan!, 1967-69, The Fantastic Four, 1967-70, The Wacky Races, 1968-70, The Adventures of Gulliver, 1969-70, The Perils of Penelope Pitstop, 1969-71, The Cattanooga Cats, 1969-71, Dastardly and Muttley in Their Flying Machines, 1969-71, Scooby-Doo, Where Are You?, 1969-74, Where's Huddles?, 1970-71, The Harlem Globetrotters, 1970-73, Josie and the Pussycats, 1970-76, Pebbles and Bamm Bamm, 1971-72, Help! It's the Hair Bear Bunch, 1971-72, The Funky Phantom, 1971-72, Wait Til Your Father Gets Home, 1972, Sealab 2020, 1972-73, The Roman Holidays, 1972-73, The Amazing Chan and the Chan Clan, 1972-74, The Flintstones Comedy Hour, 1972-74, Josie and the Pussycats in Outer Space, 1972-74, Speed Buggy, 1971-74, Butch Cassidy and the Sundance Kids, 1973-74, Peter Puck, 1973-74, Inch High, Private Eye, 1973-74, Yogi's Gang, 1973-75, Jeannie, 1973-75, Goober and the Ghost Chasers, 1973-75, The Addams Family, 1973-75, Super Friends, 1973-83, Wheelie and the Chopper Bunch, 1974-75, The Partridge Family: 2200 A.D., 1974-75, Hong Kong Phooey, 1974-76, These Are the Days, 1974-76, Devlin, 1974-76, Valley of the Dinosaurs, 1974-76, The Scooby-Doo/Dynomutt Hour, 1976-77, Mumbly, 1976-77, Jabberjaw, 1976-78, The Skatebirds, 1977-78, The Tom and Jerry/Great Grape Ape Show, 1977-78, Scooby's All-Star Laff-a-Lympics, 1977-78, Fred Flintstone and Friends, 1977-78, Captain Caveman and the Teen Angels, 1980, The Scooby-Doo and Scrappy-Doo Show, 1980-82, The Drak Pack, 1980-82, Fonz and the Happy Days Gang, 1980-82, The Richie Rich Show, 1980-82, The Kwicky Koala Show, 1981-82, Trollkins, 1981-82, Laverne and Shirley in the Army, 1981-82, The Smurfs, 1981-90 (Emmy award 1982, 83), Laverne and Shirley with the Fonz, 1982-83, Scooby, Scrappy, and Yabba Doo, 1982-83, Snorks, 1984-86, The Funtastic World of Hanna-Barbera, 1986-87,87-88, Pound Puppies, 1986-87, The Flintstone Kids, 1986-87, Wildfire, 1986-87, Foofur, 1986-87, Popeye and Son, 1987-88, The Completely Mental Misadventures of Ed Grimley, 1988-89; animated spls. include Alice in Wonderland, 1966, Jack and the Beanstalk, 1967 (Emmy award 1967), Last of the Curlews, 1972 (Emmy award 1973), My Smurfy Valentine, 1982, Smurfily-Ever-After, 1985, The Flintstones' 25th Anniversary Celebration, 1986, The Jetsons Meet the Flinstones, 1987, Hanna-Barbera's 50th: A Yabba Dabba Doo Celebration, 1989, I Yabba Dabba Doo!, 1993; live action spls. include The Runaways, 1974 (Emmy award 1974); live action TV movies include Hardcase, 1972, Shootout in a One-dog Town, 1974, The Gathering, 1977 (Christopher award 1978, Emmy award 1978), The Gathering Part II, 1979, Stone Fox, 1987; animated feature films include Hey There, It's Yogi Bear, 1964, A Man Called Flintstone, 1966, Charlotte's Web, 1973 (Annie award 1977), Heidi's Song, 1982, Once Upon a Forest, 1993; live action feature films C.H.O.M.P.S., 1979, The Flinstones, 1994; co-creator Huckleberry Hound, Yogi Bear, Flintstones, Jetsons, Top Cat, Jonny Quest, Scooby-Doo; author: (with Alan Axelrod) My Life in Toons, 1994. Recipient TV Acad. Gov.'s award, 1988, Hall of Fame award Acad. Arts and Scis., 1993, Movie Guide award Tom & Jerry the Movie, 1993, The Flintstones, 1994. *I have a simple goal; make people laugh.*

BARBERA, THOMAS P., health care company executive; Vice chmn., exec. v.p. govt. heatlh svcs. divsn. Mid Atlantic Med. Svcs., Inc., Rockville, Md., pres., CEO, 1999—. Office: Mid Atlantic Med Svcs Inc 4 Taft Ct Rockville MD 20850

BARBER-FREEMAN, PAMELA TELIA, mathematician, educator, researcher; d. Lewis Eugene and Lucille Evans Barber; children: Leonardo Eugene Freeman, Lance Esonn Freeman, Lucyll Elizabeth Freeman. PhD, U. of Okla., Norman, 1993. Math tchr. Millwood Pub. Schools, Okla. City, 1972—85; counselor/dir. Rose State Coll., Midwest City, Okla., 1985—88; assoc. prof. Miss. State U., 1993—2000, Prairie View A&M U., Tex., 2000—. Editor: (jour.) Jour. of Rsch. Assn. of Minority Professors; contbr. articles to profl. jours. Del. Dem. Party, Okla., 1985, chairperson precinct 240, precinct chair, 1984—88, chairperson for ho. dist. 101, del. Okla. City, 1985; tchr. and facilitator Brookhollow Bapt. Ch., Houston, 2001—03, disciple Ch. Without Walls, 2001—03. Nominee HL Bd. of Trustees Black History Month Program, Miss. State U., 1996—97; named Oustanding African Am. Faculty, Miss. State U. African Am. Student Body, 1998; named to Order of Endowed Scholars, Miss. State U., 1997; recipient Tchr. Edn. Equity Project Ctr. for Advanced Study in Edn., CUNY - NSF, 1994; fellow Acad. of Excellence, Tex. A&M U., Tex. A&M U. Sys. Regents' Initiative, 2004; grantee Office of Rsch., Miss. State U., 1994, Miss. Insts. of Higher Learning, 1996—99, Miss. State U., 1997, Prairie View A&M BioMedical and Behavorial Scis. Rsch. Program, 2003. Fellow: Tex. A&M U. Sys. Acad. for Educator Devel. (assoc.). Achievements include research in MATH-PLACE resource ctr. funded through Dwight D. Eisenhower grant; tchr. networking, tng. and design (TR3); African Am. parental support (BAIT); multicultural evaluation (MERGES). Avocations: pencil art, piano. Office: Assoc Prof PO Box 4349 Prairie View TX 77446 E-mail: pamela_freeman@pvamu.edu.

BARBERI, ROBERT OBED, lawyer; b. Chelsea, Mass., July 15, 1945; s. Matthew and Maryhannah Finch (Slingerland) B.; m. Margarita Dominguez Ibarra, Aug. 8, 1981; children: Robert Obed Jr., Jeffery Hayes, Susan Finch. BA cum laude with honors, Amherst Coll., 1967; JD, Columbia U., 1970. Bar: N.Y. 1972, U.S. Ct. Appeals (2d cir.) 1974, U.S. Dist. Ct. (so. and ea. dists.) N.Y. 1975, U.S. Supreme Ct. 1974, Conn. 1988, U.S. Dist. Ct. Conn. 1992. Assoc. Chadbourne & Parke, N.Y.C., 1970-75; counsel Timex Corp., Middlebury, Conn., 1975-77, asst. gen. counsel, 1977-79; v.p., gen. counsel, sec. Risdon Corp., Naugatuck, Conn., 1979-86, Caradon Inc., Westport, Conn., 1986—. Mem. bd. advisors Jour. Environ. Law and Practice, 1993-2000. Assoc. class agt. alumni fund Amherst (Mass.) Coll., 1978-84, 92—; bd. dirs. Rehab. Ctr. Waterbury (Conn.) Inc., 1983-86; pres. Weston Soccer Club, Inc., 1994-2000. Capt. USAR, 1970-78. Mem. ABA, Assn. Bar City N.Y., Am. Corp. Counsel Assn., Yale Club (N.Y.C.), Phi Delta Phi. Office: Levett Rockwood PC PO Box 5116 Westport CT 06881-5116 Office Phone: 203-222-3114. Business E-Mail: rbarberi@levettrockwood.com.

BARBERIE, JILLIAN, newscaster, meteorologist; b. Ontario, Can., Sept. 26, 1966; m. Bret Barberie (div.). BA in broadcast journalism, Mohawk Coll. of Applied Arts & Tech. Weathercaster The Weather Network, Canada, 1990—92, WSVN, Miami, 1992—93, KTTV Fox 11 10 O'clock news, Los Angeles, 1993—95; co-anchor, weathercaster Morning News and Good Day LA, KTTV Fox 11, 1995—. Newscaster NFL on Fox, 2000—. Actress: (TV series) V.I.P., 1999—2002; guest apperances Clueless, 1996; Live! with Regis and Kathy Lee, 2000; Fastlane, 2002. Office: KTTV Fox 11 1999 S Bundy Dr Los Angeles CA 90025-5235

BARBER-WESTIN, SUE, research scientist; b. Hamilton, Ohio, Dec. 6, 1960; d. Robert Dane and Lois Woodward Barber; m. Richard E Westin, Dec. 26, 1992; children: Teri Westin, Alexander Westin. BS, Union Coll. Dir. clin. rsch. Cin. Sports Medicine Rsch. and Edn. Found., 1983—. Pres. Westin Rsch. Cons., Fort Myers, Fla., 2004—; rev. Am. Jour. Sports Medicine; lectr. in field various. Contbr. 62 articles to med jours., textbooks. Independent. Achievements include development of Cincinnati knee rating system. Avocations: golf, tennis, bicycling, swimming, reading. Office Phone: 239-561-7335. Personal E-mail: sbwestin@csmref.org.

BARBEZAT, EUGENE LAVAR, computer engineer, retired military officer; b. St. Johns, Ariz., Sept. 28, 1936; s. Fred Eugene Barbezat and Madge (Gibbons) Kindall; m. Karen Elizabeth Leichner, Dec. 22, 1970; children: Michele Lynn, Sean Michael. BS in Sociology, Brigham Young U., 1963; MA in Internat. Rels., U. So. Calif., 1980. Probation officer Ada County Probate Ct., Boise, Idaho, 1963-65; state probation officer 9th Dist. Ct., Ogden, Utah, 1965-66; commd. 2d lt. U.S. Air Force, 1966, advanced through grades to lt. col., 1981; chief Intelligence Report Ctr., 497th Reconaissance Tech. Group, Wiesbaden, Fed. Republic Germany, 1968-73; staff officer 7/13 Air Force, Nakon Phenom, Thailand, Def. Intelligence Agy., Washington, 1973-77, 84-85, Hdqrs. U.S. European Command, Vaihaingen, Fed. Republic Germany, 1977-80; chief Indications and Warning Ctr., Hdqrs. Mil. Airlift Command, Scott AFB, Ill., 1980-84; liaison offer to USCG DIA, 1984—85; staff officer Def. Intelligence Agy., Washington, 1984—85; ret., 1985; staff integration and test software engr. Martin Marietta, Denver, 1985-92; documentation specialist Computer Data Systems Inc., Lakewood, Colo., 1992—98. Staff mem. com. on imagery and exploitation Dept. Def., 1975-77, mem. indications and warning study group, 1980-84. Commr., scoutmaster Boy Scouts Am., Denver, 1986-92, commr., Ft. Collins, 1994-98; mem. Operation Santa Claus, Denver, 1987-92; pres. Homeowners Assn., 1994-95. Mem.: DAV (life), Order of Arrow, Am. Legion, Denver Zool. Found., Denver Mus. Natural History, Air Force Assn., Assn. Former Intelligence Officers, Mil. Officer Assn. of Am. (life). Republican. Mem. Lds Ch. Avocations: camping, skiing, fishing, reading, music. Home: 2144 Andrews St Fort Collins CO 80528 Office Phone: 970-282-8851. E-mail: ebarbezat@earthlink.net.

BARBIE, CATHY THERESE, middle school educator; b. Ottumwa, Iowa, Apr. 29, 1955; d. Willard Eugene and Andree Marie (Joseph) Watts; m. Billy Joe Barbie, July 26, 1986; children: Bryan Michael Joseph (dec.), Joshua Ryan. BA, U. No. Iowa, Cedar Falls, 1977. Cert. tchr. English, speech, theatre, social studies, U.S. history. Tchr. Alburnett (Iowa) H.S., 1978-79, Salmon (Idaho) H.S., 1980-82, Shishmaref (AK) H.S., 1982-84, Emmonak (AK) H.S., 1984-86, Rocky Boy (Mont.) Tribal Sch., 1986-87; instr. English Big Sandy (Mont.) Schs., 1987-89; mid. sch. instr. social studies Eagle Valley Mid. Sch., Carson City, Nev., 1989—, head dept. social studies. Avocation: professional crafter/designer. Home: 5300 Goni Rd Carson City NV 89706-0352

BARBIERI, CHRISTOPHER GEORGE, professional society administrator; b. Bklyn., Jan. 9, 1941; s. Nicholas Joseph and Marie Anne (Bacigalupo) B.; m. Joanne Lee Barnett, Jan. 30, 1965 (div. 1980); children— Matthew, Deborah, Lisa; m. Laurel E. Praet, July 6, 1985 BS, Cornell U., 1962; MS, U. Vt., 1964. Adminstrv. asst., asst. new products mgr., new products mgr., retail sales mgr. H.P. Hood & Sons, Boston, 1964-69; pres. Vt. C. of C., Montpelier, 1969—2003, internat. trade v.p. Shanghai, 2003—. Dir. Vt. World Trade Office, 2001—. Past mem. adv. bd. Congl. Travel and Tourism Caucus; bd. dirs. Union 32 H.S., 1977-80; del. White House Conf. on Better Librs., 1979; mem. Vt. Travel and Recreation Coun., 1988-91; chmn. Vt. Metric Coordinating Coun., past chair Vt. Employer Support for Guard and Res. Com.; past bd. dirs. New Eng. Trade Adjustment Assistance Ctr.; past chmn. New Eng.-USA Found., 1990-92; adv. coun. U. Vt.; former mem. Washington County Rep. Com.; past bd. dirs. Vt. Employers Health Alliance; trustee Ea. States Expdn.; active Vt. State Rep. Exec. Com. With Air N.G., 1964-70. Mem. Vt. Assn. Execs. (pres. 1972), Vt. Assn. Chamber Execs. (pres. 1971), Small Bus. Adv. Coun. (past chmn.), Vt. Auto Enthusiasts (dirs.), Coun. State C. of C. (chair 1996-98). Lodges: Kiwanis (pres. Burlington 1972-73). Roman Catholic. Office: PO Box 37 Montpelier VT 05601-0037 E-mail: cbarbieri@vtchamber.com, chrisvt@granco.com.cn.

BARBO, DOROTHY MARIE, obstetrician, gynecologist, educator; b. River Falls, Wis., May 28, 1932; d. George William and Marie Lillian (Stelsel) B. BA, Asbury Coll., 1954, DSc (hon.), 1981; MD, U. Wis., 1958. Diplomate Am. Bd. Ob-Gyn. Resident Luth. Hosp. Milw., 1958-62; instr. Sch. Medicine Marquette U., Milw., 1962-66, asst. prof., 1966-67; assoc. prof. Christian Med. Coll. Punjab U., Ludhiana, India, 1968-72; assoc. prof. Med. Coll. Pa., Phila., 1972-87, prof., 1988-91, U. N.Mex., Albuquerque, 1991-99, prof. emerita, 1999—; med. dir. Women's Health Ctr., Albuquerque, 1991-99. Acting dept. chair Christian Med. Coll., Punjab U., 1970; dir. Ctr. for Mature Woman Med. Coll. Pa., 1983-91; examiner Am. Bd. Ob-Gyn, 1984-97; bd. dirs. Ludhiana Christian Med. Coll. Bd., Colorado Springs., Colo., chair, 2005, Svc. Master Co. Ltd., Downers Grove, Ill., 1982-91; bd. trustees Asbury Coll., 1996—, vice chair bd. trustees, chair acad. com. Co-author: Care of Post Menopausal Patient, 1985; editor: Medical Clinics of N.A., vol. 71, 1987; assoc. editor, contbg. author: Textbook of Women's Health, 1998; contbr. chpt. to book. Student chpt. sponsor Christian Med. and Dental Soc., Phila., 1973-93, trustee, 1991-95, pres., chair bd. trustees, 1997-99, chair com. for continuing med. and dental edn.; tchr., elder Leverington Presbyn. Ch., Phila., 1988-91; interviewer Readers Digest Internat. fellowships, Brunswick, Ga., 1982—; bd. dirs. Phila. chpt. Am. Cancer Soc., 1980-86, vol., 1984. Named sr. clin. trainee USPHS, HEW, 1963-65, one of Best Woman Drs. in Am. Harper Bazaar, 1985. Fellow ACS (sec. Phila. chpt. 1990), ACOG, Am. Fertility Soc.; mem. Obstet. Soc. Phila. (pres. 1989-90), Phila. Colposcopy Soc. (pres. 1982-84), Philadelphia County Med. Soc. (com. chmn. 1989-90), Alpha Omega Alpha. Avocations: gardening, travel, collecting antiques.

BARBOLLA, ANDREW MICHAEL, literature educator; b. Van Nuys, Calif., Mar. 18, 1966; s. Michael Richard Barbolla and Diane Barber Everett. Degree in Broadcast Mgmt., Pepperdine U., 1988; degree in English Composition, San Diego State U., 1990. Prof. San Diego Sch. of Creative And Performing Arts, 1991—, chmn. Dept. English, 1998—. Workshop presenter in field; adv. journalism San Diego Sch. of Creative and Perfoming Arts, 1996—, peer advisor, 2001—02, counseor life skills, 1994—2001; adv. in field; advisory bd. Union Tribune. Author: How To Speak Spanish, 2004, Caged, 2005; editor: Ink Drop/Shattered Silence/Sticks Stones/Papercut, 2001—05. Named Premiere Author, Sterling House Pub., 2005; recipient First Choice Critique award, San Diego (Calif.) Writers Conf., 1998, Best Tchg. Practices award, Urban League, 2005, Local Author award, San Diego Mayoral, Pub. Libr., 2005. Avocations: surfing, snowboarding. Home: 4585 Cochise Way San Diego CA 92117 Office: San Diego School Creative and Performing Arts 2425 Dusk Dr San Diego CA 92139 Personal E-mail: sensibolla@yahoo.com.

BARBOR, GRETCHEN KUNST, secondary school educator, theater educator, director; b. Pitts., Dec. 28, 1956; d. Paul Martin and Elsie Warhol Kunst; m. John Howard Barbor, Mar. 20, 1982; children: Peter Howard, Katherine Suzanne. BS in Comms., Slippery (Pa.) Rock U., 1978; MA in English Lit., Ind. U. of Pa., 1985. Cert. tchr. Pa. Dept. Edn., 1983. Tchr. English, drama Indiana (Pa.) Area Sch. Dist., 1978—; musical choreographer Indiana Sr. H.S., 1978—, drama dir., 1983—. Cons. in field. Dir.: Ind. U. Pa. Dance Theatre; editor: Ind. Arts Coun. Literary Mag., 1994—96. Grantee, Ind. Area Sch. Dist., 1988, 1990—92, 2001—04. Fellow: Nat. Writing Project; mem.: AAUW, NEA, Pa. Coun. Tchrs. English and Lang. Arts, Nat. Coun. Tchrs. English, Ind. Area Edn. Assn., Pa. State Edn. Assn., Ind. (Pa.) Hosp. Auxilliary, Kappa Gamma, Kappa Delta Pi, Alpha Psi Omega. Office: Indiana Area Senior High School 450 North Fifth Street Indiana PA 15701 Office Phone: 724-463-8562. Business E-Mail: gbarbor@iasd.cc.

BARBOSA, RUBENS ANTONIO, former ambassador; b. Sao Paulo, June 13, 1938; s. Jose Orlando and Lice (Farina) B.; m. Maria Ignez Correa da Costa, June 13, 1969; children: Joao Bernardo, Mariana. BA in Law, U. Sao Paulo; BA in Diplomacy, Brazil's Fgn. Svc. Acad.; MA in Latin Am. Politics, London Sch. Econs./Polit. Sci. 3rd sec. Brazil's Ministry of Fgn. Rels., Brasilia, Brazil and London, 1962-66; 2d sec. Brazilian Embassy, London, 1966-73, counselor, 1976-79, min., 1979-84; chief of staff to min. of fgn. rels., 1985-86; undersec. gen. for multilateral and spl. polit. affairs Ministry of Fgn. Rels., 1986-87; sec. for internat. affairs Brazilian Fin. Ministry, 1987-88; Brazilian amb. Latin Am. Integration Assn., 1988-91, pres. com. of reps., 1991-92; undersec. gen. for trade, regional integration/econ. affairs Ministry of Fgn. Rels., 1991-93, v.p. permanent com. on fgn. trade, 1992-93; Brazilian amb. to the Ct. of St. James London, 1994-99; Brazilian amb. to the U.S., 1999—2004; sr. dir. Stonebridge International LLC, Washington, 2004—. Brazilian govt. coord. Mercosul Issues, 1991-93; exec. sec. com. on trade with East European Countries, 1976-83. Author: American Latina em Perspectiva: a Integraçao Regional da Retórica à Realidad, 1991, Panorama visto de Londres, 1998, The Mercosur Codes, The British Institute of International and Comparative Law, 2000, O Brasil dos Brasilianistas, Um Guia dos Estudos sobre o Brasil nos Estados Unidos (1945-2000), 2002; contbr. articles to profl. jours. and newspapers. Mem. Assn. of Coffee Producing Countries (pres. 1994-99). Avocations: tennis, classical music. Office: Stonebridge Internat LLC 555 13th St NW Ste 300 W Washington DC 20004 Office Phone: 55-11 3039 6330. E-mail: rubens@rbarbesaconsult.com.br.

BARBOUR, ALAN GEORGE, microbiologist, physician; b. Los Angeles, Jan. 15, 1946; s. George Johnson and Mary Anita (Jones) B.; m. Ann Wolcott Condon, Dec. 30, 1969; children: Nathan, Evan. MD, Tufts U., 1972; student, U. Calif., Berkeley, 1967. Diplomate Am. Bd. Internal Medicine. Med. resident Dartmouth Coll., Hanover, N.H., 1972-74; epidemic intelligence service officer Ctrs. for Disease Control, Atlanta, 1974-76; chief med. resident LDS Hosp., Salt Lake City, 1976-77; fellow in infectious diseases U. Utah, Salt Lake City, 1977-80; sr. staff fellow Rocky Mountain Labs., Hamilton, Mont., 1980-84, chief arthropod-borne diseases, 1984—. Cons. WHO, New Delhi, 1975. Contbr. sci. articles to profl. jours. Served as sr. surgeon USPHS, 1974-76, 1985—. Fellow Infectious Diseases Soc. Am.; mem. ACP, Am. Soc. Microbiology. Office: Rocky Mountain Labs Nih Hamilton MT 59840

BARBOUR, ALTON BRADFORD, retired human communication studies educator; b. San Diego, Oct. 13, 1933; s. Ancel Baxter and Mary Jane (Fay) B.; m. Betty Sue Burch, Aug. 19, 1961 (div. 1991); children: Elizabeth, Christopher, Damon, Meagan; m. Jacqueline Moorhead, Feb. 29, 1996. BA, U. No. Colo., 1956; MA, U. Denver, 1961, PhD, 1968; postdoctoral, Moreno Inst., 1976. Diplomate Am. Bd. Psychotherapy. Lectr. Colo. Sch. Mines, Golden, 1964-65; instr. U. Denver, 1965-68, asst. prof. human comm. studies Denver, 1968-71, assoc. prof., 1971-77, prof., 1977—, chairperson dept. human comm. studies, 1980—98. Vis. lectr. Swiss Inst. for Group Psychotherapy, Switzerland, 1992, Remin U., China, 1999, Chinese U. of Hong Kong. Co-author: Interpersonal Communication: Teaching Resources, 1972, Louder Than Words: Nonverbal Communication, 1974, Assessing Functional Communication, 1978; editor: Free Speech Yearbook, 1974-76; contbg. editor Internat. Jour. Action Methods, Psychodrama, Skill Tng., and Role Playing, Psychodrama Network News; contbr. articles to profl. jours. With USN, 1956-58. Recipient Intellectual Freedom award, Nat. Coun. Tchrs. English, 1997, William McBride Writing award, Colo. Lang. Arts Soc., 1998, William McBride award for Poetry, 2004, Outstanding Alumni award, U. No. Colo., 2003, Outstanding Educator award, 2005, Disting. Alumni in Edn., 2005. Fellow: Counseling and Psychotherapy, Internat. Acad. of Behavorial Medicine, Am. Bd. of Med. Psychotherapists, Am. Soc. for Group Psychotherapy and Psychodrama (Disting. Profl. Svc. award 1998, Outstanding Scholar award 2002); mem.: Am. Bd. Examiners in Group Psychotherapy (sec. 1983—93, chair 1997—98). Avocation: trapeze catcher and flier. Home: 1195 S Vine St Denver CO 80210-1830 Office: Univ Denver Human Comm Studies Denver CO 80208-0001 Business E-Mail: abarbour@du.edu.

BARBOUR, ARTHUR J., artist; b. Paterson, NJ, Aug. 23, 1926; One-man shows include Beumont Mus. Art, Tex., 1965, exhibitions include Nat. Acad. Design, NYC, Am. Watercolor Soc., Am. Artists Profl. League, Wolf Gallery, Franklin, NJ, 1973, Fritchman Galleries, Boise, Idaho, 1974, U.S. Navy Dept., Marietta Coll., Norfolk Mus. Arts and Sci., Prudential Life Ins. Co., others; author: Watercolor: The Wet Technique, 1978, Painting Buildings in Watercolor, 1973, Painting the Seasons in Watercolor, 1980. Recipient Silver Medal Honor, Audubon Artists, 1988. Mem.: Nat. Soc. Painters Casein and Acrylic, Allied Artists, Painters and Sculptors Soc. NJ, NJ Watercolor Soc., Am. Watercolor Soc. (Gold Medal 1965, Mary S. Litt award 1983). Address: 29 Voorhis Pl Ringwood NJ 07456*

BARBOUR, CATHERINE JEAN, actress, set designer, performance artist, director; b. Dover, Del., Nov. 8, 1932; d. Peter Joseph Callovini and Lydia Clara Shane; m. Alan Gregory Barbour, June 18, 1960. Cert., Am. Acad. Dramatic Arts, 1960; BA magna cum laude, Marymount Manhattan Coll., 1987; MFA, NYU, 1991. Tchr., dir. Am. Acad. Dramatic Arts, N.Y.C., 1963-71; asst. dir., performer, tchr., dir. The Am. Mime Theatre, N.Y.C., 1965—. Adminstrv. asst. Internat. Mimes and Pantomimists, N.Y.C., 1973-74. Set piece design for Music Box; performances with The Am. Mime Theatre include Dreams, Evolution, Sludge, Six, Couplings, Abstraction, Peepshow, Unitaur, Pageant; appeared in Captain Celluloid vs. The Film Pirates (film), 1968; appeared on The Today Show, 1975, TV Tokyo-Asayan, 1999; watercolor exhbn. Nat. Arts Club, N.Y.C., 2001, 02, 03, 04; sculpture exhbn. Sauander-O'Reilly Galleries, N.Y.C., 2001 Recipient Jehlinger award Am.

Acad. Dramatic Arts, N.Y.C., 1960, Merit award, Art Students League of NY, 2004. Mem. Am. Watercolor Soc. (assoc.), Rehoboth Art League, Inc., Art Students League N.Y. (Merit award 2004—), 1100 Watercolor Soc., Sons of the Desert, Nat. Movement Theater Assn., Drama League of N.Y. Avocations: art, sculpture, writing, set designing. Office: The American Mime Theatre 61 4th Ave New York NY 10003-5204 Office Phone: 212-777-1710. E-mail: AmMime@aol.com, Mimestar@aol.com.

BARBOUR, CELIA, editor; With Bride mag., Martha Stewart Living, N.Y.C., assoc. editor, baby/weddings editor; editor Hallmark Mag. Time Inc. Custom Pub., 2003—. Office: 20 W 43d St 25th Fl New York NY 10036-7400

BARBOUR, CLAUDE MARIE, minister, educator; b. Brussels, Oct. 2, 1935; came to U.S., 1969; Diploma d'État d'Infirmières, École d'Infirmières, Paris, 1956; diploma d'Études Religieuses, Faculté Libre de Théolog, Paris, 1958; MST, N.Y. Theol. Sem., 1970; DST, Garrett Evang. Theol. Sem., 1973. Ordained to ministry Presbyn. Ch., 1974. Youth counselor Young Women's Christian Assn., Geneva, 1959-61, Edinburgh, 1965-67; missionary Paris Evang. Missionary Soc., So. Africa, 1962-64; deaconess Ch. of Scotland, Edinburgh, 1967-69; from asst. to assoc. pastor First United Presbyn. Ch., Gary, Ind., 1974-80; from asst. to assoc. prof. Cath. Theol. Union, Chgo., 1976-86, prof., 1986—, McCormick Theol. Sem., Chgo., 1990-96. Founder, dir. Shalom Ministries and Community, Chgo., 1975—; parish assoc. First Presbyn. Ch., Evanston, Ill., 1983—. World Coun. Chs. scholar, Geneva, 1969, United Presbyn. Ch. Commn. on Ecumenical Mission and Rels., N.Y., 1972; recipient Laskey award United Meth. Ch. Womens Div. the Bd. Global Ministries, N.Y., 1972, Civic award Ind. Women's Coun., 1976, Challenge of Peace award Chgo. Ctr. for Peace Studies, 1991, Martin P. Wolf O.F.M. award Justice, Peace and Integrity of Creation Coun. of the English-Speaking Conf. of the Order of Friars Minor, 1996. Mem. AAUW, Internat. Assn. for Mission Studies, Nat. Assn. Presbyn. Clergywomen, Am. Soc. Missiology, Assn. Prof. Mission, Midwest Fellowship Prof. Mission, Assn. Presbyn. in Cross-Cultural Mission. Home: 1649 E 50th St Apt 21A Chicago IL 60615-6110 Office: Catholic Theological Union 5401 S Cornell Ave Chicago IL 60615-5664 Business E-Mail: barbour@chi.edu.

BARBOUR, DAVID A., lawyer; b. Austin, Tex., June 17, 1948; Student, Stanford U.; BBA with highest honors, U. Tex., 1971, JD with honors, 1974. Bar: Tex. 1974. Ptnr. Winstead, Sechrest & Minick, PC, Dallas; ptnr., Corp./Securities Practice Andrews Kurth LLP, Dallas, mem. mgmt. com. Del. US Brazil Aspen Global Housing Forum. Fellow: So. Methodist U. Inst. Internat. Banking & Fin. (sr.); mem.: Dallas Bar Assn., State Bar Tex., ABA (Bus. Law Sect., Develop. in Bus. Financing Com., Securitization of Assets Subcom.), Chancellors U. Tex., Order of Coif, Phi Delta Phi, Beta Gamma Sigma, Phi Kappa Phi. Office: Andrews Kurth LLP 1717 Main St Ste 3700 Dallas TX 75201 Office Phone: 214-659-4444. Office Fax: 214-659-4401. Business E-Mail: dbarbour@andrewskurth.com.

BARBOUR, HALEY REEVES, governor; b. Yazoo City, Miss., Oct. 22, 1947; m. Marsha Barbour; children: Sterling, Reeves. JD, U. Miss., 1973. Bar: Miss. 1973. Exec. dir. Miss. Rep. Party and So. Assn. Rep. State Chairmen, 1973-76; ptnr., of counsel Henry, Barbour and DeCell, 1981-93; spl. asst. to the Pres., Office of Polit. Affairs, Washington, 1985-86, dep. asst. to Pres. for polit. affairs, 1986; sr. Presdl. campaign advisor, 1988; chmn., CEO, founder, ptnr. Barbour, Griffith & Rogers, Washington and Yazoo City, 1986—92; chmn. Republican Nat. Com., Washington, D.C., 1993-97; gov. State of Miss., Jackson, 2004—. Bd. dirs. Deposit Guaranty Nat. Bank, Mobil Telecomms. Techs., Inc. Regular appearances on Crossfire, Larry King Live, Face the Nation, Nightline, The Today Show and The Capitol Gang. Republican nominee U.S. Senate, Miss., 1982; mem. Rep. Nat. Com., Miss., 1984—; exec. dir. Miss. Rep. Party. Republican. Presbyterian. Office: Office of the Gov PO Box 139 Jackson MS 39205*

BARBOUR, JOHN, retail executive; b. Scotland; Degree, U. Glasgow. With sales and mktg. Procter and Gamble, M&M Mars; with Universal Matchbox Group; CEO, pres. OddzOn Products; with Satellite Bus. Group Entrepreneurial Divsn. Hasbro, CEO OddzOn Divsn.; from exec. v.p., CEO Toysrus.com to pres. Toys "R" Us Internat. Toys "R" Us, Inc., Wayne, NJ, 1999—2002; pres. Toys R Us Internat. Toys R Us, Inc., 2002—04, pres., Toys R Us US, 2004—. Office: Toys R Us Inc 1 Geoffrey Way Wayne NJ 07470-2030*

BARBOUR, LARRY GREGORY, lawyer; b. Brookhaven, Miss., Mar. 25, 1950; s. Russell Clyde Barbour Jr. and Rhoda Ann (Cox) Benson; m. Carol Christine Cronin, June 28, 1980; children: Barrell Christine, Charles Beveridge, Mary Hester. AB in Econs., Princeton U., 1972; MBA, NYU, 1974; JD, U. Tex., 1977. Bar: Tex. 1977, U.S. Ct. Appeals (5th cir.) 1978. Credit analyst Mfrs. Hanover Trust, N.Y.C., 1972-74; assoc. Vinson & Elkins LLP, Houston, 1977-85, ptnr., 1985—. Fellow Houston Bar Found.; mem. ABA, Tex. Bar Assn., Tex. Assn. Bank Counsel, Houston Bar Assn., Order of Coif. Office: Vinson & Elkins LLP First City Tower 1001 Fannin St Ste 3300 Houston TX 77002-6706 E-mail: lbarbour@velaw.com.

BARBOUR, MICHAEL G(EORGE), botanist, educator, ecologist, consultant; b. Jackson, Mich., Feb. 24, 1942; s. George Jerome and Mae (Dater) B.; m. Norma Jean Yourist, Sept. 30, 1963 (div. 1981); m. Valerie Ann Whitworth, Jan. 25, 1987; children: Julie Ann, Alan Benjamin, Steven Allan Whitworth. BS in Botany, Mich. State U., 1963; PhD in Botany, Duke U., 1967. Asst. prof. botany U. Calif., Davis, 1967-71, assoc. prof., 1971-76, prof., 1976—, chmn., 1982-85, prof. environ. horticulture, 1993—; ptnr. Ecolabs Cons., Davis, 1969—. Vis. prof. botany dept. Hebrew U., Jerusalem, 1979-81; vis. prof. marine scis. dept. La. State U., Baton Rouge, 1984; vis. prof. plant biology dept. Complutense U., Madrid, 1999, U. de la Laguna, Canary Islands, 2003. Co-author: Coastal Ecology, Bodega Head, 1973, Botany, Terrestrial Vegetation of California, 1977, 2d edit., 1988, Terrestrial Plant Ecology, 1980, 3d edit., 1998, North American Terrestrial Vegetation, 1988, 2d edit., 2000, California's Changing Landscapes, 1993, Plant Biology, 1998, An Introduction to Plant Biology, 3d edit., 2005. Fulbright Found. fellow Adelaide, Australia 1964, Evora, Portugal, 2005; Guggenheim Found. fellow, 1978; NSF rsch. grantee, 1968-78, MAB/NSF rsch. grantee, 1989-92, USDA rsch. grantee, 1992—. Mem. Ecol. Soc. Am., Brit. Ecol. Soc., Internat. Assn. Vegetation Sci., Sigma Xi. Democrat. Jewish. Office: U Calif Plant Scis Dept Davis CA 95616 Office Phone: 530-752-2956. Business E-Mail: mgbarbour@ucdavis.edu.

BARBOUR, WILLIAM RINEHART, JR., retired book publisher; b. N.Y.C., Mar. 2, 1922; s. William Rinehart and Mary (McKelvey) B.; m. Mary Munsell, Nov. 17, 1951; children: Bruce R., Elizabeth M., Alan W. Student, Mich. State Coll., 1941-42. With Fleming H. Revell Co., 1944-83, pres., 1968-80, chmn., 1980-83. Co-author: (with wife) Trading Places, 1991, Home Exchange Vacationing, 1996, What Kids Say About Life, Love, and God, 2001. Served with USAAF, 1942-44. Named Pub. of Year Religious Heritage Am., 1974 Home: Shell Point Village 6810 Turban Ct Fort Myers FL 33908-1669

BARBUR, PETER T., lawyer; b. Westfield, Mass., Nov. 6, 1960; BA magna cum laude, Dartmouth Coll., 1983; JD cum laude, NYU, 1987. Bar: NY 1989. Law clk., Hon. Hugh H. Bownes U.S. Ct. of Appeals, 1st Cir., 1987—88; assoc. Cravath, Swaine, Moore LLP, NYC, 1988—94, ptnr., litig., 1994—. Articles editor NYU Law Rev. Named a Root-Tilden Scholar. Mem.: Assn. Bar of City of NY (civil rights com.), Order of Coif. Office: Cravath Swaine & Moore LLP Worldwide Plz 825 Eighth Ave New York NY 10019-7475 Office Phone: 212-474-1058. Office Fax: 212-474-3700. Business E-Mail: pbarbur@cravath.com.

BARCA, GEORGE GINO, winery executive, financial investor, consultant; b. Sacramento, Jan. 28, 1937; s. Joseph and Annie (Muschetto) B.; m. Maria Sclafani, Nov. 19, 1960; children: Anna, Joseph, Gina and Nina (twins). AA, Grant Jr. Coll.; student, LaSalle U., 1963. With United Vintners, U.S.A., St. Helena, Napa Valley, Calif., 1960—. Chmn., pres. Barca Internat., USA, Barca Internat. USA, Calif. Grape Growers, USA, Calif. Vintage Wines, USA, Am. Vintners, USA, Barca Internat. Wineries and Vineyards USA, Barca Investment Co. USA. Named Best Prodr. of Sales, United Vintners, U.S.A. Mem. KC. Roman Catholic. Achievements include creation of international wine and liquor trademark brands and trademarks. Office Phone: 916-786-0770, 916-967-0770. Business E-Mail: E.-Gino@BarcaWines.com.

BARCA, JAMES JOSEPH, fire department administrative services executive; b. New London, Conn., Feb. 20, 1944; s. Mariano and Angeline (Curzio) B.; m. Elizabeth Drake Garrison, Mar. 28, 1969 (div. Jan. 1983); m. Janet Louise Shields, Jan. 14, 1984. BSE in Indsl. Engring., U. Cen. Fla., 1972. Launch tech. IBM Corp., Cape Canaveral, Fla., 1968-69; indsl. engr. Honeywell, Inc., St. Petersburg, Fla., 1972-75, Tampa, Fla., 1975; mgr. mgmt. div., budget & mgmt. dept. City of St. Petersburg, 1975-81; mgr. fire adminstrv. svcs. St. Petersburg Fire and Rescue Dept., 1981-2000, ret., 2000. Exec. mem. Pinellas County (Fla.) Disaster Adv. Com., 1981-2000; mem. ARC Disaster Com., St. Petersburg, 1985-94, adv. coun., Pinellas, 1994-2000. Author: Disaster Planning for Adult Congregate Living Facilities, 1985, St. Petersburg Disaster Operations Plan, 1986-2000. Guest speaker representing St. Petersburg Emergency Mgmt. program at various civic assn. mtgs., 1981-2000. With USN, 1962-66. Recipient NASA Apollo Achievement award for Apollo 11 Moon landing participation. Democrat. Roman Catholic. Avocations: computers, photography, home video. Personal E-mail: jbarca2@tampabay.rr.com.

BARCAN, STEPHEN EMANUEL, lawyer; b. Buffalo, July 10, 1942; s. Abe and Goldie (Irom) Barcan; m. Bettye Ann Grossman, June 13, 1965; children: Sara Ellen, Daniel Jonathan, Adam Michael. AB, Columbia Coll., 1963; JD cum laude, Rutgers U., 1966. Bar: N.J. 1966, U.S. Dist. Ct. N.J. 1966, U.S. Ct. Appeals (3d cir.) 1971. Law sec. to presiding judge Appellate divsn. N.J. Superior Ct., 1966—67; assoc. Wilentz, Goldman & Spitzer, PA, Woodbridge, NJ, 1967—74, ptnr., 1974—, adminstrv. shareholder, 1999—, chmn. land use and environ. law practice group, 2004—. Pres. Westfield Symphony Orch., 1999—2001, Temple Emanu-El, Westfield, NJ, 1984—86. Mem.: Middlesex County Bar Assn., N.J. Bar Assn. (chmn. land use sect. 1997—98). Democrat. Jewish. Office: Wilentz Goldman & Spitzer PO Box 10 90 Woodbridge Ctr Dr Ste 900 Woodbridge NJ 07095-1142 Office Phone: 732-855-6055. Business E-Mail: sbarca@wilentz.com.

BARCELO, JOHN JAMES, III, law educator; b. New Orleans, Sept. 23, 1940; s. John James Jr. and Elfrida Margaret (Bisso) B.; m. Lucy L. Wood, July 14, 1974; children— Lisa, Amy, Steven. BA, Tulane U., 1962, JD, 1966; SJD, Harvard U., 1977. Bar: La. 1967, D.C. 1974, U.S. Supreme Ct. 1974, N.Y. 1975. Fulbright scholar U. Bonn, Germany, 1966-67; prof. law Cornell U. Law Sch., Ithaca, N.Y., 1969—, A. Robert Noll. prof. of law, 1984-96, William Nelson Cromwell prof. internat. and comprative law, 1996—, Reich dir., Berger internat. legal studies, 1972-88, 90—. Cons. Import Trade Adminstrn., Dept. Commerce Author: (with others) Law: Its Nature, Functions and Limits, 3rd edit., 1986, International Commercial Arbitration, 1999, 2d edit., 2003; co-editor: Lawyers' Practice and Ideals: A Comparative View, 1999, A Global Law of Jurisdiction and Judgments: Lessons from the Hague, 2002; contbr. articles to profl. jours. Mem. Am. Assn. for Comparative Study of Law (bd. dirs.), Am. Soc. Internat. Law, Am. Soc. Comparative Law, Maritime Law Assn. U.S. Office: Cornell U Law Sch Myron Taylor Hall Ithaca NY 14853

BARCENAS, CAMILO GUSTAVO, physician; b. Managua, Nicaragua, Sept. 18, 1944; came to U.S., 1969; s. Camilo and Margarita (Levy) B.; M.D., U. Nicaragua, 1968; m. Aurora Cardenas, Dec. 22, 1969; children: Margarita, Marcela, Camilo. Diplomate Am. Bd. Internal Medicine. Intern, Managua (Nicaragua) Gen. Hosp., 1967-68, Mt. Sinai Hosp., U. Conn., 1969; resident internal medicine Baylor Coll. Medicine, Houston, 1970-72; chief resident St. Luke's Episcopal Hosp., Houston, 1971; chief resident VA Hosp., Houston, 1972; fellow nephrology U. Tex. Health Sci. Ctr., Dallas, 1972-74; practice medicine specializing in nephrology, Dallas, 1974-76, Houston, 1976—; chief home dialysis unit VA Hosp., Dallas, 1974-75, chief hemodialysis unit, 1975; chief nephrology sect. St. Luke's Episcopal Hosp., Houston, 1976—; chief nephrology Tex. Heart Inst., dir. renal transplant svc.; asst. prof. medicine U. Tex. Health Sci. Ctr., Dallas, 1974-75; clin. asst. prof. medicine Baylor Coll. Medicine, Houston, 1976-79, clin. asso. prof., 1979-85, clin. prof., 1985— . Gen. sec. Juventud Social Christiana, 1968. Fellow A.C.P.; mem. Internat. Soc. Nephrology, Houston Soc. Internal Medicine, Am. Soc. Nephrology, Harris County Med. Soc., Tex. Med. Assn., Colegio Medico Nicaraguense. Roman Catholic. Contbr. articles on nephrology to med. jours. Office: 6624 Fannin St Ste 2510 Houston TX 77030-2337 also: 9197 Winkler Dr Ste D Houston TX 77017-5970

BARCHAS, JACK D., psychiatrist, medical researcher, educator, behavioral molecular neurobiologist; b. LA, Nov. 2, 1935; s. Samuel Isaac and Cecile Margaret (Pasarow) Barchas; m. Patricia Ruth Corbitt, Feb. 9, 1957 (dec.); 1 child, Isaac Doherty; m. Rosemary Anne Stevens, Aug. 9, 1994; stepchildren: Carey T. Stevens, Richard N. Stevens. BA, Pomona Coll., 1956; MD, Yale Med. Sch., 1961. Lic. NY, Va. Med. intern Pritzker Sch. Medicine, Chgo., 1961—62; rsch. assoc. Nat. Inst. Health, Bethesda, Md., 1962—64; resident in psychiatry Stanford Med. Sch., Palo Alto, Calif., 1964—67; dir. lab. behavioral neurochemistry Dept. Psychiatry, Stanford Med. Sch., 1964—76; asst. prof. psychiatry Stanford Med. Sch., Palo Alto, 1967—71, assoc. prof., 1971—76, Nancy Friend Pritzker prof. psychiatry, dir. Nancy Pritzker Lab. Behavioral Neurochemistry, 1976—89, assoc. chair dept. psychiatry, 1982—87; prof. psychiatry UCLA Sch. Medicine, 1990—93, dean neuroscience and rsch. develop., 1990—93; Barklie McKee Henry prof., chair dept. psychiatry, psychiatrist-in-chief Weill Cornell Med. Coll., NY, 1993—, N.Y. Presbyn. Hosp., NY, 1993—. Past chair Stanford Psychiatry Residency Program Stanford Med. Sch., past chair Deanship Search com., past chair Com. on Endowed Chairs; founder, co-chair sci. adv. bd., mem. bd. dirs. NEUREX CORP., Menlo Park, Calif., 1984—90; exec. dir. Pritzker Network on Depression, NY, 1996—. Assoc. editor Clinical Neuroscience Research, Elsevier, Amsterdam, 2002—; author over 300 publ.; co-editor: (numerous monographs and publ. including) Serotonin and Behavior, Psychopharmacology from Theory to Practice, Neuroregulators and Psychiatric Disorders, Biological Aspects of Substance Abuse, Clinical Neuroscience of Depression, Advances in Situ Hybridization Methodolgy; editor: Archives of General Psychiatry, 1994—2001; mem. editl. bd. Jour. of the AMA, 1994—2001. Mem., bd. trustees Hatos Found., Los Angeles, 1993—; mem., sci. adv. bd. Nat. Alliance for Rsch. on Schizophrenia and Depression, 1987—; pres. & chair bd. dirs. Robert J. and Claire Pasarow Found., 2000—; chair Pasarow Med. Rsch. Awards Prog., Los Angeles, 2000—; chair, bd. dirs. Assn. for Rsch. on Nervous and Mental Disorders (ARNMD), New York, 1998—; chair, bd. trustees New York Acad. of Medicine, 2001—. Lt. Comdr. US Public Health Service, 1962—64. Recipient Bennett Rsch. Award and Lifetime Achievement Award, Soc. of Biological Psychiatry, Efron Rsch. Award, Am. Coll. of Neuropsychopharmacology, Career Tchr. Award, Rsch. Scientist Devel. Award & Rsch. Scientist Award, Nat. Inst. of Mental Health, Sachar Award in Psychiatry, Columbia U., Lehmann Award for Psychiatric Rsch., NY State Office of Mental Health, Thomas William Salmon Medal, NY Acad. Medicine; grantee for rsch. on mental illness, drug abuse, and alcohol abuse, Nat. Insts. of Heath, Office of Navel Rsch., NASA, Nat. Sci. Found. Fellow: (dist.) Am. Psychiatric Assn. (life; past chair Coun. on Rsch., past chair Disting. Service Awards Com., Award for Rsch. in Psychiatry); mem.: AMA (editor Archives of General Psychiatry 1994—2001), Inst. Med. of Nat. Acad. Scis. (chair IOM Bd. of Biobehavioral Scis. and Mental Disorders 1982—94, past mem. Prog. Com. and Mem. Com., past chair Psychiatry-Neurology Sect., past chair for report requested by White House and Executive Branch), Acad. Behavioral Med. Rsch., Am. Assn. for Advancement of Sci., Am. Med. Assn., Am. Soc. for Neurochemistry, Am. Psychopathological Assn., Am. Physiological Soc., Am. Soc. for Pharmacology and Experimental Therapeutics, Am. Psychosomatic Soc., Soc. for Neuroscience, NY Psychiat Soc. (mem. Salmon Awards Com.), Vidonian Club, Phi Beta Kappa. Achievements include research in investigation of neuroregulators to identify previously unrecognized substances; the formation and inactivation of neuroregulators, and determination of their role in brain, behavior, and mental disorders; differential changes of neuroregulators in the brain with stress; the neurobiology and psychobiology of depressive illness through the Pritzker Network and new projects in sociophysiology. Avocations: photography, High Haven Music, the Shenandoah Valley, current history. Office: Cornell U Weill Med Coll Dept Psychiatry 1300 York Ave Box 171 Rm F-1231 New York NY 10021

BARCHET, STEPHEN, obstetrician, gynecologist, retired military officer; b. Annapolis, Md., Oct. 25, 1932; s. Stephen George and Louise (Lankford) B.; m. Marguerite Joan Racek, Aug. 9, 1965. Student, Brown U., 1949—52; MD, U. Md., 1956. Diplomate Am. Bd. Ob-Gyn.; cert. physician exec. Commd. ensign M.C. USN, 1955, advanced through grades to rear adm., 1978; intern Naval Hosp., Chelsea, Mass., 1956-57, resident in ob-gyn., 1958-61, resident in gen. surgery Portsmouth, Va., 1957-58; fellow Harvard Med. Sch., 1959-60; obstetrician-gynecologist Naval Hosp., Naples, Italy, 1961-63, Portsmouth, NH, 1963-64, Beaufort, SC, 1964-66, Bremerton, Wash., 1967-70, chief ob-gyn. Boston, 1970-73; asst. head, tng. br. Bur. Medicine and Surgery, Washington, 1973, head, 1973-75; dep. spl. asst. to surgeon gen. USN, 1975; assoc. dean Sch. Medicine, Uniformed Svcs. U. Health Scis., Bethesda, Md., 1976-77, exec. sec. bd. regents, 1976-77; spl. asst. to surgeon gen. for med. dept. edn. and tng. Bur. Medicine and Surgery, Navy Dept., Washington, 1977-79, insp. gen., 1979-80; comdg. officer Naval Health Scis. and Edn. and Tng. Command, Nat. Naval Med. Ctr., Bethesda, 1977-79; asst. chief planning, resources BUMED, 1980-82; dep. surg. gen., dep. dir. naval medicine Dept. Navy, 1982-83; ret., 1983; with Pacific Med. Ctr., Seattle, 1985-91; cons. Mil. Health Care, Seattle, 1987—; prin. MSA Programs, Seattle, 1995—; mng. ptnr. Benefit Payment $olutions, 1998—; coord. Health Plan for Life, 2003—. Clin. asst. prof. Boston U. Sch. Medicine, 1971—; alt. regent Nat. Libr. Medicine, Bethesda, 1977-79; asst. prof. health care scis. George Washington U. Sch. Medicine and Health Scis., Washington, 1978—; ex officio mem. grad. med. edn. nat. adv. com. HEW, 1978-79; chmn. med.-dental com. Intersvc. Tng. Rev. Orgn., Washington, 1977-79; chmn. Washington Med. Savs. Accounts Project, 1994; bd. dir. Hope Heart Inst. Contbr. articles to med. jours. Sec. The Rainier Club, 1992-93; bd. dirs. North Seattle C.C. Found., 1992-95. Decorated Bronze Star, others. Fellow Am. Coll. Obstetricians and Gynecologists, Am. Coll. Physician Execs.; mem. AMA, Assn. Mil. Surgeons U.S., Soc. Med. Cons. Armed Forces, Wash. State Med. Assn., King County Med. Assn., N.W. Mil. Health Benefit Assn. (exec. dir. 1991-94). Home and Office: 18601 SE 64th Way Issaquah WA 98027-8616 *Lasting achievements depend not only upon knowledge well applied but also upon doing what ought to be done.*

BARCHI, ROBERT LAWRENCE, clinical neurologist, neuroscientist, educator; b. Phila., Nov. 23, 1946; s. Henry John and Elizabeth (Pesci) B.; children: Jonathan Robert, Jennifer Elizabeth. BS, Georgetown U., 1968, MS, 1969; PhD, U. Pa., 1972, MD, 1973. Diplomate Am. Bd. Neurology and Psychiatry, Am. Bd. Med. Examiners. Resident in neurology U. Pa. Hosp., 1973-75; asst. prof. biochemistry U. Pa. Med. Sch., Phila., 1974-75, asst. prof. neurology and biochemistry, 1975-78, assoc. prof., 1978-81, prof., 1981—, David Mahoney prof. neurol. scis., 1985—2002, Fairhill prof. medicine emeritus, 2004—, chmn. neurosci. grad. program, 1983-89, dir. Mahoney Inst. Neurol. Scis., 1983-96, vice-dean rsch. sch. medicine, 1989-91, chmn. dept. neurosci., 1992-95, chmn. depts. neurology and neurosci., 1995-99; provost and chief acad. officer U. Pa., Phila., 1999—2004; pres. Thomas Jefferson U., 2004—. Mem. med. adv. bd. Muscular Dystrophy Assn., 1982—94, Soc. To Prevent Blindness, 1999—2001, Cephalon Inc., 1992—; mem. sci. adv. bd. Phila. Ventures Inc., 1992—95, TransMolecular, Inc., 1996—; bd. mgrs. The Wistar Inst., 2000—; bd. dirs., vice chair Pa. BioAdvance, Inc., 2002—; bd. dirs. The Lauder Inst., Benjamin Franklin Partnership, Covance, Inc. Author: (with Rosenberg, Prusiner, DiMauro) Molecular and Genetic Basis of Neurological Disease, 3 edits.; mem. editorial bd. Muscle and Nerve Jour., 1981-82, 95—, Jour. Neurochemistry, 1981-90, Jour. Neurosci., 1988-91, Ion Channels, 1988—, Current Opinion Neurology and Neurosurgery, 1992—, The Neuroscientist, 1993—, Neurobiology of Disease, 1994—; contbr. chpts. to textbooks, numerous articles to profl. jours. Recipient Lindback award U. Pa., 1979, Javits award NIH, 1985, Sci. Achievement award Am. Heart Assn., 1997, Disting. Grad. award U. Pa. Med. Sch., 2000. Fellow AAAS, Am. Acad. Neurology, Am. Neurol. Assn. (bd. councillors 1992-94); mem. Inst. Medicine of the NAS, Biophys. Soc., Soc. for Neurosci. (pub. lectr. 1985), Am. Soc. Clin. Investigation, Assn. Am. Physicians, Phila. Coll. Physicians, Phi Beta Kappa, Alpha Omega Alpha. Avocation: antiquarian horology. Office: U Pa Office of Provost 122 College Hall Philadelphia PA 19104 Business E-Mail: barchi@mail.med.upenn.edu.

BARCLAY, DOLORES, editor, writer; d. Harold Mason Barclay and Louise Blanding Quick. BA, Elmira Coll., 1966. Asst. editor Scholastic Books, N.Y., 1967—69; assoc. editor Matthew Bender & Co., N.Y., 1969—71; from gen. assignment reporter to arts editor The Associated Press, N.Y., 1971—85, arts editor, 1985—. Adj. prof. Sch. Journalism Rutgers U., Newark, 1977—81. Author: Believe in Yourself, 1989, Starting Over, 1990; co-author: Sammy Davis Jr.: My Father, 1996, A Girl Needs Cash, 1997; collaborator: Secrets of a Sparrow, 1993. Nominee Pulitzer prize, 2001, Robert F. Kennedy prize, 1977; recipient Aronson prize, Hunter Coll., 2001, Excellence in Comm. award, Multiple Sclerosis, 1992, Griot award, Nat. Assn. of Black Journalists, 2002. Mem.: Girl Friends Inc. (fin. sec. N.Y. chpt. 1997—). Avocations: sailing, gardening, bridge, cooking, fishing. Office: Associated Press 50 Rockefeller Plaza New York NY 10020

BARCLAY, GEORGE N., lawyer; b. 1951; BA, Brown U.; JD, Boston U., 1977. Bar: DC. Asst. corp. counsel DC Govt., 1978—82; assoc. gen. counsel, personal property Gen. Services Admin., Washington, spl. counsel, FTS2000, asst. gen. counsel., acting gen. counsel, 2004—. Recipient Federal 100 award, Presidential Rank award. Office: US General Services Admin 1800 F St NW Washington DC 20405

BARCLAY, H(UGH) DOUGLAS, ambassador, lawyer; b. N.Y.C., July 5, 1932; s. Hugh and Dorothy Barclay; m. Sara Seiter, Aug. 15, 1959; children: Kathryn D., David H., Dorothy G., Susan M., William A. BA, Yale U., 1955; JD, Syracuse U., 1961; LLD (hon.), St. Lawrence U., 1980; ScD (hon.), Clarkson Univ., 1981; LLD (hon.), SUNY, 1990, Syracuse U., 1997. Bar: N.Y. 1962. Ptnr. Hiscock & Barclay and predecessors, Syracuse, NY, 1961—2003; amb. to El Salvador US Dept. State, San Salvador, 2003—. Sec., gen. counsel KeyCorp and subs., Albany, N.Y., 1971-89; mem. N.Y. State Senate, 1965-84, chmn. Judiciary com., chmn. Select Task Force on Ct. Reorgn., chmn. senate codes com.; dir., chmn. bd. Syracuse Supply Co; chmn. bd. Eagle Media, Inc. Mem. N.Y. State Econ. Power Allocation Bd., N.Y. Racing Assn., bd. trustees; pres. Met. Devel. Assn.; trustee, former chmn. Syracuse U., chair chancellor search com.; vice chmn. N.Y. State George Bush for Pres., 1988; chmn. N.Y. State Bush-Quayle campaign, 1992; mem. policy coun. Gov. Pataki's Transition Team; bd. visitors Syracuse U. Coll.; chmn., bd. trustees, Syracuse U., 1992-98; mem. Onondaga C.C. Found.; bd. dirs. Overseas Pvt. Investment Corp., 1990-93; mem. panel of conciliators, Internat. Ctr. of Settlement of Investment Disputes, 2002. Lt. arty. U.S. Army, 1955-57, Korea. Mem. ABA, N.Y. State Bar Assn. Office: Hiscock & Barclay PO Box 4878 221 S Warren St Syracuse NY 13202-1633 also: American Embassy Unit 3116 APO AA 34023 San Salvador El Salvador

BARCLAY, KATHLEEN S., automotive executive; b. Milw. B in Bus., Mich. State U., 1978; MBA, MIT, 1991. With GM, Detroit, 1978—81; retail mgr. Southland Corp., Reno, Chgo.; human resource compensation mgr. Allen-Bradley Co., Milw.; with GM, Warren, Mich., 1985—, mgr. salaried personnel corp. staffs, 1987—88; mgr. labor rels. Chevrolet-Pontiac-GM Can., 1988—91, mgr. exec. compensation, 1991; dir. compensation GM, 1992—95, dir. human resources vehicle sales svc., 1995, gen. dir. human resources mgmt. N.Am. ops., 1996—98, v.p. global human resources, 1998—. Bd. dirs. Cowdrick Group, Mich. Virtual Univ. Bd. govs. MIT; alumni bd. dirs. Mich. State U. Sloan fellow, MIT, 1991. Fellow: Nat. Acad.

Human Resources (bd. dirs.); mem.: Detroit Women's Econ. Club. Office: GM Corp 300 Renaissance Ctr Detroit MI 48265-3000 Office Phone: 313-556-5000, 313-556-1988. Fax: 248-696-7300.*

BARCLAY, MARTHA JANE, science educator, research scientist; b. Warren County, Ill., July 5, 1948; d. George Leonard and Edna Virginia Ault; children: Brad children: Austin. BS, U. Ill., 1970; MS, Ind. U., 1972; PhD, U. Tenn., 1979. Registered dietitian. Asst. prof. U. Iowa, Iowa City, 1979—86; prof. Western Ill. U., Macomb, 1986—. Rschr. Coun. Food and Agrl. Rsch., Champaign/Urbana, 1997—2003, McDonough County Extension Coun. Treas. McDonough County Teen Ct. Bd., Macomb, 2000—02. Named Hospitality Educator of Yr., Illinois Hotel and Lodging Assn., 2001-2002. Mem.: Ill. Assn. Family and Consumer Scis., Am. Assn. Family and Consumer Scis., Ill. Dietetic Assn., Am. Dietetic Assn., Midwest CHRIE (pres. 1990—91), Internat. CHRIE. Office: Western Ill U 1 University Cir Macomb IL 61455 Office Phone: 309-298-1775. Business E-Mail: MJ-Barclay@wiu.edu.

BARCLAY, MATTHEW T., educational administrator, educator; b. San Luis Obispo, Calif., June 3, 1965; s. Charles V. and Jacqueline V. Barclay; m. Carol Ann Parker, July 31, 1993. BA, U. Calif., Santa Barbara, 1989; MPA, Monterey Inst. Inter. Studies, 1998. Crop diversification specialist U.S. Peace Corps, Quetzaltenengo, Guatemala, 1989-92; investigative asst. U.S. EEO Commn., San Francisco, 1992-94; instr. English Japan Exch. Tchg. Program, Sendai, Japan, 1994-96; ednl. cons. Monterey (Calif.) Dept. Rehab., 1998-2000; prof. polit. sci. Hartnell Coll., Salinas, Calif., 1999-2000; sch.-to-career coord., 1999-2000; regional dir. Ednl. Partnership Ctr. U. Calif., Santa Cruz, 2000—. Cons., grant writer Hartnell Coll., Salinas, 2000-2001. Jazz musician. Workshop facilitator Profile Monterey, 1999-2000; writing coach, English lang. tutor Naval Postgrad. Sch., Monterey, 1999-2000. Carl Perkins Tech.-Prep. grantee Calif. C.C. Chancellor's OFfice, 2000. Mem. Nat. Assn. Returned Peace Corps Vols., Friends of Guatemala. Democrat. Roman Catholic. Avocations: travel, music.

BARCLAY, WARREN M., human resources specialist, researcher; b. New Bedford, Mass., Feb. 27, 1952; s. Emil Barclay, Alice (Stamler) Barclay. BA, U. Bridgeport, 1974; MPA Maxwell Sch., Syracuse U., 1975. Cert. Pub. Mgr. State of N.J., 1999. Bur. chief divsn. EEO and Affirmative action N.J. Dept. Pers., Trenton, 1977—93, chief rsch. projects Office Planning and Rsch., 1993—. Chair State Data Ctr. Adv. Com. N.J. Dept. Labor, Trenton, 1992—96; chair Employee Action Com. N.J. Dept. Pers., Trenton, 1991—98; adj. instr. Mercer County C.C., Trenton, 1983. Author (profl. monthly newspaper): PA TIMES, 1991; author: (jour.) Pub. Adminstrn. Rev., 1979; editor (employee monthly newsletter): N.J. Dept. Pers., 1986—90. Pres. Condo Assn. Soc. Hill at Hamilton, Hamilton, NJ, 1987—88; mem. Mercer County Exploring com. Boy Scouts Am., Trenton, NJ, 1984—93; pres. Greater Princeton Jaycees, Princeton, NJ, 1982—83; rec. sec. religious institution, Trenton, NJ, 1992—96, youth advisor, 1980—82. Co-recipient Teamwork Partnership award, NJ Dept. Personnel; named Outstanding Young Man Am., 1985; recipient Profl. Achievement award, State of NJ, 2004. Mem.: Am. Soc. Pub. Adminstrn. (Nat. Coun. 1997—98, Pres. N.J. chpt. 1998—99, chair nat. steering group 2001—02, chair internat. award com. 2004—05, Joseph E. McLean Chpt. Svc./Devel. award 1995), Acad. Polit. Sci., Commonwealth Assn. Pub. Adminstrn. and Mgmt., Soc. Human Resource Mgmt., Internat. Pub. Mgmt. Assn. Human Resources, Am. Soc. Notaries (life), Friends NJ State Libr., Old Barracks Assn., Trenton Hist. Soc., NJ Hist. Soc., Friends NJ State Mus. Avocation: travel, photography, antiques, history, flea markets. Office: New Jersey Dept Personnel PO Box 319 Trenton NJ 08625 Office Phone: 609-777-0935. Office Fax: 609-984-0442. Business E-Mail: warren.barclay@dop.state.nj.us.

BAR-COHEN, AVRAM, mechanical engineering educator; b. Bklyn., Jan. 19, 1946; s. Simon and Dorothy (Halperin) Markowitz; m. Annette Pavony, Sept. 11, 1966; children: Barak, Raanan, Talia Dvora. SB, SM, MIT, 1968, PhD, 1971. Sr. engr. Raytheon Co., Bedford, Mass., 1968-73; lectr. dept. mech. engring. Ben Gurion U., Beer Sheva, Israel, 1973-75, sr. lectr., 1975-77, 79-81; assoc. prof. Ben Gurion U. of the Negev, Beer Sheva, Israel, 1981-84, prof., 1988; vis. assoc. prof. U. Minn., 1984-85, adj. prof., 1985-87, 89, assoc. prof., 1989-91, prof. dept. mech. engring., 1992—2002, dir. Thermodynamics and Heat Transfer divsn., 1992-98, James J. Renier vis. chair Tech. Leadership, 1996-99, exec. dir. Ctr. Devel. Tech. Leadership, 1998—2002, H.W. Sweatt chair in technol. leadership, 2000—02; chair dept. of mech. engring. U. Md., 2002—. Vis. assoc. prof. MIT, Cambridge, 1977-78; adj. prof. Naval Postgrad. Sch., Monterey, Calif., 1982; exec. cons. Control Data Corp., Mpls., 1985-89. Author: (with A.D. Kraus) Thermal Analysis and Control of Electronic Equipment, 1983, Design and Analysis of Heat Sinks, 1995; editor: (with A.D. Kraus) Advances in Thermal Modeling of Electronic Components and Systems, vol. I, 1988, vol. II, 1990, vol. III, 1992, vol. IV, 1998; contbr. articles to profl. jours. Fellow ASME (v.p. rsch. 1998—2001, recipient Edwin F. Church medal 1994, Heat Transfer meml. award 1999, Worcester Reed Warner medal 2000), IEEE (editor-in-chief Transaction on Components and Packaging Technologies 1995—, award 2002); mem. N.Y. Acad. Scis., Sigma Xi, Pi Tau Sigma, Tau Beta Pi. Office Phone: 301-405-3173. Business E-Mail: abc@umd.edu.

BARCUS, BENJAMIN FRANKLIN, lawyer; b. Tacoma, June 24, 1960; s. George Eldon Barcus and Gwendolyn (Evans) Johnson. BBA, U. Wash., 1982; JD, U. Puget Sound, 1985. Bar: Wash. 1986, U.S. Dist. Ct. (we. dist.) Wash. 1986, U.S. Ct. Appeals (9th cir.) 1986, U.S. Supreme Ct. 1991. Customer svc. rep. Tacoma News Tribune, 1979-80; claims rep., investigator Office Atty. Gen. State of Wash., Seattle, 1980-81; ind. svc. contractor Am. Express Co. Inc., Seattle, 1981-85; assoc. Talbot, Orlandini, Waldron & Hemmen, Tacoma, 1986-88; pvt. practice, Tacoma, 1989—. Precinct committeeman Wash. Dem. Com., Tacoma, 1982-88. Mem. ABA, ATLA, Wash. State Bar Assn., Wash. State Trial Lawyers Assn., Wash. Assn. Criminal Def. Lawyers, Tacoma-Pierce County Bar Assn., Mopars Unltd. (treas. Tacoma chpt. 1982-88), Ferrari Owner's Club, Ferrari Club Am., Mercedes Benz Club Am., Rolls Royce Owners Club, Fircrest Golf Club, Tacoma Yacht Club. Congregationalist. Avocations: collecting and restoring automobiles, soccer, running, water-skiing, tennis. Home: 2223 E Day Island Blvd W Tacoma WA 98466-1816 Office: 4303 Ruston Way Tacoma WA 98402-5313

BARCUS, ROBERT GENE, retired educational association administrator; b. Oct. 22, 1937; s. Harold Eugene and Marjorie Irene (Dilling) B.; m. Mary Evelyn Shull, Aug. 9, 1959; children: Jennifer Sue, Debra Lynn. BPE, Purdue U., 1959; MA, Ball State U., 1963; postgrad., Ind. U., summer 1966; supts. lic., Butler U., 1967. Tchr., coach Wabash (Ind.) Jr. H.S., 1959-63; tchr. Wabash H.S., 1963-64; tchr., coach North Cen. H.S., Indpls., 1964-65; salary cons. Ind. State Tchrs. Assn., Indpls., 1965-67, asst. dir. rsch., 1967-68, dir. spl. svcs., 1968-70, exec. asst., 1971-72, adminstrv. asst., 1972-73, asst. exec. dir. spl. svcs. and tchr. rights, 1973-82, asst. exec. dir. adminstrn., pers. and governance, 1982-85, asst. exec. dir. labor rels. and adminstrn., 1985-93, assoc. exec. dir. labor rels. and adminstrn., 1993—2002, ret., 2003. Clk. Ch. of the Brethren, 1966-74, chmn., 1979-83, 87, 92-96, 97-98, 98-99, fin. sec., 2000; mem. Ind State Libr. and Hist. Bd., 2000, bd. trustees Manchester Coll., 2004. Alumni scholar Purdue U., 1959. Mem. NEA, Wabash City Tchr. Assn. (past pres.), Washington Twp. Tchr. Assn. (past pres.), Indpls. Press Club, Nat. Edn. Assn., Ind. State Tchrs. Assn., Phi Delta Kappa Home: 2230 Brewster Rd Indianapolis IN 46260-1521 Office: 150 W Market St Indianapolis IN 46204-2806 Business E-Mail: rbarcus@ista-in.org.

BARCZYNSKI, JOHN LESLIE, periodontist; b. Bethlehem, pa., July 19, 1956; s. John Peter and Theresa Marie (Mariano) B.; m. Lisa Kay Christner, May 29, 1982; children: John Edward, Heather Lynn and Kristen Marie (triplets). BS in Chemistry summa cum laude, Lehigh U., 1978; DMD, U. Pitts, 1982, MDS, 1987. Periodontist Sto-Rox Health Corp., McKees Rocks, Pa., 1982, 84-87, 1987—, dental dir., 1988—, clin. dir., 1990—; gen. dentist USPHS, Phila., 1982-84; periodontist Highland Dr. Med. Ctr., Pitts., 1986—; periodontal instr. U. Pitts. Dental Sch., 1989—. Dental cons. Pa. Forum Clin. Svcs. Com., Wormleysburg, 1991—, Alma Ilery Med. Ctr., Pitts., 1998-2000; cons., bd. dirs. Cmty. Integrated Network of Pa., Wormleysburg, 1996—. Capt. USPHS, 1982-84, Res., 1984—. Recipient Fellowship award AGD, 1987, Healthcare State Recognition award Pa. Forum Primary Health Care, 1991, Dr. Nealon Pub. Health award, 1998. Mem. ADA, Am. Acad. Periodontology, Internat. Assn. Dental Rsch., Clin. Regional Adv. Network, Pa. Dental Assn., Dental Soc. Western Pa., Northeastern Soc. Periodontists, Pa. Soc. Periodontologists, Pitts. Acad. Periodontology (pres. 1995-96, exec. com. 1993-97), Am. Assn. Dental Rsch., Am. Dental Soc. Anesthesiology, Acad. Gen. Dentistry (affiliate), USPHS Commissioned Officer's Assn., Nat. Network Oral Health Access, Am. Legion, Elks, Am. Philatelic Soc., Tau Beta Pi, Omicron Kappa Upsilon, Psi Omega, Delta Sigma Phi. Avocations: reading, piano, collecting. Office: Sto-Rox Health Corp 710 Thompson Ave Mc Kees Rocks PA 15136-3808

BARD, ELLEN MARIE, former state legislator, retired small business owner; b. Mpls., Jan. 11, 1949; d. James Donald and Elaine (Frank) B.; m. Robert George Stiratelli, 1973; 1 child, Allison. BA, Pomona Coll., 1971; MS, Boston U., 1972, MIT, 1980. Rsch. analyst Mass. Parole Bd., Boston, 1972-78; dir. market rsch. Bay Banks, Inc., Boston, 1978-79; rsch. assoc. Internat. Coal Refining Co., 1980-82; owner, founder Techlink Corp., Jenkintown, Pa., 1982—2000; mem. Pa. Ho. of Reps., Harrisburg, 1994—2004; ret., 2004. Writer, spkr., TV prodr., host Bard Means Business. Twp. commr., Abington, Pa., 1990-94; bd. dirs. Montgomery County Lands Trust, 1993—; founder, bd. dirs. Earth Right, 1990—; founder Abington Trails Adv. Com., 1995—; mem. coun. of pres.'s assocs. Manor Jr. Coll., 1995—; mem. adv. bd. Abington Coll., Pa. State U., 1998—. Named Legislator of Yr., Pa. Tax Collectors Assn., 1996, Policymaker Yr., Penn Future, 2002, Legislator of Yr., Pa. Ortho. Soc., 2002; recipient Cmty. Svc. award Willow Grove C. of C., 1996, Friend of Edn. award Abington Sch. Dist. Republican. also: PO Box 202020 Harrisburg PA 17120-2020 Personal E-mail: ebard@ellenbard.com.

BARD, JUDY KAY, retired librarian; b. Topeka, Kans., May 10, 1943; d. Wilbur Dean and Kathryn Lucille (Bauer) White; m. Nelson Parker Bard Jr., June 20, 1965; children: Daniel Oliver, Nathaniel Arthur. BA in English cum laude, Hiram (Ohio) Coll., 1965; MA, U. Va., 1968; MLS in Libr. Sci., Ind. U., 1984. Prof. ESL Internat. Lang. Inst., Elkins, W.Va., 1974-84; prof. English Davis & Elkins Coll., W.Va., 1975-85; sch. libr. Harman Sch., W.Va., 1985-86; libr. Lancaster County Libr., Pa., 1988-92, Harrisburg Area C.C., Lebanon, Pa., 1992—2005; ret., 2005. Sec. faculty coun. Harrisburg Area C.C., Lebanon, Pa., 1997-98, exec. com. faculty coun., 1997-99, strategic planning com., 1998, 2003-05, affirmative action com., 2000-05, coll. strategic plan, 2002-05, co-chmn. multicultural events, 1992-2005; exec. com. Middle States Re-Accreditation Self-Study, 1996, strategic planning com., 1998, 2003—, joint budget adv. com., 1999-2002, affirmative action com. 2000-05, mid. states mid-term report com. 2000-02; charter mem. Lebanon County Mediation Svcs., 1999-2002, sec. 1999-2000; chair One World Festival, 2003 Advisor Campus Literacy Jour., 2005; compiler, editor Historic Beverly booklet, 1970. Charter mem., sec., Randolph County Creative Arts Coun., Elkins, 1969-86, Beverly (W.Va.) Cmty. Action, 1969-86; delivery person Randolph County Meals on Wheels, Elkins, 1970-85; deacon Elizabethtown Ch. of Brethren, 1986-2003; nominating com. N.E. Atlantic Ch. of Brethren, 2000-03; vol. Lancaster County Meals on Wheels, 2005—, Lancaster County Coun. Chs., 2005— Recipient award for Excellence in Cmty. Coll. Tchg., Nat. Inst. Staff and Orgnl. Devel., 2002. Mem.: Assn. Coll. Librs. Ctrl. Pa. (sec. 2000—02, Make a Difference award 2000, 2004, Flo award 2004), Pa. Libr. Assn. (chair South Ctrl. chpt. 1995, co-chair ann. conf. bookstore 1998, chair ann. conf. registration 2000, chair scholarship com. 2001, past preservation round table chair, past regional sec.). Avocations: kayaking, biking, needlecrafts, modern dance. Personal E-mail: bardnp@etown.edu.

BARDACH, JOAN LUCILE, clinical psychologist; b. Albany, N.Y., Oct. 3, 1919; d. Monroe Lederer and Lucile May (Lowenberg) B. BA, Cornell U., 1940; AM in Psychology, NYU, 1951; PhD in Clin. Psychology, 1957; cert. in psychoanalysis and psychotherapy, NYU, 1970. Supr. clin. psychologist NYU Rusk Inst. Rehab. Medicine, 1959-61; asst. chief and acting chief psychologist Rusk Inst. Rehab. Medicine, 1962-65, dir. psychol. services, 1965-82; research psychologist, mem. faculty N.Y. Med. Coll., 1961-62, clin. prof. rehab. medicine (psychology), 1976—; supr. postdoctoral program psychoanalysis and psychotherapy NYU, 1978—; pvt. practice clin. psychology and psychoanalysis N.Y.C., 1957—. Non-govtl. orgn. rep. to UN Internat. Ctr. Sociol., Penal and Penitentiary Rsch. and Studies, Messina, Italy, 1985—; prin. investigator NIMH, 1976-81; mem. adv. bd. Coalition Sexuality and Disability, Planned Parenthood, 1983-89; cons. in field. Contbr. articles to profl. jours., chpt. to books. Recipient 3 awards for ednl. film, Choices: In Sexuality With Physical Disability, Internat. Film Festivals, Pioneer award for Sexual Attitude Reassessment Workshops The Coalition on Sexuality and Disability, 1989; NIMH fellow Inst. Sex Rsch., U. Ind., 1976. Fellow Am. Orthopsychiat. Assn.; mem. APA, Am. Congress Rehab. Medicine, Sex Info. and Edn. Council U.S., Nat. Register Health Service Providers in Psychology, Eastern Psychol. Assn., N.Y. State Psychol. Assn. Home and Office: 50 E 10th St New York NY 10003-6223 Office Phone: 212-673-2436.

BARDACK, PAUL ROITMAN, cultural organization administrator; b. N.Y.C., Nov. 13, 1953; s. Lawrence Stanley and Charlotte (Sebold) B.; m. Esther Roitman, May 27, 1979; children: David, Avi, Daniella. BA, Yale U., 1975; JD, Am. U., 1978. Bar: D.C. 1980. Atty. U.S. Dept. HUD, Washington, 1978-79; gen. counsel to U.S. congressman Robert Garcia, Washington, 1979-81; atty. Barrett Smith Schapiro Simon & Armstrong, N.Y.C., 1981-83; mgr. econ. devel. dept. City of Cleve., 1983-84; chief exec. officer, gen. counsel Econ. Devel. Resources, Inc., Phila. and Washington, 1984-86; sr. policy advisor Gov. Thomas Kean, Trenton, N.J., 1986-89; dep. asst. sec. for econ. devel. HUD, Washington, 1989-93; v.p. Nat. Mentoring Partnership, Washington, 1993-99; cons. Booz Allen Hamilton, McLean, Va., 1999—2004; CEO My Jewish Learning, Inc., Rockville, Md., 2004—. Mem. ABA, D.C. Bar Assn., U.S. Distance Learning Assn. Jewish. Home: 105 Dunloggin Dr Rockville MD 20850-5615 Office: My Jewish Learning 966 Hungerford Dr Rockville MD 20850 Office Phone: 301-217-0145. Business E-Mail: prbardack@myjewishlearning.com.

BARDACKE, PAUL GREGORY, lawyer, retired federal official; b. Oakland, Calif., Dec. 16, 1944; s. Theodore Joseph and Frances (Woodward) B.; children: Julie, Brynn, Francheska, Chloe. BA cum laude, U. Calif.-Santa Barbara, 1966; JD, U. Calif.-Berkeley, 1969. Bar: Calif. 1969, N.Mex. 1970. Lawyer Legal Aid Soc., Albuquerque, 1969; assoc. firm Sutin, Thayer & Browne, Albuquerque, 1970-82; atty. gen. State of N.Mex., Santa Fe, 1982-86; ptnr. Sutin, Thayer & Browne, 1987-90, Eaves, Bardacke, Baugh, Kierst & Kiernan, P.A., 1991—2003, Eaves, Bardacke, Baugh, Kierst & Larson, 2003—. Adj. prof. N.Mex. Law Sch., Albuquerque, 1973—; mem. faculty Nat. Inst. Trial Lawyers Advocacy, 1978— Bd. dirs. All Faiths Receiving Home, Albuquerque; bd. dirs. Friends of Art, 1974, Artspace Mag., 1979-80, Legal Aid Soc., 1970-74; bd. trustees Albuquerque Cmty. Found., 2001-. Reginald Heber Smith fellow, 1969 Fellow Am. Coll. Trial Lawyers; mem. ABA, Calif. Bar Assn., N.Mex. Bar Assn., Am. Bd. Trial Advocates (pres. N.Mex. chpt. 1992-93). Democrat. Office: Eaves Bardacke Baugh Kierst & Larson PO Box 35670 Albuquerque NM 87176-5670 Office Phone: 505-888-4300.

BARDAYAN, DAN WAYNE, nuclear scientist, physicist; b. Frankfurt, Germany, Sept. 2, 1970; arrived in US, 1972; PhD, Yale U., 1999; BS in physics, Tenn. Tech. U., 1993. Rsch. assoc. U. NC, Chapel Hill, NC, 1999—2001; nuc. physicist Oak Ridge (Tenn.) Nat. Lab., 2001—. Mem.: Am. Phys. Soc. (Dissertation award 2001). Office: Oak Ridge National Laboratory Bethel Valley Road Oak Ridge TN 37831-6354 Home: Knoxville TN Office Phone: 865-300-1774. E-mail: danbardayan@yahoo.com.

BARDELAS, JOSE ANTONIO, allergist; b. Havana, Cuba, Feb. 3, 1948; came to U.S., 1961; s. Jose A. and Georgina (Leyva) B.; m. Sallie Young, July 3, 1971; children: Joseph, Mary. BA in Human Biology, Johns Hopkins U., 1970, MD, 1973. Intern, then resident in pediats. Johns Hopkins Hosp., Balt., 1973-75; fellow in allergy and immunology Nat. Jewish Ctr., Denver, 1975-77; pvt. practice Greensboro, N.C., 1977—. Asst. clin. prof. pediats. U. N.C., Chapel Hill, 1979—. Fellow Am. Acad. Allergy and Immunology; mem. AMA, N.C. Soc. Allergy and Immunology (pres. 1982), N.C. Med. Soc. (mem. exec. coun. 1990, 91), High Point Med. Soc. (pres. 1989). Roman Catholic. Avocations: golf, reading. Home: 400 Edgedale Dr High Point NC 27262-2908 Office: 100 Westwood Ave High Point NC 27262-4320 Office Phone: 336-883-1393. E-mail: synardelas@aol.com.

BARDELLI, FREDERICK KETCHELL, artist, art educator; b. Apr. 22, 1940; s. Guido Firpo Bardelli and Mary Widitz-Bardelli. Student, U. Mont., 1958—59, student, 1970, student, 1991, U. Oreg., 1960—61; BA in Fine Arts, Whitworth Coll., 1964; postgrad., Loyola Marymount U., 2001. Edn. credential secondary art Idaho Dept. Edn. Art tchr. Wallace (Idaho) H.S., 1967—2001. Exhibitions include Nat. Art Edn. Assn. Conf., N.Y.C., 2001. Activist Sierra Club, Kalispell, Mont., 1992, Defenders of Wildlife, Silverton, Idaho, 1997, Nat. Resources Def. Coun., Spokane, Wash., 2000. Mem.: Nat. Art Edn. Assn. Roman Catholic. Avocations: hiking, studying Renaissance drawings, boxing history, photography, writing. Mailing: PO Box 124 Osburn ID 83849-0124

BARDEM, JAVIER, actor; b. Las Palmas de Gran Canaria, Gran Canaria, Canary Islands, Spain, Mar. 1, 1969; s. Pilar Bardem. Attended, Escuela de Artes y Officios. Actor: (TV series) Segunda Ensenanza, 1986, El Dia por delante, 1989—90; (films) The Ages of Lulu, 1990, High Heels, 1991, Jamon, Jamon, 1992, Numbered Days, 1994, The Detective and Death, 1994, Mouth to Mouth, 1995, Dance with the Devil, 1997, Torrente, the Stupid Arm of the Law, 1998, Before Night Falls, 2000 (award Nat. Bd. Review, 2000), Without News From God, 2001, The Dancer Upstairs, 2002, Mondays in the Sun, 2002, Collateral, 2004, The Sea Inside, 2004 (European Film award, 2004), others. Achievements include first Spanish actor to be nominated for an Academy award. Office: co Fine Line Features 116 N Robertson Blvd Los Angeles CA 90048

BARDEN, GEORGE V., county official, watershed specialist; b. Penn Yan, NY, Jan. 20, 1948; s. Gerald and Helen Lou Barden (div.); children: Peter, Thomas. Assoc., Agrl. & Tech. Coll., Canton, N.Y., 1968. Cert. profl. soil erosion and sediment control specialist. Gen. farm laborer Ej-Lo Farms, Penn Yan, 1963-66; gen. constrn. laborer Penn Yan Builders, 1967-68; designer, design draftsman MRB Group, Rochester, N.Y., 1969-78, Sear Brown Assocs., Rochester, 1979-83; owner, operator Barden Tech. Svcs., Penn Yan, 1984-90; watershed inspector Canandaigua Lake, Ontario County Soil & Water Conservation Dist., Canandaigua, N.Y., 1991—. Rep. Watershed Task Force, Canandaigua Lake Watershed Commn. rep. Watershed Task Force. Pres. Finger Lakes Concert Band, 1984—87. Recipient map competition award N.Y. State Assn. Profl. Land Surveyors, 1980, spl. project award N.Y. State Conservation Dist. Employees Assn., 1994, Merit award N.Y. State Conservation Dist. Employees Assn., 1996, recognition award Canandaigua Lake Watershed Task Force, 1998. Mem.: Finger Lakes Water Works Assn., N.Y. State Bldg. Ofcls. Assn., Am. Water Works Assn., Finger Lakes Bldg. Ofcls. Assn., Am. Design Drafting Assn., Am. Inst. Design and Drafting. Avocations: music, woodworking, furniture refinishing, vegetable gardening. Office: Ontario County Soil & Water Conservation Dist 480 N Main St Canandaigua NY 14424-1049 Office Phone: 585-396-9716. E-mail: ontswcd6@rochester.rr.com.

BARDEN, LARRY A., lawyer; b. 1956; BS, Miami Univ., Ohio, 1978; JD magna cum laude, Washington and Lee Univ., 1982. With Sidley Austin Brown & Wood LLP, Chgo., 1982—, ptnr., mergers and acquisitions, 1989—, mem. exec. com., 1999—. Former faculty Northwestern Univ. Garrett Inst. Trustee Hadley Sch. for Blind; rep. Greater Chgo. Food Depository. Fellow: Am. Bar Found.; mem.: ABA, Chgo. Bar Assn., Order of Coif. Office: Sidley Austin Brown & Wood LLP Bank One Plz 10 S Dearborn St Chicago IL 60603 Office Phone: 312-853-7785. Office Fax: 312-853-7036. Business E-Mail: lbarden@sidley.com.

BARDEN, ROBERT CHRISTOPHER, lawyer, writer, psychologist, educator; b. Richmond, Va., June 7, 1954; s. Elliott Hatcher and Jane Elizabeth Cole (Ferris) B.; m. Robin Jones, Nov. 14, 1987. BA summa cum laude, U. Minn., 1976, PhD in Clin. Psychology, 1982; postgrad., U. Calif., Berkeley, 1977; JD cum laude, Harvard U., 1992. Lic. cons. psychologist, Minn., Tex.; diplomate Am. Bd. Forensic Examiners. Project asst. NSF, 1978-79; intern in psychology VA Med. Ctr., Stanford Med. Ctr., Palo Alto, Calif., 1979-80; dir. psychology Internat. Craniofacial Surg. Inst., Dallas, 1980-87; corp., civil litigation, family and health law atty. Lindquist and Vennum, Mpls., 1992-96; psychologist, lawyer, expert witness, pub. policy analyst R.C. Barden & Assocs., 1996—. Asst. prof. psychology So. Meth. U., Dallas, 1980—84; asst. prof., coord. child clin. psychology U. Utah, Salt Lake City, 1984—87, rsch. faculty dept. surgery, 1987—93; vis. faculty, asst. prof. psychology Gustavus Adolphus Coll., St. Peter, Minn., 1988; pres. Optimal Performance Sys., Inc., Cambridge, 1989—; mem. Minn. Bd. Psychology, 1993—97; adj. prof. law U. Minn. Law Sch., 1995—97; cons. and spkr. in field. Consulting editor Devel. Psychology, 1989; editor Harvard Jour. Law and Pub. Policy, 1990-91; contbr. to profl. publs. Project dir. ch. cmty. svc. projects, Mpls. and Cambridge, 1988—; mem. Minn. Bd. Psychology, 1993-97, Higher Edn. Coordinating Bd., 1993-94; rep. Minn. Sixth Congl. Dist.; mem. Commn. for Sci. Medicine and Mental Health, 2004—. Recipient Young Scholar award Found. for Child Devel., Faculty Scholar award W.T. Grant Found., 1987-89; NSF fellow, 1978, NIMH fellow, 1976, 77. Mem. ABA, Am. Psychol. Soc., Soc. for Rsch. in Child Devel., Internat. Soc. Clin. Hypnosis, Harvard Law Sch. Soc. Law and Medicine, Lowell House Commons Rm. Harvard U., Nat.Assn. for Consumer Protection in Mental Health Practices (pres. 1995—), Sigma Xi, Phi Beta Kappa. Avocations: church and service work, tennis, martial arts, mountain climbing, music. Office: RC Barden and Assocs 1093 Duffer Ln North Salt Lake UT 84054-3313 Office Phone: 888-947-6281. Personal E-mail: rcbarden@aol.com.

BARDI, MASSIMO, anthropologist, educator; s. Nello Bardi and Lidia Ligi; m. Rosanna Lauriola, Mar. 7, 1998. B in Natural sci., U. of Pisa, Italy, 1992; MS, U. of Pisa, 1994; PhD in Phys. Anthropology, U. of Cagliari, Italy, 1998. Vis. rsch. fellow New Eng. Regional Primate Rsch. Ctr. - Harvard U., Cambridge, Mass., 1995—96; rsch. fellow Primate Rsch. Inst. - Kyoto U., Inuyama, Japan, 1999—2001, vis. assoc. prof., 2001—02; staff scientist S.W. Found. Biomed. Rsch., San Antonio, 2002—. Author: (novel) Solo posti in piedi, Signiori! (Hon. Mention, Biblioteca Penne d'Autore, 1998); contbr. articles to profl. jours. Mem. Democratici di Sinistra, Pisa, Italy, 1991—. Named Expert of the Field, U. of Pisa, 1998; fellow Doctoral fellow, Italian Ministry of Edn., U. and Rsch., 1995—98. Mem.: Primate Soc. of Japan (mem. 1999—), Associazione Primatologica Italiana (mem. 1996—), Internat. Primatological Soc. (mem. 1998—). Avocations: reading, travel, music, swimming, sailing. Office: Southwest Fnd Biomedical Research PO Box 760549 San Antonio TX 78245-0549 Office Phone: 210-258-9556. E-mail: mbardi@icarus.sfbr.org.

BARDIN, CLYDE WAYNE, biomedical researcher; b. McCamey, Tex., Sept. 18, 1934; s. James A. and Nora Irene (Barnett) Bardin; m. Bonnie Lambdin, June 24, 1958 (div.); children: Charlotte E., Stephanie F.; m. Dorothy Kreiger, Aug. 11, 1978 (dec. Apr. 2, 1985); m. Beatrice MacDonald, June 12, 1987. BA in Biology, Rice U., 1957; MS with honors, MD with honors, Baylor U., 1962; Docteur (hon.), U. de Caen, France, 1990, U. Pierre et Marie Curie, Paris, 1997, U. Helsinki, Finland, 2000. Lic. physician Tex., 1962, N.Y., 1963, Pa., 1970. Resident in medicine N.Y. Hosp., N.Y.C., 1962-64; clin. assoc. NIH, Bethesda, Md., 1964-67; sr. investigator NCI, Bethesda, Md., 1967-70; assoc. prof. Milton S. Hershey Med. Ctr., Pa. State U., Hershey, 1970-72, prof. medicine, 1972—78; v.p. The Population Coun., N.Y.C., 1978-95; pres. Bardin LLC, N.Y.C., 1996—; pres., CEO Thyreos Corp., Newark, 1997—2003. Adj. prof. Rockefeller U., NYC, 1978-2004, Cornell Med. Ctr., NYC, 1985-2004; cons. WHO, 1972-73; chmn. bd. sci. counselors Nat. Inst. Child Health and Human Devel., Bethesda, 1982-83;

chmn. endocrine study sect. NIH, Bethesda, 1977-79; nat. prostate cancer task force Nat. Cancer Inst., 1973-78; endocrinologist Nat. Inst. Child Health and Human Devel., NIH, 1996-97; bd. dirs. Harris and Harris Group, Inc. Editor 18 books on medicine and endocrinology; mem. editl. bd. 16 sci. jours.; contbr. over 500 articles to profl. jours. Advisor internat. divsn. Ford Found., NYC, 1975-79; bd. dirs. Internat. Assn. Axel Munthe Awards, 1982-92; chmn. bd. dirs. Hormone Found., 1997-98. Decorated comdr. Order of Lion (Finland); recipient Transatlantic medal Brit. Endocrine Socs., 1988; fellow Josiah Macy Jr. Found., 1976-77; named Disting. Alumnus Rice U., 1994, Disting. Alumnus N.Y. Hosp.-Cornell Med. Ctr., 1992. Mem. Am. Assn. Physicians, Am. Soc. Clin. Investigation, Am. Soc. Andrology (coun., v.p., pres. 1984-89, Serono award 1984, Disting. Andrologist award 1992), Endocrine Soc. (coun. 1976-79, pres. 1993-94, Sidney H. Ingbar Disting. Svc. award 1996), Internat. Soc. Andrology (exec. coun. 1981-85), Internat. Com. Contraception Rsch. (chmn. 1978-95), Inst. Medicine. Democrat. Achievements include studies of male reproduction, hormone action; maturation of germ cells and inhibition of cancer growth as well as direction of a team of scientists that developed seven contraceptives and treatments for menopause and cancer. Office Phone: 212-876-1830. Personal E-mail: cwbardin@aol.com.

BARDIN, DAVID JONAS, lawyer; b. N.Y.C., June 2, 1933; s. Shlomo and Ruth (Jonas) Bardin; m. Livia Goldeen, Mar. 12, 1961; children: Jacob, Matthew, Joseph, Sarah. AB, Columbia U., 1954, JD, 1956. Bar: N.Y. 1956, D.C. 1966, Israel 1970. Atty., dep. gen. counsel FPC, Washington, 1958-69; asst. to atty. gen. Israel, Jerusalem, 1970-72; counsel Israel Environ. Protection Svc., Jerusalem, 1973; commr. N.J. Dept. Environ. Protection, Trenton, 1974-77; dep. adminstr. FEA, Washington, 1977; adminstr. Econ. Regulatory Adminstrn., Dept. Energy, Washington, 1977-80; of counsel, mem. Arent Fox Kintner Plotkin & Kahn PLLC, Washington, 1980-2001, ret., 2001. Lectr. law Bar-Ilan U., Tel Aviv U., U. Va. Ext. Co-author: AGA Select Gas Use Handbook: Natural Gas for Environmental Control, 1985; contbr. chpts. on internat. energy trade and U.S. regulation of intenat. trade in energy law and transactions, (treatise) Matthew Bender, 1990; author: Psychological Coercion and Human Rights, 1994. Mem. Mayor's Coun. on Environment, 1999—2001, D.C. Zoning Adv. Com., 2003—; bd. mgrs. Adas Israel Congregation, 1998—99; trustee The Found. Jewish Studies, 1991—99; moot ct. panel Nat. Assn. Atty. Gens., 1993—; trustee Liberty State Pk. Devel. Corp., 1990—2000, Pinelands Preservation Alliance, 1991—99, Mental Health Liaison Group, 1993—2005; adv. neighborhood commr. of D.C., 1999—2005; mem. Mayor's Com. on Adoption Law, 2000—01; bd. dirs. D.C. Water and Sewer Authority, 2000—; mem. D.C. Bldg. Code Adv. Com., 2002—. Served with U.S. Army, 1956—58. Mem.: ABA, Found. for Energy Law Jour. (bd. dirs. 1987—90), Fed. Energy Bar Assn. (bd. dirs. 1985—87), Fed. Bar Assn. Democrat. Jewish. Office: Arent Fox Kintner Plotkin & Kahn 1050 Connecticut Ave NW Ste 400 Washington DC 20036-5339 E-mail: BardinD@arentfox.com. *Combine careful thought with timely action: rely on oneself, work with others, and procrastinate only if there's a very strong reason. Finally, apply this test: How will I explain my acts and omissions to a grandchild?.*

BARDIN, MARY BETH, telecommunications company executive; m. Keith Bardin; 3 children. B in Journalism, Ohio U., 1977. Reporter AP; with pub. rels. Fidelity Investments, Dallas; joined GTE, Stamford, Conn., 1988, mgr. customer comms., dir. employee comms., asst. v.p. internal comms., v.p. pub. affairs GTE telephone ops., 1994-97, v.p. pub. affairs nat. ops., 1997, sr. v.p. pub. affairs and comms., 1998—2000; (GTE and Bell Atlantic merged to form Verizon Comm., 2000); exec. v.p. pub affairs and comm. Verizon Comm. Inc., N.Y.C., 2000—. Adv. Bd. Coll. Comm. Ohio U. Office: Verizon Comm Inc 1095 Ave of the Americas New York NY 10036

BARDO, JOHN WILLIAM, university administrator; b. Cin., Oct. 28, 1948; s. John Thomas and Grace Roberta (Day) B.; m. Deborah Joan Davis, Aug. 8, 1975; 1 child, Christopher. Student, U. Southampton, Eng., 1968—69; BA in Econs., U. Cin., 1970; MA in Sociology, Ohio U., 1971; PhD in Sociology, Ohio State U., 1973. Asst. prof. Wichita (Kans.) State U., 1973-79, assoc. prof., 1979-83, chmn. dept. sociology, 1978-83; prof. Southwest Tex. State U., San Marcos, 1983-86, dean Sch. Liberal Arts, 1983-86; prof. U. N. Fla., Jacksonville, 1986-90, provost, v.p., 1986-89; prof. dept. sociology and anthropology Bridgewater (Mass.) State Coll., 1990-95, v.p. acad. affairs, 1990-95, provost, 1993-95; chancellor Western Carolina U., Cullowhee, NC, 1995—. Vis. lectr. Monash U., Clayton, Australia, 1977; vis. prof. Univ. Coll. Wales, Swansea, 1981; cons. various orgns. and govt. agys. Co-author: Urban Sociology: An Integrated Approach, 1982; editor: Defining the Mission of AASCU Institutions, 1990; contbr. articles to profl. jours. and books chpts. Co-chair N.C./Estern Band of Cherokee Indians Econ. Devel. Task Force, 1996—; bd. dirs. N.C. Arboretum, 1995—; trustee N.C. Ctr. for the Advancement of Tchg., 1995—. Recipient Humanities award Kans. Com. for Humanities, 1978; named one of Outstanding Young Men in Am., Jaycees, 1979. Mem. Am. Sociol. Assn., Assn. for Consumer Rsch., Mid-South Sociol. Assn., Am. Assn. Higher Edn., Am. Assn. State Colls. and Univs. (coll. rep. resource ctr.), Soc. Applied Multivariate Rsch. (pres.-elect 1993—), Alpha Kappa Delta, Phi Kappa Phi. Greek Orthodox. Avocations: photography, golf. Home: 10 Chancellor Dr Cullowhee NC 28723-6874 Office: W Carolina Univ Chancellor Cullowhee NC 28723 Office Phone: 828-227-7100. Business E-Mail: jbardo@email.wcu.edu.

BARDOLE, RICHARD ALLEN, music educator; b. Rippey, Iowa, Aug. 17, 1951; s. Paul Jay and Mary Elizabeth Bardole; m. Jo Lynn Taylor, Mar. 4, 1951; children: Erin Shon Englin, Shannon Jean, Andrew Paul. MusB in Edn., Westmar Coll., 1974. Cert. music edn. Iowa Dept. of Edn., 1974. 5th-12th grade instrumental music tchr. Walnut Cmty. Sch., Iowa, 1974—76, Whiting Cmty. Sch., Iowa, 1976—79; 5th and 9-12th grade instrumental music instr. West Monona H.S., Onawa, Iowa, 1979—83; 5th-8th grade music tchr. Ogden Cmty. Schs., 1984—. Ch. choir dir. Immanuel Luth. Ch., Ogden, Iowa, 1983—; bell choir dir. Cmty. United Meth. Ch., Ogden, Iowa, 1983—; adjudicator Iowa H.S. Music Assn., Boone, Iowa, 1979—, Nebr. Sch. Activities, Lincoln, Nebr., 1985—; organizer Ctrl. Dist. Choral Dirs. Assn., Fort Dodge, Iowa. Choir dir. Immanuel Luth. Ch., Ogden, Iowa, 1983—. Mem.: Iowa Choral Directors (licentiate), Iowa Bandmasters Assn. (licentiate). United Methodist. Avocations: walking, moving pianos, judging music contests. Home: 501 W Maple St Ogden IA 50212 Office: Ogden Mid Sch 313 W Sycamore St Ogden IA 50212 Office Phone: 515-275-2912. Office Fax: 515-275-2908. Personal E-mail: dbardole@ogden.k12.ia.us, dbardole@hotmail.com.

BARDSLEY, KAY, historian, archivist, dance professional; b. Port Said, Egypt, Apr. 17, 1929; arrived in U.S., 1929; d. Chris and Helen (Jones) Lanitis; m. James Calvert Bardsley, May 30, 1947 (wid. Sept. 1978); children: Wendy Jane, Amy Kim; m. Donald Marshall Kuhn, Feb. 25, 1990. Student, Duncan Dance Tng./Carnegie Hall, Steinway Hall Studios, N.Y.C., 1931—35; BA in Journalism cum laude, Hunter Coll., 1942. Dance debut Maria-Theresa Duncan Heliconiades, N.Y.C., 1934; prin. dancer Maria-Theresa Heliconiades, N.Y.C., 1935-42; Duncan tchr. Maria-Theresa Sch., N.Y.C., 1937-46; tchr. Creative Dance for Children, N.Y.C., 1960-66, Isadora Duncan-Maria-Theresa Heritage Group, N.Y.C., 1977-81; fashion editor Woman's Day, N.Y.C., 1943-46; prodr. arts and fashion segments WPIX Gloria Swanson Hour, 1948—49; writer TV Guide, 1949; writer/prodr. culture news and fashion ABC Network/Don Ameche-Langford Show, 1949-50. Syndicated film series prodr., Your Beauty Clin., 1950-60; prodr. video documentation of Duncan Repertory, 1976-80. Writer, lectr. in field:; prodr.: (documentaries) The Last Isadorable, 1988, re-issued, 1997; contbr. to profl. dance jours. and pubs. including Dance Scope, 1977, Ballet Rev., 1991, 1994, staging of ReAnimations of Duncan Masterworks, A Four-year Project, presented at Dance ReConstructed Conf., Rutgers U., 1992; author: numerous conf. presentations and earliest documentation of Isadora Duncan's 1st sch., 1979; resident dancer scholar U. Oreg., Eugene, 1997—98, staging of Duncan solos for Colo. Ballet Dancelab, 1999, Duncan's masterwork to seventh Symphony of Beethoven, 2000; owner, curator Legacy of Isadora Duncan: The Kay Bardsley Collection. Trustee Coun. for the Arts in Westchester, N.Y., 1973-76; bd. dirs. Bicentennial Com., Chappaqua, N.Y., 1973-76; co-chmn. Community Day, 1973, 75. Grantee NEA, N.Y.C., 1980; pioneer NYU/Master Tchr. Dance Tng. Inst., 1987; recipient 1997-98 Creativity award in Dance U. Oreg. Mem.: Isadora Duncan Internat. Inst. (dir., founder 1978—), Dance Critics Assn. (bd. dirs. 1997—2000), World Dance Alliance, Am. Dance Guild, Soc. Dance History Scholars. Office: 580 Capp St Ste 211 San Francisco CA 94110 Office Phone: 415-821-0754.

BARDWELL, ROSEMARY ANN, elementary school educator; b. Calif., Mo., Nov. 4, 1958; d. Willard C. and Hanorah Josephine (Leonard) Wingate; m. Mark Steven Bardwell, July 25, 1981. BS in Edn., Lincoln U., Jefferson City, Mo., 1981; postgrad., U. Mo., 1988; MAT, St. Mary's Coll., Leavenworth, Kans., 2001. Cert. elem. tchr., secondary English and social studies tchr., Mo. Tchr. St. Francis Xavier Sch., Taos, Mo., 1981-82, Annunciation Sch., California, 1982-83, St. Martins Sch., Jefferson City, 1983—. Campaigner Rohrbach for Senate Campaign, Jefferson City, 1990. Mem. Nat. Coun. Tchrs. English, Mo. Tchrs. English. Roman Catholic. Avocations: reading, crocheting, knitting, sewing, crafts. Home: 32042 Jacket Factory Rd California MO 65018-3526 Office: St Martins Sch 7206 Saint Martins Blvd Jefferson City MO 65109-3035

BARDWICK, JUDITH MARCIA, management consultant; b. N.Y.C., Jan. 16, 1933; d. Abraham and Ethel (Krinsky) Hardis; m. John Bardwick, III, Dec. 18, 1954 (div.); children: Jennifer, Peter, Deborah; m. Allen Armstrong, Feb. 10, 1984. BS, Purdue U., 1954; MS, Cornell U., 1955; PhD, U. Mich., 1964. Lectr. U. Mich., Ann Arbor, 1964-67, asst. prof. psychology, 1967-71, assoc. prof., 1971-75, prof., 1975-83, assoc. dean, 1977-83; clin. prof. psychiatry U. Calif., San Diego, 1984—; pres. In Transition, Inc. (name changed to Judith M. Bardwick, PhD, Inc., 1991), La Jolla, Calif., 1983—. Mem. population rsch. study group NIH, 1971—75. Co-author: (book) Feminine Personality and Conflict, 1970; author: Psychology of Women, 1971, In Transition, 1979, The Plateauing Trap, 1986, Danger in the Comfort Zone, 1991, In Praise of Good Business, 1998, Seeking the Calm in the Storm, 2002; mem. editl. bd. Women's Studies, 1973—, Psychology Women Quar., 1975—; contbr. articles to profl. jours. Mem. social sci. adv. com. Planned Parenthood Am., 1973. Fellow: APA; mem.: Am. Psychosomatic Soc., N.Y. Acad. Scis., Midwest Psychol. Assn., Phi Beta Kappa. Home and Office: 1389 Caminito Halago La Jolla CA 92037-7165 Office Phone: 858-456-1443. Personal E-mail: jmbwick@san.rr.com. *I am particularly grateful to the principle of academic freedom which has allowed me to pursue intellectual questions that I considered important. No other institution would have supported my pursuit of the answers to questions that seemed significant for theoretical or applied reasons before those issues were obviously important to society.*

BARDYGUINE, PATRICIA WILDE, dancer, performing company executive; b. Ottawa, Ont., Can., July 16, 1928; came to U.S., 1943; d. John Herbert and Eileen Lucy (Simpson) White; m. George Bardyguine, Dec. 14, 1953; children: Anya, Youri. Student, Profl. Children's Sch., N.Y.C. Dancer Am. Concert Ballet, N.Y.C., 1943-44, Marquis De Queras Ballet Internat., N.Y.C., 1944-45, Ballet Russe De Monte Carlo, tours nationwide, 1945-49; guest artist Roland Petit Ballet De Paris, 1949; prin. ballerina Met. Ballet, touring throughout Europe, 1950, N.Y.C. Ballet, 1950-65; dir. Harkness House, N.Y.C., 1965-67; ballet mistress Am. Ballet Theater, N.Y.C., 1969-82; ret. artistic dir. Pitts. Ballet Theatre, 1997—, advisor, tchr., 1997—. Dir. Am. Ballet Theater Sch., 1979-82; dance panelist Nat. Endowment for Arts, N.Y. State Coun. for the Arts; judge Lausanne Internat. Competition; guest tchr., coach N.Y.C. Ballet, Joffrey Ballet, Dance Theater of Harlem, The Royal Ballet of Stockholm, Internat. Summer Seminar, Cologne, Germany, Heinz Bosl Found., Munich, St. Moritz, Japan, Australia, Republic of Korea. Soloist six European tours, also tour of Orient; numerous TV appearances; commd. by N.Y. Philharm. to choreograph ballets Festival, 1964, At the Ball, 1965, Viennese Evening, 1966, Petite Suite, 1967. Adminstr. scholar fund Sch. A. Ballet Group; mem. Nat. Bd. Regional Ballet; Fulbright panelist. Recipient YWCA award for Leadership in Arts and Letters, 1990, Cultural award for Extraordinary Contbns. to Cultural Life in Region, Pitts. Ctr. for Arts, 1997, Cultural award for outstanding contbns. to cultural climate of the region Pitts. Ctr. for Arts, 1997; named Pitts. Woman of Yr. in Arts and Music, 1994. Mem. Am. Guild Mus. Artists, AFTRA, Dance/USA (bd. dirs.). Office: Pitts Ballet Theatre 2900 Liberty Ave Pittsburgh PA 15201-1511

BAREFOOT, ALDOS CORTEZ, JR., forester, educator; b. Angier, NC, Feb. 25, 1927; s. Aldos Cortez Barefoot, Sr. and Eva Kathleen (Benson) Barefoot; m. Naomi Gertrude Pugh; children: Aldos, James, Rebecca. BS, NC State Coll., 1950, Master of Wood Tech., 1951; D Forestry, Duke U., 1958. Registered forester N.C., 1981, cert. inspector Am. Tree Farm Sys., 2003, re-cert. inspector Am. Tree Farm Sys., 2005. Lab. asst. (zoology) NC State Coll., Raleigh, NC, 1948—49; supr. quality control Henry County Plywood Corp., Ridgeway, Va., 1951; grad. asst. dept. stats. N.C. State Coll., Raleigh, 1952—54; statistician Forest Products Lab., U.S. Dept. Agr., 1953; technologist and supt., wood products lab. N.C. State Coll., Raleigh, 1954—55, asst. prof. to assoc. prof. Sch. Forestry, 1955—68; advisor (utilization), forest products rsch. inst. Internat. Cooperation Agy., US State Dept., Chittagong, Bangladesh, 1959—61; prof. wood and paper sci. N.C. State U., Raleigh, 1968—86; leader, wood products sect. Coop. Ext. Svc., NC State U., Raleigh, 1972—75; head divsn. interdisciplinary studies N.C. State U., Raleigh, 1975—82; chief of party, reforestation and watershed mgmt. project, U. of Ga., SECID, Chapel Hill, NC, Colombo, Sri Lanka, 1982—84; prof. emeritus of wood and paper sci. and multidisciplinary studies N.C. State U., Raleigh, 1986—. Cons.; tree-rings, statis. quality control, and wood identification, Raleigh, NC, 1955—; dendrochronologist Winchester Rsch. Unit, Winchester and Oxford, England, 1964—; dir., vis. scientist program, soc. of wood sci. and tech. NSF, Raleigh, 1968—74; chmn. pres.'s adv. com. U. N.C., Chapel Hill, 1970—71; owner, developer, sales Hampton Hills Subdivsn., Raleigh, NC, 1954—; ptnr. Southerm Pine Mgmt. Co., Indian Ridge Co., Creek Co., 1954—2004; trustee Horseshoe Mountain Co., 1996—2004. Chmn. tchr.'s and state employee's benefits study commn. Gen. Assembly N.C., Raleigh, 1969—71, mem. commn. on pre-paid health benefits, 1979—81; mem. health adv. com. to the state treas. and bd. of trustees of the tchr. and state employee's retirement sys. The State Treas. Office, State of NC, Raleigh, 1971—81. Served in USN, 1945—46. Recipient 'Second-Mile' award, N.C. Assn. of Educators, 1971, outstanding contbn. award, State Employees Assn., 1972, Conservation Farmer of the Yr., Wake County, NC, 1960, Disting. Leadership Citation, Club Master of the Yr., Boy Scouts of Am., 1964; grantee Fulbright-Hayes Rsch. Scholarship, United States-UK Ednl. Commn., 1973—74, The Furniture R & D Inst., NSF, 1973—78. Fellow: The Inst. of Wood Sci.; mem.: TAPPI (chmn. ann. biology conf. 1966), N.C. Govtl. Ret. Employees' Assn., N.C. State U. Club, Tree-Ring Soc., Forest Products Soc., Kiwanis (trustee). Democrat. Baptist. Avocation: hunting, hiking, travel, bridge, dancing. Home: 3401 Hampton Road Raleigh NC 27607-3131 Office: Ext Forestry Coll of Nat Resources Campus Box 8003 NC State Un Raleigh NC 27695-8003 E-mail: barefoot@bellsouth.net.

BARENBERG, MARK, law educator; BA, Harvard U., 1977, JD, 1982; MSc, London Sch. Econs., 1978. Tchr. social theory, comparative econ. history and labor rels. Harvard U., 1979—82; law clk. to Hon. Eugene H. Nickerson, US Dist. Ct. (ea. dist.) NY, 1982—83; atty. Rabinowitz, Boudin, Standard, Krinsky & Lieberman; prof. Columbia Law Sch., NYC, 1987—. Vis. prof. Peking U., 1995, Yale U., 1997. Contbr. articles to law jours. Mem.: Industrial Rels. Rsch. Assn., Law and Soc. Assn., Internat. Commn. on Labor Rights. Office: Columbia Law Sch 435 W 116th St New York NY 10027 Office Phone: 212-854-2260. Office Fax: 212-854-7946. E-mail: mb15@columbia.edu.

BARENBOIM, DANIEL, conductor, pianist; b. Buenos Aires, Nov. 15, 1942; s. Enrique and Aida (Schuster) Barenboim; m. Jaqueline DuPre, June 15, 1967 (dec.); m. Elena Bashkirova, Nov. 28, 1988; 2 children. Student, Mozarteum, Salzburg, Austria, Accademia Chigiana, Siena, Italy; grad., Santa Cecilia Acad., Rome, 1956. Music dir. Chgo. Symphony Orch., 1991—; gen. music dir. Deutsche Staatsoper Berlin, 1992—. Debut with Israel Philharm. Orch., 1953, Royal Philharm. Orch., 1953, debut as pianist Carnegie Hall, N.Y.C., 1957, Berlin Philharm. Orch., 1963, N.Y. Philharm. Orch., 1964, 1st U.S. solo recital, N.Y.C., 1958, as pianist performed in N.Am., South Am., Europe, Soviet Union, Australia, New Zealand, Near East, condr., 1962—, conducted English Chamber Orch., London Symphony Orch., Israel Philharm. Orch., N.Y. Philharm. Orch., Phila. Symphony, Boston Symphony, Chgo. Symphony Orch., others, musical dir. Orch. de Paris, 1975—89, Staatsoper Berlin, 1992—, artistic advisor Israel Festival, 1971—74, over 100 recs. as pianist and condr., debut as pianist at age 7, Buenos Aires. Named to Legion of Honor, France, 1987; recipient Beethoven medal, 1958, Harriet Cohen Paderewski Centenary prize, 1963. Office: 29 rue de la Coulouvreniere 1204 Geneva Switzerland also: Chgo Symphony Orch c/o Synneve Carlino 220 S Michigan Ave Chicago IL 60604-2596 Office: Unter den Linden 7 D-10117 Berlin Germany*

BARFIELD, H. LEE, II, lawyer; b. Macon, Ga., July 22, 1946; s. L. Bayne and Corinne (Cole) B.; m. Mary Louis Frist, Jan. 31, 1968; children: Mary Lauren, Dorothy, Corinne, Cole. BA, Vanderbilt U., 1968, JD, 1974. Bar: Tenn. 1974, U.S. Dist. Ct. (mid. dist.) Tenn., U.S. Ct. Appeals (6th cir.). Assoc. Bass Berry & Sims, Nashville, 1974—78, ptnr. litig., healthcare practices, 1978—, mem. exec. com., 1994—97. Adj. prof. Vanderbilt Univ.; pres. Bd. Law Examiners, State of Tenn., 1986—2000; mem. adv. commn. on rules of civil procedures Tenn. Supreme Ct., 1982—86. Bd. dirs. Am. Retirement Corp., Met. Nashville YMCA, Ensworth Sch., Nashville, 1980-86, Harpeth Hall Sch., Nashville, 1986—, Montgomery Bell Acad., Frist Visual Arts Ctr. & WPLN. Served to lt. USNR, 1968-71. Fellow Am. Bar Found., Tenn. Bar Found.; mem. ABA, Tenn. Bar Assn., Nashville Bar Assn. (pres. 1985). Presbyterian. Avocations: tennis, golf, jogging, swimming. Home: 1026 Chancery Ln S Nashville TN 37215-4524 Office: Bass Berry & Sims Ste 2700 315 Deaderick St Nashville TN 37238 Office Phone: 615-742-6202. Office Fax: 615-742-2702. Business E-Mail: lbarfield@bassberry.com.

BARFIELD, ROBERT F., mechanical engineer, educator, retired dean; b. Thomaston, Ga., Feb. 8, 1933; s. Jason Malcome and Nettie Lee Barfield; m. Marion Janelle Neill, June 25, 1953 (div. Jan. 1980); children: Kimberly Faith, Robert Frederick Jr.; m. Sara de Saussure Davis, Nov. 27, 1981 (div. Jan. 1984); m. Leonette Walker, May 1990 (div. June 1994). B.M.E., Ga. Inst. Tech., 1956, MSM.E., 1958, PhD, 1965. Diplomate: registered profl. engr. Preliminary design engr. AiResearch Corp., Los Angeles, 1957-59; asst. prof. mech. engring. Ga. Inst. Tech., Atlanta, 1959-65; corp. mech. engr. Thomaston Mills Corp., Ga., 1965-67; prof. mech. engring. U. Ala., Tuscaloosa, 1967-94, prof. emeritus, 1994, dean of engring., 1982-94, dean emeritus, 1994. Dir., sr. adv. Shiraz Tech. Int., Iran, 1975-77; gen. bd. Assn. Internt. practical Tng., 1980-85; dir. Capstone Engring. Soc., 1982-94; head mech. engring. program, dir. Oil Testing Ctr., U. Petroleum and Minerals, Dhahran, Saudi Arabia, 1971-73; advisor King Saud U., Riyhad, Saudi Arabia, 1982-89, U. Jordan, 1984, Yarmouk U., Jordan, 1986, Birzeit U., Israel, 1985, Kabul U., Afghanistan, 1963; mem. Accreditation Bd. for Engring. and Tech., visitor in Mech. engring., 1982-94; mem. Ala. Commn. High Tech. Bd. dirs. Salvation Army Ala., 1996—, Turning Point, Inc., 1995—. Recipient Disting. Service award Inperial Orgn. for Social Services, Tehran, Iran, 1977, U. Ala. Faculty Senate, 1980, Engr. of Yr. award Ala. Soc. Profl. Engrs., 1987, Liberty Bell award Ala. Law Assn., 1987; inductee Engring. Hall of Fame, 1998. Fellow ASME; mem. Am. Soc. Engring. Edn., Nat. Soc. Profl. Engrs., Ala. Acad. Sci., Tuscaloosa C. of C., Sigma Xi, Tau Beta Pi, Pi Tau Sigma, Phi Kappa Phi, Upsilon Pi Epsilon, Tau Alpha Pi. Presbyterian. Home: 703 Shallow Creek Rd Tuscaloosa AL 35406-2085 Office: Univ Ala PO Box 870200 Tuscaloosa AL 35487-0200 Office Phone: 205-752-3675.

BARFIELD, TIM, manufacturing executive; b. Baton Rouge, La. 4 children. Atty. Vinson & Elkins LLP; Sr. v.p., spl. projects The Shaw Group Inc., Baton Rouge, 1994, asst. to J.M. Bernhard, Jr., sec., gen. counsel, mng. dir. England; pres. The Shaw Group Inc. APP; pres, Shaw Environ. and Infrastructure, Inc., 2002—03; pres., COO The Shaw Group, Inc., 2003—. Named one of Top 40 Under 40 to Watch, Bus. Report Mag., 2002. Office: The Shaw Group Inc 4171 Essen Ln Baton Rouge LA 70809

BARFIELD, W. LEON, federal judge; b. Moultrie, Ga., Sept. 8, 1947; m. Lennie Shore. AA, Abraham Baldwin Agrl. Coll., 1971; BS (magna cum laude), Univ. of Ga. Law Sch., 1973, JD, 1976. Law clk. Hon. Elie L. Holton Ga. Superior Ct., Waycross, 1976-77; asst. dist. atty. City of Augusta, Ga., 1979-81; asst. U.S. atty. So. Dist. Ga., 1981-93; magistrate judge U.S. Dist. Ct. (so. dist.) Ga., Augusta, 1993—. Served with U.S. Army, 1967-69. Office: 500 Ford St E Augusta GA 30901-2358

BARGAGLIOTTI, LILLIAN ANTOINETTE, nursing educator, dean; b. Millington, Tenn., Dec. 29, 1949; d. Benard Wood and Georgeanne (Lowe) McIllwain; m. Ronald M. Prentice, Apr. 24, 1970 (div. 1975); m. bill L. Bargagliotti, July 8, 1978; 1 child, William Benard. RN, Tacoma Gen. Hosp., 1971; BSN, U. Tenn., 1976; MS, U. Calif., San Francisco, 1978; D in Nursing Sci., U. Calif., 1984. Staff nurse Tacoma (Wash.) Gen. Hosp., 1971, St. Joseph's Hosp., Tacoma, 1971-75, City of Memphis Hosp., 1975-76; instr. N.W. Miss. Jr. Coll., Senatobia, 1976-78; inservice coord. Eden Hosp., Castro Valley, Calif., 1978-79; instr. Ohlone Coll., Fremont, Calif., 1979-84; assoc. prof. nursing San Francisco State U., 1984-85; assoc. dean, prof. nursing U. San Francisco, 1985-89, interim dean, prof. nursing, 1989-91; assoc. DON Davies Med. Ctr., 1992; dean, prof. nursing Loewenberg Sch. Nursing, U. Memphis, 1992—. Clin. evaluator SUNY Western Performance Assessment Ctr., Long Beach and Palo Alto, Calif., 1982-85; program evaluator Collegiate Commn. for Nursing Edn. Contbr. articles to profl. jours. Capt. USAR, 1976-78. Mem. ANA, Tenn. Nurses Assn., Assn. Oper. Rm. Nurses (mem. jour. editl. bd. 1987-90), Nat. League for Nursing (program evaluator, pres.-elect 2003-05, pres., 2005, bd. govs., trustee found. bd.), Tenn. Assn. Deans/Dirs. Nursing (pres. 1997-99, 99-2001), Sigma Theta Tau. Republican. Mem. Ch. of Christ. Home: 7423 Wood Rail Cv Memphis TN 38119-9007 Office: U Memphis 102 Newport Hall Memphis TN 38152-3740 Business E-Mail: tbargagl@memphis.edu.

BARGER, DONALD GORDON, JR., automotive products company executive; b. Hamilton, Ohio, Feb. 8, 1943; s. Donald Gordon and Mary Elizabeth (Sizemore) B.; m. Linda A. Liveralt, July 25, 1971; children: Neill, Charity, Austin. BS, U.S. Naval Acad., 1965; MBA, U. Pa., 1972. Fin. analyst Irwin Mgmt. Co., Columbus, Ind., 1972-73; various positions The B.F. Goodrich Co., Akron, Ohio, 1973-76; dir. analysis The B.F. Goodrich Co. Tire Group, Akron, 1976-77, dir. product mktg., 1977-78; dir. planning The B.F. Goodrich Co. Chem. Group, Akron, 1978-82, v.p. planning and control, 1982-84. The B.F. Goodrich Co. Tire Group, Akron, 1984-86; v.p., contr. The B.F. Goodrich Co., Akron, 1986—93; v.p., CFO Worthington Industries, Columbus, Ohio, 1993—98, Hillenbrand Industries, Inc., Batesville, Ind., 1998—2000; sr. v.p., CFO Yellow Roadway Corp., Shawnee Mission, Kans., 2000—. Served to lt. USN, 1965-70. Office: Yellow Roadway Corp PO Box 7270 Shawnee Mission KS 66207-0270

BARGER, DONALD RAY, JR., minister; b. Birmingham, Ala., May 30, 1971; s. Donald Ray and Kathy Butler B.; m. Jennifer Dawn Simpson, June 25, 1994; children: Chloe Madison, Caroline Grace. BS in Acctg., U. Ala., 1993; MDiv, Southwestern Bapt. Theol. Sem., 1997; diploma, Spanish Inst. Lengua Espanol, 1999. Congrl. aid U.S. Congressman Spencer Bachus, Birmingham, 1994; missionary, ch. planter Internat. Mission Bd., Monte Cristi, Dominican Rep., 1999—. Home: 144 Dee Hendrix Rd Hueytown AL 35023 Office: Internat Mission Bd PO Box 6767 Richmond VA 23230-0767 Fax: (954)301-6351.

BARGER, JAMES EDWIN, physicist; b. Manhattan, Kans., Dec. 28, 1934; s. Edgar Lee and Carolyn Marie (Grantham) B.; m. Mary Elizabeth Rupp, Aug. 24, 1957; children: Elaine Marie Fleckenstein, Carolyn Ruth Hanson, James Rupp, Corinne Elizabeth Noordzij. BS, U. Mich., 1957; MS, U. Conn., 1960; MA in Applied Physics, Harvard U., 1962, PhD, 1964. Teaching asst.

Harvard U., Cambridge, 1961-64; v.p. BBN Techs. (formerly Bolt Beranek & Newman, Inc.), Cambridge, Mass., 1965-75, chief scientist, 1975—. Trustee Winchester Savs. Bank. Mem. Methods and Procedures Com., Town of Winchester, 1967-71; trustee Winchester Hosp., 1972—; corp. mem. Mt. Vernon House, 1979—. Program officer USN, 1957—60. Recipient Disting. Engring. Alumni award U. Conn., 2002; named to Acad. Disting. Engrs., U. Conn.; NSF fellow, 1960-64. Fellow AAAS, Acoustical Soc. Am.; mem. Marine Tech. Soc., Indsl. Noise Control Engring., Winchester Country Club, Cosmos Club, Tau Beta Pi, Pi Tau Sigma. Congregationalist (deacon). Home: 3 Lakeview Rd Winchester MA 01890-3801 Office: BBN Techs 70 Fawcett St Cambridge MA 02138-1110

BARGER, RICHARD WILSON, hotel executive; b. Cleve., Aug. 16, 1934; s. Harold Wilson and Blanche (Smith) B.; m. Barbara K. Schroeder, July 20, 1963; children: Scott Wilson, Christopher Armon. BS, Cornell U., Ithaca, N.Y., 1956. Resident mgr. Sheraton Cleve. Hotel, 1964-67; gen. mgr. Sheraton Biltmore Hotel, Providence, 1967-68, Sheraton Peabody Hotel, Memphis, 1968-69, Sheraton Boston Hotel, 1969-72; v.p., regional mgr. Sheraton Corp., Boston, 1972-79; chmn. Barger Hotel Corp., Boston, 1979—, Conf. Planning Assoc., 1987—. Cons., lectr. hotel adminstrs. Mem. coun. Cornell U. Mem. Boston C. of C., Boston Conv. Bur. (dir.), Cornell U. Alumni Fund, Sigma Chi. Republican. Episcopalian. Home and Office: Barger Hotel Corp 63 Neptune St # A Beverly MA 01915-4746 Office Phone: 978-922-9500. E-mail: bargerhotel@comcast.net.

BARGER, ROBERT DANIEL, collections company executive; b. St. Louis, Feb. 13, 1970; s. Jerry Donald and Cheryl Anne Barger; m. Kelli Louise LoCigno, Sept. 21, 1996; children: Katelyn Brynn, Courtney Brooke. MBA, Webster U., St. Louis, 2002. Sr. mgr. collections Fleishman-Hillard Inc., St. Louis, 1997—2003; pres., CEO Rapid Collections, LLC, St. Louis, 2003—. Sr. ptnr. Collection Bids, St. Louis, 2004—. Office: Rapid Collections LLC Ste 310 9109 Watson Rd Saint Louis MO 63126 Office Phone: 866-581-3636. Office Fax: 314-918-9803. E-mail: rbarger@rapidcollectionsllc.com.

BARGER, VERNON DUANE, physicist, educator; b. Curllsville, Pa., June 5, 1938; s. Joseph F. and Olive (McCall) Barger; m. M. Annetta McLeod, 1967; children: Victor A., Amy J., Andrew V. BS, Pa. State U., 1960, PhD, 1963. Rsch. assoc. U. Wis., Madison, 1963-65, from asst. prof. to assoc. prof., 1965-68, prof. physics, 1968—, J.H. Van Vleck prof., 1983—, dir. Inst. Elem. Particle Physics Rsch., 1984—, Hilldale prof., 1987-91, Vilas prof., 1991—. Vis. prof. U. Hawaii, 1970, 79, 82, U. Durham, 1983, 84; vis. scientist CERN, 1972, Rutherford Lab., 1972, SLAC, 1975, Kavli Inst. for Theoretical Physics, U. Calif., Santa Barbara, 2003. Co-author: (book) Phenomenological Theories of High Energy Scattering, Classical Mechanics, Classical Electricity and Magnetism, Collider Physics. Recipient Alumni Fellow award, Pa. State U., 1974; Guggenheim fellow, 1972, Fermilab Frontier fellow, 1999. Fellow: Am. Phys. Soc. Methodist. Achievements include research in elementary particle theory and phenomenology; classification of hadrons as Regge recurrences; analyses of neutrino scattering and oscillations; weak boson, Higgs boson and heavy quark production; electroweak models; supersymmetry and grand unification; future collider physics; cosmology. Office: U Wis Dept Physics 1150 University Ave Madison WI 53706-1302

BARGER, WILLIAM JAMES, management consultant, educator; b. Los Angeles, Nov. 1, 1944; s. James Ray and Aylene M. (Skinner) B.; m. Jane A. Cox, Jan. 30, 1988. BA, U. So. Calif., 1966; MA, Harvard U., 1970, PhD, 1972. Asst. prof econs. U. So. Calif., Los Angeles, 1971-76; v.p. Bank Am., Los Angeles, 1976-81; sr. v.p. Gibraltar Savs. Co., Beverly Hills, Calif., 1981-84, exec. v.p., 1984-88; pres. High Point Acad., Pasadena, Calif., 1995—2001; dir. Maxson Young Assocs., San Francisco, 1995—2004. Mem. Phi Beta Kappa.

BARGMANN, ROLF ERWIN, computer scientist, educator; b. Glückstadt, Schleswig, Germany, May 13, 1921; arrived in U.S., 1955, naturalized, 1962; s. Erwin Bargmann and Martha (née)Bargmann; m. Ilse Heckenbach, May 24, 1920; children: Monika Brown, Evelyn, Cornelia, Dorie. PhD in stats, U. N.C., 1958. Ct. interpreter Nuremberg Trials, Office of Chief of Counsel for War Crimes, Nürnberg, Germany, 1947—48; fellow, Rockefeller Found. Psychometrics Lab., U. Chgo., 1951—52; rsch. asst., head stats. dept. Inst. for Internat. Edn. Rsch., Frankfurt, Germany, 1952—55; rsch. asst. Psychometric Lab, U. N.C., Chapel Hill, 1955—57; prof. stats. Va. Poly. Inst., Blacksburg, 1957—61; rsch. staff mem., mgr. info. scis. IBM Thomas J. Watson Rsch. Ctr., Yorktown Heights, NY, 1961—65; prof. of stats. and computer sci. U. Ga., Athens, 1965—, prof. stats. and computer sci., emeritus dept. stats., 1990—. Vis. lectr. Institut nat. d'études démographiques; U. of Paris, 1965; exch. prof. U. Erlangen/Nürnberg, Bavaria, Germany, 1978; vis. prof. U. Dortmund, Rhineland Westphalia, Germany, 1980; rsch. fellow US Dept. of Agr., Washington, 1990. Assoc. editor: Psychometrica, 1957—74, Jour. Statistical Computation, 1970—74. Pres. U. Ga. chpt. AAUP, Athens, 1975—77. Fellow: AAAS, Am. Statis. Assn.; mem.: Am. Assn. for Computing Machines, Internat. Statis. Inst., Sigma Xi. Lutheran. Avocations: music (piano, accordion), travel. Office: Univ Ga Dept Stats Athens GA 30602-1952 Home: 1320 Branchlands DR Apt 3L Charlottesville VA 22901-5706 E-mail: reb2@stat.uga.edu.

BARHAM, CHARLES DEWEY, JR., electric power industry executive, lawyer; b. Goldsboro, N.C., July 7, 1930; s. Charles Dewey and Helen Wilkinson (Douglass) Barham Hughes; m. Margaret Wright Crow, June 17, 1960; children: Margaret Douglass, Charles Dewey III. BS, Wake Forest U., 1952, JD, 1954. Bar: N.C. 1954. Asst. atty. gen. N.C. Dept. Justice, Raleigh, 1958-66; assoc. gen. counsel Carolina Power & Light Co., Raleigh, N.C., 1966-73; ptnr. Douglass & Barham, Raleigh, 1974-80; v.p., sr. counsel Carolina Power & Light Co., Raleigh, 1981-82, sr. v.p., gen. counsel, 1982-87, sr. v.p., 1982-90, exec. v.p. 1990-95; bd. of dir., 1990—95; ptnr. Douglass & Barham, 1995—. Chmn. bd., pres. Nuclear Mut., Ltd., Hamilton, Bermuda, 1981-86, bd. dirs. 1973-95; bd. dirs. Nuclear Elec. Ins. Ltd., 1987-95 Hamilton; gen. counsel World Nuclear Fuel Mkt., Atlanta, 1974-80; gen. counsel Meredith Coll., Raleigh, 1977-80, trustee, 1984-87, 90-93, 95—2001; mem. regional bd. dirs. Wachovia Bank of N.C., 1990-95. Pres. Raleigh YMCA, 1982-92; bd. vis. Sch. Law Wake Forest U., 1998—. Capt. USNR, 1955-77. Mem.: ABA, N.C. Bar Assn., Glen Forest Club (pres. 1977), Raleigh Civitan Club (dir. 1974—77, 1999—).

BARHAM, TERRY J., music educator; b. Antlers, Okla., June 1, 1940; s. Joe C and Carlene Barham; m. Susan L Horle, Feb. 18, 1953; 1 child, Kate E. PhD, U. Okla., 1970. Choral dir. Elmwood Park H.S., Ill., 1964—68; choral dir./music theory tchr. U. Wis.-La Crosse, 1970—78; choral dir. Viterbo Coll., La Crosse, 1978—82; asst. dir. choral activities U. Ariz., Tucson, 1982—87; dir. choral activities Emporia State U., Kans., 1987—. Conductor NC Jr. H.S. All State Chorus, 2004, Ala. Young Voices Hon. Choir, 2004, Mo. ACDA Jr. H.S. All State Choir, 2004, Fla. ACDA Jr. H.S. Boys All State Choir, 2004, Fla. Jr. High All-State Choir, 2005. Author: Strategies for Teaching Junior High & Middle School Male Singers-Master Teachers Speak; co-author: The Boy's Changing Voice-New Solutions for Today's Teachers; music arranger (choral music) Down by the Riverside, Vive L'Amour; editor: (S.W. divsn. newsletter) Am. Choral Dirs. Assn. Recipient Golden Apple award for Outstanding Cmty. Svc. and Excellence in Tchg., Emporia C. of C., 2000. Mem.: Music Educators Nat. Conf., Am. Choral Dirs. Assn. (life; nat. coord. of state newsletters 2004—). Office: Emporia State U Dept Music 1200 Commercial Emporia KS 66801 Office Phone: 620-341-5436. Business E-Mail: barhamte@emporia.edu.

BARHAM, WARREN SANDUSKY, horticulturist; b. Prescott, Ark., Feb. 15, 1919; s. Clint A. and Hannah Jane (Sandusky) B.; m. Margaret Alice Kyle, Dec. 27, 1940 (dec. 1997); m. Evelyn M. Csongradi, Dec. 5, 1998 (dec. 2003); children: Barbara E., Juanita S., Margaret Ann, Robert W. BS in Agr., U. Ark., 1941; PhD, Cornell U., 1950. Grad. asst. in plant breeding Cornell U., Ithaca, N.Y., 1942-45; assoc. prof. horticulture N.C. State U., Raleigh, 1949-58; dir. raw material R & D Basic Vegetable Products, Inc., Vacaville, Calif., 1958-76; prof. Tex. A&M U., College Station, 1976-82, head dept., 1976-80; v.p. Castle & Cook Techniculture, Watsonville, Calif., 1982-84; dir. watermelon R & D Tom Castle Seed Co., Morgan Hill, Calif., 1984-86; CEO Barham Seeds Inc., Gilroy, Calif., 1987—; v.p. Kyle and Barham LLC, La Quinta, Calif., 1996—. Cons. Basic Vegetable Products, Inc., Vacaville, 1976-78, U.S. AID, Central Am., 1977, Egypt and U.S., 1980-82, Gentry Foods & Gilroy Foods, 1978-93, Fed. Republic Germany Govt., Ethiopia, 1984; industry rep. adv. com. Onion Rsch. Program USDA, 1960-70. Contbr. articles to profl. jours. Bd. dirs., pres. Vacaville Sch. Bd., 1964-74. Sgt. USAF, 1942-45, ETO. Fellow Am. Soc. Hort. Sci. (pres. 1982, bd. dirs. 1979-83, fellows nominating com. 2002-04, chair 2004); mem. Sons in Retirement (bd. dirs. 1992-95, v.p. 1993, pres. 1994), Rotary Inernat. (bd. dirs. 1964), Elks Club. Achievements include development of 34 varieties and hybrids of processing onions, 15 triploid and 8 diploid hybrid watermelons, 2 cucumber varieties, 13 fresh market hybrid onions and 1 tomato variety. Home and Office: 7401 Crawford Dr Gilroy CA 95020-5421

BARI, PAOLA, application developer; b. Melzo, Italy, June 9, 1960; arrived in U.S., 1996; d. Gino Bari and Maria Pedrazzini; m. Jeffrey D. Aman, Apr. 2, 1999. Grad. H.S., Milan. IT specialist IBM Italy, Milan, 1981—96; adv. programmer IBM Corp., Poughkeepsie, NY, 1996—. Mem., co-founder River Winds Gallery, Beacon, NY, 2003. Exhibited in group shows at Denise Bibro Fine Art, N.Y.C., exhibitions include Barnes & Noble, Poughkeepsie, 2001, Byrdcliffe Barn Pottery, N.Y.C., 2002, Denise Bibro Fine Art, 2002, 2003, Village Gallery Katonah, N.Y., 2003, Les Bohemes, Troy, N.Y., 2003, Casa Del Arte N.Y., Highland, 2002, 2003, 2004, IBM Corp., Poughkeepsie, 2004, 2005. Mem.: Internat. Porcelain Artists and Tchrs., Highland Cultural Ctr. Arts. Home: 40 Prestwick Ct Poughkeepsie NY 12603

BARICEVIC, JOHN LALANDE, nun, mathematician, educator; b. East St. Louis, Ill., Jan. 3, 1947; d. Charles and Florence Baricevic. BS, Notre Dame Coll., St. Louis, 1969; MS, U. Ill., Urbana-Champaign, 1989. Tchr. math. Mater Dei H.S., Breese, Ill., 1985—99; adj. faculty Southwestern Ill. Coll., Belleville, Ill. Mem. Camp Ondessonk, Ozark, Ill., 1986—92. Roman Catholic. Avocations: technology, sports, reading. Office: Southwestern Illinois College 2500 Carlyle Ave Belleville IL 62221 Office Phone: 618-235-2700. Personal E-mail: baricevicssnd@yahoo.com. E-mail: sister.baricevic@swic.edu.

BARIL, NANCY ANN, gerontological nurse practitioner, consultant; b. Paterson, N.J., May 10, 1952; d. Kenneth Gerald and Jeanette Elenore (Girodet) Keiser; m. Joel Mark Baril, Apr. 15, 1984; children: Jason Kenneth, Jennifer Jean. AA, Gulf Coast C.C., 1976; BSN, Fla. State U., 1978; MSN, UCLA, 1983. Registered pub. health nurse, Calif.; ANA cert. gerontol. nurse practitioner. Charge nurse, nurse preceptor Cedar Sinai Med. Ctr., L.A., 1979-83; nurse Nursing Svcs. Inc., Sherman Oaks, Calif., 1980-83; nurse practitioner Santa Monica (Calif.) Peer Counseling Ctr., 1983; nurse cons., gerontol. nurse practitioner Summit Health Ltd., Burbank, Calif., 1983-85; nurse cons. Geriatric Assocs., Granada Hills, Calif., 1983-85; nurse cons., gerontol. nurse practitioner ARA Living Ctrs., Glendale, Calif., 1986-87; DON, gerontol. nurse practitioner Astoria Convalescent Hosp. Sign of the Dove, Sylmar, Calif., 1988-91; gerontol. nurse practitioner Balboa Plz. Med. Group, 1991-98, Absolute Health Care, Mission Hills, Calif., 1998-2000, Ctr. Sr. Health, Akron, Ohio, 2000—01, Health Strata, Nashville, 2001—03, Dr. Martin Freimer, East Stroudsburg, Pa., 2003—. Mem. PTA, Granada Hills, 1985. Mem. ANA, Calif. Coalition Nurse Practitioners, Calif. Nursing Assn., Gerontol. Soc., Sigma Theta Tau (rec. sec. 1983-85). Democrat. Episcopalian. Home: 115 Ledgeview Dr Hawley PA 18428 Office: 100 Plz Ct East Stroudsburg PA 18301 Office Phone: 570-424-6763. E-mail: nannynp@aol.com.

BARILICH, THOMAS ANTHONY, risk management consultant; b. South Bend, Ind., Sept. 24, 1955; s. John Joseph and Agnes B. (Sostritz) Barilich. AS in Bus., Ind. U., 1977, BA, 1977, M in Safety, 1979; AS in Risk Mgmt., Ins. Sch. of Chgo., 1985, AS in Mgmt., 1996. Engring. rep. Aetna Life & Casualty, Chgo., 1980-85; sr. loss control rep. Hartford Ins., Chgo., 1985-87; loss control specialist Continental Ins., Chgo., 1987-93; sr. tech. specialist constrn. divsn. AIG Cos., Chgo., 1993—. Instr. first aid Aetna Life & Casualty, 1983—84, instr. def. driving, 1984—85. Contbr. articles to Ski-smoke newsletter. Club instr. Chgo. Met. Ski Coun., 1990—91. Mem.: Constrn. Safety Assn. Am., Am. Soc. Safety Engrs., Sundowner Ski Club (chmn. racing bd. dirs. 1991—, Male Racer of the Yr. 1991). Roman Catholic. Avocations: sports officiating, basketball, volleyball, softball, stamp collecting/philately. Home: 113 Augusta Dr Gilberts IL 60136-4045

BARINGER, SANDRA KAY, literature educator; b. Ames, Iowa, Dec. 18, 1951; d. Maurice Edmund Baringer and Dorothy Mae Schlensig; children: William Maurice Schwartz, Joseph Thayendanegea Schwartz. BA in Lit., Antioch Coll., Yellow Springs, Ohio, 1976; JD, U. Denver, 1980; MA in English, U. Mo., 1991; PhD in English, U. Calif., Riverside, 1999. Pvt. practice, Milwaukie, Oreg., 1981—84; mng. atty. Lincoln County Legal Svcs./Oreg. Legal Svcs., Newport, 1984—87; grad. instr. English dept. U. Mo., Columbia, 1989—91; instr. English dept. Palomar Coll., San Marcos, Calif., 1992—2001, 2004—05; lectr. English dept. U. Calif., Riverside, 2000—. Adj. prof. bus. law Westminster Coll., Fulton, Mo., 1988—91; adj. prof. prison program Moberly (Mo.) Jr. Coll., 1988—89; adj. prof. bus. law Columbia (Mo.) Coll., 1989—90; steering com. Coalition of Contingent Academic Labor - Calif., Santa Rosa, 2003—04; field rep. UC-AFT Local 1966, 2004—. Author: The Metanarrative of Suspicion in Late Twentieth Century America, 2004; editor: CPFA News, 2001—; contbr. articles to profl. jours. Editing and pub. rels. Nat. Lawyers Guild, Portland, Oreg., 1981—84. Postdoctoral fellow, U. Calif. Humanities Rsch. Inst., 1999—2000. Mem.: MLA (mem. exec. com. part-time faculty discussion group 1999—2004), Calif. Part-time Faculty Assn. (dir. publs. 2001—), Am. Studies Assn. Office: Dept English Univ Calif Riverside CA 92521

BARIO, PATRICIA YAROCH, retired public relations executive; b. Kinde, Mich., Aug. 12, 1932; d. Edmund T. and Marie L. (Meagher) Yaroch; widowed; children: Gianfranco Edmundo and Marco Alessandro. BA in Journalism, Mich. State U., 1954. Reporter The Detroit Free Press, 1954-55; reporter, editor The Detroit News, 1955-61; dir. comm. Senator Philip Hart, Washington, 1963-76; dep. press sec. Pres. Jimmy Carter, Washington, 1977-81; pres., owner Patricia Bario Assocs., Washington, 1981-83; v.p. Burson Marsteller, Washington, 1983-85; pres., owner Patricia Bario Assocs., Washington, 1985—2003. Recipient Writing award AP, 1952; named Outstanding Citizen, Mich. State U., East Lansing, 1980; winner Silver Anvil Pub. Rels Soc. Am., 1989, 91, 94. Democrat. Roman Catholic.

BARISH, BARRY C., physics professor, researcher; b. Omaha; BA in physics, U. Calif., Berkeley, 1957; PhD in exptl. high energy physics, Berkeley, 1962. Maxine and Ronald Linde prof. physics Calif. Inst. Tech., Pasadena, 1991—; former chmn. commn. particles and fields Internat. Union Pure and Applied Physics (IUPAP), chmn. US liaison com.; bd. dirs. Nat. Sci. Bd.; spkr. in field. Recipient Klopsteg award, Am. Assn. Physics Tchrs., 2002. Fellow: AAAS, Am. Physics Soc.; mem.: NAS. Achievements include research in high-energy neutrinos important in demonstrating the quark substructure of the nucleon; search for magnetic monopole predicted in theories of Grand Unification. Office: LIGO Lab Calif Inst Tech MS 18 34 Pasadena CA 91125 Office Phone: 626-395-3853. Office Fax: 626-793-9594. Business E-Mail: barish@ligo.caltech.edu.

BARISH, CHARLES FRANKLIN, internist, gastroenterologist, researcher; b. Franklin, N.J., Jan. 5, 1955; s. Philip and Laura (Freedman) Barish; m. Debrah Lee Kaufman, Aug. 13, 1977; children: Philip, Stefanie, Jacob. BS in Chemistry with honors, U. Fla., 1976, MD, 1980. Diplomate in internal medicine and gastroenterology Am. Bd. Internal Medicine. Resident, fellow Wake Forest U. Sch. Medicine, Winston-Salem, N.C., 1980-85; physician Wake Internal Medicine Cons., Raleigh, N.C., 1985—; pres., founder Wake Rsch. Assocs., Raleigh, 1985—; clin. asst., prof. medicine U. N.C. Sch. Medicine, Chapel Hill, 1985—. Co-founder Peak Rsch., 1998; chmn. nutritional care com. Rex Hosp., Raleigh, 1987—97. Co-author: Gastroesophageal Reflux Disease, 1985; contbr. numerous sci. articles to med. jours. Pres. Jewish Cmty. Ctr., Raleigh, 1995—97; v.p. Raleigh-Cary Jewish Fedn., 1993—97, bd. dirs., 1990—. Fellow: ACP, Am. Coll. Gastroenterology; mem.: AMA, Crohn's and Colitis Found. (bd. dirs.), Wake County Med. Soc., N.C. Med. Soc., Am. Liver Found., Am. Soc. Gastrointestinal Endoscopy, Am. Coll. Physician Execs., Am. Gastroenterol. Assn., B'nai Brith, Alpha Epsilon Delta, Phi Kappa Phi, Alpha Omega Alpha. Avocation: Avocations: golf, skiing, gardening. Office: Wake Internal Medicine Cons 3100 Blue Ridge Rd Ste 300 Raleigh NC 27612-8035 E-mail: CFBGastro@aol.com.

BARISH, LAWRENCE STEPHEN, nonpartisan legislative staff administrator; b. Bklyn., Nov. 30, 1945; s. Louis C. and Anna (Sanders) B.; m. Sharon Lee Shapiro, July 2, 1967; 1 child, Lauren. BS in Polit. sci., U. Wis.-Madison, Wis., 1967; MA in Govt., U. Ariz., 1970. Legis. analyst Legis. Reference Bur., Madison, Wis., 1971-87; dir. reference and info. svcs. Wis. Legis. Reference Bur., Madison, 1987—. Chmn. rsch., comm. staff sec. Nat. Conf. State Legislatures, Denver, 1995-97; redistricting cons. Wis. Legis. and Local Govt. units, 1980—. Editor State Almanac, 1987—; contbr. articles to profl. jours. Home: 1429 W Skyline Dr Madison WI 53705-1134 Office: Wis Legis Reference Bur 1 E Main St Ste 200 Madison WI 53701-2037 Business E-Mail: larry.barish@legis.state.wi.us.

BARIST, JEFFREY, lawyer; b. Jersey City, Dec. 29, 1941; s. Irving and Lillian (Finkelstein) B.; m. Joan Elaine Travers, Feb. 19, 1967; children: Jessica, Alexis. AB summa cum laude, Rutgers U., 1963; JD cum laude, Harvard U., 1966. Bar: N.Y. 1967, U.S. Ct. Appeals (2d cir.) 1968, U.S. Dist. Ct. (so. dist.) N.Y. 1969, U.S. Supreme Ct. 1975. Law sec. U.S. Dist. Judge Irving Ben Cooper, N.Y.C., 1966-67; ptnr., chmn. nat. litigation group Milbank, Tweed, Hadley & McCloy, N.Y.C., 1996—. Author: Commercial Arbitration Law and Clauses, 1994; contbr. articles to profl. jours. Bd. trustees Lawyers Com. for Civil Rights Under Law; mem. N.Y.C. Panel of Disting. Neutrals, Ctr. for Public Rsch. Fellow Am. Coll. Trial Lawyers, Am. Bar Found.; mem. Am. Law Inst.; Phi Beta Kappa. Office: Milbank Tweed Hadley McCloy 47th Fl 1 Chase Manhattan Plz Fl 47 New York NY 10005-1413 Office Phone: 212-530-5115. Office Fax: 212-822-5115. Business E-Mail: jbarist@milbank.com.

BARITZ, LOREN, history professor; b. Chgo., Dec. 26, 1928; s. Joseph Harry and Helen (Garland) B.; m. Phyllis L. Handelsman, Dec. 26, 1948; children: Tony, Joseph. BA, Roosevelt U., 1953; MA, U. Wis., 1954, PhD, 1956. Asst. prof. history Wesleyan U., Middletown, Conn., 1956-62; assoc. prof. Roosevelt U., Chgo., 1962-63; prof. U. Rochester, 1963-69, chmn. dept. history, 1964-67; leading prof. SUNY, Albany, 1969-71; exec. v.p. Empire State Coll., exec. dir. univ. commn. on purposes and priorities, 1975-76; from exec. v.p. to provost SUNY, 1971-79; dir. N.Y. Inst. Humanities; prof. history NYU, 1979-80; provost, vice chancellor for acad. affairs U. Mass., Amherst, 1980-83, prof. history, 1980-91, prof. emeritus, 1991—. Vis. lectr. U. Wis.-Madison, 1959-60; cultural cons. to UNESCO, Paris, 1968-71; mgmt. cons. Balykchy Inst. of Bus. and Law, Kyrgyzstan, 1997, 99, Slovak U. of Tech., Bratislava, Slovak Republic, 1997, Comenius U., Bratislava, 1998. Author: City on a Hill, 1964, Servants of Power, 1960, Sources of the American Mind, 2 vols., 1966, The Culture of the Twenties, 1970, The American Left, 1971, Backfire, 1985, 98, The Good Life, 1989. Co-chmn. policy coun. rsch. and svc. Assembly Univ. Goals, Am. Acad. Arts and Scis., 1969-70; del. Dem. Nat. Conv., 1968; bd. govs. chmn. com. on acad. affairs Haifa U., 1975-92; mem. exec. bd. Nat. Com. for Labor, Israel, 1984-94; mgmt. cons. Am. Stock Exchange, 1994-95, 97. Rsch. Tng. fellow Social Sci. Rsch. Coun., 1955-56, grantee, 1960; grantee Am. Council Learned Socs., 1963. Home: 12 Glennana Way Sheffield MA 01257 E-mail: lbaritz@earthlink.net.

BARK, NIGEL MARTYN, psychiatrist; b. Tarporley, Eng., July 3, 1941; s. Oliver and Gwen B.; m. Helen (McQuaid) B., OCt. 3, 1970; children: Lesley Bark-Marzec, Philippa Bark-McHugh, Charles. BA in Natural Sci., Cambridge U., 1962, MA, 1986, MB, BChir., 1966; MS in Psychiat. Epidemiology, Columbia U., 1986. Diplomate Am. Bd. Psychiatry and Neurology; cert. in psychopharmacology Am. Soc. Clin. Psychopharmacology, 2000. Surg. intern Worcester (Eng.) Royal Infirmary, 1967; med. intern Univ. Coll. Hosp., London, 1967; resident in obstetrics Rotunda Hosp., Dublin, 1968; resident in pediatrics Our Lady's Hosp. for Sick Children, Dublin, 1969; resident in psychiatry St. Patrick's Hosp., Dublin, 1970-73, psychiat. registrar, 1970-75; dep. med. dir. Daus. of Charity Svcs. for Mentally Handicapped, Dublin, 1973-76; rsch. assoc. Nathan S. Kline Inst. for Psychiat. Rsch., Orangeburg, 1981-90; pvt. practice NYC, 1981—90; pvt. practice psychopharmacology NYC and Orangeburg, NY, 1976—; assoc. med. dir. schizophrenia rsch. unit Bronx (NY) Psychiat. Ctr., Albert Einstein Coll. Medicine, 1990-95, dep. med. dir., 1995, dir. schizophrenia rsch. unit, 1996—. Cons. psychiatrist Summit Park Hosp. and Robert L. Yeager Health Ctr., Pomona, N.Y., 1982-90; attending psychiatrist Gracie Sq. Hosp., N.Y.C., 1981-90; asst. attending psychiatrist Good Samaritan Hosp., Suffern, N.Y., 1985-89, St. Luke's Roosevelt Hosp., N.Y.C., 1983-86, Harlem Hosp., N.Y.C., 1983-84; med. dir. St. Luke's Day Hosp., N.Y.C., 1982; postdoctoral fellow psychiat. epidemiology tng. program Columbia U., N.Y.C., 1981-82; unit chief in rsch. and rehab. Rockland Psychiat. Ctr., 1978-81; rsch. psychiatrist Rockland Rsch. Inst., 1976-78; adj. psychiatrist Lenox Hill (N.Y.) Hosp., 1985-90. Editor: Internat. Jour. Mental Health on Risk Factors Schizophrenia and Prevention, 2000-01; contbr. about 30 sci. articles to profl. jours.; contbr. chpts. to books. Fellow Am. Psychiat. Assn. (pub. affairs rep. W. Hudson dist. br. 1985-91, pres. 1987-89, organizer, chair Internat. Psychiat. symposia ann. meetings); mem. Royal Coll. Psychiatrists (hon. sec. mental handicap sect. Irish div. 1974-76, organizer, chair ann. meetings 2001-05), Brit. Med. Assn. Home: 117 Constitution Dr Orangeburg NY 10962-2733 Office: Bronx Psychiat Ctr 1500 Waters Pl Bronx NY 10461 Home Fax: 718-862-4889; Office Fax: 718-862-4889. Personal E-mail: nbark1@pol.net. Business E-Mail: brmdnbb@omh.state.ny.us.

BARKAN, JOEL DAVID, political science professor; b. Toledo, Apr. 28, 1941; s. Manuel and Toby (Wolfe) B.; m. Sandra Lynn Hackman, Sept. 9, 1962; children: Bronwyn Michelle, Joshua Manuel. AB, Cornell U., 1963; MA, UCLA, 1965, PhD, 1970. Asst. prof. polit. sci. U. Calif., Irvine, 1969-72; asst. prof. polit. sci. U. Iowa, Iowa City, 1972-76, assoc. prof., 1976-81, prof., 1981—2005, chmn. dept. polit. sci., 1985-87, dir. ctr. internat. and comparative studies, 1981-83, prof. emeritus, 2005—. Vis. rsch. fellow Makerere U., Uganda, 1966—67, U. Dar es Salaam, Tanzania, 1973—74, Fondation Nat. des Scis. Politiques, Paris, 1978—79, U. Nairobi, Kenya, 1979, 80, Ctr. Study of Developing Socs., New Delhi, 1984, Cornell U., 1990, U.S. Inst. Peace, 1997—98, Nat. Endowment for Democracy, 2000, 2003—, Woodrow Wilson Internat. Ctr., 2001—02, U. Cape Town, 2004; regional governance advisor for Ea. and So. Africa USAID, 1992—94; sr. cons. on governance World Bank, 2000—. Co-author, editor: Politics and Public Policy in Kenya and Tanzania, 1979, rev. edit., 1984, Beyond Capitalism Versus Socialism in Kenya and Tanzania, 1994; co-author: The Legislative Connection, 1984; author: An African Dilemma, 1975; contbr. articles to profl. jours. Pres. Iowa City Fgn. Rels. Coun., 1989—90. Fellow, Social Sci. Rsch. Coun., 1966—68, Fulbright Found., 1978—79, 2005, Indo-Am. fellow, 1984, Randolph fellow, 1997—98, Woodrow Wilson fellow, 2001—02, Reagan-Facell fellow, 2005—; grantee, Rockefeller Found., 1973—74, US-AID, 1978—81, Ford Found., 1992—99. Mem. Am. Polit. Sci. Assn., African Studies Assn. (bd. dirs. 1990-93), Coun. Fgn. Rels. Office: U Iowa Dept Polit Sci Iowa City IA 52242 Office Phone: 319-335-2358. Business E-Mail: joel-barkan@uiowa.edu.

BARKEMA, DAVID VICTOR, retired secondary school educator; b. Grand Rapids, Mich., Feb. 11, 1940; s. Frank and Grace Rebecca (Redman) b.; m. Diane Wilma Lemery, Dec. 24, 1960 (div. Mar. 1983); children: Susan Diane Barkema Andrews, Robert David; m. Marianna Penton Merizon, Sept. 2, 1983; children: Stephanie Merizon Worden, John Merizon. AB in

English/Edn., Ctrl. Mich. U., 1962; MSW, Grand Valley State U., 1981. Cert. tchr., Mich. Tchr. White Cloud (Mich.) Pub. Schs., 1962; tchr. secondary lang. arts Grand Rapids Pub. Schs., 1962—2000; ret., 2000. Mem. Grand Rapids Edn. Assn. (treas. 1967-68, v.p. 1968-70, pres. 1970-72). Home: 3984 Keeweenaw Dr NE Grand Rapids MI 49525-2008 E-mail: bar3984@aol.com.

BARKER, AL(BERT) C(HARLES), artist; b. West Paterson, N.J., June 19, 1941; s. Albert C. and Ann (Downey) B.; m. Ann Goddard, Apr. 1968, (div. Jan. 1972); children: Laura Downey, Jason H.G. BS in Forestry, W.Va. U., 1964; MS in Horticulture, R.I.U., 1969; PhD, Rutgers U., 1972. Instr. Essex Agrl. Inst., Danvers, Mass., 1969-70; fellow Rutgers U., New Brunswick, N.J., 1970-72; tchr. Hightstown (N.J.) High Sch., 1972-80; artist Bordentown, N.J., 1980—. Illustrator: Grizzly Book, 1983, Deer Book, 1983, Book of Small Flies, 1984. Cover artist, Easton (Md.) Waterfowl Festival, 1982. Mem. Salmagundi Club (bd. dirs. 1983-84, Graham prize, 1983, Franklin Williams prize, 1983), Miniature Artists of Am., Miniature Soc. N.J., Artist Fellowship, Whiskey Painters Am. Avocations: hunting, fishing, soccer, baseball cards, old cars. Home and Office: PO Box 703 224 Prince St Bordentown NJ 08505-1320

BARKER, BARBARA ANN, ophthalmologist; b. Paterson, NJ, Nov. 10, 1943; d. Earle Louis and Dorothy Louise (Williamson) Barker; m. Joel Ira Papernik, July 28, 1972; children: Deborah Papernik, Ilana Papernik. BA magna cum laude, Conn. Coll., 1965; BS, Yale U., 1967; MA, Rutgers Med. Sch., 1974; MD, Mt. Sinai Sch. Medicine, 1976. Diplomate Am. Bd. Ophthalmology. Intern Beth Israel Med. Ctr., 1977; resident Mt. Sinai Sch. Medicine/Beth Israel Med. Ctr., 1980, fellow in glaucoma, 1980-81, fellow cornea, refractive surgery, 1981-82; pvt. practice medicine specializing in ophthalmology, N.Y.C., 1983—. Rsch. technician The Rockefeller U., N.Y.C., 1965—66; tchr. Riverdale Country Sch., N.Y.C., 1967—68; rsch. asst. Sloan Kettering Inst., N.Y.C., 1969—72; asst. clin. prof. Mt. Sinai Sch. Medicine, N.Y.C., 1982—; mem. staff N.Y. Eye and Ear Hosp., Beth Israel/St. Luke's/Roosevelt Hosp. Recipient Resident Best Paper award, Beth Israel Med. Ctr., 1989, Honor award, Am. Acad. Ophthalmology, 1955; grantee Beth Israel Rsch. grant, 1983, NSF, 1966. Fellow: ACS, N.Y. Acad. Medicine; mem.: AMA, N.Y. County Med. Assn., Women's Med. Soc. NYC, Am. Med. Women's Assn., Phi Beta Kappa. Home: 11 E 86th St New York NY 10028-0501 Office: 70 E 96th St New York NY 10028 Office Phone: 212-289-2244. Personal E-mail: bbarkermd@aol.com.

BARKER, BARBARA YVONNE, nursing home administrator; b. Whittier, Calif., Apr. 19, 1951; d. Donald Wayne and Ruth Berta (Hagen) Schutt; m. Jimmy D.W. McWilson, Feb. 23, 1974 (div. Sept. 1980); m. Richard Alexander Barker, Aug. 01, 1987; 1 child, Christina Nicole. AS in Respiratory Therapy, Mt. San Antonio Coll., Walnut, Calif., 1971; BSBA, U. Redlands, 1989; MPA, Marist Coll., 1996. Lic. nursing home adminstr., Calif., Iowa; registered respiratory therapist; lic. respiratory care practitioner. Neonatal respiratory therapist U. Calif.-San Diego Med. Ctr., 1971-74; respiratory therapy supr. Hillside Hosp., 1974-75; asst. dir. ops. J.D.W. McWilson and Assocs., 1975-77; sales rep. Baxter-Travenol Home Respiratory Therapy, 1984-86; clin. application specialist Infrasonics, Inc., 1987-88; respiratory therapist/clin. coord., nursing home adminstr. Sharp Health Care, 1977-84, 88-90; nursing home adminstr. Care West Anza, 1990, Brighton Pl. Spring Valley, San Diego, 1990-91; dir. respiratory care No. Dutchess Hosp., Rhinebeck, N.Y., 1991-98; adminstr. Dubuque (Iowa) Nursing and Rehab Ctr, 1998—. Cons. health care delivery sys. various acute and long-term care orgns., Dutchess County, N.Y., 1991-98; developer quality assurance program long-term care facility, San Diego, 1990; med. products rschr. devel. neonatal ventilator device FDA, San Diego, 1988; coord. regional healthcare seminar, Dutchess County, Marist Coll. Author quality assurance protocol durable med. equipment cos., San Diego Am. Lung Assn., 1989; developer instrnl. manuals for patients with chronic lung disease and asthma, San Diego, 1990. Bd. mem. San Diego chpt. Calif. Assn. Health Facilities, 1990-91; participant Christmas in April civic rebldg. program, Poughkeepsie, N.Y., 1992-93. Mem. Am. Assn. Respiratory Therapy, Calif. Soc. Respiratory Therapy (treas., bd. mem., ednl. developer 1986-90), Calif. Assn. Health Facilities, Mid Hudson Repiratory Care Dirs. Assn. Democrat. Lutheran. Avocations: boating, cross country skiing. Office: Dubuque Nursing and Rehab Ctr 2935 Kaufmann Ave Dubuque IA 52001-1656 E-mail: bybarker@dubuque.net.

BARKER, CELESTE ARLETTE, computer scientist; b. Redding, Calif., Apr. 19, 1947; d. Edwin Walter Squires and Rachel (Kinkead) Layton; m. Julius Jeep Chernak, Sept. 13, 1970, (div. 1980); children: Sean Matthew, Bret Allen; m. Jackson Lynn Barker, Oct. 8, 1988. BA in Art, San Francisco State U., 1970; AA in Engring. Tech., Coll. Marin, 1980; MBA in Mgmt., Golden Gate U., 1988. Cert. netware engr. Art tchr. San Rafael (Calif.) Schs., 1971-75; owner, photographer Julius Chernak Photography, Novato, Calif., 1970-76; draftsman Donald Foster Drafting, San Rafael, 1975-76; surveyor Parks Dept. State Calif., Inverness, 1976; electric draftsman Pacific Gas & Electric, San Rafael, 1976-78, electric engring. estimator, 1978-79, mktg. rep. Santa Rosa, 1980-85, valuation analyst San Francisco, 1985-86, budget analyst, 1986-88, budget system project mgr., 1988-89, fin. asset mgr. Vallejo, Calif., 1989-90; ops. mgr. San Francisco Mus. Modern Art, 1990-91; cons. CB Cons., Atlanta, 1991-93; computer local area network mgr. Ga. Inst. Tech., Atlanta, 1993-94; systems integrator Bank South, Atlanta, 1994-95; mgmt. info. sys. mgr. Dinwiddie Constr., San Francisco, 1995-96; process/project mgr. Sybase, Inc., Emeryville, Calif., 1996-98; Wintel delivery mgr. Fair-Isaac Cos., San Rafael, Calif., 1998—2000; dir. support Kabira Techs., San Rafael, Calif., 2000—01; dir. profl. svcs. and tech. support PC Guardian, San Rafael, Calif., 2002—. Dir. Mariner Green Townhomes Assn., treas. 1987-88. Mem. Sierra Club. Avocations: photography, painting, backpacking. Home: 29 Woodside Way San Rafael CA 94901-1439 Office Phone: 415-259-3165. Business E-Mail: cbarker@pcguardian.com.

BARKER, CHRISTOPHER B., lawyer; AB magna cum laude, Brown Univ., 1982; JD, Harvard Univ., 1985. Bar: Mass. 1985. Project mgr. engring., construction firm; atty. Nagashima Ohno & Tsunematsu, Tokyo, 1990—91; ptnr., real estate dept. Goodwin Procter LLP, Boston, chair, real estate group, mem., exec. com. Frequent lectr., writer in field. Mem.: ABA. Office: Goodwin Procter LLP Exchange Pl 53 State St Boston MA 02109 Office Phone: 617-570-1462. Office Fax: 617-523-1231. Business E-Mail: cbarker@goodwinprocter.com.

BARKER, CLIVE, artist, film director, film producer, scriptwriter; b. Liverpool, Eng., 1952; s. Len and Joan B. Student, U. Liverpool, Eng. Author: (plays) Incarnations (Frankenstein in Love, History of the Devil, Colossus), Forms of Heaven (Paradise Street, Subtle Bodies, Crazyface); (short story collection) Books of Blood I-VI (books IV, V, and VI released in U.S. as The Inhuman Condition, 1986, In the Flesh, 1986, Cabal; (TV movie) Saint Sinner, 2002; (novels) The Damnation Game, 1985, Weaveworld, 1987, Cabal, 1988, The Great and Secret Show, 1989, Imajica, 1991, The Thief of Always, 1992, Everville, 1994, Sacrament, 1996, A-Z of Horror, 1997, Galilee, 1998, The Essential Clive Barker, 1999, Coldheart Canyon, 2001; prodr. Hellraiser II: Hellbound, 1990, Candyman, 1992, Hellraiser III: Hell on Earth, 1992, Candyman II: Farewell to the Flesh, 1995, Hellraiser: Bloodline, 1996, Gods & Monsters, 1997, (Fox TV) Spirits and Shadows, 1997; writer and dir. (screenplays) Hellraiser, 1987, Nightbreed, 1990, Lord of Illusions, 1995, Art Exhibition, 1998, Clive Barker's Freaks, 1998, Undying, 2001. Home: Los Angeles CA Mailing: PO Box 691829 West Hollywood CA 90069*

BARKER, CLYDE FREDERICK, surgeon, educator; b. Salt Lake City, Aug. 16, 1932; s. Frederick George and Jennetta Elizabeth (Stephens) B.; m. Dorothy Joan Bieler, Aug. 11, 1956; children: Frederick George II, John Randolph, William Stephens, Elizabeth Dell. BA, Cornell U., 1954, MD, 1958. Diplomate Am. Bd. Surgery. Intern Hosp. U. Pa., Phila., 1958-59, resident in surgery, 1959-64, fellow in vascular surgery, 1964-65; fellow in med. genetics U. Pa. Sch. Medicine, Phila., 1965-66, assoc. in surgery, 1964-68, assoc. in med. genetics, 1966-72; attending surgeon Hosp. U. Pa., Phila., 1966—; chief div. transplantation U. Pa. Sch. Medicine, Phila., 1966—2001, asst. prof. surgery, 1968-69, assoc. prof. surgery, 1969-73, prof. surgery, 1973—, J. William White prof. surg. research, 1978-82, chief div. vascular surgery, 1982—2001, Guthrie prof. surgery, 1982—, John Rhea Barton prof. surgery, 1983—2001, chmn. dept. surgery, 1983—2001; chief surgery Hosp. U. Pa., Phila., 1983—2001. Dir. Harrison dept. surgery rsch. U. Pa., Phila., 1983-2001; immunobiology study sect. NIH; chmn. clin. practices U. Pa., 1987-89; v.p. United Network for Organ Sharing, 2001-02, pres., 2002-- Mem. editl. bd. Jour. Transplantation, 1977-2001, Clin. Transplantation, 1988—, Jour. Surg. Rsch., 1979-85, Jour. Diabetes, 1981-86, Archives of Surgery, 1987-96, Transplantation Procs., 1990-2001, Surgery, 1991-95, Cell Transplantation, 1991—, Postgrad. Gen. Surgery, 1991-95, Jour. ACS, 1994—, Annals of Surgery, 1995—; contbr. articles to profl. jours. and textbooks. Markle Found. Scholar, 1968-74; NIH grantee, 1974—; recipient Merit award NIH, 1987-95. Fellow AOA, NAS (Inst. Medicine), ACS (com. Forum on Fundamental Surg. Problems 1983-88, vice chmn. 1987-88, bd. govs. 1994-2001, pres. Phila. chpt. 1991-92), Coll. Physicians Phila., Royal Coll. Surgeons Eng. (hon.), Royal Coll. Surgeons Ireland (hon.); mem. AMA, Royal Coll. Surgeons of Ireland (hon.), Assn. Acad. Surgery, Am. Diabetes Assn., Am. Soc. Artificial Internal Organs, Am. Fedn. Clin. Rsch., Juvenile Diabetes Found., Soc. Univ. Surgeons, Am. Surg. Assn. (recorder 1991-96, pres. 1996-97, medallion for sci. achievement 2003), Soc. Clin. Surgery (chmn. membership 1984-85), Halsted Soc. (chmn. membership 1984-85, v.p. 1985-86, pres. 1986-87), Surg. Biology Club II, Soc. Vascular Surgery, Internat. Cardiovascular Soc., Internat. Surg. Group (treas. 1988-94, pres. 1994-95), Internat. Soc. Surgery (v.p. U.S. chpt. 1995-97, pres. 1997-99), Transplantation Soc. (councilman 1978-84, 94—), Am. Soc. Transplant Surgeons (chmn. membership 1980-81, treas. 1988-91, pres. 1992-93), Unitd Network for Organ Sharing (v.p. 2001-02), (pres. 2002-03), Am. Acad. Arts and Scis., Assn. Am. Physicians, Phila. Acad. Surgery (program chmn. 1984-86, v.p. 1986-88, pres. 1988-89), Greater Delaware Valley Soc. Transplant Surgeons (pres. 1978-80), Am. Philos. Soc. (coun. 2003—, v.p. 2005—) Home: 3 Coopertown Rd Haverford PA 19041-1012 Office: Hosp Univ Pa Dept Surgery 3400 Spruce St Philadelphia PA 19104-4206

BARKER, EDWIN BOGUE, musician; b. Tucson, Apr. 14, 1954; s. Francis Hustis and Mary Jeanne (Austin) B.; m. Pamela Paikin, 1980; children: Rachel Leigh, Ilana Michelle. Studies with Henry Portnoi, Peter Mercurio, Angelo LaMariana, Richard Stephan, David Perleman, 1965—76; student, Music Acad. of the West, Santa Barbara, Calif., 1969—71; MusB with honors, New Eng. Conservatory Music, 1976. Prin. bass Lake George Opera Orch., NY, 1971-72; substitute mem. N.Y. Philharm., 1976; mem. Chgo. Symphony Orch., 1976-77; prin. bass Boston Symphony, 1977—; mem. Boston Symphony Chamber Players, 1977—; instr. double bass New Eng. Conservatory Music, 1977-90, 98—, Boston Conservatory Music, 1980-83; instr. double bass and chamber music Tanglewood Music Ctr., 1978—; instr. double bass Boston U., 1983—2002; assoc. prof. Boston U. Coll. Fine Arts, Sch. Music, 2002—. Bass and string clinics Am. String Tchrs. Assn. and U. Mich., Ann Arbor, 1982, 83; instr. double bass Teton Orchestral Tng. Seminar, Wyo., 1984-86; prin. bass and faculty mem. Georg Solti Orchestral Tng. Project, Carnegie Hall, 1994—; prin. bass UN Orch. Musicians of the World, Geneva, 1995—; master classes Nat. Orchestral Inst., U. Md., 1991-, U. Ga., 1997, Juilliard Sch., 1999, New World Symphony, 2003; concert tours in N.Am., Europe, and Asia. Solo appearances with Boston Symphony Orch., Tanglewood, New England Conservatory Symphony Orch., Bergen (Norway) Music Festival, Carnegie Recital Hall, N.Y.C., 1984, 85, others; concerto performance with Boston Symphony, Madrid, 1993; other performances include: Concerto for Double Bass and Chamber Orch. by Gunther Schuller, Boston premiere with Pro Arte Chamber Orch., 1987, Concerto for Double Bass and Chamber Orch. by James Yannatos, premiere performance, 1986, Concerto for Double Bass and Orchestra by Edward Tubin, with Boston Symphony Orch., Boston premiere, 1994, Juilliard Quartet, Libr. of Congress, 1992, Muir Quartet, 1998, 99, premiere performance James Yannatos' Variations for Solo Contrabass, 1998, premier performance with Lydian String Quartet of Serenade in D by Harold Shapiro, for String Quartet and Double bass, 1999, World Premiere of Concertino for Double Bass and Chamber Orch. with Pro Arte Chamber Orch., 2000; soloist with Boston Symphony Orch., 2001; recs. include Three Sonatas for Double Bass, 1998, Variations for Solo Contrabass, 2000. Mem. Am. Youth Symphony, 1961-69, UCLA Symphony, 1968-69; mem. Players com. Boston Symphony, 1988-92, mem. music dir. search com., 2000-. Recipient Benjamin H. Delson award Berkshire Music Ctr., 1975, Chadwick medal New Eng. Conservatory of Music, 1976; named one of Outstanding Young Men of Am., 1986, Most Outstanding Alumni New Eng. Conservatory of Music, 1993. Mem. Am. Fedn. Musicians., Internat. Soc. Bassists (dir. 1983) Office: Symphony Hall Boston MA 02115

BARKER, HAROLD GRANT, surgeon, educator; b. Salt Lake City, June 10, 1917; s. Frederick George and Elizabeth Jennetta (Stephens) B.; m. Kathleen Butler, July 29, 1949; children: Janet Stephens, Douglas Reid. AB, U. Utah, 1939, postgrad., 1939-41; MD, U. Pa., 1943. Diplomate Am. Bd. Surgery. Intern. Hosp. U. Pa., 1943-44, asst. resident in surgery, 1947-51, sr. resident in surgery, 1951-52, asst. attending surgeon, 1952-53; also asst. instr., research fellow U. Pa., 1946-51, instr., research fellow, 1951-52, assoc. in surgery, 1952-53; asst. prof. surgery Columbia U., 1953-57, assoc. prof., 1957-68, prof., 1968-82, prof. emeritus, 1982—. Asst. attending surgeon Presbyn. Hosp., 1953-57, assoc. attending surgeon, 1957-69, attending surgeon, 1969-89, cons. surgeon, 1989—, dir. med. affairs, 1974-82; pvt. practice, Phila., 1952-53, N.Y.C., 1953-88. Contbr. articles med. jours. Served from 1st lt. to capt., M.C. AUS, 1944-46, ETO. Fellow ACS; mem. Soc. U. Surgeons, N.Y. Surg. Soc., Am. Physiol. Soc., Soc. Exptl. Biology and Medicine, AMA, Halsted Soc., N.Y. State (chmn. surg. sect. 1961-62), N.Y. County med. socs., Am. Surg. Assn., N.Y. Gastroent. Assn., Société Internationale de Chirurgie, Soc. Surgery Alimentary Tract, Allen O. Whipple Surg. Soc., Am. Assn. History Medicine, Collegium Internationale Chirurgiae Digestivae, Century Assn., Manursing Island Club, Am. Yacht Club. Home: 5009 Theall Rd Rye NY 10580

BARKER, HAROLD KENNETH, former university dean; b. Louisville, Apr. 14, 1922; s. J.M. and Fannie Mae (Elliott) B.; m. Elizabeth Johns, Mar. 11, 1948 (dec.); children: Leslie Ann, Glenn Lewis.; m. Beverly Williams, Feb. 28, 1984. AB, U. Louisville, 1948, MA, 1949; PhD, U. Mich., 1959. Instr. Gunfire Prep. Sch., Hanau, Germany, 1946; sch. psychologist, vis. tchr. Bay City (Mich.) Pub. Schs., 1949-52; also instr. Bay City Jr. Coll.; sch. psychologist Ypsilanti (Mich.) Pub. Schs., 1952-53; instr. Eastern Mich. U., 1954-58; asst. dir. Bur. Appointments and Occupational Info., U. Mich., 1954-59; assoc. exec. sec. Am. Assn. Colls. Tchr. Edn., Washington, 1959-66, dir., 1972—; dean Coll. Edn., U. Akron, 1966-85, asst. to pres., 1985-87, dean emeritus, 1987. Bd. dirs. World U., San Juan, P.R., 1966—, Joint Council Econ. Edn., 1979 Editor: AACTE Handbook of International Education Programs, 1963; contbr. articles to profl. jours. and periodicals. Chmn. bd. dirs. Edwin Shaw Hosp., 1989; trustee U. Akron Found., 1994—. Recipient award outstanding profl. svc. Am. Assn. Colls. Tchr. Edn., 1966; named Hon. Alumni U. Akron, 1992. Mem. Phi Delta Kappa (internat. commn. 1962-69) Home: 1811 Brookwood Dr Akron OH 44313-5061 Office: Dept Devel Martin Univ Ctr U Akron Akron OH 44325-2603

BARKER, HILDA JEAN, retired library director; b. New Hill, N.C., Aug. 12, 1938; d. John Hollie and Vila Belle (Melton) Barker; children: Rheth Alexander Fish, Hollie Ann Fish. BS, East Carolina U., 1960; MS in Edn., N.C. Agrl. and Tech. U., 1979; MLS, U. N.C., Greensboro, 1990. Cert. librarian, N.C. Bus. tchr. Contentnea H.S., Kinston, N.C., 1960-61; math. tchr. Great Bridge (Va.) Jr. H.S., 1961-62; spl. edn. tchr. Craddock Jr. H.S., Portsmouth, Va., 1962-63; sec. Dan River Mills, Danville, Va., 1963-64; bus. tchr. Bartlett Yancey H.S., Yanceyville, N.C., 1964-67, Rockingham C.C., Wentworth, N.C., 1967-72; dir. vols. Annie Penn Meml. Hosp., Reidsville, N.C., 1973-78; librarian Caswell County Schs., Yanceyville, 1978-87; bibliographer Elem. Sch. Libr. Collection, Greensboro, 1987-89; reference librarian Franklin County Libr., Louisburg, N.C., 1991, libr. dir., 1991-2001. Contbr. video revs. to Libr. Jour. Treas. Franklin County Partnership for Children, Louisburg, 1994—2001; vol. program com. and facilities improvement com. Friends of Pittsboro Libr., NC; ch. vol., 2001—. Avocations: sewing, crafts. E-mail: hildajeanbarker@aol.com.

BARKER, JAMES F., academic administrator; b. Kingsport, Tenn. BArch, Clemson U., 1970; M in Arch. and Urban Design, Washington U., 1973; PhD (hon.), S.C. State U., Mars Hill Coll. Dean Sch. Arch. Miss. State U.; dean Coll. Arch. Clemson (S.C.) U., 1986—95, dean Coll. Arch., Arts and Humanities, 1995—99, pres., 1999—. Fellow: AIA; mem.: Assn. Collegiate Schs. Arch. (past pres., Nat. Disting. Prof. award). Office: Clemson Univ 201 Sikes Hall Clemson SC 29634

BARKER, JAMES REX, water transportation executive, director; b. Cleve., Aug. 3, 1935; s. William Wardel and Elizabeth Ranghild (Wandler) B.; m. Kaye Elizabeth Schumacher, Aug. 3, 1957; children: James Arthur, Karen Elizabeth, Mark William. BA, Columbia U., 1957; MBA with distinction, Harvard U., 1963; DSc (hon.), Maine Maritime Acad., 1978. Planning exec. Pickands Mather & Co., Cleve., 1963-67; v.p. Harbridge House, Boston, 1967-69; founder, exec. v.p. Temple, Barker & Sloane, Wellesley, Mass., 1970-71; chmn. bd. Moore McCormack Resources, Inc., Stamford, Conn., 1971-87, chief exec. officer, 1971-87; vice chmn., founder, co-owner Mormac Marine Group Inc., Stamford, Conn., 1987—; chmn., prin. Interlake Steamship Co., Stamford, 1987—. Vice chmn., prin. owner Moran Towing Co.; owner, chmn. New England Fast Ferry Inc.; bd. dirs. Brink's Co., Verizon. Lt. (j.g.) USCG, 1957-61. Mem. Am. Bur. Shipping (bd. mgrs.) Clubs: Wee Burn Country, Noroton Yacht, N.Y. Yacht, Rolling Rock, Union, Links. Episcopalian. Home: 180 Long Neck Point Rd Darien CT 06820-5816 Office: Mormac Marine Group Inc 1 Landmark Sq Stamford CT 06901-2501

BARKER, JOHN ROY, lawyer; b. St. Joseph, Mo., Mar. 9, 1947; s. Frank Otis and Ella Mae (Wiley) B.; m. Mary Lucille Smith, Apr. 17, 1971; children: Sarah J., Kathryn W., Mary E. BA, U. Mo., 1969; JD, U. Mich., 1974. Bar: U.S. Dist. Ct. (no. dist.) Okla. 1974, Okla. 1974, U.S. Ct. Appeals (10th cir.) 1974. Lawyer Gable Gotwals, Tulsa, Okla., 1974—2004; sr. v.p., gen. counsel ONEOK, Inc., Tulsa, Okla., 2004—. Pres. Jenks (Okla.) Pub. Schs. Found., 1989-91; sec. St. Simeon's Episcopal Home, Tulsa, 1991-96, v.p., 1996-98, pres., 1998-2001; pres St. Simeon's Home Found., 2002-04; vice chmn. Sutton Avian Rsch. Ctr., Bartlesville, Okla., 1994-96; pres. Arts and Humanities Coun., Tulsa, 1994-96, pres., 1993-95. Served in U.S. Army, 1969—71. Mem. ABA, Okla. Bar Assn. (Outstanding Young Lawyer 1978, chair Young Lawyers 1978), Tulsa County Bar Assn., Tulsa Title and Probate (pres. 1987-88). Episcopalian. Avocations: running, bicycling. Office: ONEOK Inc 100 W Fifth St Tulsa OK 74103 Office Phone: 918-588-7946. Business E-Mail: jbarker@oneok.com.

BARKER, JOSHUA, information technology executive; BS in Econs., Va. Tech. U., 1990. Contracts Management U. Va., 2002. Analyst ICF Resources, Fairfax, Va., 1990—92; v.p. Intelligent Decisions, Chantilly, Va., 1992—96; exec. v.p. Xram, Chantilly, 1996—2001; sr. v.p. Superlative Technologies, Inc., McLean, Va., 2001—. Named Small Businessman of Yr., Def. Supply Svc., Wash., 1996; recipient Letter of Commendation, Met. Police Dept., Washington, 2002. Mem.: Nat. Contract Mgmt. Assn., Army Navy Country Club. Episcopalian. Avocations: skiing, tennis. Office: Superlative Technologies Inc 8300 Greensboro Dr Mc Lean VA 22102 Office Phone: 703-821-3732. Office Fax: 703-821-3743.

BARKER, KEITH RENE, investment banker; b. Elkhart, Ind., July 28, 1928; s. Clifford C. and Edith (Hausmna) B.; children by previous marriage: Bruce C., Lynn K.; m. Elizabeth S. Arrington, Nov. 24, 1965; 1 child, Jennifer Scott. AB, Wabash Coll., 1950; MBA, Ind. U., 1952. Sales rep. Fulton, Reid & Co., Inc., Ft. Wayne, Ind., 1951—55, office, 1955—59, asst. v.p. then v.p., 1960, dir., 1961, asst. sales mgr., 1963, sales mgr., 1964, dir. Ind. ops.; sr. v.p. Fulton, Reid & Co., 1966—75; pres., CEO Fulton, Reid & Staples, Inc., 1975—77; ptnr. William C. Roney & Co., 1977—79; exec. com. Cascade Industries, Inc.; assoc. A.G. Edwards & Sons, Inc., 1984—89, v.p. investments, 1989—. Dir. Fulton, Reid & Staples, Inc., Craft House Corp., Nobility Homes, Inc. Pres. Historic Ft. Wayne, Inc.; cons. to Mus. Historic Ft. Wayne; nominee, trustee Ohio Hist. Soc.; mem. Smithsonian Assocs.; mem. fin. com. E. Tenn. Hist. Soc., dir., treas. collections com.; v.p. Ft. Wayne Hist. Soc.; bd. dirs. Ft. Wayne YMCA, 1963-64; cons. of collections East Tenn. Hist. Soc. Recipient Achievement cert. Inst. Investment Banking, U. Pa., 1959. Mem. Alliance Française, VFW (past comdr.), Co. Mil. Historians, Cleve. Grays, Am. Soc. Arms Collectors, 1st Cleve. Cavalry Assn., Nat. Assn. Securities Dealers (bus. conduct com.), Beaver Creek Hunt Club, Cleve. Athletic Club, Rockwell Springs Club, Hill and Dale Club, Masons, Phi Beta Kappa. Episcopalian. Home: 15812 E 28th Street Ct S Independence MO 64055

BARKER, KENNETH NEIL, pharmacy administration educator; b. Spring Valley, Ohio, Mar. 25, 1937; s. Kenneth Clyde and Marjorie Dorothy (Smith) Barker; m. Louise Arlene Ferguson, Aug. 17, 1957; children: Bradford Neil, Linda Louise, Douglas Adams. BS, U. Fla., 1959, MS, 1961; PhD, U. Miss., 1971. Mgr. sterile products pharmacy svc. U. Ark. Med. Center-Little Rock, 1961-62, project dir. drug systems rsch., 1962-66; projects coord. Sch. Pharmacy, U. Miss., 1966-70; dir. adminstrv. rsch. U.S. Pharmacopeia, 1970-72; assoc. prof. pharmacy adminstrn., assoc. dir. Rsch. Inst. Sch. Pharmacy, N.E. La. U., 1972-75; Sterling prof., dir. Ctr. Pharmacy Opers. Design Sch. Pharmacy, Auburn U., Ala., 1975—; pres. K.N.B. Inc., Auburn, Ala., 1980—. Co-inventor unit dose dispensing concept for hosps., 1959. Recipient commendation HEW, 1974, Harvey A.K. Whitney award Am. Assn. Hosp. Pharmacists, 1981, A. Richard Bliss, Jr. citation of appreciation Nat. Kappa Psi Pharm. Fraternity, 1998, Cheers award for medication error rsch. Inst. for Safe Med. Practices, 1999; named Outstanding Grad. prof. Auburn U., 1992-93. Mem. Am. Pharm. Assn. (Remington Honor medal 1998), Acad. Pharm. Scis., Am. Soc. Hosp. Pharmacists (research award 1973, 85, 87), Am. Assn. Colls. Pharmacy, Ala. Pharm. Assn., Am. Assn. Pharm. Sci., Ala. Soc. Hosp. Pharmacists, Rho Chi. Presbyterian. Home: 1371 Lakeshore Ln Auburn AL 36830-6332 Office: Auburn U Dept Pharmacy Auburn AL 36849

BARKER, LARRY LEE, communications educator; b. Wilmington, Ohio, Nov. 22, 1941; s. Milford and Ruth Maxine (Garringer) B.; children: Theodore Allen., Robert Milford. BA, Ohio U., 1962, MA, 1963, Ph. D, 1965. Asst. prof. So. Ill. U., Carbondale, 1965-66, Purdue U., West Lafayette, Ind., 1966-69; assoc. prof. Fla. State U., Tallahassee, 1969-71, prof., 1971—95; prof. emeritus Auburn (Ala.) U., 1995—. Pres. Spectra Inc., New Orleans, 1979—2000. Author: (with R. Kibler) Conceptual Frontiers in Speech Communication, 1969, Behavioral Objectives and Instruction, 1970, Listening Behavior, 1971, Speech Communication Behavior, 1971, Communication Vibrations, 1974, Speech— Interpersonal Communication, 1974, (with R. Edward) Intrapersonal Communication, 1980, (with R. Kibler) Objectives for Instruction and Evaluation, 1981, Communication, 1982, Communication in the Classroom, 1982, (with others) Effective Listening, 1982, (with L. Malandro) Nonverbal Communication, 1983, (with K. Wahlers) Groups in Process, 1983, (with others) Intrapersonal Communication Processes, 1987, (with K. Watson) Interpersonal and Relational Communications, 1989, Listen Up, 2000, Fishing Florida's Top Ten Bass Lakes: Vol. I, 2003, Vol. II, 2004, vol. III, 2005; contbr. articles to profl. jours. Recipient outstanding award in discussion Tau Kappa Alpha, 1962, outstanding tchr. award Ctrl. States Speech Assn., 1969, Robert J. Kibler Meml. award Speech Comm. Assn., 1986. Mem. APA, Internat. Comm. Assn. (v.p. 1972-74), Internat. Listening Assn. (chmn. rsch. com. 1979-82, pres. 1986-87). Methodist. Home: 30617 US Hwy 19 N Ste 630 Palm Harbor FL 34684 Personal E-mail: lbarker933@excite.com.

BARKER, LLYLE JAMES, JR., management consultant, educator, journalism educator, retired military officer; b. Columbus, Ohio, July 28, 1932; s. Llyle James and Mabel Lucile (Johnson) B.; m. Maxine Ruth Metcalf, Jan. 15, 1956; children: Llyle J., Daryl Alan. BS, Ohio State U., 1954; postgrad., U. Wis., 1961; MS in Mass. Comm., Shippensburg State Coll., 1975. Commd. officer U.S. Army, advanced through grades to maj. gen.; served in Korea,

Vietnam, Thailand and Germany; pub. affairs officer Hawaii, 1957-59, NORAD, 1961-63, Dept. Army, 1966-69, 7th Army, 1969-71, Joint Casualty Resolution Ctr., 1974, European Command, 1975-77, U.S. Army Europe, 1979-80; dep. chief info. Dept. Army, 1980-81, chief pub. affairs, 1981-84; prof. Sch. Journalism Ohio State U., Columbus, 1984-98. Cons. mgmt. comm.; assoc. Gannett Ctr. Media Studies (now Freedom Forum Media Studies Ctr.), Columbia U. Contbr. articles to profl. jours. Decorated D.S.M., Legion of Merit, others. Mem. World Future Soc., Pub. Rels. Soc. Am., Assn. Edn. Journalism and Mass Comm. Office: Ohio State U Sch Journalism 242 W 18th Ave Columbus OH 43210-1107 E-mail: llylej@aol.com.

BARKER, LYNN M., manufacturing executive; BS in Physics, MS in Physics, U. Ariz. Co-founder, pres. Valyn Internat., Albuquerque. Mem. Am. Phys. Soc., Soc. Exptl. Mechanics, Internat. Soc. Optical Engring., Aeriballistoc Range Assn., Sigma Pi Sigma, Pi Mu Epsilon, Phi Beta Kappa, Sigma Xi. Office: Valyn VIP 3926 Simms Ave SE Albuquerque NM 87108-4338

BARKER, NANCY LEPARD, university official; b. Owosso, Mich., Jan. 22, 1936; d. Cecil L. and Mary Elizabeth (Stuart) Lepard; m. J. Daniel Cline, June 6, 1960 (div. 1971); m. R. William Barker, Nov. 18, 1972; children: Mary Georgia Harker, Mark L. Cline, Richard E., Daniel P., Melissa B. Van Arsdel, John C. Cline MD, Helen Grace Garrett, Wiley D., James G. BSc, U. Mich., Ann Arbor, 1957; DHum (hon.), Northwood U., 2001. Spl. edn. instr. Univ. Hosp. U. Mich., Ann Arbor, 1958-61; v.p. Med. Educator, Chgo., 1967-69; asst. to chmn., dir. careers for women Northwood U., Midland, Mich., 1970-77, asst. prof., chmn. dept. fashion mktg. and merchandising, 1972-77, dir. arts programs and external affairs, 1972-77, v.p. univ. rels., 1978-2001, office of the pres., 2001—. Bd. dirs. Alden B. Dow Creativity Ctr., Midland; cons., lectr. in field. Co-author: (children's books) Wendy Well Series, 1970-72; contbr. chpts. to books, articles to profl. jours. Advisor Mich. Child Study Assn., 1972—; chmn. Matrix: Midland Festival, 1978; bd. dirs. Nat. Coun. of Women, 1971—, pres., 1983-85, chmn. centennial com., 1988; mem. exec. bd. Mich. ACE Network for Women Leaders in Higher Edn., 2001—; bd. dirs. ArtServe, Mich., 2003—, Family and Children's Svcs., Internat. Coun. Women, Paris. Nominee, (3) Mich. Women's Hall of Fame; named 1st ann. Disting. Educator of Yr., Am. Coun. on Edn./MI Network, 2001; named one of Outstanding Young Women in U.S. and Mich., 1974; recipient Hon. award, Ukrainian Nat. Women's League, 1983, Disting. Woman award, Northwood U., 1970, Outstanding Young Woman award, Jr. C. of C., 1974. Mem. Internat. Coun. Women (bd. dirs. Paris 1991—), The Fashion Group, Internat. Furnishings and Design Assn. (pres. Mich. chpt. 1974-77), Mich. Women's Studies Assn. (founding mem.), Arts Midland Coun. (pres. 2 terms, 25th Anniversary award), Internat. Women's Forum, Mich. Women's Forum, Contemporary Rev. Club, Midland County Lawyers' Wives, Zonta, Phi Beta Kappa, Phi Kappa Phi, Alpha Lambda Delta, Phi Lambda Theta, Phi Gamma Nu, Delta Delta Delta. Office: Northwood Univ 209 Revere Midland MI 48640-4255 Office Phone: 989-631-9864. E-mail: barkermid@aol.com.

BARKER, RICHARD ALEXANDER, organizational psychologist; b. San Diego, Aug. 11, 1947; s. Alexander Markewich and Donna Lee Barker; m. Barbara Yvonne Schutt, Aug. 1, 1987; children: Jaime Lynn, Cory Richard AB in Psychology, San Diego State U., 1974, MS in Indsl. and Organizational Psychology, 1976; EdD, U. San Diego, 1990. Statis. analyst U.S. Navy Pers. R & D Center, San Diego, 1974-75; pers. and testing analyst City of San Diego, San Diego, 1976, cons. various orgns., 1976-78; employment mgr. Computer Scis. Corp., San Diego, 1978; indsl. psychologist Gen. Dynamics Corp., San Diego, 1978-91; instr. music San Diego City Coll., 1976-91; lectr. psychology, mgmt. sci., stats., orgnl. behavior U. Redlands, 1978-91; asst. prof. bus., chair mgmt. dept. Marist Coll., Poughkeepsie, N.Y., 1991-98; assoc. prof. bus. Clarke Coll., Dubuque, Iowa, 1998-2000, Upper Iowa Univ., Fayette, Iowa, 2000—. Author: On the Nature of Leadership, 2002, Horses's Hoofs, 2003, At Story Time - The Story of Charles Coleman Parker and Upper Iowa University, 2003, Misplaced Faith, 2005; mem. editl. bd. Jour. Leadership Studies, 1994—; contbr. articles to profl. jours. Bd. dirs. San Diego Youth Svcs., Inc., chmn. pers. com., 1978-81. Served with USNR, 1968-69 Mem. APA, Computer Automated Systems Assn./Soc. Mfg. Engrs., Nat. Mgmt. Assn., Am. Fedn. Musicians, Psi Chi. Office: Upper Iowa Univ 605 Washington St Fayette IA 52142 E-mail: barkerr@uiu.edu.

BARKER, ROBERT WILLIAM (BOB BARKER), television personality; b. Darrington, Wash., Dec. 12, 1923; s. Byron John and Matilda Kent (Tarleton) B.; m. Dorothy Jo Gideon, Jan. 12, 1945 (dec. Oct. 1981). BA in Econs. summa cum laude, Drury Coll., 1947. Founder DJ&T Found., Beverly Hills, Calif., 1995. Host: (radio show) The Bob Barker Show; (TV series) Truth or Consequences, 1956-75, The Price is Right, 1972—, Bob Barker Fun and Games Show, 1978; (TV specials) Miss Universe Beauty Pageant, 1966-87, Miss U.S.A. Beauty Pageant, 1966-87, Pillsbury Bake-Off, 1969-85, Rose Parade, CBS, 1969-88; appeared in (TV series) Bonanza, 1960, The Nanny, 1994, Something So Right, 1996, 1997, Martial Law, 1998, Futurama (voice), 2000, Yes Dear, 2001, Family Guy (voice), 2001, The Bold and the Beautiful, 2002; (feature films) Happy Gilmore, 1996. Served to lt. (j.g.) USNR, 1943-45. Recipient Emmy award for Best Audience Participation Host, 1981-82, 83-84, 86-87, 87-88, 89-90, 90-91, 91-92, 93-94, 94-95, 95-96, 99-00, 00-01, Lifetime Achievement Emmy award for Daytime Television, 1999, Carbon Mike award of the Pioneer Broadcasters. Mem. AGVA, AFTRA, Screen Actors Guild. inducted, Acad. of Television and Arts & Sciences Hall of Fame, 2004. Office: The Price is Right care CBS TV 7800 Beverly Blvd Los Angeles CA 90036-2112*

BARKER, SARAH EVANS, judge; b. Mishawaka, Ind., June 10, 1943; d. James McCall and Sarah (Yarbrough) Evans; m. Kenneth R. Barker, Nov. 25, 1972; 3 children. BS, Ind. U., 1965, LLD (hon.), 1999; JD, Am. U., 1969; LLD (hon.), U. Indpls., 1984; D in Pub. Svc. (hon.), Butler U., 1987; LLD (hon.), Marian Coll., 1991; LHD, U. Evansville, 1993; LLD (hon.), Wabash Coll., 1999, Hanover Coll., 2001; D of Civil Law (hon.), 2003. Bar: Ind. 1969, U.S. Dist. Ct. (so. dist.) Ind., 1969, U.S. Ct. Appeals (7th cir.) 1973, U.S. Supreme Ct., 1978. Legal asst. to senator U.S. Senate, 1969-71; spl. counsel to minority, govt. ops. com. permanent investigations subcom., 1971-72; dir. rsch. scheduling and advance Senator Percy Re-election Campaign, 1972; asst. U.S. atty. So. Dist. Ind., 1972-76, 1st asst. U.S. atty., 1976-77, U.S. atty., 1981-84; judge U.S. Dist. Ct. (so. dist.) Ind., 1984—, chief judge, 1994—2000. Assoc., then ptnr. Bose, McKinney & Evans, Indpls., 1977-81; mem. long range planning com. Jud. Conf. U.S., 1991-96, exec. com., 1989-91, standing com. fed. rules of practice and procedure, 1987-91, dist. judge rep., 1988-91; mem. jud. coun. 7th cir. Ct. Appeals, 1988-2000, jud. fellows commn. U.S. Supreme Ct., 1993-98; jud. adv. com., sentencing commn., 1995-97, bd. advisors, Ind. U., Purdue U., Indpls., 1989—; mem. pres.'s cabinet Ind. U., 1995—; bd. visitors Ind. U. Sch. of Law, Bloomington, 1984—; bd. dirs. Clarian Health Ptnrs., 1996—, Christian Theol. Sem., 1999-2001; bd. dirs. Einstein Inst. for Sci., Health and the Cts., 2001— Recipient Peck award Wabash Coll., 1989, Touchstone award Girls Club of Greater Indpls., 1989, Leach Centennial 1st Woman award Valparaiso Law Sch., 1993, Most Influential Women award Indpls. Bus. Jour., 1996, Paul Buchanan award of excellence Indpls. Bar Found., 1998, Thomas J. Hennessy award Ind. U., 1995, Disting. Citizen fellow Ind. U., 1999-2001; named Ind. Woman of Yr., Women in Comm., 1986, Ind. Univ. Disting. Alumni, 1996, Disting. Citizen fellow Ind. U., 1999-2001, Singing Hoosiers Disting. Alumni award Ind. U., 2000, Man for All Seasons award St. Thomas More Soc., 2000. Mem. ABA, Ind. Bar Assn., Indpls. Bar Assn. (Antoinette Dakin Leach award 1993), Fed. Judges Assn. (exec. com., bd. dirs. 2001—), Com. on Budget (judicial conf. 2001-), Einstein Inst. Sci., Health and Cts. (bd. dirs. 2001-), U.S. Judicial Conf. (spl. redaction rev. panel 2000-), Christian Theol. Sem. (bd. trustees 1999-), Lawyers Club, Kiwanis. Republican. Methodist. Office: US Dist Ct 210 US Courthouse 46 E Ohio St Indianapolis IN 46204-1903

BARKER, THOMAS CARL, retired health facility administrator; b. Cedar Rapids, Iowa, May 25, 1931; s. Carl Edward and Bertha Olive (Simons) B.; m. Mary Irene Beorkrem, Sept. 1, 1952 (dec. 1995); children: Cheryl Lynn, Thomas Carl Jr. (dec.), Laura Ann, David Edward; m. Patricia Blount Moore, May 2, 1998. Student, Loras Coll., 1949-50, Coe Coll., 1950-51; BS, U. Iowa, 1954, MA, 1960, PhD, 1963. Acct. Wilson & Co., Cedar Rapids, Iowa, 1951-54; contract adminstr. Collins Radio Co., Cedar Rapids, 1956-57; with customer rels. The Cryovac Co., Cedar Rapids, 1957-58; bus. officer Mercy Hosp., Iowa City, Iowa, 1958-59; rsch. asst. U. Iowa, 1959-60, tchg. asst., 1961-63, asst. prof., 1963-64; adminstrv. assoc. U. Iowa Hosp., 1960-62; rsch. assoc. UAW Internat. Union, Detroit, 1964-67; dir. Mich. Health and Social Security Rsch. Inst., Detroit, 1964-67; adj. assoc. prof. health econs. Wayne State U., Detroit, 1966-67; Arthur Graham Glasgow prof., dir. Sch. Hosp. Adminstrn. Med. Coll. Va., Richmond, 1967-71; prof., dean and CEO Sch. Allied Health Professions Va. Commonwealth U., Richmond, 1969-96, dean emeritus, prof. emeritus, 1996—. Mem. com. on allied health edn. and accreditation AMA, chmn. com., 1988-91; served as mem. or cons. to various pub. health svcs., including NIH, Health Resources Adminstrn., VA, HEW agys.; mem. dean's com. VA Med. Ctr., Richmond, 1974-96; mem. Ctrl. Va. Health Sys. Agy., 1976-88, pres., 1979-80; mem. Va. Health Coord. Coun., 1986-88. Contbr. articles to profl. jours. With USN, 1949-56; capt. Res., ret. Named Hon. Alumni, Med. Coll. Va. Fellow APHA, Am. Soc. Allied Health Professions (pres. 1975-76); mem. Am. Health Planning Assn., Assn. Univ. Programs in Health Adminstrn., Soc. Sons. Revolution in State of Va., Va. Assn. Allied Health Professions, Va. Hosp. Assn., Rotary (pres. Richmond club 1991-92), Phi Kappa Phi. Roman Catholic. Home: 2251 Winterfield Rd Midlothian VA 23113-4145 Office: The Grant House PO Box 980203 Richmond VA 23298-0203 Office Phone: 804-828-1892. Office Fax: 804-828-1894. Business E-Mail: tcbarker@hsc.vcu.edu.

BARKER, VERLYN LLOYD, retired minister, educator; b. Auburn, Nebr., July 25, 1931; s. Jack Lloyd and Olive Clara (Bollman) B. AB, Doane Coll., 1952, DD, 1977; BD, Yale U., 1956, STM, 1960; postgrad., U. Chgo., 1960-61; PhD, St. Louis U., 1970. Ordained to ministry United Ch. of Christ, 1956. Instr. history, chaplain Doane Coll., Crete, Nebr., 1954-55; pastor U. Nebr., 1956-59; sec. ministry higher edn. United Ch. Bd. Homeland Ministries, N.Y.C., 1961-96, ret. Cleve., 1996. Author: Premises about Education, 1981, Creationism, the Church and Public Education, 1981, Health and Human Values: A Ministry of Theological Inquiry and Moral Discourse, 1987; editor: The Church and the Public School, 1980, Science, Technology and the Christian Faith, 1990; contbg. author: Campus Ministry, 1964, Religious Colleges in America: A Selected Bibliography, 1988, The New Faith-Science Debate, 1989; mem. editorial adv. com. Jour. Current Social Issues; contbr. articles to various publs. Pres. United Ministries in Higher Edn., N.Y.C., 1971-77. Mem.: ACLU, AAAS, Nat. Assn. for Sci., Tech. and Society, Soc. Health and Human Values, Am. Acad. Polit. and Social Sci., Acad. Polit. Sci., Am. Studies Assn., Am. Assn. Higher Edn., Doane Coll Alumni Assn. (pres. 1957—58), Yale Club N.Y.C.

BARKER, WALTER LEE, thoracic surgeon; b. Chgo., Sept. 9, 1928; s. Samuel Robert, M.D., and Esther (Meyerovitz) B.; m. Betty Ruth Wood, Apr. 4, 1967 AB cum laude, Harvard U., 1949, MD, 1953. Diplomate Am. Bd. Surgery, Am. Bd. Thoracic Surgery. Intern, resident in gen. and thoracic surgery Cook County Hosp. and Presbyn. St. Luke's Med. Ctr. and affiliated hosps., Chgo., 1953-62; practice medicine specializing in thoracic surgery Chgo., 1962-95; clin. prof. surgery U. Ill.; prof. emeritus, 1998; head sect. thoracic surgery Cook County Hosp., 1972-93, cons. sect., 1993-98; chmn. dept. surgery St. Joseph Hosp., Chgo., 1982-97. Researcher on tuberculosis, pleural infections, lung cancer Author: The Post Operative Chest, 1977; editl. bd. Chest, 1984-89; cons. to editor, 1989—; contbr. articles to profl. jours. Served with M.C., USNR, 1955-57 Fellow Am. Coll. Chest Physicians (credentials com. 1984-89), ACS; mem. Am. Assn. Thoracic Surgery, AMA (rep. to HS of dels. 1988-94), Boylston Med. Soc., Chgo. Med. Soc., Ill. Med. Soc., Chest Club, Chgo. Surg. Soc. (v.p. 1990-91, chmn. membership com. 1991-92), Ill. Surg. Soc., Central Surg. Soc., Inst. Medicine, Soc. Thoracic Surgeons (founding mem., cons. editor Ann. Thoracic Surgery), Sigma Xi Home: 2912 N Commonwealth Ave Apt 11C Chicago IL 60657-6215 Fax: 773-525-0561. E-mail: b.b.barker@worldnet.att.net.

BARKER, WILLIAM DANIEL, hospital administrator; b. New Orleans, July 21, 1926; s. William Daniel and Ada (Will) B.; m. Nancy Pool, Sept. 23, 1949; children: Nancy Louise, Julia Ann, William Daniel III, Marion DeVilbiss. B in Bus. Adminstrn., Emory U., 1949; M in Hosp. Adminstrn., Ga. State U., 1966. Bus. office mgr. Emory U. Hosp., Atlanta, 1949-50; asst. adminstr. Griffin (Ga.) Spalding County Hosp., 1950-51; adminstr. Winder-Barrow (Ga.) Hosp., 1951-52; hosp. field rep. Ga. Dept. Pub. Health, Atlanta, 1952-54, hosp. cons., 1954-55; asst. adminstr. Tri-County Hosp., Ft. Oglethorpe, Ga., 1955-60; asst. dir. Crawford Long Hosp. Emory U., Atlanta, 1960-73, adminstr., 1973-84, dir. hosps., 1984-90, exec. dir. hosp., 1987-90; ret., 1991; prof. Emory U., Atlanta, 1988-93. Bd. dirs. Ga. Fed. Bank, Atlanta, Blue Cross Blue Shield Ga., Inc.; provider affairs com. Blue Cross Blue Shield Assn., United Network for Organ Sharing, bd. dirs., 1991—; bd. govs. SunHealth, Charlotte, N.C., chmn., 1988-89; bd. commrs. Joint Commn. on Accreditation of Healthcare Orgns., 1981-86; v.p. Greater Atlanta Coalition on Health Care, 1983-84; mem. Gov.'s Coun. Malpractice Ins., 1975-83, Medicaid Adv. Com. Ga. Dept. Human Resources, 1973-77, Health Facilities Planning Com. Met. Atlanta Coun. for Health, 1971-74, Atlanta Regional Commn. Emergency Med. Task Force 1969-73, Gov.'s Commn. on Nursing, 1970-71, adv. commn. Internat. Implant Registry, 1989—, vice-chmn., 1991, chmn., 1992; pres. Health Careers of Ga., Inc., 1969-70, Ga. Coun. Paramed. Edn., 1968. Contbr. articles to profl. jours. With U.S. Army, 1944-46. Recipient R.C. Williams award Ga. State U., 1966, Disting. Alumni award, Ga. State U., 1979, Disting. Svc. award, Ga. Med. Assn. Atlanta, 1980; Disting. Guest Lectr. Ga. State U., 1978. Fellow Am. Coll. Healthcare Execs. (regent 1972-75); mem. Am. Hosp. Assn. (chmn. 1979, Speaker of Ho. 1980, Disting. Svc. award 1987), Ga. Hosp. Assn. (pres. 1966-79, Gold Honor award of Excellence 1980), Ansley Golf Club. Baptist. Home: 50 S Prado NE Atlanta GA 30309-3309 Personal E-mail: dbarker@emory.edu.

BARKER, WILLIAM M., state supreme court justice; b. Chattanooga, Sept. 13, 1941; married; 3 children. BS, U. Chatanooga, 1964; JD, U. Cin., 1967. Bar: Tenn. 1967. Pvt. practice, 1967-83; cir. ct. judge, 1983-95; justice Ct. of Appeals, 1995-98, Tenn. Supreme Ct., 1998—. Adj. prof. U. Tenn., Chatanooga, 1984—. Chmn. bd. deacons 1st Presbyn. Ch. Chattanooga, 1995-97. Served in USMC, 1967—69. Fellow Tenn. Bar Found., Chattanooga Bar Found.; mem. Am. Legion, Alpha Soc., U. Tenn. Chattanooga Alumni Coun., Chattanooga Rotary Club. Office: Tenn Supreme Ct 540 Mccallie Ave Ste 410 Chattanooga TN 37402-2096

BARKER, WILLIAM THOMAS, lawyer; b. Feb. 28, 1947; s. V. Wayne and Cordelia (Whitten) B.; m. June K. Robinson, Jan. 30, 1981. BS, MS, Mich. State U., 1969; JD, U. Calif., Berkeley, 1974. Bar: Calif. 1975, Ill. 1976. Assoc. programmer-analyst Control Data Corp., Sunnyvale, Calif., 1969-71; law clk. Pa. Supreme Ct., Erie, 1974-75; assoc. Sonnenschein Carlin Nath & Rosenthal, Chgo., 1975-82, ptnr., 1982—. Moderator Ill. Ins. Law Forum, Counsel Connect, 1994-98; co-moderator Nat. Ins. Law gen. forum, 1996-98; moderator Ins. Law Forum, Lexis One, 2001. Bd. editors: Def. Counsel Jour., 1987—; editor Bad Faith Law Report, 1999-2001, contbg. editor 1990-99; mem. editl. bd. Ins. Litigation Reporter, 1987—, editl. dir. and sr. contbg. editor, 2001—; editor Covered Events, 1995-96, editor emeritus, 1996—; ins. law publs. bd. Def. Rsch. Inst., 1992-97; contbr. articles to profl. jours. Fellow Am. Bar Found. (life); mem. ABA (chair-elect com. on appellate advocacy, tort and ins. practice sect. 1994-95, chair 1995-96, chair gen. comm. bd. 1996-97), Internat. Assn. Def. Counsel (Yancey Meml. award for best article 1995, chair spl. com. on Amicus Curie 1996-97, chair ad hoc com. on interstate practice 2000-03), Chgo. Coun. Lawyers (sec. 1987-88, bd. govs. 1989-91, chair com. profl. responsibility 1990-95), Chgo. Bar Assn. (chmn. com. constl. law 1984-85), Def. Rsch. Inst., Assn. Profl. Responsibility Lawyers (chair com. on internat. trade in legal svcs. 2002-03), Am. Law Inst. Home: 132 E Delaware Pl Apt 5806 Chicago IL 60611-4951 Office: Sonnenschein Nath Et Al 8000 Sears Tower 233 S Wacker Dr Ste 8000 Chicago IL 60606-6491 Office Phone: 312-876-8140. E-mail: wbarker@sonnenschein.com.

BARKETT, ROSEMARY, federal judge; b. Ciudad Victoria, Tamaulipas, Mex., Aug. 29, 1939; arrived in U.S., 1946, naturalized, 1958; BS summa cum laude, Spring Hill Coll., 1967; JD, U. Fla., 1970; LLD (hon.), Stetson U., St. Petersburg, Fla., 1987; LHD (hon.), Fla. Internat. U., Miami, 1987; LLD (hon.), John Marshall Law Sch., Chgo., 1990; LHD (hon.), U. So. Fla., Tampa, 1990; DCL (hon.), Spring Hill Coll., Mobile, Ala., 1990; LLD (hon.), Rollins Coll., Orlando, Fla., 1992, Nova U., Ft. Lauderdale, Fla., 1992. Bar: Fla., U.S. Dist. Ct. (so. dist.) Fla., U.S. Ct. Appeals (5th cir.), U.S. Supreme Ct. Pvt. practice, West Palm Beach, Fla., 1971—79; judge 15th Jud. Cir. Ct., Palm Beach County, Fla., 1979—82, administrative judge civil divsn., 1982—83, chief judge, 1983—84; appellate judge 4th Dist. Ct. Appeal, West Palm Beach, Fla., 1984—85; justice Supreme Ct. Fla., Tallahassee, 1985—92, chief justice, 1992—94; cir. judge U.S. Ct. Appeals (11th cir.), Miami, 1994—. Bd. dirs. Lawyers for Children, U.S. Assn. Constl. Law; faculty U. Nev., Reno, Nat. Jud. Coll., Fla. Jud. Coll., Appellate Judges Seminar, Inst. Jud. Adminstrn., NYU; lectr. in field; vis. com. Miami U. Law Sch.; bd. visitors St. Thomas U. Mem. editl. bd.: The Florida Judges Manual. Named Women of Distinction, Crohn's & Colitis Found., 1997; named to Fla. Women's Hall of Fame, 1986, Miami Centennial Hall of Fame, 1996; recipient Woman of Achievement award, Palm Beach County Commn. on Status of Women, 1985, Hannah G. Solomon award, Nat. Coun. Jewish Women, 1991, Lifetime Achievement award, Latin Bus. Profl. Women, 1992, Breaking the Glass Ceiling award, Fla. Fedn. Bus. Profl. Women's Clubs, Inc., 1993, Disting. Jurist award, Miss. State U., 1995, Margaret Brent Women Lawyers of Achievement award, ABA Commn. Women in Profession, 1996, Harriette Glasner Freedom award, ACLU, 1999. Fellow: ABA (Minority Justice Honoree 1992); mem.: Fla. Commn. on Status of Women, Dade Marine Inst., Fed. Judges Assn., Am. Law Inst., Assn. Trial Lawyers Am. (Achievement award 1986), Acad. Fla. Trial Lawyers (Achievement award 1988, Rosemary Barkett award named in her honor 1992), Palm Beach Marine Inst., Nat. Assn. Women Judges (Honoree of Year 1999), Fla. Assn. Women Lawyers (Judge Mattie Belle Davis award 1991, Rosemary Barkett Outstanding Achievement award named in her honor 1999), Am. Acad. Matrimonial Lawyers (award 1984), Palm Beach County Bar Assn., Fla. Bar Assn. Office: US Ct of Appeals (11th cir) Fla 99 NE 4th St Rm 1223 Miami FL 33132-2140*

BARKIN, ELAINE RADOFF, composer; b. N.Y.C., Dec. 15, 1932; m. George J. Barkin, Nov. 28, 1957; 3 children. BA in Music, Queens Coll., 1954, MFA in Composition, 1956; PhD in Composition and Theory, Brandeis U., 1971; Cert. in Composition and Piano, Berlin Hochschule Musik, 1957; studied with Karol Rathaus, Irving Fine, Boris Blacher, Arthur Berger. Lectr. in music Queens Coll., 1964-70, Sarah Lawrence, 1969-70; from asst. to assoc. prof. music theory U. Mich., 1970-74; from asst. prof. to prof. composition and theory U. Calif., L.A., 1974-97. Vis. asst. prof. Princeton (N.J.) U., 1974; lectr. in field. Asst. to co-editor: Perspectives of New Music, 1963-85; composer String Quartet, 1969, Sound Play for violin, 1974, String Trio, 1976, Plein Chant, alto flute, 1977, Ebb Tide, 2 vibraphones, 1977, ...the Supple Suitor...for soprano and five players, 1978, (chamber mini opera) De Amore, 1980, Impromptu for violin, cello, piano, 1981, (theatre piece) Media Speak, 1981, At the Piano, piano, 1982, For String Quartet, 1982, Quilt Piece graphic score for 7 instruments, 1984, On The Way To Becoming for 4-track Tape Collage, 1985, Demeter and Persephone for violin, tape, chamber ensemble, dancers, 1986, 3 Rhapsodies, flutes and clarinet, 1986, Encore for Javanese Gamelan Ensemble, 1986, Out of the Air for Basset Horn and Tape, 188, To Whom It May Concern 4 track tape collage, reader and 4 players, 1989, Legong Dreams, oboe, 1990, Gamélange for harp and mixed gamelan band, 1992, Five Tape Collages, Open Space CD #3, 1993, "for my friends' pleasure," soprano and harp, 1994, numerous improvised group and duo sessions on tape; produced cassette and video: New Music in Bali, 1994; "touching all bases" for electronic bass, electronic percussion, and Balinese gamelan, 1996, e: an anthology (music, texts and graphics) 1975-95, "poem" for wind ensemble, 1999, (Chamber Music and Improvisations) Open Space, 2000, (CDs) Song for Sarah for Violin, 2001, Ballade for Violoncello, 2002, Tambellan, 2004, Open Space, 2004, Colors for mixed gamelan, 2004. Recipient Fulbright award, 1957, awards NEA, 1975, 79, awards Rockefeller Found., 1980, Meet the Composer award, 1994. Home: 12533 Killion St Valley Village CA 91607-1533

BARKIN, MARVIN E., lawyer; b. Winter Haven, Fla., Nov. 9, 1933; s. Isadore and Jean (Epstein) B.; m. Gertrude Parnes, Sept. 20, 1959; children: Thomas I., Michael A., Pamela L. AB, Emory U., 1955; LLB cum laude, Harvard U., 1958. Bar: Fla. 1958, U.S. Dist. Ct. (mid. and so. dists.) Fla., U.S. Ct. Appeals (5th and 11th cirs.), U.S. Supreme Ct. Research aide Dist. Ct. Appeal Fla., Third Dist., Miami, 1958-60; assoc., then ptnr. Fowler, White, Collins, Gillen, Humkey & Trenam, Tampa, 1960-69; mgr. Trenam, Kemker, Scharf, Barkin, Frye, O'Neill & Mullis, Tampa, 1970—; mem. Fla. Bd. Bar Examiners, 1979-84, chmn., 1982-83. Chmn. corp., banking and bus. law sect. Fla. Bar, 1974-75, chmn. appellate ct. rules subcom., 1972-73 Mem. Am. Law Inst., Am. Bar Found., Nat. Conf. Bar Examiners (bd. mgrs. 1985-95, chmn. 1993-94, 11th cir. ct. appeal com. on lawyer qualifications and conduct, chair 2001—), Fla. Bar, Omicron Delta Kappa. Democrat. Jewish. Home: 1605 Culbreath Isles Dr Tampa FL 33629-4824 Office: Trenam Kemker Scharf Barkin Frye O'Neill & Mullis 101 E Kennedy Blvd Ste 2700 Tampa FL 33602-5179 Office Phone: 813-223-7474. Personal E-mail: mebarkin@trenam.com.

BARKLEY, ANDREW PAUL, economics professor; b. Manhattan, Kans., Feb. 5, 1962; s. Paul Weston and Lela Mel (Kelly) B.; m. Mary Ellen Cates, July 14, 1984; children: Katherine Ann, Charles Kelly. BA in Econs., Whitman Coll., 1984; MA in Econs., U. Chgo., 1986, PhD in Econs., 1988. Asst. prof. Kans. State U., Manhattan, 1988-93, assoc. prof., 1993—. Coffman chair for outstanding tchg. scholars Kans. State U., 2003—; vis. prof. Quaid-I-Azam U., Islamabad, Pakistan, 1990, U. Ariz., Tucson, 1994—95, U. Cambridge, England, 2002; faculty advisor Pakistan Student Assn., Kans. State U., Agrl. Econs. Club, 1989—94. Assoc. editor Review of Agrl. Econs., 1993—. Recipient Agrl. and Rural Transp. Rsch. Paper award, 1994; named CASE Kans. Prof. of Yr., 1993. Mem.: Western Agrl. Econs. Assn. (Outstanding Undergrad. Tchg. award 1994), Nat. Agrl. Coll. Tchrs. Assn. (Knight Outstanding Jour. Article award 1992, Ctrl. Region Outstanding Tchr. 1994, Tchr. fellow 1994), Am. Agrl. Econs. Assn. (nat. advisor student sect. 1993—95, Outstanding Undergrad. Tchg. award 1995). Avocations: running, reading, travel. Home: 925 Wildcat Rdg Manhattan KS 66502-2927 Office: Kans State U Dept Agrl Econs Waters Hall Manhattan KS 66506

BARKLEY, BRIAN EVAN, lawyer, political organization worker, consultant; b. Teaneck, N.J., Jan. 30, 1945; s. Henry E. and Alice M. (Schultz) Barkley; m. Pamela A. Martin, May 5, 1979; children: Leigh Elizabeth, Christine Elizabeth, Brett Evan. BA, U. Md., 1967; JD with honors, George Washington U., 1970. Bar: Md. 1970, D.C. 1976, U.S. Dist. Ct. Md. 1973. Assoc. Everngam & Goldstein, Silver Spring, Md., 1970—72; pvt. practice Silver Spring, 1972—80, Rockville, Md., 1980—86; spl. asst. Rep. Michael Barnes, Washington, 1981—84; sr. ptnr. Barkley and Kennedy, Chartered, 1987—. Vice chmn. Nat. Capital chpt. Nat. Multiple Sclerosis Com., Washington, 1980—86, Nat. Multiple Sclerosis Soc., Washington, 1998—2001, chmn. chpt. svcs. com., 1985—2001; chmn. Montgomery County Multiple Sclerosis Com., Rockville, Md., 1980; major gifts chmn. Shady Grove Hosp., 1980; chmn. Nat. Capital chpt. Nat. Multiple Sclerosis Com., 2001—03; del. Dem. Nat. Conv., 1984; campaign mgr. Barnes for Congress, Rockville, 1980, campaign chmn., 1982—84; campaign mgr. Montgomery County for Mondale, 1984; vice chmn. Montgomery County for Dukakis, 1988. Recipient Humanitarian award, Nat. Multiple Sclerosis Soc., 1989, Hope award, 2003. Mem.: Montgomery County Bar Assn., Md. Bar Assn., Rockville C. of C. (pres. 1996—97), Bethesda Country Club, Masons. Democrat. Home: 12405 Copenhaver Ter Potomac MD 20854-3028 Office: 51 Monroe St Ste 1407 Rockville MD 20850-2408 Office Phone: 301-251-6600.

BARKLEY, CHARLES WADE, retired professional basketball player, sportscaster; b. Leeds, Ala., Feb. 20, 1963; Student, Auburn U., 1981—84. With Phila. 76ers, 1984—92, Phoenix Suns, 1992—96, Houston Rockets, 1996—2000, ret., 2000; co-host Inside the NBA, TNT, 2001—; host Listen Up, TNT, 2002—. Mem. U.S. Olympic team, 1992, 96. Co-author (with Roy S. Johnson): Outrageous! The Fine Life and Flagrant Good Times of Basketball's Irresistible Force, 1992; co-author: (with Rick Reilly) Sir Charles: The Wit and Wisdom of Charles Barkley, 1994; author: I May Be Wrong But I Doubt It, 2002, Who's Afraid of a Large Black Man, 2005; actor: (films) Forget Paris, 1995. Named to All-Rookie team, 1985, NBA All-Star team, 1988—93; recipient Schick Pivotal Player award, 1986—88, IBM award, 1986—88, NBA All-Star Game Most Valuable Player award, 1991, NBA Most Valuable Player award, 1993. Achievements include holding single game records for most offensive rebounds in one quarter-11, 1987; holding single game record for most offensive rebounds in one half-13, 1987.

BARKLEY, HENRY BROCK, JR., research and development engineering executive; b. Raleigh, N.C., Apr. 5, 1927; s. Henry Brock and Thelma Maurine (Dutt) B.; m. Edith Sumner Stowe, June 24, 1950; children: Margaret Susan, Henry Brock III, Jane Stowe. Student, U. N.C., 1944-45; BS, U.S. Naval Acad., 1949; BSEE, U.S. Naval Postgrad. Sch., 1954, MSEE, 1955. Commd. ensign USN, 1949, advanced through grades to lt. comdr., 1960; ret., 1961; supr. space power sect. Bendix, Ann Arbor, Mich., 1962-63; chief reactor divsn. Lewis Rsch. Ctr. NASA, Sandusky, Ohio, 1963-73; asst. gen. mgr., dir. power reactors EG&G Idaho, Inc., Idaho Falls, 1973-81; mgr. internat. bus. Babcock & Wilcox Co., Lynchburg, Va., 1981-83, mgr. 205 plant project svcs., 1983-87, mgr. space power and propulsion, 1987-89, dir. space and def. sys., 1989-92; cons., 1992—. Dir. Devel. Workshop, Inc., Idaho Falls., 1977-81; IEEE disting. lectr. in S.Am. and C.Am., 1984. Bd. dirs. Sandusky Concert Assn., 1965-73; chmn. Huron (Ohio) Sch. Levy Campaigns, 1970. Lt. comdr. USN, 1960. Mem. IEEE, Am. Nuc. Soc., Am. Guild Organists. Presbyterian. Home: 501 VES Rd Apt WG25 Lynchburg VA 24503-4638 E-mail: brock.barkley.jr@att.net.

BARKLEY, MARLENE A. NYHUIS, nursing educator; b. Waupun, Wis., Aug. 31, 1934; d. Fred and Esther Elsie (Leu) Nyhuis; m. Peter Don Barkley, Sept. 1, 1956; children: Peter Scott, John Fredric. Dipl. nursing, Milw. County Hosp., 1955; cert. nurse practitioner, U. Miami, Fla., 1976; AA, Miami Dade C.C., Fla., 1983; BSN cum laude, U. Miami, 1985; MSN, Barry U., 1996. RN, Fla.; cert. advanced RN, ANCC. Nurse Waupun (Wis.) Meml. Hosp., 1956-57; nurse coord. Courtland Med. Ctr., Milw., 1958-61, Planned Parenthood, Bloomington, Ind., 1971-74; nurse practitioner Miami VA Med. Ctr., 1976-83, program dir., 1983-98, cons. on home care, 1997—; adj. prof. Barry U., Miami Shores, Fla., 1997; cons. on home care Miami VA Med. Ctr., 1997; clin. adj. faculty ARNP program Barry U., Naples, Fla., 1997—; asst. dir. nursing Nursing Network of Naples, 2001—. Mem.: ANA, U. Miami Alumni Assn., Fla. Nurses Assn., Advanced Practice Coun., Am. Acad. Nurse Practitioners, Honor Soc. Fla. Gulf Coast U. Sch. Nursing, Sigma Theta Tau. Presbyterian. Avocations: rollerblading, bicycling. Home: 321 31st St NW Naples FL 34120-1705 Personal E-mail: mnbnp28@aol.com.

BARKLEY, PAUL HALEY, JR., architect; b. Washington, Sept. 24, 1937; Paul Haley Sr. and Mary Barrett (Brewer) B.; m. Jeanette Frances Nickerson, Dec. 20, 1975. Student, Ecole D'Art Americaines, Fontainebleau, France, 1959; BArch, U. Va., 1960. Registered architect, Va., Md., D.C. Archtl. designer Strang & Childers Architects, Annandale, Va., 1960-61; project designer Alan J. Lockman Architect, Washington, 1962-63; design assoc. D.G. Chase & Assocs., Alexandria, Va., 1964; pres. Barkley Pierce Assocs., Falls Church, Va., 1965-94; sole practice Paul H. Barkley, FAIA, Architect, Falls Church, Va., 1994—. Bd. dirs. Hist. Falls Church; lectr. archtl. divsn. continuing edn., 1966-91; mng. ptnr. Village Ctr. Assocs., Falls Church, 1983-99. Prin. works includes Falls Ch. Community Ctr., 1967, Vega Precision Labs., 1972, 1st Va. Bank, Arlington, 1979, Sullyfield Commerce Ctr., 1986, Rigg's Nat. Bank, McLean, Va., 1988; contbr. articles to profl. jours. Chmn. Falls Church Bus. Devel. Commn., 1987—93; mem. exec. com. Citizens for a Better City, Falls Church, 1987—92; mem. Falls Church Econ. Devel. Authority, 2002, Falls Church Pvt. Pub. Partnership, 1991—98, bd. dirs., 1991—98, pres., 1993—94. With USAF, 1960—63. Recipient excellence in design award Falls Church Village Preservation and Improvement Soc., 1979, Indsl. Devel. Vol. of Yr. award So. Indsl. Devel. Coun., 1982, Bus. Person of Yr. award City of Falls Church, 1988; Margaret Thompson Biddle fellow U. Va., 1959. Fellow AIA (bd. dirs. 1986-89, pres. Va. Soc. 1984, regional rep. Coll. of Fellows 1993-95, chair Coll. Fellows Reg. Reps. 2002-05, numerous other offices, Disting. Svc. award 1983, Outstanding Svc. award No. Va. chpt. 1982, award of recognition of outstanding achievement 1988, Noland award 1991, Leslie N. Boney Spirit of Fellowship award 2005); mem. Falls Church C. of C. (bd. dirs. 1973-75, 99—, pres. 1976, 3d v.p. 1977-79, vice chmn. 2003-04 Pillar of the Cmty. award 1977), Va. Found. for Arch. (pres. 1988-89, trustee 1993-99). Avocations: photography, travel, collecting art. Home and Office: 311 Chestnut St Falls Church VA 22046-2404 Office Phone: 703-532-8500. Personal E-mail: pbarkley@cox.net.

BARKLEY, TERRELL WAYNE, school librarian, archivist, curator; b. Tokyo, July 22, 1950; arrived in U.S., 1950; s. Hillard Rhoda and Violet Beatrice (Taylor) Barkley. BS, U. N. Ala., 1973; MA, The Citadel, 1974; MLS, U. Ala., 1987; grad. cert. in mus. studies, Harvard U., 1990. Cert. tchr. Ala., 1975, Va., 1978. Tchr. social studies Randolph Sch., Huntsville, Ala., 1975—78; chmn. Social Studies Dept. Augusta Mil. Acad., Ft. Defiance, Va., 1978—83; tchr. social studies Huntsville City Schs., 1984—86; asst. archivist Birmingham Pub. Libr., Ala., 1988—89; spl. collections libr. Ala. A&M U., Huntsville, 1990—92; archivist and mus. curator Bridgewater Coll., Va., 1993—. Editl. asst.: The Brethren Encyclopedia, 1996—97, rsch. asst., 2001—; author: One Who Served Brethren Elder Charles Nesselrodt, 1996; contbr. articles to profl. jours.; musician: Ala. Music Hall Fame (drums), 1999. Mem. com. Valley Brethren Mennonite Cultural Ctr., Harrisonburg, Va., 1998—2001, Shenandoah Valley Battlefields Found., New Market, Va., 2000—02; chmn. Shenandoah Dist. Hist. Com. Ch. of the Brethren, 1996—99; mem. exec. bd. Shenandoah Valley Civil War Roundtable, 1993—98. Advanced Army grad. ROTC, 1973. Mem.: ALA, Am. Assn. Mus., Soc. Am. Archivists, Rockingham Area Hist. Assn., Contemporary Longrifle Assn., Lincoln Soc. Va. (charter), Nat. Soc. Scabbard and Blade, Phi Alpha Theta. Avocations: music, history, travel. Office: Box 147 Bridgewater College Bridgewater VA 22812 Home: 117-B S Main St Bridgewater VA 22812 Office Phone: 540-828-5414, 540-828-5462. Business E-Mail: tbarkley@bridgewater.edu.

BARKMEIER, WAYNE W., academic administrator; b. Friend, Nebr., Mar. 29, 1944; m. Carolyn A. Johnsen; children: Kimberly, Jennifer, Wayne Jr. Postgrad., U. Nebr., Lincoln, 1962—65; DDS, U. Nebr. Med. Ctr. Coll. Dentistry, 1965—69; MS, U. Tex. Health Sci. Ctr., Houston, 1973—75. Asst. prof., oral surgery Creighton U., 1978—79; pvt. practice Omaha, 1978—82; asst. prof., operative dentistry Creighton U., 1979—82; rsch. dentist L.D. Caulk Divsn., Dentsply Internat., Milford, Del., 1982—85, intramural rsch. mgr., 1985; asst. dean rsch. and assoc. prof. operative dentistry, Sch. Dentistry Creighton U., 1985—87, dir., Ctr. Oral Health Rsch., 1986—95, assoc. dean rsch., Sch. Dentistry, 1991—94, prof., operative dentistry, Sch. Dentistry, 1991—2000, prof. gen. dentistry, Sch. Dentistry, 2000—, dean, Sch. Dentistry, 1994—. Cons. on dental materials Nat. Bd. Test Constrn. Com. for Joint Commn. on Nat. Dental Exams.; past mem. Am. Dental Assn. Coun. on Dental Rsch. Contbr. more than 130 articles to profl. jours.; mem. editl. bd. Operative Dentistry, article rev. cons. Jour. Am. Dental Assn., Am. Jour. Dentistry, Dental Materials, Jour. Dentistry, Quintessence Internat., Jour. Dental Edn., Mil. Medicine. Active duty USAF, 1969—78, brig. gen. USAFR, 1991—94. Office: 2500 Calif Plza Omaha NE 68178 Office Phone: 402-280-5061.

BARKOFF, RUPERT MITCHELL, lawyer; b. New Orleans, May 7, 1948; s. Samuel and Martha B.; m. Susan Joyce Levitt, May 31, 1970; children: Stuart, Jeffrey, Lisa. BA in Econs. with high distinction, U. Mich., 1970, JD magna cum laude, 1973. Bar: Ga. 1973. Assoc. Kilpatrick Stockton LLP, Atlanta, 1973-80, ptnr., 1980—. Contbr. articles to profl. jours. Mem. ABA (bus. law sect., antitrust sect., forum on franchising, panelist ann. forums 1980-92, chmn. 1989-92, assoc. editor Franchise Law Jour. 1981-86), Ga. Bar Assn. (corp. and banking sect.), Atlanta Bar Assn., Phi Beta Kappa. Democrat. Jewish. Home: 5215 Vernon Springs Trl NW Atlanta GA 30327-4511 Office: Kilpatrick Stockton LLP 1100 Peachtree St NE Ste 2800 Atlanta GA 30309-4530 Office Phone: 404-815-6366. Business E-Mail: rbarkoff@kilpatrickstockton.com.

BARKSDALE, CLARENCE CAULFIELD, banker; b. St. Louis, June 4, 1932; s. Clarence M. and Elizabeth (Caulfield) B.; m. Emily Catlin Keyes, Apr. 4, 1959; children: John Keyes, Emily Shepley. AB, Brown U., 1954; postgrad., Washington U. Law Sch., St. Louis, 1957-58, Stonier Grad. Sch. Banking, Rutgers U., 1964, Columbia U. Grad. Sch. Bus., 1968; LLD (hon.), Maryville Coll., St. Louis, 1976, Westminster Coll., Fulton, Mo., 1982, St. Louis U., 1989. From asst. cashier to chmn. bd., CEO Centerre Bank NA (formerly 1st Nat. Bank), St. Louis, 1960—76, chmn. bd., chief exec. officer, 1976-88; vice chmn. Bank of Am. (formerly Boatmen's Bancshares, Inc.), St. Louis, 1988-89; vice chmn. bd. dirs. Washington U., St. Louis, 1989—. Bd. dirs. SBC Comms., Inc. Bd. dirs. Mo. Bot. Gardens, Alzheimers Assn., Grand Ctr. Inc., Washington U., Mus. Contemporary Art, St. Louis Boy Scouts, Girls, Inc. With M.I., U.S. Army, 1954-57. Mem. St. Louis Club, St. Louis Country Club, Noonday Club, Bogey Club of St. Louis, Harbor Point Golf Club, Little Harbor Club, Wequetosing Golf Club (Harbor Springs, Mich.), Ocean Club, Gulfstream Golf Club, Gulf Stream Bath and Tennis Club (Delray Beach, Fla.), Alpha Delta Phi. Office: Washington U 7425 Forsyth Blvd Saint Louis MO 63105-2161 Office Phone: 314-935-4389. Personal E-mail: cedgy@aismail.wustl.edu.

BARKSDALE, JAMES LOVE, communications company executive; b. Jackson, Miss., 1943; married. Grad., U. Miss., 1965. V.p. Cook Industries, Inc., 1973-79; former pres. ISD, Inc.; sr. v.p. info. systems, chief info. officer Fed. Express Corp., Memphis, 1979-83, exec. v.p., COO, 1983-92, also dir.; pres., COO McCaw Cellular Commns.; CEO AT&T Wireless Svcs. (merger McCaw Cellular Comms. and AT&T Wireless Svcs.); pres., CEO Netscape Comms. Corp., Mountain View, Calif., 1995—, also bd. dirs. Bd. dirs. 3Com Corp., @Home, Harrah's Entertainment, Robert Mondavi Winery.

BARKSDALE, MARY ALICE, education educator; b. Roanoke, Va., Feb. 12, 1954; d. Byrd H. and Mary Anne (St. Clair) Barksdale. BA in Elem. Edn., Clemson U., 1976, MEd in Reading Edn., 1979; EdD in Curriculum and Instrn., Va. Tech., 1988. Tchr. Greenville (S.C.) Schs., 1976-81, Bedford (Va.) County Schs., 1981-83; grad. asst. Va. Tech., Blacksburg, 1983-88; prof. W.Va. U., Morgantown, 1988-94, U. South Fla., Tampa, 1994—2001, Va. Tech., Blacksburg, 2001—. Presenter in field. Co-editor Jour. Computing in Childhood Edn., 1995-97; contbr. articles to profl. jours.; reviewer publs. in field. Fulbright scholar 1995. Mem. Internat. Reading Assn. (Albert J. Harris award 1995), Nat. Reading Conf., Coll. Reading Assn., Ea. Ednl. Rsch. Assn., Fulbright Assn., Phi Delta Kappa. Office: 107 War Meml Hall Va Tech Blacksburg VA 24061 Office Phone: 540-231-3166. E-mail: mbarksda@vt.edu.

BARKSDALE, RHESA HAWKINS, federal judge; b. Jackson, Miss., Aug. 8, 1944; s. John Woodson Jr. and Mary Bryan (Saunders) Barksdale. BS, U.S. Mil. Acad., 1966; JD, U. Miss., 1972. Law clk. to Hon. Byron R. White U.S. Supreme Ct., 1972—73; assoc., then ptnr. Butler, Snow, O'Mara, Stevens & Cannada, Jackson, 1973—90; judge U.S. Ct. Appeals (5th cir.), Jackson, 1990—. Instr. U. Miss. Sch. Law, Jackson, 1975—76, Miss. Coll. Sch. Law, Jackson, 1976. Chmn. Miss. Vietnam Vets. Leadership Program, Jackson, 1982—85; del. Rep. Nat. Conv., New Orleans, 1988; elector election of Pres. of U.S., Jackson, 1988. Capt. U.S. Army, 1966—70, Vietnam. Decorated Silver Star, Bronze Star for Valor, Purple Heart, Cross of Gallantry with silver star (Republic of Vietnam). Mem.: Phi Delta Phi (Nat. Grad. of Yr. 1972). Episcopalian. Office: US Ct Appeals 5th Cir James O Eastland Courthouse 245 E Capitol St Ste 200 Jackson MS 39201-2414

BARKSDALE, RICHARD DILLON, civil engineer, educator; b. Orlando, Fla., May 2, 1938; s. William Spruil and Lucile Dillon B.; m. Bonnie Alice McClung, Nov. 16, 1962; children— Cheryl Lynn, Richelle Denise. A.S., So. Tech. Inst., Marietta, Ga., 1958; B.C.E., Ga. Inst. Tech., 1962, MS, 1963; PhD, Purdue U., 1966. Registered profl. engr., Fla., Ga., S.C., N.C., Ala., Tenn., La. Asst. prof. civil engring. Ga. Inst. Tech., Atlanta, 1965—69, assoc. prof., 1969—75, prof., 1975—95, prof. emeritus, 1995—. V.p. Soil Systems, Inc., Marietta, 1972-79, Soil Systems of the Carolina, 1976-79; spl. lectr. So. Tech. Inst., 1958-60; mem. com. longterm pavement performance Strategic Hwy. Rsch. Program. Contbr. articles in field to profl. jours. Co-pres. Briarcliff High Sch. Booster Club, 1983-84, Briarcliff High Sch. PTA, 1985-86 Recipient Ga. Engring. Soc. award, 1961, ICAR/AFTRE Disting. Rsch. award, 2003; co-recipient Croda prize Instn. Highway Engrs., 1989; NSF grantee, 1966-67; rsch. fellow Brit. Sci. and Engring. Rsch. Coun., 1988. Mem. ASCE (Norman medal 1978, pres. Ga. sect. 1975-76, chmn. nat. com. structural design of roadways), Nat. Stone Assn. (prof. of yr. 1996), Appalachee Sportsman Club (pres. 1974-95), Phi Kappa Phi (pres. Ga. Tech. chpt. 1979). Republican. Baptist. Office: Ga Tech Inst Sch Civil Engring Atlanta GA 30332-0001 Personal E-mail: rbarksda@mindspring.com.

BARKUS, BRUCE, health products executive; Pharmacist/mgr. Eckerd Corp., 1978; with Family Dollar Stores, 1999—2005, exec. vice-pres., 2003—05; pres., CEO GNC Corp., 2005—. Office: GNC 300 Sixth Ave Pittsburgh PA 15222 Office Phone: 412-288-4600. Office Fax: 412-288-4764.*

BARKUS, MARIONA MARCIA, artist; d. John and Bertha Anne Barkus. BA, Northwestern U., 1970; postgrad., UCLA, 1971—72, Pepperdine U., 1973—74. Cert. elem. tchr., secondary tchr. Calif. Part-time tchr. Los Angeles Schs., 1972—. Contbr. to art pubs.; one-woman shows include Beyond Baroque Gallery, Venice, Calif., 1979, Founder's Gallery, Knox Coll., Ill., 1979, Freeport Art Mus., Ill., 1980, Eastern Wash. State U., 1986, So. Oreg. State Coll., 1989, U. Calif. Berkeley Ext., 1991, Sushi, San Diego, 1991, Antioch U., L.A., 1992, Mcpl. Art Gallery, Las Vegas, 1994, exhibited in group shows at Triforium Galleries, San Diego, 1975, Annenberg Sch. Communication, L.A., 1977, Golden West Coll., Huntington Beach, Calif., 1978, Traction Gallery, L.A., 1981, L.A. Contemporary Exhbns., 1982, Conejo Valley Art Mus., Long Beach Mus. Art, 1983, N.Y. State Mus., Pratt Graphics Ctr., Otis Art Inst., Parsons Sch. Design, 1984, Southwestern Coll., Chula Vista, Calif., 1984, Hampshire coll., Mass., 1985, U. Calif.-Riverside, 1985, Ariz. State U., 1985, Woman's Bldg., L.A., 1985, Hampshire Coll., 1985, Occidental Coll., 1986, New Works Gallery U. Ill., Chgo., 1986, UCLA Art Libr., 1986, Fresno Art Ctr. & Mus., 1987, Fla. State U., 1988, Palos Verdes Art Ctr., L.A., 1988, A.R.C. Gallery, Chgo., 1990, Security Pacific, L.A., 1990, U. Calif.-Santa Barbara, 1991, Pierce Coll., L.A., 1991, Mt. St. Mary's Coll., L.A., 1991, Korean Cultural Ctr., L.A., 1993, SUNY, 1994, Tex. State U., 1994, Yale U., 1995, Mcpl. Art Gallery, L.A., 1995, Kresge Art Mus., Mich., 1996, U. Toledo, 1997, Represented in permanent collections Freeport Art Mus., Ill., Sch. KFAC, L.A., one-woman shows include Eastern Wash. State U. Libr., Represented in permanent collections Calif. Inst. Art, Libr. of the Mus. of Modern Art, represented in various mags., books, slide registries and art archives, in pub. (collections), Getty Rsch. Inst., U. Toledo, Ind. Purdue U., prin. works include in pub. (collections) Inst. of the Arts Libr., Calif., Libr. of the Mus. of Modern Art, N.Y.C., Yale U. Art Gallery, Libr. Art Inst., Chgo., So. Oreg. State Coll., commisioned poster, Women's Studio Workshop, N.Y., 1990, street banner, Fullerton, Calif., 1991. Artist-in-residence grantee, Women's Graphic Ctr., 1984, Artists Book grantee, 1985, 1986, Artists' Book Grant, N.Y. Arts Coun. and NEA, 1985, Women's Studio Workshop, N.Y., 1986, Individual Artist's grantee, City of L.A., 1991. Mem.: Artists Equity Assn., L.A. Inst. for Contemporary Art, Women's Caucus for Art (membership coord. 1979—80). Office: PO Box 34785 Los Angeles CA 90034-0785 E-mail: mbarkus@earthlink.net.

BARLAND, CHARLES JOHN, music educator; b. Eau Claire, Wis., Mar. 21, 1968; s. John and Judith McEvoy Barland. BA, Carroll Coll., Waukesha, Wis., 1990; MA, U. of Iowa, 1993; D of Mus. Arts, U. of Kans., 1998. Min. of music Holy Trinity Luth. Ch., Dubuque, Iowa, 1998—2003; asst. prof. of music and dept. chair U. of Dubuque, 2003—. Organist and youth choir dir. St. Luke's United Meth. Ch., Dubuque, Iowa, 2003—; organist First English Luth. Ch., Platteville, Wis., 2003—; bd. mem. Dubuque Symphony Orch., Dubuque, Iowa, 2001—. Musician: (recitalist) Organ Recitals. Vol. Big Bros. / Big Sisters, Dubuque, Iowa, 1998—2005. Co-recipient Outstanding Grad. Tchg. Asst., U. of Kans., 1998; named Grad. of the Last Decade, Carroll Coll., 1999; recipient West Ctrl. Divsn. Winner in Organ Performance, Music Teachers Nat. Assn., 1992. Mem.: Coll. Music Soc., Assn. of Luth. Ch. Musicians, Am. Choral Dir. Assn., Am. Guild of Organists (dean 1996—98), Phi Mu Alpha (life; v.p. 1992—93). Lutheran. Avocations: swimming, travel, reading. Home: 994 Patricia Ann Dr Dubuque IA 52003 Office: University of Dubuque 2000 University Ave Dubuque IA 52001 Office Phone: 563-589-3564. E-mail: cbarland@dbq.edu.

BARLAR, REBECCA NANCE, music educator; b. Lawrenceburg, Tenn., Mar. 3, 1950; d. Harold Wilford and Freda Eleanor (Bailey) Nance; m. Douglas Garland Barlar, June 14, 1969; children: Jennifer, Nancy, Jonathan, David. BS, Mid. Tenn. State U., 1972; M in Music, U. South Fla., 1979. Pvt. practice, Franklin, Tenn., 1972-76; piano instr. Dept. of Continuing Edn. U. South Fla., Tampa, Fla., 1979-82; prof. of music theory Fla. Coll., Temple Terrace, 1979—, prof. of piano, 1986—. Pvt. piano tchr., Tampa, 1976—; chmn. Fla. Coll. Life Enrichment Com., 1992—; faculty sponsor Collegiate Music Educators Nat. Conf., 1992—. Mem. Greco Jr. High PTSA, 1987-89, King High Sch. PTSA, 1986-92, 94-2000; v.p. King High Music Club, 1988-89. Named U. South Fla. Fine Arts fellow 1977, One of Outstanding Young Women Am., 1984. Mem. Music Tchrs. Nat. Assn. (profl. cert. in piano 1987), Mid-State Music Tchrs. Assn. (sec. 1980-82, treas. 1986-98, pres. 1998-2002), Fla. State Music Tchrs. Assn. (cert. of experience in piano 1986, dist. sec. 1985-87), Music Educators Nat. Conf., Fla. Music Educators Assn., Fla. Coll. Music Educators Assn., Nat. Piano Found., Delta Omicron Profl. Music Frat. (life). Mem. Ch. of Christ. Avocations: walking, needlecrafts, reading. Office: Fla Coll 119 N Glen Arven Ave Temple Terrace FL 33617-5527 Home: 11406 W Queensway Dr Tampa FL 33617-2451 Office Phone: 813-899-6793. Business E-Mail: barlarb@floridacollege.edu.

BARLEY, JOHN ALVIN, lawyer; b. Jacksonville, Fla., Oct. 16, 1940; s. Lewis Alvin Barley and Catherine Alberta (Curran) McKendree; m. Mary Freida Szarowicz, Nov. 30, 1974 (div. Dec. 1991); children: Jared Scott, Jessica Lauren; m. Debora Ann Barber Brown, July 11, 1998. BS, Fla. State U., 1963; JD, U. Fla., 1968. Bar: Fla. 1969, U.S. Dist. Ct. (mid. and no. dists.) Fla. 1973, U.S. Ct. Appeals (5th and 11th cirs.) 1973, U.S. Supreme Ct. 1973. Law clk. to judge U.S. Dist. Ct. (so. dist.), Miami, Fla., 1968-69; exec. asst. to Hon. Ray C. Osborne Lt. Gov. Fla., Tallahassee, 1969-70; asst. dir. div. of labor Fla. Dept. Commerce, Tallahassee, 1971; assoc. Maquire, Voorhis & Wells, Orlando, Fla., 1972-73; asst. atty. gen. Dept. of Legal Affairs, Tallahassee, 1974-75; gen. counsel Dept. of Gen. Services, Tallahassee, 1976-78; pvt. practice, Tallahassee, 1978—. Mem. Tallahassee Leon County Architectural Rev. Bd., 1994, 96. Mem. ABA, Fla. Bar Assn. (pub. contract law com., bd. govs. young lawyers div. 1974, rules of civil procedure com. 1974-88, 91-92), Tallahassee Bar Assn., Am. Judicature Soc., Phi Delta Phi. Roman Catholic. Avocations: camping, hunting, fishing, swimming, running. Home: 4927 Heathe Dr Tallahassee FL 32309-2134 Office: 400 N Meridian St Tallahassee FL 32301-1254 also: PO Box 10166 Tallahassee FL 32302-2166

BARLOW, ANNE LOUISE, pediatrician, medical researcher; b. Skipton-in-Craven, Eng., Jan. 28, 1925; came to U.S., 1951, naturalized, 1954; m. Howard Cadwell, May 19, 1951; children: Barbara Anne, John James Stewart; m. Alastair Ramsay, Dec. 19, 1969. MB BS, London (Royal Free Hosp.) Sch. Medicine for Women, U. London, 1948; diploma in child health, Royal Colls. Eng., 1950; MPH with honors, Yale U., 1952. House physician North Lonsdale Hosp., Barrow-in-Furness, Lancashire, Eng., 1948-49; house surgeon Royal Infirmary (Glasgow), Scotland, 1949; resident to profl. unit of child health Royal Hosp. for Sick Children, Glasgow, 1949-50; jr. hosp. med. officer Knightswood Infectious Diseases Hosp., Glasgow, 1950; Rotary Found. Internat. fellow U. Toronto Med. Sch., Ont., Can., 1950-51; research asst. Yale U. Sch. Pub. Health, New Haven, 1952-53; clinic physician in cancer prevention Arlington, Va., part-time 1953-54; resident, staff physician William H. Maybury Tb Sanatorium, Northville, Mich., 1954-56; research dir. Detroit Feeding Study with the Detroit City Health Dept., 1954-56; research asst., instr. sch. health U. Pitts. Grad. Sch. Pub. Health, 1957-62; pvt. practice medicine specializing in pediatrics Pitts., 1959-62; mem. courtesy staff St. Margaret Hosp., Pitts., 1959-62; research assoc. Tice Lab for Tb research, Cook County Hosp., Chgo., Ill., 1962; med. writer product info. Abbott Labs., North Chicago, Ill., 1963-66, med. specialist antibiotic medicine, 1966-68; mgr. clin. devel. pharm. products div. Abbott Lab., North Chicago, Ill., 1968-71, asst. med. dir., 1971-72, mgr. parenteral nutrition hosp. products div., 1972-73, med. dir., 1973-80, v.p. med. affairs hosp. products div., 1980-84; pres. Albamed, Inc., 1985—; asst. clin. prof. Med.Coll. Pa., 1988. Cons. maternal, child and sch. health, dir. well baby clinic Lake County (Ill.) Health Dept., 1963-76; pres. Tb Sanatorium Bd. Lake County Health Dept., Ill., 1976-79; dir., pres. Lake County Bd. Health, 1979-82; health officer Village of North Barrington, Ill., 1964-67; physician-adviser Head Start Lake County Community Action Project, 1970-84; chmn. profl. adv. com. Lake County Health Dept., 1972-84; preceptor Pediatric Nurse Assoc. Program; chmn. bd. Sutton Place Behavioral Health Inc., 2000—. Contbr. articles on maternal and infant care, pediatrics and nutrition; patentee high calorie solution of low molecular weight glucose polymer mixtures useful for intravenous adminstrn. Bd. dirs. Heart Assn. of Lake County, 1979-84, chmn. nutrition com. 1980-82, v.p. 1982-83, pres., 1983-84; mem. sch. bd. Grant Twp. Cmty. H.S. (Ill. Dist. 124), 1973-79; sec. to governing bd. Spl. Edn. Dist. of Lake County, 1977-79; assoc. Nat. Coll. Edn., Evanston, Ill., 1976-84; chmn. Am. Women's Hosp. Svc., 1986-95, 2004-; vol. Guardian ad Litem, 1989-2004. Recipient Charlotte Danstrom award for excellence Women in Mgmt., 1984, award of merit for outstanding contns. to pub. health Ill. Pub. Health Assn., 1975; recipient award of merit for outstanding community service to Lake County Community Action Project, 1976, award for outstanding and dedicated service as pres Lake County TB Sanatorium Bd., 1979, TWIN award YWCA, 1983. Mem. AAAS, NOW, LWV, AMA (chair sr. physician gov. com. 1996-2005), Am. Med. Women's Assn. (councilor for orgn. and mgmt. 1977-79, treas. 1980, 1st v.p. 1981, pres. 1983, chair found. 1992-95, Elizabeth Blackwell medal 1992), Fla. Med. Assn. (vice chair Internat. Med. Grad. sect. 1998-2004, coun. on pub. health 2000-05), Med. Women's Internat. Assn. (v.p. N. Am. 1993-95), Pan-Am. Med. Women's Alliance (pres. 2000), Nassau County Med. Soc. (pres. 2002-03). Home and Office: 20 S 19th St Fernandina Beach FL 32034-2767 Personal E-mail: czardaska@aol.com.

BARLOW, AUGUST RALPH, JR., minister; s. August Ralph and Kathryn Viola (Adams) B.; m. Elizabeth Evone Anderson, Aug. 27, 1960; children: Paul Martin, Andrew Ralph, Ann Kathryn. BA, Haverford Coll., 1956; BD, Yale U., 1959, STM, 1964. Ordained to ministry Meth. Ch., 1959. Pastor Fox Chapel Meth. Ch., Pitts., 1959—60, Butler St. Meth. Ch., Pitts., 1961—62, Lawrenceville Cmty. Ch., Pitts., 1962—63; intern Cleve. Inner City Protestant Parish, 1960—61; from tchg. min. to pastor Beneficent Congl. Ch., Providence, 1964—97, pastor emeritus, 1997—. Bd. govs. Beneficent House, 1970-97, Beneficent Commons Housing, Providence, sr. min., devel. team, 1991-95; bd. dirs. Pastoral Counseling Ctr., Greater Providence, v.p., 1984-86, pres., 1995-97; pres. Steere House, Providence, 1983-86, past bd. dirs.; bd. dirs. Home Health Svcs. of R.I., 1986-93, chmn. ch. in soc. com., 1985-86; mem. R.I. Conf., United Ch. of Christ, 1964—, mem. com. on ministry, 1981-83, past bd. dirs.; mem. urban divsn. R.I. Coun. Chs., 1979-82. Editor-in-chief: jour. Expanding Horizons, 1996—; contbr. articles to profl. jours., newspapers and mags.; Religious Broadcasting Sta. WEAN, 1964—87. Adv. coun. Providence Pub. Libr., 1968-71; bd. dirs. Mouthpiece Coffee House, Providence, 1969-75, pres., 1974-75; bd. dirs. Citizens United

Renewal Enterprises, 1972-77; alumni class agt. for scholarship funds Haverford Coll. and Yale U. Div. Sch., 1979-95; corp. mem. R.I. Hosp. Corp., 1980-95. Rsch. fellow Yale U. Div. Sch., 1979; recipient Alumnal Bd. award Yale U. Div. Sch., 1997. Mem. Providence Intown Chs. Assn., Mins. Assn. R.I. Conf. United Ch. of Christ, Dodeka Symposium, Rotary (trustee Rotary Charities Found. 1977-82, Paul Harris fellow), Beneficent Order of Spike, Phi Beta Kappa. Democrat. Home and Office: 103 Angell Rd Lincoln RI 02865-4710 E-mail: a.r.barlow@att.net.

BARLOW, BARBARA ANN, surgeon; b. Lancaster, Pa., June 20, 1938; d. William Barlow and Esther Stoll Barlow Lowry; m. Andre Zmurek. BA in psychology, Vassar Coll.; MA in psychology, Columbia U.; MD, Albert Einstein Coll. Medicine, 1967. Diplomate Am. Bd. Surgery. Intern Bronx (N.Y.) Mcpl. Hosp., 1967-68, resident in surgery, 1968-73; resident in pediatric surgery Columbia-Presbyn. Med.-Babies Hosp., N.Y.C., 1973-75; chief pediatric surgery Harlem Hosp., N.Y.C., 1975—2000, chief of surgery, 2000—; prof. surgery and epidemiology Columbia U. and Mailman Sch. Pub. Health, N.Y.C.; founder, exec. dir. Injury Free Coalition for Kids, 1988—. Recipient Safe Cmty. Award, US Dept. Transp., 1996, David E. Rogers award, Assn. Am. Med. Colleges, 2001, Disting. Career Award, Injury Ctrl. and Health Svcs. Sect., APHA, 2001, Pub. Svc. Award, Alfred P. Sloan Found., 2003. Mem. ACS, Am. Acad. Pediatrics (Injury and Poison Prevention Fellow Achievement Award, 1997), Am. Assn. for Surgery of Trauma, Am. Pediatric Surg. Assn., N.Y. Surgery Soc. Achievements include Featured in the Nat. Libr. Medicine exhibit "Changing the Face of Medicine" honoring women physicians, 2003. Office: Columbia U Mailman Sch Pub Health 722 W 168th St Rm 1709 New York NY 10032

BARLOW, CARROLEE, physician, scientist, educator; b. Page, Ariz., Sept. 24, 1963; d. Eslie and Carrol (Burham) B.; m. Kleanthis Gabriel Xanthopoulos, June 10, 1989. BA, U. Utah, 1985, MD, 1989; PhD, The Karolinska Inst., Stockholm, 1995. Diplomate Am. Bd. Endocrinology, Am. Bd. Internal Medicine. Study rsch. fellow Sch. Medicine U. Utah, Salt Lake City, 1986-89, The Rockefeller U., N.Y.C., 1988; resident N.Y. Hosp.-Cornell Med. Ctr.-U. Utah Med. Ctr., N.Y.C. and Salt Lake City, 1989-91; clin. assoc. NIH, Bethesda, Md., 1995-98; asst. prof. The Salk Inst., San Diego, 1998—. Presenter in field. Contbr. numerous articles to profl. jours. Recipient Caine scholarship U. Utah, 1988-89, Olga A. Logan scholarship, 1986-89, scholarship Nat. Panhellenic Assn., 1984-85, U. Utah Women's Club, 1982-83. Mem. Am. Women's Med. Assn. (Outstanding Women in Medicine award 1989), Alpha Omega Alpha, Phi Beta Kappa. Avocations: skiing, rollerblading, gardening.

BARLOW, JESSE LOUIS, computer scientist, educator; b. Lawrence, Kans., July 8, 1955; s. Richard Lewis and Elizabeth Marie (McCaffrey) B.; m. Ramsey Stade, Jan. 10, 1981; children: Hilary, Zachary. BA in Computer Sci. and Math., U. Kans., 1977; MS in Computer Sci., Northwestern U., 1979, MS in Stats., 1980, PhD, 1981. Asst. prof. computer sci. Pa. State U., University Park, 1981-87, assoc. prof. computer sci., 1987-92, prof. computer sci., 1992—. Vis. prof. U. Manchester, Eng., 1996, Courant Inst. Math. Sci., 1988, CUNY Grad. Ctr., 2002; vis. Inst. of Math. and It's Applications, Inst. Math. Scis. Contbr. articles to profl. jours. NSF grantee, 1982-84, 84-86, 87, 90-2002, Air Force Office of Sci. Rsch., grantee, 1988-90; recipient 2d prize L. Prize Meeting, London, 1986. Mem. Soc. Indsl. and Applied Math., IEEE Computer Soc., Assn. for Computing Machinery, Phi Beta Kappa. Office: Pa State U Computer Sci & Engring Dept University Park PA 16802 Home: PO Box 10221 State College PA 16805-0221 Office Phone: 814-863-1705. Business E-Mail: barlow@cse.psu.edu.

BARLOW, JIM B., retired columnist, writer; b. Port Arthur, Tex., Aug. 19, 1936; s. Joseph B. and Goldie (Johnson) B.; m. Karleen Ann Smith, Aug. 24, 1968 (div. Jan. 1974); 1 child, Samantha Lynn; m. Susan Ann Bischoff, June 20, 1975. BA, U. North Tex., Denton, 1972. Newsman KPAC-TV, Port Arthur, Tex., 1959-61; news dir. KPNG-Radio, Port Neches, Tex., 1962-63; reporter Beaumont (Tex.) Enterprise, 1963-64, Denton Record-Chronicle, 1964-66; asst. city mgr. City of Denton, 1967; staff writer U. North Tex., Denton, 1968; newsman AP, Dallas-Houston, 1968-75; dir. info. svcs. Houston Ind. Sch. Dist., 1975-77; reporter Houston Chronicle, 1977-87, columnist, 1987—2002; ret., 2002. Co-author: Big Town, Big Money, 1974, The Woodlands, 2004. With U.S. Army, 1956-59. Avocations: reading, cooking, exercise. Home: # 112 2929 Buffalo Speedway Houston TX 77098 Office Phone: 713-303-8874. Personal E-mail: JimB3333@aol.com.

BARLOW, JOHN ADEN, lawyer; b. Columbus, Ohio, June 8, 1942; s. William Willard and Eleanore (Johnson) B.; m. Patricia Ann Mowry, Oct. 17, 1970 (div. Aug. 1982); children: William P., Allison J., Jonathan A.; m. Patricia Marion Palmer, Sept. 3, 1982. BSc in Edn., Ohio State U., 1963, JD cum laude, 1968. Bar: Ohio 1969, Wash. 1969, U.S. Dist. Ct. (we. dist.) Wash. 1969, U.S. Dist. Ct. (ea. dist.) Wash. 1992. Assoc. Skeel McKelvey Henke Evenson & Betts, Seattle, 1968-70; ptnr. Walstead Mertsching Husemoen Donaldson & Barlow, Longview, Wash., 1970—. Mem. Wash. State Ins. Commr.'s Tort Reform Com., 1987. Contbg. author to 2 books. Named Boss of Yr., Cowlitz County Legal Secs. Assn., 1989. Fellow Am. Coll. Trial Lawyers; mem. Am. Bd. Trial Advocates, Wash. State Trial Lawyers Assn. (bd. dirs. 1981-90, v.p. for west 1989-90), Cowlitz County Bar Assn. (pres. 1974-75), Longview C. of C. (bd. dirs. 1977-80), Kiwanis (pres. Longview 1973). Democrat. Avocations: golf, antiques. Home: 1506 23d Ave Longview WA 98632-3616 Office: Walstead Mertsching Husemoen Donaldson & Barlow 1000 12th Ave Ste 2 Longview WA 98632-2500 Office Phone: 360-423-5220.

BARLOW, JOHN LEON, retired retail executive; b. Donalsonville, Ga., Mar. 24, 1941; s. Charles Leon Barlow and Virtie Lee Faircloth; m. Ethel A. Ruppenthal (div.); 1 child, Leon John; m. Ellen Faye Allen, Sept. 5, 1971. BA in Bus. Mgmt., Kings Coll., 1976, AAS in Acctg., 1977. Lic. ins. broker N.C.; real estate broker N.C. Enlisted USMC, Viet Nam, Cuban Missle crisis, 1961, advanced through grades to sgt., 1973; retail mgmt. A&P, NC, 1972—88, Kroger, NC, 1988—2001; ret. Author: (novels) For Love and Honor, 2001, The Fine Print-Consumer Debt in America, 2004, Missing!, 2004, One Man's Treasure, 2004, Casualty of War, 2005, Headin' West, 2005. Fundraiser Boy Scouts Am., Hawaii, 1964; collector Toys for Tots, NC, 1973—74. Mem.: Assoc. Auctioneers Am. (past editor, past spkr.). Protestant. Avocations: carpentry, deep sea fishing, long-range target practice. E-mail: johnlbarlow@earthlink.net.

BARLOW, JOHN PERRY, writer, former rancher, advocate; b. Wyo., Oct. 3, 1947; m. Elaine Parker (div. 1996); children: Leah Justine, Anna Winter, Amelia. Degree in comparative religion with honors, Wesleyan U., 1969. Mgr. Bar Cross Land and Livestock Co., Cora, Wyo., 1971-88; co-founder, vice chmn. Electronic Frontier Found., 1990—. Bd. dirs. WELL; cons. Vanguard Group of CSC, Global Bus. Network. Contbg. editor numerous publs. including Comm. of the ACM, Microtimes, Mondo 2000; contbg. writer Wired; co-writer songs for The Grateful Dead, 1971-95. Berkman fellow Harvard Law Sch., 1998—; named Thomas Jefferson of Cyberspace, Yahoo Mag. Internet Life, 1996, one of 25 Most Influential People in Fin. Svcs., Future Banker Mag., 1999, Office: Electronic Frontier Foundation 168 S Franklin Pinedale WY 82941-1009 also: 203 Grand St #2 New York NY 10013 E-mail: barlow@eff.org.*

BARLOW, JOHN SUTTON, neuroscientist; b. Raleigh, NC, June 10, 1925; s. David Henry and Anne Mary (Sutton) B.; m. Sibylle E. Jahrreiss, Aug. 5, 1950; children: Thomas Walter, Robert Sutton, Lisa Katharine. BS, U. NC, 1944, MS, 1948; MD, Harvard U., 1953. Diplomate Am. Bd. EEG. Clin., rsch. fellow, asst. resident neurology Mass. Gen. Hosp., Boston, 1953-57; clin., rsch. fellow Harvard Med. Sch., 1953-57; rsch. assoc. in elec. engring. MIT, Cambridge, 1954-64, rsch. affiliate Rsch. Lab. of Electronics, 1964-99; asst. neurology Mass. Gen. Hosp., Boston, 1957-61, neurophysiologist neurology svc., 1961—; rsch. assoc. neurology Harvard Med. Sch., 1961-69, prin. rsch. assoc., 1969-78, sr. rsch. assoc. neurology, neurophysiology, 1979—. Mem. neurology study sect. NIH, Bethesda, Md., 1966-70; mem. rev. panel on neurol. devices FDA, Washington, 1974-76; cons. dept. neurology VA Med. Ctr., Boston, 1979-89, part-time staff, 1989-98; cons. dept. neurology New Eng. Med. Ctr., Boston, 1979-89. Author: The Electroencephalogram: Its Patterns and Origins, 1993, A Chinese-Russian-English Dictionary, 1995, A Pocket Chinese-Russian-English Dictionary, 2000, The Cerebellum and Adaptive Control, 2002; editor: (with Karenina Kollmar-Paulenz) Otto Ottonovich Rosenberg and his Contribution to Buddhology in Russia, 1998; cons. editor EEG Clin. Neurophysiology, 1970-86; translator/editor books from the Russian, Czech, Polish and Chinese; contbr. articles and revs. to profl. jours. Ensign, lt. (j.g.) USN, 1944—46. Recipient Rsch. Career Devel. award NIH, 1962-71, Sr. Scientist award Alexander von Humboldt Found., Göttingen, Germany, 1979, Sr. Scientist Exch. award NAS, USA, USSR Acad. Scis., Moscow, 1982, 83, 88; rsch. grantee NIH, 1962-88; Fogarty Internat. fellow, 1979. Mem. Internat. Brain Rsch. Orgn., Am. EEG Soc. (pres. 1975-76), Am. Neurol. Assn., Am. Acad. Neurology, Soc. Neurosci., Am. Geophys. Union, Ea. Assn. EEG (pres. 1971-72), Assn. Asian Studies, European Assn. Chinese Studies, Dictionary Soc. North Am., Phi Beta Kappa. Avocations: music, rail travel, foreign languages, international relations.

BARLOW, WILLIAM KYLE, lawyer, state legislator; b. Smithfield, Va., Mar. 13, 1936; s. Gordon E. and Gladys (Holleman) B.; 1 child, Todd R.; m. Taylor Rowell; 1 child, Amy Elizabeth Barlow Britt. MS in Agrl. Econs. with honors, Va. Poly. Inst., 1958; LLB, U. Va., 1965. Assoc. Law Office of A. E. S. Stephens, Va., 1965-72; ptnr. Delk and Barlow, Smithfield, Va., 1972-87, Barlow, Councill & Riddick, Smithfield, Va., 1987-92; pres. Barlow & Riddick, Smithfield, Va., 1992—2002, Barlow, Riddick & Farmer, 2002—; mem. Va. Ho. of Dels., 1991—2001, mem. fin., agr., sci. & tech., general law, mem. cts. of justice, gen. laws, militia, police, pub. safety, 2001—. Past mem. PTA; past chmn. Isle of Wight County Dem. Com., past chmn. bd. selection commn., mem. C. of C.; past trustee Walter Cecil Rawls Regional Libr., Courtland Va.; mem. Smithfield Bapt. Ch., past chmn. bd. deacons, trustee, ch. moderator; former Little League baseball coach; former mem. and chmn. bd. trustees Walter Cecil Rawls Regional Libr.; mem. bd. dirs. Obici Hosp., Suffolk, Va.; legal advisor Isle of Wright County Rescue Squad. With USAF, 1958-62. Mem. Va. Tech. Alumni Assn. (past pres., bd. dirs.; mem. Peanut Alumni chpt.), Isle-Wight County-Smithfield C. of C., Rotary (past pres.), Ruritan Club, Phi Alpha Delta. Office Phone: 757-357-9720. E-mail: del_barlow@house.state.va.us.

BARLOW, WILLIAM PUSEY, JR., accountant; b. Oakland, Calif., Feb. 11, 1934; s. William P. and Muriel (Block) B. Student, Calif. Inst. Tech., 1952-54; AB in Econs., U. Calif., Berkeley, 1956. CPA, Calif. Acct. Barlow, Davis & Wood, San Francisco, 1960-72, ptnr., 1964-72, J.K. Lasser & Co., 1972-77, Touche Ross & Co., San Francisco, 1977-78; self employed acct., 1978-89; ptnr. Barlow & Hughan, 1990—. Co-author: Collectible Books: Some New Paths, 1979, The Grolier Club, 1884-1984, 1984; editor: Book Catalogues: Their Varieties and Uses, 2d edit., 1986, Officially Sealed Notes, 1996—; contbr. articles to profl. jours. Fellow Gleeson Libr. Assocs., 1969, pres., 1971-74; mem. coun. Friends Bancroft Libr., 1971-98, chmn., 1974-79; bd. dirs. Oakland Ballet, 1982-99, pres., 1986-89, chmn., 1995-98. Recipient Sir Thomas More medal Gleeson Libr. Assocs., 1989, Herbert Howe Bancroft award Bancroft Libr., U. Calif., 2004; named to Water Ski Hall of Fame, 1993. Mem. Am. Water Ski Assn. (bd. dirs., regional chmn. 1959-63, pres. 1963-66, chmn. bd. 1966-69, 77-79, hon. v.p. 1969—), Machine Cancel Soc. (pres., 2003—), Internat. Water Ski Fedn. (exec. bd. 1961-71, 75-78), Bibliog. Soc. Am. (coun. 1986-92, pres. 1992-96), Grolier Club (N.Y.C.), Roxburghe Club (San Francisco), Book Club of Calif. (bd. dirs. 1963-76, pres. 1968-69, treas. 1971-83). Home: 1474 Hampel St Oakland CA 94602-1346 Office: 1182 Market St Ste 400 San Francisco CA 94102-4922 Office Phone: 415-522-2490. Business E-Mail: wpbjr@barlowandhughan.com.

BARLOW-WARE, JACQUELINE SUE, music educator; d. F. John and Dorothy Marx Barlow; m. Michael Brian Ware, Aug. 11, 2001; children: Christopher Barlow Dearing, Brian Michael Ware, Jonathan Edward Ware, Jennifer Christine Ware, David Ray Ware. MusB, Lawrence U. Conservatory, Appleton, Wis., 1978; MusM, MA, Ohio State U., 1982. Cert. Massage Therapist Ohio. Adj. instr. U. Va., Charlottesville, 1973—76; instr. Lawrence U., Appleton, 1976—78; voice instr. Barlow Studio, Columbus, 1978—; mezzo soprano soloist First Cmty. Ch., Columbus, 1982—; instr. Capital U. Cmty. Music Sch., Columbus, 1990—2002; adj. assoc. prof. Capital U. Conservatory Music, Columbus, 1999—. Tchg. assoc. Ohio State U., Columbus, 1978—81. Mem.: Nat. Assn. Tchrs. of Singing (assoc.; v.p., bd. dirs. 2005—, over 75 awards for winning students at nat. competition 1991—2005). Achievements include former students who are now performing on Broadway and international and national Broadway tours, and singing with major opera companies. Avocations: travel, languages, reading, decorating. Office: Capital Univ Conservatory Music 1 Main and College Columbus OH 43209 Personal E-mail: jackie@barlowstudio.com. E-mail: jbarlow@capital.edu.

BARMANN, LAWRENCE FRANCIS, historian, educator; b. Maryville, Mo., June 9, 1932; s. Francis Lawrence and Clary Weber (LaMar) B. BA, St. Louis U., 1956, Ph.L., 1957, S.T.L., 1964; MA, Fordham U., 1960; postgrad., Princeton, 1965-66; PhD, Cambridge U., Eng., 1970. Tchr. history St. Louis U. High Sch., 1957-59; asst. prof. history St. Louis U., 1970-73, asso. prof., 1973-78, prof., 1978—, asst. dir. Am. Studies Program, 1981-83, prof. Am. studies, 1981-01, dir. Am. Studies Program, 1983-88, chair dept. Am. studies, 1999—2000, prof. theol. studies, 1996-01, ret., 2001, prof. emeritus, 2002—. Author: Newman at St. Mary's, 1962, Baron Friedrich von Hügel and the Modernist Crisis in England, 1972, The Letters of Baron Friedrich von Hügel and Professor Norman Kemp Smith, 1982; editor Sanctity and Secularity, 1999; contbr. articles profl. jours. Recipient award Mellon Faculty Devel. Fund, 1987, 92, 94, Emerson Electric Outstanding Tchr. award, 1999; rsch. grantee Am. Philos. Soc. PHila., 1971, Beaumont Fund, 1977, 82; Danforth assoc., 1978—. Mem.: Am. Acad. Religion, Cambridge Soc. (founding 1977), Am. Cath. Hist. Assn., Phi Beta Kappa. Home: The Lindell Ter 12-A 4501 Lindell Blvd Saint Louis MO 63108-2038 Office: 221 N Grand Blvd Saint Louis MO 63103-2006 Home: 5435 Vicar Ct Saint Louis MO 63119 *I have found for myself that the meaning of life is the joy of continuous discovery in unending intellectual, emotional and spiritual growth, and the satisfaction which comes from sharing my vision and concerns with the young people who will lead the next generation.*

BARNA, JAMES FRANCIS, lawyer; b. Brentwood, N.Y., May 4, 1969; s. Thomas John and Ellen Veronica (Byrne) B.; m. Jennifer Baggett, Aug. 22, 1992; children: Helen Veronica, James Nicholas. BA in Multidisciplinary Studies, Stony Brook U., 1992; JD, Washington U., 1996. Bar: Tenn. 1996, Miss. 2001, U.S. Dist. Ct. (we. dist.) Tenn. 1998, U.S. Ct. Appeals (6th cir.) 1998, U.S. Dist. Ct. (So. dist.) Miss. 2002, U.S. Supreme Ct. 2000. Law clk. Mary Anne Sedey & Assocs., St. Louis, 1994, Stokes & O'Malley, St. Louis, 1995-96; assoc. Ford & Harrison, LLP, Memphis, 1996-98; pvt. practice Memphis, 1998-99; assoc. Weintraub, Stock & Grisham, Memphis, 1999—. Articles editor Washington U. Jour. Urban and Contemporary Law, 1994-96. Rschr. So. Justice Inst., Durham, N.C., 1992. Sgt. USAR, 1990-93. Mem. ABA, Tenn. Bar Assn., Memphis Bar Assn., Phi Delta Phi, SHRM. Democrat. Roman Catholic. Avocations: fly fishing, camping, cooking. Office: Weintraub Stock & Grisham Ste 512 1715 Aaron Brenner Dr Memphis TN 38120

BARNA, PETER, chemical company financial executive; b. Hackensack, N.J., Oct. 12, 1943; s. Michael Sr. and Eva (Chomiak) B.; m. Eva Lynn Kaseta, Aug. 16, 1964; children: Lisa Marie, Peter Anthony. BSBA in Acctg., Seton Hall U., 1964. CPA, N.J. Staff acct. Price Waterhouse and Co., Newark, 1964-66; mgr. Peat, Marwick, Mitchell and Co., Newark, 1966-74; treas., prin. acctg. officer Crompton and Knowles Corp., Stamford, Conn., 1974—. Mem. Nat. Assn. Accts., N.J. Soc. CPA's, Fin. Execs. Inst., Nat. Assn. Treas. Republican. Roman Catholic.

BARNACK, TONY, art educator; b. Alexandria, Minn., June 24, 1976; s. Dennis and Julie Barnack; m. Rebecca Walther, June 21, 1997; children: Ben, Sam, Dan. BS in art Edn., Mankato State U., 1997. Art tchr. K-8 Emmons Pub. Sch., Emmons, Minn., 1997—2001; art tchr. 7-12 Montgomery Lonsdale HS, Montgomery, Minn., 2001—. Head football coach Montgomery Lonsdale HS, Montgomery, Minn., 2003—, Glenville Emmons HS, Blenville, Minn., 2000—02. Office Phone: 507-364-8111.

BARNARD, ANNETTE WILLIAMSON, educational association administrator; b. Phoenix, Nov. 29, 1948; d. Water Albert and Geraldine Williamson; m. Richard W. Heinrich, Sept. 1969 (div.); 1 child, Jennifer Anne; m. Charles Jay Barnard, June 6, 1981. AA, Mesa C.C., 1979; BA in Spl. Edn., Elem. Edn., Ariz. State U., 1981, postgrad., 1989; M in Edn. Leadership, 1996, No. Ariz. U., 1996. Cert. tchr., prin. Ariz. Tchr. spl. edn. Tempe (Ariz.) Sch. Dist., 1981-83, tchr. Indian community, 1983-84; tchr. elem. sch. Kyrene Sch. Dist., Tempe, 1984-97; sch. dist. mentor coord., 1994-96; tchr. Chandler (Ariz.) Sch. Dist., 1986-89; v.p. Pendergast Elem. Sch., Phoenix, 1997-98; prin. Arredondo Elem. Sch., Tempe Sch. Dist., 1999—. Chair profl. stds. and cert. com. Ariz. Bd. Edn., Phoenix, 1990-94; chair facilitator Kyrene Legis. Action Community, 1991-94; mentor Kyrene Sch. dist., 1990—; commencement spkr. Ariz. State U., 1981; design. team. mem. Quality Cert. Employee Appraisal System; speaker in field. Contbg. author: Environmental Education Compendium for Energy Resources, 1991, System of Personnel Development, 1989; contbr. articles to profl. jours. Bd. dirs. Ariz. State Rep. Caucus, Phoenix, 1990-93, precinct committeewoman, Tempe, 1990-92. Recipient Profl. Leadership award Kiwanis Club Am., Tempe, 1984; nominee to talent bank Coun. on Women's Edn. Programs U.S. Dept. Edn., 1982; named Tchr. of Yr., local newspaper, 1993. Mem. ASCD, Kyrene Edn. Assn. (chair legis. com. 1990-94), Kappa Delta Pi, Phi Kappa Phi, Phi Theta Kappa, Pi Lambda Theta. Achievements include being featured in PBS Cornerstones video, 1994. Home: 3080 S Greythorne Way Chandler AZ 85248-2149

BARNARD, DEBORAH E., lawyer; b. Boston, Apr. 8, 1962; BA cum laude, Smith Coll., 1984; JD magna cum laude, Boston U., 1987. Bar: Mass. 1987, Ill. 1991. Ptnr. Holland & Knight LLP, Boston, mem. dir. com., nat. chair, Women's Initiative. Instructor, first year rsch. and writing program Boston U. Sch. Law. Contbr. articles to profl. jours. Participated in LeadBoston Nat. Conf. for Cmty. and Justice; bd. dir. The City Sch.; class agent Milton Acad. Class of 1980. Mem.: ABA. Office: Holland & Knight LLP 10 St James Ave 11th Fl Boston MA 02116 Office Phone: 617-619-9240. Business E-Mail: dbarnard@hklaw.com.

BARNARD, DONALD ROY, medical and veterinary entomologist; b. Santa Ana, Calif., June 7, 1946; s. Alan Whittaker and Ethel Mae (Kennedy) B.; m. Priscilla Margaret Grier, Aug. 12, 1967; children: Jennifer Erin, David Michael. BS in Zoology, Calif. State U., 1969, MA in Biology, 1972; PhD in Entomology, U. Calif., Riverside, 1977. Postdoctoral fellow Colo. State U., Ft. Collins, 1977-79; rsch. entomologist agrl. rsch. svc. USDA, Poteau, Okla., 1979-85, supervisory rsch. entomologist, 1985-88, rsch. leader agrl. rsch. svc. Gainesville, Fla., 1988—. Adj. prof. entomology Okla. State U., 1988—, U. Fla., 1991—; tech. reviewer NIH, 1989-96, NSF, 1995-96, Ctrs. for Disease Control and Prevention, 1990. Ill. Soybean Program Operating Bd., 1995-96; mem. USDA, NRI Competitive Grants Program, 1994—, Dept. Def., Def. Logistics Agy., 1995-96; cons., tech. reviewer WHO/FAO, 1980—, USAID, Somali Dem. Republic, 1981—, Dept. of Def., AFPMB, 1985—, Republic South Africa, 1988—, State-of-Fla., DOACS, DAI, DOH, 1992—, Unilever Rsch., 1999—, Consumers Union, 2000—, USDA, APHIS, 1996—, EPA, 2000—; external reviewer U. Orange Free State, Republic South Africa, 1995-96, Tripura U., India, 1999—, Kongunadu Coll., India, 2001—, Ministry of Health, Brazil, 1988—; active Fla. Coordinating Coun. for Mosquito Control.; rsch. adv. com. Fla. Mosquito Control Assn. Contbr. chpts. to books, articles to profl. jours.; editor Jour. of Med. Entomology, 2000—; mem. editl. bd. Bull. of the Soc. Vector Ecologists. Mem. Am. Mosquito Control Assn., Internat. Orgn. Biol. Control, Entomol. Soc. Am., Entomol. Soc. Can., Ecol. Soc. Am., Internat. Soc. Travel Medicine, Am. Soc. Tropical Medicine and Hygiene. Office Phone: 352-374-5930. Business E-Mail: dbarnard@gainesville.usda.ufl.edu.

BARNARD, GEOFFREY W., magistrate judge; b. Batavia, NY, Apr. 4, 1945; Diploma, Univ. of Madrid, Spain, 1965; BA, Alleghany Coll., 1966; JD, Cornell Univ. Sch. of Law, Ithaca, 1969. Magistrate judge for V.I., U.S. Magistrate Ct., Charlotte Amalie, St. Thomas, 1986—. Chair Com. of Bar Examiners. Office: US Magistrate Ct 345 US Courthouse 5500 Veterans Dr Charlotte Amalie VI 00802-6424 also: Territorial Ct Virgin Islands PO Box 70 St Thomas VI 00804

BARNARD, KEVIN FRANCIS, lawyer; b. N.Y.C., June 1, 1951; s. Frank Louis and Marie Evelyn (Mangin) B.; m. Leigh Elaine Eckmann, Sept. 29, 1979; children: Lorraine, Paul, Maryclaire. BA, Fordham U., 1973; JD, NYU, 1976. Bar: N.Y. 1977. Dep. supt., gen. counsel N.Y. State Banking Dept., N.Y.C., 1982-83; of counsel White & Case, N.Y.C., 1984-85, ptnr., 1985—, global mgmt. bd., 2004—. Spl. counsel Temp. State Commn. on Banking, Ins., and Fin. Svcs., N.Y., 1984, Supts. Adv. Com. Transp. Banking, N.Y., 1992; dir. Apple Bank, 2001- Decorated Knight of Malta, Am. Assn. Sovereign Mil. Order. Mem. Assn. of Bar of City of N.Y. Republican. Roman Catholic. Avocations: sailing, woodworking. Office: White & Case Bldg Ll 1155 Avenue Of The Americas New York NY 10036-2787 E-mail: kbarnard@whitecase.com.

BARNARD, PATRICIA A., human resources specialist; b. Dayton, Ohio, Mar. 24, 1949; BS in Sci., Elem. Edn. and English, U. Dayton, 1971; MS in Human Resources Adminstrn. and Orgnl. Effectiveness, Ctrl. Mich. U., 1996. With audit dept. Fla. Power and Light, Miami, Fla., 1972; fin. analyst, pers. adminstrn., asst. to CEO Mead Corp., Dayton, 1972—82, and 401(k) ops., 1982—85, mgr. coll. recruiting and rels., exempt ops. supr., retirement plans and 401(k), 1985—87; dir. compensation, benefits, staffing and EEO Zellerbach, Dayton, 1987—94; dir. spl. projects Georgia-Pacific Corp., Atlanta, 1994, dir. human resources, comm. papers, 1994—95, group dir. human resources, paper, 1995—97, group dir. human resources, paper and chemicals, 1997—98, v.p. compensation and benefits, 1998—99, sr. v.p. human resources, 1999—2001, exec. v.p. human resources, 2001—. Mem., mentor Ga. 100; mem. HR Leadership Forum, HR Roundtable, Ga. State U.; bd. dirs. Metro Atlanta Recovery Residences, Inc., Big Bros. and Big Sisters, N.W. Ga. Girl Scout Coun., Inc., Leukemia and Lymphoma Soc., Salvation Army. Mem.: Soc. for Human Resources Mgmt. (chmn. bd. Atlanta chpt.), Exec. Mgmt. Assn. Office: Georgia Pacific Corp 133 Peachtree St NE Atlanta GA 30303

BARNARD, ROBERT N., lawyer; b. Madison, Wis., Dec. 15, 1947; s. Robert Julian and Dorothy Jane (Nichol) B.; m. Katherine Elaine Chott, Mar. 1, 1980; children: Suzanna Katherine, Sarah Elizabeth. AB, Harvard U., 1969; JD, Stanford U., 1975. Bar: Ill. 1975, U.S. Dist. Ct. (no. dist.) Ill. 1975, N.Y. 2003. Assoc. Mayer, Brown & Platt, Chgo., 1975-81, ptnr. London, Eng., 1982-88, Chgo., 1988—2001, New York, NY, 2001—. Trustee U. Notre Dame, London, 1986-88. Lt. U.S. Army, 1969-72. Office: Mayer Brown Rowe & Maw LLP 1675 Broadway New York NY 10019-5820 Business E-Mail: rbarnard@mayerbrownrowe.com.

BARNEA, URI N., conductor, musician; b. Petah-Tikvah, Israel, May 29, 1943; came to U.S., 1971; s. Shimon and Miriam Burstein; m. Lizbeth A. Lund, Dec. 15, 1977; 2 children. Tchg. cert., Oranim Music Inst., Israel, 1966; postgrad., Hebrew U., Israel, 1969-71; MusB, Rubin Acad. Music, Israel, 1971; MA, U. Minn., 1974, PhD, 1977; D (hon.), Rocky Mountain Coll., 1999. Music dir. Jewish Cmty. Ctr., Mpls., 1971-73; condr. Youval Chamber Orch., Mpls., 1971-73; asst. condr. U. Minn. Orchs., Mpls., 1972-77; music dir., condr. Unitarian Soc., Mpls., 1973-78, Kenwood Chamber Orch., Mpls., 1974-78, Knox-Galesburg Symphony, 1978-83, Billings (Mont.) Symphony Soc., 1984—2004, Mont. Ballet Co., 1993, 1994, 1998—2004; asst. prof. Knox Coll., Galesburg, Ill., 1978-83; violinist, violist Yellowstone Chamber players, Billings, 1984—2004; violist Tri-City Symphony, Quad-Cities, 1983—84; condr. Cedar Arts Forum String Camp, Cedar Falls, Iowa, 1981—82. Guest condr., Ark., Calif., Colo., Fla., Ill., Iowa, Maine, Mich., Minn., Mont., Pa., SD, Va., Wis. European conducting debut, London, Neuchatel and Fribourg, Switzerland, 1986; Can. conducting debut No. Music Festival, North Bay, Ont., 1989; Violin Concerto, 1990; Russian conducting debut Symphony Orch., Kuzbass, Kemerovo, 1993; recordings include: W. Piston's Flute and Clarinet Concertos, Mario Lombardo's Oboe Concerto, two compact discs of Am. music; composer numerous compositions including String Quartet (1st prize Aspen Composition Competition 1976), Sonata for Flute and Piano, 1975 (Diploma of Distinction 26th Viotti Internat. Competition, Italy 1975), Ruth, a ballet, 1974 (1st prize Oberhoffer Composition Contest 1976). Music adv. panel Ill. Arts Coun., 1980-83; v.p. Cmty. Concert Assn., Galesburg, 1980-83; bd. dirs. Knox Coll. Credit Union, Galesburg, 1982-83, Radio Sta. KEMC, Billings, 1984—, Fox Theater Corp., Billings, 1984-86. Recipient Friend of the Arts title Sigma Alpha Iota, 1982, Mont. Gov. Arts award for the arts, 2003, The Tuney award 2004, The Freeman Lacey award 2004; Ill. Arts Coun. grantee, 1979; Hebrew U. Jerusalem scholar, 1972-74, Hebrew U. and Rubin Acad. Mus. scholar, 1969, 70; Individual Artist fellow Mont. Arts Coun., 1986. Mem. NEA (music adv. panel 1990-95), ASCAP, Am. Composers Forum, Condrs. Gukld, Am. String Tchrs. Assn. Home: 1104 Poly Dr Billings MT 59102-1834

BARNEBEY, KENNETH ALAN, food company executive; b. Fremont, Nebr., Apr. 16, 1931; s. Hoyt F. and Mae S. (Mott) B.; m. Faith Price, May 10, 1969; children: Robert, Mark, Holiday, Cindy, Kendra, Valerie, Bonnie, Laurel, Susan. Student, U. Md., 1950, U. Tampa, 1951; BA in Transp., U. Wash., Seattle, 1953; grad. advanced mgmt. program, Harvard U., 1977. With Tropicana Products, Inc., Bradenton, Fla., 1955-80, gen. sales mgr., then v.p. mktg. and sales, 1957-77, exec. v.p., 1977, pres., chief adminstrv. officer, 1977-79, chmn. bd., chief exec. officer, 1979-81, also dir.; corp. v.p. Beatrice Foods, Inc., 1979-81; pres., dir., dep. chmn. Am. Agronomics Corp., Tampa, Fla., 1981-86; bus. acquisition cons. Bradenton, Fla., 1981—. Bd. dirs. Dependable Ins. Group Inc. Am., Exmart, Cmty. Bank Holding Co.; mem. sch. mktg. program Fla. Citrus Dept., 1973—; dir. First Union Bank. Bd. dirs., pres. Am. Acad. Achievement; bd. dirs. Manatee Jr. Coll., Asolo State Theatre, Blowing Rock (N.C.) Hosp., Blowing Rock Stage Co. Theater; mem. Fla. Coun. of 100; adv. coun. Fla. State U.; exec. svc. corp. pres. Manasota Basin Bd. Served with U.S. Army, 1953-55. Mem. Am. Mgmt. Assn. (lectr.), NAM (mktg. adv. com., dir.), Fla. Canners Assn. (mktg. adv. com.), Manatee County C. of C. (dir., chmn. econ. devel. com.) Clubs: Manatee County Exchange (past pres.), Bradenton Country, Blowing Rock Country (past pres.), State of Fla. Govs. Coun. of 100. Home and Office: 2302 63d St W Bradenton FL 34209

BARNER, BRUCE MONROE, retired state agency administrator, not-for-profit developer; b. Delaware, Ohio, Jan. 16, 1951; s. Charles Ray and Annabel (Monroe) B. BA in Philosophy with honors, Muskingum Coll., 1973; postgrad., Cleve. State U., 1975-77. Adminstrv. researcher Dept. Pub. Safety State of Ohio, Columbus, 1980—98; bd. chmn. ALIVE Ministries, Inc., Columbus, Ohio, 1999—. Fatal crash analyst Nat. Hwy. Traffic Safety Adminstrn., Washington, 1982-83, 85, Nat. Accident Sampling System, 1983; researcher study on motorcycle/moped crash trends, 1985, study on driving edn. in Ohio, 1987, study on semi-truck crash trends, 1986, 87, 88, study on child safety seat usage in Ohio, 1989, study on driver errors in serious heavy truck crashes in Ohio, 1989, studies on shoulder belt usage by roadway functional class in Ohio, 1991, 92, 93, 94, study on fatal crash involvement of repeat DWI offenders in Ohio, 1991-93. Contbr. articles to profl. jours. Co-founder Ohio Safety Belt Coalition, 1983-84; adminstrv. rschr. gov.'s motor carrier adv. com. State of Ohio, 1986-90, adminstrv. rschr. Ohio hwy. safety elderly driver task force, 1990, DWI task force, 1992, 93; advisor Safety Mgmt. Sys., 1994, 95. Mem. Assn. Advancement Automotive Medicine, Planetary Soc., World Future Soc., Nat. Space Soc., Search for Extra-Terrestrial Intelligence Inst., Saved by the Belt Club. Avocations: distance running, internet web-page design, extemporaneous music, chess. Home: PO Box 510 Galloway OH 43119-0510

BARNES, A. JAMES, academic dean; b. Napoleon, Ohio, Aug. 30, 1942; s. Albert James and Mary Elizabeth (Morey) Barnes; m. Sarah Jane Hughes, June 19, 1976; children: Morey Elizabeth, Laura LeHardy, Catherine Farrell. BA with high honors, Mich. State U., 1964; JD cum laude, Harvard U., 1967. Asst. prof. bus. adminstrn. Ind. U., 1967—69; trial atty. Dept. Justice, 1969—70, asst. to dep. atty. gen., 1973; asst. to adminstr. EPA, 1970—73; campaign mgr. for Gov. Milliken of Mich., 1974; ptnr. Beveridge, Fairbanks & Diamond, Washington, 1975—81; gen. counsel Dept. Agr., 1981—83; adj. prof. Georgetown U. Sch. Bus. Adminstrn., Washington, 1978—80; gen. counsel to dep. adminstr. EPA, 1983—85, dep. adminstr., 1985—88; dean Sch. Pub. Environ. Adminstrn., prof. pub. and environ. affairs Ind. U., 1988—2000, prof. pub. and environ. affairs, 1988—, adj. prof. law, 2001—. Spl. counsel Beveridge, Fairbanks & Diamond, Washington, 1988—97; cons., mediator, expert witness Nat. Acad. Pub. Adminstrn., 1988—; adj. prof. law Ind. U., 2001—. Co-author: Essentials of Business Law, 1994, Law of Commercial Transactions and Business Associations, 1995, Bus. Law and the Regulatory Environment, 2000, Law for Bus., 2005, Bus. Law: The Ethical, E-Commerce and Internat. Environ., 12th edit., 2004. Del. Ind. Rep. Conv., 1968, Mich. Rep. Conv., 1974. Named Sagamore of Wabash, 2000; recipient Outstanding Tchg. award, Ind. U., 1969. Fellow: Nat. Acad. Pub. Adminstrn.; mem.: Sagamore of Wabash, Vineyard Haven Yacht Club (Mass.), Edgartown (Mass.) Yacht Club, Met. Club (Washington). Office: Ind U SPEA 418 Bloomington IN 47405 Office Phone: 812-856-2188. Business E-Mail: barnesaj@indiana.edu.

BARNES, ANDREW EARL, former newspaper executive; b. Torrington, Conn., May 15, 1939; s. Joseph and Elizabeth (Brown) B.; m. Marion Otis, Aug. 26, 1960; children: Christopher Joseph, Benjamin Brooks, Elizabeth Cheney. BA, Harvard U., 1961. Reporter, bur. chief Providence Jour., 1961-63; from reporter to edn. editor Washington Post, 1965-73; met. editor, asst. mng. editor St. Petersburg Times, Fla., 1973-75, mng. editor, 1975-84; editor, pres. St. Petersburg (Fla.) Times, 1984-99, CEO, 1988—2004. Chmn. bd. dirs. Congl. Quar., Times Pub. Co., Poynter Inst.; chair Pulitzer prize bd., 2004-05. With USAR, 1963-65. Alicia Patterson fellow, 1969-70 Mem. Newspaper Assn. Am. (chair 2000-01), Am. Soc. Newspaper Editors, Fla. Soc. Newspaper Editors (pres. 1980-81), Internat. Press Inst. Home: 15724 Puckett Rd Dade City FL 33525-7066 Office: Saint Petersburg Times 490 1st Ave S PO Box 1121 Saint Petersburg FL 33731-1121 Office Phone: 727-821-9400. E-mail: abaines@poynter.org.

BARNES, BRENDA C., food products executive; m. Randall C. Barnes; 3 children. BA in econ., Augustana Coll., 1975, LHD (hon.), 1997; MBA, Loyola U., 1978. With PepsiCo, 1975—98, v.p. mktg. Frito-Lay, bus. mgr. Wilson Spring Sporting Goods; pres. Pepsi-Cola S., 1992; COO Pepsi-Cola N. Am., 1993—96, pres., CEO, 1996—98; interim pres., COO Starwood Hotels & Resorts Worldwide Inc., 1999—2000; COO Sara Lee Corp., Chgo., 2004—05, pres., 2004—, CEO, 2005—. Adj. prof. Kellogg Grad. Sch. Mgmt.; guest lectr. N. Central Coll., 2002; bd. dirs. Avon Products Inc., NY Times Co., Sears Roebuck & Co., Staples Inc., Lucas Film, LTD, Sara Lee Corp., 2004—. Chair bd. trustees Augustana Coll. Named one of Most Powerful Women, Forbes mag., 2005. Office: Sara Lee Corp 3 First Nat Plz Chicago IL 60602 Office Phone: 312-726-2600.*

BARNES, CARLYLE FULLER, manufacturing executive; b. Bristol, Conn., Feb. 16, 1924; s. Fuller Forbes and Myrtle (Ives) B.; m. Elizabeth Anne May, Oct. 1, 1949; children: Lynne Elizabeth, Janis Lee, Joan Wells, Fuller Forbes. AB, Wesleyan U., 1948. Staff asst. Wallace Barnes Co. div. Barnes Group Inc., 1948-50, gen. mgr., 1951-53, dir., 1951-92, pres., 1953-64, chmn. bd., 1964-77, chmn. exec. com., 1977-94, ret., 1994. Bd. dirs. Bushnell Meml. Hall. Home: Peacedale St Bristol CT 06010

BARNES, CHARLES ANDREW, physicist, researcher; b. Toronto, Ont., Can., Dec. 12, 1921; came to U.S., 1953, naturalized, 1961; m. Phyllis Malcolm, Sept., 1950. BA, McMaster U., 1943; MA, U. Toronto, 1944; PhD, Cambridge U., 1950. Physicist Joint Brit.-Canadian Atomic Energy Project, 1944-46; instr. physics U. B.C., 1950-53, 55-56; mem. faculty Calif. Inst. Tech., 1953-55, 56—, prof. physics, 1962-92; prof. emeritus physics, 1992—. Guest prof. Niels Bohr Inst., Copenhagen, 1973-74. Editor, contbr. to profl. books and jours. Recipient medal Inst. d'Astrophysique de Paris, 1986, Alexander von Humboldt U.S. Sr. Scientist award, Fed. Republic of Germany, 1986; NSF sr. fellow Denmark, 1962-63. Fellow AAAS, Am. Phys. Soc. Office: Calif Inst Tech 1201 E California Blvd Pasadena CA 91125-0001

BARNES, DENNIS NORMAN, lawyer; b. Kingston, Pa., Feb. 10, 1940; s. Leslie Orland and Mary Whitney (Brown) B.; m. Ingrid Daubitz, Oct. 5, 1961; children: Richard, Kendra. AB, Dartmouth Coll., 1962; JD, Georgetown U., 1965. Bar: D.C. 1966, U.S. Ct. Appeals (D.C. cir.) 1966, U.S. Supreme Ct. 1995. Assoc. Morgan, Lewis & Bockius LLP, Washington, 1970-75, ptnr., 1975-2000; v.p. regulatory affairs Sun Country Airlines, Washington, 2000—. Capt. JAGC, U.S. Army, 1966-70. Mem. D.C. Bar Assn., Maritime Adminstrv. Bar Assn. (pres. 1991), Assn. Transp. Practitioners. Office: Sun Country Airlines Inc 1875 Connecticut Ave NW Ste 1100 Washington DC 20009 E-mail: dbarnes@suncountry.com.

BARNES, DONALD MICHAEL, lawyer; b. Hazleton, Pa., June 15, 1943; s. Donald A. and Margaret Barnes; m. Mary Catherine Gibbons, June 3, 1967; children: Donald M., Stephanie A., Susan E. BS in Indsl. Engring., Pa. State U., 1965; JD cum laude, George Washington U., 1970. Bar: D.C. 1970, U.S. Dist. Ct. D.C. 1970, U.S. Ct. Appeals (D.C. cir.) 1970, U.S. Supreme Ct. 1975, U.S. Ct. Appeals (5th cir.) 1980, U.S. Ct. Appeals (4th cir.) 1980, U.S. Ct. Appeals (8th cir.) 1981, U.S. Ct. Appeals (6th cir.) 1993, U.S. Ct. Appeals (10th cir.) 2003. Assoc. Arent, Fox, Kintner, Plotkin & Kahn, Washington, 1970-78, ptnr., 1978-97; mng. shareholder Jenkens & Gilchrist, Washington, 1997-2000; ptnr. Seyfarth Shaw, Washington, 2000—02, Porter Wright Morris & Arthur, LLP, Washington, 2002—. Notes editor: George Washington Law Rev., 1969—70. Mem.: ABA (criminal justice, antitrust, litigation and adminstrv. law sects.), DC Bar Assn., Order of Coif, Phi Delta Phi. Office: Porter Wright Morris & Arthur LLP Ste 500 1919 Pennsylvania Ave NW Washington DC 20006-3434 Office Phone: 202-778-3056. Business E-Mail: dbarnes@porterwright.com.

BARNES, FRANCIS V., school system administrator; BS, Slippery Rock U., 1971; MS, U. Pitts., 1983, PhD, 1986. Dept. chair person, tchr. Pitts. Pub. Bd. of Edn., 1971—85; dean of students Allegheny Middle Sch., 1985—87; asst. HS prin. / dist. staff recruiter North Allegheny Sch. Dist., 1987—88, prin., dist. staff recruiter, 1987—91; supt. Hopewell Area Sch. Dist., 1991—94, Huntingdon Area Sch. Dist., 1994—98, Palisades Sch. Dist., Kintnersville, 1998—2004; sec. of edn. Pa. Dept. Edn., 2004—. Mem. Huntingdon County United Way Edn. Com.; trustee Grandview Hosp. Mem.: AASA (governing bd. mem., membership com.), Pa. Assn. of Sch. Adminstr. (pres. elect 2004, bd. govs.), Phi Delta Kappan. Office: Pa Dept Edn 333 Market St Harrisburg PA 17101-2210 Office Phone: 717-787-5820.*

BARNES, FRANK STEPHENSON, electrical engineer, educator; b. Pasadena, Calif., July 31, 1932; s. Donald Porter and Thedia (Schellenberg) B.; m. Gay Dirstine, Dec. 17, 1955; children: Stephen, Amy. BS, Princeton U., 1954; MS, Stanford U., 1955, PhD, 1958. Fulbright prof. Coll. Engring., Baghdad, Iraq, 1957-58; rsch. assoc. Colo. Rsch. Corp., Broomfield, 1958-59; assoc. prof. U. Colo., Boulder, 1959-65, prof. dept. elec. engring., 1965—, chmn. dept., 1964-81, faculty rsch. lectr., 1965, acting dean Coll. Engring. and Applied Sci., 1980-81, disting. prof., 1997—, dir. interdisciplinary telecom. program, 1971-75, 88-89, 1996-99; pres. Video Accessory Corp., Boulder, Colo., 2001—. Disting. lectr. IEEE Elec. Device Soc., 1994-01. Regional editor Electronics Letters of Brit. Instn. Elec.Engrs., 1970-75; exec. editor Ann. Rev. Telecom. Bd. dirs. Accreditation Bd. Engring. and Tech., 1980-82. Recipient cert. of merit Internat. Comm. Assn., 1989, Meritorious Svc. award IEEE Edn. Soc., 1993, Leon Montgomery award Internat. Comm. Assn., 1994, Univ. Colo. Centennial Celebration Engring. Recognition award, 1994, Catalyst award Colo. Inst. Tech., 2004; fellow Internat. Engring. Consortium, 1995. Fellow AAAS, IEEE (editor Student Jour. 1967-70, mem. G-Ed Adcom 1970-77, v.p. publ. activities 1974-75, pres. device soc. 1974-75, ednl. activities bd. 1976-82, editor IEEE Transactions on Edn. 1988-94, mem. press bd. 1989-90, ednl. activities bd., cert. of merit, Centennial medal, Millennium medal 2000, Edn. Soc. Achievement award 2003); mem. NAE (Bernard M. Gordon prize 2004), Am. Soc. Engring. (Elec. and Computer Engring. Disting. Educator award 2002), Soc. Lasers in Medicine, Engrs. Coun. Profl. Devel. (dir. 1976-82, chmn. com. on advanced level accreditation 1976-78), Bioelectromagnetics Soc. (bd. dirs. 1982-84, 96-98, pres. 2000-01), Engring. Info. (bd. dirs. 1984-90). Home: 225 Continental View Dr Boulder CO 80303-4516 Office: Video Accessory Corp 2450 Central Ave StG Boulder CO 80301 Personal E-mail: barnes@colorado.edu. *There are always more interesting problems to solve than time to solve them. The trick is to find important problems which can be solved with an effort which is small compared to the value of the results and where one can have a good time learning new ideas at the same time.*

BARNES, FREDERIC WOOD, JR., journalist, political analyst; b. West Point, N.Y., Feb. 1, 1943; s. Frederic W. and Rosa (Miller) B.; m. Barbara Beatty, Sept. 2, 1967; children: Karen, Sarah, Grace, Frederic W. III. BA in History, U. Va., 1965. Reporter Charleston (S.C.) News Courier, 1965-67, Washington (D.C.) Star, 1967-77, 78-79, Balt. Sun, 1979-85; sr. editor, White House corr. The New Republic, Washington, 1985-95; co-founder, exec. editor The Weekly Standard, Washington, 1995—. Nieman fellow Harvard U., 1977-78; panelist Presdl. debate, Louisville, 1984; regular panelist The McLaughlin Group (TV), Washington, 1988-98; moderator, host Issues in the News on Voice of America, Washington, 1988-; host (syndicated radio show) What's the Story?, 1992-; polit. analyst (TV) CBS This Morning, 1990-99; co-host (TV) Beltway Boys, FOX News Channel, 1998-; polit. contbr. FOX News Channel, 1996-; regular contbr. (TV) Special Report with Brit Hume, FOX News Channel; chief corr. (TV Series) National Desk, PBS; nat. polit. corr. Sun; writer "Presspatch", American Spectator. Editor: A Cartoon History of the Reagan Years, 1988; host (syndicated radio show) What's the Story?, 1992-;contbr. article to Reader's Digest, NY Times, Wall Street Jour., Spectator, Washingtonian, The Public Interest, Policy Review, Sunday Telegraph and Sunday Times of London; nat. polit. corr. Sun; writer "Presspatch", American Spectator; guest appearances include Nightline, Meet the Press, Face the Nation, and NewsHour with Jim Lehrer. With U.S. Army, 1960-62. Named Father of Yr., Father's Day Com., 1994. Mem.: Washington Speakers Bur. Office: The Weekly Standard 1150 17th St NW Ste 505 Washington DC 20036-4617

BARNES, HARPER HENDERSON, critic, editor, writer; b. Greensboro, NC, July 2, 1937; s. Bennett Harper and Cora Emmaline Barnes; m. Janice Stauffacher, May 10, 1961 (div. 1985); m. Roseann Marie Weiss, May 31, 1986. Critic, reporter St. Louis Post-Dispatch, 1965-70, editor, critic, 1973-97; editor The Phoenix, Boston, 1970-72, St. Louis mag., 1997-99; pvt. practice St. Louis, 1999—. Instr. Washington U., St. Louis, 1990, 94. Author: Blue Monday, 1991, Standing on a Volcano, 2001. With U.S. Army, 1959-62. Avocations: bicycling, fishing. Office Phone: 314-535-9393. Personal E-mail: hbarnesl@mindspring.com.

BARNES, HARRIS H., III, (TRIP BARNES), tax lawyer; b. Clarksdale, Miss., Sept. 17, 1946; s. Harris Hastings and Jamye (Haskins) B.; m. Sandra S. Barnes, June 21, 1969; children: Patrick S., Elizabeth Blair, Bryan Parrish. BA, Miss. State U., 1968; JD, U. Miss., 1972; LLM, U. Fla., 1980. Atty. Barnes, Broom, Dallas & McLeod, PLLC, Jackson, Miss., 1996—. Author: Financial Survival in the 80's, 1985, Financial Survival After Tax Reform, 1986. Chmn. Salvation Army Adv. Bd., Gulfport, Miss., 1984, 85, 87, vice chmn., Jackson, Miss., 1991, chmn., 1992. Named Outstanding Young Man of Am. Nat. Jaycees, 1979; fellow, Miss. Bar Found. Mem. Miss. State Bar Assn. (chmn. taxation sect. 1987-88), Miss. Tax Inst. (trustee, past chmn.), Hinds County Bar Assn. (sec/treas., pres. 1999, pres. 1999), Miss. State U. Law Alumni (pres. 1990—), Kiwanis (vice chmn.), Rotary (sgt.-at-arms, bd. dirs.). Republican. Presbyterian. Avocations: reading, weightlifting, running, tennis, golf. Office: 5 River Bend Pl Ste A Flowood MS 39232-7618 Office Phone: 601-981-6336. Office Fax: 601-981-7075. Business E-Mail: TBarnes@wealthmanagement.net.

BARNES, HARRY FRANCIS, federal judge; b. Memphis, May 14, 1932; m. Mary Milburn Mann, four children. Student, Vanderbilt U., 1950-52; BS, U.S. Naval Academy, 1956; LLB, U. Ark., 1964. With Pryor & Barnes, Camden, Ark., 1964-66, Barnes & Roberts, Camden, 1966-68, Gaughan, Laney, Barnes & Roberts, Camden, 1968-78, Gaughan, Laney & Barnes, Camden, 1978-82; mcpl. judge Camden and Ouachita Counties, 1975-82; circuit judge 13th jud. dist. State of Ark., 1982-93; judge U.S. Dist. Ct. (we. dist.) Ark., 1993—. Mem. Ark. Jud. Discipline and Disability Commn. With USMC, 1956-86, col. res. ret. Named Outstanding Trial Judge in Ark., Ark. Trial Lawyers Assn., 1986, 2000. Mem. ABA, Ark. Bar Assn., Ark. Jud. Coun. (bd. dirs.). Office: US Dist Ct We Dist PO Box 1735 El Dorado AR 71731-1735 Office Phone: 870-862-1303.

BARNES, HARRY G., JR., advocate; b. St. Paul, June 5, 1926; s. Harry George and Bertha Pauline (Blaul) B.; m. Elizabeth Ann Sibley; children: Pauline, Adrienne, Douglas, Sibley. BA summa cum laude, Amherst Coll., 1949, LLD (hon.), 1984; MA in History, Columbia U., 1968; PhD in Engring. (hon.), Stevens Inst., 1985; LLD (hon.), Monterey Inst. Internat. Studies, 1989. With fgn. service U.S. Dept. State, 1951-88; vice-consul Bombay, 1951-53; vice consul, 2d sec. Prague, Czechoslovakia, 1953-55, Moscow, 1957-59; polit. officer Office of Soviet affairs, Dept. State, Washington, 1959-62; dep. chief mission Kathmandu, Nepal, 1963-67; dep. chief of mission Bucharest, Romania, 1968-71; chief jr. officer program Dept. State, Washington, 1971-72, dep. exec. sec., 1972-74; amb. to Romania Bucharest, 1974-77; dir. gen. fgn. service, dir. pers. Dept. State, Washington, 1977-81; amb. to India, New Delhi, 1981-85, Chile, Santiago, 1985-88; ret.; exec. dir. Critical Langs. and Area Studies Consortium, 1989-94; dir. conflict resolution and human rights programs The Carter Ctr., Atlanta, 1994—2000, chmn. rights com., 1997—2000; sr. advisor Asia Soc., 1999—. Cyrus Vance vis. prof. internat. rels. Mt. Holyoke Coll., spring 1990; Sol Linowitz vis. prof. internat. rels. Hamilton Coll., fall 1990; James and Joan Warburg vis. prof. internat. rels. Simmons Coll., fall 1991-spring 1993; sr. fellow World Wild Life Fund-Conservation Found., 1989-91; interim dir. Human Rights Program Career Ctr., 1993-94, dir. human rights and conflict resolution programs, 1995-2000; chmn. bd. dirs. Romanian-Am. Enterprise Fund, 1996—; pres. Peacham Cmty. Housing, Vt., 2003-. With U.S.Army, 1944-46. Decorated Grand Cross, Order of Bernardo O'Higgins (Chile), 1990; recipient Pres.' Meritorious Svc. award, 1983, 88, Pres.' Disting. Svc. award, 1987. Fellow AAAS. Presbyterian. Home: PO Box 73 Peacham VT 05862-0073 Office Phone: 802-592-3206. Office Fax: 802-592-3046. Personal E-mail: hgbarnes@attglobal.net.

BARNES, HELEN JOYCE, elementary school educator; b. San Antonio, Mar. 8, 1949; d. Robert Pinckney and Wilma Dean (Keel) Ramsay; m. Rodney James Barnes, May 29, 1971; children: Robert James, Pamela Joyce. BA in Elem. Edn., St. Mary's U., San Antonio, 1971; MA ed. adminstrn., Univ. of Tex., San Antonio, Tex., 1996. Tchr. Ysleta Ind. Sch. Dist., El Paso, Tex., 1972-74; tchr. Pearsall Ind. Sch. Dist., Tex., 1978-80, Fabens Ind. Sch. Dist., Tex., 1982-84, S.W. Ind. Sch. Dist., San Antonio, 1984—88, El Monte City Elem. Sch., Calif., 1988-89, Compton Unified Sch. Dist., Calif., 1989-92, SW Ind. Sch. Dist., San Antonio, 1992—. Mem. NEA, Calif. Tchr. Assn., Compton Edn. Assn., Tex. State Tchr. Assn., S.W. Edn. Assn. Republican. Baptist. Avocations: soloist church choir, camping, hiking, family, sewing. Home: 11527 Woollcott St San Antonio TX 78251-3259 Office: Spl Programs The Rose SWISD 11914 Dragon Ln San Antonio TX 78252-2612 Address: 11527 Woollcott St San Antonio TX 78251-3259 Office Phone: 210-622-4351. E-mail: hbarnes@swisd.net.

BARNES, HOWARD G., communications executive, film producer; b. N.Y.C., Dec. 27, 1913; m. Joan Lesavoy, Jan. 9, 1949 (div. Nov. 1957); foster children: Marshall Alan (dec.), Denis Joy; m. Mary Ellena Mock, Dec. 7, 1958 (div.); children: Christie Ann, Paul Louis Lloyd; m. Patricia Lee Sills, August 4, 1965 (div.); children: Paxton Louise, Gillian Leigh. AB, U. Mich., 1935. Announcer radio sta. WIP, Phila., 1935, KYW, Phila., WHN, N.Y.C., 1936; producer WOR Mut., 1936-38; exec. producer MCA, 1938; producer, writer, exec. CBS, N.Y.C., 1938-46; v.p. in charge network programs CBS Radio, 1955-60; dir. programs CBS-TV, Hollywood, 1960-63; producing independently, 1946-48; v.p. in charge radio and TV Dorland, Inc., N.Y.C., 1948-51; pres. Gen. Entertainment Corp., 1949-60; TV exec. Ashley Famous Agy., Inc., 1963-66; dir. film prodn. Westinghouse Broadcasting Co., N.Y.C., 1966-67, exec. v.p. Group W Films, 1967-73, also dir. parent co.; ind. producer, 1973-89; gen. mgr., dir. advt. The Walking Ctr., Beverly Hills, Calif., 1989-91. Pres. Ragazza Inc., Washington, Conn., 1980-81; bd. govs. Dramalites, Washington, Conn., 1979-89; dir. Trio Films, Ltd., London, 1973-79; ptnr. The Barnes/Sabinson Partnership, 1976-84; exec. dir. Entertainment Hall of Fame Found., 1974-77; cons. film and video Conn. State Dept. Edn., 1985-89; lectr. Sch. Comm., San Diego State U., 1996-97. Lt. USNR, 1942-45. Home and Office: 1930 W San Marcos Blvd Spc 358 San Marcos CA 92078-3930

BARNES, HUBERT LLOYD, geochemistry educator; b. Chelsea, Mass., July 20, 1928; s. George Lloyd and Mary Ellen (MacPherson) B.; m. Mary Talbot Westergaard; children: Roy Malcolm, Catherine Patricia. BS, MIT, 1950; PhD, Columbia U., 1958. Registered Profl. Geologist Pa. Resident geologist Peru Mining Co., Hanover, N.Mex., 1950-52; lectr. geology Columbia U., N.Y.C., 1952-54; postdoctoral fellow Geophys. Lab. Carnegie Inst., Washington, 1956-60; prof. Pa. State U., University Park, 1960-96, dir. ore deposits rsch. sect., 1969-96, emeritus, 1997. Vis. prof. Mineralogy-Petrology Inst., Heidelberg, 1974, Academia Sinica, 1983, U. Sydney, 1987, U. Witwatersrand, 1990; Crosby lectr. MIT, Cambridge, 1983, mem. geophysics rsch. bd. NRC, 1976-80; mem. U.S. Nat. Com. on Geology, 1983-86; cons. numerous corps.; dir. NATO Advanced Study Inst., Salamanca, 1987; gen. chmn. 1st Goldschmidt Conf., Balt., 1988, co-chmn. PA. State U., 1995; chmn., sec. Internat. Symposium on Hydrothermal Reactions, Pa. State U., 1985; guest prof. Nanjing U., People's Republic of China, 1996; Air-India disting. lectr. Indian Inst. Tech., Bombay, 1996; hon. prof., disting. vis. fellow U. Wales, 1996-2001; pres. Applied Rsch. & Exploration, 1994—. Author: Uranium Prospecting, 1956. Editor: Geochemistry of Hydrothermal Ore Deposits, 1967, 79, 97; co-editor: Hydrothermal Experimental Techniques, 1987; consulting editor Internat. Geol. Rev., 1999—. Vice-pres. Pa. chpt. Humboldt Found., 1996-99. N.L. Britton scholar, 1955-56; Guggenheim fellow, 1966-67, Japan Soc. Promotion Sci. fellow, 1997; lecturer, World Famous Scientists Forum, Nanjing, 2002; recipient Sr. Humboldt prize Humboldt Found. Germany, 1988; named Disting. Prof. Geochemistry Pa. State U., 1990; Can. Inst. Mining and Metallurgy lectr., 1969, C.F. Davidson lectr., St. Andrews, Scotland, 1971. Fellow Mineral Soc. Am., Geol. Soc. Am., Geochem. Soc. (councillor 1970-73, v.p. 1983, pres. 1984-85, Disting. Svc. award 2003); mem. Soc. Econ. Geologists (councilor 1981-84, Thayer Lindsley lectr. 1980-81), Am. Geologic Inst. (governing bd. 1981-83), Soc. Econ. Geology (Penrose Gold medal, 2002), U.S. Nat. Geochemistry Com. (chmn. 1976-78). Democrat. Avocations: skiing, carpentry, classical music, travel. Home: 213 E Mitchell Ave State College PA 16803-3655 Office: Pa State U Dept Geoscis 405 Deike Bldg University Park PA 16802-2711 Office Phone: 814-865-7573. Business E-Mail: barnes@geosc.psu.edu.

BARNES, JAMES GARLAND, JR., lawyer; b. Ga., Mar. 3, 1940; s. James Garland Sr. and Carolyn L. (Stewart) B.; m. Lucy Curtis Ferguson, Nov. 1976; children: Susan Whitney, David Lawrence, Matthew Martin. BA, Yale U., 1961; LLB, U. Mich., 1966. Bar: Ill. 1967. With firm Baker & McKenzie, Chgo., 1966—, ptnr., 1973—. Co-author: The ABCs of the UCC Article 5: Letters of Credit. Mem. adv. com. Ill. Sec. of State's Corp. Acts, 1981-95; U.S. del. to UN Commn. on Internat. Trade Law, Internat. C. of C., 1994-2000. Mem. ABA (chmn. letter of credit subcom. 1991-96), Ill. Bar

Assn. (chmn. corp. and security law sect. 1977-78), Chgo. Bar Assn. (chmn. corp. law com. 1982-83, chmn. profl. responsibility com. 1983-84), Legal Club Chgo. Office: Baker & McKenzie 1 Prudential Pla 130 E Randolph St Ste 3700 Chicago IL 60601-6342 E-mail: james.g.barnes@bakernet.com.

BARNES, JAMES JOHN, historian, educator; b. St. Paul, Nov. 16, 1931; s. Harry George and Bertha (Blaul) B.; m. Patience Rogers Plummer, July 9, 1955; children— Jennifer Chase, Geoffrey Prescott BA, Amherst Coll., 1954, New Coll., Oxford, 1956, MA, 1961; PhD, Harvard U., 1960; DHL, Coll. of Wooster, 1976, Amherst Coll., 1999. Instr. history Amherst Coll., 1959-62; asst. prof. history Wabash Coll., Crawfordsville, Ind., 1962-67, assoc. prof. history, 1967-76, prof. history, 1976—, chmn. dept. history, Hadley prof., 1979-97. Author: Free Trade in Books: A Study of the London Book Trade since 1800, 1964, Authors, Publishers and Politicians: The Quest for an Anglo-American Copyright Agreement 1815-54, 1974, (with Patience P. Barnes) Hitler's Mein Kampf in Britain and America 1930-39, 1980, (with Patience P. Barnes) James Vincent Murphy: Translator and Interpreter of Fascist Europe, 1880-1946, 1987, (with Patience P. Barnes) Private and Confidential Letters from British Ministers in Washington to the Foreign Secretaries in London, 1849-67, 1993, (with Patience P. Barnes) Nazi Refugee turned Gestapo Spy: The Life of Hans Wesemann, 1895-1971, 2001, (with Patience P. Barnes) The American Civil War through British Eyes: Dispatches from British Diplomats, vol. 1: Nov. 1860-Apr. 1862, 2003, vol. 2: April 1862-February 1863, 2005, vol. 3: February 1863-December 1865, 2005; (with Patience P. Barnes) Nazis in Pre-War London 1930-1939: The Fate and Rule of German Party Members and British Sympathizers, 2005; contbr. articles to profl. jours. Mem. Rhodes Scholar Selection Com. for Ind., 1965-89, Crawfordsville Community Action Coun., 1966-69, Crawfordsville Community Day Care Com., 1966-67; mem. vestry St. John's Episcopal Ch., 1966-69; mem. Ind. Adv. Com. State Rehab. Svcs. for Blind, 1979-81; trustee Ind. Hist. Soc., 1982—. Recipient Disting. Alumni award St. Paul Acad. and Summit Sch., 1989; Rhodes scholar, 1954-56, Fulbright scholar, 1978; Woodrow Wilson fellow, 1956-57, Kent fellow, 1958, Great Lakes Colls. Assn. Teaching fellow, 1958, Great Lakes Colls. Assn. Teaching fellow, 1975; rsch. grantee Amherst Coll., 1960-61, Social Sci. Rsch. Coun., 1962, 70, Wabash Coll., 1962—, Am. Coun. Learned Socs., 1964-65, 80, Am. Philos. Soc., 1964, 68, 76, 91; named Hon. Alumnus, Wabash Coll., 1994. Mem. Am. Hist. Assn., Ouiatenon Literary Soc., Conf. Brit. Studies, Rsch. Soc. Victorian Periodicals, Am. Rhodes Scholars, Soc. Historians Am. Fgn. Rels., Ind. Hist. Soc., Montgomery County Hist. Soc., Midwest Victorian Studies Assn. (pres. 1989-91), Ind. Assn. Historians, N.E. Victorian Studies Assn., Soc. for History of Authorship, Reading and Pub., Am. Coun. of Blind, United Oxford and Cambridge Club of London, Phi Beta Kappa. Home: 7 Locust Hl Crawfordsville IN 47933-3347 Office: Wabash Coll History Dept Crawfordsville IN 47933 Office Phone: 765-361-6319. Business E-Mail: barnesj@wabash.edu.

BARNES, JAMES MILTON, physics professor, astronomy professor; b. Ypsilanti, Mich., July 5, 1923; s. J. Milton and Elsie (Fischer) B.; m. Marjorie Ruth Petersen, Dec. 17, 1949. BS, Eastern Mich. U., 1948; MS, Mich. State U., 1950, PhD, 1955. Asst. prof. Ea. Mich. U., Ypsilanti, 1955—58, assoc. prof., 1958—61, prof., 1961—88, head, dept. physics and astronomy, 1961—74, prof. emeritus, 1988—; ret., 1988. Served with AUs, 1942—46. Mem. A.A.A.S. (life), Nat. Sci. Tchrs. Assn. (life), Am. Assn. Physics Tchrs., Sigma Xi, Sigma Pi Sigma, Pi Mu Epsilon. Clubs: Ann Arbor (Mich.) Country. Home: 4872 N Whitman Cir Ann Arbor MI 48103-9774 Office: Eastern Mich U Physics Dept Ypsilanti MI 48197

BARNES, JANET LYNN, artist; b. Balt., Mar. 9, 1959; d. Edwin Lee and Mary Magdeline B. BA in Visual and Performing Arts, U. Md., 1979. Prin., owner Crop Cir. Ceilings, Balt. Author: Brunch with Beethoven, 2002; one-woman shows include City Hall, Balt., 1998, John Hopkins Space Telescope, 1998, book cover, Poe's Last Supper, 1998. Hon. bus. chmn. adv. coun. Nat. Rep. Congl. Com., 2003. Recipient Nat. Leadership award, Nat. Rep. Congl. Com., 2003. Mem.: Nat. and World Wildlife, Artists Equity NY, Md. Hist. Soc., Nat. Trust Hist. Preservation, Wash. Soc. Jungian Psychology, Md. Hang Glider Assn., Catherine Lorillard Wolfe Art Club, Salmagundi Club, Delta Pi Alpha. Republican. Avocations: hang-gliding, reading, writing, house renovation, African grey parrot. Home: 236 S Castle St Baltimore MD 21231

BARNES, JAY WILLIAM, JR., architect, rancher; b. Austin, Tex., Aug. 26, 1924; s. Jay William Sr. and Helen Vera (Colvin) B.; m. Eva Hoop, Apr. 12, 1952; children: Jay William III, Sherrill Ann. BS in Civil Engring., U. Tex., 1950. Registered architect, Ariz., Nev., La., Okla., Mont., N.Mex.; registered structural engr., Tex. Draftsman Preston Geren, Architect, Ft. Worth, 1950-55; architect, ptnr. Barnes, Landes & Goodman, Austin, 1955-58, Barnes Landes Goodman Youngblood, Austin, 1958-83; owner, rancher J Bar E Investments, Austin, 1983—. Chmn., trustee Tex. Archtl. Found., Austin, 1973-83; chmn. Am. Inst. Archtl. Rsch., Washington, 1978; lectr. U. Tex., Austin, 1988-91. Prin. works include Austin H.S., First Bapt. Ch., Brackenridge Hosp., Jr. Sr. H.S. Hopi Nation, Second Mesa, Ariz. Mem. Performance Certification Bd., Tex., 1972-73; vice-chmn. Conv. Ctr. Com., Austin. Sgt. U.S. Army, 1943-46, ETO, Asia. Fellow AIA (treas., dir. 1974-78); mem. Tex. Soc. Architects (pres., dir. 1961-92, Llewelyn W. Pitts award 1986), Austing C. of C. (bd. dirs., v.p., 1972-74), Nat. Coun. Architects Registration Bd., Austin Country Club, Lions (pres. 1955-80), Masons, U. Tex. Ex-Students Assn., Littlefield Soc. Republican. Baptist. Avocations: golf, fly fishing. Home: 3905 Belmont Park Dr Apt A Austin TX 78746-1168

BARNES, JHANE ELIZABETH, fashion design company executive, designer; b. Balt., Mar. 4, 1954; d. Richard Amos and Muriel Florence (Chase) B.; m. Howard Ralph Feinberg, Dec. 12, 1981 (div.); m. 2d, Katsuhiko Kawasaki, Feb. 12, 1988. A.S., Fashion Inst. Tech., 1975. Pres., designer Jhane Barnes for ME, N.Y.C., 1976-78; pres., designer, owner Jhane Barnes Inc., N.Y.C., 1978—; owner Jhane Barnes Textiles, LLC, 1998—. Recipient Coty award Menswear Am. Fashion Critics, 1980, 1984, Contract Textile award Am. Soc. Interior Designers, 1983, 84, Product Design awards Inst. Bus. Designers and Contract Mag., 1983-86, 94, Outstanding Am. Menswear Designer award Woolmark, 1990, Dalmore, 1990, Good Design award 1997, 98, 99, Best of Neo Con award. I.D. 40, 1996, 97, 98, 99, 2000; named Most Promising Designer Cutty Sark, 1980, Outstanding Designer, 1982, Outstanding Menswear Designer, Coun. of Fashion Designers Am., 1982, Design Resources Coun., 1989, 94, Designer of Yr., Neckwear Assn. Am., 1997. Office: Jhane Barnes Inc 119 W 40th St Fl 20 New York NY 10018-2500 Fax: 212-575-2506.

BARNES, JUDITH ANN, real estate executive; b. Milw., Mar. 10, 1949; d. Einar and Eleanor Svea (Russell) B.; divorced; children: Krista Svea, Erik Leif. BA, Gustavus Adolphus Coll., 1970; grad., Wis. Sch. Real Estate, Milw., 1979; postgrad., Carroll Coll., 1980, U. Wis., 1978—80, postgrad., 1992. Tchr. Oak Grove Mid. Sch., Bloomington, Minn., 1970—71, Mukwonago H.S., Wis., 1971—72; sales mgr. Lincoln Park Homes, West Allis, Wis., 1972—73, v.p., 1973—74, pres., 1974—97, Palm Coast, Fla., 1997—2000; assoc. Coldwell Banker Comml. (Nicholson-Williams), 2000—01; with Hammock Dunes Real Estate Co., 2001—. Chmn. Mfrd. Housing Subdivision S.E. Wisc., Madison, 1978-80; sec. Southeastern Wis. Housing, Milw., 1981-82, treas., 1982-84. Bd. dirs. Waukesha YMCA, 1985-87, v.p. 1987-89; bd. dirs. YMCA Heritage Found., 1994-97; bd. dirs. Waukesha County United Way, 1984-87; coun. pres. Stetson U., 1996-2000; mem. alumni bd. Gustavus Adulphus Coll., St. Peter, Minn., 1974-80; trustee The Cooper Inst., Naples, Fla., 1987-93, mem. adv. bd., 1993—. Recipient Dedicated Svc. award Wis. Mfrd. Housing, 1975-84, 88, Vol. of Yr. award Univ. Lake Sch., 1995. Mem. Wis. Mfrd. Housing Assn. (bd. dirs. 1975-80), Ind. Bus. Assn. Wis. (trustee U. Lake 1991-96), Merrill Hills Country Club (chair golf 1991), Milw. Women's Dist. Golf Assn. (bd. dirs. 1993, v.p. 1994, pres. 1995-96), Vasa Lodge, Hammock Dunes Country Club (adv. bd.). Republican. Lutheran. Avocations: golf, photography. Home: 3 Anastasia Ct Palm Coast FL 32137-2273 Office Phone: 386-446-6319. Personal E-mail: jbhd@bellsouth.net.

BARNES, KAREN KAY, lawyer; b. June 22, 1950; d. Walter William and Vashti (Greenlee) Sessler; m. James Alan Barnes, Feb. 12, 1972; children: Timothy Matthew, Christopher Michael. BA, Valparaiso U., 1971; JD, DePaul U., 1978, LLM in Taxation, 1980. Bar: Ill. 1978, U.S. Dist. Ct. (no. dist.) Ill. 1978. Ptnr. McDermott, Will & Emory, Chgo., 1978-88; prin. William M. Mercer, Inc. and predecessor firm, Chgo., 1989-93; staff dir. legal dept. McDonald's Corp., Oak Brook, Ill., 1993-95, home office dir. legal dept., 1995-97, regulatory practice group leader and mng. counsel, 1998—. Instr. John Marshall Grad. Sch. Law, Chgo., 1986-87; mem. adv. bd. John Marshall Sch. Law, 1996-2004; bd. dirs. Flutes Unlimited; mem. adv. bd. dirs. Plan Sponsor Mag., 2000-; mem. defined contbn. adv. bd. Internat. Bus. Forum, Inc., 2004-. Contbr. case note to DePaul Law Rev., 1976, note and comment editor DePaul Law Rev., 1976-77, editor Taxation For Lawyers, 1986-88. Mem. Am. Coll. Employee Benefit Attys., Chgo. Bar Assn. (chair employee benefits com. 1991-92, chgo. symphony orch. 1999-2001), Midwest Pension Conf. (name chged to Midwest Benefits Coun.), WEB (pres. Chgo. chpt. 1986-88, v.p. nat. bd. 1988, pres. 1989-90, mem. adv. bd. 2001—), Profit Sharing Coun. Am. (legal and legis. com. 1994—, bd. dirs. 1997-2004, 2d vice chair 1997-98, 1st vice chair 1998-2000, chair 2000-02). Lutheran. Home: 586 Crescent Blvd # 402 Glen Ellyn IL 60137 Office: McDonald's Corp 2915 Jorie Blvd Oak Brook IL 60523 Business E-Mail: karen.barnes@mcd.com.

BARNES, KAY, mayor; BS in Secondary Edn., U. Kans.; MS in Secondary Edn. and Pub. Adminstrn., U. Mo., Kansas City. Staff mem. Westport area Cross-Lines Coop. Coun.; pres. Kay Waldo, Inc., human resources devel. co., Kansas City, Mo.; mayor City of Kansas City, Mo., 1999—. Condr. over 400 pub. seminars Nat. Seminars, Inc.; cons., keynote spkr. 14 reginal confs. through U.S., Am. Bus. Women's Assn.; former co-host, prodr. cable TV show Let's Talk; former instr. U. Mo., Kansas City, U. Kans., Ctrl. Mich. U. Author: About Time! A Woman's Guide to Time Management. Co-founder Ctrl. Exch.; vol. Cross-Lines Coop. Coun.; a founder women's resource svc. U. Mo., Kansas City; developer multicultural women's speaking panels through western U.S.; mem. Jackson County (Mo.) Legislature, from 1974; mem. Kansas City City Coun., from 1979; chmn. Tax Increment Financing Commn., 1993-97; pres. bd. dirs. Women's Employment Network; mem. or dir. numerous other orgns., including Women's Found. Greater Kansas City, Greater Kansas City Sports Commn.; mem. chancellor's adv. bd. of Women's Ctr., U. Mo., Kansas City; co-chair of the US Conf. of Mayors Small Business/Partner America Task Force, mem. of the Conference's Community Development and Housing Standing Com.; serves Nat. Adv. Coun. of Fannie Mae. Named One of 7 Outstanding Women in Kansas City, 1977. Mem. Greater Kansas City C. of C. (com.). Office: Mayor's Office City Hall 29th Fl 414 E 12th St Ste 2902 Kansas City MO 64106-2778 Office Fax: 816-513-3518. Business E-Mail: mayor@kcmo.org.*

BARNES, KEITH LEE, electronics executive; b. San Francisco, Sept. 14, 1951; s. Arch Lee and Charlotte Mae (Sanborn) B.; m. Sharon Ann Tosaw, June 9, 1986; children: Allecia, Alexandra, Wyatt. BS, Calif. State U., San Jose, 1976. Mgr. engring. and mktg. Gould, Inc., Rolling Meadow, Ill., 1976-79; v.p., gen. mgr. Kontron Electronics, Mountain View, Calif., 1979-85; v.p. Valley Data Scis., Mountain View, 1985-86; pres., CEO Integrated Measurement Sys., Beaverton, Oreg., 1986-2000, chmn., CEO, 2000—. Bd. dirs. Data Io Corp., LWG, Inc., Clarity Visual Systems, Inc. Patentee in field. Bd. dirs. Am. Electronics Assn., 1992-93, chmn. Oreg. bd., 1993; trustee Oreg. Grad. Inst. for Sci. and Industry, 1996—; vice chair Oreg. Growth Account, 1998; regent U. Portland, 2000. Mem. IEEE, PGC. Republican. Roman Catholic. Office: Integrated Measurements Systems, Inc 5975 NW Pinefarm Pl Hillsboro OR 97124-8563

BARNES, LARRY GLEN, journalist, editor, educator; b. Louisville, July 10, 1947; s. Roy Glen and Phyllis Jane (Dunn) Barnes; m. Susan Gayle Morrow, Dec. 27, 1969 (dec. July 1973); 1 child, Brian; m. Mary Frances Meiman, July 14, 1979. Student, Murray State U., 1965-68, 71-73, Def. Info. Sch., 1968. Journalist, editor various locations U.S. Dept. Army, 1968-71; staff writer Louisville Courier-Jour., 1972-75, Lexington (Ky.) Herald-Leader, 1975; mng. editor Corydon (Ind.) Harrison County Press, 1976-77; assoc. editor Ky. Sports World, Louisville, 1977-81; editor Publs. Divsn., Ft. Knox, Ky., 1981-82, Inside the Turret, Ft. Knox, 1982—. Editor: Army's Best Newspaper, 1984, 1986, 1991, 1993, 1996, 1998 (named Army's Dean of Newspaper editors, 2000), DOD Newspaper, 1986. With U.S. Army, 1968—71. Named Editor of the Yr., Army Tng. & Doctrine Command, 1982; recipient Naismith citation, Atlanta Tipoff Club, 1981, Thomas Jefferson award, Dept. Def., Washington, 1982, 1986, 1st pl. commentary writing, Tng. & Doctorine Command, Ft. Monroe, Va., 1985, Journalist award, Dept. Army, Washington, 1986, 1st pl. commentary writing, Tng. & Doctorine Command, Ft. Monroe, Va., 1987—90, Master Craftsman award, 2002. Mem.: Am. Fedn. Govt. Employees, Soc. Profl. Journalists. Democrat. Baptist. Avocations: photography, movies, collecting 45 r.p.m records, reading. Home: 2220 Manchester Rd Louisville KY 40205-3044 Office: Pub Affairs Office PO Box 995 Fort Knox KY 40121-0995 Business E-Mail: turret@ftknox-emh3.army.mil.

BARNES, MARK JAMES, lawyer; b. Oak Park, Ill., Jan. 10, 1957; s. James W. and Lorraine (Brady) B.; m. Ellice Halpern, 1988; children: Julia Elizabeth, Katherine Claire, John Halpern. BS in Polit. Sci. summa cum laude, Ariz. State U., 1978; JD, UCLA, 1981. Staff atty. Senator Ted Stevens U.S. Senate, Washington, 1981-83, chief counsel Senator Ted Stevens, 1983-84; assoc. Davis, Wright & Jones, Anchorage, 1984-86; dep. gen. counsel U.S. Office of Personnel Mgmt., Washington, 1986-87; assoc. dir. adminstrn. U.S. Office Personnel Mgmt., Washington, 1988-89; counsel to sec. for drug abuse policy HHS, Washington, 1989-93; pvt. practice Washington, 1993—. Alaska ambassador organizing com. Anchorage Olympics, 1986; mem. exec. com., World Forum on Future of Sport Shooting Activities, 1998—. Mem. ABA, Alaska Bar Assn., Ariz. Bar Assn., D.C. Bar Assn., Phi Beta Kappa. Republican. Roman Catholic. Avocations: travel, movies, stamps. Office: 1350 Eye St NW Ste 1255 Washington DC 20005-3390 Office Phone: 202-626-0089. Personal E-mail: markb17@aol.com.

BARNES, MARYLOU RIDDLEBERGER, retired academic administrator, educator; b. Bridgewater, Va., Feb. 27, 1930; d. Hensel Dorsey Riddleberger and Ruby Elizabeth Heltzel; children: Tenley Elizabeth, Rachel Patricia. BS, Madison Coll., 1952; MS, Med. Coll. Va., 1957; MA, James Madison U., 1968; EdD, W. Va. U., 1975; DSc (hon.), U. Indpls., 1993. From staff phys. therapist to dir. clin. edn. Woodrow Wilson Rehab. Ctr., Fishersville, Va., 1958-64, dir clin. edn., 1964-67; chief phys. therapy Rockingham Meml. Hosp., Harrisonburg, Va., 1958-59; prof., dir., chair dept. phys. therapy W. Va. U., Morgantown, W. Va., 1968-79; from prof., chair dept. phys. therapy to prof. emeritus Ga. State U., Atlanta, 1979-95, ret., 1995, prof. emeritus, 1995—. Adv. bd. Perry Inst., Strafford, Pa., 1993-95; co-chair program com. Joint Am.-Can. Phys. Therapy Annual Conf. Author: Patient at Home, 1972, Neurophysiological Basis of Physical Therapy Care, vol. I, 1973, vol. II, 1977, Physical Therapy, 1989, Motor Control and Motor Learning in Rehabilitation, 1993; contbr. articles to profl. jours. Vol. Centennial Olympic Games, Atlanta, 1996, Goodwill Industries Book Ctr., Atlanta, 1999. Mem. Am. Phys. Therapy Assn. (nat. survey pool for accreditation of schs. 1974-95, pres. neurology sect. 1985-87, task force on profl. devel. 1994, chair continuing edn. bd. 1994-95, Mary McMillan Lectr. award 1992, Catherine Worthingham fellow 1994, leadership in edn. award 1995, svc. to neurology sect. award 1998, Lucy Blair Svc. award 1988). Presbyterian. Avocations: amateur archaeologist, travel, reading, tree climbers of am. Home: 133 Santolina Park Peachtree City GA 30269-3245 E-mail: mloubarnes@mindspring.com.

BARNES, MELVER RAYMOND, retired chemist; b. Salisbury, N.C., Nov. 15, 1917; s. Oscar Lester and Sarah Albertine (Rowe) B. AB in Chemistry, U. N.C., 1947; D of Physics (hon.), World U., 1983; DSc in Chemistry (hon.), Assoc. Univs., 1987, PhD (hon.) of Chemistry, 1990, Albert Einstein Internat. Acad. Found. and Associated Univs., 1990. Chemist Pitts. Testing Labs., Greensboro, NC, 1948—49, N.C. State Hwy. and Pub. Works Commn., Raleigh, 1949—51, Edgewood Arsenal, Md., 1951—61, Dugway Proving Ground, Utah, 1961—70. Recipient Albert Einstein Bronze medal, 1988, Alfred Nobel Medal award Albert Einstein Internat. Acad. Found., 1991, Albert Einstein Acad. Found. Cross of Merit, 1992. Mem. AAAS, Am. Statis. Assn., Am. Chem. Soc., Am. Phys. Soc. Home and Office: 1486 Swicegood Rd Linwood NC 27299-9386

BARNES, PAUL MCCLUNG, lawyer; b. Phila., June 27, 1914; s. Andrew Wallace and Luella Hope (Andrew) B.; m. Elizabeth McClenahan, Dec. 28, 1940 (dec.); children: Andrew M., Margaret L. Lenart, James D., John R. (dec.). BA, Monmouth (Ill.) Coll., 1936; JD, U. Chgo., 1939. Bar: Colo. bar 1939. Assoc. Bannister & Bannister, Denver, 1939-40, Foley & Lardner, Milw., 1940-47, ptnr., 1948-88, of counsel, 1988—. Dir. Wis. Public Service Corp., 1974-77, Kickhaefer Mfg. Co., 1965-85, Attys. Liability Assurance Soc., Ltd., 1979-87; sec. Sta-Rite Industries, Inc., 1965-73 Mem. adv. bd. Milw. Protestant Home, 1975-87. Served with USNR, 1942-45. Mem. ABA, Wis. Bar Assn., Order of Coif. Office: Foley & Lardner 777 E Wisconsin Ave Ste 3800 Milwaukee WI 53202-5367 Personal E-mail: pbarnes@webtv.net.

BARNES, PETER, federal official; b. Cambridge, Mass., Apr. 13, 1940; s. Tracy Barnes and Janet (White) Lawrence; m. Jan Adair; children from previous marriage: K. Tracy, John E. BA magna cum laude, Yale U., 1962; LLB cum laude, Harvard U., 1965. Bar: DC 1966, Md. 1984. Assoc. Leva, Hawes, Symington, Martin & Oppenheimer, Washington, 1965-71, ptnr., 1972-83, Venable, Baetjer & Howard, Balt., 1983-86; shareholder Swidler & Berlin, Chtd., Washington, 1987—98; mem. Swidler Berlin Shereff Friedman, LLP, Washington, 1998-99, counsel, 1999—2001; spl. asst. to gen. counsel US Govt. Printing Office, Washington, 2004—. Mem.: Elkridge Club, Met. Club. Home: 4 Deep Run Ct Cockeysville MD 21030-1600 Personal E-mail: ptrbrs@aol.com.

BARNES, PETER J., JR., assemblyman; b. East Providence, R.I., Sept. 12, 1928; BA in Polit. sci., Providence Coll.; studied, Kean Coll. Assemblyman N.J. Gen. Assembly, 1996—; majority whip, 2002—. Spl. agt. FBI, 1954—81; Edison dir. pub. safety, 1991—93. Pvt. Mil. Police U.S. Army, 1946—48. Democrat. Office: 1967 Rt 27 Ste 20 Edison NJ 08817 Business E-Mail: AsmBarnes@njleg.org.

BARNES, RICHARD DALE, college basketball coach; b. Hickory, NC, July 17, 1954; m. Candace, July 31, 1976; children: Nicholas, Caroline. Degree in Health Physical Edn., Lenoir-Rhyne Coll., 1977. Head coach North State Acad., 1977-78; asst. coach Davidson, 1978-80, George Mason, 1980-85, Ala., 1985-86, Ohio State, 1986-87; head coach George Mason, 1987-88; head basketball coach Providence Coll., 1988-94, Clemson U., 1994-98, U. Tex., Austin, 1998—. Named to Hall of Fame, Lenoir-Rhyne Coll., 2002; recipient Disting. Alumnus award, 1997. Office: U Tex Intercoll Athletics-Men Campus Mail Code E2400 Austin TX 78712

BARNES, RICHARD GEORGE, physicist, researcher; b. Milw., Dec. 19, 1922; s. George Richard and Irma (Ott) B.; m. Mildred A. Jachens, Sept. 9, 1950; children: Jeffrey R., David G., Christina E., Douglas A. BA, U. Wis., 1948; MA, Dartmouth Coll., 1949; PhD, Harvard U., 1952. Teaching fellow Harvard, 1950-52; asst. prof. U. Del., 1952-55, asso. prof., 1955-56, Iowa State U., 1956-60, prof., 1960-88, chmn. dept. physics, 1971-75, prof. emeritus, 1988—; sr. physicist Ames Lab., U.S. Dept. Energy, 1960-88; assoc. Ames lab. US Dept. Energy, 1988—; chief physics divsn. Ames lab. AEC, 1971-75. Vis. rsch. prof. Calif. Inst. Tech., 1962-63; guest profl. Tech. U. Darmstadt, Germany, 1975-76; vis. prof. Cornell U., 1982-83; program dir. solid state physics NSF, 1988-89, condensed matter physics NSF, 1995; chmn. Metal Hydrides Gordon Rsch. Conf., 1987. Served with USAAF, 1942-43; C.E. AUS, 1944-46 (Manhattan Project). Recipient U.S. Sr. Scientist award Alexander von Humboldt Found., 1975-76 Fellow Am. Phys. Soc. Office: Iowa State U Physics Dept Ames IA 50011-0001

BARNES, ROBERT F, agronomist; b. Estherville, Iowa, Feb. 6, 1933; s. Chester Arthur and Pearl Adella (Stoelting) B.; m. Bettye Jeanne Burrell, June 25, 1955; children: Bradley R., Rebecca L. Reinalda, Roberta K. Nixon, Brian L. AA, Estherville Jr. Coll., 1953; BS, Iowa State U., 1957; MS, Rutgers U., 1959; PhD, Purdue U., 1963. Rsch. agronomist USDA-Agrl. Rsch. Svc., West Lafayette, Ind., 1959-70, lab. dir. University Park, Pa., 1970-75, staff scientist nat. program staff Beltsville, Md., 1975-79, assoc. dep. adminstr. So. region New Orleans, 1979-84, dep. adminstr. So. region, 1984-86; exec. v.p. Am. Soc. Agronomy, Madison, Wis., 1986-99; exec. dir. Agronomic Sci. Found., exec. dir. emeritus, 1999—; also fellow Am. Soc. of Agronomy, Madison, Wis. Asst. prof. Purdue U., West Lafayette, 1963-66; assoc. prof., 1966-70; adj. prof. Pa. State U., University Park, 1966-70; adj. prof. agronomy U. Wis., Madison, 1986-99; pres. Internat. Grassland Congress, Lexington, Ky., 1981; cons. Agronomic Sci. Found., Am. Soc. Agronomy. Editor: Forages, 1973, 85, 95, 2003; contbr. articles to profl. jours. With U.S. Army, 1953-55, Germany. Recipient H.S. Stubbs Meml. Lecture award Tropical Grassland Soc., Brisbane, Australia, 1984, Henry A. Wallace award Iowa State U., 1991; Grad. Edn. Award for forage and grazing lands established in his name, 2004. Fellow AAAS, Crop Sci. Soc. Am. (pres. 1984-85); mem. Am. Forage and Grassland Coun. (medallion 1981, Disting. Grasslander award 2001), Grazing Lands Forum (pres. 1986-87), Forage and Grassland Found. (pres. 1993-97). Avocations: walking, reading. Personal E-mail: rbarnes0206@sbcglobal.net.

BARNES, ROBERT MYRRDYN, artist, educator; b. Washington, Sept. 24, 1934; s. Mahlon and Marjorie Barnes; m. Lia Sayers, 1957 (div. 1971); 2 children; m. Nancy Morgan, 1972; 2 children. B.F.A., Art Inst., Chgo., 1956, U. Chgo., 1956; postgrad., Columbia U., 1957, Hunter Coll., 1957-60, U. London, 1961-63. Former boxer; prof. fine arts Ind. U., Bloomington, 1965—, Ruth N Halls prof. fine arts, emeritus. Vis. artist Ind. U., Bloomington, 1960-61, Kansas City Art Inst., 1963-64, U. Wis. Milw., 1968. One-man shows, Allan Frumkin Gallery, N.Y.C., 1963, 65, 69, 75, 77, 79, 83-85, Frumkin Struve Gallery, Chgo., 1960, 63, 64, 71, 78, 81, 84, 86, 89, 92, Herron Mus. Art, 1967, 68, Gallerie du Dragon, Paris, 1967, Galleria Il Fante di Spade, Rome, 1973, Galleria La Parisina, Turin, Italy, 1974, Marianne Friedland Gallery, Ont., Can., 1978, Renaissance Soc., Chgo., 1986, Nicholson Gallery, Madison, Wis., 1989, Sonia Zaks Gallery, Chgo., 1996, 98, 2000, 02, Zails Gallery, 2004, others; group shows include Art Inst. Chgo., 1955, 58-60, 61, 63, 64, 80, Am. Fedn. Arts, 1961, 65, Galerie Du Dragon, Paris, 1962, Whitney Mus. Am. Art, 1962, 65, 80, Mus. Modern Art, N.Y.C., 1963, 65, Museo Civico, Bologna, Italy, 1965, Ravenna Festival, Italy, 1968, Galleria Il Fante di Spade, 1972, Mus. Contemporary Art, Chgo., N.Y., 1972, Galleria Communale d'Arte Contemporanea, Arezzo, Italy, 1973, Le Stanze Galeria Giulia, Rome, 1976, Am. Acad. Inst. Arts and Letters, N.Y., 1981, 89, Mus. Contemporary Art, Chgo., 1982, Artist's Choice Mus., N.Y.C., 1983, Struve Gallery, Chgo, 1986, 88, 92, Indpls. Mus. Art, 1986, Allen Frumkin Gallery, N.Y.C., 40th anniversary celebration 1987, Art Against Aids, N.Y.C., 1987, Art Adv. Coun. Mus. Modern Art for GE Corp., 1989, Va. Beach Ctr. for Arts, Va. Beach, Va., 1994, Oakton Cmty. Coll., Chgo., 1995, Ind. U., Bloomington, 1996, Mus. Art U. Chgo., 1997, Fort Wayne Mus. Art, Ind., 2000, others; travelling one man show, Ill., Ga., S.D., Ind., 1971—, Miyagi Mus. Art, Sendal, Tokushima Modern Art Mus., Sogu Museum Modern Art, Yokohama, Mus. Modern Art, Shiga, Kochi prefectural Mus., Japan; retrospective exhbns. include Artist Choice Mus. N.Y., 1985, Herron Gallery Art, Indpls., 1986, Madison Art Ctr., 1986, Hyde Park Art Ctr. and Renaissance Soc., Chgo., 1986, Fla. Internat. U., Miami, 1986; represented in permanent collections Mus. Modern Art, N.Y.C., Mus. Contemporary Art, Chgo., Whitney Mus. Am. Art, N.Y.C., Art Inst. Chgo., Pasadena (Calif.) Mus. Art, Albrecht Gallery, St. Joseph, Mo., Weatherspoon Art Gallery, Chapel Hill, N.C., Nat. Gallery Art, Smithsonian Inst., Washington, Fla. Internat. U. Art Gallery, Mus. Contemporary Art, Chgo., Yale U. Art Gallery, others. Fulbright grantee, 1961-63, NEA grantee, 1982, grantee Nat. Endowment for Arts, 1982; recipient Child Hassam award Am. Acad. Arts and Letters, 1971, Guri Siever award Art Inst. Chgo., 1963, New Talent award Art in Am. Mag., 1962, Copley Found. award, 1961. Mem.: Am. Acad. Design. Office: PO Box 438 Searsport ME 04974-0438 Business E-Mail: nabobs@adelphia.net.

BARNES, ROBERT VERTREESE, JR., construction executive; b. Dallas, Oct. 7, 1946; s. Robert Vertreese and Doris Corinne (Haffen) B.; m. Deborah Dee Brown, May 31, 1968; children: Robert V. III, John David, Leslie Shannon. BS in Indsl. Tech., Tex. A&M U. Commerce, 1976. Registered bldg. contractor, Ariz., 1992; registered and cert. bldg. contractor, Fla., 1994; gen. comml. contractor, Ariz. Salesman Sears, Roebuck and Co., Dallas, 1965-66, dept. mgr., 1967-69; estimator Dee Brown Masonry, Inc., Dallas, 1969—75, contract adminstr., 1976-77, v.p. Houston, 1980-85, exec. v.p., 1985—89; v.p. Cardinal Masonry Co., Houston, 1978-79; exec. v.p. Dee Brown, Inc., Houston, 1986—89, pres., COO, 1990-99, chmn., pres., CEO, 2000—. V.p., sec./treas., dir. Shiloh Investment Co., 1974-99, chmn., pres., dir. 2000—; mem. exec. com. Contrn. Rsch. Ctr. U. Tex., Arlington, 1992-, vice chmn., 1994, chmn. elect, 1995, chmn., 1996; pres. Stone Erectors, Inc., 1989-93; exec. v.p. Dee Brown Masonry/Hatch, Inc., 1989-90, chmn. 2000—; pres., CEO, dir. Masonry Tech., Inc., 1993-95, chmn., pres., CEO, 1996-2002; dir. Stone Anchors, Inc., 1993-2003; ptnr. Pacific Waterjet, LLC, 1996-2003, Skinner Marble and Granite LLC, 1997-99; mng. ptnr. Kepco & DBI, LLC, 1995-; mng. dir. Salesmanship Club Dallas, 1997—; trustee, chmn. Bricklayers Health and Welfare, 1983-85, Bricklayer Pension Fund, Houston, 1983-85; pres. Youngblood Masonry, Inc., 2000—; mem. arch. and constrn. com. Dallas Arboretum, 2000—, chmn., 2003—, exec. com., 2003—; dir. Innovative Masonry, Inc., 2003-. Coach Katy Youth Soccer Assn., 1978-81, mem., pres., 1980-81, Richardson Youth Soccer Assn., 1976-77; team mgr. Solar "74" Soccer Club, 1986-88, Diggers Soccer Club, 1989-92; mem. bd. White Rock Ch.'s Ath. Assn., 1972-77, commr. baseball, 1976-77; trustee, chmn. Bricklayer Health and Welfare, Houston, 1983-85; bishop warden, com. St. Cuthbert's Episcopal Ch., 1985-86, vestry mem., fin. com., 1999-2001, chmn. fin. com., 2000-2001; bd. dirs. St. John's Episcopal Sch., 1987-93, v.p., 1988-89, sch. fin. com., health, safety and ins. com., bldg. facility com., chmn. bldg. and grounds com., 1988-90, co-chmn. devel. com., vestry mem., fin. com., ath. dir., 1999-2001, co-chmn. bldg. campaign, 2003-; trustee Episcopal Found. Diocese, Dallas, 2000—, Gaston Episcopal Hosp. Found., Dallas, 2000—, John Charles Brown Parish Scholarship Fund, 1996—; exec. adv. bd. mem. Cir. Ten coun. Boy Scouts Am., 2000—, chmn. camping facilities, 2002; mem. exec. com. camp coun. facilities Cir. Ten Coun. BSA, 2002-, chmn., 2003-; mem. bd. Ctr. Brain Health U. tex.-Southwestern Med. Sch., 2004-, East Dallas Young Life, 1990-. Mem. ASTM (mem. C-12, C-15, C-18 coms. 1990—), TPC, Mason Contractors Assn. Am. (contract rsch. com. 1982-83, chmn. labor com., codes and stds. com., 1999-2001, state chmn. Tex. 2002-2004, liaison com., regional v.p. 2004), Tex. Masonry Coun. (bd. dirs. 2003-) Marble Inst. Am., Constrn. Specification Inst., Associated Gen. Contractors (chpt. Dallas 1970-, mem. bd. dirs. 1995-96, subcontractor rels. com. 1988-89, mktg. com. 1990-93, co-chmn. gen. contractor/subcontractor rels. com. 1993-94, bd. dirs. 1995-98, transition com. AGC/ABC 1995-96, nat. assn. bd. dirs. 1995-2000, assoc. mem. AGC 1995-98, Quoin, No. Tex. chpt. bd. dirs. 2002-, sec. exec. com. 2004, vice chmn. exec. com. 2005), Masonry Alliance Codes and Stds. (treas. 1996-2000), Constrn. Edn. Found. (trustee, mem. bd. dirs. 1996-98), Baylor Inst. Rehab. (mem. bd. dirs., trustee 1996-2003, vice chmn. 1998-2000, chmn. 2001-2003, v.p. 1998-2000), Assn. Masonry Contractors Tex. (pres. 1983, sec./treas. 1981-82, v.p. 1990-91), So. Bldg. Congress, Nat. Bldg. Environment and Thermal Envelope Counsel, Assn. Masonry Contractors Houston (pres. 1982-84, v.p. 1981), Am. Subcontractor Assn. (v.p. 1982-83, bd. dirs. chpt. Houston 1982-85, also mem. nat. coms., bd. dir. north Tex. chpt. 1995-97), Bldg. Stone Inst., United Masonry Contractors Dallas (dir. constrn. edn. found. 1996-98, bd. dirs. 2003-, mem. program com. 1996-98, bd. dirs. 2003—, pres. 1982-84), Dallas Exec. Assn., Houston C. of C., N.W. Houston C. of C., Dallas C. of C., East Dallas Younglife (bd. dirs. 1990—), Tex. A&M U. Alumni Assn., Tex. A&M U.-Commerce Found., Tex. A&M U. Commerce (amb. 1999-), John Brown U. Parents' Cabinet (founder, pres. 1989-93), Dallas County Pioneers Assn., Baylor Health Care Sys. Found. (mem. bd. dirs. 2003-), Pine Forest Country Club (Houston), Dallas Athletic Club, Baylor Health Club, Salesmanship Club (Dallas), Tom Landry Ctr., Dallas Country Club, Delta Sigma Pi (life mem. 1967-). Republican. Home: 6531 Meadow Rd Dallas TX 75230

BARNES, ROBERT VINCENT, retired elementary and secondary school art educator; b. Flint, Mich., May 27, 1948; s. Albert J. and Mary Elizabeth (Morey) B.; m. Sandra E. Mathews-Barnes, Dec. 20, 1986; 1 child, Kathryn R. BA, Adrian Coll., 1970; postgrad., U. Mich., 1973-75, Ctrl. Mich. U., 1976-80, Getty Ctr. Edn. Arts, Cin. Art Mus., Cranbrook Acad. Art, Marygrove Coll., Cranbrook Acad. Art, 1995—; MA, Marygrove Coll., 1997. Cert. tchr. art grades kindergarten through 12, Mich. Tchr. art Flushing (Mich.) Cmty. Schs., 1971—2002; instr. Flint Inst. Arts, 1975-76; tchr. genealogy adult edn. program Mott C.C., Flushing, Fenton and Grand Blanc, Mich., 1976-84; pvt. art tchr., 2002—. Tchr. pvt. art lessons. Author: Flushing Area Families, 1981, Fenton Area Families, 1984; editor Flint Geneal. Quar., 1981. Past pres. Flint Geneal. Soc., Fenton Hist. Soc.; bd. dirs., past pres. Flushing Area Hist. Soc.; pres. Fenton Mus. Bd., 1984-86; chmn. Fenton 150th Com., 1984; co-chmn. Fenton Civic Com. for New Mus., 1985-86; com. mem. Genesee County Sesquicentennial, Flint, 1986; mentor for jr. h.s. youth Logas program Fenton United Meth. Ch., mem. edn. commn., 2000—. Recipient 1st prize Flushing Art Fair, Flushing Jr. Women's League, 1975, 78, Orren Hart award Flushing Area Hist. Soc., 1983. Mem. NEA, Mich. Edn. Assn., Nat. Art Edn. Assn., Mich. Art Edn. Assn., Ohio Geneal. Soc., Ohio Hist. Soc. Methodist. Avocations: pottery, painting, family history research. E-mail: bbarnes48@charter.net.

BARNES, ROBIN, historian, educator; b. NYC, Mar. 1, 1951; s. William Alexander Barnes and Shirley Anna Mayer; m. Ann Lee Bressler, June 28, 1980; children: Molly Leeanna, Morgan Bruce. BA, Colby Coll., 1973; MA, U. Va., 1975, PhD, 1980. Asst. prof. history Davidson (NC) Coll., 1980—88, assoc. prof. history, 1988—94, prof. history, 1994—. Author: Prophecy and Gnosis, 1988; editor: Books Have Their Own Destiny, 1998; contbr. chpt. to Ency. Apocalypticism, 2000; assoc. editor: Sixteenth Century Jour., 1994—2003. Mem.: Soc. Reformation Rsch. (pres. 2000—01), Sixteenth Century Soc. and Conf. (mem. exec. com., medal 2003), Am. Hist. Assn. Office: Davidson Coll Dept History Box 6906 Davidson NC 28035-6906 Office Phone: 704-894-2286. Fax: 704-894-2005. Business E-Mail: robarnes@davidson.edu.

BARNES, SAMUEL HENRY, political science professor; b. Miss, Jan. 20, 1931; s. Eugene Ludlow and Christine (Thompson) B.; m. Annabelle Bivona, Nov. 30, 1954; children: Christopher F.E., Michael Andrew, Catherine Ann. BA, Tulane U., 1952, MA, 1954; PhD, Duke U., 1957; postgrad. (Fulbright scholar), Institut des Hautes Etudes Politiques, Paris, 1956—57. Instr. polit. sci. U. Mich., Ann Arbor, 1957-60, asst. prof. polit. sci., 1960-64, assoc. prof., 1964-68, prof., 1968-91, James Orin Murfin prof. polit. sci., 1982-85, acting chmn. dept. polit. sci., 1968-69, chmn. dept., 1977-82, rsch. assoc. Survey Rsch. Ctr., 1969-70, program dir. Ctr. for Polit. Studies, 1970-91; prof. Comparative European Politics, dir. Ctr. for German and European Studies Georgetown U., Washington, 1991—2003, Graf Goltz emeritus prof. and dir., 2003—. Fulbright lectr. U. Florence, Italy, 1962-63, U. Rome, 1967-68; Ctr. Advanced Study in Behavioral Scis. fellow Stanford U., 1982-83, Hoover Instn. fellow Stanford U., 1989. Author: Party Democracy: Politics in an Italian Socialist Federation, 1967, Representation in Italy: Institutionalized Traditions and Electoral Choice, 1977, (with Max Kaase and others) Political Action: Mass Participation in Five Western Democracies, 1979, Politics and Culture, 1989, (with others) Continuities in Political Action, 1990 (with others) Cultural Dynamics of Democratization in Spain, 1998; contbr. articles to profl. publs., chpts. to books. Trustee Duke U., 1989-2001. Served with USN, 1949-50. Mem. Am. Polit. Sci. Assn. (sec. 1972-74), Conf. Group for Italian Polit. Studies (v.p. 1975-77, pres. 1977-79), Cosmos Club (Washington).

BARNES, SANDRA HENLEY, publishing company executive; b. Seymour, Ind., Jan. 15, 1943; d. Ray C. and Barbara Henley; m. Ronald D. Barnes, Sept. 3, 1961; children: Laura, Barrett and Garrett (twins). Student, Ind. State U., 1962-63. Asst. sales mgr. Marquis Who's Who, Indpls., 1973-79, sales, svc. mgr., 1979-82, mktg. ops. mgr., 1982-84, mktg. mgr. Chgo., 1984-86, dir. mktg. Wilmette, Ill., 1986-87; v.p. mktg. Macmillan Directory Div., Wilmette, 1987-88; group v.p. product mgmt. Marquis Who's Who, Wilmette, 1988-89, pres., 1989-92; v.p. Reed Reference Pub., New Providence, N.J., 1992-96; v.p., fulfillment Reed Elsevier-New Providence, 1996-97, LEXIS-NEXIS, Dayton, Ohio, 1997-98, Lexis Law Pub., Charlottesville, Va., 1997-98, Congrl. Info. Svc., Bethesda, Md., 1997-98; sr. v.p. Ednl. Comms., Inc., Lake Forest, Ill., 1998—2001; gen. mgr. Marquis Who's Who, New Providence, NJ, 2002—. Republican. Avocation: reading. Office: 121 Chanlon Road New Providence NJ 07974 Home: 214 N Hills St Meridian MS 39305-2235

BARNES, STEVEN W., diagnostic equipment company executive; BS, Syracuse U., 1982. Various exec. level positions Executone Bus. Solutions; dir. Miltex Instruments; pres., COO, dir. Holson Burnes Group Inc.; exec. v.p. Bain Capital, 1996; COO Dade Behring, Deerfield, Ill., 1996—97, CEO, 1997—2000; mng. dir Bain Capital, Boston, 2000—. Office: Bain Capital 111 Huntington Ave Boston MA 02199

BARNES, SUSAN LEWIS, lawyer; b. Palo Alto, Calif., June 11, 1943; d. Prof. and Mrs. L.J. Lewis; m. Sanford C. Barnes; 1 child, Jason Bullard Barnes. BS, Stanford U., 1965; JD, U. Wash., 1968. Law clk. Ariz. Ct. Appeals, Tucson, 1968-71, U.S. Atty.'s Office, Seattle, 1971-96, 1st asst. U.S. atty., 1994-96, interim U.S. Atty., 1993, 1st asst. U.S. Atty., 1991-93, chief civil divsn., 1982-91; ptnr. McKay Chadwell PLLC, Seattle, 1996—. Pres. Fed. Bar WDWN, 1995; lawyer's rep. 9th cir. Office: McKay Chadwell PLLC 600 University St Ste 1601 Seattle WA 98101-4124

BARNES, TED D., art educator; b. Little Rock, Dec. 10, 1950; m. Debra Smith Barnes, Jan. 1, 1977; children: Whitney Smith, Tyler Smith. BA in Studio Art, Ouachita Bapt. U., Arkadelphia, Ark., 1969—72; MA in Art Edn., Western Ky. U., Bowling Green, 1976—77; MFA in Painting, U. Ark., Fayetteville, 1977—79. Asst. prof., art Ouachita Bapt. U., Arkadelphia, Ark., 1980—84; prof., art and design La. Coll., Pineville, 1986—. Asst. art dir. Halblieb & Moll Assocs. Advt. Agy., Louisville, 1984—86; curator, collections and exhibitions, part-time Alexandria Mus. Art, La., 2004—. Exhibitions include Bangles, Jangles, Beeswax, and Clay, Nicholls State U., Thibodeaux, La., 12th Ann. Art with a Southern Drawl, U. Mobile, Ala., Southeastern Juried Exhibn., Mobile Mus. Art, Ala., one-man shows include Personal Problems: Ted Barnes Recent Work, Northwestern State U., Natchitoches, La., Bootleggers, Modernists, & Bolsheviks: Recent Work, Samford U., Birmingham, Ala., Blame It On Cain: A Mid-Career Retrospective, River Oaks Square Art Ctr., Alexandria, La., exhibited in group shows at Debra Smith Barnes & Ted Barnes: Recent Work, Spalding U., Louisville, Personal Icons & Fantasy Landscapes, Alexandria Mus. Art, La., Gumbo Yumbo, U. Ky., Lexington. Mem. River Oaks Sq. Arts Ctr., Alexandria, La., 2003—05. E-4 U.S. Army, 1972—74, Ft. Leonard Wood, Mo. Grantee, La. Coll. Faculty Devel. Com., 1994, 2001, 2005, La. Divsn. Arts, 1995, 1997, 2001, 2002, Miley Endowment, La. Coll., 2002. Liberal. Baptist. Avocations: baseball, music. Office: La Coll Art Dept 1140 College St Pineville LA 71359 Office Phone: 318-487-7435. Business E-Mail: barnes@10college.edu.

BARNES, THOMAS G., law educator; b. 1930; AB, Harvard U., 1952; DPhil, Oxford U., 1955. From asst. prof. to assoc. prof. Lycoming Coll., Williamsport, Pa., 1956-60; from lectr. to prof. history U. Calif., Berkeley, 1960—, humanities rsch. prof., 1971-72, prof. history and law, 1974—, co-chmn. Canadian studies program, 1982—. Dir. legal history project Am. Bar Found., 1965-86; com. mem. on ct. records 9th Cir. Ct. Author: Somerset 1625-1640: A County's Government During the Personal Rule, 1961, List and Index to Star Chamber Procs., James I, 3 vols., 1975, Lawes and Libertyes of Massachusetts, 1975, Hastings College of Law: The First Century, 1978; mem. editl. bd. Gryphon Legal Classics Libr.; editor Pub. Record Office. Huntington Libr. fellow, 1960, Am. Coun. Learned Socs. fellow, 1962-63, John Simon Guggenheim Found. fellow, 1970-71. Fellow Royal Hist. Soc.; mem. Selden Soc. (councillor, state corr.), Assn. Canadian Studies (pres. 2001-03, past pres., 2003-05). Office: U Calif Sch Law 454 Boalt Hl Berkeley CA 94720-7200 Office Phone: 510-642-1780. Business E-Mail: barnest@law.berkeley.edu.

BARNES, THOMAS JOHN, lawyer; b. Grand Rapids, Mich., Apr. 1, 1943; s. James and Adeline (Molenda) B.; m. Lynn Marie Owens, Aug. 19, 1967; children: Nicolle, Cynthia. BA in Acctg., Mich. State U., 1965, BA in Polit. Sci., 1966; JD, Wayne State U., 1972. Bar: Mich. 1972, U.S. Dsit. Ct. (ea. and we. dists.) Mich. 1972, U.S. Ct. Appeals (6th cir.) 1974, U.S. Dist. Ct. (no. dist.) Ind. 1994, U.S. Ct. Appeals (7th cir.) 1995. Ptnr. Varnum, Riddering, Schmidt & Howlett, Grand Rapids, 1972—. Arbitrator Mich. Employment Rels. Commn.; spkr. in field. Editor-in-chief Wayne Law Rev.; contbr. articles to profl. jours. Fellow Coll. Labor and Employment Lawyers; mem. ABA (nat. labor rels. bd. practice and procedures com.), Am. Employment Law Coun., Mich. Bar Assn. (labor coun., sec., treas. 1987-88, chmn. 1989-90), Grand Rapids Bar Assn. (former chair labor sect.) Roman Catholic. Avocations: reading, horse racing, sports. Office: 333 Bridge St NW Grand Rapids MI 49504-5356 Office Phone: 616-336-6621. Business E-Mail: tibarnes@varnumlaw.com.

BARNES, THOMAS JOSEPH, writer; b. St. Paul, June 18, 1930; s. Ralph Weikert and Helen (O'Connor) B.; m. Mai Tang; children: An, Kim, Kevin; children by previous marriage: Christopher, Ross, Karen, Shannon. BA, U. Minn., 1950, MA, 1951. With fgn. service, 1957-80; vice consul Saigon, Vietnam, 1958—60; prin. officer Am. consulate, Hue, Viet Nam, 1960-61; polit. officer Bangkok, 1962-64, Vientiane, Laos, 1964-67; province sr. adviser Binh Long, Vietnam, 1967-68; country officer for Laos State Dept., 1968-70; prin. officer Am. Consulate, Udorn, Thailand, 1970-71; assoc. dir. AID, Nhatrang, Vietnam, 1971-72; consul gen. Tangier, Morocco, 1972-73, Can Tho, Vietnam, 1973; polit. counselor Bangkok, 1973-75; sr. staff mem. for East Asia Nat. Security Council, 1975-76; student Sr. Seminar in Fgn. Policy, State Dept., 1976-77; regional refugee coordinator Bangkok, 1977-78; diplomat-in-residence U. Hawaii, 1978-79; dir. Interagy. Working Group on Kampuchea, Dept. State, Washington, 1979-80; with UN High Commn. for Refugees, 1980—90, dep. rep. Somalia, 1980—82, chief S.W. Asia sect. Geneva, 1982-86, head supplies and food aid service, 1986-87, head orgn. and mgmt., 1987-90; coord. for ops. and program devel. Internat. Cath. Migration Commn., Geneva, 1991—95. Author: (novel) Tay Son: Rebellion in 18th Century Vietnam, 2000, Coping with Lust and the Colonel: Wartime Korea From Sokchang-ni, 2000, Vietnam When the Tanks Were Elephants, 2005, (memoir) Anecdotes of a Vagabond: The Foreign Service, The UN, and a Volag, 2000, (photographic art book) Southeast Asian Portraits, 2002. Capt. AUS, 1951-56. Decorated UN Svc medal, Korean Svc. medal, Bronze Star with 2 oak leaf clusters, Nat. Def. Svc. medal; recipient Award for Valor, Meritorious Honor award State Dept., Superior Honor awards State Dept, AID. Home: 15005 Solera Drive Austin TX 78717-4449

BARNES, VIRGIL EVERETT, II, physics professor; b. Galveston, Tex., Nov. 2, 1935; s. Virgil Everett and Mildred Louise (Adlof) B.; m. Barbara Ann Green, 1957 (dec. 1964); 1 son, Virgil Everett III; m. Linda Dwight Taylor, 1970; children— Christopher Richard Dwight, Charles Jeffrey, Daniel Woodbridge. AB magna cum laude with highest honors, Harvard U., 1957; PhD, Cambridge (Eng.) U., 1962. Rsch. assoc. Brookhaven Nat. Lab., Upton, N.Y., 1962-64, asst. physicist, 1964-66, assoc. physicist, 1966-69; mem. faculty Purdue U., 1969—, prof. physics, 1979—; asst. dean Purdue U. (Sch. Sci.), 1974-78. Cons. in field. Author papers on exptl. high energy particle physics. NSF predoctoral fellow Gonville and Caius Coll., Cambridge U., 1959-62; Marshall scholar Cambridge U., 1957-59; recipient Perkin Elmer prize Harvard U., 1956. Mem. AAAS, AAUP, Am. Phys. Soc., N.Y. Acad. Scis., Phi Beta Kappa, Sigma Xi. Home: 801 N Salisbury St West Lafayette IN 47906-2715 Office: Purdue U Dept Physics West Lafayette IN 47907

BARNES, WALLACE, manufacturing executive; b. Bristol, Conn., Mar. 22, 1926; s. Harry Clarke and Lillian (Houbertz) B.; m. Audrey Kent, June 14, 1947; children: Thomas Oliver, Jarre Ann Betts; m. Mrs. Frederick B. Hollister, Jr.; 1 adopted son, Frederick Hollister; m. Joan C. Fierri, Mar. 3, 1973; m. Barbara Hackman Franklin, Nov. 29, 1986. BA, Williams Coll., 1949; LLB, Yale U., 1952; grad., Advanced Mgmt. Program, Harvard, 1973; LLD (hon.), U. Hartford, 1988; LLD (hon.), Briarwood Coll., 2002. Bar: Conn. 1952. Pres. Nutmeg Air Trans. Inc., 1949-55; asst. to treas. Northeast Airlines Inc., Boston, 1951; assoc. firm Beach, Calder & Barnes (and predecessor), Bristol, 1952-55, partner, 1956-62; exec. v.p. Assoc. Spring Corp. (name changed to Barnes Group Inc.), 1960-64, pres., 1964-77, chmn., chief exec. officer, 1977-91, chmn. bd., 1991-95, ret., 1995; chmn. bd. Rohr Inc., Chula Vista, Calif., 1995-98; chmn. Coun. Employment and Tng. Commn. State of Conn., 1997—; sr. ptnr. Sky Bight Ptnrs. Bd. dirs. TeraBit Comms., LLC, Del Global Techs. Corp.; chmn. bd. Tradewind Turbines Corp., 1994—; ptnr. Green Acres Farm, 1986—. Pres. Bristol Cmty. Chest, 1956; bd. dirs., mem. exec. com. Bristol Boys Club, pres., 1965-68; bd. regents U. Hartford, 1961-94, lifetime regent, 1995, chmn., 1988-93; trustee Bristol Girls' Club Assn.; bd. dirs. New Eng. Legal Found., 1986-90, New Eng. Coun., 1980-83, Jr. Achievement North Ctrl. Conn., 1980-90; nominee for Congress, 1st Congl. Dist. Conn., 1954; Rep. town chmn. Bristol, 1953-55; mem. Conn. Senate from 5th Dist., 1958-62, 8th Dist., 1966-70, minority leader, 1969; Gov.'s Clean Water Task Force, 1966-67; bd. dirs. Cmty. Coun. of Capital Region, 1975-77, Hartford Symphony Soc., 1971-78, Coun. on Employment and Fair Taxation, 1978-80, Bus. Coalition on Health, 1983-88, Conn. Pub. Expenditure Coun., 1979-85; trustee Am. Clock and Watch Mus., Environ. Learning Ctrs. Conn. Inc., The Family Ctr.; bd. trustees New Eng. Air Mus.; corporator Inst. of Living, Hartford, Bristol Hosp., St. Francis Hosp., Hartford Hosp.; co-chair Conn. Children's Med. Cap. Campaign, chmn. CBIA, 1982-93; bd. dirs. Conn. Econ. Devel. Corp. Served as aviation cadet USAAF, 1944-45. Recipient Disting. Svc. award Bristol Jaycees, Keystone award Boys Clubs Am., 1967, Humanitarian award Tunxis C.C., 1982, Human Rels. award Nat. Conf. Christians and Jews, 1985, Hon. Alumnus award U. Hartford, 1985, Salute to Wallace Barnes Bristol C. of C., 1991, Hall of Fame award Jr. Achievement North Ctrl. Conn., 1996, Exec. Philanthropist of Yr. Nat. Soc. Fund Raising Exec., 1996; Bartels fellow U. New Haven, 1992. Mem. ABA, Conn. Bar Assn., Am. Judicature Soc., Am. Arbitration Assn., Bristol Hist. Soc., Newcomen Soc., Conn. Bus. and Industry Assn. (past chmn., dir.), Metro Hartford C. of C. (bd. dirs., exec. com. 1991—), Am. Legion, Elks, Econ. Club N.Y.C., Yale Club, Williams Club, Farmington Country Club, Chippanee Golf Club. Home and Office: Sky Bight 1875 Perkins St Bristol CT 06010-8910

BARNES, WALLACE RAY, retired lawyer; b. Easton, Pa., Nov. 7, 1928; s. Charles Hicks and Erma (Saylor) B.; m. Helen Honey Bartley, July 2, 1958; children: Charles Calvin, Elizabeth McKee, Douglas Wittmer. AB, Duke U., 1950; LLB, Harvard U., 1957. Bar: Pa. 1958, Ohio 1973. Atty. Allegheny Ludlum Steel, Pitts., 1957-62, Columbia Gas, Md., N.Y., Pa., Pitts., 1962-73, sec., gen. counsel Ky., Md., N.Y., Ohio, Pa., Va., W.Va., Columbus, Ohio, 1973-78, sr. counsel, 1978-81, assoc. gen. counsel, 1981-88, dep. gen. counsel, 1988-96, ret., 1996. Corp. dir. Columbia Gas Ohio, 1973-78, N.Y., 1973-78 Bd. dirs. Pitts. Better Bus. Bur., 1972—74. With USN, 1947—54. Mem. FBA (pres. chpt. 1961), ABA, Ohio Bar Assn., Fox Chapel Racquet Club, Racquet Club of Columbus, Sawmill Athletic Club, S&R Club of Columbus, Phi Beta Kappa. Home: 2438 Sandover Rd Columbus OH 43220-2845 Address: Les Devoliviers La Fossette France E-mail: wallacerbarnes@hotmail.com.

BARNES, WESLEY EDWARD, energy and environmental executive; b. Chgo., Sept. 11, 1937; s. Donald Edson and Helen Mary (Popovich) B.; m. Constance Arlene Simpson, Nov. 9, 1957; children: Dawn Ellen, Wesley Edward II. Grad., Indsl. Coll. of Armed Forces, 1973; BS, Cen. Mich. U., 1976, MBA, 1981. Chief warrant officer USN, 1955-68; sr. mktg. rep. UNIVAC, Washington, 1968-70; regional mgr. Weismantel Assocs. Inc., Washington, 1970-71; dir. computer ops. U.S. SBA, Washington, 1971-75; asst. dir. legis. affairs U.S. ERDA, Washington, 1975-77; dir. bus. rels. U.S. Dept. Energy, 1977-80, dir. major projects, 1980-83; chief exec. officer Western Rsch. Inst., Laramie, Wyo., 1983-90; pres., chief exec. officer Mktg. Bus. Assocs., Ltd., Washington, 1990-94; project mgr. Dept. of Energy, Yucca Mountain Project, 1995-97; energy and environ. cons. Dagsboro, Del., 1997—. Bd. dirs. Econ. Devel. Corp., Laramie, 1986-90. Mem. Rep. Nat. Com. Mem. Am. Mgmt. Assn. (pres.'s assn.), Cripple Creek Country Club, K. of C. (lector 1981-82). Roman Catholic. E-mail: barnes188@mchsi.com.

BARNES, WILLIAM DOUGLAS, advertising executive; b. Washington, Sept. 1, 1953; s. Berry Carter and Virginia Mae (Keeler) Barnes; m. Jeannette Avendano, July 3, 1990; 1 child, Chadsworth. BBA, U. Miami, Fla., 1980, MBA, 1984. Staff acct. Arthur Andersen & Co., Miami, 1980-81; sr. acct. Storer Comm., Miami, 1981-84; pres., personnel cons. Profl. Resources, Miami, 1984-86; acct. exec. Miami Herald, 1986-90; pres. Barnes & Assoc. Advt., Ft. Lauderdale, 1990-97; acct. exec. Sun-Sentinel, 1991—97; CEO Strategic Resource Group, Inc., Ft. Lauderdale, 1997—2004; dir. bus. devel. Am. Home Guides, Hollywood, Fla., 1999—2005; nat. sales mgr. NewHomeGuide.com/Primedia, Hollywood, 2005—. Mem. Beta Alpha Psi (chmn. alumni com. 1980). Republican. Home: 1146 Hidden Valley Way Weston FL 33327 E-mail: wjcbarnes@bellsouth.net.

BARNES, WILLIAM WAYNE, geographer, writer; b. Cleve., Apr. 14, 1953; s. William Joseph and Ann Marie Casciato; m. Pamela Rose Hopkins, Sept. 24, 1985 (div. May 1991); m. Mary Ann Traeger, Dec. 7, 1991. BA, Cleve. State U., 1975. Cert. Hypnotherapist Internat. Assn. of Regression Rsch. and Therapies, Minn., 2003. Lang. tchr. St. Edward H.S., Cleve., 1975—77; geographer Dept. of Def., Washington, 1979—; freelance lectr. Gila Bend, Ariz., 1996—; screenwriter NR9 Studios, Phoenix, 2003; storyboard writer R.E. Coil Prodns., Phoenix, 2003. Author: (book) Thomas Andrews: Voyage Into History, 2000, (newspaper series) In My Viewpoint, 2002, (films) Maledizione, 2003. Facilitator, annexation com. Town of Gila Bend, Ariz., 2003. Mem.: Internat. Assn. Regression Rsch. and Therapies (newsletter com. 2002—, scholarship com. 2003), Sigma Delta Pi. Independent. Roman Catholic. Avocation: horseback riding. Office: PO Box 1907 Gila Bend AZ 85337 E-mail: titanicbuilder@direcway.com.

BARNESCHI, JANET B., music educator, assistant principal; b. New Britain, Conn., Feb. 8, 1942; d. Raymond John and Nellie Catherine Szymanoweki; m. Armond John Barneschi, Nov. 11, 1967; children: Vanessa Corrinne, Damian Raymond. B of Music Edn., U. Hartford, 1964; MEd, Tufts U., 1965. Tchr. music Chamberlain Sch., New Britain, Conn., 1965—, asst. to prin., 1999—. Mem.: Internat. Soc. Tole and Decorative Painters, Alpha Delta Kappa (historian, pres. elect, pres. 1994—2000). Avocations: painting, gardening. Home: 328 Lamplighter Ln Newington CT 06111 Office: Chamberlain Sch 120 Newington Ave New Britain CT 06051

BARNES-KEMPTON, ISABEL JANET, retired microbiologist, dean; b. Union City, N.J., Sept. 22, 1936; d. Carl Robert and Isabel Sarah (Cappelletti) B.; m. John D. Bowman, June 15, 1978 (dec. Nov. 1986); m. Arnold J. Kempton, Feb. 5, 2000. BS, Pa. State U., 1958; MS, Cornell U., 1960; PhD, Hahnemann Med. Coll., 1969; postgrad., Inst. Ednl. Mgmt. Harvard U., 1991. Asst. prof. microbiology Hershey Med. Ctr., Pa. State U., 1968-73; asst. prof., then assoc. prof. Sangamon State U., Springfield, Ill., 1973-76; assoc. prof. med. tech. U. Wis., Madison, 1976-85; interim dean Sch. Allied Health Professions, 1981-84; prof. med. tech. Ferris State U., Big Rapids, Mich., 1985-2000; dean Coll. Allied Health Scis., 1985-2000, acting v.p. Acad. Affairs, 1992-93. Mem. Mich. Bd. Podiatric Medicine and Surgery, 1995—2002. Bd. dirs. Mecosta County Gen. Hosp., 1988-99, sec. 1991-94, pres., 1996-97, v.p. 1997-99, Alliance for Health, 1993-2002, Mich. Hemophilia Found., 1989-95, 97—2005, sec. 1991-94; active Mecosta Health Svcs., 1998-2002, Mecosta County Cmty. Found., 2000—, pres, 2005—; coord. St. Andrews Manna Food Pantry, 2002—; mem. Tamarack Dist. Libr. Bd., 2003—; pres. bd. Tamarack Dist. Libr., 2003—. Fellow Assn. of Schs. of Allied Health Professions (bd. dirs. 1989-91); mem. Coll. Health Deans (pres. 1988-90).

BARNESS, LEWIS ABRAHAM, physician; b. Atlantic City, N.J., July 31, 1921; s. Joseph and Mary (Silverstein) B.; m. Elaine Berger, June 14, 1953 (dec. Jan. 1985); children: Carol, Laura, Joseph; m. Enid May Fischer Gilbert, July 5, 1987; stepchildren: Mary, Elizabeth, Jennifer, Rebecca. AB, Harvard U., 1941, MD, 1944; MA (hon.), U. Pa., 1971; DS U. Wis. (hon.), 2002. Intern Phila. Gen. Hosp., 1944-45; resident Boston Children's Hosp., 1947-50; asst. chief, then chief dept. pediatrics Phila. Gen. Hosp., 1951-72; vis. physician U. Pa. Hosp., 1952-57, acting chief, then chief, 1957-72. Mem. faculty U. Pa. Sch. Medicine, 1951-72, prof. pediat., 1964-72; chmn. dept. U. So. Fla. Med. Sch., Tampa, 1972-88, prof. pediat., 1988—, Disting. Univ. prof., 2000—; vis. prof. Univ. Wis., 1987-92, prof. emeritus, 1993—. Author: Pediatric Physical Diagnosis Yearbook, edits. 1-6, 1957—; editor: Advances in Pediatrics, 1976-2004, Pediatric Nutrition Handbook, 3d edit., 1991; asst. editor Pediatric Gastroenterology and Nutrition, 1981-91; editl. bd. Cons., 1960-84, Pediatrics, 1978-83, Core Jour. Pediatrics, 1980-96, Contemporary Pediatrics, 1984—, Jour. Clin. Medicine and Nutrition, 1985-95, Nutrition Rev., 1985-87. Served to capt. AUS, 1945-46. Recipient Lindback Teaching award U. Pa., 1963; Borden award nutrition, 1972; Noer Disting. Prof. award, 1980, Joseph B. Goldberger award in clin. nutrition, 1984, Joseph St. Geme Leadership award 7 pediatric socs., 1991, U. So. Fla. Svc. award, 1997, President's Award, U. So. Fla., 2000, Distinguished Prof. award, 2000; inductee Phila. Pediat. Soc. Hall of Fame, 1996. Fellow Am. Inst. Nutrition; mem. AAAS, Am. Pediatric Soc. (recorder-editor 1964-75, pres. 1985-86, John Howland award 1993), Soc. Pediatric Rsch., Am. Acad. Pediatrics (chmn. com. on nutrition 1974-81), Abraham Jacobi award 1991, Hon. Internat. disting. fellow pediatric soc. Thailand, 2004, Med. Edn. Lifetime Achievement award, 1995, Sigma Xi, Alpha Omega Alpha. Home: 3301 Bayshore Blvd Unit 403 Tampa FL 33629-8841 Office: U South Fla Dept Pediat 17 Davis Blvd Tampa FL 33606 Business E-Mail: lbarness@hsc.usf.edu. *Most people, when given the opportunity, try to be unselfish and prefer to do good. The human brain is a fantastic instrument, which when exercised, can solve most problems.*

BAR-NESS, YEHESKEL, electrical engineer, educator; b. Baghdad, Iraq, Apr. 28, 1932; arrived in Israel, 1950; came to U.S., 1978; m. Varda Bar-Ness, Aug. 21, 1952; children: Yael, Yaron, Yegal. BEE, Technion U., Haifa, Israel, 1958, MEE, 1963; PhD, Brown U., 1969. Chief engr. Elscint Inc., Haifa, 1971-75; assoc. prof. Tel-Aviv U., 1973-78; vis. prof. Brown U., 1978-79, U. Pa., Phila., 1979-81; prof. elec. engring. Drexel U., Phila., 1981-83; tech. staff mem. AT&T Bell Lab., Holmdel, N.J., 1983-85; disting. prof. elec. and computer engring. N.J. Inst. Tech., Newark, 1985—, dir. ctr. communication and signal processing rsch., 1985—, found. chair comm. and signal processing, 2000—. Vis. prof. elec. engring. Tech. U. Delft, The Netherlands, 1993-94, Stanford U., 2000-01. Recipient Kaplan Price award Gov. of Israel, 1974. Fellow IEEE; mem. Communication Soc. of IEEE (sec. communications systems engring. com. 1985-87, vice chmn., 1987-89, chmn. 1990-91, editor IEEE transaction on comm., founder and editor-in-chief IEEE Comm. Letters). Home: 2 Etna Ct Marlboro NJ 07746-1307 Office: NJ Inst of Tech 323 King Blvd Newark NJ 07102-1824

BARNET, PETER, curator; BA, Bennington Coll., 1973; MA in Art History, Boston U., 1976; MPhil, Yale U., 1978. Grad. asst., dept. Medieval Art and The Cloisters Met. Mus. Art, NYC, 1977, Chester Dale fellow, dept. Medieval Art and The Cloisters), 1981—82, Michel David-Weill curator in charge, dept. Medieval Art and The Cloisters, 1998—, grants com., 2000—03, co-chair grants com., 2002—, dir.'s adv. com. on conservation and sci., 2002—; Nat. Endowment for the Arts intern Detroit Inst. Arts, 1982—83, asst. curator, European Sculpture and Decorative Arts dept., 1983—88, assoc. curator in charge, European Sculpture and Decorative Arts dept., 1988—89, assoc. curator, European Sculpture and Decorative Arts dept., 1989—98, collection mgmt. sys. com., long range planning task force on acquisitions, mktg. com., adv. com. for publ. Bd. advisors Internat. Ctr. Medieval Art, 1986—88, nom. com., 1988—89, bd. dirs., 1995—98, chair publ. com.; art instr. U. Mich., Ann Arbor, 1995, Bard Grad. Ctr., 2005; spkr. in field. Co-author (with MaryAnn Wilkinson): Decorative Arts 1900: Highlights from Private Collections in Detroit, 1993; editor: Images in Ivory: Precious Objects of the Gothic Age, 1997; contbr. articles and chptrs. to books and jours. Recipient State Hermitage Mus. Exchange Program, Met. Mus. Art and Trust for Mutual Understanding, 2000; Samuel H. Kress Summer Travel grant, 1975, Art History fellowship, Samuel H. Kress Found., 1978—80, John J. McCloy fellowship, 1985—86. Mem.: Assn. Art Mus. Curators (founding bd. mem. 2002—). Office: Met Mus Art 1000 Fifth Ave New York NY 10028

BARNET, ROBERT JOSEPH, cardiologist, philosopher; b. Port Huron, Mich., Apr. 27, 1929; s. John A. and Ruth Elizabeth (Wittliff) B.; children: Benedict, Maria, Antonia, Peter, Elizabeth, Rebecca, Christina, Jacqueline, Ann. Student, Port Huron Jr. Coll., summers 1947, 49; MD, Loyola U., Chgo., 1951; BS in Chemistry magna cum laude, U. Notre Dame, 1954; MA in History, U. of Nev., 1986; MA in Philosophy, U. Notre Dame, 1988. Diplomate Am. Bd. Internal Medicine, Nat. Bd. Med. Examiners. Intern Boston City Hosp., 1954—55; rotating intern Mercy Hosp., Chgo., 1955; asst. resident in medicine Boston City Hosp., 1958-59; clin. and research fellow in cardiology Children's Med. Center and House of the Good Samaritan, Boston, 1959-60; cons. fellow in rheumatic fever pediatric service Boston City Hosp., 1959-60; research fellow in pediatrics Harvard U., Boston, 1959-60; clin. fellow in cardiology Mass. Meml. Hosps., Boston, 1960-61; physician-in-charge St. Francis Mission Hosp., Solwezi, No. Rhodesia, 1961-62; dir. clinics, assoc. in medicine Stritch Sch. Medicine, Loyola U., Chgo., 1962-65; physician-in-charge Cardiac Clinic, Loyola U., Chgo., Fantus Outpatient dept. Cook County Hosp., Chgo., 1962-65, Hypertension Clinic, Fantus Outpatient dept. Cook County Hosp., 1962-65; assoc. attending physician dept. medicine Cook County Hosp., 1962-63, attending physician, 1963-65; practice medicine specializing in cardiology Reno, 1965-87; med. staff Washoe Med. Center, 1965—, St. Mary's Hosp., 1965—; assoc. clin. prof. cardiology U. Nev.; also assoc. dir. Lab. Environ. Patho-Physiology, Desert Research Inst., U. Nev., Reno, 1965-68; dir. Cardiac Care unit Washoe Med. Center, 1965-83, exec. com., 1967-71, 73-77, vice chief dept. medicine, 1969, chief, 1970-71, 78, chief dept. emergency services, 1973-77. Vis physician Solwezi Boma Rural Hosp., 1961-62; cons. in cardiology disability determination unit State of Nev., 1966-87, Crippled Children's Svc., 1966-76, Reno VA Hosp., 1967-80; asst. clin. prof. med. edn. U. Utah, 1968-71; cons. Churchill Pub. Hosp., Fallon, Nev., 1969-87, Pershing Gen. Hosp., Lovelock, Nev., 1969-87; clin. assoc. U. Nev., Reno, 1971-72, assoc. clin. prof. medicine, 1973-77, prof., 1978—; vis. scholar U. Notre Dame, 1989-90, 96-97; prof. med. ethics St. Louis U., 1993-95; med. reviewer, cons. Nev. State Bd. Med. Examiners, 1994—; affiliated scholar Ctr. Clin. Bioethics, Georgetown U., 2000—; lectr. in electrocardiography and cardiology Loyola U., Chgo., 1962-65. Contbr. articles to med. jours. Served with U.S. Army, 1955-58. Recipient Clin. Faculty Honor award Loyola U., 1963-64. Fellow A.C.P. (bd. govs. 1980-85), Am. Coll. Cardiology (bd. govs. 1974-77), Am. Coll. Chest Physicians; mem. Nev. Heart Assn. (bd. dirs., exec. com., pres. 1974-75) Home: 166 Greenridge Dr Reno NV 89509-3927 Personal E-mail: phbobmd@aol.com. *I have tried to dedicate my life to the service of all and the betterment of the community while striving for professional excellence without compromise of my moral and religious principles.*

BARNET, WILL, artist, educator; b. Beverly, Mass., May 25, 1911; s. Noah and Sarah (Toahnich) B.; m. Mary Sinclair, Feb., 1935 (div.); children: Peter George, Richard Sinclair, Todd Williams; m. Elena Ona Ciurlys, Mar. 4, 1953; 1 dau., Ona Willa. Student, Boston Mus. Fine Arts Sch., 1927-30, Art Students League, N.Y.C., 1930-33; DFA (hon.), Mass. Coll. Art, 1989. Instr. painting Art Students League, NYC, 1946—; faculty Cooper Union, NYC, 1945—, prof., 1965—; instr., critic Pa. Acad., Phila., 1967—; faculty Famous Artists Painting Course, Westport, Conn., 1954—, Mont. State Coll., summer 1951, Summer Artists Workshop, Regina Coll., U. Sask., Canada, 1957; instr. advanced painting U. Minn. at Duluth, summer 1959, Wash. State U., Spokane, summer 1963, Pa. State U., summer 1965, Des Moines Art Center, summer 1965. Distinguished vis. prof. Pa. State U., 1965-66; vis. critic Yale, 1952-53; vis. prof. Cornell U., 1968-69; condr. grand art tour of, Europe, April, 1959, Ford Found. artist in residence program, 1964 Contbr. to: Art Students League Mag; one-man shows, Hudson D. Walker Gallery, 1938, Galerie St. Etienne, 1943, Berthe Schaefer Gallery, Arthur Harlow & Co., Inc., all NYC, 1946, U.S. Nat. Mus., Washington, 1946, Bertha Schaefer Gallery, NYC, 1947, 48, Krasner Gallery, NYC, Gallery Trastevere, Rome, 1960, Terry Dintenfass Gallery, NYC, 1982, Kennedy Galleries, NYC, 1984, 86, 88, retrospective, Inst. Contemporary Art, Boston, 1961, Mary Harriman Gallery, Boston, 1963, 64, Va. Mus., Richmond, 1964, Waddell Gallery, NYC, 1965, 66, 68, 70, Des Moines Art Center, 1965, Pa. Acad. Phila., 1969, Fairweather Hardin Gallery, Chgo., 1971, David and David, Phila., 1972, print retrospective, Asso. Am. Artists, NYC, 1972-79, Hirschl & Adler Galleries, Inc., 1973, 76, 81, Essex Inst., Salem, Mass., 1980, painting retrospective, Neuberger Mus., Purchase, N.Y., 1979, 94, Ringling Mus., Sarasota, Fla., 1980, Wichita Art Mus., Wichita, Kans., 1983, traveling mus. retrospective, Currier Gallery Art, Manchester, N.H., 1984, Huntsville Mus. Art, Ala., 1984, Minn. Mus. Art, St. Paul, 1984-5, Art Gallery of Hamilton, Ont., Can., 1985, Farnsworth Libr. and Art Mus., Maine, 1985, Meek-Harmon Gallery, Naples, Fla., 1990, Terry Dintenfass Gallery, 1991, 94, Butler Inst., Youngstown, Ohio, 1992, Philharm. Ctr. Arts, Naples, Fla., 1994, Ogonquit Mus. Am. Art, Maine, 1994, Worcester Art Mus, Mass., 1995, Nat. Mus. Am. Art, Washington, 1995, Terry Dintenfars Gallery, 1996; drawing retrospective Ark. Art Ctr., Little Rock, 1991—; The Farnsworth Art Mus., Maine, 2002; exhibited, Art USA, 1959, Glenn Horowitz Bookseller, inc., East Hampton, NY, 1997, Nat. Acad. Mus., NYC, 1997, Maine Coast Artists, 1998, Tabor De Nagy Gallery, NYC, 1998, Retrospectives Montclair Art Mus., NJ, 2000, Boca Raton Mus. Art, Fla., 2000, Portland Mus. Art, Maine, 2000, Retrospective Ark. Art Ctr., 2001, Alexandre Gallery, NY, 2002, Harmon-Meek Gallery, Naples, Fla., 2003; represented in permanent collections, Minn. Inst. Arts, Met., NYC, Fogg Art Mus., Library of Congress, Art Gallery, U. ND, U. Art Gallery, Berkeley, Calif., Cin. Art Mus., Duncan Phillip Meml. Mus., Washington, Phila. Art Mus., Honolulu Acad., Mus. Modern Art, Bklyn. Mus., Mont. State Coll., Whitney Mus. Am. Art, Mus. Fine Arts, Boston, Guggenheim Mus., NYC, Farnsworth Mus. Maine, Butler Inst., Ohio, Ashmolean Mus., Oxford, Eng., Brit. Mus., London, Pulmer Mus. of Art, 2003, Alexander Gallery, 2003, Babcock Gallery, 2005; exhibited in museums throughout, US, including, Art Inst. Chgo., Los Angeles Mus., Portland Mus., John Herron Inst., Carnegie Inst., Virginia Mus. Fine Arts, Columbia (SC) Mus. Art (1st Biennial); pub. Will Barnet 27 Master Prints, 1982; illustrator The World in a Frame; subject of Robert Doty work: Publisher Abrams, 1984. Recipient Bronze medal, 3d prize Corcoran Biennial, 1961, Benjamin Altman 1st prize NAD, 1977, Medal of Honor, Nat. Arts Club, 1990, The Winthrop Rockefeller Meml. award, 1992, The Butler Medal for Life Achievement in Am. Art award Butler Inst. of Am. Art, 1992, Arts & Tourism Coun. Killy Carlisle Hart award, 1999; named to Gallery of Honors, Art World Mag., 1990. Fellow Royal Soc. Arts; mem. Art Students League (life), NAD (life), Am. Abstract Artists, Soc. Am. Graphic Artists, Inc., Fedn. Modern Painters and Sculptors, Century Assn. Liberal, Am. Acad. and Inst. Arts and Letters, NY Acad. of Art, Dr. of Fine Arts, 2002, and the Lyme Acad. Coll. of Fine Arts, 2003. Unitarian Universalist. Home: 15 Gramercy Park S New York NY 10003-1705

BARNETT, AMY DUBOIS, editor-in-chief; BA, Brown U.; MFA, Columbia U. Mng. editor Fashion Almanac Mag., 1996—98; editor-in-chief Edition Inside NY, 1999; mng. editor Fashion Planet Website; columnist, features editor Total NY Website; editor Essence Mag., 1999—2000; editor-in-chief Honey Mag., 2000—03; mng. editor Teen People, 2003—. Office: Teen People/Time Inc 1271 Ave of the Americas New York NY 10020-1393 Office Fax: 212-467-4633. E-mail: amy.barnett@teenpeople.com.*

BARNETT, BENJAMIN LEWIS, JR., retired physician, educator; b. Woodruff, SC, July 22, 1926; s. Benjamin Lewis and Mattie Bernice (Skinner) B.; m. Annalyne Louise Hall, Oct. 25, 1958; children: Benjamin Lewis III, Jane Kristen. BS, Furman U., 1946, LLD, 1978; MD, Med. U. S.C., 1949. Diplomate Am. Bd. Family Practice. Intern Protestant Episcopal Hosp., Phila., 1949-50; pvt. practice Woodruff, 1950-70; from assoc. prof. family practice to asst. dean and prof. Med. U. S.C., Charleston, 1970—75, asst. dean for student affairs, 1975—77; clin. staff Med. U. Hosp., Charleston County Hosp., 1970-77; from prof. to prof. emeritus U. Va. Med. Sch., 1977—2000, prof. emeritus, 2000—; family medicine physician-in-chief U. Va. Med. Ctr. Hosp., 1977-96. Admissions com. U. Va. Med. Sch., 1997-99; Stoneburner lectr. Med. Coll. Va., 1975; Daniel Drake lectr. U. Cin., 1976; Robert P. Walton lectr. Med. U. SC, 1978; Goodlark prof. U. Tenn., 1979; Roy J. Gerard lectr. Mich. State U., 1992; vis. scholar U. Mich. Med. Sch., 1984; vis. lectr. Med. Coll. of Ga., 1982; vis. prof. Case Western Res. Sch. Medicine, 1984, U. Vt., 1988, U. N.Mex., 1991, U. SC Sch. Medicine, 1999; spkr. baccalaureate address U. Va., 1986, 2000; Mack Lipkin vis. prof. U. Oreg., 1987, U. Utah, 1989; Donald J. Welter Meml. lectr. Med. Coll. Wis., 1989; Frederick Lytel Meml. lectr., Abington, Pa., 1989; Bradford Strock lectr. Harrisburg (Pa.) Gen. Hosp., 1989; 7th Leland Blanchard Meml. lectr. Soc. Tchrs. Family Medicine ann. meeting, Nashville, 1985; health officer, Town of Woodruff, 1950-54; keynote speaker Assn. Depts. Family Medicine, Clearwater, Fla., 1991; commencement speaker U. Va. Med. Sch., 1992, 97; Grand Prof. Rounds St. Margaret's Hosp., Pitts., 1993; Julian Keith lectr. Bowman Gray Sch. Medicine, 1993; keynote speaker leadership conf. Fla. Med. Assn., Ponta Vedra, 1994, AHEC conf. SC Family Practice, Myrtle Beach, 1994; B. Leslie Huffman lectr. Med. Coll. Ohio, Toledo, 1994; lectr. Atlanta Med. Ctr., 2000—; grad. speaker McLennan County Med. Edn. and Rsch. Found., Waco, Tex., 1995; Inaugural Buck Crockett lectr., Roanoke, Va., 2000; founder's prof. U. Okla. Health Scis. Ctr., Tulsa, 2000; Harlan Thomas Meml. lectr.; Hiram B. Curry Meml. lectr. MUSC, 1990, 2001; lectr. and cons. in field. Author: Between the Lines (Reflections of a Family Physician), 1989, Pebbles in the Water, 2003; editor: S.C. Family Physician, 1973—74; contbr. articles to med. jours. and chpts. to textbooks. Mem. Spartanburg County Bd. Edn., 1968-70, sec. 1969-70; trustee Bethea Bapt. Home for Aged, Darlington, S.C., 1972-73; mem. bd. trustees Furman U., 1994-99; dir. Marietta-Lost Mtn. Kiwanis, 2003—; mentor character curriculum Kennesaw Mountain HS, 2002—. Named Citizen of Year Woodmen of World, 1968; recipient Golden Apple award for clin. teaching Student AMA, 1973; Thomas W. Johnson award Am. Acad. Family Physicians, 1976, Disting. Alumnus award Med. U. S.C., 1993; endowed Barnett Professorship in Family Medicine established U. Va. Bd. Visitors, 1997; Thomas Jefferson award U. Va., 1997. Mem. AMA (mem. residency rev. com. for family practice 1974-79), Am. Bd. Family Practice (exam. bd. 1975-81, dir. 1976-81, exec. com. 1979-81, pres. 1980-81), Va. Med. Soc., Albemarle County Med. Soc., Soc. Tchrs. Family Medicine (v.p. 1974, sec.-treas. 1975, dir. 1981-85, Cert. of Excellence 1983, F. Marian Bishop award 1996), Am. Acad. Family Physicians, S.C. Acad. Family Physicians (v.p. 1973, pres. 1975-76), Spartanburg County Med. Soc. (v.p. 1968), Am. Philatelic Soc., Coun. Acad. Socs., Furman U. Alumni Assn. (dir. 1972-77), U. Va. Raven Soc., Kiwanis (dir.), Alpha Omega Alpha (faculty councilor, vis. prof. U. S.C. Sch. Medicine 1999), Alpha Kappa Kappa (pres. 1948), Kappa Alpha (v.p. 1944) Baptist (deacon, chmn. bd.). Home: 4734 Talleybrook Dr NW Kennesaw GA 30152-5484

BARNETT, BERNARD, accountant; b. N.Y.C., Oct. 14, 1920; s. Abraham L. and Rose (Albert) B.; m. Helen Salla, July 9, 1953; children: Susan Barnett Christiansen, Douglas (dec.). BBA magna cum laude, CCNY, 1941. CPA, N.Y., Mich., La., N.C., Va. Ptnr. Apfel & Englander, CPAs, N.Y.C., 1941-69, Seidman & Seidman, CPAs, N.Y.C., 1970, sr. ptnr., nat. dir. tax practice, 1971-86; sr. cons. BDO Seidman, LLP, N.Y.C., 1987—; pres. Found. Acctg. Edn., 1977-78; exec. dir. Fiduciary Income Tax Inst., 1986—. Adv. commn. to commr. IRC; mem. N.Y. State Bd. Pub. Accountancy; mem. faculty, mem. adv. com. Inst. Estate Planning, U. Miami (Fla.) Law Sch., 1972—; mem. adv. bd. Tax Mgmt. Inc.; mem. faculty Am. Law Inst/ABA Estate Planning Course, 1978-91, Nat. Trust Sch. of Am. Bankers Assn.; cons. CBS News Ann. Income Tax Program, 1977-90; pres. N.Y.C. Estate Planning Coun., 1967-68. Co-author: Estate Planning and the CPA, 1958, Attorneys Handbook of Accounting, 2d edit., 1979, 3d edit., 1991, Analysis of the Tax Reform Act of 1969, 1970; mem. editorial bd. Trusts and Estates, 1979—, Tax Adviser, 1970-94, emeritus, 1994—, Taxation for Accts., 1973-98, Practical Tax Strategies, 1999—. Pvt. to capt. AUS, 1942—46, maj. USAF, 1951—52. Mem. AICPA (gov. coun. 1971-80, chmn. task force on estate and gift tax reform 1979-83, chmn. joint disciplinary trial bd. 1982-84, chmn. task force on income taxation of trusts and estates 1983-87, v.p. 1985-86, bd. dirs. 1985-86, chmn. joint trial bd. divsn. 1984-93, mem. nat. rev. bd. 1984-88, trustee benevolent fund 1983-86, AICPA Disting. Svc. award for CPA in tax practice 1984, chmn. liaison AICPA tax divsn. with ABA tax sect., mem. faculty ann. adv. estate planning conf.), N.Y. State Soc. CPAs (pres. 1976-77), Nat. Conf. Lawyers and CPAs (co-chmn. 1978-81), Accts. Club Am. (pres. 1977-80), Royal Berkshire Golf Club (res., Ascot, Eng.). Office: BDO Seidman LLP 330 Madison Ave New York NY 10017-5001

BARNETT, BONNIE ALLYN, lawyer; b. Phila., 1958; BA summa cum laude, Temple Univ., 1979, JD summa cum laude, 1982. Bar: Pa. 1982, NJ 1996. Law clerk, Hon. James T. Giles US Dist. Ct. (ea. dist), Pa., 1982—84; joined Drinker Biddle & Reath LLP, Phila., 1984, ptnr., chair, environ. practice group. Articles editor Temple Law Rev., lectr. in field. Named a Pa. Super Lawyer, 2004. Office: Drinker Biddle & Reath LLP One Logan Sq 18th & Cherry Sts Philadelphia PA 19103-6996 Office Phone: 215-988-2916. Office Fax: 215-988-2757. Business E-Mail: bonnie.barnett@dbr.com.

BARNETT, CAROL CONNER, lawyer; b. Otterbein, Ind., Apr. 18, 1955; d. Stephen Robert and Eleanor Ann (Fullenwider) Conner; m. Jerrold Eugene Barnett, Aug. 27, 1977; children; Aaron, Ross. BA cum laude, Purdue U., 1977; JD cum laude, U. Ill., 1983. Bar: Mo. 1984, Ill. 1983, U.S. Ct. Appeals (8th cir.) 1995, U.S. Dist. Ct. (we. dist.) Mo. 1984, U.S. Ct. Appeals (10th cir.) 2001, U.S. Dist. Ct. Kans., 2001. Law clk. to justice Robert Underwood Ill. State Supreme Ct., Bloomington, 1983-84; assoc. Kranitz & Kranitz, St. Joseph, Mo., 1984-85; staff atty. Legal Aid of Western Mo., Kansas City, Mo., 1985-86; asst. prosecutor Buchanan County, St. Joseph, 1986-91; ptnr. Shughart, Thompson and Kilroy, St. Joseph, 1991—. Legal instr. Mo. Western State Coll., St. Joseph, 1989-91. Mem. Mo. Bar Assn., St. Joseph Bar Assn. Office: Snughart Thomson and Kilroy 3101 Frederick Ave Saint Joseph MO 64506-2911 Office Phone: 816-364-2117. Business E-Mail: cbarnett@stklaw.com.

BARNETT, CRAWFORD FANNIN, JR., internist, educator, cardiologist, travel medicine specialist; b. Atlanta, May 11, 1938; s. Crawford Fannin and Penelope Hollinshead (Brown) B.; m. Elizabeth McCarthy Hale, June 6, 1964; children: Crawford Fannin III, Robert Hale. Student, Taft Sch., 1953—56, U. Minn., 1957; AB magna cum laude, Yale U., 1960; postgrad., Oxford (Eng.) U., 1963; MD, Duke U., 1964. Intern in internal medicine Duke U. Med. Ctr., Durham, NC, 1964-65, resident, 1965; resident in internal medicine Wilmington (Del.) Med. Ctr., 1965-66; dir. Tenn. Heart Disease Control Program, Nashville, 1966-68; pvt. practice medicine in internal/travel medicine Atlanta, 1968—. Dir. Travel Immunization Ctr., Atlanta; mem. staff Crawford Long Hosp., Atlanta, Northside Hosp., Atlanta, Grady Meml. Hosp., Atlanta, West Paces Hosp., Atlanta, Piedmont Hosp., Atlanta, North Fulton Hosp., Atlanta; mem. tchg. staff Vanderbilt Med. Ctr., Nashville, 1966-68, Crawford Long Meml. Hosp., 1969—; clin. instr. internal medicine, dept. medicine Emory U. Med. Sch., Atlanta, 1969—. Contbr. articles to profl. publs. Bd. govs. Doctors Meml. Hosp., 1971-80; bd. dirs. Atlanta Speech Sch., 1976-80, 92—. Hist. Oakland Cemetery, 1976-86, So. Turf Nurseries, 1977-92, Tech Industries, 1978-92; bd. dirs. Am. Chestnut Found., 1990, bd. trustees Mary Brown Found. of Atlanta, 1998—, Woodward Found., 2001—. Surgeon USPHS, 1966-68. Fellow Am. Geog. Soc., Royal Soc. of Tropical Medicine and Hygiene, Royal Geog. Soc., Royal Soc. Medicine, Explorers Club (life, NYC); mem. Am. Soc. Tropical Medicine and Hygiene, Am. Fedn. Clin. Rsch., Coun. Clin. Cardiology, AMA, Ga. Med. Assn., Atlanta Med. Assn., Am. Heart Assn., Ga. Heart Assn., Am. Soc. Internal Medicine, Am. Assn. History Medicine, Ga. Hist. Soc., Atlanta Hist. Soc. (bd. govs. 1976-84), Ga. Trust for Hist. Preservation, Nat. Trust Hist. Preservation, Internat. Hippocratic Found. Soc. (Greece), Faculty of History of Medicine and Pharmacy Worshipful Soc. Apothecaries of London, Atlanta Com. on Fgn. Rels. (chmn. exec. com. 1972-88), So. Coun. Internat. and Pub. Affairs, Newcomen Soc., Atlanta Clin. Soc., Wilderness Med. Soc., Internat. Soc. Travel Medicine (founding), Travelers Century Club, Circumnavigators Club, South Am. Explorers Club, Victorian Soc. Am. (bd. advisers Atlanta chpt. 1971-86), Mensa, Gridiron, Piedmont Driving Club, Yale Club (dir. 1970-74), Nine O'Clocks Club, Pan Am. Drs. Club, Phi Beta Kappa. Episcopalian. Home: 2739 Ramsgate Ct NW Atlanta GA 30305-2817 Office: Ste 302 3193 Howell Mill Rd NW Atlanta GA 30327-2100 Office Phone: 404-262-1414. Personal E-mail: cfbarne@comcast.net.

BARNETT, DAVID PHILIP, horticulturist; b. Jacksonville, N.C., Nov. 18, 1956; s. Frederick D. and Janet (Holdridge) B.; m. Eileen Nickerson, Aug. 19, 1978; children: Jake, Marie. BS, U. Conn., 1978; MS, U. Calif., Davis, 1983, PhD, 1987. Collections crew leader The Morton Arboretum, Lisle, Ill., 1978-81; asst. dir. Planting Fields Arboretum, Oyster Bay, N.Y., 1986-93; dir. horticulture Mt. Auburn Cemetery, Cambridge, Mass., 1993-99, dir. ops. and horticulture, 1999—. Asst. scoutmaster Boy Scouts Am., Boxborough, Mass., 1996—. Mem. Am. Assn. Botanical Gardens & Arboreta (bd. dirs. 1995-98, chmn. N.Am. plant collections consortium 1998-2002), Worcester County Horticultural Soc. (chmn. Cary award plant selection com. 1995-2001), Internat. Dendrology Soc., Internat. Soc. Arboriculture, N.Y. Hortus Club (v.p. 1990-93), Horticultural Club Boston (chair program com. 1996-00). Avocations: running marathons, hockey, camping, hiking, gardening. Office: Mt Auburn Cemetery 580 Mount Auburn St Cambridge MA 02138-5529

BARNETT, EDWARD WILLIAM, lawyer; b. New Orleans, Jan. 2, 1933; s. Phillip Nelson and Katherine (Wilkinson) B.; m. Margaret Mauk, Apr. 3, 1933; children: Margaret Barnett Stern, Edward William. BA, Rice U., 1955; LL.B., U. Tex.-Austin, 1958. Bar: Tex. 1958. Mem. Baker Botts LLP, Houston, 1958—2004, mng. ptnr., 1984-98, sr. counsel, 1998—2004. Bd. dirs., chmn. Cen. Houston, Inc., 1989-91. Trustee Rice U., Houston, 1991-2005, chmn. bd. trustees, 1996—; trustee St. Luke's Episcopal Health System; life trustee U. Tex. Law Sch. Found.; bd. dirs. Greater Houston Partnership 1989-, former chmn., 1992; bd. dirs. Ctr. Houston's Future, 2000-, Reliant Energy, Inc., 2002-, Enterprise GP, LLC, 2005-; chmn. Houston Zoo, chmn., 2002-04. Fellow Am. Coll. Trial Lawyers; mem. ABA (chmn. sect. antitrust law 1981-82), State Bar Tex., Houston Bar Assn., Coronado Club (pres. 1989), Houston Country Club, Old Baldy Club, Riverhill Country Club. Office: Baker Botts LLP 3000 One Shell Plaza Houston TX 77002

BARNETT, ELIZABETH HALE, organizational consultant; b. Nashville, Mar. 17, 1940; d. Robert Baker and Dorothy (McCarthy) Hale; m. Crawford F. Barnett Jr., June 6, 1964; children: Crawford F. III, Robert H. BA, Vanderbilt U., 1962. Receptionist, sec. U.S. Atty. Gen. Robert F. Kennedy, Washington, 1962-64; free-lance cons. Atlanta, 1973-76; pres. E.H. Barnett & Assocs. orgnl. cons., trainers, Atlanta, 1976-86; trustee The Ga. Conservancy, Atlanta, 1978-92, chmn. bd. trustees, 1986-88, chmn. adv. bd., 1994-98; legis. asst. to Senator Michael J. Egan Ga. State Senate, Atlanta, 1990-93. Bd. dirs. Jr. League Atlanta, 1973-75, Atlanta Mus. Art, High Mus. Art, Atlanta, 1977—; bd. dirs. United Way Met. Atlanta, 1981-84, ARCS Found., Atlanta chpt., found. mem.; bd. dirs. White House Fellows Southeastern Region Selection Panel, 1995-96; chmn., pres. bd. dirs. Vol. Coms. Art Mus. U.S. and Can., 1976-79; chmn. bd. dirs. Met. Atlanta chpt. ARC, 1978-80, hon. bd. dirs., 1980—; cmty. adv. com. NW Ga. Coun. Girl Scouts Am., 1979-83; coun. mem. USO Ga., 1981-1993; bd. sponsors Atlanta Women's Network; apptd. to Ga. Clean and Beautiful Citizens Adv. Com., 1990, Ga. Solid Waste Mgmt. Commn., 1990; appt. sec. to Gov.'s Environ. Edn. Coun., 1992—; sci. coun. Ga. Coalition for Sci. Tech. and Math. Edn., 1993-, Student Aid Found., Atlanta, 2002-(bd. dirs.). Named One of 10 Outstanding Young Women of Am., 1977, Outstanding Young Woman of Ga., 1977; honored by Ga. State Legis., Atlanta, 1978. Mem. LWV. Episcopalian. Avocations: gardening, travel, hiking, snorkeling, politics.

BARNETT, FLORENCE CARSLEY, neurosurgeon; b. Atlanta, Sept. 29, 1958; d. Joseph Carl Jr. and Ruth Naomi (Partridge) B.; m. Robert A. Jones Jr., 1978 (div. 1982); children: Leslie Taryn Jones, Karyn Leigh Jones. AA in

Art History, Fleming Coll., Florence, Italy, 1977; BS in Biology, Kennesaw Coll., 1988; MD, Med. Coll. Ga., 1992. Resident surgery Carraway Hosp., Birmingham, Ala., 1992-94; resident neurosurgery Med. Coll. Ga., Augusta, 1994—. Presenter in field. Contbr. chpt. to book and articles to profl. jours. Mem. AMA, ACS (candidate), Congress Neurol. Surgeons, Am. Assn. Neurol. Surgeons, Alpha Omega Alpha. Republican. Presbyterian. Office: Spectrum Neurological Specialists 2500 Hosp Blvd Ste 310 Roswell GA 30076

BARNETT, GENE HENRY, neurosurgeon; b. Phila., Feb. 2, 1955; s. Edgar Tryon and Anne Shirley (Wenner) B.; m. Kathleen Marie Seng, May 9, 1984 (div. Sept. 1989); 1 child, Alexander; m. Cathy Ann Sila, Dec. 9, 1990; children: Austin, Addison. BA summa cum laude, Case Western Res. U., 1976, MD, 1980. Intern Cleve. Clinic Found., 1980-81, neurosurgery resident, 1981-86, staff neurosurgery, 1987—, co-dir. residency program, 1992-95, vice chmn. dept. neurosurgery, 1993—2002, program dir. dept. neurosurgery, 1995—, dir. Brain Tumor Ctr., 1995—2001, chmn. Brain Tumor Inst., 2001—, dir. Gamma Knife Ctr., 1997—. Hon. registrar U. Edinburgh, Scotland, 1985; fellow Harvard Med. Sch., Mass. Gen. Hosp., 1986-87; cons. in field. Editor: Image Guided Neurosurgery: Clinical Applications of Surgical Navigation Systems, 1998; contbr. over 120 articles to profl. jours., 27 chpts. to books. Grantee Epilesy Found. Am., 1979, NINDS, 1995; clin. and rsch. fellow Harvard Med. Sch., Mass. Gen. Hosp., Boston, 1986-87. Office: Cleve Clinic Found 9500 Euclid Ave Cleveland OH 44195-0001

BARNETT, GUY OCTO, physician, educator; b. Chula Vista, Calif., Sept. 18, 1930; married; 3 children. BA, Vanderbilt U., 1952; MD, Harvard U., 1956. Resident Peter Bent Brigham Hosp., 1956—61; clin. assoc. Nat. Heart Inst., 1958—60; investigator Am. Heart Assn., 1961—67; physician, prof. medicine, dir. computer sci. lab Mass. Gen. Hosp., 1979—; prof. medicine Harvard U., 1980—. Lectr. elec. engring. MIT, 1972—. Recipient Morris F. Colleen award. Fellow: Inst. Medicine-NAS; mem.: ACP, IEEE, Am. Med. Informatics Assn. (bd. dirs. 1984—), Biomed. Engring. Soc., Assn. Computing Machinery. Office: Mass Gen Hosp Lab Computer Sci 50 Staniford St Boston MA 02114-2517*

BARNETT, JEFFREY ADAM, academic administrator; b. Mt. Kisco, NY, May 3, 1978; s. Donald Jay and Christine Lynn Barnett. BS, Stony Brook U., 2000; MA, Columbia U., 2005. Cert. human rights rschr. Stony Brook U., 2001. Rsch. asst. child behavioral study psychology dept. Stony Brook U., 1998—2000, coll. advisor, 2003—, residence hall dir., 2000—03, co-founder & coord. residential tutoring ctrs., 2000—03. Vol. 'Tis the Season, Stony Brook, 2000—03, Stony Brook U. Blood Dr., 2000—03. Recipient Undergraduate Rsch. award, Stony Brook U., 2000, Disting. Svc. in Student Devel. award. Mem.: APA (assoc.), Assn. of Coll. & U. housing Officers (assoc.), Nat. Assn. of Student Personnel Adminstrs. (NASPA) (assoc.), Am. Coll. Personnel Assn. (ACPA) (assoc.; program reviewer 2003—05), Kappa Delta Pi (assoc.), Golden Key Nat. Honors Soc. (assoc.). Independent. Episcipal. Office: Acac Advising Ctr Melville Lib E-2360 Stony Brook NY 11790 Home Fax: 631-632-6997; Office Fax: 631-632-6997. E-mail: jeffrey.barnett@stonybrook.edu.

BARNETT, JONATHAN, urban planner, educator, architect; b. Boston, Jan. 6, 1937; s. David and Josephine Barnett; m. Nory Miller, Mar. 19, 1983. BA magna cum laude, Yale U., 1958, MArch, 1963; MA Mellon fellow, U. Cambridge, Eng., 1960. Designer Haines, Lundberg & Waehler, Archts., N.Y.C., 1963, 64; assoc. editor Archtl. Record, N.Y.C., 1964-67; cons. New City Exhbn. Mus. Modern Art, 1966, 67; prin. urban designer N.Y.C. Planning Dept., 1967-68, dir. urban design group, 1969-71; prof., dir. grad. program in urban design CCNY, 1971-98; prof. city and regional planning, dir. urban design program U. Pa., Phila., 1998—; prin. Wallace, Roberts and Todd, LLC, 2002—. Planning cons., 1971—2002; mem. vis. com. Sch. Architecture Yale U., 1974—80, William Henry Bishop prof., 1983; mem. vis. com. Harvard U. Grad. Sch. Design, 1976—81, UCLA, 1990, MIT Planning Dept., 1999; vis. prof. U. Wis., Milw., 1981; Kea disting. vis. prof. U. Md., 1988, 89; Sam Gibbons eminent scholar U. S. Fla., 1991—94; lectr. in field; cons. in field. Editor: (book) Pespecta 8, 1968; co-author: New Zoning, 1970, Collaborations: Artists and Architects, 1981, The Practice of Local Government Planning, 1988, 3d edit., 2000, Cities in Our Future, 1997, Charter of the New Urbanism, 1999; author: Urban Design as Public Policy, 1974; author: (with John C. Portman, Jr.) The Architect as Developer, 1976; author: Introduction to Urban Design, 1982, The Elusive City, 1986, The Fractured Metropolis, 1995, Planning for the New Century, 2000, Redesigning Cities, 2003; editl. cons. Archtl. Record, 1968—90, mem. adv. bd. Jour. Urban Design, 1996—; contbr. articles to profl. jours. Mem. adv. bd. Environment and Behavior, 1968—78; bd. dirs. DC Preservation League, 1996—2000; mem. Com. 100 Fed. City, 1997—2002. Fellow: AIA, Am. Inst. Cert. Planners; mem.: Congress New Urbanism (bd. dirs. 1995—), N.Y. Landmark Conservancy (bd. dirs. 1972—97), Berzelius Soc., Inst. Urban Design (bd. dirs. 1989—99), Mcpl. Art Soc. (bd. dirs. 1970—78, 1981—86), Archtl. League N.Y. (v.p. 1968—70, dir. 1975—98, pres. 1977—81), Century Assn., Elizabethan Club Yale, Yale Club. Unitarian Universalist. Home: 225 S Bonsall St Philadelphia PA 19103 Office: Dept of City and Regional Planning Univ Pa Philadelphia PA 19104

BARNETT, JOYCE LYNDEL, freelance/self-employed writer; b. Louisville, Ky., Apr. 21, 1956; d. Otis and June LaVern Cleveland; m. Lloyd Barnett; children: Luciene, Lloyd Jr. Travel agent diploma, Walters Coll., Louisville, Ky., 1989; BSBA, Barrington U., Birmingham, Ala., 2001. Mental health nurse Vis. Nurses Assn.; sales and mktg. staff Time Life Books, Washington. Motivational spkr. For the Spirit, Inc., Louisville; lectr. on autism Jewish Hosp., Louisville; speaker Vis. Nurses Assn. Author: (Book) Understanding the Autistic Person, 1994, For the Spirit, 1998, While on My Journey, 2000, (Poem) Strange Fruit, 1993. Avocation: story telling. Home: 5403 Red Leaf Rd Louisville KY 40218 E-mail: bchaplainL@aol.com.

BARNETT, KENNETH HAROLD, paramedic; b. Oklahoma City, Jan. 30, 1956; s. Harold Dean and Betty Elaine Barnett; m. Linda Sue Organ, June 6, 1975; children: Erika Lane, Sarah Joy, Kenneth Ryan, Tracy Renea. Cert. paramedic Ark., 1994, Okla., 1994. Drywall carpenter, Little Rock, 1969—74; drywall subcontractor Ft. Smith, Ark., 1974—78; constrn. foreman Nat. Specialities, Ft. Smith, 1978—88, Clark Interiors, Ft. Smith, 1988—93; paramedic Med-Tech EMS, Van Buren, Ark., 1993—96, Logan County EMS, Paris, Ark., 1996—99; flight paramedic Air Evac Lifeteam 4, Springdale, Ark., 1998—2001; lead flight paramedic Air Evac Lifeteam 22, Paris, 2001—. Paramedic program adv. com. Ark. Tech U., Ozark, 2004—. County employee activist Logan County EMS, Paris, 1994—98; patient care adv. Air Evac Lifeteam 22, Paris, 2001—05. Independent. Baptist. Achievements include first to placement of medical helicopter in Arkansas River Valley. Avocations: hunting, fishing, repelling, backpacking, automobile restoration. Office Phone: 479-963-6018.

BARNETT, MARILYN, advertising agency executive; b. Detroit; d. Henry and Kate (Boesky) Schiff; children: Rhona, Ken. BA, Wayne State U. Founder, part-owner, pres. Mars Advt. Co., Southfield, Mich. Bd. dirs. Mich. Strategic Fund; apptd. to Mich. bi-lateral trade team with Germany. Named Outstanding Retail Woman of Yr., Outstanding Retail Mktg. Exec., Oakland U., Entrepreneur of Yr., Oakland Exec. of Yr.; named to Mich.'s Top 25 Women Bus. Owners List. Mem. AFTRA (dir.), SAG, Exec. Women Am., Am. Women in Radio & TV (Top Agy. Mgmt. award, Outstanding Woman of Yr.), Internat. Women Forum, Com. of 200, Women's Econ. Club (Ad Woman of Yr.), Adcraft. Office: Mars Advt 23777 Southfield Rd Southfield MI 48075-3435 Office Phone: 248-936-2234. Business E-Mail: barnettm@marsusa.com.

BARNETT, MARTHA WALTERS, lawyer; b. Dade City, Fla., June 1, 1947; d. William Haywood and Helen (Hancock) Walters; m. Richard Rawls Barnett, Jan. 4, 1969; children: Richard Rawls, Sarah Walters. BA cum laude, Tulane U., 1969; JD cum laude, U. Fla. Coll. Law, 1973; LLD (hon.), Flagler Coll., 1995, Stetson U., 2000, Nova Southwestern U., 2000; LHD (hon.), DePaul U., 2001; LLD (hon.), Wake Forest U., 2003. Bar: Fla. 1973, U.S. Dist. Ct. (mid. and so. dists.) Fla. 1973, U.S. Ct. Appeals (3d, 4th and 11th cirs.) 1975, DC 1989. Assoc. Holland & Knight LLP, Tallahassee, 1973—78, ptnr., 1979—, chair, dirs. com., past chair. pub. law dept. Bd. dirs., v.p. Fla. Lawyers Prepaid Legal Svc. Corp., 1978—80, pres., 1980—82, legis. com., 1983—84, mem. commn. on access to justice, 1984—86, exec. coun. tax sect., 1987—88, exec. coun. pub. interest. sect., 1989—91; active Fla. Commn. Ethics, 1984—87, chairperson, 1986—87, Fla. Taxation and Budget Reform Commn., 1989—; legal adv. bd. Martindale-Hubbell/Lexis-Nexis, 1990—; chair Ho. of Dels., 1994—96; spkr., lectr. in field. Governor's appointee to the Fla. Commn. on Ethics State Fla., 1984—88, chair, Fla. Commn. on Ethics, 1986—87, mem. Governor's Select Com. on Workforce 2000, 1988—89, Governor's appointee to Constitutional Taxation & Budget Reform Commn., 1990—94, Governor's appointee to Constitution Revision Commn., 1997—98; mem. exec. com. Fla. Tax Watch, 2002; bd. dirs. Lawyers Com. Civil Rights Under Law; bd. adminstrs. Tulane Ednl. Fund; mem. Fla. Commn. on Human Rels., 1977—79; bd. trustee Fla. Tax Watch, 1983—; trustee U. Fla. Coll. Law, 1996—; mem. adv. coun. U. Fla. Law Ctr.; mem. Fla. Blue Key; founding mem., bd. dir. Fla. Women's Alliance; founding mem., past pres. Capital Women's Network, 1977—79; vice-chair Fla. Sales Tax on Svcs. Study Commn., 1986—87; mem. Fla. Coun. Econ. Edn., 1989—96, Fla. Edn. Found., 1991—96, Fla. Supreme Ct. Historical Soc.; bd. govs. Fla. Chamber, 2001. Named Nat. Women of Distinction, Girl Scouts U.S.A., 2002; named one of The 50 Most Influential Women Lawyers in Am., Nat. Law Jour., 1998; recipient Arabella Babb Mansfield award, Nat. Assn. Women Lawyers, 1996, Hillary Clinton Glass Cutter award, 1996, Alumnae of Distinction, U. Fla., 1997, Nat. Assn. Pub. Interest Law award, 1998, Newcomb Coll. Outstanding Alumna, 1999, Kate Stoneman award, Albany Law Sch., 1999, Nat. Legal Aid and Defender Assn. award, 2000, Disting. Alumna award, Tulane U., 2001, Medal of Honor award, Fla. Bar. Found., 2002, Rosemary Barkett award, Fla. Assn. Women Lawyers. Fellow: Am. Bar Found. (life); mem.: ABA (exec. coun. sect. on individual rights and responsibility 1974—86, chair, sect. individual rights and responsibilities 1984—85, task force on minorities in profession 1984—86, House of Delegates 1984—, mem. FJE Resources Com. 1985—89, commn. on legal problems of the elderly 1986—88, bd. govs. 1986—89, 1986—89, consortium on legal svcs and the pub. 1987—89, commn. on women in profession 1987—90, chair bd. govs. fin. com. 1988—89, chair, bd. govs. fin. com. 1988—89, long range planning com. 1988—91, chair commn. on pub. understanding about the law 1990—93, chair, commn. on pub. understanding about the law 1990—93, bd. editors ABA Jour. 1990—94, exec. coun. sect. legal edn. and admission to bar 1990—94, bd. editors, ABA Jour. 1990—96, chair, assembly resolutions com. 1991—94, ex-officio, Am. Bar Endowment 1994—96, ex-officio, Am. Bar Found. 1994—96, bd. govs. 1994—96, chair, Consortium on Legal Services and the Public 1996, exec. coun. sect. legal edn. and admission to bar 1996—99, mem. FJE Coun. 1996—99, Ctrl. European and Eurasian Law Initiative (CEELI) Exec. Bd. 1997—, pres.-elect 1999—2000, bd. govs. 1999—2001, bd. editors ABA Jour. 1999—2001, pres. 2000—01, mem. standing com. on legal aid to indigent defendents, mem. standing com. on prepaid legal svcs.), Tallahassee Women Lawyers Assn., Nat. Assn. Women Lawyers, Am. Judicature Soc. (bd. dir. 1986—89), Bar DC, Tallahassee Bar Assn., Fla. Bar Assn. (exec. coun. pub. interest law sect. 1989—91, mem. legis. com., mem. commn. on access to justice, exec. coun. of the tax sect.), Am. Law Inst., Nat. Inst. Dispute Resolution (sec.-treas. 1988—94, bd. dirs. 1988—94, Gov. appt. Fla. Constitution revision Commn. 1997—98), Phi Delta Phi, Phi Kappa Phi. Office: Holland & Knight LLP 315 S Calhoun St Ste 600 Tallahassee FL 32301 Office Phone: 850-425-5620. Business E-Mail: martha.barnett@hklaw.com.*

BARNETT, MARY LOUISE, elementary school educator; b. Exeter, Calif., May 1, 1941; d. Raymond Edgar Noble and Nena Lavere (Huckaby) Hope; m. Gary Allen Barnett, Aug. 9, l969; children: Alice Marie, Virginia Lynn. BA, U. of Pacific, 1963; postgrad., U. Mont., 1979-82, U. Idaho, 1984—. Cert. life elem. tchr., Calif.; standard elem. credential, Idaho; elem. tchr., Mont. Tchr. Colegio Americano de Torrean, Torreon, Coahuila, Mexico, 1962-63, Summer Sch. Primary Grades South San Francisco, 1963-66, Visalia (Calif.) Unified Sch. Dist., 1966-69, Sch. Dist. # 1, Missoula, Mont., 1969-73, Fort Shaw-Simms Sch. Dist., Fort Shaw, Mont., 1976-83, Sch. Dist. #25, Pocatello, Idaho, 1983-93, Greenacres Elem., Pocatello, 1993-94; tchr. 2d grade Bonneville Elem., Pocatello, 1994-95; tchr. Windsong Presch., Missoula, Mont., 1995-98, Headstart of Missoula, 1998-99; dir. Mary's Munchkins Presch., Missoula, 1999—. Beauty cons. Mary Kay. Foster mom Ednl. Found. Fgn. Students, Pocatello, Idaho, 1986-89; vol. Am. Heart Assn., Am. Cancer Soc., Pocatello, 1986-88, Bannock March of Dimes, Pocatello, 1988, Pocatello Laubach Lit. Tutoring, 1989; state v.p. membership, del. to P.W. Australian Mission Study; vice moderator Kendall Presbyn. Women, moderator, 1991—; moderator Kendall P.W. 1990-92; deacon, dean, treas. Presbyn. Ch., 1997—. Recipient scholarship Mont. Delta Kappa Gamma Edn. Soc., Great Falls, Mont., 1976, Great Falls AAUW, 1980, Great Falls Scottish Rite, 1981, Five Valleys Reading Assn., Missoula, Mont., 1982. Mem. AAUW (v.p. 2002—, mem. com. Idaho divsn. 1990-92, book chair 1995—, pres. Missoula chpt. 1998-2003, v.p. membership Missoula chpt. 2002—), ASCD, NEA, Nat. Coun. Tchrs. English, Internat. Reading Assn., Assn. Childhood Edn. Internat., Mont. Assn. Early Childhood Edn., Laubach Literacy Tutors (sec. 1993—), Bus. and Profl. Women Pocatello (sec. 1993—, contact advisor Missoula After 5 1999—), Mortar Bd., Alpha Lambda Delta, Delta Kappa Gamma (state fellowship chmn., corr. sec. Pocatello chpt. 1986-88, 2d v.p. 1994-96, chmn. Western expansion, 200-03), Moose (musician 1981-82), Order Eastern Star (musician 1984-85), Gamma Phi Beta (sec. Laubach Tutors 1993-95), Delta Kappa Gamma (2d v.p. chpt. 1996—, pres. 2000—). Democrat. Presbyn. Avocations: music, aquacise, aerobics, crafts, cross stitch. Home: 103 E Crestline Dr Missoula MT 59803-2412 Office: Lewis and Clark Sch 2901 Park Missoula MT 59801 Office Phone: 406-542-4035. E-mail: Gabmarybarnett@surfmk.com.

BARNETT, MEGAN A., lawyer; b. Columbus, Ohio, Feb. 21, 1971; BA, U. Va., 1993; JD, Yale Law Sch., 1997. Bar: S.C. Bar 1998, D.C. Bar 1999. Analyst Solomon Bros., N.Y., 1993—94; law clerk Hon. R. Lanier Anderson, 11th Cir. Ct. Appeals, Macon, Ga., 1997—98; assoc. Gibson, Dunn & Crutcher, Washington, 1998—2002; dean admissions Yale Law Sch., New Haven, 2002—. Editor: Yale Law Jour., 1995—97. Office: Yale Law Sch 127 Wall St New Haven CT 06511

BARNETT, MICHAEL, professional sports team executive; b. Olds, Alta., Can., Oct. 9, 1948; came to U.S., 1988; s. Terence R. and Mary M. Barnett; children: Jesse, Joey, Justin, Janie, Jenna. Student, St. Lawrence U., 1968-70; BS in Health and Phys. Edn., U. Calgary, 1973. Registered agent Nat. Hockey League Players Assn., Sports Lawyers Assn. Profl. hockey player L.I. Cougars (NAHL), 1973—74, Roanoka-Valley Rebels (SHL), 1974—75; founder, CEO Corpsport Internat. (merged with IMG), 1980—90; pres. hockey divsn. Internat. Mgmt. Group, 1990—2001; gen. mgr., alt. gov. Phoenix Coyotes, 2001—. Gen. mgr. Ninety-Nine All Stars. Named one of Top 100 Most Powerful in Sports, The Sporting News, 1994, 95, 96, 98, 99, 2000, One of Twelve Most Powerful in Hockey, Hockey News, 1995. Mem. U.S.A. Hockey, U.S. Golf Assn. Achievements include former agent for NHL players such as Wayne Gretzky, Brett Hull, Jaromir Jagr, and Sergei Federov. Avocations: golf, running. Home: 8130 N Via de Lago Scottsdale AZ 85258 Office: Glendale Arena 9400 W Maryland Ave Glendale AZ 85305 Business E-Mail: mike.barnett@phoenixcoyotes.com.

BARNETT, PATRICIA ANN, development professional; b. Culver City, Calif., Jan. 25; d. Howard Taft and Sarah (Ross) B. BJ, U. Tex., 1978; MLA, So. Meth. U., 2002. Program specialist Dallas C. of C., 1978-79, comm. specialist, 1979-81; mgr. pub. rels. Trailways Corp., Dallas, 1981-82, dir. pub. rels., 1982-85; sr. account exec. Keller-Crescent Co., Dallas, 1985-87; dir. comm. Office of Pvt. Sector Initiatives The White House, Washington, 1987-89; dir. pub. affairs United Way Am., Alexandria, Va., 1989-91; dir. pub. rels. Dally Advt., Ft. Worth, 1992-94; dir. corp. and found. rels. So. Meth. U., Dallas, 1994-96, dir. major gifts, 1996—2001; dir. devel. Dedman Coll., 2001—. Mem.: Jr. League Dallas. Republican. Avocations: history, travel, literature, folk art, bookbinding. Office: So Meth U PO Box 750402 Dallas TX 75275-0402 Office Phone: 214-768-2691. E-mail: tbarnett@smu.edu.

BARNETT, PATRICK SHAWN, music educator; b. Woodstock, Ill., Oct. 13, 1965; s. Arlis Wade and Clara Marie Barnett; m. Lisa Maureen Kiener-Barnett; 1 child, Sophie. B of Music Edn., No. Ill. U., 1987; M of Music Edn., DePaul U., 1993. Cert. tchg. Mid. sch. music tchr. Round Lake (Ill.) Area Schools, 1988—89, Villa Park (Ill.) Sch. Dist. 45, 1989—90; organist St. Johns Luth. Ch., Woodstock, 1980—83, Messiah Luth. Ch., Chgo., 1983—84; music dir. 1st Presbyn. Ch., Woodstock, 1985—87, St. Lukes Luth. Ch., Glen Ellyn, Ill., 1987—88, Luth. Ch. of St. Phillip, Glenview, Ill., 1988—91; organist Redeemer Luth. Ch., Highland Park, Ill., 1993—94; assoc. music dir. Holy Cross Cath. Ch., Deerfield, Ill., 1994—98; min. of music St. Michaels Luth. Ch., LaGrange Park, Ill., 1998—99; assoc. music dir. Divine Savior Parish, Downers Grove, Ill., 1999—2000; choral dir. Maine Twp. H.S. East, Park Ridge, Ill., 1990—; assoc. music dir. Gloria Dei Luth. Ch., Downers Grove, Ill., 2001—03, dir. music, 2003—. Dir. of choir Ill. Ambs. Music, Littleton, 1998—2000. Mem. Boy Scouts Am. Mem.: NEA, Ill. Music Educators Assn. (chair dist. 7 chorus 1999—2002), Am. Guild of Organists, Am. Choral Dirs. Assn. (chair youth and student activitites 1991—95, dir. youth and student activities 1991—95). Liberal. Avocation: home rehabbing. Office: Maine Twp H S E 2601 W Dempster St Park Ridge IL 60068

BARNETT, PEGGY G., music educator; b. Dallas, Sept. 15, 1935; d. Garnald Morris and Thelma Christean (Turner) Gregory; m. John Curtis Jones, Aug. 24, 1957 (div. June 1980); children: Lewis Gregory, Michael Wayne, Scott Carlton, Cynthia Luanne; m. Edward Ralph Burnett, Aug. 31, 2002. BS in Home Econs., Baylor U., 1956; MS in Housing and Interior Design, Okla. State U., 1957; student, Rykyu Classical Acad., 1964—68, Hampton Inst., 1968—70. Nat. cert. tchr. music; cert. profl. master. Pvt. practice piano tchr., 1964—2002; founder, dir., tchr. piano, thcr. music theory Music Arts Conservatory, Albuquerque, 1984—2002; ret., 2002. Mem. piano faculty Summer Piano Camp at Mary Hardin-Baylor U., Belton, Tex., summers 1980, 86. Performed two-piano and duet music, 1980-85; performed with ptnr. in master classes for well-known duettists. Choir dir., pianist and organist various chs., Okinawa, 1964-68, Hampton, Va., 1969-72, Las Vegas, Nev., 1972-74; talent judge Miss Teen Pageant, Albuquerque, 1993-96. Mem. Profl. Music Tchrs. N.Mex. (state membership chair 1982-83, pres. 1986-88, adjudicator 1975—, Tchr. of Yr. 1998), Music Tchrs. Nat. Assn., Nat. Guild Piano Tchrs., Tex. Music Tchrs. Assn., Abilene Music Tchrs. Assn. Avocations: downhill skiing, hiking, gardening.

BARNETT, PHILIP, librarian, educator; b. N.Y.C., May 26, 1946; s. Paul and Beatrice (Blume) Barnett; m. Sarah Ellen Friend; children: David, Reena. BS in Chemistry, Bklyn. Coll., 1967; MLS, Columbia U., 1981; PhD in Biochemistry, Rutgers U., 1973. USPHS postdoctoral fellow NYU, Tuxedo, 1972-74; postdoctoral staff assoc. Columbia U., N.Y.C., 1974-81; indexer H. W. Wilson Co., Bronx, NY, 1981-82; info. scientist Ayerst Labs., N.Y.C., 1982-87; corp. libr. Becton Dickinson Inc., Franklin Lakes, NJ, 1987-88; sr. info. scientist Warner-Lambert Co., Morris Plains, NJ, 1988-90; assoc. prof. CUNY, N.Y.C., 1990—. Author (with others): Methods Enzymology, 1982; contbr. articles to sci. jours. Mem.: AAAS, Am. Chem. Soc. Democrat. Jewish. Office: CUNY Sci Engring Libr Convent Ave and 138th St New York NY 10031-9127 Business E-Mail: pbarnett@ccny.cuny.edu.

BARNETT, PRESTON B., lawyer, communications executive; b. Monroeville, Ala., Aug. 4, 1946; m. Billie Barnett. BA in History, B in Bus., Birmingham-So. Coll.; JD, U. Ala. Bar: Ala., Ga. With various acctg. firms; v.p., gen. tax counsel Cox Enterprises, Atlanta, 1979—. Mem.: Tax Execs. Inst. (pres. Atlanta chpt. 1991—92, regional v.p. 1996—97), Ga. Bar Assn., Ala. Bar Assn., Birmingham-So. Coll. Nat. Alumni Assn. (pres. 2000—01). Office: Cox Enterprises 6205 Peachtree Dunwoody Rd Atlanta GA 30328*

BARNETT, R(ALPH) MICHAEL, theoretical physicist, educational agency administrator; b. Gulfport, Miss., Jan. 25, 1944; s. Herbert Chester and Lisa Margaret (Kielley) B.; children: Leilani Pinho, Julia Alexandra, Russell Alan. BS, Antioch Coll., 1966; PhD, U. Chgo., 1971. Postdoctoral fellow U. Calif., Irvine, 1972-74; rsch. fellow Harvard U., Cambridge, Mass., 1974-76; rsch. assoc. Stanford (Calif.) Linear Accelerator Ctr., 1976-83; vis. physicist Inst. Theoretical Physics U. Calif., Santa Barbara, 1983-84; staff scientist Lawrence Berkeley Nat. Lab., 1984-89, sr. scientist and head particle data group, 1990—; co-dir. QuarkNet Ednl. Project, 1999—. V.p. Contemporary Physics Edn. Project, 1987-98, pub. info. coor. Am. Phys. Soc. Dvsn. of Particles and Fields, 1994-97; edn. coord. ATLAS experiment at CERN, Geneva; prodr. film: The Atlas Experiment, 2000. Author: Teachers' Resource Book on Fundamental Particles and Interactions, 1988, Review of Particle Physics, 1990, 6th edit., 2002, Particle Physics—One Hundred Years of Discoveries, 1996, Guide to Experimental Particle Physics Literature, 1993, 2d edit., 1996, The Charm of Strange Quarks, Mysteries and Revolutions of Particle Physics, 2000, (chart) Fundamental Particles and Interactions, 1987, 4th edit., 1999, World-Wide Web feature, The Particle Adventure, 1995, rev. edit. 2000, (CD ROM) The Quark Adventure, 2000. Fellow Am. Phys. Soc. (pub. info. coord. divsn. particles and fields 1994-97, taskforce on informing the public, chair-elect Calif. sect.), Am. Assn. Physics Tchrs. (v.p., sect. North Calif.). Achievements include research on the Standard Model and its extensions, including studies of nature and validity of quantum chromodynamics; analyses of neutral current couplings; calculations of the production of heavy quarks; predictions of properties and decays of supersymmetric particles and higgs bosons. Office: Lawrence Berkeley Nat Lab MS-50-308 1 Cyclotron Rd Berkeley CA 94720-0001

BARNETT, RICHARD CHAMBERS, historian, educator; b. Davenport, Fla., Apr. 27, 1932; s. Jones Richard and Helen June (Chambers) B.; m. Betty May Tribble, Oct. 18, 1957; children— Amelia Carlton, Colin Warwick BA, Wake Forest Coll., 1953; M.Ed., U. N.C., 1954, PhD, 1963. Instr., acting chmn. dept. social sci. Gardner-Webb Coll., 1956-58; instr. history Wake Forest U., Winston-Salem, N.C., 1961-62, asst. prof., 1962-67, assoc. prof., 1967-76, prof., chmn. dept. history, 1968-75, 83-87, acting dean Grad. Sch., 1979; retired. Contbg. author history and polit. sci. vols., also articles and book revs. Pres Winston-Salem-Forsyth PTA, 1969-71; bd. mgrs. N.C. PTA, 1971-73, exec. com., 1972-73, life mem.; adv. com. N.C. Bd. Edn., 1973-76. Served with CIC, AUS, 1954-56 Southeastern Inst. Medieval and Renaissance Studies fellow, summer 1974 Mem. Am. Hist. Assn. (pres. elect N.C. conf. 1991-92, pres. 1992-93), AAUP, Carolinas Symposium Brit. Studies (pres. 1979-80), So. Conf. Brit. Studies (pres. 1990-92), N.Am. Conf. Brit. Studies (coun. 1990-92), Danforth Assocs. Home: 2130 Royall Dr Winston Salem NC 27106-5234

BARNETT, ROBERT BRUCE, lawyer, educator; b. Waukegan, Ill., Aug. 26, 1946; s. Bernard and Betty Jane (Simon) Barnett; m. Rita Lynn Braver, Apr. 10, 1972; 1 child, Meredith Jane. BA, U. Wis., 1968; JD, U. Chgo., 1971. Bar: D.C. 1971. Law clk. to Hon. John Minor Wisdom U.S. Ct. Appeals (5th cir.), 1971-72; law clk. to assoc. justice Byron R. White U.S. Supreme Ct., Washington, 1972-73; legis. asst. Sen. Walter F. Mondale, Washington, 1973-75; assoc. Williams & Connolly, Washington, 1975-78, ptnr., 1979—. Adj. prof. Georgetown Law Sch., 1973—80. Trustee John F. Kennedy Ctr. Performing Arts, 1994—2004, sr. counsel, 2005—; mem. bd. visitors Sanford Inst. of Pub. Policy, Duke U., 1998—2001, U. Chgo. Law Sch., 2001—04; mem. bd. visitors LaFollette Sch. Pub. Affairs U. Wis., 2004—. Named an 75 Best Lawyers, Washingtonian mag., 2002. Office: Williams & Connolly LLP 725 12th St NW Washington DC 20005-5901 Office Phone: 202-434-5034.

BARNETT, ROBERT GLENN, lawyer; b. Oxford, Miss., July 30, 1933; s. Arden and Vera (Turner) B.; m. Rae Ragsdale, Apr. 21, 1962; children: Laura Lee, Mary Melissa. BA, U. Miss., 1959, JD, 1961. Ptnr. Houston & Barnett, Southaven, Miss., 1961-63, Neal, Houston, Elliott & Barnett, Jackson, Miss., 1963-65, Barnett & Barnett, Jackson, Miss., 1965-70; legal counsel Deposit

Guaranty Nat. Bank, Jackson, 1970-79, gen. counsel, sec. to bd., 1979-95; counsel Butler, Snow, O'Mara, Stevens and Cannada, Jackson, 1996—. Vis. prof. U. Miss. Law Sch., Oxford, Miss., 1978-79, 85; banking law course coord., lectr. Sch. Banking of the South, Baton Rouge, 1978-79. Pres. Family Services Assn., Jackson, 1970-71; bd. dirs. Community Services Assn., 1968-70; bd. govs. Jackson Symphony Orch. Assn., 1981-85. Lt. (j.g.) USNR, 1954-58; capt. USNR, 1979. Fellow Young Lawyers of Miss. Bar (pres. 1995-96); mem. ABA (banking law com. 1982—), Miss. Bar Assn. (2d v.p. 1968-69), Jackson Legal Aid Bd. Trustees (pres. 1965-67), Miss. Bankers Assn. (chmn. bank lawyers com.), Miss. Jr. Bar Assn. (pres. 1967-68), Miss. Corp. Counsel Assn. (pres. 1988), So. Conf. Bank House Counsel (chmn. 1989), Lions (pres. North Jackson chpt. 1967-68), River Hills Tennis Club (dir. 1979-82, Patrick Farm Golf Club, Whisper Lake Golf Club, Oxford U. Club. Baptist. Office: PO Box 22567 Jackson MS 39225-2567 E-mail: bbarnett@netdoor.com.

BARNETT, ROCHELLE, accountant; M in Acct., C.W. Post Coll. CPA N.Y., Fla., Conn. With Mark Paneth & Shron LLP, 1979, ptnr. Woodbury, NY, 1991—. Adv. bd. Touro Law Sch. Named Woman of Distinction, March of Dimes, 1995. Mem.: AICPA, Nat. Assn. Women Bus. Owners (former exec. v.p., former treas. Long Island chpt., chairperson comm. of 100), Long Island Assn., N.Y. State Soc. CPA (former chair coop. with bankers & other credit grantors com., former bd. dirs.), N.Y. Oil Heat Assn., Ail Heat Inst. Long Island. Office: Marks Paneth & Shrun LLP 88 Froehlich Farm Blvd Woodbury NY 11797 E-mail: sbarnett@markspaneth.com.

BARNETT, ROSALIND CHAIT, psychologist; m. Nat Durlach, Aug. 21, 1988. BA, Queens Coll., 1959; MA, Harvard, 1962; PhD, Harvard U., 1964. Rsch. fellow Harvard Bus. Sch., Soldier's Field, Mass., 1964—72; rsch. assoc. Radcliffe Inst., Cambridge, Mass., 1973—77; sr. rsch. assoc. Heller Grad. Sch. Brandeis U., Waltham, Mass., 1977—80; sr. rsch. assoc. Wellesley (Mass.) Coll., Ctr. Rsch. on Women, 1979—96; sr. fellow in residence Radcliffe Inst. Advanced Study, Cambridge, 1993—2001; exec. dir. Cmty., Families and Work Program, Brandeis U.; sr. scientist Women's Studies Rsch. Ctr. Brandeis U., Waltham, Mass., 1996—. Author: Same Difference: How Gender Myths are Hurting Our Relationships, Our Children, and Our Jobs (Goldsmith Rsch. Award, Harvard U., Kennedy Sch. of Govt., 1999), Gender and Stress, She Works, He Works (Nat. Books for a Better Life Award, 1996), Behavioral Science Concepts in Case Analysis: The Relationship of Ideas to Management Action, 1968, The Competent Women: Perspectives on Socialization, 1978, Beyond Sugar and Spice, 1979, Lifeprints: New Patterns of Love and Work for Today's Women, 1985; contbr. articles to profl. publs. Mem. Dem. Town Com., Weston, Mass., 2004—. Recipient award for Outstanding Rsch., Am. Pers. and Guidance Assn., 1972, Grad. Soc. Disting. Achievement medal, Radcliffe Coll., 1988, Nat. Books for a Better Life award, Multiple Sclerosis Found., 1996, Best Paper award, Jour. Orgnl. Behavior, 1997, citation of excellence, ANBAR, 1997, Goldsmith Rsch. award, Harvard U., Kennedy Sch. of Govt., 1999; grantee, NIMH, 1988—92, Alfred P. Sloan Found., 1996—99, Nat. Inst. Occupl. Safety and Health, 1999—2002, Alfred P. Sloan Found., 2001—04, 2004—; hon. fellow, Woodrow Wilson Found., 1959. Fellow: APA; mem.: Coun. on Contemporary Families, Nat. Coun. Family Rels. Office: Brandeis U WSRC Mailstop 079 515 South Street Waltham MA 02453-2720 Office Phone: 781-736-2287. E-mail: rbarnett@brandeis.edu.

BARNETT, SAMUEL TREUTLEN, personnel director, consultant; m. Rena H. Earnhardt, Sept. 22, 2001; children: Elizabeth L., Katharine T., Emily R., Alexander W. BA, Wesleyan U., 1969; MEd, Temple U., 1973, EdD, 1975. Tchr. The Haverford Sch., 1969-74; leadership devel. specialist Phila. Sch. Dist., 1974-75; freelance cons., 1971-76; tng. cons. U.S. Office Personnel Mgmt., Pa., 1976-79; founder, chief cons. Barnett Internat. a subsidiary PAREXEL Internat., Media, Pa., 1979-99; lead ptnr. N.Am. pharm. sector mgmt. consulting svcs. Pricewaterhouse Coopers, Phila., 1999—2002; lead ptnr. Am. Life Sci. Pharm. Practice IBM Bus. Consultancy Svcs., Phila., 2002—05, ret., 2005; bd. dirs. Astalis Ltd., Fairfield, NJ, 2004—, Medifacts Internat., Rockville, Md., 2005—. Mem. adv. bd. PharmaStar Ltd.; spkr. in field. Contbr. articles to profl. jours. Mem.: Drug Info. Assn. Home: 230 S Ridley Creek Rd Media PA 19063-4216 Personal E-mail: sam.barnett3@verizon.net.

BARNETT, SUE, nurse; b. Waukegan, Ill., Apr. 8, 1956; d. Jackie Laverne and Catherine Mary (LaMarche) B. AAS in Nursing, Elgin (Ill.) C.C., 1977. RN, Ill.; ANCC cert. in psychiat. and mental health nurse. Home health nurse Adv. Health Care, Oak Brook, Ill., 1977-97; staff nurse Fox Valley Nursing Home, South Elgin, Ill., 1978-79, Elgin Mental Health Ctr., 1979—. Music min., vol. St. John Neumann Ch., St. Charles, Ill., 1977—; vol. Labarus House Shelter, St. Charles, 1997—. Mem. Ill. Nurses Assn. (local unit sec. 1981-84, local unit grievance rep. 1984-96, local unit vice chair 1984-94, conv. rep. 1990-92). Roman Catholic. Avocations: reading, singing, volunteer work. Office: Elgin Mental Health Ctr-Gahagan Unit 750 S State St Elgin IL 60123-7692

BARNETT, THOMAS GLEN, manufacturing executive; b. Olney, Ill., Aug. 15, 1946; s. Burl and Florence Ann (Gant) B.; m. Diana Kay O'Dell, Jan. 27, 1968; children— Kevin Thomas, Kelli Lyn. BS in Acctg., Millikin U., Decatur, Ill., 1968. C.P.A., Mo., Ill. Staff acct. Arthur Young & Co. (C.P.A.'s), Chgo., 1968-70, sr. acct., 1970-73, audit mgr., 1973-75; dir. internal audit Chromalloy Am. Corp., St. Louis, 1975-76, asst. controller, 1976-78, v.p., controller, 1978-80, exec. v.p. fin., 1979-87; chief fin. officer Marsh Co., Belleville, Ill., 1987-92, pres., chief operating officer, 1992—99; pres., CEO Union Fin. Group, 1999—2002; pres. Barnett & Assocs., LLC, 2002—04; pres., COO Jims Formal Wear, 2004—. Bd. dir. Jr. Achievement Gateway East, Belleville, 1988-95, United Way Metro East, Belleville, 1988-95, Meml. Hosp., 1991—, Mem. Found., Inc., 1990-95. Mem. AICPA, Fin. Execs. Inst., Mo. Soc. C.P.A.s, St. Clair Country Club (pres. 1988-89). Republican. Presbyterian. Office: One Tuxedo Park Trenton IL 62293 Office Phone: 618-224-9211 ext. 3131. Business E-Mail: tombarnett@jimsfw.com.

BARNETT, VIVIAN ENDICOTT, curator; b. Putnam, Conn., July 8, 1944; d. George and Vivian (Wood) Endicott; m. Peter Herbert Barnett, July 1, 1967; children: Sarah, Alexander. AB magna cum laude, Vassar Coll., 1965; MA, NYU, 1971; postgrad., CUNY, 1979—81. Research asst. Solomon R. Guggenheim Mus., N.Y.C., 1973-77, curatorial assoc., 1978-79, assoc. curator, 1980-81, rsch. curator, 1981-82, curator, 1982-91; dir. Roethel Benjamin Archive at Guggenheim Mus., N.Y.C., 1991—. Author: (book) The Guggenheim Museum: Justin K. Thannhauser Collection, 1978, The Guggenheim Museum Collection 1900-1980, Kandinsky at the Guggenheim, 1983, 100 Works by Modern Masters from the Guggenheim Museum, 1984, Kandinsky and Sweden, 1989, Kandinsky in Major Collections in the West, 1989, Kandinsky Watercolours: Catalogue Raisonnè, vol I 1900-1921, 1992, Kandinsky Watercolours: Catalogue Raisonnè, vol II 1922-1944, 1994, Kleine Freuden, 1992, Das bunte Leben: Kandinsky in Lenbachhaus, 1995, The Blue Four: Feininger, Jawlensky, Kandinsky, Klee in the New World, 1997, The Blue Four Collection at the Norton Simon Museum, 2002; contbg. author: Kandinsky in Paris: 1934-44, 1985, Exiles and Emigres: 1933-1945, 1997, The Joy of Color: The Merzbacher Collection, 1998, Mies in America, 2001, Die Brucke in Dresden, 2001, Art of Tomorrow: Hilla Rebay and Solomon Guggenheim, 2005, Ari of Tomorrow: Hilla Rebay and Solomon R. Guggenheim, 2005. Fellow John Simon Guggenheim, 1990, Inst. Advanced Study, Princeton, 2003—04. Mem.: Coll. Art Assn. Am., Internat. Coun. Museums, Soc. Kandinsky (sec. 1992—2001). Office: Solomon R Guggenheim Mus 1071 5th Ave New York NY 10128-0112 Personal E-mail: vbarnett@att.net.

BARNETT, WILLIAM ARNOLD, economics professor; b. Boston, Oct. 30, 1941; s. Marcus Jack and Elizabeth Leah (Forman) B.; m. Melinda Gentry, Sept. 1, 1991. BS, MIT, 1963; MBA, U. Calif., Berkeley, 1965; MS, Carnegie Mellon U., 1972, PhD, 1974. System devel. engr., Apollo Project, Rocketdyne div. Rockwell Internat. Corp., Canoga Park, Calif., 1963-67; research econometrician Bd. Govs., Fed. Reserve System, Washington, 1973-81; Stuart Centennial prof. econs. U. Tex., Austin, 1981-90; prof. econs. Washington U., St. Louis, 1990—; Oswald Disting. prof. macroeconomics U. of Kans., 2002—. Vis. prof. econs. U. Aix-Marseille, Aix-en-Provence, France, 1979, Duke U., Durham, N.C., 1987-88; organizer ann. symposia in econ. theory and econometrics; assoc. dir. Ctr. for Econ. Rsch., U. Tex., Austin, 1981-90. Author: Consumer Demand and Labor Supply, 1981; editor three spl. edits. Jour. of Econometrics, 1979, 80, 85, Cambrige U. Press Monograph series, 1985—, Cambridge U. Press Jour. Macroeconomic Dynamics, 1997—; assoc. editor Jour. of Bus. and Econ. Stats., 1982-97; contbr. approx. 75 articles to profl. jours. Contract selection panel mem. NIH, Washington, 1983; cons. World Bank, Washington, 1985. R.K. Mellon Found. fellow, 1971-73; rsch. grantee NSF, Washington, 1977-89, Hogg Found., Houston, 1983. Fellow ICC Inst. (sr., editor 1983—), Am. Statis. Assn. (assoc. editor 1982—, fellow 1989—, program chair 1992—), Jour. Econometrics (charter fellow 1989—); mem. Inst. Math. Stats., Econometric Soc. (contbr. to jour.), Am. Econ. Assn., MIT Club (St. Louis). Home: 1904 Inverness Dr Lawrence KS 66047-1832 Office: U Kans Dept Econs Lawrence KS 66045

BARNETT, WILLIAM DAVID, retired surgeon; b. Thornton, Tex., Jan. 24, 1928; MD, U. Tex. Med. Br., 1952. Cert. colon and rectal surgery, surgery. Intern Kans. City Gen. Hosp., 1952-53; resident Parkland Meml. Hosp., Dallas, 1955-59; fellow in colon rectal surgery Dr. R.J. Rowe, Dallas, 1959-60; with Baylor U. Med. Ctr., Dallas, Presbyn. Hosp., Tex., St. Paul Med. Ctr., Tex., Drs. Hosp., Tex., Baylor-Garland (Tex.) Med. Ctr. With U. Tex. S.W. Med. Ctr. Mem. ACS, AMA, Am. Soc. Colon Rectal Surgery, So. Surg. Assn., Western Surg. Assn., Tex. Surg. Assn. Office: 6211 W Northwest Hwy G226 Dallas TX 75225

BARNETTE, CURTIS HANDLEY, steel company executive, lawyer; b. St. Albans, W.Va., Jan. 9, 1935; s. Curtis Franklin and Garnett Drucella (Robinson) Barnette; m. Loris Joan Harner, Dec. 28, 1957; children: Curtis Kevin, James David. AB with High Honors, W.Va. U., 1956; postgrad. (Fulbright scholar), U. Manchester, 1956—57; JD, Yale U., 1962; grad. advanced mgmt. program, Harvard U., 1974—75; LLD (hon.), W.Va. U., 1995, DeSales U., 1996, U. Charleston, 1998, Lehigh U., 1999, Moravian Coll., 2002. Cert. Conn., 1962, Pa., 1968, D.C., 1988, W.Va., 1990. Atty. Wiggin & Dana, New Haven, 1962—67, Bethlehem (Pa.) Steel Corp., 1967—92, sec., 1976—92, gen. counsel, 1977—92, sr. v.p., 1985—92, chmn., CEO, 1992—2000, also bd. dirs., 1986—2000; of counsel Skadden, Arps, Slate, Meagher & Flom, LLP, 2000—. Lectr. U. Md., 1958—59; law tutor Yale U., 1962—67; chmn. bd. dirs. Am. Iron and Steel Inst., 1997, dir., 1992—2000; bd. dirs. Met Life Ins. Co., MetLife Inc., Lehigh Valley Partnership; chmn. Internat. Iron and Steel Inst., 1994—95, dir., 1992—2000; Comenius prof., exec. in residence, trustee Moravian Coll., 2000—. Trustee Lehigh U., 1993—2004; Pa. Soc., 1993—; mem. Adminstrv. Conf. U.S., 1988—89; bd. govs. W.Va. U., 2002—, chmn. bd. govs., 2002—04; dir. W.Va. U. Found., 1982—, chair, 1987—88; mem. pres.'s adv. com. Trade Policy and Negotiations, 1989—2001; mem. adv. com. Coal Commn., 1990, Pa. 21st Century Environ. Com., 1997—98. With Counterintelligence Corps U.S. Army, 1957—59, maj. USAR, 1959—67. Mem.: ABA, Pa. Soc. (dir.), Nat. Mus. Indsl. History (chmn.), Pa. Pk. Found., Pa. Bus. Roundtable (dir. 1986—2000, chmn. 1994—95), Bus. Roundtable (policy com. 1992—2000), Bus. Coun., Pa. Chamber Bus. and Industry (dir. 1985—93), Am. Law Inst., Am. Soc. Corp. Secs. (chmn. 1986), Assn. Gen. Counsel (pres. 1988—90), W.Va. Bar Assn., DC Bar Assn., Northampton County Bar Assn., Conn. Bar Assn., Pa. Bar Assn., Met. Club Washington, Univ. Club Washington, Blooming Grove Hunting and Fishing Club, Bethlehem Club, Lobolly, Links, Saucon Valley Country Club, Yale Club NYC, Phi Beta Kappa, Phi Delta Phi, Phi Alpha Theta, Beta Theta Pi. Home: 1112 Prospect Ave Bethlehem PA 18018-4914 Office: 1170 8th Ave Bethlehem PA 18016-7699 also: 1440 New York Ave NW Washington DC 20005-2111 Office Phone: 202-371-7252. E-mail: hbarnett@skadden.com.

BARNEVIK, PERCY NILS, electrical company executive; b. Simrishamn, Sweden, Feb. 13, 1941; s. Einar and Anna Barnevik; m. Aina Orvarsson, 1963; 3 children. MBA, Gothenburg Sch. Econs., Sweden, 1964; postgrad., Stanford U., 1965-66; TechnDr honoris causa, U. Linkoping, Sweden, 1989; Econ. Dr. honoris causa, U. Gothenburg, Sweden, 1991; JD (hon.), Babson Coll., 1995; Sci. Dr. honoris causa, Cranfield U., 1998; D (hon.), U. Manches, 1999. With The Johnson Group, Sweden, 1966-69, Sandvik AB, Sandviken, Sweden, 1969-80, group controller, 1969-75; pres. U.S. affiliate, 1975-79; exec. v.p. Sandvik, Sweden, 1979-80; pres., chief exec. officer ASEA, 1980-87; chmn. Sandvik AB, 1983—2002, hon. chmn., 2002—; pres., CEO Asea Brown Boveri Ltd., 1988-96, chmn., CEO, 1996-97; chmn. Investor AB, Sweden, 1997—2002, ABB Ltd., 1997—2001, AstraZeneca PLC, U.K., 1999—. Bd. dirs. GM, Detroit. Office: Astra Zeneca PLC 15 Stanhope Gate W1G 5NQ London England also: Investor AB S-10332 Stockholm Sweden

BARNEWALL, MARILYN MACGRUDER, retired banker; b. Indpls. d. Robert Danforth MacGruder and Hester Bruce Wooden Brown; m. Gordon Grovsnor Barnewall, Aug. 1970 (div. Jan. 1973); children: John Clyde, Katherine Barnewall Coomer. Graduate degree, Colo. U., 1978. Reporter Wyoming Eagle, Cheyenne, 1956—57; mgr. Combined Ins. Co., Denver, 1961—65; dir. public relations Nat. Camera, 1966—68; mag. editor, asst. to pub. Bell Publs., 1968—70; v.p. mgr. United Bank, Denver, 1972—79; pres., CEO MacGruder Agency Inc., Cin., 1979—93; editorialist Grand Junction (Colo.) Free Press, 2003—, Bus. Reform, 2004—. Expert witness for equal credit for women Colo. State Legis., 1977. Author: A Banker's Pragmatic Approach to the Upscale, 1982, Profitable Private Banking: The Complete Blueprint, 1986, National Private Banking Profitability Survey, 1987, Warren, Gorham & LaMont National Private Banking Profitability Survey, 1987, Profitable Private Bankning: The Complete Blueprint, 1989. Bd. mem. Camp Fire Girls, Colo. State U. Family Action Ctr., Am. for Effective Law Enforcement, United Negro Coll. Fund, Metro Denver Urban Coalition, Big Brothers. Mem.: Leukemia Soc. of Am. (chair, fundraiser 1976). Avocations: writing, photography, genealogy, travel, cooking. Home: 679 Brentwood Dr Palisade CO 81526 Personal E-mail: marilynmacg@gmail.com.

BARNEY, AUSTIN DUNHAM, II, real estate developer; b. Hartford, Conn., Apr. 27, 1945; s. Philip Cushman and Elizabeth Cole (Freeman) B.; m. Susan C. Rumney, Aug. 26, 1976 (div. Mar. 1998); children: Austin C. D. III, Amanda Brandegee. BA in Polit. Sci., Yale U., 1967; MPA, Syracuse U., 1969. Lic. real estate broker, Conn., N.Y., Mass.; lic. life/health ins., securities, Conn.; cert. ins. cons., risk profl. Mgmt. asst. U. Hartford, Conn., 1967-68; jr./sr. planner Hartford Police Dept., 1969-70; sr. planner Commn. on City Plan City of Hartford, 1970; sr. adminstrv. analyst fin. dept. City of Hartford Budget and Rsch. Divsn., 1970-71, prin. adminstrv. analyst fin. dept., 1971-72; dir. land use policy planning State of Conn., Dept. Environ. Protection, 1972-73; exec. dir. Environ. Ctrs. Inc., 1973-75; pvt. practice cons., 1975-76; dir. natural resources mgmt. and community design Westledge Ctr. for Edn., 1976-78; sr. cons. corp. citizenship Cigna Corp. (Conn. Gen. Ins. Corp.), 1979-82; dir. contbns. and civic affairs Cigna Corp., Conn. Gen. Ins. Corp., 1982-84; pres., founder Farmvest, Inc., 1984—; prin. Bus. Planning Assocs., 1991-96; pres. Life Legacy Advisors, LLC, West Simsbury, Conn., 1996—. Dir. Spiritus Wines, Inc., Aid to Artesans; ptnr. Folly Farm Assocs., 1983-90; pres. Folly Farm, Inc., 1983-90. Zoning commr. Town of Simsbury, Conn., 1976—, sec., 1993—; del. People's Republic China, Yale-China Assn., fall 1979, 80; corporator Hartford Pub. Libr., 1981—; corporator The Ctr. Families and Children, 1996—; bd. dirs., exec. com. Riverfront Recapture, Inc., 1981-90; bd. trustees Hartford Art Sch., 1969-2003, pres. 1984-86, 96-2003, hon. trustee, 2003—; bd. dirs. Conn. Trust for Hist. Preservation, 1982-85, The Nature Conservancy, treas. 1986-89, vice-chmn., 1989-2000, Oak Leaf award, 1995; bd. dirs. U. Conn. Found., 1988-92, Ensign-Bickford Found., 1987-93, v.p., 1989-93; bd. dirs. Ea. States Expo., 1989--; chmn. Conn. trustees 1993-96; elector Wadsworth Atheneum, 1983—; bd. dirs., chmn. fin. com. Conn. Earth Day 20, Inc., 1990; regent U. Hartford, 1980-86, 90-2003; mem. Simsbury Open Space Preservation Commn., 2002—. Recipient Oak Leaf award Nature Conservancy, 1995, Pubs. Svc. award State of Conn., 2001, Gold medal for outstanding leadership excellence Hartford Art Sch., 2003. Mem. Nat. Assn. Life Underwriters, Am. Assn. Life Underwriters, Conn. Assn. Life Underwriters, Hartford Assn. Life Underwriters, Conn. Life Leaders. Personal E-mail: acdb2@att.net.

BARNEY, CAROL ROSS, architect; b. Chgo., Apr. 12, 1949; d. Chester Albert and Dorothy Valeria (Dusiewicz) Ross; m. Alan Fredrick Barney, Mar. 22, 1970; children: Ross Fredrick, Adam Shafer, John Ross. BArch, U. Ill., 1971. Registered architect, Ill. Assoc. architect Holabird & Root, Chgo., 1972-79; prin. architect Orput Assoc., Inc., Wilmette, Ill., 1979-81; prin. architect, pres. Ross Barney & Jankowski, Inc., Chgo., 1981—, also bd. dirs. Studio prof. Ill. Inst. Tech., Chgo., 1993-94; asst. prof. U. Ill., Chgo., 1976-78. Prin. works include Cesar Chavez Elem. Sch., Chgo., Glendale Heights (Ill.) Post Office, Little Village Acad. Pub. Sch., Fed. Bldg., Oklahoma City. Plan commr. Village of Wilmette, 1986-88, mem. Econ. Devel. Commn., 1988-90, chmn. Appearance Rev. Commn., 1990-2000; trustee Children's Home and Aid Soc. Ill., Chgo., 1986—; mem. adv. bd. Small Bus. Ctr. for Women, Chgo., 1985—. Recipient Fed. Design Achievement award, 1992; Francis J. Plym travelling fellow, 1983. Fellow AIA (bd. dirs. Chgo. chpt. 1978-80, v.p. 1981-82, Disting. Svc. award Chgo. chpt. 1978, Ill. Coun. 1978, Firm award 1995, Honor award 1991, 94, 99, 2002, Thomas Jefferson award 2005); mem. Nat. Coun. Archtl. Registration Bds. (cert.), Chgo. Women in Architecture (founding pres. 1978-79), Chgo. Network, Cliff Dwellers Club (bd. dirs. 1995). Home: 601 Linden Ave Wilmette IL 60091-2819 Office: Ross Barney & Jankowski Inc 10 W Hubbard St Chicago IL 60610 E-mail: crossbarney@rbjarchitects.com.

BARNEY, DONNA NADYNE, writer; d. Sadie Barney. MS in Agronomy, Iowa State U., 2003. Mem. adv. bd. Jocelyn Project, Chgo., 2001—; cons. Houghton-Mifflin, Itasca, Ill., 2000—02. Author: The Carver's Gift. Bacterial Rsch. grantee, NIH, 1995, Ecol. Devel. grantee, Ill. Natural Resource, 1999, Ill. Dept. Natural Resources, 1998—2000. Achievements include invention of electronic voting machine and software. Avocations: gardening, reading, biking, camping, watching sports.

BARNEY, JOHN CHARLES, lawyer; b. Nov. 18, 1939; s. Harold Lamont and Sara Eleanor (Johnston) B.; m. Joyce Marie Ebbinge; children: John C., Karen E., William L. BA, Wesleyan U., 1961; LLB, Columbia U., 1964. Bar: N.Y. 1964, U.S. Dist. Ct. (so. and ea. dists.) N.Y. 1966, U.S. Dist. Ct. (no. and we. dists) N.Y. 1977, U.S. Ct. Appeals (2d cir.) 1973, U.S. Supreme Ct. 1979. Assoc. Donovan, Leisure, Newton and Irvine, N.Y.C., 1964-66; staff atty. N.Y. State Law Revision Commn., Ithaca, 1966-68; ptnr. Barney, Grossman, Dubow & Marcus, Ithaca, 1968—. Asst. dist. atty. Tompkins County, N.Y., 1968-70; mem. N.Y. State Com. on Profl. Standards, 3d Jud. Dept., 1984-90, chmn. 1989-90. Chmn. Bd. Zoning Appeals, Lansing, N.Y., 1975-92; mem. Bd. Edn., Lansing, 1981-96, v.p., 1983-89, pres., 1989-96; bd. edn. Tompkins-Seneca-Tioga Bd. Coop. Ednl. Svcs., 1997, v.p., 2000—; bd. dirs. Challenge Industries (sheltered workshop), Ithaca, 1970-80. Mem. Tompkins County Bar Assn. (pres. 1983-84), N.Y. State Bar Assn. Republican. Unitarian Universalist. Home: 12 Stormy View Rd Ithaca NY 14850-9774 Office: Barney Grossman Dubow & Marcus 119 E Seneca St Ithaca NY 14850-4352

BARNEY, KLINE PORTER, JR., engineering company executive, consultant; b. Dec. 16, 1934; s. Kline Porter and Doris (Nielsen) B.; m. Cheryl Kathleen Taylor, June 14, 1957; children: Peter, Suzanne, Cathleen, Patrick, Andrew. BS, U. Utah, 1957; MPA, San Diego State U., 1971. Registered profl. engr., 7 states. Asst. engr. Fallbrook (Calif.) Pub. Utility Dist., 1960-63; pres. Engring. Sci., Inc., Arcadia, Calif., 1963-85, Parsons Mcpl. Svcs., Inc., Pasadena, Calif., 1985-89; sr. v.p. Parsons Engring. Sci., Inc., Pasadena, 1989-97; cons., 1997—; owner Kline Barney Engrs., 1999—. Presenter on field of privatization, 1983—; environ. cons. Contbr. articles to profl. jours. Mem. exec. bd. San Gabriel coun. Boy Scouts Am., 1981-96. Capt. USMC, 1957-60. Mem. ASCE, Am. Acad. Environ. Engrs. (diplomate), Am. Waterworks Assn., Water Environ. Fedn., Tau Beta Pi, Chi Epsilon, Phi Eta Sigma. Republican. Mem. Lds Ch. Avocations: hiking, astronomy. Home: 800 Juniperpoint Dr Salt Lake City UT 84103-3331 Office Phone: 801-519-0335. Personal E-mail: kline.barney@usa.net.

BARNEY, MICHAEL E., lawyer; b. Petersburg, Va., Apr. 20, 1947; s. Jack Hansford and Maxine (Scott) B.; m. Roslyn Ann Weiner, June 7, 1970; children: Jason Ross, Scott Ryan. BA, U. Va., 1969; JD, U. Richmond, 1972. Bar: Va. 1972. Ptnr. Kaufman & Canoles P.C., Norfolk, Va., 1972—. Lectr. in field. Contbr. articles to profl. jours. Officer, bd. dirs. Jewish Community Ctr. of Tidewater, Norfolk, 1980-86, Beth El Congregation, Norfolk, 1988-90. Capt. USAR, 1971-79. Mem. Va. State Bar (bd. govs. real property sect., chairperson real property sect. 1988), Va. Bar Assn. (coun. real property sect.), Virginia Beach Bar Assn., Norfolk and Portsmouth Bar Assn., Am. Coll. Real Estate Lawyers, Tidewater Builders Assn. (assoc.), Va. Assn. Realtors (assoc.). Avocations: hunting, golf, fishing, boating. Office: Kaufman and Canoles PO Box 626 Virginia Beach VA 23451-0626 Office Phone: 757-491-4040. Business E-Mail: mebarney@kaufcan.com.

BARNEY, THOMAS MCNAMEE, lawyer; b. Indpls., Mar. 14, 1938; s. John R. and Helen (Adams) B.; m. Marjorie Joan Eckhert, Sept. 9, 1961; children: Lynn M., Thomas M. Jr., Katherine J. BA, Cornell U., 1960; JD, Ind. U., 1966; LLM in Taxation, NYU, 1967. Bar: Ind. 1966, N.Y. 1967, Fla. 1977. Assoc. Barney & Hughes, Indpls., 1966-67, Dewey, Ballantine, Bushby, Palmer & Wood, N.Y.C., 1967-69, Phillips, Lytle, Hitchcock, Blaine & Huber, Buffalo, 1969-74, ptnr., 1975—99, of counsel, 2000—. Lectr. in taxation SUNY, Buffalo, 1969-82, mem. adv. bd. grad. tax. cert. program, 1981-2000. Author: Major Changes in Estate Tax, 1981. Sec. Upstate N.Y. Synod. Evang. Luth. Ch. Am., Syracuse, 1987-96; bd. dirs. Luth. Theol. Sem., Phila., 1988-91, Niagara Luth. Home Found., 1988—. Lt. (j.g.) USN, 1960-63. Mem. Erie County Bar Assn. (chmn. tax com. 1981-84), Fla. Bar Assn., Ind. Bar Assn., Am. Coll. Trust and Estate Counsel. Office: Phillips Lytle Hitchcock Blaine & Huber 3400 HSBC Ctr Buffalo NY 14203-2887

BARNHARDT, ROBERT ALEXANDER, dean; b. Jenkins Township, Pa., Sept. 21, 1937; s. Daniel T. and Janet A. (MacCartney) B.; married. BS in Textile Engring., Phila. Coll. Textiles and Sci., 1959; MS, Inst. Textile Tech., 1961; MEd, U. Va., 1970, EdD, 1974. Assoc. prof. fabric tech. Phila. Coll. Textiles and Sci., 1961-64, chmn. dept. textiles, 1964-66; dir. edn. Inst. Textile Tech., Charlottesville, Va., 1966-69, dean and dir. edn., 1972-76, dir. rsch. and edn., 1977-78, v.p. rsch. and edn., 1978-84, exec. v.p., chief oper. officer, 1984-87; dean Coll. Textiles NC State U., Raleigh, 1987—2004, interim chancellor, 2004. Bd. dirs. Textile/Clothing Tech. Corp., Raleigh, Harriet & Henderson Yarns, Inc., N.C., So. Textile Assn. Mem. Curry Sch. Found., U. Va. Fellow Textile Inst. Gt. Britain (medal 1988); mem. Am. Soc. Engring. Edn., Nat. Coun. for Textile Edn. (pres. 1990—), Internat. Conf. Textile Edn., Phi Kappa Phi. Episcopalian. Avocations: tennis, skiing, singing, golf, gardening. Office: NC State U Coll Textiles Box 8301 4700 Hillsborough St Raleigh NC 27606-1428

BARNHARDT, ZEB ELONZO, JR., lawyer, mediator, arbitrator; b. Winston-Salem, N.C., Dec. 28, 1941; s. Zeb Elonzo and Katie Sue (Taylor) B.; m. Pam Hall; children: Daniel Black, Kathleen Martin. AB, Duke U., 1964; JD, Vanderbilt U., 1969. Bar: N.C. 1969; cert. mediator, N.C. Assoc. Womble Carlyle Sandridge & Rice, PLLC, Winston-Salem, 1969-75, mem., 1975-97, of counsel, 1997-98; owner, mgr. Barnhardt & Assocs., Inc., Leland, NC, 1998—; pvt. practice law, Leland, 1998—; mediator N.C. Superior Ct., 2003—. Arbitrator Nat. Assn. Securities Dealers, 1992—, mediator, 2004—. Alumni admissions adv. com. Duke U., 1970-72; bd. dirs. Industries for Blind, Winston-Salem, 1973-85, vice chmn., 1983-84, chmn., 1985; bd. dirs. Goodwill Industries, Winston-Salem, 1973-80, BarCARES of N.C., Inc., 1999-, The Little Theatre, Winston-Salem, 1979-85, asst. treas., 1980, treas., 1981-82, v.p., 1983-84, pres., 1984-85; adv. bd. Salvation Army, Winston-Salem, 1973-85, chmn., 1979-80, Leadership Winston-Salem, 1984-92, v.p. adminstrn., 1988-89, pres. 1989-90; com. mem. Winston-Salem Found., 1975-84, vice chmn., 1978-80, chmn., 1983-84; trustee High Point U., 1984-96; chmn. Second Journey Inc., 2002-2003. With USN, 1964—66.

Recipient Disting. Service award as Young Man of Yr. Winston-Salem Jaycees, 1974; Disting. Alumni award Duke U., 1979 Mem. ABA (bus. law sect., 1969—, dispute resolution sect., 2003—, Commn. on Lawyer Assistance Programs 2002-), N.C. Bar Assn. (mem. bus. law. sect., 1969—, chmn. securities regulation com. 1985-87, vice chmn. bus. law sect. 1987-89, chmn. bus. law sect. 1989-91, mem. dispute resolution sect., 2003—, bd. govs. 1991-94, chair membership recruitment and retention com. 1997-2000, chair lawyer effectiveness and quality of life com. 2001—04), Winston-Salem Jaycees (life, pres. 1973-74), N.C. Jaycees (regional dir. 1974-75, legal counsel 1975-77), Greater Winston-Salem C. of C. (bd. dirs. 1973-74), Rotary. Democrat. Methodist. Office: Barnhardt & Assocs Inc 1158 Willow Pond Ln Leland NC 28451 Office Phone: 910-383-3175. E-mail: zbarnhardt@ec.rr.com.

BARNHART, BETSY DEMPF, volunteer; b. Orange, N.J., Sept. 5, 1924; d. Joseph Maxmillian Dempf and Gertrude (Rowntree) Talbot; m. Paul Edgar Barnhart, Feb. 25, 1945 (dec. Jan. 1996); children: Nancy, Bruce, Barbara. BA, Calif. State U., Dominguez Hills, 1980, MA, 1990. Vol. placement sec. Vol. Ctr., Torrance, Calif., 1975-77; vol. coord. Fedn. Head Start, Carson, Calif., 1977-88; coord. vols. Harbor Interfaith Shelter, San Pedro, Calif., 1988-89; coord. student vols. Marymount Coll., Rancho Palos Verdes, Calif., 1989-93. Editor newsletter Peninsula-Harbor Ecumenical Cluster, 1973-89; editor newsletters for various orgns. Founder, dir. Peninsula Harbor FISH, San Pedro, Calif., 1974-80; pres. adv. bd. L.A. County Toy Loan, 1983-87; co-founder, bd. mem. Harbor Interfaith Shelter, San Pedro, 1984-88; founder, pres. Shelter for Homeless Women With Addictions, San Pedro, 1989-93; vol. Cardiff (Calif.) Pub. Libr., 1994—; tutor Paul Ecke Elem. Sch., Encinitas, Calif., 1996—; chair Endorsed Projects Com. for Presbytery, San Diego, 1996—; elder Christ Presbyn. Ch., Carlsbad, Calif, 1995—. Named Laywomen of Yr. South Coast Ecumenical Coun., Long Beach, Calif., 1984. Mem. AAUW, PTA Webster Elem. Sch. (hon. life), Phi Kappa Phi. Democrat. Presbyterian. Avocations: travel, reading, walking. Home: 2247 Wales Dr Cardiff By The Sea CA 92007-1509

BARNHART, CHARLES ELMER, zoology educator; b. Windsor, Ill., Jan. 25, 1923; s. Elmer and Irma (Smysor) B.; m. Norma McCarty, Dec. 28, 1946 (dec. Dec. 25, 1970); children: John D., Charles E., Norman R.; m. Jean M. Hutton, Jan. 12, 1973; stepchildren: Mark, David, Bonnie, Beth Hutton. BS in Agr., Purdue U., 1945; MS, Ia. State U., 1948, PhD, 1954. Mem. faculty U. Ky., Lexington, from 1948, assoc. prof. animal sci., 1955-57, prof., 1957-88, prof. emeritus, 1988—, dean, dir. exptl. sta. and coop. extension service, 1969-88, dean emeritus, 1988—. Pres. So. Assn. Agrl. Scientist, 1982-83 Patentee in field. Bd. dirs. Ky. Bd. Agr., 1966-88, Ky. State Fair and Expn. Ctr., 1969-88, Ky. Tobacco Rsch. Bd., Farm Credit Svcs. Mid Am., 1988-93, Ky. Farm Bur., 1969-76; mem. Gov.'s Coun. on Agrl., 1971-80. Named Man of Yr. in Ky. Agr. Progressive Farmer, 1962, Man of Yr. for Ky. Agr. Ky. Agrl. Communicators, 1979; elected to Saddle and Sirloin Portrait Gallery, 1987. Mem. Am. Soc. Animal Sci., Ky. Hist. Soc., Farmhouse Fraternity, Masons (32 deg.), Shriners, Epsilon Sigma Phi, Gamma Sigma Delta., Omicron Delta Kappa, Sigma Xi. Methodist. Address: 5013 Southern Pine Cir Venice FL 34293-4245

BARNHART, CYNTHIA, engineering educator, researcher; BS in Civil Engring., U. Vt., 1981; MS in Transp., Mass. Inst. Tech., 1985, PhD in Transp. and Civil Engring., 1988. With Mass. Inst. Tech., 1992—, co-dir. ctr. transp. and logistics, leader engring. systems group, asst. prof. to prof. civil and environ. engring. Founder Large-Scale Optimization Group Mass. Inst. Tech., 1997; bd. dirs. Inst. Ops. Research Mgmt. Scis. (INFORMS); spkr. in field. Assoc. editor: Operations, Research, and Transportation Science; contbr. articles to profl. jours. Recipient Jr. Faculty Career award, Gen. Electric Found., Presdl. Young Investigator award, NSF. Achievements include research in models and algorithms to improve carrier operations (focusing on airlines). Office: Mass Inst Tech 77 Massachusetts Ave Bldg 1-229/E40-149A Cambridge MA 02139 Office Phone: 617-253-3815. Business E-Mail: cbarnhar@mit.edu.

BARNHART, FORREST GREGORY, lawyer; b. Alpine, Tex., Sept. 11, 1951; s. F. Neil and Jody (Ogg) B. AB, Vassar Coll., 1973; JD, Cornell U., 1976. Bar: Fla. 1976, U.S. Dist. Ct. (so. dist.) Fla. 1977, U.S. Ct. Appeals (5th and 11th cirs.) 1977; cert. civil trial lawyer. Assoc. Levy, Plisco, Perry, Shapiro, Kneen & Kincade, West Palm Beach, Fla., 1976-78, Montgomery Searcy & Denney, P.A., West Palm Beach, 1978-81, ptnr., 1981-89, Searcy, Denney, Scarola, Barnhart & Shipley, P.A., West Palm Beach, 1989—. Lectr. in field; moderator TV show Call the Lawyer, 1983-85; dir. WXEL-TV and FM, Pub. Radio and TV, West Palm Beach. Contbr. chpt. to The Advocates Primer, 1991. Spkr., com. mem. Floridians Against Constnl. Tampering, 1984; mem. Jud. Nominating Commn., 1986-90; trustee Fla. Lawyers Action Group; bd. dirs., sec. 1000 Friends of Fla., Legal Aid Soc. Palm Beach County. Recipient Al J. Cone award; mem. Eagle Hall of Fame, 1991. Fellow ATKA, ABA, FBA (treas. 1983-84, sec., v.p. 1984-85, pres. 1986-87), Fla. Bar, Palm Beach County Bar Assn. (vice chmn. fed. ct. practice com. 1981-82, media law com. 1981-82, bench bar com. 1980-81, chmn. pub. rels. com. 1983-84, TV com. 1984—), Palm Beach Trial Lawyers Assn. (founding dir.), Acad. Fla. Trial Lawyers (sec. 1990-91, treas. 1991-92, pres.-elect 1992-93, pres. 1993—, bd. dirs. 1986-90, chmn., key man legis. com. 1986—, mem. coll. of diplomates, steering counsel continuing edn. com., Eagle Benefactor, Disting. Lectr. in Jurisprudence 1988, sec. 1990-91), Fla. Lawyers Action Group (chair bd. trustees), Cornell Club. Home: 236 Miraflores Dr Palm Beach FL 33480-3618 Office: Searcy Denney Scarola Barnhart & Shipley 2139 Palm Beach Lakes Blvd West Palm Beach FL 33409-6601

BARNHART, JO ANNE B., federal agency administrator; b. Memphis, Aug. 26, 1950; d. Nelson Alexander and Betty Jane (Fitzpatrick) Bryant; m. David Lee Ross, Feb. 14, 1976 (div. June 1983); m. David Ray Barnhart, May 24, 1986. Student, U. Tenn., 1968—70; BA, U. Del., 1975. Space and time buyer DeMartin-Marona & Assocs., Wilmington, Del., 1970—73; adminstrv. asst. Mental Health Assn., Wilmington, 1973—75; dir. SERVE nutrition program Wilmington Sr. Ctr., 1975—77; legis. asst. to Sen. William V. Roth, Jr., Washington, 1977—81; dep. assoc. commr. Office Family Assistance, HHS, Washington, 1981—83, assoc. commr., 1983—86; rep. staff dir. U.S. Senate Govt. Affairs Com., 1987—90; asst. sec. family support HHS, Washington, 1990—91, asst. sec. for children and families, 1991—92; staff U.S. Sen. William V. Roth, 1993—; comnr. Social Security Admin., Baltimore, Md., 2001—. Mem. adv. bd. on welfare indicators U.S. Dept. HHS, 1996—. Campaign mgr. U. S. Sen. William V. Roth, 1988, 1994; polit. dir. Nat. Rep. Senatorial Com., 1995—97, polit. and pub. policy cons., 1997—2001; mem. Social Security adv. bd., 1997—2001; commr. Social Security, 2001—. Republican. Methodist. Office: Social Security Admin Office of Commr Altmeyer Bldg 6401 Security Blvd Baltimore MD 21235-6401

BARNHART, MARY C., health facility administrator; b. Milw., Mar. 7, 1951; d. Zenon and Olga Soblewski; m. Clayton F. Barnhart, Feb. 22, 1997 (dec.); children: Clayton D., Lucille. BA, U. Wis. - Milw., 2002; MA in Bioethics, Med. Coll. Wis., 2004. Certified IRB Mgr. Nat. Assn. of IRB Managers, 2001, Certified IRB Profl. Pub. Responsibility in Medicine, 2002. Sec. Milw. County Children's Ct., 1986—96; mgr. internal revenue bd. programs Oakwood Healthcare Sys., Dearborn, Mich., 1996—2005; coord. internal rev. bd. St. John Hosp. and Med. Ctr., Detroit, 2005—. Contbr. newsletter articles Nat. Assn. of IRB Managers Newsletter, newsletter articles Med. Ethics Rsch. Network of Mich.; editor: (jour.) Oakwood Healthcare Rsch. Quar., (newsletter) Ch. Newsletter, author short stories, poetry. Exec. bd. mem. Allen Pk. Bapt. Ch., Mich., 1996—2005. Mem.: Nat. Assn. Internal Rev. Bd. Mgrs. (assoc. program dir. 2001—05). Baptist. Avocations: reading, poetry, music, travel, graphic design. Home: 5137 Jackson Rd Trenton MI 48183 Office: St John Hosp and Med Ctr 22101 Moross Detroit MI 48236 Office Phone: 313-343-8314. Personal E-mail: barnharm@wideopenwest.com. Business E-Mail: mary.barnhart@stjohn.org.

BARNHILL, CHARLES JOSEPH, JR., lawyer; b. Indpls., May 22, 1943; s. Charles J. and Phyllis (Landis) Barnhill; m. Elizabeth Louise Hayek, Aug. 14, 1971; children: Eric Charles, Colin Landis. BS in Econs., U. Pa., 1965; JD, U. Mich., 1968. Bar: Ill. 1968, U.S. Dist. Ct. (no. dist.) Ill. 1968, U.S. Ct. Appeals (7th cir.) 1969, U.S. Supreme Ct. 1972. Assoc. Kirkland & Ellis, Chgo., 1968; Reginald Heber Smith fellow Chgo. Legal Aid, 1968-69; assoc. Katz & Friedman, Chgo., 1969-72; ptnr. Davis, Miner, Barnhill & Galland, P.C. (now Miner, Barnhill & Galland), Madison, Wis., 1972—. Spl. master Fed. Dist. Ct. (no. dist.) Ill. Asst. editor: Mich. Law Rev., 1968. Chmn. Wis. Ctr. Tobacco Rsch. and Intervention, 1996; bd. dirs. Combined Health Appeal, Legal Assistance Found., Chgo., 1972—74, Old Town Triangle Assn., Chgo., 1972—75. Fellow: Am. Coll. Trial Lawers; mem.: ABA (chmn. employment litig. litig. section 1975—78), Order of Coif, Barristers Soc., Chgo. Coun. Lawyers (bd. dirs. 1974—76), Greater Madison Area Tennis Assn. (pres.). Office: Miner Barnhill & Galland 44 E Mifflin St Ste 803 Madison WI 53703-2800 Office Phone: 608-255-5200. Business E-Mail: cbarnhill@lawmbg.com.

BARNHILL, G. MICHAEL, lawyer; b. Rocky Mount, NC, July 16, 1956; BA cum laude, Davidson Coll., NC, 1978; JD, Wake Forest U. Sch. Law, 1981. Bar: NC 1981, admitted to practice: US Dist. Ct. (We., Mid. & Ea. Dists. NC), US Ct. Appeals (4th Cir.), US Supreme Ct. Jud. clerk to Chief Judge Woodrow W. Jones US Dist. Ct. (We. Dist.), NC, 1981—83; mng. mem., bus. litig. dept. Womble Carlyle Sandridge & Rice, PLLC, Charlotte, NC, mem. mgmt. com. Lectr. Wake Forest U. Sch. Law Ann. Review, 1999—2000. Mem.: NC Assn. of Def. Attys., ABA (mem. litig. sect., mem. tort & litig. sect.), NC Assn. of Police Attys., NC State Bar Assn. (mem. legal svc. planning com. 1987—90), NC Bar Assn. (mem. litig. sect., mem. labor & employment sect.), Mecklenburg County Bar Assn. Office: Womble Carlyle Sandridge & Rice PLLC One Wachovia Center Ste 3500 301 S College St Charlotte NC 28202-6037 Office Phone: 704-331-4960. Office Fax: 704-338-7829. Business E-Mail: mbarnhill@wcsr.com.

BARNHILL, GREGORY HURD, investment banker; b. Balt., Feb. 20, 1953; s. Robert Bell and Margaret Katheryn (Hurd) B. Student, Inst. d'Etudes Européennes, 1974, Banque Nat. de Paris, 1974; BA in Econs., Brown U., 1975; postgrad., Inst. Fin., NYC, 1975. Lic. N.Y. Stock Exch./NASD series 7, 9, 10, 63, 65. Mng. dir. internat. investment banking Deutsche Bank Securities Inc., Investment Bankers, Balt., 1975—2003; ptnr. Brown Adv. Securities, LLC, Balt., 2003—, also bd. dirs. Bd. dirs. Agora Press, BTAB-Cook Overseas Ltd., BTAB-Stark Ltd. Partnership/AB-Stark Overseas Ltd., Captel-Nat. Cap. Telesvcs., L.L.C., View Tech., NASA/Goddard Space Flight Ctr. Balt. Incubator, Innovative Med. Svc.; corp. co-chair Miss USA, 2005. Mem. adv. bd. Inst. d'Etudes Européennes; affiliate Balt. Mus. Art, Walters Art Gallery; chmn. fundraising com. Balt. Arts Festival, 1980-84; bd. dirs. Palm Beach Maritime Mus., Balt. Heritage Inc., 1981-83, Md. Ballet, 1982-83, Nat. Taxpayers Union Found., 1984-1998, The Netherlands-Am. Amity Trust, Inc., Balt. Columbus 500, Md. Art Place, 1982-90, pres. 1982-86, pres. bd. trustees, 1985-86; co-chmn. Businesspeople for Mayor Schaefer's Re-election, 1982-83; mem. fin. com. Congresswoman Helen Delich Bentley; mem. Balt. Operation Sail (chmn. fin. com., bd. dirs., pres. 1988-93), hon. mem. Christopher Columbus Quincentennary Commn., 1989—; mem. Nat. Rep. Fin. Com., 1991—; vice chmn. bd. dirs. Greater Balt. Med. Ctr., 1992-2002; trustee Md. Internat. Ctr. Md., 1993—; mem. bd. govs. Faberge Arts Found., 1992—; mem. 2000 com. Walters Art Gallery, 1978—; nat. vice-chmn. The Pres.'s Dinner, 1989—; mem. mayor's adv. com. internat. affairs, 1988—; mem. gov's bus. com. for Md.-St. Petersburg, 1993—; trustee St. Paul's Sch., 2000—, Alexander Brown Charitable Found., 2002—; chmn. Found. for Govt. House, 2003—; apptd. to Md. Racing Commn., 2004—; chmn. bd. UMBC Alex P. Brown Enterprenuership Ctr., 2005—. Mem. Bond Club Md., Balt. Hist. Soc. (trustee), Md. Hist. Soc. (trustee 1992-2004, co-chmn. MHS 150 1993—), Md. Soc. Preservation of Antiquities (dir. 1981-83), Mcpl. Arts Soc. (trustee 1985—, dir.), Md. Acad. Scis. (bd. dirs), Brown U. Club of Md. (pres. 1976-81), McDonogh Sch. Alumni Assn. (dir.), Nature Conservancy (bd. dirs.), SAR, Soc. Colonial Wars, Md. Club (bd. govs., treas. exec. com, bd. dirs. 1995), Volvo Ocean Race Chesapeake (formerly Whitbread Ocean Race Chesapeake) (chmn. 1998—), Order of Crown of Charlemagne, Baronial Order of Magna Charta, U.S.A, Newport Reading Rm. Club, Greenspring Valley Hunt Club, N.Y. Yacht Club, Ocean Reef Club, Rehoboth Country Club, Henlopen Acres Beach Club, Sigma Chi. Republican. Home: 10801 Stevenson Rd Stevenson MD 21153-0679 Office: Brown Adv Securities LLC 901 S Bond St 4th Fl Baltimore MD 21231 Office Phone: 410-537-5527. Business E-Mail: gbarnhill@brownadvisory.com.

BARNHILL, HENRY GRADY, JR., lawyer; b. Buena Vista, Ga., Aug. 24, 1930; s. Henry Grady and Imogene (Hogg) B.; m. Sarah Carolyn Haire, Oct. 29, 1953; children: Grady Michael, Stephen Drew, Kevin Scott, Carol Kelly. JD, Wake Forest U., Winston-Salem, N.C., 1958. Bar: N.C. 1958, U.S. Dist. Ct. (ea., mid. and we. dists.) N.C. 1958, U.S. Ct. Appeals (4th cir.) 1961, U.S. Supreme Ct. 1983, U.S. Ct. Appeals (fed. cir.) 1985. Assoc. Womble Carlyle Sandridge & Rice, Winston-Salem, 1958-61, ptnr., 1961—. Bd. visitors Sch. of Law Wake Forest U. Lt. USAF, 1951-55. Fellow Am. Coll. Trial Lawyers (state chmn. 1986-88, Named to Best Lawyers in Am. 1984-); mem. Am. Bd. Trial Advs., N.C. Assn. Def. Attys., N.C. Bar Assn. (litigation sect.), 4th Cir. Jud. Conf., Forsyth County Bar (pres. 1979-80), Inns of Ct. (Chief Justice Joseph Branch). Democrat. Presbyterian. Avocation: tennis. Home: 3121 Robinhood Rd Winston Salem NC 27106-5610 Office: Womble Carlyle Sandridge & Rice PLLC One W 4th St Winston Salem NC 27101 E-mail: gbarnhill@wcsr.com.

BARNHILL, JAMES ORRIS, theater educator; b. Sumner, Miss., May 23, 1922; s. James Arthur and Louise (Sullivan) B. BA, Yale U., 1947, MFA, 1954; MA, NYU, 1949; MA (hon.), Brown U. Instr. in English Brown U., Providence, 1954-56, from asst. prof. to assoc. prof., 1956-70, prof., 1970-78, prof. in theater arts, 1978-86, prof. emeritus, 1986—. Vis. prof. English R.I. Sch. Design, Providence, 1987-88, 93-94, Tougaloo (Miss.) Coll., 1989; actor Trinity Square Repertory Theatre, Providence, 1971-73. Lt. (j.g.) USNR, 1943-46, PTO. Fulbright prof. English M.S. U. Baroda, India, 1984-85, St. Xavier Coll., Ahmedabad, India, 1988-89, Am. Lit. Univ. Punjab, Pakistan, 1994-96. Mem. Univ. Club, Players Club. Baptist. Avocations: hobbies, calligraphy, sculpture. Home: 81 Transit St Providence RI 02906-1022 Office: Brown U Dept Theatre Arts PO Box 1897 Providence RI 02912-1897

BARNHOLDT, TERRY JOSEPH, industrial engineer, chemical engineer; b. Wiota, Iowa, Sept. 22, 1921; s. Claus Edward and Leona (Consaul) B.; m. Martha Francis Cannon, 1946 (dec. 1975); children: Martha Jane, Terry (Ted) Joseph Jr. BChE, Clarkson Coll. Tech., 1943; postgrad. degree in chem. engring. and adminstrn. engring., Cornell U., 1947; MBA (hon.), U. N.C., Charlotte, 1967; JD, Atlanta Law Sch., 1981. Project, process engr. Std. Oil Co., Richmond, Calif., 1947-49; Perth Amboy, N.J., 1949-51; br. mgr. The Clorox Co., Charlotte, N.C., 1949-51; pres., gen. mgr. Allied Prodrs. Supply Co., Charlotte, 1959-66; mgr. mfg. and engring. BASF Wyandotte, Charlotte, 1966-68; sales mgr. Detrex Chem. Industries, Charlotte, 1969-70; chem. mfg. sales rep. Valchem Chem. United Mchts., Charlotte, 1970-74; sales, mfg. rep. Star Chemicals Co., Macon, Ga., 1976-78; mgr. shipping Pepsi-Cola Beverage Corp., Atlanta, 1979; project engr. Metro Atlanta Rapid Transit Authority, 1981-84; comml. real estate specialist Gen. Svc. Adminstrn., Atlanta, 1984-85; gen., indsl. engr. Def. Logistics Agy., Manassas, Alexandria and Ft. Belvoir, Va., 1986—. 1st lt. U.S. Army, 1943-46. Mem. NSPE, AIChE, ATLA, Am. Chem. Soc., Assn. Energy Engrs., Def. Acquisition Corps, Alpha Chi Sigma. Republican. Presbyterian. Avocations: running, handball, free weights, golf. Office: Def Logistics Agy DLSC-BIS 8725 John J Kingman Rd Ste 2533 Fort Belvoir VA 22060-6217 Home: 3729 Midvale Ave Philadelphia PA 19129-1743

BARNHOLT, BRANDON K., retail executive; COO, exec. v.p. mktg. Clark USA Inc. (now Clark Retail Group Inc.); CEO, pres. Clark Retail Group, Inc., Glen Ellyn, Ill., 1999—. Office: Clark Retail Group Inc 3003 Butterfield Rd Oak Brook IL 60523

BARNHOLT, EDWARD W., computer company executive; b. NYC, 1943; BEE, MEE, Stanford U. R&D engr., mktg. engr., product mgr. Hewlett-Packard, Palo Alto, Calif., 1966—73, product mktg. mgr. Stanford Pk. divsn., 1973—76, mktg. mgr. Santa Clara divsn., 1976—80, gen. mgr. divsn. microwave and commns. group, 1980—84, gen. mgr. electronic instruments group, 1984—88, v.p., 1988—90, gen. mgr. test and measurement orgn., 1990—93, sr. v.p., 1993—96, exec. v.p., gen. mgr., measurement orgn., 1996—99; pres., CEO Agilent, Palo Alto, Calif., 1999—, chmn., 2002—. Dir. KLA-Tencor Corp., Agilent Technologies Inc., Palo Alto, Calif., 1999—; serves on adv. com. NY Stock Exchange Listed Co. Recipient Medal of Achievement award, AeA, 2002, Excellence in Leadership Communication (EXCEL) Award, Internat. Assn. Bus. Communicators, 2003. Mem.: N.Y. Stock Exch. (listed co. adv. com.). Address: Agilent Technologies 3000 Hanover St Palo Alto CA 94304-1112

BARNICK, HELEN, retired judicial clerk; b. Max, ND, Mar. 24, 1925; d. John K. and Stacy (Kankovsky) Barnick. BS in Music cum laude, Minot State Coll., 1954; postgrad., Am. Conservatory of Music, Chgo., 1975-76. With Epton, Bohling & Druth, Chgo., 1968-69; sec. Wildman, Harrold, Allen & Dixon, Chgo., 1969-75; part-time assignments for temporary agy. Chgo., 1975-77; sec. Friedman & Koven, Chgo., 1977-78; with Lawrence, Lawrence, Kamin & Saunders, Chgo., 1978-81; sec. Hinshaw, Culbertson et al., Chgo., 1982; sec. to magistrate judge U.S. Dist. Ct. (we. dist.) Wis., Madison, 1985-91; dep. clk., case adminstr. U.S. Bankruptcy Ct. (we. dist.) Wis., Madison, 1992-94; ret., 1994. Chancel choir 1st Bapt. Ch., Mpls., Fourth Presbyn. Ch., Chgo., Covenant Presbyn. Ch., Madison; choir, dir. sr. high choir Moody Ch., Chgo.; dir. chancel choir 1st Bapt. Ch., Minot, ND; active Festival Choir, Madison; bd. dirs., sec.-treas. Peppertree at Tamarack Owners Assn., Inc., Wisconsin Dells, Wis., Wis. Mem.: Bus. and Profl. Women Assn., Christian Bus. and Profl. Women (chmn.), Madison Civics Club, Symphony Orch. League, Sigma Sigma Sigma. Home: 7364 Old Sauk Rd Madison WI 53717-1213

BARNITZ, ANDREW JAMES, music educator; b. Brunswick, Maine, Mar. 14, 1969; s. Thomas C. Jr. and Madeline Carol B. B, U. No. Colo., Greeley, Colo., 1994. Cert. K-12 piano, vocal and gen. music tchr. 1999. K-12 music dir. Kiowa (Colo.) Sch., 1994—96; k-5 gen. music tchr. Grace Best Elem. Sch., Monument, Colo., 1996—. Singer (tenor): Colo. Symphony Chorus, 1994, Colo. Springs Symphony Chorus, 1996; dir.: (children's choir) The Sound Bearers, children's handbell choir. Mem.: Am. Orff - Schulwerk Assn., Music Educators Nat. Conf. Roman Catholic. Office: Lewis Palmer Sch Dist #38 66 Jefferson St Monument CO 80132 Personal E-mail: aj_bar@msn.com. E-mail: abarnitz@lpsd.k12.co.us.

BARNO, DAVID W., career military officer; Grad., U.S. Mil. Acad., West Point, 1976. Advanced through grades to lt. gen. U.S. Army, 2003, commd. infantry officer, 1976, various positions, 1976—2000, dep. dir. ops. U.S. Pacific Command Schofield Barracks, Hawaii, 2000—02, commanding gen., US Army Training Ctr. Ft. Jackson, SC, 2002—03; comdr. Combined Forces Command, Afghanistan, 2003—05.

BARNOFF, ROBERT MARK, civil engineering educator; b. Punxsutawney, Pa., Aug. 28, 1926; s. Joseph A. and Ruth A. (Morris) B.; m. Norma Gugliemi; children: Joni, Janice, Mark, Joseph. BS, Pa. State U., 1951, MS, 1956; PhD, Carnegie Inst. Tech., 1966. Steel detailer Am. Bridge Co., 1951-52; constrn. engr. John Mohr & Sons, 1952-53; bridge designer Gannett Fleming Corddry & Capenter, 1953-55; from instr. to prof. civil engring. Pa. State U., University Park, 1955-79, prof., chmn. dept. civil engring., 1979-85. Vis. prof. Bucknell U. Contbr. articles to profl. jours. With USNR, 1944-46. Sci. Faculty fellow NSF, 1965-66. Mem. ASTM, ASCE, Am. Concrete Inst., Sigma Xi, Tau Beta Pi, Chi Epsilon. Achievements include patents on concrete testing device and bridge deck systems. Home and Office: 606 Nimitz Ave State College PA 16801-6415 Office Phone: 814-237-5123.

BARNUM, BARBARA STEVENS, retired nursing educator, writer; b. Johnstown, Pa., Sept. 2, 1937; d. William C. and Freda Inzes (Claycomb) Burkett; m. H. James Barnum (dec.); children: Lauren, Elizabeth, Catherine, Anne (dec.), Shauna, Sallee, David. AA in Nursing, St. Petersburg Jr. Coll., 1958; BPh, Northwestern U., 1967; MA, DePaul U., 1971; PhD, U. Chgo., 1976. RN, Ill., N.Y. Dir. nursing svcs. Augustana Hosp. and Health Care Ctr., Chgo., 1970-71; dir. staff edn. U. Chgo. Hosps. and Clinics, 1971-73; prof. U. Ill., Chgo., 1973-79; dir. div. health svcs., sci. and edn. Columbia U. Tchrs. Coll., N.Y.C., 1979-87; editor Nursing & Health Care Nat. League for Nursing, N.Y.C., 1989-91; editor div. nursing Columbia-Presbyn. Med. Ctr., Columbia U., N.Y.C., 1991-95; prof. Sch. Nursing Columbia U., N.Y.C., 1995-98; ret., 1998. Chmn. bd. Barnum & Souza, N.Y.C., 1989-92; civilian cons. to surgeon gen. USAF, 1980-87. Author: Nursing Theory, Analysis, Application and Evaluation, 4th edit., 1994, Writing for Publication: A Primer for Nurses, 1995; author: (with K. Kerfoot) The Nurse as Executive, 4th edit., 1995; author: Spirituality and Nursing: From Traditional to New Age, 1996, 2d edit., 2003, Teaching Nursing in the Era of Managed Care, 1999, The New Healers: Minds and Hands in Complementary Medicine, 2002, (fiction) The Haunting of Lisa Tilden, 1999; editor: Nursing Leadership Forum, 1994—98. Mem. governing bd. Nurses House, 1979-86, Nat. Health Coun., 1981-90, others. Fellow Am. Acad. Nursing (governing bd. 1982-84); mem. Sigma Theta Tau (Founders' award 1979). Home: 80 Park Ave Apt 15G New York NY 10016-2547 Personal E-mail: barbbarnum@aol.com.

BARNUM, JOHN WALLACE, lawyer; b. N.Y.C., Aug. 25, 1928; s. William Wallace Atterbury and Frances (Long) Barnum; m. Nancy Russell Grinnell, Sept. 13, 1958; children: Alexander Stone, Sarah Kip, Cameron Long. BA, Yale U., 1949; LLB, Yale U., Inst. Derecho Internat. y Comparativo, Havana, Cuba, 1957. Bar: Conn. 1957, N.Y. 1958, D.C. 1977; on Brussels fgn. lawyer list, 1995. Adminstrv. asst. Cerro de Pasco Copper Corp., Lima, Peru, 1946; jr. asst. purser Grace Lines, 1946; analyst 1st Banking Corp., Tangier, Morocco, 1950; reg. rep. Bache & Co., London and Paris, 1951-52; assoc. Cravath, Swaine & Moore, N.Y.C., 1957-62, ptnr., 1963-71; gen. counsel U.S. Dept. Transp., Washington, 1971-73, undersec., 1973-74, dep. sec., 1974-77; resident fellow Am. Enterprise Inst. for Pub. Policy Rsch., Washington, 1977-78, vis. fellow, 1978-86; ptnr. White & Case, Washington, 1978-94, McGuireWoods, LLP, Brussels, 1995—; pres. McGuireWoods Internat. LLC, Brussels, 1999—; mng. ptnr. McGuireWoods Kazahhstan LLP, Almaty, 1999—. U.S. del. Inter-Am. Comml. Arbitration Commn., 1969—71; del. NATO Com. for Challenges to Modern Soc., 1973—76; adv. mem. Coun. on Wage and Price Stability, 1974—77; mem. Coun. Adminstrv. Conf. U.S., 1973—77. Bd. editors Regulation: AEI Jour. on Govt. and Soc., 1977-86. Chmn. bd. Internat. Play Group, 1962-77; bd. dirs., mem. exec. com. N.Y C. Ctr. Music and Drama, 1969-75; trustee Washington Drama Soc. (Arena Stage), 1983-93; bd. overseers Corcoran Gallery of Art, Washington, 1994-2000; pres. U.S. Fedn. Friends Mus., 2002-. Mem.: Am. Arbitration Assn. (exec. com. 1968—72, bd. dirs. 1968—98), Nat. Def. Transp. Assn. (chmn-.mil. airlift com. 1983—94, bd. dirs. 1988—94), Am. Bar Found., D.C. Bar Assn., N.Y. State Bar Assn. (exec. com., chmn. antitrust law sect. 1979—80), Internat. Bar Assn., N.Y. Yacht Club, Amateur Ski Club, Chevy Chase Club, Met. Club, Watersportvereniging Noord-Beveland, Cercle Royal Gaulois Artistique et Litteraire, Am. Club of Brussels (gov., v.p. exec. com.). Home: 182 Ave Franklin Roosevelt 1050 Brussels Belgium also: 2029 Connecticut Ave NW Washington DC 20008-6141 Office: McGuireWoods LLP 250 Ave Louise, Bte 64 1050 Brussels Belgium Office Phone: 011 32-2 629 4230. E-mail: jbarnum@mcguirewoods.com.

BARNUM, WILLIAM DOUGLAS, retired communications executive; b. Denton, Tex., July 28, 1946; s. Billie Douglas and Leticia Christina Barnum; m. Mary Ann Mook, Aug. 10, 1968. BSBA in Econs. with distinction, Georgetown U., 1967; MBA, Fairleigh Dickinson U., 1985. Acct. RCA Corp., Cherry Hill, NJ, 1967-68, Andros Island, 1968-70, budget and cost analyst Cherry Hill, 1970, adminstr. tel. sys., 1970-73; mgr. project adminstrn. white sands radar project RCA Svc. Co., Holloman AFB, N.Mex., 1973-74; coord. profit ctr. acctg. RCA Global Comms., N.Y.C., 1974-76, adminstr. globcom. sys., 1976-77, mgr. spl. project and accts. payable, 1978-79; mgr. fin. RCA

Globcom Sys., Inc., N.Y.C., 1979-81; mgr. gateway ops. RCA Global Comms., Edison, NJ, 1982, dir. field support svcs., 1982-88; sr. mgr. network svcs. MCI Internat., Piscataway, NJ, 1988-90, sr. mgr. sys. support and adminstrn., 1990-92, sr. mgr. messaging and marine ops., 1992-93, sr. staff internat. alliances, 1994; owner, sr. cons. Lake Road Assocs. Consulting, Far Hills, NJ, 1994-99; ret., 1999. Author: Kroodley Made Knife Catalog, 1977. Mem. Am. Security Coun., 1981—92, Far Hills (N.J.) Bd. Health, 1993—99, vice-chmn., 1994—95, chmn., 1996—99; adviser Jr. Achievement, Cherry Hill, NJ, 1968—69, Cherry Hill Jaycees, 1973—74; mem. spl. commn. Far Hills Police Dept., 1993, 1998; sustaining mem. Rep. Nat. Com., 1984—2005; bd. dirs. United Cerebral Palsy Somerset/Morris County, 1989. Mem.: NRA (life), Knifemakers Guild (hon.), RCA Commn. Retirees Assn., Mensa, S.C. Waterfowl Assn., J. Edgar Hoover Found. (life), Am. Knife Throwers Alliance (hon.), Woodcreek Country Club, Wildewood Country Club, Delta Mu Delta, Delta Phi Epsilon. Presbyterian. Home: PO Box 23329 Columbia SC 29224

BARNUM, WILLIAM MILO, architect; b. June 17, 1927; s. Phelps and Catharine (Davis) B.; m. Katharine Miller, Aug. 10, 1971; children: Anne Lyttleton, Catharine Hollerith, William Milo, Nathaniel Phelps, Caleb Townsend; 1 stepchild, Elizabeth Pierce. BA, Yale U., 1950; MArch, U. Pa., 1952. Archtl. asst. job capt. Eggers & Higgins, 1952-54; job capt. W. Stuart Thompson & Phelps Barnum, archs., 1954-58, jr. ptnr., 1958-60; sr. ptnr. Phelps Barnum & Son, N.Y.C., 1960-68; pres. William Milo Barnum Assocs., Inc., N.Y.C., 1968—. Cons. to judges com.; interior designer new U.S. Courthouse Ho., 500 Pearl St., N.Y.C., Scudder Stevens & Clark 5 Fls. Prin. works include Westminster Sch. Chapel, 1961, Westminster Sch. Acad. Ctr., 1964, Howmet Office Bldg., Greenwich, Mfrs. Hanover Bank, Bklyn., Pickwick Pla., Greenwich, R.T. Vanderbilt Corp. Hdqs., Norwalk, Conn., Union Trust Sq., Greenwich, Gen. Host. Corp. Hdqs., Stamford, Conn., Gateway Ctr., Greenwich, The Boatyard Condominium, City Island, N.Y., Gorham Island Office Bldg., Westport, Conn., N.Y. Offices Scudder Stevens and Clark, Mason Place Mixed Use Hist. Restoration, Greenwich, Shawmut Bank offices and Br. Landmark Sq. Bldg., Stamford, Shawmut br., New Canaan, St. Andrews by the Sea Episcopal Ch. Renovation and Reconstruction, Little Compton, R.I. Chmn. Archtl. Rev. Bd., Greenwich, Conn.; mem. selectmen's com. H.S. Property, Greenwich, 1964-68; bd. dirs. Cmty. Chest, Greenwich, 1964-68; mem. alumni coun. Phillips Acad., Andover, Mass., 1965-68; v.p. bd. trustees Putnam Indian Field Sch., vice-chmn.; bd. dirs. Episcopal Ch. at Yale; bd. dirs. Episcopal Ch. Bldg. Fund. With USNR, 1945-46, PTO. Mem. AIA (N.Y. chpt. office practices com.), Concrete Industry Bd. (bd. dir.), Met. Builders Assn. (liaison com.), Andover Alumni Assn. N.Y.C. (pres. 1964-65), Hist. Soc. Greenwich (v.p.), Soc. Colonial Wars, Yale Club (coun. 1958-79, pres. 1970-72) (N.Y.C.), Acoaxet Club, Providence Art Club, St. Andrews-By-The-Sea (vestry), Spindle Rock Club. Office: 32 Custom House St Providence RI 02903-2614 Office Phone: 401-276-9100. E-mail: WMBarnum@hotmail.com.

BARNWELL, FRANKLIN HERSHEL, zoology educator; b. Chattanooga, Oct. 4, 1937; s. Columbus Hershel and Esther Bernice (Ireland) B.; m. Adrienne Kay Knox, June 13, 1959; 1 child, Elizabeth Brooks. BA, Northwestern U., 1959, PhD, 1965. Instr. biol. sci. Northwestern U., Evanston, Ill., 1964, research assoc., 1965-67; asst. prof. U. Chgo., 1967-70; from asst. prof. to prof. zoology, ecology and behavioral biology U. Minn., Mpls., 1970—, head dept. ecology, evolution and behavior, 1986-93. Mem. adv. panel NASA, 1963-67, NSF, Washington, 1980; faculty Orgn. for Tropical Studies, San Jose, Costa Rica, 1966-85, bd. dirs.; Nat. Confs. on Underground Rsch., bd. dirs., treas., 1990-96; investigator rsch. R/V Alpha Helix, various locations, 1979, vis. scientist. Contbr. articles on zoology to profl. jours. NSF fellow, 1965; named Minn. Coll. Sci. Tchr. of Yr., Minn. Acad. Sci. and Minn. Sci. Tchrs. Assn., 1997, dist. tchg. prof. of ecology, U. Minn., 1997. Fellow Linnean Soc. London, AAAS; mem. Soc. Intergrative and Comparative Biology, Soc. for Rsch. on Biol. Rhythms, Assocs. Orgn. for Tropical Studies, Crustacean Soc. (founding and sustaining mem., bd. dirs., sec. 1991-98), Phi Beta Kappa, Sigma Xi. Office: U Minn Dept Ecology Evol & Behav 1987 Upper Buford Cir Saint Paul MN 55108-1051 E-mail: fhb@umn.edu.

BAROFF, GEORGE STANLEY, psychologist, educator; b. Bronx, N.Y., Nov. 27, 1924; s. Irving and Ida (Herman) B.; m. Rose Kislin, June 15, 1952 (dec. May 1992); children: Marina Binet, Roy James. BS in Zoology, George Washington U., 1948, MA in Psychology, 1950; PhD in Clin. Psychology, NYU, 1955. Research psychologist dept. med. genetics N.Y. State Psychiat. Inst., 1952-60; chief clin. psychologist Vineland (N.J.) Tng. Sch., 1960-63; asso. prof. psychology U. N.C., Chapel Hill, 1963-67, prof., 1967-2000, prof. emeritus, 2000—, dir. devel. disabilties tng. inst., 1964-2000. Forensic psychologist with criminal defendants who may be mentally retarded, 1987—. Author: Mental Retardation: Nature, Cause and Management, 1974, 3d edit., 1999, Developmental Disabilities: Psychosocial Aspects, 1991; contbr. articles to profl. jours. With U.S. Army, 1943—45. Mem. APA, Assn., Am. Assn. Mental Retardation. Jewish. Home: 417 Granville Rd Chapel Hill NC 27514-2723 Office Phone: 919-942-3044. E-mail: gbaroff@earthlink.net.

BAROFF, LYNN ELLIOTT, management consultant; b. Oklahoma City, Feb. 22, 1949; s. Phillip Dee and Estelle Claire (Reiss) B.; m. Beverly Ann Wolf, Mar. 21, 1970 (div. Dec. 1978); m. Janice Kazue Obita, Apr. 7, 1979; children: David Masanori, Steven Hideaki. BA in Mass Communications, Mundelein Coll., 1971. Producer, dir. Sta. WCIU-TV, Chgo., 1970-76; prodn. mgr. Sta. KWHY-TV, L.A., 1976-79; gen. mgr. Baroff Cons. Group, Inc., Santa Monica, Calif., 1979-92; coord. mgmt. devel. Jet Propulsion Lab., Pasadena, Calif., 1992-2000, sys. arch. for human sys. space mission planning, 2000—; liaison between Jet Propulsion Lab and US Air Force Space and Missile Sys. Ctr. Adj. prof. U. So. Calif. Internat. Tng. Trainers, L.A., 1985, 86, Antioch U. Grad. Sch., L.A., 1989—. Author poetry. Mem. adv. com. L.A. Valley Coll., 1977, Calif. State U., L.A., 1979-80, Antioch U., 1989—, Internat. Coun. Sys. Engring., 2000-. Recipient Honor Resolution, L.A. City Coun., 1976. Mem. Am. Soc. for Tng. and Devel. (v.p. 1983, pres. 1984, creator and developer HR 2000 conf. 1990), L.A. Orgn. Devel. Network, Delta Kappa Epsilon. Office: Jet Propulsion Lab 4800 Oak Grove Dr Pasadena CA 91109-8001 Office Phone: 818-393-1998. E-mail: lynn.e.baroff@jpl.nasa.gov.

BAROLINI, HELEN, writer, translator, educator; b. Syracuse, NY, Nov. 18, 1925; m. Antonio Barolini, Nov. 8, 1950 (dec.); children: Teodolinda, Susanna, Nicoletta. AB magna cum laude, Syracuse U., 1947; MLS, Columbia U., 1959. Lectr. Pace U., Pleasantville, N.Y., 1990—. Lectr., Padua, Italy, Westchester CC, Valhalla, NY, 1988; writer-in-residence Quarry Farm, Elmira Coll., 1989; resident scholar Rockefeller Found.'s Bellagio Study Ctr., Lake Como, Italy, 1991; vis. artist Am. Acad. Rome, 2001. Author: Umbertina, 1979, 2d edit., 1999, The Dream Book, 1985, 2d edit., 2000, Love in the Middle Ages, 1986, Festa, 1988, 2d edit., 2002, Aldus and His Dream Book, 1991, Chiaroscuro, 1999, More Italian Hours, and Other Stories, 2001, Rome Burning, 2004; contbr. chapters to books, articles to profl. jours.; scholar-cons., advisor: (films) Tarantella. Recipient Lifetime Achievement award, Soc. for Study of Multi-Ethnic Lit. US, 2000, Susan Koppelman award, Am. Culture Assn., 1987, Am. Book award, 1986, Marina-Velca Journalism prize, Italy, 1970, Sons of Italy Lit. Award, 2003; fellow, MacDowell Colony, 1974; grantee, Nat. Endowment for Arts, 1976. Mem.: Hudson Valley River Writers Assn., Authors Guild, PEN Am. Ctr., Phi Beta Kappa. Home and Office: 445 Broadway #2-0 Hastings On Hudson NY 10706 E-mail: helenbarolini@juno.com.

BAROLINI, TEODOLINDA, literary critic; b. Syracuse, NY, Dec. 19, 1951; d. Antonio and Helen (Mollica) B.; m. Douglas Gardner Caverly, June 21, 1980 (dec. Nov. 1993); 1 child: William Douglas; m. James J. Valentini, Feb. 10, 2001. BA, Sarah Lawrence Coll., 1972; MA, Columbia U., 1973, PhD, 1978. Asst. prof. Italian U. Calif., Berkeley, 1978-83; assoc. prof. Italian NYU, 1983-89; prof., 1989-92; chmn. dept. Italian Columbia U., N.Y.C., 1992—2004, Lorenzo Da Ponte prof. Italian, 1999—. Author: Dante's Poets, 1984, transl. into Italian as Il miglior fabbro 1993, (Howard R. Marraro prize MLA 1986, John Nicholas Brown prize Medieval Acad. Am. 1988), The Undivine Comedy, 1992, transl. into Italian as La Commedia senza Dio, 2003; editor (with H.W. Storey) Dante for the New Millennium, 2003; contbr. articles to profl. jours. AAUW fellow, 1977, ACLS fellow, 1981, NEH fellow, 1986, Guggenheim fellow, 1998. Fellow Medieval Acad. Am., Am. Acad. Arts and Scis., Am. Philos. Soc.; mem. MLA, Dante Soc. Am. (v.p. 1983-86, 91-94, 95-97, pres. 1997-2003), Renaissance Soc. Am. Office: Columbia U Dept Italian 510 Hamilton Hall New York NY 10027 Business E-Mail: tb27@columbia.edu.

BARON, CHARLES HILLEL, lawyer, educator; b. Phila., Aug. 18, 1936; s. Samuel A. and Rose (Balinky) B.; m. Irma Elaine Frankel, June 15, 1958 (dec. 1985); children: Jessica Susan, Ira Benjamin, David Hume; m. Dianne M. Quartarone, Sept. 9, 1988; 1 child, Samuel Guy. AB in Philosophy with honors, U. Pa., 1958, PhD in Philosophy, 1972; LLB, Harvard U., 1961. Bar: Pa. bar 1967, U.S. Supreme Ct. bar 1970, Mass. bar 1972. Asst. prof. law U. Pa., 1965-66; assoc. firm Blank Rome Klaus & Comisky, Phila., 1966-68; chief law reform, consumer's adv. Community Legal Svcs., Inc., Phila., 1968-70; assoc. prof. law Boston Coll., 1970-74, prof., 1974—, assoc. dean, 1972-74. Exec. dir. Resource Ctr. Consumers Legal Svcs., 1975-77. Author: (with M. Saks) The Use, Nonuse, and Misuse of Applied Social Research, 1980, Droit Constitutionnel et Bioéthique: L'Expérience Americaine, 1997; contbr. articles to profl. jours. Chmn. Cheltenham Twp. (Pa.) Dem. Party, 1966-68; mem. Mass. Health Facilities Appeals Bd., 1974-75; chmn. Mass. Gov.'s Adv. Com. on Prepaid Legal Svcs., 1978-86; bd. dirs. CEPA Found., Death With Dignity Nat. Ctr., Washington, 2001—; mem. bd. overseers Mass. Supreme Jud. Ct. Hist. Soc., 1999—. Recipient various community awards; U. Pa. fellow, 1961-63 Mem. ABA, Am. Assn. Law Schs., Soc. Am. Law Tchrs., Am. Soc. Law and Medicine (bd. editors Am. Jour. Law and Medicine 1978—, bd. dirs.), Civil Liberties Union Mass. (bd. dirs., pres. 1989-91, trustee Mass. Civil Liberties Found.), ACLU. Jewish. Home: 60 Grove Hill Ave Newton MA 02460-2335 Office: Boston Coll Law Sch 885 Centre St Newton MA 02459-1148 Office Phone: 617-552-4376. Business E-Mail: baron@bc.edu.

BARON, DENNIS E., English language educator; b. NYC, May 9, 1944; s. R.C. Roy and Sylvia (Mayer) Baron; m. Iryce White, Oct. 21, 1979; children: Cordelia, Rachel, Jonathan. AB, Brandeis U., 1965; MA, Columbia U., 1968; PhD, U. Mich., 1971. Cert. tchr. English, N.Y., Mass. Tchr. English Francis Lewis High Sch., N.Y.C., 1966-68, Wayland (Mass.) High Sch., 1968-69; asst. prof. English Ea. Ill. U., Charleston, Ill., 1971-73, CCNY, N.Y.C., 1973-74; asst. prof. English/linguistics U. Ill., Urbana, 1975-81, assoc. prof. English/linguistics, 1981-84, prof. English/linguistics, 1984—, head English dept., 1997—2003. Author: Grammar and Good Taste, 1982, Grammar and Gender, 1986, Declining Grammar, 1989, The English-Only Question, 1990, Guide to Home Language Repair, 1994. Fulbright fellow CIES, France, 1978-79, fellow Ctr. for Advanced Study, U. Ill., 1984-85, program for study of cultural values and ethics, U. Ill., 1992, NEH, 1989. Mem. MLA, Am. Dialect Soc. (editor monograph series 1984-93), Nat. Coun. Tchrs. English (commn. on lang. 1984-87, chmn. commn. on pub. policy 2003—), Linguistic Soc. Am. (com. on lang. and the schs. 1992-95), Coun. Writing Program Adminstrs., Conf. on Coll. Composition and Comm. Avocations: reading, writing, art. Office: Univ Ill Dept English 608 S Wright St Urbana IL 61801-3630 Office Phone: 217-244-0568. Business E-Mail: debaron@uiuc.edu.

BARON, EDWARD, astronomer; b. Chgo., Oct. 29, 1959; s. Harold and Paula Baron; m. Marcia Haag, June 10, 1951; 1 child, Andrew. PhD, Stony Brook U., 1985. Assoc. prof. U. Okla., Norman, 1996—2001, prof. physics and astronomy, 2001—. Contbr. scientific papers to profl. jours. Pres. Sooner Swim Club, Norman, 2001—02. Grantee, NASA, 1993—. Mem.: Am. Astron. Soc., Am. Phys. Soc. (life). Achievements include research in Supernovae. Office: U Okla 440 W Brooks Rm 131 Norman OK 73019-2061 Office Phone: 405-325-3961. Office Fax: 405-325-7557. Personal E-mail: baron@nhn.ou.edu.

BARON, FREDERICK M., lawyer; b. Cedar Rapids, Iowa, June 20, 1947; m. Lisa Blue. BA, U. Tex., 1968, JD, 1971. Assoc. editor Tex. Law Rev., 1969—71; founder, ptnr. Baron & Budd P.C., Dallas, 1977—. Trustee U. Tex. Law Sch., 2002—04. Mem.: ABA, Am. Law Inst., Trial Lawyers for Pub. Justice (founder, pres. 1997), Dallas Trial Lawyers Assn. (pres. 1980), Tex. Trial Lawyers Assn, Assn. Trial Lawyers of Am. (pres. 2000—01, chmn., environ. law sect. 1981, bd. govs. 1995—98, v.p. 1998—99), Am. Bd. Trial Advocates, State Bar of Tex., Dallas Bar Assn. Office: Baron & Budd PC 3102 Oak Lawn Ave Ste 1100 Dallas TX 75219

BARON, JEFFREY, retired pharmacologist; b. Bklyn., July 10, 1942; s. Harry Leo and Terry (Goldstein) Baron; m. Judith Carol Rothberg, June 27, 1965; children: Stephanie Ann, Leslie Beth, Melissa Leigh. BS in Pharmacy, U. Conn., 1965; PhD in Pharmacology, U. Mich., 1969. Rsch. fellow in biochemistry U. Tex. Southwestern Med. Sch., Dallas, 1969-71, rsch. asst. prof. biochemistry and pharmacology, 1971-72; from asst. prof. pharmacology to prof. emeritus U. Iowa, Iowa City, 1972—2002, prof. emeritus, 2002—. Mem. chem. pathology study sect. NIH, Bethesda, Md., 1983—87, mem. environ. health scis. rev. com., Nat. Inst. Environ. Health Scis., Research Triangle Park, NC, 1990—94. Contbr. chapters to books, articles to profl. jours. Recipient Rsch. Career Devel. award, NIH, 1975—80. Mem.: Internat. Soc. Study Xenobiotics, Soc. Toxicology, Am. Assn. Cancer Rsch., Am. Soc. Biochem. and Molecular Biology, Am. Soc. Pharmacology and Exptl. Therapeutics. Jewish. Achievements include discovery of of the role of heme synthesis in regulating the induction of cytochrome P450 in liver; participation in the discovery of oxygenated cytochrome P450; research in immunohistochemical localization of cytochromes P450 and other xenobiotic-metabolizing enzymes in liver and extrahepatic tissues. Personal E-mail: jeffrey-baron@uiowa.edu.

BARON, JOSEPH MANDEL, hematologist; b. Oak Park, Ill., 1938; BS in BioChemistry, U. Chgo., 1958; MD, U. Chgo. Pritzker Sch. Medicine, 1962; MS in Pharmacology, U. Chgo., 1962. Diplomate Am. Bd. Internal Medicine, Am. Bd. Hematology, Am. Bd. Med. Oncology. Intern U. Chgo. Hosps., 1962—63, resident in internal medicine, 1963—64, 1966—68, fellow in hematology, 1967—68; assoc. prof. medicine U. Chgo. Office: Univ Chgo MC 2115 5841 S Maryland Ave Chicago IL 60637 Office Phone: 773-702-6114.

BARON, LEE ANN, chemist, educator; d. Albert Leonard and Marion Jean Fisher; m. Keith Wayne Baron, Aug. 12, 1978; children: Kendra Elizabeth, Caitlin Constance. BA in Chemistry, Wittenberg U., 1977; MS in Chemistry, U. Mich., 1979, PhD in Chemistry, 1984, postgrad., 1986—88. Tchg. asst. organic and gen. chemistry Wittenberg U., 1975—76, tchg. asst. gen. chemistry, 1977, U. Mich., 1977, tchg. asst. organic chemistry, 1978, 1979, 1981, tchg. asst. organic chemistry Interflex Program, 1978—80, tchg. asst. honors organic chemistry, 1980, 1981, rsch. asst., 1979—84, lectr. organic chemistry, 1984—86, post-doctoral fellow, 1986—88; asst. prof. chemistry Adrian (Mich.) Coll., 1988—89, Hillsdale (Mich.) Coll., 1989—93, assoc. prof. chemistry, 1993—2003, prof. chemistry, 2003—, chair dept. chemistry, 2000. Contbr. articles to profl. jours. Mem.: Ctrl. Assn. of the Health Professions, Nat. Assn. Advisors for the Health Professions, Midwest Assn. Chemistry Tchrs. at Liberal Arts Colls., Am. Chem. Soc., Phi Lambda Upsilon, Sigma Zeta. Achievements include research in effects of alcohol on membrane fats and water-soluble metabolites in developing chick embryos using 13C NMR; diffusion and adsorption of dichlortiazyl dyes by chitin; development of laboratories used during the Hillsdale College Summer Science Camp and a K-12 science curriculum. Avocations: reading, gardening, volleyball. Office: Hillsdale Coll 33 E College Hillsdale MI 49242 Office Phone: 517-607-2466.

BARON, MARTIN, editor; BA, MBA, Lehigh U., 1976. State reporter, bus. writer Miami Herald, 1976—79; with LA Times, 1979—96, bus. editor, 1983—91, asst. mng. editor "column one" polls & spl. projects, 1991—93, editor Orange County Edit., 1993—96; joined NY Times, 1996, assoc. mng. editor nighttime news ops., 1997—99; exec. editor Miami Herald, 1999—2001; editor Boston Globe, 2001—. Named Editor of Yr., Editor & Pub. Mag., 2001. Mem.: Phi Beta Kappa. Office: Boston Globe PO Box 2378 135 Morrissey Blvd Boston MA 02107-2378*

BARON, MELVIN FARRELL, pharmacy educator; b. L.A., July 29, 1932; s. Leo Ben and Sadie (Bauchman) B.; m. Lorraine Ross, Dec. 20, 1953; children: Lynn Baron Friedman, Ross David. PharmD, U. So. Calif., 1957, MPA, 1973. Lic. pharmacist, Calif. Pres. Shield Health Care Ctrs., Van Nuys, Calif., 1957-83; dir. externship program U. So. Calif., L.A., 1991—; v.p. Shield Health Care Ctrs., Inc. (C.R. Bard, Inc. subsidiary), 1983-86; pres. Merit Coll., 1988-92, PharmaCom., L.A., 1990—; assoc. prof. clin. pharmacy U. So. Calif., L.A., 1991—, asst. dean pharm. care programs, 1995—97, dir. PharmD/MBA program, asst. dean programmatic advancement, 1998—; prin. New Horizon Pharmacy Cons. Adj. asst. prof. U. without Walls, Shaw U., Raleigh, NC, 1973; project dir. Haynes Found. Drug Rsch. Ctr., U. So. Calif., L.A., 1973; assoc. dir. Calif. Alcoholism Found., 1973—75; adj. asst. prof. clin. pharmacy Sch. Pharmacy, U. So. Calif., 1981—91; cons. Topanga Terr. Convalescent Hosp., 1970—80, Calif. Labor Mgmt. Plan of alcoholism programs and coords., 1974, Office of Alcoholism, State of Calif., Nat. In-Home Health Svc., 1975, Continuity of Life Team, 1975, Triad Med., Longs Drug Stores, HealthTek, others; vis. prof. Tokyo Coll. Pharmacy, 1994, Sandoz Pharm. Co., 1995, Clin Oscar Romero, 2000; lectr. Meijo U., Nagoya U., Japan, 1994; presenter Nat. Pharmacy Dir. Conf., 1995; cons., mem. sci. adv. bd. Leiner Health Products, 1998—; cons. Prime Care Pharmacy, 1998—, Jackson Meml. Hosp., 1998, New Horizon Pharmacy, Avalon Hosp., Queenscare Family Clinics; cons., mem. adv. bd. Medpin, 2001; chair nominating com. CPHA, 1998; co-developer Trends in Healthcare Svcs.; presenter in field. Adv. bd. Pharmacist Newsletter, 1980—. Chmn. Friends of Operation Bootstrap, 1967-77; svc. chmn. tng. coord. Am. Cancer Soc., San Fernando Valley, Calif., 1980; mem. adv. bd. L.A. VNA, 1982; bd. dirs. pres. QSAD, 1987-88; pres. bd. Everywoman's Village, 1988-89; bd. dirs. Life Svcs., 1988-94; pres. bd. counselors, U. So. Calif., 1988-92, co-chmn. good neighborhood campaign Sch. Pharmacy, 1998; mem. Calif. Bd. Pharmacy Com. on Student/Preceptor Manual, 1991-92. Named Disting. Alumnus of Yr., U. So. Calif., Sch. of Pharmacy Alumni Assn. 1983, U. So. Calif. Torchbearer, 1990-91, Hon. Tchr. of Yr. U. So. Calif. Sch. Pharmacy, 1997. Fellow Am. Coll. Apothecaries, Calif. Pharmacist Assn. (chair edn. com.); mem. Am. Pharm. Assn., Am. Soc. Health Sys. Pharmacists, Am. Soc. Pub. Adminstrn., Am. Assn. Colls. of Pharmacy (spkr. ann. meeting 2000), Phi Kappa Phi, Phi Lambda Sigma (hon., faculty advisor), Rho Chi. Home: 1245 Wellesley Ave Apt 201 Los Angeles CA 90025-1170 Office: 1985 Zonal Ave Los Angeles CA 90089-0105 Office Phone: 323-442-2686. Business E-Mail: mbaron@usc.edu.

BARON, MITCHELL NEAL, lawyer; b. N.Y.C., Nov. 8, 1947; s. Norman and Ruth (Schliftman) B.; m. Sharon Hefler, Feb. 7, 1971; 1 child, Amanda. BS, Boston U., 1969; JD, Columbia U., 1973. Bar: N.Y. 1974. Assoc. Kaye, Schuler, Fierman, Hays & Handler, N.Y.C., 1973-79; ptnr. Golberg & Abrams, N.Y.C., 1979-87, Morgan, Lewis & Bockius LLP, N.Y.C., 1987—, dep. leader firm real estate group. Mem. N.Y. Bar Assn., N.Y.C. Bar Assn.-property law sect. Office: Morgan Lewis & Bockius LLP 101 Park Ave Fl 44 New York NY 10178-0060 Office Fax: 212-309-6001. Business E-Mail: mbaron@morganlewis.com.

BARON, PATRICIA BURRELL, university director; b. Glen Ridge, N.J., Dec. 16, 1949; d. Leo Duncan and Mollie Amelia (Scard) B.; m. William Robert Baron, June 17, 1972. BA, Allegheny Coll., 1972; MA in Librarianship, U. Denver, 1973; MEd in Ednl. Adminstrn., U. Maine, 1980; EdD in Ednl. Adminstrn., No. Ariz. U., 1987. Reference libr. U. Maine, Orono, 1975, asst. to grad. dean, 1976-80, asst. to acad. v.p., 1980-82; asst. to grad. dean No. Ariz. U., Flagstaff, 1982-87, asst. grad. dean, 1987-93, assoc. grad. dean, dir. grad. admissions, 1993—. Contbr. articles to profl. jours., 1998-. Active commn. on status of women Ariz. Bd. of Regents, Phoenix, 1989-91. Recipient Pres.'s Achievement award No. Ariz. U., 1993, 2005; named Woman of Distinction, Soroptimist Internat., 1993. Mem. AAUW, Nat. Assn. Grad. Admissions (exec. bd. 1998-2004, Pres.'s Achievement award 1995, 2005), Univ. Career Women (founder, chair 1991-92), Phi Kappa Phi. Avocations: needlecrafts, gardening. Office: No Ariz U PO Box 4125 Flagstaff AZ 86011-4125

BARON, ROBERT CHARLES, publishing executive; b. LA, Jan. 26, 1934; s. Leo Francis and Marietta (Schulze) Baron; m. Charlotte Rose Persinger, Nov. 29, 1986; 1 child, Kristen Persinger 1 stepchild, Brett Persinger. BS in Physics, St. Joseph's Coll., 1956. Registered profl. engr., Mass. Engr. RCA, Camden, N.J., 1955-57, Computer Control Co., Framingham, Mass., 1959-61, program mgr. Mariner II and IV space computers, 1961-65, engring. mgr., 1965-69; worldwide systems mgr. Honeywell Minicomputer, Framingham, 1970-71; founder, pres., CEO Prime Computer, Framingham, 1971-75; pvt. practice Boston, 1976-83; founder and pres. Fulcrum Pub., Golden, Colo., 1984—. Bd. dirs. Prime Computer, Framingham, Mass., Alling-Lander, Cheshire, Conn., Oxion, Hugoton, Kans., Fulcrum Pub., Golden, Colo. Author: Digital Logic and Computer Operations, 1966, Micropower Electronics, 1970, America in the Twentieth Century, 1995, Footsteps on the Sands of Time, 1999, What Was It Like Orville: The Early Space Program, 2002, Hudson: The Story of a River, 2004, Pioneers and Plodders, 2004; editor: The Garden and Farm Books of Thomas Jefferson, 1987, Soul of America: Documenting Our Past, 1942-1974, 1989, Colorado Rockies: The Inaugural Season, 1993, Thomas Hornsby Ferrill and the American West, 1996. Vice chmn. bd. dirs. Mass. Audubon Soc., Lincoln, 1980—85; bd. dirs. Rocky Mountain Women's Inst., Denver, 1987—90, Denver Pub. Libr. Friends Found., 1989—96, pres., 1994—96; trustee Lincoln Filene Ctr., Tufts U., Medford, Mass., 1982—84. Mem.: Hakluyt Soc., Western History Assn., Mass. Hist. Soc., Thoreau Soc., Am. Antiquarian Soc. (bd. dirs., chmn. 1993—2003), Internat. Wilderness Leadership Found. (bd. dirs. 1990—, chmn. 1994—2000, 2003—), Explorer's Club, Grolier Club. Avocations: writing, reading, sports, gardening, collecting clocks. Office: Fulcrum Pub Ste 300 16100 Table Mountain Pkwy Golden CO 80403-1672 Business E-Mail: bob@fulcrum-books.com.

BARON, ROBERT HOWARD, lawyer; b. Bethpage, N.Y., Nov. 5, 1957; AB, Princeton U., 1978; JD, Harvard U., 1981. Bar: N.Y. 1982, U.S. Dist. Ct. (so. dist.) N.Y. 1982. Assoc. Cravath, Swaine & Moore, N.Y.C., 1981-88, ptnr., litig., 1988—. Office: Cravath Swaine & Moore 825 8th Ave Fl 38 New York NY 10019-7475 Office Phone: 212-474-1422. Office Fax: 212-474-3700. Business E-Mail: rbaron@cravath.com.

BARON, ROBERT M., architecture educator; b. Portland, Oreg., June 8, 1949; BArch, U. Oreg., 1972; MArch, U. Wash., 1973; MS in Arch., U. Pa., 1990. Registered arch., Wash., cert. Nat. Coun. Archtl. Registraton Bds. Arch. Jeppsen, Miller and Tobias, Corvallis, Oreg., 1970, Balzhiser, Longwood, Smith, Paul and Anderson, Eugene, Oreg., 1971—72, Durham, Anderson and Freed, Seattle, 1973, Paul Thiry, FAIA, Seattle, 1973—74; asst. prof. U. Idaho Sch. Arch., Moscow, 1974—79, assoc. prof., 1979—84, prof., 1984—2003, chair dept. arch., 1990—93, 1999—2003; assoc. dean, prof. U. Tex. Sch. Arch., San Antonio, 2003—. Presenter in field. Contbr. articles to profl. jours. Recipient Disting. Tchg. award, U. Idaho Dept. Arch., 1982, Outstanding Faculty award, Associated Students of the U. Idaho, 1983, Alumni Assn. Excellence in Tchg. award, U. Idaho, 1994, 1998. Office: U Tex San Antonio Divsn Arch and Interior Design 501 W Durango Blvd San Antonio TX 78207

BARON, SAMUEL HASKELL, historian; b. N.Y.C., May 24, 1921; s. James and Dinah (Bader) B.; m. Virginia Wilson, Dec. 22, 1949; children—Sheila, Carla, Laura. BS, Cornell U., 1942; MA, Columbia U., 1948; PhD, 1952. Instr. history U. Tenn., 1948-53; vis. lectr. Northwestern U., 1953-54, U. Mo., 1954-55, U. Nebr., 1955-56; from asst. prof. to prof. Grinnell (Iowa)

Coll., 1956-66; prof. U. Calif.-San Diego, 1966-72; Alumni Disting. prof. history U. N.C., Chapel Hill, 1972-91, prof. emeritus, 1991—; chmn. Conf. Slavic and Ea. European History, 1976. Author: Plekhanov: The Father of Russian Marxism, 1963, The Travels of Olearius in Seventeenth Century Russia, 1967, Muscovite Russia: Collected Essays, 1980, Explorations in Muscovite History, 1991, Plekhanov in Russian History and Soviet Historiography, 1994, Bloody Saturday in the Soviet Union: Novocherkassk, 1962, 2001; co-editor: Windows on The Russian Past: Essays on Soviet Historiography since Stalin, 1977, Introspection in Biography: The Biographer's Quest for Self-Awareness, 1985, Religion and Culture in Early Modern Russia and Ukraine, 1997, Adventures in Russian Historical Research, 2003. Served from pvt. to capt. AUS, 1942-46. Ford Found. fellow, 1958-59, Guggenheim Found. fellow, 1970-71, Nat. Endowment Humanities fellow, 1976; chair named in his honor U. N.C., 1994. Mem. AAUP (council 1962-65), Am. Hist. Assn., Am. Assn. Advancement Slavic Studies, Early Slavic Studies Assn. (pres. 1991). Office: U NC Dept History Chapel Hill NC 27599-0001 E-mail: shbaron@email.unc.edu.

BARON, SHELDON, research and development company executive; b. Bklyn., May 13, 1934; s. Harry and Edna (Schleifer) B.; m. Doris Earl Rudd, Aug. 11, 1961; 1 son, David. BS, Bklyn. Coll., 1955; MA, Coll. William and Mary, 1961; PhD, Harvard U., 1966. Simulation engr. USAF-NACA, Hampton, Va., 1955-57; aerospace technologist NASA, Hampton, 1958-65, Cambridge, Mass., 1965-67; mgr., researcher Bolt Beranek & Newman, Cambridge, 1967-71, mgr., prin. scientist, 1971-79, v.p., 1979-94, sr. v.p., 1994-98; ind. cons. Lexington, Mass., 1999—. Mem. sci. adv. bd. U.S. Army Missile Command, Huntsville, Ala., 1975-77; mem. working group on simulation, 1982-84; chmn. working group on human performance modelling Nat. Acad. Scis.-NRC, 1983-87; bd. vistors BBN Techs., 1998-2000; bd. councillors U. S.C. Integrated Media Systems Ctr., 1998—; cons. U.S. Army Sci. Bd., 2000-02. Assoc. editor: Jour. Cybernetics and Info. Scis., Washington, 1976-81. Served to 1st lt. USAF, 1955-57. Fellow (life) IEEE; mem. Control Systems Soc. (sec., treas. 1982-84), AIAA, Harvard Soc. Engrs. and Scientists (pres. 1976-78) Home: 7 Birch Hill Ln Lexington MA 02421-7445

BARONDES, SAMUEL HERBERT, psychiatrist, educator; b. Bklyn., Dec. 21, 1933; s. Solomon and Yetta (Kaplow) B.; m. Ellen Slater, Sept. 1, 1963 (dec. Nov. 22, 1971); children: Elizabeth Francesca, Jessica Gabrielle; m. Louann Brizendine, Sept. 14, 2002. AB, Columbia U., 1954, MD, 1958. Intern, then asst. resident in medicine Peter Bent Brigham Hosp., Boston, 1958-60; sr. asst. surgeon USPHS, NIH, Bethesda, Md., 1960-63; resident in psychiatry McLean and Mass. Gen. hosps., Boston, 1963-66; asst. prof., then assoc. prof. psychiatry and molecular biology Albert Einstein Coll. Medicine., Bronx, N.Y., 1966-69; prof. psychiatry U. Calif., San Diego, 1969-86, prof., chmn. dept. psychiatry, dir. Langley Porter Psychiat. Inst. San Francisco, 1986-94, dir. Ctr. Neurobiology and Psychiatry, 1994—, Jeanne and Sanford Robertson Prof. Neurobiol. and Psychiatry, 1996—. Pres. McKnight Endowment Fund for Neurosci., 1989-98; sci. adv. com. Rsch. Am.; governing coun. Internat. Brain Rsch. Orgn., 1994-2000; bd. sci. counselors NIMH, 1997-2002, chair, 2000-02. Author: Molecules and Mental Illness, 1993, Mood Genes, 1998, Better Than Prozac, 2003; mem. editl. bd. profl. jours.; contbr. articles to profl. jours. Recipient Rsch. Career Devel. award USPHS, 1967, Elliott Royer award, 1989, P.H. Stillmark medal Estonia, 1989; Fogarty Internat. scholar NIH, 1979; J. Robert Oppenheimer lectr., 2000. Fellow AAAS, Am. Psychiat. Assn., Am. Coll. Neuropsychopharmacology; mem. Inst. Medicine Nat. Acad. Sci. Office: U Calif-San Francisco Langley Porter Psychiat Ins 401 Parnassus Ave San Francisco CA 94143-0984 Business E-Mail: barondes@cgl.ucsf.edu.

BARONDESS, JEREMIAH ABRAHAM, physician; b. NYC, June 6, 1924; s. Benjamin and Dora (Greenberg) B.; m. Sue Kaufman, Nov. 22, 1953 (dec. 1977); 1 child, James Joseph; m. Linda Hiddemen, Dec. 10, 1982. MD, Johns Hopkins U., 1949; DSc (hon.), Albany Med. Coll., Union U., 1978; LittD (hon.), N.Y. Inst. Tech., 1992; DMedSci (hon.), Med. Coll. Pa., 1993; DSc (hon.), N.Y. Med. Coll., 1998. Diplomate Am. Bd. Internal Medicine (bd. govs., council gen. internal medicine 1975-81). Intern, then asst. resident in medicine Osler Med. Svc. Johns Hopkins Hosp., 1949-51; asst. medicine Johns Hopkins U. Med. Sch., 1950-51; mem. virology sect., research div. Children's Hosp., Phila., also; rsch. fellow virology U. Pa. Med. Sch., 1951-53; asst. resident, then chief resident in medicine N.Y. Hosp.-Cornell U. Med. Center, 1953-55; mem. faculty Cornell U. Med. Coll., 1953—, clin. prof. medicine, 1971-78, prof. clin. medicine, 1978-87, Irene F. and I. Roy Psaty Disting. Prof. Clin. Medicine, 1987-89, William T. Foley Disting. Prof. in Clin. Medicine, 1989-90, adj. prof. clin. medicine, 1990, prof. emeritus, 1993—; mem. staff N.Y. Hosp., 1953—, attending physician, 1971—; chief pvt. med. svc., 1971-92; hon. staff mem. N.Y. Hosp., 1992—; assoc. chmn. dept. medicine, 1983-90; asst. vis. physician Bellevue Hosp., 1960-67; cons. medicine Meml. Hosp. Cancer and Allied Diseases, 1972-90; Alpha Omega Alpha vis. prof. U. P.R. Med. Sch., 1972; Meyerowitz meml. lectr. U. Rochester Sch. Medicine, 1980. Disting. lectr. U. N.C., 1982; vis. prof. medicine U. Ill. Med. Sch., 1974, U. Va. Med. Sch., 1976, Mayo Clinic and Med. Sch., 1978, U. Iowa Sch. Medicine, 1979, U. Tex. Med. Ctr., 1986, 90, U. Pa., 1986, U. Va., 1989, N.Y. Med. Coll., 1990, SUNY Health Sci. Ctr., Bklyn., 1992; mem. nat. resources com. Johns Hopkins U., 1965—, trustee, 1977-94, trustee emeritus, 1994—, chmn. vis. com. Sch. Medicine, 1978-92. Author: (with A.M. Harvey and J. Bordley) Differential Diagnosis, (with J. McGovern and C. Roland) The Persisting Osler, 1985, (with A.H. Samiy and R.G. Douglas) Textbook of Diagnostic Medicine, 1987, (with C. Roland) The Persisting Osler II, 1994, (with C. Roland) The Persisting Osler III, 2002; editor: Diagnostic Approaches to Presenting Syndromes, 1971; co-editor Differential Diagnosis, 1994; mem. editl. bd. Forum on Medicine, Pharos, Internat. Jour. Technol. Assessment in Health Care, Jour. Royal Soc. Med.; contbr. articles to profl. jours. Bd. dirs. Am. Fedn. Aging Rsch., 1996—. Served with AUS, 1943-46; Served with USPHS, 1951-53. Recipient Wiggers award Albany Med. Coll. Union U., 1978, Alfred Stengel award ACP, 1983; named Hon. Alumnus Cornell U. Med. Coll., 1974. Fellow AAAS, Am. Acad. Arts and Scis., Royal Coll. Physicians London, ACP (chmn. bd. govs. 1973-75, bd. regents 1975—, pres. 1978-79, pres. emeritus 1988), Federated Coun. Internal Medicine, Royal Soc. Medicine, Royal Soc. Health, Royal Coll. Physicians Ireland (hon.); mem. Am. Clin. and Climatol. Assn. (coun. 1975-78, pres. 1994), Am. Osler Soc. (pres. 1983-84), Am. Fedn. Clin. Rsch., APHA, Assn. Am. Physicians, Harvey Soc., N.Y. Heart Assn., Inst. Medicine NAS (coun. 1979-81, co-chair coun. on health care tech., chair com. on managed care and chronic disease 1996, chair com. on musculoskeletal disorders and the workplace 1999-2001, mem. com. in spinal cord injury, 2004-05), N.Y. Acad. Scis., N.Y. Acad. Medicine (pres. 1990—), Internat. Soc. Internal Medicine, Phi Beta Kappa, Alpha Omega Alpha (dir. 1978-79, pres. 1987-89), Century Club (N.Y.C.), Cosmos Club (Washington). Jewish. Home: 544 E 86th St New York NY 10028-7536 Office: NY Acad Medicine 1216 5th Ave New York NY 10029-5202 Business E-Mail: jbaronde@nyam.org.

BARONE, ANGELA MARIA, artist, researcher; b. Concesio, Brescia, Italy, June 29, 1957; arrived in U.S., 1983; d. Giuseppe and Adelmina (D'Ercole) Barone. Laurea cum laude in geol. scis., U. Bologna, Italy, 1981; PhD in Marine Geology, Columbia U., 1989; cert. in profl. photography, N.Y. Inst. Photography, 1992; cert. in fine art painting and drawing, N. Light Art Sch., Cin., 1993. Collaborative asst. Marine Geology Inst., Bologna, 1981-83, Inst. Geology and Paleontology, Florence, Italy, 1982-83, Sta. de Geodynamique, Villefranche, France, 1982; grad. rsch. asst. Lamont-Doherty Geol. Obs., Palisades, N.Y., 1983-89, postdoctoral rsch. asst., 1989; postgrad. rschr. Scripps Instn. of Oceanography, La Jolla, Calif., 1990-92; artist San Diego, 1993—. Contbr. articles to profl. jours. Mem.: Am. Geophys. Union (co-pres. meeting session 1990), Nat. Mus. Women Arts (assoc.). Home: 7540 Charmant Dr Apt 1222 San Diego CA 92122-5044 Office Phone: 858-453-6417.

BARONE, MICHAEL D., political correspondent, writer, editor; b. Highland Park, Mich., Sept. 19, 1944; s. C. Gerald and Alice Katherine (Darcy) B.; m. Joan S. Barone, Feb. 14, 1975 (dec. Mar. 1985); 1 child, Sarah. AB, Harvard U., 1966; LLB, Yale U., 1969. Bar: Mich., D.C. Law clk. to Judge Wade H. McCree, Jr. U.S. Ct. Appeals, Detroit, 1969-71; v.p. Peter D. Hart Research Co., Washington, 1974-81; editorial writer, columnist The Washington Post, 1981—88; sr. staff editor Reader's Digest, Washington, 1996—98; sr. writer U.S. News & World Report, Washington, 1989—96, 1998—. Regular panalist McLaughlin Group; polit. contbr. FOX News Channel, 1998—. Principal co-author (books) The Almanac of American Politics, 1972, 14th edit., 1998, 2002 edit.; Author (books) Our Country: The Shaping of America From Roosevelt to Reagan, 1990, The New Americans: How the Melting Pot Can Work Again, 2001, Hard America, Soft America: Competition vs. Coddling and the Competition for the Nation's Future, 2004; contbr. to the following publs.: The Economist, The NY Times, Detroit News, Detroit Free Press, Weekly Standard, New Rupublic, National Review, American Spectator, American Enterprise, Times Literary Supplement, and Daily Telegraph of London; contbr. (chapters in books) including Beyond the Godfather, Our Harvard and several others. Office: US News & World Report 1050 Thomas Jefferson St NW Washington DC 20007 E-mail: michaelbarone@michaelbarone.com.*

BARONE, ROSE MARIE PACE, writer, retired educator; b. Buffalo, Apr. 26, 1920; d. Dominic and Jennie (Zagara) Pace; m. John Barone, Aug. 23, 1947 BA, U. Buffalo, 1943; MS, U. So. Cal., 1950; cert. advanced study, Fairfield (Conn.) U., 1963. Tchr. Angola (N.Y.) High Sch., 1943-46, Puente (Calif.) High Sch., 1946-47, Jefferson High Sch., Lafayette, Ind., 1947-50; dir. Warren Inst., Bridgeport, Conn., 1951-53; instr. U. Bridgeport, 1953-54; tchr. bus. subjects Bassick H.S., Bridgeport, 1954-74, Harding H.S., Bridgeport, 1974-80; instr. Fairfield U., Conn., 1969; freelance writer, 1980—. Chair State Poetry Festival, 1987. Founder Pet Rescue; chmn. comty. affairs com. Area Coun. Cath. Women, 1988-90, sec., 1990-91, chmn. family affairs com., 1991, v.p., 1992-93; chmn. comty. affairs Ch. Women United, 1992—, state area chmn., 1995-97, sec., 2003, state UN chair, 1997—. Pace-Barone Minority yearly scholarship Fairfield U., Auerbach Found. scholar, 1956; recipient Playwriting prize Conn. Federated Women's Clubs, 1955, 1st prize for poetry, 1985, Short Story award Federated Women Conn., 1987, 88, 90, Citizen award Bridgeport Dental Assn., 1982, State/Town Hero award, 1986, Anniversary medal and marble statuette Fairfield U., Cmty. Care Successful Aging award, 1992, Salute to Women award YWCA, 1993, Woman of Substance award, 1994, State Commission Arts award, 2000, RSVP award, 2001. Mem. NEA, AAUW (treas. 1957-58, named gift grant 1989, cultural and poetry chair 1992—, rec. sec. 1992-93, internat. rels. 1993-94, v.p. program 1995-97, contest chair 1995—, Conf. of Women award 1997, Fairfield Citizen, Vol. Extraordinaire, 2001), Am. Assn. Ret. People (v.p. 1987-88, pres. 1988-89, 94-95, instr. 55 Alive, cmty. affairs chair 1990—), Owl (sec. 1987-89, pres. 1989-90), Nat. League Am. PEN Women (Bridgeport historian 1966-84, state historian 1983—, treas. br. 1985-88, state pres. 1986-88, state lit. chair 1988-95, br. membership chair 1990, Nat. Historian award 1976, 88), Fairfield Area Poets (founder, pres. 1990—, editor 5 vols. Conn. poets), UN Assn. USA (pres. Bridgeport 1964-66, 68-70, v.p. 1988—, chmn. area UN Days 1960—, pres. Conn. 1971—, state chmn. UNICEF to 1984, area UNICEF Ctr. 1984—, state historian 1984—, chair Internat. Kite Fly), Conn. Bus. Tchrs., Bridgeport Edn. Assn. (sec. 1966-68), VFW (aux. 1989—), Am. Legion (aux. contest chair 1989—, historian 1993-95, Aux. Nat. Cmty. Svc. award 1993), Fairfield Arts Coun., Fairfield Philatelic Soc. (sec. 1971-78, founder advisor Philatelic Jrs. 1972-80), Fairfield U. Women's Club (founder, pres. 1950, 74—, v.p. 1973-74), Southport Women's Club (garden dept. sec. 1981-85, chmn. 1985-87), John & Rose Marie Barone Resource Ctr. St. Vincent's Coll., Pi Omega Pi. Home: 1283 Round Hill Rd Fairfield CT 06430-7329

BARONI, MICHAEL L., lawyer; b. NYC, Dec. 26, 1967; m. Lisa Lynnette. BA, Boston Coll., 1990; JD, Hofstra U., 1993. Bar: NY 1994, Calif. 2001. Of counsel Jacobson & Colfin, NYC; in-house counsel Gen. Media, Inc., 1995—97; gen. counsel Henry Holt & Co., 1997—98; with law dept. Metromedia Fiber Network Svcs., White Plains, NY, 1998—2003; gen. counsel, sec. BSH Home Appliances Corp., Huntington Beach, Calif., 2003—. Mem.: ABA (mem. antitrust sect., forum on franchising), Assn. Corp. Counsel, State Bar Calif. (mem. antitrust unfair competition sect., bus. law sect.), NY State Bar Assn. (mem. com. literary works and related rights 1995), Orange Co. Bar Assn. (mem. product liability sect., bus. and corp. law sect., corp. counsel). Office: BSH Home Appliances Corp Legal Dept 5551 McFadden Ave Huntington Beach CA 92649

BARON-MALKIN, PHYLLIS, artist, art educator; b. Newark, Apr. 15, 1927; d. Jack and Sadie Green; m. Milton Malkin (div.); m. Murray Baron; children: Kim, Robin, Jacki, Dara. Student, Culinary Sch. N.Y., 1947, Nat. Acad. Design, N.Y.C., 1970—76, Sch. Interior Design, Miami, Fla., 1978. Owner, designer Kirojada Sugar Creations, 1960—70; prin., owner Dade County Taxi, 1961—78, Jewelers, Ft. Lauderdale, Fla. Judge numerous art shows; ran outdoor art shows. Exhibited in group shows at Internat. Fine Arts Exhibit, Calif., Nat. Acad. Design, 1970—76, Newark Pub. Libr., Lever House, N.Y., Bernardsville State Show, Salmagundi Club, Nat. Arts Club, Miniature Show N.J., Catherine Larriland Wolfe Club, N.Y., Coun. Jewish Women, Teaneck, N.J., Greenwich Village, N.J. State Show, East Orange, Audonbon Show, Newark Mus., Jersey City Mus., one-woman shows include South Orange Gallery, N.J., Originique Gallery, Korby Gallery, Bloomfield Gallery, Delaney Gallery, Ft. Lauderdale, Tattum Gallery, represented in numerous pvt. collections. Apptd. Broward County Art Coun.; mem. arts counsel Broward County, 1974. With Air Svc. Command, 1945—46. Mem.: Nat. Pastel Soc. (selected to form organization). Democrat. Achievements include paintings being hung in galleries and private collections in Europe and nationwide in the U.S. Home: 7042 Golf Pointe Cir Tamarac FL 33321

BAROODY, MICHAEL ELIAS, trade association executive; b. Washington, Sept. 14, 1946; s. William J. and Nabeeha (Ashooh) B.; m. Mary Cecilia Patton, Dec. 16, 1967; children— Michael Elias, Timothy, Catherine, Matthew, Peter, Meghan BA in Polit. Sci., U. Notre Dame, 1968. Legis. asst. Senator Roman Hruska, Washington, 1970-71; speech writer, exec. asst. Senator Bob Dole, Washington, 1972-75; congl. liaison FEA, Washington, 1975-77; dir. pub. affairs Republican Nat. Com., Washington, 1977-81; exec. asst. to U.S. trade rep. William Brock, Washington, 1981; dep. asst. to Pres., dir. pub. affairs The White House, Washington, 1981-85; asst. sec. for policy Dept. Labor, Washington, 1985-89; sr. v.p. for policy and comms. Nat. Assn. Mfrs., 1990-93; pres. nat. policy forum A Rep. Ctr. for Exch. of Ideas, 1993-94; v.p. pub. affairs Nat. Assn. Mfrs., Washington, 1994-96, sr. v.p. pub. affairs, 1997-99, sr. v.p. policy comm. and pub. affairs, 1999-2001, exec. v.p., 2001—. Editor-in-chief: Commonsense: A Republican Jour. Thought and Opinion, 1978-80, 94, Rep. Platform, 1980. Chmn. bd. Nat. Ctr. for Neighborhood Enterprise, 1997—2002. Lt. (j.g.) USN, 1968-70 Greek Catholic Home: 4628 Newcomb Pl Alexandria VA 22304-1505

BAROTT, PAT ROBERT, broadcast technician; b. St. Paul, Minn., Oct. 26, 1953; s. Robert Wilfred Barott and Erma Janet Hagman. Grad. HS, Forest Lake HS, Forest Lake, Minn., 1972. Reporter Skywarn, 2005—. Contbr. Forest Lake,Minn.: Columbus Township. Emergency comacetions; mem. Amature Radio Emergency Svc. Mem.: AAAS, R.E.A.C.T., Skywarn, Mpls. Assn. Radio Operators, N.Y. Acad. Scis., Twin Cities Repeater Club, Anoka County Radio Club. Avocations: ham radio, astro physics. Home: 13702 Jordell St Lino Lakes MN 55014-2049 Personal E-mail: kbooli@msn.com.

BAROUCH, DAN HUNG, research scientist, educator, epidemiologist; b. Gottingen, Germany, Feb. 4, 1973; s. Eytan and Winifred Wendy B.; m. Fina Canas, May 15, 1999. BA summa cum laude, Harvard U., 1993; PhD, Oxford (U.K.) U., 1995; MD summa cum laude, Harvard U., 1999. Cert. internal medicine & infectious diseases. Rschr. HIV immunology and vaccines Oxford U., 1993-95; rschr. Beth Israel Deaconess Med. Ctr., Boston, 1995—; resident physician in internal medicine, fellow in infectious diseases Mass. Gen. Hosp., Brigham & Women's Hosp., Boston, 1999—2001, fellow infectious disease, 2001—04, staff physician infectious disease, 2004—; clin. fellow in medicine Harvard Med. Sch., Boston, 1999—2002, instr. in medicine, 2002—04, asst. prof., 2004—. Investigator HIV Vaccine Trials Network, Boston, 2000—. Contbr. articles to profl. jours. British Marshall scholarship Marshall Commn., 1993-95, Barry M. Goldwater scholarship U.S. Govt., 1991-93, USA Today Coll. scholar, 1993, Ptnrs. in Excellence award Mass. Gen. Hosp., 2002, Maxwell Finland Investigator award Mass. Infectious Diseases Soc., 2004. Mem.: AAAS, ACP, AMA, Mass. Med. Soc., Infectious Diseases Soc. Am., Mass. Infectious Diseases Soc. Avocations: calligraphy, violin, skiing, travel. Office: Beth Israel Deaconess Med Ctr Rsch E 113 Divsn Viral Pathogenesis 330 Brookline Ave Boston MA 02215 Home: 2 Saint Paul St Apt# 107 Brookline MA 02446 Office Phone: 617-667-4434. Business E-Mail: dbarouch@bidmc.harvard.edu.

BAROUDY, BAHIGE MOURAD, biochemist, researcher; b. Beirut, July 1, 1950; came to U.S., 1973, naturalized, 1988; s. Mourad Bahige and Ludmila Adelheid (Obermuller-Haddad) BSc, Am. U. of Beirut, 1972; PhD, Georgetown U., 1978. Teaching asst. Wesleyan U., Middletown, Conn., 1973-74; rsch. asst. Georgetown U., Washington, 1974-78, fellow, 1982, rsch. assoc. prof., 1985-89; dir. molecular virology div. James N. Gamble Inst. Med. Rsch., Cin., 1989-95; assoc. dir. antiviral therapy Schering-Plough Rsch. Ins., Kenilworth, N.J., 1996-2000, dir., 2000—01, group dir., 2001—02, group dir. antiviral and antimicrobial therapy, 2002—03; v.p. drug discovery Avance Pharma, Laval, Canada, 2003—. Vis. fellow scientist NIH, Bethesda, Md., 1979-81, vis. assoc. scientist, 1982-85. Contbr. articles to profl. jours., chpts. to books. Mem. Am. Assn. for Study of Liver Diseases, Am. Chem. Soc., Am. Soc. Biochemistry and Molecular Biology, Am. Soc. for Microbiology, Am. Soc. for Virology, N.Y. Acad. Scis., NIH Alumni Assn., Sigma Xi. Lutheran. Avocations: fencing, viola, skiing. Office: Drug Discovery Avance Pharma 500 Cartier Blvd W 4th Fl Laval PQ Canada H7V 5B7 Office Phone: 450-973-2777 206. E-mail: bahige.baroudy@avancepharma.com.

BARQUERO, PEDRO B., mathematician, researcher; b. Barcelona, Apr. 18, 1973; s. Benjamin Barquero and Maria Carmen Salavert. BSc, U. Bath, Eng., 1996; MA, UCLA, 1998, PhD, 2000. Lectr. Calif. State U., Dominquez Hills, 2001—02; prof. N.Y. Inst. Tech., N.Y.C., 2003—; assoc. prof. Santa Monica Coll., Calif., 2000—03; rsch. scholar CUNY. Textbook reviewer Brooks/Cole Pub., 2003—; spkr. in field. Contbr. articles to profl. jours. Fellow Chancellor's fellow, Dept. Math., UCLA; scholar UCLA scholar, 1996, CUNY, Grad. Ctr., NYC. Mem.: Internat. Assn. Cryptology Rsch., Math. Assn. Am., Am. Math. Soc. Office: NYIT-Manhattan Campus Math Dept 1855 Broadway New York NY 10023 Office Phone: 212-261-1623.

BARQUIN, RAMON CARLOS, III, political scientist, consultant; b. Boston, June 26, 1973; s. Ramón Carlos II and Rebecca (Torres) B. BA in L.Am. Studies, BA in Econs., BS in Politics, Brandeis U., 1996; student in law, U. P.R., Guaynabo, 1997-2000, Interam. U. P.R., 1997—; MBA in Global Mgmt., U. Phoenix, 2003. Pres. B&B Importers, Inc., Lexington, Mass., 1993-97; law intern Castro, Delgado-Cadilla & Assocs., Hato Rey, P.R., 1994; exec. dir. Instituto de Formación Democrática, Guaynabo, 1994—; bus. cons. and ethnic program dir. New Eng. Ethnic Prodn., Chelsea, Mass., 1996-97; bus. cons. OPPED, Inc.-Compare Supermarkets, Mass., 1997; founder, CEO, BGR Computer Learning Ctr., Inc., Millennium Technologies Assocs. Corp., 1997—, Alturas Torrimar-Oeste, Guaynabo, P.R.; editor in chief Computerworld Mag. & PC World (Caribbean Editions). Exec. dir., dir. pub. affairs Instituto de Formación Democrática, P.R., 1993—; pub. affairs and polit. cons. Hispanic Am. C. of C., Boston, 1996—, Latino, Boston, 1996, La Coperativa-Promotions 2000, Chelsea, Mass., 1997; ind. polit. analyst WUNR-1600 AM Radio Adv. Bd., Boston, 1997; founder Inst. Internat. Trade and Fgn. Policy, 1997—. Author: Think Tanks and Governance, 1995, Cuba in Transition: Comparison of IMF and World Bank Conditionalities and Cuba's Econ Reforms, 1996, Governance and Latin America, 1997, The Castro Regime Under the Bretton Woods Economic System, Cuban Communism 9th edit., 1998; contbr. to San Juan Star newspaper, 1998. Avocations: Judo, sailing, poetry, reading. Home and Office: M31 Ave Lomas Verdes Torrimar Guaynabo PR 00966-3147 Office Phone: 787-273-6724. Personal E-mail: Rbarquin3@prtc.net.

BARQUIST, DAVID LAWRENCE, curator; AB, Harvard U., 1979; MA, U. Del., 1981; PhD, Yale U., 2001. Asst. curator Am. Decorative Arts Yale U. Art Gallery, New Haven, 1983—90, assoc. curator Am. Decorative Arts, 1990—2004; curator Am. Decorative Arts Phila. (Pa.) Mus. Art, 2004—. Dir. Am. Friends Attingham Summer Sch., N.Y., 2000—03, New Haven (Conn.) Colony Hist. Soc., 1986—89. Recipient Charles F. Montgomery prize, Decorative Arts Soc., 1993. Office: Philadelphia Museum of Art Benjamin Franklin Parkway Philadelphia PA 19101 Office Phone: 215-684-7522.

BARR, ANN HELEN, director; d. John Roger and Hester Ann (Davis) Barr. B in Music Edn., Coll. Wooster, 1964; MA in Music Edn., UCLA, 1972. Tchr. music Huber Heights (Ohio) Schs., 1964—67; reconciliation specialist Merrill Lynch Pierce, Fenner & Smith, LA, 1968—72; tchr. Dayton (Ohio) Pub. Sch., 1978—98; flight dir. Challenger Learning Ctr., Dayton, 1998—2000, lead flight dir., 2000—. Hunger fund chair Westminster Presbyn. Ch., Dayton, 1984—; mem. Westminster Choir. Named Aerospace Tchr. of Yr. in Ohio, AFA, 2004; recipient 1000 mission award, Challenger Ctr., 2004; Kettering Found. grantee, 1983, Electronic Data Sys. grantee, 1999. Mem.: Civil Air Patrol, White Shrine of Jerusalem (worthy high priestess 1984). Avocations: gardening, travel, quilting, bridge, softball. Office: Challenger Learning Ctr 1401 Leo St Dayton OH 45404 Office Phone: 937-547-6196. Personal E-mail: ahbarr@juno.com.

BARR, CATHY BROWN, secondary school educator, consultant; b. ElDorado, Kans., May 21, 1952; d. Mack Elwood and Vera Mae Brown; m. Bruce William Barr, Nov. 12, 1983; children: Megan Cathleen, Brittany Beth. BA in Edn., Wichita State U., 1974; MS in Edn., U. Kans., 1987. Cert. tchr. Mo. Tchr. Hickman Mills Sch. Dist., Kansas City, Mo., 1974—2001; curriculum coord. Ctr. Sch. Dist., Kansas City, 2001—04; cons. Mo. Dept. Elem. and Secondary Edn., Jefferson City, 2004—. Mem.: ASCD (bd. dirs. Mo. chpt. 2004—), Show-Me Curriculum Adminstrs. Devel. Coun., Internat. Reading Assn. (bd. dirs 2004—), Mo. Assn. Tchrs. English, Nat. Staff Devel. Coun. Methodist. Avocations: reading, writing, cooking, gardening, art. Office: Missouri Dept of Elem and Secondary Ed PO Box 480 Jefferson City MO 65102-0480 Office Phone: 573-751-4898. Personal E-mail: cathy.barr@dese.mo.gov.

BARR, CHARLES F., lawyer, insurance company executive; BA, Boston Coll., 1972; JD, Suffolk U., 1976. Bar: Mass. 1977, Conn. 1993; CPCU. Counsel Comml. Union Ins. Cos., 1977-81; asst. gen. counsel Reliance Ins. Cos., 1981-87; v.p., gen. counsel United Pacific Life Ins. Co., 1984-87; gen. counsel Gen. Accident Ins. Co., 1987-89, Gen. Reins. Corp., Stamford, Conn., 1989-94, sr. v.p., gen. counsel, sec., 1994-2000; gen. counsel Benfield Blanch, Inc., Westport, Conn., 2000—. E-mail: charles.barr@benfieldgroup.com.

BARR, CYNTHIA MARIE, accountant; b. Lancaster, Pa., Sept. 16, 1966; d. Edwin F. and Mary C. (McLaughlin) B. BS, Elizabethtown (Pa.) Coll., 1989. CPA, Pa. Supr. Ross Buehler Falk & Co., Lancaster, Pa., 1989—. Mem. AICPA, Pa. Inst. CPA, Inst. of Mgmt. Accts., Alpha Lambda Delta, Sigma Mu Delta. Roman Catholic. Office: Ross Buehler Falk & Co 1500 Lititz Pike Lancaster PA 17601-6531

BARR, DONALD ROY, statistics and operations research educator, statistician; b. Durango, Colo., Dec. 10, 1938; s. Russell Wesely and Elizabeth Joanette B.; m. Loudean Suttle, June 14, 1958; children: Mark Edward, Bryan Michael. BA, Whittier Coll., 1960; MS, Colo. State U., 1962, PhD, 1965. Instr. Colo. State U., 1964-65; asst. prof. math. U. Wis.-Oshkosh, 1965-66; prof. stats. and ops. rsch. Naval Postgrad. Sch., Monterey, Calif., 1966-87; v.p. Evaluation Tech. Inc., 1987-88, pres. Monterey, 1988-89; v.p. VRC Corp., Monterey, 1988-89; prof. math. Naval Postgrad. Sch., Monterey, CA, 1990-93; prof. systems engring. U.S. Mil. Acad., West Point, N.Y., 1993-99; ret., 1999—. Liaison scientist London br. Office Naval Rsch., 1982-83; vis. prof. systems engring., U.S. Mil. Acad., West Point, N.Y., 1992-93. Author: College and University Mathematics, 1968, Finite Statistics, 1968, Probability, 1971, Analytic Geometry: A Vector Approach, 1971, Probability: Modeling Uncertainty, 1981, Statistics by Calculator, 1983; contbr. articles to profl. jours. Recipient Rist prize for best paper in mil. ops. rsch. Mil. Ops. Rsch. Soc., 1996, Payne award for ops. rsch. U.S. Army, 1997, Wilks award for Stats., 2004. Mem. Am. Stat. Assn., Ops. Research Soc. Am., Internat. Test and Evaluation Assn., Sigma Xi. Home: PO Box 2071 Paradise CA 95967-2071 Personal E-mail: dbarrz@comcast.net.

BARR, DOUGLAS A., lawyer; b. San Francisco, Aug. 1, 1947; BA, Whittier Coll., 1969; MS, Stanford U., 1971; JD, Golden Gate U., 1975. Bar: N.Mex. 1976, U.S. Dist. Ct. N.Mex. 1978, U.S. Ct. Appeals (10th cir.) 1978. Atty. N.Mex. Pub. Defender's Office, Santa Fe, 1976-78; ptnr. Lill, Bova & Barr, Albuquerque, 1979-83; mem. staff Sandia Nat. Labs., Albuquerque, 1984-91; pvt. practice Albuquerque, 1984-91, 94—; ptnr. Messersmith, McNeil, Schoen & Barr, Albuquerque, 1992-94; pres. The Barr Law Firm, P.C., Albuquerque, 1994—. Author: Legal Self-Help Manual for Dogs, 1992. Pres. Albuquerque Coun. for Internat. Visitors, 1994-95, dir., 1994—. Mem. N.Mex. Trial Lawyers Found., Albuquerque Bar Assn. Avocations: piano, skiing, birds. Office: The Barr Law Firm PC 3005 Louisiana Blvd NE Albuquerque NM 87110-2700 E-mail: barrlaw@aol.com.

BARR, EMILY L., television station executive; BA in Film Studies, Carleton Coll., 1980; MBA in Mktg., George Washington U., 1986. News editor KSTP-TV, St. Paul, Minn., 1980-81, news promotion specialist, 1981-82; writer, prodr. WJLA-TV, Washington, 1983-85; advtg. & promotion mgr. KHOU-TV, Houston, 1985-87, dir. creative svcs., 1987-88; dir. broadcast ops. WMAR-TV, Balt., 1988-93, acting gen. mgr., 1993, asst. gen. mgr., 1993-94; pres., gen. mgr. Sta. WTVD, Raleigh, N.C., 1994-97, Sta. WLS-TV, Chgo., 1997—. Grad. leadership program Greater Balt. Com., 1990; active NAPTE, 1988—, BPME, 1983-93, CBS Promotion Caucus, 1987-88. Vol. Mus. Broadcast Comms.; bd. dirs. United Cerebral Palsy-Chgo., Children's Meml. Hosp. Found.; commr. Chgo. State St. Commn. Recipient Dante award Joint Civic com. for Italian Americans, 1998. Mem. Ill. Broadcast Assn., Chgo./Midwest TV Acad., Chgo. C. of C. (bd. dirs.), Chgo. Cen. Area Com. (bd. dirs.). Office: 190 N State St Chicago IL 60601-3302

BARR, FREDERICK REICHERT, JR., marketing executive; b. Phila., July 3, 1956; s. Frederick R. and Edythe H. (Girvin) B.; m. Karen Wojtas, July 18, 1981; children: David A., Katie L. BA in Econs., Hobart Coll., 1978; MBA in Mktg., Roosevelt U., 1986. Advt. mgr. Chamberlain Group, Elmhurst, Ill., 1981-83, product mgr., 1983-86; mktg. mgr. Evans Rule Co., Charleston, S.C., 1986-89; mgr. product mktg. Protor-Silex, Inc., Glen Allen, Va., 1989-91; dir. mktg. Chamber Door Industries, Inc., Hot Springs, Ark., 1991-2000; v.p. sales and mktg. Century Industries, Little Rock, 2000—. Mem. Am. Mgmt. Assn., Delta Chi. Republican. Presbyterian. Avocations: weightlifting, woodworking, outdoor sports. Home: 107 Four Oaks Ln Hot Springs National Park AR 71901-8961 Office: Century Industries Inc 2300 145th St Little Rock AR 72206-5898

BARR, J. JAMES, company executive; With Am. Water Works Co., Inc., Voorhees, N.J., 1961—, CEO, 1991—, pres., CEO, 1998—, also bd. dirs. Mem. Nat. Assn. Water Cos. (chmn. bd. dirs.) Office: Am Water Works Co Inc 1025 Laurel Oak Rd Kirkwood Voorhees NJ 08043

BARR, JAMES, III, telecommunications company executive; b. Oak Park, Ill., Mar. 2, 1940; s. James Jr. and Florence Marie (Erichsen) B.; m. Joan Benning, Aug. 12, 1961; children: James IV, Brett Christopher, Heather Kathryn, Stephanie Alexandra. BS in Engring., Iowa State U., 1962; MBA, U. Chgo., 1967. Engr. Ill. Bell Tel. Co., Chgo., 1962-66, staff mgr. for regulatory affairs, 1966-69; dist. mgr. for planning AT&T, N.Y.C., 1969-72, dir. regulatory affairs, 1975-80, dir. product mgmt. Basking Ridge, N.J., 1980-85, sales v.p. N.Y.C., 1985-90; gen. mktg. mgr. Bell Can., Ottawa, Ont., 1972-75; pres., CEO, TDS TELECOM, Madison, Wis., 1990—. Exec. vp., bd. dirs. NY Bd. Trade, 1985—90; bd. dirs. Tel. and Data Sys., Chgo., Ctr. for Telecom. Mgmt., L.A., TDS Telecom, Madison, Wis. Mem. dean's adv. coun. Bus. Sch. U. Wis., 1997— Republican. Roman Catholic. Office: 525 Junction RD Madison WI 53717-2152

BARR, JAMES HOUSTON, III, lawyer; b. Louisville, Nov. 2, 1941; s. James Houston Jr. and Elizabeth Hamilton (Pope) Barr; m. Sarah Jane Todd, Apr. 16, 1970 (div.); 1 child, Lynn Jamison; m. Cindy Ann Jeffries, May 31, 1997; children: Worden Pope Washington, Augustine Washington Jeffries. Student, U. Va., 1960-63, U. Tenn., 1963-64; BSL, JD, U. Louisville, 1966. Bar: Ky. 1966, U.S. Ct. Appeals (6th cir.) 1969, U.S. Supreme Ct. 1971, U.S. Ct. Mil. Appeals 1978. Law clk. Ky. Ct. Appeals, Frankfort, 1966-67; asst. atty. gen. Ky. Frankfort, 1967-71, 79-82; asst. U.S. atty. U.S. Dept. Justice, Louisville, 1971-79, 83—; 1st asst. U.S. Atty., 1978-79; asst. dist. counsel U.S. Army C.E., Louisville, 1982-83. Lt. comdr. USNR, 1967-81, lt. col. USAR, 1981-91. Mem. FBA (pres. Louisville chpt. 1975-76, Younger Fed. Lawyer award 1975), Ky. Bar Assn., Louisville Bar Assn., Soc. Colonial Wars, SAR, Washington Family Soc., Pendennis Club, Louisville Boat Club (pres. 2004-05), Filson Club, Delta Upsilon. Republican. Episcopalian. Home: 100 Westwind Rd Louisville KY 40207-1520 Office: US Atty 510 W Broadway Ste 1000 Louisville KY 40202-2281 Office Phone: 502-582-5911.

BARR, JAMES NORMAN, federal judge; b. Kewanee, Ill, Oct. 21, 1940; s. James Cecil and Dorothy Evelyn (Dorsey) B.; m. Trilla Anne Reeves, Oct. 31, 1964 (div. 1979); 1 child, James N. Jr.; m. Phyllis L. DeMent, May 30, 1986; children: Renae, Michele. BS, Ill. Wesleyan U., 1962; JD, Ill. Inst. Tech., 1971. Bar: Ill. 1972, Calif. 1977. Assoc. Pretzel, Stouffer, Nolan & Rooney, Chgo., 1974-76; claims counsel Safeco Title Ins. Co., L.A., 1977-78; assoc. Kamph & Jackman, Santa Ana, Calif., 1978-80; lawyer pvt. practice Law Offices of James N. Barr, Santa Ana, 1980-86; judge U.S Bankruptcy Ct. Ctrl. Dist. Calif., Santa Anna, 1987—. Adj. prof. Chapman U. Sch. Law, 1996—. Lt. USN, 1962-67, Vietnam. Mem. Fed. Bar Assn. (Orange County chpt. bd. dirs. 1996-2000), Orange County Bar Assn. (cmty. outreach com.), Nat. Conf. Bankruptcy Judges, Orange County Bankruptcy Forum (bd. dirs. 1989—), Peter M. Elliott Inn of Ct. (founder, first pres. 1990-91), Warren J. Ferguson Am. Inn of Ct. (founder). Office: US Bankruptcy Ct 411 W 4th St Santa Ana CA 92701-4500 Office Phone: 714-338-5470.

BARR, JOHN BALDWIN, chemist, research scientist; b. Niagara Falls, N.Y., Nov. 8, 1932; s. Lorne Haworth and Myra (Baldwin) B.; m. Patricia Jane Kromer, Sept. 18, 1954; children: Mark Kromer, John Robert, Kathryn Jean, Karen Patricia. BA, U. Buffalo, 1954; MS, U. Mich., 1956; PhD, Pa. State U., 1961. Rsch. chemist Corning Glass Works (N.Y.), 1961-62; sr. rsch. chemist Union Carbide Corp., Parma, Ohio, 1962-71, rsch. scientist, 1971-82, sr. rsch. scientist, 1982-86, Amoco Performance Products, Parma, 1986-90, Alpharetta, Ga., 1990-91, assoc. rsch. scientist, 1991-95; cons. Rsch. Opportunities, Inc., Torrance, Calif., 1996—2001; cons. for carbon fiber industry, 2002—. Contbr. articles to profl. jours.; patentee in field. Shell Oil Co. fellow, 1959' recipient Am. Chem. Soc., 2003. Mem.: N. Am. Thermal Analysis Soc., Am. Carbon Soc., Am. Chem. Soc. (award 2003), Pi Lambda Upsilon, Sigma Xi. Republican. Episcopalian.

BARR, JOHN MONTE, lawyer; b. Mt. Clemens, Mich., Jan. 1, 1935; s. Merle James and Wilhelmina Marie (Monte) Barr; m. Marlene Joy Bielenberg, Dec. 17, 1954; children: John Monte, Karl Alexander, Elizabeth Marie. Student, Mexico City Coll., 1955; BA, Mich. State U., 1956; JD, U. Mich., 1959. Bar: Mich. 1959. Mem. Ellis B. Freatman, Jr., Ypsilanti, Mich., 1959—61; ptnr., chief trial atty. Freatman, Barr, Anhut & Moir and predecessor firm, Ypsilanti, Mich., 1961—63; pres. Barr, Anhut, Assoc. PC, Ypsilanti, Mich., 1963—2001, Barr, Anhut, Gilbreath, Ypsilanti, Mich., 2001—. City atty. City of Ypsilanti, 1981—, City of Belleville, 2000—; lectr. bus. law Eastern Mich. U., 1968—70. Contbr. articles to boating mags. Pres. Ypsilanti Family Svc., 1967; mem. Ypsilanti Pub. Housing Com., 1980—84, State Boundry Commrs., 2000—; sr. adviser Explorer law post Portage Trail coun. Boy Scouts Am., 1969—71, commr. Potawatomi dist., 1973—74, commr. Washtenong dist., 1974—75, dist. committeeman, 1984, wolverine coun. v.p., 1992, v.p. Great Saulk Trail coun., 1995—97; sec. High/Scope Ednl. Rsch. Found., 1998—2004; mem. Ypsilanti Election Commn., 1981—; pres. Ypsilanti Emmanuel Luth. Ch., 2002—03; bd. dirs. Mich. Mcpl. League Legal Def. Fund, pres., 1989—90; past pres. Washtenaw 100 Club, 1980—; mem. Mich. State Boundary Commn., 2003—. Served with AUS, 1959—60. Recipient Silver Beaver award, Boy Scouts Am., 1992, Mich. Mcpl. League award of Merit, Mcpl. League Legal Def., 1992. Mem.: ABA, Mich. Mcpl. Attys. Assn. (pres. 1989—90, dist. mcpl. atty. award 1993), Washtenaw County Trial Lawyers Assn., Washtenaw County Bar Assn. (pres. 1975—76, profl. and civility award 1998), Ypsilanti Bar Assn., State Bar Mich. (grievance bd. hearing panel 1969—97, state rep. assembly 1977—82, bd. commrs. 1993—2003, grievance bd. hearing panel 2005—), Ann Arbor Power Squadron (comdr. 1972—73), U.S. Power Squadron (instr. piloting, seamanship, sail), Washtenaw Country Club. Lutheran. Home: 1200 Whittier Rd Ypsilanti MI 48197-2152 Office: 105 Pearl St Ypsilanti MI 48197-2611

BARR, JOHN ROBERT, retired lawyer; b. Gary, Ind., Apr. 10, 1936; s. John Andrew and Louise (Stentz) Barr; m. Patricia A. Ferris, July 30, 1988; children: Mary Louise, John Mills, Jennifer Susan. BA, Grinnell Coll., 1957; LLB cum laude, Harvard U., 1960. Bar: Ill. 1960. Assoc. Sidley Austin Brown & Wood, Chgo., 1960—69, ptnr., 1970—99, sr. counsel, 2000—02; ret., 2002. Mem. Commn. Presdl. Scholars, Washington, 1975—77, Ill. Ho. of Reps., 1981—83, Ill. Electric Utility Property Assessment Task Force, 1998—99. Chmn. Ill. Student Assistance Commn., 1985—; trustee Evanston Hist. Soc., 2001—, Steppenwolf Theatre Co., Chgo., 1992—; chmn. Rep. Ctrl. Com. Cook County, Chgo., 1978—85; mem. Rep. state ctrl. com. 9th Congl. Dist. Ill., 1986—93; chmn. Ill. Bd. Regents, 1971—77; mem. Ill. Bd. Higher Edn., 1971—77, 1986—; trustee Grinnell Coll., 1996—. Mem.: ABA (chmn. task force utility deregulation state and local tax com. 1996—2003), Ill. State Bar Assn. (chmn. state tax sect. coun. 1986—87), Nat. Assn. State Bar Tax Sects. (sec-treas. 1989—90, vice chmn. 1990—91, chmn. 1991—92), Civic Fedn. (bd. dirs. 1993—97), Taxpayers Fedn. Ill. (mem. exec. com. 1983—, treas. 1990—92, vice chmn. 1992—95), Chgo. Bar Assn. (chmn. com. state and mcpl. taxation 1974—75), Emil Verban Soc., Selden Soc., Chgo. Club, Lawyer's Club Chgo., Phi Beta Kappa. Episcopalian. Home: 1144 Asbury Ave Evanston IL 60202-1137 Office: Sidley Austin Brown & Wood Bank One Plz 10 S Dearborn Chicago IL 60603 Office Phone: 312-853-7447. Business E-Mail: jrbarr@sidley.com. E-mail: barrbob@comcast.net.

BARR, JOHN W., investment company executive, foundation administrator; b. Omaha, Jan. 28, 1943; s. Robert Edward and Lois (Kurtz) B.; m. Penny Glassman, July 13, 1968; children: Nathan, Christian, Jenny BA with honors, Harvard U., 1965, MBA (Baker scholar), 1972. Assoc. Morgan Stanley & Co., N.Y.C., 1972-76, v.p., 1977-80, prin., 1981-83, mng. dir., 1984—90; founder, chmn. U.S. Natural Gas Clearinghouse (now Dynegy Corp.), Houston, 1983—89; co-founder, mng. dir. SG Barr Devlin, 1990—. Bd. dirs. Yaddo, 1987—2005. Author: The Hundred Fathom Curve, 1997, Grace, 1999. Chmn. Bennington Coll. Mem. Poetry Soc. Am. (bd. trustees 1984-2004, chmn. 1987-99, bd. govs. 1986-2000, pres. 1996-2000), Century Assn., Union League Club, Chgo. Yacht Club, Grolier Club, Arts Club of Chgo., Poetry Found. (pres. 2004-). Office: Poetry Foundation 1030 N Clark St Ste 420 Chicago IL 60610 also: SG Barr Devlin 1221 Ave of Americas New York NY 10020

BARR, LESLIE GLEN, family practice physician; b. Ft. Benning, Ga., Aug. 1, 1965; d. Glen Woodard Smith and Barbara Jean Mills; children: Shannon Leslie, Chelsea Patricia. BA, SUNY, Buffalo, 1993, MD, 1998; MBA, Niagara U., N.Y., 2000. Diplomate Nat. Bd. Family Practice, Minn. Bd. Med. Practice. Resident U. Buffalo, 1998—2001; family physician Mayo Health Sys., Waseca, Minn., 2001—; clin. instr. dept. family practice and cmty. health U. Minn. Med. Sch. Contbr. chpt. Sexism and Stereotypes in Modern Society, 1999. Mem.: AMA, Minn. Acad. Family Practice (del.), Am. Bd. Family Practice, Minn. Med. Assn., Rotary Internat. (bd. dirs. for internat. svcs.), Phi Beta Kappa. Roman Catholic. Avocation: teaching church school. Home: 2101 4th St NE Waseca MN 56093

BARR, LORENA DALESE, banker; b. Tacoma, Wash., Sept. 15, 1962; d. Leo Faye Gene Hopkins and Joan Antonia Perra; 1 child, Toni Fedchun. Cert. of completion, Digital U., 2002. Sr. loan processor Advantage Home Lending, Tacoma, 2002—02, Kitsap Mortgage, 2001—02; prin., owner Northwest Processing Svcs., 2003—. Processing trainer. Author: (text book) Basic Processing. Achievements include created processing methods that may be used universally by all lenders. Avocations: motorcycling, horseback riding, painting. Office: Northwest Processing Services Ste D 4113 Bridgeport Way West University Place WA 98466 Office Phone: 253-460-6509. E-mail: nwprocessing1@comcast.net.

BARR, MARTIN, science educator, academic administrator; b. Phila., Nov. 11, 1925; s. Louis and Bella (Moskowitz) B.; m. Nancy Lipschutz, July 15, 1951; children: Lawrence Allen, Richard Andrew, Debra Ann, Steven Bruce. B.Sc. in Pharmacy, Temple U., 1946; M.Sc. in Pharmacy, Phila. Coll. Pharmacy and Scis., 1947; PhD, Ohio State U., 1950. Grad. asst., then instr. Ohio State U. Coll. Pharmacy, 1947-50; from asst. prof. pharmacy to prof. phys. pharmacy and pharm. research Phila. Coll. Pharmacy and Sci., 1950-61; prof. pharmaceutics Wayne State U. Coll. Pharmacy, 1961-87, prof. emeritus, 1987—, chmn. dept., 1961-63, dean, 1963-72, v.p. spl. assignments, 1972-76, v.p., sec. to bd. govs., 1976-78, sec. to bd. govs., acting v.p. for health affairs, 1978-80, v.p., dep. provost, 1980-82, dean Coll. Pharmacy and Allied Health Professions, 1982-87; exec. v.p. corp. bus. and med. devel. Mich. Health Care Corp., Detroit, 1987-90, v.p. bd., profl. rels., 1990-92, v.p. continuous quality improvement, 1992-95. Cons. HEW, 1964-69 Contbg. author: Pharmacy, Compounding and Dispensing, 2d edit, 1956, Remington's Practice of Pharmacy, 11th edit, 1956, 12th edit., 1965; Profl. editor: Mid-Atlantic Apothecary, 1953-64, Apothecary, 1953-64, Central Pharm. Jour, 1961-64. Chmn. Mayor's Com. for Narcotics Rehab., Detroit, 1971-73; pres. Oakland County unit Mich. Heart Assn., 1970-72. Recipient Disting. Service award, Disitng. Alumnus award Alumni Assn. Coll. Pharmacy, Temple U., 1957, Disting. Alumnus award Temple U., 1964, Alpha Zeta Omega award, 1979, Meritorious Service award Wayne State U. Pharm. Alumni Assn., Ann. Alumus award Phila. Coll. Pharmacy and Sci., 1983, John H. Webster award Met. Detroit Pharmacist Assn., 1985, Disting. alumnus award Pharmacy Alumni Assn., 1987, Jack L. Beal Postbaccalaureate award Ohio State U. Coll. Pharmacy Alumni Assn., 1989, Disting. Svc. award Wayne State U. Pharmacy Alumni Assn., 1993, Advocate award Detroit Occupl. Therapy Assn., 1995. Fellow Am. Coll. Apothecaries, Acad. Pharm. Scis.; mem. Am. Pharm. Assn. (pres. Phila. 1954-55, chmn. sci. sect. 1959-60, Ebert medal 1956), Am. Soc. Hosp. Pharmacists, Mich. State Pharm. Assn. (pharmacist of yr. 1971), Am. Assn. Colls. Pharmacy (chmn. sect. tchrs. pharmacy 1959-60, chmn. conf. tchrs. pharmacy 1961-62), Vis. Nurse Assn. S.E. Mich. (chmn. 1999-2002), Vis. Nurse Assn. Inc. (chmn. 2004—), Sigma Xi, Rho Chi. Home: 7430 Tall Timbers West Bloomfield MI 48322-1082 Office Phone: 248-624-7974. Personal E-mail: mbarr@nshore.net.

BARR, MARY SINGLETON, educational consultant; b. Canton, N.Y., Mar. 3, 1947; d. Dennis Conley and Mary Louise Barr; m. Reginald Lee Sapp, Aug. 10, 1996; 1 child, Alem Brahan Sapp. BA, Ithaca Coll., 1969; MA in Humanities, Hofstra U., 1974; Profl. Degree Adminstrn., So. Conn. U., 1990. Tchr. lang. arts Half Hollow Hills Sch. Dist., Dix Hills, NY, 1969—2002; ednl. cons./mentor Hillside Resource and Mgmt. Corp., Roxbury, Mass., 2004—. Supervisory bldg. asst., asst. coach speech debate, coach 6 sports, asst. dir. drama, advisor yearbook, lit. mag Burr's Ln. Jr. H.S. /West Hollow Mid. Sch., Dix Hills. Vol. cons./mentor Hillside Resource and Mgmt. Corp., Roxbury, Mass., 2004—05. Recipient The Jenkins award, West Hollow PTA, 2002. Mem.: ASCD, RI Retreads, Ocean State BMW Riders. Avocations: carpentry, motorcycling, sailing, reading, photography. Home: 62 County Road 29 Canton NY 13617 Business E-Mail: msbarr@hillsideresource.org.

BARR, M.E. See BIGELOW, MARGARET

BARR, MICHAEL CHARLES, management consultant, lawyer; b. White Plains, NY, Nov. 2, 1947; s. Charles Yerger and Joan Tames (Biggar) B.; m. Helen June Rumsey, Mar. 17, 1973. Student, Washington and Lee U.; BA summa cum laude, Rutgers Coll., 1969; JD, Columbia U., 1972, MBA, 1980. Bar: N.J. 1976, N.Y. 1978, U.S. Supreme Ct. 1976. Assoc. McCarter & English, Newark, 1976-77, Conboy, Hewitt, O'Brien & Boardman, N.Y.C., 1977-78; investment banker Kidder, Peabody & Co., Inc., N.Y.C., 1980-82; v.p. Mfrs. Hanover Trust Co., N.Y.C., 1982-90, A-L Assocs., N.Y.C., 1990-92; corp. sec., dir. H. Rivkin & Co., Inc., N.Y.C., 1992-93; securities analyst Standard & Poor's Corp., N.Y.C., 1993-98; Russian securities specialist H. Rivkin & Co., Inc., N.Y.C., 1998-99; emerging markets specialist HP Capital Mkts. Group, N.Y.C., 1999-2000; fin. cons. AXA Advisors, Inc., N.Y.C., 2000; corp. bond corr. Dow Jones and Co., N.Y.C., 2001—03; prin. Barr & Co., Far Hills, NJ, 2003—. Guest commentator on Russia CNN, 1998—2000. Actor: (films) The Interpreter, 2004; (TV series) Law & Order: Trial By Jury, 2005. Adv. bd. Washington and Lee Alumni Coll., 1996-98; 30th Reunion planning com. Columbia Law Sch. Class of 1972, 2002. Lt. USN, 1972-76. Recipient Loyal Son award, Rutgers Alumni Assn., 1976. Mem.: U.S. Polo Assn., Phi Beta Kappa.

BARR, MICHAEL S., law educator; BA summa cum laude, Yale U., 1987, JD, 1992; MPhil, Oxford (Eng.) U., 1989. Bar: NY, DC. Clk. Justice David H. Souter, Supreme Ct., 1993—94; spl. adviser and counselor Policy Planning Staff U.S. State Dept., 1994—95; spl. asst. Treasury Sec. Robert E. Rubin, 1995—97; dep. asst. sec. of the Treasury for cmty. devel. policy, 1997—2001; spl. adviser to the Pres., 1999—2001; asst. prof. law U. Mich. Law Sch., Ann Arbor, 2001—. Sr. fellow Brookings Instn., 2001—. Recipient Human Rights award, Am. Immigration Law Assn., 1992, Charles G. Albom prize for appellate advocacy, Yale Law Sch., 1992; Rhodes scholar, Oxford U., 1989. Office: Univ Mich Law Sch 300G Legal Rsch 625 S State St Ann Arbor MI 48109-1215

BARR, PETER JOHN, art historian, educator, art gallery director; b. Bellefonte, Pa., Sept. 20, 1960; s. Homer James and Blanche Shurgarts Barr; m. Kimberly Dawn Roller, May 14, 1983; children: Alamanda Lorraine, Hannah Irene. BPhil in Arts Adminstrn., Pa. State U., 1983; MA in Art History, Boston (Mass.) U., 1989, PhD in Art History, 1997. Asst. dir. gallery Harcus Gallery, Boston, 1984—87; lectr. gallery Mus. Fine Arts, Boston, 1988—90; instr. art history Northeastern U., Boston, 1990, U. Mass., Boston, 1990—97, Boston (Mass.) U., 1997—97; asst. prof. art history Siena Heights U., Adrian, Mich., 1997—2002, assoc. prof. art history, 2002—. Dir. Klemm Gallery Siena Heights U., 1997—; curator exhibits; spkr. in field. Author: (website) 19th-Century Adrian Architecture (Spl. Recognition cert. Imagining Mich., 2005); contbr. articles to profl. jours. Commr. City Adrian (Mich.) Planning Commn., 2001; vol. reader Alexander Elem. Sch., Adrian, 2001; trustee Lenawee County Hist. Soc., Adrian, 2004. Grantee, Sage Found., 2001—03, Teagle Found., 2004, Siena Heights U., 2005. Mem.: Midwest Art History Assn., Coll. Art Assn., Toledo Mus. Art. Methodist. Avocation: gardening. Office: Siena Heights University 1247 E Siena Heights Dr Adrian MI 49221-1796 Office Phone: 517-264-7863.

BARR, RICHARD STUART, computer science and management science educator; b. Austin, Tex., Sept. 3, 1943; s. Howard Raymond and Margaret (Pressler) B.; m. Mary Shipp Sanders, Mar. 10, 1990; 1 child, Johnathan Austin. BSEE, U. Tex., 1966, MBA, 1972, PhD, 1978. Assoc. dir. Coll. of Bus. Computer Ctr. U. Tex., Austin, 1968-72; exec. v.p. Analysis, Rsch. & Computation, Inc., Austin, 1975-76; asst. prof. mgmt. info. scis. So. Meth. U., Dallas, 1976-80, assoc. prof., 1980-84, assoc. prof. ops. rsch. and engring. mgmt., 1984-89, assoc. prof. computer sci. and engring., 1989-2001, dir. parallel processing lab., 1989-97, dir. telecomm. mgmt. rsch. lab., 1997—, assoc. prof., chair dept. engring. mgmt., info. and sys., 2001—; co-founder, pres. Teloptica, Inc., Dallas, 1996-99. Cons. Dept. Treas., Dept. Agr., Dept. Health and Human Svcs.; vis. fellow Dept. Treas., 1977-78; vis. scholar, Princeton (N.J.) U., 1984, U. Colo., Boulder, 1992. Mem. editl. bd. Jour. of Heuristics; area editor Jour. on Computing; contbr. articles to profl. jours. Recipient Rsch. Excellence award So. Meth. U. Sch. Bus., 1980, Outstanding Grad. Instr. award, 1983; named Outstanding Instr., Nat. Tech. U., 1991-99, 2001-02; grantee NSF, 1993-2002. Mem. Inst. for Ops. Rsch. and Mgmt. Scis., INFORMS, Computing Soc. (chmn. 1997-98). Home: 6812 Velasco Ave Dallas TX 75214-3763 Office: So Meth U Sch Engring Dallas TX 75275-0123 E-mail: barr@engr.smu.edu.

BARR, ROBERT LAURENCE, JR., lawyer; b. Iowa City, Iowa, Nov. 5, 1948; s. Robert Laurence and Beatrice Emily (Radenhausen) B.; children: Adrian Robert, Derek Ryan; m. Jerilyn Dobbin, Dec. 31, 1986. BA in Internat. Rels., U. So. Calif., 1970; JD, Georgetown U., 1977; MA, George Wash. Univ., 1972. Bar: Ga. 1977, Fla. 1979. Analyst, atty., chief legis. staff CIA, Washington, 1970-78; assoc. Law Offices of Edwin Marger, Atlanta, 1979-81; pvt. practice Marietta, Ga., 1981-85, 91-94; ptnr. Brock & Barr, Marietta, 1985-86; U.S. atty. for No. Ga., 1986-90; mem. U.S. Congress from 7th Ga. dist., Washington, 1995—2003. Mem. banking and fin. svcs., govt. reform and oversight, and judiciary coms., chmn. subcom. on Comml. and Adminstrv. Law, 2001-02; gen. counsel Cobb County Rep. Com., 1981-83, 1st vice-chmn., 1983-85, chmn., 1985-86; pres. Southeastern Legal Found., Atlanta, 1990-91; mem. long-term strategy project for preserving security and democratic norms in the war on terrorism Kennedy Sch. Govt. Harvard U.; bd. dirs. Met. Atlanta Coun. Alcohol and Drugs, 1989-91. Mem. editl. staff Am. Criminal Law Rev., 1974-77; host weekly radio show on Radio Am. network Bob Barr's Laws of the Universe; writer UPI, Creative Loafing; contbg. editor Am. Spectator; contbr. CNN. Chmn. youth leadership tng. Leadership Inst., Arlington, Va., 2004—; 21st century liberties chair for freedom and privacy Am. Conservative Union; hon. chair Citizens United; bd. dirs. Patrick Henry Ctr. Disting. fellow, Freedom Alliance, 2003. Mem. NRA (bd. dirs.), Ga. Bar Assn., Fla. Bar Assn., Kiwanis, Phi Alpha Delta, Delta Phi Epsilon, Tau Kappa Epsilon. Republican. Methodist. Home: 2256 Parkwood Pl Smyrna GA 30080 Office: 255 E Paces Ferry Rd Ste 350 Atlanta GA 30305

BARR, RONALD JEFFREY, dermatologist, pathologist; b. Mpls., Jan. 5, 1945; s. Maxwell Michael and Ethel Deana (Ring) B.; m. Ulla Elisabet Edstam; children: Anna, Jessica, Sara. BA, Johns Hopkins U., 1967, MD, 1970. Diplomate Am. Bd. Pathology, Am. Bd. Dermatology. Intern U. Calif., San Diego, 1970-71, resident in pathology, 1971-75, resident in dermatology Irvine, 1975-78, fellow in dermatopathology, 1975-78, asst. prof. dermatology, 1977-83, assoc. prof. dermatology and pathology, 1983-86, prof. dermatology and pathology, 1987—, dir. Dermatopathology Lab., 1979—, prof., chmn. dept. dermatology Davis, 1986-87. Bd. dirs. Am. Bd. Dermatology, 1989—, pres., 1997. Contbr. more than 10 chpts. to books. more than 130 articles to profl. jours. Lt. USN, 1971-73. Fellow Am. Soc. Dermatopathology (pres. 1988-89); mem. Internat. Soc. Dermatopathology, Internat. Com. for Dermatopathology (sec.-treas. 1987-91, pres. 1992-93). Office: U Calif Irvine Med Ctr Dermatopathology Lab 101 The City Dr S Orange CA 92868-3201

BARR, ROSEANNE See ROSEANNE

BARR, SOLOMON EFREM, allergist, educator; b. Washington, Mar. 24, 1929; s. Barney and Jennie Florence (Brickman) B.; m. Rita Zeasla Cohan, June 20, 1954; children: Linda, Steven, Carol, Sharon. BA, George Washington U., 1951, MD, 1954. Diplomate Am. Bd. Internal Medicine, Am. Bd. Allergy and Immunology. Intern Phila. Gen. Hosp., 1954-55; resident D.C. Gen. Hosp., 1957-58, George Washington U., 1959-60; practice medicine specializing in allergies Silver Spring, Md., 1978—. Mem. staff Holy Cross Hosp. Contbr. articles to med. publs., most recent in insect sting allergy. Served as capt. M.C., U.S. Army, 1955-57. Emma K. Carr scholar, 1948-49, Maria M. Carter scholar; recipient Freshman award in chemistry Alpha Chi Sigma, 1948, award in chemistry Sigma Kappa, 1948, John Ordronaux award in medicine George Washington U., 1954. Fellow Am. Acad. Allergy, ACP, Am. Coll. Allergists, Am. Assn. Cert. Allergists; mem. Washington Allergy Soc., Montgomery County, Md. State med. socs., AMA (Physician's Recognition award 1974-77, 77-80), Smith-Reed-Russell, William Beaumont,

Jacobi Med. soc. Washington, Phi Beta Kappa, Alpha Omega Alpha. Club: Phi Delta Epsilon Grad. of Washington (pres. 1971-72). Home: 5713 Magic Mountain Dr Rockville MD 20852-3233

BARR, THOMAS D., lawyer; b. Kansas City, Mo., Jan. 23, 1931; m. Cornelia Harrington, Sept. 26, 1953; children: Daniel C., Phoebe Anne Hotz, Robert A., Sara E. BA, U. Mo., Kansas City, 1953; LL.B., Yale U., 1958. Bar: N.Y. State 1959, U.S. Supreme Ct. 1964. Assoc. firm Cravath, Swaine, & Moore, N.Y.C., 1958-65, ptnr. firm, 1965—. Bd. dirs. Salzburg Seminar Dep. dir. Nat. Commn. on Causes and Prevention of Violence, 1968-70; mem. exec. com. Lawyers' Com. for Civil Rights Under Law, nat. co-chmn., 1977-79; trustee Milton S. Eisenhower Found. Served to lt. USMC, 1953-55. Mem. Am., N.Y. State Bar Assn., Assn. Bar of City of N.Y., Am. Coll. Trial Lawyers, Internat. Acad. Trial Lawyers, Am. Bar Found., Am. Law Inst., Coun. Fgn. Rels. Home: 6200 N Yucca Rd Paradise Valley AZ 85253-4291 Office: Cravath Swaine & Moore Worldwide Plz 825 8th Ave Fl 38 New York NY 10019-7475

BARR, WILLIAM PELHAM, lawyer, former United States attorney general; b. NYC, May 23, 1950; s. Donald and Mary (Ahern) B.; m. Christine Moynihan, June 23, 1973; 3 children. AB, Columbia U., 1971, MA, 1973; JD, George Washington U., 1977. Bar: Va. 1977, DC 1978, NY. Staff officer CIA, Washington, 1973-77; law clk. to presiding judge Cir. Ct., Washington, 1977-78; assoc. Shaw, Pittman, Potts & Trowbridge, Washington, 1978-82, 83-84, ptnr., 1985-89, 93-94; dep. asst. dir. domestic policy staff The White House, Washington, 1982-83; asst. atty. gen. Office Legal Counsel, US Dept. Justice, Washington, 1989-90, dep. atty. gen., 1990-91, atty. gen., 1991-93; sr. v.p., gen. counsel GTE Corp., Washington, 1994—97, exec. v.p. govt. & regulatory advocacy, gen. counsel, 1997—2000; exec v.p., gen. counsel Verizon Communications, New York, 2000—. Mem. bd. Davis Selected Advisers. Vice chmn. bd. dirs. The Coll. of William and Mary. Mem. ABA, Va. State Bar Assn., DC Bar Assn., KC. Republican. Roman Catholic. Office: Verizon Communications Legal Dept 38th Fl 1095 Avenue of the Americas New York NY 10036

BARRACANO, HENRY RALPH, retired oil company executive, consultant; b. Bklyn., Apr. 8, 1926; s. Ralph Henry and Josephine (Chianese) B.; m. Dorothy Sue Bartlow, Aug. 19, 1945; children: Ralph Robert, Susan Jo Barracano Ratterree, Linda Joyce Barracano Swartz. BSEE, Pa. State U., 1948. Registered profl. engr., Okla. Distbn. engr. Pub. Svc. Co. Okla., Tulsa, 1948-51; elec. engr. W.R. Holway & Assocs., Tulsa, 1951-56; from staff engr. to asst. to sr. v.p. engring. and constrn. Arabian Am. Oil Co., 1956-83; ind. cons., 1983-89; sr. project mgr. Hudson Engring. and Project Mgmt. Corp., 1990-91; ind. cons., 1992—. Mem. grievance com. State Bar Tex., 1994-99; arbitrator NASD, 1994—. Precinct chair Dem. Party, Harris County, Tex., 1984-98; precinct judge Harris County, 1984-90; bd. dirs. The Pinemont Apts., 2002-2003. 1st Lt. Signal Corps U.S. Army, 1943-59. Named Outstanding Engring. Alumnus, Pa. State U., 1993, Alumni Fellow award, 1997, Pa. State Pioneer, 1998. Mem. IEEE (life sr. mem., various offices held), Petroleum Club Houston (resident mem.), Northgate Country Club. Avocation: travel. Home and Office: 7723 Allegro Dr Houston TX 77040-2508 E-mail: barracano@ieee.org.

BARRACK, WILLIAM SAMPLE, JR., petroleum company executive; b. July 26, 1929; s. William Sample and Edna Mae (Henderson) B.; m. Irene Ball, Sept. 12, 1953; children: William, Elizabeth. BS, U. Pitts., 1950; postgrad., Dartmouth Coll. With Texaco, Inc., N.Y., 1953—, mktg. mgr. Northeast, 1953-62, dist. mgr. Portland, Maine, 1962-65, asst. mgr. distbn. and devel. N.Y., 1965-66, asst. mgr. mktg. research and project devel., 1966-67, asst. div. mgr. Norfolk, Va., 1967-68, area dir. Brussels, Belgium, 1968-70; v.p. Texaco Europe Ltd., N.Y., 1970; asst. to chmn. bd. Texaco, Inc., N.Y.C., 1971, v.p. internat. Europe, 1971-76, v.p. producing Eastern hemisphere, 1976-77, v.p. personnel and corp. services White Plains, N.Y., 1977-80; chmn., chief exec. officer Texaco Ltd., London, Eng., 1980-83; sr. v.p. Texaco Inc., White Plains, N.Y., 1983-92, ret., 1992. Bd. dirs. Standard Comml. Corp., Wilson, N.C., Consol. Natural Gas Co., Pitts., Dominion Resources Inc., Richmond, Va.; mem. Naval War Coll. Found., Newport, R.I.; bd. vis. U. Pitts. Sch. Engring.; dir. Arabian Am. Oil Co., 1977-78; sr. dir. Caltex Petroleum Corp., 1983-92. Trustee Manhattanville Coll.; bd. dirs. Texaco Found. Inc., Mary Rose Soc., Disting. Alumni U. Pitts., Internat. Exec. Svc. Corps. Comdr. USNR, 1951-53. Mem. Fgn. Policy Assn. N.Y. (gov.). Clubs: N.Y. Yacht; Ida Lewis Yacht; North Sea Yacht (Belgium); Woodway Country, Ox Ridge Hunt; Clambake (Newport, R.I.); Australian (Sydney), 25 Yr. Club of The Petroleum Industry; The Pa. Soc., Naval War Coll. Found.

BARRAGÃN, CELIA SILGUERO, elementary school educator; b. Corcoran, Calif., Feb. 4, 1955; d. Frutoso Silguero and Olinda Gonzalez S.; m. Mario Barragãn Jr., Nov. 12, 1977; children: Maricela Aimē, Mario Armando. BS, S.W. Tex. State U., 1976, MA, 1977. 3rd grade tchr. Crockett Elem. Sch., San Marcos, Tex., 1977—78, Bowie Elem. Sch., San Marcos, 1978—84; 5th grade tchr. Travis Elem. Sch., San Marcos, 1984—94, Hernandez Intermediate Sch., San Marcos, 1994—99; asst. prin., bilingual coord. Bonham Elem. Sch., San Marcos, 1985—86, title I reading tchr., trainer, cons., 1995—99; coord., tchr. AVID Miller Jr. H.S., San Marcos, Tex., 1999—2000; ESL/Dyslexia tchr. Miller Jr. High, 2000—01; ESL/dyslexia tchr. Goodnight Jr. H.S., 2001—04; 4th grade bilingual tchr. Comal Intermediate Sch., New Braunfels, Tex., 2004—. Winter High ability program tchr. S.W. Tex. State U.; project math trainer, migrant tchr., Princeville, Ill.; cons., nat. trainer Lang. Cir. Project Read, Minn. Recipient Latino award for cmty. recognition S.W. Tex. State U.; named Tchr. of Yr., Canyon Intermediate Sch., 2005 Mem. Internat. Reading Assn., Tex. Reading Assn., Tex. State Tchrs. Assn., Tex. Assn. Bilingual Edn., Tex. Classroom Tchrs. Assn., San Marcos (Tex.) Assn. Bilingual Edn. (v.p. 1990-91, 94—, pres. 1995—, Bilingual Tchr. of Yr. 1991, Travis Elem. Tchr. of Yr. 1993, Hernandez Intermediate Tchr. of Yr. 1995, Secondary Tchr. of Yr. 1995, Canyon Intermediate Tchr. of Yr. 2005), Orton Dyslexia Soc., Nat. Coun. Tchrs. Math., Nat. Assn. Bilingual Educators, Ill. Migrant Edn. Assn., Tex. Assn. Gifted and Talented, N.J. Writing Project, Assn. Comprehensive Edn. in Tex. Roman Catholic. Home: 1763 Loma Verde Dr New Braunfels TX 78130-1297 Office: Comal Intermediate Sch New Braunfels TX 78130 Business E-Mail: c_barragan77@hotmail.com, celia.barragan@comalisd.org.

BARRAGAN, HUGO, retail executive; b. Cali, Colombia, Feb. 15, 1969; s. Hugo and Rosa Barragan; married. BS, Eckerd Coll., 1991. Account exec. Intercontinental Agy., Miami, Fla., 1991—92; CEO Sir Speedy Printing, Miami, 1992—. Dir. Downtown Homestead, Inc. Avocations: travel, art, cooking. Office: Sir Speedy Printing 9400 S Dixie Hwy Miami FL 33156

BARRAGRY, MARY ANN, librarian; b. Chgo., Jan. 13, 1948; d. John James and Dorothy Mae (Cylkowski) B. BS in Chemistry, Mundelein Coll., 1970; MS in Libr. Sci., U. Ill., 1971, 1971; cert. in computer studies, Alverno Coll., 1996. Cert. lay ministry St. Francis Sem., 2002. Asst. sci. libr. Northwestern U., Evanston, Ill., 1971-76; indexer ADA, Chgo., 1976-78, head indexer, 1978-80; info. analyst Am. Hosp. Supply Corp., Evanston, 1980-85; asst. libr. Wis. Electric Power Co., Milw., 1985-88, libr., 1988—2001; team leader rsch. ctr. WE Energies, Milw., 2001—. Pres. Club MSO, Milw. Symphony Orch., 1989-90; chairperson Edison Electric Inst. Libr. Svcs. Com., 1996-97, 2002-2003. Fellow Beta Phi Mu; mem. Spl. Librs. Assn. (pres. Wis. chpt. 1992-93). Avocations: classical music, opera, choral music, irish culture. Office: WE Energies 231 W Michigan St Milwaukee WI 53203-2918

BARRAM, DAVID J., federal agency administrator; BA, Wheaton Coll., 1965; MBA, Santa Clara Univ., 1973. Staff acct. Price Waterhouse and Co., Boston, 1965-66; various fin. and mktg. positions Hewlett-Packard, 1970-83, contr. computer products group; v.p. fin. and adminstrn., CFO Silicon Graphics, Inc., 1983-85; v.p. fin., CFO, and v.p. corp. comm. Apple Computer, Inc., 1985-93; dep. sec. Dept. Commerce, Washington, 1993-95; adminstr. GSA, Washington, 1996—2001; bd. dir. Net IQ, 2002, lead ind. dir., 2003. Chair Calif. Commn. Pub. Sch. Adminstrn. and Leadership; bd. dir. Nat. Ctr. Edn. and Economy. Served in USN, 1966-69. Recipient Disting. Svc. Award Assn. Calif. Sch. Adminstr.

BARRAN, THOMAS PAUL, language educator; b. Warren, Ohio, July 8, 1946; s. Paul Thomas and Sophia Catherine Barran; m. Barbara Caplan, June 5, 1983. AB, Columbia Coll., 1968; PhD, Columbia U., 1984. Preceptor Columbia U., N.Y.C., 1978—79; prof. Russian Bklyn. Coll., N.Y.C., 1986—. Vis. prof. Hunter Coll., N.Y.C., 1991; bd. dirs. Classic Rug Collection, Inc., N.Y.C.; cons. in field; expert witness in field; lectr. in field. Author: Russia Reads Rousseau 1762-1825, 2002; contbr. articles to profl. jours. Bd. dirs. ROSAS Neighborhood Assn., Bklyn., 1998—2002. Fellow, U.S. State Dept., 1972—74, Internat. Rsch. & Exchanges Bd., 1976—77. Mem.: N.Y. Pub. Libr., Slavic Lang. Profl. Assn., Modern Lang. Assn. Am., Bigelow Soc. Avocations: deep sea fishing, archaeology. Home: 417 16th Street Brooklyn NY 11215 Office: Brooklyn College CUNY Bedford Ave at Ave H Brooklyn NY 11210

BARRANGER, MILLY SLATER, theater educator, writer; b. Birmingham, Ala., Feb. 12, 1937; d. C. C. Slater and Mildred (Hilliard) Hinson; m. G. K. Barranger, 1961 (div. 1984); 1 child, Heather Dalton Barranger Case. BA, U. Montevallo, 1958; MA, Tulane U., 1959, PhD, 1964. Lectr. La. State U., New Orleans, 1964-69; asst. to assoc. prof. Tulane U., New Orleans, 1969-82, chmn. dept. theatre, 1971-82, Alumni disting. prof., 1997—2003, Alumni disting. prof. emerita, 2003—; prof. U. N.C., Chapel Hill, 1982—2003, chmn. dramatic art, 1982-99; producing dir. PlayMakers Repertory Co., Chapel Hill, 1982-99. Pres. Am. Theatre Assn., 1978-79; disting. vis. assoc. prof. U. Tulsa, 1981; vis. young prof. in humanities U. Tenn., Knoxville, 1981-82; scholar-in-residence Yale Sch. Drama, New Haven, Conn., 1982. Author: Theatre: A Way of Seeing, 1980, 1986, 1991, 1995, 2002, 2005, Theatre: Past and Present, 1984, rev. edit., 2001, Understanding Plays, 1990, 1994, 2004, Jessica Tandy, 1991, Margaret Webster, 1994, Margaret Webster: A Life in the Theater, 2004; co-editor: Generations: An Introduction to Drama, 1971, Notable Women in American Theatre, 1989; contbr. articles to profl. jours. Trustee The Paul Green Found., 1982—. Recipient New Orleans Bicentennial award for achievement in the arts, 1976, award for profl. achievement S.W. Theatre Conf., 1978, Pres.'s award U. Montevallo, 1979. Mem. Coll. of Fellows of the Am. Theatre (bd. dirs. 1998-2001); Nat. Theatre Conf. (pres. 1991-93), League Profl. Theatre Women N.Y. Avocations: film, travel.

BARRATT, ERNEST STOELTING, psychologist, educator; b. North Charleroi, Pa., Mar. 31, 1925; s. Robert Duff and Marie Agnes (Stoelting) B.; m. Karen Marie Creel, Dec. 18, 1968; 1 son, Christopher Robert; 1 dau. by previous marriage, Robin Rhein. BA, Tex. Christian U., 1947, MA, 1949; PhD, U. Tex., 1952. Asst. prof. U. Del., Newark, 1951-57; prof. Tex. Christian U., Fort Worth, 1957-62; prof., chief psychophysiology lab. and psychology sect. U. Tex. Med. Br., Galveston, 1962—, Marie B. Gale Centennial prof. psychiatry, 1998—. Contbr. articles to profl. jours. Trustee Galveston Ind. Sch. Dist., 1971-89. Served with USN, 1943-46. Spl. fellow UCLA Brain Research Inst., 1961-62 Fellow APA, Am. EEG Soc., Soc. for Personality Assessment, Am. Psychol. Soc., Internat. Orgn. Psychophysiology; mem. Soc. for Neurosci., Soc. Psychophysiol. Rsch., Soc. Biol. Psychiatry, Internat. Soc. for Study Individual Differences (pres. 1989-91), Internat. Soc. for Rsch. on Impulsivity and Impulse Control Disorders (pres., 2005-). Roman Catholic. Home: 2641 Gerol Dr Galveston TX 77551-1529 Office: U Tex Med Br Dept Psychiatry & Behavioral Sci Galveston TX 77555-0189 Office Phone: 409-747-9681. E-mail: ebarratt@utmb.edu.

BARRÉ, LLOYD MILTON, retired religion educator, researcher, writer; b. Regina, Sask., Can., Jan. 7, 1952; s. Vern Victor and Alexandra Eva Barré; 1 child, Linda. BA, San Jose State U., 1979; C of Christian Studies, Regent Coll., 1980; MA, Vanderbilt U., 1983, PhD, 1986. Rschr., tchg. asst. U. B.C., Can., 1979; tchg. asst. Vanderbilt U., 1982, instr. bibl. Hebrew, 1983-84; asst. prof. So. Meth. U., 1984—85. Author: The Rhetoric of Political Persuasion: The Narrative Artistry and Political Intentions of 2 Kings 9-11, 1988, El and Yahweh: The Early History and Formative Traditions of Ancient Israel, 1998, A Brilliant Deceit and Other Essays, 2001; Tradition and History in Early Israel, 2001; contbr. articles to profl. jours. Recipient Beach Carré fellowship, 1982-83.

BARRE, STEVEN CRAIG, lawyer; b. N.Y.C., Nov. 11, 1959; s. Gerald J. and Roslyn P. (Fink) B.; m. Rachel Brody, Aug. 21, 1983; 3 children. BS, Cornell U., 1981; JD, Columbia U., 1984. Bar: N.Y. 1985. Assoc. Weil Gotshal & Manges, N.Y.C., 1984-88; asst. gen. counsel Hanson Industries, Iselin, NJ, 1988-92, assoc. gen. counsel, 1993-95, U.S. Industries Inc., 1995-2000, v.p., gen. counsel, sec., 2000—01, sr. v.p., gen. counsel, sec., 2001—03, Jacuzzi Brands Inc. (U.S. Industries Inc.), West Palm Beach, Fla., 2003—. Pub. jour. Bus. Law Today, 1993. Book rev. editor Columbia Jour. of Environ. Law, 1983-84. Com. mem. Cornell U. Alumni Ambassadors, Ithaca, N.Y., 1981—. Harlan Fiske Stone scholar, 1984, Cornell Nat. scholar, 1977. Mem. ABA, N.Y. State Bar Assn. Avocation: bicycling. Office: Jacuzzi Brand Inc 777 S Flagler Dr Ste 1100W West Palm Beach FL 33401

BARRECA, CHRISTOPHER ANTHONY, lawyer; b. Pittsfield, Mass., Sept. 15, 1928; s. Christopher Joseph and Jennie (Cannici) B.; m. Alice Hazlehurst, Sept. 5, 1953. AA, Boston U., 1950, JD, 1953; LLM, Northwestern U., 1968. Bar: Mass. 1954, Ky. 1969, U.S. Dist. Ct. Ky. 1970, U.S. Dist. Ct. Mass. 1995, U.S. Ct. Appeals (6th cir.) 1970, Conn. 1988. With Gen. Electric Co., Fairfield, Conn., 1953-93, labor arbitration and litigation counsel, 1971-80, sr. labor and employment law counsel, 1980-93; ptnr., office chair Paul, Hastings, Janolsky & Walker LLP, Stamford, Conn., 1993-99, sr. counsel, 1999—. Mem. arbitration services adv. com. Fed Mediation and Conciliation Service, 1973—; adj. prof. U. Louisville, 1970-71, U. Bridgeport (Conn.) Sch. of Law, 1986-90; selectman Weston, 1997-00. Co-author, editor: Labor Arbitrator Development, 1983, A Practical Guide for Advocates, 1990; contbr. articles to profl. jours. Chmn. Weston (Conn.) Bd. Edn., 1977-82; trustee, vice chair exec. com., chmn. com. legal affairs, sec. bd., 2001, vice chair bd., 2002-2003, chmn. bd., Boston U., 2003-2004. Served with AUS, 1946-47. Mem. ABA (chmn. labor and employment law sect. com. labor arbitration advocacy, elected to governing council of labor and employment law sect. 1986—, chair 1996-97, elected to governing coun. dispute resolution sect. 2001-2002), Boston U. Sch. Law Alumni Assn. (Silver Shingle award 1982), Aspetuck Valley Country Club (Weston, pres. 1995-96). Home: 6 Aspetuck Hill Ln Weston CT 06883-2601 Office: Paul Hastings Janolsky & Walker LLP 1055 Washington Blvd Stamford CT 06901-2216 Office Phone: 203-961-7466. Business E-Mail: christopherbarreca@paulhastings.com.

BARREDO, RITA M., auditor; b. Torrington, Conn., June 24, 1953; d. Avelino and Josephine (DiNoia) B. BA, U. Conn., 1975; BS, Post Coll., 1981; MS in Acctg., U. Hartford, 1984, MBA, 1990. CPA Conn.; cert. info. sys. auditor; cert. in homeland security, diplomate Am. Bd. Forensic Accts., Am. Bd. Forensic Examiners. Timekeeper Timex Corp., Waterbury, Conn., 1976-85; auditor Def. Contract Audit Agy., Lowell, Mass., 1985—. Mem. AICPA, Am. Coll. Forensic Examiners, Am. Womens Soc. CPAs, Conn. Soc. CPA (continuing profl. edn. com. 1989-95, 97— social and recreation com. 1996-97), Inst. Mgmt. Accts. (sec. Waterbury chpt. 1994—), Inst. Internal Auditors, Info. Sys. Audit and Control Assn. Home: 130 Dawes Ave Torrington CT 06790-3627 Office: Def Contract Audit Agy 400 Main St East Hartford CT 06108-0968 Personal E-mail: rbarredo01@snet.net.

BARREDO, RONALD DE VERA, physical therapist, educator; b. Quezon City, Philippines, Apr. 24, 1969; s. Rodolfo Garcia and Josefina De Vera Barredo; m. Maria Adora Simpas, Aug. 7, 2001; children: Rubric Michael children: Ryan Christopher. BS in Phys. Therapy, U. of the Philippines, Manila, 1990; MA in Orgnl. Mgmt., Trevecca Nazarene U., Nashville, 1995, EdD in profl. Practics, 2002. Diplomate Am. Bd. Phys. Therapy Specialties; lic. physical therapist Tenn., Okla., Ark. Program dir., phys. therapist asst. and massage therapy programs Kaskaskia Coll., Centralia, Ill., 2000—05; assoc. prof. grad. program in physical therapy Ark. State U., State University, 2005—. Vis. faculty mem. phys. therapy program Langston (Okla.) U., 2003—; bd. dirs. Fgn. Credentialing Commn. in Phys. Therapy, Alexandria, Va., 2002—, Christian Phys. Therapists Internat., NJ, 2000—. Recipient President's Disting. Pub. Svc. Award, Tenn. State U., 1999. Mem.: Am. Phys. Therapy Assn. (chmn. awards com. 2003—04), Toastmasters Internat. (dist. gov. 1999—2000, Select Disting. Dist. Gov. 2000, Disting. Toastmaster award 1997). Office: Ark State Univ Grad Program in Phys Therapy PO Box 910 State University AR 72467 Office Phone: 870-972-3610. Business E-Mail: rbarredo@astate.edu.

BARREIRA, BRIAN ERNEST, lawyer; b. Fall River, Mass., Sept. 1, 1958; s. Ernest R. and Lillian (Rego) B. BS in Ops. Mgmt., Boston Coll., 1980; JD, Boston U., 1984, LLM in Taxation, 1990. Bar: Mass. 1985. Estate settlement specialist State Street Bank and Trust Co., Boston, 1985-87; assoc. Barron & Stadfeld, Boston, 1987-88, Winokur, Winokur, Serkey, Rosenberg, & Hingham, P.C., Plymouth, 1988-96; pvt. practice, Plymouth and Hinghham, Mass., 1996—. Contbr. articles to profl. jours. Mem. ABA (chmn. elder law com. 1990-95, chmn. long-term health care issues com. 1992-96), Nat. Acad. Elder Law Attys., Mass. Bar Assn. (coun. probate sect. 1993-94, 95-97). Home: 6 Cobblestone Ln Hanover MA 02339-1940 E-mail: bb@lawyers.com.

BARREIRO, ELIAS, music educator, researcher; b. Santiago de Cuba, Cuba, Sept. 5, 1930; arrived in U.S., 1966; s. Elias Barreiro and Consuelo Diaz; m. Juana Tellez, June 26, 1960; children: Yolanda, Roberto. M, Conservatory of Music, Havana, Cuba, 1965; student, master class, Maestro Andres Segovia, 1968. Instr. music Tulane U., New Orleans, 1967—85, adj. prof. music, 1986—. Dir. guitar programs Tulane U., 1967—; jury mem. several internat. classical guitar competitions. Author (arranger, editor): Guitar Music Books and Methods for Classical Guitar, 1979—; composer: (solo classical guitar LPs) SMC Records, 1967—75, (solo classical guitar CDs) Mastersound Records, Intersound/Fanfare and Elan Recordings, 1995—99. Recipient Mentor award, Guitar Found. of Am., 1992, award, New Orleans Internat. Music Colloquium, 2000, Proclamation for outstanding svc., City of New Orleans, 2000. Mem.: New Orleans Classical Guitar Soc. (pres. 1968—85), Am. Philatelic Soc., U.S. Chess Fedn., Cuban Profl. Club. Republican. Baptist. Avocations: travel, fishing, camping, reading. Home: 107 Magnolia Ln Covington LA 70433 Office: Tulane U 6823 St Charles Ave New Orleans LA 70118 E-mail: ebarreiro@aol.com.

BARRELL, DAWN HOLMAN, marketing specialist; b. Chattanooga, Dec. 7, 1940; d. Eldridge Martin Sr. and Althea Lois (Smead) B.; m. John MacMillin Barrell, Oct. 7, 1972 (dec. Sept. 1996). Student, U. Ga., 1958-62. Sec. Dr. Wm. Benton U. Ga., 1960-62; sec. supt. Delta Air Lines, 1963-93; terr. mgr. Panasonic, Atlanta, 1995-96, Delta Staff Svcs., Atlanta Airport, 1997-98, mgr. placement, 1998—; dir., treas. Barrell Investments Inc., Atlanta, 1986-96. Author numerous poems. Del. Conty and State Rep. Conv., 1984-86; mem. adminstv. bd. First United Meth. Ch., Peachtree City, Ga., 1998. Named Lt. Col. aide-de-camp Gov. State Ga., 1979, Dame of Grand Cross of Order St. Stanislaus, Dame Merit Order of St. John Jerusalem, Holder of Cross of Holy Land, Dame of Justice Sovereign Order of Oak. Mem. DAR. Avocations: stamp collecting/philately, waterskiing, antiques. Home: 101 Parkway Dr Peachtree City GA 30269 E-mail: deltadawn12@juno.com.

BARREN DE SERRES, BRUCE WILLARD (H.R.H. THE DUKE BRUCE WILLARD BARREN DE SERRES), merchant banker; b. Olean, NY, Jan. 28, 1942; s. James Lee and Marion Frances (Willard) Barren; children: James Lee, Christina Roseanne. Student, The Hun Sch. of Princeton, 1959; BS, Babson Coll., 1962; MS, Bucknell U., 1963; grad. cert., Harvard U., 1967, Cambridge U., England, 1968. Exec. v.p. Am. Extract Co., 1960—62; sr. cons. Price Waterhouse, NY, 1963-67; v.p. Walston & Co., Inc., NY, 1967-70; sr. v.p. Delafield Childs, Inc., NY, 1970-71; chmn. The EMCO/Hanover Group Ltd., LA, 1971—; sr. v.p. Goodway, Inc., 1972-73; pres. Park West Med. Group, Inc., 1980-81; CEO First Pacific Bank, 1984-85; exec. editor The Mgmt. Gazette, 1988-98; chmn., mem. exec. adv. com. Vitafort Internat. Corp., LA, 1996-97. CEO Four Winds Enterprises Inc., San Diego 1985-87, F.W. Myers & Co., Rouses Point, NY, 1990-91; vice chmn., CEO Hydro-Mill Co., Chatsworth, Calif., 1996-98; bd. dirs. various US and internat. cos., 1978-95; author, instr. CPA, CPE courses, Tex., Calif. and NY; mem. editl. adv. bd. Prentice-Hall, 2001-02; US rep. Transatlantic Bio-scis. Fund, London, 1988-91; instr. loan documentation and valuation procedures Sanwa Bank, 1995-96; CEO, dir. Potomac Worldwide, 1998-2000; chmn. Tech. Asset Mgmt. Ltd., Eng., 2000-01; lectr. exec. MBA program UCLA, 1988-98, U. SC Grad. Sch., Pepperdine Exec. MBA Program. Whittier Sch. Law, Chapman U. Sch. Law; mem. Calif. Small Bus. Adv. Com., 1990-92. Contbr. over 100 articles to profl. jours. including CFO, Contr. Alert, KPMG Banking Insider. Decorated Grand Cross Order of the Cross of Constantinople; recipient numerous Disting. Svc. awards: current or former Govs.: NJ, Pa. (plus its two US Senators and State Legislature), Tenn. along with Ky.; also Calif. State Senate and State Assembly, 1985-2004, Office of Gov., 1999, 2004, Office of State Treas., Counties of LA and Orange, Calif., San Diego, City of LA and Mayor; Congl. Tribute, 1988, 90, 2004, US Senate (9 times, including former Gov. Tenn.), 1986-2005, US Ho. of Reps. (5 times); Office of US Pres. (Clinton and Bush) and separately, by their respective v.p. (Gore and Cheney), 1999, 2001-02; recipient Disting. Alumni award Princeton U., 2005; named to Athletic Hall of Fame, HUN/Princeton, 1999. Mem.: Am. Mgmt. Assn. (author, instr. 1991—92), Byzantine Heraldic Soc., Blue Book Social Registry (LA and S.W.), Order of Constantinople (dep. grand chancellor), St. Andrews Soc., Ordo Supremus Militaris Templi Hierosolymitani (a.k.a. Templars) (chevalier), Grand Sovereign Dynastic Hospitalier Order St. John Knights of Malta (knight comdr.), Mil. and Hospitalier Order St. Lazarus of Jerusalem (comdr.). Roman Catholic. Avocation: writing. Home: London England Office: 11740-11 West Sunset Los Angeles CA 90049 Office Phone: 310-471-3735. Personal E-mail: barren@verizon.net.

BARRERA, SUSAN CRISTINA, secondary school educator; b. Bradford, Pa., Sept. 25, 1952; BS in Edn., St. Bonaventure U., Olean, N.Y., 1974; MS in Edn., State U. Coll., Buffalo, 1976; PhD in Adminstrn. and Supervision Phys. Edn. and Athletics, U. Iowa, 1994. Cert. tchr., N.Y., Pa. 5th grade and jr. high sch. English tchr. Tchr. Corps, Lackawanna, N.Y., 1974-75; tchr. ESL Peace Corps, Kabul, Afghanistan, 1975-76, Colegio Abraham Lincoln, Bogota, Colombia, 1977-78; tchr. phys. edn. and 4th grade Colegio Nueva Granada, Bogota, 1978-80; tchr. ESL Colegio Americano de Quito, Ecuador, 1980-81; in sales N.Y. and Pa., 1981-84; Spanish tutor U. Iowa Athletic Student Svcs., Iowa City, 1990—; tchr. Spanish City High Sch., Iowa City, 1992—; tchr. Spanish and Phys. Edn. Iowa City Community Sch. Dist., 1993-94. Recipient Beyond War award Peace Corps, 1987; Fulbright Lecturing scholar, Honduras, 1989-90. Mem. AAHPERD, Pi Beta Delta. Avocations: travel, sports. Home: 209 College Ct Iowa City IA 52245-4401

BARRERE, CLEM ADOLPH, business brokerage company executive; b. Bradford, Pa., Jan. 5, 1939; s. Clem A. and Ruth Eleanore (Brauner) B.; m. Jamie Elizabeth Newton, Aug. 30, 1969; 1 child, John Coleman Barrere. B Engring., Yale U., 1960; PhD in Chem. Engring., Rice U., 1965; postgrad., Emory U., 1975. Registered profl. engr., Tex., Okla.; bd. cert. broker; cert. bus. intermediary. Group leader rsch. dept. Conoco, Inc., Ponca City, Okla., 1965-69, dir. gas engring. Houston, 1969-72, dir. gas ops., 1972-77, mgr. loss control, 1977-81; mgr. Dupont-Transp. Svc., Houston, 1981-87, Dupont-Safety and Environ., Houston, 1987-89; pres. Barrere & Co. Ventures, Houston, 1989—. Dir. Barrere & Co. Realtors, Houston, 1978—. Contbr. articles to profl. jours.; 7 patents in field. Mem. Mus. Fine Arts, Houston, Zool. Soc., Houston, Mus. Natural Sci., Houston, 1970-96; dir. Bus. Intermediary Edn. Found., 2005—. Recipient Citations for Svc., Am. Petroleum Inst., 1988, Gas Processors Assn., 1989; NSF rsch. grantee, 1963-65. Fellow Internat. Bus. Brokers Assn. (dir. 1998-2003, Pres. award, 2002); mem. Tex. Bus. Brokers Assn., Houston Gas Processors Assn. (pres. 1981-82), Tex. Rolls-Royce Assn. (dir. 1987-96, Spl. award 1991), Houston Gun Collectors (pres. 1964), Houston Area Realtors, Petroleum Club, Lakeside Country

Club, Phi Lambda Upsilon. Republican. Methodist. Avocations: golf, travel, sailing, genealogy, car restorations. Office: Barrere & Co Ventures 5652 Doliver Dr Houston TX 77056-2322 Office Phone: 832-452-5652. E-mail: clembarrere@earthlink.net.

BARRERE, JAMIE NEWTON, real estate executive; b. Russellville, Ark., June 7, 1946; d. James Edward Jr. and Martha (Spillers) Newton; m. Clement Adolph Barrere Jr., Aug. 30, 1969; 1 child, John Coleman. BA in Math., U. Ark., 1968; grad., Realtor Inst., 1984. Cert. real estate brokerage mgr.; grad. Realtor Inst.; accredited relocation coord. Asst. programmer, analyst Conoco, Ponca City, Okla., 1968-69; programmer, analyst Bonner & Moore Assocs., Houston, 1969-70; tchr. math. Lamar Consol. H.S., Rosenberg, Tex., 1970-72; assoc. broker Betty James, Realtors, Houston, 1972-78; pres. Barrere & Co., Realtors, Houston, 1978-96, Barrere Relocation Svcs. affiliate Heritage Tex. Properties, Houston, 1996—2002; assoc. broker Heritage Tex. Properties, Houston, 2002—. Adv. bd. Western Bank-Westheimer, Houston. Active Tex. Real Estate Polit. Action Com., Harris County Heritage Soc., Houston, Houston Jr. Forum, Am. Heart Assn. Guild, Houston Zool. Soc.; guild mem. Mus. Fine Arts, Houston, Covenant House; trustee St. Luke's United Meth. Ch.; bd. dirs., adv. bd. children's dept., tchr. and pianist Moores Sch. Music Soc. U. Houston; past cub scout leader Boy Scouts Am. Mem. Nat. Assn. Realtors (past equal opportunity com.), Tex. Assn. Realtors (bd. dirs. 1989-98, chmn. Multiple Listing Svc. com. 1985-90), Houston Assn. Realtors (bd. dirs. 1986-89, 93-95, v.p. 1993), Houston C. of C. (amb.), DAR, U. Ark. Alumnae Assn. (life, v.p. Houston chpt.), RELO Internat. Relocation Network, Lakeside Country Club, Petroleum Club, Tanglewood Garden Club (officer), Delta Delta Delta (past pres. Houston alumnae), Tri Delta Art Show for Charity (past pres., adv. bd.). Office: Heritage Tex Properties 1177 West Loop South Ste 1200 77027 Office Phone: 713-341-1677. Business E-Mail: jbarrere@heritagetexas.com.

BARRETO, BERNARDO, artist; b. Lima, Peru, Sept. 30, 1959; s. Juan Barreto and Sara Valverde. Student, Cath. U. Sch. Fine Arts, Lima, Peru, 1977—80. Cert. electronic technology Ctr. For The Media Arts, N.Y.C., 1992. Art supr. Fine Arts Decorating, N.Y.C., 1984—88; art studio mgr. R.B.S. Fabrics, N.Y.C., 1990—92; fine art studio artist Novo Arts, N.Y.C., 1999—2001. Art cons. Randa Corp., N.Y.C., 1992—2000; press corr. The Illus. Wild One Mag., N.Y.C., 1994—. Mem.: Graphic Artists Guild N.Y. (assoc.; bd. mem. 1993—96).

BARRETO, HECTOR V., federal agency administrator; b. Kans. City, Mo., May 13, 1961; m. Robin Barreto; 3 children. BSBA, Rockhurst U., Kans. City, Mo. Area mgr. Miller Brewing Co.; founder and pres. Barreto Ins. and Fin. Svcs., Calif.; adminstr. U.S. Small Bus. Adminstrn., 2001—. Past chmn. bd. Latino Bus. Assn., L.A. Vice chmn. bd. U.S. Hispanic C. of C. Office: US Small Bus Adminstrn 409 3rd St SW Washington DC 20416

BARRETT, BARBARA MCCONNELL, ranch owner, community leader, lawyer; b. Indiana County, Pa., Dec. 26, 1950; d. Robert Harvey and Betty (Dornheim) McC.; m. Craig R. Barrett, Jan. 19, 1985. BS, Ariz. State U., 1972, MPA, 1975, JD, 1978, LHD (hon.), 2000. Bar: Ariz. 1978, U.S. Dist. Ct. Ariz. 1979, U.S. Supreme Ct. Ariz. 1979. Atty. The Dial Corp., Phoenix, 1976-80; assoc. gen. counsel, asst. sec. Southwest Forest Industries, Inc., Phoenix, 1980-82; vice chmn. CAB, Washington, 1982-83, mem., 1983-84, vice chmn., 1984-85; ptnr. Evans, Kitchel & Jenckes, P.C., Phoenix, 1985-88, 1989; dep. adminstr. FAA, Washington, 1988-89; pvt. practice internat. bus. and aviation law Paradise Valley, Ariz., 1989—; pres., CEO American Mngmt. Assn., N.Y.C., 1997-98, Triple Creek Ranch, Mont., 1993—; fellow Inst. Politics, Kennedy Sch. Harvard U., 1999. Chmn. bd. dirs. Valley Bank Ariz., 1997-03; chmn. nominating com. The Lovelace Inst., 1995-99, U.S.-Afghan Women's Coun., 2003—, mem. US Adv. Commn. Pub. Diplomacy, 2003—, past mem. Adv. Com. on Women in the Services, nominated as Sec. USAF, 2003; treas. Asia-Pacific Econ. Cooperation Edn. Found., 1995-99; mem. exec. com., vice chairperson career opportunities subcom. US Dept. Def., 1989-93; mem. adv. com. Gov.'s Regional Airport, Pres.'s Adv. Com. on Trade Negotiations; mem. Adminstrv. Coun. US, 1982-85; chmn. US Sec. of Commerce Export Leaders Conf., 1988, Transp. Cluster Gov.'s Strategic Partnership for Econ. Devel., 1992-94; mem. Ariz. Disease Control Rsch. Commn., 1991-93; v.p. East Valley Partnership, 1992-94; v.p. Internat. Women's Forum, 1991-99, pres., 1999-01, mem. coun. fgn. rels., 1994—; mem. Phoenix Coun. Fgn. Rels., 1991; mem. steering com. Thunderbird Internat. Symposium, 1992-99; mem. global dispute resolution Global Ctr. Dispute Resolution, 1999—; mem. adv. bd. China Mist Tea Co., 1998-99, Harvard Leadership Bd., 1999-02; bd. dirs. numerous orgns. Chmn. Ariz. Dist. Export Coun., 1985-92, Ronald W. Reagan Scholarship Program, mentor, 1984-86, Airshow Can. Symposium, 1989, 91; chmn. World Trade Ctr. Ariz., 1992-94, chmn. emerita; bd. dirs. Nat. Air and Space Mus. Smithsonian Inst., 1988-89, Palms Clinic and Hosp. Corp., 1987-00, Goldwater Inst., 1991-02; trustee, devel. com., chairperson Thunderbird Garvin Sch. Internat. Mgmt., Glendale, Ariz.; trustee, nominating and devel. com. Embry-Riddle Aeronaut. U., Prescott, Ariz., Daytona Beach, Fla., 1989-97; pres. World Affairs Ariz., 1987-88; vice chmn. Kid's Voting USA, 1991-98; trustee Lovelace Inst., 1995-99; bd. dirs., chairperson nominating com. Ctrl. Ariz. chpt. ARC, 1993-99; mem. Gov.'s Task Force Canamex Corridor, 1998-01; pres. bd. Maricopa Colls. Found., 1997-98; sr. adv. com. Inst. Politics, Harvard, 1999—; vice regent, trustee George Washington's Fredericksburg Found., 1997—; mem. numerous bd. dirs. Named Woman of Yr., Ariz. State U., 1971, named to Hall of Fame, Coll. Pub. Programs, 1989, Coll. Liberal Arts, 1997; recipient Disting. Achievement award Ariz. State U., 1987, Coll. Bus., 1994, Woman Who Made a Difference award Internat. Women's Forum, 1988, Dick Cheney citation U.S. Sec. of Def., 1992, FAA Adminstr.'s award, 1989, Woman of the Yr. Network of Women in Hospitality, 1998, Horatio Alger award, 1999, Beta Gamma Nationwide Achievement award, 2000, Girl Scouts Today and Tomorrow award, 2000, Homeroom Hero award Teach for Am., 2002, Disting. Women's award Northwood U., 2001, Medal of Hon. DAR, 2003; named to Internat. Forest Friendship Hall of Fame, 2003; named one of 100 Women Who Made A Difference in Aviation, 2003; Dubois scholar, 1977. Mem. Am. Mgmt. Assn. (truste, chmn. exec. com., pres. N.Y.C. 1997-98, Lifetime Achievement award, 2002), Nat. Assn. Corp. Dirs. (faculty 1999, bd. dirs. 2000-02), Ariz. State U. Law Soc. (bd. govs. 1990-93), Ariz. State U. Found. (bd. dirs., program chair 1996—), Ariz. Women in Internat. Trade (bd. dirs., exec. com. 1987-93), Phoenix C. of C. (bd. dirs. 1987-93), Reagan Alumni Assn., Nat. Policy Forum, Econ. Club of Phoenix (past pres. 1990—).

BARRETT, BERNARD MORRIS, JR., plastic and reconstructive surgeon; b. Pensacola, Fla., May 3, 1944; s. Bernard Morris and Blanche (Lischkoff) B.; children: Beverly Frances, Julie Blaine, Audrey Blake, Bernard Joseph. BS, Tulane U., 1965; MD, U. Miami, 1969. Diplomate Am. Bd. Plastic Surgery. Surg. intern Meth. Hosp. and Ben Taub Hosp., Houston, 1969-70; resident in gen. surgery Baylor Coll. Medicine, Houston, 1970-71, UCLA, 1971-73; resident in plastic surgery U. Miami (Fla.) Affilated Hosps., 1973-75, chief resident in plastic surgery, 1975; fellow in plastic surgery Clinica Ivo Pitanguy, Rio de Janeiro, 1973; instr. surgery Baylor Coll. Medicine, 1970-71, clin. instr. plastic surgery, 1977-80, clin. asst. prof., 1980-90, clin. assoc. prof., 1991-97, clin. prof. surgery, 1997—; instr. surg. emergencies L.A. County Paramedics, 1972-73; plastic surgery coord. for jr. med. students Sch. Medicine U. Miami, 1975; practice medicine specializing in plastic and reconstructive surgery Houston, 1976—. Pres., chmn. bd. dirs. Plastic and Reconstructive Surgeons, P.A., 1978—; chmn. Tex. Inst. Plastic Surgery, Houston; assoc. chief plastic surgery St. Luke's Episcopal Hosp., Houston, 1991—; attending physician Jr. League Clinic, Tex. Children's Hosp., Houston, 1977—; active staff St. Luke's Hosp., Houston, Meth. Hosp., Houston; clin. assoc. in plastic surgery U. Tex. Med. Sch., Houston, 1976—; instr. surg. emergencies Harris County C.C.; dir. Am. Physicians Ins. Exch., Austin, 1976-2003, vice chmn., bd. dirs., 1995—; bd. dirs. Advocate M.D. Ins., Austin, 2004—; past chief of staff, chief plastic surgery Travis Centre Hosp., Houston, 1985—; dir. Physicians for Peace, Norfolk, Va., 1991—; cons. physician Houston Oilers, 1978-97; attending physician Ontario Motor Speedway, Calif., 1972-73. Author: Patient Care in Plastic Surgery, 1982, 2d edit., 1996, Manuel de Ciudados en Cirugia Plastica, 1985, Atencion al Paciente de Cirugia Plastica, 1998; contbr. articles to med. publs., presentations to profl. confs.; inventor Barrett sterling surgigrip. Bd. dirs. Plastic Surgery Ednl. Found., Chgo.; mem. Fed. Coun. on Aging, Washington, 1991-93, Pres.'s Coun. U. Miami, 1997—; adv. bd. Johnson & Johnson, New Brunswick, N.J. Lt. comdr. M.C., USNR, 1969-74. Recipient Outstanding Tchg. Plastic Surgeon award Baylor Coll. Medicine, 2003; Surg. exch. scholar to Royal Coll. Surgeons, London, 1968; hon. dep. sheriff Harris County, Tex. Fellow ACS; mem. Am. Assn. Plastic Surgery, Am. Soc. Plastic Surgeons, Royal Soc. Medicine, Michael E. DeBakey Internat. Cardiovascular Surg. Soc., Am. Soc. for Aesthetic Plastic Surgery, Denton A. Cooley Cardiovascular Surg. Soc., Tex. Med. Assn., Tex. Soc. Plastic Surgery, Harris County Med. Soc., Houston Soc. Plastic Surgery, D. Ralph Millard Plastic Surg. Soc. (pres. 1993-94, v.p. 1977-79, sec., treas. 1975-77, historian 1980—), U. Miami Sch. Medicine Nat. Alumni Assn. (bd. dirs. 1975-77, pres. coun. 1997—), Houston City Club, Houstonian Club, Royal Biscayne Racquet Club, Commodore Club, Coral Beach and Tennis Club, Sweetwater Country Club, Alpha Kappa Kappa (pres. 1968-69). Office: 6624 Fannin St Ste 2200 Houston TX 77030-2334 Office Phone: 713-790-9000. Personal E-mail: bmb-tips@swbell.net.

BARRETT, BRUCE RICHARD, physics professor; b. Kansas City, Kans., Aug. 19, 1939; s. Buford Russell and Miriam Aileen (Adams) B.; m. Gail Louise Geiger, Sept. 3, 1961 (div. Aug. 1969); m. Joan Frances Livermore, May 21, 1979. BS, U. Kans., 1961; postgrad., Swiss Poly., Zurich, 1961-62; MS, Stanford U., 1964, PhD, 1967. Rsch. fellow Weizmann Inst. Sci., Rehovot, Israel, 1967—68; postdoctoral rsch. fellow, rsch. assoc. U. Pitts., 1968—70; asst. prof. physics U. Ariz., Tucson, 1970—72, assoc. prof., 1972—76, prof., 1976—, assoc. chmn. dept., 1977—83, mem. faculty senate, 1979—83, 1988—90, 1991—97, program dir. theoretical physics NSF, 1985—87, mem. tech. transfer com., 1996—97, 1998—99, mem. grad. coun., 1998—2000. Chmn. adv. com. Internat. Scholars, Tucson, 1985-96; chmn. rsch. policy com. U. Ariz. Faculty Senate, 1993-94, 95-96; affiliate prof. U. Wash.-Seattle, 2000—; mem. adv. com. Nat. Inst. for Nuc. Theory, 2005—. Woodrow Wilson fellow, 1961-62; NSF fellow, 1962-66; Weizmann Inst. fellow, 1967-68; Andrew Mellon fellow, 1968-69; Alfred P. Sloan Found. research fellow, 1972-74; Alexander von Humboldt fellow, 1976-77; Japan Soc. for Promotion of Sci. rsch. fellow, 1998; NSF grantee, 1971-85, 87—; Netherlands F.O.M. research fellow Groningen, 1980; recipient sr. U.S. scientist award (Humboldt prize) Alexander von Humboldt Found., 1983-85. Fellow Am. Phys. Soc. (publs. com. divsn. nuclear physics 1983-86, program com. 1993-94, 2002—03, chmn. steering com. for Nuclear Physics Summer Sch. 1996-98, mem. exec. com. four corners sect. 1998-2004, chair 2003, chmn. forum on internat. physics 2002, chmn. com. internat. sci. affairs 2003, mem. com. 2001-04), Phi Beta Kappa (pres. Alpha Ariz. chpt. 1992, 2000-02, nat. senate 2000—), Sigma Pi Sigma, Omicron Delta Kappa, Beta Theta Pi. Office: U Ariz Dept Physics PO Box 210081 Tucson AZ 85721-0081 Office Phone: 520-621-2979. Business E-Mail: bbarrett@physics.arizona.edu.

BARRETT, CATHERINE L., state representative; b. Cin., June 14, 1941; married; 3 children. BA in Bus. Adminstrn., Union Inst., Cin.; grad., Ctr. Policy Alternatives Flemming Fellows Inst.; fellow, Coun. State Govts. Bowhay Inst. Legis. Leadership Devel. Former mayor, Forest Park, Ohio; state rep. dist. 32 Ohio Ho. of Reps., Columbus, 1998—, ranking minority mem., human svcs. subcom., edn. mem., health, and ins. coms. Past councilwoman Forest Park City Coun. Recipient Ohio Hunger Heroine award, Ohio Assn. 2d Harvest; Harvard JFK Sch. Govt. Sr. Execs. in State and Local Govt. fellow, Eleanor Roosevelt Global Leadership Inst. fellow. Mem.: LWV, Negro Women Coun., Ohio, Ky. and Ind. Regional Coun. Govts., Forest Park Bus. Assn., Cin. Woman's Polit. Caucus, Cin. C. of C., Forest Park Women's Club, Delta Sigma Theta. Democrat. Office: 77 S High St 10th fl Columbus OH 63215-6111

BARRETT, COLLEEN CROTTY, air transportation executive; b. Bellows Falls, Vt., Sept. 14, 1944; AA with highest honors, Becker Jr. Coll., 1964. Legal sec. Oppenheimer Rosenberg Kelleher & Wheatley, San Antonio, 1968—72, adminstrv. asst., paralegal, 1972—78; corp. sec. Southwest Airlines, Dallas, 1978, exec. asst. to pres. and chmn., 1980—85, v.p. adminstrn., 1985—90, exec. v.p. customs, 1990—2001, pres., 2001—, COO, 2001—04. Bd. dir. Southwest Airlines, 2001—, JC Penney Co., 2004—. Named one of most powerful women, Forbes mag., 2005. Mem.: Leadership Tex. Roman Catholic. Office: SW Airlines Co PO Box 36611 Dallas TX 75235-1611 Office Phone: 214-792-4112. E-mail: vickie.shuler@unco.com.

BARRETT, CRAIG R., electronics company executive; b. San Francisco, Aug. 29, 1939; m. Barbara Barrett, 1985; 2 children. BS, Stanford U., Palo Alto; MS in Materials sci., PhD in Materials sci., Stanford U. NATO postdoctoral fellow Nat. Physical Lab., 1964—65; assoc. prof., dept. materials sci. and engring. Stanford U., 1965-74; with Intel Corp., Chandler, Ariz., 1974—, tech. develop mgr., 1974—84, v.p. components tech. and mfg. group, 1984—87, sr. v.p., gen. mgr. components tech. and mfg. group, 1987—90, exec. v.p., mgr. components tech., 1990—93, COO, 1993—97, pres., 1997—98, CEO, 1998—2005, bd. chmn., 2005—. Bd. dirs. Intel, 1992—, Qwest Comms. Internat. Inc., US Semiconductor Industry Assoc., Silicon Valley Mfg. Group; co-chmn. Bus. Coalition for Excellence in Edn.; chmn. Computer Systems Policy Project; bd. trustee US Coun. for Internat. Bus. Author: Principles of Engineering Materials, of over 40 tech. papers dealing with the influences of microstructure on the properties of materials. Bd. dirs. Nat. Forest Found., Achieve. Grantee Fulbright Fellow, Danish Tech. U., 1972. Mem.: NAE (chair 2004—). Office: 2200 Mission College Blvd Santa Clara CA 95054-1537*

BARRETT, DAVID A., lawyer; b. Altoona, Pa., Aug. 12, 1950; s. Arthur L. and Mary (Bell) B.; m. Diane DeWitt, May 23, 1981; children: Alexander, Annabel. AB, Harvard U., 1971; JD, Columbia Law Sch., 1974. Bar: N.Y. 1975, U.S. Dist. Ct. (so. dist.) N.Y. 1975, U.S. Dist. Ct. (ea. dist.) N.Y. 1987, U.S. Dist. Ct. (no. dist.) N.Y. 1992, U.S. Ct. Appeals (2d cir.) 1975, U.S. Ct. Appeals (6th cir.) 1979, U.S. Ct. Appeals (D.C. cir.) 1980, U.S. Ct. Appeals (3d cir.) 1987, U.S. Ct. Appeals (5th cir.) 1993, U.S. Ct. Appeals (11th cir.) 1994, U.S. Supreme Ct. 1979. Law clk. to Hon. Wilfred Feinberg U.S. Ct. Appeals (2d Cir.), N.Y.C., 1974-75; Karpatkin fellow ACLU, N.Y.C., 1975-76; law clk. to Hon. Thurgood Marshall U.S. Supreme Ct., Washington, 1976-77; spl. counsel U.S. Dept. Justice, Office Legis. Affairs, Washington, 1977-79; assoc. Cravath, Swaine & Moore, N.Y.C., 1979-85; assoc. prof. Rutgers U. Law Sch., Newark, 1985-87; ptnr. Barrett Gravante Carpinello & Stern LLP, N.Y.C., Albany, 1987-2000, Boies, Schiller & Flexner LLP, N.Y.C., 2000—. Author: (with others) NYU Inst. State and Local Taxation, 1987, Reforming Libel Law, 1992. Mem. Senator Charles Schumer's Judicial Screening Comm., 1999—, Spence-Chapin Services for Children & Families (bd. dir., 2000—). Mem. Columbia Law Sch. Bd. Vis., 1996—. Office: 1585 Broadway New York NY 10036-8200 also: 100 State St Albany NY 12207 E-mail: dbarrett@bsfllp.com.

BARRETT, DAVID F., lawyer; b. LA, Oct. 6, 1962; s. Frederick H. and E. Fern (Wagoner) Barrett; m. Teresa Lynn Emmert, Feb. 14, 1998; 1 child, Abigail Lynn. BS, Calif. State U., L.A., 1987; JD, MBA, Brigham Young U., 1992. Bar: Mo. 1993, Kans. 1993, U.S. Dist. Ct. (we. dist.) Mo. 1993, U.S. Dist. Ct. Kans. 1993. Police officer City of Alhambra, Calif., 1983-89; pvt. practice Independence, Mo., 1993—98; Joplin City prosecutor, 1998—2000; asst. atty. gen., 2001—. Editor: Trust Law, 1990, Mo. Employment Discrimination Law, 2000; author: Municipal Court Proceedings, Chapter 11 of Mo. Local Govt. Law, 2002, Criminal Aspects, Chapter 17 of Mo. Workers Compensation Law, 2004; contbr. articles to profl. jours. Scholar Brigham Young U., 1990-92. Mem. Mo. Bar, Kans. Bar. Republican. Avocations: reading, racquetball. Office: Missouri Atty Gen's Office PO Box 899 Jefferson City MO 65102

BARRETT, DAWN DILLON, counseling administrator, journalist, editor; b. Tylertown, Miss., Apr. 12, 1937; d. Rufus E. "Todd" and Vivian Duffee Dillon; m. John Clifton Barrett, June 21, 1959 (div. Nov. 15, 1973); children: John Todd, Charles Christopher. BS in Edn., Miss. Coll., 1959; EdM, U. So. Miss., 1979. Cert. secondary tchr./counselor Miss., La. Libr. Walthall County Libr., Tylertown, Miss., 1973; secondary English tchr. Tylertown H.S., 1974—77, sch. counselor, 1982—2000, Salem-Dexter High Schs., Tylertown, 1977—80; mng. editor The Tylertown Times, 1980—81; sch. counselor Mt. Hermon H.S., Franklinton, La., 1981—82; assoc. editor The Magnolia (Miss.) Gazette, 2000—02, contbg. editor, columnist, 1999—. Commr.,chmn. Mental Health/Mental Retardation Bd., Miss., 1981—94. Recipient Best in State award for newspaper column, Miss. Press Assn., 1981, Best in State award for feature writing, 1999, Best in State award for personal newspaper column, 2000; Grant for building STAR classroom for long-distance learning, Miss. ETV. Mem.: Miss. Counseling Assn. (life). Republican. Methodist. Avocations: creative writing, reading, swimming, public speaking, music. Home: 809 Harvey Dr Tylertown MS 39667

BARRETT, ELIZABETH ANN MANHART, nursing educator, psychotherapist, consultant; b. Hume, Ill., July 11, 1934; d. Francis J. and Grace C. (Manhart) Fridy; children: Joseph B., Jeffrey F., Paula G. Brown, Pamela M. Temple, Scott D. BSN summa cum laude, U. Evansville, 1970, MA, 1973, MSN, 1976; grad., Gestalt Assocs. Psychotherapy, 1982; PhD in Nursing, NYU, 1983; grad., Am. Inst. for Mental Imagery, 1995. From instr. to asst. prof. nursing U. Evansville, Ind., 1970-76; staff nurse Welborn Bapt. Hosp., Evansville, 1975-76, Bellevue Psychiat. Hosp., N.Y.C., 1976-79; clin. tchr. CUNY, 1977-82; asst. prof. Adelphi U., 1979-80; group practice Nurse Healers, 1979-82; pvt. practice psychotherapy, 1980—. Nurse rschr. Mt. Sinai Med. Ctr., N.Y.C., 1982-86, asst. dir. nursing, 1983-86; assoc. prof. Hunter Coll., N.Y.C., 1986-89, prof., 1994-2001, prof. emerita, 2001—, dir. grad. studies, 1989-92, coord. Ctr. for Nursing Rsch., 1993-2001; cons. Internat. Soc. Univ. Nurses; co-chair adv. com. Martha E. Rogers Ctr. for Study of Nursing Svc., 1994-96; sec., treas. Am. Inst. for Mental Imagery, 2002—; com. mem. Regional Health Planning Coun., Evansville, 1974-77. Mem. editl. bd. Alt. Therapies in Health and Medicine, 1995—. Recipient Disting. Nursing Alumnus award NYU, 1994, Disting. Nurse Rschr. award Found. N.Y. State Nurses Assn., 1995. Fellow Am. Acad. Nursing; mem. ANA (cert. psychiat.-mental health), NOW, Nat. League Nursing, Ea. Nursing Rsch. Assn. (charter), Ea. Nursing Rsch. Soc., Soc. Rogerian Scholars (co-founder, 1st pres. 1988-90), Phi Kappa Phi, Sigma Theta Tau (Upsilon chpt. pres. 1986-88), Alpha Tau Delta, Sigma Xi. Home: 415 E 85th St Apt 9E New York NY 10028-6358 Office: 16 E 96th St Ste 1 A New York NY 10128 Office Phone: 212-861-8228.

BARRETT, EUGENE JOSEPH, physician, educator, researcher; b. Jersey City, N.J., May 22, 1946; s. Joseph Francis and Margaret (Harney) B.; m. Paul Marie Quiricani, Jan. 31, 1976; children: Nora, Matthew. BS in Physics, St. Peters Coll., Jersey City, N.J., 1968; MD, PhD in Biophysics, U. Rochester, 1975. Intern in medicine Strong Meml. Hosp., Rochester, N.Y., 1975-76, asst. resident in medicine, 1976-77; fellow in endocrinology and metabolism Yale U. Sch. Medicine, New Haven, Conn., 1977-80, asst. prof. medicine, 1980-85, assoc. prof. medicine, 1985-91, chief diabetes unit, 1988-91; prof. internal medicine and pediats. U. Va. Sch. Medicine, Charlottesville, 1991—; dir. U. Va. Diabetes Ctr., 1991—. Dir. diabetes unit Yale U. Sch. Medicine, 1987-91; dir. diabetes ctr. U. Va., 1991—. Contbr. over 70 articles to profl. jours. Recipient Rsch. Career award NIH, 1981-85. Mem. NIH (mem. metabolism study sect. 1993-96), Am. Diabetes Assn. (bd. dirs. Va. affiliate 1993-96, pres.-elect 2002, mem. nat. profl. practice com., rsch. award 1996), Am. Heart Assn. (Established Investigator 1987-92, mem. Coun. affiliate grant rev. panel 1985-90, mem. grant rev. panel New Eng. region 1986-91, chair 1991), Am. Fedn. Clin. Rsch., Am. Soc. Clin. Investigation. Roman Catholic. Avocations: sailing, tennis. Office: U Va Sch Medicine Diabetes Rsch Ctr PO Box 801410 Charlottesville VA 22908

BARRETT, EVELYN CAROL, retired secondary school educator; b. Ocean Springs, Miss., Feb. 6, 1928; d. Charles Edward and Irene Effie (Hopkins) Engbarth; m. Arthur James Barrett, June 10, 1951; children: George Stanley, Ruth Anne, James Sidney, Carolyn Jean. Diploma with honors, Jr. Coll. (now Miss. Coast Coll.), Perkinston, Miss., 1945; BS in Commerce with high honors, Miss. So. Coll. (now U. So. Miss.), 1947; MBA in Acctg., La. State U., 1950; also numerous continuing edn. courses, 1950-82. Bookkeeper-sec. Non-Commn. Officers Club, Kessler AFB, Miss., summer 1947; asst., secretarial practice office and divsn. rsch.; instr. in typing Coll. Commerce, La. State U., 1947-50; instr. Miss. So. Coll., summer 1950; clk.-stenographer dept. physics U. Ill., Urbana, 1951-52; instr. in shorthand Ill. Comml. Coll., 1951-52; tchr. Milford (N.H.) H.S., 1957-58; tchr. bus. edn. Merrimack (N.H.) H.S., 1958-90, head dept. bus. edn., 1971-81; ret., 1990. Grad. asst. La. State U., 1947-50; instr. auditing Rivier Coll., 1982; registered rep. R. Danais Investment Co., Manchester, N.H.; account exec. John, Edward & Co., Lebanon, N.H.; ind. beauty cons. Mary Kay Cosmetics, Merrimack; tutor in shorthand, acctg.; cons. acctg. sys. Organizer, 1st pres. Merrimack Group Hillsborough County Ext. Svc., 1957-58; active Girl Scouts U.S.A., including Cadette leader, 1959-63, sr. troop leader Switwater coun., 1970-72, adult vol. trainer, 1964-66, troop program cons., 1963-64. Mem. AAUW, NEA, N.H. Edn. Assn., N.H. Bus. Educators Assn. (v.p. 1964-65, pres. 1965-67, rep. to N.H. Vocat. Assn. 1986-87, sec. 1967-68, treas. 1973-75, historian 1986-87), N.H. Supervisory Union 27 (sec.-treas. 1961-62), Merrimack Tchrs. Assn. (sec. 1984-85, Disting. Educator award 1980, Excellence in Edn. award 1985), New Eng. Bus. Educators Assn., Assn. Career Tech. Edn., N.H. Assn. Computer Edn. Statewide, Ea. Bus. Edn. Assn., Nat. Bus. Edn. Assn., Manchester User's Group of Apple Computers (treas. 2000), Delta Zeta, Phi Theta Kappa, Pi Omega Pi, Delta Pi Epsilon, Alpha Delta Kappa (chpt. award of appreciation 1980, historian N.E. region 1981-83, sec. N.E. region 1995-97, v.p. N.H. Alpha chpt. 1978-79, pres. N.H. Alpha chpt. 1979-82, N.H. state sgt.-at-arms 1982-84, N.H. state treas. 1984-88, N.H. state membership chmn. 1988-92, N.H. state chaplain 1992-94, N.H. state pres. elect 1994-96, N.H. state pres. 1996-98, N.H. state immediate past pres. 1998-2000), Audubon Soc. N.H., Delta Sigma Epsilon (chpt. corr. sec.), Gen. Electric Women's Club, Reeds Ferry Women's Club, Manchester Coll. Women's Club, Our Lady of Mercy Ladies Guild (v.p. 1999, pres. 2000), Merrimack Sr. Citizen Club, Manchester Area Ret. Educators Assn., Nashua Area Ret. Educators Assn., N.H. Ret. Educators Assn., Embroiderers' Guild Am. (libr. No. New Eng. chpt. 1999-2004). Roman Catholic.

BARRETT, FRANK JOSEPH, lawyer, insurance company executive; b. Greeley, Nebr., Mar. 2, 1932; s. Patrick J. and Irene L. (Printy) B.; m. Ruth Ann Nealon, Aug. 20, 1956; children: Patrick, Mary, Anne, Karen, Thomas. BS in Law, U. Nebr., 1957; LLB, Nebr. Coll. Law, 1959. Bar: Nebr. 1959, U.S. Supreme Ct. 1976, arbitrator. Asst. gen. counsel, asst. sec. Nebr. Nat. Life Co., 1957-61; dir. ins. State of Nebr., Lincoln, 1961-67; exec. v.p., sec., gen. counsel Ctrl. Nat. Ins. Group of Omaha, 1967-75; exec. v.p., chief counsel Mut. of Omaha (and Affiliates), 1975-81; pres., CEO Ctrl. Nat. Ins. Co. of Omaha, 1981-89, Ins. Rsch. Svc. Co., Omaha, 1989—; of counsel Lamson, Dugan & Murray, Omaha, 1990—. Bd. dir. Am. Family Life Assurance Co. State organizational chmn. 3 Nebr. gubernatorial campaigns. Served in U.S. Army, 1953-55, Korea. Recipient service citation Am. Nat. Red Cross, 1964, 65 Mem. ABA, Am. Arbitration Assn., Fedn. Ins. Counsels, Nebr. Bar Assn., Omaha Bar Assn., Consumer Credit Ins. Assn. (past pres. and dir.), Nat. Assn. Ind. Insurers (gov., past chmn.), Nat. Assn. Ins. Commrs. (past pres.), Am. Legion, Irish-Am. Cultural Soc., KC., ARIAS-U.S. (cert. arbitrator, cert. umpire) Democrat. Roman Catholic. Home: 516 S 119th St Omaha NE 68154-3115 Office Fax: 402-397-8450. Business E-Mail: fbarrett@ldmlaw.com.

BARRETT, HERBERT, performing company executive, management consultant; b. N.Y.C., May 31, 1910; s. John and Mollie (Pike) B.; m. Betty Palash, May 29, 1937; children: Nancy, Katherine. BA, Cornell U., 1930. Pub. rels. counsel Cadillac Car Co., N.Y.C., 1934—, GM, N.Y.C., 1935—; mgr., pres. Herbert Barrett Mgmt. (artists mgmt. assn.), N.Y.C., 1940—; mgr. inaugural Great Performers series Avery Fisher Hall, Lincoln Center for Performing Arts, N.Y.C., 1965. Mem. adv. com. Town Hall, N.Y.C., 1970—; mem. recommendation bd. Avery Fisher Artist Program, Lincoln Center

Performing Arts; mem. nat. adv. bd. Van Cliburn Internat. Quadrennial Piano Competition. Recipient Patrick Hayes award for outstanding svc. to Internat. Soc. for the Performing Arts Found., 1997, IAMA Lifetime Mem. award, 2005. Mem. Little Orch. Soc. (treas. 1970—, mgr. 1967—), Internat. Assn. Festival and Concert Mgrs. (exec. bd. 1969—), Phi Beta Kappa. Home: 15 W 72nd St New York NY 10023-3402 Office: Fl 20 266 W 37th St New York NY 10018-6648 Office Phone: 212-245-3530.

BARRETT, IZADORE, retired science administrator; b. Vancouver, B.C., Can., Oct. 4, 1926; came to U.S., 1956; s. Samuel Barrett and Rose (Hyatt) Gordon; m. Fulvia Mercedes Quesada, July 5, 1958; children: Marcus, Byron, Norman, Dora. BA, U. B.C., 1947, MA, 1949; postgrad., U. Toronto, 1949-52; PhD, U. Wash., 1980. Chief hatchery biologist B.C. Game Commn., Vancouver, 1952-56; scientist Inter-Am. Tropical Tuna Commn., La Jolla, 1956-67; chief biologist UNDP Fisheries Devel. Project, Santiago, Chile, 1967-69; fisheries advisor FAO, Santiago, 1969-70; dep. dir. S.W. Fisheries Ctr., La Jolla, 1970-77, dir., 1977-88; sci. and research dir. S.W. region, Nat. Marine Fisheries Svc., 1988-92; ret., 1992. Rsch. assoc. Scripps Inst. Oceanography, La Jolla, 1977-98; mem. sci. and statis. com. Pacific Fisheries Mgmt. Coun., Portland, Oreg., 1977-90; chmn. sci. and statis. com. Western Pacific Fisheries Mgmt. Coun., Honolulu, 1976-79. Contbr. articles to profl. jours. Bd. govs. San Diego Oceans Found., 1985-95; chmn. Mayor's San Diego/La Jolla Underwater Park Com., 1978-92; mem. adv. coun. Inst. Marine Resources U. Calif., La Jolla, 1979-85; bd. govs. San Diego Sci. Fair, 1984-92. Fellow Am. Inst. Fisheries Rsch. Biologists (v.p. 1973-76), U. Calif. San Diego Retirement Assn. (pres. 2004-05). E-mail: ibarrett@ucsd.edu.

BARRETT, J. CARL, cancer researcher, molecular biologist; b. Portsmouth, Va., Dec. 28, 1946; s. Jacob Weaver and Dixie Wike (Ring) B.; m. Roberta Mick, June 8, 1968; children: James, Paul, Lia. BS in Chemistry, Coll. of William and Mary, 1969; PhD in Biophysical Chemistry, Johns Hopkins U., 1974. Postdoctoral fellow divsn. biophysics Johns Hopkins U., Balt., 1974-77; sr. staff fellow lab. pulmonary function and toxicology Nat. Inst. Environ. Health Scis., Rsch. Triangle Park, N.C., 1977-82, group leader environ. carcinogenesis group, 1977-87, rsch. chemist, 1982-87, chief lab. molecular carcinogenesis, 1987-2000, dir. program environ. carcinogenesis div. intramural rsch., 1992-96, sci. dir., 1995-2000; dir. divsn. basic scis. Nat. Cancer Inst., Bethesda, Md., 2000—. Adj. prof. dept. pathology U. N.C., 1978—, dept. epidemiology, 1992—; adj. mem. genetics curriculum U. N.C., 1979—, toxicology curriculum, 1985—; adj. sr. fellow Ctr. Study of Aging and Human Devel. Duke U. Med. Ctr., 1993—; mem. study sections NIH, Nat. Cancer Inst., Nat. Cancer Inst. Can.; ad hoc reviewer; vis. prof. Sun Yat-Sen U., People's Rep. China, 1987, Inst. Zoology Academia Sinica, Taiwan, 1992, NYU, 1992; keynote speaker, organizer, chair numerous symposia, conferences, workshops; invited speaker more than 125 symposia, conferences, univs. worl dwide, 1986—; mem. Task Force Health Effects of Synthetic Fuels Dept. Energy, 1980; mem. workshop Internat. Program Chem. Safety, 1982; mem. working group WHO, 1983, Internat. Agy. Rsch. Cancer, France, 1985, 86, peer rev. com. sci. coun., 1988; mem. adv. panel Calif. Biotech., Inc., 1990, Greenwall Found., 1989; mem. various adv. bds., coms. Nat. Coun. Radiation Protection & Measurements, Am. Health Found., Nat. Cancer Inst., U.S. EPA, Health Effects Inst.-Asbestos Rsch. Com., Chem. Industry Inst. Toxicology, also external expert, ad hoc mem.; cons. Abbott Labs., 1989-91, Chem. Industry Inst. Toxicology, 1991-92; chmn. sci. coun. Internat. Agy. for Rsch. on Cancer, 1998. Author: Mechanisms of Environmental Carcinogenesis: Volume I-Role of Genetic and Epigenetic Changes, 1987, Vol. II-Multistep Models of Carcinogenesis, 1987; co-author: Carcinogenesis-A Comprehensive Survey: Volume 9, Mammalian Cell Transformation: Mechanisms of Carcinogenesis and Assays for Carcinogens, 1985, Comparative Molecular Carcinogenesis: Volume 376-Progress in Clinical and Biological Research, 1992; editor-in-chief Molecular Carcinogenesis, 1992—, mem. editl. bd., 1988—; assoc. editor Cancer Rsch., 1984—, Mutagenesis, 1985-88, Toxicology in Vitro, 1986-90; mem. editl. bds. profl. jours., 1988—; contbr. over 405 articles to profl. jours. Recipient merit awards NIH, 1989, 94, 97, Dir.'s award, 1995, 96, Ramazzini award Collegium Ramazzini, Italy, 1995, Secretary's award for Disting. Svc., Dept. Health and Human Svcs., 1996; NSF grantee, 1966; Dow Chem. Co. fellow, 1968. Mem. AAAS, Am. Chem. Soc., Am. Assn. Cancer Rsch. (program com., Rhodes award com., chair spl. membership com., bd. dirs. 1998—), Internat. Soc. Diffrentiation (bd. dirs. 1998—). Office: Nat Cancer Inst Bldg 37 Rm 5032 37 Convent Dr Bethesda MD 20892 E-mail: barrett@mail.nih.gov.

BARRETT, JAMES GRESHAM, congressman; b. Oconee, S.C., Feb. 14, 1961; m. Natalie Barrett; 3 children. BS in Bus. Adminstrn., The Citadel, 1983. Operator Barrett's Furniture, 1987; mem. S.C. Ho. Reps., 1996—2002, U.S. Ho. Reps. from 3rd S.C. dist., 2003—; mem. budget and fin. svcs. com. U.S. Ho. Reps. SME chair Oconee Boy Scouts, 1995, chmn.; mem. S.C. GOP steering com. Pres. George W. Bush Candidacy, 2000. Capt. U.S. Army, 1983—87. Mem.: Oconee County C. of C. (pres.), Westminster Rotary Club (pres.). Republican. Baptist. Office: 1523 Longworth HOB Washington DC 20515*

BARRETT, JAMES THOMAS, retired immunologist, educator; b. Centerville, Iowa, May 20, 1927; s. Alfred Wesley and Mary Marjorie (Taylor) B.; m. Barbro Anna-Lill Nilsson, July 31, 1967; children— Sara, Robert, Annika, Nina BA, State U. Iowa, 1950, MS, 1951, PhD, 1953. Asst. prof. bacteriology and parasitology U. Ark. Sch. Medicine, Little Rock, 1953-57; asst. prof. microbiology U. Mo. Sch. Medicine, Columbia, 1957-59, assoc. prof., 1959-67, prof., 1967-94, St. George's (Grenada, W.I.) U. Sch. Medicine, 1994—2002; prof. emeritus U. Mo. Sch. Medicine, 1994—, ret., 2003. Exchange prof. U.S. and Romanian Acads. Sci., 1971; vis. scientist Spanish Ministry Edn. and Sci., 1986. Author: Textbook of Immunology, 5th edit., 1988, Basic Immunology and Its Medical Application 2d edit., 1980, Medical Immunology, 1991, Microbiology and Immunology Casebook, 1995, Microbiology and Immunology Concepts, 1998; editor: Contemporary Classics in the Life Scienes, 1986, Contemporary Classics in Clinical Medicine, 1986, Contemporary Classics in Plant, Animal and Environmental Sciences, 1986. Served with USN, 1944—45. NIH Fogarty sr. fellow, 1977—78, Fulbright scholar, 1984. Mem. Am. Assn. Immunology, Am. Soc. Microbiology. Home: 901 Westport Dr Columbia MO 65203-0741 Personal E-mail: barrettj@mchsi.com.

BARRETT, JANE FRANCES, lawyer; b. Monterey, Calif., Sept. 13, 1952; d. Harle V. Barrett and Lucille M. Richstatter. BA in Polit. Sci., Loyola Coll., Balt., 1973; JD, U. Md., 1976. Bar: Md., D.C., U.S. Dist. Ct. Md. 1986, U.S. Ct. Appeals (4th cir.) 1987, U.S. Dist. Ct. Washington 1998. With U.S. Environ. Protection Agy., Washington, 1976—81; asst. atty. gen. State of Md., Balt., 1981-86; asst. U.S. atty. U.S. Atty. Office Dist. Md., Balt., 1986—98; ptnr., head, white collar & corp. defense practice Dyer Ellis & Joseph, Washington, 1998—2003; ptnr., chair, white collar internal and govt. investig. group Blank Rome LLP, Washington, 2003—. Adj. prof. U. Md., Balt., 1990-97. Contbr. articles to profl. jours. Mem. adv. working group environ. sanctions U.S. Sentencing Commn., Washington, 1992-93; bd. dirs. Women's Housing Coalition, Balt., 1998-99. Recipient Bronze medal U.S. EPA, 1997, Commdrs. award Army Corps. Engrs., 1998. Mem. ABA (vice-chair environ. crimes enforcement subcom. 1995—), WISTA, Fed. Bar Assn. of Md. (bd. govs.), Assn. Trial Lawyers of Am., Nat. Assn. Women Lawyers, Nat. Assn. Criminal Defense Lawyers, Maritime Law Assn., Women's Internat. Shipping & Trade Assn. Office: Blank Rome LLP 600 New Hampshire Ave NW Washington DC 20037 Office Phone: 202-772-5907. Office Fax: 202-772-5908. Business E-Mail: barrett@BlankRome.com.

BARRETT, JANE HAYES, lawyer; b. Dayton, Ohio, Dec. 13, 1947; d. Walter J. and Jane H. Barrett BA, Calif. State U.-Long Beach, 1969; JD, U. So. Calif., 1972. Bar: Calif. 1972, U.S. Dist. Ct. (cen. dist.) Calif. 1972, U.S. Ct. Appeals (9th cir.) 1982, U.S. Supreme Ct. Assoc. Lawler, Felix & Hall, L.A., 1972—84; ptnr. Arter & Hadden, L.A., 1984—94; mng. ptnr. Preston, Gates & Ellis, L.A., 1994—2002; ptnr. DLA Piper, L.A., 2002—. Lectr. bus. law Calif. State U., 1973-75. Mem. adv. bd. Harriet Buhai Legal Aid Ctr., 1991-96, mem. bd. pub. counsel, 1996-98; pres. Pilgrim Parents Orgn. 1990-91; chmn. fin. Our Mother Good Counsel Sch.; bd. regents Loyola, H.S., 2000—; mem. adv. coun. Ctr. on Ethnic and Racial Diversity. Named Outstanding Grad. Calif. State U., Long Beach, 1988, Outstanding Alumnae Polit. Sci., 1993, So. Calif. Super Lawyer, L.A. Mag., 2003, 04. Fellow Am. Bar Found.; mem. ABA (bd. govs. 1980-84, chmn. young lawyers divsn. 1980-81, com. on delivery of legal svcs. 1985-89, exec. coun. legal edn. and admissions sects. 1985-89, fin. sec. torts and ins. practice 1982-83, adv. mem. fed. judiciary com. 9th circuit rep. 2000—05, mem. minority and ethnic diversity bd., v.p. 1997—, Am. Bar Endowment 1999, bd. dirs. 1990—, sec. 1993-95, v.p. 1998-99, pres., 1999-2000, bd. fellows young lawyers divsn. 1992—, del 9th cir. jud. conf., atty. del. U.S. Dist. Ct. ctrl. dist. Calif. Atty. Conf. 2002—, U.S. Dist. Ct. Ctrl. Dist. Calif. (discipline com. 2004—, admissions com. 2005—), 9th Cir. Atty. Conf. (del. 2003), Calif. State Bar (com. adminstrn. of justice, editl. bd. Calif. Lawyers 1981-84), Legion Lex (bd. dirs. 1990-93), Los Feliz Homeowners Assn. (bd. dirs.). Democrat. Office: DLA Piper 1999 Ave of the Stars Los Angeles CA 90067 Office Phone: 310-595-3030. Business E-Mail: jane.barrett@dlapiper.com.

BARRETT, JOHN ANTHONY, publishing and printing company financial executive; b. Phila., Aug. 12, 1942; s. Stephen Francis and Margaret (Walsh) B.; m. Joan Victoria Lyncheski, Oct. 21, 1967; children: John Anthony Jr., Stephanie Lea. BSBA, Mt. St. Mary's Coll., Emmitsburg, Md., 1964; postgrad., Drexel U., 1980. Mgr. mfg. acctg. Scott Paper Co., Phila., 1968-77; contr. W.B. Saunders Co. div. CBS Inc., Phila., 1977-82; v.p., contr., chief fin. officer Diversified Printing Corp., Atglen, Pa., 1982-87; v.p. sales ops. Maxwell Communication Corp., Greenwich, Conn., 1987-89; v.p. fin. planning and control Arcata Graphics Co., Balt., 1989-94; bus. cons. Washington, 1994-95; sr. v.p., CFO Univ. Press Am., Inc., Lanham, Md., 1995-97, Nat. Book Network, Inc., 1995-97; bus. cons., 1997—; v.p., CFO BDP Internat., Inc. Global Logistics and Transp., Phila., 1997—. Lt. USN, 1964-68; Vietnam. Mem. Fin. Execs. Inst. Roman Catholic. Office: Gepapeak Bay Business Park 141 Log Canoe Cir Stevensville MD 21666-2127

BARRETT, JOHN F., insurance company executive; BBA, U. Cin. Coll. Bus. Adminstrn., 1971. Pres., CEO Bank NY; with Western & Southern Life Ins. Co., Cin., 1987—, exec. v.p., CFO, 1987—89, pres., COO, 1989—94, pres., CEO, 1994—, chmn., 2002—; pres., CEO Western & Southern Fin. Group, Cin., 2000—, chmn., 2002—. Dir. Fifth Third Bancorp, The Andersons Inc. Associated with Am. Coun. Life Ins., Catholic Inner City Schools, Cin., Cin. Bus. Com., Downtown Cin., Nat. Underground R.R. Freedom Ctr., Young President's Orgn. Mem.: Am. Bus. Roundtable. Office: Western & So Life Ins Co 400 E 4th St Cincinnati OH 45202*

BARRETT, JOHN J(AMES), JR., lawyer; b. Phila., May 19, 1948; s. John J. and Carmela (DiJohn) B.; m. Rosemary A. Campagna, Aug. 23, 1969; children: Jeffrey, Kristin, Jacqueline. BA, Temple U., 1970, JD, 1973. Bar: Pa. 1973, N.J. 1987, U.S. Dist. Ct. (ea. dist.) Pa. 1973, U.S. Ct. Appeals (3rd cir.) 1975, U.S. Dist. Ct. (mid. dist.) Pa. 1986, U.S. Supreme Ct. 1986, U.S. Dist. Ct. N.J. 1987. Assoc. Saul, Ewing, Remick & Saul, Phila., 1973-80; ptnr. Saul Ewing LLP, Phila., 1980—. Mem. Nat. Assn. R.R. Trial Counsel, Phila. Assn. Def. Counsel. Office: Saul Ewing LLP 3800 Centre Sq W 1500 Market St Philadelphia PA 19102 Office Phone: 215-972-7767. Business E-Mail: jbarrett@saul.com.

BARRETT, KATHERINE, author, journalist, state policy analyst, multimedia producer; b. N.Y.C., May 24, 1954; d. Herbert and Betty (Palash) B.; m. Richard H. Greene, Feb. 21, 1982; children: Benjamin, Sandra. BS in Journalism, Northwestern U., 1976. Reporter Comml. Appeal, Memphis, 1976-78; assoc. editor, sr. writer, sr. editor Ladies' Home Jour., N.Y.C., 1980-84, contbg. editor, 1984-98; free-lance writer, columnist numerous publs., 1984—; prodr. Walt Disney Family Edn. Found., San Francisco, 1996—; correspondent Governing mag., Washington. Spkr. on state and city mgmt., 1992—; mem. adv. bd. Govtl. Acctg. Stds. Bd., Norwalk, Conn., 1996—; curator Walt Disney Family Mus. web site; sr. project coord. Pew Ctr. on the States, 2005— Author: The Man Behind the Magic, 1991, Frankly, My Dear, 1996, Powering Up, 2000, Inside the Dream, 2001; co-prodr.: (plays, CD-ROM) Walt Disney: An Intimate History, 1998; co-prodr., writer (TV documentary) Walt: The Man Behind the Myth, 2001; contbr. articles to Redbook, Reader's Digest, Glamour, Ladies Home Jour., Newsweek., others. Recipient award for excellence N.Y. Soc. CPA's, 1991, Children's Choice award Internat. Reading Assn., 1992, Washington Monthly Journalism award, 1999, Folio Editorial Excellence award, Folio Mag., 2002, Excellence in Health Care Reporting award Nat. Inst. Health Care Mgmt., 2004

BARRETT, KIRK ROBERT, environmental engineer, educator; b. Bartlesville, Okla., May 19, 1960; BSc, Kans. State U., Manhattan, 1978—82; MSc, Kans. State U., 1982—85; PhD, Northwestern U., Evanston, Ill., 1992—96. Cert. Profl. Engr., Mass., 1997, Wis., 1994; Profl. Wetland Scientist Soc. Wetland Scientists, 1995. Rsch. environ. engr. Des Plaines River Wetlands Demonstration Project, Wadsworth, Ill., 1988—92; water resources engr. The Bioengineering Group, Inc., Salem, Mass., 1996—99; rsch. dir. Rutgers U. Meadowlands Environ. Rsch. Inst., Newark, 1999—2004; founding dir. Passaic River Inst., Montclair (N.J.) State U., 2004—. Contbr. chapters to books, articles. Commr. Essex County Environ. Commn., Newark, 2003—; chair design com. Main St. South Orange, NJ. Named South Orange Man Yr., South Orange Lions Club, 2003; fellow Walter P. Murphy Fellowship, Northwestern U., 1989, Infrastructure Fellowship, US Dept. Edn., 1992; grantee Rsch. grant, US Army Corps Engrs. Waterways Expt. Sta., 1992, US EPA, 2002. Mem.: Am. Water Resources Assn. (founding chair, wetlands tech. com. 2000—01), Am. Soc. Civil Engrs. (wetlands hydrology com. 2003—). Office: Coll Sci and Math 1 Normal Ave Montclair NJ 07043 Office Phone: 973-655-7117. Business E-Mail: kirk.barrett@montclair.edu.

BARRETT, LIDA KITTRELL, mathematics professor; b. Houston, May 21, 1927; d. Pleasant Williams and Maidel (Baker) Kittrell; m. John Herbert Barrett, June 2, 1950 (dec. Jan. 1969); children: John Kittrell, Maidel Horn, Mary Louise. BA, Rice U., 1946; MA, U. Tex., Austin, 1949; PhD, U. Pa., 1954. Instr. math. U. Conn., Waterbury, 1955-56; vis. appointment U. Wis., Madison, 1959-60; lectr. U. Utah, Salt Lake City, 1956-61; assoc. prof. U. Tenn., Knoxville, 1961-70, prof., 1970-80, head math. dept., 1973-80; assoc. provost No. Ill. U., DeKalb, 1980-87; dean, arts and scis. Miss. State U., Mississippi State, 1987-91; sr. assoc. Edn. and Human Resources Directorate NSF, Washington, 1991-95; prof. math. U.S. Mil. Acad., West Point, N.Y., 1995-98; adj. prof. U. Tenn., 1998—2001. Math. and math. edn. cons., Knoxville, Tenn., 1964-80, 98—. Contbr. articles on topology, applied math. and math. edn. to profl. jours. Mem. Math. Assn. Am. (pres. 1989, 90), Am. Math. Soc., Soc. Indsl. and Applied Math., Nat. Coun. Tchrs. Math., Am. Assn. Higher Edn., Phi Kappa Phi, Sigma Xi. Episcopalian. E-mail: lida-k-barrett@att.net.

BARRETT, MARY KATHLEEN, secondary school educator; b. Brighton, Mass., July 31, 1952; d. Patrick Joseph and Rosanna Carmel (Meunier) Leonard; m. Stephen Michael Barrett, Aug. 9, 1980; children: Patrick Mark, Christopher Francis. AA, Massasoit C.C., 1972; BA, Bridgewater State Coll., 1974. Instrnl. aide Easton Jr. H.S., North Easton, Mass., 1977-78, tchr. history, 1978. Parent com. chmn. Boy Scouts of Am. Troop 22, 2000—. Mem. Mass. Tchrs. Assn., Easton Tchrs. Assn., Holbrook Hist. Soc. (v.p. 1985-87), Weymouth Hist. Soc., Mass. Fedn. Women's Clubs (internat. affairs chmn. 1978-80), Braintree Jr. Philergians Club (newsletter chmn. 1975-76, pres. 1977-78). Roman Catholic. Avocations: antiques, deepsea fishing, bowling, Classic Auto Shows. Home: 74 Harvey St Taunton MA 02780-1218 Office: Easton Jr HS Col Ave Easton MA 02356

BARRETT, MICHAEL BAKER, historian, educator; b. Honolulu, Oct. 12, 1946; s. John P. and Bernice (Baker) B.; m. Sara Harriet McKerley, Sept. 20, 1969; 1 child, Michael M. AB, The Citadel, 1968; MA, U. Mass., 1969, PhD, 1977; student, U.S. Army Command and Gen. Staff Coll., U.S. Army War Coll. Lectr. history U. Mass., Amherst, 1973-74, 75-76; instr. history The Citadel, Charleston, S.C., 1976-78, asst. prof., 1978-82, assoc. prof., 1982—, dean of grad. studies, 1985—. Contbr. articles to profl. jours. Brig. gen. U.S. Army, 1969—2001, comdr. 941st TC Co. U.S. Army, comdr. 812th TC bn. U.S. Army, comdr. 1182d TC Brigade U.S. Army, comdr. 1186th TC Brigade U.S. Army. Recipient Legion of Merit, U.S. Army, others; Fulbright fellow, 1974-75, Citadel Devel. Found. fellow, 1977, 82, NDEA fellow, 1977. Mem. Am. Hist. Assn., Am. Mil. Inst., So. History Assn., S.C. History Assn., Soc. Mil. History, Hibernian Soc., S.C. Agrl. Assn., U.S. Army Armor Assn., Transp. Corps. Officers Assn., Fulbright Alumni Assn., Phi Alpha Theta, Phi Kappa Phi, Delta Phi Alpha. Office: The Citadel Grad Studies Office Of The Dean Charleston SC 29409-0001 Mailing: 1170 Chersonese Rd Mount Pleasant SC 29464-9506 Office Phone: 843-953-4855. Business E-Mail: barrettm@citadel.edu.

BARRETT, MICHAEL HENRY, civil engineer; b. Dove Creek, Colo., June 20, 1932; s. Frank Ace and Carrie Ethel (Snyder) B.; m. Barbara Jane Kreutz, Aug. 7, 1954; children: Robert, Mary, Bonnie, William. BS in Civil Engring, U. Colo., 1955, postgrad., 1955-64; MBA, U. Denver, 1979. Registered profl. engr., Colo., Calif., Fla., Wis., N.C., Minn., N.Mex., Utah. Design engr., then partner Ketchum & Konkel, Denver, 1955-69; pres. Ketchum, Konkel, Barrett, Nickel, Austin, Denver, 1969-79, chmn. bd., 1979-85, pres., chmn., 1986-88; prin., cons. Martin/Martin, 1988—2003, prin. emeritus, 2003—. Bd. dirs. Testing Cons., Inc., Martin Assoc. Group, Restruction Corp.; faculty U. Colo., 1963-64, U. Denver, 1968-69; lectr. Civil Def., 1962-68; cons. MMFX Steel Co., 2000—. Patentee in field. Exec. bd. Denver Area council Boy Scouts Am., 1970-, pres., 1974-75, area v.p., 1976-82, area pres., 1982; mem. Westminster (Colo.) Planning Commn., 1971-72; chmn. bd. dirs. Denver Boys, Inc. Served with USNR, 1951-54, USAR, 1955-63. Recipient Lincoln Arc Welding award, 1966, 68, award Am. Inst. Steel Constrn., 1969, Disting. Engring. Alumnus award U. Colo., 1984, Honor award Colo. Engring. Coun., 1984, Silver Beaver award Boy Scouts Am., 1977, Silver Antelope award, 1983. Fellow ASCE (life); mem. NSPE, Am. Concrete Inst., Soc. Exptl. Stress Analysis, Profl. Engrs. Colo. (pres. 1970), Am. Cons. Engrs. Coun. (life; 1st place award 1973, pres. Colo. chpt. 1982, Orley Phillips award 1992, com. of fellows 1993, peer reviewer 1984—, George Washington Leadership award 1998), Cert. Cons. Engrs. of Colo. (life), Structural Engrs. Assn. Colo., Am. Arbitration Assn., Harvard Bus. Sch. Club, Denver C. of C., Rotary (hon., bd. dirs. 1976-78). Office: Martin & Martin Inc 12499 W Colfax Ave Lakewood CO 80215 Office Phone: 303-431-6100. Business E-Mail: mbarrett@martinmartin.com.

BARRETT, MICHAEL JOHN, anesthesiologist; b. Milw., Feb. 27, 1954; s. Walter Joseph and Valerie Clara (Wisniewski) Baclawski; m. Joan Marie Rowley, May 28, 1983; children: Michael J. Jr., Jessica Marie, Monica Jane. BS in Math. with honors, U. Wis., 1974; MD, Med. Coll. Wis., 1981; MBA, U. Toledo, 1998. Diplomate Am. Bd. Anesthesiology, Nat. Bd. Medicine and Surgery, Nat. Bd. Med. Examiners, Am. Acad. Pain Mgmt., Am. Bd. Anesthesiology Pain Mgmt. Intern Med. Coll. Wis. Affiliated Hosps., Milw., 1981, resident in anesthesiology, 1982—84; dir. anesthesiology Putnam Cmty. Hosp., Palatka, Fla., 1984—92, dir. Putnam Pain Ctr., 1985—92; clin. asst. prof. anesthesiology Ohio U. Coll. Osteo. Medicine; chief dept. anesthesia Putnam Cmty. Hosp., Palatka, 1984—92. Pres. Putnam Anesthesia Assocs., Palatka, 1985-92, Associated Anesthesiologists Toledo, 2005—; staff anesthesiologist St. Vincent Med. Ctr., Toledo, 1992—, vice chmn. dept. anesthesia, 2001-05 dir. Pain Mgmt. Ctr., 1994—; ptnr. Assn. Anestheseologists of Toledo, 1993—, fiduciary pension plan, 1999—, pres., 2005—. Bd. dirs. Round Lake Park Homeowners Assn., Palatka, 1986-88. Walter Zeit fellow; recipient St. Vincents Physician Excellence award, 1996. Mem. AMA, Internat. Anesthesia Rsch. Soc., Am. Soc. Anesthesiologists, Am. Soc. Regional Anesthesiologists, Ohio Med. Assn., Acad. Medicine of Toledo and Lucas County, Am. Neuromodulation Soc., Ohio Soc. Anesthesiologists, Assoc. Anesthesiologists Toledo, Putnam County Med. Soc. (pres. 1989-91), Phi Beta Kappa, Phi Kappa Phi. Republican. Roman Catholic. Avocations: boating, private pilot, swimming. Home: 8646 Plum Hollow Pt Holland OH 43528-8487 Office: Assoc Anesthesiologists 2409 Cherry St Ste 305 Toledo OH 43608-2600 Office Phone: 419-251-4715. Business E-Mail: mjbjmb@ameritech.net.

BARRETT, MINNA SARA, psychologist, educator; b. Bklyn., Mar. 13, 1948; d. Leslie Raymond and Rita (Wilner) B.; m. Theodore David Goldfarb, Dec. 21, 1969 (div. May 1984); 1 child, Gretchen Lee. BA in Psychology cum laude, SUNY, Stony Brook, 1969, MA in Psychology, 1972, PhD in Psychology, 1978. Lic. psychologist, N.Y., Calif. Clin. cons. psychologist childcare svcs. SUNY, Stony Brook, 1975-80, assoc. prof. Old Westbury, 1975—, chair social work dept., 1984—; chair social work concentration Wayside Home for Girls, Old Westbury, 1984-90; cons. nat. non-collegiate edn. Albany Ednl. Ctr. N.Y. Bd. Regents, 1984—; prof. L.I. Pathway to Acheivement, 1988—. Asst. clin. adj. prof. social welfare SUNY, Stony Brook, 1980-82. Author (2 chpts.) China Science Walks on Two Legs, 1974; contbr. articles to profl. jours. Chmn. local chpt. Sci. for the People Coalition, Stony Brook, 1969-75, L.I. Safe Energy Coalition, Port Jefferson, N.Y., 1970-82; mem. Suffolk County Occupational Health SUNY, Stony Brook, 1969-75, Suffolk County Child Care Coun., 1970-75; journalist U.N. Conf. Govt. and Devel., Rio de Janeiro, 1992; rsch. advisor L.I. Breast Cancer Action Coalition, 1995—; bd. dirs. Compassion in Dying, 1998—, Nat. Breast Cancer Coalition, 1998—; dirs. liaison consumer advocacy assoc. NIH, 1998; mem. cmty. adv. coun. Brookhaven Nat. Lab., 1998—; mem. Suffolk County Rhabdomyocarcomic Com., 2001—, Nassau County Pesticide Adv. Bd., 1995—, Nassau County Cancer Adv. Bd., 1998—. Recipient Henri Dunant Humanitarian award ARC, 1995, Women of Distinction award March of Dimes, 1999; rsch. fellow Hearst/Avon Publs., 1972, SUNY, 1983, 85, N.Y. State Regents fellow, Spence Found. fellow, 1998; United Univ. Profls. scholar, 1985, 92, Learning and Leadership award State U. of NY, 2002. Mem. Am. Psychol. Assn., Assn. Women in Devel., N.Y. State Psychologists, ARC (Nassau County Humanitarian of Yr. 1994), UN Decade For Women, United Farm Workers Am., Prince William Sound Conservation Alliance. Avocations: skiing, swimming, reading. E-mail: barrettm@oldwestbury.edn.

BARRETT, NANCY SMITH, academic administrator; b. Balt., Sept. 12, 1942; d. James Brady and Katherine (Pollard) Smith; children: Clark, Christopher. BA, Goucher Coll., 1963; MA, Harvard U., 1965, PhD, PhD, Harvard U., 1968. Dep. asst. dir. Congl. Budget Office, Washington, 1975-76; sr. staff Council of Econ. Advisors, Washington, 1977; prin. research assoc. The Urban Inst., Washington, 1977-79; dep. asst. sec. U.S. Dept. Labor, Washington, 1979-81; instr. Am. U., Washington, 1966-67, asst. prof. econs., 1967-70, assoc. prof., 1970-74, prof., 1974-89; dean Coll. of Bus. Adminstrn. Fairleigh Dickinson U., Teaneck, N.J., 1989-91; provost, v.p. acad. affairs Western Mich. U., Kalamazoo, 1991-96, U. Ala., Tuscaloosa, 1996—2003, Wayne State U., Detroit, 2003—. Author: Theory of Macroeconomic Policy, 1972, 2d rev. edit., 1975, Theory of Microeconomic Policy, 1974, (with G. Gerardi and T. Hart) Prices and Wages in U.S., 1974; contbr. articles on econs. to profl. jours. Woodrow Wilson fellow, 1963-64; Fulbright scholar, 1973. Mem.: Am. Econs. Assn., Phi Beta Kappa. Office: Wayne State Univ 4092 Faculty Adminstrn Bldg Detroit MI 48202 Home: 2033 Shorepointe Grosse Pointe Woods MI 48236 Office Phone: 313-577-2200. E-mail: nancy.barrett@wayne.edu.

BARRETT, O'NEILL, JR., medical educator; b. Baton Rouge, Mar. 21, 1929; s. O'Neill and Hazel (Lohman) B.; m. Elois Stone; children: Deborah Ann, Michael, William. BS in Biology, La. State U., 1949; MSc in Medicine, Baylor U., 1958; MD, La. State U., New Orleans, 1953. Diplomate Am. Bd. Internal Medicine, Am. Bd. Med. Oncology, Am. Bd. Hematology. Commd. 2d lt. U.S. Army, 1953, advanced through grades to col., 1968; intern Brooke Army Med. Ctr., San Antonio, 1953-54, med. resident, 1955-58; chief gen. medicine Madigan Army Hosp., Tacoma, 1960-62; asst. chief medicine Letterman Army Hosp., San Francisco, 1963-68; chief dept. medicine Tripler Army Med. Ctr., Honolulu, 1968-71, Walter Reed Army Med. Ctr., Washington, 1971-73, ret., 1973; chmn. dept. comprehensive medicine U. So. Fla. Sch. Medicine, Tampa, 1973-76; dir. div. gen. medicine U. S.C. Sch.

Medicine, Columbia, 1976-86, chmn. dept. medicine, 1987-92, dir. clin. curriculum, 1992-94, disting. prof. emeritus, 1994—. Assoc. counselor So. Med. Assn. Editor: Internal Medicine in Vietnam, 1982; mem. editorial bd. Med. History Vietnam-U.S. Army, 1972—, Archives of Internal Medicine, 1980-91; asst. editor Southern Med. Assn. Jour.; contbr. articles to profl. jours. Recipient 5 Outstanding Tchr. of Yr. awards U. S.C. Sch. Medicine. Fellow ACP, Am. Coll. Clin. Pharmacology; mem. Am. Soc. Hematology, Am. Soc. Clin. Oncology. Avocations: sailing, birding. Home: 2810 Chatsworth Rd Columbia SC 29223-1804 Office: U SC Sch Medicine Med Libr Bldg Garver's Ferry Rd Ste 316 Columbia SC 29201

BARRETT, PATRICIA LOUISE, mathematician, educator; b. Pitts., July 11, 1947; d. Walter James and Helen Louise (Booty) White; m. Jan F. Segovis, Aug. 2, 1970 (dec. Aug. 1984); m. Telford H. Barrett, Jr., Nov. 15, 1985; stepchildren: Joseph Keith and Telford Lee (twins). BS, Valdosta State Coll., 1969, MEd, 1970; EdS, Ga. So. Coll., 1985. Tchr. math. Lowndes High Sch., Valdosta, 1970-83, 86—; math. coord. Lowndes County Schs., Valdosta, 1983-86. Instr. math. Valdosta State Coll., 1975—; registrar Ga. Math. Conf., Eatonton, Ga., 1985-89, chmn., 1990. Mem. adult choir lst Bapt. Ch., 1966—, dir. children III Sunday sch., 1972—, pianist presch. choir, 1988-92, dir., 1992—. Recipient Star Tchr. award Valdosta C. of C., 1976, 82. Mem. NEA, Nat. Coun. Tchrs. Math., Ga. Coun. Tchrs. Math. (dist. chmn. 1981-83, Gladys M. Thompson dist. award 1986, state treas. 1992-94, sec. 1999-2003), Ga. Assn. Educators, Lowndes Assn. Educators (treas. 1979-80, pres. 1981-82), AAUW. Avocations: reading, teaching, travel. Home: 114 Fairway Dr Valdosta GA 31605-6431 Office: Lowndes High Sch 1112 N St Augustine Rd Valdosta GA 31601-3545

BARRETT, REGINALD HAUGHTON, wildlife management educator; b. San Francisco, June 11, 1942; s. Paul Hutchison and Mary Lambert (Hodgkin) Barrett; m. Katharine Lawrence Ditmars, July 15, 1967; children: Wade Lawrence, Heather Elizabeth. BS in Game Mgmt., Humboldt State U., 1965; MS in Wildlife Mgmt., U. Mich., 1966; PhD in Zoology, U. Calif., Berkeley, 1971. Rsch. biologist U. Calif., Berkeley, 1970—71, acting asst. prof., 1971—72; rsch. scientist divsn. wildlife rsch. Commonwealth Scientific and Indsl. Rsch. Orgn., Darwin, Australia, 1972—75; from asst. prof. to prof. U. Calif., Berkeley, 1975—, George and Wilhelmina Goertz disting. prof. wildlife mgmt., 2002—. Author (with others): Report on the Use of Fire in National Parks and Reserves, 1977, Research and Management of Wild Hog Populations, Proceedings of a Symposium, 1977, Sitka Deer Symposium, 1979, Symposium on Ecology and Management of Barbary Sheep, 1980, Handbook of Census Methods for Birds and Mammals, 1981, Wildlife 2001: Populations, 1992; contbr. abstracts, reports to profl. jours. Recipient Outstanding Achievement award, Humboldt State U. Alumni Assn., 1986, Bruce R. Dodd award, 1965, Howard M. Wight award, 1966; Undergrad. scholar, Nat. Wildlife Fedn., 1964, NSF Grad. fellow, 1965—70, Union Found. Wildlife Rsch. grantee, 1968—70. Fellow: Calif. Acad. Sci., Explorers Club; mem.: AAAS, Orgn. Wildlife Planners, Calif. Bot. Soc., Am. Inst. Biol. Scis., Internat. Union Conservation Nature (life), Am. Soc. Mammalogists (life), Soc. Range Mgmt. (life), Australian Mammal Soc., Soc. Am. Foresters, Ecol. Soc. Am. (cert. sr. ecologist), Wildlife Soc. (pres. Bay Area chpt. 1978—79, pres. western sect. 1997—98, cert. wildlife biologist, R. F. Dasmann Profl. of the Yr. award western sect. 1989), Sigma Xi, Xi Sigma Pi. Episcopalian. Avocations: hunting, fishing, photography, camping, backpacking. Office: U Calif 137 Mulford Hall Berkeley CA 94720-3114 Office Phone: 510-642-7261. Business E-Mail: rbarrett@nature.berkeley.edu.

BARRETT, RICHARD DAVID, university director, consultant, retired bank executive; b. Cin., Sept. 27, 1931; s. Oscar Slack and Helen Rust (Kaiper) B.; m. Pamela P. Soldwedel, Feb. 25, 1971; children: David, Kimball, Randall. Grad., Choate Sch.; BA, Yale U., 1953; postgrad., George Washington U., NYU. Prodn. control Reynolds Metals Co., 1954-56; v.p. ops. Nat. Bank Washington, 1956-66; officer Irving Trust Co., N.Y.C., 1966-70; v.p. mktg. First Am. Bank, N.A., Washington, 1970-74, sr. v.p., 1974—, head internat. div., head retail ops. and mktg. group, v.p. internat. and pvt. banking group, exec. v.p. mktg. and community rels.; dir. planned giving Georgetown U., Washington; pres. Barrett Planned Giving, Inc., Washington. Past mem. Bankers Assn. Fgn. Trade, Greater Washington Area Bd. Trade Internat. Com. Author: (with Molly E. Ware) Planned Giving Essentials: A Step-by-Step Guide to Success, 2d edit., 2002. Past trustee Meridian House Internat.; past bd. dirs., treas. Hospice Care of D.C., Watergate South Inc.; past trustee Washington Hosp. Ctr.; past chmn., past mem. bd. dirs. Nat. Capitol Area Health Care Coalition, Hospice Care of D.C. Lt. (j.g.) USNR, 1953-54. Mem. Assn. Fundraising Profls., Nat. Com. on Planned Giving, Yale Club, Met. Club, Chevy Chase Club (Md.). Home: 700 New Hampshire Ave NW # 906 Washington DC 20037-2406 Office Phone: 202-349-3812. E-mail: richard@barretplannedgiving.com.

BARRETT, ROBERT JAMES, III, investment banker; b. Bangor, Maine, July 23, 1944; s. Robert James and Catherine Pauline (Rogan) B.; m. Susan Hopkins Vander Poel, July 26, 1975 (div.); children: Robert James IV, Graham Halsted; m. Catherine Moore Tankoos, Apr. 22, 1995. BA cum laude, Georgetown U., 1966; JD, Columbia U., 1969; MBA with honors, Harvard U., 1971. Bar: N.Y., 1969, Maine 1970. Assoc. Morgan Stanley, N.Y.C., 1971-76; sr. v.p. E.F. Hutton & Co. Inc., N.Y.C., 1976-83; dir. Prudential-Bache Securities, N.Y.C., 1983-90; ptnr. Barrett & Whitman., N.Y.C., 1991-92; sr. fin. cons. Merrill Lynch, 1992-95; vice chmn. Apex Ptnrs., 2002—. Dir. Senator George Mitchell Inst.; founder Bar Harbor Preservation Trust; trustee Husson Coll., Bangor, 1989—96, U. Maine, R.J. Barrett, Beatrix J. Farrand Fund, Landscape Hort. Mem.: Beach Club (Palm Beach, Fla.), Bear Lakes Club (West Palm Beach, Fla.), Northeast Harbor Club(Bar Harbor, Maine), Union Club (N.Y.C.). Republican. Roman Catholic. Avocations: tennis, squash, hunting, fishing, golf. Home: 913 S Lakeside Place Lantana FL 33462-1777 E-mail: bob@barrett3.com.

BARRETT, ROBERT MATTHEW, lawyer, educator; b. Bronx, N.Y., Mar. 18, 1948; s. Harry and Rosalind B. AB summa cum laude, Georgetown U., 1976, MS in Fgn. Svc., JD, 1980. Bar: Calif. 1981. Assoc. Latham & Watkins, L.A., 1980—82, Morgan, Lewis & Bockius, L.A., 1982—84, Skadden, Arps, Slate, Meagher & Flom, L.A., 1984—86, Shea & Gould, L.A., 1986—87, Donovan, Leisure, Newton & Irvine, L.A., 1988—90; ptnr. Barrett & Zipser, L.A., 1991—93; prof. law U West L.A. Law Sch., Woodland Hills, Calif., 1993—2004; prof. bus. U. La Verne, Calif., 2004—. Civilian vol. L.A. Sheriff's Dept., 1997-99. Mem. State Bar Calif. (standing com. on profl. responsibility and conduct 1995-99, chair 1997-98, spl. advisor 1998-99), L.A. Bar Assn. (bd. advisors vols. in parole com. 1981—). Address: 21300 Oxnard St Woodland Hills CA 91367-5058 Office Phone: 818-883-0529 x 112. Business E-Mail: robertbarrett@charter.net.

BARRETT, ROGER WATSON, lawyer; b. Chgo., June 26, 1915; s. Oliver R. and Pauline S. B.; m. Nancy N. Braun, June 20, 1940; children— Victoria Barrett Bell, Holly, Oliver. AB, Princeton U., 1937; JD, Northwestern U., 1940. Bar: Ill. 1940. Mem. firm Poppenhusen, Johnson, Thompson & Raymond, Chgo., 1940-43; 45-50; charge documentary evidence Nuremberg Trial, 1944-45; regional counsel Econ. Stablzn. Agy., Chgo., 1951-52; ptnr. Mayer, Brown & Platt, Chgo., 1952-91, of counsel, 1991—. Life trustee Mus. Contemporary Art, Chgo. With AUS, 1943-45. Mem. ABA, Ill. Bar Assn., Chgo. Bar Assn., Am. Coll. Trial Lawyers, Indian Hill Club (Winnetka), Old Elm Club, Commonwealth Club (Chgo.), Caxton Club (Chgo.). Home: 84 Indian Hill Rd Winnetka IL 60093-3934 Office: Mayer Brown Rowe & Maw 190 S La Salle St Chicago IL 60603-3410

BARRETT, ROLIN FARRAR, JR., mechanical engineer, consultant; b. Raleigh, N.C., May 18, 1962; s. Rolin Farrar and Dixie Hobbs Barrett; m. Petra Arabaszova Barrett, Feb. 27, 2001. BSEE, N.C. State U., 1986, BS in Mech. Engring., 1991; MS in Mech. Engring., La. Tech. U., 1996. Registered profl. engr., N.C. Engr. Barrett Engring., Raleigh, 1986—. Rschr. N.C. State U., Raleigh, 2001—. V.p. bd. dirs. Ruston (La.) Symphony, 1992—94; mem., fundraiser Krewe of Janus, Monroe, La., 1994—97. Named Duke, Krewe of Janus, Monroe, 1997. Mem.: Triangle Soc., Cardinal Club, Sir Walter Gun Club (bd. dirs. 1997—). Achievements include patents for guided bullet and firearm bolt assembly; patents pending for electronic aid for visually impaired; gun sight. Office: Barrett Engring Ste 280 3141 John Humphries Wynd Raleigh NC 27612

BARRETT, RONALD W., biopharmaceutical executive; PhD in Pharmacology, Rutgers U. Various positions to sr. v.p. Affymax Rsch. Inst., Palo Alto, Calif., 1989—99; co-founder, chief scientist XenoPort, 1999, CEO, 2001—. Recipient Newcomb-Cleve. prize, 1996-97. Office: XenoPort 3410 Central Expressway Santa Clara CA 95051 Office Phone: 408-616-7200. Office Fax: 408-616-7210.

BARRETT, THOMAS J., career military officer; b. Lynbrook, NY; m. Sheila Walker; 4 children. BS in Biology, LeMoyne Coll.; JD (with hons.), George Washington U.; grad., Army War Coll., Carlisle, Pa., 1989. Advanced through grades to vice admiral US Coast Guard, 2002, dep. chief, Office of Personnel & Training, 1994—96, dep. comdr., Maintenance & Logistics Command Atlantic Norfolk, Va., 1996—97, dir., reserve & training Washington, 1997—99, comdr., 17th Coast Guard Dist., 1999—2002, vice comdt., 2002—04. Decorated 5 Legion of Merit, Meritorious Svc. medal, 2 Coast Guard Commendation medal, Coast Guard Achievement medal.

BARRETT, THOMAS M., mayor, former congressman; b. Milwaukee, Wis., Dec. 8, 1953; m. Kristine Barrett; children: Thomas John, Anne Elizabeth. BA in Economics, U. Wis., 1976, JD with honors, 1980. Atty. Smith & O'Neill, Milw., 1982-84; mem. Wis. State Assembly, 1984-89, Wis. State Senate from 5th Dist., 1989-92, U.S. Congress from 5th Wis. dist., Washington, 1993—2002; mem. energy and commerce com.; mayor City of Milwaukee, 2004—. Bd. dirs. Sojourner Truth House, Shalom High Sch., Transcenter Home for Youth. Recipient Circle of Friends award Milw. Advocates for Retarded Citizens, 1989, Health Leadership award State Med. Soc., Govt. Leadership award Rehab. for Wis.; named to Clean Sixteen list for environ. voting record by Wis. Environ. Decade, 1987, 89, 90. Mem. Wis. Bar Assn., Phi Beta Kappa. Democrat. Office: 200 E Wells St City Hall Rm 201 Milwaukee WI 53202*

BARRETT, TINA, professional golfer; b. Balt., June 5, 1966; d. Barbara Smith; m. Dan Friedman, Nov. 27, 1993. BA cum laude, Longwood Coll., 1988. Winner Eastern Amateur, 1987, Md. State Amateur, 1988; golfer Ladies Pro Golf Assn., 1988—. Avocation: Baltimore Orioles and Pheonix Suns fan. Office: c/o LPGA 100 International Golf Dr Ste B Daytona Beach FL 32124-1082

BARRETT, WILLIAM GARY, advertising and marketing executive; b. N.Y.C., Oct. 24, 1943; s. Herbert Mark and Toni Eileen (Craig) B.; m. Christina Louise Sjogren, Sept. 11, 1977 (div. 1980); m. Donna Lou Barnes, May 11, 1984; 1 child, Daniel Martin. BA, U. Buffalo, 1964. Sr. media planner Grey Advt., N.Y.C., 1966-69; v.p., supr. network rels. Batten, Barton, Durstine & Osborn Advt., N.Y.C., 1969-71; v.p., media dir. Martin Landey, Arlow, N.Y.C., 1971-74; v.p. media and mktg. Shaller-Rubin Assocs., N.Y.C., 1974-77; sr. v.p., dir. media and mktg. svcs. Young & Rubicam and Dentsu, Young & Rubicam, N.Y.C., 1977-86; exec. v.p., dir. communications svcs. Earle Palmer Brown, Washington, 1986-88; exec. v.p., COO S.F.M./Havas Media, MPG, LLC, Real Time Direct, N.Y.C., 1988-2000; founding ptnr., specialist in mktg./comm. Barrett Consulting LLC, 2001—. Bd. dirs. Price Comparison website, Area TV Holobrand Cons. Lt. U.S. Army, 1964-65. Avocations: skiing, golf, photography, scuba diving, wine collecting. Home: 297 Miller Rd Hudson NY 12534 Office: PO Box 249 Claverack NY 12513-0249 Personal E-mail: 105132.157@compuserve.com.

BARRETT-CONNOR, ELIZABETH LOUISE, epidemiologist, educator; b. Evanston, Ill., Apr. 8, 1935; m. James D. Connor; 3 children. BA in Zoology, Mt. Holyoke Coll., 1956; MD, Cornell U., 1960; DCMT in clin. medicine of tropics, London Sch. Hygiene and Tropical Medicine, 1965; DSc (hon.), Mt. Holyoke Coll., 1985; PhD (hon.), U. Utrecht, The Netherlands, 1996, U. Bergen, Norway, 1996, U. Helsinki, Finland, 2000. Diplomate Am. Bd. Internal Medicine, 1968, Nat. Bd. Med. Examiners, lic. Fla., 1965, Calif., 1970, cert. advanced epidemiology U. Minn., 1967, genetics Johns Hopkins U., 1968. Intern Parkland Meml. Hosp., Dallas, 1960—61, resident, 1961—63; resident infectious disease Jackson Meml. Hosp., Miami, Fla., 1963—64; instr. medicine U. Miami, Fla., 1965-68, asst. prof. medicine, 1968-70; asst. prof. community and family medicine U. Calif., San Diego, 1970-74, assoc. prof. community and family medicine, 1974-81, prof. community and family medicine, 1981—, acting chair dept. community and family medicine, 1981-82, chmn. dept. family and preventative medicine, 1982-97. Mem. hosp. infection control com. VA Med. Ctr., San Diego, 1971-81; Kelly West Meml. lectr. Am. Diabetes Assn., Indpls. 1987; vis. prof.Royal Soc. Medicine, London, 1989; John Rankin lectr. U. Wis., 1989; Don McLeod Meml. lectr., Halifax, N.S., Can., 1990; Elizabeth Blackwell lectr., Rochester, Minn., 1991; Lila Wallace vis. prof. N.Y. Hosp.-Cornell Med. Ctr., N.Y.C., 1992; Donald P. Shiley vis. lectr. Scripps Clinic and Rsch. Found., La Jolla, Calif., 1993; Leonard M. Schuman lectr. U. Mich., 1993; disting. vis. U. Western Australia, 1997; disting. lectr. geriatrics Duke U. Med. Ctr., Durham, N.C., 1998; Heath Clark lectr.,London, 1989, Pickering lectr., Cambridge, England, 2000. Contbr. articles to profl. jours. Recipient Frederick Murgatroyd prize, 1965, Kaiser award for excellence in tchg., 1982, Dr. of Yr. award San Diego Health Care Assn., 1987, merit award Nat. Inst. Aging, 1987, Making a Difference for Women's Health award Soroptimists, La Jolla, 9195, clin. svc. award Soc. for Advancement Women's Health Rsch., 1997, health award NIH, 1999, Stokes award Am. Soc. Preventative Cardiology, 2003; grantee NIH 1970—. Master: ACP (pubs. com. 1988—90, James D. Bruce Meml. award 1994); fellow: Am. Coll. Preventive Medicine (Katharine Boucot Sturgis lectr. 1986), Royal Soc. Medicine, Am. Coll. Nutrition, Am. Coll. Epidemiology (hon.), Royal Soc. Health, Am. Heart Assn. (chmn. budget com. coun. on epidemiology 1987—88, chmn. coun. on epidemiology 1989, Ancel Keys lectr. 1995, Elizabeth Barrett-Connor rsch. award 1995, Merit award 1998); mem.: APHA (chmn. epidemiology sect. 1989—90, Wade Hampton Frost lectr. 1993), Am. Soc. Preventive Medicine, N.Y. Acad. Scis., Internat. Bone and Mineral Soc., Am. Geriat. Soc., Am. Diabetes Assn., Western Assn. Physicians, Calif. Acad. of Preventative Medicine, Assn. Practitioners in Infection Control, Am. Soc. Tropical Medicine and Hygiene (emeritus), Internat. Epidemiol. Assn., Infectious Disease Soc. Am., Am. Fedn. Clin. Rsch., Am. Venereal Disease Assn. (v.p. 1977—78), Soc. Epidemiol. Rsch. (pres. 1983, Cassell Meml. lectr. 1997), Inst. Medicine, Assn. Tchrs. Preventive Medicine (bd. dir. 1987—99, Outstanding Educator award 1992), Sigma Xi, Phi Beta Kappa. Office: U Calif San Diego Family and Preventive Medicine 9500 Gilman Dr # Mc0607 La Jolla CA 92093-0607

BARRETTE, JEAN, physicist, researcher; b. Montreal, May 1, 1946; s. Bertrand and Marguerite Ducharme B. BSc, U. Montréal, 1967, MSc, 1968, PhD, 1974. Postdoctoral fellow Max-Planck Inst., Heidelberg, Germany, 1974-76; physicist Brookhaven Nat. Lab., Upton, N.Y., 1976-82; engring. physicist Commissariat a l'energie Atomique, Saclay, France, 1982-87; prof. McGill U., Montréal, 1987—, chair dept. physics, 1997—2002; dir Foster Radiation Lab., Montréal, 1988-97. Mem.: Can. Assn. of Physicists, Am. Physical Soc. Achievements include research in nucleus-nucleus reactions and heavy-ion physics with particular interest in the study of reaction mechanism at intermediate and relativistic bombarding energies. Office: McGill U Dept Physics 3600 University St Montreal PQ Canada H3A 2T8 Office Phone: 514-398-7030. Business E-Mail: jean.barrette@mcgill.ca.

BARRETTE, LINDA JONES, retired dean; b. Johnson City, Tenn., Mar. 30, 1946; d. Horace Easterly Jones and Una Mae Scott; m. Pierre Philip Barrette, Aug. 20, 1977. BS, East Tenn. State U., 1967; MSLS, Cath. U. Am., 1977; PhD, So. Ill. U., 1992. Cert. distance learning adminstr. profl., VTEL ESA installation, operation and svc. Libr. Park Rd. Elem. Sch., Charlotte, NC, 1967—69; hed libr. Williamsburg Jr. High, Arlington, Va., 1969—77; libr. Harrisonburg (Va.) Jr. High, 1977—78; dean for learning resources John A. Logan Coll., Carterville, Ill., 1981—2002; pres. Learning, Tech. and Librs., Inc., Carbondale, 1982—91; sec.-treas. IPDN, Inc., St. Louis, 2000—02; ret. Trainer-cons. So. Ill. Collegiate Common Market, Herrin, Ill., 1998-2000, mem. tech. adv. bd., 1998—; mem. adv. bd. Ill. State Libr., Springfield, 1998-2000, Ill. Digital Acad. Libr., Champaign, 1999—. Author: (software program) CARDPREP: Microcomputer Catalog Card, Label, Proofsheet and List Writer, 1985. Del. Ill. Regional White Ho. Conf. on Libr. and Info. Svcs., Carterville, 1990; bd. trustees Grace United Meth. Ch., 2002-2003 Recipient Outstanding Regional Leadership award Chair Acad., 1999, Excellence award John A. Logan Coll. Ctr. for Excellence in Tchg., Learning and Leadership, 2000, 02. Fellow Postdoctoral Acad. Higher Edn.; mem. A Consortium of Midwest Colls. and Univs. (pres. 1999-2000), Am. Libr. Assn., So. Ill. Learning Resource Consortium (sec. 2000-01), Ill. Coun. C.C. Adminstrs. (sec. 1993-94, bd. dirs. 1993-96, pres. 1994-95), Ill. Libr. Assn., Rotary (pres. Carbondale-Breakfast chpt. 1992-93, award of merit 1996, Paul Harris fellow 1988, 99), Carbondale C. of C. (bd. dirs. 2001, chair online com. 1998), Phi Kappa Phi, Phi Kappa Delta. Methodist. Avocations: golf, swimming, crafts, cruising. Home: 10551 Diamante Way Fort Myers FL 33913-7011 E-mail: ljb@onemain.com.

BARRICK, DONNA MATZ, music educator; b. Seoul, Korea, Jan. 6, 1975; arrived in U.S., 1975; d. Donald Carl and Marilee Margaret Matz. BS in Music Edn., Bob Jones U., Greenville, S.C., 1996; M.Elem.Edn., Converse Coll., Spartanburg, S.C., 1997. Cert. tchr. in elem., spl. edn., learning disabilities, music edn., piano and early childhood S.C. Music tchr. Lake Forest Elem. Sch., Greenville, SC, 1996—98, Houston Elem. Sch., Spartanburg, SC, 1998—. Pianist Grace Bapt. Ch., Landrum, SC, 1993—; mem. Spartanburg Youth Theatre Adv. Bd., 2000—. Mem.: S.C. Music Educators Assn., Music Educators Nat. Conf. Office: Houston Elem Sch 1475 Skylyn Dr Spartanburg SC 29307

BARRICK, MARLA CARYN, music educator; b. Henderson, Tex., Dec. 1, 1966; d. Jerry Don and Toni Peterson Hale; m. Stephen Carl Barrick, Dec. 23, 1989; children: Christopher Weldon, Kaitlyn Nicole. EdM, U. of Tex., Austin, Tex., 1993—96; MusB edn., Baylor U., Waco, Tex., 1987—90; AA, Kilgore Jr. Coll., Kilgore, Tex., 1985—87. Cert. All-Level Music Edn. Tex., 1990, All Level Special Edn. Tex., Elem. Comprehensive Educ. Tex., ED/Autism Endorsement Tex. Music educ. specialist Temple ISD, Temple, Tex., 1990—94; music edn. specialist Copperas Cove ISD, Copperas Cove, Tex., 1994—2003, target reading tchr., 2003—. Children's choir dir. First Bapt. Ch., Copperas Cove, Tex., 1999—. Contbr. clinician Time Mgmt. for Music Educators/Tex. Music Educators Assn. Com. chair First Bapt. Ch., Copperas Cove, Tex., 2001—03. Recipient Semi-Finalist, Excellence in Tchg., HEB, 2003, Tchr. of the Week, Toyota, 2003, Excellence in Tchg., Killeen Daily Herald, Tchr. of the Month, Applebees. Mem.: Growing Minds Club, Assn. of Tex. Prof. Educators (campus rep. 1994—2003), Music Educators Nat. Conf., Tex. Music Educators Assn. Home: 2501 Dennis St Copperas Cove TX 76522 Office: CR Clements Intermediate School PO Box 580 Copperas Cove TX 76522 Office Phone: 254-547-2235. Personal E-mail: barrick@vvm.com. E-mail: marla@ccisd.com.

BARRIE, JOHN PAUL, lawyer, educator; b. Burbank, Calif., Oct. 7, 1947; s. John and Virginia (Feagans) B.; children: Sean, Tyler. AB in Pol. Sci., UCLA, 1969; JD, U. Calif., San Francisco, 1972; LLM in Tax, NYU, 1973. Bar: Calif. 1972, D.C. 1975, Mo. 1977, N.Y., 2001. Atty. advisor to judge U.S. Tax Ct., Washington, 1973-75; atty. office of gen. counsel Renegotiation Bd., Washington, 1975-77; assoc. Lewis & Rice, St. Louis, 1977-82, ptnr., 1982-86, Gallop, Johnson & Neuman, St. Louis, 1986-93, Bryan Cave L.L.P., St. Louis, 1993-98, Washington and NYC, 1998—. Adj. prof. Washington U. Sch. Law, St. Louis, 1979-99, Georgetown Law Ctr., 1999—; past mem. IRS Dist. Dirs.'s Liaison Group, Practitioners Coun., IRS Kansas City Svc. Ctr. Liaison Group, Mo. Dept. Rev. Adv. Group, past chmn. Editor Mo. Bar Ct. and CLE Bull.; editl. advisor Jour. Multistate Taxation; contbr. articles on tax to profl. jours. Commr., Commn. Bot. Garden Subdist., St. Louis, 1989-99. Recipient Dir.'s award IRS, 1993. Fellow Am. Coll. Tax Counsel, Exec. Inst. for Advanced Study Washington U., St. Louis Tax Lawyers Group (past chmn.), St. Louis Corp. Tax Group (chmn.), St. Louis Internat. Tax Group; mem. ABA (tax sect., chmn. com. on govtl. submissions, past chmn. com. on affiliated corps.), Am. Tax Policy Inst. (life, sponsor), Mo. Bar Assn. (tax. sect., past chmn. tax com., Pres.'s award 1983), Calif. Bar Assn. (tax sect.), DC Bar Assn. (tax sec., steering com. 2001—, vice chair), NY Bar Assn. (tax sect.), Bar Assn. Met. St. Louis (tax sect.), Nat. Assn. State Bar Tax Sects. (chmn. 1983-84), Noonday Club, City Club (Washington). Episcopalian. Home: 420 7th St NW Apt 1010 Washington DC 20004-2215 Office: Bryan Cave LLP 700 13th NW Ste 700 Washington DC 20005 also: 1290 Ave of the Americans 35th Flr New York NY 10104 Office Phone: 202-508-6051, 212-541-1184, 202-508-6051. E-mail: jbarrie@bryancave.com.

BARRIENTOS, GONZALO, advertising executive, public relations executive, state legislator; b. Galveston, Tex., July 20, 1941; m. Emma Serrato; children: Joseph, Angelina, Alicia, Adelita, Veronica. Student, U. Tex. Mem. Tex. Ho. of Reps., 1975-85, Tex. Senate, 1985—, chair com. of the whole on legis. and congl. redistricting, mem. edn. com., mem. fin. com., mem. nominations com.; vice chair natural resources com., others. Mem. nat. bd. Cmtys. in Schs.; chmn. bd. Mexican Am. State Legislators Policy Inst.; cmty. organizer Nat. Urban League; program officer VISTA/Peace Corps; trainer Leadership Inst. for Cmty. Devel., Washington. Recipient Tex. Outstanding Pub. Servants award, Tex. Rehab. Assns. Legislative Excellence award, Austin Groups for the Elderly 1995 Achievement award, Matt Garcia Pub. Svc. award Mexican Am. Legal Def. and Ednl. Fund, 1996; named Outstanding Legislator of Yr., Tex. Pub. Employees Assn. Democrat. Office: PO Box 12068 Austin TX 78711-2068

BARRINGER, JOAN MARIE, counselor, educator, artist, writer; b. Washington, Sept. 30, 1955; d. John Thomas and Maria Reginia Barringer. BA in Latin Am. Studies, George Mason U., 1981; grad. in Creating and Selling Short Stories, Inst. Childrens Lit., 1995; MA in Edn. and Counseling, George Mason U., 1999. Translator and receptionist Brazilian Embassy, Cultural Inst., Washington, 1975—83; dir. and founder day care Rainbow City Army-Navy Country Club, Arlington, Va., 1983—87; visitors svcs. Nat. Gallery Art, Washington, 1991—94; workshop and leadership conf. asst. Women's Ctr., Vienna, Va., 1996—2000; career counselor Dept. Rehab. Svcs., Alexandria, Va., 1998—99, Ind. Art. Bus. Studio of Nat. Arts, 2002—. Author: (book of poems) Metronome, 1979; contbr. poetry: Great Contemporary Poetry, 1978; designer CD cover, singer Gift of Love; Fairfax (Va.) Jour., 1992, Montgomery (Va.) Jour., 1992, exhibitions include Graffiti Gallery, 2002, Greenbelt Cmty. Ctr., 2003, Joanne Rose Gallery, 2003, Rehoboth Art League, 2004, Angel Eyes, 2004, Mimi's American Bistro, 2004, Represented in permanent collections Inova Hosp. Pres. Hampton Roadrunners, 2004—; election officer U.S. Govt., Va., 2001; fundraiser Unity Ch. Recipient award, Vienna Photo Show, 2004, 2005. Mem.: Vienna Photog. Soc., Assn. Rsch. and Enlightenment (wayshower 2001—), Women's Caucus for Art (editor, lay out designer, writer, photographer newsletter 1999—2001), Sigma Pi Alpha. Avocations: genealogy, travel, interior decorating, yoga, photography, Oceanography. Home: 11107 Hampton Rd Fairfax Station VA 22039 Personal E-mail: joanmarie5@aol.com.

BARRINGER, PAUL BRANDON, II, lumber company executive; b. Sumter, S.C., Aug. 22, 1930; s. Victor Clay and Gertrude (Hampton) B.; m. Merrill Underwood, May 27, 1957; children: Merrill U., Victor Clay, Ann Hampton. BS, U. Va., 1952; postgrad., George Washington U., 1954. With Human Relations Lab., Washington, 1954; with Coastal Forest ResouLces Co., Weldon, NC, 1954—, chmn. bd., CEO, 1967—. Bd. dirs. BB&T Corp., Sea Pines Co., Inc.; mem. Pres.'s Task Force on Internat. Pvt. Enterprise, Industry Policy Adv. Com. for trade policy matters; mem. U. Va. Exec. Com. Capital Fund Campaign, 1994-2000. Mem. coll. bd. trustees U. Va., 1995-96. With USAF, 1952-54. Mem.: NAM (bd. dirs.), Chief Execs. Orgn. (dir.), Farmington Country Coub, Sea Pines Country Club, Chockyotte Country

Club, Lamda Chi, Sigma Delta Psi, Zeta Psi. Episcopalian. Home: 14 S Calibogue Cay Rd Hilton Head Island SC 29928-2912 Office: Coastal Lumber Co PO Box 829 Weldon NC 27890-0829

BARRINGER, WILLIAM CHARLES, retired chemist; b. Cleve., Feb. 28, 1934; s. Donald Frederick and Elsa (Smith) Barringer; m. Vera Evelyn Dodge, July 8, 1955; children: Laura Elizabeth, Donna Lee, Mary Jane, Judy Lynn. BS in Chemistry, Denison U., 1956; MS in Chemistry, NYU, 1964, PhD of Chemistry, 1968. Devel. chemist, group leader Lederle Labs., Pearl River, NY, 1957—95; sr. rsch. scientist Wyeth-Ayerest Rsch., Pearl River, 1995—2000; ret., 2000. Adj. prof. King's Coll., Briarcliff Manor, NY, 1969—71. Contbr. articles to profl. jours. Mem.: N.Y. Acad. Scis., Am. Chem. Soc. Achievements include patents in field. Avocations: gardening, sports, travel, photography. Home: 155 Pearce Pkwy Pearl River NY 10965

BARRINGTON, LEONARD BARRY, chemist, educator, writer; b. Hutchinson, Kans., Jan. 21, 1924; s. August Leroy and Alice Amanda (Goodenough) B.; m. Katharine Lucy Cibes, Dec. 26, 1945 (div. 1975); 1 child, Belinda; m. Sharyn Marie Carlson, Oct. 3, 1975. BSc, DePaul U., Chgo., 1951; PhD in Biochemistry, U. Chgo., 1955. Exec. sec. Congl. Office of Tech. Assessment, Washington, 1976-79; exec. study dir. NRC, Washington, 1979-81; mgr. tech. planning Atlantic Richfield/Arco Metals, Rolling Meadows, Ill., 1981-84; prin. Cue Systems, Chgo., 1980—; sr. assoc. Pugh Roberts Assocs., Cambridge, Mass., 1983-86; dir. tech. ctr. U. Ill., Chgo., 1986-87, dir. tech. devel., 1987-93; mem. tchg. staff Prairie Crossing Charter Sch. Author/editor: Strategies/Applied Research Management, 1978; columnist Arlington Heights (Ill.) Post; contbr. articles to profl. jours. Panelist World Conf./Rsch. Pks., Chgo., 1990. AEC fellow, 1951-54. Fellow Am. Inst. Chemists; mem. ASTM (acad. mem.), Japan Soc. Chgo., Futurist Soc., Ind. Writers of Chgo., Chgo. Literary Club, Irish Inst. Chemistry, Nat. Silver-Haired Congress, Sigma Xi, Beta Beta Beta. Achievements include development of production process for polyurethane foam structural panels; patents on cultivation of micro-organisms, food safe inhibitors of polymerization. Home: 1525 Portia Rd Grayslake IL 60030-3544 Personal E-mail: osobarry1@aol.com.

BARRINO, FANTASIA, singer; b. High Point, NC, June 30, 1984; 1 child. Contestant American Idol, 2004; singer J Records, 2004—. Singer: (songs) I Believe, 2004 (Top Selling Single of Yr., Billboard Music Awards, 2004, Top Selling R&B/Hip-Hop Single of Yr., Billboard Music Awards, 2004), Summertime, 2004, Chain of Fools, 2004, (albums) Free Yourself, 2004; guest appearances The Tonight Show with Jay Leno, 2004, Live with Regis and Kelly, 2004, The Today Show, 2004. Winner, American Idol, 2004. Office: c/o J Records 745 Fifth Ave New York NY 10151*

BARRIO, SOLEDAD, dancer; b. Madrid; m. Martin Santangelo; children: Gabriela Goldin Garcia, Stella Goldin Garcia. Founder mem., dancer Noche Flamenca, N.Y.C. Recipient Bessie award, 2001. Office: Noche Flamenca 168 W 86th St New York NY 10024 E-mail: marting@arrakis.es.

BARRIOS, GEORGE G., colon and rectal surgeon; b. Zamboanga, The Philippines, Apr. 24, 1943; came to U.S., 1973; s. Donaciano and Nemesia (Gatchalian) B.; m. Olga Cruz, Dec. 11, 1969; children: Kurt, Karl, Erik, Katrina. BA, Ateneo de Manila, Quezon City, The Philippines, 1963; MD, U. The Philippines, Manila, 1968. Diplomate Am. Bd. Surgeons, Am. Bd. Colon and Rectal Surgeons. Resident in gen. surgery SUNY, Buffalo, 1975-78; resident in colon/rectal surgery, Buffalo Gen. Hosp., 1978-79; colon rectal surgeon Buffalo (N.Y.) Med. Group. Clin. asst. prof. dept. surgery SUNY, Buffalo. Fellow ACS, Am. Soc. Colon and Rectal Surgeons. Office: Buffalo Med Group 85 High St Buffalo NY 14203-1149 Office Phone: 716-857-8602. E-mail: gbarrioimd@aol.com.

BARRIOS, RICHARD (JOHN), freelance/self-employed writer, film historian; b. Houma, La., July 2, 1954; s. Manny Clement and Gladne Marie (Thibodeaux) B. MusB in Music History magna cum laude, Loyola U., New Orleans, 1980; MusM in Music History and Lit., U. Houston, 1984; MA in Cinema Studies, NYU, 1986. Fin. asst. Houston Grand Opera, 1981-82; opera promotion staff Boosey & Hawkes, Inc., N.Y.C., 1986-91; freelance writer, rschr., historian N.Y.C., 1991—. Cons., program annotator Kino Video, N.Y.C., 1997—; film programmer, lectr. Am. Film Inst., Washington, 1996, Film Forum, N.Y.C., 1996; lectr. Smithsonian Inst., Washington, 1995, U.S. Army Band, Ft. Myer, Va., 1998. Author: A Song in the Dark: The Birth of the Musical Film, 1995 (Theatre Libr. Assn. prize 1996), Screened Out: Playing Gay in Hollywood from Edison to Stonewall, 2002; contbr. articles to profl. jours.; appeared in and narrator: (film) Busby Berkeley: Going Through the Roof, 1997; appeared in: (films) Fascinatin' Rhythm, 2001, Lullaby of Broadway: Opening Night on 42nd Street, 2001. Co-chmn. reconciling congregation com. Ch. of St. Paul and St. Andrew, N.Y.C., 1996-2000, staff-parish com., 1994-98, lay del. to ann. conf., 1998-2000. Mem. Met. Opera Guild, Soc. for Cinephiles, Lesbian and Gay Cmty. Svcs. Ctr. (advocate). Democrat. Methodist. Avocations: travel, opera, exercise, cooking. Home: 15900 Riverside Dr W Apt 3K New York NY 10032-1006

BARRIS, ROBERT, music educator, musician; m. Joan Barris; children: Eric Heller, Rachel Heller. B of Music Edn., U. Mich., 1965, MusM, 1970. Bassoonist Toledo Orch., 1963—65, Dallas Symphony Orch., 1965—66, Detroit Symphony Orch., 1966—69; bassoon prof. Ctrl. Mich. U., Mt. Pleasant, 1971—84; bassoon instr. Interlochen Arts Acad., Interlochen, 1978—87; bassoon prof. Northwestern U., Evanston, Ill., 1984—. Guest performer N.Y. Philomusica, N.Y.C., 1978—93; resident artist Swannanoa Chamber Players, NC, 1978—85; substitute bassoonist Chgo. Symphony Orch., 1997—. Mem.: Internat. Double Reed Soc. (v.p. 1997—99). Home: 36 St Charles Pl Highland Park IL 60035 Office: Northwestern Univ 60 Arts Circle Dr Evanston IL 60208 Office Phone: 847-491-7228. Business E-Mail: rab@northwestern.edu.

BARRITT, EVELYN RUTH BERRYMAN, nurse, educator, dean; b. Detroit, Sept. 4, 1929; d. George C. and Ruby (Mathews) Berryman; m. Ward LeRoy Barritt, Oct. 28, 1951; 1 dau., Kelli Jo. AA, Graceland Coll., 1949; diploma, Independence (Mo.) Sanitarium and Hosp. Sch. Nursing, 1952; BSN., Ohio State U., 1956, MA, 1962, PhD, 1971. Asst. instr. nursing Atlantic City Hosp., 1952-53; staff nurse Shore Meml. Hosp., Somers Point, N.J., 1953-54, Ohio State U. Hosp., Columbus, 1954-55; instr. White Cross Hosp., Columbus, 1955-57; asso. dir. nursing service Riverside Meth. Hosp., Columbus, 1957-64; asst. exec. dir. Ohio Nurses Assn., Columbus, 1964-65; dean Capital U. Sch. Nursing, Columbus, 1965-72, Coll. Nursing, U. Iowa, Iowa City, 1972-79, prof. nursing, 1972-80; prof. Sch. Nursing U. Miami, Fla., 1980—, dean, 1980-85. Bd. dirs. Health Coun. South Fla., 1988—, pres., 1990-92; bd. dirs. So. Fla. Perinatal Network, Inc., 1980-89, pres., 1984-86; mem. Fla. Bd. Ind. and Pvt. Colls. and Univs., 1980; co-chmn. Dade County Indigent Care Task Force, 1991-93. Author: Florence Nightingale: Her Wit and Wisdom, 1975; author, editor: Thoughts on CareGiving, 1998; contbr. articles to profl. jours. Mem. ANA, Ohio Nurses Assn. (pres. dist. 1966-68), Iowa Nurses Assn., Fla. Nurses Assn., Graceland Univ. Alumni Assn., Am. Assn. Higher Edn., Am. Assn. Colls. Nursing (pres. 1976-78). Home: 416 Park Blvd N Venice FL 34285-1332

BARR-KUMAR, RAJ, architect; b. Colombo, Ceylon, Feb. 5, 1946; arrived in U.S., 1974; s. Alexander Hamilton Barr-Kumarakulasinghe and Francesca ThangaRanee (Winslow) Barr-Kumar; m. Athina Kambouri, 1975 (dec. Feb. 1977); m. Bernadette Dipica Wikramanayake, 1994. BS, U. Ceylon, Colombo, 1971; grad. diploma in architecture, U. London, 1974; MArch, U. Kans., 1975; postgrad., Harvard U., 1978; D of Arch., U. Hawaii, 2003. Lic. architect Washington, N.Y., Va., Md., Fla., Kans.; cert. Nat. Coun. Archtl. Registration Bds. Designer Panditaratna & Adithiya RIBA, Ceylon, 1967-71, Jon Prescott RIBA, Hong Kong, 1971-72, NE Met. Regional Hosp. Bd./Watkins Gray Internat., London, 1972-73, Llewellyn-Davies Assocs., London, 1973-74, Patty Berkebile Nelson Assocs./Seligson Assocs., Kansas City, Mo., 1975-78; sr. designer Barret Daffin & Carlan, Tallahassee, 1979-80; mgr. computer aided design Wolfberg, Alvarez, Taracido Assocs., Rosslyn, Va., 1982-83; pres. Barr-Kumar Architects Engrs., Washington, 1981—; asst. prof. U. Kans., Lawrence, 1975—79; assoc. prof. Fla. A&M U., Tallahassee, 1979—85, dir., assoc. prof. Arch. Ctr. Washington, 1981—84; assoc. prof. Howard U., Washington, 1986—94. Vis. prof. Washington Alexandria Ctr. Va. Polytech. Inst., 1984—86, 1998, Cath. U. Am., 2003—, U. Md., 2004—; Emens disting. vis. prof. Ball State U., 1999; spkr., panelist Smithsonian Inst., Washington, 1982—, Nat. Bldg. Mus., Washington, 1985—, Corcoran Art Gallery, 1998—, Lambda Alpha Internat., 1994—; mem. adv. coun. on arch. No. Va. C.C.'s, 1983—; apptd. mem. FIDER Nat. Interior Design Accrediting Bd., 1986—92; chair Anne Arundel County Devel. Design Awards, Md., 1985—90; examiner Nat. Coun. Archtl. Registration Bd., 1990; lectr. in field. Author: Green Architecture - Strategies for Sustainable Development, 2003. Chair archtl. group Luther Pl. Shelter for Homeless, Washington, 1990—; co-chair DC-HOME Housing Assistance Team, Washington, 1990—; pres. Sri Lanka Assn., Washington, 1991-93; mem. bldg. and preservation coms. Washington nat. Cathedral, 1995—. Recipient County Exec. Appreciation cert. Anne Arundel County, Md., 1990. Fellow AIA (bd. dirs. Washington chpt. 1984-97, pres. 1990, host chpt. chair nat. conv. 1988-91, nat. bd. dirs. 1991-97, nat. v.p. 1994, nat. pres. 1997, Outstanding Svc. award Washington chpt. 1990, Walter Wagner fellow 1992, Richard Upjohn fellow 1994, Nat. citation for exceptional svc. 1997), Bahamian Inst. Architects, Japan Inst. Architects (hon.), Philippine Inst. Architects (hon.), United Architects of Philippines (hon.), Sri Lanka Inst. Architects (hon.), Royal Archtl. Inst. Can. (hon.), Mex. Soc. Architects (hon.), Pan Am. Fedn. Architects (hon.); corp. mem. Royal Inst. Brit. Architects. Office: Barr-Kumar Architects Engrs PC 1825 I St NW Ste 400 Washington DC 20006-5415 Business E-Mail: info@BARRarchitects.com.

BARRON, BLANCA E., language educator; b. Monterrey, Nuevo Leon, Mex., Apr. 15, 1964; d. Meliton Barron and Maria Isabel Sanchez; m. Salvador Pliego, Oct. 6, 1989; children: Isis Pliego, Itzel Pliego. B in Computers, 1993. Tchr. Inst. Regional Mex., Monclova, Mexico, 1985—87, Tex. So. U., Houston, 1999—2002; lang. arts tchr. Inst. Oahuilense, Saltillo, 1990—92; bilingual tchr. Garden Oaks Elem., 1999—. Scholarship, Spain Embassy and Garden Oaks Elem., 2003, grant, Funds for Tchrs., 2004.

BARRON, BRIGID, education educator; BS in Psychology, U. Calif., Santa Cruz, 1984; MA in Psychology, Vanderbilt U., 1989, PhD in Clin. Developmental Psychology, 1992. Intern in child clin. psychology U. Wash., 1991—92; instr. Peabody Coll., Vanderbilt U., 1992—93; sr. rsch. assoc. Learning Tech. Ctr., Vanderbilt U., 1992—95; asst. prof. edn. Stanford (Calif.) U., 1996—. Mem. adv. bd. tech. task force SPEAK-UP! Leadership Program for Girls; cons. Plugged-In Tech. Access Ctr., Comty. Kids Children's Program. Office: Stanford U Sch Edn 485 Lasuen Mall Stanford CA 94305-3096*

BARRON, DAVID JEREMIAH, law educator; b. Washington, July 7, 1967; AB in History, Harvard U., 1989, JD, 1994. Bar: NY 1996. Law clk. to Judge Stephen Reinhardt US Ct. Appeals 9th Cir.; law clk. to Justice John Paul Stevens US Supreme Ct.; atty.-advisor Office Legal Counsel US Dept. Justice; asst. prof. law Harvard Law Sch., Cambridge, Mass., 1999—2004, prof., 2004—. Office: Harvard Law Sch 1563 Massachusetts Ave Cambridge MA 02138 Office Phone: 617-495-8218. Office Fax: 617-495-4863. Business E-Mail: dbarron@law.harvard.edu.

BARRON, HAROLD SHELDON, lawyer; b. Detroit, July 4, 1936; s. George Leslie and Rose (Weinstein) B.; m. Roberta Yellin, Nov. 17, 1963; children: Lawrence Ira, Jean Louise. AB, U. Mich., 1958, JD, 1961. Bar: N.Y. 1963, Mich. 1961, Ill. 1983, Pa. 1992. Pvt. practice, N.Y.C., 1962-68; practice in Southfield, Mich., 1968-83, Chgo., 1983-93, Pa., 1991—2002; atty. Hughes Hubbard & Reed, 1962-68; corp. counsel Bendix Corp., 1968-69, sec., assoc. gen. counsel, 1969-72, sec., gen. counsel, 1972-83, v.p., 1974-83; ptnr. Arnstein, Gluck, Lehr, Barron & Milligan, Chgo., 1983-86, Seyfarth, Shaw, Fairweather & Geraldson, Chgo., 1986-91; v.p., gen. counsel Unisys Corp., Blue Bell, Pa., 1991-92, sr. v.p., gen. counsel, 1992-94, sr. v.p., gen. counsel, sec., 1994-99, sr. v.p., gen. counsel, 1999-2001, vice chmn., 2001—02; counsel McDermott, Will & Emery, 2002—04. Mem. nat. adv. coun. and faculty Practising Law Inst., N.Y.C.; bd. dirs. Royal Maccabees Life Ins. Co., Southfield, 1983—94; chmn. bd. F.A. Tucker Group, Inc., 1991—95. Editor: The Business Lawyer. Com. visitors U. Mich. Law Sch.; trustee Children's Hosp. Mich., Detroit, 1976-84; mem. Census Adv. Com. on Privacy and Confidentiality, 1975-76; mem. governing bd., adv. coun. Purdue U. Info. Privacy Rsch. Ctr.; bd. dirs. Citizens Rsch. Coun. of Mich., 1982-83, Greater Phila. Econ. Devel. Coalition. Served with AUS, 1961-62. Mem. ABA (coun. bus. law sect., bus. law sect., chmn. 2002-03, standing com. on fed. judiciary, editor The Bus. Lawyer, Latin Am. legal initiatives coun., chmn. com. of corp. gen. counsel, sect. bus. law coun., com. corp. law and taxation, internat. bus. law com., com. devels. in investment svcs., com. long-range issues affecting bus. law practice, com. on corp. laws, commn. on asbestos litigation), Am. Arbitration Assn., Am. Soc. Corp. Secs. (securities law com.), Internat. Inst. Conflict Prevention and Resolution (exec. com., nat. panel disting. neutrals), Am. Law Inst., Mich. Bar Assn., Assn. Bar City NY (com. corp. law depts.), Carlton Club, Chgo. Club, Bryn Mawr Country Club (Chgo.), The Reserve (Indian Wells, Calif.). Office: 980 N Michigan Ave Ste 1400 Chicago IL 60611 Office Phone: 312-214-3908. Business E-Mail: hal@barronadr.com.

BARRON, HOWARD ROBERT, lawyer; b. Chgo., Feb. 17, 1930; s. Irwin P. and Ada (Astrahan) B.; m. Marjorie Shapira, Aug. 12, 1953; children: Ellen Barron Feldman, Laurie A. PhB, U. Chgo., 1948; BA, Stanford U., 1950; LLB, Yale U., 1953. Bar: Ill. 1953. Assoc. Jenner & Block, Chgo., 1957-63, ptnr., 1964-97; assoc. Schiff Hardin, Chgo., 1953, of counsel, 1997—. Contbr. articles to profl. jours. and books. Mem., then pres. Lake County Sch. Dist. 107 (now Dist. 112) Bd. Edn., Highland Park, 1964-71; pres. Lake County Sch. Bd. Assn., 1970-71; mem. Lake County High Sch. Dist. 113 Bd. Edn., Highland Park, 1973-77; mem. Highland Park Zoning Bd. Appeals, 1984-89. Lt. (j.g.) USNR, 1953-57. Mem.: ABA (com. corp. counsel litigation sect. 1983—2002, co-chmn. subcom. labor and employment law), Yale Club (N.Y.C.), Met. Club, Internat. Bar Assn., Yale Law Sch. Assn. of Ill. (pres. 1962), Yale Law Sch. Assn. (v.p. 1978—81), Chgo. Bar Assn., Fed. Bar Assn., Ill. State Bar Assn. (chmn. antitrust sect. 1968—69, sr. counselor 2003), Standard Club. Democrat. Home: 1366 Sheridan Rd Highland Park IL 60035-3407 Office: Schiff Hardin LLP 6600 Sears Tower Chicago IL 60606 Office Phone: 312-258-5558. Personal E-mail: hrb1366@aol.com. Business E-Mail: hbarron@schiffhardin.com.

BARRON, ILONA ELEANOR, secondary school educator, consultant; b. Sept. 19, 1929; m. George Barron; 1 child, Fred. Cert. elem. tchg., No. Mich. U., 1951; BS in Elem. Edn., Ctrl. Mich. U., 1961; MA in Edn., U. Mich., 1966; postgrad., Mich. State U. Cert. reading specialist. Tchr. Elem. Schs., 1952—67; dir. Title I reading Saginaw Twp. Cmty. Schs., Mich., 1967—68, reading cons., 1971—. Cons. elem. intern Mich. State U., East Lansing, 1968—71; cons. elem. reading Saginaw Twp. Pub. Schs., 1972—. Mem.: NEA, Saginaw Area Reading Coun., Saginaw Twp. Edn. Assn., Mich. Edn. Assn. Achievements include development of methods of teaching developmental reading skills and enrichment. Home (Winter): 35702 Clubber Ct Zephyrhills FL 33541 Home (Summer): 25366 W State Hwy M 64 Ontonagon MI 49953

BARRON, JAMES TURMAN, journalist; b. Washington, Dec. 25, 1954; s. James Pressley and Leirona Faith (Turman) B.; m. Jane-Iris Farhi, Apr. 1, 1995. AB cum laude, Princeton U., 1977. Copy person N.Y. Times, N.Y.C., 1977-78, rsch. asst., 1978-79, reporter, 1979—, acting editor, The Living Sect., 1996-97; broadcast corespondent Sta. WQXR-FM, N.Y.C., 1987—, Sta. WQEW-AM, N.Y.C., 1992-98; writer Pub. Lives column N.Y. Times, 1998—2001; writer Boldface Names column, 2001—02; writer, narrator "Page One" Discovery Times Channel, 2005—. Contbr. to books. Mem. Princeton Club of N.Y., Deadline Club N.Y. (asst. treas. 1993-95, v.p. 1995-99). Methodist. Office: NY Times 229 W 43rd St New York NY 10036-3959

BARRON, JEROME AURE, law educator; b. Tewksbury, Mass., Sept. 25, 1933; s. Henry and Sadie (Shafmaster) B.; m. Myra Hymovich, June 18, 1961; children: Jonathan Nathaniel, David Jeremiah, Jennifer Leah AB magna cum laude, Tufts Coll., 1955; JD, Yale U., 1958; LL.M., George Washington U., 1960. Bar: Mass. 1959, D.C. 1960. Law clk. to chief judge U.S. Ct. Claims, Washington, 1960-61; assoc. firm Cross, Murphy & Smith, Washington, 1961-62; asst. prof. law U. N.D., Grand Forks, 1962-64; vis. assoc. prof. U. N.Mex., Albuquerque, 1964-65; dean Syracuse U. Coll. Law, 1972-73; assoc. prof. George Washington U., from 1965, prof., 1973—, dean, 1979-88, Lyle T. Alverson prof. law, 1987-2000, Harold H. Greene prof. law, 2000—. Author: (with Donald Gillmor and Todd Simon) Mass Communication Law, Cases and Comment, 6th edit., 1998, First Amendment in a Nutshell, 3d edit. 2004, Constitutional Law: Principles and Policy, 6th edit., 2002, (with C. Thomas Dienes, Wayne McCormack and Martin Redish) Constitutional Law In A Nutshell, 5th edit., 2002; contbr. articles, chpts. to profl. publs. Served with U.S. Army, 1959-60 Mem. ABA, D.C. Bar, Cosmos Club, Phi Beta Kappa. Office: George Washington U 2000 H St NW Washington DC 20006-4234 Office Phone: 202-994-6954.

BARRON, JOHN, editor; BA in Journalism, Marquette U. Asst. editor Crain's Chgo. Bus., 1980—84; with Detroit Monthly, 1984—95, editor, 1991—94; positions including reporter, Sunday Showcase editor, dep. features editor, features editor Chgo. Sun-Times, 1995—2003, exec. mng. editor, 2003—05, editor-in-chief, 2005—. Office: Chgo Sun Times 350 N Orleans Chicago IL 60654 Office Phone: 312-321-3000. Business E-Mail: jbarron@suntimes.com.

BARRON, KEVIN DELGADO, physician, educator; b. St. John's, Nfld., Can., Apr. 21, 1929; s. S. John Augustine and Mercedes (Delgado) B.; m. Elizabeth E. Grossmann, June 14, 1956; children— Kevin Lawrence, Sheila Christine. Student, Meml. Univ. Coll., St. John's, 1945-47; MD, C.M., Dalhousie U., Halifax, N.S., Can., 1947-52. Diplomate: Am. Bd. Psychiatry and Neurology. Intern Victoria Gen. Hosp., Halifax, 1951-52, asst. resident in internal medicine, 1952-53, Queen Mary Vets. Hosp., Montreal, Que., Can., 1953-54; asst. resident in neurology Montefiore Hosp., N.Y.C., 1954-55, chief resident in neurology, 1955-56, fellow in neuropathology, 1956-59, adj. attending physician dept. neurology, 1956-59; instr. neurology Columbia U., N.Y.C., 1957-59; asso. in neurology and psychiatry Northwestern U. Med. Sch., Chgo., 1959-61, asst. prof., 1961-63, asso. prof., 1964-67, prof., 1968-69; prof., chmn. dept. neurology, prof. pathology Albany, N.Y., 1969-93; clin. prof. neurology and adj. prof. pathology, 1993-99; prof. emeritus neurology Albany Med. Coll., 2000—. Cons. neurologist Beth Abraham Home, N.Y.C., 1957-59; asst. attending neurologist Morrisania City Hosp., N.Y.C., 1958-59; attending neurologist, neuropathologist VA Hosp., Hines, Ill., 1960-62, sect. chief neurology svc., dir. electron microscope lab., 1962-64, chief neurology svc., dir. neuropathology rsch. svc., 1964-69; neurologist-in-chief Albany Med. Center Hosp., 1969-93; dir. neuropathology rsch. sect. rsch. svc. VA Hosp., Albany, 1969-93; cons. to numerous hosps.; chmn. medicine search com. Albany Med. Coll., 1980-81, mem. med. bd., 1980-81, bd. govs., 1980-82. Contbr. articles to various publs. Fulbright fellow, 1976; sr. U.S. Sci. Humboldt Found., 1976-77. Fellow Am. Acad. Neurology; mem. Am. Neurol. Assn. (councillor), Am. Assn. Neuropathologists, Assn. Univ. Profs. Neurology, Soc. Neurosci., Chgo. Neurol. Soc. (v.p. 1967) Office: 251 New Karner Rd Ste 800 Albany NY 12205-4689

BARRON, MYRA HYMOVICH, lawyer; b. July 5, 1938; d. Leo and Lillian Estelle (Berman) Hymovich; m. Jerome Aure Barron, June 18, 1961; children: Jonathan Nathaniel, David Jeremiah, Jennifer Leah. AB cum laude, Smith Coll., 1959; student, L'Institut des Hautes Etudes, Geneva, 1957—58; MA, Johns Hopkins U., 1961; JD, Georgetown U., 1970. Bar: Va. 70, DC 72, NY. Instr. econs. U. ND, Grand Forks, 1962—64; econ. rsch. asst. U. N.Mex., Albuquerque, 1964—65; legal aid staff atty. Fairfax County, Va., 1971—72, asst. county atty., 1974—81; assoc. Melvin & Melvin, Syracuse, NY, 1973; counsel Fairfax County Redevel. and Housing Authority, Fairfax, Va., 1981—88; ptnr. Sprenger & Lang (formerly Weissbrodt, Swiss & Mc Grew), 1989—98, Weinberg & Jacobs, Rockville, Md., 1998—2000, of counsel, 2001—04. Dep. gen. counsel Housing and Devel. Law Inst., 1988—94, of counsel, 1994—2000. Editor: Jour. Affordable Housing and Cmty. Devel. Law, ABA, 1993—99; contbr. articles to housing jours.; mem.: Georgetown Law Jour., 1967—68. Recipient Samuel Bowles award, Smith Coll., 1959. Mem.: LWV (local chmn. nat. events 1962—64), ABA (mem. governing com. 1994—99, co-chmn. profit practice group 2000—03, mem. forum on affordable housing and cmty. devel. law). Home: 3231 Ellicott St NW Washington DC 20008-2061 Personal E-mail: mhbarron@earthlink.net.

BARRON, (RICHARD) NEIL, librarian; b. Hollywood, Calif., Mar. 23, 1934; s. James Charles and Dorothy (Terrell) Barron; m. Dorothy Susan Weiss, Jan. 29, 1966 (div. Jan. 1976); children: Craig, Felicia; m. Carolyn Ann Goyer, Aug. 19, 1968 (dec. Sept. 2002); stepchildren: Karen, Linda, Susan, Lisa, Jonathon; m. Anne Stone, Mar. 10, 2004. AB, U. Calif., Riverside, 1961; MLS, U. Calif., 1964. Reference, reader adv. libr. Queens Borough Pub. Libr., Jamaica, NY, 1964—65; asst. to assoc. dir. libr. Columbia U., NYC, 1965—67; asst. libr. for tech. svcs. Calif. State U., Sacramento, 1967—70; asst. dir. for tech. svcs. U. South Fla., Tampa, 1972—73; tech. libr. Woodward-Clyde Cons., San Diego, 1989—96; reference libr. San Diego County Libr., 1996—. Reference libr. Calif. Western Sch. Law, San Diego, 1989—90, San Diego City Libr., 1991—96; interlibr. loan libr. Gemological Inst. Am., Carlsbad, Calif., 1999—2003; book reviewer in field. Editor: Gale Group, 1990—; contbr. chapters to books, articles to profl. jours. Pres. Friends of the Libr., Vista, Calif., 1999—2001. With U.S. Army, 1954—56. Recipient Pilgrim award, SFRA, 1982. Avocations: reading, music, travel. Home: 231 N College Dr Apt B4 Santa Maria CA 93454 Office Phone: 805-348-3790. Personal E-mail: writeneil@peoplepc.com.

BARRON, PEGGY PENNISI, management consultant; b. Chgo., Jan. 27, 1958; d. Louis Legendre and Jane Harriet (Peters) Pennisi; m. Stan Barron, May 3, 1986; children: Brian Alexander, Christine Deanna. BS with honors, U. Ill., Chgo., 1979. Data processing mgr. Oasis Aviation, Inc., L.A., 1980-87; pres. Millennium Enterprises, L.A., Calif., 1987—. Author: Broken Bloodlines, 1997, The Big Daddy, 1999. Mem. NAFE, Phi Beta Kappa, Phi Kappa Phi. Avocations: scuba diving, sky diving, cooking and travel. Personal E-mail: peggybarron@comcast.net.

BARRON, ROS, artist; b. Boston, July 4, 1933; d. Louis and Ida (Titel) Myers; m. Harris Barron, Apr. 19, 1953; children: Matt Lewis, Nina Rebecca. B.F.A., Mass. Coll. Art, 1954. Fellow Bunting Inst., Harvard U., 1966-68; co-dir. Zone Visual Theater Co., 1970; assoc. prof. art U. Mass.-Harbor Campus, Boston, 1974—. Vis. artist U. Colo., Boulder, 1983; presenter Arts at the Bunting, 1997. Producer numerous video performance tapes.; one-woman shows include North Hall Gallery, Mass. Coll. Art, Boston, 1988, Watson Gallery, Wheaton Coll., Norton, Mass., 1989, Harbor Gallery U. Mass., Boston, 1990, Mobius, Boston, 1993, Brick Bottom Gallery, Boston, 1996; exhbns. include Whitney Mus. Am. Art, 1967-68, Helen Shlien Gallery, Boston, 1979, 82, Mus. Modern Art, N.Y.C., 1980, 84, Le Nouveau Musee, Lyon, France, 1979, Montevideo Gallery, Amsterdam, Holland, 1979, World Wide Video Festival, Kijkhuis, Holland, 1984, Hirschhorn Mus., Washington, 1984, North Hall Gallery; travelling group exhbns. include Project Rembrandt Biennial, 1991-92, Women's Caucus for Art, 1992; represented in permanent collections Mus. Fine Arts, Boston, Harvard U., Smith Coll. Collection, Worcester Art Mus., Addison Gallery Am. Art., Inst. Contemporary Art, Boston, Samuel P. Harn Mus. Art, U. Fla., Gainesville, Mus. of Modern Art, N.Y.C., Mus. Modern Art, N.Y.C.; performance Art: (with Harris Barron) Mr. & Mrs. Zone: Art Life Art, Mobius Theatre, Boston, 1987, Performance Art: (with Harris Barron) Mr. & Mrs. Zone Again, Mobius Theatre, Boston, 1997, Eartheart and other video works, Mobius Theatre, Boston, 1999, Eagle Air,

The Life and Work of Harris Barron, 2001. Bd. dirs. Boston Performance Artists. Recipient Design award HUD, 1968; N.Y. Found. for Arts grantee, 1972; Guggenheim Found. grantee, 1972; Nat. Endowment Arts grantee, 1975; Rockefeller Found. grantee, 1978-80; Mass. Council Arts grantee, 1981-82, 83 Address: 30 Webster Pl Brookline MA 02445-7937 Office Phone: 617-232-9544. *I am a visual artist. As a painter and video artist, my work involves how I see and transform reality. My life force feels the ontological mystery, an intense state of wonder, and the endlessness of seeing. Strategies of surrealism and the transformational process provide emotional, intellectual, and metaphysical coherence to my work.*

BARRON, STEPHANIE, curator; AB, Barnard Coll., Columbia U., 1972; student, Harvard Inst. Arts Adminstrn., 1973; MA, Columbia U., 1974; postgrad., CUNY, 1975-76. Intern, curatorial asst. Solomon R. Guggenheim Mus., 1971-72; Nat. Endowment Arts intern in edn. Toledo Mus. Art, 1973-74; exhbn. coord. Jewish Mus., N.Y.C., 1975-76; assoc. curator modern art L.A. County Mus. Art, 1976-80, curator Twentieth Century art, 1980-94, coord. curatorial affairs, 1993-96, sr. curator Twentieth Century art, 1995—, v.p. edn. and pub. programs, 1996—2003; chief curator Modern and Contemporary Art, 2002—. Lectr., panelist in field. Contbr. articles to profl. jours. Mem. art adv. panel IRS, 1996—; advisor U.S. Holocaust Mus., 1996—; trustee Scripps Coll., 1996—; mem. steering com. Villa Aurora, 1994—; mem. bd. Stiftung Mortizburg, Halle, Germany, 2005-, Magritte Assn., 2005-. Decorated comdr.'s cross Fed. Republic of Germany, Order of Merit (Germany); recipient George L. Wittenborn award ARLIS, 1991, award for best Am. exhbn. of yr. Assn. Internat. Critics Art, 1991, 97, Theo Wormland Kunstpreis, 1992, George L. Wittenborn award, 1992, Alfred H. Barr Jr. award Coll. Art Assn., 1992, E.L. Kirchner prize, Switzerland, 1997, First Pl. award Am. Assn. Art Mus., 1998, Hon. Mention, ARLIS, 1998; named Woman of Yr., Bus. and Profl. Women of UJA, Jewish Fedn., 1991, Friends of Tel Hashomer, 1991; Nat. Endowment of Arts fellow, 1986-87; John J. McCloy fellow in art, 1981. Fellow Am. Acad. Arts and Scis.; mem. Am. Assn. Mus., Internat. Mus. Modern Art (internat. com. mus.), Internat. Coun. Mus., Internat. Com. for Mus. and Collections of Modern Art, Art Table. Office: LA County Mus Art 5905 Wilshire Blvd Los Angeles CA 90036-4597 Office Phone: 323-857-6025. E-mail: sbarron@lacma.org.

BARRON, THOMAS WILLIS, real estate broker; b. Newnan, Ga., Apr. 9, 1949; s. Lindsey Hand and Genet Louise (Heery) B.; m. Margaret Rose MacLennan, Aug. 17, 1973; children: Catharine Lindsey, Thomas Willis Jr., John Taliaferro Gaines. BA, Emory U., 1971; JD, Mercer U., 1974. Assoc. Sanders, Mottola, Haugen, Wood, Goodson and Odom, Newnan, 1974-77; v.p. Lindsey's, Inc., Newnan, 1977—; pres. Coweta Developers, Inc., Newnan, 1977—. Dir., mem. local adv. bd. BB&T (formerly First Citizens Bank); dir., mem. exec. com. Ga. Multi-List Inc., Atlanta; mem. exec. com. Ga. MLS. Dir., sec.-treas. Newnan Hosp., 1992—2005, chmn. bd., 1997—2002, past chmn.; trustee Mercer U., Macon, Ga., 1990—95, 1996—97, 2002—, Coweta Cmty. Found., 1999; past pres. Newnan-Coweta United Way, 1982—; past pres. Newnan Coweta chpt. ARC, 1980—; chmn. deacons Bapt. Ch., 1988—89, 1995—96, 2004—05. Mem. Newnan-Coweta Bd. Realtors (past pres. 1984—, Realtor of Yr. 1991, Million Dollar Club 1989—, Phoenix award 1999), Newnan Country Club (past dir.), Newnan Kiwanis Club (past pres.), Sigma Chi (life, past consul), Newnan-Coweta C. of C. (chmn. bd. 1994). Baptist. Avocations: sports, history, historical autographs. Office: Lindseys Inc Realtors 14 Jackson St Newnan GA 30263-1929 Office Phone: 770-253-6990. Business E-Mail: chipb@lindseysrealtors.com.

BARRON, WILLIAM M., physician, educator; b. Cin., Ohio, June 6, 1950; MD, U. So. Calif., L.A., 1976; MMM, Carnegie Mellon U., Pitts., 2001. Lic. Internal Medicine Am. Bd. of Internal Medicine, 1979. Asst. prof. medicine U. Chgo., 1984—91, assoc. prof. medicine Ill., 1991—94; prof. medicine Loyola U. Stritch Sch. of Medicine, Maywood, Ill., 1994—; exec. med. dir., ctr. clin. effectiveness Loyola U. Health Sys., Maywood, Ill., 1997—2004; dir., divsn. gen. internal medicine Loyola U. Stritch Sch. of Medicine, Maywood, Ill., 1994—97, v.p. quality and patient safety, 2004—. Editor Hypertension in Preganncy, 1990—97; chair Internat. Scientific Com. for the 11th World Congress of the Internat. Soc., Seattle, 1996; invited participant Nat. Forum Workshop on "Hosp. Quality Measures", Wash. Editor: Medical Disorders in Pregnancy. Adv. bd. Alliance of Chgo. Health Svcs., Chgo., 2003—03; bd. mem. Provena Health Sys., Mokena, Ill., 2003—. Recipient Chgo. Top Drs., Chgo. Mag., 1997, 2000, Chgo. Metro Area Top Drs., Castle Connelly, 2003, Best Drs. in Am., 2003; grantee Integrated Advanced Info. Mgmt. Sys., Nat. Libr. of Medicine, 2003, Lab. Testing in Preeclampsia, Agy. for Health Care Policy and Rsch., 1994-1996, Regulation of Blood Pressure During Pregnancy, Am. Heart Assn. of Methropolitan Chgo., 1990-92, Vasopressin Sect. and Osmoregulation in Pregnancy, NIH, 1986-1991, Clin. Investigator Award: Vasopressin Secretion and Osmoregulation in Pregnancy, 1984-1989. Fellow: ACP; mem.: Am. Coll. of Physician Exec., Alpha Omega Alpha, Phi Kappa Phi. Avocations: exercise, fishing, gardening. Office: Loyola Univ Med Ctr 2160 South First Ave Maywood IL 60153 Office Phone: 708-216-7862.

BARRON-DRUCKREY, ELEANOR, psychologist; b. Whittier, Calif., Oct. 27, 1943; d. José María Barrón and Catalina Bravo Barrón; m. Randall Robert Druckrey, Mar. 14, 1993. BA in History, U. Calif., Berkeley, 1978; MS in Counseling, San Francisco State, 1985; PhD in Clin. Psychology, Ctr. Psychol. Studies, Albany, Calif., 2001. Pupil pers. svcs. credential Calif. Founder and exec. dir. Maui Ctr. Attitudinal Healing, Kahului, Hawaii, 1987—89; coord., cons., social worker San Francisco Bay Area Schools, 1992—2002; instr. family issues San Francisco CC Dist., 1997—99; instr. Coll. of Marin, Kentfield, Calif., 2003—; pvt. practice psychotherapy and edn. Novato, 1986—; west region multicultural coord. Matrix Alliance, 2003—. Cons. Vallejo City Unified Sch. Dist., Calif., 1996—99; regional and nat. spr. spl. edn. underrepresented families. Author: Corn Woman Sings, 2004. Mem.: Marin County Leadership Network, Coun. Exceptional Children. Democrat. Roman Catholic. Achievements include research in cross cultural issues in clinical psychology; development of ednl. models focusing on cultural history, tradition and sociol. perspectives for youth and families. Home: 22 Margh Rd Tiburon CA 94920

BARROS, PAULINO R., communications executive; b. Sao Paulo, Brazil; Degrees in mech. and elec. enginrg.; MBA, Wash. U., 1991. Corp. v.p. Latin Am. group personal comm. Motorola, 1996—2000; pres. BellSouth Latin Am. group BellSouth, 2000—04, chief product officer, 2005—. Office: 2180 Lake Blvd Ste 1237 Atlanta GA 30319

BARROW, CHARLES HERBERT, investment banker; b. Evanston, Ill., July 23, 1930; m. Patricia Wandelt, Dec. 27, 1952; children: Paula, Carla, Barbara. AB, Princeton U., 1952; MBA, U. Chgo., 1956. With No. Trust Co., Chgo., 1952-86, v.p., 1962-68, sr. v.p., 1968-74, exec. v.p., 1974-78, sr. exec. v.p., 1978-81, pres., 1981-86, also dir.; with Blunt Ellis & Loewi, Inc. Kemper Securities, Inc., Chgo., 1987-91, sr. dir., 1987-91; mng. dir. Everen Securities, Inc. (formerly Kemper Securities, Inc.), 1991-99; sr. advisor Howe Barnes Investments, 1999—. Sr. advisor Sumitomo Trust and Banking Co., 1989-93; life mem. adv. coun. J.L. Kellogg Grad. Sch. of Mgmt., Northwestern U. Bd. dirs. Planned Parenthood Assn., Chgo., 1965-81, pres., 1972-73; bd. dirs. Rehab. Inst. Chgo., 1974—, chmn., 1982-83; trustee McCormick Theol. Sem., Chgo., 1984-95, treas., 1988-92, chmn., 1992-95, nat. trustee, 1995-96, trustee, 1996-2004, life trustee, 2004—. Mem. Comml. Club, Univ. Club, Commonwealth Club, Econ. Club, Bankers Club (pres. 1979-80), Bond Club, Glen View Club (Ill.), Michigan Shores Club (Wilmette, Ill.), Ocean Reef Club (Key Largo, Fla.), Pentwater (Mich.) Yacht Club. Presbyterian. Office Phone: 312-655-2976.

BARROW, CLYDE WAYNE, social sciences educator; b. Alice, Tex., Feb. 15, 1956; s. Floyd Smith and Wanda Ruth (Conner) B. BA in Polit. Sci., Tex. A&I U., 1977; MA in Polit. Sci., UCLA, 1979, PhD in Polit. Sci., 1984. Teaching fellow UCLA, 1978-82, dir. instrnl. devel., 1982-84; vis. asst. prof. U. Tex., San Antonio, 1984-85, Tex. A&M U., College Station, 1985-87; from asst. prof. to prof. polit. sci. U. Mass. at Dartmouth, North Dartmouth, 1987-96, prof., 1996—2003, acting chmn. dept., 1992-93, 95, sr. rsch. assoc. Ctr. for Policy Analysis, 1993-94, dir. Ctr. for Policy Analysis, 1994—, chancellor prof. policy studies, 2004—. Mem. adv. bd. Arnold Dubin Labor Edn. Ctr., North Dartmouth, 1988—; policy cons. Office of Mayor, City of Fall River, Mass., 1993—, New Bedford CEO Club, 1994—99, Fall River Sch. Dept., 1995—, Sandwich Sch. Dept., 1996—2004, New Bedford Housing Authority, 1999—2004, Lowell Sch. Dept., 2003—04; exec. staff analyst Gov.'s Commn. on Commonwealth Port Devel., Mass., 1994, Gov.'s Regional Econ. Devel. Strategies Project, 1996, 2000—01; regional analyst Mass. Benchmark Project, 1997—; pub. mem. Cranberry Mktg. Com., 2003—; chmn., bd. dirs. Fund Higher Edn. Rsch., 2003—. Author: Universities and the Capitalist State, 1990, Critical Theories of the State, 1993, More Than a Historian: The Political and Economic Thought of Charles A. Beard, 2000, Economic Impacts of the Textile and Apparel Industries in Massachusetts, 2000, Portuguese-Americans and Contemporary Civic Culture in Massachusetts, 2002; co-author: Globalisation Trade Liberalisation and Higher Education in North America, 2003; mem. bd. editors Acad. Labor 2003-, Sociol. Inquiry, 1992-95, Jour. Politics, 1993-97; mng. editor New England Jour. Pub. Policy, 1994-97; also articles. Recipient Fontera Meml. award Arnold Dubin Labor Edn. Ctr., 1991, Disting. Svc. award Mass. Fedn. Tchrs., 2001. Mem. Am. Polit. Sci. Assn., Western Polit. Sci. Assn., Caucus for a New Polit. Sci., Policy Studies Orgn., U. Mass. Faculty Fedn. (treas. 1991-96, 2002-03, pres. 1998-2000). Office: U Mass Ctr Policy Analysis 285 Old Westport Rd North Dartmouth MA 02747-2356 Office Phone: 508-999-9265. Business E-Mail: cbarrow@umassd.edu.

BARROW, FREDERICA HARRISON, education educator, social worker; b. Monroe, N.C., Apr. 10, 1939; d. Frederick Perry Crowell and Hattie Berthenia Alexander; m. Lionel Ceon, Jr. Barrow, Sept. 5, 1992; m. Claude McKinely Harrison, July 2, 1960 (dec. June 1980); children: Emily Harrison Smith, Brenda M. Feliciano, Rhonda Patricia Liquori, Aurea Adams, Kirsten Erin, Lia Barrow Ward, Laura Elaine Harrison. BA (cum laude), N.C. Coll., 1960; M in Social Work, Atlanta U., 1962; M in Administr. sci., Johns Hopkins U., Balt., 1980; PhD, Howard U., Washington, DC, 2001. LCSW Md., 2004, lic. Independent Social Worker D.C., 2003. Rsch. adminstrn., social policy The Social Security Adminstrn., Balt., 1995—2002; asst. prof. U. of South Fla., Tampa, 2002—. Clincal social worker U. of N.C. Child Psychiatry, Chapel Hill, 1962—66; dir. sch. social work program Durham Edn. Improvement Program, NC, 1966—70; clin. social worker Duke U., Divsn. of Child Psychiatry, Durham, NC, 1970—73, Linwood Children's Ctr., Ellicott City, Md., 1974—75; coord. child and adolescent svcs. Md. Dept. of Health & Hygiene, Balt., 1976—85; dir. social work dept. The Sheppard & Enoch Pratt Hosp., Balt., 1982—85; employee assistance br. chief Social Security Adminstrn., Balt., 1985—91. Author: (dissertation) The Social Welfare Career and Contributions of Forrester Blanchard Washington, A Life Course Analysis, (book chpt.) How can ethnic, cultural issues be integrated into EAP supervisory/management and union training and into Employee Assistance program delivery. In An Emerging Paradigm, EAPs and the New American Workorce; co-author: Work and Wellbeing. The Occupational Social Work Advantage. Mem. bd. dirs. Long Reach Village Bd., Columbia, Md., 1977—80; mem. Howard County Coordination Coun. for Criminal Justice, Ellicott City, Md., 1979—80, Handel Choir, Howard County Social Svcs. Bd., Ellicott City, Md., 1982—84, USO of Ctrl. Md., Balt., 1984—85, Girl Scouts of Ctrl. Md., Balt., 1984—86. Fellow NIMH, Atlanta U., 1960—62; grantee Svc. Learning Grant, The U. of South Fla., 2002. Mem.: Sch. Social Work Assn. of Am., Coun. on Social Work Edn., NASW, N.C. Ctrl. U. Alumni Assn. (life), Delta Sigma Theta, Inc. (life). Democrat. Episcopalian. Avocations: African Am. family devel. and history, art collecting, gardening, choral singing. Home: 17842 Arbor Greene Dr Tampa FL 33647 Office: U of South Fla 4202 E Fowler Ave MGY 132 Tampa FL 33620-6600 Personal E-mail: fhbarrow@aol.com. E-mail: fbarrow@chuma1.cas.usf.edu.

BARROW, JOHN J., congressman, lawyer; b. Athens, Ga., Oct. 31, 1955; s. James and Phyllis (Jenkins) B.; m. Victoria Pentlarge, Dec. 19, 1953. AB, U. Ga., 1976; JD, Harvard U., 1979. Bar: Ga., U.S. Dist. Ct. (no. and mid. dists.) Ga., U.S. Ct. Appeals (11th cir.), U.S. Ct. Appeals (5th cir.). Clk. to Hon. Tom Clark U.S. Ct. Appeals, Tampa, Fla., 1979-81; assoc. Winburn & Assocs., Athens, Ga., 1981-83; ptnr. Winburn, Lewis Barrow & Stolz, PC, Athens, Ga., 1983—2004; mem. U.S. Ho. Reps., 109th Congress, 12th Dist Ga., 2005—, mem. edu. and workforce com., agriculture com. & small bus. com., ranking mem. subcom. on rural enterprise, agriculture, and tech. Mem. rev. panel State Bar Disciplinary Bd., 1997-99; mem. Ga. Com. on Continuing Lawyer Competency, 1984-87. Commr. Athens-Clarke County Commn., Athens, 1990-2004. Mem. Ga. Trial Lawyers Assn., Assn. Trial Lawyers Am. Democrat. Baptist. Avocations: politics, tennis, backpacking, sports. Office: US Ho of Reps 226 Cannon House Office Bldg Washington DC 20515 also: Dist Office 400 Mall Blvd Ste G Savannah GA 31406 Office Phone: 202-225-2823.*

BARROW, LIONEL CEON, JR., communications consultant, marketing consultant; b. N.Y.C., Dec. 17, 1926; s. Lionel Ceon and Wilhelmina Barrow; m. Frederica Harrison; children: Lia, Kirsten Erin; stepchildren: Brenda Marie, Aurea Nellie, Rhonda Patricia, Emily Harrison Smith, Laura Harrison. BA in English, Morehouse Coll., 1948; MA in Journalism, U. Wis., 1958, PhD in Mass Communications, 1960. Reporter Richmond Afro-Am., Va., 1953-54; teaching and research asst. U. Wis., Madison, 1954-60; asst. prof. dept. communication Mich. State U., Lansing, 1960-61; research project dir. Bur. Advt., N.Y.C., 1961-63; research project supr. Kenyon & Eckhardt Advt. Agy., N.Y.C., 1963-64; research group head Foote Cone & Belding, N.Y.C., 1964-68, assoc. research dir., v.p., 1968-71; chmn. dept. Afro-Am. studies U. Wis., Milw., 1971-72, 74-75, prof. mass comms. and Afro-Am. studies, 1971-75; dean Sch. Communications Howard U., Washington, 1975-85, prof. communications, 1975-86; pres. The Barrow Info. Group, Columbia, Md., 1986—. Vis. prof. Stanford U., 1971, Ohio State U., 1986; pres. Journalism Coun. Inc., 1971-79; sec. elected advs. Md. Conf. on Small Bus., 1987-89. Contbr. articles to profl. jours. Active Higher Edn. Group Washington, 1985-92. Served with AUS, 1945-47, 50-53. Recipient media citation Journalism Edn. Assn., 1974; recipient radio pioneer award Medgar Evers Coll., 1979 Mem. Assn. for Edn. in Journalism and Mass Comms. (founder, first head minorities and comm. divsn. 2003, chair commn. on the status of minorities 2003-05), Nat. Assn. Black Journalists, Soc. Profl. Journalists, Capitol Press Club, NAACP (life), 24th Inf. Regimental Combat Team Assn. (life, Combat Inf. badge). Home: 17842 Arbor Greene Dr Tampa FL 33647-3136

BARROW, RICHARD EDWARD, architect; b. Birmingham, Ala., Feb. 3, 1940; s. Ralph A. and Hazel C. (McElroy) B.; m. Sylvia Ann Scherl, Sept. 28, 1963; children: Lisa Dawn, Kathryn Heather. BArch, Auburn U., 1963; postgrad., U. Utah, 1967-69. Reg. architect Ala., Utah. Draftsman Edward M. Paul Architects, Birmingham, 1960-63, Paul Lemoine Architects, Salt Lake City, 1967-68, Dean Gustavson, FAIA, Salt Lake City, 1968-69; project mgr. Marcellous Wright & Ptnrs., Richmond, Va., 1969-71; project architect Cobb, Adams, & Benton, Birmingham, 1971-77; ptnr. Arnold & Barrow Architects, Birmingham, 1977-84, Waters, Barrow & Assocs., Inc., Birmingham, 1984-89; pvt. practice Birmingham, 1989-93; pres. Richard E. Barrow Architects, Inc., Birmingham, 1994—. Mem. Ala. Bd. for Registration of Architects, Montgomery, 1988-2000, chair, 1992-93, 99; mem. archtl. adv. com. Auburn U., 1982-89, chair, 1988, 95-96; bldg. com. Wesley Student Ctr. Jacksonville (Ala.) State U., 1991; R&D subcom. Nat. Coun. Archtl. Registration Bds., Washington, 1992-95, coord. graphics, 1995, archtl. registration exam. subcom., 1996-98, coord., 1997, profl. devel. program com., 1999-2000, mem. interior design task force, 2000; renovations include Women's Pavillion, U. Ala. at Birmingham Hosp., 1985, Cahaba Heights United Meth. Ch., 1989; architect new facilities including Asbury United Meth. Ch., 1986, Sumatanga Retreat Ctr., 1992, Green Acres Mid. Sch., 2000. Bd. dirs. So. region Nat. Coun. Archtl. Registration Bds., 1996-99, New Life Harvest Mission, Birmingham, 1990-96, Blue Lake (Ala.) Emmaus Cmty., 1990-91, Ala. Young Adult Chrysalis, treas. 1995-97; mem. adv. bd. WBHM Pub. Radio, 1996-98. Capt. USAF, 1963-67. NIH fellow, 1967. Fellow AIA (Richard Upjohn fellow 1992, Pres.'s award 1979, 81, 82, Henry Adams Book award). Republican. Methodist. Avocations: flying, golf. Office: PO Box 661496 Birmingham AL 35226 E-mail: reb@rebarrow.com.

BARROW, ROBERT EARL, retired agricultural products executive; b. Swansea, Mass., Jan. 30, 1930; s. Charles H. and Etta (Campbell) B.; m. Dolores A. Pannoni, Jan. 30, 1954; children: Kyle A. Kawa, Susan E. Gregory. Grad. high sch., Swansea, 1948. Sr. v.p. 1st Fed. Savs. & Loan Assn., Providence, 1949-77; mgr. Old Red Bank, Fall River, Mass., 1978-79; mgr. bookkeeping Uncle Matty's Tropical Gardens, Warwick, R.I., 1980-87; sec. Nat. Grange, Washington, 1983-85, lectr., program dir., 1985-87, pres., 1987-95; sec. Mass. State Grange, 1997—2001. Master Swansea Grange #148, 1959-60, Bay State Pomona #33, 1965-66, Mass. State, 1981-85. Mem. Bretton Woods Com., 1988—, Agrl. Policy Adv. Com., 1988-94, transp. alternatives group Transp. 2020, 1988, 4-H Coun., 1988—, Bd. Hwy. Users Fedn., 1988—, Nat. Farm Coalition, 1988—, Coalition for Fiscal Restraint, 1988—. With U.S. Army, 1951-53. Avocations: singing, gardening, bell collecting.

BARROW, SALLY SETTLE, media specialist, librarian; b. Moore Haven, Fla. m. John Guy Barrow, III, June 15, 1969 (div. Jan. 19, 2001); children: Mollie Susan Barrow-Huggins, John Daniel. BA, Fla. State U., Tallahasee, FL, 1969; MSLS, Fla. State U., Tallahassee, FL, 1987. Cert. in Mental Retardation Fla. State U., 1974. Tchr. Duval County Sch. Bd., Duval County, Fla., 1970—72, media specialist, 1970—72; educator Jefferson County Sch. Bd., Jefferson County, Fla., 1974—88; media specialist Duval County Sch. Bd., Long Br. Elem., Jacksonville, Fla., 1988—93, Duval County Sch. Bd., Ctrl. Riverside Elem., Jacksonville, Fla., 1993—. Tchr. rep. Demse Title III. Contbr. co-author for curriculum guide; author: In the Shadow of the Lone Cypress, 2003. County coord. Fla. Spl. Olympics, Fla., 1982—86, Fla. Big Bend Spl. Arts Festival, Fla., 1983—88; educator First Nazarene Ch., Monticello, Fla., 1984—88, libr., 1984—88; active First Presbyn. Ch., Fernandina Beach, Fla., 2000—, libr.; vacation bible sch. tchr. and coord. First United Meth. Ch., Monticello, Fla., 1970—89; tchr. Nassau Nazarene Ch., Yulee, Fla., 1984—88, coord. social teas Yulle, Fla., 1993—99. Recipient Outstanding Young Women Award, Outstanding Young Women Award, 1982, Selected Participant, Teachers' Seminar Fla. Humanities Coun., 1996. Mem.: Duval County Media Educators In Action, Fla. Humanities Coun., Duval County Reading Coun., Alpha Delta Kappa, Beta Phi Mu Libr. Sci. Honor Frat. D-Liberal. Presbyterian. Avocation: studying Florida history. Office: Central Riverside Elementary School 2555 Gilmore Street Jacksonville FL 32204 Home: PO Box 2362 Yulee FL 32041-2362 Personal E-mail: barrows2@net-magic.net.

BARROW, THOMAS DAVIES, oil and mining company executive; b. San Antonio, Dec. 27, 1924; s. Leonidas Theodore and Laura Editha (Thomson) B.; m. Janice Meredith Hood, Sept. 16, 1950; children: Theodore Hood, Kenneth Thomson, Barbara Loyd, Elizabeth Ann BS, U. Tex., 1945, MA, 1948; PhD, Stanford U., 1953; grad. advanced mgmt. program, Harvard U., 1963. With Humble Oil & Refining Co., 1951-72, regional exploration mgr. New Orleans, 1962-64, sr. v.p., 1966—70, pres., 1970-72, also bd. dirs.; exec. v.p. Esso Exploration, Inc., 1964-65; sr. v.p. Exxon Corp., N.Y.C., 1972-78; chmn., CEO Kennecott Corp., Stamford, Conn., 1978-81; vice chmn. Std. Oil Co., Ohio, 1981-85; investment cons. Houston, 1985-89; chmn. GX Tech., Houston, 1990—2004; pres. Thomson-Barrow, 1989—; sr. chmn., bd. dir. GeoQuest Internat. Holdings, Inc., Houston, 1990-97; pres. Tecolotita, Inc., 1991—, T-BAR-X, Houston, 1995—. Chmn. bd. dirs. GPS Tech. Corp., Houston, 1986—98, Petroleum Info./Dwights, 1994—97, Tobin Internat., 1998—2003; mem. commn. on natural resources NRC, 1973—78, commn. on phys. sci., math. and natural resources, 1984—87, bd. on earth scis., 1982—84; trustee Woods Hole Oceanog. Instn., 20th Century Fund-Task Force on U.S. Energy Policy. Pres. Houston Grand Opera, 1985-87, chmn., 1987-91; trustee Am. Mus. Natural History, 1972-82, Stanford U., 1980-90, Tex. Med. Ctr., 1983—, Geol. Soc. Am. Found., 1982-87; trustee Baylor Coll. Medicine, 1984—, vice chmn bd. trustees, 1991-99. Served to ensign USNR, 1943—46. Recipient Disting. Achievement award Offshore Tech. Conf., 1973, Disting. Engring. Grad. award U. Tex., 1970, Disting. Alumnus, 1982, Disting. Geology Grad., 1985, Disting. Natural Sci. Grad., 1990; named Chief Exec. of Yr. in Mining Industry, Fin. World, 1979. Fellow N.Y. Acad. Scis.; mem. NAE, Am. Mining Congress (bd. dirs. 1979-85, vice chmn. 1983-85), Am. Assn. Petroleum Geologists, Geol. Soc. Am., Internat. Copper Rsch. Assn. (bd. dirs. 1979-85), Nat. Ocean Industry Assn. (bd. dirs. 1982-85), AAAS, Am. Soc. Oceanography (pres. 1970-71), Am. Geophys. Union, Am. Petroleum Inst., Am. Geog. Soc., Houston Country Club, The Hills Club, Petroleum Club, River Oaks Country Club, Houston Club, Sigma Xi, Tau Beta Pi, Sigma Gamma Epsilon, Phi Eta Sigma, Alpha Tau Omega Episcopalian. Office: 6363 Woodway Ste 630 Houston TX 77057

BARROW, THOMAS FRANCIS, artist, educator; b. Kansas City, Mo., Sept. 24, 1938; s. Luther Hopkins and Cleo Naomi (Francis) Barrow; m. Laurie Anderson, Nov. 30, 1974; children: Melissa, Timothy, Andrew. BFA, Kansas City Art Inst., 1963; MS, Ill. Inst. Tech., 1965. With George Eastman House, Rochester, NY, 1966-72, asst. dir., 1971-72; assoc. dir. Art Mus. U. N.Mex., Albuquerque, 1973-76, assoc. prof., 1976-81, prof., 1981—2001, Presdl. prof., 1985-90. Author: The Art of Photography, 1971; sr. editor: Reading into Photography, 1982; contbr. to Brit. Ency. Am. Art, 1973, A Hundred Years of Photographic History: Essays in Honor of Beaumont Newhall, 1975, Experimental Vision, 1994; forward The Valiant Knights of Daguerre, 1978; contbr. articles to profl. jours.; one-man shows include Light Gallery, N.Y.C., 1974-76, 79, 82, Amarillo Art Ctr., 1990, Andrew Smith Gallery, Santa Fe, 1992, Laurence Miller Gallery, N.Y.C., 1996, U. N.Mex. Art Mus., 1997, Richard Levy Gallery, Albuquerque, 2000; exhibited in group shows including Pace Gallery, N.Y.C., 1973, Hudson River Mus., Yonkers, N.Y., 1973, Internat. Mus. Photography, Rochester, 1975, Seattle Art Mus., 1976, Mus. Fine Arts, Houston, 1977, Retrospective exhbn. L.A. County Mus. Art, 1987—; represented in permanent collections Nat. Gallery Can., Mus. Modern Art, Getty Ctr. for Arts and Humanities. Nat. Endowment for Arts fellow, 1971, 78. Business E-Mail: tfbarrow@unm.edu.

BARROWS, FRANCINE ELEANOR, early childhood educator; b. Bridgeport, Conn., Nov. 16, 1948; d. Joseph John and Eleanor Sylvia (Torok) Csonka; m. Robert Lynn Barrows, Oct. 8, 1983; children: Joshua Lyn, Craig Scott (twins). BA, Sacred Heart U., 1970; postgrad., Fairfield U., 1978. Cert. profl. tchr., Conn. Sales head, asst. office head Howland-Steinbach, Fairfield, Conn., 1967-86; tchr. elem. grades Wheeler Sch., Bridgeport, Conn., 1970-71, Garfield Sch., Bridgeport, 1971—2005; sec. RC Hobbies of Conn., Inc., Milford, Conn., 1983-92. Assoc. Regional Lab. Grantee Bridgeport Pub. Edn. Fund, 1985, 89. Mem. NEA, Conn. Edn. Assn., Bridgeport Edn. Assn., Pi Sigma Phi. Roman Catholic. Avocation: collecting dinosaur memorabilia. Office: Garfield Sch 655 Stillman St Bridgeport CT 06608-1331

BARROWS, FRANK CLEMENCE, journalist; b. Lewes, Del., Nov. 2, 1946; m. Mary S. Newsom, Nov. 16, 1985; 1 child, Margaret S. BA, St. Andrews Coll., 1968. Reporter, columnist Charlotte (N.C.) Observer, 1969-72, 76-81, asst. sports editor, 1981-82, asst. met. editor, 1982-83, exec. sports editor, 1983-84, 86, dep. features editor, 1985, dep. met. editor, 1986-87, asst. mng. editor, 1987-88, dep. mng. editor, 1988-92, mng. editor, 1992—2005. Contbr. articles to mags. Recipient Ethel Fortner Writer and Cmty. award, 2000, Reporting awards, NC Press Assn., 1972—80. Mem.: NC Open Govt. Coalition (pres. 2004—), Investigative Reporters and Editors, Soc. News Design, Am. Soc. Newspaper Editors. Home: 1810 Shoreham Dr Charlotte NC 28211-2134 Business E-Mail: fcbarrows@aol.com.

BARRS, JAMES THOMAS, linguistics educator; b. Danville, Ga., Sept. 2, 1904; s. Andrew Robert and Dollie Lee (Brown) B.; m. Vida Fitz Randolph, Sept. 2, 1931; children: Dorothy Caroline, Ann Radcliffe, Andrew Fitzrandolph. AB summa cum laude, U. Ga., 1927; AM, Harvard U., 1932, PhD, 1936; student, Mercer U., 1928. Registrar, tchr. English South Ga. Coll., Douglas, 1937-42, dean, 1940-42; asst. prof. English Washington Coll.,

Chestertown, Md., 1943-45; from asst. prof. to prof. English Northea. U., Boston, 1945-71, prof. emeritus, 1971—. Lectr. Sta. WAYX, Waycross, Ga., 1940-42, Sta. WBZ-WBZA, Boston and Springfield, Mass., 1959-60, Stas. WEEI, WCRB, WILD, Boston and Concert Network, 1960s, Sta. WGBH-TV, Boston, 1958-59. Contbr. to scholarly publs. Recipient Cert. of Distinction Assn. Coll. Honor Socs., 2000. Mem. MLA (life), N.E. MLA (chmn. linguistics sect. 1972-73), Nat. Coun. Tchrs. of English (bd. dirs. 1969-70, chmn. semantics sect. 1972, mem. com. on pub. and profl. rels. 1967-70, mem. com. on semantics in sch. programs 1960-71), N.Y. Acad. Scis., Coll. English Assn. (bd. dirs. 1962-65), Conf. on Coll. Composition and Comm., New England Assn. Tchrs. of English (adv. mem. exec. bd. 1960-70, chmn. sch. and coll. liaison com. 1962-65, chmn. nominating com. 1966-69), Phi Beta Kappa (sec. Newton com. 1972-97, pres. Northea. U. assocs. 1965-68), Phi Kappa Phi (copy editor nat. forum, copy editor extraordinaire award 2000). Home and Office: PO Box 215 Onset MA 02558

BARRUS, CHARLES LAMAR, JR., music educator; b. Sugar City, Idaho, July 22, 1935; s. Charles LaMar and Ruth Hammond Barrus; m. Carol Ruth Walters, Sept. 12, 1958; children: Connie Barrus Barton, Katherine Barrus Kesler, Deborah Barrus Stoddard, Kent LaMar. BA, MusM, U. Utah, PhD, 1968. Violinist Utah Symphony Orch., Salt Lake City, 1953—65; prof. music Ricks Coll., Rexburg, Idaho, 1960—99; mgr., program dir. Pub. Radio Sta. KRIC-FM, 1982—99. Condr. Rexburg Tabernacle Orch., 2004—, Idaho Falls Symphony Orch., 1965—70. Musician: (choral symphony) Ode to Libertad (Award of Merit, Idaho Fedn. of Music Clubs, 1969). Patriarch LDS Ch., Rexburg, 2002—. Recipient Exemplary Faculty award, Ricks Coll. Faculty Assn., 1983—84, Eliza R. Snow award in Arts, Ricks Coll. Alumni Assn., 1991, Exemplary Employee award, Ricks Coll., 1996, Disting. Tchg. award, 1998, Lifetime Achievement award, Rexburg C. of C., 2000. Home: 260 S 3rd E Rexburg ID 83440 Personal E-mail: lamarb@cableone.net.

BARRY, ALAN H., consumer products company executive; m. Karen Barry. Contr. brass craft mfg. unit Masco Corp., Taylor, Mich., 1972, pres. divsn., 1988, group pres., 1996, pres., COO, 2003—. Bd. dirs. H.W. Kaufman Fin. Group, Arch Aluminum & Glass Co., Inc.; exec. bd. mem. Plumbing Mfg. Inst., 1985—2000, chmn., 1994; exec. bd., assoc. mem. divsn. Am. Supply Assn., 1995—96. Office: Masco Corp 21001 Van Born Rd Taylor MI 48180

BARRY, ALLAN RONALD, ship pilot, corporate executive; b. Chgo., Jan. 28, 1945; s. Robert Edward and Stella Yvonne (Pellonari) B.; m. Ellen Conerly, May 1, 1971; 1 child, Elizabeth Anne. BS, U.S. Mcht. Marine Acad., 1967. Unltd. masters lic., Houston Ship Channel pilot's lic. USCG; commd. branch pilot Galveston Bar and Houston Ship Channel, State of Tex. Ship's officer Lykes Bros. S.S. Co., Inc., New Orleans, 1967-74; ship's pilot Houston Pilots, 1975—; pres., chief exec. officer Allan Barry, Inc., Houston, 1979—. Commd. to office of br. pilot, Galveston Bar and the Houston Ship Channel by State of Tex. Lt. USNR, 1967-82. Mem. U.S. Mcht. Marine Acad. Alumni Assn. (leadership contbr. 1978—), Nat. Audubon Soc., Houston Audubon Soc., Nat. Maritime Hist. Soc., Coun. Am. Master Mariners, Am. Pilots Assn., Am. Mcht. Marine Vets., Propeller Club (bd. govs. Port of Houston 1986-88), Nature Conservancy, Nat. Wildlife Fed. Republican. Office: Houston Pilots 8150 South Loop E Ste 118 Houston TX 77017-1796

BARRY, ANNE M., public health officer; BA in Occupl. Therapy, Coll. St. Catherine; JD, William Mitchell Coll. Law; MPH, U. Minn. Dep. commr. health Minn. Dept. Health, Mpls., commr. health, 1995—99; dep. fin. commr. Minn., 1999—; acting commr. fin., 2002. Office: Dept Fin 400 Centennial Bldg 658 Cedar St Saint Paul MN 55155

BARRY, BRENT ROBERT, professional basketball player; b. Dec. 31, 1971; s. Rick Barry. Diploma, Oreg. State U., 1995. Guard L.A. Clippers, 1995—. Ranked 1st among rookies in 3-point field goal percentage, 1995-96; winner Nestle Slam-Dunk competition, 1996. Avocations: video collecting, internet exploration, golf. Office: LA Clippers 1111 S Figueroa St Ste 1100 Los Angeles CA 90015-1300*

BARRY, CAMILLE T., health and human services director; BS in Nursing, U. Akron; MS in Mgmt., PhD in Health Policy and Adminstrn., George Mason U. Staff nurse, nurse mgr. various acute care ctr. hosps.; sr. program analyst Sec.'s Commn. on Nursing, 1988; program analyst former Nat. Ctr. for Nursing Rsch. at NIH, Bethesda, Md.; spl. asst. for health policy Sec., Dept. Vets. Affairs; sr. drug policy advisor, counselor to Sec. Shalala U.S. Dept. Health and Human Svcs., Rockville, Md., now dep. dir. Ctr. for Substance Abuse Treatment. Adj. asst. prof. George Mason U., Fairfax, Va.; ofcl. del. to UN Commn. on Narcotic Drugs, Vienna; US. del. to Internat. Fedn. Non-Govt. Orgns., Malaysia; cons. divsn. govtl. affairs Am. Nurses' Assn. Author: Redesigning Patient Care Delivery, 1990; contbr. articles to profl. jours.

BARRY, DAVE, columnist, writer; b. Armonk, N.Y., July 3, 1947; m. Michelle Kaufman, 1996; children: Robert, Sophie. BA English, Haverford Coll., 1969. Reporter, editor Daily Local News, West Chester, Pa., 1971-75; with AP, instr. bus. writing Phila., 1975-83; columnist The Miami (Fla.) Herald, 1983—. Author: Taming of the Shrew: Several Million Homeowner's Problems Sidestepped, 1993, Babies and Other Hazards of Sex, 1984, Bad Habits: A One Hundred Percent Fact Free Book, 1985, Stay Fit and Healthy Until You're Dead, 1985, Dave Barry's Guide to Marriage and/or Sex, 1987, Claw Your Way to the Top, 1987, Dave Barry's Greatest Hits, 1988, Dave Barry Slept Here, 1989, Dave Barry Turns 40, 1990, Dave Barry Talks Back, 1991, Dave Barry's Only Travel Guide You'll Ever Need, 1991, Dave Barry Does Japan, 1992, Dave Barry Is Not Making This Up, 1994, Dave Barry's Complete Guide to Guys, 1995, Dave Barry in Cyberspace, 1996, Dave Barry is from Mars and Venus, 1997, Dave Barry Turns 50, 1998, Dave Barry is Not Taking This Sitting Down, 2000, Dave Barry Hits Below the Beltway, 2001, Boogers Are My Beat, 2003, (novels) Big Trouble, 1999, Tricky Business, 2002, (non-fiction) Homes and Other Black Holes, 1988, Dave Barry's Gift Guide to End All Gift Guides, 1994, Dave Barry's Book of Bad Songs, 1997, My Teenage Son's Goal in Life is to Make Me Feel 3,500 Years Old' and Other Thoughts on Parenting from Dave Barry, 2001, The Greatest Invention in the History of Mankind is Beer And Other Manly Insights From Dave Barry, 2001; co-author (with others): Mid-Life Confidential, 1994, Naked Came the Manatee, 1996; co-author: (with Ridley Pearson) Peter and the Starcatchers, 2004. Recipient Disting. Writing award, Soc. Newspaper Editors, 1987, Pulitzer prize for commentary, 1988. Office: Miami Herald 1 Herald Plz Miami FL 33132-1693

BARRY, DENNIS M., lawyer; b. Washington, DC, Jan. 16, 1951; BA, Ohio Wesleyan U., 1972; JD, U. Va., 1975. Bar: Tex. 1976, DC 1983. Ptnr., co-head Health Sect. Vinson & Elkins LLP, Washington, DC. Mem.: Am. Health Lawyers Assn. Office: Vinson & Elkins LLP Willard Office Bldg 1455 Pennsylvania Ave NW, Ste 600 Washington DC 20004 Office Fax: 202-639-6791. E-mail: DBarry@velaw.com.

BARRY, DESMOND THOMAS, JR., lawyer; b. N.Y.C., Mar. 26, 1945; s. Desmond Thomas and Kathryn (O'Connor) B.; m. Patricia Mellicker, Aug. 28, 1971; children: Kathryn, Desmond Todd. AB, Princeton U., 1967; JD, Fordham U., 1973. Bar: N.Y. 1974, U.S. Dist. Ct. (so. and ea. dist.) N.Y. 1974, U.S. Ct. Appeals (2d cir.) 1974, U.S. Ct. Appeals (9th cir.) 1980, U.S. Ct. Appeals (5th cir.) 1983, U.S. Ct. Appeals (3d cir.) 1984, U.S. Supreme Ct. 1985. Assoc. Condon & Forsyth, N.Y.C., 1973-79, ptnr., 1979—. Trustee Canterbury Sch., New Milford, Conn., 1970-80. Capt. USMC, 1967-70, Vietnam. Decorated Navy Commendation medal with combat V, Combat Action medal, 1969, Vietnamese Cross of Gallantry, 1969. Fellow: Am. Coll. Trial Lawyers; mem.: ABA (chmn. aviation and space law com. 1996—97), Internat. Assn. Def. Counsel (exec. com.), Assn. Bar City NY, NY State Bar Assn., US. Srs. Golf Assn., Queenwood Golf Club (London), Hawk's Nest Golf Club (Vero Beach, Fla.), Winged Foot Golf Club (bd. govs. 1999—2001), Univ. Club N.Y.C. Republican. Roman Catholic. Home: 40 Charter Oak Ln New Canaan CT 06840-6705 Office: Condon & Forsyth LLP Times Sq Tower 7 Times Sq New York NY 10036 Office Phone: 212-894-6770. Business E-Mail: dbarry@condonlaw.com.

BARRY, ESSIE MARILYN, elementary school educator, writer; b. Greenwood, Miss., June 9, 1913; d. Otho and Lula Hill (Montgomery) Thurmond; m. Essie Marilyn Thurmond, June 17, 1934; children: Gloria, Francine, Carlita. BA, CUNY, 1971. Lic. practical nurse, N.Y., 1964. Lic. practical nurse Bklyn. Hosp., 1963—64; social svc. investigator Dept. Social Svc., N.Y.C., 1971—72; tchr. State Edn. Dept., N.Y.C., 1972—85; nursery and grades K-6 tchr. Mich. State Dept. Edn., Lansing; lic. tchr. NYU and Columbia U., 1975—, ednl. adminstr., 1975—2005; pres. Barryelectronics, Farmington Hills, Mich. Internet cons. Am. Assn. of On-line Ad Agys., San Francisco, 1996. Author: Deep Dark Secrets of a Preacher's Daughter. Mem. Better Bu. Bur., 2004; founder Essie Barry Scholarship fund Steinhart Sch. Edn., NYU, 2003. Recipient Internet Recognition award, Am. On-Line Ad Agys., 1999, Jefferson cup, Steinhart Sch. Edn., NYU, 2004. Mem.: NYU Alumni Group, So. Poverty Law Ctr. Democrat. Roman Catholic. Achievements include patents for scouring gloves. Avocations: quilting, crafts, tutoring children. Home: 29606 Middlebelt Rd Unit 2801 Farmington Hills MI 48334 Office: Info Express Ad Agy 29606 Middlebelt Rd #2801 Farmington Hills MI 48334 Office Phone: 248-539-7734. Personal E-mail: e4115@aol.com.

BARRY, FRANCIS JULIAN, JR., lawyer; b. New Orleans, Oct. 7, 1949; s. Francis Julian and Bertha Anna (Lion) B.; m. Janice Leigh Gonzales, May 8, 1976; children: Francis III, Marianna. BA, Tulane U., 1970, JD, 1973. Bar: La. 1973, U.S. Dist. Ct. (ea. dist.) La. 1973, U.S. Ct. Appeals (5th cir.) 1973, U.S. Dist. Ct. (we. dist.) La. 1978, U.S. Ct. Appeals (11th cir.) 1982, U.S. Supreme Ct. 1991. Assoc. Deutsch, Kerrigan & Stiles, New Orleans, 1973-78, ptnr., 1978—. Editor Admiralty Law Inst. Symposium Tulane U., New Orleans, 1973. Adv. editor Tulane Maritime Law Jour. (formerly The Maritime Lawyer), 1975—. Served to capt. USAR. Mem. Fed. Bar Assn., La. Bar Assn., New Orleans Bar Assn., Maritime Law Assn. U.S. (proctor, carriage of goods com. 1982-87, com. offshore industries 2004—, com. marine ins. and gen. average 2004—), Admiralty Law Inst. New Orleans (mem. planning com. 1998—, mem. program com. 2000—, chmn. program com. 2004—), U.S. Naval Inst., Southeastern Admiralty Law Inst., La. Assn. Def. Counsel, Def. Rsch. Inst., Assn. Average Adjusters London, Assn. Average Adjusters U.S., Am. Legion, Navy League U.S., Army-Navy Club (Washington), La. Landmarks Soc., Bienville Club, Univ. Club (N.Y.C.), Plimsoll Club, Mariners Club, The Round Table Club. Republican. Roman Catholic. Home: 4301 Dumaine St New Orleans LA 70119-3617 Office: Deutsch Kerrigan & Stiles 755 Magazine St New Orleans LA 70130-3672 Office Phone: 504-581-5141. Business E-Mail: fbarry@dkslaw.com.

BARRY, HENRY FORD, chemical company executive; b. Detroit, June 25, 1923; s. William H. and Antoinette (Griese) B.; m. Helen A. Sasso, Aug. 27, 1947 (dec. Dec. 1983); children: Henry V., John M., Robert C., Christine M., Elizabeth M., Catherine A. BS in Chemistry, Stanford U., Palo Alto, Calif., 1950; MS in Chem. Engring., U. Mich., 1952, MBA in Mktg., 1978. Registered profl. engr., Ind., Colo. Researcher Amoco Oil Co., Whiting, Ind., 1952-59; tech. dir. Haviland Products Co., Grand Rapids, Mich., 1960-62; supr. Climax Molybdenum Co., Detroit, 1962-66, mgr. chem. rsch. Ann Arbor, Mich., 1966-76, dir. chem. devel., 1977-82; v.p. tech. Shattuck Chem. Co., Denver, 1983—. Editor: Chemistry/Uses of Mo., Vol. III, 1979, Vol. IV, 1982. With U.S. Army, 1943-46. Mem. Am. Chem. Soc., Nat. Assn. Corrosion Engrs., Soc. Tribology and Lubrication Engrs. Achievements include 6 U.S. and 4 foreign patents. Home: 3519 Meadow Grove Trl Ann Arbor MI 48108-9313 Office: Shattuck Chem Co Inc 1805 S Bannock St Denver CO 80223-3699

BARRY, HERBERT, III, psychologist, educator; b. N.Y.C., June 2, 1930; s. Herbert and Lucy Manning (Brown) Barry. BA, Harvard U., 1952; MS, Yale U., 1953, PhD, 1957. USPHS-NIMH rsch. fellow Yale U., 1957-59, asst. prof. psychology, 1960-61, U. Conn., Storrs, 1961-63; rsch. assoc. prof. pharmacology Sch. Pharmacy U. Pitts., 1963-70, prof., 1970-87, prof. pharm. scis., 1995—2001, prof. emeritus, 2001—, prof. pharmacology and physiology Sch. Dental Medicine, 1987-94. Mem. alcohol rsch. rev. com. Nat. Inst. Alcohol Abuse and Alcoholism, 1972—76; mem. sociobehavioral subcom. AIDS rsch. rev. com. Nat. Inst. Drug Abuse, 1988—89. Author (with H. Wallgren): (book) Actions of Alcohol, 1970; author: (with A. Schlegel) Adolescence: An Anthropological Inquiry, 1991; field editor: jour. Psychopharmacology, 1974—91; contbr. articles to profl. jours. Bd. dirs. Schalkenbach Found., 1996—, Ctr. Study Econs., 1988—; mem. Allegheny County Dem. Com., 1984—. Recipient Rsch. Scientist Devel. award, NIMH, 1967—77. Fellow: APA (coun. reps. 1975—76, pres. divsn. psychopharmacology 1980—81), AAAS; mem.: Am. Coll. Neuropsychopharmacology, Psychonomic Soc., Am. Name Soc. (mem. exec. com. 2000—03), Sigma Xi, Phi Beta Kappa. Unitarian Universalist. Home: 552 N Neville St Apt 83 Pittsburgh PA 15213-2830 Office: Univ Pitts 534 Salk Hall Pittsburgh PA 15261-1905 Office Phone: 412-624-3330. Business E-Mail: barryh@pitt.edu. *I believe that the contrasting behaviors of persistence and innovation both contribute to effective learning and creativity. Awareness of the need for both contrasting behaviors may help people to avoid the failures caused by overemphasis of either one.*

BARRY, JAMES P(OTVIN), editor, writer; b. Alton, Ill., Oct. 23, 1918; s. Paul Augustine and Elder (Potvin) B.; m. Anne Elizabeth Jackson, Apr. 16, 1966 BA cum laude, Ohio State U., 1940. Commd. 2d. lt. Arty. U.S. Army, 1940, advanced through grades to col., served ETO, 1944-46; adviser to Turkish Army, 1951-53; detailed Army Gen. Staff, Washington, 1953-56; ret., 1966; adminstr. Capital U., Columbus, Ohio, 1967-71; freelance writer, editor Columbus, 1971-77; dir. Ohioana Library Assn., 1977-88; editor Ohioana Quar., 1977-88; sr. editor Inland Seas, 1984—; photographer, documentary and book illustrator, 1968—. Author: Georgian Bay: The Sixth Great Lake, 1968, 3rd edit., 1995, The Battle of Lake Erie, 1970, Bloody Kansas, 1972, The Noble Experiment, 1972, The Fate of the Lakes, 1972, The Louisiana Purchase, 1973, Henry Ford and Mass Production, 1973, Ships of the Great Lakes, 1973 (Dolphin Book Club selection), Ships of the Great Lakes, rev. edit., 1996, The Berlin Olympics, 1975, The Great Lakes: A First Book, 1976, Wrecks and Rescues of the Great Lakes, 1981 (Dolphin Book Club selection), Georgian Bay: An Illustrated History, 1992, Old Forts of the Great Lakes, 1994, Hackercraft, 2002, American Powerboats, 2003; contbr. articles to mags. and jours.; over 300 photographs accepted for permanent collection Inst. Gt. Lakes Rsch. Recipient award Am. Soc. State and Local History, 1974, Nonfiction History award Soc. Midland Authors, 1982; named Gt. Lakes Historian of Yr., Marine Hist. Soc. Detroit, 1995. Mem. Internat. Assn. Gt. Lakes Rsch., Assn. Gt. Lakes Maritime History, Can. Nautical Rsch. Soc., Gt. Lakes Hist. Soc., Marine Hist. Soc., Ohio Hist. Soc., World Ship Soc., Antique and Classic Boat Soc., Royal Can. Yacht Club, Columbus Country Club, Capital Club, Phi Beta Kappa. Home: 353 Fairway Blvd Columbus OH 43213-2507

BARRY, JAN, journalist, poet; b. Ithaca, NY, Jan. 26, 1943; s. John Henry and Virginia (Graham) Crumb; m. Paula Kay Haslocher, Jan. 30, 1975 (dec. Jan. 9, 2002); children: Kim, Nikolai. BA, Ramapo Coll. of NJ, 1992. Rschr. CBS News, N.Y.C., 1971; coeditor, pub. 1st Casualty Press/East River Anthology, Bklyn., 1972—76; reporter Daily Record, Morristown, NJ, 1976—80; pub. info. officer YWCA of USA Nat. Bd., N.Y.C., 1981—87; staff writer The Record (Bergen Co.), Hackensack, NJ, 1987—. Journalist in residence North Jersey Media Group, Rutgers U., 2005. Author: (poetry collection) Earth Songs, 2003, A Citizen's Guide to Grassroots Campaigns, 2000; editor: (literary anthology) Peace Is Our Profession, 1981, (poetry anthology) Demilitarized Zones, 1976, Winning Hearts & Minds: War Poems by Vietnam Veterans, 1972. Founding pres. Vietnam Veterans Against the War, N.Y.C., 1967—71. With U.S. Army, 1962—65, Vietnam. Recipient Cmty. Svc. Award, Soc. of Silurians, 2003. Mem.: Authors Guild, Soc. Profl. Journalists, Vietnam Veterans Am. Office: The Record 150 River St Hackensack NJ 07601-7172 Office Phone: 201-646-4100. E-mail: barry@northjersey.com.

BARRY, JOHN MAYNARD, urologist; b. Winona, Minn., Mar. 14, 1940; MD, U. Minn., 1965. Intern SUNY, Syracuse, 1965-66; resident U. Oreg. Med. Sch., Portland, 1969-73; prof., chmn. urology Oreg. Health Sci. U., Portland, 1980—, dir. renal transplantation, 1976—, chmn. abdominal organ transplantation, 2000—02. Office: Oreg Health Sci U Divsn Urology 3181 SW Sam Jackson Park Rd Portland OR 97239

BARRY, JOYCE ALICE, dietician, consultant; b. Chgo., Apr. 27, 1932; d. Walter Stephen and Ethel Myrtle (Paetow) B. Student, Iowa State Coll., 1950—52, Loyola U., 1952—58; BS, Mundelein Coll., 1955; postgrad., Simmons Coll., 1963—64, U. Ga., 1979, Calif. We. U., 1980. Registered dietitian. Prodn. supr. Marshall Field & Co., Chgo., 1955-59; dir. food svcs. Women's Ednl. and Indsl. Union, Boston, 1959-62, Wellesley Pub. Schs., Mass., 1962-70; regional dietitian Canteen Corp., Chgo., 1970-83; gen. mgr. bus. devel. Plantation-Sysco, Orlando, Fla., 1983-87; dir. product devel., corp. quality assurance, procurement Marriott Internat. Hdqrs., Washington, 1987-95; owner food svc. cons. svc., 1995—. Cons. Stokes Food Svcs., Newton, Mass., 1960-70; vis. lectr. Affiliate Produce for Better Health Found. Mem.: AAUW, Nat. Hist. Trust, Sch. Nutrition Svcs., Cons. Dieticians in Healthcare Facilities, Am. Dietetics Assn. (career adv. cons.), Food and Culinary Profls., Dietitians in Bus. and Comm., Smithsonian Instn. (assoc.), Washington Opera Guild, Met. Opera Guild. Republican. Roman Catholic. Home and Office: 1009 Pearce Dr Apt 102 Clearwater FL 33764-1107 Office Phone: 727-669-6454. Personal E-mail: joyce4374@yahoo.com.

BARRY, LANCE LEONARD, judge; b. Boston, Dec. 18, 1965; s. Leonard and Theodora Ann Pawlak. BEE, Cath. U. Am., 1988; MS, Johns Hopkins U., 1991; JD, George Mason U., 1995. Bar: Va. 1995, U.S. Ct. Appeals (fed. cir.) 1995, bar: D.C. 1998. Engring. analyst RCI Internat., Vienna, Va., 1987; engring. aide MPR Assocs., Washington, 1987; engring. technician BBN Labs., Arlington, Va., 1988; cons. Booz, Allen & Hamilton, Bethesda, Md., 1988-90, sr. cons., 1990—91; patent examiner U.S. Patent and Trademark Office, Arlington, Va., 1991-95, primary examiner, 1996-99, adminstrv. patent judge, 1999—. Spkr. Va. State Bar, Richmond, 1998—; instr. U.S. Patent and Trademark Office, Arlington, 1996-97, curriculum com., 1999—; law lectr. U.S. Patent and Trademark Office, Arlington, 1997-99, 2005—, EEO counselor, 1999 Pub. adv. com. mem. Lawyers Coop. Pub., Raleigh, N.C., 1995; contbr. articles to profl. jours. Head tutor St. Francis Xavier Sch., Washington, 1997-2001; cmty. svc. v.p. St. Mary's Ch., Alexandria, Va., 2001; vol. Greater D.C. Cares, Washington, 1999-; social officer Holy Trinity Ch., Washington, 1997-98; tutor kids and chemistry program Am. Chem. Soc., 2002-; lector Our Lady of Lourdes Ch., 2002-03; vol. Alexandria Christmas in April, 2000-, house capt., 2003, Camp Invention, 2004-; judge sci. fairs, 2003— Mem. IEEE (manuscript referee Potentials mag. 1989—), Am. Intellectual Property Law Assn., Patent and Trademark Office Soc. (rep. 1996-98), Mensa, Phi Theta Kappa, Tau Beta Pi. Avocations: volunteering, Italian, birdwatching, travel, skiing. Office: US Patent and Trademark Office PO Box 1450 Alexandria VA 22313-1450

BARRY, MARILYN WHITE, retired special education educator, dean; b. Weymouth, Mass., Sept. 12, 1936; d. Harland Russell and Alice Louise (Dwyer) White; m. Dennis Edward Barry, July 11, 1959; children: Dennis Edward, Christopher Gerard. BS in Edn., Bridgewater State Coll., 1958; EdM in Spl. Edn., Boston U., 1969, EdD in Spl. Edn., 1974. Tchr. Weymouth (Mass.) pub. schs., 1958-60; spl. edn. instr. Boston U., 1972-74; ast. prof. in spl. edn. Bridgewater (Mass.) State Coll., 1974-79, assoc. prof., 1979-83, prof., 1983-87, chmn. spl. edn. dept., 1979-87, coord. dept. grad. programs, 1979-87, adminstr. bilingual spl. edn., 1983-86, dean Grad. Sch., 1987-98; ret., 1998. Co-author human svc. workers curriculum materials. Recipient 3 Disting. Svc. awards Bridgewater State Coll., 1980, 82, 85; Bilingual Spl. Edn. grantee, 1980, 83; Boston U. fellow, 1967-74 Mem. CEC (Mass. chpt. founder, past pres., learning disabilities chpt.), Mass. Assn. Children with Learning Disabilties (past v.p.), Phi Delta Kappa, Pi Lambda Theta. Democrat. Roman Catholic. Home: 138 Bedford St Lakeville MA 02347-1351

BARRY, MARY H., college official; BS in Speech and Drama, Bowling Green State U.; M Mgmt., Northwestern U.; JD, Western State U. V.p. 1st Nat. Bank, Chgo.; dir. Citibank, S.D.; sr. v.p. Marquette Banks, until 1990; dir. Nat. Coll., 1990-91; dir. acad. affairs, adminstrn. and Calif. Ctr. Profl. Edn., U. Phoenix, 1992-98; v.p. edn. Corinthian Colls., Inc., postsecondary edn. co., Santa Ana, Calif., 1998—. Maj. USMC, 1971—79. Office: Corinthian Colls 6 Hutton Centre Dr Ste 400 Santa Ana CA 92707-5764

BARRY, MARYANNE TRUMP, federal judge; b. NYC, Apr. 5, 1937; d. Fred C. and Mary Trump; m. John J. Barry, Dec. 26, 1982; 1 child, David W. Desmond. BA, Mt. Holyoke Coll., 1958; MA, Columbia U., 1962; JD, Hofstra U., 1974, LLD (hon.), Seton Hall U.; LLD (hon.), Caldwell Coll.; LLD (hon.), Kean Coll. Bar: N.J. 1974, N.Y. 1975, U.S. Ct. Appeals (3d cir.), U.S. Supreme Ct. Asst. U.S. Atty., 1974-75; dep. chief appeals div., 1976-77; chief appeals div., 1977-82; exec. asst. U.S. Atty., 1981-82; 1st asst., 1981-83; judge U.S. Dist. Ct., N.J., 1983-99, U.S. Ct. Appeals (3d cir.), Newark, 1999—. Chmn. Com. on Criminal Law Jud. Conf. of U.S., 1994-96. Recipient Sandra Day O'Connor Medal of Honor, 2004. Fellow Am. Bar Found.; mem. ABA, N.J. Bar Assn., Am. Judicature Soc. (bd. dirs.), Assn. Fed. Bar of NJ (pres. 1982-83); mem. NY Bar Assn. Office: US Ct Appeals PO & Courthouse Bldg Rm 333 PO Box 999 Newark NJ 07101-0999*

BARRY, MIRANDA ROBBINS, internet and television producer, writer, educator; b. NYC, Jan. 18, 1951; d. Philip Semple and Patricia Allen (White) B. AB, Stanford U., 1972; postgrad., Columbia Law Sch., N.Y.C., 1978-79, Bank St. Coll. Edn., 2003—. Prodn. rsch. coord. The Best of Families/CTW, N.Y.C., 1975-77; freelance story analyst CBS Inc., N.Y.C., 1976-81; asst. mgr. spl. programs devel. Sta. WNET 13, N.Y.C., 1977-78; exec. coord. Nat. TV Theatre, N.Y.C., 1981-82; story editor Am. Playhouse, N.Y.C., 1982-83, dir. program devel., 1983-87, exec. story cons., 1987; dir. internat. prodn. McNeil/Allyn Films, London, 1987-88; sr. prodr. (TV series) Ghostwriter CTW, 1990, supervising prodr., 1991-94; tchg. fellow N.Y.C. Bd. Edn., 2002—; dir. Mirror Repertory Co., Arts in Edn., 2003—. Instr. TV writing New Sch. Social Rsch., N.Y.C., 1982-83; instr. screen writing Womens Interart Ctr., N.Y.C., 1981-83; adj. assoc. prof. Columbia U. Sch. Film, 1986-87, prof., 1988, 94-96; writer One Life to Live, ABC-TV, N.Y.C., 1994-95; co-dir., organizer TV Theater Workshop Sta. KTCA, Mpls., 1983; creator TV series Mom and Dad/Embassy-NBC, 1983; v.p., lic. support Zing Sys. LP, Denver, 1995; cons. feature film Children's TV Workshop, 1996—; exec. in charge of devel. JP Kids, 1996-97, v.p. creative affairs, 1997-99, sr. v.p. creative affairs, 2000-03; exec. dir. Loire Valley Internat. Theatre Festival, 2003—. Author: Time for Kids Readers, 2003; (play) Friends and Relations, 1981, (TV adaptation) A World to Care For, (TV series) Med-School, 1980, (TV miniseries) Sara and Gerald, 1988, Who is Max Mouse?, 1993; co-author: Quincy Script Blood Ties, 1980, Basil, 1990; (screenplay) Pinkerton's Angel, 1989; scriptwriting resource person Sundance Inst., 1984-86; story editor Eugene O'Neill Nat. Playwright's Conf., 1984—; co-exec. prodr. (TV series) Green Wilma, 1997; exec. prodr. Yahooligans, 1999—; project dir. Going Global, KQED and World Affairs Coun., 1999-2000; dir. Romeo and Juliet, Mirror Repertory Co., 2003. Rape victim counselor St. Luke's Hosp., N.Y.C., 1979-81; mem. alumnae bull. com. Miss Porter's Sch., 1979-84, vol. Children's Aid Soc.; exec. dir. Loire Valley Internat. Youth Theatre Festival, Pontlevoy, France, 2003-. McKnight grantee Playwright's Ctr., Mpls., 1983. Mem. Writers Guild Am-East, Dramatists Guild, N.Y. Women in Film (sec., bd. dirs. 1984-85, 90-91). E-mail: mirandabarry@earthlink.net.

BARRY, NANCY MARIE, bank executive; b. Kansas City, Kans., Aug. 2, 1949; d. John Joseph and Lorna Marie Barry. BA in Econs., Stanford U., 1971; MBA, Harvard U., 1975. Divsn. chief pub. sector mgmt. World Bank, Washington, 1986-87, divsn. chief indsl. devel., 1987-90; pres. Women's World Banking, NYC, 1990—. Founding mem. World Bank Consultative Group to Assist the Poorest-Policy Advisory Group, Washington; adv. com. Harvard Social Enterprise, Mass. Named one of 100 Most Powerful Women in World, Forbes mag., 2005. Mem. Harvard Club. Office: Women's World Banking 8 W 40th St Fl 9 New York NY 10018-3993 Office Fax: 212-768-8519. E-mail: nmbarry@swwb.org.*

BARRY, PHILLIP OWEN, former college president; b. Chgo., May 24, 1951; m. April Lee Rank, Nov. 21, 1971; children: Patrick, Collin. Diploma, Edgewater Hosp., 1971; AAS, Morraine Valley Community Coll., 1973; BS, Chgo. Med. Sch., 1975; M. Edn. Adminstrn., Wichita State U., 1978; PhD, Kans. State U., 1983. Registered radiologic technologist Am. Registry Radiologic Technologists. With health care Med. Ctrs., Chgo., 1971-75; with faculty Hutchinson (Kans.) C.C., 1975-80; dir. Labette C.C., Parsons, Kans., 1980-83, assoc. dean, 1983-85, dean, 1985-87; pres. Salem C.C., Carneys Point, N.J., 1987-92, Hawkeye C.C., Waterloo, Iowa, 1992-95. Mem. grad. faculty Kans. State U., Manhattan, 1984-87, Glassboro (N.J.) State U., 1989-92, Small/Rural Coll. commn., Washington, 1989-92, mem. editorial bd., 1989—. Author: Radiography of Facial Bones, 1979; contbr. articles to profl. jours.; researcher in field. Mem. multiple positions Boy Scouts Am., Kans. N.J., 1975-91, Salem County Youth Commn., 1989-91, Coun. County Colls., 1987—; chmn. Ducks Unltd., Parsons, 1981-86; vice chmn. Econs. Devel. Com., Salem County, N.J., 1988-91; mem. exec. com. Healthy Heart Coalition, Salem County, 1990-91; bd. dirs. Waterloo C. of C., 1993-95, Cedar Valley Econ. Devel. Corp., 1993-95; trustee Silos and Smokestacks, 1992-95. Recipient Disting. Svc. award Ducks Unltd., 1985. Mem. Am. Assn. Community and Jr. Colls. (Outstanding Community Coll. Alumni 1991), Greater Salem C. of C., Rotary, Kiwanis (exec. 1985-87), Jaycees (Outstanding Young Men of Am. 1981). Avocations: horticulture, pomology.

BARRY, RICHARD FRANCIS, retired life insurance company executive; b. N.Y.C., Aug. 28, 1917; s. Thomas Francis and Gertrude Mary (Spillane) B.; m. Irene Patricia Schulties, July 24, 1948. BBA, St. John's U., Bklyn., 1948; JD, Fordham U., 1953. Bar: N.Y. 1954. With Met. Life Ins. Co., N.Y.C., 1937-82, v.p., office of pres., then v.p. human resources, 1979-80, sr. v.p. human resources, 1980-81, sr. v.p. office of chmn., 1981-82, ret. 1982. Mem. faculty St. John's U., 1955-60 Bd. dirs. Urban Acad. for Mgmt., Inc., 1979-82, Met. Life Found., 1981-82; sec. Nat. Assn. Drug Abuse Problems, N.Y.C., 1979-82; mem. Coop. Edn. Commn. N.Y.C., 1979-82. Served with AUS, 1943-45. Mem. Adminstrv. Mgmt. Soc. (pres. N.Y.C. chpt. 1972-73), Life Office Mgmt. Assn., Bar Assn. State N.Y., N.Y. C. of C. and Industry. Republican. Roman Catholic. Home: 237 Berry Hill Rd Syosset NY 11791-2105

BARRY, RICHARD FRANCIS, III, publishing executive; b. Norfolk, Va., Jan. 18, 1943; s. Richard F. and Mary Margaret (Perry) B.; m. Carolyn Ann Kennett, Aug. 7, 1965; children: Carolyn Michelle, Christopher David. BA, LaSalle Coll., 1964; JD, U. Va., 1967. Bar: Va. 1967. Assoc. Kaufman, Oberndorfer & Spainhour (now Kaufman and Canoles), Norfolk, 1967-71, ptnr., 1972-73; corp. sec. Landmark Comm., Inc., Norfolk, 1973—84, pres., COO, dir., 1978—84, CEO, 1984-91, vice chmn., 1991—; pres. Roanoke Times & World-News, Va., 1974-76, The Virginian-Pilot and The Ledger-Star, Norfolk, 1976-78, pub., 1983-90. Bd. dirs. The Weather Channel, Greensboro News and Record, Inc., Times World Corp., Trader Pub. Co., Capital Gazette Comm. Inc., AutoTrader.com LLC. Trustee or past trustee Norfolk Acad., Chrysler Mus., U. Va. Colgate Darden Bus. Sch. Found., Cath. H.S. Found., Old Dominion Univ. Ednl. Found., Suffolk Ctr. for Cultural Arts; bd. dirs., past pres., campaign chmn. United Way of South Hampton Rds.; bd. visitors, past rector Old Dominion U., co-chmn. capital campaign. Office: Landmark Comm Inc 150 W Brambleton Ave Norfolk VA 23510-2018

BARRY, SANDRA, school system administrator; Degree, Neb.-Wesleyan U., Calif. State U., Fullerton. Educator and adminstr. Buena Pk. Sch. Dist., 1968—97; supt. Anaheim (Calif.) City Sch. Dist., 2000—. Office: Anaheim City Sch Dist 1001 South East St Anaheim CA 92805 Office Phone: 714-517-7510.

BARRY, STEVE, sculptor, educator; b. Jersey City, June 22, 1956; s. Thomas Daniel and Lorraine (Lowery) B. BFA, Sch. Visual Arts, N.Y.C., 1980; MFA, Hunter Coll., N.Y.C., 1984. Adj. lectr. Hunter Coll., 1984-89; assoc. prof. U. N.Mex., Albuquerque, 1989—. Kohler Arts and Industry Residency, 1996; bd. dirs. Albuquerque Ctr. Contemporary Arts. Exhbns. include Bklyn. Army Terminal, N.Y.C., 1983, City Gallery, N.Y.C., 1986, 90, Storefront for Art and Architecture, 1988, Artists Space, N.Y.C., 1989, Santa Barbara Art Mus., 1990, Kohler Arts Ctr., Sheboygan, Wis., 1991, Hirshhorn Mus., Washington, 1990, Fla. State U., 1992, Contemporary Art Mus., Houston, 1992, CAFE Gallery, Albuquerque, 1993, Charolette Jackson, Santa Fe, 1993, Ctr. for Contemporary Arts, Santa Fe, 1994, U. Wyo. Art Mus., 1995, Site Santa Fe, 1996, Sheldon Art Mus., Lincoln, Nebr., 1997, U. N.Mex. Art Mus., Albuquerque, 1997, Cedar Rapids (Iowa) Mus. of Art, 1998, Albuquerque Contemporary Art Ctr., 2000, Plan B, Santa Fe, 2000, Downey Gallery, Albuquerque, 2004. Grantee Clocktower Nat. Studio, 1985, NEA, 1986, 88, 90, N.Y. State Coun. for the Arts, 1987, N.Y. Found. for the Arts, 1988, Rsch. grantee Coll. Fine Arts N.Mex., 2002; recipient AVA award, 1990. Home: PO Box 1046 Corrales NM 87048-1046 Office: U NMex Dept Art & Art History Albuquerque NM 87131-0001 Office Phone: 505-277-5861. Business E-Mail: sbarry@unm.edu.

BARRY, TERESA TRUPIANO, history educator; b. Marshall, Mich., Jan. 15, 1950; d. Stephen Frank and Ernestine Viola (Lake) Trupiano; m. David Nathan Barry, Oct. 1, 1988. BS in Education, Ea. Mich. U., 1972; MA in History, We. Mich. U., 1985. Tour dir. Marshall (Mich.) Hist. Soc., 1983; intern Charlton Pk. Village & Mus., Hastings, Mich., 1984, edn. curator, 1985-89; instr. Kellogg Community Coll., Battle Creek, Mich., 1987—; lectr. Nazareth Coll., Kalamazoo, 1989—. Contbr. articles to profl. jours. State of Mich. scholar., 1968, Mich. Mus. Assoc., 1983, Fellow Kellogg Found. Field Mus., 1986. Mem. AAUW, Am. Assn. State Local Hist. Socs., Hastings Woman's Club, Barry County Geneal. Soc.

BARRY, THOMAS CORCORAN, investment advisor; b. Cleve., Feb. 9, 1944; s. Willard Corcoran and Harriet (Mullin) Barry; m. Patricia Ryan, Feb. 14, 1976; children: Hannah McGrath(dec.), Ryan Nichols(dec.), Oliver Mullin, Lillian Nicholson, Michael Corcoran. BA in Latin Am. Studies, Yale U., 1966; MBA, Harvard U., 1969. Chartered fin. analyst. Market research analyst Corning Glass Works, Brazil and Japan, 1966-67; investment analyst T. Rowe Price Assos., Inc., Balt., 1969-70; partner Cole, Thompson and Barry, Inc., Cleve., 1971-73; pres. Rowe Price New Horizons Fund, Balt., 1973-81, Saratoga Assocs., 1981-83; pres., CEO Rockefeller and Co. Inc., 1983-93; pres. Zephyr Mgmt., L.P., 1994—. Dir. numerous cos. Mem. Yale Pres.'s Coun. on Internat. Activities; mem. dean's coun. Harvard U.-Kennedy Sch. Govt.; chair NYC Summer Search; trustee Hotchkiss Sch., 2003—, Univ. Sch., Cleve., 1998—; bd. dirs. Harvard Bus. Sch. Alumni Assn. Office: 320 Park Ave New York NY 10022-6815 Office Phone: 212-508-9410.

BARRY, WILLIAM ANTHONY, priest, writer; b. Worcester, Mass., Nov. 22, 1930; s. William and Catherine (McKenna) B. AB, Boston Coll., 1956, STL, 1963; MA, Fordham U., 1960; PhD, U. Mich., 1968. Joined S.J., Roman Cath. Ch., 1950, ordained priest, 1962. Tchr. high sch. Fairfield (Conn.) Prep., 1956-58; lectr. U. Mich., Ann Arbor, 1968-69; from asst. to assoc. prof. Weston Jesuit Sch. of Theology, Cambridge, Mass., 1969-78; rector Jesuit community Boston Coll., Chestnut Hill, Mass., 1988-91; vice provincial S.J. of New Eng., Boston, 1978-84, asst. novice dir., 1985-88, provincial, 1991-97; co-dir. S.J. Tertianship, 1997—. Dir. staff Ctr. for Religious Devel., Cambridge, 1971-78; trustee Boston Coll., Chestnut Hill, 1988-91, adj. assoc. prof., 1989-91. Co-author: Communication, Conflict, Marriage, 1974, The Practice of Spiritual Direction, 1982, Contemplatives in Action, 2002; author: God and You, 1987, Seek My Face, 1989, Now Choose Life, 1990, Paying Attention to God, 1990, Finding God in All Things, 1991, Spiritual Direction and the Encounter with God, 1992, 2d, rev. edit., 2004, God's Passionate Desire and Our Response, 1993, Allowing the Creator to Deal with the Creature, 1994, What Do I Want in Prayer?, 1994, Who Do You Say I Am?, 1996, Our Way of Proceeding, 1997, With an Everlasting Love, 1999, Letting God Come Close, 2001; editor-in-chief (quar. jour.) Human Development, 2003—. Mem. Phi Beta Kappa, Phi Kappa Phi. Democrat. Roman Catholic. Avocations: reading, writing. Home and Office: Campion Ctr 319 Concord Rd Weston MA 02493-1310 Office Phone: 781-788-6800. Business E-Mail: frbarry@bc.edu.

BARRY, WILLIAM GARRETT, III, publishing company executive; b. NYC, Aug. 16, 1955; s. William Garrett Jr. and Mary Theresa (Harrington) B.; m. Jeanne Maureen Sweet, Oct. 10, 1981; children: Emily Katherine, Maura Regina, Liam Sun-Ho. BA, Cathedral Coll., 1977. Editorial sec. Doubleday Pub. Co., NYC, 1979-80; corp. research analyst Doubleday & Co., Inc., NYC, 1980-83, bus. assoc., 1983-84, mng. editor, 1984-87, assoc. pub., 1987-90, v.p., 1989-96, dep. pub., 1990-95; dir. pub. ops. Bantam Doubleday Dell Pub. Group, Inc., 1995-96, sr. v.p. ops., 1996; pres. Hungry Minds, DK Publishing; v.p., pub. Doubleday Religion, NYC, 2005—. Mem.: Conn. Beekeepers' Assn. Office: Doubleday Religion Random House 1745 Broadway New York NY 10019*

BARRYMORE, DREW, actress; b. Culver City, Calif., Feb. 22, 1975; d. John and Jaid Barrymore; m. Jeremy Thomas, Mar. 20, 1994 (div. Feb. 1995); m. Tom Green, July 7, 2001 (div. Oct. 15, 2002). Co-owner Flower Films, 1995—. Appearances include (films) Altered States, 1980, E.T.: The Extra-Terrestrial, 1982, Irreconcilable Differences, 1984, Firestarter, 1984, Cat's Eye, 1985, Poison Ivy, 1992, Bad Girls, 1994, Boys on the Side, 1995, Batman Forever, 1995, Mad Love, 1995, Wishful Thinking, 1996, Scream, 1996, Like a Lady, 1996, Everyone Says I Love You, 1996, All She Wanted, 1997, Best Men, 1997, Never Been Kissed, 1998 (also prodr.), Home Fries, 1998, The Wedding Singer, 1998, Ever After: A Cinderella Story, 1998, Never Been Kissed (also exec. prodr.), 1999, Olive, the Other Reindeer, 1999 (voice & exec. prodr.), Titan A.E., 2000 (voice), Charlie's Angels, 2000 (also prodr.), Donnie Darko (also exec. prodr.), 2001, Riding in Cars With Boys, 2001, Confessions of a Dangerous Mind, 2002, Charlie's Angels: Full Throttle (also prodr.), 2003, Duplex, 2003 (also prodr.), 50 First Dates, 2004, Fever Pitch (also prodr.), 2005; (TV episodes) Amazing Stories, 1985, Con Sawyer and Hucklemary Finn, 1985, 2000 Malibu Road, 1992; (host) Hansel and Gretel, 1986; (TV movies) Suddenly Love, 1978, Bogie, 1980, The Screaming Woman, 1986, Babes in Toyland, 1986, Conspiracy of Love, 1987, Beyond Control: The Amy Fisher Story, 1993; (TV spls.) Screen Actors Guild 50th Anniversary, 1984, Night of 100 Stars II, 1985, Happy Birthday, Hollywood, 1987, Disney's 30th Anniversary, 1987; co-auther (book) Little Girl Lost. Named one of 50 Most Powerful People in Hollywood, Premiere mag., 2004—05; recipient Star, Hollywood's Walk of Fame, 2004. Office: Creative Artist Agency 9830 Wilshire Blvd Beverly Hills CA 90212*

BAR-SADEH, MADELEINE KAY, writer; d. Harry and Anne Kay; 1 child, Daniel Harry. BA (cum laude), Boston U., 1967; MA, U. Miami, 1975. Creative project mgr. Allyn & Bacon Pub., Boston, 1967; instr. English Tel Aviv U., 1969—71, U. Miami, 1972—78; media dir. Garber & Goodman Advt., 1978—80; pres., creative dir., owner Erica Knight Assocs., Inc., 1981—96; advt. exec., cons., 1997—; writer, lifestyle/career coach. Spkr., cons. in field. Author: Living Serrendipitously...Keeing the Wonder Alive, 2003 (Best Seller, 2004). Fellow: Pubs. Mktg. Assn. Avocations: dance, travel, hiking, theater, films. Home: Chrysalis Pub PO Box 675 Flat Rock NC 28731 E-mail: mkay@livingserendipitously.com.

BARSALONA, FRANK SAMUEL, theatrical agent; b. S.I., N.Y., Mar. 31, 1938; s. Peter and Mary (Rotunno) B.; m. June Harris, Sept. 1, 1966; 1 dau., Nicole. BA, Wagner Coll., S.I., 1958; postgrad., Herbert Berghof Sch., N.Y.C., 1959-60. Agt. Gen. Artists Corp., N.Y.C., 1960-64; founder, since pres. Premier Talent Agy. (merged with William Morris Agy.), N.Y.C., 1964—2002; co-founder, pres. Phila. Fury, 1977-80. Lectr., moderator music industry; founding ptnr. Precision Media Corp., 1984-97. Bd. govs., trustee Rock & Roll Hall of Fame Mus., Cleve. Named to Performance Mag. Hall of Fame, 1988; recipient numerous awards (cover subject spl. issue), Billboard Publs., 1984, Silver Clef award, Nordoff Robbins, 2002, Inducted into the Rock & Roll Hall of Fame Life Time Achievement award, 2005. Mem. Mus. Am. Folk Art. (internat. adv. bd.). Office: William Morris Agy 1325 Ave of Ams New York NY 10019

BARSAN, ROBERT BLAKE, dentist; b. Akron, Ohio, Apr. 7, 1948; s. Emil O. and Letitia (Dobrin) B.; m. Cheryl Lee Adams, Dec. 16, 1972; children: Erin Lee, Kathleen Letitia. BS, U. Cin., 1970; DDS, Ohio State U., 1974. Resident U. Chgo., 1976; gen. practice dentistry Cuyahoga Falls, Ohio, 1976—. Contbr. editor Modern Dental mag., 1984-89. Bd. dirs. Akron Civic Theatre, 1996-2004. Fellow Acad. Gen. Dentistry (v.p. Ohio chpt. 2004—); mem. ADA (chmn. CPR 1984-90), Akron Gnathological Soc. (pres. 1986), Am. Acad. Cosmetic Dentistry, Canton Akron Cleve. Orthodontic Study Club (pres. 1994-98). Home: 3084 Silver Lake Blvd Silver Lake OH 44224-3033 Office: 330 Stow Ave Cuyahoga Falls OH 44221-2516

BARSAN, WILLIAM GEORGE, emergency physician; b. Akron, Aug. 1950; m. Mary Barsan. MD, Ohio State U., 1975. Diplomate Am. Bd. Emergency Medicine. Intern U. Va. Hosp., Charlottesville, 1975-76, resident in radiology, 1976-77; resident in emergency medicine U. Cin. Hosp., 1977-79; resident coordinator U. Cincinnati, 1981—92; prof. dept. emergency medicine Med. Sch. U. Mich., Ann Arbor, 1992—, dir. surgery, 1992—. Mem. AMA, Soc. Tchrs. Emergency Medicine, U. Assn. Emergency Medicine, Inst. Medicine, 2004. Office: U Mich Hosp Sect Emergency Medicine UH/BIC 255/0014 1500 E Med Ctr Dr Ann Arbor MI 48109-0014

BARSANO, CHARLES PAUL, medical educator, dean; BS in Biology, Loyola U., Chgo., 1969; PhD in Pathology, U. Chgo., 1974, MD, 1975. Diplomate Am. Bd. Internal Medicine. Resident internal medicine Barnes Hosp./Washington U., St. Louis, 1975-77; fellow endocrinology U. Chgo. Sch. Medicine, 1977-79, rsch. assoc. endocrinology, 1979-80; asst. prof. medicine Northwestern U. and Lakeside VA Med. Ctr., 1980-85, U. Health Scis./Chgo. Med. Sch. and North Chgo. VA Med. Ctr., 1985-87, assoc. prof., 1987-92, prof. medicine, 1992-98, assoc. prof. pharmacology and molecular biology, 1992-94, prof. pharmacology and molecular biology, 1994-98, acting dean Med. Sch., 1998—99, sr. assoc. dean for clin. affairs, vice-chmn. dept. medicine, 1999—2001, interim dean, 2001—03; staff physician med. svc./endocrinology sect. North Chgo. VA Med. Ctr. Mem. editl. bd. Thyroid, 1990-95; mem. adv. bd. Toxic Substance Mechanisms, 1993-99. Recipient Bausch and Lomb Nat. Sci. award, 1965, Individual Nat. Rsch. Svc. award, 1979-80. Mem. Internat. Coun. for Control of Iodine Deficiency Disorders, Assn. Am. Med. Colls. (group on ednl. affairs sect. on resident edn.), Am. Assn. Clin. Endocrinologists, Am. Thyroid Assn. (fiscal com. 1982-85, pub. health com. 1986-88, membership com. 1990-93, chmn. membership com. 1993, local organizing com. 1994, bylaws com. 1995—), Endocrine Soc., Chgo. Endocrine Club (pres. 1984-85), Sigma Xi, Alpha Omega Alpha. Office: Office Clin Affairs Finch Univ Health Scis Chgo Med Sch North Chicago IL 60064 E-mail: charles.barsano@rosalindfranklin.edu, cbflyer@aol.com.

BARSE, DAVID M., financial services executive; Lawyer; gen. counsel M.H. Whitman, Inc., N.Y.C., 1991; pres., COO Daniel Holding Corp., N.Y.C., 1996—, also bd. dirs. Office: MJ Whitman Adivsers 622 3RD Ave FL 32 New York NY 10017-6715

BARSHAK, EDWARD JOEL, lawyer; b. Boston, May 21, 1924; s. Samuel and Lillian (Kahn) B.; m. Regina Winder; children: Danielle, Rachelle, Joel. AB, Tufts Coll., 1945; LLB, Columbia U., 1949. Bar: Mass. 1949, U.S. Dist. Ct. Mass. 1950. Ptnr. Sugarman, Rogers, Barshak & Cohen, Boston, 1955—. Lt. (j.g.) USN, 1942-45, PTO. Avocations: running, writing. Office: Sugarman Rogers Barshak & Cohen 101 Merrimac St Ste 9 Boston MA 02114-4719

BARSHAY, SCOTT A., lawyer; b. Manhasset, NY, Dec. 12, 1965; BA in Polit. Sci, magna cum laude, Colgate Univ., 1988; JD, Columbia Univ., 1991. Bar: NY 1992. Assoc. Cravath, Swaine, & Moore LLP, NYC, 1991—99, ptnr., corp., 1999—. Assoc. editor Journ. Transnational Law, Columbia Univ. Named a Stone Scholar; named one of Top 40 Under 40 Lawyers, Nat. Law. Jour., 2005. Mem.: ABA, Bar Assn. of City of NY, NY Bar Assn., Phi Beta Kappa. Office: Cravath, Swaine & Moore LLP Worldwide Plz 825 Eighth Ave New York NY 10019-7475 Office Phone: 212-474-1009. Office Fax: 212-474-3700. Business E-Mail: sbarshay@cravath.com.

BARSHEFSKY, CHARLENE, lawyer, former diplomat; b. Aug. 11, 1950; BA with honors, U. Wis., 1972; JD, Catholic U., 1975. Ptnr. Steptoe & Johnson, Washington, 1975-93; dep. U.S. trade rep. Exec. Office of the Pres. of the U.S., Washington, 1993-96, U.S. trade rep., 1996—2001; pub. policy scholar Woodrow Wilson Internat. Ctr., Washington, 2001; sr. internat. ptnr. Wilmer, Cutler, & Pickering, Washington, 2001—. Mem.: bd. dirs., Intel Corp., 2004-. Office: Wilmer Cutler & Pickering 2445 M St Washington DC 20037-1420 Office Phone: 202-663-6130. Office Fax: 202-663-6363.*

BARSNESS, RICHARD WEBSTER, management educator, academic administrator; b. Elbow Lake, Minn., Apr. 26, 1935; s. Russel E. and Joanna (Warga) B.; m. Dorothea L. Gother, Aug. 22, 1964; children: Karen Louise, Erik Richard. BS, U. Minn., 1957, MA, 1958, MAP.A., 1960, PhD, 1963. Budget analyst U.S. Bur. Budget, Washington, 1960-61; instr., asst. prof. Northwestern U., Evanston, Ill., 1962-69, assoc. prof., 1969-78, assoc. dean, 1972-78; dean, prof. Lehigh U., Bethlehem, Pa., 1978-92, prof., 1978—, Iacocca prof. bus., 1992-93, exec. dir. Iacocca Inst., 1992-95, Univ. disting. svc. prof. mgmt., 1995—. Exec. sec. Lexington Group in Transport History, 1969-89; pres. Bus. History Conf., 1981-82, Lexington Group, Inc., 1997-2005; lectr. Transp. Ctr., Evanston, Ill., 1964-84; editl. cons. Contbr.: articles to profl. jours.; editor: Lexington Newsletter. Mem. Gov.'s Adv. Coun. State of Ill., 1969—72; gen. chmn. United Way Lehigh U., 1981; v.p., bd. dirs. Episcopal House, Allentown, Pa., 1999—, pres., 2003—05. Recipient R.R. and E.C. Hillman award, Lehigh U., 1991. Mem.: Acad. Internat. Bus., Internat. Assn. for Bus. and Soc., Bus. History Conf. (trustee 1978—81, pres. 1981—82), Transp. Rsch. Forum, Acad. Mgmt., Phi Beta Kappa, Beta Gamma Sigma. Republican. Episcopalian. Home: 769 Apollo Dr Bethlehem PA 18017-2556 Office: Lehigh U Coll Bus 621 Taylor St Bethlehem PA 18015-3117 Office Phone: 610-758-4355. E-mail: rwb0@lehigh.edu.

BARSON, ROSS J., music educator, assistant principal; s. Vaughn P. and Gertrude M. Pat Barson; m. Peggy B. Bowen, June 3, 1982; children: Sarah, Crystal, Steven. MusB, Boise State U., 1985; MEd in Adminstrn., U. Idaho, 2000. Cert. Idaho Secondary Educator 1985, Idaho Sch. Adminstr. 2000. Dir. bands/choirs Shelley Sch. Dist., Shelley, Idaho, 1985—86; dir. bands Sugar-Salem Sch. Dist., Sugar City, Idaho, 1986—91; dir. bands Minidoka County Sch. Dist., Rupert, Idaho, 1991—2005; asst. prin. Paul (Idaho) Elem. Sch., 2002—03, West Minico Mid. Sch., 2003—05; dir. bands Burley Jr. High Sch., Idaho, 2005—, asst. prin., 2005—. Dir.(All-State Jr. High Band): Idaho Music Educators Assn. All-State Conf./Insvc., 2000 (I.M.E.A. Cert., 2000); guest condr.: Magic Philharm. Orch., 2004, 2005. Mem.: ASCD, Assn. Supervision and Curriculum Devel., Idaho Music Educators Assn. (pres. Dist. VI 1990—91, pres.-elect Dist. IV 2002, dir. Dist. VI jr. high honor band 2004), Music Educators Nat. Conf. Mem. Lds Ch. Avocations: fishing, hiking, camping, travel. Home: 1951 15th St Heyburn ID 83336-9650 Office Phone: 208-878-6613.

BARST, ROBYN JOAN, pediatric cardiologist, educator, researcher; b. Los Angeles, July 19, 1950; d. Stanley S. and Ruth (Piltzer) Walters; m. Samuel M. Barst, Aug. 24, 1980; children: Nomi, Lindsey. B.A., U. Rochester, 1972; M.D., U. N.C., 1976. Diplomate Am. Bd. Pediatrics and Pediatric Cardiology. Resident in pediatrics Columbia U., N.Y.C., 1976-79, pediatric cardiology fellow 1979-81, pediatric pulmonary fellow, 1981-83, asst. prof. pediatrics, 1983-85; asst. prof. pediatrics and pharmacology N.Y. Med. Coll., Valhalla, 1985— . Contbr. articles to med. jours. Recipient Clinican Sci. award Am. Heart Assn., 1984-87; Parker B. Francis Found. pulmonary research fellow, 1983-84; Nat. Heart, Lung and Blood Inst. grantee, 1984, clin. investigator award, 1984— . Mem. Am. Heart Assn., Am. Thoracic Soc., N.Y. Acad. Scis., N.Y. Heart Assn., Alpha Omega Alpha. Democrat. Jewish. Home: 31 Murray Hill Rd Scarsdale NY 10583-2827

BARSTOW, CHRISTOPHER R., state representative; b. Biddeford, Maine, Aug. 24, 1977; s. Douglas W. Lawrence and Karen L. Barstow; m. Rebecca J. Dever, Aug. 24, 2001; 1 child, Alexa. Grad. high sch., Gorham, Maine. Notary pub. 2001. Mem. Maine Ho. of Reps., Gorham, 2001—, chmn. tate and local govt. com., 2001—. Mem. Commn. Performance Budgeting, Maine, 2003—. Trustee Baxter Meml. Libr., Gorham, 2001—; mem. Gorham Recreation Adv. Bd., 2001—; moderator Little Falls Bapt. Ch., 2001—. Mem.: Gorham Hist. Soc. Democrat. Home: 180 Main St Gorham ME 04038 Office: Maine Ho of Reps 2 State House Sta Augusta ME 04333 Office Phone: 207-287-1289. E-mail: crbarstow@verizon.net.

BARSUGLI, JESSE BENJAMIN, lab administrator; b. Pasadena, Calif., Mar. 29, 1972; s. Norman L. and Adelfa F. Barsugli. BS in biology, BS in psychology, Liberty U., 1999. Lab. / tchg. asst. Liberty U. - Chemistry Dept., Lynchburg, Va., 1993—94; med. nursing technician Centra Health - Lynchburg Gen. Hosp., Lynchburg, Va., 1996—98; prodn. lab. technician ARC Blood Services, Los Angeles, Calif., 2001—02, lab. supr. Irvine, Calif., 2002—04, Pomona, Calif., 2004—. Spiritual life dir. Liberty U. Student Affairs Dept., Lynchburg, Va., 1993—96; vol. / pre-med rotation Riverside Regional Med. Ctr., Riverside, Calif., 1991. Named Employee of Mo., ARC, 2004; recipient Outstanding Young Men of Am., OYA, 1996, Outstanding Student Citizen, LA Times/ LA Dodgers Orgn., 1988, Outstanding Achievement in Promoting Profession of Lab. Medicine, Am. Soc. Clin. Pathology, 2003—04, Recognition award for Most Knowledgeable with Blood Svcs. Directives, ARC, 2003—04. Mem.: Nat. Forensic League (life; spkr./debator 1989—90, Degree of Merit 1990). Conservative. Bapt. Avocations: travel, hiking, camping, sports, photography. Home: 1120 Euclid Ave San Gabriel CA 91776-3011 Office: ARC So Calif Region 100 Red Cross Cir Pomona CA 91768 Personal E-mail: phoenixlight@hotmail.com. E-mail: barsuglij@usa.redcross.org.

BART, PETER BENTON, editor, film producer, writer; b. N.Y.C., July 24, 1932; m. Leslie Cox; children: Colby, Dilys. BA, Swarthmore Coll., 1954; MA, London Sch. Econs., 1956. Staff reporter The Wall Street Jour., N.Y.C., 1956-57, The N.Y. Times, N.Y.C., 1957-67; v.p. Paramount Pictures, Los Angeles, 1967-74; pres. Bart Palevsky Prodn., L.A., 1974-77, Lorimar Film Co., Los Angeles, 1977-82; sr. v.p., film producer Metro Goldwyn Mayer/United Artists, L.A., 1982-85; v.p., editorial dir. Variety and Daily Variety, L.A., 1989—, editor-in-chief. Author: Destinies, 1980, Thy Kingdom Come, 1983, Fade Out: The Calamitous Final Days of MGM, 1990; prodr.: (films) Fun with Dick and Jane, Islands in the Stream, Youngblood. Office: Variety 5700 Wilshire Blvd Ste 120 Los Angeles CA 90036-3644

BART, ROGER, actor; b. Norfolk, Conn., Sept. 29, 1962; Actor(with Broadway/first nat. tour credits including:): You're a Good Man, Charlie Brown (Tony award, Drama Desk award), The Producers, 2001,:, 2005, (with Broadway/first nat. tour credits including:): Triumph of Love, The Who's Tommy, (London's West End, U.S. Tour, German prodns. of:): King David, How to Succeed in Business, The Secret Garden, Big River, (off-Broadway) Henry IV, Parts I and II, Up Against It, role of Whizzer in Falsettos; singing voice title role of Walt Disney's animated feature Hercules, other canine credits include singing voice of Scamp in Disney's Lady and the Tramp Part II, acting role in The George Carlin Show, Fox TV; actor: (George St. prodn.)

Ancestral Voices, 2002; (TV series) Alice and Bram, 2002, Law & Order: Special Victims Unit, 1999; (films) The Insider, 1999, The Stepford Wives, 2004. Office: c/o SAG 360 Madison Ave #12 New York NY 10017-7111*

BART, SUSAN THERESE, lawyer; b. 1961; BA, Grinnell Coll., 1982; JD, U. Mich., 1985. Bar: Ill. 1985, U.S. Ct. Appeals (7th cir.) 1985. Law clk. to Hon. Richard D. Cudahy, Fed. Ct. Appeals (7th cir.), 1985—86; with Hopkins & Sutter, 1986—94, ptnr., 1992—94, Sidley Austin Brown & Wood LLP (formerly Sidley & Austin), 1994—. Articles editor U. Mich. Law Review, Ann Arbor, 1984-85; sec., bd. dirs. The Next Theatre. Author: Education Planning and Gifts to Minors, 2004; co-author: Illinois Estate Planning: Forms and Commentary, 1997 (Outstanding Achievement award Assn. for Continuing Legal Edn., 1998), rev., 2002; asst. editor: ACTEC Jour. Mem. Chgo. Estate Planning Coun.; mem. bd. dirs., exec. com. Ill. Inst. Continuing Legal Edn.; sec., bd. dirs. The Next Theatre. Mem. Chgo. Estate Planning Coun., Phi Beta Kappa, Order of the Coif. Avocations: classics, literature, theater. Office: Sidley Austin Brown and Wood LLP Bank One Plz 10 S Dearborn St Chicago IL 60603

BARTALINI, C. RICHARD, judge; b. Kincaid, Ill., Sept. 25, 1931; s. Chester Richard and Florinda (Galli) B.; m. Anne M. Evanoff, June 4, 1955; children: Robert Charles, Denise Anne, David Chester. BA, U. Calif., Berkeley, 1954; JD, U. Calif, San Francisco, 1957. Bar: Calif. 1957. Practice law, Oakland, 1957-66, Alameda, 1966-77; dep. dist. atty. Alameda County, 1957-59; chief def. counsel Transit Casualty Co., 1959-60; chief trial atty. Alameda/Contra Costa Transit Co., 1960-61; asso. Nichols, Williams, Morgan & Digardi, 1961-66; partner Davis, Craig & Bartalini, 1966-77; judge Superior Ct. Calif., 1977-93; ret., 1993. Atty., counselor Supreme Ct. U.S.; del. Calif. Bar Conf., 1963-68; cons. U.S. Dept. Justice, U.S. Dept. Edn.; faculty Nat. Inst. for Trial Advocacy, Ctr. for Trial and Appellate Advocacy, Hastings Coll. Law, Calif. Ctr. for Jud. Edn. and Rsch. Chmn. Alameda Youth Activities Com., 1958-63, Nat. Coun. on Mental Health and Retardation, 1965-69; mem. President's Coun. on Youth Opportunity, 1965-70; pres. Alameda Bd. Edn.; pres., v.p., bd. dirs. Alameda Boys Club; bd. dirs. Alameda Develop. Corp.; mem. exec. com. Nat. Found. March of Dimes; chmn. No. Calif. Area coun., mem. Nat. Commn. for Constl. Revision and mem. nat. area coun. com. Boys Clubs Am.; chmn. bd. dirs. Moreau High Sch., Hayward, Calif., Alameda Hosp. Found.; mem. adv. bd. Partners Program, The Close-Up Found., CY Press Mandela Wist Tng. Ctr.; mem. civil svc. bd. City of Alameda, 1992-96, mem. housing authority, 1996—; mem. Alameda County Grand Jury, 1997-98, chair Measure A oversight com., superintendents edn. adv. com.; bd. dirs. Alameda Devel. Corp., Alameda Friendly Visitors. Recipient Service award Nat. Congress Parents and Tchrs., 1972, Disting. Svc. award Alameda Unified Sch. Dist., 1972, Man and Boy award Boys Clubs Am., 1975, Bronze Keystone award Boys Club Am., 1979, Bronze Keystone and Svc. Bar awards Boys and Girls Clubs of Am., 1989, Cross & Anchors award, Moreau Cath. HS; named Young Man of Yr. City of Alameda, 1965, Outstanding Civic Leader of Am., 1967. Mem. ATLA, ABA, Calif. Bar Assn., Alameda County Bar Assn. (dir.), Criminal Cts. Bar Assn., Com. for Advancement and Support of Edn., Nat. Assn. Ind. Schs., Alameda Collaborative for Children, Youth and Their Families, Alameda County Lawyers Club (past pres.), Calif. C. of C. (past dir.), Alameda Jaycees (past pres.), U.S. Jaycees (past legal counsel), Elks, Eagles, Kiwanis, Alameda Rod and Gun Club, Commonwealth Club, Chabot Gun Club, Phi Alpha Delta. Home: 1224 Bay St Alameda CA 94501-3914

BARTALO, THERESA MARIE, elementary school educator; b. Frankfort, Germany, May 21, 1966; d. John Michael Bustos and Frances Eileen Stokes; m. Kenneth Michael Bartalo, July 11, 1992; children: Christina, Nathaniel. BS in elem. edn., Chadron State Coll., 1984—88. Lit. resource tchr. Will Rogers Elem., Colo. Springs, 2000—, Patrick Henry Elem., Colo. Springs, 2000—01; tchr. Glenrose Elem. Sch., Colo. Springs, 1988—2000. Recipient Crystal Apple award, Sch. Dist. #41, 1999—2000. Avocations: scrapbooks, counted cross stitch, music. Office: Will Rogers Elem 110 S Cirlce Colorado Springs CO 80910

BARTEE, NEALE, music educator, musician, conductor; b. Springfield, Mo., Feb. 23, 1947; s. Josephus Christian and Thelma Ruby Bartee; m. Debra Elaine Austin. BS in Edn., U. Ill., 1969, MEd, 1970, PhD, 1977. Tchr. instrumental music pub. schs., Norman, Okla., 1972—73; prof. music Ark. State U., Jonesboro, 1973—. Condr. Delta Symphony Orch., Jonesboro, 1975—; trombonist ch. music programs, Ark., Mo., Tenn., 1973—. Condr. Internat. Trombone Festivals. Condr. Clinician fellow, Coll. Band Dirs. Nat. Assn., Austin, Tex., 1989, Bapt. Nat. Music Conf., Glorietta, N.Mex., 1992, Friend of the Arts fellow, Sigma Alpha Iota, Epsilon Gamma chpt., 1999. Mem.: Music Edn. Nat. Conf. (assoc.; state pres. 1997—98). Baptist. Home: 3713 Burdyshaw Jonesboro AR 72401 Personal E-mail: nebartee@cox-internet.com.

BARTEE, THOMAS CRESON, computer scientist, educator; b. Moberly, Mo., Dec. 18, 1926; s. Thomas Monroe and Verna Miller (Tippett) B.; m. Mildred Higdon, Sept. 5, 1953; 1 child, Thomas Quentin. BA, Westminster Coll., 1949. Mem. staff computer research M.I.T.-Lincoln Lab., Lexington, Mass., 1955-63; Gordon MacKay lectr. in computer engring. Harvard U., Cambridge, Mass., 1963-69, dir. electronic design center, 1969-72, Gordon MacKay prof. computer engring., 1970—. Cons. Nat. Acad. Scis., IDA, IBM, Honeywell, Raytheon; IEEE disting. computer sci. lectr., 1972-74 Author: (with G. Birkhoff) Modern Applied Algebra, 1971, Introduction to Computer Science, 1972, Digital Computer Fundamentals, 7th edit., 1989, Basic Computer Programming, 1981, 2d edit., 1985, Data Communications, Networks and Systems, 1985, 2d edit., 1992, Digital Communications, 1986, Expert Systems in AI, 1987, ISDN, SNA AND DECNET, 1989; editor: IEEE-IRE Computer Jour., 1963-66. Recipient Disting. contbn. in computer sci. award Westminster Coll., 1980 Mem. IEEE (chmn. N.E. computer group 1973-74), Am. Math. Soc. Office: Aiken Computation Lab Harvard Univ Cambridge MA 02138 Home: 2534 S Walter Reed Dr Apt A Arlington VA 22206-1287 Personal E-mail: tcbartee@hotmail.com.

BARTEE, WAYNE C., humanities educator, department chairman; b. Springfield, Mo., Jan. 11, 1936; s. Josephus Christian and Thelma Ruby (Clark) Bartee; m. Alice Fleetwood; children: Wayne Clark III, George Fleetwood. BA cum laude, SW Mo. State U., 1958; MA, Columbia U., 1959, PhD, 1966. Asst. prof. history Okla. Bapt. U., Shawnee, 1964—67; prof. history SW Mo. State U., Springfield, 1967—, head dept. history, 1976—91. Contbr. articles to profl. jours. Pres. County Hist. Soc., 1973—76; trustee Judson Coll., Elgin, Ill., 2002—; sec., exec. com. Dem. Ctrl. Com., Greene County, 2002—; bd. dirs. Hist. Preservation Soc., Green County, Mo., 1970—78. Capt. U.S. Army, 1961—62. Recipient Heritage award, Heritage Coun., 1988; fellow, Woodrow Wilson Found., 1958—59; Fulbright fellow, US Govt., 1962—63. Democrat. Baptist. Avocations: reading, gardening. Home: 3033 E Carlisle Cir Springfield MO 65804 Office: SW Mo State Univ Dept History 901 S National Ave Springfield MO 65804 Office Phone: 417-836-6959. Business E-Mail: wcb777f@smsu.edu.

BARTEK, DENNIS J., lawyer; b. Akron, Ohio, July 31, 1946; s. Joseph and Julia Abraham Bartek; m. JoAnn Garver, May 26, 1978; 1 child, Wendy Nelson. BA, U. Akron, 1968, JD, 1971. Bar: Ohio, U.S. Ct. Appeals (6th cir.), U.S. Dist. Ct. (no. dist.) Ohio, S.C., W.Va., Fla., Idaho, Ill. Claims rep. Travelers Ins., Akron, 1967—71; asst. Summit County prosecutor Summit County Prosecutors Office, Akron, 1971—73; acting judge by periodic assignment Cuyahoga Falls (Ohio) Mcpl. Ct., 1977—91; pvt. practice Akron, 1973—. Leader numerous seminars, courses, workshops, and confs.; mem. Fed. Ct. Panel for Alt. Dispute Resolution for No. Dist. Ohio; mem. merit selection panel U.S. Dist. Ct. (no. dist.) Ohio, 1993, 94, 96. Past mem. parish coun. St. Joseph Cath. Ch., Akron; past mem., bd. govs. Cuyahoga Falls Comty. Oktoberfest Com.; past chair, mem. Cuyahoga Falls Civil Svc. Commn.; past mem., bd. dirs. Summit County Mental Health Assn. Named Master of Bench, Charles F. Scanlon Inn of Ct., Outstanding Alumnus, U. Akron Sch. Law, 2003, Leading Lawyer, Inside Bus. Mag., 2001, 2002, 2003, 2004, 2005; named one of Ohio's Super Lawyers, Law & Politics Mag. and Cin. Mag., 2003, 2004. Mem.: ATLA, Am. Coll. Barristers (sr. counsel), Summit County Trial Attys. (bd. trustees 1998—2001), Akron Bar Assn. (pres. elect 1998—99, pres. 1999—2000, sec. 1996—98, bd. trustees 1996—2001, past mem. exec. com., chair nominating com. 2000—01, 2001—02, 2002—03), Ohio Assn. Civil Trial Attys., Ohio Assn. Trial Lawyers, Nat. Assn. Criminal Def. Lawyers, Ohio State Bar Assn. (past mem. coun. dels. 1989), U. Akron Law Sch. Alumni Assn. (life; sec. 1996—97, bd. trustees 1994—97, 1997—2000). Avocations: travel, running, hiking, bicycling. Office: Bartek Law Office Ste E 2300 E Market St Akron OH 44312

BARTEL, DAVID, biology professor, researcher; PhD, Harvard U., 1993. Whitehead fellow Whitehead Inst., 1994, assoc. mem., 1996, current mem.; asst. prof. biology MIT, 1996, prof. biology; investigator Howard Hughes Med. Inst. Contbr. articles to profl. jours. Named Searle Scholar, 1997; recipient Newcomb Cleveland prize, AAAS, 2002, Molecular Biology award, NAS, 2005, Institut de France's Louis-D. prize, 2005. Achievements include made major contributions to the discovery and understanding of microRNAs, small RNS molecules that are important in gene regulation; created ribozyme (RNA enzyme) that synthesizes pieces of RNA, bolstering the "RNA world" theory; designed RNA sequence that can fold into either of two ribozymes; aided early work in RNAi, including moving the technique to mammalian cells. Office: Whitehead Inst Nine Cambridge Center Room WI 601B Cambridge MA 02142-1479 Office Phone: 617-258-5287. E-mail: dbartel@wi.mit.edu.*

BARTELL, ANGELA GINA BALDI, judge; b. Milw., Jan. 25, 1946; d. John Batiste and Marie Alma (Rank) Baldi; m. Jeffrey Bruce Bartell, Aug. 31, 1968; children: Jessica Marie, Carey Laurel, Chad Gerald, Dana Joyce, Nicholas John. BA, U. Wis., 1969, JD, 1971. Bar: Wis. 1972, U.S. Dist. Ct. (we. dist.) Wis. 1972. Intern Wis. Dept. Justice, Madison, 1970; law clk. to Hon. James E. Doyle U.S. Dist. Ct. (we. dist.) Wis., Madison, 1971-72; assoc., then ptnr. LaFollette Sinykin Law Firm, Madison, 1973-78; county judge Dane County Ct., Madison, 1978-79; chief judge Wis. Fifth Jud. Dist., 1982-88; cir. judge Dane County Cir. Ct., Madison, 1979—. Mem. Professionalism Commn., Madison, 1990-93; mem. Legal Edn. Commn., 1994-95; mem. adv. bd. Scan Child Abuse Prevention Project, Madison, 1988-90; assoc. dean Wis. Jud. Coll., 1999—. Jud. editor Wisconsin Judician Benchbooks, 3 vols., 1980-92 (Supreme Ct. award 1992), Wisconsin Jury Handbook, 1983; contbr.: State Bar Civil Forms Manual, 1992-99, Wisconsin Jury Instructions-Criminal, 1992-2002. Pres. Young Lawyers divsn. Wis. State Bar, Madision, 1974; bd. dirs. Dane County United Way, 1995-2001, chair bd., 2000-01. Fellow: Am. Bar Found.; mem.: Nat. Assn. Women Judges, Am. Law Inst., Rotary Club Madison (pres. 2003—04), Phi Beta Kappa. Office: Dane County Cir Ct 210 Martin Luther King Jr Blvd Madison WI 53709-0002 Office Phone: 608-266-4460.

BARTELL, ERNEST, economist, educator, priest; b. Chgo., Jan. 22, 1932; PhB, U. Notre Dame, 1953; AM, U. Chgo., 1954; MA, Coll. Holy Cross, 1961; PhD, Princeton U., 1966; LLD (hon.), China Acad., Taipei, Taiwan, 1975, St. Joseph's Coll., 1983, King's Coll., 1984, Stonehill Coll., 1992. Ordained priest Roman Cath. Ch., 1961. Instr. econs. Princeton (N.J.) U., 1965-66; asst. prof. econs. U. Notre Dame, Ind., 1966-68, assoc. prof., 1968-71, chmn. dept. econs., 1968-71, dir. Ctr. Study of Man in Contemporary Soc., 1969-71, prof. econs., 1981—2003, prof. emeritus, 2003—; exec. dir. Helen Kellogg Inst. Internat. Studies, Ind., 1981—97, fellow, 1997—; pres. Stonehill Coll., North Easton, Mass., 1971-77; dir. Fund for Improvement Post Secondary Edn. U.S. Dept. Health, Edn. and Welfare, Washington, 1977-79; dir. Project 80 Assn. Cath. Colls. and Univs., Washington, 1979-80; overseas mission coord. Priests of Holy Cross, Ind. Province, 1980-84, assoc. dir. Holy Cross Mission Ctr., 1984-95; asst. to pastor St. Anthony Ch., Ft. Lauderdale, Fla., 1993—2003. Active Inst. East-West Securities Studies Working Group on Sources in Instability, 1989-90, Internat. Ctr. Devel. Policy Commn. on U.S.-Soviet Rels., 1988-89, Overseas Devel. Coun., 1988-2000, The Bretton Woods Com., 1992-2002; mem. policy planning commn. Nat. Inst. Ind. Colls. and Univs., 1982-85; bd. dirs. Ctr. for Health Promotion, Internat. Life Scis. Inst.; hon. trustee Stonehill Coll., 2002—. Author: Costs and Benefits of Catholic Elementary and Secondary schools, 1969; co-editor: Business and Democracy in Latin America, 1995, The Child in Latin America, 2000; contbr. articles to profl. jours. Bd. regents U. Portland, Oreg., 1984-2004; bd. dirs. Missionary Vehicle Assn. Am., 1981-88, Big Bros. and Big Sisters Am., 1978-80, Brockton Community Housing Corp., 1974-77, The Brighter Day, 1974-77, Brockton Hosp., 1973-77, King's Coll., Wilkes-Barre, Pa., 1969-82; bd. trustees Emmanuel Coll., 1977-78, U. Notre Dame, 1974-2002, bd. fellows, 1974-2002; bd. trustees Regis Coll., 2002—; adv. bd. Brockton Art Ctr., 1974-77; exec. com. Opera New Eng., 1977. Recipient Fenwick Alumni Recognition award, 1974; named to Fenwick Hall of Fame, 1990; faculty fellow Kellogg Inst., 1997—. Fellow Soc. Values in Higher Edn.; mem. Am. Econ. Assn., Am. Assn. Higher Edn., Nat. Cath. Ednl. Assn. (chmn. govtl. rels. com. 1976-77, vice chmn. exec. com. 1976-77, chmn. mgmt. and planning com. 1974-76), Assn. Soc. Econs., Latin Am. Studies Assn., Young Pres. Orgn. (sec. 1974-77), Delta Mu Delta (hon.). Home: 211 Corby Hall Notre Dame IN 46556-5680 Office: U Notre Dame Kellogg Inst 211 Hesburgh Ctr Notre Dame IN 46556-5677 Business E-Mail: ebartell@nd.edu.

BARTELL, HARRY ROBERT, JR., retired finance educator, consultant; b. St. Louis, Jan. 25, 1935; s. Harry Robert and Jean Suzanne (Hyman) B.; m. Anita Marie Brown, Aug. 28, 1958 (div.); children: H. Robert III, Gregory Brent, Suzanne Louise, Edith Simms; m. Nancy Owens Bartell, Sept. 28, 1988. MBA, Washington U., 1958; PhD, Columbia U., 1963. Cert. fin. examiner. Commr. banks and trust cos. State of Ill., Springfield, 1971-74; pres., CEO, Fed. Home Loan Bank, Chgo., 1974-80, Mortgage Asset Mgmt. Assocs., Sausalito, Calif., 1981-85; chmn., CEO, PMI Mortgage Ins. Group, San Francisco, 1980-81, San Jacinto Savings Bank, Houston, 1985-89; prof. fin. San Francisco State U., 1982-85; chair banking, prof. fin. Ea. Tenn. State U., Johnson City, 1989—99. Cons. US AID, numerous others, Washington, 1990—. Author: Community Bank Membership in the Federal Home Loan Bank System, 1991; co-author: Financial Planning and Control, 1995. Mem. Fin. Mgmt. Assn., Soc. Fin. Examiners (cert.), Midwest Fin. Assn. (v.p., bd. dirs. 1980-82). Methodist. Avocation: sailing. Home: 9794 Martingham Cir # 11 Saint Michaels MD 21663 Personal E-mail: bartellh@aol.com.

BARTELL, LAWRENCE SIMS, chemist, educator; b. Ann Arbor, Mich., Feb. 23, 1923; s. Floyd Earl and Lawrence (Sims) B.; m. Joy Hilda Keer, Aug. 16, 1952; 1 son, Michael Keer. BS, U. Mich., 1944, MS, 1947, PhD, 1951. Research asst. Manhattan project U. Chgo., 1944-45; mem. faculty Iowa State U., 1953-65, prof. chemistry, 1959-65, U. Mich., 1965—, Philip J. Elving prof. chemistry, 1987-94, prof. emeritus, 1994—. Vis. prof. Moscow State U., 1972, U. Paris XI, Orsay, France, 1973, U. Tex., 1978, 86; cons. Gillette Co., Chgo., 1956-62, Mobil Oil Corp., Paulsboro, NJ, 1960-84; mem. commn. on electron diffraction Internat. Union Crystallography, 1966-75 Assoc. editor: Jour. Chem. Physics, 1963-66; mem. editorial bd.: Jour. Computational Chemistry, 1979-90, Chem. Physics Letters, 1981-84. Served with USNR, 1945. Recipient Disting. Faculty Achievement award U. Mich., 1981, Disting. Faculty award Mich. Assn. Governing Bds., 1982, Creativity award NSF, 1982, Metz-Stark award, 2004. Mem. Am. Chem. Soc. (petroleum rsch. fund adv. bd. 1970-73), Am. Phys. Soc. (chmn. divsn. chem. physics 1977-78), Am. Crystallographic Assn., AAAS, Phi Beta Kappa, Sigma Xi, Phi Kappa Phi, Phi Lambda Upsilon, Alpha Chi Sigma. Home: 381 Riverview Dr Ann Arbor MI 48104-1847 Office Phone: 734-764-7375. Business E-Mail: lbart@umich.edu.

BARTELS, BRUCE MICHAEL, health facility administrator; b. Chgo., Oct. 13, 1946; s. John Phillip Frederick and Margaret Florine (Michael) B.; children: Sarah, Jennifer, Rebecca. BA, U. Wis., 1969; MBA, U. Chgo., 1975. Adminstrv. asst. U. Chgo. Hosp., 1975-77; asst. adminstr. Meth. Hosp., Indpls., 1977-81; exec. v.p. Med. Ctr. Hosp. Vt., Burlington, 1981-88; pres. York (Pa.) Hosp. and Found., 1988-95, York Health Sys., 1995-99, WellSpan Health, York, 1999—. Contbr. articles to profl. jours. Bd. dirs. York County chpt. YMCA, York, 1989-98, chmn., 1994-96; bd. dirs. ARC, 1990-96, 2003—, United Way, 1991-96, WITF, Inc., Ctrl. Pa. Pub. Broadcasting, 1994-2002, chmn., 1999-2001; bd. dirs. Pa. Trauma Systems Found., Mechanicsburg, 1990-2003, chmn., 1997-99; bd. dirs. Novation, Inc., 2003—, Alliance Ind. Acad. Med. Ctrs., 2005—. With U.S. Army, Korea. Fellow Am. Coll. Healthcare Execs. (membership com. 1990-93); mem. Am. Hosp. Assn., Hosp. Assn. Pa. (bd. dirs., chmn.), York C. of C., U. Chgo. Health Adminstrn. Alumni Assn. (exec. com. 1991-95), Rotary. Avocations: reading, running, travel. Office: WellSpan Health 45 Monument Dr Ste 200 York PA 17403-3676 Office Phone: 717-851-2121. Business E-Mail: bbartels@wellspan.org.

BARTELS, JEAN ELLEN, nursing educator; b. Two Rivers, Wis., July 15, 1949; m. Terry D. Bartels, Aug. 14, 1971; children: Justin Dean, Ashlee Jill. Diploma, Columbia Hosp. Sch. Nursing, 1970; BSN with honors, Alverno Coll., 1981; MSN, Marquette U., 1983; PhD in Nursing, U. Wis., 1990. Staff nurse ICU Columbia Hosp., Milw., 1970-76; prof. nursing Alverno Coll., Milw., 1983-99, dean nursing, 1990-99; chair Sch. Nursing Ga. So. U., Statesboro, 1999—. Asst. edn. editor Jour. Profl. Nursing; contbr. articles to profl. jours. Mem. ANA, AACN (pres.), Internat. Soc. for Sci. Study Subjectivity, Am. Assn. Collegiate Schs. Nursing, Am. Ednl. Rsch. Assn., Am. Assn. Higher Edn., Sigma Theta Tau, Phi Kappa Phi. Home: 912 Brittany Ln Statesboro GA 30461-4499 Office: Ga So U PO Box 8158 Statesboro GA 30460-1000 Business E-Mail: jbartels@georgiasouthern.edu.

BARTELS, ROBERT EDWIN, aerospace engineer; b. Des Moines, May 24, 1955; s. Everett M. and Iola J. (Van Wyck) B. BS, Iowa State U., 1977; MDiv cum laude, N.W. Baptist Sem., Tacoma, Wash., 1983; MS, Iowa State U., 1992, PhD, 1994. Sr. engr. Boeing Comml. Airplane Co., Seattle, 1984—87; teaching asst. Iowa State U., Ames, 1987—92, grad. rsch. fellow NASA, 1992—94; NRC rsch. assoc. NASA Langley Rsch. Ctr., Hampton, Va., 1994—97, aerospace engr., 1997—2003, sr. rsch. engr., 2003—. Adj. prof. Tidewater C.C., 1998. Bd. dirs., treas. Second Wind Contemporary Dance Co., 1996-98. Recipient Grad. Student Tchg. Excellence award Iowa State U., 1991. Mem. AIAA (sr.), ASME, Phi Kappa Phi. Office: Nasa Langley Rsch Ctr Hampton VA 23681-0001

BARTELS, STANLEY LEONARD, investment banker; b. N.Y.C., Sept. 1, 1927; s. Abraham and Anna (Schultz) B.; m. Linda Lauretz; children: Jonathan Scott, Nancy Merrill, Diane Brooke, Elizabeth Cara. BS, NYU, 1954, MBA, 1956; grad., N.Y. State Maritime Acad., 1947. Examiner Mfrs. Hanover Bank, N.Y.C., 1948-50; security analyst Standard & Poor's Corp., N.Y.C., 1950-53; sr. financial analyst internat. div. Ford Motor Co., N.Y.C., 1953-56; asst. treas. W.R. Grace, Inc., N.Y.C., 1956-57; v.p. Tex. McCrary, Inc.; also controller, asst. to pres. N.Y.C., 1957-60; gen. partner, mem. mgmt. com., mem. N.Y. Stock Exchange J.R. Williston & Beane, N.Y.C., 1960-63; pres., dir. Electrocopy Corp., 1963-66; sr. v.p., dir. Shaskan & Co., Inc.; mem. N.Y. Stock Exchange, 1966-73; pres. J.D. Winer & Co., Inc.; mem. N.Y. Stock Exchange, 1973-74; v.p. L.M. Rosenthal & Co., Inc.; mem. N.Y. Stock Exchange, 1974-75; sr. v.p. Weinrich Zitzmann Whitehead, St. Louis, 1981-82, Laidlaw Adams & Peck, Inc., N.Y.C., 1982-84; exec. v.p., founding dir. Yorke McCarter Owen & Bartels, Inc., N.Y.C., 1984-91; exec. v.p. Hampshire Securities Corp., N.Y.C., 1991-94, Coleman and Co. Securities, Inc., 1995-2000; sr. v.p. Auerbach, Pollak & Richardson, Inc., 2000—. Trustee, chair fin. com. Maritime Industry Mus. N.Y. State Maritime Coll., 1994—. Served to lt. comdr. USNR. Mem. Securities Industry Assn. (mem. nat. investment banking com. 1993-96), N.Y. Soc. Security Analysts, Bond Club of N.Y., Naval Order of the U.S., Phi Alpha Kappa. Clubs: Univ. of N.Y. Home: Farley Rd Short Hills NJ 07078 *Only those projects that are of a beneficial nature to society have the tendency to survive.*

BARTELS, URSULA BRENNAN, lawyer; b. Abington, Pa., Aug. 22, 1957; life ptnr. Laura Zucker; children: Benjamin, Julia. AB, Bryn Mawr Coll., 1979; JD, U. Va., 1983. Bar: Pa. 1983, Conn. 2002. Assoc. Stradley, Ronon, Stevens & Young, Phila., 1983-88; assoc. gen. counsel, v.p. SmithKline Beecham, Phila., 1988-99; v.p., gen. counsel, sec. Boehringer Ingelheim Corp., Ridgefield, Conn., 1999—2004; v.p., gen. counsel Chiron Corp., Emeryville, Calif., 2004—. Bd. trustees Food & Drug Law Inst., Washington, 1996-99, mem. fin. & audit com. Mem.: ABA, Pa. Bar Assn., Phila. Bar Assn. Office: Chiron Corp 4560 Horton St Emeryville CA 94608

BARTER, MARY F., academic administrator; BA, U. Minn., 1964; MS, U. Wis., Milw., 1969, PhD, 1975. Supt. Three Village Cen. Sch. Dist., L.I., NY, 1992—99, Durango (Colo.) Sch. Dist. 9-R, 1999—. Recipient Disting. Supt. and Outstanding Supt. awards, Suffolk County and N.Y. Coun. Sch. Supts. Mem.: Horace Mann League, N.Y. Assn. for Women in Adminstrn. (bd. dirs.), Wis. Elem. Kindergarten Nursery Educators (pres.), N.Y. Coun. Sch. Supts. (pres.), Am. Assn. Sch. Adminstrs. (exec. com., women adminstrs. adv. com., fed. policy and legis. com., exec. dir.'s adv. com., del. assembly). Office: Durango Sch Dist 9-R 201 E 12th St Durango CO 81301

BARTFELD, DANIEL D., lawyer; b. Washington, D.C., 1968; BA, Univ. Mich., 1990; JD, George Washington Univ., 1993. Bar: N.Y. 1994. Ptnr. Global Project Fin. Dept. & mem. recruiting com. Milbank Tweed Hadley & McCloy, N.Y.C. Office: Milbank Tweed Hadley & McCloy 1 Chase Manhattan Plz New York NY 10005-1413 Office Phone: 212-530-5185. Office Fax: 212-530-5219. Business E-Mail: dbartfeld@milbank.com.

BARTGES, HANS, investment company executive; Pres. International Nederlanden, N.Y.C., BHF German Bank, N.Y.C. Office: BHF Bank Inc 590 Madison Ave Fl 28 New York NY 10022-2524

BARTH, DAVID KECK, wholesale distribution executive, consultant; b. Springfield, Ill., Dec. 7, 1943; s. David Kleck and Edna Margaret (Keck) B.; m. Dian Oldemeyer, Nov. 21, 1970; children— David, Michael, John. BA cum laude, Knox Coll., Galesburg, Ill., 1965; MBA, U. Calif., Berkeley, 1971. With data processing div. IBM Corp., Chgo., 1966; with No. Trust Co., Chgo., 1971-72; mgr. treasury ops., then treas. fin. services group Borg-Warner Corp., Chgo., 1972-79; treas. W.W. Grainger, Inc., Skokie, Ill., 1979-83, v.p., 1984-90; pres. Barth Smith Co., 1991—2001. Mem. faculty Lake Forest (Ill.) Grad. Sch. Mgmt., 1994—; bd. dirs. Indsl. Distbn. Group Inc., Atlanta. Served to lt. USNR, 1966-69. Mem. Econ. Club Chgo., Beta Gamma Sigma, Phi Delta Theta. Lutheran. Personal E-mail: davidbarth@sbcglobal.net.

BARTH, ELMER ERNEST, manufacturing executive; b. Phila., May 15, 1922; s. Paul Adolph and Anna (Miller) B.; m. Ruth Bradstreet Stone, Sept. 18, 1943 (dec. Aug. 1990); 1 dau., Rebecca Barth Gallucci; m. Barbara E. Burbridge, Jan. 25, 1992. Ed., Bentley Sch. Accounting, 1947-51; BBA, Northeastern U., 1956. Asst. treas. Hayward Hosiery Co., Ipswich, Mass., 1945-56; v.p. ops. Rockbestos Co.; Mem. Marmon Group, New Haven, 1956-86; sec., treas., dir. Applied Data, Inc., North Haven, 1961-97. Trustee Ipswich Savs. Bank, 1947-56 Bd. govs., vice chmn. fin. com. Children's Center, Hamden, Conn., 1965-68. Served with USNR, 1942-45. Recipient Charles D. Scott Disting. Career award New Eng. Wire & Cable Club. Mem.: Branford Yacht (commodore 1976), Ipswich Outboard, Inc. (sec., bd. dirs. Commodore 1988-89), Masons (excellent high priest Ipswich-Ferson chpt. 2003—04). Home: 1 Riverside Dr Ipswich MA 01938-2427 E-mail: ElmereBarth@aol.com.

BARTH, FRANCES, artist; b. N.Y.C., July 31, 1946; BFA, Hunter Coll., 1968, MA, 1970. Instr. Princeton U., 1975—79, Sarah Lawrence Coll., Bronxville, NY, 1979—85; prof. Yale U., New Haven, 1986—2004; dir. Mt. Royal Sch. of Art, Md. Inst. Coll. of Art, 2004—. One-woman shows include, N.Y.C., 1974—, Jan Cicero Gallery, Chgo., 1981, 1985, U. Mass. Amherst, 1994, E.M. Donahue Gallery, N.Y.C., 1994, 1997, 2000, Millersville Coll., Pa., 1995, Marcia Wood Gallery, Atlanta, 1998, 2001, 2002, Moravian Coll., Pa., 1999, Donahue Sosinski, N.Y.C., 2000, Dartmouth Coll., N.H., 2005, exhibited in group shows at Moore Coll. Art, 1970, Whitney Mus. Am. Art, N.Y.C., 1972—73, Houston Mus. Contemporary Art, 1972, Corcoran Gallery Art, Washington, Bard Coll., Annandale-on-Hudson, N.Y.C., 1973, Trenton

State Coll., 1974, Princeton U. Art Mus., 1975, High Mus. Art, Atlanta, 1976, Bennington Coll., 1976, San Francisco Art Inst., 1978, U. Pa., 1978, MIT, 1978, Jan Cicero, CHI, 1995, Moravia Coll., Pa., 1999, William Patterson Coll., Wayne, N.J., 1979, NYU, 1979, Va. Commonwealth U., Richmond, 1980, Sarah Lawrence Coll., 1981, Mus. Modern Art, 1981, Cleve. Mus. Art, 1983, Indpls. Mus., 1984, 1985, Princeton U., 1985, Hunter Coll., 1986, Yale U., 1987, Bennington Coll., 1991, Am. Acad. Arts and Letters, 1988 (Purchase award, 2004), Met. Mus. Art, 1990, Andre Emmerich Gallery, 1991, La Viglie, Nimes, France, 1995, Charles Cowles Gallery, N.Y.C., 1996, Am. Acad. Arts and Letters, 1999, 2004, Tucson Mus. Art, 2003, Am. Acad. Arts and Letters, 2004, Represented in permanent collections New 20th Century Wing, Met. Mus. Art, N.Y.C., Mus. Modern Art, Akron Art Inst., Albright-Knox Gallery, Am. Can Co., Greenwich, Conn., Amerada Hess Corp., N.Y.C., Chase Manhattan Bank, Cornell U., IBM Corp., N.Y.C., Mobil Oil Corp., Prudential Inst. Co., N.J., Whitney Mus. Am. Art, Lehman Bros., N.Y.C. and Chgo., Isham, Lincoln & Beale, Chgo., Security Pacific Nat. Bank, L.A., Swiss Bank Corp., N.Y.C., Cameron Iron Works, Houston, Mus. Modern Art, N.Y.C., Paul Haim Found., Paris, Humana, Inc., Louisville, Coudert Bros., N.Y.C., Dallas Mus. Art, Tucson (Ariz.) Art Mus. Grantee Creative Artists Pub. Svc., 1973, NEA, 1974, 82, N.J. State Coun. on Arts, 1987, Adolph and Esther Gottlieb Ind. Support, 1993; John Guggenheim fellow, 1977; recipient Joan Mitchell Found. award, 1995.

BARTH, JOHN M., manufacturing executive; With Johnson Controls, Inc., Milw., 1969—, pres., COO, 1997—2002, dir., 1997, pres., CEO, 2002—, chmn. bd. dirs., 2004. Office: Johnson Controls Inc 5757 N Green Bay Ave Milwaukee WI 53209-4408 Office Phone: 414-524-1200. Office Fax: 414-524-2077.

BARTH, JOHN ROBERT, language educator, priest; b. Buffalo, Feb. 23, 1931; s. Philip C. and Mary K. (Eustace) B. AB, Bellarmine Coll., 1954, PhL, 1955; MA, Fordham U., 1956; STB, Woodstock Coll., 1961, STL, 1962; PhD, Harvard U., 1967. Joined Soc. of Jesus, Roman Cath. Ch., 1948; tchr. English, French, Latin Canisius H.S., Buffalo, 1955-58; asst. prof. English Canisius Coll., Buffalo, 1967-70, Harvard U., Cambridge, Mass., 1970-74; assoc. prof. English U. Mo.-Columbia, 1974-77, prof., 1977-79, Catherine Paine Middlebush prof. English, 1979-82, prof. English, chmn. dept., 1980-83, prof. English, 1983-85, 1986-88; Thomas I. Gasson prof. English Boston Coll., 1985-86, dean Coll. Arts and Scis., 1988-99, James P. McIntyre prof. English, 1999—. Author: Coleridge and Christian Doctrine, 1969, 2d edit., 1987, The Symbolic Imagination: Coleridge and the Romantic Tradition, 1977, 2d edit., 2000 (Book of Yr. award, Conf. on Christianity and Lit. 1977), Coleridge and the Power of Love, 1988 (U. Mo. Curators Publ. award 1989), Romanticism and Transcendence: Wordsworth, Coleridge, and the Religious Imagination, 2003; editor: Religious Perspectives in Faulkner's Fiction, 1972, The Fountain Light: Studies in Romanticism and Religion, 2002; co-editor: Marginalia in Collected Works of Samuel Taylor Coleridge, 1984—92, Coleridge, Keats and the Imagination: Romanticism and Adam's Dream, 1990; mem. bd. advisors Wordsworth Circle, Phila., 1976—; mem. editl. bd. cons. Thought, 1980-93, mem. adv. bd. Studies in Romanticism, 1981—, European Romantic Rev., 1990—, Renascence, 1993—; mem. editl. adv. bd. Christianity and Literature, 1989—; mem. editl. planning bd. Religion and the Arts, 1996—. Trustee St. Louis U., 1974-79, St. Peter's Coll., 1985-91, Coll. of the Holy Cross, 1989-93, Canisius Coll., 1992-98. Recipient Howard Mumford Jones prize Harvard U., 1967; Dexter fellow, 1967; NEH summer grantee, 1969; Am. Coun. Learned Socs. grantee, 1970; Harvard U. rsch. grantee, 1973. Mem. AAUP, Conf. on Christianity and Lit. (dir. 1980-83), MLA (del. assembly 1979-83, exec. com. romantic divsn. 1975-79, exec. com. religious approaches 1983-87), N.Am. Soc. Study Romanticism, Wordsworth-Coleridge Assn. (v.p. 1978, pres. 1979), Keats-Shelley Assn., Friends of Coleridge. Address: St Mary's Hall Boston College Chestnut Hill MA 02467 Office: Boston Coll Dept English 24 Quincy Rd Chestnut Hill MA 02467-3937 Business E-Mail: robert.barth@bc.edu.

BARTH, JOHN SIMMONS, writer, educator; b. Cambridge, Md., May 27, 1930; s. John Jacob and Georgia (Simmons) B.; m. Harriette Anne Strickland, Jan. 11, 1950 (div. 1969); children: Christine Anne, John Strickland, Daniel Stephen; m. Shelly I. Rosenberg, Dec. 27, 1970. BA, Johns Hopkins U., 1951, MA, 1952; LittD (hon.), Univ. Md., 1969; DHL (hon.), Pa. State U., 1996. Instr. English Pa. State U., 1953-56, asst. prof. English, 1957-60, assoc. prof. English, 1960-65; prof. English SUNY, Buffalo, 1965-73; prof. creative writing Johns Hopkins U., Balt., 1973-91, prof. emeritus creative writing, 1991—. Author: The Floating Opera, 1956 (Nat. Book award nomination 1956), The End of the Road, 1958, The Sot-Weed Factor, 1960, Giles Goat-Boy, 1966, Lost in the Funhouse, 1968 (Nat. Book award nomination 1968), Chimera, 1972 (Nat. Book award 1973), Letters, 1979, Sabbatical: A Romance, 1982, The Literature of Exhaustion, and The Literature of Replenishment, 1982, The Friday Book: Essays and Other Nonfiction, 1984, Don't Count on It: A Note on the Number of the 1001 Nights, 1984, The Tidewater Tales: A Novel, 1987, The Last Voyage of Somebody the Sailor, 1991, Once Upon a Time: A Floating Opera, 1994, Further Fridays: Essays, Lectures, and Other Non-fiction, 1984-94, 1995, On with the Story, 1996, Coming Soon!!!, 2001, The Book of Ten Nights and a Night, 2004, Where Three Roads Meet, 2004. Recipient Brandeis Univ. Creative Arts award, 1965, F. Scott Fitzgerald award, 1997, PEN/Malamud award, 1998, Lifetime Achievement award Lannan Found., 1998, Lifetime Achievement in Letters award Enoch Pratt Soc., 1999; Rockefeller Found. grantee, 1965-66, Nat. Inst. Arts and Letters grantee, 1966. Mem. AAAL, Am. Acad. Arts and Scis. Office: Writing Seminars Johns Hopkins U Baltimore MD 21218

BARTH, KARL LUTHER, retired seminary president; b. Milw., Nov. 7, 1924; s. G. Christian and Louise A. (Schneemann) B.; m. Jean L. Kelly, June 8, 1947; children: Linda, Karl, Laurel, Kurt, Lisa. BA, Concordia Sem., 1945, M.Div., 1947; D.D. (hon.), Concordia Theol. Sem., 1975. Ordained to minstry, Lutheran Ch., 1947. Asst. pastor First English Lutheran Ch., New Orleans, 1947-50; pastor Trinity Evan. Lutheran Ch., Centralia, Ill., 1950-52, St. Paul's Lutheran Ch., West Allis, Wis., 1956-70; pres. So. Wis. Dist. Luth. Ch. Mo. Synod, Milw., 1970-82, bd. for mission svcs., 1982-90, bd. dirs., 1992—2004; pres. Concordia Sem., St. Louis, 1982-90. Exec. dir. 150th Anniversary Luth. Ch. Mo. Synod. Contbr. articles to profl. jours. Vice pres. So. Wis. dist. Lutheran Ch., Mo. Synod, 1966-70; chmn. Com. on Theology and Ch. Relations, St. Louis, 1974-82; denominational rep. Div. Theol. Studies Lutheran Council U.S.A., N.Y.C., 1975-81; mem. adv. bd. Wis. Citizens Concerned for Life, 1976-82. Mem. Badger Assn. of the Blind (adv. coun. 2000—03), Luth. Blind MIssion Soc. (bd. dirs. 2004—). Republican. Home: Apt 208 8220 Harwood Ave Milwaukee WI 53213

BARTH, MICHAEL CARL, economist; b. Newark, Apr. 3, 1941; s. Abe and Frances (Keller) B.; m. Marilyn Levy, Dec. 11, 1966; children: Christopher Jay, Karen Barth Simon. BA, Harpur Coll., Binghamton, N.Y., 1962; MA, U. Ill., Champaign, 1963; PhD, CUNY, 1971. Rsch. assoc. CCNY Rsch. Found., N.Y.C., 1965-67; lectr. econs. CCNY, 1966-68; economist Pres's. Commn. on Income Maintenance, Washington, 1968-69, Office Econ. Opportunity, Washington, 1969-73; dir. income sec. policy/analysis U.S. Dept. HEW, Washington, 1973-75; vis. assoc. prof. econs. U. Wis., Madison, 1975-76; dep. asst. sec. U.S. Dept. HHS, Washington, 1976-80; prin. ICF Inc., Washington, 1980-87, sr. v.p., 1987—; pres. ICF Info. Tech. Inc., Washington, 1992-95; exec. v.p. ICF Cons., Fairfax, Va., 1995—. Bd. dirs. ICF Info. Tech., Inc, ICF Resources. Author: (with G. Carcagno and J. Palmer) Toward an Effective Income Support System: Problems, Prospects and Choices, 1974; editor: Greenhouse Effect and Sea Level Rise, 1984 contbr. articles to profl. jours. Recipient Sec.'s Spl. citation HEW, 1975, Sec.'s Outstanding Achievement award, 1977 Mem. Am. Econ. Assn., Am. Evaluation Assn. Home: 3818 Military Rd NW Washington DC 20015-2704 Office: ICF Cons 9300 Lee Hwy Fairfax VA 22031-1207 Office Phone: 703-934-3090. Business E-Mail: mbarth@icfconsulting.com.

BARTH, ROBERT HENRY, nephrologist, educator; b. Newark, Oct. 31, 1944; s. Robert Henry and Wilma Elizabeth (Van Ness) B.; m. Elettra Nerbosi, May 10, 1976. BA in Chemistry, Cornell U., 1967; MD cum laude, U. Bologna, Italy, 1976. Diplomate Am. Bd. Internal Medicine, Am. Bd. Nephrology. Chemist Sandoz, Inc., Hanover, Basel, N.J., Switzerland, 1967-68, 70, Internat. Flavors and Fragrances, Union Beach, N.J., 1968-69; resident Berkshire Med. Ctr., Pittsfield, Mass., 1976-80; fellow, rsch. assoc. Rogosin Kidney Ctr. N.Y. Hosp.-Cornell U. Med. Ctr., 1980-83; assoc. dir. Baumritter Kidney Ctr. Albert Einstein Coll. Medicine, Bronx, N.Y., 1983-86; physician, chief nephrology, chief dialysis VA N.Y. Harbor Healthcare Sys., Bklyn., 1986—. Instr., asst. prof. Albert Einstein Coll. Medicine, Bronx, 1983-86, attending physician, 1983-86; asst. prof., assoc. prof. SUNY Health Sci. Ctr., Bklyn., 1986—; attending physician Bronx Mcpl. Hosp. Ctr., 1983-86. Contbr. chpts. in books and articles to profl. jours.; software program developer. Pres. Bklyn. VA Med. Ctr. Med. Soc., 1996—. Mem. Am. Soc. for Artificial Internal Organs (bd. trustees 1996-2000, program chmn. 1998, ann. meeting), Am. Soc. Nephrology (abstract reviewer 1993 ann. meeting session chmn.), Internat. Soc. Nephrology, Nat. Kidney Found. (exec. bd., coun. on Dialysis 1990-94), N.Y. Soc. Nephrology, Physicians for Nat. Health Program, Adirondack Mountain Club. Avocations: hiking, skiing, photography, jazz. Home: 392 11th St Brooklyn NY 11215 Office: VA Med Ctr 800 Poly Pl Brooklyn NY 11209-7104 Office Phone: 718-630-3752. Personal E-mail: ebarth@ix.netcom.com. Business E-Mail: robert.barth@med.va.gov. E-mail: rhbarth@verizon.net.

BARTH, ROLF FREDERICK, pathologist, educator; b. N.Y.C., Apr. 4, 1937; s. Rolf L. and Josephine Barth; m. Christine Ferguson, Oct. 30, 1965; children: Suzanna, Alison, Rolf, Christopher. AB, Cornell U., 1959; MD, Columbia U., 1964. Diplomate Am. Bd. Pathology. Surg. intern Columbia-Presbyn. Med. Ctr., N.Y.C., 1964-65; postdoctoral fellow Karolinska Inst., Stockholm, 1965-66; rsch. assoc. Nat. Inst. Allergy and Infectious Diseases, NIH, Bethesda, Md., 1966-68; resident pathology br. Nat. Cancer Inst., 1966-68, Nat. Inst. Health, 1968-70; Prof. dept. pathology and oncology U. Kans. Med. Ctr., Kansas City, 1970-77; clin. prof. dept. pathology Med. Coll. Wis. and U. Wis., Madison, 1977-79; prof. dept. pathology Ohio State U., Columbus, 1979—. Contbr. articles to profl. jours. Sr. asst. surgeon USPHS, 1966-70, inactive Res., 1970-2002. Grantee NIH. Mem. Am. Assn. Exptl. Pathology, Am. Assn. Immunologists, Am. Assn. Cancer Rsch., Internat. Soc. for Neutron Capture Therapy, Sigma Xi, Phi Kappa Phi. Office: Ohio State U Dept Pathology 165 Hamilton Hall 1645 Neil Ave Columbus OH 43210-1218 Office Phone: 614-292-2177. Business E-Mail: barth.1@osu.edu.

BARTH, UTA, artist, educator; b. Berlin, Jan. 29, 1958; BA, U. Calif., Davis, 1982; MFA, UCLA, 1985. From asst. prof. to assoc. prof. art dept. U. Calif., Riverside, 1990—. One-woman shows include Galleria by the Water, L.A., 1985, Frederick S. Wight Gallery, L.A., 1985, Addison Gallery of Am. Art, Andover, Mass., 1990, Howard Yezersky Gallery, Boston, 1990, Rochester (N.Y.) Inst. Tech., 1993, Calif. Mus. Photography, Riverside, 1993, Wooster Gardens, N.Y.C., 1994, Mus. Contemporary Art, L.A., 1995, ACME, Santa Monica, Calif., 1995, 98, Tanya Bonakdar Gallery, N.Y.C., 1996, London Projects, London, 1996, 98, S.L. Simpson Gallery, Toronto, Ont., Can., 1996, Mus. Contemporary Art, Chgo., 1997, Andrehn-Schiptjenko, Stockholm, 1997, 99, Tanya Bonakdar Gallery, N.Y., 1998, Lawing, Houston, 1998, Rio Hondo Coll. Art Gallery, Whittier, Caifl., 1998, Bonakdar Jancou Gallery, N.Y., 1998, 99, Rena Branston Gallery, San Francisco, 1999, ACME, L.A., 1999, Galerie Camargo Vilaça, São Paulo, 1999, Lannan Found., Santa Fe, N. Mex., 1999, Henry Art Gallery, Seattle, Washington, 2000, Kunstmuseum Wolfsburg, Germany, 2000; group shows include 56th Ann. Crocker Kingsly Exhbn., Crocker Art Mus., Sacramento, Calif., 1982, Five Photographers, Joseph Dee Mus. of Photography, San Francisco, Calif., 1982, Proof and Perjury, L.A. Inst. Contemporary Art, 1986, Artist Exbhn., Beverly Hills, 1987, Thick and Thin-Photgraphically Inspired Painting, Fahey/Klein Gallery, L.A., 1989, Spirit of Our Time, Contemporary Arts Forum, Santa Barbara, Calif., 1990, Abstraction in the 90's, Jan Kesner Gallery, L.A., 1992, Tom Solomon's Garage, L.A., 1994, Long Beach (Calif.) Mus. Art, 1994, Mus. De Beyard, Netherlands, 1994, L.A. County Mus. Art, 1994, San Bernardino County Mus., 1994, The New Mus., N.Y.C., 1995, Mus. Modern Art, N.Y.C., 1995, Rooseum-Ctr. for Contemporary Art, Malmo, Sweden, 1996, Magasin 3 Stockholm Konsthall, 1996, Wexner Ctr. for Art, Columbus, Ohio, 1997, Mus. Contemporary Art, Miami, 1997, Whitney Mus. Art, N.Y.C., 1997, 98, Mus. Contemporary Art, L.A., 1998, Matthew Marks Gallery, N.Y.C., 1997, Parco Gallery, 1997, De Appel Found., Amsterdam, The Netherlands, 1997, IKON Gallery, Birmingham, Eng., 1998., Mus. Fine Arts, Houston, 1998, Worcester (Mass.) Art Mus., 1999, Laband Art Gallery, L.A., 1999, Conceptual Art as Neurobiological Praxis, Thread Waxing Space, N.Y., 1999, Photography: An Expanded View, Recent Acquisitions, Guggenheim Mus., N.Y., 1999, Shift, ACME, L.A., 1999, Kerlin Gallery, Dublin, Ireland, 1999, Apposites Opposites, Mus. Contemporary Art, Chgo., 1999; featured in Photography at Princeton, TimeOut, Flash Art, Arforum, Art in Am., Art Monthly, Art & Text, The Birmingham Post, Jour. of Contemporary Art, L.A. Times, Paper Mag., others. Grantee NEA, 1990-91, 94-95, Art Matters Inc., 1992-93, 95; Fellow Nat. Arts Assn., 1983-84, Nat. Endowment for the Arts, 1990-91, 1994-95, Guggenheim Meml. Found., 2004. Home and Office: 3411 Colbert Ave Los Angeles CA 90066-1234*

BARTHA, DANIELA C., music educator; b. Erding, Germany, Sept. 7, 1967; d. Manfred and Monika B. BMus in Piano Performance, U. Denver, 1992; MMus in Piano Performance, U. Kansas City, 1994; postgrad., U. Cin. Teaching asst. U. Cin., 1996-99; instr. music Muskingum Coll., New Concord, Ohio, 1999-2000; lectr. of music U. N.Mex., Albuquerque, 2000—. Contbr. articles to profl. publs. Music Activity grantee U. Denver, 1988-92; recipient Non Resident Chancellor's award U. Kansas City, 1992-94; grad. scholarship U. Cin., 1994-96. Avocation: pets. Office: U NMex Albuquerque NM 87111 E-mail: dcbartha@yahoo.com.

BARTHEL, WILLIAM FREDERICK, JR., electrical engineer; b. Washington, July 14, 1940; s. William Frederick and Eva (Buday) Barthel; m. Barbara Joan Adams, Nov. 18, 1961; 1 child, William Frederick III. BS, McNeese State U., 1972. Shop mgr. Electronic Unltd., Lake Charles, La., 1968; engr. quality control Rockwell Internat., Cedar Rapids, Iowa, 1974—79, mgr. quality assurance, 1979, sr. engring. scientist, process control devel., 1980—81; engring. mgr. process reliability Digital Equipment Corp., Andover, Mass., 1981—87, engring. mgr. performance assurance, 1987—91; dir. quality Gables Engring., Inc., Coral Gables, Fla., 1991—93, v.p. ops., 1993—. With USAF, 1958—62. Mem.: Am. Inst. Chemists, Am. Chem. Soc. Republican. Home: 745 SE 25th Ln Homestead FL 33033-5234 Office: Gables Engring Inc 247 Greco Ave Miami FL 33146-1808 Office Phone: 305-442-2578.

BARTHELMAS, NED KELTON, brokerage house executive; b. Circleville, Ohio, Oct. 22, 1927; s. Arthur and Mary Bernice (Riffel) B.; m. Marjorie Jane Livezey, May 23, 1953; children: Brooke Ann, Richard Thomas. BS in Bus. Adminstrn., Ohio State U., 1950. Stockbroker Ohio Co., Columbus, 1953-58; pres. First Columbus Securities Corp., 1958—; pres., dir. Ohio Fin. Corp., Columbus, 1960—; pres. Thwirs, Inc., Columbus, 1986—. Trustee, chmn. Am. Guardian Fin., Republic Fin.; bd. dirs. Nat. Foods, Midwest Capital Corp., Capital Equity Corp., Midwest Nat. Corp., 1st Columbus Realty Corp., Dublin Nat. Corp. (all Columbus). Served with Adj. Gen.'s Dept., AUS, 1944-47. Recipient Merit award, State of Ohio, 2001. Mem. Nat. Assn. Securities Dealers (past vice chmn. dist. bd. govs.), Investment Bankers Assn. (exec. com. 1973), Investment Dealers Ohio (sec., treas. 1956-72, pres. 1973), Nat. Stock Traders Assn., Young Pres.'s Orgn. (pres. 1971), World Bus. Coun., Columbus Pres.'s Assn., Nat. Investment Bankers (pres. 1973), Internat. Real Estate Inst., Columbus Jr. C. of C. (pres. 1956), Ohio C. of C. (trustee 1957-58), World's Pres.'s Assn. (Exec. Hall of Fame award 1993), Columbus Area C. of C. (dir. 1956, named an Outstanding Young Man of Columbus 1962), Newcomen Soc., Coun. for Ethics in Econs., Coun. of Orgn. of Am. States, Winston Churchill's Wisdom Hall of Fame, Internat. Soc. Financiers, Oxford Club, Nat. Assn. Appraisers Execs. Club, Pres.' Club (Ohio State U.), Internat. Platform Assn., Stock and Bond Club (past pres.), named top 25 corp. Dirs. (1984-90), Columbus Club, Scioto Country Club, Crystal Downs Country Club, Ohio State U. Faculty Club, Kiwanis (legion of honor 1992), Am. Legion, Columbus Admirals Club, Alpha Kappa Psi, Phi Delta Theta (Golden Legion award). Office: 1241 Dublin Rd Columbus OH 43215-7000

BARTHELME, FREDERICK (RICK), writer, literature educator; b. Houston, Oct. 10, 1943; Student, Tulane U., 1961—62, U. Houston, 1962—65, student, 1966—67, Mus. Fine Arts, Houston, 1965—66; MA, Johns Hopkins U., 1977. Prof. U. So. Miss., 1977—, dir. Ctr. for Writers, 1978—, editor Mississippi Review. Author: (screenplays) Second Marriage, 1985, Tracer, 1986, (novels) War and War, 1971, Second Marriage, 1984, Tracer, 1985, Two Against One, 1988, Natural Selection, 1989, The Brothers, 1993, Painted Desert, 1995, Bob the Gambler, 1997, Elroy Nights, 2003, (short stories) Rangoon, 1970, Moon Deluxe, 1983, Chroma, 1987, The Law of Averages: New & Selected Stories, 2000; author: (with Steven Barthelme) Double Down: Reflections on Gambling and Loss, 1999; exhibitions include La. Gallery, Houston, 1965, 1967, Mus. Normal Art, N.Y.C., 1967, Seattle Art Mus., 1969, Mus. Modern Art, N.Y.C., 1970. Recipient Eliot Coleman award, Johns Hopkins U., 1976—77; grantee, Nat. Endowment for the Arts, 1979, 1980. Office: Univ So Miss Dept English Box 5037 Hattiesburg MS 39406-5037

BARTH MENZIES, KAREN ANN, lawyer; b. Dubuque, Iowa, Dec. 8, 1966; d. Henry Victor and Janet Marie Barth. BA, Colo. State U., 1989; JD, U. Calif., Davis, 1995. Bar: Calif. 1995, U.S. Dist. Ct. (cen. dist.) Calif. 1995, U.S. Dist. Ct. (so. dist.) Calif. 1999, U.S. Ct. Appeals (9th cir.) 1999, U.S. Dist. Ct. (ea. and western dists.) Ark. 2003, U.S. Dist. Ct. (so. dist.) Ill. 2003, U.S. Dist. Ct. Colo. 2003, U.S. Ct. Appeals (5th cir.) 2005. Law clk. Colo. Atty. Gen.'s Office, Denver, 1993; law clk. to Justice Davis, Calif. 3d Dist. Appellate Ct., Sacramento, 1994; legal intern Calif. Atty. Gen.'s Office, Sacramento, 1994, Sacramento Dist. Atty.'s Office, Sacramento, 1995; shareholder Baum, Hedlund and predecessor firms, L.A., 1995—. Lectr. in field; lead coun., plaintiff's steering com. MDL 1574 Paxil Products liability litig. Contbr. articles to profl. jours. Named Calif. Lawyer of Yr., Calif. Mag., 2004, Lawyer of Yr., Lawyer's Weekly, 2004; named one of Top 40 Lawyers Under 40, Nat. Law Jour., 2005. Mem. ATLA, ABA (litig. sect. Trial and Ins. sect.), State Bar of Calif., Nat. Assn. Women Lawyers, Consumer Attys. Calif., L.A. Women Lawyers Assn., George McBurney Complex Litigation Inn of Ct. Avocations: rock climbing, diving, skiing, basketball, volleyball. Office: Baum Hedlund A Profl Corp 12100 Wilshire Blvd Ste 950 Los Angeles CA 90025-7107 Office Phone: 310-207-3233. E-mail: kbmenzies@baumhedlundlaw.com.

BARTHOLD, JULIA SPENCER, urologist, researcher; b. Parkersburg, W.Va., Apr. 6, 1957; d. R. Donald and Janina R. Spencer; m. Steve Jensen Barthold, July 3, 1993; children: Christopher, Laura. BA, Northwestern U., 1979, MD, 1981. Resident in surgery McGaw Med. Ctr. Northwestern U., 1981—84, resident in urology McGaw Med. Ctr., 1984—88; fellow pediat. urology Children's Hosp. Mich., 1988—89; fellow rsch. Med. Coll. Cornell U., 1989—91, asst. prof. Med. Coll., 1991—92; attending urologist N.Y. Hosp., 1991—92; pediat. urologist Ark. Children's Hosp., Little Rock, 1992—95, Children's Hosp. Mich., Detroit, 1995—99; assoc. chief urology A. I. duPont Hosp., Wilmington, Del., 2000—. Asst. prof. U. Ark. for Med. Scis., Little Rock, 1992—95; assoc. prof. Wayne State U., Detroit, 1995—99, Thomas Jefferson U., Phila., 2000—. Contbr. articles to profl. jours. Fellow: Soc. for Pediat. Urology, Am. acad. Pediat. (exec. com. Mid-Atlantic sect. 2002—); mem.: Am. Urol. Assn. Avocations: swimming, skiing, music. Office: A I duPont Hosp for Children Box 269 1600 Rockland Rd Wilmington DE 19899

BARTHOLET, ELIZABETH, law educator; b. NYC, Sept. 9, 1940; d. Paul and Elizabeth (Ives) Bartholet; divorced; children: Derek DuBois, Christopher, Michael. BA in English Lit., cum laude, Radcliffe Coll., 1962; JD magna cum laude, Harvard U., 1965. Bar: US Supreme Ct. 1969, Mass. 1978. Staff counsel Pres.'s Commn. on Law Enforcement and Adminstrn. of Justice, Washington, 1966—67; staff atty. NAACP Legal Def. & Ednl. Fund, Inc., NYC, 1968-72; counsel VERA Inst. of Justice, NYC, 1972-73; pres., dir. Legal Action Ctr., NYC, 1973-77; asst. prof. law Harvard Law Sch., Cambridge, Mass., 1977-83, prof., 1983—, Morris Wasserstein pub. interest prof. law, 1996—, faculty dir. child advocacy program, 2004—. Civil Rights Reviewing Authority US Dept. Edn., 1979—81; adv com. on intercountry adoption US Dept. State, 1990—2000. Author: Family Bonds: Adoption and the Politics of Parenting, 1993, pub. in 1999 as Family Bonds: Adoption, Infertility, and the New World of Child Production; contbr. articles to profl. journals. Mem. overseers com. to visit Harvard Law Sch., 1971-77; bd. overseers Harvard Coll., 1973-77; mem. assisted reproductive tech. ethics com. Brigham and Women's Hosp., 1990—; mem. IVF ethics com. Boston Fertility & Gynecology Assn., 1991—; mem. adv. com. Internat. Concerns Com. for Children, 1993-; mem New Eng. com. NAACP Legal Def. & Ednl. Fund, Inc., 1994-98; mem. adv. coun. Appleseed Found., 1996-; bd. dirs. Legal Action Ctr., 1977—, vice chair bd., 1998-. Recipient Friends of Adoption Award for Adoption Lit., Adoptive Parents Com., 1993, Media Achievement Award, Cath. Adoptive Parents Assn., 1994, Friends of Adoption Award, Open Door Soc., 1994, Alumnae Recognition Award, Radcliffe Coll., 1997, Award for Advocacy on Behalf of Foster Children, Mass. Appleseed Ctr., 1998. Mem. Assn. Bar City of NY (exec. com. 1973-77), Am. Arbitration Assn. (labor panel 1980-, comml. panel 1995-), Soc. Am. Law Teachers (bd. dirs. 1977-89), Fed. Mediation and Conciliation Svc. Roster Arbitrators, Am. Acad. Adoption Attorneys (hon.), Harvard Club. Democrat. Office: Harvard Law Sch 1563 Massachusetts Ave Cambridge MA 02138 Office Phone: 617-495-3128. Office Fax: 617-496-4947. Business E-Mail: ebarthol@law.harvard.edu.*

BARTHOLOMAUS, BRETT WILLIAM, small business owner; b. Milw., Jan. 19, 1944; s. Weber and Beatrice (Elmergreen) B.; m. Joan Anne Cavosi, Feb. 19, 1977 (dec.); children: Laura, Thomas, Eric. Student, Milw. tech. Coll. Lic. pvt. security Wis. Motorcycle sales rep. Vic Panetti & Sons, Milw., 1963-75; maint. supr. U. Wis., Milw., 1977; owner North Trail Inn Supper Club, Tigerton, Wis., 1978-82; security supr. Sentinal Detective agy., Wausau, Wis., 1988—. Author: (poetry book) Moments Beautiful, Moments Bright, 1993, (novel) Reflection of Evil, 1998; poetry pub. various pubs.; numerous poetry readings. Vol. numerous charitable orgns. Recipient Golden Poets award World of Poetry, 1988, 89, 90, 92. Democrat. Lds Church. Avocations: motorcycling, backpacking, weightlifting, family. Address: Wildwood Apts 100 Wall St Apt 1 Bowler WI 54416

BARTHOLOMAY, WILLIAM C., insurance brokerage company executive, professional baseball team executive; b. Evanston, Ill., Aug. 11, 1928; s. Henry C. and Virginia (Graves) B.; m. Sara Taylor, 1950, (div. 1964); children: Virginia, William T., Jamie, Elizabeth, Sara; m. Gail Dillingham, May 1968 (div. Apr. 1980). Student, Oberlin Coll., 1946-49, Northwestern U., 1949-50; BA, Lake Forest Coll., 1955. Ptnr. Bartholomay & Clarkson, Chgo., 1951-63; v.p. Alexander & Alexander, Chgo., 1963-65; pres. Olson & Bartholomay, Chgo. and Atlanta, 1965-69; sr. v.p. Frank B. Hall & Co. Inc., N.Y.C. and Chgo., 1969-72, exec. v.p., 1972-73, pres., 1973-74, vice chmn., 1974-90; chmn. bd., dir. Atlanta Braves, 1966—2004, chmn. emeritus, chmn. exec. com., 2004—; pvt. practice Chgo., 1990—91; pres. Near North Nat. Group, 1991—2003; vice chmn., chmn. exec. com. Turner Broadcasting Sys., Inc., Atlanta, 2001—; vice chmn. Willis Group Holdings (NYSE), Chgo., 2003—. Bd. dirs. WMS Industries Inc., Chgo., Midway Games, Inc., Exec. Coun. Maj. League Baseball, Maj. League Baseball Players Pension Plan; dir. Internat. Steel, 2002—. Commr. Chgo. Park Dist., 1980-2002, Chgo. Pub. Bldg. Commn., 1989-2003; bd. dirs. Chgo. Maternity Ctr., Lincoln Park Zool. Soc.; trustee Adler Planetarium, Mus. Sci. and Industry, Roosevelt U., Chgo., Ill. Inst. of Tech.; past trustee Lake Forest (Ill.) Coll., Ogelthorpe Coll., Atlanta, Marymount Manhattan Coll., NY With USNR, 1951-54. Mem. Chief Execs. Orgn., World Pres.'s Orgn., Chgo. Pres.'s Orgn., Nat. Assn. CLU, Chgo. Assn. CLU, Chgo. Club, Racquet Club, Saddle and Cycle Club, Econ. Club, Onwentsia Club, Shoreacres Club (Lake Forest), Brook Club, Links Club, Racquet & Tennis Club, Doubles Club (N.Y.C.), Piedmont Driving

Club, Atlanta Country Club, Peachtree Golf Club, Commerce Club. Episcopalian. Home: 180 E Pearson St Chicago IL 60611-2130 Office: Willis Group Holdings 10 S LaSalle St Ste 3000 Chicago IL 60603 also: Atlanta Braves PO Box 4064 Atlanta GA 30302-4064 E-mail: bartholomay_wi@willis.com.

BARTHOLOMEW, DEBRA LEE, publishing executive; b. Cobleskill, NY, Sept. 11, 1958; d. Donald Walter Mochrie, Sr. and Jean Marie (Hamm) Mochrie; m. Richard Ray Bartholomew, July 8, 2001; children: Kerry Hartuny, Kris Manchester children: Robert Wayne Kucienski, Jr. Author: Hope: Discovering the Power of 'No' (Merit from the Writer's Digest, 2001), Who Am I? My Tree of Hope, 2003, Who Am I? My Tree of Konwledge, 2003; composer: (song) Believing in Myself, 2002, Angel in the Sky, 2003; contbr. poetry to lit. publs. Organizer fundraiser poster contest War against Terrorism, 2001, For the children, boost the moral of the soldiers, Richmondville, NY, 1991. Recipient Dirs. award of merit, 2002—03. Mem.: Internat. Soc. Poets (Silver Cup, Bronze Medallion, Outstanding Achievement award 2003). Home: 297 Main St Richmondville NY 12149-0150 Office Phone: 518-294-8860. Personal E-mail: debilee@capital.net.

BARTHOLOMEW, GILBERT ALFRED, retired physicist; b. Nelson, Can., Apr. 8, 1922; s. Alfred and Anna (Lenzman) B.; m. Rosalie May Dinzey, Apr. 19, 1952 (dec. Dec. 10, 1990); m. Anna Lubicz-Luba, July 24, 1992. BA, U. B.C., 1943; PhD, McGill U., 1948. With Atomic Energy of Can., Ltd., 1948-83, head neutron physics br., 1962-71, dir. physics div., 1971-83. Contbr. articles to profl. jours. Fellow AAAS, Royal Soc. Can., Am. Phys. Soc.; mem. Can. Assn. Physicists, Can. Nuclear Soc., Assn. for Baha'i Studies, Sigma Xi. Home: PO Box 150 Lions Bay BC Canada V0N 2E0 E-mail: gabarth@telus.net.

BARTHOLOMEW, LINCOLN EDWIN, physician; b. Oct. 12, 1954; MD, U. Pa., 1981; MPH, Columbia U., 1999. Dir. primary care St. Albans (N.Y.) VA Med. Ctr.; med. dir. Montefiore Rikers Island Health Svcs. Home: 401 E 74th St # 8 New York NY 10021-3919

BARTHOLOMEW, LLOYD GIBSON, physician; b. Whitehall, N.Y., Sept. 15, 1921; s. Emerson F. and Minnie (Swinton) B.; m. Elisabeth Thrall, Dec. 27, 1943; children: Suzanne, Lynne, Lloyd Gibson, Deborah, Douglass Thrall. AA, Green Mountain Jr. Coll., 1939; BA, Union Coll., Schenectady, 1941; MD, U. Vt., 1944; MS in Internal Medicine (fellow), U. Minn., 1952; LHD (hon.), Green Mountain Coll., 1984. Diplomate Am. Bd. Internal Medicine, subsplty. bd. gastroenterology. Intern Mary Hitchcock Meml. Hosp., Hanover, N.H., 1944-45, resident, 1945-46, 48-49; asst. internal medicine Dartmouth, 1948-49; 1st asst. div. internal medicine Mayo Clinic, Rochester, Minn., 1949-52, asst. to staff div. internal medicine, 1952-53; practice medicine, specializing in gastroenterology Rochester, 1952—; instr. internal medicine Mayo Found., U. Minn., 1952-58, asst. prof., 1958-63, assoc. prof. internal medicine, 1963-67, prof. medicine, 1967—, Mayo Med. Sch., 1973—. Attending physician St. Mary's, Meth. hosps., Rochester, 1952; mem. adv. bd. to surgeons gen. of armed forces and asst. sec. def., 1978-86; mem. policy bd. Bush Found., 1978-87. Contbr. articles profl. publs. Trustee Green Mountain Coll. Poultney, Vt., 1991—, chmn. bd. trustees, 1997-2003, trustee emeritus, 2003—. Capt. M.C. AUS, 1946-47; col. M.C., 1960-86, ret. Recipient Woodbury prize in medicine, 1944, Carbee prize in obstetrics, 1994, disting. svc. award U. Vt. Coll. Medicine, 1977, Henry J. Plummer disting. clinician award Mayo Found. Internal Medicine, 1992, disting. svc. award Green Mtn. Coll. Alumni Assn., 1995. Mem. AMA (sec. gastroenterology sect. 1962-68, vice chmn. gastroenterology sect. 1968-69, chmn. 1969-70, mem. council sci. assembly 1969, chmn. program planning com. 1971-75, chmn. council sci. assembly 1974-76, chmn. council continuing physician edn. 1976-77), Minn. Med. Assn. (del. ho. dels. 1964—, chmn. scholarship and loan com. 1967—, alt. del. to AMA 1974-77, 85—, del. to AMA 1978-83, Pres.'s award 1983, Disting. Service award 1987), So. Minn. Med. Assn. (pres. 1963-64), Zumbro Valley Med. Soc. (sec.-treas. 1969-70, v.p. 1970-71, pres. 1971-72), Soc. Med. Cons. to Armed Forces (mem. governing council 1980-86, pres. 1984, del. to AMA 1984-92), Am. Gastroent. Assn. (com. on procedures 1970-72, presdl. comm. on future of assn. 1973-74, com. on constn. and by-laws 1980-85), Minn. Soc. Internal Medicine, Sigma Xi. Office: Mayo Med Sch 200 1st St SW Rochester MN 55902

BARTHOLOMEW, MERVIN JEROME, geologist, educator; b. Altoona, Pa., Nov. 22, 1942; s. Mervin Wilbur Bartholomew and Catherine Clara Morris. BS, Pa. State U., 1964; MS, U. So. Calif., 1968; PhD, Va. Tech. U., 1971. Lic. geologist N.C. Bd. Licensing of Geologist, 2005. Asst. engring. geology Std. Oil Co., L.A., 1965—68; field geologist Atlantic Richfield Oil Co., Bakersfield, Calif., 1968; instr. geol. scis. Va. Tech. U., Blacksburg, Va., 1971—72; asst. prof. geoscis. N.C. State U., Raleigh, NC, 1972—75; geologist, wae Va. Divsn. of Mineral Resources, Charlottesville, Va., 1976—79; supr. geologist Va. Tech Office Va. Divsn. Mineral Resources, Blacksburg, 1979—83; chief Geology and Mineral Resources Divsn. Mont. Tech. Mont. Bur. Mines and Geology, Butte, Mont., 1983—90; rsch. scientist Earth Scis. and Resources Inst U. S.C., Columbia, SC, 1992—2002; chmn. Dept. Earth Scis. U. Memphis, 2002—. Geol. cons. Wintergreen (Va.) Inc., 1969—71; assoc. prof. Mont. Bur. Mines and Geology, Butte, 1983—88, prof., 1988—92; contract geologist NC Divsn. Land Resources, Raleigh, 1975—80; dir. grad. program Earth and Environ. Resources Mgmt. Program U. S.C., Columbia, SC, 1994—2001. Editor: The Grenville Event in the Appalachians and Related Topics, 1984, Characterization and Comparison of Ancient and Mesozoic Continental Margins, 1992; co-editor: Proterozoic Tectonic Evolution of the Grenville Orogen in North America, 2004; contbr. articles to profl. jours. Fellow: Geol. Soc. Am.; mem.: Basement Tectonics Assn., Inc. (bd. trustees 1989—94), Am. Geophys. Union (life), Soc. Pa. Archaeology (life). Independent. Avocations: fishing, genealogy, archaeology. Office: Earth Sciences University of Memphis 001 Johnson Hall Memphis TN 38152-3550 Office Phone: 901-678-4536. Office Fax: 901-678-2178. E-mail: jbrthlm1@memphis.edu.

BARTILUCCI, ANDREW JOSEPH, university administrator; b. N.Y.C., Nov. 29, 1922; s. Rocco and Philomena (Innello) B.; m. Lucy Ann Fulvio, June 10, 1950; children— Mary Ann, Phyllis, Eugenie. BS, St. John's U., 1944; MS, Rutgers U., 1949; PhD, U. Md., 1953. Analytical chemist Armed Services Med. Procurement Lab., War Dept., 1947-48; assoc. research pharmacist, research and devel. div. Merck & Co., 1949-50; prof. pharmacy, asst. dean Coll. Pharmacy St. John's U., 1952-56, dean, 1956-88, v.p. for health professions, clin. svc. and rsch., 1979-91; acting dean St. John's Coll. Liberal Arts & Scis., 1989-91, exec. v.p., 1991-96, spl. asst. to pres., 1996—2002. Fellow Am. Found. Pharm. Edn., 1950-52 Served as pharmacist's mate USNR, 1944-46; ensign 1949-57; Pharmacist dir. USPHS(R), 1957-98. Fellow AAAS; mem. Am. Coll. Apothecaries, N.Y. Acad. Scis., N.Y. Acad. Pharmacy, Am. Pharm. Assn., N.Y. State Bd. Pharmacy, Sigma Xi, Rho Chi, Phi Delta Chi. Home: 115 Roosevelt St Garden City NY 11530-2309 Office: Saint Johns Univ 8000 Utopia Pkwy Jamaica NY 11432-1343 E-mail: bartilua@stjohns.edu.

BARTIZAL, DENISE, psychologist; b. Naperville, Ill., Oct. 14, 1963; d. H. J. and Dolores Underwood Bartizal; m. Jeff Ellis, Oct. 5, 2002. BA, Tulane U., 1984; MS, NOVA Southeastern U., 1993; PsyD, Caribbean Ctr. Advanced Studies, 1998. Nat. bd. cert. behavior analyst. Mental health technician NOVA Geriatric Inst., Lauderhill, Fla., 1992—93; behavior analyst Dept. Children and Families, Ft. Lauderdale, Fla., 1993—97; psychologist intern Fed. Correctional Instn., Petersburg, Va., 1997—98; sr. psychologist Ctrl. State Hosp., Petersburg, 1998—2001, Southside Va. Tng. Ctr., Petersburg, 2000—01; dir. dept. psychology Catawba State Hosp., Va., 2001—. Spkr. in field. Mem.: APA, Aerobics and Fitness Assn. Am., Assn. Behavior Analysis. Republican. Episcopalian. Avocations: travel, classic fiction, exercise. Office: Catawba State Hosp PO Box 200 Catawba VA 24070

BARTKUS, BARBARA R., finance educator; b. Ill. BSBA, Hawaii Pacific U., 1987, MBA, 1989; PhD, Tex. A&M U., 1997. Asst. prof. of mgmt. Old Dominion U., Norfolk, Va., 1997—2003, assoc. prof. of mgmt., 2003—. Office Phone: 757-683-3000.

BARTKUS, RICHARD ANTHONY, magazine publisher; b. Chgo., Mar. 14, 1931; s. Anthony J. and Mary (Petraitis) B.; m. Betty Ann Luetke, Jan. 2, 1954; children: Susan Kimberly, David Richard. Student, U. Ill., 1949-55. Circulation trainee Chgo. Tribune, 1955-58; asst. advt. mgr. Kilner Pub. Co., Chgo., 1958-59; advt. mgr. Cox Publs., Arcadia, Calif., 1959-60, Bond Pub. Co., 1960, western advt. mgr., advt. dir., 1969-75; pub. Road & Track mag., Newport Beach, Calif., 1975-91; v.p. CBS Publs., 1977-91. With USMC, 1951-53. Mem. Univ. Athletic Club. Home: 18681 Via Torino Irvine CA 92612-3438 E-mail: bartkusra@sbcglobal.net.

BARTKUS, ROBERT EDWARD, lawyer; b. Kearny, NJ, Sept. 30, 1946; s. Edward Charles and Dorothy Agnes (Konschott) B.; m. Mary Bartkus. BA with honors, Swarthmore Coll, 1968; JD, Stanford U., 1976. Bar: Calif. 1976, N.J. 1977, N.Y. 1977, U.S. Supreme Ct (3d, 2d cirs.), U.S. Dist. Ct. N.J., U.S. Dist. Ct. (so. and ea. dist.) N.Y. Spl. counsel Schulte, Roth & Zabel, N.Y.C., 1985-88; ptnr. Dillon, Bitar, & Luther, LLC. Tchg. asst. Stanford U. Law Sch., 1976; mem. Dist. X Ethics Com., 1992-97, chair, 2002-03; lectr. N.J. Inst. for Continuing Edn., 1988—; master John J. Gibbons Intellectual Property Inn of Ct. Articles co-editor Stanford Law Rev., 1974-76; author Innovation Competition 28 Stanford Law Rev. 1976; author, editor: New Jersey Federal Civil Practice, 1992, N.J. Federal Civil Procedure, 1999; mem. editl. bd. N.J. Law Jour. (Alfred C. Clapp award 1995). Atty. Community Law Office, 1976-79, Legal Aid Soc., 1979-87; mem. alumni coun. Swarthmore Coll., 1977-78. Lt. USNR, 1968-73. Mem. ABA (ethics com. Dist. X), Nat. Assn. Securities Dealers (arbitrator), N.J. Bar Assn. (chair fed. practice com.), Assn. Fed. Bar of State of N.J., Am. Arbitration Assn. (arbitrator), Delta Upsilon. Home: 6 Terrill Dr Califon NJ 07830-3443 Office: Dillon Bitar & Luther LLC 53 Maple Ave Morristown NJ 07963-0398 Office Phone: 973-539-3100. Business E-Mail: rbartkus@dbl-law.com.

BARTLEMAN, JAMES K., lieutenant governor; b. Orillia, Ont., Dec. 24, 1939; m. Marie-Jeanne Rosillon, 1975; children: Anne-Pascale, Laurent, Alain. BA in History, U. Western Ont., 1963, LLD (hon.). Lt. gov., Ont., 2002—; amb. to Cuba, 1981—83; amb. to Israel, 1986—90; high commr. to Cyprus, 1986—90; amb. to North Atlantic Coun. NATO, 1990—94; high commr. to Australia, 1999—2000; Can.'s amb. to European Union, 2000—02. Author: (memoirs) Out of Muskoka, 2002, On Six Continents, 2004, Roller Coaster, 2005. Named Knight of Justice in Order of St. John, hon. chief, Toronto Police Svc.; named to Order of Ont.; recipient Golden Jubilee Medal in Commemoration of Queen Elizabeth II, Nat. Aboriginal Achievement award, 1999, Anishinabek Lifetime Achievement award. Office: Lt Gov of Ont Queen's Park Toronto ON Canada M7A 1A1

BARTLETT, ALEX, lawyer; b. Warrensburg, Mo., Aug. 7, 1937; s. George Vest and May (Woolery) B.; m. Sue Gloyd, June 5, 1961 (div. June 1978); children: Ashley R., Nathan G.; m. Eleanor M. Veltrop, Oct. 27, 1978. BA, Cen. Mo. State U., 1959; LLB, U. Mo., 1961. Bar: Mo. 1962, U.S. Ct. Mil. Appeals 1963, U.S. Supreme Ct. 1965, U.S. Dist. Ct. (we. dist.) Mo. 1966, U.S. Ct. Appeals (8th cir.) 1968. From assoc. to ptnr. Hendren & Andrae, Jefferson City, Mo., 1965-79; mem. Bartlett, Venters, Pletz & Toppins, P.C., Jefferson City, 1980-87; pvt. practice Jefferson City, 1987-90; mem. Husch & Eppenberger, LLC, Jefferson City, 1990—. With Transit Casualty Co. Receivership, 1986-90, commr. claims, 1986-87, spl. claims counsel, 1987-89, dir. legal affairs dept., 1989-90; lectr. law U. Mo., Columbia, 1965-66. Contbr. editor Mo. Law Rev., 1960-61. Served to capt. JAGC, U.S. Army, 1962-65. Mem. ABA, FBA, Mo. Bar Assn. (chmn. young lawyers sect. 1972-73, ct. modernization com. 1972-74, jud. reform com. 1974-76, chmn. cts. and jud. com. 1978-79, legis. com. 1981-84, President's award 1976, Smithson award 1976), Cole County Bar Assn., Am. Coll. Trial Lawyers (chmn. Mo. 1994-96), Order of Coif. Democrat. Office: Husch and Eppenberger PO Box 1251 235 E High St Jefferson City MO 65102-3236 Office Phone: 573-635-9118.

BARTLETT, ALLEN LYMAN, JR., retired bishop; b. Birmingham, Ala., Sept. 22, 1929; s. Allen Lyman and Edith Buell (West) B.; m. Jerriette L. Kohlmeier, Dec. 28, 1957; children: Christopher, Stephen, Catherine. BA, U. of South, 1951, D.D. (hon.), 1988; M.Div., Va. Theol. Sem., 1958, D.Min., 1980, D.D. (hon.), 1986. Ordained to ministry Episcopal Ch. 1958, ordained priest 1959. Vicar St. James' Ch., Alexander City, Ala., 1958-61, St. Barnabas Ch., Roanoke, Ala., 1958-61; rector Zion Ch., Charles Town, W.Va., 1961-70; dean Christ Ch. Cathedral, Louisville, 1970-85; ordained bishop, 1986; bishop coadjutor Diocese of Pa., Phila., 1986-87, bishop, 1987-98; assisting bishop Diocese of Washington, 2001—04. Dep. Episcopal Gen. Convention, 1964-67, 73-85; mem. exec. coun. Episcopal Ch., 1979-85. Lt. (j.g.) USN, 1952-55. Mem.: Union League, Phi Beta Kappa. Democrat. Episcopalian. Avocations: tennis, hiking. Home: 316 S 10th St Philadelphia PA 19107-6149

BARTLETT, ARTHUR EUGENE, real estate company executive; b. Glens Falls, N.Y., Nov. 26, 1933; s. Raymond Ernest and Thelma (Williams) Bartlett; m. Collette R. Bartlett, Jan. 9, 1955 (dec.); 1 child, Stacy Lynn; m. Nancy Sanders Bartlett, Feb. 12, 2005. Sales mgr. Forest E. Olson, Inc., 1960-64; co-founder, v.p. Four Star Realty, Inc., Santa Ana, Calif., 1964-71, v.p., sec., 1964-71; founder, pres. Comps, Inc., Tustin, Calif., 1971-81; co-founder, chmn. of bd., pres., CEO Century 21 Real Estate Corp., Tustin, 1980—; pres. Larwin Sq. LLC Shopping Ctr, Tustin, 1979—2002. Chmn. bd. dirs. United Western Med. Ctrs., 1981—87. Mem.: Internat. Franchise Assn. (v.p., bd. dirs. 1975—80, Hall of Fame 1987), Masons.

BARTLETT, BRUCE REEVES, economist, columnist; b. Ann Arbor, Mich., Oct. 11, 1951; s. Frank and Marjorie (Stern) B.d BA, Rutgers U., 1973; MA, Georgetown U., 1976. Spl. asst. to Congressman Jack F. Kemp, Washington, 1977-78; chief legis. asst. to U.S. Senator Roger Jepsen, Washington, 1979-80; dep. dir. Joint Econ. Com., U.S. Congress, Washington, 1981-83, exec. dir., 1983-84; v.p. Polyconomics, Inc., Morristown, N.J., 1984-85; sr. fellow Heritage Found., Washington, 1985-87; sr. policy analyst The White House, Washington, 1987-88; dep. asst. sec. for econ. policy Dept. Treasury, 1988-93; sr. fellow CATO Inst., Washington, 1993, Alexis de Tocqueville Instn., 1993-94, Nat. Ctr. for Policy Analysis, 1995—. Author: Coverup: The Politics of Pearl Harbor, 1941-46, 1978, Reaganomics: Supply Side Economics in Action, 1981; co-editor: The Supply Side Solution, 1983; syndicated columnist Creators Syndicate, L.A., 1997—; contbr. articles to Washington Post, N.Y. Times, Wall Street Jour., numerous others. Served with USAF, 1973. Mem. Am. Econ. Assn. Republican. Home: 439 Seneca Rd Great Falls VA 22066-1113 Office: Nationla Center for Policy Analysis 601 Pennsylvania Ave NW Ste 9005 Washington DC 20004-3615 E-mail: bartlettb@cox.net.

BARTLETT, CHARLES LEFFINGWELL, foundation executive; b. Chgo., Aug. 14, 1921; s. Valentine C. and Marie (Frost) B.; m. Josephine Martha Buck, Dec. 16, 1950; children: Peter B., Michael V., Robert S., Helen B. Student, St. Mark's Sch., Southboro, Mass., 1934-39; AB, Yale U., 1943. Reporter Chattanooga Times, 1946-62, Washington corr., 1948-63; editor News Focus Service, 1958-63; columnist Field Syndicate, 1962-80, Chgo. Sun-Times, 1963-75, Chgo. Daily News, 1975-78, Field Syndicate, 1978-81; pres. Jefferson Found., 1982—; editor Coleman/Bartlett's Washington Focus, 1988—. Author: (with Edward Weintal) Facing the Brink, 1957. Served as lt. USNR, 1943-46. Recipient Pulitizer prize for nat. reporting, 1955 Mem.: Gridiron, Federal City. Roman Catholic. Home: 4615 W St NW Washington DC 20007-1515 Office: Washington Focus 2208 46th St NW Washington DC 20007-1031 Office Phone: 202-234-3681.

BARTLETT, CHERYL ANN, public health service administrator; b. Norwich, Conn., June 28, 1954; d. William Jr. and Frances (Fredette) B.; m. Rogers Washburn Cabot Jr., June 5, 1982 (div. July 1995); m. Bruce Templin Miller, Sept. 10, 1995. ASN, Quinnipiac Coll., 1979; student healthcare adminstrn., Stonehill Coll. Cert. Infection Control, dialysis nursing, HIV/AIDS nursing. Nursing supr. Nantucket (Mass.) Cottage Hosp., 1981-95, dir. nursing, 1995, dir. clin. svcs., 1995-97; public health officer Public Health Assocs. of Nantucket, Southeastern, Mass., 1989—; exec. dir. Nantucket AIDS Network, 1989—. Spkr. in field. Bd. dirs. Nantucket Housing Authority Properties Inc., Nantucket, 1997—; apptd. pres. Cmty. Action Com., Cape Cod and Islands, 1993—; selectman Town of Nantucket, 1993-96, county commr., 1993-96, chmn. Nantucket Bd. Health, 1992-94; mem. Coun. for Health and Human Svcs., 1990-93, chmn., 96—, chmn., 1998-99; pres. bd. dirs. Family and Children's Svc. Recipient Cmty. Recognition award AIDS Action Com. of Mass., 1996, Outstanding Cmty. Health Program, U.S. Dept. of Health and Human Svcs., 1993, Outstanding Citizens award Nantucket Rotary Club, 1992, Recognition for Dedication and Commitment for the Care of AIDS Patients, Mass. State Senate, 1991, Mass. House of Reps., 1991. Mem. ANA, Assn. of Nurses in AIDS Care (govt. rels. com. 1997, chmn. govt. rels. com. 1999), Assn. of Infection Control Practitioners (nominating com. 1991-92, bd. dirs.), Mass. Nurses Assn., Alpha Sigma Lambda. Avocations: reading, gourmet cooking, 3rd world travel, public health volunteer work. Office: Nantucket AIDS Network 35 Old South Rd Nantucket MA 02554-2895 E-mail: cbartlett@nanet.org.

BARTLETT, CLIFFORD ADAMS, JR., lawyer; b. N.Y.C., Mar. 17, 1937; s. Clifford Adams and Frances (Burke) B.; m. Eileen Marie McCarthy; children: Elizabeth, Kathleen, Clifford III, Christopher, Karen, Charles, Eileen, Kevin, Jamison. BA, St. Francis Coll., N.Y.C., 1959; JD, St. John's U., N.Y., 1962. Bar: N.Y. 1963, U.S. Dist. Ct. (so. dist.) N.Y. 1964, U.S. Supreme Ct. 1966. Ptnr. Bartlett, McDonough, Bastone & Monaghan, Mineola, N.Y., 1992—. Mem. faculty Nassau Acad. Law, Mineola, N.Y. & N.Y.C., 1984—. Mem. ABA, N.Y. State Bar Assn., Nassau County Bar Assn., Nassau-Suffolk Trial Lawyers Assn., Suffolk County Bar Assn. Avocations: golf, skiing, swimming. Office: 300 Old Country Rd Mineola NY 11501-4198 also: 230 Park Ave New York NY 10169 also: 81 Main St White Plains NY 10601-1711 Office Phone: 516-877-2900, 516-877-2900. E-mail: clifford.bartlett@bmbm.com.

BARTLETT, CODY BLAKE, retired lawyer; b. Syracuse, N.Y, Apr. 21, 1939; s. Stanley Jay and Izora Elizabeth (Blake) B.; m. Claudine Germaine Bouthillette, Dec. 27, 1968; 1 child, Cody Blake. AAS, Auburn C.C., 1960; BA with high honors, Mich. State U., 1963; JD, Harvard U., 1966. Bar: Mich. 1967, N.Y. 1967, Colo. 1993, U.S. Dist. Ct. (ea. dist.) Mich. 1967, U.S. Dist. Ct. (no. dist.) N.Y. 1967, U.S. Supreme Ct. 1984, U.S. Dist. Ct. (we. dist.) N.Y. 1985, U.S. Ct. Appeals (2d cir.) 2002, U.S. Tax Ct. 1999, U.S. Ct. Fed. Claims 1999. Law clk. Onondaga County Dist. Atty.'s Office, Syracuse, 1965; assoc. Touche, Ross, Bailey & Smart, Detroit, 1966; law clk. Onondaga County Family Ct., Syracuse, 1967; assoc. Melvin & Melvin, Syracuse, 1967; budget and accounts officer Appellate Divsn., 4th Dept., Rochester, N.Y., 1967-69, dep. dir. adminstrn., 1969-72, dir. adminstrn., 1972-80; chief atty. State Commn. on Jud. Conduct, 1980-84; ptnr. Newman, Kehoe, Wunder and Bartlett, Lyons, N.Y., 1984-91, Kehoe, Bartlett & Kehoe, Wolcott, N.Y., 1992-94, Bartlett Law Offices, Wolcott, 1994—2005; ret., 2005. Spl. adminstr. N.Y. State Dangerous Drug Program, Western N.Y., 1973-75; adj. prof. polit. sci. dept. SUNY, Brockport, 1983-85, Grad. Sch. Pub. Adminstrn., 1985-90; adj. prof. Syracuse U. Coll. Law, 1980-84, Coll. Criminal Justice, Rochester Inst. Tech., 1979-80; grad. asst. polit. sci. dept. Mich. State U., 1962-63; lectr. jud. ethics and discipline Office Ct. Adminstrn., 1990. Author: Staying Fit Past Fifty, 1992; contbr. articles on legal issues and sports and fitness to publs.; drafter numerous legis. bills that became law. Mem. adv. com. Regional Criminal Justice Edn. and Tng. Ctr., Monroe C.C., Rochester, 1974-80; divsn. leader YMCA, Midtown Rochester membership drive, 1976; mem. East Bloomfield Planning Bd., 1984-87, chmn., 1985-87; trustee Village of East Bloomfield, 1985-87; mem. Sodus Point (N.Y.) Zoning Bd. Appeals, 1986-87; mem. adv. bd. Sodus Bay Hist. Soc., 1992; justice Sodus Point Village, 1994-95; mem. adv. bd. Wolcott C. of C., 1993; mem. Circuit of Reebok Profls. and Specialists, 1992-94. Recipient Disting. Alumni award Assn. Bds. Trustees SUNY, 1980; named nat., regional and state powerlifting and bench press champion, 1982, 83, 96-2002; N.Y. State and Am. nat. and world bench press record holder, 1996-2004, world bench press champion, 2004. Mem. N.Y. State Bar Assn. (spl. com. on jud. conduct 1984-90, profl. sports com. 1988-90), Wayne County Bar Assn., Onondaga County Bar Assn. (chmn. Syracuse City Ct. com. 1968-72), Nat. Strength and Conditioning Assn. (cert. strength and conditioning specialist, bd. dirs., lectr. 1989-96), Phi Kappa Phi, Pi Sigma Alpha. Home: 54 Little Spring Run Fairport NY 14450

BARTLETT, DAN, federal official; BA, U. Tex. With Karl Rove and Assocs., Austin, Tex.; dep. to policy dir. Office of Gov., Tex., 1994—98, issues dir. gov.'s re-election campaign, 1998; sr. spokesman, dir. Rapid Response Bush for Pres. campaign; dep. asst. to Pres., dep. to counselor to Pres. The White House, 2001—02, comm. dir., 2001—05, counselor to Pres., 2005—. Office: The White House 1600 Pennsylvania Ave Washington DC 20001*

BARTLETT, DAVID, management consultant; b. Bethlehem, Pa., Mar. 23, 1946; s. Bertram Francis and Sally Caroline (Lewis) Bartlett; m. Joan Carol Benevelli, Dec. 27, 1975. BA, Trinity Coll., Hartford, Conn., 1969. News dir. WRC Radio, Washington, 1979-81; mng. editor Metromedia TV news, Washington, 1981-83; dir. news and English broadcasts Voice of Am., Washington, 1984-85; program dir. NBC Radio Networks, N.Y.C., 1986-88, v.p., 1988-89; pres. Radio-TV News Dirs. Assn., Washington, 1989-97; dir. global news svcs. Worldspace Corp., Washington, 1998-2000; ptnr. Rowan & Blewitt, Washington, 2000—. Office Phone: 703-234-4428.

BARTLETT, DAVID CARSON, state legislator; b. New London, Conn., Feb. 2, 1944; s. Neil Riley and Susan Marion (Carson) B.; m. Barbara Hunting, July 14, 1973 (div. 1974); m. Janice Anne Wezelman, Feb. 11, 1979; children: Daniel Wezelman, Elizabeth Anne. Student, Wesleyan U., Middletown, Conn., 1962-64; BA, U. Ariz., 1966, MA, 1970; JD, Georgetown U., 1976. Teaching asst. U. Ariz., Tucson, 1967-69; program analyst U.S. Dept. Labor, Washington, 1970-76; assoc. Snell & Wilmer, Tucson, 1976-77; pvt. practice Tucson, 1976-79; assoc. Davis, Eppstein & Hall, Tucson, 1979-85; mem. Ariz. Ho. of Reps., Tucson, 1983-88, Ariz. State Senate, 1989-92; chief counsel for civil rights Ariz. Atty. Gen.'s Office, Tucson, 1993-99, spl. couns., 1999—2002. Democrat. Home: 3236 E Via Palos Verdes Tucson AZ 85716-5854

BARTLETT, DAVID FARNHAM, physics professor; b. N.Y.C., Dec. 13, 1938; s. Frederic Pearson and Margaret Mary (Boulton) B.; m. Roxana Ellen Stoessel, Nov. 19, 1960; children: Andrew, Susannah, Christopher, Jennifer AB, Harvard U., 1959; AM, Columbia U., 1961, PhD, 1965. Instr. Princeton U., N.J., 1964-67, asst. prof., 1967-71; assoc. prof. physics U. Colo., Boulder, 1971-82, prof., 1982—2003, prof. emeritus, 2004—. Editor: The Metric Debate, General Relativity and Gravitation, 1989; contbr. articles to profl. jours. Fellow Am. Phys. Soc.; mem. Am. Assn. Physics Tchrs., Am. Geophys. Union., Am. Astronomical Soc. Democrat. Home: 954 Lincoln Pl Boulder CO 80302-7234 Office: U Colo Dept Physics PO Box 390 Boulder CO 80309-0390 Office Phone: 303-492-6960. Business E-Mail: david.bartlett@colorado.edu.

BARTLETT, DEDE THOMPSON, association executive; m. James Wesley Bartlett; children: Katherine Morgan, John Eriksen. BA, Vassar Coll.; MA, NYU. V.p., corp. sec. Philip Morris Cos. Inc., 1991-94, v.p. corp. affairs programs, 1995—2002; comms. cons., 2002—; now pres. Women's Forum of N.Y. Mem. adv. bd. infrastructure, safety and environ. RAND Corp. Chair adv. bd. Nat. Domestic Violence Hotline; mem. adv. coun. Woodrow Wilson Nat. Fellowship Found.; bd. dirs. Corp. Alliance to Edn Ptnr. Violence. Recipient honors, YWCA, N.Y.C., Nat. Ctr. for Victims of Crime, Plays for Living, Nat. Coun. Jewish Women, Ctr. Against Domestic Violence, Lifetime TV. Home: 643 Oenoke Ridge New Canaan CT 06840 Office Phone: 203-966-8948.

BARTLETT, DESMOND WILLIAM, engineering company executive; b. Southampton, Eng., Feb. 11, 1931; came to U.S., 1971; s. Walter Hayward and Gladys (Akerman) B.; m. Joan Margaret Mitchell, July 19, 1952; children: Jennie Claire. Grad. Marine Engring., U. Coll., Southampton, 1951; diploma, Shippingport Nuclear Sch., Pitts., 1961; exec. devel. diploma, Cornell U., 1978. Registered profl. engr., Europe; chartered engr. U.K.; lic. chief engr., U.K. Ministry of Transport, nuclear power plant operator, U.K. Ministry of Def. Engr. officer Cunard Steamship Co., Liverpool, Eng., 1952-57; engr. Vickers Armstrong Ltd., Southampton, 1957-59; project mgr. Rolls Royce & Assocs., Derby, Eng., 1959-65; chief engr. Cammell Laird Shipbuilders & Engrs., Birkenhead, Eng., 1965-71; cons. Gibbs & Hill, Inc., N.Y.C., 1971-72; project dir. Westinghouse Electric Co., Pitts., 1972-79; pres. Dravo Engrs. Inc., Pitts., 1979-85, C.F. Braun, Inc., Alhambra, Calif., 1986-89; v.p. bus. devel. Raytheon Engrs. and Constructors, Inc., Phila., 1991-95; v.p. Corp. Ventures Flour Daniel, Irvine, Calif., 1995-98, Bartlett Consulting Ltd., Sewickley, Pa., 1998—. Bd. dirs. Dravotec spa, Milan, Italy, F.C. de Weger Bv, Rotterdam, Dravo-Still, Inc., Pitts., Worley Santa Fe Ltd., London, Santa Fe Braun (UK) Ltd, London, Biomechanics Corp. Am. Melville, N.Y., Badger Catlytic Ltd., New Malden, England, Catalytic Svcs., Caracas, Venequela, Cosa United C.A., Caracas, United Yemen, Sana Yemen. Decorated officer Order Brit. Empire (Eng.). Fellow Inst. Marine Engring. Sci. and Tech.; mem. ASME, Am. Nuclear Soc., Am. Mgmt. Assn., Project Mgmt. Inst., Am. Petroleum Inst., Coun. on Fgn. Rels. (L.A. com. on fgn. relations). Clubs: Duqesne. Office Phone: 412-749-0313. E-mail: bartlettobe@aol.com.

BARTLETT, ELIZABETH SUSAN, audio-visual specialist; b. Bloomington, Ind., Sept. 11, 1927; d. Cecil Vernon and Nell (Helfrich) Bartlett; m. Frederick E. Sherman, July 8, 1955 (div. 1978). Student, Ind. U., 1946—48. Traffic-continuity dir. WTTS-Radio, Bloomington, Ind., 1947—48; traffic continuity dir. WTTV-TV, Indpls., 1949—57, program dir., 1958—59; creative dir. Venus Advt. Agy., Indpls., 1960—68; prodn. mgr. Nat. TV News, Detroit, 1968—71; owner, prodr. Susan Sherman Prodns., Greenwich, Conn., 1971—73; audiovisual officer NSF, Washington, 1973—2001, cons., 2001—. Cons. NSF, 2001—; lectr. in field. Concept writer/prodr. film: The Observatories, 1981; prodr.: Science: Woman's Work, 1982, Keyhole of Eternity, 1975, What About Tomorrow?, 1978, The American Island, 1970, The New Engineers, 1986, Discover Science, 1988, A Brain, Books and a Curiosity, 1992, Radio Astronomy: Observing the Invisible Universe, 1999, Breaking the Code: The Arabidopsis Genome, 2000, others. Recipient Silver award Internat. Film and TV Festival of N.Y., 1970, 74, 2001, Gold medal Nat. Ednl. Film Festival, 1982, 89, Chris Bronze plaque Columbus Film Festival, 1982, Bronze award Internat. Film & TV Festival of N.Y., 1982, Gold award 1976, Gold Camera award U.S. Indsl. Film Festival, 1982, Silver Cindy award, Info. Film Prodrs. Assn., 1982, award for creative excellence U.S. Indsl. Film Festival, 1975, Techfilm Festival award, 1979, 80, 88, Gold award Houston Internat. Film Festival, 1987, Art Direction Mag. Creativity award, 1988, Videographer award of Distinction, 2001, Silver award, 2001, Aurora Festival Gold award, 2001; named Outstanding Woman for Contbn. in Arts, Federally Employed Women, 1984. Mem.: Am. Women in Radio and TV (chpt. pres. 1953—56, 1969—70), Coun. on Internat. Non-Theatrical Events (adv. bd., Golden Eagle award 1970, 1974, 1976—79, 1982, 1987, 1999), Washington Film and Video Coun. (pres. 1978—79). Home: 809 S Columbus St Alexandria VA 22314-4206 Office Phone: 703-292-7726.

BARTLETT, JAMES LOWELL, III, investment company executive; b. Boston, May 26, 1945; s. James Lowell and Shirley Victoria (Wyatt) B.; m. Shannon Mara McMillion, May 4, 1979; children: James Lowell IV, Zachary Morgan, Matthew Wyatt. BS, U. Calif., Berkeley, 1967, MBA, 1968. Loan officer nat. div. Bank of Am., Los Angeles, 1968; fin. mgr. Psychology Today mag., Del Mar, Calif., 1969; pres. Forum Communications Corp.; pub. Cuisine, Politics Today, Volleyball mags., N.Y.C., 1970-82; pres. Bartlett & Co., Santa Barbara, Calif., 1982—. Commr. Internat. Volleyball Assn., 1977-80 Mem. Lds Ch. Office: 5662 Calle Real Santa Barbara CA 93117-2317

BARTLETT, JAMES WILSON, III, lawyer; b. Pasadena, Calif., Mar. 21, 1946; s. James Wilson Jr. and Helen (Archbold) B.; m. Jane Edmunds Graves; children: Matthew Archbold, Polly Graves. BA, Washington & Lee U., 1968; JD, Vanderbilt U., 1975. Bar: Md. 1975, U.S. Dist. Ct. Md. 1975, U.S. Dist. Ct. (no. dist.) Ohio, 1992, U.S. Ct. Claims 1984, U.S. Ct. Appeals (4th cir.) 1976, U.S. Ct. Appeals (6th cir.) 1992, U.S. Supreme Ct. 1995. Assoc. Semmes, Bowen & Semmes, Balt., 1975-85; pvt. practice Balt., 1985-86; ptnr. Kroll & Tract, Balt., 1986-87, Wilson, Elser, Moskowitz, Edelman & Dicker, Balt., 1987-98, mng. ptnr., 1998-2001; ptnr. Semmes, Bowen & Semmes, Balt., 2001—. Permanent mem. jud. conf. 4th Cir.; bd. dirs. Balt. Maritime Exch., 2001—. Assoc. editor: Am. Maritime Cases, 1997—; contbr. articles to profl. jours. Chmn. law firm campaign United Fund, Balt., 1979; bd. dirs. Roland Park Civic League, 1987-90, Balt. (Md.) Maritime Exchange, 2001—. 1st lt. U.S. Army, 1969-71. Mem.: ABA (vice chmn. 1985—88, chmn. admiralty and maritime law tort and ins. practice sect. 1990—91, vice chmn. 1992—95, chmn. admiralty and maritime litig. com. litig. sect. 1997—99, vice chmn. 1999—), Assn. Average Adjusters U.S., Assn. Average Adjusters (Eng.), Md. Def. Counsel Inc., Def. Rsch. Inst., Maritime Law Assn. U.S. (proctor, bd. dirs. 1998—2001, chair practice and proc. com. 2000—04, sec. 2004—), Balt. City Bar Assn., Md. Bar Assn., St. Andrews Soc., Am. Boat and Yacht Coun., Tupenny Club, Propeller Club U.S. (gov. Balt. chpt. 1984—87, v.p. 1987—88, exec. v.p. 1988—89, pres. 1989—90, nat. regional v.p. 1991—92, nat. 3d v.p. 1995—96, gov. Balt. chpt. 1997—2003), Md. Club. Republican. Presbyterian. Home: 307 Edgevale Rd Baltimore MD 21210-1913 Office: Semmes Bowen & Semmes 250 W Pratt St Baltimore MD 21201 Office Phone: 410-576-4833. E-mail: jbartlett@semmes.com.

BARTLETT, JENNIFER LOSCH, artist; b. Long Beach, Calif., Mar. 14, 1941; BA, Mills Coll., 1963; B.F.A., Yale U., 1964, M.F.A., 1965; studied with Jack Tworkvov, James Rosenquist, Al Held, Jim Dire. Instr. Sch. Visual Arts, N.Y.C. One-woman shows include Mills Coll., Oakland, Calif., 1963, Reese Paley Gallery, N.Y.C., 1972, Paula Cooper Gallery, N.Y.C., 1974, 76, 77, 79, 81, 82, 83, 85, 87, 88, 90, 91, 92, 94, Saman Gallery, Genoa, Italy, 1974, 78, John Doyle Gallery, Chgo., 1975, Contemporary Art Ctr., Cin., 1975, Dartmouth Coll., 1975, Wadsworth Atheneum, Hartford, Conn., 1977, San Francisco Mus. Modern Art, 1978, U. Calif., Irvine, 1978, Hansen-Fuller Gallery, San Francisco, 1978, Balt. Art Mus., 1978, Art Mus. South Tex., Corpus Christi, 1978, Margo Leavin Gallery, Los Angeles, 1979, 81, 83, U. Akron, 1979, Carleton Coll., 1979, Heath Gallery, Atlanta, 1979, 83, Galerie Mukai, Tokyo, 1980, Akron Art Inst., 1980, 89, 92, Albright-Knox Art Gallery, Buffalo, 1980, Joslyn Art Mus., Omaha, 1982, Tate Gallery, London, 1982, McIntosh/Drysdale Gallery, Houston, 1982, Gloria Luria Gallery, Bay Harbor Islands, Fla., 1983, Rose Art Mus., Brandeis U., Waltham, Mass., 1984, Long Beach Mus. Art., Calif., 1984, Univ. Art Mus., U. Calif.-Berkeley, 1984, Knight Gallery, Charlotte, N.C., 1985, Walker Arts Ctr., Mpls., 1985, Nelson-Atkins Mus. of Art, Kansas City, Mo., 1985, Bklyn. Mus., 1985, La Jolla Mus. Coll. Art, Calif., 1986, Mus. of Art, Carnegie Inst., Pitts., 1986, Whitechapel Art Gallery, London, 1986, Cleve. Mus. Art, 1986, Greg Kucera Gallery, Seattle, 1986, 92, Harvard U. Grad. Sch. of Design, Cambridge, Mass., 1987, Milw. Art Mus., 1988, John Berggruen Gallery, San Francisco, 1988, 90, 93, Knoedler Gallery, London, 1989, 90, Richard Gray Gallery, Chgo., 1991, 93, 96, Maier Mus. Randolph-Macon Women's Coll., Lynchburg, Va., 1992, Nancy Drysdale Gallery, Washington, 1992, Santa Fe Inst. Fine Arts, 1993, Gallery Camino Real, Boca Raton, Fla., 1994, Orlando (Fla.) Mus. Art, 1994, Locks Gallery, Phila., 1995, Gagosian Gallery, Beverly Hills, Calif., 1996, 97, others; group exbhns. include Mus. Modern Art, N.Y.C., 1971, 77, 78, 79, 80, 81, 83, 85, Whitney Mus. Am. Art, N.Y.C., 1972, 73, 77, 78, 79, 81, 82, 83, 86, 89, 91, Walker Art Ctr., Mpls., 1972, Kunsthaus, Hamburg, Fed. Republic Germany, 1972, Paula Cooper Gallery, N.Y.C., 1972, 73, 74, 76, 77, 78, 81, 83, 84, 85, 86, 87, 88, 90, 93, Corcoran Gallery Art, Washington, 1975, Art Inst. Chgo., 1975, 76, 86, Kunstmuseum, Dusseldorf, Fed. Republic Germany, 1976, Kassel, Fed. Republic Germany, 1977, Contemporary Arts Mus., Houston, 1980, Am. Acad. Arts and Letters, N.Y.C., 1981, 83, 85, 92, Sarah Lawrence Art Gallery, Bronxville, N.Y., 1984, Archer M. Hunting Art Gallery, U. Tex.-Austin, 1984, Hudson River Mus., Yonkers, N.Y., 1984, Tucson Mus. Art, 1984, Leo Castelli Gallery, N.Y.C., 1984, Gerald Peters Gallery, Dallas, 1994, Numark Gallery, Washington, 1995, others; represented in permanent collections, Mus. Modern Art, N.Y.C., Met. Mus. Art, N.Y.C., Whitney Mus. Am. Art, N.Y.C., Phila. Mus. Art, Walker Art Ctr., Mpls., Yale U. Art Gallery, New Haven, Art Mus. S.Tex., Corpus Christi, R.I. Sch. Design, Providence, Art Gallery S. Australia, Adelaide, Goucher Coll., Balt., Amerada Hess, Woodbridge, N.J., Dallas Mus. Fine Arts, Richard B. Russell Fed. Bldg. and U.S. Courthouse, Atlanta, others. Recipient Harris prize Art Inst. Chgo., 1976, 86; recipient Creative Arts award Brandeis U., 1983, award Am. Acad. Arts and Letters, 1983, AIA award, 1986; Creative Artists Public Services fellow, 1974; Lucas vis. lectr. award Carleton Coll., 1979 Address: 134 Charles St # 114 New York NY 10014-2538 also: Paula Cooper Inc 534 W 21st St New York NY 10011-2812 also: c/o Gagosian Gallery 456 N Camden Dr Beverly Hills CA 90210

BARTLETT, JOHN LAURENCE, lawyer; b. L.A., June 9, 1942; s. Oswald and Sarah Elisabeth (Caldwell) B.; m. Jane Helen Dormann, June 22, 1963; children: Jennifer Lynn, George Andrew. AB, UCLA, 1963; LLB, Stanford Law Sch., 1967; ThM, Va. Theological Studies, 2004. Bar: D.C. 1967, U.S. Dist. Ct. D.C. 1968, U.S. Ct. Appeals (D.C. cir.) 1969, U.S. Ct. Appeals (4th cir.) 1976, U.S. Supreme Ct. 1976, U.S. Ct. Appeals (2d cir.) 1977. Assoc. Kirkland & Ellis, Washington, 1967-72, ptnr., 1972-83, Wiley, Rein & Fielding, Washington, 1983—. Bd. dirs. Arinc Inc., Aeronautical Radio, Inc., Cmty. Residences Found., chmn. 1995—. Bd. dirs. Found. for Ministry of the Laity, Inc. Mem. ABA, Fed. Comm. Bar Assn. Home: 2757 N Nelson St Arlington VA 22207-5033 Office: Wiley Rein & Fielding 1776 K St NW Washington DC 20006-2304 Office Phone: 202-719-7070. Business E-Mail: jbartlett@wrf.com.

BARTLETT, JOHN WESLEY, consulting firm executive; b. Camden, N.J., Oct. 18, 1935; s. William W. and Naomi Verna (Snook) B.; m. Helen Barbara Boulas, Mar. 2, 1968 (dec. Feb. 1986); children: Larah, Tanya; m. Joan R. Field, June 21, 2000. BSChemE, U. Rochester, 1957; MChemE, Rensselaer Poly. Inst., 1959, PhD, 1962. Staff engr. Knolls Atomic Power Lab., Schenectady, N.Y., 1957-62; asst. prof. U. Rochester, N.Y., 1962-68; Fulbright prof. nuclear engring. Istanbul (Turkey) Tech. U., 1968-69; program mgr. Pacific N.W. Labs., Richland, Va., 1969-78; presdl. exch. exec. Nat. Bur. Standards, Washington, 1973-74; dir. energy and environment Analytic Scis. Corp., Reading, Mass., 1978-89; cons. to sec. U.S. Dept. Energy, Washington, 1989-90, dir. Office Civilian Radioactive Waste Mgmt., 1990—; pres. The Bartlett Co., Vienna, Va., 1993-96, SC&A, McLean, Va., 1996—. Contbr. articles to profl. jours. Mem. Sch. Bd., Richland, 1970-73; mem., mayor pro tem City Coun., Richland, 1974-78; vice chair Conservation Commn., Lynnfield, Mass., 1979-89. Rsch. grantee NSF, 1963-64, NIH, 1965-68, recipient Robert E. Wilson award, AIChE, 1993. Mem. AAAS, Am. Nuclear Soc. (exec. com. 1976-80, 86-90), Rotary (bd. dirs. Richland club 1976-78), Sigma Xi. Republican. Avocations: model shipwright, piano. Home: 1300 Crystal Dr #403 Arlington VA 22202 Office: SC&A Inc 1200 Penn Ave Washington DC 20460 Office Phone: 202-564-0311. Personal E-mail: jbvienna@aol.com.

BARTLETT, JOSEPH WARREN, lawyer; b. Boston, June 14, 1933; s. Charles W. and Barbara (Hastings) B.; m. May Parish, Apr. 28, 1956 (div.); children: Charles, Susan, Henry; m. Barbara Bemis, Sept. 20, 1980. AB, Harvard U., 1955; LLB, Stanford U., 1960. Bar: Mass. 1962, D.C. 1969, N.Y. 1981. Law clk. Chief Justice Warren, U.S. Supreme Ct., 1960-61; pvt. practice Boston, 1961-66; ptnr. Gaston & Snow, Boston, 1966-80, Gaston & Snow (formerly Gaston Snow Beekman & Bogue), N.Y.C., 1980-90, of counsel, 1990-91; ptnr. Mayer, Brown & Platt, 1991-96, Morrison & Foerster, N.Y.C., 1996—2002; of counsel Fish & Richardson P.C., N.Y.C. Counsel Mass. Commn. Adminstrn., 1964-65; gen. counsel, under sec. Dept. Commerce, Washington, 1967-69; prin. adviser on universal social security coverage Sec. of HEW, Washington, 1978-79; acting prof. Stanford U., 1978; trustee, mem. fin. com. Montefiore Med. Ctr.; mem. Council on Fgn. Relations; adj. prof. NYU Law Sch. Served to 1st lt. U.S. Army, 1956—57. Fellow Am. Bar Found.; mem. Am. Law Inst., Am. Bar Assn., Boston Bar Assn. (pres. 1977-78) Democrat. Episcopalian. Home: 200 E 71st St Apt 16C New York NY 10021-5147 Office: Fish and Richardson PC Citi Group Ctr 153 E 53rd St 52nd Fl New York NY 10022 Office Phone: 212-641-2285. E-mail: bartlett@fr.com.

BARTLETT, KATHARINE TIFFANY, dean, law educator; b. New Haven, Feb. 16, 1947; d. Edgar Parmelee and Elizabeth (Clark) B.; m. Christopher H. Schroeder, Aug. 13, 1975; children: Emily, Ted, Elizabeth. BA, Wheaton Coll., 1968; MA, Harvard U., 1969; JD, U. Calif., Berkeley, 1975. Bar: Calif. 1975, N.C. 1980, U.S. Dist. Ct. (no. dist.) Calif. 1975, U.S. Dist. Ct. (mid. dist.) N.C. Law clk. to presiding justice Calif. Supreme Ct., San Francisco, 1975-76; atty. Legal Aid Soc. of Alameda County, Oakland, Calif., 1976-79; A. Kenneth Pye prof. of law Duke U., Durham, NC, 1979—; dean, 2000—. Vis. prof. UCLA, 1985-86, Boston U., 1990. Grad. prize fellow Harvard U., 1968-69, fellow Nat. Humanities Ctr., 1992-93. Mem. Am. Law Inst., Soc. Am. Law Tchrs., N.C. Women Attys., Am. Law Inst. (reporter for principles of family dissolution), Phi Beta Kappa. Democrat. Office: Duke Univ Law Sch Sci Dr and Towerview Rd Box 90362 Durham NC 27708-0362 Office Phone: 919-613-7001. E-mail: bartlett@law.duke.edu.

BARTLETT, LEONARD LEE, retired communications educator, advertising executive; b. Mountain Home, Idaho, May 31, 1930; s. Harold Roberts and Alma Martina (Nixon) B.; m. Sue Ann Kipfer, Nov. 5, 1966; children: Jennifer, Deborah; children by previous marriage: Linda Lee, Cynthia, Nancy, Pamela, William Charles. BA, Brigham Young U., Provo, Utah, 1957, MA, 1989. Advt. mgr. Steiner Co., Chgo., 1957-59; sr. v.p. Marsteller Inc., Chgo., 1959-67; vice chmn. Cole & Weber, Inc., Seattle, 1966-84; chmn. Cole & Weber Calif., San Francisco, 1984-86, Los Angeles, 1986-87; assoc. prof. communications Brigham Young U., Provo, 1989-2000; ret., 2000. Acting chmn. dept. comms. Brigham Young U., Provo, 1995—96, chmn. dept. comm., 1996—97, asst. to pres. univ. comms., 1997—2000. Mem. Am. Assn. Advt. Agys. (chmn. Western region 1980, nat. bd. 1980-81). Republican. Mem. Ch. Jesus Christ of Latter-day Saints. Home: 1211 East 2080 North Provo UT 84604-2123 Personal E-mail: leebar30@comcast.net.

BARTLETT, LYNN CONANT, English literature educator; b. Bethlehem, Pa., Dec. 14, 1921; s. Fay Conant and Marie Agnes (McGuiness) B.; m. Margaret Emma Johnson, June 29, 1946; 1 dau., Anne Elston. BA, Lehigh U., 1943; A.M., Harvard, 1947, PhD, 1957; B. Litt., Oxford U., Eng., 1952. Instr. English Lehigh U., 1946; teaching fellow Harvard, 1948-50; instr. Vassar Coll., 1952-57; asst. prof., 1957-62; asso. prof., 1962-70; prof., 1970-92; prof. emeritus, 1992—; asst. dean coll., 1958-61; sec. coll., 1966-76. Editor: (with W.R. Sherwood) The English Novel, Background Readings, 1967. Served with AUS, 1943-46. Decorated Bronze Star. Mem. Phi Beta Kappa, Sigma Phi Epsilon. Clubs: Harvard (N.Y.C.), Circumnavigators Club. Home: 170 College Ave Poughkeepsie NY 12603-2806 Personal E-mail: Lcbartlett6@aol.com.

BARTLETT, MICHAEL JOHN, lawyer; b. Paterson, N.J., June 8, 1943; s. Ernest John and Alice Edith (Schrell) B.; children: Tara Christine, Jessica Simons, Darren Michael. BA cum laude, Amherst Coll., 1965; JD, U. Va., 1969. Bar: Va. 1969, D.C. 1971, U.S. Supreme Ct. 1976. Atty. Office Gen. Counsel, NLRB, Washington, 1969-71; atty. law offices Joseph C. Wells, Washington, 1971-74; assoc. Vedder, Price, Kaufman, Kammholz & Day, Washington, 1974-76, ptnr., 1976-80; ptnr. (Michael J. Bartlett, P.C.) Ogletree, Deakins, Nash, Smoak & Stewart, Washington, 1980-86; staff v.p. employee rels. Ea. Airlines, Inc., 1986-87; shareholder Verner, Liipfert, Bernhard, Mc Pherson and Hand, Chartered, 1987-94; pvt. practice, 1994-98; dir. labor law policy U.S. C. of C., 1998—2002; mem. NLRB, Washington, 2002—. Contbr. articles to profl. jours. Mem. exec. bd. Arlington (Va.) YMCA, 1982-86, treas., 1984-86. Andrew D. Lawrie scholar, Amherst Coll., 1964-65; Am. Jurisprudence award in labor law Lawyer Coop. Pub. Co., 1969. Mem. ABA (sect. on labor law), Va. State Bar, D.C. Bar. Home: 4650 Washington Blvd Apt 926 Arlington VA 22201-5776 Office: 1099 14th St NW Washington DC 20570-2000

BARTLETT, NEIL, chemist, emeritus educator; b. Newcastle-upon-Tyne, Eng., Sept. 15, 1932; s. Norman and Ann Willins (Vock) B.; m. Christina Isabel Cross, Dec. 26, 1957; children: Jeremy John, Jane Ann, Christopher, Robin. B.Sc., Kings Coll., U. Durham, Eng., 1954; PhD in Inorganic Chemistry, Kings Coll., U. Durham, 1957; D.Sc. (hon.), U. Waterloo, Can., 1968, Colby Coll., 1972, U. Newcastle-upon-Tyne, 1981, McMaster U., Can., 1992; D.Univ. (hon.), U. Bordeaux, France, 1976, U. Ljubljana, Slovenia, 1989, U. Nantes, France, 1990; LLD, Simon Fraser U., Can., 1993; Dr. rer. nat. (hon.), Freie U., Berlin, 1998. Lectr. chemistry U. B.C., Vancouver, Canada, 1958—63, prof., 1963—66; prof. chemistry Princeton U., NJ, 1966—69, U. Calif., Berkeley, 1969—99; guest sr. scientist chem. sci. divsn. LBNL, Berkeley, 1999—. Mem. adv. bd. on inorganic reactions and methods Verlag Chemie, 1978—; mem. adv. panel Nat. Measurement Lab., Nat. Bur. Stds., 1974-80; E.W.R. Steacie Meml. fellow NRC, Can., 1964-66; Miller vis. prof. U. Calif., Berkeley, 1967-68; 20th G.N. Lewis Meml. lectr., 1973; William Lloyd Evans Meml. lectr. Ohio State U., 1966; A.D. Little lectr. Northeastern U., 1969; Phi Beta Upsilon lectr. U. Nebr., 1975; Henry Werner lectr. U. Kans., 1977; Jeremy Musher Meml. lectr., Israel, 1980, Randolph T. Major Meml. lectr. U. Conn., 1985, J.C. Karcher lectr. U. Okla., 1988; Brotherton vis. prof. U. Leeds, Eng., 1981; Erskine vis. lectr. U. Canterbury, New Zealand, 1983; Wilsmore fellow Melbourne U., Australia, 1983; vis. fellow All Souls Coll., Oxford U., 1984; Miller prof. U. Calif.-Berkeley, 1986-87; George H. Cady lectr. U. Wash., Seattle, 1994; Leermakers lectr. Wesleyan U., 1995; Davis Meml. lectr. U. New Orleans, 1997, Pierre Duhem seminaires, U. Bordeaux, 1998. Bd. editors Inorganic Chemistry, 1967-79, Jour. Fluorine Chemistry, 1971-80, Synthetic Metals, Revue Chimie Minerale; mem. adv. bd. McGraw-Hill Ency. Sci. and Tech. Recipient Rsch. Corp. prize; E.W.R. Steacie prize, 1965; Elliott Cresson medal Franklin Inst., 1968; Kirkwood medal Yale U. and Am. Chem. Soc. (New Haven sect.), 1969; Dannie-Heinemann prize The Gottingen acad. 1971; Robert A. Welch award in chemistry, 1976; Alexander von Humboldt Found. award, 1977; medal Jozef Stefan Inst., Slovenia, 1980; Moissan medal, 1986; Prix Moissan, Paris, 1988; Grand Prix de la Fondation de la Maison de la Chimie, 2004; fellow Alfred P. Sloan Found., 1964-66; Bonner Chemiepries, Bonn, 1991; Berkeley citation, 1993. Fellow Royal Soc. (Davy medal, 2002), Royal Soc. Chemistry (U.K., hon.), Am. Acad. Arts and Scis., Chem. Inst. Can. (1st Noranda lectr. 1963), Royal Soc. Can.; mem. NAS (fgn. assoc.), Leopoldina Acad. (Halle, Salle), Akademie der Wissenschaften in Gottingen, Associé Etranger, Academia Europaea, Académie des Sciences, Institut de France, Am. Chem. Soc. (chmn. divs. fluorine chemistry 1972, inorganic chemistry 1977, award in inorganic chemistry 1970, W.H. Nichols award N.Y. sect. 1983, Pauling medal of Pacific N.W. sects. 1989, Disting. Svc. award 1989, award for Creative Work in Fluorine Chemistry 1992), Phi Lambda Upsilon (hon.) Home: 6 Oak Dr Orinda CA 94563-3912 Office: Bldg 70A c/o Rm 3307 LBNL Berkeley CA 94720 Business E-Mail: nbartlett@lbl.gov.

BARTLETT, NORMA THYRA, retired administrative assistant; b. Raymond, S.D., June 7, 1922; d. Wilhelm Emil and Olga Sophie (Mailand) Claussen; m. Fred Otis Metcalf, Mar. 29, 1941 (dec. Apr. 1963); children: Linda E. Lepak, Barry Otis (dec. Feb. 2000); m. Francis Grindal Bartlett, Dec. 27, 1963 (dec. Jan. 2004). BA, U. Wash., 1969; Diploma, Inst. of Children's Lit., 1997. Cert. profl. sec. Office mgr. Fed. Old Line Ins. Co., Everett, Wash., 1949-55; supr. office svc. Scott Paper Co., Everett, Wash., 1958-63; tchr. bus. edn. Canyon Park Jr. H.S., Seattle, 1969, Bellevue (Wash.) C.C., 1969; exec. asst. Peoples Bank, Starkville, Miss., 1970-76; prin. Satellite Steno Svc., Starkville, Miss., 1976-77; office mgr. Donald Wiley & Assocs., Sydney, Australia, 1977-80. Bd. dirs. United Cmty. Fund Snohomish County, Everett, Wash., 1961-62; pres. Scott Paper Co. Fellowship Fund, Everett, 1961. Hon. life mem. United Luth. Ch. Women, Everett, Wash., 1958—; organizer, charter pres. Starkville Bus. and Profl. Women, 1972-74; pres. Welcome Wagon Club, Ocean Springs, Miss., 1982-83; tutor Jackson County Literacy, Ocean Springs, 1985-88; organizer Discourse, Ocean Springs, 1985-86. Norma T. Bartlett scholarship named in her honor Starkville Area Bus. and Profl. Women, 1978. Mem.: AAUW (Gig Harbor br. media rep. 1997—99), Intertel, Mensa (local sec. 1989—91, editor newsletter 1987—89), U. Wash. Alumni Assn. Democrat. Lutheran. Avocations: needlecrafts, reading, writing, travel. Home: 1305 N Highlands Pkwy Apt C1 Tacoma WA 98406-2171 E-mail: fgbart@comcast.net.

BARTLETT, RAYMOND L., music educator; b. Walton, N.Y., Oct. 23, 1962; s. Robert Hoyt and Sarah Alta Bartlett; m. Jennifer Lynn Carlson, Aug. 13, 1983; children: Josiah Douglas, Rebekah Lynn, Caleb Joseph. MusB Edn., Houghton Coll., 1984; MusM Edn., Ithaca Coll. Sch. of Music, 1989. Music tchr. Walton Ctrl. Sch., NY, 1984—. Deacon First Bapt. Ch., Walton, NY, 1998—2004. Mem.: NYSSMA. Home: 4433 Pines Brook Rd Walton NY 13856 Office: Walton Ctrl Sch 47 - 49 Stockton Ave Walton NY 13856

BARTLETT, RICHARD ADAMS, retired history professor; b. Boulder, Colo., Nov. 23, 1920; s. John Thomas and Margaret Emily (Abbott) Bartlett; m. Marie Regina Cosgrove, Dec. 26, 1945; children: Richard, Margaret, Thomas, Mary. BA, U. Colo., 1942, PhD, 1953; MA, U. Chgo., 1947. Instr. Tex. A&M U., College Station, 1945-51; asst. prof. Fla. State U., Tallahassee, 1955-63, assoc. prof., 1963-67, prof., 1968-89, prof. emeritus, 1989—. Author: Great Surveys of the American West, 1962, 1966, paperback, 1993, The Wilderness and the Indians: Challenges in the New World, 1970, Nature's Yellowstone, 1974, The New Country: A Social History of the American Frontier, 1776-1890, 1974, paperback, 1986, Freedom's Trail, 1979, 2d edit., 1981, Yellowstone: A Wilderness Besieged, 1985;; paperback, 1989, From Cody to the World: The First Seventy-Five Years of the Buffalo Bill Memorial Association, 1992, Troubled Waters: Champion International and the Pigeon River Controversy, 1995, Yellowstone Holiday, 1998; editor: The Gilded Age: America, 1865-1900, 1969, Rolling Rivers: An Encyclopedia of America's Rivers, 1984; contbr. articles and bookr revs. to profl. jours. Fellow, Am. Philos. Soc., 1967; grantee, Fla. State U.; Hungtington Libr. fellow, 1967, Woodrow Wilson fellow, Smithsonian Inst., 1979—80. Mem.: Fla. Coll. Tchrs. History (pres. 1974—75), Western History Assn. (governing coun. 1976—79, mem. editl. bd. The Am. West 1980—82), Phi Alpha Theta. Episcopalian. Home: 2205 Mendoza Ave Tallahassee FL 32304-1319 Personal E-mail: rbartlet@mailer.fsu.edu.

BARTLETT, RICHARD CHALKLEY, writer, conservationist; b. L.A., May 23, 1935; s. Theodore Lester Bartlett and Maud (Colley) Newsom; m. Joanne Krieger; children: Lisa, Christopher. BS in Communications, U. Fla., 1956. With advt. sales dept. The Miami (Fla.) Herald, 1958; internat. sales and mgmt. exec. for home parties div. Tupperware Inc., Orlando, 1959-65; v.p. advt. and sales promotion Vanda Beauty Counselor div. Dart Industries, Orlando, Fla., 1965-71; exec. v.p. mktg. Dynasty Industries Inc., Dallas, 1971-73; dir. mktg. svcs. Mary Kay Inc., Dallas, 1973-76, v.p. mktg., 1976-85, exec. v.p. mktg., 1986-87, pres., COO, 1987-93, vice-chmn., 1993—. Chmn. U.S. Direct Selling Assn., Washington, 1991-93, U.S. Direct Selling Edn. Found., Washington, 1993-94, bd. dirs.; vice chmn. edn. World Fedn. Direct Selling, 1997-99; bd. dirs. Vital Voice Global Partnership, 2001-03; adv. bd. U. Fla. Ctr. for Retailing Edn. and Rsch., Gainesville; adv. coun., bd. dirs. mem. adv. coun. U. Tex. Press; mem. adv. com. Coll. Agrl. Sci. and Natural Resources, Tex. Tech. U.; chmn. bd. dirs. Nat. Environ. Edn. and Tng. Found.; bd. dirs. Nat. Coun. Sci. and the Environment. Author: The Direct Option, 1994, Saving the Best of Texas: A Partnership Approach to Conservation, 1995; co-author: The Sportsman's Guide to Texas, 1988. Chmn. Tex. Environ. Edn. Partnership Fund Bd.; bd. dirs. Better Bus. Bur. Met. Dallas, The Aldo Leopold Found., Nature Conservancy N.Mex.; hon. trustee The Nature Conservancy of Tex.; chmn. edn. and outreach adv. com. Tex. Parks and Wildlife Dept. With U.S. Army, 1957. Named Outstanding Marketer of Yr., Southwestern Mktg. Assn., 1991, Chief of Exec. of Yr., Internat. TV Assn., 1992; named to U.S. Direct Selling Assn. Hall of Fame, 1994, U.S. Direct Selling Edn. Found. Circle of Honor, 1995, Pi Kappa Phi

Nat. Hall of Fame, 1996; recipient Oak Leaf award Nature Conservancy, 1997. Mem. Acad. Mktg. Sci. (Disting. Marketer of Yr. 1995). Avocations: conservation work, performing arts. Office: Mary Kay PO Box 799045 Dallas TX 75379-7045

BARTLETT, RICHARD JAMES, lawyer; b. Glens Falls, N.Y., Feb. 15, 1926; s. George Willard and Kathryn M. (McCarthy) Bartlett; m. Claire E. Kennedy, Aug. 18, 1951; children: Michael, Amy. BS, Georgetown U., 1945; LLB, Harvard U., 1949; LLD (hon.), Union Coll., 1974; ScD (hon.), Albany Med. Coll., 1986. Bar: N.Y. 1949. Pvt. practice, Glens Falls, 1949-73; mem. NY Assembly, 1959—66; with Clark Bartlett & Caffry, 1962-73; justice N.Y. State Supreme Ct., 1973-79; chief adminstr. cts. N.Y. State, 1974-79; dean Albany (N.Y.) Law Sch., Union U., 1979-86; mem. Bartlett, Pontiff, Stewart, & Rhodes P.C., Glens Falls, 1986—. Com. mem. Revising Pend Law, 1961—70; mem. N.Y. Bd. Law Examiners, 1986—2001, chair, 1998—2001; chmn. N.Y. Jud. Commn. Justice for Children, 1988—90; trustee Nat. Conf. Bd. Examiners, 1987—97, chair, 1996; dir. Nat. Conf. Bar Founds., 2001—03; del. N.Y. Constl. Conv., 1967. Trustee Hyde Collection, Glens Falls, 1967—98. Capt. USAF, 1951—53. Fellow: Am. Bar Found.; mem.: ABA (ho. dels. 1997—2001), N.Y. State Bar Assn. (ho. dels. 2002—, Gold medal 2004), N.Y. Bar Found. (bd. dirs. 1989—, pres. 2000—03), Am. Law Inst. (life), Warren County Bar, Assn. Bar City of N.Y. Republican. Roman Catholic. Office: 1 Washington St PO Box 2168 Glens Falls NY 12801-2168 Office Phone: 518-792-2117. Business E-Mail: rjb@bpsrlaw.com.

BARTLETT, ROBERT HAWES, surgeon; b. Ann Arbor, Mich., May 8, 1939; BA, Albion (Mich.) Coll., 1960; MD cum laude, U. Mich., 1963. Diplomate Nat. Bd. Med. Examiners, Am. Bd. Surgery (examination cons. 1989-90), Am. Bd. Thoracic Surgery. Intern in surgery Peter Bent Brigham Hosp., Boston, 1963-64, asst. resident/sr. asst. resident, 1964-67, chief resident in thoracic surgery, 1968, chief resident surgeon, 1969; rsch. fellow in surgery Harvard Med. Sch., Boston, 1968, Arthur Tracy Cabot Teaching fellow in surgery, 1969; Harvey Cushing fellow and rsch. fellow in surgery Peter Bent Brigham Hosp./Harvard Med. Sch., Boston, 1969-70; asst. prof. surgery U. Calif., Irvine, 1970-73, assoc. prof. surgery, 1973-77, prof. surgery, 1977-80, U. Mich., Ann Arbor, 1980—. Asst. in surgery Peter Bent Brigham Hosp., 1969-70; attending staff U. Calif.-Irvine/Orange County Med. Ctr., 1970-80, asst. dir. surg. svcs., 1970-80, dir. burn ctr., 1971-80; attending staff St. Joseph Hosp., Orange, Calif., 1970-80, Children's Hosp. of Orange County, 1970-80, VA Hosp., Long Beach, 1970-80, Wayne County Gen. Hosp., 1980-84, Westland Med. Ctr., 1984-85; attending staff U. Mich. Med. Ctr., 1980—, dir. SICU, 1980—, gen. surgery sect. head, 1981-87, dir. grad. edn., 1980-91, trauma/critical care divsn. chief, 1980-91, critical care divsn. chief, 1991—, program dir. surg. critical care fellowship, 1991—, dir. extracorporeal life support program, 1980—; lectr. in field; cons. in field to NIH, Nat. Heart and Lun Inst., Calif. Heart Assn., March of Dimes Found., numerous others. Editl. bd. Perfusion, 1985—, Critical Care, 1985—, Trans ASAIQ, 1986—, Internat. Jour. Biomaterials, Artificial Cells and Artificial Organs, 1987, Jour. Thoracic and Cardiovascular Surgery, 1992-94, SESATS; reviewer Sci., 1974, Chest, 1974-79, 83—, Jour. Applied Physiology, 1977, Heart and Lung, 1978—, New Eng. Jour. Medicine, 1981, 87-88, Surgery, 1984—, Am. Rev. Respiratory Disease, 1985—, Jour. Thoracic and CArdiovascular Surgery, 1987—, Artificial Organs, 1987—, Pediatrics, 1987—, Intensive Care Medicine, 1987—, Jour. Parenteral and Enteral Nutrition, 1988—, Jour. Critical Care, 1989—, Jour. AMA, 1993—, Am. Jour. Respiratory and Critical Care Medicine, 1993—; patentee in field; contbr. over 243 articles to profl. jours., chpts. to books; author: Mechanical Devices for Cardiopulmonary Assistance, Advances in Cardiology, Vol. 6, 1971, Hematological Analysis of extracorporeal Membrane Oxygenation, 1974, Extracorporeal Circulation for Cardiopulmonary Failure, Current Problems in Surgery, Vol. 15, 1978, Extracorporeal Life Support for Cardiopulmonary Failure, Current Problems in Surgery, Vol. 27, 1990; co-editor: Biologic and Synthetic Vascular Protheses, 1982, Life Support Systems in Invensive Care, 1984, Medical Education: A Surgical Perspective, 1986; editor: Respiratory Care of the Surgical Patient, 1980. Rsch. grantee Orange County Heart Assn., 1971, Donald E. Baxter Found., 1970-71, Calif. TB and Respiratory Disease Assn., 1971-72, NIH, 1972-75, 74-77, 76-79, 78-80, 81-84, 84-85, 84-85, 85-90, 90-92, Hearst Found., 1976-78, 79-80, 89-93, Thoratec Inc., 1983, Mead-Johnson, 1983, GM Corp., 1984-85, others; recipient Gibbon award Am. Soc. Extra-Corporeal Tech., 1992, Dwight E. Harken award Temple U., 1992, Kaiser Permanente Excellence in Teaching award, 1993. Mem. ACS, Am. Surg. Assn., Am. Assn. Thoracic Surgery, Am. Assn. for Surgery of Trauma, Assn. for Acad. Surgery, Ctrl. Surg. Soc., Coller Surg. Soc., Soc. Univ. Surgeons, Surg. Biology Club II, Surg. Infection Soc., Western Thoracic Surg. Assn., Am. Burn Assn., Am. Assn. History of Medicine, Am. Physiol. Soc., Am. Coll. Chest Physicians, Am. Soc. for Artificial Internal Organs (bd. trustees 1986-87, regulatory affairs com. 1985—, pres. 1984, others), Am. Thoracic Soc., Am. Trauma Soc., Extracorporeal Life Support Orgn., Internat. Soc. Artificial Organs, Mich. Soc. Critical Care, Perinatal Assn. Mich., Soc. Critical Care Medicine, Am. Inst. for Med. and Biol. Engring. (charter mem.), Beta Beta Beta, Alpha Omega Alpha, Galens Hon. Med. Soc., Inst. Medicine, 2004. Office: U Mich 1500 E Medical Ctr Dr #2920 Ann Arbor MI 48109-0999

BARTLETT, ROBERT WATKINS, metallurgist, educator, consultant; b. Salt Lake City, Jan. 8, 1933; s. Charles E. and Phyllis (Watkins) B.; m. Betty Cameron, Dec. 3, 1954; children: John C., Robin Parmley, Bruce R., Susanne. BS, U. Utah, 1953, PhD, 1961. Registered profl. engr., Calif. Group leader ceramics SRI Internat., Menlo Park, Calif., 1964-67; assoc. prof. metallurgy Stanford U., Palo Alto, Calif., 1967-74; mgr. hydrometallurgy Kennecott Minerals Co., Salt Lake City, 1974-77; dir. materials lab. SRI Internat., Menlo Park, Calif., 1977-80; v.p. rsch. Anaconda Minerals Co., Tucson, 1980-85; mgr. materials tech. Idaho Sci. and Tech. Dept., Idaho Falls, 1985-87; dean Coll. Mines and Earth Resources, U. Idaho, Moscow, 1987-97. Dir. Idaho Geol. Survey, Moscow. Author approximately 100 rsch. publs. in metallurgy; 12 patents in field; 1 textbook. Served to lt. (j.g.) USN, 1953-56. Recipient Turner award Electrochem. Soc., 1965, McConnell award AIME, 1985. Mem. Nat. Acad. Engring., Metall. Soc. (pres. 1989, EPD lecturer 1997), Soc. Mining Engrs. (disting. mem., Wadsworth award 1996), Sigma Xi, Tau Beta Pi. Office: 2505 Loch Way El Dorado Hills CA 95762 Personal E-mail: bobnbettybartlett@sbcglobal.net.

BARTLETT, ROSCOE G., congressman; b. Moreland, Ky., June 3, 1926; married; 10 children. BA, Columbia Union, 1947; MS, U. Md., 1948, PhD, 1952. Asst. prof. Loma Linda Med. Sch., 1952-54, Howard Med Sch., 1954-56; rschr. NIH, 1956-59; engr. Naval Aerospace Med. Inst., 1959-62, 62-67; dir. Space Life Scis. Divsn. Johns Hopkins U., 1968-74; dir. rsch. devel. IBM, 1975-87; owner Roscoe Bartlett & Assocs.; mem. U.S. Congress from 6th Md. Dist., 1993—, mem. armed svcs. com., sci. com., vice chmn. small bus. com. Republican. Office: US Ho of Reps 2412 Rayburn House Ofc Bldg Washington DC 20515-0001*

BARTLETT, SHIRLEY ANNE, accountant; b. Gladwin, Mich., Mar. 28, 1933; d. Dewey J. and Ruth Elizabeth (Wright) Frye; m. Charles Duane Bartlett, Aug. 16, 1952 (div. Sept. 1982); children: Jeanne, Michelle, John, Yvonne. Student, Mich. State U., 1952-53, Rutgers U., 1972-74. Auditor State of Mich., Lansing, 1951-66; cost acct. Templar Co., South River, N.J., 1968-75; staff acct. Franco Mfg. Co., Metuchen, N.J., 1975-78; controller Thomas Creative Apparel, New London, Ohio, 1978-80; mgr. gen. acctg. Ideal Electric Co., Mansfield, Ohio, 1980-85; staff acct. Logangate Homes, Inc., Girard, Ohio, 1985-88; pvt. practice acctg. Youngstown, 1985—; acct. Universal Devel. Enterprises, Liberty Twp., Ohio, 1987-88. V.p. Lang Industries, Inc., Youngstown, 1984-93. Author: (play) Our Bicentennial-A Celebration, 1976. Mem. various orchs., Mich., Va., Ohio, soloist, Mich., Va.; mem. Human Rels. Commn., Franklin Township, 1971-77, Friends of Am. Art; treas. Heritage Found., New Brunswick, N.J., 1973-74, New London Proceeds Corp., 1979-83; commr. Huron Park Commn., Ohio, 1979-83; elected Dem. com. mem., N.J., Ohio, 1970-82; vol. IRS for small bus., 1988-94; mem. planning com. Youngstown State U. Tax Insts., 1990-95, presenter, 1990098; bd. dirs., treas. Discovery Place, Inc., 1991-95; mem. planning com. for Children's Miracle Network Telethon, Tod's Children's Hosp., Youngstown, 1985-2001; mem. citizens adv. bd. of the Mahoning County Juvenile Ct., 2004—; bd. dirs., treas. Youngstown Arts and Entertainment Dist. Assn., 2003—; founder Youngstown Farmer's Market, 2003—; mem. Mahoning Valley Children's Mus., 2004—; apptd. to citizens' adv. bd. Mahoning Ct., 2004—; treat. Youngstown Arts and Entertainment Dist. Assn., 2005—. Mem.: NOW (treas. Youngstown chpt. 1986—93), NAFE, Am. Soc. Notaries, Am. Soc. Women Accts. (bd. dirs. 1986—88, v.p. 1988—89, pres. 1989—91, scholarship com. 1991—2001, chair chpt. devel. 1995—96, bd. dirs. 1996—2001, bd. dirs. 1996—, chair program com. 1997—2001), Youngstown Arts & Entertainment Dist. Assn., Chataqua Lit. and Sci. Cir., Friends of Am. Art, Citizen's League Greater Youngstown, Bus. and Profl. Women (v.p. 1980—2001), Nat. Women's Polit. Caucus, Women's Jour. Network, Internat. Platform Assn., Youngstown Opera Guild, Sci. Cir. Club (pres. 1979—), Chataqua Literary Club, Franklin JFK Club (treas. 1970—72, v.p. 1973—78), Investment Club (pres. 1997—99, treas. 1999—2001). Democrat. Unitarian Universalist. Avocations: music, knitting, needlecrafts. Office Phone: 330-788-8638. E-mail: sbartlett328@hotmail.com, sbartlett328@zoominternet.net.

BARTLETT, THOMAS ALVA, retired educational administrator; b. Salem, Oreg., Aug. 20, 1930; s. Cleave Wines and Alma (Hanson) B.; m. Mary Louise Bixby, Mar. 20, 1954; children: Thomas Glenn, Richard A., Paul H. Student, Willamette U., 1947—49, DCL (hon.), 1986; AB, Stanford U., 1951, PhD, 1959; MA, Oxford (Eng.) U., 1953; LHD (hon.), Colgate U., 1977, Mich. State U., 1978, Union Coll., 1979; DCL (hon.), Pusan Nat. U., Korea, 1985, U. Ala., 1983, U. N. Ala., 2001; DHL (hon.), Am. U., Cairo, 2004. Mem. U.S. Permanent Mission to UN, 1956-63; advisor Gen. Assembly Dels., 1956-63; pres. Am. U., Cairo, 1963-69, Colgate U., Hamilton, NY, 1969-77, Assn. Am. Univs., Washington, 1977-82; chancellor U. Ala. Sys., 1982-89, Oreg. State Sys. of Higher Edn. Office, Eugene, 1989-94, SUNY, 1994-96; ret., 1996; interim pres. Am. U., Cairo, 2002—03. Mem. UAR-U.S. Ednl. Exch. Commn., 1966-69; mem. Task Force on Financing Higher Edn. in N.Y. State (Keppel Commn.), 1972-73; chmn. Commn. Ind. Colls. and Univs. N.Y., 1974-76; bd. dirs. Nat. Assn. Ind. Colls. and Univs., 1975-76; trustee Univs. Field Staff Internat., 1985-87; mem. NASA Comml. Space Adv. Com., 1988-90. Mem. nat. bd. examining Chaplains Episcopal Ch., 1978-91; trustee Gen. Theol. Sem., 1977-82, Am. U., Cairo, 1978-2002, vice chair 1998-2002; trustee U.S.-Japan Found., 1988-2001, chmn. 1996-2001; bd. mem. Internat. Assn. of Univs., 1995-2000; trustee Am. U. Kuwait, 2004—. Rhodes scholar, Oxford U., 1953. Mem. Coun. Fgn. Rels., Century Assn., Phi Beta Kappa. Home: 1209 SW 6th Ave Apt 904 Portland OR 97204 E-mail: t-mbartlett@att.net.

BARTLETT, THOMAS FOSTER, management consultant; b. Oklahoma City, Nov. 28, 1918; s. Martin Johnson and Clara Nell (Mattingly) Bartlett. BS, Harvard U., 1943, MBA, 1948; cert., Sorbonne, Paris, 1987, Oxford (Eng.) U., 1988, Cambridge (Eng.) U., 1989, U. Salamanca, Spain, 1993, U. Genoa, Italy, 1994; grad., US Command and Gen. Staff Coll, Ft. Leavenworth, Kans., 1945. Asst. to pres. Am. Express Co., N.Y.C., 1948-50; export promotion specialist Dept. of State, Paris; mem. U.S. Mission to NATO Dept. Def., London and Paris; econ. cons. Am. Embassy, Rome, 1950-55; exec. asst. to pres. for internat. devel. Kaiser Industries, Oakland, Calif., 1955-56; mktg. specialist Bigelow-Sanford Inc., N.Y.C., 1957-59; pres. Internat. Mgmt. Cons. Thomas F. Bartlett & Assocs., N.Y.C., 1959—. Cons. UN, U.S. Govt., fgn. govts., corps., other orgns. Capt. U.S. Army, 1943—46, maj. USAFR. Mem.: Am. Mktg. Assn., Am. Mgmt. Assn., Am. Soc. Profl. Cons., Harvard Club. Avocations: travel, photography, lecturing. Office: Thomas F Bartlett & Assoc 330 E 52nd St New York NY 10022-6718

BARTLETTE, DONALD LLOYD, social worker, consultant; b. Walhalla, N.D., Dec. 17, 1939; s. Abraham Bruno and Lily Alice (Houle) B.; m. Julie Gay Poer, Feb. 1, 1969; children: Lisa Maaca, Joanna Leigh, Andrea Gay, Marisa Anne,m Laura Bethany, Sara Elizabeth, Seth VanAdams, Vanessa Joy. PhB, U. N.D., 1962; MA, N.D. State U., 1966; PhD, CPU, 1981. Camp worker, program dir. Camp Grassick, N.D., 1957-62; unit supr., counselor Cambridge State Sch. and Hosp., 1963-64; group worker Children's Village, Fargo, N.D., 1964-65; supr. Meth. Children's Village, Detroit, 1966-68; program dir. Mich. Children's Inst., Ann Arbor, 1968-70; exec. program dir. Madison County (Ind.) Assn. for Retarded, 1970-71; dir. program and social work svcs. Outreach Cmty. Ctr., Mpls., 1972-73; exec. dir. Minn. Epilepsy League, St. Paul, 1974-75; pvt. cons. in retardation, 1972-75; coord. spl. svcs., adviser Human Rights Commn. City of Bloomington, Minn., 1975-78; assoc. pastor, dir. social svcs. Am. Indian Evang. Ch., Mpls., 1978-79; dir. social svcs. Stark County (Ohio) Bd. Mental Retardation, 1979-80; field work instr. Sch. Social Work U. Minn., Augsburg Coll., Mpls., 1972-73; off-campus tchr. in retardation and social work Anderson Coll., 1970-71; adj. faculty Univ. Without Walls, U. Minn., 1972-73. Author presentation: Macaroni at Midnight; film participant Believing for the Best in You, 1985; film subject When Nobody Loves You, 1988; focus of play Macaroni at Midnight, Erie, Pa., 1986. Pres. Nat. Minority Affairs Coalition, 1977-78, sec., 1976-77; mem. Met. Developmental Disabilities Task Force, 1975; chmn. Pub. Info. Coalition Project on Developmental Disabilities Task Force, 1974-75; vol. mem. Pres.'s Minn. Gov.'s coms. on employment handicapped; task force minority affairs Pres.'s Com. Mental Retardation; bd. dirs. N.W. Hennepin Human Svcs. Coun., 1975-76; bd. dirs., chmn. poverty com. Anoka County Assn. for Retarded, 1974-79; bd. dirs. Family and Children's Svcs. of Greater Mpls., Stark County Mental Health Bd., Citizen Advocacy Program of Stark County; cons. People First of Stark County; adv. Indian Children Coun. for Exceptional Children; patron and com. mem. Lake Ctr. Christian sch., Hartville, Ohio; trustee Cuyahoga Valley Christian Acad., 1985-86; patron Heritage Christian Sch., 1986-94, Good Shepherd Christian Sch., 1994-2000; bd. dirs. Pretty Shield Found., 1999—; spkr. Fellowship of Christian Athletes; adv. cons. Christian Berets, Keystone Acad. and Navajo Missions; spkr. Assn. Christian Schs. Internat.; founder travel ministry, 1974—; cons. Children's Harbor, Ala.; nat. bd. dirs. Teen Ranch, Mich.; mem. Nat. Assn. Native Am. Children of Alcoholics; lectr. Nat. Edn. Svcs., Insts. Drug Addictions and Alcoholism; guest lectr. Jennings Inst. Outstanding Educators in Ohio; spkr. Promise Keepers; lectr. series spkr. Staley Found.; prayer breakfast spkr. Ashtabula County Concerts of Prayer, Ohio; spkr. Concerned Women of Am., Old Time Gospel Hour, Bill Gaither Family Fest, Gaither Gathering. Recipient Hon. Grad. award Chemawa Indian Sch., Hon. Citizen award W.Va., Ark.; Don Bartlette Day proclaimed by City of Cin. and N.D. Fellow Acad. Ednl. Disciplines. Mem. Am. Acad. Mental Retardation, Nat. Assn. Christian Social Workers, Nat. Assn. Retarded Citizens (bd. dirs., chmn. com. on poverty and mental retardation 1973-74), Internat. Platform Assn., Assn. Am. Indian Social Workers, Soc. for Protection Unborn through Nutrition (life mem.), Focus on Family, Civitan Club (hon.), Internat. Inst. for Christian Sch. Tchrs., Christian Home Educators Ohio, Christian Coun. on Disabilities, The 700 Club, Phi Delta Kappa, Kappa Delta Pi. Home: 2602 Ocelot St NE Canton OH 44721-2144

BARTLEY, BURNETT GRAHAM, JR., oil industry executive; b. Pitts., Nov. 10, 1924; s. Burnett Graham and Helen (McKee) McKenney B.; m. Mary Lou Gilbert, Aug. 7, 1947; children: Burnett III, Davison Wittmer, Richard McKenney, Parker Bowen, Heather Swinston, Tiffany Gilbert; m. Wendy K. Keyes, May 12, 2001; 1 child, Timothy Lee Vogler. BA, Yale U., 1949; grad. advanced mgmt. program, Harvard U., 1967. Rep. sales Koppers Co. Inc., Pitts., 1949-52, dist. mgr. sales, 1952-56, v.p. sales, 1956-58, v.p., gen. mgr. forest products, 1958-69, dep. chmn. bd., 1969-79, exec. v.p., 1979-88; chmn., chief exec. officer chems. and coatings Kop-coat, Inc., Pitts., 1988-90; chmn., chief exec. officer Anegada Group, Inc., Pitts., 1990—. Chmn., CEO Ameritex Chem. and Coatings Co., Irving, Tex.; chmn. Bridgewater Steel Corp., N.J., Trans-Ocean Trading Corp., Ltd.; chmn. bd. Edgewater Marine Corp., Morgantown, W.Va. Dir. World Affairs Coun., Pitts., 1987; Trustee Rehab. Ctr. Pitts., 1989, Children's Hosp., Pitts., 1989, Mich. Inst. Tech., 1989; chmn. bd. trustees Point Park Coll., Pitts., 1989; bd. dirs. Penn. Economy League, 1989; pres. Health Rsch. and Svcs. Found., Pitts., 1989. Lt. inf. U.S. Army, 1943-45, ETO. Mem. Am. Wood Preservers Inst. (pres. 1970), Am. Wood Preserver's Assn. (pres. 1975), So. Pressure Treaters Assn. (pres. 1974), Harvard-Yale-Princeton Club, Duquesne Club, Fox Chapel Golf Club, Annapolis Yacht Club, Buffalo Launch Club, Rolling Rock Club, Laurel Valley Golf Club, Pitts. Athletic Club, St. John (V.I.) Yacht Club, St. Thomas (V.I.) Yacht Club, Chautauqua Lake Yacht Club (Lakewood, N.Y.). Republican. Presbyterian. Avocations: hydroplanes, flying, sailing, fishing, motorcycling. Office: Anegada Group Inc 2335 Koppers Bldg Pittsburgh PA 15219 also: Fairwinds Estate PO Box 248 Mayville NY 14757-0248 also: Villa # 4113 Virgin Grand, Great Cruz Bay Cruz Bay VI 00830

BARTLEY, GEORGE B., ophthalmologist, surgeon; b. Warren, Ohio, Nov. 12, 1955; B in Zoology, Miami U., Oxford, OH; MD, Ohio State U., 1981. Intern Riverside Methodist Hosp., Columbus, Ohio, 1981—82; resident in ophthalmology Mayo Clinic, Rochester, Minn., 1982—85, staff mem., 1986—2003, chmn. ophthalmology, 1992—2001, prof. ophthalmology Coll. Medicine, 1996—; fellow in ophthal. plastic and orbital surgery Wright State U. Sch. Med., Dayton, 1985—86. CEO Mayo Clinic, Jacksonville, Fla., 2002—; mem. bd. trustees Mayo Found., Rochester, Minn.; dir. Am. Bd. Ophthalmology. Mem.: Am. Acad. Ophthalmology (Senior Achievement award 2003). Office: Mayo Clinic 4500 San Pablo Rd Jacksonville FL 32224 Office Phone: 904-953-2100.

BARTLEY, JACQUELINE PRIOR, public relations executive, journalist; b. Augusta, Ga., Mar. 10, 1947; d. Jim Henry Neal Prior and Sarah Cathleen Hennemeire; m. Benny Douglas Bartley, Sept. 11, 1970; 1 child, Heather Diana. BA in Journalism, U. S.C., 1969. Copy editor The Augusta Chronicle, 1972—79, news corr., 1979—85; publicity dir. Beech Island (S.C.) Hist. Soc., 1990—. Editor, contbg. writer: (newsletter) Four Centuries & More, 1995—. Pres. Beech Island Hist. Soc., 2003—, v.p., 1995—2002; bd. dirs. Region III S.C. Heritage Corridor, Aiken, SC, 2001—03. Recipient Vol. award, Beech Island Hist. Soc., 2001. Mem.: Aiken County Hist. Soc., Archaeol. Soc. S.C. (Vol. award 2001). Avocations: cross country skiing, snorkeling, biking. Office: Beech Island Hist Soc 144 Old Jackson Hwy Beech Island SC 29842 Office Phone: 803-867-3600.

BARTLEY, LINDA L., musician, music educator; b. Amarillo, Tex., 1948; MusB in Edn., MusM, D of Musical Arts, Mich. State U. Asst. prof. clarinet SUNY, Fredonia, NY, 1974—75, Ark. Tech U., Russellville, 1981—83; assoc. prof. clarinet Ctrl. Mich. U., Mt. Pleasant, 1987—92; prof. clarinet U. Wis., Madison, 1992—. Vis. prof. clarinet U. Western Ont., London, 1975—81; prin. clarinet London Symphony Orch., 1975—81, Madison Symphony Orch.; clarinetist Grand Teton Music Festival, Jackson Hole, Wyo., 1989—2001, Powers Woodwind Quintet, Mt. Pleasant, 1987—92, Wingra Woodwind Quintet, Madison, 1992—; internat. soloist/recitalist, adjudicator, US, Europe, Japan, Canada. Musician: (performance) soloist/recitalist International Clarinet Association numerous national and international symposiums, recital and concerto tours of US, Canada, Europe and Japan; contbr. articles various profl. jours. and CD reviews. Mem.: Chamber Music Am., Coll. Music Soc., Internat. Clarinet Assn. (state chair, grants com. mem., young artist competition judge). Office: School of Music University of Wisconsin 455 N Park St Madison WI 53706-1483 Office Phone: 608-263-1910. E-mail: lbartley@wisc.edu.

BARTLEY, MURRAY HILL, retired dental educator; b. Jamestown, N.Y., June 15, 1933; s. Merle Campbell and Doris Ann (Keller) B.; m. Anita Estelle Glatfelter, July 29, 1956; children: Todd L., Brian C., Kathleen A. Student, Lewis & Clark Coll., 1951-54; DMD, U. Oreg., 1958; PhD, U. Utah, 1968. Cert. in oral pathology. Teaching fellow U. Oreg. Dental Sch., Portland, 1961-64; assoc. dir. rsch. D.N. Sharp Hosp., San Diego, 1964-65; postdoctoral fellow dept. anatomy Sch. Medicine U. Utah, Salt Lake City, 1965-68; acting assoc. prof. oral biology and pathology UCLA, 1968-69; assoc. prof. oral pathology Dental Sch. U. Oreg., Portland, 1969-77; prof. oral pathology Sch. Dentistry Oreg. Health Sciences U., Portland, 1977—95, prof. emeritus, 1995—, chmn. dept. oral pathology, 1972—76, 1980—95. Cons. Wadsworth VA Hosp., 1968-69, Barnes VA Hosp., Vancouver, Wash., Portland Med. Ctr., 1968—, Coun. on Hosp. Dental Svcs., ADA, Chgo., 1970, Oreg. State Dental Assn. Biohazards Com., Portland, 1976-82, chmn. dental care counsel, 1992—, Oreg. Dept. Health AIDS Task Force, Portland, 1981-91, Project Hope-Stomatology Faculties, Peoples Republic of China, 1984, Mich. AMC. Contbr. sci. articles to profl. jours. Mem. com. ORE div., profl. edn. Am. Cancer Soc., Portland, 1974—; bd. dirs. Oreg. regional med. program O.C.C.P., Portland, 1973-81. Col. USAR, 1958-92. USPHS Tchr.'s Tng. grantee NIH, Portland, 1961-64; Post-Doctoral Teaching fellow NIH, 1965-68; recipient Presdl. citation Oreg. Dental Assn., 1979, 89; decorated U.S. Army Meritorious Svc. medal, 1981. Mem. AAAS, ADA, Am. Acad. Oral Pathology, Soc. Mil. Surgeons, Sigma Xi, Omicron Kappa Upsilon (chpt. pres. 1988-89), Delta Sigma Delta. Avocations: watercolor, wood working, sculpture. Home: 6020 SW Arrow Wood Ln Portland OR 97223-7700 Office: OHSU Sch Dentistry Dept Oral Pathology 611 SW Campus Dr Portland OR 97201-3001

BARTLEY, ROBERT PAUL, management consultant; b. Worcester, Mass., Oct. 17, 1926; s. Harry Eugene and Helen (Hamilton) B.; m. Joan Anne Leahy, 1952; children: Robert, Brian, Maureen, Michael, Bridget, Timothy, Terrence, Patricia. BS, U.S. Naval Acad., 1952; MBA, U.S. Air Force Inst. Tech., 1959. Cert. Energy Mgr. Commd. 2d lt. U.S. Air Force, 1952, advanced through grades to capt., 1972, ret., 1972; mng. dir. Del. Soc. for Prevention of Cruelty to Animals, Newark, 1975; fiscal asst. Pres.'s Office Del. Tech. and Community Coll., Dover, 1976-77; dir. Del. State Energy Conservation Plan Office of Mgmt. and Budget and Planning, Dover, 1977-79; asst. dir. Del. Energy Office, Dover, 1979-81, acting dir., 1982, asst. dir. for energy div. facilities mgmt., 1982-91; prin. Cavalier Mgmt. Cons. Svcs., 1991—. Instr. U. Dayton (Ohio), 1959; presenter 2d Mid-Atlantic Energy Conf. Contbr. articles to profl. jours. Chmn. com. on devel. and enforcement of energy savings in pub. schs., 1977-78; mem. citizens adv. group on regional transp., Kent County, Del., 1969; mem. tuition guidelines com. Holy Cross Sch., 1971-74. Decorated Air medal. Mem. Del. Assn. Pub. Adminstrn., Mcpl. Fin. Officers Assn., Del. Assn. Govt. Fin. Officers (treas. 1978-79, sec. 1982-83, exec. com. 1984), Nat. Assn. State Energy Ofcls., Assn. Energy Engrs., U.S. Dept. Energy Commn. Alternative Fin., Cavaliers of Del. Club, Blue and Gold Club, Ft. Delaware Soc. (bd. dirs. 1996—). Roman Catholic. Office: 1401 Pennsylvania Ave Wilmington DE 19806-4124

BARTLEY, WILLIAM CALL, science administrator; b. Mason, Mich., Dec. 4, 1932; s. Hugh Jerome and Daisy Ione (Call) B.; m. W. Dee Gray, July 14, 1956; children: Carol Sue Gourlas, Gregory William Bartley, Christopher Gray Bartley. BS in Electircal Engring., Mich. State U., 1955, MS in Electircal Engring., 1959. Registered Profl. Engr., Tex.; commercial pilot/instr., FAA. Rsch. scientist/dir. space-sci. lab. U. Tex., Richardson, 1963-67; exec. sec. Fed. Coord. Coun. Sci., Engring. and Tech. The White House, Washington, 1967—74; sr. staff dir. Nat. Acad. Sci., Washington, 1974-78; asst. dir. Office Energy Rsch. U.S. Dept. Energy, Washington, 1978-82; min.-counselor for health and sci. Geneva, 1982-88; spl. asst. to FDA commr., 1988-89; sr. advisor to U.S. Trade Rep. The White House, Washington, 1989-91; sr. adv. to asst. sec. oceans, environ., sci. U.S. State Dept., Washington, 1991-95; chmn./CEO Bartley Tech., Inc., Bandera, Tex., 1995—; founder, co-owner TreeLife Tech., Boerne, Tex., 1998—2000. Co-investigator NASA, U. Tex., Richardson, Tex., 1965-67, study dir./exec. dir. Nat. Acad. Sci., Washington, 1969-74. Contbg. author: International Orbital Debrie, 1994; patentee in field. Mem. panel on trends in aviation Davos World Econ. Forum, Switzerland, 1987, vice-chmn., Bandera County Federated Libr. Bd., 1999-2001; pres. bd. trustees Bandera Libr., 2000-01; chmn. Kronkosky Libr. of Bandera County Expansion Com., 2001-03; chmn. Bandera Frontier Times Mus. Expansion Com., 2003-; rectory renovation project leader Vestry of St. Christopher's Ch., 2002-03; delagate coun. Diocese of West Tex., 2003-, mem., task Force on Mission and Ministry, Diocese of West Tex., 2003-, Vestry St. Christopher's Ch., 2005-; chmn. Power of One Capital Campaign/Regional Found., 2005—. Recipient Certificate of Appreciation, U.S. State Dept., Geneva, Switzerland, 1984, 86, Washington, 95; named disting. mil. grad. ROTC-USAF, Libya, 1955-58.

Mem. NY Acad. Sci., Am. Geophysical Union, Am. Men an Women Sci., Free Trade Alliance. Episcopalian. Avocations: tennis, skiing, travel, historical restoration, aviation. Home: PO Box 2246 2628 English Crossing Rd Bandera TX 78003-2246 Office: Bartley Tech Inc PO Box 821 Bandera TX 78003-0821 Office Phone: 830-796-7643. Business E-Mail: bartleytech@yahoo.com.

BARTLIT, FRED HOLCOMB, JR., lawyer; b. Harvey, Ill., Aug. 1, 1932; s. Fred Holcomb and Agnes Marie (Rahn) Bartlit; m. Jana Cockrell, Feb. 28, 1987. BS in engring., US Mil. Acad., 1954; JD, U. Ill., 1960. Bar: Ill. 1960, US Ct. Appeals 7th cir. 1962, US Ct. Appeals 6th cir. 1969, US Ct. Appeals 10th cir. 1970, US Supreme Ct. 1970, US Ct. Appeals 8th cir. 1971, US Ct. Appeals 3rd cir. 1973, US Ct. Appeals 5th cir. 1978. Assoc. Kirkland & Ellis, Chgo., 1960—64, ptnr., 1964—93, Bartlit, Beck, Herman, Palenchar & Scott, Chgo., 1993—. Lectr. in field; mem. faculty Nat. Inst. Trial Advocacy, 1975—. Served U.S. Army, 1954—58. Fellow: Internat. Acad. Trial Lawyers, Am. Coll. Trial Lawyers; mem.: Chgo. Bar Assn., Ill. Bar Assn., Castle Pines Golf, Mid-Am., Glen View. Republican. Presbyn. Office: Bartlit Beck Herman Palenchar & Scott Courthouse Pl 54 W Hubbard St Chicago IL 60610-4645*

BARTLO, SAM D., lawyer; b. Cleve., Oct. 5, 1919; BBA, Case Western Res. U., 1941; JD, Cleve.-Marshall Law Sch., 1950. Bar: Ohio, 1950, U.S. Supreme Ct., 1958. Mem. firm Buckingham, Doolittle & Burroughs, Akron, Ohio, 1971-90. Capt. U.S. Army, 1942-46. Fellow Am. Bar Found. (life), Ohio Bar Found. (life, pres. 1981-82, trustee 1976-81); mem. ABA (bd. govs. 1989-92, ho. of dels. 1977-94, state del. 1981-89, exec. com. 1990-92, chair ops. com. 1991-92, trustee FJE resource coun. 1992-94), Akron Bar Assn. (pres. 1967-68, exec. com. 1968-7), Ohio State Bar Assn. (coun. dels. 1970-86, pres. 1977-78, exec. com. 1973-79), Am. Judicature Soc., Nat. Conf. Bar Presidents (trustee 1979-82), Ohio Legal Ctr. Inst. (pres. 1979-81, trustee 1977-81). Office: Buckingham Doolittle Burroughs PO Box 1500 Akron OH 44309-1500

BARTLOW, GENE STEVEN, professional society administrator, retired military officer; b. Alva, Okla., Dec. 19, 1939; s. C. Merle and Mildred Violet (Stevens) B.; m. Carolyn F. Strickland, Dec. 31, 1960 (div. Apr. 4, 1962); 1 child, Karie Jean Bartlow Parsons; m. Karin C. Jacobsen, Jan. 13, 1967; children: Christina K., Erik K. BA in Ednl. Comm., N.W. Okla. State U., 1962; disting. grad., Indsl. Coll. Armed Forces, Washington, 1972; MPA, Ball State U., 1978; grad., Air War Coll., Maxwell AFB, Ala., 1984; MS in Computers and Info. Mgmt., Webster U., St. Louis, 1995. Cert. assn. exec. Am. Soc. Assn. Execs. Tchr. speech, debate coach Liberal (Kans.) Pub. H.S., 1962-63; commd. 2d lt. USAF, 1964, advanced through grades to full col.; chief logistics plans divsn. 68th tactical air support group Tactical Air Command, Shaw AFB, S.C., 1971-73; chief logistics plans inspection br. Hdqs. Tactical Air Command, Langley AFB, Va., 1973-76; chief NATO logistics plans br. Hdqs. USAF in Europe, Ramstein Air Base, Germany, 1976-80; dep. comdr. for resource mgmt. 474th tactical fighter wing Tactical Air Command, Nellis AFB, Nev., 1980-83; chief congl. activities divsn. Office Asst. Sec. Air Force (Acquisition), Washington, 1984-87; dean adminstrn., prof. sys. acquisition mgmt. Indsl. Coll. Armed Forces, Nat. Def. U., 1987-90; ret., 1990; asst. exec. dir., CFO, Assoc. Cath. Charities, Archdiocese of Washington, 1990-91; dep. exec. dir. Internat. Assn. for Dental Rsch.-Am. Assn. for Dental Rsch., Washington, 1991-94; pres., CEO, Am. Wood Preservers Inst., Fairfax, Va., 1995-97; exec. v.p., COO, Painting and Decorating Contractors Am., 1998-2000; exec. dir., COO Assn. Old Crows, Alexandria, Va., 2002—05. Adj. prof. mgmt. Nat.-Louis U., McLean, Va., 1989-97, U. Md. U. Coll., 1998-99; lectr. congl. liaison activities exec. mgmt. course Def. Sys. Mgmt. Coll., Ft. Belvoir, 1986-92. Contbr. articles to profl. jours. Decorated Legion of Merit, others. Mem.: Greater Washington Soc. Assn. Execs., Air Force Assn., Mil. Officers Assn. Republican. Congregationalist. Avocations: Am. Civil War history, photography, music, politics. Home: 6501 Tiburon Ct Springfield VA 22152-2824 E-mail: eagle85@cox.net.

BARTNICK, HARRY WILLIAM, artist, art educator; b. Newark, July 30, 1950; s. Harry William and Gertrude (Johnson) B.; 1 child, Noah. BFA, Temple U., 1972; MFA, Syracuse U., 1974. Instr. Lake Placid Sch. Art, N.Y., 1974-78; prof. New Eng. Sch. Art and Design Suffolk U., Boston, 1979—. Permanent collections include De Cordova Mus., Hyde Collection, also numerous pvt. collections. Artists fellow State of Mass., 1981, New England Found. for Arts, 1992; Creative Artists Pub. Svc. grantee State of N.Y., 1977, Mass. Artists Fellowship grantee, 1981, New Eng. Found. Arts, 1992, 96, John Simon Guggenheim Grant, 2001. Avocations: travel, Italian studies. Home: 14 Prospect St Beverly MA 01915-3524

BARTNIKAS, RAYMOND, electrical engineer, educator; b. Kaunas, Lithuania, Jan. 25, 1936; s. Andrius and Eugenia (Kanisauskas) B.; m. Margaret McLachlan, Aug. 19, 1967; children: Andrea Marie, Thomas Benedict. BASc, U. Toronto, 1958; M in Engring., McGill U., Montreal, 1962, PhD, 1964; D in Engring. (hon.), U. Waterloo, 2002. Rsch. engr. No. Electric Co. (now Nortel), Lachine, Canada, 1958—63; mem. sci. staff phys. scis. divsn. No. Electric R&D Labs. (now Nortel Techs.), Ottawa, Canada, 1963—68; research scientist, sci. dir. materials sci. research div., Disting. Sr. Scientist Hydro-Quebec Inst. Rsch., Varennes, Que., 1968-98; rschr. emeritus Hydro-Quebec Inst. Research, 1998—. Adj. prof., lectr. theory of dielectrics McGill U., 1968—; adj. prof. Fleming Found., visitor dept. elec. and computer engring. U. Waterloo, Ont., 1969—; adj. prof. dept. engring. physics Ecole Poly. U. Montreal, 1982—; vis. prof. U. Rome, 1994—; cons. Cepel Inst. Rsch., Rio de Janeiro, 1973-84; mem. Task Force on Long Term Performance of Insulating Materials Nat. Acad. Scis., 1976-77; mem. elec. engring. com. Nat. Scis. and Engring. Rsch. Coun. Can., 1987-90; mem. Commn. de la recherche universitaire Conseil des Universites, Que., 1989-93. Author, editor: ASTM book series on Engring. Dielectrics, 1979, Elements of Cable Engineering, 1980, Power Cable Engineering, 1987, Power and Communication Cables, 1999; contbr. articles on dielectric and discharge loss mechanisms in elec. insulating systems to profl. jours. Decorated officer Order of Can.; recipient Golden Jubilee medal Can. Fellow IEEE (mem. energy com. 1978—, mem. insulated condrs. com. 1966—, mem. awards and recognition com. 1984-88, mem. electric machinery materials com. 1993--, IEEE Thomas Dakin Disting. Sci. Achievement award 1980, Centennial medal 1984, Herbert Whitehead Meml. award 1987, Morris Leeds award 1989, MacNaughton Gold medal 1993, 3d Millennium medal 2000), ASTM (chmn. elec. insulation com. 1979-85, mem. editl. bd. Jour. Testing and Evaluation 1985—, award of merit 1985, Charles Dudley medal, appreciation award, Arnold Scott award), Can. Acad. of Engring., Inst. Elec. Engrs. Japan (Disting. hon. lectr. symposium on elec. insulating materials 1983), Inst. Physics (U.K.), Royal Soc. Can. Acad. Scis. (Thomas W. Eadie medal 1994); mem. Dielectrics and Elec. Insulation Soc. of IEEE (pres. 1976-78, mem. editl. bd. Elec. Insulation Mag. 1984-91), Internat. Electrotech. Commn. (mem. com. insulation materials, chmn. subcommittee on tests 1993—), Order Engrs. Que., Can. Stds. Assn. (Merit award 1986, John Jenkins award 1989), Can. Elec. Assn., Can. Stds. Coun. (J.P. Carrière award 1992), French-Can. Assn. for Advancement of Scis. (Urgel Archambault award 1993), U. Toronto Engring. Alumni Assn. (engring. medal 1993). Roman Catholic. Office: Hydro-Québec Inst Rsch 1800 Boul Lionel-Boulet CP 1000 Varennes PQ Canada J3X 1S1

BARTNOFF, JUDITH, judge; b. Boston, Apr. 14, 1949; d. Shepard and Irene F. (Tennenbaum) B.; m. Eugene F. Sofer, Sept. 10, 1978; 1 child, Nelson Bartnoff Sofer. BA magna cum laude, Radcliffe Coll., 1971; JD (Harlan Fiske Stone scholar), Columbia U., 1974; LLM, Georgetown U., 1975. Bar: D.C. 1975, U.S. Dist. Ct. D.C. 1975, U.S. Ct. Appeals (D.C. cir.) 1980, U.S. Ct. Appeals (fed. cir.) 1985, U.S. Ct. Appeals (11th cir.) 1988, U.S. Ct. Appeals (3d cir.) 1989, U.S. Claims Ct. 1991. Fellow Inst. Pub. Interest Representation Georgetown Law Ctr., Washington, 1974—75; staff atty. Coun. Pub. Interest Law, Washington, 1975—77; spl. asst. to asst. atty. gen. criminal divsn. Dept. Justice, Washington, 1977—78, assoc. dep. atty. gen., 1978—80; spl. asst. U.S. atty. Office of U.S. Atty., Washington, 1980—81, asst. U.S. atty., 1982—85; assoc. Patton, Boggs & Blow, 1987—87, ptnr., 1988—94, assoc. ind. counsel, 1993—94; assoc. judge Superior Ct. of D.C., Washington, 1994—. Mediator U.S. Dist. Ct. D.C., 1991-94; mem. com. on pro se litig. U.S Dist. Ct., 1991-94. Mem. D.C. Bar Task Force on Children at Risk, 1997—98, D.C. Child Support Guidelines Commn., 2003—. Fellow Am. Bar Found.; mem. Nat. Assn. Women Judges, D.C. Bar, Women's Bar Assn. Office: 500 Indiana Ave NW Washington DC 20001-2131 Office Phone: 202-879-1988. Business E-Mail: bartnofj@dcsc.gov.

BARTO, CHARLES O., JR., lawyer; b. Altoona, Pa., Aug. 12, 1946; s. Charles O. and Ernestine I. (Styers) B.; m. Marsha D. Packer, July 31, 1971; 1 child, Megan Suzanne. BA, Pa. State U., 1968; JD, Dickinson Sch. of Law, 1971. Bar: Pa. 1971, U.S. Dist. Ct. (mid. dist.) Pa. 1971, U.S. Supreme Ct. 1975, U.S. Ct. Appeals (3d cir.) 1979, U.S. Tax Ct. 1985, U.S. Dist. Ct. (we. dist.) Pa. 2001, U.S. Ct. Vets. Appeals 2001. Asst. pub. defender Dauphin County Pub. Defender's Office, Harrisburg, Pa., 1971-73; assoc. Killian, Gephart & Snyder, Harrisburg, 1971-74; ptnr. Killian & Gephart, Harrisburg, 1975-83; prin. Charles O. Barto, Jr. & Assocs., Harrisburg, 1983—. Gen. counsel Pa. Health Care Assn., Harrisburg, 1971—; conflicts counsel Hosp. Assn. Pa., Harrisburg, 1990—. Contbr. articles to books in field. V.p. St. Thomas Civic Assn., Linglestown, Pa., 1976-87; pres. consistory St. Thomas United Ch. of Christ, Linglestown, 1989, 92; chair constn. com. Pa. Coun. Chs., Harrisburg, 1990—, parliamentarian, 1990—; mem. Pa. Forestry Assn. Recipient Better Life award Pa. Health Care Assn., 1988, award of merit Health Care Facilities Assn. Pa., 1977, Boss of Yr. award Dauphin County Legal Secs. Assn., 1985-86. Mem. ABA, Pa. Bar Assn., Dauphin County Bar Assn., Am. Health Lawyers Assn. (bd. dirs. 1994—, pres. 1997-98), Kiwanis (lt. gov. divsn. 13N Pa. dist. 2001—, Kiwanian of Yr. 2004), Koons Pool and Swim Club (pres. 1994—). Democrat. Avocations: tennis, skiing, coaching softball, computers, pen collecting. Office: Charles O Barto Jr & Assocs 608 N 3rd St Harrisburg PA 17101-1102 Office Phone: 717-236-6257. E-mail: cbarto13@aol.com.

BARTO, DEBORAH ANN, physician; b. West Chester, Pa., July 27, 1948; d. Charles Guy and Jeannette Victoria (Golder) B. BA, Oberlin Coll., 1970; MD, Hahnemann U., 1974; Reiki III, N.W. Sch. Healing, 2003. Cert. Reiki master. Intern, resident Kaiser Permanente Hosp., San Francisco, 1974-77; dir. med. oncology Evergreen Hosp., Kirkland, Wash., 1980-85, head oncology quality assurance, 1992-94; med. dir. Cmty. Home Health Care Hospice, Seattle, 1981-84. Mem. hosp. ethics com. Evergreen Hosp., 1995-98, mem. integrative care com., 1996-2001. Mem. Evergreen Women's Physicians, Reiki III. Democrat. Buddhist. Avocation: horseback riding. Office: Evergreen Profl Plz 12911 120th Ave NE Ste E60 Kirkland WA 98034-3047

BARTO, SUSAN CAROL, writer; b. Bklyn., June 21, 1941; d. William O. and Ida (Birra) Forcellon; m. Harry W. Barto, Mar. 11, 1960; 1 child, William M. Cert., Katherine Gibbs, 1960; student, Union Coll., 1979-82. Sec. dean of students Montclair (N.J.) State Coll., 1960; sec. Presbyn. Synod of N.J., East Orange, N.J., 1961-62; exec. sec. Union County Rep. Com., Westfield, N.J., 1971-79; legis. aide State Senator James Vreeland-Morris County, N.J., 1977-79. Author of short stories. County com. woman Union County Rep. Com., Westfield, 1970-82; active New Providence (N.J.) Libr. Bd., 1979-86. Recipient plaque of appreciation New Providence (N.J.) Libr. Bd., 1986. Mem. Friends of the Hunterdon Mus. of Art (pres. 1996-99). Presbyterian. Home and Office: 1 Fisher Ct Lebanon NJ 08833-2107

BARTOES, RICHARD ALAN, agricultural products executive; b. Norwich, Conn., July 29, 1928; s. Francis Florian and Katherine Brown Bartoes; m. Nancy Pettice Smith, June 22, 1952; children: Daniel Ryland, Janet Elizabeth, Karen Francis, Marilyn Pettice, Richard Smith. BS in Geology, Trinity Coll., Hartford, Conn., 1951. Plant expediter Charles C. Hart Seed Co., Wethersfield, Conn., 1951—91, sales mgr., 1960—91, prodn. mgr.; purchasing dir. Helen's Greenhouses, Aquebogue, NY, 1980—; owner, v.p. Blue Ridge Garden Ctr. INc., Charlottesville, Va., 1992—99. Justice of Peace Town of Rocky Hill, Conn., 1960—62; spkr. in field. Scoutmaster Boy Scouts Am.; exec. bd. Stonwall Jackson BSA. Recipient Silver Beaver, Boy Scouts Am., 1989. Mem.: Lions Club (pres. Rocky Hill chpt. 1988). Episcopalian. Avocations: collecting ships and lighthouses, gardening, running, swimming. Home: 1050 Earlysville Forest Dr Earlysville VA 22936-9550

BARTOK, LE ANN, painter, sculptor, filmmaker; b. Martins Ferry, Ohio, Mar. 1, 1937; d. Joseph and Margaret (Dvoracek) B.; m. Bernard L. Wilchusky, July 18, 1959 (div. 1987); children: Shari, Mark, Dennis, Jayne. R.N., Mercy Sch. Nursing, 1958; student, Carnegie Mus. Art, 1958-59, Carnegie Mellon U., 1968-69. Actress Japanese Films, Tokyo, 1960; model, 1960; tchr. Universities Tokyo, 1960; artist Pitts., N.Y.C., 1968—. Lectr. Edinboro Coll., Pa., 1977, Carnetie Mus., Pitts., 1969, PNB Bank, Pitts., 1969. Film screenings include Banff Fine Arts Ctr., Alta., Can., Eye Music, San Francisco Millennium, 1978, Monterey Coll., Carnegie Mus., Carnegie-Mellon U., Pitts., 1974-77, Annenberg Internat. Film Festival, Phila., 1978, numerous others throughout U.S., Can., Spain, Italy. Exhibited in group shows at Pa. State U., 1975, 3 Rivers Art Festival, Pitts., 1976-77, Carlow Coll., Pitts., 1975, Carnegie Mus., 1969, Carnegie-Mellon U., 1974, 77, 15th Ann. Avant Garde Art Exhibit, N.Y.C., 1980. Conceptual artist Antiobject Art Issue in Pioneer Book, 1975 (named Pioneer in Field); artist, dir. on conceptual "Skyworks" drops, 1977 (Tallest Piace of Art in World), 1973-77, film Skyworks documentary (Golden Fleece award 1977-78), 1973-77; artist, painter 48 acrylic collages (postmodern Stonehenge and Black Arc projects), 1980-89, 169 Views of Mt. Fuji (Sacred Space series), Turquoise Plante Pole Circle., 1998-2001; artist, filmmaker: An Introduction to American Underground Fmil, 1975; patentee in field. NEA grantee; painting prize Carnegie Mus. Art Exhbn., 1959, Pitts. Filmmakers, 1977; prodn. cons. short subject A Quarter Till..., 1987; screenwriter The Salvage Merchants, 1988. Mem. Guggenheim Mus. (assoc. com. 1983-85), N.Y. Filmmakers Co-op, Canyon Cinema Co-op, Japan Soc., Internat. Platform Assn. Clubs: Ikebana Internat. (Tokyo). Mem. Baha'i Faith. Avocations: vintage collectibles, writing, poetry. Studio: Bartok Artworks-Bartok Filmworks 425 W Broadway Apt 6D New York NY 10012-3751 also: PO Box 280 Laurel Mountain Pk Walnut Rd Laughlintown PA 15655

BARTOL, THERESA MARIE, artist, curator; b. Bklyn., Oct. 14, 1941; d. Joseph and Marie Domenica (Ciancotti) Antonelli; m. Joseph William Bartol, Nov. 21, 1964 (div. Oct. 1989). BA, Bklyn. Coll., 1965, MFA, 1973; student, N.Y. Studio Sch., 1968-70. Exhbn. curator Mallete Gallery, Garden City, N.Y., 1997—. Exhbns. included in Duane Gallery, N.Y.C., 1972, Bowery Gallery, N.Y.C., 1974, Patricia Keane Mason Gallery, N.Y.C., 1980, Haber Theodore Gallery, N.Y.C., 1981, Blue Mountain Gallery, N.Y.C., 1982-86, Semion Gallery, Laguna Beach, Calif., 1992-96. Art chairperson Unitarian Universalist Congregation, Garden City, 1997—. Recipient The Critic's Choice Exhibit award, 1983, 2d prize The Artist mag. ann. competition, 1991. Home: 97-20 161 Ave Queens NY 11414

BARTOLI, CECILIA, soprano; b. Italy, 1967; d. Pietro Angelo and Silvana B. Attended, Academia de Santa Cecilia. Recording artist Decca/London, 1986—. Stage debut, Verona, 1987; appearances include La Scala, Met. Opera, Opéra Bastille, Carnegie Hall, Berlin, Nantes, Warsaw, Naples, Zürich, Orch. Hall, Chgo.; albums: include Rossini Recital, 1990, Mozart Arias, 1991, Rossini Heroines, 1992, Arie Antiche, 1992, The Impatient Lover: Italian Songs by Beethoven, Schubert, Mozart, Haydn, 1993 (Grammy award for best classical vocal performance, 1994), Mozart Portraits, 1995, An Italian Songbook, 1997 (Grammy award for best classical vocal performance, 1997), Vivaldi album, 1999 (Grammy award for best classical vocal performance, 2000), Gluck Italian Arias, 2001 (Grammy award for best classical vocal performance, 2001), The Salieri Album, 2003. Named Musical America's Vocalist of Yr., 1993.

BARTOLI, JILL SUNDAY, reading and language arts researcher and educator; b. Carlisle, May 17, 1945; d. Harvey Preston and Helen Elizabeth (Hershey) Sunday; m. James Carl Bartoli, June 26, 1971; children: David Carl, Daniel Joseph, Stephen Mario, Catherine Elizabeth, Patrick Preston. BA in English and Speech, U. Ky., 1966, MA in English, 1967; MEd in Reading, Shippensburg U., 1977; PhD in Lang. Arts and Family Literacy, U. Pa., 1986. Cert. supr. comm., cert. reading specialist, Pa. Tchr. English and speech Cumberland Valley H.S., Mechanicsburg, Pa., 1969-73; lectr. English Pa. State U., York, 1968-69; rsch. assoc. U. Pa., Phila., 1988-89, lectr., 1987-89; assoc. prof. Elizabethtown (Pa.) Coll., 1990—. Coll.-sch. partnership dir. Elizabethtown and Steelton Sch. Dist., 1989—, rsch. grant dir., writer, 1992—, partnership with Harrisburg Sch. Dist., 2002—. Author: Unequal Opportunity, 1995, Celebrating City Teachers, 2001; co-author: Reading/Learning Disability, 1988; contbr. articles to profl. jours.; rschr. on successful inner-city schs. Organizer, mem. Social Justice Coalition, Carlisle, Pa., 1990—; mem. cmty. svc. com. Elizabethtown Coll., 1992—. Mem. NAACP, Nat. Coun. Tchrs. of English (mem. nominating com. 1980-92, presenter), Nat. Assn. for Edn. of Young Children, Am. Ednl. Rsch. Assn. (session chairperson 1985-96), Internat. Reading Assn., Kappa Delta Pi (counselor 1992—), Phi Delta Kappa. Home: 316 Garland Dr Carlisle PA 17013-4229 Office: Elizabethtown Coll 1 Alpha Dr Elizabethtown PA 17022-2298 Office Phone: 717-361-1379. E-mail: bartoljs@etown.edu.

BARTOLINI, BRUCE ANTHONY, real estate executive; b. Framingham, Mass., Mar. 4, 1950; s. Benjamen A. and Eleanor H. (Connery) B.; m. Elaine A. Dowd, Dec. 30, 1990; 1 child, Bethany Nicole. Student, Northeastern U., Boston, 1967-69, postgrad., 1986-88; BA in Biology, Framingham State Coll., 1971; postgrad., Keene State Coll., 1972. Cert. in hematology. Sci. instr. Orford (N.H.) Acad., 1971-73; biology, chemistry instr. J.P. Keefe Tech. Sch., Framingham, 1973—; pres. Bartolini Motor Sales, Inc., Medway, Mass., 1979—. Trustee Milford Realty Devel., 1979—, Blackstone Realty Trust, 1980, Bartolini Realty Trust, High Rock Realty Trust, Lake Williams Realty Trust, Worcester Realty Trust; securities investor A.G. Edwards & Sons; mem. Adesa Auto Auctions, 1979—. Contbr. articles to profl. jours. With USAR, 1984—, Op. Desert Storm, Operation Iraqi Freedom, 2003-. Decorated Army Achievement medal, Nat. Def. medal, Combat Life Savor medal, Liberation of Kuwait medal. Mem. NEA, Am. Soc. Clin. Pathologists, Keefe Tech. Tchrs. Assn., Mass. Tchrs. Assn. Clubs: Southboro Rod and Gun (Mass.), Framingham Militia, Chatham Yacht Club. Republican. Roman Catholic. Avocations: skeet and trap shooting, skiing, sailing.

BARTOLINI, ROBERT ALFRED, electrical engineer, researcher; b. Waterbury, Conn., Apr. 4, 1942; s. Alfred N. and Maria D. (Cartoceti) B.; m. Janice M. Daly, June 13, 1964; children: Jill C., Ellen G., Robin M. BSEE, Villanova U., 1964; MSEE, Case Western Res. U., 1966; PhD, U. Pa., 1972. Rsch. scientist RCA Labs., Princeton, N.J., 1966-79, leader optical sys., 1979-83, head optoelectronic rsch., 1983-87; head laser diode rsch. David Sarnoff Rsch. Ctr., Princeton, 1987-89, dir. integrated cir., 1989-96, sr. dir. inegrated cir. lab., 1996-97; v.p. integrated cir. lab. Sarnoff Corp., Princeton, 1997—2001, v.p. internat. ops., 2001—02, sr. v.p. comm. ops., 2002—. Chmn. elect. engring. dept. LaSalle U., 1982-90. Contbr. 35 articles to jours. in field; presenter 65 profl. presentations. Chmn. Sewer Oper. Com., West Windsor, N.J., 1974-82, chmn. assessment bd., West Windsor, N.J., 1984; vice chmn. Stony Brook Regional Sewerage Authority, Princeton, N.J., 1980-96, chmn., 1997—. Recipient 3 labs. achievement awards RCA Labs., 1970, 76, 80, Outstanding Paper award Soc. Internat. Display, 1979, Engring. Alumni award Villanova U., 1986, Sarnoff award RCA Corp., 1986, Career Engring. award Villanova U., 2002. Fellow IEEE (Centennial medal 1984), Optical Soc. Am. (chmn. laser conf. 1987-91); mem. Sigma Xi (nat. lectr. 1983-84), Tau Beta Pi, Eta Kappa Nu. Achievements include patents in field; research in embossable holographic devel., optical data storage media devel., optical data storage system devel., surface emitting diode laser devel. Office: Sarnoff Corp 201 Washington Rd Princeton NJ 08540-6449 Business E-Mail: rbartolini@sarnoff.com.

BARTON, ALAN JOEL, lawyer; b. N.Y.C., Sept. 2, 1938; s. Sidney and Claire (Greenfield) B.; m. Ann Rena Beral, Jan. 29, 1961; children: Donna Frieda Olsen, Brian Joseph. AB, U. Calif., Berkeley, 1960, JD, 1963. Assoc. Nossaman, Krueger & Mash, L.A., 1963—70, ptnr., 1970—80, Paul, Hastings, Janofsky & Walker, LLP, LA, 1980—2002, sr. counsel L.A., 2002—. Lectr. UCLA Sch. Law, 2001—; lectr. corp. and securities law U. Calif. Continuing Edn. Bar, 1980—; lectr. venture capital and securities law Practicing Law Inst., 1986—. Assoc. editor U. Calif. Law Rev., 1963. Dir. Ctr. for Study of Young People in Groups, L.A., 1988-2004, Planned Parenthood, L.A., 1999-2004; trustee Dubnoff Ctr. for Ednl. Therapy, North Hollywood, Calif., 1976-80. Mem. ABA (com. on fed. regulation of securities), Calif. Bar Assn. (com. on corps.), Order of Coif, The Calif. Club. Republican. Jewish. Avocations: movies, Torah study, contemporary art, tennis, travel. Office: Paul Hastings Janofsky & Walker LLP 515 S Flower St Fl 25 Los Angeles CA 90071-2300

BARTON, BERNARD ALAN, JR., lawyer; b. Glens Falls, N.Y., Aug. 13, 1948; s. Bernard A. Sr. and Geraldine (Bushey) B.; children: Lindsey, Kylie. BA, U. Fla., 1969, JD, 1975, LLM, 1976. Bd. cert. tax lawyer. Ptnr. Holland & Knight, Tampa, Fla., 1976—. Editor, contbg. author Florida Taxation, State Taxation Series, 1994. Mem. ABA, Nat. Assn. Bond Attys., Fla. Bar Assn. (exec. coun. tax sect., chmn. various coms. 1980-99). Republican. Episcopalian. Office: Holland & Knight PO Box 1288 Tampa FL 33601-1288 Office Phone: 813-227-6539. Business E-Mail: bernie.barton@hklaw.com.

BARTON, BETTY LOUISE, school system administrator; b. Shawnee Mission, Kans., Jan. 12, 1931; d. David and Dora Elizabeth (Grother) Schulteis; m. William Clayton Barton, Aug. 11, 1951; children: Linda Ann, Sharon Elaine. BA, Washburn U., 1951; MS in Curriculum and Instrn., Kans. U., 1976, EdD, 1983. Cert. ednl. adminstrn., curriculum and instrn., Kans. Classroom tchr. Topeka Pub. Schs., 1951-52; music tchr. Shawnee Mission Schs., 1959-62, classroom tchr., 1962-65, 69-72, asst. prin., 1976-83, prin., 1983—96; elem. adminstr. DeSoto (Kans.) Schs., 2001—. Bd. dirs. Headstart, Shawnee Mission, 1991—, Child Abuse Coalition, Shawnee Mission, 1984-94, Parents as Tchrs., Shawnee Mission, 1989-93, Srs. Serving Schs., Shawnee Mission. Bd. dirs. Multidisciplinary Team, Johnson County, Kans., 1992-94; mem. early childhood adv. com. Johnson County C.C., 1988-93. Named Adminstr. of Yr., Shawnee Mission Schs., 1996; recipient award for outstanding dissertation, Internat. Reading Assn., 1984. Mem. ASCD, Shawnee Mission Adminstrs. Assn. (pres., Adminstr. of Yr. 1990), Phi Delta Kappa. Lutheran. Avocations: music, writing, gardening, reading. Home: 9301 High Dr Leawood KS 66206-1918 Office: Cherokee Elem Sch 8714 Antioch Rd Shawnee Mission KS 66212-3698

BARTON, BRUCE ANDREW, lawyer; b. Detroit, May 30, 1934; s. Michael Andrew and Mary Watson (Strain) B.; m. Barbara Ann Haener, Feb. 3, 1962; children: Anne M. Blackport, Colleen M. Davis, Scott A. Barton, Kevin A. Barton. B of Philosophy, U. Detroit, 1958, JD, 1961. Bar: Mich. 1961, U.S. Dist. Ct. (ea. dist.) Mich. 1973, U.S. Supreme Ct. 1973, U.S. Dist. Ct. (we. dist.) Mich. 1974, U.S. Claims Ct. 1990. Pvt. practice, Jackson, Mich., 1962, 77-79; asst. prosecuting atty. County of Jackson, 1962-65, prosecuting atty., 1965-76; ptnr. Barton Benedetto & Bishop, Jackson, 1979-93, shareholder, 1994-95; pvt. practice Jackson, 1996—. Chair State Bar Rep. Assembly, 1984-85, elected assembly mem., 1978-85, 91-94, 98—04. Dist. adminstr. Mich. Little League Dist. 3, S.E. Mich., 1987—; chmn. Jackson Rep. Party, 1995-96; pres. Exch. Club of Jackson, 1988-89. Roman Catholic. Office: 414 S Jackson St Jackson MI 49201-2261 Office Phone: 517-780-0800.

BARTON, GERALD LEE, food products executive; b. Modesto, Calif., Feb. 24, 1934; s. Robert Paul and Alice Lee (Hall) B.; m. Janet Murray, June 24, 1955; children: Donald Lee, Gary Michael, Brent Richard. BA with distinction, Stanford U., 1955. Owner, pres. Barton Ranch, Escalon, Calif., 1961—; v.p. R.P. Barton Mfg. Co., Escalon, 1963-86; chmn. bd. Diamond Walnut Growers Inc., 1976-81, chmn. emeritus, 1981—, pres., 1986-90; chmn. GoldRiver Orchards, 2004—. Chmn. Growers Harvesting Com., Modesto, 1976-77, Diamond-Sunsweet Co., Stockton, Calif., 1978-80, Sun Diamond Growers, Inc., 1980-81; bd. dirs. Calif. Fin. Holding Co., Stockton; vice-chmn. Fed. Land Bank, Modesto, 1976-81; pomology rsch. adv. bd. U.

Calif., Davis, 1968-74, Walnut Mktg. Bd., Sacramento, 1971-73, 77-2000; mem. Calif. Walnut Commn., 1987-99; agribus. adv. bd. U. Santa Clara, 1979-89; dir. Ross Hort. Found.; ext. adv. bd. San Joaquin County U. Calif. Chmn. bd. edn. Escalon Unified Sch. Dist., 1963—75; vice chmn. San Joaquin County Sch. Bds. Assn., 1965; trustee Yosemite Assn., 1999—2005, The Cortopassi Inst., 2004—; elder Trinity United Presbyn. Ch., Modesto, 2002—05; bd. dirs. St. Joseph's Healthcare Corp., 1991—95; bd. dirs., v.p. Stanislaus River Flood Control Assn., 1965—. With U.S. Army, 1956—58. Decorated Order of the Golden Walnut, 1990; named Outstanding Young Farmer in San Joaquin County C. of C., 1965, Farmer of Yr. Escalon C. of C., 1979; recipient U. Calif. Friend of Ext. award, 1992; named to San Joaquin County Agrl. Hall of Fame, 1993; recipient Disting. Svc. award Calif. Walnut Commn., 1998; named Co-op Farmer of Yr. Agrl. Coun. Calif., 2001. Mem. Stanford U. Alumni Assn., Delta Chi. Republican. Presbyterian. Office: 22398 McBride Rd Escalon CA 95320-9637

BARTON, GREGORY MARK, Olympic athlete; b. Jackson, Mich., Dec. 2, 1959; BS in Mech. Engring., U. Mich., 1983. Olympic kayak racer, 1000 meter singles, L.A., 1984; Olympic kayak racer, 1000 meter singles and doubles Seoul, Korea, 1988; Olympic kayak racer, 1000 meter singles Barcelona, Spain, 1992. Recipient Bronze medal 1000 meter kayak singles Olympics, L.A., 1984, Gold medal 1000 meter kayak singles Olympics, Seoul, 1988, Gold medal 1000 meter kayak doubles Olympics, Seoul, 1988, Bronze medal 1000 meter kayak singles Olympics, Barcelona, 1992.

BARTON, HUGH PERRY, bank executive; b. Modesto, Calif., Apr. 6, 1932; s. Robert Paul and Alice B.; m. Sheila Grieve, Dec. 29, 1954; children: Elizabeth, James. BS, U. Calif., Berkeley, 1954. Pres., CEO R.P. Barton & Co., Escalon, Calif., 1955-91; chair bd. Modesto (Calif.) Banking Co., 1977-94, Barton McLean & Waters, San Francisco, 1992-97; dir. Bank of Los Altos, Calif., 1994—, Heritage Commerce Corp., San Jose, Calif., 2000—02; vice-chmn., dir. Pvt. Bank of the Peninsula, Palo Alto, Calif., 2003—. Mem. Carmel Valley Ranch Golf Club, Pebble Beach Tennis Club, Old Capitol Club. Republican. Episcopalian. Home: 9906 Club Place Ln Carmel CA 93923-8507 Office: PO Box 222097 Carmel CA 93922-2097 Personal E-mail: pavpawbean@sbcglobal.net.

BARTON, JEAN MARIE, psychologist, educator; b. Pitts., Mar. 24, 1945; d. Joseph Paul and Jean Marie (Anderson) Adamchic; m. Robert L. Barton, Jr., Aug. 14, 1965; children: Robert Joseph, Katherine Anne. BS summa cum laude, U. Pitts., 1965; MEd, Boston U., 1969; CAGS, Cath. U. Am., 1985, PhD in Ednl. Psychology, 1988. Cert. sch. psychologist, Md., nationally cert. sch. psychologist. Tchr./curriculum Wellesley (Mass.) pub. schs., 1965-69; lectr. U. R.I./R.I. Coll., Providence, 1969-72; curriculum specialist/tchr. St. Jane DeChantal Sch., Bethesda, Md., 1977-83, computer prog. dir., 1982-84; psychology assoc. Long Assocs., Bethesda, 1988—; psychol. cons. gifted unit Montgomery County Pub. Schs., Rockville, Md., 1985-99; sch. psychologist various schs. Archdiocese of Washington (Md.), 1987—; adj. mem. faculty Cath. U. Am., Washington, 1989—2004. Mem. evaluation team Cath. Schs. Studies, 1987-92; dir. Profl. Devel. Inst., Cath. U. Am., 1985-86; mem. adv. com., chairperson identification com. Jacob Javits Grant, Montgomery County Pub. Schs., 1989-92, project coord. Jacob Javitz grant, 1992-95, supt. adv. com. on Edn. of Gifted, 1992-96, on Spl. Edn.; assoc. dir. Ctr. for Advancement Cath. Edn. at Cath. U. Am., 1998-2004; mem. adv. com. on gifted edn. Md. State Dept. Edn., 1999-2000. Contbr. articles to profl. jours. U. Pitts. scholar, 1962-65. Mem. APA, ASCD, NASP, Md. Sch. Psychologists Assn., Pi Lambda Theta. Home: 5008 Benton Ave Bethesda MD 20814-2804 E-mail: docjeanbarton@cs.com. *Meaningful achievements consist of recognizing one's unique talents, working hard to develop them to the fullest, and then striving to seize opportunities to use them so that in some small way humanity is better for one's having lived.*

BARTON, JOE LINUS, congressman; b. Waco, Tex., Sept. 15, 1949; s. Larry Linus and Bess Wynell (Buice) Barton; children: Bradley Linus, Allison Renee, Kirsten Elizabeth. BS in Indsl. Engring., Tex. A&M U., 1972; MS in Indsl. Adminstrn., Purdue U., 1973. Asst. to v.p. Ennis (Tex.) Bus. Forms, 1973-81; White House fellow, aide to energy sec. James B. Edwards Washington, 1981-82; cost control cons. ARCO, Dallas, 1982-84; mem. U.S. Congress from 6th Tex. dist., 1985—; chmn. energy and commerce com., 2004—; mem. sci. com.; chmn. energy and air quality subcom. of commerce com.; mem. Rep. steering com. Mem. Assn. Former Students Tex. A&M U. (councilman at large 1985—) Republican. Methodist.*

BARTON, JOHN JOSEPH, obstetrician, gynecologist, educator, health facility administrator, researcher; b. Rockford, Ill., Mar. 19, 1933; s. L. David and Helen M. (Fox) B.; m. Lois Maltby, 1959 (div. 1965); children: Mary Katherine, Karen Ann. BA in History, U. Ill., 1957; BS in Medicine, U. Ill., Chgo., 1959, MD, 1961; student Law, Loyola U., Chgo., 1966-69. Diplomate Am. Bd. Ob.-Gyn.; cert. Advanced Cardiac Life Support. Rotating intern Cook County Hosp., Chgo., 1961-62, resident in ob.-gyn., 1962-65; fellow gynecologic pathology Northwestern U., Chgo., 1963, clin. asst. ob.-gyn., 1963-64, clin. instr. ob.-gyn., 1964-65, assoc. in ob.-gyn., 1965-71; prof. ob.-gyn. Cook County Grad. Sch. of Medicine, Chgo., 1965—; dir. ob.-gyn. rsch. and edn. Cook County Hosp., Chgo., 1965-69; chmn. ob.-gyn. Ill. Masonic Med. Ctr., Chgo., 1970—2001; assoc. prof. ob.-gyn. U. Ill. Coll. Medicine, Chgo., 1971-83, prof., 1983-93, lectr. in ob.-gyn., 1993—; prof. ob.-gyn. Rush Med. Coll., Chgo., 1993—; chmn. emeritus ob-gyn Ill. Masonic Med. Ctr., 2002—. Clin. clerkship subcom. U. Ill. Coll. Medicine, 1974-90, acad. senate 1977-91, 85-87, perinatal steering com., 1977-92, admissions com. 1985-91, screening subcom. 1988-89; ad hoc com. on rules for governance, Rush Med. Coll., Chgo., 1993—, curriculum com. 1993, com. on student evaluation and promotions, 1994—, core ckerkship subcom. of curriculum com. 1995—; editl. bd. Jour. Obstetrics and Gynecology, Am. Jour. Obstetrics and Gynecology, Internat. Jour. Obstetrics and Gynecology Contbr. numerous articles to profl. jours., chpts. to books. including Laparoscopy in Gynecologic Practice, 1972, Guidelines for Perinatal Care, 1983, Antepartum HIV Screenings: A Comparison of Methodologies, 1990. Vol. cons. Ob.-Gyn. Claremore (Okla.) Indian Hosp., 1979-80, 86, Fort Defiance (Ariz.) Indian Hosp., 1981, Red Crescent Soc., Heliopolis, Cairo, Egypt, 1987; vol. surgeon Internat. Red Cross and Red Crescent Soc. Vols., West Beirut, Lebanon, 1982; mem. Ill. Gov.'s AIDS adv. coun.; advisor, expert witness Atty. Gen. State of Ill. on Standards of Practice in Ob.-Gyn.; mem. com. formation of outcome-oriented surveillance systems for Ill. Dept. of Pub. Health, adv. com. to Health Planning Com. for Chgo., perinatal adv. com. Ill. Dept. Health, steering com. Mayor Washington's Infant Mortality Reduction Initiative and others. Sgt. USMC, 1950-55, Korea. Fellow Am. Coll. Obstetricians and Gynecologists (adv. coun. 1977-81, adv. coun. dist. VI 1977-81, chmn. Ill. sect. 1977-78, com. on profl. liability 1989-92, Jr. Fellow Rsch. prize award 1991), Ctrl. Assn. Obstetricians nd Gynecologists (ctrl. travel club, sci. awards com. 1985-89. chmn. 1987-89, Ann. prize award 1988), Chgo. Gynecol. Soc. (exec. com. 1994—, pres. 1995-96), Am. Coll. Surgeons, Soc. Contemporary Medicine and Surgery, Am. Soc. Clin. Hypnosis, Chgo. Inst. Medicine, Royal Soc. Medicine (London); mem. Ill. Assn. Maternal and Child Health, Assn. Profs. Gynecology and Obstetrics, Am. Pub. Health Assn., Phi Kappa Phi, Nu Sigma Nu. Avocations: rancher quarter horses, exotic animals, hounds, harleys. Home: Bar T Ranch 20516 Bunker Hill Rd Marengo IL 60152-8003 Office: Ill Masonic Med Ctr 836 W Wellington Ave Chicago IL 60657-9224 Office Phone: 815-943-6823. Personal E-mail: barthand2@aol.com.

BARTON, JONATHAN MILLER, clergyman; b. Elizabeth, N.J., June 26, 1952; s. Douglas William and Deborah (Gray) B.; m. Elizabeth Dora Rinehart, May 19, 1985 (div. June 1990); 1 child, Katherine Nicole (dec. 2003); m. Elizabeth Wood Stark, July 17, 1994; stepchildren: Liza, Archer Blair. Student, Union Coll., 1970-72; BA in Psychology, Kean Coll., 1974; MDiv, Drew U, 1978. Ordained to ministry Presbyn. Ch., 1981. Asst. chaplain Drew U., Madison, N.J., 1976-78, resident dir., 1977-81; hunger action enabler Elizabeth, Newark, Newton presbyteries United Presbyn. Ch. U.S.A., 1978-82; cons. World Hunger Edn. Svc., Washington, 1983; assoc. regional dir. Ch. World Svc., Rocky Hill, N.J., 1983-85, regional dir. Richmond, Va., 1985-2000; gen. min. Va. Coun. Churches, Richmond, 2000—. Mem. Nat. IMPACT Briefings, Washington, 1978-84; mem. coord. com. N.J. State Food Conf., 1979; spl. asst. to coord. U.S. Nat. Com. for World Food Day, 1981-83; mem. 4th World Food Issues Conf., Cornell U., 1982; testifier Senate Subcom. on edn., ARts and Humanities, 1982; mem. NGO Com. for UN Internat. Conf. on Population Consultation, 1984, UN/NGO Com. on Food and Rural Devel. Food Forum, 1985, UN/NGO Consultation on African Crisis, 1985; mem. Summer Inst. in Devel. Edn., Tao, N.Mex., 1986; mem. prep. com. for visit Dir.-Gen. UN/FAO on FAO's 50th anniversary commemoration, Washington, 1993; attended US AID Conf. Global Edn., Williamsburg, Va., 1989; mem. Gov.'s Conf. Infant Mortality, Richmond, Va., 1986. Regional editor Va. Steps, Ch. World Svc., 1985-2000; contbr. articles to various publs. in field. Co-chair grant com. Va. Hands Across Am., 1986; co-founder, chair Madison, N.J. chpt. Amnesty Internat., 1976-80; chair program adv. com. Ch. World Svc., 1987-89; chair Divsn. Mission and Svc., Presbytery of James, 1992-93; bd. dirs. Va. Interfaith Ctr. Pub. Policy, 1987-93; bd. dirs. Direct Ministries, Va. Coun. Chs., 1986-94, mem. Va. refugee adv. coun., 1992—; co-founder, convener Va. Congress on Hunger, 1987-93; founding mem. bd. dirs. Va. Hunger Found., 1992-95. Recipient C.J. Helen svc. award Miquin Lodge #68, 1967, Virgil honor Order of the Arrow, 1968, Lighthouse award Foodbank S.E. Va., 1993. Mem. Internat. Platform Assn. Office: Va Coun Churches 1214 W Graham Rd Ste 3 Richmond VA 23220-1409 Business E-Mail: barton@vcc-net.org.

BARTON, LESLIE L., physician; b. N.Y.C., N.Y., Feb. 22, 1943; d. Raymond and Beatrice Liebesman; m. William Holmes; 1 child, Todd Barton. BA cum laude, Hunter Coll., 1963; MD, U. Chgo., 1966. Diplomate Am. Bd. Pediat. Combined pediat.-medicine intern Cook County Hosp., Chgo., 1966-67; resident Boston Children's Hosp. Med. Ctr., 1967-69; fellow in rsch. virology Nat. Children's Hosp. Med. Ctr., Washington, 1969-70; instr. pediat. Washington U. Sch. Medicine, St. Louis, 1971-73, asst. prof. pediat., 1973-76, St. Louis U. Sch. Medicine, 1977-81, assoc. prof. pediat., 1981-88, prof. pediat., 1988-90; prof. pediat., dir. pediat. housestaff U. Ariz. Sch. Medicine, Tucson, 1990—. Pediat. cons. Montgomery County Health Dept., Rockville, Md., 1970-71; cons. Malcolm Bliss Mental Health Ctr., St. Louis, 1977-85; asst. dir. pediat. St. Louis County Hosp., 1971-73, dir. pediat., 1974-76; dir. pediat. St. Louis City Hosp., 1977-85; mem. ambulatory divsn. Cardinal Glennon Children's Hosp., St. Louis, 1985, joint appt. infectious disease and ambulatory divsn., 1986, interim dir. divsn. infectious diseases, 1989-90; med. staff U. Med. Ctr., Tucson, 1990, Tucson Med. Ctr., 1990. Reviewer numerous pediat. and infectious disease jours., 1978—; contbr. articles to profl. jours. N.Y. Pub. Health Rsch. fellow, 1963. Fellow: Infectious Diseases Soc. Am., Am. Acad. Pediat. (editl. bd.); mem.: Assn. Pediat. Program Dirs., Pediat. Infectious Diseases Soc., Phi Beta Kappa. Avocations: gardening, music, reading. Business E-Mail: llb@peds.arizona.edu.

BARTON, LEWIS, food products executive, consultant; b. N.Y.C., Mar. 9, 1940; s. Louis and Mary (Mosca) Bologna; m. Barbara Joan Hummell, Sept. 6, 1964; children: Glenn Scott, Gregory Jon. Student, Adelphi U., 1957-59. Sales rep. Olivetti Corp., N.Y.C., 1962-64, W. Ralston Co., Chgo., 1964-65, Milprint Co., N.Y.C., 1965-66; pres., founder Sigma Quality Foods, Farmingdale, N.Y., 1966-88, Sigma Star Food Corp., N.Y.C., 1993-98; pres. The Barton Group, Inc., N.Y.C., 1998—. Lectr. various confs. Patentee several package design constructions and methods. With USAF, 1961-62. Named to Pres. Coun. for Ednl. Distinction, Adelphi U. Mem. Nat. Single Svc. Food Assn. (charter, chmn. 1977-79, Svc. award 1982), Assn. Dressings and Sauces, Dwight D. Eisenhower Soc. (founder), Columbus Citizen's Found., Internat. Orgn. Packaging Profls., NY Athletic Club. Home: 45 Sutton Pl S New York NY 10022-2444 Office Phone: 212-588-1043. E-mail: lb@consultbarton.com.

BARTON, NOREEN DUFFY, secondary school educator; b. Phila., June 7, 1926; d. John Joseph and Mary Josephine (McDonough) Brett; m. Thomas Francis Duffy, Feb. 22, 1960 (div. June 1971); children: Thomas B., John F., Joseph D.; m. Patrick Joseph Barton, Nov. 11, 1995. BA, Montclair (N.J.) State Coll., 1948; MEd, U. Va., 1966. Cert. secondary math., bus. and acctg. tchr., N.J. Tchr. math. and bus. Egg Harbor (N.J.) City High Sch., 1948-55, coach girls basketball, 1948-51; instr. math. North Adams (Mass.) Coll., 1964-65, Frostburg (Md.) State Coll., 1969-70; tchr. math. So. Regional High Sch., Manahawkin, N.J., 1964-65, 75—, chmn. dept., 1958-60; chess coach, 1979—. Tchr. confrat. Christian doctrine Star of Sea Sch., Atlantic City, 1958-60, Holy Spirit High Sch., Absecon, N.J., 1975-86; tchr., prin. Assumption Sch., Ponoma, N.J., 1971-75. Scholar NSF, 1959-60. Mem. NEA, Nat. Coun. Tchrs. Math., N.J. Math. Assn., N.J. Edn. Assn., So. Regional Tchrs. Assn. (assoc. rep. 1988—). Roman Catholic. Avocations: chess, watching baseball, basketball and football. Home: 739 Bayview Dr Absecon NJ 08201-1208 Office: So Regional High Sch RR 9 Manahawkin NJ 08050

BARTON, PAUL J., lawyer; b. Price, Utah, Sept. 24, 1946; s. John O. and Mae L. Barton; m. Elaine L. York, Oct. 12, 1974 (div. Sept. 1997); children: Susan, John, James. BA in Econs., Brigham Young U., 1970; JD, U. Utah, 1973; LLM in Taxation, Washington U., 1974. Pvt. practice, Salt Lake City, 1973—; real estate broker Utah and Mo., 1979—; investment advisor Utah, 1988—. Contbr. articles to profl. jours. With U.S. Army, 1969. Scholar Hinckley Inst., 1971, John A. Widtsoe Meml. scholar, 1972-73. Mem. Internat. Assn. Fin. Planners, Estate Planning Coun., Utah State Bar Assn. (probate and tax sect. 1974-2003, unauthorized practice law sect. 1994-99, advt. com. 1994-99). Mem. Ch. Jesus Christ Latter Day Sts. Avocations: basketball, hunting. Office: 345 E 400 S Ste 201 Salt Lake City UT 84111-2971 Office Phone: 801-322-2300.

BARTON, RICHARD N., computer company executive; BS in Indsl. Engring., Stanford U., 1989. Strategy cons. Alliance Consulting Group, 1989-91; with Microsoft Corp., Redmond, Wash., 1991-94; gen. mgr. traveler bus. unit, founder Expedia, a div. Microsoft Corp., Redmond, Wash., 1994—99; pres. CEO, dir. Expedia, Inc., Bellevue, Wash., 1999—2003. Bd. dirs. Netflix, Ticketmaster, InterActiveCorp (formerly USA Interactive), AtomShockwave, Inc. Office: InterActiveCorp 152 W 57th St 42nd Fl New York NY 10019

BARTON, ROBERT H., III, automotive executive; BS in Civil and Elec. Engring., Lehigh U.; postgrad., Carnegie Mellon U. With Alcoa, 1955—96, various mktg. mgmt. positions including industry mgr.-bldg. constrn., N.Y. dist. sales mgr., gen. mgr. Alcoa Export, Alcoa gen. mgr. mktg. sales and distbn. European region, pres. Alcoa Conductor Products Co.; pres. Alcoa Fujikura Ltd., Mexico; non-exec. chmn. J.L. French Holdings, 1996—99; CEO Meridian Automotive Sys. Inc., Dearborn, Mich., chmn., pres., CEO, chmn., 2002—. Mem. internat. supplier adv. coun. Ford Motor Co.; bd. dirs. U.S. Alumweld Co., Outlook Nashville, Japan-Tenn. Soc.; chmn. Tenn. Del. S.E. Govs. U.S.-Japan Orgn. Capt., flight examiner USAF. Mem.: ASCE, Soc. Automotive Engrs. Office: Meridian Automotive Systems 550 Town Center Dr Dearborn MI 48126 Office Fax: (313) 336-4184.

BARTON, ROBERT LEROY, JR., judge, educator; b. Ballston Spa, NY, June 19, 1943; s. Robert L. Sr. and Bertha (Di Pasquale) B.; m. Jean M. Adamchic, Aug. 14, 1965; children: Robert Joseph, Katherine Anne. BA, U. Pitts., 1965; JD, Boston Coll., 1969. Bar: Mass. 1969, R.I. 1970, D.C. 1972, U.S. Ct. Appeals (1st cir.) 1970, U.S. Ct. Appeals (D.C. cir.) 1973, U.S. Dist. Ct. R.I., 1971, U.S. Dist. Ct. D.C. 1973, U.S. Dist. Ct. Md. 1973. Law clk. U.S. Dist. Ct. R.I., Providence, 1969-70; staff atty. R.I. Legal Svcs., Providence, 1970-71; spl. asst. to solicitor U.S. Dept. Labor, Washington, 1971-72; assoc. Sherman, Dunn, Cohen & Leifer, Washington, 1972-75; trial atty. FTC, Washington, 1975-88; judge Pa. Office of Hearing & Appeals, Pitts., 1988-90, Office of Hearings, Washington, 1990-95, Office of Chief Adminstv. Hearing Officer, U.S. Dept. Justice, Falls Church, 1995—2005, Office of Adminstrv. Law Judges, U.S. Internat. Trade Commn., Falls Church, 2005—. Trial instr. Nat. Inst. Trial Advocacy, Washington, 1982-86, U.S. Dept. Justice, Washington, 1986-96. Chair com. Cath. League for Religious Rights, Milw., 1983-84. Master Am. Inn of Ct.; Fed. Adminstrn. Law Judges Assn. (exec. com.), Nat. Lawyers Assn. Roman Catholic. Avocations: travel tennis, swimming. Office: Office Adminstrv Law Judges 500 E St SW Ste 317 Washington DC 20436 Office Phone: 202-708-4051. Business E-Mail: robert.barton@usitc.gov.

BARTON, STANLEY FAULKNER, retired management consultant; b. Halesowen, Worcestershire, Eng., Dec. 30, 1927; came to U.S., 1957, naturalized, 1963; s. Lazarus and Alice (Faulkner) B.; m. Marion Brittain, Dec. 20, 1952; children: Carolyn Francesca, Andrea Elizabeth. B.Sc. (hons.), U. Birmingham, Eng., 1949; PhD, U. Birmingham, 1952. Group leader Naval Rsch. Establishment, Halifax, N.S., Can., 1953-56; project coord. Def. Rsch. Chem. Labs., Ottawa, Ont., Can., 1956-57; devel. engr. Procter & Gamble, Cin., 1957-58, R & D group leader, 1958-59, R & D sect. head, 1959-69; tech. dir. food products-natural resources ITT, N.Y.C., 1969-76; sr. v.p. tech. and quality ITT Rayonier, Inc., Stamford, Conn., 1976-90; v.p., dir. Spectrum Internat. Assocs., Inc., Tucson, 1990-92; ret., 1992. Pres. Catalina Cons., 1990—. Mem. Am. Theater Organ Soc. Home and Office: Catalina Cons 4051 N Circulo Manzanillo Tucson AZ 85750-1879 Personal E-mail: stanb@prodigy.net.

BARTON, STANLEY L., ophthalmologist, consultant; b. Columbia Station, Ohio, May 30, 1920; 1 child, Randal L. BA, Bowling Green State U., 1943; MD, Wayne State U., 1946. Cert. Am. Bd. Ophthalmology. Capt. U.S. Army, 1946—49, Korea. Mem.: AMA (life), Wayne County Med. Soc., Mich. State Med. Soc. Home: 17400 Ft St Riverview MI 48192-6646 Office: Troy Med Clinic 1663 Stephenson Hwy Troy MI 48083 Office Phone: 248-689-7100. Office Fax: 248-689-5571.

BARTON, THOMAS HEISLER, management consultant; b. Chgo., Apr. 12, 1924; s. Jay and Agnes Heisler Barton; m. Jo Jeanne Millon, Apr. 5, 1952; children: Avril Barton Moore, Brooke Millon. BS, Northwestern U., 1945, BSEE, 1946; postgrad., Navy Russian Lang. Sch., Boulder, Colo., 1945—46; MBA, Harvard U., 1948. Asst. to pres. Automatic Electric Co., Chgo., 1948—49; dist. sales mgr. Beckman Instruments, Inc., Fullerton, Calif., 1949—52; govt. mktg. staff BG Corp., N.Y.C., 1952—53; asst. to pres. Nickel Cadmium Battery Co., N.Y.C., 1953—55; v.p. Barrington & Co., Inc., N.Y.C., 1955—65, Am. Express Co., N.Y.C., 1965—71; fin. cons. A.T. Kearney, Inc., N.Y.C., 1971—73; pres. Thomas H. Barton & Co., Inc., N.Y.C., 1973—. Author: Japanese Technology for the Graphic Arts, 1986; contbr. articles to profl. jours. Trustee St. Vincents Hosp., N.Y.C., 1973—2000. Lt. j.g. USNR, 1942—46. Mem.: AAAS, IEEE, Union Club City N.Y., Tau Beta Pi. Roman Catholic. Avocations: travel, languages. Home: 1192 Park Ave New York NY 10128

BARTON, THOMAS J., lawyer; b. Allentown, Pa., 1962; BA, Coll. William & Mary, 1984; JD, Boston Coll., 1987. Bar: Pa. 1987, NJ 1991. Ptnr., co-chair, labor, employment practice group Drinker Biddle & Reath LLP, Phila. and Princeton. Office: Drinker Biddle & Reath LLP One Logan Sq 18th & Cherry Sts Philadelphia PA 19103-6996 Office Phone: 215-988-2834. Office Fax: 215-988-2757. Business E-Mail: thomas.barton@dbr.com.

BARTON, THOMAS JACKSON J., chemistry professor, researcher; b. Dallas, Nov. 5, 1940; s. Ralph and Florence (Whitfield) Barton; m. Elizabeth Burton, Oct. 1, 1966; children: Ralph, Brett. BS, Lamar U., 1962; PhD in Organic Chemistry (hon.), U. Fla., 1967. NIH postdoctoral fellow Ohio State U., 1967; mem. faculty Iowa State U., Ames, 1967—, prof. chemistry, 1978—, disting. prof., liberal arts and scis., 1984—, program dir. Ames Lab., 1986—88, dir. Ames Lab (US Dept. Energy), 1988—, dir. Inst. for Phys. Rsch. and Tech., 1998—. Assoc. prof. U. Montpellier, France; exch. scientist NAS, Former Soviet Union, 1975, NATO, France; mem. coun. on materials scis. Dept. Energy, 1992—97; lectr. Japan Society for the Promotion of Science. Contbr. rsch. papers to profl. publs., editl. bd. Organometallics. Recipient Fredric Stanley Kipping award in organosilicon chemistry, 1982, Gov.'s medal for sci. tchg., 1983, Excellence in Tchg. faculty achievement award, Burlington No. Found., 1988, Outstanding Sci. Accomplishment in Materials Chem. award, Dept. Energy, Materials Sci. Rsch. Competition, 1989, Lab. Dir. of Yr. for Tech. Transfer, Fed. Lab. Consortium, 2003. Fellow: Japan Soc. Promotion of Sci.; mem.: Am. Chem. Soc. (Midwest award 1995). Methodist. Home: 815 Onyx Cir Ames IA 50010-8429 Office: Iowa State Univ Dept Chemistry 1605 Gilman Hall Ames IA 50011-3111 E-mail: barton@ameslab.gov.

BARTON-COLLINGS, NELDA ANN, political organization worker, bank executive; b. Providence, Ky., May 12, 1929; m. Harold Bryan Barton, May 11, 1951 (dec. Nov. 1977); children: William Grant (dec.), Barbara Lynn, Harold Bryan, Stephen Lambert, Suzanne; m. Jack C. Collings, Mar. 28, 1992 (dec. Feb. 2000). Student, Western Ky. U., 1947-49; grad., Norton Meml. Infirmary Sch. Med. Tech., 1950; student, Cumberland Coll., 1978, LLD (hon.), 1991. Lic. nursing home adminstr.; registered med. technician. Pres. Barton & Assocs. Inc., Corbin, Ky., 1977—2002; past pres., now chmn. Hazard Nursing Home Inc., Ky., 1977—2002, Health Sys. Inc., Corbin, Ky., 1978—2002, Corbin Nursing Home Inc., 1978—2002, Williamsburg Nursing Home, Inc., 1978—2002; pres. Key Distbg. Inc., 1980—, pres., chmn. bd., 1981-97; past pres., now chmn. The Whitley Whiz Inc., Williamsburg, 1983—2002; chmn. bd. dirs., now dir. Tri-County Nat. Bank., 1985-97; bd. dirs., now chmn. Harlan Nursing Home, Inc., 1986—2002; chmn. bd. dirs. Knott Co. Nursing Home, Inc., 1986; pres. Tri-County Bancorp, Inc., 1987—2002; chmn. bd. Instl. Pharmacy, Corbin, Ky., 1990—2002; past pres., now chmn. bd. Wolfe County Health Care Ctr., 1990—2002; pres. Bretors, LLC, 2004—; chmn. Tri-County Cineplex, LLC, 2004—. Mem. exec. com. Corbin Deposit Bank, 1982-84; bd. dirs. Greensburg (Ky.) Deposit Bank, Williamsburg (Ky.) Nat. Bank, Campbellsville Nat. Bank, McCreary Nat. Bank, Tri County Nat. Bank, Somerset Nat. Bank, Laurel Nat. Bank; chmn., organizer, dir. Green County Bancorp Inc., 1987—2002; organizer, dir. Laurel Nat. Bank, 1996—2002; mem. nat. adv. com. SBA, 1990-92; active Nat. Policy Forum, 1994—96. Mem. Fedn. Coun. on Aging, 1982-87; bd. dirs. Leadership Ky., 1984-88, adv. com., 1987—92; bd. dirs. Cumberland Coll. Found., 1995, mem. devel. bd., 1981—; v.p. Southeastern Ky. Rehab. Com., 1981-93; mem. Fair Housing Task Force, Corbin, 1981-84, Ky. Mansions Preservation Found. Inc., 1970-2004, Corbin Comty. Devel. Com., 1970-83; cub scout den mother, 1965-67; pres. Corbin Cen. Elem PTA, 1963-65; vice chmn. 9th dist. PTA, 1958-59; Rep. nat. committeewoman for Ky., 1968-96, sec., 1993-96; del. Rep. Nat. Conv., 1976, 88, 96, 2000, 04; vice-chmn. Rep. Nat. Com., 1984-93; sec.-treas. Nat. Rep. Inst. Internat. Affairs, 1984-86; bd. mem. Ky. Econ. Devel. Fin. Auth., 2000-03, Ky. Econ. Devel. Partnership Bd., 2003-; active numerous other polit. orgns. Recipient Ky. Woman of Achievement award Ky. Bus. and Profl. Women, 1983, Recognition award Joint Rep. Leadership, U.S. Congress, Dwight David Eisenhower award, 1970, John Sherman Cooper Disting. Svc. award Ky. Young Reps. Fedn., 1987, Outstanding Layperson award Ky. Med. Assn., 1992, Nelda Barton Comty. Svc. award Ky. Assn. Health Care Facilities, 1992, 5th Dist. Rep. Party Recognition award, 1996, Tribute to Nelda Barton-Collings Rep. Party of Ky. and 5th Dist. Lincoln Club, 1997, Disting. Recognition award Ky. State Senate, 2002, Hon. Lifetime award Ky. Mansion Preservation Found., 2004; Nelda Barton Collings Rep. internship award established by Rep. Party of Ky., 1997, Jefferson County Ky. Office for Women Hall of Fame, 1999, Ky. State Senate Cert. for Outstanding Women in Bus. and Leadership, 1999; named Ky. Col., 1968, Ky. Rep. Woman of Yr., Ky. Fedn. Rep. Women, 1969; named to 5th Dist. Lincoln Club Hall of Fame, 1996; Nelda Barton Day proclaimed by Mayor of Corbin, 1973; Western Ky. U. Acad. scholar, 1947-49. Mem. Am. Coll. Nursing Home Adminstrs., Ky. Assn. Health Care Facilities (legis. com. 1980-97, Ira O. Wallace award 2002), Ky. Assn. Nursing Home Adminstrs. (bd. dirs., polit. action com. 1979—), Ky. Med. Aux. (chmn. health edn. com. 1975-77), Ky. Commn. on Women, Women's Aux. So. Med. Assn. (Ky. counselor), Whitley County Med. Aux. (pres. 1959-60), Aux. Ky. Med. Assn., Ky. Mothers Assn. (parliamentarian 1970—, hon. Mother of Ky. award 1983), Ky. C. of C. (bd. dirs. 1983—, v.p. Region 5 1985—, 1st vice chmn. 1989, chmn. 1990-91). Avocations: fishing, painting. Home: 1311 7th Street Rd Corbin KY 40701-2207

BARTOSIC, FLORIAN, lawyer, educator; b. Danville, Pa., Sept. 15, 1926; s. Florian W. and Elsie (Woodring) B.; m. Eileen M. Payne, 1952 (div. 1969); children: Florian, Ellen, Thomas, Stephen; m. Alberta C. Chew, 1990. BA, Pontifical Coll., 1948; B.C.L., Coll. William and Mary, 1956; LL.M., Yale U., 1957. Bar: Va. 1956, U.S. Supreme Ct. 1959. Asst. instr. Yale U., 1956-57; assoc. prof. law Coll. William and Mary, 1957, Villanova U., 1957-59; atty. NLRB, Washington, 1956, 57, 59; counsel Internat. Brotherhood of Teamsters, Washington, 1959-71; prof. law Wayne State U., 1971-80, U. Calif., Davis, 1980-92; recalled to tchg., 1994-99; prof. emeritus law U. Calif., Davis, 1993—, dean law, 1980-90. Adj. prof. George Washington U., 1966-71, Cath. U. Am., 1960-71; mem. panel arbitrators Fed. Mediation and Conciliation Service, 1972—; hearing officer Mich. Employment Relations Commn., 1972-80, Mich. Civil Rights Commn., 1974-80; bd. dirs. Mich. Legal Services Corp., 1973-80, Inst. Labor and Indsl. Relations, U. Mich., Wayne State U., 1976-80; mem. steering com. Inst. on Global Conflict and Cooperation, 1982-83; mem. adv. bd. Assn. for Union Democracy Inc., 1980—, adv. coms. Calif. Jud. Council, 1984-85, 87; vis. scholar Harvard Law Sch., 1987, Stanford Law Sch., 1987; sr. rsch. scholar ILO, 1990-91; acad. visitor Oxford U., London Sch. Econs., 1991; mem. exec. bd. Pub. Interest Clearinghouse, 1988-90. Co-author: Labor Relations Law in the Private Sector, 1977, 2d edit., 1986; contbr. articles to law jours. Mem. ABA (sec. labor rels. law sect. 1974-75), Fed. Bar Assn., Am. Law Inst. (acad. mem. labor law adv. com. on continuing profl. edn.), Soc. Profls. in Dispute Resolution (regional v.p. 1979-80), Indsl. Rels. Rsch. Assn., Internat. Soc. Labor Law and Social Legis., Internat. Indsl. Rels. Assn., Lawyers Guild, ACLU (dir. Detroit chpt. 1976-77), Order of Coif (hon.), Scribes. Home: 235 Ipanema Pl Davis CA 95616-0253 Office: U Calif Sch Law Mrak Hall Dr Davis CA 95616 Office Phone: 530-752-2889. Business E-Mail: fbartosic@ucdavis.edu.

BARTOSSIK, NIKOLAI, artist; b. Ivanky, Cherkasa oblast, Ukraine, Apr. 5, 1951; arrived in U.S., 1995; s. Gryigoriy Bartossik and Maria Svyistun; m. Ludmila Perova, Aug. 21, 1976 (dec. July 1995); children: Julia, Pavel. BFA, Coll. Arts Kyiv, 1970; MFA, Inst. Applied Arts Kharkiv, 1975. By the Sources, Kyiv, Ukraine, 1987 (Honor award, 1987), Meteorite, Dnipropetrovsk, Ukraine, 1983 (Medal and award, 1983). Mem.: Ukrainian Nat. Soc. Artists, United Scenic Artists Local 829. Home: 400 E 84th St Apt 7E New York NY 10028

BARTOW, BARBARA JENÉ, university program administrator; b. Buffalo, June 26, 1950; d. Nicholas Michael Bojack and Lillian Lenore Bennett; m. Michael Hartzell Bartow; children: Barbara Simmons, Edward Michael Hagen. AA in Journalism, Miami Dade Jr. Coll., 1970; M. in Non-fiction Writing, USAF Air U., 1975, M. Adminstrn. Auto. mechanic Amoco, Miami, Fla., 1969-70; cargo dispatcher McKinley Transport Worldwide, Ont., Can., 1970-72; office adminstr. Modernage Furniture, Miami, 1972-74. Social svc. rep. Vets. Adminstrn. and DAV and Am. Legion, 1976—; commdr. DAV and Am. Legion, 1985-86; deputy chief of staff DAV, 1986. Contbr. poetry to World of Poetry, Internat. Soc. Poets, Internat. Libr. of Poetry, Libr. of Congress, 1990—. Active crisis intervention CASA, Fla., 1984-86; foster parent DCFS, Ill.; Dem. polit. activist, Ill., Fla., N.Y., Pa., 1976—. Sgt USAF, 1974-80. Recipient citation of merit DAV, Fla., 1985. Roman Catholic. Avocations: writing, social work, wheelchair racing. Home: 1515 Lantern Ln Joliet IL 60433-2910

BARTOW, DIANE GRACE, marketing and sales executive; b. Maspeth, NY, Apr. 20, 1948; d. Alfred Otto and Charlotte Florence (Bronnenkant) Bruggeman; m. Eugene A. Bartow, aug. 29, 1992; children: Jason, Trudi. AAS, Queensborough C.C., 1967; BS, Nova Southeastern U., 1979. Jr. acct. Exxon, N.Y.C., 1967-69; acct. BRM Assocs., N.Y.C., 1969, Texaco, N.Y.C., 1969-74; supr. Eutectic, Flushing, N.Y., 1974-76; regional industry dir. Am. Express, N.Y.C., 1976-83; v.p. Eastern Exclusives, Boston, 1983-85; pres. The Mktg. Dept., 1985-86; sr. v.p., gen. mgr. Rogers Merchandising Inc., 1986-92; exec. v.p., COO Bartow Ins. Agy., Inc., 1992—. Seminars Marketing to Win. Author tng. manual, travel newsletter, 1982, Ins. Update, 1992. Trustee, v.p. Murray Hill Neighborhood Assn., 1982, pres., 1997—; trustee 7 E 35th Corp., 1983; chmn. judging Promotion and Advt. awards, 1990, awards chair, 2001-02. Mem. Nat. Assn. Advt. and Promotional Allowances (judging chair 1996-00), Am. Soc. Travel Agts. (tour rels. com. 1983), Am. Hotel and Motel Mgmt. Assn., Am. Film Assn., Am. Mgmt. Assn., Life Underwriters, Sigma Mu Omega (pres. Bayside (N.Y.) 1966-67). Home: 7 E 35th St New York NY 10016-3810 Office Phone: 631-242-4745.

BARTRAM, RALPH HERBERT, physicist; b. N.Y.C., Aug. 16, 1929; s. Herbert L. and Grace L. Bartram; m. Ellen Anderson Devlin, Oct. 9, 1953; children: Ellen Ruth, Robert Arthur. Student, Northwestern U., 1948-49; BA cum laude, NYU, 1953, MS, 1956, PhD, 1960. Engr. Sylvania Electric Products Inc., Kew Gardens, NY, 1953-56; advanced rsch. physicist GTE Labs., Inc., Bayside, NY, 1956-61, cons., 1961-85; mem. faculty U. Conn., Storrs, 1961—, prof. physics, 1971-92, dept. head, 1986-92, prof. emeritus, 1992—. Rsch. assoc. Atomic Energy Rsch. Establishment, Harwell, England, 1967—68; vis. prof. U. Oxford, England, 1978; sr. vis. fellow U. Strathclyde, Scotland, 1993; cons. U.S. Army, 1966—71, Am. Optical Co., 1966—78, Brookhaven Nat. Lab., 1971—85, Timex Corp., 1981—82, Polaroid Corp., 1987—88, Boston U., 1993—99, ALEM Assocs., 1996—, Photonics Materials Ltd., 2002—03. Author (with J. M. Spaeth and J. R. Niklas): (book) Structural Analysis of Point Defects in Solids, 1992; author: (with B. Henderson) Crystal-Field Engineering of Solid-State Laser Materials, 2000; contbr. articles to profl. jours. With USN, 1946—48. Grantee, U.S. AEC, 1963—69, U.S. Army Rsch. Office, 1971—78, 1982—92, NSF, 1974—77, 1983—91, NATO, 1985—90. Fellow: Am. Phys. Soc.; mem.: AAUP, Conn. Acad. Sci. Engring., Optical Soc. Am., Phi Beta Kappa, Phi Eta Sigma, Sigma Pi Sigma, Phi Kappa Phi, Sigma Xi. Achievements include patents in field. Home: 67 Independence Dr Mansfield Center CT 06250-3259 Office: U Conn Dept Physics Storrs Mansfield CT 06269-3046 Personal E-mail: RHBartram2@aol.com.

BARTREM, DUANE HARVEY, retired military officer, residential designer, building consultant; b. Lansing, Mich., June 4, 1928; s. Harvey Theodore and Ruby Leola (Thomas) B.; m. Frances Lillie Bushee, Sept. 12, 1948 (dec. Jan.19, 2000); children: Lawrence Duane, Jeffrey Earl. BA in Bus. Adminstrn., Columbia Coll., Mo., 1976. Enlisted U.S. Army N.G., Lansing, 1948, commd. 2d lt., 1951, advanced through grades to col., 1951-76, comdr. battery, 1956-60; facilities engr. Mich. Nat. Guard, Lansing, 1960-69, chief engr., 1969-76, comdr. 119 FA Bn., 1971-75, comdr. 46th Brigade, 1975-76, comptr., 1976-83, ret., 1983; prin. residential design office Lansing, 1955-60, Grand Ledge, Mich., 1967—. Leader local and regional levels Boy Scouts of Am.; chmn. congregation Bretton Woods Covenant Ch., Mich., 1986—89, v.p. congregation, 1995—. With USNR, 1946—48. Decorated Army Commendation with 3 clusters, Meritorious Svc. medal with 2 clusters, Legion of Merit. Mem. Mil. Officers Assn., Mil. Order Fgn. Wars (sr. vice comdr. gen., 2003-05, comdr. gen. 2005—), Assn. of the U.S. Army (mem. resolutions com. 1973, 74, chair resolutions com. 1975, area v.p. 1976—, mem. adv. bd. 1978—, chair by-laws com. 1978—, past state pres., past region pres. 1988-92, coun. of trustees 1992-96, Pres.'s medal 1998), Grand Lodge Rotary (pres. 1989-90, Paul Harris award 1992), Boy Scouts Am. (pres. 1973-79, exec. bd. 1970—; disting. Eagle Scout 1989, Silver Beaver award 1969, Silver Antelope 1983, God and Svc. award 1992, James E. West fellow, 1910 Soc., Ernest Thompson Seton Mem. 1999). Avocation: golf. Office Phone: 517-627-9072. Personal E-mail: dhbartrem@aol.com.

BARTSCHAT, KLAUS RICHARD WILHELM, physics professor; b. Steinfurt, Westfalen, Germany, June 17, 1956; s. Richard Ewald and Helmine Angela Käthe (Busch) Bartschat; m. Teresa Elisabeth Zweerman, Aug. 13, 1988; children: Nicholas, Erika. Diploma in physics, U. Münster, Germany, 1981; PhD, U. Münster, 1984, Habilitation, 1989. Rsch. scientist U. Münster, 1984-88; asst. prof. physics Drake U., Des Moines, 1988-91, assoc. prof. physics, 1991-94, prof. physics, 1994-2000, Ellis and Nelle Levitt Disting. prof. physics, 2000—. Author: Computational Atomic Physics, 1996, Polarization, Alignment, and Orientation in Atomic Collisions, 2000; contbr. over 200 articles to profl. jours. Grantee NSF, 1991—, NATO, 1990, 93, 2000, Rsch. Corp., 1989. Fellow Am. Phys. Soc.; mem. Deutsche Physikalische Gesellschaft, Theoretical Atomic, Molecular and Optical Cmty. (chair 1998-2000), Internat. Conf. Photonic, Electronic, and Atomic Collisions (sec. 2001—). Am. Baptist. Avocations: family, exercise, travel. Home: 4301 101st St Urbandale IA 50322 Office: Drake U Dept Physics and Astronomy Des Moines IA 50311 Office Phone: 515-271-3750. E-mail: klaus.bartschat@drake.edu.

BARTTER, BRIT JEFFREY, investment banker; b. Berea, Ohio, Dec. 27, 1949; s. Lynn Martin Bartter and Scharlie Ellen (Watson) Handlan; m. Marilyn McCullough, Aug. 25, 1973; children: Bryndl Lynn and Blake McCullough (twins). AB in Econs., Duke U., 1972; MS in Fin., Cornell U., 1976, PhD in Fin., 1977. Asst. prof. computer sci. Grad. Sch. Bus. Cornell U., Ithaca, N.Y., 1976; asst. prof. fin. Grad. Sch. Mgmt. Kellogg Grad. Sch. Mgmt., Northwestern U., Evanston, Ill., 1977-79; assoc., then v.p. Merrill Lynch Capital Markets, Chgo., 1979-83; v.p. The First Boston Corp., Chgo., 1983-87, dir., 1988-89, mng. dir., 1989-94, Merrill, Lynch Investment Banking, Chgo., 1995—2004, vice chmn., 2004—. Bd. dirs. Coun. for Young Profls., Chgo., 1985-87. Contbr. articles to Jour. of Fin., Fin. Mgmt. Bd. dirs. Cornell Coun. Chgo., 1987-88, Duke Campaign Chgo., 1987-88. Mem. Econ. Club Chgo., Northwestern U. Assocs., Glen View Golf Club, Chgo. Club, Naples Nat. Golf Club, Merit Club. Home: 221 Apple Tree Rd Winnetka IL 60093-3703 Office: Merrill Lynch Investment Banking 1 N Wacker 19th Fl Ste 1900 Chicago IL 60606 Office Phone: 312-869-6252. Business E-Mail: brit_j_bartter@ml.com.

BARTUNEK, JEAN MARIE, management educator; b. Cleve., Oct. 25, 1944; d. Robert Richard Bartunek and Clare Elizabeth Lonsway. PhD, U. Ill., Chgo., 1976. Vis. asst. prof. orgnl. behavior U. Ill., Urbana, 1976—77; asst. prof., assoc. prof., prof., Robert A. and Evelyn J. Ferris chair orgn. studies Boston Coll., Chestnut Hill, Mass., 1977—. Author: Creating alternative realities at work: The quality of worklife experiment at FoodCom, 1990, Insider-Outsider team research, 1996, Organizational and educational change: The life and role of a change agent group, 2003; editor: Hidden conflict in organizations: Uncovering behind the scenes disputes, 1992, Church Ethics in its Organization Context; co-editor: Non-Traditional Rsch. Jour. Mgmt. Inquiry, 1994—97; assoc. editor: Jour. Applied Behavioral Sci., 2005—, mem. editl. bd.: Adminstrv. Sci. Quar., 1997—, Jour. Orgnl. Behavior, 1999—. Recipient Best Manuscript award, Mass. Soc. CPAs, 1980; grantee, Marion and Jasper Whiting Found., 1997—99, Soc. for Orgnl. Learning, 1998—99. Fellow: Acad. Mgmt. (exec. com., chmn. orgn. and devel. change divsn. 1986—91, exec. com. women in mgmt. divsn. 1993—96, editl. bd. Acad. Mgmt. jour. 1997—2001, officer 1998—2003, pres. 2001—02, coord. external rels. 2002—03, editl. bd. Acad. Mgmt. jour. 2004—, Best Practice-Related Paper orgn. devel. and change divsn. 1996); mem.: Ea. Acad. Mgmt. (bd. dirs. 1993—96), Soc. for Orgnl. Learning, Am. Ednl. Rsch. Assn. Roman Catholic. Office: Boston Coll 140 Commonwealth Ave Chestnut Hill MA 02467-3808 Business E-Mail: bartunek@bc.edu.

BARTUS, RAYMOND THOMAS, neuroscientist, writer, pharmaceutical executive; b. Chgo., May 19, 1947; s. Frank A. and Katherine (Bogus) B.; m. Cheryl Marie Gyure, Feb. 11, 1967; children: Raymond T., Kristin Marie. BA, California State U. Pa., 1968; MS, N.C. State U., 1970, PhD, 1972. NRC postdoctoral fellow, research assoc. Naval Med. Rsch. Lab., Groton, Conn., 1972; scientist Parke-Davis Rsch. Labs., Ann Arbor, Mich., 1973-75, sr. scientist, 1975-78, Lederle Labs., Am. Cyanamid Co., Pearl River, N.Y., 1978-79, group leader neuroscience, dir. geriatric discovery program, 1979-88; sr. v.p. R & D, chief sci. officer Cortex Pharms. Inc., Irvine, Calif., 1988-91, interim pres., 1990, exec. v.p., chief oper. officer, 1991-92, chief sci. officer, 1988-92; sr. v.p. neurobiology Alkermes Inc., Cambridge, Mass., 1992-96, sr. v.p. preclin. R&D, 1996—2001; sr. v.p. Worldwide Life Sci. R&D, 2001—02; v.p., rsch. and devel. Ceregene Inc., San Diego, 2002—04, sr. v.p., COO, 2004—. Bd. dir. Net Met; prof. N.Y.U. Med. Ctr., 1979—; adj. prof. Tulane U., 1978—87, U. Calif., Irvine, Calif., 1988—92, Tufts U., 1992—. Editor-in-chief, founder, Neurobiology of Aging, 1980-89; contbr. articles on neurosci. to profl. jours. Fellow Am. Coll. Neuropsychopharmacology; mem. Alzheimers Assn. (sci. med. bd. 1986-92), Soc. Neurosci., N.Y. Acad. Sci., Brain Tumor Soc., Am. Assn. Pharm. Sci., Am. Soc. Pharmacology and Exptl. Biology. Office: Ceregene Inc 9381 Judicial Dr #130 San Diego CA 92121 Business E-Mail: rtbartus@ceregene.com.

BARTUSKA, ANN, government official, biologist; b. Phila. BS in Biology, Wilkes Coll., 1975; MS in Botany, Ohio U.; PhD in Biology, W.Va. U. Program mgr. nat. acid precipitation assessment program N.C. State U., Raleigh; asst. dir. Southeastern Forest Expt. Sta., Forest Svc., USDA, Asheville, N.C., acting dir. ecosys. mgmt. Washington, spl. asst. chief, liaison to Nat. Biol. Survey, dir. forest health protection state and pvt. forestry orgn., dir. forest mgmt., 1998—2001, dep. chief rsch. and devel., 2004—; exec. dir. Invasive Species Initiative The Nature Conservancy, Va., 2001—04. Mem. Ecol. Soc. Am. (v.p. for pub. affairs). Office: USDA Forest Svc Auditors Bldg 201 14th St SW Washington DC 20250-0001 Fax: 202-205-1045. E-mail: fm.wo@fs.fed.us.

BARTZ, CAROL, software company executive; b. Alma, Wis., Aug. 29, 1948; m. William Marr; 1 child. BS in Computer Sci. with honors, U. Wis., 1971; DSc (hon.), Worcester Poly. Inst.; LittD (hon.), William Woods U. With sales mgmt. dept. 3M Corp., Digital Equipment Corp., 1976-83; mgr. customer mktg. Sun Microsys., 1983-84, v.p. mktg., 1984-87, v.p. customer svc., 1987-90, v.p. worldwide field ops., exec. officer, 1990-92; chmn. bd., CEO, pres. Autodesk, Inc., San Rafael, Calif., 1992—. Pres. Sun Fed., from 1987; bd. dirs. AirTouch Comm., Bea Sys., Cadence Design Sys., Cisco Sys., Inc.; mem. President's Export Coun., 1994, President's Coun. Advisors on Sci. and Tech.; adv. coun. bus. sch. Stanford U. Bd. dirs. U. Wis. Sch. Bus., Nat. Breast Cancer Rsch. Found., Found. for Nat. Medals Sci. and Tech.; mem. adv. coun. Stanford U. Bus. Sch.; mem. Com. of 200; adv. for women's health issues; former mem. Ark. of Gov.'s Econ. Summit, Little Rock. Recipient Donald C. Burnham Mfg. Mgmt. award Soc. Mfg. Engrs., 1994, Horatio Alger Award, 2000, named one of 100 Most Influential Women in Business, San Francisco Bus. Times, 2004, 100 Most Powerful Women in World, Forbes mag., 2005, World's 30 Most Respected CEOs, Barron's mag., 2005. Mem. Calif. C. of C. (bd. dirs.). Avocations: gardening, tennis. Office: Autodesk Inc 111 McInnis Pkwy San Rafael CA 94903-2700*

BARUA, RAJAT S., medical association administrator; MD, Nalanda Med. Coll., India, 1995; PhD, U. Surrey, Eng., 2003. Cert. USMLE Step I Fedn. of State Med. Bds., USMLE Step II Fedn. of State Med. Bds., USMLE Step III Fedn. of State Med. Bds., Edn. Commn. for Fgn. Med. Grad. Med. intern Nalanda Med. Coll. Hosp., Bihar, India, 1996—97, resident house physician, 1997—98; rsch. assoc. dept. medicine, divsn. cardiology St. Vincents Cath. Med. Ctrs. N.Y., NYC, 1999—2003; resident house officer dept. medicine Bronx VA Med. Ctr., 2003—. Manuscript reviewer Circulation, 2002—, Annals of Allergy, Asthma & Immunology, 2002—. Contbr. articles to profl. jours. Scholar, Interdisciplinary Ctr. Comparative Rsch., 1989—95. Mem.: Soc. for Exptl. Biology and Medicine, NY Acad. Sci., Am. Heart Assn. Achievements include research in acute coronary lesions and troponin I elevation in unstable angina or non ST elevation acute myocardial infarction; impaired mitochondrial function induced by serum from septic shock patients is attenuated by inhibition of nitric oxide synthase and poly (ADP-ribose) synthase; peripheral left bundle block in patients with left ventricular dysfunction; reactive oxygen species are involved in smoking-induced dysfunction of nitric oxide biosynthesis and upregulation of endothelial nitric oxide synthase in human coronary artery endothelial cells; PARS activation mediates inhibition of mitochondrial respiration in patients with septic shock; pathophysiology of smoking and cardiovascular disease; serum from patients with septic shock inhibits normal mitochondrial respiration and decreases endothelial cell proliferation and induces apoptosis, inhibits ATP production; Reactive oxygen species are involved in smoking-induced dysfunction of nitric oxide biosynthesis and upregulation of endothelial nitric oxide synthase in human coronary artery endothelial cells; Endogenous free radical generating sources are involved in smoking-mediated dysfunction of nitric oxide biosynthesis in human coronary artery endothelial cells: an in vitro demonstration; Attenuation of platelet-neutrophil interactions in sepsis with combinations of blocking antibodies; IIIa inhibitors, abciximab versus tirofiban, on thrombin generation during percutaneous coronary intervention; Bismuth-ethanedithiol modulates TNF and IL-10 in septic mice; Monophosphoryl lipid A stimulated up-regulation of reactive oxygen intermediates in human monocytes in vitro; Smoking is associated with altered endothelial-derived fibrinolytic and anti-thrombotic factors: An in vitro demonstration; heavy and light cigarette smokers have similar dysfunction of endothelial vasoregulatory activity: An in vivo and in vitro correlation; Mechanism of platelet-neutrophil interactions and effects on cell filtration in septic shock; dysfunctional endothelial nitric oxide biosynthesis in healthy smokers with impaired endothelium-dependent vasodilatation. Office: Bronx VA Med Ctr 130 W Kingsbridge Rd Bronx NY 10468 Office Phone: 718-584-9000. Office Fax: 718-898-7116.

BARUAH, PUNDARIKAKSHA, industrial engineer, researcher; s. Manindra Kumar and Sonmai Baruah. BS in Engring., Nat. Inst. Tech., Karnataka, India, 2000; postgrad., Wayne State U., 2001—. Mgmt. trainee PEC Ltd, India, New Delhi, 2000—01; rsch. fellow Wayne State U., Detroit, 2001—02, rsch. asst. indsl. engring., 2002—. Cons. Efficientbiz.com, Detroit, 2003—. Contbr. articles to profl. jours. and sci. conf. proceedings. Higher edn. cons., Detroit, 2004. Grantee, Wayne State U. Coll. Engring., 2004; scholar, Wayne State U., 2002—04; Thomas C. Rumble fellow, 2001—02. Achievements include development of diagnostic and prognostic framework for condition-based maintenance. Office Phone: 313-577-5293. Office Fax: 313-577-8833.

BARUCH, EDUARD, management consultant; b. Bklyn., Dec. 19, 1907; s. Emile and Grace (Willis) B.; m. Dorothy Hurd, Sept. 8, 1934 (dec. Aug. 1994); 1 child, Hurd. Mech. engr., Rhenania Coll., Switzerland, 1924-26; AB, Columbia U., 1930; postgrad., Law Sch., 1933. Trust adminstr. spl. loan div. Irving Trust Co., N.Y.C., 1933-39; sales exec. Bankers Life Co., Des Moines, 1939-42; v.p. charge sales James H. Rhodes & Co., 1942-47; nat. sales mgr. vending div. Pepsi Cola Co., 1947-49; v.p. Heli-Coil Corp., Danbury, Conn., 1949-55, exec. v.p., 1955-56, pres., 1956-70; indsl. commr. State Conn., 1973-75; corp. cons., 1970—2005. Exec. com., mem. bd. Barden Corp. (acquired by F.A.G. Schinefert Germany), Danbury, Conn.; bd. dirs. Savs. Bank, Danbury. Comdr. Conn. State Police Aux., 1967-70. Recipient Cecil J. Previdi Meml. award for civic accomplishment, leadership and entrepreneurial spirit State of Conn. Gen. Assembly and City of Danbury, 2000. Mem. Soc. Automotive Engrs., Rotary (past pres., Paul Harris fellow), Masons, Shriners, Jesters, KT (Bridgeport, Conn.), Wings Club (NYC), Coral Ridge Yacht Club (gov.), Tower Club, Lago Mar Beach and Tennis Club, Navy League (Ft. Lauderdale), Danbury Hosp. Pres. Coun., Psi Upsilon, Phi Delta Phi. Presbyterian. Home: Tucson, Ariz. *I learned from yesterday, it is past. Today is my gift to use - it is a present.Both will prepare me for tomorrow, the future.* Died June 6, 2005.

BARUCH, HURD, retired lawyer; b. N.Y.C., Nov. 29, 1937; s. Eduard and Dorothy (Hurd) B.; m. Mary Ellen Kinney, July 8, 1964; children: Edward, Michael, Amy. BA, Hamilton Coll., 1957; LLB, Yale U., 1960; MBA, Columbia U., 1961. Bar: Conn. 1960, N.Y. 1966, D.C. 1971, Pa. 1972, Ill. 1988, U.S. Supreme Ct. 1964. Ptnr. Winston & Strawn, Chgo. Spl. counsel divsn. trading and markets, SEC, 1969-72. Author: Wall Street Security Risk, 1971, Light on Light, 2004. Treas. dir. Venture Canyon Com Assn.; bd. dir. Beads Courage, Inc. Capt. USAF, 1961—64. Mem. Ill. State Bar Assn., KM, Order of Coif, Phi Beta Kappa, Beta Gamma Sigma, Ventana Canyon Golf

BARUCH, JORDAN JAY, retired management consultant; b. N.Y.C., Aug. 21, 1923; s. Solomon L. and Minnie (Kessner) B.; m. Rhoda Wasserman, June 3, 1944; children: Roberta, Marjory, Lawrence. BS, MS, Mass. Inst. Tech., 1948, Sc.D., 1950. V.p., dir. Bolt, Beranek & Newman, Inc., Cambridge, Mass., 1949-66, dir., 1949-77, Boston Broadcasters, 1963-77, 81-83, Inst. for Mental Health Initiatives, Washington, 1982—, treas., 1982-98; dir. Gould Corp., 1985-88, Baupost Group, Cambridge, Mass., 1984-98; asst. prof. elec. engring. MIT, Cambridge, 1950-53, lectr., 1954-70; lectr. bus. adminstrn. grad. sch. bus. adminstrn. Harvard U., Boston, 1970-74; prof. Amos Tuck Sch. Bus. Adminstrn., Thayer Sch. Engring., Dartmouth Coll., Hanover, N.H., 1974-77; asst. sec. sci. and tech. Dept. Commerce, Washington, 1977-81; pres. Jordan Baruch Assocs., Washington, 1981—; ret. Mem. bd. sci. and tech. for internat. devel. Nat. Rsch. Coun.; advisor to U.S./Israel Hightech Commn.; founder Nat. Ctr. Indsl. Sci. & Tech., Dalian, China; founder, U.S. advisor U.S./Israel Bianational Indsl. R&D Found., 1978—; regent Nat. Libr. Medicine, Washington, 1998-2001. Contbr. articles to books and profl. jours.; patentee loudspeakers, acoustical treatments, automotive mufflers. Bd. dirs. Inst. Mental Health Initiatives, Washington. Served with AUS, 1942-46. Named Outstanding Young Elec. Engr. Eta Kappa Nu, 1956 Fellow Acoustical Soc. Am., IEEE, AAAS, Nat. Acad. Engring. (Augustine sr. scholar 2001-03), Am. Acad. Arts and Scis. Patentee loudspeakers, acoustical treatments, automotive mufflers. Home and Office: 5630 Wisconsin Ave Apt 905 Chevy Chase MD 20815-4456 Office Phone: 301-907-3601. E-mail: jbaruch@alum.mit.edu.

BARUCH, RALPH M., communications executive; came to U.S., 1940, naturalized, 1944; s. Bernard and Alice B.; m. Jean Ursell de Mountford, June 9, 1963; children by previous marriage: Eve, Renee, Alice, Michele. Student, Sorbonne, U. Paris. Account exec. SESAC, 1947-50, Dumont TV, 1950-54; Eastern Sales mgr. Enterprises, N.Y.C., 1954-59, v.p. internat. sales, 1959-67, v.p., gen. mgr., 1967-70; group pres. CBS, 1970-71; pres., chief exec. officer Viacom Internat. Inc., N.Y.C., 1971-78, chmn. bd., mem. office of chief exec., 1979-87; sr. fellow Gannett Ctr. for Media Studies Columbia U., 1988. Cons. Adv. Commn. on Comm., USIA, 1979-86. Bd. dirs., vice chmn. exec. com. Internat. Rescue Com., N.Y.C., 1975-88; mem. Pres.'s Coun. for Internat. Youth Exch., 1982; trustee Mus. of TV and Radio, Carnegie Hall, Lenox Hill Hosp., 1980-94, Thirteen-WNET, Carnegie Hall; adv. Mayor's Coun. on Cultural Affairs, N.Y.C., 1994. Fellow Internat. Council TV Acad. Arts and Scis. (pres. 1973-76, 85-87, dir. 1976—); mem. Internat. Radio and TV Soc. (pres., past pres. Found.), Nat. Acad. Cable Programming (chmn. emeritus), Nat. Assn. Broadcasters (task force on pub. broadcasting, chmn. program producers and distbrs. com.), Cable TV Edn. Found. (chmn.). Office: Viacom Inc 1633 Broadway New York NY 10019-6708

BARUSCH, LAWRENCE ROOS, lawyer; b. Oakland, Calif., Aug. 23, 1949; s. Maurice Radston and Phyllis (Rose) B.; m. Susan Amanda Smith, Aug. 7, 1983; children: Nathaniel M., Ariana G. BA summa cum laude, Harvard U., 1971, JD cum laude, 1975. Bar: Calif. 1975. Assoc. Cotton, Seligman & Ray, San Francisco, 1975-77; gen. counsel Jones & Guerrero Co., Inc., Agana, Guam, 1977-82; ptnr. Klemm, Blair & Barusch, PC, Agana, Guam, 1982-85; assoc. Davis, Graham & Stubbs, Salt Lake City, 1986-87; counsel Parsons, Behl & Latimer, Salt Lake City, 1987-89, shareholder, 1989—; counsel Guam Tax Code Commn., 1990-94. Adj. prof. U. Utah Coll. Law, 1998-99, 2000—, vis. assoc. prof., 1999-2000; mem. com. U.S. activities of foreigners and tax treaties, tax sect. ABA, 1994—; mem. tax rev. commn. Utah, 2000—. Contbr. articles to profl. jours. including Guam Bar Jour., Utah Bar Jour., Offshore Investment, Tax Management Internat. Jour., Tax Notes. Chmn. Dem. Party, Davis County, Utah, 1997-99; mem. bd. dirs. The Road Home, 2002—. Recipient Billings prize, U. Utah S.J. Quinncy Coll. Law, 2004; Sheldon fellow, Harvard U., 1971. Mem. Guam Bar Assn. (pres. 1982-84), No. Marianas Bar Assn., Utah Bar Assn. (chmn. tax sect. 1994-95), Calif. Bar Assn., Utah Tax Review Comm., Phi Beta Kappa. Office: Parsons Behle & Latimer 201 S Main St Ste 1800 Salt Lake City UT 84111-2218 Office Phone: 801-532-1234. Business E-Mail: lbarusch@pblutah.com.

BARUSCH, RONALD CHARLES, lawyer; b. Oakland, Calif., Sept. 6, 1953; s. Maurice Radston and Phyllis Rose (Roos) B.; m. Cynthia Jean Dahlin, May 28, 1977; children: Margaret Camilla Dahlin Barusch, Christopher Charles Barusch Dahlin, Julia Rose Barusch Dahlin. AB, Harvard U., 1974, JD, 1978; M in Pub. Policy, J.F. Kennedy Sch. Govt., 1978. Bar: Mass.

1978, U.S. Ct. Appeals (1st cir.) 1979, U.S. Dist. Ct. Mass. 1979, U.S. Ct. Appeals (D.C. cir.) 1981, U.S. Dist. Ct. D.C. 1982, Va. 2000. From assoc. to ptnr. Skadden, Arps, Slate, Meagher & Flom LLP, Boston, 1978-81, Skadden, Arps, Slate, Meagher & Flom, Washington, 1981-96, ptnr. Sydney, Australia, 1996-99, Skadden Arps Slate Meaghen & Flom, Washington, 1999-2000, Skadden, Arps, Slate, Meagher & Flom, Reston, Va., 2000—03, Skadden, Arps, Slate, Meghen & Flom LLP, Washington, 2003—. Democrat. Office: Skadden Arps Slate Meagher & Flom 1440 New York Ave NW Washington DC 20005 Office Phone: 202-371-7990. E-mail: rbarusch@skadden.com.

BARVE, KUMAR P., state legislator; b. Schenectady, N.Y., Sept. 8, 1958; s. Prabhakar R. and Neera S. (Gokhale) B. BS, Georgetown U., 1980. Precinct chmn. Dist. 17 Dem. Caucus; del. Dist. 17 State of Md., Annapolis, 1991—, majority leader, 2003—. Campaign mem. Robert Hacken for Del., 1974, Barnes for Congress, 1980-84, Bruce Adams and Ike Leggett for County Coun., 1986, Barnes for Senate, 1986, Franchot for Congress, 1988, Dukakis for Pres., 1988; treas. Montgomery County Young Dem.; mem. house facility and econ. matters coms., workers compensation subcom.; vice chair Montgomery County del., 1993—. Treas., bd. dirs. Md. Nat. Abortion Rights Action League; del. GCI Consumer Coop.; fin. analyst. Mem. Md. Citizen Action, Washingtonian Towns Civic Assn., Sierra Club, Indian Culture Coord. Com., Gaithersburg and Upper Montgomery County C. of C. Office: Md Ho of Deleg Lowe Ho Off Bldg 84 Coll Ave Annapolis MD 21401*

BARWICK, WILLIAM D., lawyer; b. Atlanta, June 4, 1949; BA, Amherst Coll., 1971; JD, U. Ga., 1974. Bar: Ga. 1974. With Sutherland Asbill & Brennan LLP, Atlanta. Mem.: Def. Rsch. Inst., Atlanta Bar Assn. (bd. dirs. 1986—90, sec.-treas. 1990—91, pres. 1992—93), State Bar Ga. (pres. 2003, mem. young lawyers sect., exec. coun. 1980, sec. 1981—83, pres. 1984—85, sec. 2000—01, bd. govs. 1987—91, 1993—), Phi Delta Phi. Office: Sutherland Asbill & Brennan LLP 999 Peachtree St NE Atlanta GA 30309-3996

BARWIG, REGIS NORBERT JAMES, priest; b. Chgo., Jan. 16, 1932; s. Ladislas-Joseph and Josepha Agnes (Neugebauer) B. AB, St. Procopius Coll., 1954; postgrad., Georgetown U., 1957, Pontifical Lateran U., Rome, 1959-61. Ordained priest Roman Cath. Ch., 1959. Sec. to abbot of Lisle, 1955-61; sec. gen. Christian Unity Apostolate, 1961-64; founding prior Claremont Priory, Cedarburg, Wis., 1964-67; prior Community of Our Lady, Oshkosh, Wis., 1968—. Co-chmn. 1st Festival Faith, Milw., 1966; chmn. Ecumenical Conf. Spiritual and Liturgical Renewal Religious Life, 1969—; mem. Green Bay Diocese Ecumenical Commn., 1970-73; theol. cons. Consortium Perfectae Caritatis, 1974—; preacher, U.S. and Europe; U.S. liaison for beatification of Pope Pius IX, 1975—; assoc. Wanda Landowska Music Ctr., Lakeville, Conn., 1969; bd. dirs. Inter-Cath. Press Agy., N.Y., 1967-72. Author: Changing Habits, 1971, Waiting for Rain, 1975, Reflections on Spiritual Life for Order of Malta, 1982; translator: His Will Alone, 1971, Wanda Landowska Diaries, 1971, Pius XI-A Close-up, 1975, Pius IX-More than a Prophet, 1977, Writings of Blessed Maximilian Maria Kolbe, 1977, Evaluations of the Possibility of Constructing a Christian Ethic on the Assumptions of the Philosophy of Max Scheler, 1982; editor: Conferences of Mother Mary of Jesus, 1968; contbr. articles to religious publs. Decorated Bruderschaft, Collegio Teutonico, Vatican City, Knight Comdr., Order Isabel la Catolica, Spain, Grand Cross of Merit, Sovereign Mil. Order of Malta, Magistral Chaplain, Conventual Grand Cross Chaplain of Honor, Prelatial Councillor, Chief of Chaplains, Polish Assn., Sovereign Mil. Order of Malta, knight comdr. Ecclesiastical Grace, Gold Benemerenti medal Sacred Mil. Constantinian Order of St. George-Bourbon Two Sicilies, Chaplain Am. Del., knight Order of Francis I, Bourbon-Two Sicilies, Knight Comdr. Equestrian Order Holy Sepulcher of Jerusalem, Grand Priory of Poland, Comdr., Order of Merit, Republic of Poland, Gold Cross Merit Primate of Poland, hon. Canon, Royal Coll. Chpt., Wilanow-Warsaw, Archbishop Weber HS Madonna award, Skowyrow Found. award Pastoral Inst. Cath. U. Lublin, Spl. Fgn. award Warsaw Soc. Civitas Christiana, Person of Yr. award St. John Cantius Soc. Chgo., Gold Cross Merit Polish Cath. Mission Eng. and Wales, Meml. medal Cardinal Stefan Wyszynski, Merit medal Arch. Warsaw. Mem. Selden Soc., Queen Mary Coll., Polish-Am. Assn. Wis. (chaplain 1979—), Polish Arts Club. Home and Office: 2804 Oakwood Ln Oshkosh WI 54904-8406 *From my Roman Catholic faith and my Polish heritage I imbibed early a sense of the importance of Divine Providence in one's life. In this context, then, regret and disappointment are both futile and destructive emotions. Everything can be redeemed. Radical eternalism makes one look Above and Beyond.*

BARYSHNIKOV, MIKHAIL, ballet dancer, actor; b. Riga, Latvia, Jan. 28, 1948; arrived in US, 1974, naturalized, 1986; s. Nicholai and Aleksandra (Kisselov) B.; 4 children: Aleksandra, Peter, Anna Katerina, Sofia-Luisa. Student, Ballet Sch. of Riga, Kirov Ballet Sch., Leningrad, Russia; DFA (hon.), Yale U., 1979; DHL (hon.), Columbia U., 1985. Mem. Kirov Ballet Co., 1969-74; prin. dancer Am. Ballet Theatre, 1974-78, N.Y.C. Ballet, 1978-79; dir. designee Am. Ballet Theatre, 1979-80, artistic dir., 1980-90; founder White Oak Dance Project, 1990—. Since 1974 guest artist with leading ballet cos. throughout world including Nat. Ballet of Can., Royal Ballet, Hamburg (Germany) Ballet, Ballet Victoria, Australia, Stuttgart (W.Ger.) Ballet, appeared at, Covent Garden, Spoleto (Italy) Festival; dances premier danseur roles in the traditional repertory; other repertory includes: Le jeune homme et la morte, Vestris, Medea, Push Comes to Shove, Hamlet Connotations, Other Dances, Pas de Duke, Santa Fe Saga, Pique Dame, Four Seasons, Opus 19, Rhapsody Apollo, Configurations, The Wild Boy, The Little Ballet, Follow the Feet, Sinatra Suite, Requiem; ballets staged for the Am. Ballet Theatre include The Nutcracker, 1976, Don Quixote (Kitri's Wedding), 1978, Cinderella, 1983, A Month in the Country, 1985, Drink to Me Only with Thine Eyes, 1988, Wonderland, 1989, Duo concertante, 1992, Three Preludes, 1992; motion pictures include The Turning Point, 1976 (Acad. award nomination best supporting actor 1976), When I Think of Russia (voice), 1980, White Nights, 1985, That's Dancing, 1985, Dancers, 1987, The Cabinet of Dr. Ramirez, 1991, Company Business, 1992, Russian Holiday, 1992, Le mystere Babilee, 2001; actor on Broadway: Metamorphosis, 1989 (Theatre World special award, Outer-Circle Drama Critics award 1989), Forbidden Christmas, or the Doctor and the Patient, 2004; numerous TV appearances including Dance in America series, Baryshnikov at the White House (Emmy award 1979), Baryshnikov on Broadway (Emmy award 1980), Baryshnikov in Hollywood, Baryshnikov by Tharp, A Salute to Fred Astaire, A Salute to Gene Kelly, Dance in America: Baryshnikov Dances Balanchine (Emmy award 1989); co-creator (with choreographer Mark Morris): White Oak Dance Project, 1990; author: Baryshnikov at Work: Mikhail Baryshnikov Discusses His Roles, 1976, Baryshnikov in Color, 1980; toured in Cutting Up (choreographed by Twyla Tharp), 1992-93; guest appearance Sex and the City, 2003-2004. Gold medal, Internat. Ballet Competition, Bulgaria, 1966, Gold medal, First Internat. Ballet Competition, Moscow, 1969, Nijinsky prize, Internat. Ballet Competition, Paris Academy, 1969, Dance Mag. award, 1978, Ellis Island medal of honor, Nat. Ethnic Coalition of Orgn., 1986, Hasty Pudding award, Hasty Pudding Theatricals, 1987, Nat. Merit award from U.S. President Bill Clinton, 2000, John F. Kennedy Ctr. Honor, 2000. *The dancer who would grow in his art must seek to explore and develop new phases of his talent, and to expand his performing horizons in terms of both the new and existing repertoire.*

BARZA, HAROLD A., lawyer; b. Montreal, Que., Can., July 28, 1952; came to U.S., 1969; s. Solomon A. and Evelyn (Elkin) B. BA, Boston U., 1973; JD, Columbia U., 1976. Bar: N.Y. 1977, Calif. 1978, U.S. Dist. Ct. (ctrl. dist.) Calif. 1978. Law clk. to Hon. Milton Pollack U.S. Dist. Ct. (so. dist.) N.Y., 1976-77; assoc. Munger, Tolles & Rickershauser, L.A., 1978-81; ptnr. Gelles, Singer & Johnson, L.A., 1982-83, Gelles, Lawrence & Barza, L.A., 1983-87, Loeb & Loeb, L.A., 1987-99, Quinn, Emanuel, Urquehart, Oliver and Hedges, L.A., 1999—. Adj. prof. mass comm. law Southwestern U. Sch. Law, L.A., 1979-82; judge pro tem., L.A. Mcpl. Ct., 1985—. Mem. bd. editors Columbia Law Rev., 1975-76. Mem. steering com. Jewish Nat. Fund, L.A., 1983. James Kent scholar, 1974-76, Harlan Fiske Stone scholar, 1973-74. Mem. ABA (mem. com. on antitrust litigation), Los Angeles County Bar Assn. (trial lawyers, litigation and intellectual property sects.). Office: Quinn Emanuel Urquhart Oliver and Hedges 865 S Figueroa St Los Angeles CA 90017-2543 E-mail: hab@qeuo.com.

BARZDA, SUSAN MARIE, special education educator, art educator; d. John Anthony and Verona Jewel (Brickner) Barzda. MusB, Heidelberg Coll., 1974; postgrad., Muskingum Coll., 2003—. Lic. tchr. music k-12 Ohio Dept. Edn., 1974, Qualified Mental Retardation Professional (QMRP) Ohio Dept. of Mental Retardation, Devel. Disability, 1980. Instr. instrumental and vocal music Rolling Hills Local Sch. Dist., Byesville, Ohio, 1974—76; tchr. music, supr. Cambridge Devel. Ctr., 1976—87; dir. high sch. band, tchr. music appreciation Bishop Rosecrans Cath. High Sch., Zanesville, 1981—85; adminstrv. asst. II Cambridge Devel. Ctr., 1987—93, 1989—93, qualified mental retardation profl., 1993—. Dir., instr. majorettes, drill team, and fife and drum corps Rolling Hills Local Sch. Dist., Byesville, Ohio, 1974—76, instr. Meadowbrook unit Guernsey county bicentennial fife and drum corps, 1975—76; dir. YMCA Y-ettes Baton Twirling Corps, 1978—81; coord. Spl. Olympics Cambridge Devel. Ctr., 1981—84, mem. devel. centers mini-team improve quality of svcs. individuals with mental retardation, 1977—79, mem. Ohio's mini-teams devel. centers, 1977—79, adult basic edn. grant coord., 1986—90. Play selection com. chair Cambridge Pertorming Arts Ctr., 1986—2003; sec. Cambridge City Band, 1980—81, Zanesville Meml. Concert Band, Zanesville, 2002—03; S.E.Ohio regional rep. Ohio Cmty. Theatre Assn., Columbus, 1999—2002, bd. mem.-at-large, 2002—, sec., 2004; clarinettist Dominic Greco Concert Band, Dover, 2002—03; tenor saxophone player Dick Simcox Big Band, Cambridge, 1981—85; clarinetist Southeastern Ohio Symphony, New Concord, 1982—84; mem., pit orch. mem., actress, dancer, choreographer, prodr., dir., musical dir., Cambridge Performing Arts Centre, 1977—2003; clarinettist Zanesville Meml. Concert Band, 1982—2003, Coshocton Cmty. Band, 2002—03. Recipient Jean Lisle Meml. award, Alliance Music Study Club, 1970, Dick Beal Outstanding Regional Rep. award, Ohio Cmty. Theatre Assn., 2002; scholar, Quota Club Alliance, Ohio, 1970; Rhodes-King scholar, Heidelberg Coll., 1970—71. Mem.: Philalethean Women's Soc. Alumni (life). Independent. Avocations: clarinet, acting, genealogy, travel. Office: Cambridge Developmental Ctr 66737 Old 21 Rd Cambridge OH 43725 Personal E-mail: subar@cambridgeoh.com.

BARZELATTO, JOSE S., social welfare organization executive; b. Santiago, Chile, Apr. 6, 1926; arrived in U.S., 1989; s. Jose Q. Barzelatto and Veronica G. Sanchez; m. Juanita Ramirez Barzelatto, Jan. 8, 1950 (dec. Nov. 21, 1999); children: Veronica, Ana Maria, Jovan, Marcos, Cristina, Virginia. MD, U. Chile, 1949. Lic. physician Fla. Mem. faculty U. Chile, Santiago, 1950—68; postgrad. trainee Mass. Gen. Hosp., Boston, 1951—53, rsch. fellow, 1959—60; spl. advisor OAS, Washington, 1968—75; med. officer, dir. WHO, Geneva, 1975—89; dir. reproductive health The Ford Found., N.Y.C., 1989—97; v.p. Ctr. for Health & Social Policy, N.Y.C. and San Francisco, 1997—. Founder, exec. sec. Chile's Nat. Coun. Sci. and Tech., Santiago, 1967—68; mem. coun. Pugwash Conf. Sci. and World Affairs, 1971—82; mem. ethics com. Internat. Fedn. Ob-Gyn., London, 1997—2004; pres. directive coun. Civil Soc. Forum of the Ams., Rio de Janeiro, 2000—05. Author (with Anibal Foundes): The Drama of Abortion Seeking a Consensus, 2004; co-editor: Ethics and Human Values in Family Planning, 1989; contbr. articles to profl. jours., chapters to books. Mem.: Latin Am. Assn. Rsch. in Human Reprodn. (hon.). Avocations: family, politics. Home: 5800 Nicholson Ln Apt 1201 Rockville MD 20852 Office: Ctr Health & Social Policy 847 25th St San Francisco CA 94121 E-mail: josebarzel@aol.com.

BARZILAY, JUDITH MORGENSTERN, federal judge; b. Russell, Kans., Jan. 3, 1944; d. Arthur and Hilda Morgenstern; m. Sal (Doron) Barzilay, Aug. 19, 1973; children: Ilan, Michael. Student, Stern Coll., 1961—62; Bachelors, Wichita State U., 1965; MLS, Rutgers U., 1971, JD, 1981. Bar: N.J. 1981. Tchr. English Wichita (Kans.) H.S., 1965-67; editor Carter Wallace Pharms., Cranbury, N.J., 1967-68; tchr. English Hamilton Sch., Hamilton Twp., N.J., 1968-69; ref. libr. Suffolk County Coll., Selden, N.J., 1971-74, Somerset Coll., Somerville, N.J., 1975-76, East Brunswick (N.J.) Libr., 1977-78; law clk. to Hon. Robert Tarleton N.J. Superior Ct., Jersey City, 1982-83; atty. Williams, Caliri, Miller & Otley, Wayne, N.J., 1982-83, US Dept. Justice, N.Y.C., 1983-86, Siegel, Mandell & Davidson, N.Y.C., 1986-88; sr. atty. Sony Electronics, Park Ridge, NJ, 1988—89, v.p. import-export ops., 1989—95, v.p. govt. affairs, 1996—98; judge U.S. Ct. Internat. Trade, N.Y.C., 1998—. Mem. Treasury Sec.'s Com. on Comml. Ops. of U.S. Customs Svc., Washington, 1996-98. Bd. trustees Ramapo Coll., Mahwah, N.J., 1996-98. Recipient Tribute to Women and Industry award YWCA of Bergen County, N.J., 1993, Disting. Alumna award Wichita State U., 1996. Mem. Am. Assn. Exporters and Importers (exec. bd. dirs. 1992-98). Jewish. Office: US Ct Internat Trade One Federal Plz New York NY 10278 Fax: 212-264-5487.*

BARZILAY, ZVI, real estate executive; BArch, U. Md.; M in Urban Design/Real Estate Devel., Harvard U. Chief ctr. city planner Phila. City Planning Commn.; with Toll Bros., Inc., Huntingdon Valley, Pa., 1980—, pres., COO, also bd. dirs. Mem. Urban Land Inst., Phila. Dist. Coun. Avocations: sailing, fishing, outdoors. Office: Toll Bros 250 Gibraltar Rd Horsham PA 19044 Office Phone: 215-938-8228.

BARZUN, JACQUES, writer, literary agent; b. Créteil, France, Nov. 30, 1907; came to U.S., 1920, naturalized, 1933; s. Henri Martin and Anna-Rose B.; m. Mariana Lowell, Aug. 1936 (dec. 1979); children: James Lowell, Roger Martin, Isabel; m. Marguerite Davenport, June 1980. Ed., Lycée Janson de Sailly, Paris; AB, Columbia U., 1927, MA, 1928, PhD, 1932. From lectr. history to assoc. prof. Columbia U., N.Y.C., 1927-45, prof., 1945, dean grad. faculties, 1955-58, dean faculties and provost, 1958-67, prof. emeritus, spl. adviser on arts, 1967-75; lit. adviser Scribner's, N.Y.C., 1975-93. Author: The French Race, 1932, Teacher in America, 1945, Berlioz and the Romantic Century, 1950, 3d edit., 1969, Pleasures of Music, 1951, 2d edit., 1977, God's Country and Mine, 1954, Music in American Life, 1956, Darwin, Marx, Wagner, 1941, The Energies of Art, 1956, Of Human Freedom, 2d edit, 1964, Race: A Study in Superstition, 1937, The Modern Researcher, 1957, 6th edit., 2003, The House of Intellect, 2d edit, 1975, Classic, Romantic and Modern, 1961, Science: The Glorious Entertainment, 1964, The American University, 1968, 2d edit., 1995, A Catalogue of Crime, 1971, 2d edit., 1986, On Writing, Editing and Publishing, 1971, The Use and Abuse of Art, 1974, Clio and the Doctors, 1974, Simple and Direct, 1975, 2d edit., 1993, Critical Questions, 1982, A Stroll With William James, 1983, A Word or Two Before You Go, 1986, The Culture We Deserve, 1989, Begin Here: On Teaching and Learning, 1990, An Essay on French Verse, 1991, From Dawn to Decadence: 1500 Years of Western Cultural Life, 2000, A Jacques Barzun Reader, 2001, What Is a School?, 2002; mem. editl. bd. The American Scholar, 1946-76, Ency. Brit, 1979—; editor: Selected Letters of Lord Byron, 1953, Nouvelles Lettres de Berlioz, 1954, The Selected Writings of John Jay Chapman, 1957, Follett's Modern American Usage, 1966. Trustee NY Soc. Libr., 1968-97; adv. coun. U. Buckingham. Decorated Legion of Honor; recipient Presdl. medal of Freedom; Extraordinary fellow Churchill Coll., U. Cambridge (Eng.). Fellow Royal Soc. Arts, Royal Soc. Lit.; mem. Soc. Am. Historians, Mass. Hist. Soc. (corr.), AAAL (pres. 1972-75, 77-78), Am. Philos. Soc., Am. Acad. for Liberal Edn. (hon. pres.), Acad. Delphinale (Grenoble), Century Assn., Phi Beta Kappa.

BAS, HERNAN, artist; b. Miami, Fla., 1978; Degree, New World Sch. Art, Miami. One-man shows include Slim Fast, Frances Wolfson Gallery, Miami Dade Cmty. Coll., 2000, Hernan's Merit & the Nouveau Sissies, Fredric Snitzer Gallery, Miami, 2001, It's Super Natural, Mus. Contemporary Art, Miami, 2002, Love in Vein, Sandroni Rey, Venice, Calif., 2002, First Comes the Blood, Then Come the Boys, Fredric Snitzer Gallery, Miami, 2002, Sometimes With One I Love, Daniel Reich Gallery, NY, 2004, exhibited in group shows at Frank: an Agl. Connoting...Superfantastic, Baltimore, Md., 1997, Fashion Issue: four simple steps towards younger looking skin, Fredric Snitzer Gallery, Miami, 1998, Superfantastic 7, The Dirt Room, Kansas City, Ohio, 1999, Departing Perspectives, Espirito Santo Building, Miami, 2000, Ob-la-di-Ob-la-da, Art Ctr./South Fla., 2000, Making Art in Miami:Travels in Hyperreality, Mus. Contemporary Art, Miami, 2000, Humid, Mus. Contemporary Art, Chgo., 2001, Fast Forward, Projects Nash Hotel Art Fair, Miami Beach, 2001, Champion, Zinc Gallery, Stockholm, Sweden, 2002, Dangerous Beauty, Jewish Cmty. Ctr., Manhattan, 2002, Friends & Family, Lombard-Fried Fine Arts, NY, 2002, AOP 2002: 37th Art on Paper Exhbn., Weatherspoon Art Mus., U. NC, 2002, In the Place of Revolution, Great Hall of The Cooper Union, 2002, Drawing Conclusions, Buena Vista Bldg., Miami, 2002, Made in Miami, Fredric Snitzer Gallery, Miami, 2003, Whitney Biennial Am. Art, Whitney Mus. Am. Art, 2004, Sixth Ann. Altoids Curiously Strong Collection, New Mus. Contemporary Art, NY, 2004. Mailing: c/o MOCA Grand Ave 250 South Grand Ave Los Angeles CA 90012*

BASAÑEZ, MIGUEL EBERGENYI, political scientist, educator; b. Tuxpan, Ver, Mex., Oct. 24, 1947; came to U.S., 1995; s. Miguel Sorcini and Magdalena Ebergenyi Basáñez; m. Tatiana Beltran, Feb. 7, 1970; children: Tatiana, Alejandro, Pamela, Nicolas. BA in Law, UNAM, Mexico City, 1969; MA in Adminstrn., U. Warwick, Coventry, Eng., 1974; PhD in Polit. Sci., London Sch. Econs., 1991. Prof. U Nat. Autonoma Mex., U. Autonoma Estado Mex., Inst. Tech., Mexico City and Toluca, 1975-95; atty. gen. State of Mex., Toluca, 1985-86; chief of staff Ministry of Energy, Mexico City, 1986-88; pres. Mori-Mexico, Mexico City, 1988—2002; vis. prof. U. Mich., Ann Arbor, 1995-96; sr. v.p. MORI-Internat., Princeton, NJ, 1996—98; CEO MORI-USA, Princeton, 1998-2000; CEO, Global Quality Rsch. Corp., Princeton, 2000—. Pub. Este Pais mag., Mexico City, 1990-95; bd. dirs. Serfin Bank, Mexico City, 1986-88, Mexican-Am. Binat. Found., Mexico City/Washington D.C., 2002. Co-author: Human Beliefs and Values, 2004, North American Trajectories, 1996; author: El Pulso de Los Sexenios, 1990, La Lucha por La Hegemonia, 1981, Asia Barometer, 2005. Pres. Acude-Alianza Democratica, Mexico City, 1992-93, LSE Alumnai in Mex., Mexico City, 1980-83; del. PRI, Mex., 1970-72. Recipient Nat. prize Nat. Pub. Adminstrn. Inst., 1982. Mem. World Assn. for Pub. Opinion Rsch. (pres. 1999-2000, Nelson award 1993), Am. Polit. Sci. Assn., Am. Assn. for Pub. Opinion Rsch., Latin Am. Studies Assn. Avocations: photography, waterskiing, computers, films. Office: Global Quality Rsch Corp 116 Village Blvd Ste 200 Princeton NJ 08540-5740 Office Phone: 609-818-1531.

BASAVAPPA, RAVI, biophysical science educator; b. Bangalore, India, Feb. 7, 1961; arrived in U.S., 1968; BS, Duke U., 1980; MS, Clemson U., 1983; PhD, U. Chgo., 1991. Postdoctoral fellow Harvard Med. Sch., Boston, 1991—95; asst. prof. dept. biochemistry and biophysics U. Rochester (N.Y.) Med. Ctr., 1995—2002, assoc. prof., 2002—04; program dir. NIH, 2004—. Rsch. scholar Leukemia and Lymphoma Soc. Am. Contbr. articles to sci. jours. Postdoctoral fellow NIH, 1992-95, rsch. grantee, 1998—. Mem. Am. Crystallographers Assn. Achievements include research in biochemistry and biophysics. Office: NIH Gen Scis 2AS 19C 45 Center Dr Bethesda MD 20892

BASCOM, C. PERRY, retired foundation administrator; b. Boston, July 30, 1936; s. William Richardson and Jean Ames (Hall) B.; m. Sally Cissel Greenwood, July 18, 1995; children: Elisabeth Brooke, Heather Ames, Sarah Duff Greenwood, Amy Greenwood Dunaway. BA, Yale U., 1958; LLB, Harvard U., 1961. Assoc. Bryan Cave, St. Louis, 1962-72, ptnr., 1972-95; adminstr. Gateway Found., St. Louis, 1995—2001, ret., 2001. Judge St. Louis Night Housing Ct., 1970-72; lectr. on various topics, including Truth in Lending, Real Estate Settlement Procedures Act, techniques in comml. bank lending, devels. in Mo. banking law, electronic funds transfers. Sr. warden Trinity Ch., St. Louis, 1974-78. Served with USAR, 1961-68. Mem. Mo. Bar Assn. Home: 4650 Pershing Pl Saint Louis MO 63108-1908 Personal E-mail: scgcpb@earthlink.net.

BASCOM, RUTH F., retired mayor; b. Ames, Iowa, Feb. 4, 1926; d. Frederick Charles and Doris Hays Fenton; m. John U. Bascom, June 14, 1950; children: Lucinda, Rebecca, Ellen, Thomas, Paul, Mary. BS, Kans. State U., Manhattan, 1946; MA, Cornell U., 1949. Tchr. Dickinson County Cmty. H.S., Kans., 1946-48, Nat. Coll. Edn., Chgo., 1949-51. Co-chair Cascadia High Speed Rail, 1995-98. Chair City and State Bicycle Com., 1971-83; mem., chair Met. Park Bd., Eugene, 1972-82; past bd. pres. Youth Symphony, 1962-68; city councilor City of Eugene, Oreg., 1984-92, coun. v.p., pres., 1988-90, mayor, 1993-97; v.p., pres. LWV, Eugene, 1967-69; chair, Oreg. Passenger Rail Com., 2000—; state bd. 1000 Friends of Oreg., 1999-2005. Recipient Gold Leaf award Internat. Soc. Arboriculture, 1993; dedicated Ruth Bascom Riverbank Trail Sys., 2003. Democrat. Congregationalist. Avocations: music, tree farm, bicycling. Home: 2114 University St Eugene OR 97403-1542 E-mail: jbascomr@pacinfo.com.

BASDEN, CAMERON, ballet mistress, dancer; b. Dallas; Scholarship student, The Joffrey Ballet Sch., 1976-77. Dancer Dallas Ballet, 1975-76, Joffrey II Dancers, N.Y.C., 1977-79, The Joffrey Ballet, N.Y.C., 1979—, asst. ballet mistress, 1990-93, ballet mistress N.Y.C., Chgo., 1993—. Prof. dance Manhattanville Coll. Actor: (films) The Company, 2003. Office: Joffrey Ballet 70 E Lake St Fl 1300 Chicago IL 60601-5917

BASE, GRAEME ROWLAND, illustrator, author; b. Amersham, Eng., Apr. 6, 1958; s. Geoffrey Donald and Elizabeth Enid (Philips) B.; m. Robyn Anne Paterson, Aug. 1, 1981; children: James Geoffrey, Katherine Gabrielle, William Alexander. Art diploma, Swinburne Inst. Tech., 1978. Author (illustrator): My Grandma Lived in Gooliguich, 1983, Animalia, 1983 (Australian Children's Book award Children's Book Coun. Australia, 1987, Kids Own Australia Literature award, 1988), The Eleventh Hour: A Curious Mystery, 1988 (Australian Children's Book award Children's Book Coun. Australia, 1989, Book Design award Australian Book Pub. Assn., 1988, Young Australian Best Book award, 1989, Kids Own Australia Literature award, 1989), The Sign of the Seahorse, 1992, The Disovery of Dragons, 1996, The Worst Band in the Universe, 1999, The Water Hole, 2001, Truckdogs, 2003; illustrator Adventures with My Best Worst Friend, 1982, The Island Bike Business, 1982, Jabberwocky From "Through the Looking Glass", 1985; author (illustrator): Jungle Drums, 2004. Office: Penguin Australia 250 Camberwell Rd Camberwell VIC 3124 Australia

BASEFSKY, STUART MARK, law librarian, library and information scientist, journalist, educator; b. Denver, Oct. 31, 1949; s. Stanley S. and Ilene U. (Sunshine) Basefsky; m. Claire M. Germain, Aug. 16, 1976; 1 child, Nicolas. Student, U. Erlangen, Fed. Republic of Germany, 1969-70; BA, U. Colo., 1971; MA in Tchg., Duke U., 1975; MSLS, U. N.C., 1979. Info. specialist N.C. Sci. & Tech. Rsch. Ctr., Research Triangle Park, NC, 1980; documents libr. N.C. State U., Raleigh, 1980-83, Duke U., Durham, NC, 1983-93; reference libr. Sch. Indsl. & Labor Rels., Cornell U., Ithaca, NY, 1993—, editor, dir. IWS news bur., 2002—, lectr. human resource studies, 2004—. Adj. instr. sch. info. and libr. sci. U. N.C., Chapel Hill, 1990—92; mem. adv. bd. Washington Alert Svc. Congl. Quar. Inc., 1990—; pres. Ithaca Pub. Edn. Initiative, 1996—2003; mem. adv. bd. HR Advisor West Group, 1998—. Contbr. articles to profl. jours. Recipient Key Vol. award, Durham County, 1978, Indsl. and Labor Rels. Recognition award, 1999, H. W. Wilson Co. award, Spl. Librs. Assn., 2002, Chancellor's award, SUNY, 2005. Mem.: ALA, Can. Assn. Journalists, Internat. Platform Assn., Am. Assn. Law Librs. (founder, chmn. citation reform com. 1980—83), Patent Documentation Soc., N.C. Libr. Assn. (mem. exec. bd. 1984—85, lobbyist 1987). Democrat. Avocation: swimming. Home: 10 Wedgewood Dr Ithaca NY 14850-1063 Office: Cornell U Sch Indsl & Labor Rels Catherwood Lib Ives Hall Ithaca NY 14853-3901 E-mail: smb6@cornell.edu.

BASEHORE, NICHOLAS FREDERICK, church musician; b. Lebanon, Pa., Feb. 6, 1981; s. Frederick Allen Basehore, Jr. and Sharon Marie Youtz Zechman, Pamela Rae Broome Basehore (Stepmother) and Paul Daniel Zechman (Stepfather); m. Alexis Elizabeth Hileman, May 28, 2005. MusB, Clarion U. Pa., 2003. Assoc. dir. music and liturgy St. Petronille Cath. Ch., Glen Ellyn, Ill., 2003—. Recipient Meritorious Achievement in Musical Direction, Kennedy Ctr., Am. Coll. Theater Festival, 2003. Mem.: Nat. Assn. Pastoral Musicians, Am. Guild Organists, Phi Mu Alpha Sinfonia (songleader

2002—03). Roman Catholic. Avocations: motorcycling, crafts, reading, travel, cooking. Office: St Petronille Cath Ch 420 Glenwood Ave Glen Ellyn IL 60137 Office Phone: 630-469-0404 2105. Business E-Mail: basehoren@stpetschurch.org.

BASERGA, RENATO LUIGI, pathology educator; b. Meda, Milan, Italy, Apr. 11, 1925; came to U.S., 1949; s. Alessandro and Giuseppina (Annoni) B.; m. Jane Conrad, Dec. 23, 1954 (div. Sept. 1974); children: Susan Jane, Janice Rene; m. Beverly Lange, Oct. 12, 1974. MD, U. Milan, 1949. Diplomate Am. Bd. Pathology. Resident U. Milan, 1949-51; intern Columbus Hosp., Chgo., 1952-53; assoc. in onocology Chgo. Med. Sch., 1953-54; resident pathology St. Luke's Hosp., Chgo., 1955-58; instr. pathology Northwestern U., Chgo., 1958-60, asst. prof., 1960-64, assoc. prof., 1964-65; prof. Temple U., Phila., 1965-91, chmn. dept. pathology, 1980-91; prof. microbiology Thomas Jefferson Univ., Phila, 1991—2000, disting. prof., 2000—; dep. dir. Kimmel Cancer Ctr., 1991—2004, interim dir., 2004—. Cons. Argonne (Ill.) Nat. Lab., 1959-65; sr. investigator Fels Rsch. Inst., Temple U., 1965-91; Louis Gross Meml. lectr. NYU, 1974; Searle lectr. Brit. Soc. Cell Biology, 1976; Wellcome vis. prof., 1984. Author: Autoradiography Techniques and Applications, 1969, Multiplication and Division in Mammalian Cells, 1976, The Biology of Cell Reproduction, 1985; editor: The Cell Cycle and Cancer, 1971. Served with vol. forces, 1943-45, Italy. Recipient rsch. career devel. award USPHS, 1964-65, Samuel Noble Found. award, 1989, Rous-Whipple award, 1990, Fred Stewart award, 1990; Maria Antoinetta Della Casa scholar, Milan, 1951; sr. rsch. fellow USPHS, 1958-60, Schiffer Meml. Lectr. Internat. Cell Soc. award, 1992, Susan Swerling lectureship Dana-Farber Cancer Ctr., 1993. Fellow AAAS. Office: Kimmel Cancer Inst Bluemle Life Scis Bldg 233 S 10th St Fl 6 Philadelphia PA 19107-5541*

BASH, FRANK NESS, astronomer, educator; b. Medford, Oreg., May 3, 1937; s. Frank Cozad and Kathleen Jane (Ness) B.; m. Susan Martin Fay, Sept. 10, 1960; children: Kathryn Fay, Francis Lee BA, Willamette U., 1959; MA in Astronomy, Harvard U., 1962; PhD, U. Va., 1967; DSc (hon.), Willamette U., 2000. Staff scientist Lincoln Lab. MIT, 1962; assoc. astronomer Nat. Radio Astronomy Obs., Green Bank, W.Va., 1962-64; rsch. asst. U. Va., 1965-67; postdoctoral faculty assoc. U. Tex., Austin, 1967-69, asst. prof. astronomy, 1969-73, assoc. prof., 1973-81, prof., 1981—, Frank N. Edmonds Regents prof., 1985—, chmn. dept. astronomy, 1983-86, dir. W.J. McDonald Obs., 1989—2003. Mem. astronomy adv. panel NSF, 1988-91; chmn. vis. com. Nat. Radio Astronomy Obs., 1990, mem., 1990-93; mem. vis. com. Arecibo Obs., 1990-95, chmn., 1994; mem. planning com. NASA Astrophys. Data Systems, 1991-95; bd. dirs., mem. rep. Assoc. Univs. for Rsch. in Astronomy, 1995-2000; chmn. bd. dirs. Hobby-Eberly Telescope, So. African Large Telescope. Author: (with Daniel Schiller and Dilip Balamore) Astronomy, 1977; contbr. articles to profl. jours. Grantee NSF, 1967—, The Netherlands NSF, 1979, W.M. Keck Found., 1988. Mem. Am. Astron. Soc. (councillor 1996-98), Astron. Soc. Pacific (bd. dirs. 1995-97, v.p. 1997-99, pres. 1999-2000), Internat. Astron. Union, Internat. Sci. Radio Union, Tex. Assn. Coll. Tchrs. (pres. U. Tex. chpt. 1980-82), Tex. Philos. Soc., Town and Gown Club (Austin). Office: U Tex McDonald Obs Mail Code C1402 Austin TX 78712 Office Phone: 512-471-3373. Business E-Mail: FNB@astro.as.utexas.edu.

BASH, PHILIP EDWIN, publishing executive; b. Huntington, Ind., Aug. 13, 1921; s. Philip Purviance and Nell (Johnson) B.; m. Flora Wiley Oberg, Mar. 11, 1944; children: Barbara, Kingsley, Roger, Amy. BA, DePauw U., 1943. Account exec. Leo Burnett Co., Inc., Chgo., 1947-54; account supr., v.p., sr. v.p. mktg. services Clinton E. Frank Inc., Chgo., 1954-64, pres., 1964-72, Barrington (Ill.) Press, Inc., 1972-86, also bd. dirs. Bd. dirs. Fla. Family Inst. Co. Chmn. bd. trustees Shimer Coll., 1989—; trustee Garrett Theol. Sem., 1976—, chmn. bd., 1989-95. Served to lt. (j.g.) USNR, 1943-46, PTO. Mem. Am. Assn. Advt. Agys. (bd. govs. Chgo. council), Am. Mktg. Assn., Sigma Chi. Methodist (trustee). Clubs: University (Chgo.), Economics (Chgo.); Barrington Hills Country. Office: 200 James St Barrington IL 60010-3328 Business E-Mail: bash@megsinet.nsi.

BASHAM, GARLYN ARGABRIGHT, retired academic administrator; b. Delano, Calif., Feb. 20, 1913; s. William Everett Basham and Bessie Jane Argabright; m. Dixie Mildred Tarwater, Sept. 3, 1934 (dec. Mar. 2003); children: Roger Erryl, Laurence Anthony. BA, Santa Barbara (Calif.) State Coll., 1936; MA, U. So. Calif., 1940; EdD, St. John's U., Ambur, India, 1965. Tchr., counselor, dir. student activities Taft (Calif.) Union H.S. and Jr. Coll., 1936—50; dist. supt. West Kern C.C. Dist., Taft, 1950—75; pres. Taft Coll., 1950—75; ret. Author: Collected Writings, 2003. Lt. comdr. USNR, 1943—46. Mem.: Calif. Ret. Tchrs. Assn., Nat. Sojourners (pres. 1978), Kiwanis (pres. 1970), Masons (capt. 1943—2003, mem. Order of the Shrine 1975—, chair bd. dirs. Childhood Lang. Disorders Clinic 1980—90). Republican. Avocations: public speaking, reading, writing, coin collecting/numismatics.

BASHAM, LLOYD MOMAN, manufacturing service company executive; b. Paris, Tex., June 30, 1947; s. Ralph Allen and Faye (Frith) B.; m. donna Jean Walker, aug. 27, 1965; children: Jason, Adam. BBA, Tex. A&M U., Commerce, 1968; MBA, 1970; MA in Internat. Corp. Mgmt., U. Tex., Dallas, 1979. Divsn. cost mgr. Tex. Instruments, Inc., Dallas, 1973—75; corp. fin. analyst, 1975—76; divsn. contr., 1977—78; subs. corp. contr. Ciba Geigy, Richardson, Tex., 1979—80, also bd. dirs.; v.p. fin. Cable & Wireless N.Am., Dallas, 1981—85; v.p. ops., 1985—87; exec. v.p., 1987—88; contr. gen. sys. sector field svc. ops. Motorola, Inc., 1988—92; v.p. N.Am. svc. ops., 1992—93; v.p. worldwide svc. ops., 1993—94; v.p. customer svc. multimedia comms. sys. Nortel, Richardson, 1994—95; v.p. bus. devel. enterprise and wireless networks Nortel Networks, 1995—96; corp. v.p. ATM svc. U.S. Brinks Co., Irving, Tex., 1996—2001; pres. LMB LLC, 2001—03; corp. contr. King Supply Co., Inc., 2003—. Online faculty mem. U. Phoenix; adj. instr. Tex. A&M U., Commerce, Tex. State adv. to U.S. Adv. Bd. Fgn. Policy Nat. Security and Internal Affairs, Rep. Presdl. Task Force; bd. dirs., mem. adv. bd. Coll. Bus. and Tech. Tex. A&M U., Commerce. With USAF, 1970-73. Mem. Nat. Assn. Wholesalers Distbrs. Fin. Execs. Inst., Nat. Assn. Corp. Treas., Nat. Assn. Corp. Dirs., Nat. Assn. Purchasing Mgmt., Am. Mgmt. Assn., Assn. MBA Execs., Nat. Assn. Accts., Assn. Svcs. Mgmt. Internat., Rotary Internat. Republican. Avocation: cattle rancher. Home: Box 3615 Commerce TX 75429 Office: LMB LLC Mgmt Cons PO Box 450912 Garland TX 75045 E-mail: ibasham777@aol.com.

BASHAM, W. RALPH, federal agency administrator; b. Owensboro, Ky. m. Judith A. O'Bryan; three children. BA in Bus. Adminstrn., Southeastern U. Various positions to deputy asst. dir. for trng. U.S. Secret Svc., Washington, 1993-94; spl. agent in charge Office of Investigations Washington, Louisville, 1970-74, 76-79, 86-87, 90-92; spl. agt. of Protective support Divsn. U.S. Secret Svc., Washington, 1974-76; spl. agt., asst. spl. agt. in charge Vice Presdl. Protective Svc. Washington, 1979-83; dep. chief Fin. Mgmt. Divsn. U.S. Secret Svc., Washington, 1983-85; spl. agt. in charge of Vice Presdl. Protective Svc. U.S. Svc., Washington, Cleve., 87-89, 92-93; spl. agt. in charge of Dignitary Protective Divsn. U.S. Secret Svc., Washington, 1989-90, asst. dir. for Adminstrn., 1994-98; insp. Office of Inspections Washington, 1985-86; dir. Fed. Law Enforcement Tng. Ctr. U.S. Dept. Treasury, 1998—2001; chief of staff Transp. Security Adminstrn., Washington, 2002—03; dir. US Secret Svc., Washington, 2003—. Recipient Meritorious Presidential Rank award, 1992, 2000. Mem. Sr. Exec. Svc. Office: US Secret Svc Comm Ctr PO Box 6500 Springfield VA 22150

BASHINSKI, SUSAN MARGARET, education educator, consultant; d. Francis Joseph Bashinski and Margaret Elizabeth Muir; 1 child, Christopher Andrew Neal. BS in Edn., U. Mo., 1973, MEd in Spl. Edn., 1982; PhD, U. Kans., 1996. Asst. prof. Mo. Western State Coll., St. Joseph, Mo., 1985—86, U. Tex., Tyler, 1987—91; project assoc. U. Kans., 1992—97; specialist curriculum adaptation Unified Sch. Dist. 497, Lawrence, Kans., 1998—2001; asst. rsch. prof. U. Kans., Lawrence, Kans., 2001—. Grantee, U.S. Dept. Edn., 2003—, Kans. State Dept. Edn., 2005—. Mem.: Am. Soc. Curriculum Devel., Am. Assn. on Mental Retardation, The Assn. Persons with Severe Handicaps (founding mem. Mo. state chpt., Nat. Alice H. Hayden award 1993), Phi Delta Kappa, Phi Kappa Phi. Office: University of Kansas 1200 Sunnyside Avenue Lawrence KS 66045 Office Fax: 785-864-7605. E-mail: sbashins@ku.edu.

BASHKIN, LLOYD SCOTT, marketing and management consultant; b. Bridgeport, Conn., July 11, 1951; s. Jules Bernard and Luella (Kobre) B.; children: Marisa Elizabeth, Carly Michelle. BS in Fin., Syracuse U., 1973, MBA in Mktg. and Acctg., 1974; postgrad., Columbia U., 1975-78. Corp. staff mktg. cons. RCA, N.Y.C., 1974-77, mgr. entertainment, indsl. mktg. and nat. sales Cherry Hill, N.J., 1977-79; v.p. mktg. and sales CCA Electronics Corp. div. Singer Co., Cherry Hill, 1979-80; pres. Lloyd Scott & Co., Cherry Hill, 1980—, Sydex, Cherry Hill, 1987-88. Adj. instr. Temple U. Grad. Sch., Phila., 1980-82; adj. prof. Drexel U. Grad. Sch., Phila., 1982—; speaker in field. Trustee, chmn. mktg. com. Food Bank South Jersey, 1985—; mem. Camden County Pvt. Industry Coun., 1989-90; mem. cabinet World Affairs Coun., 1989, Community Leaders Recognition Com., 1991—. Recipient Commendation award Gov. of N.J., 1981, SBA, 1983, Nat. Distbn. and Logistics Honorary award Delta Nu Alpha, 1973, Nat. Broadcasting Honorary award Alpha Epsilon Rho, 1979. Mem. Am. Mktg. Assn., C. of C. of So. N.J. (chmn. small bus. action com. 1982-85, strategic planning and mktg. com. 1985—, bd. dirs. 1984—, chmn. programming com. 1989-92), Greater Cherry Hill C. of C. (chmn. small bus. coun. 1982-83), Rotary (bd. dirs. Garden State club 1980-81). Avocations: skiing, photography, guitar. Office: Lloyd Scott & Co Commerce Ctr Ste 192 1820 Chapel Ave W Cherry Hill NJ 08002 E-mail: lbashkin@lloydscott.com.

BASHKOW, JACK SIMON, musician; b. Bklyn., Dec. 7, 1954; s. David and Sylvia Bashkow; m. Lorraine Shemesh, Sept. 12, 1993. Student, Queens Coll., 1972—74, Columbia U., 1991—93. Mem. orch. West Side Story traveling road co., 1978—79, Richard III with Kevin Kline, N.Y.C., 1984, Big River Broadway co., N.Y.C., 1985, Grease Broad co., N.Y.C., 1997—98, Footloose Broad co., N.Y.C., 1999, Fosse Broadway co., N.Y.C., 2000, Annie Get Your Gun Broadway co. with Reba McEntire, N.Y.C., 2001, Hairspray -Broadway co., N.Y.C., 2002—03, Laughing Room Only - Broadway co., 2003—, Bklyn. - The Musical - Broadway Co., 2004—05. Music prodr. Moo Music Prodns. Recording credits include albums with: Jane Olivor, 1982, Keith Richards, 1992, Lionel Hampton, 1999, performed with: Aretha Franklin, The Temptations, The Four Tops, Cyndi Lauper, Natalie Cole, Manhattan Transfer, Michael Bolton, Darlene Love, Peter Allen, others, musician for numerous TV commls.:. Nominee Helen Hayes award for Outstanding Musical Direction. Home and Office: 22 W 30th St # 4-5 New York NY 10001-4423 Office Phone: 212-517-1000. E-mail: JBashkow@aol.com.

BASHKOW, THEODORE ROBERT, electrical engineering consultant, former educator; b. St. Louis, Nov. 16, 1921; s. Maurice Louis and Caroline (Davidson) B.; m. Delphina Brownlee, Sept. 12, 1960; 1 stepdau., Lynn Michele. BS, Washington U., St. Louis, 1943; MS, Stanford U., 1947, PhD, 1950. Mem. tech. staff David Sarnoff Research Labs., RCA, 1950-52, Bell Telephone Labs., 1952-58; mem. faculty Columbia U., 1958-91, prof. elec. engring., 1967-79, prof. computer sci., 1979-91, chmn. dept. elec. engring., 1968-71, mgr. Sch. Engring. Computing Center, 1961-64. Cons. to industry, 1959—; dir. MSI Inc., Woodside, N.Y., 1961—; chmn. tech. program 1968 Spring Joint Computer Conf.; chmn. sci. sect. Internat. Fedn. Info. Processing Congress, 1965 Author articles, chpts. in books. Served to 1st lt. USAAF, 1943-45. Mem. Assn. Computing Machinery, IEEE, Profl. Group Circuit Theory and Electronic Computers. Home: 92 Jay St Katonah NY 10536-3729

BASHOUR, FOUAD ANIS, cardiology educator; b. Tripoli, Lebanon, Jan. 3, 1924; s. Anis E. and Mariana (Yazigi) B.; m. Val Imm, Sept. 28, 1978. BA, Am. U. of Beirut, Lebanon, 1944, MD, 1949; PhD, U. Minn., 1957. Intern Am. U. of Beirut Hosp., Beirut, 1949-50; med. officer UNRWA, 1950-51; resident in internal medicine U. Minn. Hosps., 1951-54; rsch. fellow U. Minn. Med. Schs., 1954-55; instr. in medicine U. Minn., 1955-57; rsch. assoc. Am. U. Med. Sch., Beirut, 1957, asst. prof. medicine cardiopulmonary lab. sect., 1957-59; instr. internal medicine U. Tex. Southwestern Med. Ctr., Dallas, 1959-60, assoc. prof. internal medicine, 1963-71, dir. Cardiovascular Inst., 1967-78, prof. medicine, 1971-85, prof. medicine and physiology, 1985-95; mem. staff Parkland Meml. Hosp., Dallas; prof. emeritus of physiology and internal medicine, 1995-99; mem. staff Zale-Lipshy Univ. Hosp., Dallas, Ashbel Smith prof. medicine and physiology, 1999—. Founder, pres. Cardiology Fund, Inc., 1972-93; program dir. consultation agreement lectrs. Univ. Kuwait, U. Tex., 1977-85; mem. chancellor adv. coun. U. Tex., 1982—; mem. bd trustees of coms. on promotions and med. sch. Am. U. Beirut, 1996—; cons. in field. Mem. editorial bd. Chest, 1963-69, Lebanese Med. Jour., 1957-59, cited in the Warren Commn. Pub., 1963; contbr. more than 200 articles to profl. publs. Elder Christ Luth. Ch., Dallas. Recipient Americanism award DAR, 1970; named Knight Order of Holy Cross Jerusalem; Fouad Bashour ann. lectr. disting. physiologist in their honor, 1974—, Fouad A. and Val Imm Bashour distinguished chair in physiology in his honor, 1990, eminent scholar, Tex., 1985, Wisdom Hall of Fame, eminent Wisdom fellow, 1998. Fellow Am. Coll. Chest Physicians (emeritus), Am. Physiol. Soc. (circulation group), Am. Heart Assn. (coun. on basic sci., coun. on circulation); mem. Am. Fedn. Clin. Rsch. (emeritus), Ctrl. Soc. Clin. Rsch. (emeritus), So. Soc. Clin. Investigation (emeritus), Tex. Med. Assn., Dallas County Med. Assn., Am. Soc. Internal Medicine, Tex. Med. Found., Order of Cedars of Lebanon (officer 1971), cons. Tex. Bd. of Med. Examiners. Office: U Tex Southwestern Med Ctr 5323 Harry Hines Blvd Dallas TX 75390-9040 Home: 6831 Stichter Ave Dallas TX 75230-5316 Fax: 214-648-9376.

BASHSHUR, RASHID L., health facility administrator, educator; arrived in U.S., 1956; s. Lutfallah M. and Yamna D. Bashshur; m. Naziha S. Sima'an, Sept. 15, 1957; children: Ramona R., Noura R. PhD, U. Mich., 1962. Prof. health mgmt. and policy U. Mich., Ann Arbor, 1977—; dir. telemedicine U. Mich. Health Sys., Ann Arbor, Mich., 1998—. Staff assoc. Inst. of Medicine, NAS, Washington, 1970—72. Editor in chief: eHealth Internat. Jour. Pres. Am. Telemedicine Assn., Washington, 2000—02, pres. emeritus. Grantee Effects of Telemedicine on Cost, Quality and Access, Health Care Financing Adminstrn., 1996—98. Achievements include first original evaluation of telemedicine in the U.S. Avocations: watercolor painting, swimming. Office: Telemedicine Resource Ctr 300 N Ingalls 8807 Ann Arbor MI 48109-0402 Office Phone: 734-647-3089.

BASHWINER, STEVEN LACELLE, lawyer; b. Cin., Aug. 3, 1941; s. Carl Thomas and Ruth Marie (Burlis) B.; m. Arden J. Lang, Apr. 24, 1966 (div. 1978); children: Heather, David; m. Donna Lee Gerber, Sept. 13, 1981; children: Margaret, Matthew. AB, Holy Cross Coll., 1963; JD, U. Chgo., 1966. Bar: Ill. 1966, U.S. Dist. Ct. (no. dist.) Ill. 1967, U.S. Dist. Ct. (ea. dist.) Wis. 1988, U.S. Dist. Ct. (no. dist.) Calif. 1994, U.S. Dist. Ct. (ea. dist.) Mich. 2003, U.S. Ct. Appeals (7th cir.) 1968, U.S. Ct. Appeals (4th cir.) 1990, U.S. Supreme Ct. 1970. Assoc. Kirkland & Ellis, Chgo., 1966-72, ptnr., 1972-76, Friedman & Koven, Chgo., 1976-86, Katten Muchin Rosenman LLP, Chgo., 1986—. Bd. dirs. Constl. Rights Found., Chgo. Served to sgt. USAFR, 1966-72. Mem. ABA, 7th Cir. Bar Assn., Chgo. Bar Assn., Chgo. Inn of Ct. (pres. 2004-05), Lawyers Club Chgo. Home: 834 Green Bay Rd Highland Park IL 60035-4630 Office: Katten Muchin Rosenman LLP 525 W Monroe St Ste 1900 Chicago IL 60661-3693 Office Phone: 312-902-5330. Business E-Mail: steven.bashwiner@kattenlaw.com.

BASICHIS, GORDON ALLEN, writer, scriptwriter, marketing consultant, media consultant; b. Phila., Aug. 23, 1947; s. Martin and Ruth (Gordon) B.; m. Marcia Hammond; 1 child, Casey James. BS, Temple U., 1969. Reporter Phila. Bull., 1969; writer, reporter Santa Fe News, 1971-72; with advt., pub. rels. Jay Bernstein Pub. Rels., L.A., 1978-80; screenwriter MGM Feature Films, Culver City, Calif., 1982—83; exec. dir. media and mktg. Laclede, Inc., 2002—04. Exec. v.p. Antigua Rd. Prodns., 1996; sr. v.p. market Nextworld Entertainment Zone; pres. Big Venus Entertainment, 2003; co-founder CorraGroup, 2005. Author: Constant Travelers, 1978, Beautiful Bad Girl: The Vicki Morgan Story, 1985, Spook, 2005, Sleeping with Snakes, Notes from the Los Angeles Underbelly, 2005; screenwriter: Breach of Trust, 1995; exec. prodr.: Land of Dreams, 2001. Mem. ASCAP, Writers Guild Am. West, Am. Film Inst., Nat. Sports Mktg. Assn., Simon Wiesenthal Inst., Ellis Island Found. Office: PO Box 1511 Beverly Hills CA 90213-1511 Office Phone: 310-966-1556. Business E-Mail: gordonb@corragroup.com.

BASIL, DOUGLAS CONSTANTINE, writer, educator; b. Vancouver, BC, Can., May 30, 1923; s. William and Christina (Findlay) B.; m. Evelyn Margaret Pitcairn, 1950; 1 dau., Wendy Patricia. B.Commerce, U. B.C., 1949; BA, 1949; PhD, Northwestern U., 1954; postgrad., London Sch. Econs., 1950. Instr. Marquette U., 1951-54; asst. prof. Northwestern U., 1954-57; asso. prof. U. Minn., 1957-61; prof. mgmt. U. So. Calif., 1961-88, prof. emeritus, 1988—. Cons. mgmt. devel.; lectr., Brussels, Caracas, Bogota, Paris, London, others. Author: Executive Development, 1964, (Paul Cone, John Fleming) Effective Decision Making Through Simulation, 1972, Organacao E Controls Da Pequena Empresa, 1968, La Direccion de la Pequena Empresa, 1969, Managerial Skills for Executive Action, 1970, Leadership Skills for Executive Action, 1971, Women in Management: Performance, Prejudice, Promotion, 1972, Autorite Personnelle et Efficacite des Cadres, 1972, Conduccion y Liderazgo, 1973, Developing Tomorrow's Managers, 1973, Management of Change, 1974, others.; Contbr. (Paul Cone, John Fleming) articles to profl. jours. Served to capt. Canadian Army, 1943-46. Home: 2201 Warmouth St San Pedro CA 90732-4532 Office: U So Calif Grad Sch Bus Adminstrn Los Angeles CA 90007

BASILE, JOSEPH LAWRENCE, humanities educator; b. Arlington, Mass., Sept. 1, 1946; s. Joseph Mario Basile and Charlene Cecil Chesteen; m. Katherine Ann Evans, Dec. 18, 1971 (div. Sept. 1977). BA in English cum laude, Boston Coll., 1968; MA in English, La. State U., 1970, PhD in English, 1972. Instr. English La. State U., Baton Rouge, 1971—72; asst. prof. English U. S.D., Vermillion, 1972—77, assoc. prof. English, 1977—2004, chair dept. English, 1978—81, prof. emeritus, 2004—. Contbg. author: Artist and Citizen Thoreau, 1971; contbr. articles to profl. jours. 2d v.p. Friends of W.H. Over Mus., Vermillion, 1976. Avocations: baseball, fishing, photography, travel. Home: 220 Spruce St # 7 Vermillion SD 57069

BASILI, VICTOR ROBERT, computer science educator; b. Bklyn., Apr. 13, 1940; s. Basil Lucien Basili and Marie Grace Tesoriero; m. Patricia Ann D'Amato, Dec. 27, 1967; children: Brian, Theodore, Alexander. BS in Mathematics, Fordham Coll., 1961; MS in Mathematics, Syracuse U., 1963; PhD in Computer Science, U. Tex., 1970; Laurea Honoris Causa in Informatic Engring. (hon.), U. Sannio Benevento, Italy, 2004; D in Natural Sci. (hon.), Fachbereich Informatik, Tech. U. Kaiserslautern, Germany, 2005. Prof., computer sci. dept. and inst. for advanced computer studies U. Md., College Park, 1970—, exec. dir., Fraunhofer Ctr., 1998—2004; co-director, prin. NASA/GSFC Software Engring. Lab., 1976—2001. Contbr. articles to profl. jours., chapters to books; editor-in-chief: IEEE Transactions on Software Engring., co-editor-in-chief: Jour. of Empirical Software Engring. Program chair, gen. chair 6th and 15th Internat. Conf. on Software Engring.; cons. NSF Com. Visitors, IEEE Software Process Achievement Awards Com., ACM Fellow Com. Recipient IEEE Computer Soc. Outstanding Paper award, IEEEE Trans. on Software Engring., 1981, Harlan D. Mills award, IEEE Computer Soc., 2003, Group Achievement award, NASA, Outstanding Contributions to Math. and Computer Sci. award, Wash. Acad. Sciences, Outstanding Rsch. award, ACM SIGSOFT, 2000; grantee, NASA, NSF, 2004—05. Fellow: ACM, IEEE. Achievements include research in measuring, evaluating and improving software development process and products; development of methods for improving software quality including goal question metric approach, quality improvement paradigm and experiencer factory organization. Office: U Md Dept Computer Sci 4111 AV Williams Bldg College Park MD 20742 Office Phone: 301-405-2668. Office Fax: 301-405-3691. Business E-Mail: basili@cs.umd.edu.

BASINGER, KIM, actress; b. Athens, Ga., Dec. 8, 1953; d. Don Basinger; m. Ron Snyder-Britton, 1980 (div. 1988); m. Alec Baldwin, August 19, 1993 (div. 2002), 1 child. Student, Neighborhood Playhouse, N.Y.C. Model Eileen Ford Agy., N.Y.C., 1972-77; ind. actress, 1977—. (feature films) Hard Country, 1981, Mother Lode, 1982, Never Say Never Again, 1983, The Man Who Loved Women, 1983, The Natural, 1984, Fool for Love, 1985, 9 1/2 Weeks, 1986, No Mercy, 1986, Blind Date, 1987, Nadine, 1987, My Stepmother Is an Alien, 1988, Batman, 1989, The Marrying Man, 1991, Final Analysis, 1992, Cool World, 1992, The Real McCoy, 1993, Wayne's World 2, 1993, The Getaway, 1994, Ready to Wear (Prêt-à-Porter), 1994, L.A. Confidential (Golden Globe award for best supporting actress, 1998) (Academy Award for best supporting actress, 1998), 1997, I Dreamed of Africa, 2000, Bless the Child, 2000, 8 Mile, 2002, People I Know, 2002, The Door in the Floor, 2004, Elvis Has Left the Building, 2004, Cellular, 2004; (TV series) Dog and Cat, 1977; TV films include Katie-Portrait of a Centerfold, 1978, The Ghost of Flight 401, 1978, Killjoy, 1981; (TV miniseries) From Here to Eternity, 1980; (TV appearances) Gemini Man, 1976, Charlie's Angels, 1976, The Six Million Dollar Man, 1977, McMillan and Wife, 1977, Vega$, 1978, The Simpsons (voice only), 1998, 2002. Office: c/o Ron Meyer CAA 11288 Ventura Blvd #414 Studio City CA 91604

BASINGER, WILLIAM DANIEL, computer programmer; b. Washington, Feb. 14, 1952; s. James Samuel and Eleanor (Freeburger) B.; m. Martha Kecskes, July 1, 1978 (div. 1983); m. Mary Teresa Richardson, June 11, 1988. BA in Linguistics, U. Md., 1974; MS in Linguistics, Georgetown U., 1977; MS in Computer Sci., Johns Hopkins U., 1989. Programmer Evaluation Techs., Arlington, Va., 1977—78; programmer, analyst, cons. Vitro Corp., Silver Spring, Md., 1978—84, 1987—88; programmer, analyst Tracor Applied Scis., Rockville, Md., 1984—88, PRC, Inc., McLean, Va., 1988—89; sr. programmer, analyst Systems & Computer Tech. group George Washington U., Washington, 1989—95; sr. programmer, statistician PRC, Inc., Reston, 1996—97; sr. sys. analyst, Yr. 2000 Assessment Project M-Cubed Info. Sys., Rockville, 1997—2000; sr. computer specialist, statistician VGS, Fairfax, Va., 2000—01; statistician U.S. Dept. Transp., 2001—02; sr. computer specialist Ajilon Cons., Rockville, 2002—03, Sci. Applications Internat. Corp., San Diego, 2003—. Cons. applications software dept. geology George Washington U., Washington, 1990-91, 93—. Contbr. articles to profl. jours. Contbr., sponsor Statue of Liberty/Ellis Island Found., N.Y.C., 1985—. Md. State Sen. scholar U. Md., 1970-74. Mem. Assn. Computing Machinery, Am. Geophys. Union, Am. Statis. Assn., N.Y. Acad. Scis., Math. Assn. Am., Nat. Assn. Pastoral Musicians. Republican. Roman Catholic. Avocations: viola, violin, bridge, poetry, philosophy. Home: Apt 203 11342 Cherry Hill Rd Beltsville MD 20705-3735 Office: US Dept Commerce Suitland Federal Ctr Beta Test Site Suitland MD 20746 Office Phone: 301-763-8925. Personal E-mail: wdbasinger@hotmail.com.

BASINSKI, ANTHONY JOSEPH, lawyer; b. Pitts., Apr. 11, 1947; s. Anthony F. and Emily C. (Klocko) B.; m. Elisabeth Fawcett, Oct. 4, 1980; children: Ann Elisabeth, Robert Anthony. BA, U. Pitts., 1969, JD, 1974. Bar: Pa. 1974, U.S. Dist. Ct. (we. dist.) Pa. 1974, U.S. Ct. Appeals (3d cir.) 1981, U.S. Ct. Appeals (4th cir.) 1992, U.S. Ct. Appeals (fed. cir.) 1995. Law clk. to presiding justice Pa. Supreme Ct., Pitts., 1974-76; ptnr. Reed, Smith, Shaw and McClay, Pitts., 1976—2004; spec. counsel Pietragallo, Bosick & Gordon, Pitts., 2004—. Served with U.S. Army, 1969-71, Vietnam. Mem. Allegheny County Bar Assn., Am. Arbitration Assn. (arbitrator 1983—). Democratic. Roman Catholic. Home: 1749 Taper Dr Pittsburgh PA 15241-2623 Office: Pietragallo Bosick & Gordon One Oxford Centre 38th Fl Pittsburgh PA 15219 Office Phone: 412-263-4346. Business E-Mail: ajb@pbandg.com.

BASISZTA, MARTIN WINSTON, lawyer; b. Antioch, Calif., Jan. 10, 1943; m. Catherine Dawn Czarnecki, Mar. 3, 1978; children: Kelly Jane, Meghan Aileen. BA summa cum laude, U. Calif.-Davis, 1968; JD, U. Calif.-Berkeley, 1972. Bar: Calif. 1973. Assoc. McNamara, Lewis & Craddick, Walnut Creek, Calif., 1973—75, Maloney, Chase, Fisher & Hurst, San Francisco, 1975—76; ptnr. Van Voorhis & Skaggs, Walnut Creek, 1976—78; sole practice law Walnut Creek, 1978—83; ptnr. Basiszta & Daniels, Hayward, Calif., 1983—. Assoc. editor: Calif. Law Rev., 1971—72; contbr. articles to legal jours. Served with submarine service USN, 1960—63.

Recipient deptl. citation German studies, U. Calif.-Davis, 1968; vis. scholar John Woodward Ayer fellow in law, 1971—72; regents scholar, U. Calif., 1966—68, German Govt. grad. grantee, German Govt. Grad. Exchange Program, 1969, Alexander Von Humboldt grad. fellow in law, 1982, hon. Woodrow Wilson fellow, 1968. Mem.: Def. Rsch. Inst., Assn. Def. Counsel, Contra Costa/Alameda Trial Lawyers Assn., Calif. Trial Lawyers Assn., San Mateo Bar Assn., Santa Clara Bar Assn., Mt. Diablo Bar Assn., Contra Costa County Bar Assn., Bar Assn. San Francisco, Barristers Club San Francisco, Lawyers Club San Francisco, Phi Beta Kappa, Phi Kappa Phi, Alpha Gamma Sigma.

BASKA, JAMES LOUIS, wholesale grocery company executive; b. Kansas City, Kans., Apr. 3, 1927; s. John James and Stella Marie (Wilson) B.; m. Juanita Louise Carlson, Oct. 14, 1950; children: Steven James, Scott David. BSBA, U. Kans., 1949; JD, U. Mo., 1960. Bar: Kans. 1960. Pres., chief exec. officer Baska Laundry Co., Kansas City, 1951-62; ptnr. Rice & Baska, Kansas City, 1962-76; corporate sec., gen. counsel Assoc. Wholesale Grocers Inc., Kansas City, 1976-77, v.p., sec., gen. counsel, 1977-79, exec. v.p., chief fin. officer, sec., gen. counsel, 1979-84, pres., chief exec. officer, 1984-92; pres. emeritus, 1992. Mem. SDC com. Wakefern Food Corp., 1998—; bd. dirs. Raley's, Riverwood Homes, Inc. Served as staff sgt. U.S. Army, 1944-46. Mem. Nat. Grocers Assn. (bd. dirs. 1980-89, chmn. 1987-88), Food Mktg. Inst. (bd. dirs. 1988-93). Republican. Roman Catholic. Avocations: hunting, golf. Office: Assoc Wholesale Grocers Inc PO Box 2932 5000 Kansas Ave Kansas City KS 66106-1135 *There is always room at the top and my objectives whatever they may be and no matter how big or wild, are always attainable. The only questions are— am I ready to make the move and willing to pay the price?.*

BASKERVILLE, CHARLES ALEXANDER, geologist, educator; b. Jamaica, N.Y., Aug. 19, 1928; s. Charles H. and Annie M. (Allen) Baskerville; children: Mark Dana, Shawn Allison, Charles Morris, Thomas Marshall. BS, CCNY, 1953; MS, NYU, 1958, PhD, 1965. Cert. profl. geologist Maine. Asst. civil engr. N.Y. State Dept. Transp., Babylon, 1953-66; prof. engring. geology CUNY, N.Y.C., 1966-79, dean sch. of gen. studies, 1970-79, prof. emeritus, 1979—; project rsch. geologist U.S. Geol. Survey, 1979-90; prof. geology Ctrl. Conn. State U., New Britain, 1990—, dept. chmn., 1992-94. Commonwealth vis. prof. George Mason U., Fairfax, Va., 1987-89; mem. U.S. Nat. Com. on Tunnelling Tech., NRC, chmn. subcom. on edn. and tng.; mem. Am. del Internat. Tunnelling Assn. to Internat. Colloquim of Tunnelling and Underground Works, Beijing, People's Republic of China, 1984; geol. cons. N.Y.C. Dept. Environ. Protection Water Tunnel #3; guest lectr. various colls., 1964—; geol. program evaluator for colls. seeking continued mid. states accreditation. Author numerous sci. papers. Mem. com. for minority participation in the geoscis. U.S. Dept. Interior, 1972-75; panelist Grad. Fellowship Program NRC; chmn. Minority Grad. Fellowship Program, 1979-80; mem. com. of visitors for edn. and human resources program divsn. earth scis. NSF, 1991; mem. N.Y. State Low Level Radioactive Waste Com. NAS, 1994-96. Recipient Founders Day award N.Y. U., 1966, 125th Anniversary medal The City Coll., 1973, award for excellence in engring. geology Nat. Consortium Black Profl. Devel., 1978, Recognition award Nat. Assn. Black Geologists and Geophysicists, 1998. Fellow Geol. Soc. Am. (sr., com. on minorities in geoscis., chmn. com. on coms. 1989), N.Y. Acad. Scis., Geol. Soc. Washington, Am. Inst. Profl. Geologists, Assn. Engring. Geologists (rep. to nat. bd. dirs. 1973-74, chmn. N.Y.-Phila. sect. 1973-74), Internat. Assn. Engring. Geology, Yellowstone-Bighorn Rsch. Assn., Sigma Xi. Office: Ctrl Conn State Univ 1615 Stanley St New Britain CT 06050-4010 Business E-Mail: baskerville@ccsu.edu.

BASKETTE, ROGER DUVAL, SR., lawyer; b. Nashville, Dec. 12, 1924; s. Robert Lee and Sarah Elizabeth (Norman) B.; m. Thetis Lorena Peacock, Nov. 4, 1950; children: Roger DuVal Jr., Pamela Leigh, Lizbeth Rene, Marsha Elane. LLB, Cumberland U., 1947; LLD, Samford U., 1973. Bar: Tenn. 1948. Ptnr. Baskette & Baskette, Nashville. Active Met. Coun., Nashville, 1970-74. With U.S. Army, 1943-46, ETO. Mem. Nashville Bar Assn., Hugenot Soc. Am., SAR (Andrew Jackson chpt., pres. 1976-77, Gold Good Citizenship medal), Magna Carta Barons (Somerset chpt.). Republican. Mem. Ch. Christ. Avocations: golf, playing tennis, gardening, boating, stamp collecting/philately. Office: Baskette & Baskette 223 Cavalier Bldg 95 White Bridge Rd Nashville TN 37205-1497

BASKIN, C. R., civil engineer; b. Houston, Mar. 6, 1926; s. Charles Todd and Bessie Emma (Heilig) B.; m. Peggy June Holden, Dec. 31, 1952; children: Richard Karl, Sheila Frances. BSCE, La. State U., 1953. Design engr. City-Parish Dept. Pub. Works, Baton Rouge, 1953-57; city engr. City of Plaquemine, La., 1957-58; sect. head, asst. chief engr. Tex. Bd. Water Engrs., Austin, 1958-62; asst. chief engr. Tex. Water Commn., Austin, 1962-65; asst. chief engr., chief engr. Tex. Water Devel. Bd., Austin, 1965-77; dir. data and engring. svcs. divsn. Tex. Dept. Water Resources, Austin, 1977-83; spl. asst. Office of Asst. Dir. Info. Sys./U.S. Geol. Survey, Reston, Va., 1983-92; ret., 1992. Chmn. Tex. Mapping Adv. Com., 1968-83; chmn. water oriented data programs sect. Tex. Interagy. Council on Natural Resources and the Environment, 1968-72, Tex. Natural Resources Info. System Task Force, 1972-83; mem. Non-Fed. Adv. Com. on Water Data for Public Use, 1970-83; chmn. Water Data Coordination Task Force, Interstate Conf. on Water Problems, 1975-83. Contbr. articles to profl. jours. With U.S. Army, 1944-47, POW; commd. Adm. Tex. Navy, 1961. Recipient John Wesley Powell award U.S. Geol. Survey, 1972, Combat Inf. badge. Mem.: Am. Ex-POWs, Sigma Tau Sigma (pres. 1950), Phi Eta Sigma, Chi Epsilon, Tau Beta Pi (chpt. pres. 1950), Phi Kappa Phi. Adventist (elder). Avocations: photography, walking. Home: 304 N Woodlake Dr Columbia SC 29229-8932

BASKIN, JOHN SPENCER, physicist; b. Waco, Tex., Aug. 9, 1954; s. Roy Howard Jr. and Lowrey (Burleson) Baskin; m. Qian Li Baskin, Aug. 19, 2000; 1 child, Bernice Lowrey. BS in Physics, Ga. Inst. Tech., 1976, MS in Physics, 1983; PhD in Applied Physics, Calif. Inst. Tech., 1990. Tchr. physics Inst. Kizito, Isiro Zaire, 1978—81; rsch. scientist King Fahd U. Petroleum and Minerals, Dhahran, Saudi Arabia, 1989—92; rsch. assoc. U. Houston, 1992—95; rsch. fellow Calif. Inst. Tech., Pasadena, 1995—98, sr. rsch. fellow, 1998—2004, staff scientist, 2004—. Named Disting. Alumnus, Waco Ind. Sch. Dist. Edn. Found., 1998. Republican. Home: 1213 Cordova St #5 Pasadena CA 91106 Office: Calif Inst Tech Caltech 127-72 Pasadena CA 91125

BASKIN, JON A., biology professor, researcher; b. Boston; s. Meyer and Beverly Baskin; m. Christine Baskin. BA, NYU, 1970; MS, U. Ariz., 1975; PhD, U. Fla., 1979. Prof. Tex. A&M U., Kingsville, 1980—. Author: (monograph) Systematic Revision of Ctenodactylidae (Mammalia, Rodentia) from the Miocene of Pakistan; contbr. chapters to books, articles to profl. jours. Mem.: Southwestern Assn. Naturalists, Paleontol. Soc., Soc. Vertebrate Paleontology. Achievements include 2 fossil rodents, Bensonomys baskini and Sayiyms baskini, named in his honor. Office: Texas A&M U-Kingsville MSC 158 Kingsville TX 78363 Office Phone: 361-593-3580. E-mail: kfjab02@tamuk.edu.

BASKIN, MAURICE, lawyer; b. Miami, Fla., June 25, 1954; BA magna cum laude, Harvard U., 1975; JD with honors, U. Fla., 1978. Bar: DC, Md., Fla., US Dist. Ct. Md., US Dist. Ct. DC, US Ct. Appeals (1st, 3d, 4th, 6th, 7th, 9th cirs.), US Supreme Ct., US Ct. Appeals (8th cir.), US Ct. Appeals (DC cir.). Assoc. Pierson, Ball & Dowd, Washington, 1978-81, Venable LLP, Washington, 1981-87, ptnr. Labor & Employment Dept., 1987—. Mem. Labor & Employment Lawyers Adv. Com., Nat. Assn. Mfrs.; legal sect. governing coun. ASAE; adj. prof. labor law Georgetown U. Law Ctr., 1981—87; moderator labor and employment law Counsel Connect. Mem. ABA (chmn. labor rels. divsn. constrn. industry forum 1992-95, chm. constrn. labor com. pub. contract law sect.), U.S. C. of C. (labor rels. com.). Office: Venable LLP 575 7th St NW Washington DC 20004 Office Phone: 202-344-4823. Office Fax: 202-344-8300. E-mail: mnbaskin@venable.com.

BASKIN, RONALD JOSEPH, biophysicist educator, dean; b. Joliet, Ill., Nov. 25, 1935; s. Mack Robert and Evelyn Josephine (Rudzinski) B.; m. Lydia Olga Lendl, Mar. 29, 1957; children— Ronald James, Thomas William. AB, UCLA, 1957; MA, 1959, PhD, 1960. Asst. prof. biology Rensselaer Poly. Inst., Troy, N.Y., 1961-64; asst. prof. zoology U. Calif., Davis, 1964-67, assoc. prof., 1967-71, prof., 1971—, chmn. dept. zoology, 1971-78, assoc. dean coll. letters and sci., 1986-90. Mem. editorial bd. U. Calif. Press. Contbr. articles to sci. publs. Nat. Heart Inst. predoctoral fellow, 1957-60 Mem. Biophys. Soc., Soc. Cell Biology, Am. Physiol. Soc., N.Y. Acad. Scis., Sigma Xi. Office: Molecular & Cellular Biology Sect U Calif Davis CA 95616 Office Phone: 530-752-1554. E-mail: rjbaskin@ucdavis.edu.

BASKIN, SCOTT DAVID, lawyer; b. N.Y.C., Oct. 24, 1953; s. George and Anne (Strauss) B.; m. Sherry Nahmias, Mar. 13, 1982; children: Jonathan, Felicia. BA, Stanford U., 1975; JD, Yale U., 1978. Bar: Calif. 1978, U.S. Dist. Ct. (ctrl., ea., so. and no. dists.) Calif. 1979, U.S. Appeals (2d and 9th cirs.) 1979. Law clk. Hon. Herbert Choy, 9th Cir. Ct., Honolulu, 1978-79; ptnr. Irell & Manella, Newport Beach, Calif., 1979—. Lectr. Calif. Continuing Edn. of the Bar, 1985—. Contbr. articles to profl. publs. Office: Irell & Manella 840 Newport Center Dr Ste 400 Newport Beach CA 92660-6323 Office Phone: 949-760-5239, 949-760-0991. Business E-Mail: sbaskin@irell.com.

BASKIN, WILLIAM GRESHAM, counselor, vocalist, music educator; b. Cameron, Tex., July 14, 1933; s. James Dollar and Ruth (McKinney) B.; m. Margaret Lee Williams, Mar. 26, 1959; 1 child, Susan Elizabeth. Student, U. Tex., 1951-54; B of Music Edn., S.W. Tex. State U., 1955; postgrad., Ea. Wash. U., 1956; MEd, S.W. Tex. State U., 1961. Cert. life elem. and secondary tchr., profl. music tchrs., provisional vis. techr., profl. counselor, profl. prin., Tex.; lic. profl. counselor, Tex.; nat. cert. counselor; nat. cert. career counselor; nat. cert. sch. counselor. Choral dir. San Marcos (Tex.) Bapt. Acad., 1957-58, Carrizo Springs (Tex.) Ind. Sch. Dist., 1958-62, Victoria (Tex.) High Sch., 1962-68; counselor Brazosport Ind. Sch. Dist., Freeport, Tex., 1968—. Music dir. 1st Bapt. Ch., Carrizo Springs, 1958-62, Bapt. Temple, Victoria, 1962-64; interim music dir. 1st Bapt. ch., Victoria, 1965, Freeport, 1972-73, 87-88, 89, Lake Jackson, Tex., 1978-79, Temple Bapt. Ch., Clute, Tex., 1990; mem. Music Educators Nat. conf., 1958-68; del. Am. Mental Health Counselors Assn. and Citizen Amb. Program People to People Internat. to Chinese Assn. Mental Health and Chinese Assn. for Sci. and Tech. of People's Republic of China in Beijing, Shanghai and Kunming, 1994; del. from Am. Sch. Counselor's Assn. and Citizen Amb. Program of People to People Internat. to 1st U.S./Russia Joint Conf. on Edn., Moscow, 1994. Mem. Victoria Fine Arts Assn. (pres. 1964-66), 1963-68; mem. Brazosport Fine Arts Coun., Lake Jackson, 1970-73, Brazoria County Hist. Mus., Angleton, Tex., 1990—; del. Tex. Gov.'s Conf. on Arts, Austin, 1966-68; del. Dem. Precinct Conv., Lake Jackson, 1976, 77, 93, Brazoria County Dem. Conv., Angleton, 1977, Tex. Dem. Conv., San Antonio, 1977; deacon 1st Bapt. Ch., Lake Jackson, 1989, also youth worker. Scholar PTA, Victoria, 1966. Mem. Music Educator's Nat. Conf., NEA (del. 1977-79), Am. Sch. Counselors Assn., Nat. Career Devel. Assn., Assn. for Specialists in Group Work, Assn. for Measurement and Evaluation in Counseling and Devel., Tex. Assn. for Measurement and Evaluation in Counseling and Devel., Tex. Career Guidance Assn., Tex. Sch. Counselors Assn., Tex. Assn. for Counseling and Devel. (senator 1979-82, legis. com. 1984-87), Tex. Music Educators Assn. (state bd. dirs. 1964-68, dist. choral chmn. 1964-68), Tex. State Schrs. Assn., Brazosport Edn. Assn. (pres. 1977-78), Brazoria County Assn. Counseling and Devel. (legis. chmn. 1984—), Rotary (Brazosport club, Paul Harris fellow 1988). Avocations: gardening, flying. Home: 111 Oyster Bend Ln Lake Jackson TX 77566-3105 Office: PO Box Z Freeport TX 77542-1926

BASKINS, ANN O., lawyer, computer company executive; b. Red Bluff, Calif., Aug. 5, 1955; AB, Stanford U., 1977; JD, UCLA, 1980. Bar: Calif. 1980. Assoc. Crosby, Heafey, Roach & May, 1980—81; atty. Hewlett-Packard Co., Palo Alto, Calif., 1982—85, sr. atty., 1985—86, assist. sec., 1985—99, corp. counsel, 1986—99, corp. sec., 1999—, sr. v.p., gen. counsel, 2000—. Mem.: ABA, State Bar Calif., Assn. Gen. Counsel, Am. Soc. Corp. Secs., Am. Corp. Counsel Assn. Office: Hewlett Packard Co Mail Stop 1069 3000 Hanover St Palo Alto CA 94304

BASKIR, LAWRENCE M., federal judge; b. N.Y.C., Jan. 10, 1938; s. Philip and Florence B.; m. Marna S. Tucker, May 13, 1973; children: Cecily Elizabeth, Micah Tucker. AB magna cum laude, Princeton U., 1959; LL.B., Harvard U., 1962. Bar: N.Y. 1963, D.C. 1964, U.S. Supreme Ct. 1968. Assoc. Weaver and Glassie, 1963-65; counsel Ho. of Reps. Judiciary Com., 1965-66; chief counsel Constl. Rights Subcom., U.S. Senate, 1968-74; dir. Presidential Clemency, Bd., 1974-75; faculty fellow U. Notre Dame, 1975-77; dep. asst. sec. US Dept. Treasury, Washington, 1977-79; legis. dir. Senator Bill Bradley, 1979-80; sole practice Washington, 1981-93; prin. dep. gen. counsel US Army, 1994-98; judge US Ct. Fed. Claims, Washington, 1998—, chief judge, 2000—02. Adj. prof. Georgetown Law Center, Cath. U. Law Sch.; cons. U.S. Senate Intelligence Com., ABA Contbr. articles to profl. jours.; author: Reconciliation After Vietnam, 1977, Chance and Circumstance: The Draft, the War and the Vietnam Generation, 1978. Grantee, Ford Found., 1975—77. Office: 717 Madison Pl NW Washington DC 20439-0002*

BASLAW-FINGER, ANNETTE, education educator, consultant; b. Paris, Oct. 11, 1929; arrived in U.S., 1943; d. David and Shulamit Notik Szer; m. Seymour Maxwell Finger, June 12, 1988; m. Alfred A. Baslaw, Feb. 11, 1951 (dec. July 6, 1978); children: Robin, Michele Friedman, David. BA, Bklyn. Coll., 1951; MA, Hofstra U., N.Y., 1965; PhD (with distinction), NYU, 1969. Exec. sec. L.R. Dooley, Inc., N.Y.C., 1951—52; French copywriter Morse Internat., N.Y.C., 1952—54; French tchr. Glen Cove (N.Y.) HS, 1958—65, Roslyn (N.Y.) HS, 1969; dir. French edn. Columbia Tchrs. Coll., N.Y.C., NY, 1969—73; chairperson fgn. lang. and internat. edn. NYU, 1973—77, dir. fgn. lang. and bilingual edn., 1977—94; ret., 1994. Contbr. articles to profl. jours. Ann. spkr. Long Island and N.J. Schs., 1995—2003, Temple Sholom, Pompano Beach, Fla., 1998—2003. Decorated Order Palmes Academiques France; Danforth fellow, 1965—69. Mem.: MLA (bd. dirs.), N.Y. State Assn. Fgn. Lang. Tchrs. (bd. dirs.), Am. Assn. Tchrs. of French (pres. LI chpt.), Mus. Jewish Heritage, Inst. on Mediterranean Affairs at UN (dep. to pres.), Pi Delta Phi, Kappa Delta Pi (pres.), Phi Beta Kappa, Pi Lambda Theta (pres. chpt.). Avocations: travel, ballet, theater, art, books. Home: 50 Sutton Pl S New York NY 10022 also: 133 N Pompano Beach Blvd Pompano Beach FL 33062

BASLER, THOMAS G., librarian, educator; b. Cleve., Mar. 8, 1940; s. Gordon Fred and Bertha Elizabeth (Gerspacher) B.; m. Samille Jones, Nov. 25, 1986; children from previous marriage: William T., Elizabeth E., Charles G. BEd, U. Miami, Coral Gables, Fla., 1962; MS, Fla. State U., 1964; PhD, Laurence U., Santa Barbara, Calif., 1977. Intern Emory U., Atlanta, 1965; asst. prof., librarian Insts. Marine Scis., Miami, Fla., 1966-68; librarian Am. Mus. Natural History, N.Y.C., 1968-70, N.Y. Acad. Medicine, N.Y.C., 1970-72; prof., dir. library Med. Coll. Ga., Augusta, 1972-91; dir. libr. and learning resources ctrs. Med. U. S.C., Charleston, 1991—, dir. environ. hazards assessment program info. sys., 1994—, chair dept. of libr. sci. and informatics. Cons. Abbott Pharm. Co., North Chicago, Ill., 1973-83; chmn. Regents Acad. Com. on Libraries, Univ. System Ga., 1984-85; mem. adv. council SE Atlantic Regional Med. Library, 1984— Author: Health Science Librarianship, 1977, Medical School Library Directorship, 1977, also articles Mem. Consortium So. Biomed. Libraries, Inc. (sec.-treas. 1983—) Home: 1205 Manor Ln Mount Pleasant SC 29464-5188 Office: Med U SC 171 Ashley Ave Charleston SC 29425-0001 Office Phone: 843-792-9211. E-mail: basler@mwsc.edu.

BASMAJIAN, JOHN VAROUJAN, medical researcher, educator; b. Constantinople, Turkey, June 21, 1921; came to Can., 1923, naturalized, 1927; s. Mihran and Mary (Evelian) B.; m. Dora Belle Lucas, Oct. 4, 1947; children: Haig, Nancy, Sally. MD with honors, U. Toronto, 1945; LLD (hon.), Queen's U., 1999; DSc (hon.), McMaster U., 2001. Intern Toronto Gen. Hosp., 1945; surg. resident Sunnybrook Hosp. and Hosp. for Sick Children, Toronto, 1946-48; from lectr. to prof. U. Toronto, 1949-57; prof. anatomy, chmn. dept. anatomy Queen's U., Kingston, 1957-69; prof., dir. regional rehab. rsch. and tng. ctr. Emory U., Atlanta, 1969-77; prof. medicine McMaster U., Hamilton, 1977-86, prof. emeritus, 1986—2004; dir. rehab. ctr. Chedoke-McMaster Hosps., 1977-86; ret. Exec. sec. Banting Rsch. Found., Toronto, 1954-57; chmn. rsch. com. Fitness Coun. Can., Ottawa, Ont., 1965-69; spl. cons. med. rsch. Ga. Inst. Tech., Atlanta, 1984-90; dir. rsch. and tng. grants Ea. Seal Rsch. Inst., Toronto, 1990-95; bd. dirs. Can. Physiotherapy Found., Toronto, 1984-89; lectureships in Europe, Asia, South Am., Australia, Japan, others. Author 11 med. sci. and clin. books in multiple edits. and transls., 1953—; editor 9 med. clin. books in multiple edits., and transls., 1977—; series editor: Rehabilitation Medicine Library, 24 vols., 1977—; editl. bd. Am. Jour. Phys. Medicine, 1968-90, Am. Jour. Anatomy, 1971-74, Electromyography and Clin. Neurophysiology, 1966-85, Electro-diagnostic-therapy, Physiotherapy Can., 1979-84, Jour. Motor Behavior, 1980—, Med Post; assoc. editor Anat. Record, 1970-73, 77—, BMA Audiotape Series, 1970-77; contbr. articles to profl. jours.; prodr. several motion pictures; inventor sci. and med. devices and techniques. Mem. and chmn. Bd. Edn., Kingston, Ont., 1960-68; founding chmn. bd. govs. St. Lawrence Coll. Applied Arts and Tech., Ont., 1964-69. Served to capt. M.C., Can. Army, 1943-46 Decorated officer Order of Ont., officer Order of Can.; recipient awards including Starr Gold medal U. Toronto, 1957, Kabakjian award Armenian Youth Fedn., 1967; NRC (Can.) vis. scientist Soviet Acad. Scis., 1963, Henry Gray Laureate, 1991,. Fellow Am. Acad. Angiology, Royal Coll. Physicians (Can.), Royal Coll. Physicians and Surgeons (Glasgow, hon.), Royal Coll. Physicians (Edinburgh, hon.), Physicians Coll. Rehabilitative Medicine (Australia, hon., Edinburgh, hon.); mem. Am. Assn. Anatomists (pres. 1985-86, Henry Gray Laureate award 1991), Can. Assn. Anatomists (founding, sec. 1965-69, J.C.B. Grant award 1985), Am. Congress Rehab. Medicine (Gold Key award 1977, Coulter lectr. 1988), Biofeedback Soc. Am. (founding, pres. 1978-79), Internat. Soc. Electromyographic Kinesiology (founding, pres. 1955-60), Order St. John of Jerusalem (hon. life mem.), Am. Orthopedic Foot Soc. (hon. life), Australian Biofeedback Soc. (hon. life), Venezuelan Biofeedback Soc. (hon. life), Mex. Soc. Anatomy (hon. life), Columbian Assn. Phys. Medicine (hon. life), Physiotherapy Assn. North Greece (hon. pres. 1995—). Avocations: travel, music, gardening, writing.

BASNETT, MARGARET G., reading and language arts educator, consultant; b. Avoca, Iowa, Oct. 7, 1946; d. Fay and Mary Gertrude (Grote) Osborn; m. Richard John Socwell, Mar. 11, 1971 (div. May 1979); 1 child, Benjamin Adam; m. William C. Basnett, Dec. 19, 1999. BS, Ohio State U., Columbus, 1968; MS, U. Wis., 1979. Cert. reading specialist, libr. media specialist, Spanish and French tchr., Ariz. Tchr. French Mason (Ohio) Pub. Schs., 1969-70; tchr. Spanish and French St. Matthias Cath. Girls H.S., L.A., 1970-71; tchr. French Whitewater (Wis.) Pub. Schs., 1971-72, tchr. Spanish, 1972-78; reading specialist Chilton (Wis.) Pub. Schs., 1978-79, Tolleson (Ariz.) Elem. Schs., 1979-80; tchr. reading and Spanish Deer Valley Unified Schs., Phoenix, 1980-88; tchr. reading Rio Salado C.C., Phoenix, 1987-91, tchr. lang. arts, 1989-93, tchr. social studies, 1993-96, libr. media specialist, 1996-2000. State forensics judge Whitewater Pub. Schs., 1974—; test designer Deer Valley Reading Curriculum Com., Phoenix, 1986-87, participant lang. arts pilot program Deer Valley Unified Sch. Dist., 1989; designer integrated social studies curriculum, Hillcrest Mid. Sch., Deer Valley Unified Pub. Schs., Phoenix, 1994-96; ret. Deer Valley Unified Sch. Dist., 2000. Recipient grant Deer Valley Edn. Found., Inc., 1992. Mem.: Ariz. Quilters Guild (cmty. svcs. coord. Calico Cut-Ups chpt. 2002, pres. Calico Cut-Ups chpt. 2003—04). Democrat. Avocations: reading, quilting, embroidery, cross stitch, travel.

BASOLO, FRED, chemistry professor; b. Coello, Ill., Feb. 11, 1920; s. John and Catherine (Marino) Basolo; m. Mary P. Nutley, June 14, 1947; children: Mary Catherine, Freddie, Margaret-Ann, Elizabeth Rose. BE, So. Ill. U., 1940, DSc (hon.), 1984; MS, U. Ill., 1942, PhD in Inorganic Chemistry, 1943; LLD (hon.), U. Turin, 1988; Laurea Honoris Causa (hon.), U. Palermo, Italy, 1997. Rsch. chemist Rohm & Haas Chem. Co., Phila., 1943—46; mem. faculty Northwestern U., Evanston, Ill., 1946—, prof. chemistry, 1958—, Morrison prof. chemistry, 1980—90, chmn. dept. chemistry, 1969—72; Charles E. and Emma H. Morrison prof. emeritus Nortwestern U., Evanston, Ill., 1990—. Guest lectr. NSF summer insts.; chmn. bd. trustees Gordon Rsch. Conf., 1976; pres. Inorganic Syntheses, Inc., 1977—81; mem. bd. chem. scis. and tech. NRC-NAS; adv. bd. Who's Who in Am., 1983; cons. in field. Co-author (with Ralph G. Pearson): (books) Mechanisms of Inorganic Reactions, A Study of Metal Complexes in Solution, 1958, 1967; co-author: (with Ronald C. Johnson) Coordination Chemistry, 1964; co-author: (with John L. Burmeister) On Being Well-Coordinated, A Half Century of Research on Transition Metal Complexes, 2002; author: (autobiography) From Coello to Inorganic Chemistry, A Lifetime of Reactions, 2002. Recipient Ballar medal, 1972, So. Ill. U. Alumni Achievement award, 1974, Dwyer medal, 1976, James Flack Norris award for Outstanding Achievement in Tchg. of Chemistry, 1981, Oesper Meml. award, 1983, IX Century medal, Bologna U., 1988, Mosher award, 1990, Padova U. medal, 1991, Distinction Bicentenaria medal, Univ. Los Andes, Merida, 1991, Chinese Chem. Soc. medal, 1991, G.C. Pimental award, 1992, Chem. Pioneer award, 1992, Humboldt Sr. US Scientist award, 1992, Gold medal, Am. Inst. Chemists, 1993, Josiah Willard Gibbs medal, 1996, Joseph Chatt medal, Royal Soc. Chemistry, 1996, Inauguration mem. Hall of Fame, Chem. Dept. So. Ill. U., 1996, SIU Obelisk Leadership award, 2000, Priestly medal, 2001; fellow Guggenheim, 1954—55, NSF, 1961—62, NATO sr. scientist, Italy, 1981. Fellow: AAAS (chmn. chemistry sect. 1979), NAS, Am. Acad. Arts and Scis.; mem.: Am. Inst. Chemists, Nat. Acad. Lincei (Italy), Italian Chem. Soc. (hon.), Royal Soc. Chemistry (Joseph Chatt medal 1996), Am. Chem. Soc. (assoc. editor jour. 1961—64, chmn. divsn. inorganic chemistry 1970, pres. 1983, bd. dirs. 1982—84, award for rsch. in inorganic chemistry 1964, Disting. Svc. award in inorganic chemistry 1975, N.E. regional award 1971, award in chem. edn. 1992, Chem. Pioneer award 1992, Gold medal 1993, Willard Gibbs medal 1996), Sigma Xi (Monie A. Ferst medal 1992), Kappa Delta Phi, Phi Kappa Phi, Alpha Chi Sigma, Phi Lambda Upsilon, Phi Lambda Theta (hon.). Office: Northwestern U Chemistry Dept Rm GG40 2145 Sheridan Rd Evanston IL 60208-0834

BASOMBRIO, JUAN C., lawyer; b. 1964; BA in Polit. Sci., Univ. Houston, 1986; JD, Ind. Univ., 1989. Bar: Minn. 1989, Calif. 1991, US Supreme Ct. 1992. Ptnr.-in-charge, So. Calif. off. Dorsey & Whitney LLP, Irvine, Calif., 2001—03, ptnr., trial dept., and mem. policy com., 2003—. Office: Dorsey & Whitney LLP 38 Technology Dr Irvine CA 92618-5310 Office Phone: 949-932-3650. Office Fax: 949-932-3601. Business E-Mail: basombrio.juan@dorsey.com.

BASON, GEORGE R., JR., lawyer; b. N.Y.C., 1954; AB magna cum laude, Harvard U., 1975, JD cum laude, 1978. Bar: N.Y. 1979, U.S. Dist. Ct. (so. and ea. dists.) N.Y. 1979; cert. Avocat à la Cour de Paris 1992. Assoc. Davis Polk & Wardwell, N.Y.C., 1978-85, assoc.-Paris Office, 1980—83, ptnr. N.Y.C., 1986—, co-head mergers & acquisitions practice group. Mem. ABA, Bar Assn. City N.Y., Phi Beta Kappa. Office: Davis Polk & Wardwell 450 Lexington Ave New York NY 10017-3982 Office Phone: 212-450-4340. Office Fax: 212-450-3340.

BASQUIN, MARY SMYTH (KIT BASQUIN), museum administrator; b. NYC, July 3, 1941; d. Joseph Percy and Virginia Sandford (Gibbs) Smyth; m. Maurice Hanson Basquin, Feb. 4, 1967 (div. Feb. 1984); children: Susan, Peter Lee, William. BA, Goucher Coll., Balt., 1963; MA, Ind. U., 1970. Asst. dir. pub. rels. Indpls. Mus. Art, 1971-72; dir. Washington Gallery, Frankfort, Ind., 1972-79, Indpls., 1977-79, Kit Basquin Gallery, Milw., 1981-83; curator edn. Haggerty Mus. Marquette U., Milw., 1988-95; dir. outreach Milw. Wis. Humanities Coun., 1995-98; curator Marvin Lowe Retrospective, Ind. U. Art Mus., 1998; mktg. William Doyle Galleries, NYC, 1999, exhbn. mgr., 2000; rsch. assoc. Bklyn. Mus. Art, 2000; asst. print study rm. Met. Mus. Art, NYC, 2000—. Instr. art history Concordia U., Mequon, Wis., 1991, instr. Marquette U., Gaza, 1996; pres. contemporary art soc. Milw. Art Mus., 1986-87, prints and drawings subcom., 1991-99, pres. Print Forum, 1996-97; mem. program com. Midwest Mus. conf., Milw., 1992. Wis. editor: New Art Examiner, 1980—81; mem. St. Barts Singers, 1999—; contbr. articles to profl. jours.

Trustee Ten Chimneys Found., Genesee Depot, Wis., 1997-99; mem. adv. bd. Ten Chimneys Found., 2000-01. Mem. Univ. Club NY, Univ. Club Milw. Episcopalian. Avocations: singing, fashion, theater, swimming. Home: 1675 York Ave Apt 19A New York NY 10128-6756

BASS, AARON, school system administrator; b. Phila., May 26, 1950; m. Jade King, July 3, 1999; children: Naja Killebrew, Clyde Killebrew, Aaron III, Jared, Sharita. BA in Psychology, Lincoln U., 1972; MA in Social Psychology, Temple U., 1974; AA in Data Processing, Phila. C.C., 1982; MDiv, Luth. Theol. Sem., 1998. Learning specialist Urban Career Edn. Ctr., Phila., 1974; rsch. asst. Sch. Dist. Phila., 1974-94, rsch. assoc., 1994-96, rsch. asst., 1996-2000, analyst pupil data, 2000—05; specialist rsch and assessment William Penn Sch. Dist., 2005—. Author numerous studies and evaluations. Tchr. Germantown Cmty. Photography Workshop, Phila., 1972-74; elder Eagles Nest Christian Fellowship, Phila., 1999-2001, Mt. Airy Ch. of God in Christ, 2001—; mem. Phila. Interfaith Action; mem. Germantown 1st Presbyn. Ch. Temple U. scholar, 1972; recipient award Most Unique Reporting Technique for Career Edn. Accumulative Report, Am. Ednl. Rsch. Assn., 1980. Mem.: Phila. Interfaith Action, Evang. Tng. Assn., Phi Delta Kappa, Omega Psi Phi. Avocations: running, biking, swimming, reading, travel. Home: 6025 Morton St Philadelphia PA 19144 Office Phone: 610-284-8005 x259. Personal E-mail: abass@voicenet.com. Business E-Mail: abass@phila.k12.pa.us.

BASS, CHARLES F., congressman; b. Boston, Jan. 8, 1952; s. Perkins and Katharine J. Bass; m. Lisa L.; children: Lucy, Jonathan. AB, Dartmouth Coll., 1974. Field worker Congressman William S. Cohen, 1974; legis. asst. Congressman David F. Emery, 1975-76, chief of staff, 1976-79; v.p. High Std., Inc., Dublin, N.H., 1980-94; chmn. Columbia Archtl. Products, Beltsville, Md., 1980-94; mem. U.S. Congress from 2d N.H. dist., 1995—; mem. ho. budget com., energy and commerce com.,mem. working groups on nat. security and govt. reform; vice chmn. subcom. on civil svc., subcom. on govt. mgmt., info. and tech. Trustee N.H. Higher Edn. Assistance Found., Monadnock Conservancy, N.H. Humanities Coun. Mem. Monadnock Rotary (pres. 1992-93), Amoskeag Vets., Masons. Republican. Office: US Ho of Reps 2421 Rayburn HOB Washington DC 20515-2902 also: 142 N Main St Concord NH 03301-4917 also: 170 Main St Nashua NH 03060-2731 also: 78 Main St Littleton NH 03561-4012*

BASS, DAVID STEVEN, law educator, arbitrator, mediator, financial consultant; b. Bklyn., Dec. 10, 1946; s. Joseph and Thelma (Feingold) B.; m. Carol W. Palevsky, Aug. 17, 1969; children: Adam Brett, Wayne Jonathan. BA, Bklyn. Coll., 1967; JD, NYU, 1971, LLM in Labor Rels., 1975. Bar: N.Y. 1972, U.S. Dist. Ct. (ea. dist.) N.Y. 1975. Atty. Office Labor Rels. and Collective Bargaining N.Y.C. Bd. Edn., 1973-80, dep. dir., 1980-84, dep. exec. dir., 1984—2002. Adj. prof. edn. law, finance and pers. adminstrn. City Coll. CUNY, 1992—, Touro Coll., 2001—. Mem. N.Y. State Bar Assn. (labor and employment law section); appointed to various arbitration panels in N.Y. and N.J. Jewish. Home and Office: 31 Whitney Dr Marlboro NJ 07746-1249 Office Phone: 732-972-1114.

BASS, FRANKLIN F., lawyer; b. NYC, Mar. 9, 1951; BA, NYU, 1972; JD, Bklyn. Law Sch., 1976. Bar: NY 1977, US Dist. Ct. So. Dist. NY, US Dist. Ct. Ea. Dist. NY, US Ct. Appeals 2nd Cir., US Ct. Appeals 3rd Cir., US Supreme Ct. Ptnr. Wilson, Elser, Moskowitz, Edelman & Dicker LLP, NYC. Assoc. prof. real estate inst. Sch. Continuing & Profl. Studies, NYU, 1980—87. Mem.: ABA, NY State Trial Lawyers Assn., NY State Bar Assn. (chmn. aviation law com. of torts, ins. & compensation law sect.), Aircraft Owners and Pilots Assn., Warbirds of Am., Exptl. Aircraft Assn., Wings Club, Aviation Ins. Assn. Office: Wilson Elser Moskowitz Edelman & Dicker LLP 23rd Fl 150 E 42nd St New York NY 10017-5639 Office Phone: 212-490-3000 ext. 2405. Office Fax: 212-490-3038. Business E-Mail: bassf@wemed.com.

BASS, GARY D., advocate, director; PhD in Psychology, U. Mich. Creator RTK NET, 1989—; pres. Human Svcs. Info. Ctr.; dir. liaison Internat. Yr. Dasabled Persons; dir. OMB Watch, Washington. Spl. asst. task force on investigation and prevention of abuse in residential instns. Mich. Gov. Office: OMB Watch 1742 Connecticut Ave NW Washington DC 20009

BASS, GEORGE FLETCHER, retired archaeology educator; b. Columbia, S.C., Dec. 9, 1932; s. Robert Duncan and Virginia (Wauchope) B.; m. Ann Singletary, Mar. 19, 1960; children: Gordon Wauchope, Alan Joseph. MA, Johns Hopkins U., 1955; PhD, U. Pa., 1964; PhD (hon.), Bogazici U., Istanbul, Turkey, 1987, U. Liverpool, 1998. Asst. prof. U. Pa., Phila., 1964-68, assoc. prof., 1968-73; prof. archaeology Tex. A&M U., College Station, 1976-80, disting. prof., 1980-2000, George T. and Gladys H. Abell prof. nautical archaeology, 1986-2000, Yamini Family prof., 1994-2000, prof. emeritus, 2001—. Dir. excavations of ancient shipwrecks off Turkish coast, 1960-2003; pres. Inst. Nautical Archaeology, 1972-82, 96-98. Author: Archaeology Under Water, 1966, Cape Gelidonya, 1967, History of Seafaring, 1972, Archaeology Beneath the Sea, 1975, Yassi Ada I, 1982, Ships and Shipwrecks of the Americas, 1988, Serce Limani I, 2004; adv. editor Am. Jour. Archaeology, 1987-99, Archaeology, 1987—, Internat. Jour. Nautical Archaeology, 1987—, Nat. Geog. Rsch., 1987-94. Lt. U.S. Army, 1957-59, Korea. Recipient Centennial award Nat. Geog. Soc., 1988, La Gorce Gold medal, 1979, Lowell Thomas award Explorers Club, 1986, Nat. Medal of Sci., 2002 (presented by Pres. George W. Bush); named one of Outstanding Young Men of Yr., Jaycees, 1967. Mem. Inst. Nautical Archaeology (pres. 1973-82), Archaeol. Inst. Am. (Gold medal for disting. archaeol. achievement 1986), Soc. for Hist. Archaeology (J.C. Harrington medal 1999), Nat. Maritime Hist. Soc., Mothers Against Drunk Driving. Presbyterian. Avocation: classical music. Home: 1600 Dominik Dr College Station TX 77840-3623 Office: Tex A&M U Nautical Archaeology College Station TX 77843-4352 Business E-Mail: gfbass@neo.tamu.edu.

BASS, HAROLD MICHAEL, plastic surgeon; b. NYC, Mar. 17, 1942; s. Albert and Rose Bass; m. Iris Marilyn Schoen, Aug. 30; children: Aviva Bass-Varsalona, Sheryl Tracy. BS, Rensselaer Poly. Inst., 1962; MD, Albany Med. Coll., 1966. Diplomate Am. Bd. Plastic Surgery, Nat. Bd. Med. Examiners. Surg. intern Nassau County Med. Ctr., Hempstead, NY, 1966—67; resident to chief resident surgery Winthrop Med. Ctr., Mineola, 1967—71; resident to chief resident plastic surgery Ctrl. Fla. Med. Ctr., Orlando, Fla., 1971—73; attending plastic surgeon U. Hosp., Tamarac, 1975—, Holy Cross Hosp., Ft. Lauderdale, 1999—, North Ridge Med. Ctr., 1999—, Oakridge Outpatient Ctr., 2000—. Vis. fellow Western Pa. Hosp., Pitts., 1963, Finsen Inst. And Radium Ctr., Copenhagen, 1972, Jewish Hosp. and U. Louisville Affiliated Hosps., 1973; vis. faculty Ctrl. Fla. Regional Hosp., Orlando, 1973—74. Med. cons. Salvation Army, Albany, 1965—66, Freeport Speedway, NY, 1967—69. Recipient cert. of appreciation, Fla. Med. Assn., 1995. Fellow: ACS; mem.: Broward County Soc. Plastic Surgeons (pres. 1993—95), Fla. Soc. Plastic Surgeons (pres. 1995—96), Southeastern Soc. Plastic and Reconstructive Surgeons, Am. Soc. Aesthetic Plastic Surgery, Am. Soc. Plastic Surgeons. Avocations: computers, sports, technology, acting. Office: Bass Ctr Aesthetic Surgery Ste 415 5601 N Dixie Hwy Fort Lauderdale FL 33334 Office Phone: 954-267-9030. Office Fax: 954-267-9952.

BASS, HAROLD NEAL, pediatrician, medical geneticist; b. Chgo., Apr. 14, 1939; s. Louis A. and Minnie (Schachter) B.; m. Phyllis Appell, June 25, 1961; children: Laura Renee, Alana Suzanne. Student, U. Ill., 1956—59; MS in Pharmacology, MD, U. Chgo., 1963. Diplomate Am. Bd. Pediat., Am. Bd. Med. Genetics, Nat. Bd. Med. Examiners. Intern Children's Meml. Hosp., Chgo., 1963-64, resident, 1964-65, chief resident, 1965-66, fellow in med. genetics, 1965-66; chief pediat. and profl. svcs. Norton AFB Hosp., Calif., 1966-68; attending pediatrician/med. geneticist Kaiser Permanente Med. Ctr., Panorama City, Calif., 1968—; dir. med. genetics prog. Kaiser Permanente Med. Care Program So. Calif., 1987—2003; clin. prof. pediat. and human genetics UCLA Med. Sch., 1970—. Pres. med. staff Kaiser Permanente Med. Ctr., 1989-2004; bd. dirs. So. Calif. Permanente Med. Group, 1998-04; adj. prof. biology Calif. State U., Northridge, 1995—. Contbr. articles to profl. jours. Mem. mayor's adv. com. San Fernando Valley, City of L.A., 1973-78. Capt. USAF, 1966—68. Founding Fellow Am. Coll. Med. Genetics, Western Soc. Pediat. Rsch., Brady Handgun Control, ACLU, Am. Soc. Human Genetics, Amnesty Internat. Democrat. Jewish. Avocations: civic affairs, music, writing. Home: 11922 Dunnicliffe Ct Northridge CA 91326-1324 Office: Kaiser Permanente Med Ctr 13652 Cantara St Panorama City CA 91402-5497 Office Phone: 818-375-2248. Business E-Mail: harold.n.bass@kp.org.

BASS, HENRY ELLIS, physics educator; b. Tulsa, Aug. 31, 1943; s. HenryUlyses Bass and Hazel (Ellison) Harrell; m. Ruby Lee Wright (div. 1977); children: Belinda Sue Heflin, Christine Annette Ware, Henry E. Jr.; m. Judy Cathy Sneed, 1978; 1 child, John Duncan. BS, Okla. State U., 1965, PhD, 1970. Barnard prof. physics U. Miss., University, 1970—. Dir. Nat. Ctr. for Phys. Acoustics, 1992—. Recipient Headway Educator award Miss. State Legis., 1988. Fellow Acoustical Soc. Am. (Bienniel award 1978). E-mail: pabass@olemiss.edu.

BASS, HILARIE, lawyer; b. NYC, Nov. 22, 1954; BA magna cum laude, George Washington Univ., 1972; JD summa cum laude, Univ. Miami, 1981. Bar: Fla. 1981, US Dist. Ct. (so., middle districts) Fla., US Ct. Appeals (11th cir.), US Supreme Ct. Shareholder, chair nat. litig. practice group Greenberg Traurig LLP, Miami, Fla. Adj. prof. litig. Univ. Miami. Mem., exec. com. United Way, Dade County, 1995—, chair, bd. dir., 1997—99; bd. trustees Univ. Miami, 2003—. Named Bus. Woman of Yr., So. Fla. Bus. Jour., 2001; named one of So. Florida's Top Lawyers, So. Fla. Legal Guide, 2001—05, Best of the Best Rainmakers, Coral Gables Living Mag., 2003, Legal Elite, Fla. Trend Mag., 2004; recipient Dorothy Shula award for volunteerism, United Way of Miami-Dade, 2000. Mem.: ABA (bd. gov. 1990—93, chair, coun. for fund for justice and edn. 2000—02, mem., ho. of del. 1988—95, 2000—), Fla. Bar Found. (bd. dir. 1988—93, pres.). Office: Greenberg Traurig LLP 1221 Brickell Ave Miami FL 33131 Office Phone: 305-579-0745. Office Fax: 305-579-0717. Business E-Mail: bassh@gtlaw.com.

BASS, JAMES ORIN, SR., lawyer; b. Sumner County, Tenn., July 12, 1910; s. Francis Marion and Sadie (Dunn) B.; m. Susanne Warner, June 9, 1937; children: James Orin, Edwin Warner, Francis Marion II, Susan Richardson. BA, U. of South, 1931; LL.B., Harvard, 1934. Bar: Tenn. 1934. Ptnr. Bass, Berry & Sims, Nashville, 1937—. Mem. Tenn. Ho. of Reps. from Davidson County, 1936-38, Tenn. Senate, 1940-42. Served to lt. col. AUS, 1942-45, ETO. Mem. ABA, Tenn. Bar Assn., Nashville Bar Assn. (pres. 1952), Am. Coll. Trial Lawyers. Presbyterian. Home: 4412 Georgian Pl Nashville TN 37215-4528 E-mail: jbasssr@bassberry.com.

BASS, JAY MICHAEL, lawyer; b. Valdosta, Ga., Aug. 27, 1963; BA, Valdosta State Coll., 1985; JD, U. Ga., 1988. Bar: Ga. 1988, U.S. Dist. Ct. (mid. dist.) Ga. Asst. solicitor Ga. State Solicitor's Office, Athens, 1989-90; ptnr. Closson, Bass & Tomberlin, Valdosta, 1991—. Bd. dirs. Nat. Criminal Def. Coll., 1992. Mem. Nat. Assn. Criminal Def. Lawyers, Ga. Assn. Criminal Def. Lawyers (v.p. 1998—2000), Valdosta Assn. Criminal Def. Lawyers (founder, pres. 1998-99). Avocations: golf, fishing, model rocketry, blues music, travel. Office: Closson Bass & Tomberlin PO Box 159 112-114 W Valdosta GA 31603-0159 Office Phone: 912-244-7171. E-mail: m.bass@cbt-law.com.

BASS, JOSEPH OSCAR, retired minister; b. Vicksburg, Miss., Jan. 23, 1933; s. Sylvester and Jeanette (Sims) B.; m. Charline Delores Sanders, June 5, 1955; children: Karen Sue, Julie Yvette. BRE, Western Bapt. Coll., Kansas City, Mo., 1956; BA, Nat. Coll., Kansas City, 1958; MRE, Cen. Bapt. Sem., Kansas City, Kans., 1959; MA, U. Mo., 1969, postgrad., 1975-76; MDiv, Mo. Sch. Religion, Columbia, 1971; LHD (hon.), Va. Coll., Lynchburg, 1974; PhD, Walden U., Naples, Fla., 1976. Ordained to ministry Am. Bapt. Chs. in U.S.A., 1954. Pastor chs., Kans., Mo., 1955-62; indsl. missionary to Thailand Am. Bapt. Conv., 1962-69, assoc. exec. dir. world mission support, 1969-72; nat. dir. fund of renewal Progressive Nat. Bapt. Conv., Am. Bapt. Conv., Valley Forge, Pa., 1972-74; exec. dir. home mission bd. Progressive Bapts.; pastor, founder Alpha Bapt. Ch., Alpha Acad. Christian Growth, Willingboro, NJ, 1977—2005. Mem. adv. coun. internat. affairs Nat. Coun. Chs., Washington, 1974-81; mem. exec. coun. Am. Bapt. Chs., mem. gen. bd.; founder Bankok's Inter-racial Coun. Author: These Are They, 1970, The History of the Progressive National Baptist Convention, 1976; co-author: One in Nine Americans Is Black, 1973, The Black American Experience, 1974. Mem. men's com. Japan Internat. Christian U., 1972; pres. Burlington County (N.J.) Cmty. Action Program, 1972-73, pres. 1973—; bd. dirs. Burlington County United Way Campaign; vice-chmn. N.J. Chaplaincy Cons. Com.; founder Ptnrs. in Edn.; gen. bd. A.B.C. Ch.; chaplain Family Svcs. Burlington County. Mem. Am. Sociol. Assn., Nat. Doctoral Assn. Educators, World Wide Acad. Scholars., Willingboro Clergy Assn. (pres. 1987—), Congress of Willingboro (chair), Willingboro Hall of Fame (pres.), Rotary Internat. Achievements include youngest Am. to become pres. of AFL-CIO Local 221 at age 16; first Am. to meet PhD lang. requirements in Thai; instituted international director school to work program, 1998; graduate Leadership N.J., 1998. Home: 2 Normont Ln Willingboro NJ 08046-1321 *Since nothing in this life is forever, I have made a quality decision to accept every moment of life I have left as an unearned gift from God the Creator-giver and translate it into service to humanity.*

BASS, JUDY MARSHA, artist, educator; b. Balt., Mar. 17, 1946; d. Charles Sam and Anne (Epstein) B. BA, U. Md., 1967; MFA, George Washington U., 1974. Lectr. Mt. Vernon Coll., Washington, 1979-84; vis. asst. prof., vis. painter U. N.Mex., Albuquerque, 1981-82; instr. art Md. Inst. Art, Balt., 1983-84; prof. art Marymount U., Arlington, Va., 1984—, dir. Barry Gallery, 1989—. One-woman shows The Phillips Collection, Washington, 1980, Mateyka Gallery, Washington, 1984, 85, 88, The Barry Gallery, Marymount U., Arlington, Va., 1993, Mt. Vernon Coll., Washington, 1996, Bird-In-Hand Gallery, Washington, 2000; represented in pemanent collection The Phillips Collection, Art-in-Embassies, Program, Botswana, George Washington U., Marymount U. Mem. Coll. Art Assn., Southeastern Coll. Art Conf. Office: Marymount U 2807 N Glebe Rd Arlington VA 22207-4299 Office Phone: 703-284-1561. Business E-Mail: jbass@marymount.edu.

BASS, LYNDA D., retired medical/surgical nurse, nursing educator; b. Suffolk, Va. d. H.M. and Katie Lea Bass. BSN, NC Agrl. and Tech. State U., Greensboro, 1968; MSN, Cath. U. Am., Washington, 1974. Med.-surg. nurse Kenner Army Hosp., Ft. Lee, Va., 1968—71, Walter Reed Army Med. Ctr., Washington, 1968—71; staff nurse Providence Hosp., Washington, 1971—73, clin. educator, 1988—94; gen. surgery clin. specialist George Washington U. Hosp., Washington, 1974—77; clin. nurse specialist Walter Reed Army Hosp., Washington, 1977—78; coord. clin. staff devel. Mt. Vernon Hosp., Alexandria, Va., 1978—79; clin. nurse preceptor Greater SE Cmty. Hosp., Washington, 1979—81; instr. clin. nursing edn. Suburban Hosp., Bethesda, Md., 1980—83; edn./tng. quality assurance coord. Howard U. Hosp., Washington, 1983—88; edn. specialist Vets. Affairs Md. Healthcare Sys., Balt., 1995—2002. Adj. faculty Cath. U. Am., 1975—76. Active Women in Mil. Svc. for Am. Meml. Found. Capt. USAR, 1967—71, Vietnam. Mem.: Nat. Nursing Staff Devel. Assn., Vietnam Vets. Am., Chi Eta Phi.

BASS, NANCY AGNES, airport executive; b. Beaver Falls, Pa., Feb. 26, 1937; d. John Joseph and Kathleen Lillian (Retzer) Paff; m. Lee Herbert Bass, Jan. 10, 1959; children: Thomas Andrew, Marilee, Laura Kathleen. Student, Clarion State Coll., 1954-56. Purchasing clk. Orange County Purchasing Dept., Santa Ana, Calif., 1957-60; bookkeeper Cal Gas, Ridgecrest, Calif., 1975-78; interline mgr. C and M Airlines, Inyokern, Calif., 1978-82; mgr. CLC Engring and Surveying, Ridgecrest, Calif., 1982-86; gen. mgr. Indian Wells Valley Airport Dist., Inyokern, Calif., 1985—, Ridgecrest (Calif.) Redevel. Agy., 1989-90. Chair Kern County Aviation Transp. Tech. Adv. Com., Bakerfield, Calif., 1989, 92; mem. tech. adv. com. for aeronautics State of Calif. Transp. Commn., 1994—. Bd. dirs. Ridgecrest Bd. of Appeals, 1986-90, dir. High Desert Child Abuse Prevention Coun., Ridgecrest, 1985-87, Am. Cancer Soc., Ridgecrest, 1988—, sec. Airport Dist. Formation Com., Ridgecrest, 1983-85; planning commr. City of Ridgecrest, 1990—, vice-chair, 1992-94, chair 1995—; dir., treas. Ridgecrest Area Conv. & Visitor Bur., 1992-94, chair., 1995—. Mem. Calif. Assn. Airport Execs., Am. Assn. Airport Execs. (cert.), Altrusa. Home: 600 W Coral Ave Ridgecrest CA 93555-5214 Office: IWV Airport Dist PO Box 634 Inyokern CA 93527-0634

BASS, NORMAN HERBERT, neurologist, educator, research scientist, hospital administrator, academic administrator; b. N.Y.C., July 10, 1936; s. Julius and Celia (Annex) B.; m. Kathleen Bass; children: Joel Martin, Rebecca Pier, Robert Farrell. BS (Ford Found. scholar 1953, N.Y. State Regents scholar 1954), Swarthmore (Pa.) Coll., 1958; MD, Yale U., 1962. Diplomate: Am. Bd. Psychiatry and Neurology. Intern Med. U. Wash. Hosp., Seattle, 1962-63; resident in neurology U. Va. Hosp., Charlottesville, 1963-65; clin. fellow in neurology Mass. Gen. Hosp., Boston, 1965-67; NIH fellow Harvard U. Med. Sch., 1965-67; from asst. prof. to prof. neurology U. Va. Med. Sch., Charlottesville, 1967-79, dir. Clinic Neurosci. Rsch. Ctr., 1973-79; prof. neurology, chmn. dept. Albert B. Chandler Med. Center, U. Ky., Lexington, 1979-85; neurologist in chief Univ. Hosp., 1979-85; dir. lab. neurochemistry Sanders-Brown Ky. Rsch. Ctr. Aging, 1979-85; dean Sch. Medicine, prof. dept. Neurology Med. Coll. Ga., 1985-86; prof. neurology, rehab. medicine, chief div. rehab. medicine U. Md. Sch. Medicine, Balt., 1986-89; prof. neurology, rehab. medicine U. Pitts., 1989-92; sr. v.p., chief med. officer Harmarville Rehab. Ctr. Inc., Pitts., 1989-92; prof. pediatrics and neurology Sch. Medicine, Boston U., 1992—; sr. v.p. med. affairs Franciscan Childrens Hosp. and Rehab Ctr., 1992-94; pvt. practice Cape and Islands, 1994—. Cons. neurology VA Med. Ctr., Lexington, Augusta, Balt., Pitts., Boston; chmn. nat. rsch. program merit rev. bd. in neurobiology VA, 1978-81; mem. bd. sci. advisers Delta Regional Primate Ctr., Tulane U., 1978-81, chmn., 1979-81; chmn. profl. adv. bd. Epilepsy Assn. VA Ky., 1978-82; chmn. study sect. Nat. Inst. Disability and Rehab. Rsch., 1986-89; program surveyor Commn. on Accreditation of Rehab. Facilities, 1987-92; mem. panel co-chari Task Force Med. Rehab. Rsch. Office Sci. Policy, NIH, 1990; vis. prof. pharmacology U. Goteborg, Sweden, 1972-73. Assoc. editor Neurochem. Rsch. Jour., Jour. Neurol. Rehab.; mem. editorial bd. Stroke jour.; contbr. numerous articles to med. jours. Served to maj. M.C. USAR, 1963-69. Recipient Rsch. Career Devel. award NIH, 1971-75, Nat. Inst. Neurologic Disease rsch. fellow in neurochemistry, 1965-67; Markle scholar in acad. medicine, 1969-74 Fellow Am. Acad. Neurology (S. Weir Mitchell rsch. award 1967, chmn. sect. on geriatrics 1986, sect. on neurol. rehab. 1987), AAAS, Stroke Coun. of Am. Heart Assn., Am. Acad. Cerebral Palsy and Devel. Medicine; mem. Am. Assn. U. Profs. Neurology (v.p. 1980-81), Am. Assn. Anatomists, Am. Soc. Neurochemistry, Am. Soc. Neuro. Rehab., Soc. Neurosci., Internat. Soc. Neurochemistry, Child Neurology Soc., Am. Neurol. Assn., Assn. Rsch. Nervous and Mental Disease, Nat. Head Injury Found., Inc., AMA, Am. Congress Rehab. Medicine, Nat. Assn. Rehab. Facilities Inc., Nat. Multiple Sclerosis Soc., Nat. Head Injury Found., Alpha Omega Alpha. Office: PO Box 1050 West Falmouth MA 02574

BASS, PERKINS, retired lawyer, congressman; b. East Walpole, Mass., Oct. 6, 1912; s. Robert P. and Edith (Bird) Bass; m. Katherine Jackson (dec.); children: Alexander, Katherine, William J., Charles F., Roberta, Roberta; m. Rosaly S. Riley, Sept. 30, 1973. AB, Dartmouth Coll., 1934; LLB, Harvard U. Law Sch., 1938. Bar: N.H. 1938. Lawyer Sheehan, Phinney, Bass & Green PLC, Manchester, NH, 1938—95, of counsel, 1995—2005; rep. N.H. Gen. Ct., Concord, 1949—63; mem. U.S. Ho. Reps., Washington, 1954—63. Trustee New Hampshire Savings Bank, Concord, 1950—80; bd. dirs. Bird & Son, Inc., East Walpole, Mass., 1946—84. Trustee Franklin Pierce Coll., Rindge, NH, 1972—87; trustee, pres. Monadnock Cmty. Hosp., 1948—54; Rep. Nat. Committeeman from N.H., 1964—68; selectman Peterborough, 1972—75. Major USAF, 1942—45, Far Eastern Theater. Decorated Bronze Star USAF, Yun Ma medal Disting. and Meritorious Svc. Nat. Govt. China (now Taiwan). Home: PO Box 210 Peterborough NH 03458 Office: Peterborough Hist Bldg Grove St Peterborough NH 03458 Office Phone: 603-924-3303.

BASS, ROBERT MUSE, financier; b. Ft. Worth, 1948; s. Perry Richardson and Nancy Lee (Muse) B.; m. Anne Thaxton Bass, 1970; 3 children. BA, Yale U., 1970; MBA, Stanford U., 1974. V.p., bd. dirs. Bass Bros. Enterprises Inc., Ft. Worth, until 1985; pres. Robert M. Bass Group Inc. (now The Keystone Group), Ft. Worth, 1985—; founder Oak Hill Capital Partners. Named one of world's richest people Forbes mag. Mem. collector's com. Nat. Gallery, Washington; chmn. emeritus Nat. Trust Historic Preservation; bd. trustees Stanford U. (chmn., 1996-), 1989—, Rockefeller U., Groton Sch., Middlesex Sch., Amon Carter Mus.; commr. Tex. State Hwy. and Pub. Transp. Commn., 1986—87. Office: Keystone Inc 201 Main St Ste 3100 Fort Worth TX 76102

BASS, RONALD, screenwriter; b. Los Angeles, 1943; Screenplays include Code Name: Emerald, 1985, Black Widow, 1987, Gardens of Stone, 1987, (with Barry Morrow) Rainman, 1988 (Academy award best original screenplay 1988), Sleeping with the Enemy, 1991, (with Amy Tan) The Joy Luck Club, 1993; screenwriter, exec. prodr.: (with Al Franken) When a Man Loves a Woman, 1994, Dangerous Minds, 1995, (with Terry McMillan) Waiting to Exhale, 1995, My Best Friend's Wedding, 1997, What Dreams May Come, 1998, Stepmom, 1998, How Stella Got Her Groove Back, 1998, Entrapment, 1999, Snow Falling on Cedars, 1999, Passion of Mind, 1999, The Lazarus Child, 2004. Office: Creative Artists Agency care Beth Swofford 9830 Wilshire Blvd Beverly Hills CA 90212-1825

BASS, RUTH MARY HASKINS, journalist; b. Springfield, Mass., July 18, 1934; d. Ralph Warner and Hilda Marie (Allen) Haskins; m. Milton R. Bass, May 27, 1960; children: Michael Jon, Elissa Allen, Amy Brunell. AB in English, Bates Coll., 1955; MS in Journalism, Columbia U., 1956. Police and ct. reporter The Berkshire Eagle, Pittsfield, Mass., 1956-61; freelance writer, editor Berkshire Week mag., Pittsfield, Mass., 1963-68; editor Berkshire Sampler, Pittsfield, Mass., 1977-87; assoc. sunday editor Berkshire Eagle, Pittsfield, Mass., 1987-90; Sunday editor Pittsfield, Mass., 1990-96; columnist Berkshire Eagle, Pittsfield, 1996—. Freelance travel writer, 1996—; Elder Hostel instr. Berkshire C.C., 2000—. Author: (book series) Herbal Sweets, Herbal Salads, Herbal Bread, Herbal Soups, Tomatoes Love Herbs, Peppers Love Herbs, Onions Love Herbs, Mushrooms Love Herbs, 1996; co-author: Teen Career Guide, 1962; editor The Paper, 1997-2002. Selectman Town of Richmond, 1972-77, mem. fin. com., 1990—, chmn., 1993—; mem. bd. health, 1972-90; leader Girl Scouts US, Richmond, 1982-2000. Recipient Best Column in New Eng. award UPI, 1988, Charles and Mary Kusik Citizenship award, Richmond, 1994, New England Press Assn. hall of Fam for Cmty. Journalism, 2004. Avocations: tennis, gardening, photography, bird watching, needlecrafts.

BASS, SID. R., investment company executive; b. 1943; m. Mercedes Bass; 2 children. BA, Yale Univ., 1965; MBA, Stanford Univ., 1969. Founder Buena Venture Associates, 1998—. V.p. & dir. Sid. W. Richardson Found. Former sr. fellow of the corp. Yale Univ.; vice chmn. bd. trustees Mus. Modern Art, N.Y.C. Mailing: Buena Venture Associates 1201 Washington Terrace Fort Worth TX 76107*

BASS, STEVEN CRAIG, computer science educator; b. Indpls., July 29, 1943; s. Leland Ellsworth and Isabelle Frances (Ross) B.; m. Sara Ann Hiday, Sept. 4, 1965 (div. Apr. 1988); children: Leland Kai, Marshall Lynn; m. Kevyn Anne Salsburg, Jan. 2, 1989. BSEE, Purdue U., 1966, MSEE, 1968, PhD in Elec. Engring., 1971. Prof. elec. engring. Purdue U., Lafayette, Ind., 1971-88; prof. elec. and computer engring. George Mason U., Fairfax, Va., 1988-91; prin. engr. Mitre Corp., McLean, Va., 1988-91; prof. computer sci. and engring., chmn. dept. U. Notre Dame, Notre Dame, Ind., 1991-2000. Cons. Magnovox Co., Ft. Wayne, Ind., 1971-73, Admiral Corp., Chgo., 1973-76, Kimball Internat., Jasper, Ind., 1978-84, Tektronix Corp., Wilsonville, Oreg., 1987-88. Contbr. over 25 articles to profl. jours., delievered over 35 papers at sci. confs. Rescue officer Stockwell (Ind.) Vol. Fire Dept.,

1985-88. Recipient numerous grants from NSF, USAF, IBM, Mitre Corp., others. Fellow IEEE (v.p. circuits and sys. soc. 1981, 91-93, mem. audio engring. soc.); mem. Tau Beta Pi. Roman Catholic. Achievements include 3 U.S. and 6 fgn. patents in the field of digital signal processing. E-mail: bass@cse.nd.edu.

BASS, STEVEN MURRAY, public television executive; b. Atlantic City, N.J., Feb. 27, 1957; s. Walter and Catherine (Stump) B.; m. Sara Traut, May 12, 1984; children: Catherine Elizabeth, Caroline Anne. BA, Bucknell U., 1979; MA in Bus., U. Wis., 1981. Mgr. spl. projects Sta. WHA-TV, Madison, 1981-82, asst. dir. membership devel., 1982; assoc. dir. devel. Pub. Broadcasting Svc., Washington, 1982-86, dir. devel., 1986-87, dir. nat. corp. support, 1987-91; v.p., gen. mgr. Sta. WGBY-TV, Springfield, Mass., 1992-96; v.p., mgr. WGBH-TV, Boston, 1996-98; pres., CEO Nashville Pub. TV, 1998—. Mem.: Assn. Am.'s Pub. TV Stas. (bd. dirs. 2001—), Greater Nashville C. of C. (bd. dirs. 2002—). Avocations: sailing, scuba diving. Home: 9220 Foxboro Dr Brentwood TN 37027-6123 Office: Nashville Pub TV 161 Rains Ave Nashville TN 37203-5330 E-mail: sbass@wnpt.net.

BASSAM, BASSAM A., neurologist, medical educator; b. Aynata, Lebanon, Jan. 9, 1947; s. Ali Bassam and Seikneh Bazzi. MD, Aleppo (Syria) U., 1973; postgrad., Wayne State U., 1981. Diplomate Am. Bd. Psychiatry and Neurology. Dir. neurology sect. Wayne County Gen. Hosp., Westland, Mich., 1982—85; asst. prof. medicine U. Mich., Ann Arbor, 1982—85; dir. neuromuscular program U. South Ala., Mobile, 1985—, prof. neurology, 1998—. Contbr. articles to profl. jours., chpts. to books. Fellow: Am. Acad. Neurology; mem.: So. Fedn. Syrian-Lebanese Ams. (Ala. state pres. 1998—), Mobile Neurol. Soc. (sec. 1995—), Am. Assn. Electrodiagnostic Medicine (mem. faculty com.). Avocations: sports, soccer, travel. Office: U South Ala Dept Neurology Ste 205 3401 Medical Park Dr Bldg # 3 Mobile AL 36693

BASSANO, C. LOUIS, state legislator, fuel oil company executive; b. Newark, Oct. 29, 1942; s. Charles and Mildred (Tortoriello) B.; m. Joan DeFlores, May 25, 1984; children: Charles Louis II, Jennifer Ann, Kimberly Claire, Jeffrey Alan. Student, Bloomfield Coll., 1961-63. V.p. H & I Bassano Fuel Oil, Kenilworth, N.J.; mem. N.J. Gen. Assembly, 1972-74, 76-81, N.J. Senate, Dist. 21, Trenton, 1981—; asst. minority whip, 1987-88; minority whip, 1989; asst. senate minority leader, 1990-91. Mem. senate law, pub. safety and def. com., senate instns., health and welfare com.; chmn. senate health and human svcs. com.; mem. senate family svcs. com. (vice chmn.), senate law and pub. safety com., 1994; chmn. senate sr. citizens, vet. affairs and human svcs. com., 1994—; mem. health com., 1996—, women's issues, children and family svcs. com., 1996—; chmn. legis. caucus on Israel; co-chmn. joint legis. task force to study adult diagnostic and treatment ctr., vice chair women's issues, children and family svcs. com., 1994—, health com., 1996—; active N.J. Intergovtl. Rels. Commn. Chmn. Sammy Davis, Jr. Liver Inst.; past mem. N.J. Monorail Legislation Commn., Senate Rep. Task Force on Liability Ins. Reform, Hazardous Waste Minimization Task Force, Law Enforcement Tng. Acad. Study Commn., Nat. Com. for Treatment of Intractable Pain; bd. dirs. Children's Specialized Hosp.; past chmn. fund drive Meml. Gen. Hosp.; past chmn. Union Township Epilepsy Fund; past co-chmn. Cancer Crusade; mem. bd, dirs. NJ Mental Health Assn.; bd. dirs. Bridgeway Found. for Mental Health. Recipient cert. of recognition Bd. Dirs. Home Health Agy. Assembly N.J./N.J. Home Care Coun., Outstanding Community Svc. award Cancer Care, Inc./Nat. Cancer Found., PTA Safety award State PTA, B'nai B'rith Youth Svc. award, Pub. Safety award N.J. Tire Dealers Assn., Good Govt. award Township of Union Gov. Body, Disting. Svc. award Jr. Achievement, certs. of appreciation Union County March of Dimes, LWV of Cranford, Pres. award N.J. Assn. Rehab. Facilities, 1994; named Unico Man of Yr. by Union chpt. Unico, Senator of Yr. by N.J. Builders Assn., Outstanding Rep. Legislator, Legislator of Yr., Assn. Schs. and Agens. for Handicapped, 1994, N.J. Organ and Tissue Sharing Network, 1994; honored by N.J. State Nurses Assn., N.J. Psychol. Assn., 1996; recipent legis. svc. award Union County C. of C., 1994, outstanding svc. award ARC, 1994, pub. svc. award COSAC, 1995, spl. distinction award Mental Health Assn., legis. recognition award N.J. Alliance for Mentally Ill, 1996, Cmty. Access Unltd. Humanitarian award 1996, Legislator of Yr. Crohn's and Colitis Found. of Ams. N.J. chpt. 1997; named senator of yr. 1996 Garden State Pharmacy Owners. Mem. Elks, K.C.

BASS DE MARTINEZ, BERNICE, academic administrator, consultant; b. Denver, Sept. 23, 1948; d. Arthur and Beatrice Bass. BA, U. No. Colo., 1970, MA, 1972; PhD, U. Fla., 1975. Dept. chair Calif. State U., Fresno, 1987—91; dean edn. and human svcs. Seton Hall U., South Orange, NJ, 1991—93; assoc. provost Mills Coll., Oakland, Calif., 1993—96; sr. assoc. v.p., dean grad. sch. Ind. State U., Terre Haute, 1996—2000; spl. asst. pres., prof. Calif. State U., Sacramento, 2000—. Interim exec. dir., CEO Leadership Am., Alexandria, Va., 2002—02; rschr. Women of Color Rsch., Phoenix, 2003—. Editor: (educational text/book) Prespectives in Multicultural Education. Supporter Nat. Found. for Women Legislators, 2002; chair, recruitment com. Leadership Am., Dallas, 2000; state liaison ACE/OWHE Women's Network, Washington, 1999; dir. internat. edn. euro-American Women's Coun., Athens, 2002. Fellow: Assn. Am. Colls. and Univs.; mem.: Alpha Kappa Alpha (chpt. pres. 1996—2000). Democrat. Roman Catholic. Avocations: walking, travel, reading, networking. Office: Calif State U 6000 J St Sacramento CA 95819-6016 Office Phone: 916-928-2440. Home Fax: 916-928-8478. Personal E-mail: babed4sure@aol.com. E-mail: bbdem@csus.edu.

BASSECHES, ROBERT TREINIS, lawyer; b. NYC, Jan. 24, 1934; s. Jacob Thomas and Paula (Treinis) B.; m. Harriet Itkin, July 6, 1958; children: K.B., Joshua, Jessica. BA, Amherst Coll., 1955; LLB, Yale U., 1958. Bar: D.C. 1962, U.S. Ct. Appeals (D.C. cir.) 1962, U.S. Ct. Appeals (2d cir.) 1978, U.S. Ct. Appeals (4th cir.) 1998. Law clk. to judge David L. Bazelon U.S. Ct. Appeals (D.C. cir.), Washington, 1958-59; law clk. to justice Hugo L. Black U.S. Supreme Ct., Washington, 1959; assoc. Shea & Gardner, Washington, 1959-63, ptnr., 1963—2004, adminstrv. ptnr., 1980-86, chmn., exec. com., 1988-93; sr. counsel Goodwin Procter LLP, Washington, 2004—. Trustee Green Acres Sch., Rockville, Md., 1971-76, pres., chmn. bd. trustees, 1973-75; pres. Chevy Chase (Md.) Village Citizens Assn., 1976. Mem. Maritime Adminstrv. Bar Assn. (pres. 1969-71, sec. 1967-69), Phi Beta Kappa. Office: Goodwin Procter LLP 901 New York Ave NW Washington DC 20001

BASSEN, NED HENRY, lawyer; b. NYC, June 8, 1948; s. Harold Russell and Annette (Frankfeldt) B.; m. Susan Millington Campbell, July 2, 1999; children: Amanda Lee, Susannah Spence. BS, Cornell U., 1970, JD, 1973. Bar: N.Y. 1974, U.S. Dist. Ct. (so. and ea. dists.) N.Y. 1974, U.S. Dist. Ct. (ea. dist.) Mich. 1990, U.S. Dist. Ct. (we. dist.) N.Y. 1999, U.S. Dist Ct. (no. dist.) N.Y. 2004, U.S. Ct. Appeals (11th cir.) 1984, U.S. Ct. Appeals (2d cir.) 2001. Assoc. Baer Marks & Upham, N.Y.C., 1975-80, Kelley Drye & Warren, N.Y.C., 1973-75, 80-83, ptnr., 1983-92; ptnr., labor group head Mudge Rose Guthrie Alexander & Ferdon, N.Y.C., 1993-95; ptnr., chair labor and employment group Hughes Hubbard & Reed LLP, N.Y.C., 1995—. Note and comment editor Cornell Law Rev., 1972—73. Fellow Coll. Labor and Employemnt Lawyers; mem. ABA (labor and employment law sect., com. devel. of law under the nat. legal rels. act), US Coun. Internat. Bus., Indsl. Rels. Com., Indsl. Rels. Rsch. Assn., NY State Bar Assn. (labor law sect., com. on equal employment opportunity law), NY State Mgmt. Attys. Conf. Office: Hughes Hubbard & Reed LLP 1 Battery Park Plz Fl 12 New York NY 10004-1482 Office Phone: 212-837-6090. Business E-Mail: bassen@hugheshubbard.com.

BASSETT, ANGELA, actress; b. N.Y.C., Aug. 16, 1958; m. Courtney Vance, 1997. BA in African-Am. studies, Yale U., 1980; MFA, Yale Sch. of Drama, 1983. Appeared in (plays) Colored People's Time, 1982, The Mystery Plays, 1984-85, The Painful Adventures of Pericles, Prince of Tyre, 1986-87, Joe Turner's Come and Gone, 1986-87, (Broadway) Ma Rainey's Black Bottom, (Broadway) Joe Turner's Come and Gone, 1988, King Henry IV Part I, 1987; (TV movies) Line of Fire: The Morris Dees Story, 1991, The Jacksons: An American Dream, 1992, A Century of Women, 1994, Ruby's Bucket of Blood, 2001 (also producer), The Rosa Parks Story, 2002 (also exec. producer); guest appearances (TV Series) The Cosby Show, 1985, 1988, Spenser: For Hire, 1985, A Man Called Hawk, 1989, Tour of Duty, 1989, 227, 1989, thirtysomething, 1989, Alien Nation, 1990, The Flash, 1991, Nightmare Café, 1992, The Bernie Mac Show, 2003; (films) F/X, 1986, Kindergarten Cop, 1990, Boyz N the Hood, 1991, City of Hope, 1991, Innocent Blood, 1992, Malcolm X, 1992, Passion Fish, 1992, What's Love Got to Do with It, 1993 (Acad. award nominee for best actress 1993, Golden Globe award best actress in a musical or comedy 1994), Strange Days, 1995, Panther, 1995, Waiting to Exhale, 1995, A Vampire in Brooklyn, 1995, Contact, 1997, How Stella Got Her Groove Back, 1998, Wings Against the Wind, 1999, Cosm, 1999, 50 Violins, 1999, Music of the Heart, 1999, Supernova, 2000, Whispers: An Elephant's Tale, 2000 (voice), Boesman and Lena, 2000, The Score, 2001, Sunshine State, 2002, Masked and Anonymous, 2003, The Lazarus Child, 2004, Mr. 3000, 2004; exec. prodr. Our America, 2002. Office: care Doug Chapin Mgmt # 430 9465 Wilshire Blvd Beverly Hills CA 90212 also: Creative Artists Agy Wilshire Blvd Beverly Hills CA 90212-2613

BASSETT, CHARLES WALKER, literature and language professor; b. Aberdeen, SD, July 7, 1932; s. Wilfred Walker and Angela (Jewett) B.; m. Carol Hoffer, Sept. 15, 1956 (dec. Feb. 5, 1995); children— David, Elizabeth. BA, U. S.D., 1954, MA, 1956; PhD, U. Kans., 1964; LHD (hon.), U. S.D., 2000. Asst. instr. English U. S.D., 1954-56, U. Kans., 1958-64; instr. U. Pa., Phila., 1964-66, asst. prof., 1966-69; asst. prof. English Colby Coll., Waterville, Maine, 1969-74, assoc. prof., 1974-80, prof., 1980-83, Charles A. Dana prof. Am. studies and English, 1983-93, Lee Family prof. Am. studies and English, 1993-99, dir. Am. studies Waterville, 1971-87, 89-96, chmn. dept. English, 1987-89, Lee family prof. Am. Studies & English emeritus, 1999—. Book rev. editor Am. Quar., 1983—91, assoc. editor Ency. of Polit. Parties and Elections in the U.S., 1991; contbr. articles to profl. jours. Recipient Charles Bassett/Sr. Class Tchg. award, 1993, Charles Bassett award for dedicated svc. Colby Alumni Assn., 1997, Student Assn. award for outstanding dedication to the students of Colby Coll., 1981; S.L. Whitcomb fellow, 1961-62, U. Kans. fellow, 1962-63; U. Pa. Faculty Rsch. grantee, 1966-68; Humanities and Mellon grantee, 1973-96. Mem. MLA (New Eng. rep. del. assembly), Am. Studies Assn. (Mary C. Turpie award 1994). Democrat. Roman Catholic. Home: 9 Martin Ave Waterville ME 04901-4625 Office: Colby Coll Dept English Waterville ME 04901 Office Phone: 207-872-3298. Business E-Mail: cwbasset@colby.edu.

BASSETT, ELIZABETH EWING (LIBBY BASSETT), writer, editor, consultant; b. Cleve., July 22, 1937; d. Ben and Eileen Grace (Ewing) B.; m. Robert Richter, Feb. 20, 1994. AA, Bradford Jr. Coll., Mass., 1957. Girl Friday Time-Life, animated film cos., others, 1957-63; asst. producer, stage mgr. N.Y. State Pavilion at N.Y. World's Fair, 1963-64; writer, reporter, editor AP, N.Y.C., 1965-72; free-lance corr. AP, Newsweek, Voice of America, UNICEF, ABC Radio, Africa, 1972-74; resident corr. ABC News, Cairo, 1974-77; dir. publs. and comm. World Environment Ctr., N.Y.C., 1978-85; cons. writer, editor, editorial designer Women's Environ. and Devel. Orgn., 1989—98, UN orgns. and others, 1985—2000; co-organizer Project on Religion and Human Rights, 1994-95. Guest lectr. Am. U. Cairo, Rutgers U., Columbia U., L.I. U., Hunter Coll., CUNY; press officer Global Survival Conf., Oxford, Eng., 1988; press coord. Global Forum on Environ. and Devel., Moscow, 1990, Parliamentary Earth Summit, Rio de Janeiro, 1992; info. officer Internat. Green Cross/Global Forum, Kyoto, Japan, 1993; comm. coord. World Women's Congress for a Healthy Planet, Miami, 1991; press. coord. WEDO Web, NGO Forum on Women, China, 1995. Author: The Growth of Environment in the World Bank, World Environment Center, 1982, UNEP N.Am. News, 1986-91, Shared Vision, 1988-92, The Global Forum Decade, 1995, Earth and Faith: A Book of Reflection for Action, 2000, also others; editor, designer: Women in African Economies--From Burning Sun to Boardroom, 2000, Liberian Women Peacemakers, 2004; assoc. editor, designer: The Bella Abzug Reader, 2003; cons. writer, editor Inst. for Pvt. Investors, 1999—. Mem.: Soc. Profl. Journalists, Soc. Environ. Journalists.

BASSETT, JOHN E., academic administrator, language educator; b. Washington, May 12, 1942; s. J. Earl and Frances E. (Walker) B.; m. Kay E. Hobart, Sept. 5, 1964; children: Laura, Gregory. BA in History, Ohio Wesleyan U., 1963, MA in English, 1966; PhD in English, U. Rochester, 1970. Instr. U. Rochester, N.Y., 1969-70; asst. prof. Wayne State U., Detroit, 1970-75, assoc. prof., 1975-84; prof., head dept. English No. Carolina State U., Raleigh, 1984-93; dean Coll. Arts and Scis., prof. English Case Western Res. U., Cleve., 1993-2000; pres. Clark U., Worcester, 2000—. Author: William Faulkner: An Annotated Checklist of Criticism, 1972, Faulkner: The Critical Heritage, 1975, Faulkner: A Checklist of Recent Criticism, 1983, Vision and Revisions: Essays on Faulkner, 1989, Faulkner in the Nineties: A Bibliography of Criticism, 1991, A Heart of Ideality in My Realism and Other Essays on Howells and Twain, 1991, Harlem in Review: Critical Reactions to Black American Writers 1917-1939, 1992, Defining Southern Literature, 1997, Thomas Wolfe: An Annotated Bibliography of Criticism, 1996, Sherwood Anderson, 2005; contbr. articles to profl. jours. Mem. MLA, Mark Twain Soc., Thomas Wolfe Soc., Soc. for Study of So. Lit., Assn. Depts. of English (pres. 1990-91), Phi Beta Kappa, Phi Kappa Phi, Phi Alpha Theta. Office: Clark U 950 Main St Worcester MA 01610-1477 Business E-Mail: jbassett@clarku.edu.

BASSETT, LAWRENCE C, management consultant; b. N.Y.C., Dec. 11, 1931; s. David Isaac and Genia Esther Bassett; m. Charlotte Corinne Margolis, Jan. 24, 1960; children: Wendy Jill, Craig Henrid, Heidi Jill, Evan Henrid. BA, NYU, 1953, MBA, 1958. Pers. mgr. Republic Carloading & Distbg. Co., N.Y.C., 1956-61; dir. pers. Clay Adams Inc., N.Y.C., 1961-63; asst. dir. pers. Montefiore Hosp. and Med. Ctr., N.Y.C., 1963-65; dir. pers. Hosp. for Joint Diseases and Med. Ctr., N.Y.C., 1965-67; sr. cons. Orgn. Resources Counselors Inc., N.Y.C., 1967-76; pres. Applied Leadership Tech. Inc., Bloomfield, N.J., 1976-86, The Bassett Cons. Group Inc., Thornwood, N.Y., 1986—. Adj. prof. NYU, 1978—, N.Y. Med. Coll., 1992, Fairleigh Dickenson U., Teaneck, N.J., 1964-86; instr. Helene Fuld Sch. for RN's, N.Y.C., 1966-67. Author: Achieving Excellence, 1986; producer & presenter audio & video tape tng. albums; contbr. articles to profl. jours. Pres., v.p. Mt. Pleasant Bd. Edn., Thornwood, N.Y., 1973-76, 81-87; docent Am. Mus. Natural History. With U.S. Army, 1953-55. Mem. Soc. Profl. Mgmt. Cons. (bd. dirs., v.p.), Inst. Mgmt. Cons. (cert. mgmt. cons.), Am. Soc. for Tng. and Devel., Am. Hosp. Assn., Am. Arbitration Assn., Nat. Speakers Assn., Masons. Avocations: clock making, baking, beekeeping, skiing, orchid growing. Home and Office: The Bassett Cons Group Inc 1 Ilana Ln Thornwood NY 10594-2001

BASSETT, LESLIE RAYMOND, composer, educator; b. Hanford, Calif., Jan. 22, 1923; s. Archibald Leslie and Vera (Starr) B.; m. Anita Elizabeth Denniston, Aug. 21, 1949; children— Wendy Lynn (Mrs. Lee Bratton), Noel Leslie, Ralph (dec.). BA in Music, Fresno State Coll., 1947; M.Music in Composition, U. Mich., 1949, A.Mus.D., 1956; student, Ecole Normale de Musique, Paris, France, 1950-51. Tchr. music pub. schs., Fresno, 1951-52; mem. faculty U. Mich., 1952—, prof. music, 1965—. Albert A. Stanley disting univ. prof., 1977—, chmn. composition dept., 1970, Henry Russel lectr., 1984, emeritus, 1992. Guest composer Berkshire Music Center, Tanglewood, Mass., 1973 Served with AUS, 1942- 46. Fulbright fellow, 1950-51; recipient Rome prize Am. Acad. in Rome, 1961-63; grantee Soc. Pub. Am. Music, 1960, Nat. Inst. Arts and Letters, 1964, Nat. Council Arts, 1966; Guggenheim fellow, 1973-74, 80-81; recipient Pulitzer prize in music for Variations for Orch., 1966; citation U. Mich. regents, 1966; Walter Naumburg Found. rec. award for Sextet, 1974; Disting. Alumnus award Calif. State U., Fresno, 1978; Disting. Artist award Mich. Council Arts, 1981; Citation of Merit, U. Mich. Sch. Music Alumni, 1980 Mem. Am. Composers Alliance, Mich. Soc. Fellows, Am. Acad. of Arts and Letters, Pi Kappa Lambda, Phi Kappa Phi, Phi Mu Alpha. Methodist.

BASSETT, PETER Q., lawyer; b. Buenos Aires; s. John Jewett and Helen (Gibbs) B.; m. Wendy O. Bassett, Sept. 2, 1972; children: Elisabeth E., Laura G. AB, Princeton U., 1971; JD, George Washington U., 1975. Assoc. Alston, Miller & Gaines, Atlanta, 1975-81; ptnr., litig. Alston & Bird LLP, Atlanta, 1981—. Mem. Ga. Bar Assn., Atlanta Bar Assn. Avocation: motorcycles. Office: Alston & Bird LLP One Atlantic Ctr 1201 W Peachtree St NW Ste 4200 Atlanta GA 30309-3449 Office Phone: 404-881-7343. Business E-Mail: pbassett@alston.com.

BASSETT, ROBERT ANDREWS, lawyer; b. Pitts., Dec. 7, 1946; s. Ralph Harris and Mary (Andrews) B.; m. Victoria Ann Panettiere, June 15, 1969; children: Robert Anthony, Christopher James. Student, San Diego State U., 1964-65; BS in Engring., U.S. Mil. Acad., 1969; postgrad., MIT, 1974-75; JD, Quinnipiac Sch. Law, 1991. Bar: Conn. 1991. Commd. 2d lt. U.S. Army, 1969, advanced through grades to capt., 1971; assigned to Air Def. Arty., El Paso, Tex., 1969, Ansbach, Germany, 1969-72, Kunsan and Osan, Republic of Korea, 1972-73, Stewart AFB, N.Y., 1973-74; resigned, 1974; mktg. mgr., product mgr. Linde divsn. Union Carbide Corp., N.Y.C., 1975-82, bus. mgr. Danbury, Conn., 1982-92; corp. counsel, asst. sec. Praxair, Inc., Danbury, 1992—. Mem. proxy fees adv. com. N.Y. Stock Exch., 1995. Contbr. articles on corp. governance to law jours. Chmn. goals com. Newtown (Conn.) Bd. Edn., 1986; chmn. music devel. adv. com. C.H. Booth Pub. Libr., Newtown, 1998—. Mem.: Am. Soc. Corp. Secs. (dir., mem. exec. com., corp. practices com. 1993—, chmn. publs. subcom. 1994—). Home: 10 Monitor Hill Rd Newtown CT 06470-2243 Office: Praxair Inc 39 Old Ridgebury Rd Ste M-1 Danbury CT 06810-5103 E-mail: bob_bassett@praxair.com.

BASSETT, TINA, communications executive; b. Detroit; m. Leland Kinsey Bassett; children: Joshua, Robert. Student, U. Mich., 1974, 76-78, 81, Wayne State U., 1979-80. Advt. dir. Greenfield's Restaurant, Mich. and Ohio, 1972-73; dir. advt. and pub. rels. Kresco, Inc., Detroit, 1973-74; pub's. rep. The Detroiter mag., 1974-75; pub. rels. dir. Detroit Bicentennial Commn., 1975-77; prin. Leland K. Bassett & Assocs., Detroit, 1976-86; intermediate job devel. specialist Detroit Coun. of the Arts, 1977; project dir. Detroit image campaign dept. pub. info. City of Detroit, 1975, spl. events dir., 1978, dep. dir. dept. pub. info., 1978-83, dir. dept. pub. info., 1983-86; pres., prin. Bassett & Bassett, Inc., Detroit, 1986—. Publicity chmn. Under the Stars IV, V, VI, VII, VIII, IX and X, Benefit Balls, Detroit Inst. of Arts Founders Soc., 1983-88, Detroit Inst. of Arts Founders Centennial Ball, 1985, publicity chmn. Mich. Opera Theater, Opera Ball, 1987; program lectr. Wayne County Close-Up Program, 1984; mem. ctrl. planning com. Am. Assn. Mus.; mem. Founders Soc., Detroit Inst. Arts, 1988—; mem., publicity chair Grand Prix Ball, 1989; co-chair, prodr. Mus. Hall Ctr. for Performing Arts; bd. dirs. arts coun. Detroit Inst. Arts, 1996, bd. dirs. cinema arts coun., 1996—; bd. dirs. Weizman Inst. Sci., 1996-97. Named Outstanding Woman in Agy. Top Mgmt., Detroit chpt. Am. Women in Radio and TV, 1989, one of Most Powerful Women in Mich., CORP Mag., 2002. Mem. AIA (hon., pub. dir. 1990-91, Richard Upjohn fellowship 1991), Detroit Hist. Soc., Internat. Women's Forum, Music Hall Assn., Pub. Rels. Soc. Am. (Advt. Woman of Yr. 1989), Woman's Advt. Club Detroit, Cinematic Arts Coun., DIA (bd. dirs. 1996-99). Home: 30751 Cedar Creek Dr Farmington Hills MI 48336-4989 Address: Bassett & Bassett 1502 Randolph St Ste 200 Detroit MI 48226-2295 Office Phone: 313-965-3010.

BASSETT, WILLIAM, JR., regional analyst; b. St. Louis, July 4, 1956; s. William Bassett and Lois Mae (Vincent) Valentine, Edgar Laurence Valentine (Stepfather). BA, Ctrl. Mo. State U., 1983; MA, Tchrs. Coll. Columbia U., 1988; diploma, U. Dijon, France, 1982. Math, sci. tchr. US Peace Corps, Moabi, Gabon, 1983—85; peace corps fellow NYC Bd. of Edn. and Tchrs. Coll., Columbia U., 1986—88; cartographer Def. Mapping Agy. Dept. of Def., Bethesda, Md., 1988—92; database mgr. Def. Mapping Agy., Nat. Imagery and Mapping Agy., 1992—2000; regional analyst NIMA Nat. Geospatial-Intelligence Agy., Washington, 2000; staff officer Pentagon, Arlington, Va., 2003—04. *In 2000, successfully founded and implemented a martial arts program in Washington, DC church, which helps students clarify the courage and self-denial inherent in turning the other cheek when it is not the obvious option. Through teachings and community outreach, emphasizes the true focus of the martial artist — to obtain victory without combat and to seek justice through the resolution of conflict.* Sgt. USMC, 1974—78, US., Republic of Philippines. Recipient Letter of Appreciation, Def. Mapping Agency, 1990, 1991, 1992, Spl. Act award, Def. Mapping Agency, NIMA, 1993, 1996, 1997, 1998, 1999, 2000, Quality Improvement award, Def. Mapping Agency, 1994, Editor's Choice award, Nat. Libr. Poetry, 1995, Tradecraft award - For Excellence in Current Intelligence, Nat. Geospatial Intelligence Agy., 2004, Nat. Intelligence Meritorious Unit Citation, Nat. Fgn. Intelligence Cmty., 2003, Brick award For Outstanding Svc. and Dedication, Alliance of the Guardian Angels, 2001, 2002, Performance award, Dept. Def., 1991, 1992, 1993, 1994. Mem.: Assn. Symbolic Logic, Mensa, Internat. High IQ Soc., Kappa Delta Pi, Alpha Mu Gamma, Phi Theta Kappa. Avocations: martial arts, reading. Home: 1131 University Blvd West #515A Silver Spring MD 20902 Personal E-mail: lefty21@earthlink.net.

BASSETT, WILLIAM AKERS, retired geologist, educator; b. Bklyn., Aug. 3, 1931; s. Preston Rogers and Jeanne Reed (Mordorf) B.; m. Jane Ann Kermes, Sept. 8, 1962; children: Kari Nicalo, Jeffrey Kermes, Penelope North. BA, Amherst Coll., 1954; MA, Columbia U., 1956, PhD, 1959. Research assoc. Brookhaven Nat. Lab., 1960-61; Asst. prof. U. Rochester, NY, 1961-65, asso. prof., 1965-69, prof. geology, 1969-77, Cornell U., Ithaca, NY, 1978—99, ret., 1999. Vis. prof. Brigham Young U., 1967-68; Crosby vis. prof. MIT, 1974 Research, publs. on the devel. of techniques for investigation of properties of minerals at pressures and temperatures within the earth's interior Recipient Bridgman award Internat. Assn. for Rsch. at High Pressure and Temperature, 1997; NSF grantee; Guggenheim fellow, 1985. Fellow Geol. Soc. Am., Mineral. Soc. Am. (Roebling medal 1994, Bridgman award 1997), Am. Geophys. Union, AAAS; mem. Sigma Xi (pres. Rochester chpt. 1977-78). Home: 765 Bostwick Rd Ithaca NY 14850-9310 Office Phone: 607-272-5387. E-mail: bassett@geology.cornell.edu.

BASSETT, WOODSON WILLIAM, JR., lawyer; b. Okmulgee, Okla., Nov. 7, 1926; s. Woodson William and Bee Irene (Knerr) B.; m. Marynm Shaw, Dec. 16, 1950; children: Woodson William III, Beverly M., Tod Corbett. JD, U. Ark., 1949. Bar: Ark. 1949. Employed in New Orleans and Monroe, La., 1949-51; claims examiner Employers Group Ins. Cos., 1949-51; mgr. Light Adjustment Co., 1951-56; v.p. legal dept. Preferred Ins. Cos., 1957-62; sr. partner Bassett Law Firm, 1962—. Spl. chief justice Ark. Supreme Ct., 1991—; mem. Ark. Bd. Law Examiners Mem. editorial staff: Ark. Law Review, 9. Pres. Sherman Lollar Boys Baseball League, 1962; v.p. Babe Ruth Baseball Assn., 1968; chmn. bd. dirs. Fayetteville Public Library, 1975-79. Served with AUS, 1950-51. Fellow Am. Coll. Trial Lawyers; mem. ABA, Ark. Bar Assn., Washington County Bar Assn. (pres. 1973-74), Am. Bd. Trial Advs., Delta Theta Phi, Kappa Sigma. Home: 2210 E Manor Dr Fayetteville AR 72701-2640 Office: Bassett Law Firm 221 N College Ave Fayetteville AR 72701-4238 Business E-Mail: b.bassett@bassettlawfirm.com.

BASSI, SUZANNE HOWARD, retired secondary school educator, volunteer; b. Santa Ana, Calif., Feb. 26, 1945; d. David Gould and Marian (Matthews) H.; Roger Joseph Bassi, Aug. 25, 1973; children: Carrie, Steven, Gregory. BA, Rosary Coll., River Forest, Ill., 1966; MA in Teaching, U. Ill., Champaign, 1973. Tchr. Resurrection HS, Chgo., 1966-67, Proviso Twp. HS, Hillside, Ill., 1967-76; home day care operator Palatine, Ill., 1980-84; mem. bd. Palatine Elem. Sch. Dist. # 15, 1987-95. Rep. candidate for state rep. dist. 54, Ill., 1996, 98, state rep., 54th Dist., 1998—; vice chmn. Ed-Red, Park Ridge, Ill., 1993, chmn., 1994-96; legis. chmn. Ill . Assn. of Sch. Bds., North Cook divsn., Lombard, Ill., 1994-96. Named Those Who Excel, Ill. State Bd. Edn., 1992. Mem. LWV (former bd. dirs., legis. chair), Palatine Rep. Women's Orgn. Republican. Roman Catholic. Home: 2509 Honeysuckle Ln Rolling Meadows IL 60008

BASSIN, GILBERT SHELDON, manufacturing executive, engineer; b. NYC, June 7, 1932; m. Doreen Bassin; children: Pamela, Elisabeth, William. BME, NYU, New York, NY, 1953. Cert. Professional Engineer, NY, 1957. Engr. Cornel Dubilier Electric Co, Cambridge, Mass., 1953—56; chief engr. Litton Industries-Components Div, Mt Vernon, NY, 1956—61; pres., owner

Bassin Tech. Sls. Co, Mamaroneck, NY, 1961—, Logicomp Electronics Inc, Mamaroneck, NY, 1967—, Pres:Air:Trol Corp, Mamaroneck, NY, 1977—. Mem. bd. of trustees Neuberger Mus. of Art, Purchase, NY, 1994—. Recipient Pi Tau Sigma, Hon. Engring. Frat., 1952. Mem.: ASME. Achievements include patents for Fluid Actuated Control-1988,Control Housing-1993, Bellows Switch Actuator-1999, Bellow Actuator-2000. Avocations: boating, art collecting. E-mail: presair@aol.com, dorbert@aol.com.

BASSIN, JULES, foreign service officer; b. N.Y.C., Apr. 16, 1914; s. Abe and Bessie (Brooks) B.; m. Beatrice M. Kellner, Dec. 25, 1938; children: Arthur Jay, Nelson Jay. BS, CCNY, 1936; JD, N.Y.U., 1938; student, Criminal Investigation Sch., U.S. Army, 1943, Security Intelligence Sch., 1944, Mil. Govt. Sch., U. Va., 1944, Far East Civil Affairs, Harvard, 1945; grad., Armed Forces Staff Coll., 1960. Bar: N.Y. bar 1939. Dir. law div. Gen. Hdqrs., Supreme Comdr. Allied Powers, Tokyo, Japan, 1945-51; legal attache Am. embassy, Tokyo, 1951-56; also spl. asst. to ambassador for politico-mil. affairs; spl. asst. to ambassador for mut. security affairs Am. Embassy, Karachi, 1956-59; State Dept. faculty adviser Armed Forces Staff Coll., Norfolk, Va., 1960-62; chief titles and rank br. Dept. State, 1962-63, chief functional assignments br., 1963-65, dir. functional personnel program, 1965-67, spl. asst. to dep. undersec. state for adminstrn., 1967-69, exec. sec. Bd. Fgn. Service, 1967-69; dep. rep. of U.S. to European office UN and other internat. orgns.; also dep. chief U.S. mission with personal rank of minister, Geneva, Switzerland, 1969-74; cons. on refugee and migration affairs Dept. State, 1974—; cons. USIA, 1975-76. Served from 2d lt. to col., Judge Adv. Gen. Corps. AUS, 1942-46; col. Res. Mem. Am. Fgn. Service Assn. Clubs: American Internat. (Geneva) (exec. com.). Home: 2891 Audubon Ter NW Washington DC 20008-2309

BASSINGTHWAIGHTE, JAMES BUCKLIN, physiologist, educator, medical researcher; b. Toronto, Sept. 10, 1929; s. Ewart MacQuarrie and Velma Emeline B.; m. Joan Elizabeth Graham, June 18, 1955; children: Elizabeth Anne, Mary, Alan, Sarah, Rebecca. BA, U. Toronto, 1951, MD, 1955; postgrad., Med. Sch. London, 1957-58; PhD, Mayo Grad. Sch. Medicine U. Minn., 1964. Intern Toronto Gen. Hosp., 1955-56; physician Internat. Nickel Co., Sudbury and Matheson, Ont., 1956-57; house physician Hammersmith Hosp., London; postgrad. Med. Sch. London, 1957-58; teaching asst. physiology U. Minn., Mpls., 1961-62; fellow Mayo Grad. Sch. Medicine, Rochester, Minn., 1958-64, instr., 1964-67, asst. prof., 1967-69, assoc. prof., 1969-72; vis. prof. Pharmacology Inst., U. Bern, Switzerland, 1970-71; asso. prof. bioengring. U. Minn., 1972-75; prof. physiology Mayo Grad. Sch. Medicine, 1973-75, prof. medicine, 1975; prof. bioengring., radiology and biomath U. Wash., Seattle, 1975—; dir. Ctr. for Bioengring., 1975-80; vis. prof. medicine and physiology McGill U., 1979-81; affiliate prof. physiology Limburg U., Maastricht, The Netherlands, 1990—. Mem. study sect. NIH, 1970-74, 80-83, chmn., 2004; chmn. Biotech. Resources Adv. Com., 1977-79, chmn. 1st Gordon Rsch. Conf. on Water and Solute Transport in Microvasculature, 1976; chmn. workshop on metabolic imaging Nat. Heart, Lung and Blood Inst., 1985; bd. dirs. Nat. Space Biomed. Rsch. Inst., NASA, 2002—; adv. bd. mem. Burroughs Wellcome Fund, 2004-; Lewellen-Thomas lectr., U. Toronto, 1991; Coulter lectr. U. N.C., 1995; Oxford lectr. Internat. Soc. Magnetic Resonance Medicine, 1996. Author: (with L.S. Liebovitch and B.J. West) Fractal Physiology, 1994; contbr. over 250 articles to profl. publs. Recipient NIH Rsch. Career Devel. award, 1964-74, Louis and Artur Lucian award McGill U., 1979, Witzig award Cardiovasc. Sys. Dyamics Soc., 1982, Faculty Achievement award for outstanding rsch. U. Wash. Coll. Engring., 1993; Edmund Hustinx chair Maastricht U., 1999. Mem. AAAS, Am. Heart Assn. (coun. on circulation 1976—), Biophys. Soc. (assoc. editor Biophys. Jour. 1980-83), Biomed. Engring. Soc. (dir. 1971-74, pres. 1977-78, Alza award 1986, editor-in-chief Annals of Biomedical Engring. 1993—, Disting. Svc. award 1999), Microcirculatory Soc. (mem. coun. 1975-78, 80-83, pres. 1990-91, Landis award 1995), Nat. Acad. Engring., Am. Physiol. Soc. (mem. circulation group, editorial bd. 1972-76, 79-83, mem. edn. com.), Internat. Union Physiol. Scis. (U.S.A. nat. com. 1978-86, U.S. del. to assembly 1980, 83, 86, chmn. 1983-86, chmn. Commn. on Bioengring. and Clin. Physiology 1986-97, chmn. satellite to 30th Congress on Endothelial Transport 1986, co-chmn. satellite on microvascular networks 1989, chmn. satellite on Physiome Project 1997). Achievements include research in cardiovascular physiology and bioengineering, biomathematics and computer simulation with emphasis on ion and substrate exchange in heart, fractals in physiology, integrative biology and originator of the Physiome Project. Home: 3150 E Laurelhurst Dr NE Seattle WA 98105-5333 Office: U Wash Dept Bioengring PO Box 35-7962 Seattle WA 98195-7962 Office Phone: 206-685-2005. Business E-Mail: jbbe@u.washington.edu.

BASSIS, MICHAEL STEVEN, academic administrator; b. N.Y.C., Sept. 8, 1944; s. Lewis and Barbara (Fay) B.; m. Mary Suzanne Wilson, Dec. 27, 1977; children: Anne Elizabeth, Christina, Jessica, Nicholas. BA with honors, Brown U., 1967; MA, U. Chgo., 1968, PhD, 1974. Asst. dir. acad. potential project Brown U., 1966-67; rsch. assoc. Ctr. for the Study of the Acts of Man U. Pa., 1968; instr., asst. prof.-assoc. prof. dept. sociology and anthropology U. R.I., 1971-81, acting asst. dean Coll. Arts and Scis., 1977-78; assoc. Harvard U. Grad. Sch. Edn., 1980-81; assoc. dean faculty U. Wis., Parkside, 1981-85, assoc. prof. sociology, 1981-86, interim asst. chancellor ednl. svcs., 1985-86; v.p. acad. affairs Ea. Conn. State U., 1986-89; exec. v.p., univ. provost Antioch U., Yellow Springs, Ohio, 1989-93; pres. Olivet (Mich.) Coll., 1993-98; dean, warden New Coll., U. South Fla., Sarasota, 1998—2001; president Westminster Coll. of Salt Lake City, 2002—. Presenter in field. Author (with W.R. Rosengren) The Social Organization of Nautical Education: The U.S., Great Britain and Spain, 1976, (with R.J. Gelles and A. Levine) Sociology: An Introduction, 4th edit., 1991, Social Problems, 1982; editor Teaching Sociology, 1982-85; contbr. articles to profl. jours. NIMH grantee, 1967-71, Exxon Edn. Found. grantee, N.Y.C., 1975, Fund for Improvement of Post-Secondary Edn. grantee, Washington, 1978. Mem. Am. Sociol. Assn. (undergrad. edn. sect., membership com. 1979-81, coun. 1980, 82, 86-89, teaching resources group 1984-86, publs. com. 1985, chair 1987-88), Am. Assn. Higher Edn., Nat. Soc. Experiential Edn. Office: Office of the President Westminster College 1840 South 1300 East Salt Lake City UT 84105 E-mail: mbassis@westminstercollege.edu.

BASSIST, DONALD HERBERT, retired academic administrator; b. Dallas, Oct. 28, 1923; s. Ellis and Adele (Gutz) B.; m. Norma Dale Andersen, Oct. 14, 1950; children: Matthew Perry, Bradford Beaumont. AB, Harvard U., 1948; MBA, Portland State U., 1975; grad., U.S. Army Command and Gen. Staff Coll., 1967. Pres. Bassist Coll., Portland, Oreg., 1963-98; ret. Chmn. ednl. adv. bd. pvt. vocat. schs., Salem, Oreg., 1972-78; active Oreg. Ednl. Coordinating Coun., 1970-73. Writer, dir. (film) Fashion: The Career of Challenge, 1969 (N.Y. Internat. Bronze award). Lt. A.C., U.S. Army, 1943-46; 14th AF, 1944, lt. col. Corps of Engrs., ret., 1972. Mem. Nat. Assn. Scholars, Japanese Garden Soc. (bd. dirs. 1988-93), Portland Advt. Fedn. (bd. dirs. 1969-72). Avocations: Japanese gardening, travel.

BASSLER, BONNIE, molecular biologist; BS, U. Calif., Davis, 1984; PhD, Johns Hopkins U., 1990. Rsch. scientist Agouron Inst., La Jolla, Calif., 1993—94; faculty dept. molecular biology Princeton U., 1994—96, faculty environ. inst., 1996—. Contbr. articles to profl. jours. Recipient Inventor of the Yr., New York Intellectual Property Law Assn., 2004; fellow Rsch. fellow, Agouron Inst., 1990—93, MacArthur Found. fellow, 2002. Achievements include research in quorum sensing. Office: Princeton U 329 Lewis Thomas Lab Princeton NJ 08544*

BASSLER, ROBERT COVEY, artist, educator; b. N.Y.C., Nov. 9, 1935; s. Robert Stein and Joan (Covey) B.; m. Linda Marie Allen, June 14, 1964. BA, Bard Coll., 1957; MFA, U. So. Calif., 1960. Instr. sculpture Occidental Coll., 1960-64; prof. sculpture Calif. State U., Northridge, 1964-97, prof. emeritus, 1998—. Artist in residence Calif. Inst. Tech., 1970-71; art film tour Arts Coun. Gt. Britain. Solo exhbns. include Comara Gallery, L.A., 1961, 63, Occidental Coll., L.A., 1961, 70, Calif. State U. Bakersfield, 1964, L.A. Mcpl. Art Gallery, Barnsdall Park, 1965, 81, Calif. State U., Northridge, 1965, Santa Barbara (Calif.) Mus. Art, 1968, Molly Barnes Gallery, L.A., 1969, Baxter Art Gallery, Calif. Inst. Tech., 1971, Galerie La Demeure, Paris, 1972, Amerika-Haus, West Berlin, 1972, Wenger Gallery, L.A., 1988, Security Pacific Pla., L.A., 1989-90, Calif. State U., Northridge, 1997, Orlando Gallery, Sherman Oaks, Calif., 1997; exhibited in group shows at Jewish Mus., N.Y.C., Milw. Art Ctr., San Francisco Mus. of Art, Los Angeles County Mus. of Art, Pasadena Mus. of Art, Long Beach (Calif.) Mus. of Art, LaJolla (Calif.) Mus. of Art, San Francisco Mus. of Art, Newport Harbor Art Mus., Oakland Mus. of Art, Esther Bear Gallery, Santa Barbara, Houston Mus. of Art, Ackland Meml. Art Ctr., Chapel Hill, N.C., Mus. Fine Arts, St. Petersburg, Fla., Jacksonville (Fla.) Art Mus., Musée d'Art Moderne, Paris, Galerie La Demeure, Paris, Redfern Gallery, London, U.S. Embassy, London, Wenger Gallery, L.A., Calif. Inst. Tech., Amerika Haus, Berlin, Century City, Calif., Fine Arts Gallery, San Diego, Art Park, L.A., Design Ctr., L.A., Washington Sq., Washington, Fine Arts Bldg., L.A., Valerie Miller Gallery, Palm Desert, Calif., Tom Bradley Terminal, L.A. Internat. Airport, Finegood Art Gallery, West Hills, Calif., Pacific Design Ctr., L.A., L.A. Contemporary Exhibitions; represented in permanent collections including Atlantic Richfield Corp., Container Corp. Am., Quinn & Assocs., L.A., Security Pacific Nat. Bank, Carter Hawley Hale Stores Inc., Home Savs. & Loan, The Ahmanson Collection, Chgo. Convention Ctr., Arts Coun. of Gt. Britain, U. So. Calif., Bard Coll., N.Y., Kirk O' The Valley, Reseda, Calif., Calif. State U., Northridge. With AUS, 1959-62. Recipient Pres.'s Creativity award Calif. State U., Northridge, 1978, Meritorious Performance award, 1989, 96. Achievements include developing technique for casting clear polyester resin. Address: 8329 Melvin Ave Northridge CA 91324-4132 E-mail: robert.c.bassler@csun.edu. *My current work explores visual phenomena created by light and structural juxtapositions and their resulting effects upon one's concept of reality. Most recently painted interpretations of our planet's atmospheric patterns have been incorporated as provocative elements of beauty, fragility, order and chaos.*

BASSOUL, SELIM A., food products executive; MBA, Northwestern U. From pres. Southbend to pres., CEO Middleby Corp., Elgin, Ill., 1996—2001, pres., 2001—, CEO, 2001—; pres. Middleby Marshall Inc., 2001—, CEO, 2001—. Office: Middleby Corp 1400 Toastmaster Dr Elgin IL 60120

BASSUK, ELLEN LINDA, psychiatrist; b. N.Y.C., Feb. 8, 1945; d. Irving and Molly (Pakarow) B.; children: Daniel, Sarah. BA, Brandeis U., 1964; MD, Tufts U., 1968; Dr.P.S. (hon.), Northeastern U., 1993. Diplomate Am. Bd. Psychiatry. Intern Mt. Auburn Hosp., Cambridge, Mass., 1968-69; resident psychiatry Univ. Hosp., Boston, 1969-70, Boston State Hosp., Boston, 1970-71, Beth Israel Hosp., Boston, 1971-73, dir. psychiat. emergency svcs., 1974-82; fellow Bunting Inst., Cambridge, Mass., 1982-84; assoc. prof. psychiatry Harvard Med. Sch., Boston, 1983—. Founder, pres. Nat. Ctr. on Family Homelessness, Newton, Mass., 1988—; mem. Com. on Health Care of Homeless Persons Inst. of Medicine, Washington, 1986-88. Editor: The Practitioners Guide to Psychoactive Drugs, 1977, 83, 91, 97; editor-in-chief Am. Jour. Orthopsychiatry, 1994-98; contbr. numerous articles to profl. jours. Fellow Am. Psychiat. Assn.; mem. Mass. Psychiat. Soc. Office: Nat Ctr Family Homelessness 181 Wells Ave Newton MA 02459-3332 Home: 70 Montvale Rd Newton MA 02459 Office Phone: 617-964-3834 14. E-mail: ellen.bassuk@familyhomelessness.org.

BAST, ROBERT CLINTON, JR., medical researcher; b. Washington, Dec. 8, 1943; s. Robert Clinton and Ann Christine (Borland) B.; m. Blanche Amy Simpson, Oct. 21, 1972; 1 child, Elizabeth Simpson Bast. BA cum laude, Wesleyan U., Middletown, Conn., 1965; MD magna cum laude, Harvard U., 1971. Diplomate Am. Bd. Internal Medicine, Am. Bd. Med. Oncology, Am. Bd. Hematology. Predoctoral fellow dept. pathology Mass. Gen. Hosp., Boston, 1967-69; intern Johns Hopkins Hosp., Balt., 1971-72; rsch. assoc. biology br. Nat. Cancer Inst., NIH, Bethesda, Md., 1972-75; asst. resident Peter Bent Brigham Hosp., Boston, 1975-76; fellow med. oncology Sidney Farber Cancer Inst., Boston, 1976-77; asst. prof. medicine Harvard U. Med. Sch., Boston, 1977-83, assoc. prof., 1983-84; prof. Duke U. Med. Ctr., Durham, N.C., 1984-92, Wellcome clin. prof. medicine in honor of R. Wayne Rundles, 1992-94, co-dir. div. hematology-oncology, 1984-94; dir. clin. research programs Duke U. Comprehensive Cancer Ctr., Durham, 1984-87; dir. Harry Carothers Wiess chair cancer rsch. U. Tex. M.D. Anderson Cancer Ctr., 1994—2004, Harry Carothers Wiess disting. Univ. chair, 2004—, head divsn. med., 1994-2000, v.p. translational rsch., 2000—; dir. divsn. med. oncology dept. medicine U. Tex. Health Sci. Ctr., Houston, 1994-2000. Hosp. appointments include asst. in medicine Peter Bent Brigham Hosp., 1976-77; jr. assoc. in medicine Brigham and Women's Hosp., 1977-82; cons. oncologist Boston Hosp. Women, 1978-80; physician Duke U. Med. Ctr., 1984-94; internist M.D. Anderson Cancer Ctr., 1994—; mem. biol. response modifiers decision network com. Nat. Cancer Inst., 1984-87, exptl. immunology study sect., 1983-84, 90-92; mem. grant rev. com. Leukemia Soc. Am., 1985-87, adv. com. oncologic drugs FDA, 1985-89, chmn. 1988-89; bd. dirs. Cancer and Leukemia Group B., 1986-88, Am. Council Transplantation, 1985-87; mem. grant rev. com. Am. Cancer Soc., 1987, com. on biomechanics study sect., 2003--; numerous other coms.; Edward G. Waters Meml. lectr., 1987; John Ohtani Meml. lectr., 1991; D. Nelson Henderson lectr., 1991; Stolte Meml. lectr., 1992; Arnold O. Beckman Disting. Lectureship, 1993; Robert C. Knapp lectr., 1996; Alan Dembo Meml. Keynote lectr., 1997, George Willbanks lectr., 2000. Contbr. numerous articles on tumor immunology, immunodiagnosis and immunotherapy of cancer and cellular immunology to profl. jours. Served as surgeon USPHS, 1972-75. Named Disting. Spkr., Chao Family Comprehensive Cancer Ctr. Symposium, U. Calif., Irvine, 2002; recipient Dominus award, 1984, Robert C. Knapp award, 1990, Recognition Outstanding Leadership and Advocacy award, Nat. Coalition for Cancer Rsch., 1995, Smith Kline Beecham Clin. Labs. award, Clin. Ligand Soc., 1996, award of Achievement, Ptnrs. in Courage, ACS, 1998, Abbott award, Internat. Soc. Oncodevelopmental Biology and Markers, 2001, ISOBM Abbott award, 2001, Highly Cited Investigator award, Inst. Sci. Info., 2003; grantee, Nat. Cancer Inst., NIH, HHS, 1978—; scholar, Leukemia Soc. Am., 1978—83. Fellow: AAAS, ACP; mem.: Am. Clin. and Climatological Assn., Am. Soc. Hematology, Soc. Biol. Therapy (bd. dirs. 1984—86), Internat. Soc. Immunopharmacology, Am. Soc. Clin. Investigation, Am. Fedn. Clin. Rsch., Am. Soc. Clin. Oncology, Assn. Am. Physicians, Am. Assn. Immunologists, Am. Assn. Cancer Rsch., Am. Soc. Microbiology, The Reticuloendothelial Soc., Internat. Gynecol. Cancer Soc. (coun. 1997—2002), Soc. Gynecol. Oncology (assoc.; trustee Helene Harris Meml. trust). Achievements include development of monoclonal antibodies to react with human ovarian cancer, leading to CA125 blood test; techniques for selective elimination of tumor cells from human bone marrow; identification of molecular changes associated with malignant transformation of ovarian epithelium. Office: U Tex MD Anderson Cancer Ctr 1515 Holcombe Blvd # 355 Houston TX 77030-4009 Office Phone: 713-792-7743. Business E-Mail: rbast@mdanderson.org.

BASTIAANSE, GERARD C., lawyer; b. Holyoke, Mass., Oct. 21, 1935; s. Gerard C. and Margaret (Lally) B.; m. Paula E. Paliska, June 1, 1963; children: Elizabeth, Gerard. BSBA, Boston U., 1960; JD, U. Va., 1964. Bar: Mass. 1964, Calif. 1970. Assoc. Nutter, McClennen & Fish, Boston, 1964-65; counsel Campbell Soup Co., Camden, N.J., 1965-67; gen. counsel A&W Internat. (United Fruit Co.), Santa Monica, Calif., 1968-70; ptnr. Kindel & Anderson, Los Angeles, 1970—. Mem. ABA, Calif. Bar Assn., Mass. Bar Assn., Japan Am. Soc., Asia Soc., World Trade Ctr. Assn. Clubs: California (Los Angeles); Big Canyon Country (Newport Beach, Calif.). Home: 2 San Sebastian Newport Beach CA 92660-6828 Office: Kindel & Anderson 2030 Main St Ste 1300 Irvine CA 92614-7220

BASTIAN, DONALD NOEL, retired bishop; b. Estevan, Sask., Can., Dec. 25, 1925; s. Josiah and Esther Jane (Millington) B.; m. Kathleen Grace Swallow, Dec. 20, 1947; children: Carolyn Dawn, Donald Gregory, Robert Wilfrid, John David. BA, Greenville Coll., 1953, DST (hon.), 1974; BD, Asbury Theol. Sem., 1956, DD (hon.), 1991, Seattle Pacific U., 1965; DHL (hon.), Roberts Wesleyan Coll., 1990. Ordained to ministry Free Meth. Ch. N.Am., 1954; pastor chs. Lexington, Ky., 1953-56, New Westminster, B.C., Can., 1956-61; pastor College Free Meth. Ch., Greenville, Ill., 1961-74; bishop Free Meth. Ch. N.Am., Toronto, Ont., Can., 1974-90, mem. bd. adminstrn., 1964-90, exec. editor Light and Life mag., 1974-84, chmn. editorial adv. com. Light and Life mag., 1980-86; bishop Free Meth. Ch. in Can., 1990-93. Author: The Mature Church Member, 1960, Along the Way, 1974, Belonging, 1974; editor: The Joy of Christian Fathering: Five First Person Accounts, 1979, Counterfeit: The Lie of Living Together Unmarried, 1988. Recipient Disting. Svc. award Asbury Theol. Sem., 1974; Presdl. award Greenville Coll., 1972; Donald N. and Kathleen G. Bastian chair Wesley studies established at Tyndale Sem., Toronto, 2000. Mem. Can. Holiness Fedn. (pres. 1977, 78), Christian Holiness Assn. (v.p. 1977-78), Evang. Fellowship of Can. (pres. 1989-91). Mem. Free Methodist Ch. Home: 63 Adirondack Cres Brampton ON Canada L6R 1E5 Personal E-mail: dnbasti@aol.com. *I live by the conviction that, however durable it may seem, evil is by nature unstable. Righteousness, by contrast, gives stability to life in the long pull.*

BASTIAN, EDWARD H., air transportation executive; BBA, Bonaventure U. CPA. Strategic planning ptnr. Price Waterhouse, NY, ptnr., audit practice; v.p., fin., controller Frito Lay Internat.; v.p., bus. process re-engring. for Frito Lay Pepsico; v.p., finance Delta Air Lines, Inc., Atlanta, 1998—2000, sr. v.p., finance, controller, 2000—05, exec. v.p., chief fin. officer, 2005—. Office: Delta Air Line Inc PO Box 20706 Atlanta GA 30320-6001 Office Phone: 404-715-2600.*

BASTIANICH, LIDIA MATTICCHIO, chef, food service executive; b. Italy, 1947; Owner Buonavia Restaurant, Forest Hills, NY, 1972—81, Villa Secondo, Fresh Meadows, NY, 1979—81, Felidia Restaurant, NY, 1981—; co-owner Becco Restaurant, NY, 1993—, Lidia's Restaurant, Kansas City, Mo., 1998—; founder, pres. Esperienze Italiane Travel, 1996—. Founder, owner Lidia's Flavors of Italy, 1988—; host, chef Lidia's Italian Table, 1998—2001, Lidia's Italian Am. Kitchen, 2001—, Lidia's Family Table, PBS Series. Author: (montly syndicated column) on Italian food, (cookbooks) La Cucina di Lidia, 1990, Lidia's Italian Table, 1998, Lidia's Italian American Kitchen (and host of PBS series of same name), 2001, Lidia's Family Table, 2004. Established Lidia Matticchio Bastianich Found., 1999. Office: Felidia Restaurant 243 E 58th St New York NY 10022 Office Phone: 212-758-1479. Business E-Mail: info@lidiasitaly.com.

BASTRENTA, BRIGITTE ELISABETH, school administrator; b. Moutiers, Savoie, France, Jan. 7, 1952; came to U.S., 1979; d. Marcel Rinaldo and Jeanne Eulalie (Chaville) B.; m. Rudolph Andrew Walter, Dec. 27, 1979; children: Laurie Nicole Walter, Julian Thomas Walter. BA, U. Paul Valéry, Montpellier, France, 1973, MA, 1974. Tchr. French Marin Acad., San Rafael, Calif., 1980-83, Arrowsmith Acad., Berkeley, Calif., 1989-96, dir. admission and devel., 1996—2004; devel. assoc. Katherine Delman Burke Sch., San Francisco, 2004—. Tchr. French Diablo Valley Coll., Pleasant Hill, Calif., 1990-95; mem. WASC Accreditation Commn., 1998—. Editor (newsletter) Arrowsmith in Action, 1999—. Co-pres. East Bay French-Am. Sch. PTA, Berkeley, 1991-93; mem. Natural Resources Def. Coun. Mem. Amnesty Internat., Doctors Without Borders, So. Poverty Law Ctr., The Carter Ctr. Democrat. Avocations: swimming, skiing, hiking, travel, cooking. Home: 333 Scottsdale Rd Pleasant Hill CA 94523 Office: Katherine Delman Burke Sch 7070 Calif St San Francisco CA 94121

BATA, RUDOLPH ANDREW, JR., lawyer; b. Akron, Ohio, Jan. 9, 1947; s. Rudolph Andrew and Margaret Eleanor (Ellis) Bata; m. Genevieve Ruth Brannan, Aug. 25, 1968 (div. May 1985); 1 child, Seth Andrew; m. Linda Lee Waldo, Apr. 7, 1985; 1 child, Sarah Ariel. BS, So. Coll., Collegedale, Tenn., 1969; JD, Emory U., 1972. Bar: D.C. 1973, N.C. 1978, U.S. Dist. Ct. N.C. 1991, U.S. Ct. Appeals (4th cir.) 1991, U.S. Supreme Ct. 2004, cert.: Adminstrv. Office of Cts. (arbitrator, mediator). Assoc. ICC, Washington, 1972-73; in house counsel B.F. Saul Real Estate Investment Trust, Chevy Chase, Md., 1973-74; staff atty. Martha, Cafferky, Powers & Jordan, Washington, 1974-75; asst. corp. counsel Hardee's Food Systems, Inc., Rocky Mount, N.C., 1975-78; ptnr. Bata & Blomeley, Murphy, N.C., 1978-87, 88-90, Bata & Sumpter, Murphy, 1987-88; sole practice, 1990—. Bd. dirs. Cherokee County United Fund, Murphy, 1981—83. Mem. ABA, N.C. Bar Assn., D.C. Bar Assn., 30th Jud. Dist. Bar Assn., So. Soc. of Adventist Attys. (pres. 1984-85), Cherokee County C. of C. (bd. dirs. 1980-82). Avocations: golf, tennis, hiking. Office: 225 Valley River Ave Ste A Murphy NC 28906-3000 Office Phone: 828-837-8684. Personal E-mail: batalaw@yahoo.com.

BATAILLE, GRETCHEN, academic administrator; B of English, M of English Edn., Calif. Polytech. State U.; DA, Drake U. Chair dept. English Ariz. State U., assoc. dean acad. personnel, until 1994; provost U. Calif., Santa Barbara, 1994-97; provost, acad. v.p. Wash. State U., Pullman, 1997-2000; sr. v.p., v.p. acad. affairs U. NC Sys., Chapel Hill, 2000—; interim chancellor NC Sch. Arts, Winston-Salem, 2005—. Author: Living the Dream in Arizona: The Legacy of Martin Luther King, Jr., 1992, Native American Women: A Biographical Dictionary, 1994, Ethnic Studies in the United States, 1998, others. Office: U NC PO Box 2688 Chapel Hill NC 27515-2688 also: NC Sch Arts 1533 S Main St Winston Salem NC 27127-2188 Office Phone: 919-962-4614. Business E-Mail: bataille@northcarolina.edu.

BATALDEN, PAUL BENNETT, pediatrician, educator; b. Mpls., Dec. 4, 1941; s. Abner Bennett and Martha (Bjornstad) B.; m. LaVonne Marie Olson; children: Maren, Sonja. BA, Augsburg Coll., 1963; MD, BS, U. Minn., 1967. Diplomate Am. Bd. Pediatrics. Clin. assoc. Nat. Cancer Inst., Bethesda, Md., 1969; med. dir. Job Corps, Washington, 1970-72; dir. Community Health Svc., Rockville, Md., 1972-73; dir., Bur. Community Health Svc., Rockville, 1973-75; pediatrician Park Nicollet Med. Ctr., Mpls., 1975-86, quality assurance dir., 1976-84, chief oper. officer, 1984-86; v.p. med. care, head quality resource group Hosp. Corp. of Am., Nashville, 1986-94; Breech chmn. Dept. Health Care Quality Improvement Edn. and Rsch. Henry Ford Health Sci. Ctr., 1990—2000; prof. pediatrics and cmty. family medicine Dartmouth Med. Sch., prof., dir. Ctr. Healthcare Improvement Leadership Devel. Founding chmn., bd. dirs., sr. v.p. health profl. development Inst. for Healthcare Improvement; dir. preventive medicine residency DHMC; cons. Acct. COun. Grad. Med. Edn. Author: Quality Assurance in Ambulatory Care, 1980, Clinical Improvement Action Guide, 1998; contbr. articles on quality in healthcare and aspects of pediatric practice to profl. jours. Regent Augsburg Coll., Mpls., 1978-90. Recipient Guild of Honor, 1963, Pub. Svc. award Nat. Med. Assn., 1974, Disting. Alumnus award Augsburg Coll., 1984, Award of Honor, Am. Hosp. Assn., 1997, Codman award, 1998, Nemours Found. award for improving quality, 2002. Mem. Inst. of Medicine of NAS, Am. Acad. Pediatrics, Minn. Med. Assn., Tenn. Med. Assn., N.H. Med. Assn., Alpha Omega Alpha Office Phone: 603-650-6513.

BATALI, MARIO, chef; m. Susi Cahn; children: Benno, Leo. Student, Rutgers U., Le Cordon Bleu, London. Owner, chef Babbo Ristorante e Enoteca, N.Y.C., 1998—; co-owner, chef Lupa, N.Y.C.; owner Italian Wine Merchants, N.Y.C.; owner, chef Esca, N.Y.C., 2000—; co-owner, chef Otto Enoteca Pizzeria, N.Y.C., NY, 2003—. Challenger Iron Chef TV cooking series. Author: Simple Italian Food, 1998, Mario Batali Holiday Food, 2000, The Babbo Cookbook, 2002, Molto Italiano: Simple Italian Recipes for Cooking at Home, 2005; host Molto Mario, Food Network, Mario Batali's Italy. Named Man of Yr. in chef category, GQ Mag., 1999; recipient Best New Restaurant award for Babbo, James Beard Found., 1998, Best Chef: NYC award, 2002. Office: Babbo Ristorante e Enoteca 110 Waverly Pl New York NY 10011-9109*

BATAMACK, PATRICE THEODORE DESIRE, chemistry professor, researcher; b. Douala, Littoral, Cameroon, Nov. 1, 1962; s. Joseph Etote Robert and Philomene Claire (Ngo Batadjam) B.; m. Ndjee Aurélie, Apr. 25, 1998. Grad. in chem. engring., Poly. Inst. Loraine, Nancy, France, 1988; cert. in computer sci., Indsl. Computer Sci. Inst., Brest, France, 1989; PhD in Chemistry, U. Pierre et Marie Curie, Paris, 1991; MBA, Nat. Conservatory Arts & Craft, 2000; diploma for directing postgrad. works, U. Pierre et Marie

Curie, 1999. Postdoctoral fellow Loker Hydrocarbon Inst. U. So. Calif., L.A., 1992-94; lectr. chemistry U. Pierre et Marie Curie, 1994—2004. Vis. scholar Loker Hydrocarbon Inst., U. So. Calif., L.A., 2002—03, rsch. assoc., 2003—. Contbr. articles to profl. jours. Mem.: French Chem. Soc. (prize catalysis divsn. 1995), Am. Chem. Soc. Avocations: reading, meditation, sports. Office: Loker Hydrocarbon Rsch Inst USC Univ Pk Los Angeles CA 90089-1661 E-mail: pba@ccr.jussieu.fr.

BATAVIA, MITCHELL, physical therapist, educator; b. Bklyn., Nov. 8, 1959; s. Gabriel and Renée (Hyman) Batavia; m. Evgenia Yakovleva, Aug. 12, 2001; 1 child, Michael Andrew. BS, U. of Del., 1978—81; MA, Columbia U., 1986; PhD, N.Y. U, 1994—97. Lic. Physical Therapist N.Y. State, 1981. Staff phys. therapist Inst. for Rehab. Medicine, NY U. Med. Ctr., 1981—84; home care phys. therapist Vis. Nurse Svc. of NY, 1984—86; pediatric phys. therapist NY Foundling Hosp., 1986—91; phys. therapy cons. Terence Cardinal Cooke Health Care Ctr., N.Y.C., 1989—97; adj. lectr. Hunter Coll. Phys. Therapy Program, N.Y.C., 1992—93, 1996; asst. prof. of phys. therapy NYU, 1998—2004, assoc. prof. phys. therapy, 2004—. Manuscript reviewer Neurology Sect., Am. Phys. Therapy Assn., Alexandria, Va., 2000—; manuscript reviewer for book submissions Butterworth-Heinemann, Boston, 1999—2001. Author: (book) The Wheelchair Evaluation: A Practical Guide, Clinical Research for Health Professionals: A User Friendly Guide; contbr. articles to profl. jours. Vol., food distbr. Coalition for the Homeless, N.Y.C., 2002. Recipient NY U. Arch award, NY U., 1997; DeWitt Wallace Reader's Digest fellow, Inst. for Rehab. Medicine; NY U. Med. Ctr., 1978, Trainee for Phys. Therapy Clin. Rsch. in Doctoral Studies, Nat. Inst. for Disabilities Rsch. in Rehab., NY U., 1993—97, Robert Salant Post Doctoral fellow, Dept. of Phys. Therapy, NY U., The Inst. for Rehab., NY U. Med. Ctr., 1997—98, Rsch. Challenge fund, NY U., Sch. of Edn., 2000. Mem.: Neurology Sect. of the Am. Phys. Therapy Assn., Am. Phys. Therapy Assn. Achievements include constructed a functional rotation test to measure a person's rotation ability; construction of a mechanical stretch reflex model for teaching; construction of a tissue compliance meter for research. Avocation: music. Office: New York U 380 Second Ave 4th floor New York NY 10010 Office Phone: 212-998-9409. Business E-Mail: mitchell.batavia@nyu.edu.

BATCHELDER, ALICE M., federal judge; b. Wilmington, Del., Aug. 15, 1944; m. William G. Batchelder III; children: William G. IV, Elisabeth. BA, Ohio Wesleyan U., 1964; JD, Akron U., 1971; LLM, U. Va., 1988. Tchr. Plan Local Sch. Dist., Franklin County, Ohio, 1965-66, Jones Jr. High Sch., 1966-67, Buckeye High Sch., Medina County, 1967-68; assoc. Williams & Batchelder, Medina, Ohio, 1971-83; judge U.S. Bankruptcy Ct., Ohio, 1983-85, U.S. Dist. Ct. (no. dist.) Ohio, Cleve., 1985-91, U.S. Ct. of Appeals (6th cir.), Cleveland, 1991—. Editor-in-chief Univ. Akron Law Rev., 1971. Mem. ABA, Fed. Judge's Assn., Fed. Bar Assn., Medina County Bar Assn.

BATCHELDER, ANNE STUART, retired publishing executive, political organization worker; b. Lake Forest, Ill., Jan. 11, 1920; d. Robert Douglas and Harriet (McClure) Stuart; m. Clifton Brooks Batchelder, May 26, 1945; children: Edward, Anne Stuart, Mary Clifton, Lucia Brooks Student Lake Forest Coll., 1941-43. Clubmobile driver ARC, Eng., Belgium, France, Holland and Germany, 1943-45; pub., editor Douglas County Gazette, 1970-75, 79-90. Bd. dirs. Firstier Bank Omaha; dir., treas. U.S. Checkbook Com. Mem. Rep. Ctrl. Com. Nebr., 1955-62, 70-83, vice chmn. Ctrl. Com., 1959-64, chmn., 1975-79, mem. fin. com., 1957-64; chmn. women's sect. Douglas County Rep. Fin. Com., 1995, vice chmn. com., 1958-60; v.p. Omaha Woman's Rep. Club, 1957-58, pres., 1959-60; alt. del. Nat. Conv., 1956, 72, del., 1980, 84, 88; mem. Rep. Nat. Com. for Nebr., 1964-70; asst. chmn. Douglas County Rep. Ctrl. Com., 1971-74; 1st v.p. Nebr. Fedn. Rep. Women, 1971-72, pres., 1972-74; chmn. Nebr. Rep. Com., 1975-79; vice-chmn. Bldg. Fedn. Rep. Women, 1998—; mem. Nebr. State Bldg. Commn., 1979-83; Rep. candidate for lt. gov., 1974. Sr. v.p. Nebr. Founders Day, 1958; trustee Hastings Coll., 1977—; bd. dirs. YWCA, 1983-89, Omaha Libr. Found., 1991-2000, Libr. Found., 2000—; past trustee Brownell Hall, Vis. Nurse Assn.; past pres. Nebr. chpt. Freedoms Found. at Valley Forge; chmn. fin. George Bush for Pres., Nebr., 1987-88; apptd. Kennedy Ctr. Performing Arts, 1989, 94, Pres.' Adv. Com. on the Arts, 1990-92, Nat. Com. for the Performing Arts, 1992—; mem. Nebr. Rep. State Fin. Com., 1990, Nat. Fin. Com. Bush-Quayle, 1992; active Omaha Meth. Hosp. Found., Brownell-Talbot Sch. Found.; mem. Uta Halee Home for Girls, 1980—. Elected to Nebr. Rep. Hall of Fame, 1984; named Citizen of the Yr. Midlands Coun. Boy Scouts Am., 1997; recipient Silver Beaver, Boy Scouts Am., Spirit award Uta Halee Home for Girls, 1999. Mem. Mayflower Soc., Colonial Dames, P.E.O., Nat. League Pen Women Omaha Country, Omaha, Halee Spirit of Youth. Presbyterian. Home: 6875 State St Omaha NE 68152-1633

BATCHELDER, DRAKE MILLER, lawyer; b. Indpls., Dec. 12, 1941; s. Keith Drake and Anna (Miller) B.; divorced; children: Brian, Michael, David. BS in Indsl. Engring., U. Fla., 1965, JD with honors, 1969. Bar: Fla. Assoc. Mershon, Sawyer, Johnston, Dunwody & Cole, Miami, 1969-71; ptnr. Rimes, Greaton, Murphy & Batchelder, Ft. Lauderdale, Fla., 1971-79, English, McCaughan & O'Bryan, Ft. Lauderdale, 1979-86, Finley, Kumble Wagner, Ft. Lauderdale, 1986-88, Heinrich, Gordon, Batchelder, Hargrove & Weihe, Ft. Lauderdale, 1988-95, Tripp, Scott, Conklin & Smith, Ft. Lauderdale, 1995-98, Akerman, Senterfitt & Eidson, Ft. Lauderdale, 1998—. Editor U. Fla. Law Rev., 1969. Trustee Fla. Oaks Sch. Bd., Ft. Lauderdale, 1981-87, chmn. sch. bd., 1985-86; trustee St. Thomas Aquinas Found., Ft. Lauderdale, 1982-87. Mem. Broward County Bar Assn. (pres. young lawyers sect. 1973-74), Fla. Bar Assn. (bd. of govs. 1974-78, 79-84, chmn. merit retention commn. 1981-82), Ft. Lauderdale C. of C. (chmn. task force 1981-82). Republican. Roman Catholic. Clubs: Touchdown (pres. Ft. Lauderdale 1980-81), Lauderdale Yacht, Lago Mar County. Home: 9301 S Orchard Rd N Davie FL 33328 Office: Akerman Senterfitt & Eidson Ste 1600 350 E Las Olas Blvd Fort Lauderdale FL 33301-2292 E-mail: dbatchelder@akerman.com.

BATCHELDER, SAMUEL LAWRENCE, JR., retired corporate lawyer; b. Boston, Apr. 3, 1932; s. Samuel L. and May W. (Read) B.; m. Jane B. Borden, 1955 (div. 1965); children: John H., Benjamin A.; m. Marion C. Thomas, 1967; children: Timothy C., Lily L. AB, Harvard U., 1954, LLB, 1960. Bar: Mass., 1960, U.S. Dist. Mass. 1961. Assoc. Goodwin, Procter LLP, Boston, 1960-67, ptnr., 1968-97, of counsel, 1997—. Active ARC, bd. dirs. local orgns., Boston, 1966-2003, chmn. Mass. Bay unit, 1979-83, mem. various nat. coms., 1981-98, chmn. resolutions com., 1998, NE Blood Svcs., 1981-92; mem. grad. coun. Milton Acad., 1986-91, chmn., 1989-91, trustee, 1989-92; trustee Mass. Continuing Legal Edn., 1995-2004; dir. Exec. Svc. Corps. N.E., 1998—, chair, 2003-05. 1st lt. U.S. Army, 1954—57. Mem. ABA, Mass. Bar Assn., Boston Bar Assn. (chmn. corp. law com. 1985-88, mem. gov. coun. 1988-91, legal edn. com. 1995-2000), Brookline Cmty. Fund (trustee 1998-2004). Clubs: The Country Club (Brookline, Mass.). Democrat. Avocations: tennis, skiing, gardening, music, art. Office: 66 Laurel Rd Chestnut Hill MA 02467-2211 also: Goodwin Procter LLP Exchange Pl Boston MA 02109-2803 Office Phone: 617-566-5752.

BATCHELLER, JOE ANN, entrepreneur; b. Jacksonville, Fla., Dec. 11, 1932; d. Osmer St. Clair and Lorena (Jones) Deming; m.David Springsteen Batcheller, Aug. 8, 1957; children: Elizabeth Batcheller Whalen, Osmer Deming, John Alden. AA, Stephens Coll., Columbia, Mo., 1952; BA, U. N.C., 1955. Sec. Seminole Oil Co., Miami, Fla., 1957-61, pres., bd. dirs., 1961-65; pres., chmn. Blue Water Mobile Home Sales, Inc., Tavernier, Fla., 1967-76; dir. Miami Heart Inst., Miami Beach, 1973—, v.p., 1975—, exec. v.p., 1986-89, pres., chief exec. officer, 1989-93. Sec., bd. dirs. Bluegrass Plant Foods, Inc., Cynthiana, Ky., 1958-72; chmn. Superior Plant Foods, Inc., Lakeland, Fla., 1958-60; v.p., bd. dirs. Pensacola Petroleum Co., Inc., Miami, 1961-65, Top Power Stas., Miami, 1961-65, Atico Savs. Bank, Miami, 1987-88, Pan Am. Bank, Miami, 1984-87; bd. dirs. Intercontinental Bank; vice chmn. Miami Heart Rsch. Inst., Inc., 1993—. Bd. dirs. Am. Heart Assn., Miami, 1989-91; mem. adv. bd. Convent of Sacred Heart, Miami, 1973-77; mem. parents adv. bd. Furman U., Greenville, S.C., 1979-83. Mem. Surf Club on Miami Beach (pres. bd. govs. 1993-97, vice chmn. 1997-99), Surf Club Debutante Com. (chmn. 1976-82, 86, 87), Bay Point Property Owners Assn. (pres. 1991-96), Young Patronesses of Opera, English Speaking Union, DAR. Episcopalian. Avocations: reading, boating, Beaux Arts. Home: 4595 Sabal Palm Rd Miami FL 33137-3363

BATCHELOR, BARRINGTON DE VERE, civil engineer, educator; b. Lucea, Jamaica, W.I., July 2, 1928; s. Reginald Augustus and Vera Louise (O'Connor) B.; m. Alison Yvonnie Johnston, Sept. 14, 1960; children: Roger, Nicola, Wayne. B.Sc. with honors (Elias Issa scholar), U. Edinburgh, 1956; PhD (Commonwealth scholar), U. London, 1963; student, Nat. Def. Coll. Can., 1982-83. Registered profl. engr., Ont. Asst. engr. Sir William Halcrow & Partners, London, 1956-58; exec. engr. Ministry Edn., Jamaica, 1958-63, sr. exec. engr., 1963-64; ptnr. Franks & Batchelor, cons. engrs., Kingston, Jamaica, 1964-66; asst. prof. civil engring. Queen's U., Kingston, Ont., Can., 1966-68, assoc. prof., 1968-72, prof., 1972-93, prof. emeritus, 1993—. Bd. govs. Kingston Gen. Hosp. Fellow Engring. Inst. Can., Can. Soc. Civil Engrs.; mem. ASCE, Am. Concret Inst., Instn. Engrs. Jamaica, Instn. Engrs. Ont. Home: 150 Collingwood St Kingston ON Canada K7L 3X5 Office: Queen's U Dept Civil Engring Kingston ON Canada K7L 3N6 Personal E-mail: drdevb@aol.com.

BATCHELOR, JAMES KENT, lawyer; b. Long Beach, Calif., Oct. 4, 1934; s. Jack Morrell and Edith Marie (Ottinger) Batchelor; m. Jeanette Lou Dyer, Mar. 27, 1959 (div.); children: John, Suzanne; m. Susan Mary Leonard, Dec. 4, 1976. AA, Sacramento City Coll., 1954; BA, Calif. State U., Long Beach, 1956; JD, U. Calif., 1959. Bar: Calif. 1960, U.S. Dist. Ct. (ctrl. dist.) Calif. 1960, U.S. Supreme Ct. 1968, cert.: Calif. Bd. Legal Specialization (family law specialist) 1980. Dep. dist. atty., Orange County, Calif., 1960-62; assoc. Miller, Nisson, Kogler & Wenke, Santa Ana, Calif., 1962-64; ptnr. Batchelor, Cohen & Oster, Santa Ana, Calif., 1964-67, Kurilich, Ballard, Batchelor, Fullerton, Calif., 1967-72; pres. James K. Batchelor, Inc., 1972—. Instr. paralegal sect. Santa Ana City Coll.; lectr. family law Calif. Continuing Edn. Bar, 1973—; judge pro-tem Superior Ct., 1974—. Contbr. articles to profl. jours. Named one of Best Lawyers in Am., 1989—. Fellow: Am. Acad. Matrimonial Lawyers (pres. So. Calif. chpt. 1989—90); mem.: ABA, Orange County Bar Assn. (pres. family law sect. 1968—71, plaque sec. 1977), Calif. State Barristers (v.p., plaque 1964), Orange County Barristers (founder, pres. plaque 1963), Calif. State Bar (plaque chmn. family law sect. 1975—76, advisor 1976—78). Republican. Methodist. Office: 765 The City Dr S Ste 270 Orange CA 92868-6908 Office Phone: 714-750-8388. Personal E-mail: batchelorlaw@aol.com.

BATCHELOR, KAREN LEE, English language educator; b. Oregon City, Oreg., June 17, 1948; d. Jewel Elaine Durham; m. Luis Moncado, Mar. 17, 1978 (div. Aug. 1988); children: Virginia, Travis. BA in English, San Fransicso State U., 1971, MA in English, 1980. Vol. U.S. Peace Corps, Andong, Republic of Korea, 1972-74; tchr. English as second lang. City Coll. San Francisco, 1975—; tchr. trainer U. Calif., Berkeley, 1986—; acad. specialist USIA, 1991—; lectr. English Sonoma State U., Rohnert Pk., Calif., 1999—. Speaker in field. Co-author: (textbooks) Discovering English, 1981, In Plain English, 1985, More Plain English, 1986, The Writing Challenge, 1990, The English Zone, Books 1-4, 1998; contbr. articles to profl. jorus. Mem. Tchrs. English to Speakers of Other Langs., Calif. Tchrs. English to Speakers of Other Langs. Office: Sonoma State Univ 1801 E Cotati Ave Rohnert Park CA 94928 Office Phone: 415-239-3425. Business E-Mail: kbatchel@ccsf.edu.

BATCHVAROVA, MADLEN TODOROVA, music educator, conductor; d. Todor Bachvarov and Stefka Bachvarova. MusB, Acad. for Music and Dance Art, Bulgaria, 1991; MusM in Choral Conducting, Ga. state U., 1997; Mus D, U. of Ala., 2000. Condr. Plovdiv Choral Soc., Bulgaria, 1992—94; piano accompanist Secondary Music Sch., Plovdiv, Bulgaria, 1992—94; grad. tchg. asst. U. of Ala., Tuscaloosa, 1997—2000; asst. prof. music Columbus State U., Ga., 2000—01; asst. prof. music, dir. choral programs Hanover Coll., Ind., 2001—. Mem. internat. jury Internat. Choral Festival, Preveza, Greece, 2002. Singer: (CD recording) John Adams (GRAMMY for Best Choral Performance, 1997); singer: (chorus) (music performance at carnegie hall) Brahms, Requiem. Mem.: Am. Choral Dirs. Assn., NARAS, Pi Kappa Lambda. Office: Hanover Coll POBox 890 Hanover IN 47243 E-mail: batchvarova@hanover.edu.

BATE, BRIAN R., retired psychologist; b. Cleve., July 4, 1940; s. Paul A. and Claire N. B.; children: Jennifer Bate Tyler, Julia L. Bate-Poxon. BA in English, Western Res. U., 1963, MS in Psychology, 1965; PhD in Psychology, Case Western Res. U., 1972. Instr. Cuyahoga C.C. Western Campus, Parma, Ohio, 1969, from asst. prof. to prof. of psychology, 1970—2004; pvt. practice, Cleve., 1972-96. Contbr. articles to profl. jours. Nat. Merit Scholar Princeton U., 1958-61, Western Res. U., 1962-63; USPHS fellow, 1963-67. Mem. APA, Am. Fedn. Musicians, Edelweiss Ski Club, Cleve. Buddhist Temple. Achievements include devel. and tchg. of the first underclass-level behavior modification course in the world, 1970-1977. Home: 8498 Vera Dr Cleveland OH 44147-2204 also: The Apartelle Apt 201 N Escario St Cebu City Philippines 6000 Office Fax: 440-526-0166.

BATEH, ABRAHAM ISSA, lawyer; b. Jacksonville, Fla., Jan. 13, 1955; m. Renee Bajalia Bateh, Aug. 25, 1996. BSBA with high honors, U. Fla., 1976; JD, Stetson U., 1979. Bar: Fla. 1980, U.S. Dist. Ct. (mid. and no. dists.) Fla. 1981, U.S. Ct. Appeals (5th and 11th cir.) 1981. Assoc. Boyer, Tanzler, Blackburn & Boyer, Jacksonville, Fla., 1980-82, Edwards, Abbott & Willis, Jacksonville, Fla., 1983; partner Abbott & Bateh, Jacksonville, Fla., 1984-86; pvt. practice Jacksonville, Fla., 1986-88; partner Bateh & Clark, Jacksonville, Fla., 1988—. Lectr. Jacksonville Bar Assn. Law Week, 1992, 93, 94, 95. Bd. dirs. AHA, Jacksonville, 1991-93. Mem. Jacksonville Bar Assn. (chmn. lawyer referral svc., 1988—), Jacksonville Trial Lawyers Assn., Inc. (treas. 1996-98, pres.-elect 1998, pres. 1999). Avocations: water sports, biking, college football. Office: Bateh and Clark 1558 San Marco Blvd Jacksonville FL 32207-2944

BATEMAN, JASON, actor; b. Rye, NY, Jan. 14, 1969; s. Kent Bateman; m. Amanda Anka, July 3, 2001. Actor: (films) Teen Wolf Too, 1987, Necessary Roughness, 1991, Love Stinks, 1999, The Sweetest Thing, 2002, Starsky & Hutch, 2004, Dodgeball, 2004; (TV films) Just a Little More Love, 1983, The Fantastic World of D.C. Collins, 1984, Poison Ivy, 1985, The Thanksgiving Promise, 1986, Bates Motel, 1987, Confessions: Two Faces of Evil, 1994, Hart to Hart: Secrets of the Hart, 1995; (TV series) Little House on the Prairie, 1981—82, Silver Spoons, 1982—84, It's Your Move, 1984—85, The Hogan Family, 1988—91, Simon, 1995—96, Chicago Sons, 1997, George & Leo, 1997—98, Some of My Best Friends, 2001, Arrested Development, 2003— (Golden Globe for best actor in musical or comedy, 2005); actor, dir.: Valerie, 1986—88; dir.: Family Matters, 1989—98, For Your Love, 1998—2002, Brother's Keeper, 1998—99; TV appearances include Knight Rider, 1984, Mr. Belevdere, 1986, St. Elsewhere, 1986, Matlock, 1987, Burke's Law, 1995, Rude Awakening, 2000. Office: Internat Creativde Mgmt Inc 8942 WilshireBlvd Beverly Hills CA 90211-1934*

BATEMAN, JOHN JAY, classics educator; b. Elmira, N.Y., Feb. 17, 1931; s. Joseph Earl and Etha M. (Edwards) B.; m. Patricia Ann Hageman, July 5, 1952; children: Kristine M., Kathleen A., John Eric. BA, U. Toronto, 1953; MA, Cornell U., 1954, PhD, 1958. Lectr. Univ. Coll., U. Toronto, 1956-57; lectr., then asst. prof. U. Ottawa, 1957-60; mem. faculty U. Ill., Urbana, 1960—, prof. classics and speech, 1968-93; prof. emeritus, 1993—; head dept. classics U. Ill., 1966-73, chmn., 1988-92, acting dir. Sch. Humanities, 1973-74. Author, editor books and articles. Dem. precinct committeeman, 1964-68; sec. Champaign Dem. Central Com., 1965-66. Mem.: Am. Philol. Assn. (sec.-treas. 1968—73), Renaissance Soc. Am. Home: 1723 W Royal Tern Ln Fort Pierce FL 34962-6012 E-mail: jjbateman@aol.com.

BATEMAN, MAUREEN SCANNELL, lawyer; b. N.Y.C., July 27, 1943; d. Daniel Thomas and Gertrude Rose (Lally) Scannell; m. Frank Coffroth Bateman, June 26, 1971; 1 child: Daniel Frank. AB, Manhattanville Coll., 1964; JD, Fordham U., 1968. Bar: N.Y. 1969, Mass. 1998. Assoc. attorney Willkie Farr & Gallagher, N.Y.C., 1968-69, Davis Polk & Wardwell, N.Y.C., 1969-78; asst. resident counsel Morgan Guaranty Trust Co., N.Y.C., 1978-80; v.p., counsel Bankers Trust Co., N.Y.C., 1980-90; mng. dir., gen. counsel U.S. Trust Corp. N.Y., N.Y.C., 1990-97; exec. v.p., gen. counsel State St. Bank & Trust Co., Boston, 1997—2003; ptnr. Holland & Knight, NYC, 2004—. Office: Holland & Knight 195 Broadway 24th Fl New York NY 10007 Business E-Mail: maureen.bateman@hklaw.com.

BATEMAN, PAUL TREVIER, mathematician, educator; b. Phila., June 6, 1919; s. Harold John and Anna (Yeager) Bateman; m. Felice Hilda Davidson, June 25, 1948; 1 child, Sarah Elizabeth. AB, U. Pa., 1939, AM, 1940, PhD, 1946. Lectr. Bryn Mawr Coll., 1945-46; instr. Yale U., 1946-48; mem. Inst. Advanced Study, 1948-50; mem. faculty U. Ill., Urbana, 1950-89, prof. math., 1958-89, head dept., 1965-80; ret. Vis. prof. U. Pa., 1961—62, CUNY, 1964—65, U. Mich., 1980—81. Sr. Postdoctoral fellow, NSF, 1956—57. Mem.: Am. Math. Soc. (assoc. sec. 1966—83, trustee 1971—75, mem.-at-large coun. 1961—63), London Math. Soc., Math. Assn. Am. (problems editor Am. Math. Monthly 1986—91). Home: 108 Meadow Dr Urbana IL 61801-5822

BATEMAN, PAUL WILLIAM, federal agency administrator; b. Whittier, California, Feb. 28, 1957; s. John William and Glenus Bernice (Redman) B.; m. Marguerite (Cameron); children: Ellen Ryan, Nancy Cameron, Greer Aidan. BA, Whittier Coll., 1979. Asst. to former pres. Office of Richard Nixon, N.Y.C. and San Clemente, Calif., 1979—81; dep. dir. adminstrv. ops. div. The White House, Washington, 1981—82; exec. asst. to asst. sec. econ. devel. U.S. Dept. Commerce, Washington, 1982—84, dep. asst. sec. econ. devel., 1984—85; dep. treas. U.S. Dept. Treasury, Washington, 1985—88; sr. v.p. New Eng. Coun., Inc., Boston, 1988—89; dep. asst. to Pres. The White House, Washington, 1989—93; dir. pub. affairs Gold Inst., Washington, 1994—95; v.p. Klein and Saks, Inc., 1995—96; exec. v.p. Gold Inst., Washington, 1995—99; pres. Klein and Saks, Inc., 1996—2002, Gold Inst., Washington, 2000—02, KSG, LLC, 2003—. V.p. George Washington Boyhood Home Found., 1994-96; exec. dir. Silver Inst., 1996-2003. Trustee Whittier Coll., 2000-05; mem. Adv. Coun. on Hist. Preservation, 1989-93; bd. dirs. Internat. Cyanide Mgmt. Inst., 2002-03. Mem.: Econ. Club NY (pres. 2004—). Republican. Episcopalian. Home: 490 Ft Williams Pky Alexandria VA 22304-1810 Office: 1200 G St NW Ste 800 Washington DC 20005-4818

BATEMAN, ROBERT MCLELLAN, artist; b. Toronto, Ont., Can., May 24, 1930; s. Joseph Wilbur and Ann (McLellan) Bateman; m. Suzanne Bowerman, June 1961; children: Alan, Sarah, John; m. Birgit Freybe, Aug. 1975; children: Christopher, Rob. BA in Geography with honors, U. Toronto, 1954; postgrad., Ont. Coll. Edn., 1955; DSc (hon.), Carleton U., Ottawa, 1982; LLD (hon.), Brock U., St. Catherine, Ont., 1982; D Letters for Fine Arts (hon.), McMaster U., Hamilton, Ont., Can., 1983; LLD (hon.), U. Guelph, Ont., 1984; LittD (hon.), Lakehead U., Thunder Bay, Ont., 1986; LLD (hon.), Laurentian U., Sudbury, Ont., 1987, U. Victoria, B.C., 2003; DFA (hon.), Colby Coll., 1989, Northeastern U., 1991; DSc (hon.), McGill U., Montreal, 1995. Tchr. Nelson H.S., Burlington, 1958-63, 65-69; tchr. geography Nigeria, 1963-65; tchr. art Lord Elgin H.S., Burlington, 1970-76. One-man shows include Tryon Gallery, London, 1975, 79, Beckett Gallery, Hamilton, 1978, 87, Smithsonian Instn., 1987, Nat. Mus. Natural Sci., Ottawa, 1981-82, Everard Read Gallery, Johannesburg, South Africa, 2000, Beckett Fine Art Gallery, Toronto, 2002, Retrospective Tour, USA, 2002-03, Gerald Peters Gallery, Santa Fe, 2004, also touring U.S. and Can., Can. Embassy, Tokyo, 1992; represented in permanent collections Govt. Ont. Art Collection, Toronto Bd. Trade, Hamilton Art Gallery, Leigh Yawkey Woodson Art Mus., Wausau, Wis., H.R.H. The Prince of Wales, H.R.H. Prince Phillip, The Late Princess of Monaco, Am. Artists Collection, Gilcrease Mus., Tulsa, Art Gallery of Greater Victoria; commd. World Wildlife Fund, 1971, Endangered Species Silver Bowl, 1971, Endangered Species Postage Stamp Series, 1976-81, Northern Reflections - Loon Family, 1981, Govt. Can. wedding gift to Prince of Wales, 1981, Can. Post Office, Royal Can. Mint-Platinum Polar Bear series, 1990, Nat. Capital commn. Canadiana Fund; subject of the Art of Robert Bateman, 1981, A Day in the Life of Robert Bateman, 1985, The World of Robert Bateman, 1985, Robert Bateman An Artist in Nature, 1990, Natural Worlds: Robert Bateman, 1996, The Life and Times of Robert Bateman, 1997, Safari, 1998, Thinking Like a Mountain, 2000, Birds, 2002, Bateman's Backyard Birds, 2005. Bd. dirs. Elsa Wild Animal Appeal, Toronto, 1975—; hon. dir. Long Point Bird Obs.; hon. chmn. Harmony Found., Ottawa. Decorated Queen Elizabeth Silver Jubilee medal Govt. of Can., 1977, Officer of Order of Can., 1984; recipient award of excellence Soc. Animal Artists, 1979, 80, 86, 90, Gov. Gen. award for conservation, Quebec City, Can., 1987, Lescarbot award Can. Govt., 1992, Rachel Carson award, 1996, Golden Plate award Am. Acad. Achievement, 1998; named Artist of Yr., Am. Artist Collection, 1980, Master Artist, Leigh Yawkey Woodson Mus., Wausau, Wis., 1982, Environ. Hero, Nat. Aububon Soc., 1998, others. Mem. Order B.C., Jane Goodall Inst. (bd. dirs.), Audubon Soc. (hon. life), Royal Can. Acad. Arts, Can. Wildlife Fedn. (hon. life), Sierra Club (hon. life), Kenya Wildlife Fund (hon. dir.), Sierra Legal Def. Fund (hon. dir.), Ecotrust (adv. coun.), Pollution Probe (adv. coun.). E-mail: rb@gulfislands.com.

BATEMAN, SHARON LOUISE, public relations executive; b. St. Louis, Oct. 18, 1949; d. Frank Hamilton and Charlotte Elizabeth (Hogan) Bateman. Student, Drury Coll., 1967-69; BJ, U. Mo., 1971. Asst. dir. pub. rels. Cardinal Glennon Hosp. Children, St. Louis, 1971-76; staff asst. pub. rels. Ozark Air Lines, St. Louis, 1976-80; mgr. corp. rels. Kellwood Co., St. Louis, 1980-83; mgr. corp. comm. May Dept. Stores Co., St. Louis, 1983-86, dir. corp. comm., 1986-94, v.p. corp. comms., 2000—; mgr. comm. Arthur Andersen, St. Louis, 1995-96; mgr. editl. and adminstrv. svcs. Falk Design Group, St. Louis, 1996—2000. Bd. dirs. St. Michael's Houses, 1996—97, Gateway Greening, 1999—2001, The Wellness Cmty., 2004—. Recipient Best Regional Airline Employee Publ. award, Editor's Assn. Am. Transp. Assn., 1978. Mem.: Pub. Rels. Soc. Am. (sec.St. Louis chpt. 1983, bd. dirs. 1988—90, v.p. 1991), Internat. Assn. Bus. Comms. (pres. St. Louis chpt. 1977). Office: May Dept Stores Co 611 Olive St Saint Louis MO 63101-1721

BATEMAN, THOMAS ROBERT, lawyer; b. Winchester, Mass., Dec. 9, 1944; s. Richard Holt and Phyllis (Brown) B.; m. Katherine Elizabeth Elliott, Sept. 9, 1972; children: Kyra Elizabeth, Richard Holt, Robert Elliott. BA, Harvard U., 1967; JD, NYU, 1971. Bar: N.Y. 1972, U.S. Dist. Ct. (so. dist.) N.Y. 1973, U.S. Ct. Appeals (2d cir.) 1974, Mass. 1978, U.S. Dist. Ct. Mass. 1978, U.S. Ct. Appeals (1st cir.) 1978. Assoc. Winthrop, Stimson, Putnam & Roberts, N.Y.C., 1971-77, Skadden, Arps, Slate, Meagher & Flom, Boston, 1977-79, ptnr., 1980—. Class agent Phillips Exeter Acad., N.H., 1969—; class steering com. Harvard U., Cambridge, Mass. 1985—. Mem.: ABA, Assn. of Bar of City of N.Y., N.Y. State Bar Assn., Somerset Club, Harvard Club (Boston). Episcopalian. Home: 33 Bullard Rd Weston MA 02493-2203

BATES, ALLAN CHARLES, playwright, educator; b. Cleve., May 20, 1929; s. Abram Allan and Ruth Barnes Bates; m. Laura Raidonis, Dec. 31, 1989; children: Allan, Jeffrey, Kirsten, Ruth, Gregory. BA in Sociology, Ohio Wesleyan U., 1951; PhD in English, U. Chgo., 1967. Instr. Lake Forest (Ill.) Coll., 1958—62; asst. prof. Chgo. (Ill.) State U., 1962—66; prof. N.E. Ill. U., Chgo., 1967—92. Instr. playwriting Victory Gardens Theater, Chgo., 1980—88; playwright in residence Raven Theater, Chgo., 1990—96. Author: (plays) Red Badge of Courage, 1989, YellowHeat (Van Gogh in Arles), 1988, Ninny, 2002. Vol. instr. Ind. Dept. Correction, Rockville, Ind., 1998—2003. Recipient Playwriting award, Ill. Arts Coun., 1988. Avocation: farming. Home: 9309 N 525 W Tangier IN 47952 E-mail: allanb@allanbates.com.

BATES, BARBARA J. NEUNER, retired municipal official; b. Mt. Vernon, NY, Apr. 8, 1927; d. John Joseph William and Elsie May (Flint) Neuner; m. Herman Martin Bates, Jr., Mar. 25, 1950; children: Roberta Jean Bates Jamin, Herman Martin III, Jon Neuner. BA, Barnard Coll., 1947. Confidential clk. to supr. Town of Ossining, N.Y., 1960-63, receiver of taxes, 1971-90; ret.; pres. BNB Assocs., Briarcliff Manor, N.Y., 1963-83, Upper Nyack Realty Co., Inc., Briarcliff Manor, 1966-71. V.p. Ossining (N.Y.) Young Rep. Club, 1958; pres. Young Womens Rep. Club Westchester County (N.Y.), 1959-61; regional committeewoman N.Y. State Assn. Young Rep. Clubs, 1960-62; mem. Westchester County Rep. Com., 1963-95; mem. Ossining Women's Rep. Club, 1960-92, pres., 1984-85; mem. Westchester County Women's Rep. Club, 1957-92. Mem. DAR, Jr. League Westchester-on-Hudson, Receivers Taxes Assn. Westchester County (legis. liaison, v.p., pres. 1984-85), Hackley Sch. Mothers Assn. (pres. 1968), R.I. Hist. Soc., Ossining Hist. Soc., Westchester County Hist. Soc., Landmark Preservation Soc. of S.E., Ossining Woman's Club. Home: 23 Bloomer Rd Brewster NY 10509-1026 also: 663 Reynolds Rd Chepachet RI 02814-1629 Office Phone: 401-968-9021.

BATES, BETSEY, artist; b. Dobbs Ferry, N.Y., Nov. 29, 1924; d. Homer Morgan and Dorothy (Graef) Smith; m. Guy C. Bates, Aug. 30, 1947 (div. 1965); children: Carleton Jane, Leslie Collins; m. Joseph M. Gerhart, June 13, 1978. BFA magna cum laude, Beaver Coll., 1946. Artist; b. Dobbs Ferry, N.Y., Nov. 29, 1924; d. Homer Morgan and Dorothy (Graef) Smith; B.F.A. magna cum laude, Beaver Coll., 1946; m. Guy C. Bates, Aug. 30, 1947 (div. 1965); children: Carleton Jane, Leslie Collins; m. Joseph M. Gerhart, June 13, 1978. Designer, painter, illustrator, printmaker for advt. agys., corps. and publs.; works include: Christmas card Easter Seal Soc., 1974, mural for RCA TV Studio, Switzerland, 1977; represented in collections: Washington Hilton Hotel, Houston Marriott, Syracuse Marriott, Chgo. Marriott, Texaco, World Book, Lynell, Grad. Hosp. of Phila, Butler Inst. Am. Art, Danskin, Inc., Episcopal Acad., Hahnemann Hosp., Friends Central Sch., Continental Bank, Fed. Res. Bank, Free Library Phila., Germantown Hosp., Montgomery Hosp. (13), Smith Kline Pharm. Labs., McNeil Pharm. Corp. (2); designer collectible Christmas plates for World Book Publishers, Chgo., 1979-91, designer Beach/Contempo paper products, 1960-89. Recipient cert. of merit Nat. Consumer Fin. Assn., 1963; cert. of excellence Phila. Art Dirs. Club, 1964; award Nat. Community Arts Program, Golden Disc, Beaver Coll., 1975; Best of Show award Norristown Borough (Pa.) Council of Arts, 1980. Mem. Plymouth Art Guild, Duxbury Art Assn., Cape Cod Art Assn. Designer, painter, illustrator, printmaker for advt. agys., corps. and publs.; works include: Christmas card Easter Seal Soc., 1974, mural for RCA TV Studio, Switzerland, 1977; represented in collections: Washington Hilton Hotel, Houston Marriott, Syracuse Marriott, Chgo. Marriott, Texaco, World Book, Lynell, Grad. Hosp. of Phila., Butler Inst. Am. Art, Danskin, Inc., Episcopal Acad., Hahnemann Hosp., Friends Central Sch., Continental Bank, Fed. Res. Bank, Free Library Phila., Germantown Hosp., Montgomery Hosp. (13), Smith Kline Pharm. Labs., McNeil Pharm. Corp. (2); designer collectible Christmas plates for World Book Publishers, Chgo., 1979-91, designer Beach/Contempo paper products, 1960-89. Recipient cert. of merit Nat. Consumer Fin. Assn., 1963; cert. of excellence Phila. Art Dirs. Club, 1964; award Nat. Community Arts Program, Golden Disc, Beaver Coll., 1975; Best of Show award Norristown Borough (Pa.) Council of Arts, 1980. Mem. Plymouth Art Guild, Duxbury Art Assn., Cape Cod Art Assn. Home: 146A Westerly Rd Plymouth MA 02360-4534

BATES, BEVERLY JO-ANNE, artist, educator; b. Pitts., Jan. 29, 1938; d. Joseph Whitfield and Thelma Alease (McMullen) Loftin; divorced; children: Roy F. Jr., Brian Whitfield, Stephen Jeffrey. BS in Art Edn., W.Va. State Coll., 1959; MEd in Art Edn., U. Pitts., 1973, postgrad., 1985-88, Temple U., 1963-64, RISD, 1984. Art tchr. Pitts. Pub. Sch. System, 1959, 70-75, print tchr. Brashear High Sch., 1975-78, coord. art dept., printmaking tchr. Pitts. High Sch., 1970—; art tchr. N.J. Pub. Schs., Camden, N.J., 1961; print instr. Selma Burke Art Ctr., Pitts., 1971, Pitts. Arts and Crafts Ctr., 1972; panel mem. visual arts Pa. Coun. on Arts, Harrisburg, 1979—. Com. mem. Links Inc. Nat. Art Com., Washington, 1992—; mem. adv. bd. Manchester Craftsman's Guild, Pitts., 1985—, Visions, 1990—. Author: (catalogues) Black American Art, 1977 (Meade award 1977), 1978 (W. Pa. Prize 1978); one-person shows include Westmoreland Mus., 1991, Visual Arts Gallery, C.C. of Allegheny County, 1991, Kipp Gallery, Indiana U. Pa., 1991, Westminster Coll. Art Gallery, 1991, others; exhibited in group shows at Pitts. Ctr. for Arts, 1982, 83, 84, 85, 87, 88, 90, 91, 92, Carnegie Mus., 1982, 86, 90, 92, S.G. Galleries, 1992, LaTeste, France, 1992, U. Pitts. Kimbo Gallery, 1990, 91, 92, Carson St. Gallery, 1991, others. Bd. trustees Pitts. Ctr. for Arts, 1989—; bd. dirs. Soc. Contemporary, Pitts., 1990—, Soc. Arts and Crafts. Honors fellow R.I. Sch., Providence, 1984; recipient Frick Fellowship award Pitts. Bd. Edn., 1975, Outstanding Art Edn. award Pitts. Bd. Edn., 1984, Youth Arts award Pa. Art Edn. Assn., Pitts., 1988, Outstanding Art Edn. award Pratt Inst., Bklyn., 1989, Jurors award Pitts. Print Group, 1991, Images show U. Pitts., 1992. Mem. The Links Inc. (bd. mem. nat. arts com.), Nat. Art Edn. Assn., Pa. Art Edn. Assn., Pa. Coun. on Arts (past panel mem.), Pitts. Print Group (past bd. mem.), Associated Artists Pitts. (past bd. mem.), Nat. Conf. Artists, Pa. Alliance for Art Edn. (bd. mem.). Avocations: art, printmaking, reading, travel. Home: 6922 Meade St Pittsburgh PA 15208-2402 Office: Pitts High Sch 925 Brushton Ave Pittsburgh PA 15208-1613 Personal E-mail: jbates6220@aol.com.

BATES, CHARLES WALTER, human resources executive, lawyer; b. Detroit, June 28, 1953; s. E. Frederick and Virginia Marion (Nunneley) B. BA in Psychology and Econs. cum laude, Mich. State U., 1975, M in Labor and Indsl. Rels., 1977; postgrad., DePaul U., 1979-80; JD, William Mitchell Coll. Law, 1984. Bar: Wash. 1990, U.S. Dist. Ct. (we. dist.) Wash. 1992, U.S. Ct. Appeals (9th cir.) 2002; cert. sr. profl. in human resources. Job analyst Gen. Mills, Inc., Mpls., 1977—78, plant pers. asst. II Chgo., 1978—80, plant asst. pers. mgr., 1980—81, pers. mgr. consumer foods mktg. Mpls., 1981—82, pers. mgr. consumer foods mktg. divsns. and Saluto Pizza, 1982—84; mgr. human resources We. divsn. Godfather's Pizza, Inc., Costa Mesa, Calif., 1984—85, mgr. human resources we. U.S. and Can. Bellevue, Wash., 1985—91; dir. human resources Royal Seafoods, Inc., Seattle, 1991—92, dir. human resources and employee rels. counsel, 1992—94, dir. human resources and counsel, 1994—95; sr. internal auditor PACCAR, Inc, Bellevue, Wash., 1995—97; dir. field human resources PACCAR Automotive, Inc., Renton, 1997, dir. human resources, 1997—2000; dir. human resources Centralia (Wash.) ops. TransAlta USA, Inc., 2000—02; dir. adminstrn., corp. sec. TransAlta USA Inc., Centralia, 2002—04; dir. human resources Wash. State Ferries Washington State Dept. Transp., 2005—. Instr. employee labor rels. Lake Washington Tech. Coll., 1992-94, Key Bank Profl. Devel. Ctr. U. Wash., Tacoma, 2005; bd. dirs., TransAlta USA Inc., 2000-01, TransAlta Investments LLC, 2000-01, Olympia Symphony Orch., 2001-02. Candidate for lt. gov. of Minn., 1982; mem. East Bellevue (Wash.) Transp. Study Adv. Com., 1989-92, Sammamish Cmty. Coun., Bellevue, 1990-93, Bellevue Civil Svc. Commn., 1997-2000, vice chmn., 1999, chmn., 2000; commr. Scott Lake Drainage Dist., 2002-05; asst. scoutmaster Boy Scouts Am., 1971-. Recipient Scouter's Tng. award Boy Scouts Am., 1979, Vantage Recruiting award Recruitment Today mag., 1989, Vigil Honor award Order of the Arrow, Boy Scouts Am., 1990, Dist. Award of Merit, Boy Scouts Am., 1991; finalist Wash. Atty. Award of Excellence Butch Blum/Wash. Law and Politics mag., 2003. Mem. Wash. State Bar Assn., Soc. Human Resource Mgmt., Nat. Eagle Scout Assn. Office: Wash State Ferries 2911 2d Ave Seattle WA 98121-1012 Personal E-mail: charlie_bates@hotmail.com.

BATES, DAVID WESTFALL, internist, educator, medical researcher; b. Madison, Wis., June 5, 1957; s. Robert and Patricia Bates; m. Carol Kurtz; children: Michael, Sarah. BS, Stanford U., 1979; MD, Johns Hopkins U., 1983; MSc, Harvard U., 1990. Diplomate Am. Bd. Internal Medicine. Intern and resident internal medicine Oreg. Health Scis. U., Portland, 1983-86; house physician Vancouver (Wash.) Vets. Hosp., 1984-87, Kaiser Sunnyside Hosp., Portland, 1984-86; assoc. physician Oreg. Health Scis. U. Hosp., Portland, 1986-87; rsch. fellow medicine Harvard Med. Sch., Boston, 1988-90; rsch./clin. fellow medicine Brigham and Women's Hosp., Boston, 1988-90, assoc. physician, 1989-91, attending physician holding unit, 1990-95, attending physician med. consultation svc., 1990-97, attending physician Brigham Internal Medicine Assocs., 1990—, mem. Ctr. for Applied Med. Info. Sys. Rsch., 1993—. Physician Wallace Med. Concern, Portland, 1985-87, Tumu-Tumu Hosp., Karatina, Kenya, 1987-88; instr. medicine Oreg. Health Scis. U., 1986-87, Harvard Med. Sch., 1990-93, asst. prof. medicine, 1993-97, assoc. prof. medicine, 1997—; joint appt. Harvard Sch. Pub. Health, Dept. Health Policy and Mgmt., 2000—; house physician St. Luke's Hosp., New Bedford, 1989-91; mem. program project grant com. Nat. Cancer Inst. Can., 1996; mem. quality care coun. Ptnrs. Cmty. Health Care Inc., 1996—, mem. coronary disease prevention task force, 1996-98, mem. drug therapy team, 1996-98, mem. med. mgmt. com., 1996—; med. dir. Brigham and Women's Physician Hosp. Orgn., 1996-97, Ptnrs. Clin. Data Warehouse, 1997-99; med. dir. clin. and quality analysis Ptnrs. Healthcare Sys., 1997—; mem. Nat. Acad. Clin. Biochemistry, Stds. for Lab. Practice, 1997, Improving Prescribing Practices Initiative, Inst. for Health Care Improvement, 1997-98; chief divsn. Gen. Internal Medicine, 1998—; sci. advisor SCRIPT project Health Care Financing Adminstrn. and Joint Commn. for Accreditation of Healthcare Orgns., 1998—; chair abstract selection com. SGIM N.E. Region, 1999; mem. Consensus Devel. Panel on the Safety of Intravenous Drug Delivery Sys., Latiolais Leaderhip Program, 1999; trustee Inst. for Safe Medication Practices, 2000; mem. steering com. Nat. Quality Forum, 2000—; mem. safe medication use expert com. U.S. Pharmacopeia, 2000—; mem. Harkness Fellows in Health Care Policy, The Commonwealth Fund, 2000—; presenter in field; many others. Mem. editl. bd. Jour. Evaluation in Clin. Practice, 1997—, The Joint Commn. Jour. on Quality Improvement, 1997—; contbr. numerous articles to profl. jours. Recipient Nat. Rsch. Svc. award Agy. for Health Care Policy and Rsch., 1990, Young Investigator of the Yr. award Soc. for Med. Decision-Making, 1993. Fellow ACP; mem. AMA (mem. medication error reducation initiative 1996-98), Am. Soc. for Clin. Pharmacology and Therapeutics, Am. Med. Informatics Assn. (mem. editl. bd. jour. 1997—, awards com. 2000—), Am. Fedn. Clin. Rsch. (Henry Christian award for excellence in rsch. 1992), Assn. for Health Svcs. Rsch., Soc. for Med. Decision Making, Soc. for Gen. Internal Medicine (Clin. Investigator of Yr. award N.E. region 1993). Office: Brigham and Womens Hosp 75 Francis St Boston MA 02115

BATES, DENA BETH, shop owner; b. Pomona, Calif., Aug. 21, 1965; d. James Garfield and Patsy Lorriane Pride; m. Michael Lynn Bates, Nov. 11, 2003; children: Cullena Brittany Clement, Valorie Rose Clement. Diploma, Sch. Tax Preparation, Atlanta, 1997; AAS in Constrn. Mgmt., C.C. So. Nev., 2004; Assoc. Divinity, 2004. Asst. to gen. mgr. Lassen Internat., Las Vegas, 1994—97; vacation coord. Vegas Golfer, Las Vegas, 1998—99; office mgr. Evergreen Corp., 1999—2000; project asst. R & O Constrn., 2000—04; owner Dena Woodworks, 2004—; with MP Constrn., 2004—. Editor (pub.): (booklet of poems) Just a Few Poems. Notary pub. State of Nev., 1999—; deacon Seventh-Day Adventist Ch. Mem.: Constrn. Mgmt. Assn. Am., Phi Theta Kappa (notary pub. 1999—2004). Republican. Avocations: woodworking, sewing, music, crafts, race cars. Personal E-mail: cowgirl_865@hotmail.com.

BATES, GEORGE WILLIAM, obstetrician, gynecologist, educator; b. Durham, N.C., Feb. 15, 1940; s. George W. and Lillian M. (Streete) B.; m. Susanne Rayburn, Oct. 18, 1969; children: Jonathan Rayburn, Jeffrey William, Robert Wiser. BS, U. N.C., 1962, MD, 1965; SM, MIT, 1984. Diplomate Am. Bd. Ob-Gyn. (examiner 1984-93). Intern U. Ala., Birmingham, 1965-66; resident ob-gyn U. N.C., Chapel Hill, 1966-70; prof., chmn. ob-gyn U. Tenn., Knoxville, 1972-76; fellow reproductive endocrinology U. Tex., Dallas, 1976-78; prof., dir. reproductive endocrinology U. Miss. Med. Ctr., Jackson, 1978-86; prof. ob.-gyn. Coll. Medicine, Med. U. S.C., Charleston, 1986-90, dean, 1986-89; v.p. med. edn. Greenville (S.C.) Hosp. System, 1990-96; exec. v.p., chief med. officer Prin.Care, Inc., Brentwood, Tenn., 1996-98; v.p. devel. Vanderbilt U. Med. Ctr., Nashville, 1998—. CEO digiChart, Inc. Co-author: Obstetrics and Gynecology for Medical Students, 1992, 95; editor: Manual of Clinical Problems in Obstetrics and Gynecology, 1982, 86, 90; contbr. numerous articles to profl. publs. Commr. coun. Boy Scouts Am., 1989-90, v.p. adminstrn., 1992, pres., 1993-94, bd. dirs. Mid. Tenn. Coun., 2002--; elder Mt. Pleasant Presbyn. Ch., Westminster Presbyn. Ch.; mem. pres.'s adv. coun. Mars Hill Coll., Presbyn. Coll., Nat. Devel. Coun., U. N.C. Maj. USAF, 1970-72. Morehead scholar, 1958; NIH rsch. trainee, 1976-78; Sloan fellow, 1983; recipient Eagle Scout award, 1955, Henry Fordham award, 1966, Golden Apple award, 1987, Silver Beaver award, 1989, Hon. Alumnus award Med. U. S.C., 1990, Disting. Eagle Scout award, 1991; named Prof. of Yr., U. Miss., 1980, Top 100 Healthcare Exec., 2002. Mem. ACOG (chmn. fin. com. 1990-94, health care commn. 1994-97, Jr. Fellow Profl. of Y. award dist. IV 1991), AMA, AAAS, Assn. Profs. Ob-Gyn. Found. (bd. dirs. 1993), Am. Gyn.-Ob. Soc., Nat. Bd. Med. Examiners, Gynecol. Investigation, Am. Fertility Soc. (bd. dirs. 1991-94, treas. 1994-96), Soc. Gynecol. Surgeons, Accreditation Coun. Grad. Med. Edn., So. Atlantic Assn. Obstetricians and Gynecologists, Ctrl. Assn. Obstetricians and Gynecologists, Endocrine Soc., Rotary, Alpha Omega Alpha. Office: digiChart Inc 102 Woodmont Blvd Ste 500 Nashville TN 37205-5254 Office Phone: 615-777-2727.

BATES, GERALD EARL, bishop emeritus; b. Caldwell, Ohio, Sept. 12, 1933; s. Earl and Lillian Inez (Merritt) B.; m. Marlene Rachel Parsons, Aug. 21, 1954; children: David Earl, William Randall, Elizabeth Ann. AA, Spring Arbor Coll., 1953; AB, Greenville Coll., 1955; MDiv, Asbury Theol. Sem., 1958; ThM, Western Theol. Sem., 1964; PhD, Mich. State U., 1975; DD (hon.), Roberts Wesleyan Coll., 1986, Greenville Coll., 1998. Missionary with Gen. Missionary Bd. Free Meth. Ch. of N.Am., Winona Lake, Ind., 1957-85, area adminstrv. asst. for Cen. Africa, 1973-85, bishop Indpls., 1985-99, bishop emeritus, 1999—. Adj. prof. Union Inst. U., Cin., West Africa Theol. Sem., Nigeria. Author: Soul Afire, 1981, 2d edit., 1993; chmn. bd. editors: Book of Discipline, 1985. Trustee Spring Arbor U., Mich., bd. vice chair, chair strategic plan oversight com.; bd. dirs. India Missionary Tng. Bd., Ctr. for Study of Wesley and Society; pres. Free Meth. World Fellowship, 1989-95; pres. U.S. bd. Hope Africa U., Burundi. Recipient Alumnus of Yr. award Spring Arbor Coll., 1974, Goodwill Amb. award Noble County C. of C., 1988, Alumnus of Yr. award Asbury Theol. Sem., 1991, Disting. Alumnus Greenville Coll., 2005. Mem. Am. Soc. Missiology, Phi Kappa Phi. Republican. Mem. Free Methodist Ch. Avocations: reading, travel, photography. Home: 6715 Oak Lake Dr Indianapolis IN 46214-2038 E-mail: nijewe@cs.com.

BATES, HAROLD MARTIN, lawyer; b. Wise County, Va., Mar. 11, 1928; s. William Jennings and Reba (Williams) B.; m. Audrey Rose Doll, Nov. 1, 1952 (div. Mar. 1978); children: Linda, Carl; m. Judith Lee Farmer, June 23, 1978 (div. Feb. 2002); m. Helen H. Herndon, May 1, 2004. BA in Econs., Coll. William and Mary, 1952; LLB, Washington and Lee U., 1961. Bar: Va. 1961, Ky. 1961. Spl. agt. FBI, Newark and N.Y.C., 1952-56; tech. sales rep. Hercules Powder Co., Wilmington, Del., 1956-58; investigator U.S. Def. Dept., Lexington, Va., 1959-62, Louisville, 1959-62; practice law Louisville, 1961-62; sec.-treas., dir., house counsel Life Ins. Co. of Ky., Louisville, 1962-66; practice law Roanoke, Va., 1966—; sec., dir. James River Limestone Co., Buchanan, Va., 1970-96; sec. Eastern Ins. Co., Roanoke, 1984-87. Pres., Skil, Inc., orgn. for rehab. Vietnam vets., Salem, Va., 1972-75; freshman football coach Washington and Lee U., 1958-60. With airborne U.S. Army, 1946—47. Mem. Va. Bar Assn., Roanoke Bar Assn., William and Mary Alumni Assn. (bd. dirs. 1972-76), Soc. Former Spl. Agts. of FBI (chmn. Blue Ridge chpt. 1971-72). Republican. Home: 8705 Shadwell Dr Roanoke VA 24019 Office: 320 Elm Ave Roanoke VA 24016 Office Phone: 540-982-1616. E-mail: hbates6802@aol.com.

BATES, JAMES EARL, academic administrator; b. Ligonier, Pa., Aug. 10, 1923; s. Earl Barrington and Margaret (Kinsey) B.; m. Lauralou Courtney, Apr. 15, 1950; children: Susan Bates Jaren, Sara Bates Hudson, James Barrington, Willa Bates Leitten. DSc, Temple U., 1946; DPM, Pa. Coll. Podiatric Medicine, 1970, LHD (hon.), 1996; EdD (hon.), Franklin Pierce Coll., 1972; DSc (hon.), Calif. Coll. Podiatric Med., 1995; LLD, Barry U., 1995; LHD (hon.), Pa. Coll. Podiatric Medicine, 1996. Practice podiatric medicine, Phila., 1946-71; assoc. prof. roentgenology Temple U., Phila., 1948-60; prof., pres. Pa. Coll. Podiatric Medicine, Phila., 1962-95, chancellor, 1995-96, chancellor, CEO, 1997-98; cons. to dean Sch. Podiatric Medicine Temple U., 1998—; chancellor Temple Sch. Podiatric Medicine. Cons. BHRD Region IX, HEW, San Francisco, 1973-74, Region V, Chgo., 1974-75; del. Nat. Commn. on Certifying Health Manpower; mem. health adv. com. HEW, 1972-73; adv. panel for podiatry Inst. Medicine, Nat. Acad. Scis., 1972-74; adv. council for comprehensive health planning Pa. Dept. Health, 1972-75, health manpower task force edn. com., 1976; task force on health manpower distbn. Nat. Health Council, 1973, com. on manpower, 1976-83; mem. Nat. Adv. Council on Health Professions Edn., 1983-87; cons. team So. Regional Ednl. Bd. Feasibility Study for So. Podiatry Sch., 1975-76; mem. Statewide Profl. Standards Rev. Council, 1976-82, Greater Phila. Com. for Med.-Pharm. Scis. Contbr. articles to profl. jours. Trustee First United Meth. Ch. of Germantown, 1965-72, past chmn. fin. com.; v.p. bd. Germantown Businessmen's Assn., Disting. Service award, 1964; chmn. 277th and 278th Ann. Germantown Week, 1958-59; dep. service dir. Phila. CD Council, 1966-73; mem. Health Adv. Commn., Phila., 1976; past pres., bd. mgrs. Germantown YMCA; v.p. Phila. Boosters Assn.; trustee Univ. City Sci. Center, Phila. Served with M.C. AUS, WWII. Recipient citation, Pa. Coll. Podiatric Medicine, 1970, Gov. Pa., 1973, Lifetime Achievement award, Podiatric Mgmt. Mag., 1993, Disting. Svc. citation, Am. Podiatric Med. Assn., 2004. Fellow Internat. Acad. Preventive Medicine (dir. 1973-78), Brit. Soc. Podiatric Medicine (hon.), Royal Soc. Health (Eng.), Am. Coll. Foot Roentgenologists (pres. 1958-59), Coll. Physicians Phila.; mem. Am. Podiatry Assn. (Merit award 1962, gen. chmn. Region Three Ann. Conv. 1975—), Pa. Podiatry Assn. (pres. 1959-60, Man of Yr. award 1961, Spl. citation 1973), Greater Phila. Podiatry Soc. (pres. 1955-56), Fedn. Assns. Schs. of Health Professions (pres. 1975-76), Am. Assn. Colls. Podiatric Medicine (pres. 1969-72), Pi Epsilon Delta, Pi Delta. Clubs: Greate Bay Country, Union League, Pyramid Club. Republican. Office: Pa Coll Podiatric Medicine 810 N Race St Philadelphia PA 19107-2496

BATES, JAMES T., chief of staff; b. Jan. 4, 1958; BA magna cum laude, Pepperdine U., 1981; MPP, Claremont Grad. U., 1984. Mgmt. sys. analyst, adminstrv. asst. 1 dept. water and power City of LA, 1985; budget analyst, adminstrv. asst. II Dept. Gen. Svcs., 1986—87; budget analyst US Ho. Reps., Com. on Budget, 1988—90, counsel Washington, 1990—94, chief counsel, 1995—2000, dep. staff dir., chief counsel, 2001—04, chief of staff, 2004—. Office: Committee on Budget Cannon House Office Bldg Rm 309 Washington DC 20515-6065

BATES, JOHN CECIL, JR., lawyer; b. Buffalo, May 27, 1936; s. John C. and Geraldine K. Bates; m. Ellen Clare Eyler, June 28, 1964; children: Andrew, Jeremy, Eliot, Emily. AB magna cum laude, Harvard U., 1958; JD, U. Mich., 1961; LLM, NYU, 1962. Bar: N.Y. 1962, D.C. 1977. Assoc. Milbank, Tweed, Hadley & McCloy, N.Y.C., 1963-72; spl. asst. tax policy Treasury Dept., Washington, 1973-76; ptnr. Squire, Sanders & Dempsey, Washington, 1977-84, Reid & Priest, Washington, 1984-91, Foley & Lardner, Washington, 1992-94; tax policy advisor Dept. Treas. Tech. Assistance Program (Ctrl. and Eastern Europe), 1995-98; cons. to fgn. govts. on taxation and decentralization, 1998—. Tax and fin. cons. state and local govts., also others, 1977—; adj. prof. Fordham U. Grad. Sch. Bus. Administrn., 1992. Co-author: Federal Law of Public Finance, 1988; contbr. numerous articles on tax, energy and fin. to profl. jours. Fellow: Internat. Law Inst. (sr.); mem.: ABA (chmn. com. tax sect. 1981—83), D.C. Bar Assn., Harvard Club. Avocations: historic preservation, environmental protection, music. Home: PO Box 293 Tenants Harbor ME 04860-0293 Office Phone: 207-372-8815. Personal E-mail: batesconsult@aol.com.

BATES, JOHN WYTHE, III, lawyer; b. Richmond, Aug. 22, 1941; s. John Wythe, Jr. and Virginia (Wellington) B.; m. Beverly Jane Estes, June 20, 1964; children: Elizabeth Puller, Kathryn Wellington. BS, Va. Tech., 1963; LLB, U. Va., 1966. Assoc. McGuire Woods Battle & Boothe, L.L.P., Richmond, 1966-71, pntr., 1971—, mng. ptnr., 1989-96. Mem. Va. Racing Commn., 1997-2000; chmn. Richmond Renaissance, Inc., 1998—2001. Chmn. United Way Gtr. Richmond, 1975-76; pres. Family and Children's Svc. Richmond, 1978-80; trustee St. Paul's Coll., 1989-96, Va. Found. Ind. Colls., 1994—; sr. warden St. Stephen's Ch., 1985-86, 2002; mem. exec. com. Va. Tech. Found. Bd., 1994-2000. Va. Law Found. fellow, 1997. Mem. Am. Coll. Real Estate Lawyers, Richmond Real Estate Group, Forum Club, River Rd. Citizens Assn. (pres. 1983-84), Country Club Va. (pres. 1987-88), Bull and Bear Club (pres. 1980-81), Commonwealth Club. Episcopalian. Avocations: golf, waterfowl hunting. Office: McGuire Woods LLP One James Ctr 901 E Cary St Richmond VA 23219-4057 E-mail: jbates@mcguirewoods.com.

BATES, KATHY, actress; b. Memphis, June 28, 1948; d. Langdon Doyle and Bertye Kathleen (Talbot) Bates; m. Anthony Campisi, 1991 (div. 1997). BFA, So. Meth. U., 1969. Actor: (plays) Vanities, 1976, Semmelweiss, Crimes of the Heart, The Art of Dining, Goodbye Fidel, 1980, Chocolate Cake and Final Placement, 1981, 5th of July, 'night, Mother, 1983 (Tony nomination, Outer Critics Circle award), Two Masters: The Rain of Terror, 1985, Curse of the Starving Class, Frankie and Johnny in the Clair de Lune (OBIE award 1988), The Road to Mecca; (films) Taking Off, 1971, Straight Time, Come Back to the Five and Dime, Jimmy Dean, Jimmy Dean, Summer Heat, Arthur 2: On the Rocks, Signs of Life, High Stakes, Men Don't Leave, Dick Tracy, White Palace, Misery, 1990 (Acad. award for Best Actress 1990, Golden Globe award), At Play in the Fields of the Lord, 1991, Fried Green Tomatoes, 1991 (Golden Globe nomination, BAFTA nomination), The Road to Mecca, 1992, Prelude to a Kiss, 1992, Used People, 1992, A Home of Our Own, 1993, North, 1994, Curse of the Starving Class, 1994, Dolores Claiborne, 1994, Angus, 1995, Diabolique, 1996, The War at Home, 1996, Primary Colors, 1998, Swept from the Sea, 1998, Titanic, 1998, The Waterboy, 1998, Baby Steps, 1999, Dash and Lilly, 1999, My Life as a Dog, 1999, Bruno, 2000, Rat Race, 2001, American Outlaws, 2001, About Schmidt, 2002, Love Liza, 2002, Dragonfly, 2002, Around the World in 80 Days, 2004, The Bridge of San Luis Rey, 2004; (TV series) All My Children, 1984; (TV films) Johnny Bull, 1986, Murder Ordained, 1987, Roe vs. Wade, 1989, No Place Like Home, 1989, Hostages, 1993, Talking with, 1995, The West Side Waltz, 1995, The Late Shift, 1996, Annie, 1999, My Sister's Keeper, 2002, Warm Springs, 2005; dir. (TV films) Fargo, 2003; actor, exec. prodr. The Ingrate, 2004; TV guest appearances include The Love Boat, 1978, St. Elsewhere, 1986, 87, China Beach, 1989, LA Law, 1989, 3rd Rock from the Sun, 1999, (voice) King of the Hill, 2001, Six Feet Under, 2003-05. Office: Susan Smith & Assocs 121 N San Vicente Blvd Beverly Hills CA 90211-2303*

BATES, LEO JAMES, artist; b. Pitts., Apr. 12, 1944; s. Leo Thomas and Rose (Paiano) B.; m. Ellen Arch Levinson, Aug. 23, 1971. Student, Yale U., 1965; BFA, Carnegie-Mellon U., 1966. One-man shows include Albright-Knox Art Gallery, 1975, Picker Art Gallery, Dana Arts Ctr., Colgate U., 1975, Harriman Coll., 1978; exhibited in group shows including Joe and Emily Lowe Art Gallery, Syracuse U., 1978, Terry Dintenfass, Inc., N.Y.C., 1980, others; represented in permanent collections Albright-Knox Art Gallery, Bklyn. Mus., Carnegie Mus. Art, Pitts., Columbia Mus. Art, S.C., N.J. State Mus., Trenton. Creative Artists Pub. Scv. grantee N.Y. State Coun. Arts, 1974. Home: 499 11th St Brooklyn NY 11215-4303

BATES, MARCIA JEANNE, information scientist educator; b. Terre Haute, Ind., July 30, 1942; d. Robert Joseph and Martha Jane B. BA, Pomona Coll., 1963; MLS, U. Calif., Berkeley, 1967; PhD, U. Calif., 1972. Peace corps vol., Saraburi, Thailand, 1963-64, Nongkhai, Thailand, 1964-65; jr. specialist Inst. Libr. Rsch., U. Calif., Berkeley, 1968; acting instr. U. Calif., Berkeley, 1969-70; asst. prof. U. Md., College Park, 1972-76, U. Wash., Seattle, 1976-80, assoc. prof., 1980-81, U. Calif., Los Angeles, 1981-91, prof., 1991—, prof. and dept. chmn. libr. and info. sci. Cons. U.S. Libr. Congress, Washington, 1986, 91, 2002-03, Getty Art Hist. Info. Program, Santa Monica, Calif., 1988-91, Info. Access Co., Foster City, Calif., 1992-95; mem. editl. bd. Jour. of Asis &T, 1989—, Libr. Quar., 1993-2001. Co-author: For Information Specialists, 1992; contbr. articles to profl. jours. Recipient Distinguished Lectureship award N.J. Am. Soc. for Info. Sci., New Brunswick, 1991. Fellow AAAS (sect. T electorate nominating com. 1980-84, chmn. 1983-84, sect. T com. mem.-at-large, 2001-04), mem. ALA (Frederick G. Kilgour award, 2001), Am. Soc. Info. Sci. and Tech. (bd. dirs. 1973-74, Best Jour. Article Yr.

award, 1980, 99, Rsch. award 1998), Assn. Records Mgrs. Adminstrs., Calif. Libr. Assn. (mem. task force on future of Libr. profession, 1993-95), Phi Beta Kappa. Achievements include design of information systems and interfaces for search and subject access in information retrieval systems. Office: Grad Sch Edn & Info Studies UCLA 405 Hilgard Ave Los Angeles CA 90095-1520

BATES, MARGARET P., historian; BA, Barnard Coll.; MA, Wash. U., St. Louis. Dir. Coun. Basic Edn., Washington. Internat. bd. advisors Monterey Inst. Internat. Studies; bd. trustees York Sch., Carmel/Monterey, Calif.; mem. pres.'s coun. Calif. State U. Monterey Bay; former trustee Barnard Coll.; former mem. Calif. State Bd. Edn.

BATES, ROBERT C., academic administrator; m. Wendy Bates. BS in Biology, Lewis & Clark Coll., 1966; MS in Bacteriology and Pub. Health, Wash. State U., 1969; PhD in Virology, Colo. State U., 1972. Asst. prof. Va. Poly. Inst. and State U., 1972—78, assoc. prof., 1978—85, prof., 1985—2002, assoc. dean for rsch., facilities and grad. studies, 1987—94, dean Coll. Arts and Scis., 1994—2002; provost, exec. v.p. Wash. State U., Pullman, 2002—. Contbr. chapters to books, articles to profl. jours. Mem.: AAAS, Am. Soc. for Virology, Am. Soc. Biol. Chemists, Sigma Xi. Office: Office of Provost Wash State Univ PO Box 641046 Pullman WA 99164-1046 Office Phone: 509-335-5582. Business E-Mail: bates@wsu.edu.

BATES, SHAWN M., lawyer; b. Falmouth, Mass., Mar. 16, 1965; s. Robert and Elaine Childs Bates; m. Leticia Villarreal, Apr. 29, 1995; children: Christopher Shawn, Nicole Marie, Patrick Michael. BA, Loyola Coll., Balt., 1987; JD magna cum laude, Georgetown U., 2000. Def. analyst Sci. Applications Internat. Corp., McLean, Va., 1989—92; sr. auditor U.S. Dept. of State, Washington, 1995—97; sr. evaluator U.S. GAO, Washington, 1992—95, 1997—99; atty. Yetter & Warden, LLP, Houston, 2000—. Editor, pub.: mag. The Original Fishermen's Almanac. Lector St. Anne's Cath. Ch., Houston, 2004. Recipient law fellowship, Georgetown U. Law Ctr., 1998. Mem.: Order of Coif. Home: 8115 Stony Dell Ct Houston TX 77061 Office: Yetter & Warden LLP Ste 3600 909 Fannin Houston TX 77010 Office Phone: 713-632-8019. Office Fax: 713-632-8002. E-mail: sbates@yetterwarden.com.

BATES, WALTER ALAN, retired lawyer; b. Wadsworth, OH, Oct. 27, 1925; s. Edwin Clinton and Gertrude (Connor) B.; m. Aloise Grasselli O'Brien, Feb. 9, 1957; children: Charles, Aloise, Walter Alan Jr., Thomas, David. BS cum laude, Harvard U., 1945, LLB, 1950. Bar: Ohio 1950, U.S. Dist. Ct. (no. dist.) Ohio 1954, U.S. Ct. Appeals (6th cir.) 1965, U.S. Ct. Appeals (7th cir.) 1966, U.S. Dist. Ct. Conn. 1976, U.S. Ct. Appeals (2nd cir.) 1977, U.S. Dist. Ct. Minn. 1978, U.S. Ct. Appeals (8th cir.) 1980, U.S. Ct. Appeals (5th cir.) 1984, U.S. Dist. Ct. (no. dist.) Tex. 1988, U.S. Supreme Ct. 1989. Assoc. McKeehan, Merrick, Arter & Stewart, Cleve., 1950-60; ptnr. Arter & Hadden, Cleve., 1960-94; ret., 1994. Chmn. bd. trustees Cleve. Inst. Music, 1980-85, hon. trustee, 1985—; assoc. v.p., chmn. new programs com. United Way Svcs., Cleve., 1982-85, trustee, 1985-88; mem. Cleve. panel Ctr. for Pub. Resources; trustee Apollo's Fire, 1998—. Lt. USN, 1945—46, lt. USN, 1951—53. Mem. ABA (antitrust sect.), Ohio State Bar Assn. (chmn. bd. govs. antitrust sect. 1987-91), Cleve. Bar Assn. (joint com. on bar admissions 1990-97, cert. grievance com. 1992-95), Kirtland Country Club (sec., bd. dirs. 1981-86), Mentor Harbor Yachting Club (emeritus, bd. dirs. 1980-89, commodore 1988), Tavern Club, Harvard Club (Cleve. pres. 1968-69). Republican. Roman Catholic. Avocations: sailing, golf, travel. Home: 2684 Sulgrave Rd Shaker Heights OH 44122 E-mail: sailor74@adelphia.net.

BATES, WILLIAM, III, lawyer; b. Phila., May 1, 1949; s. William and Elizabeth (Martin) B. BA, Yale U., 1971; JD, Stanford U., 1974. Bar: Calif. 1974, U.S. Dist. Ct. (no. dist.) Calif. 1976, U.S. Dist. Ct. (ea. dist.) Calif. 1978, U.S. Dist. Ct. (ctrl. dist.) Calif. 1984, U.S. Ct. Appeals (9th cir.) 1986, U.S. Dist. Ct. (so. dist.) Calif. 1987, U.S. Supreme Ct. Law clk. to chief judge U.S. Dist. Ct. Conn., Hartford, 1974—75; assoc. McCutchen, Doyle, Brown & Enersen, San Francisco, 1975—81; ptnr. Bingham, McCutchen (formerly McCutchen, Doyle, Brown & Enersen), 1981—. Bd. visitors Stanford Law Sch., 2003—. Mem. ABA (mem. bus. bankruptcy com.), State Bar Calif. (chair rules of ct. com. 1979-80, mem. uniform comml. code com. 1985-88, mem. debtor/creditor rels. com. 1989-92), San Francisco Bar Assn. (chair comml. law and bankruptcy sect. 1991-92). Democrat. Episcopalian. Avocations: wine tasting, bicycling, travel. Office: Bingham McCutchen 1900 University Ave East Palo Alto CA 94303-2223 Office Phone: 650-849-4400. E-mail: bill.bates@bingham.com.

BATES, WILLIAM HUBERT, lawyer; b. Lexington, Mo., Apr. 14, 1926; s. George Hubert and E. Norma (Comer) B.; m. Joy LoRue Godbehere, Oct. 20, 1956; children: William Brand, Joy Ann. BA, U. Mo., 1949; JD, U. Mich., 1952. Bar: Mo. 1952. With Lathrop & Gage L.C., Kansas City, Mo., 1952—, chmn., 1988-95. Mem., pres. bd. curators U. Mo. Multi-Campus U., 1983-89. Sgt. U.S. Army, 1943-46, ETO. Recipient Brotherhood award NCCJ, 1984; Disting. Alumni award U. Mo., 1989, Geyer award for pub. svc., 1991. Fellow Am. Bar Found. (state chmn. 1990-97); mem. ABA (ho. of dels. 1990-93), Mo. Bar Assn. (bd. dirs. 1982-91, v.p., pres. 1988-91), Kansas City Bar Assn. (pres. Found. 1985-87), Lawyers Assn. Kansas City (Charles Evans Whittaker award 1990), Mo. C. of C. (chmn., bd. dirs. 1983-85), Greater Kansas City C. of C. (bd. dirs., chmn. 1975-92), Van Guard Club, Mercury Club, Beta Theta Pi (Man of Yr. award Kansas City 1985, Oxford Cup 1996). Democrat. Methodist. Avocations: golf, swimming, music. Home: 310 W 49th St Apt 1002 Kansas City MO 64112-3400 Office: Lathrop & Gage L C 2345 Grand Blvd Ste 2600 Kansas City MO 64108-2617 Office Phone: 816-292-2000. Business E-Mail: bbates@lathropgage.com.

BATESON, MARY CATHERINE, anthropology educator emerita; b. N.Y.C., Dec. 8, 1939; d. Gregory and Margaret (Mead) B.; m. J. Barkev Kassarjian, June 4, 1960; 1 child, Sevanne Margaret. BA, Radcliffe Coll., 1960; PhD, Harvard U., 1963; DHL (hon.), Fordham U., 1994, U. Redlands, 1996, DePaul U., 1998, Marygrove Coll., 1999, Mills Coll., 2000. Instr. Arabic Harvard U., 1963-66; assoc. prof. anthropology Ateneo de Manila U., 1966-68; sr. rsch. fellow psychology and philosophy Brandeis U., 1968-69; assoc. prof. anthropology Northeastern U., Boston, 1969-71; rschr. U. Tehran, 1972-74; vis. prof. Northeastern U., 1974-75; prof. anthropology, dean grad. studies Damavand Coll., 1975-77; prof. anthropology, dean social sci. and humanities U. No. Iran, 1977-79; vis. scholar Harvard U., 1979-80; dean faculty, prof. anthropology Amherst Coll., 1980-87; Clarence J. Robinson prof. anthropology and English George Mason U., 1987—2002, prof. emerita, 2002—. Pres. Inst. Intercultural Studies, 1979—; vis. prof. Spelman Coll., 1996; scholar in residence, Radcliffe Inst. Advanced Studies, Harvard U., 2000-01; Harvard Grad. Sch. Edn., 2001-04. Author: Arabic Language Handbook, 1967, 2d edit., 2003, Structural Continuity in Poetry: A Linguistic Study of Five Early Arabic Odes, 1970, Our Own Metaphor: A Personal Account of a Conference on Consciousness and Human Adaption, 1972, 3d edit., 2004, With a Daughter's Eye: A Memoir of Margaret Mead and Gregory Bateson, 1984, 3d edit., 2001, Composing a Life, 1989, 3d edit., 2001, Peripheral Visions: Learning Along the Way, 1994, Full Circles, Overlapping Lives: Culture and Generation in Transition, 2000, Willing to Learn: Passages of Personal Discovery, 2004; co-author: Angels Fear: Towards an Epistemology of the Sacred, 1987, 2d edit., 2005, Thinking AIDS, 1988; co-editor: Approaches to Semiotics: Anthropology, Education, Linquistics, Psychiatry and Psychology, 1964. Mem. adv. bd. Cities at Peace Nat. Fellow Ford Found., 1961-63, NSF, 1968-69, Wenner-Gren Found., 1972, Bunting Inst., 1983-84, Guggenheim Found., 1987-88. Mem. Am. Anthrop. Assn., Lindisfarne Assn., Nat. Ctrs. Atmospheric Rsch. (adv. bd.), Phi Beta Kappa. E-mail: mcatb@attglobal.net.

BATES STOKLOSA, EVELYNNE (EVE BATES STOKLOSA), educational consultant, educator; b. Camden, N.J., Mar. 13, 1946; d. Linwood T. and Eve Mary (Widzenas) Bates; m. Leslie E. Stoklosa, Apr. 15, 1968; children: Phillip J., Kristine L. BS in Home Econs. Edn., Buffalo State U. Coll., 1968, MS in Home Econs. Edn., 1971, Cert. Advanced Studies, 1994. Cert. sch. dist. adminstr. Tchr. Parkside Elem. Sch., Kenmore, N.Y., 1968-69, Kenmore West High Sch., 1968-71, 73-75, Kenmore Jr. High Sch., 1977-80, Ken-Ton Continuing Edn., Kenmore, 1980-87, Kenmore Mid. Sch., 1981—2001. Owner, pres. EBS Decors, Tonawanda, N.Y.; edn. cons. Villa Maria Coll., Buffalo, 1980-2000; adv. bd. interior design dept.; facilitator student of the month award program Kenmore Mid. Sch., 1982—, active mem. sch. planning team, 1984—, facilitator design team, 1990—; participant Buffalo Summits, 1994; ind. fashion cons. Editor parent informational pamphlet, 1992, faculty informational newsletter, 1992-94. Vol., Frankl Loyd Wright Found. of the Martin House Restoration Corp., 1999—; vol. various charitable functions and events in and around Buffalo; mem. Amateur Chamber Music Players, 2000—, Buffalo Philharmonic Orch. Women's Com. Found., 2000—. Erie County Nutrition Assn. grantee. Mem. AAUW (bd. dirs. 1992-94), ASCD, DAR (life), Family and Consumer Scientists Am. (life), Am. Vocat. Assn., Am. Fedn. Tchrs., N.Y. State Home Econs. Tchrs. Assn. (Tchr. of Yr. 1992-93, Most Outstanding Leadership and Creativity award 1987), N.Y. State Assn. Family and Consumer Sci. Educators (life), N.Y. State United Tchrs., Western N.Y. Women in Adminstrn., Kenmore Tchrs. Assn. (bldg. rep.), Opera Buffs Western N.Y. (life), Amatuer Chamber Mus Soc., Chautaqua Lit. and Sci. Cir. (life), Phi Delta Kappa, Phi Upsilon Omicron. Avocations: travel, singing, swimming, golf, piano.

BATEY, DOUGLAS LEO, lawyer; b. Portland, Oreg., Oct. 23, 1947; s. Frank and Dorothy Frances (Hoffman) B.; m. Patricia Johnson, May 27, 1967 (div. 1982); 1 child, Jonathan Samuel; m. Marian Virginia Gaynor, Sept. 24, 1983; children: Thomas Gaynor, Leland Franklin, Ramsey Calhoun, Lucas Gabriel. BS summa cum laude, U. Wash., 1972, JD with honors, 1980. Bar: Wash. 1980, U.S. Dist. Ct. (we. dist.) Wash. 1980. Prin. Stoel Rives LLP, Seattle, 1980—. Served to sgt. USMC, 1965-69. Mem. Wash. Bar Assn., Seattle-King Bar Assn., Phi Beta Kappa. Address: Stoel Rives LLP 600 University St Ste 3600 Seattle WA 98101-4109 Office Phone: 206-624-0900.

BATH, JOANNE MCMATH, music educator; b. Seattle, Dec. 28, 1935; d. Roy Jayne and Anne Catherine (Bergstrand) Mc.; m. Charles Frederick Bath, Aug. 23, 1958; children: Pamela, Patricia, Stephen, Andrea. MusB, Denison U., Granville, Ohio, 1957; MusM, U. Mich., 1959. Violinist Wichita (Kans.) Symphony, 1961-66; violin tchr. Bath Sch. of Music, Greenville, N.C., 1966—, dir., 1966—. Bd. dirs. Suzuki Assn. of Ams., 1991-95, registered tchr. trainer, 1989—; dir. Suzuki Violinists of Ea. N.C., 1980—; pres. Greenville (N.C.) Suzuki Assn., 1985—, N.C. Suzuki Assn., 1980—; Hardy disting. prof. suzaki pedagogy East Carolina U. Sch. Music, Greenville, 1993—; violinist Bath Duo, 1958—. Contbr. articles to profl. jours. Bd. dirs. Eastern Carolina Orch. and Chamber Music Assn., Greenville, N.C., 1978—, pres., 1980-84; bd. dirs. Greenville Choral Soc., N.C. Sinfonia, 1990-92. Recipient Fine Arts award, N.C. Gov., 1996, Learning Cmty. award, Suzuki Assn. of Americas, 2002. Mem.: Am. String Tchrs. Assn. (state sec. 1972—74), Music Tchrs. Nat. Assn. (chmn. 1982—84, chmn. state string sect. 1990). Episcopalian. Office: Sch Music East Carolina Univ Greenville NC 27858-5231 Office Phone: 252-328-6907. Business E-Mail: bathj@mail.ecu.edu.

BATHAEE, SOUSSAN, engineering technician; b. Tehran, Iran, Jan. 23, 1953; arrived in U.S., 1983; d. Mohammad Bathaee and Farokhlagha Hassanpour. BSCE, Calif. State U., Fullerton, 2002; postgrad., 2004—. Overseas supr. Atomic Energy Orgn., Tehran, Iran, 1972—80; overseas drafts person London, 1980—83; drafts person Earl Walls Assocs., San Diego, 1984—85; job capt. Rsch. Facilities Design, San Diego, 1985—90; engring. svc. technician County of San Bernardino, Calif., 1991—2002, ret., 2002; freelance engr. LDIC, San Jose, Calif., 2002—. Mem.: AIA, ASCE, Great Riverside C. of C. Moslem. Home: 42045 Kaffirboom Ct Temecula CA 92591

BATHE, KLAUS-JURGEN, mechanical engineering educator; BSc, U. Cape Town, South Africa, 1967; MSc, U. Calgary, Can., 1969; PhD, U. Calif., Berkeley, 1971. Prof. mech. engring. MIT, Cambridge, Mass., 1975—; founder, dir. ADINA R&D, Inc., Watertown, Mass., 1986—. Author: (book) Finite Element Procedures, 1996; contbr. articles to profl. jours.; editor: Computers & Structures. Mem.: ASME, ASCE, Soc. for Indsl. and Applied Math. Achievements include research in structures and CFD; finite element methods. Office: MIT Dept Mech Engring Rm 3-356 Cambridge MA 02139

BATHURST, DEBRA LYNNETTE, physical therapist assistant; d. John Howard and Marcia Bernice Bathurst. AA, Lake City (Fla.) C.C., 1984, AS, 1988, Miami (Fla.) Dade C.C., 1996. Bd. lic. phys. therapist asst. Asst. supt. Turkey Creek Country Club, Gainesville, Fla., 1988—89, Jack Nicklaus home, West Palm Beach, Fla., 1989—90, The Falls Country Club, Lake Worth, Fla., 1990—92, Boca Rio Country Club, Boca Raton, Fla., 1992—94; phys. therapist asst. Broward Inst. Orthop. Spltys., Hollywood, Fla., 1996—. Author: Paradise Found, 2003, Indiscretions, 2003, Commitments, 2003. Mem.: Am. Phys. Therapy Assn. Avocations: sports, writing, travel, video editing. Home: 4712 NW 82d Ave Lauderhill FL 33351 E-mail: bly1313@yahoo.com.

BATIE, LONA R., music educator; d. LeRoy W. and Phyllis A. Busching; m. Dwight R. Batie, June 28, 1975; children: Sara L. Batie Vollmer, Ann L. Ede, Jeffrey D. BS, Moorhead (Minn.) State U., 1971. Tchr. K-12 vocal music Raymond (Minn.) Sch., 1972—73; tchr. K-6 vocal music Sisseton (N.D.) Sch., 1973—75; tchr. K-12 vocal and instrumental music Summit (S.D.) Sch., 1975—79; tchr. K-8 vocal music Big Stone City (S.D.) Sch., 1979—81; tchr. K-12 vocal and instrumental music Veblen (S.D.) Pub. Sch., 1981—90; tchr. 7-12 vocal music Britton (S.D.)-Hecla Sch., 1990—. Pvt. piano instr., 1979—; organist and choir dir. First Luth. Ch., Britton, 1990; Whetstone Choral Festival accompanist Sisseton Kiwanis, 1989—. Bd. dirs. S.D. All-State Chorus, 2004. Named Sisseton Outstanding Young Educator, Sisseton Sch., 1975; recipient Sword of Honor, Sigma Alpha Iota, 1971. Mem.: S.D. Bandmasters Assn. (grade instrumental contest mgr. 2003—, piano contest mgr. 1992—), Nat. Fedn. Interscholastic Music Assn, Am. Choral Dirs. Assn. (choral reading clinic accompanist). Home: PO Box 436 1007 5thSt Britton SD 57430 Office: Britton-Hecla Sch 759 5th St Britton SD 57430 Office Phone: 605-448-2234. Personal E-mail: ldbatie@sbtc.net. E-mail: lona.batie@k12.sd.us.

BATKA, JOHN, education educator, consultant; b. Springfield, Ohio, Sept. 20, 1969; s. Joseph and Catherine Batka; m. Jennifer Melzer, Dec. 2, 1969. BS, Ohio State U., Columbus, Ohio, 1991—91; MS, Wright State U., Dayton, Ohio, 1994; PhD, Tenn. State U., Nashville, Tenn., 1999. Lic. Psychologist Okla., 2001. Asst. prof. psychology So. Utah U., Cedar City, Utah, 1998—99, Cameron U., Lawton, Okla., 1999—. Cons. Self-employed, Lawton, Okla., 2000—. Contbr. articles pub. to profl. jour. Recipient Advisor of the Yr., Cameron U., 2000-2001, Spirit of Human Rights Award, Cameron U. P.R.I.D.E., 2000-2001; scholar Milton Cudney Scholarship, Western Mich. U., 1997-1998. Mem.: ACA, APA, Okla. Psychol. Soc., Am. Psychol. Soc., Chi Sigma Iota, Psi Chi (advisor 1999—2005). Roman Cath. Avocation: scuba diving. Office: Cameron Univ 2800 W Gore Lawton OK 73505 Office Phone: 580-581-2567.

BATLA, RAYMOND JOHN, JR., lawyer; b. Cameron, Tex., Sept. 1, 1947; s. Raymond John and Della Alvina (Jezek) B.; m. Susan Marie Clark, Oct. 1, 1983; children: Sara, Charles, Michael, Traci. BS with highest honors, U. Tex., 1970, JD with honors, 1973. Bar: Tex. 1973, D.C. 1973, N.Y. 2004, U.S. Dist. Ct. (so. dist.) Tex. 1982, U.S. Ct. Appeals (D.C. cir.) 1974, U.S. Ct. Appeals (5th cir.) 1982, U.S. Ct. Appeals (10th cir.) 1978, U.S. Supreme Ct. 1977; registered Fgn. Lawyer, Law Soc. of Eng. and Wales, 2000. Structural engr. Tex. Hwy. Dept., Austin, 1970; assoc. Hogan & Hatson, Washington, 1973-82, gen. ptnr., 1983—, mng. ptnr.-internat. offices. Mem. Am. Endowment for Democracy Internat. Observer Del. to Czechoslovakia, 1990; sec. Coun. on Alt. Fuels, 1987-97. Author: Petroleum Regulation Handbook, 1980, Natural Gas Yearbook, 1991; columnist, mem. editorial bd. Natural Gas mag., 1984-91, Energy Law Jour., 1991-93; contbr. articles to profl. jours. Mem. ABA (mem. spl. com. for energy fin., vice chmn. energy com. 1981), Fed. Energy Bar Assn. (chmn. internat. energy transactions com. 1993-94), Fed. Bar Assn., D.C. Bar Assn., State Bar Tex., N.Y. State Bar Assn., City Club of Wash., London Capital Club, Order of Coif, Chi Epsilon, Tau Beta Pi. Home: 12406 Shari Hunt Grv Clifton VA 20124-2056 also: 5 Half Moon St London W1Y 7RA England Office: Hogan & Hartson 555 13th St NW Ste 800W Washington DC 20004-1109 also: Hogan & Hartson One Angel Ct London EC2R 7HJ England Office Phone: 202-637-5745. E-mail: rjbatla@hhlaw.com.

BATLIN, ROBERT ALFRED, retired newspaper editor; b. San Francisco, Aug. 24, 1930; S. Philip Alfred and Lavenia Mary (Barnes) B.; m. Diane Elise Giblin, July 4, 1956; children— Lisa, Philippa. BA, Stanford U., 1952, MA, 1954. Reporter San Bruno Herald, 1952-53; copy editor, then dept. editor San Francisco News, 1956-59; dept. editor San Francisco News-Call Bull., 1959-65; feature editor San Francisco Examiner, 1965-74, arts editor, 1974-85, asst. style editor, 1985-2001; copy editor San Francisco Chronicle mag., 2001—02, ret., 2002. Served with AUS, 1954-56. Mem. Soc. of Profl. Journalists. Home: 91 Fairway Dr Daly City CA 94015-1215

BATMAN, SHIRLEY DE PORTER, music educator; b. Carr, Colo., Aug. 10, 1931; d. Arthur Triphon and Mabel Etta (Gallatin) De Porter; m. Larry Gene Batman, Nov. 25, 1952; children: Christine Dee, Elena Jeanne. AB, U. No. Colo., 1952, MA, 1969; postgrad., U. N.Mex., 1967, Colo. State U., 1982. Cert. tchr. Colo. Tchr. music, lang. arts Pierce (Colo.) Cons. Schs., 1952-57; pvt. practice music tchr. Albuquerque, 1958-67, Greeley, Colo., 1967—. Choir dir. Asbury Meth. Ch., Albuquerque, 1960-67; pubs. specialist Aims Community Coll., Greeley, 1982-85, music tchr., 1982—, basic communication skills tchr., 1984—; clinician-adjudicator Federated Music Clubs, Albuquerque, 1964-67. Mem. publicity com., vocal soloist Mosiac Choir, Albuquerque, 1982-86; mem. publicity and fund raising coms. 4-H Clubs, Washington and Weld County, Colo., 1977-79; chmn. Dem. precinct, Greeley, 1982—, Albuquerque, 1964-67. Mem. Standard Quarter Horse Assn. (cir. nat. youth activities 1982-84), Colo. Music Educators Assn. (bd. dirs. 1984—, chmn. ann. conv. 1987, speaker), Delta Omicron (province pres. 1955-57, nat. officer 1957—), U. No. Colo. Alumni Assn. (v.p. Weld chpt. 1986—, reunion chmn. 1982—), Fortnightly Mus. Club (pres. 1977-78, publicity com. and historian 1975-76). Presbyterian. Home: 5037 Kiowa Dr Greeley CO 80634-9322

BATMASIAN, MARTA TERSAKIAN, investment company owner; b. Istanbul, Turkey, Oct. 4, 1949; came to U.S., 1970. Garo and Anjel Tersakian; m. James H. Batmasian, Aug. 10, 1974; children: Jimmy, Armen. Student, Robert Coll., Istanbul, 1966-69, Leiden (The Netherlands) U., 1969-70; BA, Emerson Coll., 1972; MA, Brandeis U., 1975, postgrad., 1972-76; MBA, Barry U., 1987. Supt. Sahag Mesrob Sch., Watertown, Mass., 1974-75; lectr., prof. U. Mass., Boston, 1975-83; owner, pres. Mar-Mel Travel, Ins. and Real Estate, Cambridge, Mass., 1979-83; co-owner Investments Ltd., Boca Raton, Fla., 1983—. Co-owner Investments Ltd., Cambridge, Mass., 1983—. Mem. Elem. Sch. Bd. of Watertown, 1979-81, Boca Raton Hist. Soc., South Fla. Symphony, Boca Raton Mus. Art, St. David's Armenian Ch.; bd. dirs. Boca Delray Sci. Mus., 1986-88; rec. sec. Fla. Symphonic Pops-Pro-Pops, 1986-87; v.p. Friends of Children's Mus. Boca Raton, 1987-89; Rep. nominee for Mass. Senate, 1982; bd. dirs. YMCA of Boca Raton, 1988-92; founder, v.p. Children's Sci. Explorium, Boca Raton, pres., chmn. bd., 1989—; active Men's Rep. Club of Baca Raton, Cystic Fibrosis Assn., St. Andrew's Sch. PTA; bd. trustees Am. Assembly, 1986—, Caldwell State Theater, 1990—, Children's Mus. of Boca Raton, 1986-90; founder, pres. Caldwell Theater Guild, 1991—; active Humanitarian Soc., 1989—; founder, bd. dirs. Boca Raton Literary Soc., 1991—. Mem. Nat. Assn. Armenian Studies and Rsch., Boca Raton C. of C., Jr. League of Baca Raton, AGBU Pres.'s Club, Allegro Soc. Club, Pro Pops (founder), Poinciana Women's Rep. Club (legis. chair 1985-87), YMCA Y's Women's Club (v.p. 1987—), Daus. of Vartan Lodge (treas. 1983—). Armenian Apostolic. Avocations: jogging, music, theater, stamp collecting/philately. Office: Investments Ltd 215 N Federal Hwy Ste 1 Boca Raton FL 33432-3992

BATOR, FRANCIS MICHEL, economist, educator; b. Budapest, Hungary, Aug. 10, 1925; came to U.S., 1939, naturalized, 1944; s. Victor and Franciska Elisabeth (Sichermann) B.; m. Micheline Charlotte Martin, June 30, 1949; children: Nina, Christopher Francis. Grad., Groton Sch., 1943; BS, MIT, 1949, PhD, 1956; MA (hon.), Harvard U., 1967. Exec. asst. to dir. Center Internat. Studies, MIT, 1951-54; sr. research staff Center Internat. Studies, Mass. Inst. Tech., 1954-63, asst. prof. econs., 1957-60, assoc. prof., 1960-63; sr. econ. adviser AID, Dept. State, 1963-64; sr. staff NSC, 1964-65; dep. asst. to Pres. for nat. security affairs White House, 1965-67; prof. polit. economy John F. Kennedy Sch. Govt. Harvard U., 1967-87, Ford Found. prof. internat. polit. economy John F. Kennedy Sch. Govt., 1987-92; Lucius N. Littauer prof. polit. economy John F. Kennedy Sch. Govt., Harvard U., 1992-96, emeritus Lucius N. Littauer prof. polit. economy, 1996—. Cons. Rand Corp., Inst. Def. Analysis, Office Sec. Treasury, 1961-63, under sec. state for econ. affairs, 1961; U.S. mem. consultative group on econ. projections UN, 1962, on internat. monetary arrangements, 1969; spl. cons. sec. treasury, 1967-69; mem. Pres.'s Adv. Com. Internat. Monetary Arrangements, 1967-69; vis. fellow Collegium Budapest Inst. Advanced Study, 1993. Author: The Question of Government Spending, 1960; co-author: Energy, the Next Twenty Years, 1979; contbr. Agenda for the Nation, 1968, Employment and Growth, 1987, The Theory of Market Failure, 1998; contbr. articles to profl. jours. Fgn. affairs task force Dem. Adv. Coun. Elected Ofcls., 1974-76; nat. adv. bd. Ctr. Nat. Policy, 1981-90; adv. bd. Scudder New Europe Fund, 1990-92, McKinsey and Co. Global Inst., 1991-95; bd. dirs. Hungarian-Am. Enterprise Fund, 1994—. 1st lt. inf. AUS, 1944-46. Recipient Disting. Service award Treasury Dept., 1968; Guggenheim fellow, 1959; named to US Army Officer Candidate Sch. Hall of Fame. Fellow Am. Acad. Arts and Scis.; mem. Coun. Fgn. Rels., Am. Econ. Assn., Century Assn. (NYC), Harvard Club (NYC). Home: 17 Farrar St Cambridge MA 02138-2007 Office: Harvard U 79 Jfk St Cambridge MA 02138-5801 Business E-Mail: Francis_Bator@Harvard.edu.

BATOR, MARTHA ZACHRY MAYSON, artist; b. Atlanta, Feb. 12, 1930; d. James Lucian and Jane Crawford (Hancock) Mayson; m. Edmund Alexander Bator, June 11, 1952; children: Jane Crawford, Zachry Mayson. BA, Oglethorpe U., 1951; studies in painting, Helsinki (Finland) U.; studies in sculpture and pastel, various artists. Tchr. Dekalb County Schs., Atlanta, 1951-53, Prince Georges County Schs., Mt. Ranier, Md., 1954-56, D.C. Schs., 1967-70; pres. Design Studio, Kuwait, 1975-79; artist Atlanta, 1980—. One-woman shows at Mercer U., Oglethorpe U. Mus., Goodyear Ho.; two-person shows at DeKalb C.C., Quinlan Fine Arts Gallery; represented in corp. collections including King and Spaulding, Atlanta, McRae and Holloway, Atlanta, Ganek, Wright and Dobkin, Atlanta, Ga. Coun. for Arts, Children's Hosp., Macon, Ga., Kuwait Embassy, Washington, Heathrow Country Club, Sarasota, Fla., John C. Campbell Folk Sch., Brasstown, N.C., Art Pl., Kuwait and Dubai, Oglethorpe U. Mus., Kaiser Permanente, Jean and Mack Henderson Women's Ctr. at Kennestone Hosp.; works included in publs. including So. Homes Mag., Peachtree Mag., Pastel Jour., 200 Great Painting Ideas for Artists (Carole Katchen), The Best of Pastel and A Gallery of Marine Art, others. Mem. Dekalb Coun. for Arts, 1982—. Recognized for Achievement by Ga. Woman in Visual Arts, Sec. of State, 1997; recipient 1st prize Ann. Heritage Fine Arts Competition, 3 Nat. Juried Best of Show awards, various nat. and internat. awards. Mem. Pastel Soc. Am. (signature), Southea. Pastel Soc. (v.p. 1987—), Knickerbocker Artists, U.S.A., Atlanta Artist's Ctr. (gallery chmn. 1986, 87, Mem. of Excellence), Art Sta., Plein Air Painters of Ga. Avocations: travel, photography. Home: 3432 Stratfield Dr NE Atlanta GA 30319-2567 E-mail: bator@artshow.com.

BATRA, ROMESH CHANDER, engineering educator, researcher; b. Dherowal, Panjab, India, Aug. 16, 1947; came to U.S., 1969; s. Amir Chand and Dewki Bai (Dhamija) B.; m. Manju Dhamija, June 26, 1972; children: Monica, Meenakshi. BSME, Panjabi U., Patiala, India, 1968; MASc, U. Waterloo, Ont., Can., 1969; PhD, Johns Hopkins U., 1972. Postdoctoral rsch. assoc. Johns Hopkins U., Balt., 1972-73; rsch. assoc. McMaster U., Hamilton, Ont., 1973-74; asst. prof. U. Ala., Tuscaloosa, 1976-77; asst. prof. engring. mechanics U. Mo., Rolla, 1974-76, assoc. prof., 1977-81, prof., 1981-94;

Clifton C. Garvin prof. Va. Poly. Inst. and State U., Blacksburg, 1994—. Bd. dirs. Midwestern Mechanics Conf., 1989—93, mem. editor procs., 1991; mem. NRC Panel on Armaments, 1996—99, NRC Panel on Survivability and Lethality, 2001—; organizer, co-chair Mechs. and Mats. Conf., 1999; lectr. S.W. Mechanics Series, 2000; Michael L. Sadowski mechanics lectr. Rensselaer Poly. Inst., 2000; hon. prof. Nanjing (China) U. Sci. and Tech., 2004—; co-chair 1st internat. conf. Mechanical Engring. & Mechanics, Nanjing, China. Co-editor-in-chief: Internat. Jour. Computational Methods, 2004-; editor: Contemporary Research in Engineering Science, Springer Verlag, 1995, Handbook on Smart Materials/Structures, 2004; co-editor: Contemporary Research in the Mechanics and Mathematics of Materials, Internat. Ctr. for Numerical Methods in Engring., 1996, Constitutive Laws, Experiments and Numerical Implementation, Internat. Ctr. for Numerical Methods in Engring., 1995, Material Instabilities, Theory and Applications, 1994, Impact, Waves and Fracture, 1994, Contemporary Research in Mechanics, 2002; mem. editl. bd. Internat. Jour. Plasticity, 1989-2003, Internat. Jour. Engring. Design and Analysis, 1992—, Continuum Mechanics and Thermodynamics, 1993-2004, Computational Mechanics, 1994—, Jour. Engring. Materials and Tech., 1996-2001, Polish Jour. Theoretical and Applied Mechanics, 2000—, Computer Modeling in Engring. and Sci., 2003—; editor: Mathematics and Mechanics of Solids, 1995—; author: Elements of Continuum Mechanics, AIAA Publ., 2005; reviewer for various jours. in field; contbr. articles to profl. jours. Grantee NSF, 1980-83, 87—, Army Rsch. Office, 1985—, Office of Naval Rsch., 1994—; recipient Alexander von Humboldt award for sr. scientists, 1992, Jai Krishna award Indian Geotech. Soc., 1994, Eric Reissner medal Internat. Congress in Computational Engrg. Sci., 2000; inducted into Hopkins Soc. Scholars, 1993. Fellow ASME (chair elasticity com. 1995-2000, co-editor symposium procs. 1991, 94-95, co-editor meeting procs. 1999, awards nominating com. 1997—), Am. Acad. Mechanics (awards nominating com. 2002—, sec. 2003—), Am. Soc. Engring. Edn. (Centennial award 1993), Soc. Engring. Sci. (bd. dirs. 1991-96, editor meeting procs. 1982, v.p. 1995, pres. 1996); Soc. Natural Philosophy (treas. 1987-89, editor meeting procs. 1981), U.S. Nat. Congress Theoret. and Applied Mechs. (organizer, co-chmn. 2002). Office: Va Polytech Inst & State U Dept Engring Sci & Mechanics 220 Norris Hall Blacksburg VA 24061-0219 Business E-Mail: rbatra@vt.edu.

BATROUNEY, CLIVE M., corporate financial executive; With Victoria Funds Mgmt. Co.; chmn., dir. Telstra Superannuation Fund, Melbourne, 2003—. Office: Telstra Super Pty Ltd 215 Spring St Level 3 Melbourne VIC 3000 Australia Office Phone: 03-96536000.

BATSAKIS, JOHN GEORGE, pathology educator; b. Petoskey, Mich., Aug. 14, 1929; s. George John and Stella (Vlahkis) B.; m. Mary Janet Savage, Dec. 28, 1957; children: Laura, Sharon, George. Student, Va. Mil. Inst., 1947, Albion Coll., Mich., 1948-50; MD, U. Mich., 1954. Diplomate Am. Bd. Pathology. Intern George Washington Univ. Hosp., Washington, 1954-55; resident in pathology U. Mich. Hosp., Ann Arbor, 1955-59; prof. pathology U. Mich., Ann Arbor, 1969-79; chmn. dept. pathology M.D. Anderson Hosp. U. Tex., Houston, 1981-96, chm. and prof. emeritus dept pathology, 1996—. Ruth Legett Jones prof. U. Tex., Austin, 1982-96; adj. prof. oral pathology U. Tex. Dental Br., Houston; cons. Armed Forces Inst. Pathology, 1972—, VA Hosp., Ann Arbor, 1968-79; Hayes Martin lectr. Am. Soc. for Head and Neck Surgery, 1994; Gunnar Holmgren lectr. Swedish Nat. Ear, Nose, Throat Meeting, 1994; William Christopherson lectr. U. Louisville Dept. of Pathology, 1995; external examiner U. Hong Kong Dental Sch., 1995—; Francis A. Sooy lectr. dept. otolaryngology, head and neck surgery U. Calif., San Francisco, 1997; 2d Matthews lectr. dept. pathology Emory U., 1997; spkr. in field. Author: Tumors of the Head and Neck, 2d edit., 1979; co-author: Surgical Pathology of the Head and Neck, 2000; editor: Clin. Lab. Ann., 1981—86; co-editor: Advances in Anatomic Pathology, 1994—98, Oral Cancer, 2003, Comprehensive Management of Head and Neck Tumors, 1999; contbr. articles to profl. jours. Bd. trustees, v.p. Mike Hogg Found., Houston, 1991—; trustee George C. Marshall Found., Lexington, Va., 1995-00, emeritus trustee, 2000—. Capt. U.S. Army, 1959-61. Recipient William H. Rorer award Am. Coll. Gastroenterology, 1972, Disting. Alumnus award Albion Coll., 1987, Reviewer of the Decade award AMA Archives Orolaryngology Head Neck Surgery, 1990, Presdl. award Am. Soc. Head and Neck Surgery, 1991, Harlan Spjut award Houston Soc. Clin. Pathologists, 1992, Honor award Am. Laryngologic Assn., 1995; Spl. Honored Guest of Am. Soc. for Head and Neck Surgery, 1993. Fellow ACP, Am. Soc. Clin. Pathologists, Coll. Am. Pathologists (Disting. Svc. award 2002), Am. Acad. Otolaryngology (assoc., honor award 1994), Royal Soc. Medicine. Republican. Episcopalian. Home: 1701 Hermann Dr Unit 3304 Houston TX 77004-7373

BATSHAW, MARK LEVITT, pediatrician; b. Montreal, Que., Can., Sept. 19, 1945; s. Manuel G. and Rachel (Levitt) B.; m. Karen N. Korman, June 29, 1969; children: Elissa, Michael, Andrew. BA, U. Pa., 1967; MD, U. Chgo., 1971. Diplomate Am. Bd. Pediatrics. Resident in pediatrics Hosp. for Sick Children, Toronto, 1971-73; fellow in developmental pediatrics Kennedy Krieger Inst., Johns Hopkins U. Sch. Medicine, 1973-75; instr. Johns Hopkins U. Sch. Medicine, Balt., 1975-76, asst. prof., 1976-80, assoc. prof. pediatrics, 1980-88; W.T. Grant prof. pediatrics and neurology U. Pa. Sch. Medicine, Phila., 1988-98; chief div. child devel. and rehab. Children's Hosp. of Phila., 1988-98; physician-in-chief Children's Seashore House, Phila., 1988-98; chief acad. officer Children's Nat. Med. Ctr., Washington, 1998—; chmn. pediats. George Washington U. Med. Ctr., 1998—; dir. Children's Rsch. Inst., 1998—. Mem. NIH study NICHD, 1991-95. Author: Children with Disabilities, 4th edit., 1997, Your Child Has a Disability, 1991. Johns Hopkins U. fellow, 1973-75; Kennedy scholar, Kennedy Inst., 1983-86. Fellow Royal Coll. Physicians; mem. Am. Pediatric Soc. Office: Children's Nat Med Ctr 111 Michigan Ave NW Washington DC 20010-2916

BATSON, DAVID WARREN, lawyer; b. Wichita Falls, Tex., Jan. 4, 1956; s. Warren M. Batson and Jacqueline (Latham) B. BBA, Midwestern State U., 1976; JD, U. Tex., 1979. Bar: Tex. 1980, U.S. Dist. Ct. (no. dist.) Tex. 1981, U.S. Tax Ct. 1981, U.S. Ct. Appeals (5th cir.) 1983, U.S. Ct. Appeals (D.C. cir.) 1983, U.S. Ct. Claims 1984, U.S. Supreme Ct. 1984. Atty. Arthur Andersen & Co., Ft. Worth, 1980-81; tax atty. The Western Co. of N.Am., Ft. Worth, 1981-85; sr. tax atty. Alcon Labs., Inc., Ft. Worth, 1985; gen. counsel Data Tailor, Inc., Ft. Worth, 1985-87; sr. tax atty. Arco, 1988-90; atty. pvt. practice, Wichita Falls, Tex., 1990—99; pvt. practice Stephenville, Tex., 1999—. Lectr. U. of Tex., Arlington, 1984-85; of counsel Means & Means, Corsicana, Tex., 1985-86. Contbr. articles to profl. jours. Speaker A Wish With Wings, Arlington, Tex., 1984-85, Habitat for Humanity (bd. dirs. 1999-). Fellow Tex. Bar Found.; mem. ATLA, Tex. Bar Assn., Christian Legal Soc., Tex. Trial Lawyers Assn., Phi Delta Phi. Avocations: negotiations, camping, self improvement. Address: PO Box 585 Stephenville TX 76401-0585 Office Phone: 254-918-7400. E-mail: batson@itexas.net.

BATSON, RICHARD NEAL, lawyer; b. Nashville, May 1, 1941; s. John H. and Mildred (Neal) B.; m. Jean Elizabeth Flanagan; children: John Hayes, Richard Davis. BA cum laude, Vanderbilt U., 1963, JD, 1966. Bar: Ga. 1967. Law clk. to Judge Griffin B. Bell U.S. Ct. Appeals (5th cir.), Atlanta, 1966-67; assoc. Alston & Bird (formerly Alston, Miller & Gaines), Atlanta, 1967-71, ptnr., 1971—. Spkr. Nat. Conf. Bankruptcy Judges, 1982, 86, 87, 88, 94, 96, Bank Lending Inst., 1986-87, also other instns. and assns.; adj. prof. Emory U. Sch. Law, 1994-95; co-lectr. Ga. State U., fall 1984; mem. bankruptcy rules com. Jud. Conf. U.S., 1993-99. Co-author: Problem Loan Strategies, 1985, rev. 1998; contbg. author Bankruptcy Litigation Manual, 1990—; contbg. editor Norton Bankruptcy Law and Practice, 1990—. Sgt. USAF, 1967-73. Fellow Am. Coll. Trial Lawyers, Am. Coll. Bankruptcy (bd. dirs., pres. 1997-2001, chmn. bd. dirs. 2001-03); mem. Atlanta Bar Assn. (pres. 1979-80), Am. Law Inst., Southeastern Bankruptcy Law Inst. (bd. dirs., pres. 1986-87), Nat. Bankruptcy Conf. Avocations: hiking, outdoor activities. Office: Alston & Bird One Atlantic Ctr 1201 W Peachtree St Atlanta GA 30309-3400 Office Phone: 404-881-7267. Business E-Mail: nbatson@alston.com.

BATSTONE, JOANNA L., physicist; BSc in Chem. Physics, PhD in Physics, U. Bristol. Computer scientist IBM Thomas J. Watson Rsch. Ctr., Hawthorne, NY. Mem. adv. bd. Bio IT Coalition. Recipient Robert Lansing Hardy Gold Medal award Minerals, Metals & Materials Soc., 1991, Cosslett award Microbeam Analysis Soc., 1989, Burton award Microscopy Soc. Am., 1995. Mem.: NY Acad. Scis. Womens Investigators Network. Office: IBM Life Scis Rt 100 Somers NY 10589 E-mail: batstone@us.ibm.com.

BATT, NICK, property and investment executive; b. Defiance, Ohio, May 6, 1952; s. Dan and Zenith (Dreher) B. BS, Purdue U., 1972; JD, U. Toledo, 1976. Asst. prosecutor Lucas County, Toledo, 1976-80, civil divsn. chief, 1980-83; village atty. Village of Holland, Ohio, 1980-91; law dir. City of Oregon, Ohio, 1984-91; spl. counsel State of Ohio, 1983-93; pres. Property & Mgmt. Connection, Inc., Toledo, 1993—2002, All Rental Property Mgmt. Co., 2002—. Mem. Maumee Valley Girl Scout Coun., Toledo, 1977-80; bd. mem. Bd. Cmty. Rels., Toledo, 1975-76; mem. Lucas County Dem. Exec. Com., 1981-83. Named One of Toledo's Outstanding Young Men, Toledo Jaycees, 1979. Mem. KC, Elks. Democrat. Roman Catholic. Office: All Home Group PO Box 292 Holland OH 43528 Office Phone: 419-490-4582. E-mail: nickbatt@toast.net.

BATT, RONALD ELMER, gynecologist, researcher, historian; b. Buffalo, Sept. 24, 1933; s. Elmer Lawrence and Mary Catherine (Roll) B.; m. Carol Mary Schaab, Dec. 28, 1957; children: Paula, Douglas, Thomas, Neil, Jennifer, John; m. 2d, Kathleen Over Cansdale, May 19, 1982; stepchildren: William, James, Suzanne, Timothy, John, Mark. BS in Biology, Niagara U., 1954; MD, U. Buffalo, 1958; MA in History, SUNY Buffalo, 2002. Intern Millard Fillmore Hosp., Buffalo, 1958—59; resident in ob-gyn SUNY, Buffalo, 1959—60, SUNY Buffalo, 1962—66; rsch. fellow Harvard U. Med. Sch., 1963—64; asst. in surgery Peter Bent Brigham Hosp., Boston, 1963—64; fellow in gynecologic surgery Mayo Clinic, 1965; practice gynecology specializing in endometriosis and reproductive surgery Buffalo, 1966—98; rschr., 1966—. Prof. clin. gynecology, clin. prof. social and preventive medicine SUNY Buffalo. Co-author: Another Era: A Pictorial History of the School of Medicine and Biomedical Sciences, State University of New York at Buffalo 1846-1996; contbr. chpts. to books, articles to profl. jours. With M.C., USN, 1960-62. Recipient Lifetime Career Achievement award Med. Alumni Assn. Sch. Medicine and Biomed. Scis. SUNY, 1998, ACOG-Ortho/McNeil fellow in the history of Am. Obstetrics and Gynecology, 2004. Fellow ACS, Royal Coll. Surgeons Can., Am. Coll. Obstetricians and Gynecologists; mem. Am. Soc. Reproductive Medicine, Soc. Reproductive Surgeons, Am. Assn. History Medicine, Internat. Soc. History Medicine, Am. Assn. Gynecol.Laparoscopists. Office: 5648 Broadway Lancaster NY 14086-2317

BATTAGLIA, ANTHONY SYLVESTER, lawyer; b. Binghamton, N.Y., Aug. 21, 1927; s. Sylvester Anthony and Helen B.; m. Catherine Jean, Oct. 1, 1972; children: Christina, Marc Anthony; children by previous marriage—Anthony, Sandra, Brian, Brenda Lee. AA, U. Fla., 1948, BA, 1949, LL.B., 1953, JD, 1967. Bar: Fla. 1953, U.S. Dist. Ct. (mid. and so. dists.) Fla., U.S. Ct. Appeals (5th, 11th cirs.), U.S. Tax Ct., U.S. Ct. Appeals (D.C. cir.), U.S. Ct. Mil. Appeals; cert. ct. approved abritrator U.S. Dist. Ct., U.S. Supreme Ct. 1966. Asst. to U.S. dist. atty., So. Dist. Fla., 1953-56; ptnr. Parker, Parker & Battaglia, St. Petersburg, Fla., 1953-56, Parker, Battaglia & Ross, St. Petersburg, 1965-73, Parker, Battaglia, Parker, Ross & Ross, St. Petersburg, 1973-75, Battaglia, Parker, Ross, Parker & Stolba, St. Petersburg, 1975-76, Battaglia, Ross & Stolba, 1976-77, Battaglia, Ross, Stolba & Forlizzo, 1977-78, Battaglia, Ross & Forlizzo, 1978-80, Battaglia, Ross, Hastings, Dicus & Andrews, 1980-93, Battaglia, Ross, Dicus & Wein PA, 1993—. Mem. Fla. Pub. Svc. Commn., 1971; chmn. bd. Metrocare, Inc., 1975-78; mem. grievance com. U.S. Dist. Ct., 1985-88; pres. Asst. U.S. Attys. Assn. for Mid. Dist. Fla., 1994; guest lectr. Stetson U., 1994; bd. dirs. Intervest Bank, 1st Bankers Tampa Bay, N.A., St. Petersburg, Nat. Bank Fla., St. Petersburg, Operation PAR, Inc.; chmn. adv. bd. 1st Union Nat. Bank, South Pinellas, Fla. Republican nat. committeeman, Fla., 1956-64, bd. dirs., Tampa div.; bd. dirs. San Carlo Opera Fla., 1972-74, pres., chmn. bd. dirs., Pinellas County div., 1974-76; bd. dirs. St. Petersburg Opera Co., 1976-77; chmn. bd. Pinellas County Arthritis Found., 1985; founding sponsor Civil Justice Found.; trustee Ctr. Against Spouse Abuse, 1999. Elected to U. Fla. Hall of Fame and Fla. Blue Key, 1951 Master Ferguson-White Am. Inn of Ct.; fellow Am. Coll. Mortgage Attys.; mem. ABA, ATLA (sustaining), Fla. Bar Assn. (bd. govs. 1993-99), St. Petersburg Bar Assn. (pres. 1990), Fed. Bar Assn. (v.p. Mid. Fla. dist.), U.S. Attys. Assn. for Mid. Dist. Fla. (pres. 2001), Internat. Bar Assn., Hillsborough County Bar Assn., Acad. Fla. Trial Lawyers (judge student competition 1985), Am. Judicature Soc. (Supreme Ct. Hist. Soc. 1985-89), Nat. Assn. Criminal Def. Lawyers, Acad. Criminal Justice Scis., Fla. Criminal Def. Trial Lawyers, Criminal Def. Lawyers Hillsborough County, Pinellas County Trial Lawyers Assn. Roscoe Pound Am., Trial Lawyers Found. (judicial nominating com.), U. Fla. Nat. Alumni Assn., St. Petersburg C. of C. (gov.), Pinellas Inns Ct. (master bench), Herbert G. Goldberg Criminal Law Am. Inn Ct., Fla. Bar Bd. of Govs. Clubs: Treasure Island Tennis and Yacht (bd. dirs.), Suncoast Tiger Bay, St. Petersburg Yacht, Nat. Italian Am. Found., Italian-Am. Unico Internat. Lodges: K.C. Roman Catholic. Office: 980 Tyrone Blvd N Saint Petersburg FL 33710-6333 Office Phone: 727-381-2300. E-mail: abatt@brdwlaw.com.

BATTAGLIA, FREDERICK CAMILLO, physician; b. Weehawken, N.J., Feb. 15, 1932; m. Jane B. Donohue; children: Susan Kate, Thomas Frederick. BA, Cornell U., 1953; MD, Yale U., 1957; DSc (hon.), U. Ind. Diplomate Am. Bd. Pediat. Intern in pediat. Johns Hopkins Hosp., 1957—58; USPHS postdoctoral fellow biochemistry Cambridge (Eng.) U., 1958—59; Josiah Macy Found. fellow in physiology Yale U. Med. Sch., 1959—60; asst. resident, fellow in pediat. Johns Hopkins Hosp., 1960—61, resident, fellow, 1961—62; USPHS surgeon lab. perinatal physiology NIH, San Juan, PR, 1962—64; asst. prof. Johns Hopkins Med. Sch., 1963—65; mem. faculty U. Colo. Med. Sch., Denver, 1965—, prof. pediat., prof. ob-gyn., 1969—2003, prof. pediat., ob-gyn. emeritus, 2003—, dir. divsn. perinatal medicine, 1970—74, chmn. dept. pediat., 1974—89. Attending pediatrician Children's, Denver Gen., Fitzsimons Gen. Hosps. Editor (assoc.): Pediatrics; med. progress contbg. editor Jour. Pediat., 1966—74, editl. bd. European Jour. Ob-Gybn., 1971—, assoc. Jour Perinatal, med. editor Biol. Neonate, 1979—; contbr. numerous articles to med. jours. Mem.: Inst. Medicine NAS, Soc. Exptl. Biology and Medicine, Internat. Congress Perinatal Medicine (pres. 1996), Am. Pediatric Soc. (pres. 1996, John Howland medal 2004), Soc. Gynecol. Investigation (coun. 1969—72), We. Soc. Pediatric Rsch. (pres. 1987—), Perinatal Rsch. Soc. (pres. 1974—75), Soc. Pediatric Rsch. (pres. 1976—77), Am. Gynecologic and Obstetric Soc., Am. Acad. Pediat. (E. Mead Johns award 1969), Assn. Am. Physicians, Sigma Xi, Phi Beta Kappa. Home: 2975 E Cedar Ave Denver CO 80209-3211 Office: Fitzsimons Bldg 260 MS F441 PO Box 6508 Aurora CO 80010 Office Phone: 303-724-0546. Business E-Mail: fred.battaglia@uchsc.edu.

BATTAGLIA, LYNNE ANN, judge; b. Buffalo, 1946; BA in Internat. Relations, Am. U., 1967, MA, 1968; JD, U. Md., 1974; JD (hon.), U. Baltimore Sch. of Law, 2001. Asst. US atty. Dist. Md., 1978—82; sr. trial atty. special litigation US Dept. of Justice, 1984—88; chief criminal investigations div. Office of Atty. Gen., 1988—91; chief of staff Office of U.S. Sen. Barbara A. Mikulski, 1991—93; US atty. Dist. Md., 1993-2001; judge Md. Ct. Appeals, 2001—. Adjunct prof. U. Md. Sch. of Law, 1983—; mem. Task Force on Sentencing & Intermediate Sanctions, 1995—96, Md. Alternative Dispute Resolution Commn., 1998—2000. Author: Obeisance to the Separation of Powers, and Protection of Individuals' Rights and Liberties: The Honorable John C. Eldridge's Approach to Constitutional Analysis in the Court of Appeals of Maryland, 2003. Co-chair Women's Health Promotion Council, 1999—2001; mem. Safe Schools Interagency Steering Com., 1999—2001; vice-chair Md. Commn. for Women, 2000—01. Named one of Maryland's Top 100 Women, Daily Record, 1996, 1999, 2001; recipient Dorothy Beatty Memorial award, Women's Law Ctr. of Md., 1994, Margaret Brent-Juanita Jackson Mitchell award, 2002—03, Md. Leadership in Law award, Daily Record, 2003, Professional Legal Excellence award, Md. Bar Foundation, 2004. Mem.: James MacGill Am. Inns of Ct., Howard County Bar Assn., Baltimore City Bar Assn. (chair gender issues subcom., former chair jud. administration com.), Md. State Bar Assn. (vice-chair jud. administration council 2004—, mem. gender equality com., mem. civility task force). Office: Robert C Murphy Ct Appeals Bldg 361 Rowe Blvd Annapolis MD 21401*

BATTAH, HAMMAM JAMIL, civil engineer, utilities executive; b. Kirkuk, Nov. 11, 1939; arrived in US, 1994; s. Jamil Gergies and Nadene Joseph (Massa) Battah; m. Haifa Jecob Battah, June 26, 1969; children: Hani, Basil. BSCE, Coll. Engring., Baghdad, 1962, MSCE, 1968. Registered profl. engr., Mich. Field civil engr. Modern Constrn. Co., Lebanon, Iraq, 1964—70; from head engr. to tech. mgr., v.p. Orient Engring. Co., Iraq, 1970—79; owner, pres. Hammam Modern Constrn. Co., Iraq, 1980—92; field engr. Henessy Engrs. and SBG Constrn. Co., Mich., 1994—97; assoc. civil engr. City of Detroit, 1998—. CEO, pres. Solar Water Energy LLC, Mich., 2004—. Achievements include patents for solar distillation sys; patents pending for wave breaker sys; solar thermal energy conversion sys. Office: Solar Water Energy LLC 16445 W Twelve Mile Rd Ste 100 Southfield MI 48076 Office Phone: 248-559-0968. Business E-Mail: hammam@solarwaterenergy.com.

BATTEN, ALAN HENRY, astronomer; b. Tankerton, Kent, Eng., Jan. 21, 1933; emigrated to Can., 1959, naturalized, 1975; s. George Cuthbert and Gladys (Greenwood) B.; m. Lois Eleanor Dewis, July 30, 1960; children: Michael Henry John, Margaret Eleanor. BSc with 1st class honors, U. St. Andrews, Scotland, 1955, DSc, 1974; PhD, U. Manchester, Eng., 1958. Rsch. asst. in astronomy, jr. tutor St. Anselm Residence Hall, U. Manchester, 1958-59; postdoctoral fellow Dominion Astrophys. Obs., Victoria, B.C., Can., 1959-61, mem. staff, 1961-91, assoc. rsch. officer, 1970-76, sr. rsch. officer, 1976-91, guest scientist, 1991—. Lectr. astronomy U. Victoria, 1961-64; guest investigator Vatican Obs., 1970, Inst. Astronomia y Fisica del Espacio, Buenos Aires, 1972; lectr. history U. Victoria, 2003-04; rsch. awards com. Craigdarroch, 2003—. Author: Binary and Multiple Systems of Stars, 1973, Resolute and Undertaking Characters: The Lives of Wilhelm and Otto Struve, 1988; editor: Extended Atmospheres and Circumstellar Matter in Spectroscopic Binary Systems, 1973, Algols, 1989, Astronomy for Developing Countries, 2001; sr. author: Eighth Catalogue of the Orbital Elements of Spectroscopic Binary Systems, 1989; co-editor: The Determination of Radial Velocities and Their Applications, 1967; translator: L'Observation des Etoiles Doubles Visuelles par P. Couteau, 1981; contbr. articles to profl. jours. Pres. Willows Elem. Sch. PTA, Victoria, 1971-73; active Anglican Ch. Can. Diocesan Synod, B.C., 1966-68, 74; adv. coun. Ctr. Advanced Studies in Religion and Soc., U. Victoria, 1993-2002, chmn., 1997-2000. Recipient Queen's Silver Jubilee medal, Can., 1977; Erskine Vis. fellow, U. Canterbury, New Zealand, 1995. Fellow Royal Soc. Can. (convenor interdisciplinary sect. 1980-81, mem. coun. 1980-81), Royal Astron. Soc., Explorers Club; mem. Internat. Astron. Union (v.p. 1985-91, pres. commn. 30 1976-79, pres. commn. 42 1982-85, chmn. nat. orgn. com. XVII Gen. Assembly 1975-79), Royal Astron. Soc. Can. (pres. 1976-78, hon. pres. 1993-98, editor jour. 1981-88), Astron. Soc. Pacific (v.p. 1965-68), Can. Astron. Soc. (pres. 1972-74), Am. Astron. Socs., Ancient Soc. Coll. Youths. Home: 2987 Westdowne Rd Victoria BC Canada V8R 5G1 Office: Dominion Astrophys Obs 5071 W Saanich Rd Victoria BC Canada V9E 2E7 E-mail: alan.batten@nrc.gc.ca.

BATTEN, FRANK, newspaper publisher, cable broadcaster; b. Norfolk, Va., Feb. 11, 1927; s. Frank and Dorothy (Martin) B.; m. Jane Neal Parke; children: Frank, Mary, Dorothy. Grad., Culver Mil. Acad., 1945; AB, U. Va., 1950; MBA, Harvard U., 1952; LittD (hon.), Washington and Lee U., 1996. Reporter The Norfolk Ledger-Star; with advt. and circulation depts. The Virginian-Pilot and Norfolk Ledger-Star newspapers; v.p. The Norfolk Virginian-Pilot and Norfolk Ledger-Star newspapers, 1953, pub., 1954—; chmn. bd. Landmark Comm., Norfolk, 1967-97, chmn. exec. com., 1998—; also chmn. Greensboro (N.C.) News & Record; chmn. Roanoke (Va.) Times, KLAS-TV; dir. Capital-Gazette Communications Inc., Annapolis, Md.; 2d vice chmn. AP, 1977-79, 1st vice chmn., 1979-81, chmn. bd., 1982-87; founder The Weather Channel, 1982. Formerly chmn. AP Pension, Tech., Fgn. ops. coms.; past chmn. AP Nominating Com., Va. AP Members; former dir. So. Newspapers Pubs. Assn.; former chmn. bd. Newspaper Advt. Bur. Trustee Culver Ednl. Found., U.S. Naval Acad. Found., So. Newspaper Pubs. Found., U. Va. Grad. Bus. Sch. Sponsors, Hollins Coll.; past chmn. bd. Old Dominion U.; past vice chmn. State Coun. Higher Edn. for Va.; past pres. and campaign chmn. Norfolk Area United Fund; chmn. com. for Internat. Naval Rev., 1957; mem. bd. visitors Coll. William and Mary. With U.S. Merchant Marine, World War II, also USNR. Recipient Norfolk's First Citizen award, 1966, Alumni Achievement award Harvard Bus. Sch., 1998. Mem. Newspaper Assn. of Am. (dir.), Delta Kappa Epsilon. Episcopalian. Office: Landmark Communications Inc 150 W Brambleton Ave Norfolk VA 23510-2018

BATTEN, KIMBERLY JANE, Olympic athlete; b. McRae, Ga., Mar. 29, 1969; Grad., Fla. State U., 1991. Winner 2d place NCAA 400 meter hurdles, 1990, 3rd place 400 meter hurdles, 1991, 1st place 400 meter hurdles Mobil/USA Championships, 1991, 5th place World Championships, 1991, 4th place, 1992, Silver medal 400 meter hurdles Atlanta Olympics, 1996, World Bronze medalist, 1997, World Cup Bronze medalist, 1998, competed in Sydney Olympics, 2000, 6-time U.S. outdoor champion.

BATTENBERG, J. T., III, automotive company executive; BS in Indsl. Engring., Kettering U.; MBA Columbia U.; grad. advanced mgmt. program, Harvard U. With GM, 1986, mng. dir. GM Continental divsn., gen. mgr. overseas truck ops., v.p. Buick-Oldsmobile-Cadillac group, 1986, v.p., group exec. Buick-Oldsmobile-Cadillac, v.p., group exec. automotive components group, 1992, sr. v.p., pres. group, 1992-95, exec. v.p., 1995; pres., CEO, chmn. bd. Delphi Corp. (formerly ACG Worldwide), Troy, Mich., 1995—. Mem. GM's Pres. Coun.; nat. adv. bd. Chase Manhattan Corp. Bd. trustees Kettering U.; bd. overseers Columbia U. Bus. Sch.; exec. bd. Detroit area Coun. of Boy Scouts Am.; exec. bd. Oakland County Automation Alley; bd. dirs. For Inspiration and Recognition of Sci. and Tech.; mem. Coun. on Competitiveness; adv. bd. Covisint; mem. Bus. Roundtable and Bus. Coun. Named Internat. Bus. Coun. World Trader of the Yr. Detroit Regional Chamber, 1998. Mem. Soc. of Automotive Engrs., Soc. of Body Engrs., Engring. Soc. of Detroit, Exec. Leadership Coun., Automobile Nat. Heritage Area, Econ. Club of Detroit. Office: Delphi Corp 5725 Delphi Dr Troy MI 48098-2815

BATTENFELD, JOHN LEONARD, JR., secondary school educator, journalist, editor; b. Norwalk, Conn., Aug. 25, 1943; s. John Leonard and Mary Florence Fay B.; m. Yasuyo Aso, Apr. 23, 1977; children: John O., Sachiko C. BA, NYU, 1969; MFA, New Sch. Social Rsch., 1998. Journalist UPI, N.Y.C., 1969-76; asst. press sec. Mayor's Office, N.Y.C., 1976-81; editor UPI, N.Y.C., 1981-83, fgn. corr. Tokyo, 1983-85, Reuters Ltd., Hong Kong, New Delhi, & Seoul, 1985-95; lectr. NYU, N.Y.C., 1999—2000, Boston U., 1998—99, Purchase Coll., SUNY, 1999—; tchr. English and social studies Truman H.S., Bronx, NY, 2000—01, Chestnut Ridge Mid. Sch., NY, 2001—02, Warren Harding H.S., Bridgeport, Conn., 2002—. With USNR, 1965-67. Mem. MLA, Soc. Profl. Journalists, Nat. Coun. for the Social Studies, Vietnam Vets. Am., Nat. Coun. Tchrs. English. Democrat. Roman Catholic.

BATTERMAN, BORIS WILLIAM, physicist, educator, academic administrator; b. N.Y.C., Aug. 25, 1930; children: Robert W., William E., Thomas A. Student, Cooper Union Coll., 1949-50, Technische Hochschule, Stuttgart, Germany; SB, MIT, 1952, PhD, 1956. Mem. tech. staff Bell Tel. Labs., Murray Hill, N.J., 1956-65; assoc. prof. Cornell U., Ithaca, N.Y., 1965-67, prof. applied and engring. physics, 1967—, dir. Sch. Applied and Engring. Physics, 1974-78, dir. Synchrotron Radiation Lab. (CHESS), 1978-97, Walter S. Carpenter Jr. prof. engring., 1985—2001, Walter S. Carpenter Jr. prof. emeritus, 2002—. Mem. staff Lawrence Berkeley Lab., 1998—, Stanford Linear Accelerator Ctr., 1999—; mem. U.S.A. Nat. Com. Crystallography, NAS, 1969—72. Assoc. editor Jour. Crystal Growth, 1964—74. Fulbright scholar, 1953-54; Guggenheim fellow, 1971, Fulbright Hayes fellow, 1971, Alexander von Humboldt fellow, 1983. Fellow: AAAS, Am. Phys. Soc. Office: 150 Lombard St #603 San Francisco CA 94111 E-mail: bwb1@cornell.edu.

BATTERMAN, STEVEN CHARLES, engineering mechanics and bioengineering professor, consultant; b. Bklyn., Aug. 15, 1937; s. Jacob and Anna (Abramowitz) B.; m. Judith Wilpon, Mar. 29, 1959; children: Scott David, Risa Karen, Daniel Adam. BCE, Cooper Union, 1959; ScM (NSF fellow), Brown U., 1961, PhD, 1964; MA (hon.), U. Pa., 1971. Bd. cert. diplomate Internat. Inst. Forensic Engring. Scis. Mem. faculty U. Pa., 1964-97, prof. mech. engring. and applied mechanics, 1974-79; assoc. prof. orthopaedic surgery rsch. U. Pa. Sch. Medicine, 1972-74, prof. orthopaedic surgery rsch., 1974-97; prof. biomechanics in vet. medicine U Pa Sch. Vet Medicine, 1975-84, prof. bioengring., 1974-97; emeritus prof. Sch. Engring. and Applied Sci., Sch. Medicine U. Pa., 1997—; mng. ptnr. Batterman Engring., LLC, Cherry Hill. Forensic enring. and biomechanics cons. to govt., industry, ins. cos., attys.; mem. adv. bd. Cyril H. Wecht Inst. Forensic Sci. and Law, Duquesne U. Contbr. numerous articles to profl. jours. Recipient S.R. Warren Disting. Teaching award, U. Pa., 1982. Fellow ASME; mem. ASCE, Am. Acad. Mechanics, Am. Soc. Engring. Edn., Biomed. Engring. Soc., Soc. Exptl. Mech., Soc. Automotive Engrs., Am. Soc. Safety Engrs., Am. Acad. Forensic Scis. (Founder's award 1992, 2004, pres.-elect 1993-94, pres. 1994-95, Disting. Fellow 2001), Assn. for Advancement Automotive Medicine, Sigma Xi, Tau Beta Pi, Chi Epsilon. Jewish. Achievements include patent for apparatus for acoustically determining periodontal health. Home: 109 Charlann Cir Cherry Hill NJ 08003-2906 Office Phone: 856-424-3775. Personal E-mail: batterman@aol.com. Business E-Mail: batterma@seas.upenn.edu.

BATTERSBY, HAROLD RONALD, retired anthropologist, archaeologist, linguist; b. Guildford, Surrey, Eng., Nov. 16, 1922; arrived in US, 1960, naturalized, 1972; s. Eric and Lillian (Darnell) B.; m. Betty Yertchenig O'Hannesian, Apr. 22, 1944. BA in Modern Near Eastern Studies, U. Toronto, Can., 1960; PhD in Altaic Studies-Anthropology Linguistics, Ind. U., 1969. Corr. Surrey Times, London-Guildford, 1947-55; adv. dir. Turkish Post, Istanbul, 1949-53; instr. English Istanbul Med. Faculty, 1948-49, Amerikan Lisan ve San'at Dersanesi, Istanbul, 1948-54, Pangalti Ermeni Orta Okulu, Istanbul, 1949-56; coordinator athletic events USO, Istanbul, 1948-54; asst. Royal Ont. Mus., Toronto, 1957-59; asst. mgr. City of Toronto, 1957-59; research asst. in med. anthropology U. Pitts., 1960-62; asst. Ind. U., Bloomington, 1962-69; assoc. prof. anthropology SUNY-Geneseo, 1970-98, dir. linguistics program, 1978-98, adj. prof., 1999-2001; ret. Author: Anatolian Archaeology: A Comprehensive Bibliograph, 2 vols., 1976; sect. editor: Altaic and Uralic Studies, Ultimate Reality and Meaning, 1982—; contbr. articles to profl. jours., translations, proofreading and editing of Biblical ethnographic and linguistic texts into Altaic langs. and from Altaic langs. into English. Served with RAF Vol. Res., 1939—46. NDEA fellow; Ind. U. grantee; Geneseo Found. grantee, 1973, 77, 78— Fellow Royal Anthrop. Inst. Gt. Brit. and Ireland, Am. Anthrop. Assn., Royal Asiatic soc.; mem. Am. Oriental Soc., Royal Ctrl. Asian Soc., Royal Soc. Asian Affairs, Hakluyt Soc., Internat. Soc. Oriental Rsch., Middle East Inst., Chgo. Anthrop. Soc., Inst. Ency. of Human Ideas on Ultimate Reality and Meaning, Brit. Inst. Archaeology at Ankara, Am. Oriental Soc., Am. Soc. Study People of Ea. Europe and No. and Ctrl. Asia, Linguistic Soc. Am., Niagara Linguistic Soc., N.Y. State Coun. Linguistics, Soc. Armenian Studies, Zoryan Inst., Ind. U. Alumni Assn., The Smithsonian Assocs., The Wilson Ctr. Assocs., Lambda Alpha. Clubs: Ind. U. Linguistics. Republican. Episcopalian. Avocations: reservation birds, cats, ducks, ethnolinguistics. Home: PO Box 80 Groveland NY 14462

BATTERSBY, JAMES LYONS, JR., language educator; b. Pawtucket, RI, Aug. 24, 1936; s. James Lyons and Hazel Irene (Deuel) B.; m. Lisa J. Kiser, Aug. 6, 1990; 1 child, Julie Ann. BS magna cum laude, U. Vt., 1961; MA, Cornell U., 1962, PhD, 1965. Asst. prof. U. Calif., Berkeley, 1965-70; assoc. prof. English Ohio State U., Columbus, 1970-82, prof., 1982—. Cons. Ohio State U. Press, U. Ky. Press, U. Calif. Press, Prentice-Hall, McGraw Hill, Fairleigh Dickinson U. Press, U. Mich. Press, U. Ala. Press. Author: Typical Folly: Evaluating Student Performance in Higher Education, 1973, Rational Praise and Natural Lamentation: Johnson, Lycidas and Principles of Criticism, 1980, Elder Olson: An Annotated Bibliography, 1983, Paradigms Regained: Pluralism and the Practice of Criticism, 1991, Reason and the Nature of Texts, 1996, Unorthodox Views: Reflections on Reality, Truth, and Meaning in Current Social, Cultural, and Critical Discourse, 2002, 7 Poets, 2005; contbg. author: Domestick Privacies: Samuel Johnson and the Art of Biography, 1987, Fresh Reflections on Samuel Johnson: Essays in Criticism, 1987, Criticism, History and Intertextuality, 1988, Beyond Poststructuralism: The Speculations of Theory and the Experience of Reading, 1996; contbr. articles to profl. jours. With U.S. Army, 1954—57. Woodrow Wilson fellow, 1961-62, 64-65, Samuel S. Fels fellow, 1964-65, U. Calif. Summer Faculty fellow, 1966, Humanities Research fellow, 1969; recipient Kidder Medal U. Vt., 1961. Mem. MLA, Am. Soc. 18th Century Studies, Midwest Soc. 18th Century Studies, Royal Oak Found., Phi Beta Kappa, Phi Kappa Phi, Kappa Delta Pi. Home: 472 Clinton Heights Ave Columbus OH 43202-1277 E-mail: batterjay@msn.com.

BATTESTIN, MARTIN CAREY, retired language educator; b. N.Y.C., Mar. 25, 1930; s. Martin Augustus and Marion (Kirkland) B.; m. Ruthe Rootes, June 14, 1963; children: David (dec. 1999), Catherine. BA summa cum laude, Princeton U., 1952, PhD, 1958. English master Westminster Sch., Simsbury, Conn., 1952-53; instr. Wesleyan U., Middletown, Conn., 1956-58, asst. prof., 1958-61, U. Va., Charlottesville, 1961-63, assoc. prof., 1963-67, prof., 1967-75, William R. Kenan, Jr. prof. English, 1975-98, emeritus prof., 1998—, chmn. dept. English, 1983-86. Vis. prof. Rice U., Houston, 1967—68; assoc. Clare Hall, Cambridge (Eng.) U., 1972. Author: The Moral Basis of Fielding's Art, 1959, 1975, The Providence of Wit, 1974, 1989, Henry Fielding: A Life, 1989, 2d edit., 1993, New Essays by Henry Fielding, 1989, 1993, A Henry Fielding Companion, 2000; editor: Joseph Andrews (Henry Fielding), 1961, 1967, Shamela (Henry Fielding), 1961, Tom Jones (Henry Fielding), 1974, 2d edit., 1975, Amelia (Henry Fielding), 1983, Tom Jones: A Collection of Critical Essays, 1968, British Novelists, 1660-1800, 1985, Tobias Smollett, translator Cervantes' Don Quixote, 2003; co-editor: The Correspondence of Henry and Sarah Fielding, 1993. Am. Coun. Learned Socs. fellow, 1960-61, 72; Guggenheim fellow, 1964-65; Sr. fellow Coun. Humanities, Princeton U., 1971; Ctr. for Advanced Studies fellow U. Va., 1974-75; NEH Bicentennial Rsch. fellow, 1975-76. Mem. MLA (chmn. sec. VII 1967, adv. editor publs. 1982-86), South Atlantic Modern Lang. Assn., Internat. Assn. Univ. Profs. English (chmn. sect. V 1990-92), Assn. Lit. Scholars and Critics, East Ctrl. Am. Soc. Eighteenth Century Studies, Nat. Assn. Scholars, The Johnsonians. Mem. Ch. of England. Home: 1832 Westview Rd Charlottesville VA 22903-1648 Personal E-mail: mcb9g@virginia.edu.

BATTEY, JAMES F., JR., federal agency administrator, neurologist; BS in Physics with honors, Calif. Inst. Tech.; MD, PhD, Stanford U. Mem. staff, then head molecular structure sect. lab. biol. chemistry Nat. Cancer Inst., NIH, 1983—88; chief molecular neurosci. sect. lab. neurochemistry Nat. Inst. Neurol. Disorders and Stroke, 1988—92; chief molecular structure, lab. of biological chemistry Nat. Cancer Inst., NIH, 1992—95; acting dir. divsn. intramural rsch. Nat. Inst. Deafness and Other Comm. Disorders, Bethesda, Md., 1995—98, dir., 1998—. Chmn., Stem Cell Task Force, Nat. Inst. Health, 2002-; adj. prof. George Washington U. Sch. Medicine Author: (with Leonard Davis and Michael Kuehl) Basic Methods in Molecular Biology; contbr., co-contbr. over 120 rsch. articles to profl. jours. Recipient Commendation medal Pub. Health Svc., 1990, Outstanding Svc. medal, 1994; postdoctoral fellow Harvard Med. Sch. Office: Nat Inst Deafness & Comm Disorders 31 Center Dr Msc 2320 Bldg 31 Bethesda MD 20892-0001

BATTIE, DAVID ANTHONY, art appraiser; b. Oct. 22, 1942; s. Donald Charleson and Peggy Joan Battie; m. Sarah Battie; children: Henrietta Victoria, Eleanor Harriet. Attended, King James I Sch., Knaresborough, UK. Dir. Sotheby's, NYC, 1976—99; expert BBC-TV; appraiser Antiques Roadshow, 1977—. Lectr. in field. Author: Price Guide to 19th & 20th Century British Procelain, 1975, Sotheby's Concise Encyclopedia of Porcelain, 1990, Sotheby's Concise Encyclopedia of Glass, 1991, Treasures In Your Home, 1994, Pottery & Porcelain, Antiques Roadshow Pocket Guides, 1995.*

BATTILEGA, JOHN A., research and development company executive; b. Portland, Oreg., Nov. 25, 1941; s. Ercole Anthony and Odelia Francis Battilega; m. Nancy Ann Scott, May 2, 1964; children: Catherine, Edward, Michael, David. BS, Gonzaga U., 1963; PhD, Oreg. State U., 1967. Rsch. asst. Tektronix, Beaverton, Oreg., 1961—62, Sandia Nat. Lab., Livermore, Calif., 1965; staff engr. Martin Marietta Corp., Denver, 1971—73; corp. v.p., gen. mgr., rsch. dir. Sci. Applications Internat. Corp., Englewood, Colo., 1973—99; pres. John Battilega Assocs., Littleton, Colo., 1999—. Adj. prof., sr. lectr. Grad. Sch. Internat. Studies U. Denver, 2000—; mem. U.S. Def. Sci. Bd., Washington, 1984—85; dir. Fgn. Sys. Rsch. Ctr., Sci. Applications Internat. Corp., Englewood, Colo., 1978—99; dir. strategic rsch. on def. policy and planning and internat. issues U.S. govt. nat. security orgns., Washington, 1973—; mem. modeling and simulation rev. com. U.S. Space Command, Colorado Springs, Colo., 1986; mem. U.S. strategic def. initiative Soviet red team Dept. Def., Washington, 1985—90; sr. cons. various U.S. govt. agys., Washington, 1973—; adj. prof. U.S. Def. Intelligence Coll., Washington; mem. several adv. panels U.S. govt., Washington, 1980—; seminar developer over 20 seminars on def. planning topics, Washington, 1973—; lectr. def. and intelligence colls., 1978—; mem. AirLand Battle Future Spl. Study Group U.S. Army, Ft. Leavenworth, Kans., 1988; mem. select com. on computer tech. Nat. Def. U., Washington, 1983. Author, editor: book The Military Applications of Modeling, 1984; contbr. book chpts., articles, rsch. monographs. Coach youth baseball, Lakewood and Littlewood, Colo., 1975—98; Pres. parish coun. St. Jude Cath. Ch., Lakewood, Colo., 1972—74. Maj. U.S. Army, 1963—71. Decorated Meritorious Svc. medal, Bronze star, Vietnamese Cross of Gallantry. Mem.: AIAA, IEEE, Denver Coun. Fgn. Rels., U.S. Mil. Ops. Rsch. Soc. (bd. dirs. 1983—85), Inst. for Ops. Rsch. and Mgmt. Sci., Internat. Inst. Strategic Studies. Roman Catholic. Avocations: travel, reading, fishing, baseball, bridge. Home: 7706 S Forest St Littleton CO 80122 E-mail: j.battilega@worldnet.att.net.

BATTIN, PATRICIA MEYER, librarian; b. Gettysburg, Pa., June 2, 1929; d. Emanuel Albert and Josephine (Lehman) Meyer; m. William Thomas Battin, June 16, 1951 (div. 1975); children: Laura, Joanna, Thomas BA, Swarthmore Coll., 1951; MS in LS, Syracuse U., 1967. Asst. libr. SUNY-Binghamton, 1967-69, asst. dir. for reader svcs., 1969-74; dir. libr. svcs. Columbia U., N.Y.C., 1974-78, v.p., univ. libr., 1978-87; interim pres. Research Libraries Group, Palo Alto, Calif., 1982, also dir., 1974-87; pres. Commn. on Preservation and Access, Washington, 1987-94. Trustee Coun. on Libr. Resources, Washington, 1984-94, EDUCOM, Princeton, N.J., 1982-88, Lehigh U., 1989-98, CAUSE, Boulder, Colo., 1993-96; mem. adv. com. on coun. on libr. and info. resources Frye Leadership Inst. Contbr. articles to profl. jours., Co-author: The Mirage of Continuity: Reconfiguring Academic Information Resources for the 21st Century, 1998. Recipient Nat. Medal for the Humanities, 1999. Mem. ALA, Assn. Rsch. Librs. (trustee 1982-85), Phi Beta Kappa, Beta Phi Mu.

BATTIN, RICHARD HORACE, aeronautical engineer; b. Atlantic City, Mar. 3, 1925; s. Horace Leslie and Martha Esther (Scheu) B.; m. Margery Katheryn Milne, Aug. 25, 1947; children: Thomas, Pamela, Jeffrey. BS, MIT, 1945, PhD, 1951; DSc (hon.), Tex. A&M U., 1999. Instr. math. MIT, Cambridge, 1946-51, research mathematician Instrumentation Lab., 1951-56, adj. prof. aero. and astronautics, 1979-95, sr. lectr., 1995—. Sr. staff mem. Ops. Research Group, Arthur D. Little, Inc., Cambridge, 1956-58; tech. dir. Apollo Mission Devel.; assoc. dir. Instrumentation Lab., 1958-73; assoc. head NASA program dept. Charles Stark Draper Lab., Inc., 1973-87, mem. aerospace safety adv. panel, 1980-86. Author: (with J.H. Laning, Jr.) Random Processes in Automatic Control, 1956, Astronautical Guidance, 1964, An Introduction to the Mathematics and Methods of Astrodynamics, 1987; Mem. editorial com.: Celestial Mechanics, 1968-74. Pres. Project Impact, 1981-90; Mem. Lexington (Mass.) Town Meeting, 1956—; mem. Lexington Appropriations Com., 1958-64. Lt. (j.g.) Supply Corps USNR, 1945-46. Recipient Superior Achievement award, Inst. of Navigation, 1980, 1st Tycho Brahe award, 2000, Tchg. award, dept. aeros. and astronautics MIT, 1981. Fellow: AIAA (hon.; assoc. editor jour. 1967—87, chmn. astrodynamics tech. com. 1978—80, dir. tech. 1979—82, Louis W. Hill Space Transp. award 1972, Mechanics and Control of Flight award 1978, Pendray Aerospace Lit. award 1987, von Karman Disting. Lectureship award in astronautics 1989, Summerfield Book award 2002, Aerospace Guidance, Nav. and Control award 2002), Am. Astronautical Soc. (Dirk Brouwer award 1996); mem.: Celestial Mechanics Inst., Internat. Acad. Astronautics, Nat. Acad. Engring., Hancock Men's Club (pres. 1974—76), Sigma Xi. Home: 15 Paul Revere Rd Lexington MA 02421-6632 Office: MIT' 9-335 77 Massachusetts Ave Cambridge MA 02139-4307 Office Phone: 781-862-3639. Business E-Mail: battin@alum.mit.edu.

BATTINO, RUBIN, retired chemistry professor; b. N.Y.C., June 22, 1931; s. Sadik and Anna (Decastro) B.; m. Charlotte Alice Ridinger, Jan. 30, 1960; children— David Rubin, Benjamin Sadik BA, CCNY, 1953; MA, Duke U., 1954, PhD, 1957; MS, Wright State U., 1978. Lic. profl. clin. counselor, Ohio. Research chemist Leeds & Northrup Co., Phila., 1956-57; asst. prof. Ill. Inst. Tech., Chgo., 1957-66; prof. Wright State U., Dayton, Ohio, 1966-95, ret., 1995, prof. emeritus, 1995—. Vis. prof. U. Vienna, Austria, Oxford U., Eng., Hebrew U. Jerusalem, Ben Gurion U., U. New Eng., Australia, U. Canterbury, N.Z., Okayama U. Sci., Japan, Rhodes U., U. Turku, Finland. Author: (with S.E. Wood) Thermodynamics-An Introduction, 1968; Oxygen and Ozone, 1981, Nitrogen and Air, 1982, (with S.E. Wood) The Thermodynamics of Chemical Systems, 1990, (with T.L. South) Ericksonian Approaches, A Comprehensive Manual, 1999, Guided Imagery and other Approaches to Healing, 2000, Coping: A Practical Guide for People Who Have Life-Challenging Diseases and Their Caregivers, 2001, Meaning: The Life of Viktor E. Frankl, 2002, Metaphoria: Metaphor and Guided Metaphor for Psychotherapy and Healing, 2002; mem. editl. bd. Solubility Data Series, Jour. Chem. and Engring. Data; contbr. tech. papers to profl. jours. Fulbright fellow, 1979; recipient Outstanding Tchr. award Wright State U., 1979, 93, Outstanding Engr. award Engring. and Sci. Found., Dayton, 1985, Bd. Trustees award Wright State U., 1985. Mem. AAAS, Am. Chem. Soc., Internat. Union Pure and Applied Chemistry (commn.), Sigma Xi, Phi Lambda Upsilon Democrat. Jewish. Office: Wright State U Chemistry Dept Dayton OH 45435 Business E-Mail: rubin.battino@wright.edu.

BATTIS, EMERY JOHN, actor; b. Arlington, Mass., May 30, 1915; s. Floyd Rumney and Myrtle Evelyn (Davis) Battis; m. Elaine Goodell (dec.); children: Christopher, Michael, Peter, Robert, Wendy; m. Elizabeth Neuman. BA, Harvard U., 1942; MA, Columbia U., 1948, PhD, 1959; hon. degree, Clark U., 2001. Assoc. prof. history Rutgers U., New Brunswick, N.J., 1948-68; actor Guthrie Theatre, Mpls., 1968-72, Long Wharf Theatre, New Haven, Conn., 1972-84, The Shakespeare Theatre, Washington, 1984—. Recipient Helen Hayes award for Disting. Lifetime Achievement in Theatre. Address: 324 S Carolina Ave SE Washington DC 20003

BATTISTA, PAUL DAVID, construction executive, investor; b. West Long Branch, NJ, Dec. 31, 1975; s. Wayne David and Angelina Battista; m. Holly Marie Battista, July 24, 2003; 1 child, Gracie. BS in Bus., Monmouth U., 1997; MS in Bus. Adminstrn., Rutgers U., 1998. Apprentice K. Hovnanian, Newark, 1997—99, cmty. constrn. mgr. Manalapan, NJ, 1999—2003, regional constrn. mgr. Jersey City, 2003—05; v.p. cmty. constrn. K. Hovnanian at Meriks, Greenville, 2005—. Investor various comml. and residential bldgs. and homes nationwide, 2000—. Columnist Construction Monthly, 2004—; contbr. articles to profl. magazines. Vol. Coalition Housing & Homeless Orgns., Va., 2004—05. Recipient Outstanding Young Profl. award, Bus. Execs. of Am., 2003, Upcoming Exec. of Yr., K. Hovnanian, 2004. Mem.: Confederation of Internat. Constrn. Assns. (vice-chair 2003—), Professional Construction Estimators Association, Constrn. Fin. Mgmt. Assn. (bd. dirs. 2004—, Named one of Best Bus. Execs. of Yr. 2004). Democrat. Roman Catholic. Achievements include being the youngest executive in Monmouth County, NJ to execute and complete the most high-end tasks for two-consecutive years for K. Hovnanian construction company. Avocations: baseball, cooking, hunting. Home: 172 Ralph St Greenville SC 29611 Office: K Hovnanian at Meriks 5 Welcome View Dr Greenville SC 29611-7756 Office Phone: 908-778-2235. Personal E-mail: davidbattista@comcast.net. Business E-Mail: pd.battista@khovnanian.com.

BATTISTA, RICHARD, entertainment company executive; m. Brenda Battista. BS in bus. adminstrn., Georgetown U.; MBA, Harvard Bus. Sch. Fin. analyst Morgan Stanley; with Fox Entertainment Group (formerly Fox, Inc.), 1990—99, 2001—04; v.p. fin. and adminstrn. Morning Studies (sub. Fox Circle Prodn.); sr. v.p. fin. and ops. Fox Circle Prodn.; exec. v.p. Fox/Liberty Networks, 1997—98; head Fox Sports Internat., 1997—98; exec. v.p. Fox Channels Group, 1998—99, Fox TV, 2001—03, Fox Networks Group, 2003—04; exec. v.p. bus. devel. and strategy Fox Entertainment Group, 2004; co-founder, CEO iFUSE, 1999—2001; CEO Gemstar-TV Guide International Inc., LA, 2004—. Bd. dirs. Nat. Geographic Channel US, Nat. Geographic Channels Internat.; founder, chmn. Georgetown Entertainment and Media Alliance. Bd. gov. Georgetown U.; bd. dirs. Hands of Change. Office: Gemstar-TV Guide Internat Inc 6922 Hollywood Blvd 12th Fl Los Angeles CA 90028

BATTISTELLA, EDWIN L., dean; m. Maureen Battistella. BA, Rutgers Coll., 1976; MA in linguistics, PhD in linguistics, CUNY, 1981. Divsn. head for humanities Wayne State Coll., Wayne, Nebr., 1993—2000; dean, sch. of arts and letters So. Oreg. U., Ashland, Oreg., 2000—. Rev. editor Lang., 1997—2002; assoc. editor Linguistic Abstracts, 2002—; vis. tchr. Vilem Mathesius Workshop on Linguistics, Charles U., Czech Republic, 1993; vis. scientist IBM Thomas J. Watson Rsch. Ctr., 1989—90; vis. asst. prof. Linguistic Soc. Am. Summer Inst., 1986. Author: The Logic of Markedness, Bad Language: Are Some Words Better than Others?, Markedness: The Evaluative Superstructure of Language. Fellow Summer Seminar for Coll. Teachers, NEH, 1984, Summer Seminar, 1992; Fellowship for Ind. Study, 1986, China Studies Travel grant, ACLS, 1987, Ind. Study fellowship, NEH, 1993. Office: So Oregon U 1250 Siskiyou Blvd Ashland OR 97520 Office Phone: 541-552-6520.

BATTISTI, PAUL ORESTE, retired municipal official; b. Herkimer, N.Y., Mar. 16, 1922; s. Oreste and Ida (Fiore) B.; m. Constance Muth Drais, May 18, 1985; children— Paul J., Kate, Deborah, Thomas, Daniel, Melora, Stephen. Student, Cornell U., Ithaca, N.Y., 1947-48, U. Neb., 1951-52. With VA, 1946-75; dir. VA Hosp., Martinez, Calif., 1969-73; western region dir. San Francisco, 1973-75; adminstr. State Vets. Home Calif., 1976-86; supr. County of Napa, 1989-97. Chmn., CEO Medam., Inc.; dir. Med. Am. Corp.; health care cons. 1975-88; chmn. Bay Area Air Quality Mgmt. Dist.; mem. exec. bd. Assoc. Bay Area Govts.; chmn. Bay Area Regional Planning Com.; mem. exec. bd. Bay Area Econ. Forum; chmn. Napa River Flood Control Dist. Fellow Am. Coll. Hosp. Adminstrs.; mem. Hosp. Conf. No. Calif. (pres.), Nat. Assn. State Vets. Homes (pres.). Home: Silverado Country Club 117 Milliken Creek Dr Napa CA 94558-1240

BATTLE, ALLEN OVERTON, JR., psychologist, educator; b. Memphis, Nov. 19, 1927; s. Allen Overton and Florence Louise (Castelvecchi) B.; m. Mary Madeline Vroman, June 14, 1952; 1 son, Allen Overton, III. BS, Siena Coll., 1949; MA, Cath. U. Am., 1953, PhD, 1961; certificate in clin. psychology, U. Tenn. Coll. Medicine, 1953. Diplomate: in clin. psychology Am. Bd. Profl. Psychology, 1971. Instr. dept. psychiatry U. Tenn. Coll. Medicine, 1956-61, asst. prof., 1961-67, asso. prof., 1966-72, prof., 1972—; chief clin. psychologist U. Tenn. Mental Health Center, 1971-78, chief div. clin. psychology, 1974—. Vis. lectr. Southwestern U. at Memphis, 1962-84; vis. prof. Rhodes Coll., 1984—2001 . Author: Clinical Psychology for Physical Therapists, 1975, Suicide and Crisis Intervention Training Manuals, 1978, The Psychology of Patient Care: A Humanistic Approach, 1979; contbr. articles to profl. jours. Cons. USPHS, Suicide and Crisis Intervention Svc.; mem. Mayor's Commn. on Alcohol and Drug Abuse, 1974-77; bd. dirs. Runaway House, St. Peter's Home for Children, De Neuville Heights Sch. Family Svc. Decorated knight Russian Imperial Order; knight Order St. John of Jerusalem; recipient Disting. Svc. award Tenn. Dept. Mental Health, 1971, Jefferson award, Am. Inst. for Pub. Svc., 2001. Mem. Am., Tenn. psychol. assns., Am. Anthrop. Assn., N.Y. Acad. Sci., AAAS, Brit. Soc. Projective Techniques, Sigma Xi. Home: 2220 Washington Ave Memphis TN 38104-3025 Office: 135 N Pauline St Memphis TN 38105-4619 Office Phone: 901-448-4556. E-mail: meijen@midsouth.rr.com.

BATTLE, HILARY HOWARD, minister, educator; b. Cleve., July 1, 1936; s. Joseph Battle and Alice Lee Thomas-Battle; m. Kathleen Ann Harris-Battle, July 4, 1987; 1 child, Rubin. AB, Cuyahoga CC, 1972; BA, Cleve. State U., 1975; MDiv, Princeton (NJ) Theol. Sem., 1978; post grad., U.S. Army Chaplain Sch., 1987. Cert. U.S. Army Chaplain Sch., 1987, ordained Mt. Olive Miss. Bapt. Ch., Cleve., 1975. Chaplain (major) U.S. Army, 1955—96, ret.; pastor Mt. Olive Bapt. Ch., Highstown, NJ, 1977—78; substance abuse counselor Cleve. Treatment Ctr., 1978—80; Hosp. chaplain Ohio Dept. of Mental Health, Cleve., 1981—96, U.S. Army 256 Comat Support, Parma, Ohio, 1982—96. Substitute tchr. Cleve. Pub. Sch., 1974—81; chaplain V.A. Hosp., East Orange, 1977—78; adj. prof. Ashland Theol. Sem., Cleve., 1985—88; clin. privileges Cleve. Psychiat. Inst.; instr. Am. Bapt. Coll., Cleve., 1992—; founder 4 annual conf. Tchg. Techniques for Ch. Educators, 1999—2003; presenter in field. Author: Thee of Come Things All, 2002; founder, chief author: church in-house manual. Founder, dir. instl. choir Cleve. Psychiat. Hosp., 1989—91; choir dir. several ch. choirs, 1955—85; 2 v.p. Ohio State Chaplain Assn., Cleve., 1994—96; chaplain North Coast chpt. Tuskegee Airmen, Beachwood, Ohio, 1996—. Avocations: music, skating. Home: 436 Partridge Ct Macedonia OH 44056 E-mail: kathleen@buckeyeweb.com.

BATTLE, LUCIUS DURHAM, retired academic administrator, retired diplomat; b. Dawson, Ga., June 1, 1918; s. Warren Lazarus and Jewel Beatrice (Durham) B.; m. Betty Jane Davis, Oct. 1, 1949; children: Lynne, John, Laura, Thomas. AB, U. Fla., 1939, LL.B., 1946; LL.D.; L.H.D., Fla. State U. Mgr. student staff U. Fla. Library, 1940-42; assoc. adminstrv. analyst War Dept., 1942-43; fgn. affairs specialist Dept. State, Washington, 1946-49, spl. asst. to sec. of state, 1949-53, 61-64, also exec. sec., 1961-62; asst. sec. of state for ednl. and cultural affairs, 1962-64; 1st sec. Am. Embassy, Copenhagen, 1953-55; dep. exec. sec. NATO, Paris, 1955-56; ambassador to UAR, 1964-67; asst. sec. state for Nr. Eastern and South Asian affairs Washington, 1967-68; v.p. corp. affairs Communications Satellite Corp., 1968-73, sr. v.p. corp. affairs, 1974-80; dir. COMSAT Gen. Corp., 1974-80; chmn. Fgn. Policy Inst., Sch. Advanced Internat. Studies, Johns Hopkins U., 1980-84; pres. Middle East Inst., Washington, 1973-74, 86-91, bd. dirs., 1973-81. Chmn. UNESCO Gen. Conf., Paris, 1962; pres. Found. for Mid. East Peace, 1994—. V.p. Colonial Williamsburg, Inc., Williamsburg Restoration, Inc., 1956-61; chpt. mem. Protestant Episcopal Cathedral Found., Washington; chmn. bd. St. Albans Sch., 1973-76; vice chmn. Meridian House Internat., 1976-77; trustee George C. Marshall Research Found., Am. U., Cairo, 1970-79; chmn. vis. com. Ctr. for Middle Eastern Studies, Harvard, 1973-76; bd. dirs. Fgn. Policy Assn., 1974-84, Sch. Advanced Internat. Studies, 1975—, World Council of Washington, 1980, Smithsonian Assocs., 1981-85; Am. Near East Refugee Aid, 1985—; mem. fine arts com. Dept. State, 1973-77; mem. Nat. Study Commn. on Records and Documents Fed. Ofcls., 1975-76; pres. Bacon House Found., 1975-85, v.p. DACOR Bacon House Found. adv. bd. Ctr. for Contemporary Arab Studies, Georgetown U., 1976-86; mem. founders council Inst. for Study of Diplomacy, 1978-87; chmn. nat. com. to honor 14th centennial of Islam, 1979-84; chmn. Am. Inst. Islamic Affairs, 1984-87; pres. Found. for Middle Eastpeace, 1994. Served to lt. USNR, 1943-46. Decorated Order of Republic 1st class Egypt; recipient Fgn. Service Cup, Diplomatic and Consular Officers Ret., 1984, Founders award Sch. Advanced Internat.

Studies. Mem. Am. Fgn. Service Assn. (pres. 1962-63), Order of Coif, Phi Beta Kappa, Alpha Tau Omega, Phi Delta Phi. Clubs: Met. (Washington); Alibi. Home: 4856 Rockwood Pky NW Washington DC 20016-3249

BATTLE, MICHAEL A., federal agency administrator, former prosecutor, lawyer; b. 1955; Grad., Ithaca Coll., SUNY, Buffalo. Asst. U.S. atty. (we. dist.) NY US Dept. Justice, 1985—92; asst. pub. defender Fed. Pub. Defender's Office, We. Dist. N.Y., 1992—95; asst. atty. gen. 8th Jud. Cir., NY State Atty. Gen.'s Office, 1995—96; judge Erie County Family Ct., Buffalo, 1996—2002; US atty. (We. Dist.) NY US Dept. Justice, 2002—05, dir., Exec. Office US Attys. (EOUSA), 2005—. Bd. dir. YMCA Greater Buffalo, NY, Greater Niagara Frontier Council of Boy Scouts of Am., NY; dean's adv. council SUNYat Buffalo Law Sch., NY. Mem.: Minority Bar Assn. We. NY (pres.). Office: Exec Office for US Attorneys US Dept Justice 950 Pennsylvania Ave NW Rm 2616 Washington DC 20530-0001 Office Phone: 202-514-2121. Office Fax: 202-616-2278.*

BATTLE, TURNER CHARLES, III, art educator, educational association administrator; b. Oberlin, Ohio; s. Turner and Annie (McClellan) B.; m. Carmen Helena Gonzalez Castellanos; children: Anne E., Turner C. IV, Conchita Yvonne, Carmen Rosario. Student, Andrews U.; BA, Oakwood Coll.; postgrad., Wagner Inst. Sci., Cheyney State Coll., Temple U., Columbia U., NYU; MFA, Temple U.; HHD, Wiley Coll. Instr. art Oakwood Coll., Huntsville, Ala.; auditor, acct. Navy Regional Acct. Office; instr. art Phila.; dir. Sch. Art League Sch. Gifted Children, Phila.; asst. prof. art Elmira Coll., NY; assoc. prof. art Moore Coll. Art, Phila.; vis. assoc. prof. NYU, NY; tchg. fellow. Vis. assoc. prof., dir. program Westminster Choir Coll.; art cons., lectr. pvt. and pub. orgns.; edn. cons. cmty. planners group U.S. Office Edn.; cons. E. Africa, Mid. E. Exhibited in group shows ea. U.S., including Bucknell U., Phila. Art Alliance, Newport (R.I.) Art Assn., Phila. Mus. Art, Susquehanna U., Atlantic City Boardwalk Show, Greenwich Village, N.Y.C., numerous others; represented in pvt. collections throughout U.S., India, Eng., Africa, Japan. Exec. dir. Higher Edn. Coalition Southeastern Pa.; dir. Open Door Program, LaSalle U.; asst. exec. dir., corp. sec. United Negro Coll. Fund, N.Y.C., pres. ednl. devel. svc., 1994—. Mem. Am. Assn. Higher Edn., Tyler Sch. Temple U. Alumni Assn. (pres. 1965-66), Am. Mus. Natural History, Smithsonian Inst., Sierra Club, Phi Delta Kappa. Home: 1519 W Turner St Allentown PA 18102-3634 E-mail: turnercbattle3@cs.com.

BATTLE, VINCENT M., former ambassador; b. Teaneck, N.J., Sept. 1940; MA, Columbia U., 1967, PhD, 1974. Consular officer U.S. Fgn. Svc., Manama, Bahrain, 1977—79; head of Immigrant Visa sect., Port-au-Prince, Haiti, 1985—88; polit. officer Muscat, Oman, 1983—85; consular officer Bur. of Near East Affairs, Damascus, Syria, 1980—83; various to dep. chief of mission U.S. Embassy, Cairo, 1996—99; U.S. amb. to Lebanon US Dept. State, Beirut, 2001—04.

BATTLE, WILLIAM ROBERT (BOB BATTLE), retired publishing executive; b. Nolensville, Tenn., Dec. 25, 1927; s. William Robert and Cleo (Smith) B.; m. Elizabeth Ogilvie, Dec. 23, 1948; children: Valerie Elizabeth Kienzle, William Robert III. Student, George Peabody Coll., 1946-49. Exec. offcl. Nashville Banner, 1943-98, police beat, county polit. beat, 1943-53, city editor, 1953-64, movie columnist, 1955-72, mng. editor, 1964-71, exec. editor, 1971-75, asst. to editor, 1975-78, regional editor, 1978-80, sr. editor, 1980-84, v.p., bus. editor, 1984-89, v.p., sr. bus. editor, 1989-98; staff writer Country Style mag., Livin Country. Columnist Williamson A.M., Tennessean; mem. exec. bd. Tenn. Dept. Agr. Agrl. Mus., 2002—. Appeared as newspaperman in: film Teacher's Pet, 1957, also in Country Music on Broadway, 1963; contbr. World Book Ency., numerous articles to nat. publs. Supt. gates and admissions Tenn. State Fair, 1953-64; pub. rels. chmn. Davidson County Coun. for Retarded Children, 1961-66; mem. exec. bd. Mid. Tenn. coun. Boy Scouts Am.; mem. 4-H Club Found.; exec. bd. dirs., past sec. Nashville Boys Club, now life mem. bd. dirs.; bd. dirs. College Grove Sr. Enrichment Ctr., 2002—; mem. exec. coun. Coll. Grove Sr. Recreational Ctr., 2002—; bd. mem. Tenn. Agricultural Mus. Recipient Big Story award NBC-TV, 1956; named Man of Yr., 4-H Club, 1974, Man of Yr., Future Farmers Am., 1975, Silver Beaver award Boy Scouts Am., 1997; Robert Battle scholarship established in his honor Belmont U. Sch. Bus., By Opryland, U.S.A., 1989. Mem. Nashville Area C. of C., Tenn. Press Assn., Nat. Screen Coun., Country Music Assn., Masons (33d deg., knights commdr. ct. of honor), Shriners (potentate 1976), Royal Order of Jesters (former dir.), Elks (former chmn. scholarship com.), Sigma Delta Chi (former chmn. scholarship com., former pres.). Methodist. Home: 8889 Horton Hwy College Grove TN 37046-9280 Office Phone: 615-368-2353. Personal E-mail: bobbattle@aol.com.

BATTLES, JOHN MARTIN, lawyer; b. Pitts., Pa., May 10, 1957; s. John and Rosemarie B.; m. Mary Ann Battles; children: John David, Katherine Rose. BA, U. Pitts., 1978; BA in Bus. Adminstrn., U. Cin., 1980, JD, 1990. Asst. corp. counsel Cincom Systems, Cin.; now corp. counsel Lexis-Nexis Group, divsn. Reed Elsevier Inc., Dayton, Ohio. Home: 7 Crescent Ct Fort Thomas KY 41075-2113 Office: Lexis Nexis Group Div Reed Elsevier Inc 9443 Springboro Pike Miamisburg OH 45342-4425

BATTLES, ROXY EDITH, novelist, consultant, educator; b. Spokane, Wash., Mar. 29, 1921; d. Rosco Jirah and Lucile Zilpha (Jacques) Baker; m. Willis Ralph Dawe Battles, May 2, 1941 (dec. 2000); children: Margaret Battles Holmes, Ralph, Lara. AA, Bakersfield (Calif.) Coll., 1940; BA, Calif. State U., Long Beach, 1959; MA, Pepperdine U., 1976. Cert. tchr. English, adult basic edn. and elem. edn., Calif. Freelance writer 50 nat. and regional mags., 1940—; tchr. elem. Torrance (Calif.) Unified Schs., 1959-85; tchr. adult edn. Pepperdine U., Torrance, 1969-79, 88-89; freelance children's author, 1966—; mystery novelist Pinnacle Publs., NYC, 1980; with Tex. A&M U., 1988. Instr. Mary Mount Coll., Harbor Coll., 1995; author-in-residence Young Authors Festival, Am. Sch. Madrid, 1991; participant First Educators to Japan Exch., 1973; lectr. in field. Author: Over the Rickety Fence, 1967, The Terrible Trick or Treat, 1970, 501 Balloons Sail East, 1971, The Terrible Terrier, 1972, One to Teeter-Totter, 1973, 2d edit., 1975, Eddie Couldn't Find the Elephants, 1974, reprints, 1982, 84, 88, What Does the Rooster Say, Yoshio?, 1978, reprinted in Swedish, German, French, 1980, The Secret of Castle Drai, 1980, The Witch in Room 6, 1987, 3d edit., 1989, The Chemistry of Whispering Caves, 1988, rev. edit., 1997, Computer Encryptions in Whispering Caves, 1997; playwright: Roxy, 1995, The Lavender Castle, 1996, mus. version, 1997, Sacred Submarine, 2000, Embarking on Rebellion, 2001. Active So. Calif. Coun. on Lit. for Children and Young People, 1973-80, 87—. Recipient Commendation UN, 1979. Mem. S.W. Manuscripters (founder), Surfwriters. Home: 560 S Helberta Ave Redondo Beach CA 90277-4353 Personal E-mail: groxy@aol.com. *However I rail at prejudice, some prejudgment is inevitable and, except in extremity, foreseeable. Whether caused by neglect or studied plan, negatives are noticed. When the fixable remains unfixed, I deserve to be judged for my part, however I blame my adjudicator.*

BATTOCCHI, RONALD SILVIO, lawyer; b. Hartford, Conn., Sept. 28, 1947; s. Silvio Romano and Elda (Ferrari) B.; m. Mary Therese Bell, June 18, 1977; children: Keith, Scott, Julia. BA, Amherst Coll., 1970; JD, U. Maine, 1974. Bar: Maine 1974, D.C. 1983, U.S. Supreme Ct. 1987. Spl. asst. to chmn. Nat. Transp. Safety Bd., Washington, 1974-76, atty. advisor, 1976-80, spl. asst. and counsel to chmn., 1980-81, atty. advisor, 1981-90, dep. gen. counsel, 1990-94, dep. mng. dir., 1994-99, gen. counsel, 1999—. Office: Nat Transp Safety Bd Rm 6401 490 L'Enfant Plz SW Washington DC 20594-0001 Office Phone: 202-314-6080. Office Fax: 202-314-6090. Business E-Mail: battocr@ntsb.gov.

BATTON, BEAU JACOB, pediatrician; s. Daniel Gene and Nelda Lei Batton; m. Angela Lynn Rabl, May 10, 2002. MD, Loyola U. Chgo., Stritch Sch. Medicine, 2002. Pediatrician William Beaumont Hosp., Royal Oak, Mich., 2002—. Home: 694 Colonial Ct Birmingham MI 48009 Office Phone: 248-898-5000. Office Fax: 248-551-2032.

BATTS, ALICIA J., lawyer; AB, Harvard Coll., 1987; JD, Columbia U. Law Sch., 1990. Bar: NY 1991, DC 1993. Assoc. Howrey Simon Arnold & White LLP, Skadden, Arps, Slate, Meagher & Flom LLP; atty.-advisor to Fed. Trade Commr. Mozelle W. Thompson, 1998—2000; ptnr. Foley & Lardner, 2000—04, Dickstein Shapiro Morin & Oshinsky LLP, DC, 2004—. Contbr. articles to law jour.; editl. bd. Antitrust Law Jour.; co-editor: Clayton Act Com. Newsletter. Bd. dirs. Appleseed Found. Named one of Am. Top Black Attys., Black Enterprise, 2003. Mem.: ABA, DC Bar, Nat. Black Bar Assn. (regular panelist), Minority Corp. Counsel Assn. (regular panelist). Office: Dickstein Shapiro Morin & Oshinsky LLP 2101 L St NW Washington DC 20037-1526 Office Phone: 202-777-4411. Business E-Mail: BattsA@dsmo.com.

BATTS, DEBORAH A., federal judge; b. Phila., Apr. 13, 1947; d. James A., Jr. and Ruth Violet (Silas) Batts; 2 children. BA, Radcliffe Coll., 1969; JD, Harvard U., 1972. Summer atty. Foley, Hoag & Eliot, Boston, Mass., 1970, Kaye, Scholer, Fierman, Hays & Handler, N.Y.C., 1971; law clerk to Hon. Lawrence W. Pierce U.S. Dist. Ct. (so. dist.) N.Y., N.Y.C., 1972-73; assoc. atty. Cravath, Swaine & Moore, N.Y.C., 1973-79; asst. U.S. atty. criminal divsn. U.S. Dist. Ct. (so. dist.) N.Y., N.Y.C., 1979-84; assoc. prof. law Fordham U., 1984-94, adj. prof. law, 1994—; spl. assoc. counsel dept. investigation N.Y.C., 1990-91; commr. law revision com. State of N.Y., 1990-94; judge U.S. Dist. Ct. (so. dist.) N.Y., N.Y.C., 1994—. Bd. trustees Cathedral Sch., N.Y.C., 1990-96; mem. faculty Corp. Counsel Trial Advocacy Program, 1988-94. Contbr. articles to legal jours. Trustee Spence Sch., 1987-95. Mem. ABA, Second Cir. Fed. Bar Coun., Assn. Bar. City N.Y., Lesbian and Gay Law Assn. Greater N.Y., Met. Black Bar Assn. Office: US Courthouse 500 Pearl St Rm 2510 New York NY 10007-1316*

BATTS, MICHAEL STANLEY, German language educator; b. Mitcham, Eng., Aug. 2, 1929; s. Stanley George and Alixe Kathleen (Watson) B.; m. Misao Yoshida, Mar. 19, 1959; 1 dau., Anna. BA, U. London, 1952, BA with honors, 1953, LittD, 1973; PhD, U. Freiburg, Germany, 1957; MLS, U. Toronto, 1974. Mem. faculty U. Mainz, Germany, 1953-54, U. Basel, Switzerland, 1954-56; Mem. faculty U. Wurzburg, Germany, 1956-58; instr. German U. Calif., Berkeley, 1958-60; mem. faculty dept. German U. B.C., Canada, 1960-91, prof., 1967-91, head dept., 1968-80; ret., 1980. Author: Die Form der Aventiuren im Nibelungenlied, 1961, Bruder Hansens Marienlieder, 1964, Studien zu Bruder Hansens Marienliedern, 1964, Das Hohe Mittelalter, 1969, Das Nibelungenlied-Synoptische Ausgabe, 1971, Gottfried von Strasburg, 1971, A Checklist of German Literature, 1945-75, 1977, The Bibliography of German Literature: An Historical and Critical Survey, 1978, A History of Histories of German Literature, 1835-1914, 1993, Germanic Studies at Canadian Universities From the Beginning to 1995, 1998; editor: Seminar, 1970-80. Served with Brit. Army, 1947-49. Alexander von Humboldt fellow, 1964-65, 83; Can. Coun. Sr. fellow, 1964-65, 71-72; Killam fellow, 1981-82. Fellow Royal Soc. Can.; mem. Can. Assn. Univ. Tchrs. German (pres. 1982-84), Modern Humanities Rsch. Assn., Alcuin Soc. (exec. v.p. 1972-79, pres. 1979-80), Internat. Assn. for Germanic Studies (pres. 1990-95). Office: U BC German Dept Vancouver BC Canada V6T 1Z1 E-mail: msb@interchange.ubc.ca.

BATTS, WARREN LEIGHTON, retired manufacturing executive; b. Norfolk, Va., Sept. 4, 1932; s. John Leighton and Allie Belle (Johnson) B.; m. Eloise Pitts, Dec. 24, 1957; 1 dau., Terri Allison. BEE, Ga. Inst. Tech., 1961; MBA, Harvard U., 1963. With Kendall Co., Charlotte, N.C., 1963-64; exec. v.p. Fashion Devel. Co., Santa Paula, Calif., 1964-66; dir. mfg. Olga Co., Van Nuys, Calif., 1964-66; v.p. Douglas Williams Assocs., N.Y.C., 1966-67; co-founder Triangle Corp., Orangeburg, S.C., 1967, pres., chief exec. officer, 1967-71; v.p. Mead Corp., Dayton, Ohio, 1971-73, pres., 1973-80, chief exec. officer, 1978-80; pres., chief operating officer Dart Industries, Inc., L.A., 1980-81, Dart & Kraft, Inc., Northbrook, Ill., 1981-86; chmn., chief exec. officer Premark Internat. Inc., Deerfield, 1986-96, chmn., 1996-97; chmn., CEO Tupperware Corp., Orlando, Fla., 1996-97.

BATULE, ROBERT JOHN, priest, writer; b. Bklyn., May 23, 1958; s. Robert Philip and Ann Marie (Reilly) B. BA in Sociology, Cathedral Coll., 1980; MDiv, Immaculate Conception, 1985; MA in Sociology summa cum laude, Adelphi U., 1990; MA in Theology summa cum laude, St. Johns U., 1996. Ordained priest Roman Cath. Ch., 1985. Parish priest St. Boniface Roman Cath. Ch., Elmont, NY, 1985-90, St. Martha Roman Cath. Ch., Uniondale, NY, 1990-93, Corpus Christi Roman Cath. Ch., Mineola, NY, 1993—2002, adminstr., 2001—, 2001—02; Monsignor, 2004—; Pastor Holy Family RC Church, Hicksville, NY, 2004—. Del. for Pastoral Intervention, 2002—, chmn., moderator Cath. Youth Orgn. Nassau and Suffolk, Hicksville, NY, 1997-2000; adj. faculty St. Vincent's Coll. divsn. humanities, dept. theology, St. John's U., 1996-99. Contbr. Cath. Ency., 1991, 98, Cath. Dictionary, 1993; columnist, The Catholic Answer, 1987-96, The Catholic Transcript, 1993-95, The Long Island Cath. Newspaper; contbr. numerous homilies, revs. and articles to profl. jour. 2d lt. USAF, 1981-82. Mem. Fellowship of Cath. Scholars, Soc. Cath. Social Scientists, Nat. Assn. of Scholars. Roman Catholic. Avocations: athletics, reading. Home and Office: Holy Family RC Ch 5 Fordham Ave Hicksville NY 11801 Office Phone: 516-938-3846.

BATZLI, GEORGE OLIVER, ecology educator; b. Mpls., Sept. 23, 1936; s. Oscar H. and Bertha M. B.; m. Sandra Lou Scharf, Jan. 2, 1959; children—Jeffrey, Samuel. BS in Psychology, U. Minn., 1959; MA in Biology, San Francisco State U., 1965; PhD in Zoology (Ecology), U. Calif., Berkeley, 1969. Research assoc. U. Calif., Davis, 1969-71, lectr. biology Santa Cruz, 1971; asst. prof. zoology U. Ill., Urbana, 1971-76, assoc. prof. ecology, 1976-80, prof. ecology, 1980—2004, prof. emeritus, 2004—, head dept. ecology, ethology and evolution, 1983-88, 95-97. Sr. scientist research in arctic environs., 1976-78, mem. ecology program adv. panel NSF, 1984-87, 2003, long term econ. rsch. adv. panel alpine tundra, 1988, arctic tundra, 1992, tall grass prairie, 1999; research scientist DSIR, N.Z., 1979; chmn. ecology program U. Ill., 1976-82. Contbr. articles on ecology to profl. jours.; spl. issue editor Arctic and Alpine Research, 1980, Oikos, 1983; mem. editorial bd. Ecology, Ecol. Monographs, 1981-84. Fellow NSF, 1962-63, NIH, 1967-69, 69-71, Zool. Inst. U. Oslo, Norway, 1982. Fellow AAAS; mem. Am. Inst. Biol. Scis., Am. Soc. Mammalogy (C. Hart Merriam award 2002), Ecol. Soc. Am., Intecol. Office: U Ill Shelford Vivarium 606 E Healey St Champaign IL 61820-5502 Business E-Mail: g-batzli@life.uiuc.edu.

BATZLI, TERRENCE RAYMOND, lawyer; b. Dec. 28, 1946; s. Marion Raymond and Kathryn Velma (Hudran) Batzli; m. Sharon Lee Heinatz, Aug. 2, 1969; children: Catherine Barrett, Jonathan Raymond. BS, U. Richmond, 1974, JD, 1975. Bar: Va. 1975, U.S. Dist. Ct. (ea. dist.) Va. 1975, U.S. Dist. Ct. (we. dist.) Va. 1983, U.S. Ct. Appeals (4th cir.) 1984. Ptnr. Mays & Valentine and predecessor firms, Richmond, 1982-93, Durrette & Bradshaw, Richmond, Va., 1993-96; prin. Barnes & Batzli, PC, 1996—2004, Batzli Wood & Stiles, 2004—. Mediator McCammon Group; adj. prof. law Reynolds C.C., Richmond, 1980—82; lectr. in field. Mem. adv. bd. Nat. Head Injury Found., 1988—, VA Head Injury Found., 1990—91. Capt. U.S. Army, 1966—70. Named Best Divorce Atty. in Richmond in a pub. opinion poll, Richmond Mag., 2000; named one of Top Three Family Law Lawyers in Richmond in a survey of lawyers, 1999, Top 5 Family Law Attys. in State of Va., 2000, 2001, 2002, 2003, 2004. Fellow: Internat. Acad. Matrimonial Lawyers, Am. Acad. Matrimonial Lawyers; mem.: Hanover Assn. Bus. (pres. 1989, bd. dirs.), Va. State Bar (bd. govs. family law sect. 1996—, sec. 1997, vice-chair 1999, chair 2000—), Metro Richmond Family Law Bar Assn. (founding pres. 1994), Hanover County Bar Assn. (treas. 1997, sec. 1998, pres.-elect 1999, pres. 2000), Richmond Bar Assn. (chmn. family law sect. 1982—83, exec. com. 1982—83), Ruritan Club (pres., zone gov., dist. sec.), Rotary (bd.dirs. 1980—84). Republican. Methodist. Home: 11910 Aberdeen Landing Ter Midlothian VA 23113-1394 Office: Batzli Wood & Stiles Ste 200 10900 Nuckols Rd Glen Allen VA 23060 Office Phone: 804-545-9800.

BAUCH, JONATHAN MARC, literature educator, writer; b. Bklyn., July 12, 1968; s. Ira and Lynn Carol Bauch; m. Elisa Fraidkin, Nov. 25, 1996. BA in English, CUNY, S.I., N.Y., 1990; MA in English, CUNY, 1992; MFA in Fiction, U. of Nev., Las Vegas, 2005. Prodn. asst. Avon Books, N.Y.C., 1992—93; adj. instr. English The Coll. of Staten Island/CUNY, 1993—96; sr. editor/writer Equinox Internat., Las Vegas, 1996—97; part time instr. English U. of Nev., Las Vegas, 1997—2000, grad. tchg. asst./part time instr., 2000—. Asst. to the Ben Jonson jour. English Dept.; U. of Nev. Las Vegas, Las Vegas, Nev., 1998—99. Assistant to editor (book) Cambridge Companion to Brian Friel. Mem.: N.Am. Soc. of Pipe Collectors, Phi Kappa Phi Honor Soc.

BAUCH, THOMAS JAY, financial consultant, retired lawyer, retired apparel executive; b. Indpls., May 24, 1943; s. Thomas and Violet (Smith) B.; m. Ellen L. Burstein, Oct. 31, 1982; children: Chelsea Sara, Elizabeth Tree. BS with honors, U. Wis., 1964, JD with highest honors, 1966. Bar: Ill. 1966, Calif. 1978. Assoc. Lord, Bissell & Brook, Chgo., 1966-72; lawyer, asst. sec. Marcor-Montgomery Ward, Chgo., 1973-75; spl. asst. to solicitor Dept. Labor, Washington, 1975-77; dep. gen. counsel Levi Strauss & Co., San Francisco, 1977-81, sr. v.p., gen. counsel, 1981-96, of counsel, 1996-2000; pvt. practice, Tiburon, Calif., 1996-2000; mng. dir. Offit Hall Capital Mgmt. LLC, San Francisco, 2000—04; ret., 2004. Cons. prof. Stanford (Calif.) U. Law Sch., 1997-2004; ptnr. Ika Enterprises. Mem. U. Wis. Law Rev., 1964-66. Bd. dirs. Urban Sch., San Francisco, 1986-91, Gateway H.S., San Francisco, Charles Armstrong Sch., Belmont, Calif., 1998-2001, San Francisco Opera Assn., 1998-2001, Telluride Acad., 1996-2000, Corinthian Acad.; bd. visitors U. Wis. Law Sch., 1991-95. Mem. Am. Assn. Corp. Counsel (bd. dirs. 1984-87), Bay Area Gen. Counsel Assn. (chmn. 1994), Univ. Club, Villa Taverna Club, Corinthian Yacht Club, Order of Coif, San Francisco Yacht Club. Office: Offit Hall Capital Mgmt One Maritime Plz Ste 500 San Francisco CA 94111

BAUCOM, SIDNEY GEORGE, lawyer; b. Salt Lake City, Oct. 21, 1930; s. Sidney and Nora (Palfreyman) B.; m. Mary B., Mar. 5, 1954; children: Sidney, George, John JD, U. Utah, 1953. Bar: Utah 1953. Pvt. practice, Salt Lake City, 1953-55; asst. city atty. Salt Lake City Corp., 1955-56; asst. atty. Utah Power and Light Co., Salt Lake City, 1956-60, asst. atty., asst. sec., 1960-62, atty., asst. sec., 1962-68, v.p., gen. counsel, 1968-75, sr. v.p., gen. counsel, 1975-79, exec. v.p., gen. counsel, 1979-89, dir., 1979-89; of counsel Jones, Waldo, Holbrook & McDonough, Salt Lake City, 1989—. Past chmn. Utah Coordinating Coun. Devel. Svcs., Utah Taxpayers Assn.; past pres. Utah State Fair Found.; past dir. Utah Power & Light Co., El Paso Electric Co., vice chmn. Mem. Alta Club, Lions, Phi Delta Phi Mem. Lds Ch. Home: 2248 Logan Ave Salt Lake City UT 84108-2715 Office: Jones Waldo Holbrook & McDonough 1500 Wells Fargo Bank Bldg 170 S Main St Salt Lake City UT 84101-1605 Office Phone: 801-521-3200. Business E-Mail: sbaucom@joneswaldo.com.

BAUCUS, MAX S., senator; b. Helena, Mont., Dec. 11, 1941; s. John and Jean (Sheriff) Baucus; m. Wanda Minge, Apr. 23, 1983; 1 child. BA, Stanford U., 1964, LLB, 1967. Bar: D.C. 1969, Mont. 1972. Staff atty. CAB, Washington, 1967-68; lawyer SEC, Washington, 1968-71, legal asst. to chmn., 1970-71; sole practice Missoula, Mont., 1971-74; mem. Mont. Ho. of Reps., 1973-74, 94th-95th congresses from 1st Dist. Mont., 1975-79, mem. com. appropriations; senator from Mont. U.S. Senate, 1979—, ranking minority mem., mem. environ. and pub. works com., mem. fin. subcom. on internat. trade, mem. health com., taxation and IRS oversight com., mem. agrl./nutrition and forestry coms., mem. intelligence/joint com. on taxation, mem. Senate Dem. steering and coordination com. Democrat. Avocation: motorcycling. Office: US Senate 511 Hart Senate Bldg Washington DC 20510-0001 also: District Office 207 N Broadway Billings MT 59101*

BAUDE, PATRICK LOUIS, law educator; b. Independence, Kans., Apr. 7, 1943; s. E.L. Andre and Jane (O'Brien) B.; m. Deborah Robinson, June 1, 1963 (div. Oct. 1977); children: Virginia, Leora; m. Julia Lamber, Feb. 27, 1981; children: William, Jonathan. AB, U. Kans., 1964, JD, 1966; LLM, Harvard U., 1968. Bar: Wis. 1966, Ind. 1990, U.S. Supreme Ct. 1969. Assoc. Foley & Lardner, Milw., 1966-67; fellow Harvard Law Sch., Cambridge, Mass., 1967-68; prof. law Ind. U., Bloomington, 1968-2001, Ralph F. Fuchs prof. law, 2001—. Vis. prof. U. Warsaw, Poland, 1993, U. Paris, 2000; mem. Ind. Bd. Law Examiners, Indpls., 1990-01, pres., 1997-99. Office: Indiana Univ Law Sch Bloomington IN 47465 E-mail: baude@indiana.edu.

BAUDO, SERGE, conductor; b. Marseille, France, July 16, 1927; s. Etienne and Genevieve (Tortelier) B.; student Conservatory of Paris; m. Madelein Reties, June 16, 1947; children: Stephane, Catherine. Music dir. Radio Nice, France, 1957-59; condr. Paris Opera Orch., 1962-66; titular condr., interim orch. dir. Paris Orch., 1968-70; music dir. Opera de Lyon, 1969-71; music dir. Orch. of Lyon, 1971-87; condr. many internat. orchs. including Tonhalle Orch. Zurich, Orchestre de la Suisse Romande, Berlin Philharm., La Scala, Met. Opera, Dallas Orch., Deutsche Oper Berlin, London Philharm. Orch., Yomiuri Nippon Orch., Prague (Czechoslovakia) Philharm., Stockholm Philharm., Met. Opera, Dallas Orch., Indpls. Orch., Detroit Orch., Statoper Wien, Wiener Philharm., Tokyo NHK Orch., Opera de Zurich, Opera de Paris/Bastille, R.S.O. Berlin, London Philharm., others; founder Berlioz Festival, Lyon, 1979—, mus. dir., 1989—. Decorated chevalier Ordre National du Merite; officier des Arts et des Lettres; recipient numerous Grand Prix du Disque, 1976-90. Office: 211 Gough St Ste 112 San Francisco CA 94102

BAUDOIN, PETER, family business consultant; b. Breaux Bridge, La., Dec. 23, 1946; s. Roy Paul and Carrie (Broussard) B.; m. Donna Renz, Apr. 17, 1971; 1 child, Jonn Pierre. BS in Bus. Adminstrn., U. Southwestern La., 1968. CPA; cert. mgmt. acct.; cert. in succession assurance. Ops. auditor Firestone Tire & Rubber Co., Akron, Ohio, 1969-71; sr. acct. Unishops of Clarkins, Inc., Akron, Ohio, 1972-73; cons. supr. Ernst & Young, Cleve., 1973-78; ptnr. Baudoin & Hamza CPAs, Lafayette, La., 1978-82; pres. Peter Baudoin Cons., Lafayette, La., 1982—; founder, mng. dir. Family Bus. Accts. and Advisors, Lafayette, La., 1990—. Bd. dirs., treas., exec. com., mem. body of knowledge task force Family Firm Inst., Boston, 1990—, chair 1997 internat. conf. in New Orleans; dir. programming Acadiana Family Bus. Forum, 1992—; spl. advisor Family Bus. Forum, La. State U., adj. prof. entrepreneurship and family bus.; vis. advisor Family Bus. Forum, Tex. A&M U. Contbr. numerous articles to profl. jours. Founding pres. Rocky River (Ohio) Jaycees, 1976; former chmn. adv. bd. Charity Depot, an agy. of Lafayette Cath. Svcs. Ctr., Inc.; retreat capt. Our Lady of the Oaks Retreat House, Grand Coteau, La. With Spl. Forces, USAR, 1968-75. Named hon. Paramount Chief Zokai of Liberia, bestowed by Mandingo Tribe, 1975. Mem. Fin. Execs. Internat., Inst. Mgmt. Accts. (nat. v.p. 1998-00, nat. bd. 1993-95, pres. Gulf South Coun. 1996-97), Serra Club of Lafayette (pres. 1999-2000), Secretariat of Fin. of Redemptorist Vice-Provincial New Orleans, Carmelite Men's Guild Lafayette. Republican. Roman Catholic. Home: 101 Florida Ct Lafayette LA 70503-2005 Office: Peter Baudoin Cons 158 Industrial Pky Lafayette LA 70508-8309 E-mail: pbaudoin@aol.com.

BAUE, ARTHUR EDWARD, surgeon, educator, retired health facility administrator; b. St. Louis, Oct. 7, 1929; s. Arthur Christian and Viola (Wegener) B.; m. Rosemary Dysart, Nov. 24, 1956; children: Patricia Sage Baue Nizen, Arthur Christian II, William Dysart. AB summa cum laude, Westminster Coll., 1950; MD cum laude, Harvard, 1954; M Honoris Privatum, Yale U., 1975; MD honoris causa, Ludwig Maxmillian U., Munich, Germany, 2000. Diplomate Am. Bd. Surgery (dir.), Am. Bd. Thoracic Surgery (dir.). Cpt. asst. chief of surgery USAF Hosp., Philippine Islands, 1955-57; from intern to chief resident surgery Mass. Gen. Hosp., Boston, 1954-61; asst. prof. surgery U. Mo. Sch. Medicine, 1962-64; sr. registrar in thoracic surgery Bristol, Eng., 1961-62; from asst. prof. to assoc. prof. surgery U. Pa. Sch. Medicine, Phila., 1964-67; Harry Edison prof. surgery Washington U. Sch. Medicine, St. Louis, 1967-75; surgeon-in-chief, dir. dept. surgery Jewish Hosp., St. Louis, 1967-75; chief of surgery Yale-New Haven Hosp., 1975-85; prof., chmn. dept. surgery Yale U., 1975-85, Donald Guthrie prof. surgery, 1977-85; assoc. dean for clin. affairs St. Louis U. Sch. Medicine, 1985-86;

v.p. for the med. ctr. St. Louis U., 1986-90, prof. surgery, 1986-97, prof. emeritus, v.p. emeritus for the med. ctr., 1997. Dir. surg. edn. St. Mary's Health Ctr., 1990-97; cons. surgery Nat. Bd. Med. Examiners; cons. to chief of staff VAMC, St. Louis, 1994-97; chmn. NIH surgery B study sect., 1978-82; bd. dirs., med. dir. Healthcare Mgmt., Inc.; vis. prof. various colls.; hon. pres., Internat. Symposium Critical Care Medicine, Trieste, 2003, 04; spkr. in field. Chief editor Archives of Surgery, 1977-88, sr. cons. editor, 1989-93; editor: Parameters of Health Care, 1986-90; mem. editl. bd. JAMA, 1977-88, Circulatory Shock, Am. Jour. Physiology, 1975-87, Postgrad. Gen. Surgery, Jour. Shock, 1994—; sr. editor: Glenn's Thoracic and Cardiovascular Surgery; editor and/or author 13 books; contbr. more than 660 articles to profl. jours. Life trustee Westminster Coll.; trustee Nat. Commn. for Quality Health Care, 1986-92, Health Care Leadership Coun.; bd. dirs. United Way. Capt. USAF, 1959-69. John and Mary R. Markle scholar acad. medicine, 1963; recipient Rsch. Career Devel. award USPHS, 1965-68, Scientist of Yr. award Sigma Xi, 1991, Internat. Health Prof. of Yr. award, 2005. Mem. ACS, AMA (trustee jour., editl. bd. jour.), Assn. Am. Med. Colls. (coun. acad. socs.), Am. Assn. Thoracic Surgery, Am. Coll. Cardiology, Am. Coll. Chest Physicians (Pres.'s citation), Assn. Acad. Surgery, New Eng. Surg. Soc., New Eng. Vascular Soc., Internat. Cardiovasc. Soc., Soc. Thoracic Surgeons, Soc. Univ. Surgeons, Soc. Vascular Surgery, Shock Soc. (scientific achievement award 2003), Internat. Fedn. Shock Socs. (pres. 1992-95), Internat. Vascular Soc. Surgery, Am. Assn. for Surgery of Trauma, Am. Assn. Artificial Internal Organs, Organ Failure Acad. (Trieste, Italy, hon. pres. 1983—), Surg. Biol. Club, Soc. U. Surgeons, Am. Physiol. Soc., Sr. Physiol. Commn., Soc. Critical Care Medicine, Am. Surg. Assn., Ctrl. Surg. Assn., Halsted Soc., Societé Internat. de Chirurgie, Soc. of Clin. Surgery, Surg. Infection Soc., James IV Assn. of Surgeons, Southern Thoracic Surg. Soc., Soc. for Surgery Alimentary Tract, St. Louis Surg. Soc. (hon.), Soc. Grad. Surgeons L.A. County-U. S.C. Med. Ctr. (hon.), Assn. VA Surgeons (hon.), Colombia Surg. Soc. (hon.), Chgo. Surg. Soc. (hon.), L.A. Surg. Soc. (hon.), Mpls. Surg. Soc. (hon.), Fla. Assn. Gen. Surgeons, Indonesian Shock Soc. (hon.), Organ Failure Soc. (hon. pres.), Alpha Omega Alpha. Home and Office: PO Box 396 Fishers Island NY 06390 Office Phone: 631-788-5571. Office Fax: 631-788-5591.

BAUER, A. ROBERT, JR., (AUGUST ROBERT BAUER JR.), surgeon; b. Dec. 23, 1928; s. A(ugust) Robert and Jessie Martha-Maynard (Monie) Bauer; m. Charmaine Louise Studer, June 28, 1957; children: Robert, John, William, Anne, Charles, James. BS, U. Mich., 1949, MS, 1950, MD, 1954; M in Med. Sci.-Surgery, Ohio State U., 1960. Diplomate Am. Bd. Surgery. Intern Walter Reed Army Med. Ctr., 1954—55; resident in surgery Univ. Hosp., Ohio State U., Columbus, also instr., 1957—61; pvt. practice medicine, specializing in surgery Mt. Pleasant, Mich., 1962—74; chief surgery Ctrl. Mich. Cmty. Hosp., Mt. Pleasant, 1964—65, vice chief of staff, 1967, chief of staff, 1968; clin. faculty Mich. State Med. Sch., East Lansing, 1974; mem. staff St. Mark's Hosp., Salt Lake City, 1974—91; pvt. practice surgery Salt Lake City, 1974—91. Clin. instr. surgery U. Utah, 1975—91; rschr. surg. immunology. Contbr. articles to profl. publs. Trustee Rowland Hall, St. Mark's Sch., Salt Lake City, 1978—84; mem. Utah Health Planning Coun., 1979—81. With M.C. U.S. Army, 1954—57. Fellow: ACS, Southwestern Surg. Congress; mem.: AAAS (affiliate), AMA, Zollinger Surg. Soc., Pan Am. Med. Assn. (affiliate), Salt Lake Surg. Soc., Utah Med. Assn. (various coms.), Salt Lake County Med. Soc., Phi Rho Sigma, Sigma Phi Epsilon. Episcopalian. Office: PO Box 17533 Salt Lake City UT 84117-0533 Address: 1366 Murray Holladay Rd Salt Lake City UT 84117-5050

BAUER, BARBARA A., financial consultant; Student, Syracuse U., 1973—75, Wilma Boyd Airline Travel Sch., 1975. Script editor various networks, L.A., 1976—88; v.p. You, Inc., Palos Verdes Estates, Calif., 1980—83; cons. Pub. Broadcasting Sys., L.A., 1981—89; fin. cons., pres. Fin. Diversified Mgmt., Laguna Niguel, Calif., 1989—. Founder Bauer Living Fulfillment Found., 1992—, sr. health homecare and estate cons., 1993—, sr. health and rehab. cons. svcs., 1994—; mem., adv. Commn. Human Rights, 2003—. Fashion model at charitable events, 2000—; advocate Disabled Am. Vets., 2003—. Mem. ACLU, NAFE, Orange County Bus. Women, Entrepreneurs of Am., Delta Delta Delta. Office: Fin Diversified Mgmt 28241 Crown Valley Pkwy Suite F-600 Laguna Niguel CA 92677-4441

BAUER, BARBARA ANN, marketing consultant; b. Fairfield, Ohio, Dec. 4, 1944; d. Charles P. and Grace J. (Peteka) B.; m. Joseph J. Strojnowski. AA, So. Sem. Jr. Coll., Buena Vista, Va., 1964; BA, Am. U., 1966. Pub. relations, advt. specialist Sta. WOR-AM-FM-TV, N.Y.C., 1966-67; pub. relations mgr. Continental Corp., N.Y.C., 1967-68; dir. corp. communications Am. Internat. Group, N.Y.C., 1968-80; dir. mktg. mgmt. infos. CIGNA Corp., Phila., N.Y.C., 1980-83; asst. v.p. Citicorp Credit Services Inc., N.Y.C., 1983-87; v.p., dir. mktg. Skandia Am. Group, N.Y.C., 1987-88, v.p. corp. communications, 1988-89; pres. Bauer Mktg. and Communications, Goshen, N.Y., 1989—. Mem. Reinsurance Cons. Network. Lifetime mem. Girl Scouts U.S. Mem.: Ins. Media Assn. (adv. bd.), Assn. Profl. Ins. Women (chair pub. rels., advisor bd. dirs.), Pub. Rels. Soc. Am. (accredited, counselors' acad.). Office Phone: 845-294-3550. E-mail: barbarabauer@pioneeris.net.

BAUER, CHARLES WIDMAYER, lawyer, judge; b. Hartford, Conn., Nov. 26, 1943; s. Phillip John and Ruth Olive (Widmayer) B.; m. Sophia Godfrey, Feb. 27, 1978; children: Stephanie Widmayer, Justin Frederick. BA, Hamilton Coll., 1965; JD, U. Conn., 1968. Bar: Conn., U.S. Dist. Ct. Conn., U.S. Ct. Appeals (2d cir.), U.S. Supreme Ct. Staff atty. Pub. Interest Law Firm Phila., 1972-73; vol. U.S. Peace Corps, Botswana, Africa, 1968-71; judge probate Town of Burlington (Conn.), 1978—, town counsel, 1981—; ptnr. Eisenberg, Anderson, Michalik & Lynch, New Britain, Conn., 1973—2004, Michalik, Bauer, Silvia & Ciccarillo, LLP (formerly Eisenberg, Anderson, Michalik & Lynch, LLP), New Britain, 2004—. Mem. Dem. Town Com., Burlington, 1988—2003; pres. Leadership New Britain, 1989-90; bd. dirs. United Cmty. Svc., New Britain, 1989—; incorporator Hosp. for Spl. Care, 1989—. Mem. New Britain Bar Assn., New Britain C. of C. (v.p. membership 1990—). Home: 7 Hart Ridge Dr Burlington CT 06013-1817 Office: Michalik Bauer Silvia & Ciccarillo LLP 35 Pearl St Ste 300 New Britain CT 06051 Office Phone: 860-225-8403. Business E-Mail: charlesbauer@eaml.com. E-mail: cbauer@mbsclawyers.com.

BAUER, CHRIS MICHAEL, banker; b. Milw., Sept. 2, 1948; s. Heinz Gerald and Maria (Weber) B.; m. Susan Marie Branton, June 28, 1969. BBA, U. Wis., 1970; MBA, Marquette U., 1976. Mgmt. trainee 1st Wis. Nat. Bank, Milw., 1970-72, spl. enterprise officer, 1972-74, asst. mgr., 1974-75; v.p. 1st Wis.-Racine, 1976-78; pres. 1st Wis.-Brookfield, 1978-84; 1st v.p. Firstar Corp. (formerly 1st Wis. Corp.), Milw., 1984-86, sr. v.p., 1986-89; pres., COO Firstar Bank Milw. (formerly 1st Wis. Nat. Bank), Milw., 1989-91, chmn., CEO, 1991-99, 1999—; chmn, CEO Business Banc Group Ltd.; also bd. dirs. Firstar Bank Milw. (formerly 1st Wis. Nat. Bank). Bd. dirs. Aurora Health Care Metro Region, Milw. Pub. Libr. Found., J.A. of Wisconsin, Inc., Next Door Found., Siebert Lutheran Found., The Auto Club Group Inc., AAA Wisconsin; mem. Greater Milw. Com. Mem. Milw. Country Club, Univ. Club, Westmoor Country Club. Lutheran. Office: Bus Banc Group Ltd 18500 W Corporate Dr Ste 170 Brookfield WI 53045-6309

BAUER, DAVID WOODFIN, history professor; b. Selma, Ala., Mar. 28, 1937; m. Edith Crane Bauer, June 21, 1960; children: Stephen Woodfin, Amanda Bauer Ingram. BS, U.S. Mil. Acad., 1960; MA in Tchg., U. Fla., 1972; grad., U.S. Army Command and Gen. Staff Coll., 1976. Cert. tchr. Ala., N.C. Asst. commandant Marion Mil. Inst., 1984—93, history instr., 1993—94, chair history and social sci. dept., 1994—. Assoc. prof. history U.S. Mil. Acad., West Point, NY, 1976—79; prof. mil. sci. Davidson Coll., NC, 1982—84. Tchr. Sunday sch. St. Wilfrid's Episcopal Ch., Marion, 1995—, Eucharistic minister, vestry mem., 1984—. Lt. col. U.S. Army, 1960—84, Italy, Korea, Vietnam. Mem.: Assn. Grads., Assn. U.S .Army, Ala. Hist. Assn. Episcopalian. Avocations: reading, travel. Office: Marion Mil Inst 1101 Washington St Marion AL 36756 Office Phone: 334-683-2371.

BAUER, DOUGLAS F., retired lawyer; b. Lackawanna, N.Y., Nov. 20, 1942; s. Ellsworth W. and Gloria G. (Fakler) B. AB magna cum laude, Princeton U., 1964; JD cum laude, Harvard U., 1967. Bar: N.Y. 1967, D.C. 1979, U.S. Supreme Ct. 1979. Assoc. Chadbourne & Parke, N.Y.C., 1967—71; assoc. counsel Gulf & Western Industries, Inc. (Paramount Communications, Inc.), N.Y.C., 1971—75; gen. counsel Amerace Corp., N.Y.C., 1975—86; gen. counsel, corp. sec. Bowne & Co., Inc., N.Y.C., 1986—2002; ret., 2002. Author: The Grolier Club 1884-1984, 1984; editor: The Bowne Family of Flushing, N.Y., 1987; contbr. articles to profl. jours. Mem. Fellows of the Pierpont Morgan Libr., N.Y.C., 1984—; trustee Bowne House Hist. Soc., Flushing, N.Y., 1986-2003, pres., 1996-2002; sec.-treas., trustee Robert Bowne Found., N.Y.C., 1986-2002; coun. Friends of the Princeton U. Libr., 1980—; chmn. bd. trustees Am. Printing History Assn., 1991-94. Mem. ABA, Assn. of Bar of City of N.Y. (non-profit com. 1997-2001), N.Y. State Bar Assn. (corp. law com. 1982—), Nat. Assn. Corp. Dirs., Am. Soc. Corp. Secs. Clubs: Princeton, Grolier. Republican. Lutheran. Home: 300 Rector Pl New York NY 10280-1416

BAUER, EUGENE ANDREW, dermatologist, educator; b. Mattoon, Ill., June 17, 1942; s. Eugene C. and Madge L. (Armer) B.; m. Gloria Anne Hehman, Feb. 19, 1966; childen: Marc A., Christine A., J. Michael, Amanda F. BS, Northwestern U., 1964, MD, 1967. Diplomate Am. Bd. Dermatology, Nat. Bd. Med. Examiners. Intern Barnes Hosp., St. Louis, 1967-68; resident, fellow divsn. dermatology Washington U. Med. Ctr., St. Louis, 1968-70; instr. Washington U., St. Louis, 1971-72, asst. prof. dermatology, 1974-78, assoc. prof., 1978-82, prof., 1982-88; prof., chmn. Stanford (Calif.) U. Sch. Medicine, 1988-95, dean, 1995-2001; program dir. Gen. Clin. Rsch. Ctr., 1990-93; v.p. med. affairs Stanford U., 1997-2000, v.p. Med. Ctr., 2000—01. Mem. adv. coun. Nat. Inst. Arthritis and Musculoskeletal and Skin Diseases, 1997—2000; bd. dirs. U. Calif. San Francisco-Stanford Health Care, Connetics Corp., Reconstructive Techs., Arbor Vita Corp., Medgenics. Contbr. numerous articles to profl. jours. Served to lt. comdr. USNR, 1972-74. Recipient Alumni Merit award Northwestern U., 1999. Fellow Am. Acad. Dermatology; mem. Am. Fedn. Clin. Rsch., Am Soc. Clin. Investigation, Am. Dermatol. Assn., Soc. Investigative Dermatology (bd. dirs. 1981-86, assoc. editor Jour. Investigative Dermatology 1982-87, pres.-elect 1994-95, pres. 1995-96), Ctrl. Soc. Clin. Rsch., Assn. Am. Physicians, Inst. Medicine of NAS, Am. Clin. and Climatol. Assn. Office: Stanford U Sch Medicine Office of the Dean M121 Stanford CA 94305 Office Phone: 310-226-6378. E-mail: eugene.bauer@stanford.edu.

BAUER, FRED D., lawyer; b. Cleve., Oct. 27, 1965; BA, BS magna cum laude, U. Pa., 1987; JD cum laude, Harvard U., 1990. Bar: Ohio 1990, U.S. Dist. Ct. Ohio (No. dist.) 1991. Assoc. Baker & Hostetler, 1990—92; assoc. corr. counsel Bearings, Inc., 1992—94; asst. gen. counsel, asst. sec. Applied Indsl. Technologies, Inc., Cleve., 1994—2002, v.p., gen. counsel, sec., 2002—. Mem.: Am. Corp. Counsel Assn., Am. Soc. Corp. Secretaries, Ohio State Bar Assn., Cleve. Bar Assn. Office: Applied Indsl Technologies Inc One Applied Plz Euclid Ave at E 36th St Cleveland OH 44115-5015 Office Phone: 216-426-4753. Office Fax: 216-426-4804. E-mail: fbauer@applied.com.

BAUER, HENRY HERMANN, chemistry and science educator; b. Vienna, Nov. 16, 1931; came to U.S., 1965, naturalized, 1969; s. Martin Josef and Anne (Rafael) B.; m. Barbara Bush, Aug. 25, 1986; children from previous marriage: Helen Suzanne, Judith Ann. B.Sc., U. Sydney, 1952, M.Sc., 1953, PhD, 1956. Rsch. assoc. U. Mich., 1956-58, vis. scientist, 1965-66; lectr., sr. lectr. U. Sydney, 1958-66; assoc. prof., prof. U. Ky., 1966-78; vis. prof. Southampton (Eng.) U., 1972-73; dean Coll. Arts and Scis. Va. Poly. Inst. and State U., Blacksburg, 1978-86, prof. chemistry and science studies Coll. Arts and Scis., 1986-99. Author: Alternating Current Polarography and Tensammetry, 1963, Electrodics, 1973, Instrumental Analysis, 1978, Beyond Velikovsky, 1984, Enigma of Loch Ness, 1986, (under pseudonym Josef Martin) To Rise Above Principle, 1988, Scientific Literacy and the Myth of the Scientific Method, 1992, Science or Pseudoscience, 2001, Fatal Attractions: The Troubles with Science, 2001; editor-in-chief Jour. Sci. Exploration, 2000—. Fulbright fellow, 1956-58; Japan Soc. fellow for promotion of sci., 1974 Mem. Soc. Sci. Exploration (founding mem.), Internat. Soc. Cryptozoology. Unitarian Universalist. E-mail: hhbauer@vt.edu.

BAUER, HERBERT, retired physician; b. Vienna, Jan. 21, 1910; came to U.S., 1940; s. Fritz and Irma (Lindenfeld) B.; m. Hanna Goldsmith, 1939; children: Timothy, Christopher. MD, U. Vienna, Austria, 1936; MPH, U. Calif., Berkeley, 1948. Chief county physician San Luis Obispo County, San Luis Obispo, Calif., 1942-47; med. dir. Sacramento Health Dept., 1948-52; pub. and mental health dir. Yolo County, Calif., 1952-72; clin. prof. U. Calif., Davis, Calif., 1972-92; ret. Recipient Liberty Bell award Bar Assn. Woodland, Calif., 1955, Peace and Justice award City of Davis, Calif., 1991. Mem. AMA, APHA, Am. Psychiat. Assn., Am. Acad. Child Psychiatry, Am. Acad. Psychiatry and Law, Calif. Med. Assn. Democrat. Unitarian Universalist. Avocations: reading, music, chess. Home and Office: 831 Oeste Dr Davis CA 95616-1856

BAUER, IRENE SUSAN, elementary school educator; b. Elyria, Ohio; m. Robert D. Bauer; 1 child, Jacquelyn I. BS in Edn., Ohio U., 1973. Tchr. OBerlin Pub. Schs., Ohio; owner Puti's, Amherst; tchr. Country Day Sch., Charles Town, W.Va., head. Office: The Country Day Sch Rt 51 W PO Box 659 Charles Town WV 25414 E-mail: headofschool@citynet.net.

BAUER, JOEL J., surgeon, educator; b. NYC, Aug. 16, 1942; s. David W. and Toby B.; m. Judy Bauer (Siegel), Dec. 3, 1967; children: Dana, Ross. BS, U. Vt., 1963; MD, NYU, 1967. Lic. physician, N.Y.; cert. Am. Bd. Surgery. Intern in surgery Mt. Sinai Hosp., N.Y.C., 1967-68, resident in surgery, 1968-72, chief resident in surgery, 1972-73, clin. asst. surgery, 1973-77, asst. attending surgeon, 1977-81, assoc. attending surgeon, 1981-88, attending surgeon, 1988—; instr. surgery to asst. clin. prof. to clin. prof. surgery Mt. Sinai Sch. Medicine, N.Y.C., 1972—; vice chmn., dept. surgery Mt. Sinai Hosp., 2001—. Presenter in field. Contbr. articles to profl. jours. Fellow Am. Coll. Surgeons; mem. AMA, Assn. Acad. Surgery, Am. Coll. Gastroenterology, Am. Coll. Colon & Rectal Surgery, Soc. for Surgery for the Alimentary Tract, N.Y. Acad. Scis., N.Y. County Med. Soc., N.Y. Acad. Gastroenterology, N.Y. Soc. Colon & Rectal Surgeons, N.Y. Surg. Soc., N.Y. Acad. Medicine (sec. surg. sect. 1986-87, pres. surg. sect. 1987-88). Office: 25 E 69th St New York NY 10021-4925 Office Phone: 212-517-8600.

BAUER, JUDY MARIE, minister; b. South Bend, Ind., Aug. 24, 1947; d. Ernest Camiel and Marjorie Ann (Williams) Derho; m. Gary Dwane Bauer, Apr. 28, 1966; children: Christine Ann, Steven Dwane. Ordained to ministry Christian Ch., 1979. Sec. adminstrv. asst. Bethel Christian Ctr., Riverside, Calif., 1975-79; founder, pres. Kingdom Advancement Ministry, San Diego, 1979—; co-pastor Bethel Christian Ctr., Rancho Bernardo, Calif., 1991—2004; coll. funding advisor, 2002—03. Trainer, mgr., cons. Tex., Ariz., Calif., Oreg., Wash., Alaska, Okla., Idaho, Rep. South Africa, Guam, Egypt, The Philippines, Australia, Can., Mozambique, Malawi, Mex., Zimbabwe, Poland, Guatemala, Israel, Scotland, Ireland, Japan, Eng., others, 1979—; pres. Witty Outerwear Distbrs. Internat., Inc., 1993—96; mktg. exec. Melaleuca, 1999—2002; founder, co-pastor Bernardo Christian Ctr., San Diego, 1981—91; adult tchr. Bethel Christian Ctr., 1973—81, undershepherd minister, 1975—79, evangelism dir., 1978—81; chaplain La Mesa Fed. Penitentiary, Tijuana, Mexico, 1998—2001; bd. dirs. Strong Tower Rehab. Ministry, San Diego; pres., founder Bethel Christian Ctr., Ranco Bernardo, Calif., 1991—2004; condr. leadership tng. clinics, internat. spkr., lectr. in field. Author syllabus, booklet, tng. material packets. Pres. Bernardo Christian Ctr., San Diego, 1981-91. Mem. Internat. Conv. Faith Ministries, Inc. (area bd. dirs. 1983-88). Address: 40335 Winchester Rd E283 Temecula CA 92591 also: Kingdom Advancement Min PO Box 501711 San Diego CA 92150-1711 E-mail: jbauer2@ix.netcom.com, kam@kingdomadvancementministries.org.

BAUER, MARION DANE, writer; b. Oglesby, Ill., Nov. 20, 1938; d. Chester and Elsie (Hempstead) Dane; m. Ronald C. Bauer, June 25, 1959 (div. Dec. 1988); children: Peter Dane, Elisabeth Alison. AA, LaSalle-Peru-Oglesby Jr. Coll., 1958; student, U. Mo., 1958—59; BA in Lang. Arts, U. Okla., 1961, postgrad., 1961—62. Author: Shelter from the Wind, 1976 (Notable Children's Book ALA, 1976), Foster Child (Golden Kite Honor Book award Soc. Children's Book Writers, 1977), Tangled Butterfly, 1980, Rain of Fire, 1983 (Tchrs.' Choices award Nat. Coun. Tchrs. of English, 1984, Revs. Choice award ALA Booklist, 1983, Children's Book award Jane Addams Peace Assn., 1984), Like Mother, Like Daughter, 1985, On My Honor, 1986 (Newbery Honor Book, 1987, Notable Children's Book ALA, 1986, Best Books of 1986 Sch. Libr. Jour., Editors' Choice Booklist, 1986, Pub.'s Weekly Choice the Yrs.'s Best Books, 1986, Flicker Tale Children's Book award, N.D., 1989, Golden Archer award, Wis., 1989, William Allen White Children's Book award, Kans., 1989, BBY, IRA selection for Janusc Korczak Lit. Competition Poland, 1990), Touch the Moon, 1987, A Dream of Queens and Castles, 1990, (drama) God's Tears: A Woman's Journey, Face to Face, 1991 (Children's Book of Distinction, Hungry Mind Rev., 1992), What's Your Story? A Young Person's Guide to Writing Fiction, 1992 (Notable Children's Book ALA, 1992), Ghost Eye, 1992, A Taste of Smoke, 1993, A Question of Trust, 1994; editor: Am I Blue? Coming Out from the Silence, 1994, When I Go Camping With Grandma, 1995, A Writer's Story, From Life to Fiction, 1995, Alison's Wings, 1996, Our Stories, A Fiction Workshop for Young Authors, 1996, Alison's Puppy, 1997, If You Were Born a Kitten, 1997, Turtle Dreams, 1997, Alison's Fierce and Ugly Halloween, 1997, Bear's Hiccups, 1998, Christmas in the Forest, 1998, An Early Winter, 1999, Sleep, Little One, Sleep, 1999, Jason's Bears, 2000, Grandmother's Song, 2000, My Mother is Mine, 2001, If You Had a Nose Like an Elephant's Trunk, 2001, Frog's Best Friend, 2002, Love Song for a Baby, 2003, Runt, 2002, Land of the Buffalo Bones, 2003, Toes, Ears and Nose, 2003, Why Do Kittens Purr, 2003, Wind, 2003, Snow, 2003, Rain, 2004, Clouds, 2004, The Double-Digit Club, 2004 (CBC Best Books award, 2004), The Very Best Daddy of All, 2004, A Recipe for Valentine's Day, 2004, Easter is Coming, 2005, The Blue Ghost, 2005, A Bear Named Trouble, 2005, If Frogs Made Weather, 2005, Waiting for Christmas, 2005; contbr. short stories to mags. and books in field. Mem.: Soc. Children's Book Writers and Illustrators, Authors League Am., Authors Guild. Democrat. Home: 8861 Basswood Rd Eden Prairie MN 55344-7407 Office: Clarion 215 Park Ave S New York NY 10003-1603 Office Phone: 952-941-3102. Personal E-mail: mdanebauer@aol.com. *Children are our future, of course, but they are also the touchstone for our present. To discover who we are and how we are doing we need only check our reflections in our children's eyes.*

BAUER, MICHAEL ANTHONY, computer scientist, educator; b. Dayton, Ohio, Feb. 18, 1948; married; 2 children. BSc, U. Dayton, 1970; MSc, U. Toronto, 1971, PhD in Computer Sci., 1978. Rschr. artificial intelligence Edinburgh U., 1974-75; prof. computer sci. U. Western Ont., 1975—, chmn. dept., 1991-96, 2002—, assoc. v.p. IT, 1996—2001. Cons. Geac Computers Internat., 1984—88, IBM, 1991—94; advisor IBM Ctr. Advanced Studies, 1990—91, vis. scientist, 1991—2003. Mem.: Assn. Computing Machinery (bd. dirs. 1989—94), Can. Info. Processing Soc. (bd. dirs. 1984—88). Achievements include research in in distributed computing, especially distributed systems and applications management, distributed algorithms, correctness, languages for distributed computing, verfication; software engineering, including methodologies, testing, formal specifications, development environments. Office: University of Western Ontario Middlesex College Rm 355 London ON Canada N6A 5B7 Office Phone: 519-661-3562. Business E-Mail: bauer@csd.uwo.ca.

BAUER, MONICA MARY, artist; b. Kenmare, N.D., June 17, 1950; d. Albert Matthew and Anna Mary (Antonich) B. BFA, U. Mont., 1979, MFA, 1990; MA, Sch. Art Inst. Chgo., 1996. Artist Pre-Vue Publs., Billings, Mont., 1980-84; instr. No. Mont. Coll., Great Falls, 1991-92; instr. MFA program Vt. Coll. Norwich U., Montpelier, 1991-94; adj. lectr. mus. edn. Art Inst. Chgo., 1995—2004; instr. Robert Morris Coll., Chgo., 1996—2000; instr. Graham Sch. U. Chgo., 1997—99. Mem., newsletter coord., German liaison A.R.C. Gallery, 1995—. Editor art criticism F NewsMagazine, 1993-95; writer, reviewer New Art Examiner, 1996-2000; group exhbns. include Sch. Art Inst., Chgo., 1996, 98, 99, Atelierhof Galerie, Bremen, 1999—, Amos Eno, N.Y., Hamburg, 2001; one-woman shows include Art Mus., Missoula, 1990, Lewistown Art Ctr., 1991, Dahl Gallery, Great Falls, 1992, A.R.C. Gallery, 1997, 99, 2002, Lisa Cosone Gallery, 2003; contbr. revs. to publs. Bertha Morton scholar U. Mont., 1990; Lectr. fellow Sch. Art Inst. Chgo., 1995, Ox-Bow residency, 1995, 98; Artist's Refuge resident, 2002, Jentel resident, 2004, Chgo. Dept. Cultural Affairs CAAP grants, 1999, 2000, 2004. Mem. Coll. Art Assn., Sch. Art Inst. Chgo. Alumni Assn., U. Mont. Alumni Assn. Home: 73 Gold St Brooklyn NY 11201 Office Phone: 718-858-3095. E-mail: bauermonica@netscape.net.

BAUER, OTTO FRANK, academic administrator, communications executive, educator; b. Elgin, Ill., Dec. 1, 1931; s. Otto Leland and Cora Dorothy (Berlin) B.; m. Jeanette L. Erickson, May 27, 1956; children: Steven Mark, Eric Paul. BS, Northwestern U., 1953, MA, 1955, PhD, 1959; D of Humanitarian Svcs. (hon.), Clarkson Coll., 1999. Instr., then asst. prof. English USAF Acad., Colo., 1959-61, dir. debate, 1959-61; instr. to prof. Bowling Green State U., Ohio, 1961-71, dir. grad. admissions and fellowships, 1965-69, asst. dean Grad. Sch., 1967-69, asst. v.p., 1970-71; ACE fellow U. Calif.-Berkeley, 1969-70; prof. communication U. Wis.-Parkside, Kenosha, 1971-79; vice chancellor U. Wis. -Parkside, Kenosha, 1971-76; acting chancellor U. Wis.-Parkside, 1974-75; vis. prof. communication, spl. asst. to chancellor U. Wis., Madison, 1976-77; vice chancellor for acad. affairs U. Nebr., Omaha, 1979-94, prof. communication, 1979—2000, vice chancellor emeritus, 1995. Mem. Commn. on Instns. Higher Edn., North Ctrl. Assn. Colls. and Schs., 1975-77, 84-88, cons., evaluator, 1976—; cons. in field. Author: Fundamentals of Debate, 1966, rev. edit., 1999, Lower Moments in Higher Education, 1997, Trust and Distrust, 2005; co-author: Guidebook for Student Speakers, 1966; editor: Introduction to Speech Communication, 1968. Bd. dirs. United Way Kenosha County, Wis., 1973-79, Kenosha County coun. Girl Scouts U.S., 1977-79; chmn. spkrs. bur. United Way Midlands, Omaha, 1983, mem. allocations coms., 1985-93, steering com., 1989-93; bd. dirs. Fontenelle Forest Assn., 1987-94, v.p., 1990-92; bd. dirs. Clarkson Coll., 1992-2000, vice-chair, 1995-97, chair, 1997-2000. Recipient Faculty Disting. Svc. award U. Wis., Parkside, 1978, Chancellor's medal U. Nebr., Omaha, 1994, Disting. Svc. award U. Nebr. Aviation Inst., Omaha, 1994, named in his honor, 2000; named Faculty Man of Yr., Bowling Green State U., 1967, Exec. of Yr., Nat. Secs. Assn., Omaha, 1980; Clarion DeWitt Hardy scholar, 1949-53; humanitarian svc. award named in his honor Clarkson Coll., 1999. Mem. Am. Coun. on Edn. (exec. com. coun. of fellows 1982-85), Nat. Comm. Assn., Rotary.

BAUER, PETER F., publishing executive; Degree, U. Colo. Advertising sales rep. People Mag., Boston, 1986—88, NYC, 1988—90, advertising sales mgr., 1990, advertising dir., head, Eastern advertising sales ops., 1994—96, assoc. pub., 1996—98, pub., 1998—2002, pres., 2002—05; pub. Life Mag., 2004—05; pres. Time Mag., 2005—. Office: People/Time Inc 1271 Ave of Americas New York NY 10020-1393 Office Phone: 212-627-0222. Office Fax: 212-522-0076.

BAUER, R. ANDRE, lieutenant governor; b. Charleston, SC, Mar. 20, 1969; s. William R. and Saundrea J. Bauer. BS, U. S.C., 1991. Rep. S.C. Ho. of Reps., 1997—99; senator S.C. State Senate, Columbia, 1999—2003; lt. gov. state of S.C., 2003—. Sec.-treas. freshman caucus SC Ho. of Reps., 1997; with SC State Senate. Mem. Union Meth. Ch. Mem. SAR, TKE. Republican. Office: State House 1st Fl PO Box 142 Columbia SC 29202 E-mail: ltgov@scstatehouse.net.

BAUER, RALPH GLENN, lawyer, arbitrator; b. Bellevue, Pa., May 22, 1925; m. Rosemary Larson. BS, Yale U., 1946; BSE, U. Mich., 1948, JD, 1951. Bar: Mich. 1951, N.Y. 1952. Assoc. Haight, Gardner, Poor & Havens, N.Y.C., 1951-69, ptnr., 1970-94. Arbitrator, N.Y.C., 1973—; speaker Soc.

Maritime Arbitrators, N.Y.C., 1978—; tchr. World Trade Inst., N.Y.C., 1986—; adj. prof. Cardozo Law Sch., 1992—, Hofstra Law Sch., 1995—. Author: Poor on Charter Parties, (supplement), 1974, Tiberg on Demurrage, 4th edit., 1995; contbr. articles to Tulane Law Rev., Lloyds Press, Congress Maritime Arbitrators and Jour. Maritime Law and Commerce. Ensign USN, 1943-46, PTO. Mem. ABA (chmn. com. 1986-88), Internat. Bar Assn., Maritime Law Assn. (chmn. com. 1993-95), London Maritime Arbitrators Assn. (supp.), Soc. Naval Architects (assoc.), Yale Club (N.Y.C.), Raritan Yacht Club (Perth Amboy, N.J.). Episcopalian. Avocation: boating. Office: Haight Gardner Holland & Knight 195 Broadway Rm 2400 New York NY 10007-3189

BAUER, RAYMOND GALE, sales professional; b. Merchantville, N.J., June 19, 1934; s. Robert Iwrin and Florence Winifred (Guyer) B.; m. Jayne Whitehead, Feb. 15, 1955; 1 child, Linda Joan. AA, Monmouth Coll., 1955; BBA, U. Miami, 1958. Divsn. mgr. R.J. Reynolds Tobacco Co., Winston-Salem, N.C., 1959-68; mgr. Mid-Atlantic U.S. Envelope Co., Springfield, Mass., 1968-74; divsn. sales mgr. Eastern Tablet Corp., Albany, N.Y., 1974-75; owner Ray Bauer Assocs., mfrs. reps., Haddonfield, N.J., 1975—. With USAFR, 1959-64; officer USAF Aux. Mem. Friends of Haddonfield Libr., Haddonfield Civic Assn., Smithsonian Assn., U. Miami Alumni Assn., Monmouth U. Alumni Assn., Nat. Philatelic Soc., Am. Security Coun., Air Force Assn., Am. Conservative Union, Am. Mgmt. Assn., Internat. Platform Assn., Sch. and Home Office Products Assn., Am. Legion, Rep. Club Haddonfield, U.S. Sentatorial Club, Arrowhead Racquet Club, Iron Rock Swim and Country Club, Lambda Sigma Tau, Lambda Chi Alpha. Home and Office: 132 Maple Ave Haddonfield NJ 08033-1432 Office Phone: 856-428-6371. E-mail: RayGBauer@aol.com, raygbauer@hotmail.com.

BAUER, RICHARD CARLTON, nuclear engineer; b. Batavia, N.Y., July 15, 1944; s. Willard Ronald and Ethel Bauer; m. Madeline Joy Amreich, June 28, 1969; children: Jason Todd, Cheryl Robyn. BS in Chem. Engring., Clarkson Coll. Tech., 1966; M in Engring., Cornell U., 1968; PhD in Nuclear Sci., Engring., Carnegie-Mellon U., 1974. cert. in bus. mgmt. Am. Mgmt. Assn. Extension Inst., 1989; registered profl. engr., Pa.; cert. fallout shelter analyst, multiprotection designer. Technician Graham Mfg. Co., Batavia, summer 1965; engr. Linde divsn. Union Carbide Corp., Tonawanda, N.Y., summer 1966; hot cell operator asst. Cornell U., Ithaca, N.Y., 1967; engr. Bettis Atomic Power Lab, Inc., West Mifflin, Pa., 1968-73, sr. engr., 1973-78, staff engr., 1978, mgr. AIW performance analysis, 1979-82, AIW/S5G performance analysis, 1982-86, mgr. centralized safety and plant analysis support, 1986-93, mgr. centralized thermal hydraulic devel. group, 1994—2002, mgr. centralized thermal hydraulic advanced analysis methods devel. group, 2002—. Employee tng. lectr. reactor safety, mem. and sec. lab. reactor ops. safety com. Contbr. articles to sci. jours. Chmn. Cornell Secondary Schs., Pitts., PEI Pitts. Clarkson Trustee scholar; Regents fellow, 1962, Bettis Doctoral Program fellow, AEC spl. fellow, 1967. Mem. Nat. Soc. Profl. Engrs., Pa. Soc. Profl. Engrs. (chmn. sustaining assocs. com., dir. chpt. 1981-83, 2d v.p. 1984, 1st v.p. 1985, chpt. pres. 1987, chpt. past pres. 1988, alt. state dir. 1989, state dir. 1990-94, Mathcounts com. 1984, chpt. award for meritorious svc. 1984, restructuring task force 1992-93, chpt. award dedicated svc. 2000), Cornell Soc. Engrs. (regional v.p. 1970-83), Am. Nuclear Soc., N.Y. Acad. Scis., Am. Inst. Chem. Engrs., Tau Beta Pi, Sigma Xi, Omega Chi Epsilon, Triangle Fraternity.

BAUER, RICHARD LEROY, music educator, musician; b. Fairfield, Iowa, Mar. 8, 1949; s. LeRoy Otto and Gertrude Elizabeth Bauer; m. Gretchen Marie Hagen, Sept. 6, 1951; children: Liesel Hagen, Johanne Marie, Peter Hagen. MusB, U. Idaho, 1972; MusM, Ohio State U., 1974. Dir. orchestras Pendleton Jr. H.S., Oreg., 1975—84, North Salem H.S., Oreg., 1984—86, South Salem H.S., Oreg., 1986—. Violist Spokane Symphony Orch., Wash., 1969—72, Columbus Symphony Orch., Ohio, 1972—74; violin/viola tchr. Oreg. Suzuki Inst., Forest Grove, 1975—; prin. viola Portland Opera Orch., Oreg., 1985—98, Oreg. Festival of Am. Music Orch., Eugene, 1998—2002; viola tchr. Advanced Suzuki Inst. at Stanford, Palo Alto, Calif., 2000—; prin. viola Portland Chamber Orch., Oreg., 2000—. Pres. Oreg. String Tchr.'s Assn., Salem, 1995—97. Recipient Oreg. Music Educator of the Yr. award, Oreg. Symphony Assn., 2001. Mem.: Am. Viola Soc., Oreg. Music Educator's Assn., Suzuki Assn. of the Americas, Am. String Teaher's Assn., Music Educator's Nat. Conf. Achievements include South Salem High School Orchestra, 1st pl., Oregon State Orchestra Competition, 2001, 2003; South Salem High School Orchestra performed at The Midwest Clinic, 2003. Avocations: family, travel. Home: 4554 12th Ave S Salem OR 97302 Office: South Salem HS 1910 Church St SE Salem OR 97302 Business E-Mail: bauer_dick@salkeiz.k12.or.us.

BAUER, RICHARD P., lawyer; b. Pitts., Nov. 17, 1951; BS, US Mil. Acad., 1973; JD, Cath. U., 1984. Bar: Va. 1984, DC 1985. Ptnr. Katten Muchin Zavis Rosenman, Washington, DC. Mem.: DC Bar Assn., Va. Bar Assn., Am. Intellectual Property Law. Office: Katten Muchin Zavis Rosenman East Lobby, Ste 700 1025 Thomas Jefferson St, NW Washington DC 20007 Office Phone: 202-625-3507. Office Fax: 202-298-7570. E-mail: richard.bauer@kmzr.com.

BAUER, ROBERT F., lawyer; b. NYC, Feb. 22, 1952; BA magna cum laude, Harvard U., 1973; JD, U. Va., 1976. Bar: Pa. 1976, DC 1977. Ptnr., Polit. Law Practice Area Perkins Coie LLP, Washington, mng. ptnr. DC office. Author: US Federal Election Law, 1982, Soft Money Hard Law — A Guide To The New Campaign Finance Law, 2002, More Soft Money Hard Law: The Second Edition Of The Guide To The New Campaign Finance Law, 2004. Nat. adv. bd. Jour. Law & Polit., U. Va. Mem.: ABA. Office: Perkins Coie LLP 607 Fourteenth St NW Washington DC 20005-2011 Office Phone: 202-434-1602. Office Fax: 202-434-1690. Business E-Mail: rbauer@perkinscoie.com.

BAUER, ROGER DUANE, chemistry professor, consultant; b. Oxford, Nebr., Jan. 17, 1932; s. Albert Carl and Minnie (Lueking) B.; m. Jacquelyn True, Aug. 10, 1956; children— Lisa, Scott, Robert. BS, Beloit Coll., 1953; MS, Kans. State U., 1957, PhD, 1959. Asst. prof. chemistry Calif. State U., Long Beach, 1959-64, assoc. prof., 1964-69, prof., 1969-92; dean Calif. State U. (Sch. Natural Scis.), 1975-88. Served with U.S. Army, 1954-56. USPHS fellow, 1966; Am. Coun. on Edn. fellow, 1971 Mem. Am. Chem. Soc., Radiation Rsch. Soc., Sigma Xi, Phi Lambda Upsilon. Home: 6320 E Colorado St Long Beach CA 90803-2202 Office: Calif State U Coll Natural Sci Long Beach CA 90840-0001 Office Phone: 562-985-8640. Business E-Mail: rdbauer@csulb.edu.

BAUER, ROSS, composer, music educator; b. Ithaca, N.Y., Nov. 19, 1951; s. Simon H. and Miriam R. Bauer; m. Carla Wilson, Mar. 31, 1990; children: Nicholas Wilson, Isaac Benjamin. PhD, Brandeis U., 1984. Lectr. music Stanford (Calif.) U., 1986—88; prof. music U. Calif., Davis, 1988—. Founder and dir. Empyrean Ensemble, Davis, 1988—2002; rec. with New World, GM, and Centaur Recordings; condr. more than 100 performances including numerous world premieres; rec. conductor with Empyrean Ensemble in the music of Mario Davidovsky and David Rakowski; guest composer Wellesley Composers Conf., 2001. Composer: (chamber concerto, cello and 14 players) Thin Ice (Commd. by Sequitur, 2004), (concerto for bassoon and orchestra) Icons (Commd. by the Berkeley Symphony, Kent Nagano, Music Dir., 1997), (orchestral piece) Romanza for Violin and Orchestra (Commd. by the Santa Cruz Symphony, John Larry Granger, Music Dir., 1996), (song cycle) Eskimo Songs (Written for Christine Schadeberg, 1996), (chamber music) Stone Soup (Commd. by the NY New Music Ensemble, 1995), (song cycle) Ritual Fragments (Commd. by the Fromm Found. at Harvard U., 1991), (chamber music) Octet (Written for Empyrean Ensemble, 1994), (orchestral) Halycon Birds (Commd. by the Serge Koussevitzky Music Found. in the Libr. of Congress, 1993), (chamber music) Aplomb (for violin and piano) (Commd. by Dan Kobialka), Tributaries (for cello, percussion, piano) (Commd. by the Core Ensemble, 1992), Anaphora (flute, string trio, piano) (Commd. by the Earplay Ensemble, 1990), Piano Quartet (Commd. by SUNY Stony Brook, 2004), (concerto) Concerto for Piano and Chamber Orchestra (Commd. by Wellesley Coll., 1990), (chamber music) Chimera (Commd. by Alea III, Theodore Antoniou, Music Dir., 1987), (solo piano) Tonarten (Commd. by Christopher Keyes, 1982), (orchestral) Dusk (Commd., Calif. Youth Symphony, 2002), (concerto, saxophone, winds, percussion) This, That, and the Other (Commd. by Nat. Assn. of Coll. Wind and Percussion Instructors, 2001), (chamber concerto, flute and 8 players) Fast and Loose (Fromm Found., Harvard U., 2001), (chamber music for solo flute) Nimbus (Commd. by Perspectives of New Music, 2000), (chamber music) String Quartet No. 3 (Commd. by Stanford Lively Arts for the Alexander Quartet, 2000), Pulse (Commd. by the Left Coast Ensemble, 1999), Motion (for piano trio) (Commd. by the Triple Helix Trio, 1998). Mem. exec. bd. Griffin Music Ensemble, Boston, 1984—90. Recipient award, Am. Acad. Arts and Letters, 2005, Speculum Musicae's Third Annual Composition Competition, Walter Hinrichsen award, Am. Acad. Arts and Letters, 1984, prizes, Internat. Soc. Contemporary Music; fellow, Wellesley Composer Conf., Djerassi Found., Wurlitzer Found., Guggenheim Found., 1988, MacDowell Colony, 1984, 1985, 1987, 1989, 1996; composition fellow, Nat. Endowment Arts, 1986. Democrat. Avocations: hiking, reading, coaching baseball. Office: U Calif Davis Dept Music Davis CA 95616 Office Phone: 530-752-4487. Personal E-mail: rmbauer@ucdavis.edu.

BAUER, THOR ERIK, lawyer; b. Detroit, Apr. 5, 1969; s. James Edward and Coralie Elizabeth Bauer; m. Amy Bauer, Dec. 28, 2002; 1 child, TJ. BA in History, Virginia Mil. Inst., 1991; JD, Capital U., Columbus, Ohio, 1999. Bar: Colo. Supreme Ct. 1999, Colo. US Dist. Ct. 2000. U.s. naval officer U.S. Navy, Yokosuka, Japan, 1991—94; assoc. Crespin, Kerns & Furman LLC, Fort Morgan, Colo., 1999—2002; ptnr. Furman, Kerns & Bauer LLC, Fort Morgan, Colo., 2002—. Treas. Ct. Apptd. Spl. Advs. 13th Jud. Dist., Fort Morgan, Colo., 2002—04. Lt. USN, 1991—94, Yokosuka, Japan. Mem.: Nat. Assn. of Criminal Def. Lawyers (assoc.), Colo. Criminal Bar Assn. (assoc.), Colo. Bar Assn. (assoc.; dist. rep. 2004—), 13 Jud. Bar Assn. (assoc.; pres. 2004—). Avocation: golf. Home: 325 Euclid Fort Morgan CO 80701 Office: Furman Kerns & Bauer LLC 526 Meeker St Fort Morgan CO 80701 Office Phone: 970-867-4460. Office Fax: 970-867-4489. Personal E-mail: tbauer@twol.com.

BAUER, WILLIAM JOSEPH, federal judge; b. Chgo., Sept. 15, 1926; s. William Francis and Lucille (Gleason) Bauer; m. Mary Nicol, Jan. 28, 1950; children: Patricia, Linda. AB, Elmhurst Coll., 1949, LLD, 1969; JD, DePaul U., 1952, LLD (hon.), 1993; LLD, John Marshall Law Sch., 1987; LLD (hon.), Roosevelt U., 1994. Bar: Ill. 1951. Ptnr. Erlenborn, Bauer & Hotte, Elmhurst, Ill., 1953—64; asst. state's atty. Du Page County, Ill., 1952—56; 1st asst. state's atty., 1956—58; state's atty., 1959—64; judge 18th Jud. Cir. Ct., 1964—70; U.S. dist. atty. No. Ill. Chgo., 1970—71; judge U.S. Dist. Ct. (no. dist.), Chgo., 1971—75, U.S. Ct. Appeals (7th cir.), 1975—86, chief judge, 1986—93, sr. judge Chicago, 1994—. Instr. bus law. Elmhurst Coll., 1952—59; adj. prof. law DePaul U., 1978—91; former mem. Ill. Supreme Ct. Com. on Pattern Criminal Jury Instrns.; chmn. Fed. Criminal Jury Instrn. Com. 7th Cir.; mem. Am. Judicature Soc., Ill. Assn. of Cir. and Appellate Ct. Judges, Ill. States Attys. Assn., Nat. Dist. Attys. Assn. Trustee Elmhurst Coll., 1979—, DePaul U., 1984—, DuPage Meml. Hosp.; bd. advisors Mercy Hosp. With U.S. Army, 1945—47. Mem.: FBA (former bd. dirs.), ABA, Chgo. Bar Assn., DuPage County Bar Assn. (past pres.), Ill. Bar Assn., Legal Club (Chgo.), Law Club, Union League Club. Roman Catholic. Office: US Ct Appeals 219 S Dearborn St Ste 2754 Chicago IL 60604*

BAUER-KING, CHARLES F., clergyman; b. East St. Louis, Ill., July 30, 1936; s. Charles Francis and Lydia Amanda King; m. Jean G. King (div.); children: Karen Beth, David Charles, Gayle Crista; m. Nancy L. Bauer, May 5, 1990. BA, Ohio Wesleyan U., 1958; MDiv, Garrett Theol. Sem., Evanston, Ill., 1962; M Internat. Studies, Am. U., 1970. Ordained to ministry United Meth. Ch., 1959. Asst. pastor 1st Meth. Ch., West Allis, Wis., 1959-62; pastor La Paz (Bolivia) Cmty. Ch., 1963-68, Trinity United Meth. Ch., Racine, Wis., 1969-75; sr. pastor Oconomowoc (Wis.) United Meth. Ch., 1975-82; co-pastor 1st United Meth. Ch., Appleton, Wis., 1982-89, lead pastor Kenosha, Wis., 1989-2000. Trustee Oconomowoc Pub. Libr., 1976-82, Appleton Pub. Libr., 1985-88. Mem. Racine Theater Guild. Avocation: drama. Home: 5110 Darby Pl Racine WI 53402-2325

BAUERLE, JAMES ERNEST, oral surgeon; b. Hamilton Pool, Tex., Sept. 24, 1923; s. Ernest and Nancy Ima Bauerle; m. Frances Irene Tankers, June 25, 1945 (div. Sept. 1979); children: Frances Diane, Nancy Lea, Janet Elizabeth; m. Charlotte Margaret Ehlers, May 27, 1983. BS in Pharmacy, U. Tex., 1943; DDS, St. Louis U., 1946; MS in Oral Surgery, U. Pitts., 1950; LLD, U. Tex., 1969. Regent U. Tex. System, Austin, 1973—79, chmn. bldg. & grounds, 1975—79; clin. prof. oral surgery U. Tex. Health Sci. Ctr., San Antonio, 1979—; Bauelre prof. U. Tex. Coll. Pharmacy, Austin, 1982. Capt. U.S. Army, 1950—52. Recipient Alumni Merit award, St. Louis U., 1973. Fellow: Am. Coll. Dental & Maxilofacial Surgeons, Internat. Coll. Dentists, Am. Coll. Dentists, Royal Soc. Health (life); mem.: San Antonio Assn. Oral and Maxillofacial Surgeons, Soc. Advancement Gen. Anesthesia in Dentustry (life), Tex. Dental Assn. (life), Fedn. Dentaire Internat. (life), Tex. Pharm. Assn. (hon.), Am. Assn. Oral and Maxillofacial Surgeons, Tex. State Bd. Dental Examiners, San Antonio Breakfast Club (pres. 1968—2003), Scottish Rite, Masons, Rho Chi, Delta Sigma Delta. Republican. Prsbyterian. Avocation: ranching. Home: 150 Oak Park San Antonio TX 78209 Office: Oral & Maxillofacial Surgery 1100 NW Look 410 Ste 500 San Antonio TX 78213

BAUERLY, RONALD JOHN, marketing educator; b. Monroe, Wis., Oct. 31, 1953; s. Jack Leroy and Josephine (Wiegel) B.; m. Robin Rochelle Kramer, Aug. 8, 1981; children: Shannon Marie, Thomas Joseph. BBA, U. Iowa, 1975, MBA, 1977; DBA, Southern Ill. U., Carbondale, 1989. Asst. mgr. K-Mart Corp., Racine, Wis., 1977-78; instr. Metropolitan Tech. Community Coll., Omaha, 1978, Loras Coll., Dubuque, Iowa, 1979-81, Northwest Mo. State U., Maryville, 1981-82; asst. prof. Brescia Coll., Owensboro, Ky., 1983-86; asst. prof. mktg. Western Ill. U., Macomb, 1987-91, assoc. prof., 1991-96, prof., 1996—. Editor Jour. of Contemporary Business Issues; contbr. articles to jours. Mem. Am. Acad. Advt., Am. Mktg. Assn., Assn. for Consumer Rsch., Acad. Mktg. Sci., Mktg. Mgmt. Assn., Phi Kappa Phi, Beta Gamma Sigma. Office: Western Ill U 424 Stipes Macomb IL 61455 Office Phone: 309-298-1592. Business E-Mail: rj-bauerly@wiu.edu.

BAUERSFELD, CARL FREDERICK, lawyer; b. Balt., June 9, 1916; s. Emil George and Irene Marie (Hulse) B.; m. Ann Yancey, Mar. 3, 1944 (div.); children: Elizabeth Bauersfeld Garnett, Carl F. Student, George Washington U., 1937-42; LLB, Am. U., 1937. Bar: D.C. 1937, U.S. Dist. Ct. D.C. 1937, U.S. Ct. Appeals (D.C. cir.) 1937, U.S. Supreme Ct. 1941, U.S. Ct. Claims 1946, U.S. Tax Ct. 1946, Md. Ct. Appeals 1957, U.S. Ct. Appeals (5th cir.) 1947, (9th cir.) 1956, (3d cir.) 1958, (8th cir.) 1960, (4th cir.) 1966, (2d cir.) 1970. Practiced in, Washington, 1937—; ptnr. Bauersfeld, Burton, Hendricks & Vanderhoof, L.L.C., 1956—. Lectr. on fed. taxation at various univs. Lt. comdr. USNR, 1942-46. Mem. ABA, Md. Bar Assn., Bar Assn. D.C., Congl. Country Club, Burning Tree Club, Sigma Nu Phi, Phi Sigma Kappa. Lutheran. Office: 7101 Wisconsin Ave Bethesda MD 20814-4805 Office Phone: 301-986-8600. Business E-Mail: c.bauersfeld@bbhv.net.

BAUGH, BRADFORD HAMILTON, occupational and environmental health advisor; b. Seattle, Jan. 18, 1943; s. Sheppard McReynolds and Naomi Emma (Hugel) B.; m. Karyl Eileen Onstad, June 8, 1974; children: Taggart, Darin, Robyn, Patrick, Tracy. BS in Zoology, BS in Psychology, Wash. State U., 1972; MS in Biology, Ea. Wash. State U., 1976, BSN, 1983, MS in devel. psychology, 1992; PhD in Environ. Engring., Kennedy-Western U., 2002; student, U. Fla., 2002—. Cert. med. lab. technician, cmty. health nurse, safety specialist, registered sanitarian, cert. environ. health specialist. Environ. chemist, research and devel. USCG, Groton, Conn., 1975-76, occupational health advisor Alameda, Calif., 1983—; adj. prof. Whitworth Coll., Spokane, Wash., 1973-82; counselor Morning Star Ranch, Spokane, 1982-83; instr. Chapman Coll., Alameda, 1983—; indsl. hygienist, fire chief VA, American Lake, Wash., 1986-87; child mental health specialist Tamarack Ctr., Spokane, Wash., 1987-92; occupational and environ. health cons., Nine Mile Falls, Wash., 1987—; indsl. hygienist Wash. State U., Pullman, 1990-93; environ. protection specialist no. cluster USDA Agr. Rsch. Svc., Pullman, 1993—. With USCGR, 1961-93. Mem. Am. Med. Techs., Nat. Environ. Health Assn. (registered environ. health specialist and sanitarian), Am. Conf. Govt. Indsl. Hygienists World Safety Orgn., Assn. Profl. Indsl. Hygienists, Am. Indsl. Hygiene Assn. (Pacific N.W. sect.). Mem. Lds Ch. Home: PO Box 209 Nine Mile Falls WA 99026-0209 Office: USDA Agr Rsch Svc Pullman WA 99164-0001 E-mail: conquest@sisna.com.

BAUGH, JEREMY RICHARD, music educator; b. Indlps., Sept. 6, 1977; s. Richard Allen Baugh and Kathryn Carmel Morrow, Robert Joseph Morrow, Jr. (Stepfather) and Gloria Baugh (Stepmother); m. Tamara Joy Irwin, June 16, 2001. B, Ind. State U., 1995—2000. Music specialist North Putnam Cmty. Sch. Corp., Bainbridge, Ind., 2000—02, Pittsboro Elem. Sch., Ind., 2002—. Musician: Terre Haute Symphony Orchestra. Creative & Performing Arts award, Ind. State U., 1995—99, Robert L. Hotchkins award, Robert L. Hotchkins Found., 1995—99, Robert Amos Outstanding Jr. award, Ind. State U., 1998. Mem.: Percussive Arts Soc., Music Educator's Nat. Conf., Omicron Delta Kappa (life), Delta Sigma Phi, Phi Mu Alpha Sinfonia (pres. 1998—99, Man of Sinfonia 1999). United Methodist. Home: 1301 Brownswood Dr Brownsburg IN 46112-1909

BAUGH, KIM CLARKE, music educator; M in Music Edn., Shenandoah Conservatory, Winchester, Va., 1985. Band dir. Massanutten Acad., Woodstock, Va., 1983—84; music tchr. Atlantic Friends Sch., Northfield, NJ, 1985—86; band dir. St. Pauls Coll., Lawrenceville, Va., 1986—88, Brunswick H.S., Newport News, Va., 1988—99, Denbigh High Schoo, Newport News, Va., 1999—2000; music tchr. Eppes Elem., Newport News, Va., 1999—2000, South Morrison Elem., Newport News, Va., 2000—01; band dir. Warwick H.S., Newport News, Va., 2000—. Office Phone: 757-591-4700 1180. E-mail: kim.baugh@nn.k12.va.us.

BAUGH, RANDY DAVID, literature and language educator; s. Millard Ivan Eyler and June Pauline Clauson; m. Carol Jean Fleischman, Sept. 18, 1970; children: Trina Wind, Camas Rain. BA, Whitworth Coll., 1981; MEd, U. Portland, 1992. Tchr. English Shelton High Sch., Wash., 1988—, Ctrl. Wash. U., Ellensburg, 2002—. Chair English dept. Shelton High Sch., 1994—. Author: (CD's) The Road Is Promising, 2000, Talking To Machines, 2002. Music entertainment Relay for Life, Shelton, 2004. Mem.: NEA, Phi Kappa. Avocations: surfing, guitar. Home: PO Box 588 Union WA 98592 Office: Rock Ship Recording PO Box 588 Union WA 98592

BAUGHAM, SAMUEL MCCOY, actor, painter; s. Samuel Glenn and Margaret (McCoy) Baugham. BFA in Drama, NC Sch. Arts, 1968; BA in Arts Mgmt., E. Carolina U., 1983; grad., Columbia Sch. Broadcasting, spl. cert. of completion in radio announcing, 1969. Cert. tchr. of theatre arts NC Dept. Public Instrn. Prin. actor Berkshire Regional Ednl. Theatre, Pittsfield, Mass., 1968, CBS T.V., NYC, 1970, Theatre Ctr. Miss., Jackson, 1971, Theatre Four, NYC, 1971; tchr. theatre arts Hertford County Schs., Ahoskie, NC, 1987—90, Warren County Schs., Warrenton, 1990—92; portrait & landscape painter Baugham Art Studio, Rich Square, 1992—. Fine arts announcer/prodr. WTEB Pub. Radio, New Bern, NC, 1985—87; asst. dir. devel. Brevard Music Ctr., 1983—85. Organist Rich Square United Meth. Ch., NC, 1987—; choir dir. Rich Square United Methodist Ch., 1987—; bd. dirs. Northampton Co. Mus., Jackson, NC, 1987—. Mem.: Actors' Equity Assn. Home and Office: 209 Bryantown Rd Rich Square NC 27869 Office Phone: 252-578-5716.

BAUGHER, PETER V., lawyer; b. Chgo., Oct. 2, 1948; s. William and Marilyn (Sill) Baugher; m. Robin Stickney, Nov. 25, 1978; children: Julia Allison, Britton William Herbert. AB, Princeton U., 1970; JD, Yale U., 1973. Bar: Ill. 1974, U.S. Dist. Ct. (no. dist.) Ill. 1974, U.S. Ct. Appeals (7th cir.) 1974, U.S. Supreme Ct. 1987. Law clk. to judge U.S. Ct. Appeals (7th cir.), Chgo., 1973-74; from assoc. to ptnr. Schiff Hardin & Waite, Chgo., 1974-85; ptnr. Adams, Fox, Adelstein & Rosen, Chgo., 1985-89, Schopf & Weiss, Chgo., 1989—. Trustee Sta. WTTW Channel 11, Chgo., 1976—81, Kendall Coll., Evanston, 1980—92, WBEZ, Chgo. Pub. Radio, 1992—98, Ill. Humanities Coun., 1997—2003; pres. Chgo. Internat. Dispute Resolution Assn., 1997—. Mem. adv. com. Rep. Nat. Conv., Detroit, 1980; bd. dirs. Protestants for the Common Good, 2001—; mem. adv. com. Northwestern U. Sch. Law Ctr. Internat. Human Rights; bd. dirs. Sabre Found.; pres. Chgo. Lincoln Inn of Ct., 1994—96. Mem.: ABA, Chgo. Coun. Fgn. Rels., Am. Law Inst., Chgo. Bar Assn. (chair internat. and fgn. law com., chair fed civil practice com.), Ripon Soc. (chmn. 1975—76), Am. Coun. Germany, Mich. Shores Club, Econ. Club Chgo., Univ. Club. Home: 1310 Sheridan Rd Wilmette IL 60091-1834 Office: Schopf & Weiss 312 W Randolph St Chicago IL 60606-1721 Office Phone: 312-701-9300. E-mail: baugher@sw.com.

BAUGHMAN, J. ROSS, photographer, writer, educator; b. Dearborn, Mich., May 7, 1953; s. Charles T. and Patricia Jane (Hill) B.; m. Jonalyn Sue Schuon, May 9, 1987 (div. 1995); 1 child, Henry Marshall. BA cum laude; BA (J. Winton Lemen Photojournalism scholar), Kent State U., 1975. Staff photographer, writer Lorain (Ohio) Jour., 1975-77; contract photographer, writer AP in, Africa & Mid. East, 1977-78; co-founder Ind. Visions Internat., Inc., 1978; pres. Visions Photo Group, N.Y.C., 1978-97; dir. photography The Day Publ. Co., New London, Conn., 1997-98; dep. dir. photography The Washington Times, 1999—2003, dir. photography, 2003—. Mem. faculty New Sch. for Social Research, N.Y.C., 1979-97, NYU, 1980-82; co-founder, program dir. Focus Photography Symposiums, N.Y.C., 1981-88; adj. prof. U. Mo. Grad. Program in Journalism, N.Y.C., 1984-86. Author: Graven Images: a thematic portfolio, 1976, Forbidden Images: a secret portfolio, 1977, Some Ancestors of the Baughman Family in America: Tracing Back Twelve Generations from Switzerland through Virginia, 1989, Harvest Time, 1994, Apart From the World, 1997, A Lake Beneath the Crescent Moon, 2000, The Chain Rejoined, 2003. Recipient Pulitzer prize in journalism for feature photography, 1978; finalist Pulitzer prize in journalism for news photography, 2003. Mem. Nat. Press Photographers Assn., Photographers Gallery, Am. Soc. Mag. Photographers (sustaining 1984—), White House News Photographers' Assn. (edn. chair), Sigma Delta Chi. Office: The Washington Times 3600 New York Ave NE Washington DC 20002-1996 E-mail: j_ross_baughman@hotmail.com.

BAUGHMAN, JAMES CARSON, minister, sports official; b. Stanford, Ky., July 12, 1938; s. William Henry Baughman and Mary Elizabeth Carson; m. Katherine Ann Roach, Nov. 27, 1994; children: James Carson Jr., Helen Elizabeth Lewis, William Graham. BA, U. of Ky., Lexington, 1960; BD, Coll. of the Bible, Lexington, 1963; MDiv, Lexington Theological Sem., 1967, D of Ministry, 1972. Ordained min. Ravenna Christian Ch., Ky., 1963—65; sr. min. Middletown Christian Ch., Ky., 1965—88; cert. tennis official US Tennis Assn., White Plains, NY, 1966—. Nat. workshop leader Christian Ch. (Disciples of Christ), 1975—90. Author: Keeping Your Worms Warm, 1976, Behind the Pulpit, 1996, From the Pulpit, 1998. Bd. mem. Net Results, Sr. Citizen, Middletown Adv., Louisville, 1973—80; chaplain Ky. Colonels basketball team, Louisville, 1974—75. Pvt. U.S. Army, 1960, Ft. Knox, Ky. and San Antonio, Tex. Recipient Ky. Tennis Hall of Fame, 1998. Mem.: Logan's Fort Restoration Bd. (v.p. 2002—). Disciples Of Christ. Achievements include founding pres. of Louisville area KA Alum. Assn. Avocations: tennis, bridge. Home: 985 US Highway 27 South Stanford KY 40484 Office Phone: 606-365-2305.

BAUGHMAN, KENNETH LEE, cardiologist, educator; b. Kansas City, Mo., Oct. 8, 1946; m. Cheryl Jean Cain, Aug. 10, 1968; children: Matthew Tyler, Christopher Rolle. AB in Chemistry, U. Mo., 1968, MD, 1972; MA (hon.), Harvard U., 2003. Diplomate in internal medicine and cardiovasc. disease Am. Bd. Internal Medicine. Resident in internal medicine Johns Hopkins Hosp., Balt., 1972—75, asst. chief Osler Med. Svc., 1975—77; clin. and rsch. fellow divsn. cardiology Mass. Gen. Hosp., Boston, 1977—79; asst. prof. Johns Hopkins U. Sch. Medicine, Balt., 1979—2001, asst. dean postdoctoral programs and faculty devel., 1985—91; dir. cardiology divsn. Johns Hopkins Hosp., 1992—2001; sr. physician Brigham and Women's Hosp., Boston, 2002—, dir., adv. heart disease sect., 2003; prof. medicine

Harvard Med Sch., Boston, 2003—. Various com. assignments Johns Hopkins Hosp., 1979—2001, bd. mem., 1985—91, chmn., joint com. house staff and postdoctoral program, 1985—91; leadership devel. for Physicians in Academic Health Ctrs. Harvard Sch. Pub. Health, 2001; lectr. in field. Mem. editl. bd. New Eng. Jour. Medicine, 2003—; reviewer: profl. jours. Mem.: Assn. Univ. Cardiologists, Assn. Profs. Cardiology, Am. Fedn. Clin. Rsch., Assn. Subsplty. Profs. (sec.-treas. 2001), Heart Failure Soc., Am. Clin. and Climatologic Assn., Internat. Soc. Heart Transplantation, Paul Dudley White Soc., Am. Coll. Cardiology (nat. program com. 1992—93, gov. 1994—97, bd. govs. steering com., chmn. bd. govs. working group on acad. issues 1995—97, co-chmn. Bethesda conf. 1998, editl. bd. 1999—2003), Am. Heart Assn. (fellow coun. clin. cardiology 1980—, program com. 1995—98). Office: Brigham and Women's Hosp Divsn Cardiology 75 Francis St Bldg A 3rd Fl AB 362 Boston MA 02115 Home: 83 Beethoven Ave Waban MA 02468 Office Phone: 617-732-8970. Business E-Mail: kbaughman@partners.org.

BAUGHMAN, PAULINE CLARA, librarian; b. Portland, Oreg., July 29, 1971; d. John Junior and Norma Winifred (Strohschein) Baughman. BA in English, Oreg. State U., 1993; MLS, U. Ariz., 1994. Libr., asst. prof. U. Idaho, Moscow, 1995—97; reference libr., team leader sci., bus. dept. Multnomah County Libr., Portland, 1998—. Reviewer for libr. jours., mags. for librs. Vol. gardener Hinson Meml. Bapt. Ch., Portland, Oreg., 2002—, music, arts camp instr., 2002. Grantee U. Ariz, 1996, Multnomah County Libr., 2000. Mem.: ALA (comm. adv. com. 2001—02, chmn. 2003—05), Pub. Libr. Assn. Achievements include creator of the Knowmobile a mobile reference desk. Avocations: art, piano, cooking. Office: Multnomah County Libr 801 SW 10th Ave Portland OR 97205

BAUGHMAN, R(OBERT) PATRICK, lawyer; b. Zanesville, Ohio, Nov. 18, 1938; s. Robert G. and Kathryn E. B.; m. Joyce Hall, June 17, 1959; 1 child, Patricia. BS, Ohio State U., 1960, JD, 1963. Bar: Ohio 1963. Assoc. firm Sindell & Sindell, Cleve., 1964-71, Jones, Day, Reavis & Pogue, Cleve., 1972-73; asst. atty. gen. State of Ohio, Columbus, 1971-72; pres., prin. firm Baughman & Assocs., Cleve., 1973—. Mem. ABA, Ohio Bar Assn., Cuyahoga County Bar Assn., Nat. Coun. Self-Insurers, Internat. Assn. Indsl. Accident Bds. and Commns., Internat. Platform Assn., Columbia Hills Country Club. Episcopalian. Office: Baughman & Assocs 55 Public Sq Ste 2215 Cleveland OH 44113-1996 E-mail: rpaf38@aol.com.

BAUGHMAN, ROBERT PHILLIP, physician, educator; b. Warren, Ohio, Oct. 31, 1951; s. George May and Ellen (Van Huffel) Baughman; m. Elyse Ellen Lower, May 25, 1984. BS, Yale U., 1973; MD, Case Western Res. U., 1977. Intern, resident U. Cin., 1977-80, prof. Editor: Bronchoalveolar Lavage, 1990. Fellow: ACP, Am. Coll. Chest Physicians; mem.: European Respiratory Soc., Am. Thoracic Soc., Ctrl. Soc. Roman Catholic. Office: U Cin 1001 Holmes Eden Ave Cincinnati OH 45267-0565 Business E-Mail: bob.baughman@uc.edu.

BAUGHN, ROBERT ELROY, microbiology educator; b. Jan. 31, 1940; s. Berryman Thomas and Delia Louise (Smith) B.; m. Myra Donell Phillips, Dec. 12, 1965; children: Heather Lynne, Brenna Gayle. BS, The Citadel, 1963; MS (USPHS fellow), U. Tenn., 1966; PhD (NIH fellow), U. Cin., 1975; MBA, Houston Bapt. U., 1980. Microbiologist Hutcheson Meml. Tri-County Hosp., Ft. Oglethorpe, Ga., 1969-71, Parkridge Hosp., Chattanooga, 1971; instr. dept. dermatology and dept. microbiology & immunology Baylor Coll. Medicine, Houston, 1975-77, asst. prof., 1977-83, assoc. prof., 1983-93, prof., 1993—; with dept. med. tech. Sch. Allied Health Scis. U. Tex., Houston, clin. assoc. prof., 1985—; assoc. career rsch. scientist VA, Houston, 1990-98. Mem. editl. bd. Infect, Immunity, Jour. Microbial Methods. Home: 3903 Crystal Lake Cir S Pearland TX 77584-2574 Office: VA Hosp Bldg Dept Infectious Diseases 2002 Holcombe Blvd Houston TX 77030-4211 E-mail: rbaughn@bcm.tmc.edu.

BAUKNIGHT, CLARENCE BROCK, construction executive, consultant, retail executive; b. Anderson, S.C., May 14, 1936; s. John Edward and Theodosia (Brock) B.; m. Harriet League, June 29, 1959; children: Harriet League, Clarence Brock. BS, Ga. Inst. Tech., 1958. Exec. v.p. Builder Marts Am., Inc., Greenville, SC, 1965-87, pres., chief exec. officer, 1970—88, chmn. bd. dirs., 1987—2003. Chmn. bd. dirs. Enterprise Computer Sys., Inc. Mem. policy adv. bd. Joint Ctr. Urban Studies Harvard U., 1982-87; trustee Buncombe St. United Meth. Ch., 1985-90, chmn., 1989-90, Greenville Hosp. System, 1987-93, chmn., 1991-92; bd. dirs. Greenville Health Corp., 1994-97. Mem. Chief Exec. Orgn., Greenville Country Club, Cullasaja and Highlands, Masons, Shriners, Phi Delta Theta. Methodist. Home and Office: PO Box 2183 Greenville SC 29602-2183

BAUKOL, RONALD OLIVER, retired finance company executive; b. Chgo., Aug. 11, 1937; s. Oliver Peter and Clara Marie (Haugstad) B.; m. Gay Lynn Gollan, Aug. 29, 1959; children: David, Andrew, Kathlyn. BSChemE, Iowa State U., 1959; MSChemE, MIT, 1960. Engr., group leader Procter & Gamble, Cin., 1960-66; lab. supr. 3M Co., 1966-70; White House fellow Washington, 1970-71; dept. mgr. dental, new enterprises, diagnostic depts. Minn. Mining & Mfg. Co., St. Paul, 1972-82; v.p., gen. mgr. 3M/Riker Labs., 1982-86; mng. dir., CEO 3M U.K. PLC, 1986-89; mng. dir. 3M Ireland, 1988-89; group v.p. Pharms. and Dental Products Group, 3M Co., St. Paul, 1989-90, Med. Products Group, 1990-91; v.p. Asia Pacific, 1991-94, Asia Pacific Can. and L.Am., 1994-95, exec. v.p. internat. ops., 1996—2002; ret., 2002. Bd. dirs. The Toro Co.; mem. exec. bd. Internat. C.of C., 2001-. Chmn. bd. ARC St. Paul, 1979-81, dir. regional blood com., 1972-86; mem. alumni assn. bd. dirs. Iowa State U., 1974-76, gov. found., 1990—; trustee Minn. Med. Found., 1990-93, Children's Hosp., St. Paul, 1993-95; trustee U.S. Coun. Internat. Bus., 1994—, vice-chmn., 2000—; mem. adv. coun. U. St. Thomas Ctr. Health and Med. Affairs, Minn., 1990-97, internat. programs adv. coun. Carlson Sch. Mgmt., U. Minn., 1998—, Children's Hosps. and Clinics Fedn., Minn., 2003; bd. dirs. Children's Health Care, St. Paul, 1995-97. Named Outstanding Young Alumnus, Iowa State U., 1969. Mem. Brit. Inst. Mgmt. (companion 1988-89). Methodist. Avocation: tennis. Office: 30 Seventh St East Ste 3050 Saint Paul MN 55101 Office Phone: 651-221-0582. Personal E-mail: robaukol@hotmail.com.

BAUM, AXEL HELMUTH, lawyer; b. Berlin, July 14, 1930; came to U.S., 1933; s. Stefan H. and Gertrud (Goette) B.; m. Elisabeth K. Nordwall, Dec. 11, 1982; children: Nicholas S., Andreas S. BA cum laude, Amherst Coll., 1952; LL.B., Yale U., 1957. Bar: Conn. 1957, N.Y. 1958, U.S. Supreme Ct. 1976; Conseil Juridique, France, 1971; Avocat à la Cour (Paris) 1992. Assoc. Hughes, Hubbard & Reed, N.Y.C., 1957-64; fgn. atty. Lovell, White & King, London, 1959-60; ptnr. Hughes, Hubbard & Reed, N.Y.C., 1964—2002, ptnr.-in-charge European office Paris, 1966—2002, counsel, 2002—. Lectr., spkr. various internat. forums and seminars, France, Germany, U.S., Mid. East, 1970—; arbitrator, U.S. mem. Internat. Ct. of Arbitration of ICC, Paris, 2000—; CPR Panel of Disting. Internatl. Mediators. Mng. editor Yale Law Jour., 1957; contbr. articles to profl. jours. Bd. dirs. Am. Aid Soc., France, 1981, chmn. 1995—, Am. Ch. Com. France, 1991-96, World Monuments Fund France, 1989-; Bd. trustees, Amer. Libr. of Paris 1999-2002, Served to lt. USNR, 1952-54. Mem. Am. Arbitration Assn., U.S. Coun. Internat. Bus., ICC Commn. Internat. Arbitration, Coll. Commn. Arbitrators, London Ct. Internat. Arbitration, German Inst. Arbitration, Swiss Arbitration Assn., French Comite Arbitrage, Internat. Arbitration Inst., Coll. of Commn. Arbitration (U.S.), Polo Club (Paris), Yacht Club France, Swedish Cruising Club, Yale Club of N.Y.C. Avocations: sailing, tennis, swimming. Home: 8 Rue des Dames Augustines 92200 Neuilly Seine France Office: Hughes Hubbard & Reed 47 Ave Georges Mandel 75116 Paris France Office Phone: 33-1-44058000. Business E-Mail: baum@hugheshubbard.com.

BAUM, BERNARD HELMUT, sociologist, educator; b. Giessen, Germany, Apr. 18, 1926; arrived in U.S., 1933, naturalized, 1934; s. Theodor and Beatrice (Klee) Baum; m. Barbara B. Eisendrath, June 13, 1953; children: David Michael, Jonathan Klee, Victoria, Lisa Baum Kritz. PhB, U. Chgo., 1948, MA, 1953, PhD, 1959. Qualifications rating examiner, bd. adviser U.S. CSC, Chgo., 1952-54; instr. human relations, psychology Chgo. Police Officers' Coll. Edn. Program, 1955-59; dir. orgnl. analysis CNA Ins., Chgo., 1960-66; assoc. prof. mgmt. and sociology U. Ill., Chgo., 1966-69, assoc. dean Coll. Bus. Adminstrn., 1967-68, prof. mgmt. and sociology, 1969—2002, prof. mgmt. and sociology emeritus, 2002—, prof. health policy and adminstrn. Sch. Pub. Health, 1973—2002, prof. emeritus, 2002—, dir. health policy and adminstrn. Sch. Pub. Health, 1977-92. Lectr. Roosevelt U., 1955—66, U. Chgo., 1961—68, Northwestern U., 1968—70, U. Colo., 1971—76; mem. spkr.'s bur. Adult Edn. Coun. Greater Chgo., 1963—76; team leader joint evaluation mission UN devel. program WHO primary health care and health mgmt. devel. projects in South Pacific, 1985; vis. scholar Chiang Mai U., Thailand, 1988. Author: Decentralization of Authority in a Bureaucracy, 1961, As If People Mattered: Dignity in Organizations, 2005; co-author: Basics for Business, 1968; co-editor: Intervention: the Management Use of Organizational Research, 1975; contbr. articles to profl. jours. Bd. dirs. Selfhelp Home for Aged, Chgo. With AUS, 1944—46, brig. gen. Ill. Army N.G., ret. Decorated Legion of Merit, Bronze Star; recipient Bus. Adminstrn. and Social Sci. Doctoral Dissertaion award, Ford Found., 1960. Mem.: APHA, AAAS, Acad. Mgmt., Am. Acad. Polit. and Social Sci., Am. Sociol. Assn., Sigma Xi. Office: U Ill Sch Pub Health M/C 923 Chicago IL 60680 Home: Apt 3B 2610 Central St Evanston IL 60201-1354 Office Phone: 312-996-5760. Business E-Mail: bhbaum@uic.edu.

BAUM, BERNARD RENE, research scientist; b. Paris, Feb. 14, 1937; s. Kurt and Martha (Berl) B.; m. Danielle Habib, May 24, 1961; 1 child, Anat. BS, MS, Hebrew U., Jerusalem, 1963, PhD, 1966. Research scientist Agr. Can., Ottawa, Ont., 1966-74, sr. research scientist, 1974-80, prin. research scientist, 1980—, chief vascular plants sect. Biosystematics Research Inst., 1981—89. Author: Oats: Wild and Cultivated, 1977, Monograph of Tamarix, 1978, World Registry of Avena Cultivars, 1972, World Registry of Barley Cultivars, 1985, World Registry of Triticale, (on Internet), 1994; assoc. editor Can. Jour. Botany, 1986-2004, Euphytica, 1987—, Plant System Evolution, 1992-2000, Genetic Resources and Plant Evolution, 1992—, Kurtziana, 1999—. Fellow Acad. Sci.-Royal Soc. Can.; mem. Can. Bot. Assn. (Lawson medal 1979), Bot. Soc. Am., Am. Soc. Plant Taxonomists, Internat. Assn. Plant Taxonomists, Classification Soc., Linnean Soc. London, Orgn. Plant Taxonomy of the Mediterranean Area Home: 15 Murray St Ste 408 Ottawa ON Canada K1N 9M5 Office: Ea Cereal & Oil Seed Rsch Ctr Agrl Food Can Rsch Br Cen Exptl Farm Ottawa ON Canada K1A 0C6 Office Phone: 613-759-1821. E-mail: baumbr@agr.gc.ca, baumbd@allstream.net.

BAUM, BRANDON, lawyer, law educator; AB, U. Calif., Berkeley, 1982; JD, Hastings Law, 1985. Bar: Calif., U.S. Internat. Trade Commn., U.S. Ct. Appeals (5th, 9th and Fed. Cirs.). Ptnr. Cooley Godward LLP, Palo Alto, Calif., 1996—2004, Mayer Brown Rowe and Maw LLP, Palo Alto, Calif., 2005—. Adj. prof. Hastings Law, San Francisco, 2001—. Pub. adv. Calif. Child Advocates, Martinez, 1985—90. Avocation: horology. Office: Mayer Brown 2 Palo Alto Square 3000 El Camino Real Palo Alto CA 94306-2112 Office Phone: 650-331-2000. Business E-Mail: bbaum@mayerbrown.com.

BAUM, CARL EDWARD, electrical engineer, researcher; b. Binghamton, N.Y., Feb. 6, 1940; s. George Theodore and Evelyn Monica (Bliven) B. BS with honors, Calif. Inst. Tech., 1962, MS, 1963, PhD, 1969; Dr.-Ing.E.h. (hon.), Otto-von-Guericke U., 2004. Commd. 2d lt. USAF, 1962, advanced through grades to capt., 1967, resigned, 1971; project officer Air Force Rsch. Lab. (formerly Phillips Lab.), Kirtland AFB, N.Mex., 1963-71, sr. scientist for electromagnetics, 1971—2005; prof. dept. elect. and computer engrng. U. N.Mex., Albuquerque, 2005—. Pres. SUMMA Found.; U.S. del. to gen. assembly Internat. Union Radio Sci., Lima, Peru, 1975, Helsinki, Finland, 78, Washington, 81, Florence, Italy, 84, Tel Aviv, 87, Prague, Czech Republic, 90, Kyoto, 93, Lille, France, 96, Toronto, Canada, 99, Maastricht, Netherlands, 2002; mem. Commn. B U.S. Nat. Com., 1975—, Commn. E, 1982—, Commn. A, 1990—. Author: (with others) Transient Electromagnetic Fields, 1976, Electromagnetic Scattering, 1978, Acoustic, Electromagnetic and Elastic Wave Scattering, 1980, Fast Electrical and Optical Measurements, 1986, EMP Interaction: Principles, Techniques and Reference Data, 1986, Lightning Electromagnetics, 1990, Modern Radio Science, 1990, Recent Advances in Electromagnetic Theory, 1990, Scattering, 1992, Direct and Inverse Methods in Radar Polarimetry, 1992, (with A.P. Stone) Transient Lens Synthesis: Differential Geometry in Electromagnetic Theory, 1991; editor: (with H.N. Kritikos) Electromagnetic Symmetry, 1995, (with L. Carin and A.P. Stone) Ultra-Wideband, Short-Pulse Electromagnetics 3, 1997, Detection and Identification of Visually Obscured Targets, 1998, Scattering, 2002; contbr. articles to profl. jours. Recipient award Honeywell Corp., 1962, R & D award USAF, 1970, Harold Brown award Air Force Systems Command, 1990; Air Force Rsch. Lab. fellow, 1996; Electromagnetic pulse fellow. Fellow IEEE (Harry Diamond Meml. award 1987, Richard R. Stoddart award 1984); mem. Electromagnetics Soc. (pres. 1983-85), Electromagnetics Acad., Sigma Xi, Tau Beta Pi. Roman Catholic. Home: 5116 Eastern Ave SE Apt D Albuquerque NM 87108-5618 Personal E-mail: carl.e.baum@ieee.org.

BAUM, ELEANOR, electrical engineering educator, academic administrator; b. Poland, Feb. 10, 1940; came to U.S., 1942; d. Sol and Anna (Berkman) Kushel; m. Paul Martin Baum, Sept. 2, 1962; children: Elizabeth, Jennifer. BSE.E., CUNY, 1959; M.E.E., Poly Inst. N.Y., 1961, PhD, 1964; DS (hon.), Union Coll., 1993, Notre Dame, 1995. Engr. Sperry Gyrosoope Co., N.Y.C., 1960-61; instr. Poly. Inst. N.Y., N.Y.C., 1961-64; asst. prof. elec. engring. Pratt Inst., N.Y.C., 1964-67, assoc. prof., 1967-71, prof., chmn. dept. elec. engrng., 1971-84, dean Sch. Engring., 1984-87; dean Sch. Engring., Cooper Union for Advancement Sci. and Art, N.Y.C., 1987—; exec. dir. Cooper Union Rsch. Found., N.Y.C., 1987—. Cons. engring. to various corps.; accreditation visitor Accreditation Bd. Engrng. and Tech., 1983—, bd. dirs., fellow, 1994; organizer career confs. for careers in engring., careers for women, N.Y.C., 1970—; chair bd. examiners Grad. Record Exam., 1984-90; bd. dirs. Alleghany Powers Systems, U.S. Trust Co., Avnet, Inc.; commr. Engrng. Workforce Commn., 1990—; mem. engring. adv. bd. NSF, 1989-94; mem. adv. bd. Duke U., Rice U., U.S. Mcht. Marine Acad., 1992—; mem. U.S./Japan Engrng. Edn. Task Force, 1994—. Contbr. tech. articles and articles on engring. careers and edn. to profl. jours. Recipient Disting. Alumnus award Poly. Inst. N.Y., 1986, Alumni Achievement award CCNY, 1986, Emily Warren Roebling award Womens' Hall of Fame, 1988, Achievement award Mich. State U., 1992, Outstanding Woman Scientist award, 1992 Assn. Women Sci. Fellow IEEE (Steinmetz award 1990), Soc. Women Engrs. (Upward Mobility award 1990, Achievement award engrs. joint com. L.I. 1995); mem. Am. Soc. Engring. Edn. (bd. dirs. 1989—, v.p. 1992-93, pres. 1995—, various nat. task forces), Nat. Engring. Deans Coun. (bd. dirs. 1987—, chair 1990-93), N.Y. Met. Deans Assn. (chmn. 1985-90), N.Y. Acad. Scis. (bd. govs. 1994—), Order of Engr. (bd. govs. 1985-92, competitiveness policy coun. subcom. critical techs. 1992—, nat. rsch. coun. bd. engring. edn. 1991-95), Eta Kappa Nu, Tau Beta Pi (Achievement award Mich. Tech. U. 1995).

BAUM, ELIZABETH CLARK, retired elementary school educator; b. Jackson, Miss., Oct. 29, 1942; d. Moses Hamilton and Isabel (Hayes) Clark; m. Robert Jefferson Marsh II, Aug. 23, 1963 (div. Feb. 1973); children: Robert Jefferson III, Christopher Hamilton; m. Jerome Stephen Baum, Dec. 28, 1977; children: Garrett Adam, Courtney Jill. BS in Edn., U. Ga., 1964; MEd, Ga. State U., 1979. Tchr. Atlanta Pub. Schs., 1964—65, Gwinnett County (Ga.) Schs., Ga., 1965—71, DeKalb County (Ga.) Schs., DeKalb County, 1971—77; rep. elem. curriculum coun. Jefferson County Schs., Colo., 1978—81, citizen chmn. com. external audit for instrnl. programs, 1980—84, mem., 2d v.p. bd. of edn., 1985—87, mem., treas. bd. edn., 1987—89; exec. dir. Le Festivale, Denver, 1989—90; sales assoc. Neiman-Marcus, Denver, 1990—93; tchr. Wailuku Elem. Sch. Hawaii Dept. Edn., Maui, 1994—96; tchr. Kamalii Elem., 1996—99; tchr. Compton Elem. Cobb County Dept. Ed., Ga., 1999—2000; tchr. Allgood Elem. Paulding County Dept. Edn., Ga., 2000—03, ret., 2003. Mem. AAUW, ASCD, LWV, PTA (nominee Phoebe Apperson Hearst Outstanding Educator award 1985), Phi Delta Kappa, Alpha Delta Kappa Avocations: travel, ski, read.

BAUM, GORDON LEE, lawyer, non-profit organization administrator; b. St. Louis, Aug. 24, 1940; s. James Paul and Johnnie Thelma (Thompson) B.; m. Georgia Dee Thompson, Sept. 12, 1959 (div. 1977); children: Gordon Lee II, Mark Evans Sterling, Duane Russell Stuart; m. Linda Gaye Gulledge, Feb. 10, 1978; children: Laura Leigh, Renee Gabrielle. Grad., U. Mo., 1965; JD, St. Louis U., 1969. Bar: Mo. 1969, U.S. Dist. Ct. Mo. 1969. Sr. inspection clk. Chevrolet Divsn. GM Corp., St. Louis, 1961-65, work standards engr., 1965-69; field dir. mid-west Citizens Coun. Am., Jackson, Miss., 1969-84; pvt. practice civil law St. Louis, 1969—. CEO, Coun. Conservative Citizens, St. Louis, 1985—, Conservative Citizens Found., St. Louis, 1985—; dir. St. Louis Met. Area Citizens Coun. Assoc. editor (newspaper) Citizens Informer, 1971—; talk show host WGNU Radio, St. Louis, 1995-2005. State Coord. Wallace Presdl. Campaign, Mo., 1972, 76; del. Dem. Party State Conv., 1976. Yeoman 2d class petty officer USN, 1958-61. Mem. Mo. Bar Assn., Phi Alpha Delta, MENSA, NRA, Sons of Confederate Vets., Hist. Soc. Berks County, Pa., Ger.-Am. Heritage Soc., Am. Legion. Lutheran. Avocations: politics, history, hunting, gardening, travel. Home: 2412 Park Ave Saint Charles MO 63301 Office: Coun of Conservative Citizens PO Box 221683 Saint Louis MO 63122-8683 Office Phone: 636-940-8475. Personal E-mail: glb1940@hotmail.com.

BAUM, HERBERT MERRILL, consumer products company executive; b. Chgo., Dec. 6, 1936; s. Jack William and Ruth Frances (Ginsburg) Baum; m. Diane Jean Kale, Nov. 1, 1975 (div. Sept. 1977); m. Karen Rochelle Oberman, Dec. 22, 1983. BSBA, Drake U., 1958. Account exec. Stern, Walters & Simmons, Chgo., 1962-66, Doyle, Dane & Bernbach, Chgo., 1966-69; v.p., account dir. Needham, Harper & Steers, Chgo., 1969-78; assoc. dir., dir. new products Campbell Soup Co., Camden, NJ, 1978, v.p. mktg., gen. mgr. soup div., 1978-84, exec. v.p. U.S. divsn., 1984-85; pres. Campbell USA, Camden, NJ, 1985-90, sr. v.p., 1986-89, exec. v.p., 1989-93; pres. Campbell N.Am., Camden, NJ, 1990-92, Campbell North & South Am., Camden, NJ, 1992-93; chmn., CEO Quaker State Corp., Irving, Tex., 1993-98; pres., COO Hasbro Inc., Providence, R.I., 1999-2000; chmn., CEO Dial Corp., Scottsdale, Ariz., 2000—05; exec. chmn. Action Performance Companies, Tempe, Ariz., 2005—. Bd. dirs. Meredith Corp., Pepsi Ams. Inc., Action Performance Cos. Inc., Am. West Airlines, Playtex Product Co., Inc. With U.S. Army, 1958—59. Mem.: Am. Mktg. Assn. Home: 702 Ocean Dr Juno Beach FL 33408-1911 Office: Action Performance Companies 1480 S Hohaken Dr Tempe AZ 85218 Office Phone: 480-754-6870, 602-331-3700. Business E-Mail: basilhb@bellsouth.net.

BAUM, INGEBORG RUTH, librarian; b. Berlin, Sept. 20; d. Ella Koch; Oberlyceum (scholar), Kassel, Germany, 1926-33; postgrad. Georgetown U., 1963-70; m. Albert Baum, Feb. 16, 1938 (div. 1960); children: Harro Siegward, Helma Sigrun (Mrs. George Meadows). Came to U.S., 1951, naturalized, 1957. Export corr. Bitter-Polar, Germany, 1933-35, Henschel Locs, Germany, 1936; exec. sec. Fieseler Airplane Mfrs., Germany, 1936-38; interpreter, sec. UNRRA, Germany, 1946-48; payroll supr., civilian dept. U.S. Army, Wetzlar PX, Germany, 1948-51; asst. librarian Supreme Council, Ancient and Accepted Scottish Rite, Washington, 1951-70, librarian and museums curator, 1970-93, ret., 1993; appraiser rare books and documents; v.p. Merical Elec. Contractors, Inc., Forestville, Md., 1974-83. Mem. Am. Soc. Appraisers, Calligraphers Guild. Mem. Ch. Jesus Christ of Latter-day Saints. Free-lance contbr. to Pabelverlag, Rastatt, Germany, Harle, Ofcl. Publs., Inc., Soc. for Contemporary Am. Lit. in German, others. Avocations: travel, art. Office: 1733 16th St NW Washington DC 20009-3103

BAUM, JOHN, physician; b. N.Y.C., June 2, 1927; s. Louis Israel and Lilian (Treitman) B.; m. Erna Rose Bailis, Jan. 28, 1950; children: Nina, Jane, Carl, Antonia, Theodore. BA, NYU, 1949, MD, 1954. Intern Baltimore City Hosp., 1954-55; resident in medicine Lenox Hill Hosp., N.Y.C., 1955-56, VA Hosp., N.Y.C., 1956-57; NIH clin. trainee N.Y.U.-Bellevue Hosp., 1957-58; NIH research fellow Rheumatism Research Unit, Taplow, Eng., 1958-59; asst. prof. medicine U. Tex. Southwestern Med. Sch., 1962-68; dir. arthritis clinic Parkland Meml. Hosp., Dallas, 1959-68, dir. med. clinics, 1965-67; co-dir. pediatric arthritis clinic Scottish Rite Hosp., Dallas, 1960-68; mem. faculty U. Rochester (N.Y.) Med. Sch., 1968—, prof. medicine pediatrics and rehab., 1972-93, prof. medicine emeritus, 1993—, chmn. rsch. subjects rev. bd., 1987-96, prof. orthopedics (rehabilitation), 1991-93, prof. pediatrics, 1997—. Vis. prof. rheumatology, hon. sr. rsch. fellow U. Birmingham, Eng., 1988-89; vis. prof. U. Kiev Med. Sch., 1995; dir. arthritis and clin. immunology unit Monroe Cmty. Hosp., 1968-93; dir. pediatric arthritis clinic Strong Meml. Hosp., 1970—; mem. drug efficacy panel NRC-NAS, 1960-65; mem. rsch. rev. bd. immunology VA, 1970-76; adv. panel U.S. Pharmacopeia, 1975—; coord. therapeutics U.S.-USSR Program Rheumatology, 1974—; mem. test com. for rheumatology Am. Bd. Internal Medicine, 1971-76; locum pediat. rheumatologist Princess Margaret Hosp. for Children, Perth, Australia, 1999-2000. Mem. editl. bd. Clin. Rheumatology (Brussels), Jour. Rheumatology (Can.), Japanese Rheumatology, 1984-93; contbr. articles to profl. jours., chpts. to books. Served with AUS, 1944-46. Recipient award of merit Rochester Acad. Medicine, 1999, Sr. Role Model award, 2000, Earl Brewer award, Am. Juvenile Arthritis Orgn., 2002; Fulbright scholar, 1958; clin. scholar rheumatology Arthritis Found., 1964-69. Mem. Am. Coll. Rheumatology (master 1993, coun. pediat. rheumatology 1975-80, 85-00), Heberden Soc., Am. Fedn. Clin. Rsch., Am. Soc. Human Genetics, Am. Assn. Immunologists, Reticuloendothelial Soc., So. Soc. Clin. Investigation, Tex. Rheumatism Assn., Brit. Soc. Rheumatology, Midlands Rheumatology Soc. (Eng.), Polish Rheumatol. Soc. (hon.), La Found. Rheum Argentina (Dr. Oswaldo Garcia Morteo int. sci. com. 1997—), Great Lakes Interurban Club, Sigma Xi. Home: 1470 East Ave Rochester NY 14610-1619 Office: Strong Meml Hosp 601 Elmwood Ave Rochester NY 14642-0002 Business E-Mail: john_baum@urmc.rochester.edu. *If what I have achieved is called success, it is not because it has been my goal. As a clinician, teacher and researcher, I realize that success comes mostly with the latter, but my greatest satisfaction, which must have been my "secret goal," has been with the personal contacts that come through taking care of people and sharing my knowledge with students. The lagniappe of a supportive wife and fascinating children makes achieving the goals more worthwhile.*

BAUM, JULES LEONARD, ophthalmologist, educator; b. N.Y.C., Mar. 13, 1931; children from previous marriage: Jeffrey Stuart, Alison Rachel; m. Laura Klabin, 1990; stepchildren: Alexander Matthew, Samantha Merrill. AB, Dartmouth Coll., 1952; MD, Tufts U., 1956. NIH fellow in rsch. in ophthalmology NYU, 1958-59, rschr. in ophthalmology, 1961-62; asst. prof. NYU Med. Sch., 1965-68; resident in ophthalmology Bellevue Hosp., N.Y.C., 1962-64; mem. faculty Tufts U. Med. Sch., 1968—, prof. ophthalmology, 1974-91; sr. surgeon New Eng. Med. Ctr. Hosp., Boston, 1973-91; rsch. prof. Tufts U. Med. Sch., 1991—2002, prof. ophthalmology emeritus, 2002—. Assoc. editor Ophthalmic Lit., 1967-85; mem. editl. bd. Investigative Ophthalmology and Vision Sci., 1978-82, Survey of Ophthalmology, 1970-79, Am. Jour. Ophthalmology, 1985-91, Ophthalmic Surgery, 1985-95, Cornea Jour., 1989-98; contbr. articles to profl. jours. Served to capt. M.C. AUS, 1959-61. Recipient William Warner Hoppin award N.Y. Acad. Medicine; Alcon Rsch. Inst. award, 1991; NIH fellow, 1958-59, 64-65; Nat. Eye Inst. grantee. Fellow: Royal Coll. Ophthalmologists; mem.: Ocular Microbiology Immunology Group (pres. 1990—91, Thygeson lecture 2001), Mass. Ophthalmology Soc. (sec. 1974—76), Castroviejo Soc. (exec. sec., treas. 1979—87, v.p. 1987—89, pres. 1989—91, Castroviejo Corneal medalist 1997), Assn. Rsch. in Vision and Ophthalmology (trustee 1981—86, v.p. 1986), Am. Acad. Ophthalmology (bd. councillors 1981—83, honor award 1979, sr. honor award 1990), Confrerie des Chevaliers du Tastevin, Internat. Wine and Food Soc., Phi Beta Kappa. Jewish. Personal E-mail: julesbaum@verizon.net.

BAUM, KERRY ROBERT, retired military officer, director; b. LaGrande, Oreg., May 25, 1939; s. Guy Hiatt Baum and Niola (Anderson) Jones; m. Lynda Sue Christian, Dec. 18, 1964; children: Kerry Jr., Tatia D., Christian H., Buffy Jo, Patrick H., Britta Sue, Natalie A. BA in History, Brigham Young U., 1967; MBA in Mktg., Murray State U., 1978; postgrad., Webster Coll., St. Louis, 1979-80; MA in Nat. Security & Strategic Studies, U.S. Naval War

Coll., 1986. Cert. bus. continuity planner Disaster Recovery Inst. Internat., recovery planner Harris Recovery Group. Commd. 2d lt. U.S. Army, 1957, advanced through grades to col., 1990; mgr. emergency preparedness Brigham Young U., 1993—. Joint staff rep. LIVE OAK, 1986—90; U.S. rep. Maj. NATO Comdrs. Alert Conf., 1987—90. Author, editor: book NATO Alert Procedures for Joint Staff, 1988, Focal Point Procedures Manual, 1989. Mem., past pres. Utah Campus Safety Assn.; apptd. mem. Utah Seismic Safety Commn., 2001; bishop Mormon Ch., Hopkinsville, Ky., 1974—78, councilor, bishopric Newport, RI, 1985—86; bishop Mormon Ch. BYU 185th Ward, 1996—99. Decorated Bronze Star, Army Commendation medal, Air Force Commendation medal, Def. Superior Svc. medal; named Mem. of the Yr., Utah Emergency Mgmt. Assn., 2000; recipient Peak award, Nuskin Internat., 2005. Mem.: Internat. Assn. Emergency Mgrs. (cert. emergency mgr., cert. bus. continuity planner Disaster Recovery Inst.), Assn. Contingency Planners (Utah chpt. past treas.), Res. Officers Assn. Home: 10938 N 5870 W Highland UT 84003-9487 Office Phone: 801-422-8142. Business E-Mail: kerry_baum@byu.edu.

BAUM, M(ARY) CAROLYN, occupational therapist; b. Chgo., Mar. 26, 1943; d. Gibson Henry and Nelle (Curry) Manville; 1 child, Kirstin Carol. BS, U. Kans., 1966; MA, Webster Coll., 1979; PhD, Washington U., St. Louis, 1993. Occupl. therapist U. Kans. Med. Ctr., 1966-67; staff occupl. therapist Rsch. Med. Ctr., Kansas City, Mo., 1967, dir. occupl. therapy, 1967-73, dir. phys. medicine and rehab., 1973-76; dir. occupl. therapy and clin. svcs. Washington U. Sch. Medicine, St. Louis, 1976—88, from assoc. prof. to prof. occupl. therapy and neurology, 1988—, dir. program on occupl. therapy, 1988—. Vis. prof. NYU, U. Mo., 1985—87; mem. adv. com. Nat. Ctr. Med. Rehab. Rsch. NIH; allied health rep. AMA Health Policy Agenda for Am. People; mem. com. on assessing rehab. sci. and engring. Inst. Medicine; bd. dirs. Rehab. Inst. St. Louis; pres. Occupl. Therapy Certification Bd., 1986—93. Author: Understanding the Prospective Payment System: A Business Perspective, 1986, Occupational Therapy: Overcoming Human Performance Deficits, 1991, Occupational Therapy: Enabling Function and Well Being, 1997, Occupational Therapy: Performance, Participation and Wellbeing, 2005, Measuring Occupational Performance: Supporting Best Practice in Occupational Therapy, 2001, Occupation-Based Practice: Fostering Performance and Participation, 2001, 2nd edit., 2005, Occupational Therapy: Performance, Participation and Well-Being; editor Jour. OTJR; Occupation, Participation and Health; contbr. articles to profl. jours. Coord. St. Louis Ind. Living Coun., 1980-81; mem. nominating com. Greater Kansas City Health Sys. Agy.; vice-chmn. Village Ch. Accessibility Task Force, 1974-76; bd. dirs. Rehab. Inst. St. Louis. Named Employee of Yr., Rsch. Hosp., 1974, Kans. Occupl. Therapist of Yr., 1975, Outstanding Alumni Sch. Allied Health U. Kans., 1999. Fellow Am. Occupl. Therapy Assn. (chmn. stds. and ethics commn. 1973-77, nat. v.p. 1978-82, pres. 1982-83, pres. 2004—, Eleanor Clarke Slagel Lectureship award 1980, award of Merit 1984); mem. Mo. Occupl. Therapy Assn. (Occupl. Therapy Clinician of Yr. 1985), Mo. Assn. Rehab. Facilities (bd. dirs.), St. Louis Med. Rehab. Soc. (pres. 1987). Office: Program Occupl Therapy Wash U Sch Medicine 4444 Forest Park Ave Saint Louis MO 63108-2212 Office Phone: 314-286-1618. Business E-Mail: baumc@wustl.edu.

BAUM, MICHAEL LIN, lawyer; b. Clinton, Okla., Apr. 10, 1952; s. William Eldon and Patricia (Schumacher) B.; m. Colleen Margaret Condon, Apr. 6, 1991; children: Elizabeth, Alexandra, Kevin. BA summa cum laude, UCLA, 1982, JD, 1985. Bar: Calif. 1985, D.C. 1993, U.S. Dist. Ct. (ctrl. dist.) Calif. 1986, U.S. Dist. Ct. (ea. and no. dists.) Calif. 1989, U.S. Dist. Ct. (we. dist.) Mich. 1991, U.S. Dist. Ct. (no. dist.) Ohio 1993, U.S. Dist. Ct. (no. dist.) N.Y. 1996, U.S. Ct. Appeals (9th cir.) 1990, U.S. Ct. Appeals (4th cir.) 1996, U.S. Ct. Appeals (7th cir.) 1997, U.S. Supreme Ct. 1991. Assoc. Kananack, Murgatroyd, Baum & Hedlund,and predecessors, L.A., 1985-87; ptnr., shareholder Baum, Hedlund, A Profl. Corp., L.A., 1987—. Mem. discovery and trial teams MDL 817 United Airlines 1989 aircrash at Sioux City, Iowa, Chgo.; mem. plaintiffs' steering com. MDL 891 Northwest Airlines 1990 aircrash at Detroit Met. Airport, Ill. State Ct. procs. for USAir 427 crash near Aliquippa, Pa., 1994, MDL 1041 USAir 1994 crash at Charlotte, N.C.; trial team for consolidated hemophilia-AIDS cases, New Orleans, 1999. Recipient Safety award, Nat. Air Disaster Found., 2002. Mem. State Bar Calif., D.C. Bar, Bar Assn. D.C., Consumer Attys. Calif., Consumer Attys. L.A. Office: Baum Hedlund A ProfessionalCorp 12100 Wilshire Blvd Ste 950 Los Angeles CA 90025-7107 Office Phone: 310-207-3233. Business E-Mail: mbaum@baumhedlundlaw.com.

BAUM, PAUL FRANK, mathematics professor; b. N.Y.C., July 20, 1936; s. Mark and Celia (Frank) B.; m. Barbara Alice Bigelow, June 21, 1961; children: Sarah Alice, Michael Eli, Jessica Louise. AB, Harvard U., 1958; PhD, Princeton U., 1963. Vis. mem. Inst. for Advanced Study, Princeton, N.J., 1964-65, 76-77; asst. prof. math. Princeton U., 1965-67, vis. assoc. prof. math., 1967-68; assoc. prof. math. Brown U., Providence, 1967-71, prof. math., 1971-87, Pa. State U., University Park, 1987-91, disting. prof. math., 1991—. Speaker at conf., seminar in field. Contbr. articles to profl. publs. Japan Soc. for Promotion of Scis. fellow, 1986; NSF rsch. grantee, 1965—. Mem. Am. Math. Soc. (profl. editorial com. 1983-86). Jewish. Office: Pa State U 206 Mcallister Bldg University Park PA 16802-6401

BAUM, RICHARD THEODORE, engineering executive; b. NYC, Oct. 3, 1919; m. Jean Knapp, June 15, 1946 (dec. Sept. 1, 1994); children: Kathryn, Judith. BA, Columbia U., 1940, BS, 1941, MS, 1948. Registered profl. engr., N.Y., D.C., and 20 other states, Nat. Bur. Engring. Registration. Engr. Electric Boat Co., Groton, Conn., 1941-43; with Jaros, Baum & Bolles, N.Y.C., 1946—, ptnr., 1958-86, ptnr. emeritus, cons. to firm, 1986—. Mem. adv. coun., faculty of engring. and applied sci. Columbia U., N.Y.C., 1972—. 1st lt. USAAF, 1943-46. Egleston medalist Columbia U., 1985 Fellow ASME, ASHRAE, AAAS, Am. Cons. Engrs. Coun.; mem. NAE (mech. engring. peer com. 1991-93), NSPE, N.Y. Acad. Scis., Nat. Soc. Energy Engrs., NRC (chmn. bldg. rsch. bd. 1987-91), Am. Arbitration Assn. (panel arbitrators 1973—), Coun. on Tall Bldgs. and Urban Habitat (vice chmn. N.Am. chpt.), Univ. Club N.Y.C. Home: 9 Ivy Hill Rd Chappaqua NY 10514-1805 Office: Jaros Baum & Bolles 80 Pine St New York NY 10005-1702 Office Phone: 212-530-9300.

BAUM, ROGER S., writer; b. LA, Mar. 21, 1938; s. Joslyn S. and Elizabeth Baum; m. Charlene S. Baum. Author: Lion of Oz and The Badge of Courage, 1997, Dorothy of Oz, 1990, Green Star of Oz, 2001, (short stories) SillyOZbul Trilogy, 1991—93, Rewolf of Oz, 1998, Toto in Candy Land of Oz, 2002, Wizard of Oz and The Magic Merry Go Round, 2003, ToTo of Oz and the Surprise Party, 2004, The Oz Odyssey, 2005, (novella) Longears and Tailspins Adventure, 1962, (musical) Lion of Oz, 2001. Schools/hospitals. Po 3 U.S. Navy, 1958—61. Achievements include Animated Musical - Lion of Oz/ Sony Wonder; Legends of Oz / CD Rom. E-mail: roger_baum@tototooinc.com.

BAUM, STANLEY, radiologist, educator; b. N.Y.C., Dec. 26, 1929; s. Herman and Fannie (Harris) B.; m. Jeanne Masch, June 29, 1958; children: Richard Arthur, Laura Dianne, Carol Lisa. BA, NYU, 1951; MD, U. Utrecht, Holland, 1957. Intern Kings County Hosp., N.Y.C., 1957-58; resident in radiology Grad. Hosp., U. Pa., Phila., 1958-61; trainee Nat. Cancer Inst., Bethesda, Md., 1958-61; fellow cardiovascular radiology Stanford (Calif.) U., 1961-62; instr. radiology U. Pa., Phila., 1962-63, asst. prof., 1963-66, assoc. prof., 1966-70, prof., 1970—, Eugene P. Pendergrass prof. radiology, 1977-96, chmn. dept. radiology, 1975-96; chmn. med. bd. Hosp. of U. Pa., 1983-86; chief cardiovascular radiology Mass. Gen. Hosp., Boston, 1971-75; prof. radiology Harvard Med. Sch., Boston, 1971-75. Cons. Radiation Effects Research Found., Hiroshima, Japan, 1975-76; mem. cardiovasc. rev. bd. Am. Heart Assn., 1970-90. Editorial bd.: Investigative Radiology, 1970-80, New Eng. Jour. Medicine, 1975-76, Radiology, 1975-85, Gastrointestinal Radiology, 1975-79, Jour. Continuing Edn., 1978-80, Postgrad. Radiology, 1980-90; editor-in-chief: Acad. Radiology, 2000—. Fellow Am. Coll. Radiology, Am. Coll. Cardiology; mem. Inst. Medicine Nat. Acad. Sci., Soc. Cardiovascular Radiology (pres. 1974-76), Soc. Chmn. Acad. Radiology Depts. (pres. elect 1985-86, pres. 1986), Acad. Radiol. Rsch. (pres. 1997-2000, editor-in-chief Acad. Radiology 2000—). Home: 401 W Moreland Ave Philadelphia PA 19118-4207 Office: U Pa 3400 Spruce St Philadelphia PA 19104-4206 Office Phone: 215-662-2028. E-mail: baum@oasis.rad.upenn.edu.

BAUM, STANLEY DAVID, lawyer; b. Bklyn., Feb. 22, 1954; s. Irwin and Muriel A. (Margolis) B.; m. Ilyne Rhona Fried, June 9, 1979; children: Andrew, Miranda. BS, U. Pa., 1976, JD, 1980; LLM, NYU, 1984. Bar: N.Y. 1981, U.S. Tax Ct. 1993. Lawyer Carter, Ledyard & Milburn, N.Y.C., 1988-98; of counsel Swidler, Berlin, Shereff, Friedman, LLP, N.Y.C., 1998—2004; counsel Dechert LLP, N.Y.C. 2005—. Contbr. articles to profl. jours. Mem. N.Y. State Bar Assn. (com. on employee benefits tax sect.). Office Phone: 212-698-3838. E-mail: stanley.baum@dechert.com.

BAUM, STEPHEN L., utilities company executive; Grad., Harvard U.; JD, U. Va. Sr. v.p., gen. counsel N.Y. Power Authority, 1982-85; various positions with SDG&E, 1985-93, exec. v.p., 1993-96; pres., CEO Enova Corp., 1996-97, chmn., CEO, 1998; vice-chmn., pres., CEO Sempra Energy, San Diego, 1998—2000, chmn., pres., CEO, 2000—. Bd. dirs. Computer Sci. Corp., mem. audit com. Capt. USMC, 1966—69. Office: Sempra Energy 101 Ash St San Diego CA 92101-3017

BAUM, WILLIAM ALVIN, astronomer, educator; b. Toledo, Jan. 18, 1924; s. Earle Fayette and Mable (Teachout) B.; m. Ester Bru, June 27, 1961. BA summa cum laude, U. Rochester, 1943; PhD magna cum laude, Calif. Inst. Tech., 1950. Physicist U.S. Naval Research Lab., Washington, 1946-49; astronomer Mt. Wilson and Palomar observatories, Pasadena, Calif., 1950-65; dir. Planetary Research Center, Lowell Obs., Flagstaff, Ariz., 1965-90; rsch. prof. astronomy dept. U. Wash., Seattle, 1990—97, rsch. prof. emeritus, 1998—. Adj. prof. astronomy Ohio State U., 1969-91; adj. prof. physics No. Ariz. U., 1973-91; rsch. prof. astronomy U. Wash., Seattle, 1990-97, prof. emeritus, 1997—; cons. physics, astronomy, optics; cons. U.S. Army Research Office, Durham, N.C., 1967-74; vis. prof. Am. Astronomy Soc., 1961-98; adv. com. Nat. Acad. Sci., 19 58-67; mem. optical instrumentation panel adv. Air Force, 1967-76; coms. and panels NSF and NASA Office Space Scis., 1967-91; mem. NASA Viking Orbiter Imaging Team, 1970-79, Hubble Space Telescope Camera Team, 1977-96. *In 1946 Baum was a member of the team that made the very first successful astrophysical observation above the earth's atmosphere by installing an ultraviolet spectrograph in a German V2 rocket. Later, he designed and used a photoelectric "Photon counter" at Palomar Observatory to extend reliable photometry of stars and galaxies about 4 magnitudes fainter than previously possible. Over the years, Baum's publications have dealt with topics ranging from planetary science to cosmology. In the 1990s, he used the Hubble Space Telescope to investigate globular star clusters, the cosmic distance scale, and the age of the universe.* Contbr. articles to tech. publs. Served to lt., jr. grade USNR, 1943-46. Guggenheim fellow, 1960-61; Asteroid 4174 named Billbaum, 1990. Mem. Am. Astron. Soc. (chmn. div. planetary scis. 1976-77), Royal Astron. Soc., Astron. Soc. Pacific, Internat. Astron. Union, Phi Beta Kappa, Sigma Xi, Theta Delta Chi. Achievements include asteroid 4175 named "Billbaum" in his honor, 1990. Home: 2124 NE Park Rd Seattle WA 98105-2422 Office: U Wash Dept Astronomy Seattle WA 98195-1580 E-mail: baum@astro.washington.edu.

BAUMAN, DALE ELTON, nutritional biochemistry professor; b. Detroit, Dec. 26, 1942; s. Elton Blaine and Waneta Mary (Taylor) B.; m. L. Marie Vinande, Aug. 28, 1965; children: Rebecca, Todd, Jeffrey. BS, Mich. State U., 1964, MS, 1968; PhD, U. Ill., 1969. Asst. prof., assoc. prof. U. Ill.-Urbana, 1969-78; vis. prof. Mich. State U., East Lansing, 1978; assoc. prof., then prof. Cornell U., Ithaca, N.Y., 1979—, Liberty Hyde Bailey prof., 1987. Chmn. NAS/NRC Bd. Agr., 1990-97. Contbr. articles to profl. jours. Leader and scoutmaster Boy Scouts Am., Mich., N.Y., 1978-83. Recipient N.Y. Farmers award, 1982, Alexander von Humboldt award, 1985, USDA Superior Svc. award, 1986, U. Ill. Alumni award, 1995, Cornell Alumni Faculty award, 2000, Disting. Scientist, U.S. Libr. of Congress, 2001, Outstanding Alumni award Mich. State U., 2003, Disting. Alumni award, 2004. Mem. NAS, Am. Dairy Sci. Assn. (Nat. Student award 1967, Nutrition Rsch. award 1982, Biotech. award 1987, Physiology Rsch. award 1994), Am. Soc. Animal Sci. (Young Scientist award 1977, Growth Biology award 1996, Fellow Rsch. award 1999, Morrison award 2004), Am. Soc. Nutritional Sci. (pres-elect 2002, pres. 2003, past pres. 2004), Coun. Agr. Sci. Tech. (Black award 1995), Fed. Animal Sci. Soc. (New Frontiers award 2004). Methodist. Home: 2 Eagleshead Rd Ithaca NY 14850-9659 Office: Cornell U 262 Morrison Hall Ithaca NY 14853-4801 Office Phone: 607-255-2262. Business E-Mail: deb6@cornell.edu.

BAUMAN, FRANK ANTHONY, retired lawyer; b. Portland, Oreg., June 10, 1921; s. Frank Anthony and Josephine Louise (Carolan) Bauman; m. Mildred Inez Packer, Sept. 9, 1950 (dec. June 1997); children: Todd Anthony, Patricia Jean; m. Jane Carter, Aug. 15, 1998 (div. July 29, 2003). Student in Japanese, U.S. Naval Sch. U. Colo., 1943-44; AB, Stanford U., 1944; JD, Yale U., 1949; postgrad., U. London, 1951-52. Bar: Oreg. 1950, U.S. Dist. Ct. Oreg. 1950. Assoc. Wilbur Beckett Oppenheimer Mautz & Souther, Portland, 1950-51; pvt. practice Portland, 1952-55, 68-71, 1978-91; ptnr. Veatch Bauman Lovett, Portland, 1955-63, Keane Haessler Bauman & Harper, Portland, 1963-68; rep. UN, Australasia, 1971-76, New Zealand, 1971—76, 1971-73. Property advisor Frank M. Packer Trust, Dallas, 1971—; adj. prof. internat. law Lewis and Clark Sch. Law, Portland, 1979—80; advisor Lillian Baumann Fund, Portland, 1985—; co-trustee Mildred P. Bauman Trust, Portland, 1997—. Past trustee, pres. World Affairs Coun., Oreg., 1954—; mem. Portland Com. Fgn. Rels., 1978—, past chmn., bd. dirs.; mem. English Speaking Union, Portland, 1992—2001, pres., 1991—2001; bd. dirs., mem. exec. com. English Speaking Union U.S., N.Y.C., 1997—; bd. dirs., past pres. English Speaking Union, Portland, 1991—2001. Recipient World Peace award, Assembly of the Bahia's, 1985, MacNaughton Civil Liberties award, ACLU, 1998. Mem.: ABA, UN Assn. U.S., UN Assn. Oreg., Internat. Law Assn. (Am. br.), Am. Soc. Internat. Law (patron), Yale Club N.Y.C. (class of 1949 reunion co-chmn. 2004), Arlington Club, Univ. Club (past pres. scholarship found.), Masons (past master). Democrat. Christian Scientist. Office: Ladd Carriage Ho 1331 SW Broadway Portland OR 97201 Office Phone: 503-224-1195.

BAUMAN, JOHN DUANE, lawyer; b. Kaskaskia, Ill., Aug. 22, 1930; s. Louis Wells and Veronica Genevieve (Schmerbauch) B.; m. Avis Crysella Moore, Sept. 15, 1956; children: Mark Duane, Thomas Jon, Jeffery Paul. BA, S.E. Mo. U., 1952; JD, Washington U., St. Louis, 1957. Bar: Mo. 1957, Ill. 1957. Assoc. Baker, Kagy & Wagner, East Saint Louis, Ill., 1957-62; ptnr. Wagner, Bertrand, Bauman & Schmieder, Belleville, Ill., 1962-86, Hinshaw & Culbertson, Chgo. and Belleville, 1986—. Bd. dirs. Breeders Cup/Nat. Thoroughbred Racing Assn. Pres. Ill. Thoroughbred Breeders and Owners Found., 2001—03; gen. counsel Okaw Valley coun. Boy Scouts Am., 1980—90. With U.S. Army, 1952—54. Mem. ABA, Ill. Bar Assn., Internat. Assn. Ins. Counsel (state membership chmn.), Assn. of Def. Trial Counsel (pres. 1975-76), St. Clair County Bar Assn. (pres. 1972-73), Horsemen's Benevolent and Protective Assn. (v.p. 1989-98), Ill. Thoroughbred Breeders and Owners Found. (bd. dirs. 1999-2002, v.p. 1996-99, sec.-treas. 1999-2000, pres. 2000—), Bradenton Country Club, St. Clair Country Club (pres. 1972-74), Paducah Country Club, Elks, Mo. Athletic Club (emeritus 1998). Roman Catholic. Avocations: horse racing, golf. Office: Hinshaw & Culbertson PO Box 509 521 W Main St Belleville IL 62220-1533 Office Phone: 618-277-2400. Personal E-mail: jb222555@aol.com.

BAUMAN, JOHN E., JR., chemistry professor; b. Kalamazoo, Jan. 18, 1933; s. John E. and Teresa A. (Wauchek) B.; m. Barbara Curry, June 6, 1964; children— John, Catherine, Amy BS, U. Mich., 1955, MS, 1960, PhD, 1962. Chemist Midwest Research Inst., Kansas City, Mo., 1955-58; research assoc. U. Mich., Ann Arbor, 1958-61; prof. chemistry U. Mo., Columbia, 1961-97, prof. emeritus, 1997—. Active Mo. Symphony Soc. Recipient Faculty Alumni award, 1969, Amoco Teaching award, 1975, Purple Chalk award, 1980, all U. Mo. Mem. Am. Chem. Soc. (nat. lectr.), Mo. Acad. Sci., U. Mo. Retirees Assn. (pres. 2000—), Kiwanis, Sigma Xi, Alpha Chi Sigma. Roman Catholic. Home: 3703 S Woods Edge Rd Columbia MO 65203-6607 Office: Univ Mo 125 Chemistry Building Columbia MO 65211-7600 E-mail: baumanj@missouri.edu.

BAUMAN, JONATHAN HUGH, psychiatrist; b. Bklyn., June 28, 1948; s. Morris and Rachel (Fialkoff) B.; m. Carol Ann Weiss, Dec. 22, 1973; children: Emily, Jacob. BA, U. Rochester, 1970; MD, Georgetown U., 1974. Diplomate Am. Bd. Psychiatry and Neurology, Am. Bd. Adolescent Psychiatry, Am. Bd. Med. Examiners. Resident U. Va. Hosp., Charlottesville, 1974-75, Georgetown U. Hosp., Washington, 1975-77; acting clin. dir. Upper Montgomery Community Mental Health Ctr., Olney, Md., 1977-79, cons. psychiatrist, 1977-84; clin. asst. prof. Georgetown U. Sch. of Medicine, Washington, 1977-84; med. staff Montgomery Gen. Hosp., Olney, 1977-84; staff psychiatrist Four Winds Hosp., Katonah, N.Y., 1984-85, program dir., 1985-92, med. dir., 1992—; asst. prof. Albert Einstein Coll. Medicine, N.Y.C., 1997—. Fellow Am. Psychiat. Assn. Jewish. Avocations: bicycling, skiing, hiking, photography. Office: Four Winds Hosp 800 Cross River Rd Katonah NY 10536-3549 E-mail: jbauman@fourwindshospital.com.

BAUMAN, LAURIE JULIA, sociologist, researcher; b. Rockville Center, N.Y., May 18, 1949; d. Maurice Joseph and Madelon Joan (Broz) Bauman; m. Richard Henry Pereira Mendes, Mar. 5, 1983. BA in Polit. Sci., CUNY, 1970; MA in Sociology, Columbia U., 1975, MPhil in Sociology, 1981, PhD in Sociology, 1984. Rsch. asst., field dir. Bur. Applied Social Rsch. Columbia U., N.Y.C., 1970-75, rsch. staff assoc. Ctr. for Social Scis., 1975-77, rsch. staff assoc. grad. sch. bus., 1977-85; rsch. assoc. Meml. Sloan Kettering Cancer Ctr., N.Y.C., 1982-86; asst. prof. Albert Einstein Coll. Medicine, Bronx, 1986-91, assoc. prof., 1991-95, prof. pediat., 1996—, co-dir. Preventive Intervention Rsch. Ctr., 1986—2000, dir. Preventive Intervention Rsch. Ctr., 2000—. Assoc. editor Jour. Devel. and Behavioral Pediat., 1992-96; contbr. articles to profl. jours. Recipient Lela Rowland Prevention award Nat. Mental Health Assn., 1992, Robert Wood Johnson Investigator award, 2000—. Fellow N.Y. Acad. Medicine; mem. Am. Assn. Pub. Opinion Rsch. (bd. dirs. pubs. 1993-95), Am. Sociol. Assn. Avocations: needlepoint, bird watching. Office: Albert Einstein Coll of Med PIRC NR 7 South 21 1300 Morris Park Ave Bronx NY 10461-1926 Office Phone: 718-918-4421. Business E-Mail: bauman@aecom.yu.edu.

BAUMAN, STEPHEN ADRIAN, lawyer; b. LA, Jan. 25, 1935; BSBA, UCLA, 1956; JD, Stanford U., 1959; LLM, Harvard U., 1960. Bar: Calif. 1960; cert. taxation specialist Calif. State Bar Bd. Legal Specialization. Ptnr. Seyfarth Shaw, LA, 1987—2001; of counsel Mitchell, Silberberg & Knupp, LA, 2002—. Lectr. tax law and estate planning U. So. Calif. Law Ctr. Advanced Profl. Program; U. So. Calif. Tax Inst., Calif. Continuing Edn. of Bar, Practising Law Inst. Mem. State Bar Calif. Office: Mitchell Silberberg & Knupp 11377 W Olympic Blvd Los Angeles CA 90064 Office Phone: 310-312-3269. Business E-Mail: sab@msk.com.

BAUMAN, SUSAN JOAN MAYER, mayor, lawyer; b. NYC, Mar. 2, 1945; d. Curt H. J. and Carola (Rosenau) Mayer; m. Ellis A. Bauman, Dec. 29, 1968. BS, U. Wis., 1965, JD, MS, 1981; MS, U. Chgo., 1966. Bar: Wis. 1981, U.S. Dist. Ct. (we. dist.) Wis. 1981, U.S. Ct. Appeals (7th cir.) 1983, U.S. Dist. Ct. (ea. dist.) Wis. 1985. Tchr. Madison (Wis.) Pub. Sch., 1970-78; research asst. U. Wis. Law Sch., Madison, 1981; ptnr. Thomas, Parsons, Schaefer & Bauman, Madison, 1981-84; sole practice Madison, 1984-85; ptnr. Bauman & Massing, Madison, 1985-87; pvt. practice, Madison, 1987-97; mayor City of Madison, 1997—2003; mem. Wis. Employment Rels. Commn., 2003—. Alderman Madison Common Coun., 1985-97, coun. pres., 1989-90; commr. equal opportunities com. City of Madison, 1985-89; mem. Econ. Devel. Commn., 1986-87, chmn. human resources com., 1987-90, mem. affirmative action com., 1988-93; mem. Cmty. Action Commn., 1988-97, pres., 1991-96; mem. Pub. Health Commn., 1991-97, Monona Terr. Conv. and Cmty. Ctr. Bd., 1993-97; pres. South Madison Health and Family Ctr., Inc., 1993-97; bd. visitors U. Wis. Coll. Letters and Scis., Madison, 1997—2003; mem. exec. com. Wis. Alliance Cities, 1996-2003; mem. adv. bd. U.S. Conf. Mayors, 1999—2003; dir. Safe Cmtys. Coalition Madison County. Mem. Wis. Bar Assn., Dane County Bar Assn., Wis. Indsl. Rels. Alumni Assn. (pres. 1985-86), Madison Civics Club. Democrat. Avocations: knitting, reading, backpacking, cross country skiing. Home: 125 N Hamilton St # 407 Madison WI 53703 Office: Wis Employment Rels Commn 18 S Thornton Ave Madison WI 53709 E-mail: sjmbauman@aol.com.

BAUMAN, WENDALL CARTER, JR., ophthalmologist, career officer; b. Oklahoma City, Nov. 7, 1956; s. Wendall C. and Donna M. (Kolzow) B. BS, Nebr. Wesleyan U., 1979; MD, Uniformed Svcs. U. Health Sci., 1983. Med. lic., Tex. Commd. USAF, 1979, advanced through grades to lt. col., 1995; resident in internal medicine Wright-Patterson Med. Ctr., Wright-Patterson AFB, Ohio, 1983-85; chief hosp. svc. USAF Hosp., Kunsan Air Base, Korea, 1985-86; staff physician USAF Clinic, Izmir, Turkey, 1986-87; resident in ophthalmology Wilford Hall Med. Sch., Lackland AFB, Tex., 1987-90; retina fellow Mass. Eye and Ear Infirmary Med. Sch. Harvard U., Cambridge, 1990-92, chief fellow retina svc., 1991-92; chief retina svc. Brooke Army Med. Ctr., Ft. Sam Houston, Tex., 1992—, asst. chief dept. surgery, 1996—. Contbr. articles to profl. jours. Recipient Investigators award Barcelona Med. Soc., 1991. Fellow Am. Acad. Ophthalmology; mem. AAAS, Tex. Med. Assn., Mass. Med. Assn. Methodist. Avocations: camping, hiking, fishing, gardening, stamp collecting/philately. Home: 137 Primrose Pl San Antonio TX 78209-3832 Office: Ophthalmology Svc Brooke Army Med Ctr 2851 Roger Brooke Dr Fort Sam Houston TX 78234

BAUMANN, CAROL EDLER, retired political scientist; b. Plymouth, Wis., Aug. 11, 1932; d. Clarence Henry and Beulah Hanetta (Weinhold) E.; m. Richard Joseph Baumann, Feb. 28, 1959; children: Dawn Carol, Wendy Katherine. BA in Internat. Rels., U. Wis., 1954; PhD in Internat. Rels., London Sch. Econs./Polit. Sci., 1957. Chmn. internat. rels. major U. Wis., Milw., 1962-79; dep. asst. sec. Bur. of Intelligence and Rsch./Dept. of State, Washington, 1979-81; prof. U. Wis., Milw., 1972-95, dir. internat. studies and programs, 1982-88, prof. emeritus, 1995—; dir. Inst. of World Affairs, Milw., 1964-97, dir. emeritus, 1997—. Internat. edn. adv. coun. U. Wis. Milw., 2000—. Author: Program Planning About World Affairs, 1991, The Diplomatic Kidnappings, 1973; editor: Europe in NATO: Deterrence, Defense, and Arms Control, 1987, Western Europe: What Path to Integration?, 1967. Mem. Gov.'s Commn. on the UN, 1964-79, 82-89, 2004—; Dem. candidate 9th Congl. Dist., 1968; mem. World Affairs Coun. of Milw., 1964-75; bd. dirs. Wis. World Trade Ctr., 1987-2001, Wis. Dist. Export Coun., 1987-2003, Ea. Shores Libr. Sys., 1999—, Inst. World Affairs, U. Wis., Milw., 2000—. Recipient Pub. Svc. Achievement award Common Cause, Wis., 1991, World Citizen of Yr. award Internat. Inst. Wis, 2004; Marshall scholar, 1954-57. Mem. Coun. on Fgn. Rels., Fgn. Policy Assn. (bd. dirs. 1990—, editl. adv. com. 1977-79, 82-88), Nat. Coun. World Affairs Orgns. (pres. 1977-79, bd. dirs. 1992-96), UN Assn. of USA (bd. dirs. 1977-79, 82-89), Soc. for Citizen Edn. in world Affairs (pres. 1977-79), Phi Kappa Phi, Phi Beta Kappa. Democrat. Lutheran. Avocations: walking, swimming, reading, travel, writing fiction. Home: W6248 Lake Ellen Dr Cascade WI 53011-1322 Personal E-mail: cbaumann@excel.net.

BAUMANN, DANIEL E., publishing executive; b. Milw., Apr. 10, 1937; s. Herbert F. and Agnes V. (Byrne) B.; m. Karen R. Weinkauf, Apr. 29, 1961; children: James W., Jennifer R., Colin D. BJ, U. Wis., 1958, MA in Polit. Sci., Cert. in Russian Area Studies, U. Wis., 1962. Reporter South Milwaukee (Wis.) Voice Jour., 1958-59, East St. Louis (Ill.) Jour., 1959-60; pub. relations rep. Credit Union Nat. Assn., Washington, 1962-64; reporter Paddock Publs., Inc., Arlington Heights, Ill., 1964-66, mng. editor, 1966-68, exec. editor, 1968-70, editor and pub. Paddock Circle newspapers, 1970-75, v.p., editor, 1975-83, sr. v.p., gen. mgr., editor, 1983-86, pres., editor, 1986-90, dir., 1986—, pres., chief operating officer, 1990—2002, chmn., pub., 2002—. Recipient William Alan White award U. Kans., 1976. Avocation: travel. Office: Paddock Publs Daily Herald 155 E Algonquin Rd Arlington Heights IL 60005-4617

BAUMANN, EDWARD ROBERT, environmental engineering educator; b. Rochester, N.Y., May 12, 1921; s. John Carl and Lillie Minnie (Roth) B.; m. Mary A. Massey, June 15, 1946; children: Betsy Louise, Philip Robert. BSCE, U. Mich., 1944; BS in San. Engring, U. Ill., 1945, MS, 1947, PhD, 1954; NSF faculty fellow, U. Durham, Eng., 1959-60. Research assoc. U. Ill., 1947-53; assoc. prof. civil engring. Iowa State U., 1953-56, prof., 1956-91, Anson Marston Disting. prof. engring., 1972-91, emeritus Disting. prof., 1991—. Cons. Water Quality Office of EPA, Culligan Internat., Lakeside Engring. Co., Bolton & Menk, many cities and industries. Author: Sewerage and Sewage Treatment, 1958; mem. editorial bd.: Internat. Jour. Air and Water Pollution, London, 1960-67; asst. editor: San. Engr. Newsletter of ASCE, 1962-74; contbr. articles to profl. jours. V.p., treas. Water Found., Inc., 1978-83; mem. Iowa Bd. Health, 1975-76, Iowa State U. Rsch. Found., 1975-78, 83-91. With C.E., AUS, 1944-46. Recipient George B. Gascoigne medal Water Pollution Control Fedn., 1962, 80, Publs. award, 1963, Purification divsn. award Am. Water Works Assn., 1965, Anson Marston medal Iowa Engring. Soc., 1966, Disting. Svc. award, 1968, Gold medal Filtration Soc. Eng., 1970, Bedell award, 1977, Rsch. award, 1978, Philip F. Morgan award Water Pollution Control Fedn., 1986; named Water Works Man of Yr., 1972, Disting. Alumni award U. Ill. Alumni Assn., 1992. Fellow ASCE (life), Iowa Acad. Scis. (disting. sci. 1990), Am. Filtration Separations Soc. (F.M. Tiller award 1994); mem. NSPE (nat. bd. dirs.), AAUP, Am. Water Works Assn. (hon., life, internat. bd. dirs. 1978-80), Assn. Environ. Engring. Profs. (pres. 1967-70, 86-87, Nalco award, Founders award 1991), Am. Soc. Engring. Edn., Am. Inst. Chem. Engrs., Am. Acad. Environ. Engring. (diplomate), Filtration Soc. (Eng., bd. dirs., tech. editor, vice chmn. 1993, chmn. 1994, Fluid/Particle Separation Jour.), Rotary, Sigma Xi, Phi Kappa Phi (Centennial medal 1997), Chi Epsilon. Home: 1627 Crestwood Cir Ames IA 50010-5520 Business E-Mail: rbaumann13@mchsi.com, robertba@bolton-menk.com. *It isn't enough to build a "big pie"; we must also protect its quality and learn how to cut it fairly.*

BAUMANN, ERNST FREDERICK, retired college president; b. N.Y.C., Oct. 4, 1943; s. Ernst and Grace (Crowley) B.; m. Kathleen Ann Brennan, June 17, 1967 (dec. jan. 1999); children: Ernst Frederick Jr., Lori Ann, Macushla, Katrinka, Victoria, Greta. BA, Harvard U., 1967; postgrad., Colo. U. Observer, rsch. asst. High Altitude Obs., Nat. Ctr. for Atmospheric Rsch., Boulder, Colo., 1967-69; uranium geologist, grade control engr. Kerr-McGee Corp., Casper, Wyo., 1969-71; mine geologist engr. Am. Smelting and Refining Co., Leadville, Colo., 1975; chief geologist, engr. Leadville (Colo.) Lead Corp., 1976-79; dir. adult basic edn. and gen. ednl. devel., counselor Upper Ark. Area Coun. Govts., Cañon City, Colo., 1987-96; corr. officer, supr. C.T.C.F./D.O.C., Cañon City, 1979-99; pres., chmn. Coll. of the Cañons, Cañon City, 1987-96, ret., 1996. Officer Colo. Territorial Correctional Facility, Dept. Corrections, Cañon City; recruiter Harvard U., Cañon City; pres., chmn. bd. Working in SETI Search for Extra-Terrestrial Intelligence. Co-author: Toward a New World: Powerful Proof of the Existence of God, 1995; editor: The Crucifixion; patentee mil. mountaineer's collapsible ski. Mayoral candidate City of Cañon City, 1983, 85. Maj. CAP, USAF Aux., 1980-99. Mem. K. of C. (scribe; Grand Knight). Republican. Roman Catholic. Achievements include patents in field. Home: PO Box 118 Twin Lakes CO 81251-9705

BAUMANN, HANS D., engineering executive; PhD, Columbia Pacific U. Registered profl. engr. Internat. cons., corp. v.p. Masoneilan Internat. Inc.; mgr. R&D Worthington S/A; dir. engring. CASHCO Inc.; chief engr. W & T Co.; founder H. D. Baumann Assoc. Ltd.; sr. v.p. Fisher Controls Internat., St. Louis. Bd. dirs. E&J Cating Inc., H.D. Baumann Inc. Author 4 books; co-author 5 books; contbr. numerous articles to profl. jours.; patentee 140 patents in field. Bd. govs. Palm Beach Opera Co. Fellow ASME, ISA (life); mem. Abenaqui Country Club, Govs. Club (Palm Beach). Office: HD Baumann Inc 130 International Dr Portsmouth NH 03801-6809

BAUMANN, JULIAN HENRY, JR., lawyer; b. Ft. Leavenworth, Kans., Feb. 20, 1943; s. Julian Henry and Helene (Claiborne) B.; m. Karen Ann Hofmann, July 14, 1973; children: Andrew H., Allison C. BS, Clemson U., 1965; postgrad., U. Tenn., 1966; JD, U. S.C., 1968; LLM in Taxation, NYU, 1975. Bar: S.C. 1968, Del. 1976. Assoc. Richards, Layton & Finger, Wilmington, Del., 1975-80, dir., 1980—. Served to capt., JAGC, U.S. Army, 1969-74. Fellow Am. Coll. Tax Counsel; mem. ABA, S.C. Bar Assn., Del. State Bar (chmn., sec. taxation 1990-91), Wilmington Tax Group (chmn. 1988-89), The Com. of 100 (pres. 1994-96), Bd. of Mgrs., The Nemours Found., Wilmington Club. Democrat. Roman Catholic. Home: 8 Brendle Ln Wilmington DE 19807-1300 Office: Richards Layton & Finger One Rodney Sq 10th & King Sts Wilmington DE 19801 Office Phone: 302-651-7774. Business E-Mail: baumann@rlf.com.

BAUMANN, MARTIN F., savings and loan association executive; BA in Acctg., Queens Coll.; MBA in Fin., Baruch Coll.; degree in Bus. Adminstrn., Columbia U. CPA. With PricewaterhouseCoopers, 1969—2003, ptnr., 1980—2003, World Fin. Svcs. Practice, dep. chmn.; exec. v.p. for fin. Freddie Mac, McLean, Va., 2003, exec. v.p., 2003—, CFO, 2003—. Recipient Humanitarian of the Year award, Catholic Community Services of Newark, NJ, 2001. Office: Freddie Mac 8200 Jones Branch Drive Mc Lean VA 22102-3110*

BAUMANN, RICHARD GORDON, lawyer; b. Chgo., Apr. 7, 1938; s. Martin M. and Harriet May (Granof) B.; m. Terrie Bemel, Dec. 18, 1971; children: Michelle, Alison. BS cum laude, U. Wis., 1960, JD, 1964. Bar: Wis. 1964, Calif. 1970, U.S. Supreme Ct. 1973; bd. cert. creditors rights specialist. Congressional intern U.S. Senator Hubert H. Humphrey, 1959; assoc. firm Kohner, Mann & Kailas, Milw., 1964-69, Sulmeyer, Kupetz & Alberts, L.A., 1969-73; mem. firm Sulmeyer, Kupetz, Baumann & Rothman, L.A., 1973—2003, SulmeyerKupetz, L.A., 2003—. Judge pro tem L.A. Superior Ct., 1980—. Assoc. editor Comml. Law Jour., 1991—. Fellow Comml. Law Found. (bd. dirs.); mem. Nat. Inst. on Credit Mgmt. (bd. dirs.), Am. Bd. Cert. (bd. dirs.), Acad. Comml. and Bankruptcy Law Specialists (bd. dirs.), Comml. Law League (pres. 1990-91, bd. govs. 1986-92, chmn. Western Region Mem. Assn. 1982-83). Office: 333 S Hope St 35th Fl Los Angeles CA 90071 Office Phone: 213-626-2311. Business E-Mail: rbaumann@sulmeyerlaw.com.

BAUMANN, ROBERT JAY, child neurology educator; b. Chgo., Oct. 22, 1940; s. Stephen S. and Evelyn (Hellerstein) B.; m. Judith Kravitz, Oct. 1964; children: Barbara, Stephen, Lauren. BS magna cum laude, Tufts U., 1961; MD, Western Res. U., 1964. Diplomate Am. Bd. Psychiatry and Neurology (examiner 1976—). Intern, resident in pediatrics and neurology U. Chgo. Hosps., 1965-69, fellow in child neurology, 1971-72; asst. prof. neurology U. Ky., Lexington, 1972-78, assoc. prof., 1987-92, prof., 1992—, assoc. prof. rehab., 1987—, assoc. prof. pediatrics, 1989-92, prof., 1992—, dir. regional neurology program, 1972—, dir. child neurology program, 1979—. Cons. U.S. Commn. for Control Epilepsy, Washington, 1976; reviewer, cons. Nat. Inst. Neurol. Disease and Stroke, Bethesda, Md., 1979-95; neuroepidemiology cons. Ky.-Ecuador Ptnrs. of Ams., Quito, 1987-91, Am. Acad. Pediatrics, 1991—, Instituto de Investigaciones, Facultad de Ciencias Medicas, U. Ctrl. Del Ecuador, Quito, 1991-93; cons. Min. of Health, Ecuador, 2000—, Shandong Med. Ctr., Jinan, China, 2001—; vis. lectr. Pan Am. Health Orgn., Quitos, Ecuador, 2000—. Chmn. United Jewish Appeal Campaign, Lexington, 1986-87; v.p. Cen. Ky. Jewish Fedn., Lexington, 1988-92. Capt. M.C., USAF, 1969-71. Mem. Child Neurology Soc., Am. Acad. Neurology, Am. Acad. Pediatrics (neuroepidemiologic cons. 1992—), Am. Coll. Epidemiology, Soc. for Epidemiologic Rsch., Profs. Child Neurology (bd. dirs. 1988-92). Office: U Ky Dept Neurology Ky Clinic 800 Rose St Dept L409 Lexington KY 40536-0284 Office Phone: 859-323-6702 x242.

BAUMANN, THEODORE ROBERT, aerospace engineer, consultant, military officer; b. Bklyn., May 13, 1932; s. Emil Joseph and Sophie (Reiblein) B.; m. Patricia Louise Drake, Dec. 16, 1967; children: Veronica Ann, Robert Theodore, Joseph Edmund. B in Aerospace Engring., Poly. U., Bklyn., 1954; MS in Aerospace Engring., U. So. Calif., L.A., 1962; grad., US Army C&GS Coll., 1970, Indsl. Coll. of Armed Forces, 1970, US Army War Coll., 1979, Air War Coll., 1982. Structures engr. Glenn L. Martin Co., Balt., 1954-55; structural loads engr. N.Am. Rockwell, L.A., 1958-67; dynamics engr. TRW Systems Group, Redondo Beach, Calif., 1967-71, systems engr., 1971-75, project engr., 1975-84, sr. project engr., 1984-92. Cons. SAAB-Scania Aerospace Div., Linkoping, Sweden, 1981-82; asst. dir. Dir. Weapons Systems, U.S. Army, Washington, 1981-85, staff officer Missile & Air Def. System div., 1975-81. Contbr. articles to Machine Design, tech. publs., tech. symposia. Asst. scoutmaster Boy Scouts Am., Downey, Calif., 1985-93; instr. Venice Judo Boys Club, 1966-86. Served from 2d lt. U.S. Army to col. USAR, 1954-88. Decorated Legion of Merit. Mem. AIAA; mem. Soc. Am. Mil. Engrs (life), Am. Legion, Res. Officers Assn. (life), U.S. Judo Fedn., Nat. Rifle Assn, Knights of Columbus. Republican. Roman Catholic. Achievements include developing a new method for the analysis and classification of random data; contbr. to air force ballistic missile program; devel. procedure for design of prestressed joints and fittings. Office: Theodore R Baumann & Assoc 7732 Brunache St Downey CA 90242-2206

BAUMBERGER, CHARLES HENRY, lawyer; b. Port Huron, Mich., Sept. 13, 1941; s. Peter Julius and Evelyn Margaret (Jackson) B.; m. Martha Carolyn Megathlin, Aug. 8, 1969; children: Peter Scott, Charles Henry Jr. BA, Vanderbilt U., 1963; JD, U. Fla., 1966. Bar: Fla. 1966, U.S. Dist. Ct. (so. dist.) Fla. 1967; cert. civil trial lawyer. Atty. Stephens, Demos & Magill, Miami, Fla., 1967-68; ptnr. Hastings, Goldman & Baumberger, Miami, Fla., 1969-74; founding ptnr. Rossman & Baumberger P.A., Miami, Fla., 1974—. Lectr. various continuing legal edn. programs; guest on numerous radio, TV talk shows, 1987—. Contbr. articles to profl. jours. Mem. Gov's. Task Force on Emergency Room and Trauma Care, 1987; So. Fla. Health Action Coalition, Inc., 1984; task force on trauma and trauma systems Dept. Transp., 1987—. Served to 1st lt. U.S. Army Res., 1966-72. Mem. ABA, ATLA (past chair of Profl. Negligence Sect.), Dade County Bar Assn. (bd. dirs. 1977-88, pres. 1989-90), Fla. Bar (exec. coun. trial lawyers sect. 1983-89, chmn. 1990-91), Acad. Fla. Trial Lawyers (bd. dirs. 1980-89), Dade County Trial Lawyers Assn. (founding mem. bd. dirs. 1981-84), Am. Bd. Trial Advocates (Miami chpt. past pres.), Fla. Lawyers Action Group, So. Trial Lawyers Assn., Trial Lawyers for Pub. Justice (founding mem. 1982—), Am. Coll. Trial Lawyers, Internat. Soc. Barristers, Coral Reef Yacht Club. Democrat. Methodist. Home: 5755 Suncrest Dr Miami FL 33156-5704 Office: Rossman Baumberger Reboso & Spier 44 W Flagler St Fl 23 Miami FL 33130-1808 Office Phone: 305-373-0708. Business E-Mail: Baumberger@rbrlaw.com.

BAUMBUSCH, PETER L., lawyer; b. Aug. 5, 1944; B cum laude, Dartmouth Coll., 1956; student, Magdalen Coll., Oxford, Eng., 1965—66; JD magna cum laude, Harvard Univ., 1972. Bar: US Tax Ct., DC Ct. of Appeals. Joined Gibson Dunn & Crutcher LLP, 1972—, now ptnr. tax dept. Washington. Past bd. dir. Fair Tax Found.; mem. exec. com. Gibson Dunn & Crutcher LLP. Mem. Harvard Law Rev., 1971—72. Mem.: ABA, Calif. Bar Assn. (past chair, tax section com. on fgn. activities of US taxpayers), Phi Beta Kappa. Office: Gibson Dunn & Crutcher LLP 1050 Connecticut Ave NW Washington DC 20036 Office Phone: 202-995-8530. Office Fax: 202-530-9529. Business E-Mail: pbaumbusch@gibsondunn.com.

BAUMEL, HERBERT, violinist, conductor; b. N.Y.C., Sept. 30, 1919; s. Leon and Fannie (Beckerman) B; m. Rachael Bail, Oct. 17, 1949 (div. Nov. 1970); children: Susan, Samuel, Mary Elizabeth (dec.); m. Joan Patricia French, July 11, 1971. Student, Mannes Sch. of Music, 1932-34; diploma, Curtis Inst. of Music, 1937-42; postgrad., Santa Cecilia, Accademia Chigiana, Rome and Siena, 1954-56. Violinist, concertmaster, conductor with orchs., chamber groups, Broadway shows, jazz ensembles, ballets, operas worldwide, 1939—. Baumel-Booth-Smith Trio (1st integrated classical trio to tour deep south), 1968-71; Baumel-Booth Duo, 1968-96; violinist/storyteller, 1970—, co-dir., Baumel Assocs., Yonkers, N.Y., 1984—; judge Fulbright Nat. Screening Com., 1965-67; guest artist Sponsors' Concerts of Dallas Chamber Music Soc., 1991, Internat. Piano Archives U. Md., College Park, Beveridge Webster Celebration Concert, 1991; lectr. and violinist with Dr. Joan French Baumel, 1991—, Yonkers Pub. Libr., 1992, Greenburgh (N.Y.) Pub. Libr., 1992, Waverly Heights, Gladwyne, Pa., 1993, 94, 95, Alliance Francaise, Westchester, N.Y., 1993, 94, 95, 96, 1st Unitarian Soc. Westchester, 1994, Workmen's Circle Lodge, Sylvan Lake, N.Y., 1994, Thomas Paine/Huguenot/New Rochelle (N.Y.) Hist. Soc., 1995, 96, others; commentator All Things Considered, Nat. Pub. Radio, 1999—; contbr. (mag.) Opera News, 2000—. Violinist Phila. Orch. with Ormandy, Toscanini, Walter, Monteux, Mitropoulos, Szell; first to play Samuel Barber's Violin Concerto with Curtis Symphony (Reiner), 1939 and Phila. Orch. (Ormandy); concert artist with: Stokowski, Stravinsky, Copland, Bernstein, Benny Goodman; concertmaster Phila. Opera, N.Y.C. Opera, N.Y.C. Ballet, Joe Bushkin Jazz Ensembles, (original Broadway musicals) New Girl in Town, Fiorello!, She Loves Me, Fiddler on the Roof, A Little Night Music, Rex, Dancin', also three Presdl. galas with Marilyn Monroe, Bill Cosby, Woody Allen, Jack Benny, Johnny Carson, Rudolph Nureyev, Margot Fonteyn; recs. with Heifetz, Horowitz, Rubinstein, Leonard Warren, Frank Sinatra, Edith Piaf, Tallulah Bankhead, many others; writer script and music ednl. audio-visual program The Art of Listening, 1972—; composer: Fiddlers Two, 1976, Caprice #48 1/2, 1978, Sentiment America, 1984, arranger selections from Fiddler on the Roof, 1971, 2001. Mem. adv. bd. Mark Brent Dolinsky Found., White Plains, N.Y., 1982—; played benefits for Westchester Assn. Retarded Citizens, 1982—, Coalition for the Homeless,Westchester County, N.Y., 1986—. Recipient Silver medal New York Music Week Assn., 1928, Gold medal New York Music Week Assn., 1929; 2-time Fulbright scholar to Rome, 1954-56; chosen for both Stokowski All-American Youth Orch. tours, S.Am., U.S., 1940, 41; chosen to organize, present and play concerts for U.S. Embassy and Cultural Offices throughout Italy with Anna Moffo, Ezio Flagello, Ivan Davis, Gimi Beni, and in honor of Queen Elisabeth of Belgium, 1954-56, Phila. Drama Guild Lectr. Series, 1978. Mem. Am. Fedn. Musicians, Curtis Inst. of Music Alumni Assn., Phila. Orch. Retirees and Friends. Democrat. Jewish. Avocations: tennis, gardening, reading, photography, chess. Home and Office: Baumel Assocs 86 Rosedale Rd Yonkers NY 10710-3033

BAUMEL, JOAN PATRICIA FRENCH, writer, educator; b. Winona, Minn., Mar. 12, 1930; d. William Oswald and Gertrude Marie (Fitzgerald) French; m. Herbert Baumel, July 11, 1971. Student, l'Ecole du Louvre, France, 1950-51; student with high honors, Inst. Phonétique Sorbonne, Paris, 1950-51; BA magna cum laude, Douglass Coll., 1952; postgrad., U. Detroit, 1952-55, Case Western Reserve U., 1960, U. Akron, 1962, U. Notre Dame, 1963, Manhattanville Coll., 1971; MA in French, Rutgers U., 1965; PhD in Modern Langs., Fordham U., 1985. Tchr. French lang. and culture, elem. and coll. levels various schs. including Mother House of Religious of the Sacred Heart, Kenwood, Albany, N.Y., Ohio, Mich., 1955-66; tchr. French White Plains (N.Y.) Pub. High Sch., 1966-86; curricula creator Akron (Ohio) Pub. Schs., 1962-63; co-dir. Baumel Assocs., Yonkers, N.Y., 1984—, Concerts and Lectures with Herbert Baumel, 1991—, Words and Music Programs with Herbert Baumel, 1991—, Yonkers Pub. Libr., 1992, Waverly Heights, Gladwyne, Pa., 1993-95, Workmen's Circle Lodge, Sylvan Lake, N.Y., 1994, Thomas Paine/Huguenot Hist. Soc., New Rochelle, N.Y., 1995—. Lectr. French lang. and culture Yonkers (N.Y.) Pub. Libr., 1992, Greenburgh (N.Y.) Pub. Libr., 1992; lectr. anti-semitism CUNY Grad. Ctr., 1988—, B'nai B'rith Internat. Mus., Washington, 1st Unitarian Soc., Westchester, N.Y., Rockland (N.Y.) Ctr. for Holocaust Studies, Unitarian Ch. of All Souls, N.Y.C., Temple Beth Israel, Port Washington, N.Y., Holocaust Resource Ctr. and Archives, Queensborough C.C., CUNY, 1991, Women's Am. ORT, Midchester Jewish Ctr., Yonkers, 1992, 2000, Ctrl. Queens YM & YWCA, N.Y.C., 1992, 2000, Jewish Cmty. Ctr., Scarsdale, N.Y., 2001. Author: Paul Claudel and the Jews: A Study in Ambivalence, 1985; lectr. topics include French Anti-Semitism; The Gallic Road to the Concentration Camp; Klaus Barbie and the Children of Izieu, Kristallnacht Remembered, numerous others. Mem. adv. bd. Mark Brent Dolinsky Meml. Found. Recipient Woodrow Wilson fellowship, 1958-59, Yearbook Dedication award White Plains (N.Y.) Pub. H.S., 1980. Mem. Am. Assn. Tchrs. French, White Plains Tchrs. Assn., N.Y. State Assn. Fgn. Lang. Tchrs., French Inst./Alliance Francaise, Alliance Francaise Westchester, Phi Beta Kappa. Avocations: tennis, gardening, music, reading. Home and Office: Baumel Assocs 86 Rosedale Rd Yonkers NY 10710-3033

BAUMER, BEVERLY BELLE, journalist; b. Hays, Kans., Sept. 23, 1926; d. Charles Arthur and Mayme Mae (Lord) B.; BS, William Allen White Sch. Journalism, U. Kans., 1948. Summer intern reporter Hutchinson (Kans.) News, 1946-47; continuity writer, women's program dir. Sta. KWBW, Hutchinson, 1948-49; dist. editor Salina (Kans.) Jours., 1950-57; commd. writer State of Kans. Centennial Year, 1961; contbg. author: Ford Times, Kansas City Star, Wichita (Kans.) Eagle, Ojibway Publs., Billboard, Modern Jeweler, Floor Covering Weekly, other bus. mags., 1962-69; owner and mgr. apts., Hutchinson, 1970—; broadcaster Reading Radio Room, Sta. KHCC-FM, Hutchinson, 1982—, columnist The Hutchinson (Kans.) Record, 1983-86; info. officer, maj. Kans. Wing Hdqrs. CAP, 1969-72; participant People to People Citizen Ambassador program, People's Republic of China, summer 1988. Mem. Republican Presdl. Task Force. Recipient Human Interest Photo award Nat. Press Women, 1956, News Photo award AP, 1952. Mem. Fellows Menninger Found., Suffolk County Hist. Soc., Nat. Fedn. Press Women, Kans. Press Women (Comm. Contest award 1986), Am. Soc. Profl. and Exec. Women, Am. Film Inst., Nat. Soc. Magna Charta Dames, Nat. Soc. Daus. Founders and Patriots Am., Nat. Soc. Daus. Am. Colonists, Kans. Soc. Daus. Am. Colonists (organizing regent Dr. Thomas Lord chpt., state chmn. insignia com.), Nat. Soc. Sons and Daus. Pilgrims (elder Kans. br.), D.A.R., Ben Franklin Soc. (nat. adv. bd.), Daus. Colonial Wars, Order Descs. Colonial Physicians and Chirurgiens, Colonial Dames 17th Century (chaplain, charter mem. Henry Woodhouse chpt.), Plantagenet Soc., Internat. Platform Soc., U. Kans. Alumni Assn., Nat. Geneal. Soc. Author book of poems, 1941; editor: A Simple Bedside Book for People Who Are Kinda, Sorta Interested in Genealogy, 1983. Home and Office: 122 Downing Rd Hutchinson KS 67502-4453 *Kindness belongs in business, the professions and the trades. It is the most sincere form of good will and leaves no one uncomfortable.*

BAUMER, EDWARD FERDINAND, finance company executive; b. Irvington, N.J., Dec. 5, 1913; s. Ferdinand Fred and Augusta Baumer (Wagemann) B.; m. Elizabeth Karl, Feb. 10, 1940 (dec. June 2002); children: Edward K. (dec.), Richard Eaton, Jane Elizabeth Woodman. B in Liberal Arts, Rutgers U., 1934, JSD, LLB, 1937. Bar: N.J. Advanced through grades to brig. gen. U.S. Army, 1973, commd., 1934, ret., 1973; dir. advt., pub. rels. Prudential Ins. Co. Am., L.A., 1934-55; v.p. McCann Erickson Comm., N.Y.C., 1955-59, Union Bank, L.A., 1959-61; sr. v.p. Great Western Fin. Corp., Beverly Hills, Calif., 1961-65; pres., CEO, E.F. Baumer & Co., L.A., 1965-87; chmn. Baumer Fin. Publ., L.A., 1987; chmn., pres., CEO, World-Wide Super Sr. Sports, L.A., 1999—. Chmn. emeritus Baumer Fin. Publ., L.A., 1997— (affiliate Imagination Publ. Chgo.); v.p. Union Bank, L.A. Named capt., USA's Billy Talbert Cup Tennis Team, 2004—; named to All-Am. Water Polo Team, 1934. Mem. Calif. Club, La Jolla Beach & Tennis Club, Internat. Lawn Tennis Club of U.S.A. Republican. Protestant. Achievements include winning 15 sr. European Tennis Championships, 2 USTA Natl. Championships and 3 World ITF Tennis Championship (doubles), 1997-99. Home and Office: # 1504 1820 Avenida Del Mundo Coronado CA 92118-4039 Office Phone: 619-435-1444. Office Fax: 619-435-2156.

BAUMER, MARTHA ANN, minister; b. Cleve., Sept. 12, 1938; d. Harry William and Olga Erna (Zenk) B. BA, Lakeland Coll., 1960; MA, U. Wyo., 1963; MDiv, United Theol. Sem., 1973; D Ministry, Eden Theol. Sem., 1990. Parish minister Congl. United Ch. of Christ, Amery, Wis., 1973-79; organizing minister United Ch. of Santa Fe (N.Mex.), 1979-85; conf. minister Ill. South Conf. United Ch. of Christ, Highland, Ill., 1985-93; pastor Windsor (Wis.) United Ch. of Christ, 1993-99; vis. prof. pastoral studies Eden Theol. Sem., St. Louis, 1999—. Trustee pension bds. United Ch. of Christ, N.Y.C., 1983—, mem., chair exec. coun., 1977-83; del. World Coun. Chs., 1961, 83; trustee Eden Theol. Sem., St. Louis, 1990-99. Contbr. articles to profl. publs. Mem. Coun. of Conf. Ministers United Ch. of Christ (sec.-treas. 1989-93). Home: 814 Amherst Dr East Alton IL 62024 Office: Eden Theol Sem 475 E Lockwood Ave Saint Louis MO 63119-3124 E-mail: mbaumer@eden.edu.

BAUMGARDNER, BARBARA BORKE, publishing consultant; b. Harrisburg, Pa., Nov. 8, 1937; d. Otto Lockhart Borke and Margaretta Mildred (Feigley) Borke Traugh; m. E. Wayne Baumgardner, July 12, 1958; children: Brian Wayne, Bruce Edward. AB, Gettysburg (Pa.) Coll., 1959; MLA, Western Md. Coll., 1976, MEd, 1982. Cert. secondary tchr., Md. Sales promoter Scott, Foresman & Co., Chgo., 1959-60; tchr. Carroll County Pub. Schs., Westminster, Md., 1964-84; cons. McDougall, Littell & Co., Evanston, Ill., 1984-91. Adj. prof. Western Md. Coll., Westminster, 1975. Mem. Savannah Symphony Women's Guild. Mem. Women's Assn. Hilton Head, Mensa, Fed. Garden Clubs of Md., Phi Mu. Republican. Presbyterian. Avocations: skiing, floral design, poetry, bridge, golf. also: PO Box 1642 6635 Silver Lake Dr Park City UT 84060

BAUMGARDNER, EDWARD, financial company executive; CEO, pres. Potters Fin. Corp., East Liverpool, Ohio, 1994—. Office: Potters Fin Corp 519 Broadway St East Liverpool OH 43920-3137 Fax: 330-385-3508.

BAUMGARDNER, JAMES LEWIS, history professor; b. Bristol, Va., Jan. 26, 1938; s. John Richard and Roxie Katherine (Lewis) B.; children: Ellen Lorena, James Michael; m. Paula Louise Jones; stepchildren: Joseph Branscome, Sarah Elizabeth Brock. AA, Bluefield Jr. Coll., 1957; BA, Carson-Newman Coll., 1959; MA, U. Tenn., Knoxville, 1964, PhD, 1968. Ordained to ministry Baptist Ch., 1955. Asst. prof. history Carson-Newman Coll., Jefferson City, Tenn., 1964-67, assoc. prof., 1967-73, prof., 1973—, chmn. history-polit. sci., dept., 1974-95. Contbr. articles to learned jours. Interim mem. Jefferson County (Tenn.) Bd. Sch. Commrs., 1978; mem. Anderson County (Tenn.) Bd. Edn., 1990-94; active interim, bivocation pastor. Served with U.S. Army, 1959-62. Named Bivocational Pastor of the Yr., Tenn. Bapt. Conv., 1997. Mem. Am. Hist. Assn., Acad. Polit. Sci., Orgn. Am. Historians, So. Hist. Assn., Bapt. History & Heritage Soc., Phi Alpha Theta. Office: Carson-Newman Coll PO Box 71929 Jefferson City TN 37760-7001

BAUMGARDNER, JOHN ELLWOOD, JR., lawyer; b. Balt., Jan. 6, 1951; s. John Ellwood and Nancy G. (Brandenburg) B.; m. Astrid Rehl, Sept. 7, 1974; children: Jeffrey Mark, Julia Alexis. AB, Princeton Univ., 1973; JD, Columbia Univ., 1975. Bar: NY 1976. Assoc. Sullivan & Cromwell, NYC, 1975-83, ptnr., 1983—, also coord. investment mgmt. practice area and mem. Fin. Institutions, Investment Mgmt. Broker-Dealer and Commodities, Futures and Derivatives Groups. Supervisory dir. The Turkish Pvt. Equity Investment Co., 1991-93; trustee JPM Advisor Funds, 1996. Vice chair gen. dir.'s coun. N.Y.C. Opera. Mem.: ABA, Assn. Bar City NY (chair com. on investment mgmt. regulation 2000—03), NY State Bar Assn., Nat. Dance Inst. (bd. dirs. 1988—89), Princeton Club. Office: Sullivan & Cromwell LLP 125 Broad St Fl 32 New York NY 10004-2498 Office Phone: 212-558-4000. Office Fax: 212-558-3588. E-mail: baumgardnerj@sullcrom.com.

BAUMGARDNER, MATTHEW CLAY, artist; b. Columbus, Ohio, Feb. 5, 1955; s. Alan Wirth and Mary Lou (Weidner) B.; m. Heather Evans; children: Zoe Klee, Eva Evans, Lila Joy, Sofi Clare. MFA, U. N.C., 1982. One-man shows include Presbyn. Coll., Clinton, S.C., 1980, Sumter (S.C.) Gallery, 1981, Wilkov/Goldfeder, N.Y.C., 1987, Wessel O'Connor Ltd., N.Y.C., 1988, 89, Howard Yezerski Gallery, Boston, 1992, Charles Cowles Gallery, N.Y.C., 1993, Gallery A, Chgo., 1995, Bentley Gallery, Scottsdale, Ariz., 1998, MD Modern, Houston, 1998, Jeffrey Coploff Fine Art, 2000, 2001, Bentley Gallery, Scottsdale, Ariz., 2000, Jeffrey Coploff Fin Art, 2001; group exhbns. include Spartenburg (S.C.) Arts Ctr., 1979, Columbia (S.C.) Mus., 1979, Clemson (S.C.) U., 1980, Greenville (S.C.) County Mus., 1980, Greater Birmingham (Ala.) Arts Alliance, 1981, Gibbes Mus., Charleston, S.C., 1981, Mint Mus., Charlotte, N.C., 1981, Ackland Mus., Chapel Hill, N.C., 1982, Huntington (W.Va.) Mus., 1982, Edward Thorp Gallery, N.Y.C., 1985 Hudson Ctr. Gallery, N.Y.C., 1985, Edward Thorp Gallery, N.Y.C., 1985, Mokotoff Gallery, N.Y.C., 1985, 86, Wilkov/Goldfeder, N.Y.C., 1987, Trenton (N.J.) City Mus., 1988, Wessel O'Connor Ltd., N.Y.C., 1989, Stephanie Theodore Gallery, N.Y.C., 1991, Art Dealers Assn. Am., N.Y.C., 1993, New Mus. Contemporary Art, N.Y.C., 1993, Trans Hudson Gallery, Jersey City, 1993, N.Y.C., 1997, Gallery A, Chgo., 1994, 95, 98, Gallerie Marie-Louise Wirth,

Zurich, Switzerland, 1995, Bentley Gallery, Scottsdale, Ariz., 1997, MD Modern, Houston, 1998, Jeffrey Coploff Fine Art, N.Y.C., 1999, 2000, Bemis Ctr., Omaha City, Nebr., 1999, LewAllen Contemporary, Santa Fe, N. Mex., 2000. Recipient Purchase awards Mint Mus., Charlotte, N.C., 1981, Gibbes Mus., Charleston, S.C., 1981; Visual Artist fellow Nat. Endowment for the Arts, Washington, 1993. Episcopalian. Office: 241 6th Ave 10-B New York NY 10014 E-mail: baumeye@hotmail.com.

BAUMGARDT, BILLY RAY, professional society administrator, agriculturist; b. Lafayette, Ind., Jan. 17, 1933; s. Raymond P. and Mildred L. Baumgardt; m. D. Elaine Blain, June 8, 1952; children: Pamela K. Baumgardt Farley, Teresa Jo Baumgardt Adolfsen, Donald Ray. BS in Agr., Purdue U., 1955, MS, 1956; PhD, Rutgers U., 1959. From asst. to assoc. prof. U. Wis., Madison, 1959-67; prof. animal nutrition Pa. State U., University Park, 1967-70, head dept. dairy and animal sci., 1970-79, assoc. dir. agrl. expt. sta., 1979-80; dir. agrl. research, assoc. dean Purdue U., West Lafayette, Ind., 1980-98; exec. v.p. Am. Registry Profl. Animal Scientists, Savoy, Ill., 1998—2003; coord. DISCOVER conf. series Am. Dairy Sci. Assn., Savoy, 1998—. Contbr. chapters to books, articles to profl. sci. jours. Recipient Wilkinson award, Pa. State U., 1979. Fellow: AAAS, Am. Soc. Nutritional Sci., Am. Dairy Sci. Assn. (pres. 1984—85, Nutrition Rsch. award 1966, award of Honor 1993, Disting. Svc. award 2003); mem.: Nat. Agrl. Biotech. Coun. (chair 1993—94), Am. Soc. Animal Sci., Am. Inst. Nutrition, Rotary, Sigma Xi. Home and Office: 2741 N Salisbury St West Lafayette IN 47906-1431 Personal E-mail: bbaum@gte.net. Business E-Mail: baumgardt@purdue.edu.

BAUMGARDT, GEORGE FRANCIS, bank executive, musician, director; b. Racine, Wis., Apr. 23, 1950; s. Richard Bernard and Blanche Marie Baumgardt; m. Mary Anne Braun, Aug. 3, 1974; children: Gretchen Marie, Erika Ann Slater, Richard Joseph, George Thomas, Gregory John. BA in Music Edn., U. Wis., Kenosha, Wis., 1974; student in Banking and Lending, Am. Banking Assn., 1988—89. 1st v.p. Bank Elmwood, Racine, Wis., 1969—. Pres. Am. Inst. Banking, Racine, 1978—88, instr., 1982—94; bd. dir. Cmty. Econ. Devel. Corp, Racine; pres. Ctr. Cmty. Concerns, Racine, 1986—95; dir. liturgical music St. Paul the Apostle Cath. Ch., Racine, 1965—80, Sacred Heart Cath. Ch., Racine, Wis., 1980—. Composer: (songs) Liturgical Music; dir.: (choir) Salzburg Mozart Music Festival, 2002, Sacred Heart Church Choir, 1999. Sec. Cmty. Econ. Devel. Corp, Racine; bd. dir. Alliance Mentally Ill, Racine, 2001—, United Way, Racine, 1994—96, Ctr. Cmty. Concerns, Racine, 1986—2004. Named Ch. Musician of Yr., Racine County, 1996, Loan Officer of Year, Racine County Economic Devel. Corp., 1996, 1997, 1998, 1999. Mem.: Nat. Assn. Pastoral Musicians, Am. Liturgical Musicians Am. (assoc.), Kenosha Country Club. Roman Catholic. Avocations: golf, travel, music. Home: 5310 Lathrop Ave Racine WI 53403 Office: Bank of Elmwood 2704 Lathrop Ave Racine WI 53405 Office Phone: 262-554-5321.

BAUMGARDT, JUSTI MICHELLE, professional soccer player; b. Federal Way, Wash., July 22, 1975; m. Tote Yamada. Student in sociology, U. Portland. Former mem. US Women's Nat. Soccer Team; mem. Wash. Freedom Women's United Soccer Assn., 2001, mem. N.Y. Power, 2002—. Named Athlete of Yr., Seattle Times, 1993, Player of Yr., State of Wash., 2-time H.S. All-Am., Most Valuable Player, U. Portland, 1994, WCC Player of Yr., 1996. Achievements include playing in Nike Victory Tour, St. Charles, Ill., 1997; Nordic Cup, Denmark, 1993; Germany, 1994. Office: US Soccer Fedn 1801-1811 S Prairie Ave Chicago IL 60616

BAUMGART, JESSICA K., librarian; d. Linda and David Baumgart, Ruth Baumgart (Stepmother). BA, Newberry Coll., Newberry, SC, 1993; MA in Libr. and Info. Studies, U. of Wis., 2000. Student asst. Wessels Libr., Newberry Coll., Newberry, SC, 1993—97; libr. project assistantship Office of News & Pub. Affairs, U. of Wis., Madison, 1997—2000; info. resources specialist Office of News & Pub. Affairs, Harvard U., Cambridge, Mass., 2000—. Author: (weblog) J's Scratchpad. Recipient SLA President's Club, Spl. Libraries Assn., 2005, Feedster Developers Contest, Feedster, 2004, Chpt. Achievement award, Spl. Libraries Assn. Boston Chpt., 2005; grantee Vormelker-Thomas Student award, Spl. Libraries Assn. News Divsn., 2000. Mem.: ALA, New Eng. News Librs. Assn., Am. Soc. for Info. Sci. & Tech., Spl. Libraries Assn., Weblog Writers Group.

BAUMGARTEN, DIANA VIRGINIA, gerontological nurse; b. Bklyn., May 24, 1943; d. Francis and Leah (Cuoghi) DeMarco; married; children: Elizabeth Salonia, Matthew, Edward. AS, Broward C.C., 1991. RN, Fla. Pediats. staff nurse North Broward Med. Ctr., Pompano Beach, Fla., 1991; staff nurse Tamarac (Fla.) Convalescent Ctr., 1992, nursing supr. Ft. Lauderdale, Fla., 1992-93; corp. nurse cons. HBA Health Mgmt. Corp., Ft. Lauderdale, Fla., 1993-94; acting DON Broward Convalescent Home, Ft. Lauderdale, 1994; acting asst. DON Springtree Walk Nursing Ctr., Sunrise, Fla., 1994; resident assessment coord., infection control officer Broward Convalescent Home, Ft. Lauderdale, 1994-95; asst. dir. nursing Adon Hillhaven Convalescent Ctr., Fla., 1995-97; dir. nursing Menorah House, 1997-98; legal nurse cons., case mgr. J.R. Health Mgmt., 1998-99; nurse specialist State of Fla., Agy. for Health Care Adminstrn., 1999—2001; geriatric care mgr. Eldercare Mgmt. Inst., 2001—; Q1 specialist Hospice and Home Care by the Sea, 2001—. Mem. ANA, Nat. Gerontol. Nurses Assn., Fla. Nurses' Assn., Phi Theta Kappa. Avocations: flute, classical music. Home: 11417 Little Bear Dr Boca Raton FL 33428-2609

BAUMGARTEN, JON A., lawyer; b. N.Y.C., Oct. 26, 1942; m. Jodi Rush, Jan. 1, 1983. BA, CCNY, 1964; LLB, NYU, 1967. Bar: N.Y. 1968, U.S. Ct Appeals (4th cir.) 1977, D.C. 1980, U.S. Supreme Ct. 1982, U.S. Dist. Ct. D.C. 1983, U.S. Ct. of Appeals, Sixth Circuit, 1994. Assoc. Parker Chapin Flattau, NYC, 1968-70, Linden & Deutsch, NYC, 1970-75; gen. counsel U.S. Copyright Office, Washington, 1976-79; ptnr. Paskus Gordon & Mandel, Washington, 1979-86; ptnr., intellectual property dept. Proskauer Rose LLP, Washington, 1986—. Mem. Internat. Copyright Panel of Adv. Com. to Dept. of State on Internat. Intellectual Property, Adv. Com. to U.S. Copyright Office, Ad Hoc Working Group on Adherence to Berne Convention, Nat. Adv. Com. to U.S. Copyright Office, Internat. Copyright Panel, U.S. State Dept. Author: U.S.-U.S.S.R. Copyright Relations Under the Universal Copyright Convention, 1973; contbr. articles to profl. jours.; mem. editorial bd. Jour. Copyright Soc. U.S.A., Patent, Trademark and Copyright Jour., World Intellectual Property Report, Computer Lawyer, Jour. Proprietary Rights. Named one of Best Lawyers in Am., Best Lawyers in Washington. Mem. ABA Patent Trademark and Copyright Law Sect. (chair various coms.), Copyright Soc. of the U.S.A. (trustee 1975-78, 1992—). Office: Proskauer Rose LLP 1233 20th St NW Ste 800 Washington DC 20036-2377

BAUMGARTEN, PAUL ANTHONY, retired lawyer; b. N.Y.C., July 31, 1934; s. Louis S. and Margaret (Karol) B.; m. Susan T., Feb. 21, 1960; children— Stephen, Michael, Lisa, Deborah BA, Swarthmore Coll., 1955; LLB, Harvard U., 1958. Bar: N.Y. Assoc. Otterbourg Steindler, Houston Rosen, N.Y.C., 1958-66; assoc. Halperin, Morris, Granett & Cowan, N.Y.C., 1960; with legal dept. Hill & Range Songs Inc., 1960-62, Warner Bros. Pictures Inc., 1962-64, Embassy Pictures Corp., 1964-70; ptnr. Krause, Hirsch & Gross, 1970-77, Rosenman & Colin, LLP, N.Y.C., 1977—2001, counsel, 2001—. Co-chmn. workshops on motion picture industry Practicing Law Inst.; trustee Copyright Soc. U.S., 1989-91. Co-author: Producing, Financing & Distributing Film (revised and expanded edition), 1992. Mem. Columbia Artists Mgmt. Inc. (dir.). Avocations: classical music, sailing, tennis. Home: 61 W Gate Blvd Plandome NY 11030-1452 Office: Katten Muchin Zavis Rosenman 575 Madison Ave New York NY 10022-2585 E-mail: paul_baumgarten@yahoo.com.

BAUMGARTEN, RONALD NEAL, lawyer; b. Chgo., May 13, 1942; s. Albert and Beatrice (Loseff) B.; m. Aloha Herman, Aug. 27, 1966; children: Brett, Reed, Jaclyn, Blake. BA, U. Ill., 1964, JD, 1966. Bar: Calif. 1970, U.S. Dist. Ct. (cen. dist.) Calif. 1970, U.S. Ct. Appeals (9th cir.) 1973, U.S. Supreme Ct. 1975. Gen. counsel, chief ops. officer Elgin Jewelry Distbrs. Inc., L.A., 1967-72, also bd. dirs.; assoc. Grobe, Rinestein, Freid & Katz P.L.C., Beverly Hills, Calif., 1972-75; ptnr. Jacobs & Baumgarten P.L.C., Beverly Hills, 1975-80; CEO Baumgarten & Greene P.L.C., Santa Monica, Calif., 1980-88; pvt. practice law Santa Monica, 1988-89, L.A., 1989—; sr. v.p. Comml. Fin. Ctr., 1991-95, also bd. dirs.; pres. Occidental Svcs., Inc., 1992-95; pres., CEO, sole shareholder Holmby Investments, Inc., 1994—, Baumgarten Property Mgmt. Svcs., Inc., 1994—; v.p., sec. Sierra Crest Equities, LLC, 1997—, Corner Stone Real Estate Investment, Inc., 1997—; CEO Sierra Sr. Cmtys. LLC, 2001—; mem. Coastal Ptnrs., LLC, 2004—. Chmn., CEO, COO, J.D. Alexander & Assocs., Inc., LA, 1980-92; asst. prof. law U. San Fernando Valley, Calif., 1974. Mem. L.A. World Affairs Coun., 1974—, L.A. Olympic Citizens Adv. Commn., 1982-84, Town Hall, 1983—; exec. v.p., gen. counsel, bd. dirs. Variety-The Children's Charity, 1974-2000, Variety Boy's and Girl's Club, L.A., pres., 1996-99, bd. dirs., 1981—; founder 1st Bus. Bank, L.A., 1981. Mem. ABA, Calif. Bar Assn., LA County Bar Assn., Beverly Hills Bar Assn., Phi Delta Phi, Auburn Rotary Club. Office: 10590 Wilshire Blvd Ste 201 Los Angeles CA 90024 also: Ste 120 2237 Douglas Blvd Roseville CA 95661 Office Phone: 916-660-0201. Personal E-mail: rbpacpal@aol.com. Business E-Mail: rbaumgarten@coastalpartners.net.

BAUMGARTEN, SIDNEY, lawyer; b. NYC, July 30, 1933; s. Abraham and Doris (Kanarick) B.; children: Douglas, Frederick, Roger, Julia. AB, Brown U., 1954; JD, NYU, 1960. Bar: N.Y. 1961, U.S. Dist. Ct. (ea. and so. dists.) N.Y. 1961, U.S. Ct. Claims 1961, U.S. Ct. Appeals (2d cir.) 1961. Asst. mgmt., field underwriter Home Life Ins. Co., 1957-61; sole practice, 1961-67; asst. dist. atty. Queens County, N.Y., 1967-68; law sec. to presiding justice State of N.Y., Queens, 1968-73; asst. to Mayor City of N.Y., 1974-77; gen. counsel Phoenix House Found., 1978-80; sr. ptnr. Baumgarten, Swiedler & Waxman, N.Y.C., 1980-88; pvt. practice N.Y.C., 1989-94; pres., CEO Spectral Biosci. Corp., 1994—. Lectr. various seminars, assns. and ednl. instns; adj. prof. law N.Y. Inst. Tech.; vis. prof. Found. U. Cardiology, Brazil, 1996. Pres. N.Y.'s Finest Found., 1993; bd. dirs., chmn. N.Y. Therapeutic Communities, Inc.; trustee Lawrence Country Day Sch. (pres. 1985-87). Served with U.S. Army, 1954—56, with Res., 1956—73, brig. gen. Army Div., 2001—, N.Y. Guard. Decorated Companion Order of Merit SMOTJ, N.Y. State Conspicuous Svc. medal. Mem.: NAHC, VFW, NRA (life), East Side C. of C. (pres. 1983—86, chmn. 1987—), Am. Legion. Office: 355 South End Ave Ste 31J New York NY 10280 Office Phone: 212-775-0190.

BAUMGARTNER, ANTON EDWARD, automotive sales professional; b. NYC, May 18, 1948; s. Hans and Carmen Maria (Figueroa) B.; m. Brenda Lee Lemmon, May 24, 1969 (div. 1990); 1 child, Anton Nicholaus; m. Virginia Thiele, 1992 (div. 2004); 1 child, Bree Alexandra. BS, Woodbury U., 1970. Sales mgr. Maywood Bell Ford, Bell, Calif., 1966-69, O.R. Haan, Inc., Santa Ana, Calif., 1969-72; pres. Parkinson Volkswagen, Placentia, Calif., 1972-77; exec. v.p. United Moped, Fountain Valley, Calif., 1975-82; pres. Automobili Intermeccanica, Fountain Valley, 1975-82; gen. mgr. Bishop (Calif.) Volkswagen-Bishop Motors, 1982-85, Beach Imports-Irvine Imports, Newport Beach, Calif., 1985-88; chmn. bd. Stan and Ollie Ins. Co., Santa Ana, Calif., 1989—92; exec. v.p. Asterism, Inc., 1992-96; chmn. Marich Acceptance Inland Empire, 1996—98; gen. mgr. Saturn Retail Enterprises, Anaheim, Calif., 1999—2005, Swedish Cars of Orange County, 2005—. Mem. faculty, Automotive World Congress, Detroit, 1980. Contbr. articles to weekly serial publs. Mem. Coachbuilders Assn. N.Am. (sec. 1975-78). Home: 29401 Port Royal Way Laguna Niguel CA 92677-7945 Office: Saturn Retail Enterprises Anaheim CA 92806 Office Phone: 714-542-7060. Personal E-mail: tbaumgartner@cox.net.

BAUMGARTNER, INGEBORG, foreign language educator; b. Horna Stubna, Czechoslovakia, Jan. 29, 1936; came to U.S., 1949; m. Jörg Baumgartner, Nov. 25, 1967; 1 child, Nicholas. BA, U. Mich., 1958, PhD, 1970; MA, U. Wis., 1959. Prof. dept. fgn. langs. Albion (Mich.) Coll., 1966—2001, assoc. provost, 1982-85, prof. emeritus, 2001—. Editor: There You Are, 1982; contbr.articles to profl. jours. Home: 411 Darrow St Albion MI 49224-2226

BAUMGARTNER, JAMES EDUMND, pediatric neurosurgeon; b. Detroit, Jan. 22, 1957; s. Ed and Mary Baumgartner; m. Linda Susan Jones, May 4, 1985; children: Alexander James, John Adam, Catherine Joyce Baumgarnter, Michael Evan. BS, U. Mich., 1979; MPhil, U. Cambridge, Eng., 1981; MD, U. Mich., 1985. Bd. Cert. in Neurosurgery Am. Bd. of Neurol. Surgery, 1998. Intern surgery U. Calif., San Francisco, 1985—86, resident neurol. surgery, 1986—91, fellow pediat. neurosurgery, 1991—92; assoc. prof. surgery U. Tex., 1992—. Chief pediatric epilepsy surgeon Tex. Comprehensive Epilepsy Program, U. Tex., 1992—; craniofacial neurosurgeon, cleft and craniofacial team U. Texas, 1992—; chief pediat. neurosurgery Shriner's Hosp., Houston, 1993—. Author (surgeon): (jour. articles) Pediatric Epilepsy Surgery/Craniofacial Surgery. Asst. scout master Boy Scouts of Am., Houston; advisor Gulf Coast Epilepsy Found., Houston, 2002—03; youth soccer coach West U. Soccer Club, Houston, 1997—2003. Mem.: Congress of Neurol. Surgeons, Am. Assn. of Neurol. Surgeons. Presbyterian. Achievements include development of novel surg. approaches to craniofacial and pediat. epilepsy surgery. Avocations: running, hiking, camping. Office: Univ of Texas-Houston 6431 Fannin St MSB 5228 Houston TX 77030 Office Phone: 713-500-7285. Personal E-mail: james.e.baumgartner@uth.tmc.edu.

BAUMGARTNER, JOHN H., gas industry executive; b. 1936; married. With Clark Oil & Refining Corp., Milw., 1956-82, retail sales rep., 1960-65, dist. mgr., 1965-72, regional mgr., 1972-74, v.p. retail mktg., asst. gen. sales mgr., 1974-75, sr. v.p. mktg., 1975-78, exec. v.p., 1978-82; pres. J.H. Baumgartner Enterprises, Brookfield, Wis., 1982—; v.p., owner Robert Kidd & Assocs. Inc., 1990—. Served with USMC, 1954-56.

BAUMGARTNER, ROBERT, investment company executive, consultant; b. Dallas, Aug. 20, 1934; s. Oren Floyd and Jessie Elizabeth (Seale) B.; m. Sabina Jumatayeva, Aug. 1, 1998; children: Janet, Cathy, Diane, Mitchell. BBA, So. Meth. U., 1956. V.p. Rep. Nat. Bank, Dallas, 1958-70, Bank of Southwest, Houston, 1970-71; v.p., treas. Marathon Mfg. Co., Inc., Houston, 1971-78; CEO Amistad Well Svc., Houston, 1978-79; treas. Anderson Clayton & Co., Inc., Houston, 1980-82; pres. Baumgartner Capital, Austin, Tex., 1982—. Mem. Assn. Corp. Growth, Fin. Execs. Inst., Beta Gamma Sigma. Republican. Methodist. Avocations: golf, travel. Home and Office: Tex Bus Svcs 12400 Wycliff Ln Austin TX 78727-5219 Office Phone: 512-453-3400. Business E-Mail: bb@onr.com.

BAUMGARTNER, VITO H., manufacturing executive; b. Zurich, Switzerland, 1940; Grad., Swiss Sch. Commerce, MIT. Various fin. positions Caterpillar, 1963, pres.; v.p., chmn. Caterpillar overseas Caterpillar, Inc., 1990, group pres. Peoria, Ill., 2003—. Bd. dirs. SKF, Geneva Internat. Airport. Mem.: Internat. Inst. Mgmt. Devel. (mem. exec. com.), Fedn. Syndiacats Patronaux (mem. mgmt. bd.), Swiss-Am. C. of C., European-Am. Indsl. Coun.

BAUMGARTNER, WILLIAM ANTHONY, cardiac surgeon; b. Covington, Ky., Apr. 18, 1947; s. Nicholas Raymond Baumgartner and Rosemary Jones; m. Betsy Reik; children: Bill Jr., Amy, Mark. BS, Xavier U., 1969; MD, U. Ky., 1973. Cert. Am. Bd. Thoracic Surg. Intern surgery Stanford (Calif.) U. Med. Ctr., 1973-74, asst. resident gen. surgery, 1974-75, asst. resident cardiothoracic surgery, 1975-76, asst. resident cardiovasc. surgery, 1976-77, chief resident cardiovasc. surgery, 1977-78, chief resident thoracic surgery, 1978, asst. resident gen. surgery, 1978-80, chief resident, 1980-81; cardiac surgeon-in-charge Johns Hopkins U. Sch. Medicine, Balt., 1993—, Vincent L. Gott prof. Editor: (book) Heart and Heart Lung Transplantation, 1990, 2001. Grantee, NIH, 1988, 1992, 1995, 2000. Mem.: ACS, Clin. Practice Assn. (pres., vice dean clin. practice 1999—), Soc. Univ. Surgeons, Am. Assn. Thoracic Surgery, Am. Soc. Transplant Surgeons, Internat. Soc. Heart and Lung Transplantation, Soc. Thoracic Surgeons (pres. 2002—03), Am. Surg. Assn. Avocation: golf. Office: Johns Hopkins Hosp 600 N Wolfe St # 618 Baltimore MD 21287-0005 Office Phone: 410-955-5248. Business E-Mail: wbaumgar@csurg.jhmi.jhu.edu.

BAUMGARTNER, WILLIAM HANS, JR., lawyer; b. Chgo., July 24, 1955; s. William H. and Charlotte Burnette (Lange) B.; m. Andrea Jean Coath, Oct. 6, 1984. B.A., U. Chgo., 1976; J.D. magna cum laude, Harvard U., 1979. Bar: Ill. 1979, U.S. Dist. Ct. No. Ill. 1979, Ea. Wis. 1994, U.S. Ct. Appeals 3rd cir. 1996, 6th cir. 1988, 7th cir. 1992, 8th cir. 1998, 11th cir. 1994, Fed. cir. 1991. Assoc. Sidley & Austin, Chgo., 1979-86, ptnr., 1986—. Mem. ABA, Chgo. Bar Assn., Phi Beta Kappa. Office: Sidley Austin Brown & Wood LLP Bank One Plz 10 S Dearborn St Chicago IL 60603 Business E-Mail: wbaumgar@sidley.com.

BAUMHART, RAYMOND CHARLES, Roman Catholic church administrator; b. Chgo., Dec. 22, 1923; s. Emil and Florence (Weidner) B. BS, Northwestern U., 1945; PhL, Loyola U., 1952, STL, 1958; MBA, Harvard U., 1953; DBA, Harvard, 1963; LLD (hon.), Ill. Coll., 1977; DHL (hon.), Scholl Coll. Podiatric Medicine, 1983, Rush U., Chgo., 1987, Northwestern U., 1993, Xavier U., Cin., 1994, Ill. Benedictine Coll., 1994. Joined Jesuit Order, 1946; ordained priest Roman Cath. Ch., 1957. Asst. prof. mgmt. Loyola U., Chgo., 1962-64, dean Sch. Bus. Adminstrn., 1964-66, exec. v.p., acting v.p. Med. Ctr., 1968-70, pres., 1970-93; cons. to Cardinal George, Cath. Archdiocese of Chgo., 2000—. Alfred Ring lectr. U. Fla., 1988; John and Mildred Wright lectr. Fairfield U., 1992; D. B. Reinhart lectr. Viterbo Coll., 2000; bd. dirs. Ceres Food Group, Inc. Author: An Honest Profit, 1968, (with Thomas Garrett) Cases in Business Ethics, 1968, (with Thomas McMahon) The Brewer-Wholesaler Relationship, 1969; corr. editor: America, 1965-70. Trustee St. Louis U., 1967-72, Boston Coll., 1968-71; bd. dirs. Coun. Better Bus. Burs., 1971-77, Cath. Health Alliance Met. Chgo., 1986-93; mem. U.S. Bishops and Pres.'s Com. on Higher Edn., 1980-84, Jobs for Met. Chgo., 1984-85, Chgo. Health Care Industry, 1990-94. Decorated cavalier Order of Merit, Italy, 1971, commendatore, 1994; recipient Rale medallion Boston Coll., 1976, Daniel Lord S.J. award Loyola Acad., Wilmette, Ill., 1992, Mary Potter Humanitarian award Little Company of Mary Hosp., Ill., 1993, Sword of Loyola Loyola U., Chgo., 1993, Theodore Hesburgh award Assn. Cath. Colls. and Univs., 1995; John W. Hill fellow Harvard U., 1961-62, Cambridge Ctr. for Social Studies Rsch. fellow, 1966-68. Mem. Comml. Club, Mid-Am. Club, Tavern Club. Roman Catholic. Business E-Mail: rbaumhart@archdiocese-chgo.org.

BAUMHEFNER, CLARENCE HERMAN, retired bank executive; b. Lester Prairie, Minn., Apr. 1, 1912; s. Walter P. and Clare A. (Jacobs) B.; m. Virginia Haight, May 11, 1941; children— Robert, Bonnie. Grad., Am. Inst. Banking, 1940; student, Grad. Sch. Banking, Rutgers U., 1951. With Bank of Am., 1940—, Bank of Am. (inspection dept.), 1940-43, insp., 1943-47, asst. chief insp., 1947-50, asst. to cashier, 1950-56, cashier and v.p., 1956-65, sr. v.p., cashier, 1965-66, exec. v.p., 1966-70, vice chmn. bd., 1970—76. Mem.: Union Pacific Club (San Francisco), Bohemian Club, Bankers Club. Home and Office: 555 California St Ste 1100 San Francisco CA 94104-1514 Business E-Mail: lisasiew@bankofAmerica.com.

BAUMKEL, MARK S., lawyer; b. Flint, Mich., Feb. 17, 1951; s. Sherwood and Marilyn (Schiff) B.; m. Julie A. Kimbrell, Oct. 20, 1978; 1 child, Molly. BA cum laude, Oakland U., Rochester,Mich., 1973; JD cum laude, Wayne State U., 1977. Bar: Mich. 1977, U.S. Dist. Ct. Mich. 1977, U.S. Ct. Appeals (6th cir.) 1985. Assoc. dist. counsel U.S. SBA, Detroit, 1977-78; asst. pros. atty. Ingham County Prosecutor's Office, Lansing, Mich., 1978-79; assoc. atty. Shifman & Goodman, P.C., Southfield, Mich., 1979-81, Kaufman & Friedman, Southfield, 1981-84; sole practitioner Troy, Mich., 1984-94; ptnr. Provizer & Phillips, P.C., Southfield, 1994—. Mem. Assn. Trial Lawyers Am. (sustaining), Mich. Trial Lawyers Assn. (PAC contbr.), Oakland County Bar Assn., Wayne County Mediation Tribunal (mediator), Am. Arbitration Assn. (arbitrator), Oakland County Mediation (mediator). Avocations: running, bicycling, guitar. Home: 3826 Lakecrest Dr Bloomfield Hills MI 48304-3040 Office: 30200 Telegraph RD #200 Bingham Farms MI 48025-4510 Office Phone: 248-642-0444. E-mail: m.baumkelm@p-ppclawfirm.org.

BAUMOL, WILLIAM JACK, economist, educator; b. NYC, Feb. 26, 1922; s. Solomon and Lillian (Itzkowitz) B.; m. Hilda Missel, Dec. 27, 1941; children: Ellen Frances, Daniel Aaron. B Soc. Sci., CCNY, 1942; PhD, London U., 1949; LLD (hon.), Rider Coll., 1965; fellow (hon.), London Sch. Econs., 1970; fellow hon. doctorate (hon.), Stockholm Sch. Econs., Sweden, 1971, U. Basel, Switzerland, 1973; D (hon.), U. Limburg, The Netherlands, 1996, U. Belgrano, Buenos Aires, 1996, U. Lille, France, 1997; LHD (hon.), Knox Coll., 1973; PhD (hon.), Hebrew U., 1999; LHD (hon.), Princeton U., 1999; D (hon.), U. Paris, 2001. With USDA, 1942-43, 46; asst. lectr. London Sch. Econs., 1947-49; asst. prof. Princeton (N.J.) U., 1949-52, assoc. prof., 1952-54, prof., 1954-92, NYU, 1971—; joint appointment Princeton U. and NYU, 1971—; prof. emeritus Princeton U., 1992—, sr. rsch. economist, 1992—. Bd. dirs. Theatre Devel. Fund; cons. for govt. and industry. Author: Economic Dynamics: An Introduction, 1951, 3d edit., 1970, Welfare Economics and the Theory of the State, 1952, 2d edit., 1965, Business Behavior, Value and Growth, 1959, 2d edit., 1966, Economic Theory and Operations Analysis, 1960, 4th edit., 1976; author: (with L.V. Chandler) Economic Processes and Policies, 1954; author: (with Klaus Knorr) What Price Economic Growth?, 1961; author: The Stock Market and Economic Efficiency, 1965; author: (with W.G. Bowen) Performing Arts: The Economic Dilemma, 1966; author: (with S.M. Goldfeld) Precursors in Mathematical Economics, 1969; author: (with W.E. Oates) The Theory of Environmental Policy, 1975, 2d edit., 1988; author: Selected Economic Writings of William Jack Baumol, 1976; author: (with W.E. Oates and S.B. Blackman) Economics, Environmental Policy and the Quality of Life, 1979; author: (with A.S. Blinder) Economics: Principles and Policy, 1979, 6th edit., 1994; author: (with J.C. Panzar and R.D. Willig) Contestable Markets and the Theory of Industry Structure, 1982, rev. edit., 1987; author: (with H. Baumol) Inflation and the Performing Arts, 1984; author: (with K. McLennan) Productivity Growth and U.S. Competetiveness, 1985; author: Superfairness: Applications and Theory, 1986 (Best Book in Mgmt. and Econs. award Assn. Am. Pubs., 1986); author: (with Sue Anne Batey Blackman and Edward N. Wolff) Productivity and American Leadership: The Long View, 1989 (hon. mention Soc. Sci., Assn. Am. Pub., 1989); author: (with Stephen M. Goldfeld, Lilli A. Gordon, Michael F. Koehn) The Ecomomics of Mutual Fund Markets: Competition Versus Regulation, 1990; author: (with Sue Anne Batey Blackman) Perfect Markets and Easy Virtue: Business Ethics and the Invisible Hand, 1991; author: (with Gregory Sidak) Toward Competition in Local Telephony, 1994; author: Entrepreneurship, Management and the Structure of Payoffs, 1993, Baumol's Cost Disease: The Arts and Other Victims, 1997; author: (with Richard R. Nelson and Edward N. Wolff) Convergence of Productivity: Cross-National Studies and Historical Evidence, 1994; author: (with J.G. Sidak) Transmission Pricing and Stranded Costs in the Electric Power Industry, 1995; author: (with Ralph E. Gomory) Global Trade and Conflicting National Interests, 2000; author: The Free-Market Innovation Machine: Analyzing the Growth Miracle of Capitalism, 2002; author: (with A.S. Blinder and E.N.Wolff) Downsizing in America: Reality, Causes and Consequences, 2003; author: (compendium of articles) Growth, Industrial Organization and Economic Generalities, 2003; editor: Public and Private Enterprise in a Mixed Economy, 1980; editor: (with W.G. Becker) Assessing Educational Practices: The Contribution of Economics, 1995; editor: (with J.G. Sidak) Transmission Pricing and Stranded costs in the Electric Power Industry, 1995; editor: (with C.A. Wilson) Welfare Economics, Vol. I, II, III, 2001; periodic mem. bd. editors jours. Am. Econ. Rev., Jour. Econ. Lit., Jour. Econ. Perspectives, Mgmt. Sci., Kyklos; contbr. numerous articles to profl. jours. Past pres. Am. Friends of London Sch. Econs.; trustee Rider Coll., Lawrenceville, 1960-70, Joint Coun. Econ. Edn.; past chmn., mem. State of N.J. Econ. Policy Coun., 1967-75. Recipient Townsend Harris medal CCNY, 1975, John Commons award Omicron Delta Epsilon, 1975, F.E. Seidman Disting. award in Polit. Economy, 1987, Best Book in Econs. and Bus. award Assn. Am. Pubs., 1986, First Sr. scholar in Arts & Scis. award NYU, 1992; Guggenheim fellow, 1957-58; Ford faculty fellow, 1965-66; named Joseph

Douglas Green '95 Prof. Econs. Princeton U., 1988. Fellow Econometric Soc., Am. Econ. Assn. (disting. fellow, mem. exec. com., v.p. 1966-67, pres. 1981); mem. Nat. Acad. Scis., AAUP (v.p., chmn. com. on econ. status of the profession 1968-70, mem. com. on hon. mems.), Am. Acad. Arts and Scis., Am. Philos. Soc., Eastern Econ. Assn. (pres. 1978-79), Assn. Environ. and Resource Economists (pres. 1979), Atlantic Econ. Soc. (pres. 1986), Econ. Assn. P.R. (disting. mem.) Home: 455 North End Ave New York NY 10282 Office: NYU New York NY 10012 Office Phone: 212-998-8943. E-mail: william.baumol@nyu.edu.

BAUMRIN, BERNARD STEFAN HERBERT, lawyer, educator; b. N.Y.C., Jan. 7, 1934; s. David and Regina (Zuckerburg) B.; m. Judith Anne Marti, Dec. 20, 1953; children: Seth, Jeanne, Rachel. Student, Marietta Coll., 1951-52, NYU, 1952-53; BA, Ohio State U., 1956; PhD, Johns Hopkins U., 1960; postgrad., Washington U., St. Louis, 1965-67; JD, Columbia U., 1970. Dir. forensics Johns Hopkins U., Balt., 1957—59; vis. asst. prof. philosophy Butler U., 1960—61, Antioch Coll., 1961; asst. prof. philosophy U. Del., Newark, 1961—64, Washington U., 1964—67; assoc. prof. philosophy Hunter Coll., CUNY, 1967—68, assoc. prof. philosophy Grad. Sch. and Lehman Coll., 1968—72, prof., 1972—, treas. univ. faculty senate, 1978—81, 1990, exec. com., 1976—84, 1987—91, 1992—93, 1998—99, 2002—; ptnr. Baumrin, Galub & Volkomer, 1979—. Adj. prof. med. edn. Mt. Sinai Sch. of Medicine, 1988—; bd. dirs. CUNY Acad. for the Humanities and Scis. Author: Philosophy of Science, 2 vols., 1963, British Moralists, 1964, Hobbes's Leviathan, 1968, Moral Responsibility and the Professions, 1983; U.S. editor: Jour. Applied Philosophy, 1986—2001, mem. adv. bd.: Jour. Philosophy Psychiatry and Psychology, 1995—; cons. editor Metaphilosophy, 1968—; contbr. articles to profl. jours. AEC fellow, 1963, U. Del. fellow, 1962, Washington U. Forsyth fellow, 1964-67; CUNY grantee, 1968, 70, 89, 91, 93, N.Y. Council for Humanities grantee, 1976, NEH grantee, 1977-79, 91, Mellon Found. grantee, 1980-84, Am. Council Learned Socs. grantee, 1987. Mem. AAAS, AAUP, ACLU, N.Y. State Bar Assn. (chmn. ethics subcom., com. on legal edn. and admission to bar 1986—2004), Mind Assn., Am. Philos. Assn. (chmn. standing com. on philosophy and medicine 1988-92, chmn. standing com. on philosophy and law 1998-2001), Soc. for Philosophy and Pub. Affairs, Internat. Assn. Philosophy of Law and Social Philosophy, Conf. on Methods in Philosophy and the Scis. (chmn. 1988-90), Internat. Hobbes Assn. (exec. com. 1986—), Internat. Soc. Econs. and Philosophy (treas. 1994—). Office: CUNY Grad Sch 365 5th Ave New York NY 10016-4334 also: Lehman Coll Philosophy Dept Bronx NY 10468 Office Phone: 718-960-8292.

BAUMRIND, DIANA, research psychologist, educator; b. N.Y.C., Aug. 23, 1927; AB, Hunter Coll., 1948; MA, U. Calif., Berkeley, 1951, PhD, 1955. Cert. and lic. psychologist, Calif. Project dir. psychology dept. U. Calif., Berkeley, 1955-58; project dir. Inst. of Human Devel., 1960—, also rsch. psychologist and prin. investigator family socialization and devel. competence project. Lectr. and cons. in field; referee for rsch. proposals Grant Found., NIH, 1970—, NSF, 1970—. Contbr. numerous articles to profl. jours. and books; author 2 monographs; mem. editorial bd. Devel. Psychology, 1986-90, Parenting: Science and Practice, 2000—. Recipient Rsch. Scientist award, NIMH; grantee NIMH, 1955-58, 60-66, Nat. Inst. Child Health and Human Devel., 1967-74, MacArthur Found., Grant Found., 1967—. Fellow Am. Psychol. Assn., Am. Psychol. Soc. (G. Stanley Hall award 1988), Soc. Research in Child Devel. Office: U Calif Inst of Human Devel 1217 Tolman Hall Berkeley CA 94720-1691 Office Phone: 510-642-3603.

BAUMSTEIN, PASCHAL M., priest; b. Coffee County, Tenn., Sept. 16, 1950; s. Josef ben-Abram and Mae (Winton) Baumstein. AA, Aquinas Coll., Nashville, 1972; AB, Holy Apostles Coll., Cromwell, Conn., 1973; MDiv, St. Meinrad Coll., Ind., 1979; AM, Ind. U., 1979. Monk Benedictine Order, 1974, ordained priest Roman Cath. Ch., 1979. Faculty Belmont Abbey Coll., Belmont, NC, 1977—80; archivist-historian Belmont Abbey/Belmont Abbey Coll., 1979—96, archivist-historian emeritus, 1996—; editor CRESCAT, Belmont, 1977—87; book editor Cistercian Studies Quar., Gethsemani, Ky., 1997—98. Chaplain Abbey Players of Belmont Abbey Coll., 1977—; calligrapher Cath. Worker, 1999—; expert, cons. on work and life of Anselm of Canterbury and Robert Hugh Benson. Author: My Lord of Belmont, 1985, Blessing the Years to Come, 1997; contbr. over 100 revs. to scholarly and profl. jours., numerous articles to scholarly and profl. jours. Mem. Pax Christi, Cath. Peace Fellowship; mem. archivists exec. bd. Cath. Libr. Assn., 1982—96; bd. trustees Belmont Abbey Coll., 1986—94. Mem.: Am. Cath. Philos. Soc., Acad. Cert. Archivists (cert. archivist), Internat. Arthurian Soc. (life), Am. Cath. Hist. Assn. (life), Phi Sigma Tau (sec. 1979—84), Delta Epsilon Sigma, Alpha Phi Gamma. Home and Office: Belmont Abbey 100 Belmont-Mount Holly Rd Belmont NC 28012-1802

BAUM-VILLAVICENCIO, LYNNE MIRIAM, lawyer; b. Waukesha, Wis., Oct. 7, 1972; d. Bernard and Julie Ann Baum. BA, U. Wis., 1994; JD, Georgetown U., 1999. Bar: (N.Y.) 2000, U.S. Dist. Ct. PR 2001, D.C. 2002. Law clk. to Hon. Jaime Pieras Jr. U.S. Dist. Ct. PR, San Juan, 1999—2001; assoc. Hogan & Hartson LLP, Washington, 2001—. Mem.: ABA, DC Bar Assn., Phi Beta Kappa. Office: Hogan & Hartson LLP 555 13th St NW Washington DC 20004 Home: 1452 Ogden St NW Washington DC 20010 Office Phone: 202-637-6636. E-mail: lynne_baum@yahoo.com.

BAUNER, RUTH ELIZABETH, library director; b. Quincy, Ill. d. John Carl and M. Irene (Nutt) B. BS in Edn., Western Ill. U., 1950; MS, U. Ill., 1956; postgrad., So. Ill. U., 1974, PhD, 1978. Asst. res. libr. Western Ill. U., Macomb, 1950; tchr., libr. Sandwich (Ill.) Twp. High Sch., 1950-54; circulation dept. asst. U. Ill. Libr., Urbana, 1955; asst. edn. libr. So. Ill. U., Carbondale, 1956-63, acting edn. libr., 1963-64, edn. and psychology libr., 1965-93, assoc. prof. curriculum and instrn. dept., 1971-93; coord. freshman yr. experience program, vis. assoc. prof. Coll. of Liberal Arts, Carbondale, 1994-96. Dir. Grad. Residence Ctr. Librs., So. Ill. U., 1973-79; subject matter expert Learning Resources Svc. Interactive Video, Carbondale, 1990-91, also scriptwriter; faculty emeritus So. Ill. U., 2004—. Co-author: The Teacher's Library, 1966; contbr. articles to profl. jours. Pres. alumni constituency bd. Coll. Edn., Carbondale, 1988—89; mem. Carbondale Bd. Ethics, 1989—2001; tchr. I Can Read Program, 2001—03; mem. Carbondale Citizens Adv. Commn., 1999—2001; bd. dirs. So. Ill. U. chpt. UN, 1985—86, 1994—97; mem. faculty bd. So. Ill. Learning in Retirement, So. Ill. U. Emeritus Assn.; bd. dirs. Jackson County AARP, 1997—99, 2001—03, So. Ill. U. Emeritus Faculty Assn., 2004—. Recipient Luck Has Nothing To Do With It award, Oryx Press, 1993. Mem.: AAUW (univ. rep. Carbondale br. 1988—89), ALA, Ill. Libr. Assn., Assn. Coll. and Rsch. Librs. (chmn. edn. and behavioral scis. sect. 1976—77, Most Active Mem. award 1968—93), AAUP (v.p. So. Ill. U. chpt. 1972—73), Delta Kappa Gamma, Phi Kappa Phi, Phi Delta Kappa (Women of Distinction award 1999). Office: 1206 W Freeman St Carbondale IL 62901-2351

BAUROTH, NANCY ANN, journalist, former marketing executive; b. Phila., Oct. 12, 1949; d. Harry William and Mary Octavia (Coffman) B. Dir. advt. and pub. rels. Doubleday & Co., N.Y.C., 1974-80; dir. product advt. Merrill Lynch & Co., N.Y.C., 1989-82, dir. mktg. comm. and cash mgmt., 1982-84; v.p., dir. mktg. direct access electronic banking Citibank, 1984-86; op-ed columnist Charlotte (N.C.) Observer, 1998—. Lectr. advt. writing CUNY, 1978, 79. Honoree Boston Soc. Fin. Analysts, 1982, creative workshop honoree Advt. Age, 1983. Mem. Fin. Comm. Soc. (honoree 1982), Pubs. Advt. Club (v.p. 1976-80). Republican. Presbyterian. Home: 11167 Foxhaven Dr Charlotte NC 28277-1492 E-mail: nan1971@mindspring.com.

BAUSCH, RICHARD CARL, writer, educator; b. Ft. Benning, Ga., Apr. 18, 1945; s. Robert Carl and Helen (Simmons) B.; m. Karen Miller, May 3, 1969; children: Wesley, Emily, Paul, Maggie, Amanda. BA, George Mason U., 1973; MFA, U. Iowa, 1975. Instr. No. Va. C.C., Annandale, Va., 1975-80; prof., Heritage chair of creative writing George Mason U., Fairfax, Va., 1980—. Vis. prof. U. Va., Charlottesville, 1985, 88, Wesleyan U., Middletown, Conn., 1986, 90, 92, 93; lectr., reader in field. Author: (stories) Spirits and Other Stories, 1987 (PEN/Faulkner award nomination 1988), The Fireman's Wife & Other Stories, 1990, Rare & Endangered Species, 1994, Modern Library Selected Stories, 1996, Someone to Watch Over Me, 1999; (novels) Real Presence, 1980, Take Me Back, 1981 (PEN/Faulkner award nomination 1982), The Last Good Time, 1984, Mr. Field's Daughter, 1989, Violence, 1992, Rebel Powers, 1993, Good Evening Mr. & Mrs. America and All the Ships At Sea, 1996, In the Night Season, 1998. Recipient Lila Wallace Reader's Best Writer's award Lila Wallace Fund, 1992, Acad. award in Lit. AAAL, 1993; grantee Nat. Endowment for the Arts, 1982; Guggenheim fellow John Simon Guggenheim Found., 1984. Fellow So. Writers; mem. PEN Am. Democrat. Roman Catholic. Avocations: songwriting, singing. Office: George Mason U Dept English 4400 University Dr Fairfax VA 22030-4444

BAUSE, GEORGE STEPHEN LONERAVEN, anesthesiologist; b. Chester, Pa., Nov. 22, 1955; BS in Biophysics cum laude, Ursinus Coll., Collegeville, PA, 1973—77; MPH in Epidemiology, Johns Hopkins U., 1980—81, MD, 1977—81. Diplomate Am. Bd. Anesthesiology. Intern Johns Hopkins Hosp., Balt., 1981-82, resident in anesthesiology, 1982-84; fellow geriatric anesthesiology Johns Hopkins Hosp.-Nat. Inst. Aging, Balt., 1984-85; attending physician Yale-New Haven Hosp., 1985-92, dir. geriatric anesthesia, 1987-92; chief dept. anesthesia West Haven (Conn.) VA Med. Ctr., 1990-92; Whitacre dir. anesthesia edn. Meridia Health Sys. of Cleve. Clinic, Ohio, 1992-96; asst. prof. Yale U., New Haven, 1985-91, assoc. prof., 1991-92; clin. assoc. prof. anesthesiology Case Western Res. U., Cleve., 1993—. Hon. curator USA's Wood Libr.-Mus. Anesthesiology, 1987—; assoc. curator USA's United Ch. of Christ, 2000—, George and Ramona Bause Collection, USA's Wood Libr. Mus., 2002, Living Hist. Anesthesiology Interviewee, 2005. Contbr. scientific papers in field. Pres. Yale Assn. Native Americans, 1988—90. St. Andrews Scholar, U. Edinburgh, 1975. Fellow: Coll. Physicians Phila., Royal Soc. Medicine, Anesthetists Internat. Coll. Surgeons (hon. William Halsted prize in Anesthesiology 1993); mem.: AMA, Anesthesia History Assn. (named Roderick Calverley Lectr. 2004), Soc. Cardiovasc. Anesthesiologists, Soc. Advancement Geriatric Anesthesia, Internat. Anesthesia Rsch. Soc., Am. Soc. Regional Anesthesia, Am. Soc. Anesthesiologists, Am. Geriat. Soc., Acad. Anesthesiology, Phi Beta Kappa (scholar 2004). Democrat. Congregationalist. Office: 5247 Wilson Mills # 282 Cleveland OH 44143-3016

BAUSELL, R. BARKER, JR., research methodology educator; s. Rufus B. and Nellie (Bowman) B.; m. Carole R. Vinograd, Jan. 6, 1978; children: Jesse T., Rebecca B. BS in Edn., U. Del., 1968, PhD in Ednl. Rsch. and Evaluation, 1975. Rsch. methodologist Med. Coll. Pa., 1975-76; prof., coord. faculty rsch. U. Md., Balt., 1976-91, dir. office rsch. methodology, 1991-94, prof. rsch., 1994-98, dir. rsch. complementary medicine program, 1998—. Sr. scientist Demarna Found. for Med. Care, 1994-98; cons., part-time dir. prevention rsch. ctr. Rodale Press, Inc.; presenter numberous seminars and confs. Author: (with C.R. Bausell and N.B. Bausell) The Bausell Home Learning Guide: Teach Your Child to Read, 1980, (with C.R. Bausell and N.B. Bausell) The Bausell Home Learning Guide: Teach Your Child to Write, 1980, (with C.F. Waltz) Nursing Research: Design, Statistics and Computer Analysis, 1981, (with C.R. Bausell and N.B. Bausell) The Bausell Home Learning Guide: Teach Your Child Math, A Practical Guide to Conducting Empirical Research, 1986, An Instructor's Manual for a Practical Guide to Conducting Empirical Research, 1986, (with C. Inlander and M. Rooney) How to Evaluate and Select a Nursing Home, 1988, Advanced Research Methodology: An Annotated Guide to Sources, 1991, Conducting Meaningful Experiments, 1994, (with Yu-Fang Li) Power Analysis for Experimental Research, 2002; editor: Evaluation and the Health Professions; author numerous monographs; contbr. numerous articles to profl. jours. Recipient Outstanding Rsch. award Nat. Wellness Conf., 1986, 87, Gov.'s award Meritorious Svc., 1992, award for Disting. Assessment Project Md. Assessment Resource Ctr., 1993. Achievements include research on documented effects of class size on student learning, effects of teacher experience on student learning, and determinants of health seeking (preventative) behavior. Home: 1311 Doves Cove Rd Baltimore MD 21286-1426 Office: U Md Complementary Med Program 2200 Kernan Dr Baltimore MD 21207-6665 E-mail: bausell@son.umaryland.edu.

BAUSER, NANCY, social worker, counselor; BS in Edn., U. Mich., 1973; MS in Social Work, U. Wis., 1976. Diplomate Am. Acad. Experts Traumatic Stress Specialists; bd. cert. disability trauma, bd. cert. expert in traumatic stress. Social worker 2 alcohol treatment programs; disability peer counselor dual-diagnosis treatment program, 1995—2002. Social worker, peer counselor; presenter BIA's 14th Ann. Symposium, 1995, Second World Congress Brain Injury, Seville, Spain, 1997. Author: Acceptance Groups for Head Injured Survivors, 1991, Acceptance Groups for Disability Survivors, 1993, Acceptance Groups for Survivors, A Guide for Facilitators, 2001; contbr. articles to profl. jours. Mem.: NASW, Am. Bd. Cert. Disability Trauma (BCETS, BCDT 2004), Acad. Cert. Social Workers (ACSW 1984), Am. Acad. Cert. Social Workers, Am. Acad. Experts Traumatic Stress Specialists (diplomate), Assn. Traumatic Stress Specialists. Home: 4260 Wabeek Lake Dr Bloomfield Hills MI 48302 Office Phone: 248-732-9939. E-mail: nancy@survivoracceptance.com.

BAUSHER, VERNE C(HARLES), retired bank executive; b. Reading, Pa. s. La Verne H. and Helen M. (Dornes) B.; m. Sandra Stamm Bausher, May 22, 1965; children: Christopher S., Gretchen S., Samantha A., Andrew P. BS, Drexel U., 1961; MBA, Northwestern U., 1962. Asst. v.p. Cen. Nat. Bank of Cleve., 1962-69; v.p. Meridian Bank (formerly American Bank and Trust Co. of Pa.), Reading, 1969-83; exec. v.p. Penn Savs. Bank, Wyomissing, 1983-87; exec. v.p., chief lending officer Germantown Savs. Bank, Bala Cynwyd, Pa., 1987—2004, ret., 2004. Trustee, v.p. Pub. Edn. Found. for Berks County, 1986—; bd. dirs. Wilson Sch. Dist., West Lawn, Pa., 1977—, pres., 1989-90; bd. dirs. Berks County Intermediate Unit, Reading, 1977—, YMCA of Reading, 1987-89. Republican. Lutheran. Avocations: reading, swimming, diving. Home: 4152 Hill Terrace Dr Sinking Spring PA 19608-9384

BAUTISTA, MANUEL QUIRAY, physician; b. The Philippines, June 19, 1947; came to U.S. s. Gil C. and Consuelo (Quiray) B. BS, U. Santo Tomas, Manila, 1966; MD, U. Santo Tomas, 1971. Diplomate Am. Bd. Emergency Medicine. Intern Hosp. St. Raphael, New Haven, Conn., 1972-73, resident in surgery, 1973-74; sr. med. staff Lawrence (Mass.) Gen. Hsop., 1975-93, White Meml. Med. Ctr., L.A., 1993—. Fellow ACEP; mem. AMA, Am. Coll. Emergency Physicians Home: 2125 Sunset Plaza Dr Los Angeles CA 90069-1204

BAVARIA, JOAN, finance company executive; b. 1944; Student, Mass. Coll. Art, U. Mass., CFA Program. Investment officer Bank of Boston, 1967—75; co-founder, pres. Social Investment Forum, 1981—86; founder, pres., CEO Trillium Asset Mgmt., 1982—. Chair Coalition Environmentally Responsible Econs. (CERES), 1989—2001; mem. bd. Earth Justice Legal Def. Fund, Ctr. Environ. Leadership, LightHawk, Social Investment Forum, 1981—89; spkr., writer in field. Chair Nat. Adv. Com. Policy and Tech. Com. (advisors to EPA); mem. dean's com. internat. devel., John F. Kennedy Sch. Govt. Harvard U.; mem. adv. bd. Greening of Industry Network; mem. adv. bd. Corp. Environ. Mgmt. Program U. Mich.; mem. bd., sec. Green Seal, 1991—99; mem. bd. Coun. Econ. Priorities, Indsl. Cooperative Assn. Loan Fund. Named Woman Yr., New Eng. Women Bus. Owners, 1994, Hero for Planet, Time Mag., 1999, Sci. Am. 50, Sci. Am. mag., 2002; recipient 2 Regional awards, Working Women mag., 1999, Entrepreneurial Excellence award, 1999, Millennium award corp. environ. leadership, Global Green and Green Cross Internat., Pres. Mikhail Gorbachev, 2000. Achievements include encouraging major companies to endorse the Coalition Environmentally Responsible Econs. principles for environmental management such as GM, BankAmerica, IT&T, Sun Company, Polaroid and Ben & Jerry's. Office: Trillium Asset Mgmt Corp 711 Atlantic Ave Boston MA 02111-2809 Office Fax: 617-482-6179.

BAVASI, PETER JOSEPH, sports management executive; b. Bronxville, N.Y., Oct. 31, 1942; s. Emil Joseph and Evit E. (Rice) B.; m. Judith Marzonie, June 13, 1964; children: Patrick, Cristina. BA in Philosophy, St. Mary's Coll., Moraga, Calif., 1964. Minor league gen. mgr. L.A. Dodgers, 1964-68; dir. minor league ops. San Diego Padres, 1968-73, v.p., gen. mgr., 1973-76; pres., CEO Toronto Blue Jays, 1976-81; pres. Peter Bavasi Sports, Inc., Tampa, Fla., 1981-84; pres., COO Cleve. Indians, 1984-87; pres., CEO Telerate Sports and SportsTicker, Jersey City, 1987-94; pres. ESPN/SportsTicker, Jersey City, 1995-96; prin. Bavasi Sports Ptnrs., LLP, La Jolla, 2001—. Office: Bavasi Sports Ptnrs LLP 1001 Genter St Unit 3G La Jolla CA 92037-5531

BAWA, AVANTIKA, artist, educator; b. Ootacamund, Tamil Nadu, India, Sept. 16, 1973; d. Parambir Singh and Shashi Bawa. MFA, Sch. Art Inst. Chgo., 1998. Prof. Ill. Inst. Art, Chgo., 1998—99, Savannah Coll. Art and Design, Ga., 1999—. Dir. Aquaspace Gallery, Savannah, 1999—2005. Installations, Navigating Spaces. Presdl. Fellowship, Savannah Coll. Art And Design, 2003. Home: 1600 Peachtree St Atlanta GA 30303 Home Fax: 912-525-5200. Business E-Mail: abawa@scad.edu.

BAWA, RAJ, biology professor, biotechnologist, biotechnology firm executive; s. Sukhdev Raj and Sudesh (Bhalla) B. BSc in Microbiology with honors, Panjab U., India, 1985; MS in Biology, Rensselaer Poly. Inst., 1987, PhD in Biology, 1990. Registered patent agent. Rsch. and tchg. asst. biology dept. Rensselaer Poly. Inst., Troy, NY, 1985-90; patent examiner Patent and Trademark Office, U.S. Dept. Commerce, Washington, 1990-96; instr. U.S. Patent Acad., Washington, 1995—2002; primary examiner, supervisory patent examiner (acting), Patent and Trademark Office U.S. Dept. Commerce, Washington, 1996—2002; pres. Bawa Biotech. Cons., LLC, Arlington, Va., 2002—; adv. office tech. commercialization Rensselaer Polytechnic Inst., Troy, 2003—; prof. natural and applied scis. No. Va. C.C., Annandale, 2004—. Spl. awards judge Intel Internat. Sci. and Engring. Fair, 1997, 98; vis. guest lectr. Sch. Sci. Rensselaer Polytechnic Inst., Troy, NY, 1998—99, vis. asst. prof., 1999—2002, adj. asst. prof., 2002—04; lectr. Am. Intellectual Property Law Assn., 2002; mem. adv. bd. UN's Online Lving Hist. Initiative for HIV/AIDS; spkr. in field; mem. editl. bd. Nanotechnology Law & Business, Risk Review, Nanomedicine; patent agent intellectual property Shire Lab., Inc., Rockville, Md., 2005—. Contbr. articles to profl. jours. and books. Recipient Talbot award U.S. Biophys. Soc., Bethesda, Md., 1988, Performance award U.S. Dept. Commerce, 1992, 93, 95, 98, 2000, Cert. Appreciation U.S. Dept. Commerce, 2001, Rensselaer Alumni Assn. Dir.'s award, 2001, Key award, 2005. Mem.: AAAS, Am. Intellectual Property Law Assn., Am. Chem. Soc., Am. Soc. Microbiology, World Future Soc. (life), Sigma Xi (Travel award 1988, 1990, life. mem.). Achievements include research in isolation and biochemical characterization of a new potassium transport protein from mammalian mitochondria, research on membrane transport of cationic anticancer drugs and polyamines in mammalian mitochondria, electron microscopy of animal sperm cells. Office: 21005 Starflower Way Ashburn VA 20147 Office Phone: 703-582-1745. Personal E-mail: bawabio@aol.com.

BAWDEN, JAMES WYATT, dental educator, dental scientist; b. St. Louis, Apr. 23, 1930; s. Leland Miller and Rose Helen (Watt) Bawden; children: Steven L., Michael J., Timothy C., David W. D.D.S., U. Iowa, 1954, MS, 1960, PhD, 1961. Gen. practice dentistry, Glenwood Springs, Colo., 1956—58; mem. faculty dept. pediatric dentistry Sch. Dentistry, U. N.C., Chapel Hill, 1961—, prof., 1965—77, Alumni disting. prof., 1977—, dean, 1966—74. Mem. faculty Sch. Dentistry, U. Lund, Malmo, Sweden, 1974—75; vis. prof. Karolinska Inst., Stockholm, 1992—93; mem. med.-dental staff N.C. Univ. Hosp., Chapel Hill, 1975—; cons. various coms. NIH, Bethesda, Md., 1979—; mem. oral medicine and biology study sect. Nat. Inst. Dental Health, Bethesda, 1982—83; mem., past pres. So. Conf. Dental Deans and Examiners, 1966—74. Contbr. articles to profl. jours., dental textbooks and studies. Chmn. bd. dirs. United Fund, Chapel Hill, 1972. Lt. Dental Corps USN, 1954—56. Named Disting. Educator, U. Iowa, 1985; recipient Disting. Svc. award, Dental Found. N.C., 1974; grantee, W.K. Kellogg Found., 1976—79, Nat. Inst. Dental Rsch., 1963—66, 1975—. Fellow: AAAS, Am. Acad. Pediat. Dentistry; mem.: ADA (coun. dental edn. 1971—74), Internat. Assn. for Dental Rsch., N.C. Dental Soc., Am. Assn. Dental Schs. (chmn. coun. of deans 1972—73), N.C. Dental Soc. (Disting. Svc. award), Am. Assn. for Dental Rsch. (pres. 1984—85), Inst. Medicine of NAS, Delta Sigma, Omicron Kappa Upsilon. Office: Univ NC Dept Pediats Dentistry Cb 7450 205 Braver Hl Chapel Hill NC 27599-0001*

BAWDEN, NINA (MARY BAWDEN), author; b. Eng., 1925; Author: Who Calls the Tune (in U.S. as Eyes of Green), 1953, The Odd Flamingo, 1954, Change Here for Babylon, 1955, The Solitary Child, 1956, Devil by the Sea, 1957, Just Like a Lady (in U.S. as Glass Slippers Always Pinch), 1960, In Honour Bound, 1961, Tortoise by Candlelight, 1963, The Secret Passage (in U.S. as The House of Secrets), 1963, On the Run (in U.S. as Three on the Run), 1964, Under the Skin, 1964, A Little Love, A Little Learning, 1966, The White Horse Gang, 1966, The Witch's Daughter, 1966, A Handful of Thieves, 1967, A Woman of My Age, 1967, The Grain of Truth, 1968, The Runaway Summer, 1969, The Birds on the Trees, 1970, Squib, 1971, Anna Apparent, 1972, Carrie's War, George Beneath a Paper Moon, 1974, The Peppermint Pig, 1975, Afternoon of a Good Woman, 1976, Rebel on a Rock, 1978, Familiar Passions, 1979, Walking Naked, 1981, Kept in the Dark, 1982, The Ice House, 1983, The Finding, 1985, Finding, 1985, Circles of Deceit, 1987, Keeping Henry, 1988, The Outside Child, 1989, Family Money, 1991, Humbug, 1992, The Real Plato Jones, 1993, In My Own Time, 1994, A Nice Change, 1997, Off the Road, 1998, Ruffian on the Stair, 2001, Dear Austen, 2005. Recipient S.T. DuPont Golden Pen award for alifetime's svc. to lit., 2004. Address: care Curtis Brown Ltd 10 Astor Pl New York NY 10003-6935 also: 22 Noel Rd London NI 8HA England also: 19 Kapodistriou Nauplion 21100 Greece E-mail: ninakrak@talk21.com.

BAWDEN, TIMOTHY TODD, geographer, educator; b. Sheboygan, Wis., Aug. 20, 1965; s. Art and Sandra (Schmidt) Bawden; m. Wendy Sue Hakari, July 25, 1992; 1 child, Max. BS, U. Wis., Oshkosh, 1988; MS, U. Wis., Madison, 1991, PhD, 2001. Instr. U. Wis., Madison, 1993—2000, prof. Eau Claire, 2001—. Office: U Wis Eau Claire 105 Garfield Ave Eau Claire WI 54702 Office Phone: 715-836-5186. Business E-Mail: bawdent@uwec.edu.

BAWENDI, MOUNGI G., chemist, educator; b. 1961; AB, Harvard U., 1982, AM, 1983; PhD in Chem., U. Chicago, 1988. Postdoctoral rsch. Bell Labs, 1988—90; asst. prof. chem. MIT, Cambridge, 1990—95, assoc. prof. chem., 1995—96, prof. chem., 1996. Recipient David & Lucile Packard Sci. & Engring Fellowship, 1991-96, Coblentz award, 1997, NSF Presidential Young Investigator award, 1991-96, Alfred P. Sloan Rsch. Fellowship, 1994-96, Raymond & Beverly Sackler prize in physical sci., 2001. Fellow: AAAS, Am. Acad. Arts & Sci.; mem.: Am. Chem. Soc. (Nobel Laureate Signature award for grad. ed. 1997). Office: MIT Dept Chemistry 77 Massachusetts Ave Rm 6-221 Cambridge MA 02139-4307

BAX, SIMON TRISTAN, film company executive; b. Bristol, Eng., Mar. 3, 1959; s. Claude Henry James and Kay (Thorn) B.; m. Briony Kay Mitchell, Apr. 19, 1986. BA with honors, Gonville & Caius Cambridge U., U.K., 1980, MA, 1983. Chartered acct. Stoy Hayward & Co., London, 1980-86, ptnr., 1986-87; v.p., dir. fin. WCRS N. Am., N.Y.C., 1987-88, CFO, 1988—90; sr. v.p. Della Femina Travisano & Ptnrs., N.Y.C., 1987—90; dir. fin. svcs. Chiat/Day Inc., Venice, Calif., 1990, sr. v.p., CFO, 1990—91, exec. v.p., CFO, 1991—94; sr. v.p., CFO Fox Filmed Entertainment, 1994—97, exec. v.p. bus. and legal affairs, CFO, 1997—99, pres. studio ops., CFO, 1999—2001; exec. v.p., CFO Pixar Animation Studios, 2004—. Chmn. bd. dirs. Wonder of Reading. Mem. Inst. Chartered Accts. of Eng. and Wales, Am. Assn. Advt. Agys., Acad. Motion Pictures Arts and Scis., Brit. Academy Film and TV Arts. Avocations: golf, woodworking. Office: Pixar Animation Studios 1200 Park Ave Emeryville CA 94608

BAXLEY, LUCY, lieutenant governor; m. Bill Baxley (div.); children: Becky Nichols, Louis; m. Jim Smith. Licensed realtor; Treas. State of Ala., 1994—2002, lt. gov., 2002—. Former spokesperson Senior Promise; Women's Philanthropy Bd. Auburn U. Recipient Senior Citizens' Golden Eagle

Statesman of Yr., Outstanding Woman Leader, Am. Assn. of U. Women. Mem.: Nat. Assn. Lt. Govs., Ala. Fedn. of Dem. Women (chair adv. coun.), U. Ala. XXXI. Democrat. Office: Ste 725 11 S Union St Montgomery AL 36130 Office Phone: 334-242-7900. Business E-Mail: lucybaxley@ltgov.alabama.gov.

BAXLEY, STEPHEN R., lawyer; b. Dallas, Aug. 23, 1967; s. Larry O. and Sondra J. (Coffee) B.; m. Kathryn M. Pumphrey, June 14, 1986; 1 child, Nicole R. B Gen. Studies, U. Nebr., Omaha, 1990; JD, U. Houston, 1995. Bar: Wash. 1996, Tex. 1997, U.S. Dist. Ct. (we. dist.) Wash. 1996, U.S. Ct. Appeals (9th cir.) 1996, U.S. Dist. Ct. (so. dist.) Tex. 1998. Atty. Boston & Assocs., PC, Houston, 1996—. With USAF, 1986-87, U.S. Army, 1993-94. Mem. ABA, Tex. Bar Assn., Wash. State Bar ASsn. Avocations: travel, photography. Office: Ste 1650 1360 Post Oak Blvd Houston TX 77056-3068

BAXT, WILLIAM GORDON, medical educator; b. Mar. 31, 1941; BA, Brown U., 1963; MD, Yale U., 1967. Diplomate Am. Bd. Internal Medicine, Am. Bd. Emergency Medicine. Intern Columbia-Presbyn. Hosp., N.Y.C., 1967-68, resident in internal medicine, 1970-71, fellow in hematology, 1971-73; from asst. prof. medicine to prof. clin. medicine & surgery U. Calif., San Diego, 1973-94; prof., chmn. dept. emergency medicine U. Pa. Med. Ctr., Phila., 1994—. Rsch. biologist U. Calif., La Jolla, 1976-77; med. dir. life flight aeromed. program U. Calif. Med. Ctr., San Diego, 1980-89, assoc. dir. divsn. emergency med. svcs., 1978-80, dir. dept. emergency medicine, 1980-94; chmn. dept. emergency medicine U. Pa. Med. Ctr., 1994—. Co-author: (with others) Cellular Modifiction and Genetic Transformation by Exogenous Nucleic Acids, 1973, The Leukemia Cell, 1979, Systems Approach to Emergency Medical Care, 1983, Trauma: The First Hour, 1985; mem. editl. bd. Emergency Care Quar., Annals of Emergency Medicine; contbr. articles to profl. jours. Surgeon USPHS, 1968-70. Leukemia Soc. Am. scholar, 1976; recipient Physicians Recognition award AMA, 1985, Best Oral Clin. Sci. Paper U. Assn. for Emergency Medicine, 1988, Best Oral Methodology Paper Soc. for Acad. Emergency Medicine, 1990. Mem. Nat. Acad. Scis., Soc. for Acad. Emergency Medicine, Phi Beta Kappa. Office: Hosp U Pa Dept Emergency Med Ground Ravdin 3400 Spruce St Philadelphia PA 19104-4206 E-mail: baxtw@uphs.epenn.edu.

BAXTER, ALMA JEAN, academic administrator; d. Joseph and Lillian Baxter; children: Ibtihal Al-Ghamdi, Hamzah Al-Ghamdi, William L. BS in Home Econ. Edn. and Edn., Fla. A&M U., 1976; postgrad., Fla. Atlantic U., 1980, Fla. State U., 1989; student, Am. U. Cairo. Asst. dir., coord. Dar Al-Haran, Jeddah, Saudi Arabia; co-owner, fashion cons. Kti'sis Unltd., Tallahassee; libr. Selby, Mizzell, Sarasota; program coord., counselor Discovery Ctr., Ft. Lauderdale, Fla.; admission rep. Century Coll., Tallahassee. Asst. mgr. Jordan Marsh, Ft. Lauderdale, 1976; instr. fashion design Prospect Hall Coll., Ft. Lauderdale, 1977; co-owner, designer, couturier A & J Cloth and Stitch, Ft. Lauderdale, 1978; neighborhood counselor, program coord. BETA Employees, 1977—80; permanent substitute, substitute tchr. Roosevelt H.S., West Palm Beach, Fla., 1980; libr. I Riviera Beach Libr., 1980—82; libr. II Mizell Libr., Ft. Lauderdale, 1982; bookmobile dir. Selby Libr., Sarasota, Fla., 1982—84; co-owner, fashion cons. Ktisis Unltd., Tallahassee, 1984—87; admission rep. Century Coll., Tallahassee, 1985—86; CEO, founder AlaBee, Inc. Author: Through theValley, 2003, When Will My Mommy Come, 2004. Mem. Am. Bus. Women, Tallahassee, 1992—2000; vol. Jay Ministries, Riviera Beach, 2002—03; choir mem., greeter Redeeming Word Christian Ctr. Internat., Ft. Lauderdale, 2000—04. Achievements include invention of dual compartment compact. Avocations: fashion design, writing, boating, bicycling. Home and Office: 17335 35th Pl N Loxahatchee FL 33470

BAXTER, BETTY CARPENTER, academic administrator; b. Sherman, Texas, Oct. 10, 1937; d. Granville E. and Elizabeth (Caston) Carpenter; m. Cash Baxter; children: Stephen Barrington, Catherine Elaine. AA in Music, Christian Coll., Columbia, Mo., 1957; MusB in Voice and Piano, So. Meth. U., Dallas, 1959; MA in Early Childhood Edn., Tchrs. Coll., Columbia, 1972, MEd, 1979, EdD, 1988. Tchr. Riverside Ch. Day Sch., N.Y.C., 1966—71; head mistress Episcopal Sch., N.Y.C., 1972—87, head mistress, emeritus, 1987—; founding head Presbyn. Sch., Houston, 1988—94; dir. Chadwick Village Sch., Palos Verdes Peninsula, Calif., 1995—; head sch. St. Margaret's Episcopal Sch., Palm Desert, Calif., 2001—02, life coach, 2004—. Author: The Relationship of Early Tested Intelligence on the WPPSI to Later Tested Aptitude on the SAT. Mem.: ASCD, LA Assn. Sch. Heads, Nat. Assn. Edn. Young Children, Ind. Sch. Assn. Admissions Greater N.Y. (former exec. bd.), Nat. Assn. Elem. Sch. Prins., Nat. Assn. Episcopal Ch. (former gov. bd., editor Network publ.), Delta Kappa Gamma, Kappa Delta Pi. Republican. Episcopalian. Office: 72-828 Joshua Tree St Palm Desert CA 92260 Office Phone: 310-291-7489. Personal E-mail: bettybaxtercoach@earthlink.net.

BAXTER, BEVERLEY VELONS, economic association administrator, educator; b. Eugene, Oreg., July 5, 1943; d. J. Clifford Baxter and O. Veloris Crenshaw; m. Doyle R. Dobbins, July 7, 1962; children: Kendall Reé Baxter Dobbins, Kalen Baxter Dobbins, Konlee Baxter Dobbins. Certificate, Graduate Sch. Ecumenical Studies, Bossey, Switzerland, 1965, William Temple Coll., Rugby, Eng., 1965; BS, Phillips U., 1966, MEd, 1967; MA, U. Del., 1971, PhD, 1976. Tchg. asst. U. Del., Newark, 1971—76; asst. prof. dept. English Temple U., Phila., 1977—79; real estate investor Wilmington, Del., 1979—83; dir. edn. programs First Unitarian Ch., Wilmington, 1983; exec. asst. to county exec. New Castle County, Wilmington, 1983—84; v.p. Blue Ball Properties, Wilmington, 1985—93; exec. dir. The Com. of 100, Wilmington, 1993—. Dir. Wilmington Area Planning Coun. Wilmington Initiatives Steering Com., 1995—; mem. Gov.'s State Planning Citizens Adv. Coun., Del., 1995—, Del. State C. of C. Small Bus. Alliance Legis. Com., 1997—; dir. Del. Bus. Pub. Edn. Coun., Wilmington, 1998—; mem. working group De. Dept. Transportation; mem. Del. Dept. Natural Resources & Environ. Control Regulatory Adv. com.; bd. dirs., treas. Wiley Coll., Marshall, Tex. Author: Diaries and Journals of Americans Held Prisoner During the Revolutionary War, 1976; editor: For Your Info., 1995. Pres. bd. dir. Montessori Cmty. Sch., Wilmington, 1996—2000; bd. dir. Unitarian Universalist Svc. Com., Cambridge, Mass., 1985—91; pres. First Unitarian Ch., Wilmington, 1979—82, bd. dir., 1979—82, Friends of Rockwood Mus., Wilmington, 1986—88. Recipient Economic Turnaround Cert. of Appreciation, Wilmington 2000, 1982, Disting. Svc. award, Unitarian Universalist Svc. Com., 1991, Liveable Cmty. award, Wilmington Area Planning Coun., 1998. Mem.: The Associates, The Bus. Group, New Castle County C. of C. (state affairs coun., county govt. coun.). Unitarian Universalist. Avocations: music, reading, gardening, skiing. Office: The Committe of 100 824 Market St Ste 612 Wilmington DE 19801

BAXTER, CECIL WILLIAM, JR., retired college president; b. Stockton, Kans., Aug. 11, 1923; s. Cecil William and Marjorie LaVerne (Fitzpatrick) B.; m. Pat Ann Layman, June 6, 1951; children: Cecil William, Michael Kent, Patrick Alan. BA, Kans. Wesleyan U., 1950; MBA, U. Denver, 1954; PhD, U. Tex., 1967. Secondary edn. tchr., then secondary sch. prin., 1951-60; bus. mgr. Cottey Coll., Nevada, Mo., 1960-65; dean instrn. Kansas City Community Jr. Coll., Kans., 1967-68, Forest Park Community Coll., St. Louis, 1968-70; pres. North Seattle Community Coll., 1970-85, pres. emeritus, 1985—; exec. dir. Coun. on Naturopathic Med. Edn., 1989-92. Mem. faculty U. Wash., 1971; mem. Comm. on Colls. N.W. Assn. Schs. and Colls., 1981-85 Bd. dirs. Sr. Citizens Orgn., Seattle, 1972. Served with AUS, 1944-46. Ford Found. fellow U. Okla.; Kellogg Found. fellow U. Tex. Mem. Phi Delta Kappa Lodges: Rotary.

BAXTER, CHARLENE ADAMS, librarian; b. Rome, Ga., May 2, 1955; d. Ralph Eugene Adams and Maudie Lee Pollard; m. Michael Alan Baxter, Aug. 20, 1976; 1 child, Kerry Elaine. BA, West Ga. U., 1975; MLS, Ga. Peabody Coll., 1976. Tech. and pub. svcs. libr. LaGrange (Ga.) Coll., 1976—. Book reviewer (jour.) Georgia Librarian. Baptist. Avocations: reading, nature. Home: 412 Park Ave Lagrange GA 30240 Office: LaGrange College 601 Broad St Lagrange GA 30240 Office Phone: 706-880-8311. Office Fax: 706-880-8040. Business E-Mail: cbaxter@lagrange.edu.

BAXTER, ELIZABETH PALM, music educator; b. Detroit, Oct. 25, 1955; d. Gerald Victor and Virginia Leech Palm; m. Timothy Edward Baxter, June 17, 1982; children: Ryan Timothy, Erin Elizabeth, Bridget Hannah. Diploma, Interlochen (Mich.) Arts Acad., 1973; MusB, Mich. State U., 1977; MusM, Northwestern U., 1979. Nat. cert. tchr. music in piano MTNA. Pvt. piano tchr., Farmington Hills, Mich., 1979—; piano accompanist Southfield (Mich.) Christian Sch., 1998—; pianist Grace Chapel Evang. Presbyn. Ch., Farmington Hills, 2001—. Musician: (multi-media presentation) Jerusalem (C. H. H. Parry). Mem.: Livonia Area Piano Tchrs. Forum, Camerata Music Club, Nat. Fedn. Music Clubs, Mich. Music Tchrs. Assn. (mem. bd. certification 2003), Music Tchrs. Nat. Assn. Presbyterian. Avocations: reading, travel.

BAXTER, GENE FRANCIS, chemical researcher, consultant; b. Sanish, Nd, July 25, 1922; s. Leslie Valentine and Frances (Ellertson) Baxter; m. Elizabeth Rose Turner, Feb. 14, 1970; children: Marsha Lynn, Michael James, Anthony Frederick. BS Chem., Univ. Wash., Seattle, WA, 1944. Rsch. chemist Adhesive Products Co., Seattle, Wash., 1944—46, Martin-Marietta Corp., Seattle, 1946—53; group leader Weyerhaeuser Co., Seattle, 1953—62, rsch. scientist, 1962—73, Georgia-Pacific Corp., Decatur, 1973—83, sr. scientist, 1983—85, cons., 1985—99. Recipient Disting. Scientist Award, Georgia-Pacific Resins Corp., 1986. Achievements include patents for 22 US patents granted between 1940-1990. Avocation: playing cards. Home: 195 Tiburon Drive Lithonia GA 30038

BAXTER, GREGORY STEPHEN, lawyer; b. Long Branch, N.J., Mar. 26, 1948; s. George Washington and Doris Louise (Bogart) B.; m. Katherine Ruth Nilsen, Apr. 15, 1972; children: David Stephen, Kevin Scott, Stephen Gregory. BBA, Wake Forest U., 1969; JD, Seton Hall U., 1972. Bar: N.J. 1972, U.S. Dist. Ct. N.J. 1972, U.S. Supreme Ct. 1982. Law sec. to judges Aikins & Arnone, Freehold, N.J., 1972-73; assoc. Saling, Moore, O'Mara & Coogan, Eatontown, N.J., 1973-79; prin., ptnr. Caruso & Baxter (formerly Saling, Gassert, Caruso & Baxter), Shrewsbury, N.J., 1979—. Bd. dirs. Ocean-Monmouth Legal Svcs., Red Bank, N.J., 1983-86; trustee Monmouth Bar Found., Freehold, 1988-94, 97—. Mem. West Long Branch Zoning Bd. Adjustment, 1980-84, Long Branch and West Long Branch County Rep. Com., 1974—. Mem. N.J. Bar Assn., Monmouth Bar Assn. (pres. 1987-88, chair jud. evaluations and reappointments com. 1995—), Legal Aid Soc. Monmouth County (pres. 1982-85, trustee 1978—). Methodist. Avocation: tennis. Home: 45 Parker Rd West Long Branch NJ 07764-1136 Office: Caruso & Baxter PA 1129 Broad St Shrewsbury NJ 07702-4333

BAXTER, JOAN ANNA PATTEN, technical writer; b. Phila., July 5, 1933; d. Frank Perc and Anna Calvert Patten; divorced; children: Stephen Paul, William Jeffrey, Timothy David. AA, Pa. State U., Lima, 1983; Cert. in Mgmt., Widener U., Chester, Pa., 1984; BS, West Chester (Pa.) U., 1987; MA Communications, West Chester U., 2004. Coord. purchases/installation Scott Paper Co., Phila., 1988-91; tech. writer McGraw Hill Pub., Delran, N.J., 1994-95; cons. PC trainer Archdiocese of Phila., 1996; quality assurance tester Bell Atlantic Graphics, Audubon, Pa., 1996-97; writer product devel. Franklin Pub. Inc., Burlington, N.J., 1997-98; tech. writer, processes Telespectrum, Phila., 1998—; coord. Y2K project Simon & Schuster, Wayne, Pa., 1998—99; system analyst Bd. Edn., Phila., 2000; tech. writer Independence Blue Cross, 2000; tech. writer processes, procedures & svc. descriptions Agere Systems, Inc., Allentown, Pa., 2002. Devel. editor Boyd & Fraser, Boston, 1992; implementor, supr. Temple U. Sch. Dentistry, Phila., 1980-84; adminstrv. asst. Brandywine Conservancy, Chadds Ford, Pa., 1976-80, Roy F. Weston Inc., West Chester; propr. Baxter Enterprises, 1994-96. Recipient Chapel of Four Chaplains award, 1982. Mem. AAUW (pub. policy com. 1991-99), U.S. Power Squadron, Delaware Blue Hen Coun. (dir. 1996-99). Republican. Christian Scientist. Avocations: tennis, music, art. Home: 926 Tyson Dr West Chester PA 19382-7571 Office Phone: 610-719-0889. Business E-Mail: baxter@baxtercommunicationsolution.com. E-mail: jpbaxter_19103@yahoo.com.

BAXTER, JOHN DARLING, internist, endocrinologist, educator, health facility administrator; b. Lexington, Ky., June 11, 1940; s. William Elbert and Genevive Lockhart (Wilson) B.; m. Ethelee Davidson Baxter, Aug. 10, 1963; children: Leslie Lockhart, Gillian Booth. BA in Chemistry, U. Ky., 1962; MD, Yale U., 1966; DSc (hon.), U. Ky. 2004. Intern, then resident in internal medicine Yale-New Haven Hosp., 1966-68; USPHS research assoc. Nat. Inst. Arthritis and Metabolic Diseases, NIH, 1968-70; Dernham sr. fellow oncology U. Calif. Med. Sch., San Francisco, 1970-72, mem. faculty, 1972—, prof. medicine and biochemistry and biophysics, 1979—, dir., Metabolic Rsch. Unit San Francisco, 1981—2000. Dir. endocrine research Howard Hughes Med. Inst., 1976-81, investigator, 1975-81; chief div. endocrinology Moffitt Hosp., 1980-97; attending physician U. Calif. Med. Center, 1972- Editor textbook of endocrinology and metabolism; Author research papers in field; mem. editorial bd. profl. jours. Recipient George W. Thorn Outstanding Investigator award, Howard Hughes Med. Inst., 1978, Disting. Alumni award U. Ky., 1980, Dautrebande prize for research in cellular and molecular biology, Belgium, 1985, Albion Bernstein award N.Y. Med. Soc., 1987, Edwin B. Astook award, US Endocrine Society, 1997; grantee NIH, Am. Cancer Soc., others. Mem. Am. Chem. Soc., Am. Soc. Hypertension, Am. Soc. Clin. Investigation, Am. Thyroid Assn., Assn. Am. Physicians, Am. Fedn. Clin. Research, Endocrine Soc., pres., 2002- Western Assn. Physicians, Western Soc. Clin. Research, Inst. Medicine, 2004.

BAXTER, KATHLEEN ANN, literary agent, consultant; b. Tracy, Minn., Mar. 22, 1944; d. John Edison and Audrey Maud Little Baxter; m. William Riley Harrison, May 21, 1992. BA, Coll. St. Catherine, 1966; MA, U. Minn., 1969. Coord. children's svcs. Anoka County Libr., Blaine, Minn., 1969—2002; tchr. children's lit. Bur. Edn. and Rsch., Bellevue, Wash., 2004—. Adv. bd. Nat. Geog. Soc., Washington, 2004—; spkr. in field. Author: Gotcha, Gotcha Again, Gotcha Covered, (column) Sch. Libr. Jour. Mem.: ALA. Dfl. Roman Catholic. Avocations: Broadway shows, reading, travel, music. Home: 50 94th Cir NW #201 Coon Rapids MN 55448 Office Phone: 763-717-2581. Home Fax: 763-717-6830. Personal E-mail: kathybaxter@gmail.com.

BAXTER, KATHLEEN BYRNE, academic administrator; b. Rockville Center, Jan. 31, 1976; d. Anthony Campbell and Margaret Regan Baxter. BA in English, Villanova U., 1997; MA in Higher Edn. and Student Pers. Adminstrn., Teachers Coll., Columbia U., 2000. Asst. dir. event planning Teachers Coll., Columbia U., N.Y.C., 1998—2000; asst. dir. programs MIT, Cambridge, 2000—02; dir. leadership and first yr. programs Simmons Coll., Boston, 2002—03; assoc. dir. Ctr. for Career Edn., Columbia U., N.Y.C., 2003—. Mem. Franciscan Children's Hosp. Young Profl. Coun., Brighton, Mass., 2000—03. Mem.: Assn. Coll. Pers. Adminstrs., Nat. Assn. Pers. Adminstrs., Kappa Delta Pi, Delta Delta Delta. R-Liberal. Catholic. Avocations: travel, running, reading. Personal E-mail: kathleenbaxter7@hotmail.com.

BAXTER, MARVIN RAY, state supreme court justice; b. Fowler, Calif., Jan. 9, 1940; m. Jane Pippert, June 22, 1963; children: Laura, Brent. BA in Economics, Calif. State U., 1962; JD, Hastings Coll. of Law, 1966. Bar: Calif. 1966. Dep. dist. atty. Fresno County, Calif., 1967-68; assoc. Andrews, Andrews, Thaxter & Jones, 1968-70, ptnr., 1971-82; apptd. sec. to Gov. George Deukmejian, 1983-88; assoc. justice Calif. Ct. Appeal (5th dist.), 1988-90, Calif. Supreme Ct., 1991—. Mem. Jud. Coun. of Calif., chmn. policy coord. and liaison com., 1996-; dir. emeritus Hastings Coll. of Law. Recipient Man of the Yr. award, Armenian Nat. Com., 1991, Armenian Professional Soc., 1993, Mentor award, Fresno County Young Lawyers Assn., 1996. Mem. Fresno County Bar Assn. (bd. dirs. 1977-82, pres. 1981), Calif. Young Lawyers Assn. (bd. gov. 1973-76, sec.-treas. 1974-75), Fresno County Young Lawyers Assn. (pres. 1973-74), Fresno County Legal Svcs., Inc. (bd. dirs. 1973-74), Fresno State U. Alumni Assn. (pres. 1970-71), Fresno State U. Alumni Trust Coun. (pres. 1970-75). Office: Calif Supreme Ct 350 Mcallister St San Francisco CA 94102-4712 Office Phone: 415-865-7080.

BAXTER, MEREDITH, actress; b. Los Angeles, June 21, 1947; d. Tom and Whitney (Blake) Baxter; m. Bob Bush, June 23, 1966 (div. 1969), children: Ted, Eva; m. David Birney, Apr. 10, 1974 (div. 1989), children: Kate, Peter and Mollie (twins), m. Michael Blodgett, Oct 21, 1995 (div. 2000). Student, Interlochen Arts Acad., Mich. Prin., Meredith Baxter Skin Care Products Actress (films) including Ben, 1972, Stand Up and Be Counted, 1972, Bittersweet Love, 1976, All the President's Men, 1976, The November Plan, 1976, (TV movies) The Cat Creature, 1973, The Stranger Who Looks Like Me, 1974, The Imposter, 1975, The Night That Panicked America, 1975, Target Risk, 1975, Little Women, 1978, The Family Man, 1979, Beulah Land, 1980, The Two Lives of Carol Letner, 1981, Take Your Best Shot, 1982, Family Ties Vacation, 1985, The Rape of Richard Beck, 1985, Kate's Secret, 1986, The Long Journey Home, 1987, Winnie, 1988, She Knows Too Much, 1989, Jezebel's Kiss, 1990, The Kissing Place, 1990, Burning Bridges, 1990, A Bump in the Night, 1991, A Mother's Justice, 1991, A Woman Scorned: The Betty Broderick Story, 1992, The Betty Broderick Story: Part 2, 1992, (also exec. prodr.) Darkness Before Dawn, 1993, My Breast, 1994, One More Mountain, 1994, For the Love of Aaron, 1994, Betrayed: A Story of Three Women, 1995, After Jimmy, 1996, Inheritance, 1997, Miracle in the Woods, 1997, Let Me Call You Sweetheart, 1997, Holy Joe, 1999, Down Will Come Baby, 1999, Miracle on the 17th Green, 1999, The Wednesday Woman, 2000, A Mother's Fight for Justice, 2001, Aftermath, 2001, Murder on the Orient Express, 2001, A Christmas Visitor, 2002, Angel in the Family, 2004, On the Rocks, 2005; (plays) Guys and Dolls, Talley's Folley, Butterflies are Free, Varieties; star (TV series) Bridget Loves Bernie, 1972-73, Family, 1976-80, Family Ties, 1982-89, The Faculty, 1996; (TV spls.) Vanities, 1981, Missing...Have You Seen This Person?, 1985, Diabetes Update, 1986, Other Mothers, 1993, TV's Funniest Families, 1994; other TV appearances include The Interns, Police Woman, Medical Story, City of Angels, McMillan and Wife, The Streets of San Francisco. Mem. Am. Diabetes Assn. Mailing: c/o Constance Freiberg Envision Entertainment Ste 300 9255 Sunset Blvd West Hollywood CA 90069*

BAXTER, NANCY, medical writer; b. Grand Rapids, Mich., Oct. 3, 1950; d. Robert Emerson and Mary (Knoblauch) B. BA in Journalism, Am. U., 1972. Asst. dir. pubs. Am. Speech, Lang. & Hearing Assn., Washington, 1973-77; mng. editor Biomedia, Inc., Princeton, N.J., 1977-79, Continuing Profl. Edn. Ctr., Inc., Princeton, 1981-82; editor A.M. Best Co., Oldwick, N.J., 1979-81; med. writer, editor Biomed Info. Corp., N.Y.C., 1982-83; pres. Baxter Med. Comms. Co., Warren, N.J., 1983—. Mem. Am. Med. Writers Assn. Home and Office: 18 Stiles Rd Warren NJ 07059-5413 Office Phone: 908-755-4589. Personal E-mail: baxmedcomm@aol.com.

BAXTER, NATHAN DWIGHT, dean; b. Coatesville, Pa., Nov. 16, 1948; s. Beigium Nathan and Augusta Ruth (Byrd) Baxter; m. Mary Ellen Walker, June 10, 1969; children: Timika Ann, Harrison David. MDiv with honors, Lancaster Theol. Sem., 1976, DMin, 1984; STD (hon.), Dickinson Coll., Carlisle, Pa., 1990; DD (hon.), St. Paul's Coll., Lawrenceville, Va., 2000; DST (hon.), Messiah Coll., Grantham, Pa., 2001; DHL (hon.), York Coll., Pa., 2002; DD (hon.), Colgate U., Hamilton, N.Y., 2003. Ordained Episcopal Ch., 1977. Curate St. John's Episcopal Ch., Carlisle, Pa., 1976—78; rector St. Cypman's Episcopal Ch., Hampton, Va., 1978—84; chaplain, prof. religious studies St. Paul's Coll., Lawrenceville, Va., 1984—86; dean, assoc. prof. church and ministry Lancaster Theol. Sem., Pa., 1986—90; adminstrv. dean, assoc. prof. pastoral theology Episcopal Div. Sch., Cambridge, Mass., 1990—91; dean Washington Nat. Cathedral, 1991—. Bd. dirs. Faith and Politics Inst., Washington, 1996; lectr., Medina Seminar Princeton U., NJ, 1997—2002; preacher Chautaugua Inst., NY, 1997—2002; bd. mem. U. Va. Ctr. on Religion & Democracy, 2002; bd. dirs. Riggs Nat. Bank, Washington, 2002. Author: Visions for the Millennium: Thoughts on Christian Living. E-5 U.S. Army, 1968—70. Decorated Vietnam Cross of Gallantry with Palm U.S. Army; fellow, Coll. of Preachers, 1990; Charles E. Merrill fellow, Harvard Div. Sch., 1998. Mem.: NAACP (life), Cosmo Club. Episcopalian. Avocations: black poetry, walking, jazz. Office: Washington Nat Cathedral Massachusetts and Wisconsin Aves NW Washington DC 20016-5098 Address: 115 N Duke St Lancaster PA 17602

BAXTER, NEVINS DENNIS, bank consultant; b. NYC, June 29, 1941; s. Sol and Beatrice B.; m. Anne Susan Hatow, July 30, 1972; children: S.J., Keith. BA, Columbia Coll., 1961; MA, Princeton U., 1962, PhD in Econs., 1964. Asst. prof. fin. U. Pa., 1965-69; v.p. Mathematica, Princeton, N.J., 1969-71; pres. Baxter & Co., Washington, 1971-75, Golembe Assocs., Inc., Washington, 1975-89; chmn. BEI Golembe Cons., Washington, 1989-90; vice chmn. BEI Holdings Ltd., Washington, 1990-93; prin. Baxter & Co., Washington, 1993—. Contbr. articles to numerous profl. jours. Office: Baxter & Co Ste 260 1667 K St NW Washington DC 20006 Office Phone: 202-337-1749.

BAXTER, RALPH H., JR., lawyer; b. San Francisco, 1946; AB, Stanford U., 1968; MA, Cath. U. Am., 1970; JD, U. Va., 1974. Bar: Calif. 1974. Chmn. Orrick, Herrington & Sutcliffe LLP, San Francisco, 1990—, ptnr., CEO, 1990—. Mem. adv. bd. Nat. Employment Law Inst.; spkr. in field. Author: Sexual Harassment in the Workplace: A Guide to the Law, 1981, Sexual Harassment in the Workplace: A Guide to the Law, 2d rev. edit., 1989, 1994, Manager's Guide to Lawful Terminations, 1983, Manager's Guide to Lawful Terminations, rev. edit., 1991; mem. editl. bd.: Va. Law Rev., 1973—74, mem. editl. adv. bd.: Employee Rels. Law Jour. Named one of 100 most influential lawyers, Nat. Law Jour., 1997, 2000, Calif. Lawyers of Yr., Calif. Lawyer Mag., 2003. Mem.: ABA-labor & employment law sect. (mgmt. co-chmn. com. employment rights & responsibilities in workplace 1987—90, com. EEO), Nat. Employment Law Inst. (adv. bd.), State Bar Calif., Employee Relations Law Jour. (editl. adv. bd.). Office: Orrick Herrington & Sutcliffe LLP The Orrick Building 405 Howard St San Francisco CA 94105 Office Phone: 415-773-5650. Office Fax: 415-773-5759. Business E-Mail: ralphbaxter@orrick.com.*

BAXTER, RANDOLPH W., history professor; b. Kingsburg, Calif., May 17, 1963; s. Phillip L. Baxter and Pamela J. Dern, Nino Yannoni (Stepfather), Sandy Robertson (Stepmother); life ptnr. Rick D. Herrera, Mar. 28, 2004. BA in History and Humanities, U. of Calif., Berkeley, 1986; MA in Internat. Affairs, Columbia U., 1990; PhD in History, U. of Calif., Irvine, 1999. Summer intern U.S. Dept. of State, Port Louis, Mauritius, 1989, Coun. on Fgn. Rels., N.Y.C., 1990; devel. asst. Columbia Univ./SIPA, N.Y.C., 1990—93; vis. lectr. in history U. of Calif., Irvine, 1999—2001; vis. lectr. in Am. studies Calif. State U., Fullerton, 2001—. Grad. rep. UCI LGB Ctr. Dir. Search, Irvine, Calif., 1995—96. Author: (article) Nebraska History (James Sellers Award, 2004), (booklet) Bible & Homosexuality. Columnist Fullerton Observer, Fullerton, Calif., 2001—03; bd. dirs. Evangelicals Concerned With Reconciliation (ECWR), Laguna Hills, Calif., 1995—98, Calvary Open Door Ministries, Long Beach, Calif., 1999—2001. Scholar James Harvey Dissertation award, U.C. Irvine, 1998. Mem.: Soc. for Historians of Fgn. Rels., Am. Hist. Assn. D-Liberal. Progressive Evangelical. Avocations: travel, genealogy, hiking. Office Phone: 714-278-2441. E-mail: rbaxter@fullerton.edu.

BAXTER, ROBERT BANNING, insurance company executive; b. Rochester, NY, Aug. 26, 1946; s. Robert Clarkson and Flora Corinne (Banning) B.; m. Sandra Anne Weber, Apr. 21, 1973; children: Matthew Hamilton, Darcy Colson, Jeffrey Ford. BA, U. Rochester, 1968. Chartered property casualty underwriter; cert. ins. counselor. Personal lines account underwriter Allstate Ins. Co., Rochester, 1973-77; asst. personal lines underwriting mgr. Reliance Ins. Co., Pitts., 1977-78, personal lines underwriting mgr. Canandaigua, N.Y., 1978-79, regional personal lines underwriting mgr. Cin., 1979-81, mktg. mgr., 1981-84, Hartford Ins. Group, Cleve., 1984-85; regional mktg. mgr. Nat. Grange Mut. Ins. Co., Syracuse, N.Y., 1985-88; asst. br. mgr., mktg. mgr. Gen. Accident Ins., Syracuse, 1988-90, br. mgr., 1990-93; CEO, gen. mgr. Dryden Mut. Ins. Co., Dryden, N.Y., 1994—. Capt. USAF, 1968—73, Thailand, West Germany. Decorated Air Force Commendation medal (2). Mem. Soc. Chartered Property Casualty Underwriters, Soc. Cert. Ins. Counselors, Ins. Mgrs. Coun., Am. Numismatic Assn., Syracuse (sec.-treas. 1992, v.p. 1993, pres. 1994-95), Ind. Ins. Agts. Assn. N.Y. (assoc.), Profl. Ins. Agts. N.Y. (assoc.), Honorable Order of Blue Goose Internat., N.Y. Ins. Assn. (bd. dirs.), Air Force

Assn., DeWitt Hist. Soc. (bd. trustees 2003-), SAR Soc. Republican. Unitarian Universalist. Avocation: coin collecting/numismatics. Home: 29 Forest Acres Dr Ithaca NY 14850-9782 Office: Dryden Mut Ins Co PO Box 635 12 Ellis Dr Dryden NY 13053 Office Phone: 607-844-8106. Business E-Mail: bob@drydenmutual.com.

BAXTER, ROBERT HAMPTON, insurance executive; b. Glassport, Pa., Mar. 27, 1931; m. Barbara Miller, Aug. 4, 1956. Student, Carnegie Inst. Tech., 1949-50; AB, U.S.C., 1954, JD, 1958. Bar: S.C. bar 1959. Trust officer Citizens & So. Nat. Bank, Charleston, S.C., 1958-60, First Citizens Bank & Trust Co., Charlotte, N.C., 1960-68; with Aetna Life & Casualty Co., Atlanta, 1968-91. Comdr. USNR, 1954—77. Mem. Bernardo Heights (Calif.) C.C., Phi Delta Phi. Presbyterian. Home: 12143 Caminito Corriente San Diego CA 92128-4569

BAXTER, ROBERT JAMES, artist; b. Nov. 30, 1933; BS, U. Wis., 1956, MS, 1959, MFA, 1960. Prof. painting San Diego State U., 1962—75. Exhibitions include Conn. Acad. Fine Arts Ann Wadsworth Atheneum, Hartford, 1962—64, Smithsonian Inst., 1963, Pa. Acad. Fine Arts, Phila., 1963, 1965, San Diego Mus., 1980—81, Gabinetto Nat. Delle Stampe La Farmesina, Rome, 1981, Milw. Art Ctr., Wis., 1981, Phoenix Mus. Art, 1981—82, Gruenwald Coll. Graphic Arts U. Calif., L.A., 1981—82, San Francisco Mus. Art, 1981—82, others, one-man shows include San Francisco Mus. Art, 1970, Represented in permanent collections Vatican Mus., Rome, Chase Manhattan Bank, San Diego Mus. Art, U. N.C., Greensboro, Wichita Falls Mus., Tex., others. Recipient Henry Clay Hofheimer award, Norfolk Mus. Arts and Sci., 1963, Howard Penrose Prize, Conn. Acad. Fine Arts; grantee, Louis Tiffany Found., 1972. Address: PO Box 620437 Woodside CA 94062*

BAXTER, RUTH HOWELL, educational administrator, psychologist; b. Washington; d. Robert R. and Georgie (Murray) Lassiter; m. Edward A. Howell; children: Robert, Astrid, Mova, Mava, Josephine. BS, D.C. Tchrs. Coll.; MA in Edn., George Washington U.; cert. (N.Am. Com. of Oslo scholar), Oslo U.; grad. Adminstr.'s Acad. Class, D.C. Public Schs. Founder, dir., propr. Jewels of Ann. Pvt. Day Sch., Washington, 1970—; tchr. Newlands Infant, Southampton, Eng.; instr. math. demonstration lessons dept. edn. Howard U. Dir. early childhood edn. workshop Brent Elem. Sch., Washington; tchr. adult edn. Air Sch., Woodbridge, Va.; founder, cons. Ask Dr. Ruth Rdnl. Cons. Group; mem. Ednl. Instn. Licensure Commn. Task Forces; mem. Mayor's Pre-White House Conf. on Libraries and Info. Services; exec. high sch. internship program D.C. Public Schs. Author: A Norwegian Birthday Party; contbr. children's stories to various publs. Mem. planning com. Eastern region Jr. Red Cross, Washington; cons. coll. youth motivation task force program Nat. Alliance for Bus.; bd. dirs. Ctr. Ednl. Change D.C. Pub. Schs. Fulbright scholar; North Atlantic scholar; named Outstanding Tchr. of Yr., Future Tchrs. Am.; recipient Outstanding Contbn. award Nat. Assn. Negro Women, Commemorative Medal of Honor. Mem. APA, EVa. Psychol. Assn., English Speaking Union, Columbia Women (sec.), Zeta Phi Beta (life), Phi Delta Kappa. Home: 13349 Delaney Rd Dale City VA 22193

BAXTER, SANDRA L., government agency administrator; BA in English, Howard U.; M in Education, Loyola Coll.; EdD in Social Policy, Harvard Grad. Sch. of Education, 1995. Sr. evaluator US Gen. Acctg. Office; exec. dir. Nat. Inst. Literacy, 2001—. Office: Nat Inst for Literacy 1775 I Street NW Ste 730 Washington DC 20006 Office Phone: 202-233-2025.

BAXTER, STEPHEN BARTOW, retired historian; b. Boston, Mar. 8, 1929; s. James Phinney 3d and Anne (Strang) B.; m. Ann Sweeney, Aug. 22, 1953; children: Clare, Persis Baxter Andrews, James, Nicholas, Stephen, Michael. AB in Econs. with honors, Harvard U., 1950; PhD, Cambridge U., 1955. Instr. history Dartmouth Coll., Hanover, N.H., 1954-57; asst. prof. U. N.C., Chapel Hill, 1958-62, assoc. prof., 1962-66, prof. history, 1966-91, Kenan prof. history, 1975-91. Vis. asst. prof. U. Mo., Columbia, 1957-58; dir. post-doctoral summer seminars Clark Meml. Libr. UCLA, 1973, 88, Clark libr. prof., 1977-78; dir. summer seminars NEH, Chapel Hill, 1974, post-doctoral seminar, 1978-79. Author: The Development of the Treasury, 1660-1702, 1957, William III and the Defense of European Liberty, 1650-1702, 1966; (with Paul R. Sellin) Anglo-Dutch Cross Currents in the Seventeenth and Eighteenth Centuries, 1976; (with others) Major Crises in Western Civilization, vol. 1, 1965, Eighteenth Century Studies Presented to Arthur M. Wilson, 1973, The Revolution of 1688 and the Birth of the English Political Nation, 1973, Biography in the Eighteenth Century, 1980, Changing Views on British History, 1984; editor: Basic Documents of English History, 1968, England's Rise to Greatness, 1660-1763, 1983; mem. editorial bd. Jour. Modern. History, 1971-77, Albion, 1982-92. Guggenheim fellow, 1959-60, 73-74; Charles Henry Fiske III scholar Trinity Coll., 1950-51.

BAXTER, VIOLET DIANE, artist; b. N.Y.C. d. Meyer and Belle (Katz) B.; m. Martin J. Leff, Apr. 25, 1971; 1 child, Mara H. Leff. Cert., Cooper Union, 1960; student, Columbia U., 1961-62, Pratt Graphic Art Ctr., 1980-81. Calligraphy mentor Pratt Inst., N.Y.C., 1974-75; guest lectr. Parsons Sch. Design, 1991 One-woman shows include Aspects Gallery, N.Y.C., 1961, Brata Gallery, N.Y.C., 1962, Ruth Sherman Gallery, N.Y.C., 1963, Pleiades Gallery, N.Y.C., 1985, 87, 89, 91, Suffolk County C.C., Riverhead, N.Y., 1986, Vista World Trade Ctr., N.Y.C., 1991, Nat. Arts Club, N.Y.C., 1999, Gallery Juno, N.Y.C., 2000, S.E. Mo. State U. Mus., Cape Girardeau, Mo., 2002; exhibited in group shows at Nabisco Brands Gallery, 1988, Sharon Creative Arts Foun. Gallery, Conn., 1987, Zenith Gallery, Washington, DC, 1987, Nexus Found., Phila., 1986, Monmouth (N.J.) Mus., 1985, Smithtown Twp. Arts Coun., St. James, N.Y., 1992, NYU, 1993, Salander-O'Reilly Galleries/Fred Hoffman, L.A., 1993, Michael Ingbar Gallery, N.Y.C., 1993, 94, GE Corp. Hdqs., Conn., 1994, Owen Gallery, N.Y.C., 1995, Mus. City of N.Y., 1996, Rockland County (N.Y.) C.C., 1996, Fordham U./Lincoln Ctr., N.Y.C., 1996, Staten Island Inst. Arts and Scis., 1997, Md. Fedn. Art, Annapolis, 1997, 98, 99, 2000, Ice Gallery, N.Y.C., 1997, 98, 99, Pelham (N.Y.) Art Ctr., 1997, Xi'an (China) Acad. Fine Arts, 1997, Badahsenzi Meml. Gallery, Nanchang, China, 1997, Marin-Price Galleries, Chevy Chase, Md., 1998, Butler Inst. Am. Art, Youngstown, Ohio, 1998, Grace Gallery N.Y.C. Tech. Coll., 1998, CUNY, 1999, Boston Ctr. Arts, 1999, Savanah Coll. Art and Design, Ga., 1999, N.Y. Law Sch., N.Y.C., 1999, Fordham U./Lincoln Ctr., N.Y.C., 2000, Butler Inst. Am. Art, Ohio, 2001, Art Students League, N.Y.C., 2001, Mercer County C.C., N.J., 2001, U. Mus. S.E. Mo. State, Cape Girardeau, 2002, Marymount Coll./Fordham U., Tarrytown, N.Y., 2003, David Findlay, Jr. Fine Art, N.Y.C., 2003, Jacqueline Casey Hudgens Ctr. for Arts, Duluth, Ga., 2004, Butler Inst. Am. Art, Youngstown, Ohio, 2005; represented in permanent collections Fidelity Investments, Coun. on Environment of N.Y.C., Mus. City of N.Y., Oppenheimer Capital Corp., Morgan Stanley Trust, Consolidated Edison of N.Y., Schroder & Co., Inc., N.Y.C., Southeast Mo. State U. Mus., Savannah Coll. Art and Design, Guy Carpenter and Co. Ins., N.Y.C.; reviewed and featured in various publs Recipient Gold medal of honor Audubon Artist, 1994, Bronze, 1995, 97, Jane Peterson Meml. award, 1996, Richard Florsheim Art Fund grant, 2002. Mem. N.Y. Artists Equity Assn. (bd. dirs. 1988—, v.p. 1991—, treas. 1997-99, v.p. 1999—), Fine Arts Fedn. N.Y. (dir. 2004—), Nat. Arts Club N.Y.C. (hon.) Home: 333 E 30th St Apt 18L New York NY 10016-6459 Office Phone: 718-482-9980. Personal E-mail: VioletBaxter@aol.com.

BAXTER, WARNER L., energy executive; BS in acctg., U. Mo. Cert. CPA. Sr. mgr. Price WaterhouseCooper, LLC, Acctg. Auditing Svcs. Dept., St. Louis, 1983—93, Price WaterhouseCooper, LLC, SEC Svcs. Dept., N.Y.C., NY; asst. contr. Union Electric, 1995—96, contr., 1996—97; v.p., contr. Ameren Corp. and Ameren Svcs. (following Union Electric and CIPSCO merger), 1997—2001; sr. v.p., fin. Ameren, St. Louis, 2001—03, exec. v.p., CFO, 2003—. Mem.: Mo. Soc. CPA's, Am. Inst. CPA's, Coll. of Bus., Dean's Adv. Bd., Chancellor's Coun., U. Mo. (v.p.), Mo. Energy Policy Coun., Wyman Ctr. (bd. of trustees). Office: Ameren 1901 Chouteau Saint Louis MO 63166-6149

BAY, JOANN REEDER, financial planner; b. Williamsport, Pa., Sept. 29, 1926; d. Rollin A. and Esther Ellen (Costello) Reeder; m. John William Bay, Sr., Aug. 22, 1948; children: John William Jr., Neil Andrew. BA in English & Psychology, Bucknell U., 1948. Cert.: Inst. Paralegal Tng., Phila. (paralegal) 1973; fin. planner Coll. Fin. Planning. Analyst HAY Assoc., Phila., 1973—75, fin. planning cons., 1975—77; prin., owner J.R. Bay Assoc., Drexel Hill, Pa., 1978—. Adv. com. Upper Darby (Pa.) Sch. Bd., 1970—72; exec. v.p. Mother's Group Upper Darby HS, 1970—71, pres. Parent's Group, 1971—72; pro bono work for financially needy women; chmn. investment com. Cmty. Y Ea. Delware County, Upper Darby, 1992—97, Cmty. Y Found., Upper Darby, 1995—97. Named one of 200 Best Fin. Adv. in U.S., Money Mag. Silver Anniversary Issue, 1987. Mem.: Fin. Planning Assn. (llic. practitioner), Delaware County Estate Planning Assn., Philadelphia County Estate Planning Assn., Delaware Valley chpt. IAFP, Women in Transition. Democrat. Presbyterian. Avocations: piano, reading, concerts, museums. Office: JR Bay Associates 5022 Sylvia Rd Drexel Hill PA 19026

BAY, MICHAEL BENJAMIN, film director; b. Los Angeles, Feb. 17, 1965; Grad., Wesleyan U. Dir. Got Milk/Aaron Burr TV commerical (Grand Prix Clio award for Commerical Dir. of Yr., Mus. of Modern Art award for Best Campaign of Yr.), various other TV commericals; (films) Bad Boys, 1995, The Rock, 1996, Bad Boys II, 2003; dir., prodr.: (films) Armageddon, 1998, Pearl Harbor, 2001, The Island, 2005; prodr. (films) The Texas Chainsaw Massacre, 2003, The Amityville Horror, 2005. Named Commerical Dir. of Yr., Directors Guild Am., 1995; named one of 50 Most Powerful People in Hollywood, Premiere mag., 2005. Address: c/o Rob Carlson William Morris Agency One William Morris Pl Beverly Hills CA 90212*

BAYARD, MICHAEL S., priest; b. Milw., Sept. 22, 1965; s. Ralph C and Donna Bayard. BA in Theology, Marquette U., 1983; MA in Christian Spirituality, Creighton U., 1995; M in Div., Weston SJ Sch. of Theology, Cambridge, Mass., 1997; M in Non-Profit Leadership, Seattle U., 2005. Cert. grant writer The Grant Inst., Calif., 2004. Tchr. Red Cloud Indian Sch., Pine Ridge, SD, 1991—93, Marquette U. H.S., 1993—94; campus min. Creighton U., Omaha, 1997—98; assoc. pastor Gesu Ch., Milw., 1998—2000; campus min. Ignatian retreats Seattle U., 2000—. Spiritual dir. SJ Retreat Ho., Oshkosh, Wis., 1994—98. Com. mem. Oreg. Province Jesuits Com. on Spirituality, Portland, Oreg., 2000—04; bd. dirs. Ignatian Spirituality Ctr., Seattle, 2004—05. Home: 924 East Cherry Street Seattle WA 98122 Office: Seattle U Campus Ministry 901 12th Ave Seattle WA 98122-1090 Office Phone: 206-296-2267. Personal E-mail: bayardm@seattleu.edu.

BAYBAYAN, RONALD ALAN, lawyer; b. Paia, Hawaii, July 4, 1946; s. Celedonio Ladresa and Carlina (Domingo) B.; m. Dianne Lea, June 14, 1969 (div. June 1985); children: Alycia Kay, Amber Lea; m. Sharyn Dee Huckins, Dec. 31, 1985 (div. Oct. 1996). BA, Coe Coll., 1968; JD, Drake U., 1974. Bar: Iowa 1977, U.S. Dist. Ct. (so. dist.) Iowa 1977, U.S. Tax Ct. 1978, U.S. Dist. Ct. (no. dist.) Iowa 1980, U.S. Ct. Appeals (8th cir.) 1985, U.S. Supreme Ct. 1985, U.S. Dist. Ct. Hawaii 1986. Asst. law librarian Drake U., Des Moines, 1974-77; assoc. Law Office Mike Wilson, Des Moines, 1977-78; sole practice Des Moines, 1978—. Bd. dirs. Berkley & Co. Amb.; presenter in field. Co-author: Paralegals in Family Law Practice in Iowa, 1995, How to Draft Wills and Trusts in Iowa, 1996, 99, A Practical Guide to Estate Administration in Iowa, 1997. Bd. dirs. Wakonda Christian Ch., 1989-90; dir. communique Victory Christian Ctr., 1991—; mem. bd. counselors Drake U. Law Sch., 1997—. Served with USAF, 1969-73. Mem. ABA, Iowa Bar Assn., Polk County Bar Assn., Am-Filipino Assn. Iowa (bd. dirs. 1986), Bass Anglers Sportsman Soc. (Iowa chpt. pres. 1979-82), Iowans for Better Fisheries (bd. dirs. 1991), Mid-Iowa Bassmasters (past pres., past v.p., past sec.). Republican. Home: 6217 Urbandale Ave Des Moines IA 50322-3541 Office: PO Box 790458 Paia HI 96779-0458

BAYDA, EDWARD DMYTRO, judge; b. Alvena, Sask, Can., Sept. 9, 1931; s. Dmytro Andrew and Mary (Bilinski) B. BA, U. Sask., 1951, LLB cum laude, 1953; LLD (hon.), 1989. Bar: Sask. 1954; created Queen's Counsel, 1966. Barrister, solicitor, Regina, Sask., 1953-72; sr. ptnr. Bayda, Halvorson, Scheibel & Thompson, 1966-72; justice Ct. Queen's Bench for Sask., Regina, 1972-74, Ct. Appeal for Sask., Regina, 1974-81; chief justice Sask., Regina, 1981—. Roman Catholic. Home: 3000 Albert St Regina SK Canada S4S 3N7 Office: Ct Appeal Sask Courthouse 2425 Victoria Ave Regina SK Canada S4P 3V7 E-mail: mrodie@sasklawcourts.ca.

BAYE, MICHAEL ROY, economics professor; b. Dallas, Apr. 6, 1958; s. Firmin Joseph and Exia (Jaynet) B.; m. M'Lissa Arlene, Aug. 6, 1977; children: Natalie, Mitchell. BS in Econs., Tex. A&M U., 1980; MS in Econs., Purdue U., 1981, PhD in Econs., 1983. From asst. prof. econs. to assoc. prof. Tex. A&M U., College Station, 1985—88; from assoc. prof. econs. to prof. econs. Pa. State U., University Park, 1991—97; Bert Elwert prof. bus. Ind. U., 1997—. Cons. in field. Author: Consumer Behavior, 1986, Managerial Economics and Business Strategy, 1994, 4th edit., 2003, Russian translation, 1999, Korean translation, 2002, Money, Banking, and Financial Markets: An Economic Approach, 1995, Indian edit., 1996; mem. editl bd. Jour. Pub. Policy and Mktg., Lecture Notes in Econs. and Math. Systems, Econs. of Governance, Advances in Applied Microeconomics, 1996-; contbr. articles to profl. jours. Recipient Alfred Chalk award, 1980, Tchg. Excellence award KBS, 1997-2000; David Ross fellow, 1982-83, NSF grantee 1984-85, Fulbright fellow 1985-86, Ctr. Economic Rsch. fellow, 1990-; vis scholar KBS, 1995-2002; named Outstanding Rschr. KBS, 1999-2000. Mem. Econometric Soc., Am. Econ. Assn., Royal Econ. Soc., European Econ. Assn. Office: Kelley Sch Bus Bloomington IN 47405

BAYER, ROBERT EDWARD, retired federal agency administrator; b. Cleve., Oct. 26, 1941; s. Charles and Pauline (Kamuf) B.; m. Mary Ellen Horrigan, Dec. 27, 1965 (div. 1981); m. Rozanne Deane Oliver, Jan. 29, 1983; children: Sylvia M., Laura A., Anne M., John C. BS in Social Sci. magna cum laude, John Carroll U., 1962; postgrad., Loyola U., 1962-63. Commd. 2nd lt. USAF, 1963, advanced through grades to lt. col., 1979, ret., 1983; mem. profl. staff Office of Sen. Sam Nunn U.S. Senate, Washington, 1983-86; mem. profl. staff Senate Com. on Armed Svcs., Washington, 1986-93; dep. asst. sec. of def. installations U.S. Dept. Def., Washington, 1993-97, ret., 1997. Mem. Creative Team Concepts LLC; cons. in field. Pastor, spiritual dir. The Seeker Ch., Washington, 1989-93; co-chair Bridge Builders Fund, 1998-2000; mem. Mt. Olivet United Meth. Ch., Arlington, Va. Nat. Def. fellow Loyola U., 1962-63. Mem.: Nat. Assn. Installation Developers, Meth. Fedn. for Social Action, Nat. Alliance for the Mentally Ill, Parents, Families and Friends of Lesbians and Gays. Methodist. Avocations: bicycling, swimming, travel, teaching. Office Phone: 703-276-2829. E-mail: roliver52@comcast.net.

BAYES, BEVERLEY JOAN, retired pediatrician; b. Regina, Can., Nov. 1, 1937; came to U.S., 1988; d. Frederick Charles and Sylvia Mae (Hickling) B.; m. Edgar Gibson Merson, May 25, 1988; children: Jennifer Alice Merson Hersberg, Andrew Charles Merson, Keith Graham Merson. MD, U. Toronto, 1961. Diplomate Am. Bd. Pediat. Intern Toronto (Can.) Gen., 1961-63; resident Hosp. for Sick Children, Toronto, 1963-64, 65-68, Royal Hosp. for Sick Children, Glasgow, Scotland, 1964-65, Children's Hosp. Nat. Med. Ctr., Washington, 1968-69; pediat. Fairfax County (Va.) Health Dept., 1972-82, North Va. Pediat. Assoc., Falls Church, 1982-99, ret., 1999. Family life edn. com. Fairfax County Coun. PTAs, 1982-84, Fairfax County Sch. Bd., 1992-94. Fellow ACP, Am. Acad. Pediat. (program chair Va. chpt. 1992-93). Presbyterian. Avocations: music, gardening, reading, travel, painting.

BAYES, RONALD HOMER, English language educator, writer; b. Freewater, Oreg., July 19, 1932; s. Floyd Edgar and Mildred Florence (Cochran) B. BS, East Oreg. State Coll., 1955, MS, 1956; postgrad., U. Pa., 1959-60; DDM, U. Delle Arti, Termi, Italy, 1982; LHD (hon.), St. Andrews Pres. Coll., 2005. Asst. prof. English Ea. Oreg. State Coll., LaGrande, 1955-56, assoc. prof. English, 1960-68; lectr. English U. Md., College Park, 1958-59, 66-67; disting. prof. creative writing St. Andrews Presbyn. Coll., Laurinburg, 1968—. Founder, exec. bd. St. Andrews Rev. & Press, Laurinburg, 1970-95; mem. N.C. State Arts Coun., Raleigh, 1987-89; master poet Atlantic Ctr. for Arts, New Smyrna Beach, Fla., 1988; cons. Nat. Coun. for Arts, Washington, 1969-71. Author: (poetry) Dust & Desire, 1961, Cages & Journeys, 1964, Child Outside My Window, 1965, History of the Turtle, 1970, The Casketmaker, 1972, Porpoise, 1974, Tokyo Annex, 1977, King of August, 1979, Fram, 1979, Beast in View, 1985, Guises, 1992, Greatest Hits 1969-2002, 2003; (fiction) Sister City, 1971. Chmn. Rep. Ctrl. Com., Union County, Oreg., 1967-68, Scotland County, N.C., 1980-81; bd. dirs. Scotland County Humane Soc., Laurinburg, 1993—. With U.S. Army, 1956-58. Named one of Outstanding Young Men of Am., 1960, master poet Atlantic Ctr. for the Arts, 1988, Disting. Prof. Creative Writing Chair named in his honor, 1999, Emeritus, 2002, Lifetime Achievement award in writing named in his honor, N.C. Writers' Network, 2001; recipient Outstanding Alumni award Ea. Oreg. State Coll., 1973, Roanoke-Chowan prize for poetry, 1973, N.C. Writers' Conf. award, 1987, N.C. award for Literature, 1989, cert. honor Poetry Coun. N.C., 1994, Honor for contr. to N.C. Writers, N.C. State Senate, 2002; fellow Woodrow Wilson Nat. fellow, 1959—60; grantee N.C. arts grantee, 1988. Mem. Danforth Found. (assoc.), Internat. House Japan, Japan Soc., N.C. Poetry Soc. (life), Oregon Poetry Assn. (life), Anti-Vivesection Soc. (life), Mason. Episcopalian. Avocations: gardening, reading, jogging, travel. Home: PO Box 206 Laurinburg NC 28353-0206 Business E-Mail: bayesron@sapc.edu.

BAYH, BIRCH EVANS, JR., lawyer, former senator; b. Terre Haute, Ind., Jan. 22, 1928; s. Birch Evans and Leah (Hollingsworth) B.; m. Marvella Hern, Aug. 24, 1952 (dec. Apr. 1979); 1 son, Birch Evans III; m. Katherine Halpin, 1981; 1 son, Christopher John. BA, Purdue U., 1951; JD, Ind. U., 1960. Bar: Ind. 1961, DC 1978. Engaged in farming, Vigo County, 1952-57; mem. Ind. Ho. of Reps. from Vigo County, 1954-62, minority leader, 1957-58, 61-62, speaker, 1959-60; U.S. senator from Ind., 1962-81; chmn. intelligence com., mem. appropriations, jud. coms.; sr. ptnr. Bayh, Connaughton & Malone PC, Washington; ptnr. Legis. and Regulatory Group, Govt. Div. Venable LLP, Washington. Mem. U. Va. Commn on Presdl. Disability & the Twenty-Fifth Amendment. Mem. Nat. Inst. Against Prejudice and Violence, Fullbright Foreign Scholarship Bd. Named Outstanding Young Man in Ind. Ind. Jr. C. of C., 1959; one of 10 outstanding Reps. in Ind. Gen. Assembly Ind. Newspaper Men and Women Vets., 1961 Mem.: Mental Health Assn. (mem. Nat. Commn. on Insanity Defense). Democrat. Office: Venable LLP 575 7th St NW Washington DC 20004 Office Phone: 202-344-4705. Office Fax: 202-344-8300. E-mail: bbayh@venable.com.

BAYH, EVAN, senator, former governor; b. Terre Haute, Ind., Dec. 26, 1955; s. Birch Evans Jr. and Marvella (Hern) B.; married. BS in Bus. Econs., Ind. U., 1978; JD, U. Va., 1981. Atty. Bingham, Summers, Welsh & Spilman; sec. of state State of Ind., Indpls., 1987-89, gov., 1989-96; ptnr. Baker & Daniel Assocs., Indpls., 1997-98; U.S. senator from Ind., 1999—. Chmn. State Recount Commn. & Corp. Law com.; mem. Nat. Edn. Goals Panel & Nat. Assessment Edn. Panel; chmn. Edn. Commn. States; vice chmn. Nat. Govs. Assn. Task Force Workforce Devel. Democrat. Office: US Senate 463 Russell Senate Office Bldg Washington DC 20510-0001 also: 10 W Market St Ste 1650 Indianapolis IN 46204-2934*

BAYLES, JENNIFER LUCENE, museum program director, educator; b. Tokyo, May 26, 1953; d. Lewis Allen Bayles and Rosemary (Beuhler) Fraser; m. Robert Steinfeld, July 4, 1992; children: Noah Isaac Steinfeld, Ezra Milton Steinfeld. BA in Art History with honors, Ind. U., Bloomington, 1976; MA in Art History, U. Mich., 1984, cert. in mus. practice, 1984. Curatorial apprentice Indpls. Mus. Art, 1976; mus. apprentice Portland (Oreg.) Art Mus., 1976-78, asst. curator edn., 1978-81; asst. curator photographic collection dept. art history U. Mich., Ann Arbor, 1981-83, rsch. and editl. asst. Mus. Art, 1982-83; intern dept. mus. edn. Art Inst. Chgo., 1983-84; curator edn. Albright-Knox Art Gallery, Buffalo, 1984—2001, educator spl. projects, 2001—. Horace H. Rackman Grad. scholar, 1981—83, Acad. scholar, U. Mich., 1982. Mem.: Am. Assn. Mus. (regional rep. edn. com. 1979—81). Office: Albright-Knox Art Gallery 1285 Elmwood Ave Buffalo NY 14222-1096 Office Phone: 716-270-8252. E-mail: jbayles@albrightknox.org.

BAYLESS, BETSEY, state official; b. Phoenix; BA in Latin Am. Studies and Spanish, U. Ariz., 1966; MPA, Ariz. State U., 1974; DHL (hon.), U. Ariz., 2001. V.p. pub. fin. Peacock, Hislop, Staley & Given, Inc., Phoenix; asst. dir. Ariz. Bd. Regents; acting dir. dept. revenue State of Ariz., dir. dept. adminstrn., sec. of state, 1997—2003; dir. Ariz. Dept. Adminstrn., 2003—. Bd. suprs. Maricopa County, 1989-97, chmn. bd., 1992, 94, vice chair, 1997; mem. Ariz. Bd. Investment, 2003—; bd. dirs. Child Help Ariz.; mem. Nat.bd. dirs. U. Ariz. Coll. of Bus. and Pub. Adminstrn.; adv. bd. Ariz. State U. West. Bd. dirs. Xavier Coll. Preparatory Found., Charter 100, Valley Leadership Class VI, Ariz. Rep. Caucus, Ariz. Women's Forum, 4-H Found., Ariz. Cmty. Found.; mem. leadership bd. U. Ariz. Health Svcs.-Phoenix Campus. Named to Hall of Fame, Ariz. State U. Coll. Pub. Programs; recipient Disting. Citizen award U. Ariz. Alumni Assn., Woman of Yr. award Capitol chpt. Bus. and Profl. Women, Disting. Achievement award NEH Fellowship, Achievement award Nat. Assn. Counties, 1993, Citizen award Bur. Reclamation, 1993, Woman of Achievement award Xavier Coll. Preparatory, 1995. Mem. Phi Beta Kappa (Freeman medal 1966). Republican.

BAYLESS, CAROLYN COTTON, nurse; b. Marietta, Ga., Aug. 16, 1948; d. John Lamar Cotton and Jeanne Walker Garriss; m. Luke Edward Bayless, Dec. 17., 1995. BSN, Brenau U., 1990; MBA, Mercer U., 1998. Cert. nurse adminstr. ANA, 1992; lic. nursing home adminstr., RN. Coord. chem. dependency unit N.E. Ga. Med. Ctr., Gainesville, 1984-90, unit dir., 1990-95; dir. NGHS LTC Svcs./Northeast Ga. Health System, Inc., Gainesville, 1995-2001; co-founder One Voice, Inc., Hiawassee, Ga., 2001—; RN Piedmont Hosp., Atlanta, 2001—02, clin. mgr. transplant unit and med./surg. unit, 2002—. Mem. Am. Coll. Healthcare Adminstrs. (Ga. chpt.), Complimentary Alternative Med. Assn., Ga. Nurses Assn., Sigma Theta Tau. Office: One Voice Inc 1435 Long Ridge Rd Hiawassee GA 30546 Home: 1435 Long Ridge Rd Hiawassee GA 30546

BAYLESS, DOLAN JAY, church music director; b. Topeka, Kans., Dec. 24, 1950; s. Jay C. and Ruth A. Bayless; m. Kathleen Susan Kirwan, Jan. 4, 1972; children: Brant, Cory, Kara. MusB, Washburn U., 1972; MusM, U. Kans., 1978. Dir. music First United Meth. Ch., Ponca City, Okla., 1978—97, dir. music ministries Lake Jackson, Tex., 1997—. Musical dir., condr. Houston Bronze Ensemble, 2001—; bd. of directors, treas., registrar Tex. Conf. Choir Clinic, Inc., Lake Jackson, Tex., 1981—; bd. dirs. Area IX, Am. Guild English Handbell Ringers, Inc., Dallas, 1993—. Home: 719 Walnut St Lake Jackson TX 77566 Office Phone: 979-297-3046.

BAYLESS, LYN NIXON, librarian; b. Little Rock, July 17, 1949; d. William Robert and Jane Carolyn (Cheairs) Nixon; m. Henry Montgomery Bayless, Mar. 13, 1976; children: Jefferson Philip, Thomas Walton. BA in History, U. Ark., 1971; MLS, George Peabody Coll., Nashville, 1974. Children's libr. Jefferson County Pub. Libr., Pine Bluff, Ark., 1971-73; libr. John W. Finney Meml. Libr. Columbia State Community Coll., Columbia, Tenn., 1974—. Bd. dirs. King's Daus.' Sch., 1982-90, 94-2003; v.p. bd. dirs., 1986-90; circle leader, Mt. Pleasant, Tenn., 1983-84, 91—; sec. Maury County Union, 1984-86; mem. adv. bd. Working Opportunities for Women, 1988-90; mem. coun. on ministries First United Meth. Ch., Mt. Pleasant, mem. subcom. chair 40th Ann. Com. Columbia State CC. Mem. Tenn. Libr. Assn., Va. Mai Kittrell Cir. of Mt. Pleasant (pres. 1983-84, 91-94), Assn. for Preservation of Tenn. Antiquities. Democrat. Methodist. Avocations: needlecrafts, reading, swimming, travel. Office: Columbia State Community Coll PO Box 1315 Columbia TN 38402-1315 Office Phone: 931-540-2559. Business E-Mail: bayless@columbiastate.edu.

BAYLESS, RICK, chef; b. Oklahoma City, 1953; m. Deann Bayless. Host PBS TV series Cooking Mexican, 1978—79; owner, chef Frontera Grill, Chgo., 1987—, Topolombampo, Chgo., 1989—; host PBS series Mexico One Plate at a Time With Rick Bayless, 2000—. N. Cheffs Collaborative 2000;

ptnr. Frontera Foods, 1995. Author: Authentic Mexican, 1987, Rick Bayless's Mexican Kitchen, 1996, Salsas That Cook, 1999; co-author (with daughter Lanie Bayless): Rick & Lanie's Excellent Kitchen Adventures, 2004; appeared on TV programs: Today, Good Morning Am., This Morning, Martha Stewart Living, Cooking Live, In Julia's Kitchen with Master Chefs, Great Chefs of Am., others; contbr. to numerous food and cooking publs.; contbg. editor: Saveur. Named Best New Chef of 1988, Food and Wine mag., Best Am. Chef: Midwest, James Beard Found., 1991; recipient Nat. Chef of Yr. award, 1995, Chef of Yr. award, Internat. Assn. Clinary Profls., 1995, Humanitarian of Yr., James Beard Found., 1998. Office: Frontera Grill 445 N Clark St Chicago IL 60610*

BAYLIS, THOMAS ARTHUR, political science educator; b. Providence, R.I., Feb. 28, 1937; s. Charles A. and Ruth Weage B.; m. Helen E. Ullrich, Aug. 28, 1969 (div. Oct. 1979), Theresa M. Kelley, Nov. 23, 1985; children: Patrick AB, Duke U., 1958; postgrad., Free U., Berlin, 1958-59; MA, U. Calif., Berkeley, 1961, PhD, 1968. Acting instr. in polit. sci. U. Calif., Berkeley, 1966-67; instr. polit. sci. Duke U., Durham, N.C., 1967-69; asst. prof. polit. sci. SUNY, Albany, 1969—74; assoc. prof. of polit. sci. U. Tex., San Antonio, 1974-90, prof. polit. sci., 1990-2000; sr. lectr. polit. sci. U. Wis., Madison, 2001—04. Vis. assoc. prof. govt. U. Tex., Austin, 1990, 2000; vis. fellow Western Socs. Program Cornell U., Ithaca, N.Y., 1984-85; fellow Inst. for Sino-Soviet Studies George Washington U., 1987-88. Author: The Technical Intelligentsia and the East German Elite, 1974, Governing by Committee, 1989, The West and Eastern Europe, 1994; contbr. articles to profl. jours. Recipient Fulbright rsch. award U.S. Govt., 1980-81, Rsch. and Publ. award 20th Century Fund, 1986-93. Mem. German Dem. Republic Studies Assn. (pres. 1986-89), Southwestern Assn. of Slavic Studies (pres. 1996-97). Avocation: music. Home: 725 Oneida Pl Madison WI 53711 E-mail: tbaylis@polisci.wisc.edu.

BAYLOR, DENIS ARISTIDE, neuroscientist, educator; b. Oskaloosa, Iowa, Jan. 30, 1940; s. Hugh Murray and Elisabeth Anne (Barbou) B.; m. Eileen Margaret Steele, Aug. 12, 1983; children: Denis Murray, Michael Randel; 1 stepchild, Michele Gonelli. BA in Chemistry magna cum laude, Knox Coll., 1961, DS (hon.), 1989; MD cum laude, Yale U., 1965. Post-doctoral fellow Yale Med. Sch., New Haven, 1965-68; staff assoc. NINDS, Bethesda, Md., 1968-70; USPHS spl. fellow Physiol. Lab. Cambridge U., England, 1970-72; assoc. prof. physiology U. Colo. Med. Sch., Denver, 1972-74, Stanford U., Calif., 1974-75, assoc. prof. neurobiology, 1975-78, prof. neurobiology, 1978—2001, chmn. dept. neurobiology, 1992-95; sr. sci. officer Howard Hughes Med. Inst., 2004—; First Annual W.S. Stiles lecturer U. Coll., London, 1989; Jonathan Magnes lecturer Hebrew U., Jerusalem, 1990; Woolsey lectr. U. Wis., 1992; E. Hille lectr. U. Wash., 1995. Mem. NIH Visual Scis. Study Sect., 1984-88, chmn., 1986-88; vis. com. med. scis. Harvard U., 1987-93; chmn. Summer conf. on Vision FASEB, 1989; Wellcome vis. prof. U. Miami, 1995; mem. sci. adv. com. Alcon Rsch. Inst., 1994-99; mem. HHMI Sci. adv. bd. 1997-2003, Med. adv. bd. 1998-01; mem. sci. adv. bd. Found. Fighting Blindness, 1998—; trustee The Grass Found., 1995-99. Mem. editorial bd. Jour. Physiology, 1977-84, Neuron, 1988-93, Jour. Neurophysiology, 1989—, Visual Neurosci., 1990-93, Jour. Neurosci., 1991—; contbr. articles to profl. jours. Recipient Sinsheimer Found. award, 1975, Mathilde Solowey award, 1978, Kayser Internat. award Retina Rsch. Found., 1988, Golden Brain award Minerva Found., 1988, Merit award Nat. Eye Inst., 1990, Alcon Rsch. Inst. award, 1991; Rank Optoelectronics prize Rank Orgn., Eng., 1980; Proctor medal Assn. Rsch. Vision & Ophthalmology, 1986, Von Sallman prize in eye rsch., 1998. Fellow Am. Acad. Arts and Scis.; mem. NAS, Royal Soc. London, Phi Beta Kappa, Alpha Omega Alpha. Avocations: golf, woodworking. Office: Stanford U Sch Med Neurobiology/Fairchild D253 835 Esplanada Way Stanford CA 94305 E-mail: dbaylor@stanford.edu.

BAYLY, JOHN HENRY, JR., judge; b. Washington, Jan. 26, 1944; s. John Henry and Salome Carole (Winters) B.; m. Barbara Jean Downey, Feb. 16, 1974 (dec. Jan. 1977); 1 child, Anne Louise; m. Katherine Bridget Kenny, Dec. 1, 1979; children: Johanna, Georgia. AB, Fordham U., 1966; JD, Harvard U., 1969. Bar: U.S. Dist. Ct. D.C. 1969, U.S. Ct. Appeals (D.C. cir.) 1969, D.C. 1971, U.S. Supreme Ct. 1974. Atty., advisor FCC, Washington, 1969-71; asst. atty. Office of U.S. Atty., Washington, 1971-75, 78-85; dep. minority counsel Senate Select Com. on Intelligence, Washington, 1975-76; acting asst. gen. counsel Corp. for Pub. Broadcasting, Washington, 1976-78; gen. counsel Legal Services Corp., Washington, 1985-87, pres., 1987-88; of counsel Stein, Mitchell & Mezines, Washington, 1988-90; judge D.C. Superior Ct., 1990—. Mem. D.C. Bar Assn., John Carroll Soc., Counsellors, Bryant Inn of Ct., Lawyers Club Washington, Phi Beta Kappa. Republican. Roman Catholic. Home: 3512 Runnymede Pl NW Washington DC 20015-2420 Office: DC Superior Ct 500 Indiana Ave NW Ste 1 Washington DC 20001-2131 Business E-Mail: baylyjh@dcsc.gov.

BAYM, NINA, literature educator; b. Princeton, N.J., June 14, 1936; d. Leo and Frances (Levinson) Zippin; m. Gordon Baym, June 1, 1958; children—Nancy, Geoffrey; m. Jack Stillinger, May 21, 1971 BA, Cornell U., 1957; MA, Harvard U., 1958, PhD, 1963. Asst. U. Calif.-Berkeley, 1962-63; instr. U. Ill., Urbana, 1963-67, asst. prof. English, 1967-69, assoc. prof., 1969-72, prof., 1972—, Jubilee prof. liberal arts and scis., 1989—, dir. Sch. Humanities Urbana, 1976-87, sr. Univ. scholar, 1985, assoc. Ctr. Advanced Study, 1989-90, permanent prof. Ctr. Advanced Study, 1997—, Swanlund Endowed chair, 1997—. Author: The Shape of Hawthorne's Career, 1976, Woman's Fiction: A Guide to Novels By and About Women in America, 1978, 2d rev. edit., 1993, Novels, Readers and Reviewers: Responses to Fiction in Antebellum America, 1984, The Scarlet Letter: A Reading, 1986, Feminism and American Literary History, 1992, American Women Writers and the Work of History, 1790-1860, 1995, American Women of Letters and the 19th Century Sciences, 2002; gen. editor: Norton Anthology of American Literature; sr. editor Am. Nat. Biography; also author essays, edits., revs.; mem. editl. bd. Am. Quar., New Eng. Quar., Legacy, A Jour. of 19th Century Am. Women Writers, Jour. Aesthetic Edn. Am. Lit., Tulsa Studies in Women's Lit., Am. Studies, Studies Am. Fiction, Am. Periodicals, Hemingway Rev., Resources for Am. Lit. Study, Am. Lit. History, Cambridge U.P. Studies in Am. Lit. and Culture; mem. editl. adv. bd. PMLA. Guggenheim fellow, 1975-76, AAUW hon. fellow, 1975-76, NEH fellow, 1982-83; rec pient Arnold O. Beckman award U. Ill., 1992-93, Hubbell Lifetime Achievement medal, Am. Let. Sect., 2000. Mem. MLA (exec. com. 19th century Am. Lit. divsn., chmn. 1984, chmn. Am. Lit. sect. 1984, Hubbell Lifetime Achievement medal 2000), Am. Studies Assn. (exec. com. 1982-84, nominating com. 1991-93), Am. Lit. Assn., Am. Antiquarian Soc., Mass. Hist. Soc., Nathaniel Hawthorne Soc. (adv. bd.), Western Lit. Assn., Mortar Bd., Phi Kappa Phi, Phi Beta Kappa. Office: U Ill Dept English 608 S Wright St Urbana IL 61801-3630 Office Phone: 217-333-2391. Business E-Mail: baymnina@uiuc.edu.

BAYMILLER, LYNDA DOERN, social worker; b. Milw., July 6, 1943; d. Ronald Oliver and Marian Elizabeth (Doern) B. Student, U. Hawaii, 1962, Mich. State U., 1965; BA, U. Wis., 1965, MSW, 1969. Vol. Peace Corps, Chile, 1965-67; social worker Luth. Social Svcs. of Wis. and Upper Mich., Milw., 1969-77, contract social worker, 1978-79; dist. supr. Childrens Svc. Soc. Wis., Kenosha, 1977-78; social work supr. Sauk County Dept. Human Svcs., Baraboo, Wis., 1979-90; sales and relief mgr.-trainee Wal-Mart, 1992-93, cashier, 1993—. Author: (with Clara Amelia Hess) Now-Won, A Collection of Feeling Poetry, 1973. Bd. dirs. Zoo Pride, Zool Soc. Milwaukee County, 1975-77, Sauk County Mental Health Assn., 1979-84; mem. Harmony chpt. Sweet Adelines, West Allis, Wis., 1970-75, pres. chpt., 1971; pres. bd. dirs. Growing Place Day Care Ctr., Kenosha, 1977-78; mem. Baraboo (Wis.) Centennial Com., 1982; pres. bd. dirs. Laubach Literacy Coun., Baraboo, 1986-88; mem. Sauk County Humane Soc., 1987—, sec., 1988-90. Mem. NASW, Acad. Cert. Social Workers, AAUW (br. sec. 1982-84), U. Wis. Alumni Assn. (life), Am. Legion Aux., DAR, Nat. Soc. Magna Carta Dames, Eddy Family Assn. (life), Nat. Soc. Ancient and Hon. Arty. Co. of Mass. (life), Wis. Soc. Daus. of 1812 (rec. sec. 1994-96), Sauk County Hist. Soc., Internat. Crane Found. (patron), Daus. Colonial Wars, Daus. Am. Colonists, Zool. Soc. Milwaukee County (life), Am. Bus. Womens Assn.(Baraboo chptr. 21), Order Eastern Star (grad. rep. Miss. in Wis. 1988-90), Order White Shrine of Jerusalem, Ladies Aux. of Fraternal Order Eagles, Cameo Club (Reedsburg chptr. 26), Queen of Sheba Order Eastern Star, Alpha Xi Delta.

BAYNE, DAVID COWAN, priest, educator, lawyer; b. Detroit, Jan. 11, 1918; s. David Cowan and Myrtle (Murray) B. AB, U. Detroit, 1939; LLB, Georgetown U., 1947, LLM, 1948; MA, Loyola U., Chgo., 1946, STL, 1953; SJD (grad. fellow), Yale, 1949; LLD (hon.), Creighton U., 1980. Bar: Fed. and D.C. 1948, Mich. 1960, Mo. 1963. Joined Soc. of Jesus, 1941; ordained priest Roman Catholic Ch., 1952; asst. prof. law U. Detroit, 1954-60; acting dean U. Detroit (Law Sch.), 1955-59, dean, 1959-60; research assoc. Nat. Jesuit Research Orgn., Inst. Social Order, St. Louis, 1960-63; vis. lectr. St. Louis U. Law Sch., 1960-63, prof. law, 1963-67; vis. prof. Mich. Law Sch., 1967, Inst. fur Auslandisches und Internationales Wirtschaftrecht, Frankfurt, 1967; prof. U. Iowa Coll. Law, Iowa City, 1967-88, prof. emeritus, 1988—. Vis. prof. U. Koln, Germany, 1970, 74 Author: Conscience, Obligation and the Law, 1966, 2d edit., 1988; The Philosophy of Corporate Control, 1986; editor legal materials; contbr. articles to profl. jours. Achievements include research in corp. law. E-mail: dcbsj@netzero.net, dcbsj@buckeye-express.com.

BAYNE, JAMES ELWOOD, financial consultant; b. Detroit, May 6, 1940; s. John David and Alice Angie (Davis) Bayne; children: James E. Jr., Laura Lee Poe. BA, Yale U., 1962; MBA, Columbia U., 1967. Investment adminstr. Bankers Trust, N.Y.C., 1962-65; fin analyst Std. Oil, N.Y.C., 1967; sr. fin. analyst Esso Internat., N.Y.C., 1967-70; asst. treas. Esso S.A.P.A., Buenos Aires, 1970-71; treas. Intercol, Bogota, Colombia, 1971-74; asst. treas. Esso InterAm., Coral Gables, Fla., 1974-77; asst. gen. mgr. Esso Ctrl. Am., Coral Gables, 1977-80; mgr. Mexican Bus. Opportunity, Coral Gables, 1980-81; treas. Exxon Chem. Europe, Brussels, 1981-86; mgr., benefits fin. and investment Exxon, Dallas, 1986-99; mgr. benefits fin. and investment Exxon Mobil, Dallas, 1999-2000; cons., advisor to fin. svcs. industry Dallas, 2001—; pres., CEO 1st & 5th Dance Ctr. Inc., 2002—05. Exec. com. CIEBA, Washington, 1994—, vice chmn., 1995—96, chmn., 1996—98; pension adv. com. N.Y. Stock Exch., N.Y.C., 1995—99; mem. adv. bd. Wharton Trading Sys., 1993—96; bd. dirs. Church Life Ins. Co.; mem. adv. com. Aslan Capital, 2001—; mem. Nat. Commn. on Retirement Policy, 1997—99. Del. 1st White Ho. Summit Retirement Savs., Washington, 1998; v.p. Incarnation Found., 1996—2003; adv. com. Asian Capital, 2001—; pres. secretariat Dallas-Ft. Worth Cursillo Movement, 1992—96; dir. Dallas-Ft. Worth Episcopal Renewal Ctr., 1994—2002; chair Episcopal Renewal Ctr., 1996—2002; mem. investment com. Episcopal Found. Dallas, 1998—2003; trustee Ch. Pension Fund, N.Y.C., 1999—, chair fin. com.; mem. steering com. Interforum, 1993—96; bd. dirs. Fin. Execs. Inst., 1996—98. Mem.: Yale Club N.Y., Yale Club Dallas, Order St. John. Episcopalian. Avocations: church work, walking, reading, travel. Home: 3401 Lee Pkwy # 1704 Dallas TX 75219 E-mail: venturejim@msn.com.

BAYNE, STEPHEN B., electronics engineer, researcher; s. Alton and Mary Bayne. BSEE, Tex. Tech U., 1993, MSEE, 1994, PhD in Elec. Engring., 1997. Rsch. asst. Tex. Tech U., 1993—97, rsch. assoc., 1997—98; electronic engr. Naval Rsch. Lab., Washington, 1998—2000, Adelphi, Md., 2000—; adj. prof. Tex. Tech U.; program evaluator Accredidation Bd. for Engr. Adj. prof. Howard U., Washington, 2001. Author: (research) Inductive Switching of 4H-SiC Gate Turn-Off Thyristors; contbr. chapters to books. With USAF, 1986—90. Central Power and Light scholar for Academic Excellence. Mem.: IEEE (sr.; mem. rev. com. 1999—), Eta Kappa Nu. Achievements include research in MOS-Gated Thyristors (MCTs) for repetitive high power switching; half-bridge inverter using 4H-SiC gate turn-off thyristors; inductive switching of 4H-SiC gate turn-off thyristors. Home: 8801 Castlebury Ct Laurel MD 20723 Office: Army Research Lab 2800 Powder Mill Rd Adelphi MD 20783 Personal E-mail: dvsbb@yahoo.com. Business E-Mail: sbayne@arl.army.mil.

BAYNES, THOMAS EDWARD, JR., retired judge, lawyer, educator; b. N.Y.C., Mar. 19, 1940; s. Thomas Edward and Ann Jane (Burke) B.; m. Maija Eva Kokko, Dec. 30, 1963; children: Cynthia Lynn, Barbara Ann. BBA, U. Ga., 1962; JD, Emory U., 1967, LLM, 1972, Yale U., 1973. Bar: Ga. 1968, U.S. Supreme Ct. 1971, Ct. of Mil. Appeals 1978, Fla. 1981. Dir. Legal Assistance to Inmates Program, Emory U., 1968-69; asst. dean, asst. prof. bus. law Ga. State U., 1969-72; acting regional dir. Nat. Ctr. for State Cts., Atlanta, 1973-74; prof. law and public adminstrn. Nova U. Law Ctr., Ft. Lauderdale, Fla., 1974-76, 77-81; jud. fellow U.S. Supreme Ct., 1976-77; speedy trial reporter U.S. Dist. Ct., So. Dist. Fla., 1977-81; ptnr. Peterson, Myers, Craig, Crews, Brandon & Mann, Lake Wales, Fla., 1981-87; U.S. bankruptcy judge for mid. dist. Fla. U.S. Bankruptcy Ct., Tampa, 1987—2005, chief bankruptcy judge, 2000—03; ret., 2005. State chmn., Ga., Nat. Council on Crime and Delinquency, 1971-72; legal counsel Reorgn. Study Commn. Ga., 1971-72 Author: (with W. Scott) Legal Aspects of Laboratory Medicine in Quality Assurance in Laboratory Management, 1978, Eminent Domain in Florida, 1979, Florida Mortgage Law, 1999, (with others) Supreme Court Justices, Illustrated Biographies, 1993; supplement editor Fla. Real Estate Law and Procedure, 1976; contbg. editor Norton Bankruptcy Law and Practice, 1995. Bd. dirs. F. Lee Moffitt Cancer Rsch Hosp., Tampa, 1989-94, 97—. Comdr. JAGC, USNR, 1960-80, ret. Sterling fellow Yale U. Law Sch., 1972-73; Harry J. Loman Found. rsch. fellow, 1979. Mem. Ga. Bar Assn., Fla. Bar Assn. (cert. cir. ct. and fed. ct. mediator and arbitrator), Am. Law Inst., Hillsborough Assn. Women Lawyers (bd. dirs. 2001-04), Fla. Acad. Profl. Mediators Inc., Supreme Ct. Hist. Soc., Am. Arbitration Assn., Nat. Adv. Com. for Bankruptcy, Ferguson-White Inn (pres. 1992-93, master), Omicron Delta Kappa. Personal E-mail: tebaynes@aol.com.

BAYONA, MANUEL, medical educator; MD, Nat. U. Mex., 1977, MSc Biostatistics, 1979; PhD in Epidemiology, Johns Hopkins U., 1985. Intern Chihuahua Gen. Hosp., Chihuahua City, Mexico, 1975; med. social svc. intern Nat. U. Mex., Mexico City, 1976; cons. epidemiologist WHO, Ouagadougou, Burkina Faso, 1985—86; cons. pub. health specialist/epidemiologist Westinghouse Corp./Guatemalan Ministry of Health and USAID, Guatemala City, 1986; epidemiologist Arthritis Rsch. Inst. Am., Clearwater, Fla., 1987; cons. epidemiologist PAHO/WHO and Sch. Malariology and Environ. Sanitation, Min. of Health Venezuela, Maracay, 1987; temp. advisor PAHO/WHO, Washington, 1988; cons. epidemiologist, vis. prof. Min. Health of Venezuela, Maracay, 1988; med. epidemiologist and program dir. UNICEF, Mexico City, 1991—92; acad. coord. Pan Am. Health Orgn. and U. South Fla., Tampa, 1993—95; dir. pub. health program Coll. Allied Health, Nova Southeastern U., Ft. Lauderdale, Fla., 1995—96; acad. coord. Sch. Malariology and Environ. Health Ministry of Health of Venezuela, Pan Am. Health Orgn. and World Bank, Maracay, 1998—2001; assoc. prof., dir. Ctr. for Internat. Health and Tropical Diseases, dir. Dr.P.H. Sch. Pub. Health U. North Tex. Health Sci. Ctr., Ft. Worth, 2000—; assoc. prof. epidemiology, dir. doctoral program, assoc. dir. rsch. Tex. Inst. Hispanic Health, Fort Worth, 2005—. Vis. prof. Ponce Sch. Medicine, Ponce, PR, 1994—, Carabobo U., Maracay, 1997—2001; adj. asst. prof. dept. internal medicine U. South Fla., Tampa, 1994—95; vis. lectr. U. Autonoma de Ciudad Juarez, Mexico, 2003; vis. prof. U. P.R. and Glaxo Wellcome Labs., 1998; cons. epidemiologist in field; vis. prof. numerous colls. and univs.; lectr. in field. Contbr. numerous articles, abstracts to profl. jours. Recipient numerous rsch. grants, fellowships; grantee, Pan Am. Health Orgn. and World Bank, 1999, Tobacco Rsch. grantee, U. N. Tex. Health Sci. Ctr., 2000. Mem.: APHA, Fla. Pub. Health Assn., Internat. Epidemiol. Assn., Internat. Biometric Soc., Soc. Epidemiologic Rsch. Achievements include invention of method and apparatus for fast and non-invasive diagnosis of malaria; spectrophotometric characterization of human blood; patents for in field. Office: Univ of North Texas Health Sci Ctr EAD 701-A 3500 Camp Bowie Blvd Fort Worth TX 76107-2699

BAYRAKTAR, ILHAN, engineer, researcher; PhD in Aerospace Engring., Old Dominion U., Norfolk, Va., 1998—2002. Rsch. engr. Langley Full Scale Tunnel, Langley Air Force Base, Va., 2001—. Recipient WP Award, Ansys, 2004. Mem.: AIAA, Soc. Automotive Engrs. Office: Langley Full Scale Tunnel PO Box 65309 Langley Afb VA 23665 Office Phone: 757-766-2266 113.

BAYRAKTAROGLU, ISMET, computer engineer; s. Nedim and Mediha Bayraktaroglu. PhD, U. of Calif, San Diego, 2001. Staff engr. Sun Microsystems, Sunnyvale, Calif., 2001—.

BAYS, JAMES C., lawyer; b. Denton, Tex., July 23, 1949; BA magna cum laude, Dartmouth Coll., 1971; JD, U. Va., 1974. Bar: Ohio 1974. Assoc. Jones, Day, Reavis & Pogue, 1974—78; counsel TRW, Inc., 1978—81, sr. counsel, 1981—85, v.p., asst. gen. counsel, 1985—92, GenCorp, Inc., 1993—96; sr. v.p., gen. counsel, chief legal officer Invensys plc, London, 1996—2001; v.p., gen. counsel Ferro Corp., Cleve., 2001—. Mem. editl. bd.: Va. Law Review, 1972—74. Mem.: ABA, Ohio State Bar Assn., Cleve. State Bar Assn. Office: Ferro Corp 1000 Lakeside Ave Cleveland OH 44114-7000 Office Phone: 216-875-6122. Office Fax: 216-696-6958. E-mail: baysj@ferro.com.

BAYS, JOHN THEOPHANIS, consulting engineer; b. Bklyn., July 17, 1947; s. Theophanis A. and Mildred Bays; m. Mindy Giardina, July 8, 1973; 1 dau., Nina. BS, N.Y. Inst. Tech., 1972; BArch, CCNY, 1974; cert. in solar design, Ohio State U., 1975. Cert. energy mgr., energy auditor, asbestos investigator, N.Y. Project mgr., head sys. designer Wormser Sci. Corp., Stamford, Conn., 1975-82, v.p. engring., 1982-85; pres. E.E. Linden Assocs., Cons. Engrs., Norwalk, Conn., 1985—. Recipient awards in solar design. Mem.: ASHRAE. Home: 18 Marion Rd Westport CT 06880-2919 Office: 110 Richards Ave Norwalk CT 06854-1622 Office Phone: 203-299-1600. E-mail: j.t.bays@eelinden.com.

BAYS, MONA RAE, retired librarian; b. Mattoon, Ill., June 16, 1950; d. Alburn Marion and Doris Madeline Reynolds Grafton; m. Michael Allan Bays, Mar. 20, 1999; children: Brent Allan, Clinton Andrew. BA in English, Ea. Ill. U., 1972; MA in Librarianship, U. Denver, 1973. Youth libr. Mattoon (Ill.) Pub. Libr., 1973-75, cataloger, 1975-76, libr., 1976-94, dir., 1994—2002. Author: A House Not Made With Hands, 1981. Elder, bd. dirs. First Christian Ch. of Mattoon. Named Best Boss in Ctrl. Ill. Decatur Herald and Rev., 1987, Young Careerist Bus. and Profl. Women's Assn., 1978. Mem. ALA, Am. Bus. Women's Assn. (Woman of Yr. Mattoon chpt. 1980, 95, Pegtown chpt. 1999), Women of the Moose, Ill. Libr. Assn. Avocations: golf, travel. E-mail: mmbays@consolidated.net.

BAYS, THERESA, music director, liturgist; b. Jersey City, June 24, 1961; d. Pat and Elizabeth Fiorito; m. Robert Alexander Bays, May 24, 2000. MusB in Music Edn., U. Hartford, 1983. Cert. tchr. NJ, in hypnosis NJ. Dir. music St. Margaret of Cortona Ch., Little Ferry, NJ, 1984—86, Our Lady of Good Coun. Roman Cath. Ch., Washington Township, NJ, 1987—88, St. Cassian's Ch., Montclair, NJ, 1988—89, Notre Dame Ch., North Caldwell, NJ, 1989—2000; dir. music and liturgy St. Patrick's Roman Cath. Ch., Carlsbad, Calif., 2000—02, St. John Vianney Roman Cath. Ch., Sedona, Ariz., 2002—. Tchr. acting through song program Magnet Sch. Gifted and Talented Program, Teaneck, NJ, 1985—86; presenter cantor workshops Diocese of Newark, Newark, 1992—2000; workshop presenter on ritual Conscious Consulting, London, 2000—; dir., founder Strolling Quartet Carolers. Singer: National Anthem soloist; singer: (role of Anita) West Side Story; singer: (role of Hodel) Fiddler on the Roof; singer: (role of Marie) The Sound of Music; singer: (one-woman show) Listen to my Heart, (solo CD) Spark of Creation. Vol. Dem. Party, Hackensack, NJ, 1985—2000, Sedona, 2004—05; dir. AMEN: A Musician's E-mail Network, Sedona, 2003—05. Mem.: Music Educator's Nat. Conf., Nat. Pastoral Musician. Democrat. Roman Catholic. Avocations: writing, travel, nature/animal life, reading, photography. Home: 21 San Jose Circle Sedona AZ 86336 Office: St John Vianney Church 180 Soldier's Pass Road Sedona AZ 86336 Office Phone: 928-282-7545. Personal E-mail: teribays@teribays.com. E-mail: tbays@sjvsedona.org.

BAYSINGER, KARA, lawyer; b. St. Cloud, Minn., Aug. 26, 1966; BA in Polit. Sci., U. Mich., 1988; JD, Loyola U., 1994. Bar: Ill. 1994, Calif. 1999. Asst. to gen. counsel Provident Ins. Co., Waukegan, Ill., 1988—90; compliance analyst Benefit Trust Life Ins. Co., Lake Forest, Ill.; asst. v.p. legal and regulatory affairs Celtic Life Ins. Co.; dir.-counsel product approval & compliance Bankers Life and Casualty Co., 1994—97; spl. counsel ins. regulatory practice group Long & Levit LLP, 1997; ptnr. Sonnenschein Nath & Rosenthal LLP, San Francisco, vice chair Ins. Practice Group. Co-chair Calif. adv. bd. BizWorld. Mem.: Chgo. Bar Assn., Ill. Bar Assn. Office: Sonnenschein Nath & Rosenthal LLP 685 Market St, 6th Fl San Francisco CA 94105 Office Phone: 415-882-2475. Office Fax: 415-543-5472. Business E-Mail: kbaysinger@sonnenschein.com.

BAYSINGER, KERRI M., mechanical engineer; b. Phoenix, Ariz., Sept. 18, 1977; d. Duane Thomas and Cynthia Kay Fradenburgh; m. Richard Allen Baysinger, May 16, 1998. BS in Math. & Edn., Grande Canyon U., 1999; MS in Engring., Wright State U., 2004. Math. instr. Paradise Valley Unified Sch. Dist., Phoenix, 1999—2000, Glendale Union HS, 2000—01; mech. engring. co-op. Air Force Rsch. Lab., Dayton, Ohio, 2002—04; mech. engr. Mitre Corp., Bedford, Mass., 2005—. Mem.: Am. Inst. Aeronautics & Astronautics, Am. Soc. Mech. Engrs.

BAYUK, THOMAS M., SR., restaurant owner, writer; b. Plainfield, NJ, June 6, 1942; s. Max and Stella A. (Sulewski) B.; m. Joyce A. Biondi, Apr. 27, 1962; children: Patricia, Thomas Jr., John, Jennifer. Student, Rutgers U., 1960-61, LeCordon Bleu, Paris, 1987-88. Owner Tom's Luncheonette, Flemington, NJ, 1970—74; real estate broker Weichert Realtors, Clinton, NJ, 1974—78; project mgr. Forest City Enterprises, Cleveland, Ohio, 1978—80; ceo West Dennis Village Deli, Inc., West Dennis, Mass., 1981—96, J & T Corp, West Dennis, Mass., 1996—; real estate broker Robert J. Bayuk Assoc., Inc., Clinton, NJ. Author: (book) Coping and Prevailing, 2002, Still Coping and Prevailing, 2004, What We Don't Talk About, 2005. With U.S. Army, 1960-61. Specialist 4th class U. S. Army N.G., 1960—63, Summit, N. J. Mem. Nat. Assn. Realtors, Nat. Restaurant Assn., Mass. Right to Life, Mus. Fine Arts, Boston Ballet. Republican. Catholic. Achievements include Founder- MS2therescue. Avocations: writing, cooking, wine tasting, travel. Home and Office: 19868 Cypres Woods Ct North Fort Myers FL 33903 Office Phone: 239-543-4105. Personal E-mail: tbayuk@comcast.net.

BAYUS, LENORE WEATHERLY, writer, public relations consultant; b. NYC, Apr. 11, 1923; d. John Bruce and Lena Catherine (Ferguson) Weatherly; m. John Daniel Bayus, Aug. 14, 1948. BS, Indiana U., Pa., 1944; postgrad., Case Western Res. U., 1945-47; MLS, U. Pitts., 1966, postgrad., 1972-73. Librarian East Palestine (Ohio) High Sch., 1947-48; substitute tchr. Gateway Sch. Dist., Monroeville, Pa., 1959-64; librarian Gateway High Sch., Monroeville, 1964-66; evaluator edn. collection Hillman Library U. Pitts., 1968-69; reference librarian Carnegie Library Pitts., 1969-72, specialist teenge services, 1972-73, pub. relations dir., 1973-82; freelance writer Pitts., 1982—. Pub. relations cons. Pitts. Civic Garden Ctr., 1986-87 Author: Beulah Presbyterian Church: 1784-1984, 1984, Pittsburgh, Building for the Future, 1988; author, editor: Monroeville: Gateway to the Future, 1986, 87; mem. editorial bd. Alive mag., 1982—; contbr. articles to mags.; staff writer Allegheny Bus. News. Bd. mgrs. Home for the Aged, 1985-97, v.p., 86-90, pres. 90-94 Recipient award Pa. Humanities Council, 1987. Mem. ALA (pub. relations council 1976, nat. library week com. 1980), AAUW, Women In Communications, Inc., Pa. Library Assn., Pitts. (Pa.) Press Club, Beta Phi Mu (pres.) Republican. Presbyterian. Home and Office: 821 Lake Port Blvd Apt S510 Leesburg FL 34748-2515 Personal E-mail: lbayus2@aol.com.

BAZ, MAHER AFIF, internist, educator, medical director lung transplant program; b. Monrovia, Liberia, Aug. 3, 1964; s. Afif Salem and Sana Baz. MD, Am. U. of Beirut, 1989. Resident internal medicine Duke U., Durham, NC, 1989—92, pulmonary fellow, 1992—95; asst. prof. of medicine U. of Fla., Gainesville, 1996—2002, assoc. prof. of medicine, 2002—. Med. dir. lung transplant program U. of Fla., Gainesville, 1996—; thoracic com. United Network for Organ Sharing. Named one of Young Leaders in Pulmonary Medicine, Boehringer-Ingelheim Pharmaceuticals, 2001. Mem.: Internat. Soc. of Heart and Lung Transplantation, Am. Thoracic Soc. Achievements include research in biology and immunosuppressive therapy of airway rejection. Office: U Fla 1600 SW Archer Rd PO Box 100395 Gainesville 32610 Office Phone: 352-265-8940. Business E-Mail: bazma@medicine.ufl.edu.

BAZANT, ZDENEK PAVEL, engineering educator; b. Prague, Czechoslovakia, Dec. 10, 1937; came to U.S., 1968, naturalized, 1976; s. Zdenek and Stepanka (Curikova) B.; m. Iva Marie Krasna, Sept. 27, 1967; children: Martin Zdenek, Eva Stephanie. Civil Engr., Tech. U., Prague, 1960; PhD in Mechanics, Czechoslovak Acad. Sci., 1963; postgrad. diploma in theoretical physics, Charles U., Prague, 1966; hon. doctorate, Czech Tech. U., Prague, 1991, Karlsruhe (Germany) U., 1998, U. Colo., 2000, Poly. Milan, 2001, Institut Nat. des Scis. Appliques, Lyon, 2004. Registered structural engr., Ill. Scientist, adj. prof. Bldg. Rsch. Inst., Tech. U., Prague, 1963-67; docent habilitation Tech. U., Prague, 1967; vis. rsch. engr. Centre d'Étude et de Recherche du Bâtiment et des Travaux Publics, Paris, 1967, U. Toronto, 1967—68, U. Calif., Berkeley, 1969; assoc. prof. civil engring. Northwestern U., Evanston, Ill., 1969-73, prof., 1973-90, Walter P. Murphy prof., 1990—, coord. structural engring. program, 1974-78, 92—; founding dir. Ctr. for Concrete and Geomaterials, 1981-86. Cons. Argonne Nat. Lab., many other orgns. Author: Creep of Concrete in Structural Analysis, 1966, Stability of Structures: Elastic, Inelastic, Fracture and Damage Theories, 1991, Concrete at High Temperatures, 1996, Fracture and Size Effect, 1997, Scaling of Structural Strength, 2002, Inelastic Analysis of Structures, 2002; editor 13 books; editor in chief Jour. Engring. Mechanics, 1989-94; regional editor Internat. Jour. Fracture, 1991—; assoc. editor Applied Mechanics Rev., 1987—, Cement and Concrete Research Internat. Jour, 1970—, Materials and Structures, 1979— Solid Mechanics Archives, 1980-91, Materials and Structures, 1981—; mem. editl. bds. of 16 hours.; contbr. (with others) over 350 articles to profl. jours.; patentee in field. Recipient Best Engring. Book of Yr. award Soc. Am. Pubs., 1992, Outstanding New Citizen award Chgo. Citizenship Coun., 1976, A. von Humboldt award, 1990, Šolín medal Czech Tech. U., Prague, 1998, Stodola gold medal Slovak Acad. Scis., 1999, Highly Cited Scientist award Internat. Sci. Index, 2001; grantee NSF, 1970—, Air Force Office Scientific Rsch., 1975—, Los Alamos Sci. Lab., 1978-80, European Power Rsch. Inst., 1980—, Office Naval Rsch., 1990—, Dept. Energy, 1984—; Ford Found. fellow, 1967-68, Guggenheim fellow, 1978-79, Kajima Found. fellow U. Tokyo, 1987, NATO fellow, Paris, 1988, Japan Soc. Promotion of Sci. fellow U. Tokyo, 1995-96. Fellow ASME (Worcester Reed Warner medal 1997), Am. Acad. Mechanics, ASCE (chmn. com. properties of materials 1976-78, 82-84, editor in chief Jour. Engring. Mechanics 1988-94, Walter L. Huber rsch. prize 1976, T.Y. Lin Prestressed Concrete award 1977, Newmark medal 1996, Croes medal 1997, Lifetime Achievement Award, 2003, von Kármán medal 2005), Am. Concrete Inst. (chmn. fracture mechanics com. 1985-92), Internat. Assn. for Fracture Mechanics of Concrete Structures (pres. 1991-93), Internat. Union Testing and Rsch. Labs. Materials Structures (chmn. com. on creep, L'Hermite gold medal 1975), Soc. Engring. Sci. (pres. 1993, Prager medal 1996); mem. NAS, NAE, Academia di Scienze e Lettere Milan, Engring. Acad. Czech Republic (fgn. mem.), Austrian Acad. Scis., U.S. Nat. Com. on Theoretical and Applied Mechanics, Internat. Assn. Structural Mechanics Reactor Tech. (coord. concrete structures divsn.), ASTM (mem. concrete com., skiing com.), Prestressed Concrete Inst., Am. Ceramic Soc. (D.M. Roy award 2001), Internat. Assn. Soil Mech. Found. Engring., Internat. Assn. Bridge and Structural Engring., Soc. Exptl. Mechanics, Am. Soc. Engring. Edn., Bldg. Rsch. Inst. Spain (hon., Torroja Gold medal 1990), Czech Soc. Civil Engring. (hon.), Czech Soc. Mechanics (award of merit 1993), Structural Engrs. Assn. Ill. (Meritorious Paper award 1992). Home: 707 Roslyn Ter Evanston IL 60201-1721 Office: Northwestern Univ Dept Civil Engring Evanston IL 60208-0001

BAZELIDES, DIANE, public relations executive; BS in Bus. Edn., U. Nebr. With dept. internal audit Enron Corp., Houston, 1976-80, with dept. pub. rels., 1980-83, comm. adminstr. dept. pub. rels., 1983-86, mgr. media rels., 1986-88, dir. media rels. dept. pub. rels., 1988-91, gen. mgr. dept. pub. rels., 1991-92, v.p. dept. pub. rels., 1992—98; mng. dir. mktg. comms. and pub. rels. Azurix, Houston, 1998—. Bd. dirs. Alley Theater, Houston, Houston Ballet; mem. exec. com., pres. bd. dirs. Alzheimer's Assn., Houston. Mem. Pub. Rels. Soc. Am., Internat. Assn. Bus. Communicators.

BAZELL, ROBERT JOSEPH, science correspondent; b. Pitts., Aug. 21, 1945; s. Irving and Beatrice (Robb) B.; m. Ilene Tanz, Sept. 11, 1966 (div.); children: Rebecca, Joshua; m. Margot Weinshel, July 31, 1979. BA, U. Calif., Berkeley, 1967; student, U. Sussex, Eng., 1968-69; postgrad., U. Calif., 1971. Writer Sci. Mag., Washington, 1971-72; reporter N.Y. Post, N.Y.C., 1972-76; network corr. NBC News, N.Y.C., 1976—. Contbr. articles to mags. Recipient over 2000 various journalistic awards. Mem. Phi Beta Kappa Office: NBC News 30 Rockefeller Plz Fl 3 New York NY 10112-0002

BAZEMORE, TRUDY MCCONNELL, librarian; d. Charlie Arthur and Elizabeth Bruns McConnell; m. John Everett Bazemore, Jr., Nov. 5, 1983. BA in Interdisciplinary studies magna cum laude, Coastal Carolina U., Conway, S.C., 2001. Libr., tech. svcs. Georgetown Pub. Libr., SC, 1978—89, libr., reference svcs., 1989—93, head, pub. svcs., 1993—2001, asst. dir., 2001—. Mem.: Nat. Geneal. Soc., Founding Families of S.C., S.C. Hist. Soc., Interagency Coun., Am. Libr. Assn., Ribbon Club of Georgetown, Phi Theta Kappa, Alpha Sigma Lambda, Phi Sigma Tau. Methodist. Avocations: genealogy, gemology, photography, travel, art. Office: Georgetown County Pub Libr 405 Cleland St Georgetown SC 29440

BAZIN, PATRICK, library director; b. Besancon, France, Feb. 23, 1950; s. Joseph Bazin and Louisette (Le Goff) Lazar; m. Denyse Clavel, May 8, 1978; 1 child, Marianne. B in Philosophy, Lyon (France) 2 Univ., 1973, M in Philosophy, 1976; grad., Nat. Upper Libr. Sch., Lyon, 1976. Curator Ecole Nat. des Mines de Paris, Paris, 1976-78, Lyon Pub. Libr., Lyon, 1978-92, dir., gen. curator, 1992—. Tchr. Nat. Upper Sch. Info. Sci. and Librs., Lyon, 1989—; vice-chmn. Rhone-Alpes Agy. for Book and Documentation, Rhone-Alpes Province, 1994—. Mem. Nat. Ctr. of Books. Office: Bibliotheque Municipale 30 Blvd VivierMerle 69431 Lyon Cedex 03 France Office Phone: 04 78 62 19 24. Business E-Mail: pbazin@bm-lyon.fr.

BAZIRJIAN, ROSANN V., dean, librarian; b. NYC, Sept. 5, 1952; d. Dickran and Rose V. Bazirjian; m. Patrick T. Burger; 1 child, Terence Burger. BA, Lehman Coll., N.Y.C., 1973; MS, Columbia U., 1980; MSSC, Syracuse U., 1993. Acquisitions libr. Syracuse U., NY, 1980—84, head acquisitions dept., 1990—91, head bibliog. svcs., 1991—95; head acquisitions and collections devel. U. West Fla., Pensacola, 1985—90; asst. dir. tech. svcs. Fla. State U., Tallahassee, 1995—99; asst. dean tech. and access svcs. Pa. State U., University Park, 1999—2004; libr. U. N.C., Greensboro, 2004—. Contbr. articles to profl. publs., chapters to books. Mem.: ALA (Leadership in Acquisitions award 2002), Assn. Library Collections and Tech. Svcs., Assn. Coll. and Rsch. Libraries, Phi Beta Kappa. Office: Univ NC Greensboro Jackson Libr 208 Jackson Greensboro NC 27402 Office Phone: 336-334-5880. Business E-Mail: rvbazirj@uncg.edu.

BAZZAZ, FAKHRI A., plant biology educator, administrator; b. Baghdad, Iraq, June 16, 1933; came to U.S., 1958; s. Abdul-Latif and Munifa Bazzaz; m. Maarib Bazzaz, Aug. 25, 1958; children: Sahar, Ammar. BS, U. Baghdad, 1953; MS, U. Ill., 1960, PhD, 1963; A.M. (hon.), Harvard U., 1984. Prof. U. Ill., Urbana, 1977-84, head dept. plant biology, acting dir. Sch. Life Scis., 1983-84; prof. Harvard U., Cambridge, Mass., 1984—, Mallinckrodt prof. biology, 1997—. Editor: Oecologia, 1983—; author: over 300 peer-reviewed sci. articles, 2 books; co-editor: 4 books. Guggenheim fellow; fellow Clare Hall, Cambridge (Eng.) U., 1981—, Imperial Coll., London, 2002, World Innovation Found., 2004; recipient Nev. medal, 2004. Fellow AAAS, Am. Acad. Arts and Scis.; mem. Ecol. Soc. Am., Brit. Ecol. Soc, Humboldt Forschungspreise, Germany (1997 award). Office: Harvard U Biol Labs 16 Divinity Ave Cambridge MA 02138-2020 Business E-Mail: maaribbazzaz@comcast.net.

BAZZETT, LISA B., surgeon; b. Traverse City, Mich. d. Bernard J. and Mary A. Bazzett. BS, U. Mich., Ann Arbor, MI, 1989; MD, Wayne State U., Detroit, 1993. Diplomate Am. Bd. Obstetrics and Gynecology, 2002, gynecologic oncology Am. Bd. Obstetrics and Gynecology, 2003. Staff physician and surgeon Ochsner Clinic, New Orleans, 2000—. Clin. asst. prof. La. State u., New Orleans, 2002—. Contbr. chapters to books, articles to profl. jour. Vol. New Orleans Med. Mission Svcs. Found., Inc., New Orleans, 2004—, bd. dir., 2004—. Recipient Women of Influence Spirit award, Gynecolgic Oncology, 2004. Fellow: Am. Coll. Obstetricians and Gynecologists; mem.: Internta. Gynecotogic Cancer Soc., Am. Assn. Cancer Rsch., Soc. Gynecologic Oncology. Avocation: travel. Office: Ochsner Clinic Dept OB/GYN 1514 Jefferson Hwy New Orleans LA 70121 Office Phone: 504-842-4165.

BAZZI, SAMER, application developer, consultant; b. Sayda, Lebanon, Jan. 8, 1968; s. Mohamad Bazzi and Sana Osseiran; 1 child, Moses. BS in Computer sci., Am. U., Washington, 1993. Software devel. cons. Arcs Tech. Solutions, Daly City, Calif., 2001—03, Sun Microsystems, Sunnyvale, Calif., 2003—04. Activist SABA, San Jose, Calif., 2003—04. Achievements include development of For the case of Sun Microsystems vs. Microsoft, developed the discovery software that allowed Sun to detect and submit millions of emails and documents to Microsoft by the court-imposed deadline. Home: PO Box 60723 Sunnyvale CA 94088 Business E-Mail: sambazzi@alum.american.edu.

BAZZONE, THERESA (TERRY) A., sales executive; Student, Bentley Coll. Sales mgr. Corp. Software, Inc., 1987—92; dir. software product mktg. div. Tech Data Corp., Clearwater, Fla., 1992—96, v.p., gen. mgr. strategic bus. dev. unit, 1996—2002, sr. v.p. US sales, 2002—. Office: Tech Data Corp 5350 Tech Data Rd Clearwater FL 33760-3122

BEA, CARLOS TIBURCIO, federal judge; b. San Sebastian, Spain, Apr. 18, 1934; Student, Menlo Jr. Coll., 1950—51; BA, Stanford U., 1956, JD, 1958. Bar: Calif. 1959. Assoc. Dunne, Phelps & Mills, 1959—66, ptnr., 1967—75; prin., owner Carlos Bea Law Corp., 1975—90; judge San Francisco (Calif.) Superior Ct., 1990—2003, U.S. Ct. Appeals, (9th cir.), San Francisco, 2003—. Office: US Ct Appeals 95 Seventh St San Francisco CA 94103*

BEA, ROBERT G., civil engineering educator; BS, U. Fla., 1959, MS, 1960. Sr. staff civl engr. Shell Oil Co., 1959-76; chief engr., v.p. Ocean Engring. Divsn., Woodward-Clyde Cons., 1976-81; v.p. PMB Sys. Engring., Inc., 1981-88; prof. dept. civil engring., naval arch. and offshore engring U. Calif., Berkeley, 1988—. Cons. prof. engring Stanford U., 1985-89. Recipient J. Hillis Miller Engring. award. Mem. ASCE (Croes medal, 1959), Nat. Acad. Engring. Achievements include projects and research in coastal, offshore and ocean engineering; development of methods to define design criteria for fixed and mobile offshor structures; development of guidelines for the requalifications and rehabilitation of marine structures and ships; evaluation of forces due to waves, currents, earthquakes, ice and sea floor slides; development of technology for evaluation of the dynamic response characteristics of marine foundations and structures. Office: U Calif 215 Mclaughlin Hall Berkeley CA 94720-1712

BEACH, ARTHUR O'NEAL, lawyer; b. Albuquerque, Feb. 8, 1945; s. William Pearce and Vivian Lucille (Kronig) B.; m. Alex Clark Doyle, Sept. 12, 1970; 1 child, Eric Kronig. BBA, U. N.Mex., 1967, JD, 1970. Bar: N.Mex. 1970. Assoc. Smith & Ransom, Albuquerque, 1970-74, Keleher & McLeod, Albuquerque, 1974-75, ptnr., 1976-78; shareholder Keleher & McLeod, P.A., Albuquerque, 1978—. Tchg. asst. U. N.Mex., 1970. Bd. editors Natural Resources Jour., 1968-70. Mem. ABA, State Bar N.Mex. (unauthorized practice of law com., adv. opinions com., med.-legal panel, legal-dental-osteo.-podiatry com., jud. selection com., specialization bd.), Albuquerque Bar Assn. (dir. 1978-82). Democrat. Mem. Christian Sci. Ch. Home: 2015 Dietz Pl NW Albuquerque NM 87107-3240 Office: Keleher & McLeod PA PO Box AA Albuquerque NM 87103 Office Phone: 505-346-9107. E-mail: aob@keleher-law.com.

BEACH, BERT BEVERLY, clergyman; b. Gland, Vaud, Switzerland, June 15, 1928; s. Walter Raymond and Gladys (Corley) B.; m. Eliane Marguerite Palange, Apr. 8, 1954; children: Danielle, Michele. BA, Pacific Union Coll., 1948; postgrad., Stanford U., 1948-49, 51; PhD, U. Paris, 1958; ThD, Christian Theol. Acad., 1986. Prin. West Liberty Union Intermediate Sch., Gridley, Calif., 1949-50, Italian Jr. Coll., Florence, Italy, 1952-58; chmn. history dept. Columbia Union Coll., Takoma Pk., Md., 1958-60; dir. edn. No. Europe-West Africa Div. of SDA, St. Albans, Eng., 1960-75, gen. sec., 1973-80; sec. Conf. of Secs. Christian World Communions, Silver Spring, Md., 1970—2002; dir. pub. affairs Gen. Conf. of Seventh-day Adventists, Silver Spring, Md., 1980-95; gen. sec. Coun. on Inter-Ch. Rels., 1980—; sec. gen. Internat. Religious Liberty Assn., Silver Spring, Md., 1980-95, pres., 1996, 2000. Sec. Internat. Acad. for Freedom of Religion, 1985—; v.p. Internat. Commn. for Prevention of Alcoholism and Drug Dependency, 1980—, pres., 1991, 1997—. Chmn. bd. John H. Weidner Found. Altruism, 1996—2005; sec. bd. Bridging Boundaries Internat., 2002—. Recipient Citation, Senate of State of Md., 1984; named Paul Harris fellow Rotary Internat., 1984, Order of Bishop Hodura, Polish Nat. Cath. Ch., 1986, Order of St. Magdalene, Polish Orthodox Ch., 1987, Honored Alumnus of Yr. Pacific Union Coll., 1997, Knight's Cross of Order of Merit of Polish Republic, 1998, Human Rights Leadership award Freedom Mag., 1998, Pres. Leadership medallion Andrews U., 1999, Distinction medal Gen. Conf. Health Ministries, 2004, Medallion of Distinction Gen. Conf. Edn. Dept., 2005, Bridge award Gen. Conf. Com. Dept., 2005. Mem. Rotary Club, Cosmos Club, SAR, Md. Assn. Founders and Patriots of Am. (gov. 1998-2000), Polish Bible Soc. (hon.). Adventist. Avocation: prestidigitation. Home: 14508 Cutstone Way Silver Spring MD 20905-7430 Office: 12501 Old Columbia Pike Silver Spring MD 20904-6601 Office Phone: 301-680-6680. Personal E-mail: bertbbeach@msn.com.

BEACH, CECIL PRENTICE, librarian; b. Knoxville, Tenn., July 12, 1927; s. Frank Alfred and Lillie Maude (Sims) B.; m. Doris Jean Pardue, Apr. 17, 1949; children: Steven Prentice, Rex Arthur, Keven Sanders, Kyle Alfred, Quentin Anthony; m. Marcia Gibson Buckley, June 20, 1969; children: Stephanie Lynn, Shannon Sue. AB, U. Chattanooga, 1950; MA, Fla. State U., 1952. Bookmobile libr. Chattanooga Pub. Libr., 1948-51; extension libr. Decatur (Ga.)-DeKalb Regional Libr., 1952-54; dir. Piedmont Regional Libr., Winder, Ga., 1954-60, Gadsden (Ala.) Pub. Libr., 1960-64, Tampa (Fla.)-Hillsborough Libr. System, 1965-72; state libr. State of Fla., Tallahassee, 1972-77; dir. div. librs. Broward County, Ft. Lauderdale, Fla., 1977-89, dir. pub. svcs. dept., 1989-93, ret., 1993; appt. bond project coord., 1999—; ptnr. Beach/Willey Cons., Tallahassee, 1993—; prof. Fla. State U. Sch. of Libr. and Infr. Studies, 1993—. Instr. dept. libr. sci. U. South Fla.; chmn. Fla. Libr. Study Commn., 1970-72; chmn. bd. dirs. Southeastern Libr. Network; chmn. S.E. Fla. Libr. Info. network; chmn. Fla. del. to The White House Conf. on Libr. and Info. Svcs., 1991; cons. libr. bldgs. and svc. Pres., Gadsden Community Coun., 1963; bd. govs. Nova U.; chmn. adv. coun. Seagull Sch. for Exceptional Children; mem. Fla. Endowment Humanities, 1972—, Ft. Lauderdale Downtown Coun.; bd. dirs. Easter Seal Soc., 1975—, Ft. Lauderdale Art Mus., Multiple Sclerosis Soc., Broward Pub. Libr. Found., Ft. Lauderdale Children's Theater. With USNR, 1944-46. Mem. ALA, Southeastern Libr. Assn. (pres. 1972—), Ala. Libr. Assn., Ga. Libr. Assn., Fla. Libr. Assn. (pres. 1969), Pub. Libr. Assn. (Allie Beth Martin award 1984), Adult Edn. Assn., Tampa C. of C., Greater Ft. Lauderdale C. of C., Fla. State U. Alumni Assn. (pres. 1967, Disting. Alumni award 1985). Lodges: Masons, Rotary. Democrat. Presbyterian. Home and Office: Apt 715 3100 NE 48th St Fort Lauderdale FL 33308-4948 Office Phone: 954-560-3000. Personal E-mail: cbeach0712@aol.com.

BEACH, CHARLES ADDISON, lawyer; b. Albany, N.Y., Apr. 21, 1945; s. Charles A.W. and Eleanor (Johnston) B.; m. Jane L. Shlionsky, June 8, 1968; children: James E. and Jonathan M. BA, Hamilton Coll., 1967; JD, Cornell U., 1973. Bar: N.Y. 1974, U.S. Dist. Ct. (no., ea., we. and so. dists.) N.Y. 1974, U.S. Ct. Appeals (2d and 10th cirs.) 1975, U.S. Supreme Ct. 1982, Tex. 1991, U.S. Dist. Ct. (no. dist.) Tex. 1993, U.S. Ct. Appeals (5th cir.) 1995, U.S. Ct. Appeals (6th cir.) 1998. Assoc. Shearman & Sterling, N.Y.C., 1973-77, 79-81, Paris, 1977-79; sr. counsel, coord. corp. litigation Exxon Mobil Corp., N.Y.C., 1981—90, Irving, Tex., 1990—. Mng. editor: Cornell Internat. Law Jour. Vol. Peace Corps., Libya and Tunisia, 1968-71; adv. coun. Cornell Law Sch. Fellow Tex. Bar Found. (sustaining life); mem. ABA, N.Y. State Bar Assn., Assn. of Bar of City of N.Y., Dallas Bar Assn., Irving Bar Assn., Am. Arbitration Assn. (adv. coun. Dallas chpt.), U.S. Coun. Internat. Bus./Internat. C. of C. (arbitration com., S.W. com. on arbitration), Inst. for Trasnational Arbitration Ctr. for Am. and Internat. Law (adv. bd.), Coll. State Bar Tex. Home: 1431 N Travis Cir Irving TX 75038-6238 Office: Exxon Mobil Corp 5959 Las Colinas Blvd Irving TX 75039-2298 Business E-Mail: charles.a.beach@exxonmobil.com.

BEACH, DOUGLAS RYDER, lawyer, educator; b. Kittery, Maine, Sept. 20, 1948; s. Raymond Homer and Carolyn (Ryder) B.; m. Deborah C.M. Henry; children: Lindsay Alison, Garrett Wesley, Katherine Henry. BS, Central Conn. State U., 1970; JD cum laude, New Eng. Sch. Law, 1973; grad. with honors, U.S. Army Judge Sch., U. Va., 1976. Bar: Mass. 1973, Mo. 1977, US Dist. Ct. (ea. and we. dists.) Mo. 1977, US Ct. Mil. Appeals, 1973. Gen. ptnr. Paule & Beach, Inc., Clayton, Mo., 1977-81, Kaveney, Beach, Russell, Bond & Mittleman, Clayton, 1981-88, Beach, Burcke & Helfers, P.C., 1988—. Instr. bus. law Washington U., St. Louis, 1980-89; atty. City Chesterfield, Mo., 1988-2005 Contbr. chpt. to Medical Records, Property Distribution, Trial Tactics in Domestic Rels., 1984, Elder Bonhomme Presbyterian Ch., Chesterfield, Mo., 1984. Treas. Y's Men's Internat., St. Louis, 1977-80; exec. bd. John Marshall Rep. Club, 1969-72; pres. Mcpl. Attys. Lawyer, 2004. Lt. col. USMCR, 1973-91 Mem. ABA, Am. Acad. Matrimony Lawyers (pres. Mo. chpt., Best Atty. US Am. 1990-2004), St. Louis County Bar Assn. (named Outstanding Young Lawyer 1983, pres. 1984-85), Met. Bar St. Louis, Trial Lawyers Assn. St. Louis. Home: 14565 Ansonborough Ct Chesterfield MO 63017-4614 Office: Beach Stuart Higgie & Mettleman 222 S Central Ave Ste 900 Saint Louis MO 63105-3575 Office Phone: 314-863-8484.

BEACH, FRANKLIN DARREL, minister; b. South Charleston, W.Va., June 24, 1938; s. Elwood James and Virgie (O'Dell) B.; m. Brenda Pauley, Oct. 4, 1968; children: Frank Jr., Deanna Dawn. Grad. high sch., Alum Creek, W.Va. Ordained min. Bapt. Ch., 1967. Welder, boilermaker Putnam Fabricators, Bandcroft, W.Va., 1972; welder South Charleston, W.Va., 1963-70; assoc. pastor, tchr. Dollie Hill Christian Acad. and God's Ch. Alum Creek, W.Va., 1973-79; min. King (N.C.) Christian Ctr., 1983—; TV min. CAT TV Channel 6, Winston-Salem, N.C., 1994—. Pres. Forsyth County Right to Life, Winston-Salem, 1993-95. With U.S. Army, 1956-61. Recipient award Concerned Citizens of Kanawha County, 1974. Avocations: private pilot, oil painting, auto mechanics. Home: 4673 Hyatt Dr Winston Salem NC 27101-2215 E-mail: darrel_b_27101@yahoo.com.

BEACH, HARRY LEE, JR., mechanical engineer, aerospace engineer; b. Richmond, Va., Aug. 16, 1944; married, 1966; 3 children. BS, N.C. State U., 1966, MS, 1968, PhD in Mech. Engring., 1970. Rsch. engr. Langley Rsch. Ctr., NASA, Hampton, Va., 1970-75, head combustion sect., 1975-77, leader performance analysis group, 1977-80, asst., 1980-81, head hypersonic propulsion br., 1981-89, head nat. aerospace plane, 1989-92, dep. dir., 1992-98; prof. dept. physics, computer sci. and engring. Christopher Newport U., 1998—2002; exec. dir. Hampton Roads Rsch. Partnership, 2002—. Asst. prof. Joint Inst. Advanced Flight Sci., George Washington U., 1977—; adj. prof. Christopher Newport Coll., 1980—. Fellow AIAA (Air Breathing Propulsion award 1997). Achievements include research in supersonic combustion ramjet propulsion, combustion fundamentals, computational fluid dynamics, combustion diagnostics, inlet and combuster conceptual design and testing, inlet-combustor component integration.

BEACH, JEAN MRHA, food products executive; BA, Wellesley Coll.; MA in Fin. and Acctg., U. Chgo. V.p. Enron Upstream Products; sr. v.p. commodity and trading risk mgmt. Tyson Foods, Inc., Springdale, Ark., 2002—. Office: Tyson Foods Inc 2210 W Oaklawn Dr Springdale AR 72762-6999

BEACH, JOHN DOUGLAS, education educator; b. N.Y.C., Nov. 10, 1948; s. Herbert Clason and Lillian June (Loehmann) B.; m. Carol Louise Geisler, Aug. 29, 1968; children: Stephanie Lillian, Margaret Cordelia, Peter Gregory. BA in French, SUNY, Oswego, 1970; MA in French, SUNY, Binghamton, 1974; MS in Elem. Sch., L.I. U., 1975; PhD in Reading, SUNY, Albany, 1988. Cert. K-12 reading tchr., 7-12 French and Russian tchr., nursery sch. and kindergarten tchr., elem. tchr., N.Y. Adj. asst. prof. C.W. Post Ctr., L.I. U., Greenvale, N.Y., 1975-82; 1st grade tchr. William Floyd Unified Sch. Dist., Shirley, N.Y., 1976-77; reading tchr. Walton (N.Y.) Ctrl. Schs., 1978-79; reading specialist Cairo (N.Y.)-Durham Schs., 1979-86; asst. prof. edn. U. Wis., Kenosha, 1986-88, U. Maine, Orono, 1988-90, U. Nev., Reno, 1990-94, SUNY, Cortland, 1994—97; assoc. prof. edn. U. Nebr., Omaha, 1997—2000, Boise (Idaho) State U., 2001—04, St. John's U., 2004—. Editl. cons. Allyn and Bacon Pubs., Needham Heights, Mass., 1988—; freelance storyteller, Cortland, 1975—; sr. assoc. for assessment N.W. Regional Ednl. Lab., Portland, Oreg., 2000. Contbr. articles to profl. publs. Cubmaster Boy Scouts Am., Cairo, 1983-86, cubmaster, leader trainer, Reno, Nev., 1990-94, summer camp dir., Dryden, N.Y., 1995. Bird and Bird Fund grantee U. Maine, 1989; NDEA Title IV fellow, 1970-72; recipient Ednl. Rsch. award Assn. Am. Pubs., 1986. Mem. Internat. Reading Assn. (mem. pubs. rev. bd., 1997—), N.Y. State Reading Assn., Nat. Coun. Tchrs. English (chair com. on storytelling 1994—). Avocations: classical piano, gardening, art, cooking, history. Home: 92-38 B Holland Ave Rockaway Beach NY 11693 Office: St John's Univ 8000Utopia Pkwy Queens NY 11439 Office Phone: 718-990-1398. E-mail: beachj@stjohns.edu.

BEACH, MARGARET SMITH, retired language educator; b. Decaturville, Tenn., Dec. 9, 1937; d. Luther Grant and Eva Irene Mallard; m. James Edward Smith (dec. 1960); children: James Edward III(dec.), John Fitzgerald; m. John D. Beach, July 26, 1975; stepchildren: John D. Jr., Michael Jerome. BA in English, Agrl. and Indsl. State U., Tenn., 1961; MS in Psychology, Tenn. State U., 1982. English and French tchr. Townsend HS, Winchester, Tenn., 1959—61, Nashville Christian Inst., 1961—63; part-time English tchr. Burt HS, Clarksville, Tenn., 1963—64; tchr. Cobb Elem. Sch., Clarksville, Tenn., 1963—69; English and French tchr. Wharton HS, Nashville, 1969—70, Neely's Bend Jr. HS, Madison, Tenn., 1970—91; ret., 1991. Chairperson English dept. Neely's Bend Jr. Mid. Sch., Madison, Tenn., 1974—76; cheerleader co-sponsor Neely's Bend Jr. HS, Madison, Tenn., 1975—76; English accreditation chairperson Neely's Bend Mid. Sch., Madison, Tenn., 1978—79, sch. newspaper sponsor, 1980—81; faculty rep. Tchrs. Union, Nashville, 1978—80; writer proficiency test items Metro. Nashville Schs., 1984—85. Author: (book) Creative Poems, 1974, Ethnic Poetry for All, 1998, Religious Poems of Faith, 2001; poet Our World's Best Loved Poems, 1983. Recipient Cert. of Appreciation, Met. Bd. of Edn., 1991, Award of Appreciation, Alumni Assn., 1992, 1996, 2002, Award of Dedication, 1996, Cert. of Appreciation, Nat. Coun. of Tchrs. of English, 1998, Cert. of Merit, Tenn. Ret. Tchrs. Assn., 2000—01. Mem.: Ret. Tchrs. Assn. Avocations: writing, reading, storytelling, poetry, performing. Office: Agape Pearl Publ PO Box 280653 Nashville TN 37228 Office Phone: 615-242-2307. E-mail: mrgrtmlmsb@aol.com.

BEACH, REGINA LEE, librarian; b. Georgetown, Ohio, Dec. 22, 1963; d. H. LeRoy and R. Jean (Wardlow) B. BSBA, BA, Ohio No. U., 1987; MLS, Kent State U., 1990; MS in Bus. Adminstrn., Miss. State U., 1999. Serials cataloger, libr. U. Mich., Ann Arbor, 1990-92; libr. Allen Correctional Inst., Lima, Ohio, 1993-94; serials cataloger, libr. Miss. State U., Mississippi State, 1994-99; head info. tech., libr. U. Ark., Little Rock, 1999—2001; head tech. svcs. and systems Tex. A&M U., Kingsville, 2001—. Mem. ALA, ASIS, Southeastern Libr. Assn., Ark. Libr. Assn. Avocations: walking, running, swimming, aerobics, camping. Office: MSC 197 Jernigan Libr Tex A&M U Kingsville TX 78363

BEACH, WALTER EGGERT, retired publishing organization executive; b. North Adams, Mass., Aug. 24, 1934; s. W. Edwards and Liselotte Josephine Sophie (von Usedom) B. BA, Dickinson Coll., 1956; MA, George Washington U., 1961. Staff assoc., asst. dir. Am. Polit. Sci. Assn., Washington, 1965-80; sr. staff mem. Brookings Instn., Washington, 1980-90; dir. Heldref Publs. Helen Dwight Reid Ednl. Found., Washington, 1990-97. Treas. D.C. Dem. Party, 1981-84; mem. adv. bd. Hubert H. Humphrey Inst. Pub. Affairs, U. Minn., Mpls., 1990-99; trustee Dickinson Coll., 1984—, Mt. Vernon Coll., 1971-97, Helen Dwight Reid Ednl. Found., 19‚ —; pres. Internat. Eye Found., 1993-95; bd. dirs. Hillwood Mus. and Gardens, 2001—; mem., bd. dirs. various polit. coms. With U.S. Army, 1956-58. Recipient Disting. Alumni award Dickinson Coll., 1991. Mem. Internat. Polit. Sci. Assn., Am. Polit. Sci. Assn. (Frank Goodnow award 1998), Ctr. Study Presidency, Hist. Soc. D.C., Midwest Polit. Sci. Assn., Nat. Capital Area Polit. Sci. Assn., Policy Studies Orgn., So. Polit. Sci. Assn., UN Assn. Nat. Capital Area, Western Polit. Sci. Assn., Cosmos Club, Pi Sigma Alpha. Democrat. Unitarian Universalist. Home: 5719 Chevy Chase Pky NW Washington DC 20015-2521 Office: Heldref Pubs 1319 18th St NW Washington DC 20036-1826 Office Phone: 202-296-6267 x1219. Personal E-mail: wbeach7421@aol.com.

BEACHELL, EILEEN JEANETTE, statistician; b. Newark, Del., Oct. 24, 1953; d. Harold Charles and Georgiana Katherine (Sorm) B. B.A., U. Del., 1975; M.S., Fla. State U., 1976. Product design engr. Ford Motor Co. Heavy Truck Div., Dearborn, Mich., 1976-84; statis. methods engr. Ford Motor Co. Transmission and Chassis Div., Livonia, Mich., 1984-87; stats. cons. J.T. LuFtig & Assocs., West Bloomfield, Mich., 1987—. Mem. Am. Statis. Assn. Avocations: sailing; gardening.

BEACHEM, MICHAEL T., IV, university/college student affairs administrator, counselor; b. Princeton, July 6, 1976; s. Linda L. (Weissenburger) Beachem and Michael T. Beachem III. BA in Comm. cum laude, Wilkes U., Wilkes-Barre, Pa., 1998; MA in Counselor Edn., Kean U., Union, NJ. Cert. Restricted Radiotelephone Operator Permit, USA FCC, 1995. Resident asst. Wilkes U., 1996—98; residence hall dir. Kean U., 1999—2001; residence dir. The Coll. of NJ, Ewing, 2001—02; resident dir. Temple U., Phila., 2002—. Editor: (yearbook) Mustang Memories, Reflections, Amnicola (Gettysburg Yearbook Experience, Best Theme Packet Layout Design and Director's Assistantship, 1996); prodr.: (video) Wilkes University Summer Orientation Video. Youth co-chairperson Middlesex County NJ March of Dimes, Cranbury, 1991—93; youth mem. NJ Commn. on Cmty. Svcs., Princeton, 1992—94; mem. Greater Phila. Profls. Network, 2003, Human Rights Campaign, Washington, 2001; first communion celebrant and confirmed mem. Ch. of Immaculate Conception - Roman Cath., Spotswood, NJ, 1979—90; mem. First Presbyn. Ch. of Wilkes-Barre, Pa., 1994—98, Ewing Presbyn. Ch., 2001; baptized mem. St. Ambrose Roman Cath. Ch., Old Bridge, NJ, 1976—79; mem. So. Poverty Law Ctr., Montgomery, Ala., 2002. Recipient Presdl. Acad. Fitness Award, US Presdl. Acad. Fitness Awards Program, 1990, Robert F. Lucas Outstanding Lt. Gov., Key Club Internat., 1994, Acad. Achievement Award, Monroe Twp. Home Sch. Assn., 1994, Middlesex County Edn. Assn. Student Recognition Award, NJ. Edn. Assn., 1994, NJ Dist. Outstanding Lt. Gov., NJ Dist. Key Club Internat., 1994, Fredd Briggs Award, NJ. Dist. Kiwanis Internat., 1994, The Caring Award, Middlesex County Guidance Counselors Assn., 1994, US Achievement Acad. Nat. Collegiate Student Govt. Awards, Wilkes U., 1998, Wilkes U. Inspirational Tchr. Award, Wilkes U. Divsn. Student Affairs, 1998, Theresa Jordan and Frank Mehm Prize, Wilkes U., 1998; Ann. Scholarship, Monroe Twp. Mother's Club, 1994, Ann. Kiwanis Student Leadership Scholarship, Rossmoor Kiwanis Club of Monroe Twp., 1994, Nat. Honor Soc. Ann. Scholarship, Monroe Twp. HS Nat. Honor Soc., 1994, Dr. Andrew Batsis Scholarship, 1994, IRTS Coll. Program Fellowship, Internat. Radio and TV Soc. Found. Inc., 1997. Mem.: ACA, Nat. Assn. Student Pers. Adminstrs., Am. Coll. Personal Assn., NJ Counseling Assn., Mid-Atlantic Coll. U. Housing Officers (Scholarship 1998), Intercollegiate Leadership Wilkes-Barre, Wilkes U. Class of 1998 Alumni Assn. (pres. 1998), Internat. Radio and TV Soc. Found. Inc. (IRTS), AFT - The Coll. of NJ. (TCNJ) Local 2364, AFT - Kean U. Local 2187, Wilkes U. Alumni Assn. (alumni mentor 2004), AFSCME - Temple U. Local 1723 (shop steward 2002), Immaculate Conception Youth Soccer League (Grad. Years of Svc. Award 1989), Kappa Delta Pi, Lamba Pi Eta (pres. Wilkes U. chpt. 1994), Phi Eta Sigma. Democrat. Achievements include Am. Cancer Soc. Top Youth Fundraiser 1992; Wilkes U. Student Commencement Speaker May 1998. Avocations: genealogy, pop culture, photography. Home: PO Box 30 Old Bridge NJ 08857-0030 Office: Temple Univ 1910 Liacouras Walk Ste 301 TU Zip 29100 Philadelphia PA 19122-6027

BEACHLEY, MICHAEL CHARLES, radiologist; b. Harrisburg, Pa., Nov. 14, 1940; s. Kenneth Gumbert and Carolyn Elizabeth (Jones) B.; m. Deborah Rowe Samson, July 27, 1963; children: Kenneth, Barbara, William. AB, Dartmouth Coll., 1962, B.MS, 1963; MD, Harvard U., 1965. Diplomate: Am. Bd. Radiology. Intern in surgery Med. Coll. Va., Richmond, 1965-66, resident in radiology, 1966-69, instr. radiology, 1970, faculty, 1972—, acting chmn. dept. radiology, 1976, prof., 1977-87, chmn. dept. radiology, 1977-82, prof. radiation scis., 1981-87, prof. biophysics, 1980-82, prof. physiology and biophysics, 1982-87, clin. prof., 1987—; clin. prof. radiology U. Pitts., 1988—; chmn. Dept. Radiology St. Margaret Meml. Hosp., Pitts., 1987-97; pres. Three Rivers Imaging Cons., Ltd., 1993-94, Duquesne Imaging Ltd., 1994-2001; med. dir. Radiology Ptnrs.; chmn. dept. radiology U. Pitts. Med. Ctr., Saint Margaret, 1997-99. Cons. McGuire VA Hosp., 1977—; fellow in radiol. pathology Armed Forces Inst. Pathology, Washington, 1969. Contbr. chpt. to book, revs. and med. articles to profl. jours. Vice-pres. College Hills Civic Assn., 1975-77. Served as maj. M.C. U.S. Army, 1970-72. Fellow Am. Coll. Radiology (pres. Va. chpt. 1982-83, chmn. com. on stds. and accreditation 1998-2004); mem. AMA, Am. Heart Assn., Radiol. Soc. N.Am. (chmn. bylaws com. 1994-96), Am. Roentgen Ray Soc., Pitts. Roentgen Soc. (chmn. com on fellowship nomination 1998-99), Pa. Radiol. Soc., Pa. Med. Soc. (alt. del., mem. med.-legal com.), Allegheny Med. Soc. (peer rev. bd. 1997-99), Pa. Radiol. MSO (chmn. by-laws com., exec. com.), Dartmouth Club Western Pa. (exec. com.), Harvard Club Western Pa. (treas.), Pitts. Field Club. Home: PO Box 331 Bakerstown PA 15007-0331 Business E-Mail: beachleymc@upmc.edu.

BEACHLEY, NORMAN HENRY, mechanical engineer, educator; b. Washington, Jan. 13, 1933; s. Albert Henry and Anna Garnet (Eiring) B.; m. Marion Ruth Iglehart, July 18, 1959; children: Brenda Ruth, Rebecca Sue, Barbara Joan. B.M.E., Cornell U., 1956, PhD, 1966. Mem. tech. staff Hughes Aircraft Co., Culver City, Calif., 1956-57; mem. tech. staff Space Tech. Labs., Redondo Beach, Calif., 1959-63; mem. faculty U. Wis., Madison, 1966—, prof. mech. engring., 1978-94, prof. emeritus, 1994—. Cons. numerous orgns., 1967— Co-author: Introduction to Dynamic System Analysis, 1978. Served with USAF, 1957-59. Sci. and Engring. Research Council Gt. Britain fellow, 1981-82 Fellow Soc. Automotive Engrs.; mem. ASME, Sigma Xi. Achievements include research in field of energy storage powerplants for motor vehicles, 1970—. Home: 2332 Fitchburg Rd Verona WI 53593-9278 Office: U Wis 1513 University Ave Madison WI 53706-1539 Business E-Mail: beachley@wisc.edu.

BEACHY, PHILIP ARDEN, molecular biology educator; b. Red Lake, Ont., Oct. 25, 1958; s. Moses Andrew and Ada Barbara (Miller) B.; m. Katrin Ingrid Andreasson, May 21, 1988. BA in Natural Scis., Goshen Coll., 1979; PhD in Biochemistry, Stanford U., 1986. Staff assoc. dept. embryology Carnegie Instn., Balt., 1986-88; asst. prof. dept. molecular biology and genetics Johns Hopkins U. Sch. Medicine, Balt., 1988—93; assoc. prof. molecular biology and genetics Johns Hopkins U., Balt., 1993—98, prof., 1998—; asst. investigator Howard Hughes Med. Inst., Balt., 1988—2000, full investigator, 2000—. Contbr. articles to sci. jours. Sloan Found. fellow, 1987-90; recipient Outstanding Young Sci. award Md., 1998. Fellow AAAS; mem. NAS (Molecular biology award 1998), Genetics Soc. Am., AAAS. Achievements include research in developmental morphogen, its processing and structure, and its covalent attachment to cholesterol; the hedgehog gene and protein, advancing the understanding of embryo development, cell differentiation and cancer development. Office Fax: 410-955-9124. Business E-Mail: pbeachy@jhmi.edu.

BEADEL, STEPHEN JAY, author; b. Sharpsburg, Iowa, Aug. 5, 1949; s. Walter Reldon and Katherine Margaret (Repplinger) B. BS, Iowa State U., 1971. Owner, mgr. Beadel Lumber, Lenox, Iowa, 1976-83; author, 1985—. Guest on numerous talk shows, 1990. Author: The Prophetic Beast, The Predicted Fall of Berlin Wall, 1989, What the Church Won't Tell You About Christmas, 1989, The Four Horseman of the Apocalypse, 1989, What Do You Mean "Born Again"?, 1990, The Pagan Rituals of Easter, 1990, Where is the True Church, 1990, The Reward for Salvation, 1990. Avocations: photography, painting. Home: 1230 70th St Windsor Heights IA 50311

BEADLE, ELIZABETH AHRENS, retired elementary school educator; b. Queens County, NY, Jan. 27, 1927; d. William Henry Ahrens and Marie Esta Strong-Ahrens; m. Harold Kenneth Beadle, Dec. 2, 1950; children: Carol Beadle Shelley, Richard Kenneth, Robert Thomas. BA in Child Study, St. Joseph Coll. for Women, Bklyn., 1948; student, Queens Coll., 1949, Hunter Coll., 1949, St. Leo Coll., Fla., 1968, U. South Fla., 1968—75; student reading improvement, Psychotechnics, Inc., 1968. Cert. tchr. NY, Fla. Tchr. kindergarten P.S. 109, Queens Village, NY, 1948—50; office mgr. Beadle Excavation/Instant Shade Inc., Zephyrhills, Fla., 1951—2000; tchr. 1st grade Pasco Elem. Sch., Dade City, Fla., 1969—70, home-sch. coord., 1974—75, tchr. kindergarten, 1970—72, tchr. 3d grade, 1975—88; tchr. kindergarten Dade City Grammar Sch. (now Cox Elem.), 1972—74; ret., 1988. Organizer Reading is Fundamental program Pasco Elem. Sch., 1974. Pres., sec., treas. Intertown Pvt. Sch. Transp., Inc., Zephyrhills, 1966—69. Mem.: DAV Aux. (organizer, pres. 1958—60), Alpha Delta Kappa. Republican. Roman Catholic. Avocations: reading, travel, birdwatching, mechanical drawing.

BEADLE, JOHN M., food products executive; With Assoc. Biscuits; gen. mgr. grocery products Can. divsn., Freshbake Foods Group subs. Campbell Soup Co.; mng. dir. Europe ltd. Schwan Food, 1991—2001, pres., COO Marshall, Minn., 2001—. Office: Schwan Food 115 W College Dr Marshall MN 56258

BEAGLE, BENJAMIN STUART, JR., columnist; b. Staunton, Va., Apr. 24, 1927; s. Benjamin Stuart Sr. and Mamie Virginia (Smith) B.; m. Mary Ann John, June 25, 1952; children: Ann Beheler, Benjamin III, Lucinda. BA in English, Roanoke Coll., 1952. Reporter Radford (Va.) News Jour.; pub. rels. asst. Roanoke Coll., Salem, Va., 1952-53; reporter Staunton News Leader, 1953-54; sr. writer Roanoke (Va.) Times & World News, 1954-92, columnist, 1957—. Author: The World I Never Made, 1986, El Viejo Writes Again, 1990, J. Lindsay Almond, Virginia's Reluctant Rebel. With U.S. Army, 1945-46, ATO. Named Disting. Alumnus Roanoke Coll., 1992. Avocations: reading, writing, outdoor work, woodworking. Home: 5571 Highfields Rd Roanoke VA 24018-4109 Office: Roanoke Times & World News 201 Campbell Ave SW # 209 Roanoke VA 24011-1100 E-mail: bbeaglejr@aol.com.

BEAGRIE, GEORGE SIMPSON, dentist, educator, retired dean; b. Peterhead, Scotland, Sept. 14, 1925; emigrated to Can., 1968, naturalized, 1973; s. George and Eliza Lawson (Simpson) B.; m. Marjorie McVie, Sept. 30, 1950; children: Jennifer, Lesley, Ailsa, Elspeth. LDS, Royal Coll. Surgeons, Edinburgh, Scotland, 1947; DDS, U. Edinburgh, 1966; DSc (hon.), McGill U., Can., 1985; DDS (hon.), U. Edinburgh, 1987; D, U. Montreal, Can., 1991. Prof., chmn. dept. restorative dentistry U. Edinburgh Dental Sch., 1963-68; prof., chmn. dept. clin. scis. U. Toronto Dental Sch., 1968-78, dir. postgrad. div., 1974-78; dean faculty dentistry U. B.C., Vancouver, Canada, 1978—88, dean emeritus, 1989—. Sci. officer grants com. dental scis. Med. Rsch. Coun. Can., 1971-76, dir. dental tng. grants programme, 1971-78; mem. Nat. Dental Examining Bd. Can.; chmn. written exams com. Nat. Dental Examining Bd., Can., 1984-93; cons. WHO, 1976-1996, in field. Contbr. over 100 articles to dental jours. Mem. United Ch. Can. Served to flight lt. RAF, 1948-50. Fellow Nuffield Found., 1957-58; grantee Med. Research Council U.K., 1962-64; grantee Med. Research Council Can., 1968; grantee Commonwealth Found., 1973 Fellow Royal Coll. Dentists Can. (pres. 1977-79), Am. Coll. Dentists, Internat. Coll. Dentists; fellow in dental surgery Royal Coll. Surgeons Edinburgh and Eng.; mem. ADA (hon.), Internat. Assn. Dental Research (pres. 1977-78), Fedn. Dentaire Internat. (chmn. commn. on dental edn. and practice 1981-87), Can. Dental Assn. (editor tape cassette program 1972-76, coord. Self-Learning, Self-Appt. C-E program for gen. practitioners, 1986-), Omicron Kappa Upsilon.

BEAHM, FRANKLIN D., lawyer; b. Independence, Kans., Jan. 18, 1953; s. Edgar Hiram and Dorothy S.; m. Tawny L. McIntyre, Jan. 7, 1994; children: F. David, Patrick Stuart, Kristin Sanders, Stephen McWilliams. BBA, So. Methodist U., 1975; JD, Tulane U., 1977. Bar: La. 1977, Colo. 1993, Tex. 2000, U.S. Dist. Ct. (ea. dist.) La. 1977, U.S. Dist. Ct. (mid. dist.) La. 1980, U.S. Dist. Ct. (we. dist.) La. 1985, U.S. Ct. Appeals (5th cir.), U.S. Tax Ct. 1989, U.S. Supreme Ct. 1993. Assoc. Manard & Scheonberger, New Orleans, 1977-80, Bourgeois, Bennett, Metairie, La., 1980, Hammett, Leake & Hammett, New Orleans, 1980-83, ptnr., 1983-85, Thomas, Hayes & Beahm, New Orleans, 1985-95, Chehardy, Sherman, Ellis, Breslin, Murray, Metairie, 1995-97, Beahm & Green, New Orleans, 1997—. Mem. Am. Health Lawyers Assn., Am. Soc. Law and Medicine, La. Assn. Def. Counsel, La. Bar Assn. (Interprofl. com. 1997-98, professionalism com. 1999—), La. Med. Soc. (Interprofl. com. 1997-98), La. Soc. Hosp. Attys. of the La. Hosp. Assn., Denver Bar Assn., Def. Rsch. Inst. (med. malpractice com., product liability com.), Beta Alpha Psi. Office: 145 Robert E Lee Blvd Ste 408 New Orleans LA 70124-2581 Office Phone: 504-288-2000. Business E-Mail: frank@beahm.com.

BEAHRS, OLIVER HOWARD, surgeon, educator; b. Eufaula, Ala., Sept. 19, 1914; s. Elmer Charles and Elsa Katherine (Smith) B.; 1 child, Gean Beahrs Landy; m. Helen Edith Taylor, July 27, 1947; children: John Randolf, David Howard, Nancy Ann Beahrs Oster. BA, U. Calif., Berkeley, 1937; MD, Northwestern U., 1942; MS in Surgery, Mayo Grad. Sch. Medicine, 1949; D of Mil. Medicine honoris causa (hon.), Uniform Svcs. U. Health Sci., 1999. Diplomate Am. Bd. Surgery. Fellow surgery Mayo Grad. Sch. Medicine, Rochester, Minn., 1942, 46-49, prof. surgery, 1966-79; Joel and Ruth Roberts prof. surgery Mayo Med. Sch., 1978-79; prof. emeritus Mayo Grad. Sch. Medicine, Rochester, Minn., 1979—; asst. surgeon Mayo Clinic, 1949-50, head sect. gen. surgery, 1950-79, vice-chmn. bd. govs., 1964-75. Bd. dirs. Rochester Meth. Hosp.; trustee Mayo Found.; mem. cancer control and rehab. adv. com. Nat. Cancer Inst., 1975-84; mem. Am. Joint Com. on Cancer, 1975-78, exec. dir., 1980-92; advisory com. Dept.Surgery Uniformed Svcs. U. Health Scis. Editor: Surgical Consultations; editorial bd.: Surgery, Surg. Techniques Illustrated; contbr. over 400 articles to profl. jours. Hon. life, bd. dirs. Am. Cancer Soc., 1975—; trustee Rochester Meth. Hosp.; adv. bd. Uniform Svcs. Univ. Health Scis.; med. cons. Pres. and Mrs. Reagan; founder Naval War Coll. Capt. USNR, 1942-64, ret. Recipient Leadership and Humanitarian awards, Am. Cancer Soc., Lifetime Achievement award, Nat. Cancer Awards Trust, 2004. Fellow Royal Coll. Surgery in Ireland (hon.), Royal Australasian Coll. Surgery (hon.); mem. AMA, ACS (mem. exec. com., bd. govs., chmn. cen. jud. com., long-range planning com., chmn. bd. govs., chmn. bd. regents, pres. 1988-89), Am. Group Practice Assn. (sec.-treas. 1974-75), Minn. Surg. Soc. (pres. 1960-61), Am. Thyroid Assn., James IV Assn. Surgeons, Am. Surg. Assn. (pres. 1979-80, chmn. com. on issues 1980-83), So. Surg. Assn., Cen. Surg. Assn., Western Surg. Assn., Soc. Head and Neck Surgeons (pres. 1966-67), Am. Assn. Endocrine Surgeons (pres. 1986-87), Am. Assn. Clin. Anatomists (pres. 1986-87), Soc. Surgery Alimentary Tract, Soc. Pelvic Surgeons (pres. 1983-84), Soc. Surg. Oncology, Am. Assn. Clin. Anatomists (pres.), Philippine Coll. Surgeons (hon.), Hellenic Coll. Surgery (hon.), Assn. Française de Chirurgie Française, Northwestern U. Alumni Assn. (Merit award), Sigma Xi, Phi Kappa Epsilon, Phi Beta Pi, Theta Delta Chi. Republican. Methodist. Home: 2253 Baihly Ln SW Rochester MN 55902-1023 Office: 200 1st St SW Rochester MN 55905-0001 Office Phone: 507-284-8655. Business E-Mail: beahrs.oliver@mayo.edu.

BEAIRD, CHARLES T., former publishing executive; b. Shreveport, La., July 17, 1922; s. James Benjamin and Mattie Connell (Fort) B.; m. Carolyn Williams, Feb. 6, 1943; children: Susan, Marjorie, John. BA, Centenary Coll., 1966; PhD in Philosophy, Columbia U., 1972. Vice pres., asst. gen. mgr. J.B. Beaird Corp., Shreveport, 1946-57; cons. in oil and investments Shreveport, 1957-59; pres. Beaird-Poulan Inc., Shreveport, 1959-73; chmn. bd. Beaird-Poulan div. Emerson Electric Co., 1973-76; pres., pub. Shreveport Jour., 1976-99; pres. Beaird Properties LLC, 2000—. Dir. Fed. Res. Bank of Dallas, 1972-78, dep. chmn., 1973-78; dir. Winrock Enterprises, Inc., Little Rock; adj. prof. Centenary Coll., Shreveport, 1969-95, prof. emeritus, bd. dirs. Mem. Caddo Parish Police Jury, 1956-60; bd. dirs. Woodrow Wilson Nat. Fellowship Found., Princeton, N.J., 1975-78 bd. dirs. Community Found. of Shreveport-Bossier, 1975-85, chmn., 1979-80 Served to capt. USMCR, 1943-46. Mem. Shreveport Club, Cambridge Club. Office: 330 Marshall St Ste 1112 Shreveport LA 71101-3015 E-mail: chasbeaird@aol.com.

BEAIRD, JAMES RALPH, law educator, dean; b. 1925. BS, U. Ala., 1949, LLB, 1951; LLM, George Washington U., 1953. Bar: Ala. 1951, D.C. 1973. Atty. U.S. Dept. Labor, 1951-56, asst. solicitor, 1956-59; assoc. gen. counsel NLRB, 1959-60; assoc. solicitor U.S. Dept. Labor, 1960-65; vis. prof. U. Ga., 1965-66, prof. law, 1967-89, prof. emeritus, dean, 1976-87, dean emeritus; John Sparkman Vis. Disting. Prof., U. Ala., 1988—; mem. Sec. Labor's Adv. Council on Welfare and Pension Plans, 1968—. Mem. adv. com. for Ga. SBA, 1969—. Mem. Farrah Order Jurisprudence. Office: U Ga Sch Law Athens GA 30602 Personal E-mail: jrb@aol.com. Business E-Mail: jrb@bbgbalaw.com.

BEAK, PETER ANDREW, chemistry professor; b. Syracuse, N.Y., Jan. 12, 1936; s. Ralph E. and Belva (Edinger) B.; m. Sandra J. Burns, July 25, 1959; children: Bryan A., Stacia W. BA, Harvard U., 1957; PhD, Iowa State U., 1961. From instr. to prof. chemistry U. Ill., Urbana, 1961—, Roger Adams prof. chemistry, 1997—2003, Jubille prof. liberal arts and sci., 1990—, James R. Eiszner chair chemistry, 2003, CAS prof. chemistry. Cons. Abbott Labs., North Chicago, Ill., 1964—, Monsanto Co., St. Louis, 1969-99, G.D. Searle Co., Ill., 1987-2001, Pharmacia, 2001-2002, Pfizer, 2003—. Contbr. articles to profl. jours. A.P. Sloan Found. fellow, 1967-69; Guggenheim fellow, 1968-69 Fellow AAAS (chmn. chemistry sect. 1999), Am. Acad. Arts and Scis.; mem. NAS, Am. Chem. Soc. (editl. and adv. bds., sec. and divsn. officer, A.C. Cope scholar 1993, Mosher award 1994, Gilman award 1997, Gassman award 2000). Home: 304 E Sherwin Ave Urbana IL 61802 Business E-Mail: beak@scs.uiuc.edu.

BEAL, BRIAN FAIRFIELD, marine ecology professor; b. Machias, Maine, Nov. 19, 1957; s. Milton Fairfield and Marie Grace Beal; m. Ruth Elizabeth Jenkins, May 10, 1980; children: Hannah Avery, Caleb Fairfield. BS, U. Maine, Machias, 1979; MS, U. NC, Chapel Hill, 1983; PhD, U. Maine, Orono, 1994. Asst. prof. U. Maine, Machias, 1989—96, assoc. prof., 1996—2001, prof., 2001—. Rsch. dir. Downeast Inst., Beals, Maine, 1987—; chmn. bd. Maine Aquaculture Ctr., Orono, Maine, 1994—2000. Contbr. articles to profl. jours. Coach Little League, Maine, 1999—. Named Tchr. of Yr., U. Maine Machias, 2000, Disting. Alumni, 2001; recipient Fulbright Scholarship, Galway, Ireland, 2000—01; Switzer Environ. Fellowship, Switzer Found., 1993—94. Mem.: Maine Dept. Marine Resources (mem. softshell clam adv. bd.). Independent. Avocations: baseball, handball, skiing, basketball, gardening. Office: Univ Maine 9 O'Brien Ave Machias ME 04654 Business E-Mail: bbeal@maine.edu.

BEAL, DONALD GORDON, clinical psychology educator; b. Phoenix, Nov. 4, 1943; s. Charles Gordon and Jane Ann (Cramer) B.; m. Rayma Carol Kirkpatrick, June 14, 1969; 1 child, Kristin Rayma. PhD, Tex. Tech U., 1978. Asst. prof. Miami U., Oxford, Ohio, 1978-82; clin. asst. prof. U. Cin. Coll. Medicine, 1982-87; assoc. prof. clin. psychology Ea. Ky. U., Richmond, 1987—. Contbr. articles to profl. jours. 1st lt. U.S. Army, 1968-70. Mem. APA, Assn. for Advancement Behavior Therapy. Avocation: photography. Home: 1977 Twain Ridge Dr Lexington KY 40514-1806 Office Phone: 859-622-1108. E-mail: donbeal@eku.edu.

BEAL, GRAHAM WILLIAM JOHN, museum director; b. Stratford-on-Avon, Eng., Apr. 22, 1947; came to U.S., 1973; s. Cecil John Beal and Annie Gladys (Barton) Tunbridge; m. Nancy Jane Andrews, Apr. 21, 1973: children: Priscilla Jane, Julian William John. BA, Manchester U., Eng., 1969; MA, U. London, 1972. Acad. asst. to dir. Sheffield City (Eng.) Art Galleries, 1972-73; gallery dir. U. S.D., Vermillion, 1973-74, Washington U., St. Louis, 1974-77; chief curator Walker Art Ctr., Mpls., 1977-83; dir. Sainsbury Ctr. for Visual Arts, Norwich, Eng., 1983-84; chief curator San Francisco Mus. Modern Art, 1984-89; dir. Joslyn Art Mus., Omaha, 1989-96, Los Angeles County Mus. Art, 1996-99, Detroit Inst. Arts, 1999—. Mem. Fed. Adv. Com. on Internat. Exhbns., 1991-94. Author: (book, exhbn. catalog) Jim Dine: Five Themes, 1984; co-author: (book, exhbn. catalog) A Quiet Revolution, 1987, David Nash: Voyages and Vessels, 1994, Sainsbury Collection Catalogue, vol. I, 1997, Joslyn Air Museum: Fifty Favorities, 1994, Joslyn Art Museum: A Building History, 1998, American Beauty: American Paintings and Sculpture from the Detroit Institute of Arts, 2002; contbg. to Apollo Mag., London, 1989-91. Trustee Djerassi Found., Woodside, Calif., 1987-89. Mem.: Am. Assn. Museums (trustee), Assn. Art Mus. Dirs. (trustee), Det⁻ it Athletic Club, Century Club. Avocations: history, cooking, music. Offic Detroit Inst Arts 5200 Woodward Ave Detroit MI 48202

BEAL, JACK, artist; b. Richmond, Va., June 25, 1931; s. Walter Henry and Marion Watkins (Baker) B.; m. Sondra Freckelton. Student, Coll. William and Mary, 1950-53, Art Inst. Chgo.; studies with Briggs Dyer, Isobel MacKinnon and Kathleen Blackshear, 1953-56; DFA (hon.), Art Inst. Boston, 1992; LittD (hon.), Hollins Coll., 1994. Vis. lectr. over 100 schs. and univs. Represented in permanent collections Whitney Mus. Am. Art, N.Y.C., Walker Art Ctr., Mpls., Art Inst. Chgo., San Francisco Mus. Fine Arts, Nat. Gallery Art, Washington, Met. Mus., N.Y.C., Del. Mus., Wilmington, Washington and Lee U., Lexington, Va., U.S. Dept. Interior, Washington; executed mural U.S. Labor Bldg., Washington; paintings exhibited Allan Frumkin Gallery, N.Y.C., 1965-93, Galerie Claude Bernard, Paris, Boston U., 1973-84, Va. Mus., 1973-74, Mus. Contemporary Art, Chgo., 1973-74, Madison (Wis.) Art Ctr., 1977-78, Art Inst. Chgo., 1977-78, Chrysler Mus., Norfolk, Va., 1980, Whitney Mus., Fairfield County, Conn., 1981, Munson-Williams-Proctor Inst., Utica, N.Y., 1982, Del. Art Mus., 1983, Galleria di Arte Moderna Udine, Italy, 1999-2003, Two Mosaic Murals: Times Sq. Subway Sta., MTA, N.Y.C., 2000-04. Mem. Youth Bd., Gouverneur, N.Y., 1970-73; bd. govs. Skowhegan (Maine) Sch., 1972-82; bd. visitors Sch. Visual Arts, Boston U; bd. trustees La Napoule Art Found., 1983-89; co-founder, advisor N.Y. Acad. Art. Recipient Neysa McMein Purchase award Whitney Mus., 1965, award Nat. Acad. & Inst. Arts and Letters, 1996; Nat. Endowment for Arts grantee, 1973; Hermitage Found. fellow, 1953-56; occupant Class of 1939 Endowed Chair Coll. William and Mary, 1992; subject of monograph by Eric Shanes, 1993. Office: care George Adams Gallery 41 W 57th St New York NY 10019-3409 Office Phone: 212-644-5665. E-mail: freckbea@dmcom.net.

BEAL, JOHN EVERETT, composer, conductor; b. Santa Monica, Calif., Jan. 20, 1947; s. Ralph Raymond and Marjory May B.; m. Helene Nina Marie Nielsen, Dec. 12, 2002. Student, San Diego State Coll., UCLA. Composer, pub. Opus Pocus Music, N. Hollywood, Calif., 1978—; pres., sr. composer Reeltime Music, Inc., Beverly Hills, Calif., 1984—. Musician, 1966—; composer (film) Zero to Sixty, 1977, The Funhouse, 1981, Terror in the

Aisles, 1984; composer, rec. artist: Coming Soon!, 1998 (Golden Score award 1998). Sgt. USMC, 1966—72, Vietnam. Decorated Air medal with bronze star, 8 Air medals, Naval Achievement with valor. Mem. ATAS, ASCAP, NARAS (gov. 1984-86), Soc. Composers and Lyricists. Avocations: film, travel, dining. Office: Reeltime Music Inc 10918 Bloomfield St Toluca Lake CA 91602-2212 E-mail: johnbeal@earthlink.net.

BEAL, JOHN M., surgeon, medical educator; b. Starkville, Miss., 1915; m. Mary Lucinda Phemister, Feb. 20, 1943 (dec. July 2005); children: John M., Bruce Phemister, Margaret Anne MD, U. Chgo., 1941. Diplomate Am. Bd. Surgery. Intern N.Y. Hosp., N.Y.C., 1941-42, asst. resident surgery, 1942-44, 46-47, surgeon, 1947-48, attending surgeon, 1953-63; chmn. tumor bd. and staff surgeon Wadsworth Gen. Hosp., West Los Angeles, 1949-50, chief surg. service, 1950-53; cons. staff St. John's Hosp., Santa Monica, Calif., 1950-53; instr. surgery Cornell U., Ithaca, N.Y., 1948-49, assoc. prof. clin. surgery, 1953-63; instr. surgery UCLA, 1949-50, asst. prof., 1950-53; J. Roscoe Miller disting. prof. Northwestern U., 1981-84, prof. emeritus, 1984—, chmn. dep. surgery, 1963-82; clin. prof. surgery U. N.C., Chapel Hill, 1984-88; chmn. dept. surgery Chgo. Wesley Meml. Hosp., 1963-69, Northwestern Meml. Hosp., 1973-82; chief surgery Passavant Meml. Hosp., Chgo., 1963-73. Chmn. Am. Bd. Surgery, 1970-71. Served to capt. M.C. AUS, 1944-46. Fellow ACS (bd. regents 1973-83, pres. 1982-83); mem. Council of Med. Splty. Socs. (sec. 1978-80), Soc. Univ. Surgeons, Soc. Clin. Surgery, AMA, Am. Surg. Assn. Address: 432 Georgetown Cir Valdosta GA 31602-4114

BEAL, MERRILL DAVID, conservationist, museum director; b. Richfield, Utah, June 26, 1926; s. Merrill Dee and Bessy (Neill) B.; m. Jean Lorraine Wood, Feb. 24, 1947; children: John David, James Merrill. BA, Idaho State Coll., 1950; MS, Utah State U., 1952. Park ranger, naturalist Yellowstone Nat. Park, 1953-60; chief park naturalist Grand Canyon Nat. Park, 1960-69; asst. supt. Great Smoky Mountains Nat. Park, Gatlinburg, Tenn., 1969-72; assoc. regional dir. Midwest region Nat. Park Service, Omaha, 1972-75, regional dir., 1975-78; supt. Gt. Smoky Mountains Nat. Park, Gatlinburg, Tenn., 1978-83; asst. dir. Ariz.-Sonora Desert Mus., Tucson, 1983-91. Author: Grand Canyon, the Story Behind the Scenery, 1967. Mem. bd. Grand Canyon Sch., 1964-69. Served with USN, 1944-46. Recipient Meritorious Svc. award US Dept. Interior, 1975. Mem. Wildlife Soc., Gt. Smoky Mountains Natural History Assn. (bd. dirs. 1993-95), S.W. Parks and Monument Assn., Ea. Nat. Park and Monument Assn. (bd. dirs. 1989-95), Sigma Xi. Personal E-mail: jbeal389@msn.com.

BEAL, MYRON CLARENCE, osteopath; b. N.Y.C., Dec. 4, 1920; s. Clarence Joseph and Birdice Elvira (Flint) Beal; m. Esther Naomi DeLong, Sept. 11, 1948; children: Rebecca Johnson, Myron Flint, Shelley Rees, Julie Wilson, Christina Beal Bailey. AB, U. Rochester, 1942; D.O., Chgo. Coll. Osteo. Medicine, 1945; MS in Physiology, U. Chgo., 1949. Asst. dir. clinics Chgo. Coll. Osteo. Medicine, 1946-49; instr. London Coll. Osteopathy, 1949-51; pvt. practice osteo. medicine Rochester, N.Y., 1951-74; prof. biomechanics Coll. Osteo. Medicine, Mich. State U., East Lansing, 1974-81, prof. family medicine, 1981-89, prof. emeritus, 1989—, acting chmn. biomechanics, 1975-77. Mem. Nat. Bd. Examiners Osteo. Physicians and Surgeons, 1960—84, cons., 1984—89; mem. N.Y. State Bd. Medicine, 1961—73. Trustee Chgo. Coll. Osteo. Medicine, 1969—93, chmn. bd. dirs., 1985—91. Fellow: Am. Acad. Osteopathy (editor 1987—2005); mem.: Chgo. Osteo. Health Sys. (bd. dirs. 1986—90), Mich. Assn. Osteo. Physicians and Surgeons, N.Y. State Osteo. Soc., Am. Osteo. Assn. Congregationalist. Office: 110 Ferris Hills Canandaigua NY 14424-3202

BEAL, ROBERT LAWRENCE, real estate executive; b. Boston, Sept. 10, 1941; s. Alexander Simpson and Leona M. (Rothstein) B. BS cum laude, Harvard U., 1963, MBA, 1965. Vice pres., ptnr. Beacon Cos., Boston, 1965-76; ptnr. The Beal Cos., Boston; pres. Beal and Co., Inc., Boston, 1976—. Corporator, dir., mem. exec. com., lending com. Provident Instn. Savs., 1975-86; chmn. bd. dirs. Mass. Devel. Fin. Agy., 1976—; instr. real estate Northeastern U., 1969-75; mem. East Cambridge rezoning adv. com., 1989—; dir. Artery Bus. Com., 1989—, chmn., 1995-99, treas., 1989-95. Bd. dirs. Boston Zool. Soc., 1972-86, pres., 1980, chmn., 1981-84, hon. chmn., 1985; mem. vis. com. Sch. Mus. Fine Arts, Boston, 1974-76, 88-89; overseer Boys Club Boston, 1975-93; mem. corp. Belmont Hill Sch.; trustee, overseer Beth Israel Deaconess Med. Ctr., 1981-2001, mem. bldg. and grounds com., 1976-82, 86-90; dir. Harvard Coll. Fund Coun., 1972-73, capital fund dir. Class '63, 1979-85, co-chmn. 25th reunion, co-chmn. 35th and 40th reunions, class gift, class sec., 2000—; exec. bd. Boston chpt. Am. Jewish Com., 1987-96, mem. bd. govs., 1989-92; bd. dirs. Boston Mcpl. Rsch. Bur., 1978—, treas., 1988-89, 92, vice chmn., 1990-93, chmn., 1994-96; bd. dirs. Met. Boston Housing Partnership, Inc., 1983-95; trustee The Partnership, Inc., 1981-89, New Eng. Aquarium, 1987—, bd. govs., 1993-98, 2002—, mem. exec. comm., 2002—, co-chair campaign steering com., 2001—; mem. adv. task force John F. Kennedy Libr., 1982; bd. overseers Mus. Fine Arts, Boston, 1988-97, 98-2001, overseer for life, 2001—; mem. vis. com. Harvard Div. Sch., 1989—, adv. com. Taubman Ctr., John F. Kennedy Sch. Govt., Harvard U., 1989—, chair, 2003—, co-chair campaign steering com., 2001—; co-chair United Way of Massachusetts Bay's Alexis de Tocqueville Soc., 2000, mem. cabinet, 2000, co-chair 2003 campaign; bd. overseers Mass. Soc. Prevention Cruelty to Animals, 1988—; chair coun. fellows Angell Meml. Animal Hosp., 1999—. Mem. Nat. Realty Com. (dir., past sec., mem. exec. com. 1974-99, v.p., vice chmn.), Mass. Assn. Realtors (dir. 1979-81), Greater Boston Real Estate Bd. (bd. dir. 1970-72, 76-90, pres. 1978-79), Am. Soc. Real Estate Counselors, Bldg. Owners-Mgrs. Assn. Boston (dir. 1970-72), Ripon Soc. (co-founder, nat. treas. 1968-73, nat. governing bd. 1979-85), Nat. Assn. Real Estate Appraiser (cert.), Mass. Taxpayers Found. (dir. 1980-86), Inst. Property Taxation (affliate), Internat. Assn. Assessing Officers (primary subscribing mem. 1982—), Beacon Hill Civic Assn. (bd. dir. 1975-79), Bostonian Soc. (life), Greater Boston C. of C. (bd. dirs.), The Vault (coord. com. 1978-97), Combined Jewish Philanthropies Greater Boston (exec. com. 1989—, vice chmn. 1992-93, chmn. com. on endowment fund 1999—, chair devel. com. 2001—, chair cmty. capital campaign 2002—, chmn. 2004—), Greater Boston C. of C. (bd. dirs. 1992—). Republican. Jewish. Home: 21 Brimmer St Boston MA 02108-1001 Office: Beal and Co Inc 177 Milk St Ste 2A Boston MA 02109-3410

BEALE, BETTY (MRS. GEORGE K. GRAEBER), columnist, writer; b. Washington; d. William Lewis and Edna (Sims) B.; m. George Kenneth Graeber, Feb. 15, 1969. AB, Smith Coll. Columnist Washington Post, 1937-40; reporter and columnist Washington Evening Star, 1945-81; weekly columnist North Am. Syndicate (formerly Field Newspaper Syndicate), 1953-89; ret., 1989. Lectr. in field. Author: Power at Play: A Memoir of Parties, Politicians and the Presidents in My Bedroom, 1993; columnist Georgetown and Country, 1998-99. Recipient Freedom Found. award, 1969; named Woman of Distinction, Birmingham So. Coll., 1987. Address: 2926 Garfield St NW Washington DC 20008-3536 E-mail: Gbetg@aol.com.

BEALE, MARK DOUGLAS, psychiatrist, educator; b. Richmond, Va., May 11, 1962; BA, U. Va., 1984; MD, Ea. Va. Med. Sch., 1989. Diplomate Am. Bd. Psychiatry and Neurology; lic. S.C. State Bd. Med. Examiners. Intern Med. U. S.C., Charleston, 1989-90, resident in psychiatry, 1989-93, fellow in electroconvulsive therapy, 1992-93, instr. dept. psychiatry and behavioral scis., 1993-94, asst. prof. dept. psychiatry and behavioral scis., 1994—98, assoc. prof., 1999—; owner, pres. Charleston Psychiat. Assocs., 2000—. Cons. electroconvulsive therapy, attending psychiatrist Inst. Psychiatry, Med. U. S.C., Charleston, 1993—2000, Ralph Johnson VA, Charleston, 1996—; cons. electroconvulsive therapy Charleston Meml. Hosp., 1993-96; lectr. in field. Author: (with others) Handbook of ECT, 1996, (book chpts.) Handbook of Child and Adolescent Psychiatry, 1996, Textbook of Consultation-Liaison Psychiatry, 1996, (jours.) Convulsive Therapy, Psychosomatics, Neuropsychiatry/Neuropsychology & Behavioral Neurology; book reviewer: Clinical Gerontologist; editl. bd. Jour. of ECT. Recipient Young Investigator award Nat. Alliance Rsch. on Schizophrenia and Depression, 1998. Mem. Am. Psychiat. Assn., S.C. Psychiat. Assn. Avocations: guitarist in the psychodymanics band, saltwater fly fishing, motorcycling. Office: Charleston Psyciatric Associates 669 St Andrews Blvd Charleston SC 29407

BEALES, RANDOLPH A., lawyer, former state attorney general; m. Julie Leftwich; 3 children. BA in Govt. with high honors, Coll. William and Mary; JD, U. Va. Assoc. Williams Mullen Christian & Dobbins, 1986—87; various pos. U.S. Dept. Education, 1987—92; dep. assoc. dir. policy devel. The White House, 1992—93; assoc. Peterson & Basha, P.C., 1993—94; exec. dir. commn. champion schs. Gov.'s Office State of Va., 1994—96; exec. dir. Va. Bus.-Edn. Partnership, 1995—98; chief dep. atty. gen. Commonwealth of Va., 1998—2001; atty. gen. Commonwealth Va., 2001—02; ptnr. Christian & Barton, LLP, 2002—. Episcopalian. Office: Christian & Barton LLP 909 E Main St Richmond VA 23219 Office Phone: 804-697-4100.

BEALKE, LINN HEMINGWAY, banker; b. St. Louis, Nov. 14, 1944; s. Charles Francis and Miriam Frances (Hemingway) B.; m. Jean Long Wells, Sept. 6, 1969; children: David Q.W., Emily R., Linn H. BA, U. Ark., 1966; MBA, Washington U., 1969. Fin. analyst Edison Brothers Stores, St. Louis, 1969-74; sr. v.p. Commerce Bank of St. Louis, 1975-78; v.p. fin. and adminstrn. Curlee Clothing Co., Lexington, Ky., 1978-80; vice chmn. County Bank of St. Louis, 1980-84, Southwest Bank of St. Louis, 1984—2004. Bd. dirs. Zoltek Cos., Inc.; bd. dirs. Miss. Valley Bancshares, pres., 1984-2002. Treas. Forsyth Sch., St. Louis, 1980-87; pres. Edgewood Childrens Ctr., Webster Groves, Mo., 1986-88; dir. Mo. Colls. Fund, Jefferson City, Mo., 1990-93. Mem. Mo. Bankers Assn. (dir. 1988-90, 99-2002), Fin. Execs. Inst. (pres. St. Louis chpt. 1989-90, dir. 1991-94), Am. Bankers Assn. Leadership Conf. (del. 1990-92), Racquet Club (v.p. 1987-89), Bellerive Country Club, St. Louis Country Club, Old Baldy Club, John's Island Club. Office: SW Bank St Louis PO Box 790178 Saint Louis MO 63179-0178

BEALL, BURTCH W., JR., architect; b. Columbus, Ohio, Sept. 27, 1925; s. Burtch W. and Etta (Beheler) B.; m. Susan Jane Hunter, June 6, 1949; children: Brent Hunter, Brook Waite. Student, John Carroll U., 1943; BArch, Ohio State U., 1949. Draftsman Brooks & Coddington, Architects, Columbus, 1949-51, William J. Monroe, Architects, Salt Lake City, 1951-53, Lorenzo Young, Architect, Salt Lake City, 1953-54; prin. Burtch W. Beall, Jr., Architect, Salt Lake City, 1954—. Vis. lectr. Westminster Coll., 1955; adj. prof. U. Utah, 1955-85, 92-97; treas. Nat. Coun. Archtl. Registration Bds., 1982-84. Restoration architect Salt Lake City and County Bldg; contbr. projects to: A Pictorial History of Architecture in America, America Restored, This Before Architecture. Trustee Utah Found. for Arch., 1985, pres., 1987-91; mem. Utah State Bd. Fine Arts, 1987-95, chmn., 1991-93; chmn. Utah State Capitol Adv. Com., 1986-90, Western States Art Fedn., Bd. trustees, 1991-94; mem. exec. residence com. State of Utah, 1991-97; mem. Utah: A Guide to the State Found. With USN, 1943-45. Recipient several merit and honor awards; Found. fellow Utah Heritage Found., 1985. Fellow AIA (jury mem. 2000-02); mem. Masons, Sigma Alpha Epsilon. Methodist. Home: 4644 Brookwood Cir Salt Lake City UT 84117-4908 Office: Burtch W Beall Jr Arch 2188 Highland Dr Salt Lake City UT 84106-2896 Office Phone: 801-464-1304.

BEALL, CYNTHIA, anthropologist, educator; b. Urbana, Ill., Aug. 21, 1949; d. John Wood and J. Alene (Beachler) Beall. BA in Biology, U. Pa., 1970; MA in Anthropology, Pa. State U., 1972, PhD in Anthropology, 1976. Asst. prof. Case Western Res. U., Cleve., 1976—82, assoc. prof. of anthropology, 1982—87, prof. anthropology, 1987—. Co-editor: Jour. of Cross-Cultural Gerontology, 1986—95; contbr. articles to profl. jours. Active Internat. Rsch. Exch. Program, 1990, 1991. Fellow Nat. Program for Advanced Study and Rsch. in China, NAS, 1986—87, 1997; grantee rsch., NSF, 1981, 1983, 1986, 1987, 1993, 1994, 1995, 1997, 2000, 2002, 2005, Am. Fedn. for Aging Rsch., 1983, 1986, Nat. Geog. Soc., 1983, 1986—87, 1993, 1995. Fellow: AAAS; mem.: NAS (coun. 2002—), Assn. for Anthropology and Gerontology, Soc. for Study Human Biology, Human Biology Coun. (exec. com. 1989—92, pres. 1992—94), Am. Assn. Phys. Antrhopology (exec. com. 1989—92), Am. Anthrop. Assn., Am. Philo. Soc. Achievements include research in in Peru, Bolivia, Nepal, Tibet, Mongolia and Ethiopia. Office: Case Western Res U Dept Anthropology 238 Mather Memorial Bldg Cleveland OH 44106-7125 E-mail: cmb2@po.cwru.edu.

BEALL, DENNIS RAY, artist, educator; b. Chickasha, Okla., Mar. 13, 1929; s. Roy A. and Lois O. (Phillips) B.; 1 son, Garm. Student, Okla. City U., 1950-52; BA, San Francisco State U., 1956, MA, 1958. Registrar Oakland (Calif.) Art Mus., 1958; curator Achenbach Found. for Graphic Arts, Calif. Palace of the Legion of Honor, San Francisco, 1958-1965; asst. prof. art San Francisco State U., 1965-69, assoc. prof., 1969-76, prof. art, 1976-92; prof. emeritus, 1992—. Numerous one-man shows of prints, 1957—, including: Award Exhbn. of San Francisco Art Commn., Calif. Coll. Arts and Crafts, 1978, San Francisco U. Art Gallery, 1978, Los Robles Galleries, Palo Alto, Calif.; numerous group shows 1960— including Mills Coll. Art Gallery, Oakland, Calif., Univ. Gallery of Calif. State U., Hayward, 1979, Marshall-Meyers Gallery, 1979, 80, Marin Civic Ctr. Art Galleries, San Rafael, Calif., 1980, San Francisco Mus. Modern Art, 1985; touring exhibit U. Mont., 1987-91, An Inner Vision, Oysterponds Hist. Soc., Orient, N.Y., 1998, Modernism in Calif. Printmaking, Annex Gallery, Santa Rosa, Calif., 1998, The Stamp of Impulse, Worcester (Mass.) Art Mus., 2001, Haverford Coll., 2001, Palm Springs (Calif.) Desert Mus., 2003, Internat. Print Ctr., N.Y.C., 2003, Cummer Mus. Art and Gardens, Jacksonville, Fla., 2003; represented in numerous permanent collections including Libr. of Congress, Washington, Mus. Modern Art, N.Y.C., Nat. Libr. of Medicine, Washington, Cleve. Mus., Whitney Mus., Phila. Mus., U.S. embassy collections, Tokyo, London and other major cities, Victoria and Albert Mus., London, Achenbach Found. for graphic Arts, Calif. Palace of Legion of Honor, San Francisco, Oakland Art Mus., Phila. Free Libr., Roanoke (Va.) Art Ctr., Worcester (Mass.) Art Mus., Whitney Mus. Am. Art, Cleve. Mus., various colls. and univs. in U.S. Served with USN, 1947-50, PTO. Office: San Francisco State Univ Art Dept 1600 Holloway Ave San Francisco CA 94132-1722 Office Phone: 707-632-5124. E-mail: chu2kar@comcast.net.

BEALL, GEORGE HALSEY, ceramics engineer; b. Montreal, Can., Oct. 14, 1935; BS in Physics, Geology with honors, McGill U., 1956, MS in Geology, 1958; PhD in Geology, MIT, 1962. Rsch. geologist/mineralogist Corning Inc., Corning, N.Y., 1962-66, mgr. glass/ceramic rsch. dept., 1966-77, rsch. fellow, 1977—. Courtesy prof. materials sci. Cornell U., 1980; vis. corp. com. materials sci. and Engring, MIT, 1981. Contbr. over 80 articles to profl. jours. Recipient award in chemistry of materials Am. Chem. Soc., 1995, Achievement award Indsl. Rsch. Inst., 2001. Fellow Am. Ceramic Soc. (George D. Morey award 1988, Samuel Geijsbeek award 1993, John Jeppson award 1993), mem. Acad. Ceramics. Achievements include research in glass crystallization and glass ceramics which are nonporous, microcrystalline ceramics formed by controlled internal nucleation and crystallization of glass; research in luminescence in transparent glass ceramics for use in photonic applications and glass-ceramics for magnetic memory discs; holder 102 U.S. patents. (Macor, Cercor, Corelle, Suprema, Cortem, Keraglas stovetops, Visions, Dicor). Home: 16 Woodland Dr Big Flats NY 14814-7914 Office: Corning Inc Glass Ceramic Res Division Sullivan Pk Fr 51 Corning NY 14831-0001 E-mail: beallgh@corning.com.

BEALL, JAMES HOWARD, physicist, educator; b. Grantsville, W.Va., May 12, 1945; s. Judson Harmon and Mary Lenore (Burns) Beall; m. Mary Ruth Clance; children: Aaron James, Tara Siobhan. BA in Physics, U. Colo., 1972; MS, U. Md., 1975; PhD, U. Md., 1979. Grad. rschr. in astrophysics Goddard Space Flight Ctr., NASA, Greenbelt, Md., 1975—78; Congl. fellow U.S. Congress Office Tech. Assessment, Washington, 1978—79; project scientist sci. and analysis divsn. BKD, Rockville, Md., 1979—81; NAS/NRC resident rsch. assoc. Naval Rsch. Lab., Washington, 1981—83; mem. faculty St. John's Coll., 1983—; sr. cons. E.O. Hulburt Ctr. Space Rsch., Naval Rsch. Lab., Washington, 1983—. Moderator Libr. Congress Symposium Sci. and Lit., 1981; project adminstr. black oral history project Folger Shakespeare Libr., Washington, 1981; mem. sci. and engring. adv. bd. High Frontier, Arlington, Va., 1991—; prof. space scis., Sch. for Computational Scis. George Mason U., Fairfax, Va., 1992—; chair adv. group. Joint Global Change Rsch. Inst., College Park, Md., 2003—. Author: (book) Hickey, the Days, 1980. Dir. edn. Environ. Action Com., U. Colo. Denver, 1971—72; Poets-in-the-Schs. participant Va. Pub. Schs., 1975—; bd. dirs. Partridgeberry Sch., Greenbelt, 1977—78. Served with USAF, 1963—67. Recipient Tchr. Excellent award, Dept. Physics and Astronomy, U. Md., 1974—75; grantee, Nat. Endowment for Humanities, 1976, 1978, NSF, 1991, 1995. Mem.: AAAS, Coun. Scholars, Am. Acad. Liberal Edn. (mem. coun. scholars 2004—), Md. Writers Coun., Am. Astron. Soc., Am. Phys. Soc., Cosmos Club, Sigma Xi, Phi Beta Kappa, Sigma Pi Sigma. Republican. Achievements include research in theoretical and observational astrophysics, renewable energy resources and public policy; discovery of 1st concurrent radio and x-ray variability of active galaxy; made first prediction of inverse compton x-ray emission from supernovae, first prediction of detectable infrared and optical emission from accretion disks around black holes; first detection of a ring of x-ray light around the earth's equator. Office: Naval Rsch Lab Code 7650 Washington DC 20375-0001 Office Phone: 410-295-6915.

BEALL, JAMES ROBERT, toxicologist, consultant; b. Stillwater, Okla., June 29, 1940; s. James Arthur and Annabel (Hess) B.; m. Sandra L. Morseth, Aug. 31, 1985; children by previous marriage: Jimmie Karlene, Sidney Sharleen, Tracy Darlene. AAS, Amarillo Coll., 1960; BS, Okla. State U., 1963; MS, U. Okla., 1965, PhD, 1970. Diplomate Am. Bd. Toxicology. Sect. leader toxicology Schering Corp., Lafayette, N.J., 1969-77; biol. sci. adminstr. EPA, Washington, 1977-79; spl. asst. OSHA, Washington, 1979-80; sr. policy advisor, toxicologist U.S. Dept. Energy, Washington, 1980-97. Cons. in toxicology Specialized Tech. Resources, Inc., 1997—; dir. Cytomed. Lab., 1970-71, Am. Bd. Toxicology, Washington, 1981-85, Toxicology Lab. Accreditation Bd., Washington, 1983-87; cons. in field. Author: Uterine Lipid Biosynthesis During Reproductive Cycles, 1970; contbr. articles to profl. jours. Mem. Ambulance Squad, N.J., 1974-76. Recipient award of appreciation Consumer Product Safety Commn., 1981, plaque of appreciation Am. Bd. Toxicology, 1985, Md. Govt. award, 1992, Mem. Soc. Toxicology, Teratology Soc., Assn. Govt. Toxicologists (pres. 1983-88, bd. dirs. 1983-88), N.Y. Acad. Scis., Sigma Xi. Avocations: backpacking, photography, writing. Office: 4804 Old Middletown Rd Jefferson MD 21755-8315 Office Phone: 301-473-5967. Personal E-mail: jbeall@fred.net.

BEALL, JULIANNE, librarian; b. Portland, Oreg., July 16, 1946; d. Marsh Flagg and Ruth Gildersleeve (Large) B.; m. William Tobin Amatruda, Jan. 6, 1979. BA, Lewis & Clark Coll., 1967; PhD in English Lit., UCLA, 1974, MLS, 1977. Decimal classification specialist Libr. of Congress, Washington, 1977-86, asst. editor Dewey decimal classification, 1986—. Prin. author: DDC 004-006 Data Processing and Computer Science, 1985; asst. editor: Dewey Decimal Classification, 22d edit., 2003, Abridged Dewey Decimal Classification, 14th edit., 2004. UCLA fellow, 1967-70. Mem. ALA, Spl. Librs. Assn., Internat. Fedn. Libr. Assns. and Instns. (affiliate), Beta Phi Mu. Office: Libr of Congress Decimal Classification Dv Washington DC 20540-4330 Office Phone: 202-707-5715. E-mail: jbea@loc.gov.

BEALL, KENNETH SUTTER, JR., lawyer; b. Evanston, Ill., Aug. 9, 1938; s. Kenneth Sutter and Helen Cantlon (Koenig) B.; m. Blair Hamilton Bissett, May 25, 1975; children: Kevina Anne, Hunter Bissett, Baret Bissett. BA, Washington and Lee U., 1961, LLB, 1963. Bar: Fla. 1964. With Gunster, Yoakley & Stewart, P.A., West Palm Beach, Fla., 1964—, ptnr., 1970—, pres., 1994—. Bd. dirs. The Whitehall Found., The Wells Family Found.; chmn. Palm Beach County Environ. Control Hearing Bd., 1970-92; mem. law coun. Washington and Lee U., 1997-2001; trustee, sec. Caribbean/Latin Am. Action. Served with USMCR, 1963-68. Mem. ABA, Fla. Bar (Pres.'s Pro Bono Svc. award 1983), Palm Beach County Bar Assn., Fed. Bar Assn. (pres. Palm Beach County chpt. 1981). Democrat. Roman Catholic. Office: 777 S Flagler Dr Ste 500E West Palm Beach FL 33401-6121 E-mail: kbeall@gunster.com.

BEALL, ROBERT JOSEPH, foundation executive; b. Washington, May 19, 1943; s. William Joseph and Louise Rachel (Tayman) B.; m. Mary Ellen O'Connor, June 24, 1967; children: Thomas Joseph, Robert Andrew. BS, Albright Coll., 1965; MA, PhD, SUNY, Buffalo, 1970. Asst. prof. dept. physiology Case-Western Reserve U., Cleve., 1971-74; asst. prof. Case-Western Reserve U. (Sch. Dentistry), 1972-74; grants asso. div. research grants NIH, 1974-75; program dir. metabolic diseases program Nat. Inst. Arthritis, Metabolism & Digestive Diseases, 1975-79; med. dir. Cystic Fibrosis Found., Rockville, Md., 1980-93, nat. dir. Bethesda, Md., 1981-84, exec. v.p., 1984-93, pres., CEO, 1994—. Recipient Merit award NIH, 1980 Mem. AAAS, N.Y. Acad. Scis., Am. Soc. Human Genetics, Sigma Xi. Presbyterian. Office: Cystic Fibrosis Found 6931 Arlington Rd Bethesda MD 20814-5231

BEALL, ROBERT MATTHEWS, II, retail chain executive; b. Fresno, Calif., Aug. 7, 1943; s. Egbert Ruffin and Lynda Topp (Matthews) B.; m. Aldona Louise Kupchella, June 15, 1943; children: Jennifer, Lydia, Alexis, Robert. BSBA, U. Fla., 1965; MBA with distinction, NYU, 1969. Asst. buyer Bloomingdale's, N.Y.C., 1969-70; mgr. to CEO/chmn. bd. Beall's, Inc., Bradenton, Fla., 1970—. Bd. Fla. Power & Light Corp., Blue Cross Blue Shield Fla., SunTrust Bank, Inc. Divsn. chmn. United Way, Bradenton, 1991; bd. dirs. St. Stephens Sch., Bradenton, 1977-80, Tilton (N.H.) Sch., 1988-92, Fla. Coun. Econ. Edn., 1992—. Capt. U.S. Army, 1965-67. Mem. Nat. Retail Fedn. (bd. dirs. 1982—), Fla. C. of C. (chmn. 1994), Fla. Coun. 100 (bd. dirs., exec. com.), Pi Kappa Phi. Episcopalian. Office: Beall's Inc PO Box 9285 Bradenton FL 34206-9285

BEALS, HERBERT KYLE, urban planner, historian, consultant; b. Portland, Oreg., July 26, 1934; s. James Herbert and Mae Adelia (Thompson) B.; m. Barbara Carol Brown, Mar. 22, 1957; children: Patricia Louise, Cheryl Ann, Steven Kyle. BA in Social Sci., Portland (Oreg.) State U., 1958, MA in History, 1983. Planner, asst. dir. Clackamas County Planning Dept., Oregon City, 1957-65; planning cons. Bur. of Govt. Rsch., U. Oreg., Eugene, 1965-70; prin. planner Columbia Region Assn. of Govs., Portland, 1970-79; housing planner Met. Svc. Dist., Portland, 1979-80; with spl. projects Oreg. Hist. Soc., Portland, 1983-90; hist. cons. Gladstone, Oreg., 1990-96; ret., 1996. Author: Gladstone, Oregon, Part One, 1992, Part Two, 1998; editor, translator: For Honor and Country, 1985, Juan Pérez on the NW Coast, 1989; editor: Seeking Western Waters, 1995. Vol. Nat. Park Svc., Ft. Vancouver, 1974, USDA Forest Svc., Portland, 1981; commr. City Planning Commn., Gladstone, 1964-67, 72-76, Portland Metro Area Boundary Commn., 1985-88, vice chair 1988; mem. Pub. Libr. Bd., Gladstone, Oreg., 1996-2004, chair 1999-2003; mem. County Hist. Rev. Bd., Clackamas, Oreg., 1990-94, 96-2003, co-chair 1999-2003; bd. dir. Columbia Gorge Interpretive Ctr., 2004—. Recipient John Lyman Book award N.Am. Soc. for Oceanic History, 1990. Mem. Oreg. Archaeol. Soc. (life; pres. 1971, 77), Oreg. Hist. Soc., Hakluyt Soc., Soc. for the History of Discoveries (bd. dirs.), Phi Alpha Theta. Avocation: coin collecting/numismatics. Home: 7005 Valley View Dr Gladstone OR 97027 Personal E-mail: barbherb@aol.com.

BEALS, KAREN MARIE, minister; b. Phila., Dec. 9, 1948; d. Garner Harris and Mae Frances (Thacker) Downey; m. Edward Roy Beals Jr., Feb. 2, 1970 (div. Apr. 2001); 1 child, Katie Adrianne Downey. AA, Peace Coll., 1969; BA, U. Colo., 1971, MA, 1977; MDiv, San Francisco Theol. Sem., 1994. Ordained Presbyterian Ch. 1994. Tchr. Pikes Peack Bd. Coop. Svcs., 1975—78; customer rels. Pacific Mut. Life, Newport Beach, Calif., 1979—81; owner, CEO Beals on Wheels, Dana Point, Calif., 1983—86; dir. Children and Family Ministry South Laguna Beach United Meth. Ch., Laguna Beach, Calif., 1987—90; min. Elkton Presbyn. Ch., Dagus Mines, Pa., Wilcox Presbyn. Ch., Pa., Ridgway Presbyn. Ch., Pa., Elk County Presbyn. Parish, 1994—99, Olivet Neighborhood Mission, Olivet Presbyn. Ch., Cedar Rapids, Iowa, 1999—. Bd. dirs. Faith in Action, Cedar Rapids. Mem.: Rotary West Side. Presbyterian. Avocations: reading, knitting, hiking, walking, contemplative prayer. Office: Olivet Presbyn Ch 237 Tenth St NW Cedar Rapids IA 52405

BEALS, NANCY FARWELL, former state legislator; b. El Paso, July 21, 1938; d. Fred Whitcomb and Katharine Doane (Pier) Farwell; m. Richard William Beals, June 30, 1962; children: Katharine, Robert, Susannah. BA in Polit. Sci., Bryn Mawr Coll., 1960; MA in Teaching, Harvard U., 1961. Group leader Exptl. Internat. Living, Putney, Vt.; jr. high sch. tchr. Wincehster (Mass.) Pub. Schs., 1961-62; high sch. tchr. Hamden (Conn.) Pub. Schs., 1962-64; state rep. Conn. Gen. Assembly, Hartford, 1993—2003; mem. adv. bd. Parenting Support Program Yale-New Haven (Conn.) Hosp., 2003—, chairperson adv. bd. Parenting Support Programs, 2005—. Mem. state adv. coun. on spl. edn., 2000-02. Mem. various local and regional offices PTA, Chgo. and Hamden, 1970-83; local pres., state bd. dirs. LWV, Conn., 1979-92; mem., sec., chmn. Hamden Bd. Edn., 1983-92; mem. citizen's adv. bd. High Meadows Residential Treatment Facility, 1993—; treas. Spring Glen Civic Assn., 2003—; bd. dirs. Hamden Edn. Found., 2001-04. Recipient Citizenship award for Conn. Philip Morris Corp., 1992, Hamden Notable award Friends of Hamden Libr., 1986, Children's Hero award Children's Trust Fund, 1995, Disting. Legislator award Conn. Assn. Bds. of Edn., 1998, Master Builder award Habitat for Humanity of Greater New Haven, 2002; named Legislator of Yr. Conn. Libr. Assn., 1994, Caucus of Conn. Dems., 1997, Conn. Coalition on Aging, 2002; Flemming fellow Ctr. for Policy Alternatives, 1995. Democrat.

BEALS, PAUL ARCHER, religious studies educator; b. Russell, Iowa, Feb. 18, 1924; s. Archer Edwin and Myrtle Mae (Kelsey) B.; m. Vivian Brown, Sept. 29, 1945; children: Lois Ruth, Stephen Paul, Samuel Archer, Timothy Joel. AB, Wheaton (Ill.) Coll., 1945; diploma, Moody Bible Inst., Chgo., 1948; ThM with high honors, Dallas Theol. Seminary, 1952, ThD, 1964. Missionary in Cen. African Republic Bapt. Mid-Missions, Cleve., 1952-64; prof. of missiology Grand Rapids (Mich.) Bapt. Seminary, 1964-97, prof. emeritus missiology, 1998—, dir. continuing edn., 1977-90. Theol. cons. Bapt. Mid-Missions, 1969-72, missionary emeritus, 2002--; conf. speaker. Author: A People for His Name, 1985, rev. edit., 1995; contbr. articles to profl. jours. Mem. Evang. Theol. Soc., Evang. Missiological Soc. (pres. 1990-93), Am. Soc. Missiology, Pi Gamma Mu. Home: 2111 Audley Dr NE Grand Rapids MI 49525-1517

BEALS, RALPH E., economist, educator; b. Lexington, Ky., Oct. 30, 1936; s. Wendell Everett and Gratia Marie (Burns) B.; m. Mildred Ann Hubbard, Sept. 3, 1960; children— Gerald E., Ellen H. BS, U. Ky., 1958; MA, Northwestern U., 1959; PhD, MIT, 1970; MA (hon.), Amherst Coll., 1971. Asst. prof. econs. Amherst (Mass.) Coll., 1962-63, assoc. prof., 1966-71, prof. econs., 1971—, Clarence Francis prof. econs., 1980—, acting dean of faculty, 1988-89, acting pres., 1991; asst. prof. econs. Northwestern U., 1963-66. Cons. Harvard U. Inst. Internat. Devel., 1973-90, project assoc., Indonesia, 1973-75, 80-82; cons. Boston Inst. for Developing Econs., 1991; cons. U.S. Treasury Office of East Europe and Former Soviet Union, 1993-95; cons. in field. Author: Statistics for Economists: An Introduction, 1972, (with others) Tax and Investment Policies for Hard Minerals: Public and Multinational Enterprises in Indonesia, 1979; also articles. Chmn. bd. Hampshire Community Action Commn., 1969-73. Mem. Am. Econ. Assn. Home: 164 Columbia Dr Amherst MA 01002-3127 Office: Amherst Coll Dept Econs Amherst MA 01002

BEALS, VAUGHN LE ROY, JR., retired motorcycle manufacturing executive; b. Cambridge, Mass., Jan. 2, 1928; s. Vaughn Le Roy and Pearl Uela (Wilmarth) B.; m. Eleanore May Woods, July 15, 1951; children: Susan Lynn, Laurie Jean. BS, M.I.T., 1948, MS, 1954. Research engr. Cornell Aero. Lab., Buffalo, 1948-52, MIT Aero Elastic and Structures Research Lab., 1952-55; dir. research and tech. N.Am. Aviation, Inc., Columbus, Ohio, 1955-65; exec. v.p. Cummins Engine Co., Columbus, Ind., 1965-70, also dir.; chmn. bd., chief exec. officer Formac Internat., Inc., Seattle, 1970-75; dep. group exec. Motorcycle Products Group, AMF Inc., Milw., 1975-77, v.p. and group exec. Stamford, Conn., 1977-81; chief exec. officer Harley-Davidson, Inc., Milw., 1981-89, chmn., 1981-96, chmn. emeritus, 1996—. Mem. Desert Mountain Club, Desert Forest Golf Club, Forest Highlands Golf Club. Home: PO Box 3260 Carefree AZ 85377-3260 Office: Harley-Davidson Inc Box 653 3700 W Juneau Ave Milwaukee WI 53208-2865

BEAM, CLARENCE ARLEN, federal judge; b. Stapleton, Nebr., Jan. 14, 1930; s. Clarence Wilson and Cecile Mary (Harvey) Beam; m. Betty Lou Fletcher, July 22, 1951; children: Randal, James, Thomas, Bradley, Gregory. BS, U. Nebr., 1951, JD, 1965. Feature writer Nebr. Farmer Mag., Lincoln, 1951; with sales dept. Steckley Seed Co., Mount Sterling, 1954—58, advt. mgr., 1958—63; from assoc. to ptnr. Chambers, Holland, Dudgeon & Knudsen, Berkheimer, Beam, et al, Lincoln, 1965—82; judge U.S. Dist. Ct. Nebr., Omaha, 1982—87, chief judge, 1986—87; cir. judge U.S. Ct. Appeals (8th cir.), 1987—. Mem. com. on lawyer discipline Nebr. Supreme Ct., 1974—82; mem. Conf. Commrs. on Uniform State Laws, 1979—, chmn. Nebr. sect., 1980—82; mem. jud. conf. com. on ct. and jud. security, 1989—93; chmn., 1992—93. Contbr. articles to profl. jours. Mem. Nebr. Rep. Ctrl. Com., 1970—78. Capt. U.S. Army, 1951—53, Korea. Scholar Regents, U. Nebr., Lincoln, 1947, Roscoe Pound scholar, 1964. Mem.: Nebr. State Bar Assn. Office: US Ct Appeals 8th Cir 435 Federal Bldg 100 Centennial Mall N Lincoln NE 68508-3859 Office Phone: 402-437-5420.

BEAM, JAMES CARROLL (JIM BEAM), retired newspaper editor; b. Cameron, La., Oct. 7, 1933; s. Charles Cleveland and Carrie (Welch) B.; m. Jo Ann Drachenberg, Aug. 20, 1954; children: Jamie Lynn Meek, Bryan Carroll. BA, McNeese State, 1955; MA, La. State, 1962. Tchr. Calcasieu Sch. Bd., Lake Charles, La., 1958-62; reporter Lake Charles (La.) Am. Press, 1962-65, city editor, 1965-81, co-editor, 1981-92, editor, 1992-98, dir. polit. and pub. affairs, 1998-99. Lt. U.S. Army, 1955-57. Recipient 1st place column La. Press Assn., 1979, Hal Boyle award La. Miss AP Assn., 1985-86, 1st place Personal Column, 1997. Mem.: Phi Kappa Phi. Democrat. Methodist. Home: 4824 Gentilly St Lake Charles LA 70607-6341

BEAM, JOEL WHITT, athletic trainer, educator; b. Asheboro, NC, Dec. 24, 1963; s. Mary Humphries Beam. BSc, East Carolina U., 1982—86; MEd, Clemson U., 1988—90; EdD, U. of North Fla., 1998—2001. Cert. Athletic Trainer Nat. Athletic Trainers' Assn. Bd. of Certification, 1987, Healthcare Provider CPR/AED Am. Heart Assn., 2003, Clinical Instructor Educator Nat. Athletic Trainers' Assn., 2002, Approved Clinical Instructor Nat. Athletic Trainers' Assn., 2001, lic. Athletic Trainer State of Fla., 1995, cert. Heartsaver First Aid Am. Heart Assn., 2005. Asst. athletic trainer/adj. instr. U. Miami, 1990—97; head athletic trainer/adj. instr. U. North Fla., Jacksonville, 1997—2000, vis. asst. prof., 2000—01, asst. prof., 2001—. Guest reviewer Jour. of Athletic Training, 2004—, Jour. of Sport Mgmt., 2005—. Contbr. articles to profl. jours. Grant, U. North Fla. Coll. Health, 2003—, U. North Fla. Undergraduate Academic Enrichment Program, 2003—, Nat. Athletic Trainers' Assn. Ethnic Diversity Adv. Coun., 2003—. Mem.: Jacksonville Sports Medicine Program, Athletic Trainers' Assn. of Fla. (Northeast regional rep. 2002—03), Nat. Athletic Trainers' Assn. D-Conservative. Office: Univ N Fla COH 4567 St Johns Bluff Rd S Jacksonville FL 32224-2673 Office Phone: 904-620-1424. E-mail: jbeam@unf.edu.

BEAM, RICHARD SQUIRES, theater educator; b. Evanston, Ill. s. Robert Edwin and Hope Squires Beam; m. Marilyn Bonnie Jordan, Dec. 27, 1966; children: Katherine, Margaret. AB, Ind. U., 1966, AM, 1969; PhD, U. Ga., 1984. Designer, tech. dir. Theater 65 children's theater, Evanston, 1969—71; prof., dir. theater Western Carolina U., Cullowhee, NC, 1971—. Dir., scenery designer and lighting: (more than 200 theatrical prodns.). Mem.: NC Theater Conf., Southeastern Theater Conf., U.S. Inst. Theater Tech. Home: 52 Smoke Rise Tr Sylva NC 28779 Office: Dept Comm Theater and Dance Western Carolina U Cullowhee NC 28723 Office Phone: 828-227-7491. Business E-Mail: beamr@wcu.edu.

BEAMAN, JOYCE PROCTOR, retired secondary and elementary school educator, writer; b. Wilson, N.C., Apr. 27, 1931; d. Jesse David and Martha Pauline (Owens) Proctor; m. Robert Hines Beaman; 1 child, Robert David. BS, East Carolina Coll., 1951, MA, 1952. English and French tchr. Stantonsburg (N.C.) H.S., 1952-53, Snow Hill (N.C.) H.S., 1953-60, Saratoga (N.C.) Ctrl., 1960—78, libr., 1972-78, Elm City (N.C.) Mid. Sch., 1978-82, Spaulding Elem. Sch., Spring Hope, N.C., 1987-92. Mem. Competency Test Commn. N.C., Raleigh, 1983-84. Author: Broken Acres, 1971, All for the Love of Cassie, 1973, Bloom Where You Are Planted, 1975, You Are Beautiful: You Really Are, 1981, Teaching: Pure and Simple, 1998. Recipient Terry Sanford Creativity and Innovation in Edn. state award, 1977. Mem. Kappa Delta Pi, Delta Kappa Gamma (state chmn. 1978-80). Home: 8427 Piney Grove Church Rd Walstonburg NC 27888-9626 Office Phone: 252-238-3455.

BEAN, BENNETT, artist; b. Cin., Mar. 25, 1941; s. William Bennett and Abigail (Shepard) B.; m. Cathy Bao, Dec. 17, 1966; 1 child, William Bao. Student, Grinnell Coll., 1959-62; postgrad., U. Iowa, 1963, U. Wash., 1963; MFA, Claremont Grad. Sch., 1966. Asst. prof. art Wagner Coll., S.I., N.Y., 1966-79. Trustee Am. Craft Enterprises, New Paltz, N.Y., 1982-85, Am. Craft Coun., N.Y.C., 1980-84; former chmn. bd. dirs. Peters Valley, Layton, N.J. One-man show Royal Marks Gallery, N.Y.C., 1969, Henri Gallery, Washington, 1969; one-person retrospective exhbn. lifetime work Ark. Arts Ctr. Decorative Arts Mus.; exhibited in numerous groups show, including Whitney Mus. Am. Art, 1968-69, Newark Mus., 1968, 80, 89, 91, Am. Craft Mus. II, 1982, 86, N.J. State Mus., 19i4, Newport Art Mus., 1984, Hunter Mus., Chattanooga, 1990; represented in permanent collections Whitney Mus. Am. Art, The White House, Washington, Boston Mus. Fine Arts, Newark Mus., N.J. State Mus., St. Louis Mus. Art, Royal Ont. Mus., Ariz. State U., Grinnell Coll., Milw. Art Mus., Crocker Art Mus., Calif., Toledo Mus. Art, Cin. Art Mus., J.P. Speed Art Mus., Ky., others. Recipient editorial award Met. Home mag., 1990; rsch. grantee Wagner Coll., 1968, 70, 77, 78; fellow N.J. Coun. on Arts, 1978, 88, Nat. Endowment for Arts, 1980. Tibetan Buddhist. Studio: 357 County Road 661 Blairstown NJ 07825-4054 E-mail: bennettbean@bennettbean.com.

BEAN, BRUCE WINFIELD, lawyer; b. Albany, N.Y., Dec. 19, 1941; s. William Joseph and Ruth Elizabeth (Lafferty) B.; m. Barbara Bryant Hunting; children: Austin Bryant, Ashley Elizabeth. AB, Brown U., 1964; JD, Columbia U., 1972. Bar: N.Y. 1973, Calif. 1981. Law clk. to judge U.S. Ct. Appeals (2d cir.), 1972-73; assoc. Simpson Thacher & Bartlett, N.Y.C., 1973-76, Patterson, Belknap, Webb & Tyler, N.Y.C., 1976-80; counsel fin. and planning Atlantic Richfield, Los Angeles, 1980-85; exec. v.p., gen. counsel AmBase Corp. (formerly The Home Group Inc.), N.Y.C., 1985-91; ptnr. Coudert Bros., Moscow, 1995—98; ptnr., head corp. dept. Clifford Chance, Moscow, 1998—2002, counsel, 2002—04. Prof. Mich. State Law Sch. Col. USAFR, 1964-86. Mem. ABA (chmn. com. Russian-Eurasia), Am. C. of C. in Russia (bd. dirs. 1996—, chmn. bd. 1998-2000), Russian Inst. of Corp. Law and Governance (dir. 2000-03).

BEAN, CATHY BAO, humanities educator, writer; b. Kweilin, China, Aug. 27, 1942; came to U.S., 1946; d. Sandys and Dora Bao; m. Bennett Bean, Mar. 25, 1941; 1 child, William Bao. BA cum laude, Tufts U., 1964; postgrad. philosophy, U. Calif., Berkeley, 1966; MA Philosophy, Claremont Grad. Sch., Calif., 1969. Mem. faculty Jersey City (N.J.) State Coll., 1968-71, Montclair State Coll., Upper Montclair, N.J., 1977-88, East Stroudsbourg (Pa.) U., 1987-92. Bus. mgr. Bennett Bean art studio; spkr. and presenter in field. Author: The Chopsticks-Fork Principle, A Memoir and Manual. Vol. various ednl. and civic orgns.; bd. dirs. N.J. Coun. for Humanities, 1993-98, Soc. for Values in Higher Edn., 1990--; bd. trustees Ridge and Valley Conservancy Inc., 1991-95. Kent fellow Danforth Found., 1965-67, 71-72; scholar Claremont Grad. Sch., 1965. Personal E-mail: cathy@cathybaobean.com.

BEAN, EDWIN TEMPLE, JR., lawyer; b. Washington, Feb. 17, 1926; s. Edwin Temple and Mary (a'Becket) B.; m. Susan Roberts, May 22, 1952; children: Douglas C., Philip O., Emelie R. Bean Ventling. BS, MIT, 1946; LLB, Georgetown U., 1950. Bar: D.C. 1950, N.Y. 1951, U.S. Dist. Ct. (we. dist.) N.Y. 1952, U.S. Ct. Appeals (2nd cir.) 1975, U.S. Supreme Ct. 1978, U.S. Ct. Appeals (fed. cir.) 1982. Examiner U.S. Patent Office, Washington, 1946-50; assoc. Bean, Brooks, Buckley & Bean, Buffalo, 1950-61; ptnr. Christel & Bean, Buffalo, 1961-78, Christel, Bean & Linihan, Buffalo, 1978-85; pres. Christel, Bean & Linihan, P.C., Buffalo, 1985-89; ptnr. Hodgson Russ LLP (formerly known as Hodgson, Russ, Andrews, Woods & Goodyear), Buffalo, 1989—. Lectr., adj. prof. Law Sch., SUNY, Buffalo, 1987—. Pres. Children's Aid, Buffalo, 1968-70; bd. dirs. Child and Family Svcs., Buffalo, 1982—; trustee emeritus Gow Sch., South Wales, N.Y., chmn., 1991-95. Mem. ABA, N.Y. State Bar Assn., Erie County Bar Assn., Am. Intellectual Property Law Assn., Buffalo Tennis and Squash Club (pres. 1974), Buffalo Yacht Club, Mid-Day Club (pres. 1972). Republican. Presbyterian. Office: Hodgson Russ LLP Ste 2000 One M&T Plz Buffalo NY 14203 Office Phone: 716-856-4000. Business E-Mail: ebean@hodgsonruss.com.

BEAN, GLEN ATHERTON, entrepreneur; b. Mpls., Aug. 30, 1962; s. Douglas Atherton Bean and Eleanor Green (Caswell) Nolan; m. Mary Catherine Slingsby, June 16, 1990. BS, Ariz. State U., 1988. Promotion specialist John Deere & Co., Waterloo, Iowa, 1987; regional mgr. Elliott Meat Co., Duluth, Minn., 1989—90; gen. ptnr. No. Star Food Brokerage, Savage, Minn., 1990—92; pres. Rochester Bus. Group, Ltd., Minn., 1993—98, Hunter Holdings Ltd., Savage, 1998—. Dir. McGab Agribus. Scholar., Ariz. State Univ., 1989—. Media coord. U.S. Olympic Festival, Mpls. 1990; vol. Multiple Sclerosis Soc., 1989-2000; founder Ariz. State Univ. Agribus. Spkrs. Bur., 1987; bd. mem. alumni assn. Phoenix County Day Sch., Phoenix, 1983-89; guarantor Minn. Orch. Mem. Nat. Cattlemens Assn., Ariz. Cattle Growers Assn., Clan MacBean in N.Am., Universidad Iberoamaericana (assoc.), Ducks Unltd. (publicity chmn. Phoenix 1986-88, dinner chmn. Burnsville 1990, 91, zone chmn. 1992-99, dist. chmn. 2000—, state conv. chmn. 1998-99), State Feather Soc. (chair 1999—), Trout Unltd., T.C. Pub. TV, U.S.A. Shooting, Nat. Geog. Soc., Minn. Waterfowl Assn., Izaak Walton League, Nat. Wild Turkey Fedn., Nat. Sporting Clays Assn., Nat. Skeet Shooting Assn., NRA, PGA Tour/Ptnrs. Club, U.S. Golf Assn., Pheasants Forever, Ducks Unltd. Can. (life), Ariz. State U. Alumni Assn., Mpls. Inst. Arts, Minn. Hist. Soc., Bell Mus. Natural History, Sci. Mus. Minn., Minn. Zoo, Mustang Club Am., Sigma Nu. Republican. Episcopalian. Avocations: hunting, camping, conservation, international travel. Office: Hunter Holdings Ltd PO Box 276 Savage MN 55378-0276

BEAN, MATT, theater educator; b. Provo, Utah, Mar. 27, 1958; s. John E. and Ruth E. Bean; m. Lisa Kirkwood, June 21, 1985; children: Jonathan, Emily, David. BA, Brigham Young U., Provo, Utah, 1983; MM, Manhattan Sch. Music, NYC, 1985; DM, Ind. U., Bloomington, 1991. Asst. prof. musical theatre and voice Brigham Young U., Provo, Utah, 1991—97; assoc. prof. musical theatre and voice Wichita State U., Kans., 1998—2000, Western Ill. U., Macomb, 2000—. Vis. asst. prof. voice and opera U. Utah, Salt Lake City, 1990—91. Dir.: (Operas) La Bohème; actor: (plays) Sweeney Todd; composer: (plays) The Emperor's New Clothes, The 101 Dalmatians; contbr. articles to profl. jour. Mem.: Nat. Assn. Humanities Edn., Coll. Music Soc. (campus rep. 2004—05), Nat. Assn. Tchrs. of Singing, Pi Kappa Lambda. Mem. Lds Ch. Office: WIU Sch of Music 1 University Cir Macomb IL 61455 Office Phone: 309-298-1422.

BEAN, MELISSA, congresswoman; b. Chgo., Jan. 22, 1962; m. Alan Bean; children: Victoria, Michelle. AA in Bus., Oakton Cmty. Coll., 1982; BA in Polit. Sci., Roosevelt U., 2002. Dist. sales mgr. DJC Corp., 1982—85; br. mgr. MTI Systems Inc. Arrow Electronics, 1985—89; dist. mgr. UDS Motorola, 1989—91; area mgr. SynOptics Comm. Inc., 1991—94; v.p. sales Dataflex Corp., 1994—95; pres. Sales Resources Inc., 1995—2004; mem. US Congress from Ill. Dist. 8, 2005—; mem. Fin. Svcs. com., Small Bus. com. Mem. Palatine C. of C.; past pres. Deer Lake Homeowners Assn. Mem.: Nat. Assn Women Bus. Owners, Barrington Area Profl. Women. Democrat. Serbian Orthodox. Office: 512 Cannon House Office Bldg Washington DC 20005 Office Phone: 202-225-3711.*

BEANE, MARJORIE NOTERMAN, academic administrator; b. Adams, Minn., Oct. 3, 1946; d. Matthias Hubert and Anna Helen (Boegeman) Noterman. BA, Marillac Coll., St. Louis, 1969; MEd, U. Ariz., 1979; PhD, Loyola U., Chgo., 1988. Tchr. St. Alphonsus Sch., Prospect Heights, Ill., 1969-73; tchr., asst. prin. St. Raphael Sch., Chgo., 1973-75; prin. St. Theresa Sch., Palatine, Ill., 1975-84; pres. Mallinckrodt Coll. of the North Shore, Wilmette, Ill., 1986-90; sr. v.p. for adminstn. Loyola U., Chgo., 1991—. Trustee Mallinckrodt Coll. of the North Shore, 1980-90; cons. Jospehinum High Sch., Chgo., 1976, St. Viator High Sch., Arlington Heights, Ill., 1986. Mem. History of Women Religious, Fedn. Ind. Ill. Colls. and Univs. (exec. com. 1989), Wilmette C. of C., Sisters of Christian Charity (councilor 1980-88). Rotary. Roman Catholic. Avocations: sewing, bicycling, swimming, travel. Office: Loyola U 820 N Michigan Ave Fl 1 Chicago IL 60611-2196

BEAR, DINAH, lawyer; b. Lynnwood, Calif., Oct. 22, 1951; d. Henry Louis and Betty Jean (Isenhart) B. BJ, U. Mo., 1974; JD, McGeorge Sch. Law, 1977. Bar: Calif. 1978, D.C. 1981, U.S. Supreme Ct. 1982. Dep. gen. counsel Council on Environ. Quality, Washington, 1981-83, gen. counsel, 1983—. Contbr. articles to profl. publs. Recipient Disting. Svc. award Sierra Club, 1993, Chmn.'s award Natural Resources Coun. of Am., 1993. Mem. ABA (chmn. standing com. on environ. law), D.C. Bar Assn. Jewish. Avocation: gardening. Office: Coun Environ Quality 722 Jackson Pl NW Washington DC 20503-0002

BEAR, GERALDINE M., nursing assistant, poet; b. Spartanburg, S.C., Mar. 6, 1926; d. Clarence Lee and Lucy Bell Hayes; m. Samuel Sidney Bear, Apr. 8, 1945; children: Diana L., Russell M., Joseph J. Student, Edgecombe Acad., 1943. Cert. nursing asst., CPR, RN home health aide. Author: (poems) Dedications of Love, 1974, The Poetry Seed, 1991. Deacon, mem. choir Grace Presbyn. Ch., Springhill, Fla., 1975—79. Avocations: painting, sewing, decorating.

BEAR, GREGORY DALE, writer, illustrator; b. San Diego, Aug. 20, 1951; s. Dale Franklin and Wilma (Merriman) B.; m. Astrid May Anderson, June 18, 1983; children: Erik William, Alexandra. AB in English, San Diego State U., 1973. Tech. writer, host Reuben H. Fleet Space Theater, 1973; freelance writer, 1975—. Author: Hegira, 1979, Psychlone, 1979, Beyond Heaven's River, 1980, Strength of Stones, 1981, The Wind From a Burning Woman, 1983, The Infinity Concerto, 1984, Blood Music, 1985, Eon, 1985, The Serpent Mage, 1986, The Forge of God, 1987, Eternity, 1988, Tangents, 1989, Heads, 1990, Queen of Angels, 1990, Anvil of Stars, 1992, Moving Mars, 1993 (Nebula award 1994), Songs of Earth and Power, 1993, Legacy, 1995, Slant, 1997, Dinosaur Summer, 1998 (Endeavor award 1999), Foundation and Chaos, 1998, Darwin's Radio, 1999 (Endeavor award 2000, Nebula award 2001), Rogue Planet, 2000, Vitals, 2002, Darwin's Children, 2003, Collected Short Stories of Greg Bear, 2003, Dead Lines, 2004; short stories: Blood Music (Hugo and Nebula awards), 1983, Hardfought (Nebula award), 1993, Tangents (Hugo and Nebula awards), 1987; editor: New Legends, 1995. Cons. Citizen's Adv. Council on Nat. Space Policy, Tarzana, Calif. Mem. Sci. Fiction Writers of Am. (editor Forum 1983-84, chmn. grievance com. 1985-86, v.p. 1987, pres. 1988-90). Avocations: book collecting, science, music, movies, history. Home: 506 Lakeview Rd Lynnwood WA 98037-2141

BEAR, LARRY ALAN, retired lawyer, educator; b. Melrose, Mass., Feb. 28, 1928; s. Joseph E. and Pearl Florence B.; m. Rita Maldonado, Mar. 29, 1975; children: Peter, Jonathan, Steven. BA, Duke U., 1949; JD, Harvard U., 1953; LLM, Columbia U., 1966. Bar: Mass. 1953, PR 1963, NY 1967. Trial lawyer Bear & Bear, Boston, 1953-60; cons. legal medicine PR Dept. Justice, 1960-65; prof. law sch. U. PR, 1960-65; legal counsel, then commr. addiction svcs. City of NY, 1967-70; dir. Nat. Action Com. Drug Edn. U. Rochester, NY, 1970-77; pvt. practice NYC, 1970-82; pub. affairs radio broadcaster Sta. WABC, NYC, 1970-82; US legal counsel Master Enterprises of PR, 1982-90. Vis. prof. legal medicine Rutgers U. Law Sch., 1969; mem. alcohol and drug com. Nat. Safety Coun., 1972—82; cons. in field of substance abuse prevention, edn. programming, 1980—; adj. prof. markets, ethics and law Stern Sch. Bus. NYU, 1986—99, vis. prof. bus. ethics, 1999—2003; pres. Found. for a Drug Free Pa., 1991—92; mem. Atty. Gen.'s Med./Legal Adv. Bd. on Drug Abuse, Pa., 1992; lectr. in legis. and ethics Wharton Sch. exec. program U. Pa., 1996—2000; vis. prof. legal, social and ethical context of bus. Athens Lab. Bus. Adminstrn., 1996. Author: Law, Medicine, Science and Justice, 1964, The Glass House Revolution: Inner City War for Interdependence, 1990, Free Markets, Finance, Ethics, and Law, 1994; contbr. articles to profl. jours. Adv. com. on pub. issues Advt. Coun., 1972-95; mem.-at-large Nat. coun. Boy Scouts Am., 1972-85; chmn. Bd. Ethics, Twp. of Mahwah (NJ), 1990-91; alumni admissions adv. com. Duke U., 1987—. Mem. ABA, NY State Bar Assn., Forensic Sci. Soc. Great Britain, Acad. Colombiana de Ciencias Medico-Forenses, Harvard Club (N.Y.C.). Home: 95 Tam Oshanter Dr Mahwah NJ 07430-1526 E-mail: rmaldona@stern.nyu.edu.

BEAR, MARK FIRMAN, neuroscientist, educator; BS, Duke U.; PhD in Neurobiology, Brown U.; postdoctoral training, Max Planck Inst. for Brain Rsch., Frankfurt, Germany. Prof. Brown U. Sch. of Medicine, 1985—2002; investigator Howards Hughes Medical Inst., 1996—; Picower prof. neurosci. MIT, 2003—. Mem. Dana Alliance for Brain Initiatives, Neuroscience Rsch. Prog. Neurosciences Inst., San Diego. Co-author (with Barry W. Connors, Michael A. Paradiso): Neuroscience: Exploring the Brain, 2000. Recipient Young investigator award, Office of Naval Rsch., Soc. for Neuroscience; grantee Fogarty Sr. Internat. Fellowship. Fellow: Am. Acad. Arts and Scis. Achievements include research in disorders ranging from mental retardation and autism to Alzheimer's disease. Office: MIT Dept Brain & Cognitive Sciences 77 Mass Ave Cambridge MA 02139-4307*

BEAR, STEPHEN E., pharmaceutical executive; Former exec. v.p. U.S. consumer products group Bristol-Myers Squibb, former pres. worldwide consumer medicines bus., sr. v.p. human resources, 2002—. Office: Bristol-Myers Squibb Co 345 Park Ave New York NY 10154-0037

BEARCE, JEANA DALE, artist, educator; b. St. Louis; d. Clarence Russell and Maria Emily Dale; m. Lawrence F. Rakovan, June 7, 1969; children: Barbara Emily, Luke, Francesca. B.F.A., Washington U., St. Louis, 1951; MA, N.Mex. Highlands U., 1954. Vis. artist, various lectureships, India, Pakistan, 1961-62, 93; founder art dept. U. Maine, Portland, 1965, chmn. and dept. rep., 1965-70, asst. prof. art, 1967-70, assoc. prof., 1970-81, prof., 1982—. Reflections South India sabbatical, 1992—93. Exhibited one-woman shows, Portland Mus. Art, Maine, 1958, U. Maine, Orono, 1958, 65, 69, 77, 80, Madras Govt. Mus., India, 1962, Gallery 65, Paris, 1964, Bristol Mus. Art, R.I., 1965, Center Gallery, N.Y.C., 1974, Benbow Gallery, Newport, R.I., 1979, Ctr. for the Arts, Chocolate Ch., Bath, Maine, 1988, USM Gallery, 1991, Main Gallery U. So. Maine, 1991, others, group show, Boston Mus. Art, Library of Congress, Phila. Print Club, Springfield Mus., Mo., Birmingham Mus. Art, Ala., others; represented permanent collection, St. Louis Art Mus., U.S. Edn. Found. in India, New Delhi, U. Maine, Orono and Portland, Bklyn. Mus. Art, Cornell U. Mus. Art, Calif. Coll. Arts and Crafts, Sarasota Art Assn., Fla., Bowdoin Coll., Brunswick, Maine; executed murals, N.Mex. Highlands U., Bowdoin Longfellow-Hawthorn Library, Brunswick, sculpture reliefs, St. Bartholomew, Cape Elizabeth, Maine, St. Charles Ch. Brunswick; retrospective, Maine Ctr. for the Arts, 1988. Mem. artist's com. Maine Art Gallery, 1957—75, 1980—87; mem. Maine com. Skowhegan Sch. Painting and Sculpture, 1972—. Recipient various awards; recipient Fannie Cook award People's Competition, 1958, 59; sabbaticals to India: Return to India-Creative Paintings and Printmaking, 1987, South India-Painting and Printmaking, 1993, The Maine to India Series USM Environ. Studies Ctr., 1996, Tibet The Maine Art Gallery, Wiscasset, 1999, Summer Invitational, Ctr. for Maine Contemporary Art, 2002, Maine Coast Artists, Rockport, 2002. Mem.: Bowdoin Coll. Mus. Assocs. Home: 327 Maine St Brunswick ME 04011-3310 Office: U So Maine College Ave Gorham ME 04038-1004

BEARD, AMANDA, swimmer, Olympic athlete; b. Irvine, Calif., Oct. 29, 1981; Student, Univ. of AZ, Tucsan. Mem. Pan Pac Team, 1995; swimmer U.S. Olympic Team, Atlanta, 1996, Sydney, 2000, Athens, 2004. Holder Am. record for 100 meter breastroke, 1996. Achievements include Gold Medal, 4x100m medley, Silver medal, 100m, 200m breast, Atlanta Olympic games, 1996; second youngest (14 years old) Gold medalist in USA swimming history, Atlanta Olympic games, 1996; Bronze medal, 200m breast, Sydney Olypmic games, 2000; Gold medal, 100m, 200m breast, Pan Pacific games, 2002; Gold medal, 200m breast, World Championships, 2003; Gold medal, 100m, 200m breast, 200m IM, U.S. Nat. Championships, 2004, 200m IM, 2003; Gold medal, 200m breast, Silver medal, 200m IM, 4x100m medley relay, Athens Olympic games, 2004. Office: US Swimming Inc One Olympic Plz Colorado Springs CO 80909

BEARD, ANN SOUTHARD, diplomat, oil industry executive; b. Denver, Jan. 13, 1948; d. William Harvey and Cora Alice Cornelia (Caldwell) Southard; m. Terrill Leon Beard, Dec. 20, 1970 (div. Oct. 1980); 1 son, Jeffery Leon; m. Rainer G. Froehlich, Feb. 12, 1988 (div. 1992). BA, Willamette U., 1970; postgrad., U. Calif., San Diego, 1981-82. Exec. asst. Kidder Peabody & Co., San Francisco, 1970-72; adminstrv. aide Arthur Anderson & Co., Portland, Oreg., 1972-73; owner, mgr. Beard's Frame Shoppes, Inc., Portland, 1973-80; dir. mktg. Multnomah County Fair, Portland, 1979; owner, CEO Ann Beard Spl. Events, San Diego, 1980-82; pres. Frame Affair, Inc., San Diego, 1982-86, Jack Oil Co., Inc., Greeley, 1982—; chancellor, v.p. programs Consular Corps. Coll., Phila., 2002—. Mem. Pres.'s Small Bus. Adv. Coun.; co-owner, v.p. Froehlich Internat. Travel, La Jolla, Calif., 1987-92; chief of protocol Mayor Susan Golding's Office, City of San Diego, 1993-2001; pres., CEO, Diplomacy & Internat. Protocol, San Diego, 2001—; chmn. 1st Nat. Protocol Officers Assn. conf. U.S. Dept. State, Washington; chmn. 1st Internat. Protocol Conf., Ottawa, Can.; v.p. 146 Co., Inc., Greeley, pres. 1970-88; mem. San Diego Consular Corps; lectr. World Trade Ctr., Alaska, Consular Corps, Alaska, 2002; cons. SBA, San Diego, 1980-85; facilitator internat. seminars, workshops, and retreats; prof. San Diego State U., 2002—, Palomar Coll., 2004—, SAIC U., 2004—, Smithsonian Inst. Assocs. Program, 2004—; internat protocol advisor to ind. film co. Molecular Pictures.com.; v.p. ceremonies Presdl. Inauguration, 2005; lectr. in field Active Civic Light Opera, Old Globe Theatre; bd. dirs. San Diego Master Chorale, 1981-92; mem. state bd. Miss. Calif. Pageant/Miss. Am., 1982-87; citizens adv. bd. Drug Abuse Task Force/Crime Prevention Task Force, San Diego, 1983-87; campaign coord. Bill Mitchell for City Coun., 1985; candidate for Congress; staff aide to dep. mayor, 1987; mem. Lead San Diego Alumni, 1988, Scripps Hosp. Aux., 1992—, Internat. Visitors Coun., 1993—, San Diego County Commn. on the Status of Women, 1993-96; mem. Internat. Affairs Bd., San Diego, 1993—; chancellor, Consular Corps Coll., Phila., 2001—; founder, nat. chmn. Nat. Protocol Resource Bd., USA, 2002—, founder, internat. pres. Protocol and Diplomacy Internat., U.S., 2002-04; bd. dirs. La Jolla Rep. Women Fedn., 1992—. Mem. Am. Mktg. Assn., World Affairs Coun., San Diego C. of C., Save Our Heritage Orgn., Charter 100 San Diego, San Diego 1988 Alumna Willamette U., 1909 Univ. Club (bd. dirs. 1992—, pres. 1996-98), Univ. Club San Diego (mktg., devel. and social dir. 1987-88), Pres., Protocol and Diplomacy Internat., Delta Gamma. Office: PO Box 1621 Solana Beach CA 92075 Home: 7220 Vistas Ln Mc Lean VA 22101 Office Phone: 858-481-5661. E-mail: bearddiplomacy@yahoo.com.

BEARD, BRUCE H., psychiatrist; m. Mary Ann Dempsey, Sept. 7, 2004. Pvt. practice psychiatry, Dallas, 1981—92. Fellow: Am. Psychiat. Assn. (licentiate Disting. fellow). Address: 10199 Vistadale Dr Dallas TX 75238-1636 Office Phone: 214-349-3029. E-mail: bruceandmary@sbcglobal.net.

BEARD, DENNIS ALTON, pastor; b. Overton, Tex., Dec. 21, 1948; s. George Alton and Edna Berneice B.; m. Diane Woodard, July 14, 1969; children: Angela Rochelle, Bradley Alton. AA, Kilgore Coll., 1969; student, Stephen F. Austin State U., 1970. Ins. mgr., Dallas; owner The Am. Agency Ins. and Equities, Dallas, 1975-80; regional v.p. Nat. Assn. Self-employed, Dallas, 1981-83; pastor, evangelist The Testimony of Jesus Christ Ch., Houston, 1985—. Founder OneGodSite.com. Author: The Errors of the Trinity and the Revelation of Jesus Christ, 1998, Behold the Real Jesus, 1999, The Mystery of the Kingdom of God, 2000. Republican. Avocations: playing piano and organ, singing, songwriting. Home: 14525 Main St Houston TX 77035 Office: The Testimony of Jesus Christ Ch 14525 Main St Houston TX 77035 E-mail: MinisterBeard@aol.com.

BEARD, ELIZABETH LETITIA, physiologist, educator; b. New Orleans, Apr. 2, 1932; d. Howard Horace and Irene (Handley) Beard. BA in Biology, Tex. Christian U., 1952, BS in Med. Tech., 1953, MS in Med. Tech., 1955; postgrad., Smith Coll., 1953-54, Vanderbilt U., 1954-55; PhD in Animal Physiology, Tulane U., 1961. Instr. dept. biol. scis. Loyola U., New Orleans, 1955-58, asst. prof., 1958-62, assoc. prof., 1962-68, prof., 1969—, chmn. premed. com., 1978—; rsch. assoc. dept. physiology Sch. Medicine Tulane U., New Orleans, 1960-63, prof. biology med. reinforcement and enrichment program, 1968-94. Vis. prof. dept. physiology and biophysics Med. Sch. Harvard U., 1983-84, dept. neuropharmacology Scripps Rsch. Inst., La Jolla, Calif., spring 2001; vis. scientist Am. Indian Rsch. Opportunities Programs at Mont. State U., 1994. Contbr. articles on rsch. in physiology to profl. publs. Project rev. com. New Orleans Health Planning Coun., 1974-77, bd. dirs., 1975-78; soprano soloist Holy Name of Jesus Ch., 1978—, pres. sch. bd., 1976-79; grad. rsch. com. La. chpt. Am. Heart Assn., 1970-72, 81-83, undergrad. rsch. com., 1978-81, 89-93; active Met. Mus. Art, New Orleans Mus. Art. NIH grantee, 1962-64, 67-69, La. Heart Assn. grantee, 1966-67, Edward Schleider Found. grantee, 1974-77, New Orleans Cancer Assn. grantee, 1962-63; Libby Rsch. fellow Sch. Medicine Tulane U., 1961. Mem. AAUP, AAAS, Am. Physiol. Soc., Soc. Exptl. Biology and Medicine, Christian Med. and Dental Soc. (participant internat. med. missions 1993—), Sigma Xi. Office: 6363 St Charles Ave New Orleans LA 70118-6143 Home: # 22 6363 Saint Charles Ave New Orleans LA 70118-6143 Business E-Mail: Beard@Loyno.edu.

BEARD, JERE S., secondary school educator; b. Sugar Hill, Ga., Oct. 24, 1972; d. Jerald T. Beard and Suzanne Beart. BS, N. Ga. Coll., 1995; MEd, U. Ga., 1999, MEd, 2005. Cert. Nat. Disc Jockey. Residence life coord. N. Ga. Coll., Dahlonega, Ga., 1995—97; grad. asst. U. Ga., Athens, Ga., 1997—99, counselor, 1999—2005; tchr. English as second lang. Meadowcreek H.S. Gwinnett County Pub. Schs., Ga., 2005—. Tutor - ESOL U. Ga., Athens, 2004—05, rsch. asst., 2005; presenter, rschr. English Literacy for Spanish Speaking Adults: Common Errors in English Literacy, 2004. Vol. Habitat for Humanity, Dahlonega, Ga., 1995—97; vol. svc. CCF, Tuarez, Mexico, 1997. Grant, SEGUE, 2004, Tell scholar, U. Ga., 2005. Mem.: Am. Coll. Personnel Assn. Democrat. Avocations: hiking, reading, music, mountain biking, travel. E-mail: jere1024@yahoo.com.

BEARD, KENNETH FRANKLIN, music educator; b. Atlanta, Ga., Mar. 18, 1954; s. Charles Edwin and Martory Arlene (Hinton) Beard; m. Cynthia Elaine Priester, Aug. 7, 1977; children: Kenneth Franklin Jr., Jonathan Andrews. MusB, Ga. State U., 1976; MusM, Eastman Sch. of Music, 1978. Cert. tchg. T-5 Ga. Asst. band dir. Forest Pk. HS, Forest Pk., Ga., 1977—80; band dir. Newton County HS, Covington, Ga., 1980—81, Fayette County Jr. HS, Fayetteville, Ga., 1981—90, Fayette County HS, Fayetteville, Ga., 1990—2005. Orch. dir. New Hope Bapt. Ch., Fayetteville, Ga., 1991—2005. Contbr. articles various profl. jours. Mem. Gideons, Fayetteville, Ga., 1983—90; band chair Ga. Music Educators Assn., Ga., 1994—96; band chmn. Chick-Flc-A Peach Band, Atlanta, 1998—2005. Recipient Citation of Excellence, Nat. Band Assn. Mem.: Profl. Assn. of Ga. Educators, Ga. Music Educators Assn., Phi Beta Mu. Republican. Bapt. Achievements include Fayetteville County HS Band performed in the Sydney 2000 Olympic Games opening ceremony. Avocation: music. Office: Fayette County HS 1 Tiger Trail Fayetteville GA 30214 Office Phone: 770-719-2112. Office Fax: 770-460-3410. E-mail: beard.ken@fcboe.org.

BEARD, LEO ROY, retired civil engineer; b. West Baden, Ind., Apr. 6, 1917; s. Leonard Roy and Barbara Katherine (Frederick) B.; m. Marian Janet Wagar, Oct. 21, 1939 (dec.); children: Patricia Beard Huntzicker, Thomas Edward, James Robert; m. Marjorie Elizabeth Pierce Wood, Aug. 30, 1974. AA, Pasadena City Coll., 1937; BS, Calif. Inst. Tech., 1939. Engr. U.S. Army C.E., Los Angeles, 1939-49; engr. Office Chief of Engrs., Washington, 1949-52; chief of Reservoir Regulation, Sacramento, 1952-64; dir. Hydrologic Engring. Center, Davis, Calif., 1964-72; prof. civil engring. U. Tex., Austin, 1972-87, prof. emeritus, 1987—. Cons. Espey, Huston & Assos., Austin, 1980-92; v.p. Internat. Commn. of Water Resource Sys.; mem. NRC Water Sci. and Tech. Bd. Editor-in-chief: Water International; Editor: Jour. of Hydrology. Served with USNR, 1945-46. Recipient Meritorious Civilian Service award U.S. Army C.E., 1972. Fellow AAAS,. Internat. Water Resources Assn. (exec. bd.), ASCE (water resources exec. com., Julian Hinds award 1981, hon. mem. 1987, Hunter Rouse award 1993, Lifetime Achievement award 2001); mem. Am. Water Resources Assn. (hon.), Am. Geophys. Union (pres. hydrology sect.), Nat. Soc. Profl. Engrs., Internat. Assn. Hydrol. Scis., World Meteorol. Orgn. (chmn. com. on hydrol. design data), U.S. Com. on Irrigation, Drainage and Flood Control, Univs. Council on Water Resources (exec. bd.), Nat. Acad. Engring. *As you spend most waking hours at your work, choose to love it. The key is to select an occupation that serves others.*

BEARD, LILLIAN B. MCLEAN, pediatrician, consultant; b. N.Y. d. Johnie Wilson and Woodie (Durden) McLean; m. Delawrence Beard. BS, Howard U., 1965, MD, 1970. MD, 1970. Pvt. practice pediat. Lillian M. Beard, Washington, 1973—; assoc. prof. pediat. George Washington U., 1983—; asst. prof. cmty. medicine Howard U., 1983—; contbg. editor Good Housekeeping Mag., N.Y.C., 1989-95; health adv. WUSA-TV, Washington, 1993-95; health and med. contbr. ABC-TV, Washington, 2000—04. Comm. cons. to industry including: Nestle Nutritional Products; mem. bd. dirs. Nat. Women's Econ. Alliance, 1993-2000, Children's Hosp., 1993-2002. Recipient Disting. Leadership award Nat. Assn. Equal Opportunity in Higher Edn., 1993, Disting. Svc. award Nat. Med. Assn., 1990, Hall of Fame in Medicine award, 1994, Healthy Babies Project "Making a Difference" award, 1995, Howard U. Alumni Achievement award, 1996. Fellow Am. Acad. Pediat.; mem. Nat. Med. Assn., Am. Acad. Pediat. (physician recognition awards 1993—). Home: 10517 Alloway Dr Potomac MD 20854-1662 Office: 10801 Lockwood Dr Ste 260 Silver Spring MD 20901

BEARD, RONALD STRATTON, lawyer; b. Flushing, N.Y., Feb. 13, 1939; s. Charles Henry and Ethel Mary (Stratton) Beard; m. Karin Paridee, Jan. 24, 1991; children: D. Karen, Jonathan D., Dana K. BA, Denison U., 1961; LLB, Yale U., 1964. Bar: Calif. 1964, U.S. Ct. Appeals (9th cir.) 1980, U.S. Dist. Ct. (ctrl. dist.) Calif. 1964. Ptnr. Gibson, Dunn & Crutcher, LA, 1964—2001, mng. ptnr., 1991—97, chmn., 1991—2001. Trustee Denison U., Granville, Ohio, 1975—, chmn., 1998—2003; mem. steering com. Calif. Minority Coun. Program, 1991—2001; mem. Constl. Rights Found., 1994—. Mem.: ABA, LA Bar Assn., Calif. Bar Assn., Coto de Caza Golf Club, Chancery Club, City Club. Avocations: sports, travel, golf. Home: 27442 Hidden Trail Rd Laguna Hills CA 92653-5876 Office: Gibson Dunn & Crutcher 4 Park Plz Ste 1700 Irvine CA 92614-8560 Office Phone: 949-451-4089. Business E-Mail: rbeard@gibsondunn.com.

BEARD, STEPHANIE GRIFFITH, lawyer; b. Tyler, Tex., Dec. 23, 1964; d. Lindley Bryant and Virginia Ann Griffith; m. David Lynn Beard, Sept. 26, 1998; children: Julie Michelle Maddox, Randi Marie Maddox. BS, U. Tex. at Tyler, 1990—93; JD, Loyola Sch. Law, 1995—98. Bar: La., U.S. Ct. Appeals (5th cir.) 1998, U.S. Dist. Ct. (ea., mid. and we. dists.) La. 1998. Classroom tchr. Frankston (Tex.) Pub. Schs., 1994—95; law clk. La. Workers' Compensation Corp., Metairie, 1996—98, collection atty. Baton Rouge, 1998—99; pres./owner Stephanie Griffith Beard, APLC, Destrehan, La., 1999—. Contract atty. 29th Jud. Dist. Ct. Indigent Defender Bd., Hahnville, La., 1999—. Mem.: La. Assn. of Criminal Def. Attorneys, La. State Bar Assn., ABA. R-Consevative. Avocations: golf, fishing, writing. Home: 65 Belle Grove Dr Destrehan LA 70047 Office: Stephanie Griffith Beard APLC PO Box 375 Destrehan LA 70047 Business E-Mail: stephgbeard@cox.net.

BEARDEN, ESTHER SHU-SHIN LEE, dean; d. Wei-chin and Phoebe Lee; m. Billy Charles Bearden; children: Faith Shu-ping Yao, Irene Shu-wei Yao. BS, Nat. Taiwan Normal U., Taipei, 1966; MS, No. Ill. U., 1969; PhD, Purdue U., W. Lafayette, Ind., 1971. Asst. prof. U. of Houston Clear Lake, Houston, 1975—79, assoc. prof., 1979—92; bd. mem. Tex. Bd. of Pardons and Paroles, Angleton, Tex., 1990; dep. dir. U.S. Dept. Edn., Washington, 1990—91; exec. prodr. of video tapes Interactive Parenting, Houston, 1996—97; syndicated columnist Interative Parenting, Houston, 1997—2002; prof. So. Ark. U., Magnolia, 1998—99; dept. chair DePauw U., Greencastle, Ind., 1999—2002; dean of the grad. sch. Troy State U. Montgomery, Montgomery, Ala., 2002—. Mem. Selective Sys. Svc. Bd., Houston, 1988—90; v.p. Orgn. of Chinese Am. Women, Washington, 1979—88; mem. Houston City Affirmative Action Adv. Commn., 1986—87, Houston's Police Adv. Com., 1983—86, Com. on Recruit Tng., Houston Police Dept., 1984—85, Criminal Justice Com. of the Houston Police Acad., 1984—85; instr. on multiculture Houston Police Dept., 1984—85; pres. and founder/advisor Houston chpt. of Orgn. of Chinese Ams., Houston, 1980—82; pres. and founder Houston chpt. of Orgn. of Chinese Am. Women, 1982—83; mem. Houston Clean (Mayor's office), 1990—90, Mayor's Houston Youth 2000, 1988—89, Gov.'s Asian Am. Adv. Com., Austin, Tex., 1987—90, State representative's Ednl. Task Force, Houston, 1982, Houston Internat. U., Houston, 1986—87; bd. mem. Associated Texans Against Crime, Dallas, 1988—91; mem. Fulbright Scholars Bd., Washington, 1992—93; commr. US Congl. Commn. for the Study of Internat. Migration and Coop. Econ. Devel., Washington, 1987—90; mem. Nat. Adv. and Coord. Coun. on Bilingual Edn. of DOE, Washington, 1985—87, Tex. Literacy Coun., Austin, Tex., 1987—90; commr. Ark. Early Childhood Commn., Little Rock, 1998—99; founder, prin. and tchr. Clear Lake Chinese Sch., Houston, 1972—79; mem. tchr. edn. coun. Ind. Profl. Standards Board, Indpls., 1999—2002; mem. Host Com. of the 1990 Econ. Summit of Industrialized Nations, Houston, 1989—90. Named Outstanding Alumni, Nat. Taiwan Normal U., 2001; recipient Disting. Edn. Alumni Award of Distinction, Purdue U., 2003, President's Disting. Svc. award, U. of Houston Clear Lake, 1988, US Presdl. Achievement award, The White Ho., 1982, Tribute award by Minority Women's Conv., Minority Women in Houston, 1982, First prize of nationwide piano contest, Taiwan, 1965; grantee numerous grants. Mem.: NCATE (bd. examiners 2001—).

BEARDEN, JAMES HUDSON, university official; b. Marion, Ala., Sept. 25, 1933; s. Joseph N. and Lula (Worrell) B.; m. Pauline Larkins, Mar. 31, 1961; children: James Hudson, Jr., Pauline B. Simonowich. BS, Centenary Coll. La., 1956; MA, East Carolina U., 1959; PhD, U. Ala., 1966. Bus. mgr. Marion Inst., 1959; mem. faculty East Carolina U., Greenville, N.C., 1959—, prof. bus. adminstrn., 1964—, dir. bur. bus. research, 1964, dean, 1968-83, dir. BB&T Ctr. for Leadership Devel., 1983—. Author articles in field. Former trustee Campbell U.; pres., trustee N.C. Council Econ. Edn. Served with AUS, 1956-58. Mem. Newcomen Soc. N.Am., Assn. Leadership Educators, Fedn. Bus. Honor Socs. (pres. 1991—), Rotary, Beta Gamma Sigma (pres. 1986-1990), Sigma Beta Delta (pres. 1994-2000). Home: 106 Crown Point Rd Greenville NC 27858-5718 Office: BB&T Ctr for Leadership Devel East Carolina U 1100 Bate Bldg Greenville NC 27858-4353

BEARDEN, RANDALL DALLAS, music educator, director; b. St. Louis, Mo., Feb. 3, 1971; s. Sharon Kay Bearden and Van Bearden, Jr.; 1 child, Isabel Savannah. MusB, S.W. Mo. State U., 1995, MusM in Edn., 2001. Cert. Tchr. K-12 Instrumental Music Mo., 2001. Vol. asst. band dir. Greenwood Lab. Sch. Springfield Pub. Sch., Springfield, Mo., 1990—94; asst. band dir. Ctrl. H.S. Springfield Pub. Sch., 1999—2000; band dir. Study Mid. Sch. Springfield Pub. Sch., 2000; music dir. Bunker R-III Sch. Dist., Bunker, Mo., 2001—. Pvt. music instr., Rolla/Springfield, Mo., 1986—2000; musician So. Mo. State U. Bands, Springfield, Mo., 1989—2001, So. Mo. State U. Tent Theater, Springfield, Mo., 1989—97, Springfield Little Theater, Springfield, 1990—98, Blue Lake Monster Jazz Band, Whitehall, Mich., 1991; counselor, music instr. Blue Lake Fine Arts Camp, Whitehall, Mich., 1991—91; musician Bobby Vinton Theater, Branson, 1996—98, Manhattan Transfer, Springfield, Mo., 1998. Rep. Bunker CTA, Bunker, Mo., 2001—. Recipient Winner, S.W. Mo. State U. Ann. Concerto Competition, 1994; fellow, SW Mo. State U., 1998—2000; scholar Wellock scholarship, S.W. Mo. State U., 1992—93. Mem.: Nat. Band Dir. Assn., Mo. Bandmasters Assn., Mo. Music Educators Assn., Internat. Assn. of Jazz Educators, Music Educator Nat. Conf., Mo. State Tchr. Assn., Phi Mu Alpha Sinfonia (v.p. 1992—94). Green Party. Office: Bunker R-III School District PO 365 Hwy 72 Bunker MO 63629 Business E-Mail: randallbearden@hotmail.com.

BEARDEN, THOMAS EUGENE, research scientist, researcher; b. Cheniere, La., Dec. 17, 1930; m. Doris Faye McDonald, 1964. BS in Math., NE La. U., 1953; MS in Nuc. Engring., Ga. Inst. Tech., 1971; PhD in Sci. (hon.), Trinity Coll., U.K., 1999. Commd. U.S. Army, 1954, advanced through grades to lt. col., intelligence specialist air def. and ABM def., 1960—75, ret.; dir. Assn. Disting. Am. Scientists, Huntsville, Ala., 1995—; ceo CTEC, Inc., Huntsville, 1995—. Fellow emeritus Alpha Found.'s Inst. for Advanced Study, 1998—2004. Author: (scientific book) Energy from the Vacuum: Concepts and Principles, 2002; contbr. articles to profl. jours. Mem.: Am. Assn. Physics Tchrs. Achievements include discovery of solution to the problem of the source charge and its associated EM fields and potentials; corrected flaw in 3-law Aristotelian logic to 5-law logic; discovery of proposed mechanism for excess antigravity accelerating expansion of the universe; extension to Becker's model of the cellular regenerative system; thermodynamics of permissible COP over 1.0 electrical power systems; co-inventor of Motionless Electromagnetic Generator; discovery of mechanism for practical antigravity; correction of Second Law of Thermodynamics to include negentropic systems; EM epigenetic reprogramming mechanism in the Prioré effect; mechanisms used in advanced Soviet energetics weapons; circuits using the nondiverged Heaviside energy flow component arbitrarily discarded by Lorentz; proposed mechanism for excess gravity holding the arms of spiral galaxies together; extension of first law of thermodynamics to include asymmetric regauging; co-invention of environmental amplication of Dirac negative energy in circuits; discovery of precursor force-free field structuring; proposed Dirac Sea hole currents produced in sharp strong gradients in cosmological processes as what dark matter is, and negative energy Emfields from dark matter as constituting dark energy; proposed mechanism for dark energy, dark matter effects and enodaus drag on NASA pioneer spacecraft; proposed models for mind dynamics and mind/body coupling mechanism. Avocations: aikido (retired, sandan), author, consultant. Office: Assn Distinguished Am Scientists PO Box 1472 Huntsville AL 35807 Personal E-mail: soliton@bellsouth.net.

BEARDSLEY, CHARLES MITCHELL, retired insurance company executive; b. Chgo., Jan. 13, 1921; s. Richard Stanley and Maude Clarice (Mitchell) B.; m. Marjorie Helen Gahan, Feb. 27, 1943; children: Helen Charlene, Karen Jeannette. AB, Depauw U., 1942; MA, U. Wis., 1947. From actuarial student to assoc. actuary Paul Revere Life Ins. Co., Worcester, Mass., 1947-55; from actuary to v.p. Security Life and Trust Co., Winston-Salem, N.C., 1955-63; actuary sr. v.p. H.W. Satchwell & Co., Columbus, Ohio, 1963-67; actuary chmn., chief exec. officer Charles M. Beardsley & Assocs., Columbus, 1967-68; from exec. v.p. to chmn. Booke and Co., Winston-Salem, 1968-85, vice chmn., 1985-91. Author Life Company Annual Statement Handbook and New Items in the Annual Statement for Life Insurance Companies, 1959-2005; contbr. articles to profl. jours. Pres. Wachovia Hist. Soc., Winston-Salem, 1981, Huguenot Soc. N.C., 1987-89; bd. dirs. Moravian Music Found., Winston-Salem. Served to lt. (j.g.) USN, 1943-46. Fellow Conf. of Cons. Actuaries (v.p. 1980-82), Soc. Actuaries (dir. 1983-86); mem. Am. Acad. Actuaries, Internat. Actuarial Assn., Internat. Assn. Cons. Actuaries (bd. dirs. 1980-89), Founders and Patriots Am. Democratic. Clubs: Forsyth Country, Twin City, Piedmont (Winston-Salem). Lodges: Masons, Kiwanis (local pres.). Avocation: music. Home: 341 Muirfield Dr Winston Salem NC 27104-3952 Office Phone: 336-748-1120. Personal E-mail: cmb2293@yahoo.com.

BEARDSLEY, JENE E, education educator; b. Mt. Vernon, NY; s. Euguene Vernon Beardsley and Beatrice Catherine (Galbina); m. Nancy Lee Chilcoat (div.). BA, Wheaton Coll, 1958; MA, U. Ill., 1959. Prof. English Eastern Coll., St. Davis, Pa., 1954—96; v.p., newsletter editor Phil. Affiliate of OCF, Bala Cynwyd, Pa., 1994—. Mem.: Acad. Am. Poetry. Christian. Avocations: gardening, cooking, piano, hiking. Personal E-mail: nemuscoot@aol.com.

BEARDSLEY, THEODORE S(TERLING), JR., professional society administrator; b. East St. Louis, Ill., Aug. 26, 1930; s. Theodore Sterling and Margaret (Kienzle) B.; m. Lenora J. Fierke, May 26, 1955; children: Theodore Sterling III, Mark A., Mary Elizabeth. BS, So. Ill. U., 1952; MA (Max Bryant fellow), Washington U., St. Louis, 1954; postgrad., U. Heidelberg, Germany, 1955-56; PhD, U. Pa., 1961; linguistic rsch., Inst. Caro y Cuervo, Bogota, Colombia, summer 1973. Asst. in English Lycee Wilson, Chaumont, France, 1952-53; mem. faculty Rider Coll., 1957-61, chmn. dept. modern lang., 1959-61; asst. prof. Spanish So. Ill. U., 1961-62, U. Wis., 1962-65. Dir. Hispanic Soc. Am., N.Y.C., 1965-95, pres., 1995—; adj. prof. NYU, 1967-69, 80, Adelphi U., 1966, 68, Columbia U., 1969, Eckerd Coll., 1997—; Fulbright lectr., Ecuador, 1974; guest lectr. U. Complutense, Madrid, 1990, 94, U. Salamanca, 1994, 99, U. Rábida, Spain, 1996; diss. dir. U. Oviedo, Spain, 1992; vis. prof. U. Wis., 1995; chmn. Museums Coun. N.Y.C., 1972-73; spl. cons. Hispanic bibliography Libr. Congress, fall 1973, N.J. State Dept. Edn., spring 1975, NEH, 1978—. Narrator Spanish lang. recorded tours, Nat. Gallery Art, Met. Mus., Mus. Natural Sci., Boston Sci. Mus., Smithsonian Instn.; continuing series on Caribbean popular music in U.S, WBGO-FM, 1979; Xavier Cugat, 1980, USA Latino, 1981, Enrique Madriguera, Spanish Nat. Radio, 1985; author: Hispano-Classical Translations, 1482-1699, 1970, Tomas Navarro Tomas, A Tentative Bibliography, 1908-1970, 1971; librettist: Ponce de Leon, 1973; also articles; recordings include: Charla con Camilo José Cela, 1966, Visita a la Hispanic Society, 1969; editor: (CD)Enrique Madriguera, 1994, Carlos Molina, 2000, Madriguera II, 2003; co-editor: Celestina: Early Text, 1997; narrator-author: 4 part series Hispanic Immigration to the United States (text pub. 1976), CBS-TV, 1972; narrator: Ponce de Leon, Charlotte Symphony, 2000; master or ceremonies: Conquistador Ball, Punta Gorda, Fla., 1998-05; Introductions for Don Quixote Suite, Charlotte Symphony, 2002, Romance de Espana, 2005; mem. adv. bd.: Hispanic Rev., Studia humanitatis, Boletín de ANLE, Hispanic Sem. of Medieval Studies, Revista Caribe. Served with AUS, 1954-56. Decorated Orden de Mérito Civil, Spain; Fulbright grantee, 1952-53; Jusserand traveling fellow, 1962; research grantee Am. Council Learned Socs., 1964; travel grantee, 1974; recipient Premio Bibliofilia Barcelona, Spain, 1973, Merit award Noticias de Arte, 1999. Mem. ASCAP, Hispanic Soc. Am., Renaissance Soc. Am. (exec. coun., acting dir. 1981-82), Acad. Norteamericana Lengua Española, Internat. Inst. (Madrid), Internat. Linguistic Assn. (exec. coun.), Hispanic Sem. Medieval Studies (bd. dirs.), Ponce De Leon Conquistadors, Sigma Delta Pi, Sigma Tau Gamma; corr. mem. Royal Spanish Acad., Real Acad. Bellas Artes San Carlos (Valencia), Acad. Guatemalteca de Lengua, Assn. Bibliofilos Barcelona, Fundacion Odón Betanzos (Rociana), Fundacion Santa Maria de la Rabida, Fundacion Universitaria Espanola (Madrid), Inst. Valencia Don Juan (bd. dirs. Madrid). Office: Hispanic Soc Am 613 W 155th St New York NY 10032-7501

BEARE, MURIEL ANITA NIKKI, public relations executive, author; b. Detroit, Mar. 7, 1928; d. Elbert Standly and Dorothy Margaret (Welch) Brink; m. Richard austin Beare, June 15, 1946; 1 child, Sandra Lee. AA, Miami Dade C.C., 1974; BA, Skidmore coll., 1979. Writer Key West (Fla.) Citizen, 1959; Miami News, 1967; field dir. Fla. Project HOPE, 1967-68; southeastern area dir., 1968-69; asst. v.p. pub. rels. I/D Assocs., Inc., Miami, 1969-70; pres. Nikki Beare & Assocs., Miami, 1971—; v.p. South Fla. office Cherenson, Carroll & Holzer, Livingston, N.J., 1973; sr. v.p. D.J. Edelman, Inc., 1981-83. Co-owner south Miami Travel Svc., 1976-78; pres. Gov.'s Sq. Travel, Inc., Tallahassee, 1979-85, Travel Is Fun, Miami, 1985-90; owner Silver Beare Travel, Inc., 1995—; bd. dirs. corp. sec. Imperial Bank. Author: Pirates, Pineapples and People: Tales and Legends of the Florida Keys, 1961, From

Turtle Soup to coconuts, 1964, Bottle Bonanza, A Handbook for Antique Bottle Collectors, 1965; prodr. cable TV program Traveler's Digest, 1986-92; moderator, prodr. Women's Powerline, Sta. wIOD, Miami, 1972-77. Chmn. adv. bd. Met. Dade County Libr., 1964; active Greater Miami Host Com., Met. Dade County Com. Status Women, 1971-76; former chmn. City of Miami Commn. Status Women, 1985-92; active Met. Gen. Land Use Master Planning Com. Employment Handicapped, 1970-72; chmn. Met. Dade Fair Housing and Employment appeals Bd., 1975-78; active Miami YWCA's; chmn. Handicapped and Elederly subcom. Met. Dade Transti Devel. Com.; mem. Fla. Ins. Commn. Task force, 1975, Dade County Dem. Exec. Com., 1972-76, south Fla. Health Planning coun., 1972-74; founding mem. Nat. Women's Polit. Caucus, 1971—; pres. Capitol Women's Polit. Caucus; v.p. Fla. Women's Polit. Caucus, NWPC, Fla.; v.p. Herstory, 1971—; candidate Fla. Senate, 1974, Fla. Ho. of Reps., 1976; past pres. adv. bd. Inst. for Women, Fla. Internat. U.; pres. Fla. Feminist Credit Union, 1975-78; bd. dirs. Cmty. Health Inst., South Dade County, 1975-77; mem. Jobs for Miami, 1980-88; chmn. Fla. Gov.'s Small Bus. Adv. Coun., 1981-83, Greater Miami Torusim Coalition, 1983-85; del. White House Conf. on Small Bus., 1980, 86; chmn. publicity com. Asta World Congress, 1989,chmn. com. travel persons with disabilities; co-chmn. Fla. Internat. U. Sch. Journalism and Mass Comms. adv. bd., 1984-92. Recipient Silver Image award Pub. Rels. Assn., 1967-68; named to Fla. Women's Hall of Fame, 1994. Mem. AAUW, LWV, NOW, Hist. Assn. So. Fla., Friends of Everglades, Women's C. of C. So. Fla., Am. Soc. Travel Agts., Women in Comms., Nat. Assn. Women Bus. Owners, Pub. Rels. Soc. Am., Fla. Pub. Rels. Assn., Women's Inst. Freedom of the Press, Antique Bottle Collectors Assn. Fla., Caribbean Tourism Orgn., South by Southeast Profl. Women In Travel, Vet. Feminists Am. Democrat. Office: Nikki Beare & Assocs Inc RR 3 Box 786 Havana FL 32333-9594 E-mail: nikkibeare@aol.com.

BEARE-ROGERS, JOYCE LOUISE, research and development company executive; b. nr. Pickering, Ont., Can., Sept. 8, 1927; d. Frederick John and Sarah May (Michell) Beare; m. Charles Graham Rogers, Dec. 30, 1961; 1 child, Anne Catherine. BA, U. Toronto, Ont., 1951, MA, 1952; PhD, Carleton U., Ottawa, Ont., 1966; DSc (hon.), U. Man., Winnipeg, Can., 1985, U. Guelph, Ont., 1993. Rsch. assoc. U. Toronto, 1952-54; instr. Vassar Coll., Poughkeepsie, 1954-56; chemist Food, Drug Directorate, Ottawa, 1956-65; rsch. scientist Health Can., Ottawa, 1965-75; rsch. mgr. Bur. Nutritional Scis., Ottawa, 1975-91. Adj. prof. U. Ottawa, 1980-92; cons. Food and Agrl. Orgn. UN, 1992-94; Hilditch lectr. U.K., 1994; trustee Nat. Inst. Nutrition (Can.), 1997-99. Editor: Methods for Nutritional Assessment of Fats, 1985, Fat Requirements for Development and Health, 1988; contbr. articles on dietary fats to profl. jours. Decorated Order of Can.; recipient Queen's Jubilee medal Govt. of Can., 1977, Medaille Chevreul award Inst. Corps Gras, 1984, Crompton award McGill U., 1986, Normann medal German Assn. for Fat Rsch., 1987, Commemorative medal for 125th Anniversary of Fedn. of Can., 1992, Queen's Golden Jubilee medal 2002. Fellow: Am. Inst. Nutrition, Royal Soc. Can. (panelist on food biotechnology 2000—01, hon. treas. 2000—04, chair com. awards and medals 2004—); mem.: Can. Biochem. Soc., Can. Soc. for Nutrition Scis. (pres. 1984—85, Bordon award 1971, McHenry award 1993), Internat. Soc. Fat Rsch. (pres. 1991—92), Am. Oil Chemists Soc. (pres. 1985—86, Lifetime Achievement award Can. sect. 1995). Avocations: hiking, canoeing, cross country skiing, reading. Home: 41 Okanagan Dr Ottawa ON Canada K2H 7E9 Personal E-mail: jbrogers@sympatico.ca.

BEARMAN, DAVID, corporate financial executive; Various positions, including CFO General Electric Co., 1970—89; exec. v.p., CFO Cardinal Health, Inc., 1989—98; sr. v.p., CFO NCR Corp., Dayton, Ohio, 1998—2003; exec. v.p., CFO Hughes Supply, Orlando, Fla., 2003—. Bd. dir. (audit com.) AtheroGenics, 2002—. Office: Hughes Supply One Hughes Way Orlando FL 32805

BEARMAN, TONI CARBO See CARBO, TONI

BEARSCH, LEE PALMER, architect, urban planner; b. Binghamton, NY, July 5, 1942; s. Frederick James and Mildred Jane (Palmer) B.; m. Christine Cromer, Dec. 31, 1972; children: Frederick Cromer, Benjamin Palmer, Peter Furlong. BArch, Clemson U., 1965; M in Planning, Leverhulme Sch. Archtl. Assn., London, 1970. Registered profl. arch., N.Y., Pa., Md., Mass., Wis. Project dir. Llewelyn-Davies Assocs., London, N.Y., Racine, Wis., 1970-75; pres. Bearsch Compeau Knudson, Archs. and Engrs., P.C., Binghamton, 1976—. Mem. N.Y. State Edn. Dept. Bd. for Arch. Lic. Bd., 1997—. Mem. Broome County Planning Adv. Bd., Binghamton, 1978-90, sec., 1986-88; bd. dirs. Broome County Small Bus. Coun., 1979-84, vice chmn., 1981-83; vestryman Christ Episcopal Ch., 1981-84; bd. dirs. Family and Childrens Soc. Broome County Inc., 1982—, pres., 1985-86; bd. dirs. Binghamton Symphony Orch., Binghamton U. Found., 2002—; mem. adv. bd. Endicott Trust divsn. Mfrs. and Traders Bank; mem. Binghamton U. Coun.; mem. N.Y. State Bd. for Arch. State Licensing Bd., 1995—, chmn., 2002, 03. Fellow AIA (area dir. 1978-79, v.p. 1979-81, chpt. pres. 1981-82, state conv. chmn. 1983, state pres. 1990, nat. bd. dirs. 1990-93, nat. documents com. 1994—, chmn., 1998-2000, nat. conv. chmn. 1996); mem. Am. Inst. Cert. Planners, N.Y. State Assn. Archs. (bd. dirs. 1985—, exec. com. 1987—, pres. 1990, mem. bd. archtl. registration 1995—), Archtl. Assn. (Eng.), Broome County C. of C. (bd. dirs. 1986—, chmn. 1990-91), Leadership Broome (adv. bd. 1988-90), Binghamton City Club (bd. govs. 1995-2000), Binghamton Country Club (bd. govs. 1999—, pres. 2002), Live Wire Club, Nat. Coun. Archtl. Registration Bds. (chmn. profl. program devel. com. 2002—). Office: Bearsch Compeau Knndson A&E PC 41 Chenango St Binghamton NY 13901-2901 Home: 1312 Robinson Hill Rd Endwell NY 13760 Office Phone: 607-772-0007.

BEART, ROBERT W., JR., colon and rectal surgeon, educator; b. Kansas City, Mo., Mar. 3, 1945; s. Robert Woodward and Helen Elizabeth (Wamsley) B.; m. Cynthia Anne, Jan. 23, 1971; children: Jennifer, Kristina, Amy. AB, Princeton U., 1967; MD, Harvard U., 1971. Diplomate Am. Bd. Surgery, Am. Bd. Colon and Rectal Surgery. Intern U. Colo., 1971-72, resident, 1972-76; prof. surgery Mayo Clinic, Scottsdale, Ariz., 1976—87, U. So. Calif., L.A., 1992—. Maj. USMC, 1972-83. Fellow Am. Soc. Colon and Rectal Surgery (pres. 1994). Office: 1441 Eastlake Ave Ste 7418 Los Angeles CA 90033 Office Phone: 323-865-3690.

BEARY, JOHN FRANCIS, III, rheumatologist, pharmaceutical executive, medical researcher; b. Melrose, Iowa, Dec. 14, 1946; s. John F. and Dorothy (McGrath) B.; m. Bianca E. Mason, May 6, 1972; children: John Daniel, Vanessa, Webster, Nina. BS summa cum laude, U. Notre Dame, 1969; MD, Harvard U., 1973; MBA, Georgetown U., 1988. Diplomate Am Bd. Internal Medicine, Am. Bd. Rheumatology, Am. Bd. Clin. Pharmacology. Flight surgeon 89th Mil. Airlift Wing (Air Force One), 1974—77; Osler medicine resident Johns Hopkins Hosp., Balt., 1977—78; rsch. fellow Cornell Med. Coll., N.Y.C., 1978—80; from asst. prof. to clin. prof. Sch. Medicine Georgetown U., Washington, 1980—2005; prin. dept. asst. sec. health affairs Dept. Def., Washington, 1981—83, appropriations task force for USNS Mercy and USNS Comfort, 1982—83; assoc. dean strategic planning Georgetown U. Sch. Medicine, Washington, 1984—87; sr. v.p. regulatory and sci. affairs Pharm. Rsch. and Mfg. Assn., Washington, 1988—97; sr. med. dir. bone and arthritis rsch. Procter and Gamble Pharma, Cin., 1997—. Steering com. Internat. Conf. on Harmonization of Pharm. Stds., 1990-97; clin. prof. rheumatology and immunology U. Cin., 1997—; mem. OMERACT Rheumatology Rsch. Com., 1998-2003; sci. com. Arthritis Found., Ohio, 1998-. Editor: Manual of Rheumatology, 1981, 5th edit., 2005; mem. editl. bd. Jour. Pharm. Medicine, 1990—, Drug Devel. Rsch., 1992-2000. Bd. dirs. Scleroderma Found., Washington, 1982—92. Served to capt. USNR, 1984—99. Recipient Disting. Mil. Grad. award, 1969, Rsch. award NY Arthritis Found., 1979, Disting. Pub. Svc. medal Dept. Def., 1983, Navy and Marine Corps Commendation medal, 1997, Georgetown Med. Vicennial medal, 2003, 6th Naval Beach Battalion Normandy award, 2004 Fellow: ACP, Am. Coll. Rheumatology; mem.: Am. Soc. for Bone and Mineral Rsch., Osteoarthritis Rsch. Soc., Am. Soc. Clin. Pharmacology and Therapeutics, Am. Geriat. Soc., Weller-Brown Assn., Mil. Officers Assn., Johns Hopkins Med. and Surg. Assn., U.S. Naval Inst., Harvard Club, Notre Dame Club (Cin.), Chevy Chase Club. Office: Procter & Gamble Pharma 8700 Mason Montgomery Rd Mason OH 45040-8006

BEASER, LAWRENCE JAY, lawyer; m. Rochelle Beaser; children: Deborah, Barbara. BA, U. Pa., 1967; JD cum laude, Harvard U., 1970. Bar: Pa. 1971. Law clk. Superior Ct. Judge H. Sydney Hoffman, Pa., 1970—71; dep. atty. gen. Commonwealth of Pa., Harrisburg, 1972—73, assoc. counsel to gov., 1971, dep. coun. to gov., 1972, acting counsel to gov., 1972—73, counsel to gov., 1973—78; ptnr. Blank Rome LLP, Phila., 1978—, also bd. dirs. Bd. dirs. Beck Inst. Cognitive Therapy and Rsch.; adv. bd. Pa. Modern Cts. Bd. mgrs., exec. com., chair program and distbn. com. Phila. Found., past chair personnel com., chair resolution and declaration trust revision com.; bd. dirs. counsel Louis D. Brandeis Law Soc. Recipient Benjamin F. Levy Cmty. Svc. award, Louis D. Brandies Law Soc., 2004. Fellow: Am. Bar Found. (life); mem.: ABA (chair health law com. 1991—95, working group health care reform 1994—95, co-chair com. state and local bar involvement 1996—99, liaison to health law sect. from bus. law sect. 1999—2004, ho. of dels. 2000—02, revised model non-profit corp. act drafting com. 2002—, mem. bus. law sect., health law sect., com. on nonprofit corps.), Phila. Bar Assn. (vice chair 1979, elected bd. govs. 1986—88, asst. sec. 1989—91, vice chancellor 1992, chancellor elect 1993, chancellor 1994, counsel bd. govs. 1997—2003, co-chmn. bylaws com. 2000, mem. bus. law sect., counsel bd. govs. 2005), Pa. Bar Assn. (ho. of dels., bus. law sect., statutory law com., gaming law com.). Office: Blank Rome LLP 1 Logan Sq Philadelphia PA 19103

BEASLEY, ANITA CLAIRE, special education educator, consultant; d. Everett Davis Nelson and Mary Pauline Stinchcomb; m. Wayne Beasley, Nov. 21, 1953; children: Chad Christopher, Kirk Justin, Eric Wayne. A in Edn., Clayton State Jr. Coll., 1977; BS, Ga. State U., 1992; M, State U. West Ga., 1999, M, 2003. Nat. bd. cert. tchr. Nat. Bd. Profl. Tchg. Stds., 2000. Tchr. Clayton County Bd. Edn., College Park, Forest Park, Ga., 1992—2000; reading tchr. Henry County Bd. Edn., Hampton, 2000—04; reading specialist Butts County Bd. Edn., Jackson, 2004—. Cons. Profl. Assn. Ga. Educators, Atlanta, 2000—, Ga. Tchr. Ctr., Kennesaw, 2000—, Ga. REA Program, Atlanta, 2001, Ga. Dept. Edn., 2003—04; family literacy com. chair Ga. Reading Assn., 2005—. Mem. Henry Heritage Reading Coun., McDonough, Ga., 2000—05. Fellow, Ga. Tchr. Ctr., 2005—; grantee, Clayton County Bd. Edn., 1996, Greater Henry County Commrs. Office, 2001, 2004, Families and Work Inst., 2003. Mem.: ASCD, Internat. Reading Assn., Delta Kappa Gamma. Avocations: reading, travel. Home: 830 Monticello Ln Mcdonough GA 30253 Office: Butts County Bd Edn/Daughtry 150 Shiloh Rd Jackson GA 30233 Office Phone: 770-504-2356. E-mail: beasleya@butts.k12.ga.us.

BEASLEY, BARBARA STARIN, sales executive, marketing professional; b. Nashville, Dec. 31, 1955; d. Donald Francis and Martha Murry (Bridges) S.; m. Johnny Mark Beasley, Oct. 22, 1983; children: John Thomas, Cara Nicole. BFA, So. Meth. U., 1976. Cert. strategic mktg. mgmt., Harvard Bus. Sch. Producer Bill Stokes Assn., Dallas, 1976-80; Mary Kay Cosmetics, Inc., Dallas, 1980-93; sr. v.p. mktg., 1987-89; exec. v.p. sales, 1990-93; sr. v.p. mktg. Nest Entertainment, Dallas, 1994-99, sr. v.p. sales and mktg., 1999-2000; freelance writer, 2000—. Mem. Leadership Tex., 1986. Avocation: birdwatching.

BEASLEY, BRUCE MILLER, sculptor; b. LA, May 20, 1939; s. Robert Seth and Bernice (Palmer) B.; m. Laurence Leaute, May 21, 1973; children: Julian Bernard, Celia Beranice. Student, Dartmouth Coll., 1957-59; BA, U. Calif., Berkeley, 1962. One-man shows include Everett Ellin Gallery, L.A., 1963, Kornblee Gallery, N.Y.C., 1964, Hansen Gallery, San Francisco, 1965, David Stuart Gallery, L.A., 1966, Andre Emmerich Gallery, N.Y.C., 1971, DeYoung Mus., San Francisco, 1972, Santa Barbara Mus. Art, 1973, San Diego Mus. Art, 1973, Fuller-Goldeen Gallery, San Francisco, 1981, Hooks-Epstein Gallery, Houston, 1990, 93, 95, 98, Pepperdine U., L.A., 1990, So. Oreg. State U., 1991, Sonoma State U., Rhonert Park, Calif., 1991, Fresno Art Mus., 1992, Oakland Mus., 1992, Utermann Gallery, Dortmund, Germany, 1993, Scheffel Gallery, Bad Homberg, Germany, 1993, Galerie Rudolfinum, Prague, 1994, Kunsthalle Mannheim, Germany, 1994, Harcourts Gallery, San Francisco, 1994, Galerie Wirth, Zurich, Switzerland, 1995, Yorkshire Sculpture Park, Eng., 1995, City Ctr., Dortmund, Germany, 1996, Atrium Gallery, St. Louis, 1997, Purdue U., West Lafayette, Ind., 1997, Solomon-Dubnick Gallery, Sacramento, 1997, Gwenda Jay Gallery, Chgo., 1998, Kouros Gall., N.Y.C., 1999, Math. Scis. Rsch. Inst., Berkeley, Calif., 2000, Gail Severn Gallery, Ketchum, Idaho, 2001, Silicon Valley Art Mus., Belmont, Calif., 2001, Solomon-Dubnick Gallery, Sacramento, 2002, Atrium Gallery, St. Louis, 2004, 45 Yr. Retrospective, Oakland Mus. Calif., 2005; exhibited in group shows at San Francisco Mus. of Modern Art, 1961, Mus. of Modern Art, N.Y.C., 1961,62, Dallas Mus. Contemporary Art, 1962, Musee d'Art Moderne, Paris, 1963, U. Art Mus., Berkeley, 1964, Fine Arts Museums, San Francisco, 1965, Guggenheim Mus., 1966, Krannert Art Mus., Ill., 1969, Jewish Mus., N.Y.C., 1970, Milw. Art Ctr., 1970, Expo '70, Osaka, Japan, Stanford Art Mus., 1972, Musee d'Art Moderne, Paris, 1973, Nat. Mus. Am. Art, 1980, Musee d'Art Contemporain Bordeaux, France, 1984, Kunsthalle Mannheim, 1984, Palace of Exhbns., Budapest, Hungary, 1987, Middleheim Sculpture Park, Belgium, 1987, Yorkshire Sculpture Park, Eng., 1984, 87, Hakone Open-Air Mus., Japan, 1993, 95, Landesgartenschau, Germany, 1994, Sculpture '97, Bad Homberg, Germany, Pier Walk '97, 98, 99, 2000, 01, Chgo., Galerie Wirth, Zurich, Switzerland, 1997, Darmstadt (Germany) Sculpture Biennale, 1998, Cairo Biennale, Egypt, 1998, Mus. Modern Art, San Francisco, 2000, Grounds for Sculpture, Hamilton, N.J., 2001, Solomon-Dubnick Gallery, Sacramento, 2002, Sigurjon Olafsson Mus., Reykjavik Iceland, 2003, U. Hawaii Art Gallery, 2003, Galleri Dionisi, Hollywood Calif., 2004; represented in permanent collections Mus. Modern Art, N.Y.C., Guggenheim Mus., N.Y.C., Musee d'Art, Paris, Nat. Mus. Am. Art, Washington, Kunsthalle Mannheim, Germany, San Franciso Mus. Modern Art, L.A. County Mus. Art, Sheldon Mem. Art Gallery, Lincoln, Nebr., Hood Mus. Art-Dartmouth Coll., Spencer Mus. Art, Lawrence, Kans., Laguna Art Mus., Franklin D. Murphy Sculpture Garden, UCLA, Crocker Art Mus., Sacramento, Seattle Art Mus., Fresno Art Mus., Xantus Janos Mus., Hungary, Fine Art Muss., San Francisco, Oakland Mus. Calif., Santa Barbara Mus. Art, San Jose (Calif.) Mus. Art, Grounds for Sculpture, Hamilton, N.J., Nora Eccles Harrison Mus., Utah State U., Logan, Sculpture Park, Isla Mujeres, Mex.; commissions include State of Calif., Oakland Mus., City San Francisco, Miami Internat. Airport, San Francisco Internat. Airport, Fed. Home Loan Bank, San Francisco, Stanford U., City Anchorage, City Salinas, Calif., Fresno Art Mus., Gateway Ctr., Walnut Creek, Calif., Village of Flossmoor, Ill., City Oakland, Calif., City of Brea, Calif., U. Oreg. Art Mus., Eugene, Miami U., Oxford, Ohio, La Jolla Crossroads, San Diego. Home: 322 Lewis St Oakland CA 94607-1236

BEASLEY, DAVID MULDROW, former governor, consultant; b. Lamar, S.C., Feb. 26, 1957; s. Richard Lee and Jacqueline Adele (Blackwell) B.; m. Mary Wood Payne. Student, Clemson U., 1976-78; BA, U. S.C., 1979, JD. Mem. Dist. 56 S.C. Ho. Reps., 1979-92, majority leader, 1987, mem. joint legis. com. on edn., vice chmn. joint legis. com. on children, 1987-88; atty., 1992-94; gov. State of S.C., 1995—99; fellow Inst. Politics Kennedy Sch. Govt. Harvard U., 1999; prin. Bingham Cons. Group, 1999—2001; partner Beasley, Ervin & Warr; chmn. Nat. Advisory Com. on Rural Health & Human Svcs., 2001—.*

BEASLEY, JAMES W., JR., lawyer; b. Atlanta, July 13, 1943; s. James W. and Sara Capal (Tucker) Beasley; m. Elizabeth Barno Marshall, Nov. 28, 1986. AB cum laude, Davidson Coll., 1965; LLB cum laude, Harvard U., 1968. Bar: N.Y. 1969, DC 1971, Fla. 1972, U.S. Supreme Ct. 1973. Assoc. Sullivan & Cromwell, N.Y.C., 1968, Wilmer, Cutler & Pickering, Washington, 1970-72; assoc., then ptnr. Paul & Thomson, Miami, Fla., 1972-78; mng. ptnr. Beasley, Olle & Downs, Miami, 1978-88; ptnr. Tew, Jordan, Schulte & Beasley, Miami, 1988-89, Cadwalader, Wickersham & Taft, Palm Beach, Fla., 1989-94, Tew & Beasley LLP, Palm Beach, 1994-97, Beasley Hauser Kramer & Leonard, P.A., West Palm Beach, Fla., 1997—. Author: Florida Corporations, 1985; contbr. articles to profl. jours. Chmn. County Conv. Ctr. Adv. Bd., 1994—95, Palm Beach Opera, 2005—. Capt. U.S. Army, 1968—70. Mem.: ATLA, ABA, Acad. Fla. Trial Lawyers, Fla. Bar Assn. (chmn. securities regulation com. bus. law sect. 1975—77). Office: Beasley Hauser Kramer and Leonard PA 505 S Flagler Dr West Palm Beach FL 33401-5923 Office Phone: 561-835-0900.

BEASLEY, JIM SANDERS See LEE, JACK

BEASLEY, MARK V., lawyer; b. Jackson, Mich., Feb. 13, 1954; m. Linda Beasley. AB with high distinction, U. Mich., 1976, JD cum laude, 1979. Bar: Texas 1979. Assoc. Johnson & Swanson, Dallas, 1979—84; counsel Zale Corp., Dallas, 1984—87; sr. v.p., gen. counsel, sec. Michaels Stores, Inc., Irving, Tex., 1987—. Mem.: ABA, State Bar of Tex. (mem. section on Bus. Law, Corp. Counsel, Labor & Employment Law), Dallas Bar Assn. (mem. sections on Corp. Counsel, Employment Law, Securities). Avocations: stargazing, piano. Office: Michaels Stores Inc Legal Dept 8000 Bent Branch Dr Irving TX 75063

BEASLEY, MAURINE HOFFMAN, journalism educator, historian; b. Jan. 28, 1936; d. Dimmitt Heard and Maurine (Hieronymus) Hoffman; m. William C. McLaughlin, May 20, 1966 (div. 1969); m. Henry R. Beasley, Dec. 24, 1970; 1 child, Susan Sook. BA in History, U. Mo., 1958; MS in Journalism, Columbia U., 1963; PhD in Am. Civilization, George Washington U., 1974. Edn. editor Kansas City (Mo.) Star, 1959—62; staff writer Washington Post, 1963—73; from asst. prof journalism to prof. U. Md., College Park, 1975—87, prof., 1987—, grad. dir. Coll. Journalism, 2000—02; sr. lectr. Fulbright Jinan U., Guangzhou, China, 2000. Author: Eleanor Roosevelt and the Media: A Public Quest for Self-Fulfillment, 1987; author: (with others) Women in Media, 1977, The New Majority, 1988, Taking Their Place! Documentary History of Women and Journalism, rev., 2002 (Outstanding Acad. Books Choice, 1994, award Text and Academic Authors Assn., 2004); editor: White House Press Conferences of Eleanor Roosevelt, 1983; co-editor: Voices of Change: Southern Pulitzer Winners, 1978, One Third of a Nation, 1981 (hon. mention Washington Monthly Book award, 1982), Eleanor Roosevelt Encyclopedia, 2000 (Editor's Choice award Booklist, 2001); mem. adv. bd. Am. Journalism, 1983—, Jour. Mass Media Ethics, —, Mass Com. Rev., —; corr. editor: Journalism History, 1995—; contbr. articles to profl. jours. Violinist Washington Conservatory Orch., 2001—; pres. Little Falls Swimming Club, Inc. 1988-89; bd. dirs. Sino-Am. Ctr. for Media Tech. and Tng., 2000—. Gannett Tchg. Fellowships Program fellow, 1977, Pulitzer Travelling fellow Columbia U., 1963; Eleanor Roosevelt studies grantee Eleanor Roosevelt Inst., 1979-80, Arthur Schlesinger rsch. fellow and grantee Roosevelt Inst., 1998; named one of nation's outstanding tchrs. of writing and editing Modern Media Inst. (Poynter) and Am. Soc. Newspaper Editors, 1981, most outstanding woman U. Md. Coll. Park Pres. Commn. on Women's Affairs, 1993; recipient Haiman award Speech Comm. Assn., 1995, Founders Disting. Sr. Scholar award AAUW Ednl. Found., 1999, Columbia U. Sch. Journalism Alumni award, 2000, Smith-Cotton H.S. Hall Fame award, Sedalia, Mo., 2000, Alumni award U. Mo., 2004. Mem.: AAUW (v.p. Coll. Pk. br. 2002—04), Am. Assn. Univ. Women, Am. Journalism Historians Assn. (pres.-elect 1988—89, pres. 1989—90, Kobre award for lifetime achievement 1997, Rsch. Paper award named in her honor 1998), Internat. Assn. Mass. Comms. Rsch., Soc. Profl. Journalists (chair nat. hist. site com. 1986—87, bd. dirs. Washington chpt. 1988—90, pres. 1990—91, dir. region 2, nat. bd. dirs. 1991—92, Disting. Local Svc. award 1994, First Amendment award (with others) 1998), Assn. Edn. in Journalism and Mass Comms. (sec. history divsn. 1986—87, vice-head 1987—88, head history divsn. 1988—89, chair profl. freedom and responsibility 1990—91, exec. com. 1990—91, nat. pres. elect 1992, pres. 1993—94, leader People-to-People delegation to China and Hong Kong 1994, exec. com. 1994—95, Outstanding Contbn. to Journalism Edn. award 1994, Disting. Leadership award 2001), Nat. Press Club, Am. News Women's Club (bd. govs. 2001—03), Am. Hist. Assn., Orgn. Am. Historians, Omicron Delta Kappa, Phi Beta Kappa (v.p. Gamma chpt. 2005—). Democrat. Unitarian Universalist. Home: 4920 Flint Dr Bethesda MD 20816-1746 Office: U Md Coll Journalism College Park MD 20742-7111 Office Phone: 301-405-2413. Business E-Mail: mbeasley@jmail.umd.edu.

BEASLEY, ROBERT PALMER, epidemiologist, dean, educator; b. Glendale, Calif., Apr. 29, 1936; AB in Philosophy, Darmouth Coll., 1958; MD, Harvard U., 1962; MSc in Preventive Medicine, U. Wash., 1969. Diplomate Am. Bd. Preventive Medicine, Am. Bd. Internal Medicine. Intern King County Hosp., Seattle, 1962-63; EIS officer CDC, USPHS, Atlanta, 1963-65; resident U. Wash., Seattle, 1965-67; resident preventive medicine U. Washington Hosp., Seattle, 1967-69; asst. prof. dept. medicine, dept. epidemiology U. Wash., Seattle, 1969-71, assoc. prof. to rsch. prof., 1972-86; prof. U. Calif., San Francisco, 1986-87; dir. Am. U. Med. Ctr., Taipei, Taiwan, 1979—; dean, Ashbel Smith prof. Sch. Pub. Health U. Tex., Houston, 1987—. Recipient King Faisal Internat. prize in medicine, 1985, Maxwell Finland Annual prize, 1987, Wade Hampton Frost prize, 1987, Prince Mahidol Found. prize in medicine, 1999; co-recipient Mott Medal GM Cancer Rsch. Found., 1987. Mem. Am. Epidemiological Soc., Am. Fedn. for Clin. Rsch., Am. Pub. Health Assn., Am. Soc. of Internal Medicine, Soc. for Epidemiological Rsch. Office: U Texas Health Sci Ctr Sch Pub Health PO Box 20186 Houston TX 77225-0186

BEASLEY, TROY DANIEL, secondary education educator; b. Whitestone, Ga., Dec. 5, 1942; s. Amos Daniel and Imogene (Duckett) B.; m. Debbie L. Jones, Feb. 23, 1985; children: Flannery Meghan, Annalise Sarah, Ammelia Katherine. BA, Ga. State U., 1973, MA, 1981. Cert. tchr., Ga. Tchr. English, drama and theatre Murray County H.S., Chatsworth, Ga., 1973—; tchr. Rinehardt Coll., Waleska, Ga., 1975-96. Del. Gov. Ga. Conf. on Edn., Atlanta, 1993. Staff sgt. USAF, 1963-68. Recipient Star Tchr. award Ga. C. of C., 1976, 77, 82, 85, 86, 94. Mem. Nat. Assn. Educators, Nat. Coun. Tchrs. English, Ga. Assn. Educators, Ga. Coun. Tchrs. English, Murray Assn. Educators (pres. 1983-85). Democrat. Roman Catholic. Avocations: theater, reading, swimming, movies. Home: 151 Sahara Ln Chatsworth GA 30705-2633 Office: Murray County HS 1001 Green Rd Chatsworth GA 30705-2011

BEASON, CHRISTOPHER M., music educator; b. Lincoln, Nebr., Jan. 13, 1975; s. Donald D. and Gene L. Beason; m. Christine F. Beason, June 13, 2004. MusB, U. Ill., 1998, M in Music Edn., 2000. Cert. Tchr. (grades K-12) Ill., 1998. Grad. asst. U. Ill. Bands, Champaign, 1998—2000; dir. of bands Mater Dei Cath. HS, Breese, 2000—. Adminstrv. asst. Smith Walbridge Clinics, Charleston, 1995—, clinician, 1996—, Granite City HS Band, 1998—2000, Rolling Meadows HS Band, 1998—99; freelance designer marching band field show, Vandalia, Ill., 1999—; judge Centralia Halloween Parade, 2001—01; band divsn. coord. - dist. 6 Ill. Music Educator's Assn., Edwardsville, 2001—03; adminstrv. asst. Midwest Percussion Clinics, Lebanon, 2001—03; saxophone instr. McKendree Coll., 2002—; mem. Music Educator's Nat. Conf. Named Outstanding Music Educator, Nat. Band Assn., 2002. Mem.: Internat. Assn. Jazz Edn., Ill. Music Educator's Assn., Phi Kappa Theta. Avocations: travel, cooking, bicycling, woodworking, music.

BEATO, CRISTINA V., government agency administrator; b. Cuba, 1958; BS, U. N.Mex., MD, 1984. Diplomate Am. Bd. Family Practice. Assoc. dean clin. affairs, chief med. officer U. N.Mex. Health Sci. Ctr., 1999—2001; med. dir. Youth Diagnostic and Devel. Ctr., 1999—2001; dep. asst. sec. health office pub. health and sci. U.S. Dept. Health and Human Svcs., 2001—02, prin. dep. sec. health, 2002—03, acting asst. sec. health, 2003—. Rear adm. USPHS. Office: US Dept Health and Human Svcs 200 Independence Ave SW Washington DC 20201 Office Phone: 202-690-7694. Business E-Mail: cheato@usphs.dhhs.gov.

BEATON, ROY HOWARD, retired nuclear energy industry executive; b. Boston, Sept. 1, 1916; s. John Howard and Mary (LaVoie) B.; m. Margaret Marchant, July 22, 1939 (dec. Oct. 4, 1978); m. Leora Lauer Schier, June 26, 1982; children: Constance Beaton Fegley, Roy Howard, Patricia Schier

Briselden, Susan Schier Craig, Mary Schier Rieber. BS, Northeastern U., 1939, DSc (hon.), 1967; DEng, Yale U., 1942. Registered profl. engr., Wash., Wis., Fla., Calif. With E.I. DuPont, 1942-46, plant tech. supr. Manhattan (Nuclear Bomb) Project, 1943-44; chief chem. devel., chief engr., gen. mgr. constrn. engring. GE, Richland, Wash., 1946-56, gen. mgr. neutron devices dept. Milw., 1957-63; gen. mgr. Apollo Systems, Daytona Beach, Fla., 1964-68; v.p., gen. mgr. def. electronics systems div. GE, Syracuse, N.Y., 1968-74, v.p., gen. mgr. energy systems and tech. div. Fairfield, Conn., 1974-75; sr. v.p. and group exec. Nuclear Energy Group, San Jose, Calif., 1975-81. Chmn. industry div. United Way Campaign, Santa Clara County, Calif., 1978-79. Fellow AAAS, Am. Inst. Chemists; mem. NSPE, Nat. Acad. Engring., Am. Ordnance Assn., Am. Nuclear Soc., Am. Inst. Chem. Engrs., IEEE, AIAA, Navy League U.S., Air Force Assn., Soc. Mil. Engrs., Santa Clara County Mfg. Group, Sigma Xi, Tau Beta Pi Home: 201 Foursome Dr Sequim WA 98382

BEATRICE, RUTH HADFIELD, hypnotherapist, retired educator, financial administrator; b. Phila., Feb. 6, 1931; d. Claude and Alice Elizabeth (Smith) Hadfield; m. Michael Joseph Beatrice, May 29, 1954 BS, West Chester State U., 1953; MS, Marywood Coll., 1978; postgrad., Temple U., Pa. State U., 1978-80; cert. clinl. hypnotherapist, Phila. Hypnosis Union Inst., 1980. Cert. hypno-anaesthesia therapist Nat. Bd. Hypnotherapy and Hypnotic Anaesthesiology, 1991. Educator Bristol Twp. (Pa.) Sch. Dist., 1953-54, Phila. Sch. Dist., 1954-55; recreation dir. Phila. Dept. Recreation, 1953-57; educator Worcester (Pa.) Sch. Dist., 1958-59, Springford (Pa.) Joint Sch. Dist., 1960-61, Souderton (Pa.) Sch. Dist., 1961-63, Ctrl. Bucks Sch. Dist., Doylestown, Pa., 1970-1993; ret., 1993; clin. hypnotherapist in pvt. practice Perkasie, Pa., 1980—; clin. hypnotherapist, pvt. practice Avalon, N.J., 1980—, Port St. Lucie, Fla., Perkasie, Pa. Bus. adminstr. Beatrice Adminstrs. Co-author books on tutoring for Ptnrs. at Learning Series, 1978, 1979, 1983. Bd. mem. Pierce Free Libr., Hilltown, Pa., 1970-75; union del. Office and Profl. Employees Internat. Union Internat. Conv., Vancouver, B.C., Can., 1995; treas. Newcomers Civic Assn., Perkasie, 1964-85; me. Avalon (N.J.) Civic Assn., avalon Sr. Assn. Mem. NEA (life), AAUW, Nat. Assn. Profl. Therapists, Am. Legion Aux., Pa. State Edn. Assn. (life), Hypnotism Soc. of Pa. (v.p. Phila. br. 1993-95), Phila. Hypnosis Union Local 476 (v.p. 1993-95), Nat. Guild of Hypnotists, Nat. Bd. for Hypnotherapy and Hypnotic Anaesthesiology, Womens Assn., Ballanlfae's Angler Assn.; clubs: Ballanlfrae Gulf & Yacht Club. Democrat. Presbyterian. Avocations: biking, fishing, golf, tennis, walking. Home and Office: 3192 Carrick Green Ct Port Saint Lucie FL 34952 also: 3192 SE Carrick Green Ct Port Saint Lucie FL 34952-6042 Office Phone: 772-337-1469, 609-368-3256. Personal E-mail: rudibea@yahoo.com.

BEATTIE, ANN, writer; b. Washington, Sept. 8, 1947; d. James and Charlotte (Crosby) B.; m. Lincoln Perry. BA, Am. U., 1969; MA, U. Conn., 1970; L.H.D. (hon.), Am. U., 1983. Vis. asst. prof. U. Va., Charlottesville, 1976-77, vis. writer, 1980; Briggs Copeland lectr. English Harvard U., Cambridge, Mass., 1977. Author: Chilly Scenes of Winter, 1976, Distortions, 1976, Secrets and Surprises, 1979, Falling In Place, 1980, Jacklighting, 1981, The Burning House, 1982, Love Always, 1985, Where You'll Find Me, 1986, Alex Katz, 1987, Picturing Will, 1990, What Was Mine, 1991, My Life Starring Dara Falcon, 1997, Park City: New & Selected Stories, 1998, Perfect Recall, 2000, The Doctor's House, 2002, Follies: And New Stories, 2005. Recipient Disting. Alumnae award Am. U., 1980, award in lit. Am. Acad. and Inst. Arts and Letters, 1980, PEN/Malamud award for excellence in short fiction, 2000; Guggenheim fellow, 1977. Mem. Am. Acad. and Inst. of Arts and Letters (v.p. lit., 1989-99), PEN, Authors Guild. Office: care Janklow and Nesbit 445 Park Ave New York NY 10022-2606

BEATTIE, DIANA SCOTT, biochemistry professor; b. Cranston, R.I., Aug. 11, 1934; d. Kenneth Allen and Lillian Francis (Barton) Scott; m. Benjamin Howard Beattie, June 30, 1956 (div. 1975); children: Elizabeth, Sara, Rachel, Ruth; m. Robert Nathan Stuchell, Feb. 6, 1976 (div. 1991). BA, Swarthmore Coll., 1956; MS, U. Pitts., 1958, PhD, 1961. Research assoc. U. Pitts., 1961-67, VA Hosp., Pitts., 1967-68; faculty Mt. Sinai Sch. Medicine, N.Y.C., 1968-85, prof. biochemistry, 1976-85; prof., chmn. dept. biochemistry W.Va. U. Sch. Medicine, Morgantown, 1985-2001, chmn. dept. biochemistry and molecular pharmacology, 2001—. Mem. grad. faculty biomed. sci. CUNY, 1968-86, biochemistry, 1971-85, biology, 1974-85; mem. grad. faculty biochemistry W.Va. U. Sch. Medicine, Morgantown, 1985—; vis. prof. U. Louvain, Belgium, 1982, U. Nairobi, Kenya, 1993, Shandong U., China, 2000, Oman Med. Coll., 2005; mem. ad hoc biochemistry study sect. NIH, 1976-77, 79-81, mem. phys. biochemistry study sect., 1981-85, 1993-97; chmn. phys. biochemistry study sect., 1983-85, 1995-97; mem. metabolic biology panel NSF, 1986-89; mem. basic sci. merit rev. panel VA, 1989-92. Contbr. articles to profl. jours.; mem. editorial bd. Archives of Biochemistry and Biophysics, 1975-78, 85-2000, Jour. Bioenergetics, 1975—. Recipient award Met. N.Y. chpt. Assn. for Women in Sci., 1979; grantee NSF, 1970-92, 97—2001, NIH, 1966-2004; Fogarty internat. fellow, 1982, Fulbright fellow, 1993. Mem. Am. Soc. Biol. Chemists (membership com. 1987-89), Am. Soc. Cell Biology, Biophysics Soc., Assn. Med. Sch. Depts. Biochemistry (exec. com. 1989-92, pres.-elect 1995, pres. 1996), Am. Assn. Med. Schs. (coun. acad. socs. 1989-2001, adminstrv. bd. 1994-99, chair 1998), Nat. Bd. Med. Examiners (biochemistry test com. 1991-93, chair 1994-95, cell biology test com. 1998-2001, mem. adv. com. for med. sch. programs 2003—), Nat. Caucus Basic Biomed. Chairs (vice chair 1991—). Home: 324 Dream Catcher Cir Morgantown WV 26508-9473 Office: WVa U Sch Medicine Dept Biochemistry Morgantown WV 26506 Office Phone: 304-293-7522. Business E-Mail: dbeattie@hsc.wvu.edu.

BEATTIE, DONALD A., aerospace scientist, consultant; b. N.Y.C., Oct. 30, 1929; s. James Francis and Evelyn Margaret (Hickey) B.; m. Ann Mary Kean, Mar. 27, 1973; children: Thomas James, Bruce Andrew. AB, Columbia U., 1951; MS, Colo. Sch. Mines, 1958. Regional geologist Mobil Oil Co., 1958-63; Apollo lunar expts. program mgr. NASA, 1963-72, dir. NASA energy systems div. Washington, 1978-82; v.p. Houston ops. BDM Corp., 1983-84; cons. on energy and space tech., 1984—; pres. Endosat Inc., 1991-96. Dir. advanced energy research and tech. NSF, 1973-75; dep. asst. adminstr. ERDA, 1975-77; acting asst. sec. Dept. Energy, Washington, 1977-78; solar energy coordinator U.S./USSR Coop. in Sci. and Tech.; U.S. rep. Vienna Inst. for Comparative Econ. Studies Workshop on Energy. Author, editor: History and Overview of Solar Heat Technologies, 1997; author: Taking Science to the Moon, 2001; contbr. numerous articles on lunar sci., energy to profl. jours. Active Boy Scouts Am., 1958-71. Served with AC USN, 1951-56. Recipient Exceptional Service medal NASA, 1971, Sr. Exec. Service and Outstanding Performance award, 1980; Superior Achievement award Dept. Energy, 1978 Fellow AAAS; mem. Geol. Soc. Am., Nat. Space Club. Home and Office: 808 Mill Pond Ct Jacksonville FL 32259-3027 Office Phone: 904-287-6322.

BEATTIE, GEORGE CHAPIN, retired orthopedist, surgeon; b. Bowling Green, Ohio, Sept. 24, 1919; s. George Wilson and Mary Turner B.; m. Nancy U. Fant, Mar. 1, 1947; children: Michael, Suzanne, Eric. BA, Bowling Green State U., 1939; MD, U. Chgo., 1943. Diplomate Am. Bd. Orthopaedic Surgery. Commd. lt. (j.g.) MC USN, 1943, advanced through grades to lt. comdr., 1951; med. officer, intern U.S. Naval Hosp., Great Lakes, Ill., 1943-44; resident, fellow in orthopaedic surgery Lahey Clinic, Boston, 1944; ward med. officer orthopaedic services Naval Hosp., Guam, 1944-46; sr. med. officer USN, Manus Island, Papua New Guinea, 1946; resident tng. in orthopaedic surgery U.S. Naval Hosp. St. Albans, N.Y.C., 1947-48; resident in orthopaedic surgery Children's Hosp., Boston, 1949; asst. chief orthopaedic surgery U.S. Naval Hosp. Oak Knoll, Oakland, Calif., 1950-52; comdg. officer med. co. 1st Marine Div. Med. Bn., Republic of Korea, 1952-53; chief orthopaedic service Dept. Phys. Medicine and Navy Amputee Ctr. U.S. Naval Hosp., Phila., 1954; resigned USN, 1954; practice medicine specializing in orthopaedic surgery San Francisco, 1954-99; ret., 1999. Co-chmn. handicapping conditions com. Health Action Study San Mateo County, 1965; 1st chmn. orthopaedic sect. surg. dept. Peninsula Hosp. and Med. Ctr., Burlingame, Calif., 1967, chmn. rehab. service, 1967-71, chmn. phys. therapy and rehab. com., 1956—, vice chmn. orthopaedic dept., 1973-76, chmn., 1977-79; med. dir. research and rehab. ctr. San Mateo (Calif.) County Soc. Crippled Children and Adults, 1958-63; mem. exec. com. Harold D. Chope Community Hosp., San Mateo, 1971-76, chief, co-chmn. orthopaedic sect., 1971-76; chief orthopaedic surg. sect. Mills Meml. Hosp., San Mateo, 1976-78; others. Contbr. articles to profl. jours. Active Indian Guides, 1972-77; pres. Calif. Easter Seal Soc., 1969-71. Decorated Bronze Star. Fellow Am. Acad. Orthopaedic Surgeons (exhibit com. 1979-86); mem. AMA (Billings Bronze medal 1954), Internat. Soc. for Prosthetics and Orthotics, Western Orthopaedic Assn. (pres., bd. dirs. 1986), Leroy Abbott Orthopaedic Soc. U. Calif. San Francisco (assoc. clin. prof.), Alpha Omega Alpha.

BEATTIE, RICHARD IRWIN, lawyer; b. N.Y.C., Mar. 24, 1939; s. Richard I. Beattie and Ruth (Fisher) McCarthy; m. Diana Lewis, Dec. 21, 1963; children: Lisa C., Nina M. BA, Dartmouth Coll., 1961; LLB, U. Pa., 1968; EdD, Bank Street Coll. Bar: N.Y. 1968, U.S. Dist. Ct. (so. and ea. dists.) N.Y. 1972, U.S. Ct. Appeals (2d cir.) 1975, U.S. Ct. Appeals (D.C. cir.) 1977, U.S. Supreme Ct. 1978, U.S. Ct. Appeals (5th cir.) 1979. Dep. gen. counsel U.S. Dept. Health, Edn. and Welfare, Washington, 1977-78, exec. asst. to sec., 1978-79, gen. counsel, 1978-79; spl. counsel to sec., dir. transition U.S. Dept. Edn., Washington, 1980; assoc. Simpson, Thacher & Bartlett, N.Y.C., 1968-75, ptnr., 1975-77, 80—, chmn. firm & mem. exec. com. Teaching fellow Harvard U., 1979-81; chmn. Commn. Reorgn. of Human Resources Adminstrn., N.Y.C., 1984-85, Commn. on Spl. Edn., N.Y.C., 1984-85; Mem. Mayor's Coun. Fgn. Rels., N.Y.C. Mem. Bd. Edn., N.Y.C, 1986-87.; bd. trustees WNET/Channel 13, N.Y.C., 1983—, Natural Resources Def. Counsel, N.Y.C., 1984-86, Carnegie Corp., 1988—; chmn. fund N.Y.C. Pub. Edn, 1989—; bd. dirs. Nat. Women's Law Ctr., Am. Ditchley Found., Am. Restaurant Group, Inst. Internat. Edn., Am.-Israel Friendship League; mem. Mayor's Task Force on AIDS. Capt. USMC, 1961-65; Mem. Hosp. Cancer & Allied Diseases; Meml. Sloan-Kettering Cancer Ctr., chmn.; New Visions Pub. Sch., founder & chmn. bd. Jet pilot USMC. Mem. Bar City N.Y. Avocations: skiing, mountain climbing. Office: Simpson Thacher & Bartlett 425 Lexington Ave Fl 15 New York NY 10017-3954 Office Phone: 212-455-2635. Office Fax: 212-455-2502. Business E-Mail: rbeatie@stblaw.com.*

BEATTIE, STEPHANIE SHANNON, human resources specialist; b. Greenville, S.C., Aug. 19, 1968; d. Jerry Nelson and Judith Farley Beattie. BS, Presbyn. Coll., Clinton, S.C., 1990; MA in Counseling, Webster U., 1997, MA in Human Resources and Devel., 2003. Residential counselor Luth. Family Svcs., Pelzer, SC, 1990—92; drug/alcohol counselor Methodone Clinic, Greenville, 1992—94; social worker Dept. Social Svcs., Greenville, 1994—2004; mgr. employee/vol. rels. The Blood Connection, Greenville, SC, 2004—. Mem. consumer adv. bd. Greenville Mental Health, 1999. Roman Catholic. Avocations: golf, skiing, landscaping. Office: The Blood Connection Greenville SC 29605 Office Phone: 864-255-5005 1008.

BEATTS, ANNE PATRICIA, writer; b. Buffalo, Feb. 25, 1947; d. Patrick Murray Threipland and Sheila Elizabeth Jean (Sherriff Scott) B. BA with honors, McGill U., Montreal, Que., Can., 1966. Contbg. editor National Lampoon mag., N.Y.C., 1970-74; writer Saturday Night Live NBC, N.Y.C., 1975-80; creator, prodr. Square Pegs CBS, Los Angeles, 1982-83; co-exec. prodr. A Different World NBC, Los Angeles, 1987-88; exec. prodr. The Stephanie Miller Show, 1994-95. Writer, creative cons. Saturday Night Live 25th Ann. Spl., 1999; exec. story cons. (WETV) Committed, 2000-01; head writer WGA Awards, 2004; adj. prof. writing divsn. Sch. Cinema-TV, U. So. Calif., 2003-05. Co-editor: (humorous books) Titters, 1976, Saturday Night, 1977; co-author: (humorous books) Titters 101, 1984, The Mom Book, 1986; author book for Broadway mus. Leader of the Pack, 1985; humor columnist L.A. Times, 1997-98. Mem. AFTRA, SAG, Writers Guild Am. (award 1976, 77, 2000), Dirs. Guild Am., Women in Film, Dramatists Guild, NATAS (2 Emmy awards, 6 Emmy award nominations 1975-80, 2000). E-mail: beattsclass@aol.com.

BEATTY, CARL, music educator; b. NYC, Feb. 5, 1956; s. Carl James and Juanita (Hunter) Beatty; m. Jacqueline M. Reid, Mar. 21, 1987; children: Zoe J., Mayrose C.; m. Cynthia Crockford, Sept. 1979 (div. Aug. 1981). BA, C.W. Post Coll., 1977. Rec. engr. Mediasound, NYC, 1979—85; ind. rec. engr., 1985—89; assoc. prof. to prof. Berklee Coll. of Music, Boston, 1989—. Mixing engr. (various performer's recordings albums). Bd. of trustees North Bennet St. Sch., Boston, 1996—2000. Avocations: photography, driving, electronics. Office: Berklee Coll of Music 1140 Boylston St Boston MA 02115

BEATTY, FRANCES, civic worker; b. Chgo., Apr. 17, 1940; d. Pasquale and Rose (Brunetti) Calomeni; m. Robert Alfred Beatty, Aug. 24, 1963; children: Bradford, Roxanna Beatty Goebel. BA, Northwestern U., 1961; MA, U. Chgo., 1967. Tchr. math. Proviso West High Sch., Hillside, Ill., 1961-66. Active Oak Brook Dist. 53 Sch. Bd., 1979-85; women's bd. Field Mus. Natural History, Chgo., 1985—, founders coun., 1988—, treas. women's bd., 1991-93; governing bd. Chgo. Symphony, 1985-92; trustee Chgo. Symphony Orch., 1992-96, life trustee, 2005—; women's bd. Ravinia Festival, Highland Park, Ill., 1987—, Northwestern U., Evanston, Ill., sec. women's bd., 1999—, libr. bd., 1990-95; women's bd. U. Chgo.; mem. coun. Wellness House, Hinsdale, Ill., 1994; com. mem. Chgo. Humanities Festival, 1999—; treas. 626 Landmark Found., 2005— Mem.: 626 Found. (sec., treas. 2005—), Merit Sch. Music, Alumnae of Northwestern U. (pres. 1996—98), The Antiquarian Soc. Art Inst. Chgo., John Evans Club, Woman's Athletic Club Chgo. (3d v.p. 1985—87, 1st v.p. 1992—94, pres. 1994—96).

BEATTY, JOHN CABEEN, JR., judge; b. Washington, Apr. 13, 1919; s. John Cabeen and Jean (Morrison) B.; m. Clarissa Hager, Feb. 8, 1943 (dec. Apr. 4 1996); children: John Cabeen III, Clarissa Jean; m. Virginia R. Campbell, May 10, 1997. AB, Princeton U., 1941; JD, Columbia U., 1948. Bar: Oreg. 1948. Pvt. practice law, Portland, Oreg., 1948-70; ptnr. Dusenbery, Martin, Beatty, Bischoff & Templeton, 1956-70, of counsel, 1985-96; judge Cir. Ct., Oreg., 1970-85, sr. judge, 1985—. Mem. Oreg. Bd. Bar Examiners, 1953-54; chmn. legis. com. Oreg. Jud. Conf., 1976-82; mem. Oreg. CSC, 1962-64, Oreg. Law Enforcement Coun., 1974-77; vice chmn. Oreg. Commn. Jud. Br., 1979-85; vice chmn. Oreg. Criminal Justice Coun., 1985-90. Author: D Day to VE Day, 1946, The Fourth Part of Gaul, 2004. Mem. legis. com. Nat. Sch. Bds. Assn., 1966-68, chmn. coun. large city sch. bds., 1967-68; counsel Dem. Party Oreg., 1956-58; co-chmn. Oreg. for Kennedy Com., 1968; bd. dirs. Portland Pub. Schs., 1964-70, chmn., 1967, 69; chmn. policy adv. com. on hazardous waste Dept. Environ. Quality, 1985-86; mem. Mayor's Spl. Rev. Commn., 1986; chmn. various adv. coms. Dept. Environ. Quality, 1987-89; chmn. tech. adv. com. Willamette River Basin Water Quality Study, 1990-94; chmn. city club study Oreg. Initiative and Referendum, 1994-95; chmn. Oreg. Initiative Com., 1996-2000. Capt. AUS, 1941-46, ETO. Decorated Bronze Star medal; recipient City Club of Portland award, 1967. Mem. ABA, Oreg. Bar Assn., Oreg. Hist. Soc. (dir. 1973-92), City Club (past pres., bd. govs.), Racquet Club. Home and Office: 3331 SW Mitchell St Portland OR 97201-1260 Personal E-mail: jcbeatty@comcast.net.

BEATTY, JOSEPH ROBERT, lawyer; b. Charlotte, N.C., July 12, 1944; s. Joe Sellers and Frances Kathleen (McCorkle) B.; m. Nancy Jane McCaskey, June 8, 1974; children: Anne Patton, Robert Locke. BA, U. N.C., 1966; JD with distinction, Duke U., 1969. Bar: N.C. 1969, U.S. Dist. Ct. (mid. dist.) N.C. 1974, U.S. Ct. Appeals (4th cir.) 1977. Staff atty. Forsyth County Legal Aid Soc., Winston-Salem, N.C., 1969-70; assoc. Nichols Caffrey Hill Evans and Murelle, Greensboro, N.C., 1974-79, ptnr., 1979-95, Hill, Evans, Duncan, Jordan & Davis, Greensboro, 1995-2000; mem. Hill, Evans, Duncan, Jordan & Beatty, LLC, Greensboro, 2001—. Capt. U.S. Army, 1970-74. Mem. ABA, N.C. Bar Assn., Greensboro Bar Assn., Phi Beta Kappa. Democrat. Methodist. Avocations: reading, history, modern lit., traveling. Office: Hill Evans Duncan Jordan & Beatty LLC 230 N Elm St Ste 1400 Greensboro NC 27401-2498

BEATTY, KENNETH ORION, JR., chemical engineer, educator; b. East Lansdowne, Pa., Dec. 18, 1913; s. Kenneth Orion and Ada Pearl (Marshall) B.; m. Mary Catharine Carter, Aug. 8, 1936; children: Susan Jennifer, Prudence Carter, Lucy Margaret. BS, Lehigh U., 1935, MS, 1937; PhD, U. Mich., 1946. Registered profl. engr., N.C. Raybestos-Manhattan fellow Lehigh U., 1935-37; chem. engr. Dow Chem. Co., Midland, Mich., 1937-39; asst. prof. chem. engring. U. R.I., Kingston, 1939-44; rsch. assoc. U. Mich., 1944-46; assoc. prof. N.C. State U., Raleigh, 1946-48, prof., 1948—, acting head dept. chem. engring., 1959-60, R.J. Reynolds Industries prof. chem. engring., 1961—, spl. cons. in forensic engring., 1982—. Dir. Carolina Cons. Scientists and Engrs., 1979-87; vis. prof. chem. engring. Ohio State U., summer 1949; vis. engr. Pratt & Whitney Co., Middletown, Conn., summer 1957; resident cons. engr. Nat. Lead Co. of Ohio, Fernald, summer 1959; mem. Max Jakob Award Com., 1963-67, chmn., 1966; mem. Nat. Heat Transfer Conf. Coordinating Com., 1965-71, chmn., 1967; coordinating chmn. 9th Nat. Heat Transfer Conf., Seattle, 1967; U.S. founding del. Assembly for Internat. Heat Transfer Conf., 1967-72; mem. sci. council Internat. Center for Heat and Mass Transfer, Yugoslavia, 1971-90. Contbr. articles to profl. jours. Mem. N.C. Gov.'s Sci. Adv. Com. Rsch. grantee NASA, NSF, Wright Air Devel. Center, AEC, Am. Soc. Refrigerating Engrs.; Princeton U. fellow, 1967-68. Fellow AIChE; mem. Am. Chem. Soc., University Park Homeowners Assn. Home: 323 Shepherd St Raleigh NC 27607-4031 Office: NC State U Dept Chem Engring Raleigh NC 27695-0001

BEATTY, LORI ELIZABETH, music educator; b. Indiana, Pa., Sept. 22, 1965; d. William Frank and Dorothy Marie Long; m. William Rue Beatty, June 8, 1991; children: Rachel Elizabeth, Eliana Renee. BS in Music Edn., Clarion U. of PA, Clarion, PA, 1983—87; degree, State of Pa., 2002. Music Edn. Pa., 1987, Elem. Edn. Pa., 1993. Music educator Kane Area Sch. Dist., Pa., 1987—. Ch. choir dir. Kane First United Meth. Ch., Kane, 1987—98. Worship leader, lead singer for contemporary svc. Warren First United Meth. Ch., Pa., 2003—; mem. Madrigals of Warren First United Meth. Ch., 2004—, Chancel Choir of Warren First United Meth. Ch., Warren, Pa., 2004—. Mem.: MENC, Pa. Music Educator's Assn. Methodist. Avocations: singing, piano. Home: 100 Brook St Warren PA 16365 Office: Chestnut St Elem Sch 226 Chestnut St Kane PA 16735 Office Phone: 814-837-7555. Personal E-mail: wbeatty@kinzua.net. E-mail: lbeatty@kasd.net.

BEATTY, MARILYN BARTON, special education educator; b. Cin., June 7, 1952; d. Robert Scott and Evelyn (Barton) B. BS, Ball State U., 1974; MEd, Xavier U., Cin., 1977. Cert. elem. tchr., spl. edn. tchr., Ohio. Spl. edn. tchr. Columbus (Ohio) Pub. Schs., 1974-75, Western Brown Local Schs., Mt. Orab, Ohio, 1975—. Mem. NEA, Oho Edn. Assn., Western Brown Edn. Assn.

BEATTY, PERRIN, business association executive; b. Toronto; married; 2 children. Student, Upper Can. Coll., Toronto, U. Western Ont. Elected mem. Parliament, 1972; cabinet min. Min. of State-Treasury Bd., 1979, Min. of Nat. Revenue, 1984; solicitor gen., 1985; min. of nat. def., 1986; min. of health, 1989; min. of comms., 1991; min. external affairs, 1993; pres., CEO Can. Broadcasting Corp., 1995-1999, Canadian Mfrs. & Exporters, Ottawa, Ont., 1999—. Former hon. vis. prof. dept. polit. sci. U. We. Ont.; former columnist Toronto Sun. Office: CME 1 Nicholas St Ste 1500 Ottawa ON Canada K1N 7B7

BEATTY, ROBERT ALFRED (R. ALFRED), surgeon, educator; b. Colchester, Vt., May 7, 1936; s. George Lewis and Leila Margaret (Ebright) B.; m. Frances Calomeni, Aug. 24, 1963; children: Bradford, Roxanna. BA, U. Oreg., 1959, BS, 1960, MD, 1961. Diplomate Am. Bd. Neurol. Surgery. Intern Rsch. and Edn. Hosp. U. Ill., Chgo., 1961—62, resident neurosurgery, 1962—66; practice neurosurgery Hinsdale, Ill., 1967—; mem. staff Hinsdale Hosp., 1967—, Cmty. Meml. Hosp., LaGrange, Ill., 1967—, U. Ill. Hosp., Chgo., 1967—, Good Samaritan Hosp., Downers Grove, Ill., Elmhurst Hosp., Ill.; clin. assoc. prof. neurosurgery U. Ill., 1967—. Founding adviser Marion Joy Rehab. Ctr., Wheaton, Ill., 1969-7; mem. State Ill. Spinal Cord Injury Adv. Coun., 1995, vice-chmn. 1997. Contbr. articles to profl. jours. Mem. founder's coun. Field Mus. Capt. USMC, AUS, 1968. Rsch. fellow St. George's Med. Sch., London, 1966-67. Mem. AMA, ACS, SAR, Ill. Med. Soc., Dupage County Med. Soc., Am. Assn. Neurol. Surgeons, N.Am. Spine Soc., Congress Neurol. Surgeons, Soc. Brit. Neurol. Surgeons, Internat. Microsurg. Soc., Nat. Assn. Spine Specialists, English Speaking Union, John Evans Club (N.W. U.), Theodore Thomas Soc., Chgo. Symphony Orch. (governing), Hinsdale Golf Club, Phi Beta Kappa, Phi Beta Pi, Phi Kappa Psi. Republican. Achievements include research on intracranial aneurysms, lumbar discs; inventor medical instruments; profl. sculptor (under name R. Alfred). Office: 333 Chestnut St Hinsdale IL 60521-3247 Office Phone: 630-986-8290.

BEATTY, ROBERT CLINTON, religious studies educator; b. Needham, Mass., May 19, 1935; s. Henry Russell and Alice Cornelia (van Schagen) B.; m. Carolyn Phyllis Caton, Oct. 5, 1957; children: Robert Russell, Daniel Clinton, Melissa Lynn, Alicia Felicity. AB in Econs., Northeastern U., 1957; MBA in Mgmt., Fairleigh Dickinson U., 1973; MDiv, Columbia Biblical Sem., 1983, MA in Bible, 1985; DMin in Orgn. Devel., Fuller Theol. Sem., 1993. Ordained to ministry Harmony Ch., 1984. Commd. 2d lt. U.S. Army, 1957, advanced through grades to lt. col., ret., 1980; dir. U.S. extension ctrs. Columbia (S.C.) Internat. U., 1983-89; assoc. prof., chmn. bus. mgmt. Miami Christian Coll., 1989-92, Trinity Internat. U., Miami, 1992-2001, undergrad. program coord., 2001—02; MAR program coord. South Fla. ext. Trinity Evang. Div. Sch., 1994—; prof. Calvary Chapel Bible Inst., 2000—. Lectr. Christian Leadership Tng. Inst., Chisinau, Moldova, 2001—; adj. prof. Embry Riddle Aero. U., Mannheim, Germany, 1976—77, City Colls. of Chgo., Mannheim, 1976—77; bible study tchr. Prison Fellowship, Columbia, 1981—89, Calvary Chapel, Ft. Lauderdale, 1996—2000; ch./ministry bd. cons., 1987—. Author: Extension Coordinator's Handbook, 1984, 1985, 1987, 1989, (student manual) Practical Applications of Biblical Hermeneutics, 1992—94, 2000, 2003—04, Human Resource Management, 1992, (manual) Business Ethics, 1991, Organization Behavior, 1991, Acts: A Sociological and Cross Cultural Communications Perspective, 1991; editor: Adjunct-Extension Faculty Handbook, 1984, 1985, 1989. Decorated Legion of Merit, Bronze Star with oak leaf cluster, Air medal, Meritorious Svc. medal, Gallantry Cross with Silver Star; recipient Vol. of Yr. award Goodman Correctional Instn., 1985, Broad River Correctional Instn., 1989, Prof. of Yr. award Trinity Internat. U., 2001. Mem.: DAV, Mil. Officers Assn. of Am., AARP. Republican. Avocation: travel. Home: 10500 NW 21st Ct Sunrise FL 33322-3509 Office: Calvary Chapel Bible Inst 2401 W Cypress Creek Rd Fort Lauderdale FL 33309 Office Phone: 954-315-4340. E-mail: bibleprof@msn.com.

BEATTY, (HENRY) WARREN, actor, producer, director; b. Richmond, Va., Mar. 30, 1937; s. Ira O. and Kathlyn (MacLean) Beaty; m. Annette Bening; 4 children, Kathlyn, Benjamin, Isabel and Ella Corrine. Student, Northwestern U., 1956, Stella Adler Theatre Sch., N.Y.C., 1957. Actor films Splendor in the Grass, 1961, The Roman Spring of Mrs. Stone, 1962, All Fall Down, 1962, Lilith, 1963, Mickey One, 1965, Promise Her Anything, 1965, Kaleidoscope, 1966, The Only Game in Town, 1969, McCabe and Mrs. Miller, 1971, Dollars, 1971, The Parallax View, 1974, The Fortune, 1975, Town and Country, 2001; actor, producer films include Bonnie and Clyde, 1967 (Acad. award nomination for best actor), Ishtar, 1987; producer, co-screenwriter, actor Shampoo, 1975 (Acad. award nomination for best screenplay); producer, co-dir., co-screenwriter, actor Heaven Can Wait, 1978 (Acad. award nominations for best actor, best dir. and best screenplay); producer, dir., co-screenwriter, actor Reds, 1981 (Acad. award for best dir.), dir., actor Dick Tracy, 1990; co-producer, actor: Bugsy, 1991; Love Affair (also producer and writer), 1994; Bulworth (also producer and writer); actor (TV) A Salute to Dustin Hoffman, 1999; TV guest appearances include Studio One, 1948, What's My Line, 1950, Vibe, 1997; appeared in Broadway play A Loss of Roses, 1960. Recipient Irving G. Thalberg Memorial award, 1999, American Soc. of Cinematographers Bd. of Governors award, 2000, BAFTA

Fellowship, 2002, Kennedy Ctr. Honors, John F. Kennedy Ctr. Performing Arts, 2004. Mem. Dirs. Guild Am. Democrat. Office: Creative Artists Agy care Risa Gertner 9830 Wilshire Blvd Beverly Hills CA 90212-1804

BEATUS, BRIAN J., lawyer; b. Queens, NY, Jan. 17, 1967; BSEE cum laude, Boston Univ., 1989, JD, 1993. Bar: NY 1992, DC 1992, Calif. 1999, Pa. (inactive), US Dist. Ct. (no. & ctrl. dist. Calif., ea. dist. Tex.), US Ct. Appeals (Fed., DC, 9th cir.). Ptnr., head Silicon Valley Intellectual Property dept. Pillsbury Winthrop Shaw Pittman, Palo Alto, Calif. Named one of Silicon Valley's Top 300 Lawyers, San Jose mag., 2003, Silicon Valley's Top Legal Eagles, 2004. Mem.: ABA, Am. Intellectual Property Law Assn. Office: Pillsbury Winthrop Shaw Pittman 2475 Hanover St Palo Alto CA 94304-1114 Office Phone: 650-233-4683. Office Fax: 650-233-4545. Business E-Mail: brian.beatus@pillsburylaw.com.

BEATY, JAMES ARTHUR, JR., federal judge; b. 1949; m. Toyoko Christine Beaty; 1 child. BA cum laude, Western Carolina U., 1971; JD, U. N.C., 1974; postgrad., U. Nev., 1985—91; LHD (hon.), Western Carolina U., 2002. With Richard C. Erwin, Winston-Salem, NC, 1974—77; atty. at law Ewrin and Beaty, Winston-Salem, 1977—78, Beaty and Friende, Winston-Salem, 1980—81; pvt. practice Winston-Salem, 1978—79; judge N.C. Superior Ct., 1981—94; dist. judge U.S. Dist. Ct. (mid. dist.) N.C., 1994—. Recipient Disting. Alumni award, Western Carolina U., 1994. Mem.: ABA, NAACP (life), N.C. Assn. Black Lawyers (sec. 1976, v.p. 1978), N.C. Acad. Trial Lawyers (named outstanding trial ct. judge of yr. 1990), Winston-Salem Bar Assn., Forsyth County and 21st Jud. Dist. Bar, N.C. State Bar, Rotary Club, Sigma Pi Phi, Alpha Phi Alpha. Office: 251 N Main St Rm 248 Winston Salem NC 27101-3914*

BEAUBIEN, ANNE KATHLEEN, librarian; b. Detroit, Sept. 15, 1947; d. Richard Parker and Edith Mildred Beaubien; m. Philip Conway Berry, Feb. 7, 2004. Student, Western Mich. U., 1965-67; BA, Mich. State U., 1969; MLS, U. Mich., 1970. Reference libr., bibliographic instr. U. Mich. Libr., Ann Arbor, 1971-80, dir. MITS, 1980-85, dir. coop. access svc., 1985—, head bus. and fin. office, 1995—2000, grants officer, 2000—. Author: Psychology Bibliography, 1980; co-author: Learning the Library, 1982; contbg. articles to profl. jour., editor, conf. proc., 1987. Mem. vestry St. Clare's Episcopal Ch., Ann Arbor, 1986—89, 2002—03; pres. Ann Arbor Ski Club, 1978—79. Recipient Woman of Yr. Award, Ann Arbor Bus. and Profl. Women's Club, 1982; Disting. Alumnus Award; Sch. Info. and Libr. Studies, U. Mich., 1987. Mem. ALA, Assn. Coll. and Rsch. Librs. (pres. 1991-92). Avocations: skiing, bicycling, ballroom dancing. Office: U Mich Libr 106 Hatcher Grad Libr Ann Arbor MI 48109 Office Phone: 734-936-2322. Business E-Mail: beaubien@umich.edu.

BEAUCHAMP, J. PATRICK, lawyer; s. James Vance and Margaret Opp Beauchamp; m. Michelle Duceung, May 14, 1975; 1 child, Robert. BA in English, Loyola U., New Orleans, La., 1970, JD, 1973. Bar: La. 1974. Assoc. Mmahat, Galiano, Metairie, La., 1974—77, Phelps, Dunbar, New Orleans, 1977—80, ptnr., 1980—92; mem. McGlinchey Stafford PLLC, New Orleans, 1993—. Uniform title stds. com. mem. La. Bar Assn., 1997—99, bar admission com. mem., 2002—. Bd. mem., pres. Farnham Pl. Assn., Metairie, La., 1989—94, Am. Heart Assn., New Orleans, 1990—94, Jefferson Parish Performing Arts Assn., Metairie, La., 1999—2004. Lt. U.S. Army, 1973—74, U.S.A. Mem.: Nat. Assn. Bond Lawyers, La. State Bar Assn., ABA. Office: McGlinchey Stafford PLLC 643 Magazine St New Orleans LA 70130

BEAUCHAMP, JESSE LEE (JACK BEAUCHAMP), chemistry professor; b. Glendale, Calif., Nov. 1, 1942; m. Patricia Margaret Beauchamp; children: Melissa Ann, Thomas Alton, Amanda Jane, Ryan Howell, Michael Andrew. BS with honors in Chemistry, Calif. Inst. Tech., 1964; PhD in Chemistry, Harvard U., 1967. Arthur Amos Noyes instr. in Chemistry Calif. Inst Tech., Pasadena, 1967-69, asst. prof. chemistry, 1969-71, assoc. prof. chemistry, 1971-74, prof. chemistry, 1974—. Panelist chem. rsch. evaluation Directorate of Chem. Scis. Air Force Office of Sci. Rsch., 1978-81, adv. panelist high energy density materials, 1988-92; exec. com. advanced light source users, LBL, 1984-87; exptl. evaluation com. TRIUMPH, U. B.C., 1985-88; grad. fellow selection panel, NSF, 1986-89; postdoctoral selection panel NATO, 1987-89; mem. com. critical techs.: role of Chemistry and Chem. Engring. Nat. Rsch. Coun., 1991-92; chmn. com. on comml. aviation security Nat. Materials Adv. Bd., Nat. Rsch. Coun., 1994-97; commr. White House commn. on aviation safety and security, 1996-97. Mem. editorial adv. bd. Chemical Physics Letters, 1981-87, Jour. Am. Chem. Soc., 1984-87, Jour Physical Chemistry, 1984-87, Organometallics, 1989-92, Interat. Jour. Chemical Kinetics, 1990—. Woodrow Wilson fellow Harvard U., 1964-65, NSF grad. fellow, 1965-67; fellow Alfred P. Sloan Found., 1967-70; tchr.-scholar Camille and Henry Dreyfus, 1971-76; meml. fellow John Simon Guggenheim, 1976-77. Fellow AAAS; mem. NAS (com. chem. scis., chem. kinetics subgroup 1980-83), Am. Chem. Soc. (award in pure chemistry 1978, exec. com. divsn. physical chem., 1980-82, Peter Debye award in phys. chemistry 1999), Am. Assn. Mas. Spectometry, Aircraft Owners and Pilots Assn., Soc. Fellows Harvard U. Office: Calif Inst Tech Dept of Chemistry Noyes Lab 127 # 72 Pasadena CA 91125-0001

BEAUCHAMP, MALCOM E., director; b. Baton Rouge, Oct. 27, 1944; s. Wallace M. and Gwendolyn N. Beauchamp; m. Suzanne P. Beauchamp, June 11, 1966; 1 child, Malcom C. MusB, George Peabody Coll., 1966, MusM, 1968; PhD, La. State U., 1980. Band dir. Stinson Jr. High, South Huntington, NY, 1970—88, Harrison (NY) HS, 1988—90, East Meadow (NY) Sch., 1990—2003. Contbr. articles to profl. jours. Home: 29 Hastings Dr Northport NY 11768

BEAUCHAMP, MILES PHILIP, editor, columnist, consultant; b. L.A., Apr. 17, 1953; s. Henry and Kathrinjo (Shelton) B.; m. Michelle Colleen Ryan, July 1, 1989. BA, San Diego State U., 1993, MA, 1994. V.p. Beauchamp Co. Hotels, San Diego, 1972-84; editor, columnist Asian Jour. newspaper, San Diego, 1985—; instr. U.S. Internat. U., San Diego, 1996—. Instr. Alliant Internat. U., 1996—, Nat. Univ., 1996—; cons. The Writing Ctr., San Diego, 1992—96, Main Street mag., San Diego, 1994—95. Co-author: The Exquisite Cadaver, 1993; author: A New Way of Looking, 1996; editor: Filipinos in America, 1992; columnist Still Amazed, 1985-96. Profl. devel. facilitator Grossmont Coll., San Diego, 1990—; tchr. writing St. Vincent De Paul Shelter, San Diego, 1992; tchr., facilitator Profls. in Schs., San Diego, 1990—. Recipient award of appreciation San Diego Journalism Edn. Assn., 1992, San Diego Pub. Libr., 1994, Georgi awards Writers Fedn. Am., 1993. Mem. Film and Video Artists Assn., Writers Haven, San Diego Press Club. Avocations: travel, boating, photography. Office: Asian Jour Newspaper 550 E 8th St Ste 6 National City CA 91950 E-mail: milespb@gncib.com.

BEAUCHAMP, ROBERT E., computer company executive; BA, Univ. Tex. Austin; MS mgmt., Houston Baptist Univ., 2001. With BMC Software, Inc., 1988—2001, pres., CEO. Mem. bd. dir. Nat. Oilwell Varco, Inc., Memorial Herman Hospital System, Tex. Med. Ctr., NYSE Listed Co. Adv. Bd. With Greater Houston Partnership, Ctr. Houston's Future; adv. Houston Tech. Ctr., Indo-Am. Chamber Commerce Greater Houston. Recipient Distinguished Alumnus, Houston Baptist Univ. Office: BMC Software Inc 2101 City West Blvd Houston TX 77042 Office Phone: 713-918-8800. Office Fax: 713-918-8000.*

BEAUDET, ARTHUR L., medical genetics researcher; b. Woonsocket, R.I., July 4, 1942; s. Louis George and Sylvia Mary (Lareau) B.; m. Marjorie Adelynn Miller, June 10, 1967; m. Nicole, Alissa. BS in Biology magna cum laude, Holy Cross Coll., Worcester, 1963; MD cum laude, Yale U., 1967. Diplomate Nat. Bd. Med. Examiners, 1968, Am. Bd. Pediatrics, 1973, Am. Bd. Med. Genetics, 1982, 93. Pediatric resident John Hopkins Hosp., Balt., 1967-69; rsch. assoc. NIH, Bethesda, Md., 1969-71; instr. Baylor Coll. Medicine, Houston, 1971-73; active staff Harris County Hosp. Dist., 1973—; active staff, chief of genetic svc. Tex. Children's Hosp., 1973—; cons. staff Methodist Hosp., 1976—; asst. prof. Baylor Coll. Medicine, Houston, 1973-77, assoc. prof., 1977-81, prof., 1981—; investigator Howard Hughes Med. Inst., Houston, 1973-80, 85—; acting chmn. dept. moledular and human genetics Baylor Coll. Medicine, Houston, 1994-95, chmn. dep. molecular and human genetics, 1995—. Mem. bd. dirs. Am. Soc. Human Genetics, Rockville, Md., 1987-90; mem. founding bd. dirs. Am. Coll. Med. Genetics, 1990-94; mem. editl. bds. Human Molecular Genetics, 1991—, Human Mutation, 1991—, Human Gene Therapy, 1994—, Gene Therapy, 1994—, Human Genetics, 1994—. Co-author: (book) The Metabolic and Molecular Bases of Inherited Disease, 7th edit., 1995; editor: (books) The Metabolic Basis of Inherited Disease, 6th edit., 1989, The Metabolic and Molecular Bases of Inherited Disease, 1995; contbr. chpts. to books, articles to profl. jours. Recipient Med. award Alpha Omega Alpha, 1966; grantee numerous orgns. including NIH, March of Dimes, Cystic Fibrosis Found., others. Mem. Am. Acad. Pediatrics, Am. Pediatrics, Am. Pediatric Soc., Am. Soc. Human Genetics (program com. 1984-86, bd. dirs. 1987-90), Am. Soc. Microbiology, Assn. Am. Physicians, Genetics Soc. Am., Tex. Pediatric Soc., Houston Pediatric Soc., Harris County med. Soc., Soc. Inherited Metabolic Disease, Soc. Pediatric Rsch., NAS Inst. Medicine. Achievements include research in the fields of molecular and human genetics, cystic fibrosis, gene therapy, inborn errors of metabolism and gene targeting; discovery of the uniparental disomy in humans. Office: Baylor Coll Med Dept Molecular/Human Genetics 1 Baylor Plz # T619 Houston TX 77030-3411*

BEAUDET-FRANCÈS, PATRICIA SUZANNE, photography editor; b. Chgo., Aug. 6, 1951; d. André Marcel and Helen Gertrude (Joiner) B.; m. Gérard Jean-Pierre Frances, June 27, 1997. Sr. photography editor Playboy Enterprises Inc., Chgo., 1970—. Contbg. photographer Rolling Stone Illustrated History of Rock and Roll, 1992; rschr., photo editor Playboy (photographs pub. 50 yrs.): The Playboy Book: Forty Years, 1994, Playboy: 50 Years The Photographs Featured; prodr. CD Instrumental Journey, 2002. Democrat. Roman Catholic. Avocations: photography, travel, cinema, workouts, reading. Home: PO Box 31351 Chicago IL 60631-0351 Office Phone: 312-373-2715. E-mail: pattyb@playboy.com.

BEAUDOIN, CAROL ANN, psychologist; b. Lowell, Mass., Mar. 30, 1949; d. Adrien P. and Rita J. (LeBlanc) B.; B.A. with honors, U. Fla., 1971; M.Ed. in Counseling, Boston U., 1973, Ed.D. in Counseling Psychology, 1979. Psychiat. aide U. Fla.-Shands Teaching Hosp., Gainesville, 1970-71; trainee VA Hosp., Gainesville, 1971-72; attendant Boston State Hosp., 1972, intern, 1973; intern Univ. Hosp., also Counseling Center, Northeastern U., Boston, 1973-74, Dorchester Mental Health Center, also Carney Hosp., 1974-75; staff psychologist Human Resource Inst., Boston, 1974-80, treatment team leader, 1975-80; pvt. practice psychology, Brookline, Mass., 1980— . Mem. Am. Psychol. Assn. Office: 1101 Beacon St Brookline MA 02446-5587 Office Phone: 617-232-3603.

BEAUDOIN, GÉRALD A(RMAND), lawyer, educator, retired senator; b. Montreal, Qué., Can., Apr. 15, 1929; s. Armand and Aldéa (St.-Arnaud) B.; m. Renée Desmarais, Sept. 11, 1954; children: Viviane, Louise, Denise, Françoise. BA summa cum laude, U. Montreal, 1950, LLL magna cum laude, 1953, MA in Law, 1954; postgrad. in comparative law (Carnegie scholar), U. Toronto, 1954-55; DESD cum laude, U. Ottawa, Ont., 1958; LLD, U. Louvain-la-Neuve, Belgium, 1989. Bar: Called to Que. bar 1954, created queen's counsel 1969. Practiced law with Paul Gérin-Lajoie, Montreal, 1955-56; adv. counsel Dept. Justice, Ottawa, 1956-65, sr. adv. counsel, 1965-69; asst. parliamentary counsel Ho. of Commons of Can., Ottawa, 1965-69; civil law dean Faculty of Law, U. Ottawa, 1969-79, prof. constl. law, 1969-89, dir. Human Rights Ctr., 1986-88; mem. Senate of Can., 1988. Mem. Goldenberg Com. on Constn., 1967, La Commn des Svcs. Juridiques du Quebec, 1972-73, Task Force on Can. Unity, 1977-79; vis. prof. U. Sorbonne, 1985; vis. prof. faculty of law U. Ottawa, 1989-94, prof. emeritus, 1994—; co-chmn. spl. joint com. of Senate and Ho. of Commons. on process for amending Constn. of Can., 1991, on a renewed Can., 1991-92; mem. Senate Spl. Com. on Euthanasia and Assisted Suicide, 1994-95. Author: Essais sur la Constitution, 1979, Le partage des pouvoirs, 1980, 3d edit., 1983, La Constitution du Canada, 1990, 2004, Le fédéralisme au Canada, 2000, Les droits et libertés au Canada, 2000; (with others) Mécanismes pour une nouvelle Constitution, 1981; co-editor: La Charte Canadienne des droits et libertés, 3d edit., 1996, Perspectives Canadiennes et Européennes des droits de la personne, 1986; editor: The Supreme Court of Can.-La Cour suprême du Can., 1986, Charter Cases, 1986-87, Your Clients and the Charter, 1988, Vues Canadiennes et Européennes des droits et libertés, 1989, As the Charter Evolves, 1990, The Charter: Ten Years Later, 1992, (with G. Robertson et al) Federalism for the Future: Essential Reforms, 1998; mem. Thémis Law Rev., 1951-52; contbr. numerous articles to Can. and fgn. law revs. Mem. spl. com. to draft Can. Constn. in French, 1985-90. Decorated officer Order of Can., officer Legion of Honor; recipient The Ramon John Hnatyshyn award, 1997, Walter S. Tarnopolsky Human Rights award, 2002. Mem. Royal Soc. Can., Acad. des Lettres du Québec, Can. Bar Assn. (nat. chmn. sect. constl. and internat. law 1971-73, 86-87), Can. Inst. Pub. Affairs, Inst. Pub. Adminstrn. (Can.), Can. Law Deans (chmn. 1972-73), Can. Inst. Inter de Droit d'Expression Française (v.p. 1973—), Que. Law Deans (chmn. 1975-76), Internat. Assn. Comparative Law, Internat. Commn. Jurists (v.p. for Can. 1987-90, pres. for Can. 1990-92). Roman Catholic. Home: 4 rue de la Guadeloupe Gatineau PQ Canada J8Y 1L4 Fax: 819-778-1729.

BEAUDOIN, ROBERT LAWRENCE, small business owner; b. Newberry, Mich., Nov. 22, 1933; s. Leo Joseph and Edith Wilhelmina (Graunstadt) B.; m. Margaret Cecelia Linck, June 20, 1953; children: Eugene Robert, Kathleen Therese, Annette Marie, Suzanne Margaret. Student, Marquette U., 1952—53. With Fisher plant GM, 1953; dock hand State of Mich., St. Ignace, 1953; sch. bus driver Engadine (Mich.) Consol. Schs., 1957-96; owner, operator Beaudoin's Texaco, Beaudoin's Cafe, Naubinway, Mich., 1956-82, Beaudoin's Cafe and Marathon, Naubinway, 1982-83, Beaudoin's Cafe, Naubinway, 1956—. Bd. dirs. Naubinway Mchts. Inc., 1985—. Mem. Naubinway July 4th Com., 1954—; past mem. Naubinway Port commn., Garfield Twp. Planning and Zoning Commn.; vol. fireman Garfield Twp. Fire Dept., Naubinway, 1980-94; mem. recreation com. Garfield Twp. Bd., Engadine, 1983; support fellow N.G. and Res., support mem. U.S. Army Recruiting Main Sta., Detroit; mem. USAF Ground Observer Corp. Recipient Cert. of Appreciation, U.S. Army Recruiting Main Sta., Detroit, 1971, Statement of Support, N.G. and Res., 1976. Mem. NRA (life; endowment mem.); mem. Internat. Platform Assn., West Mackinac C. of C., Nat. Fedn. Ind. Bus. (adv. bd. 1971—, 20 Yr. award 1985), Am. Farmland Trust, Heritage Found., Hiawatha Sportsmans Club (bd. govs. Engadine 1965-67, 89-95, apptd. security officer 1996-98, treas. coun. 7472 1998-99), Curtis C. of C., N.Am. Hunting Club (life), Engadine Trap Shooting Club, KC (grand knight 1979-83, 99-2001, coun. 7472 Naubiway membership and program dir. East Marquette diocese 1984-88, 96-98, 2002—, dist. dep. 1988-92, supreme coun. dist. dep. 1988-92, state dir. coun. activities 1992-94, dep. grand knight coun. 7472 1995-96, 2001-2003), Handyman Club Am. (life), Nat. Home Gardening Club (life), NRA Whittington Ctr. Founders Club, N.Am. Fishing Club (life), NRA Golden Eagles, Lions (3d v.p. Engadine club 1970-71), Hiawatha Sportsmans Club, Cooking Club Am. (life), Creative Home Arts Club (life), Mich. Upper Peninsula Travel and Recreation Assn Roman Catholic. Avocations: hunting, fishing. Home: PO Box 143 Naubinway MI 49762-0143 Office: Beaudoins Cafe PO Box 143 US Hwy 2 Naubinway MI 49762 Office Phone: 906-477-6292.

BEAUFAIT, FREDERICK W(ILLIAM), retired engineering educator; b. Vicksburg, Miss., Nov. 28, 1936; s. Frank W. and Eleanor Chambliss (Haynes) B.; m. Lois Mary Erdman, Nov. 27, 1964; children: Paul Frederick, Nicole. BSc, Miss. State U., 1958; MSc, U. Ky., 1961; PhD, Va. Poly. Inst., 1965. Structural engr. U.S. Army C.E., Vicksburg, 1958-59; engr. L. E. Gregg & Assocs., Lexington, Ky., 1959-60; vis. lectr. civil engring. U. Liverpool, Eng., 1960-61; prof. civil engring. Vanderbilt U., Nashville, 1965-79; prof., chmn. dept. civil engring. W.Va. U., Morgantown, 1979-83, assoc. dean Coll. Engring., 1983-86; dean Coll. Engring. Wayne State U., Detroit, 1986-95; dir. NSF Greenfield Engring. Edn. Coalition, 1996-98; pres. NYC Coll. Tech. of the CUNY, 1999—2004; ret., 2004. Vis. prof. civil and structural engring. U. Wales, Cardiff, 1975-76; cons. in field; mem. Engring. Accreditation Commn. Accreditation Bd. for Engring. and Tech., 1988-93, Engring. Manpower Commn., 1988-92; bd. dirs. Ford (Motor) Design Inst., 1991-96. Co-author: Computer Methods of Structural Analysis, 1970; author: Basic Concepts in Structural Analysis, 1977; also over 40 articles to profl. jours. Vice chmn. stewardship com. 1st Presbyn. Ch., Morgantown, 1982, elder, 1983-85, mem. long-range planning com., 1985-86; deacon Southminster Presbyn. Ch., Nashville, 1968-69, elder, 1971-73, 78-79, clk. of session, 1971-73; bd. dirs. Presbyn. Campus Ministry, Nashville, 1972-78, treas., 1972-75, pres., 1976-78; mem. citizens adv. com. Met. Sch. System, Nashville, 1978-79; bd. dirs. Independence Cmty. Found., 2001—. Decorated chevalier Ordre des Palmes Academiques (France); named Outstanding Vol. of Yr. Mich. Ctr. for High Tech., 1991; Disting. Engring. fellow Miss. State U., 1992; named to Acad. Disting. Alumni, Dept. Civil and Environ. Engring., Va. Tech, 2004. Mem. ASCE, NSPE, Mich. Soc. Profl. Engrs. (bd. dirs. Detroit metro chpt. 1987-90, vice chmn. 1991, chmn.-elect 1992, chmn. 1993, pres. profls. in engring. edn. divsn. 1990-93, state bd. dirs., treas. 1995-97, v.p. 1997-98, Outstanding Engr. in Edn. 1994), Am. Soc. Engring. Edn. (chmn. civil engring. divsn. 1992-93, Centennial medallion 1993, George K. Wadlin award of Civil Engring. Divsn. 1994), Engring. Soc. Detroit (Coll. of Fellows 1994, gold award 1997), Order of Engrs. (bd. governance 1989-97), Chi Epsilon, Tau Alpha Pi, Tau Beta Pi. Avocations: painting, reading, travel. Home: 6 Blue Heron Dr Lewes DE 19958 Business E-Mail: fbeaufait@citytech.cuny.edu.

BEAUFORD, CARTER, musician; b. Nov. 2, 1957; s. Roland and Anne Beauford; 1 child, Breanna. Student, Shenandoah Conservatory. Elem. and H.S. tchr., NC; drummer Black Entertainment TV Show BET on Jazz, 1991—95; mem. Secrets, 1984—90; mem. (drums, percussion and vocals) Dave Matthews Band, 1991—. Musician (with Dave Matthews Band): (albums) Remember Two Things, 1993, Crash, 1996, Live at Red Rocks 8.15.95, 1997, Before These Crowded Streets, 1998, Don't Drink the Water, 1998, Everyday, 2001, Busted Stuff, 2002, Central Park Concert, 2003, Gorge, 2004; musician: Running on Ice, Vertical Horizon, 1995, Best of Columbia Records Radio Hour, Vol. 2, Various Artists, 1996, Live on Letterman: Music from the Late Show, Various Artists, 1997, Scream 2 Original Soundtrack, 1997, Yin-Yang, Victor Wooten, 1999, Zygote, John Popper, 1999, Mercury, Dawn Thompson & John d'Earth, 2001, Other Side of the Mountain: Bluegrass, Newgrass and Beyond, 2002. Recipient (with Dave Matthews Band) Grammy award for Best Rock Performance by a Duo or Group with Vocal for So Much to Say, 1996, Chmns. award, NAACP Image Awards, 2004. Office: RCA Records 1540 Broadway New York NY 10036

BEAUFORD, SANDRA, registered nurse, data processing executive; b. N.Y.C., Feb. 7, 1950; d. Ethel Beauford; children: Gary, Michael, David Sumerlin-Beauford. A.S, Manhattan C.C., 1974; BSN, Herbert H. Lehman Coll., 1976. CCRN, cert. parish nurse. Critical care mgr. Botsford Hosp., Farminington, Mich., 1990—92; asst. mgr. Henry Ford Hosp., Detroit, 1992—96; clin. mgr. Taylor Ambulance, Detroit, 1996—98; o.r. quality coord. Oakwood Hosp., Dearborn, Mich., 1999—; parish nurse Oakwood Hosp. Greater Grace Temple, Detroit, Mich., 2000—01. Author: On The Road to Your New Beginning, 2000 (Bravo award, 2001, 2002). Facilitator customer svc. enhancement program Oakwood Hosp., 2002—. Lt. USAF, 1974—78, Mclaughin Air Force Base. Mem.: Am. Heart Assn. (logistic com.), American Coll. Cardiology, Soc. Thoracic Surgeons. Pentecostal. Avocations: basketball, photography, reading. Office: 18101 Oakwood Blvd Dearborn MI 48124-4089 Personal E-mail: beaufors@oakwood.org.

BEAULIEU, RODNEY JOSEPH, academic administrator, education educator; b. Van Buren, Maine, Sept. 24, 1957; s. O'Neil and Theresa (Grivois) B. BA in Psychology, U. Mass., 1980; MA in Edn. Psychology, U. Calif., Santa Barbara, 1991, PhD in Ednl. Psychology, 1995. Ind. computer cons., Santa Barbara, 1983-90; instr. U. Calif., Santa Barbara, 1989-93, rsch. assoc., 1992—; adminstr. Fielding Grad. U., Santa Barbara, 1995—95; prof., co-founder sch. of ednl. leadership and change program, 1998—. Adj. prof. Ventura (Calif.) Coll., 1998-2000, Calif. State U., 1999—, San Marcos, 2001—. Asst. editor Phenomenology and Human Scis. Jour., 1994—97; contbr. articles to profl. jours. Vol. Women's Resource Ctr., Oceanside, Calif., 2000—. Mem. Am. Ednl. Rsch. Assn., Am. Sociol. Assn. (com. on tchg. 1994—), Pacific Sociol Assn. Avocations: painting, gardening. Home: 421 S Barnwell St Oceanside CA 92054-4510 Office Phone: 760-722-2296. Business E-Mail: rjbeaulieu@fielding.edu.

BEAUMONT, MONA, artist; b. Paris; d. Jacques Hippolyte and Elsie M. (Didisheim) Marx. m. William G. Beaumont; children: Garrett, Kevin. Postgrad., Harvard U., Fogg Mus., Cambridge, Mass. One-woman shows include Galeria Proteo, Mexico City, Gumps Gallery, San Francisco, Palace of Legion of Honor, San Francisco, L'Armitiere Gallery, Rouen, France, Hoover Gallery, San Francisco, San Francisco Mus. Modern Art, Galeria Van der Voort, San Francisco, William Sawyer Gallery, San Francisco, Palo Alto (Calif.) Cultural Ctr., Galerie Alexandre Monnet, Brussels, Honolulu Acad. Arts; group shows include San Francisco Mus. Modern Art, San Francisco Art Inst., DeYoung Meml. Mus., San Francisco, Grey Found. Tour of Asia, Bell Telephone Invitational, Chgo., Richmond Art Ctr., L.A. County Mus. Art, Galerie Zodiaque, Geneva, Galerie Le Manoir, La Chaux de Fonds, Switzerland, William Sawyer Meml. Exhibit, San Francisco, 1st Internat. Flash Art Mus. Exhbn., Trevi, Italy, 1999, Masks of Venice 2, Internat. Exhbn., 1999 (silver medalist), Masks of Venice 3 Internat. Exhbn., 2000; others; represented in permanent collections Oakland (Calif.) Mus. Art, City and County of San Francisco, Hoover Found., San Francisco, Grey Found., Washington, Bulart Found., San Francisco; also numerous pvt. collections; invited artist Internat. Biennale 3, Florence, Italy, 2001. Mem. Soc. for Encouragement of Contemporary Art, Bay Area Graphic Art Coun., San Francisco Art Inst., San Francisco Mus. Modern Art, Capp Street Project, San Diego Mus. Contemporary Art, L.A. Mus. Contemporary Art. Recipient ann. painting award Jack London Square, 2 ann. awards San Francisco Women Artists, One-man Show award San Francisco Art Festival; purchase award Grey Found., San Francisco Women Artists (2), San Francisco Art Festival; included in Printworld Internat., Internat. Art Diary, Am. Artists, N.Y. Art Rev., Calif. Art Rev., Art in San Francisco Bay Area. Address: 11785 River Rim Rd San Diego CA 92126-1148

BEAUMONT, PAMELA JO, marketing professional; b. Valentine, Nebr., July 30, 1944; d. William Henry and Phyllis Faye (Zersen) (Mott) Bostrom; m. Fred H. Beaumont, Apr. 17, 1971 (div. May 1981). BS in Bus., U. Colo., 1966, MBA, 1968. Asst. product mgr. Ore-Ida Foods, Boise, Idaho, 1969-71, product mgr., 1971-73, sr. product mgr., 1973-75, gen. mgr. sales and mktg. services, 1975; v.p. consumer affairs Albertson's Inc., Boise, 1975-76, v.p. mktg., 1976-87; ptnr. Forrest/Beaumont & Andrus, Boise, 1987—; chair Garden City Urban Renewal Agy., 1995—. Home: 9304 N Pebble Falls Ln Boise ID 83714 Office: 4948 Kootenai St Ste 201 Boise ID 83705-2082 E-mail: pamb@spro.net.

BEAUPREZ, BOB, congressman; b. Lafayette, Colo., Sept. 22, 1948; m. Claudia Beauprez; 4 children. BS, U. Colo., 1970. Ptnr. Boulder Valley Holsteins, Lafayette, Colo., 1970-89; pres. Indian Peaks, Inc., Lafayette, Colo., 1989—; pres., CEO, chmn. Heritage Bank, Louisville, 1990—; state chmn. Rep. State Ctrl. Com. of Colo., 1999—2002; mem. U.S. Ho. Reps. from 7th Colo. dist., 2003—; mem. com. on Ways and Means. Pres. Ind. Bankers Colo., 1997-98, chmn. 1998, bd. dirs. 1993-99; vice chmn., policy devel. com. Ind. Com. Bankers of Am., 2000-; mem. Rep. Nat. Com. Western State Chmn. Assn., 1999—. Republican. Office: 504 Cannon Ho Office Bldg Washington DC 20515-0607

BEAUREGARD, LUC, public relations executive; b. Montreal, Que., Can., Aug. 4, 1941; s. Francois and Gertrude Beauregard; m. Michelle Beauregard; children: Valérie, Stéphanie, Francois, Philippe. BA, Coll. Stanislas, Montreal. Reporter, parliamentary corr. in Ottawa, city editor Montreal (Que.) Daily La Presse, Can., 1961-68; press sec. Que. Minister Edn., Quebec City, Que., 1968-69; founding ptnr. Beauregard, Landry, Nantel & Assocs. Pub.

Rels. Cons., Montreal; pres., pub. Montreal-Matin Daily Newspaper, 1973-76; chmn., CEO Nat. Pub. Rels., Inc., Montreal, 1976—. Chmn. Amarc, City of Montreal Corp. managing Man and His World (formerly Expo '67), 1982-86. Chmn. Montreal Better Bus. Bur., 1983—84; mem. exec. com. Montreal Mus. Contemporary Art, 1986—97, chmn., 1987—90. Found. Montreal Island Sch. Coun., 1991—97; gov. Conseil du Patronat du Que., 1992—; sec. info. commn. Que. Liberal Party, 1978—79; bd. dirs. Can. C. of C., Nouvelle Compagnie Theatrale, 1984—94, Que. Heart Found., 1983—85; bd. dirs., adv. bd. Montreal Neurological Inst. Decorated mem. Order of Can.; recipient Philip A. Novikoff award Can. Pub. Rels. Soc. Fellow Can. Pub. Rels. soc. (pres. 1984-85, chmn. Cons. Inst. 1982-83); mem. Am. Pub. Rels. Coun. (chmn. 1985-86), Can. C. of C. (bd. dirs., exec. com.), Club des Quinze, Mt. Royal Club, St. Denis Club, Knowlton Golf Club. Avocation: golf. Office: Nat Pub Rels 2001 McGill Coll Ave Ste 800 Montreal PQ Canada H3A 1G1 E-mail: lbeauregard@national.ca.

BEAUREGARD, PHILIP N., lawyer, educator; b. New Bedford, Mass., July 30, 1944; s. R. Albert Beauregard and Adrienne Champagne; m. Kate Harrison; children: Pierre, Philip, Adrienne. Student, Carnegie Inst. Tech., 1962—65; BA, U. Notre Dame, 1967; JD, Georgetown U., 1972. Assoc. Desmarais & Carey, New Bedford, Mass., 1972—76; city solicitor City of New Bedford, 1979—80; owner Beauregard Burke, New Bedford, 1980—. Adj. prof. So. New Eng. Law Sch., Dartmouth, Mass., 2003. Contbr. sects. to books. V.p. Port Soc., New Bedford, 2001—02; pres. bd. dirs. Coalition for Buzzards Bay, New Bedford, 1998—99. With U.S. Army, 1969—71. Home: One Clinton Pl New Bedford MA 02740 Office: Law Offices Beauregard Burke & Franco PO Box 952 32 William St New Bedford MA 02741 E-mail: bbf.robeson@verizon.net, andrew.robeson@verizon.net.

BEAUREGARD, RAYMOND A., mathematician, educator; b. New Bedford, Mass., Feb. 10, 1943; s. R. Albert and Adrienne Beauregard; m. Barbara A. Beauregard, Apr. 4, 1964; children: Jacqueline Robbins, David, Stephen. BA, Providence Coll., 1964; MS, U. N.H., 1966, PhD, 1968. Prof. Math. U. R.I., Kingston, 1968—. Author (textbook): Linear Algebra, 1995; contbr. articles and referee for profl. jours. Mem.: Math. Assn. Am. Home: 28 Beechwood Hill Trl Exeter RI 02822 Office: Dept Math Univ Rhode Island Kingston RI 02881

BEAUSOLEIL, DORIS MAE, federal agency housing specialist; b. Chelmsford, Mass., Jan. 9, 1932; d. Joseph Honorious and Beatrice Pearl (Smith) Beausoleil. Student, State Tchrs. Coll., Lowell, Mass., 1949-51; BA in Sociology and Psychology, Goddard Coll., Plainfield, Vt., 1954; MA in Human Rels., NYU, 1957; postgrad., CUNY, N.Y.C., 1988-97. With divsn. human rights State of N.Y., N.Y.C., 1960-69, housing dir., 1966-68; housing cons. Nat. Com. Against Discrimination Housing, N.Y.C., 1969—70, Edwin Gould Found., N.Y.C., 1970—71; human resources cons. interfaith housing strategy com., housing cons. Fedn. Prot. Welfare Agys., Inc., N.Y.C., 1971—72; housing cons., 1972—74; equal opportunity compliance specialist N.Y./N.J. HUD, N.Y.C., 1975—2000, fed. women's program coord., 1975—79, pub. trust specialist, 2000—. Br. chief Title VI Sect. 109 compliance divsn. fair housing and equal opportunity region II HUD, N.Y.C., 1979—84, coord. sect. III N.Y./N.J., 1998—. Mem. adv. panel Housing Mag., 1979. Founding mem. N.Y. State HUD Com.; cons., examiner N.Y. State Civil Svc. Commn., 1970—93; bd. dirs. Nat. Assn. Human Rights Workers, 1974—77. Mem.: Citizens Housing and Planning Coun., Goddard Coll. Alumni Assn. (sec. 1988—90), Rep. Bus. Women's Club (pres. 1985—88, bd. dirs. 1989—91). Unitarian Universalist. Home: 392 Central Park W Apt 14N New York NY 10025-5868 Office: 26 Federal Plz Rm 3532 New York NY 10278-0004 Office Phone: 212-542-7533. E-mail: doris_m._beausoleil@hud.gov.

BEAUZAY, VICTOR H(ILTON), lawyer; b. Waverly, N.Y., Mar. 28, 1924; s. Eugene Louis and Edith (Peet) B.; m. JoEllen, Apr. 17, 1946; children: Victor H. II, Victoria Ellen Beauzay. Student, Syracuse U., 1947; AB in Polit. Sci., Stanford U., 1948, JD, 1951. Bar: Calif. 1952, U.S. Supreme Ct. 1957. Pvt. practice law, San Jose. Lectr. in workers' compensation law; chmn. Workers' Compensation Adv. Commn., Calif. State Bar Specialization Program; exec. com. State BarCalif., conf. of dels. 1984-87. Served with U.S. Army, 1943-46. Recipient Golden Banana award P & L Seminar Soc., 1979, Gene Marias Lifetime Achievement award. Mem. Santa Clara County Bar Assn. (pres. 1981), Calif. Applicants Attys. Assn. (pres. 1968-69, chmn. legis. com. 1968-71). Clubs: Century (pres.), Masons (San Jose).

BEAVER, BONNIE VERYLE, veterinarian, educator; b. Mpls., Oct. 26, 1944; d. Crawford F. and Gladys I. Gustafson; m. Larry J. Beaver, Nov. 25, 1972 (dec. Nov. 1995). BS, U. Minn., 1966, DVM, 1968; MS, Tex. A&M U., 1972. Instr. vet. surgery and radiology U. Minn., 1968-69; instr. vet. anatomy Tex. A&M U., College Station, 1969-72, asst. prof., 1972-76, assoc. prof., 1976-82; prof. Tex A&M U., College Station, 1982-86, prof. vet. small animal medicine and surgery, 1986—, chief medicine, 1990-99. Mem. vet. medicine adv. com. HEW, 1972-74, nat. adv. food and drug com., HEW, 1975, com. on animal models and genetic stocks NAS, 1984-86, 87-89, panel on microlivestock NRC, 1986-87, task force on animal use study Inst. Lab. Animal Resources, 1986, adv. com. for Pew Nat. Vet. Edn. Program, Pew Charitable Trusts, 1987-92, 10th symposium on Vet. Med. Edn. Com., 1988-89; Frank K. Ramsey lects. Iowa State U., 2004. Mem. editl. bd. Applied Animal Ethology, 1981-82, 83-84, VM/SAC, 1982-85, Applied Animal Behavior Sci., 1982-84, 84-86, 86-88, 88-2000, Bull. on Vet. Clin. Ethology, 1994-1999, Jour. Am. Animal Hosp. Assn., 1995—, Jour. Vet. Behavior: Clin. Applications and Rsch., 2005—; contbr. articles to profl. jours. V.p. Brazos Valley Regional Sci. and Engring. Fair, 1974—83, dir., 1983—85; bd. dirs. Brazos Valley unit Am. Cancer Soc., 1976—83, v.p., 1976—83. Named Citizen of Week, The Press, 1981, Outstanding Woman Vet. of 1982, Disting. Practitioner, Nat. Acads. Practice; recipient Friskies PetCare award Am. Animal Hosp. Assn., 2001, Bustad Human-Animal Bond award, 2001, Elanco Disting. Lectr. award, 2002, Frank K. Ramsey Lectr. award, 2004. Mem.: AVMA (exec. bd. 1997—, chair exec. bd. 2001—02, pres.-elect 2003—04, pres. 2004—05, immediate past pres. 2005—, Animal Welfare award 1996), AAAS, Am. Horse Coun., Am. Quarter Horse Assn., Tex. Palomino Exhibitors Assn., Palomino Horse Breeders Am. (v.p. 1983—88, treas. 1984—85, pres.-elect 1988—89, pres. 1989—90), Nat. Acad. Practice, Am. Coll. Vet. Behaviorists (chair organizing com. 1976—91, pres. 1991—96, charter diplomate 1993—, exec. dir. 1996—), Animal Behavior Soc., Am. Assn. Bovine Practitioners, Am. Assn. Equine Practitioners, Am. Assn. Vet. Clinicians, Am. Vet. Soc. Animal Behavior (pres. 1975—80), Am. Animal Hosp. Assn., Brazos Valley Vet. Med. Assn., Tex. Vet. Med. Assn. (3d v.p. 1990, 2d v.p. 1991, 1st v.p. 1992, pres.-elect 1993, pres. 1994), Phi Delta Gamma (pres. 1974—75), Phi Zeta (nat. pres. 1979—81), Sigma Epsilon Sigma, Phi Sigma, Delta Soc. Office: Tex A&M Univ Coll Vet Medicine Vet Small Animal Medicine & Surgery College Station TX 77843-4474

BEAVER, CARL R., marine scientist, educator, consultant; s. Robert and Phyllis Beaver; m. Robinn Crawford, Mar. 23, 2001; 1 child, Jennifer. BS, Corpus Christi State U.; MS, Tex. A&M U., Corpus Christi; D of Wildlife and Fisheries Sci., Tex. A&M U., College Station. Rsch. assoc. Ctr. for Coastal Studies, Corpus Christi, 1993—2000; prof. Our Lady of Corpus Christi Coll., 2001—03; postdoctoral rsch. assoc. Harte Rsch. Inst. for Gulf of Mex. Sci., Corpus Christi, 2002—03; assoc. rsch. scientist Fish & Wildlife Rsch. Inst., St. Petersburg, Fla., 2003—. Chief scientist Eco-Tones, Riverview, Fla., 1999—. Author: State of the Coral Reefs of the World, Fisheries, Reefs and Offshore Development. Mem. Sci. Diving Control Bd., Tex. State Aquarium, Corpus Christi, 2000—04. Mem.: Am. Fisheries Soc. (assoc.), Am. Assn. Underwater Scientists (assoc.). Office: Fish & Wildlife Rsch Inst 100 8th Ave SE Saint Petersburg FL 33701 Office Phone: 727-896-8626. E-mail: carl.beaver@myfwc.com.

BEAVER, FRANK EUGENE, critic, historian; b. Cleve., N.C., July 26, 1938; s. John Whitfield and Mary Louise (Shell) B.; m. Gail Frances Place, June 30, 1962; children: Julia Clare, John Francis, Johanna Louise. BA, U. N.C., 1960, MA, 1966; PhD, U. Mich., 1970. Instr. speech Memphis State U., 1965-66; instr. radio-TV-motion pictures U. N.C., Chapel Hill, 1966-68; asst. prof. speech comm. U. Mich., Ann Arbor, 1969-74, assoc. prof., 1974-79, assoc. prof. comm., 1979-84, prof., chmn. dept. comm., 1987-91, Arthur F. Thurnau prof., 1989-92, dir. grad. program in telecom. arts and film, 1991-96. Advisor Muskegon (Mich.) Film Festival, 2001. Film critic radio Stas. WUOM, WVGR, WFUM, Ann Arbor, Grand Rapids, Mich., 1975-97; author: Bosley Crowther, 1974, On Film, 1983, Dictionary of Film Terms, 1983, 94 (Mandarin-Chinese translation 1993), Oliver Stone: Wakeup Cinema, 1994, 100 Years of American Film, 2001; writer, dir. documentary film Under One Roof, 1967; editor (book series) Framing Film, Peter Lang, Pub., N.Y., 1998—; commentator Mich. Today-News-e, 2004—. Bd. dirs. Mich. Theater Found., Ann Arbor, 1977-79, 86—; alumni adv. bd. Lambda Chi Alpha, Ann Arbor, 1989-94; advisor Ann Arbor Film Festival, 1975—. With M.I. Corps, U.S. Army, 1962-65, Vietnam. Recipient Playwriting award Carolina Playmakers, 1962, Major Hopwood writing awards for drama and essays U. Mich., 1969, Outstanding Tchg. award Amoco Found., Ann Arbor, 1985; fellow NEH, 1975. Mem.: Speech Comm. Assn., Soc. Cinema Scholars, Racquet Club, Azazels Club, Phi Kappa Phi, Kappa Tau Alpha. Democrat. Roman Catholic. Home: 1050 Wall St #2F Ann Arbor MI 48105 Office: U Mich Film and Video Studies 2512 Frieze Bldg Ann Arbor MI 48109-1285 Business E-Mail: fbeaver@umich.edu.

BEAVER, HILARY A., medical educator, ophthalmologist; b. Manhattan, N.Y., Oct. 4, 1965; BS in Biology, Coll. William and Mary, Williamsburg, Va., 1987; MD, U. Va., 1991. Intern Baylor Coll. Medicine, Houston, 1991—92, resident in ophthalmology, 1992—95, clin. instr. dept. ophthamology, 1995—98, clin. asst. prof., 1998—2000; asst. prof. Univ. Iowa Hosps. and Clinics, Iowa City, 2000—. Mem. Task Force on Aging Com., 2001—03. Contbr. articles to profl. jours. Recipient Janet M. Glasgow Meml. Achievement citation, U. Va. Sch. Medicine, 1991, Physicians Recognition award, AMA, 1997—2000. Mem.: Am. Acad. Ophthalmology (subcom. basic and clin. sci. course sect. 2 2003—, com. on aging 2003—), Am. Soc. Cataract and Refractive Surgery, Iowa Med. Soc., Iowa Acad. Ophthalmology. Office: Univ Iowa Hosps and Clinics Dept Ophthalmology 200 Hawkins Dr Iowa City IA 52242 Office Phone: 319-356-8118.

BEAVERS, KAREN MARJORIE, small business owner; b. Laurel, Md., Nov. 2, 1947; d. James Walter and Marjorie Lois (Fullerton) McQuaid; m. George Edward Kowalski, Aug. 30, 1969 (div.); children: Eddie, Charlie, Bill; m. Edward George Beavers Jr., Feb. 14, 1991; stepchild, Edward. Student, Art Instrn. Sch., 1970; BS in Behavioral Sci., U. Md., 1994; postgrad., Loyola Coll., 1995. Receptionist Capitol Software, Laurel, 1988-89; new accounts devel. staff Focus Telecom., Burtonsville, Md., 1989-90; CSR & tng. asst. Encore Mktg. Internat., Lanham, Md., 1990-91; office mgr. Computer Image Svc., Laurel, 1991-94; pres., owner Gifts & More, Laurel, 1994-95, Gifts & More, Inc., Laurel, 1993-2000. Author: Tippy and Freckles Great Adventures, 1996; The Development of Children's Behavior, several theories of parenting, author of poetry. Hot-line counselor Domestic Violence Ctr., Howard County, Md., 1993-94; vol. art tchr., playground and lunchroom staff St. Marys of the Mills, Laurel; team mother Prince George Gymnastics, Beltsville, Md.; actress Ann Martin's Drama Guild, Laurel. Mem. APA (grad. affiliate), AAUW, Internat. Soc. Poets, Psi Chi. Roman Catholic. Avocations: gardening, doll collecting, antique shopping.

BEAVERS, ROY LACKEY, retired utilities executive, volunteer, writer; b. Joplin, Mo., Apr. 24, 1930; s. Roy L. Sr. and Margarette Nellie (Loughlin) B.; m. Valerie Evelyn Gurney; children: Leslie Anne, Brendan G. BS in Bus., U. Mo., 1952; MA in Polit. Sci., U. Md., 1970. Commd. ens. USN, 1952, advanced through grades to comdr., 1966, retired, 1972; agt., broker ins. agy., Lebanon, Mo., 1972-77; field rep. Nat. Rural Electric Coop. Assn., Washington, 1977-84; mgr. pub. info. and legis. liaison wholesale power coop. KAMO Power, Vinita, Okla., 1984-93. With SALT I strategic arms negotiations U.S. Arms Control Disarmament Agy., 1970—72; moderator internet discussion list EMF, 1995—. Contbr. polit. and mil. essays to newspapers and other publs. including An Absence of Accountability (U.S. policy failure in Vietnam), 1976. State hdqrs. dir. Va. Com. to Re-elect Nixon, Richmond, Va., 1972; mem. Bd. Mo. Cmty. Betterment Edn. Fund, 1990-93, Bd. Okla. Acad. for State Goals, 1990-93. Decorated Bronze, Silver, and Gold medals U.S. Naval Inst., Pres. Merit Svc. medal, Navy Commendation medal Mem. U.S. Naval Inst., Bioelectromagnetics Soc. Home: Lake Shore Estates 26555 Gene Dr Lebanon MO 65536-5776 Personal E-mail: avolinch@earthlink.net. Business E-Mail: roy@emfguru.org.

BEAZLEY, HAMILTON, writer, educator; b. Houston, Dec. 21, 1943; s. Hamilton and Marjorie Beazley. BA, Yale U., 1966; MBA, So. Meth. U., 1977; PhD, George Washington U., 1998. Founder/exec. com. DyChem Internat. (U.K.) Ltd., Dallas, London, 1970-73; oil and gas industry exec., 1970—80; strategic planning cons. Houston, 1980-88; pres. Nat. Coun. on Alcoholism and Drug Dependence, N.Y.C., 1988-90; assoc. prof. orgnl. scis. George Washington U., 1999—2002; scholar-in-residence St. Edward's U., Austin, Tex., 2003—. Co-creator TV series, BBC, Secrets Out, 1984-87; co-author: (with Bishop Payne) Reclaiming the Great Commission, 2000; author: No Regrets, 2004; co-author: Continuity Management, 2002; co-editor: The Servant-Leader Within, 2003; mem. editl. bd. Internat. Jour. Servant-Leadership. Bd. dirs. Total World Corp., Houston, 1985-97; bd. trustees Ednl. Advancement Found., 1996—; mem. adv. bd. divsn. on addictions Harvard Med. Sch., 1994-98. Mem. Am. Psychol. Assn., Acad. of Mgmt., Yale Club of N.Y.C. Republican. Episcopalian. Avocation: sailing. Home: 411 W St Elmo # 24 Austin TX 78745

BEBCHUK, LUCIAN ARYE, law educator, finance educator; b. Dec. 4, 1955; m. Alma Cohen; children: Alon, Yonatan. BA in Math. and Economics, summa cum laude, U. Haifa, Israel, 1977; LLB magna cumlaude, U. Tel-Aviv Sch. Law, 1979; LLM, Harvard Law Sch., 1980, SJD, 1984; MA in Economics, Harvard U., 1992, PhD in Economics, 1993. Asst. prof. Harvard Law Sch., Cambridge, 1986—88, prof. law, 1988—94, prof. law, economics, and fin., 1994—98, William J. Friedman & Alicia Townsend Friedman prof. law, economics, and fin., 1998—, dir. program on corp. governance, 2003—. Vis. sr. prof. by spl. appointment Tel-Aviv U., 1994—; rsch. assoc. Nat. Bur. Econ. Rsch., Cambridge, 1995—; vis. prof. Tilburg U., Netherlands, 2001; bd. dirs. John M. Olin Ctr. for Law, Economics, and Bus. Harvard Law Sch. Co-author (with Jesse Fried): Pay Without Performance, 2004. Guggenheim Found. Fellow, 2004—05. Fellow: European Corp. Goverance Inst. (inaugural), Centre for Econ. Policy Rsch.; mem.: Am. Assn Law and Economics (bd. dirs. 1997—99), Am. Assn. Law Schools (chair bus. associations sect. 1999—2000), Am. Acad. Arts and Sciences. Office: Harvard Law Sch 1545 Massachusetts Ave Cambridge MA 02138 Office Phone: 617-495-3138. Office Fax: 617-496-3119. Business E-Mail: bebchuk@law.harvard.edu.

BEBER, ROBERT H., lawyer, diversified financial services company executive; b. N.Y.C., Aug. 17, 1933; s. Morris and Martha (Pollock) B.; m. Joan Parsons, June 14, 1957; children: Andrea, Judith, Deborah. AB in Econs, Duke U., 1955, JD, 1957. Bar: N.Y., N.C. With Everett, Everett & Everett, N.C., 1957-58; atty. SBA, Washington, 1961-63; with RCA, 1963-81; sr. v.p., gen. counsel, sec. GAF Corp., N.Y.C., 1981-83, exec. v.p., dir., 1983-84, dir. subs.; sr. v.p., gen. counsel, sec. Phlcorp, Inc. (formerly Baldwin United Corp.), Phila., 1984-88; asst. gen. counsel litigation W.R. Grace & Co., N.Y.C., 1988-89, v.p., dir. litigation, 1989-91, sr. v.p., gen. counsel, 1991-93, exec. v.p., 1993-98, ret., 1999, cons., 1999—. Bd. dirs. Advantage Bank. Bd. vis. Sch. Law, Duke U., 1996—; chmn. bd. Health Care Plan N.J., 1975-78; v.p. South Jersey C. of C., 1974-77; dir. Advantage Bank, Palm Beach, Fla., 1999-2003. Served with U.S. Army, 1958-61. Mem. ABA. Republican. Jewish. Home: 7228 Queenferry Cir Boca Raton FL 33496-5953 Office: WR Grace & Co 5400 Broken Sound Blvd NW Boca Raton FL 33487-3511 Personal E-mail: dhb11682@yahoo.com.

BEBO, JOSEPH ANTHONY, counselor, educator; b. Boston, Dec. 31, 1954; s. John Thomas and Leah B.; m. Frances Gail Coker, Oct. 10, 1978 (dec. Aug. 1988); children: Joseph Anthony Jr., John James; m. Patricia Ann Bebo. BA, U. Mass., 1976, MA in Sociology, 1996, postgrad. in edn., 1999—. Cert. substance abuse counselor Mass. Bd. Counselor Certification; lic. alcohol & drug counselor Mass., 2004. Substance abuse counselor Sullivan House Middlesex Human Svcs., Jamaica Plain, Mass., 1993—99; program coord. alcohol and substance abuse studies cert. and grad. cert. forensci svcs. Coll. Arts and Sci. criminal justic program U. Mass., Boston, 1997—99; lectr. U. Mass, 1999—, Rivier Coll., 1999—2000, Fitchburg State Coll., 1999—2001; alcohol and drug counselor Addiction Treatment Ctr. NE, Brighton, 2000—02; vis. lectr. Bridgewater State Coll., 2001—, Massasoit CC, 2002—. Treas. Internat. Coalition Addictions Studies Educators, 2000—, convention coord., 2000, 02, 04; alcohol and drug counselor Divsn. Youth Svcs., Phoenix Ctr., Brockton YMCA, Plymouth County Correctional Facility. Contbr. articles to profl. jours. Recipient Cert. Appreciation, Higher Edn. Ctr. Mem.: Acad. Criminal Justice Scis., Nat. Assn. Alcohol and Drug Abuse Counselors, Northeastern Assn. Criminal Justice Scis. (contbr. criminal justice edn. task force), Am. Soc. Criminology, Alpha Kappa Delta. Office: U Mass 100 Morrissey Blvd Boston MA 02125 Office Phone: 877-347-7663. E-mail: joseph.bebo@hotmail.com.

BEBOUT, ELI DANIEL, oil industry executive; b. Rawlings, Wyo., Oct. 14, 1946; s. Hugh and Dessie Bebout; m. Lorraine J. Tavares; children: Jordan, Jentry, Reagen, Taggert. BEE, U. Wyo., 1969. With U.S. Energy Co., Riverton, Wyo., 1974-75; field engr. Am. Bechtel Corp., Green River, Wyo., 1975-76; pres. NUPEC Resources, Inc., Riverton, 1976-83, Smith-Collins Pharm. Inc., Riverton, 1976-83; cons. Nucor Inc., Riverton, 1984—2004; v.p. Nucor Drilling, Inc., Riverton, 1987—2001; state legislator Wyo. Assembly; pres. Nucor Oil & Gas, 1993—2004. Past chmn. Wyo. Bus. Alliance; Wyo. Heritage Found.; former mem., mem. rules com. mgmt. coun., majority floor leader, spkr. Wyo. Ho. of Reps.; past chmn. Energy Coun. Republican. Office: Nucor Inc PO Box 112 Riverton WY 82501-0112

BECCALLI, FERDINANDO, manufacturing executive; b. Italy; M in chem. engring., Polytechnic of Torino, Italy; grad. work in bus. admin., Xavier Univ., Cin. Joined G.E.'s strategic planning group G.E. European Hdqs., Bergen op Zoom, Netherlands, 1977; mgmt. positions in splty. plastics, NORYL ® resin, LEXAN ® resin and mktg. div. G.E. Plastics Hdqs., Pittsfield, Mass., 1981; dir. of G.E. European Hdqs., Bergen op Zoom, Netherlands, 1987; mng. dir. SPE, 1990; pres. G.E. Plastics, Japan Ltd., 1993—96; v.p. gen. mgr. G.E. Plastics, Am., 1997—2001; exec. v.p. G.E. Capital Svc., 2001—02; pres., CEO, G.E. Europe G.E. Electric Co., 2002—. Office: General Electric Co 3135 Easton Turnpike Fairfield CT 06828-0001*

BECCATELLI, THERESA CECILIA, secondary school educator; b. Norristown, Pa., Nov. 10, 1949; d. Joseph F. Jr. and Elsie M. (Caruso) Decker; m. John J. Beccatelli, June 27, 1987; 1 child, Anne Marie Foley. AA, Community Coll. Phila., 1969; BS, Ea. Ky. U., 1972; MEd, Temple U., 1975, EdD, 1986. Cert. tchr., Pa. Tchr. Sch. Dist. Phila., 1972-90. Math. instr. Community Coll. Phila., 1979-82. CCD tchr., 1995-2002. Mem. Assn. of Tchrs. of Math. Phila., Kappa Delta Pi. Roman Catholic. Avocations: playing piano, songwriting, poetry, gardening. E-mail: tbecc@aol.com.

BECCHETTI, FREDERICK DANIEL, JR., physicist, researcher; b. Mpls., Mar. 3, 1943; s. Frederick Daniel and Olga Maxine Becchetti. BS, U. Minn., 1965, MS, 1968, PhD, 1969. Research assoc. Niels Bohr Inst., Copenhagen, 1969-71; research assoc. Lawrence Berkeley Lab., Calif., 1971-73; asst. prof. U. Mich., Ann Arbor, 1973-76, assoc. prof., 1976-82, prof. physics, 1982—. Contbr. articles to profl. jours. NSF fellow, 1970-71. Fellow Am. Phys. Soc.; mem. IEEE, Am. Assn. Physicists Tchrs., Am. Assn. Physicists in Medicine. Democrat. Roman Catholic.

BECERRA, ROBERT JOHN, lawyer; b. Jersey City, Jan. 26, 1962; s. Joseph Hercules and Blanche (Rosado) B.; m. Christiana Marie Carroll, Oct. 30, 1993. BBA, U. Miami, 1986, JD, 1990. Bar: Fla. 1990, U.S. Dist. Ct. (so. and mid dists.) Fla. 1991, U.S. Ct. Appeals (11th cir.) 1991, U.S. Dist. Ct. (ea. dist.) Mich. 1994, U.S. Ct. Appeals (3d cir.) 1997, U.S. Supreme Ct. 1994, U.S. Ct. Appeals (2d cir.) 2003. Assoc. Raskin & Raskin, Miami, Fla., 1990-96, ptnr., 1997—2004; sr. assoc. Sandler, Travis & Rosenberg, Miami, 2004—. Mem. Fed. Bar Assn., Dade County Bar Assn. (fed. cts. com., Certificate of Merit 1993), Phi Kappa Phi. Democrat. Roman Catholic. Avocations: sailplane pilot, scuba diving, boating, skiing. Office: Sandler Travis & Rosenberg 5200 Blue Lagoon Dr 600 Miami FL 33126 Office Phone: 305-267-9200. Personal E-mail: rbecerra@strtrade.com.

BECERRA, ROSINA MADELINE, social welfare educator; b. San Diego, Mar. 6, 1939; d. Ray and Ruth (Albanez) B. BA, San Diego State U., 1961, MSW, 1971; PhD, Brandeis U., 1975; MBA, Pepperdine U., 1981. Mathematician United Tech. Corp., Sunnyvale, Calif., 1962-63; with Peace Corps, Washington, 1963-65; probation officer San Diego County Probation Office, 1965-69; research assoc. Brandeis U., Waltham, Mass., 1973-75; assoc. prof. UCLA, 1975-81, prof., 1981—, acting dean, 1989-90, assoc. dean, 1986-89, 92, dean, 1992—, assoc. vice chancellor faculty diversity, 2002—. Author: Defining Child Abuse, 1979, Hispanic Veterans Seek Health Care, 1982, The Hispanic Elderly, 1984 (Choice Mag. Book award 1986); editor: Hispanic Mental Health, 1981; contbr. articles to profl. jours. Ford Found. award, 1980.

BECERRA, XAVIER, congressman, lawyer; b. Sacramento, Jan. 26, 1958; s. Manuel and Maria Teresa B.; m. Carolina Reyes, 1987. BA in Economics, Stanford U., 1980, JD, 1984. Atty., 1984—; dir. dist. office State Senator Art Torres, L.A.; dep. atty. gen. dept. justice, Calif., 1987-90; assemblyman, 59th dist. State of Calif., 1990-93; mem. U.S. Congress from 30th Calif. dist., 1993—. Mem. Ways and Means com.; chmn. Congl. Hispanic Caucus. Mem. Mexican-Am. Bar Assn., Calif. Bar Assn., Assn. Calif. State Attys. and Adminstrv. Law Judges. Democrat. Avocations: reading, carpentry, golf. Office: US Ho of Reps 1119 Longworth Bldg Washington DC 20515-0530 also: Dist Office 1910 Sunset Blvd Ste 560 Los Angeles CA 90026*

BECERRA-FERNANDEZ, IRMA, electrical engineer, researcher, educator; b. Havana, Cuba, Mar. 28, 1960; came to U.S., 1960; d. Daniel Ivan Becerra and Irma Maria Peiteado; m. Vicente L. Fernandez, June 29, 1985; children: Anthony John, Nicole Marie. BSEE, U. Miami, Coral Gables, Fla., 1982, MSEE, 1986; PhDEE, Fla. Internat. U., Miami, 1994. Cert. engr. in tng., Fla., 1982. Engr., corp. instr. Fla. Power and Light, Miami, 1983-90; rsch. assoc. Fla. Internat. U., Miami, 1990—94, dir., vis. prof. Coll. Engring., 1994—98, asst. prof. Coll. Bus. Adminstrn., 1998—2003, assoc. prof., 2003—. Scholar Nat. Hispanic Scholarship Fund, Miami, 1982, Unico Nat. Soc., Miami, 1978; Women's History Month honoree Coalition Hispanic Am. Women, 1997. Mem. IEEE, Assn. Cuban Engrs. (v.p. 1994-96, pres. 1996, Student of Yr. 1993, faculty advisor), Soc. Women Engrs. (faculty advisor), Eta Kappa Nu (v.p. 1981-82, Most Valuable Mem. 1982), Tau Beta Pi, Phi Kappa Phi. Roman Catholic.

BECH, DOUGLAS YORK, retired lawyer, resort executive; b. Seattle, Aug. 18, 1945; s. Albert Richard and Vera Evelyn (Peterson) B.; m. Sheryl Annette Tucker, Aug. 9, 1968; children: Kristen Elizabeth, Allison York. BA, Baylor U., 1967; JD, U. Tex., 1970. Bar: Tex. 1970, N.Y. 1993. Ptnr. Andrews & Kurth, Houston, 1970-93, Akin, Gump, Strauss, Hauer & Feld, 1994-97; mng. dir. Raintree Capital Co., Houston, 1994—. Chmn., CEO Raintree Resorts Internat., Inc., Club Regina Resorts, Inc.; bd. dirs. Frontier Oil, Pride Cos., J2 Global Comm. Sgt. USAR, 1968-74. Republican. Baptist. Avocations: running, snowskiing, travel, big game hunting, golf. Office: Raintree Resorts Internat 10000 Memorial Dr Ste 480 Houston TX 77024-3409 E-mail: dybech@raintreeresotrs.com.

BECHAMPS, GERALD JOSEPH, surgeon; b. Flushing, N.Y., 1937; MD, Georgetown U., 1963. Diplomate Am. Bd. Surgery. Intern Meadowbrook Hosp., East Meadow, N.Y., 1963-64, resident in surgery, 1964-65; fellow surgery Mayo Clinic-Found., Rochester, 1965-69; clin. instr. U.Va. Sch. Medicine, 1971; pvt. practice Winchester Surg. Clinic, Ltd., 1971—; asst. clin. prof. Va. Commonwealth U., 2003—. Past pres. Fedn. State Med. Bds. of U.S.; surgeon Winchester Med. Ctr., Surgi-Ctr. of Winchester; mem. Va.

State Bd. Medicine, pres., 1985-86, 87-88. Mem. ACS (past pres. Va. chpt.), So. Soc. Clin. Surgeons. Office: Winchester Surg Clinic Ltd PO Box 2698 Winchester VA 22604-1898 Fax: 540-722-4515. Office Phone: 540-662-0377.

BECHER, WILLIAM DON, retired electrical engineer, engineering educator, writer; b. Bolivar, Ohio, Nov. 26, 1929; s. William and Eva Vernette (Richardson) Becher; m. Helen Norma Hager, Aug. 31, 1950; children: Eric Alan, Patricia Lynn. BS in Radio Engring., Tri-State U., 1950; MSEE, U. Mich., 1961, PhD, 1968. Registered profl. engr., Mich., N.J. Project engr. Bogue Electric, Paterson, NJ, 1950-53; sr. devel. engr. Goodyear Aircraft Corp., Akron, Ohio, 1953-57; sr. systems engr. Beckman Instruments, Fullerton, Calif., 1957-58; engring. supr. Bendix Aerospace Systems, Ann Arbor, Mich., 1958-63; rsch. engr. U. Mich., Ann Arbor, 1963-68, adj. prof. elec. engring., 1978-79, 81-94, lectr. elec. engring. Dearborn, 1964-68, prof. elec. engring., 1968-78, chmn., 1971-76; engring. dept. mgr. Environ. Rsch. Inst. Mich., Ann Arbor, 1977-79, assoc. dir., 1981-87, tech. cons., 1988-90, engr. emeritus, 1990—; dean engring. Coll. Engring. N.J. Inst. Tech., Newark, 1979-81; cons. Widbec Engr, Ann Arbor, 1978—. Pres. Mich. Computers & Instrumentation, Inc., Ann Arbor, 1983—87; prof., chmn. elec. engring. Calif. State U., Fresno, 1988. Author: (book) Courses in Continuing Education for Electronics Engineers, 1975, 1976, Logical Design Using Integrated Circuits, 1977, An Ocean Between, 2000. With U.S. Army, 1953—55. Fellow GE, 1962—63. Mem.: IEEE (life; sr. mem.), Order of Engrs., Am. Soc. Engring. Edn., Tau Beta Pi, Sigma Xi, Eta Kappa Nu. Achievements include patents in field. Home and Office: Widbec Engring 691 Spring Valley Rd Ann Arbor MI 48105-1060

BECHERER, RICHARD JOHN, architecture educator; b. East St. Louis, Ill., Nov. 8, 1951; s. Adam Jacob and Agnes Evelyn (Baker) B.; m. Charlene Castellano, Aug. 13, 1982. Student Courtauld Inst., U. London, 1973; BA, BArch, Rice U., 1974; MA, Cornell U., 1977, PhD, 1981. Archtl. asst. Colin St. John Wilson and Ptnr., London, England, 1972-73; designer The Brooks Assn., Houston, 1973-74; grad. asst. Cornell U., Ithaca, N.Y., 1974-80, asst. prof. architecture, 1981; asst. prof. Auburn (Ala.) U., 1980-82, U. Va., Charlottesville, 1982-86; head grad. architecture program Carnegie Mellon U., Pitts., 1986-90, assoc. prof. architecture, 1987-96; assoc. prof. Cornell U., 1996, Am. U. Beirut, 1999—2001, Iowa State U., 2001—. Presenter seminars NEH, 1982, 88, 89, Am. Collegiate Schs. Architecture, 1988, 93, 97, 2002; lectr. Centre Canadien d'Architecture, Montreal, Carnegie Mus., Pitts., and various colls., univs. and nat. confs.; vis. assoc. prof. U. Pitts., 1997-99; assoc. prof. Am. U. Beirut, 1999—, Iowa State U.; mem. Fulbright Fellowship selection com. Author: Science Plus Sentiment; César Daly's Formula for Modern Architecture, 1984, (mus. catalogue and display) Urban Theory and Transformation, 1976, (tourist guidebook) Canandaigua: A Walking Tour, 1977; contbr. articles to profl. jours.; prin. works include interiors Michael P. Keeley House, Belleville, Ill., 1978, Robert Becherer House, Stonybrook, 1990; selected exhibitor Venice Biennale, Prato della Valle, Padua, 1985; exhibitor Heart of the Park, Houston, 1992; exhibitor installation Sioux City Ghosts, Sioux City, Iowa, 2004. Recipient Design Arts award Nat. Endowment for Arts, 1989-90, Graham Found. award, 1993; grad. fellow Cornell U., 1975-79, Eidlitz fellow, 1978, Soc. for Humanities and Mellon Found. fellow, 1984-85, NEH fellow, 1986, Paul Mellon vis. sr. fellow Ctr. for Advanced Study in Visual Arts, Nat. Gallery of Art; Travel to Collections grantee NEH, 1985. Mem. AAUP, Soc. Archtl. Historians (session chmn. ann. meeting 1989), Coll. Art Assn., Rice U. Alumni Assn. Democrat. Roman Catholic. Avocations: free-hand drawing, ballroom dancing, film. Home and Office: 119 Race St Pittsburgh PA 15218-1337 E-mail: richardbecherer@yahoo.com.

BECHTEL, JOEL RAY, small business owner; b. Sellersville, Pa., June 26, 1969; s. Raymond Styer and Marie Ellen Bechtel; m. Rachael Rae Greger, Apr. 22, 2000; children: Brandon Philip, Brooke Elizabeth. A in Engring., B in B in Bus., B in Indsl. Engring., Geneva Coll., 1991. Bus. owner Software Application Svcs., Inc., Souderton, Pa., 1996—. Office: Software Application Svcs Inc 220 North Main St Souderton PA 18969 Office Phone: 215-723-5070.

BECHTEL, RILEY PEART, engineering company executive; s. Stephen D. Jr. Bechtel. BA in Polit. Sci., Psychology, U. Calif., Davis, 1974; JD, Stanford U., 1979, MBA, 1979. Bar: Calif. 1979. With Bechtel Group, Inc., San Francisco, 1966—79, Thelen, Marrin, Johnson & Bridges, San Francisco, 1979—81; from exec. v.p. to chmn., CEO, dir. Bechtel Corp., 1987—96, chmn., 1996—, CEO, 1996—, dir., 1996—. Mem. Bus. Coun., Bus. Roundtable policy com; bd. dirs. Bechtel Corp., 1987—, J.P. Morgan Chase; adv. com. Stanford U. Grad. Sch. of Bus.; dean's adv. coun. Stanford Law Sch. Trustee Jason Found. for Edn. Fellow: Am. Acad. Arts and Scis.; mem.: Am. Soc. Corp. Execs. (conservation fund corp. coun.), Am. Soc. Civil Engrs. (hon.). Office: Bechtel Corp 50 Beale St PO Box 193965 San Francisco CA 94119-3965

BECHTEL, SHERRELL JEAN, psychotherapist; b. Birmingham, Ala., Sept. 23, 1961; d. Lewis Eugene and Sarah Rozelle (Sherrell) B. BS in Social Work, U. Ala., Birmingham, 1989; MSW, U. Ala., Tuscaloosa, 1990; DD, World Christianship Ministries, Fresno, Calif., 1997. Cert. addiction specialist; cert. group psychotherapist; lic. clin. social worker, Tenn., Ga.; ordained minister. Vol. counselor Planned Parenthood, Birmingham, 1986-88; intern Bradford Adult Chem. Dependency, Birmingham, 1989; rsch. staff asst. U. Ala., Tuscaloosa, 1989-90; intern counselor Bradford Adolescent Chem. Dependency, Birmingham, 1990; primary counselor The Crossroads, Chattanooga, 1990-92; owner S. J. Bechtel LCSW, CAS, Chattanooga, 1991—. Rschr. Ala. Commn. Youth, Montgomery, 1989-90; trainer Legal and Jud. Aspects Child Welfare, Decatur, Ala., 1989; presenter Ala. Victim Compensation, Mobile, 1990; speaker Limestone Correctional Facility, Huntsville, 1990; lectr. Grad. Sch. Social Wk., Tuscaloosa, 1990, U. Tenn., Chattanooga. Spkr. Victims of Crime and Leniency, Tuscaloosa, 1990; vol. ARC Disaster Mental Health/Direct Svcs.; broadcaster Power and Victory Ministry, 2000—; subcom. mem. Atty. Gen. Alliance Against Drug Abuse, Birmingham, 1989; mem. Tenn. Coun. on Children and Youth-Legis./Policy; planning com. Holistic Health Retreat, Birmingham, 1988. Mem. NASW (pres. student orgn. 1986-89), Tenn. Alcohol Drug Assn., Jewish Community Ctr., Phi Kappa Phi. Avocations: tennis, woodworking, softball, bowling, water sports. Office: 109A Jordan Dr Chattanooga TN 37421-6732 E-mail: sb4jc1@aol.com.

BECHTEL, STEPHEN DAVISON, JR., engineering company executive; b. Oakland, Calif., May 10, 1925; s. Stephen Davison and Laura (Peart) Bechtel; m. Elizabeth Mead Hogan, June 5, 1946; 5 children. Student, U. Colo., 1943—44, DSc (hon.), 1981; BS, Purdue U., 1946, D (hon.) in Engring., 1972; MBA, Stanford U., 1948. Registered profl. engr., N.Y., Mich., Alaska, Calif., Md., Hawaii, Ohio, D.C., Va., Ill. Engring. and mgmt. positions Bechtel Corp., San Francisco, 1941-60, pres., 1960-73, chmn. of cos. in Bechtel group, 1973-80; chmn. Bechtel Group, Inc., 1980-90, chmn. emeritus, 1990—, Fremont Group, 1995—. Former chmn., mem. Bus. Coun., life-term counselor, past chmn. Conf. Bd. Trustee, mem., past chmn. bldg. and grounds com. Calif. Inst. Tech.; mem. pres.'s coun. Purdue U.; mem. adv. coun., bd. visitors Inst. Internat. Studies, Stanford; former charter mem. adv. coun. Stanford U. Grad. Sch. Bus. With USMC, 1943-46. Decorated officer French Legion Honor; named Man Yr. Engring., News-Record, 1974; recipient Disting. Alumnus award, Purdue U., 1964, Ernest C. Arbuckle Disting. Alumnus award, Stanford Grad. Sch. Bus., 1974, Outstanding Achievement in Constrn. award, Moles, 1977, Disting. Engring. Alumnus award, U. Colo., 1979, Chmn.'s award, Am. Assn. Engring. Soc., 1982, Kenneth Andrew Roe award, 2003, Washington award, Western Soc. Engrs., 1985, Herbert Hoover medal, 1980, Nat. Medal Tech., Pres. Bush, 1991, Golden Beaver award, 1992, Oxford Cup award, Beta Theta Pi, 1997, Engr. Distinction award, U. Colo., 2000. Fellow AAAS; mem. ASCE (hon., engring. mgmt. award 1979, pres. award 1985, OPAL award for outstanding lifetime achievement in constrn. 2000), Inst. Chem. Engrs. (U.K., hon.); mem. AIME, NSPE (hon. chmn. Nat. Engrs. Week 1990), NAE (past chmn., Founder's award 1999), Calif. Acad. Scis. (hon. trustee), Am. Soc. French Legion Honor (bd. dirs., Disting. Achievement medal 1994), Royal Acad. Engring. (U.K., fgn.), Pacific Union Club, Bohemian Club, San Francisco Golf Club, Claremont Country Club, Cypress Point Club, Bear River Club (Utah), Wild Goose Club (Calif.), Chi Epsilon, Tau Beta Pi. Office: PO Box 193965 San Francisco CA 94119-3965

BECHTEL, STEPHEN E., mechanical engineer, educator; BS in Engring. summa cum laude, U. Mich., 1979; PhD in Engring., U. Calif., Berkeley, 1983. Prof. dept. mech. engring. Ohio State U., Columbus, 1983—. Reviewer design, mfg. and computer-integrated engring. divsn., fluid dynamics and hydraulics directorate, thermal transport and thermal processing directorate NSF, 1985—, USDA food characterization, process, product rsch. program; cons. Hoechst Celanese Corp., Los Alamos Nat. Lab., Battelle Meml. Inst., Corning, Inc., Proctor & Gamble. Referee Jour. Rheology, Jour. Applied Mechanics, Jour. Non-Newtonian Fluid Mechanics, others. James B. Angell scholar U. Mich., 1976-79. Fellow ASME (mem. fluid mechanics com., elasticity com., applied mechanics divsn. 1989—, rec. sec. gen. com. 1991-92, rec. sec. exec. com. 1992-93, textile engring. divsn, exec. com., 2002-, Henry Hess award 1990); mem. Am. Acad. Mechanics, Soc. Rheology, Tau Beta Pi. Achievements include research in modeling of industrial polymer processing and fiber manufacturing, viscoelastic fluid flows, free surface flows and instability mechanisms, fundamental modeling of thermal expansion, material characterization, transducer characterization in non-destructive evaluation. Office: Ohio State U Mech Engring 650 Ackerman Rd Columbus OH 43202 Office Phone: 614-292-6570. Business E-Mail: bechtel.3@osu.edu.

BECHTLE, ROBERT ALAN, artist, educator; b. San Francisco, May 14, 1932; m. Nancy Elizabeth Dalton, 1963 (div. 1982); children: Max Robert, Anne Elizabeth; m. Whitney Chadwick, 1982. BA, Calif. Coll. Arts and Crafts, Oakland, 1954, M.F.A., 1958; postgrad., U. Calif.-Berkeley, 1960-61. Graphic designer Kaiser Industries, Oakland, 1956-59; instr. Calif. Coll. Arts and Crafts, 1957-61, assoc. prof. to prof.; lectr. U. Calif.-Berkeley, 1965-66; vis. artist U. Calif.-Davis, 1966-68; assoc. prof. San Francisco State U., 1968-76, prof., 1976-99, prof. emeritus, 1999—. One-man shows Mus. of Art, San Francisco, 1959, 64, Berkeley Gallery, 1965, Richmond Art Ctr. (Calif.), 1965, U. Calif.-Davis, 1967, O.K. Harris Gallery, N.Y.C., 1971, 74, 76, 81, 84, 87, 92, 96, Berggruen Gallery, San Francisco, 1972, E.B. Crocker Art Mus., Sacramento, 1973, Univ. Art Mus., U. Calif.-Berkeley, 1979, O.K Harris Works of Art, N.Y.C., 1981, 84, 87; Daniel Weinberg Gallery, Santa Monica, 1991, Gallery Paul Anglim, San Francisco, 1991, San Francisco Mus. Modern Art, 1991, others; exhibited in group shows San Francisco Art Inst., 1966, Whitney Mus. N.Y.C., 1967, Milw. Art Ctr., 1969, Mus. Contemporary Art, Chgo., 1971, Serpentine Gallery, London, 1973, Toledo Mus. Art, 1975, San Francisco Mus. Modern Art, 1976, 1985, 2005, Pushkin Fine Arts Mus., Moscow, 1978, Pa. Acad. Fine Arts, Phila., 1981, San Antonio Mus. Art, 1981, Pa. Acad. Fine Arts, Phila, 1981, Calif. Palace of Legion of Honor, San Francisco, 1983, Mus. Contemporary Art, L.A., 1984, Univ. Art Mus., U. Calif., Berkeley, 1987, Whitney Mus., N.Y.C., 1991, Fine Arts Mus. San Francisco, 1995, Jaffe Baker Gallery, Boca Raton, Fla., 1997, Young U., Provo, Utah, others; represented in permanent collections Achenbach Found. for Graphic Arts, San Francisco, Chase Manhattan Bank, N.Y.C., E.B. Crocker Art Mus., Sacramento, Gibbes Art Gallery, S.C., High Mus. Art, Atlanta, Hunter Art Mus., Chattanooga, Library of Congress, Washington, Lowe Art Mus.-U. Miami, Coral Gables, Fla., Mills Coll., Oakland, Mus. Modern Art, N.Y.C., Met. Mus., N.Y.C., Neue Gal der Stadt Aachen, West Germany, Oakland Mus., San Francisco Mus. Modern Art, Univ. Art Mus.-U. Calif-Berkeley, Fine Arts Mus. of San Diego, Rose Art Mus., Brandeis U., Waltham, Mass., U. Nebr.-Lincoln, Whitney Mus., N.Y.C., Guggenheim Mus., N.Y.C. Served with U.S. Army, 1954-56. Recipient James D. Phelan award, 1965, Acad. award Am. Acad. Arts and Letters, 1995; named Nat. Academician, Nat. Acad. Design, 1993; Nat. Endowment for Arts grantee, 1977, 83, 89, Guggenheim grantee, 1986. Office: San Francisco State U 1600 Holloway Ave Dept Art San Francisco CA 94132-1722

BECHTOL, LARRY OWEN, pastor; b. Gordon, Ohio, Oct. 14, 1937; s. Owen S. and Maudie B. B.; m. Betty J.; children: Julie, Lori, Stephen, Joan, Melissa, Sean, Tarla. BA, Asbury Coll., 1959; MDiv, United Theol. Sem., 1963. Ordained to ministry, United Ch. of Christ. Pastor Hollansburg (Ohio) UCC Ch., 1961-64, Frankford Congrl. Ch., Phila., 1964-66, Lansdale (Pa.) Schwenkfelder, 1966-68; pastor, counselor First E and R, Vermillion, Ohio, 1976-82; prof. Cin. Christian Coll., 1989-2000, So. State C.C., Sardinia, Ohio, 2000—; pastor, counselor Matthew United Ch., Cin., 1969-76, 82—. Chaplain Boy Scouts Am., Dayton, Ohio, 1960; youth leader Schwenkfelder Youth, 1968; chair Ch. Growth and Devel., Cleve., 1979-81; bd. dirs. CY Inc. Bd. dirs. Winton Place Civic Assn., Cin., 1970-76. Mem. MLA, Am. Assn. Christian Counselors, Christian Educators Assn., Acad. Am. Poets. Avocations: writing, poems, reading, tennis.

BECHTOLSHEIM, ANDY (ANDREAS BECHTOLSHEIM), software executive; b. Germany, 1956; Grad., U. Germany; M of Computer Engring., Carnegie Mellon U., 1976; postgrad., Stanford U., 1977—82. Co-founder Sun Microsystems, 1982; founder Granite Systems, 1995; various positions including v.p., gen. Cisco Sys., 1996; founder Kealia, Inc., Palo Alto, Calif., 2003; sr. v.p., chief arch. Volume Sys. Products Group Sun Microsystems, Santa Clara, 2004—. Recipient Stanford Entrepreneur Co. of Yr. award, Smithsonian Leadership award; fellow, Fulbright Found.; scholar, German Nat. Merit Found. Office: Sun Microsystems 4152 Network Cir Santa Clara CA 95054

BECICH, RAYMOND BRICE, healthcare consultant, mediator, trainer, educator; b. Chgo., Jan. 9, 1945; s. Nicholas Gabriel and Rose Christina (Spillar) B. BA, Ind. U., 1966; MS, Columbia U., 1968. Adminstrv. officer, then hosp. dir. Indian Health Svc., Harlem, Mont., 1968-72, hosp. dir. Rapid City, S.D., 1972-78; hosp. adminstr. St. Elizabeth's Hosp., Washington, 1979-82, exec. officer, 1983-86, NIH Clin. Ctr., Bethesda, Md., 1986-94; healthcare cons., mediator, trainer, educator, 1994—. Adj. faculty Univ. Coll., U. Md., College Park, U. N.Mex., Albuquerque and Los Alamos, Coll. Santa Fe, Ctrl. Mich. U., Mt. Pleasant, U. St Francis, Joliet, Ill., 1995—. Bd. dirs. Ronald McDonald House, Washington, 1986-89; vol. Whitman-Walker Clinic, 1987-95. Fellow Am. Coll. Healthcare Execs. (life). Democrat. Episcopalian. E-mail: rbecich@ix.netcom.com.

BECK, AARON TEMKIN, psychiatrist, educator; b. Providence, July 18, 1921; s. Harry S. and Elizabeth (Temkin) B.; m. Phyllis Whitman, June 4, 1950; children: Judith, Daniel, Alice, Roy. BA, Brown U., 1942, Dr.Med.Sci. (hon.), 1982; MD, Yale U., 1946; LHD (hon.), Assumption Coll., 1995. Mem. faculty U. Pa. Med. Sch., 1954—, prof. psychiatry, 1971—, Univ. prof., 1983—; dir. Center Cognitive Therapy, 1965-94; pres. Beck Found. for Cognitive Therapy, 1995—. Mem. rev. panel NIMH, 1965-80, chmn. task force suicide prevention, 1969-80; bd. dirs. West Philadelphia Community Mental Health Consortium, 1975-77. Author: Depression: Causes and Treatment, 1967, Diagnosis and Management of Depression, 1973, Prediction of Suicide, 1973, Cognitive Therapy and the Emotional Disorders, 1976, Cognitive Theory of Depression, 1979, Anxiety Disorders and Phobias: A Cognitive Perspective, 1985, Love is Never Enough, 1988, Cognitive Therapy of Personality Disorders, 1990; co-author: Cognitive Therapy in Clinical Practice, 1989, Cognitive Therapy with Inpatients, 1992, Cognitive Therapy of Substance Abuse, 1993, The Integrative Power of Cognitive Therapy, 1997, Scientific Foundations of Cognitive Theory and Therapy of Depression, 1999, Prisoners of Hate, 1999, Bipolar Disorder: A Cognitive Perspective, 2001, Cognitive Therapy for Chronic Pain, 2003. Served as officer M.C. U.S. Army, 1952-54. Recipient rsch. award, R.I. Med. Soc., 1948, ann. award, Phila. Soc. Clin. Psychologists, 1978, Am. Psychopathol. Assn., 1983, Soc. for Psychotherapy Rsch., 1995, Calif. Psychol. Soc., 1996, Belmont Hosp. award, 1996, Disting. Sci. award, APA, 1989, rsch. award, Am. Assn. Suicidology, 1985, Am. Suicide Found., 1991, Albert Einstein Sch. Medicine award, 1992, Nathaniel Winkelman award, 1996, Heinz Found. award for the human condition, 2001, Rhoda and Bernard Sarnat Internat. Prize in Mental Health, Inst. of Medicine, 2003, Grawemeyer award for new idea in psychology, 2004. Fellow Royal Coll. Psychiatry, N.Y. Acad. Medicine (Thomas Salmon award 1992), APA (rsch. award 1993); mem. Calif. Psychol. Assn. (lifetime svc. award 1996), So. Psychotherapy Rsch. (pres. 1975-76), Am. Psychiat. Assn. (prize rsch. psychiatry 1979), Am. Assn. Suicidology (rsch. prize 1985), Assn. Advancement of Behavior Therapy (Lifetime Contbn. award 2001), Nat. Acad. Sci. Inst. Medicine (Internat. Mental Health award). Office: 3535 Market St Rm 2022 Philadelphia PA 19104-2641 Office Phone: 215-898-4102. Business E-Mail: abeck@mail.med.upenn.edu.

BECK, AL WILLIAM (ALBERT BECK), art educator, artist, writer; s. Joseph Emanual Beck and Celia Frances Garfinkle; m. Carmen Isabel Federowich, Sept. 11, 1939; children: Jeremy, Adam, Zoe. BA, Northwestern U., Evanston, Ill., 1956; MFA, Clayton U., Saint Louis, Mo., 1977. Cert. Sorbonne & Academie de la Grande Chaumiere Paris, 1956. Elem. visual arts specialist Ashtabula City Schs., Ohio, 1957—59; chmn., visual arts dept. Eastlake-North HS, Ohio, 1959—67; dean for students Kans. City Art Inst., Kansas City, Mo., 1967—68; head art dept., gallery dir. Culver-Stockton Coll., Canton, Mo., 1968—96, artist-in-residence, prof. emeritus, 1997—2004. Summer dir. water safety Camp Taconic, Hinsdale, Mass., 1959—74; film creator, 1970; midwest field rschr. Gallop Poll Princeton Rsch. Ctr., NJ, 1977—78; artist, photography, painting, design, and visual literacy educator John Wood CC, Quincy, Ill., 1976—93; coord. rsch. project of hist. photographic evidence Ill. Humanities Coun., 1982; attendee various workshops and summer programs in field. Author, artist: book Gnomes and Poems, 1992, Sight Lines, 1996, Songs From The Rainbow Worm, 1997, Beaucoup Haiku, 1999, God Is In The Glove Compartment, 2000, Survival Weapons, 2001, Warm Verse, Cold Turkey, 2002, Rapping Paper, Mythic Thundermugs, 2002, Conversations With Lizard's Bones and Wizard's Stones, 2003, Lifepsychles, 2004, folksinger: album Vintage Voices/Timeworn Tunes, 1998; contbr. articles to profl. jours. and mags. Participant ednl. evaluation teams NCA, 1967; ESL tchr. Taegu, Republic of Korea, 1955; children's swimming instr. ARC, 1958—76. Cpl. U.S. Army, 1953—55, Korea. Decorated Korean Svc. medal US Army, UN Svc. medal, Good Conduct Medal, Nat. Def. Svc. medal, Korean Conflict medallion State of Mo. Vet. Recognition award; recipient Ill. Bell award, Miss. River Exhbn., 1973, Painting and Poetry Silver medals, Mo. Bicentennial Arts, 1976, Glass Medium First prize, Muscatine Art Ctr., Iowa, 1988, Clay Sculpture prize, Mark Twain Regional Exhbn., 1990, Sculpture First prize, Raintree Art exhibit, Clarksville, Mo., 1995. Mem.: Monroe City Arts Coun., Hannibal Art Ctr. (Hannibal Sculpture prize 2000), Quincy Art Ctr. (Best in Show award 2000), Vets. Fgn. Wars (life), Korean War Vets. (life). Achievements include vase replication drawing in included at Vatican's Etruscan Museum. Avocations: plants, magic. Home and Office: 5897 County Rd 231 Monroe City MO 63456 E-mail: abeck@marktwain.net.

BECK, ALBERT, manufacturing executive; b. N.Y.C., Jan. 14, 1928; s. Albert Christian and Mabel Agnes (Dunn) B.; m. Jean Norma Russ, June 16, 1951; children— Nancy, Richard, Douglas BS, Fairleigh Dickinson U., 1950; MS, Rutgers U., 1956. Product line mgr. Tung Sol Electric Inc. div. Wagner Electric, Bloomfield, N.J., 1951-66; dir. quality control IT&T, Brussels, 1966-69, asst. dir. product ops. N.Y.C., 1969-72, dir. N.Am. staff, 1972-73; v.p. ops. Grinnell Fire Protection Co., Providence, 1973-79, exec. v.p., 1979, Grinnell Corp., 1986—2002. Mem. bd. edn. curriculum com. Wayne, N.J., 1964. Served with A.C., USN, 1945-47 Mem. Nat. Fire Sprinkler Assn. (bd. dirs. 1990), Sigma Xi. Republican. Avocations: golf, bridge, travel.

BECK, ANATOLE, mathematician, educator; b. Bronx, N.Y., Mar. 19, 1930; s. Morris and Minnie (Rosenblum) B.; m. Evelyn Torton, Apr. 10, 1954 (div.); children— Nina Rachel, Micah Daniel; m. Eve-Lynn Siegel, Nov. 30, 2003. BA, Bklyn. Coll., 1951; MS, Yale U., 1953, PhD, 1956. Instr. math. Williams Coll., Williamstown, Mass., 1955-56; Office Naval Rsch. rsch. assoc. Tulane U., New Orleans, 1956-57; traveling fellow Yale U., 1957-58; from asst. to assoc. prof. U. Wis., Madison, 1958-66, prof. math., 1966—; chair of math. London Sch. Econ./U. London, England, 1973-75. Vis. prof. Cornell U., 1960, Hebrew U., Jerusalem, 1964-65, U. Göttingen, Fed. Republic Germany, 1965, U. Warwick, 1968, Imperial Coll., U. London, 1969, U. Erlangen, Fed. Republic Germany, 1969, U. Md., 1971, Tech. U. Munich, Fed. Republic Germany, 1973, London Sch. Econs. and Univ. Coll., U. London, 1985, 91-92, 94-97, 99—; v.p. Wis. Fedn. Tchrs., 1975-83; co-founder Wis. U. Union, 1984, pres., 1988-91. Author: Continuous Flows in the Plane, 1974, (with M.N. Bleicher and D.W. Crowe) Excursions into Mathematics, 1969, 2d edit., 2000, The Knowledge Business, 1997; contbr. articles to profl. jours. Recipient Disting. Alumnus award, Bklyn. Coll., 1976. Mem. Am. Math. Soc. (council 1973-75), Math. Assn. Am., AAUP, Sigma Xi, Phi Beta Kappa, Pi Mu Epsilon. Address: 480 Lincoln Dr Madison WI 53706-1325 Office: U Wis 480 Lincoln Dr 721 Van Vleck Hall Madison WI 53706-1329 Office Phone: 608-262-2933. Personal E-mail: a.beck@lse.ac.uk. Business E-Mail: beck@math.wisc.edu.

BECK, ANDREW H., farm equipment manufacturing executive; BBA in fin., Emory U.; MBA in acctg., U. NC. Auditor Arthur Andersen; asst. treas., contr., internat. oper. AGCO Corp., chief acctg. officer, contr., sr. v.p., CFO Duluth, Ga., 2002—. Office: AGCO Corp 4205 River Green Pkwy Duluth GA 30096

BECK, ANDREW JAMES, lawyer; b. Washington, Feb. 19, 1948; s. Leonard Norman and Frances (Greif) B.; m. Carol Beck, Oct. 13, 2002; children: Carter, Lowell, Justin. BA, Carleton Coll., 1969; JD, Stanford U., 1972; MBA, L.I. U., 1975. Bar: VA. 1972, NY 1973, Pa. 1992. Assoc. Casey, Lane & Mittendorf, NYC, 1972-80, ptnr., 1980-82, Haythe & Curley, NYC, 1982-99, Torys LLP, NYC, 1999—, exec. com., 2000—03. Trustee Bklyn. Heights Synagogue, 1980-81, Bklyn. Heights Montessori Sch., 1988-92, treas., 1990-92. Mem. ABA, Va. State Bar Assn., NY State Bar Assn., Pa. Bar Assn., Assn. Bar City of NY, Nat. Stroke Assn. (gen. counsel 1992—, sec., bd. dirs. 2000—). Avocation: bridge. Home: 525 E 80th St Apt 6A New York NY 10021 Office: Torys LLP 237 Park Ave New York NY 10017-3142 Office Phone: 212-880-6010. Business E-Mail: abeck@torys.com.

BECK, BARBARA NELL, elementary school educator; b. Corpus Christi, Tex., Oct. 25, 1940; d. Marshall Joseph and Madie Ann (Spence) Robertson; m. Joel J. Beck, June 23, 1973. BA, Baylor U., 1964. Tchr. Killeen (Tex.) Ind. Sch. Dist., 1964-2001. Sunday sch. tchr., 1967—, co-treas., 2000—, ch. clk. First Bapt. Ch. of Nolanville. Mem. NEA, Tex. State Tchrs. Assn. (life), Tex. Assn. for the Gifted and Talented, Killeen Edn. Assn. (treas., past pres., bd. dirs.), Clifton Park PTA (past treas.). E-mail: jbeck1@hot.rr.com.

BECK, CHARLES MILBURN, II, analytical chemist; b. McKeesport, Pa., July 19, 1941; s. Charles Milburn and Dolly (Hoffman) B.; m. Charlotte Ayres Hastings, Sept. 7, 1968; children: John Charles, Paul Nathan. BS in Chemistry with high distinction, Worcester Poly. Inst., 1963, postgrad., 1978-80; MDiv, Princeton Theol. Sem., 1968. Analytical chemist Water Resources Adminstrn. State of Md., Annapolis, 1970-78; teaching asst. chemistry dept. Worcester (Mass.) Poly. Inst., 1978-80; analytical chemist Luvak Inc., Boylston, Mass., 1980-84; mem. tech. staff materials analysis dept. GTE Labs., Inc., Waltham, Mass., 1984-87; sr. chemist ea. divsn. Wyman-Gordon Co., North Grafton, Mass., 1987-90; rsch. chemist Nat. Inst. Stds. and Tech., Gaithersburg, Md., 1990-95, project mgr., 1995-97, rsch. chemist, 1997—2002; analytical chemist Los Alamos Nat. Lab., N.Mex., 2002—. Contbr. articles to profl. jours. Recipient Edward Condon award for excellence in tech. writing Nat. Inst. Stds. & Tech., 1994. Mem. ASTM (com. on analytical chemistry for metals, ores and related materials, John L. Hague award 1995, Lundell-Bright Meml. award 1999), Am. Chem. Soc. (chmn.-elect Ctrl. Mass. sect. 1988, chmn. 1989), Sigma Xi, Phi Lambda Upsilon. Achievements include research on history and current status of classical analysis; development and preparation of first certified rhodium standard reference material solution; development of analytical methods for certification of standard reference materials; development of chemical separation methods for radionuclides. Office: Los Alamos Nat Lab Mailstop J514 Los Alamos NM 87545 E-mail: cbeck@lanl.gov.

BECK, CHRISTINE SAFFORD, photographer, publisher, volunteer, school system administrator, academic administrator; b. Phila., July 10, 1943; d. Elisha Jr. and Margaret (Tramdack) Safford; m. Leif Christian Beck, Nov. 21, 1964; children: C. Lars, Eric S., Anders. BA in German and French, Queens Coll., 1964; MA in German Lit., Bryn Mawr Coll., 1969; postgrad., N.Y. Inst. Photography. Co-founder, pres. Nat. Jr. Tennis League of Phila., 1969-79; pres., CEO Nat. Jr. Tennis League, N.Y.C., 1979-83; owner, photographer Christine S. Beck Photography, Villanova, Pa., 1990—; pub., owner Prism Light Press, Bryn Mawr, Pa., 1995—; stock photographer Garden Image Agy., Montreal, 1999—2002; v.p. Advisory Publs., 2001—03; pres., CEO Gesu Sch., 2003—. Pres. Phila. Tennis Patrons Assn., 1985-95, mem. adv. bd., 1995—; pres. Arthur Ashe Youth Tennis Ctr., Phila., 1985-95; chair adv. coun. Esperanza Health Ctr., Phila., 1994-97. Photographer (books): Beyond Me. Voices of the Natural World, 1993, Spirit of Summit County, Colorado, 1996; producer Broadway Comes to Queens benefit concert, Charlotte, N.C., 1999. Bd. dirs. Habitat for Humanity, Phila., 1988-90; coord. vols. Jimmy Carter Workcamp, North Phila., 1988; chair stewardship campaign Bryn Mawr Presbyn. Ch., 1992; trustee Queens U. Charlotte, N.C., 1995—; trustee Gesu Sch., Phila., 1996—2003, chair devel., 2000-2003, pres., 2003—,; chair fundraising campaign Arthur Ashe Youth Tennis Ctr., 2000—; chair alumni phase fundraising campaign Queens U. Charlotte, N.C., 2000-02; trustee Penn Coun. for Relationships, 2000-02, pres./CEO, Gesu Sch. 2003-. Recipient Kennedy award Robert F. Kennedy Pro Celebrity Tennis Tournament, 1975, Jimmy Carter Hammer award Habitat for Humanity, 1988, Merit award for women Internat. Tennis Hall of Fame, 1988, Svc. Bowl, U.S. Tennis Assn., 1991, Take the Lead award Girl Scouts of Greater Phila., 1992, First Phila. Youth Tennis Jerome Laroque award, 1999. Mem. U.S. Tennis Assn. Middle States (treas. 1986-89, Mangan award 1990, Coren award 1973), N.Am. Nature Photographers Assn. (charter mem.), Nikon Profl. Svcs. Avocations: golf, tennis, hiking. Office: Gesu Sch 1700 W Thompson St Philadelphia PA 19121 Home: 6 Deggs Cir Newtown Square PA 19073-1906

BECK, DANA KENDALL, lawyer; b. Bklyn. BA, SUNY, Albany, 1987; JD, U. Bridgeport, 1991. Bar: Conn. 1992, U.S. Dist. Ct. Conn. 1998. Law clk. Conn. Superior Ct., Bridgeport, 1990-91; assoc. Schiavetti, Geisler et al, Garden City, N.Y., 1991-94; mng. atty. Beck & Beck LLC, N.Y.C. & Stratford, Conn., 1995—. Adj. prof. law Fairfield U., Albertus Magnus Coll., U. Hartford, Bridgeport, Conn., 1998-99; instr. Women's Bus. Devel. Ctr., Stamford, Conn., 1996—; legal expert Home-Based Working Moms, 1997—. Mem. Nat. Assn. Women Bus. Owners (dir.-at-large 1998—), Entrepreneurial Women's Network (v.p. 1995—). Office: Beck & Beck LLC 83 Booth St Stratford CT 06614 also: 67 Wall St New York NY 10005-3198 Fax: 203-378-5263. E-mail: DKBeck@prodigy.net.

BECK, DAVID CHARLES, lawyer; b. Kansas City, Mo., July 11, 1954; s. W. Morton and Jane Lillian (Partridge) B.; m. Susan Jane Kessler, Oct. 7, 1978; children: Miranda Jillian, Jonathan "Jake" Guthrie, S. Spencer. BA in English, U. Oreg., 1978; JD, U. Va., 1982. Atty. Peabody & Brown, Boston, 1982-85, Powers Pyles Sutter & O'Hara, Washington, 1985-86, McDermott Will & Emery, Washington, 1986-88; ptnr. Casson Harking & Lapallo, Washington, 1988-93; spl. counsel Proghauer Rose, Washington, 1993-96; ptnr. Powers Pyles Sutter & Verville, Washington, 1996—. Pres. bd. dirs. St. John's Cmty. Svc., Washington, 1995-97. Mem. D.C. Health Care Assn. (exec. dir. 1993—). Office: Powers Pyles Sutter Verville 1875 Eye St NW Ste 1200 Washington DC 20006-5420

BECK, DAVID EDWARD, surgeon; b. Geneva, Ill., May 1, 1953; s. George R. and Gloria M. (Zesch) B.; m. Sharon Mieir, Aug. 30, 1983; children: Allison, Lauren, John. BS, USAF Acad., 1975; MD, U. Miami, Fla., 1979; postgrad., USAF Aerospace Medicine Primary Course, Brooks AFB, Tex., 1978, Combat Casualty Care Course, Ft. Sam Houston, Tex., 1980, Hyperbaric Oxygen CourseB, Brooks AFB, 1982, ATLS Instr. Course, Ft. Sam Houston, 1986, Squadon Officers Sch., 1987-88, Mgmt. for Chief of Hosp. Svcs., Sheppard AFB, Tex., 1988, Sch. Pub. Health, Harvard U., 1990. Diplomate Am. Bd. Colon and Rectal Surgery. Lt. Col. USAF, 1975-93; resident in gen. surgery Wilford Hall USAF Med. Ctr., Lackland AFB, Tex., 1979-84, chief colorectal surgery, 1986-92, staff surgeon, chief colorectal surgery svc., 1986-92, asst. chmn. dept. gen. surgery, 1988, chmn. dept. gen. surgery, residency program dir., 1988-92; staff gen. surgeon Patrick AFB (Fla.) Hosp., 1984-85; fellow in colorectal surgery Cleve. Clinic Found., 1985-86; residency program dir. gen. surgery Joint Mil. Med. Command, San Antonio, 1989-91; clin. assoc. prof. surgery U. Tex. Health Sci. Ctr., San Antonio, 1990-92, F. Edward Herbert Sch. Medicine, U. Health Scis., Bethesda, Md., 1992—; chief surgery 870 USAF Contingency Hosp., RAF Little Rissington, U.K., 1993; staff colorectal surgeon Ochsner Clinic, New Orleans, 1993—, chmn. dept. colon and rectal surgery, 1994—; med. dir. Ochsner Endoscopy Ambulatory Surgery Ctr., 2003—. Cons. USAF Surgeon Gen., Washington, 1986-92. Author chpts. to books; co-editor (textbooks); (with David R. Welling) Patient Care in Colorectal Surgery, 1991, (with Steven D. Wexner) Fundamentals of Anorectal Surgery, 1992, 2nd edit., 1998, (with T.C. Hicks, F.E. Opelka, A.E., Timmcke) Complications of Colon and Rectal Surgery, 1996; editor: Handbook of Colorectol Surgery, 1997, 2d edit., 2002; mem. editl. bd. Current Surgery, 1990—; reviewer Diseases of the Colon and Rectum, 1990—, mem. editl. bd., 1992-98, So. Me. Jour., 1988-92; mem. editl. bd. Perspectives in Colon and Rectal Surgery, 1997-2000; editor-in-chief Clinics in Colon and Rectal Surgery, 2001—; contbr. articles to profl. jours. Decorated Air Force Achievement medal with oak leaf cluster, Air Force Meritorious Svc. medal with oak leaf cluster; recipient Pres. award United Ostomy Assn., 2000. Fellow ACS; mem. AMA, Am. Soc. Colon and Rectal Surgeons (mem. socioecon./legis. com. 1991-94, pub. rels. com. 1993-99, chmn. 1996-99, mem.-at-large exec. coun. 2004—, Outstanding Young Investigator award, 1992), Assn. Mil. Surgeons U.S., La. State Med. Soc., Soc. Air Force Clin. Surgeons (treas. 1989-90, v.p. 1990-92, pres. 1992-93, Excalibur award 1992), Soc. Surgery of Alimentary Tract, So. Med. Assn. (mem. colon and rectal sect., sec. 1988-91, v.p. 1990-91, pres. 1991-92), Soc. Med. Cons. to Armed forces, St. Tamminy Parish Med. Soc., Tex. Soc. Colon and Rectal Surgeons (sec. 1991-93), Air force Assn., USAF Acad. Assn. Grads. Avocations: fishing, wood working, gardening. Home: 127 Deloaks Rd Madisonville LA 70447-9597 Office: Oschner Clin Found 1514 Jefferson Hwy New Orleans LA 70121-2429 Office Phone: 504-842-4060. Personal E-mail: dbeckmd@aol.com. Business E-Mail: dbeck@ochsner.org.

BECK, DAVID PAUL, biochemist; b. Wilmington, Del., Aug. 3, 1944; s. David Franklin and Mary Jane (Lazar) B.; m. Jeanne Elaine Crawford, Nov. 19, 1966; children: Jennifer Jeanne, David Andrew. AB, Princeton U., 1966; PhD, Johns Hopkins U., 1971. Fellow Harvard U., Cambridge, Mass., 1971-74; staff scientist Md. Psychiat. Rsch. Ctr., Balt., 1974-77; health scientist, adminstr. NIH, Bethesda, Md., 1977-84; assoc. dir., sec. bd. dir. Pub. Health Rsch. Inst., NYC, 1984-91; pres. Coriell Inst. Med. Rsch., Camden, NJ, 1991—, sec. bd. trustees, 1991—. Bd. dirs. CorCell, Inc., NJ Tech. Coun., Exec. Svc. Corp. of Delaware Valley, South Jersey C. of C. Contbr. articles to profl. jours. Active Baltimore County Bd. Recreation and Pks., 1977-84; bd. dirs. Hoff-Barthelson Music Sch., Scarsdale, N.Y., 1989-91, West Jersey Chamber Music Soc., Moorestown, N.J., 1992—, Opera Co. Phila., 2003—; mem. N.J. Commn. on Sci. and Tech., 2004—. Mem.: NJ Commn. on Sci. and Tech., South Jersey C. of C. (bd. dirs. 2003—), NJ Tech. Coun. (bd. dirs.), NJ Assn. Biomed. Rsch. (bd. dirs.), Assn. Ind. Rsch. Insts. (v.p. 1989—92, pres.-elect 1993—95, pres. 1995—97, exec. v.p. 1997—99), Exec. Svc. Corps. of Delaware Valley (bd. dirs. 2003—). Office: Coriell Inst Med Rsch 403 Haddon Ave Ste 403 Camden NJ 08103-1559 Office Phone: 856-757-4820. E-mail: dabeck@umdnj.edu.

BECK, EDWARD WILLIAM, lawyer; b. Atchison, Kans., Aug. 19, 1944; s. Russell Niles and Lucille Mae (Leighton) B.; m. Marshia Ablon, June 24, 1966; children: Michael Adam, David Gordon, Stephen Jared BA cum laude, Yale U., 1967; JD cum laude, Harvard U., 1972. Bar: Calif. 1972. Assoc. firm Pillsbury, Madison & Sutro, San Francisco, 1972-77; gen. counsel Pacific Lumber Co., San Francisco, 1977-86, sec., 1978-86, v.p., 1980-86, dir., 1985-86; v.p., gen. counsel, sec. Yamamouchi Consumer Inc. (formerly Shaklee Corp.), Pleasanton, Calif., 1986-87, sr. v.p., gen. counsel, sec., 1987—2004, exec. v.p., gen. counsel, sec., 2004; sr. v.p., gen. counsel, sec. Mervyn's LLC, 2005—. Bd. dirs. Yamanouchi Consumer Inc. (formerly Shaklee Corp.), mem. audit com., 2001—04. Trustee, mem. exec. com. San Francisco Conservatory Music, 1988—, co-chmn. acad. affairs com., 1989—91, chmn. presdl. search com., 1991, chair trustees and officers com., 1993—96, exec. vice chair, 1994—, chair conservatory 2006 com., 1996—99, chmn. maj. gifts com., 1999—2001, co-chmn. instl. advancement com., 1999—2001, mem. bldg. com., 2000—05, chair new conservatory com., 2004—; mem. law com. United Way of Bay Area Campaign, 1991—2000, chmn., 1992. Mem. ABA, Calif. Bar Assn., San Francisco Bar Assn. (bd. dirs. 1991-94, nominating com. 1993), Bay Area Gen. Counsels Group (chmn. 1991), San Francisco C. of C. (leadership coun. 1987—, gen. coun., bd. dirs., exec. com. 1993-96), San Francisco Yale Alumni Assn. (schs. com.). Office: Mervyns LLC 22301 Foothill Blvd MS 4135 Hayward CA 94541-2771

BECK, GEORGE PRESTON, anesthesiologist, educator; b. Wichita Falls, Tex., Oct. 21, 1930; s. George P. and Amanda (Wilbanks) Beck; m. Constance Carolyn Krog, Dec. 22, 1953; children: Carla Elizabeth, George P., Howard W. BS, Midwestern U., 1951; MD, U. Tex., 1955. Diplomate Am. Bd. Anesthesiology. Intern John Sealy Hosp., 1955—56; resident in anesthesiology Parkland Meml. Hosp., Dallas, 1959—62, vis. staff, 1964—; pvt. practice Lubbock, Tex., 1964—. Asst. prof. anesthesiology U. Tex. Southwestern Med. Sch., Dallas, 1962—64, asst. clin. prof., 1964—71, prof., 1996—; assoc. clin. prof. anesthesiology U. Tex. Med. Br., Galveston, 1971—; pres. Gt. Plains Ballistics Corp., 1967—; clin. prof. Tex. Tech U. Sch. Medicine, Lubbock, 1986—. Pres. coun. Luth. Ch., 1965—66. With USAF, 1956—59. Fellow: Am. Coll. Anesthesiologists; mem.: Lubbock Surg. Soc., Lubbock County Med. Soc., Tex. Soc. Anesthesiologists (pres. 1974), Tex. Med. Soc., Am. Soc. Anesthesiologists. Achievements include invention of Beck Airway Airflow Monitor. Home: 4601 18th St Lubbock TX 79416-5713 Office: PO Box 16385 Lubbock TX 79490-6385 Office Phone: 806-795-2031.

BECK, GEORGE WILLIAM, retired industrial engineer; b. Dayton, Ohio, Aug. 31, 1921; s. George A. and Florence I. (Hosket) B.; m. Elizabeth A. Thatcher, Apr. 14, 1945 (died Nov. 8, 1992); children: Bruce, Christine, William. B.Indsl. Engring., Gen. Motors Inst., 1946. Registered profl. engr., Ohio. Sales rep. Inland Mfg. div. Gen. Motors Corp., Dayton, 1946-53, sr. project engr., 1953-56, staff engr., 1956, asst. chief engr., 1956-62, chief engr., 1962-80, dir. engring., 1980-85; ret., 1985. Trustee Met. YMCA, 1964-71; chmn. bd. mgmt. Kettering YMCA, 1966-70; mem. Centerville City Sch. Dist. bd. edn., 1968-74, v.p., 1973-74. Served to lt. (j.g.) USNR, 1943-45. Mem. Soc. Automotive Engrs., Dayton C. of C., Aircraft Owners and Pilots Assn. (lic. pilot). Clubs: MVMA, Sycamore Creek Country, Mission Valley Country. Lutheran. Achievements include the invention of automotive products; holder of 10 patents in field. Home: 2120 Timucua Trl Nokomis FL 34275-5306

BECK, GLENN E., information technology executive; b. Quakertown, Pa., 1952; BS in Mgmt. sci., Lehigh Univ., 1974; grad. mgmt. info. resource program, Harvard Univ., 1990. Joined Air Products and Chem., Allentown, Pa., 1974—, various positions in info. tech. ops, application devel. and project mgmt., 1974—93, dir. of IT, chem. group, 1993—2000, dir., IT bus. process, 2000—01, v.p., global info. tech., 2001—. Bd. dir. Chem. Industry Data Exchange; former bd. dir. Chem. Process Dir. Group. Mem.: Phila. Chapter, Soc. for Info. Mgmt., Lehigh County Conf. of Churches (bd. dir.). Office: VP Global Info Tech Air Products & Chem Inc 7201 Hamilton Blvd Allentown PA 18195-1501

BECK, GUY LEON, religious studies educator, music educator; b. NYC, Aug. 3, 1948; s. George Anthony and Dale Hanson Beck, Harold Rice Sincock; m. Kajal Dass, Nov. 22, 1979. MA, U. South Fla., 1983, Syracuse U., 1986, PhD, 1989. Acting asst. prof. La. State U., Baton Rouge, 1990—95; extraordinary prof. Loyola U., New Orleans, 1995—97; vis. asst. prof. Coll. of Charleston, 1997—99; vis. prof. Tulane U., New Orleans, 1999—. Vis. fellow Oxford Ctr. for Hindu Studies, 2001. Author: Sonic Theology: Hinduism and Sacred Sound, 1993 (Am. Acad. of Religion Top Five Book in South Asia Studies, 1996); editor: Alternative Krishnas, 2005; musician (pianist): (CD) Sacred Raga Indian Vocal. Sr. Rsch. grantee, Fulbright Commn. USIS, 1992—93, Rsch. grantee, Infinity Found., 2001. Mem.: Am. Acad. Religion (assoc. Rsch. Grant 1989), Masons. Office: Tulane University Religious Studies 210 Jones Hall New Orleans LA 70118 Office Phone: 504-865-5719. Office Fax: 504-862-8736. E-mail: beckg@tulane.edu.

BECK, IRENE CLARE, educational consultant, writer; b. N.Y.C., Dec. 18, 1944; d. James E. and Helen (Carroll) Clare; m. William J. Beck, Aug. 9, 1986; children: Daniel, James Chesire. BA, St. Mary's Coll., 1966; MA, Fairfield U., 1977; EdD, U. Rochester, 1982; Grad. Cert. Women's Studies, DePaul U., 1998. Cert. tchr., N.Y. Tchr. Elem. Sch., N.Y.C., 1966-68, Montessori Acad. N.Y., Bklyn., 1968-73; faculty Housatonic Community Coll., Bridgeport, Conn., 1975-77, Nazareth Coll., Rochester, N.Y., 1977-83; faculty dir. Sheppard Pratt Nat. Ctr. Human Devel., Balt., 1983-91; exec. dir. William & Irene Beck Found., 1987—. Cons. Headstart Programs, Rochester, 1980-83, Family Day Care Tng., Rochester, 1980-83; mem. women's studies faculty program DePaul U., 1999—; presenter workshops and seminars. Author: Expect Respect, Let Me Tell You (manuals), (No Hang Ups (telephone audiotape), 1987, In Tune With Teens (booklet), 1990; weekly news col. Parents and Teens, 1987-90; freelance writer, 1986—; contbr. articles to profl. jours.; sr. editor What's Working for Girls in Illinois, 1996-99. Mem. AAUW, Assn. Childhood Edn. Internat. Avocations: hiking, swimming, biking.

BECK, JAMES V., mechanical engineering educator; b. Cambridge, Mass., May 18, 1930; BS in Mech. Engring., Tufts U., 1956; SM in Mech. Engring., MIT, 1957; PhD in Mech. Engring., Mich. State U., 1964. Prof. mech. engring. Mich. State U., East Lansing, 1964-98, dir. heat transfer property measurement, prof. emeritus; pres. Beck Engring. Cons. Co., Okemos, Mich. Do-organizer Joint Am.-Russian Workshop on Inverse Problems in Heat Transfer, 1992. Contbr. articles to profl. publs. Achievements include research on inverse problem solutions for selected composite materials, development of a user-friendly three-dimensional transfer heat conduction program and measurement of temperature fields of electronic components using infrared thermography, multidimensional thermal and sensing properties of high termerature structures consisting of composites and CVD diamond films. Office: Mich State U Dept Mech Engring 2328E Engring Bldg East Lansing MI 48824 E-mail: beck@egr.msu.edu, jvb@BeckEng.com.

BECK, JEAN MARIE See WIK, JEAN

BECK, JILL, academic administrator, dance educator; b. Worcester, Mass., Aug. 10, 1949; d. John Jacob and Helen Bernadette (Provost) Lindberg; m. Robert Joel Beck, Apr. 21, 1973. BA, Clark U., 1970; MA, McGill U., 1976; PhD, CUNY, 1985. Cert. tchr. and profl. reconstructor in Labanotation. Dir. edn. Dance Notation Bur., NYC, 1980-83; sr. lectr. S. Australian Coll. Advanced Edn., Adelaide, 1983-85; guest faculty U. Mich., 1985, U. Colo, 1986, Denison U., 1987; faculty Am. Dance Festival, Durham, N.C., 1985, The Juilliard Sch., NYC, 1985, asst. dir. dance div., 1988-89; chmn. theatre and dance dept., CUNY, 1985-87, dir. grad. studies dept. dance, 1987; faculty, cons. Hartford Ballet, Conn., 1983, chmn. dance dept. Southern Meth. U., CUNY, dean, Sch. of Arts, U. Calif. Irvine, 1995-03, pres. Lawrence U., Wis., 2004-. Project dir. Ct. Coun. on the Humanities and Arts, 1989-90; cons. Universal Ballet Co. of Korea, 1988-89; project dir. Fund for Improvement Post-Secondary Edn., Washington, 1982-85, NEH, 1983-85, CUNY Research Found., 1981-82; dance dir., cons. Dance Notation Bur., NYC, 1983, mem. profl. adv. com., 1982-84, 85-88; mem. Internat. Conf. Kinetography Laban, 1982—; mem. exec. com. Internat. Movement Notators Alliance, 1984-85; co-chmn. Soc. Dance History Scholars Conf., NYC, 1985-86; dir. program in advanced studies Am. Dance Festival, 1986; stage dir. Lincoln Ctr. student programs, 1987; Dir. dance revivals Doris Humphrey choregraphy, 1981—, Anna Sokolow choreography, 1982—, founder and dir. ArtsBridge Am., 1996, daVinci Ctr. Learning through Arts, 2001. Editor Dance Notation Jour., 1983-85; author several monographs, dance textbooks, and instructional videotapes. Recipient Exhibit award CUNY, 1982, Jack Linquist award, Clara Barton award, Learning for Life award. Democrat. Avocations: travel, art collecting. Office: Off of Pres Lawrence Univ PO Box 599 Appleton WI 54912

BECK, JOHN CHRISTIAN, physician, educator; b. Audubon, Iowa, Jan. 4, 1924; s. Wilhelm and Marie (Brandt) Beck. MD, McGill U., 1947, MSc, 1951, DSc (hon.), 1994; PhD (hon.), Ben Gurion U. of the Negev. Diplomate Am. Bd. Internal Medicine (chmn., dir.). Intern Royal Victoria Hosp., Montreal, 1947—48, sr. asst. resident, 1948—49, physician-in-chief, endocrinologist Montreal, 1964—74; chmn. dept. medicine and dir. Univ. Clinic McGill U., 1964—74; prof. medicine U. Calif., San Francisco, 1974—79; dir. Robert Wood Johnson Clin. Scholars Program, 1973—78; prof. geriat. medicine and gerontology UCLA, 1979—, dir. academic geriat. resource ctr., 1984—90; dir. long term car gerontology ctr. UCLA/U. So. Calif., 1980—85; dir. Calif. Geriatric Edn. Ctr., 1987—97, emeritus dir., 1993—; dir. multicampus program in geriat. medicine and gerontology UCLA, 1979—93. Pres. Am. Bd. Med. Spltys.; vis. prof. numerous univs.; Simeone lectr. Brown U., 1977; John McCreary Meml. lectr. U. B.C., 1985; Bruce Hall Meml. lectr. Garvan Inst. Med. Rsch., U. NSW, Sydney, 1989; Allen T. Bailey Meml. lectr. U. Sask., Canada, 1989; delivered Chaikin Oration, Australian Acad. Tech. Scis. and Engring., 2004—. Editl. bd. Jour. Clin. Endocrinology and Metabolism, Current Topics in Exptl. Endocrinology, Psychiatry in Medicine, Health Policy and Edn., Jour. Am. Bd. Family Practice, cons. editor Roche Lab. Series on Geriatrics and Gerontology. Recipient Lifetime award, Ben Gurion U. of Negev, Israel, 1985, Ann. Gerontology award in edn., Jewish Homes for the Aging, 1994, commendation, City of L.A., 1994. Master: ACP (Philips award 2003); fellow: AAAS, Am. Fedn. on Aging Rsch. (Irving S. Wright award 1991), Gerontol. Soc. Am. (mem. editl. bd. jour., Joseph T. Freeman award 1990, Donald P. Kent award 2001), Am. Geriat. Soc. (Milo F. Leavitt Meml. award 1988), Western Assn. Physicians, Internat. Soc. Neuroendocrinology, Assn. Am. Med. Colls., Can. Assn. Profs. Medicine (Ronald V. Christie award 1987), Can. Physiol. Soc., McGill Osler Reporting Soc. (sec.), Royal Soc. Can., Inst. Medicine, Internat. Soc. Endocrinology (sec.-gen.), Can. Soc. Clin. Investigation (pres.), Endocrine Soc. (v.p., chmn. postgrad. assembly), Am. Fedn. Clin. Rsch. (coun. East divsn.), Can. Med. Assn. (postgrad. edn. com.), Am. Diabetes Assn., Can. Diabetes Assn., Royal Coll. Physicians Can. (mem. coun., Duncan Graham award 1990), Royal Coll. Physicians London, Montreal Physiol. Soc., Laurentian Hormone Conf. (bd. dirs.), Am. Clin. and Climatol. Assn., Can. Med. Protective Assn., Soc. Exptl. Biology and Medicine (mem. editl. bd. jour.), Alpha Omega Alpha, Sigma Xi; mem.: Australian Acad. Technol. Scis. and Engring. (chaikin oration 2004), Assn. for Gerontology in Higher Edn. (Disting. Svc. Recognition award 2001). Office: 1562 Casale Rd Pacific Palisades CA 90272-2714 Fax: 310-454-1944. Business E-Mail: egebjcb@ucla.edu.

BECK, JOHN ROBERT, pathologist, information scientist; b. Cleve., Sept. 8, 1953; s. John Edward and Maralyn Janet (Smith) Beck; children: John Benjamin, Stefan Andrew, Meredith Louise; m. Marjorie Callahan Ritchie, July 20, 2002. AB, Dartmouth Coll., 1974; MD, Johns Hopkins U., 1978. Diplomate Am. Bd. Pathology. Intern, then resident in pathology Dartmouth-Hitchcock Med. Ctr., Hanover, N.H., 1978-80, dir. bloodbank, 1984-89, dir. clin. pathology, 1987-89; fellow, clin. decision making New Eng. Med. Ctr., Boston, 1981; from asst. to assoc. prof. pathology Dartmouth Med. Sch., Hanover, 1982-89; prof., dir. biomed. info. communication ctr. Oreg. Health Scis. U., Portland, 1989-92; prof., v.p. info. tech. Baylor Coll. Medicine, Houston, 1992—2001; exec. dir. Houston Acad. Medicine-Tex. Med. Ctr. Libr., 1999—2001; sr. mem., v.p. Infotech Fox Chase Cancer Ctr., Phila., 2001—, dir. evaluation scis program, 2004—. Mem. healthcare tech. and decision scis. rev. panel Agy. Healthcare Rsch. and Quality, 2005—; bd. dirs. IDM, Inc. Editor-in-chief Med. Decision Making, 1989-94. Elder First Presbyn. Ch., Moorestown, NJ, 2005—. Recipient Rsch. Career Devel. award Nat. Libr. Medicine, 1986. Fellow: Coll. Am. Pathologists (com. vice-chair 1997—2000), Am. Coll. Med. Informatics; mem.: Leadership of Phila., Group on Info. Resources (exec. com. 1997—2000), Am. Assn. Med. Colls., Soc. for Med. Decision Making (sec.-treas. 1985—87, v.p. 1987—88, pres. 1995—96). Republican. Avocations: golf, bridge, trumpet. Office: 333 Cottman Ave Philadelphia PA 19111 Office Phone: 215-214-1697. Business E-Mail: robert.beck@fccc.edu.

BECK, JULIE RENEE, director; b. Montpelier, Ohio, Aug. 30, 1963; d. Kenneth Lamar and Colene Yvonne Beck. BA in commn., Bowling Green State U., 1985; BA in English, Mt. Olive Coll., 2000; MS in parks, rec. and tourism, MC State U., 2005. Field dir. Coastal Carolina Girl Scouts, Goldsboro, NC, 1985—89; dir. student activities Mt. Olive Coll., Mt. Olive, NC, 1989—. Former pres. NC Coll. Personnel Assn., Greenville, NC. Former pres. Mt. Olive C. of C., Mt. Olive, NC, Mt. Olive Jaycees; treas. Waylin Found.; sec., treas. NC Assn. of Festivals and Events, Lexington, NC. Named Woman of Yr., Bus. and Profl. Women, 2002; recipient Dist. Svc. award, Mt. Olive Jaycees, 1999, Key to Mt. Olive, Town of Mt. Olive, 2001. Mem.: Mt. Olive C. of C. (former pres., Outstanding Chamber Mem. award), Jaycees (former pres.). Achievements include coordinator of Kids World Playground, 2000. Avocations: travel, camping, backpacking, canoeing. Home: 634 Henderson St Mount Olive NC 28365 E-mail: jbeck@moc.edu.

BECK, KATHLEEN GODDARD-LOUISE, secondary school educator; b. Columbia, Pa., July 30, 1949; d. Goddard Frederick and Dorothy Marie (Schickling) B. BA in English/Edn., Cabrini Coll., Radnor, Pa., 1971; MS in Edn., Millersville (Pa.) U., 1980. Cert. reading specialist K-12. Tchr. Penn Manor High Sch., Millersville, 1971-75; reading specialist Lancaster-Lebanon Intermediate Unit 13, East Petersburg, Pa., 1975—. Reading and edn. cons. to various schs. in south Cen. Pa. and Laurel, Md., 1976—; lectr. in field; mem. Jane Austin Soc. of Lancaster County, 2004—. Editor:(mag.) Creativity. Founder, dir., coach Conestoga Dolphin Swim Club, 1972-73; tchr. adult scripture study Sacred Heart Ch., also bd. dirs., chair liturgy com.; tchr. High Sch. Religious Studies, Lancaster, 1971—; bd. dirs. Diocesan Pastoral Council, Harrisburg, 1982—; acad. advisors bd. Millersville U., Pa., 1988—. Mem. Internat. Reading Assn., NEA, Nat. Council of Tchrs. of English, Pa. State Edn. Assn., Keystone State Reading Assn., Lancaster-Lebanon Intermediate Unit Edn. Assn., Lancaster-Lebanon Reading Council (scholarship chmn. 1985—). Republican. Avocations: creative writing, reading, theater, needlecrafts, competitive sports. Office: Lancaster-Lebanon Intermediate Unit 13 1110 Enterprise Rd East Petersburg PA 17520-1604

BECK, KIM CHRISTOPHER, director; b. Neenah, Wis., Aug. 10, 1955; s. Benedict Christian Beck and Eileen Catherine Block; m. Pamela Jean Van Ryzin, May 27, 1989; 1 child, Benedict David. BA, St. John's U., Collegeville, Minn., 1978; MA, U. Wis., Oshkosh, 1986, U. Wis., Madison, 1989. World svc. worker YMCA, Alexandria, Egypt, 1983—84; cultural and fine arts program mgr. Naperville (Ill.) Pk. Dist., 1990—93; dir. arts, humanities and sci. U. Wis.-Milw. Sch. Continuing Edn., 1993—. Pres. Milw. Ethnic Coun. Roman Catholic. Achievements include Completed first marathon, Longford, Ireland, 2005. Avocations: family history research, architecture appreciation, cultural/educational tour leader, running marathons. Office: U Wis-Milw 161 W Wisconsin Ave Ste 6000 Milwaukee WI 53203 Office Phone: 414-227-3321. Personal E-mail: kcb@uwm.edu.

BECK, LIVIA GRÜNWALD, physician, psychiatrist; b. Bratislava, Czechoslovakia, Jan. 5, 1947; came to U.S., 1974; d. Dezider and Gizela (Reisz) G.; 1 child, Michael. MBCHB, Victoria U., Manchester, England, 1969-74. Resident in psychiatry Long Island Jewish Hosp. and Med. Ctr., N.Y.C., 1974-78, fellow in psychotherapy, 1978-80, staff psychiatrist Aftercare div., 1978-83, unit chief Adult Day Hosp., 1983—, supr. of residents, 1978-83; pvt. practice N.Y.C., 1980—. Staff psychiatrist L.I. Jewish Hosp. and Med. Ctr.

Geriatric Day Hosp., N.Y.C., 1991—, Holliswood Hosp., Jamaica Estates, N.Y., 1994—; clk. N.Y. Hosp. Queens, Flushing, N.Y., 1997—. Mem. Am. Psychiatric Assn. Jewish. Avocations: travel, theater, concerts, nature. Personal E-mail: Lilimd@aol.com.

BECK, LOIS GRANT, anthropologist, educator, author; b. Bogota, Colombia, Nov. 5, 1944; d. Martin Lawrence and Dorothy (Sweet) Grant; m. Henry Huang; 1 dau., Julia Huang. BA, Portland State U., 1967; MA, U. Chgo., 1969, PhD, 1977. Asst. prof. Amherst (Mass.) Coll., 1973-76, Univ. Utah, Salt Lake City, 1976-80; from asst. to assoc. prof. Washington U., St. Louis, 1980-92, prof., 1992—. Author: Qashqa'i of Iran, 1986, Nomad, 1991; co-editor Women in the Muslim World, 1978, Women in Iran from the Rise of Islam to 1800, 2003, Women in Iran from 1800 to the Islamic Republic, 2004. Grantee Social Sci. Rsch. Coun., 1990, NEH, 1990-92, 98, Am. Philos. Soc., 1998. Mem. Mid. East Studies Assn. (bd. dirs. 1981-84), Soc. Iranian Studies (exec. sec. 1979-82, edit. bd. 1982-91, coun. 1996-98). Office: Washington U Dept Anthropology CB114 1 Brookings Dr Saint Louis MO 63130-4899 Office Phone: 314-935-5252. Business E-Mail: lbeck@artsci.wustl.edu.

BECK, MARGARET ANN (PEGGY BECK), secondary school educator; b. Camden, N.J., Aug. 29, 1949; d. Raymond S. and Margaret Doyle Beck. B of Edn. in English, Trenton State Coll., 1971, MEd in English, 1974; MA in Sch. & Pub. Libr., Glassboro State Coll., 1989. Tchr. English Cherry Hill High Sch. East, NJ, 1971—89, chair media dept., 1989—95; media specialist Cooper Elem. Sch., 1995—2000; media facilitator Cherry Hill High Sch. East, 2000—03, medoa specialist, 2003—. Author: Glogalinks: Resources for Asian Studies, 2002. Mem.: ALA, Ednl. Media Assn. N.J. Home: 107 S Forklanding Rd Maple Shade NJ 08052

BECK, MARILYN MOHR, columnist; b. Chgo., Dec. 17, 1928; d. Max and Rose (Lieberman) Mohr; m. Roger Beck, Jan. 8, 1949 (div. 1974); children: Mark Elliott, Andrea; m. Arthur Levine, Oct. 12, 1980. AA, U. So. Calif., 1950. Freelance writer nat. mag. and newspapers, Hollywood, Calif., 1959-63; Hollywood columnist Valley Times and Citizen News, Hollywood, Calif., 1963-65; West Coast editor Sterling Mag., Hollywood, Calif., 1963-74; free-lance entertainment writer LA Times, Calif., 1965-67; Hollywood columnist Bell-McClure Syndicate, 1967-72; chief Bell-McClure Syndicate (West Coast bur.), 1967-72; Hollywood columnist NANA Syndicate, 1967-72; syndicated Hollywood columnist NY Times Spl. Features, 1972-78, NY Times Spl. Features (United Feature Syndicate), 1978-80, United Press abroad, 1978-80, Internat. Editors News and Features, Chgo. Tribune/NY Daily News Syndicate, 1980-97; columnist TV Guide, 1989—92, Creators Syndicate, 1997—. Creator, host Marilyn Beck's Hollywood Outtakes spls. NBC, 1977, 78; host Marilyn Beck's Hollywood Hotline, Sta. KFI, LA, 1975-77; Hollywood reporter Eyewitness News, Sta. KABC-TV, LA, 1981, (TV program) PM Mag., 1983-88; on-air corr. E! TV, 1993-99, CompuServe Entertainment Authority, 1994-96, eDrive Internet Authority, 1996-97, e!online Internet Hollywood Authority, 1997-2000, Compuserve, 2000—, aeNTV-.com, 2001-02; author: (non-fiction) Marilyn Beck's Hollywood, 1973, (novel) Only Make Believe, 1988; co-author: Unfinished Lives, What If...?, 1996. Recipient Citation of Merit LA City Coun., 1973, Press award Pub. Guild Am., 1974, Bronze Halo award So. Calif. Motion Picture Coun., 1982. Address: 4926 Delos way Oceanside CA 92056 *Being the best isn't everything; it's the only thing. "Life is too short to be little" (Disraeli).*

BECK, MARTHA ANN, art curator, director; BA in English Lit., Vassar Coll., 1960; postgrad., NYU, 1963-67. Editor, writer, rschr. The Frick Collection, 1962-64; curatorial asst. drawings dept. The Mus. Modern Art, 1968-75; founder, dir. The Drawing Ctr., 1975-90, The Ctr. for Internat. Exhbns., 1992—. Served on numerous juries and panels including Nat. Endowment for the Arts, SUNY Thayer Family Fellowships, The Westchester Coun. on the Arts and the Jerome Found. Fellowships; lectr. in field. Recipient NYU scholarship, 1964-65. Home: 9 Gramercy Park S New York NY 10003-1742 Office Phone: 212-473-4918.

BECK, MARYELLEN, library director; b. Amsterdam, NY; d. Henry and Annette Thelma Lessick; m. Roger Andrew Beck, Dec. 25, 1975; children: Jared Harrison, Zachary Baruch. BA, Herbert William Smith Coll., 1974; MLS, State U. of NY at Albany, 1975. Head of adult svcs. Troy Pub. Libr., NY, 1988—94; dir. libr. ops. Small Bus. Develop., Ctr. Rsch. Network, State U. of NY at Albany, 1994—97; mgr. of global info. svcs. United Technologies, East Hartford, Conn., 1997—2000; dir. of libr. Rockville Pub. Libr., Vernon, Conn., 2001—. Recipient Excellence award for pub. svc. in a large libr. in the state of Conn.; Dewey fellow, NY Libr. Assn., 1993. Mem.: Am. Libr. Assn. Office: Rockville Pub Libr Inc 52 Union St P O Box 1320 Vernon Rockville CT 06066 Business E-Mail: mbeck@biblio.org.

BECK, MORRIS, allergist; b. Miami, Fla., Oct. 12, 1927; s. Max and Anna (Luks) B.; m. Hollis Schwartz, Aug. 6, 1960; children: Gayle Beck Finan, Anne Lin. BA, UCLA, 1949; MD, U. Zurich, Switzerland, 1957. Diplomate Am. Bd. Allergy and Immunology, Am. Bd. Pediatrics. Intern Queens Hosp. Ctr., 1958, resident in pediatrics, 1959-60; preceptor in allergy U. Miami (Fla.) Med. Sch., 1961-77; pvt. practice pediatrician Miami, 1961—78; pvt. practice allergist, 1979—; chief dept. allergy Miami Children's Hosp., 1986—2003; clin. prof. pediatrics Nova U. Southeastern Med. Sch., 1998—; clin. asst. prof. U. Miami Med. Sch. With U.S. Army, 1950-52. Fellow: Am. Assn. Cert. Allergists, Am. Acad. Pediatrics, Am. Acad. Asthma, Allergy and Immunology, Am. Coll. Allergy and Immunology; mem.: Am. Coll. Chest Physicians. Republican. Jewish. Avocations: photography, fishing, travel. Office: 7800 SW 87th Ave # C-340 Miami FL 33173-3570 Office Phone: 305-595-0109. E-mail: beckmd123@aol.com.

BECK, PAUL A., lawyer; m. Nancy Flaherty; children: Jennifer, Bradford, Michael. BS, Carnegie-Mellon U., 1957; LLB, Duquesne U., 1962. Bar: Pa. 1962, U.S. Ct. Appeals (4th cir.) 1963, U.S. Supreme Ct. 1966, U.S. Ct. Appeals (2d and 3d cirs.) 1971, U.S. Ct. Appeals (7th cir.) 1974, U.S. Ct. Appeals (Fed. cir.) 1982. Ptnr. Buell, Ziesenheim, Beck & Alstadt, Pitts., 1962-88, Buchanan Ingersoll, Pitts., 1988-95; propr. Paul A. Beck & Assocs. P.C., Pitts., 1995—. Del. U.S. Ct. Appeals (3d cir.) Jud. Conf., 1983. Chmn. alumni forum com. Carnegie-Mellon U., Pitts., 1966-67. Capt. U.S. Army, 1957-59. Mem. ABA, Pa. Bar Assn., Nat. Coun. Pat. Law Assn., Allegheny County Bar Assn. (gov. 1977-79, chmn. intellectual property law sect. 1979-84), Pitts. Intellectual Property Law Assn. (bd. dirs., pres. 1989-90), Duquesne U. Law Sch. Alumni Assn. (v.p. 1997-98, pres. 1999—). Office: Paul A Beck & Assocs PC Ste 100 1575 McFarland Rd Pittsburgh PA 15216-1808 Office Phone: 412-343-9700. Business E-Mail: pbeck@pbeck.law. *Man must set principles as guided by his conscience under which he will live. He will then be accountable to mankind and God in meeting that standard.*

BECK, PAUL ALLEN, political science professor, dean; b. Logansport, Ind., Mar. 15, 1944; s. Frank Paul and Mary Elizabeth (Flanegin) B.; m. Maria Teresa Marcano, June 10, 1967; children: Daniel Lee, David Andrew. AB, Ind. U., 1966; MA, U. Mich., 1968, PhD, 1971. Asst. prof. U. Pitts., 1970-75, assoc. prof., 1976-79; prof. Fla. State U., Tallahassee, 1979-87, chmn. dept., 1981-87; prof. Ohio State U., Columbus, 1987—, chmn. dept., 1991—2004, dean Coll. Social and Behavioral Scis., 2004—. Co-author: Political Socialization Across the Generations, 1975, Individual Energy Conservation Behaviors, 1980, Electoral Change in Advanced Industrial Democracies, 1984, Party Politics in America, 10th edit., 2003. Chmn. coun. Inter-Univ. Consortium for Polit. and Social Research, 1982-83, mem., 1980-83; mem. NSF polit. sci. panel, 1988-89. Recipient Disting. Svc. award Ohio State U., 2000, Disting. Scholar award Ohio State U., 2004. Mem. Am. Polit. Sci. Assn. (exec. coun. 1981-82, 93-94, book rev. editor 1976-79, program chair 1994, chair strategic planning com. 1999-2000, Goodnow award 2005), Midwest Polit. Sci. Assn. (exec. coun. 1987-90, mem. editl. bd. 1988-90, program chair 1991, v.p. 1996-98), So. Polit. Sci. Assn. (mem. editl. bd. 1982-87), Phi Beta Kappa, Pi Sigma Alpha (exec. coun.). Democrat. Home: 7003 Perry Dr Columbus OH 43085-2815 Office: Ohio State U Coll Social and Behavioral Scis Columbus OH 43210-1341 Business E-Mail: beck.9@osu.edu.

BECK, PHILIP S., lawyer; b. Chgo., Apr. 30, 1951; BA with academic distinction, U. Wis., 1973; JD magna cum laude, Boston U., 1976. Bar: Ill. 1977. Clerk U.S. Ct. Appeals DC Cir., 1976-77; ptnr. Kirkland & Ellis, 1977—93; founding ptnr. Bartlit Beck Herman Palenchar & Scott LLP, Chgo., 1993—. Editor-in-chief Boston U. Law Review. Bd. visitors Boston U. Sch. Law; bd. dir. Northwestern U. Settlement House. Named one of Top 10 Litigators, Nat. Law Jour., 2003. Fellow: Am. Bar Found., Internat. Acad. Trial Lawyers, Am. Coll. of Trial Lawyers. Office: Bartlit Beck Herman et al Courthouse Pl 54 W Hubbard St Chicago IL 60610-4645 Office Phone: 312-494-4400. Office Fax: 312-494-4440. Business E-Mail: philip.beck@bartlit-beck.com.

BECK, PHYLLIS WHITMAN, judge; b. N.Y.C. d. Irving and Dora (Sugar) Whitman; m. Aaron T. Beck; children: Roy, Judith, Daniel, Alice. AB magna cum laude, Brown U.; JD, Temple U., 1967, hon. degrees (2), 1997. Bar: Pa. 1967. Pvt. practice law, Phila., 1967-74; assoc. prof. Temple U. Law Ctr., Phila., 1974-76; vice dean U. Pa. Law Sch., Phila., 1976-81; judge Superior Ct. Pa., 1981—. Chmn. Pa. Gov.'s Commn. on Jud. Reform, 1987—88; Phi Beta Kappa lectr. Brown U., Providence; Lindbach lectr. Bryn Mawr Coll.; bd. dirs. Mann Ctr. for Performing Arts, WHYY--Pub. Broadcasting Corp. Contbr. articles to profl. jours. Pres. Found. Cognitive Therapy, 1974—; chair bd. Independence Found.; bd.dirs. Temple Law Sch., Free Libr. of Phila., Jewish-Am. History Mus.; mem. Joint State Govt. Commn. on Domestic Rels. Law, 1995—; mem. Pennsylvanians for Modern Cts.; mem. bd. consultors Villanova Law Sch.; mem. bd. overseers U. Pa. Sch. Nursing. Named a Disting. Dau. of Pa.; recipient Leadership award, Med. Coll. Pa., Phila., William Brennan award, Phila. Bar Assn., 1997, Sandra Day O'Connor award, 2005. Mem. Am. Law Inst., Am. Bar Found., Am. Judicature Soc. (bd. dirs., Herbert Harley award 1995), Pa. Bar Assn. (Jud. award 1990, Anne Alperin award 1997), Women in the Profession, Nat. Assn. Women Judges (Murray award 1998), Disting. Dau. of Pa. 2000. Office: Pa Superior Ct GSB Bldg Ste 800 Bala Cynwyd PA 19004

BECK, RHONDA JOANN, paramedic, educator, writer; b. Hawkinsville, Ga., Apr. 20, 1965; d. Franklin Lamar and Ida (Scarborough) Woodard; m. Gary Wendell Bramlett, Apr. 9, 1983 (div. May 1995); 1 child, Gary Michael Bramlett; m. Kenneth Steve Beck, June 8, 1997. Gen. Banking Degree, Am. Inst. Banking. Cert. BTLS, CPR, PHTLS, ACLS, BLS instr. trainer, emergency med. technician-paramedic, instr. Collateral clk. Bank South, N.A., Perry, Ga., 1986-94; emergency med. technician Taylor Regional Hosp., Hawkinsville, 1993-94; paramedic Med. Ctr. Ctrl. Ga., Macon, 1994-99; emergency med. technician instr., paramedic instr. Ctrl. Ga. Tech. Coll., Macon, 1997—; paramedic Houston Med. Ctr., Warner Robins, Ga., 1997—. Instr. ACLS, Pediat. Life Support, PreHosp. Trauma Life Support, Basic Trauma Life Support, Am. Heart Assn.; reviewer Delmar Thomson, 1999—, Jones & Bartlett, 2000-, GEMS Faculty, 2003-present, Am. Geriatric Soc.; Brady, 2001—. Author: Emergency Care and Transportation of the Sick and Injured, student workbook, AAOS, 8th edit., 2001; pub. author, reviewer: Jones & Bartlett. Vol. firefighter Houston County Vol. Fire Dept., Hayneville, Ga., 1986-95. Recipient Heartsaver award Laerdal Med. Corp., 1994, Vol. Svc. award Am. Lung Assn. Ga., 1995. Democrat. Baptist. Avocations: reading, swimming, exercise, writing, coin collecting/numismatics. Office: Houston County EMS Warner Robins GA 31093 E-mail: takai_sensei@yahoo.com.

BECK, ROBERT ALFRED, hotel executive, educator; b. Boston, Nov. 1, 1920; s. Alfred and Laura Martha (Reissman) B.; m. Mary Kathryn Murray, Nov. 5, 1944; children: Susan Jane, Janice Barbara, Robin Maria. BS, Cornell U., 1942, MS in Edn., 1952, PhD, 1954. Food technologist, pers. mgr. Quincy Market Co., Boston, 1945-50; mem. faculty Sch. Hotel Adminstrn., Cornell U., 1954-84, prof., 1960-84, dean, 1961-81; dir. Internat. Inst. Hotel Mgmt., Cergy-Pontoise, France, 1981-84; prof., disting. scholar in residence Fla. Internat. U., 1984—. Vis. lectr. USAF in PTO and ETO, U.S. Army in Europe, others; bd. dirs. Carrolls Devel. Corp., Consulan AG, Switzerland; mgmt. cons. U.S. Dept. Commerce, USAF, U.S. Army, USN, Govt. of Jamaica, Govt. of Barbados, Govt. of Bahama Is., Nat. Restaurant Assn., others. Contbr. articles to trade publs. Trustee, v.p. Ednl. Inst. Am. Hotel and Motel Assn.; v.p. Nat. Inst. Foodservice Industry; trustee Caribbean Hotel Tng. Inst., Ithaca (NY) Coll.; mem. bd. advisors Nova U., Ft. Lauderdale, Fla.; bd. dirs. Culinary Inst. Am., Internat. Hotel and Tourism Tng. Inst., Basel, Switzerland; mem. governing bd. East-West Coll. Natural Medicine, Sarasota, Fla., 2000—; mem. adv. bd. U. South Fla. 1st lt. F.A., AUS, 1942-45, ETO. Decorated Purple Heart. Mem. AAUP, Croix de Guerre, Phi Kappa Phi, Phi Delta Kappa. Home: 1255 N Gulfstream Ave Apt 805 Sarasota FL 34236-8929 E-mail: beckiab815@aol.com.

BECK, ROBERT BERYL, real estate executive; b. Dalton, Ga., Feb. 25, 1935; s. Carson W. and Gladys (Gray) B.; m. Martha Lucinda Cone, June 14, 1957; children: Perkie Cone Beck Cannon, Robert B. Jr., Carson W. Student, Vanderbilt U., 1953-57; LLB, JD, Nashville Sch. Law, 1964. Salesman Southeastern Inc., Nashville, 1957-64; purchasing agt. Nashville Bd. Edn., 1965-66; pres. Beck & Beck Realty, Nashville, 1967—, Beck & Beck Ins. Co., Nashville, 1967-78, v.p., 1978—; pres. Tri-County Builders, Nashville, 1974—. Editor Grace Bapt. Monthly, 1985, real estate newsletter, 1986-87. Mem. Nashville Bd. Realtors, Lodges: Masons. Democrat. Avocations: fishing, hiking, bicycling. Home: 3500 Brick Church Pike Nashville TN 37207-2002 Office: Beck & Beck 4205 Gallatin Rd Nashville TN 37216-2111 Office Phone: 615-226-9900. E-mail: robertbecksr@msn.com.

BECK, ROBERT EDWARD, computer scientist, educator; b. Denver, June 7, 1941; s. Arthur Walter and Caroline Adelheid (Petrie) B.; m. Barbara Ruth Pennell, Aug. 21, 1965; children: Philip Arthur, Christopher William, Jennifer Grove. BS in Math., Harvey Mudd Coll., Claremont, Calif., 1963; PhD in Math., U. Pa., 1969. Instr. Villanova (Pa.) U., 1966-69, asst. prof., 1969-74, assoc. prof., 1974-78, prof. computer sci., 1978—, dept. chair, 1992—. Team chair computing accreditation commn. ABET, 1986—. Author: Elementary Linear Programming, 2d edit., 1995; editor: Computers in Nonassociative Rings and Algebras, 1978. Fulbright Exchange fellow, 1981-82. Mem. AAUP, Assn. for Computing Machinery (chair computer sci. conf. 1995, 96, chair preparing future faculty program 1998-2002), Sigma Xi. Office: Villanova U Dept Computing Sci Villanova PA 19085 Office Phone: 610-519-7307. E-mail: robert.beck@villanova.edu.

BECK, ROBERT JAMES, editor, writer, economist, consultant; b. Milw., Nov. 21, 1938; s. Walter John and Evelyn Barbara (Bigus) Beck; m. Mary Ellen Drew, Jan. 20, 1968 (div. Aug. 1978); m. Connie Sue Sparling, Aug. 2, 1988 (div. May 1994). BS in Econs. with honors, U. Wis., Milw., 1961; MS in Internat. Econs., U. Wis., 1965; postgrad., Wharton Sch., U. Pa., 1967, U. Okla., 1981. Actuarial asst. Milliman & Robertson, Milw., 1963-64; rsch. asst. U. Wis., Milw., 1964-65; economist, statistician Wis. Telephone Co., Milw., 1965-68; dir. econ. rsch. Mackay Shields Econs., N.Y.C., 1968-69; head oper. planning Oil Svc. Co. Iran, Ahwaz, 1969-79; econs. editor Oil & Gas Jour., Tulsa, 1979-2000; developer, mgr. Oil & Gas Jour. Energy Database, Tulsa, 1984—; cons. Oil & Gas Jour., 2000—, Robert J. Beck & Assocs., 2000—; contract mgr. Oil & Gas Jour. Online Rsch. Ctr., 2001—. Cons. Oil and Gas Jour. Online Rsch. Ctr., 1994—, Altec Energy, Centralia, Ill., 1986—90, Rainbow Petroleum, N.Y.C., 1986, Farrar and Assocs., Tulsa, 1985—86, Internat. Soc. Energy Advs., 2002—. Author: Oil Industry Outlook, 1983, 20th edit., 2003; developer Energy Statistics Sourcebook, 1986—; editor: Company Performance Statistics Sourcebook, 1966—, International Energy Statistics Sourcebook, 1991—, Natural Gas Statistics Sourcebook, 1993—, Refining Statistics Sourcebook, 1993—, Price Statistics Sourcebook, —; contbr. articles to mags. and newspapers. Active Wis. Gov.'s Commn. Econ. Indicators, 1967, Nature Conservancy, Tulsa, 1988—, Philbrook Mus. Art, Tulsa, 1989—, Tulsa Zoo, 1991—, Mus. Fine Arts, Houston, 1999—, Gilcrease Mus., Philbrook Art Mus., Tulsa Mayor's Energy Adv. Com., 2002—, Tulsa Com. Fgn. Rels., 2002—; bd. dirs., pres. Energy Literacy Project, 1996—; pres. Young Dems., West Allis, Wis., 1960—62. Mem.: Ind. Petroleum Assn. Am. (mem. supply and demand com., mem. cost study com.), U.S. Assn. Energy Econs., Assn. Petroleum Writers, Nat. Assn. Bus. Econs., Internat. Assn. Energy Advs., Internat. Assn. Energy Econs. (coun.). Avocations: bicycling, hiking, movies, tennis, golf. Office Phone: 918-831-9488. Personal E-mail: bbeck2138@cs.com. Business E-Mail: bobb@pennwell.com.

BECK, ROBERT N., nuclear medicine educator; b. San Angelo, Tex., Mar. 26, 1928; married, 1958. AB, U. Chgo., 1954, BS, 1955. Chief scientist Argonne Cancer Rsch. Hosp., 1957-67, assoc. prof., 1967-76; prof. radiol. sci. U. Chgo., 1976; dir. Franklin McLean Inst., 1977-94, dir. Ctr. Imaging Sci., 1986-98; prof. emeritus U. Chgo., 1998—. Cons. Internat. Atomic Energy Agency, 1966-68; mem. Internat. Com. on Radiation Units, 1968—, Nat. Coun. on Radiation, Protection & Measurements, 1970—. Recipient Aebersold award FDR, 1991. Mem. IEEE (Med. Imaging Sci. award 1996), Soc. Nuclear Med., Am. Assn. Physicists in Medicine, Soc. Magnetic Resonance. Achievements include research in development of a theory of the process by which images can be formed of the distribution of radioactive material in a patient in order to diagnose his disease. Office: U Chgo MC 2026 5841 S Maryland Ave Chicago IL 60637-1463 Business E-Mail: r-beck@uchicago.edu.

BECK, STUART EDWIN, lawyer; b. Phila., Aug. 12, 1940; s. Louis M. Beck and (Cooper) Anna; m. Elaine Kushner, June 20, 1964; children: Adam, Barry, Caroline. BSME, Drexel U., 1964; JD, George Washington U., 1968. Bar: Va. 1968, U.S. Dist. Ct. D.C. 1969, Pa. 1970, U.S. Dist. Ct. (ea. dist.) Pa. 1971, U.S. Ct. Appeals (3d cir.) 1971, U.S. Supreme Ct. 1980, U.S. Ct. Appeals (4th cir.) 1989, U.S. Patent and Trademark Office. Assoc. Seidel, Gonda & Goldhammer, Phila., 1969-73; atty. pvt. practice, Phila., 1974-79, 91—; ptnr. Trachman, Jacobs & Beck, Phila., 1979-88, Weinstein, Trachtman, Beck & Kimmelman, Phila., 1988-91. Adj. prof. patent law Rutgers U. Law Sch., Camden, N.J.; instr. patent, trademark and copyright law The Phila. Inst.; lectr. patent, trademark and copyright law Newmann Coll., 1999, lectr. U.S. trademark prosecution, seminar on U.S. trademark practice for paralegals, Phila., 2003; lectr. trademark law Halfmoon LLC, 2003, internat. patent law, 2005 Capt. Am. Cancer Soc., 1974, 75; bd. dirs. Jewish Family and Children Svc. Phila., 1973-89, legal, fin. and budget com., 1979—, spkrs. com., 1979—, bldg. and grounds com., 1980-82, trustee, 1989; bd. dirs., by-laws revision com., bldgs. and grounds com., edn. com. Temple Beth Hillel; bd. dirs. Phila. Vol. Lawyers for Arts, 1980-84, treas., 1980-82. Mem. ABA (patent trademark and copyright law sect., litigation sect., antitrust law sect.), Am. Intellectual Property Law Assn. (com. patent contracts other than govt. 1971-75), Pa. Bar Assn., Phila. Bar Assn. (com. profl. responsibility 1975-93, com. election procedures 1976-84, com. law and arts 1976-80), Phila. Patent Law Assn. (com. ethics 1977-83, com. pub. rels. 1974-77, com. profl. responsibility 1975-79). Avocations: sailing, travel. Office Phone: 215-568-6000. Personal E-mail: beckemail@aol.com.

BECK, TAMARA, association management firm executive; b. Belgrade, Yugoslavia, Feb. 7, 1947; came to U.S., 1953, naturalized, 1967; d. Jakov M. and Slava Levi; m. Burton Philip Beck, May 3, 1992. AB in English, Clark U., 1968; tchr. cert. Hunter Coll., 1971; postgrad. Columbia Tchr.'s Coll., 1973-74, Bank St. Coll., 1975-78. Cert. tchr., N.Y. Tchr. East Harlem Block, N.Y.C., 1973-78; mem. adj. faculty Bank St. Coll., N.Y.C., 1976-78; direct mkgt. svcs. mgr. Flaghouse, Inc., N.Y.C., 1980-87, pres. Clean Lists Assocs., N.Y.C., 1987—; prin. SBI Advt. and Mktg., 1984-89, N.Y.C. and South Lee, Mass., 1986-89; assoc. Classic Printers Ltd., N.Y.C., 1987-92; instr. direct mkgt. Marymount Manhattan Coll., 1985-87; instr. direct mktg., Baruch Coll., 1987-94; devel. cons. Conn. Women's Edn. and Legal Fund, Hartford, Conn., 1983-86; In Touch Networks, N.Y.C., 1982-88. Adaptor script for film, staging The Only Jealousy of Emer, 1968. Bd. dirs. Berkshire Pub. Theater, Pittsfield, Mass., 1979-81; active career resources com. Clark Alumni Assn., 1980-89. Mem. Am. Women Entrepreneurs, Women's Direct Response Group, Mcpl. Arts Soc. (co-chair membership com. fellows program 1989-91). Office: Clean Lists 122 E 42nd St Rm 1700 New York NY 10168-0002 Office Phone: 212-551-1013. Personal E-mail: cleanlists@mindspring.com.

BECK, URSULA, art educator, artist; Founding exec. dir. Taos Inst. Arts, N.Mex., Taos Art Sch. Office: Taos Art Sch PO Box 2588 Taos NM 87571 Office Phone: 505-758-0350. Office Fax: 505-758-4880. Business E-Mail: tas@laplaza.org.

BECK, VAUGHN PETER, lawyer; b. Eureka, S.D., Nov. 13, 1966; s. Floyd and Gladys M. (Zimmerman) B.; m. Julie I. Meier, Jan. 2, 1993; children: Emily I., Philip F. BS, U. S.D., 1989, JD, 1992. Bar: S.D. 1992, U.S. Dist. Ct. S.D. 1993. Legal intern Governmental Rsch. Bureau, Vermillion, S.D., 1990, S.D. Pub. Utilities, Pierre, S.D., 1991, Freiberg, Rudolf & Peterson, Beresford, S.D., 1992; staff atty. Pub. Defenders Office, Deadwood, S.D., 1992; atty. Beck Law Office, Ipswich, S.D., 1993—. Bd. dirs. Ipswich Devel. Corp., 1993—, Ipswich Comml. Club, 1993—; com. mem. Consumer Protection S.D., 1994—. Mem. Ipswich Vol. Fire Dept., 1993—; trustee, officer United Church of Christ, 1993—. Republican. Office: Beck Law Office P O Box 326 509 Bloemendaal Dr Ipswich SD 57451 Office Phone: 605-426-6319. E-mail: becklaw@valleytel.net.

BECK, WARREN RANDALL, retired glass technologist; b. Bethlehem, Pa., Feb. 14, 1918; s. Stewart Elbert and Lottie (Horn) B.; m. Lois K. Jones, Sept. 1, 1939 (div. 1964); children: Dianne Evelyn Blankenship, Kathryn Lynn Thostenson, Vicki Allison Martin, Constance Rae Stiles; m. Carol J. Anderson, Mar. 14, 1970. BS in Ceramics, Pa. State U., 1942; MS in Mineralogy, U. Minn., 1948. Staff Pa. State U., 1942-43; glass technologist 3M Co., St. Paul, 1943-48, sect. leader, 1948-55, mgr. rsch. and devel., 1955-64, corp. scientist, 1964-86, ret., 1986. Patentee in field; contbr. articles to profl. publs. Recipient Samuel Geijsbeek award for Innovation in Ceramics Am. Ceramics Soc., 1995. Fellow Am. Ceramic Soc. Home: 942 Winterberry Dr Woodbury MN 55125-9122 E-mail: wncbeck@aol.com.

BECK, WILLIAM G., lawyer; b. Kansas City, Mo., Mar. 4, 1954; s. Raymond W. Beck and Wanda Williams; m. Cheryl A. Beck; children: Collin M., Sergei M., Valentina M., Kseniya M. BA in Econs., U. Mo., Kansas City, 1974, JD, 1978. Bar: Mo. 1978, U.S. Dist. Ct. (we. dist.) Mo. 1978, U.S. Ct. Appeals (5th cir.) 1988, U.S. Dist. Ct. (ea. dist.) Mich. 1991, U.S. Dist. Ct. (no. dist.) Ill. 1992, U.S. Ct. Appeals (6th cir.) 1992, U.S. Dist. Ct. (ea. dist.) Wis. 1997, U.S. Ct. Appeals (2d cir.) 1997, U.S. Ct. Appeals (10th cir.) 1997, U.S. Supreme Ct. 1997, U.S. Ct. Appeals (1st cir.) 1998, U.S. Ct. Appeals (7th cir.) 1999, U.S. Dist. Ct. Colo. 2000, U.S. Dist. Ct. Rhode Island 2002, U.S. Dist. Ct. Mass. 2002. Shareholder Field, Gentry, Benjamin & Robertson, P.C., Kansas City, 1978-89; ptnr. Lathrop & Norquist, Kansas City, 1989-95, Lathrop & Gage, L.C., Kansas City, 1996—. Commr. Human Rels. Commn., Jackson County, Mo., 1985-89; chmn. Citizens Assn., Kansas City, 1991-92, 95-96; mem. Pub. Improvement Adv. Com., Kansas City, 1991-2001, vice chmn., 1995-98, chmn. 1998-2001, fin. chmn. cmty. infrastructure com., 1996-1997; mem. Waste Minimization Com., Kansas City, 1990-91; bd. mem. Regional Transit Alliance, 2001-03. Office: Lathrop & Gage LC 2345 Grand Blvd Ste 2800 Kansas City MO 64108-2684 E-mail: bbeck@lathropgage.com.

BECKEL, CHARLES LEROY, physicist, educator; b. Phila., Feb. 7, 1928; s. Samuel Mercer and Katherine (Linsky) Beckel; m. Josephine Ann Beck, June 27, 1958; children: Amanda S., Sarah K., Timothy C., Andrea C. BS, U. Scranton, 1948; PhD, Johns Hopkins U., 1954. Asst. prof. physics Georgetown U., 1953-59, assoc. prof., 1959-64; rsch. staff mem. Inst. Def. Analyses, Arlington, Va., 1964-66; assoc. prof. U. N.Mex., Albuquerque, 1966-69, prof., 1969-94, prof. emeritus, 1995—, asst. dean, 1971-72, acting v.p. rsch., 1972-73, acting dir. Inst. Social R&D, 1972. Cons. Ballistics Rsch. Lab., Aberdeen Proving Ground, Md., 1955—57, Inst. Def. Analyses, 1962—64, 1966—69, Dikewood Corp., Albuquerque, 1967—72, Albuquerque,

1974—80, Albuquerque Urban Obs., 1969—71, U.S. ACDA, 1981—84; Fulbright lectr. U. Peshawar, Pakistan, 1957—58, Cheng Kung U., Tainan, Taiwan, 1963—64; vis. prof. theoretical chemistry Oxford U., 1973; vis. prof. chemistry and molecular scis. U. Sussex, England, 1987; phys. sci. officer U.S. Arms Control and Disarmament Agy., 1980—81; vis. prof. physics U. Scranton, 1995. Pres. Nat. Kidney Found. N.Mex Inc., 1968—72, del. trustee, 1972—73, 1976—80, mem. exec. com., 1974—80, 1983—86, v.p., 1982—83, trustee, 1987—93; bd. dirs. Nat. Capital Area Nat. Kidney Found., 1965—66, N.Mex Combined Health Appeal, 1972—73; mem. Navajo Sci. Com., 1975—82. Recipient Vol. award, Nat. Kidney Found. N.Mex, 1988, Frank J. O'Hara award for Disting. Achievement in Sci., U. Scranton Nat. Alumni Soc., 1988, award in solic state physics materials scis., U.S. Dept. Energy, 1988, Outstanding Tchg. award, Burlington No. Found., 1989. Mem.: Biolectromagnetics Soc., Am. Phys. Soc., Nat. Eagle Scout Assn. Office: U NMex Dept Physics And Astronomy Albuquerque NM 87131-0001 Business E-Mail: clbeckel@unm.edu.

BECKEN, BRADFORD ALBERT, engineering executive; b. Providence, Oct. 5, 1924; s. Albert R. and Ruth M. (Stephenson) B.; m. Gaynelle M. Lane, Nov. 30, 1946; children: Bradford Albert, Brian A., Christian L., Anne Tracey. Student, U. R.I., 1942-43; BS, U.S. Naval Acad., 1946; BS in Electronics, U.S. Naval Postgrad. Sch., 1952; MS, UCLA, 1953, PhD, 1961. Commd. officer USN, advanced through grades to comdr.; cons. Airtronics-Spl. Warfare Lab., 1967; mgr. systems engring. lab. submarine signal div. Raytheon Co., Portsmouth, R.I., 1967-70, mgr. engring., 1970-82, dir. tech. Portsmouth Engring. Lab., 1982-94; cons., 1994—97. Author: Advances in Hydroscience, 1964. Trustee Newport Hosp., 1977, chmn. bd., 1979-84; chmn. bd. dirs. Newport Health Care Corp., 1984-93; treas. Newport Hist. Soc., 1993-94, pres., 1994-2001. Recipient Asst. Chief Bur. Ships award, 1963, Am. Def. Preparedness Assn. Gold medal, 1995, Navy Undersea Warfare Ctr. Decibel award, 1997, Capt. George W. Ringenberg award, 1999. Fellow Acoustical Soc. Am.; mem. Nat. Def. Indsl. Assn., Naval War Coll. Found., U.S. Naval Inst., U.S. Naval Acad. Alumni Assn. Episcopalian. Home: 260 Fischer Cir Portsmouth RI 02871-5400 Personal E-mail: babecken@aol.com.

BECKENSTEIN, MYRON, journalist; b. Cleve., Mar. 11, 1938; s. Irwin and Rachel (Miller) B.; 1 child: Amanda Mbuvi. BS, Northwestern U., 1959, MS, 1960. Mem. staff Chgo. Daily News, 1959-78, Balt. Sun, 1978—2002. Served with U.S. Army, 1961—64. Mem. Upper Patuxent Archeol. Group, Archeol. Soc. Md., Soc. Profl. Journalists. Home: 6817 Pineway University Park MD 20782 E-mail: myronbeck@aol.com.

BECKER, ALLIENNE R., education educator, writer; b. Dubois, Pa. d. Harold Raymond and Anne Williams Rimer; m. Isidore H. Becker; m. William Sterling Hopwood, June 9, 1947 (div. Jan. 1, 1969); children: William Hopwood, Carolyn Hopwood Blick, Richard B. Hopwood. AB, Duke Univ., Durham, N.C., 1947; MA, W.Va. Univ., Morgantown, 1970, MA, 1971; PhD, Pa. State Univ., College Park, 1984. Assoc. prof. Lock Haven (Pa.) Univ., 1970—97. Author: The Lost Worlds Romance, 1992, Visions of The Fantastic, 1996, Divine & Human Comedy of Andrew Greeley, 2000, I, Paul: The Life of the Apostle to the Gentiles, 2002, Andrew M. Greeley: The Mysteries of Grace, 2002, Eagle in Flight: The Life of Athanasius the Apostle of the Trinity, 2002; author: (with Ricardo C. Castellanos) All You Need is Love: The Way of Joy, 2003, Be Free! The Gift of Freedom, 2003; author: (with Ricardo Castellanos) Peace! Be Still: The Gift of Peace, 2004. Avocation: travel.

BECKER, BRANDON, lawyer; b. Berwyn, Ill., Mar. 19, 1954; BA summa cum laude, U. Minn., 1974; JD magna cum laude, U. San Diego, 1977; LLM, Columbia U., 1979. Bar: Calif. 1978, DC 1978, NY 2002. Atty. SEC, Washington, 1978-80, br. chief, 1980, legal asst., 1981-82, asst. dir., 1982-86, assoc. dir., 1986-91, dep. dir., 1991-93, dir. divsn. mkt. regulation, 1993-95, spl. advisor to the chmn. for internat. derivatives, 1995-96; ptnr. Wilmer Cutler Pickering Hale & Dorr, Washington, 1996—, co-chmn. Securities dept. Mem. bd. adv. Ctr. for Study of Securities Markets; instr. Am. Univ., George Mason Univ., Georgetown Univ. Editor (articles): San Diego Law Rev.; contbr. articles to profl. jours.; mem. editl. adv. bd. Internat. Finance, wallstreetlawyer.com. Mem.: ABA (chmn. subcommittee on market regulation). Avocation: chess. Office: Wilmer Cutler Pickering Hale and Dorr LLP 2445 M St NW Washington DC 20037-1435 Office Phone: 202-663-6979. Office Fax: 202-663-6363. Business E-Mail: brandon.becker@wilmerhale.com.*

BECKER, BRENDA L., federal official; Degree, Mich. State U.; MBA, Ctrl. Mich. U. Former v.p. congl. comm. Blue Cross Blue Shield Assoc.; asst. sec. legis. & intergovernmental affairs U.S. Dept. Commerce, Washington, 2001—04; asst. to the v.p. for legis. affairs The White House, Washington, 2004—. Office: 17th & Pennsylvania Ave Washington DC 20502

BECKER, CATHERINE HICKEY HANDY, retired librarian; b. Holyoke, Mass., May 10, 1932; d. Cornelius Joseph and Mary Agnes (Collins) Hickey; m. Wallace H. Handy, Nov. 1955 (dec. Nov. 1961); children: Cornelia and Roberta (twins), Mary; m. Bernhard H. Becker, Sept. 1992. BA, U. Mass., 1953; MS in LS, So. Conn. State Coll., 1965. Tchr. New Salem (Mass.) Acad., 1953-54, Londmeadow (Mass.) Jr. High Sch., 1954-56; libr. Wilson Jr. High Sch., Windsor, Conn., 1965-69; reference libr. Westfield (Mass.) State Coll., 1969-92, ret., 1992. Abstractor Libr. Currents, 1984-86. Vol. Noble Hosp., Westfield, 1977-80, LifeLink of S.W. Fla., 1996—, Venice Hosp., 1997—. Mem. AAUW, ALA (cert. sch. and acad. libr., reviewer RQ 1980-92, Choice 1984-92), Assn. Coll. and Rsch. Librs., New Eng. Libr. Assn., NEA, Mass. Tchrs. Assn., Mass. State Coll. Assn., Venice Area Audubon Soc., U. Mass. Alumni Assn., Sigma Kappa. Roman Catholic. Avocations: reading, biking, bird watching. Home: 5815 Buchanan Rd Venice FL 34293-6864

BECKER, DAVID, artist, educator; b. Milw., Aug. 16, 1937; s. Walter Gustav and Fern Bertha (Raddatz) B.; m. Catherine Claytor, Aug. 27, 1960 (div. 1981); children: Sarah Lynne, Amelia Elisabeth; m. Patricia Ann Fennell, Nov. 13, 1988; 1 child, Sloane Fennell. Student, Layton Sch. Art, 1956-58; BS, U. Wis., Milw., 1961; MFA, U. Ill., 1965. Asst. prof. Wayne State U., Detroit, 1965-71, assoc. prof., 1971-80, prof., 1980-85; assoc. prof. U. Wis., Madison, 1985-87, prof., 1987—. Vis. prof. U. Wis., Madison, 1985—87; vis. artist Utah State U., Logan, 1981; art lectr. in field; rep. by Ann Nathan Gallery, Chgo. Exhbns. include Mus. Fine Arts, Boston, 1965, 75, Butler Inst. Am. Art, Youngstown, Ohio, 1967, 68, 72, Lawrence Stevens Gallery, Detroit, 1968, Detroit Inst. Arts, 1971, 77, 86, 91, Richard Nash Gallery, Seattle, 1974, Franz Bader Gallery, Washington, 1974, 77, 80, Madison (Wis.) Art Ctr., 1975, 79, Libr. of Congress, Washington, 1975, Honolulu Acad. Arts, 1975, 83, ADI Gallery, San Francisco, 1975, London Arts Gallery, Detroit, 1976, Boston Ctr. Arts, 1976, 78, Museo de Arte Moderno, Cali, Colombia, 1976, 77, 81, Bawag Found., Vienna, Austria, 1976, Bklyn. Mus., 1976, 84, Met. Mus., Miami, Fla., 1977, 80, Habatat Galleries, Dearborn, Mich., 1977, Visual Arts Ctr. Alaska, Anchorage, 1978, 86, Cranbrook Acad. Art, Bloomfield Hills, Mich., 1980, Associated Am. Artists Gallery, Phila., 1980, Phila. Art Alliance/Phila. Print Club, 1980, Kalamazoo (Mich.) Inst. Arts, 1980, 86, Nat. Mus. Am. Art, Washington, 1982, DeCordova Mus., Lincoln, Mass., 1982, 86, USIA, 1983, Saginaw (Mich.) Mus. Art, 1984, Brockton (Mass.) Mus. Art, 1984, Mich. Gallery, Detroit, 1986, Neville-Sargent Gallery, Chgo., 1986, Intergrafic, East Berlin, 1984, 87, 9th Brit. Internat. Print Biennale, Bradford, 1986, Jane Haslem Gallery, Washington, 1987, 90, 92, 93, John Szoke Graphics, N.Y.C., 1988, Silvermine Gallery, Stamford, Conn., 1988, Elvehjem Mus. Art, Madison, 1989, Boston Printmakers 42d and 43d Nat. Print Exhbn., 1993, Fitchburg (Mass.) Mus. Art, 1990, New Orleans Mus. Art, 1990, NAD, N.Y.C., 1986, 87, 90, 91, 92, 93, 94, The Hoyt Inst. Fine Arts, New Castle, Pa., 1992, Sodarco Gallery, Montreal, 1993, Davidson Galleries, Seattle, 1993, Galleria Mesa, Mesa, Ariz., 1993, Intergrafia, Katowice, Poland, 1994, Sapporo Internat. Print Biennale, Japan, 1993, Maastricht Internat. Print Biennale, The Netherlands, 1993, Outside Art Fair, N.Y.C., 2002, Arch Chgo., Navy Pier, 2002, 03; permanent collections include: Libr. of Congress, Washington, Art Inst. Chgo., Rose Art Mus., Waltham, Mass., Elvehjem Mus. Art, Madison, Wis., Butler Inst. Am. Art, Minot (N.D.) Art Assn., Silvermine Guild Arts, New Canaan, Conn., Honolulu Acad. Arts, N.Y. Pub. Libr., Detroit Inst. Art, Museo de Arte Moderno, Bklyn. Mus., Met. Mus., Miami, Nat. Mus. Am. Art, Washington, Portland (Oreg.) Art Mus., Art Ctr., South Bend, Ind., USIA, Prague, Czech Republic, and numerous colls. and univs. 1st lt. U.S. Army, 1961-63. Creative Artist grantee Mich. Coun. Arts, 1982; NEA Visual Arts fellow, 1993-94. Fellow The MacDowell Colony; mem. NAD (nat. academician). Home: 2512 Lunde Ln Mount Horeb WI 53572-2440 Office: U Wis Art Dept 6241 Humanities Bldg Madison WI 53706 E-mail: dhbecker@facstaff.wisc.edu.

BECKER, DAVID MANDEL, law educator, author, consultant; b. Chgo., Dec. 31, 1935; m. Sandra Kaplan, June 30, 1957; children: Laura, Andrew, Scott. AB, Harvard Coll., 1957; JD, U. Chgo., 1960. Bar: Ill. 1960. Assoc. Becker and Savin, Chgo., 1960—62; instr. law U. Mich., Ann Arbor, 1962—63; from asst. prof. law to prof. Washington U., St. Louis, 1963—93, Joseph H. Zumbalen prof. law, 1993—, assoc. dean external rels., 1998—, Joseph H. Zumbalen emeritus prof. law, 2004—. Author: (with David Gibberman) Legal Checklists, 1968, and ann. supplements; Legal Checklists-Specially Selected Forms, 1977, and ann. supplements; Perpetuities and Estate Planning: Potential Problems and Effective Solutions, 1993; contbr. numerous articles to profl. jours. Recipient Founders Day award Washington U. Alumni Assn., 1973, Tchr. of Yr. award Washington U., 1980, 89, Disting. Tchr. award Washington U. Sch. Law Alumni, 1988, Deans medal, 2005. Office: Washington U Sch Law Campus Box 1120 Saint Louis MO 63130-4899 Home: 540 North and South Rd #204 Saint Louis MO 63130 Office Phone: 314-935-6492.

BECKER, DOROTHY LORETTA, education educator, librarian; b. Long Beach, Calif., May 27, 1933; d. Francis Ryan and Constance Marie Wolff; m. Paul Hermann Karl Heinz Peter Becker, Feb. 14, 1964 (div. Nov. 1971). BS, U. Calif., L.A., 1954; MLS, San Jose State U., 1981. Tchr. Monterey (Calif.) Peninsula Unified Sch. Dist., 1956—91, reading specialist, cons., 1966-78, sch. libr., 1978-81; supr. student tchrs. Chapman U., Monterey, 1991-99; reference libr. Monterey County Free Librs., Seaside, Calif., 1996—2003. Mem. Ikebana Internat., Friends of Monterey Symphony; vol. Carmel Bach Festival; elder, Stephen min., leader First Presbyn. Ch., Monterey. Mem. Calif. Ret. Tchrs. Assn., Total Reading Assn. (cons. 1966—), Delta Kappa Gamma Soc. Internat. (Calif. corr. sec. 1993-95, Calif. state exec. sec. 1995-97, Chi state strategic plan ad hoc com. 1995-99, chmn. Chi state bylaws 1999-2001), Chi State Learning Is For Everyone Found. (pres. bd. dirs. 1999-2002, bd. dirs. 1999-2005) Democrat. Avocations: travel, reading, literacy advocate, flower arranging.

BECKER, DWIGHT LOWELL, physician; b. Mercer County, Ohio, July 21, 1918; s. George and Maude R. (Purdyzz) B.; m. Mary Lauer, Sept. 6, 1942; children— Lawrence, Judith, George Edward. BA, Ohio State U., 1940, MD, 1943. Intern Christ Hosp., Cin., 1943-44; gen. practice medicine Lima, Ohio, 1946-65; emergency room practice, 1965-87; mem. staff Lima Meml. Hosp.; med. dir. Blue Cross of Lima, 1970-87; past student health dir. Ohio No. U.; med. dir. Auglaize County Health Dept., Wapakoneta, Ohio, 1994—; ret., 1999. Past chmn. bd. Ohio Med. Indemnity, Inc., Worthington; field med. cons. Ohio Vocat. Rehab.; past bd. dir. Met. Bank, Lima. Mem. Allen County Bd. Health, 1952-55; past v.p. bd. dirs. Allen County Coun. on Aging; past med. advisor Lima and Allen County Vis. Nurses Assn.; past bd. dirs. Sta WIMA, Lima. Served to capt. M.C. AUS, 1944-46. Mem. Am. Coll. Emergency Physicians, AMA, Ohio Med. Assn., Phi Beta Kappa. Clubs: Masons, Shawnee Country, Elks. Republican. Home and Office: 454 Partridge Ct Cridersville OH 45806-9626 E-mail: dlbmkl@wcoil.com.

BECKER, EDWARD ROY, federal judge; b. Phila., May 4, 1933; s. Herman A. and Jeannette (Levit) Becker; m. Flora Lyman, Aug. 11, 1957; children: James Daniel(dec.), Jonathan Robert, Susan Rose, Charles Lyman. BA, U. Pa., 1954; LLB, Yale U., 1957; LLD (hon.), Temple U., 2003. Bar: Pa. 1957. Ptnr. Becker, Becker & Fryman, Phila., 1957—70; U.S. Dist. Judge, 1970—82; judge U.S. Ct. Appeals (3d cir.), 1982—98, chief judge, 1998—2003, sr. judge, 2003—. Counsel Rep. City Com., Phila., 1965—70; mem. task force on implementation of new jud. article Joint State Govt. Commn., 1969; lectr. law U. Pa. Law Sch., 1978—83; mem. edn. adv. com. concerning Comprehensive Crime Control Act Fed. Jud. Ctr., 1981—90, Fed. Jud. Ctr. Com. on Sentencing, Probation and Pretrial Svcs., 1985—90; bd. dirs. Fed. Jud. Ctr., 1991—95; mem. faculty sr. appellate judges seminar Inst. Jud. Adminstrn., N.Y.C., 1992—94. Bd. editors: Manual for Complex Litigation, 1981—90; contbr. articles to profl. jours. Trustee Magna Carta Found., Phila.; vis. com. U. Chgo. Law Sch., 1988—91; chair Rhodes Scholarship Selection Com. Dist. II (Pa., N.Y., Vt., N.H.), 1996—98; bd. mem. Historic Phila., Inc., 2001—; bd. mem., adv. bd. Am. Soc. of Internat. Law, 2000. Mem.: ABA (jud. rep. antitrust sect. 1983—86), Jud. Conf. U.S. (com. on adminstrn. probation sys. 1979—87, chmn. com. on criminal law and probation adminstrn. 1987—90, com. on long range planning 1991—96, exec. com. 1998—2003), Am. Law Inst. (mem. ALI-ABA com. 1992—, chmn. program subcom. 1996—99, adv. com. restatement conflict of laws 2d), Am. Judicature Soc. (Devitt Disting. Svc. award 2002), Phila. Bar Assn., Phi Beta Kappa. Jewish. Office: US Ct Appeals 19613 US Courthouse 601 Market St Philadelphia PA 19106-1713 Office Phone: 215-597-9642. Business E-Mail: judge_edward_becker@ca3.uscourts.gov.

BECKER, EDWIN DEMUTH, chemist, director; b. Columbia, Pa., May 3, 1930; married, 1953; 2 children. BS, U. Rochester, 1952; PhD in Chemistry, U. Calif., 1955. Instr. U. Calif., 1955; phys. chemist NIH, Bethesda, Md., 1955—, chief sect. molecular biophysics, 1962-72, chief lab. chem. physics, 1972-80, acting dir. Fogarty Internat. Ctr., 1979-80, assoc. dir. for research services, 1980-88, chief sect. NMR, 1972-98, scientist emeritus, 1998—, mem. faculty Grad. Sch., 1963-99; sec. gen. Internat. Union Pure and Applied Chemistry, 1996—2003. Lectr. Georgetown U., 1958-97. Bd. dirs. Chem. Heritage Found., 2003—; treas. Found. for Advanced Edn. in the Scis., 2003—. NSF fellow U. Calif. Fellow AAAS; mem. Am. Chem. Soc., The Nat. Acads. (nat. assoc.), World Innovation Found. (hon.). Achievements include research in nuclear magnetic resonance, hydrogen bonding, molecular structure, infrared spectroscopy. Office: NIH Rm 128 Bldg 5 Bethesda MD 20892-0520 Office Phone: 301-496-1024. Business E-Mail: tbecker@nih.gov.

BECKER, ELIZABETH ANNE, secondary school educator; b. Winston-Salem, N.C., Aug. 27, 1959; d. Byron Gustav Becker and Shirley Anne Howard; m. Duane Allen Johnson, June 27, 1981 (div. 1991); children: Christopher, Matthew; m. Thomas Everett Edmonds, Aug. 17, 1991; step-children: Jacob, Sarah. AAS, Sauk Valley Coll., Dixon, Ill., 1979; BS in Biology summa cum laude, Radford U., 1998; postgrad. in neurobiology and anatomy, Wake Forest U., 1998-99; MS in Edn., Radford U., 2000. Registered clin. lab. scientist; lic. collegiate profl., Va. Med. lab. technician St. Joseph Hosp., Belvedere, Ill., 1980-88, Pulaski (Va.) Hosp., 1988-90; clin. lab. scientist Giles Meml. Hosp., Pearesburg, Va., 1990-95; biology tchr. Carroll County H.S., Hillsville, Va., 2000—; sci. rschr. Radford U., 1996—99. Vol., Spl. Olympics, Radford, Va., 1998; cub scout leader, Cub Scouts A., 1990, 91; coord. infant and child support group, SHARE, Belvedere, 1986, 87, 88; ednl. advisor Nat. Youth Leadership Forum Medicine, 2002. Named Internat. Woman of Yr., 2004, Internat. Educator of Yr., Internat. Biographical Ctr., 2003; named one of 2000 Outstanding Scientists of the 21st Century. Mem. AAAS, Nat. Sci. Tchrs. Assn., Nat. Cert. Agy. for Clin. Scientists, Beta Beta Beta (pres. Sigma Rho chpt. 1997-98, Excellence in Rsch. award 1998), Omicron Delta Kappa (life). Achievements include research in desert funnel-web spiders courtship behavior; discovery of male pheromone transmission. Avocations: sculpting, pen and ink, hiking, remodeling, behavior research. Home: 286 Huddle Rd Wytheville VA 24382 Office: Carroll County High Sch Rt 58 Hillsville VA 24343 Office Phone: 276-728-2125. E-mail: LizBecker@naxs.com.

BECKER, FRAWLEY, writer, dialogue director, location manager; s. Arthur A. and Mildred (Cohen) Becker. BA, U. Pa., 1950; postgrad., Oxford (Eng.) U., 1956. Asst. entertainment dir. Spl. Svcs. Hdqrs. Dept. of the Army, Paris, 1958—61; mng. dir. Paris Playhouse, 1961—63; dialogue coach, dialogue dir. various film cos., Paris, 1964—72; asst. to prodr. (film) Weingarten Prodns., LA, 1973—74; rsch. writer (t.v.) Columbia Pictures, Burbank, Calif., 1974—75; location mgr. (film) various film cos., Calif., 1976—; prodn. exec. (film) Disney Studios, Burbank, 1990—91. Founder, dir. Studio 128, Paris, 1957—61, Harlequin Guild, Paris, 1959—61; founder, dir., mng. dir. Paris Playhouse, 1961—63; French interpreter Olympic Games, 1984. Author: (screenplays) But Not A Drop to Drink, 1973, Columbo Stories, 1975, On The Way Out, 1976, The Strike, 1976, Behold the Evening Spider, 1980, The Gang's All Where?, 1989, Bonjour Homicide, 1995, (plays) Dreamhouse, 1987, The Picture They Never Made, 1987, Bashing, 1990, 411 Joseph, 1998, Never Fall in Love with A Fireman, 2001, Tiger by the Tail, 2003, short stories, (novel) Tittyboo For President, 1984, And the Stars Spoke Back, 2004. French interpreter 1984 Olympics Games. Cpl. U.S. Army, 1951—53, Korea. Avocations: cooking, travel. Home: 15016 Archwood St Van Nuys CA 91405

BECKER, FRED RONALD, lawyer; b. Phila., Apr. 7, 1937; s. Samuel and Molly (Cletter) B.; m. Judith Ellen Ettlinger, June 5, 1961 BA, U. Pa., 1958; JD magna cum laude, Harvard U., 1961. Bar: D.C. 1963. Law clk. U.S. Ct. Appeals (9th cir.), 1961-62; asst. Stanford U. Law Sch., 1962-63; atty. tax div. U.S. Dept. Justice, 1963-65; atty. Office Tax Legis. Counsel U.S. Treasury, 1965-69; ptnr. Ropes & Gray, Boston, 1969. Office: Ropes & Gray 1 International Pl Fl 4 Boston MA 02110-2624

BECKER, GAIL ROSELYN, museum director; b. Long Branch, N.J., Oct. 22, 1942; d. Joseph and Adele (Michelsohn) B. BA, Vassar Coll., 1964. Exhibit project officer U.S. Info. Agy., Washington, 1967-87, chief devel. and prodn. exhibits, 1987-91; exec. dir. Louisville Sci. Ctr. (formerly Mus. History and Sci.), 1991—. Bd. dirs. Louisville Advanced Tech. Coun., 1993-2000, Louisville Com. Fgn. Rels., Main St. Assn., 1998—, Arts and Cultural Attractions Coun., 1999—; active Leadership Louisville. Recipient Presdl. Design awards Nat. Endowment for the Arts, Washington, 1984, 88, 92, Special Achievement award U.S. Info. Agy., Washington, 1988. Mem. Am. Assn. Mus. (bd. dirs. 1994-97), Assn. Sci.-Tech. Ctrs. (bd. dirs. 1992—2003, pres. 1999-2001), Vassar Coll. Alumnae Assn., Rotary. Office: Louisville Sci Ctr 727 W Main St Louisville KY 40202-2681

BECKER, GARY STANLEY, economist, educator; b. Pottsville, Pa., Dec. 2, 1930; s. Louis William and Anna (Siskind) Becker; m. Doria Slote, Sept. 19, 1954 (dec.); children: Judith Sarah, Catherine Jean; m. Guity Nashat, Oct. 31, 1979; children: Michael Claffey, Cyrus Claffey. AB summa cum laude, Princeton U., 1951, PhD (hon.), 1991; AM, U. Chgo., 1953, PhD, 1955; PhD (hon.), Hebrew U., Jerusalem, 1985, Knox Coll., 1985, U. Ill., Chgo., 1988, SUNY, 1990, U. Palermo, Buenos Aires, 1993, Columbia U., 1993, Warsaw (Poland) Sch. Econs., 1995, U. Econs., Prague, Czech Republic, 1995, U. Miami, 1995, U. Rochester, 1995; PhD, Hofstra U., 1997, U. d'Aix-Marselles, 1999, U. Athens, 2002; PhD (hon.), Harvard U., 2003. Asst. prof. U. Chgo., 1954—57; from asst. prof. to assoc. prof. Columbia U., N.Y.C., 1957—60, prof. econs., 1960—68, Arthur Lehman prof. econs., 1968—70; prof. econs. U. Chgo., 1970—83, univ. prof. econs. and sociology, 1983—, chmn. dept. econs., 1984—85, prof. Grad Sch. Bus., 2002—. Ford Found. vis. prof. econs. U. Chgo., 1969—70; assoc. Econs. Rsch. Ctr. Nat. Opinion Rsch. Ctr., Chgo., 1980—; mem. domestic adv. bd. Hoover Instn., Stanford, Calif., 1973—91, sr. fellow, 1990—; mem. acad. adv. bd. Am. Enterprise Inst., 1987—91; rsch. policy advisor Ctr. for Econ. Analysis Human Behavior Nat. Bur. Econ. Rsch., 1972—78; mem. and sr. rsch. assoc. Monetary Policy, Min. Fin., Japan, 1988—; bd. dirs. Unext.com, 1999—2003; affiliate Lexecon Corp., 1990—2002, LEAF, Inc., 2003—. Author: The Economics of Discrimination, 1957, (2d edit.), 1971, Human Capital, 1964, (3d edit.), 1993, (Japanese transl.), 1975, (Spanish transl.), 1984, (Chinese transl.), 1987, (Romanian transl.), 1997, Human Capital and the Personal Distribution of Income: An Analytical Approach, 1967, Economic Theory, 1971, (Japanese transl.), 1976; author: (with Gilbert Ghez) The Allocation of Time and Goods Over the Life Cycle, 1975; author: The Economic Approach to Human Behavior, 1976, (German transl.), 1982, (Polish transl.), 1990, (Chinese transl.), 1993, (Romanian transl.), 1994, (Italian transl.), 1998, A Treatise on the Family, 1981, (expanded edit.), 1991, (Spanish transl.), 1987, (Chinese transl.), 1988, 2000, Accounting for Tastes, 1996, (Czech transl.), 1998, (Chinese transl.), 1999, (Italian transl.), 2000; author: (with Guity Nashat Becker) The Economics of Life, 1996, (Chinese transl.), 1997, with Guity Nashat Becker: The Economics of Life, 1998, (Spanish transl.), 2002; author: (in German) Family, Society and State, 1996; author: (in Italian) L'approccio Economico al Comportamento Umano, 1998; author: (with Kevin M. Murphy) Social Economics, 2000; editor: Essays in Labor Economics in Honor of H. Gregg Lewis, 1976; co-editor (with William M. Landes): Essays in the Economics of Crime and Punishment, 1974; columnist: Bus. Week, 1985—2004; contbr. articles to profl. jours. Named to Hall of Honor, Nat. Inst. Child Health and Devel., 2003; recipient W.S. Woytinsky award, U. Mich., 1964, Profl. Achievement award, U. Chgo. Alumni Assn., 1968, Frank E. Seidman Disting. award in Polit. Economy, 1985, Merit award, NIH, 1986, John R. Commons award, Omicron Delta Epsilon, 1987, Nobel prize in Econ. Sci., 1992, award, Lord Found., 1995, Irene Taueber award, 1997, Nat. medal Sci., 2000, Phoenix award, U. Chgo., 2000, award, Am. Acad. Achievement, 2001, Heartland prize, 2002, Hayek award, 2003, medal, Italian Presidency, 2004, medal of Italian Presidency, 2004, John Neumann Lecture award, Rojk Coll., Corvinus U., Budapest. Fellow: Am. Econ. Assn. (Disting., v.p. 1974, pres. 1987, John Bates Clark medal 1967), Am. Acad. Arts and Scis., Nat. Assn. Bus. Economists, Econometric Soc., Am. Statis. Assn.; mem.: NAE, NAS, Nat. Assn. Bus. Economists, Econ. History Assn., Pontifical Acad. Scis., Western Econ. Assn. (v.p. 1995—96, pres. 1996—97), Mont Pelerin Soc. (exec. bd. dirs. 1985—96, v.p. 1989—90, pres. 1990—92), Internat. Union for Sci. Study Population, Am. Philos. Soc., Nat. Assn. Bus. Economists, Phi Beta Kappa. Office: U Chgo Dept Econs 1126 E 59th St Chicago IL 60637-1580 Office Phone: 773-702-8168. Business E-Mail: gbecker@uchicago.edu.

BECKER, ISIDORE A., corporate financial executive; b. N.Y.C., May 10, 1926; s. Max and Eva (Chester) B.; m. Adele Sandler, Dec. 20, 1947; children: Steven Richard, Carol Ann. BA, Bklyn. Coll., 1949. Partner Herbert D. Silver & Co., N.Y.C., 1956-63; fin. v.p., chmn. financial com. Rapid-Am. Corp., N.Y.C., 1966-72, vice chmn. bd., 1967-72, 76-82, dir., 1964-82, pres., 1972-76; chief financial officer, treas. McCrory Corp., N.Y.C., 1964-70, dir., 1964-82; vice chmn. bd., dir. Glen Alden Corp., N.Y.C., 1967-72; chmn. bd., dir. Schenley Industries, Inc., 1968-82; pres. Riviera Hotel, Inc., 1973-83; chmn. bd. Shaw-Ross Internat. Importers, Inc., 1983—, Southern Wine & Spirits, 1983—. Vice chmn. bd. Boys Town Jerusalem; founder Albert Einstein Coll. Medicine; asso. chmn., bd. govs. Anti Defamation League B'nai B'rith. Served with USMCR, 1944-46. Home: 215 E 68th St Apt 17L New York NY 10021-5726

BECKER, JAMES MURDOCH, surgeon, educator; b. Cleve., Jan. 7, 1949; s. Norman O. and Mildred Edith (Murdoch) B.; m. Christine Louise Lohmann, Dec. 30, 1972; children: Alexander, Selby, Catherine, Anne. BA in Biology, Yale U., 1971; MD, Case Western Res. U., 1975. Diplomate Nat. Bd. Med. Examiners, Am. Bd. Surgery; lic. surgeon, Minn., Utah, Mo., Mass. Intern in surgery U. Utah Hosps., Salt Lake City, 1975-76, resident in gen. surgery, 1976-79, chief resident in surgery, 1979—80; research fellow in surgery U. Utah Sch. Medicine, 1977-78, asst. prof. surgery, 1982-86; NIH rsch. fellow digestive diseases Mayo Clinic, 1980-82; mem. surg. staff VA Hosp., Salt Lake City, 1982-86, chief gen. surgery, 1983-86, head nutritional support team, 1983-86; mem. cons. staff Intermountain Unit Shriners Hosps. for Crippled Children, Salt Lake City, 1984-86; assoc. prof. surgery, dir. gastrointestinal surgery Washington U. Sch. Medicine, 1986-89; assoc. prof surgery, chief divsn. gen. and gastroint. surg. Harvard Med. Sch./Brigham and Women's Hosp., Boston, 1989-94; James Utley prof. and chmn. surgeon-in-chief Boston U. Sch. Medicine/Boston Med. Ctr., 1994—. Contbr. articles to profl. jours., chpts. to books. NIH fellow, Mayo Clinic, 1980-82; grantee Johnson & Johnson Products, Inc., 1985, NIH, 1985—, Sandoz Corp., 1985-87, Ethicon, Inc., 1985-86. Mem. ACS, AMA, Am. Gastroenterol. Assn., Am. Motility Soc., Am. Pancreatic Assn., Assn. Acad. Surgery, Am. Soc. Parenteral and Enteral Nutrition, Internat. Biliary Assn., Collegium Internat. Chirurgiae Digestivae (Grassi prize 8th World Congress 1984), Soc. for Surgery Alimentary Tract, Soc. Univ. Surgeons, Yale U. Alumni Assn., Am. coll. Surgeons, Am. Surg. Assn., We. Surg. Assn., Cen. Surg. Assn., New Eng. Surg. Assn., Am. Soc. Colorectal Surgeons, Soc. Internat. Chirugiae, Soc. Surg. Oncology, Alpha Omega Alpha. Office: Boston Med Ctr 88 E Newton St Boston MA 02118-2308 Office Phone: 617-638-8600.

BECKER, JAMES RICHARD, lawyer; b. San Juan, P.R., Sept. 25, 1954; s. John Joseph and Patricia (Doherty) B.; m. Mary E. McGurk; children: Colette Anne, Robert Charles II. BA in English, Va. Tech., 1977; JD, George Mason Law Sch., 1982. Bar: Va. 1982, U.S. Dist. Ct. (ea. and we. dists.) Va. 1982, U.S. Ct. Appeals (4th cir.) 1982. Atty. pvt. practice, Middleburg and Chantilly, Va., 1982-93; assoc. atty. Nichols, Bergere & Zauzig, P.C., Woodbridge, Va., 1993-94, Joel Atlas Skirble and Assocs., Falls Church, Va., 1994-98, Anderson & Corrie, Fairfax, Va., 1998-2000; atty. pvt. practice, Chantilly, 2000, 2003—; assoc. John A. Boneta & Assocs., Falls Church, 2001—03; atty. pvt. practice Chantilly, 2003—. Editor Law Rev., 1980-82. Mem. Fairfax Bar Assn. Avocations: computers, software development. Home: 4515 Fillingame Dr Chantilly VA 20151-2820 Personal E-mail: JamesRBecker@juno.com.

BECKER, JEFFREY M., lawyer; b. San Angelo, Tex., Mar. 15, 1965; BSME with high honors, U. Tex. at Austin, 1987, JD with honors, 1990. Bar: Tex. 1990, admitted to practice: US Dist. Ct. (No. Dist.) Tex. 1990, US Ct. Appeals (Fed. Cir.) 1991, registered: US Patent and Trademark Office. Ptnr., intellectual property law Haynes and Boone LLP, Dallas. Named one of Best Lawyers in Dallas, DMagazine, 2003. Mem.: Coll. of State Bar Tex., DFW Intellectual Property Law Assn., Am. Intellectual Property Law Assn., Internat. Trademark Assn., State Bar Tex. (Intellectual Property Law Sect.), Dallas Bar Assn. (Intellectual Property Sect.), Order of Coif, Tau Beta Pi. Office: Haynes and Boone LLP 901 Main St Ste 3100 Dallas TX 75202-3789 Office Phone: 214-651-5066. Office Fax: 214-200-0558. Business E-Mail: jeff.becker@haynesboone.com.

BECKER, JOANN ELIZABETH, retired insurance company executive; b. Chester, Pa., Oct. 29, 1948; d. James Thomas and Elizabeth Theresa (Barnett) Clark; m. David Norbert Becker, June 7, 1969. BA, Washington U., St. Louis, 1970, MA, 1971. CLU, ChFC, FLMI/M, CFA. Tchr. Kirkwood (Mo.) Sch. Dist., 1971-73; devel. and sr. devel. analyst Lincoln Nat. Life Ins. Co., Ft. Wayne, Ind., 1973-77, systems programming specialist, 1977-79, sr. project mgr., 1979-81, asst. v.p., 1981-85, 2d v.p., 1985-88, v.p., 1988-91; pres., CEO The Richard Leahy Corp., Ft. Wayne, 1991-93; pres. Lincoln Nat. Corp. Equity Sales Corp, Ft. Wayne, 1993-94; v.p. portfolio mgmt. group Lincoln Nat. Investment Mgmt. Co., Ft. Wayne, 1994-97, dir. investment mgmt., sr. v.p., 1997—2005. Contbr. articles to profl. jours. Bd. dirs. Ind. Humanities Coun., Indpls., 1991-96, treas., mem. exec. com., 1994-95, mem. devel. com., 1995-96; bd. dirs. Auburn (Ind.) Cord Duesenberg Mus., 1995-2000, mem. devel. and exec. com., 1997-2000; bd. dirs. Pierst Lake Mus., 2005—. Named Women of Achievement, YWCA, Ft. Wayne, 1986, Sagamore of Wabash, Gov. State of Ind., 1990. Fellow Life Mgmt. Inst. Soc. Ft. Wayne (pres. 1983-84, honors designation 1980); mem. Life Ins. Mktg. Rsch. Assn. (Leadership Inst. fellow, mem. exec. com. 1993-94, mem. fin. svcs. com. 1993-94), Am. Mgmt. Assn., Ft. Wayne C. of C. (mem., chmn. audit-fin. com. 1989-2000).

BECKER, JOHN ALPHONSIS, retired bank executive; b. Kenosha, Wis., Jan. 26, 1942; s. Paul Joseph and Hedwig (Hammacke) B.; m. Bonny J. Anderson, July 4, 1963; children: Danial, Todd, Kathryn, Erik BS, Marquette U., 1963, MBA, 1965. Asst. v.p. 1st Wis. Nat. Bank of Milw., 1970-73, v.p., 1973-76, 1st v.p., 1976-79; pres. 1st Wis. Nat. Bank of Madison, 1979-86; exec. v.p. 1st Wis. Nat. Bank of Milw., 1986-87, pres., chief oper. officer, 1987-89, also chief exec. officer, 1988-89, chmn., chief exec. officer, 1989-91; pres. Firstar Corp., Milw., 1990-99; ret., 1999. Div. chmn. United Way, Madison, 1984; trustee Edgewood Coll., Madison, 1980—; mem. fin. com. Madison Republican Com. Served to 1st lt. U.S. Army, 1965-67. Mem. Wis. Bankers Assn. (exec. com.), Greater Madison C. of C. (chmn. bd. 1983). Clubs: Madison, Maple Bluff Country. Roman Catholic. Office: Firstar Corp 777 E Wisconsin Ave Milwaukee WI 53202-5300

BECKER, KARIN LEIGH, humanities educator; b. Toronto, Can., June 30, 1976; d. Richard S. and Joanne S. Becker; m. David Andrew Smith, June 12, 2004. BA in Comms. and Photography, U. N.D., Grand Forks; MA in Creative Writing, Ea. Mich. U., Ypsilanti. Photographer Photeo's, Traverse City, Mich.; English instr. Ea. Mich. U., Ypsilanti, Ft. Lewis Coll., Durango, Colo., testing ctr. coord. Contbr. articles to various profl. literary jours. Missionary Youth for Christ, New Zealand, 2000. Mem.: Vegetarian Soc., San Juan Writers (v.p. 2002—). Protestant. Avocations: backpacking, skiing, baking, stamp collecting/philately.

BECKER, KARL MARTIN, lawyer; b. Glenridge, NJ, May 30, 1943; s. Alfred Martin and Helen K. (Gramse) B.; m. Barbara A. Benton, Feb. 19, 1966; children— Glenn M., Mark W. AB, Yale U., 1965; JD, U. Chgo., 1968. Bar: Ill. 1968, S.C. 1994. Assoc. Vedder Price Kaufman Kammholz, Chgo., 1968-75, ptnr., 1975-78; asst. gen. counsel Esmark, Inc., Chgo., 1978-83, assoc. gen. counsel, 1983-84; v.p., gen. counsel, sec. Swift Ind. Corp., Chgo., 1985-86, sr. v.p., gen. counsel, sec., 1986; sr. v.p., gen. counsel Beatrice Cos., Inc. and BCI Holdings Corp., Chgo., 1986-87, E-II Holdings, Inc., Beatrice Co., Chgo., 1987-88, Beatrice Co., Chgo., 1988-90; dir. Mathers Fund, Inc., Bannockburn, Ill., 1991-98. Mem. S.C. Bar Assn. Avocations: skiing, sailing. Home: 31 Hearthwood Dr Hilton Head Island SC 29928-2906 Personal E-mail: KBecker1@aol.com.

BECKER, KARLA LYNN, information technology manager, consultant; b. West Point, NY, Nov. 3, 1956; d. Fred D. and Margaret Erika (Buckmann) Spinks; m. Eric Louis Becker; children: Erika Margaret Augusta Ashmore, Eric Robert. BA, Ind. U.-Purdue U. at Indpls., 1982; MS, Ind. U., 1986. Cert. software quality engr.; Hatha and Kundalini yoga tchr., registered yoga alliance tchr. Mgr. Eastside Chiropractic Clinic, Indpls., 1978-80; English tutor univ. div. Ind. U.-Purdue U. at Indpls., 1980-82, composition instr. English dept., 1982-83, tech. writer computing services, 1983-84; tech. writer Ind. U. Adminstrv. Computing, 1984-87; mgmt. info. svcs. cons., writer, support adminstr. Simon Property Group, Indpls., 1987-97; sys. cons. KFORCE.COM, Indpls., 1997-99; assoc. info. cons. Eli Lilly & Co., Indpls., 1999—. Author: Composing Technical Documents, 2000; editor: Lit. Jour., Genesis, All-Am. Mag., Am. Collegiate Press Assn., 1983; author numerous poems; contbr. articles to profl. jours. Mem. Am. Soc. Quality, Soc. Tech. Communication (Cert. of Achievement 1985), Sigma Delta Chi, Pi Lambda Theta. Democrat. Roman Catholic. Avocations: singing, yoga. Personal E-mail: karla11@hotmail.com.

BECKER, LAWRENCE CARLYLE, philosopher, educator, writer; b. Lincoln, Nebr., Apr. 26, 1939; s. Albert Carlyle and Harriette (Toren) B.; m. Charlotte Ann Burner, June 10, 1967. BA in History, Midland Coll., 1961; MA in Philosophy, U Chgo., 1963, PhD in Philosophy, 1965; LHD (hon.), Midland Luth. Coll., 1994. Instr. philosophy Hollins Coll., Roanoke, Va., 1965-67, asst. prof. philosophy, 1967-71, assoc. prof., 1971-78, prof., 1978-89, fellow of coll., 1989—, dir. summer inst. for ethics and pub. policy, 1990-92; prof. philosophy, William R. Kenan, Jr. prof. humanities Coll. William and Mary, Williamsburg, Va., 1989-2001, acting chair, 1992-93; pres. Bookwork, L.L.C., 2000—. Mem. summer conf. in metaphysics Coun. for Philos. Studies, 1968, mem. summer conf. on moral problems in medicine, 1974; vis. fellow in philosophy Harvard U., Cambridge, Mass., 1975-76; invited lectr. in field. Author: On Justifying Moral Judgments, 1973, Property Rights: Philosophic Foundations, 1977, Reciprocity, 1986, A New Stoicism, 1998; editor: (with Kenneth Kipnis) Property: Cases, Concepts and Critiques, 1984 (with Charlotte B. Becker) A History of Western Ethics, 1992, Encyclopedia of Ethics, 2 vols., 1992, 2d edit., 3 vols., 2001; mem. editl. bd. Ethics, 1979-85, 2000, assoc. editor, 1985-2000, acting editor, 1994-95, book rev. editor, 1998-2000; contbr. over 70 articles and book revs. to profl. jours. Woodrow Wilson grad. fellow, 1961-62, Danforth grad. fellow, 1961-65, Woodrow Wilson dissertation fellow (hon.), 1964-65, fellow NEH, 1971-72, 93-94, Oxford (Eng.) U., 1971-72, Harvard U., 1975-76, Am. Coun. Learned Socs., 1975-76, humanities fellow Rockefeller Found., 1982-83, Ctr. for Advanced Study in Behavioral Scis., 1983-84. Mem. Am. Philos. Assn. (com. on philosophy and law 1984-87, adv. com. to program com. ethics divsn. 1989-92, com. on status and future of profession 1993-96), Am. Soc. for Legal and Polit. Philosophy, Va. Philos. Assn. (sec. 1978-79, v.p. 1979-80, pres. 1980-81).

BECKER, LAWRENCE WILFRED, headmaster; b. Albany, N.Y., Nov. 16, 1941; s. Randall Damas and Hilda (Meuser) B.; m. Grace Marianne Zelinka, Aug. 23, 1969. BA, Amherst Coll., 1963; MA in Teaching, Harvard U., 1964. Math. instr. Hotchkiss Sch., Lakeville, Conn., 1964-86, dir. coll. counseling, 1969-80, dean admission and coll. counseling, 1980-82, dean faculty, 1982-86, asst. headmaster, 1983-86; headmaster Brooks Sch., North Andover, Mass., 1986—. Co-author: Relevant Mathematics/Algebra, 1970, Relevant Mathematics/Geometry, 1971, Relevant Mathematics/Advanced Algebra and Trigonometry, 1971. Trustee Brooks Sch., 1986—, Pike Sch., Andover, Mass., 1988-94. Mem. Univ. Club, Lanam Club, North Andover Country Club. Avocations: reading, jogging, music, musical theater, photography. Home and Office: Brooks Sch 1160 Great Pond Rd North Andover MA 01845-1206*

BECKER, LORNE ARTHUR, family physician; b. Kitchener, Ont., Can., Mar. 6, 1945; s. Percy Lorne Becker and Katie Klassen; m. Elizabeth Joy Wonnacott, June 1, 1968; children: Andrew James, Doug Scott, Lynn Marie. MD, U. We. Ont., 1969. Diplomate Am. Bd. Family Practice. Asst. prof. U. Rochester, NY, 1977—79; assoc. prof. Temple U., Phila., 1979—83, U. Okla., Oklahoma City, 1983—88, dir. family health program, 1983—88; assoc. prof. U. Toronto, Ont., 1988—94, chief family medicine, 1988—93; prof. dept. family medicine SUNY, Syracuse, 1994—2004, chair dept. family medicine, 1997—2004; prof. emeritus family medicine SUNY Upstate Med. U., Syracuse, 2004—. Founding bd. mem. Family Practice Inquiries Network; mem. steering group Cochrane Collaboration, 2004—07; mem. panel Gulf war and health Inst. Medicine, 2002—03; mem. U.S. Dept. Health and Human Svcs. Working Group on Hearing Loss in Children, 2004—; coord. Cochrane Primary Health Care Field, 1998—. Contbr. chapters to books; assoc. editor: Family Practice, 2004—. Fellow Coll. Family Physicians Can., Am. Acad. Family Physicians; mem. Soc. Tchrs. Family Medicine (chair rsch. com. 1985-89, Curtis Hames Rsch. award 2001), Ambulatory Sentinel Practice Network (bd. dirs. 1979-93). Avocations: sailing, handheld computers. Office: SUNY Dept Family Medicine 475 Irving Ave Ste 200 Syracuse NY 13210-1529 Business E-Mail: beckerla@upstate.edu.

BECKER, MARY LOUISE, political scientist; b. St. Louis; d. W. R. and Evelyn (Thompson) Becker; divorced; children: James, John. BS, Washington U., St. Louis, 1949, MA, 1951; PhD, Radcliffe Coll., 1957; postgrad., U. Karachi, Pakistan, 1953-54. Intelligence rsch. analyst Dept. State, Washington, 1957—59; internat. rels. officer AID, Washington, 1959—64, cmty. rels. officer, 1964—66, sci. rsch. officer, 1966—71, UN rels. officer, 1971—91; pres. Internat. Devel. Enterprises, Washington, 1992—. Adviser U.S. dels. 19th, 21st, 23d, 24th, 26th, 28th, 30th, 32d, 34th Governing Coun. sessions UN Devel. Program; adv. U.S. del. 3d prep. com. meeting World Conf. UN Decade for Women; adviser U.S. dels. UNICEF exec. bd. sessions, 1987—91; mem. U.S. Com. for UN Fund for Women; lectr. internat. rels. civic orgns., student groups, 1954—. Author: Muhammed Iqbal, 1965; contbg. editor: Concise Ency. of Mid. East, 1973; contbr. articles to profl. jours. Mem. adv. bd. chmn. internat. student placement Washington Citizenship Seminar Nat. YMCA-YWCA, Washington, 1961—71. Blewett fellow, Washington U., 1951, resident fellow, Radcliffe Coll., 1952—56, Fulbright scholar, U. Karachi, 1953—54. Mem.: AAUW, Nat. Press Club, Mo. Soc. Washington (sec. 1959—60), S. Asian Muslim Studies Assn. (v.p. 1992—), UN Assn. (bd. dirs. Nat. Capital area 1991—), Mid. East Inst., Asia Soc., Assn. Asian Studies, Soc. Internat. Devel., Am. Polit. Sci. Assn., Harvard Club (Washington), Chimes, Mortar Bd., Pi Sigma Alpha, Eta Mu Phi, Beta Gamma Sigma, Alpha Lambda Delta. Presbyterian. Home: 2301 E St NW Washington DC 20037-2829 Office: North Bldg Ste 700 601 Pennsylvania Ave NW Washington DC 20004-2601

BECKER, MICHAEL ALLEN, internist, rheumatologist, educator; b. N.Y.C., Oct. 3, 1940; s. David S. and Sylvia M. (Salomon) B.; m. Mary E. Baim; children: David, Jonathan, Abigail, Arielle, Daniel. BA, U. Pa., Phila., 1961, MD, 1965. Diplomate Am. Bd. Internal Medicine, Am. Bd. Rheumatology. Intern Barnes Hosp., Washington U., St. Louis, 1965-66, resident, 1969-70; asst. prof. U. Calif., San Diego, 1972-77, assoc. prof., 1977-80; prof. medicine U. Chgo. Pritzker Sch. Medicine, 1980—. Mem. biochemistry study sect. NIH, Bethesda, Md., 1991-95. Contbr. numerous rsch. articles to med. publs. Sr. asst. surgeon USPHS, 1966-69. Fellow John Simon Guggenheim Meml. Found.; mem. Am. Soc. Clin. Investigation, Assn. Am. Physicians, Am. Coll. Rheumatology. Office: U Chgo Med Ctr MC0930 Chicago IL 60637 Office Phone: 773-702-6899. Business E-Mail: mbecker@medicine.bsd.uchicago.edu.

BECKER, NANCY ANNE, state supreme court justice; b. Las Vegas, May 23, 1955; d. Arthur William and Margaret Mary (McLoughlin) Becker. BA, U.S. Internat. U., 1976; JD, George Washington U., 1979. Bar: Nev. 1979, D.C. 1980, Md. 1982, U.S. Dist. Ct. Nev. 1987, U.S. Ct. Appeals (9th cir.) 1987. Legis. cons. D.C. Office on Aging, Washington, 1979—83; assoc. Goldstein & Ahalt, College Park, Md., 1980—82; pvt. practice Washington, 1982—87; dep. city atty., prosecutor criminal div. City of Las Vegas, 1983; judge Las Vegas Mcpl. Ct., 1987—89, Clark County Dist. Ct., Las Vegas, 1989—99, chief judge, 1993—94; assoc. justice Nev. Supreme Ct., 1999—. Cons. MADD, Las Vegas, 1983—87. Contbr. articles to profl. jours. Pres. Clark County Pro Bono Project, Las Vegas, 1984—95. Mem.: NCCJ, Am. Businesswomen's Assn. (treas. Las Vegas chpt. 1985—86), Southern Nev. Assn. Women Attys. (past officer), Soroptimist Internat., Vietnam Vets. Am., Las Vegas and Latin C. of C. Office: Nevada Supreme Court Capital Complex 316 Bridger Ave Las Vegas NV 89101-5906

BECKER, NANCY MAY, nursing educator; b. Reading, Pa., July 28, 1949; d. Theodore R. and Minerva M. (Deiseroth) B. Diploma, Reading Hosp. Sch. Nursing, 1970; BS, Albright Coll., 1979; MS, U. Del., 1981. RN Pa., Del. Nurse mgr. Cmty. Gen. Hosp., Reading, 1974-76; nurse educator Albright Coll., Reading, 1980-87; clin. nurse specialist Polyclinic Med. Ctr., Harrisburg, Pa., 1987-89; asst. prof. Lehigh Carbon C.C., Schnecksville, Pa., 1989-95, dir. nursing programs, 1995-97, dean allied health/dir. nursing, 1998—, dean profl. accreditation and curriculum, dir. nursing, 2001—, interim v.p. acad. and student affairs, 2001—02, 2005—06. Mem. ANA, Nat. League Nursing, Sigma Theta Tau.

BECKER, PHYLLIS, systems analyst; b. Plainfield, N.J., Nov. 9, 1963; d. Stephen and Jean Mae Potasky; m. Andrew D. Becker, Feb. 14, 1993; 1 child, Samuel. BS in Computer Sci., Kean U., 1986; MS, Stevens Inst., 1998. Programmer ITT Def. Comms., Nutley, N.J.; sys. analyst AT&T, Somerset, N.J., CSC, Somerset. Republican. Jewish. Avocations: cat and dog care, sewing, needlecrafts. Office: CSC 500 Atrium Dr Somerset NJ 08873 Office Phone: 732-652-6205. E-mail: pbecker@csc.com.

BECKER, QUINN HENDERSON, orthopedic surgeon, military officer; b. Kirksville, Mo., June 11, 1930; s. Quinn Henry B. and Sarah Lucille (Henderson) Finley; m. Gladys Marie Roussell, Aug. 11, 1951; children: Quinn E., Terri K., Paul Eric. Grad., N.E. La. State Coll., 1952; MD, La. State U., 1956; student, Armed Forces Staff Coll., 1969-70, Command and Gen. Staff Coll., 1971, U.S. Army War Coll., 1974-75. Diplomate Am. Bd. Orthop. Surgery. Commd. 2d lt. U.S. Army, advanced through grades to lt. gen., 1985; intern Tripler Gen. Hosp., 1956-57; resident in orthopedic surgery Confederate Meml. Med. Ctr., Shreveport, La., 1958-61; orthopedic surgeon Ft. Gordon, Ga., 1962-63; chief orthopedic service Ft. Rucker, Ala., 1963-64; comdg. officer 5th Surg. Hosp. (Mobile Army), Heidelberg, W. Ger., 1964-65; surgeon 3d Inf. Div., Wurzburg, W. Ger., 1965-66; chief orthpedic surgery 33d Field Hosp., Wurzburg, 1965; asst. chief orthopedic service Walter Reed Gen. Hosp., 1966-69; chief profl. services 85th Evacuation Hosp., Vietnam, 1970; div. surgeon and bn. comdr. 15th Med. Bn. 1st Cavalry Div., Vietnam, 1970-71; chief orthopedic service and orthopedic residency tng. Tripler Army Med. Ctr., 1971-74; surgeon 18th Airborne Corps., Ft. Bragg, 1975-77; comdr. Med. Activity Womack Army Hosp., Ft. Bragg, 1976-77; dir. health care ops. Office Surgeon Gen., 1977-80; comdt. Acad. Health Scis., U.S. Army, Ft. Sam Houston, Tex., 1980-81; dep. surgeon gen. Washington, 1981-83; comdr. 7th Med. Command, Heidelberg, 1983-85; Surgeon Gen. Dept. Army, 1985-88, ret., 1988. Asst. prof. orthopedic surgery Howard U., Washington, 1967-69; clin. assoc. prof. Sch. Medicine U. Hawaii, Honolulu, 1973-74; chief of staff VA Hosp., Asheville, N.C., 1989-92, ret. 1992; mem. Congl. Commn. on Svc. Mems. and Vets. Transition Assistance, 1998. Contbr. papers to publs. and confs. in field. Decorated Legion of Merit, Meritorious Service medal, Bronze Star, Air medal, Disting. Service medal. Fellow Am. Acad. Orthopedic Surgeons (chmn. mil. affairs com. 1981-85), ACS, Am. Coll. Physician Execs. (disting.); mem. AMA (ho. of dels.), Am. Orthopaedic Assn., Masons (33d degree, Grand Cross 1993), Civitan (pres. Asheville club 1992, chmn. internat. rsch. com. 1996-98). Home: 3307 McHenry San Antonio TX 78239-3085 E-mail: mqbecker@armyresidence.net.

BECKER, RAY EVERETT, management consultant; b. Grand Rapids, Mich., Jan. 14, 1937; s. Lawson Everett and Virginia Jane (Shellman) B.; m. Mary Rita Warren, Aug. 18, 1960 (div. 1972); children: Elizabeth Anne, Catherine Virginia; m. Arlyss Ellen Roeber, Aug. 17, 1974. AB in Engring., Dartmouth Coll., 1959, MS in Engring and Bus. Adminstrn., 1960; MS in Mgmt., MIT, 1974. Project adminstr. Astro Electronics div. RCA, Hightstown, N.J., 1961-65; bus. mgr.radar lab. Missile Systems div. Raytheon Corp., Bedford, Mass., 1965-68, mgr. mgmt. systems, 1968-70, mgr. adminstrn. and data processing, 1970-73, program mgr. Lowell, Mass., 1981-85; mgr. comml. svcs. Raytheon Svc. Co., Burlington, Mass., 1974-75, dir. mktg., 1975-80; v.p., mgr. Mideast area Raytheon Overseas Ltd., Riyadh, Saudi Arabia, 1980-81; v.p., gen. mgr. Info. Svcs. div. Keane Inc., Boston, 1985-95; mgmt. cons. to info. svcs. cmty., 1995—. Avocations: skiing, reading.

BECKER, REX LOUIS, architect; b. St. Louis, May 20, 1913; s. Louis Herman and Elsie (Schroeder) B.; m. Ada Sylva Schmidt, Nov. 20, 1937; children: Susan (Mrs. Robert L. Barley), Kathryn (Mrs. Russell Kisling), Rex Louis, Roger G. B.Arch., Washington U., St. Louis, 1934, M.Arch., 1935. With archtl. firm Johnson & Maack, St. Louis, 1935-42; ptnr. Froese, Maack & Becker, St. Louis, 1946-73; pres. Becker & Flowers, St. Louis, 1973-81. Cons., mem. architects com. Luth. Ch.-Mo. Synod, 1980-96, chmn. 1986-87. Works include: Luth. Hosp., St. Louis, Civil Engring. Bldg., Math & Computer Bldg U. Mo. at Rolla, over 150 ch. projects. Pres. Council Luth. Chs. Greater St. Louis, 1960-61. Served with C.E. U.S. Army, 1942-45. Recipient Disting. Alumni award Washington U., 1995. Fellow AIA (pres. St. Louis 1956, regional dir. 1966-69, treas. 1969-71, Gold Medal award St. Louis chpt. 1998), Mo. Assn. Registered Architects (pres. 1955), Guild Religious Architecture, Scarab. Clubs: Mo. Athletic (St. Louis) (gov. 1973-76, treas. 1975-76), Engrs. (St. Louis). Home: Apt G02 701 S Laclede Station Rd Webster Groves MO 53119

BECKER, RICHARD CHARLES, retired college president; b. Chgo., Mar. 1, 1931; s. Charles Beno and Rose Mildred (Zak) B.; m. Magdalene Marie Kypry, June 19, 1954; children: Richard J., Daniel P., Douglas F., Steven G., Pamela J. BS in Elec. Engring, Fournier Inst. Tech., 1953; MS in Elec. Engring, U. Ill., 1954, MS in Math., 1956, PhD in Elec. Engring, 1959; postgrad., Harvard Inst. Ednl. Mgmt., 1976. Engr. Ill. Bell Tel. Co., Chgo., 1952, Andrew Corp., Chgo., 1953; rsch. asst. U. Ill., Urbana, 1954-58, asst. prof., 1959; sr. staff engr. Amphenol Corp., Chgo., 1959-60, sr. rsch. scientist, 1961-64, dir. program mgmt., 1965-67; dir. Amphenol Corp. (Far Eastern ops.), 1968; group v.p., corporate dir. adminstrn. Bunker Ramo Corp., Oak Brook, Ill., 1968-73; chief exec. officer and chmn. bd. Fortune Internat. Enterprises, Inc., Oak Brook, 1973-76; pres. Benedictine Univ. (formerly Ill. Benedictine Coll.), Lisle, 1976-95, pres. emeritus, 1995—. Trustee, prof. Midwest Coll. Engring., Lombard, Ill., 1968—86; trustee Ill. Benedictine Coll., Lisle, 1973—76; bd. dirs. Amphenol Tyree Proprietary, Ltd., Australia, Amphetronix, Ltd., India, Oxbow Resources, Ltd., Canada; v.p. Bonita Springs Incorporation Com., Inc., 1998—99, pres., 1999—2000; bd. dirs. Arthur J. Schmitt Found., 1970—, pres., 1995—; mem. exec. adv. bd. Internat. Engring. Consortium, 2000—. Contbr. articles and chpts. to profl. jours. and books. Gov. Brook Forest Community Assn., 1971-74; del. Oak Brook Caucus, 1970; trustee, pres. Arthur J. Schmitt Found., Ill. Benedictine Coll.; chmn. Coun. West Suburban Colls., Chgo. Met. Higher Edn. Coun., officer Fedn. Ind. Ill. Colls. and Univs.; chmn. Associated Colls. of Ill., West Suburban Regional Acad. Consortium. Named Disting. Eagle Scout, 1989, Regent Nat. Eagles Scout Assn.; Arthur J. Schmitt fellow U. Ill., 1953-56. Mem. Am. Phys. Soc., Nat. Assn. Ind. Colls. and Univs. (bd. dirs.), Albertus Magnus Guild, Rotary (Paul Harris fellow), Equestrian Order of the Holy Sepulchre of Jerusalem (knight commdr. with star), KC (4th deg. color corps), Sigma Xi, Eta Kappa Nu, Tau Beta Pi. Home: 25761 Creek Bend Dr Bonita Springs FL 34135-9523 Personal E-mail: rpapinani@aol.com.

BECKER, ROBERT A., advertising executive; b. Mar. 3, 1920; s. William and Eva (Kats) B.; m. Pearl Pehr, Aug. 22, 1948; son, David Jonathan; m. Nancy Gibbs, 1977. BS in Mktg., NYU, 1941; BS in Pharmacy, L.I. U., 1949; DCS (hon.), St. John's U., 1989. Copywriter Plough Inc., Memphis, 1941-42, Murray Breese Assocs., N.Y.C., 1944-48; profl. advt. mgr. Squibb, 1949—57; advt. dir. Nepera Pharm. Co., Yonkers, N.Y., 1953-54; v.p. Burdick & Becker Inc., N.Y.C., 1957-61; pres. Robert A. Becker, Inc., N.Y.C., 1958—88, Hosp. Publs., Inc., 1963-84. Bd. visitors Fordham U. Sch. Law, 1987-90; bd. dirs. Guild Hall Mus., East Hampton, N.Y., 1995-97, Collegiate Chorale, N.Y.C., 2000-; founder, pres. The Beethoven Soc., N.Y.C., 1976-90. Recipient Decoration of honor in Gold, Govt. Austria; officer's cross Order of Merit, Fed. Republic Germany, 1985; Distinction of Merit in Gold, City of Vienna; elected to Med. Advt. Hall of Fame, 1997. Mem. Lotos Club.

BECKER, ROBERT JEROME, allergist, consultant; b. Milw., May 29, 1922; s. Jacob and Sarah (Saxe) B.; m. June Granof, June 25, 1950; children: Scott M., Jill Becker Wilson, Jon G. BS, U. Wis., Milw., 1943; MD, Med. Coll. Wis., 1949. Intern Michael Reese Hosp., Chgo., 1949-50; resident in internal medicine VA Hosp., Wood, Wis., 1950-53; resident in allergy Roosevelt Hosp., N.Y.C., 1955-56; pvt. practice specializing in allergy Joliet, Ill., 1956-82; founder, chmn. bd. dirs. HealthCare COMPARE, 1982-90, chmn. bd. dirs. emeritus, 1990—98; cons. health care utilization co., 1982-90; founder, pres. Becker Cons. Corp., 1990—; founder, chmn. bd. dirs. Health-care Comm. Mgmt. Corp., 1990-93. Med. dir. Quad River Found. Med. Care, 1976-84; pres. Am. Assn. Profl. Stds. Rev. Orgns., 1980-82; exec. v.p. Joint Coll. Allergy and Immunology, 1978-86; mem. adv. coun. Nat. Inst. Environ. Health Scis., 1984-88; vice chmn. bd. dirs. Madison Info. Technologies, Inc.; chmn. Utilization Rev. Accreditation Commn., 1991-94, bd. dirs., 1994-96. Author articles in field. Pres. bd. edn. Joliet Twp. H.S. Dist. 204, 1969-70, 75-76; mem. bus. adv. com. U. Ill. Sch. Bus., Chgo., 1987—. Recipient Clemens von Pirquet award Georgetown U. Internat. Interdisciplinary Ctr. Immunology, 1978, Alumni Merit award Marquette U., 2003; named Entrepreneur of Yr. Arthur Young/Venture Mag., 1988. Fellow ACP, Am. Acad. Allergy, Am. Coll. Allergists (pres. 1987), Am. Coll. Chest Physicians; mem. Ill. Soc. Internal Medicine (pres. 1984-86), Asthma and Allergy Assn. Am. (bd. dirs. 1987—), Asthma and Allergy Found. Am. (bd. dirs. 1990-94), Am. Managed Care and Rev. Assn. (bd. dirs. 1989-95), Am. Assn. Preferred Providers Assn. (bd. dirs. 1989—), Utilization Rev. Accreditation Commn. (chmn. 1991-94, bd. dirs. 1991-96), Am. Assn. Preferred Provider Orgns. (bd. dirs. 1988-93), Am. Psychiat. Sys. (bd. dirs. 1994-2003), Alpha Omega

Alpha, Alpha Sigma Nu. Office: 1S 045 Spring Rd Oakbrook Terrace IL 60181 Personal E-mail: wsimed@aol.com. *Whatever success I have achieved has occurred with the following rules of my life: 1) Individual and public accountability for decisions made; 2) Kindness to all persons in my sphere of contact; 3) Hard work; 4) Humility, truth, and respect for human dignity have been uppermost elements in my interpersonal relations; and, 5) I have accepted my humanness when I fall short of these rules.*

BECKER, ROBERT JOSEPH, database consultant, application developer, educator, computer science specialist; b. Grand Rapids, Mich., Apr. 22, 1946; s. Leon Joseph and Alfreda Mary (O'Rielly) B.; m. Kathleen Zbikowski, Jan. 16, 1970; children: Steven, Michael, Kimberly, John. BS in Computer Sci., Mich. State U., 1970. Computer sci. specialist Wolverine World Wide, Rockford, Mich., 1970-73; data base adminstr. Foremost Ins. Co., Grand Rapids, 1973-80, with data base, data communications, 1980-86, mgr. data base adminstrn., 1986-88, cons. of tech. directions, 1988—; prin. info. tech. cons., 2000—. Keynote data base performance speaker U.S. and European Software AG Confs., 1973—; tchr. computer basics to elem. sch. students, 1988-93; actor cmty. theater, 1995—. Editor (data base products) Software Ag Connections, 1987-98, author performance courses, 1993—; contbr. articles to profl. jours. Community edn. instr., Wyoming, Mich., 1974-80; vol. examiner FCC, Grand Rapids, 1975-85; vol. religious edn. instr., 1980-2003; amateur radio vol. examiner, 1985—; jr. achievement instr. sch. grades 2-5, 2002—. Mem. Software AG Internat. Users Group (cert., chmn. performance spl. interest group 1978—, tech. rep. 1983-85, data base products rep. 1987-94, chmn. data base future directions 1989-99, comm. and client-server software rep. 1994-96, bd. dirs. 1996—, v.p. software exec. bd. 2002—, best presentation award 1978, 82, best speaker award 1979), Am. Radio Relay League, Nat. Train Collectors Assn. Republican. Roman Catholic. Avocations: amateur radio, commercial broadcasting, community and semi-professional theater. Home: 4560 Bremer St SW Grandville MI 49418-2238 Office: Foremost Ins Co PO Box 1233 Grand Rapids MI 49501-1233 Office Phone: 616-954-6128. E-mail: bob.becker@foremost.com, bob.becker@grnet.com.

BECKER, ROBERT OTTO, orthopedic surgery educator; b. River Edge, N.J., May 31, 1923; s. Otto and Elizabeth (Blank) B.; m. Lillian J. Moller, Sept. 6, 1946; children: Lisa, Michael, Adam. BA, Gettysburg Coll., 1946; MD, NYU, 1948. Am. Bd. Orthopedic Surgery Nat. Bd. Med. Examiners. Intern Bellevue Hosp., N.Y.C., 1948-49; resident Mary Hitchcock Meml. Hosp., Hanover, N.H., 1950-51, SUNY Downstate Med. Ctr., 1953-56; practice medicine specializing in orthopedic surgery, 1956—; prof. orthopedics SUNY Upstate Med. Ctr., Syracuse, 1966—; clin. prof. orthopedics La. State Coll. Medicine, Shreveport, 1980—; v.p. rsch. Becker Biomagnetics, 1992—. Author: Electromagnetism and Life, 1982, The Body Electric, 1985, Cross Currents, 1990; editor: Mechanisms of Growth Control, 1981; patentee electric stimulation of growth, iontophoretic method for tissue healing and regeneration. Served to 1st lt. USMC, 1951-53. Faculty exchange scholar SUNY, 1979; recipient Middletown research award VA, 1960, disting. alumnus award NYU Coll. Medicine, 1966, Nicolas Andry award Assn. Bone and Joint Surgery, 1979, Albert Einstein Internat. Acad. award 2000. Mem. AAAS, N.Y. Acad. Scis., Bioelectronics Soc., Internat. Soc. for Bioelectricity. Republican. Home: 6802 Erie Canal Rd Lowville NY 13367 Office: Becker Biomagnetics Star Route Lowville NY 13367 *Any success I have enjoyed in research has been due to the fact that it has been the most exciting and all-consuming endeavor I ever engaged in.*

BECKER, ROBERTA (BOBBIE) RAE, elementary school educator, physical education educator; b. Lockport, NY, Mar. 1, 1943; d. Charles J. and Ramona C. (Spoth) Berent; m. Frank E. Dluhy, July 29, 1967 (div. 1986); children: Dawn, Wendy; m. Vincent G. Becker, Feb. 15, 2002. BS, SUNY, Brockport, 1965; MS, SUNY, Buffalo, 1985. HS phys. edn. tchr. Royalton-Hartland Cen. Sch., Middleport, NY, 1965-67; jr./sr. high phys. edn. tchr. Kenmore Schs., Tonawanda, 1967-68; swim instr. Zwicker Aquatic Club, Lockport, 1978-80; elem. phys. edn. tchr. Gasport Elem. Sch., Royalton Hartland Schs., 1980—; jr. varsity volleyball coach Royalton Hartland HS, 1990—94, coach boys varsity tennis, 1995. Coach Jr. Varsity Volleyball, 1990—2004, boys varsity tennis, 1995—. Mem. AAHPERD (v.p. western zone 1985-89, Jump Rope for Heart rep. 1989—, Amazing Person's western zone award 1992), NY State Assn. Health, Phys. Edn., Recreation and Dance (scribe 1988—, Amazing People State Svc. award 1989). Roman Cath. Avocations: tennis, volleyball, Marian Movement of priests. Home: 4263 Lockport Rd Lockport NY 14094-9655 Office: Gasport Elem Sch Orchard Pl Gasport NY 14067 Office Phone: 716-722-2616. Business E-Mail: beckerb@royhart.org.

BECKER, SCOTT, lawyer; b. Chgo., 1964; BS in Fin. & Acctg., U. Ill., 1986; JD, Harvard U., 1989. CPA Ill.; bar: Ill. 1989, Wis. 2000. Ptnr. Ross & Hardies (merged with McGuireWoods in 2003), Chgo., 1996—2003, McGuireWoods LLP, Chgo., 2003—, co-chair health care dept., 2003—. Office: McGuireWoods LLP Ste 4100 77 W Wacker Dr Chicago IL 60601-1815 Office Phone: 312-920-6016. Office Fax: 312-920-6135. Business E-Mail: sbecker@mcguirewoods.com.

BECKER, STEPHAN E., lawyer; b. Chgo., Ill., June 29, 1957; BA, Yale Univ., 1979; JD, Columbia Univ., 1982. Bar: DC 1982, US Dist. Ct. (DC), US Ct. Appeals (7th, 9th, Fed., DC cir.), Ct. Internat. Trade, US Supreme Ct. Ptnr., co-chmn. Internat. Trade practice Pillsbury Winthrop Shaw Pittman, Washington. Adj. prof. Georgetown Univ. Law Ctr. Editor (Notes & Comments): Columbia Law Rev.; contbr. articles to profl. jours. Mem.: ABA. Office: Pillsbury Winthrop Shaw Pittman 2300 N St NW Washington DC 20037-1128 Office Phone: 202-663-8277. Office Fax: 202-663-8007. Business E-Mail: stephan.becker@pillsburylaw.com.

BECKER, STEPHEN A., physicist; b. Evanston, Ill., Sept. 11, 1950; s. John N. and Irene A. (Wlodarski) B.; m. Wendee M. Brunish, May 30, 1980. BA, Northwestern U., 1972; MS, Case Western Res. U., 1974; PhD, U. Ill., 1979. Rsch. and teaching assoc. U. Ill., Champaign, 1979-80; postdoctoral fellow Calif. Inst. Tech., Pasadena, 1980-82; dep. group leader Los Alamos (N.Mex.) Nat. Lab., 1983—. Contbr. articles to Astrophys. Jour. Recipient Recognition of Excellence award U.S. Dept. Energy, 1999, R&D 100 award, 1999. Mem. Am. Astron. Soc., Internat. Astron. Union. Roman Catholic. Office: Los Alamos Nat Lab PO Box 1663 Mail Stop T085 Los Alamos NM 87545 E-mail: sab@lanl.gov.

BECKER, STEPHEN BRADBURY, fraternal organization administrator; b. Toronto, Can., Aug. 17, 1947; s. Jack and Anne (Havill) B.; m. Trudy Ann Gaar, Dec. 27, 1968; two children. BSc, U. Fla., 1969; MEd in Human Resources Devel., Xavier U., 2002. Cert. Assn. Exec. 2005. Asst. mgr. distbn. Composers Authors & Publs. Can., Toronto, 1969-71; employee rels. adminstr. Can. Imperial Bank Commerce, Toronto, 1971-80; dir. pers. & mgmt. tng. Mother's Restaurants, Inc., Burlington, Canada, 1980-83; dist. mgr. Radio Shack, Toronto, 1983-85; mgr. devel. & cmty. rels. Oakville (Can.)-Trafalgar Meml. Hosp., 1985-88; v.p. Navion Fund Raising Cons., Toronto, 1988-92, v.p., prin., 1995-97; dir. advancement Beta Theta Pi Found., Oxford, Ohio, 1992-94; assoc. adminstrv. sec. Beta Theta Pi Frat., Oxford, 1997-98; admin. sec. Beta Theta Pi, Oxford, 1998—. Fellow Inst. Canadian Bankers; mem., Fraternity Execs. Assn, Nat. Assn. Fraternity Advisors, Am. Soc. Assn. Exec Home: 10 University Ave Oxford OH 45056-1348

BECKER, STEVEN H., lawyer; b. NYC, Nov. 21, 1956; BA, Cornell Univ., 1977; JD, Vanderbilt Univ., 1980. Bar: N.Y. 1981, D.C. 1985, US Dist. Ct. (so. & ea. N.Y.) 1981, US Ct. Internat. Trade 1982. Ptnr., co-head Global Customs & Internat. Trade practice Coudert Bros. LLP, NYC. Mem.: Customs & Internat. Trade Bas Assn. (dir., past treas., mem. Litigation & Customs & Tariffs com.). Office: Coudert Bros LLP 1114 Ave of the Americas New York NY 10036 Office Phone: 212-626-4834. Office Fax: 212-626-4120. Business E-Mail: beckers@coudert.com.

BECKER, SUSAN KAPLAN, management and marketing communication consultant, educator; b. Newark, Jan. 4, 1948; d. Charles and Janet Kaplan; m. William Paul Becker, 1969 (div. 1977). BA in English cum laude, with distinction, U. Pa., 1968, MA, 1969, PhD, 1973, MBA in Fin., 1979. Instr. English Bryn Mawr (Pa.) Coll., 1972-74; assoc. editor U. Pa., Phila., 1975, asst. dir., lectr. urban studies, 1975-77; fin. analyst Phila. Nat. Bank, 1979-82; asst. v.p. Chem. Bank, N.Y.C., 1982-84; v.p. Bankers Trust Co., N.Y.C., 1984-85; prin. Becker Cons. Svcs., N.Y.C., 1985—; adj. assoc. prof. mgmt. comm. Stern Sch. Bus. N.Y.U., 1990—. Cons./evaluator Pa. Humanities Council, Phila., 1977-78; mem. editorial bd. Mgmt. Comm. Quar., 1993-97. Author: How to Develop Profitable Financial Products for the Institutional Marketplace, 1988; contbr. articles and revs. to profl. jours. Vol. N.Y. Cares, 1989-92, N.Y.C. affiliate Am. Heart Assn., 1995-97. U. Pa. fellow, 1968-72; E.I. DuPont de Nemours fellow, 1979, N.Y. Regents Coll. Teaching fellow, 1968-70. Mem. Internat. Comm. Assn. (reviewer tech. and comm. divsn. 1991), Internat. Assn. Bus. Communicators, Fin. Women's Assn. N.Y. (profl. devel. com. 1995—), The Wharton Club N.Y. (career devel. com. 2003—) Democrat. Avocations: painting and drawing, swimming. Office: 155 E 29th St New York NY 10016-8173 Business E-Mail: skbecker@beckerconsultingsvcs.com.

BECKER, WENDY JEANNE, music educator, lyricist, singer; b. Milw., July 26, 1956; d. Arthur Becker and Muriel Jeanne (Mark) Sweet; m. Rik Howard. BFA, U. Wis., 1979. Registered music therapist. Music dir. Camp Hess Kramer, L.A., 1976-81; music tchr., dir. schs. and synagogues, L.A., 1981-90; music and choir dir. Stephen Wise Cmty. H.S., L.A., 1987-94; drama dir. Milken Cmty. H.S., L.A., 1992-97; v.p. Merrie Way Cmty., non-profit org.; producer Morphing of Am.; dir. M.Star Prodns., 2004—. Actress: Days of Our Lives, My Work is Blessed, Getting Back, Blithe Spirit; performances include (with Barbara Streisand) Dem. Nat. Conv., Barbara Streisand Farewell Tour Concert, L.A.; performer various benefits and charities; editor, sub-pub.: Jean Davoust. Music specialist Congregation Ohr Ha Torah, 1997-2003, Petite Amie Music. Recipient Tchr. of the Yr. award Morphing of Am., 1997. Mem. Nat. Assn. Music Therapy, SAG, AFTRA, Actors Equity Assn., Songwriters Guild of Am., Nat. Acad. Recording Arts and Scis., Delta Omicron. Avocations: singing, dance, violin. E-mail: wendybecker@adelphia.net.

BECKER, WILLIAM EDWARD, economist, consultant; s. William and Bernadette Becker; m. Suzanne Rita Holt, Mar. 11, 1967; children: Jennifer, Catherine, Andrea. BA, Coll. St. Thomas, 1967; MA, U. Wis., 1970; PhD, U. Pitts., 1973. Assoc. prof. econ. edn. U. Minn., Mpls., 1973—79; prof. econs. Ind. U., Bloomington, Ind., 1979—. Adj. prof. internat. bus. U. South Australia, Adelaide, Australia, 1996—. Editor: Jour. Econ. Edn., 1989—, Econ. Rsch. Network Educator, 2003—; author: 13 Books; contbr. over 100 articles to profl. jours. Recipient Marvin Bower Leadership and Svc. to Econ. Edn. award, Nat. Coun. Econ. Edn., 2003. Mem.: Am. Econ. Assn. (com. econ. edn. 1989—), Midwest Econ. Assn. (pres. 2005—). Achievements include research in contributions to the assessment and development of educational practices and valuation of human capital. Office: Indiana University 100 South Woodlawn Bloomington IN 47405

BECKER, WILLIAM WATTERS, theater producer; b. New Orleans, Apr. 1, 1943; s. Ralph Elihu and Ann Marie (Watters) B.; m. Joan A. Alper; children: Kirsten Anne, Gevry Danielle. BA, Dartmouth Coll., 1964, MBA, 1965; LLB, Harvard U., 1968. Bar: Mass. 1968, D.C. 1970, U.S. Supreme Ct. 1978, Md. 1978. Staff atty., Reginald Heber Smith fellow Community Legal Assistance Office, Cambridge, Mass., 1968-69; ptnr. Landfield, Becker & Green, Washington, 1969-89, Breed, Abbott & Morgan, 1989-92; prin. William W. Becker, Chtd., Washington, 1993—. Gen. counsel, dir. Voice Found., N.Y.C., 1976-2001; assoc. gen. counsel John F. Kennedy Ctr. Performing Arts, Washington, 1977-93, gen. counsel, 1993-2001; gen. counsel Kennedy Ctr. Prodns., Inc., 1972-2001; dir. Greater Washington Bd. Trade, 1978-92, gen. counsel, 1981-85; chmn. ShowOnDemand.com, Inc., 2000—, TheaterDreams, Inc., 2000-, The Chgo. Theatre, 2004—, The Kodak Theatre, 2005—. Prodr.: (plays) The Dinner Party, 2001, Urinetown, 2002, Into the Words, 2003, Good Vibrations, 2004. Mem. Mass. Bar Assn., D.C. Bar Assn., Fed. Bar Assn. Home: 7252 Stagecoach Dr Park City UT 84098 Office Phone: 312-462-6309. E-mail: becker@theatredreams.com.

BECKER-KLICKER, MARGARET CHAN, library director; b. Tronoh, Perak, West Malaysia; came to U.S., 1972; d. Chan Heong and Ng Tai; m. Millage W. Becker, Oct. 10, 1972 (dec. Sept. 1984); m. Alfred Klicker, June 19, 1991. Degree in bus., Bus. Inst., Ipoh, West Malaysia. Cert. libr., N.Mex. Sec. dist. and land office Malaysian Govt., Batu Gajah, 1963-72; health and social coord. Migrant Coun., Burley, Idaho, 1977-78; clk. Deming (N.Mex.) Pub. Libr., 1979-87, asst. dir., 1987-92, acting dir., 1992, dir., 1993—. Mem. N.Mex. Libr. Assn. Home: PO Box 745 Deming NM 88031-0745 Office: Deming Pub Libr 301 S Tin St Deming NM 88030-3698

BECKERMAN, MICHAEL BRIM, music educator, writer, television personality; b. New York, NY, Aug. 2, 1951; s. Bernard and Gloria Beckerman; m. Karen Palmore, May 30, 1977. PhD, Columbia U., NYC, 1974—82. Prof. of music NYU, 2002—, UC Santa Barbara, 1992—2002. Chair dept. music NYU, 2004—. Author: (writing about music) New Worlds of Dvorak, (book about music) Janacek and His World, (article about music) Smetana's Bartered Bride (Best Rev. in Notes), (articles in the New York Times) various. Recipient Laureate, Czech Music Soc., 2000, Janacek Medal, Czechoslovak Ministry of Culture, 1989, Order of Merit, Czech Parliament, 2004. Achievements include directing numerous music festivals and lecturing throughout the US and Europe. Office: New York University 24 Waverly Place Room 268 New York NY 10003 Office Phone: 212-998-8312. Business E-Mail: michael.beckerman@nyu.edu.

BECKERT, NATALIE A., artist, educator; b. Jamaica, N.Y., May 3, 1937; d. Martin Arthur and Kathryn Elizabeth (Quinn) Myerson; m. James T. Beckert, June 25, 1960; children: Suzanne, Joseph, Jason, Juliane. BA in English, CUNY, 1959; postgrad., West Conn. State U., 1972-77; MFA in Painting, Drawing, Printmaking, Winthrop U., 1990. Tchr., instr. Ctrl. Piedmont C.C., Charlotte, N.C., 1990-94, Winthrop U., Rock Hill, S.C., 1993-94; dir., mgr. Spirit Sq. Print Studio, Charlotte. Solo shows include Mooresville (N.C.) Art League, 1991, Wilkesboro (N.C.) Gallery, 1991, Christa Faut Gallery, Davidson, N.C., 1993, WSOC-TV Lobby, Charlotte, 1994, Pope Gallery, Charlotte, 1994, Union Bldg., Davidson Coll., 1994; represented in collections at Wachovia Bank, Winston-Salem, N.C., 1977, Winthrop U., Rock Hill, S.C., 1989, Nationsbank, High Point, N.C., 1991, others. Judge, registrar Mecklenburg County, N.C., 1988-90; speaker Ctrl. Piedmont C.C., Charlotte, 1990-94; bd. dirs., sec. Friends of Art at Queens Coll., Charlotte, 1990-94. Mem. Phi Kappa Phi. Avocation: gardening.

BECKETT, FAYE TRUMBO, school psychologist; b. Baton Rouge, La., Apr. 29, 1943; d. Leslie Orval and Thelma May Trumbo; m. Robert Earl Beckett, Nov. 19, 1994; children: Denisea Lynn Ray, Douglas Tracey Ray, Heather Dean Ray. BS, U. Memphis, 1981, MS, 1983. Cert. sch. psychologist. Sch. psychologist Memphis City Schs., 1983—87, Tipton & Lauderdale Counties, 1987—2004, Tipton County, 1989—. Various ch. positions, 1963—2005. Recipient Key Man Cert., Parkway Village Jaycettes, 1970, Rosetta I. Miller award, Memphis State U., 1982. Mem.: Tenn. Assn. Psychol. Examiners, Tenn. Assn. Sch. Psychologists, Assn. Sch. Psychologists.

BECKETT, THEODORE CHARLES, lawyer; b. Boonville, Mo., May 6, 1929; s. Theodore Cooper and Gladys (Watson) B.; m. Daysie Margaret Cornwall, 1950; children: Elizabeth Gayle, Theodore Cornwall, Margaret Lynn, William Harrison, Anne Marie. BS, U. Mo., Columbia, 1950, JD, 1957. Bar: Mo. 1957. Of counsel Baker, Sterchi, Cowden & Rice, LLC; instr. polit. sci. U. Mo., Columbia, 1956-57; asst. atty. gen. State of Mo., 1961-64. Mem. City Plan Commn., Kansas City, 1976-80; bd. curators U. Mo., 1995-2001, pres. 1998. 1st lt. U.S. Army, 1950-53. Mem.: ABA, Kansas City Bar Assn., Mo. Bar Assn., Newcomen Soc. N.Am., SAR, Blue Hills Country Club (Kansas City, Mo.), Order of Coif, Sigma Nu, Phi Alpha Delta. Presbyterian. Office: 2400 Pershing Rd Ste 500 Kansas City MO 64108 Office Phone: 816-471-2121.

BECKETT, VICTORIA LING, physician; m. Peter G.S. Beckett, 1954 (dec. 1974); 1 child, Paul T. (dec.); m. Joseph C. Sharp, 1996. BA, Mt. Holyoke Coll., 1945; MD, U. Mich., 1949; MA, St. Mary's U., 1995. Intern Mpls. Gen. Hosp., 1949-50; fellow Mayo Grad. Sch., 1951-55; clin. instr. Wayne State U. Sch. Medicine, Detroit, 1956-67; staff cons. internal medicine oncology svc. Henry Ford Hosp., Detroit, 1957-60; rsch. physician Darling Meml. Ctr., Detroit, 1965-69; rsch. assoc. rheumatology Trinity Coll. Dublin U., 1970-72, postgrad. tutor, 1972-73, dir., 1973-76; cons. physician in rheumatology Federated Dublin Vol. Hosps., 1973-76; staff cons. rheumatology Mayo Clinic, 1976-90, emeritus staff, 1990—; asst. prof. medicine Mayo Med. Sch., 1976-90; med. dir. Rochester (Minn.) Health Care Ctr., 1985—90. Fellow: ACP; mem.: Mayo Med. Alumni Assn., Am. Coll. Rheumatology (ret. mem.), Minn. State Med. Assn., Zumbro Valley Med. Soc., Phi Beta Kappa, Sigma Xi. Methodist. Avocations: teaching exercise class, creative writing.

BECKHAM, DAVID (DAVID ROBERT JOSEPH BECKHAM), professional soccer player; b. Leytonstone, London, May 2, 1975; s. Sandra and Ted; m. Victoria Adams; children: Brooklyn, Romeo, Cruz. Trainee Manchester (Eng.) United, 1991—94, profl. soccer player, 1995—2003, Real Madrid, Spain, 2003—. Mem. English Nat. Team, 1996—, captain, 2000—. Author (with Dean Freeman): David Beckham: My World, 2000; (with Tom Watt) Both Feet on the Ground: An Autobiography, 2003. Decorated Most Excellent Order of the British Empire (OBE) Queen Elizabeth II's Honours List; named BBC Personality of the Yr., 2001, Sportsman of the Yr., Sports Press Assn., 2001; recipient Young Player of the Yr. Award, 1997, Player of the Yr. Award, 2003. Office: Real Madrid Santiago Bernabéu Stadium Avenida de Concha Espina 1 28036 Madrid Spain*

BECKHAM, DWIGHT RUSSEL, music educator; b. Lamont, Okla., Apr. 25, 1931; s. Wick G. and Gladys Magnolia (Channel) Beckham; m. Helen June Barney, Mar. 21, 1951; children: Christine Lynn, Janice Dee, Dwight Russel Jr. B in music edn., Wichita U., 1957, M in music edn., 1958. Trumpet instr. Wichita U., Kans., 1956—58; dir. of bands Valley Ctr. USD 272, Valley Ctr., Kans., 1958—69, Newton USD 373, Newton, Kans., 1969—88, dist. music coord., 1977—88; trumpet instr. Bethel Coll., North Newton, Kans., 1984—95. Trumpet Wichita Symphony Orch., Wichita, Kans., 1947—76, Mid-Kans. Symphony Orch., Newton, Kans., 1954—. Composer various compostions for concert band, symphony orch.; contbr. articles various profl. jours. Bd. dirs. Hist. Soc., Harvey County, Kans., 1980—84. Cpl. U.S. Army, 1952—54. Named Music Educator of Yr., Kans. Federated Music Clubs, 1997; named to Hall of Fame, Kans. Tchrs., 1996; recipient Heritage award for Preservation, City Comm., 1999; Mini fellowship in music composition, Kans. Arts Comm., 2005. Mem.: NEA, ASCAP, Nat. Fed. Interscholastic Music Assn., Kans. Bandmasters Assn., Internat. Trumpet Guild, Music Educators Nat. Conf., Kans. Music Educators Assn., Wichita Musicians' Assn., Phi Beta Mu. Achievements include placed numerous sites on Nat. Register of His. Places. Avocations: bicycling, hiking. Home: 48 Lakeshore Dr Marion KS 66861 E-mail: dwighthelen@mygalaxyexpress.com.

BECKHAM, EDGAR FREDERICK, educational consultant; b. Hartford, Conn., Aug. 5, 1933; s. Walter Henry and Willabelle (Hollinshed) B.; m. Ria Haertl, Aug. 16, 1958; 1 child, Frederick Hollinshed. BA, Wesleyan U., 1958; MA, Yale U., 1959, postgrad., 1959—61; DHL, Olivet Coll., 1997, Clark U., 2000. Instr. German Wesleyan U., Middletown, Conn., 1961-66, dir. lang. lab., 1963-66, lang. lab. dir., lectr. German, 1967-69, assoc. provost, 1969-73, dean, 1973-90, dean emeritus, 1996—; program officer The Ford Found., N.Y.C., 1990-96; coord. Campus Diversity Initiative, 1996-98; sr. fellow Assn. Am. Colls. and Univs., 1998—. Lectr. English U. Erlangen, Germany, 1966-67; cons. NEH; mem. Commn. on Instns. Higher Edn., 1981-84; pres. Rockfall Corp., 1985-86; bd. dirs. Assn. Am. Colls., 1985-90; scholar-in-residence Ctr. Am. and World Cultures, Miami U., 2003-04. Chmn. Conn. Humanities Coun., 1979-80, Conn. Com. on Edn. Equity and Excellence, 1994-95, Conn. State Bd. Edn., 1993-95; mem. Dem. Town Com., Middletown, 1972-90; pres. bd. dirs. Conn. Housing Investment Fund, 1981-83; chmn. bd. dirs. Middlesex Hosp., 1983-85, dir. emeritus; trustee emeritus Vt. Acad.; chmn., bd. dirs. Conn. Pub. Broadcasting, 1990-92; chmn. bd. trustees Donna Wood Found.; trustee Mt. Holyoke Coll., 2000-05; bd. dirs. NAFSA, 2001-04; mem. adv. coun. Appalachian Coll. Assn. Inst., mem. Future of Higher Edn. Project, 2001-04. With AUS, 1954-57. Recipient Outstanding Contbn. to Higher Edn. award Nat. Assn. Student Pers. Adminstrs., 1997, Raymond E. Baldwin medal Wesleyan U. Alumni Assn., 1991, Outstanding Svc. award, 1998. Mem. MLA, Am. Assn. Tchrs. German. Office: Assn Am Colls and Univs 1818 R St NW Washington DC 20009-1604 E-mail: efbeckham@aol.com.

BECKHAM, WALTER HULL, III, lawyer; b. Boston, Feb. 12, 1948; s. Walter Hull Beckham Jr. and Ethel Brooks (Koger) Beckham. BA, Emory U., 1970, JD, 1977; MBA, U. Mich., 1972. Bar: Ga. 1977, U.S. Dist. Ct. (no. dist.) Ga. 1978, U.S. Dist. Ct. (mid. dist.) Ga. 1988, U.S. Ct. Appeals (11th cir.) 1982. Investment analyst, portfolio mgr. Life of Ga., Atlanta, 1972-74; assoc. Jessee, Ritchie & Duncan, P.C., Atlanta, 1977-81, ptnr., 1981-82; pvt. practice, Atlanta, 1982—. Bd. dirs. Cmty. Outreach YMCA, Atlanta, 1973—75; Brookhaven Boys Club Atlanta, 1976; pres. Sr. Hon. Soc. Emory U., Atlanta, 1984—85, mem. Law Sch. Coun., 1993—2001, bd. govs., 2001—05. Mem.: ABA (tort and ins. practice sect., long range planning com. 1986—90, coun. 1990—93, sect. chmn. 1995—96), Ga. Trial Lawyers Assn. (long range planning com. 1982—86), Internat. Acad. Trial Lawyers (state chmn. 2002—, internat. rels. com. 2004—), Atlanta Bar Assn. (state ct. com. 1985), Ga. Bar Assn. (co-chmn. com. on professionalism 1997—2000, jud. procedure and adminstrn. com. 2000—), Kappa Alpha (Hardeman Province Ct. of Honor). Avocations: hunting, fishing, skiing. Home: 1208 Village Run NE Atlanta GA 30319-5303 Office: Ste 2600 75 14th St Atlanta GA 30309 Office Phone: 404-873-8000.

BECKINGHAM, KATHLEEN MARY, education educator, researcher; b. Sheffield, Yorkshire, Eng., May 8, 1946; arrived in U.S., 1976; d. Philip and Mary Ellen (Flint) B.; m. Alan Edward Smith, Oct. 7, 1967 (div. Oct. 1978); m. Robert Bruce Weisman, July 25, 1986; 1 child, Caroline Mary Weisman. BA, U. Cambridge, Eng., 1967, MA, 1968, PhD, 1972. Grad. student Strangeways Rsch. Lab., Cambridge, 1967-70; postdoctoral Inst. Molecular Biology, Aarhus, Denmark, 1970-72; rsch. assoc. Nat. Inst. Med. Rsch., London, 1972-76; rsch. assoc., instr. U. Mass. Med. Sch., Worcester, 1976-80; asst. prof. Rice U., Houston, 1980-85, assoc. prof. biochemistry, cell biology, molecular biology, 1985-92, prof., 1992—. Recipient award, Camille and Henry Dreyfus Found., 1979. Office: Rice U Dept Biochemistry and Cell Biology PO Box 1892 Ms-140 Houston TX 77251-1892

BECKJORD, ERIC STEPHEN, nuclear engineer, researcher; b. Evanston, Ill., Feb. 17, 1929; s. Walter Clarence and Mary Amelia (Hitchcox) B.; m. Caroline Wendell Gardner, Feb. 28, 1953; children: Eric H., Amy W., Charles A., Sarah H. AB cum laude, Harvard U., 1951; MS in Elec. Engring., MIT, 1956; MBA, U. Chgo., 1984. Devel. engr. GE, San Jose, Calif., 1956-60, project engr. Pleasanton, Calif., 1960-63; engring. mgr. Westinghouse Electric Corp., Pitts., 1963-70, project dir., mgr. strategic planning-nuclear, 1973-75; v.p. Westinghouse Nuclear Europe, Brussels, 1970-73; dep. dir. FEA, Washington, 1975; dir. div. reactor devel. and demonstration ERDA, Washington, 1976-77; dir. nuclear power devel. Dept. of Energy, Washington, 1977-78, coordinator internat. nuclear study, 1978-80; dep. dir. Argonne Nat. Lab., Ill., 1980-84; vis. prof. nuclear engring. MIT, Cambridge, 1984-86, exec. dir. nuclear energy study, 2002—03; dir. rsch. U.S. Nuclear Regulatory Commn., Washington, 1986-95, cons., 1995—2003; chmn. com. safety of nuclear installations NEA-DECD, Paris, 1995. Author: Boiling Water Reactor Design, 1962; contbr. articles to profl. jours. Mem. vis. com. for nuclear engring. dept. MIT, 1992-98; mem. bd. visitors dept. materials and nuclear engring. U.

Md., 1995—2002. Lt. (j.g.) USNR, 1951-54. Recipient Presdl. Meritorious award, 1992. Fellow Am. Nuclear Soc. (bd. dirs. 1995-98, chair nuclear installations safety divsn. 2000-01); mem. IEEE (sr.), Sigma Xi. Avocation: history.

BECKLEY, DAVID LENARD, academic administrator; b. Shannon, Miss., Mar. 21, 1946; s. George and Georgianna (Fields) B.; m. Gemma Douglas, June 1, 1968; children: Jacqueline, Lisa. BA, Rust Coll., 1967; MEd, U. Miss., 1975, PhD, 1986. Dir. advancement Rust Coll., Holly Springs, Miss., 1967-87; pres. Wiley Coll., Marshall, Tex., 1987-93, Rust Coll., Holly Spring, Miss., 1993—. Mem. NAACP (life). Named Outstanding Alumni, U. Miss., Oxford, 1989; recipient Silver Beaver award, Yocona Area coun. Boy Scouts Am., 2002. Mem. Tex. Assn. Developing Colls. (chmn. 1991-93), Edn. Ins. Assn. (bd. dirs. 1988-93), United Negro Coll. Fund (bd. dirs. 1990—), Omega Psi Phi (Citizen of Yr. award 1986, Man of Yr. award 1984). Democrat. Methodist. Avocations: reading, travel, collecting antiques. Office: Rust Coll 150 E Rust Ave Holly Springs MS 38635-2330 E-mail: dbeckely@rustcollege.edu.

BECKLEY, HARLAN R., academic administrator, religious studies educator; b. 1943; BS, U. Ill., 1966; attended, Wesley Theol. Seminary; MDiv, Vanderbilt U., 1972, MA, 1973, PhD in Christian Theol. Ethics, 1978. Min. United Meth. Charge, Kingston Springs, Tenn., 1971—74; instr., asst. prof., assoc. prof. religion Washington and Lee U., Lexington, Va., 1984—91, adj. prof. Soc. and Professions Program, 1984—91, prof. religion, 1989—99, chair Dept. of Religion, 1989—95, dir. Shepherd Program for Interdisciplinary Study of Poverty, 1997—, Fletcher Otey Thomas prof. religion, 1999—, interim pres., 2005—. Mem. Pres. Adv. Com. Washington and Lee U., 1990—93, 1994—95, 1996—2001, 2003—05, mem. Faculty Review Com., 1996—97, co-chair, chair Task Force on Inclusiveness, 2000—01, chair Presdl. Search and Screening Com., 2001—02. Author: James M. Gustafson's Theocentric Ethics: Interpretations and Assessments, 1988, Passion for Justice: Retrieving the Legacies of Walter Rauschenbusch, John A. Ryan, and Reinhold Niebuhr, 1992; editor: The Annual of the Society of Christian Ethics, 1991—96, Economic Justice: Selections from Distributive Justice and A Living Wage, 1996; contbr. articles to profl. jours. Tchr. theology class Trinity United Meth. Ch. Recipient Va.'s Outstanding Faculty Award, State Coun. of Higher Edn., 2004; fellow U. Chgo. Div. Sch., 1981—82, Nat. Humanities Ctr., 1995—96; grantee NEH Fellowship for Coll. Tchrs., 1987—88. Mem.: Soc. Christian Ethics, Am. Acad. of Religion, Omicron Delta Kappa (hon.). Meth. Office: Sheperd Program Newcomb Hall N20 Washington and Lee U Lexington VA 24450 Home: 503 Jackson Ave Lexington VA 24450 Office Phone: 540-463-8784. E-mail: beckleyh@wlu.edu.*

BECKLEY, ROBERT MARK, architect, educator; b. Cleve., Dec. 24, 1934; s. Mark Ezra and Marie Elizabeth (Kuhl) Beckley; m. Jean Dorothy Love, Feb. 26, 1956 (div. May 1988); children: Jeffery, Thomas, James; m. Jytte Dinesen, Oct. 24, 1990. BArch, U. Cin., 1959; MArch, Harvard U., 1961. From asst. to assoc. prof. U. Mich., Ann Arbor, 1963—69; assoc. prof. 1987—97, prof., 1997—2002, prof., dean emeritus, 2002—; from assoc. prof. to prof. U. Wis., Milw., 1969—86. Exec. chair Genesee Inst., 2004—; prin. Beckley-Myers, Architects, Milw., 1980—91. Prin. works include Theater Facilities, 1980—81 (award, 1983), Theater Dist., 1981—82 (award, 1984), Bellevue Downtown Park, 1985 (1st place award, 1985). Recipient Distinction award, Milw. Art Mus., 1986. Fellow: AIA (Mich. Pres.'s award 1994), Graham Found., Inst. Urban Design; mem.: Assn. Collegiate Schs. Architecture (bd. dirs. 1987—90, pres. 1988—89, mem. Nat. Archtl. Accreditation Bd. 1990—92). Home: 1016 Scott Pl Ann Arbor MI 48105-2585 Office: U Mich Coll Arch 2000 Bonisteel Dr Ann Arbor MI 48109-2069

BECKMAN, ERICKA, artist, filmmaker; b. Hempstead, N.Y., July 7, 1951; d. Robert Beckman and Ellen (Kathrine) Von Hofen. BFA, Wash. U.; MFA, Calif. Inst. of Arts, L.A. Prof. dept. media and performing arts Mass. Coll. Art, 1983—. One-woman shows include The Kitchen, NYC, 1986, Walker Art Ctr., Mpls., 1986, 2005, Milw. Art Mus., 1987, Hirshhorn Mus., 1987, Whitney Mus., NYC, 1987, 1991, PS-1 Ctr. for Contemporary Art, 1999, MOMA, NY, 2003, exhibited in group shows at Palais Des Beaux Arts, Brussels, 1986, L.A. Mus. Contemporary Art, 1989, ICA-Boston, 1991, ICA-London, 1992, Koln (Germany) Kunstverin, 1992, Galerie Nat. du Jeu de Paume, Paris, 1992, Ctr. Pour L'Arte Contemporaine, Geneva, 2000, Whitney Mus. Art, NYC, 2000, NY Film Festival, 2002, Shanghai Duolun Mus. Modern Art, 2004, Musee D'Orsay, Paris, 2005, Met. Mus., NYC, 2005. Grantee, Nat. Endowment for the Arts, 1982, 1994, NY State Coun. on the Arts, 1983, 1990, The Jerome Found., 1983, NY Found. for the Arts, 1989, Mass. Coun. on the Arts, 1989; ArtsLink Collaborative Projects grantee, 1999. Home: 358 Broadway New York NY 10013-3922

BECKMAN, FRANK SAMUEL, computer science educator, researcher; b. N.Y.C., Apr. 10, 1921; s. Morris and Esther (Newburgh) B.; m. Shirley Cooperblum, Mar. 18, 1951; children: Susan, Denise, Jonathan. BS, CCNY, 1940; AM, Columbia U., 1947, PhD, 1965. Asst. prof. maths. Pratt Inst., 1947-51; mgr. univ. rels., assoc. dir. IBM Systems Rsch. Inst. IBM Corp., Yorktown Heights, NY, 1951-71; chmn. dept. computer sci. Bklyn. Coll. CUNY, NYC, 1971-85, exec. officer PhD program in computer sci. Grad. Ctr., 1985-88, prof. PhD program in computer sci. Grad. Ctr., 1988-93; prof. emeritus, 1993—. Cons. rsch. div. IBM Corp., Yorktown Heights, 1983-84, IBM Corp., White Plains, NY, 1989-90. Author: Mathematical Foundations of Programming, l980. Sgt. US Army, 1944-46. Grantee HEW, l974, Exxon Edn. Found., 1975, NSF, l984-85, IBM, l984-86, John Ben Snow Found., 1987. Mem. Am. Math. Soc., Math. Assn. Am., Soc. for Indsl. and Applied Math., Assn. for Computing Machinery, AAAS, Sigma Xi. Home: # 126-101 14095 Royal Vista Dr Delray Beach FL 33484-1828

BECKMAN, JAMES WALLACE BIM, management consultant, educator; s. Wallace Gerald and Mary Louise (Frissell) B. BA, Princeton U., 1958; PhD, U. Calif., 1973. Ordained elder & deacon Presbyterian Ch. Pvt. practice, Berkeley, Calif., 1962-67; cons. Calif. State Assembly, Sacramento, 1967-68; pvt. practice Laguna Beach, Calif., 1969-77; cons. Calif. State Gov.'s Office, Sacramento, 1977-80; pvt. practice real estate cons. L.A., 1980-83; v.p. mktg. Gold-Well Investments, Inc., L.A., 1982-83; pres. Beckman Analytics Internat., mgmt. cons. to bus. and govt., L.A. and Lake Arrowhead, Calif., 1983—, East European/Middle East Bus. and Govt., 1992—; prof. U. Applied Sciences, Fulda, Germany, 2003—. Adj. prof. Calif. State U. Sch. Bus., San Bernardino, 1989-2002, U. Redlands, 1992-97, U. Calif., 1998-2001. Contbr. articles to profl. jours. Maj. USMC, 1958-67; various positions C. of C., Assn. Realtors, So. Calif., 1988-99. NIMH fellow, 1971-72. Fellow Soc. Applied Anthropology; mem. Am. Econs. Assn., Am. Statis. Assn., Am. Mktg. Assn. (officer), European Econ. Assn., Nat. Assn. Bus. Economists (officer). Democrat. Presbyterian. Avocations: running, weightlifting, travel. Home and Office: Fachbereich Wirtschaft Marquartstr 35 Fulda 36039 Germany E-mail: bimbhappy@aol.com, happybim@hotmail.com.

BECKMAN, JUDITH KALB, financial counselor and planner, educator, writer; b. Bklyn., June 27, 1940; d. Harry and Frances (Cohen) Kalb; m. Richard Martin Beckman, Dec. 16, 1961; children: Barry Andrew, David Mark. BA, Hofstra U., 1962; MA, Adelphi U., 1973, cert., 1984. CFP; registered investment adviser, stockbroker. English tchr. Long Beach H.S., 1962-65; Promotion coordination pub. rels. Mandel Sch. for Med. Assts., Hempstead, N.Y., 1973-74; exec. dir. Nassau Easter Seals, Albertson, N.Y., 1974-76; dir. pub. info. Long Beach (N.Y.) Meml. Hosp., Long Beach, 1976-77; account rep. First Investors, Hicksville, N.Y., 1977-78; from sales asst. to acct. exec. Josephthal & Co. Inc., Great Neck, N.Y., 1978-81; v.p., fin. planner Arthur Gould Inc., Great Neck, N.Y., 1981-88; pres. Fin. Solutions (affiliated with Seco West Ltd., Goldner Siegfried Assocs. Inc.), Westbury, NY, 1988—2002; with Am. Portfolio Fin. Svcs., 2002—. Adj. instr. Adelphi U., Garden City N.Y., 1981-83, Molloy Coll., Rockville Ctr., N.Y., 1982-84; lectr. SUNY, Farmingdale, 1984-85; creater, presenter seminars, workshops on fin., investing, 1981—; adv. bd. L.I. Devel. Corp., 1993—; advisor investment clubs, 1996—. Fin. columnist The Women's Record, 1985-93; writer quar. newspaper The Reporter, 1987. Coord. meat boycott, L.I., 1973; mentor SUNY Old Westbury, 1989-93; co-founder, chair L.I. del. High Profile Men and Women, Colonie Hill, Hauppauque, N.Y., 1985; treas. L.I. Alzheimer's Found., 1989-93, trustee, 1993-95; apptd. to Nassau County Women's Adv. Coun. by County Exec., 1990; chief adv. coun. Ctr. for Family Resources, 1996-98; bd. dirs. L.I. Small Bus. Assistance Corp., 2003—, sec., 2003—, For Our Children, 2001—, For Our Children and Us, Inc., 2002—; adviser to 2 investment clubs. Recipient citation for leadership Town of Hempstead, N.Y., 1986, 89, L.I. Press Club award, 1987, 92, Mentor award SBA, 1989, Fin. Svcs. award SBA, 1991, L.I. Assn. Fin. Svc. Advocate award, 1991, Woman of Distinction in Bus. award Women on the Job, 1989, Bus. Leadership citation Nassau County, N.Y., 1989, Supr. award Town of Hempstead, 1989, Pathfinder Bus. award, 1997, Bus. Adv. of Yr. N.Y. Dist. award U.S. SBA, 1998, Women's Bus. Advocate award, 1998, NAWBO LI Small Bus. Entrepreneur of the Yr. award, 1998; named one of 50 Leading Bus. Women, L.I. Bus. News, 2002, 2003, one of 90 Women in 90 Yrs. Making a Difference, Girls Scouts Nassau County, 2002. Mem. Nat. Assn. Women Bus. Owners L.I. (bd. dirs. 1987-89, membership chair 1996, v.p. membership 1996-98, v.p. edn. 1998-99, v.p. R&D 2002-03), Women's Econ. Developers of L.I. (bd. dirs. 1985-92), Internat. Assn. Fin. Planners, Inst. Cert. Fin. Planners, Fin. Planning Assn. L.I., L.I. Ctr. Bus. and Profl. Women (adv. coun. 1996-98, pres. 1984-86, Pres.' award 1992, Hall of Fame Achiever inductee 2001, steering com., co-founder L.I. Women's Agenda 1998, exec. v.p. Women's Agenda 1998-2000), Art League L.I. (bd. dirs. 2002—), Kiwanis (bd. dirs. 1994-97, chair fund raising 1994, chair cmty. svcs. 1995-97, v.p. membership 1996) Republican. Jewish. Avocations: theater, classical music, opera, reading. Home: 2084 Beverly Way Merrick NY 11566-5418 Office: Fin Solutions Fin Planning Office 2084 Beverly Way Merrick NY 11566-5418 also: 400 Post Ave Ste 200 Westbury NY 11590-2226 Office Phone: 516-333-1370. E-mail: jbeck0627@aol.com.

BECKMAN, MICHAEL, lawyer; b. N.Y.C., Oct. 8, 1945; s. Albert Beckman and Cecille Bronson; m. Susan Liebowitz, June 26, 1970 (separated Dec. 1987); children: Andrew D., Jason D. Bar: N.Y. 1969, U.S. Dist. Ct. (so. dist.) N.Y. 1972. Atty. Gordon Brady Keller & Ballen, N.Y.C., 1969-71; ptnr. Wolkowitz & Beckman, N.Y.C., 1971-74; sr. ptnr. Bell Kalnick Beckman Klee & Green, N.Y.C., 1974-88; sole practice N.Y.C., 1988-92; sr. ptnr. Beckman & Millman PC, N.Y.C., 1992-96, Beckman Millman & Sanders LLP, N.Y.C., 1996—2000, Beckman, Millman, Barandes, & Douglass, LLP, N.Y.C., 2000—. Adj. prof. law NYU, 1981-93. Dir. N.Y. Jr. Tennis League, N.Y.C., 1986-95, Sports & Arts in Schs. Found. Mem. West Side Tennis Club. Avocations: tennis, skiing. Home: 437 W 24th St New York NY 10011-1253 Office: Beckman Millman & Sanders LLP 116 John St Rm 1313 New York NY 10038-3303

BECKMAN, RICHARD DAVID, publishing executive, advertising executive; b. London, Jan. 26, 1960; came to U.S., 1987; s. John Neville and Margon Lelia (Rosen) B.; m. Jane Cecilia Heaney, Nov. 5, 1983; 1 child, Alana Jane. BS (honors), U. Manchester, Eng., 1980. Sales exec. Thomson Mag., London, 1980-82; acct. mgr. Thames TV, London, 1982-83; bus. devel. mgr. Find Sup, NYC, 1983-85; pub. Conde Nast Traveler, 1994—95, Gentlemen's Quar., 1995—98; European advt. mgr. The New Yorker Mag., NYC; v.p. pub. Vogue, NYC, 1998—2002; exec. v.p., chief mktg. officer Conde Nast Publications, NYC, 2002—; pres. Conde Nast Media Group, 2004—; exec. v.p. Advance Media Group, 2004—. Mem. IAA, Foxholes. Office: The Conde Nast Publications 4 Times Sq New York NY 10036

BECKMANN, CHARLES HENRY, cardiologist, educator; b. N.Y.C., July 18, 1930; s. William and Margaret (Wellershaus) B.; m. Ardith Clara Kuehm, June 9, 1956; children: David, Eric, Diana. BS, MIT, 1952; MD, Cornell U., 1956. Diplomate Am. Bd. Internal Medicine, Am. Bd. Cardiology. Entered USAF, 1957, advanced through grades to col., 1971; asst. chief cardiology USAF Willford Hall Med. Ctr., San Antonio, 1965-70; chmn. dept. medicine Clark AFB Hosp. USAF, Philippines, 1970-73, chief cardiology Wilford Hall Med. Ctr. San Antonio, 1973-83; dir. med. ctr. San Antonio (Tex.) State Hosp., 1983-84; cardiologist Skinner Clinic, San Antonio, 1984—; clin. prof. medicine U. Tex., San Antonio, 1983—; prof. medicine Uniformed Svcs. U. Health Scis., Bethesda, Md., 1982-83. Nat. cons. to surgeon gen., USAF, 1979-83, chief cardiology Bapt. Meml. Hosp. System, San Antonio, 1992-93, chmn. dept. medicine, mem. exec. bd., 1993-94; chmn. ethics com. Baptist Meml. Hosp., 1993-94,; chmn. dept. cardiology Bapt. Hosps. Sys., San Antonio, 1996-98. Mem. editl. bd. Heart Smart mag., contbr. articles to Am. Jour. Cardiology, Jour. Nuclear Medicine, Archives Internal Medicine, Jour. Cardia Rehab., Circulation, Jour. Allergy and Clin. Immunology. Pres. Helotes (Tex.) Park Civic Assn., 1965-67, Helotes Elem. PTA, 1968-70; mem. exec. bd. So. Region Boy Scouts Am., Atlanta, 1989—; bd. dirs. San Antonio dvsn. Am. Heart Assn., 1989-92. Recipient Award of Merit Boy Scouts of Am., San Antonio, 1976, Silver Beaver medal, 1977. Fellow ACP, Am. Coll. Cardiology (bd. govs. 1979-83), Am. Coll. Preventive Medicine, Coun. Clin. Cardiology, Am. Heart Assn., N.Y. Acad. Sci., San Antonio Cardiology Soc. (pres. 1989-90), Am. Fed. Clin. Rsch. (sr.), Masons, Shriners. Lutheran. Home: 14802 Circle A Trl Helotes TX 78023-4023 Office: Skinner Clinic 124 Dallas St San Antonio TX 78205-1288

BECKMANN, JON MICHAEL, publishing company executive; b. N.Y.C., Oct. 24, 1936; s. John L. and Grace (Hazelton) B.; m. Barbara Ann Efting, June 26, 1965. BA, U. Pa., 1958; MA, NYU, 1961. Sr. editor Prentice-Hall Inc., Englewood Cliffs, N.J., 1964-68; v.p., editor Barre Pubs., Mass., 1970-73; pub. Sierra Club Books, San Francisco, 1973-94; pres. Beckmann Assocs. and Millennium Press, Sonoma, Calif., 1994—. Author: After-Dinner Drinks, 1998. Mem. Book Club of Calif. Office: Beckmann Assocs & Millennium Press 18185 7th St E Sonoma CA 95476-4797 Office Phone: 707-938-8194. E-mail: jonnytheb@vom.com.

BECKMANN, KATHLEEN ANN, music educator; b. Binghamton, N.Y., Apr. 10, 1954; d. Eugene Stickle and Mary Catherine Baxter; m. Allan Graham, Jr. Beckmann, Aug. 16, 1975; children: Allan, Carolyn, Melinda. MusB, State U. Coll. Potsdam, N.Y., 1975; MusM, SUNY, Fredonia, 2003. Music tchr. Monticello Ctrl. Sch., NY, 1975—78, Wappingers Ctrl. Sch., Wappingers Falls, NY, 1978—81, Hyde Park Ctrl. Sch., NY, 1990—. Editor: Orchestrations, 1994—98. Recipient Crane Merit award, SUNY-Potsdam, 1975. Mem.: N.Y. State Sch. Music Assn. (string adjudicator), Nat. Sch. Orch. Assn. (exec. bd. 1994—98), Nat. Condrs. Guild, Am. String Tchrs. Assn., Music Educators Nat. Conf., Sigma Alpha Iota (parliamentarian). Avocations: tennis, travel, biking. Home: 3 Robin Ln Wappingers Falls NY 12590 Office: F D Roosevelt High Sch S Cross Rd Hyde Park NY 12538 Office Phone: 845-229-4020.

BECKMEYER, HENRY ERNEST, anesthesiologist, pain management specialist, medical educator; b. Cape Girardeau, Mo., Apr. 13, 1939; s. Henry Ernest Jr. and Margaret Gertrude (Link) B.; m. Deborah Beckmyer; children: Henry IV, James, Martha, Leigh, Hillary. BA, Mich. State U., 1961; DO, Des Moines U., 1965. Diplomate Am. Bd. Med. Examiners, Am. Acad. Pain Mgmt.; cert. Am. Osteo. Bd. Anesthesiology. Chief physician migrant worker program and op. head start Sheridan (Mich.) Community Hosp., 1967-69; resident in anesthesia Bi-County Community Hosp./DOH Corp., Detroit, 1969-71, chief resident, 1968-69; staff anesthesiologist Detroit Osteo. Hosp./BCCH, 1971-75; founding chmn. dept. anesthesia Humana Hosp. of the Palm Beaches, West Palm Beach, Fla., 1975-79; assoc. prof. Mich. State U., East Lansing, 1979-88, prof. anesthesia, 1988—, chmn. dept. osteo. medicine, 1985-96; chmn. dept. osteo. surg. specialities, 1996-97; chief staff Mich. State U. Health Facilities, 1988-90, chmn. med. staff exec. and steering coms., 1988-90; chmn. of anesthesia St. Lawrence Hosp., Lansing, Mich., 1984-90, adminstrv. dir. dept. anesthesia and pain mgmt., 1994-98. Chief of staff Sheridan Cmty. Hosp., 1968-69; adminstrv. coun. Mich. State U., 1988-97, acad. coun., 1992-96, faculty coun., 1992-96, U. hearing bd., 2000-, bylaws com., 2000-04, clin. practice bd., bd. dirs. sports medicine, athletic coun., 2003--; internal mgmt. com. Mich. Ctr. for Rural Health; cons. Ministry Health, Belize C.A., 1993-97; amb. Midwestern U. Consortium Internat. Activities, 1993; chmn. com. student performance, 2002-03, com. on acad. policy, 2000-05, admissions com., 2000-2007, chmn. admissions com., 2003—, MOA-MSUCOM liaison com. chair 2005-; adv. com. on pain mgmt. State of Mich., 1999-2001; program chmn. Am. Russian Med. Exch., 1993-97; bd. dirs. Belize Med. Partnership. Spkr. Sta. WKAR, Mich. State U.; bd. dirs. Boy Scouts Am., W. Bloomfield, Mich., 1973-74, Palm Beach Mental Health, 1977-79, Care Choices HMO, Lansing, 1987-88; mem. adv. com. pain and symptom mgmt. State of Mich., 1999-2002; mem. athletic coun. Mich. State U., 2003--. Fellow Am. Coll. Osteo. Anesthesiologists; mem. AMA, Am. Osteo. Coll. Anesthesiology (chmn. commn. on colls. 1988-89), Soc. Critical Care Medicine, Internat. Anesthesiology Rsch. Soc., Am. Coll. Physician Execs., Am. Osteo. Assn. (spkr., mem. evaluators registry), Am. Acad. Pain Mgmt., Am. Arbitration Assn., Mich. State Med. Soc., Mich. Pain Soc., Mich. Peer Rev. Orgn., Mich. Osteo. Assn. (chmn. edn. com. 2002—), Ingham County Med. Soc. (edn. com.), Am. Soc. Regional Anesthesia, Soc. Security Disability Evaluation, Soc. Internat. Scholars, Phi Beta Delta. Office: Mich State U West Fee Hall East Lansing MI 48824 Office Phone: 517-353-8470. Business E-Mail: beckmey1@msu.edu. E-mail: heb@beckmeyer.com.

BECKNER, WILLIAM, mathematician; b. Kirksville, Mo., Sept. 15, 1941; s. William Horace and Bessie Mae Beckner; m. Chandra Muller; children: Amalia Marise, Chiara Lisa. BS, U. Mo., 1963; PhD, Princeton (N.J.) U., 1975. L.E. Dickson Instr. U. Chgo., 1975-76; lectr. Princeton U., 1975; asst. prof. U. Chgo., 1976-83; assoc. prof. U. Tex., Austin, 1983-90, prof., 1992—. Vis. prof. U. Chgo., 1990-91, UCLA, 1992. Contbr. articles to profl. jours. Salem prize French Math., 1975; Sloan fellowship Sloan Found., 1976-78. Mem. Am. Math. Soc., Transactions of the Am. Math. Soc., Tex. Inst. for Computational and Applied Math. Office: U Tex at Austin Dept of Math Austin TX 78712 E-mail: beckner@math.utexas.edu.

BECKSON, MACE, psychiatrist; b. N.Y.C., Aug. 6, 1959; s. Karl and Estelle Beckson; m. Ann Marie Davis, June 16, 1989. AB magna cum laude, Harvard U., 1980; MD, Cornell U., 1985. Diplomate forensic psychiatry and addiction psychiatry Am. Bd. Psychiatry and Neurology, cert. in Addiction Medicine Am. Soc. Addiction Medicine, lic. Physician State of Calif. Intern N.Y. Hosp.-Payne Whitney Clinic, N.Y.C., 1985—86; resident, chief resident UCLA Neuropsychiatric Inst., 1986—89; neurobehavior fellow UCLA Sch. Medicine, 1989—91; rsch. psychiatrist NIDA-VA Med. Devel., L.A., 1991—97; program chief alcohol and drug treatment VA Med. Ctr., L.A., 1992—95, chief intensive OPT treatment of addictions, 1995—97; med. dir. PICU VA Greater L.A. Healthcare Sys., 1998—, forensic psychiatrist, expert witness, 1998—; forensic faculty mem. UCLA, 1998—, clin. prof. dept. psychiatry, 2005—, tng. supr. psychiatry residents, 1988—. Cons. Sexual Recovery Inst., L.A., 1998—2003, Aim Healthcare Found., L.A., 1998—2001, Didi Hirsh Cmty. M.H.C., L.A., 1988—98; expert reviewer Calif. Med. Bd., 2000—. Contbr. articles and chpts. to profl. jours. Vol. psychiatrist UCLA Student Psychol. Health, 1989—91. Recipient VA Innovations of Care Recognition award, Dept. Vet. Affairs, Oskar Diethelm prize, Cornell U. Med. Coll., 1985. Fellow: Am. Psychiat. Assn. (disting. fellow); mem.: Am. Soc. Adolescent Psychiatry (chmn. task force adolescent substance abuse 2003—05), Assn. Threat Assessment Profls., Am. Assn. Suicidology, Internat. Soc. Traumatic Stress Studies, Assn. Treatment Sexual Abusers, Am. Acad. Psychiatry & Law (chmn. addiction psychiatry com.). Office Phone: 310-966-1907. Business E-Mail: becksonmd@becksonmd.com.

BECK-VON-PECCOZ, MICHELE, retired secondary school educator, writer; b. Phila., July 12, 1939; d. William Wallace Perry and Margaret Kenny; m. Stephen Beck-von-Peccoz, Jan. 8, 1972; 1 child, Lisa Michele Beck-von-Peccoz, MD. BA, Trinity Coll., 1958—62. Eng./art tchr. San Dieguito Union H.S. Dist., Encinitas, Calif., 1971—2003. Author: (teachers manual) Holt Handbook, 2001. Mem.: Trinity Coll. Alumnae Orgn. (pres. 1988—90). Achievements include invention of a method of grammar instruction copyrighted 2000: Sentence Surgery: A Systematic and Graphic Method of Grammar Instruction, based on the consistent use of eight symbols to identify grammar concepts. Avocations: e-mail Scrabble, bronze casting sculpture. Home: 636 Nardito Ln Solana Beach CA 92075-2306 Personal E-mail: michelebvp@cox.net.

BECKWITH, BARBARA JEAN, journalist; b. Chgo., Dec. 11, 1948; d. Charles Barnes (dec.) and Elizabeth Ann (Nolan) Beckwith. BA in Journalism, Marquette U., 1970. News editor Lake Geneva (Wis.) Regional News, 1972-74; asst. editor St. Anthony Messenger, Cin., 1974-82, mng. editor, 1982—. Mem. Cath. Conf. Comm. Com., 1990—92. Mem.: Cath. Union of the Press, Cath. Journalism Scholarship Fund (bd. dirs. 1993—, v.p. 1995—96, pres. 1996—99, 2001—), Nat. Cath. Assn. for Broadcasters and Communicators (bd. dirs. 1989—96, 1997—98), Fedn. Ch. Press Assns. of Internat. Cath. Union of the Press (3d v.p. 1989—92, pres. 1992—2004, 3d v.p. 2004—), Cath. Press Assn. (bd. dirs. 1986—96, v.p. 1988—90, pres. 1990—92, best interview 1982, best photo story 1985, St. Francis de Sales award for outstanding contbn. to Cath. journalism 1994, best poetry 1997). Office: St Anthony Messenger 28 W Liberty St Cincinnati OH 45202-6498 Office Phone: 513-241-5615 x 170.

BECKWITH, EDWARD JAY, lawyer; b. Paterson, NJ, July 18, 1949; s. David and Beverly Beckwith; m. Iris Kailo; children: Jessica, Jason, Jenna. BS, Pa. State U., 1971; JD, Georgetown U., 1974, ML in Taxation, 1983. Bar: D.C., U.S. Supreme Ct., U.S. Ct. Appeals (fed. cir.), U.S. Ct. Appeals (D.C. cir.), U.S. Dist. Ct. D.C., U.S. Tax Ct., U.S. Claims Ct. Staff asst. Coun. on Environ. Quality Exec. Office of Pres., Washington, 1973; assoc. Fried, Frank, Harris, Shriver & Kampelman, Washington, 1974-82, Baker & Hostetler, Washington, 1982-83, ptnr., 1984—. Adj. prof. law Georgetown U. Law Ctr., Washington, 1984—; bd. advisors Jour. Taxation Trusts and Estates, 1989-92; mem. Greater Washington Bd. Trade. Contbr. articles to profl. jours. Steering com. sect. on trusts and probate law D.C. Bar, 1985-87; chmn. planned giving adv. coun. Pa. State U., 2000—. Alumni fellow honoree Pa. State U., 1998. Fellow: Am. Bar Found., Am. Coll. Trust and Estate Counsel (state chmn. D.C. 1998—2003, chmn. philanthropy study com. 2000—03, chmn. charitable planning and exempt orgns. com. 2001—04, regent 2002—); mem.: ABA, Estate Planning Coun., Am. Law Inst., Pa. State U. Alumni Assn., Army-Navy Club (Washington), Omicron Delta Kappa. Office: Baker & Hostetler LLP 1050 Connecticut Ave NW Washington DC 20036-5304 Office Phone: 202-861-1646. E-mail: beckwith@bakerlaw.com.

BECKWITH, JOHN, musician, educator, composer; b. Victoria, B.C., Can., Mar. 9, 1927; BMus, U. Toronto, 1947, MMus, 1961; DMus (hon.), Mt. Allison U., Sackville, N.B., 1974, McGill U., Montreal, 1978, U. Guelph, Ont., 1995, U. Victoria, B.C., 1999; LLD (hon.), Queen's U., Kingston, Ont., 1998. Pvt. piano studies Alberto Guerrero, Royal Conservatory of Music, Toronto, 1945-50; pvt. composition studies Nadia Boulanger, Paris, 1950-51; pub. relations dir. Royal Conservatory of Music, Toronto, 1948-50; staff writer for radio music continuity Can. Broadcasting Corp., Toronto, 1953-55; freelance radio programmer and writer, 1955-70; spl. lectr. U. Toronto, 1952-53, lectr., 1954-60, asst. prof. music, 1960-66, assoc. prof., 1966-70, dean, 1970-77, prof., 1977-90, 1st holder Jean A. Chalmers chair in Can. music, 1984-90. Debut: Toronto, 1950; over 130 compositions including 4 operas, works for orch., chorus, etc.; 30 works published including: 4 songs to poems by E.E. Cummings, 1950; Fall Scene and Fair Dance, 1956; Music for Dancing, 1959; Jonah, 1963; Sharon Fragments, 1966; Circle, with Tangents, 1967; Gas, 1969; Taking a Stand, 1972; Musical Chairs, 1973; 3 Motets on Swan's China, 1981; Sonatina in 2 Movements, 1982; Harp of David, 1985; recorded compositions include: Music for Dancing; The Trumpets of Summer; Sharon Fragments; Circle, with Tangents; Quartet; Keyboard Practice; 3 Motets on Swan's China; Upper Can. Hymn Preludes; Taking a Stand, Etudes, Arctic Dances, Harp of David, On the Other Hand..., A Concert of Myths, Synthetic Trios, Stacey, Round and Round; recordings.: Music at Sharon, 1982; Musical Toronto, 1984, à la claire fontaine, 2000; arranger, dir. of instrumental ensemble; editor: The Modern Composer and His World, 1961; Contemporary Canadian Composers, 1975; Canadian Composer series, 1975-90, Musical Canada, 1988; Canadian Consultant, The

New Grove, London, 1980; author: Music Papers, 1997; contbr. articles to profl. jours. Recipient Can. Music Coun. ann. medal, 1972, Arts Found. of Greater Toronto ann. music award, 1994; named to Order of Can., 1987. Mem. Can. League of Composers (former sec.), Ency. of Music in Can. (bd. dirs. 1972-94), Can. Musical Heritage Soc. (editl. bd. 1981-2003). Office: 121 Howland Ave Toronto ON Canada M5R 3B4 E-mail: j.beckwith@utoronto.ca.

BECKWITH, LEWIS DANIEL, lawyer; b. Indpls., Jan. 30, 1948; s. William Frederick and Helen Lorena (Smith) B.; m. Marcia Ellen Ride, June 27, 1970; children: Laura, Gregory. BA, Wabash Coll., 1970; JD, Vanderbilt U., 1973. Bar: Ind. 1973, U.S. Dist. Ct. (so. dist.) Ind. 1973. Assoc. Baker & Daniels, Indpls., 1973-80, ptnr., 1981—. Articles editor Vanderbilt Law Rev., 1972-73. Bd. dirs. Luth. Disabilities Ministries, Inc., 2003—, Luth. Child and Family Svcs. of Ind./Ky., Inc., 2004—. Named to Ind. Superlawyers for Environ. Law, 2004. Mem. ABA (assoc. editor occupational safety & health law 2002), Ind. Bar Assn., Indpls. Bar Assn., Ind. C. of C. (com. occupational safety and health law 1982—), Associated Gen. Contractors of Ind. (com. occupational safety and health 1988—, safety and health counsel), Order of Coif, Eta Sigma Phi, Beta Theta Pi. Republican. Lutheran. Avocation: sports. Office: Baker & Daniels 300 N Meridian St Ste 2700 Indianapolis IN 46204-1782 Office Phone: 317-237-1406. Business E-Mail: lew.beckwith@bakerd.com.

BECKWITH, PETER HESS, bishop; b. Battle Creek, Mich., Sept. 8, 1939; s. Robert Edgar Sr. and Florence Catheryn (Hess) Beckwith; m. Melinda Jo Foulke, July 10, 1965; children: Peter H. II, Michael J. AB, Hillsdale (Mich.) Coll., 1961, ThD (hon.), 1988; MDiv, U. of the South, 1964, DD (hon.), 1999; STM, Nashotah Ho., 1974, LHD (hon.), 1992. Ordained deacon Episc. Ch., 1964, ordained priest Episc. Ch., 1965, ordained bishop Episc. Ch., 1992; cert. marriage counselor Mich. Asst. rector St. John's Episcopal Ch., Plymouth, Mich., 1964—66, St. Paul's Episcopal Ch., Jackson, Mich., 1966—70; rector St. Matthew's Episcopal Ch., Saginaw, Mich., 1970—78, St. John's Episcopal Ch., Worthington, Ohio, 1978—92; bishop Episcopal Diocese of Springfield, Ill., 1992—; mem. Am. Anglican Coun., 1997—, v.p., 2004—; founding mem. Anglican Communion Network, 2003—. Chaplain USNR, 1972—99; instr. Sch. of Theology Diocese of Mich., Saginaw, 1975; res. instr. Navy Chaplains Sch., Newport, RI, 1979; chaplain to Episcopal inmates So. Mich. State Prison, Jackson, 1966—70; nat. chaplain Navy League of U.S., Washington, 1992—; chaplain Marine Corps Res. Assn., Washington, 1994—96, Ill. State Police, 1995—. Chair Jackson County Cancer Crusade, 1967. Rear adm. USNR, 1996—99, dep. chief of chaplain for total force USNR. Named Hon. Seabee, U.S. Naval Constrn. Force, Washington, 1992; named to Hillsdale Coll. Athletic Hall of Fame, 2002; recipient Alumni Achievement award, Hillsdale Coll., 1982. Mem.: Am. Anglican Coun. (bd. dirs. 2000—), Navy League (pres. Columbus coun. 1990). Republican. Avocations: golf, skiing, gardening. Home: 400 Clipper Rd Springfield IL 62711-8010 Office: Episcopal Diocese of Springfield 821 S 2d St Springfield IL 62704-2694 Office Phone: 217-525-1876. E-mail: bishop@episcopalspringfield.org.

BECKWITH, SANDRA SHANK, federal judge; b. Norfolk, Va., Dec. 4, 1943; BA, U. Cin., 1965, JD, 1968. Bar: Ohio 1969, Ind. 1976, Fla. 1979, U.S. Dist. Ct. (so. dist.) Ohio 1971, U.S. Dist. Ct. Ind. 1976, U.S. Supreme Ct. 1977. Sole practice, Harrison, Ohio, 1969-77, 79-81; judge Hamilton County Mcpl. Ct., Cin., 1977-79, 81-86, commr., 1989-91; judge Ct. Common Pleas, Hamilton County Divsn. Domestic Rels., 1987-89; assoc. Graydon, Head and Ritchey, 1989-91; judge U.S. Dist. Ct. (so. dist.) Ohio, 1992—2004, chief judge, 2004—. Mem. Ohio Chief Justice's Code of Profl. Responsibility Commn., 1984, Ohio Gov.'s Com. on Prison Crowding, 1984-90, State Fed. Com. on Death Penalty Habeas Corpus, 1995—; pres. 6th Cir. Dist. Judges Assn., 1998-99; chair So. Dist. Ohio Automation Com., 1997—. Mem. advisory bd. Tender Mercies. Mem. Fed. Judges Assn., Am. Judges Assn., Am. Judicature Soc., Fed. Bar Assn. (exec. com.), Fed. Cir. Bar Assn. Office: Potter Stewart US Courthouse Ste 810 Cincinnati OH 45202 Office Phone: 513-564-7610.

BECKWITH, SIDNEY JOHNSON, program director; b. East Grand Rapids, Mich., Dec. 30, 1947; d. William Judson and Betty Dame (Bonisteel) Johnson; m. James Luther Beckwith, Aug. 17, 1974; children: Crystina Ann, Betty Bonisteel-Chaffee, William James. BS, Western Mich. U., 1969; MS in Guidance and Counseling, Boston State Coll., 1974, cert. advanced grad. studies, 1976; adminstrv. cert., Syracuse U., 1981. Cert. tchr. reading and English, N.Y.; cert. guidance counselor, Mass. Tchr. English and reading Boston Pub. Schs., 1970-76; coord. K-12 reading, lang. arts, and compensatory program Union Springs (N.Y.) Cen. Schs., 1976-91, 99, chair com. spl. edn., 1984—2004, dir. spl. programs and curriculum, 1990—2005, cons. K-12 program cons.; dir. nat. difussion network IPIMS Reading Ctr. Union Springs Cen. Schs., 1984-90. Co-dir. Wellsprings Leadership Summer Camp, 1993-2003; co-founder, co-dir. Wellsprings Leadership Curriculum and Summer Camp. Mem. Cayuga County children's com. United Way, 1983-89; bd. dirs. YMCA-WEIU, 1978-81. Grantee NDN, N.Y. State ESEA. Mem. ASCD, Midlakes Reading Coun. (pres. 1978-79), Cayuga County Prins. Assn. (sec. 1986-87), Regional Com. for Reading, Spl. Edn., Gifted and Talented, Fingerlakes Reading Assn., Phi Delta Kappa. Office Phone: 315-889-4117. Personal E-mail: sbeckwith@unionsprings.cnyric.org.

BECKWITH, STEVEN VAN WALTER, astronomy educator; b. Madison, Wis., Nov. 20, 1951; m. Susan McCormick; 2 children. BS in Engring. Physics, Cornell U., 1973; PhD in Physics, Calif. Inst. Tech., Pasadena, 1978. Asst. prof. astronomy Cornell U., Ithaca, NY, 1978-84, assoc. prof., 1984-89, prof., 1989-94; dir. Max Planck Inst. for Astronomy, Heidelberg, Germany, 1994-98, Space Telescope Sci. Inst., Baltimore, MD, 1998—; prof. physics and astronomy Johns Hopkins U., Baltimore, 1999—; dir. Space Telescope Sci. Inst., Johns Hopkins U., Baltimore, Md., 1998—. Mem. adv. com. for large telescope mirrors NSF, 1989; mem. decade report astronomy in 1990's and working group for priorities in space scis., NAS, 1989-90; Volwiler lectr. in chemistry Lake Forest (Ill.) Coll., 1985. Alfred P. Sloan Found. fellow, 1982-85; recipient Fullam award Dudley Obs., 1983. Fellow Am. Acad. Arts and Scis.; mem. AAAS, Am. Astron. Soc., Internat. Astron. Union. Office: Space Telescope Sci Inst 3700 San Martin Dr Baltimore MD 21218-2686*

BECKWORTH, JOHN B., lawyer; b. Washington, Jan. 18, 1958; s. Lindley Garrison and Eloise (Carter) B.; m. Laura Hobby, July 31, 1983; children: William Lindley, Carter Hobby, John Pettus. BA, U. Tex., 1980, JD, 1983. Tex. 1983, U.S. Dist. Ct. (so. dist.) Tex. 1984, U.S. Ct. Appeals (5th cir.) 1984, U.S. Supreme Ct. 1987, U.S. Dist. Ct. (ea. and we. dists.) Tex. 1988, U.S. Dist. Ct. (no. dist.) Tex. 1993, U.S. Ct. Appeals (9th cir.) 1997, U.S. Dist. Ct. (Ariz.), U.S. Dist. Ct. (ea. dist.) Mich.; cert. in civil trial law, personal injury trial law. Ptnr. Fulbright & Jaworski, Houston, 1983-93, Beckworth & Carrigan, Houston, 1994-2000, Watt Beckworth & Carrigan, Houston, 2001—, Watt Beckworth Thompson & Henneman, LLP, Houston, 2002—. Trustee The Kinkaid Sch., Univ. Texas Law Sch. Found. Mem. ABA, Am. Bd. Trial Advocates, Tex. Bar Assn., Houston Bar Assn., Coll. of State Bar; life fellow Tex. Bar Found., Houston Bar Found. Office: Watt Beckworth Thompson & Henneman LLP Ste 1600 1010 Lamar Houston TX 77002-6706 Office Phone: 713-650-8100. Business E-Mail: jbeckworth@wattbeckworth.com.

BECKWORTH, LINDLEY GARY, JR., lawyer; b. Washington, Apr. 29, 1943; s. Lindley and Eloise (Carter) B.; m. Martha Brindley, Aug., 1966; children: Melissa Love, Allison Louise. BA, U. Tex., Austin, 1966, LLB, 1968. Bar: Tex. 1968, U.S. Dist. Ct. (ea. dist.) Tex. 1974, U.S. Dist. Ct. (we. dist.) La. 1977, U.S. Ct. Appeals (5th cir.) 1980. Asst. counsel Consumer Credit Commn. State of Tex., Austin, 1968; asst. dist. atty. Gregg County, Longview, Tex., 1969; ptnr. Whitehead-Beckworth Law Firm, Longview, 1973-85; pvt. practice Longview, 1985—. Vis. com. dept. botany U. TEx., 1988—; v.p. Gregg Bus. Incubator, Inc., Longview, 1991—; founder record labels Making Tex. Music, Code of the West Pub. Chmn. Water Adv. Commn. City of Longview, 1981-93 Mem. Gregg County Bar Assn. (sec. 1970, v.p. 1971), State Bar of Tex. (bar jour. com., vice chmn. 1974-86), Univ. Tex. Law Alumni Assn. (dist. dir. 1987-89), Univ. Tex. Alumni Assn. (dist. dir. 1989-91), Ex-Students Assn. U. Tex. (dist. coun. mem. dist. 7 1988-91), Gregg County U. Tex. Ex-Students Assn. (pres. 1975), Coun. State Govts., Washington (yr. two participant Japan environ. study. 1991). Methodist. Office: PO Box 5276 Longview TX 75608

BECOFSKY, ARTHUR LUKE, arts administrator, writer; b. NYC, Sept. 17, 1950; s. Arthur and Frances (Oliva) B. BA in Polit. Sci., Duke U., 1972; MA in Polit. Sci., Columbia U., 1974. Adminstr. Cunningham Dance Found., N.Y.C., 1974-79, exec. dir., 1980-94; pres. Art Becofsky Associates, 1994—. World booking agt. Merce Cunningham Dance Co., N.Y.C., 1976-94; cons. Found. for Ext. and Devel. of Am. Profl. Theatre, N.Y.C., 1985, Found. for Dance Promotion, 1995-2000, Ringside/Elizabeth Streb, 1995-2001, The Armitage Found., 1995, 2002—, Cross Performance, Inc., 1995-98, Stephen Petronio Dance Co., 1995-2002, Gotham Dance, Inc., 1995, ODC/San Francisco, 1995—, Twyla Tharp, 1996, David Dorfman Dance, 1996-2001, Ballet Hispanico, 1996-2001, David Rousseve/Reality, 1996-2001, Susan Marshall Dance Co., 1996-2001, Rena Shagan Assocs., 1996-2001, Margaret Jenkins Dance Co., 1997—, Bill Young and Dancers, 1997—, Bridgehampton Chamber Music Assocs., 1997, Ananda Shankar Dance Co., Calcutta, 1997—, Nest/Tokyo, 1997—, Garth Fagan Dance, 1998—, Moving Education, 1998—, Richard Alston Dance Co., London, 1998-2004, Grupo Corpo/Brazil, 1998—, Rosy Co./Tokyo, 1998—, Siobhan Davies Dance Co., London, 1998-99, Lines Contemporary Ballet, 1998-2000, Joe Goode Performance Group, 1999-2001, Compagnie Jant-Bi, 1999—, Pentacle Help Desk, 1999-2003, Art Plus Care to Dance, 1999—, Expressions Dance Co., Brisbane, 1999-2002, Uno Man, Tokyo, 1999—, Kazco Takemoto, Tokyo, 1999—, Kenichi Tanno & Numbering Machine, Tokyo, 1999—, Jose Limon Dance Co., 1999-2002, Daniel Yeung, Hong Kong, 1999—, Compagnie Marie Chouinard, 2001—, Chunky Move, 2001-, Dance Works Rotterdam, 2002—, Compagnie Flak/Jose Navas, 2002—, Pappa Tarahumara, Tokyo, 2002—, Choreographers in Mentorship Exchange, 2004—; mem. dance panel NEA, 1983-94. Guitarist with Rhys Chatham & The Din, 1981; composer: Secretarial Suite, 1980, Track, 1983, Get Real, Cassandra, 1985, Space Into Action, 1986; author: The Road Show Abroad, 1985, On Commissioning New Art, 1989, MMerce, 1991, Lar Lubovitch: The Company We Keep, 1999. Bd. dirs. Dancing for Life, 1987; U.S. Performing Arts subcom. CULCON for U.S.-Japan cultural exch., 1989-93. Mem. Dance/U.S.A. (bd. dirs. 1983-88, 91-98, treas. 1983-86, vice chair 1993-96), World Dance Alliance (bd. dirs. 1993-97), Am. Arts Alliance (bd. dirs. 1983-87). Democrat. Avocation: photography. Home and Office: 46 Barkit Kennel Rd Pleasant Valley NY 12569 Office Phone: 845-635-9311. Personal E-mail: ckdance@aol.com.

BECRAFT, CAROLYN HOWLAND, communications executive; b. San Antonio, Aug. 17, 1944; d. Donald Roe and Jeanne (Dady) Howland; m. Peter Michael Becraft, May 10, 1969; children: Peter Howland, Jeremy Cliffor. BS in Foods and Nutrition, U. N.D., 1966; MS in Adult Edn., U. So. Calif., 1978. Registered dietitian. Cons. dietitian Breckinridge Meml. Hosp., Harrisonburg, Ky., 1972-73; dir. Resource Ctr. U.S. Army, Bad Kreuznach, Germany, 1979-80; dir. mil. project Women's Equity Action League, Washington, 1982-87; rsch. assoc. Decision Resources Corp., Washington, 1987-89; ind. cons. Women's Rsch. and Ednl. Inst., Washington, 1990-91; dir. comms. Internat. Ctr. Rsch. on Women, Washington, 1991-92; sr. policy assoc. and cons. Women's Rsch. and Ednl. Inst., 1990, 1991, 1993; dep. asst. secy. personnel support, familes and edn. Dept. of Defense, 1993-98; asst. secy for manpower and reserve affairs Dept. of the Navy, Washington, 1998—. Chair Army Family Action Com., Ft. Myer, Va., 1980-82. Contbr. chpt. to books, articles to mags. Pres. Burke (Va.) Sta. Swim Club, 1985-86; sec. Woodhirst Homeowners Assn., Burke, 1988-89. Capt. U.S. Army, 1966-71. Recipient Joyce Ott award Army Family Action Com., Alexandria, Va., 1982. Fellow Inter-Univ. Seminar on Armed Forces and Soc.; mem. Nat. Mil. Family Assn. (bd. dirs. 1983-86), Am. Soc. Assn. Execs., Am. Dietetic Assn., Women in Comms., Women in Def. (pres., treas. capital sect. 1989, 90, program chair nat. sect. 1988, 91). Episcopalian. Avocations: reading, skiing. Home: 8942 Kenilworth Dr Burke VA 22015-2175

BECTON, HENRY PRENTISS, JR., broadcasting company executive; b. Englewood, NJ, Oct. 16, 1943; s. Henry Prentiss and Jean Sprague (Coggan) B.; m. Jean Campbell Redpath, Sept. 28, 1968; children: Sara Campbell, Wilson Prentiss, Elizabeth Campbell BA magna cum laude, Yale U., 1965; JD cum laude, Harvard U., 1968. Tchr. Cambridge Sch., Weston, Mass., 1968-69; tel. producer WGBH Ednl. Found., Boston, 1970-73, program mgr., 1974-78, v.p., gen. mgr., 1978-84, pres., 1984—. Bd. dirs. Becton, Dickinson & Co., Pub. Broadcasting Svc. Bello Corp., 1988—2001, Banff Internat., TV Festival, Pub. Radio Internat.; bd. dir. Am. Pub. TV, 1997—2003, Assn. Public TV Station; trustee Scudder Funds, Conn. Coll., 1992—97; with Com. for Econ. Devel., 1992—2002, Ethics Resource Ctr., 1994—97. Bd. dirs. Mass. Com. for Prevention of Child Abuse, 1979-81; trustee Boston Ballet, 1976-78, Met. Cultural Alliance, Boston, 1974-76, New Eng. Aquarium, 1981-2003, Boston Mus. Sci., 1984—, Wang Ctr. for Performing Arts, 1985-93, 99, Concord Acad., 1993—, v.p., 1994-2002, pres., 2002-; bd. overseers Boston Mus. Fine Arts, 1990-2003, New Eng. Aquarium, 2003—. Mem. NATAS (bd. dir. New Eng. chpt. 1980-84), Mass. Bar Assn., Kollegewidgwok Yacht Club (Blue Hill, Maine), Phi Beta Kappa. Office: Sta WGBH-TV & WGBH-FM 125 Western Ave Allston MA 02134-1008

BEDARD, PATRICK JOSEPH, editor, writer, consultant; b. Waterloo, Iowa, Aug. 20, 1941; s. Gerald Joseph and Pearl Leona (Brown) B. BS in Mech. Engring, Iowa State U., 1963; M.Automotive Engring., Chrysler Inst. Engring., 1965. Product engr. Chrysler Corp., Highland Park, Mich., 1963-67; tech. editor Car and Driver mag., N.Y.C., 1967-69, exec. editor, 1969-78, editor-at-large, 1978—. Race driver, cons. in field; freelance writer mags. and TV films. Author: Expert Driving, 1987. Mem. Soc. Automotive Engrs., U.S. Ultralight Assn., Aero Sports Connection, Sports Car Club Am., Pi Tau Sigma. Roman Catholic. Achievements include first driver to win profl. road race in N.Am. in Wankel-powered car, 1973; raced at Indpls. 500, 1983-84; 1st driver to go 200 miles per hour at Indpls. in Stockblock-powered car, 1984. Home: Rt 1 Box 779 Port Saint Joe FL 32456 Office: Car and Driver 2002 Hogback Rd Ann Arbor MI 48105-9795

BEDAU, HUGO ADAM, philosophy educator; b. Portland, Oreg., Sept. 23, 1926; s. Hugo Adam and Laura (Romeis) B.; m. Jan Lisbeth Peterson Mastin, 1952 (div. 1988); children: Lauren, Mark Adam, Paul Hugo, Guy Antony; m. Constance Elizabeth Putnam, 1990. Student, U. So. Calif., 1944-45; BA summa cum laude, U. Redlands, 1949; MA, Boston U., 1951, Harvard, 1953, PhD, 1961. Instr. Dartmouth, 1953-54; instr. Princeton, 1954-57, lectr., 1958-61; assoc. prof. Reed Coll., 1962-66; prof. philosophy Tufts U., 1967—97, prof. emeritus, 1997—. Vis. prof. law faculty U. Natal, South Africa, 1981, U. Westminster, London, 1994—; vis. life fellow Clare Hall, Cambridge U., 1980; vis. fellow Wolfson Coll., Oxford, 1988; hon. rsch. fellow Bentham Project, U. London, 1997-99, 2003-04. Author: The Courts, The Constitution and Capital Punishment, 1977, Death is Different, 1987, Thinking and Writing About Philosophy, 2d edit., 2002, Killing as Punishment, 2004; co-author: Victimless Crimes, 1974, Current Issues and Enduring Questions, 1987, 7th edit., 2004, In Spite of Innocence, 1992, Critical Thinking, Reading, and Writing, 5th edit., 2004; editor: Death Penalty in America, 1964, 4th edit., 1997, Civil Disobedience, 1969, Justice and Equality, 1971, Civil Disobedience in Focus, 1991; co-editor: Capital Punishment in the US, 1976, Debating the Death Penalty, 2004; contbr. articles and essays on social, polit., and legal philosophy to books and profl. jours. Bd. dirs. Am. League to Abolish Capital Punishment, 1959—72, pres., 1969—72; bd. dirs. ACLU, Mass., 1984—87, 1988—93, 1995—98, v.p., 1987; chmn. Nat. Coalition Against Death Penalty, 1990—93. Danforth fellow, 1957-58, Liberal Arts fellow in law and philosophy Harvard U. Law Sch., 1961-62. Mem. Am. Philos. Assn., AAUP, Am. Soc. Polit. and Legal Philosophy (v.p. 1981), Phi Beta Kappa. Office: Tufts U Dept Of Philosophy Medford MA 02155 Personal E-mail: habedau@aol.com.

BEDDALL, THOMAS HENRY, lawyer; b. Pottsville, Pa., Apr. 24, 1922; s. Thomas and Martha Roberta (Gallagher) B.; m. Priscilla Kimball, July 26, 1956 (dec.); children: Laurence, Frederic, Margaret, and Katherine; m. Catherine C. Larmore, May 2, 1994. AB, Yale U., 1943; LL.B., U. Va., 1950. Bar: N.Y. 1951, D.C. 1968. Assoc. Sullivan & Cromwell, N.Y.C., 1950-57, Paul Mellon Interests, Washington, 1957-89. Dir. Carborundum Co., Niagara Falls, N.Y., 1960-78; lectr. U. Va., 1976-79 Chmn. bd. trustees Sheridan Sch., Washington, 1972-74; trustee Va. Mus. and Found., 1984-99, Nat. Mus. of Racing, 1988-2001, The Textile Mus., 1990-92, Va. State Parks Found., 1992-96; chmn. VA Tech. Equine Rsch. Sta., 2000-. Mem. Bar Assn. City N.Y., Mil. Order World Wars, Order of Coif, Raven Soc., Metropolitan Club, Phi Delta Phi, Omicron Delta Kappa, Pi Delta Epsilon, Chi Psi. Office: PO Box 914 Middleburg VA 20118-0914

BEDDOW, RICHARD HAROLD, retired judge; b. Springfield, Mass., Jan. 3, 1932; s. Richard Harold and Elizabeth Christine (Geehern) Beddow; m. Trudy C. Howells, Jan. 14, 1967; children: Catherine Elizabeth Almand, Elissa Christine. BS, U. Mass., 1953; LLB, Boston Coll, 1959. Bar: Mass. 1960. Atty. ICC, Washington, 1959-69, mem. rev. bd., 1969-73, adminstrv. law judge, 1973-81, NLRB, Washington, 1981—2002; ret., 2002. With USN, 1953—55. Roman Catholic. Avocation: landscape gardening. Home: 2406 Rockwood Rd Accokeek MD 20607-9584

BEDEIAN, ARTHUR GEORGE, business educator; b. Davenport, Iowa, Dec. 22, 1946; s. Arthur and Varsenick (Donjoian) B.; m. Lynda L. Kennon, June 29, 1968; children: Katherine Nicole Kingsmill, Thomas Arthur. BBA, U. Iowa, 1967; MBA, Memphis U., 1968; DBA, Miss. State U., 1973. Instr. mgr. Miss. State U., Mississippi State, 1969-71; asst. prof. Ga. So. Coll., Statesboro, 1971-73; adj. asst. prof. Boston U., 1973-74; Edward L. Lowder prof. mgmt. Auburn (Ala.) U., 1974-85; Ralph and Kacoo G. Olinde Disting. prof. mgmt. La. State U., Baton Rouge, 1985-96, Boyd prof., 1997—. Dir. Found. for Adminstrv. Rsch., 1982-93, pres., 1989-90; cons. in field. Author: Organizations: Theory and Design, 1991, Management Laureates, 1992, 6th edit., 2002; Standardization of Selected Management Concepts, 1986, Management, 3d edit., 1993, Management in Extension, 3d edit., 1995; editor Jour. of Mgmt., 1977-79. With USAR, 1968-73. Fellow Acad. Mgmt. (pres. 1987-89, dean 1997-99), Internat. Acad. Mgmt., So. Mgmt. Assn.; mem. APA, Inst. Decision Scis. (nat. coun. 1976-79), Southeastern Inst. Decision Scis. (pres. 1978-79), So. Mgmt. Assn. (pres. 1982-83), Am. Sociol. Assn., Beta Gamma Sigma, Delta Mu Delta, Phi Kappa Phi, Sigma Iota Epsilon. Armenian Orthodox. Home: 838 High Plains Ave Baton Rouge LA 70810-4349 Office: La State U Dept Mgmt Baton Rouge LA 70803-6312 Office Phone: 225-578-6141. Business E-Mail: abede@lsu.edu.

BEDELIA, BONNIE, actress; b. N.Y.C., Mar. 25, 1948; d. Philip and Marian (Wagner) Culkin; m. Kenneth Luber, Apr. 15, 1969; children: Yuri, Jonah. Student, Hunter Coll., N.Y.C.; studied with Uta Hager, Herbert Berghof studios; studied with Lee Strasberg, Actors Studio. Stage appearances include The Glass Menagerie, 1970, The Sea Gull, 1970, As You Like It, 1970, Midsummer Night's Dream, 1970, (T.V. series) The Division, 2001-04; Broadway appearances include Isle of Children, 1960, Enter Laughing, 1963, The Playroom, 1965, Happily Never After, 1966, My Sweet Charlie, 1967 (Theatre World award 1967); film appearances include Gypsy Moths, 1969, They Shoot Horses, Don't They?, 1969, Lovers and Other Strangers, 1970, Rosalie, 1972, Between Friends, 1973, The Big Fix, 1978, Heart Like a Wheel, 1983, Death of an Angel, 1986, The Boy Who Could Fly, 1986, Violets are Blue, 1986, The Stranger, 1987, Die Hard, 1988, Prince of Pennsylvania, 1988, Fat Man & Little Boy, 1989, Presumed Innocent, 1990, Die Hard II, 1990, Needful Things, 1993, Speechless, 1994, Judicial Consent, 1994, Homecoming, 1996, Any Mother's Son, 1997 (Cable Ace award), Bad Manners, 1998, Gloria, 1999, Anywhere But Here, 1999, Sordid Lives, 2000, Manhood, 2003, Berkley, 2004; TV series Love of Life, 1961-67, The New Land, 1974, mini-series Salem's Lot, 1979, A Season in Purgatory, 1996, Flowers for Algernon, 2000; TV films Then Came Bronson, 1969, Sandcastles, 1972, Hawkins on Murder, 1973, A Message to My Daughter, 1973, A Time for Love, 1973, Heatwave, 1974, A Question of Love, 1978, Walking Through the Fire, 1979, Fighting Back, 1980, Million Dollar Infield, 1982, Memorial Day, 1983, The Lady from Yesterday, 1985, Alex, The Life of a Child, 1986, When the Time Comes, 1987, Somebody Has to Shoot the Picture, 1990, Switched At Birth, 1991, A Mother's Right: The Elizabeth Morgan Story, 1993, The Fire Next Time, 1993, Fallen Angels (The Quiet Room), 1993 (Emmy nomination, Guest Actress - Drama, 1994), The Gift, 1994, Shadow of a Doubt, 1995, Legacy of Sin: The William Coit Story, 1995, Her Costly Affair, 1996, To Live Again, 1998, Locked in Silence, 1999, Picnic, 2000. Recipient Golden Globe award, 1983. Office: care ICM c/o Brian Bunnin 8942 Wilshire Blvd Beverly Hills CA 90211-1934

BEDELL, BARBARA LEE, journalist; b. Annapolis, Md., July 10, 1936; d. Royal Lee and Kathryn Rosalee (Alton) Sweeney; m. Raymond Lester Bedell, July 1, 1955 (div. 1979); children: Patricia Bedell Pulito, Barbara Ann Bedell Porrini, Raymond, Robert. DHL (hon.), Mt. St. Mary Coll., 2000. Dir. woman's programming, host daily talk show Sta. KLME, Laramie, Wyo., 1962-68, Sta. WKIP, Poughkeepsie, N.Y., 1968-70; asst. soc. editor, feature writer Poughkeepsie Jour., 1968-70; dir. comm. and publs. Spackenkill Sch. Dist., Poughkeepsie, 1970-73; columnist, reporter Times Herald-Record Newspaper, Middletown, N.Y., 1973—. Bd. dirs. Middletown Day Nursery, 1988—; mem. steering com. Dr. Martin Luther King Jr. Cmty. Wide Celebration, 1992—; lectr. on various topics to civic, polit., religious, social orgns., 1961—. Mem. 75th Anniversary Com., Cheyenne, Wyo., 1965; mem. Rep. Precinct Com., 1961-68, Albany County Bd. Electors, 1966-68; mem. com. history and heritage collection Orange County C.C., Middletown, 1984; mem. 100th Anniversary Com., Middletown, 1983-88; bd. dirs. divsn. marshal 1988 Parade; apptd. del. Gov. Mario Cuomo's N.Y. State Conf. on Librs., 1981; campaign chair United Way, 1996; bd. dirs. Literacy Vols. of Am.; kettle chmn. Salvation Army, 1999. Recipient 1st in N.Y. feature writing award Am. Cancer Soc., 1973, Disting. Svc. award NAACP, 1980, 96, Hadassah Myrtle Wreath award, 1979, Cmty. Svc. award Boy Scouts Am., 1990, Humanitarian award Human Rights Commn., 1997, Orange County Agr. Soc. award, Svc. awards from numerous svc. clubs and lodges, chs., assns.; named Mrs. Wyo., Mrs. Am. Pageant, 1967, N.Y. State All-Am. Family, 1972, Lions Knight of the Blind award, 1999, Pinnacle award U.S. Harness Racing Hall of Fame, 2002, Masonic DeWitt Clinton award, 2002. Mem. Nat. Fedn. Press Women (8 awards for feature writing 1967-70, top Wyo. state award for radio script writing 1966), Elks (Mother of Yr. award 1989), SAR (Woman of Yr. award 1991), Kiwanis, Lions, Rotary. Home: PO Box 458 Walker Valley NY 12588-0458 Office: Times Herald-Record PO Box 2046 Middletown NY 10940-0558 E-mail: bbedell@th-record.com.

BEDELL, DENNIS PETERS, lawyer, educator; b. Detroit, July 13, 1939; s. Charles Peters and Elnora Jane (Petersen) B; m. Janet Mae Spaeth, Aug. 19, 1961; children: Kevin Bryan, Jeffrey Allan. AB, Harvard Coll., 1961; JD, U. Mich., 1964. Bar: D.C. Ct. Appeals 1965, U.S. Tax Ct. 1979, U.S. Supreme Ct. 1980, U.S. Ct. Appeals (fed. cir.) 1982, U.S. Ct. Fed. Claims 1979. Atty. Office of Chief Counsel, IRS, Washington, 1964-67; legis. atty. Joint Com. Taxation U.S. Congress, Washington, 1967-69, asst. chief staff, 1970-71; assoc. Miller & Chevalier Chartered, Washington, 1972, ptnr., 1973—2004, of counsel, 2005—. Chmn. tax com. Amer. Mining Congress, D.C., 1974-88, counsel, 1988-95; adj. prof. Georgetown U. Law Sch., D.C. 1977—. Bd. dirs. Miller & Chevalier Charitable Found., D.C., 1990—. Fellow Amer. Coll. Tax Counsel; mem. ABA (tax sect.). Avocations: fiddle playing, boating, water and snow skiing, jogging. Home: 4142 Round Hill Rd Arlington VA 22207-4623 Office: Miller & Chevalier Chartered 655 15th St NW Ste 900 Washington DC 20005-5799 Office Phone: 202-626-5930. Business E-Mail: dbedell@milchev.com.

BEDELL, ELIZABETH SNYDER (BETTY BEDELL), editor-in-chief, marketing professional; b. Jacksonville, Fla., Mar. 26, 1940; d. Ralph Edward and Elizabeth Follin Snyder; m. David Thorpe Bedell, June 16, 1961 (div. Aug. 1974); children: Charles, Elizabeth Bedell Coyle, George. Student, Hollins U.; BA, U. North Fla. Founding editor Kalliope, A Jour. of Women's

Lit. and Art, 1978—81; tchr. Stanton Coll. Prep., Venetia Elem., 1981—84; freelance writer, editor, 1984—93, 1997—; program developer St. Vincent's Found., Inc., 1993—98; editor Betty Snyder Bedell Editl. Svcs., Jacksonville, 1999—. Chmn. garden and grounds Ximenez-Fatio Mus. House, St. Augustine, Fla.; bd. dirs. Jr. League, Jacksonville. Mem.: Colonial Dames, Fla. Yacht Club Jacksonville. Home and Office: 4242 Ortega Blvd # 21 Jacksonville FL 32210 E-mail: ebedell@bellsouth.net.

BEDELL, GEORGE NOBLE, internist, educator; b. Harrisburg, Pa., May 1, 1922; s. George Harold and Elsie Clair (Noble) B.; m. Betty Jane Goldzier, Nov. 4, 1950 (dec. Mar. 1970); children: David, Mark, Barbara, Bruce; m. Mirriel Shields Hummel, Oct. 17, 1970; step-children: Judy, Jeffrey, Eric, Deborah, Andrew. BA, DePauw U., 1944; MD, U. Cin., 1946. Intern U. Iowa, 1946-47, resident in pathology, 1947-48, resident in internal medicine, 1950-52, research fellow in internal medicine, specializing in cardiology, 1952-54; research fellow physiology Postgrad. Sch. Medicine, U., Pa., 1954-55; asst. prof. dept. medicine Coll. Medicine, U. Iowa, 1955-59, asso. prof. dept. medicine, 1959-68, prof., 1968—; dir. Pulmonary Disease div. Dept. Medicine, 1968-81. Cons. VA Hosp., Iowa City, 1954—; mem. staff U. Hosps., Iowa City Contbr. articles to profl. jours. Mem. Johnson County Democratic Central Com., 1956-69, treas., 1958-64. Served with AUS, 1948-50. NIH Spl. fellow, 1954-55; recipient Career Devel. award, 1960-70, Walter L. Bierring award Am. Lung Assn. Iowa, 1973 Mem. ACP, Am. Lung Assn. (dir. 1972-80), Am. Lung Assn. Iowa (dir. 1971-81), Am. Fedn. Clin. Research, Am. Thoracic Soc., Iowa Thoracic Soc. (v.p. 1960-61, pres. 1962-63), Iowa Tb and Health Assn. (dir. 1961-65, 67-71), AMA (vice chmn. sect. council on diseases of chest 1971-73, chmn. sec. council diseases of chest 1974-76, Am. Thoracic Soc. del. to AMA 1979-85), Iowa, Johnson County med. socs., Soc. Exptl. Biology and Medicine, Iowa Clin. Soc. Internal Medicine, Central Soc. Clin. Research, Am. Coll. Chest Physicians, Am. Physiol. Soc., Am. Soc. Clin. Investigation, A.C.P., Central Clin. Research Club. Democrat. Unitarian Universalist. Home: 903 Highwood St Iowa City IA 52246-3807 Office Phone: 319-356-2755. E-mail: george-bedell@uiowa.edu.

BEDELL, JAY DEE, small business owner, writer; b. Monterey, Calif., Oct. 20, 1946; s. John Dewhirst and Lucille (Huffman) Bedell. BA, U. Calif., Davis, 1968. Tchr. Antioch Schs., Calif., 1969—84; v.p., dir. Credit Union, 1979—81; owner Bedell Enterprises, 1986—; supr. security Chevron U.S.A., 1988—90. Mem. Adv. Coun. for Spl. Edn., Antioch, Calif., 1979-81; mem. State Dept. Conf. on Spl. Edn., 1978; staff devel. com. Office of Supt. of Schs., Contra Costa County, Calif., 1979-81; cons. in field. Author numerous poems. Deacon Adventist Ch., Antioch, Calif.; sch. bd. Hilltop Christian Sch., Antioch; honor guard Vets. Home Calif. With US Army, 1971-75. Recipient Golden Poet award, World of Poetry Press, 1985—92. Fellow Am. Biog. Inst. Rsch. Assn. (life); mem. NRA (cert. asst. rifle instr.), Sierra Club, Nature Conservancy, Internat. Platform Assn., Wilderness Soc., Libr. of Congress (assoc.), Smithsonian (assoc.), Commonwealth Club of San Francisco (assoc.), Marines Mem. Club San Francisco, Knight Sovereign Mil. Templar Order, Delta Upsilon. Democrat. Address: Vets Home of Calif PO Box 1200 Yountville CA 94599 E-mail: jaydbedell@yahoo.com.

BEDELL, KEVIN SHAWN, physicist, researcher; b. N.Y.C., July 7, 1948; s. James Raymond and Doris (Breslin) B.; m. Carmen Elizabeth Uriarte, Jan. 18, 1970; 1 child, Christopher Michael. BS in Physics, Dowling Coll., 1971; MS in Applied Math., SUNY, Stony Brook, 1972, PhD in Physics, 1979. Lab. asst. physics Dowling Coll., Oakdale, N.Y., 1971-73, instr. physics and math., 1973-74, adj. asst. prof., 1974-78, adj. assoc. prof., 1978-79; rsch. asst. physics SUNY, Stony Brook, 1975-79; rsch. assoc. physics U. Ill., Urbana, 1979-82; Inst. Theoretical Physics rsch. fellow physics SUNY, Stony Brook, 1982-85; vis. prof. Kamerlingh Onnes Lab., Leiden, The Netherlands, 1985-86; staff mem. theoretical divsn. Los Alamos (N.Mex.) Nat. Lab., 1986-95; prof., chair physics dept. Boston Coll., 1995—, Rourke prof. physics, 1999—. Adj. prof. physics Fla. State U., Tallahassee, 1991—, U. Fla., Gainesville, 1991—; mem. sci. adv. com. Nat. High Magnetic Field Lab., Tallahassee, Gainesville, Los Alamos, 1995-96; cons. Los Alamos Nat. Lab., 1996-; founding mem., bd. govs. Inst. for Complex and Adaptive Matter, 2001-. Editor 4 books, 1 conf. procs.; co-editor: Advances in Physics, 1995—; contbr. numerous articles to profl. jours. Grantee Dept. Energy, 1990-95, 97—, NSF, Dept. Edn. Fellow Am. Phys. Soc. Avocation: weight-lifting. Home: 11 Worth Cir Newton MA 02458-1945 Office: Boston Coll Dept Physics Chestnut Hill MA 02467 Office Phone: 617-552-3575. E-mail: bedell@bc.edu.

BEDENBAUGH, ANGELA LEA OWEN, chemistry educator, researcher; b. Seguin, Tex., Oct. 6, 1939; d. Wintford Henry and Nelia Melanie (Fischer) Owen; m. John Holcombe Bedenbaugh, Dec. 27, 1961; 1 child, Melanie Celeste. BS cum laude, U. Tex., 1961; PhD in Organic Chemistry, U. S.C., 1967. Geol. mapping asst. Roland Blumberg Assocs., Seguin, summer 1958, 59; chemistry lab. instr. U. Tex., Austin, 1960-61; rsch. assoc. chemistry U. So. Miss., Hattiesburg, 1966-80, rsch. assoc. prof. chemistry, 1980—, bd. mem. women's studies program, 1996-97. Co-prin. investigator Bell South Found. grant, 1998; dir. website NASA grant, 1999-00; project dir. math. and sci. ptnr. program U.S. Dept. Edn., 2004—; mem Nat. Def. Coun. Author: Nomenplayture, 1998; co-author: (with John H. Bedenbaugh) Handbook for High School Chemistry Teachers, 1985, (with John H. Bedenbaugh) Teaching First Year Chemistry, 4th edit., 1993, (with John H. Bedenbaugh) Teaching Physical Science, Vols. 1 and 2, 2003; patentee in field. Adminstrv. bd. Parkway Heights United Meth. Ch., 1974-75, women's unit leader, 1973-75, women's unit treas., 1977, Wesleyan Svc. Guild v.p., 1970, Sunday Sch. tchr., 1973-74; bd. dirs. Forrest Stone Area Opportunity Inc., 1970-72, bd. dirs. exec. com., 1972, mem. com. to rewrite pers. policies and procedures, 1971, mem. Headstart monitoring com., 1971-72, mem. pers. screening com., 1971; mem. nat. Women's Polit. Caucus, 1976—; mem. Toastmasters Internat., 1986—, club. pres., 1993, area gov., 1994; adminstr., dir. Tchr. Mentoring Initiative through Bell South Found. Grant, 1998-2000; Miss. state coord. Bldg. a Presence for Sci., 2002-; mem. Gov.'s Edn. Summit, 2004; mem. U.S. Dept. Edn. Math. and Sci. Partnership, 2004-2005. Recipient John and Angela Bedenbaugh award Coastal Miss. Assn. H.S. Chemistry Tchrs., 1996—; rsch. grantee U.S. Dept. Energy, 1980-81, U. So. Miss., 1980, NSF, U. So. Miss., 1985, Adminstrv. Dir. Rsch. grant, 1988-91, 1993-96, 2001-04, NSF, 2000—, others. Mem. NSTA (nat. resource rev. panel for rev. of instrnl. materials), LWV, AAUW, Am. Chem. Soc. (chmn. 1984-85, program chmn. 1983-84, exec. bd. 1983—, Chemist of Yr. award 1991), Miss. Sci. Tchrs. Assn. (exec. bd. 1994—, pres.-elect 1998-2000, pres. 2000-02, state bldg. a presence for sci. coord. 2002—, Disting. Sci. Tchr. award 1994), Nat. Wildlife Fedn., Wilderness Soc., Union of Concerned Scientists, Nat. Resources Def. Coun., Delta Kappa Gamma (pres. Miss. br. 1989-91, chmn. internat. rsch. com. 1980-82, chmn. internat. computer share fair at internat. conv. 1994, editor U.S. Forum Connection 2000-), Nat. Audubon Soc., Sierra Club, Commonwealth Club, Sigma Xi (charter, sec.-treas. 1967-69, treas. 1970, pres. 1973-74, program chmn. 1972-73). Arthritis Found. Democrat. Methodist. Home: 63 Suggs Rd Hattiesburg MS 39402-3639 Office: Univ So Miss 118 College Dr 8466 Hattiesburg MS 39406-1000

BEDERSON, BENJAMIN, physicist, researcher; b. NYC, Nov. 15, 1921; s. Abraham Michael and Lena (Waxlowsky) B.; m. Betty Weintraub, Jan. 20, 1956; children: Joshua Benjamin, Geoffrey Adam, Aron Gregory, Benjamin Boris. BS, CCNY, 1946; MS, Columbia U., 1948; PhD, NYU, 1950. Rsch. scientist MIT, Cambridge, 1950-52; faculty dept. physics NYU, 1952-92, prof., 1967-92, prof. emeritus, 1992—, chmn. dept., 1973-76, spl. advisor for sci. to dean Faculty Arts and Scis., 1983-86, dean Grad. Sch. Arts and Scis., 1986-89. Chmn. Internat. Conf. Physics of Electronic and Atomic Collisions, 1983-85; chmn. vis. panel Ctr. for Absolute Phys. Quantities, Nat. Bur. Standards, 1980-83. Editor-in-chief Am. Phys. Soc., 1992-96; editor Phys. Rev. A, 1978-91; assoc. editor Atomic Data and Nuclear Data Jour., 1969-98; editor (with Herbert Walther) Advances in Atomic, Molecular, and Optical Physics, 1974—2004; contbr. articles to profl. jours.; patentee in field. With U.S. Army, 1942-46, PTO. Fellow: APS (chair forum history physics 2001—02), AAAS. Home: 60 E 8th St Apt 24K New York NY 10003-6522 Office: NYU Physics Dept 4 Washington Pl New York NY 10003-6621 Office Phone: 212-998-7695. Business E-Mail: ben.bederson@nyu.edu.

BEDFORD, BRIAN, actor; b. Morley, Yorkshire, Eng., Feb. 16, 1935; s. Arthur and Ellen (O'Donnell) B. Student, Royal Acad. Dramatic Art, London. Actor: (plays) A View From the Bridge, 1958, Five Finger Exercise, 1959, The Tempest, 1959, Write Me A Murder, 1962, Lord Pengo, 1962, The Doctor's Dilemma, 1963, The Private Ear, 1963, The Knack, 1964, The Unknown Soldier and His Wife, 1967, 73, Astrakhan Coat, 1967, The Cocktail Party, 1968, The Seven Descents of Myrtle, 1968, Hamlet, 1969, Private Lives, 1969, Three Sisters, 1969, Blithe Spirit, 1970, The Tavern, 1970, School for Wives, 1971 (Tony award for Best Actor 1971), Jumpers, 1972, Butley, 1973, Measure for Measure, 1975, Twelfth Night, 1975, Equus, 1976, Richard III, 1977, The Guardsman, 1977, As You Like It, 1977, The Winter's Tale, 1978, Uncle Vanya, 1978, Death Trap, 1979, The Seagull, 1980, Much Ado About Nothing, 1980, Whose Life Is It Anyway?, 1980, The Misanthrope, 1981, Arms and the Man, 1982, Blithe Spirit, 1982, Tartuffe, 1983, Richard II, 1983, 86, A Midsummer Night's Dream, 1984, Waiting for Godot, 1984, The Real Thing, 1985, The Tempest, 1985, Private Lives, 1986, Opera Comique, 1987, No Time for Comedy, 1987, The Merchant of Venice, 1988, Educating Rita, 1988, The Relapse, 1989, The Merchant of Venice, 1989, The Lunatic, The Lover and The Poet, 1989, Macbeth, 1990, Julius Caesar, 1990, Timon of Athens, 1991, Much Ado About Nothing, 1991, School for Wives, 1991, Two Shakespearean Actors, 1991, 92 (Tony award nominee for Lead Actor in a Play 1992), Measure for Measure, 1992, Timon of Athens, 1993, 94 (Tony award nominee for Lead Actor in a Play 1994), Twelfth Night, 1994, The Molière Comedies, 1994, 95, (Tony award nominee for Lead Actor in a Play 1995), Amadeus, 1995, 96, The Little Foxes, 1996, London Assurance, 1997 (Tony award nominee for Lead Actor 1997), Equus, 1997, Much Ado About Nothing, 1998, A Midsummer Night's Dream, 1999, The School for Scandal, 1999, As You Like It, 2005; (films) Man of the Moment, 1955, Miracle in Soho, 1957, The Angry Silence, 1960, Number Six, 1961, The Pad and How to Use It, 1966, Grand Prix, 1966, Robin Hood, 1973, Nixon, 1995, others; also numerous TV appearances; dir.: (plays) Titus Andronicus, 1978, The Rivals, 1981, Coriolanus, 1981, Blithe Spirit, 1982, Phaedra, 1990, Othello, 1994, Waiting for Godot, 1996, 98, Equus, 1997, The Winter's Tale, 1998. Inducted into Theatre Hall of Fame, 1996. Address: Stratford Festival PO Box 520 Stratford ON Canada N5A 6V2 Office: PO Box 298 Hurley NY 12443-0298*

BEDFORD, STACIA C., information technology manager; BS in Sociology, SUNY; post grad. in Mgmt. Sys., Old Dominion U., Norfolk, Va.; post grad. in Internat. Rels., Armed Forces Staff Coll., Norfolk, Va. Cert. Oracle adminstr., project mgr. PMI, IBM project mgmt., BPR bus. methodology; Six Sigma. Project and documentation mgr. Cherokee Electronics, Inc., Virginia Beach, Va., 1986; dir. tng. Executrain of Ea. Va., 1989—92; internat. program dir. Firstwave, Inc., Atlanta, 1992—96; regional ops. mgr. and program mgr. Cambridge Tech. Ptnrs., Inc. (a Novell Co.), Dallas, 1996—98; industry exec. pub. sector IBM Global Svcs., 1998—2001; COO Anthem Investment Corp., 2001—03; divsn. head NETS/NEMAIS program IT tech. svcs. CACI, Inc.-Federal, 2003—. Mem.: Project Mgmt. Inst., Bus. Execs. Nat. Security. Address: 2304 Beech St Virginia Beach VA 23451

BEDINI, SILVIO A., historian, author; b. Ridgefield, Conn., Jan. 17, 1917; s. Vincent and Cesira (Stefanelli) B.; m. Gerda Hintz, Oct. 20, 1951; children: Leandra, Peter. Student, Columbia U., 1935—42; LLD, U. Bridgeport, 1970. Curator divsn. mech. and civil engring. U.S. Nat. Mus., Smithsonian Instn., Washington, 1961-65; from asst. dir. to dep. dir. Mus. History and Tech., 1965-78, keeper rare books, 1978-87; historian emeritus Smithsonian Inst., 1987—. Author: Ridgefield in Review, 1958, The Scent of Time, 1963, Early American Scientific Instruments and Their Makers, 1964; (with F.R. Maddison) Mechanical Universe, 1966; (with W. Von Braun and F.L. Whipple) Moon, Man's Greatest Adventure, 1970, The Life of Benjamin Banneker, 1972, rev. and expanded edit., 1999; (with others) The Unknown Leonardo, 1974, Thinkers and Tinkers, Early American Men of Science, 1975, The Spotted Stones, 1978, Declaration of Independence Desk: Relic of Revolution, 1981, Thomas Jefferson and His Copying Machines, 1984, At the Sign of the Compass and the Quadrant, 1984, Clockwork Cosmos, 1985, Thomas Jefferson Statesman of Science, 1990, The Pulse of Time, 1990, The Trail of Time, 1993, Science and Instruments in Seventeenth Century Italy, 1994, The Pope's Elephant, 1997, The Mace and the Gavel: Symbols of Government in America, 1997, The Jefferson Stone, 1999, Patrons, Artisans and Instruments of Science, 1999, The Life of Benjamin Banneker, The First African American Man of Science, rev. and expanded edit., 1999, With Compass and Chain, Early American Surveyors and Their Instruments, 2000, Jefferson and Science, 2002. Fellow Washington Acad. Scis.; mem. Am. Philos. Soc., Am. Antiquarian Soc., Soc. Am. Historians, History Sci. Soc., Soc. for History Tech., Astrolabe Soc. Home: 4303 47th St NW Washington DC 20016-2449 E-mail: sbedini@att.net.

BEDNAR, CHARLES SOKOL, political science professor; b. N.Y.C., Nov. 3, 1930; s. Karel and Anna (Tomcala) B.; m. Beluse Alzbeta Pokorny, Aug. 31, 1959. AB, Rutgers U., 1951, MA, 1952; PhD, Columbia, 1960. Asso. prof. Lynchburg Coll., 1958-62; prof., chmn. dept. polit. sci., asso. dean of coll. Muhlenberg Coll., 1962-99, Eve Elizabeth Muhlenberg Disting. Svc. prof., 1989-99, prof. emeritus; adj. prof. grad. program in gen. edn., chmn. social sci. panel Temple U., 1963-86. Author: Transforming the Dream: Ecologism and the Shaping of an Alternative American Vision, 2003; contbr. articles to profl. jours. Chmn. Lehigh Valley Citizens for Progress, 1972-75; pres. Allentown YMCA, 1979-80. Recipient award Lindback Found., 1965, Paul E. Empie Meml. award, 1983. Mem. Czechoslovak Acad. Arts and Scis., Phi Beta Kappa, Delta Phi Alpha, Tau Kappa Alpha, Omicron Delta Kappa, Pi Sigma Alpha. Home: 1285 Sheridan Rd Coopersburg PA 18036-1816 E-mail: beluse@aol.com.

BEDNAR, MICHAEL JOHN, architecture educator; b. Cleve., Mar. 19, 1942; s. Peter and Mary (Rohal) B.; m. Mary Kathryn Gillman; children: Richard Earl, Matthew Scott, Rachel Catherine; m. Elizabeth Waddel Lawson. BArch, U. Mich., 1964; MArch, U. Pa., Phila., 1967. Registered architect, Pa., N.Y., Va. Jr. designer I.M. Pei & Ptnrs., N.Y.C., 1965-66; project architect Geddes, Brecher, Qualls, Cunningham, Phila., 1967-68; asst. prof. Renselaer Polytech. Inst., Troy, 1968-72; assoc. prof. U. Va., Charlottesville, 1972—, co-chmn. div. of architecture, 1976-81, assoc. dean for academics, 1992-95. Prin. Michael Bednar, FAIA Architect, Charlottesville, 1973-90, Bednar Lawson Architects, 1990—. Author: Architecture for Handicapped, 1973, The New Atrium, 1986;, Interior Pedestrian Places, 1989; editor: Barrier-Free Environment, 1977. Mem., chair City Planning Commn., Charlottesville, 1982—; chmn. Urban Design Task Force, Charlottesville, 1985-88; mem. Bd. of Architectural Review, Charlottesville, 1983-86. Booth fellow U. Mich., 1972, NEA fellow, 1984, Graham Found. fellow, 1988-2003; recipient Nat. Book award Am. Assn. of Publ., 1986, Nichols award Preservation Alliance Va., 1997, Cmty. Svc. award AIA Ctrl. Va., 1997. Fellow Am. Inst. Architects (Disting. Achievemnt award 1997), Assn. for the Preservation of Va. Antiquities (bd. dirs. Jefferson chpt. 1999-2000). Avocations: jazz music, tennis, travel. photography. Home: 1201 E Jefferson St Charlottesville VA 22902-5414 Office Phone: 434-924-6364. Business E-Mail: mjb6g@virginia.edu.

BEDNAR, RUDY, television producer, director; b. Palmerton, Pa., May 31, 1951; s. Rudolph and Rita (Colan) Bednar. BA, Marquette U., 1973. Producer, dir. various TV stas., 1973—79; prodr., dir. ABC, N.Y.C., 1980—84, Good Morning Am., ABC, N.Y.C., 1984—88, 20/20 ABC, N.Y.C., 1989; prodr. Prime Time Live ABC, N.Y.C., 1990—92; sr. prodr. Turning Point ABC News, N.Y.C., 1993—98; exec. prodr. ABC News Long Form Unit, 1999—. Recipient 10 Emmy awards, Monitor award, Investigative Reports & Editors award, 3 Dupont awards. Mem.: Dirs. Guild Am. Office: ABC News 147 Columbus Ave New York NY 10023-5999

BEDNAREK, ALEXANDER ROBERT, mathematician, educator; b. Buffalo, July 15, 1933; s. Alexander G. and Bertha (Wlodarz) B.; m. Rosemary Anderson, Aug. 29, 1954 (dec.); children: Robert A., Andrew R., Thomas C., Eugene P. BS, SUNY, Albany, 1957; MA, SUNY, Buffalo, 1959, PhD, 1961. Sr. mathematician Goodyear Aerospace Corp., Akron, Ohio, 1961-62, cons. info. scis. dept., 1963-65; asst. prof. math. U. Akron, 1962-63, U. Fla., Gainesville, 1963-66, assoc. prof., 1967-69, prof., 1969—, chmn. dept. math., 1969-86, interim chmn., winter 1988, co-dir. Center Applied Math., 1974-92, prof. dept. math. Gainesville, 1993—96, prof. emeritus, 1996—. Vis. staff mem. Los Alamos Sci. Lab., 1976-85; mem. adv. bd. CRC Handbook Math. Tables; NAS exchange prof., Warsaw, Poland, 1972 Editor (with L. Cesari) Dynamical Systems, Vol. I, 1977, Vol. II, 1982; contbr. to Ency. of Libr. and Info. Sci., Vol. 3, 1970; editor (with F. Ulam) Analogies Between Analogies, 1990; contbr. articles to profl. jours. Served with U.S. Army, 1952-54. Mem. Math. Assn. Am. (past chmn. Fla. sect.). Home: 530 NE 7th Ave Gainesville FL 32601-4387 Office: U Fla Dept Math 358 Little Hall Gainesville FL 32611-2082

BEDNAREK, JANET ROSE, history educator; b. Omaha, Oct. 14, 1959; d. John Louis and Corinne Janet (Ryan) Daly; m. Michael Henry Bednarek, Mar. 23, 1991. BA, Creighton U., 1981, MA, 1983; PhD, U. Pitts., 1987. Historian USAF, Washington, 1989-92, Dayton, Ohio, 1992; prof. history U. Dayton, 1992—. Author: The Changing Image of the City, 1992, The Enlisted Experience, 1995, America's Airports, 2001, Dreams of Flight, 2003; also articles. Mellon fellow, 1985-87, U. Dayton rsch. fellow, 1993, 94, 97. Mem. Orgn. Am. Historians, Am. Hist. Assn., Urban History Assn., Aircraft Owners and Pilots Assn. Roman Catholic. Avocations: flying, aircraft restoration. Home: 7507 James Bradford Dr Centerville OH 45459-5172 Office: U Dayton Dept History 300 College Park Ave Dayton OH 45469-1540

BEDNARSKI, MARY LOU, secondary school educator, department chairman; d. Henry Bedarski and Tina Bednarski. BA, Jersey City State Coll., 1979; MA, St. Peter's Coll., 1996. Cert. Tchr. English (seventh through twelfth grades) NJ, Secondary Level Supr. NJ Dept. Edn. English tchr. St. Dominic Acad., Jersey City, 1979—93; dir. fin. aid St. Peter's Coll., Jersey City, 1993—97; English dept. head Passaic Valley HS, Little Falls, NJ, 1997—. Mem.: NCTE.

BEDNASH, GERALDINE POLLY, educational association administrator; b. San Antonio, May 6, 1943; d. David Anthony and Bernice (Brewer) Parrott; m. Thomas Francis Bednash, June 24, 1967; children: Thomas F. Jr., Joseph Andrew. B of Nursing, Tex. Women's U., 1965; M of Nursing, Cath. U. Am., 1977; PhD, U. Md., 1989. Cert. nurse practitioner. Nurse Binghamton (N.Y.) Gen. Hosp., 1967-69; instr. Broome County Community Coll., Binghamton, 1967-71; asst. prof. No. Va. Community Coll., Annandale, 1977-78, George Mason U., Fairfax, Va., 1978-86; dir. govt. rels. Am. Assn. Coll. Nursing, Washington, 1986-89, exec. dir., 1989—. Co-chmn. Nat. Com. Nursing Implementation Project, Washington, 1990-91; cons. in field. Contbr. articles to profl. jours. Polit. action chmn. Va. Nurses Assn., 1979-83; nurse clinician So Others Might Eat, Washington, 1981-83. Capt. U.S. Army, 1963-67. Primary Care fellow Robert Wood Johnson Found., U. Md., 1981-82, Nat. Rsch. Svc. fellow, Washington, 1983-87. Fellow Am. Acad. Nursing; mem. ANA, Sigma Theta Tau. Roman Catholic. Avocations: skiing, horticulture. Office: Am Assn Coll Nursing 1 Dupont Cir NW Ste 530 Washington DC 20036-1135

BEDNOFF, STUART LEON, obstetrician, gynecologist, educator; b. NYC, Aug. 31, 1936; MD, SUNY, 1961. Diplomate Am. Bd. Ob/gyn. Intern L.I. Jewish Hosp., N.Y.C., 1961-62; resident in ob/gyn. North Shore U. Hosp., Manhasset, N.Y., 1962-66, mem. staff, 1965; pvt. practice, Gt. Neck, N.Y., 1968. Clin. assoc. prof. dept. ob-gyn. NYU Sch. Medicine. Fellow ACOG, ACS; mem. Nassau Obstetricians/Gynecologists. Office Phone: 516-482-8741.

BEDRICK, ANTHONY EDWARD, oral surgeon, educator; b. Fall River, Mass., Jan. 29, 1918; s. Samuel and Ida (Snyder) Bedrick; m. Rachel Libbian Rubinstein, Jan. 21, 1945; 1 child, Jeffrey David. Grad., Durfee Tech. Inst., Fall River, Mass., 1935—37; pre-dental, Providence Coll., R.I., 1941; DDS, St. Louis Sch. of Dentistry, 1954. Textile chemist/colorist, Fall River/New Bedford, Mass., 1937—42; staff mem. Beekman Downtown Hosp., NYC, 1959—65; instr. NYU Sch. of Dentistry, NYC, 1960—2002; attending Met. Hosp., NYC, 1959—. Author: (jour.) Pharmacology, 1979. With U.S. Army, 1942—45. Fellow: Royal Soc. of Health; mem.: Am. Dental Assn., Rsch. Soc. of Am. Achievements include research in A.A.A.S. - rsch. histological staining of benign and malignant human tissues with textile dyes not previously used for staining tissue. Avocation: sci. reading. Home: 345 Webster Ave Apt 4-H Brooklyn NY 11230

BEDRICK, BERNICE, retired principal, science educator; b. Jersey City, Sept. 29, 1916; d. Abraham Lewis and Esther (Cowan) Grodjesk; m. Emanuel Arthur Bedrick, Dec. 25, 1938 (dec. 1967); children: Allen Paul, Jane Bedrick Abels; m. Samuel Milberger, Sept. 23, 1984 (dec. 1984); stepchildren: Susan Milberger Rafael, Stanford. BS, U. Md., 1938; MA, NYU, 1952. Cert. tchr., N.J. Tchr. Linden (N.J.) Pub. Sch. System, 1950-69, supr. sci. curriculum, 1969-79, sch. prin., 1979-87; ret., 1987. Co-author: A Universe to Explore, 1969; developer program of safety and survival N.J. Dept. Edn., 1975. Founder, mem., bd. dirs., v.p. edn. Temple Mekor Chayim, Linden; pres. bd. trustees Linden Pub. Libr., 1989-90, v.p., 1991; pres. Friends of Linden Libr., 1987-92, 95-97, coord. used books sales, 1990—, founder, 1987; bd. trustees Temple Beth-El Mekor Chayim, Cranford, N.J., 1999—, bd. edn., 1999—. Recipient Cmty. Vol. Svc. award B'Nai B'Rith, 1993, Outstanding Sr. Citizen of Yr., City of Linden, 1996; honored with Bernice Bedrick rm. at Sunnyside br. Linden Pub. Libr., 2001. Mem.: NEA (life), Nat. Sci. Tchrs. Assn., N.J. Sci. Tchrs. Assn., N.J. Prins. and Suprs. Assn., N.Y. Acad. Scis., Linden Edn. Found. (bd. dirs.), Am. Fedn. Sch. Adminstrs. (chpt. pres. 1984—86), Nat. Coun. Jewish Women (life), N.J. PTA (life), N.J. Edn. Assn. (life), Linden Ceramics Club (life; sec. 1991—92, 1995—99, pres. 2000—), Hadassah (life), Phi Kappa Phi, Alpha Lambda Delta, Alumni Assn. U. Md. (life). Home: 2016 Orchard Ter Linden NJ 07036-3719

BEDRIJ, OREST, investment banker, physicist; b. Ukraine, May 24, 1933; arrived in U.S., 1949, naturalized, 1955; s. Eustachy and Olha Bedrij; m. Oksana Cymbalista, Nov. 10, 1956; children: Orest W., Roksana Bedrij Arpa, Chrystyna Bedrij Stecyk. BSEE, Rochester Inst. Tech., 1956, MS in Humanities; PhD in Physics, Columbia Pacific U., 1986. Various positions IBM Corp., Poughkeepsie, N.Y., LA, 1956-68; IBM tech. dir. Space Flight Ops. facility Jet Propulsion Lab., Calif. Inst. Tech., 1962—63; founder, pres., dir. Securities Coun., Inc., 1965-83, Profit Tech., Inc., 1983-89, Griffin Capital Mgmt. Corp., N.Y.C., 1989—98; with Griffin Securities, Inc., N.Y.C., 1998—. Co-founder, dir. Advance Memory Sys. Inc. (merged with GE) as Intersil, Inc., Sunnyvale, Calif., 1968—72, Inst. Math. Physics, 1972—2001, Jour. Nonlinear Math. Physics, Kiev, 1992, Inst. for Advanced Study of I, 2001—; mem. exec. com., treas., dir. Ukranian Studies Fund Harvard U., 1959—72. Author: Yes, It's Love: Your Life can be a Miracle, 1974, One, 1977, You, 1988, La preuve scientifique de l'existence de Dieu, 2000, Seeing God Face to Face, 2005, Celebrate Your Divinity, 2005; contbr. articles to profl. jours. Trustee, treas. John E. Fetzer Found., 1987—89. With USAR, 1954—60. Mem.: Metanexus Inst., Sci. and Med. Network London, Shevchenko Sci. Soc., N.Y. Acad. Arts and Scis., Internat. Soc. Study Human Ideas Ultimate Reality and Meaning (dir.). Achievements include patents in field; research in physics and philosophy of ultimate reality and meaning.

BEDROSIAN, EDWARD, retired electrical engineer; b. Chgo., May 22, 1922; s. Charles and Hazel (Najarian) B.; m. Evelyn Patricia Gardner, Apr. 16, 1971; children— William C., Barbara A., Charles E., Edward G., Victoria G. BS, Northwestern U., 1949, MS, 1950, PhD, 1953. Aero. engr. Convair, San Diego, 1942, Hughes Aircraft Co., Culver City, Calif., 1943-44; elec. engr. Motorola, Chgo., 1953-57; sr. scientist Rand Corp., Santa Monica, Calif., 1957-98. Adj. prof. U. So. Calif., 1968-71 Contbr. articles to profl. jours.

Served with USMC, 1944-46. Fellow IEEE, Inst. Advancement Engring.; mem. Sigma Xi, Eta Kappa Nu, Tau Beta Pi. Home: 3923 Sierks Way Malibu CA 90265-5214 Personal E-mail: bedrosian@charter.net.

BEDROSIAN, GREGORY RONALD, investment banker; b. Phila., Sept. 14, 1966; s. Samuel D. and Agnes Bedrosian; m. Elena V. Mayorova; 1 child, Nicholas G. BS in Econs., U. Pa., 1988; MBA, Harvard U., 1992. Investment banker Salomon Bros., Inc., N.Y.C., 1988-90; investment banker Credit Suisse First Boston Ltd., London, Moscow, 1992-95; co-founder, mng. dir. Sputnik Funds (Renaissance Capital), Moscow, 1995-99; CEO Redwood Capital Group, NYC and London, 2000—. Mem.: Royal Inst. Internat. Affairs, Inst. Dirs. (London), Coun. on Fgn. Rels., Penn Club N.Y., Met. Club, Harvard Club of N.Y. Republican. Home: 25 Pecksland Rd Greenwich CT 06831

BEDSWORTH, WILLIAM W., judge; b. Long Beach, Calif., Nov. 21, 1947; m. Carolyn Kelly McCourt, Mar. 28, 1999. BA cum laude, Loyola U., L.A., 1968; JD, U. Calif., Berkeley, 1971. Felony trial deputy, appellate atty., mng. atty. Orange County Dist. Atty.'s Office, Calif.; judge Orange County Superior Ct., 1986-97; assoc. justice 4th Appellate Dist., Calif. Ct. of Appeals, Santa Ana, 1997—. Adj. prof. Western State U. Coll. of Law, Chapman U. Sch. of Law, Orange, Calif., Calif. Jud. Coll., Berkeley. Author: What I Saw and Heard, 1996, A Criminal Waste of Time, 2003; author nationally syndicated column A Criminal Waste of Space; contbr. articles to profl. publs. Former bd. dirs. NCCJ, Orange County Bar Assn.; bd. dirs. Fair Share 502; goal judge Nat. Hockey League, 1993—. Named Judge of Yr., Hispanic Bar Assn., 1997. Mem. Assn. Orange County Dep. Dist. Atty. (past pres.). Avocations: softball, country music, ice hockey.

BEE, ROBERT NORMAN, banker; b. Milw., Mar. 4, 1925; s. Clarence Olson and Norma Pern (Pitt) B.; m. Dolores Marie Cappelletti, Apr. 23, 1955; children: Diane, John, Leslie. PhB, Marquette U., 1949; BS in Fgn. Svc., Georgetown U., 1950, MA, 1955. With Dept. Treasury, various locations, 1950-65; fin. attache Stockholm, 1952-54, Ankara, Turkey, 1956-60; chief fin. affairs Am. embassy, Bonn, Germany, 1960-65; dep. dir. AID, Karachi, Pakistan, 1965-67; 1st. v.p. 1st Wis. Nat. Bank, 1967-71; sr. v.p. Wells Fargo Bank; also pres. Wells Fargo Internat. Investment Corp., San Francisco, 1971-78; mng. dir., CEO London (England) Interstate Bank Ltd., 1978—87; mng. dir. TSB Pvt. Bank Internat. SA, London, 1987-90; chmn. U.S. Fin. Adv. Svc., London, 1990-91, SAJ Investments Ltd., London, 1991-95; sr. advisor Porvenir Inc., San Francisco, 1998-2000. Sr. fellow Ctr. Internat. Banking Studies, Charlottesville, Va. Chmn. World Affairs Coun. Milw., 1970-71; bd. dirs. Adam Smith Inst., London, chmn., 1985-87; chmn. Am. Soc. in London, 1986-87. With AUS, 1943-46. Recipient Bronze Star, 1945. Mem. Bankers Assn. for Fgn. Trade (pres. 1977-78). Home and Office: 1940 Vallejo St Apt 5 San Francisco CA 94123-4918 Office Phone: 415-931-7520.

BEE, SAMANTHA, comedian, actress; b. Toronto, Can. m. Jason Jones. Grad., U. Ottawa, Can. Mem. sketch comedy troupe The Atomic Fireballs. Actor: (films) Ham and Cheese, 2004; (TV films) Ham I Am, 2001, Jasper, Texas; (TV series) The Endless Grind, 2001, The Daily Show with Jon Stewart, 2003. Office: The Daily Show 513 W 54th St New York NY 10019

BEEBE, ELLEN SCOTT, musicologist, music editor; b. Norfolk, Va., Feb. 21, 1947; d. George Arthur and Margaret Anne (Sterling) Beebe; m. Gerard Elie Dallal (div.); 1 child, James G.B. Dallal. BA in Humanities, Mich. State U., 1969; MPhil in History of Music, Yale U., 1972, PhD in History of Music, 1976. Music editor Broude Bros. Ltd., N.Y.C., 1978—84, Williamstown, Mass., 1984—. Presenter in field. Editor: Harmonice Musices Odhecaton A-CF7, 2001; translator: The Modes of Classical Vocal Polyphony, 1988. Mem. town com., Williamstown, 2000—; del. State Dem. Conv., 2001, 2005, alt. del., 2004; vestry mem. St. John's Episcopal Ch., Williamstown, 1993—95, 2001—03, 2005—. Mem.: Am. Guild Organists, Am. Musicolo. Soc. Democrat. Episcopalian. Avocations: reading, gardening, needlecrafts.

BEEBE, MARY LIVINGSTONE, curator; b. Portland, Oreg., Nov. 5, 1940; d. Robert and Alice Beebe; m. Charles J. Reilly. BA, Bryn Mawr Coll., Pa., 1962; postgrad., Sorbonne, U. Paris, 1962—63. Apprentice Portland Art Mus., 1962—64, Boston Mus. Art, 1964—66; curatorial asst. dept. drawing Fogg Art Mus., Harvard U., Cambridge, Mass., 1966-68; prodr. Am. Theatre Co., Portland State U., Oreg., 1969—72; exec. dir. Portland Ctr. for Visual Arts, 1972—81; dir. Stuart Collection U. Calif., San Diego, 1981—. Cons. in field; lectr. in field; mem. art steering com. Portland Devel. Commn., 1977-80, New Denver Internat. Airport, 1990-97; bd. dirs. Henry Gallery, U. Wash., Seattle, 1977-80; project cons. Nat. Rsch. Ctr. for Arts, N.Y.C., 1978-79; bd. dirs. Western Assn. Art Museums, Art Mus. Assn. San Francisco, 1978-84; bd. dirs., trustee Art Matters Inc., N.Y.C., 1984-, Balboa Art Conservation Ctr., San Diego, 2001-; trustee Russell Found., 1982-94, bd. dirs., 1983-85; hon. mem. bd. dirs. Portland Ctr. for Visual Arts, 1981-88; mem. arts adv. bd. Centre City Devel. Corp., San Diego, 1982-94, U. Calif. San Francisco Mission Bay, 1999—, Indpls. Mus. Art, Art and Nature Pk. adv. bd., 2003-, nat. adv. bd. Headlands Ctr. for the Arts, San Francisco; panel mem., cons. Nat. Endowment Arts; mem. adv. com. Port of San Diego, 1983-88, San Diego Design Ctr., 1987-88, ART/LA, 1987-94, Pearl Art Found., Portland, 1998-2000, inSITE94, inSITE97, inSITE00, inSITE03 and 05, San Diego, 1993-, Friends of Art and Preservation in Embassies Profl. Sculpture adv. com., Wash., 2003-; mem. pub. art adv. com. Harvard and Radcliffe, 1989-93, U. Wash., Seattle, 1989-96, Commn. for Arts and Culture, San Diego, 2003-; juror numerous art exhbns. Nat. Endowment Arts fellow, 1979. Author: Landmarks: Sculpture Commissions for the Stuart Collection at the University of California, San Diego, 2001; contbr. articles to profl. jours. Recipient Allied Professions award AIA, 1992, Nat. Honors award, 1994. Achievements include having the Stuart Collection featured on CBS Sunday Morning with Charles Kuralt, 1993. Office: U Calif San Diego Stuart Collection 9500 Gilman Dr La Jolla CA 92093-0010 Office Phone: 858-534-2117.

BEEBE, MIKE, state attorney general; b. Amagon, Ark., Dec. 28, 1946; s. Lester Kendall and Meadean Louise (Quattlebaum) B.; m. Ginger Croom, Mar. 2, 1979; 1 child, Kyle. BA, Ark. State U., 1968; JD, U. Ark., 1972. Bar: Ark. 1972. Ptnr. Lightle, Beebe, Raney, Bell & Simpson, Searcy, Ark., 1972—2003; mem. Ark. Senate, 1983—2003; pres. Ark. Senate, 2001—03; atty. gen. State of Ark., 2003—. Editor (in-Chief): U. Ark. Sch. of Law, 1972. Trustee Ark. State U., Jonesboro, 1974-79, chmn. bd. trustees, 1977-79; chmn. Ctrl. Ark. Gen. Hosp., Searcy, 1985-93. Named Outstanding Trial Lawyer, Ark., 1982. Mem. Ark. Mcpl. League (dist. svc. award 1985), Searcy C. of C. Democrat. Episcopalian. Avocation: golf. Office: Atty Gen 200 Tower Bldg 323 Center St Little Rock AR 72201

BEEBE, SANDRA E., retired English language educator, artist, writer; b. March AFB, Calif., Nov. 10, 1934; d. Eugene H. and Margaret (Fox) B.; m. Donald C. Thompson. AB in English and Speech, UCLA, 1956; MA in Secondary Edn., Calif. State U., Long Beach, 1957. Tchr. English, Garden Grove (Calif.) High Sch., 1957-93, attendance supr., 1976-83, ret., 1993. Tchr. watercolor courses, Asilomar, Calif., 1997; jury chmn. N.W.S., 1997. Contbr. articles to English Jour., chpts. to books; watercolor artist; exhbns. include AWS, NWS, Okla. Watercolor Soc., Watercolor West, Midwest Watercolor Soc., Butler Inst. Am. Art, Youngstown, Ohio, Kings Art Ctr., Audubon Artists N.Y.; cover artist Exploring Painting, 1990, title page Understanding Watercolor, American Artist, 1991. Mem. faculty Asilomar, 1997; chmn. of jurors N.W.S. Open, 1997. Named one of the Top Ten Watercolorists The Artists Mag., 1994; recipient Best Watercolors award Rockport Press, 1995; chosen for Design Poster selection, 1995, 97. Mem. Am. Watercolor Soc. (dir. 1999—), Nat. Watercolor Soc., Midwest Watercolor Soc., Watercolor West, Allied Artists N.Y., Knickerbocker Artists N.Y., Audubon Artists N.Y., West Coast Watercolor Soc., Rocky Mountain Nat. Watermedia Honor Soc., Jr. League Long Beach, Kappa Kappa Gamma. Republican. Home: 239 Mira Mar Ave Long Beach CA 90803-3899 Address: 239 Mira Mar Ave Long Beach CA 90803-6153 E-mail: sebeebeaws@aol.com.

BEECHER, LEE HEWITT, psychiatrist; b. Mpls., Feb. 18, 1939; s. James Morrison and Ruth Eleanor (Borgendale) Beecher; m. Mary Jane Heinen, June 10, 1978; children: James Arthur, Lynn Ruth. BA, Carleton Coll., 1961; MA, U. Minn., 1965. Lic. md State of Minn.; cert. in psychiatry ABPN, 1971, in addiction psychiatry ABPN, 1994. Psychiatrist Mpls. Clin. Psychiatry and Neurology, Golden Valley, Minn., 1972—73; self employed Lee. H. Beecher, MSPA, St. Louis Pk., Minn., 1973—; clin. assoc. prof. U. Minn., Dept. Psychiatry, Minn. Bd. dir. Alliance for the Mentally Ill, St. Paul, 1982—91; assoc. med. dir. Preferred One, Golden Valley, Minn., 1991—93. Contbr. articles numerous profl. jours. Lcdr USN, 1969—72, Hawaii. Named one of Top 100 Minn. Healthcare Leaders, Minn. Physician, 2004; recipient Pres. award, Minn. Med. Assn., 2004; Dist. Life fellow, Am. Psychiatric Assn., 2001. Mem.: Clin. Psychiatry News (edtl. adv. bd.), Minn. Physician Patient Alliance (pres. 1998—), Minn. Psychiatric Soc. (pres. 1987—89), Minn. Med. Assn. (trustee 1998—). Avocations: philosophy, swimming, family life, sci. and nature, cosmology. Home: 7574 Mariner Pt Maple Grove MN 55311-2617 Office: Lee H Beecher MD PA 6600 Excelsior Blvd Ste 121 Saint Louis Park MN 55426-4746 Office Phone: 952-935-7116. Office Fax: 952-935-0687. E-mail: leebeecher@aol.com.

BEECHER, VIRGINIA ANN, special education educator; d. George MCLane and Virginia Maxine Walker; m. Lindsey Lyndon Beecher, May 26, 1984; children: Adam, Katie, Thomas, Julie. BA in Elem. Edn., U. No. Iowa, 1985. Libr. dir. West Bend Pub. Libr., West Bend, Iowa, 1993—97; tchr. computer and lit. West Bend-Mallard Ctrl. Sch. Dist., 1997—2003; tchr. at-risk Aplington-Parkersburg Ctrl. Sch. Dist., 2003—. Pres. Dike Pub. Libr. Bd., Iowa, 2004—05; v.p. Wolverine Booster Club, 2004—05. Mem.: Iowa Talented & Gifted Assn., Iowa State Edn. Assn. Methodist. Avocation: reading.

BEECHER, WILLIAM MANUEL, management consultant; b. Framingham, Mass., May 27, 1933; s. Samuel and Gertrude (Kradelman) B.; m. Eileen Brick, June 8, 1958; children: Debbie, Diane, Lori, Nancy. BA, Harvard U., 1955; MS, Columbia U., 1956. Reporter St. Louis Globe-Democrat, 1956-59; corr. Fairchild Pubs., Washington, 1959-60, Wall Street Jour., Washington, 1960-66, N.Y. Times, Washington, 1966-73; asst. sec. def. U.S. Dept. Def., Washington, 1973-75; corr. Boston Globe, Washington, 1975-87; Washington bur. chief Mpls. Star Tribune, Washington, 1987-92; pub. affairs dir. U.S. Nuclear Regulatory Commn., Washington, 1993—2003; mem. U.S. Sr. Exec. Svc., 1993—2003; pres. Strategic Vision LLC, 2004—; prin. The Dilenschneider Group, N.Y.C., 2004—. Author: Mayday Man, 1990; co-author: (newspaper study) U.S.-Soviet Relations, 1983 (Pulitzer prize 1983); bd. of editors Foreign Svc. Jour. 2d lt. U.S. Army, 1956. Recipient Disting. Pub. Svc. medal Dept. of Def., 1975, Excellence awards Overseas Press Club, N.Y.C., 1975, 79, 86, Weintal award Georgetown U., Washington, 1983, Presdl. medal Y2K conversion, 2000; named Knight, Order of St. John of Medina, 2003. Mem. Internat. Inst. for Strategic Studies, State Dept. Corrs. Assn. (pres. 1982), Overseas Writers Assn. (pres. 1978-79), Aviation/Space Writers Assn. (pres. 1970-71), Coun. Fgn. Rels., Gridiron Club, Army and Navy Club. Home and Office: 7911 Robison Rd Bethesda MD 20817-6928 Office: The Dilenschneider Group MetLife Bldg 200 Park Ave 26th Fl New York NY 10166

BEEDLE, DAWN DANENE, marketing professional; b. Mexico, Mo., July 16, 1968; d. Ronald Wayne and Delores Kay (Eastin) B. BA, William Woods Coll., 1990. Retail mgr. Kirlins Hallmark, Columbia, Mo., 1991-94, dist. mgr. Chgo./Milw., 1994, St. Louis, 1994-96, corp. tng. mgr. Quincy, Ill., 1996-2000, dir. recruiting and tng., 2000—04; mktg. specialist Mo. Grape and Wine Program, Columbia, 2004—. Pub. speaker, cons., Quincy, 1997—. Republican. Presbyterian. Avocations: gardening, exercise, cooking, travel, family and friends. Home: 12 Broadway Village Dr Apt C Columbia MO 65201

BEEDLES, WILLIAM LEROY, finance educator, financial consultant; b. Independence, Kans., Apr. 9, 1948; s. Roy William Beedles and Opal Irene (Connor) Hunter; m. Margaret Ann Vanderlip, Dec. 21, 1974; children: Margaret Micaela, Patricia Opal, Cyrus Dean. BS, Kans. State U., 1970, MS, 1971; PhD, U. Tex., 1975. Asst. prof. Ind. U., Bloomington, 1975-78; vis. prof. Monash U., Melbourne, Victoria, Australia, 1984, U. NSW, Sydney, Australia, 1985; assoc. prof. to prof., dir. Masters program U. Kans., Lawrence, 1978—. Vis. rsch. fellow Pub. Utilities Commn., Austin, Tex., 1981 Contbr. articles to profl. jours. Capt. U.S. Army, 1970-78 Mem. Am. Fin. Assn., Western Fin. Assn., So. Fin. Assn. (assoc. editor jour. 1979-84), Fin. Mgmt. Assn. Congregationalist. Avocation: raquetball. Office: U Kans Summerfield Hall Lawrence KS 66045-7585 E-mail: wbeedles@ku.edu.

BEEGLE, EARL DENNIS, physician, medical association administrator; b. Ashland, Ohio, July 24, 1944; s. Ray Benjamin and Alice Mae (Imhoff) B.; m. Isabel Sloan-Kerr Adamson, Sept. 3, 1964; children: Ryan Benjamin, Kevin Ian. BA, Manchester Coll., 1967; MS, Purdue U., 1970; MB BChir, MD, BAO, Queen's U., Belfast, No. Ireland, 1978. Diplomate Am. Bd. Family Practice. Life scis. tchr. Elkhart (Ind.) Schs., 1967-72; house officer Nat. Health Svc. of U.K., 1978-79; resident in family practice Riverside Hosp. Med. Coll. Ohio, Toledo, 1979-81, chief resident, 1981-82; pvt. practice Everett, Wash., 1982-93; med. dir. Providence Primary Care Network, Everett, 1993-96; v.p., med. dir. Medalia Healthcare, Seattle, 1997-98, exec. v.p. managed care, 1998-99; CEO, chief med. officer Providence Physician Group (formerly Medalia Med. Group N.W. Wash.), 1999—. Credentials com. Providence Gen. Med. Ctr., 1996-2001, physician well-being com., 1997-99; med. dir. Planned Parenthood, Everett, 1983-86; chmn. utilization Providence Hosp., Everett, 1987-90, chmn. quality assurance, 1991-92; chmn. dept. family practice Providence-Gen. Med. Ctr., Everett, 1993-94; dir. Sisters of Providence Health Plans, Seattle, 1993-98; asst. clin. prof. U. Washington, 2004—. Active Friends of the Somme, No. Ireland, 1991—. NSF fellow, 1967-70. Fellow Am. Acad. Family Practice; mem. Irish and Am. Pediatric Soc., Snohomish County Med. Soc., Internat. Soc. Travel Medicine. Avocations: international travel, period furniture, antiquities.

BEEK, BARTON, lawyer; b. Pasadena, Calif., Jan. 23, 1924; s. Joseph Allan and Carroll (Brewster) B.; m. Linda McCarter, Dec. 28, 1978; children: Charles, Carroll, Barbara, Barton Jr., Joseph. BS, Calif. Inst. Tech., 1944; MBA, Stanford U., 1948; JD, Loyola U., L.A., 1955. Bar: Calif. 1955. Ptnr. O'Melveny & Myers, L.A., 1955—. Bd. dirs. Sun World Internat., Inc., Santa Monica, Calif., Fechtor, Detwiler, Mitchell & Co., Boston. Lt. (j.g.) USN, 1943-46. Mem. Newport Harbor Yacht Club. Office: O'Melveny & Myers 610 Newport Center Dr Newport Beach CA 92660-6419

BEEKE, JOEL ROBERT, minister, educator, writer; b. Kalamazoo, Mich., Dec. 9, 1952; s. John and Johanna Lucy (Van Strein) B.; m. Mary Ann Kamp, Aug. 21, 1989; children: Calvin James, Esther Idelette, Lydia Ruth. Student, Western Mich. U., 1971-73; BA, Thomas A. Edison Coll.; MDiv, Netherlands Reformed Theol. Sch., St. Catharines, Ont., Can., 1978; PhD in Reformation and Post-Reformation Theology, Westminster Theol. Sem., 1988. Ordained to ministry The Netherlands Ref. Congregations, 1978. Pastor The Netherlands Ref. Congregation, Sioux Center, Iowa, 1978-81, Ebenezer Netherlands Ref. Ch., Franklin Lakes, N.J., 1981-86, Heritage Netherlands Ref. Congregation, Grand Rapids, Mich., 1986—; instr. theology Netherlands Ref. Theol. Sch., 1986-92. Clk. The Netherlands Ref. Synod, 1980-92; v.p. The Netherlands Ref. Gen. Mission, 1980-82; pres. The Netherlands Ref. Book and Pub., 1980-93; v.p. The Netherlands Ref. Synodical Edn., 1986-93; pres. Interitance Pubs., 1987—, Macedonia Mission Soc., sermon divsn., 1990-93; v.p. Dutch Reformed Translation Soc., 1994—; lectr. Ctr. for Urban Theol. Studies, 1984-86; lectr. Westminster Theol. Sem., Phila., 1985-86, adj. prof., 1993—; pres. Stitching Studie der Nadere Reformatie, 1992-2003; editl. dir. Reformation Heritage Books, 1994—; pres., prof. systematic theology and homiletics Puritan Reformed Theol. Sem., 1995—; lectr. Westminster Theol. Sem., Calif., 1995—, The Puritan Project, Brazil, 1995—, Reformed Theol. Sem., 1995—. Author: Jehovah Shepherding His Sheep, 1982 (Korean edit. 2001), Backsliding: Disease and Cure, 1982 (Korean edit. 2004), Student Workbook on the Reformed Faith: Based on Rev. Hellenbroek's "A Specimen of Divine Truths", vol. I, 1985, Verachtering in de Genade: Kwaal en Genezing, 1989, Assurance of Faith: Calvin, English Puratinism and the Dutch Second Reformation, 1991, Holiness: God's Call to Sanctification, 1994 (Spanish, Portguese and Chinese edits. 2000), Justification by Faith: Selected Bibliography, 1995, A Tocha dos Puritanos: Evangelizacao Biblica, 1996; Heidelberg Cutechism, 5 vols., 1998; Truth that Frees, 1998; Reformed Confessions Harmonized, 1998, A Reader's Guide to Reformed Literature, 1999, The Quest for Full Assurance: Calvin and the Legacy of His Successors, 1999 (Porguese edit. 2003), Puritan Evangelism, 1999 (Chinese edit. 2001, Korean edit. 2002, Portguese edit. 2003, Gisbertus Voetius, 1999, Bringing the Gospel to Covenant Children, 2001 (Portguese edit. 2004), Family Worship, 2002, Puritan Reformed Spirituality, 2004, The Family at Church, 2004, Portraits of Faith, 2004, Overcoming the World: Grace to Win the Daily Battle, 2005; contbr. over 1500 articles to profl. jours.; co-author (with J.W. Beeke) Bible Doctrine Student Workbook, 1982; (with J.W. Beeke and Diane Kleyn) Building on the Rock, Book 1, 1989, Book 2, 1990, Book 3, 1993, (with J.D. Greendyk) Knowing and Living the Christian Life, 1997, (with D. Patrick Ramsey) An Analysis of Human Witsins's "Economy of the Covenants", 2002, (with J.W. Beeke and Diane Kleyn) Book 4, 2000 (Chinese edit. 2000); co-translator (with J.C. Weststrate) Reformed Dogmatics, vol. I, 1980, vol. II, 1983; editor: Religious Stories for the Young and Old, vol. 4, 1983, The Twenty-fifth Mission Day, 1984, Sovereign Grace in Life and Ministry, 1984, Experiential Grace in Dutch Biography, 1985, Collected Writings of Rev. William C. Lamain, vol. I, 1986, Doctrinal Standards, Liturgy and Ch. Order, 1992, Heaven Taken By Storm, 1992, The Pearl of Christian Comfort, 1997, (with H. Boorsma) God's Alphabet for Life, 2000, (with D. Kleyn) The Truths of God's Word, 2002, Daily Devotional for Children, 5 vols., 2003; gen. editor: The Poor Man's Morning and Evening Portions, 1995, Memoirs of Thomas Halyburton, 1996; co-editor (with B. Elshout) The Christian's Reasonable Service, 4 vols., 1992-95, Forerunner of the Great Awakening, 2000, The Path of True Godliness, 2003; editor periodicals Banner of Truth, 1985-93, Paul, 1984-93, Banner of Sovereign Grace Truth, 1993—, The Christian Observer, 1994—, The Gospel Trumpet, 1995—; radio pastor, 1995-2004. With U.S. Army, 1971-74. Mem. Evang. Theol. Soc., Soc. for Reformation Rsch., Calvin Studies Soc., 16th Century Studies Conf. Soc., Am. Soc. Ch. History, Colloquium on Calvin Studies, Conf. on Faith and History. Republican. Home and Office: 2965 Leonard St NE Grand Rapids MI 49525-5828 Office Phone: 616-977-0599 123. Personal E-mail: jrbeeke@aol.com.

BEEKEN, TIMOTHY K., lawyer; b. Apr. 2, 1959; BA with honors, Haverford Coll., 1983; JD, Columbia U., 1991. Assoc. Debevoise & Plimpton LLP, NYC, 1991—2002, mng. atty., 2002—. Mem.: Mng. Attys. and Clks. Assn. (exec. com. 2004—, newsletter com. 2002—), Assn. of Bar of City of NY (consumer affairs com. mem. 1999—2001), NY State Bar Assn., NY County Lawyers Assn. Office: Debevoise & Plimpton LLP 919 Third Ave New York NY 10022 Office Phone: 212-909-6518. Fax: 212-909-6836. E-mail: tkbeeken@debevoise.com.

BEEKMAN, WILLIAM BEDLOE, lawyer; b. N.Y.C., July 8, 1949; s. Robert Struthers and Mary (Marckwald) B.; m. Helen Hinckley, June 7, 1980; children: Izaak, Hugo. BA magna cum laude, Harvard U., 1971; JD, Yale U., 1980. Bar: N.Y. 1981. Assoc. Debevoise & Plimpton LLP, N.Y.C., 1980-89, ptnr., 1989—. Bd. dirs. Lafayette Studios Corp., N.Y.C. Bd. dirs. Romanian Am. Enterprise Fund. Mem. ABA, Assn. of Bar of City of N.Y., Am. Coll. Investment Counsel (bd. dirs.), N.Y. Hist. Soc. (bd.dirs.), Libr. Coun. for Mus. of Modern Art, Century Assn. Grolier Club, Romanian Am. Enterprise Fund. Democrat. Episcopalian. Home: 284 Lafayette St Apt 4B New York NY 10012-3303 Office: Debevoise & Plimpton LLP 919 3rd Ave 2d fl New York NY 10022-6225 Office Phone: 212-909-6215. Business E-Mail: wbbeekman@debevoise.com.

BEEKUN, RAFIK ISSA, education educator; arrived in U.S., 1999; s. Issa and Umdah Beekun; m. Nadiah Beekun. BA, Columbia, N.Y.; MA, Columbia U., N.Y., 1979; MBA, U. Tex., Austin, 1981, PhD, 1988. Prof. of mgmt. and strategy U. Nev., Reno, 1996—. Pres. Assn. of Muslim Social Scientists. Author: Islamic Business Ethics, 1997, Leadership from an Islamic Perspective, 1999. Mem. Rep. Party, Reno. Office: Univ Nev Mgrs /28 Reno NV 89557 Office Phone: 775-784-6993.

BEELER, JOHN FRANCIS, history educator; b. Greensboro, NC, Oct. 3, 1956; s. John Herbert Beeler and Anne Chaydeane Boise; m. Amy Elizabeth Crowson, Dec. 30, 1995. AB in History, Guilford Coll., Greensboro, N.C., 1974—78; MA in History, U. N.C., Greensboro, 1982—86; PhD in History, U. Ill., Urbana-Champaign, 1986—91. Postdoctoral fellow Yale U., New Haven, 1991—92; vis. asst. prof. Ea. Ill. U., Charleston, 1992—93; asst. prof. U. Ala., Tuscaloosa, 1993—99, assoc. prof., 1999—2004, prof., 2004—. Mem. Ala. Maritime Adv. Coun., 1998—2002. Author: British Naval Policy in the Gladstone-Disraeli Era, 1866-1880, 1997, Birth of the Battleship: British Capital Ship Design, 1870-1881, 2001; editor: Imperial Defence, 1868-1887, 2000, The Papers of Admiral Sir Alexander Milne, Vol. 1, 1820-1859, 2004; contbr. articles to profl. jours., chapters to books. Fellow: Royal Hist. Soc.; mem.: Can. Soc. for Nautical Rsch., N.Am. Conf. on British Studies, Am. Hist. Assn. Home: 4710 Old Birmingham Hwy Tuscaloosa AL 35404 Office: Univ Ala History Dept PO Box 870212 Tuscaloosa AL 35487 Office Phone: 205-348-1872. Business E-Mail: jbeeler@tenhoof.as.ua.edu.

BEELER, VIRGIL L., lawyer; b. Inpls., June 6, 1931; s. Elmer L. and Margaret Gwendolyn (Turney) B.; m. Patricia McAtee Walker; children: Stephen L., Philip E. AB in Econs., Ind. U., 1953, JD, 1959. Bar: Ind. 1959, U.S. Dist. Ct. Ind., U.S. Ct. Appeals (7th cir.), U.S. Supreme Ct., U.S. Tax Ct. Assoc. Baker & Daniels, Indpls., 1959-65, ptnr., 1966-95, of counsel, 1995—. Contbr. articles to profl. jours. 1st lt. U.S. Army, 1954—56. Fellow Am. Coll. Trial Lawyers, Ind. Bar Found.; mem. Indpls. Bar Assn., Ind. State Bar Assn., 7th Cir. Bar Assn., Order of Coif, Phi Beta Kappa. Office: Baker & Daniels 300 N Meridian St Ste 2700 Indianapolis IN 46204-1782

BEEM, CHARLES E., history educator; b. Culver City, Calif., Dec. 3, 1956; s. Dennis Bradley and Betty Lou Beem. BA, Calif. State U., 1979; MA in History, No. Ariz. U., 1990; PhD in History, U. Ariz., 2002. Asst. prof. history U. NC, Pembroke, NC, 2003—. Mem. N. Am. Conf. British Studies, 2001—. Faculty advisor Young Democrats U. NC, Pembroke. Mem.: Am. Hist. Assn. Democrat. Home: 4900 Independence Dr #17 Lumberton NC 28358 Office: Univ NC History Dept PO Box 1510 Pembroke NC 28372 Office Phone: 910-521-6443. Business E-Mail: charles.beem@uncp.edu.

BEEM, JACK DARREL, retired lawyer; b. Chgo., Nov. 17, 1931; AB, U. Chgo., 1952, JD, 1955. Bar: Ill. 1955. Assoc. firm Wilson & McIlvaine, Chgo., 1958-63; ptnr. firm Baker & McKenzie, Chgo., 1963—2004; ret., 2004. Decorated Order of the Sacred Treasure gold rays with rosette Japan. Mem. ABA, Chgo. Bar Assn., Japan-Am. Soc. Chgo. (pres. 1988-92), Am. Fgn. Law Assn. (chmn. Chgo. br.), Am. Law Inst., Univ. Club of Chgo., Tokyo Club, Tokyo Am. Club, Sons Am. Revolution, Phi Beta Kappa, Alpha Delta Phi. Home: 175 E Delaware Pl Apt 8104 Chicago IL 60611-7746 Office: Baker & McKenzie 1 Prudential Plz 130 E Randolph St Ste 3700 Chicago IL 60601-6342 Personal E-mail: abojdb@comcast.net.

BEEM, JOHN KELLY, retired mathematician, educator; b. Detroit, Jan. 24, 1942; s. William Richard and June Ellen (Kelly) B.; m. Eloise Masako Yamamoto, Mar. 24, 1964; 1 child, Thomas Kelly AB in Math., U. So. Calif., 1963, MA in Math., 1965, PhD in Math., 1968. Asst. prof. math. U. Mo., Columbia, 1968-71, assoc. prof., 1971-79, prof., 1979—2002; ret., 2002. Author: (with P. Y. Woo) Doubly Timelike Surfaces, 1969, (with P.E. Ehrlich) Global Lorentzian Geometry, 1981, (with P.E. Ehrlich and K.L. Easley), 2d edit., 96; condr. research in differential geometry and gen. relativity. Recipient Kemper Tchg. award, 1996; NSF fellow, 1965, 68. Mem.: Am. Math. Soc., Math. Assn. Am., Phi Beta Kappa. Home: 5204 E Tayside Cir Columbia MO 65203-5191

BEEMAN, JOSIAH HORTON, diplomat; b. San Francisco, Oct. 8, 1935; s. Josiah Horton and Helen Virginia (Hooper) B.; m. Susan Louise Sturman, Oct. 28, 1995; children: Olivia Louise, Josiah Horton. BA, Calif. State U., 1957. Adminstrv. asst. Congressman Phillip Burton, Washington, 1964-66; mem. San Francisco Bd. Suprs., 1967-68; sec. internat. affairs Presbyn. Ch., N.Y.C., 1969-70, dir. Washington Office, 1970-75; staff dir. Democratic Caucus U.S. Ho. of Reps., Washington, 1975; chief dep. dir. fin. State Calif., Washington, 1975-80; polit. and legis. dir. Am. Fedn. State, County and Mcpl. Employees, Washington, 1980-83; dir. Dem. Nat. Conv., San Francisco, 1983-84; pres. Beeman and Assocs., Washington, Sacramento, 1983-94; U.S. amb. to New Zealand and Samoa, 1994-99; chief of staff U.S. Broadcasting Bd. Govs., 2000-2001. Chmn. Fairfax County Cmty. Svcs. Bd., Fairfax County Coun. Homelessness. Democrat. Presbyterian. Office: 3036 Beechwood Ln Falls Church VA 22042-3138

BEEMAN, RICHARD ROY, historian, educator; b. Seattle, May 16, 1942; m. Pamela Jane Butler, Dec. 26, 1964; children: Kristin Dowds, Joshua Douglas. AB in History, U. Calif., Berkeley, 1964; MA in History, Coll. of William and Mary, 1965; PhD in History, U. Chgo., 1968. Asst. prof. history U. Pa., 1968-73, assoc. prof., 1973-82, prof., 1982—, acting chmn. dept., 1986-87, chmn., 1987-91, assoc. dean, 1991-96; vis. prof. Am. studies U. Hull, Eng., 1976-77; dean Coll. Arts and Scis. U. Pa., 1998—2003; William R. Kenan prof. history, chmn. Colby Coll., 1979-80; Vyvian Harmsworth prof. Am. history Oxford U., 2003—. Dir. Phila. Ctr. for Early Am. Studies, 1980-85. Author: The Old Dominion and the New Nation, 1788-1801, 1972, Patrick Henry: A Biography, 1974, The Evolution of the Southern Backcountry, 1984; editor: Beyond Confederation: The Origins of the American Constituion and National Identity, 1987, The Varieties of Political Experience in Eighteenth Century America, 2003; also articles and book revs. Dept. of History fellow Coll. William and Mary, 1964, Univ. fellow U. Chgo., 1966-67, Newberry Library jr. fellow, Chgo., 1967-68, U. Pa. summer research grants, 1969, 71, Am. Philos. Soc. research grants, 1971, 76, 89, Social Sci. Research Council post-doctoral fellowship, 1972-73, Nat. Book Award nominee, 1974, Fulbright sr. lectr., U.K., 1976-77, NEH basic research grant, 1983-84, summer seminar grant, 1986, sr. fellow, 1989—; fellow Inst. Advanced Study, 1989-90, Huntington Libr., 1997. Office: U Pa 213 College Hall Philadelphia PA 19104 Office Phone: 215-848-5801. E-mail: rbeeman@sas.upenn.edu.

BEEMER, JOHN BARRY, lawyer; b. Scranton, Pa., Sept. 4, 1941; s. Ellis and Rose Mary (Costello) B.; m. Diane Montgomery Fletcher, July 18, 1964 (dec. July 1999); children: David, Bruce. BS, U. Scranton, 1963; LL.B., George Washington U., 1966. Bar: Pa. 1966, U.S. Supreme Ct. 1980; cert. civil trial adv. Nat. Bd. Trial Advocacy. Law clk. U.S. Ct. Claims, 1966-67; clk. to judge U.S. Dist. Ct. (mid. dist.) Pa., 1967-68; assoc. Warren, Hill, Henkelman & McMenamin, Scranton, 1968-72; ptnr. Beemer, Brier, Rinaldi & Fendrick, 1972-77; pres. Beemer, Rinaldi, Fendrick & Mellody, P.C., Scranton, 1977-83; ptnr. Beemer & Beemer, Scranton, 1984—. Lectr. in law U. Scranton, 1969-70. Chmn. com. constn. and by-laws revision Lackawanna (county Pa.) United Fund., 1971; nat. chmn. U. Scranton Alumni Fund Drive, 1972. Mem. ABA, Pa. Bar Assn., Lackawanna Bar Assn. (bd. dirs. 1988—), Assn. Trial Lawyers Am., Pa. Trial Lawyers Assn., Phi Delta Phi. Office: 114-116 N Abington Rd Clarks Summit PA 18411 Office Phone: 570-587-0188. Personal E-mail: bbeemer123@aol.com.

BEEMER, JUDY O., English language educator; b. Maryville, Mo., June 8, 1951; d. Loyd Dean and Joanne Osburn; m. Chris Elvin Beemer, May 31, 1970; children: Christa Anne, Christopher Judson. BS in Secondary Edn., N.W. Mo. State U., Maryville, 1973. Tchr. English Wallace County H.S., Sharon Springs, Kans., 1975—83, Arkansas City (Kans.) H.S., 1983—2001, Junction City (Kans.) H.S., 2001—. Cons. and presenter in field Arkansas City H.S., 1986—2001. Named Wal Mart Tchr. of the Yr., Wal Mart, 1997, Outstanding Young Tchr., Arkansas City Jaycees, 1986; recipient Kans. Tchr. of the Yr. Finalist award, Kans. State Dept. of Edn., 1997. Mem.: ASCD, Internat. Reading Assn., PEO, Delta Kappa Gamma. Avocations: travel, interior decorating, gardening. Office: Junction City H S 800 N Eisenhower Dr Junction City KS 66441 Office Phone: 785-717-4200.

BEEMSTER, JOSEPH ROBERT, risk management consultant; b. Chgo., Nov. 11, 1941; s. Joseph Z. and Emily (Dehaus) B.; m. Judith L. Scheffers, Sept. 7, 1963; children: David, Susan. BA, DePaul U., 1962; postgrad., Ill. Inst. Tech., 1976, postgrad., 1977, U. Minn., 1979, postgrad., 1980. Mfg. mgr. Johnson & Johnson, Chgo., 1967—71, mgr. safety and security, 1971—78; corp. dir. safety and health Pacific Dunlop GNB Inc., St. Paul, 1978—88; v.p. loss control Willis of Ill., 1988—. Author: Safe Work Practices for Workers Exposed to Lead; prodr. videotapes on health and safety tng. Chmn. Bolingbrook (Ill.) Human Rels. Commn., 1971-77. Mem. Am. Soc. Safety Engrs., Am. Indsl. Hygiene Assn. Home: 1606 Hadley Ct Wheeling IL 60090-6916 Office: 10 S LaSalle St Ste 3000 Chicago IL 60603 Office Phone: 312-621-4827. Personal E-mail: jbeemster@aol.com. E-mail: beemster_jr@willis.com.

BEEN, VICKI LYNN, law educator; b. 1956; BS, Colo. State U., 1978; JD, NYU, 1983. Bar: NY 1984. Law clk. to Judge Edward Weinfeld US Dist. Ct. So. Dist. NY, NYC, 1983—84; law clk. to Justice Harry Blackmun US Supreme Ct., 1984—85; assoc. Debevoise & Plimpton, NYC, 1986—87; assoc. counsel Office of Independent Counsel for Iran/Contra Matters, Washington, 1987—88; assoc. prof. Rutgers Sch. Law, Newark, 1988—90, NYU Sch. Law, 1990—95, prof., 1995—, Elihu Root prof. law, faculty dir. Root-Tilden-Kern scholarship program, dir. Furman Ctr. Real Estate & Urban Policy. Vis. prof. law Harvard Law Sch., 1995—96. Office: NYU Sch Law Vanderbilt Hall Rm 314H 40 Washington Sq S New York NY 10012-1099 Office Phone: 212-998-6223. Office Fax: 212-995-4590. E-mail: vicki.been@nyu.edu.

BEENEY, GARRARD RUSS, lawyer; b. New Rochelle, NY, Mar. 15, 1954; s. Arthur William James and Olga Anne B. BA, Swarthmore Coll., 1976; JD, U. Pa., 1979. Bar: NY 1980. Assoc. Sullivan & Cromwell, NYC, 1979-87, ptnr., 1987—, and chair e-bus. and tech. practice area and intellectual property practice area. Mem.: ABA. Office: Sullivan & Cromwell 125 Broad St Fl 28 New York NY 10004-2489 Office Phone: 212-558-3737. Business E-Mail: beeneyg@sullcrom.com.

BEENS, RICHARD ALBERT, lawyer; b. Tracy, Minn., Sept. 7, 1941; s. Albert Charles and Dolores (Burnham) B.; m. Lynn Margaret Baker, Aug. 20, 1966 (dec. June 1973); 1 child, Jennifer Lois; m. Laura Lee Marie Geraghty, Aug. 9, 1974. BA, Coll. St. Thomas, St. Paul, 1965; JD, U. Minn., 1968. Bar: Minn. 1968, U.S. Ct. Appeals (8th cir.) 1968. From assoc. to ptnr. Babcock & Locher, Anoka, Minn., 1968-77; ptnr. Steffen, Munstenteiger, Beens & Peterson, Anoka, 1977—. Instr. U. Minn. Law Sch., Mpls., 1972-73; asst. pub. defender State of Minn., Anoka, 1977-83, State Bd. PUb. Defenders 1986—. Vol. Peace Corps, West Pakistan, 1962-64; commr. Met. Waste Control Com., St. Paul, 1974-83; mem. Aviation Adv. Task Force, St. Paul, 1984-85; chmn. adv. com. Met. Council Solid Waste, St. Paul, 1986—. Mem. Assn. Trial Lawyers Am., Minn. Trial Lawyers Assn., Minn. Bar Assn., Anoka County Bar Assn. (chmn. ethics com. 1982—, chmn. judicial evaluation com. 1987—), Am. Arbitration Assn. (arbitrator 1970—). Avocations: reading, hunting, fishing. Office: 403 Jackson St Anoka MN 55303-2372

BEER, ALAN EARL, microbiologist, educator; b. Milford, Ind., Apr. 14, 1937; s. Theo and Naoma Marguerite (Speheger) B.; m. Dorothy Gudeman, Aug. 17, 1958; children— Michael, Elizabeth, Margaret, Laura. BS, Ind. U., 1959, MD, 1962. Diplomate: Am. Bd. Ob-Gyn. Resident in Ob-Gyn Hosp. of U. Pa., Phila., 1965-68; USPHS/Ford Found. fellow Dept. Med. Genetics and Ob-Gyn, U. Pa., Phila., 1968-70; asst. prof. dept. Ob-Gyn, U. Tex. Southwestern Med. Sch., Dallas, 1971-73, assoc. prof., 1973-76, prof., 1976-79; Bates prof., chmn. dept. Ob-Gyn, U. Mich., Ann Arbor, 1979-84; prof. Ob/Gyn, dir. Reproductive Immunology Labs., 1984-87; prof. microbiology, immunology, obstetrics and gynecology Chgo. Med. Sch., 1987—. Assoc. editor: Jour. Reproductive Immunology, 1979, editor-in-chief, 1979—; contbr. articles to profl. jours. Served with USPHS, 1963-65. Recipient Lalor Found. award, 1969; Carl F. Hartman award Am. Fertility Soc., 1970 Mem. Am. Coll. Obstetricians and Gynecologists, Am. Fertility Soc., Internat. Transplantation Soc., AMA, Soc. for Study of Reprodn., Soc. for Gynecol. Investigation, Am. Assn. Ob-Gyn., Am. Soc. Immunology of Reprodn. (pres. 1985). Office: 15151 National Ave Ste 2 Los Gatos CA 95032 Office Phone: 408-356-9500. E-mail: beerdoc@aol.com.

BEER, BARRETT LYNN, historian; b. Goshen, Indiana, July 4, 1936; s. Peter J. and Mabel M. B.; m. Jill (Parker), 1965. BA, DePauw U., 1958; MA, U. Cin., 1959; PhD, Northwestern U., 1965. Instr. history Kent State U., Ohio, 1962—65; asst. prof. U. N.Mex., Albuquerque, 1965—68; assoc. prof. Kent State U., Ohio, 1968—76, prof., 1976—2002, prof. emeritus, 2002—; asst. dean Coll. Arts and Sci. U. N. Mex., Albuquerque, 1966—68; Fulbright prof. U. Tromso, Norway, 1983. Author: Northumberland: The Political Career of John Dudley, Earl of Warwick and Duke of Northumberland, 1973, Rebellion and Riot: Popular Disorder in Eng. during the Reign of Edward VI, 1982, 2nd edit., 2005; (with others) Recent Historians of Great Britain, 1990, Tudor England Observed: The World of John Stow, 1998; editor: (with S.M. Jack) The Letters of William, Lord Paget of Beaudesert, 1547-1563, 1974, The Life and Raigne of King Edward the Sixth (John Hayward), 1993, contbr., New Oxford Dictionary of Nat. Biography, 2004. Am. Philos. Soc. grantee, 1966; Am. Coun. Learned Soc. grantee, 1973; fellow Newberry Libr., 1991, Folger Shakespeare Libr., 1997. Fellow Royal Hist. Soc.; mem. Conf. on Brit. Studies, Ohio Acad. History, Phi Beta Kappa. Episcopalian. Home: 445 Dansel St Kent OH 44240-2626 Office: Kent State U Dept History Kent OH 44242-0001 Business E-Mail: bbeer@kent.edu.

BEER, CLARA LOUISE JOHNSON, retired electronics executive; b. Bisbee, Ariz., Jan. 14, 1918; d. Franklin Fayette and Marie (Sturm) Johnson; m. Philip James McElmurry, May 15, 1937 (div. July 1944); children—Leonard Franklin, Philip James Jr.; m. William Sigvard Beer, July 15, 1945 (dec. Aug. 1977); 1 son, Douglas Lee; m. Kenneth Christy Huntwork, May 1, 1982 (dec. Jan. 2003). Student, Merritt Bus. Sch., Oakland, Calif., 1935, Bus. Instrn. Sch., Palo Alto, Calif., 1955. Sec., artist M.R. Fisher Studios, Oakland, 1936-40; piano, organ instr. Anna May Studios, Palo Alto, 1948-50; pvt. piano, organ instr. Palo Alto, 1949-56; sec. Stanford Electronics Labs., Stanford U., 1955-58; corporate sec. and exec. sec. to chmn. bd. Watkins-Johnson Co., Palo Alto, 1958-88. Dir., sec. Watkins-Johnson Internat., 1968-88, Watkins-Johnson Ltd., 1971-88, Watkins-Johnson Assocs., 1977-88. Mem. Nat. Secs. Assn., Christian Bus. and Profl. Women's Coun. (sec. 1966-67, adviser 1968) Home: 24157 Hillview Rd Los Altos CA 94024-5222

BEER, ESTHER RAE, elementary school educator; b. Chgo., Feb. 16, 1949; d. Jack and Fay Beer. BS in Edn., No. Ill. U., 1971, MS in Edn., 1975. Cert. elem. tchr., cert. adminstr. 3d-4th grade tchr. Sch. Dist. 146, Oak Forest, Ill., 1971-78, 5th-6th grade tchr., 1978-88, 6th grade tchr., 1988—; gifted edn. facilitator, 1997—. Gifted instr. Sch. Dist. 146, Oak Forest, 1980—89; tchr. Lewis U., Bolingbrook, Ill., 1988, Golden Apple Scholars Summer Program, 2001—. Recipient Golden Apple award Golden Apple Found., 1988. Fellow Golden Apple Acad.; mem. Ill. Coun. for Gifted, Phi Delta Kappa. Avocations: reading, theater, travel, shopping. Office: Fierke Edn Ctr 6535 Victoria Dr Tinley Park IL 60477-4790

BEER, FRANCIS ANTHONY, political science professor; b. N.Y.C., Feb. 5, 1939; s. William Joseph and Anne (Benedikt) B.; m. Diana Darnall, June 12, 1965; children: Omar, Marie, Jeremy. AB cum laude, Harvard U., 1960; MA, U. Calif., Berkeley, 1963, PhD, 1967. Asst. prof. dept. govt. U. Tex., Austin, 1967-70, assoc. prof. dept. govt., 1970-75; prof. dept. polit. sci. U. Colo., Boulder, 1975—. Author: Integration and Disintegration in NATO: Processes of Alliance Cohesion and Prospects for Atlantic Community, 1969, Peace Against War: The Ecology of International Violence, 1981, Meanings of War and Peace, 2001; editor Alliances: Latent War Communities in the Contemporary World, 1970; co-editor: (with Ted. R. Gurr) Conflict, Violence, Peace: An International Series of Books, 1990-93, (with R. Hariman) Post-Realism: The Rhetorical Turn in International Relations, 1996, (with C. DeLandtsheer) Metaphorical World Politics, 2004; asst. editor Jour. Politics, 1968-71; contbr. articles to profl. jours. Lt. USNR, 1960-62. Fulbright fellow, 1965-66, 71, Mershon fellow, 1966-67, NEH fellow, 1990; grantee Earhart Found., 1972, Inst. World Order, 1974-77. Mem. Internat. Polit. Sci. Assn., Internat. Soc. Polit. Psychology, Am. Polit. Sci. Assn., Internat. Studies. Assn. Office: U Colo Polit Sci Dept PO Box 333 Boulder CO 80309-0333

BEER, JAMES A., air transportation executive; b. London; BS in Aero. Engring., London U.; MBA, Harvard U. With Anderson Consulting; fin. analyst Am. Airlines, 1991, mng. dir. corp. devel., mng. dir. internat. planning, v.p. fin. analysis and fleet planning, 1998—2000, treas., v.p. corp. devel., 2000—02, v.p. for Europe and Asia, 2002—03; sr. v.p., CFO AMR Corp. and Am. Airlines, 2003—. Office: PO Box 619616 Dallas TX 75261-9616

BEÉR, JANOS MIKLOS, engineering educator; b. Budapest, Hungary, Feb. 27, 1923; s. Sandor and Gizella (Trismai) B.; m. Marta Gabriella Csato, Oct. 27, 1944. Dipl. Ing., Jozsef Nador U. Tech., Budapest, 1950; PhD, U. Sheffield, Eng., 1960, DSc, 1968; Dr honoris causa, U. Miskolc, Hungary, 1987, U. Tech. Scis., Budapest, Hungary, 1997. Research engr. Heat Research Inst., Budapest, 1949-56, head combustion div., 1952-56; prin. lectr. combustion Budapest Tech. U., 1953-56; research engr. Babcock & Wilcox Ltd., Renfrew, Scotland, 1956-57; head research sta. Internat. Flame Research Found., Ijmuiden, Holland, 1960-63; prof. fuel sci. Pa. State U., 1963-65; Newton Drew prof., head dept. chem. engring. and fuel tech. U. Sheffield, 1965-76, dean engring., 1973-75; prof. chem. and fuel engring. MIT, 1976-93, prof. emeritus, 1993—, sci. dir. MIT Combustion Rsch. Facility, 1976—93. Vis. fellow Australian Commonwealth, 1972; joint com. Internat. Flame Rsch. Found., 1972-89, supt. rsch., 1972-89; bd. dirs. Combustion Inst., Pitts., 1974-86; adv. coun. rsch. and devel. fuel and power U.K. Dept. Energy, 1973-76; mem. Clean Air Coun., Dept. Environ., U.K., 1974-76; chem. tech. com. U.K. Sci. Research Coun., 1972-75; combustion sci. com. Italian Nat. Rsch. Coun., 1974—; chmn. clean coal utilization project NAS, 1987-88; adv. coun. U.S. Sec. Energy Nat. Coal Coun., 1992—. Co-author: Combustion Aerodynamics, 1972; editor: Fuel and Energy Science Monograph Series, 1972; co-editor: Heat Transfer in Flames, 1972, Industrial Flames, 1972, Combustion Technology, 1974; author articles; patentee in field. Recipient BCURA Coal Sci. Gold medal, 1986, Alfred Egerton Gold medal Combustion Inst., 1986, Axel Axelson Johnson medal Swedish Acad. Engring. Scis., 1995, AIAA Energy Sys. award, 1998, George Westinghouse Gold medal ASME Internat., 2001, Homer Lowry Gold medal, US Dept. of Energy, 2003; named Hon. Supt. Rsch., Internat. Flame Rsch. Found., 1991. Fellow ASME (Moody award 1964, Percy Nicholls award 1988, Internat. George Westinghouse Gold medal 2001), Inst. Energy (sr., Melchett medal 1985), Royal Acad. Engring. U.K.; mem. Am. Inst. Chem. Engrs., Hungarian Acad. Scis. (hon.), Hungarian Nat. Acad. Engring. (hon.), Finnish Acad. Tech. (fgn.). Office: MIT 66-301 Dept Engring Cambridge MA 02139 Office Phone: 617-253-6661. Business E-Mail: jmbeer@mit.edu.

BEER, JEANETTE MARY SCOTT, foreign language educator; b. Wellington, New Zealand; d. Alexander Samuel and Una Doreen (Castle) Scott; m. Colin Gordon Beer; children: Stephen James Colin, Jeremy Michael Alexander. BA, Victoria U., N.Z., 1954, MA 1st class, 1955; BA 1st class, Oxford U., Eng., 1958, MA, 1962; PhD (fellow), Columbia U., 1967. Asst. lectr. French Victoria U., Wellington, 1956; lectrice French and English U. Montpellier, France, 1958-59; instr. French Otago U., Dunedin, N.Z., 1963-64, Barnard Coll., Columbia U., N.Y.C., 1966-68; asst. prof. French Fordham U., Bronx, N.Y., 1968-69, assoc. prof., 1969-76, prof., 1976-80; assoc. Lady Margaret Hall Oxford U., 1992—; acting assoc. dean Thomas More Coll., 1972-73, dir. medieval studies, 1972-80; prof. French Purdue U., West Lafayette, Ind., 1980—2004, head dept. fgn. langs. and lits., 1980-83, chair Ctr. for Humanistic Studies, 1990-93. Mem. nat. bd. cons. NEH, 1977—, asst. dir. divsn. fellowships and seminars, 1983-84; coord. Purdue U. Annual Conf. of Romance Langs., Lits. and Film, 1992-2000. Author: Villehardouin -- Epic Historian, 1968, A Medieval Caesar, 1976, Narrative Conventions of Truth in the Middle Ages, 1981, Medieval Fables: Marie de France, 1981, Master Richard's Bestiary of Love and Response, 1985, Early Prose in France, 1992, Beasts of Love - Richard de Fournival's Bestiaire d'amour and a Woman's Response, 2003; editor: Medieval Translators and Their Craft, 1989, Translation and the Transmission of Culture Between 1300 and 1600, 1995, Translation Theory and Practice in the Middle Ages, 1997; gen. editor Teaching Language through Literature, 1971-88, Romance Langs. Ann., 1992-2000; contbr. articles to profl. jours. NEH grantee, 1975, rsch. fellow, 1980; summer fellow Ind. Com. for Humanities, 1985; Am. Philos. Soc. grantee, 1986, Am. Coun. Learned Socs. grantee, 1990. Mem. MLA (del. assembly 2003—), Medieval Acad., Internat. Arthurian Soc., Internat. Courtly Lit. Soc., Soc. Rencesvals, Am. Assn. Tchrs. French, Anglo-Norman Text Soc. Anglican. Home: 227 Cranbury Rd Princeton Junction NJ 08550-2805 Business E-Mail: beer@purdue.edu.

BEER, MICHAEL, biophysicist, educator, environmentalist; b. Budapest, Hungary, Feb. 20, 1926; came to U.S., 1958, naturalized, 1965; s. Paul and Lidia (Pap-Kovacs) B.; m. Margaret Terry Peters, Jan. 22, 1954; children: Nicholas, Suzanne, Wendy. MA, U. Toronto, 1950; PhD, U. Manchester, Eng., 1953. Rsch. assoc. U. Mich., Ann Arbor, 1953-56; rsch. fellow Nat. Rsch. Coun. Can., 1956-58; mem. faculty Johns Hopkins U., Balt., 1958—, prof. biophysics, 1964-96, prof. emeritus, 1996—, chmn. dept. biophysics, 1974-80, assoc. dean arts and scis., 1989-92. Mem. Biophys. Soc. (pres. 1975-76), Electron Microscopy Soc. Am. (pres. 1980), Chesapeake Bay Trust (Ellen Fraites Wagner award, 1999). Home: 4623 Wilmslow Rd Baltimore MD 21210-2549

BEER, MICHAEL, education educator, researcher; s. Kurt and Hilde Beer; m. Cynthia Ann Noles, Aug. 13, 1937; children: Thomas Noles, Shannon Laurey Belanger. PhD, Ohio State U., Columbus, Ohio, 1964. Lst lt. USAF, 1958—62; dir. of orgnaizational r & d Corning Inc., Corning, NY, 1964—75; cahners-rabb prof. of bus. adminstrn., emeritus Harvad Bus. Sch., Boston, 1975—; dir. GTECH, Greenwich, RI, 1983—89; mem. bd. of govs. Acad. of Mgmt., 1984—86; vis. prof. am. mgmt. Johann Goethe U., Frankfurt, Germany, 1989; chmn. and founder Ctr. for Orgnl. Fitness, Waltham, Mass., 1998—. Chmn. and cons. Ctr. for Orgnl. Fitness, Waltham, Mass., 1998—. Pres. Kennebunk Improvement Assn., Kennebunk, Maine, 1986—90. 1st lt. USAF, 1958—62, Dayton, Ohio. Finalist Terry Book Award, Acad. of Mgmt., 1990; recipient Johnson Smith Knisley award, Johnson Smith Knisley, 1991, Devel. of Strategic Fitness Process - an orgnl. intervention, Orgn. Devel. Inst., 1998, Top 10 orgn. devel. cons., Tng. and devel. Jour., 1985, Mem., Nat. Acad. of Human Resources, 1998; Fellow, Acad. of Mgmt., 1999, Soc. of Indsl. & Orgnl. Psychology, 1982, Divsn. of Gen. Psychology, APA, 2002. Fellow: Soc. of Indsl. & Orgnl. Psychology (exec. com., program chair 1971—77), Acad. of Mgmt. (hon.; bd.govs. 1984—86); mem.: Divsn. of Orgn. Devel. and Change, Acad. of Mgmt. (chmn. 1980—81), Nat. Acad. of Human Resources, Sigma Alpha (life), Psi Chi (life), Sigma Xi (life), Phi Kappa Phi (life). Achievements include development of Rsch. a strategic learning process by which senior teams of corp. can define a strategic and orgnl. direrction and assess orgnl. alignment; research in Research in orgnaizational effectiveness, change and human resource management. Avocations: golf, tennis, swimming. Office: Harvard Bus Sch Soldiers Field Boston MA 02163 Office Phone: 617-495-6655.

BEER, PETER HILL, federal judge; b. New Orleans, Apr. 12, 1928; s. Mose Haas and Henret (Lowenburg) B.; children: Kimberly Beer Bailes, Kenneth, Dana Beer Long-Innes; m. Marjorie Barry, July 14, 1985. BBA, Tulane U., 1949, LLB, 1952; LLM, U. Va., 1986. Bar: La. 1952. Successively assoc., ptnr., sr. ptnr. Montgomery, Barnett, Brown & Read, New Orleans, 1955-74; judge La. Ct. Appeal, 1974-79, U.S. Dist. Ct. (ea. dist.) La., New Orleans, 1979—. Vice chmn. La. Appellate Judges Conf.; apptd. by chief justice of U.S. to state-fed. com. Jud. Conf. U.S., 1985-89; apptd. by chief justice of U.S. to Nat. Jud. Coun. State and Fed. Cts., 1993—. Mem. bd. mgrs. Touro Infirmary, New Orleans, 1969-74; mem. exec. com. Bur. Govtl. Rsch., 1965-69; chmn. profl. divsn. United Fund New Orleans, 1966-69; mem. New Orleans City Coun., 1969-74, v.p., 1972-74. Capt. USAF, 1952-55. Decorated Bronze Star, Air Force Commendation medal; recipient Justice William Brennan award U. Va. Sch. Law, 2005. Mem. ABA (mem. ho. dels.), Am. Judicature Soc., Fed. Bar Assn., La. Bar Assn., Nat. Lawyers Club, So. Yacht Club, St. John Golf Club. Jewish. Home: 133 Bellaire Dr New Orleans LA 70124-1008 also: 204 3rd Ave Pass Christian MS 39571-3214 Office: US Dist Ct US Courthouse 500 Poydras St New Orleans LA 70130-3313 Office Phone: 504-589-7510.

BEER, REINHARD, atmospheric scientist; b. Berlin, Nov. 5, 1935; came to U.S., 1963, naturalized, 1979; s. Harry Joseph and Elizabet Maria (Meister) B.; m. Margaret Ann Taylor, Aug. 11, 1960. B.Sc. with Honors, U. Manchester, Eng., 1956, PhD, 1960. Rsch. asst. physics U. Manchester, 1956-60, sr. asst. astronomy, 1960-63; sr. scientist Jet Propulsion Lab., Pasadena, Calif., 1963-70, group supr. tropospheric sci., 1970—2005, sr. rsch. scientist, 1985—, mgr. atmospheric and oceanographic scis. sect., 1990-92, flight team leader, 1997—, prin. scientist, 1999—. Vis. assoc. prof. astronomy U. Tex., Austin, 1974; vis. astronomer Kitt Peak Nat. Obs., 1979-81, Mauna Kea Obs., 1982-86; prin. investigator Tropospheric Emission Spectrometer NASA Earth Observing System, 1989—, airborne emission spectrometer program NASA, 1992-2003, group supr. Tropospheric Emission Spectrometry, 2005—; co-investigator NASA Atlas 1 mission, 1992, Atlas 2, 1993. Author: Remote Sensing by Fourier Transform Spectrometry, 1992; contbr. articles to profl. jours. Hon. Turner and Newall fellow, 1961; recipient medal for exceptional sci. achievement NASA, 1974, NASA group achievement award for Pioneer Venus, 1980, Spacelab 3 ATMOS experiment and sci., 1986, group achievement award Tropospheric Emission Spectrometry, 2005 Mem. AAAS, Am. Geophys. Union, Optical Soc. Am. Achievements include discovery of extra-terrestrial deuterium (heavy hydrogen), 1972, of carbon monoxide in Jupiter, 1975. Office: 183-601 Jet Propulsion Lab Pasadena CA 91109

BEERBOWER, CYNTHIA GIBSON, lawyer; b. Dayton, Ohio, June 25, 1949; d. Charles Augustus and Sarah (Rittenhouse) Gibson; m. John Edwin Beerbower, Aug. 28, 1971; children: John Eliot, Sarah Rittenhouse. BA, Mt. Holyoke Coll., 1971; JD, Boston U., 1974; LLB, Cambridge (Eng.) U., 1976. Bar: N.Y. 1975. Assoc. Cadwalader, Wickersham & Taft, N.Y.C., 1975-76, Simpson, Thacher & Bartlett, N.Y.C., 1977-81, ptnr., 1981-93; internat. tax counsel, dept. asst. sec. Dept. Treasury, Washington, 1993-96; chmn., CEO Reeve Ct. Ins. Ltd., 1997—2001; prin. Quellos Group, 2001—04; mng. dir. XE Capital, 2004—05, Paget LLC, 2005. Mem. ABA, Assn. Bar City N.Y., N.Y. State Bar Assn. (com. co-chmn. 1987-93). Presbyterian. Home: 720 Park Ave New York NY 10021-4954

BEERBOWER, JOHN EDWIN, lawyer; b. Columbus, Ohio, Jan. 7, 1948; m. Cynthia Gibson, Aug. 28, 1971; children: John Eliot, Sarah Rittenhouse. BA, Amherst Coll., 1970; JD, Harvard U., 1973; student, Trinity Coll., Cambridge (Eng.) U. Bar: N.Y. 1975. Mem. Cravath, Swaine & Moore, LLP, N.Y.C., 1980—, ptnr., litig. Bd. govs. Mannes Coll. Music, 1993—, vice chmn., 2000—02, chmn., 2002—; com. on instl. policy New Sch. U., 2003—; trustee Madison Ave. Presbyn. Ch., 1995—2001, pres. bd. trustees, 2000—01. Mem. ABA, N.Y. State Bar Assn., N.Y. Law Inst. (mem. nominating com.), Assn. of Bar of City of N.Y. (chmn. profl. and jud. ethics com. 1990-93), Soc. of Alumni Amherst Coll. (pres. 1994-95), Union Internat. Advocats, Am. Econ Assn., Phi Beta Kappa. Office: Cravath Swaine & Moore LLP Worldwide Plz 825 8th Ave Fl 40 New York NY 10019-7416 Office Phone: 212-474-1864. Office Fax: 212-474-3700. Business E-Mail: jbeerbower@cravath.com.

BEERING, STEVEN CLAUS, academic administrator, medical educator; b. Berlin, Aug. 20, 1932; arrived in U.S., 1948, naturalized, 1953; s. Steven and Alice (Friedrichs) Beering; m. Catherine Jane Pickering, Dec. 27, 1956; children: Peter, David, John. BS summa cum laude, U. Pitts., 1954, MD,

1958, ScD (hon.), 1998; DSc (hon.), Ind. Cen. U., 1983, U. Evansville (Ind.), 1984, Ramapo Coll., 1986, Anderson Coll., 1987, Purdue U., 2000; ScD (hon.), Ind. U., 1988; LLD (hon.), Hanover Coll., 1986; LLD (hon.), Tex. Wesleyan, 2001. Intern Walter Reed Gen. Hosp., Washington, 1958—59; resident Wilford Hall Med. Center, San Antonio, 1959—62, chief internal medicine, edn. coordinator, 1967—69; prof. medicine Ind. U. Sch. Medicine, Indpls., 1969—, asst. dean, 1969—70, assoc. dean, dir. postgrad. edn., 1970—74, dir. statewide med. edn. system, 1970-83, dean, 1974—83; chief exec. officer Ind. U. Med. Center, Indpls., 1974—83; pres. Purdue U. and Purdue U. Rsch. Found., West Lafayette, Ind., 1983—2000, pres. emeritus, 2000—; dir. Purdue Rsch. Found., West Lafayette, 2000—. Prof. pharmacology and toxicology Purdue U.; bd. dirs. NISource, Inc., Am. United Life; cons. Indpls. VA Hosp., St. Vincent Hosp.; chmn. Med. Edn. Bd. Ind., 1974—83, Liaison Com. Med. Edn., 1976—81, Ind. Commn. Med. Edn., 1978—83. Contbr. articles to sci. jours. Sec. Ind. Atty. Gen.'s Trust, 1974—83; regent Nat. Libr. Medicine, 1987—91; trustee U. Pitts., 2000—. Lt. col. M.C. USAF, 1957—69. Fellow: ACP, Royal Soc. Medicine; mem.: Nat. Sci. Bd., Ind. Acad., Nat. Acad. Sci. Inst. of Medicine, Assn. Am. Univs. (chair 1995—96), Coun. Med. Deans (chmn. 1980—81), Assn. Am. Med. Colls. (chmn. 1982—83), Endocrine Soc., Am. Diabetes Assn., Am. Fedn. Med. Rsch., Meridian Hills Club, Skyline Club, Phi Rho Sigma (U.S. v.p. 1976—85), Alpha Omega Alpha, Sigma Xi, Phi Beta Kappa. Presbyterian. Home: 10487 Windemere Dr Carmel IN 46032 Office: Purdue U Office Pres Emeritus Rm 218 Memorial Union West Lafayette IN 47906-3584 Office Phone: 765-496-7555. Personal E-mail: sbeering@indy.rr.com. Business E-Mail: scb@purdue.edu.

BEERMAN, JOEL I., chemical manufacturing company executive, lawyer; b. Johnstown, Pa., 1950; BA, Boston U., 1972; JD, Seattle U., 1974. Bar: Wash. 1975, Oreg. 1975, Ga. 1983. Assoc. counsel Zidell Explorations, Inc., 1975—77; assoc. atty. Fellows, McCarthy, Zikes & Kayser, 1977—79; sr. counsel Ga. Gulf Corp., Atlanta, 1979—84, gen. counsel, 1985—, v.p., sec., 1994—. Office: Ga Gulf Corp Ste 595 400 Perimeter Center Ter Atlanta GA 30346-1232 Office Fax: 770-395-4529.

BEERMAN, JOSEPH, health educator; b. N.Y.C., Aug. 31, 1937; s. Herbert and Frances B.; m. Andrea Ellenhorn, Aug. 15, 1987; 1 child, Eric Hunter. BA, Hunter Coll., 1959; MA, NYU, 1963; diploma Tchr.'s Coll., Columbia U., 1970. Cert. in health and phys. edn., N.Y. Tchg. asst., track coach NYU, 1959-61; tchr. health edn. Herman Ridder Jr. H.S., N.Y.C., 1961-65; prof. health and phys. edn. Manhattan C.C.-CUNY, N.Y.C., 1965-96, assoc. dean faculty, 1978-79, prof. emeritus, 1996—, adj. prof., 1996—. Cons. Nat. Coun. Jr. Colls., NEA, Washington, 1965—; rep. Coun. Health Educators, CUNY, 1965—. Author: Chemical Dependency and the Minorities, 1993, Basic Tennis: Skills and Strategies, 1995. Guest speaker YMCA and sr. citizen orgns., N.Y.C., 1965—; presenter tennis clins. Ea. Tennis Patrons, N.Y.C., 1965-75; presenter seminars N.Y.C. Bd. Edn., 1961-70. Sgt. U.S. Army, 1959-61. Nat. Humanities Faculty grantee, 1978; recipient McGovern award U.S. Tennis Assn., 1987; inducted into Hunter Coll. Athletic Hall of Fame, 1993. Fellow Internat. Inst. Cmty. Svc., Friends of Penn Relay's; mem. Am. Alliance Phys. Edn., Health, Recreation and Dance (mem. various coms. 1960—), Democrat. Jewish. Avocations: stamp collecting/philately, coin collecting/numismatics, antiques, tennis. Home: 16-70 Bell Blvd Apt 113 Bayside NY 11360 Office: CUNY 199 Chambers St New York NY 10007-1044

BEERMAN, MIRIAM, artist, educator; b. Providence; d. William and Rose (Nochemsohn) Beerman; m. Julian F. Jaffe (dec. 1973); 1 child, William Jaffe. Student, Atelier 17, Paris, 1953; BFA, R.I. Sch. Design, 1945; postgrad., Art Students League, N.Y.C., 1945-46, New Sch. for Social Rsch., NYU. Prof. painting and drawing Queensborough C.C., CUNY, 1972—95; instr. Jersey City State Coll., 1973—75, Montclair (N.J.) Art Mus. Art Sch., 1974—90, Montclair State Coll., 1980—89. Artist-in-residence MacDowell Colony, 1959, Ossibaw Island, Ga., 1974, Va. Ctr. for Creative Arts, Sweet Briar, 1985-87, 89-96, 98, 2000-02, Leighton Artist's Colony, Banff Ctr., Alta., Can., 1986-87, Millay Colony, Austerlitz, NY, 1992, Blue Mountain Ctr., Blue Mountain Lake, NY, 1994, 96, 98, Camargo Found., 1980, Mid-Atlantic Arts Found., 2000, Women's Studio Workshop, 2000; vis. artist Burston Graphic Ctr., Jerusalem, 1980. One-woman shows include LI U., Bklyn., 1965, Chelsea Gallery, NYC, 1969, Benton and Bowles, NYC, 1970, Bklyn. Mus., 1971, Graham Gallery, NYC, 1972, 77, Montclair Art Mus., 1974, 87, Mus. St. John the Divine, NYC, 1977, Gallery One, Montclair State U., 1978, Camargo Found., Cassis, France, 1980, Va. Ctr. for Creative Arts, Sweetbriar, 1986, Millersville (Pa.) U., 1986, Pratt Inst., NYC, 1989, NJ State Mus., Trenton, 1991, Klarfeld Perry Gallery, NYC, 1993, Suffolk C.C., Selden, NY, 1993, Bergen (NJ) Mus., 1996, Jersey City Mus., 1997-98, Baird Ctr., South Orange, NJ, 2001, Tomasulo Gallery, NJ, 2001, U. Wis., 2002, Chautauqua Ctr. for Visual Arts, NY, 2004; exhibited in group shows at Robeson Ctr. Gallery, Newark, 1986, Contemporary Arts Ctr., New Orleans, 1986, Stadtiche Galerie, Regensburg, Germany, Monmouth Mus., 1987-88, Hunterdon Art Ctr., Clinton, NJ, 1989, Holman Hall Art Gallery, Trenton, 1989, Women's Caucus for Art, NYC, 1990, Studio Mus., NYC, 1990, Morris Mus., Morristown, NJ, 1991, Rutgers U., New Brunswick, NJ, 1991, Chgo. Art Expo, 1993, Corcoran Gallery Art, Washington, 1994, 2004, Jersey City (NJ) Mus., 1995, Newark Pub. Libr. Artist Book Collection, 1995, Ctr. for Book Arts, NYC, 1996, 98, 2002, Rutgers Ctr. for Innovative Printmaking, New Brunswick, NJ, 1997, Montclair Art Mus., 1997, Mus. Modern Art, Dominicana, Santa Domingo, 1998, Nat. Mus. Women in the Arts, Washington, 1999, NJ State Mus., Trenton, 1999, Conn. Coll., 1999, Bristol Meyers-Squibb Gallery, Lawrenceville, NJ, 2000, Sterling Art Libr., Yale U., 2000, Gallery 241, Montclair, 2001, Pacifico Fine Arts, NYC, 2002, William Paterson U., Wayne, NJ, 2004, William Paterson U. Artist Book Collection, 2005, Everson Mus., Syracuse, NY, others; represented in permanent collections U. Del., Nat. Mus. Women in Arts, Washington, Israel Mus., Jerusalem, Israel, U. Oreg., Newark Mus., Whitney Mus., Am. Art, Bklyn. Mus., Montclair Art Mus., Arnot Art Mus., Morris Mus., Met. Mus. Art, NY, Mus. Art, RISD, Providence, Queens Mus., NY, Jersey City Mus., Jewish Mus., NYC, Women's Studio Workshop, Rosendale, NY, Allen Meml. Art Mus., Oberlin, Ohio, Skirball Mus., LA, Spertus Mus., Chgo., Neuberger Mus., Purchase, NY, Bass Mus., Miami (Fla.) Beach, Kresge Mus., Lansing, Mich., Corcoran Gallery of Art, Everson Art Mus., Syracuse, Sterling Art Libr. Yale U., NJ State Mus., Trenton, 1949-1990, Smithsonian Archives of Am. Art, 1979-2005, Abraham Lincoln Ofcl. Libr. and Mus., Springfield, Ill, 2005 Recipient Childe Hassam Purchase award Am. Acad. Arts and Letters, 1977, prize 11th R.I. Arts Festival, 1969, Ives prize RISD, Disting. Artist award NJ State Coun. on Arts, 1987, Grand prize Am. Impressions Ben Shahn Galleries William Patterson U., 2003, Abraham Lincoln Presdl. Libr., Springfield, Ill.; grantee NY State Coun. on Arts, 1971, NJ State Coun. on Arts, 1978, 83, 87, Womens Rsch. and Devel. Fund, CUNY, 1986, Rutgers Ctr. for Innovative Printmaking, 1987, 97, Rutgers Ctr. for Innovative Printmaking, 1989, 98, Joan Mitchell Found., 1994, Mid Atlantic NEA, 1996, Dodge Found. artist residency, 1998, 2000, 02, Womens Studio Workshop, Rosendale, NY, 1999-2000, Pollock-Krasner Found., 2000, Midatlantic Arts Found., 2000, E.D. Found.; Fulbright fellow, Paris, 1953-55, Ossibaw Island Residency, Ga., 1975, Forest fellow Millay Colony, 1992, San Diego Art Mus., others.

BEERMANN, ALLEN J., former state official; b. Sioux City, Iowa, Jan. 14, 1940; BA, Midland Lutheran Coll., Fremont, Nebr., 1962; JD, Creighton U., Omaha, 1965; LLD (hon.), Midland Luth. Coll., 1995. Bar: Nebr. 1965. Legal counsel, adminstrv. asst. to sec. state, State of Nebr., 1965-67; dep. sec. state, 1967-71; sec. of state, 1971-95. Mem. Fed. Election Commn. adv. panel. Bd. dirs. NebraskaLand Found.; exec. bd. Cornhusker coun. Boy Scouts Am.; state chair N.E. Commn. Employer Support for Guard and Res., 1997-2002. Lt. col. U.S. Army, ret. Recipient Disting. Svc. plaque Omaha Legal Aid Soc., 1964, Silver Beaver award Boy Scouts Am., 1979, Fgn. Svc. Medallion Rep. of China, 2001, Homeland Def. Ribbon, 2001; named Outstanding Young Man Lincoln Jaycees, 1975, Outstanding Young Man Nebr. Jaycees, 1975 Mem. ABA, Nat. Assn. Secs. State (pres. 1976-77), Nebr. Bar Assn. (exec. dir. 1995—), Nebr. Press Assn., Am. Legion (fed. election commn. adv. panel, Cert. Appreciation). Republican. Lutheran. Office: Nebr Press Assn 845 S St Lincoln NE 68508-1226 Office Phone: 402-476-2851. Business E-Mail: nebpress@nebpress.com.

BEERS, CHARLOTTE LENORE, former federal agency administrator; b. Beaumont, Tex., July 26, 1935; d. Glen and Frances (Bolt) Rice; m. Donald C. Beers, 1971; 1 dau., Lisa. BS in Math. and Physics, Baylor U., Waco, Tex., 1958. Group product mgr. Uncle Ben's Inc., 1959-69; sr. v.p., dir. client services J. Walter Thompson, 1969-79; chief operating officer Tatham-Laird & Kudner, Chgo., from 1979, mng. ptnr., chmn. and chief exec officer; vice chmn. RSCG Group Roux Seguela, Cayzac & Goudard, France; chmn., CEO Ogilvy & Mather Worldwide, N.Y.C., Ogilvy Group Inc., N.Y.C., chmn. emeritus, 1997-99; chmn. J. Walter Thompson, N.Y.C., 1999-2000; under sec. for pub. diplomacy & pub. affairs US Dept. State, Washington, 2001—03. Named Nat. Advt. Woman of Yr. Am. Advt. Fedn., 1975 Mem. Am. Assn. Advt. Agencies (chmn. from 1987), Women's Advt. Club Chgo., Chgo. Network. Republican. Episcopalian.

BEERS, NATHANIEL BRITTINGHAM SAVIO, pediatrician; s. Rand Brittingham and Marian Alice Brittingham Beers; m. Lee Ann Savio Savio, June 9, 2001; 1 child, Charlotte Savio. MD, George Wash. U., 1995; Cert. in Leadership in Human Resource Devel., George Wash. U. Sch. of Edn., 2004; MPA, Harvard U., 2001, Cert. in Clin. Effectiveness, 1999. Cert. Am. Bd. of Pediat. Pediatric intern and resident Children's Nat. Med. Ctr., Washington, 1995—98; Anne Dyson fellow in child advocacy The Children's Hosp. of Boston, Boston, 1998—2000, chief fellow divsn. gen. pediat., 1999—2000, clin. instr. of pediat., 2000—01; asst. prof. of pediat. Children's Nat. Med. Ctr., Washington, 2001—, continuity clinic dir., 2003—. Bd. dirs. Syrentha Savio Endowment, Washington, 2003—, Neighbors Consejo, Washington, 2005—. Contbr. articles to profl. jours. Recipient Mel Levine Award for Devel. Behavioral Pediat., The Children's Hosp. of Boston, 2000; grantee Master Tchr., Children's Nat. Med. Ctr., 2003—. Fellow: Am. Acad. Pediat. (chair sect. on residents 1999—2000, rep. on membership com. 2002—, sec., treas. DC chpt. 2004—); mem.: Ambulatory Pediatric Assn. Democrat. Office: Children's Natl Med Ctr 111 Michigan Ave NW Washington DC 20010 Office Phone: 202-884-3948.

BEESON, ANN, lawyer; MA in Anthropology, U. Tex.; JD, Emory U. School Law, 1993. Attorney Human Rights Watch; assoc. legal dir. ACLU, 1995—. Named one of America's top 50 Women Litigators, Nat. Law Journal. Avocations: amateur pilot, singing. Office: c/o ACLU 125 Broad St 18th Floor New York NY 10004

BEESON, JACK HAMILTON, composer, educator, writer; b. Muncie, Ind., July 15, 1921; children: Christopher Sigerist (dec.), Miranda. Student, U. Rochester, Columbia U.; studied with, Béla Bartók; Mus D (hon.), Columbia U., 2002. Tchr. Juilliard Sch. Music; former chmn. dept. music, assoc. dir. opera workshop Columbia U., N.Y.C., MacDowell prof. emeritus. Former sec. Alice M. Ditson Fund; former chmn. music publ. com. Columbia U. Press.; bd. dirs. Composers Recs., Inc., others. Composer: (operas) Jonah, Hello Out There, The Sweet Bye and Bye, Lizzie Borden (commd. by Ford Found.), My Heart's in the Highlands (commd. by NET), Captain Jinks of the Horse Marines (commd. by Nat. Endowment of Arts), Dr. Heidegger's Fountain of Youth (commd. Nat. Arts Club), Cyrano, Sorry, Wrong Number, Practice in the Art of Elocution, (for orch.) Hymns and Dances, Symphony in A, Transformations, Interludes and Arias from Cyrano (for baritone and orchestra), Two Concert Arias (for soprano and orch.), (chamber music) Sonata for Viola and Piano, Interlude, Song, 4th and 5th Piano Sonatas, Two Diversions, Round and Round, Sonata Caronica for two alto recorders, Old Hundredth for Organ, (vocal works) Six Lyrics, Five Songs, Eldorado, Piazza Piece, Big Crash Out West, Indiana Homecoming, Margret's Garden Aria, To a Sinister Potato, (cycles) From a Watchtower, (bass-baritone and piano) Two by Betjeman and A Rupert Brooke Cycle, (for bass and piano) Three Viereck Songs, (countertenor and chamber ensemble) The Daring Young Man on the Flying Trapeze, (mezzosoprano and chamber ensemble) Ophelia Sings, (soprano, tenor and chamber ensemble) The Equilibrists, others, works for voice and string quartet, (choral works) Knots, Magicke Pieces, Epitaphs, In Praise of Singing, Summer Rounds and Canons. Recipient Rome prize, City of Rochester prize, Marc Blitstein Mus. Theatre award Nat. Inst. Arts and Letters, Gold medal for music Nat. Arts Club, 1976, Gt. Tchrs. award Columbia U., 1979, Alumni Achievement award U. Rochester, 1985, award for Lifetime Achievement award Nat. Opera Assn., 1998; Guggenheim fellow, Fulbright fellow to Italy. Mem. ASCAP (bd. dirs. 1991-95), AAAL (treas., v.p. for music), Phi Beta Kappa. Home: 18 Seaforth Ln Huntington NY 11743-9714 also: 404 Riverside Dr New York NY 10025-1861 Office: Columbia U Dept Music New York NY 10027

BEETON, ALFRED MERLE, lab administrator, director, biologist, educator, environmentalist; b. Denver, Aug. 15, 1927; s. Charles Frederick and Edna F. (Smith) B.; m. Mary Eileen Wilcox, July 20, 1945; children: Maureen Ann, Heather Ann, Celeste Nadine; m. Ruth Elizabeth Holland, June 4, 1966; children: Jonathan Eugene, Daniel Paul. BS, U. Mich., 1952, MS, 1954, PhD, 1958; DSc (hon.), U. Wis., Milw., 1996. Fishery biologist U.S. Bur. Comml. Fisheries, Ann Arbor, Mich., 1957-65, chief environ. research, 1960-65; prof. zoology U. Wis.-Milw., 1965-76; asst. dir. U. Wis.-Milw. (Center for Gt. Lakes Studies), 1965-69, assoc. dir., 1969-73; assoc. dean U. Wis.-Milw. (Grad. Sch.), 1973-76; dir. Gt. Lakes and Marine Waters Ctr., Mich. Sea Grant; prof. engrng. and natural resources U. Mich., Ann Arbor, 1976-86; dir. Gt. Lakes Environ. Research Lab., Nat. Oceanic and Atmospheric Adminstrn. Dept. Commerce, Ann Arbor, 1986-96, emeritus, 2002—, acting chief scientist Nat Oceanic & Atmospheric Adminstrn. Washington, 1996-97, sr. sci. advisor, 1998—2002. Instr. biology Wayne State U., 1956—57, lectr. biology, 1957—61; lectr. civil engring. U. Mich., 1961—65; U.S. chmn. Sci. Adv. Bd. Internat. Joint Commn., 1986—91; mem. Mich. Toxic Substance Control Commn., 1987—89; mem. rsch. adv. coun. Wis. Dept. Natural Resources; mem. water quality criteria com. Nat. Acad. Scis.; cons. U.S. Army C.E., 1967—73, Met. San. Dist. Chgo., 1968—76, EPA, 1973—83; adviser on projects in Ghana, Laos and Yugoslavia Smithsonian Instn., 1972—82; adviser WHO/Pan Am. Health Orgn., Venezuela, 1978; mem. environ. program com. NRC, 1976—82, internat. environ. program com., 1977—82, mem. environ. studies bd.; adj. vis. prof. Oreg.State U., 1982; mem. Coun. Great Lakes Rsch. Mgrs., 1995—97; chmn. sci. adv. bd. NOAA, 1998—2002; mem. Ocean Rsch. Adv. Panel/Nat. Oceanographic Partnership Program, 2000—02; adj. prof. Sch. Pub. Health U. Mich., 1999—. Contbr. chpts. to books; articles Ency. Brit. Mem.: Mich. Acad. Sci., Arts and Letters, Internat. Assn. Gt. Lakes Rsch., Am. Soc. Limnology and Oceanography (treas. 1962—81), Internat. Assn. Theoretical and Applied Limnology (nat. rep. for U.S. 1976—95), Detroit Audubon Soc. (bd. dirs. 2002—04). Home: 2761 Oakcleft St Ann Arbor MI 48103-2247 Personal E-mail: abeeton@netzero.net.

BEETS, LATIN RENEE, elementary school educator; b. London, Ky., Aug. 1, 1959; d. Samuel Carson and Julia Jane (Taylor) Beets. BA in Elem. Edn., Cumberland Coll., 1981, MA in Elem. Edn., 1984. Cert. elem. tchr., Ky. Tchr. Laurel County Sch. Bd., London, 1981—. Weekend head resident Cumberland Coll., Williamsburg, Ky., 1984-85. Contbr. Southwest Laurel County Kentucky Cemeteries, 1987, Branches of Laurel, 1987-93; contbr., editor, Southeast Laurel County Kentucky Cemeteries, 1991. Mem. NEA, Ky. Edn. Assn., Ky. Assn. for Gifted Edn., Ky. Tchrs. Math., Laurel County Edn. Assn. (bldg. dir. 1982-88), Laurel County Hist. Soc., Clay County Hist. Soc., Campbell County (Tenn.) Hist. Soc., Women of Moose, Knox Hist. Mus. Democrat. Avocations: genealogy, travel, flowers.

BEEVER, JAMES WILLIAM, III, biologist; b. Balt., Aug. 17, 1955; s. James William Jr. and Virginia Irene (Ruhlmann) B.; m. Lisa Britt Dodd, May 26, 1990. BS, Fla. State U., 1977, MS, 1979; postgrad., U. Calif., Davis, 1984. Environ. specialist Fla. Dept. Environ. Regulation, Ft. Myers, 1984—88; coord. resource mgmt. and rsch. South West Fla. Aquatic Preserves, Bokeelia, 1988—90; biol. scientist III Fla. Game and Fresh Water Fish Commn., Punta Gorda, 1990—98; biol. scientist IV Fla. Fish and Wildlife Conservation Commn., Punta Gorda, 1998—. Mem. tech. adv. bd. Sarasota Bay and Tampa Bay Nat. Estuary Program, Sarasota, 1989—; mem. policy com. and tech. adv. com. Charlotte Harbor Nat. Estuary Program; chair sci. com. on Mangrove Tech. Adv. Com. Fla. Dept. Environ. Protection, 1994—95; chair Fla. com. on rare and endangered plants and animals; expert witness in field, 1986—; coord. Conservation Plan for the Hillsborough River Greenway Area, 1995; founder Frog Listening Network, 1997; chair Estero Bay Agy. on Bay Mgmt., 1999—. Author: Lemon Bay Aquatic Preserve Management Plan, 1988, The Cedar Point Study, 1992, Hydric Pine Flatwoods of Southwest Florida, 1994, (computer database) Resource Inventory of Species in S.W. Fla., Coastal Conservation Corridor Plan, 1999—; contbr. articles to profl. jours. Chair Grad. Student Assn., Davis, 1981-83. Regents fellowship U. Calif, 1983-84; recipient Grad. Rsch. award, 1982-83, Outstanding Profl. Achievements award Fla. DNR, 1989, Spl. Chmn.'s award Fla. Wildlife Fedn./Nat. Wildlife Fedn., 2000, Guy Bradley award, 2001. Mem. Fla. Acad. Sci., Estuarine Rsch. Fedn., Soc. Wetland Scientists, Soc. for Conservation Biology, Ecol. Soc. Am., Phi Beta Kappa, Sigma Xi. Achievements include rsch. on mangrove tree crab and arboreal folivore, mangrove cutting, endangered species protection, red cockaded woodpeckers; hydric pine flatwoods, xeric oak scrub, regional wildlife habitat/wildlife corridor planning; designation Fla. ecosystems, hydrogeomorphic method for the Everglades. Office: Fla Fish & Wildlife Conservation Comm 29200 Tuckers Grade Punta Gorda FL 33955-2207 Office Phone: 239-338-2550 ext 216. E-mail: james.beever@myfwc.com.

BEEZER, ROBERT RENAUT, federal judge; b. Seattle, July 21, 1928; s. Arnold Roswell and Josephine (May) B.; m. Hazlehurst Plant Smith, June 15, 1957; children: Robert Arnold, John Leighton, Mary Allison. Student, U. Wash., 1946-48, 51; BA, U. Va., 1951, LLB, 1956. Bar: Wash. 1956, U.S. Supreme Ct. 1968. Ptnr. Schweppe, Krug, Tausend & Beezer, P.S., Seattle, 1956-84; judge pro tem Seattle Mcpl. Ct., 1962—76; judge U.S. Ct. Appeals (9th cir.), Seattle, 1984-96, sr. judge, 1996—. Alt. mem. Wash. Jud. Qualifications Commn., Olympia, 1981-84 1st lt. USMCR, 1951-53 Fellow Am. Coll. Trust and Estate Counsel, Am. Bar Found.; mem. ABA, Seattle-King County Bar Assn. (pres. 1975-76), Wash. Bar Assn. (bd. govs. 1980-83) Clubs: Rainier, Tennis (Seattle). Office: US Ct Appeals 1200 6th Ave Ste 301 Seattle WA 98101

BEFFORT, SUE WILSON, state legislator; b. Albuquerque; BA, So. Meth. U. Mem. N.Mex. Senate, Dist. 19, Santa Fe, 1996—; mem. fin. com. N.Mex. Senate. Republican. Home: 67 Raindance Rd Sandia Park NM 87047

BEFIS, MATTHEW PETER, music educator; b. Ridgewood, NJ, June 16, 1980; s. Philip Anthony and Sophia Cynthia Bufis. MusB, Ithaca Coll., 2002. Cert. tchg. NY, Md. Pvt. instrument tchr. Misically Yours Music Store, Calif., 2002—, 2002—; dir. of bands Great Mills HS, Great Mills, Md., 2002—; asst. coach Misericordia Swim Team, Dallas, Pa., 2005. Band conductor St. Mary's County Pub. Schs., Great Mills, Md., 2004; guest clinician Leonardtown Mid. Sch., Leonardtown, Md., 2004. Mem.: NEA, World Assn. of Syphonic BOE, So. Md. Music Conf. Avocations: running, swimming, composing, arranging. Home: 65 Marcla Rd Ringwood NJ 07456 Office: Great Mills HS 21130 Great Mills Rd Great Mills MD 20634 Office Phone: 301-863-4001 x116. Office Fax: 301-863-4006. E-mail: bufonium2002@yahoo.com.

BEFORT, CARLENE MAE, music educator; b. Capron, Okla., Aug. 31, 1935; d. Carl Wesley and Gertrude Gwendolyn (Lewis) Dunkelberger; m. Robert George Befort, Oct. 16, 1954; children: Bonnie Jean, Barbi Lynn Befort Shaler, Robert Carl. AA, MusB, San Diego State U., MA, 1980. Colleague Am. Guild Organists, 1979. Pvt. instr. piano and organ, San Diego, 1962—; organist and choirmaster St. Andrews by-the-Sea Episcopal Ch., 2001—. Instr. piano and accompanist Southwestern C.C., Chula Vista, Calif., 1983—87; recitalist. Mem.: Am. Guild Organists (dean 1990—92). Episcopalian. Avocations: reading, needlecrafts, travel. Home: 6519 Lockford Ave San Diego CA 92139 Office: St Andrews by-the-sea Episcopal Ch 1050 Thomas Ave San Diego CA 92109 Office Phone: 858-273-3022. Personal E-mail: carlenebefort@cox.net.

BEGALA, PAUL EDWARD, television personality, political scientist, consultant; b. Montclair, N.J., May 12, 1961; m. Diane Friday Begala, 1989; children: John Paul, William Travis, Patric Aaron. BA in Govt., U. Tex., Austin, 1983, JD, 1990. Bar: Pa. Ptnr., polit. cons. Carville & Begala; travel aide Lloyd Doggett Campaign for Senate, Tex., 1984; speech writer Congressman Richard Gephardt, 1987—88, speech writer presdl. campaign, 1989—91; cons. Dem. Nat. Com. and Clinton Adminstrn., 1992—95; sr. v.p. Pub. Strategies, Austin, 1995—97; asst. to pres., counselor to pres. Clinton Adminstrn., 1997—99; rsch. prof. govt. and pub. policy Georgetown U., 1999—; co-host Equal Time, MSNBC, 1999—2000, Crossfire, CNN, 2002—. Lectr. U. Tex., Austin, 1995—97; contbg. editor, columnist Capital Hillbilly George mag. Author: Is Our Children Learning?: The Case Against George W. Bush, 2001, It's Still the Economy Stupid: George W. Bush, The GOP's CEO, 2002; co-author (with James Carville): Buck Up, Suck Up and Come Back When You Foul Up: 12 Winning Secrets from the War Room, 2001; contbr. articles to profl. jours. Office: CNN Crossfire 820 1st St NE Washington DC 20002

BEGAM, ROBERT GEORGE, lawyer; b. N.Y.C., Apr. 5, 1928; s. George and Hilda M. (Hirt) B.; m. Helen C. Clark, July 24, 1949; children— Richard, Lorinda, Michael. BA, Yale U., 1949, LL.B., 1952. Bar: N.Y. bar 1952, Ariz. bar 1956, U.S. Dist. Ct. Ariz. 1957, U.S. Ct. Appeals (9th cir.) 1958, U.S Supreme Ct. 1973. Assoc. firm Cravath, Swaine & Moore, N.Y.C., 1952-54; spl. counsel State of Ariz., Colorado River Litigation in U.S. Supreme Ct., 1956-58; pres. Begam, Lewis Marks & Wolfe, P.A., Phoenix. Author: Fireball, 1987. Pres. Ariz. Repertory Theater, 1960—66; trustee Atla Roscoe Pound Found.; bd. dirs. Boys Clubs of Met. Phoenix; bd. govs. Welzmann Inst. Sci., Rehovot, Israel; pres. Am. Com. for Welzmann Inst. of Sci., 1996—98, chmn. fin. resource devel., 2000—; bd. dirs. Phoenix Theater Ctr., 1955—60, 1987—92, Ariz. Theatre Co., 2001—. Fellow: Internat. Soc. Barristers; mem.: State Bar Ariz. (cert. specialist in injury and wrongful death litigation), Am. Bd. Trial Advocates (bd. dirs.), Western Trial Lawyers Assn. (pres. 1970), ATLA (pres. 1976—77, chmn. polit. action com. 1979—86), Phoenix Country Club, Yale Club (N.Y.C.). Avocations: writing, theater, golf. Office: Begam Lewis Marks & Wolfe 111 W Monroe St Ste 1400 Phoenix AZ 85003-1787 Office Phone: 602-254-6071. Business E-Mail: rbegam@begamlaw.com.

BEGAYE, JOHNSON J. (JAY BEGAYE), art educator; b. Ganado, Ariz., Apr. 3, 1956; s. Alvin Williams and Glennabah Begaye; 1 child, Tiinesha Begay. BFA, Yavapai Coll., 1978. Tchr. Ganado Mid. Sch., 2001—. Musician: Cathedral Lake Singers; singer: (albums) Honoring Our Ways, Song of Colors. Founder Jr. Native Basketball Championship Tournament; coord. Rocky Mountain Basketball Championship. Home: PO Box 365 Ganado AZ 86505 Office: Ganado Mid Sch PO Box 1757 Ganado AZ 86505

BEGEL, THOMAS M., manufacturing executive; b. 1942; married Grad., U. Mo., Columbia. With E.I. Du Pont de Nemours and Co., 1964-66, Boise Cascade Corp., 1966-72; sr. v.p. Wheelabrator-Frye Inc., 1972-81; chmn., pres., CEO Pullman Co., 1981—88; founder, chmn., prin. TMB Industries, 1989—; chmn., CEO TTI Industries. Chmn. bd. dirs. Metalforming Technologies, Inc., Fuel Systems LLC. Office: TTI Industries 980 N Michigan Ave Ste 1000 Chicago IL 60611

BEGELL, WILLIAM, publisher; b. Wilno, Poland, May 18, 1928; came to U.S., 1947, naturalized, 1953; s. Ferdinand and Liza (Kowarski) Beigel; m. Esther Kessler, May 27, 1948; children: Frederick Paul (dec.), Alissa Maya (dec.). BChemE, CCNY, 1953; MChemE, Poly. Inst. Bklyn., 1958; postgrad., Columbia U., 1958-59; DSc, Acad. Sci. BSSR, Minsk, 1984. Engrng. mgr. heat transfer research facility dept. chem. engrng. Columbia U., 1953-59;

co-founder, exec. v.p. Scripta Technica, Inc., Washington, 1959-74; founder, pres. Hemisphere Publishing Corp., Washington, 1974-91, Begell House, Inc., Pubs., N.Y.C., 1991—; pres., chief scientist Byelocorp Sci., Inc., 1991—; dir. Supco Internat. Engring. Corp., Milan, 1994—. Lectr. pub. George Washington U., Washington, also N.Y. U.; cons. Heat Transfer Research Lab., Columbia U.; cons. in field. Editor 7 books; contbr. numerous articles on heat transfer to profl. jours.; patentee in field. Mem. nat. adv. bd. ctr. for the Book, Libr. of Congress; chmn. exec. coun. Profl. and Scholarly Pubs.; bd. dirs. Am. Fedn. for the Blind. Recipient Benjamin Gomez award book pub. div. Anti-Defamation League, 1984 Mem. AAAS, Am. Inst. Chem. Engrs., Am. Soc. for Engring. Edn., ASME (communications bd. Fellow, 1996, Disting. Svc. award 1992), Assn. Am. Publishers (dir.), N.Y. Acad. Scis. (publs. bd.), Internat. Centre for Heat and Mass Transfer, Washington Book Publishers (founder), Am. Assn. Engring. Socs. Jewish. Home: 46 E 91st St New York NY 10128-1350 Office: Begell House Inc Pubs 145 Madison Ave New York NY 10016-7802 Business E-Mail: bill@begellhouse.com.

BEGERT, WILLIAM J., lieutenant general United States Air Force; BS, U.S. Air Force Acad., 1968; grad., Squadron Officer Sch., Maxwell AFB, Ala., 1974; MPA, U. Colo., 1980; student, Air Command and Staff Coll., Maxwell AFB, Ala., 1981, Nat. War Coll., Ft. Lesley J. McNair, Washington, 1985; Mgmt. Program for Execs., U. Pitts., 1990; Program for Sr. Execs. in Nat. Security, John F. Kennedy Sch. Govt., Harvard, 1995. Pilot, aircraft comdr. 20th Mil. Airlift Squadron USAF, Dover AFB, Del., 1969-71; combat crew tng. USAF, Hurlburt Field, Fla., 1971; forward air controller, flight examiner pilot 20th tactical support squadron USAF, DA Nang Air Base, Vietnam, 1972-73; pilot, flight examiner 9th mil. airlift squadron 436th Airlift Wing, Dover AFB, Del., 1973-77; mil. instr. U.S. Air Force Acad., Colorado Springs, 1977-78, air officer commanding Cadet Squadron 20, 1978-80; comdr. and wing exec. officer 436th Mil. Airlift Wing, Dover AFB, Del., 1981-82; squadron comdr. 3d Mil. Airlift Squadron, Dover AFB, Del., 1983-84; from mobility forces programmer to chief mobility forces divsn., directorate of programs Hdqtrs. USAF, Washington, 1985-88; vice comdr. then comdr. 436th Mil. Airlift Wing USAF, Dover AFB, Del., 1988-90; comdr. 60th Mil. Airlift Wing USAF, Travis AFB, Calif.; chief of staff Hdqtrs. U.S. Transp. Command, Scott AFB, Ill., 1992-94; comdr. USAF Mobility Warfare Ctr., Air Mobility Command, McGuire AFB, N.J., 989-90; dir. ops. and logistics Hdqtrs. U.S. Transp. Command, Scott AFB, Ill., 1995-97; vice comdr. Hdqtrs. U.S. Forces in Europe, Ramstein Air Base, Germany. Decorated Defense Disting. Svc. medal, Defense Superior Svc. medal, Legion of Merit with oak leaf cluster, Disting. Flying Cross with oak leaf cluster, Meritorious Svc. medal with oak leaf cluster, Air medal with 11 oak leaf clusters.

BEGG, JOHN DANIEL, management consultant; AB, Cath. U. Am., 1976. Rsch. analyst Nat. Motor Freight Traffic Assn., Inc., Washington, 1980—81, cheif tariff divsn., 1981—84; speechwriter Am. Wayterways Operators, Inc., Arlington, Va., 1984—85, US Navy's Mil. Sealift Command, Washington, 1985—87, US Small Bus. Adminstrn., Washington, 1987—89; pvt. practice, 1989—; pub. events specialist Libr. of Congress, Washington, 1991—92; dep. dir. office external affairs Peace Corps US, Washington, 1992—93. Contbr. articles to profl. jours., local newspapers. Home: 4853 Sedgwick St NW Washington DC 20016

BEGGS, DONALD LEE, academic administrator; b. Harrisburg, Ill., Sept. 16, 1941; s. C. J. and Mary (Fitzgerald) Beggs; m. Shirley Malone, Mar. 19, 1963; children: Brent A., Pamela A. BS in Edn., So. Ill. U., 1963, MS in Edn., 1964; PhD, U. Iowa, 1966. Prof. So. Ill. U., Carbondale, 1966—98, assoc. dean grad. sch., 1970—71, asst. dean edn., 1973—75, acting asst. v.p. acad. affairs, 1975—76, assoc. dean edn., 1975—81, dean Coll. Edn., 1981—96, chancellor, 1996—98; pres. Wichita (Kans.) State U., 1998—, prof., 1999—. Cons. Ill. State Bd. Edn., 1966—, Quincy (Ill.) Pub. Schs., 1974—79, Chgo. Pub. Schs., 1977—80, Nat. Inst. Edn., Washington, 1983. Author: Measurement and Evaluation in the Schools, Evaluation and Decision Making in the Schools, 1971, Research Design in the Behavioral Sciences, 1969, Nat. Standardized Tests, 1980. Active United Way Campaign, 1978, Carbondale Schs. PTA, 1972—83; bd. dirs. NCAA, 2001—. Named Outstanding Tchr. in Edn., Coll. Edn., 1969; grantee, Ill. State Bd. Edn., 1979, Ill. Supt. Pub. Instrn., 1968, U.S. Office Edn., 1969. Mem.: Rsch. and Evaluation Adv. Council Ill. Office Edn. (chmn. 1982—83), Ill. Pub. Sch. Deans of Edn. (chmn. 1982—83), Am. Edn. Rsch. Assn. (sec. div. D. 1976—79), Phi Delta Kappa (one of 75 Young Leaders 1981). Office: Wichita State Univ Office of Pres 1845 Fairmount St Wichita KS 67260-0001*

BEGGS, WILLIAM H., microbiologist, researcher; b. Ft. Dodge, Iowa, Feb. 19, 1935; s. Harold William and Bliss Jewel (Swanstrom) Beggs; m. Nancy Florence Ost, Sept. 14, 1957 (dec. June 1995); children: John W., Margaret B. BA, U. Minn., 1956; PhD, U. Cin., 1964. Rsch. microbiologist Dept. Vets. Affairs Med. Ctr., Mpls., 1965—. Bd. dirs. Minn. Vets. Rsch. Inst., Mpls. Contbr. articles to profl. jours. and conf. procs. 1st lt. U.S. Army, 1956—58, Tex., Kans., La. Mem.: Am. Soc. Microbiology. Achievements include research in chemical properties, biological activities, modes of action and chemotherapeutic potentials of antituberculosis and antifungal drugs. Avocations: tennis, travel, hiking, music.

BEGHE, RENATO, federal judge; b. Chgo., Mar. 12, 1933; s. Bruno and Emmavve (Frymire) B.; m. Bina House, July 10, 1954; children: Eliza Ashley, Francesca Forbes, Adam House, Jason Deneen. BA, U. Chgo., 1951, JD, 1954. Bar: N.Y. 1955. Practiced in, N.Y.C.; assoc. Carter, Ledyard & Milburn, 1954-65, ptnr., 1965-83, Morgan, Lewis & Bockius, 1983-89; judge U.S. Tax Ct., Washington, 1991—2003, sr. judge, 2003—. Lectr. N.Y. U. Fed. Tax Inst., 1967, 78, U. Chgo. Fed. Tax Conf., 1974, 80, 86, also other profl. confs. Mng. editor U. Chgo. Law Rev., 1953-54; contbr. articles to profl. jours. Mem. ABA, Internat. Bar Assn., N.Y. State Bar Assn. (chmn. tax sect. 1977-78), Assn. of Bar of City of N.Y. (chmn. art law com. 1980-83), Am. Law Inst., Internat. Fiscal Assn., Am. Coll. Tax Counsel, America-Italy Soc. Inc. (bd. dirs. 1980-92), Phi Beta Kappa, Order of Coif, Phi Gamma Delta. Office: US Tax Ct 400 2nd St NW Washington DC 20217-0002

BEGLEITER, MARTIN DAVID, law educator, consultant; b. Middletown, Conn., Oct. 31, 1945; s. Walter and Anne Begleiter; m. Ronni Ann Frankel, Aug. 17, 1969; children: Wendy Cara, Hilary Ann. BA, U. Rochester, 1967; JD, Cornell U., 1970. Bar: N.Y. 1970, U.S. Dist. Ct. (ea. dist.) N.Y. 1971, U.S. Ct. Appeals (2d cir.) 1975. Assoc. Kelley Drye & Warren, N.Y.C., 1970—77; assoc. prof. Law Sch., Drake U., Des Moines, 1977—80, prof., 1980—87, 1993—2005, Richard M. and Anita Calkins disting. prof. law, 1987—93, Ellis and Nelle Levitt Disting prof. law, 2005—. Contbr. articles to legal jours. Mem. ABA (com. on estate and gift taxes, taxation sect. 1980—, com. malpractice, real property, probate and trust law sect. 1999—, com. on tax legislation and regulations, lifetime transfers, real property, probate and trust law sect. 1980-2002, study com. law reform 1996-2002, chmn. task force on spl. use valuation 1988-93, advisor Nat. Conf. Commns. on Uniform State Laws 1988-93), Iowa Bar Assn. (adviser, resource person, probate, trust sect. 1983-89, 93—), Am. Law Inst. (adviser restatement 3d trusts 1994—). Jewish. Avocations: science fiction, golf. Office: Drake U Sch Law 2507 University Ave Des Moines IA 50311 Office Phone: 515-271-2062. Business E-Mail: martin.begleiter@drake.edu.

BEGLEITER, RONNI FRANKEL, lawyer; b. Tupper Lake, NY, July 7, 1948; d. Samuel and Ruth (Kaplan) Frankel; m. Martin David Begleiter, Aug. 17, 1969; children: Wendy Cara, Hilary Ann. BA, Cornell U., 1969; MLS, Columbia U., 1971; JD, Drake U., 1982. Bar: Iowa 1983, U.S. Tax Ct. 1987. Libr. Fried Frank Harris Shriver & Jacobson, N.Y.C., 1971-74, Proskauer Rose Goetz & Mendelsohn, N.Y.C., 1974-77; reference libr. Drake U. Law Libr., Des Moines, 1977-81; clk. Iowa Supreme Ct., Des Moines, 1983-84; assoc. Davis, Hockenberg, Wine, Brown & Koehn, Des Moines, 1984-87; assoc., shareholder Pingel & Templer PC, West Des Moines, Iowa, 1987-2000; ptnr. Brown Winick, Graves, Gross, Baskerville & Schoenebaum, Des Moines, Iowa, 2000—. Adj. prof. Drake U. Law Sch., Des Moines, 1992, 95, 97. Chmn. Clive (Iowa) Mayor's Libr. Com., 1995-98; trustee Clive Pub. Libr., 1999-2001; bd. dirs. Iowa Libr. Assn. Found., 2002-2003; active Clive City Coun., 2002-03, 2004—. Nominated for Clive Citizen of Yr., 1999. Mem. Iowa State Bar Assn. (probate sect. coun. 2004—), Am. Coll. of Trusts and Estates Coun., ERISA Forum Office: Brown Winick Graves Gross Baskerville & Schoenebaum Ste 2000 666 Grand Ave Des Moines IA 50309 Office Phone: 515-242-2463. E-mail: begleiter@ialawyers.com.

BEGLEY, CHARLENE, electronics executive; married; 3 children. BS in Bus. Adminstrn. magna cum laude, U. Vt., 1988. With transp. sys. GE, 1988—90, corp. audit staff, 1990—94, v.p. ops. capital mortgage svc., 1994—97, CFO transp., 1997, dir. fin. plastics, 1998—99, v.p. corp. audit staff, 1999—2001, pres., CEO transp. sys., 2001—. Office: GE Transp Sys 2901 E Lake Rd Erie PA 16531

BEGLEY, CHRISTOPHER B., pharmaceutical executive; b. Chgo., Apr. 13, 1952; BBA, Western Ill. U.; MBA, No. Ill. U. V.p. mktg. V. Mueller Divsn., Am. Hosp. Supply Corp.; various positions Abbott Labs., Abbott Park, Ill., 1986—90, divisional v.p., gen. mgr. hosp. products bus. sector, 1990—93, v.p. hosp. products bus. sector, 1993—96, v.p. MediSense, Inc., 1996—98, v.p. Abbott HealthSystems, 1998—99, sr. v.p. chem. and agrl. products, 1999—2000, sr. v.p. hosp. products, 2000—. Office: Abbott Labs 100 Abbott Park Rd Abbott Park IL 60064-6400

BEGLEY, ED, JR., actor; b. Hollywood, Calif., Sept. 16, 1949; s. Edward James and Allene Jeanne Begley; m. Ingrid Margaret Taylor (div.); children: Amanda, Nicholas, Hayden; m. Rachelle Carson-Begley. Student, Los Angeles Valley Coll. Actor (theatre) Love Letters, The Cryptogram, The Old Neighborhood, (films) including Showdown, 1973, Citizen's Band, Stay Hungry, 1976, Blue Collar, 1978, Goin' South, 1978, The In-Laws, 1979, The One and Only, Airport 79, 1979, TPrivate Lessons, 1981, Buddy Buddy, 1981, Cat People, 1982, Protocol, 1984, Transylvania 6-5000, 1985, The Accidental Tourist, 1988, Scenes from The Class Struggle in Beverly Hills, 1989, She Devil, 1989, Meet The Applegates, 1991, Dark Horse, 1992, Mastergate, 1992, Page Master, 1994, Even Cowgirls get the Blues, 1993, Cooperstown, 1993, Sensations, Renaissance Man, Greedy, 1994, Renaissance Man, 1994, Batman Forever, 1995, Santa With Muscles, 1996, Lay of the Land, 1997, Ms. Bear, 1997, Joey, 1997, I'm Losing You, 1998, Addams Family Reunion, 1998, Best in Show, 2000, Anthrax, 2001, Bug, 2002, Ragged Point, Mighty Wind, 2003, others; (TV movies) A Shining Season, Elvis, Amateur Night at the Dixie, Dead of Night, Rascals & Robbers, Hot Rod, An American Love Affair, Spies, Lies and Naked Thighs, The Incredible Ida Early, Roman Holiday, Home, In the Best Interest of the Child, Not a Penny More, Not a Penny Less, 1990, A Change of Heart, Story Lady, Stand Off At Marion, Exclusive, World War II: When the Lions Roared, Jacks, The Late Shift, Alone, Not in This Town, Murder She Purred: A Mrs. Murphy Mystery; (TV series) Homicide: The Movie, Tale of Two Freedoms, The Practice, Mary Hartman, Mary Hartman, Battlestar Galactica, Roll Out, Room 222, St. Elsewhere, Parenthood, Winnetka Road, Todays Environment, Meego, Maggie Day, Meego, 7th Heaven, 1999—, The Web, Six Feet Under, 2001, Providence, The West Wing, Gideon's Crossing; also numerous TV commls., night club performances; dir. Enemies of Laughter, 1999; TV guest appearances include Quincy, The Love Boat, Touched by an Angel, 3rd Rock from the Sun, Star Trek: Voyager, Sabrina, The Teenage Witch, The Drew Carey Show, Ellen, The Simpsons, The Agency Titus, others. Chmn. Santa Monica Mountains Conservancy; commr. environ. affairs, L.A. Democrat. Roman Catholic. Avocations: carpentry, organic gardening, environmental concerns. Office: Sterling Winters Co 10877 Wilshire Blvd #15TH-FLR Los Angeles CA 90024-4341

BEGLEY, LOUIS, writer, lawyer; b. Stryj, Poland, Oct. 6, 1933; came to U.S., 1948, naturalized, 1953; s. Edward David Begley and Frances Hauser; m. Sally Higginson, Feb. 11, 1956 (div. May 1970); children: Peter Higginson, Amey B. Larmore, Adam C.; m. Anne Muhlstein Dujarric de la Riviere, Mar. 30, 1974. AB summa cum laude, Harvard U., 1954, LLB magna cum laude, 1959. Bar: N.Y. 1961. Assoc. Debevoise & Plimpton, N.Y.C., 1959-67, ptnr., 1968—2003, of counsel, 2004—. Author: Wartime Lies, 1991, The Man Who Was Late, 1993, As Max Saw It, 1994, About Schmidt, 1996, Mistler's Exit, 1998, Schmidt Delivered, 2000, Das Gelobte Land, 2001, Shipwreck, 2003; author: (with Anka Muhlstein) Venedig unter vier Augen, 2003; contbr. articles and revs. to newspapers and periodicals. With U.S. Army, 1954-56. Recipient Irish Times-Aer Lingus Internat. Fiction Prize, 1991, PEN/Hemingway Found. award, 1992, Prix Medicis Etranger, 1992, Harold U. Ribalow prize, 1992, award in Lit., Am. Acad. Arts and Letters, 1995, Jeanette Schocker prize, 1995, Konrad-Adenauer-Stiftung Literaturpreis, 2000, Chevalier de l'Ordre des Arts et Lettres. Mem. Am. Philos. Soc., PEN Am. Ctr. (pres. 1993-95, trustee 1995-2001), Century Assn. Democrat. Office: Debevoise & Plimpton 919 3rd Ave 46th Fl New York NY 10022-3904 Office Phone: 212-909-6273.

BEGLEY, SHARON LYNN, journalist; b. Englewood, N.J., June 14, 1956; d. John Joseph and Shirley (Wintner) B.; m. Edward Groth III, July 24, 1983; children: Sarah, Daniel. BA, Yale U., 1977. Sci. editor Newsweek, N.Y.C., 1982—. Office: Newsweek 251 W 57th St New York NY 10019-1802

BEGLEY, VINCENT JOSEPH, writer, educator; b. NYC, July 11, 1948; s. Vincent and Margaret Begley; m. Patricia Luzon Begley, Aug. 17, 1974; children: Jennifer, Jeremy, Nicholas, Kieran. Studied, Manchester Coll., Oxford, Eng., 1968—69; BA in English, Marist Coll., Poughkeepsie, N.Y., 1970; MS Ed in Secondary Edn., Mount Saint Mary Coll., Newburgh, N.Y., 2002. Mgr., mktg. comms. Amtrak, Washington, 1975—81; v.p., creative BS&A, Inc., N.Y.C., 1981—89; dir., publicity & comm. Fordham U., N.Y.C., 1989—91; assoc. to prodr. Alexander H. Cohen Prodns., N.Y.C., 1985—95; English tchr. St. Jean Baptiste H.S., N.Y.C., 1996—99; asst. dir., pub. info. Mount Saint Mary Coll., Newburgh, NY, 1999—2004, adj. prof., 1999—, dir. mktg. comms., 2004—. Writing cons. M-W Schs., Monroe, NY, 1987—91; adj. prof. Maris Coll., Poughkeepsie, NY, 1999—. Author: (books) Missing Links, 1989, Freedom's Light and Adventures of Tom Tinker, 1996, Dorothy - This Side of the Rainbow, 2002. Mem.: Kappa Delta Pi (dir., publicity 2002—). Avocations: directing plays, graphic art design, photography. Home: 19 Able Noble Dr Chester NY 10918 Office: Mount Saint Mary Coll 330 Powell Ave Newburgh NY 12550 Office Phone: 845-569-3219. Business E-Mail: begley@msmc.edu.

BEGUHN, SANDRA E., poet, writer; b. Kirksville, Mo., Nov. 3, 1942; d. Charles Elwin and Loeta Elaine (Payton) Funk; m. Lynn L. Beguhn, June 29, 1963; children: Kelly Lyn Beguhn Simpson, John Christopher. Student, MaryCrest Coll., Davenport, Iowa, 1962-63. Contbr. poetry to Capper's Weekly, Lyrical Iowa, Nat. Libr. of Poetry, Creative Arts and Enterprises. Mem.: Poetry Guild, Durango Colo. Poetry Gathering, Famous Poets Soc., Sparrowgrass Poetry Forum, Illiad Press, Mu Chi Sigma Soc. (pres.). Methodist. Avocations: travel, photography, writing. Home: 2115 W 34th St Davenport IA 52806-5301 E-mail: xalthim@mchsi.com.

BEHAN, KATHLEEN A. (KITTY BEHAN), lawyer; b. Milw., July 28, 1963; BA magna cum laude, Yale U., 1985; JD, Columbia U., 1989. Bar: Md. 1989, DC 1991. Staff counsel Nat. Security Project ACLU, 1989—90; assoc. Arnold & Porter LLP, Washington, 1990—96, ptnr., 1996—, co-chair pro bono com. Bd. dirs. probono.net, So. Ctr. for Human Rights, Atlanta, Am. Assn. People with Disabilities; bd. trustees Metrostage, Alexandria, Va.; bd. advisors Tahirih Justice Ctr., Falls Church, Va. Named one of Washington's Top 40 Lawyer's Under 40, Washingtonian Mag., 1998, The Top 50 Women Litigators, Nat. Law Jour., 2001, The Top 40 Litigators Under 40. Mem.: Women's Bar Assn. DC (bd. dirs.). Office: Arnold & Porter LLP 555 12th St NW Washington DC 20004-1206 Office Phone: 202-942-5533. Office Fax: 202-942-5999.*

BEHAR, JEFFREY STEVEN, lawyer; b. Phila., Nov. 20, 1952; s. Joseph and Helene (Richmond) B.; m. Lori R. Wolfe, July 30, 1977; children: Alexander J., Mallory R. BA magna cum laude, UCLA, 1974; JD, Loyola U., L.A., 1978. Bar: Calif. 1978, U.S. Dist. Ct. (ctrl. dist.) Calif. 1978. Ptnr. Shield & Smith, L.A., 1978-91; founding ptnr. Ford, Walker, Haggerty & Behar, Long Beach, Calif., 1991—. Mem. Am. Bd. Trial Advocates, Internat. Assn. Def. Counsel, Def. Rsch. Inst., Assn. So. Calif. Def. Counsel (bd. dirs. 1994-2000), Phi Beta Kappa. Avocations: race cars, volleyball, golf. Office: Ford Walker Haggerty & Behar One World Trade Ctr Long Beach CA 90831

BEHAR, JOY, television personality; b. Brooklyn, N.Y., Oct. 7, 1943; m. Joe Behar, 1965 (div. 1981); 1 child; m. Steven Janowitz, 1982. BS in Sociology, Queens Coll.; MA in English, SUNY, Stony Brook. Teacher Lindenhurst H.S., Long Island, NY. Corrs. Comedy Cen.; host call-in radio show on WABC. Profl. actress: (tv series) Baby Boom, (tv pilot) The Rock, (guest appearances) Dr. Katze (CableACE award), (discussion panel) Politically Incorrect; (movies) Cookie, 1989, This is My Life, 1992, Manhattan Murder Mystery, 1993, Love Is All There Is, 1996, M Word, 1996; Broadway appearances include The Food Chain, The Vagina Monologues, Comedy Tonight; author Joy Shtick or What Is the Existential Vacuum and Does It Come with Attachments?, 1999; co-host The View, 1997-. Office: 320 W 66th St New York NY 10023-6304

BEHAR, LEON ISIDORE, lawyer; b. Santa Clara, Cuba, Jan. 12, 1956; came to U.S., 1962. s. Samuel and Violeta Behar. BA in History cum laude, Yeshiva U., 1978; JD, U. Pa., 1981. Bar: N.Y. 1983, N.J. 1983, U.S. Dist. Ct. (so. and ea. dists.) N.Y. 1983, U.S. Dist. Ct. N.J. 1983, U.S. Ct. Appeals (2nd and 3rd cirs.) 1984, U.S. Ct. Claims 1985, U.S. Tax Ct. 1985, U.S. Supreme Ct. 1986, U.S. Ct. Appeals (fed. cir.) 1985; lic. real estate broker, N.Y. Assoc. Bachner, Tally & Mantell, N.Y.C., 1981—82, Balsam & Morris, N.Y.C., 1982—84, Rosenberg & Estis, P.C., N.Y.C., 1984—88, Jacobs & Zinns, N.Y.C., 1988—89; ptnr. Behar & Greer, P.C., N.Y.C., 1989—95, Leon I. Behar, P.C., N.Y.C., 1995—. Mem. ABA (litigation com.), N.Y. Bar Assn., N.J. Bar Assn., N.Y. County Lawyers Assn. (Supreme Ct. com.), Assn. of Bar of City of N.Y. (civil ct. com.), Assn. Trial Lawyers Am., N.Y. Trial Lawyers Assn. Republican. Jewish. Avocations: philosophy, real estate. Office: 330 W 38th St Ste 606 New York NY 10011 Office Phone: 212-242-0500. Office Fax: 212-242-0515. Personal E-mail: lbehar@aol.com.

BÉHAR, YVES, industrial designer; Studied indsl. design in Europe and US; BS in Indsl. Design, Art Ctr. Coll. Design. Design leader frogdesign, Calif., Lunar Design, Calif.; design prin., founder fuseproject, San Francisco, 1999—. Designer with team Footprints, Birkenstock Shoes, Jawbone, Aliph, (signature collection of lifestyle products) MINI_motion name,MINI, designer with team for Herman Miller, Nike, Microsoft, Hussein Chalayan, Toshiba, haasprojekt, Hewlett Packard, PUIG, and Philou, work can be found in permanent collections San Francisco Mus. Modern Art, Munich Mus. of Applied Arts, Cooper-Hewitt Nat. Design Mus., NY, Chgo. Athenaeum Mus., designer (one-man shows) San Francisco Mus. Modern Art, Musée de design et d'arts appliqués contemporains in Lausanne; author: Yves Béhar+fuseproject: Concept/Commerce:Commerce/Concept. Nominee Rave award for Technology, WIRED, 2005; recipient Nat. Design award for Product Design. Mem.: Indsl. Design Soc. Am. Office: Fuseproject 123 S Park St San Francisco CA 94102 Office Phone: 415-908-1493 est. 11. Business E-Mail: yves@fuseproject.com.

BEHLING, CHARLES FREDERICK, psychologist, educator; b. St. George, S.C., Sept. 8, 1940; s. John Henry and Floy (Owings) B.; m. Jennifer Crocker; children: John Charles, Andrew Crocker. BA, U. S.C., 1962, MA, 1964, Vanderbilt U., 1966, PhD, 1969. Asst. dean of students U. S.C., Columbia, 1962-63; asst. state news editor The State Newspaper, Columbia, 1963-64; asst. prof. psychology Lake Forest (Ill.) Coll., 1968-74; assoc. prof. Lake Forest Coll., 1974-88, chmn. dept., 1977-84; pvt. practice psychotherapy Lake Bluff, Ill., 1970-88, Buffalo, 1988-95; clin. assoc. prof. SUNY, Buffalo, 1988-95; dir. of undergraduate studies, 1989-95; adj. prof. U. Mich., Ann Arbor, 1995—; dir. intergroup rels., conflict and cmty., 1995—. Contbr. articles to profl. jours: Bd. dirs. Nat. Abortion Rights Action League, Planned Parenthood; mem. long-range planning com. Lake Bluff Bd. Edn. Named Outstanding Prof., Underground Guide to Colls., 1971, Birnbaum Guide, 1992, Outstanding Tchr., Lake Forest Coll., 1981, SUNY, Buffalo, 1991; NASA fellow. Mem. Am. Psychol. Assn., Soc. Psychol. Study of Social Issues, Assn. Humanistic Psychology, AAUP, Univ. S.C. Alumni Assn., Psi Chi, Sigma Delta Chi. Democrat. Office: U Mich Dept Psychology Ann Arbor MI 48109 Address: 1325 Wynnstone Dr Ann Arbor MI 48105-2894 Office Phone: 734-936-1875. E-mail: cbehling@umich.edu.

BEHLMAR, CINDY LEE, medical association administrator, management consultant; b. Smyrna, Tenn., July 4, 1959; d. James Wallace and Barbara Ann (Behlmar) Gribble. BBA, Coll. William and Mary, 1981; MBA, Old Dominion U., 1995. Cert. mgmt. acct.; cert. gen. mediator. Adminstrv. extern Hampton (Va.) Gen. Hosp., 1981-82; from mktg. rep. to supr. mktg. svcs. PruCare of Richmond, Va., 1983-85; exec. dir. PhysicianCare, Inc., Newport News, Va., 1986-89; provider rels. cons. Va. Health Network, Richmond, 1989-91; ind. cons. Tidewater Health Care, Virginia Beach, Va., 1991-92; COO Tidewater Phys. Therapy, Inc., Newport News, 1993-95; ind. cons. Yorktown, Va., 1996-97; contract mgr. Sentara Health Mgmt., Virginia Beach, 1998-99; state mgr. managed care Va. Oncology Assocs., 1999—2004; adminstr. Peninsula Emergency Physicians, Inc., 2004—. Sec., bd. dirs. Greater Peninsula Area Med.-Bus. Coalition, Newport News, 1987-89; symposium faculty mem. Am. Hosp. Assn., Orlando, Fla., 1987, Washington, 1988; profl. spkr. in field. Mem. ch. coun. St. Mark Luth. Ch., Yorktown, Va., 1988-91. Fin. Exec. Inst. scholar, 1993. Mem. Inst. Mgmt. Accts., Toastmasters Internat. (club pres. 1997-98, area gov. 1998-99, Club Toastmaster of Yr. 1997-98, Dist. Spirit Success award 1998, Dist. Area Gov. of Yr. 1998-99, Disting. Toastmaster 1999), Phi Kappa Phi, Beta Gamma Sigma. Avocations: reading, music theory and piano, art and fashion. Home: 922 Hanson Dr Newport News VA 23602-8910 Office: Peninsula Emergency Physicians Inc Ste E 11828 Canon Blvd Newport News VA 23606-4250 Office Phone: 757-599-4922. E-mail: CiLeBe@aol.com.

BEHLMER, RUDY H., JR., retired director, writer, film educator, scriptwriter; b. San Francisco, Oct. 13, 1926; s. Rudy H. and Helen Mae (McDonough) B.; 1 child by previous marriage, Curt; m. Stacey Endres, Oct. 1992. Student, Pasadena Playhouse Coll., 1946-49, Los Angeles City Coll., 1949-50. Dir. Sta. KLAC-TV, Hollywood, Calif., 1952—56; network TV dir. ABC-TV, Hollywood, 1956—57; TV comml. prodr.-dir., exec. Grant Advt., Hollywood, 1957—60; exec. prodr.-dir. Sta. KCOP-TV, Hollywood, 1960—63; v.p., TV comml. prodr.-dir. Hollywood office Leo Burnett USA, 1963—84; lectr. film Art Ctr. Coll. of Design, Pasadena, Calif., 1967—92, Calif. State U., Northridge, 1984—92, UCLA, 1988. Author: Memo from David O. Selznick, 1972, (with Tony Thomas) Hollywood's Hollywood, 1975, America's Favorite Movies-Behind the Scenes, 1982, Inside Warner Bros., 1985, Behind the Scenes: The Making of..., 1990, Memo From Darryl F. Zanuck, 1993, W.S. Van Dyke's Journal-White Shadows in the South Seas, 1996, Henry Hathaway (a Directors Guild of Am. Oral History), 2001; co-author: The Films of Errol Flynn, 1969; text on Warner Bros. Fifty Years of Film Music, 1973; editor: The Adventures of Robin Hood, 1979, The Sea Hawk, 1982 (Wis./Warner Bros. screenplay series), Warner Bros. 75 Years of Film Music, 1998; contbr. articles on film history, booklets for film music CDs; writer, narrator and on camera participant for DVDs, laserdiscs, and video documentaries. Served with AC, USNR, 1944-46. Mem. Dirs. Guild Am.

BEHM, FORREST EDWIN, glass manufacturing company executive; b. Lincoln, Nebr., July 31, 1919; s. Forrest E. and Lisle (Jacobson) B.; m. Ethel E. Groth, Aug.11, 1943; children: Courtney Ann, Douglas, Brian, Gregory. BS, U. Nebr., 1941, LLD, 1965, LHD, 1991. Foreman to plant mgr. Corning (N.Y.) Glass Works and affiliates, 1946-55; divsn., sales and mfg. mgr. Corning Glass Works, 1955-61, v.p., 1961-65; pres., bd. dirs. Corning Internat. Corp., 1965-75; sr. v.p., mem. mgmt. com., bd. dirs. Corning Glass Works, 1975-82, sr. v.p. ops., 1982-83, dir. quality, 1983-87; pvt. practice, 1987—2003; ret. Bd. examiners Malcolm Baldridge Nat. Quality award, sr. examiner, 1989, 90, judge for N.Y. State Quality award, 1991, 92. Author:

Saving a Great Company, 2001. Served to maj. AUS, 1942-46. Mem. All Am. Football at Nebr., 1940; named to Nebr. Football Hall of Fame; elected to Nat. Coll. Football Hall of Fame, 1988. Mem. Corning Country Club, Beta Gamma Sigma. Republican. Presbyterian. Home and Office: 3 Briarcliff Dr Corning NY 14830-3328

BEHM, MARK EDWARD, academic administrator, consultant; b. Balt., Apr. 21, 1945; s. Carl and Margaret Anderson (Weichman) Behm; m. Linda Ann Walker, Oct. 9, 1976; children: Scott Anderson, Craig Redgwick. BS, U. Md., 1967; MBA, Loyola Coll., Balt., 1980. Co-owner Applied Light Tech. Co., Silver Spring, Md., 1968-69; product area adminstr. Singer Co., Link Div., Silver Spring, Md., 1969-73; asst. comptroller U. Md. Balt. County, 1973—75, dir. fin. planning, 1976—85, dir. planning and budget, 1986—88, v.p. for adminstrv. affairs, 1988—2005. Chmn. bd. dirs. UMBC Tng. Ctrs., LLC. Founding mem., bd. dirs. Grant-a-Wish Found., Balt., 1979-87, Baltimore County Govt. Econ. Devel. Commn., BWI Partnership Bd.; econ. devel. subcom. Md. Info. tech. Bd.; chmn. Troop 880 com. Boy Scouts Am. Mem.: Assn. Univ. Rsch. Parks, Ea. Assn. Coll. and Univ. Bus. Officers (bd. dirs.). Home: 13809 Princess Anne Way Phoenix MD 21131-1521 Business E-Mail: behm@umbc.edu.

BEHNAVA, SHAHRIYAR, management consultant; b. Tehran, Iran, Sept. 5, 1954; s. Nasrollah Behnava and Gohar Mirfakhraee; m. Belinda Maree Bogsrud, Feb. 27, 1949; 1 child, Saman. Degree in Internat. Banking, City of London Poly., 1980; BA with hon. in Econ., London Guildhall U., 1979; MBA, Clayton U., 1986. Cert. mgmt. acctg., 1980. Mgmt. cons. Shadow Mgmt. cons., Portsmouth, England, 1984—87; CEO S & E Internat., Inc., Newport Beach, Calif., 1988—90, Irvine Analytical Lab., Irvine, Calif., 1988—91; mng. cons., dir. Blue Ocean Shipping Co., Ltd., Tehran, Iran, 1990—. Fellow: Chartered Mgmt. Inst.; mem.: Inst. of Mgmt. Cons. (assoc. mem. 1990), Amer. Acad. of Mgmt. (exec. mem. 1988). Achievements include design and construction of jetties for ro-ro vessels, Nowshahr ro-ro ramp, 1986, designed and engineered Pneumatic Grain Terminals, Caspian Sea Ports, 1998-2002. Office Phone: 9821 8875 8248. E-mail: sbehnava@blueoceanshipping.com.

BEHNEN, IAN, human services administrator; s. Richard and Boni Behnen. MS in sociology and human rels., St. Cloud State U., 2003—05. Qmrp Minn., 2004. Jud. coord. of campus life St. John's U., Collegeville, Minn., 2003—; human services technician State of Minn., 2002—. Internship Minn. Coalition for the Homeless, St. Paul, 2005—. Mem.: ACPA. Green Party. Home: 24285 193rd Ave Richmond MN 56368

BEHNEY, CHARLES AUGUSTUS, JR., veterinarian; b. Bryn Mawr, Pa., Nov. 30, 1929; s. Charles Augustus and Victoria Parks (Wythe) B.; m. Joan M. Langdon, Nov. 15, 2000; children: Charles Augustus III, Keenan F. BS, U. Wyo.; DVM, Colo. State U., 1961. Owner Cochise Animal Hosp., Bisbee, Ariz., 1961—; veterinarian, dir. S.W. Traildust Zoo, Bisbee, 1966—; owner Ultra Mini Ranch, Bisbee, 1969—. Assoc. prof. Cochise Coll.; chmn. Comprehensive Health Planning, Cochise County, Ariz., 1968. Mem. Ariz. Coun. for the Hearing Impaired, 1999. Mem. Am. Vet. Med. Assn., Soc. for Breeding Soundness, Internat. Platform Assn., Rotary, Elks. Republican. Episcopalian. Achievements include patents in ultrasound device and eye cover for treating infections, apparatus to alter equine leg conformation, external vein clamp, equine sanitation instrument; development of ear implant instrumentation system; patent for Farrier's rasp with measure. Home and Office: PO Box 4337 Bisbee AZ 85603-4337 Office Phone: 520-432-3296. E-mail: dodeeclare@aol.com.

BEHNEY, CLYDE JOSEPH, health policy researcher; b. Williamstown, Pa., May 19, 1946; s. Clyde J. Behney and Gladys Yvonne (Host) Williams; children: Lindsay, Fletcher, Taylor. BS, Lehigh U., 1968; MBA, U. Md., 1972; postgrad., George Washington U., 1975—82. Staff asst. U.S. Dept. Health, Edn., & Welfare, Washington, 1972-74, mgmt. intern, 1974-77; analyst/project dir. Office Tech. Assessment U.S. Congress, Washington, 1977-81, health program mgr. Office Tech. Assessment, 1981-93, asst. dir. Office Tech. Assessment, 1993-96; dir. divsn. health care svcs. Inst. Medicine, NAS, 1996-97, dep. dir., 1997—, interim exec. officer, 1998. Exec. dir. The Sorcerer's Apprentice Network, Washington, 1981—85, 1998—; mem. steering com. Nat. Health Policy Forum, 1998—2000; mem. quality awards adv. bd. Health Improvement Inst., 1998—; adv. com. mem. George Washington Univ. Pub. Health Program, 1999—; mem. tech. adv. bd. Millbank Meml. Fund, N.Y.C., 1998—. Co-author: Toward Rational Technology in Medicine, 1981; author/co-author chpts. in 9 books; editor: (newsletter) The Sorcerer's Apprentice, 1981-85; mem. editl. bd. Internat. Jour. Tech. Assessment in Health Care, 1985-98; contbr. articles to profl. jours. Treas. Glebe Elem. PTA, Arlington, Va., 1990—94, Swanson Mid. Sch. PTSA, Arlington, 1994—96, Yorktown H.S. PTA, 2001—02. Sgt. U.S. Army, 1969—71. Home: 2515 N Vermont St Arlington VA 22207-4125 Office: Inst Medicine 500 Fifth St NW Washington DC 20001 Business E-Mail: cbehney@nas.edu.

BEHNKE, MARYLOU, pediatrician, educator; b. Orlando, Fla., Sept. 1, 1950; d. Ernest Edmund and Elizabeth (Kolb) Behnke. BS in Chemistry, U. Fla., 1972, MD, 1976. Diplomate Am. Bd. Pediatrics, Am. Bd. Neonatology-Perinatology. Intern dept. pediat. Coll. Medicine U. Fla., Gainesville, 1976-77, resident, 1977-79, chief resident, 1979-80, fellow in neonatology, 1981-83, asst. prof., 1979-81, 83-89, assoc. prof., 1989-99, prof., 1999—, adj. asst. prof. Coll. Nursing, 1988-89, adj. assoc. prof., 1989-99, mem. senate-at-large, 1984-89, 2004—07, mem. grad. studies faculty, 1988-2000. Presenter nat. and internat. meetings, 1981—; med. dir. ICU Shands Hosp., Gainesville, 1983—89, neonatal devel. follow-up program, 1989—; ad hoc mem. spl. rev. com. human devel. rsch. NIH, 1991—96, chair, 1993, 94, mem. human devel. and aging-3 study sect., 1998—99; mem. BBBP-6 study sect., 1999—2002. Mem. editl. bd.: Death Studies, 1983—94; contbr. articles to profl. jours., chapters to books. Grantee, NIH, 1984—87, 1991—, Nat. Inst. Drug Abuse, 1991—, Ctr. Substance Abuse Treatment, 1993—95. Fellow: Am. Acad. Pediat. (sect. perinatal pediat. com. substance abuse); mem.: Am. Pediatric Soc., Fla. Soc. Neonatal Perinatologists, Fla. Interagency Coord. Coun. Infants and Toddlers, Soc. Pediatric Rsch., Nat. Perinatal Assn., Soc. Pediat. Rsch., Alachua County Med. Soc., Fla. Med. Assn. Republican. Mem. Ch. Of Christ. Avocation: reading. Home: 426 SW 40th St Gainesville FL 32607-2749 Office: J Hillis Miller Health Ctr Dept Pediatrics PO Box 100296 Gainesville FL 32610-0296 Office Phone: 352-392-4193. Business E-Mail: behnkem@peds.ufl.edu.

BEHNKE, ROY HERBERT, physician, educator; b. Chgo., Feb. 24, 1921; s. Harry and Florence Alice (MacArthur) B.; m. Ruth Gretchen Zinszer, June 3, 1944; children: Roy, Michael, Donald, Elise. AB, Hanover Coll., 1943; PhD (hon.), 1972; MD, Ind. U., 1946. Diplomate: Am. Bd. Internal Medicine. Intern Ind. U. Med. Center, 1946-47, resident, 1949-51, chief resident medicine, 1951-52; instr. medicine Ind. U. Sch. Medicine, Indpls., 1952-55, asst. prof. medicine, 1955-58, assoc. prof., 1958-61, prof., 1961-72; chief medicine VA Hosp., Indpls., 1957-72; prof. medicine U. South Fla. Coll. Medicine, Tampa, 1972—, chmn. dept. medicine, 1972-95, chmn. dept. head emeritus, 1995—. AMA rep. to residency rev. com. in internal medicine, 1970-75; mem. exec. and adv. com. Inter-Soc. Commn. Heart Disease Resources, 1968-72, chmn. pulmonary study sect., 1969-72; chmn. career devel. com. VA, 1980-83 Mem. Met. Sch. Bd. Washington Twp., 1968-72, pres., 1971; bd. dirs. Southside Community Health Center, 1968; trustee Tampa Gen. Hosp. Found., 1979-85; mem. research coordinating com. Am. Lung Assn., 1983-85, chmn., 1985-87, bd. dirs., 1983-87. Served with AUS, 1943-45, 47-49. Recipient Std. Oil Found. award Ind. U., 1971, Alumni Achievement award Hanover Coll., 1971; named Hon. Alumnus, USF Coll. Medicine, 1995; John and Mary Markle scholar, 1952, 57. Fellow and master ACP (gov. Fla. chpt. 1980-84, Laureate award 1991); fellow Am. Coll. chest Physicians; mem. AMA, Am. Fedn. Clin. Rsch., Ctrl. Soc. Clin. Rsch., So. Soc. Clin. Rsch., Alpha Omega Alpha. Office: Dept Internal Medicine 12901 N 30th St # 19 Tampa FL 33612-4742 Home: Apt D 1635 Royal Palm Dr S Saint Petersburg FL 33707-3882

BEHNKEN, WILLIAM JOSEPH, art educator, artist; b. NYC, Mar. 29, 1943; s. William Henry and Margaret Mary (Hoolan) Behnken. BA, CCNY, 1968, MA, 1995. Dir. art sch. Provincetown (Mass.) Art Assn. Mus., 1984-93; prof. art Bronx (N.Y.) C.C., 1973-83, CCNY, 1970—; instr. studio art Art Students League, N.Y.C., 1998—; instr. printmaking Sch. Fine Arts Nat. Acad. Design, 2001—. Artist print edits. lithographs, aquatints, mezzotints; represented in permanent collections at Met. Mus. Art, N.Y.C., Fitzwilliam Mus., Cambridge, Eng., Brit. Mus., N.Y. Pub. Libr. Print Divsn., Bklyn. Mus., Bowdoin Coll. Mus., Indpls. Mus. Fine Arts, Mus. Nat. Acad. Design, Jane Voorhees Zimmerli, Mus. Rutgers U., Mus. City N.Y., New Orleans Mus. Recipient Louis Lozowick awards Audubon Artists Soc., N.Y.C., 1991, 92, 1st Ann. Art Career Achievement award City Coll. Art Alumni Assn., 2004 Mem. Soc. Am. Graphic Artists (pres. 1998-2002), NAD (graphics prize 1992, Ralph Fabri Graphics prize 2003, instr. 2001—), Boston Printmakers, Phi Beta Kappa (pres. CCNY Gamma chpt. 2001). Democrat. Home: 3415 Fort Independence St Bronx NY 10463-4507

BEHR, MARION RAY, artist; b. Rochester, N.Y., Sept. 12, 1939; d. Justin Max and Sophie Gusta (Koffler) Rosenfeld. B.Art Edn., Syracuse U., 1961, M.F.A., 1962; m. Omri Marc Behr, June 24, 1962; children: Dawn Marcy Yael, Darrin Justin Mason, Dana Marisa Jana. Curator, contbr. Internat. Electrotech Print Show World of Electrotech: N.J. Print Coun. Contbr. publs. for stories, crafts, mag. covers and toy designs to nat. mags. including McCall's, Good Housekeeping, Lady's Circle, 1962-77; one-woman shows include Douglas Coll., 1983, Pargot Gallery, 1989, Eldorado Gallery, 1992, Beamsderfer Gallery, 1992, Hunterdon Art Gallery, 1993; Hunterdon Mus. Art, 1998; Inst. Cultural Peruano Norteamericano, 1999, Johnson Gallery, 2002, Discover Jersy Arts (artist of the month 2005); exhibited in group shows at Contemporary Am. Artists, Scarsdale, N.Y., 1964, Douglass Coll., 1977, John Szoke Gallery, 1989, Kanagawa Prefectual Gallery, Yokohama, Japan, 1989, 80 Washington Sq. East Gallery, N.Y.C., 1990, Juniper Gallery, Napa, Calif., 1991, Eldorado Gallery, Colorado Springs, Colo., 1992, B. Beamsderfer Gallery, Highland Park, N.J., 1992, Artsquad Gallery, Easton, 1993, Lever House, 1995, Audubon Artists, 1995, 97, 99, Cork Gallery, 1996, Cheltenham Ctr. for Arts, 1996, Krasdale Gallery, 1998, Nat. Acad. Mus., 1998, Stark & Stark, 1998, Grounds for Sculpture, 2001, Zimmerli Art Mus., Rutgers U., New Brunswick, 80th Fifth Ave Gallery, 2004, German Archtl. Ctr., Berlin, 2004, Hunteron Mus., 2005; permanent print collection Smithsonian Instn. Nat. Mus. Art History, 1995, Jane Voorhees Zimmerli Art Mus., 1993, 96, 2002, 04, 05, Piero Gallery, 2004, Thai Royal Art Collection, Bangkok, 1995, Inst. Cultural Peruano Norteamericano, Peru, 1999, Bethanien Gallery, Berlin, 2004, World of Electrotech, N.J. Print Coun., 2005; creator survey Women Working Home-the Invisible Workforce, 1978; pres. Women Working Home, Inc., Edison, N.J., 1980—; condr. workshops; author: (with others) Women Working Home: The Homebased Business Guide and Directory, 1981, 2nd edit., 1983; contbr. articles to popular mags., 1988-89, popular art jours., 1991-98, numerous articles to profl. jours.; illustrator Jewish Holiday Book, 1977; inventor (with Omri Behr) acid free, environmentally safe graphic etching process; installed Electrotech processor and taught first non toxic intaglio etching class at Stanford U., 1999; installed electroetch and established non-toxic etching in the Inuit Artists Holman Eskimo Co-op Art Center, Holman Island, NWT, Canada, 1999, U. Al Moutamid IBN Abbad, Asilah, Morocco, 2000, Howard U., Washington, Syracuse U., N.Y., 2001, U. Alaska, Juneau, U. Alaska, Fairbanks, 2001; extensive radio and TV appearances rep. Nat. Alliance Homebased Businesswomen. Mem. Kean for Gov. campaign, 1981; mem. White House Conf. on Free Enterprise Zones, 1982, Nat. Assn. of Women Artists, 1992, Soc. Am. Graphic Artists, So. Graphics Coun., 1992, Print Coun. N.J., 1993; trustee Women's Bus. Ownership Ednl. Conf., Inc., N.J., 1985; apptd. to N.J. Devel. Authority for Small, Minority and Women's Bus. Commn., 1986; Presdl. del. White House Conf. on Small Bus., 1986. Recipient N.J. Women in Bus. Advocate of the Yr. award SBA, 1984, Merit award Am. Artist Profl. League, Woman of Yr. in Bus. and Industry award, 1985, Audubon Artists Merit award, 1995; named Artist of Month (August) Discover Jersey Arts, 2005; Syracuse U. alumni grantee, 1957; Arts and Humanities grantee Charles E. Lindbergh Fund, 1993-94. Mem. Nat. Alliance Homebased Businesswomen (pres. 1980-82, legis. chair 1982-85; originator, founder), Women's Caucus for Art, Audoban Artists. Jewish. E-mail: electroetch@prodigy.net. *Father Justin Rosenfeld, born 1901 in Schopfloch, Bavaria. Studied law and economics, 1926, employed by bankers Wilhelm Vogt & CO., full responsibility for stories, casting, advertising, licensing, production and distribution of films for German speaking and foreign countries, film producer, president Orbis Film, Berlin.1936, very successfully produced film Razzia in St. Pauli and Mademoiselle Josette, Ma Femme. 1937, compelled by Nazi laws to cease operations completely. Fled to United States in 1938 with wife, Sophie Koffler Rosenfeld. Died in 1947 at 47. Mother- Sophie Koffler Rosenfeld Lustik-teacher and translator of fine languages lived to be 92.*

BEHR, OMRI M., lawyer; m. Marion Behr. BA in Chemistry with honors, Oxford U., 1956, BSc in Organic Chemistry, 1958, MA in Chemistry, 1960; PhD in Organic Chemistry, U. Glasgow, 1961; NIH postdoctoral fellow, Columbia U., 1960-61; LLB/JD, Seton Hall U., 1966. Bar: N.J. 1967, N.Y. 1968, U.S. Dist. Ct. N.J. 1967, U.S. Patent and Trademark Office 1966, U.S. Ct. Customs and Patent Appeals, 1977, U.S. Supreme Ct. 1977; Chartered Chemist U.K., European Chemist. Rsch. chemist U.S. Rubber Co., Inc., Wayne, N.J., 1961-63; patent trainee, agent, atty. Merck & Co., Rahway, N.J., 1963-67; assoc. Ostrolenk, Faber, Gerb & Soffen, N.Y.C., 1967-68; ptnr. Lerner, David & Behr, Newark, 1968-69, Cifelli & Behr, Newark, 1969-72, Omri M. Behr, Newark, 1972-74, Behr & Woodbridge, Princeton, N.J., 1974-76, Omri M. Behr, Princeton, 1976-81, Behr & Adams, Edison, NJ, 1981—2000; counsel Selitto, Behr & Kim, Metuchen, NJ, 2000—03, The Behr Office, 2003—. Contbr. articles to profl. jours.; inventor (with Marion Behr) new acid free, environ. safe graphic etching process (patent of week N.Y. Times, May 2, 1992). Del. N.J. White House Confs Small Bus., 1986; moderator N.J. Gov. Conv. Small Bus., 1986; lectr. U.S. Dept. Energy Licensing Seminars, 1983-87; legis. co-chair, mem. nom. com. Nat. Assn. Homebased Bus.; mem. N.J. Small Bus. Devel. Adv. Bd., 1988—93; mem. Edison Twp. Rent Control Bd., 1984-94; committeeman Rep. County Middlesex County, N.J., 1989-94. Charles E. Lindbergh Fund: Arts and Humanities co-grantee, 1993-94. Fellow Royal Soc. Chemistry, Royal Inst. Chemistry (U.S. sect., hon sec. 1968-74); mem. ABA, N.J. Bar Assn., Middlesex County Bar Assn., Internat. Fedn. Counsels in Indsl. Property, Am. Indsl. Property Law Assn., Phi Lambda Upsilon. Office: 325 Pierson Ave Edison NJ 08837-3123 Office Phone: 732-603-6006. E-mail: omrib@aol.com.

BEHREN, ROBERT ALAN, lawyer, accountant; b. N.Y.C., Dec. 29, 1929; s. Jeremiah E. and Sue (Windman) B.; m. Judith Sandra Morgan, Dec. 20, 1971. BBA, CUNY, 1951, MBA, 1956; JD, NYU, 1956, LLM, 1958. Bar: N.Y.; CPA, N.Y. Prof. CUNY, N.Y.C., 1957-72; pvt. practice N.Y.C., 1958—; pub., CEO, founder Inst. Continuing Profl. Devel., N.Y.C., 1967-87; CEO Behren Fin. Strategies, West Palm Beach, Fla., 1990—; ptnr. Behren & Cohen. Contbr. over 1000 articles to profl. mags., fin. pubs., newsletters. Pres. Musician's Emergency Fund, N.Y.C., 1991—. Maj., jet fighter pilot USAF, 1952-53. Recipient numerous awards, scholarships and grants. Mem. Flight Instrs. Assn., Ret. Officers Assn., U.S. Polo Assn., Mensa. Avocations: teaching aviation, skiing and sailing. Home: 2417 Golf Brook Dr West Palm Beach FL 33414-7067 Office Phone: 203-869-0200. E-mail: rbehren@aol.com.

BEHREND, ALBERT JAMES, surgeon; b. Phila., Nov. 18, 1946; MD, Jefferson Med. Coll., 1972. Cert. surgery. Intern Vanderbilt U. Hosp., Nashville, 1972-74; resident in surgery La. State U. Med. Ctr., New Orleans, 1974-76, Albert Einstein Med. Ctr., Phila., 1976-79; fellow in vascular surgery U. Ill., Chgo., 1981-82; with Grossmont Hosp., La Mesa, Calif. Vol. asst. clin. prof. surgery U. Calif., San Diego. Mem. ACS, So. Calif. Vascular Soc., Soc. Clin. Vascular Surgery. Office: 5525 Grossmont Center Dr Ste 609 La Mesa CA 91942-3009 Office Phone: 619-462-5916. E-mail: ajjeff2@juno.com.

BEHREND, DONALD FRASER, academic administrator, educator; b. Manchester, Conn., Aug. 30, 1931; s. Sherwood Martin and Margaret (Fraser) B.; m. Joan Belcher, Nov. 9, 1957; children: Andrew Fraser, Eric Hemingway, David William. BS with honors and distinction, U. Conn., 1958, MS, 1960; PhD in Forest Zoology, SUNY, Syracuse, 1966. Forest game mgmt. specialist Ohio Dept. Natural Resources, Athens, 1960; res. asst. Coll. Forestry, SUNY, Newcomb, 1960-63, res. assoc., 1963-67; dir. Adirondack ecol. ctr. Coll. Environ. Science and Forestry, SUNY, Newcomb, 1968-73; acting dean grad. studies Syracuse, 1973-74; asst. v.p. research programs, exec. dir. Inst. Environ. Program Affairs, 1974-79; v.p. acad. affairs, prof., 1979-85; prof. emeritus, 1987—; asst. prof. wildlife mgmt. U. Maine, Orono, 1967-68; provost, v.p. acad. affairs U. Alaska Statewide System, Fairbanks, 1985-87, exec. v.p., provost, 1988; chancellor U. Alaska, Anchorage, 1988-94, chancellor emeritus, 1994—. Mem. patent policy bd. SUNY, 1983-85, chmn. Res. Found. com. acad. res. devel., 1984-85; chmn. 6-Yr. planning com. U. Alaska, 1985-86; bd. dirs. Commonwealth North, 1991-92, Alaska Internat. Ednl. Found., 1997; mem. selection com. Harry S. Truman Scholarship Found.; mem. Pres.'s Commn., NCAA, 1992-95; chmn. spl. com. on student athlete welfare access and equity, 1993-95; chmn. 20th Great Alaska Shootout, 1997. Contbr. numerous articles and papers to profl. jours. Mem. Newcomb Planning Bd., 1967-69; mem., pres. Bd. Edn. Newcomb Cent. Sch., 1967-73; chmn. governing bd. N.Y. Sea Grant Inst., 1984-85; trustee U. Ala. Found., 1990-94. Served with USN, 1950-54. Mem. Alaska Internat. Edn. Found. (bd. dirs. 1997—), Wildlife Soc., Soc. Am. Foresters, AAAS, Phi Kappa Phi (hon.), Sigma Xi, Gamma Sigma Delta, Sigma Lambda Alpha (hon.). Lodges: Rotary (bd. dirs. Fairbanks club 1985-86), Lions (bd. dirs. Newcomb club 1966-67). Avocations: reading, writing, photography, fly fishing, bagpiping. Home: 22 Conifer Ln Avon CT 06001

BEHREND, LINDA, librarian, writer; d. Frederick William Behrend and Mary Fern Green; m. Wayne Franklin Akard (div.); children: Lucy Akard Seay, Mary Alison Akard, Kevin Wayne Akard, Alexander Keith Akard. BA in English summa cum laude, U. Tenn., Knoxville, 1963—67, MLS, 1987—89. Pub. rels. asst. Tenn. Eastman Co., Kingsport, 1967—69; tech. processing asst. Va. Intermont Coll. Libr., Bristol, 1984—88, tech. services libr., 1989—95; catalog libr. Sherrod Libr., E. Tenn. State U., Johnson City, 1995—96; acting tech. svcs. archivist Archives & Spl. Collections, E. Tenn. State U., Johnson City, 1996—97; tech. svcs. libr. Quillen Coll. Medicine Libr., E. Tenn. State U., Johnson City, 1998—2001; catalog libr., subject libr. for philosophy and religious studies Hodges Libr., U. Tenn., Knoxville, 2001—05, collection devel. libr. for religious studies, 2005—. News and feature writer TEC News, Tenn. Eastman Co., Kingsport, 1967—69; freelance copy editor Ctr. for Appalachian Studies and Services, E. Tenn. State U., Johnson City, 1997, fact checker, editl. asst., 2000—01; editl. bd. Appalachian Consortium Press, Boone, NC, 1998—2004. Mem. editl. bd.: Choice: Current Reviews for Acad. Librs., 2004—; contbr. articles to profl. jours. and mags. Mem. Bristol Concert Choir Tenn./Va., 1983—2000. Mem.: ALA, Assn. for Libr. Collections & Tech. Svcs., Tenn. Libr. Assn. (chair, tech. svcs. roundtable 2003—05), Online Audiovisual Catalogers, Inc., Assn. Coll. & Rsch. Librs., E. Tenn. Libr. Assn., Appalachian Studies Assn., Phi Beta Kappa. Presbyterian. Avocations: reading, creative writing. Home: 1021 Sanders Rd Knoxville TN 37923 Office: Univ Tenn 306 Hodges Libr Knoxville TN 37996-1000 Office Phone: 865-974-0392.

BEHRENDT, DAVID FROGNER, retired journalist; b. Stevens Point, Wis., May 25, 1935; s. Allen Charles and Vivian (Frogner) B.; m. Mary Ann Weber, Feb. 4, 1961 (dec. Sept 1998); children: Lynne, Liza, Sarah. BS, U. Wis., 1957, MS, 1960. Reporter Decatur (Ill.) Review, 1957-58; reporter Milw. Jour., 1960-70, copy editor, 1970-71, editorial writer, 1971-84, editorial page editor, 1984-95; Crossroads sect. editor Milw. Jour. Sentinel, 1995-98. Home: 1522 N Prospect Ave #1402 Milwaukee WI 53202

BEHRENDT, GREG, comedian; b. Calif. married; 1 child. Student, Univ. Oreg. Performer: alternative rock bands, stand-up comedy, 1986—; cons. (TV series) Sex & The City, Committed, 2005—; performer: (HBO TV special) Mantastic, 1997; co-author (with Liz Tuccillo): He's Just Not That Into You, 2004 (NY Times, Publisher's Weekly Bestseller list); performer: (TV series) Tonight Show with Jay Leno, Late Show with David Letterman. Named one of Variety's 10 Comics to Watch, 2001. Mailing: c/o Andrea Barzvi Internat Creative Mgmt 40 W 57th St New York NY 10019*

BEHRENDT, JOHN CHARLES, geophysicist researcher, writer; b. Stevens Point, Wis., May 18, 1932; s. Allen Charles and Vivian Eulaine B.; m. Donna Ebben, Oct. 6, 1961 (div.); children: Kurt Allen, Marc Russell; m. Laura Backus, May 16, 2004. Student, Cen. State Coll., Stevens Point, 1950-52; BS in Physics, U. Wis., Madison, 1954, MS in Geology, 1956, PhD in Geophysics, 1961. Cert. geophysicist, Calif. Asst. seismologist Arctic Inst. N.Am., Ellsworth Sta., Antarctica, 1956-58; rsch. assoc. U. Wis., Madison, 1958-64; rsch. geophysicist U.S. Geol. Survey, Denver, 1964—68, Liberia, West Africa, 1968-70, Denver, 1970-72; chief br. of Atlantic-Gulf of Mex. marine geology Woods Hole, Mass., 1974-77; research geophysicist, Antarctic coordinator U.S. Geol. Survey, 1977-95, geophysicist emeritus, 1995—; fellow Inst. Arctic and Alpine Rsch U. Colo., Boulder, 1996—, rsch. scientist, 1996—. Frequent pub. spkr. on Antarctica and other rsch.; advisor U.S. Depts. State and Interior, Washington, 1977—; mem. U.S. del. to Antarctic Treaty Meetings, various countries, 1977-95, various working groups NAS-NRC; rsch. on Antarctic, earthquakes in ea. U.S., Rocky Mountain tectonics, Gt. Lakes geologic structure, Atlantic continental margin of N.Am. and West Africa. Author: Innocents on the Ice: A Memoir of Antarctic Exploration, 1957, 1998 (Colo. Book award for non-fiction 1999), The Ninth Circle: A Memoir of LIfe and Death in Antarctica, 1960-1962, 2005; contbr. more than 275 articles to profl. jours. Recipient Antarctic Svc. medal U.S. Dept. Def., 1966, Meritorious Svc. award Dept. Interior, 1992, Filice Ippolito Gold medal for Antarctic Rsch., Italian Antarctic Rsch. Program and Acad. Nazionale dei Linceia, 1999. Fellow: AAAS, Geol. Soc. Am., Explorers Club; mem.: Soc. Exploration Geophysicists, Am. Geophys. Union. Avocations: photography, outdoor activities, music. Business E-Mail: behrendj@stripe.colorado.edu.

BEHRENDT, RICHARD LOUIS, academic administrator; BA in Secondary Edn., U. Pitts., 1964, MEd in Secondary Edn., 1965; PhD in Higher Edn., U. Mich., 1980. Tchr. Mt. Lebanon (Pa.) HS, 1963, Hempfield Area HS, Greensburg, Pa., 1965; departmental asst. U. Mich., Ann Arbor, 1965-66; dir. instnl. rsch. Washtenaw Community Coll., Ypsilanti, Mich., 1967; asst. to pres. Ind. State U., Terre Haute, 1967-68, dir. student rsch., 1968-69; dir. instnl. rsch. Hagerstown (Md.) Jr. Coll., 1969-74, dir. instl. rsch. and dir. personnel svcs., 1974-76, dean of supportive svcs., 1976-81; dean of coll. svcs. Clark County Community Coll., North Las Vegas, Nev., 1982-84; pres. Lincoln Trail Coll., Robinson, Ill., 1984-86, Sauk Valley Community Coll., Dixon, Ill., 1986—2005. Instr. bus. and speech U. Pitts., 1964; assoc. prof. mgmt. Frostburg (Md.) State Coll., 1971-74; mem. master planning com. Clark County Sch. Dist.; chmn. Washington County (Md.) Bd. Edn. Open versus Traditional Schs. Study Commn.; mem. Employment and Tng. Coun., Clark County, Nev., Pvt. Industry Coun., Nev., steering com. Correctional Ctr. Location, Ill. Contbr. articles to profl. jours. Bd. dirs. Community Theatre of Terre Haute, Family Svc. Agy. of Washington County (Md.), Big Bros. of Washington County, Crawford County (Ill.) Opportunities; v.p. bd. Potomac Playmakers, Md.; gen. vice chmn. United Way of Sterling-Rock Falls, 1988-89, chmn., 1989-90. Mem. Am. Assn. Higher Edn., Coll. and Univ. Pers. Assn., Assn. Instl. Rsch., Nat. Coun. on Community Svcs. and Continuing Edn., Md. Community Coll. Rsch. Group, Md. Community Coll. and Bus. Pers. Officers Assn., Nev. Assn. for Community Edn., Ill. Coun. Pub. Community Colls., Ill. Pres.'s Coun. (chmn. profl. devel. com.), Coun. North Cen. Community Jr. Colls. (sec., treas. 1987-88, 2d v.p. 1988-89, pres. 1989-90), Jaycees (Sterling, Ill. chpt.), Rotary (bd. dirs., pres.), Greater Sterling Area C. of C. (bd. dirs., v.p., pres.), Phi Delta Kappa. Address: 1878 Alistar Ct The Villages FL 32162 E-mail: behrenr@svcc.edu.

BEHRENS, ASHLEY, physician, ophthalmologist, researcher; b. Caracas, Distrito Capital, Venezuela, May 27, 1964; s. Aquiles Anibal and Bethy Behrens; m. Nathalie Morales, Nov. 28, 1997; children: Ashley Aquiles,

Nicole Nathalie Jessica. MD, Ctrl. U. Venezuela, Caracas, 1990. Chmn. dept. Ophthalmology Friends Blinds Soc., Caracas, Venezuela, 2002—03; asst. prof. ophthalmology Johns Hopkins U., Baltimore, 2003—. Editor-in-chief Venezuelan Ophthal. Jour., Caracas, 2001—. Mem. Sci. Edn. Ctr., Caracas, 2000—03. Recipient Fellowship Award, German Academic Exch. Svc., 1996, Prof. Dr. Eugen Schreck, U. Erlangen-Nuremberg, 2000, Travel award, Eye Bank Assn. Am., 2000. Fellow: Venezuelan Soc. Ophthalmology (licentiate; sci. com. 2000—02, diplomate 1994); mem.: Assn. Rsch. and Vision in Ophthalmology (assoc.), Am. Acad. Ophthalmology (assoc.). Achievements include research in microkeratome technology. Home: 6 Cross Falls Way Sparks Glencoe MD 21152 Office: Wilmer Eye Inst Johns Hopkins Hosp 600 N Wolfe St Baltimore MD 21287 Personal E-mail: ashleybehrens@verizon.net. E-mail: abehrens@jhmi.edu.

BEHRENS, BEREL LYN, physician, academic administrator, health facility administrator; b. New South Wales, Australia, 1940; MB, BS, Sydney (Australia) U., 1964. Diplomate Am. Bd. Pediatrics, Am. Bd. Allergy and Immunology. Intern Royal Prince Alfred Hosp., Australia, 1964; resident Loma Linda (Calif.) U. Med. Ctr., 1966-68, Henrietta Egleston Hosp. for Children, Atlanta, 1968—69, T.C. Thompson Children's Hosp., Chattanooga, 1969—70; faculty pediatrics Loma Linda U., 1970-72, with dept. pediatrics, 1972—, dean Sch. Medicine, 1986-91, pres., 1990—, Loma Linda U. Med. Ctr., 1999—; pres., CEO Loma Linda U. Adventist Health Scis. Ctr., 1997—. Office: 11175 Campus St Loma Linda CA 92354 E-mail: myhanna@ahs.llumc.edu.

BEHRENS, CLIFFORD ALLEN, mathematician, anthropologist; m. Susan Damberg, Sept. 21, 1974; 1 child, Stuart. BA, Mich. State U., 1972; MA, UCLA, 1975, PhD, 1984. Rsch. scientist Psychometrics, Inc., Santa Monica, Calif., 1979—84; sr. scientist, dir. Telcordia Technologies, Inc., Piscataway, NJ, 1993—. Invited com. mem. Nat. Rsch. Coun., Nat. Acad. Scis., Mapping Sci. Com., 2001—02; vis. investigator NASA, Stennis Space Center, Miss., 1988—92; vis. scientist IBM Sci. Ctr., L.A., 1986—90; adj. faculty UCLA, 1984—92. Contbr. articles to profl. jours., chpts. to books. Recipient Outstanding Grad. Student, UCLA Alumni Assn., 1984, V.P.'s Fund award, Bell Comm. Rsch., 1993; fellow, UCLA, 1971—78; grantee Shipibo Ecology and Economy, Peruvian Amazon, NSF, 1980—81, Cultural Ecology Land Use Intensification Among Barí Indians Venezuela, 1990—92, Usability and Interoperablity: A Dual Strategy for Enabling Broader Pub. Use of NASA's Remote Sensing Data on the Internet, NASA, 1994—97. Mem.: Trout Unlimited (v.p. 2004—05). Achievements include patents for -Automatic Recommendation of Products using Latent Semantic Indexing of Content; -Digital Subscriber Line Network Deployment Method; patents pending for -Distributed Latent Semantic Indexing. Avocations: fly fishing, shooting sports, canoeing, history of exploration. Office: Telcordia Techs Inc One Telcordia Dr RRC1N331 Piscataway NJ 08854-4157 Office Phone: 732-699-2619. Business E-Mail: cliff@research.telcordia.com.

BEHRENS, JAMES WILLIAM, physicist, administrator, author; b. Litchfield, Ill., Apr. 29, 1947; s. George William and Norma Clara Marie (Boeker) B.; m. Pamela Jane Breese, July 7, 1973 (div. Jan. 1980); 1 child, Jaime Rhea; m. Linda Sue Lawrence, July 5, 1984. BS in Engring. Physics, U. Ill., 1970; MS in Engring and Applied Sci., U. Calif., Davis, 1976, postgrad., 1976-78. Physicist Lawrence Livermore (Calif.) Nat. Lab., 1969-78, U.S. Dept. Commerce, Nat. Bur. Stas., Gaithersburg, Md., 1978-89; sci. tech. advisor Joint Chiefs of Staff, U.S. Dept. Def. Joint Staff, Washington, 1989-91; asst. exec. program mgr. Office Asst. Sec. Def. U.S. Dept. Def., Washington, 1991-92; sr. spl. projects mgr. U.S. Dept. Def., USN, Indian Head, Md., 1992-93; asst. dir. U.S. Dept. Def., Interagy. Tng. Ctr., Ft. Washington, Md., 1993-95; dep. dir. Interagy. Tng. Ctr. U.S. Dept. Def., Ft. Washington, Md., 1995-97; dir. U.S. Dept. Def. Ft. Washington Facility, 1997-99; sr. rsch. scientist, engr. U.S. Dept. Def., Naval Rsch. Lab., Washington, 1999—2000; sr. analyst Computer Sci. Corp., Alexandria, Va., 2004—. Tech. cons., pres. I.Q. in Nuc. Electronics Sys. & Tech., Inc., Rockville, Md., 1983-89; guest scientist Commissariat à l'Energie Atomique (CEA), Bruyere-le-Chatel, France, 1984. Author: Symbols and Fragments, 1993, Record of the House of Braunschweig-Illinois-Hannover, 1995, The 1995 Behrens Chronicle: A Complete Work, 1996, The 1995 Boeker Chronicle: A Complete Work, 1996, The 1996 Behrens-Boeker Chronicles: A Combined Work, 1997; co-editor: Fifty Years with Nuclear Fission, 1989; contbr. tech. articles to profl. pubs. Mem. Nat. Geneal. Soc., Nat. Writers Assn., Internat. Platform Assn., Nat. Audubon Soc., Nat. Wildlife Fedn., Am. Nuc. Soc. (cert. Appreciation 1989). Independent. Lutheran. Achievements include investigation of fast neutron-induced fission cross section measurements of the actinide elements, improvement of accuracy of neutron-induced fission cross section values which are used in broad areas of applied nuclear physics.

BEHRENS, JOHN (JACK), editor, writer, columnist, educator; b. Lancaster, Ohio, Feb. 7, 1933; s. Charles H. and Dorothy Margaret (Pairan) Behrens; m. Patricia Ann Beaty; children: Cynthia Sue Daugherty, Mark Andrew. BS in Journalism, Bowling Green State U., 1955; MA in Journalism, History, Pa. State U., 1956. Corr. Korea Bur. Pacific Stars and Stripes, 1957—58; sports editor SAC Times, Korea, 1957—58; sports and wire editor Lancaster (Ohio) Eagle-Gazette, 1958—62; instr., chmn. dept. journalism Ohio Wesleyan U., 1962—63; interim mng. editor Marysville (Ohio) Jour.-Tribune, 1962—63; asst. prof. dept. journalism Marshall U., Huntington, W.Va., 1963—65; summer desk editor Ashland Daily Ind., Ky., 1963—65; asst. prof., publs. editor Utica Coll. Syracuse U., 1965—86; adminstrv. asst. on media rels. to Rep. Walter H. Moeller, 1965—68; Reader's Digest Found. prof. mag. journalism Utica Coll. Syracuse U., 1969—97; adminstrv. aide to Dr. Virgil Crisafulli, del. to N.Y. Constnl. Conv., 1969—85; editor UC Pioneer Mag., 1969—85; editing cons., 1985—2001; dir. pub. rels./journalism programs Utica Coll. Syracuse U., 1986—92; editor Commerce Commentary Quar., 1969—; bus. columnist The Elks Mag., 1976—; assoc. editor Am. Printer Mag., 1978—2000; editor HomeBus. Jour. Mag., 1995—2001. Curator CMA Student Press Archives, 1968—; host, founder CBS/WIBX/Utica Coll. Roundtable Sunday, 1994—; assoc. editor Coll. Press Review, Am. Journalism History, 1970—89; editor Laubach's Literacy Advance Mag., 1984—86. Author: The Writer's Handbook, 1968; author: (with Allan Neuharth) Reporting Worktext, 1974; author: The Typewriter Guerrillas, 1977; author: (with Alex Haley) The Writing Business, 1992; author: Pioneering Generations, 1946-1997, 1997, The Big Band Days: A Memoir and Source Book, 2003; editor: Wood and Stone: Landmarks of the Mohawk Valley, 1972, School of Art: The First Fifty Years, 1991; contbr. (over 11,000 articles to profl. jours. and mags.). Trustee Village of Clinton, 1992—; mem. Village Planning Bd., Clinton, 1980—92. With U.S. Army, 1956—58, Korea. Named Journalist of Yr., Fairfield County (Ohio) Friends of Libr., 1984; named to Hall of Fame, Lancaster (Ohio) H.S., 1995; recipient Outstanding Writer award, Nazareth Coll., 1971, Outstanding Comm. award, St. Bonaventure, 1972, Nat. Disting. Svc. award, NCCPA, 1975, Gold Key award, Columbia U. Scholastic Press Assn., 2000. Mem.: Am. Soc. Journalists and Authors, Oneida County Hist. Soc. (bd. dirs., chmn. membership com. 1998—), Mohawk Valley Inst. of Learning in Retirement. Avocations: big band historian, power cruiser enthusiast. Home: 57 Stebbins Dr Clinton NY 13323

BEHRENS, M. KATHLEEN, medical researcher; PhD in Microbiology, U. Calif., Davis. With Robertson Stephens Mgmt. Co., 1983—99, gen. ptnr., 1986-93; mng. dir. RS Investments, San Francisco, 1999—. Bd. dirs. Abgenix Inc., HealthTrio; mem. President's Coun. Advisors on Sci. and Tech. Mem. Nat. Venture Capital Assn. (pres. elect 1999—). Office: RS Investments 388 Market St San Francisco CA 94111 also: Abgenix Inc 7601 Dumbarton Cir Fremont CA 94555-3616

BEHRINGER, REINHOLD WERNER, physicist, researcher; arrived in U.S., 1996; MA in Physics, SUNY, 1988; diploma in Physics, U. Wuerzburg, 1990; PhD, U. Bundeswehr Muenchen, 1996. Rschr. U. Bundeswehr Muenchen, Neubiberg, Germany, 1990—96; rsch. scientist Rockwell Sci., Thousand Oaks, Calif., 1996—. Pres. SciAutonics, LLC, Thousand Oaks, Calif., 2003—. Composer: (songs) Romantic Suite, 2001, Elegia, 2005. Lt. Signal Corps German Army, 1982—84. Mem.: IEEE (Project of Yr. award 2005), Deutsche Physikalische Gesellschaft. Achievements include patents for augmented reality system. Office: Rockwell Scientific 1049Camino Dos Rios Thousand Oaks CA 91360

BEHRMAN, BRUCE WARD, social sciences educator; b. Peoria, Ill., Sept. 15, 1934; s. Carl Martin and Elwin Ward Behrman; m. Rileyne Elizabeth Brown; children: Zachary, Matthew, Mark. *Father, Carl Martin Behrman, was an Illinois state senator and federal judge.* BA, Bradley U., 1956, MA, 1957; JD, Northwestern U., 1962; PhD, Purdue U., 1967, MA, 1977. Tchg. asst., grad. instr. Purdue U., 1965—66; asst. prof. Calif. State U., Sacramento, 1967—70, assoc. prof., 1970—77, prof., 1978—. Cons. in field, 1980—. Contbr. articles to profl. jours. Mem.: Am. Psychology & Law Soc., Am. Psychol. Soc., Phi Kappa Phi. Independent. Presbyterian. Office: Calif State U Dept Psychology 6000 J St Sacramento CA 95819

BEHRMAN, EDWARD JOSEPH, biochemistry educator; b. N.Y.C., Dec. 13, 1930; s. Morris Harry and Janet Cahn (Solomons) B.; m. Cynthia Fansler, Aug. 29, 1953; children: David Murray, Elizabeth Colden, Victoria Anne. BS, Yale, 1952; PhD, U. Calif. at Berkeley, 1957. Research asso. biochemistry Cancer Research Inst., Boston, 1960-64; bd. tutors biochem. scis. Harvard, 1961-64; asst. prof. chemistry Brown U., Providence, 1964-65; mem. faculty Ohio State U., Columbus, 1965—, asso. prof. biochemistry, 1967-69, prof., 1969—. Rschr. in peroxydisulfate and nucleotide chemistry. Contbr. articles to profl. jours. USPHS fellow, 1955-56, 57-60; NSF grantee, 1966-73; NIH grantee, 1973-81 Mem. Am. Chem. Soc., Royal Soc. Chemistry, Phi Beta Kappa, Sigma Xi. Home: 6533 Hayden Run Rd Hilliard OH 43026-9642 Office: Ohio State U Dept Biochemistry Columbus OH 43210 Office Phone: 614-292-9485. E-mail: behrman.1@osu.edu.

BEHRMAN, HAROLD RICHARD, endocrinologist, physiologist, educator; b. Sask., Can., Nov. 26, 1939; s. Henry Fred and Minnie Alice (Waslenko) B.; m. Carol Hope O'Rourke, Aug. 8, 1981; children: Tracy Lee, Terri Lynne, Russell Norman, Kevin Michael, Kathleen Hope. BS, U. Man., (Can.), 1962, MA, 1965; PhD, N.C. State U., 1967; MS (hon.), Yale U., 1982. Research fellow Harvard U. Med. Sch., Boston, 1967-71, asst. prof., 1971-72; dir. reproductive biology Merck Inst., Rahway, N.J., 1972-75; assoc. prof. gynecology and pharmacology Yale U., New Haven, 1975-81, prof. ob-gyn. and pharmacology, 1981—, dir. reproductive biology sect., 1975—. Cons. NIH, 1978-83, 91-95, USDA, 1985, NSF, 1985, Med. Rsch. Coun. Can., 1990-91. Recipient Research award Lalor Found., 1971-72; Fulbright-Hays Disting. prof., 1978; MRC Can. fellow, 1967-70; recipient Alta. Heritage Vis. Prof. award, 1983 Mem. AAAS, Am. Physiol. Soc., Endocrine Soc., Soc. Study of Reprodn., Soc. Endocrinology, Can. Physiol. Soc. Home: 790 Green Hill Rd Madison CT 06443-2404 Office: Yale U Dept Ob-Gyn 1303A Yale Sta New Haven CT 06520

BEHRMAN, JERE RICHARD, economics professor; b. Indpls., Mar. 2, 1940; s. Robert Wilbur and Mary Jane (Krull) B.; m. Barbara Ann Ventresco; children: Kennedy Robert, Julia Andrea, Emily Louise. Student, Russian Lang. Inst., Ind. U., 1960-61; BA summa cum laude, Williams Coll., Williamstown, Mass., 1962; PhD in Econs., Mass. Inst. Tech., 1966. Asst. prof. econs. U. Pa., Phila., 1965-68, asso. prof., 1968-71, prof., 1971—, chmn. dept. econs., 1973-79, research asso. Center for Population Studies, 1979—, William P. Kenan, Jr. prof. econs., 1983—, assoc. dir. Lauder Inst. Mgmt. and Internat. Studies, 1983-87; co-dir. Ctr. for Analysis Developing Economies, 1982-95; Ctr. for Household and Family Econs., War Cannon, prof. econ, 1982—; South Asian Studies Ctr., 1983-95; acting dir. Population Studies Ctr., 1992-93, dir., 1998—. Faculty assoc. NSF sponsored project, 1965-68; vis. seminar coord. U. Catolica, Santiago, Chile, 1969; vis. lectr. pub. and internat. affairs, Princeton U., 1973; rsch. assoc. Nat. Bur. Econ. Rsch., 1975-79; hon. fellow dept. econs. U. Wis., 1976-77; rsch. assoc. Ctr. Latin Am. Devel. Studies, Boston U., 1978-79; cons. econs. dept. IBRD, Washington, 1966-69, Devel. Rsch. Ctr., 1972-73; rsch. assoc.; cons. MIT-ODEPLAN-Ford project Office Nat. Econ. Planning, Santiago, 1968-71; cons. Wharton Econ. Forecasting Assocs., Inc., 1970-71, U.S. Treasury, 1972, U.S. Treasury Brookings-SIECA-BID project on Cen. Am. Common Market, 1973-78, UN Com. on Trade and Devel. World Commodity Models, 1974, Harvard Inst. Internat. Devel., Cen. Bank Nicaragua Econ. Modeling Project, 1975, ILPES-NBER-UN Project on Short Term Policy in Latin Am. Econs., 1975, AID, 1976-77, Dept. of Treasury, 1977, ECIEL, 1978, Internat. Crops Rsch. Inst. for Semi-Arid Tropics, 1980-87, UN, 1982, Botswana Ministry at Planning, 1982, Ncaer India, 1980, World Bank, 1981—, Thai Devel. Rsch. Inst., 1987-91, Indonesian Ministry of Planning, 1987-88, Internat. Rice Rsch. Inst., 1987-89, Malaysian project ILO, 1989, humanresource and devel. project ILO/ARTEP, 1989-90, World Bank Mellon Brazilian edn. project, 1990, Pakistan rural edn. project Internat. Food Policy Rsch. Inst., 1989-95, World Bank Productivity Project, 1990, HIID Bolivia project on social sectors, 1992-94, World Bank project on Pakistan in 2010, Internat; internat. expert Unido Social Summit, 1994-95, cons. UNPP human resources, 1995; prin. investigator on NSF project, 1972-75, 95—, AID, 1977-80, Ford-Rockefeller, 1977-78, 16 project NIH, 1981—, Population Coun., 1982-86, Pew Charitable Trust, 1988—; vis. scholar NAS, Am. Coun. Learned Socs., Social Sci. Rsch. Coun., People's Republic of China, 1987-88; Arnold Bernhard Disting. vis. prof. econs. Williams Coll., 1990-91. Autor 25 books and monographs; co-editor Jour. Devel. Econs., 1985-95; contbr. more than 240 articles and book revs. to profl. jours. Recipient Benedict prize as outstanding math. student Williams Coll., 1960, Grosvenor Cup as outstanding mem. class of, 1962; award of merit for outstanding research in agrl. econs. Am. Farm Econ. Assn., 1967; Nat. Merit scholar, 1958-62; Tyng Found. fellow, 1958-64; Carnegie fellow, 1961; Danforth Found. fellow, 1962-66; NSF fellow, 1962-63; Mass. Inst. Tech. Center for Internat. Studies fellow, 1964-65; Ford Found. Faculty fellow, 1971-72; Guggenheim Found. Faculty fellow, 1979-80; Compton Found. Population fellow, 1980-81; Fulbright 40th Anniversary Disting. fellow, 1987. Fellow Econometric Soc.; mem. Am. Econ. Assn., L.Am. Studies Assn., Population Assn. Am., Phi Beta Kappa. Home: 320 Mallwyd Rd Merion Station PA 19066-1411 Office: U Pa Dept Econs 3718 Locust Walk Philadelphia PA 19104-6209 E-mail: jbehrman@econ.sas.upenn.edu.

BEHRMAN, RICHARD ELLIOT, pediatrician, neonatologist, university dean; b. Phila., Dec. 13, 1931; s. Robert and Vivian (Keegan) Behrman; m. Ann Nelson, Aug. 14, 1954; children: Amy Jane, Michael Jameson, Carolyn Ann, Hillary. AB, Amherst Coll., 1953; JD, Harvard U., 1956; MD, U. Rochester, 1960; DSc (hon.), Med. Coll. Wisc., 2000. Diplomate Am. Bd. Pediat. (examiner). Intern Johns Hopkins Hosp., Balt., 1960—61, resident in pediat., 1963—65; asst. prof. pediat. U. Oreg. Sch. Medicine, Portland, 1965—67, assoc. prof., 1967—68; prof. U. Ill. Coll. Medicine, Chgo., 1968—71; prof., chmn. dept. pediat. Columbia U. Coll. Physicians and Surgeons, N.Y.C., 1971—76; prof., chmn. dept. Case Western Res. U. Sch. Medicine, Cleve., 1976—81, dean Sch. Medicine, 1980—89; prof. clin. pediat. Stanford U., 1989; v.p. med. affairs Case Western Res. U. Sch. Medicine, Cleve., 1987—89; dir. dept. pediat. Rainbow Babies and Children's Hosp., Cleve., 1976—81; dir. Ctr. for Future of Children, 1989—99; sr. v.p. med. affairs Lucile Packard Found. for Children's Health, Palo Alto, Calif., 1999—2002, chmn. bd., 1996—99; dir. Lucile S. Packard Children's Hosp./Stanford Health Svcs., Stanford, UCSF-Stanford Health Care; exec. chair pediat. edn. steering com. Fedn. Pediat. Orgns., 2002—. Author: Neonatology: Diseases of the Fetus and Infant, 1973, Neonatal-Perinatal Medicine, 1977; editor: Nelson's Textbook of Pediatrics, 1978, 1983, 1987, 1992, 1995, 2000, 2003, Essentials of Pediatrics, 1989, 1993, 1997, 2001; editor-in-chief: The Future of Children, 1990—2005, mem. editl. bd., sect. editor fetal and neonatal medicine: Jour. Pediat., 1970—85, assoc. editor, mem. editl. bd., cons. editor: Pediat. Rsch. Jour., 1971—80. With USPHS, 1961—63. Fellow, Wyeth pediat., 1963—65; scholar, Whipple, 1960—61, Univ., U. Rochester, 1960. Fellow: Am. Acad. Pediat.; mem.: Soc. Gynecol. Investigation, Perinatal Rsch. Soc. (coun. 1970—73), Inst. Medicine of NAS, Soc. Pediat. Rsch. (v.p. 1976—77), Century Assn., Sigma Xi. Episcopalian. Home: PO Box 1338 Belvedere Tiburon CA 94920-2433 Office Phone: 650-839-1911. Business E-Mail: rbehrman@fopo.org.

BEHRMANN, JOAN GAIL, newspaper editor; b. N.Y.C. d. Jerome and Jeanette (Silberman) Metzner; m. Larry Jinks, Oct. 2, 1960 (div. 1970); children: Laura Jinks Kastigar, Daniel Carlton; m. Nicolas Lee Behrmann, Dec. 21, 1972. BA, Queens Coll., 1956; MS, Columbia U., 1958. Reporter Charlotte (N.C.) Observer, 1958-60, Miami (Fla.) Herald, 1960-64, Miami News, 1965-66; asst. prof. Miami Dade C.C., 1968-72; assoc. prof. Boston U., 1975-78; Sunday editor The Saratogian, Saratoga Springs, NY, 1979-80; editor Gannett Westchester, Westchester County, N.Y., 1981-83; page one editor, entertainment editor USA Today, Rosslyn, Va., 1983-87; exec. editor The Desert Sun, Palm Springs, Calif., 1987-95; arts editor The Detroit News, Detroit, 1996-2000; ret., 2000; freelance writer Trash or Treasure column, theater revs. Detroit News, Detroit, 2001—05. Co-author: Questioning Media Ethics, 1978. Bd. dirs. Coll. of the Desert Found., Palm Desert, 1993-95, Jewish Family Svcs., Palm Springs, 1994-95, Palm Springs Opera Guild, 1989-91, Adult Well-Being Svcs., Detroit, Mich., 1997-2000, Mich. Opera Theatre, 2000-2005; founder Every Women's Coun., Glens Falls, N.Y., 1978-80. Recipient Athena award Palm Springs C. of C., 1991. Mem. Assn. Press Mng. Editors Orgn. (bd. dirs. 1991-96, com. chair 1996-97), Am. Soc. Newspaper Editors. Avocations: travel, reading. Personal E-mail: jbehrmann@aol.com.

BEHRNS, KEVIN E., heptobiliary and pancreatic surgeon; s. Eugene J. and Donna J. Behrns; m. Patricia J. Lee, Jan. 24, 1961; children: Andrew E., Brittany L., Callista J. MD, Mayo Med. Sch., 1988. Diplomate Am. Bd. Surgery. Prof. surgery U. N.C., Chapel Hill, 1995—2003, U. Fla., Gainesville, 2005—. Rsch. grantee, NIH, 1999—. Mem.: ACS, Am. Surg. Assn., Am. Gastroent. Assn., Am. Assn. Study of Liver Diseases, Soc. Univ. Surgeons, Soc. Surgery of the Alimentary Tract. Achievements include NIH-funded basic science laboratory that studies growth control of normal and cirrhotic hepatocytes. Office: Univ Fla PO Box 100286 1600 SW Archer Gainesville FL 32610 Office Phone: 352-265-0761.

BEIDER, MARLYS ANNA, hotel executive, writer; b. Hannover, Germany, Feb. 7, 1945; d. Walter Schroeder and Elfriede (Ellen) Pallenberg-Schroeder; m. Harold Beider, Apr. 21, 1971 (dec.); children: Jacqueline Lee Shear, Kenneth Harry, Kelly Tema Rubin, Daniel Ayal. Bus., Buhmann Fachschule, 1960—63. V.p. Mid Am. Hotel Corp., Chgo., 1975—90, pres., 1990—. Author: (novels) Fateful Parallels, Continuum. Woman's bd. mem. North Shore Country Day Sch., Winnetka, Ill., 1981—91; adv. bd. The Theatre Sch. DePaul U., Chgo.; v.p. To Protect Our Heritage PAC, Chgo., 1985—90. Mem.: Royal Melbourne. Avocations: writing, opera, golf, hiking.

BEIDLER, MARSHA WOLF, lawyer; b. Bridgeton, N.J., Feb. 29, 1948; d. Benjamin and Esther (Lourie) Wolf; m. John Nathan Beidler, Aug. 18, 1974; children: Dora E., Evan A. BA, Dickinson Coll., Carlisle, Pa., 1969; JD, Rutgers U., Camden, N.J., 1972; LLM in Taxation, NYU, 1979. Bar: Pa. 1972, Fla. 1973, N.J. 1975; Fla. bar bd. cert. tax lawyer. Estate and gift tax atty. IRS, Phila., 1972-74, Trenton, N.J., 1974-76; atty. McCarthy & Hicks, Princeton, N.J., 1976-81; ptnr. Pinto & Beidler, Princeton, 1981-83; prin. Smith, Lambert, Hicks & Miller, Princeton, 1983-88; ptnr. Drinker, Biddle & Reath, Princeton, 1988—. Sec. Mercer County Estate Planning Council, 1977-86; prof. paralegal studies Rider Coll., Trenton, 1982; lectr. estate planning various corps. and univs. Bd. dirs. Birth Alternatives, Princeton, 1980; bd. dirs. Mercer Council on Alcoholism, Trenton, 1985-86. Fellow Am. Coll. Trusts and Estate Counsel; mem. ABA (taxation sect., real property, probate and trust sect.), Fla. Bar Assn., N.J. Bar Assn. (taxation sect.). Office: Drinker Biddle & Reath 105 College Rd E PO Box 627 Princeton NJ 08542-0627 Office Phone: 609-716-6515. Business E-Mail: marsha.beidler@dbr.com.

BEIDLER, PETER GRANT, language educator; b. Bethlehem, Pa., Mar. 13, 1940; s. Paul Henry and Margaret (Grant) B.; m. Anne E. Gilbert, June 15, 1963; children: Paul, Kurt, Gretchen, Nora. BA, Earlham Coll., 1962; MA, Lehigh U., 1965, PhD, 1968. Asst. prof. English Lehigh U., Bethlehem, Pa., 1968-72, assoc. prof., 1972-77, prof., 1977—, Lucy G. Moses Disting prof. English, 1978—, acting v.p. for student affairs, 1982-83; Robert Foster Cherry disting. tchg. prof. Baylor U., 1995-96. Author: Fig Tree John: An Indian in Fact and Fiction, 1977; co-author: (bibliography) The Indian in American Short Fiction, 1979; editor: John Gower's Literary Transformations, 1982, Ghosts, Demons and Henry James, 1989, Writing Matters, 1992, Henry James's The Turn of the Screw: Case Studies in Contemporary Criticism, 1995, 2d edit., 2004, Geoffrey Chaucer's The Wife of Bath: Case Studies in Contemporary Criticism, 1996, Masculinities in Chaucer, 1998, Chaucer's Wife of Bath: Prologue and Tale: An Annotated Bibliography, 1990-1995, 1998, A Reader's Guide to the Novels of Louise Erdrich, 1999, 2d edit., 2005, Native Americans in the Saturday Evening Post, 2000, The Native American in Short Fiction in the Saturday Evening Post, 2001, Why I Teach, 2002. Served with USAF, 1962-68. Named Nat. Prof. of Yr. Coun. for Advancement and Support of Edn., 1983; Fulbright lectr. Sichuan U., Chengdu, Peoples Republic of China, 1987-88; recipient Robert Foster Cherry Disting. Teaching chair Baylor U., 1995-96. Mem. MLA, New Chaucer Soc., Medieval Soc. Am., Phi Beta Kappa, Phi Beta Delta. Office: Lehigh U English Dept 35 Sayre Dr Bethlehem PA 18015-3116 E-mail: pgb1@lehigh.edu.

BEIER, ANITA P., air transportation executive; BS in Bus. Adminstrn., MBA, U. Md. Economist Fed. Railroad Adminstrn., 1979—81; various fin. positions in econ. and fin. analysis, budgeting and acctg. CSX Corp., 1981—96, v.p. fin. planning, 1998; CFO Am. Comml. Lines, 1997—98; v.p., contr. US Airways Group, Inc., US Airways, Inc., Arlington, Va., 1999—2004, sr. v.p., contr., 2004—. Office: US Airways 2345 Crystal Dr Arlington VA 22227

BEIER, CAROL ANN, state supreme court justice; b. Kansas City, Kans., Sept. 27, 1958; Student, Benedictine Coll., 1976-77, The Poynter Inst., 1979; BS, U. Kans., 1981, JD, 1982-85; ML in Judicial Process, U. Va. Sch. Law, 2004. Bar: Kans., 1985, D.C., 1988; U.S. Dist. Kans., 1985; U.S. Ct. Appeals (10th cir.) 1986. With Balloun & Bodinson, Olathe, Kans., 1983; jud. clk. U.S. Ct. Appeals (10th cir.), Olathe, 1985-86; staff atty. Nat. Women's Law Ctr., Washington, 1986-87; assoc. Arent, Fox, Kintner, Plotkin & Kahn, Washington, 1987-88, Foulston & Siefkin, Wichita, Kans., 1988-93; lectr. Wichita State U., 1994—; ptnr. Foulston & Siefkin, Wichita, 1993—2000; judge Kansas Ct. of Appeals, 2000—03; justice Kans. Supreme Ct., 2003—. Dir. Kans. Defender Project, Lawrence, 1989-90, Kans. Appellate Clinic, Lawrence, 1989-90; vis. asst. prof. U. Kans. Sch. of Law, Lawrence, 1989-90, lectr. Wichita State U., 1994; fellow Georgetown Women's Law and Pub. Policy Program, Washington, 1986-87. Articles editor U. Kans. Law Rev., 1984-85. Pres. Wichita Women Atty.'s Assn., 1993-94; bd. dirs. Kans. Civil Liberties Union, Wichita, 1990-94. Recipient Bernard Kilgore award, Soc. Profl. Jours., U. Kans., 1980, Louise Mattox Atty. of Achievement award, 2003. Fellow Kans. Bar Found., ABA, Sam A. Crow inn of Ct. (master); mem. ABA, Kans. Bar Assn., D.C. Bar, Wichita Bar Assn., Women's Atty. Assn. Topeka, Order of the Coif. Office: Kansas Supreme Ct 301 W 10th Topeka KS 66612

BEIERLE, ANDREW W.M., journalist, writer; b. Bklyn., Aug. 5, 1951; s. Arthur W. and Margaret Beierle. BA, Pa. State U., University Park, 1969—73. Reporter Orlando Sentinel, Fla., 1973—77; editor, signs & symptoms Brown U., Providence, 1977—80; editor Emory mag. Emory U., Atlanta, 1980—. Author: (novels) The Winter of Our Discotheque (Lambda Lit. Award, 2002), (short stories) Pump Jockey, Rebel Yell: Stories by Contemporary Gay Southern Authors, Gravity, Harrington Gay Men's Fiction Quarterly (First runner up, Richard Hall Meml. Short Story Contest, 2001). Mem.: Coun. for Advancement and Support of Edn., Omicron Delta Kappa, Kappa Tau Alpha.

BEIERWALTES, WILLIAM HENRY, physician, educator; b. Saginaw, Mich., Nov. 23, 1916; s. John Andrew and Fanny (Aris) B.; m. Mary Martha Nichols, Jan. 1, 1942; children: Andrew George, William Howard, Martha Louise. AB, U. Mich., 1938, MD, 1941. Diplomate: Am. Bd. Internal

Medicine and Nuclear Medicine. Intern, then asst. resident medicine Cleve. City Hosp., 1941-43; mem. faculty U. Mich. Med. Center, 1944-87, prof. medicine, 1959-87, prof. emeritus, 1987—; dir. nuclear medicine, also dir. Thyroid Research Lab., 1952-86, cons., 1987-95. Cons. nuclear medicine depts. St. John Hosp., Detroit, Wm. Beaumont Hosp., Royal Oak and Troy, Mich., 1987-95, The UpJohn Co. Rsch. div., 1952-65, The Abbott Labs. Rsch. div., 1960-67; sr. med. cons. MD (Med. Fedn.), Bagdad, Iraq, 1963; mem. exec. com. Inst. Sci. and Tech., 1963; lectr. Nat. Naval Med. Ctr., 1964-88, Ctr. for Environ. Health Mich. State Dept. Health, 1988-89; Peter Heimann lectr. 34th meeting Internat. Congress Surgery, Stockholm, Sweden, 1991; adv. panel on radionuclide labeled compounds for tumor diagnosis Internat. AEC, 1974-75; mem. Mich. State Radiation Bd., 1980-84; co-chmn. Nat. Coop., Thyroid Cancer Therapy Group, 1978-81 Author: Clinical Use of Radioisotopes, 1957, Manual of Nuclear Medicine Procedures, 1971, Love of Life Autobiog. Sketches, 1996; contbr. numerous articles to profl. jours.; assoc. editor Jour. Lab. and Clin. Medicine, 1954-60; editl. bd. Jour. Nuclear Medicine, 1964-69, assoc. editor, 1975-81; editl. bd. Jour. Clin. Endocrinology and Metabolism, 1963; adv. bd. Annals of Saudi Medicine, 1986-90; patentee for monoclonal antibodies to HCG, and radionuclide in vivo biochem. imaging of endocrine glands, 1951; first to treat a patient for cancer with radio labeled antibodies, 1951; co-inventor radiopharms, 1971; originator of radioimmunodetection of human cancer; first description of cytogenetic evolution of thyroid cancer; first description of fall of serum antithyroid antibodies during pregnancy with rise after delivery, other med. techniques. Guggenheim fellow, 1966-67; Commonwealth Fund fellow, 1967; recipient Hevesy Nuc. Medicine Pioneer award, 1982, Disting. Faculty award U. Mich., 1982, Johann-Geor-Zimmerman Trust for Cancer Rsch. Sci. prize for greatest contbn. to treatment of thyroid cancer, 1983, WWJ 950 Detroit Citizen of Week award, 1994; named Internat. Man of Yr. Internat. Biog. Ctr., Cambridge, Eng., 1992-93. Mem. AMA (Outstanding Scientific Achievement award 1994), ACP, Am. Fedn. Clin. Rsch. (pres. 1954-55), Soc. Nuclear Medicine (pres. 1965-66, Disting. Educator's award 1989, The Best Doctors in Am. award 1993-95), Ctrl. Clin. Rsch. Club (pres. 1958-59), Am. Thyroid Assn. (v.p. 1964-65, 66-67, Disting. Svc. award 1972), Ctrl. Soc. Clin. Rsch. (councillor 1964-67, 67-71), Galens Med. Soc., Assn. Am. Physicians, Mich. Med. Soc., Am. Endocrine Soc., Am. Soc. Clin. Oncology. Home: Independence Village 965 Hager Dr Apt 327 Petoskey MI 49770-8748

BEIERWALTES, WILLIAM HOWARD, physiologist, educator; b. Ann Arbor, Mich., Oct. 6, 1947; s. William Henry and Mary-Martha (Nichols) B.; m. Patricia Sue Olson, July 11, 1982; children: William N., Peter L., Nora R. BA, Kalamazoo Coll., 1969; PhD, U. N.C., 1978. Instr. Mayo Med. Sch., Rochester, Minn., 1979-81; sr. staff scientist Henry Ford Hosp., Detroit, 1981—. Prof. Wayne State U. Sch. Medicine, Detroit, 2004—. Contbr. articles to profl. jours. With U.S. Army, 1971—72. Mem. Am. Physiol. Soc., Am. Heart Assn. (fellow coun. on high blood pressure 1992, fellow coun. on high blood pressure rsch. 2001, honor roll coun. on kidney 1988, chair rsch. fellowship com. Mich. chpt. 1987-90, 92-94, established investigator 1983-88), Am. Soc. Nephrology, Inter-Am. Soc. Hypertension, Mich. Soc. Med. Rsch. (bd. dirs. 1988-94, pres. 1992-94), Nat. Kidney Found. Mich. (rsch. rev. com. 1984-85, 88, 2004). Presbyterian. Avocation: collecting antique toy soldiers. Home: 750 Lakepointe St Grosse Pointe Park MI 48230-1706 Office: Henry Ford Hosp 2799 W Grand Blvd Detroit MI 48202-2689 Office Phone: 313-916-7494. Business E-Mail: wbeierw1@hfhs.org.

BEIGHEY, LAWRENCE JEROME, packaging company executive; b. Akron, Ohio, June 24, 1938; s. Jac Laverne and Martha Rose (Vestal) B.; m. Carole Anne LaFlamme, Dec. 11, 1970; children: Basil, Susan, Thomas, Timothy, Elizabeth, Anne. BS in Indsl. Engring., Pa. State U., 1960. Registered profl. engr., Pa.; cert. data processor. Mgr. internat. div. Brockway (Pa.), Inc., 1968-76, mgr. energy div., 1976-78, project mgr., 1978-79, plant mgr., 1979-81, mgr. mfg. staff and services, 1981-83; exec. v.p. Brockway Standard, Atlanta, 1983-86, pres., 1986-89; v.p. Brockway, Inc., Jacksonville, Fla., 1986-89; pres. Transition Mgmt. Resources, Atlanta, 1989; v.p., gen. mgr. All-Pak, Inc., Decatur, Ga., 1990; pres. Plastite Corp., 1990-95; mfg. cons., 1995—. Bd. dirs. Boy Scouts Am., DuBois, Pa., 1978-80, YMCA, DuBois, 1981-83; mem. sch. bd. Brockway Area Sch. Dist., 1981-83; pres. Jaycees, DuBois, 1964. Mem. Steel Shipping Container Inst. (bd. dirs. 1986), Data Processing Mgmt. Assn. (bd. dirs. 1966-68), Alpena Country Club, Amelia Island (Fla.) Ocean Club. Avocations: golf, tennis. Personal E-mail: LJBeighey@aol.com.

BEIGHLE, DOUGLAS PAUL, retired aerospace transportation executive; b. Deer Lodge, Mont., June 18, 1932; s. Douglas Paul Beighle and Clarice Janice (Driver) Kiefer; m. Gwendolen Anne Dickson, Oct. 30, 1954 (dec. Jan. 1996); children: Cheryl, Randall, Katherine, Douglas J. BS in Bus. Adminstrn., U. Mont., 1954; JD, U. Mont, 1958; LL.M., Harvard U., 1960. Bar: Mont. 1958, Wash. 1959, U.S. Supreme Ct. 1970. Assoc. Perkins & Coie, Seattle, 1960-67, ptnr., 1967-80; v.p. contracts Boeing Co., Seattle, 1980-81, v.p. contracts, gen. counsel, sec., 1981-86, sr. v.p., 1986-97; chief legal counsel Puget Energy, Inc., Bellevue, Wash., 1970-80, chair, 2002—05; exec. dir. Wash. State, U.S. West Comm., Denver, 1990-95; ret., 2005. Bd. dirs. Washington Mut. Inc., Seattle, 1989—, Simpson Investment Co., Seattle, Active Voice Corp., Seattle, Infrastrux Group, Bellevue, Wash.; bd. dirs. KCTS-9 TV, chair 1996—2005. Nat. bd. dirs. Jr. Achievement, Colorado Springs, 1981-95; bd. dirs. Greater Puget Sound Jr. Achievement, 1983—, Intiman Theatre, Seattle, 1991-93; trustee Mcpl. League Seattle, 1983-88, U. Mont. Found., Missoula, 1983-91, Mansfield Found., Missoula, 1990-95, Pacific Sci. Ctr., Seattle, 1992—, pres. 1996; trustee Corp. Coun. for the Arts, Seattle, 1994—, chair, 1995-96. 1st lt. USAF, 1954-56. Harvard U. Law Sch. fellow, 1959 Mem. Wash. State Bar Assn. (chmn. adminstrv. law sect. 1979-80), Nat. Assn. Mfrs. (bd. dirs., regional vice chmn. 1988-93), Greater Seattle C. of C. (chair 1994-95), Rainier Club Seattle, Seattle Yacht Club. Republican. Presbyterian. Office: 1000 2nd Ave Ste 3700 Seattle WA 98104-1053

BEIHL, FREDERICK, retired lawyer; b. St. Joseph, Mo., Jan. 26, 1932; s. Ernst F. and Evelyn E. (Kline) B.; m. Lillis Prater, Mar. 3, 1962. AB, U. Mo., 1953, LLB, 1955. Bar: Mo. 1955, U.S. Supreme Ct. 1968. With Shook Hardy & Bacon, Kansas City, 1955-99, ptnr., 1961-99, shareholder, 1992-99; ret., 1999. Chmn. bd. dirs. UMKC Conservatory of Music, Kansas City, 1988-91, Visiting Nurses Assn., Kansas City, 1977-79; pres. Heart of Am. Family and Children Svcs., Kansas City, 1982-84, Friends of Art Nelson Mus., Kansas City, 1979-81. Avocations: tennis, skiing, art collecting. Office: Shook Hardy & Bacon 2555 Grand Blvd Kansas City MO 64108-2613 Business E-Mail: fbeihl@shb.com.

BEILENSON, PETER LOWELL, public health official; b. L.A., Feb. 6, 1960; s. Anthony Charles and Dolores (Martin) B.; m. Christina Weininger; children: Valerie, Alex, Jane, Jack. AB, Harvard U., 1981; MD, Emory U., 1987; MPH, Johns Hopkins U., 1990. Family practice intern U. Md., Balt., 1987-88; resident in preventive medicine Johns Hopkins U., Balt., 1989-91, chief resident, 1991-92; commr. Balt. City Health Dept., 1992—. Mem. AMA, APHA (Milton and Ruth Roemer award for creative pub. health 1996). Avocations: sports, coaching youth sports. Office: Balt City Health Dept 210 Guilford Ave Baltimore MD 21202-3621 E-mail: pbeilenson@baltimorecity.gov.

BEILMAN, GREG J., medical educator, researcher; b. Kans. MD, U. Kans. Assoc. prof. surgery U. Minn., Mpls., 1995—. Col. USAR. Office: Univ Minnesota 420 Delaware St SE Minneapolis MN 55455 Office Phone: 612-625-7911.

BEIM, DAVID ODELL, investment banker, educator; b. Mpls., June 2, 1940; s. Raymond Nelson and Moana (Odell) B.; m. Elizabeth Lucile Artz, Aug. 29, 1964; children— Amy Marie, Nicholas Frederick. BA with honors, Stanford U., 1963; MPhil (Rhodes scholar), Oxford (Eng.) U., 1965. With First Boston Corp., N.Y.C., 1966-75, v.p., 1971-75, head project finance, 1973-75; exec. v.p. Export-Import Bank U.S., Washington, 1975-77; head corp. fin. Bankers Trust Co., N.Y.C., 1978-87, sr. v.p., 1978-79, exec. v.p., 1979-86, mem. mgmt. com., 1986-87; mng. dir. Dillon Read & Co., 1987-89; prof. Bus. Sch. Columbia U., N.Y.C., 1990—; dir., audit com. chair, Cluster D Funds Merrill Lynch Investment Mgrs., 2001—. Chmn. Wave Hill, Inc.; trustee Phillips Exeter Acad. Mem. Coun. Fgn. Rels. Home: 4684 Dodgewood Rd Bronx NY 10471-3604 Office: Columbia U Uris Hall 711 New York NY 10027

BEIM, NORMAN, playwright, actor, theater director, writer; b. Newark; s. Herman and Frieda (Thau) B.; m. Virginia Rapkin (div.). Student, Ohio State U., Hedgerow Theatre Sch., Phila., Inst. Contemporary Art, Washington. Appeared in Broadway play Inherit the Wind, 1956-58, off-Broadway play Coriolanus, 1953, Black Visions, 1973; nat. touring prodn. Tribute, 1980; plays include The Deserter, (Samuel French award) 1979, Success, 1983, Pygmalion and Galatea, 1984, Archie's Comeback, 1986, Jewel Thieves, 1990, On a Darkling Plain (James Ellis Meml. award 1992), Death Amid the Rich and Famous, 1991, Cri de Coeur, 1991, Dreams (No Empty Theater New Play award 1993), Shakespeare Revisited (Maxim Mazumdar New Play award 1993); author: Six Award Winning Plays, Plays at Home and Abroad, My Family, The Jewish Immigrants, 1997, (novel) Hymie and the Angel, 1998, Giants of the Old Testament, 2001, Infamous People, 2004. Mem. Bronx Coun. of the Arts. Served with F.A. U.S. Army. Mem. SAG, AFTRA, Dramatists Guild Am., Actors Equity Assn. Home: 425 W 57th St New York NY 10019-1764 Office Phone: 212-265-6284. Personal E-mail: normanbeim@aol.com.

BEINART, PETER, editor; BA, Yale Univ, 1993; MPh, University Coll, Oxford, England, 1995. Mng editor The New Republic, 1995—97, sr editor, 1997—99, editor, 1999—. Columnist Washington Post, Time Magazine. Contbr. columns in newspapers, commentary on CNN, NPR, PBS and other radio & TV programs. Rhodes scholar, Marshall scholar (declined). Office: The New Republic Suite 700 1331 H St NW Washington DC 20005*

BEINECKE, CANDACE KRUGMAN, lawyer; b. Paterson, N.J., Nov. 26, 1946; d. Martin and Sylvia (Altshuler) Krugman; m. Frederick W. Beinecke II, Oct. 2, 1976; children: Jacob Sperry, Benjamin Barrett. BA, NYU, 1967; JD, Rutgers U., 1970. Bar: N.Y. 1971. Assoc., then ptnr. Hughes, Hubbard & Reed, N.Y.C., 1970—, chair, 1999—. Bd. dirs. First Eagle Funds, N.Y.C., 1996—, chair bd. dirs., 2004—; bd. dirs. ASTROM, 2001—. Bd. dirs. Merce Cunningham Found., N.Y.C., Jacob's Pillow Dance Festival, Lee, Mass., The N.Y.C. Partnership; mem. vis. com. Met. Mus. Art Watson Libr. Mem. ABA, Assn. Bar City of N.Y., River Club, Women's Forum. Office: Hughes Hubbard & Reed One Battery Park Plaza New York NY 10004-1466

BEINECKE, FREDERICK WILLIAM, investment company executive; b. Stamford, Conn., June 3, 1943; s. William S. and Elizabeth (Gillespie) B.; m. Candace Krugman, Oct. 2, 1976; children— Jacob Sperry, Benjamin Barrett BA, Yale U., 1966; JD, U. Va., 1972; PMD, Harvard U., 1977. Bar: N.Y. 1973. Assoc. firm Hughes Hubbard & Reed, N.Y.C., 1972-73; gen. counsel South Street Seaport Mus., N.Y.C., 1973-75; with Sperry and Hutchinson Co., N.Y.C., 1975-82; pres. Gunlocke Co. subs., 1979-80, corp. v.p., 1977-80, pres., 1980-82, dir., 1977-82; pres. Antaeus Enterprises, Inc., 1982—, also bd. dirs. Chmn. bd. Catalina Mktg. Corp. Trustee Phillips Acad., Andover, Mass., 1980—2000, Wildlife Conservation Soc., 1984—, Outward Bound USA, 1987—2000; trustee coun. Nat. Gallery of Art, 2004—; trustee Sterling and Francine Clark Art Inst., 2000—, Trudeau Inst., Saranac Lake, NY, 1971—98, chmn., 1984—91, 1995—97, chmn. emeritus, 1998—2004; bd. dirs. Close Encounters with Music, 1995—, pres., 1995—2003; bd. dirs. Prospect Hill Found., 1962—, Samuel H. Kress Found., 1997—, N.Y.C. Ballet, 1978—88, 1992—2000, 2001—, pres., 2003—; bd. dirs. Sperry Fund, 1977—, pres., 1982—; bd. visitors Yale Sch. Music, New Haven, 1997—. Capt. USMC, 1966—69. Decorated Bronze Star. Mem. Assn. Bar City N.Y., River Club, Sky Club, Yale Club, Hollenbeck Club, Clove Valley Club, Knickerbocker Club. Office: Antaeus Enterprises Rm 2200 99 Park Ave New York NY 10016-1601

BEINECKE, WILLIAM SPERRY, retired consumer products company executive; b. N.Y.C., May 22, 1914; s. Frederick William and Carrie (Sperry) B.; m. Elizabeth Barrett Gillespie, May 24, 1941; children: Frederick W. II, John B., Sarah S., Frances G. BA, Yale U., 1936, MA (hon.), 1971; LL.B., Columbia U., 1940; LL.D. (hon.), Southwestern U., 1967, Cath. U. Am., 1972, Yale U., 1986. Former asso. firm Chadbourne, Wallace, Parke & Whiteside; co-founder firm Casey, Beinecke & Chase; became gen. counsel The Sperry and Hutchinson Co., N.Y.C., 1952, v.p., 1954-60, pres., 1960-67, chmn. bd., chief exec. officer, 1967-80. Bd. dirs. Antaeus Enterprises, Inc. Chmn. bd. dirs. The Prospect Hill Found.; chmn. emeritus Hudson River Found. for Sci. and Environ. Rsch.; bd. dirs. The Sperry Fund; hon. trustee Am. Mus. Natural History, The Pingry Sch.; life trustee Ctrl. Park Conservancy. Served to comdr. USNR, World War II. Recipient Alumni medal Alumni Fedn. Columbia U., 1971, Yale medal, 2000, Frederick Law Olmsted award, 1986. Mem. Yale U. Club, Sky Club, Baltusrol Golf Club, Eastward Ho Country Club, Gulf Stream Golf Club, Ocean Club, Little Club. Home: 21 E 79th St New York NY 10021-0125 Office: Antaeus Enterprises Inc 99 Park Ave #2200 New York NY 10016-1601 Office Phone: 212-370-1144.

BEINEKE, LOWELL WAYNE, mathematics professor; b. Decatur, Ind., Nov. 20, 1939; s. Elmer Henry and Lillie Agnes (Snell) B.; m. Judith Rowena Wooldridge, Dec. 23, 1967; children: Jennifer Elaine, Philip Lennox. BS, Purdue U., 1961; MA, U. Mich., 1962, PhD, 1965. Asst. prof. Purdue U., Ft. Wayne, Ind., 1965-68, assoc. prof., 1968-71, prof., 1971-86, Jack W. Schrey prof., 1986—. Tutor Oxford (Eng.) U., 1974, The Open U., Milton Keynes, England, 1974, 75; vis. lectr. Poly. North London, 1980—81; vis. scholar Wolfson Coll., Oxford U., 1993—94, 2000—01; mem. SCR Keble Coll., 2000—01. Co-author (co-editor): Selected Topics in Graph Theory, 3 vols., 1978, 1983, 1988, Applications of Graph Theory, 1979, Graph Connections, 1997, Topics in Algebraic Graph Theory, 2004; assoc. editor Jour. Graph Theory, 1977—80, mem. editl. bd., 1977—, Internat. Jour. Graph Theory, 1991—95; editor: The Coll. Math. Jour.; co-editor: Congressus Numerantium, Vols., 1963—64, 1988; contbr. numerous articles to profl. jours. Corp. mem. Bd. for Homeland Ministries, United Ch. of Christ, N.Y., 1988-91, del. Gen. Synod, 1989, 91. Recipient Outstanding Tchr. award AMOCO Found., 1978, Friends of the Univ., 1992, Outstanding Rsch. award Ind. U.-Purdue U. Ft. Wayne, 1999; Fulbright Found. grantee London, 1980-81, rsch. grantee Office Naval Rsch., Washington, 1986-89; fellow Inst. Combinatorics and its Applications, 1990—. Mem. AAUP, Math. Assn. Am. (chairperson Ind. Sect. 1987-88, bd. govs. 1990-93, 2004—, Disting. Tchg. award Ind. Sect. 1997, Disting. Svc. award Ind. sect. 1998), Am. Math. Soc., London Math. Soc., Common Cause, Amnesty Internat., Summit Book Club, Internat. Affairs Forum, Sigma Xi (club pres. 1984-86, chpt. pres. 1997-98), Phi Kappa Phi (chpt. pres. 1993), Pi Mu Epsilon. Achievements include characterization of line graphs and thickness of complete graphs; enumeration of multidimensional trees. Home: 4529 Bradwood Ter Fort Wayne IN 46815-6028 Office: Ind U-Purdue U Dept of Math Scis 2101 E Coliseum Blvd Fort Wayne IN 46805-1445 Office Phone: 260-481-6223. Business E-Mail: beineke@ipfw.edu.

BEIRNE, MARTIN DOUGLAS, lawyer; b. NYC, Oct. 24, 1944; s. Martin Douglas and Catherine Anne Beirne; m. Kathleen Harrington; children: Martin, Shannon, Kelley. BS, Spring Hill Coll., 1966; JD with honors, St. Mary's U., 1969. Bar: Tex. 1969, U.S. Dist. Ct. (ea. dist.) Tex. 1972, U.S. Dist. Ct. (so. dist.) Tex. 1971, U.S. Dist. Ct. (no. dist.) Tex., U.S. Dist. Ct. (we. dist.) Tex., U.S. Dist. Ct. DC, U.S. Ct. Appeals (5th and 11th cirs.) 1974, U.S. Dist. Ct. (ea. dist.) Calif., U.S. Supreme Ct. 1975. Ptnr. Fulbright & Jaworski, Houston, 1971-85; mng. ptnr. Beirne, Maynard & Parsons, Houston, 1985—. Editor-in-chief St. Mary's Law Rev. Bd. dirs. St. Thomas U., Houston Law Rev. Found., NCCJ. Capt. U.S. Army, 1969-71. Fellow Am. Bar Found., Tex. Bar Found.; mem. ABA, Tex. Bar Assn., Houston Bar Assn., Coronado Club, Houstonian Club, Legatus-U. Houston Law Sch. Found. Am. Law Inst., Inst. for Transnat. Arbitration, Houston Bar Found. (bd. dirs.). Roman Catholic. Office: Beirne Maynard & Parsons LLP 1300 Post Oak Blvd Fl 25 Houston TX 77056-3028 Office Phone: 713-623-0887.

BEIRNE, OWEN ROSS, dental educator, researcher; b. Santa Maria, Calif., Jan. 18, 1947; s. Owen and Themla Beirne; m. Sheryl Martha Schochet; children: Samuel, Deborah. BA, U. Calif., Berkeley, 1968; DMD, Harvard U., 1972; PhD, U. Calif., San Francisco, 1979. Cert. in oral and maxillofacial surgery, diplomate Am. Bd. Oral and Maxillofacial Surgery, Nat. Dental Bd. Anesthesiology. Asst. prof. U. Calif., San Francisco, 1979—85, assoc. prof., 1985—85; assoc. prof. Sch. Dentistry U. Wash., Seattle, 1985—93, prof., 1993—, dir. residency tng. dept. oral and maxillofacial surgery, 1985—99, chmn. dept. oral and maxillofacial surgery, 1999—. Mem. oral biology and medicine II study sect. Nat. Inst. Dental Rsch., Bethesda, Md., 1988—91; abstract reviewer Internat. Jour. Oral and Maxillofacial Implants, 1988—, cons., 1989—, ADA Commn. Dental Accreditation, Chgo., 1997—2003; mem. examination com. Am. Bd. Oral and Maxillofacial Surgery, 1997—2001. Sect. editor Principles of Oral and Maxillofacial Surgery, 1992; contbr. articles to profl. jours., chpts. to books; assoc. editor: Jour. Oral Implantology, 1992—; mem. editl. bd. Jour. Evidence Based Dental Practice, 2001—. Mem. editl. bd. Anesthesia Progress, 2003—; mem. boundary com. Northshore Sch. Dist., Bothell, 1996—98. Recipient Distinction in Tchg. award, U. Calif.-San Francisco, 1984. Fellow: Am. Coll. Dentists, Am. Dental Soc. Anesthesiology (pres. Wash. State 1996—2005); mem.: Am. Assn. Oral and Maxillofacial Surgeons (chmn. adv. com. on rsch. and tech. 1999—2000), Am. Assn. Dental Rsch. (councilor 1992—2004), Phi Beta Kappa, Omicron Kappa Upsilon (pres. Supreme chpt. 2000—01). Office: Univ Washington Oral Maxillofacial Surgery Box 357134 Seattle WA 98195-7134 Business E-Mail: slsb@u.washington.edu.

BEISNER, JOHN HERBERT, lawyer; b. Salina, Kans., Feb. 24, 1953; s. Herbert J. and Matilda (Cordel) B.; m. Diane G. Klinke, Apr. 26, 1980; 1 child, Laura Ann. BA with honors, U. Kans., 1975; JD with honors, U. Mich, 1978. Bar: Calif. 1978, U.S. Dist. Ct., Central Dist. Calif., 1978, D.C. 1980, U.S. Dist. Ct., DC 1980, U.S. Supreme Ct., 1985. Assoc. O'Melveny & Myers LLP, Washington, 1978-85, ptnr., 1985—, mng. ptnr., Washington office, 2000—, office head, class action practice, mem. policy com. Mem. Litigation Dept. of Yr. American Lawyer; lectr. in field. Contbr. articles to profl. jours.; administrv. editor Mich. Law Review, 1977—78, assoc. editor, 1976—77. Mem. State Colls. Coord. Com. Kans. Bd. Regents, 1974-75. Mem. ABA, DC Bar, State Bar Calif., Am. Law Inst., Fed. Comm. Bar Assn., Phi Beta Kappa. Office: O'Melveny & Myers LLP 1625 Eye St NW Washington DC 20006-4001 Office Phone: 202-383-5370. Office Fax: 202-383-5414. Business E-Mail: jbeisner@omm.com.*

BEISSER, WILLIAM CONRAD, secondary school educator, painter; b. Fort Dodge, Iowa, Feb. 21, 1960; s. Louie Fredrick and Corrine Anne Beisser; m. Chunli Zhang, Mar. 18, 2002; children: Jessica, Allen Fredrick. BA in Spl. Studies with honors and distinction in ceramics, Cornell Coll., Mount Vernon, Iowa, 1983. Cert. secondary tchr. Ariz. Dept. Edn., 2002, indsl. arts Ariz. Dept. Edn., 2002, music Ariz. Dept. Edn., 2002, art Ariz. Dept. Edn., 2002. Art tchr. Mesa (Ariz.) Sch. Dist., 2001—02; indsl. arts, music and art tchr. Paridise Valley Unified Sch. Dist. #69, Phoenix, 2002—. Chair attendance com. Phoenix Unified Sch. Dist., 1999—2000. Prin. works include Large Cactus. At-risk student mentor Paradise Valley Unified Sch. Dist. #96, Phoenix, 2002—. Mem.: Ariz. Edn. Assn. (assoc.). Independent-Republican. Christian. Avocations: painting, travel, photography, guitar, swimming. Office: Polaris High Sch 3950 East Bell Rd Phoenix AZ 85032 Office Phone: 602-787-5015. Office Fax: 602-867-5153. Personal E-mail: wbeisser@hotmail.com.

BEISTLINE, EARL HOOVER, mining consultant; b. Juneau, Alaska, Nov. 24, 1916; s. Ralph H. and Catherine (Krinach) B.; m. Dorothy Ann Hering, Aug. 24, 1946; children— Ralph Robert, William Calvin, Katherine Noreen, Lynda Marie. B. Mining Engring., U. Alaska, 1939, E.M., 1947, LL.D. (hon.), 1969. Mem. faculty U. Alaska, 1946-82, dean Sch. Mines, 1949-61, dean Coll. Earth Sci. and Mineral Industry, 1961-75, provost Coll. Earth Sci. and Mineral Industry, 1970-75, exec. officer no. region, 1970-73, dean Sch. Mineral Industry, 1975-82, dean emeritus, prof. mining engring. Sch. Mineral Industry, 1982—; mining cons. Served to maj. AUS, 1941-46. Fellow AAAS, Explorers Club; mem. NSPE, Am. Inst. Mining and Metall. Engrs., Mining and Metall. Soc. Am., Arctic Inst. N.Am., Am. Soc. Engring. Edn., N.W. Mining Assn., Alaska Mining Assn., Pioneers of Alaska. Home and Office: PO Box 80148 Fairbanks AK 99708-0148

BEITLER, STEPHEN, investment company executive, venture capitalist; s. Stanley and Arline Beitler; m. Deborah, Jan. 1982; children: Grace, Elinore. BA, cert. Asian Study, Am. U. Sch. Internat. Studies, 1977; postgrad., U. Chgo., 1977—78; MS, Def. Intelligence Coll., 1986. Legis. aide U.S. Ho. Reps., Washington, 1975—77; commd. 2d lt. U.S. Army, 1977, advanced through grades to maj., 1989; intelligence briefing officer Sec. Def. and Chmn. Joint Chiefs of Staff, Washington, 1984—86; asst. to asst. sec. of def. Office Sec. Def., Washington, 1987—88, asst. to undersec. of def., 1988—89; resigned U.S. Army, 1989; mgr. ops. devel. Helene Curtis, Inc., Chgo., 1989—90, corp. mgr. strategy and devel., 1990—92, dir. strategy and devel., 1993; nat. mgr. operational planning and info. Sears Merchandise Group, Hoffman Estates, Ill., 1993—95; sr. dir. fin. processes and sys. Sears, Roebuck and Co., Hoffman Estates, 1995—97, asst. corp. contr., 1997—98, v.p. Chgo., 1998; sr. mng. dir., gen. ptnr. Trident Capital, Chgo., 1998—2002; gen. ptnr., sr. mng. dir. Dunrath Capital, Chgo., 2002—. Comdr. 305th psychol. ops. bn. USAR, Arlington Heights, Ill., 1992-96; comdr. 16th psychol. ops. bn. USAR, Ft. Sheridan, Ill., 1996-98; cons. MGA, Inc., Chgo., 1985—; founding chmn. Conf. Bd. Coun. Competitive Analysis; former bd. dirs. Brightroom, Inc.; bd. dirs. ReachMD Inc.; bd. adv. ARXAN, Inc., Salon 123 Inc., Questra Inc.; former bd. observer The Revere Group, Ltd; entrepreneurial adv. bd. Grad. Sch. Bus., Univ. Chgo., 2003—. Contbg. author: The Military Intelligence Community, 1986; contbr. articles to profl. publs. Bd. dirs. United Way of Highland Park-Highwood, 1999-2002; vol. Bus. Vols. for Arts, Chgo., 1991-94; bd. dirs. Spl. Ops. Warrior Found. Decorated Green Beret for valor and svc. Fellow Inter-univ. Seminar on Armed Forces and Soc., Soc. Competitive Intelligence Profls. (bd. dirs. 1991-94), Ill. Venture Capital Assn. (founding mem., bd. dirs., sec. 2001, vice chmn. 2002, chmn. 2003-2004); mem. Spl. Forces Club, Army and Navy Club, Union League Club Chgo., Execs. Club Chgo., Fin. Execs. Inst., The Birchwood Club, Carleton Club, Met. Club City of Washington D.C., Economic Club Chgo. Office Phone: 888-287-3459. Business E-Mail: steve@dunrath.com.

BEITTENMILLER, J. GORDON, small business owner; CFO, exec. v.p., treas. Comfort Sys. USA, Inc., Houston. Office: Comfort Syss USA Inc Ste 500 777 Post Oak Blvd Houston TX 77056

BEIZER, LANCE KURT, priest, lawyer; b. Hartford, Conn., Sept. 8, 1938; s. Lawrence Sidney and Victoria Merriam (Kaplan) B. BA in Sociology, Brandeis U., 1960; MA in English, San Jose State U., 1967; JD, U. San Diego, 1975; MDiv, Ch. Divinity Sch. Pacific, 2005. Bar: Calif. 1975; Ordained to ministry Episcopal Ch. as priest, 2005. Selective svc. affairs coord. U. Calif., 1969-73, vet. affairs coord., 1973-75; vet. outreach coord. San Diego Community Coll. Dist., 1975-76; dep. dist. atty. Santa Clara County, Calif., 1976—2002; Episcopal priest, 2005—. Bd. mgrs. Santa Clara Valley S.W. YMCA, Saratoga, Calif., 1988—, chair, 1991-93; bd. dirs. Lumen Found., San Francisco, 1985—; bd. dirs. Fedn. Cmty. Ministries, Calif., 1992—, chmn., 1996—. Lt. USNR, 1961-65. Mem. Nat. Assn. Counsel for Children, Am. Weil Soc., Mensa, Commonwealth Club. Republican. Episcopalian. Office: PO Box 1121 Campbell CA 95009-1121 Personal E-mail: lbeizer@yahoo.com.

BEJ, EMIL, retired dean; b. Stryj, Ukraine, Apr. 26, 1925; U.S., 1949; m. Vera A. Szwabiuk, Oct. 7, 1961; children: Mark D., Andrew E. JD, Abitur, LLB, Ukrainian Free U., Munich, 1949, 1962; BA Comml. Sci., Detroit Bus. Inst., 1957; MA in Econ., U. Detroit, 1966; PhD in Econ. cum laude, Ukrainian Free U., 1970. From asst. prof. to prof. Shippensburg (Pa.) U., 1969-98; assoc. dean faculty law and econ. Ukrainian Free U., 1995-97. Vis. prof. U. Manitoba, Winnipeg, Canada, 1976, Ukrainian Free U., 1974, 79, 81, 1994—98, Dickinson Coll., Carlisle, Pa., 1983, Lviv (Ukraine) Inst. Mgmt.,

1992. Author: Outline of Economic Geography of Ukraine, 1977, Theory of International Integration, 1985, Political Economy of European Communities, 1992, International Economics Theory, 1995; mem. editl. bd. Studien zu Nationalitatenfragen, 1986—94; contbr. articles to profl. jours. Fellow, Shippensburg U., 1992. Mem.: Ukrainian Acad. Arts and Scis., Internat. Social Sci. Honor Soc. (life). Home: 9730 Alvin Dr Shippensburg PA 17257-9228

BEJA, MORRIS, English literature educator; b. NYC, July 18, 1935; s. Joseph and Eleanor (Cohen) B.; children: Andrew Lloyd, Eleni Rachel; m. Ellen Carol Jones, 1990. BA, CCNY, 1957; MA, Columbia U., 1958; PhD, Cornell U., 1963. From instr. to prof. English Ohio State U., Columbus, 1961-2000, prof. emeritus, 2001—. Vis. prof. U. Thessaloniki, Greece, 1965-66, Univ. Coll. Dublin, 1972-73. Author: Epiphany in the Modern Novel, 1971, Film and Literature, 1979, Joyce the Artist Manqué and Indeterminacy, 1989, James Joyce: A Literary Life, 1992; editor: Virginia Woolf's Mrs. Dalloway, 1996, Joyce in the Hibernian Metropolis, 1996, Perspectives on Orson Welles, 1995, Samuel Beckett: Humanistic Perspectives, 1983, James Joyce Newestlatter, 1977—, James Joyce's Dubliners and Portrait of the Artist, 1973; editor: (with E.C. Jones) Twenty-First Joyce, 2004. Pres. Internat. James Joyce Found., 1982-90, sec. 1990—; dir. Internat. James Joyce Symposia, 1982, 86, 92, 2004. With USAR, 1958-63. Guggenheim fellow, 1972-73; Fulbright lectr., 1965-66, 72-73. Mem. MLA, Internat. Virginia Woolf Soc. (trustee 1976-84), Am. Conf. Irish Studies. Jewish. Avocations: photography, travel, bicycling. Home: 1135 Middleport Dr Columbus OH 43235-4060 Office: Ohio State U Dept of English 164 W 17th Ave Columbus OH 43210-1326 E-mail: beja.1@osu.edu.

BEJAN, ADRIAN, mechanical engineering educator; b. Sept. 24, 1948; married; 3 children. SB in Mech. Engring., SM in Mech. Engring., MIT, 1972, PhD Mech. Engring., 1975; PhD (hon.), Poly. U. Bucharest, 1992, U. Galati, Romania, 1995, U. Constantza, 1997. Engr. Sci. Energy Systems, Inc., Watertown, Mass., 1972; rsch. asst. dept. mech. engring. MIT, 1971-74, lectr., rsch. assoc., dept. mech. engring., 1975-76; fellow Miller Inst. Basic Rsch. Sci., U. Calif., Berkeley, 1976-78; asst. prof., dept. mech. engring. U. Colo., Boulder, 1978-81; Croft prof. U. Colo. Coll. Engring., 1981-82; assoc. prof., dept. mech. engring. U. Colo., Boulder, 1981-84; prof., dept. mech. engring. and materials sci. Duke U., Durham, NC, 1984-89, J.A. Jones prof., dept. mech. engring., 1989—. Author: Entropy Generation Through Heat and Fluid Flow, 1982, Convection Heat Transfer, 1984, 2d edit., 1995, Advanced Engineering Thermodynamics, 1988, Heat Transfer, 1993, Entropy Generation Minimization, 1996; co-author: Convection in Porous Media, 1992, Thermal Design and Optimization, 1996; hon. editorial bd.: International Journal of Heat and Mass Transfer, 1992, International Communications in Heat and Mass Transfer, 1992, Termotehnica, 1993; bd. editors: Internat. Journal for Engineering Analysis and Design; adv. editor: Heat Transfer Japanese Rsch., 1990, Internat. Jour. Heat and Fluid Flow, 1988, Numerical Heat Transfer, 1995, Jour. Non-Equilibrium Thermodynamics, 1996, Energy-The Internat. Jour., 1997, Revue Générale de Thermique, 1997; reviewer manuscrips for numerous jours.; contbr. over 260 articles to profl. jours. Recipient Ralph R. Teetor award Soc. Automotive Engrs., 1980, De Florez award MIT, 1969, Heat Transfer Meml. award, 1994, Worcester Reed Warner medal 1996; Faculty fellow U. Colo., 1984-85; F. Mosey Vis. scholar U. Western Australia. Fellow ASME (Gustus L. Larson award 1988, James Harry Potter Gold medal 1990); mem. Am. Acad. Mechanics, Tau Beta Pi, Pi Tau Sigma. Office: Duke U Box 90300 Dept Mech Engring Sc Durham NC 27708-0300 Office Phone: 919-660-5309. Business E-Mail: dalford@duke.edu.

BEKAVAC, NANCY YAVOR, academic administrator, lawyer; b. Pitts., Aug. 28, 1947; d. Anthony Joseph and ELvira (Yavor) Bekavac. BA, Swarthmore Coll., 1969; JD, Yale U., 1973. Bar: Calif. 1974, U.S. Dist. Ct. (cen. dist.) Calif. 1974, U.S. Dist. Ct. (no. dist.) Calif. 1975, U.S. Ct. Appeals (9th cir.) 1975, U.S. Dist. Ct. (so. dist.) Calif. 1976, U.S. Surpeme Ct. 1979, U.S. Ct. Appeals (8th cir.) 1981. Law clk. at large U.S. Ct. Appeals (D.C. cir.), Washington, 1973-74; assoc. Munger, Tolles & Rickershauser, L.A., 1974-79, ptnr., 1980-85; exec. dir. Thomas J. Watson Found., Providence, 1985-87, cons., 1987-88; counselor to pres. Dartmouth Coll., Hanover, N.H., 1988-90; pres. Scripps Coll., Claremont, Calif., 1990—. Adj. prof. law UCLA Law Sch., 1982—83; mem. Calif. Higher Edn. Roundtable, 1996—; trustee Am. Coun. Edn., 1994—97; bd. dir. Electro Rent Corp. Author: (books) Imagining the Real Future, 1996. Bd. mgrs. Swathmore Coll., 1984—; trustee Wenner-Gren Found. Anthrop. Rsch., 1987—94; bd. trustees Am. Coun. Edn., 1994—97; chair Assn. Ind. Colls. and Univs., 1996—97. Recipient Human Rights award, LA County Commn. Civil Rights, 1984; fellow Woodrow Wilson fellow, Thomas J. Watson fellow, 1969. Mem.: WestEd. (bd. dir.), Women's Coll. Coalition, Am. Assn. Ind. Calif. Colls. and Univs. (chair 1996), Commn. on White House Fellowships (chmn., selection com. 1993—94), Seaver Found. (bd. dir.), Sierra Club. Avocations: hiking, reading, travel. Office: Scripps Coll Office of Pres 1030 Columbia Ave Claremont CA 91711-3986

BEKEY, GEORGE ALBERT, computer scientist, educator; b. Bratislava, Slovakia, June 19, 1928; arrived in U.S., 1945, naturalized, 1956; s. Andrew and Elizabeth Bekey; m. Shirley White, June 10, 1951; children: Ronald Steven, Michelle Elaine. BS with honors, U. Calif., Berkeley, 1950; MS, UCLA, 1952, PhD, 1962. Rsch. engr. UCLA, 1950-54; mgr. computer ctr. Beckman Instruments, LA and Berkeley, Calif., 1955-58; mem. sr. staff, dir. computer ctr. TRW Systems Group, Redondo Beach, Calif., 1958-62; mem. faculty U. So. Calif., LA, 1962—, prof. elec. and biomed. engring. and computer sci., 1968—2003, chmn. dept. elec. engring. systems, 1978-86, dir. Robotics Lab., 1983-98, chmn. computer sci. dept., 1984-89, dir. Ctr. for Mfg. and Automation Rsch., 1987-94, assoc. dean Sch. Engring., 1996-2001. Chair computer sci. Gordon Marshall, 1990—2002; cons. to govt. agys. and indsl. orgns. Author (with W. J. Karplus): Hybrid Computation, 1968; author: (with K. Goldberg) Robotics and Neural Networks, 1994; author: Autonomous Robots, 2005; editor: 6 books; mem. editl. bd.: 3 profl. jours., founding editor: IEEE Trans. Robotics and Automation; contbr. articles to profl. jours.; editor-in-chief Autonomous Robots Jour. With U.S. Army, 1954—56. Recipient Disting. Faculty award, 1977, Sch. Engring. Svc. award, U. So. Calif., 1990, Presdl. medallion, 2000, Engelberger prize in robotics, 2001. Fellow: IEEE (3d Millennium medal 2000), AAAS, Am. Assn. Artificial Intelligence, Am. Inst. Med. and Biol. Engring.; mem.: NAE, Biomed. Engring. Soc., Soc. Computer Simulation, Assn. Computing Machinery, IEEE Robotics and Automation Soc. (pres. 1996—97, Pioneer in Robotics and Automation award 2002, Disting. Svc. award 2004), Tau Beta Pi, Eta Kappa Nu. Achievements include patents in field. Office: U So Calif Computer Sci Dept Los Angeles CA 90089-0781

BEKKER, ALEX Y., anesthesiologist, educator; b. Thilisi, Georgia, USSR, Apr. 18, 1953; came to U.S., 1978; s. Anatoly and Plly (Kapustinsky) B.; m. Karen Dorros, Aug. 17, 1986; children: Andrew, Tanya, William. MS in Chemistry, Thilisi State U., 1975; PhD in Biomed. Engring., N.J. Inst. Tech., 1987; MD, U. Medicine and Dentisty N.J., 1991. Diplomate Am. Bd. Anesthesiology. Intern St. Joseph's Hosp. and Med. Ctr., Paterson, N.J.; resident Columbia-Presbyn. Med. Ctr., N.Y.C.; rsch. chemist Inst. Stable Isotopes, Thilisi, 1975-78; vis. scholar Columbia U., N.Y.C., 1979-81; rsch. engr. Allied-Signal Corp., Morristown, N.J., 1981-86; resident Columbia-Presbyn. Med. Ctr., N.Y.C., 1991-95; asst. prof. NYU Med. Ctr., N.Y.C., 1995—; dir. Neuroanesthesia Svc., 1995—. Lectr. Glaxo-Wellcome, Research Triangle Park, N.C., 1997—. Contbr. articles to profl. jours.; patentee in field. Bd. adv. Starting Place, Inc., Pearl River, N.Y., 1987—. Am. Heart Assn. fellow, 1987-88; N.J. Inst. Tech. scholar, 1986; Rsch. grantee Glaxo-Wellcome, Research Triangle Park, N.C., Sanofi Pharms., N.Y.C., Merck Co., N.Y.C. Mem. Am. Soc. Anesthesiologists, Internat. Anesthesia Rsch. Soc., Soc. TEch. Anesthesiology, Soc. Intravenous Anesthesiology, Tau Beta Pi. Avocations: soccer, tennis, computer analysis. Office: NYU Med Ctr 550 1st Ave New York NY 10016-6402 E-mail: abekkes@anes.med.nyu.edu.

BEKKERS, JOHN, food products company executive; b. Arnhem, The Netherlands; arrived in U.S., 1962, naturalized, 1983; Student, The Netherlands, Harbor Jr. Coll., San Pedro, Calif.; grad., Duke U. Dir. Poultry Group Mgmt. Sys., Atlanta, 1985-87; mgr. N.E. Ala. Poultry divsn. Boaz, 1987-94, exec. v.p., 1994-95; exec. v.p., mem. exec. com. Gold Kist Inc., Atlanta, pres., COO, 1995—2001, pres., CEO, 2001—. With U.S. Army, Vietnam. Office: Gold Kist Inc 244 Perimeter Ctr Pkwy NE Atlanta GA 30346*

BEKRENEV, ANATOLIY, physicist; b. Shuya, Russia, Feb. 24, 1944; s. Nikolai and Anna Bekrenev; m. Ludmila Kudysh, Sept. 16, 1972; children: Vlada, Sergei. MS, Petrozavodsk State U., Russia, 1966; PhD, Kharkov State U., Ukraine, 1971; DSc, Materials Sci. Inst., Ukraine, 1985. From asst. prof. to 1st v.p. Samara State Tech. U., 1970—96; cons. Phys. Tech. Co., 1996—99; prof. Nat. Am. U., 1999—. Author: Small-angle X-ray Scattering, 1991, Post Deformation Processes, 1992, Physics Problems with Solutions, 1996, Diffusion Along Dislocations, 1996, Phase Transformations and Mass Trnasport Under Pulse Reactions, 2001, Mass Transport Under Pulse Reactions, 2002, Laser Treatment of Materials, 2005. Mem.: Internat. Higher Edn. Acad. Sci., St. Petersburg Acad. Sci. for Strength Problems, N.Y. Acad. Sci. Avocations: singing, gardening, reading, history. Home: 13951 Wellington Dr Eden Prairie MN 55347 Office: Nat Am Univ W112 W Market Bloomington MN 55425-5521 Personal E-mail: bekrenev@pro-ns.net.

BELAG, ANDREA SUSAN, artist; b. NYC, Nov. 21, 1951; d. Julius Belag and Harriet (Goldberg) Belag-Lange; m. James Cole Bowness, Apr. 20, 1980 (div. Aug. 1989). Student, N.Y. Studio Sch., 1971-74. Lectr. visual arts program Princeton (N.J.) U., 1995; instr. Sch. Visual Arts, 1995—, SUNY., Purchase, 1992, Md. Inst. Coll. of Art, Baltimore, 1993; resident Bellagio Study Ctr. Curator Eight Painters, Jersey City Mus., 1980, 1981 Invitational, Selected Drawings, 1983, Ralph Hilton 1946-84, 1985, Mystery Show, 1985, The Mirror in Which Two Are Seen as One, 1989, Drawn Out, Kansas City (Mo.) Art Inst., 1987.; vis. artist N.Y. Studio Sch., 1983, Bard Coll., 1984, N.J. Coun. of Arts (fellowship juror), 1985, Kansas City Art Inst., 1987, N.Y. Feminist Art Inst., 1989, RISD, Providence, 1993, Hampshire Coll., 1999, Concordia U., Montreal, Que., Can., 1999. One-person shows include Jersey City Mus., 1979, N.J. State Mus., Trenton, 1984, John Davis Gallery, Akron, 1985, N.Y.C., 1987, 88, David Beitzel Gallery, N.Y.C., 1991, (monotypes), Richard Anderson Fine Arts, N.Y.C., 1992, 93, 94, Rutgers U., New Brunswick, N.J., 1995, Littlejohn Contemporary Art, N.Y.C., 1996, Bill Maynes Gallery, N.Y.C., 1998, 2000, 02, Galerie Heinz Holtmann, Cologne, Germany, 1998, 2000, 02, Bill Maynes Gallery, N.Y.C., N.Y., 2003; numerous group shows include Westport Arts Ctr., Conn., Mead Art Mus. & U. Gallery, U. Mass., Amherst, Warren Robbins Gallery, The U. Mich. Sch. Art & Design, Ann Arbor, Pratt Inst., NY, Rhona Hoffman Gallery, Chgo., Newhouse Ctr. Contemporary Art, Snug Harbor Cultural Ctr., Staten Island, NY, Graham Modern Gallery, NY, Tibor de Nagy Gallery, NY, Newark Museum; represented in mus. collections including Newark Mus., N.J. State Mus., Moriss Mus. of Arts and Scis.; work represented in numerous publs. Fellow N.J. Coun. for Arts, 1984, Nat. Endowment for Arts, 1987, Mariposa Found. fellow Corp. of YADDO, 1994; grantee Blue Mountain Ctr., 1993; Guggenheim fellow, 1999, Bellagio Study Ctr. fellow Rockefeller Found., 2003. Studio: 137 W Broadway New York NY 10013 Personal E-mail: abelag@earthlink.net.

BELAGA, DEBRA S., lawyer; b. Fairborn, Ohio, 1954; AB magna cum laude, Brown U., 1975; JD, Stanford U., 1978. Bar: Calif. 1978, US Ct. Appeals (9th Cir.), US Dist. Ct. (No., Ea. So., and Central Districts of Calif.), US Claims Ct. Head litigation dept. O'Melveny & Myers LLP, San Francisco, mem. class action practice group, firmwide head, environmental class action practice group, mem. policy com. Faculty mem., deposition skills tng. program Practicing Law Inst., 1986, 87, 88; evaluator, early neutral evaluation program US State Dist. Ct. (No. Dist. Calif.). Sr. editor Stanford Jour. of Internat. Law, 1977—78. Mem.: Am. Arbitration Assn. (arbitrator), San Francisco Bar Assn., ABA (mem., sect. on litigation, mem., sect. tort and insurance), Phi Beta Kappa. Office: O'Melveny & Myers LLP Embarcadero Ctr West 275 Battery St San Francisco CA 94111-3305 Office Phone: 415-984-8750. Office Fax: 415-984-8701. Business E-Mail: dbelaga@omm.com.

BELAIR, RAYMOND WILLIAM, lawyer; b. Washington, Mar. 31, 1948; s. Raymond Felix and Mary Alice (Moher) B.; m. Sarah Anne Edmonds, June 24, 1972; children: Raymond Farrell, David Robert, John William. AB cum laude, Assumption Coll., Worcester, Mass., 1970; JD, Fordham U., 1973. Bar: N.Y. 1974, U.S. Dist. Ct. (ea. dist. and so. dist.) N.Y. 1974, U.S. Ct. Appeals (2d cir.) 1974, U.S. Ct. Appeals (1st cir.) 1979, U.S. Dist. Ct. (no. dist.) N.Y. 1986; diplomate and cert. Am. Bd. Profl. Liability Attys. with spl. competence in med. profl. liability, 1997; cert. civil trial advocate Nat. Bd. Trial Advocacy, 1996. Assoc. Condon & Forsyth, N.Y.C., 1973-76; assoc. Kroll, Edelman, Elser & Wilson, N.Y.C., 1976-79, Morris & Duffy, N.Y.C., 1979-85; ptnr. (sr. founding) Belair & Evans, N.Y.C., 1985—. Mem. Med. Malpractice Mediation Panel, N.Y.C., 1982-92. Contbr. chpt.: Medical Malpractice in New York, 1992, 2d. edit. 1999; spkr. on Sexual Harrassment and Discrimination by Restaurant Operators: Prevention, Risk and Ins. Mgrs. Soc. Conv., San Francisco, 1995. Mem. ABA, ATLA, N.Y. State Bar Assn., Westchester County Bar assn. (mem. medico-legal com.), N.Y. State Trial Lawyers Assn. (mem. ins. and compensation law sects., trial lawyers sect.), Def. Rsch. Inst. and Trial Lawyers Assn., Cath. Lawyers Guild. Republican. Roman Catholic. Avocations: horology, golf, sailing. Home: 90 Overhill Rd Bronxville NY 10708-5136 Office: Belair & Evans 61 Broadway Rm 1320 New York NY 10006-2701

BELAND, MATTHEW ROBERT, library assistant; b. Victorville, Calif., Oct. 7, 1973; s. Robert David and Marilyn Beland; m. Rachel Lorraine Calman, Apr. 25, 2000; 1 child, David Arthur. BA, James Madison U., 1992—96; MA, Drew U. Caspersen Sch. of Grad. Studies, 1997—2001, MPhil, 2001—02. Grad. student Drew U. Caspersen Sch. of Grad. Studies, Madison, NJ, 1998—; libr. asst. Drew U. Libr., Madison, NJ, 2000—. Mem.: Am. Hist. Assn. (assoc.). Home: 67 Park Ave Apt 1 Madison NJ 07940 Office: Drew Univ Library 36 Madison Ave Madison NJ 09740 Office Phone: 973-408-3925. Personal E-mail: mr_beland@msn.com. E-mail: mbeland@drew.edu.

BELANGER, GERARD, economics professor; b. St. Hyacinthe, Que., Can., Oct. 23, 1940; s. Georges and Cecile (Girard) B.; 1 child, Marie-Jose. BA, U. Montreal, 1960; B in Social Sci., Laval U., 1961, M in Social Sci., 1967; MA, Princeton U., 1966. Asst. prof. econs. Laval U., 1967-71, assoc. prof., 1971-77, prof. econs., 1977—; rsch. coord. Howe Inst., Montreal, 1977-79; mem. fin. com. Coun. Univs., 1971-73. Co-author: The Price of Health, 1974, Le Prix du Transport au Quebec, 1978; author: L'economique du secteur public, 1981, Croissance du secteur public et fédéralisme, 1988. Woodrow Wilson scholar, 1964-65; Walter N. Rothchild scholar, 1965-66. Fellow Royal Soc. Can. Office: Université Laval Dept D'eco Pav Desève Quebec City PQ Canada G1K 7P4 Office Phone: 418-656-5363. Business E-Mail: gebe@ecn.ulaval.ca.

BÉLANGER, MAURIL, member of parliament; b. Mattawa, Ontario, Can., June 15, 1955; m. Catherine Hidasy BA in English Lit., U. Ottawa, Ontario, Can., 1977. Legis. asst., spl. asst. Canadian Mem. Parliament and Canadian Minister of Transport, Ottawa, Ontario, Can., 1980-84; rep. Investment Broker, Ottawa, 1985-89; legis. asst. Canadian Mem. Parliament, Ottawa, 1989-91; chief of staff Chmn. Regional Municipality Ottawa-Carleton, Ottawa, 1991-95; elected to Can. Parliament, Ottawa, 1995—, dep. leader of the Govt. in the Ho. Commons, 2003—; parliamentary sec. to min. Canadian heritage Govt. of Can., 1998—2000. Vice-chair Com. Canadian Heritage, 1995—. Office: Canadian Parliament Rm 835 Confederation Bldg Ottawa ON Canada K1AO86 Home: 504 -168 rue Charlotte St Ottawa Ontario Canada K1N8K6

BELANGER, WILLIAM JOSEPH, chemist, consultant; b. Chgo., Mar. 20, 1925; m. Keltah Long, Feb. 1, 1947; children: William Joseph, Thomas, Kathryn, Michael, Jeanne, Judith, Elizabeth, John, Anne. BS in Chemistry, St. Louis U., 1948; PhD in Organic Chemistry, Notre Dame U., 1951. Research chemist duPont Co., 1951-53; research chemist, then tech. service mgr. Devoe & Reynolds Co., 1953-60; tech. mgr. resin devel. Celanese Coatings & Specialties Co., Louisville, 1960-69; v.p. tech. and engring. Celanese Polymer Specialties Co., Jeffersontown, Ky., 1970-79; v.p. Specialties Group, Celanese Plastics & Specialties Co., 1979-82; Splty. polymer applications cons., 1982—. Tchr. polymer chemistry U. Louisville, 1957; tchr. organic chemistry Ind. Univ. Southeast, 1986. Patentee in field. Vice chmn. Jefferson County Housing Authority, 1975-78; trustee Audubon Hosp., 1979-82. Served with USNR, 1943-45. Mem. Am. Chem. Soc., Nat. Paint and Coatings Assn. Home and Office: 1208 Creighton Hill Rd Louisville KY 40207-2244 Office Phone: 502-895-8936. E-mail: bllbel@juno.com.

BELASCO, STEVEN RONALD, lawyer; b. Bklyn., Jan. 16, 1947; s. Philip Robert and Edythe (Barbell) B.; m. Claire Belasco, Aug. 14, 1969 (div. Feb. 1984); children: Daniel, Judith; m. Frances Schwartz, May 3, 1987; 1 child, Sara. BS cum laude, Bklyn. Coll., 1967; JD, U. Va., 1970; LLM in Taxation, NYU, 1974. Bar: N.Y. 1971. Assoc. Jackson, Nash, Brophy, Barringer & Brooks, N.Y.C., 1973-76; sr. tax atty. Colgate-Palmolive Co., N.Y.C., 1976-78, v.p. taxation, 1987-95, v.p. taxation and real estate, 1996—. Contr. articles to profl. jours. Mem. zoning bd. appeals, Greenburgh, NY, 1993—; chmn., 2000—. Mem. ABA, N.Y. Bar Assn., Assn. of Bar of the City of N.Y., NYU Tax Soc. (v.p. 1986—2001). Avocation: stamp collecting/philately. Home: 287 Evandale Rd Scarsdale NY 10583-1505 Office: Colgate-Palmolive Co 300 Park Ave Fl 14 New York NY 10022-7402 Office Phone: 212-310-3032. E-mail: Steve_Belasco@colpal.com.

BELATÈCHE, LYDIA, language educator; b. Rabat, Morocco, Sept. 27, 1962; d. Messaoud and Rita (Kelsh) B.; m. John Marshall Graham, May 15, 1990. BA in French, Vassar Coll., 1984; MA in French, Yale U., 1986, MPhil in French, 1988, PhD in French, 1993. Acting instr. dept. French Yale U., New Haven, 1987-88, 89-90; tchg. asst. English lang. and lit. Lycee Fenelon, Paris, 1988-89; vis. lectr. dept. Romance langs. U. Mich., Ann Arbor, 1991-94; asst. prof. French dept. fgn. langs. Miss. State U., Starkville, 1994—97; lectr. dept. French and Italian U. Minn., Mpls., 1997. Instr. French Breck Mid. Sch., Golden Valley, Minn., 1997—98. Contbr. articles, reviews to profl. jours. Mem. Am. Assn. Tchrs. French, Internat. Assn. Multidisciplinary Approaches and Comparative Studies, MLA, Midwest Modern Lang. Assn. Office: U Minn Dept French & Italian 260 Polwell Hall 9 Pleasant St SE Minneapolis MN 55455-0122

BELAY, ERMIAS D., epidemiologist; s. Belay Dagnachew and Kelemua Worku; m. Mahlet Mekonnen, Feb. 11, 1990; children: Yokabed Ermias, Sarah Ermias, Zanna Ermias. MD, Addis Ababa U., Ethiopia, 1988. Trained as an epidemic intelligence svc. officer Ctrs. for Disease Control and Prevention, 1996. Epidemic intelligence svc. officer Ctrs. for Disease Control and Prevention, Atlanta, 1994—96, med. epidemiologist, 1996—. Mem., transmissible spongiform encephalopathy adv. com. FDA, Wash., 1999—2003. Author: (articles in jours.) Annual Rev. of Public Health, Emerging Infectious Diseases, Public Health Reports, Pediatrics, Pediatric Infectious Diseases, Neurology, Disasters, Clinics in Lab. Medicine, Pediatric Infectious Diseases, Emerging Infectious Diseases, Archives of Pediatrics and Adolescent Medicine, Archives of Neurology, Jour. Am. Med. Assn., Pediatric Infectious Diseases, Archives of Pediatrics and Adolescent Medicine, Neuroepidemiology, New Eng. Jour. of Medicine, Annual Rev. of Microbiology, Pediatric Infectious Diseases Jour., Jour. Infectious Diseases. Bd. chmn. Covenant Gospel Ministry, Alexandria, Va., 1996—2004. Recipient Adv. Com. Svc. award, FDA, 1999-2003, Noteworthy Publ. 2001, 42nd Interscience Conf. on Antimicrobial Agents and Chemotherapy, 2002. Mem.: APHA. Christian. Achievements include research in the possible transmission to humans of animal prion diseases; the occurrence of Kawasaki syndrome, a childhood disease with unknown cause, to determine epidemiologic features and associated risk factors that may lead to discovery of a causative agent. Office Phone: 404-639-3091.

BELAY, HALEFOM, economist, educator; b. Mekelle, Tigray, Ethiopia, Oct. 5, 1959; s. Belay Asres, Emabaynesh Sebhatu (Stepmother). PhD, Binghamton U., Binghamton, N.Y., 1996. Lectr. Kotebe Tchrs. Coll., Addis Ababa, Ethiopia, 1987—89; assoc. prof. econs. Whitman Coll., Walla Walla, Wash., 1996—. Author: (outstanding feature article of the year) Bayesian VAR forecasts fail to live up to their promise, 2000; contbr. articles to profl. jours. Recipient Abramson Scroll award, Nat. Assn. Bus. Econs., 2000. Mem.: Am. Econ. Assn. Office: Whitman College 345 Boyer Ave Walla Walla WA 99362 Office Fax: 509-527 5026. Business E-Mail: belayh@whitman.edu.

BELAY, STEPHEN JOSEPH, lawyer; b. Joliet, Ill., May 30, 1958; s. Donald L. and Miriam A. (Madden) B.; m. Trudy L. Patterson, Nov. 7, 1987; children: Jacob, Katherine. BA, U. Iowa, 1980, JD, 1983. Bar: Iowa 1983, U.S. Dist. Ct. (no. dist.) Iowa 1985. Pvt. practice, Cedar Rapids, Iowa, 1983-88; asst. county atty. State of Iowa, Burlington, 1988-89, Decorah, 1989-92, 95—; assoc. Anderson, Wilmarth & Van Der Maaten, Decorah, 1993-96; ptnr. Anderson, Wilmarth, Van Der Maaten & Belay, Decorah, 1997—. Chair Winneshiek County Rep. Party, Decorah, 1992-94. Mem. ABA (chair juvenile justice com. young lawyers divsn. 1992-93), Iowa State Bar Assn. (chair juvenile law com. young lawyers divsn. 1992-94), Lions (bd. dirs. 1991-93). Roman Catholic. Avocations: trout fishing, bicycling, camping. Home: 903 Pine Ridge Ct Decorah IA 52101-1135 Office: Anderson Wilmarth Van Der Maaten & Belay PO Box 450 Decorah IA 52101-0450

BELAZELKOSKA, KATERINA, school system administrator; b. Stip, Macedonia, July 28, 1956; d. Dragan Gajdardziski and Cvetanka Gajdardziska; m. Ljubencho Belazelkoski, Apr. 28, 1984; children: Ana, Vera. BSc in Elec. Engring., U. Skopje, 1981; MSc in Ednl. Adminstrn., postgrad, U. Wis., 2001—. Tchg. Cert. U. Skopje, 1988. Secondary sch. prin. Secondary Tech. Sch. Vlado Tasevski, Skopje, Macedonia, 1999—2001; project asst. U. Wis., Milw., 2001—. Tchr. Milw. Achiever and Huntington Learning Ctr., 2003—. Sch. bd. dir. Two Secondary and one Elem. Sch., Skopje, Macedonia, 1988—99. Recipient Chancellor's award, U. Wis., 2002—04, 2004—05, 2005—, David Clark Scholar, 2005; Day Finch Meml. scholar, U. Wis. Sch. of Edn., 2002—03. Mem.: Urban Edn. Doctoral Com. (assoc.). Avocations: travel, camping, skiing. Home: 3131 W Coldspring Rd Greenfield, Milwaukee WI 53221 Office: Univ Wis Enderis Hall 644 Milwaukee WY 53201 Office Phone: 414-229-5771. Office Fax: 414-229-5300. Personal E-mail: katebela@yahoo.com. E-mail: katerina@uwm.edu.

BELCASTRO, PATRICK FRANK, pharmacist, researcher; b. Italy, June 3, 1920; came to U.S., 1927, naturalized, 1943; s. Samuel and Sarah (Mosca) B.; m. Hanna Vilhelmina Jensen, July 6, 1963; children— Helen Maria, Paul Anthony. BS, Duquesne U., 1942; MS (Am. Found. Pharm. Edn. fellow), Purdue U., 1951, PhD in Pharmacy and Pharm. Chemistry (Am. Found . for Pharm. Edn. fellow), 1953. Instr. pharmacy Duquesne U., 1946-49; asst. prof. pharmacy Ohio State U., 1953-54; prof. indsl. pharmacy Purdue U., 1954-90, prof. emeritus, 1990—. Author: Physical and Technical Pharmacy, 1963; contbg. editor: (with others) Pharm. Tech, 1977—; contbr. to: (with others) Jour. Pharm. Scis. Served with U.S. Army, 1942-46. Mem. Am. Pharm. Assn., Rho Chi, Phi Lambda Upsilon. Roman Catholic. Home: 327 Meridian St West Lafayette IN 47906-2603 Office: Purdue U Sch Pharmacy and Pharm Scis West Lafayette IN 47907 E-mail: pbelcas1@purdue.edu.

BELCHER, ANGELA, engineering educator; BS, U. Calif. Santa Barbara, 1991, PhD, 1997; postdoctoral fellow, 1997—99. Faculty, dept. chem. and biochemistry U. Tex., Austin, Tex., 1999—2002; John Chipman Career Devel. assoc. prof. materials sci. and engring. MIT, Cambridge, Mass., 2002—. Author: numerous rsch. articles, including in Science and Nature. Named a MacArthur Fellow, 2004. Office: Biological Engring 16-244 MIT 77 Mass Ave Cambridge MA 02139-4307

BELCHER, CHARLES WILLIAM, education educator; b. Independence, Mo., Sept. 29, 1954; s. Daniel Marvin and Florence Marie Belcher; m. Rebecca Sue Newcom, May 10, 1985. AA in Music, Nebr. Western Coll., 1974; B Music Edn., Park U., 1985; MA in Ednl. Adminstrn., N.Mex. State U., 1992, PhD, 2005. Profl. spl. educator Coun. Exceptional Children, 1998, cert. music tchr. Mo., N.Mex., spl. edn. tchr. Mo., N.Mex., edn. admnstrn. Mo., spl. edn. admnstrn. Mo. Part-time faculty mem. N.Mex. State U., Las Cruces, 1991—92, grad. asst., 1992—94; spl. edn. tchr. Las Cruces Pub. Schs., 1994—99, head spl. edn. dept., 1995—96; dir. spl. svcs. Cole County R-II Schs., Jefferson City, Mo., 1999—2000; instr. William Woods U., Fulton, 2000—03, adj. faculty, 2003—; pastor Cmty. of Christ, 2003—. Cons. Cmty. Tutors, Jefferson City, 2002—03; program asst. in spl. edn. N.W. R3gional Profl. Devel. Ctr., Maryville, Mo., 2002—. Bd. dirs. Mo. Impact, 2001—. Mem.: Mo. Profl. Devel. Coun., Nat. Staff Devel. Coun., Mo. Coun. Exceptional Children (v.p. tchr. edn. divsn. 2001—), Phi Delta Kappa. Avocations: reading, music performance, music composition. Office Phone: 660-562-1413. E-mail: charles@mail.nwmissouri.edu.

BELCHER, DENNIS IRL, lawyer; b. Wheeling, W.Va., Aug. 24, 1951; s. Finley Duncan Belcher and Ellen Jane (Huffman) Good; m. Vickie Marie Early, Aug. 2, 1975; children: Sarah Anne, Matthew Irl, Benjamin Scott. BA, Coll. William and Mary, 1973; JD, U. Richmond, 1976. Bar: Va. 1976, U.S. Tax Ct. 1978. Assoc. McGuire, Woods, Battle & Boothe, Richmond, Va., 1976-83, ptnr., 1983—, mem. exec. com., 1996—2001. Adj. prof. taxation Va. Commonwealth U., Richmond, 1985-88. Co-author: Business Tax Planning Forms for Businesses and Individuals, 1985. Chmn. Richmond chpt. Am. Heart Assn., 1984-85; trustee St. Christopher's Sch., 1993-2003. Fellow Am. Coll. Trust and Estate Counsel (bd. regents 1999-2005, sec. 2005—); mem. ABA (real property and probate sect., sec. 1997-98, chmn. marital deduction com., vice chmn. lifetime transfers com., ho. of dels. 1998-99, vice chair probate divsn. 1999-2001, chair 2002-03), Va. Bar Assn. (wills and trusts and taxations sects.), Country Club of Va., Kinloch Golf Club Presbyterian. Avocations: golf, farming. Office: McGuire Woods LLP One James Ctr 901 East Cary St Richmond VA 23219 Office Phone: 804-775-4304. Business E-Mail: dbelcher@mcguirewoods.com.

BELCHER, DOROTHY S., state correctional department administrator; b. Macon, Ga., Sept. 3, 1954; d. Lawyer B. Stanley and Lena Mae Montgomery; divorced; children: Ayotunde Ronke Ware, Aziza Asha Belcher. BA, U. Wis., 1976. Cert. correctional probation officer, correctional officer inspector, Fla. Probation and parole officer I State of Fla. Dept. of Corrections, Miami, 1978-80, probation and parole officer II, 1980-83, pub. svc. officer, 1983-87, gold program coord., 1987-89, probation and parole supr., 1989-90, correctional probation sr. supr., 1990-91, correctional officer, sr. inspector, 1991-97, correctional probation sr. supr. Ft. Lauderdale, 1997-98, correctional probation dep. adminstr. Miami, 1998-99, correctional probation sr. cir. adminstr., 1999—. Fellow Eta Phi Beta; mem. 100 Black Women, Fla. Coun. on Crime and Delinquency, Criminal Justice Inst. (hon.). Democrat. Pentecostal. Avocations: reading, writing, singing, playing piano, gardening. Home: 17731 NW 32d Ave Opa Locka FL 33056 Office: State of Fla Dept Corrections Probation and Parole 3552 Okeechobee Rd Fort Pierce FL 34947-4597 Personal E-mail: virtuousone1954@aol.com.

BELCHER, LEE BEVERLY, elementary school educator; b. Greenville, N.C., June 4, 1952; d. Robert Lee and Agnes Smith Belcher. BS, Winston-Salem State U., 1974. Tchr. Edna Andrews Elem., Hamilton, NC, 1974, AG Cox Mid. Sch., Winterville, NC, 1980—87, WH Robinson Elem., Winterville, NC, 1987—. Mem.: Winston-Salem State U. Alumni Assn. (Pitt County chpt. treas. 1995—2001). Roman Catholic. Home: 203 Singletree Dr Greenville NC 27834 Office Phone: 252-756-3707.

BELCHER, LOUIS DAVID, marketing professional, retired mayor; b. Battle Creek, Mich., June 25, 1939; s. Louis George and Josephine (Johnson) B.; children: Debora Louise, Sheri Lynn, Stacy Elizabeth; m. Jane Elisabeth Dillon, May 8, 1987. Student, Kellogg Community Coll., 1959; BS, Eastern Mich. U., 1962. With GM, Livonia, Mich., 1962; adminstr. U. Mich., Ann Arbor, 1962-63; with NCR, Lansing, Mich., 1963-69, Veda, Inc., Ann Arbor, 1969-72; owner, v.p., treas. First Ann Arbor Corp., 1972-83; owner, chief fin. officer Third Party Services, Inc. and Data Scan, Inc., Ann Arbor, Mich., 1983-84; pres., chief exec. officer Data Scan, Inc., Ann Arbor, 1984-86, Ann Arbor Rod & Gun Co., 1986-88; ptnr. Shipman, Corey, Belcher, Ann Arbor, 1984-86; sr. asst. to pres. and dir. tech. svcs. Environ. Rsch. Inst. Mich., Ann Arbor, 1988-93; owner, prin. L. D. Belcher and Assocs. Mgmt. Cons., Ann Arbor, 1993—; v.p. Cybernet Syss. Corp., Ann Arbor, 1996-97; pres., CEO, owner, dir. Innovative Rsch. Corp., Ann Arbor, 1999—. Bd. dirs. The Geosat Com., Inc., Washington; corp. dir. M.W. Microwave, Inc., Ann Arbor, Environment Tech. Corp., Ann Arbor, Innovative Rsch. & Svcs., Inc.; adv. bd. dirs. Mich. Consol. Gas Co.; mem. exec. com. Ann. Conf. Earth Observations and Decision Making - A National Partnership, Washington, 1988—, Ann. Internat. Symposium on Remote Sensing of Environment, 1990—, Thematic Conf. Geol. Remote Sensing, 1990, Ann. Thematic Conf. Coastal and Marine Environment, 1992—; co-founder, dir. Ann Arbor IT Zone, 1999. Mem. City Coun., Ann Arbor, 1974-78, mayor pro tem, Ann Arbor, 1976-78, mayor, 1978-85; mem. adv. coun. region 5 SBA, Detroit, 1982-86; pres. bd. dirs. U. Mich. Theatre, 1983-85; bd. dirs. Marcel Marceau World Ctr. for Mime, Inc., Ann Arbor, 1986-89, Mich. Theatre Found., Ann Arbor, 1986-92; mem. nat. Rep. campaign team, 1980. Served to capt. Air N.G., 1956-70. Recipient Outstanding Alumni awards Kellogg C.C., Outstanding Alumni awards Ea. Mich. U. Coll. Bus., Silver Elephant award Rep. Party, Commendation Adminstr. Vets. Affairs, Commendation Ann Arbor Vets. Hosp.; Bügermedaille, City of Tübingen, Fed. Republic Germany; elected Mayor's Hall of Fame, 1995. Mem. Air Force Assn., U.S. Conf. Mayors (past pres.), Mich. Conf. Mayors (chmn.), Am. Soc. for Photogrammertry and Remote Sensing, Ann Arbor Club. Republican. Mem. Ch. of Christ. Home: 1352 Cobblestone Ct Ann Arbor MI 48108-9553 Office: IRIS Corp 4220 Varsity Dr Ste E Ann Arbor MI 48108-2263 *I have had incredible luck - I was born an American and given the opportunity and freedom to chase my dreams.*

BELCHER, MAX, social services administrator, dean; b. East Lynn, W.Va., Mar. 16, 1942; s. George H. and Ella D. (Dickerson) B.; m. Linda L. Frey, Aug. 8, 1964; children: Kipling, Babbette, Andrew, Raleigh, Perry. BA, Berea (Ky.) Coll., 1969; ThM, Trinity Theol. Sem., 1972; ThD, Trinity Theol. Sem., 1973; MA, Liberty (Va.) U., 1994; DD, LLD (hon.), Internat. Free Prof. Episc. U., London, 1966; PhD, U. San Jose, 1996. Cert. cognitive behavioral therapist, rational marriage and family therapist, rational sex therapist. From case-worker to dist. mgr. Mich. Dept. Social Svcs., Flint, 1964-97, dist. mgr., 1992-97; mem. faculty dept. psychology Baker Coll., Flint, 1987-98, 99—, dean for gen. edn., 1998-99. Bd. dirs. Consortium on Child Abuse and Neglect, Flint, 1993-97, 99. Recipient Cert. of Merit in Youth Employment, Genesee Intermediate Sch. Dist., 1979, Cert. of Appreciation, Health Care Access Project, 1990. Mem. Nat. Assn. Cognitive Behavioral Therapists, Am. Assn. Christian Counselors, Intercollegiate Studies Inst. (faculty advocate), Mich. County Social Svcs. Assn. (life). Home: 9421 McAfee Rd Montrose MI 48457-9123 Office: Baker Coll 1050 W Bristol Rd Flint MI 48507-5508 Office Phone: 810-766-4130. Business E-Mail: max.belcher@baker.edu.

BELCK, NANCY GARRISON, dean, educator; b. Montgomery, Ala., Aug. 1, 1943; d. Lester Moffett and Stella Mae (Whaley) Garrison; m. Jack Belck, May 27, 1976; 1 child, Scott Brian. BS, La. Tech. U., 1964; MS, U. Tenn., 1965; PhD, Mich. State U., 1972. Cert. tchr., La. State textile specialist coop. extension svc. U. Ga., Athens, 1965-67, chair, dir. Tucson, 1976-79; asst. prof./instr. Mich. State U., East Lansing, 1967-73; family econ. researcher USDA Agrl. Res. Svcs., Hyattsville, Md., 1973-75, nat. extension evaluation coord. Washington, 1978-79; dean, prof. Coll. Human Ecology U. Tenn., Knoxville, 1979-87; dean, prof. Coll. Edn. Cen. Mich. U., Mt. Pleasant, 1987—91, interim provost, v.p. acad. affairs, 1988-89; provost, vice chancellor academic affairs La. State U., 1991—93; chancellor So. Ill. U., Edwardsville, 1994—97, U. Neb., Omaha, 1997—. Author: Development of Egyptian Universities Linkages, 1985, Mid-Career Administrators, 1986, Textiles for Consumers, 1990. Mem. exec. com. Mich. Milescular Inst., Midland, strategic planning team Pub. Schs., Mt. Pleasant, 1989—; chair Women's Networking Group, Mt. Pleasant, 1990—. Mem. Am. Home Econs. Assn., Am. Assn. for Higher Edn., Am. Assn. for Colls. Tchr. Edn., Am. Home Econs. Assn., Rotary, Sigma Iota Epsilon, Omicron Nu, Phi Delta, Kappa, Omicron Delta Kappa, Phi Kappa Phi. Avocations: gardening, walking, travel, international food tasting. Office: U of Nebraska at Omaha Office of the Chancellor Omaha NE 68182

BELDA, ALAIN J. P., metal products executive; b. Meknes, Morocco; Degree in bus. adminstrn., MacKenzie U. With Alcoa Aluminio, Brazil, 1969—79, pres., 1979—94; v.p. Alcoa Inc., 1982—94, pres. Latin Am., 1991, exec. v.p. Pitts., 1994—97, vice chmn., 1995—97, pres., COO, 1997—99; CEO Alcoa, Inc., Pitts., 1999—, chmn. bd. dirs., 2001—. Bd. dirs. Citigroup, Coopers Industries. Office: Alcoa Inc 201 Isabella St Pittsburgh PA 15212-5858

BELDEN, DAVID LEIGH, professional society administrator, engineering educator; b. Mpls., Jan. 9, 1935; m. Lois Marion Lind, June 14, 1956; children: Richard Alan, Grant David. B in Gen. Edn., U. Omaha, 1961; MS in Indsl. Engring., Stanford U., 1963, PhD, 1969; grad., Indsl. Coll. Armed Forces, 1973; DSc (hon.), Manhattan Coll., 1992. Registered profl. engr., Calif. rated navigator, aviator. Enlisted U.S. Air Force, 1954, commd. 2d lt., 1956, advanced through grades to col., 1973; served Thailand; asst. for procurement mgmt. to Sec. Air Force, Washington; ret., 1976; exec. dir. Inst. Indsl. Engr., Norcross, Ga., 1976-87, ASME, NYC, 1987—2002, United Engring. Found., 2003—. Adj. prof. Far East divsn. U. Md., 1970; asso. prof. George Washington U., 1974 Author articles in field. Bd. dirs. NYC Indsl. Tech. Assistance Corp. Decorated Legion of Merit, Meritorious Svc. medal, Commendation medal (3); recipient Nat. Engring. Leadership award Ariz. State U., 2000. Fellow ASME, Instn. of Engrs. of Ireland, Hong Kong Instn. of Engrs., Inst. Indsl. Engrs., Inst. Prodn. Engrs. (Eng., life); mem. Am. Assn. Engring. Socs. (bd. govs. 1980-2002, Kenneth Andrew Roe award), Coun. Engring. and Sci. Soc. Execs. (pres. 1984-85, Leadership award), N.Y. Soc. Assn. Execs. (bd. dirs. 1996-2004, vice chair 2000-01, chair 2002-03, Outstanding Assn. Exec. award), Am. Soc. Assn. Execs. (found. bd. 1992-94, bd. dirs. 1994-97), United Engring. Found. (bd. dirs. 1998-2002, pres. 2002), Australian Inst. Indsl. Engrs. (hon.), Japan Mgmt. Soc. (assoc.), Israeli Soc. Mech. Engrs. (hon.), Nat. Eagle Scout Assn. (Disting. Eagle Scout 1987), Alpha Pi Mu, Tau Beta Pi. Republican. Office: United Engring Found PO Box 70 Mount Vernon VA 22121-0070 Office Phone: 973-244-2328. Business E-Mail: beldend@asme.org.

BELDEN, SANFORD ADAMS, banker; b. Hatfield, Mass., Sept. 28, 1942; s. Luther Adams and Mary Evelyn (Ladd) B.; m. Elizabeth Louise Graham, Jun. 20, 1964; children: Jean, Douglas, Kathryn. BS, Purdue U., 1964, MS, 1967, PhD, 1971. Asst. prof. Cornell U., Ithaca, N.Y., 1970-72; v.p. Farm Credit Banks, Springfield, Mass., 1972-75, sr. v.p. St Louis, 1980-84; gen. mgr. Farm Credit Svcs., Auburn, Maine, 1975-78; chief exec. officer Farm Credit Banks, Midland, Mich., 1984-85; dep. gov. Farm Credit Adminstr., Washington, 1978-80; sr. v.p. First Bank Systems, Mpls., 1985-88, mng. dir., 1988—. Bd. dirs. First Bank System Polit. Party Program. Co-author: Productivity in the Food Industry, 1972. Mem. adv. bd. Natl Future Farmers Am. Found., Madison, Wis., 1986-87; cons. Ho. Reps. Agrl. Commn., Washington, 1985; chmn. stewardship Wayzata (Minn.) Community Ch., 1986-88; trustee Am. Inst. Coops., Washington, 1983. Named One of Outstanding Young Men Am. 1974; recipient Spl. Sr. award Robert Morris Assn., 1985. Mem. Am. Agrl. Econs. Assoc., Minn. Bankers Assn. (exec. bd. 1987—), Minn. Agrl. Growth Council (exec. bd. 1986—). Office: Community Bank Systems Inc 5790 Widewaters Pky De Witt NY 13214

BELDOCK, DONALD TRAVIS, investor; b. N.Y.C., May 29, 1934; s. George and Rosa (Tribus) B.; m. Lucy Geringer, Apr. 23, 1971; children: John Anthony, Gwen Ann, James Geringer. BA, Yale U., 1955. Mdse. and fin. exec. R. H. Macy & Co., N.Y.C., 1955-60; mng. ptnr., fin. cons., chmn. D. T. Beldock & Co., N.Y.C., 1961-66; pres., chief exec. officer, chmn. fin. com. BASIX Corp. (formerly Basic Resources Corp.), N.Y.C., 1966-69, chmn. bd., pres., chief exec. officer, 1970-88; chmn., dir. White Shield Greece Oil Corp., N.Y.C., 1969—98; chmn., chief exec. officer Fundamental Properties, Inc., N.Y.C., 1989—, also bd. dirs.; chmn., pres., chief exec. officer Primavera Labs, 1989—; also bd. dirs. CRA Inc, Phoenix, 1982-89. Chmn., CEO Packard Press Corp., Phila., 1987-88, bd. dirs., 1977-88; founding ptnr. Transp. Infrastructure Adv. Group; mng. dir. Hellenic Oil Co., 1989—; chmn., CEO AGB2, Inc., 1999—; bd. dirs. Amromco Energy, LLC. Patentee in field. Chmn. bd. trustees Strang Cancer Rsch. Ctr.-Preventive Medicine Inst., 1985-89, chmn. emeritus, 1989—, chmn. investment com., 1996-; mem. bd. advisors Chem. Bank, 1983-88; bd. dirs. Renewable Energy Inst., 1981-86; trustee Am. Symphony Orch., 1979-96; chmn. bd. dirs. Teamwork Found., 1980-89, trustee, 1989—; mem. com. Nat. UN Day, 1978-87; mem. N.Y. Gov.'s Commn. on Voluntary Enterprise, 1985-88; chmn. N.Y. Gov.'s Commn. Subcom. on Foster Care, 1986-88, Foster Care Ind. Living, 1986-89; bd. advisers Free Fellowship program U. Hawaii, 1982-86; mem. pvt. sector adv. panel on infrastructure financing of budget com. U.S. Senate, 1984-88; mem. devel. bd. Yale U., 1983-93, mem. exe. com., 1984-88. Honoree testimonial dinner United Jewish Appeal, 1960, 1986, testimonial gala, 2005, Vol. Svc. Leadership award, NY State Gov. Mario Cuomo, 1983, Outstanding Entrepreneur, Pres. Ronald Reagan, 1983, Innovation Leadership award, US Sec. Commerce Malcolm Baldridge, 1984, Outstanding Leadership award, Strang Cancer Rsch. Ctr. & Preventive Medicine Inst., 2005. Mem. Am. Mgmt. Assn., Fgn. Policy Assn., Assn. Yale U. Alumni (nat. class rep. 1983-86, bd. govs. 1986-89), Alumni Assn. N.Y. (hon., bd. dirs.), Yale Club, Westchester Country Club, Lotos Club. Office: Fundamental Properties Inc 575 Madison Ave New York NY 10022

BELDOCK, MYRON, lawyer; b. N.Y.C., Mar. 27, 1929; s. George J. and Irene (Goldstein) B.; m. Elizabeth G. Pease, June 28, 1953 (div. 1969); children: David, Jennifer, Hannah, Benjamin, Adam Schmalholz; m. Karen L. Dippold, June 19, 1986. BA, Hamilton Coll., 1950; LLB, Harvard U., 1958. Bar: (N.Y.) 1958, N.Y. (U.S. Dist. Ct. (ea. and so. dists.)) 1960, (U.S. Ct. Appeals (2d cir.)) 1960, (U.S. Supreme Ct.) 1973. Asst. U.S. Atty. U.S. Atty's Office, Eastern Dist., N.Y., 1958-60; assoc. Geist, Netter & Marx, N.Y.C., 1960-62; sole practice N.Y.C., 1962-64; ptnr. Beldock Levine & Hoffman LLP, N.Y.C., 1964—. Bd. dirs., v.p. Brotherhood-In-Action, N.Y.C., 1972—; bd. dirs. Brookdale Revolving Fund., N.Y.C., 1973-76. Served with U.S. Army, 1951-54. Recipient Milton S. Gould award for outstanding oral advocacy, Office of Appellate Defender, 2004. Mem. N.Y. State Bar Assn. (award 2002), Assn. Bar City N.Y. (spl. com. penology 1974-80, com. on judiciary 2000-03), N.Y. County Lawyers Assn., Bklyn. Bar Assn., Kings County Criminal Bar Assn. (Humanitarian of Yr. 1989), N.Y. County Criminal Bar Assn. (award for Excellence 2000), N.Y. State Assn. Criminal Def. Lawyers (Pres.'s commendation 2004), Nat. Assn. Criminal Def. Lawyers, Nat. Lawyers Guild.

BELDON, SANFORD T., publisher; b. Scranton, Pa., Nov. 9, 1932; s. Benjamin and Evelyn (Jacobson) B.; m. Jeanne Sherman, June 25, 1967 (dec. Nov. 1992); m. Patricia Wood, Feb. 4, 1995; children: Mary, Kenneth, Emily. BBA, CCNY, 1955; postgrad., NYU Grad. Sch. Bus., 1956-57. Publicist Prentice-Hall, Inc., N.Y.C., 1956-59; publicity dir. Fawcett Publs., Inc., N.Y.C., 1959-62; asst. dir. public relations Crowell-Collier-Macmillan, N.Y.C., 1963-65; dir. advt. and public relations, edn. group Litton Industries, White Plains, N.Y., 1966-68; dir. promotion Baker & Taylor divsn. W.R. Grace Co., 1968-71; dir. mktg. book div. Rodale Press, Inc., Emmaus, Pa., 1971-74; dir. advt. Organic Gardening mag., Emmaus, 1974-78, v.p., 1974-82, pub., 1978-86, group v.p., 1982-91, sr. v.p., 1991-98. Pub. New Shelter mag., 1984-86, Pub. Prevention Mag., 1986-91, sr. v.p., 1991-99; bd. dirs. Second Harvest Food Bank of Lehigh Valley, 1996—, chmn., 2002—. Pres. ecology adv. com. Allentown (Pa.) City Coun., 1972-75; bd. dirs. Lehigh Valley Child Care, Allentown, 1974-82, pres. bd., 1976-80; bd. dirs. Lehigh Valley Conservancy, Allentown, 1976-77, Planned Parenthood Lehigh County, Pa., 1977-78, Lehigh County Youth and Childrens Office, 1999-2002, Jewish Family Svc. Lehigh Valley, 2000-2003; mem. bd. assocs. Cedar Crest Coll., 1985—; trustee, mem. corp. com., chmn. mktg. coms. Allentown Art Mus., 1992—, pres. bd. trustees, 1997—; mem. Pa. Housing Adv. Commn., 1997-2002. Democrat. Jewish. Personal E-mail: sbeldon@yahoo.com.

BELENY, KAREN K., secondary school educator; b. Tiffin, Ohio, Oct. 10, 1960; d. Junior and Luella King; m. Dave Beleny, June 20, 1992; children: David, Alexander. BM, Bowling Green State U., Ohio, 1982; MEd, Ashland U., Ohio, 1992. Vocal, instrumental music tchr. Ridgewood H.S., Mt. Blanchard, Ohio, 1982—87; vocal music tchr. Riverdale H.S., Mt. Blanchard, 1987—89, Clearview H.S., Lorain, Ohio, 1989—93; vocal, instrumental music tchr. Old Fort H.S., Ohio, 1993—. Mem.: NEA, Ohio Edn. Assn., Internat. Assn. Jazz Educators, Music Educators Nat. Conf., Ohio Music Educators Assn. Home: 4240 W Co Rd 48 Tiffin OH 44883 Office: Old Fort HS 7635 N Co Rd 51 Old Fort OH 44861 Office Fax: 419-992-4293. Business E-Mail: kbeleny@old-fort.k12.oh.us.

BELEU, STEVE (DAN BELEU), librarian; b. Shawnee, Okla., June 6, 1952; s. Dan Lewis and Ann Beleu; m. Debbie Dougherty, June 7, 1977 (div. Jan. 1991). BA, Okla. Bapt. U., 1975; MLS, U. Okla., 1977. Ref. libr. Okla. Dept. Librs., Oklahoma City, 1979-86, regional depository libr., head U.S. govt. info. divsn., 1986—. Fellow Nat. Ctr. for Edn. Stats., 2002—; coord. Norman Yoga Tchrs. Assn., 2004—05. Author: Yoga Asanas for the Relief and Prevention of Carpal Tunnel Syndrome, 2001; compiler: Forty-Six Important Federal Publications About Oklahoma, the 46th State, 2001, American Indian Materials in the Federal Depository Libraries of Oklahoma, 2002, Oklahoma Directory of Depositories for United States and State of Oklahoma Government Publications, 2002, Yoga in Norman--A Guide to Yoga Teachers and Classes in Norman, Oklahoma, 2003, 2d edit., 2005; contbr. poetry to small press periodicals; author various musical compositions; contbr. articles to profl. jours. Mem. Ctrl. Okla. Grotto (sec. 1994—), Metrodocs (coord. 1986—). Democrat. Avocations: poetry, composing music, teaching yoga, caving, backpacking. Home: 1609 E Boyd St Norman OK 73071 Office: Okla Dept Libraries 200 NE 18th St Oklahoma City OK 73105-3298 Office Phone: 405-521-2502. E-mail: sbeleu@oltn.odl.state.ok.us.

BELEW, JOHN SEYMOUR, academic administrator, chemist; b. Waco, Tex., Nov. 3, 1920; s. George H. and Mary (Seymour) B.; m. Ruth Edna McAtee, June 3, 1944; children— James Seymour, Janet Elizabeth. BS, Baylor U., 1941; MS, Wichita State U., 1947; PhD, U. Wis., 1951; LLD, Hong Kong Bapt. U., 1995. Instr. U.S. Army Air Corps Tech. Tng. Command, 1941-43; rsch. assoc. Brown U., Providence, 1951-53; acting. asst. prof. U. Va., 1953-56; asst. prof., then assoc. prof. and prof. chemistry Baylor U., Waco, Tex., 1956-91, prof. emeritus, 1991—, assoc. dean Coll. Arts and Scis., 1973-74, dean Coll. Arts and Scis., 1974-79, chief acad. officer, 1979-91, Jo Murphy chair in internat. edn., 1990-96, provost emeritus, 1991—. Vis. fellow Manchester Coll., Oxford U., summer 1995; mem. team advs. to Tech. U. Liberec, Czech Rep., 1999. Mem. various cmty. bds.; trustee Midway Ind. Sch. Dist., Waco, 1962-72; bd. dirs. Tex. High Speed Rail Authority, 1992—; del. Nat. Dem. Conv., 2000. With USAAF, 1943-46. Wilton Park fellow, 1976; recipient Disting. Alumnus award Baylor U., 1993. Mem.: Royal Soc. Chemistry, Am. Chem. Soc., Turner Soc. London, Grolier Club, Sigma Xi. Office: Provost Emeritus Baylor Univ Waco TX 76798-7121 E-mail: seymourbelew@earthlink.net.

BELFIGLIO, VALENTINE JOHN, political science professor; b. May 28, 1934; s. Edmond Liberato and Mildred Elizabeth (Sherwood) B.; 1 child by previous marriage, Valentine Edmond; m. Ellie K. Belfiglio; stepchildren: Andy, Kevian Navid. BS, Union U., 1956; MA, U. Okla., Norman, 1967; PhD, U. Okla., 1970. Registered pharmacist, Fla., Okla., Tex.; cert. cons. pharmacist. Grad. asst., instr. U. Okla., 1967-70; prof. polit. sci., instr. drug law and policy Tex. Woman's U., Denton, 1970—; cons. pharmacist West Dallas Pharmacy. Author: The United States and World Peace, 1971, American Foreign Policy, 1979, The Italian Experience in Texas, 1983, The Best of Italian Cooking, 1985, Alliances, 1986, Go for Orbit, 1987, Pride of the Southwest, 1991, Italian Experience in Texas: A Closer Look, 1994, Honor, Pride, Duty: A History of the State Guard, 1995, They Came from the Sea, 2000, A Study of Ancient Roman Amphibious and Offensive Sea-Ground Task Force Operations, 2001; contbr. articles to profl. jours.; contbr. textbooks in internat. politics Holbrook Press, Boston, 1973-75. With USAF, 1959-67. Decorated knight Order of Merit, Republic of Italy; recipient Guido Dorso prize U. Naples, 1985, C.K. Chamberlain award East Tex. Hist. Assn., 1990, Cornaro award Tex. Woman's U., 2003, Faculty Devel. leave, Rome, 2001, Cornaro award Tex. Woman's U., 2003; Instnl. Rsch. grantee Tex. Woman's U., 1973-74, 76-77, NEH grantee, 1978; postdoctoral fellow Republic of South Africa, 1976; Faculty Devel. fellowship, Rome, 2001 Mem. AAUP, Internat. Studies Assn. (sec.-treas. region 1974-76), Am. Polit. Sci. Assn., Am. Italian Hist. Assn., Tex. State Def. Forces, Fourth degree Knight of Columbus, Mensa, Kappa Psi Republican. Roman Catholic. Avocations: chess, dance, gourmet cookery. Office: Tex Woman's U PO Box 425889 Denton TX 76204-5889 Home: 11505 Sonnet Dr Dallas TX 75229-2629 Office Phone: 940-898-2144. Business E-Mail: vbelfiglio@twu.edu.

BELFORT-CHALAT, JACQUELINE, art educator, sculptor; b. Mt. Vernon, NY, Feb. 23, 1930; d. Jacob Samuel and Mildred (Belfort) Chalat; m. Warren Leigh Ziegler, Sept. 17, 1950 (div. 1979); children: David Matthew, Catherine Amalia. Student, Frederick V. Guinzburg, 1943, Ruth Nickerson, 1944, Oronzio Maldarelli, Ettore Salvatore, Columbia U., 1947, Stuart Klonis, Art Students League, 1948, Fashion Inst. Tech., 1948-50, Royal Acad. Fine Arts, Copenhagen, 1960-62; BA, U. Chgo., 1948. Prof., chair fine arts Moyne Coll., Syracuse, NY, 1969—2003, visual chair, 2004—. Lectr. Cath. U., Howard U., Lorton Prison, Smithsonian Instn., Syracuse U., Govt. of Nigeria, others; presenter in field. One-woman shows include Le Moyne Coll., 1969, 73, 83, St. Peter's Gallery, Soc. Art, Religion and Culture, N.Y.C., 1975, Everson Mus., Syracuse, 1979, City Hall, Syracuse, 1981, Schweinfurth Meml. Art Ctr., Auburn, N.Y., 1983, Yager Art Mus., Oneonta, 1985; exhibited in group shows at Charlottenborg Slot, Copenhagen, 1962, Nat. Collection Fine Arts, Washington, 1963, Washington Gallery Art, Washington, 1966, Everson Mus., Syracuse, 1972-74, Munson-Williams-Procter Mus., Utica, N.Y., 1974, Boston Coll., Chestnut Hill, 1974, St. Joseph's Coll., Phila., 1976, Internat. Art Fair, Boston, 1980, Festival of Arts, St. David's Ch., Syracuse, 1969—; prin. works include statue of Mary monument, Life-size Christ, sports paintings; appeared in videos; writer in field. Bd. dirs. Cultural Resources Coun. Mem. Am. Aesthetic Soc., Coll. Art Assn. Am., Nat. Soc. Am. Pen Women, Internat. Sculpture Ctr., Internat. Women's Writing Guild, Syracuse Ceramic Guild, Soc. for Art, Religion and Culture, Theta Chi Beta. Republican. Roman Catholic. Home: 321 Hurlburt Rd Syracuse NY 13224-1822 Office: Le Moyne Coll Dept Fine Arts Syracuse NY 13214-1399 Office Phone: 315-445-4147. Business E-Mail: belfortj@lemoyne.edu. E-mail: belfort@belarts.com.

BELFORTE, DAVID ARTHUR, electronics executive; b. Framingham, Mass., Oct. 25, 1932; s. Arthur David and Jean Louise (Purcell) B.; m. Virginia Elizabeth Crowley, Aug. 2, 1958; 1 child, Steven, David. BS, Northeastern U., 1963, MS, 1970. Staff scientist Raytheon Co., Waltham, Mass., 1957-65; v.p. Thomson Gen. Corp., Lynn, Mass., 1965-70; dir. mktg. Am. Optical Corp., Southbridge, Mass., 1970-73; mgr. Ferranti Elec. Inc., Sturbridge, 1973-76; dir. mktg. Avco Everett Metal Working Lasers, Somerville, Mass., 1976-81; pres. Belforte Assocs., Sturbridge, 1982—. Pub., editor-in-chief: Industrial Laser Handbook, 1986-92; editor Indsl. Laser Rev., 1986-98; pub., editor-in-chief Indsl. Laser Solutions, 1999—. Recipient Arthur L. Schawlow award Laser Institute of America, 1995. Fellow Laser Inst. Am. (Pres.'s award 1988, Arthur L. Schawlow Award, 1995); mem. Am. Welding Soc. (life), Soc. Mfg. Engrs., Ukranian Acad. Engring. Scis. Office: Belforte Assocs PO Box 245 Sturbridge MA 01566-0245 E-mail: belforte@pennwell.com.

BEL GEDDES, JOAN, writer; b. L.A. d. Norman and Helen (Sneider) Bel G.; m. Barry Ulanov, Dec. 16, 1939 (div. 1968); children: Anne, Nicholas, Katherine. BA, Barnard Coll. Columbia U., 1937. Researcher and theatrical asst. to Norman Bel Geddes, Inc., N.Y.C., 1937-41; publicity dir. Compton Advt., Inc., N.Y.C., 1942, new program mgr., 1943-47; pub. info. officer UNICEF, N.Y.C., 1970-76, chief editl. and publs. svcs., 1976-79, cons. devel. edn., promoter Universal Children's Day (over 100 countries), 1979-85, editor Almanac World's Children, 1985-90; editor Pate Inst. Bull., 1988-94. Tchr. drama Birch Wathen Sch., N.Y.C., 1950; mem. faculty Inst. Man and Sci., Rensellaerville, N.Y., 1969. Interviewer-hostess: weekly radio program Religion and the Arts, NBC, 1968; author: Small World: A History of Baby Care from the Stone Age to the Spock Age, 1964, How to Parent Alone: A Guide for Single Parents, 1974, To Barbara With Love--Prayers and Reflections by a Believer for a Skeptic (Catholic Press Assn. award 1974), Are You Listening, God?, 1994, Childhood and Children, a Compendium of Customs, Superstitions, Theories, Profiles, and Facts, 1998, Children Praying, Why and How to Pray with Your Children, 1999, (with others) Art, Obscenity and Your Children, 1969, American Catholics and Vietnam, 1970, The Future of the Family, 1971, Holiness and Mental Health, 1972, The Children's Rights Movement, 1977, And You, Who Do You Say I Am?, 1981; translator: (with Barry Ulanov) Last Essays of Georges Bernanos, 1955; editor: Magic Motorways (Norman B. Geddes), 1940, Earth: Our Crowded Spaceship (Isaac Asimov), 1974; editor in chief: My Baby mag, 1954-56, Congratulations mag, 1954-56. Rep. Balkan-Ji-Bar Internat. Orgn. for Child and Youth Welfare of the World, UN. Mem. Authors League Am., Assn. Former Internat. Civil Servants, The Coffee House, Teilard de Chardin Assn., Mcpl. Arts Soc. N.Y., Internat. Inst. Rural Reconstrn. (mem. internat. coun.), Thomas More Soc. (pres. 1966), Barnard Coll. Alumnae Assn. (class v.p. 1972-76, 92—, pres. 1976-82), N.Y. City Mission Soc., Guilford Friends of Music, Pate Inst. Human Survival (bd. dirs. 1989-95, editor bi-monthly bull. 1990-93), The Charles A. and Anne Morrow Lindbergh Fund, Citizens Against Govt. Waste. Roman Catholic. Office: 60 E 8th St New York NY 10003-6514 *The longer I live the more I relish life. People praise and envy youth but, to my great surprise, I find that growing older is even better than being young. Pleasures taken for granted before become valued, enlarged, prolonged. Like a baby chortling joyfully at seeing things for the first time, I marvel at seeing things for the hundredth or last time. I don't think of life as a right one can in any way earn or deserve but as an inexplicably, unbelievably amazing gift to enjoy and to use and to learn from — so each day is, to me, wondrous, surprising, full of unimagined possibilites.*

BELGOROD, BARRY MILES, surgeon, educator; b. NYC, Mar. 27, 1953; s. Howard H. and Madeline (Bloom) B. BA summa cum laude, Queens Coll., 1973; MD, U. Pa., 1977. Diplomate Am. Bd. Ophthalmology, Nat. Bd. Med. Examiners. Intern in internal medicine Pa. Hosp., 1977-78; resident in ophthalmology Manhattan Eye, Ear and Throat Hosp., N.Y.C., 1978-81, assoc. attending surgeon, 1981—; asst. attending ophthalmologist N.Y. Hosp., 1982—. Clin. instr. dept. ophthalmology Cornell U. Med. Coll., NYC; pres. BMB Patent Holding Corp.; med. coun. U. Pa., 1973-76; cons. in field. Bd. dirs. Soc. Salk Scholars, 1983—88. Fellow NSF, 1972; recipient Ira M. Goldin award, 1973, Charles A. Oliver Meml. prize in ophthalmology, 1977; scholar N.Y. States Regents, 1969-73, Jonas Salk Found., 1973-77. Fellow ACS, Am. Acad. Ophthalmology, NY Acad. Medicine, NY State Ophthal. Soc.; mem. U. Pa. Alumni Assn., Phi Beta Kappa, Sigma Xi, Beta Delta Chi. Achievements include patents for electronic photochromic lens. laser corneal surgery, analgesics. Office: 115 E 61st St New York NY 10021-8183 Office Phone: 212-753-2020.

BELICH, JOHN PATRICK, SR., journalist; b. Peekskill, N.Y., Dec. 6, 1938; s. John Andrew and Iris Patricia (Brown) B.; m. Louise Daniel, June 4, 1971; children: Mary Louise, John P., Andrew J. Student, N.Y. Inst. Photography, St. Petersburg Jr. Coll. Staff news photographer UPI, 1963-69; So. div. photo mgr. Atlanta, 1969-72; photo editor, dir. photography St. Petersburg Times and Evening Independent, 1972-87, mgr. newsroom projects, 1987-94, asst. to pres., 1994—. V.p., bd. dirs. N.W. Fla. Little Maj. League Assn.; mem. photography adv. com. St. Petersburg Vocat. Tech. Inst.; guardian ad litem 6th Jud. Ctr., Fla.; Skywarn vol. Amateur Radio Emergency Svc. Corp., Nat. Weather Svc.; bd. advisors Coll. Comm., Fla. State U. Recipient Pres.'s medal Nat. Press Photographers Assn., 1978, citation of excellence, 1979 Mem. Nat. Press Photographers Assn. (bd. dirs., chmn. info. com. 1978), Atlanta Press Photographers Assn. (past treas., v.p.), Fla. News Photographers Assn., Nat. Press Photographers Found., Am. Meteorol. Soc., Nat. Weather Assn., Am. Radio Relay League, Amateur Radio Satellite Corp., NRA, Clearwater Amateur Radio Soc., Soc. Newspaper Design, Bass Anglers Sportsman Soc., Fla. Assn. Lic. Investigators (bd. dirs. 2004), Am. Soc. Indsl. Security, Computer Security Inst., Info. Sys. Security Assn., Sigma Delta Chi. Office: 490 1st Ave S Saint Petersburg FL 33701-4204 Business E-Mail: jbelich@sptimes.com.

BELICH, KAY S., music educator; d. Robert W. and Lorna O. Schoenfeld; m. Sam M. Belich, Aug. 16, 1975; children: Aaron F., Eva A. MusB, The U. of Wis., 1970—74; MusM, The Juilliard Sch., 1974—77. Lic. Teacher Dept. of Pub. Instrn., Wis., 1991. Singer NYC Opera Co., 1977—90; elem. sch. music tchr. Kenosha Unified Pub. Sch. Dist., Wis., 1991—96, West Allis/West Milw. Pub. Sch. Dist., 1996—; studio vocal and instrumental tchr. freelance, N.Y. and Milw., NY, 1968—, opera and concert singer N.Y. and Milw., 1972—; u. instr. Cardinal Stritch U., Milw., 1999—. Apprentice singer Ctrl. City Opera Co., Colo., 1975; union del. NYC Opera Touring Co., 1990; cooperating tchr. for student tchr. Carthage Coll., Kenosha, Wis., 1993—94; mentor West Allis/West Milw. Pub. Sch. Dist., 2001—02; cooperating tchr. for student tchr. Cardinal Stritch U., Milw., 2002—03. Singer performances include Cami Hall recital. Ch. coun. mem. Grace and St. Paul's Luth. Ch., NYC, 1980—81; various positions Mt. Hope Luth. Ch., West Allis, Wis., 1991—. Recipient Regional Finalist, Met. Opera, 1978, First Pl., Wis. Fedn. of Music Clubs, 1974; Full Tuition scholarship, The U. of Wis., 1970—74. Mem.: Music Educators' Nat. Conf., Take Off Pounds Sensibly (treas. 1998—). Lutheran. Achievements include Solo Debuts: with New York City Opera, 1982; with Music Under the Stars, 1991; with Skylight Opera Theatre, 1993; with Racine Symphony, 1996; with Waukesha Symphony, 1997. Avocation: organic gardening. Home: 2141 South 105 St West Allis WI 53227-1211 Office: Hoover School 12705 West Euclid Ave New Berlin WI 53151-4611 also: Cardinal Stritch Univ 6801 North Yates Rd Milwaukee WI 53217-3985

BELICHICK, BILL (WILLIAM STEPHEN BELICHICK), professional football coach; b. Nashville, Apr. 16, 1952; m. Debbie Belichick April 30, 1977; Children: Amanda, Stephen, Brian. BS in Econ., Wesleyan U., 1975; LHD, Boston U., 2004, New England Inst. Tech., 2004. Spl. asst to the coaching staff Balt. Colts, 1975; asst. spl. teams coach Detroit Lions, 1976—77, tight ends & receivers coach, 1977—78; asst. spl. teams coach & asst. to defensive coord. Denver Broncos, 1978-79; spl. teams coach N.Y. Giants, 1979—81, spl. teams & linebackers coach, 1981—83, linebackers coach, 1983—85, defensive coord., 1985-91, defensive backs coach, 1989—91; head coach Cleve. Browns, 1991-95; asst. head coach, defensive backs coach New England Patriots, Foxboro, Mass., 1996-97, head coach, 2000—; asst. head coach, defensive backs coach N.Y. Jets, 1997-99. Named Coach of the Yr., Dallas Morning News, 2002, 2003, NFL Coach of the Yr., AP, 2003, NFL Alumni, 2003, Coach of the Yr., NFL.com, 2003, The Sporting News, 2003; named one of TIME's 100 Most Powerful & Influential People in the World, TIME mag., 2004; recipient Baldwin medal, Wesleyan U., 2002, Tom Landry award: AFC Coach of the Yr., USA Today, 2002, Amos Alonzo Stagg Coaching award, US Sports Acad., 2004. Defensive coord., Super Bowl Champion New York Giants, 1986, 1990, Head coach, Superbowl Champion New England Patriots, 2002, 2004, 2005. Achievements include holds the NFL record for the best postseason coaching record, 2005. Office: New England Patriots One Patriots Pl Foxboro MA 02035-1388

BELIC WEISS, ZORAN, artist, design educator, director; b. Beograd, Srbija, Yugoslavia, Apr. 24, 1955; arrived in U.S., 1989, naturalized, 2000; s. Milan and Ljubinka (Vidosavljevic) B. BFA in Painting/Mixed media, U. Arts, Belgrade, Yugoslavia, 1981; BA in Philosophy, U. Belgrade, 1985; MFA in Multi-media, Rutgers U., 1991. Pvt. practice, Irvine, Calif.; art dir. D'Arcy, Masius, Benton & Bowles, Inc., N.Y.C., 1991-93; prof. Miss. State U., 1993-96, U. Denver, 1996-97, Laguna Coll. Art and Design, 1997—2005; chair design program Laguna Coll. of Art and Design, Laguna Beach, 2001—05; prof. U. Calif., Irvine, 1997—2005; dir. gen. Imperium deSign, Irvine-Cosmopolis, 1998—; chmn. design pub. rels. Savannah (Ga.) Coll. Art and Design, 2005—. Tchr. Internat. Aikido Fedn., Irvine, 1988—; juror numerous exhbns., art event proposals for art programs; curator, co-curator 17 exhbns.; lectr. in field. Author: Academy of Arts and Sciences Dictionary of Visual Arts, 1989; editor: Mental Space, 1983—87, Dragon Series, 1988—89; one-man shows include SKC, Belgrade, 1977, 1978, 1979, 1980, 1984, 1994, New Gallery, Zagreb, Yugoslavia, 1979, Gallery Rhinoceros, Novi Sad, Yugoslavia, 1984, Collegium Artisticum, Sarajevo, Yugoslavia, 1984, Gallery AUT, Groznjan, Yugoslavia, 1989, Jewish Hist. Mus., Belgrade, 1989, Rutgers U., New Brunswick, NJ, 1990, 1991, Gallery Sebastian, Belgrade, 1994, McCommas Gallery, Miss. State U., 1996, Asbury Gallery, Denver, 1997, OCCCA Gallery, Santa Ana, Calif., 2002, exhibited in group shows at White Palace, Genoa, Italy, 1979, The Apple, Amsterdam, Holland, 1979, Mus. Modern Art, Paris, 1980, Mus. Arch., Wroclaw, Poland, 1981, Bilbao, Spain, 1982, Mus. Modern Art, Brussels, 1982, Mus. Contemporary Art, Belgrade, 1983, Mimar Sinan U., Istanbul, Turkey, 1983, Modern Mus., Stockholm, 1983, Art Space, Hamburg, Germany, 1985, Skenderija, Sarajevo, 1989, Franklin Furnace, N.Y.C., 1989, Mus. Modern Art, Tampere, Finland, 1989, Gallery ULUS, Belgrade, 1990, Zimmerly Mus., New Brunswick, 1991, Gallery V, N.Y.C., 1991, Anthology Film Archives, 1992, Art in Gen., 1993, Sherry Frumkin Gallery, Santa Monica, Calif., 1995, Barutana, Belgrade, 1997, Seven Degrees, Laguna Beach, 2003, others, Represented in permanent collections Mus. Contemporary Art, Belgrade, ULUS, Nat. Mus., Wroclaw, Poznan, Poland, others; contbr. over 55 articles to profl. jours. Recipient 2d award Internat. Drawing Triennial, Wroclaw, Poland, 1981, 4th award Internat. Drawing Biennial, Rijeka, Yugoslavia, 1988; Robert Watts Meml. scholar Rutgers U. 1989; ULUS fellow Beograd, Yugoslavia, 1986-87; rsch. grantee U.S. Dept. Interior, Washington, 1995. Mem. Internat. Assn. Aesthetics, Internat. Assn. Philosophers, Internat. Aikido Fedn., Coll. Art Assn., Udruzenje Likovnih Umetnika Srbije (v.p. 1987-89, pres. expanded media chpt. 1986-89, cons. program bd. 1987-89), Serbian Assn. Aesthetics, Assn. Spacial Rsch. (Belgrade). Avocation: Aikido (2d degree black belt). Home: 2253 Martin St # 204 Irvine CA 92612 Office: Imperium Design Ste 204 2253 Martin St Irvine CA 92612 Office Phone: 949-280-5029. E-mail: zbelic@imperiumdesign.com.

BELIN, FRANCES, music educator; b. Bklyn., Oct. 11, 1936; d. Max Trube and Doris Shapiro; 1 child, Anina. Student, Hunter Coll., NYC, 1954—55, Concord Coll., 1974, Adamant Music Sch., 1977, student, 2001—. Pvt. piano instr., NYC, 1956—71, W.Va., 1972—. Adjudicator Radford U., 2002, 03; builder creator, dir. Indian Creek Sch. Arts, Greenville, W.Va., 1980—. Photographer Internat. Theatre Inst., 1972; performer: Carnegie Hall, 2002, 2004; contbr. articles to newspapers. Mem.: Music Tchrs. Nat. Assn.

BELINGER, HARRY ROBERT, retired food service executive; b. Phila., Sept. 16, 1927; s. Harry and Florence (McGovern) B.; m. Jean Marie O'Neill, Nov. 30, 1957 (dec. Aug. 1998); 1 child, Lizanne. BS, Temple U., 1957. Reporter UPI, Phila., 1957-62, Phila. Daily News, 1962-63, asst. city editor, 1963-66, city editor, 1966-68, 70-71, Phila. Inquirer, 1968-70; city rep., dir. commerce City of Phila., 1972-76; v.p. pub. affairs ARAMARK Inc., Phila., 1976-95; ret., 1995. Pres. Great Flag Gateway, Inc., 2002. Former ex-officio mem. City Planning Commn.; former v.p. Phila. Indsl. Devel. Corp.; past dir., mem. exec. com. Phila. Port Corp.; former mem. sch. bd. Archdiocese of Phila.; past bd. dirs., mem. exec. com. Conv. and Tourist Bur., Phila.; past bd. dirs. Phila. Civic Ctr., Mercy Fitzgerald Hosp. With inf., AUS, 1950-52. Mem. Phila. Press Assn. (bd. dirs. 1964-66). Home: 830 Strawberry Ln Wynnewood PA 19096-1644

BELINSKY, RACHEL, mathematician, educator; b. St. Petersburg, Russia; arrived in U.S., 1992; d. Mendel and Polina Yekhilevsky; children: Natalia Cohen, Velvel. BS, MS, Leningrad U., PhD, 1971. Lectr., asst. prof., assoc. prof. Leningrad Naval Tech. U., St. Petersburg, 1971—92; assoc. prof. Morris Brown Coll., Atlanta, 1993—2003; lectr. Ga. State U., 2003—. Contbr. articles to profl. jours. Business E-Mail: rbelinsk@gsu.edu.

BÉLISLE, PAUL CHARLES, Canadian government official; b. St. Joachim, Ont., Can., Nov. 14, 1950; m. Danielle Parent; children: Ariane, Alexia. B in Social Sci. (hon.), U. Ottawa, Ont., 1974, cert. in pub. adminstrn., 1975, LLL, 1980. Bar: Que. Clk. Coms. and Pvt. Legis. Directorate, 1979-84, asst. dir., 1984-94; sec. gen. Can.-France Interparliamentary Assn., 1989-91; clk. of the Senate, clk. of the Parliaments Senate of Canada, Ottawa, Ont., 1994—. Mem. editl. bd. Can. Parliamentary Rev. Recipient l'Ordre de la Pleiade award. Mem. Assn. Clks.-at-the-Table Can., Commonwealth Parliamentary Assn. (exec. sec. treas.), Assn. of Secs. Gen. of Parliaments. Office: Senate of Canada Parliament Bldgs Centre Block Rm 185-S Ottawa ON Canada K1A 0A4 Fax: 613-992-7959. Office Phone: 613-992-2493.

BELITZ, PAUL EDWARD, lawyer; b. Omaha, July 11, 1951; s. Edward Paul and Jo Anna Beverly (Brown) B.; m. Joanne Deborah Nilson, June 9, 1973; children: Nicholas P., Christopher T. BS with high distinction, U. Nebr., 1973; JD magna cum laude, Creighton U., 1976. Bar: Nebr. 1976, Colo. 1982. Assoc., then ptnr. Kutak Rock LLP, Omaha, 1976-81, ptnr. Denver, 1982—. Bd. dirs. Fleischer Found., Scottsdale, Ariz., 1986—. Mem.: ABA, Denver Bar Assn., Colo. Bar Assn., Nebr. Bar Assn., Glenmoor Country Club (Cherry Hills Village, Colo.) (bd. dirs.). Avocations: reading, skiing, golf. Office: Kutak Rock LLP 1801 California St Ste 3100 Denver CO 80202 Office Phone: 303-297-2400. E-mail: paul.belitz@kutakrock.com.

BELK, F. NORMAN, librarian; b. Greenville, S.C., June 8, 1947; s. Francis Norman and Louellen Vinny (Davis) B. BA, Furman U., 1969; MLS, U. S.C., 1975. Reference librarian Greenville County Libr., 1970-77, br. libr. mgr., 1977-84, outreach librarian, 1984-85, audiovisual sect. mgr., 1985-86, acquisitions-automation librarian, 1986-89, coord. cmty. rels., 1989-98, coord. main libr. svc., 1998-2000, interim dir., 2000—. Rschr., contbr.: Tales from the Dark Corner: Documenting the Oral Tradition, 2 vols., 1995; contbr. articles to profl. jours. Mem. ALA (mem. intellectual freedom com. 1997—), Pub. libr. Assn. (mem. audiovisuals com. 1995—), S.C. Libr. Assn. (chair awards com. 1988-91, chair intellectual freedom com. 1991-93, Outstanding Librarian award 1994), Met. Arts Assn., Palmetto Soc. of United Way, Greenville East Rotary (program chair 1996-97, bd. dirs. 1995—), Furman Club (founder), S.C. Libr. Assn. (v.p., pres.-elect 1999, pres. 2000). Home: 107 Richbourg Rd Greenville SC 29615-1354 Office: Greenville County Libr 300 College St Greenville SC 29601-2015

BELK, JOAN PARDUE, language educator; b. Lancaster, S.C., Oct. 4, 1933; d. William Hazel and Alfleda Steele Pardue; m. Joe Harvey Belk, Sr.; children: Joe Harvey Jr., Jennifer Elizabeth. Degree, Winthrop U., 1954; BA summa cum laude, U. Houston, 1957. Cert. tchr. Tex. Asst. to dir. librs. U. Houston, Houston, 1957—61; tchr. English Galena Park H.S., Galena Park, Tex., 1961—62; tchr. English (advanced placement) Meml. H.S., Houston, 1962—96; instr. English Houston C.C., 1996—2002. Musician, piano accompanist, piano tchr. Editor articles for profl. pubs. Mem. Royal Spring Civic Assn., Houston, 1989—, newsletter editor, 2002—; mem. Happy Hide-a-Way Civic Assn., Crosby, 1972—, Cancer Fighters Houston, Inc., 1998—, bd. dirs., 2003—, Woman's Club of Houston, 2004—; chmn. evaluations com. Expanding Your Horizons (conf. jr. HS girls), Houston, 1997—2003; mem. Chancel Choir; accompanist children's choir, elder Spring Branch Presbyn. Ch., Houston. Recipient Excellence in Tchg. award, So. Meth. U., 1992, Mrs. James P. Houstoun Found. award, 1957, Phi Mu Alumnae award, 1957; Friedheim Found. scholar, Winthrop U., 1954. Mem.: AAUW (com. chair 1997—2003), NEA, Spring Br. Coun. Tchrs. English, Spring Br. Edn. Assn., Tex. State Tchrs. Assn., Spring Branch Ind. Sch. Dist. Minority Lit. Reading and Discussion Group (discussion leader 1990—96), U. Houston Reading and Discussion Group (sec. 1990—), Tex. Coun. Tchrs. English, Nat. Coun. Tchrs. English, Outstanding Lit. Book Club, Les Belles Lettres Club (pres. 1967—68), Shadow Oaks Garden Club (v.p. 1958—60, pres. 1960—61), En Amie Book Rev. Club, Kappa Delta Pi (award 1957), Phi Kappa Phi (treas. 1958—60, award 1957), Delta Kappa Gamma (rsch. com. chair 1998—2002, yearbook com. chair 2004—). Presbyterian. Avocations: piano, bridge, travel, crocheting. Home: 2014 Southwick Dr Houston TX 77080 Personal E-mail: joebelksr@aol.com.

BELK, JOHN R., retail executive; s. Thomas M. Belk and Katherine Belk Cook. BA in Economics, Political sci., U. NC, Chapel Hill; MBA, U. Va. With Irving Trust Co., 1981—83; mgmt. trainee Belk Inc., NC, 1986, buyer, merchandise mgr. Matthews Belk store, 1986—89, store mgr. Monroe Belk store, 1989—90, v.p., dir. Charlotte, NC, 1990—92, sr. v.p., 1992—97, pres. fin., sys. and ops., 1998—2004, pres., COO, 2004—. Bd. dirs. Alltel Corp., Bank of Am. Corp., Ruddick Corp. Bd. dirs. Ctrl YMCA, United Way Ctrl. Carolinas. Office: Belk Inc 2801 W Tyvola Rd Charlotte NC 28217

BELK, LEOTIS S., language educator; b. Lancaster, SC, Jan. 8, 1934; s. Samuel David and Mabel Cora Belk; m. Johnnie Ruth Alexander (div.); 1 child, Shayila Nicole Adela. BA, Queens Coll., 1955; MDiv, Va. Union U., 1958; MA, U. San Carlos, 1963; PhD, Temple U., 1975. Instr. J.C. Smith U., Charlotte, NC, 1958—63, Bishop Coll., Dallas, 1963—69; chair, philosophy of religion Colgate-Rochester Divsn. Sch., NY, 1969—75; pastor New Hope Bapt. Ch., Niagara Falls, 1977—80; assoc. prof. Shaw U., Raleigh, NC, 1991—93; adj. prof. Campbell U., Buies Creek, NC, 1998—2000; asst. prof. St. Augustines Coll., Raleigh, 2000—. Bd. mem. Charlotte symposium of World Affairs, NC, 1962—63; chmn. Colgate-Rochester Div. Sch., Philos. Religion Dept., 1971—72; cons. NY State Correctional Sys., Albany, NY, 1974—75; vice-chair Love Canal Revitalization Agy., Niagara Falls, 1980—90; adj. prof. U. Rochester, NY, 1965—69, U. Buffalo, NY, 1977—. Contbr. Outstanding Black Sermons; author: A Record of the Carey Mungo Family and Kin Families of SC. Exec. dir. HUD of Niagara Falls, 1982—83; bd. mem. Criminal Justice Task Force, Niagara County, NY, 1978—79. Grantee Study grant for Mex., J.C. Smith U., 1956. Mem.: NAACP, Raleigh Area Theo. Soc., Martin Luther King Fellows Inc. Democrat. Baptist. Avocations: genealogy, badminton, languages, anthropology, second hand books. Office: St Augustines Coll 1315 Oakwood Ave Raleigh NC 27610 E-mail: belkleo@aol.com.

BELK, THOMAS MILBURN, JR., (TIM BELK), apparel executive; s. Thomas Milburn and Katherine (McKay) Belk. With Belk Inc., Charlotte, NC, 1981—, pres. store div., 1998—2004, chmn., CEO, 2004—. Trustee NC Blumenthal Performing Arts Ctr.; mem. adv. bd. Kenan-Flagler Bus. Sch., Univ. NC, Chapel Hill, Univ. NC, Charlotte; bd. mem. Carolinas Healthcare Sys., Rsch. Triangle Found. NC. Office: Belk Inc 2801 W Tyvola Rd Charlotte NC 28217*

BELKIN, BORIS DAVID, violinist; b. Sverdlovsk, USSR, Jan. 26, 1948; s. David Boris and Anna Alexandre Belkin; children: Alexander, Maïa. Student, Central Music Sch., Moscow, 1969, Moscow Conservatory, 1969-74; studied with, Yankelevitch and Andrievsky. Violinist; appeared with orchs. throughout world, including, N.Y. Philharm., Israel Philharm., Chgo. Symphony Orch., Los Angeles Philharm., Cleve. Symphony Orch., Boston Symphony Orch., Berlin Philharm., Royal Philharm., Phila. Symphony Orch., Paris National, Vienna Symphony, London Philharm., Pitts. Symphony Orch., Concertgebouw, Tokyo Philharm., Phila. Orch.; recs. include Prokofiev Concertos, Brahms, Sibelius, Strauss, Paganini, Shostakovich, Bruch, Glazunov. Recipient 1st prize Nat. Violin Competition USSR, 1973 Office: care Terry Harrison Artists Mgmt The Orchard Market St Charlbury 0X7 3PJ England Office Phone: 0044 1608 810330. Business E-Mail: artists@terryharrison.force9.co.uk.

BELKNAP, MICHAEL H. P., real estate developer; b. South Bend, Ind., Oct. 27, 1940; s. Paul E. and Mary Elizabeth (Gibb) B.; m. Dorothy Callaway, Aug. 12, 1967 (div. Dec. 1989); children: Michael, Jenny Warner, Matthew Gibb; m. Martha Burke-Hennessy, May 25, 1996; stepchildren: Hélène Lesterlin, Roland Lesterlin. BA, Harvard U., 1963, JD, 1967; LLB, Cambridge (Eng.) U., 1965. Bar: N.Y. 1969. Assoc. Sullivan & Cromwell, N.Y.C., 1967-70; dir. Coun. on Environment, Office of Mayor City of N.Y., 1970-72; v.p., gen. counsel Corp. Property Investors, N.Y.C., 1972-75; v.p. Levitt & Sons Inc., Greenwich, Conn., 1975-78; pres. Belknap Co. Ltd., Canaan, N.Y., 1978—. Adj. prof. Western New Eng. Coll. Sch. Law. English Speaking Union fellow, 1963-64. Mem. Berkshire Natrual Resources Coun. (trustee), Harvard Club. Democrat. Episcopalian. also: 45 E End Ave New York NY 10028-7953 Office: 41 Warner Crossing Rd Canaan NY 12029-2807 Office Phone: 518-781-4646.

BELKNAP, NORTON, foundation administrator; b. Topeka, June 17, 1925; s. Paul Edward and Twila Norton Belknap; m. Mary Lonam, June 7, 1950; children: Paula Belknap Reynolds, David Barrett, Randall Page. BS, MIT, 1950, MS, 1951. Various tech. and supervisory positions Exxon, 1951-60; v.p., dir. Esso Japan, 1961-65; chmn., mng. dir. Esso Australia, 1966-69; v.p., exec. v.p., dir. Esso Europe, 1969-73; v.p. corporate planning Exxon Corp., N.Y.C., 1973-79; sr. v.p. Exxon Internat., N.Y.C., 1979-82; trustee Carnegie Hall, N.Y.C., 1974—, mng. dir., 1983-88. Petroleum cons., 1982-2003; bd. dirs. So. Pacific Petroleum USA, 1989-2003; dir. So. Pacific Petroleum NL, 1999-03. Pres. dirs. Paul Taylor Dance Co. 1st lt. USAAF, 1943—46. Decorated Air medal with oak leaf cluster. Mem. Union Club, Century Assn., Met. Opera Club. (N.Y.C.), Tau Beta Pi, Alpha Tau Omega. Home: 563 Park Ave New York NY 10021-7314 Personal E-mail: nbelknap@aol.com.

BELKNAP, ROBERT LAMONT, literature educator; b. NYC, Dec. 23, 1929; s. Chauncey and Dorothy (Lamont) B.; m. Josephine E. Hornor, Aug. 20, 1955 (separated 1992); children: Lydia Duff, Ellen Belknap, Abigail Krueger; m. Cynthia H. Whittaker, Aug. 24, 1997. AB, Princeton U., 1951; postgrad., U. Paris, 1951-52; MA, Columbia U., 1954; cert., Russian Inst., 1957, PhD, 1960; postgrad., Leningrad U., 1963-64; PhD (hon.), Petrozavodsk U., 2001. Instr. Russian, Columbia U., 1957-60, asst. prof., 1960-63, chmn. freshman humanities, 1963, 67-68, 88-91, assoc. prof., 1963-68, assoc. dean student affairs, 1968-69, prof., 1968—2001, acting dean of Coll., 1976-77; dir. Russian Inst., 1977-80; prof. emeritus Columbia U., 2001—. Vis. assoc. prof. Russian Ind. U., 1966, 67; adj. prof. Russian Yale U., 1967; vis. foreign scholar, Hokkaido U., 1999-2000; dir. Columbia U. Seminars, 2001—. Author: The Structure of the Brothers Karamazov, 1967, reprint, 1989, Russian translation, 1997, The Genesis of The Brothers Karamazov, 1990, Russian translation, 2003; co-author: General Education and the Reintegration of the University, 1977; editor, Russianness, 1990. Pres. bd. trustees Brearley Sch., N.Y.C., 1981-87; trustee Whiting Found., 1985—, pres. 2001—; with U.S. Army, 1953-55. Fellow Kennan Inst., 1987-88, Guggenheim, 1994-95. Office: Univ Seminars Columbia Univ New York NY 10027 Office Phone: 212-854-2389. Business E-Mail: rb12@columbia.edu. *Students rarely learn anything they are told. They often learn the things they say themselves. Good teaching wrestles them into saying sensible, verifiable, interesting, and sometimes important things.*

BELKOV, MEREDITH ANN, landmark administrator; b. Chgo., Sept. 26, 1939; d. Louis and Sylvia (Charak) B. Student, U. Md. Recreation dir. Dept. Pks. and Recreation, Washington, 1960-69; outdoor recreation specialist Nat. Pk. Svc., Washington, 1971-73; chief disvn. recreation Golden Gate Nat. Recreation Area, San Francisco, 1973-75; chief interpretation and visitor svcs. Nat. Visitor Ctr., Washington, 1975-78, Dept. Interior Mgmt., Washington, 1978-79; supt. Chickamauga (Ga.) and Chattanooga (Tenn.) Nat. Mil. Park, 1979-87, Jean Lafitte Nat. Hist. Pk. and Preserve, New Orleans, 1987-90, Statue of Liberty, Ellis Island, N.Y.C., 1990—. Bd. dirs. N.Y. Conv. and Visitors Bur., Greater New Orleans Tourist and Conv. Commn., Inc., New Orleans Jazz and Heritage Found. V.p. Chattanooga Symphony and Opera, U. Tenn. Roundtable, Chattanooga Audubon Soc. Fellow NCCJ; recipient Freedom Found. award. Mem. Nat. Pk. and Recreation Assn., Hist. Soc., Mus. Coun. N.Y. Jewish.

BELL, ALBERT JEROME, lawyer; b. Columbus, Ohio, Apr. 24, 1960; s. Albert Leo and Jean Marie (DeFino) B.; m. Carla Jean Hudak, June 7, 1986; 2 children, Brian Albert, Kristin Elizabeth. BA, Ohio State U., 1982; JD, Capital U., 1985. Bar: Ohio 1985. Writer Battelle Meml. Inst., Columbus, 1982-84; pvt. practice law Columbus, 1985-86; vice-chmn., chief adminstrv. officer Big Lots Inc., Columbus, 1987—2004; CEO Moochie & Co., 2005—. Mem. devel. coun. St. Anthony's Hosp., 1990; mem. adv. bd. devel. comm. chair, Annual Fund St. Charles Prep. H.S. Mem. ABA, Ohio Bar Assn., Columbus Bar Assn., Assn. Trial Lawyers Am., Internat. Assn. Corp. Real Estate Execs., Ohio State U. Alumni Assn. Roman Catholic. Avocations: golf, skiing, exercising, basketball.

BELL, ANDREW C., music educator; b. New Orleans, Oct. 9, 1964; s. Clark B. and Maxine P. Bell; m. Angela W. Bell, June 3, 1989; children: Andee, Alayna. B in Music Edn., Glenville State Coll., 1987; M in Music Edn., VanderCook Coll. Music, 1997. Band dir. Washington Middle Sch., Cairo, Ga., 1987—93, Screven County H.S., Sylvania, Ga., 1993—2000, Ctrl. H.S., Macon, Ga., 2000—04; prof. Ga. Mil. Coll., Warner Robins; band dir. Crisp County H.S., Cordele, Ga., 2004—. Mem.: Music Educators Nat. Conv., Condrs. Guild, Ga. Music Educators Assn. (dist. band chair 1997—2000, state rsch. and advocacy chmn. instrumental 1999—2002), Nat. Band Assn. Avocations: movies, reading, Star Trek. Home: 865 Malwood Dr Macon GA 31204 Office: Crisp County HS 2402 Cougar Alley Cordele GA 31015 Business E-Mail: abell@crisp.k12.ga.us.

BELL, BRADLEY J., water treatment company executive; b. 1952; BS, U. Ill., 1974; MBA, Harvard U., 1978. Fin. analyst G.E., 1974-76; mgr. treasury analysis Bendix Corp., 1978-80; treas. Bundy Corp., 1983-87, v.p., treas., 1987; treas. Whirlpool Corp., Benton Harbor, Mich., 1987—97, v.p., 1990—97; sr. v.p., CFO Rohm & Haas Co., 1997—2003; exec. v.p., CFO Nalco Co., Naperville, Ill., 2003—. Bd. dirs. Idex Corp., Compass Minerals Internat. Office: Nalco Co 1601 W Diehl Rd Naperville IL 60563-1198

BELL, BURWELL BAXTER, III, general United States Army; b. Oak Ridge, Tenn., Apr. 9, 1947; BS in Bus. Adminstrn., U. Tenn.; MS in Systems Mgmt., U. So. Calif.; grad. armor officer advanced course, U.S. Army Armor Sch, Fort Knox, Ky., 1976; student, Army Command, Gen. Staff Colls, Fort Leavenworth, Kans., 1980-81, Nat. War Coll., Fort McNair, N.J., 1987-88. Commd. 2d lt. U.S. Army, 1969, advanced through grades to gen., 2002; from platoon leader to exec. officer Troop M, 14th Cavalry U.S. Army Europe and Seventh Army, Germany; comdr. L troop, 3d Reconnissance Squadron, 14th Cavalry U.S. Army Europe and Seventh Army, Germany, 1971-72; comdr. D troop 5th Cavalry Squadron 1st Indivual Tng. Brig. U.S. Army Armor Sch., Ft. Knox, Ky., 1974-75; chief individual tng. dept. U.S. Army Armor Ctr., Ft. Knox, Ky., 1975-76; staff officer modernization coord. office Office Chief of Staff, Army, Washington, 1981-83; cmmdr. 2d squadron, 9th cavalry, 24th infantry divsn. U.S. Army, Ft. Stewart, Ga., 1984-87; exec. officer to cmdr.-in-chief U.S. Ctrl. Command Operation Desert Shield/Desert Storm, Saudi Arabia, 1990-91; comdr. 24th infantry divn., 2nd brigade, Ft. Stewart, Ga., 1991—93; chief of staff 3d infantry divsn. U.S. Army Europe and Seventh Army, Germany, 1993-94; asst. div. comdr. 1st infantry divn. (mech.), Bamberg, Germany, 1995—96; chief of staff V Corps U.S. Army Europe and Seventh Army, Germany, 1996-97, dep. chief of staff for ops., 1997-98, chief of staff, 1998-99; comdg. gen. U.S. Army Armor Ctr., and Ft. Knox, Ft. Knox, Ky., 1999—2001, III Corps. and Fort Hood, Ft. Hood, Tex., 2001—02, U.S. Army, Europe & 7th Army, Heidelberg, Germany, 2002—. Decorated Legion of Merit with 2 Oak Leaf Clusters, Bronze Star medal, Army Commendation medal with 2 Oak Leaf Clusters, Defense Superior Svc. medal, Meritorious Svc. medal with 2 Oak Leaf Clusters.*

BELL, CARL COMPTON, psychiatrist, researcher; b. Chgo., Oct. 28, 1947; s. William Yancy and Pearl Louise (Debnam) Bell; m. Joanne Scott, Jan. 1, 1969 (div. Apr. 1971); 1 child, Cristin Carol; m. Dora Dixie, Dec. 1984 (div. May 1989); m. Tyra Taylor, Mar. 19, 1991 (div. Oct. 2003); children: Briatta Honore, William Yancy Bell IV; m. Phyllis West, Mar. 18, 2005. BS in Biology, U. Ill.-Chgo., 1967; MD, Meharry Med. Coll., 1971. Diplomate Am. Bd. Psychiatry and Neurology (examiner). Intern Ill. State Psychiat. Inst., Chgo., 1971-72, resident, 1972-74; pvt. practice medicine specializing in psychiatry Chgo., 1974—; dir. psychiat. emergency svcs. Jackson Park Hosp., Chgo., 1976-77, assoc. dir. divsn. behavioral and psychodynamic medicine, 1979-82, mem. staff, 1972—; staff psychiatrist Human Correctional and Svcs. Inst., Chgo., 1977-78, Chgo. Bd. Edn., 1977-79, Chatham Avalon Mental Health Ctr., Chgo., 1977-79, Cmty. Mental Health Coun., Chgo., 1977-79, med. dir., 1983-87, exec. dir., 1987—; pres., CEO Cmty. Mental Health Coun. and Found., 1993—; assoc. prof. to prof. clin. psychiatry U. Ill., 1983—, prof. pub. health, 1993—. Cons. Cmty. divsn. Lilly Endowment; cons. editl. bd. Jour. Prison and Jail Health, 1990-92, Cmty. Mental Health Jour., 1989—, Jour. Hosp. and Cmty. Psychiatry, 1990-94, Jour. Nat. Med. Assn., 1994-98, Psychiat. Svcs., 1994-98, Jour. Correctional Health Care, 1997-2000, Jour. Health Care to Poor and Underserved, 1991—, Jour. Infant, Child and Adolescent Psychotherapy, 1997—, Clin. Psychiatric News, 2000—; cons. in field. Prodr.(creator animation): Book Worm, 1984; author: Psychiatric Aspects of Violence: Issues in Prevention and Treatment, 2000, Sanity of Survival: Reflections on Community Mental Health and Wellness, 2004; co-author: Suicide and Homicide Among Adolescents, 1994; mem. editl. bd.: Am. Psychiat. Pub., Inc., 2001—; contbr. articles to profl. jours.; prodr.(creator): (video) Eight Pieces of Brocade, 2000—; talk show host: Sta. WVON-AM, 1987—90; Sta. WJPC-FM, 1992—93. Profl. adv. panel Mental Health Assn. Greater Chgo., 1983—; adv. com. funded grant on Aggressors, Victims and Bystanders, 1989-92; bd. dirs. Ill. Coun. Against Handgun Violence, 1990—, Nat. Commn. on Correctional Health Care, 1983—, chmn. 1992; lectr. U. Chgo., 1986—, Chgo. Med. Sch., 1987—; tchr. martial arts, 1973—; apptd. to violence against women adv. coun., 1995-2000; mem. White House strategy session on Children, Violence and Responsibility, 1999; mem. surgeon gen. report on mental health-Culture, Race and Ethnicity Working Group, 2000; mem. Surgeon Gen. report on youth violence working group, 2000—; mem. Chgo. Bd. Health, 2002—. Lt. comdr. USN, 1974-76. Named Top Doctor, Chgo. mag., 1997, 2001; named to Guide To Am.'s Top Psychiatrists, Consumers Rsch. Coun. Am., 2004—05; recipient plaque in recognition and appreciation, Chatham-Avalon Mental Health Ctr., 1979, Div. Behavioral Medicine, 1982, Social Action award, Chgo. chpt. Black Social Workers, 1988, Mental Health award, Englewood Cmty. Health Orgn., 1988, Scholastic Achievement award, Chgo. chpt. Nat. Assn. Black Social Workers, 1980, Ellen Quinn Meml. award, 1986, Monarch award, Alpha Kappa Alpha, 1986, Alumnus of Yr. award, Meharry Med. Coll., 1991, Cmty. Psychiatry award, Am. Assn. Cmty. Psychiatrists, 1992, Lifetime Achievement award, Black Psychiatrists of Am., 1994, Freddye Smith award, Cmty. Mental Health Coun., 1997, Blanche F. Ittleson award Lifetime Contbns., Am. Ortho Psychiatric Assn., 2000, Lifetime Achievement award, Cmty. Behavioral Healthcare Assn. Ill., 2001, Living Legacy award, Provident Found., 2001, Dr. Jeanne Spurlock Lectr. award, Am. Acad. Child and Adolescent Psychiatrists, 2002, George B. Nash, Sr. Pub. Edn. award, Nat. Alliance for Mentally Ill, Chgo., 2003, Disting. Psychiatrist Lecture Award Outstanding Achievement in Psychiatry, Am. Psychiat. Assn., 2003, Minority Mental Health award, Am. Psychiat. Found., 2003, Minority Svcs. award, 2004, Welcome Back award, Eli Lily Co., 2003, From Whence We Came award, Allstate Ins. Co., 2004; fellow Inst. Medicine Chgo., 2004; grantee, NIMH, 2001—; Goldberger fellow, 1969, Dr. Martin Luther King Jr. fellow, 1970—71. Fellow Am. Coll. Psychiatrists (com. Laughlin fellows 1989-92, com. on fins. 1993-96, com. on pub. edn. 1994-96, com. membership devel. 1996-00, com. strategic planning 2000—, bd. regents 2005-, Bowis Disting. Svc. award 2002), Am. Psychiat. Assn. (disting.; Falk fellow 1972-73, task force-delivery psychiat. svcs. to proverty areas 1972-73, com. black psychiatrists, 1988-90, chmn. black caucus 1990-92, vice chair task force psychiat. aspects of violence 1997—, joint commn. on pub. affairs 2000—, com. on psychiat. diagnosis and assessment 2003—, Spl. Presdl. Commendation 1997, Disting. Psychiatrist Lecture award 2003); mem. Nat. Med. Assn. (local chmn. sect. on neurology and psychiatry 1983, conv., nat. chmn. sect. on psychiatry and behavioral scis. 1985-86, E. Y. Williams Disting. Sr. Clin. scholar psychiatry sect. 1992), Black Psychiatrists Am. (editor Bottom Line newsletter 1977-82, v.p. 1980-82), Cook County Physicians Assn., Prairie State Physicians, Ill. Psychiat. Soc., Am. Assn. Cmty. Mental Health Ctr. Psychiatrists (bd. dirs. 1985-89), Am. Coll. Psychiatry, Nat. Coun. Cmty. Health Ctrs. (sec. bd. dirs. 1986, sec., treas. 1987), Underwater Explorers Soc., Shorei Goju Karate Soc. (6th degree Black Belt), Martial Arts Karate Assn., Alpha Omega Alpha. Office: Community Mental Health Coun 8704 S Constance Ave Chicago IL 60617-2756 also: Jackson Park Hosp 7531 S Stony Island Ave Chicago IL 60649-3993 Office Phone: 773-734-4033 ext. 204. Business E-Mail: carlcbell@pol.net.

BELL, CAROLYN SHAW, economist, educator; b. Framingham, Mass., June 21, 1920; d. Clarence Edward and Grace (Wellington) Shaw; m. Nelson S. Bell, Aug. 26, 1953; 1 dau. by previous marriage, Tova Maria. AB magna cum laude, Mt. Holyoke Coll., 1941; PhD, London Sch. Econs., 1949; LHD (hon.), Babson Coll., 1983, Denison U., 1988, North Adams State Coll., 1991. Economist OPA, 1941-45; rsch. economist London Sch. Econs., 1946-47, Social Sci. Rsch. Coun., Harvard, 1950-53; mem. faculty Wellesley Coll., 1950-89, prof. econs., 1962-89, chmn. dept., 1962-65, 79-82, Katharine Coman prof. econs., 1970-89, Katharine Coman prof. econs. emeritus, 1989—; cons. Lexington, Mass., 1989—. Pub. mem. Fed. Adv. Coun. on Unemployment Inc., 1974-77, chmn., 1975-77; bd. econ. advisors Pub. Interest Econ. Ctr.; bd. overseers Amos Tuck Grad. Sch. Bus. Adminstrn., Dartmouth, 1973-79; mem. econs. policy coun. UN Assn., 1976-85, trustee, 1981-90; trustee Joint Coun. Econ. Edn., 1975-83, Tchrs. Ins. and Annuity Assn., 1977-85, Symmes Life Care, Inc., 1994-2001, NEADS, Inc., 1994—; mem. NRC Com. for Behavioral & Social Scis., 1977-83; bd. adv. Internat. Labour Rev. Author: Consumer Choice in the U.S. Economy, 1967, The Economics of the Ghetto, 1970; co-author: (with W.W. Cochrane) Economics of Consumption, 1956; co-author: Coping in A Troubled Society, 1974; contbr. articles to profl. jours.; radio and TV commentator; mem. bd. editors Challenge Mag. Mem. Hearing Dog Adv. Coun., 1990-93. Recipient Disting. Achievement award The Boston Club, 1996, WERT award for Tchg. Excellence, 1997, Acad. of Women Acheivers, YWCA, 1997. Mem. AAUP (pres. Wellesley chpt. 1965-66). AAUW (Shirley Farr fellow 1961-62), ACLU, Assn. for Advancement Socio-Econs., Manhattan Inst. (adv. bd.), Am. Econs. Assn. (chmn. com. on status women in econs. profession 1972-74, exec. com. mem. 1975-77), Assn. Evolutionary Econs. (bd. dirs. 1973-75), Ea. Econs. Assn. (exec. bd. 12983-85), Phi Beta Kappa (pres. Eta Mass chpt. 1978-80), Delta Soc. (svc. dog. adv. bd. 1994-95). Home and Office: 1010 Waltham St Apt 8F Lexington MA 02421-8061 E-mail: cbell@wellesley.edu.

BELL, CHARLES EUGENE, JR., retired industrial engineer; b. N.Y.C., Dec. 13, 1932; s. Charles Edward and Constance Elizabeth (Verbella) Bell; m. Doris R. Clifton, Jan. 14, 1967; 1 child, Scott Charles. B.Engring., Johns Hopkins U., 1954, MS in Engring., 1959. Registered Calif. Indsl. engr. Signode Corp., Balt., 1957—61, asst. to plant mgr., 1961—63, plant engr., 1963—64, divsn. indsl. engr. Glenview, Ill., 1964—69, asst. to divsn. mgr., 1969—76, engring. mgr., 1976—93; cons., 1993—2004; ret., 2004. Host committeeman Internat. Indsl. Engring. Conf., Chgo., 1984, Chgo., 92. With U.S. Army, 1955—57. Mem.: NSPE, Soc. Plastics Engrs., Tenn. Soc. Profl. Engrs., Indsl. Mgmt. Club Ctrl. Md. (pres. 1964), Am. Inst. Indsl. Engrs. (pres. 1981), Druid Hills Country Club. Republican. Roman Catholic. Home: 207 Markham Ln Crossville TN 38558

BELL, C(LYDE) R(OBERTS) (BOB BELL), foundation administrator; b. Balt., Apr. 12, 1931; s. William and Rachel (Roberts) B.; m. Carol Ann Murphy, June 14, 1980 (dec. Aug. 1997); children: Diane, Nancy, Mary Lynn, Catherine, Robert, Brian, Douglas, Jeffrey, Lawrence, Laura; m. Jean Creighton Chapman, Feb. 13, 1999. BS with distinction, U.S. Naval Acad., 1953. Registered profl. nuclear engr. Commd. ensign USN, 1953, advanced through grades to vice adm., 1987, ret., 1988; pres. Greater Omaha C. of C., 1989—. Bd. dirs. Ctr. for Human Nutrition, Omaha, WELCOM, Omaha. Trustee Boy Scouts Am., Omaha, 1990—; bd. dirs. NCCJ, Omaha, 1991—. Mem. Omaha Country Club, Omaha Club (Man of Yr. 1991), Omaha Plaza Club, Omaha Press Club. Avocations: golf, reading, the arts, family. Office: Greater Omaha C of C 1301 Harney St Omaha NE 68102-1832 E-mail: gocc@accessomaha.com.

BELL, DANIEL JOSEPH, elementary school educator; b. Leominster, Mass. s. Daniel Joseph and Marie Bell; m. Buffy Clifford Bell, Dec. 30, 1983; children: Amy Foss, Lucas Foss, Derek. BS in nautical sci., Mass. Maritime Acad., 1972; M in edn., Antioch U., 1998. 2d grade tchr. Bernice A. Ray Sch., Hanover, Mass., 1990—95, 5th grade tchr., 1996—2004. Ensign1975 naval, 1972. Avocations: canoeing, bicycling, fishing. Home: 318 Delano Rd Reading VT 05062 Personal E-mail: danbell@sover.net.

BELL, DANIEL MARK, music educator; b. Omaha, Aug. 17, 1962; s. Ron and Nancy Bell; 1 child, Ryan. MusB, U. Iowa, 1985; MusM, Colo. State U., 1988. Tchr. Ft. (Colo.) Lupton HS, 1988—94, Rangeview HS, Aurora, Colo., 1994—97, Cheyenne Mt. Jr. HS, Colo. Springs, Colo., 1997—; freelance musician Colo., 1985—. Band dir. Colo. Music Educators Conf., 2000—03. Mem.: Am. Sch. Band Dirs. Assn., Colo. Music Educator's Assn., Phi Beta Mu Band Dirs. of Excellence Music Frat. Avocation: skiing. Home: 7716 Barn Owl Dr Fountain CO 80817-4211 Office Phone: 719-475-6120. Business E-Mail: bell@cmsd.k12.co.us.

BELL, DAVID ARTHUR, advertising agency executive; b. Mpls., May 29, 1943; s. Arthur E. and Frances (Tripp) B.; m. Gail G. Galvani; children: Jennifer L., Jenny L., Jeffrey D., Ashley Tripp, Andrew Joseph. BA in Polit. Sci., Macalester Coll., 1965. Account exec. Leo Burnett, Chgo., 1965-67; pres. Knox Reeves, Mpls., 1967-74; pres. Atlantic div. Bozell & Jacobs, 1974-85; pres. Bozell, Jacobs, Kenyon & Eckhardt, 1986-92; chmn., CEO Bozell Worldwide Inc., 1995—98, True North Comm., Inc., 1998—2001; vice chmn. Interpublic Group of Companies, Inc., N.Y.C., 2001—03, chmn., 2003—. CEO, 2003—05, co-chmn., 2005. Bd. dirs. Bus. Publs. Audit, Primedia, Inc., mem. corp. governance and compensation com., 2003; chmn. Am. Advt. Fedn. Nat. com. coord. United Way Am., Minn., 1975—; trustee Macalester Coll., 1986—88, trustee emeritus, 1998—, Sacred Heart Acad., NY; chmn. Advt. Ednl. Found., Ad Coun., 2002—; bd. dirs. True North, 1998—2001, Warnaco, 2003—, Nat. Forest Fedn., 2002—, chmn., 2004—; mem. corp. coun. Interlochen Ctr. Arts, 2003—. Recipient charter centennial medallion Macalester Coll., 1974; named disting. alumnus Macalester Coll., 1978; recipient Minn. Airman of Yr. award, 1967 Mem. Am. Advt. Fedn. (chmn. nat. bd. dirs. 1988-91), Am. Assn. Advt. Agys. (chmn. 1996-97. Republican. Presbyterian. Office: Interpublic Group of Companies Inc 1114 Avenue of the Americas New York NY 10036

BELL, DAVID GUS (BUDDY BELL), professional baseball manager; b. Pitts., Aug. 27, 1951; s. Gus B.; m. Gloria Eysoldt Bell; children: David, Michael, Ricky, Kristi Marie, Tracy. Player in minor leagues, 1969-71; outfielder, 3d baseman Cleve. Indians, 1972-78, minor league hitting instr., 1990, coach, 1994-95; 3d baseman Tex. Rangers, 1979-85, 89; with Cin. Reds, 1985-88; player Houston Astros, 1988; dir. minor league instrn. Chgo. White Sox, 1991-93; mgr. Detroit Tigers, 1996-98, Colo. Rockies, Denver, 1999—2002; bench coach Cleve. Indians, 2002—05; head coach Kansas City Royals, 2005—. Mem.: Am. League All-Star Team, 1973, 80-82, 84. Recipient Gold Glove award, 1979-84; Lou Gehrig Mem. award, 1988; named to Tex. Baseball Hall of Fame, 1988. Office: c/o Kansas City Royals 1 Royal Way Kansas City MO 64129

BELL, DAVID MAXWELL, music educator, consultant; b. Waukehsa, Wis., Nov. 8, 1954; s. Vernon Leigh Bell and Enid Ruth Morrison-Bell; m. Lois Jean Tams, May 30, 1979; children: Lauren Elizabeth, Amanda Leigh, Eric William. BA, No. Ill. U., 1975; MusM, U. Cin., 1979. Cert. tchr. Ohio Dept. of Edn., 1979. Vocal music tchr. Dayton City Schs., 1979—82; fine arts facilitator and head choral dir. Winton Woods City Schs., Cin., 1982—; music dir. Dayton Liederkranz-Turner Soc., Ohio, 1979—87; founding music dir. Sing Cin.! Cin. Arts Festival, 1994; guest clinician Miami U., Oxford, Ohio, 2001; guest clinician Coll.-Conservatory of Music U. Cin., 2002. Bd. mem. Ohio Alliance for Arts Edn., Columbus, Ohio; mem. arts edn. adv. com. Ohio Dept. of Edn., Columbus, Ohio, 1997—99, mem. adv. bd. state content standards for fine arts, 2001—03; co-chmn. ednl. leadership team Winton Woods HS, Cin., 2000—; arts in edn. partnerships adv. panel Ohio Arts Coun., Columbus, 2000—01; adv. panel fine arts field test Nat. Coun. of Exec. State Sch. Officers, Washington, 1998—98; adv. panel Ohio dept. of edn. Ednl. Testing Svcs., Princeton, NJ, 1999—99; cons. WLWT TV, Cin., 1996; founding adv. com. May Festival Youth Honors Chorus, Cin., 1988—88, Muse Machine Youth Arts Orgn., Dayton, 1981—82. Contributing conductor: TV series Cin. Pops Holiday: Fourth of July from the Heartland; contributing conductor (TV series) Cin. Olympic Torch Ceremony, (albums) Cin. Pops Mega Movies (Premiered at number fourteen on the Billboard Mag. classical-crossover charts, 2000), (TV series) Tall Stacks Farewell Ceremony (Emmy award, 1995); singer: (albums) Verdi's Requiem with Chicago Symphony and Symphony Chorus (Grammy award, 1978), Beethoven's Missa Solemnis with Chicago Symphony and Symphony Chorus (Grammy award, 1979), Verdi's Four Sacred Pieces with Chicago Symphony and Symphony Chorus (Grammy award, 1980); contbr. articles to profl. jours. Scholar, U. of Cin. College-Conservatory of Music, 1977—79. Mem.: Winton Woods Teachers Assn. (bldg. rep. 1984—86), Ohio Music Edn. Assn. (choral affairs chair for state conf. 1992—93), Ohio Choral Dirs. Assn. (pres. 1999—2001), Pi Kappa Lambda (hon.). Avocations: family, reading, golf. Home: 7695 Chelsea Court Hamilton OH 45011 Office: Winton Woods City Schools 1231 West Kemper Road Cincinnati OH 45240 Office Phone: 513-619-2438. E-mail: Bell.David@Winterwoods.org.

BELL, DELORIS WILEY, physician; b. Solomon, Kans., Sept. 30, 1942; d. Harry A. and Mildren H. (Watt) Wiley; children: Leslie, John. BA, Kans. Wesleyan U., 1964; MD, U. Kans., 1968. Diplomate Am. Bd. Ophthalmology. Intern St. Luke's Hosp., Kansas City, Mo., 1968-69; resident U. Kans. Med. Ctr., Kansas City, 1969-72; practice medicine specializing in ophthalmology Overland Park, Kans., 1973—. Mem. AMA, Kans. Med. Soc. (pres. sect. ophthalmology 1985-86, spkr. house 1994-97), Am. Acad. Ophthalmology (councillor 1988-93, chmn. state govtl. affairs 1993-97, bd. trustees 2000-03), Kans. Soc. Ophthalmology (pres. 1985-86), Kansas City Soc. Ophthalmology and Otolaryngology (sec. 1984-86, pres.-elect 1988, pres. 1989). Avocations: photography, travel. Office: 7000 W 121st St Ste 100 Shawnee Mission KS 66209-2010 Office Phone: 913-498-2015. Personal E-mail: cd2cdb@gmail.com.

BELL, DONNA LOUISE, music educator; b. Houston, Oct. 25, 1953; d. Jewell Stanley and Hazel (Rogers) Rush; m. Stephen Ray Bell, June 4, 1983; children: Melissa Lynn, Jered Stephen. BS in Elem. Edn. and Music, Howard Payne U., Brownwood, Tex., 1976. Cert. in early childhood edn., ESL instr. Elem. tchr. Klein Ind. Sch. Dist., Houston, 1976-77, Inwood Bapt. Sch., Houston, 1977-79, Cen. Ind. Sch. Dist., Pollok, Tex., 1983-84, Liberty Christian Sch., Denton, Tex., 1986-87; elem. tchr. music Cypress-Fairbanks Ind. Sch. Dist., Houston, 1979-83; pvt. tchr. voice, Lewisville, Tex., 1988—; music tchr., choir dir. Liberty Christian Sch., Denton, 1994—; early childhood tchr. Magnolia Ind. Sch. Dist., 2001—. Former vocalist Continental Singers, Singing Texans, Eng., Scotland; soloist local chs., Dallas, 1985—; dir. children's choirs, Lewisville, 1985—. Mem. Community Chorus Ft. Worth, 1990—. Baptist. Avocations: singing, playing piano, drawing.

BELL, ERNEST LORNE, III, retired lawyer; b. Boston, June 12, 1926; s. Ernest L. and Ellamay (Currier) B.; m. Margaret Van Nostrand Depue, Apr. 14, 1951 (dec. Oct. 1988); children: David E., Robin E., Roseanne Margaret; m. Sally Leavitt Cheney, Nov. 25, 1989. BA cum laude, Harvard Coll., 1949; JD, U. Mich., 1952. Bar: N.H. 1952, U.S. Supreme Ct. 1962. Pvt. practice, Keene, N.H., 1952; ptnr. firm Bell & Falk, P.A., 1972-99; sole practice law Keene, NH, 1999—2003; ret., 2003. Author: An Initial View of Ultra as an American Weapon in World War II. Mem. exec. bd. Daniel Webster coun. Boy Scouts Am., 1970-79, 93—; chmn. bd. advisers Colony House Mus., 1984-91; trustee, treas. Keene Pub. Libr.; del. N.H. Constl. Conv., 1964, 74; mem. World War II Studies Assn.; mem. N.H. Aero. Commn., 1980-86. Recipient Silver Beaver award Fellow Am. Bar Found. (N.H. chair 1993-99); mem. ABA, N.H. Bar Assn (pres. 1978-79), N.H. Bar Found. (sec., bd. dirs. 1985-90, chmn. 1991-93), Cheshire County Bar Assn., Lawyer Pilots Bar Assn. (founding dir. 1962-68), Def. Rsch. Inst. (v.p. 1969-73, sec. 1973-76), Am. Kennel Club (del. 1979-81), Std. Schnauzer Club Am., Harvard Club (Boston). Episcopalian. Home: 35 Felt Rd Keene NH 03431-2103 Personal E-mail: tutt_b@verizon.net.

BELL, FRANCES LOUISE, medical technologist; b. Milton, Pa., Apr. 28, 1926; d. George Earl and Kathryn Robbins (Fairchild) Reichard; m. Edwin Lewis Bell II, Dec. 27, 1950; children: Ernest Michael, Stephen Thomas, Eric Leslie. *Edwin Lewis Bell II, BS, MS, PhD, an emeritus professor of biology at Albright College, continues to research and publish about amphibians and reptiles. Ernest, BS Rensselaer Polytechnic Institute 1974, MS 1975, is an electrical engineer. His wife Christine Luddy, BS Simmons College 1974, MS 1977, is a medical librarian. Stephen, BS Franklin and Marshall College 1976, MD Jefferson Medical College 1980, is a cardiologist. His wife Wendy Stabolepszy, BS in business management Franklin and Marshall College 1979, is currently a homemaker and volunteer. Eric, BS Bucknell University 1977, MS Cornell University 1980, PhD 1985, is a research chemist. His wife Linda Kaszczuk, BS University of Connecticut 1981, MBA University of Rochester 1991, is a research scientist. Mrs. Bell has eight grandchildren.* BS in Biology cum laude, Bucknell U., 1948; MT, Geisinger Meml. Hosp., 1949. Registered med. technologist. Med. technologist Burlington County Hosp., Mt. Holly, N.J., 1949-50, Robert Packer Hosp., Sayre, Pa., 1950, Carle Hosp./Clinic, Urbana, Ill., 1951-52, St. Joseph Hosp., Reading, Pa., 1972-83. Vol. Crime Watch, City Hall, Reading, 1985-90, Am. Heart Assn., Reading, 1956-2000, March of Dimes, Reading, 1956-72, Am. Cancer Soc., Reading, 1956-71, Multiple Sclerosis, Reading, 1956-72, Reading Musical Found., 1985-90, Hist. Soc. Berks County; corr. sec. women's aux., 1986-90; fin. sec. aux. Albright Coll., 1988-95; hospitality co-chmn. women's com. Reading Symphony Orch., 1985-90, editor yearbook women's com., 1992-96; editor yearbook Reading Symphony Orch. League, 1996-2003; chmn. hospitality Reading-Berks Pub. Librs., 1988-91; mem. Friends Reading Mus., Berks County Conservancy. Mem. AAUW (assoc. editor bull. 1961-63, cultural interests rep. 1967-68), Woman's Club of Reading (treas. 1986-88, fin. sec. 1991-2004), United Meth. Women, World Affairs Coun. Berks County, Libr. Soc. Albright Coll., Phi Beta Kappa. Republican. Methodist. Avocations: music appreciation, photography, postcard art prints. Home: 1454 Oak Ln Reading PA 19604-1865 *Life and grace are cherished gifts to each one of us from our creator. We are spiritual beings, so our nature is to be loving, kind, understanding, forgiving and compasssionate in all our relations with others.*

BELL, FRANK OURAY, JR., lawyer; b. San Francisco, Aug. 13, 1940; s. Frank Ouray Sr. and Clara Belle (McClure) Bell; m. Sherrie A. Levie, Mar. 29, 1981; children: Aimee, David;children from previous marriage: Carin, Laurie. AB, San Francisco State U., 1963; JD, U. Calif., San Francisco, 1966. Bar: Calif. 1966, U.S. Dist. Ct. (no. dist.) Calif. 1967, U.S. Ct. Appeals (9th cir.) 1967, U.S. Supreme Ct. 1973. Dep. atty. gen. Calif. State's Atty.'s Office, Sacramento, 1966-68; ptnr. Goorjian & Bell, San Francisco, 1968-70; chief asst. Fed. Pub. Defender's Office, San Francisco, 1970-82; dir. Calif. State Pub. Defender's Office, 1984-87; pvt. practice law San Francisco, 1982-84; sr. litig. assoc. Olimpia, Whelan & Lively, San Jose, Calif., 1987-89; pvt. practice San Mateo and Redwood City, Calif., 1989—. Mem.: Calif. Pub. Defenders Assn. (bd. dirs. 1986—87), San Mateo County Bar Assn. Democrat. Jewish. Office: 303 Bradford St Ste C Redwood City CA 94063 Office Phone: 650-365-8300. Business E-Mail: FrankBell@FrankBellLaw.com.

BELL, GARY LYNN, owner production company, video and audio producer; b. Coffeyville, Kans., Oct. 11, 1949; s. Robert Hayes Bell and Nadine Owens; m. Karen Elizabeth Miller, Feb. 1, 1997; 1 child, Eric; m. Bertha Ruth May (div. Sept. 0, 1978); children: Gregory, Jeremy. Sonar technician USN, Long Beach, Calif., 1969—73; ind. prodr., musician L.A., 1973—92; news cameraman, editor Jones Intercable TV, Palmdale, Calif., 1997—99; owner, CEO Gig 2 Me Music & Video, Lancaster, Calif., 1999—2002. Prodr. Dabany

Productions, Hollywood, Calif., 1986—94. Prodr.: (musical composition) I'm Telling You, 1998 (named most popular song on Indie.com, 2000). Com. mem. Lancaster C. of C., 1999—2002, Palmdale C. of C., 2000—02; mem. Quartz Hill Chamber Of Commerce, 2001—02. Recipient appreciation award, Palmdale C. of C., 2001. Office: Gig 2 Me Music & Video 43568 Yaffa St Lancaster CA 93535 Business E-Mail: gary@gig2me.com.

BELL, GEORGE F., computer company executive; b. England; BME, U. Newcastle-upon-Tyne; MA in Bus. Mgmt., Durham (Eng.) U. With IBM, England; from mng. dir., CEO Australian Group to v.p., pres. European Group Computer Scis. Corp., El Segundo, Calif., 1998—2003, v.p., 2003—, pres. European Group, 2003—.

BELL, GRIFFIN BOYETTE, lawyer, former United States attorney general; b. Americus, Ga., Oct. 31, 1918; s. A. C. and Thelma (Pilcher) Bell; m. Mary Foy Powell, Feb. 20, 1943 (dec.); 1 child, Griffin; m. Nancy Duckworth Kinnebrew, June 8, 2001. Student, Ga. Southwestern Coll.; LL.B. cum laude, Mercer U., 1948, LL.D., 1967. Bar: Ga. 1947. Pvt. practice law, Savannah, Rome, Ga., 1947-53; ptnr. firm King & Spalding, Atlanta, 1953—58, mng. ptnr., 1959-61, sr. ptnr., 1976—77, 1979—2004, sr. counsel, 2004—; chief of staff to Gov. Ernest Vandiver State of Ga., Atlanta, 1959-61; judge U.S. Ct. Appeals (5th cir.), 1961-76; atty. gen. U.S. Dept. Justice, Washington, 1977-79. Mem. vis. com. Vanderbilt U. Law Sch.; head Am. del. Madrid Conf. Security and Coop. Europe, 1980. Co-chmn. Nat. Task Force Violent Crime, 1981, Pres. Bush's Com. Fed. Ethics Law Reform, 1989; mem. Sec. of State's Adv. Com. South Africa; mem. rev. panel U.S. Office Mil. Commn. for mil. tribunals at Guantanamo Bay, Cuba, 2003—; chmn. Atlanta Commn. Crime Delinquency, 1965—66; bd. dirs. Fed. Jud. Ctr., 1974—76; trustee Mercer U., Ga. Served to maj. U.S. Army, 1941—46. Recipient Thomas Jefferson Meml. Found. award for Excellence in Law, 1984. Mem.: ABA (chmn. divsn. jud. adminstrn. 1975—76), Am. Law Inst., Am. Coll. Trial Lawyers (pres. 1985—86), Order of Coif. Baptist. Office: King & Spalding LLP 191 Peachtree St NE Atlanta GA 30303-1740 Office Phone: 404-572-4879. E-mail: gbell@kslaw.com.

BELL, HANEY HARDY, III, lawyer; b. Staunton, Va., Aug. 20, 1944; s. Haney Hardy Jr. and Maud (Deekens) B.; m. Alice Tester, Feb. 17, 1968; 1 child, Landon D. BA, U. Va., 1966; JD cum laude, U. Wis., 1973. Bar: Va. 1974. Group ins. rep. Prudential Ins. Co. Am., Milw., 1969-70; assoc. Woods, Rogers & Hazlegrove, Roanoke, Va., 1973-78; assoc. counsel R.J. Reynolds Industries, Inc., Winston-Salem, N.C., 1978-79; sec., gen. counsel RJR Foods, Inc., 1979-80; sr. internat. counsel R.J. Reynolds Tobacco Internat., Inc., 1980-87; assoc. gen. counsel Fieldcrest Cannon Inc., Eden, N.C., 1987-95, Lorillard Tobacco Co., Greensboro, 1996—2002, Santa Fe (N.Mex.) Natural Tobacco Co., 2002—. Lt. AUS, 1967-69. Mem. Va. State Bar, Order of Coif. Office Phone: 505-438-1335. E-mail: hbell@sfntc.com.

BELL, HELEN LAVIN, artist; b. Allentown, Pa. d. Thomas Joseph and Anna Helen Lavin; m. Paul Edward Bell, June 10, 1950; children: Celine Butler, Sharon Neiman, Paul Jr., Christine Schlacter. Student, Western Md. Coll., 1945-47, Md. Inst. Art, 1947-48, Telfair Acad. Arts, 1958-59, U. Calif., Riverside, 1970-71, 80-81. Asst. art dir. Davison's, Atlanta, 1950-51. One-woman shows include Riverside (Calif.) Art Mus., 1980, 2003-04, Rizzoli Internat., Costa Mesa, Calif., 1987, Zola Fine Art, Beverly Hills, Calif., 1990, EOS Gallery, Redlands, Calif., 2003, Riverside Art Mus., Calif., 2003-2004, Mission San Juan Capitrano, Calif., 2005, Sandstone Gallery, Laguna Beach, Calif., 2005, others; group shows include City of Riverside, Calif., 1975, Riverside County Mus., Beaumont, Calif., 1976, 90, Calif. Poly. U., Pomona, 1987, Corp. Rental program L.A. County Mus. Art, 1989-95, Calif. Small Works, Santa Rosa, 1992, 93, Carte Blanche, 1996, Made in Calif., Brea, 1997, Echoes and Visions II, V, 2002, Laguna Niguel, Calif., 1998, Millard Sheets Small Works Gallery, 2001, EOS Gallery, Redlands, Calif., 2003, Riverside Art Museum, Riverside, Calif., 2003, J. Wayne Stark Gallery, Tex. A & M U. Coll. Station, 2004. Event chair Nat. Charity League, Riverside, Calif., 1979-83; trustee Riverside Art Mus., 1979-82. Merit scholar Telfair Acad. Arts and Scis., Savannah, Ga., 1958. Mem. Redlands Art Assn. (trustee 1985-87, 91-95, sec.), Art Alliance (pres. 1979-80, com. chairs 1978, 81, 82, 2000), Nat. Assn. Women Artists, Inc., Calif. Art Club (painting patron), So. Calif. Plein Air Painters Assn. Republican. Roman Catholic. Avocations: swimming, travel. Studio: 6359 Dulcet Pl Riverside CA 92506 Office Phone: 951-682-9289.

BELL, JACQUELINE DELORES, management consultant; b. Cleveland, Ohio, Feb. 28, 1951; d. Gwendolyn Cherry Marks and William Glover; children: Corey, Shaun. AB, Atlanta Area Tech. Coll., 1970. Dir. bus. devel. Dreamsan, Inc., College Park, Ga., 2001—; mgr. customer svc. Denon Digital Industries, Madison, Ga., 1987—2001. Mem. Monticello City Coun., Monticello, Ga., 1992—2002; pres. 5th dist. Ga. Mcpl. Assn., Atlanta, 2001—02; bd. dirs. Funderburg Park Commn., Monticello, Jasper County Family Connection, Monticello; mem. exec. bd. Ga. Assn. Black Elected Ofcls., Atlanta, 1998—2002; bd. dirs. Ga. Mcpl. Assn., Atlanta. Named One of 50 Most Influential Black Women in Ga., Ga. Informer News Publ., 2000-2001; recipient Racial Barrier Breaker - History Maker award, The James Wimberly Inst. Black Studies & History Inc., 2002. Mem.: Nat. League Cities (cmty. devel. policy com. 2002). Democrat. Avocation: travel. Home: 778 Funderburg Dr Monticello GA 31064 Office Phone: 404-559-9700.

BELL, JAMES A., aerospace transportation executive; b. L.A. m. Mary Bell. B in Acctg., Calif. State U., L.A. Joined as acct. Rockwell, 1972, various positions including corp. senior internal auditor, mgr. acctg. and mgr. gen. and cost acctg., 1972—86, dir. acctg., Rocketdyne, 1986—92; dir. bus. mgmt., Space Station Electric Power System, Rocketdyne unit Rockwell (acquired by The Boeing Co.), Chgo., 1992—96; v.p. contracts and pricing Boeing Space and Comm. The Boeing Co., Chgo., 1996—2000, sr. v.p. fin., corp. contr., 2000—03, CFO, 2004—, interim CEO, pres., 2005. Bd. dirs. New Leaders for New Schools, L.A. Urban League, Joffrey Ballet; past bd. dirs. Charles Drew U. Medicine and Sci. Mem.: World Bus. Chgo. (bd. dirs.). Office: The Boeing Co 100 N Riverside Plz Chicago IL 60606-2609*

BELL, JAMES FREDERICK, retired lawyer; b. New Orleans, Aug. 5, 1922; s. George Bryan and Sarah Barr (Perry) B.; m. Jill Cooper Arden, Apr. 14, 1951; children: Bradley Cushing, Sara Perry, Ashley Arden. AB cum laude, Princeton U., 1943; LL.B., Harvard U., 1948. Bar: D.C. 1949. Assoc. Pogue & Neal, Washington, 1948-53, ptnr., 1953-88, cons., 1988-89; ret., 1988. Gen. counsel Conf. State Bank Suprs., 1951-87. Chmn. com. on canons and other bus. Episcopal Diocese of Washington, 1960-78; pres. Episc. Ctr. for Children, Washington, 1966-67. Lt. USNR, 1943-46. Mem. ABA, D.C. Bar Assn. Home: 2103 R St NW Washington DC 20008-1933 *The fragmentation of human thought into an increasing number of disciplines has proliferated standards of judgment as to the rightness or wrongness of human conduct to a point where consensus as to viable guidelines becomes impossible.*

BELL, JAMES THOMAS, housing authority official; b. NYC, Oct. 17, 1949; m. Leslie Toombs, June 25, 1977; children: Guy K., Colin J., Kate E. BA in English Edn. cum laude, Boston Coll., 1971; MPA, L.I. U., 1985. Cert. tchr., N.Y., Conn., Mass. With pers. office Town of Oyster Bay, N.Y., 1971-72; with pub. info. office Town of Oyster Bay, N.Y., 1972-76, dir. cmty. rels., 1977-80, founding mem., vice chmn. Indsl. Devel. Agy., 1980-82, exec. asst. to town supr., 1980-82, dep. town supr., 1982-87, comptr., 1988-97, chmn. town geog. info. sys. commn., 1995-97, dep. town supr., 1998—2002; exec. dir. Town of Oyster Bay Housing Authority, 2002—. Instr. LI U.-C.W. Post, 1998—, adv. coun. health care and pub. adminstrn. dept. Exec. com. Sea Cliff (NY) Rep. Com.; del. 10th Jud. Dist. Rep. Conv.; trustee Inc. Village Sea Cliff, 1978-80. Recipient Fin. Reporting Achievment award Govt. Fin. Officers Am. and Can., 1996. Mem. Am. Soc. for Pub. Adminstrn. (exec. coun. L.I. chpt.), Sea Cliff Civic Assn., Met. Boston Coll. Club N.Y., North Shore Kiwanis, Pi Alpha Alpha Home: 9 Leonard Pl Sea Cliff NY 11579-2011 Office: Town of Oyster Bay Housing Authority PO Box 351 115 Central Park Rd Plainview NY 11803 Office Phone: 516-349-1000.

BELL, JAMES WINFRED, retired publishing executive; b. Little Rock, Sept. 27, 1929; s. Thacher Winfred and Edna Hafner; m. Ruth Naomi Fletcher, July 1, 1951; children: Susan, Anne, Elizabeth, Charlotte. BS in Bus. Adminstrn., Northwestern U., 1951. V.p Bush-Caldwell Co., Little Rock, 1961—72; pres. Pub. Bookshop, Inc., Little Rock, 1972—94; ret. Moderator Word Spinners Ink-Mainstream, 2000—05. Author: Pulaski County Handbook, 1980; editor: (newsletter) Toast of the South, 1994—95. Pres. Hi-Noon Toastmasters Club, Little Rock, 1994—95. Named Hi-Noon Toastmaster of the Yr., Hi-Noon Toastmasters Club, 1991—92. Mem.: Fiction Writers Ctrl. Ark. (treas. 2002—03, pres. 2005), Pulaski County Hist. Soc. (past pres. 1998, 1999), Little Rock Toastmaster Club (divsn. gov. 1995—96, Dist. 43 Toastmaster of the Yr. 1995—96, Divsn. Gov. of the Yr. 1995—96). Unitarian Universalist. Avocation: writing historical fiction. Home: 7611 Briarwood Cir Little Rock AR 72205-4810 E-mail: j22bell@comcast.net.

BELL, JANET S., product designer, interior designer; b. Ft. Campbell, Ky., Feb. 13, 1954; d. Mack Carson Smith and Walburga Maria Franz; m. David Michael Bell, June 9, 1979. Mem. dir. for Jacques Cousteau, N.Y.; owner Janet S. Event Prodr., Builder, Interior Designer, Va. Beach, Va., Design Firm, Va. Beach, Va., Mike Bell Bldg. Cpr., Va. Beach, Va., Va. Beach Conservatory of Arts, Va. Beach, Va. Prodr. mem. Mus. of Art, Norfolk, Va. Founder Cat Found., Va. Beach. Home: 1539 Mccullough Ln Virginia Beach VA 23464

BELL, JERRY ALAN, science education association administrator; b. Davenport, Iowa, June 28, 1936; s. Walter Samuel and Lilah Mae (Mergy) B.; m. Dorothy Alice Rodgers, June 10, 1961 (div. Dec. 1981); children: Allan Tracy (dec.), John Leonard; m. Mary Ann Stepp, Mar. 21, 1984; children: Christina Marie, Allison Rachel. AB, Harvard U., 1958, PhD, 1962. Asst. prof. U. Calif., Riverside, 1962-67; assoc. prof., prof. Simmons Coll., Boston, 1967-92; dir. sci. edn. program AAAS, Washington, 1992—99; sr. scientist Edn. divsn. Am. Chem. Soc., Washington, 1999—. Mem. adv. bd. Merck Inst. for Sci. Edn., Newark, 1993-99. Author: Chemical Explorations, 1993; editor, author: Chemical Principles in Practice, 1967, Chemistry, 2004. Recipient Catalyst award Mfg. Chemists Assn., 1977, John Timm award New Eng. Assn. Chemistry Tchrs., 1986. Fellow AAAS, Am. Chem. Soc. (sec. div. chem. edn. 1977-82, chmn. 1988, vis. scientist western Conn. sect. 1979, Norris award northeastern sect. 1992, George C. Pimentel award in Chem. Edn., 2000). Avocations: carpentry, gardening. Office: Am Chem Soc 1155 16th St NW Washington DC 20036 Business E-Mail: j_bell@acs.org.

BELL, JERRY ARCH, JR., lawyer; b. Austin, Tex., Oct. 9, 1951; s. Jerry Arch and Beverly (Nash) B.; m. Mary Hooper, March 29, 1980; children: Julia, John, Molly. BA, U. Tex., 1974, JD, 1977. Bar: Tex. 1977, bd. cert.in Health Law, Tex. Bd. Legal Specialization, 2002. Ptnr. Fulbright & Jaworski LLP, Houston, and head, health law bus. and regulatory dept. Adj. faculty Univ. Houston Law Sch., 1992-93. Recipient Philip Overton Annual Lectureship award Tex. Med. Assn., Austin, 1993, named on of nation's 12 Outstanding Hosp. Lawyers, 2004, One of Texas Super Lawyers, Tex. Monthly Mag., 2003, 2004. Mem. State Bar Tex. (officer health law sect. chmn. 1993-94), Am. Acad. Healthcare Attys. (chair managed care com. 1993-94, bd. dirs. 1995—). Roman Catholic. Office: Fulbright & Jaworski LLP 1301 McKinney St Ste 5100 Houston TX 77010-3031 Office Phone: 713-651-5151. Office Fax: 713-651-5246. Business E-Mail: jbell@fulbright.com.

BELL, JOHN PERRY, minister, religious organization administrator; b. Columbia, La., Feb. 8, 1948; s. John Dixon and Laverne (Beck) B.; m. Gwendolyn Jean McKay, Dec. 18, 1971; children: Felicia, Peter, Rachel. BA, N.E. La. U., 1970, MA, 1971; ThM, So. Meth. U., 1973; DMin, Garrett Evang. Sem., 1989. Ordained to ministry United Meth. Ch., 1974. Min. youth United Meth. Ch., Athens, Tex., 1972, pastor Argyle, Wis., 1973-76, Sheboygan Falls, Wis., 1976-84, Waupaca, Wis., 1984-91; assoc. conf. min. United Ch. of Christ, 1991-97; exec. dir. United Meth. Found., 1998-2000. Bd. dirs. Bell Press, Waupaca, 1990—; sec. Coun. on Fin. Adminstrn., Sun Prairie, Wis., 1984-92; del. World Meth. Conf., Honolulu, 1981, Nairobi, 1986, New World Mission, Bangalore, India, 1989, UNCED, Rio de Janeiro, 1992, UN Conf. on Population, Cairo, Egypt, 1994. Pres. Am. Cancer Soc., Waupaca, 1988-90, Mental Health Assn., Waupaca, 1988-91. Recipient Superior award Am. Cancer Soc., 1989-90. Mem. World Future Soc., Kiwanis (local pres. 1983). Democrat. Home: 2212 Stockton Dr Springfield IL 62703-5268 Office Phone: 815-865-5314. E-mail: gnanny50@aol.com. *Life is both internal and external. We have to place equal emphasis on both. Our internal life needs as much care as any other part of life. How we think and feel will determine what we do and say. Faith, then, is the foundation for life.*

BELL, JOHN WILLIAM, lawyer; b. Chgo., May 3, 1946; s. John and Barbara Bell; m. Deborah Bell, Aug. 25, 1974; children: Jason, Alicia. Student, U. So. Calif., 1964-65; BA, Northwestern U., 1968; JD cum laude, Loyola U., Chgo., 1971. Bar: Ill. 1971. Assoc. Kirkland & Ellis, Chgo., 1972-75; ptnr. Johnson & Bell, Ltd. (formerly Johnson, Cusack & Bell, Ltd.), Chgo., 1975—. Mem. ABA (vice chmn. products, gen. liability and consumer law com. sect. tort and ins. practice 1986-87, 88—, com. on torts and ins. practice sect.), Ill. Bar Assn., Chgo. Bar Assn. (tort liability sect., aviation com. 1982—, chmn. med.-legal rels. com. 1994-95), Internat. Assn. Ins. Def. Counsel, Ill. Def. Coun. (faculty mem. trial acad. 1994), Soc. Trial Lawyers Am., Ill. Trial Lawyers Assn., Am. Coll. Trial Lawyers, Fed. Trial Bar.

BELL, JONATHAN ROBERT, lawyer; b. Bklyn., Oct. 2, 1947; s. Saul A. and Hope R. (Rosenblat) B.; children: Gabriel J., Nicholas R.; m. Catherine Janow, May 5, 1989. BA, Yale U., 1969; JD, Harvard U., 1973. Bar: Mass. 1974, U.S. Tax Ct. 1977, N.Y. 1978, U.S. Dist. Ct. (so. dist.) N.Y. 1980. Assoc. Nutter, McClennen & Fish, Boston, 1973-77, Debevoise & Plimpton, N.Y.C., 1977-83, ptnr., 1984-93, Paul, Weiss, Rifkind, Wharton & Garrison, N.Y.C., 1993—2001, Duane Morris, N.Y.C., 2002—. Bd. dirs. United Way, N.Y.C., 1984-95, N.Y.C. Ballet, 1995-2003, 04—; bd. dirs. Studio in A School, 1988—, vice chair, 2003—. Fellow Am. Coll. Trust and Estate Counsel; mem. N.Y. State Bar Assn. (trusts and estates law sect.), Assn. Bar City N.Y. (chair trusts, estates and surrogate cts. com. 1995-98). Home: 99 Jane St New York NY 10014-7221 Office: Duane Morris LLP 380 Lexington Ave New York NY 10168 Office Phone: 212-692-1088. E-mail: jrbell@duanemorris.com.

BELL, JOSEPH CHARLES, lawyer; m. Ruth Greenspan, June 9, 1968; children: Samuel Robert, Johanna Rebecca. BA summa cum laude, U. Colo., 1962; AM in econs., Harvard U., 1965; JD, Yale U., 1968. Bar: D.C. 1977, Mass. 1968. Legal asst. Cabinet Task Force on Oil Import Control, Washington, 1969-70; atty. advisor Antitrust divsn., Dept. of Justice, Washington, 1970-72; asst. prof. Duke U., Durham, N.C., 1972-74; asst. gen. counsel Fed. Energy Adminstrn., Washington, 1974-77; assoc. Hogan & Hartson, Washington, 1977-79, ptnr., 1979—, energy practice group dir. Gen. counsel Citizens Energy Corp., 1979-88; advisor on privatization State Ministry of Property and Entrepreneurship, Ukraine Republic, 1991; adv. bd. Program on Econ. Reform in Ukraine, Harvard U., 1990-92; spl. counsel Ministry of Fin., Republic of Poland, 1989-91; resident ptnr. Warsaw, Poland, Hogan and Hartson, 1991-93; economist Office of Tax Analysis, Treasury Dept., summer 1965, Office of Internat. Tax Affairs, summer 1966. Contbr. articles to profl. jours. Mem. Wilson Coun., World Affairs Coun. of Washington. Mem. ABA (internat., adminstrv. and bus. sects.), Am. Econ. Assn., Fed. Energy Bar Assn., Phi Beta Kappa, Harvard Club. Office: Hogan and Hartson Columbia Sq 555 13th St NW Ste 800E Washington DC 20004-1161 Office Phone: 202-637-5780. Office Fax: 202-637-5910. Business E-Mail: jcbell@hhlaw.com.

BELL, JOSEPH R., finance educator; BA, Bloomsburg U.; MBA in Fin., Mich. State U.; JD, T.M. Cooley Law Sch. In-ho. counsel Warren Real Estate Group, 1987; securities atty. Dept. Commerce State of Mich., 1988—93; asst. prof. entrepreneurship, fin., strategic planning law Mesa State Coll., 1993—94; dir. Small Bus. Devel. Ctrs., 1994—96; state dir. Colo. Small Bus. Devel. Ctrs./Gov.'s Office, 1996—97; dir., instr. U. Colo., Denver, 1997—2000; asst. prof., dir. Entrepreneurship Ctr. at Monfort Coll. Bus. U. No. Colo., 2000—. Contract COO C-TEK Angels, 2002; pres.-elect, v.p. programs and conf. coord. Small Bus. Inst., 2004; mem. steering com. Colo. Entrepreneurial Hothouse Initiative, 2004—; instr. advanced tchr. trrack Youth Entrepreneurship Conf., Milw., 2003, lead instr. tchr. track, Greeley, Colo., 03; track chair S.W. Acad. Mgmt., 2003; founder The Creation Club, Denver, 2003—; lead spkr. DaVinci Inst., 2002; regional judge Small Bus. Adminstrn. Advocacy Awards, 1996, 97; mem. adv. bd. Rockies Venture Club, 1997—; cons., presenter in field. Contbr. articles to profl. jours. Recipient McGraw-Hill/Irwin Outstanding Paper award, ASBE Conf., Albuquerque, 2004. Mem.: U.S. Assn. Small Bus. and Entrepreneurship (v.p. membership 2002—03, chair audit com. 2001, panelist 1997, 2000), State Bar Mich. Address: 924 E 22d Ave Denver CO 80205

BELL, JOY ANN, librarian; b. Cross Plains, Tenn., June 9, 1944; d. James Ausie and Evelyn Trevenia (Yates) Carpenter; m. George Carter Bell, Sept. 4, 1966. BA cum laude, Western Ky. U., 1964; MS in Libr. Sci., Simmons Coll., 1972. Asst. catalog libr. U. Tex. Health Sci. Ctr., San Antonio, 1973; cataloger, instr. Trinity U. Libr., San Antonio, 1974, spl. collections cataloger, instr., 1974-75; asst. libr., asst. prof. Rosenstiel Sch. Marine & Atmospheric Sci., U. Miami, Fla., 1976-79; med. librarian St. Francis Hosp., Miami Beach, Fla., 1979-82; tech. info. specialist US Army Health Care Studies and Clin. Investigation Activity, Ft. Sam Houston, Tex., 1984-86; libr. cons., researcher San Antonio, 1986—. Researcher Blackwell, Walker, Gray, Powers, Flick & Hoehl Law Offices, Miami, 1978-81 Named to Hon. Order Ky. Cols. Commonwealth of Ky., 1975. Mem. NAFE, Med. Libr. Assn. Methodist. Home and Office: 2622 Oak Leigh San Antonio TX 78232-4208

BELL, KAREN A., dean; BA in sociol., SUNY Potsdam; MFA in dance, Sarah Lawrence Coll. Prof. SUNY Potsdam, Elmira Coll., Wells Coll.; visiting asst. prof. Cornell U.; prof. Ohio State U., 1980—; chairperson Dept. Dance, Ohio State U., 1995—; assoc. dean Coll. Arts. Ohio State U., 1995—2001, interim dean, 2001—02, dean, 2002—. Individual Artist Fellowship, Ohio Arts Coun., Academic Leadership Fellow, Com. Instl. Cooperation, 1991—92. Mem.: Nat. Assn. Sch. Dance (commn. accreditation, evaluator), Am. Coll. Dance Festival Assn. (bd. dirs., northeast regional rep.). Office: Office of Dean OSU Coll Arts 152 Hopkins Hall 128 North Oval Mall Columbus OH 43210 Office Phone: 614-292-5171. Office Fax: 614-292-5218. E-mail: bell.1@osu.edu.*

BELL, KENNETH B., State Supreme Court Justice; married; 4 children. Bachelor's degree, Davidson Coll., N.C.; JD cum laude, Fla. State U., 1982. Pvt. practice real estate atty.; trial judge 1st Jud. Cir. Fla.; justice Fla. Supreme Ct., Tallahassee, 2002—. Mem. cir. com. on professionalism Supreme Ct., 2000—. Founding pres. of bd. dirs. Friends of Children's Hosp. at Sacred Heart, Inc.; bd. dirs. Escambia County 4-H Found., Waterfront Rescue Mission; c-founder Yan-Bian Chinese-Korean Tech. U., China. Mem.: Escambia-Santa Rosa Bar Assn. Office: Supreme Ct Fla 500 Duval St Tallahassee FL 32399

BELL, KRISTOPHER ALLAN, telecommunications executive; b. Ogdensburg, N.Y., Sept. 24, 1966; s. Allan John and Nancy Elaine (Bice) B. Student, Heuvelton Ctr. Sch., 1983-84; BA, SUNY, Potsdam, 1988, MA in English/Lit., 1989; postgrad., Rensselaer Poly. Inst., 1994-95. Part-time instr. Marist Coll., 1991; instr. English North Country C.C., 1992-94, Dutchess C.C., Poughkeepsie, N.Y., 1995-99; curriculum leader BellAtlantic, Poughkeepsie, N.Y., 1997-98; course designer Hekimian Labs., Rockville, Md., 1999-2000, course devel. supr., 2000—. Adj. instr. Ulster County C.C., 1990-92. Mem. bldg. com. North Franklin Theatre Group; mem. Coachouse Players. Mem. MLA, Internat. Soc. of Anglo-Saxonists, N.Y. Coll. English Assn., Sigma Tau Delta Internat. Democrat. Presbyterian. Avocations: theatrical work, running, photography, tennis, medieval studies. Office: Spirent Comms Hekimian Divsn 15200 Omega Dr Rockville MD 20850 Address: 2353 Sorrel Ct Baltimore MD 21209-4628 E-mail: Kristopher.Bell@mac.com.

BELL, LARRY STUART, artist; b. Chgo., Dec. 6, 1939; s. Hyman David and Rebecca Ann (Kriegmont) B.; three children. Student, Chouinard Art Inst., L.A., 1957-59. One man exhbns. include Stedelijk Mus., Amsterdam, 1967, Pasadena (Calif.) Art Mus., 1972, Oakland (Calif.) Mus., 1973, Ft. Worth Art Mus., 1975, Santa Barbara (Calif.) Mus. Art, 1976, Washington U., St. Louis, 1976, Art Mus. So. Tex., Corpus Christi, 1976, Erica Williams, Anne Johnson Gallery, Seattle, 1978, Hayden Gallery, MIT, Cambridge, Mass., 1977, Hudson River Mus., Yonkers, N.Y., 1981, Newport Harbor Art Mus., 1982, Marian Goodman Gallery, N.Y.C., 1982, Ruth S. Schaffner Gallery, Santa Barbara, Calif., Arco Ctr. Visual Arts, L.A., 1983, Unicorn Gallery, Aspen, Colo., 1983, Butler Inst. Am. Art, Youngstown, Ohio, 1984, Leigh Yawkey Woodson Art Mus., Wausau, Wis., 1984, Colorado Springs, Colo. Fine Arts Ctr., 1987, Cleve. Ctr. for Contemporary Art, Ohio, 1987, Mus. Contemporary Art, L.A., 1987, Am. Acad. and Inst. Arts and Letters, N.Y.C., 1987, Boise (Idaho) Gallery Art, 1987, Gilbert Brownstone Gallery, Paris, 1987, Braunstein/Quay Gallery, San Francisco, 1987, 89, Fine Arts Gallery, N.Mex. State Fairgrounds, 1987, Laguna Art Mus., Laguna Beach, Calif., 1987, High Mus. Art, Atlanta, 1988, Sena Galleries West, Santa Fe, 1989, Kiyo Higashi Gallery, L.A., 1989, 90, 94, 2002, Musee D'Art Contemporain, Lyon, France, 1989, Contemporary Art Ctr., Kansas City, Mo., 1989, San Antonio Art Inst., 1990, New Gallery, Houston, 1990, Braunstein/Quay Gallery, San Francisco, 1990, Galerie Rolf Ricke, Koln, Fed. Republic Germany, 1990, Galerie Montenay, Paris, 1990, 95, The Works Gallery, L.A., 1990, Galerie Kammer, Hamburg, Germany, 1990, Tony Shafrazi Gallery, N.Y.C., 1991, Tucson Mus. Art, 1991, New Gallery, Houston, 1991, Janus Gallery, Santa Fe, 1992, Kiyo Higashi Gallery, L.A., 1992, 93, New Gallery, Houston, 1992, Tampa Mus. Art, 1992, Kiyo Higashi Gallery, L.A., 1993, 94, New Directions Gallery, Taos, N.M., 1993, Dartmouth St. Gallery, Albuquerque, 1994, Braunstein/Quay Gallery, San Francisco, 1994, Leedy/Voulkos Gallery, Kansas City, 1994, Kiyo Higashi Gallery, L.A., 1994, U. Wyo. Art Mus., Laramie, 1995, Denver Art Mus., 1995, Indigo Gallery, Boca Raton, Fla., 1995, Harwood Mus. U. N. Mex., Taos, 1995, Galerie Montenay, Paris, 1995, Joy Tash Gallery, Scottsdale, Ariz., 1996, Kiyo Higashi Gallery, L.A., 1996, Boulder Mus. Contemporary Art, 1996, Braunstein/Quay Gallery, San Francisco, 1996, Art et Industrie Gallery, N.Y.C., 1996, The Albuquerque Mus., 1997, The Reykjavik Mcpl. Art Mus., Iceland, 1997, Bergen (Norway) Kunstmus., 1998, Seljord (Norway) Art Assn., 1998, Wood Street Galleries, Pitts., 1999, Mus. Moderner Kunst Landkreis Cuxhaven, Otterndorf, Germany, 1999, Kiyo Higashi Gallery, 1999, Center Galleries, Detroit, 2000, Larry Bell Studio Annex/New Directions Gallery, Taos, N.Mex., 2000, Mus. Moderner Kunst Landkreis Cuxhaven, Otterndorf, Germany, 2000, New Gallery, Houston, 2001, Gallery Gan, Tokyo, 2001, Skovridder AS, Oslo, Norway, 2001, Roswell Mus. and Art Ctr., 2002, New Gallery, Houston, 2002, Off Main Gallery, Santa Monica, Calif., 2003, St. John's Coll., Santa Fe, 2003, Harwood Art Mus. U. N.Mex., Taos, N.Mex., 2004, Bernard Jacobson Gallery, U. Tenn., Chattanooga, 2005; numerous group exhbns. including most recently Calif., 2000, Peggy Guggenheim Collection, Venice, Italy, 2000, Guggenheim Mus. Bilbao, Spain, 2000, La. Mus. Art, Humlebaek, Denmark, 2000, L.A. County Mus. Art, 2000, Solomon R. Guggenheim Mus., N.Y., 2001, Bernard Jacobson Gallery, London, 2001, Museu Serralves, Porto, Portugal, 2002, The Contemporary Mus., Honolulu, 2002, Yale U. Art Gallery, New Haven, Conn., 2002, Denver Art Mus., 2002, Gagosian Gallery, N.Y.C., 2002, Franklin Parrasch Gallery, N.Y.C., 2003, Gagosian Gallery, N.Y.C., 2002, Stephen Stux Gallery, N.Y.C., 2002, Harwood Mus. U. N.Mex., Taos, 2004, Bernard Jacobson Gallery, London, 2005, Sintra Mus. Modern Art, Portugal, 2003, Contemp. Art Ctr., New Orleans, 2003, Guggenheim Mus. Art, N.Y., 2003, MOCA, L.A., 2004, U. Pa., Phila., 2004, L.A. (Calif.) County Mus. Art, L.A., 2004, Miami Art

Mus., 2004, Mus. Contemporary Art, San Diego, 2004, Marian Goodman Gallery, N.Y., 2004, Jacobson-Howard Gallery, N.Y., 2004, Frederick R. Weisman Art Mus., U. Minn., 2005, others; represented in permanent collections including Nat. Collection Fine Arts, Musee de Art Contemporaine, Lyon, France, Mus. of Fine Arts, Santa Fe, N.Mex., Whitney Mus. Am. Art, N.Y.C., Laguna Gloria Mus., Austen, H & W Bechtler Gallery, Charlotte, Calif. Crafts Mus., San Francisco, Parrish Art Mus., Southampton, Tate Gallery, London, Gallery New South Wales, Australia, Albright-Knox Gallery, Buffalo, Art Inst. Chgo., Denver Art Mus., Dallas Mus. Fine Arts, Guggenheim Mus., Houston, L.A. County Mus., Victoria and Albert Mus., London, San Antonio Mus. Art, The Menil Collection, Houston, Mpls. Inst. Arts, Mus. Ludwig, Koln, Albuquerque Mus., Mpls. Inst. Arts, others; instr. sculpture, U. South Fla., Tampa, U. Calif., Berkeley, Irvine, So. Calif. Inst. of Architecture, Taos (N.Mex.) Inst. of Art, City of Albuquerque, Art in Pub. Places, 1999, Myers Devel. Co., 1999, Billingsley Co., Carrolton, Tex., Mus. Abteiberg, Monchengladbach, Germany, Centex Homes, South Coast Divsn., Brea, Calif., MOCA, LA, Calif., Great Eagle Devel. and Mgmt. Ltd., Hong Kong. Copley Found. grantee, 1962; Guggenheim Found. fellow, 1970; Nat. Endowment Arts grantee, 1975; recipient Gov.'s award for excellence in visual arts, N.Mex., 1990. Office: Box 4101 Taos NM 87571-9998 Office Phone: 505-758-3062. Business E-Mail: bell@newmex.com.

BELL, LAWRENCE T., lawyer; b. 1948; BBA, St. Bonaventure U., 1970; JD, William Mitchell Coll. Law, St. Paul, Minn., 1979. Bar: Minn. 1979. Joined Ecolab Inc., St. Paul, 1979, internat. v.p. - adminstrn., 1986—91, named gen. counsel, 1998, now sr. v.p., gen. counsel, sec. Mem. bd. Twin Cities Pub. TV, St. Paul Chamber Orch.; bd. dirs. VocalEssence, 2002—; bd. trustees William Mitchell Coll. Law, 2004—. Office: Ecolab Inc 370 Wabasha St N Saint Paul MN 55102

BELL, LEE PHILLIP, television personality, television producer; b. Chgo. d. James A. and Helen (Novak) P.; m. William Joseph Bell, Oct. 23, 1954; children: William J., Bradley, Lauralee. BS in Microbiology, Northwestern U., 1950. With CBS-TV, Chgo., 1952-86; pres. Bell-Phillip TV Prodns., 1985—. Bd. dirs. William Wrigley, Jr. Co., Chgo. Bank Commerce, Phillips Flowers Inc. TV and radio shows include Lee Phillip Show, Chgo., from 1952, Lady and Tiger Show WBBM Radio, from 1962, WBBM TV from 1964; hostess Noon Break, numerous TV Spls. including Forgotten Children, The Rape of Paulette (nat. Emmy award, duPont Columbia award); Children and Divorce (Chgo. Emmmy award) co-creator: (with William Bell) The Young and the Restless CBS-TV daytime drama, 1973 (Emmy award); co-creator, exec. producer The Bold and the Beautiful, 1987—. Bd. dirs. United Cerebral Palsy, Chgo. Unlimited, Northwestern U. Hosp., Chgo. Heart Assn., Nat. Com. Prevention of Child Abuse, Mental Health Assn., Children's Home and Aid Soc., Salvation Army, Chgo., Family Focus; mem. Chgo. Maternity Ctr.; life mem. Northwestern U. Bd. Trustees. Recipient 16 Chgo. Emmys; Top Favorite Female award TV Guide mag., 1956, Outstanding Woman of Radio and TV award McCall's mag., 1957-58, 65, bd. govs. award Chgo. chpt. Nat. Acad. TV Arts and Scis., 1977, William Booth award for community svc. Salvation Army, 1990; named Person of Yr. Broadcast Advt. Club, Chgo., 1980. Mem. Am. Women Radio and TV (Golden Mike award 1968, Broadcaster of Yr. 1993), Acad. TV Arts and Scis. (bd. dirs.), Chgo. chpt. Acad. TV Arts and Scis., Women's Athletic Club of Chgo., Comml. Club, Delta Delta Delta. Home: 9955 Beverly Dr Beverly Hills CA 90210 Office: CBS c/o Bold and Beautiful 7800 Beverly Blvd Los Angeles CA 90036-2188 Office Phone: 323-575-2812. E-mail: dianemoss@boldandbeautiful.tv.

BELL, LEO S., retired physician; b. Newark, Nov. 7, 1913; s. Alexander M. and Marie (Saxon) B.; m. Edith Lewis, July 3, 1938; children: Jewyl Linn, David Alden. AB, Syracuse U., 1934, MD, 1938. Diplomate Am. Bd. Pediatrics. Intern N.Y.C. Hosp., 1938, Bklyn. Hosp., 1939-40; resident Sea View Hosp., N.Y.C., 1940-41, N.Y.C. Hosp., 1941-42; pediatrician pvt. practice, San Mateo, Calif., 1946-84. Staff mem. Mills Meml. Hosp., San Mateo, Peninsula Hosp. & Med. Ctr., Burlingame, Children's Hosp., San Francisco; assoc. clin. prof. pediatrics U. Calif. Med. Sch., San Francisco; prof. clin. emeritus Stanford Med. Sch., Palo Alto; mem. curriculum & ednl. affairs com. U. San Francisco Med. Sch., adminstrv. coun. Columnist San Mateo Times; contbr. articles to profl. jours. Bd. dirs. Mills Hosp. Found., San Mateo, U. Calif. San Francisco Hosp., San Mateo County Heart Assn., Hillsborough Schs. Found. (Calif.), 1980-83. Capt. USAAF, 1942-46. Recipient bronze and silver medals Am. Heart Assn. Fellow Am. Acad. Pediatrics, Am. Pub. Health Assn.; mem. AMA (alt. del. to ho. of dels), U. Calif. San Francisco Clin. Faculty Assn. (pres.), Calif. Fedn. Pediatric Socs. (pres.), Am. Fedn. Pediatric Socs. (pres.), Calif. Med. Assn., Am. Pub. Health Assn., Air Force Assn., Calif. Med. Assn. (ho. of dels.), San Mateo County Med. Assn. (vice chmn. quality assurance com. San Mateo county health plan), Internat. Snuff Bottle Soc., Hong Kong Snuff Bottle Soc., San Francisco Gem and Mineral Soc., World Affairs Coun. San Francisco, U. San Francisco Med. Sch. Clin. Faculty Assn. (coun., pres.), Peninsula Golf & Country Club, Commonwealth Club. Office: PO Box 1877 San Mateo CA 94401-0946

BELL, LEWIS CLAY, economics professor, government administrator; b. New Dorp, NY, Mar. 29, 1928; s. Samuel Virgil and Ruth Bell; m. Dolores Eva Bell, Dec. 19, 1951; children: Brent, David, Daniel. BA in Econs., Berea Coll., 1953; postgrad., Emory U., 1953—54; PhD in Econs., U. Ky., 1957. Rsch. asst. Bur. Bus. Rsch. U. Ky., 1954—55, rsch. assoc., 1956—57; asst. dir. purchases Commonwealth of Ky., 1957, dir. purchases, 1957—60; assoc. prof. U. Miss., 1960—63, assoc. prof. econs., econs. rsch. analyst, 1963—64, prof. econs., sr. rsch. analyst, 1964, prof. econs., 1964—65; dir. Tax Rsch. Ctr., prof. econs. Western Ky. U., 1965—66, dir. Tax Rsch. Ctr., Office of Rsch. and Svcs., prof. econs., 1966—68; prof. econs. fiscal cons. to W.Va. Legis., 1968—70; dir. legis. fiscal studies W.Va. U., 1969—70, prof. econs., 1969—88, dir. grad. programs econs., 1978—83, prof. emeritus, 1988—; exec. dir. W.Va. Coun. Econ. Edn., 1985—87; prof. econs. Christian Sci. Practitioner, 1988—. Author (with D.H. McKinney): The Role of Third-Structure Taxes in the Highway-User Tax Family, 1968; contbr. articles to profl. jours., chapters to books. Active Ky. Efficiency Task Force, 1966—68; Ky. col.; treas. Support Our Schs., Morgantown, 1971; chmn. com. on publ. for W.Va. Christian Sci., 1975—91; counsel, advisor Christian Sci. Coll. Orgn. W.Va. U., chmn. bd.; 1st reader, Sunday sch. supt. Christian Sci. Ch.; advisor Sch. Bonds. Com., Morgantown, 1971. Mem.: Mountain State Econ. Assn. (pres. 1980), W.Va. Tax Inst. (pres. 1973), So. Econs. Assn., Tax Inst. Am., Nat. Tax Assn., Am. Econ. Assn., Rotary (pres. 1983—84), Beta Gamma Sigma, Phi Kappa Phi. Democrat. Christian Scientist. Home and Office: 1287 Colonial Dr Morgantown WV 26505-2437

BELL, LORETTA MAE, elementary school educator; b. Chana, Ill., Dec. 13, 1936; d. Floyd R. and Ida Ruth (Hepfer) Long; m. Donald Lee Bell, Aug. 18, 1962; children: Robert, John, Linda. BS in Edn., No. Ill. U., 1960, MEd, 1967. Cert. tchr., Ill. Tchr. Rochelle Twp. H.S., Ill., 1960—64, Steward Elem. Sch., Ill., 1967—69, Eswood Elem. Sch., Lindenwood, Ill., 1976—2000; ret., 2000—. Recipient Outstanding Tchr. award Ill. Math. and Sci. Acad., Aurora, Ill., 1992. Mem.: Ill. Ret. Tchrs. Assn. (pres. Ogle-Lee unit 3 2004—).

BELL, M. JOY MILLER, financial planner, real estate agent; b. Enid, Okla., Dec. 29, 1934; d. H. Lee and M.E. Madge (Hatfield) Miller; m. Richard L.D. Berlemann, July 21, 1957 (div. Nov. 1974); children: Richard Louis, Randolph Lee; m. Donald R. Bell, Aug. 17, 1996; children: Jeri, Johnna, Nolan, Charles, Mary. BSBA, N.Mex. State U., 1956. CFP; grad. Realtors Inst.; fellow Life Underwriting Tng. Coun. Tchr. bus. and math. Alamogordo (N.Mex.), Las Cruces (N. Mex.) and Omaha Pub. Schs., 1956-63; tchr., dir. Evelyn Wood Reading Dynamics So. N.Mex. Inst., 1967-68; registered rep. Westamerica Fin. Corp., Denver, 1968-76; gen. agt. Security Benefit Life, Topeka, 1969—2001, Delta Life & Annuity, Topeka, 1969—2001; registered rep. AGF Sponsors, Inc., Denver, 1976—; pres., broker Fin. Design Corp. R.E. (name changed to Bell, Inc. 1997), Las Cruces, 1977—; with Allianz L.I. Co. N.Am., 2000—. Mrs. U.S. Savings Bonds ofcl. goodwill amb. U.S. Treasury, U.S. Savs. Bond Divsn., Washington, 1968-70. Contbr. articles to profl. jours. V.p. programs Dona Ana County Fedn. Rep. Women. Recipient Top Sales Person award Investment Trust and Assurance, 1976-77; named Outstanding Young Woman of N.Mex., 1970, Outstanding Young Women of Am., 1970. Mem. Nat. Assn. Realtors, Nat. Assn. Ins. and Fin. Advisors, Nat. Assn. Ret. Fed. Employees (v.p. programs local chpt.), Internat. Assn. Registered Fin. Planners, Fin. Planners Assn., S.W. N.Mex. Assn. of Ins. and Fin. Advisors (treas. 1990-91, pres.-elect 1991-92, pres. 1992-93), Las Cruces Assn. Realtors (bd. dirs.), Multiple Listing and Info., Inc. (pres.-elect 2004, pres. 2005), Las Cruces City Alumnae Panhellenic, Altrusa, Order Ea. Star, Delta Zeta. Presbyterian. Home: 4633 Lamar Rd Las Cruces NM 88005-3558 Office: Bell Inc PO Box 577 Las Cruces NM 88004-0577 Office Phone: 505-526-9166. E-mail: joybell@bellinc.com.

BELL, MARC H., investment company executive; s. Robert and Ruth Bell; m. Ruti K. Kon, Oct. 22, 1996; children: Rachel J., David B. BS, Babson Coll., 1988; MS, NYU, 1989. Chmn., CEO Globix Corp., N.Y.C., 1989—2002; mng. ptnr. Marc Bell Capital Ptnrs. LLC, Boca Raton, Fla., 2002—. Bd. trustees NYU, N.Y.C., 2001—, Babson Coll., Babson Park, Mass., 2001—; mem. NYU Sch. Medicine Found., N.Y.C., 2002—. Office: Marc Bell Capital Ptnrs LLC 6800 Broken Sound Pkwy Boca Raton FL 33487 Office Phone: 561-988-1700.

BELL, MARK GERALD, physician, surgeon; b. Winfield, Kans., Dec. 29, 1950; s. Gene LeRoy and Erma Lorraine (Marshall) B.; m. Joyce Linda Rumsey, Jan. 9, 1971 (div. Feb. 1980); 1 child, Tara Kimberly; m. Joy Elaine Bermel, June 22, 1980 (div. Oct. 1992); children: Tamera Michelle, Tia Joanna; m. Sherie Ann McAdams Hall, Feb. 20, 1993; 1 stepchild, Evan Hall; 1 child, Kyler Michael Bell. BA in Biology, Kans. State U., 1972; MD, U. Kans. Med. Sch., 1975. Cert. Am. Bd. Otolaryngology. Resident gen. surgery St. Luke's Hosp., Kansas City, Mo., 1975-77; resident otolaryngology Kans. U. Med. Ctr., Kansas City, 1977-80; chief dept. otolaryngology U.S. Naval Regional Med. Ctr., Okinawa, Japan, 1980-83; mem. staff Salina (Kans.) Regional Health Ctr., 1983—; co-founder Salinas Cares Indigent Clinic, 1995, med. dir., 1995—98. Chmn. emergency room-intensive care unit com. U.S. Naval Regional Med. Ctr., Okinawa, 1981-83; chief of med. staff St. John's Asbury Hosp., 1990. Mem. Horizon Fifty Cultural Patrons, Salina, 1986-95; leader Boy Scouts Am. Served to lt. comdr. USN, 1980-83. Recipient Resident Teaching award St. Luke's Hosp., Kansas City, Mo., 1977, Service Commendation award U.S. Naval Regional Med. Ctr., Okinawa, 1983, Golden Rule award J.C. Penney, 1996. Mem. AMA, Am. Acad. Otolaryngology, Kans. Med. Soc. (resolution reference com. 1986, 90, 96, constitutional sec. 1989-94), Salina County Med. Soc. (del. Kans. Med. Soc. 1984-2005, pres. 2004). Republican. Avocations: gun collecting, photography, tennis, flying, hunting. Home: 7 Crestview Dr Salina KS 67401-3587 Office: Ctrl Kans ENT Assocs PA 520 S Santa Fe Salina KS 67401-2201 Office Phone: 785-823-7225.

BELL, MARK ROBERT, strategy consultant; b. Pasadena, Calif., Dec. 16, 1975; s. Mark Robert and Patricia Moffitt Bell; m. Bianca Camac, May 22, 2004. Doctorate, Oxford (Eng.) U., 2002. Lectr. Oxford U., 2000—02; sr. assoc. D.C. Shaw, N.Y.C., NY, 2002—. Author: Apocalypse How. Marshall scholar, Parliament, Eng., 1998—2002. Roman Catholic. Home: 6 St Dunstan's Garth Baltimore MD 21212

BELL, MARTIN ALLEN, investment company executive; b. N.Y.C., Apr. 29, 1951; s. Bernard B. and Helene (Spiro) Bell; m. Alison D. Brown, Dec. 1, 2002; 1 child, Olivia Joan;children from previous marriage: Daniel Warren, Frances Annelies. BA, U. Mich., 1974; JD, NYU, 1977. Bar: N.Y. 1978. Ptnr. Finley, Kumble, Wagner, Heine, Underberg, Manley & Casey, N.Y.C., 1977-85; pres. Svc. Resources Corp., N.Y.C., 1985-90; gen. counsel D.H. Blair Investment Banking Corp., N.Y.C., 1991—, vice chmn., 1995—. Bd. dirs. Venus Exploration Corp., Rand Pub. Corp., News Comm., Inc. Democratic. Jewish. Home: 1035 5th Ave New York NY 10028-0135 Office: D H Blair Investment Banking Corp 44 Wall St New York NY 10005-2401 E-mail: mab10355@aol.com.

BELL, MARVIN HARTLEY, poet, language educator; b. N.Y.C., Aug. 3, 1937; s. Saul and Belle (Spector) B.; m. Mary Mammosser, 1958 (div.); m. Dorothy Murphy; children: Nathan Saul, Jason Aaron. BA, Alfred U., 1958, LHD (hon.), 1986; MA, U. Chgo., 1961; MFA, U. Iowa, 1963. Mem. faculty, Writers' Workshop U. Iowa, Iowa City, 1965—, Flannery O'Connor prof. of letters, 1986—, Iowa poet laurete, 2000—04. Vis. lectr. Goddard Coll., 1970; disting. vis. prof. U. Hawaii, 1981; vis. prof. U. Wash., 1982; Lila Wallace-Reader's Digest Writing fellow U. Redlands, 1991-92, 92-93; Woodrow Wilson vis. fellow St. Mary's Coll. of Calif., 1994-95, Nebr. Wesleyan U., 1996-97, Pacific U., 1996-97, Hampden-Sydney Coll., 1998-99, W.Va. Wesleyan Coll., 2000-2001, Birmingham So. U., 2000-2001, Ill. Coll., 2002-03, Bethany Coll., 2003-04; judge Lamont Award-Acad. Am. Poets, 1989-91, Pushcart Prizes, 1991, 97, Western Book Awards-Western States Arts Fedn., 1991, Nat. Poetry Series, NEA, N.C. Arts Coun., Coordinating Coun. Lit. Mags., Discovery Contest-Poetry Ctr. of 92nd St Y, N.Y.C., Poetry Soc. Am., Hopwood Awards, Tulsa Arts Coun., Anhinga Poetry Prize-Fla. State U. Press, numerous others; disting. poet-in-residence Wichita State U., 2004, Prague Seminar, 2002, 04. Author: (poems) Things We Dreamt We Died For, 1966, A Probable Volume of Dreams, 1969 (Lamont award Acad. Am. Poets 1969), The Escape into You, 1971, 94, Residue of Song, 1974, Stars Which See, Stars Which Do Not See, 1977 (Nat. Book award finalist 1977), 92, These Green-Going-To-Yellow, 1981, Drawn by Stones, by Earth, by Things That Have Been in the Fire, 1984, New and Selected Poems, 1987, Iris of Creation, 1990, The Book of the Dead Man, 1994, Ardor: The Book of the Dead Man, vol. 2, 1997, Wednesday: Selected Poems, 1998, Poetry for a Midsummer's Night, 1998, Nightworks: Poems 1962-2000, 2000, Ashes Poetica, 2002, Rampant, 2004; (essays) Old Snow Just Melting: Essays and Interviews, 1983; (anthology) A Marvin Bell Reader, 1994; co-author: Segues: A Correspondence in Poetry, 1983, Annie-Over, 1988, editor, pub. Statements, 1959-64; poetry editor The Iowa Rev., 1969-71, guest poetry editor, 1980, 2005; poetry editor The Pushcart Prize, vol. XXI, 1996-97, editor-at-large vol. series, 1994-96, series editor, poetry, 1997—; columnist The Am. Poetry Rev., 1975-78, 90-92; contbr. and commd. poetry to numerous mags. and anthologies. Fellow Guggenheim Found., 1977, NEA, 1978, 84; Sr. Fulbright scholar to Yugoslavia, 1983, Sr. Fulbright scholar to Australia, 1986; recipient Bess Hokin award Poetry, 1969, Emily Clark Balch prize Va. Quar. Rev., 1970, Am. Poetry Rev. prize, 1982, Lit. award Am. Acad. Arts and Letters, 1994, Shestack prize Am. Poetry Rev., 2003; Poet Laureate of Iowa, 2000-05. also: PO Box 1759 Port Townsend WA 98368-0180 Office: U Iowa Writer's Workshop Dey House Iowa City IA 52242

BELL, MAXINE TOOLSON, state legislator, librarian; b. Logan, Utah, Aug. 6, 1931; d. John Max and Norma (Watson) Toolson; m. H. Jack Bell, Oct. 26, 1949; children: Randy J. (dec.), Jeff M., Scott Alan (dec.). Assocs. in Libr. Sci., Coll. So. Idaho; CSI, Idaho State U., 1975. Librarian Sch. Dist. 261, Jerome, Idaho, 1975-88; mem. Idaho Ho. of Reps., 1988—. Bd. dirs. Idaho Farm Bur., 1976-77; rep. western states Am. Farm Bur. Women, 1990-93, vice chmn., 1993—; vice chmn. Am. Farm Bur., 1993-2005, chmn. appropriations com., 1999—; mem. Jerome County Rep. Precinct Com., 1980-88. Recipient Pres. medallion award, Idaho State U., 2005. Home: 194 S 300 E Jerome ID 83338-6532 Personal E-mail: mbell@magielink.com.

BELL, MICHAEL A., investment company executive; BS in Econ., U. Pa.; MBA, Harvard Bus. Sch. Founding dir. Monitor Co., 1983—2002; founding and mng. dir. Monitor Clippers Ptnrs., Inc., 1997—; sr. exec. v.p. John Hancock Fin. Svcs., Inc., 2001—, John Hancock Life Ins. Co., 2001—; chmn. and CEO John Hancock Variable Life Ins. Co., 2002—. Bd. dirs. John Hancock Subs., Ptnrs. HealthCare Sys., Inc., Brigham and Women's Hosp., Veridian Corp., Medicalis, IGI/Earth Color, Smart Mail. Chmn. bd. trustees Brigham and Women's Hosp. Office: John Hancock Fin Svcs Inc John Hancock Pl PO Box 111 Boston MA 02117*

BELL, MICHAEL D., artist, educator; b. Balt., Apr. 10, 1971; s. Alex and Alma Vallery Bell; m. Lisa Ann Molinaro. MEd, Towson (Md.) U., 2004. Advanced profl. cert. State Dept. of Edn., Md. Art tchr. So. H.S., Harwood, Md., 1995—; gifted visual arts program instr. Anne Arundel County Pub. Schs., Annapolis, Md., 2000—. Named Tchr. of Yr., So. High, 2000—01, Md. Tchr. of Yr., Md. State Dept. Edn., 2004—05, Tchr. of Yr., Anne Arundel Pub. Schs., 2004—05. Mem.: Nat. Art Educators Assn. (assoc.; Md. Art Edn. Assn. secondary divsn. dir. 2000—02, Art Educator of Yr. 2000). Avocations: painting, drawing, photography, graphic arts, travel. Home: PO Box 61 Abingdon MD 21009 Personal E-mail: michaelbell@mbellart.com.

BELL, MICHAEL JOSEPH, business and information technology educator; s. Jonathan C. and Victoria L. Bell. BSBA, Longwood Coll., 1996. Cert. CCNA Cisco Systems. Bus. and info. tech. educator Page County Pub. Schs., Luray, Va., 1998—. Future Bus. Leaders Am. chpt. adviser Page County Tech. Ctr., Luray, Va., 1998—, SkillsUSA chpt. adviser, 2001—. Mem. Luray Indsl. Devel. Authority, 2002. Mem.: NEA, ASCD, Nat. Genealogical Soc., Va. Edn. Assn., Va. Bus. Edn. Assn., Johnny Appleseed Soc., Muskingum County Ohio Geneal. Soc., Phi Kappa Phi. Office: Page County Tech Ctr 525 Middleburg Rd Luray VA 22835 Office Phone: 540-778-7282. E-mail: mbell@pagecounty.k12.va.us.

BELL, MICHAEL W., insurance company executive; B in Actual Sci. summa cum laude, U. Ill. Various positions with Cigma Corp., 1984—94; v.p., chief fin. officer Cigna Intracorp, 1994—95; v.p., actuary Cigna HealthCare, 1995—97; v.p. corp. acctg. and planning Cigna, 1997—2000; exec. v.p., chief fin. officer Cigna Corp., Phila., 2002—. Fellow: Soc. Actuaries. Office: Cigna Corp 1 Liberty Pl Philadelphia PA 19192-1550

BELL, NANCY LEE HOYT, real estate investor, middle school educator, volunteer; b. L.A., Oct. 25, 1929; d. James and Mabel Ruth (Lockard) Hoyt; m. Ralph Rogers Bell, July 3, 1953; children: Linda Lee, John Curtis, James Hoyt, Martha Chambers, Ralph Rogers II, Nancy Lee II. Student, Whittier Coll., 1948, San Jose State Coll., 1949; BA in Edn., U. Calif., Santa Barbara, 1950; postgrad., San Francisco State Coll., 1952, UCLA, 1953; MS in Edn., U. So. Calif., 1955. Tchr. John Adams Jr. H.S., Santa Monica, Calif., 1950-54; real estate investor. Pres. Santa Clarita Cmty. Concerts, Saugus, Calif., 1968-69; vol. worker USO, YWCA, 1944-45, Cancer Crusade, Calif. and Wash., 1960-90. Mem. AAUW (charter life; pres.), Big Bear Valley Hist. Soc. (life; sec.), DAR (charter life; treas.), Gen. Soc. Mayflower Descs. (life; bd. dirs.), Alpha Delta Pi. Republican. Methodist. Avocations: world travel, collecting antiques, genealogy researcher, music. Home: 615 Main St Apt B Edmonds WA 98020-3804

BELL, NORMAN HOWARD, endocrinologist, educator; b. Gainesville, Ga., Feb. 11, 1931; s. Kenneth Rush and Henrietta Maria (Howard Rankin) Bell; m. Claude Handy Bell, June 27, 1959 (dec. 1967); children: Douglas Howard, Julianne Rankin; m. Mary Virginia Baughman, Aug. 24, 1968 (div. July 1927); m. Ledlie Laird Dinsmore, Dec. 16, 1972; 1 child, Baynard Gardiner. AB, Emory U., 1951; MD, Duke U., 1955. Intern Duke U. Med. Ctr., Durham, N.C., 1955-56, resident, 1956-57; clin. assoc. Nat. Inst. Allergy and Infectious Diseases, NIH, Bethesda, Md., 1957-59; mem. staff clin. endocrinology br. Nat. Heart, Lung and Blood Inst., NIH, Bethesda, 1959-63, assoc. in medicine, 1963-65; asst. prof. medicine Northwestern U. Sch. Medicine, Chgo., 1965-68; assoc. prof. Ind. U. Med Sch., Indpls., 1968-71, prof., 1971-79; prof. medicine and pharmacology Med. U. S.C., Charleston, 1979—, disting. univ. prof., 1998—. Mem. gen. medicine B study sect. NIH, Bethesda, 1982—86, chmn., 1985—86, mem. spl. grants rev. com. Nat. Inst. Arthritis, Musculo-Skeletal and Skin Diseases, 1990—95, chmn., 1993—94. Mem. editl. bd. Calcified Tissue Internat., 1978—83, 1994—2002, Jour. Clin. Endocrinology and Metabolism, 1982—87, Jour. Bone and Mineral Rsch., 1989—93, Italian Jour. Mineral and Electrolyte Metabolism, 1990—, Current Drug Targets-Immune, Endocrine and Metabolic Disorders, 2000—, Reviews in Endocrine & Metabolic Disorders, 2000—. Trustee Nat. Osteoporosis Found., Washington, 1984—88, chmn. sci. adv. bd., 1985—88. With USPHS, 1957—63. Recipient Career Devel. award, USPHS, 1965—68, VA Med. Investigator award, 1979, 1981—87, Thomas A. Roe Found. award, S.C. Med. Assn., 1982, William S. Middleton VA award, 1983, Frederic C. Bartter award, Am. Soc. Bone and Mineral Rsch., 1992, Career Recognition award, Vitamin D Workshop, 1997. Mem.: Endocrine Soc., Assn. Osteobiology (councillor 1997—98, sec.-treas. 1999, pres. 2000—02), Assn. Am. Physicians, Am. Soc. Pharmacology and Exptl. Therapeutics, Am. Soc. Bone and Mineral Rsch. (sec.-treas. 1978—85, pres. 1986—87, Shirley Hohl Svc. award 1998), Am. Soc. Clin. Investigation, Alpha Omega Alpha. Democrat. Episcopalian. Home: 1 Johnson Rd Charleston SC 29407-7514 Office: Strom Thurmond Rsch Bldg 114 Doughty St Charleston SC 29425 Business E-Mail: belln@musc.edu.

BELL, PATRICIA ANN, photographer, artist, writer; b. Sumter, SC, Oct. 21, 1952; d. Clarence Allen Bell, Jr. and Virgina Mae Verhoeven; m. John Edgar Terry, Sept. 9, 1969 (div.); 1 child, Daryl Allen Terry. AAS in Visual Comm. cum laude, Ivy Tech State Coll., Terre Haute, 2000; BFA in Photography, Art History minor magna cum laude, Ind. State U., Terre Haute, 2004. Accounts rep. Gt. Western Unifreight, Compton, Calif., 1978—81; prodn. asst. location/stage layout/ fabrication Renaissance Pleasure Faire, Novato and San Bernardino, Calif., 1989—96; CEO Ann Bell: Photography and Fine Art, 2005—. Exhibitions include Photography Granny's Vine (Ind. State U. Permanent Art Collection Purchase award, 2003), A Few of My Favorite Things (Ind. State U. Presdl. Merit award, 2002), Dried Flowers (First Pl./Wabash Valley Art Guild Spring Show at The Meadows, 2000), exhibitions include photography Rose Hulman Inst. Tech., Terre Haute, 2004—05, exhibitions include Wallflowers (Juried entry/Swope Museum's 57th Ann. Wabash Valley Exhbn.), Starving Artists Bread and Water Art Show (Best of Show, 2000), Rebirth: A Mile In My Shoes. Mem.: Ladies' Aux., VFW, Marine Corps League (assoc.), Phi Kappa Phi. Office Phone: 812-236-4425. Personal E-mail: patriciaa1@hotmail.com.

BELL, PATRICIA WRIGHT, music educator; b. Balt., Mar. 4, 1955; d. Henry Leroy and Mary Ann Wright; children: Mary Catherine, Joseph Christopher. Assocs. Degree, Anne Arundel C.C., Arnold, Md., 1977; BS in Music Edn., Towson State U., 1982; Master's Equivalency, Western Md. Coll., 1992. Advanced profl. cert. Anne Arundel County Pub. Schs. Music tchr. Old Mill Mid. Sch. South, Millersville, Md., 1984—94, Chesapeake Bay Mid. Sch., Pasadena, Md., 1994—. Chairperson Mid. Sch. All County Chorus for Anne Arundel County, 2000—. Mem.: Music Educators Nat. Conf., Mid. Sch. Choral Dirs. Anne Arundel County (spokesperson 2000—). Avocations: music, tennis, golf, boating, singing. Office: Chesapeake Bay Mid Sch 4804 Mountain Rd Pasadena MD 21122

BELL, PHILIP WILKES, accountant, economist, educator; b. NYC, Oct. 24, 1924; s. Samuel Dennis and Miriam Ball (Wilkes) B.; m. Katherine Elizabeth Hubbard, June 16, 1945 (div. May 1980); children: Susan, Geoffrey, Mary Ellen, James; m. Virginia Wood Crozier, June 14, 1980 (dec. Nov. 1998); stepchildren: Thomas, Steven, Peter; m. Jean Grady Wyeth, Oct. 24, 1999. BA, Princeton U., 1947; MA, U. Calif., Berkeley, 1949; PhD, Princeton U., 1954. Instr. Princeton (N.J.) U., 1948-51; rsch. assoc. Inst. for Advanced Study, Princeton, 1951-52; asst. prof. Haverford (Pa.) Coll., 1952-56, assoc. prof., then prof., 1960-68; assoc. prof. U. Calif., Berkeley, 1957-60; prof. Merrill Coll., U. Calif., Santa Cruz, 1968-79, provost, 1968-72; William A. Kirkland prof. Rice U., Houston, 1979-89; prof. acctg. and econs. Boston U., 1989-92; ret. Assoc. dir. Rockefellor Found., 1963-68; chmn., prof. econ. Makerere U. Coll., Uganda, 1963-65; chmn. econ., Fisk U., 1965-66; dir. Edn. Abroad Program U. Calif., Kenya, 1972-74; vis. prof. Univ. Sains Malaysia, Penang, 1976-77, Norges Handelshoyskole, Bergen, Norway, spring 1982, U. Pa., Phila, fall 1982. Author: Sterling Area in the Postwar World, 1956, Toward Greater Logic and Utility in Accounting: The Collected Writings of Philip W. Bell, 1997; co-author: (with Edgar O. Edwards) Theory and Measurement of Business Income, 1961, (with Edgar O. Edwards and L. Todd Johnson) Accounting for Economic Events, 1979, (with Michael H. Granof) Financial Accounting: Principles and Issues, 1992; contbr. articles to profl. jours. 2d lt. USAF, 1943-45. Social Sci. Rsch. Coun. rsch. fellow, London, 1956-57, Ford Found. fellow, Berkeley, 1959. Mem. Am. Acctg. Assn., Brit. Acctg. Assn., European Acctg. Assn., Royal Econ. Soc. (U.K.), Acctg. Assn. Australia and New Zealand (elected to Acctg. Hall of Fame, Columbus, Ohio, 2003). Mem. Soc. Of Friends. Home: 30 Lonsdale Ln Cartmel Kennett Square PA 19348-2045 Personal E-mail: philjean@kennett.net.

BELL, PHILLIP JACKSON, federal agency administrator; b. Portsmouth, Va., Dec. 31, 1941; s. John Henry and Lois Belle (Hendrix) B.; m. Virginia Phillips Inman, Apr. 11, 1981; children by previous marriage: Scarlett Lee Talamantes, Christopher J. Bell, John R. Bradley, Lynda I. Kleene. BSBA, Northwestern U., 1963; MA, U. S.C., 1964. Mgmt. cons. McKinsey & Co., Washington, 1967-73; dir. corp. planning Washington Post Co., 1973-77; asst. to pres. Allegheny Airlines, Washington, 1977-78; v.p.-long range planning USAir Inc, Washington, 1978-83, sr. v.p.-fin., CFO, 1983-86, exec. v.p.-fin., 1986-89; v.p.-fin., chief fin. officer USAir Group, 1984-89; exec. v.p., chief fin. officer Burlington Northern Inc., Ft. Worth, 1989-91; sr. v.p. planning Am. Airlines Inc., Ft. Worth, 1991-92, sr. v.p. strategic programs, 1992-93; exec. v.p., CFO Conner Peripherals Inc., San Jose, Calif., 1993-96; exec. v.p., CFO, chief adminstrv. officer Adobe Systems, Inc., San Jose, 1996-98, venture advisor, 1998—2003; dep. under sec. Dept. Army, Washington, 2005; dep. under. sec. for logistics & material readiness US Dept. Def., Washington, 2005—. Chief of staff Afghanistan Reconstruction Group of US State Dept., 2003-04; Served to capt. USMC, 1964-67, Vietnam. Office: US Dept Def 3500 Def Pentagon Rm 3E808 Washington DC 20301

BELL, RANDALL WILLIAM, ophthalmic surgeon; b. N.Y.C., Jan. 20, 1938; s. William Randall; children: Randall, Deborah, Kevin, Thomas, James; m. Maryanne Gallagher. BS, U.S. Mil. Acad., 1959; MD, Cornell U., 1966; grad., U.S. Army War Coll., 1983. Diplomate: Am. Bd. Ophthalmology, Nat. Bd. Med. Examiners. Commd. 2d Lt. U.S. Army, 1959, advanced through grades to brig. gen. Res., 1975, intern Walter Reed Gen. Hosp. Washington, 1966-67, resident Walter Reed Gen. Hosp., 1967-70, chief ophthalmology Valley Forge (Pa.) Gen. Hosp., 1970-72; practice medicine specializing in ophthalmology USAR 338th Med. Group, Wayne, Pa., 1972-83; comdg. gen. 2290th U.S. Army Hosp., Washington, 1981-85. Mem. Surgeon's Gen.'s Adv. Council; mem. staff Scheie Inst., Presbyn. U. Pa. Med. Ctr., assoc. attending surgeon Wills Eye Hosp., Phila., Jefferson Hosp., Phila., Bryn Mawr (Pa.) Hosp.; sr. attending opthalmologist, mem. exec. com. Sacred Heart Hosp., Norristown; asst. prof. Thomas Jefferson U., Phila., 1972-76, U. Pa., 1978. Contbr. articles on ophthalmology to profl. jours. Bd. dirs. West Point Fund and Soc. Fellow ACS, Pa. Acad. Opthalmology and Otolaryngology, Am. Acad. Opthalmology, Phila. Coll. Physicians; mem. AMA, Pa. Med. Soc., Del. County Med. Soc., Assn. Research in Vision and Ophthalmology, Soc. Contemporary Ophthalmology, Soc. Mil. Ophthalmologists, Ophthalmic Club Phila. (pres. 1981-83), West Point Soc. Phila. (bd. govs. 1975—, pres. 1981-82), Assn. U.S. Army (life), Soc. Med. Cons. Armed Forces Clubs: Merion Cricket, Merion Golf, Union League of Phila, Cornell, Racquet Club Phila. Home: 124 Bloomingdale Ave Wayne PA 19087-3929 Office Phone: 610-687-6888. Personal E-mail: genrwbellmd@aol.com.

BELL, REBECCA, psychotherapist, journalist; b. N.Y.C., Dec. 20, 1942; d. Hiram Charles Bluming and Mildred Ann Good; m. Martin Bell, Feb. 7, 1986 (div. Apr. 1993); children: Michael Sobel, Jessica Sobel. BA, UCLA, 1993, MSW, 1995. Lic. clin. social worker. Reporter Hollywood Citizens News, L.A., 1969-70; news writer Sta. KTLA-TV, L.A., 1970-71; assignment editor Sta. KHJ-TV, L.A., 1971-72; anchor, reporter Sta. WXYZ-TV, Detroit, 1972-76; reporter Sta. WCAU-TV, Phila., 1976-78; anchor Sta. WNET-TV, N.Y.C., 1978; corr. NBC, N.Y.C., 1978-86; corr. war coverage, White House reporter NBC Network, London, N.Y., Washington, 1978-86; pvt. practice as psychotherapist Beverly Hills, Calif., 1995—. Author: (book) The Strange Disappearance of Jimmy Hoffa, 1974. Recipient Emmy award Am. Fedn. Radio and TV Artists, 1983, Deadline award, 1978, Golden Mike award, 1974. Mem. NASW. Avocations: painting, horseback riding.

BELL, RICHARD EUGENE, grain and food company executive; b. Clinton, Ill., Jan. 7, 1934; s. Lloyd Richard and Ina (Oglesby) B.; m. Maria Christina Mendoza, Oct. 22, 1960; children— David Lloyd, Stephen Richard. BS with honors, U. Ill., 1957, MS, 1958. Internat. economist Dept. Agr., Washington, 1959-60, dir. grain div., 1969-72; agrl. attache Am. embassies in Ottawa, Can., Brussels, and Dublin, Ireland, 1961-68; asst. sec. agr. internat. affairs and commodity programs, 1973-77; pres. Riceland Foods Inc., Stuttgart, Ark., 1977—, now also chief exec. officer. Bd. dirs. First Comml. Corp., GTE S.W. Inc., Fed. Res. Bank St. Louis; pres., dir. Commodity Credit Corp., also Fed. Crop Ins. Corp., 1975-77; exec. sec. Pres.'s Agrl. Policy Com., 1976-77; rep. Internat. Wheat Coun., London, 1970-77; adviser World Food Conf., Rome, 1974; trustee Ark. State U., 1997—. Recipient Disting. Service award Dept. Agr., 1975 Mem. Alpha Gamma Rho, Alpha Zeta. Republican. Mem. Christian Ch. (Disciples Of Christ). Office: Riceland Foods Inc PO Box 927 2120 S Park Ave Stuttgart AR 72160-6822

BELL, RICHARD THOMAS, lawyer; b. Houston, Tex., Aug. 31, 1972; s. James Ronald Bell and Carolyn Sue Thrasher; m. Catherine Stokes, Dec. 9, 1995; 1 child, Travis Stokes. BA, Southwestern U., 1994; JD, South Tex. Coll. Law, 1997. Bar: Tex. 1997, U.S. Dist. Ct. (so. dist.) Tex. 1997, U.S. Ct. Appeals (5th cir.) 1997, Wis. 2000. Assoc. Allan A. Cease and Assocs., Sugar Land, Tex., 1995—99; ptnr. Cease and Bell, Sugar Land, 1999—. Prof. Legal Studies Alvin C.C., Alvin, Tex., 1997—. Mem. Pro Bono Coll. Tex., Austin, 2001—; bd. dirs. Fort Bend County Law Libr., Richmond, Casey Cease Outreach,Inc., Sugar Land. Mem.: ATLA, Fort Bend County Bar Assn. (pres. 2003, sec. 2001), Fort Bend County Criminal Def. Lawyers Assn., Tex. Criminal Def. Lawyers Assn. Baptist. Avocations: golf, reading, exercise, teaching Sunday school. Office: Cease and Bell PLLC 2507 Williams Trace Blvd Ste 103 Sugar Land TX 77479

BELL, ROBERT, literature educator; b. 1946; BA, Dartmouth Coll., 1967; PhD, Harvard U., 1972. Prof. Williams Coll., Williamstown, Mass., 1972—, founder, dir. Project for Effective Tchg., 1994—, William R. Kenan, Jr., Prof. English. Host The Book Show, Northeast Pub. Radio, 1996—98. Author: Jocoserious Joyce: The Fate of Folly in Ulysses, Bertrand Russell and the Eliots, Blushing Like the Morn: Milton's Human Comedy in Paradise Lost, Metamorphoses of Spritual Autobiography, James Boswell's Notes Toward a Supreme Fiction, David Hume's Fables of Identity, Dryden's Aeneid as English Augustan Epic, Sterne's Etristramology, Rousseau: Prophet of Sincerity, Shakespeare in Cyberspace, Critical Essays on Kingsley Amis, Bob Dylan and the Language that He Used, Shakespeare's Anatomy of Folly, A Teacher for All Seasons, Hades Episode: Notes and Annotations; editor-in-chief Berkshire Review. Recipient Exemplary Tchr. award, Am. Assn. Higher Edn., 1994, Robert Foster Cherry Award, 1998, Outstanding Baccalaureate Coll. Prof. of Yr., Coun. for Advancement and Support of Edn. & Carnegie Found. for Advancement of Tchg., 2004; grantee Danforth Found. Fellowship, 1967—72. Avocations: jazz, theater, films, history. Office: Stetson Hall Williams Coll Williamstown MA 01267 E-mail: Robert.H.Bell@williams.edu.

BELL, ROBERT CECIL, lawyer; b. San Francisco, June 1, 1951; s. Robert Elmer and Lillian Marie (Petrik) B. BJ, U. Nev., 1973; JD, U. Pacific, 1980. Bar: Nev. 1980, Colo. 1993, U.S. Dist. Ct. Nev. 1980, U.S. Bankruptcy Ct. 1981, U.S. Ct. Appeals (9th cir.) 1982, U.S. Supreme Ct., 1988. Investigator, legal asst. Washoe County Dist. Atty.'s Office, Reno, 1975-77; law clk. to presiding justice Washoe County Dist. Ct., Reno, 1980-81; sole practice Reno, 1981—. Judge pro tem Reno Mcpl. Ct., 1985—, Sparks Mcpl. Ct, 1986—; adminstrv. law judge, Reno; bd. dirs. Washoe Legal Svcs., Reno. Bd. dirs. March of Dimes, Reno, 1985—; mem. Supreme Ct. Hist. Soc. Mem. ABA, Washoe County Bar Assn., Assn. Trial Lawyers Am., Nev. Trial Lawyers Assn., Reno Rodeo Assn., Reno Air Races, U. Pacific McGeorge Sch. Law Alumni Assn. (bd. dirs. 1986—). Democrat. Lutheran. Avocations: photography, flying, skiing, golf, guitar. Office: 20 Winter St Reno NV 89503 Office Phone: 775-333-9977.

BELL, ROBERT EUGENE, anthropology educator; b. Marion, Ohio, June 16, 1914; s. Harry Thew and Clara (Stouffer) B.; m. Emily Virginia Merz, Aug. 31, 1938; children— Patricia (Mrs. Paul Lindsey), David Eugene. Student, Ohio State U., 1936-38; BA with honors, U. N.M., 1940; MA, U. Chgo., 1943, PhD, 1947. Asst. prof. anthropology U. Okla., 1947-51, assoc. prof., 1951-55, prof., 1955-69, George L. Cross Research prof., 1969-80, emeritus, 1980—. Chmn. dept., 1947-55, 61-64; head curator Stovall Mus., 1947-85; dir. Mississippi Valley Dendochronology Lab. U. Chgo., 1942-43, 46-47, Oklahoma River Basin Salvage Lab., 1962-78 Author: Oklahoma Archaeology: an Annotated Bibliography, 1969, 2d edit., 1978, The Harlan Site, CK-6, A Prehistoric Mound Center in Cherokee County, Eastern Oklahoma. Archaeol. investigations at site of El Inga, Ecuador, Ferdinandina: Biography of a French-India Trading Community on the Southern Plains, 2004; editor: Am. Antiquity, 1966-70, Bull. Okla. Anthrop. Soc, 1963-66, Prehistory of Oklahoma, 1984. Served with M.C. AUS, 1943-46. Recipient Clarence H. Webb award Outstanding Contbns. to Caddoan Archeology, 1985, Presentation in Recognition of Outstanding Contbn. to Ecuadorian Archeology, Govt. of Ecuador, 1986; subject of Festschrift Okla. Anthrop. Soc., Okla. Archeol. Survey, 1983, Shirk Meml. award for Hist. Preservation, 1987; named to Okla. Hist. Soc.'s Hall of Fame, 1994, Plains Anthropol. Soc. Disting. Svc. award 1994; Fulbright fellow, New Zealand, 1955-56. Mem. Am. Anthrop. Assn., Am. Assn. Phys. Anthropology, AAAS, Okla. Hist. Soc., Am. Ethnol. Soc., Soc. for Am. Archaeology (50th Anniversary award 1985), Mo., Ark., Tex., Kans. archaeol. socs., Inst. Gt. Plains, Southeastern Archaeol. Conf., Polynesian Soc., Soc. for Hist. Archaeology, Soc. for Conservation Archaeology, Explorers Club, Phi Beta Kappa (hon.), Sigma Xi. Home: 1120 Berry Cir Norman OK 73072-6307

BELL, ROBERT FRED, German language educator; BA in German, U. Ill., 1959, MA in German, 1962, PhD, 1969. Fulbright teaching asst. German high schs., Munich, 1959-60; grad. instr. U. Ill., 1964-65; instr. Purdue U., 1965-68, U. Ky., 1968-69, asst. prof., 1969-72, U. Ala, Tuscaloosa, 1972-76, assoc. prof., 1976-82, prof., 1982—, chair dept. German and Russian, 1976-78, acting chair dept. German and Russian, 1994-95, summer acting chair dept. Modern Langs. and Classics, 1998. Mem. exec. com. Ky. Fgn. Lang. Conf., U. Ky., 1970-72, chair German 3 sect., 1986; co-organizer symposium German exile lit. U. Ala., 1975; chair sect. German war novels South Atlantic Modern Lang. Convention, Atlanta, 1979. Co-editor: Protest-Form-Tradition: Essays on German Exile Literature, 1979, Exile: The Writer's Experience, 1982; consulting editor Critique: Studies in Modern Fiction, 1983—; mem. editorial adv. bd. Classical and Modern Lit.: A Quar., 1981-99; contbr. over 50 articles, revs. and papers to profl. jours., confs.; translator poems. Grantee U. Ala. Rsch. Grants Com., 1973. Mem. MLA (organizer spl. sect. ann. meeting 1982, 83, del. assembly 1989-93, South Atlantic affiliate, sec. German II sect. 1969-70, chmn. German II sect. 1970-71, sect. nominating com. 1971-74, chmn. nominating com. 1973-74, exec. com. 1974-77, sec. German III sect. 1980-81, chmn. 1981-82, sect. nominating com. 1982-85, chmn. sect. nominating com. 1984-85, presider German gen. session 1984, 86, 95, 97, SAMLA studies award com. 1985-88, chmn. ad hoc com. on constitution and by-laws, 1996, exec. dir. 1989-94, editor South Atlantic Rev. 1989-94), Am. Assn. Tchrs. German (sec. SAMLA region 1979-80, pres. 1980-81), Soc. for Exile Studies, German Studies Assn. (moderator session 71 16th ann. conf. 1992), Ala. Assn. Fgn. Lang. Tchrs. (v.p. 1979-80, pres. 1980-81), Phi Beta Kappa (3 term exec. com. U. Ala. chpt. 1982-85, 90-92, 98—, v.p. 1983-84, pres. 1984-85), Delta Phi Alpha (faculty sponsor U. Ala. chpt. 1975, 76, 79—), Phi Kappa Phi. Home: 708 Greystone St Northport AL 35473-2648 Office: U Ala Dept Modern Langs and Classics PO Box 870246 Tuscaloosa AL 35487-0154

BELL, ROBERT HOLMES, federal judge; b. Lansing, Mich., Apr. 19, 1944; s. Preston C. and Eileen (Holmes) B.; m. Helen Mortensen, June 28, 1968; children: Robert Holmes Jr., Ruth Eileen, Jonathan Neil. BA, Wheaton Coll., 1966; JD, Wayne State U., 1969. Bar: Mich. 1970, U.S. Dist. Ct. (we. dist.) Mich. 1970. Asst. prosecutor Ingham County Prosecutor's Office, Lansing, Mich., 1969-72; state dist. judge Mich. State Cts., 1973-78, state cir. judge Mason, 1979-87; judge US Dist. Ct. (we. dist.) Mich., Grand Rapids, Mich., 1987-2001, chief judge, 2001—. Office: US Dist Ct 402 Fed Bldg 110 Michigan St NW Grand Rapids MI 49503-2363 E-mail: kim@miwd.uscourts.gov.

BELL, ROBERT JEFFREY, lawyer; b. L.A., June 1, 1947; AB, U. Calif., Santa Cruz, 1969; JD summa cum laude, Loyola U., L.A., 1976. Bar: Calif. 1976. Ptnr. Luce, Forward, Hamilton & Scripps, San Diego, mng. ptnr., 2004—. Chief note and comment editor: Loyola U. L.A. Law Rev., 1975-76. Mem. ABA, State Bar Calif. (chair sales and brokerage subsect., mem. exec. com. real property law sect. 1990-93). Office: Luce Forward Hamilton & Scripps LLP 600 W Broadway Ste 2600 San Diego CA 92101 E-mail: rbell@luce.com.

BELL, ROBERT LLOYD, retired neurosurgeon; b. McKeesport, Pa., Sept. 3, 1923; s. Samuel Lowry and Nellie Pearl Bell; m. Helen Louise Matthews, Oct. 13, 1951; children: Robert Matthews, Louise Helen. BS, Washington and Jefferson Coll., 1944; MD, U. Pitts., 1947. Jr. intern Shady Side Hosp., Pitts., 1945—47; intern Western Pa. Hosp., Pitts., 1947—48; resident in surgery Aspin Wall Pa. Hosp., Pitts., 1948—49; resident in neurosurgery Bklyn. Hosp., 1949—50, Kings County Hosp., Bklyn., 1950—51, chief neurosurg. resident, 1953—54; chief neurosurgery 98th GH Hosp., Munich, 1951—53; from instr. to assoc. prof. SUNY, Bklyn., 1954—59; chief neurosurgery Wadsworth (Kans.) VA Hosp., 1959—64, Coatesville (Pa.) VA Hosp., 1964—69, Chester County Hosp., West Chester, Pa., 1969—83; chair nuc. medicine VA Hosp. Coatesville, 1983—91. 1st lt. col. USMC, 1951—53. Fellow: ACS, Am. Coll. Nuc. Medicine (gold medal 1989); mem.: AMA, SAR (compatriot), Chester County Med. Soc., Pa. Med. Soc., Am. Legion. Presbyterian. Home: 51 S 12th St Coatesville PA 19320

BELL, ROBERT M., judge; b. Rocky Mount, N.C., July 6, 1943; AB with honors, Morgan State Coll., 1966; JD, Harvard U., 1969. Bar: Md. 1969. Judge Md. Dist. Ct. Dist. 1, Balt., 1975-79; former judge Cir. Ct. Md. 8th Jud. Cir.; assoc. judge Md. Ct. Spl. Appeals, 1980-91, Md. Ct. Appeals, Balt., 1991-96, chief judge, 1996—. Mem. exec. com. Md. Jud. Conference, 1996—2000, chair, 1996—, mem. jud. compensation com., 1996—; chair Library Com. State Law Library, 1996—; mem. Judges, Masters & Juvenile Justice Com., 1996—; chair Com. on Bldg. Public Trust & Confidence in Justice System, 1998—99, Md. Alternative Dispute Resolution Commn., 1998—2001, Hall of Records Commn., 1998—, Technology Oversight Bd., 1999—; mem. State Commn. on Criminal Sentencing Policy, 1999—2000, Juvenile Justice Coord. Council, 2000—02; chair Public Trust & Confidence Implementation Com., 2000—, Jud. Cabinet, 2000—; chair jud. council Md. Jud. Conference, 2000—; chair advisory bd. Md. Mediation & Conflict Resolution Office, 2001—; mem. Task Force to Study Criminal Offender Monitoring by Global Positioning Systems, 2004—. Recipient Legal Excellence award, Md. Bar Foundation, 1999, Rosalyn B. Bell award, Women's Law Ctr. of Md., 1999, Louis M. Brown award, ABA, 2000, Access to Justice Tribute award, Pro Bono Resource Ctr., 2001, Md. Top Leadership in Law award, Daily Record, 2001, D'Alemberte/Raven award, ABA, 2003. Mem. ABA, Nat. Bar Assn., Md. State Bar Assn. (Special award 1998), Inc., Bar Assn. Balt. City, Monumental City Bar Assn. Office: Court of Appeals 634 Courthouse East 111 N Calvert St Baltimore MD 21202-1904*

BELL, ROBERT MATTHEW, pharmaceutical company consultant; b. London, Dec. 3, 1932; came to U.S., 1972; s. George Frederick and Patricia (Brusso) B.; m. Jeanette Edna Head, Sept. 17, 1955; children: Adrian R., Colette M. Pharm. diploma, Portmouth Coll., England, 1954; MB,ChB, Birmingham U., Eng., 1968. Diplomate Am. Bd. Family Practice. Relief mgr. Boots Chemists, Eng., 1955-57; owner Bell's Pharmacy, Rhodesia, 1958-61; joint owner Strachan's Pharmacy, Rhodesia, 1962-69; asst. lectr. Godfrey Huggins Sch. Medicine, Rhodesia, 1970-72; clin. project dir. Sterling Winthrop Rsch. Inst., Renesselaer, 1973-75; chief clin. pharmacology ICI Americas, Wilmington, Del., 1975-78; pres., owner RAMA Med. Clinic, Charlotte, N.C., 1980-86; from assoc. dir. to sr. dir. healthcare info. svcs. Searle, Inc., Skokie, Ill., 1986-96; prin. Bell and Assocs., Sedona, Ariz., 1996—. Mem. drug rev. com. Drugs Control Coun. of Rhodesia, Salisbury, 1971—72; mem. adv. bd. Upjohn Healthcare Svcs., Charlotte, NC; chmn. adv. bd. med. office asst. program Piedmont C.C., Charlotte, NC; chief dept. family practice Charlotte Meml. Hosp., 1983—84; trustee Am. Acd. Pharm. Physicians, Apex, NC, 1995—96; mem. Pharm. Soc. of Great Britian, 1955—72. Co-author: (book) The Practical Management of Renal Failure, 1969; co-editor: (book) The Endorphins, Marcel Dekker, N.Y., 1982. Grantee Malvern Trust, Rhodesia, 1963; named Metrolina Vol. of Yr., Am. Lung Assn., N.C., 1985. Mem. AMA, Drug Info. Assn.(Outstanding Svc. award 1997), Am. Acad. Pharm. Physicians (Life Hon. Membership award 2002, Certs. of Appreciation 1999, 2000), Am.-Zimbabwe Med. Assn. (chmn. 1996-98). Avocations: postal history, reading, exercising. Office: Bell & Assocs PO Box 3668 Sedona AZ 86340-3668

BELL, ROBERT MORRALL, lawyer; b. Graniteville, SC, Feb. 15, 1936; s. Jonathan F. and Ruby Lee (Carpenter) B.; m. Cecelia Richardson Coker, June 11, 1965 (dec.). AB, U. S.C., 1958, LLB, 1965. Bar: S.C. 1965, U.S. Dist. Ct. S.C. 1965, U.S. Ct. Appeals (4th cir.) 1970. With Watkins, Vandiver, Kirven & Long, Anderson, S.C., 1965-67; sr. law clk. to chief judge U.S. Dist. Ct. S.C., Greenville, 1967-69; mem. Abram, Bowen & Townes, Greenville, 1969-71, Bell, Surasky and Brown, P.A., Langley, S.C., 1971-76, sr. ptnr., 1976—2003; pvt. practice Graniteville, 2004—. County atty. Aiken County (S.C.), 1982—. Mem. SC Hwy Commn., 1982-86; state exec. committeeman SC Dem. Com., 1980-86; active SC Bd. Chiropractic Examiners, 1978-80, Svc. Coun. of Aiken County, 1976-82, Aiken County Planning Commn., 1976-80; chmn. Aiken County Transp. Com., 1993-96; bd. dirs. Aiken County Crippled Children's Soc., 1976-82; bd. dirs. Gregg-Graniteville Found., 1984—, chmn., 1998—; del. gen. and jurisdictional confs. United Meth. Ch., 1988-92; mem. SC Midlands Citizens Com. on Jud. Qualifications, 1996—. With USAR, 1959-60. Named to Order Ky. Cols., 1989—. Mem. ABA, ATLA, Aiken County Bar Assn., S.C. Bar Assn., S.C. Trial Lawyers Assn., Masons, Shriners, Am. Legion, Beech Island Agrl. Club, Kappa Sigma Kappa, Tau Kappa Alpha, Phi Delta Phi, Chi Psi (nat. visitor, 1960-62, nat. dir. scholarship, 1962-65, nat. exec. coun., 1987-90, Nat. Disting. Svc. award, 2004). Democrat. Office: PO Box 421 Ste 9 Masonic Shopping Ctr 50 Canal St Graniteville SC 29829-0421 Office Phone: 803-232-0300. Business E-Mail: robert.bell@scbar.org.

BELL, RONALD MACK, university foundation administrator, consultant; b. Atlanta, Mar. 4, 1937; m. Deborah Jean Slaton, Dec. 28, 1989. BS in Indsl. Mgmt., Ga. Inst. Tech., 1959; MBA, U. Mich., 1965; attended, Cornell U., 1980. Commd. USN, 1959, advanced through grades to capt., 1979, ret., 1985; assoc. dir. rsch. contracts Ga. Inst. Tech., Atlanta, 1985-88; v.p., gen. mgr. Ga. Tech. Rsch. Corp., Atlanta, 1988-97; exec. dir. S.C. Rsch. Inst., Columbia, 1997-2001; v.p., bd. dirs. Pisgah Astrol. Rsch. Inst., 1999—2003; pres., CEO UCRF Support Assoc., St. Simons Island, Ga., 1998—. Bd. dirs., past pres., now dir. emeritus Nat. Supply Corps. Assn.; cons. Wesvaco/Post, Buckley, Coastal Cons., Inc., also others, 1985—; expert witness ELSCO, U. Tenn., others, 1987-90; nat. chmn. Univ. Connected Rsch. Found., 1990-91. Past chmn., dir. emeritus Naval Supply Corps. Sch. Mus. Com., Athens, mem., 1983—; mem. Exec. Roundtable, Atlanta, 1985-97; resource staff Gov.'s Com. Tech. & Devel., Atlanta, 1992-97; bd. dirs. Ga. Tech. Sch. Mgmt., 1995-98; bd. grad. studies advisors Ga. So. U., 2004—. Decorated Legion of Merit (2), Meritorious Svc. medal (2), Navy Commendation medal (2). Mem. Soc. Rsch. Adminstrs. (nat. coms., chair regional com. 1985-2002), Licensing Execs. Soc., Nat. Coun. Univ. Rsch. Adminstrs. (chair regional com., nat. panelist 1985-2001), Coun. Rsch. and Tech. (dir. workshop, tax com. 1986-92), Ga. Tech. Nat. Alumni Assn. (various coms.), Nat. Conf. on the Advancement of Rsch. (conf. com. 2000), Assn. Univ. Tech. Mgrs., Theta Chi (past chpt. pres.), Phi Kappa Phi, Beta Gamma Sigma. Avocations: golf, woodworking. Home: 113 Thompson Cv Saint Simons Island GA 31522-3768 Office: UCRF Support Assoc PO Box 20272 Saint Simons Island GA 31522 E-mail: bellssi@earthlink.net.

BELL, ROSONALD RENAE, toxicologist; b. Gainesville, Fla., July 8, 1959; s. Gerome Bell, Sarah Dollie Stewart; m. Michelle Angela Crane; children: Maya, Sharon. MS, PhD, Fla. A&M U., 1992. Diplomate Am. Bd. of Toxicology 1996. Bil. lab. technigian insects affecting man and animals rsch. lab. USDA/Agrl. Rsch. Svc., Gainesville, Fla., 1981—86; grad. rsch. asst. toxicology lab. Fla. A&M U., 1986—92; grad. summer intern new molecule rsch. divsn., pulmonary pharmacolog 3M Pharms., St. Paul, 1989, profl. intern new drug discovery rsch. divs., 1990—91; postdoctoral rsch. scientist Pharmacia Corp., Kalamazoo, 1992—94; study dir. reproductive and gen. toxicology Novartis Pharms. Corp., Summit, NJ, 1994—96; study dir. gen. toxicology Novartis Pharms. Corp.Ciba Pharms., East Hanover, NJ, 1997—98; sr. toxicologist Pharmacia Corp./GD Searle, Skokie, Ill., 1998—. Contbr. numerous articles to profl. jours. Fellow Patricia Robert Harris fellow, Patricia Robert Harris Found., 1991—92, Doctoral fellow, McKnight Found.-Fla. Endowment Fund, 1988—91, inority Biomed. Rsch. Support fekkiw, Fla. A&M U., 1986—88; scholar 3M Scholarship, 3M Pharms., 1990—92. Mem.: Mid-West Teratology Assn., Soc. of Toxicology, Nat. Soc. of Toxicology, Teratogy Soc., Kappa Psi, Rho Chi (VP 1990—91, National Honor Society 1988), Alpha Kappa Mu (National Honor Society, Highest GPA - Graduate Student 1991-1992). Avocations: basketball, softball, travel, exercise. Office: Pharmacia Corporation 4901 Searle Pkwy Rm J203A Skokie IL 60077 Business E-Mail: rosonald.r.bell@pharmacia.com.

BELL, SAMUEL H., federal judge, educator; b. Rochester, N.Y., Dec. 31, 1925; s. Samuel H. and Marie C. (Williams) B.; m. Joyce Elaine Shaw, 1948 (dec.): children: Henry W., Steven D.; m. Jennie Lee McCall, 1983 BA, Coll. Wooster, 1947; JD, U. Akron, 1952. Pvt. practice, Cuyahoga Falls, Ohio, 1956-68; asst. pros. atty. Summit County, Ohio, 1956-58; judge Cuyahoga Falls Mcpl. Ct., Ohio, 1968-73, Ct. of Common Pleas, Akron, Ohio, 1973-77, Ohio Ct. Appeals, 9th Jud. Dist., Akron, 1977-82, U.S. Dist. Ct. (no. dist.) Ohio, Akron, 1982-2000, sr. status, 1996; sr. judge. Adj. prof. Coll. Wooster, 1987-2003, Bell disting. lectr. in law, 1998—; adj. prof., adv. bd. U. Akron Sch. Law, past trustee Dean's club; bd. dirs. Jos. R. Miller Found; co-owner Bell Letters Ltd. Co-author: Federal Practice Guide 6th Cir., 1996. Recipient Disting. Alumni award U. Akron, 1988, St. Thomas More award, 1987. Fellow Akron Bar Found. (trustee 1989-94, pres. 1993-94); mem. Fed. Bar Assn., Akron Bar Assn., Akron U. Sch. Law Alumni Assn. (Disting. Alumni award 1983), Charles F. Scanlon Akron Inn Ct. (pres. 1990-92), Masons, Phi Alpha Delta. Republican. Presbyterian. Office: US Dist Ct 433 US Court House Fed Bldg 2 S Main St Akron OH 44308-5836 E-mail: sbell2@neo.rr.com.

BELL, SANDRA ELIZABETH, commercial and investment banker; b. Toronto, Ont., Can., Apr. 23, 1957; came to U.S., 1961; d. Alexander James Bell and Marion Ann (Scaysbrook) Robinson. BA in Econs., Ohio State U., 1979; MBA, Harvard U., 1983. Mgmt. trainee, systems analyst First Nat. Bank of Cin., 1979-81; asst. v.p. E.F. Hutton & Co., N.Y.C., 1983-87; v.p. The Deerpath Group, Lake Forest, Ill., 1988-91; mng. dir. N.Y. br. Deutsche Bank AG, N.Y.C., 1991—2004; exec. v.p., CFO Fed. Home Loan Bank of Cin., 2004—. Mem. Phi Beta Kappa. Avocations: skiing, tennis, reading. Office: Fed Home Loan Bank 221 E 4th St Fl 10 Cincinnati OH 45202

BELL, SHARON KAYE, small business owner; b. Lincoln, Nebr., Sept. 14, 1943; d. Edwin B. and Evelyn F. (Young) Czachurski; m. James P. Kittrell (div. Sept. 1974); children: Nathan James, Nona Kaye; m. Joseph S. Bell, June 5, 1976; stepchildren: Eugene, Patricia, Bobbie, Linda. Continuing edn./active tax preparer/interviewer assoc., H&R Block, Laguna Hills, 1987—. Various positions mgmt., bookkeeping, 1961-71; bookkeeper Internat. Harvester, Chesapeake, Va., 1971-73, Cheat'AH Engring., Santa Ana, Calif., 1973-74, Fre Del Engring., Santa Ana, Calif., 1974-75; bookkeeper/mgr. Tek Sheet Metal Co., Santa Ana, Calif., 1975-79; owner, bookkeeper Bell's Bookkeeping, Huntington Beach, Calif., 1979-86, Fountain Valley, Calif., 1986—, Laguna Hills, Calif., 1986—2002; tax preparer H&R Block, Laguna Hills, 1989—98, Bell's Bookkeeping, Laguna Hills, 1998—, Oceanside, Calif., 2002—. Mem. Inst. Mgmt. Accts. (bd. dirs.

1985-86, sec. 1986-87, v.p. 1987-90, dir. manuscripts 1990-91), Nat. Notary Assn., NAFE, Wives of Submarine Vets. World War II (v.p. L.A. chpt. 1986-87, treas. 1990-92), Nat. Soc. Pub. Accts., Internat. Platform Assn. Republican. Avocations: gardening, dance, grandchildren and great grandchildren, rv travel.

BELL, SHARON L., retired elementary school educator; b. Lancaster, Pa., Sept. 16, 1949; d. Harry W. and Lillian A. (Hall) Garner; m. Marvin W. Bell, Dec. 21, 1974. BSE, Millersville State Coll., 1971, MEd in Elem. Edn., 1974. Cert. tchr., Pa. Tchr. Sch. Dist. Lancaster, Pa., 1971—2004; ret., 2004. Mem.: Lancaster Assn. Sch. Retirees, Pa. Assn. Sch. Retirees.

BELL, STEPHEN ANDREW, humanities educator; b. Chipping, Lancashire, United Kingdom, Apr. 18, 1956; s. Stanley Edward and Elizabeth Margaret Bell. BA with honors, Queen's Coll., Oxford U., 1978; MA, U. Toronto, 1980, PhD, 1991. Asst. prof. UCLA, Dept. of Geography, LA, 1999—; rsch. assoc. McGill U., Dept. of Geography, Montreal, Canada, 1989—99. Author: (research monograph) Campanha Gaucha: A Brazilian Ranching System, 1850-1920 (Stanford University Press, 1998) (Warren Dean Meml. Award of the Conf. on Latin Am. History, 1999). Office: Dept of Geography UCLA 1255 Bunche Hall 405 Hilgard Avenue Los Angeles CA 90095-1524 Office Phone: 310-825-1071. Office Fax: 310-206-5976. E-mail: sbell@geog.ucla.edu.

BELL, STEPHEN D., lawyer; b. 1951; AB, Dartmouth Coll., 1974; JD, Univ. SD, 1978. Bar: SD 1978, Minn. 1980, Mont. 1984, Colo. 1993. Ptnr., trial group Dorsey & Whitney LLP, Denver, and mem., policy com. Office: Dorsey & Whitney LLP Ste 4700 Republic Plz Bldg 370 17th St Denver CO 80202-5647 Office Phone: 303-629-3405. Office Fax: 303-629-3450. Business E-Mail: bell.steve@dorsey.com.

BELL, STEPHEN KEITH, psychologist; b. Ft. Mclellan, Ala., Oct. 8, 1968; s. William Charles and Janice Elizabeth Bell; m. Melissa Ann Likens-Bell, July 21, 2001; 1 child, William Elijah. BA, M of Acctg., Auburn U.; PhD in Clin. Psychology, U. Memphis. CPA Ga., 1993; lic. psychologist Ala., 2002. Staff auditor Ernst & Young, Atlanta, 1991—93; staff psychologist Children's Health Sys., Birmingham, Ala., 2002—. Cons. in field. Contbr. articles to profl. jours. Mem. prescription privileges com. Assn. Lic. Psychologists Ala., 2004—; mem. early warning panel Mountain Brook Sch. Sys., 2003—; bd. dirs. Project I'm Just Like You Ala. Epilepsy Found., 2005—. Recipient Dudley award, Auburn U., 1986, Rsch. Travel award, U. Memphis, 1999, Philip McElroy Excellence award, Auburn U., 1989; fellow, U. Fla., Gainesville, 2001—02; Kilgore scholar, Auburn U., 1986. Mem.: APA, Ala. Psychol. Assn., Phi Kappa Phi, Phi Eta Sigma. Methodist. Avocations: hiking, running. Home: 159 Redwood Dr Trussville AL 35173 Office: Childrens Hosp 1600 7th Ave S Ste 500 Birmingham AL 35233 Office Phone: 205-939-9193.

BELL, STEPHEN ROBERT, lawyer; b. Menominee, Mich., July 10, 1942; s. John Martin and Catherine Irene (Goodman) B.; m. Linden Tucker, May 22, 1976. AB, Georgetown U., 1964; JD, U. Wis., 1967. Bar: D.C. 1971, Minn. 1967, Wis. 1967, U.S. Ct. Appeals (4th and 5th cirs.), U.S. Supreme Ct. Assoc. Dorsey & Whitney, Mpls., 1967—68; ptnr. Wilkinson, Cragun & Barker, Washington, 1971—82, Squire, Sanders & Dempsey, Washington, 1982—96, Willkie, Farr & Gallagher LLP, Washington, 1996—. Contbr. articles to profl. jours. Lt. USNR, 1968—71. Mem. ABA, D.C. Bar Assn., Fed. Communications Bar Assn., Computer Law Assn. (bd. dirs. 1987-93), Order of Coif. Office: Willkie Farr & Gallagher LLP 1875 K St NW Washington DC 20006-1238 Office Phone: 202-303-1102. Personal E-mail: sbell@willkie.com.

BELL, STEPHEN SCOTT (STEVE BELL), journalist, educator; b. Oskaloosa, Iowa, Dec. 9, 1935; s. Howard Arthur and Florance (Scott) B.; m. Joyce Dillavou, June 16, 1957; children: Allison Kay, Hilary Ann. BA, Central Coll., Pella, Iowa, 1959, PhD (hon.), 1969; MS in Journalism, Northwestern U., 1963. Announcer Radio Sta. KBOE, Oskaloosa, 1955-59; reporter WOI-TV, Ames, Iowa, 1959-60; news writer WGN Radio-TV, Chgo., 1960-61; reporter, anchorman WOW-TV, Omaha, 1962-65; anchorman Radio Sta. WNEW, N.Y.C., 1965-66; corr. ABC News, 1967-86, assignments include Vietnam War corr., 1970-71, polit. corr., 1968, 72, chief Asia corr., 1972-73, White House corr. Washington, 1974-75; news anchorman World News This Morning and Good Morning Am., 1975-86; news anchor KYW-TV, Phila., 1987-91, USA Network Updates, 1989-92; prof. telecomm. Ball State U., Muncie, Ind., 1992—. Recipient Emmy nominations, 1965, 73, Overseas Press Club award, 1969, Headliner award, 1975 Mem. AFTRA, Council Fgn. Relations. Presbyterian (elder). Office: Ball State U Dept Telecommunications Muncie IN 47306-0001 *As a journalist, the older I get, the less inclined I am to "play God.".*

BELL, STEVEN DENNIS, lawyer; b. Akron, Ohio, Feb. 11, 1953; s. Sam H. and Joyce E. (Shaw) B.; m. E. Jane White (div. Feb. 1995); children: Colleen, Patrick. BA, U. Notre Dame, 1975; JD, U. Akron, 1978. Bar: Ohio 1979, D.C. 1989, U.S. Dist. Ct. (no. dist.) Ohio 1980, U.S. Ct. Appeals (6th cir.) 1980, U.S. Ct. Appeals (D.C. cir.) 1987, U.S. Supreme Ct. 1989, U.S. Dist. Ct. (so. dist.) Ohio 1990, U.S. Dist. Ct. (ea. dist.) Mich. 1996. Pvt. practice, Akron, 1979-81; chief trial atty. City of Akron, 1981-84; asst. U.S. atty. no. dist. Ohio U.S. Atty.'s Office, Cleve., 1984-88, chief civil divsn., 1986-88, chief appellate litigation, 1987; ptnr. Janik & Bell, Cleve., 1988-91, Ulmer & Berne LLP, Cleve., 1991—. Mem. ABA, Ohio State Bar Assn., Nat. Health Lawyers Assn. Office: Bond Ct Bldg 1300 E 9th St Lbby 9 Cleveland OH 44114-1503

BELL, STOUGHTON, computer scientist, mathematician, educator; b. Waltham, Mass., Dec. 20, 1923; s. Conrad and Florence Emily (Ross) Bell; m. Mary Carroll O'Connell, Feb. 26, 1949 (div. 1960); children: Karen, Mark; m. Laura Joan Bainbridge, May 24, 1963 (div. 1979); children: Nathaniel Stoughton, Joshua Bainbridge; m. Edna Casman, July 25, 2001. Student, Harvard U., 1946-49; AB, U. Calif., Berkeley, 1950, MA, 1953, PhD, 1955. Mem. staff Sandia Corp., Albuquerque, 1955-66, div. supr., 1964-66; vis. lectr. U. N.Mex., 1957-66, dir. computing center, 1966-79, assoc. prof. math., 1966-71, prof. math. and computer sci., 1971-92, prof. emeritus, 1992—. Vis. lectr. N.Mex. Acad. Scis., 1965—. Co-author: (book) Linear Analysis and Generalized Functions, 1965, Introductory Calculus, 1966, Modern University Calculus, 1966, Mathematical Analysis for Modeling, 1999. With AUS, 1943—44. Mem.: Ops. Rsch. Soc. Am., Am. Statis. Assn., Soc. Indsl. and Applied Math., Math. Assn. Am., Am. Math. Soc., Assn. Computing Machinery (nat. lectr. 1972—74). Office: U NMex Computer Sci Dept Albuquerque NM 87131-1386 Business E-Mail: sto@cs.unm.edu.

BELL, SUSAN JANE, nurse; b. Columbus, Ohio, July 24, 1946; d. Donald Richard Bell and Martha Jane (McDowell) Nichols; m. Robert Earlin Ward, Oct. 24, 1964 (div. 1984); children: Duane Allen Ward, Melissa Jane Ward, Bryan Thomas Ward. Degree in nursing, Columbus Sch. Practical Nursing, 1986; ADRN, Columbus State C.C., 1989; student, Franklin U., 1993, Edn. Direct Nutrition and Fitness. RN, Ohio; cert. CPR. Nurse's asst. Riverside Meth. Hosp., Columbus, 1970-80, Norworth Convalescent Ctr., Columbus, 1980-86; nurse, charge nurse Heartland Thurber Care Ctr., Columbus, 1986-89; staff nurse Am. Nursing Care, Columbus, 1989—; medicare home visitation, staffing and pvt. duty nurse Telemed, Columbus, 1989—; asst. head nurse Northland Terr., Columbus, 1989; supr. Elmington Manor, Columbus, 1989; staff nurse cardiac step down unit Grant Hosp., Columbus, 1989-92; nurse med. ICU, CCU and pediatric ICU, 1992-93; charge nurse critical-skilled unit First Cmty. Village Health Care Ctr., Columbus, 1992-95; supr., charge nurse St. Rita's Home; charge nurse Mother Angeline McCrory Manor, 2005—. Pres. Bell Mktg. Distbrs., pvt. duty ALS ventilator patients Med. Pers. Poole. Sponsor Childreach. Mem. NAFE, ASPCA, World Wildlife Found., Nature Conservancy, Ohio Hist. Found. (archives/libr. divsn.), Nat. Audubon Soc., Environ. Def. Fund, Nat. Wildlife Fedn., Humane Soc. U.S., Am. Assn. Individual Investors, Columbus Met. Mus. Art (supporting), Internat. Assn. Global Execs., Nat. Notary Assn., Nat. Mus. of Women in the Arts, Ohio Hist. Soc.-Archives Libr., Omtermat/ Exec. Guild, Rotary, Sierra Club. Avocations: body building, power lifting, swimming, music, crocheting. Personal E-mail: bellcanine@aol.com.

BELL, THEODORE AUGUSTUS, writer, former advertising executive; b. Tampa, Fla., July 3, 1946; s. Theodore A. and Mary Trice (Howell) B.; m. Evelyn Byrd Lorentzen, Mar. 31, 1978; 1 child, Evelyn Byrd. BA in English, Randolph-Macon Coll., 1969; DFA (hon.), Kendall Coll., 1990. Copywriter Wilson, Haight, Welsh Advt., Hartford, Conn., 1970-71, Tinker, Dodge & Delano, NYC, 1971-72; v.p., creative dir. Doyle Dane Bernbach, NYC, 1972-82; pres., chief creative officer Leo Burnett USA, Chgo., 1982-93; vice-chmn., worldwide creative dir. Young & Rubicam, NYC, 1993—2000. Creative cons. Heart of Am. America's Cup Challenge, Chgo., 1985-86. Author (novels) Hawk, 2003, Assassin, 2004. Bd. dirs. Lincoln Park Zoo, 1988—, Prentice Women's Maternity Ctr. Northwestern Meml. Hosp., Chgo., 1981—. Recipient Gold Lion award Cannes (France) Internat. Festival du Film Publicitaire, 1988. Mem. Racquet Club (Chgo. and N.Y.C.), Field Club (Greenwich, Conn.). Republican. Episcopalian. Avocations: sailing, golf, screenwriting, gamebird hunting. Office: c/o Atria Books 1230 Av of Am New York NY 10020

BELL, W. DONALD, electronics company executive; BSEE, U. AL. V.p., sales and mktg. Texas Instruments; pres and CEO Electronic Arrays (now NEC Microelectronics); sr. vp memory & microprocessors, mktg. v.p., exec. v.p. Am. Microsystems Inc.; exec. V.P. Kierulff Electronics, 1980-81, pres., 1981-86; pres and COO Docummun, Inc., 1986-88; pres., CEO, chmn. Bell Microproducts, San Jose, CA, 1988—. Mem. bd. dir. Sand Hill Capital, Eng. Leadership Bd. for the U. of AL. Disting. Eng. Fellow of U of AL. Office: Bell Microproducts 1941 Ringwood Ave San Jose CA 95131-1721

BELL, WALLACE EDWARD, minister, insurance agent; b. Jackson, Tenn., Feb. 23, 1950; s. William and Marvelyne Eugenia (Wallace) B.; m. Johnnie Mae Mitchell, Sept. 12, 1974; children: Jonathan Edward, Candace Michelle. BS, Union U., 1972. Lic. to ministry Ch. of Christ (Holiness) U.S.A., 1973; ordained, 1979. Assoc. minister Christ Temple Ch. of Christ (Holiness) U.S.A., Jackson, 1978—79; bus. tax inspector Madison Cty. Clk., Jackson, 1978—87; pastor Christ Temple Ch. of Christ (Holiness) U.S.A., Jackson, 1979—87, Greater Peace Ch. of Christ, Aurora, Colo., 1987—88, Christ Temple Ch. of Christ (Holiness) U.S.A., Kans. City, Kans., 1988—95; agt. Am. Nat. Life Ins. Co., Shawnee Mission, Kans., 1995—97, Woodmen Accident & Life Ins. Co., Kans. City, Mo., 1997; personal ins. cons. Sitel Corp., Shawnee Mission, 1997—98; pastor First Ch. of Christ, Kans. City, Mo., 1998—2001; ins. lic. trainer Sitel Corp., Shawnee Mission, 1998—2001; pastor Mount Zion Ch. of Christ (Holiness) U.S.A., Inc., Gilbert, La., 2001—. Trustee C.M. & I. Coll. Nat. Bd., Jackson, 1980-92; sec. Northcentral Diocese, St. Louis, 1982-90; dir. comms. Nat. S.S. Congress CoCHUSA, Jackson, 1989-96; career agt. Am. Nat. Life Ins., 1995-97; agt. Woodmen Accident & Life, 1997; personal ins. cons. Sitel, 1997-98; dist. chmn. midwest dist. Ch. of Christ (Holiness) USA, Kansas City, Mo., 1997-2001, dist. pres. 1997-2001, chmn Nat. Bd. Claimants, 2000-; ins. licensing trainer, 1998-2001; lic. trainer Sitel Corp., 1998—. Bd. dirs. Aspell Manor, Jackson, 1985-87. Recipient E.M. Wills award Tenn.-Ky. Dist., 1986. Mem. Jaycees (chaplain 1984-85). Office: Mt Zion Ch of Christ (Holiness) 7140 Hwy 15 Gilbert LA 71336 Home: PO Box 367 Winnsboro LA 71295 Personal E-mail: wallbell@yahoo.com.

BELL, WAYNE S., lawyer, state agency official; b. L.A., June 24, 1954; s. Joseph and Jane Barbara (Barsook) B.; m. M. Susan Modzelewski, Apr. 1, 1989; 1 child, Seth Joseph Bell. BA magna cum laude, UCLA, 1976; JD, Loyola U., L.A., 1979; Advanced Mgmt. Program, Rutgers U., 1992. Bar: Calif. 1980, U.S. Dist. Ct. (cen. dist.) 1981, U.S. Tax Ct. 1981, U.S. Ct. Appeals (9th cir.) 1981, U.S. Dist. Ct. (so. and no. dists.) Calif. 1983, U.S. Supreme Ct. 1984, D.C. 1986, Tex. 1995; lic. real estate broker, Calif. Intern office of gov. State of Calif., Sacramento, summer 1976; assoc. Levinson, Rowen, Miller, Jacobs & Kabrins, L.A., 1980-82; sr. assoc. Montgomery, Gascou, Gemmill & Thornton, L.A., 1982-84; counsel, project developer Thomas Safran & Assocs., L.A., 1984-85; of counsel Greenspan, Glasser & Medina, Santa Monica, Calif., 1984-86; assoc. gen. counsel Am. Diversified Cos., Costa Mesa, Calif., 1985-88; legal cons. Project Atty., L.A., 1988-89; sr. counsel, asst. sec. Ralphs Grocery Co., L.A., 1989-99, v.p., sr. counsel, asst. sec., 1999; dep. sec., gen. counsel Calif. Bus., Transp. and Housing Agy., Sacramento, 1999—2003, spl. counsel to Gov.'s Legal Affairs Sec., 1999—2003, provisional undersecretary, 2001—03; dir. Homeownership Calif. Housing Fin. Agy., 2003—; spl. assignment Office of Gen. Counsel, 2005—. Judge pro tem Mcpl. Ct. South Bay Jud. Dist., 1987, L.A. Superior Ct., 1991, 94, 97; settlement officer L.A. Mcpl. Ct., Settlement Officer Program, 1990-92; spl. master State Bar Calif., 1991-92; fellow Program Sr. Execs. State & Local Govt., Fannie Mae Found., Harvard. Chief note and comment editor Loyola U. Law Rev., 1978-79; contbr. articles to profl. jours. and gen. pubs. Vol. atty. Westside Legal Svcs., Santa Monica, 1982-87; legal ombudsman Olympics Ombudsman Program L.A. County Bar Assn., 1984; gov. apptd. mem. Calif. adv. coun. Legal Svcs. Corp., 1982-88, Autism Soc. Am., Amnesty Internat.; contbg. mem. Dem. Nat. Com.; mem. leadership coun. So. Poverty Law Ctr.; charter mem. presdl. task force Ams. for Change; bd. dirs. Am. Theatre Arts, Hollywood, Calif., 1983-84; pres., exec. com., bd. dirs. Programs for the Developmentally Handicapped, Inc., L.A., 1987-92; chmn. bd. appeals handicapped accommodations City of Manhattan Beach, 1986-88; bd. dirs. The Foodbank of So. Calif., 1991-94, sec., 1993; legal oversight com. Legal Corps L.A., 1995-97; sec. bd. trustees The Ralphs/Food 4 Less Found., 1995-99; vol. L.A. County Bar Assn., Barristers Homeless Shelter Advocacy Project, 1996-99, exec. com. labor and employment law sect., 1997-99; mem. coordinating com. Calif. Lake Tahoe Interagy Coun., 2001-05; mem. San Francisco Bay Conservation and Devel. Commn., 2002-05 Mem. Calif. Bar Assn. (legal svcs. sect. standing com. legal problems of aging 1983-86, chmn. legis. subcom. 1984-86, conf. dels. alternate 1987), D.C. Bar Assn., Legal Assistance Assn. Calif. (bd. dirs., mem. exec. com., legis. strategy com. 1984-86), Loyola Law Sch. (advocate), Phi Beta Kappa. Democrat. Avocations: sailing, hiking, human behavior study, photography, travel. Office: Calif Housing Finance Agency 1121 L Street 7th Floor Sacramento CA 95814 Office Phone: 916-324-9054. Business E-Mail: wbell@calfha.ca.gov.

BELL, WENDELL, sociologist, educator, futurist; b. Chgo., Sept. 27, 1924; s. Wendell and Blanche (Leiferman) B.; m. Lora-Lee Edwards, June 15, 1947; children: Karen Ann, Sharon Lee (dec. 2001), David Howard. BA with highest honors, Calif. State U., Fresno, 1948; MA, UCLA, 1951, PhD, 1952; MA (hon.), Yale U., 1963. Asst. prof. sociology, acting dir. survey rsch. facility Stanford U., 1952-54; assoc. prof. sociology Northwestern U., 1954-57; from assoc. prof. to prof. sociology, dir. West Indies study program UCLA, 1957-63; prof. sociology Yale U., New Haven, 1963-95, chmn. dept., 1965-69, dir. comparative sociology tng. program, 1969-77, dir. undergrad. studies, 1976-83, dir. grad. studies, 1984-89, 94; prof. emeritus, 1995—. Sr. rsch. scientist, Yale Ctr. for Comparative Studies, 2000-05; mem. divsn. behavioral scis. NRC, 1966-69, mem. exec. com., 1968-69; tng. grant dir. in comparative sociology NIMH, 1969-77; vis. fellow Inst. Advanced Studies, The Australian Nat. U., 1985. Author: (with E. Shevky) Social Area Analysis, 1955; (with R.J. Hill and C.R. Wright) Public Leadership, 1961; (with I. Oxaal) Decisions of Nationhood, 1964, Jamaican Leaders, 1964, Foundations of Futures Studies, Vol. I. History, Purposes, and Knowledge, 1997, paperback edit., 2003, Chinese transl., 2004, Vol II Values, Objectivity, and the Good Society, 1997, paperback edit., 2004, Chinese translation, 2005; editor, contbr.: The Democratic Revolution in the West Indies, 1967; (with James A. Mau) The Sociology of the Future, 1971; (with Walter Freeman) Ethnicity and Nation-Building, 1974; editor Internat. Studies in Polit. and Social Change, 1966-76; assoc. editor Am. Sociol. Rev., 1958-61; mem. editl. adv. bd. Sage Profl. Papers in Internat. Studies, 1972-84, Sage Rsch. Papers in Social Sci., Series Social Orgn. of Cmty., U. Iowa, 1974-84, Futurics, 1976—, Cultural Futures Rsch., 1976-87, Technological Forecasting and Social Change, 1995-96; editl. cons. Sociometry, 1959-61; mem. editl. bd. Internat. Studies Quar., 1970-80, Plantation Soc. in the Americas, 1978-90, Political Behavior, 1978-80, Jour. Conflict Resolution, 1980-97, Futures Rsch. Quar., 1992—, The Jour. of Contingencies and Crisis Management, 1992-2004, Jour. Futures Studies, 2000—, Foresight, 1998-2004; cons. editor D.C. Heath and Co., 1971-84, cons., U.S. Commn. on National Security/21st Century, 1999. Gov.'s appointee Commn. on Conn.'s Future, 1987-89; mem. adv. coun. Inst. for Global Ethics, 1990—. Aviator USNR, 1943-46, CBI. Recipient Disting. Alumnus award Calif. State U., Fresno, 1988, W. Bloomberg award for promoting a vision of future based on social justice, 2000; rsch. tng. predoctoral fellow Social Sci. Rsch. Coun., 1951-52, faculty fellow, 1956-59, fellow Ctr. for Advanced Study Behavioral Scis., 1963-64; rsch. grantee, Soc. Sci. Rsch. Coun., 1978, grantee Carnegie Corp. N.Y., 1960-63, NSF, 1969-70. Mem. AAUP, Internat. Sociol. Assn., Am. Sociol. Assn., Eastern Sociol. Soc., Pacific Sociol. Assn. (v.p. 1960-61), Sociol. Rsch. Assn., Internat. Studies Assn. (v.p. 1970-71), Caribbean Studies Assn. (v.p. 1978, pres 1979, Meritorious Service award 1985, mem. coun. 1988-89), World Future Soc., World Futures Studies Fedn. Home: 364 Sperry Rd Bethany CT 06524-3542 Office: Yale U Dept Sociology PO Box 208265 New Haven CT 06520-8265 Office Phone: 203-432-4322. Business E-Mail: wendell.bell@yale.edu.

BELLA, DANTINA CARMEN QUARTAROLI, human services consultant; b. Providence, May 11, 1922; d. Bernardo and Jennie (Zinno) Quartaroli; m. Salvatore J. Bella, Dec. 30, 1946; children: Theresa, Joseph, Jennifer. BA, Bryant Coll.; MA in Psychology, Alfred U., 1952; MS in Adminstr., U. Notre Dame, 1973; postgrad., U. Mich., 1977. Cert. social worker. Rehab. counselor R.I. Dept. Edn., 1942-46; admission counselor Coll. Bus. Adminstrn., Boston U., 1946-49; asst. to dean Coll. of Ceramics, Alfred U., 1949-53; dir. pupil personnel svcs., asst. prin. Marian H.S., Mishawaka, Ind., 1968-74; registrar, admissions officer Ind. Vocat. Tech. Coll., South Bend, 1974-76; resident counselor, dir. Forever Learning Inst., Harvest House, South Bend, 1977-84; pres., owner Potentials for Greying Ams., Notre Dame, Ind., 1984—; exec. dir. Battell Sr. Workers, Inc., Mishawaka, 1985—97. Textbook cons. South Bend Community Sch. Corp., 1974-77; lectr., workshop coordinator, 1974-80. Writer, prodr. TV series Pub. Broadcasting System; Better Understanding of Self Through Literature, 1978, Mothers of the Depression, 1979. Columnist Sr. Life, 1987—; therapist older adult specialist Cath. Social Svc., 1989—; bd. dirs. Cath. Social Svc. Ctr., 1968-90, Women Career Ctr., 1974; pres. South Bend Commn. on Status of Women, 1975-78; mem. Older Adult Legislature, Ind., 1995-96. Named to, South Bend Cmty. Hall of Fame, 2001. Mem. AACD, AAUW, Beta Gamma Sigma. Democrat. Roman Catholic. Home: 1029 Clermont St South Bend IN 46617-1801

BELLA, JONATHAN NORIEGA, cardiologist; b. Cotabato City, The Philippines, Apr. 12, 1965; came to U.S., 1991; s. Primitivo Jr. and Patrocinio (Noriega) B. BA in Humanities, U. of Philippines, Manila, 1985; MD, U. of East, Manila, 1989. Cert. Am. Bd. Internal Medicine, Am. Bd. Cardiovasc. Disease. Intern Atlantic City Med. Ctr., N.J., 1991-92; resident Montefiore Med. Ctr., N.Y.C., 1992-94; fellow in cardiology N.Y. Hosp.-Cornell Med. Ctr., 1994-97; instr. medicine Weill Med. Coll. Cornell U.; fellow in echocardiography N.Y. Hosp.-Cornell Med. Ctr., 1997-98; instr. Weill Med. Coll. Cornell U.; dir. echocardiology Louis Stokes Cleve. VA Med. Ctr., 1998-2000; asst. prof. medicine Sch. Medicine Case Western Res. U., Cleve., 1998-2000; dir. echocardiology Bronx-Lebanon Hosp. Ctr., Bronx, N.Y., 2000—; assoc. prof. medicine Albert Einstein Coll. Medicine, 2000—; chief cardiology Bronx Lebanon Hosp. Ctr., 2005—. Fellow Am. Coll. Cardiology; mem. Am. Heart Assn., Am. Soc. Echocardiography. Roman Catholic. Office: Bronx-Lebanon Hosp Ctr 1650 Grand Concourse Bronx NY 10457 Home: 500 E 83rd St Apt 2L New York NY 10028-7243

BELLACK, ALAN SCOTT, clinical psychologist; b. N.Y.C., Nov. 27, 1944; s. Jack and Yetta B.; m. Barbara Bartlett, Nov. 16, 1969; children: Jonathan, Adam. BS, CCNY, 1965; MS, St. John's U., 1967; PhD, Pa. State U., 1970. Diplomate Am. Bd. Profl. Psychology. Asst. prof. psychology Pa. State U., 1970; mem. faculty U. Pitts., 1971-82, prof. psychology and psychiatry, 1980-82; prof. psychiatry Med. Coll. Pa., Phila., 1982-95, U. Md., 1995—; vice chmn., dir. clin. psychology Med. Coll. Pa., Phila.; dir. VA Capitol Health Care Network MIRECC. Chmn., dir. clin. psychology; prof. psychiatry U. Md. Sch. Medicine, dir. VISN5 Mental Illness Rsch., Education and Clinical Ctr.; cons. in field. Author: Behavioral Assessment: A Practical Handbook, 1976, 2nd edit., 1981, 3rd edit., 1988, Behavior Modification: An Introduction, 1977, Introduction to Clinical Psychology, 1980, The Clinical Psychology, Handbook, 1983, 2nd edit., 1991, others; editor: Clin. Psychology Rev., 1981—, Behavior Modification, 1977—; contbr. articles to profl. jours. USPHS fellow, 1968-70 Mem. Am. Psychol. Assn., Assn. Advancement Behavior Therapy Office: Univ of Maryland at Balt Dept Psychiatry 737 W Lombard St Fl 5 Baltimore MD 21201-1009

BELLAH, LISA DANIELLE, psychologist, educator; b. El Paso, Tex., Feb. 5, 1973; d. Luis Alfonso and Josefita Velarde; m. Christopher Garth Bellah, Oct. 26, 2001. BA, St. Mary's U., San Antonio, 1991—95; MA, U. Tex., El Paso, 1995—97; PhD, La. Tech U., Ruston, 1997—2001. Psychology intern Fed. Bur. of Prisons, Butner, NC, 2000—01, staff psychologist Oakdale, La., 2001—; adj. faculty Northwestern State U., Natchitoches, La., 2001—. Contbr. articles to profl. jours. Mem.: APA. Roman Catholic. Avocations: reading, travel. Office: Fed Correctional Instn PO Box 5050 East Whatley Rd Oakdale LA 71463 Personal E-mail: lisavelar@yahoo.com. E-mail: lvelarde@bop.gov.

BELLAH, ROBERT NEELLY, sociologist, educator; b. Altus, Okla., Feb. 23, 1927; s. Luther Hutton and Lillian Lucille (Neelly); m. Melanie Hyman, Aug. 17, 1949; 4 children. BA, Harvard U., 1950, PhD, 1955. Rsch. assoc. Inst. Islamic Studies, McGill U., Montreal, Can., 1955-57; with Harvard U., Cambridge, Mass., 1957-67, prof., 1966-67; mem. faculty dept. sociology U. Calif., Berkeley, 1967-97, Elliott prof. emeritus, 1997—. Author: Tokugawa Religion, 1957, Beyond Belief, 1970, The Broken Covenant, 1975 (Sorokin award Am. Sociol. Assn. 1976), (with Charles Y. Glock) The New Religious Consciousness, 1976, (with Phillip E. Hammond) Varieties of Civil Religion, 1980, (with others) Habits of the Heart, 1985, (with others) The Good Society, 1991, Imagining Japan, 2003. With U.S. Army, 1945-46. Fulbright fellow, 1960-61; recipient Harbison award Danforth Found., 1971, Nat. Humanities medal, 2000. Mem. Am. Acad. Arts and Scis., Am. Sociol. Assn., Am. Acad. Religion, Am. Philos. Soc. Episcopalian. Office: U Calif Dept Sociology Berkeley CA 94720-1980

BELLAIRS, HERBERT JACK, social worker; b. Rochester Hills, Mich., Jan. 2, 1941; s. Herbert Henry and Lottie Pearl Bellairs; m. Elizabeth Ruth Davis, July 4, 1991; m. Kathleen Sue Ernsberger, June 9, 1962 (div. Jan. 12, 1990); children: Marti Lorraine Daly, Colleen Sue Mayard, Charles Kevin Sieracki, Peggy Ann Kimminau, Rebecca Lynn Smith. BRE, Grand Rapids Bapt. Coll., 1963; MSW, Wayne State U., 1972. Lic. minister First Bapt. Ch., Rochster, MI, 1963, ordained to ministry First Bapt. Ch., Lake Orion, MI, 1973; lic. master social worker Tex., 2003. Asst. pastor First Bapt. Ch., Rochester, Mich., 1964—66; supr. clin. social work Clinton Valley Ctr., Pontiac, Mich., 1972—74; dir. social work Meml. Hosp. South Bend, Ind., 1975—84; clin. social worker VA Med. Ctr., Dallas, 1989—; founder and min. Bellairs Wedding Bells, Mansfield, Tex., 1996—; dir. social svcs. Regular Bapt. Children's Agy., St. Louis, Mich. Asst. instr. in social work Bethel Coll., Mishawaka, Ind., 1976—85; field instr. U. of Mich. Sch. of Social Work, Ann Arbor, 1970—74, U. of Tex. Sch. of Social Work, Arlington. Author: (newspaper column) Reflections; co-author (booklet) Seven Ways to Ruin A Perfectly Good Wedding; contbr. articles to profl. jours. Mem.: NASW, Acad. Cert. Social Workers, Am. Assn. Spinal Cord Injury Psychologists and Social Workers. Independent. Evangelical. Avocations: poetry, reading, history. Home: 628 Plainview Mansfield TX 76063 Personal E-mail: wedvows@yahoo.com.

BELLAMY, CAROL, international organization administrator; b. Plainfield, NJ, Jan. 14, 1942; BA in Psychology, Gettysburg Coll., 1963; JD, NYU, 1968. Asst. commr. Dept. Mental Health and Mental Health Retardation Svc., NYC; with Peace Corps., Guatemala, 1963—65; assoc. Cravath, Swaine & Moore, NYC, 1968—71; mem. NY State Senate, 1973—77; pres. NYC Coun.,

1978—85; prin. Morgan Stanley & Co., NYC, 1986—90; mng. dir. Bear Stearns, NYC, 1990—93; dir. Peace Corps., Washington, 1993-95; exec. dir. UNICEF, 1995—2005; pres., CEO World Learning, Brattleboro, Vt., 2005—, pres. Sch. Internat. Training, 2005—. Former trustee, NYC Pension Sys., mem., NY Met. Transit Authority, First v.p. Nat. League of Cities. Fellow, Harvard U. Kennedy Sch. Govt. Mem.: Phi Alpha Alpha. Avocation: Mets baseball fan. Office: World Learning PO Box 676 Kipling Rd Brattleboro VT 05302-0676

BELLAMY, JAMES CARL, retired insurance company executive; b. Detroit, Oct. 15, 1926; s. Robert Maxwell Belllamy and Mamie (Moery) B.; m. Marie Alice Brakebill, Jan. 20, 1951; children: James Carl, Janet Marie. BS, U. Tenn., 1950. C.L.U. Agt., asst. mgr. Nat. Life & Accident Ins. Co., Chattanooga, Louisville, 1950-58, dist. mgr. Little Rock, Nashville, 1958-73, 2d v.p. Nashville, 1973-78, v.p., 1978-82; sr. v.p., dir. Am. Gen. Life & Accident Ins. Co., Nashville, 1982-87; sr. v.p. mktg. Southlife Holding Co., Nashville, 1987-91, ret., 1991. Exec. v.p. mktg. Pub. Savs. Life Ins. Co., Charleston, S.C.; vice chmn. Security Trust Life Ins. Co., Macon, Ga., bd. dirs.; pres. Southlife Gen. Agys., Nashville; bd. dirs. Pub. Savs. Life Ins. Co., Charleston. Solicitor United Way, Nashville, 1968-74; solicitor Boy Scouts Am., 1968-74. Served with USNR, 1944-46, PTO. Mem. Nat. Assn. Life Underwriters, Nashville Assn. Life Underwriters (pres. 1970-71), Nashville Gen. Agts. and Mgrs. Assn. (pres. 1967), Ins. Mktg. Research Assn. (exec. com.), Hillwood Country Club (bd. dirs.), Univ. Club, Kiwanis, Sigma Chi. Republican. Baptist. E-mail: jasbellamy@aol.com.

BELLAMY, JENNIFER WIGGINS, artist; b. Clio, S.C., Aug. 9, 1944; d. Leland and Myrtle Lee (Wise) Wiggins; married; 1 child, Audrey Katherine Rollins. BA in Art & Performance magna cum laude, U. Tex., 1989, postgrad., 1992-93, 95-99. Cert. interior decorator 2002. Dist. sec. Corning Glass Works, Richardson, Tex., 1977-80; adminstrv. asst. The Chase Manhatten Bank, Dallas, 1981-85; owner The Bellamy Studio, Richardson, Tex., 1990—, Interiors by Jennifer Rachelle Wiggins, 2003—. Recipient tchg. assistantships U. Tex., Dallas, 1993. Mem. Phi Theta Kappa. Avocations: writing, gardening, cooking, walking.

BELLAMY, JOHN A.A., lawyer; b. 1962; BA in English summa cum laude, King Coll., 1984; JD with honors, U. Tenn., 1990. Bar: Tenn. 1990. Staff atty. King Pharmaceuticals, Bristol, Tenn., exec. v.p. legal affairs, gen. counsel, asst. sec., 1998—. Mem.: Assn. Corp. Counsel Tenn. Chpt. (bd. dirs. East region). Office: King Pharmaceuticals 501 5th St Bristol TN 37620 Office Phone: 423-989-8000. Office Fax: 423-989-6282. E-mail: john.bellamy@kingpharm.com.

BELLAMY, LILLIAN MILES, secondary school educator, writer; b. Drakes Branch, Va., Dec. 11, 1935; d. William James and Jannie Betty Miles; m. Paul L. Bellamy, Jr., Jan. 23, 1964; children: Nikki Danièlle Johnson, Paul Lawrence III. BA, Bennett Coll., Greensboro, N.C., 1958; postgrad. studies, George Washington U., D.C., 1962—64, Howard U., 1963, U. Va., Charlottesville, 1964—72; cert. of Attendance, Univs. Bordeaux and Toulouse, Pau, France, 1962. Tchr. Dillon County Schs., Dillon, SC, 1958—59, Fairfax County Schs., Fairfax, Va., 1959—91, substitute tchr., 1991—. Translator, tutor. Author: Defaming Teddy, 2004, My Love Affair with the French, 2005. Mentor Alpha Kappa Alpha reading programs for children, Alexandria-Arlington, Va., 1972—. Grantee, Washington Post, 1988—89, Fairfax County Minority Achievement grant, Fairfax County Sch. System, 1990—91. Mem.: Fairfax County Tchrs. Assn., Va. Tchrs. Assn., Nat. Tchrs. Assn., Zeta Chi Omega (philacter 1973—74). Democrat. Roman Catholic. Avocations: reading, travel, writing. Home: 9637 Courthouse Rd Vienna VA 22181 Personal E-mail: lmiles2222@aol.com.

BELLAMY, WALTER, retired basketball player; Student, Ind. U., 1957-61. With Chgo. Packers, 1961-62, Balt. Bullets, 1963-66, N.Y. Knicks, 1966-68, Atlanta Hawks, 1970-74. Mem. U.S. Olympic Basketball Team, 1960. Mem. Atlanta Police Athletic League, Ga.; trustee Gate City Day Nursery Assn.; founder, 1st pres. Men of Tomorrow, Inc., Md.; bd. dirs. S.W. Youth Bus. Orgn.; membership chmn. Campbelltown/Cascade YMCA Men Internat. Club; chmn. Atlanta Labor Day Weekend Football Classic; vice chmn. College Park Bus. and Devel. Authority, Metro Atlanta Respite Svc.; bd. dirs. Gate City Day Nursery Assn. Named Rookie of Yr., 1962, Basketball Hall of Fame, 1993; winner Gold medal U.S. Olympics, 1960; named to U.S. Olympic Hall of Fame, N.C. Sports Hall of Fame, 100% Wrong Club Atlanta Hall of Fame, Ind. U. Sports Hall of Fame, NBA Hall of Fame. Mem. Ind. U. Alumni Club, Alpha Phi Alpha, Alpha Phi Omega. Achievements include mem. gold-medal-winning U.S. Olympic Team, 1960, holds single-season record for most games played-88, 1969. Address: PO Box 42751 Atlanta GA 30311-0751

BELLANCA, JOSEPH PAUL, engineering construction executive; b. Rochester, N.Y., Nov. 25, 1936; s. Sam and Anna (Cani) B.; m. Joy Eleanor Gaston, Dec. 5, 1964 (dec.); children: Joseph Jr., Victoria Ann Gordon, Lizabeth Ann Wilbur, Lorraine Thacker. BSCE, Purdue U., 1958. Registered profl. engr., D.C. and 10 states. Assoc./project mgr. TAMS Cons., Dallas/Ft. Worth, 1968-73, assoc./resident mgr. Washington, 1973-77; pres. Bellanca Engrng. Cons., Atlanta, 1977-85; dir. Schal Assocs., Chgo., 1985-86; v.p. Greiner, Inc., Orlando (Fla.), Denver, 1986-88, Bechtel Internat. Inc., Vienna, Va., 1988-92, Turner Constrn. Co., Atlanta, 1992-98; exec. v.p. Bovis Lend Lease, Atlanta, 1998—2002; v.p. Heery Internat., 2002—. Lobbyist Airport Cons. Coun. Editor Airports--Challenges of the Future, 1973; (design compendium) World Travel Center--Detroit Met. Airport (Design award for $1 billion new air terminal complex). Named Young Engr. Yr. Mid-Cities chpt. Tex. Soc. Profl. Engrs., 1971. Mem. ASCE (sec. 1973, vice-chmn. 1979, exec. com., air transport divsn.), NSPE, Tex. Soc. Profl. Engrs. (pres. Mid-Cities chpt. 1972-73). Achievements include aifield pavement design for future 2 million pound aircraft at Dallas-Ft. Worth airport; executive-level involvement in airport development programs for Dallas-Ft. Worth, Atlanta, Chicago, Denver, Barcelona, 2-Jordan, 4-Saudi Arabia, New Seoul, and Detroit Downtown People Mover. Home: 9295 Heatherton Walk Duluth GA 30097-2492 Office: Heery Internat 999 Peachtree St Atlanta GA 30309 E-mail: jbellanca@mindspring.com.

BELLANGER, FLORIAN, food service executive, educator; Grad., L'Ecole de Paris des Métiers de la Table. With La Maison du Chocolat, Fauchon; pastry chef Le Bernardin, N.Y.C. Tchr. classes on chocolate desserts French Culinary Inst.

BELLANGER, SERGE RENÉ, bank executive; b. Vimoutiers, France, Apr. 30, 1933; s. René Albert and Raymonde Maria (Renard) Bellanger. MBA, Paris Bus. Sch., 1957. With Citibank, 1966-73, mem. Paris br., 1966-69, world corp. rels. officer for Europe N.Y.C., 1969-73, asst. v.p., 1969-71, v.p., 1972-73; sr. v.p., gen. mgr. Crédit Industriel et Commercial, N.Y.C., 1974-79, exec. v.p., gen. mgr., 1979—; U.S. gen. rep. CIC Group, N.Y.C., 1973—, mem. exec. com., 1998—. Prof. banking French Banking Inst., 1961—64; mem. adv. com. French House Columbia U., 1976—, chmn., 1996—, mem. internat. adv. bd. Inst. Study Europe, 2002—; mem. Nat. Com. Fgn. Trade Advisors France, 1978—, exec. v.p. U.S. nat. com., 1985—93, bd. dirs. nat. com., 1987—2002, v.p. U.S. nat. com., 1992—93, mem. Paris exec. com., 1994—95; chmn. internat. banking course New Sch. Social Rsch., N.Y.C., 1981—83; dir. Am. Ctr. Paris, 1985—93; mem. adv. com. Ctr. Study French Civilization and Culture NYU, N.Y.C., 1988—2000; mem. adv. bd. French Inst. Culture and Tech. U. Pa., 1992—, chmn. adv. bd., 1992—95; mem. adv. bd. Lycée Francais, NY, 2000—; mem. Adv. Coun. French Abroad, 2000; mem. exec. com. Fedn. French Vets., 2001—; bd. dirs. Ubifrance, 2002—, French Ctr. Fgn. Trade, Banque Transatlantique, 2002—; pres. Grand Marnier Found., 2004—. With French Air Force, 1958—60. Decorated Algeria Commemorative medal, comdr. Legion of Honor, Nat. Order of Merit. Mem.: Bank Adminstrn. Inst. (mem. editl. bd. World Banking Mag. 1981—87, columnist Banker's Mag. 1986—96), N.Y. Cotton Exch. (bd. dirs. fin. instrument exch. divsn. 1985—95), N.Y. Futures Exch. (dir. 1980—87, chmn. fgn. exch. com. 1981—82), Banque de l'Union Européenne (bd. dirs. 1989—90), Assn. Promotion French Sci., Industry and Tech. (pres. 1986—91), Lyonnaise de Banque (bd. dirs. 1986—89), Inst. Internat. Bankers (trustee 1975—77, v.p. 1977—79, chmn. legis. and regulatory com. 1977—79, chmn. 1979—80), French Overseas Assn., European-Am. Bus. Coun. (bd. dirs. Washington 1991—), Food and Wine France (bd. dirs. 1983—93), N.Y.C. Partnership and C. of C. (ptnr. 1991—), Assn. French C. of C. and Industry Abroad (adminstr. 1984—, v.p. 1989—95, 1st v.p. 1995—99, pres. 1999—), N.Y. C. of C. (mem. internat. bus. initiative 1994—95), French-Am. C. of C. (councillor 1973—74, mem. exec. com. 1974—80, v.p. 1980—82, exec. v.p. 1982—83, nat. pres. 1983—, pres. N.Y. chpt. 1983—), European-Am. C. of C. (pres., CEO 1990—96, hon. chmn. 1996—), Automobile Club de France, River Club, Univ. Club. Home: 860 U N Plz Apt 23/24C New York NY 10017-1810 Office: 37th Floor 520 Madison Ave New York NY 10022-4213 Office Phone: 212-715-4444. Business E-Mail: sbellanger@cicny.com.

BELLAS, ALBERT CONSTANTINE, investment company executive; b. Steubenville, Ohio, Sept. 15, 1942; s. Constantine Michael and Kiki (Michalopoulos) B.; m. Kay Mazzo, Dec. 21, 1978; children: Andrew James, Kathryn Kiki. BA, Yale U., 1964; JD, U. Chgo., 1967; MBA, Columbia U., 1968. Summer intern The White House, Washington, 1963; assoc. Dillon, Read & Co., Inc., N.Y.C., 1968-72; v.p. Goldman Sachs & Co., N.Y.C., 1973-76; gen. ptnr. Loeb Rhoades & Co., N.Y.C., 1976-78; sr. exec. v.p. Shearson Lehman Bros., N.Y.C., 1979—91; mng. dir. Offitbank, N.Y.C., 1992—2000; chmn., CEO Neuberger Berman Trust Co., N.Y.C., 2000—03; mng. dir. Neuberger Berman, LLC, N.Y.C., 2000—03; CEO The Solaris Group, LLC, 2004—. Allied mem. N.Y. Stock Exch., 1976-92; bd. dirs. 1128 Park Ave. Corp. Trustee St. Mary's Found. for Children, 1999—2002, Lenfest Found., 2000—03, Statue of Liberty-Ellis Island Found., 2002—, investment com. NYC, 2002—; day sch. com. Brick Ch., N.Y.C., 1985—88; bd. regents, investment com. Mercersburg Acad., Pa., 1992—, exec. com., 1993—, chmn. fin. com., 1994—; bd. dirs. Lincoln Ctr. for Performing Arts, N.Y.C., 1987—, audit com., 1989—; bd. dirs. Sch. Am. Ballet, N.Y.C., 1975—86, chmn., 1987—2004, chmn. emeritus, 2004—; bd. dirs. Guild Hall, East Hampton, NY, 1990—96, 1998—, fin. com., 1998—. McKinsey scholar, 1968 Mem.: ABA, Ohio Bar Assn., Brook Club, Univ. Club, Century Assn., Maidstone Club. Avocation: tennis. Home: 1130 Park Ave New York NY 10128-1255 Office: 598 Madison Ave 15th Fl New York NY 10022

BELLATTI, LAWRENCE LEE, lawyer; b. Oklahoma City, Apr. 19, 1944; s. Lawrence Fitzhugh and Esther Lee (Swank) Bellatti; m. Barbara Gail Wolfinger, June 25, 1977; children: Julie M., Jenny E., Jill N. BS, Okla. State U., 1966; JD, Okla. U., 1969. Bar: Okla. 1969, Tex. 1974, U.S. Dist. Ct. (so., we, ea. and no. dists.) Tex., U.S. Dist. Ct. (no., we. and ea. dists.) Okla., U.S. Ct. Mil. Appeals, U.S. Ct. Appeals (8th cir., 10th and 11th cirs.). Assoc. Andrews, Kurth, Campbell & Jones, Houston, 1974-80; ptnr. Andrews Kurth LLP, Houston, 1980—. Bd. dirs. Samaritan Counseling Ctrs., Inc., Houston, 1984—2001. Mem. Harris County Flood Control Dist. Task Force, Houston, 1984. Lt. comdr. JAGC USNR, 1969—74. Mem.: Houston Bar Assn., Okla. Bar Assn., Tex. Bar Assn., Order of Coif, Phi Delta Phi, Sigma Chi, Phi Kappa Phi. Republican. Baptist. Office: Andrews Kurth LLP 600 Travis St Ste 4200 Houston TX 77002-2910 Office Phone: 713-220-4196.

BELLAVANCE, MARIA ISABEL, librarian; b. Lisboa, Portugal, July 24, 1946; came to US, 1966; d. Adriao Garcia and Maria de Lourdes (Serrao) B.; m. David Walter Bellavance, Sept. 28, 1969 (div. Aug. 1999); 1 child, Angela Maria Bellavance. BS in Elec. Engring., Brown U., Providence, RI, 1969; MLS, North Tex. U., Denton, 1985. Tech. staff Bell Lab., Murray Hill, NJ, 1970-72; parish libr. All Saints Cath. Ch., Dallas, 1985—; libr. specialist Ctr. Info. Processing Southern Meth. Univ., 1996—. Part-time staff dir. All Saints Parish Resource Libr., Dallas. Mem. Ch. and Synagogue Libr. Assn. (Outstanding Congl. Libr. award 1993), Tau Beta Pi, Beta Phi Mu. Roman Cath. Avocations: reading, sewing, knitting, bible study, travel. Home: 1225 Danville Dr Richardson TX 75080-5809 Office: So Meth U Ctrl U Librs Ctr Info Processing PO Box 750135 Dallas TX 75275-0135 Personal E-mail: maria_b_75080@yahoo.com. Business E-Mail: mbellava@smu.edu.

BELLE, GREGG ANTHONY, forensic specialist, psychologist; b. Boston, Sept. 14, 1972; s. Ray and Margaret Belle. BS, Brown U., 1994; MA, Wash. U., 1996, PhD, 2001. Lic. psychologist Bd. Registration, Mass., 2004, designated forensic psychologist Mass., 2004. Intern psychology Med. Sch. Harvard U., Cambridge, Mass., 1999—2000; intern psychology Brockton (Mass.) VA Med. Ctr., 1999—2000; postdoctoral fellow forensic psychology Law and Psychiatry Program Med. Sch. U. Mass., Worcester, Mass., 2000—01, forensic psychologist Med. Sch., 2001—; forensic psychologist Bridgewater (Mass.) State Hosp., 2001—. Recipient Boys State award, Gov. of Mass., 1989; fellow Chancellor's fellowship, Wash. U., 1994—99. Mem.: APA. Office: Bridgewater State Hospital 20 Administration Road Bridgewater MA 02324 Office Phone: 508-279-4500 4820. Personal E-mail: gabelle@alumni.brown.edu. Business E-Mail: gregg.belle@umassmed.edu.

BELLE-ISLE, DAVID RICHARD, organization and management consultant; b. Springfield, Mass., Mar. 26, 1950; s. Richard Alfred and Eda (Carra) Belle-Isle; divorced; children: Justin, Melissa, Michelle, Megan. AA, Kendall Coll., 1969; BS magna cum laude, Springfield Coll., 1971, MEd, 1972; PhD, U. North Colo., 1975; postgrad., MIT, 1979-80. Asst. dean Western New Eng. Coll., Springfield, 1972-73, U. No. Colo., Greeley, 1973-75, W.Va. Inst. Tech., Montgomery, 1975-76; sr. cons. Digital Equipment Corp., Maynard, Mass., 1976-80; dir. corp. planning Martin Marietta Corp., Bethesda, Md., 1980-84; exec. dir. Sara Lee Corp., Chgo., 1984-86; sr. v.p. Electrolux Corp., Stamford, Conn., 1986-87; pres. David Belle-Isle Corp., Fairfield, Conn., 1987-88; chief human resources officer Epic Health Care Group, Dallas, 1988-94; pres. Tex. chpt. Nat. Esop Assn., 1992-94, Insight Consulting, Inc., 1994—. Prof. Suffolk U., Boston, 1976-78, Clark U., Worcester, Mass., 1977-79, U. Mich., Ann Arbor, 1985-87; bd. dirs. Mgmt. Techs., Houston. Mem. Grace Commn., U.S. Presdl. Pvt. Sector Study on Cost Control, Washington, 1983-84. Mem. Psi Chi Nat. Honor Soc. Republican. Avocations: reading, skiing, aerobic training. Home and Office: Belle-Isle Insight Cons Inc 2100 Parker Lawe Austin TX 78741 E-mail: belle_isle_insight@msw.com.

BELLER, GARY A., lawyer, finance company executive, insurance company executive; b. NYC, Oct. 16, 1938; s. Charles W. and Jeanne A. B.; m. Carole P. Wrubel, Nov. 22, 1967; 1 child, Jessie Melissa. BA, Cornell U., 1960; LLB, NYU, 1963, LLM, 1971. Bar: N.Y. 1963. Various positions gen. counsel's office Am. Express Co., NYC, 1968-82, exec. v.p. and gen. counsel, 1983-94; exec. v.p., chief legal officer Met. Life Ins. Co., NYC, 1995—2003; sr. legal counsel Marsh & McLellan Cos. Inc., NYC, 2004—. Bd. dirs. Lenox Hill Neighborhood Assn.; bd. dirs., chmn. Citizens' Crime Commn. N.Y. Mem. ABA, Assn. Bar City N.Y. Office: Marsh & McLellan 1166 Ave of Americas New York NY 10036-2774

BELLER, GEORGE ALLAN, medical educator; b. NYC, 1940; MD, U. Va., 1966. Diplomate Am. Bd. Internal Medicine. Intern U. Wis. Hosp., Madison, 1966-67, resident, 1967-68; resident in medicine Boston Med. Svc., 1968-69; fellow in cardiology Thorndike Meml. Lab. Harvard Med. Unit/Boston City Hosp., 1969-70; mem. staff cardiac unit Mass. Gen. Hosp., Boston, 1973-77; instr. medicine Harvard U., Boston, 1974-75, asst. prof., 1975; prof. medicine U. Va., Charlottesville, 1977—, chief cardiovascular divsn., 1977—2004, vice-chmn. dept. medicine, 1997-99, pres. med. staff, 1998—2005. Maj. M.C., U.S. Army, 1970-73. Mem. Am. Soc. Clin. Investigation, Am. Fedn. Clin. Rsch., Assn. Am. Physicians, Am. Coll. Cardiology (chmn. bd. govs. 1994-95, pres. 2000), Assn. Profs. Cardiology (pres. 1995). Office: U Va Med Ctr Dept Cardiology PO Box 800158 Charlottesville VA 22908-0158

BELLER, HARRY R., microbiologist, chemist, researcher; BA in Environ. Sci., Wesleyan U., Middletown, Conn.; MS in Chem. Oceanography, Oreg. St. U., Corvallis, Oreg.; PhD in Civil/Environ. Engring., Stanford U., Stanford, Calif. Rsch. asst. Oreg. St. U., Corvallis, Oreg., 1982—85; environ. chemist Tetra Tech, Inc., Bellevue, Wash., 1985—87; sr. environ. chemist PTI Environ. Svcs., Bellevue, Wash., 1987—89; rsch. asst. Stanford U., Calif., 1989—95, postdoctoral scholar, 1995—98; sr. environ. scientist Lawrence Livermore Nat. Lab., Livermore, Calif., 1998—. Adj. assoc. prof., dept. chem. engring. & applied chemistry U. Toronto, Ontario, Canada, 2003—. Switzer Found. Environ. Fellow, 1991, 1992. Mem.: Am. Geophys. Union, Am. Soc. for Microbiology, Am. Chem. Soc. (ACS Award for grad. students in environ. chemistry 1994), Sigma Xi. Office: Lawrence Livermore Nat Lab 7000 East Ave PO Box 808 L-542 Livermore CA 94551

BELLER, HERBERT N., lawyer; b. Ill., 1943; BSBA, Northwestern U., 1964, JD cum laude, 1967. Bar: Ill. 1967, D.C. 1969; CPA, Ill. Law clk. to Hon. Theodore Tannenwald, Jr. U.S. Tax Ct., 1967-68; ptnr. Sutherland, Asbill & Brennan, Washington. Adj. prof. law Georgetown U., Washington, 1972-81. Editor-in-chief: The Tax Lawyer, 1993-96. Mem. ABA (mem. sect. taxation, vice chair 1993-96, chair 2002-03, mem. coun. 1989-92, liaison to AICPA tax div. 1998-2000, chmn. govt. submissions com. 1988-89, chmn. closely held corps. com. 1981-83), Am. Coll. Tax Counsel (regent), D.C. Bar Assn., Ill. State Bar Assn., Nat. Conf. Lawyers and CPAs (co-chair 2003-), Am. Tax Policy Inst. (trustee 2003—). Office: Sutherland Asbill & Brennan LLP 1275 Pennysylvania Ave NW Washington DC 20004

BELLER, LUANNE EVELYN, retired accountant; b. Ft. Dodge, Iowa, Feb. 5, 1950; d. Gerald L. and Evelyn E. (Liston) Heyl; m. Stephen M. Beller, June 28, 1970; children: Clancy Dee, Corby Lu. BA, Oreg. State U., 1977; MBA, Rochester Inst. Tech., 1981. CPA, Ill. Plant acct. DuBois Plastic Products, Avon, N.Y., 1977-79; coll. acct. SUNY, Geneseo, 1979-81; gen. acctg. supr. Master Foods, USA (formerly M&M/Mars, Inc.), Cleveland, Tenn., 1981—83, Hackettstown, NJ, 1983—84, sales rep. Jacksonville, Ill., 1984—86, terr. sales supr., 1986—88; gen. acctg. coord. Masterfoods USA (formerly Kal Kan Foods, Inc.), Columbus, Ohio, 1988-90, fin. info. coord., 1990-92, gen. acctg. supr., 1992-97, site svc. and fin. mgr., 1997—2004; ret., 2004. Vol. Girl Scouts U.S.A., Jacksonville, 1985—88, Bexley, Ohio, 1988—2004; mem. sound control com. Bexley United Meth. Ch., 1989—2001, chair edn. com., 1998—2001, mem. edn. com., 1996—2004, LOGOS vol., 1996—2002, mem. diversity team, 2001—02; com. mem. Meth. Theol. Sch. Ohio Partnership, 2001—02; vol. children's programs St. John's United Meth. Ch., Corpus Christi, 2005—. Mem. Phi Kappa Phi, Beta Gamma Sigma, Beta Alpha Psi. Democrat. Avocations: children, pets, reading. E-mail: lbeller@stx.rr.com.

BELLER, MARTIN LEONARD, retired orthopaedic surgeon; b. NYC, Apr. 30, 1924; s. Abraham Jacob and Ida (Fishkin) B.; m. Wilma Gertrude Kjelgaard, June 29, 1947; children: Alan Lewis, Beatrice Ann Beller Foreman Heck, Peter James. AB with honors, Columbia U., 1944, MD, 1946. Diplomate Am. Bd. Orthopaedic Surgery. Intern Mt. Sinai Hosp., N.Y.C., 1946-47; resident in orthopaedic surgery Hosp. Joint Diseases, N.Y.C., 1949-52; pvt. practice Phila., 1952-87; asst. prof. orthopaedic surgery U. Pa. Sch. Medicine, Phila., 1967-72, assoc. prof., 1972-80, clin. prof., 1980-87; ret., 1987. Attending orthopaedic surgeon Hosp. U. Pa., 1963-87; assoc. attending orthopaedic surgeon Albert Einstein Med. Center, Phila., 1960-70; chmn. dept. orthopaedic surgery Albert Einstein Med. Center (Daroff divsn.), 1970-79. Author (with I. Stein and R. O. Stein): Living Bone in Health and Disease, 1955; author: (with I. Stein) Clinical Densitometry of Bone, 1970. Vestryman Episcopal Ch., 1966—87, 1990—93, 1996—99, 2002—05; trustee St. Paul's Episcopal Ch., Wellsboro, Pa., 1999—. Am. Orthopaedic Assn. exchange fellow, Gt. Britain, 1963. Fellow ACS, Am. Acad. Orthopaedic Surgeons (bd. councilors 1978-81, Pa. rep. commn. on trauma 1984-87), Internat. Soc. Orthopaedic Surgery and Traumatology; mem. Am. Orthopaedic Assn., Pa. Orthopaedic Soc. (pres. 1975-77), Orthopaedic Rsch. Soc., Am. Coll. Rheumatology, N.Y. Acad. Sci., Phi Beta Kappa, Alpha Omega Alpha, Phi Delta Epsilon (nat. pres. 1975-76, chmn. bd. trustees 1984-85, assoc. exec. sec. 1991-95, exec. com. 1995—), Union League Phila. (life), Tyoga Country Club (Wellsboro, Pa.). Republican. Home: 2415 Rt 6 Gaines PA 16921-9505

BELLER, STEPHEN MARK, retired university administrator; b. Chgo., Aug. 14, 1948; s. I.E. and De Vera (Jameson) B.; m. Luanne Evelyn Heyl, June 28, 1970; children: Clancy Dee, Corby Lu. BS, U. Ill., 1970; MS, Western Ill. U., 1972; PhD, Oregon State U., 1977. Asst. head ed. Awards of Rotary Found., Evanston, Ill., 1972-73; asst. dean of students SUNY, Geneseo, N.Y., 1977-81; dean of student svcs. Tenn. Wesleyan Coll., Athens, 1981-83, MacMurray Coll., Jacksonville, Ill., 1984-88, Capital U., Columbus, Ohio, 1988-99, v.p., dean of student svcs., 1999—2003, v.p. emeritus, 2003—. Mem.: Phi Delta Kappa, Phi Kappa Phi. Methodist. Avocations: railroading, photography. Home: PO Box 18268 Corpus Christi TX 78480-8268 E-mail: sbeller@stx.rr.com.

BELLET, PAUL SANDERS, pediatrician, educator; b. Phila., June 28, 1945; BA, Johns Hopkins U., 1967; MD, U. Rochester, 1971. Diplomate Am. Bd. Pediat. Intern in pediat. Cleve. Met. Gen. Hosp., 1971-72; resident in pediat. Case Western Res., Cleve., 1972-73, fellow in pediat. cardiology, 1973-75; pediatrician USAF/Maxwell AFB Regional Hosp., Montgomery, Ala., 1975-77; asst. prof. pediat. U. Ala., Tuscaloosa, 1977-81, assoc. prof. of pediat., 1981-83; assoc. prof. pediat. Children's Hosp. Med. Ctr./U. Cin. Coll. Medicine, Cin., 1983-94, prof. pediat., 1994—. Author: The Diagnostic Approach to Symptoms and Signs in Pediatrics, 2d edit., 2002. Fellow Am. Acad. Pediat.; mem. Ambulatory Pediat. Assn., Cin. Pediat. Soc. Office: Cin Children's Hosp Med Ctr 3333 Burnet Ave Cincinnati OH 45229-3039 Office Phone: 513-636-4506. Business E-Mail: paul.bellet@cchmc.org.

BELLEVILLE, PHILIP FREDERICK, lawyer; b. Flint, Mich., Apr. 24, 1934; s. Frederick Charles and Sarah (Adelaine) B.; m. Geraldean Bickford, Sept. 2, 1953; children: Stacy L., Philip Frederick II, Jeffrey A. BA in Econs. with high distinction and honors, U. Mich., 1956, JD, 1960, MS in Psychology CCU, 1997. Bar: Calif. 1961. Assoc. Latham & Watkins, LA., 1960-68, ptnr. L.A. and Newport Beach, Calif., 1968-98, chmn. litigation dept., 1973-80, ptnr. L.A., Newport Beach, San Diego, Washington, 1980-98, Chgo., 1983-98, N.Y.C., 1985-98, London and San Francisco, 1990-98, Moscow, 1992-98, Hong Kong, 1995-98, Tokyo, 1995-98, Singapore, 1997-98, Silicon Valley, 1997-98. Past mem. So. Calif. steering com. NAACP Legal Def. Fund, Inc.; cmty. adv. bd. San Pedro Peninsula Hosp., Calif., 1980—88; bd. dirs. Harbor Interfaith, 2001—, chmn. bd., 2004—; bd. dirs. House of Hope, 2004—. James B. Angell scholar U. Mich., 1955-56 Mem. ABA, State Bar Calif. (LAP evaluation com.), L.A. County Bar Assn., Order of Coif, Portuguese Bend (Calif.) Club, Palos Verdes (Calif.) Golf Club, Caballeros, Phi Beta Kappa, Phi Kappa Phi, Alpha Kappa Psi. Republican. Avocations: antique and classic autos, public service, sports, art, antiques.

BELLEW, KEVIN MICHAEL, biologist; s. Mara James and Helen C. Bellew; m. Lisa D. D'Egidio. BS in Biology, Cath. U. Am., 1991; MS in Biology, Villanova U., 2000. Assoc. dir. clin. devel. GlaxoSmithKline, King of Prussia, Pa., 1992—. Scholar, Immaculata U., 2004. Roman Catholic. Office Phone: 800-877-7074.

BELLIN, HOWARD, management consultant company executive; b. N.Y.C., Oct. 30, 1933; arrived in Australia, 1961; s. Paul and Anna (Sterner); m. Barbara Ann Box, May 12, 1962; children: Sara Lea, Paul. BSMetE, Carnegie Mellon U., 1955. Trainee Great Lakes Steel Corp., Detroit, 1955; dept. mgr. Kelsey Hayes Corp., Detroit, 1955-57; from indsl. engr. to dept. mgr. Gillette Co., Boston, 1957-64; factory mgr. Allied Corp., Richmond, Va., 1964-65, Sydney, Australia, 1966-67; mng. dir. Avin Plating, Melbourne, Australia, 1967-69; founder, chmn. IF Cons., Melbourne, 1969—. Presenter in field. Mem. editl. bd. Jour. Mktg. Channels; contbr. articles to profl. jours. Active Franchising Cons. div., Indsl. Consumer & Corp. Commn. With U.S.

Army, 1957. Mem. Am. Club. Liberal. Jewish. Avocations: exercise, jogging, photography, reading, history. Home: 17 Moule Ave, Brighton 3186 Victoria Australia Office: I F Cons 390 St Kilda Rd 3004 Melbourne Victoria Australia Office Phone: 61-3-9596-0074. E-mail: hbellin@i-f.com.

BELLINA, JOSEPH HENRY, obstetrician, gynecologist; b. New Orleans, La., Jan. 30, 1942; s. Philip Vincent and Sue Ethyl Bellina; m. Deborah Ann Thomas, Mar. 11, 2000; children: Shawn Vincent, Christopher Todd. MD, LSU Sch. of Medicine, 1961—65. Diplomate Bd. Cert. Am. Bd. of Obstetrics and Gynecology, 1971, cert. Am. Bd. of Laser Surgery, 1986. Pres. Gynecologic Laser Soc., New Orleans, 1979—82; nat. advisor Nat. Inst. of Health Child Health and Human Devel. Coun., Washington, 1984—88; pres. Jefferson Soc. of Obstetrics and Gynecology, Metairie, La., 1982—83; rsch. assoc. in electroscience and biophysics rsch. lab. Tulane U., New Orleans, 1978. Prof. La. State of Medicine Dept. of Obstetrics and Gynecology, New Orleans, 1980. Editor: (medical textbook) Gynecologic Laser Surgery; author: (book) You Can Have a Baby. Editl. bd. Laser in Surgery and Medicine Jour., NY, 1981. Ensign NAVY, 1963—65, Pensicola. Recipient William B Mark award for Outstanding Contbn. to Laser Tech., Am. Soc. for Laser Medicine and Surgery, Inc., 1985, Hon. Membership, Tulane U. Conrad Collins Soc., 1982, First prize, Am. Coll. of Obstetrics and Gynecology Dist. VII, 1970, First Prize in Obstetrics and Gynecology, AMA, 1975, Prize For Outstanding Exhibit, Am. Coll. of Obstetrics and Gynecology, 1979, Am. Assn. of Gynecologic Laparoscopists, 1979, Exhibit of JULIE Capsule of NASA Flight 661, Smithsonian Air and Space Mus., 1983, Exhibit of Laser in Medicine - First Gynecologic Surgery in Am., Smithsonian Inst., 1982. Fellow: Am. Coll. of Obstetrics and Gynecology; mem.: Am. Urology Assn. (assoc.), Am. Urogynecologic Soc. (assoc.). R-Consevative. Methodist. Achievements include patents for signal baloon dispensing apparatus; laser surgery drape; operating room design with intergrated laser system. Avocations: mountain climbing, sailing, travel. Home: 713 W Francis St Aspen CO 81611 Office: Omega Hosp 2525 Severn Ave Metairie LA 70002 E-mail: jbellina@omega-institute.com.

BELLINGER, EDGAR THOMSON, lawyer; b. N.Y.C., Sept. 23, 1929; s. John and Margaret (Thomson) B.; children from previous marriage: Edgar Jr., Robert, Margaret; m. Ann Clark, Feb. 25, 1989. BA, Haverford Coll., 1951; JD with honors, George Washington U., 1955. Bar: D.C. 1955, Md. 1955. Law clk. to chief judge U.S. Dist. Ct. D.C., 1955-57; asst. U.S. aty for Washington, 1957-59; ptnr. Pope, Ballard & Loos, Washington, 1959-81, Zuckert, Scoutt and Rasenberger, Washington, 1981-94, Bellinger & Assocs., Washington and Md., 1995—. Chmn. unauthorized practice com. D.C. Ct. Appeals, 1972-78; mem. D.C. jud. conf., 1972-90; bd. mgrs. Chevy Chase Village, 1983-86. Mem. ABA (mem. fidelity and surety com., mem. forum on constrn. industry, past chmn. bonds, liens and ins. divsn.), Am. Arbitration Assn. (panel of arbitrators), D.C. Bar Assn. (D.C. Ct. Appeals orgn. com. 1972), Md. Bar Assn., Talbot County Bar Assn., Nat. Assn. Securities Dealers (panel of arbitrators), Met. Club, Chevy Chase Club (bd. govs. 1972-77, pres. 1976-77). Office: PO Box 739 Easton MD 21601-8914 Home: 4791 Sailors Retreat Rd Oxford MD 21654

BELLINGER, JOHN B., III, lawyer; b. Paris, Mar. 28, 1960; s. John B. Bellinger Jr. and Anne Taliaferro (Tynes) B.; m. Caroline Dawn Renzy, June 9, 1984; children: Catharine Meade, Ann Thomson. AB, Princeton U., 1982; JD, Harvard U., 1986; MA, U. Va., 1991. Assoc. Shaw, Pittman, Potts & Trowbridge, Washington, 1986—88; spl. asst. to dir. CIA, Washington, 1988-91; assoc., then spl. counsel Wilmer, Cutler & Pickering, Washington, 1991-95; gen. counsel, commn. on the roles and capabilities of U.S. Intelligence Cmty., Washington, 1995-96; spl. counsel senate select com. on intelligence U.S. Senate, Washington, 1996; sr. counsel for nat. security matters criminal divsn. US Dept. Justice, Washington, 1997-2001; sr. assoc. counsel to Pres., The White House, Washington, 2001—05, legal adviser to Nat. Security Coun., 2001—05; sr. advisor to sec. U.S. Dept. State, Washington, 2005, legal advisor, 2005—. Vestryman St. Mary's Episcopal Ch., Arlington, Va., 1991-94, sr. warden, 1993-94; bd. govs. St. Albans Sch., Washington, 1997-2004; mem. Coun. on Fgn. Rels., Am. Coun. on Germany. Fellow, Brit.-Am. Project. Office: US Dept State Harrry S Truman Bldg 2201 C St NW Rm 6423 Washington DC 20520 Office Phone: 202-647-9598.

BELLINGHAM, ROGER GERRY, librarian, researcher, consultant; b. Cin., Aug. 10, 1945; s. Charles Albert and Helen Mildred (Weiss) Bellingham. BS, U. Cin., 1973, MS, 1983; MEd, Xavier U., 1975; MLS, U. Ky., 1989; M in Environ. sci., Miami U., 1990. Chemist DuBois Chem. Co., Cin., 1967—74; rsch. assoc. U. Cin., 1978—84; cons. Foto Technicks Group, 1983—2002; libr. dir. Margrave Rsch. Libr., 1992—. Mem.: AAAS, NY Acad. Sci. Achievements include consulting expertise in light microscopy-quantitive color work. Avocation: history. Office: Margrave Rsch Libr 8307 Jadwin St Cincinnati OH 45216 E-mail: toad175@members.nyas.org, frogg115@netzero.net.

BELLINI, FRANCESCO, chemist; b. Ascoli, Piceno, Italy, Nov. 20, 1947; s. Berardino Bellini; m. Marisa Bellini; children: Roberto, Carlo. Diploma in chem. engring., I.T.I.S., Italy, 1967; BSc in Chemistry, Coll. Loyola, Montreal, Que., Can., 1972; PhD in Organic Chemistry, U. N.B., Can., 1977. Rsch. asst. Ayerst Labs., 1968-74, postdoctoral fellow, 1977-79, sr. scientist, 1979-81, rsch. assoc., 1981-84; dir. biochems. divsn. Institut Armand Frappier, Laval, Que., 1984-86; pres., CEO Biochem Pharma Inc., Laval, Canada, 1986—2001; chmn., CEO Biochem. Pharma Inc., Laval, Canada, 2001—, Picchio Pharma and Picchio Internat., 2001—; chmn., pres., CEO Neurochem, 2002—. Chmn. Adaltis, 1992—, Innodia, 2003—, Virochem, 2004—; bd. dirs. Molson-Coors Inc. Contbr. numerous articles to profl. jours. Achievements include patents on angiotensin conberting enzyme inhibitors; discovery of 6-(lower alkoxy)-5- (trifluoromenthyl) -1-naphtalene -carboxylic acid, known and Tolrestat, used as an aldose reductase inhibitor; co-author of 20 patents.

BELLIS, ARTHUR ALBERT, financial executive, government official; b. Worcester, Mass., June 16, 1928; s. Frank Clayton and Ruth Porter (Gordon) B.; m. Barbara Swift, Feb. 22, 1952 (div. 1969); children: Bradford, Susan; m. E. Deborah Shea, May 28, 1972 (div. 1997); children: Cynthia, Michael. BSBA, Boston U., 1952. Asst. credit mgr. Procter & Gamble, N.Y.C., 1955-56; asst. supr. capital budget Western Union, N.Y.C., 1956-58; corp. budget analyst CBS, N.Y.C., 1958-64; account exec. Edwards & Hanley, N.Y.C., 1964-66, Spencer Trask, Worcester, 1966-70; sr. securities compliance examiner SEC, Boston, 1970-90; retired, 1990; treas., CFO, chief compliance officer Burlington Securities Corp., Chatham, Mass., 1993-97. Advisor Explorer program Mohegan council Boy Scouts Am., 1966-70; mem. Worcester Rep. Com., 1952-53, Rep. Presdl. Task Force, 1984-85; mem. fin. com. Town of Yarmouth, 1982-86; v.p. Sheriff's Cmty. Patrol, 1997—; extraordinary min. of Holy Communion, Roman Cath. Ch., 2004. Recipient Superior Performance award SEC, 1976, 1986; Medal of Merit, Pres. of U.S., 1985. Mem. Masons (treas. Howard lodge 1988-91, trustee 1992-97), Pine Run High Twelve Club (sec. 2003, leader cmty. emergency response team, 2003-), Ea. Star Roman Catholic. Avocations: flying, hiking, camping, keyboard, painting. Address: 9701 e Highway 25 #32 Belleview FL 34420 Personal E-mail: lebrta@aol.com.

BELLIS, CARROLL JOSEPH, surgeon, educator; b. Shreveport, La. s. Joseph and Rose (Bloome) B.; m. Mildred Darmody, Dec. 26, 1939; children: Joseph, David. BS summa cum laude, U. Minn., 1930, MS in Physiology, 1932, PhD in Physiology, 1934, MD, 1936, PhD in Surgery, 1941. Diplomate Am. Bd. Surgery, cert. Internat. Bd. Proctology, Internat. Bd. Surgery. Fellow in physiology U. Minn., Mpls., 1930-34; resident in surgery U. Minn. Hosps., Mpls., 1937-41; pvt. practice surgery Long Beach, Calif., 1945-95. Prof., chmn. dept. surgery Calif. Coll. Medicine, 1962—; surg. cons. to surgeon gen. U.S. Army; adj. prof. surgery U. Calif. Author: Fundamentals of Human Physiology, A Critique of Reason, Lectures in Medical Physiology; contbr. numerous articles on surgery and physiology to profl. jours. Served to col. M.C. AUS, 1941-46. Recipient Charles Lyman Green prize in physiology, 1934, prize Mpls. Surg. Soc., 1938, ann. award Mississippi Valley Med. Soc., 1955; Alice Shevlin fellow U. Minn., 1932-34. Fellow: ACS, Peripheral Vascular Soc. Am. (founding), Internat. Acad. Proctology, Nat. Cancer Inst., Phlebology Soc. Am., Gerontol. Soc., Am. Med. Writers Assn., Internat. Coll. Surgeons, Royal Soc. Medicine, Am. Coll. Gastroenterology, Internat. Coll. Angiology (sci. coun.), Am. Soc. Abdominal Surgeons; mem.: AAAS, Pan Am. Med. Assn. (diplomate), Indsl. Med. Assn., Pan Pacific Surg. Assn., Am. Assn. History Medicine, Irish Med. Assn., Am. Geriatrics Soc., Hollywood Acad. Medicine, N.Y. Acad. Scis., Miss. Valley Med. Soc., Am. Assn. Study Neoplastic Diseases, Alpha Omega Alpha, Sigma Xi, Phi Beta Kappa. Home: PMB 808 904 Silver Spur Rd Rolling Hills Estates CA 90274 Office Phone: 310-377-6343.

BELLISARIO, DOMENIC ANTHONY, lawyer; b. Pitts., May 14, 1953; s. Domenic and Mary (Murgia) B. BA, U. Pitts., 1975, JD, 1978. Bar: Pa. 1978, U.S. Dist. Ct. (we. dist.) Pa. 1978, U.S. Dist. Ct. (no. dist.) Ohio 1999, U.S. Ct. Appeals (3d cir.) 1985, U.S. Ct. Appeals (6th cir.) 2002. Trial atty. Nat. Labor Rels. Bd., Pitts., 1978-83; human resource counsel Western Res. Care Sys., Youngstown, Ohio, 1986-89; ptnr. Bellisario & Pontier, Pitts., 1984-90; pvt. practice Pitts., 1991—. Author: Preventing and Defending Sexual Harassment Claims in Pennsylvania, 1996, Basic Wage and Hour Law in Pennsylvania, 1997. Mem. coun. Nat. Italian Am. Found., Washington, 1991. Mem. ABA, Am. Arbitration Assn. (arbitrator), Nat. Italian Am. Found., Pa. Bar Assn., Allegheny County Bar Assn., Pa. Trial Lawyers Assn., Italian Cultural Heritage Soc. West Pa. Avocations: travel, skiing. Office: 1000 Law & Finance Bldg Pittsburgh PA 15219 Office Phone: 412-471-6463. Business E-Mail: domenic@bellisario.com.

BELLISARIO, KRISTEN MARIE, music educator; b. Putnam, Conn., Nov. 4, 1968; d. Joseph William Bellisario and Deborah Dorothy Phelps; m. Timothy Brian O'Donnell, Feb. 13, 1999; children: Iris Aemilia O'Donnell Bellisario, Noah Quinn Bellisario O'Donnell. MFA, U. Calif., Irvine, 1998. Exec. dir. Irvine Youth Symphony (Four Seasons Symphony), Calif., 1996—99; founder, exec. dir. So. Ind. Youth Symphony, Inc., Bloomington, Ind., 2000—04; adj. faculty Sch. Music Ind. U., Bloomington, Ind., 2002—; exec. dir. New World Youth Orchs., Indpls., 2005—. Imp faculty sponsor Ind. U., Individualized Maj. Program, Bloomington, Ind., 2003—. Prodr.: (media design) Azerbaijan, Music and Culture DVD; prodr., flutist, developer (media arts) Quadrivium Interactive Composition; musician: (performances) Flute Recital Series, Nonyx by Christopher Dobrian, Master's Recital - George Crumb, Vox Bolanae, (performance) Copland, Due for Flute and Piano with Robert Hatten, IU Professor of Music, (performance, recording) Phase Reflections by Timothy O'Donnell; composer: Lost Boy (based on a poem by Robert Blake), Bandit. Vista vol. Area 10 Agy. on Aging, Ellettsville, Ind., 2002—03; vol. edn. dir. Bloomington (Ind.) Symphony Orch., 1999—2000; youth activity vol. Eager Beaver/Adventurer's Club, Bloomington, 2003—05; at large mem. Musical Arts Youth Orch. (So. Ind. Youth Symphony, Inc.), Bloomington, 2004—05; edn. chair Cmty. Chamber Music Assn., Bloomington, 2000—04. Recipient German Cultural Soc. award, German Cultural Assn., 1986, Women's Club award, Norwich Free Acad., 1986; grantee, Ind. Arts Commn., NEA, 2001, Ind. U., Bloomington, Dept. US Edn., 2004; scholar, Norwich Free Acad., 1986, Calif. State U., Long Beach, 1993—96; Regent fellow, U. Calif., Irvine, 1996—98, Walter and Katie Navick Meml. Fund scholar, Norwich Free Acad., 1986. Mem.: Pi Kappa Lambda (hon.), Pi Kappa Phi (life), Golden Key (life). Conservative. Avocations: backpacking, vegetarianism, classical music. Home: 2455 N Pennsylvania St Indianapolis IN 46204 Office: New World Youth Orch Inc 32 E Washington St Ste 950 Indianapolis IN 46205 Office Phone: 317.229-2365. Personal E-mail: kbellisa@indiana.edu. E-mail: bellisario@nwyso.org.

BELLISSIMO, MARY F., art educator; b. Ellwood City, Pa., Oct. 26, 1955; d. James J. and Inese Bellissimo. BSEd Art Edn., Indiana U. of Pa., 1977; MSEd Classroom Tech., Wilkes U., 2004. Long range planner and tchr. of gifted Laurel Sch. Dist., Pa., 1978—79; art tchr. Easton Area Sch. Dist., 1979—. Mem.: Lehigh Valley Arts Coun., Easton Edn. Assn., NEA, St. Jane Frances de Chantal Ch., Pa. State Edn. Assn. Avocations: gardening, travel, social orgns. Home: 2529 Madison Ave Bethlehem PA 18017-3872 Office: Easton Area Sr High Sch 2601 William Penn Hwy Easton PA 18045

BELLIVEAU, GERARD JOSEPH, JR., librarian; b. Waltham, Mass., May 27, 1940; s. Gerard Joseph and Mary Teresa (Reilly) B. BA in English Lit., Boston Coll., 1963; MA in Philosophy, Boston U., 1972; MLS in Libr. Svc., Rutgers U., 1973. Lectr. U. Rouen (France), 1965-66; philosophy bibliographer Boston Pub. Libr., Boston, 1967-68; asst. libr. Racquet & Tennis Club: Libr. of Sport, N.Y.C., 1971-78, head libr., 1979—; libr. gen. rsch. div. N.Y. Pub. Libr., N.Y.C., 1973-79, libr. in charge gen. rsch. div., 1980-81, asst. chief pub. catalog sect. gen. rsch. div., 1981-88, asst. chief libr. gen. rsch. div., 1988-95. Mem. coop. acquisitions program com. METRO Ref. and Rsch. Libr. Agy., N.Y.C., 1984-88, chair coop. acquisitions program com., 1985-86, mem. resources devel. com., 1986-89. Bd. dirs. Peabody-Mason Music Found., Boston, 1972-87. Mem. Williams Club. Democrat. Avocations: architecture, travel, french medieval history. Office: Racquet & Tennis Club Libr 370 Park Ave New York NY 10022-5968

BELLIVEAU, KATHRIN PAGONIS, lawyer; b. Fall River, Mass., Aug. 25, 1968; d. Constantine Peter and Betty (Jamoulis) Pagonis; m. James Joseph Belliveau, June 20, 1998. BA magna cum laude, Wellesley Coll., 1990; JD, Boston Coll., 1993. Bar: R.I. 1993, U.S. Dist. Ct. R.I. 1994. Assoc. Tillinghast Collins & Graham, Providence, 1993-96, Adler Pollock & Sheehan, Providence, 1996-97; mng. atty. Hasbro, Inc., Pawtucket, RI, 1997—. Bd. dirs. Children's Mus., Providence, 1998—, Caritas House, Pawtucket, 1997—. Mem. ABA, Wellesley Club of R.I. (bd. dirs. 1996—), Phi Beta Kappa. Greek Orthodox. Avocations: tennis, golf, skiing, cooking. Office: Hasbro Inc 1027 Newport Ave Pawtucket RI 02861-2500

BELLIZZI, JOHN J., law enforcement association administrator, pharmacist, educator; b. N.Y.C., July 26, 1919; s. Francis X. and Carmela (Bruno) B.; m. Celeste Morga, Sept. 1, 1942; children: John J. Jr., Robert F. PhG, St. John's U., N.Y.C., 1939; LLB, Albany Law Sch., 1960; JD, Union U., 1968; LLD, St. John's U., 1981. Pharmacist St. Luke's Hosp., N.Y.C., 1939-44; police officer N.Y.C. Police Dept., 1944-53; narcotics agt. N.Y. Bur. Narcotics Enforcement, N.Y.C., 1953-59, dir. Albany, 1959-81; exec. dir. N.Y. State Drug Abuse Commn., Albany, 1981-84, Internat. Narcotics Enforcement Assn., Albany, 1984—. Prof. pharmacy law St. John's U., N.Y.C., 1962-76; lectr. in field. Contbr. articles to profl. jours. Recipient Papal medal Vatican, 1965. Mem. Internat. Narcotics Enforcement Officers Assn. (pres. 1960-62, Anslinger medal 1979, chmn. law enforcement com. Paramount Pictures, 1972-75, Svc. award 1975), Ft. Orange Club, Albany Country Club, Univ. Club (Albany), Am. Friends of Law Enforcement Found. (bd. dirs., sec. Japanese), Phi Alpha Delta, Phi Sigma Chi (pres. 1939), Sigma Chi (fellow). Office: Internat Narcotics Enforcement Officers Assn 112 State St Albany NY 12207-2005 Office Phone: 518-463-4569.

BELLM, JOAN, civic worker; b. Alton, Ill., June 20, 1934; d. Harvey Jacob and Alma Lorene (Roberts) Goldsby; m. Earl David Bellm, Oct. 1, 1955; children: David, Lori, Michael. Bd. dirs. Drug Watch Internat., 1991-02, lifetime hon. dir., 1998—; exec. dir. Ctr. for Drug Info., 1998—. Editor Best of IDEA newsletter, 1991-96, Drug Watch World News, 1996-02; chmn. Drug Watch Internat. editl. rev. com., 1996-02; columnist weekly newspaper, 1998—. Organist, dir. jr. choir St. Mary's Cath. Ch., 1958-78; mem. adv. bd. Carlinville (Ill.) Area Hosp., 1981-86; trustee Blackburn Coll., Carlinville, 1983-86; bd. dirs. Cath. Children's Home, Diocese of Springfield, Ill., 1986—; founder, bd. dirs., state networker Ill. Drug Edn. Alliance, 1982-86, pres., 1987-89; bd. dirs., nat. networker Nat. Fedn. Parents for Drug-Free Youth, Washington, 1984-86; mem. Ill. Gov.'s Adv. Coun. on Alcoholism and Substance Abuse, 1989-93; dir. Ctr. for Drug Info., 1998—; founder Drug Watch Internat., 1991, Internat. Drug Strategy Inst., 1993, invited participant Internat. Private Sector Conf. on Drugs, Seville, 1993, advisor U.N. Internat. Drug Ctrl. Program, 1994; numerous others. Recipient letter of endorsement Pres. of U.S., 1981, citation of recognition Ill. Dept., Am. Legion, 1981, Meritorious Svc. award, 1982, award Ill. Drug Edn. Alliance award, 1984, Southwestern Ill. Law Enforcement Commn., 1984, Carlinville Sch. Bd., 1985, Outstanding Svc. award Nat. Fedn. Parents, 1986, award Ill. Alcohol and Drug Dependence Assn., 1986, Optimist Internat., 1987, Ill. Drug Edn. Alliance, 1988, Outstanding Citizen award Blackburn U., 1989, Citizen of Yr. award, Carlinville, 1990; Leadership award Drug Watch Internat., 2001. Home: PO Box 227 Carlinville IL 62626-0227

BELLO, JUDITH HIPPLER, lawyer, trade association administrator; b. Alexandria, Va., May 31, 1949; BA in history summa cum laude, U. NC, 1971; JD, Yale Law Sch., 1975. Bar: D.C. 1975. Office legal adviser Dept. State, Washington, 1977-82; from dep. to gen. counsel, US trade rep. Sec. Commerce for Import Adminstrn., Washington, 1982—89; ptnr. Sidley & Austin, Washington, 1989-96; joined Pharm. Rsch. and Mfrs. Am. (PhRMA), 1996—, exec. v.p. policy and strategic affairs Washington, 1996—2001. Mem. Pres. Commn. on Federal Ethics Law Reform; policy official and atty. Dept. Commerce and State; editl. adv. bd. Am. Jour. Internat. Law, Georgetown Law and Policy in Internat. Bus., George Wash. Jour. Internat. Law and Econ.; adv. bd. and com. US Export-Import Bank, Syracuse U. Maxwell Sch. Citizenship and Pub. Affairs, Atlantic Coun., Brookings Instn. Coun. on Pub. Policy Edn.; vis. lectr. in field. Author: (with Alan F. Holmer) The Antidumping and Countervailing Duty Laws: Key Legal and Policy Issues, 1987, Guide to US-Can. Free-Trade Agreement, 1990; editor: North American Free Trade Agreement, 1994; contbr. numerous articles to profl. jours. Recipient Overall Excellence award DC Bar Com., 1985, Meritorious Pub. Svc. award USCG, 1978; named one of 100 Most Powerful Women in Wash., Washingtonian mag., 2001. Mem. ABA (internat. sect. co-chmn. trade com. 1986-90, couns. 1987-90), DC Bar (internat. sect., chmn. steering com. 1987-88; co-chmn. trade com. 1983-86), Am. Soc. Internat. Law (editl. adv. bd. 1982-89, coun. 1994-96, bd. dirs. 1995-2000), Coun. on Fgn. Rels., Aspen (Colo.) Strategy Group, Phi Beta Kappa. Office: PhRMA 100 15th St NW Washington DC 20005 E-mail: jbello@phrma.org.

BELLO, MARIA ELANA, actress; b. Norristown, Pa., Apr. 18, 1967; 1 child, Jackson Blue McDermott. BS in Polit. Sci., Villanova U. Actress: (off-Broadway plays) include The Killer Inside Me, Small Town Gals With Big Problems, Urban Planning; (films) Maintenance, 1992, Permanent Midnight, 1998, Payback, 1999, Coyote Ugly, 2000, Duets, 2000, Sam the Man, 2000, China: The Panda Adventure, 2001, Auto Focus, 2002, 100 Mile Rule, 2002, The Cooler, 2003, Nobody's Perfect, 2004, Secret Window, 2004, Silver City, 2004, Assault on Precinct 13, 2005; (TV films) The Commish: In the Shadow of the Gallows, 1995; (TV series) Mr. & Mrs. Smith, 1996, ER, 1997-98 (Screen Actors Guild award for outstanding performance by an ensemble in a drama series, 1997). Co-founder Dream Yard Drama Project for Kids, Harlem, N.Y.C. Office: Creative Artists Agy 9830 Wilshire Blvd Beverly Hills CA 90212*

BELLO, MARY, physician; b. Paterson, N.J., Dec. 27, 1954; d. John Vincent and Rose (Piccirilli) B.; m. Michael Mutter, June 3, 1984; children: Michael Mutter, Jonathan Mutter. BA, Rutgers Coll., 1977; BS, L.I. U., 1980; MD, Ross U., 1984. Diplomate Am. Bd. Family Practice. Intern St. Joseph's Hosp., Paterson, N.J., resident; family physician pvt. practice, 1985—; clin. asst. prof. family medicine UMDNJ. Fellow Am. Acad. Family Physicians. Republican. Roman Catholic. Avocation: antique doll collecting. Office: 400 Franklin Tpke Ste 106 Mahwah NJ 07430-3517 Office Phone: 201-327-3333.

BELLON, VENETIA ROCHELLE, financial consultant, educator; b. Beaufort West, Cape, South Africa, July 24, 1941; arrived in U.S., 1965; d. Michael and Roslyn (Sklaar) Bellon; m. Barry Fenroy Bass, Jan. 17, 1963 (div. Aug. 15, 1977); children: Tracey Bass Shilling-Hysjulien, Dayana Bass; m. Andrew Jackson Ponton, III, Oct. 2004. Cert., U. Capetown, South Africa, 1960; BA in History, U. Tex., 1981, MA, LBJ, U. Tex., 1984. Tchr. Ellerton Jr. Sch., Capetown, 1961—63, Girls' HS, Pietermartizburg, South Africa, 1964; mktg. mgr. Austin Mag., 1978; officer corp. Bank Am., Va., 1987—91; mortgage cons. Penn Nat. Bancshares, McLean, Va., 1993—95, Access Nat. Mortgage, Reston, 1995—99, Countrywide Home Loans, Alexandria, Va., 2001—. Conf. coord. Third World Militarization, 1984; mem. Amnesty Internat.; mem. task force Gov. State of Tex., 1984. Mem.: AAUW, So. Poverty Law Ctr., Tex. Execs., Nat. Yiddish Book Ctr. Democrat. Jewish. Avocations: abstract expressionism, travel, crossword puzzles. Home: PO Box 1755 Alexandria VA 22313 Office: Countrywide Home Loans 5830 Kingstowne Ctr Alexandria VA 22315 Office Phone: 703-924-9236 235. Business E-Mail: venetia_bellon@countrywide.com.

BELLOSPIRITO, ROBYN SUZANNE, artist, writer; b. Glen Cove, N.Y., Sept. 11, 1964; BA, L.I. U., 1986. Asst. Slide Libr. The Met. Mus. Art, N.Y.C., 1987-88, The Frick Art Reference Libr., N.Y.C., 1988-89; pub., editor The Exhibitioner Art Mag., Old Brookville, N.Y., 1993—, curator exhbns., 1994—. Exhbns. include Crystal Art Gallery, N.Y.C., 1988, Hutchins Gallery, Greenvale, N.Y., 1990, 91, Nassau County Mus. Art, Roslyn, N.Y., 1990, Sakura Gallery, Kennedy Airport, N.Y.C., 1992, PAAS Gallery, N.Y.C., 1992, Ward-Nasse Gallery, N.Y.C., 1992, 94, Outrlimits Art Gallery, Franklin Square, N.Y., 1993, Sea Cliff (N.Y.) Gallery, 1993, 94, Prince St. Gallery, N.Y.C., 1994, Foster Freeman Gallery, San Antonio, 1994, UN 4th Conf. on Women, Beijing, 1995, Ticknor Gallery/Harvard U., 1996, Fine Arts Mus. L.I., Hempstead, 1996, Islip (N.Y.) Art Mus., 1996, Galerie Observatoire 4, Montreal, 1996, Hillwood Art Mus., Brookville, N.Y., 1997, Fitton Ctr. for Creative Arts, Hamilton, ohio, 1997, Ghost Fleet Gallery, Nags Head, N.C., 1997, Watchung (N.J.) Arts Ctr., 1997, Barnes & Noble, N.Y.C., 1998, Soc. Illustrators, N.Y.C, 2001, IMAC, Huntington, NY, 2002, Oyster Bay Hist. Soc., N.Y., 2003-2004, others; permanent collections include Nat. Mus. Women in Arts, 1-800-Flowers, Inc., and pvt. homes. Grantee Puffin Found., 1997. Personal E-mail: bellspirit@aol.com.

BELLOWS, CARL D., lawyer; b. Bklyn., Sept. 29, 1944; BA, Columbia U., 1966; JD cum laude, NYU Sch. Law, 1969, LLM in Taxation, 1974. Bar: NY 1969, US Tax Court 1969, US Ct. Fed. Claims 1969. With Weil, Gotshal & Manges LLP, NYC, 1969—, ptnr., co-chair trusts and estate dept. Lectr. NYC Bar Assn., NY State Bar Assn. Contbg. editor Review of Taxation of Individuals, 1978—82; co-author: (treatise) Partnership Buy-Sell Agreements, 1995. Mem.: NY State Bar Assn. (mem. com. on Income Taxation, Estates and Trusts Law Section 1971—), Order of the Coif. Office: Weil Gotshal & Manges LLP 767 Fifth Ave New York NY 10153 Office Phone: 212-310-8134. Office Fax: 212-310-8007. Business E-Mail: carl.bellows@weil.com.

BELLOWS, CHARLES FREDERICK, III, surgeon, educator; b. Auburn, N.Y., Sept. 12, 1963; s. Charles Frederick Bellows, Jr. and Nancy Jane Bellows; m. Renee Jeanette Rabalais, June 29, 2001. BS, U. R.I., 1986; M in Liberal Arts, Harvard U., 1990; MD, Med. Coll. Pa., Phila., 1995. Diplomate Am. Bd. Gen. Surgery. Resident in surgery Tulane U., New Orleans, 1995—2001; asst. prof. surgery U. Fla., Jacksonville, Fla., 2001—04, Baylor Coll. Medicine, Houston, 2004—; chief laparoscopic surgery Michael E. DeBakey VA Med. Ctr., Houston, 2004—. Editl. bd. Duval County Med. Soc. Journal, Jacksonville, 2001—. Contbr. articles to profl. jours., including Jour. Surg. Rsch. Recipient Krementz Rsch. award, Tulane U., 1999, Rsch. award, Assn. Acad. Surgery, 1995. Mem.: ACS, Soc. Am. Gastrointestinal Endoscopic Surgeons, Soc. Surgery of the Alimentary Tract. Business E-Mail: cbellows@bcm.tmc.edu.

BELLOWS, HOWARD ARTHUR, JR., corporate financial executive; b. N.Y.C., Mar. 10, 1938; s. Howard Arthur and Rita Jennie (Maffitt) B.; m. Mary Josephine Boyd, Sept. 7, 1968; children— Maffitt Vodrey, Alexander Scott, Hillary Newland, Jennifer Pacheteau. BA, Princeton U., 1960; MBA, Harvard U., 1964. Dir. mktg. Olga Co., Van Nuys, Calif., 1964-66; chmn. bd., co-chief exec. officer Triangle Corp., Stamford, Conn., 1967-71, chmn. bd., pres., chief exec. officer, 1971-95; pres. Audits & Surveys Worldwide, Inc., N.Y.C., 1995—99; chmn. The Finance Network, LLC, 2000—. Bd. dirs. Haxcel Corp., Beacon Roofing Supply, Inc. Trustee Western Res. Acad.,

Hudson, Ohio. Served to lt. (j.g.) USNR, 1960-62. Mem. Links Club, Blind Brook Club, Round Hill Club, Eagle Springs Golf Club, Univ. Cottage Club (bd. govs.), McArthur Golf Club. Office Phone: 203-552-1745. E-mail: artbellows@earthlink.net.

BELLOWS, LAUREL GORDON, business lawyer; m. Joel J. Bellows. BA, U. Pa., 1969; JD, Loyola U., Chgo., 1974. Bar: Ill. 1974, Fla. 1975, U.S. Dist. Ct. (no. dist.) Ill. 1975, U.S. Dist. Ct. (no. dist.) Ga. 1980, Calif. 1981, U.S. Dist. Ct. (cen. dist.) Calif. 1980. Ptnr. Bellows and Bellows, Chgo., 1975—. Editor Loyola U. Law Rev., 1973-74; co-author: Trial Techniques in Business and Commercial Cases, 1988-2000. Past pres. women's bd. Traveller's Aid Soc., Chgo.; past chmn. Chgo. Network, 1992—; mentor Woman of Destiny program, 1990-91. Mem. ABA (bd. govs. 2001—, sec.-treas. 1991-92, past chmn. commn. on women 1993-95, mem. fed. jud. com. 1999—), Ill. Bar Assn., Chgo. Bar Assn. (bd. mgrs. 1983-85, sec. 1987-89, pres. 1991-92), Women's Bar Assn. Ill., Women's Bar Assn. Ill. Found. (bd. dirs. 1988—), Am. Arbitration Assn. (arbitrator 1976—, award 1990). Office: Bellows and Bellows 209 S LaSalle St Chicago IL 60604 Office Phone: 312-332-3340. E-mail: lbellows@bellowspc.com.

BELLOWS, MICHAEL DONALD, foreign service officer; b. Spirit Lake, Iowa, Mar. 7, 1952; s. Donald Morris and Dolores Elizabeth (Thiesen) B.; m. Toni Leder, July 27, 1974; 1 child, Melissa Elizabeth. BA in History, Morningside Coll., Sioux City, Iowa, 1974; diploma, Nat. Def. U., 1990. Vice consul U.S. Embassy, Manila, 1975-77, U.S. Consulate Gen., Frankfurt, Germany, 1978-80, dep. prin. officer Halifax, Can., 1980-82; consul U.S. Embassy, Suva, Fiji, 1982-84, polit. officer, 1985-87; polit. and econ. officer U.S. Dept. State, Washington, 1987-89; consul gen. U.S. Consulate Gen., Auckland, New Zealand, 1990-93; dean Auckland Consular Corps, 1992-93; dir. Office Pub. and Diplomatic Liaison Dept. State, Washington, 1994-96; spl. asst. Bur. of Consular Affairs Dept. State, Washington, 1996—; min.-counselor U.S. Embassy, Ottawa, Can., 1997—; sr. advisor Bur. Consular Affairs, Dept. State, Washington, 2001—. Vis. fellow Inst. Nat. Strategic Studies, Nat. Def. U., 1993-94; sr. advisor Summit Planning Orgn., 2003-04; policy info. coord. Bur. Internat. Orgn. Affairs, 2004-05. Editor: Asia in the 21st Century: Evolving Strategic Priorities, 1994. Mem. Am. Fgn. Svc. Assn., Am. Defenders of Bataan and Corregidor. Avocations: reading, music. Office: US Dept State Fgn Svc Lounge Washington DC 20520-0001

BELLOWS, THOMAS JOHN, political scientist, educator; b. Chgo., Aug. 15, 1935; s. Charles Everett and Dorothy (Morrison) B.; m. Marilyn Denise Corbell; children: Scott Anthony, Justin Thomas, Trevor Cullen, Ethan Forrest; children by previous marriage: Roderick Alan, Adrienne Marie, Jeannine Louise, Derek John, Marshall Everett. Student, Am. U., 1956, UCLA, 1956-57; BA, Augustana Coll., 1957; MA, U. Fla., 1958, Yale U., 1960, PhD, 1968. From asst. prof. to prof. polit. sci. U. Ark., Fayetteville, 1967-81, chmn. dept., 1971-78; dir. divsn. social policy scis. U. Tex., San Antonio, 1981-88, prof. polit. sci., 1981—. Vis. lectr. depts. history, polit. sci. Nanyang U., Singapore, 1965; vis. prof. Nat. Chengchi U., Taiwan, 1979. Author: The People's Action Party of Singapore: Emergence of a Dominant Party System, 1970; (with S. Erikson and H. Winter) Political Science: Introductory Essays and Readings, 1971, Taiwan's Foreign Policy in the 1970's, 1976, (with H. Winter) People and Politics: An Introduction to Political Science, 1985, Bridging Tradition and Modernization: The Singapore Bureaucracy, 1989, Conflict and Compromise, 1992; Taiwan and Mainland China, 2000; (with Felix Almaraz), Modern Texas, 2003, The Republic of China's Legislative Yuan: A Study of Institunional Evolution, 2003; editor Am. Jour. Chinese Studies, 1999— Mem.: Am. Assn. for Chinese Studies (pres. 1998—2000), Assn. Asian Studies, S.W. Conf. Asian Studies (pres. 1995), Phi Beta Kappa, Phi Kappa Phi. Methodist. Office: U Tex Dept Polit Sci San Antonio TX 78249 Office Phone: 210-458-4628. Personal E-mail: tbellows@juno.com. Business E-Mail: thomas.bellows@utsa.edu.

BELLUOMINI, FRANK STEPHEN, accountant; b. Healdsburg, Calif., May 19, 1934; s. Francesco and Rose (Giorgi) B.; m. Alta Anita Gifford, Sept. 16, 1967; 1 child, Wendy Ann. AA, Santa Rosa Jr. Coll., 1954; BA with honors, San Jose State U., 1956. CPA, Calif. Staff acct. Hood, Gire & Co., CPA's, San Jose, Calif., 1955-60, ptnr., 1960-66, Touche Ross & Co., CPA's, San Jose, 1967-89, ptnr.-in-charge San Jose office, 1971-85, sr. ptnr., 1985-89; ptnr. Deloitte & Touche, San Jose, 1989-95. Bd. dirs. Santa Clara Valley chpt. ARC, 1993-200 chmn. bd. dirs. 1995-97; adv. bd. Salvation Army, San Jose, 1979-85, San Jose Children's Coun., 1982-89; citizens adv. coun. Via Rehabiliation Svcs., Inc., 1989-94, bd. dirs., 1995-2002, sec./treas., 1996-98, vice chair, 1998-99, chair, 1999-2000; trustee Santa Clara County (Calif.) United Way, 1979-95, v.p. planning and allocations, 1981-83, vice chmn., 1985-87, chmn. 1987-89; bd. dirs. San Jose Mus. Art, 1984-86; mem. Presentation HS Devel. Bd., 1989-92; dean's adv. coun. San Jose State U. Bus. Schl., 1990-95, adv. bd. Acad. of Fin., 1992-94. Named Disting. Alumnus, San Jose State U. Sch. Bus., 1978. Mem. AICPA (chmn. state and local govt. com. 1976-79), Santa Clara County Estate Planning Coun. (pres. 1979-80), Calif. Soc. CPA's (pres. chpt. 1968-69, state v.p. 1976-77), San Jose State Alumni Assn. (treas. 1960-61, dir. 1961-62, exec. com. 1961-62), San Jose State Acctg. Round Table (bd. dirs., treas. 1982-87, 92-97, pres. 1994-95), Beta Alpha Psi (San Jose State U. Outstanding Alumnus award 1986), Rotary (dir. 1979-81, dir. San Jose Rotary Endowment 1976-83, 2000-01, pres. 2001-03).

BELLUSCHI, ANTHONY C., architect; b. Portland, Oreg., Aug. 2, 1941; s. Pietro and Helen (Hemila) B.; m. Helen Risom, June 25, 1966 (div. 1975); children: Pietro Antonio, Catharine Camilla; m. Martha Mull Page, July 17, 1992. BArch, R.I. Sch. Design, 1966. Lic. arch. 28 states including N.Y., Mass., R.I., Calif., N.J., Oreg., Ill., Fla., Ga. Draftsman Ernest Kump Assocs., San Francisco, 1964; designer Zimmer-Gunsel-Frasca, Portland, 1965; assoc. Jung/Brannen Assocs., Boston, 1968-73; prin., treas. Belluschi/Daskalakis Inc., Boston, 1973-77; sr. v.p. Charles Kober Assocs., L.A., 1977-84; mng. ptnr. Kober/Belluschi Assocs., Chgo., 1984-87; pres. Anthony Belluschi Assocs. Inc., 1984-87; founder Anthony Belluschi Archs., Ltd., Chgo., 1988-2000; pres. Belluschi-OWP&P Arch. Inc., Chgo., 2000—03; cons. architect Chgo., 2003—. Archtl. cons. U.S. Peace Corps, El Salvador, 1966-68; trustee R.I. Sch. Design, 1986—, vice chmn., 1995-2000, chair bd., 2000-04. Bd. adv. Inland Arch. Mag., 1992-95. Bd. dirs. Friends of the Park, Chgo., 1993—; chair bd. trustees R.I. Sch. Design, 2000-04. Recipient First prize sculpture contest RKO & Redevel. Agy., Boston, 1973, award of merit Mass. Commn. Housing, 1975, Alumni of Yr. award RISD, 1982-83. Mem. AIA (award of excellence 1997), Urban Land Inst. (award of excellence 1997), Internat. Coun. Shopping Ctrs. (design awards for Erieview Galleria, Clevel., Bridgewater Commons, N.J., 1989, Sportsgirl Office/Retail Hirise Bldg., Melbourne, Australia, 1991, Park Meadows Retail Resort, Denver, Univ. Retail Ctr., Tampa, Fla., 1996, The Falls, Miami, 1996, Northwood Cafe, Appleton, Wis., 1999), RISD Alumni Assn. (founder Chgo. chpt.). Avocations: travel, automobiles, hunting. Home: The Coach House 119 W Chestnut St Chicago IL 60610-3254

BELLUZZO, RICK, information technology executive; BS in Acctg., Golden Gate U. Various positions including gen. mgr. Laser Jet Divsn., Hewlett-Packard, exec. v.p.; CEO Silicon Graphics Inc.; group v.p. Personal Svcs. and Devices Group, group v.p. consumer group Microsoft Corp., Redmond, Wash., 1999—2001, pres., COO, 2001—02; chmn. bd., CEO Quantum Corp., San Jose, Calif., 2002—. Mem. Sr. Leadership Team, Bus. Leadership Team, Microsoft Corp.; bd. dir. PMC-Sierra, JDS Uniphase. Bd. trustee Golden Gate Univ. Avocations: running, scuba diving, skiing. Office: Quantum Corp 1650 Technology Dr Ste 800 San Jose CA 95110-1382*

BELL-VILLADA, GENE H., literature educator, writer; b. Port-au-Prince, Haiti, Dec. 5, 1941; came to U.S. 1959; s. Gene H. Bell and Carmen (Villada) Romero; m. Audrey M. Dobek, Aug. 9, 1975. BA, U. Ariz., 1963; diploma, U. Paris, 1966; MA, U. Calif., Berkeley, 1967; PhD, Harvard U., 1974. Instr. SUNY, Binghamton, 1971-73; lectr. Yale U., New Haven, 1973-74; from asst. to prof. dept. romance langs. Williams Coll., Williamstown, Mass., 1975—, chair dept., 1993-95, 1997—2000. Instr. Middlebury (Vt.) Coll., summer 1971-72; reader, grader Advance Placement Readings, Ednl. Testing Svc., 1978-85, 94—; vis. prof. Wellesley (Mass.) Coll., 1984-85, 89-90; resident dir. Acad. Yr. in Spain program Hamilton Coll., Madrid, 1986-87, 95-96; freelance editl. cons., 1987—. Author: Borges and His Fiction, 1981, Garcia Marquez, 1990 (Best Book award New England L.Am. Studies 1991), The Carlos Chadwick Mystery, 1990, Art for Art's Sake and Literary Life, 1996 (finalist Nat. Book Critics Cir. award 1997), The Pianist Who Liked Ayn Rand: A Novella & 13 Stories, 1998; editor: Gabriel Garcia Marquez's One Hundred Years of Solitude: A Casebook, Overseas American: Growing Up Gringo in the Tropics, 2005; contbr. articles to profl. jours. and gen. interest mags. Nat. Endowment for Humanities fellow, 1979; Am. Philos. Soc. grantee, 1982. Mem. MLA, Latin Am. Studies Assn., Am. Assn. Tchrs. Spanish and Portuguese. Avocations: music, travel, films, swimming. Office: Williams Coll Dept Romance Langs Williamstown MA 01267 Office Phone: 413-597-2045.

BELLVILLE, MARGARET (MAGGIE BELLVILLE), communications executive; B in Social Scis., SUNY, Binghamton; grad. advanced mgmt. program, Harvard U. With GTE Wireless/Contel Cellular, Inc., 1986—93; sr. v.p. Century Comm., L.A., 1993—95; from v.p. ops. to exec. v.p. ops. Cox Comm., Inc., 1995—2001; pres., CEO Incanta, Atlanta, 2001—02; exec. v.p. ops. Charter Comm., Inc., St. Louis, 2002—03, exec. v.p., COO, 2003—04. Mem. exec. vom., bd. dirs. Calif. Cable TV Assn.; bd. dirs. Cable Positive, Women in Cable and Telecomm. Found.; advisor Nat. Cable and Telecomm. Assn. Task Force on Diversity. Named Woman of Yr., Women in Cable, Calif. chpt., Woman to Watch, Women in Cable, Atlanta chpt., Woman of Yr., Women in Cable nat.; named one of Top 10 Women in Bus. in Atlanta. Office: Charter Comm Inc 12405 Powerscourt Dr Saint Louis MO 63131

BELL WILSON, CARLOTTA A., state official, consultant; b. Detroit, Dec. 7, 1944; d. Albert Powell (dec.) and Elfrieda (Bertram) Bell; divorced; children: Lizette C. Wilson, SaMia M. Wilson, Shira M. Ingram. AA, Wayne County C.C., Detroit, 1975; BS, Wayne State U., 1979; MEd, Bowling Green State U., 1983. Dental asst. Fred Colvard, DDS, Detroit, 1968-73; edn. coord. Merrill Palmer Inst., Detroit, 1979-81; head start evaluator Cmty. Devel. Inst., Wayne County, 1981; grad. asst. Bowling Green (Ohio) State U., 1981-83; child care worker Meth. Children's Village, Detroit, 1984-85; tchr. New Calvary Head Start, Detroit, 1985; child welfare specialist Mich. Dept. Social Svcs., Detroit, 1985-93; resource program analyst teen parent program Family Independence Agy., Lansing, Mich., 1993—2002. Conf. presenter U. Mich., Ann Arbor, 1995, Mich. Assn. Cmty. and Adult Edn., Bellaire, 1995, Baker Coll., Flint, Mich., 1996. Mem. Mich. Profl. Soc. on Abuse of Children, Internat. Assoc. Infant Massage (cert. infant massage instr.). Roman Catholic. Avocations: gardening, pottery, cultural activities, travel. Home: 2110 Chene Detroit MI 48207

BELMONT, LARRY MILLER, retired public health executive; b. Reno, Apr. 13, 1936; s. Miller Lawrence and Madeline (Echante) B.; m. Laureen Metzger, Aug. 14, 1966; children: Miller Lawrence, Rebecca Madeline, Amie Echante, Bradley August. BA in Psychology, U. Nev., 1962; MPH, U. Mich., 1968; cert. in environ. mgmt., U. So. Calif., 1978; MPA, U. Idaho, 1979. Rep. on loan to city health depts. USPHS, Los Angeles and Long Beach, 1962-63, advisor pub. health on loan to Alaska dept. health & welfare Anchorage, 1963-64, Juneau and Anchorage, 1964-67; dep. dir. Wash./Alaska Regional Med. Program, Spokane, Wash., 1968-71; dir., sec.-treas. bd. of health Panhandle Health Dist., Coeur d'Alene, Idaho, 1971-98; ret., 1998. Past adj. faculty Whitworth Coll., Spokane; presenter in field. Contbr. articles to newspapers. Past chmn. nominating com. Kootenai Econ. Devel. Coun., Idaho, 1985, bd. dirs. 1981-86; mem. adv. com. Kootenai County Coun. Alcoholism, 1979-80; regional coord. Gov.'s Com. Vol. Svcs., Idaho, 1979-80; chmn. Montessori Adv. Bd., Idaho, 1975-79; chmn. pers. com. North Idaho Hospice, 1985-88, bd. dirs. 1985-88; bd. dirs. North Idaho Spl. Svcs. Agy., 1972-76; bd. dirs., vice-chmn. Pub. Employees Credit Union, 1990-95; bd. dirs. United Way of Kootemai County, Inc., 1990-91; mem. nat. steering com. APEX/PH, 1987-91; others; past treas. Friends of Head Start Bd. Area Aging Agy. Legis. Com.; mem. Newspaper Adv. Coun., 1998-2002, tactical chair, cmty. svc. coun.; congl. dist. II coord. AARP; treas. Friends of Head Start. USPHS trainee U. Mich., 1967-68, EPA trainee U. So. Calif., 1978. Mem. APHA, AARP (past chair comty. svcs. network, mem. state legis. com.), Nat. Assn. Home Health Agys. (chmn. legis. com. 1979-82, bd. dirs. 1978-81), Nat. Assn. County Health Ofcls. (bd. dirs. 1986-88, registry com. 1990), Idaho Pub. Health Assn. (bd. dirs. 1998-2002, treas. 1973-77, 98-00, 00—, Award of Merit 1999), Idaho Conf. Dist. Health Dirs. (bd. dirs. 1998, vice-chmn. and chmn. 1993-95), Idaho Forest Owners Assn. (tree farmer), Kootenai County Environ. Alliance, Idaho Conservation League, Area Agy. on Aging (past mem. legis. com., adv. coun.), Newspaper Adv. Coun., Idaho Rural Health Coalition, The Nature Conservancy, Ducks Unltd., Dem. Club (natural resources com.), Senior Coalition. Democrat. Avocations: hunting, fishing, wood carving, music, boating.

BELMONTE, STEVEN JOSEPH, hotel chain executive; b. Oak Park, Ill., Aug. 25, 1952; s. Silvio J. and Vilma (Giannini) B.; m. Dwyonia Conrad; children: Gino Anthony, Kellie Rose, Michael Steven. BA in Hotel Mgmt., Wright Coll., Chgo., 1974; student, Holiday Inn U., Memphis, 1974; BM in Innkeeping, Harper Coll., Rolling Meadows, Ill., 1981; D Applied Pub. Svc. (hon.), Hocking Coll., 1993. Gen. mgr., regional dir. Holiday Inns, Chgo., 1972-84; pres., CEO Equity Hotel Corp., Rolling Meadows, 1984-91, Ramada Franchise Sys., Inc., 1991—. Chmn. Ramada Inns Nat. Assn.; founding sponsor Childreach; speaker Ill. Budget for Tourism, 1978-81. Bd. advisors Wright Jr. Coll.; mem. Joint Civic Com. Italian Ams.; hon. chmn. Childreach Plan Internat., 1996; bd. dirs. Chgo. chpt. Inner City Games, 1998—, chmn., 2000—; active fund raiser for various charities and retirement homes; chmn., lodging chair Am. Hotel Found., 2000—. Recipient citation Italo-Am. War Vets, U.S., 1980, Humanities award PLAN Internat. Charities, 1994, Ambassador of Peace Humanitarian award Am. Friends of Neve Shalom/Wahat-Al-Salam, 1999. Fellow Hotel and Catering Internat. Mgmt. Assn. (hon.); mem. Am. Soc. Travel Agts., Am. Hotel and Motel Assn. (bd. trustees ednl. inst.), Am. Hotel Fedn., Hotel Sales Mgmt. Assn., Soc. Mng. Execs., Chgo. Innkeepers Assn. (v.p. 1979-81), Am. Hotel Found. (exec. com. 1997—, chmn. devel. com. 1997-2000). Office: Ramada Franchise Sys Inc 1 Sylvan Way Parsippany NJ 07054-3878

BELNAP, DAVID F., journalist; b. Ogden, Utah, July 27, 1922; s. Hyrum Adolphus and Lois Ellen B.; m. Barbara Virginia Carlberg, Jan. 17, 1947. Student, Weber Coll., Ogden, 1940. Asst. city editor Seattle Star, 1945-47; bur. chief UP Assns., Helena, Mont., 1947-50, Honolulu, 1950-52; regional exec. Pacific N.W., 1952-55, dir. Latin Am. services, 1955-67; Latin Am. corr. L.A. Times, 1967-80, asst. fgn. news editor, 1980-93. Recipient Overseas Press Club Am. award for best article on Latin Am., 1970, Maria Moors Cabot prize, 1973 Mem. Overseas Press Club Am., LA Press Club, Audiophile Soc. Clubs: Am. of Buenos Aires; Phoenix of Lima (Peru). Home and Office: 1134 W Huntington Dr Arcadia CA 91007-6308

BELOFF, ZOE, filmmaker, educator, photographer; b. Edinburgh, Scotland; arrived in N.Y.C., 1980; Student, Edingburgh (Scotland) U.; MFA in Film, Columbia U., 1983. Tchr. digital media Pratt Inst.; adj. prof. City Coll. N.Y., 1989—, Coll. SI. Prodr.: (CD-ROM) include The Vanishing Machine of Miss Natalija A., Illusions, Where There There There Where, Beyond (First prize Apple QuickTime VR Competition, 1998); (film performances) include Claire and Don in Slumberland, A Mechanical Medium, Lost, Life Underwater; (films) include Echo, A Trip to the Land of Knowledge, Shadow land or light from the other side, Lost, Wonderland USA, Nightmare Angel. Work has been exhibited at MoMA, N.Y. Film Festival, Rotterdam Film Festival, Pacific Film Archives, Pompidou Ctr., others. Recipient Finishing Funds Award, Experimental TV Ctr., 1996, 2000, 2002, Found. Contemporary Performance Arts Fellowship, N.Y. Found. for the Arts, 1997; grantee, Art Matters Inc., 1986, 1989, 1997, The Jerome Foundations Inc., Apparatus Prodns., 1992, Nat. Endowment for the Arts, 1993, Individual Artist Grant, N.Y. State Coun. for the Arts, 1996, 2001, Guggenheim Found., 2003.

BELONGIE, MICHAEL EUGENE, English language educator, poet; b. Escanaba, Mich., Nov. 1, 1946; s. Cyril and Anne (Strazzinski) B.; m. Jane Comerford, Apr. 15, 1974; children: Shaun, Ryan. BS, U. Wis., Oshkosh, 1970. Instr. English, curriculum and staff devel. facilitator Randolph (Wis.) Sch. Dist., 1970—2004; ret., 2004. Mem. adv. bd. Scholastic, Inc., N.Y.C., 1979-86; instr. interactive TV, broadcaster South Cen. Instrnl. Network Group, 1995—; drama critic Beaver Dam Daily Citizen, 1978—. Author: (poetry collection) All Things Living, Mighty and Small, 2005. Sgt. USAR, 1970-76. Recipient Congl. Tchg. award Congressman Scott Klug, 1991, 95. Mem. ASCD, Wis. Fellowship of Poets (life, pres. 1992-95), So. Edn. Inservice Orgn. (pres. 1995-96, 2004-05), Phi Delta Kappa. Avocations: supporting the arts, exercise. Home: 1421 Hiawatha Dr Beaver Dam WI 53916-1041 Office: Randolph Sch Dist 110 Meadowood Dr Randolph WI 53956-1318

BELSHAW, GARY D., music educator, composer; b. Washington, Mar. 17, 1949; s. Walter Dwinnell Belshaw and Virginia Louise Barlow, Robert L. Barlow (Stepfather); m. Renée Reinholt, Aug. 21, 1975; children: Benjamin David, Bethany Louanne Reinecke, Micah Paul. B.M., Tex. Tech U., 1991, MusM, 1994, PhD, 2000. Asst. prof. piano pedagogy Wayland Bapt. U., Plaiview, Tex., 2000—. Composer: Spirit of the Llano Estacado, A Concerto in One Movement for Piano and Orchestra, 1994, Weekend Stories for Trombone and Piano, 1995, Wind Sculptures for Trombone and Band, 2000, Oldest and Finest Concert March, 2002, At a Lake for Solo Trombone and Trombone Quartet, 2002, Constellations for Solo Trombone and Trombone Choir, 2003. Mem.: ASCAP, Tex. Music Educators Assn., Soc. Composers, Inc., Am. Music Ctr. Home: 513 Raleigh Plainview TX 79072 Office: Wayland Baptist Univ 1900 W Seventh St Plainview TX 79072 Personal E-mail: garydbelshaw@yahoo.com. E-mail: belshawg@wbu.edu.

BELSHAW, GEORGE PHELPS MELLICK, bishop; b. Plainfield, N.J., July 14, 1928; s. Harold and Edith (Mellick) B.; m. Elizabeth Wheeler, June 12, 1954; children: Richard, Elizabeth, George. BA, U. of South, 1951; STB, Gen. Theol. Sem., N.Y.C., 1954, STM, 1959, DD (hon.), 1975, U. of South, 1994, Hamilton Coll., 2003. Ordained to ministry, Episcopal Ch., consecrated bishop. Vicar St. Matthew's Ch., Waimanalo, Hawaii, 1954-57; fellow, tutor Gen. Theol. Sem., N.Y.C., 1957-59; rector Christ Ch., Dover, Del., 1959-65, St. George's Ch., Rumson, N.J., 1965-75; suffragan bishop Diocese of N.J., Trenton, 1975-83, bishop of N.J., 1983-94. Vis. lectr. Gen. Theol. Sem., 1969, 70; governing bd. Episc. Urban Caucus, 1982—, pres., 1986-89; mem. Commn. Peace of Episc. Ch., 1979-85, Econ. Justice Implementation Com., Episc. Ch., 1988-95. Editor: Lent with Evelyn Underhill, 1964, Lent with William Temple, 1966; contbr. articles to theol. jours. Trustee Gen. Theol. Sem., 1975—, chmn. 1992-2000, acting dean, pres., 1997-98; trustee Westminister Choir Coll., 1976-82. Mem. Am. Teilhard de Chardin Assn. (bd. dirs. 1976—), N.J. Coalition Religious Leaders (pres. 1986), Bd. Anglican Theol. Rev. (1993—), Coalition for Peace Action (chmn. 1999-2004). Episcopalian. Home: 15 Boudinot St Princeton NJ 08540-3007 E-mail: gpmbelshaw@aol.com.

BELSITO, DONALD VINCENT, dermatologist, educator; b. Worcester, Mass., Aug. 27, 1950; s. Robert John and Florence Mary (Corey) B.; m. Maria del Carmen Tapia, Aug. 23, 1980; children: Monica, Vanessa, Christina. BS, Georgetown U., 1972; MD, Cornell U, 1976. Diplomate Nat. Bd. Med. Examiners, Am. Bd. Internal Medicine, Am. Bd. Dermatology. Med. residency Case Western Reserve Univ. Hosp., Cleve., 1976-79; dermatol. residency NYU Med. Ctr., N.Y.C., 1979-82, instr. dept. dermatology, 1982-84, asst. prof. dept. dermatology, 1984-87, assoc. prof. dept. dermatology, 1987—, assoc. prof. dept. pathology, 1990—. Dir. allergy clinic, skin and cancer unit NYU Med. Ctr., N.Y.C., 1983—. Author several chpts. in dermatologic texts; contbr. articles to profl. jours. Recipient Parkhurst award Young Dermatologist of Yr. Am. Dermatologist Assn., 1986. Fellow Am. Coll. Physicians, Am. Acad. Dermatology; mem. AMA, Am. Dermatol. Assn., Am. Assn. Immunology, Soc. for Investigative Dermatology, Cosmetic Ingredient Rev. Com., Phi Beta Kappa, Alpha Omega Alpha. Roman Catholic. Avocation: gardening. Office: NYU Med Ctr Dept Dermatology 550 1st Ave New York NY 10016-6402

BELSKY, JOSEPH L., endocrinologist; b. Newark, Mar. 14, 1927; m. Jane Belsky. BA in Chemistry, cum laude, Drew U., 1949; MA in Chemistry, Wesleyan U., 1951; MD, Albany Med. Coll., 1955. Diplomate Am. Bd. Internal Medicine, Am. Bd. Endocrinology and Metabolism, cert. advanced achievement in internal medicine 1987. Intern Tufts Med. Svc., Boston City Hosp., 1955—56; asst. resident Boston City Hosp., 1956—57; asst. resident, internal medicine (metabolism) VA Hosp., Boston, 1957—58, resident, internal medicine, 1958—59, staff physician, med. svc., 1959—61; pvt. practice Ridgefield, Conn., 1961—64; dir. med. edn. Danbury Hosp., Conn., 1964—69; chief of medicine Atomic Bomb Casualty Commn., Hiroshima/Nagasaki, Japan, 1969—72; chief of medicine, program dir. internal medicine Danbury Hosp., 1972—80, chief of endocrinology and metabolism, 1980—96, part-time endocrinologist, 1994—. Vis. staff, internal medicine Yale New Haven Hosp., 1962—; attending physician, medicine Danbury Hosp., 1961—, asst. attending physician, lab. medicine, 1968—, cons. pediat., 1981—; tchg. fellow to clin. instr. medicine Tufts U. Sch. Medicine, 1957—61; clin. asst., medicine Harvard Med. Svc., Boston City Hosp., 1958; clin. instr. to assoc. clin. prof. medicine Yale U. Sch. Medicine, 1962—86, clin. prof. medicine, 1986—. Spkr. Med. Town Meetings; participant regular health broadcasts local radio, Ridgefield, 1966—95; mem. Bd. Edn. Town of Ridgefield, 1965—69, sch. bldg. com., 1964—69, bd. ethics, 1994—2004. Served USN, 1945—46. Recipient Alumni Achievement award, Drew U., 1981. Master: ACP (gov.'s coun. Conn. chpt. 1975—93, sec.-treas., v.p., pres. 1975—82, gov. for Conn. 1985—89, chmn. assocs. subcom. 1988—89, Laureate award Conn. chpt. 1990); mem.: Am. Diabetes Assn. (bd. dirs. Conn. affiliate 1981—84), Am. Soc. Internal Medicine, Nat. Bd. Med. Examiners (adv. com. 1976), Lawson Wilkins Pediatric Endocrine Soc., Conn. Endocrine Soc. (v.p. 1975—77, 1980—83, pres. 1983—85), Endocrine Soc., ACGME (residency rev. com. internal medicine 1990—93, appeals panel 1993—96), Am. Fedn. Clin. Rsch., Alpha Omega Alpha, Sigma Xi (assoc.). Office: 25 Germantown Rd Danbury CT 06810 Office Phone: 203-731-2020. Business E-Mail: joseph.belsky@danhosp.org.

BELSKY, MARTIN HENRY, law educator, dean; b. May 29, 1944; s. Abraham and Fannie (Turnoff) Belsky; m. Kathleen Waits, Mar. 9, 1985; children: Allen Frederick, Marcia Elizabeth. BA cum laude, Temple U., 1965; JD cum laude, Columbia U., 1968; cert. of study, Hague Acad. Internat. Law, The Netherlands, 1968; diploma in Criminology, Cambridge U., England, 1969. Bar: Pa. 1969, Fla. 1983, N.Y. 1987, U.S. Dist. Ct. (ea. dist.) Pa. 1969, U.S. Ct. Appeals (3d cir.) 1970, U.S. Supreme Ct. 1973. Chief asst. dist. atty. Phila. Dist. Atty.'s Office, Pa., 1969—74; assoc. Blank, Rome, Klaus & Comisky, Phila., 1975; chief counsel U.S. Ho. of Reps., Washington, 1975—78; asst. adminstr. NOAA, Washington, 1979—82; dir. ctr. for govtl. responsibility, assoc. prof. law U. Fla. Holand Law Ctr., 1982—86; dean Albany Law Sch., 1986—91, dean emeritus, prof. law, 1991—95; dean U. Tulsa Coll. of Law, Okla., 1995—2004, dean emeritus, prof. law, 2004—. Chmn. Select Commn. on Disabilities, NY, Spl. Commn. on Fire Svcs.; bd. advs. Ctr. Oceans Law and Policy; mem. corrections task force Pa. Gov.'s Justice Commn., 1971—75; adv. task force on cts. Nat. Adv. Commn. on Criminal Justice Standards and Goals, 1972—74; mem. com. on proposed standard jury instrns. Pa. Supreme Ct., 1974—81; lectr. in law Temple U., 1971—75; mem. faculty Pa. Coll. Judiciary, 1975—77; adj. prof. law Georgetown U., 1977—81. Author (with Steven H. Goldblatt): (non-fiction) Analysis and Commentary to the Pennsylvania Crimes Codes, 1973; author: Handbook for Trial Judges, 1976, Law and Theology, 2005, (non-fiction) Rehnquist Court: A Retrospective, 2002; editor (in chief): (jour.) Jour. Transnat. Law, Columbia Law Sch., 1968; editor: The Rehnquist Court: Farewell to the Old Order in the Court, 2002; contbr. articles to legal pubs. Chmn. N.Y. region, mem. D.C. bd. Anti-Defamation League, 1977—78, chmn. N.Y. region, mem. nat. leadership coun.; exec. v.p. Urban League Northeastern N.Y. and Tulsa Urgan League; state chair exec. com. Okla. Anti-Defamation League; mem. Okla. Ethics Commn.; mem. magnet schs.

task force Tulsa Pub. Schs., 2000, mem. woods task force, 2003—04; bd. dirs. Nat. Jewish Coun. on Pub. Affairs; pres. Tulsa Met. Ministry, Jewish Fedn. Tulsa; bd. dirs. Coun. on Aging and Disability; pres. Jewish Fedn.; mem. exec. com Nat. Conf. for Cmty. and Justice. Fellow Intenat., Columbia U. Law Sch.; scholar Stone. Mem.: ABA (del. young lawyers sect. exec. bd. 1973—75), Fund for Modern Cts. (bd. dirs.), Am. Law Inst., Am. Arbitration Assn. (referee N.Y. State Commn. on Jud. Discipline), Am. Soc. Internat. Law, Nat. Dist. Attys. Assn., Am. Judicature Soc. (bd. dirs.), Fed. Bar Assn., Fla. Bar Assn., Pa. Bar Assn. (exec. com. young lawyers sect. 1973—75), Phila. Bar Assn. (chmn. young lawyers sect. 1974—75), Albany County Bar Assn., N.Y. State Bar Assn., United Jewish Fedn. Northeastern N.Y. (v.p., pres. elect), Cardoto Soc., B'nai B'rith (v.p. lodge 1973—75), Sword Soc., Hudson-Mohawk Assn. Coll. and Univs. (v.p.), Temple U. Liberal Arts Alumni Assn. (v.p. 1971—75). Office: U Tulsa Coll Law 3120 E 4th Pl Tulsa OK 74104-2418 Office Phone: 918-631-3199. Business E-Mail: martin-belsky@utulsa.com.

BELSON, ABBY AVIN, writer; b. Bklyn., Apr. 1, 1935; d. Raphael and Molly Avin; m. Joel Jay Belson, June 17, 1956; children: Gabrielle Belson Rattner, Nicole Belson Goluboff. BA, Barnard Coll., N.Y.C., 1956; MA, Columbia U., N.Y.C., 1959. Tchr. N.Y.C. Sch. Sys., 1956—59; adj. lectr. Queens Coll., CUNY, 1961—64; freelance writer, 1970—83; editor med. pubs. Mount Sinai Med. Ctr., N.Y.C., 1983—94; freelance writer, 1994—. Bd. dirs. Conservative Synagogue of Jamaica Estates, Jamaica, NY, 1993—96. Recipient MacEachern award, Pub. Rels. Soc. Am., 1989, Med. Journalism award 1st prize, Sandoz Pharms., 1989, Med. Journalism award, 1991. Mem.: Nat. Assn. Sci. Writers. Avocations: gardening, swimming.

BELSON, JAMES ANTHONY, judge; b. Milw., Sept. 23, 1931; s. Walter W. and Margaret (Taugher) B.; m. Rosemary P. Greenslade, Jan. 11, 1958; children: Anthony James, Marie Taylor, Elizabeth Ann, Stephen Griffin. AB cum laude, Georgetown U., 1953, JD, 1956, LLM, 1962. Bar: D.C. 1956, Md. 1962. Law clk. US Ct. Appeals (DC cir.), 1956-57; assoc. Hogan & Hartson, Washington, 1960-67, ptnr., 1967-68; trial judge DC Superior Ct., Washington, 1968-81, chmn. rules com., 1971—81, presiding judge civil divsn., 1978-81, assoc. judge, 1981-91; sr. judge DC Ct. Appeals, Washington, 1991—. Faculty Nat. Jud. Coll., 1973-80; bd. dirs. Coun. for Ct. Excellence, 1981—; bencher Am. Inn of Ct. VI, 1983-90. Bd. editors Georgetown Law Jour., 1955-56. Bd. dirs. Project SHARE D.C., Inc., 1992—, chmn., 1997-99; bd. dirs. Cath. Legal Immigration Network, 1994-98. With JAGC, U.S. Army, 1957-60. Mem. ABA, Bar Assn. of D.C. (bd. dirs. 1966-67, chmn. jr. bar 1965-66), Am. Judicature Soc. (bd. dirs. 1980-85), Am. Bar Found., John Carroll Soc. (bd. govs. 1978-85, 1st v.p. 1989-91), Sovereign Mil. Order of Malta Fed. Assn. (pres. 1991-94, bd. dirs. 1988-95, 97-2003, chmn. task force on Cuba 1994-2000). Home: 12 W Severn Ridge Rd Annapolis MD 21401-5844 Office: DC Ct Appeals 500 Indiana Ave NW Washington DC 20001-2131 Business E-Mail: jbelson@dcca.state.dc.us.

BELTH, JOSEPH MORTON, retired business educator; b. Syracuse, N.Y., Oct. 22, 1929; s. Irving and Helen Rose (Bright) B.; m. Marjorie Helen Lavine, June 12, 1955; children: Ann Irene, Michael Irving, Jeffrey Edward. AAS., Cayuga Community Coll., 1958; BS summa cum laude, Syracuse U., 1958; PhD, U. Pa., 1961. CLU, CPCU. Asst. purchasing agt. Onondaga Supply Co., Syracuse, N.Y., 1947-53; agt. Continental Am. Life Ins. Co., Syracuse, 1953-58; asst. dir. continuing edn. Am. Soc. Chartered Life Underwriters, Bryn Mawr, Pa., 1961-62; asst. prof. Ind. U., Bloomington, 1962-65, assoc. prof., 1965-68, prof., 1968-93, prof. emeritus, 1993—. Author: Participating Life Insurance Sold by Stock Companies, 1965, The Retail Price Structure in American Life Insurance, 1966; Life Insurance: a Consumer's Handbook, 1973, 2d edit., 1985, The A.L. Williams Replacement Empire, 1987, 2d edit., 1989, Viatical Transactions, 2000; editor newsletter The Ins. Forum, 1974— (George Polk award 1990). Mem. Am. Risk and Ins. Assn. (pres. 1973-74, Elizur Wright award, 1966, Jour. Risk and Ins. awards 1962,64,65,67,71,79), Huebner Gold medal, 1999, AAUP, Beta Gamma Sigma, Phi Kappa Phi. Democrat. Jewish. Home: 5125 N Starnes Rd Bloomington IN 47404-9358

BELTING, HANS, art historian, educator, writer; b. Andernach, Germany, 1935; PhD, U. Mainz, Germany, 1959; LittD (hon.), Courtauld Inst. U. London, 2003. Prof. art history U. Heidelberg, Germany, 1970—80, U. Munich, Germany, 1980—93; prof. art history and media theory Staatliche Hochschule Fur Gestaltung, Karlsruhe, Germany, 1993—2002, prof. emeritus, 2002—; European Chair College de France, 2002—03; Mary Jane Crowe Prof. Art History Northwestern U., Chgo., 2003—. Has held vis. appointments Harvard U., Columbia U.; Getty Vis. Prof., Buenos Aires, 2002. Co-author: Mosaics and Frescoes of St. Mary Pammakaristos (Fethiye Camii) at Istanbul, 1978, Patronage in Thirteenth-Century Constantinople: An Atelier of Late Byzantine Book Illumination and Calligraphy, 1978; author: The End of the History of Art?, 1987, Max Beckmann: Tradition as a Problem in Modern Art, 1990, Likeness and Presence: A History of the Image Before the Era of Art, 1993, The Germans and Their Art: A Troublesome Relationship, 1998, The Invisible Masterpiece: The Modern Myths of Art, 2001, Hieronymus Bosch: The Garden of Earthly Delights, 2002, Art History After Modernism, 2003, Image and Its Public in the Middle Ages: Form and Function of Early Paintings of the Passion, others. Recipient Disting. Lifetime Achievement Award for Writing on Art, Coll. Art Assn., 2004. Mem.: Academia Europaea, Heidelberger Akademie der Wissenschaften, Orden pour le merite fur Wissenschaften und Kunste, Germany, Inst. Advanced Study, Berlin, Am. Acad. Arts and Sciences, Medieval Acad. Am. Office: Northwestern U Dept Art History Kresge Centennial Hall 1880 Campus Dr Evanston IL 60208-2208*

BELTON, BETTY KEPKA, retired art educator, artist; b. Wilson, Kans., Mar. 11, 1934; d. Frank and Rose Betty (Kepka) Hochman; m. Glen S. Belton, 1969 (div. 1974); 1 child, Risa-Marie. BS in Art Edn., Emporia State U., 1956; MS in Art Edn., Ft. Hays State U., 1966. Cert. art tchr., Kans. Jewelry apprentice Ursula Letovsky, Omaha, 1957-60; designer Hallmark Cards, Kansas City, Mo., 1960-62; art tchr. Linn (Kans.) Unified Sch. Dist. 223, 1966-69; murals, design Parsons (Kans.) Jr. High Sch., 1974-75; freelance writer, designer, artist Better Homes and Gardens, Creative Crafts, Woman's Day, Popular Crafts, Eng., 1975-77; inspector El Kan, Ellsworth, Kans., 1977-79; dist. coord., art tchr. Unified Sch. Dist. 328, Wilson, Kans., 1979-98, ret., 1998. Adv. bd. Wilson C. of C., 1980-84, Kans. Scholastic Art Awards, 1991-94; mem. Inst. for Improving Visual Arts in Edn., The Getty Ctr., Cin. Art Mus.; participant, cultural contbr. Smithsonian Instn., Nat. Park Svc., Washington, 1976; workshop leader Kans. State U., Manhattan, 1983; nat. folk art contbr. Kans. Future Homemakers, Reston, Va., 1988; panelist Southwest Regional Rural Arts Conf., Garden City, Kans., 1989, Arts in Edn., Kans. Arts Commn., Salina, 1991; cons. DeCordova Mus. Art, Lincoln, Mass., 1990. Author: Egg Lap Studio and Batiking Method for Making Czechoslovakian Kraslice, 1984; contbr. Crafts in America, 1988, American Folk Masters, 1992; prepresented in collection Internat. Mus. Folk Arts, Santa Fe; atentee lap studio for Czech Kraslice, 1984. Recipient Nat. Heritage fellowship Nat. Endowment Arts, Washington, 1988, Gov.'s award Kans. Gov. Joan Finney, Topeka, 1992, Master Folk Artist Apprenticeship Program, Kans. State Hist. Soc., 1985-86, 87-88, 91-92, Disting. Alumni award Emporia State U., 2002 Mem. NEA, Kans. Art Edn. Assn. (Art Enhancer award 1985), Czech Soc. Arts and Scis., Ellsworth Area Arts Coun. (v.p. 1992-94, adv. bd.). Avocations: czech folklore, history, giving workshops, public speaking, prairie grasses. Home: PO Box 1214 Midland MI 48641 Office Phone: 989-687-6861.

BELTON, ROBERT, law educator; b. 1935; BA, U. Conn., 1961; JD, Boston U., 1965. Bar: N.Y. 1966, N.C. 1970, Tenn. 1980. Asst. counsel legal def. fund NAACP, N.Y.C., 1966-70; ptnr. Chambers, Stein, Ferguson & Lanning, Charlotte, N.C., 1970-75; lectr., dir. fair employment clinic Vanderbilt U., Nashville, 1975-77, assoc. prof., 1977-82, prof., 1982—. Vis. prof. Harvard U. Law Sch., Cambridge, Mass., 1986-87, U. No. Car., 1990-91, Charles Hamilton Houston Disting. vis. prof. N.C. Ctrl. Law Sch., 1997. Author: Remedies in Employment Discrimination Law, 1992; co-author Casebook on Employment Discrimination Law, 1999; contbr. articles to profl. jours. Fellow Coll. Labor and Employment Lawyers, Inc.; mem. ABA, Nat. Bar Assn., Am. Assn. Law Schs. (exec. com. 1991-94), Am. Law Inst., Nat. Employment Lawyers' Assn. (exec. bd. 1996—). Office: Vanderbilt U Sch Law 131- 21st Ave S Nashville TN 37203-1181

BELTON, SHEILA JAN, minister, writer; b. Columbia, S.C., Aug. 18, 1965; d. Albert and Eloise Gibbs Belton. AA, Midlands Tech. Coll., S.C., 1992. Lic. ins. agent. Claims examiner IV Blue Cross & Blue Shield, Columbus, Ohio, 1991—95; ins. rep. Colonial Life & Accident Co., Columbia, SC, 1997—98; ins. sales rep. Conseco Ins. Co., Dallas, 1999—2000; ins. exec. Ind. Contractor, Columbia, SC, 2000—01; assoc. pastor Greenhill Bapt. Ch., Elgin, SD, 2001. Tchr. Greenhill Bapt. Ch., Elgin, SC, 2000—; conf. spkr. Bread of Heaven Ministries, Elgin, SC, 2000—, tchr., radio broacaster, 2001—02. Author: (book) Take Your Mountain, 2003. Food distbr., vol. Harvest Hope Food Bank, Greenhill Bapt. Ch., Elgin, SC, 2002—; conf. spkr. Bread of Heaven Ministries, SC, 2000—. Mem.: Nat. Prog. Bapt. Assn. Baptist. Avocations: reading, travel, music, writing, movies. Home: 11 Mayzola Ct Elgin SC 29045

BELTRAM, NOVELINE ELAINE, assistant principal; b. Providence; d. Henry William and Glennis Elaine Beltram; BS in Music Edn., RI Coll., Providence, 1978; MBA in Mgmt., Bryant U., Smithfield, Conn., 1985; profl. cert. in adminstrn., Sacred Heart U., Fairfield, Conn., 2001. Music educator Thompson Pub. Sch., North Grosvenordale, Conn., 1978—2002; asst. prin. Thompson Middle Sch., North Grosvenordale, 2002—. Mem.: ASCD, Am. Band Dirs. Assn., Conn. Assn. Schs. Avocations: flute, skiing, tennis, gardening, swimming. Home: 1237 Putnam Pike Chepachet RI 02814 Office: Thompson Pub Sch 785 Riverside Dr North Grosvenordale CT 06255

BELTRAN, CARLOS, professional baseball player; b. Manati, P.R., Apr. 24, 1977; m. Jessica Lugo. Player Kansas City Royals, 1998—2004, Houston Astro's, 2004, New York Mets, 2005—. Named to, Am. League All-Star Team, 2004, Nat. League All-Star Team, 2005; recipient Am. League Rookie of the Yr. award, 1999. Office: c/o New York Mets 123 01 Roosevelt Ave Flushing NY 11368

BELTRAN, EUSEBIUS JOSEPH, archbishop; b. Ashley, Pa., Aug. 31, 1934; s. Joseph C. and Helen Rita (Kozlowski) Beltran. Grad., St. Charles Sem., Overbrook, Pa. Ordained priest Roman Cath. Ch., 1960. Consecrated bishop, 1978; pastor various chs., Atlanta and Decatur, Ga., 1960; notary, then vice officialis Atlanta Diocesan Tribunal, 1960—62; vice chancellor Archdiocese Atlanta, 1962; officialis Archdiocesan Tribunal, 1963—74; pastor various chs., Atlanta and Rome, Ga., 1963—66; vicar gen. Archdiocese of Atlanta, 1971—78; pastor St. Anthony's Ch., Atlanta, 1972—78; bishop of Tulsa, 1978—92; archbishop Archdiocese of Okla. City, 1992—. Liturgy com. Nat. Conf. Cath. Bishops; com. mem. Am. Coll., Louvain, Belgium; bd. regents Conception Sem.; bd. dirs. St. Gregory's Coll., Shawnee, Okla. Mem.: NCCJ, Equestrian Order Holy Sepulchre, K.C. Office: Archdiocese of Oklahoma City 7501 NW Espressway Oklahoma City OK 73132-2180*

BELTZ, CHARLES ROBERT, retired engineering executive; b. Pitts., Feb. 23, 1913; s. Charles Fred and Ester (Johnston) B.; m. Amy Margaret Ferguson, Oct. 23, 1935; children: Charles R., A.M. Bonnie Beltz Hatch, Homer F., William T., Carol E. Beltz Marks, M. Joy Beltz O'Keefe. Student, Greenbrier Mil. Sch., 1930-33; MSE, Cornell U., 1934; MS in Aero. Engring., U. Pitts., 1937. Engr. Crane Co., 1937-39; design engr. Stout Skycraft Corp., 1939-43; project engr. Cycle-Weld Labs., 1943-44; project engr., mgr. Fairchild E&A Corp., Roosevelt Field, 1944-46; corp. engr. Chrysler Corp., 1946-47; pres. Charles R. Beltz & Co., Detroit, 1947-85, Beltz Engring., 1950-2001, Beltemp, Inc., 1969-81. Author: Ice Skating, Skating Weather or Not, ABC's Air-conditioning, Roatable Aircraft; designer in field. Mem. Nat. Aero. Assn. (past pres.), Air Conditioning Inst. (past pres.), Inst. Aero. Scis. (vice chmn.), ASHRAE (contbg. author), Engring. Soc. Detroit, Air Force Assn., Grosse Pointe Hist. Soc., English Speaking Union, Air Force Found., Yankee Air Force, Toledo Zool. Soc., Am. Philatelic Soc., Aero Club (bd. dirs.), Econ. Club, Curling Club (Detroit), Grosse Pointe Yacht Club, Lost Lake Woods Club. Address: 500 Lakeland St Grosse Pointe MI 48230-1655

BELTZNER, GAIL ANN, music educator; b. Palmerton, Pa., July 20, 1950; d. Conon Nelson and Lorraine Ann (Carey) Beltzner. BS in Music Edn. summa cum laude, West Chester State U., 1972; postgrad., Kean State Coll., 1972, Temple U., 1972, Westminster Choir Coll., 1972, Lehigh U., 1978. Tchr. music Drexel Hill Jr. H.S., 1972-73; music specialist Allentown (Pa.) Sch. Dist., 1973—; tchr. Corps Sch. and Cmty. Devel. Lab., 1978-80, Corps Cmty. Resource Festival, 1979-81, Corps Cultural Fair, 1980, 81. Mem. bd. assocs. Lehigh Valley Hosp. and Health Network. Mem. Mus. Fine Arts, Boston, aux. Allentown Art Mus., aux. Allentown Hosp.; mem. woman's com. Allentown Symphony, The Lyric Soc. of the Allentown Orch.; mem. Allentown 2nd and 9th Civilian Police Acads.; bd. dirs. Allentown Area Ecumenical Food Bank, Allentown Arts Commn; mem. Growing with Sci. partnership—Air Products and Chems., Inc. and Allentown Sch. Dist., Good Shepherd Home Aux. Decorated Dame Comdr., Ordre Souverain et Militaire de la Milice du St. Sepulcre; recipient Cert. of Appreciation, Lehigh Valley Sertoma Club; Excellence in the Classroom grantee Rider-Pool Found., 1988, 91-92. Mem. AAUW, NAFE, ASCD, Am. String Tchrs. Assn., Am. Viola Soc., Internat. Reading Assn., Internat. Platform Assn., Allentown Edn. Assn., Music Educators Nat. Conf., Pa. Music Educators Assn., Am. Orff-Schulwerk Assn., Orgn. Am. Kodaly Educators, Am. Recorder Soc., Phila. Area Orff-Schulwerk Assn., Soc. Gen. Music, Am. Assn. Music Therapy, Internat. Soc. Music Edn., Internat. Tech. Edn. Assn., Assn. for Tech. in Music Instrn., Civil War Roundtable Ea. Pa., Choristers Guild, Lenni Lenape Hist. Soc., Lehigh Valley Arts Coun., Allentown Symphony Assn., Midi Users Group, Pa.-Del. String Tchrs. Assn., Nat. Sch. Orch. Assn., Lehigh County Hist. Soc., Confedn. Chivalry (life mem. of merit, grand coun.), Maison Internat. des Intellectuels Akademie, Order White Cross Internat. (apptd. dist. comdr. for Pa./U.S.A. dist., nobless of humanity), Airedale Terrier Club of Greater Phila., Kappa Delta Pi, Phi Delta Kappa, Alpha Lambda. Republican. Lutheran. Home: PO Box 4427 Allentown PA 18105-4427

BELUSHI, JAMES A., actor; b. Chgo., June 15, 1954; s. Adam and Agnes Belushi; m. Sandra Davenport, May 17, 1980 (div.); 1 child; m. Marjorie Bransfield, Sept. 22, 1990 (div. 1992); m. Jennifer Sloan, May 2, 1998; 2 children. Student, Coll. DuPage; grad., So. Ill. U. Mem., musician James Belushi & The Sacred Hearts, Blues Brothers Band. Mem. Second City comedy troupe, 1977-78, 80; co-owner (with Dan Aykroyd) House of Blues clubs. Actor: (plays) Under Milkwood, Born Yesterday, Dubwaiter, Sexual Perversity in Chicago, 1979, Baal in the Twenty-first Century, 1980, Pirates of Penzance, 1982, True West, 1983, Moon Over Miami, 1987; (films) About Last Night, 1986—, Little Shop of Horrors, 1986, K-9, 1989, Taking Care of Business, 1990, Mr. Destiny, 1990, Only the Lonely, 1991, Curly Sue, 1991, Diary of a Hitman, 1991, Once Upon a Crime, 1992, Trace of Red, 1992, Separate Lives, 1995, Race the Sun, 1996, Gang Related, 1997, Angel's Dance, 1999, The Florentine, 1999, Made Men, 1999, K-911, 1999, Return to Me, 2000, Joe Somebody, 2001, (also dir.): (TV series) According to Jim, 2001—,: (films) Easy Six, 2003, Behind the Smile, 2004, DysEnchanted, 2004; actor (voice) (films) Nuttiest Nutcracker, 1999, Snow Dogs, 2002; voice overs: (TV series) Bad Baby; Mighty Duck's Duckman; Ahh, Monsters; Animaniacs; Superman; Pinky and the Brain; 3 Little Pigs; Real Monsters; Looie and Louie; Cow & Chicken; voiceovers (TV series) Legend of the Lost Tribe, 2002; voice overs: (TV series) Life with Louie; (films) The Pebble and the Penguin, 1995; Dog's Best Friend, 1997; Babes In Toyland, 1997; Hey Arnold!, 1997; Gargoyles; Felix the Cat; Timon and Pumbaa; The Tick; Bruno the Kid; Hercules; Greedy Show; voiceover (films) Pinocchio, 2002; actor(voiceover): (films) Snow Dogs, 2002; co-author: (films) Number One With a Bullett; writer: TV series Saturday Night Live, 1983—85, TV films Birthday Boy, 1986, films Greedy Show, 2001. Mem. Actors Equity Assn., Screen Actors Guild, AFTRA, Writers Guild Am., Acad. Motion Picture Arts and Scis., Acad. TV Arts and Scis. Office: care ICM 8942 Wilshire Blvd Beverly Hills CA 90211-1934*

BELYTSCHKO, TED, engineering educator; b. Proskurov, Ukraine, Jan. 13, 1943; arrived in U.S.A., 1950; s. Stephan and Maria B.; m. Gail (Eisenhart), Aug. 1967; children: Peter, Nicole, Justine. BS in Engring. Sci., Ill. Inst. Tech., 1965, PhD in Mechanics, 1968; PhD (hon.), U. Liege, 1997; Doctorate (hon.), Ecole Ctrl., Paris, 2004. Asst. prof. structural mechanics U. Ill., Chgo., 1968—73, assoc. prof., 1973—76, prof., 1976—77; Walter P. Murphy prof. civil and mech. engring. Northwestern U., Evanston, Ill., 1977—, chair mech. engring., 1998—2002. Editor (assoc.): (jour.) Computer Methods in Applied Mech. and Engring., 1977—, Jour. Applied Mechanics, 1979—85; editor: Nuc. Engring. and Design, 1980—88, Engring. with Computers, 1984—98, Internat. Jour. Numerical Methods in Engring., 1998—. Chmn. US Nat. Com. on Theoretical and Applied Mechanics, 2005—. NDEA Fellow, 1965-68; recipient Thomas Jaeger prize Internat. Assn. Structural Mechanics in Reactor Tech., 1983; Japanese Soc. Mech. Engr. Computational Mechanics Award, 1993; Gold medal Internat. Conf. on Computational Engring. and Sci., 1996; Computational Mechanics Award, Internat. Assn. for Computational Mechanics, 1998; Gauss Newton medal, 2002. Fellow: ASME (chmn. applied mechanics divsn. 1991, Pi Tau Sigma Gold medal 1975, Timoshenko medal 2001), Am. Acad. Arts and Scis.; mem.: NAE, ASCE (chmn. engring. mechanics divsn. 1982, Walter Huber Rsch. Prize 1977, Structural Dynamics and Materials Award 1990, Theodore von Karman medal 1999), Am. Acad. Mechanics (pres. 2004), Shock and Vibration Inst. (Baron medal 1999), U.S. Assn. Computational Mechanics (pres. 1992—94, von Neumann medal 2001, Computational Structural Mechanics Award 1997). Office: Northwestern Univ Mech Engring Dept 2145 Sheridan Rd Evanston IL 60208-3111 Office Phone: 847-491-7270. Business E-Mail: tedbelytschko@northwestern.edu.

BELZ, ANGELA M., accountant; b. Neceda, Wis., Dec. 31, 1978; d. Joseph R. and Mary A. Zwirlein; m. Matthew R. Belz, July 10, 2004; 1 child, Logan N. Woods. BBA (hon.), Ottawa U., 2004. Specialist accounts receivable Kleen Test Products, Port Washington, Wis., 2002—04; acct. Bus. Office Concordia U., Mequon, Wis., 2004—. Mem.: Wis. Coll. Pers. Administrs. (assoc.), Nat. Assn. Student Pers. Administrs. (assoc.). Home: 678 South 7th Ave West Bend WI 53095 Office Phone: 262-243-4556.

BELZ, JULIE ANNE, language educator; b. Ill. BS, U. of Ill., 1986; MA, U. of Calif., 1990, PhD, 1997. English instr. Fulbright Tchg. Fellowship, Vienna, 1987—88; german instr. U. of Calif., Berkeley, 1988—93; rschr. Berkeley (Calif.) Lang. Ctr., 1996—97; dir. german lang. program U. of Ariz., Tucson, 1997—98; asst. prof. of applied linguistics and german Pa. State U., U. Pk., Pa., 1998—. Rschr. Ctr. for Lang. Acquisition, U. Pk., 2000—; rschr. Ctr. for Advanced Lang. Proficiency Edn. and Rsch. Pa. State U., 2002—. Guest editor: Lang. Learning and Tech.: Telecollaboration, 2003; author: Foreign Language Play and the Discursive Construction of Identity; contbr. articles to profl. jours.;, editor volumes. Fellow Fgn. Lang. and Area Studies fellowship, U.S. Dept. of Edn., 1991—92, U. of Calif. at Berkeley, 1996, Instrnl. Devel. fellowship, Berkeley (Calif.) Lang. Ctr., U. of Calif., 1996—97; grantee Internat. Studies and Rsch. grant, U.S. Dept. of Edn., 2000—03, Nat. Fgn. Lang. Rsch. Ctr. grant, 2002—; scholar, The Rotary Found. Internat., 1986—87, Fulbright Found., 1987—88, Deutscher Akademischer Austauschdienst, 1995. Mem.: MLA (exec. com. of the divsn. on applied linguistics 2001—), Am. Assn. for Applied Linguistics, Am. Assn. of Tchrs. of German, Phi Beta Kappa. Office: Penn State University 311 Burrowes Building University Park PA 16802 E-mail: jab63@psu.edu.

BELZER, IRVIN V., lawyer; b. Kansas City, Apr. 6, 1948; BA, Oberlin Coll., 1970; JD cum laude, U. Mo., Kansas City, 1976. Bar: Mo. 1976. Atty. Smith, Gill, Fisher & Butts, Kansas City; mng. ptnr., group co-leader comml. litig. Bryan Cave LLP, Kansas City. Mem. bd. editors: U. Mo. at Kansas City Law Rev., 1975-76; cases and statutes editor: The Urban Lawyer, 1975-76. Mem. ABA, Mo. Bar, Lawyers Assn. Kansas City, Comml. Law League Am., Order of Bench and Robe. Office: Bryan Cave LLP One Kansas City Pl 1200 Main St, Ste 3500 Kansas City MO 64105 Office Phone: 816-391-7677. E-mail: ivbelzer@bryancave.com.

BEMENT, ARDEN LEE, JR., science foundation director; b. Pitts., May 22, 1932; s. Arden Lee and Edith Ardelia (Bigelow) B.; m. Mary Ann Baroch, Aug. 24, 1952 (dec.); children: Kristine, Kenneth, Vincent, Cynthia, Mark, David, Paul, Mary; m. Louise Coquestrain, June 15, 2001. Degree of Engr. in Metallurgy, Colo. Sch. Mines, 1954; MSMetE, U. Idaho, 1959; PhD, U. Mich., 1963; PhD honoris causa, Cleve. State U., 1997, Case Western Res. U., 2002. Rsch. metallurgist Hanford Labs., GE, Richland, Wash., 1954-65; sr. rsch. mgr. Pacific N.W. Lab., Battelle Meml. Inst., Richland, 1965-70; prof. nuc. materials MIT, 1970-76; dir. Def. Advanced Rsch. Projects Agy. Office Materials Sci., DARPA, DOD, Washington, 1976-79, dep. undersec. rsch. and advanced tech., 1979-80; v.p. tech. resources TRW, Lyndhurst, Ohio, 1980-89, v.p. sci. and tech., 1990-92; Basil S. Turner disting. prof. engring. Purdue U., West Lafayette, Ind., 1992-98, head sch. nuc. engring., 1998—2001; dir. Nat. Inst. Standards & Tech., Gaithersburg, Md., 2001—04; acting dir. NSF, Arlington, Va., 2004, dir, 2004—. Tech. assistance expert to Mexico UNI-AEA, 1974-76; cons. NRC, Taiwan, 1975; mem. Nat. Sci. Bd., 1988-94; mem. sci. adv. com. Electric Power Rsch. Inst., 1987—, Advanced Tech. Inc., 1993—. Author publs. in field; editor: Biomaterials: Structural and Biomedical Bases for Hard Tissue and Soft Tissue Substitutes, 1971; co-editor: Dislocation Dynamics, 1968, Creep of Zirconium Alloys in Nuclear Reactors, 1983; mem. editl. bd. Jour. Nuclear Materials, 1970-77, Materials Tech., 1987-99; contbr. articles to profl. jours. Chmn. bd. health Mental Health/Mental Retardation, Benton-Franklin Counties, Wash., 1968-70; mem. Richland, Wash. city coun., 1968-70; pres. Arts Coun., Richland, Pasco and Kennewick, Wash., 1968-70; bd. dirs. Cleve. Opera Bd., treas., 1982-86, v.p., 1986-91, nat./internat. bd. mem., 1992—; bd. dirs. LaFayette Symphony, 1998—; bd. overseers Fermi Nat. Accelerator Lab., 1999—. Lt. col. USAR, 1954-79. Recipient Outstanding Achievement award Colo. Sch. Mines, 1984, Melville F. Coolbaugh award, 1991, Disting. Engr. award UCLA, 1987, Honor Roll award U. Idaho Alumni Assn., 1991, Engring. Alumnus of Yr. award U. Mich. Alumni Assn. (Cleve. br.), 1992, Merit award U. Mich. Alumni Assn., 1993, Nat. Mats. Adv. award Fedn. of Mats. Socs., 1997. Fellow Am. Nuclear Soc., Am. Soc. Metals (Disting. Life mem. 1998), Am. Inst. Chemists; mem. Nat. Acad. Engrs., ASTM, AIME, Am. Acad. Arts & Sci., Metals Soc. of AIME (Leadership award 1988, life mem. 2000), Sigma Xi, Tau Beta Pi, Sigma Gamma Epsilon. Republican. Roman Catholic. Office: NSF Office Legis Pub Affairs 4201 Wilson Blvd Arlington VA 22230 Office Phone: 301-975-2300.*

BEMIS, MARY FERGUSON, magazine editor; b. N.Y.C., Dec. 28, 1961; d. Edmund Augustus and Anne Adoian (Nalbandian) Bemis. BFA in Writing, Johnson State Coll., 1983. Co-editor, co-pub. Ave. Literary Rev. Ave. Publs. Inc., Burlington, Vt., 1983-85; editor Unique Hair and Beauty Mag., 1994; editor Lady's Circle Mag. Lopez Publs., N.Y.C., 1987-94, editor, 1989-94; freelance editor, writer Mus. Sci., Boston, 1991-93; freelance editor Woman's Day Spl. Interest Publs., 1996—98; sr. editor Am. Salon and Am. Spa Mags., 1988—; editor-in-chief Am. Spa Mag., 1998—2003; bd. dirs. Internat. Spa Assn., 2003; spa reporter, founder Founder Insider's Guide to Spas, 2004—. Spa adviser Shape mag., 2004. Co-editor: The Green Mountain Rev., 1982—83, Nature Through Her Eyes: Art and Literature by Women, 1994, Journey Into the Wilderness, 1994; contbg. editor: Luxury Spa Finder mag., 2004. Mem.: Am. Soc. of Mag. Editors. Democrat. Unitarian Universalist. Home and Office: 532 W 25th St #FL 2 New York NY 10001-5502 E-mail: MFBEMIS@aol.com.

BEMIS, MICHAEL B., utility company executive; b. Pascagoula, Miss., Mar. 24, 1947; s. James E. and Mary I. (Rowell) Loris; m. Elizabeth Ann Welfare, May 2, 1982 BS, U. So. Miss., 1969. C.P.A., Ark., La., Miss., N.C. Staff acct. Deloitte Haskins & Sells, New Orleans, 1970-72, sr. acct., 1972-75, mgr., 1975-79, ptnr., 1979-81, ptnr. in charge acctg. and audit services, 1981-82; sr. v.p., sec., asst. treas. Ark. Power & Light Co., Little Rock, 1982—. Vice chmn. Econ. Devel. Council, Little Rock C. of C.; bd. dirs. Ark.

Arthritis Found., First Ark. Devel. Fin. Corp., Little Rock. Mem. Am. Inst. C.P.A.s, Ark. Soc. C.P.A.s Avocation: golf. Office: Ark Power & Light Co PO Box 551 Little Rock AR 72203-0551 also: Miss Power & Light Co PO Box 1640 Jackson MS 39215-1640

BENABOU, ROLAND JEAN-MARC, economist, educator; Degree in Engring., Ecole Poly., 1980, Ecole Nat. des Ponts et Chaussées, 1982; PhD, MIT, 1986. Prof. econs. and pub. affairs Princeton (N.J.) U., 1999—; chargé de rsch. Ctr. Nat. de la Rsch. Sci., CEPREMAP, Paris, 1986—88; asst. prof. econs. MIT, Mass., 1988—92, assoc. prof. econs., 1992—94, NYU, NY, 1994—96, prof. econs., 1996—99; prof. econs. and pub. affairs dept. econs., Woodrow Wilson Sch. Pub. and Internat. Affairs Princeton (N.J.) U., 1999—. Vis. prof. U. Paris X-Nanterre, France, 1995, IDEI, Toulouse, France, 1997—99, CERAS, Paris, 1997—99; mem. Sch. Social Sci., Inst. for Advanced Studies Princeton U., NJ, 2002—03; lectr. in field. Assoc. editor: Jour. Econ. Growth, 1995—, Macroeconomic Dynamics, 1997—, Quarterly Jour. Econs., 1997—2001, QR Jour. Macroeconomics, 2000—, Jour. Pub. Econs., 2000—, Jour. European Econ. Assn., 2003—, fgn. editor: Rev. Econ. Studies, 1993—2001, overseas assoc. editor: European Econ. Rev., 1994—2000, mem. editl. bd.: Annals d'Economie et de Statistique, 1993—. Fellow, Guggenheim Found., 2003; grantee, NSF, 1990—92, 1992—94, 1996—99, 2001—; sr. fellow, Bur. for Rsch. and Econ. Analysis of Devel., 2002—. Fellow: Econometric Soc.; mem.: Inst. for Rsch. on Poverty (assoc.). Office: Woodrow Wilson Sch Pub and Internat Affairs Princeton Univ Princeton NJ 08544

BENACERRAF, BARUJ, pathologist, educator; b. Caracas, Venezuela, Oct. 29, 1920; arrived in US, 1939, naturalized, 1943; s. Abraham and Henriette (Lasry) Benacerraf; m. Annette Dreyfus, Mar. 24, 1943; 1 child, Beryl. B es L, Lycee Janson, 1940; BS, Columbia U., 1942; MD, Med. Sch. Va., 1945; MA, Harvard U., 1970; MD (hon.), U. Geneva, 1980; DSc (hon.), NYU, 1981, Va. Commonwealth U., 1981, Yeshiva U., 1982, U. Aix-Marseille, 1982, Columbia U., 1985, Adelphi U., 1988, Weizmann Inst., 1989, Harvard U., 1992, U. Bordeaux, 1993, U. Vienna, 1995. Intern Queens Gen. Hosp., NYC, 1945—46; rsch. fellow dept. microbiology Med. Sch. Columbia U., 1948—50; charge de recherches Centre Nat. de Recherche Scientique Hosp. Broussais, Paris, 1950—56; asst. prof. pathology Sch. Medicine NYU, 1956—58, assoc. prof. Sch. Medicine, 1958—60, prof. Sch. Medicine, 1960—68; chief immunology Nat. Inst. Allergy and Infectious Diseases NIH, Bethesda, Md., 1968—70; Fabyan prof. comparative pathology, chmn. dept. Med. Sch. Harvard U., 1970—91; ret. Med. Sch., Harvard U., Cambridge, Mass., 1991. Pres, CEO Dana-Farber Cancer Inst, 1980—91, Dana-Farber Inc, 1990—95; mem immunology study sect NIH; pres Fedn Am Socs Experimental Biol, 1974—75; chmn sci adv comt Centre d'Immunologies de Marseille, France. Bd govs Weizmann Inst Med; mem sci adv comt Children's Hosp, Boston; mem award comt GM Cancer Research Found, chmn selection comt Sloan Prize, 1980. Capt MC AUS, 1946—48. Recipient T Duckett Jones Meml Award, Helen Hay Whitney Found, 1976, Rabbi Shai Shacknai Lectr and Prize, Hebrew Univ Jerusalem, 1974, Waterford Award, 1980, Nobel Prize, 1980, Corr, Emerite de l'Institut de la Sante et de la Rcherche Scientifique, Nat Medal Sci, NSF, 1990. Fellow: Am Acad Arts and Scis; mem.: NAS, Int Union Immunology Socs (pres 1980—83), French Soc Biol Chemistry, Brit Asn Immunology, Am Asn Immunologists (pres 1973—74), Nat Inst Med. Office: Dana-Farber Cancer Inst 44 Binney St Boston MA 02115-6084

BENACK, CLAUDIA JANE, music educator (voice), singer; b. Pitts., Oct. 10, 1958; d. John Francis and Dorothy Margaret (Schnorr) C.; m. Ben Edward Benack, Jr.; children: Laura Emily, Ben Edward III. BFA, Carnegie-Mellon U., Pitts., 1980, MFA, 1983. Adj. instr. Carnegie Mellon U., Pitts., 1980-86, 94-96; singer, chorus leader Benny Benack Band, Pitts., 1976—; leading soprano Opera Theatre of Pitts., Pitts., 1982—; chorister and small roles Pitts. Opera, 1980-86; soprano soloist Rodef Shalom Temple, Pitts., 1983-92, Shadyside Presbyn., Pitts., 1992-98; pvt. voice instr. Pitts., 1980—; singer Dear Friends, Pitts., 1986—; lectr. in voice Carnegie-Mellon U., Pitts., 1997—. Probation counselor Carnegie Mellon, Pitts., 1997—. Mem. Welcome Wagon, 1987-94, Newcomers of Upper St. Clair, Pa., 1987-93, pres. 1991-92. 1st prize Nat., MTNA, 1983; 8th prize NSAL, 1987, 1st prize Regionals, NATS, 1979, 80. Mem. Music Tchrs. Nat. Assn. (1st prize Nats. 1983), Nat. Soc. Arts Letters (8th prize 1987), Nat. Assn. Tchrs. Singing (1st prize regionals 1979, 80), Sigma Alpha Iota. Democrat. Presbyterian. Home: 2500 Corteland Dr Pittsburgh PA 15241-2528 Office: Carnegie-Mellon U Drama Dep 5000 Forbes Ave Pittsburgh PA 15213-3815

BEN-AKIVA, MOSHE EMANUEL, civil engineering educator; b. Tel Aviv, June 11, 1944; came to U.S., 1968; s. Eliezer and Rivka (Reiner) B.A.; children: Ori, Lea, Danna, Elana, Erez. BSCE, Technion-Israel Inst. Tech., Haifa, 1968; MSCE, MIT, 1971, PhD in Transp. Systems, 1973; docteur honoris causa, U. Lumiere Lyon, France, 1992; Doctorate (hon.), U. of the Aegean, 2000. Registered profl. engr., Israel. Edmund K. Turner prof. civil engring. MIT, Cambridge, Mass., 1973-96. Vis. prof. Technion-Israel Inst. Tech., Haifa, 1978—79, Haifa, 1981—82, Tel Aviv, 1981—82; vis. scholar NTT Rsch. Labs., 1988; cons. Am. Airlines, 1987; Atty. Gen. Mass., Boston, 1985—88, The Hague Cons. Group, 1985—2000, Cambridge Systematics, Inc., 1972—, RAND, 2001—. Editor-in-chief: Transport Policy; assoc. editor: Transp. Science Lady Davis fellow Technion-Israel Inst. Tech., 1978. Mem. Transp. Rsch. Bd., Transp. Rsch. Forum, Regional Sci. Assn., Ops. Rsch. Soc. Am. (award 1973), World Conf. on Transp. Rsch. Soc. Office: MIT 77 Massachusetts Ave Rm 1-181 Cambridge MA 02139-4307 E-mail: mba@mit.edu.

BENAMATI, DENNIS CHARLES, librarian, editor, consultant; b. Orlando, Fla., Oct. 30, 1948; s. Thomas Guy and Ann (Clements) B.; m. Evelina Estella Lemelin, Aug. 19, 1983; children: Suzette, Alicia, Marcus. BA, St. Francis Coll., Loretto, Pa., 1970; MA, Fordham U., 1974; MLS, So. Conn. State U., 1975. Law libr. Conn. State Libr., Stamford, 1976-78; reference libr. U. Bridgeport (Conn.) Sch. Law, 1979; asst. law libr. for tech. svcs. U. Maine Sch. Law, Portland, 1979-83; asst. law libr. Aetna Life & Casualty Co., Hartford, Conn., 1983-84; head cataloging U. Conn. Sch. Law, Hartford, 1984-88; dir. The Dewey Grad. Libr. SUNY, Albany, 1988-93; adj. faculty Sch. Criminal Justice, SUNY, Albany, 1993—95; vis. elec. info. svcs. libr., instr. advanced legal rsch. U. S.C. Sch. Law, 1995—97; asst. libr. dir. Marist Coll., 1997—2002, adj. instr. criminal justice dept., interim libr. dir., adj. instr. Sch. Mgmt., 2000—02; libr. Sacred Heart U., Fairfield, Conn., 2002—. Ptnr. Lemelin & Benamati; cons., Nassau, N.Y., 1985—; cons. to various law firms, Lawyers Coop. Pub. Co., European Inst. for Crime Prevention and Control. Co-author: Publication Opportunities for Law Librarians, 1995, Criminal Justice Information: How to Find It, How to Use It, 1998; rapporteur World Criminal Justice Libr. Network Conf., 1997, 99, 2001, 04; contbr. articles to profl. jours. Mem. ALA, Assn. Coll. & Rsch. Librs., Am. Assn. Law Librs., Law Librs. New England (bd. dirs. 1985-87). Roman Catholic. Mailing: 358 Kingman Rd Nassau NY 12123 Office Phone: 203-371-7700. E-mail: benamatid@sacredheart.edu.

BEN-AMI, LEORA, lawyer; BS, SUNY, Stony Brook; JD cum laude, SUNY, Buffalo. Law clk. to Sr. Circuit Judge Philip Nichols, Jr., US Ct. Appeals Fed. Circuit, 1984—85; ptnr. Clifford Chance, chair Am. Intellectual Property Group; ptnr. Kaye Scholer LLP, 2003—. Spkr. on patent law at conferences and seminars. Contbr. articles in field. Named one of 45 under 45, Am. Lawyer Media, 2003. Mem.: Am. Intellectual Property Law Assn., NY Patent, Trademark and Copyright Law Assn., Fed. Circuit Bar Assn., NY State Bar Assn. Office: 425 Park Ave New York NY 10022-3598 Office Phone: 212-836-8000. Office Fax: 212-836-8689. Business E-Mail: lbenami@kayscholer.com.

BEN-ARIE, RONIT PELEG, elementary school educator; arrived in U.S., 1989; d. Israel and Edith Popovich; m. Jezekiel Ben-Arie, Nov. 17, 1983. BA, Haifa (Israel) U., 1985; postgrad., Oranim Tchrs. Sem., Israel, 1986; MA, Lesley Coll., 1988. Music and art therapist in charge of expressive arts rehab. programs Fliman Rehab. Geriatric Hosp., Haifa, 1985—89; music and arts therapist Ill. Masonic Hosp. Ctr., Warren Barr Pavilion, Chgo., 1989—92; instr. tchrs. Jewish Fedn., Chgo., 1998—2000; tchr., kindergarten curriculum developer Solomon Schechter Day Schs., Skokie and Northbrook, 1992—. Composer included in nat. curricula Union of Am. Hebrew Congregations; presenter, spkr. in field. *Currently recording "Hello World," a collection of songs for young children. These songs teach math, English poetry and social studies through music, drama, movement and games.* Composer: Songs in Easy Hebrew, 1996, Hebrew in Song, 2000 (No. 1 rating in Jewish and Yiddish music, Amazon.com, 01, No. 1 rating in Israeli style music, Amazon.com, 01), Hello World, 2005. Advocacy group organizer, convenor Conf. on Alternatives in Jewish Edn., Chgo., 2002. Lt. Israeli Def. Forces, 1977—80. Recipient songs selected to be part of nat. music curricula, Union Am. Hebrew Congregations. Avocations: ceramic sculpture, painting, reading, ballroom dancing, bicycling. Home: 155 N Harbor Dr Apt 2011 Chicago IL 60601 Office: Solomon Schechter Day Schs 3210 Dundee Rd Northbrook IL 60062 Office Phone: 847-412-5600. E-mail: rbenarie@yahoo.com.

BENARIO, HERBERT WILLIAM, classicist, educator; b. NYC, July 21, 1929; s. Frederick and Ilse (Kessler) Benario; m. Janice M. Martin, Dec. 23, 1957; children: Frederick M., John H. BA, CCNY, 1948; MA, Columbia U., 1949; PhD, Johns Hopkins U., 1951. Instr. Greek and Latin Columbia U., 1953-58; asst. prof. Greek and Latin Sweet Briar Coll., 1958-60; mem. faculty Emory U., Atlanta, 1960—, prof. classics, 1967-87, chmn. dept., 1968-73, 76-78, prof. emeritus, 1987, disting. fellow emeritus, 2001—02. Dir. Vergilian Soc. Summer Sch., Italy, 1963, Italy, 67, Italy, 73, Italy, 81, asst. dir., Italy, 57, Italy, 59; dir. Roman Britain Tour, 1977, 86, Roman Germany Tour, 1981, 88, Rome and North Italy, 1982, Roman Germany Tour Mediterranean Soc., 1998, North Italy Tour Mediterranean Soc., 1999; vis. prof. Intercollegiate Ctr. Classical Studies, Rome, 1967, co-prof. in charge, 1984—85; vis. prof. U. Colo., 1969, Brigham Young U., 1999; Fulbright Sr. prof. U. Passau, Germany, 1990; co-exec. sec. Vergilian Soc., 1992—93; mem. Latin achievement test com. Coll. Entrance Exam. Bd., 1963—66. Author: (book) Tacitus, Agricola, Germany, Dialogue on Orators, 1967, Tacitus, Agricola, Germany, Dialogue on Orators, rev. edit., 1991, An Introduction to Tacitus, 1975, A Commentary on the Vita Hadriani in the Historia Augusta, 1980, Tacitus Annals 11 and 12, 1983, The Classical Association of the Middle West and South, 1989, Caesaris Augusti Res Gestae et Fragmenta, 1990, Thusnelda: A German Princess in Ancient Rome, 1993, Tacitus Germany, 1999; co-editor: Basil Lanneau Gildersleeve: An American Classicist, 1986. With AUS, 1951—53. Fellow Am. Coun. Learned Soc., 1978, Heilbrun, Emory U., 2002; grantee Fulbright, 1956, Rsch., Am. Philos. Soc. Mem.: Classical Soc. Am. Acad. Rome (pres. 1965), Am. Classical League, Vergilian Soc. Am. (trustee 1960—65, 1969—73, pres. 1980—82), Classical Assn. Midwest and South (pres.so. sect. 1968—70, pres. 1971—72), Am. Philological Assn., Phi Beta Kappa (pres. Emory U. chpt. 1968—69). Home: 1717 N Decatur Rd NE #119 Atlanta GA 30307 Office: Emory U Classics Dept Atlanta GA 30322-0001 Personal E-mail: hwbenario@yahoo.com.

BEN-ASHER, DANIEL LAWRENCE, retired legislative staff member, photojournalist; b. Newark, Apr. 15, 1946; s. Jerry and Florence (Tasoff) Ben-Asher; m. Michele Lauren Cohn, July 16, 1978; children: Sarah, Joshua. AB, Rutgers Coll., 1968; MA, U. Minn., 1970. Plant pers. adminstr. Tanatex Chem. Co. divsn. Sybron Corp., Lyndhurst, NJ, 1970-71; rsch. asst. Office Legis. Svcs. N.J. State Legislature, Trenton, 1971-76, rsch. assoc., 1976-87, sr. rsch. assoc., 1987-98, sr. rsch. analyst, 1999—2003; freelance photojournalist NJ, 2005—. Staff N.J. Assembly Labor Com., 1974—81, Assembly Commerce and Industry Com., 1981—82, Assembly Drug and Alcohol Abuse Policy Com., 1990—91, Assembly Housing Com., 1995; mem. N.J. Tobacco Age-of-Sale Enforcement Task Force, 1994—96; mem. politics and govt. judges panel Best in Am. spl. edit. U.S. News and World Report, 1990. Mem. Ewing Twp. (N.J.) Rent Control Bd., 1976—77; fin. coord. Lawrence Twp. (N.J.) Hist. Preservation Adv. Com., 1985—92; twp. chmn. Guide Lawrenceville's Hist. Landmarks, 1991—93; mem. nat. alumni adv. com. admissions Rutgers U., New Brunswick, alumni admissions rep., 1994—2001, chmn. Mason Gross Presdl. Meml., 1992—94. Recipient Loyal Son award for Extraordinary Svc. to Alma Mater, Rutgers Alumni Assn., 1995. Home: 11 Bennington Dr Lawrenceville NJ 08648-1536 E-mail: Legisdan@aol.com.

BEN-ASHER, M. DAVID, physician; b. Newark, June 18, 1931; s. Samuel Irving and Dora Ruth (Kagan) Ben-Asher; m. Bryna S. Zeller, Nov. 22, 1956. BA, Syracuse U., 1952; MD, U. Buffalo Sch. Med., 1956. Intern E.J. Meyer Mem. Hosp., Buffalo, 1956-57; resident Jersey City Med. Ctr., 1957-58; asst. chief med. service U.S. Army Hosp., Ft. McPherson, Ga., 1958-60; resident Madigan Gen. Hosp., Tacoma, 1960-62; chief gen. med. service Walson Army Hosp., Ft. Dix, NJ, 1962-64; attending staff St. Mary's Hosp., Tucson, 1964—; pvt. practice, 1964—. Bd. dir. Tucson Symphony, 1971-73; mem. Ariz. State Bd. Med. Examiners, 1978-88, joint bd. for regulation of physicians' assts., 1990-97; bd. trustees United Synagogue Am., 1981-87, nat. adv. bd., 1987-91. Fellow ACP; mem. AMA, Pima County Med. Soc. (bd. dir. 1971-77, pres. 1976), Ariz. Med. Assn., Am. Soc. Nephrology. Democrat. Avocations: health club, music, computers. Home: 3401 N Tanuri Dr Tucson AZ 85750-6735 Office: So Ariz Med Specialists 4733 N 1st Ave Tucson AZ 85718-5610 Office Phone: 520-888-3032.

BENATAR, LEO, packaging company executive; b. Atlanta, Feb. 21, 1930; s. Morris H. and Mary (Levy) B.; m. Louise Cure, Sept. 2, 1956; children: Morris L., Ann Marie, Ruth Eileen. B. Indsl. Engring., Ga. Inst. Tech., 1951; postgrad., Rochester Inst. Tech., 1956, Harvard Bus. Sch., 1970. Formerly pres. Mead Packaging Co., Atlanta; chmn. Engraph, Inc., Atlanta. Bd. dirs. Sonoco Products Co., Johns Manville Corp., Interstate Bakeries Corp., Mohawk Industries, Inc., Aaron Rents, Inc.; past mem. internat. adv. coun. Trust Co. Ga., Trust Co. Bank; past mem. adv. bd. Arkwright-Boston Ins.; past chmn. Fed. Res. Bank Atlanta. Past bd. dirs. Rsch. Atlanta, Jr. Achievement, ARC, Nat. Minority Purchasing Coun., Keep Am. Beautiful, Peachtree Corners; past bd. visitors Emory U.; bd. dirs. Atlanta Partnership Bus. and Edn., Ga. Coun. on Econ. Edn.; steering com. Nat. Found. Ileitis and Colitis; past indsl. mgmt. adv. coun., nat. adv. bd. Ga. Inst. Tech.; mem. adv. coun. Coll. Bus. Adminstrn., Ga. State U.; mem. alumni adv. bd. Sch. Indsl. and Systems Engring. Ga. Tech.; bd. trustees Ga. Tech. Found.; past chmn. Pvt. Industry Coun.; past mem. DeKalb Reorgn. Com., Ga. Bd. Industry and Trade. With USN, 1951-53. Recipient Arcdiocesan medal of St. Paul Greek Orthodox Archdiocese of North and South Am.; Lion of Judah award, Cmty. Achievement award ORT. Mem. Bus. Coun. Ga., Nat. Alliance Bus. (past chmn. Met. Atlanta, bd. dirs.), Japan-Am. Soc. Ga., Commerce Club, Standard Club, Buckhead Club. Home and Office: 121 Burdette Rd NW Atlanta GA 30327-4803*

BENATAR, PAT (PAT ANDRZEJEWSKI), rock singer; b. Bklyn., 1953; m. Neil Geraldo; 1 child, Haley. Albums include: In the Heat of the Night, 1979, Crimes of Passion, 1980, Precious Time, 1981, Get Nervous, 1982, Live From Earth, 1983, Tropico, 1984, Seven the Hard Way, 1985, Wide Awake in Dreamland, 1988, Best Shots, 1989, True Love, 1991, Gravity's Rainbow, 1993, All Fired Up: The Very Best of Pat Benatar, 1994, Heartbreaker: 16 Classic Performances, 1996, Innamorata, 1997, 8-15-80, 1998, Synchronistic Wanderings: Recorded Anthology 1979-99, 1999, Live at Electric Ladyland, 2002, Greatest Hits Live, 2003, Go, 2003; popular recs. include Treat Me Right, Hit Me With Your Best Shot, Love is a Battlefield, Hell is for Children. Recipient Grammy award for best female rock vocal performance, 1981, 82, 83, 84 Office: 584 N Larchmont Blvd Los Angeles CA 90004 also: Gold Mountain Mgmt care Danny Goldberg 2575 Cahuenga Blvd W # 470 Los Angeles CA 90068-2102

BENAVENTE, DIEGO T., lieutenant governor; b. Saipan, Apr. 21, 1959; Grad., Northern Mariana Islands Police Academy, 1977; stud., College of S. Idaho. Mem. N. Mariana Islands Leg., 1990—2002, spkr., 1996—2002; lt. gov. Commonwealth of No. Marianas Islands. Republican. Office: Office of the Governor Isa Dr Capitol Hill Caller Box 10007 Saipan MP 96950

BENAVENTE, JAVIER EDGAR, venture technology executive; b. Chgo., July 20, 1959; s. Javier and Rebecca (Davis) B.; m. Theresa Lucille Augsback, July 28, 1984; children: Javier Christopher, Alexandria Joann, Jeremy Edward. B Aero./Astron.Engring., Purdue U., 1986, M in Astron. Engring., 1987; M Engring. Mgmt., Fla. Inst. Tech., 1989, MBA, 1990. Restaurant mgr. Orlando (Fla.) Marriott Inn, 1980, 81; asst. food and beverage dir. Holiday Inn Fannies, Richmond, Va., 1981; innkeeper Holiday Inn Beachside, Panama City Beach, Fla., 1981-82; mem. tech. staff Hughes Space and Comms., El Segundo, Calif., 1986-87; engr. mgr. Dynacs Engring. Co., Inc., Clearwater, Fla., 1988-92, sr. engr., mgr. bus. devel., 1992-93, v.p., gen. mgr., 1993-95; pres. Dynacs Digital Studios, L.A., 1995—98; v.p. Dynacs Inc., 1998—2000; CEO, pres. Tech-Lind Solutions, LLC, 2001—. Program mgr./tech. lead on numerous engring. projects inluding the devel. of systems engring. analysis tools, docking and berthing dynamics, multi-body dynamic simulation software, neural network techs., computer animation, multi-media technologies and telecomms. technologies, interactive media, digital ink and paint and film colorization; bd. dirs. CST Entertainment. Contbr. papers, revs. to profl. jours. and mags. Mentor Pinellas County Intership, Clearwater, 1993; coach Countryside Little League, Clearwater, 1993, 94, Countryside Soccer Assn., Clearwater, 1993, 94; mem. Pinellas County Urban League, St. Petersburg, Fla., 1994. Fellow Hughes Aircraft, 1986-87, Ford Found., 1988. Mem. AIAA, IEEE. Avocations: skiing, scuba diving, travel, camping, robotics. Home: 2738 Poppyseed Ct Clearwater FL 33761-1221 Office: Dynacs Engring 28870 Us Highway 19 N Ste 405 Clearwater FL 33761-2593

BEN-AVI, SIMON STEPHEN, biomedical researcher, educator; s. Harold Barber and Annabelle Cynthia Bevan; m. Nina Ben-Avi (div.); children: Julia Caroline, Emma Hannah. BS with honors, U. Manchester Inst. Sci. and Tech., 1972, MS, 1973; PhD, Queen Victoria U. Manchester, 1979. Prof. computer sci. N.Y. Inst. Tech., N.Y.C.; prof. elec. engring. Cooper Union, 1984—; ednl. cons. AT&T Bell Labs., Holmdel, 1986—92; biomedical cons. Lenox Hill Hosp., N.Y.C., 1994—; assoc. dean engring. Cooper Union Sci. and Art, 1998—. Rschr. Lenox Hill Hosp., 1986—. Musician: (organist) Church Organist. Dir. curf Cooper Union Rsch. Found., N.Y.C., 2000—. Grantee, NSF, 1985—2005. Mem.: IEE, ACM, IEEE, Inst. Elec. and Radio Engineers, Brit. Computer Soc. Achievements include research in Multiple Research Papers; Biomedical research. Office: The Cooper Union Sci and Art 51 Astor Pl New York NY 10023 Office Phone: 212-353-4346. Home Fax: 212-353-4341; Office Fax: 212-353-4341. Personal E-mail: benavi@cooper.edu.

BENAVIDES, CHRISTOPHER, special education educator; b. Oregon, Ohio, Aug. 4, 1960; s. Henry and Nancy Benavides. BA, U. Southern Calif., 1983; MEd, Fla. Atlantic U., 1993. Cert. profl. educator, profl. achieve. cert. Nat. Assn. for Gifted Children. Tchr. Palm Beach County Sch. Dist., West Palm Beach, Fla., 1993—94, enrichment tchr., 1994—2002, gifted resource tchr., 2002—03, resource tchr., 2003—. Mem. Nat. Assn. for Gifted Children Edn. Commn., Wash., DC, 2005—. Adv. bd. mem. Do Something Nat. Educators, 2000—02. Named Hispanic Tchr. of Yr., USA Today, 2002, Boca Raton Tchr. of Yr., Boca Raton Rotary Club, 2001; recipient Palm Beach County award, Hispanic Human Resources Coun., 2003. Mem.: Nat. Assn. for Gifted Children, Kappa Delta Pi. Cath. Avocation: travel. Home: 9442 Aegean Dr Boca Raton FL 33496 Office: Sch Dist of Palm Beach County 3372 Forest Hill Blvd B101 West Palm Beach FL 33406 Office Phone: 561-977-0105. Office Fax: 561-434-7378. E-mail: benavides@palmbeach.k12.fl.us.

BENAVIDES, DEBORAH ANN, academic advisor; d. Willie A. and Theresa L. Benavides. BA in Theatre, Incarnate Word Coll., 1983; MA in Edn., U. Tex., San Antonio, 2002. Bldg. supr. univ. ctr. ops. office U. Tex., San Antonio, 1988—96, internat. student program coord. office multicultural programs, 1996—99, academic advisor Coll. Liberal and Fine Arts, 1999—2002, academic advisor Sch. Arch., 2002—. Vol. Esperanza Peace and Justice Ctr., San Antonio, 1995—2001. Mem.: Tex. Academic Advisors Network. Avocations: music, reading, art, photography. Office: U Tex 501 W Durango Blvd San Antonio TX 78207 Office Phone: 210-458-3010. E-mail: dabenavides@utsa.edu.

BENAVIDES, FORTUNATO PEDRO (PETE BENAVIDES), federal judge; b. Mission, Tex., Feb. 3, 1947; BBA, U. Houston, 1968, JD, 1972. Atty. Rankin, Kern & Martinez, McAllen, Tex., 1972—74, Cisneros, Beery & Benavides, McAllen, 1974, Cisneros, Brown & Benavides, McAllen, 1975, Cisneros & Benavides, McAllen, 1976; pvt. practice McAllen, 1977; judge Hidalgo County Ct.-at-Law # 2, Edinburg, Tex., 1977—79; prin. Law Offices of Fortunato P. Benavides, McAllen, 1980—81; judge 92nd Dist. Ct. of Hidalgo County, Tex., 1981—84, 13th Ct. Appeals, Corpus Christi, Tex., 1984—91, Tex. Ct. Criminal Appeals, Austin, 1991—92; atty. Atlas & Hall, McAllen, 1993—94; judge U.S. Ct. Appeals (5th cir.), Austin, 1994—. Commr. Tex. Juvenile Probation Commn., 1983—89; vis. judge to cts. in Tex., 1993. Active Mustangs of Corpus Christi, 1990—91, hon. mem., 1992; active Mex.-Am. Dems. of Tex., 1990—92; mem. St. Michael Episc. Ch., Austin, 1992—. Mem.: ABA, Hidalgo County Bar Assn., State Bar Tex. Office: US Ct Appeals 5th Cir Homer Thornberry Judicial Bldg 903 San Jacinto Blvd Rm 450 Austin TX 78701 Office Phone: 512-916-5796.*

BENAVIDES, GRETA LOUISE, elementary school educator, entrepreneur; b. Denver, July 28, 1956; d. Edwin M. and Mariam Jayne Randall; m. Francisco Vega Benavides, July 3, 1994; children: Dane David Fredericksen children: Robyn G. Fredericksen, Masi Brede Fredericksen. BA in Fine Arts with honors, Calif. State U., Fullerton, 1996; MA in Edn., Biola U., 2000. Cert. tchr. Calif. 2d grade tchr. South Whittier (Calif.) Sch. Dist., 1997—; supr. Herbalife, L.A., 2003—. Supr. Home Sch., Buena Park, Calif., 1984—, young adult fine art instr., 1994—2003; tutor disabled students South Whittier Sch. Dist., 1999—2003. Exhibitions include Santa Ana Coll., 1984, Irvine Fine Arts Ctr., 1986; prodr.: (compact disc) Sing the Wondrous Story, 2003. Union rep. Calif. Tchrs. Assn., Whittier, 1997—2003; mem. chorus St. Linus Ch., 2000—03. Recipient Best in Show award, 1984; advanced classroom instrn. grantee, Whittier Credit Union, 2002. Democrat. Roman Catholic. Achievements include original research in the effects of reading comprehension on colored paper for persons with scotopic sensitivity. Avocations: painting, photography, promoting healthy nutrition, promoting public awareness of important political issues. Office: Los Altos Sch 12001 Bona Vista Ln Whittier CA 90605 Personal E-mail: teacher714@hotmail.com, gretafrancisco@adelphia.net.

BENBENISTY, KEITH M., dermatologist; b. Atlanta, June 11, 1973; s. Lewis M. Benbenisty and Carol Leet Bush; m. Siobhan C. Briscoe; children: Noah Lewis, Jacob Anthony. BS, U. Ga., Athens, 1991—95; MD, Med. Coll. Ga., Augusta, 1996—2000. Cert. physician USMLE, 2000. Immunodermatology fellow Duke U., Durham, NC, 2001—02; dermatology resident MUSC Dermatology, Charleston, SC, 2002—. Mem.: AMA, Celiac Sprue Assn., So. Med. Assn., Am. Acad. Dermatology (RFC com. mem., sports com. mem. 2002—). Office: MUSC Dermatology 135 Rutledge Ave 11th Fl Charleston SC 29425 Office Phone: 843-792-5858. Office Fax: 843-792-9936. E-mail: benbeni@musc.edu.

BENBOW, CAMILLA PERSSON, dean, psychology professor; b. Lund, Sweden, Dec. 3, 1956; came to U.S., 1965, naturalized, 1985; m. David Lubinski; children: Wystan R., Bronwen G., Trefor A., Evan M., Lovisa D., G. Byron, Lena C. BA in Psychology with honors, Johns Hopkins U., 1977, MA in Psychology, 1978, MS in Edn. of the Gifted, 1980, EdD with distinction in Edn. of Gifted, 1981. Dir. Office of Precollegiate Programs for Talented & Gifted Iowa State U., 1987-98, Johns Hopkins U., Balt., 1977-79, asst. dir. Study of Mathematically Precocious Youth, 1979-81, assoc. dir., 1981-85, co-dir., 1985-86, dir., 1986—, assoc. rsch. scientist dept. psychology, 1981-86, asst. prof. sociology, part-time, 1983-86; assoc. prof. psychology Iowa State U., Ames, 1985-90, prof. psychology, 1990-95, chair dept. psychology, 1992-98, disting. prof., 1995-98, interim dean coll. edn., 1996-98; dean Peabody Coll. of Edn. and Human Devel., Vanderbilt U., Nashville, 1998—. Sr. editor: Academic Precocity: Aspects of Its Development, 1983,

Intellectual Talent: Psychometric and Social Issues, 1996; contbr. articles to profl. jours. Recipient John Curtis Gowan prize Nat. Assn. Gifted Children, 1980, 81; Rsch. award Am. Ednl. Rsch. Assn., 1982; Spencer fellow, alt., 1984, 85, 86, Rsch. paper award Mensa, 1985, 86, 89, 94, 95 Mensa Lifetime Achievement award, 2004; Early Scholar award Nat. Assn. Gifted Children, 1985, Disting. Scholar award 1992, George A. Miller award APA, 1999. Mem. Johns Hopkins Soc. Scholars, Phi Beta Kappa, Sigma Xi. Office: Vanderbilt Univ Peabody Coll Edn/Human Devel Deans Office Box 329 Peabody Sta Nashville TN 37203 E-mail: camilla.benbow@vanderbilt.edu.

BENBUNAN-FICH, RAQUEL, information scientist, educator; Degree in Computer Engring., U. Simon Bolivar, Venezuela, 1986; MBA, IESA, Caracas, Venezuela, 1989; PhD, Rutgers U., 1997. Asst. prof. Seton Hall U., South Orange, NJ, 1998—2001; asst. prof. Baruch Coll. CUNY, N.Y., 2001—. Recipient Faculty Excellence award, Seton Hall U., 2001, Outstanding Paper of Yr. award, Jour. Mktg. Edn., 2001, Best Paper in Mgmt. Edn. award, Acad. Mgmt. Meeting, 2003; scholar, Baruch Coll., CUNY, 2003—05; Eugene Lang Jr. Faculty fellowship, 2004. Office: Baruch College CUNY One Bernard Baruch Way Box 11-220 New York NY 10010 Office Phone: 646-312-3350.

BENCHLEY, PETER BRADFORD, author; b. NYC, May 8, 1940; s. Nathaniel Goddard and Marjorie Louise (Bradford) Benchley; m. Winifred B. Wesson, Sept. 19, 1964; children: Tracy, Clayton, Christopher. BA cum laude, Harvard U., 1961. Gen. assignment reporter Washington Post, 1963; assoc. editor Newsweek mag., N.Y.C., 1963—67; staff asst. to Pres. White House, Washington, 1967—69; freelance writer, 1969—. Mem. Nat. Coun. Environ. Def.; mem. bd. advisors Bermuda Underwater Exploration Inst. Author: (books) Time and a Ticket, 1964, Shark Trouble, 2002, (novels) Jaws, 1974, The Deep, 1976, The Island, 1978, The Girl of the Sea of Cortez, 1982, Q Clearance, 1986, Rummies, 1989, Beast, 1991, White Shark, 1994; author: (with others) (screenplays) Jaws, 1975 (Brit. Acad. Award nomination), The Deep, 1977, The Island, 1979; co-author Ocean Planet, 1995; writer, narrator, host (episodes) The Am. Sportsman TV show, 1974—83, Galapagos TV spl., 1987, host, narrator Expedition Earth TV series, 1990—93, co-creator Dolphin Cove TV series, 1989, exec. prodr. Beast miniseries, 1996, host, narrator Ocean Reports pub. radio series, 1997—2000, creator, co-exec. prodr. (syndicated TV series) Peter Benchley's Amazon, 1999—2000, co-creator, co-prodr., co-writer, narrator New Eng. Aquarium's World of Water film series, 1998—; contbr. articles to newspapers and mags., including Nat.Geographic, N.Y.Times. With USMCR, 1962—63. Recipient Diver of Yr. award, Sea Rovers Assn., 2002, Lowell Thomas Gold award for adventure-travel writing, 2003, 2004, Daniel B. Stone award, N.E. Aquarium, 2005. Office: care ICM 40 W 57th St New York NY 10019-4001

BENCHOFF, JAMES MARTIN, manufacturing executive; b. Hagerstown, Md., May 18, 1927; s. J. Thompson and Marie (Hickey) B.; m. Brigitte R. Puhringer, July 1, 1978 (div.); children by previous marriage— Helen Marie, James Martin II. Student, U. Pa., 1944-45. With Grove Mfg. Co. div. Hanson Industries, Shady Grove, Pa., 1954—, v.p., 1962-66, 1st v.p., 1966, 1st v.p., asst. gen. mgr., 1966-68, exec. v.p., gen. mgr., 1968-69, pres., chief exec. officer, 1969-80, chmn., chief exec. officer, 1980-88, chmn. emeritus, 1988—. Pres. Monta Vista Inc., Waynesboro, Pa., 1959—; pres., chmn. Ben Mar Holdings Ltd., Waynesboro, 1970—. Mem.: Waynesboro Country; Fountain Head Country (Hagerstown, Md); Met. (N.Y.C.). Office: PO Box 308 Waynesboro PA 17268-0308

BENCINI, SARA HALTIWANGER, concert pianist; b. Winston Salem, N.C., Sept. 2, 1926; d. Robert Sydney and Janie Love (Couch) Haltiwanger; m. Robert Emery Bencini, June 26, 1954; children: Robert Emery, III, Constance Bencini Waller, John McGregor. Mus. B., Salem Coll., 1947; postgrad. grad. Juilliard Sch. Music, 1948-50; M.A., Smith Coll., 1951; D In Mus. Arts, U. N.C., Greensboro, 1989. Head piano dept. Mary Burnham Sch. for Girls, Northampton, Mass., 1949-51; pianist, composer dance and drama dept. Smith Coll., 1951-52; head music dept. Walnut Hill Sch. for Girls, Natick, Mass., 1952-54; pvt. piano tchr., High Point, N.C., 1954-66; concert pianist appearing in Am. and Europe, 1948—; duo-piano performances with PBS-TV, Columbia, S.C., 1967, Winston Salem Symphony, N.C., 1964-68, Ea. Mus. Festival, Greensboro, N.C., 1969. Democrat. Presbyterian.

BENCIVENGO, CATHY ANN, lawyer; BA, Rutgers Univ., 1980, MA, 1981; JD magna cum laude, Univ. Mich., 1988. Bar: Calif. 1988, US Dist. Ct. (no., ea., so. Calif. dist.), US Ct. Appeals (9th, Fed. cir.), US Supreme Ct. Ptnr., co-chmn. Patent Litigation practice group DLA Piper Rudnick Gray Cary, San Diego. Adj. faculty Univ. San Diego Law Sch., 1999; judge pro tem San Diego County Small Claims Ct.; dir. San Diego Mediation Ctr., 1999—2000. Eagleton Inst. of Politics Fellow. Mem.: San Diego Bar Found. (dir.), ABA, Fed. Bar Assn., Fed. Cir. Bar Assn., San Diego County Bar Assn. (co-chmn. Intellectual Property sect. 1993—94, dir. 1996—98, treas. 1997, v.p. 1998, chmn., lawyer referral & info. svc.), Order of the Coif. Office: DLA Piper Rudnick Gray Cary Suite 2000 401 B St San Diego CA 92101 Office Phone: 619-699-3616. Office Fax: 619-699-2701. Business E-Mail: cathy.bencivengo@dlapiper.com.

BENCLOSKI, JOSEPH W., geography educator; BS in Edn., Indiana (Pa.) U., 1964, MA, 1970; PhD, Pa. State U., 1976. Grad. teaching asst. dept. geography Pa. State U., University Park, 1970-72; vis. asst. prof. Ohio State U., Columbus, 1976-77; temp. asst. prof. U. Ga., 1978-83, asst. prof., 1983-85; asst. prof. dept. geography and regional planning Indiana (Pa.) U., 1988—. Vis. prof. dept. geoscis. Pa. State U., 1988; vis. assoc. prof. U. N.C., Greensboro, 1985-87; researcher in field. Contbr. articles to profl. jours. Recipient Teaching Excellence award Teaching Excellence Ctr., 1993. Mem. AAAS, Nat. Coun. Geographic Edn. (dep. exec. dir. 1988—, editor Perspective, 1988—, coord. svc. coords. program 1988-91, ad hoc mem. long range planning com. 1989-91, awards com. 1983-86, chair awards com. 1985-86, Disting. Teaching Achievement award 1990), Assn. Am. Geographers (population geography specialty group, climatology specialty group), Nat. Collegiate Honors Coun., Pa. Geographic Soc. (Devel. Exemplary Teaching Materials award 1993), Kappa Delta Pi, Sigma Xi, Phi Delta Kappa, Pi Gamma Mu, Gamma Theta Upsilon. Office: Indiana U Pa Dept Geography & Regional Planning 1011 S Drive 1C Leonard Hall Indiana PA 15705-0001

BENDELIUS, ARTHUR GEORGE, engineering firm executive; b. Passaic, NJ, May 21, 1936; s. Arthur Leopold and Lydia Ella (Flach) B.; m. Virginia Brown, June 21, 1958; children: Linda Ellen Newlin, Bonnie Sue, Heidi Ann Mitchell. BE, Stevens Inst. Tech., 1958, MMS, 1966. Registered profl. engr., NY, NJ, Mich., Minn., Ga., Fla., Tex. Ala., Ky., NC, SC, Miss., Tenn., La., Ohio, Ark., Okla., Md., Utah, Colo., Wyo., W.Va., Pa. Engr. Syska & Hennessey, NYC, 1958-60, Parsons Brinckerhoff Quade & Douglas, Inc., NYC, 1960-62, Nat. Biscuit Co., NYC, 1962—63; asst. dept. head Parsons Brinckerhoff Quade & Douglas, Inc., NYC, 1963-68, dept. head, 1968-70, project mgr., 1970-73, regional mgr. Atlanta, 1973-76, asst. v.p., 1976-78, v.p., 1978-82, sr. v.p., 1982-89; regional mgr. Energy Sys. Group, NYC, 1989-93, prin. profl. assoc., 1991—2004, sr. v.p., 1989—, tech. dir., 1992—2004. Divsn. mgr. PBES, NYC, 1994-96, Parsons Brinckerhoff Quade & Douglas, Inc., NYC, 1996-2002, Atlanta, 2002-04; pres. A & G Cons., Inc., 2004—; presenter in field. Co-author: Tunnel Engineering Handbook, 1982, 2d edit., 1996, ASHRAE Handbook Applications, 1978, 5th edit., 2003, Fire Protection Handbook, 19th edit., 2003, Handbook of Tunnel Fire Safety, 2005; co-editor Equipment and Systems for Fire Smoke Control in Road Tunnels, 2005; contbr. articles to profl. jours. Pres. Brookside Home Sch. Orgn., Westwood, NJ, 1972-73; co-v.p. Dunwoody Band Booster Club, Ga., 1975-76, co-pres., 1976-77. Named Atlanta Engr. of Yr. in Pvt. Practice, 1978; recipient Harold R. Fee Alumni award, 1978. Fellow Soc. Am. Mil. Engrs. (pres. Atlanta chpt. 1978-79, nat. bd. dirs. 1983-86), ASHRAE (chmn. tech. com. 1975-79, rsch. promotion com. 1980-82, tech. com. 5.0 1982—); mem. NSPE, Ga. Soc. Profl. Engrs. (bd. dirs. 1976-78), Nat. Coun. Examiners Engring. and Surveying (cert.), Ga. Engring. Found. (life 1983-, bd. dirs. 1977-89, sec. 1979, v.p. 1980, pres. 1982, 83), Steven's Alumni Assn., ASME, Brit. Tunneling Soc., Transp. Assn. SC (bd. dirs. 1987, treas. 1987-89), Nat. Fire Protection Assn. (tech. com. 130, 1992-2004, task group ventilation, tech. com. 502 1993—, chair NPPA 502 subcom. 1994-97, chair tech. com. 502, 1996-2004, World Road Assn. (PIARC) (tech. com. C5 and C3.3 on Rd. Tunnel Operation, 1999-, working group Fire & Smoke 1992—, chmn., 1999-), Aircraft Owners and Pilots Assn., Tau Beta Pi, Sigma Nu (pres. alumni assn. 1966-70, comdr. 1971-73), Ansley Golf Club, Atlanta Stevens Club (pres. 1974-90, 2002-). Lutheran. Office: A&G Consultants Inc 11391 Big Canoe Big Canoe GA 30143-5108 Office Phone: 706-268-1965. E-mail: bendelius@tds.net.

BENDER, BETTY BARBEE, food service professional; b. Lexington, Ky., Apr. 29, 1932; d. Richard Carroll and Sarah Elizabeth (Rodes) Barbee; m. David H. Bender, Dec. 14, 1957; children: Bruce, Carroll. BA in Home Econs., Mont. State U., 1954; MS in Food Service Mgmt., Miami U., Oxford, Ohio, 1980. Adminstrv. dietitian Mass. Gen. Hosp., Boston, 1955—56; asst. chief dietitian Meth. Hosp., Indpls., 1957—61; chief dietitian Cmty. Hosp., Indpls., 1961—63; supervising dietitian Chgo. area ARA, 1963—67; asst. supr. food svc. Dayton Bd. Edn., Ohio, 1969, mgr. food svc., 1969—98. Cons. Nat. Frozen Food Assn., Washington, 1983, Crescent Metal Products Co., Cleve., 1985; nat. food svc. mgr. Meat Inst., 1998-2003; clin. nutritionist Jessamine County Health Dept., 2003—. Contbr. articles to profl. jours. Recipient 26th Ann. Foodsvc. Facilities Design award Instrs. Mag. for Commissary Design, 1972, Silver and Gold Plate awards Internat. Foodsvc. Mfrs. Assn., 1985, Pres.'s award Ohio Sch. Food Svc. Assn., 1987, FAME Golden Star award, 1992; recognized for outstanding contbns. to child nutrition program Ohio Ho. of Reps., 1972, 84. Mem. Am. Sch. Food Svc. Assn. (nat. pres. 1983, chmn. 1978-80, maj. city sect.), Ohio Sch. Food Svc. (pres. 1977), Dayton Sch. Adminstr. Assn., Dayton Sch. Mgmt. Assn. (pres. 1993-94), Am. Dietetic Assn. (cert., chair dietary practice group 1990-91, award for Excellence in Mgmt. Practice 1992, Food Svc. Dir. Yr. 1994), Ohio Dietetic Assn., Dayton Dietetic Assn., Soc. Nutrition Edn. (panel 1983). Democrat. Avocations: bridge, golf, swimming. Home: 1953 E Hickman Rd Nicholasville KY 40356-8838 E-mail: bbender831@aol.com.

BENDER, BETTY WION, librarian; b. Mt. Ayer, Iowa, Feb. 26, 1925; d. John F. and Sadie A. (Guess) Wion; m. Robert F. Bender, Aug. 24, 1946. BS, N.Tex. State U., Denton, 1946; MA, U. Denver, 1957. Asst. cataloger N. Tex. State U. Library, 1946-49; from cataloger to head acquisitions So. Meth. U., Dallas, 1949-56; reference asst. Ind. State Library, Indpls., 1951-52; librarian Ark. State Coll., 1958-59, Eastern Wash. Hist. Soc., Spokane, 1960-67; reference librarian, then head circulation dept. Spokane (Wash.) Public Library, 1968-73, library dir., 1973-88. Vis. instr. U. Denver, summers 1957-60, 63, fall 1959; instr. Whitworth Coll., Spokane, 1962-64; mem. Gov. Wash. Regional Conf. Libraries, 1968, Wash. Statewide Library Devel. Council, 1970-71 Bd. dirs. N.W. Regional Found., 1973-75, Inland Empire Goodwill Industries, 1975-77, Wash. State Library Commn., 1979-87, Future Spokane, 1983-88, vice chmn., 1986-87, pres., 1987-88. Recipient YWCA Outstanding Achievement award in Govt., 1985 Mem. ALA (mem. library adminstrn. and mgmt. assn. com. on orgn. 1982-83, chmn. nominating com. 1983-85, v.p./pres.-elect. 1985-86, pres. 1986-87), Pacific N.W. Library Assn. (chmn. circulation div. 1972-75, conv. chmn. 1977), Wash. Library Assn. (v.p./pres.-elect 1975-77, pres. 1977-78), AAUW (pres. Spokane br. 1969-71, rec. sec. Wash. br. 1971-73, fellowship named in honor 1972), Spokane and Inland Empire Librarians (dir. 1967-68), Am. Soc. Pub. Adminstrn. Clubs: Zonta (pres. Spokane chpt. 1976-77, dist. conf. treas. 1972). Republican. Lutheran. Home: 221 E Rockwood Blvd Apt 504 Spokane WA 99202-1274

BENDER, BRUCE F., book publishing executive; b. Toledo, Ohio, Oct. 4, 1949; s. Richard S. and Joan B. Bender; m. Margaret Norris, Sept. 4, 1971; children: Courtney, Meghan. BA, Musklingum Coll., 1971; MBA, Rutgers U., 1972. Supr. Coopers & Lybrand CPA's, N.Y.C., 1972-76; pres. Lyle Stuart, inc., Secaucus, N.J., 1989—; also bd. dirs.; pres. Carol Pub. Group, N.Y.C., 1989-2000; mng. dir. Citadel Press, N.Y.C., from 2000, Kensington Pub. Corp., N.Y.C., 2000—04; CFO Book Club Am., 2004—. Pres. Brightwood Assn.; bd. dirs. Westfield Symphony. Mem. AICPA, Pub. Fin. Round Table, N.J. Inst. CPAs, Echo Lake Club, Royal Poinciana Club. Office: Book Club America 100 Marcus Blvd Hauppauge NY 11788 Office Phone: 631-235-4644. Business E-Mail: brucebender@bookclubusa.com.

BENDER, BYRON WILBUR, linguistics educator; b. Roaring Spring, Pa., Aug. 14, 1929; s. Ezra Clay and Gertrude Magdalene (Kauffman) B.; m. Lois Marie Graber, Aug. 25, 1950; children: Susan Alice, Sarah Marie, Catherine Anne, Judith Lee, John Richard. BA, Goshen Coll., 1949; MA, Ind. U., 1950, PhD, 1963. Edn. specialist Trust Terr. of Pacific Islands, Majuro, Marshall Island, 1953-59, Saipan, Marianas Island, 1962-64; asst. prof. Goshen Coll., Ind., 1960-62; assoc. prof. linguistics U. Hawaii at Manoa, Honolulu, 1964-69, prof., 1969-99, chmn. dept., 1969-95, prof. emeritus, 2000—. Bd. dirs. U. Hawaii Profl. Assembly, Honolulu, 1978-88, 92-98, pres., 1982-88. Author: Spoken Marshallese, 1969, Linguistic Factors in Maori Education, 1971, (with others) Marshallese-English Dictionary, 1976; editor Oceanic Linguistics Spl. Publ., 1965—, Studies in Micronesian Linguistics, 1984, Oceanic Linguistics, 1991—; mng. editor Oceanic Linguistics, 1965-90. Trustee Hawaii Pub. Employees Health Fund Bd., 1987-95; regent U. Hawaii Bd. of Regents, 2003-. Recipient Merit awards U. Hawaii 1971, 76, 86. Mem. NEA (standing com. higher edn. 1985-89), Linguistic Soc. Am. (dir. Linguistic Inst. summer 1977, program com. 1987-89, parliamentarian 1994-97). Mem. Soc. Of Friends. Home: Apt 1504 6710 Hawaii Kai Dr Honolulu HI 96825-1548 Office: U Hawaii Dept Linguistics 1890 E West Rd Honolulu HI 96822-2318 Office Phone: 808-956-8374. Personal E-mail: bender@hawaii.rr.com. Business E-Mail: bender@hawaii.edu.

BENDER, CARL MARTIN, physics professor, consultant; b. Bklyn., Jan. 18, 1943; s. Alfred and Rose (Suberman) B.; m. Jessica Dee Waldbaum, June 18, 1966; children— Michael Anthony, Daniel Eric AB summa cum laude with distinction, Cornell U., 1964; AM, Harvard U., 1965, PhD, 1969. Mem. Inst. for Advanced Study, Princeton, N.J., 1969-70; asst. prof. math. MIT, Cambridge, 1970-73, assoc. prof., 1973-77; prof. physics Washington U., St. Louis, 1977—; research assoc. Imperial Coll., London, 1974. Cons. Los Alamos Nat. Lab., 1979—; vis. prof. Imperial Coll., London, 1986-87, 95-96, 2003-04, Technion Israel Inst. of Technology, Haifa, Israel, 1995; fellow Engring. and Phys. Scis. Rsch. Coun., U.K., 2003—. Author: Advanced Mathematical Methods for Scientists and Engineers, 1978; editor: Am. Inst. Physic series on math. and computational physics; mem. editl. bds. Jour Math. Physics, 1980-83, Advances in Applied Math., 1980-85, Jour. Physics A, 1999-2003; editor-in-chief, Jour. Physics A, 2004—; contbr. more than 200 articles to sci. jours. Trustee Ctr. for Theoretical Study of Phys. Sys., Clark Atlanta U. Recipient Burlington No. Found. Faculty Achievement award, 1985, Fellows award Acad. Sci. St. Louis, 2002; Telluride scholar, 1960-63, NSF fellow, 1964-69, Woodrow Wilson fellow, 1964-65, Sloan Found. fellow, 1973-77, Fulbright fellowship to U.K., 1995-96, Lady Davis fellowship to Israel, 1995, Rockefeller Found. grantee to visit Bellagio Study and Conf. Ctr., 1999; Guggenheim Fellow, 2003-04, fellow Engring. and Physical Scis. Rsch. Coun., London, 2003-04. Fellow: St. Louis Acad. Sci., Am. Phys. Soc. (vice chmn. Danny Heineman prize selection com., chmn. Danny Heineman prize selection com.); mem.: Inst. of Physics (U.K.), Phi Kappa Phi, Phi Beta Kappa. Home: 509 Warren Ave Saint Louis MO 63130-4155 Office: Washington U Dept Physics Saint Louis MO 63130 Office Phone: 314-935-6216. Business E-Mail: cmb@wustl.edu.

BENDER, CAROL TILL (PINKY BENDER), minister; b. Charleston, S.C., Apr. 21, 1937; d. Wallace Conrad and Erna Louise (von Postel) T.; m. Michael Swift Bender; children: Louise, Katherine, David. BA in Journalism, Winthrop U., 1960; MDiv, Erskine Theol. Sem., 1984; DMin, Columbia Sem., 1993. Writer Presbyn. Ch. (USA), Louisville, 1983—; prof. Queens Coll., Charlotte, N.C., 1985-93; pastor McQuay Meml. Presbyn. Ch., Charlotte, 1986-97; parish assoc. Plz. Presbyn. Ch., Charlotte, 1998—2002. Chair ARC Blood Svcs., Charlotte, 1991-95, Clergy Assn. Bd., Charlotte, 1995-96. Author (curriculum) Bible Discovery, 1983-93; editor (study books) Presbyterian Women, 1990-92. Mem. bd. mgrs. Harris YMCA. Mem. AAUW (life, Ednl. Found. Program grantee 1983), Presbyn. Writers Guild. Home: 5001 Belford Ct Charlotte NC 28226-7801

BENDER, CHARLES CHRISTIAN, retail home center executive; b. Bklyn., July 4, 1936; s. Charles C. and Virginia R. (Rahlfs) B.; m. Jean Ann Couper; children: Lori Ann Grenier, Hallie Couper Fivecoat. BA, Hillsdale Coll., 1959; MBA, U. Mich., 1960. Buyer Target, Detroit, 1962-69; v.p., gen. mdse. mgr. Wickes Lumber, Saginaw, Mich., 1969-81; gen. mgr. Wickes B.V., Utrecht, Netherlands, 1981-84; chmn., CEO, owner Busy Beaver Bldg. Ctrs., Pitts., 1984—. Mem. adv. bd. Home Ctr. Industry Pres. Coun., 1986—; mem. Coun. of Exec. Officers; chmn. bd. dirs. Home Ctr. Inst., 1998. With U.S. Army, 1960—61. Mem.: Pitts. Field Club, Rotary. Republican. Presbyterian. Avocations: golf, sailing. Home: 310 Buckingham Rd Pittsburgh PA 15215-1527 Office: Busy Beaver Bldg Ctrs Inc 3130 William Pitt Way Pittsburgh PA 15238-1360 Home: 3830 Sawgrass Way Naples FL 34112

BENDER, CHARLES WILLIAM, lawyer; b. Cape Girardeau, Mo., Oct. 2, 1935; s. Walter William and Fern Evelyn (Stroud) Bender; m. Carolyn Percy Gavagan, June 20, 1961 (div. 1983); children: Theodore Marten, Christopher Percy; m. Betty Lou Port, May 5, 1983; stepchildren: Courtney Elizabeth, Cameron Ann. AB magna cum laude, Harvard U., 1960, LLB magna cum laude, 1963. Bar: Calif. 1965, U.S. Dist. Ct. (ctrl. dist.) Calif. 1965, U.S. Ct. Appeals (9th cir.) 1969, U.S. Supreme Ct. 1979, DC 1984. Assoc. O'Melveny & Myers, LA, 1965—71, ptnr., 1972—84, mng. ptnr., 1984—92, chmn., 1993—2001. Editor: Harvard U. Law Rev., 1961—62; articles editor:, 1962—63. Trustee LA Legal Aid Found., 1971, Lawyers' Com. for Civil Rights Under Law, Washington, 1985—2001; advisor campaign Alan Cranston for Senator, Calif., 1968, 1974, 1980; mgr. campaign Jess Unruh for Gov., Calif., 1970. Served with U.S. Army, 1956—57. Fellow Sheldon Traveling, Harvard U., 1963—64. Democrat. Home: 2831 The Strand Hermosa Beach CA 90254-2400 Office: O'Melveny & Myers 400 S Hope St Los Angeles CA 90071-2899

BENDER, DAVID RAY, retired library director; b. Canton, Ohio, June 12, 1942; s. John Ray and Mary Elizabeth (Witmer) B.; children: Robert Ray, Scott David, Lori Jo Ryan. BS, Kent State U., 1964; MS in LS, Case Western Res. U., 1969; PhD, Ohio State U., 1977. Librarian South High Sch., Willoughby, Ohio, 1964-68; cons. sch. library services Ohio Dept. Edn., Columbus, 1969-70; grad. research asso. Ohio State U., Columbus, 1970-72; br. chief sch. library media services Md. Dept. Edn., Balt., 1972-79; exec. dir. Spl. Librs. Assn., Washington, 1979-2001, exec. dir. emeritus, 2001—; ret., 2001. Lectr. Rutgers U., New Brunswick, N.J.; vis. prof. Towson State U., Balt.; cons., project dir. various state depts. edn. and colls. and univs., profl. assns. also internat., state and local orgns.; mem. adv. com. on naval history, USN, 1991-95. Author: Learning Resources and the Instructional Program in Community College, 1980, Library Media Programs and the Special Learner, 1981; co-author (with others): Nat. Information Policies: Strategies for the Future, 1991; contbr. numerous articles to profl. jours. Mem. adv. coun. Kent (Ohio) State U. Sch. of Libr. and Info. Sci., 1991-99, Washington Nat. Cathedral Fund Com., 1998—, libr. com., 2005—; CWRU Libr. ann. gift fund chair, 1999-2002; bd. dirs. Dresden Condominium, 2002-05 (dir., pres. 2004-); mem. sr. medicare error patrol project AARP, 2002-. Recipient award for outstanding svc. Md. Ednl. Media Orgn., 1980, H.W. Wilson Co. award, 1989. Mem. Spl. Librs. Assn. (President's award 1986, John Cotton Dana award 2001, David R. Bender Endowment Fund for Internat. Devel. 2001), Nat. Libr. and Info. Assns. (chmn. 1990-91), Internat. Fedn. Libr. Assns. and Instns. (chmn. round table for Mgmt. of Libr. Assn. 1993-99), Am. Soc. Assn. Execs. Found. (chmn. 1988), Greater Wash. Soc. Assn. Execs. (chair CEO adv. coun. 2000-2001, Five Smart Assn. CEO's 2001), Kappa Sigma. Republican. Episcopalian. Home: Unit 34 2126 Connecticut Ave NW Washington DC 20008-1729

BENDER, DEAN, public relations executive; Ptnr. Bender/Helper Impact (formerly Bender, Goldman & Helper), LA, 1986—. Office: Bender/Helper Impact 11500 W Olympic Blvd Ste 655 Los Angeles CA 90064-1530 Address: Bender/Helper Impact 220 Fifth Ave #1502 New York NY 10001 Office Phone: 212-689-6360. Office Fax: 310-478-4727, 212-689-6601.

BENDER, JACK SINCLAIR, III, retired lawyer; b. Kansas City, Mo., July 12, 1944; s. Jack Sinclair Jr. and Ruby June (Blake) B.; m. Donna Lou LaMar, Aug. 28, 1965; children: Kelley Ann, Heather Christine, Marcia Lynn. BA, Washburn U., 1966, JD, 1969; grad., Air Command and Staff Coll., 1979, Air War Coll., 1989. Bar: Kans. 1969, U.S. Dist. Ct. Kans. 1969, U.S. Supreme Ct. 1973. Asst. atty. gen. State of Kans., 1969; sr. atty. Boeing Co., Wichita, Kans., 1974-90, constrn. mgmt., 1990-99; ret., 1999. Cons. Boeing Employees' Assn., 1976-99, Boeing Mgmt. Club Bd. of Control, 1986-88; mobilization augmentee to gen. counsel Def. Logistics Agy., 1994-96. Author: The Law Can Help You, 1973. Ch. officer, 1st Presbyn. Ch., Wichita, 1981-87; trustee Hertzler Rsch. Found., 2001—, Civil War lectr.; active disaster svcs. human resources sys. ARC. Capt. JAG, USAF, 1966-74; col., JAG-USAFR, 1974-96 (ret.), USAF Acad. Liaison Officer, 1994—. Recipient Younger Fed. Lawyer award Fed. Bar Assn., 1973, Outstanding Air Force Res. Lawyer of Yr. award, 1983. Mem. ABA, Kans. Bar Assn., Wichita Bar Assn., Corp. Counsel Soc. Wichita (v.p. 1975-76, pres. 1976-77, 85-86), Am. Platform Assn., Wichita Civil War Round Table, Kans. State Hist. Soc., Halstead Hist. Soc., Res. Officers Assn., Jaycees (bd. dirs. 1978-80, Pres.'s award 1979), Air Force Assn. (life), Veteran's Affairs (Wichita v.p. 2005-), Air War Coll. Alumni Assn., U.S. Golf Assn., Wichita Geneal. Soc., Am. Legion, Assn. Ret. Persons, Washburn Alumni Assn., Phi Alpha Delta Home: 9431 Epping Ln Halstead KS 67056-9355 Personal E-mail: galaxy2010@aol.com.

BENDER, JAMES J., oil industry executive, lawyer; b. Aurora, Ill., 1956; m. Kristin Bender; 3 children. JD, U. Minn. Law Sch.; undergraduate degree in math., St. Olaf Coll. Bar: Minn., Colorado. Law clerk fed. dist. ct., St. Paul; assoc. Gibson, Dunn & Crutcher; ptnr. Masion, Edelman, Borman & Brand, 1983—88, Loenard, Street, & Deinard, 1993—94; sr. counsel Pfizer, Inc., 1989—93; asst. gen. counsel AlliedSignal, 1996—97; sr. v.p., gen. counsel NRG Energy, 1997—2002, The Williams Inc., Tulsa, 2002—. Spkr. in field. Div. chair United Way, Tulsa; bd. mem. YMCA, Minn.; conducted pro-bono legal work Interfaith Outreach, Minn. Mem.: Am. Corp. Coun. Assn., Minn. State Bar Assn., Am. Bar Assn. Office: Williams One Williams Ctr Tulsa OK 74172

BENDER, JOEL CHARLES, lawyer; b. Bklyn., Dec. 12, 1939; s. Harry and Edna (Bogolowitz) B.; m. Terry Bender; children: Lisa, Andrew, Gary. BA, Cornell U., 1961; JD, NYU, 1964. Bar: N.Y. 1964, U.S. Supreme Ct. 1970, Fla. 1980; diplomate Am. Coll. Family Trial Lawyers. Ptnr. Bender, Jenson & Silverstein, LLP, White Plains, N.Y., 1999—. Councilman Greenburgh, N.Y. 1977-89; dep. supv., police commr. Greenburgh, 1979-89. Fellow Am. Assn. Matrimonial Lawyers, Internat. Acad. Matrimonial Lawyers; mem. ABA (mem. faculty Trial Advocacy Inst.), Am. Acad. Matrimonial Lawyers (pres. N.Y. chpt. 1999-2001, former officer, bd. mgrs.), N.Y. State Bar Assn., Fla. Bar, Westchester County Bar Assn. Democrat. Office: Ste 104 120 Bloomingdale Rd White Plains NY 10605-1518 E-mail: jbender@jcbender.com.

BENDER, JOHN CHARLES, lawyer; b. N.Y.C., May 17, 1940; s. John H. and Cecilia B.; m. Helen Hadjiyannakis; 1 child, Marianna Celene. BSME, Northea. U., 1964; JD, NYU, 1968, LLM, 1971. Bar: N.Y. 1968, U.S. Dist. Ct. (so. dist.) N.Y. 1972, U.S. Supreme Ct. 1997. Atty. Marshall, Bratter, Greene, Allison and Tucker, 1968-69; asst. dir. NYU Ctr. for Internat. Studies, N.Y.C., 1969-71; atty. Poletti Freidin Prashker Feldman & Gartner, N.Y.C., 1971-75; spl. counsel Moreland Act Commn. on Nursing Homes and Residential Facilities, N.Y.C., 1975-76; gen. counsel N.Y. State Fin. Control Bd., N.Y.C., 1976-80; v.p., gen. counsel News Am. Pub. Inc., N.Y.C., 1980-85; group v.p., gen. counsel Simon & Schuster Inc., N.Y.C., 1985-90; sr. v.p., dir., gen. counsel Maxwell Macmillan Group, 1991-95; dir. Black Book Mktg. Group, Inc., 1994-96. Chmn., trustee Trust for Cultural Resources of

City of N.Y., 1981-99; chmn., trustee Mary McDowell Ctr. for Learning, 1993—. Mem. ABA, Assn. of Bar of City of N.Y. (mem. com. on comm. law 1981-85, mem. spl. com. on edn. and the law 1982-85, mem. com. on bioethics). Home: 27 W 67th St New York NY 10023-6258 Office: 10 E 40th St New York NY 10016 Office Phone: 212-813-0999. Business E-Mail: jcb@benderlaw.net.

BENDER, JOHN HENRY, JR., (JACK BENDER), editor, cartoonist; s. John Henry and Wilma (Lowe) B.; divorced; children: Thereza, John Henry IV, Anthony; m. Carole R. Suggs, 1995. BA, U. Iowa, 1953; postgrad., Art Inst. Chgo., 1956, Washington U., St. Louis, 1957; MA, U. Mo., 1962. Art dir., asst. editor Commerce Pub. Co., St. Louis, 1953-54, 56-58; editor Florissant Reporter, 1958-61; editl. cartoonist Waterloo Courier, 1962-84, assoc. editor, 1975-83; art. dir., editor Alpha VII Corp., Tulsa, 1984-87; head dept. prodn. art Platt Coll., Tulsa, 1987-92; cartoonist Don Martin Studio, Miami, Fla., 1989-92; artist Alley Oop comic strip United Media Syndicate, NYC, 1991—. Sports cartoonist Basketball Weekly, Baseball Digest Mag., U. Iowa, others. Author: Pocket Guide to Judging Springboard Diving, (with Dick Smith) Inside Diving, (with Ed Gagnier) Inside Gymnastics; exhibited at Grout Mus., Waterloo, Iowa, 2002 USAFR 1953-1983 (active duty 1954-56; col., ret. 1983). Recipient Best Editl. award Mo. Press Assn., 1960, Grenville Clark Editl. Page award, 1968, Freedoms Found. award, 1969, 75, Freedoms Found. Honor medal, 1971, Ignatz award Orlandocon, 1992, Air Force Commendation medal, 1981; named to Hall of Fame East H.S., Waterloo, Iowa, 1972, Names on Main, Cedar Falls, Iowa, 1997. Mem. Assn. Am. Editl. Cartoonists, Nat. Cartoonists Soc., Comic Art Profl. Soc., Sigma Chi. Office: RR 1 Box 540 Terlton OK 74081-9740 Home: 7424 E 31st Pl Tulsa OK 74145

BENDER, KIM K., academic administrator, educator; b. New Salem, ND, Jan. 31, 1955; s. John A. and Esther H. Bender; m. Carolyn Pullem Bender (div.); m. Mary Ellen Lake, July 6, 2000. BA, U. Mary, 1978; PhD, U. Okla., 1996. Cert. US Profl. Tchg. Assoc. Dir. assessment Colo. State U., Ft. Collins, Colo.; assessment coord. Fla. Atlantic U., Boca Raton, Fla.; rsch. acad. policy Okla. State Regents Higher Edn., Okla. City; dir. tennis ctr. for Okla. City; history instr. Rose State Coll. SP U.S. Army, 1974—77, Germany. Recipient Govs. Commendation award, Okla., 1999. Mem.: US Profl. Tchg. Assn. Independent. Avocations: tennis, running, backpacking, history. Home: 1512 Ashroott Dr Longmont CO 80501 Office: Colo State U 108 Adminstrn Fort Collins CO 80523 Office Phone: 970-491-2043.

BENDER, MICHAEL LEE, state supreme court justice; b. NYC, Jan. 7, 1942; s. Louis and Jean (Waterman) B.; m. Judith Jones, Feb. 27, 1967 (div. Mar. 1977); children: Jeremy, Aviva; m. Helen H. Hand, Sept. 10, 1977; children: Maryjean Hand-Bender, Tess Hand-Bender, Benjamin Hand-Bender. BA in Philosophy, Dartmoutn Coll., 1964; JD, U. Colo., 1967. Bar: Colo. 1967, D.C. 1967, U.S. Supreme Ct. 1980. Pub. defender City and County Denver, 1968-71; assoc. regional atty. EEOC, 1974-75; supr. atty. Jefferson County Pub. Defender, 1975-77; divsn. chief Denver Pub. Defender, Denver, 1977-78; atty. Gibson, Dunn & Crutcher, LA, 1979-80; ptnr. Bender & Treece PC, Denver, 1983-93; pres., shareholder Michael L. Bender PC, 1993-97; justice Colo. Supreme Ct., 1997—. Adj. faculty U. Denver Coll. Law, 1981-86, chair. ABA Criminal Justice sect., Washington, 1990-91, NACD Lawyers Assistant Com., 1989-90, U. Colo. Sch. of Law, 2004; dir. Nat. Assn. Criminal Def. Lawyers, 1984-90; mem. practitioner's adv. com. U.S. Sentencing Com., 1990-91; mem. com. for Criminal Justice Act for Dist. Colo. U.S. Dist. Ct., 1991-93, domestic rels. reform com.; liaison mem. Colo. Pub. Edn. com., Ct. Svcs., 1998—, atty. regulation adv. com., 1998-99; co-chair civil justice com. Supreme Ct., 1998-; liaison Supreme Ct. Standing Com. Colo. Rules Profl. Conduct, 2003-. Contbr. articles to profl. jours. Bd. govs. Colo. Bar, 1989-91. Recipient Fireman award Colo. State Pub., 1990; Robert C. Heeney Meml. award Nat. Assn. Criminal Def. Lawyers, 1990; Named Vol. of Yr. Denver Bar Assn., 1988. Mem. Colo. Bar Assn. (ethics com. 1980—), ABA (chair criminal justice sect. 1990-91, criminal justice standards com. 1997—). Democrat. Jewish. Avocations: aerobics, skiing, bicycling, camping. Office: Colo Supreme Ct State Jud Bldg 2 E 14th Ave Fl 4 Denver CO 80203-2115*

BENDER, PATRICIA ANN, secondary school educator; b. Chardon, Ohio, Mar. 28, 1953; d. Ernest Steven Bender and Norma Lee (Custer) Doing. AA, Lakeland CC, 1973; BS, Culver Stockton U., 1978; MA, N.E. Mo. State U., 1980; MEd, U. Mo., St. Louis, 2004. Cert. tchr. Mo. Phys. edn. tchr. Hannibal (Mo.) Pub. Schs., 1980-83; math. and sci. tchr. Green City (Mo.) R-1 Schs., 1983—. Staff sgt. USAF, 1975—80. Mem.: Green City Tchrs. Assn. (pres. 1984—86, 1991—93), Green City Cmty. Tchrs. (pres. 1984—86, 1991—), Mo. State Tchrs. Assn. (mem. resolutions com. 1986—92, mem. exec. com., N.E. dist. 2d v.p., pres. N.E. dist. 1995—96), Delta Kappa Gamma, Phi Kappa Phi. Methodist. Avocations: golf, bowling, interior decorating, reading, crafts. Home: 26266 Spring Lake Tr Kirksville MO 63501 Office: Green City R-1 Schs 301 N East St Green City MO 63545-1005 Office Phone: 660-874-4127.

BENDER, PEGGY WALLACE, charitable gift planning consultant; b. Athens, Ohio, Apr. 29, 1957; d. Allen Riley and Carol Jean (Jago) Wallace; children: Meghan Elizabeth, Erin Michelle. AS, Ohio U., 1986, BA, 1988. Cert. Fund Raising Exec., 1988. Asst. to dean Ohio U. Col. Bus. Admin., Athens, 1981-86; asst. dir. planned giving U. Cin. Found., 1986—88; dir. planned/major gifts Western Md. Col., Westminster, 1988-89; dir. planned giving Am. Red Cross, Cleve., 1991-93; pres. Strategies for Planned Giving, Cleve., 1993—. Bd. dirs. Nat. Com. Planned Giving, Indpls. Bd. dirs. Nat. Com. Planned Giving, 1998-2000. Named Outstanding Fund Raising Exec. No. Ohio Planned Giving Coun./NSFRE Cleve./Ohio Coun. Fundraising Execs., 1997. Mem. Northern Ohio Planned Giving Council (pres., 1993-96, bd. dirs.), Nat. Soc. Fund Raising Execs. (v.p., 1992), Ohio Council Fund Raising Execs., Ohio Assn. Healthcare Philanthropy. Avocations: reading, travel, horses. Office: Strategies Planned Giving PO Box 665 Columbia Station OH 44028 Home: 27724 Ann Dr Columbia Station OH 44028-9536 E-mail: giftplan@aol.com.

BENDER, ROSS THOMAS, minister; b. Tavistock, Ont., Can., June 25, 1929; came to U.S., 1960, naturalized, 1966; s. Christian and Katie (Bender) B.; m. Ruth Eileen Steinmann, Dec. 22, 1950 (dec. Dec. 1997); children: Ross Lynn, Elizabeth, Michael, Lenore, Anne. BA, Goshen Coll., 1954, BD, 1956; MA, Yale U., 1961, PhD, 1962. Ordained to ministry Mennonite Ch., 1958. Prin. Rockway Mennonite sch., Kitchener, Ont., 1956-60; prof. Christian edn. Associated Mennonite Bibl. Sem., Elkhart, Ind., 1962-96, dean, 1964-79, dean emeritus, 1996; dir. Inst. Mennonite Studies, 1990-97; ret. Pres. Mennonite World Conf., 1984-90. Author: The People of God, 1969, Christians in Families, 1982, Education for Peoplehood, 1997; co-editor: Baptism, Peace and the State in the Reformed and Mennonite Traditions, 1991. Rockefeller doctoral fellow, 1960-61; Am. Assn. Theol. Schs. fellow, 1961-62; NIMH postdoctoral fellow U. Pa., 1970-71 Mennonite.

BENDER, STEVEN D., dental educator; b. Waterloo, Iowa, Mar. 11, 1959; BSc, Stephen F. Austin State U., 1981; DDS, Baylor Coll. Dentistry, 1986. Cert. in orofacial pain U. Medicine and Dentistry N.J., 2003. Asst. clin. prof. Baylor Coll. Dentistry, Dallas, 2001—03; pres., dir. North Tex. Ctr. for Head, Face & TMJ Pain, Plano, 2003—. Cons., spkr. Daiichi Pharm.; med., dental adv. Pain.com. Mem.: ADA, Orgn. Understanding Cluster Headaches, Am. Acad. Orofacial Pain, Internat. Sleep Medicine Assn., Am. Coll. Clin. Pharmacology, World Soc. Pain Clinicians, Serotonin Club, The Sci. Adv. Bd., Internat. Anesthesia Rsch. Soc., Internat. Soc. Anesthesia Pharmacology, Am. Headache Soc., Am. Pain Soc., Internat. Myopain Soc., Acad. Gen. Dentistry, Am. Acad. Craniofacial Pain, Am. Equilabration Soc., Am. Acad. Pain Mgmt., Pankey Alumni Assn., New Eng. Headache Coop., Dallas County Dental Soc., Dallas Acad. Gen. Dentistry (dir. 2003), Tex. Acad. Gen. Dentistry, Tex. Dental Assn., Am. Acad. Sleep Medicine, Internat. Headache Soc., Am. Acad. Neurology, Nat. Headache Found. Avocations: student ministies, golf, weightlifting, continuing education, book collecting. Office: North Tex Ctr Head Face & TMJ Ste 100 5068 W Plano Pkwy Plano TX 75093 Office Phone: 214-291-8063. E-mail: b.steve@benderdds.com.

BENDER, THOMAS, historian, educator; b. Redwood City, Calif., Apr. 18, 1944; s. Joseph Charles and Catherine Frances (McGuire) B.; m. Sally Hill, June 8, 1966 (div. 1983); 1 child, David William; m. Gwendolyn Wright, Jan. 14, 1984; 1 child, Sophia Wright BA, U. Santa Clara, 1966; MA, U. Calif.-Davis, 1967, PhD, 1971. Asst. prof. history and urban studies U. Wis., Green Bay, 1971-74; asst. prof. history NYU, N.Y.C., 1974-76, assoc. prof. history, 1976-77, prof. history, 1977—, Samuel Rudin prof. humanities, 1977-82, Univ. prof. humanities, 1982—, dean for the humanities, 1995-98, dir. Internat. Ctr. for Advanced Studies, 1996—. Rsch. planning com. N.Y.C. Social Sci. Rsch. Coun., 1985-88. Author: Toward an Urban Vision, 1975 (Frederick Jackson Turner prize 1975), Community and Social Change in America, 1978, (with Edwin Rozwenc) The Making of American Society, 1978, New York Intellect, 1987, Intellect and Public Life, 1993, The Unfinished City: New York and the Metropolitan Idea, 2002; co-author: The Education of Historians for the Twenty-First Century, 2004; editor: Democracy in America, 1981, Intellectual History Group Newsletter, 1978-85, The University and the City, 1988, The Anti-Slavery Debate: Capitalism and Abolitionism as a Problem in Historical Interpretation, 1992; co-editor: (with Carl Schorske) Budapest and New York: Studies in Metropolitan Transformation 1870-1930, 1994, (with Carl Schorske) The Tranformation of American Academic Culture, 1998, (with Michael Peter Smith) City and Nation: Rethinking Identity and Place, 2001, Rethinking American History in a Global Age, 2002; cons. editor New Studies in American Intellectual and Cultural History, 1981-94; mem. editl. bd. Readers Encyclopedia of American History, 1988-91, Am. Hist. Rev., 1991-94, Modern Intellectual History, 2002—; assoc. editor Am. Nat. Biography, 1990-97. Bd. dirs. Mcpl. Art Soc. N.Y., N.Y.C., 1983-84, N.Y. Coun. for the Humanities, 1989-96, chair, 1992-95; mem. gov. coun. Rockefeller Archives Ctr., Pocantico Hills, N.Y., 1987-92; trustee Grace Sch., N.Y.C., 1987-94. N.Y. Inst. Humanities fellow, 1977-88; Guggenheim fellow, 1980-81; Rockefeller Found. fellow, 1984-85; Getty scholar Getty Ctr. for Study of Art and Humanities, 1992-93; Mel and Lois Tukman fellow Cullman Ctr. for Scholars and Writers, N.Y. Pub. Libr., 2002-2003, Ctr. for Advanced Study in the Behavioral Scis. fellow, 2005-06. Fellow Am. Acad. Arts and Scis.; mem. Am. Hist. Assn., Orgn. Am. Historians, Soc. Am. Historians, Writers Guild, PEN. Democrat. Office: NYU Dept History 53 Washington Sq S New York NY 10012-1098

BENDER, VIRGINIA BEST, computer scientist, educator; b. Rockford, Ill., Feb. 10, 1945; d. Oscar Sheldon and Genevieve Best; m. Robert Keith Bender, July 19, 1969; children: Victoria Ruth, Christopher Keith. BS in Chemistry, Math., No. Ill. U., 1967; postgrad., U. Ill., 1967-69; MBA, Loyola U., Chgo., 1973. Cert. computer profl. Sr. sys. rep. Burroughs Corp., Chgo., 1969-73; sys. analyst Marshall Field & Co., Chgo., 1973-74; project leader Fed. Home Loan Bank, Chgo., 1974-76; sr. sys. analyst United Air Lines, Elk Grove Village, Ill., 1976-78; supr. Kemper Group, Long Grove, Ill., 1978-82; prof. computer info. sys., coord. computer info. sys. William Rainey Harper Coll., Palatine, Ill., 1982—2002, prof. emeritus, 2002—. Spkr. Midwest Computer Conf., DeKalb, Ill., 1988, moderator, 91; exch. prof. Maricopa CC, Mesa, Ariz., 1990, rsch. sabbatical, 93, 98; spkr. conf. info. tech. League for Innovation, Kansas City, Mo., 1995; steering com. Midwest Computer Conf., 1995—99; facilitator ToolBook User's Conf., Colorado Springs, Colo., 2000, presenter, Colo. Springs, 2001—03; adj. prof. SUNY/Westchester C.C., Valhalla, 2003—. Nat. chief mother-dau. group Indian Maidens YMCA, Des Plaines, 1982—83; mem. Vols. Pks. Environ. Edn. Westchester County Dept. Pks., Recreation and Conservation, NY, 2002—; mem. Master Singers of Westchester, 2005—; choir Kingswood United Meth. Ch., Buffalo Grove, Ill., 1982—2002, asst. organist, 1982—89; choir 1st Congl. Ch., Chappaqua, NY, 2002—, bell choir, 2003—. Named Tchr. of the Month, Burroughs Corp., Chgo., 1972. Mem.: No. Ill. Computer Soc., Ill. Assn. Data Processing Instrs., Inst. Cert. Computer Profls. (life), No. Ill. Alumni Assn. (life), Mortar Bd., Sigma Zeta, Phi Theta Kappa. Avocations: swimming, needlecrafts, playing piano, organ, and marimba. Personal E-mail: vbender@hotmail.com.

BENDERLIOGLU, ZEYNEP A., psychologist, researcher; b. Ankara, Turkey, Jan. 10, 1965; d. Erol E. and Nurten Benderlioglu; m. Thomas Kerler, Mar. 28, 2003. MA, Ohio State U., 1998, PhD, 2003. Program assoc. UN, Aankara, Turkey, 1989—91; rschr. Ohio State U., Columbus, Ohio, 1991—. Musician solo piano recital. Fellow, Ohio State U., 2002; grantee, NSF, 2000-2002; Mershon Ctr. Rsch. Fellow, Ohio State U., 2000-2002. Fellow: Internat. Soc. for Rsch. on Aggression, Human Biology Assn. Achievements include research in Asymmetrical characters are linked to temper, aggression; Birth Season Is Linked To Development Of Body Asymmetry; Male Typical Morphology In Females Is Linked To Aggression. Office: Ohio State Univ 251 Journalism Bldg 242 West 18th Ave Columbus OH 43210

BENDES, BARRY JAY, lawyer; b. NYC, Sept. 8, 1950; s. Arnold R. and Shirley Bendes; m. Tamara Shulman, Jan. 14, 1984; children: David Laurence, Jessica Haley. BA cum laude, Queens Coll., 1971; JD, NYU, 1974, cert. in real property law, 1980. Bar: NY 1975, US Dist. Ct. (so. and ea. dists.) NY 1975, US Ct. Appeals (2d cir.) 1975, US Supreme Ct. 1978, US Ct. Internat. Trade 1985, NJ 1988, US Dist. Ct. NJ 1988, US Tax Ct. 1988, US Ct. Appeals (7th cir.) 1997, US Ct. Appeals (3rd cir.) 1999. Assoc. Leon, Weill & Mahony, NYC, 1974—78, Washington, 1974—78, Certilman Haft Balin Buckley Kremer & Hyman and predecessors, NYC, LI, Boca Raton, Fla., 1978-82, ptnr., 1983-88, Rivkin, Radler, Dunne & Bayh, NYC, Chgo., LA, LI, Washington, 1988-89; shareholder, coun. Parker Duryee Rosoff & Haft, PC, NY, NJ, 1989-93; ptnr. Kane Kessler, PC, NYC, NJ, 1994—97, Vedder Price Kaufman & Kammholz, NYC, Chgo., Livingston, NJ, 1997—2003, Wolf, Block, Schorr & Solis-Cohen LLP, NYC, Roseland and Cherry Hill, NJ, Phila., Wilmington, Del., Boston, 2003—. Sr. v.p. adminstrn. and gen. counsel Emerson Computer Corp. & Emerson Tech. LP, 1989-92, gen. coun., 1990-92, sec., 1991-92, Emerson Radio Corp.; spkr. in field. Author: Accounting Terms in Legal Documents, 2000, 2001, PLI; rsch. editor NYU Rev. Law and Social Change, 1972-74; contbr. articles to profl. publs. Organizing new bus. NJ Bar Found., 1994—2005. Mem. ABA (com. on computer contracting, sect. sci. and tech. 1983-98), Am. Arbitration Assn. (nat. panel arbitrators 1978-98), Assn. Bar City NY (computer law com. 1986-89, chmn. sub-com. software liability 1987-89, uniform state laws 1990-94, 97-2001, sec., task force ltd. liability cos. 1993-94), NY State Bar Assn., NJ Inst. CLE (organization and sale of businesses 2001-05, negotiation exec. compensation and employments agts. 2001-02), NJ State Bar Assn., Bus. Law Sect. (dir. 1998—, vice chair, 2000-2004, sec. 2004—) com. on third party opinions 1989—, chair 1998—, computer and internet related law 1993—, third party legal opinions in acquisitions and mergers 1995-2000, in secured financings under and outside ABA accord 1993, UN convention internat. sale of goods, drafting documents with accounting tems, third party legal opinions 1st ann. bus. law symposium 2000, drafting agts. using acctg. terminology, 2d ann. bus. law symposium 2001, negotiation of exec. corp. agreements 2002), Am. Corp. Counsel Assn. (dir. greater NY chpt. 1990-2003, sec. 1995-2002, chair com. on third party legal opinions 1992-2002, moderator corp. counsel roundtable 1993-2003, v.p. 1998-2001), Am. Soc. Corp. Secs. (corp. practice com. 1992—), NJ Inn Transactional Counsel (trustee, bd. dirs. 2003-). Office: Wolf Block Schorr & Solis-Cohen 250 Park Ave New York NY 10177 also: 101 Eisenhower Pkwy Roseland NJ 07068 Office Phone: 212-883-4965. Business E-Mail: bbendes@wolfblock.com.

BENDICH, JUDITH ELLEN, lawyer; b. N.Y.C., Jan. 17, 1945; m. Arnold J. Bendich, Aug. 2, 1964; 1 child, Justin Bendich. BA, U. Md., 1966; JD, U. Wash., 1975. Bar: Wash. 1975, U.S. Dist. Ct. (we. dist.) Wash. 1975, U.S. Ct. Appeals (9th cir.) 1975, U.S. Ct. Appeals (D.C. cir.) 1986, U.S. Supreme Ct. 1979. Ptnr. Bendich, Stobaugh & Strong, Seattle, 1975—; lectr. U. Wash., Seattle, 1975-76; commr. Seattle Civil Svc. Commn., 1985-87. Pres. ACLU of Wash., Seattle, 1980-83; bd. dirs. Nat. ACLU, N.Y.C., 1983—, mem. exec. com., 1987-97. Mem. FBA, King County Bar Assn., Washington Women Lawyers, Washington State Trial Lawyers Assn., Nat. Employment Lawyers Assn. Office: Bendich Stobaugh & Strong PC 900 4th Ave Ste 3800 Seattle WA 98164-1044

BENDICKSON, MARCUS J., engineering company executive; BS, Iowa State U.; MS, Columbia U.; PhD, U. Ala., 1980. Rschr. signal and com. lab Bell Labs; mgr. radio bulk filtering br. Teledyne Brown Engring.; pres., CEO Dynetics, Inc., Ala., 1989—. Mem. adv. bd. U. Ala., Colonial Bank; bd. dirs. Huntsville-Madison County C. of C. Address: Dynetics Inc 1000 Explorer Blvd NW Huntsville AL 35806-2806*

BENDIG, WILLIAM CHARLES, editor, artist; b. Corry, Pa., Dec. 1, 1927; s. William Charles and Hazel Grace Mae (Dailey) B. BA with honors, Trinity Coll., 1953; postgrad., U. London, 1955-56. Founding editor Erie (Pa.) Tribune, 1944-48; mgr. Nat. Symphonic Choir, Erie, 1946-49; program mgr. Erie Philharmonic Orch., 1947-49; instr. Cheshire (Conn.) Acad., 1953-54, Brunswick Sch., Greenwich, Conn., 1954-55; editor in chief, pub. theARTgallery Mag., Ivoryton, Conn., 1957-84; prin., pub. Hollycroft. Pubs., Ivoryton, 1987—; editor in chief Botswana Rev., Ivoryton and Gaborone, 1988-90; curator, archivist theARTgallery Archive, 1990—; pres. Hollycroft Found., 1992—; cons. Kuwait Info. Office, Washington, 1993-96; chief curator The Sculpture Mile Exhbns., Madison and Middletown, Conn., 2001—. Cons. Submarine Force Libr. & Nautilus Mus., Groton, Conn., 1994—; dep. dir. U.S.-Africa Arts Found., Gaborone, 1988-93, life trustee; trustee Contemporary Sculptors Guild, 1994-95; dep. dir. Sculptors Guild, N.Y.C., 1997—; juror nat. art exhbns.; lectr. univs. and mus. Designer, fabricator Pentecost rose window All Sts.' Episcopal Ch., Ivoryton, 1988; contbr. works in various art exhbns. V.p. Essex Art Assn., 1960-62; founding v.p. Ivoryton Village Assn.; mem. Essex Landmark Commn., 1981-82; trustee Ivoryton Pub. Libr., Ivoryton Playhouse Found. (founding); dir. art seminar program. Episcopal Conf. Ctr., Ivoryton, 1982-92. Recipient Greater New Haven Arts Coun. aard, 2003. Mem. Mediaeval Acad. Am., Africa Studies Assn., Friends of Trinity Libr., Naval Submarine League, Trinity Coll. Alumni Assn. (pres. New London chpt. 1963-67), Grad. Club, New Haven Club. Episcopalian (vestryman 1970-92). Home and Office: Hollycroft Found Main St Ivoryton CT 06442-0278

BENDIKSEN, ODDVAR OLAV, aerospace engineer, educator; b. Tennskjer, Troms, Norway, July 7, 1945; s. Albert and Mally Bendiksen; m. Ellen Berit Myklebust, Oct. 24, 1964; children: Lene, Aage. BS, Northrop Inst. Tech., 1968; MS, UCLA, 1975, PhD, 1980. Airframe and power plant lic. FAA, 1968. Engring. sys. analyst The Fluor Corp., LA, 1968—69; power plant engr. TWA, Kansas City, Mo., 1969—70; engring. systems analyst Pacific Airmotive Corp., Burbank, Calif., 1970—72, project engr., 1972—75, sr. project engr., 1975—76, dir. engring., 1976—77, dir. of project engring., 1977—80; asst. prof. U. So. Calif., LA, 1980—81, Princeton U., 1981—88; assoc. prof. U. Calif., LA, 1988—94, prof., vice chmn., 1994—99, prof., 1999—. Aviation and aerospace engring. cons.; assoc. editor AIAA Jour., 1983—86. Contbr. numerous articles to profl. jours. Recipient Structures and Materials award, ASME, 1990, 1992. Fellow: AIAA (assoc.). Office: UCLA Mech and Aerospace Engring Los Angeles CA 90095-1597 Office Phone: 310-205-5453.

BENDINER, ROBERT, writer, editor; b. Pitts., Dec. 15, 1909; s. William and Lillian (Schwartz) B.; m. Kathryn Rosenberg, Dec. 24, 1934; children: David, William (dec.), Margaret. Student, CCNY, 1928-33; LHD (hon.), L.I. U., 1994. Mng. editor The Nation, N.Y.C., 1937-44, assoc. editor, 1946-50, free-lance writer, 1951-68, 78—. Lectr., program chmn. Wellesley Summer Inst. Social Progress, 1946-53; mem. faculty Salzburg Sem. in Am. Studies, 1956; vis. lectr. journalism Wesleyan U. (Conn.), 1983 Contbg. editor The Reporter, N.Y.C., 1956-60; U.S. corr. New Statesman, London, 1959-61; mem. editorial bd. N.Y. Times, 1969-77; author: The Riddle of the State Department, 1942, White House Fever, 1960, Obstacle Course on Capitol Hill, 1964, Just Around the Corner, 1967, The Politics of Schools, 1969, The Fall of the Wild, The Rise of the Zoo, 1981, TV documentary NBC White Paper, The Man in the Middle, The State Legislator, 1961. Served with AUS, 1944-45. Guggenheim fellow, 1962-63; grantee Carnegie Fund; recipient Benjamin Franklin Mag. award U. Ill., 1955, NEA award, 1960 Mem. Nat. Press Club. Clubs: Coffee House (N.Y.C.). Home and Office: Southampton Estates 238 Street Rd Apt PC205 Southampton PA 18966-3128 Office Phone: 215-942-9487.

BENDINGER, GARY FREDERICK, lawyer; b. Sioux City, Iowa, Jan. 28, 1950; s. Warren Frederick and Joann (Janssea) B.; m. Christina Ruth Griffith (div.); m. Lorie Jean Carter, Sept. 17, 1981; children: Zelda Fay, Alton Mandel, Bernard Nathaniel. BA, Hastings Coll., 1972; JD, U. San Francisco, 1975. Bar: UT 1975, N.D. 1975, U.S. Ct. Appeals (10th cir.), U.S. Supreme Ct. 1981. Assoc. ptnr. Berman & Giauque, Salt Lake City, 1975-80; v.p. Biauque, Holbrook, Bendinger & Gurmankin, Salt Lake City, 1980-81, Giauque & Williams's, Salt Lake City, 1981—, Giauque, Williams, Wilcox & Bendinger, Salt Lake City, 1987; ptnr., litig. practice Bendinger Crockett Peterson Greenwood & Casey, Salt Lake City. Fellow Am. Coll. Trial Lawyers; mem. ABA (litigation and antitrust sects.), State Bar of Utah (litigation sect.). Democrat. Lutheran. Avocation: golf. Office: Bendinger Crockett Peterson Greenwood & Casey Ste 400 170 S Main St Salt Lake City UT 84101 Office Phone: 801-350-7835. Office Fax: 801-531-1486.

BENDITT, THEODORE MATTHEW, humanities educator; b. Phila., Oct. 23, 1940; m. Anne Rosamond Shaw, Feb. 3, 1968; 1 child, David Shaw. AB, U. Pa., 1962, JD, 1965, MA, 1967; PhD, U. Pitts., 1971. Instr. Duke U., Durham, N.C., 1970-71, asst. prof., 1971-75, U. So. Calif., Los Angeles, 1975-78; assoc. prof. U. Ala., Birmingham, 1978-83, prof., 1983—, dean, Sch. Arts and Humanities, 1984-98. Author: Law as Rule and Principle, 1978, Rights, 1982, The Virtue of Pride: Jane Austen as Moralist, 2003. Recipient Younger Humanist Fellowship, NEH, 1974-75. Mem. Am. Philos. Assn., Am. Soc. for Polit. and Legal Philosophy, Amintaphil. Office: Univ of Ala at Birmingham Dept Philosophy Birmingham AL 35294-1260

BENDIX, HELEN IRENE, lawyer; b. N.Y.C., July 24, 1952; d. Gerhard Max and Eva Gabriela (Sternberger) B.; m. John A. Kronstadt, Nov. 29, 1974; children: Jessica Claire Kronstadt, Erik Bendix Kronstadt, Nicola Eva Kronstadt. BA, Cornell U., 1973; JD, Yale U., 1976. Bar: Calif. 1976, D.C. 1978, U.S. Dist. Ct. D.C. 1980, U.S. Dist. Ct. (ctrl. dist.) Calif. 1986, U.S. Ct. Appeals (D.C. cir.) 1981, U.S. Ct. Appeals (9th cir.) 1987, U.S. Dist. Ct. (so. dist.) Calif. 1990. Law clk. to Hon. Shirley M. Hufstedler U.S. Ct. Appeals (9th cir.), L.A., 1976-77; assoc. Wilmer Cutler & Pickering, Washington, 1977-79; asst. prof. law UCLA, 1979-80; from assoc. to ptnr. Leva Hawes Symington Martin & Oppenheimer, Washington, 1980-85; of counsel Gibson Dunn & Crutcher, L.A., 1986-89; ptnr. Heller Ehrman White & McAuliffe, L.A., 1989-96; sr. v.p., gen. counsel KCET Cmty. TV of So. Calif., 1996—; judge Mcpl. Ct. L.A. Jud. Dist., 1997-2000, Superior Ct. L.A., 2000—. Vis. prof. law UCLA, 1985-86; chair ADR com. L.A. Superior Ct., 2004. Co-author: Moore's Federal Practice, Vols. X and XI, 1976, Vols. XII and XIII, 1979; contbr. articles to profl. jours. Violinist Palisades Symphony, Pacific Palisades, Calif., 1989—. Mem. European Union Ctr. of Calif., (mem. exec. adv. bd., 2003—), Am. Law Inst., D.C. Bar Assn., Calif. State Bar Assn. (chairperson internat. law sect. 1990-91), Calif. Judges Assn., L.A. County Bar Assn. (past pres. dispute resolution svcs.), Jud. Coun. Calif. (mem. ad hoc com. on canon 6D 1998, working group on mediator ethics 2000, mem. access and fairness adv. com.), Nat. Charity League (past chmn. 12th grade class), Chancery Club, Phi Beta Kappa. Office: Dept 18 111 N Hill St Los Angeles CA 90012-3014

BENDIX, JANE, artist, writer, illustrator; b. Lansing, Mich., Oct. 20, 1920; d. Helmer and Violet Walstrum; m. Reinhard Bendix, July 5, 1940 (dec. Feb. 1991); children: Karen, Erik, John. BA, U. Chgo., 1941; postgrad., Art Inst. Chgo., 1941-43. Freelance artist, 1941—. Author: Mi'ca, 1987 (Kinderbuch prize 1987), Mi'ca, Buffalo Hunter, 1992, Türkishöhle, 1990, Chaco. The Anasazi Mystery, 1997, The Secret Map, 2000; exhbns. San Francisco, 1988, Oakland, Calif., 1979, Goldern, Switzerland, 1965, Oxford, Eng., 1966, Washington, 1975, Berlin, Germany, 1990. Mem. Calif. Watercolor Assn. Home: 3 Orchard Ln Berkeley CA 94704-1821

BEN-DOR, GISSELLE, conductor, musician; b. Montevideo, Uruguay; came to U.S., 1982; m. Eli Ben-Dor; children: Roy, Gabriel. Student, Acad. of Music, Tel Aviv; artist diploma, Rubin Acad. Music, Tel Aviv; M, Yale Sch. of Music, 1982. Music dir. Annapolis Symphony, Md., Pro Arte Chamber Orch. of Boston; condr. Norwalk (Conn.) Youth Symphony; conducting fellow L.A. Philharm. Inst., 1984, Tanglewood Music Ctr., 1985; resident condr. Houston Symphony, 1991; music dir. Santa Barbara Symphony, Calif., 1994—. Resident condr. Houston Symphony; condr. variety conducting activities including prestigious summer festivals, competitions, 1983-87, Hungarian Nat. Symphony, Budapest Philharm., others; guest condr. orchs. in Uruguay, Ea. Europe, Israel and U.S. including Barvarian Radio Orch., Boston POPS, New World Symphony, Women's Philharm, San Francisco, Minn. Orch. in Summerfest Festival, 1986, N.Y. Philharm., 1993, 95, Orquestra del Teatro Nacional, Brazil, Ulster Orch., Israel Philharm., 1991, Carnegie Hall, 1991, others; past music dir. Houston Youth Symphony; past acting orch. dir. Shepherd Sch. Music Rice U.; music dir. Boston ProArte Chamber Orch., Annapolis Symphony. Condr. Israel Philharm. Orch. (play) The Rite of Spring; recs. with London Symphony, Israel Chamber Orch., (CD) London Symphony Orch., Sofia Soloists, Boston ProArte Chamber Orch.; numerous TV appearances. Am.-Israel Cultural Found scholar, Frances Wickes scholar; Leonard Bernstein fellow; recipient Bartók prize Hungarian TV Internat. Condrs. Competition, 1986. Office: Santa Barbara Symphony Orch Arlington Theatre 1900 State St Ste G Santa Barbara CA 93101-8424 also: Del Rosenfield Assoc 714 Ladd Rd Bronx NY 10471-1204 E-mail: delrosdra@aol.com.

BENDOR, JONATHAN, economics professor, researcher; BA, U. Calif., 1972, MA, 1973, PhD, 1980. With Stanford U., 1979—; Walter and Elise Haas prof. polit. economics and organizations. Faculty dir. Stanford U.; mem. electoral bd. Am. Polit. Sci. Rev., Am. Jour. Polit. Sci. Contbr. articles to profl. jours. Fellow: Am. Acad. Arts and Scis.; mem.: Am. Polit. Sci. Assn. Office: Stanford Grad Sch Bus 518 Meml Way Stanford Univ Stanford CA 94305-5015*

BENDOR, SUSAN JULIA, social worker, educator; b. Budapest, Feb. 5, 1937; arrived in U.S., 1959, naturalized, 1968; d. David and Elizabeth Blum; m. Edgar Bendor, Nov. 29, 1959; children: Jane Melissa, Catherine Anne. BS in Math. and Physics, Bishops U., Lennoxville, Que., Can., 1968; M in Social Svc., Adelphi U, 1962; PhD in Social Welfare, CUNY, 1986. Caseworker Jewish Childcare Assn., NYC, 1962—64; psychiat. social worker Mt. Sinai Hosp., NYC, 1964—65; chief psychiat. social worker Nassau County Med. Ctr., East Meadow, NY, 1968—75; assoc. dir. field devel. SUNY, Stony Brook, NY, 1971—75; dir. social work Molloy Coll., Rockville Centre, NY, 1977—81; assoc. dir. social svcs. dept Montefiore Med. Ctr., Bronx, NY, 1981—86; assoc. prof., dir. gerontology program Yeshiva U., NYC, 1988—. Co-chair Coun. On Aging, NYC, 1994—; head start cons. OEO, DC, 1966—68; sr. tng. cons. sch. social work Hunter Coll., NYC, 1977—80; adv. social work com. Am. Ctr. South. Contbr. articles to profl. jours. Chair social action com., mem. bd. dirs. Temple Isaiah, Great Neck, NY, 1995. Master; NASW (licentiate; exec. bd. 2001—03, chair 1999—2001, Citations from County Execs. 2001, Social Worker of Yr. 1975). Avocations: folk dancing, swimming. Home: 38 Allenwood Road Great Neck NY 11023-2127 Office: Wurzweiler School Of Social Work-Yeshiva 2495 Amsterdam Avenue New York NY 10033

BENEDEK, MELINDA, television executive; BA, Oxford U., 1972; JD, Columbia U., 1977; French Law Degree, 1974. Owner High Wire Ltd., 1981—84; ptnr. Pollock, Bloom & Dekom; exec. v.p. Imagine Films; exec. v.p. bus. affairs Twentieth Century Fox, L.A.; exec. v.p. bus. affairs and prodn. Showtime Networks, L.A. Office: ShowtimeNetworks 1633 Broadway Fl 37 New York NY 10019-6708 also: Showtime Networks Inc Ste 1600 10880 Wilshire Blvd Los Angeles CA 90024-4116 Fax: 310-234-5397.

BENEDETTO, ANTHONY DOMINICK See BENNETT, TONY

BENEDETTO, JENNIFER A., elementary school educator; b. Queens, N.Y., July 5, 1972; d. Thomas E. Lobacz and Josephine Montgomery. AA in Liberal Arts, SUNY, Farmingdale, 1992; BS in Elem. Edn., L.I. U., 1995, MS in Spl. Edn., 1997. Substitute tchr. Lindenhurst (N.Y.) Pub. Schs., 1995—96, tchr., 1996—2005. Vol. big sister Big Bros./Big Sisters, 2003—. Avocations: travel, exercise.

BENEDICK, RICHARD ELLIOT, diplomat; b. NYC, May 10, 1935; s. Lester and Jean (Shamski) B.; m. Hildegard Schulz, 1957 (div.); children: Andreas, Julianna; m. Helen Freeman, 1983 (div.); m. Irene Federwisch, 1997. AB summa cum laude, Columbia U., 1955; MA with honors, Yale U., 1956; DBA, Harvard U., 1962; DSc (hon.), N.C. State U., 2004. Program economist AID U.S. Dept. State, Washington, 1958, Tehran, Iran, 1959-61, Karachi, Pakistan, 1962-64; economist OECD, Paris, 1964-66; 1st sec. Am. Embassy, Bonn, Germany, 1966-71; dir. Office Devel. Fin., Washington, 1971-75; counselor for econ. and comml. affairs Am. Embassy, Athens, Greece, 1975-77; mem. sr. seminar Dept. State, Washington, 1977-78; coord. population affairs with rank amb. U.S. Dept. State, Washington, 1979-84, dep. asst. sec. for environ., health and natural resources, 1984-87; sr. fellow World Wildlife Fund, 1987-98; dep. dir. Battelle Pacific N.W. Nat. Lab., 1998—; sr. adv. Battelle/Joint Global Change Rsch. Inst./U. Md., 2001—. Spl. advisor to sec. gen. UN Conf. on Environ. and Devel., 1990-92, Internat. Conf. on Population and Devel., 1993-94; pres. Nat. Coun. for Sci. and Environ., 1994—; vis. prof. Acad. Internat. l'Environnement, Geneva, 1992-96; lectr. in field; head U.S. del. to confs.; chief U.S. negotiator Montreal Protocol on protection of ozone layer, 1985-87; bd. dirs. Population Resource Ctr., Pacific Inst., Environ. and Energy Study Inst.; internat. adv. bd. Battelle, 1994-97, Environ. Tech. Ctr., Berlin, 1996, Climate Policy Ctr., 2002—; v.p. OECD Environ. Com., 1984-87; v.p. Transboundary Air Pollution Conv., Econ. Commn. for Europe, 1985-87; vis. fellow Nat. Ctr. Atmospheric Rsch., 1988-89, Ostwestwirtschafts Akademie, Berlin, 1991-96, Wissenschaftszentrum Berlin, 1995—; Stimson fellow Yale U., 2001; faculty Fgn. Svc. Inst., U.S. Dept. State, 1999—; cons. in field. Author: Industrial Finance in Iran, 1964, The High Dam and the Transformation of the Nile, 1979, Ozone Diplomacy, 1991, rev. edit., 1998; contbr. articles to profl. jours. Recipient Presdl. Meritorious Svc. award, 1984, 90, Superior Honor medal Dept. State, 1985, 87, John Jacob Rogers award, 1993, Presdl. Disting. Svc. award, 1988, ann. award Climate Inst., 1988, UN Global Ozone award, 1997; Evans fellow Oxford U., 1956, Population Ref. Bur. hon. fellow, 1986. Fellow World Acad. of Art and Sci. (elected 1991), Am. Acad. Diplomacy (elected 2002); mem. Toenissteiner Kreis (Germany), Phi Beta Kappa. Home: 4111 27th St N Arlington VA 22207-5211 Office: Joint Global Change Rsch Inst 8400 Baltimore Ave College Park MD 20470 Business E-Mail: richard.benedick@pnl.gov.

BENEDICT, BARRY ARDEN, university administrator; b. Wauchula, Fla., Feb. 7, 1942; s. Clifford Allen and Caroline Mae (Watzke) B.; m. Sharon Gail Parker; children: Erin, Beau, Brooke, Mark. BCE, U. Fla., 1965, MS in Engring., 1967, PhD in Civil Engring., 1968. Rsch. assoc. U. Fla., Gainesville, 1968-69, prof., 1980-86; asst. prof. Vanderbilt U., Nashville, 1969-72, assoc. prof., program dir., 1972-75; assoc. prof. Tulane U., New Orleans, 1975-77, U. S.C., Columbia, 1978-80; prof., dept. head La. Tech. U., Ruston, 1986-88, dean., Jack Thigpen prof., 1988-98; v.p. acad. affairs Rose-Hulman Inst. Tech., Terre Haute, Ind., 1998—. Project dir. La. NSF-EPSCoR, 1989-94; cons. to numerous industries; dir. Inst. Micromanufacturing, 1997-98. Contbr. articles to profl. jours. and chpts. to books. Mem. NSPE (gov.-at-large profl. engrs. in edn. divsn.), La. Dept. Econ. Devel., La. Transp. Rsch. Ctr. (vice chair 1993-98). Methodist. Avocation: jogging. Office: Rose-Hulman Inst Tech 5500 Wabash Ave Terre Haute IN 47803-3999 E-mail: barry.a.benedict@rose-hulmon.edu.

BENEDICT, BURTON, retired museum director, anthropologist; b. Balt., May 20, 1923; s. Burton Eli Oppenheim and Helen Blanche (Deiches) B.; m. Marion MacColl Steuber, Sept. 23, 1950; children: Helen, Barbara MacVean AB cum laude, Harvard U., 1949; PhD, U. London, 1954. Sr. rsch. fellow Inst. Islamic Studies, McGill U., Montreal, Que., Can., 1954-55; sociol. rsch. officer Colonial Office, London and Mauritius, 1955-58; sr. lectr. social anthropology London Sch. Econs., 1958-68; prof. anthropology U. Calif., Berkeley, 1968-91, prof. emeritus, 1991—, chmn. dept., 1970-71, dean social scis., 1971-74, dir. Hearst Mus. Anthropology, 1989-94; dir. emeritus Hearst Mus. Anthropology, 1994—. Dir. U. Calif. Study Ctr. for U.K. and Ireland, London, 1986-88 Author: Indians in a Plural Society, 1961; author and editor: Problems of Smaller Territories, 1967, (with M. Benedict) Men, Women & Money in Seychelles, 1982, The Anthropology of World's Fairs, 1983; contbr. numerous articles to profl. jours. Trustee East Bay Zool. Soc. Sgt. USAF, 1942-46. Recipient Western Heritage award Nat. Cowboy Hall of Fame, 1984; rsch. fellow Colonial Office, 1955-58, 60, U. Calif., Berkeley, 1974-75; grantee NEH, 1981-83. Fellow Royal Anthrop. Inst. (mem. coun. 1962-65, 67-68, 86-89), Am. Anthrop. Assn.; mem. Assn. Social Anthropologists of Brit. Commonwealth, Athenaeum Club (London) Avocations: museums, the zoo, birdwatching, collecting postcards, world fairs. Office: U Calif Berkeley Dept Anthropology Berkeley CA 94720-0001

BENEDICT, Mrs. COLEMAN HAMILTON See WOLFE, ETHYLE

BENEDICT, DOROTHY JONES, genealogist, researcher; b. Bronxville, NY, Mar. 23, 1916; d. Harry Edwin and Katherine Jones; m. Mark Charles Benedict; children: Ann Benedict Johnson, Sharon Benedict Bash, Gail Benedict Bain, Faye. BA, Goucher Coll., 1938. Statistician E.W. Axe Co., N.Y.C., 1938; with Nat. Labor Rels. Bd., N.Y.C., 1938-39. Leader Girl Scouts of Am., Glastonbury, Conn., 1957-64; creator convalescent homes Sunday mini-svc. Asbury Ch., Glastonbury, 1960-70. Mem. Nat. Soc. Magna Carta Dames, DAR, Delta Delta Delta, Phi Beta Kappa. Methodist. Avocations: golf, walking, art. Home: 100 S Interlachen Ave Winter Park FL 32789-4438

BENEDICT, GAIL CLEVELAND, music educator; b. Rockville Ctr., N.Y., Dec. 15, 1942; d. Walter Charles and Louise Cleveland; m. Donald Alexander Davis, July 4, 1967 (div. Apr. 14, 1980); 1 child, Scott Paul Davis; m. Robert Lorin Benedict, July 6, 1983. BS in Music Edn., SUNY, Fredonia, 1964; MS in Adminstrn. and Supervision, Nova U., 1980; EdD, U. Sarasota, Fla., 1982. Cert. tchr. Fla., N.Y. Music tchr., dept. chair North Country Elem. Sch., Stony Brook, NY, 1964—66; music tchr., chorus dir. Narimasu Elem. Sch., Tokyo, 1966—67; vocal music tchr. Mineral Wells (Tex.) H.S., 1967—68; music tchr., chorus dir. Park Ave. Elem. Sch., Amityville, NY, 1968—70; music tchr., resource tchr. Magruder Elem. Sch., Newport News, Va., 1970—72; music specialist Skyview Elem. Sch., Pinellas Park, Fla., 1979—; adj. instr. Nova Southea. U., Tampa, Fla., 1991—. Gen. mgr. V.I. Properties, St. Petersburg, Fla., 1989—. Author: (book) Cruzan Child, 2002. Grantee, Pinellas County Arts Coun., 2001. Mem.: Pinellas Co. Music Educators Assn. (vocal chair 1980—83), Fla. Elem. Music Educators Assn. (chair Dist. III 1979—84), Music Educators Nat. Conf. Avocations: travel, reading, history, writing. Home: 6712 Cardinal Dr S Saint Petersburg FL 33707 Office: Skyview Elem Sch 8601 60th St N Pinellas Park FL 33782 E-mail: drmommusic@aol.com.

BENEDICT, JAMES NELSON, lawyer; b. Norwich, N.Y., Oct. 6, 1949; s. Nelson H. and Helen (Wilson) B.; m. Janet E. Fagal, May 8, 1982. BA magna cum laude, St. Lawrence U., 1971; JD, Albany Law Sch. of Union U., 1974. Bar: N.Y. 1975, U.S. Dist. Ct. (no., ea. and so. dists.) N.Y. 1975, U.S. Ct. Appeals (2d cir.) 1975, U.S. Ct. Appeals (8th cir.) 1977, U.S. Ct. Appeals (10th cir.) 1978, U.S. Ct. Appeals (11th cir.) 1982, U.S. Supreme Ct. 1978. Assoc. Rogers & Wells, N.Y.C., 1974-82; ptnr. Clifford Chance, N.Y.C., 1982—2004, Milbank Tweed, Hadley & McCloy, N.Y.C., 2004—. Mem. bd. contbg. editors and advisors The Corp. Law Rev., 1976-86; contbr. articles to profl. jours. Bd. dirs. Reece Sch., N.Y.C., 1984-89, Stanley Isaacs Neighborhood Ctr., N.Y.C., 1984-89; trustee St. Lawrence U., Canton, N.Y., 1985-91. Mem. ABA (chmn. securities litigation subcom. on 1940 Act matters 1984-86, 96—), Fed. Bar Coun. N.Y. State Bar Assn., Assn. Bar City N.Y. (com. on securities regulaton, fed. legislation com., fed. cts. com.), Am. Soc. Writers on Legal Subjects, Sky Club (N.Y.C.), Scarsdale Golf Club, Phi Beta Kappa. Home: 26 Kensington Rd Scarsdale NY 10583-2217 Office Phone: 212-530-5696. E-mail: jbenedict@milbank.com.

BENEDICT, JOSEPH HAROLD, JR., academic administrator, management consultant; b. Albany, N.Y., Aug. 13, 1941; s. Joseph Harold Sr. and Frances Ellen (Long) B.; m. Elizabeth Ann Roberts, July 8, 1968 (div.); children: Brian Arthur, Timothy Joseph. BS in Edn., SUNY, Brockport, 1965; MS in Edn. Adminstrn., SUNY, Albany, 1967; MS in Pub. Adminstrn., L.I. U. C.W. Post Campus, Brookville, 1985. Coord. student activities Rockland (N.Y.) Cmty. Coll., 1966-67; assoc. dir. student activities SUNY, Farmingdale, 1967-72; dir. student life L.I. U., 1972-90; mgmt. cons. Henn & Green Assocs. Inc., Williston Park, N.Y., 1984—; exec. dir. Bklyn. Coll. Student Svcs. Corp., Bklyn., 1990—. Mem. Assn. Coll. Unions Internat. (pres. 1986, v.p. regional affairs 1981-84, regional rep. 1984-85, Butts-Whiting award 1992), Nat. Assn. Campus Activities (chair commn. for vols. 1987-88). Democrat. Roman Catholic. Avocations: boating, bicycling, cross country skiing. Home: Apt 511 140-18 Burden Crescent Briarwood NY 11435

BENEDICT, KENNETTE MARI, foundation executive, researcher; b. NYC, Jan. 19, 1948; d. Donald LaVerne Benedict and Ann Kennette Cnare; m. Jonathan David Casper, Aug. 2, 1980 (div. 2002); 1 child, Sarah Casper. AB, Oberlin Coll., 1971; PhD, Stanford U., 1981. Rschr. Gov.'s Com. Law Enforcement/Adminstrn. Criminal Justice, Boston, 1971; asst. prof. Rutgers U., New Brunswick, N.J., 1980-81, U. Ill., Urbana-Champaign, 1981-85; dep. dir. peace and internat. cooperation MacArthur Found., Chgo., 1989-92, dir. internat. peace and security, 1992—, sr. advisor on philanthropy, 2002—. Cons. Compton Found., Menlo Park, 1998-2000, bd. dirs.; adv. coun. Stanley Found., Muscatine, Iowa, 2001-, Ctr. for Effective Philanthropy, 2003—; advisor Rockefeller Bros. Fund, NYC, 1996-97, com. mem. Leonard Rieser Prize, Chgo., 2000— Contbr. articles to profl. jours. Bd. trustees mem. Oberlin Coll., 2004—; bd. dirs. Compton Found., 2003—. Lena Lake Forrest fellow Bus. and Profl. Women's Found., 1977-78. Mem. Coun. on Fgn. Rels., Internat. Inst. Strategic Studies, Chgo. Coun. on Fgn. Rels. Avocations: hiking, music. Office: MacArthur Found 140 S Dearborn St Chicago IL 60603

BENEDICT, LAWRENCE NEAL, foreign service officer; b. Independence, Mo., Dec. 17, 1942; s. Albert Michael and Audentia Elizabeth (Thomas) B.; m. Gloria Kay Bruning, July 2, 1966. BA, Calif. State U., Long Beach, 1974. V.p. A.M. Benedict & Assocs., Long Beach, 1966-72; vice consul Am. Embassy, Dahka, Bangladesh, 1974-77; comml. officer Am. Consulate Gen., Rio de Janeiro, 1977-79; desk officer for Bangladesh U.S. Dept. State, Washington, 1979-80, desk officer for Turkey, 1980-82, dep. dir. devel. fin., 1986-89; fin., devel. officer Am. Embassy, Ankara, Turkey, 1982-86, counselor econ. affairs Islamabad, Pakistan, 1989-92, dep. chief of mission Khartoum, Sudan, 1992-95, amb. Praia, Cape Verde, 1996—. Staff sgt. U.S. Army N.G., 1963-69. Mem. Am. Fgn. Svc. Assn. Avocations: tennis, reading, collecting books and wine. Address: Am Embassy London PSC 801 Box 34 FPO AE 09498 Personal E-mail: benedict_li@hotmail.com.

BENEDICT, MANSON, chemical engineer, educator; b. Lake Linden, Mich., Oct. 9, 1907; s. C. Harry and Lena I. (Manson) Benedict; m. Marjorie Oliver Allen, July 6, 1935 (dec. 1995); children: Mary Hannah (Mrs. Myran C. Sauer, Jr.), Marjorie Alice (Mrs. Martin Cohn). B in Chemistry, Cornell U., 1928; MS, MIT, 1932, PhD, 1935. NRC fellow chemistry, 1935—36; rsch. assoc. geophysics Harvard, 1936—37; rsch. chemist M.W. Kellogg Co., 1938—43; in charge process design gaseous diffusion plant for uranium-235 Kellex Corp., 1943—46; dir. process development Hydrocarbon Rsch., Inc., 1946—51; tech. asst. to gen. mgr. AEC, 1951—52; prof. nuclear engring. MIT, 1951—69, Institute prof., 1969—73, prof. emeritus, 1973—, head dept. nuclear engring., 1958—71; dir. Burns & Roe, Inc., 1979—85. Sci. advisor Nat. Rsch. Corp., 1951—58, dir., 1962—67; mem. gen. adv. com. AEC, 1958—68, chmn., 1962—64; dir. Atomic Indsl. Forum, 1966—72; mem. energy R & D adv. coun. FEA, 1973—75. Co-editor: Engineering Developments in the Gaseous Diffusion Process, 1949; co-author: Nuclear Chemical Engineering, 1981. Recipient Indsl. and Engring. Chemistry award, Am. Chem. Soc., 1962, Perkin medal Soc. Chem. Industry, Robert E. Wilson award in nuclear chem. engring., 1968, Fermi award, AEC, 1972, John Fritz medal, Engring. Founder Socs., 1974, Nat. Medal Sci., 1975, Henry D. Smyth Nuclear Statesman award, Atomic Indsl. Forum, 1979, Washington award, Western Soc. Engrs., 1982. Fellow: AIChE (William H. Walker award 1947, Founders award 1965), Am. Philos. Soc., Am. Acad. Arts and Scis., Am. Nuclear Soc. (pres. 1962—63, Arthur H. Compton award); mem.: NAS, Nat. Acad. Engring. (Founders award 1976), Country Club Naples (Fla.), Weston Golf Club (Mass.), Sigma Xi. Office: MIT Nuclear Engng Dept 77 Mass Ave Cambridge MA 02139-4307*

BENEDICT, MARK J., marketing professional, lawyer, real estate consultant; b. San Antonio, Oct. 1, 1951; s. Irvin J and Loraine H. (Layer) B. AA cum laude, San Antonio Coll., 1970; BA summa cum laude, Trinity U., 1973; JD, U. Tex., 1977. Bar: Tex. 1978, Tex. (U.S. Dist. Ct. (we. dist.)) 1979, (U.S. Ct. Appeals (5th cir.)) 1980, (U.S. Supreme Ct.) 1980; lic. real estate salesperson Tex., Va. Legis. aide Tex. State Rep., San Antonio, 1977—79; ptnr. Nowlin and Benedict, San Antonio, 1977—79; atty., owner Law Offices of Benedict, San Antonio, 1980—86; sr. mgmt. Rasamny Group, NYC, 1986; residential and comml. broker Shannon and Luchs, Washington, 1987-88; v.p. mktg. Microlaw/MLX, Washington, 1987-88; comml. broker Century 21 Real Estate, Fairfax, Va., 1988-91, ReMax, Alexandria, Va.; v.p. mktg. Shared Equity Cons., Annandale, Va., 1988-91; owner, pres. PreMar Cons., Austin, Tex., 1986—, PreMar Internat., Fredericksburg, Tex., 1990—; exec. v.p. Equity Ventures Group, Inc., Washington, San Francisco, 1990-91. Cons. Resolution Trust Corp., Washington, 1989-91; mktg. aide Fairfax C. of C., 1988-91; mem. No. Va. Bd. Realtors, Fairfax, 1987—; sr. analyst U.S. Presdl. Com. for Disabled, Washington, 1991-2001; policy analyst USDA/Food Safety Inspection Svc., Washington, 2001-04, staff officer, 2004-; v.p. programs USDA Assoc. People with Disabilities in Agr., 2001-02, pres., 2004-. Rsch. editor Tex. Internat. Law Jour., 1972-73, Am. Jour. Criminal Law, 1972-73; contbr. articles to jours. and newspapers. Active Big Bros. and Sisters, San Antonio, 1979—80, Young Republicans. Benedict fellow, 1973; named one of Outstanding Young Men of Am., 1980, Top Broker, U.S. C. of C., 1979, Top Prodr. San Antonio C. of C. Pres. Club, 1977-83. Mem.: ABA, Tex. State Soc., Tex. Soc. City Attys., USDA Toastmasters (pres. 2003—, Advanced Toastmaster 2004—, competent leader, competent toastmaster, area gov. 2004—), Optimist Club San Antonio, U. Tex. Ex-Student Assn. (life), Alpha Chi, Phi Alpha Delta, Phi Theta Kappa, Phi Beta Kappa. Republican. Lutheran. Avocations: chess, travel, tennis, sailing, food and wine. Office: 477 Summit Cir Fredericksburg TX 78624-5042

BENEDICT, STEWART H., writer, playwright; Author (editor): (book) Tales of Terror and Suspense, 1963, Harper's English Grammar, 1964, The Crime Solvers, 1966, A Teacher's Guide to Senior High School Literature, 1966, Famous American Speeches, 1967, A Teacher's Guide to Modern Drama, 1967, A Teacher's Guide to Poetry, 1969, Blacklash: Black Protest in Our Time, 1970, Twelfth Night and Your Own Thing, 1970, Making a Difference, 1971, A Teacher's Guide to Contemporary Teenage Fiction, 1973, A Teacher's Guide to Jonathan Livingston Seagull, 1973, A Teacher's Guide to Fireweed, 1973, A Teacher's Guide to the Faraway Lurs, 1973, The Literary Guide to the United States, 1981, Street Beat, 1982, Curtain Going Up, 2002; contbr. chapters to books; author: (plays) One Day in the Life of Ivy Dennison, 1967, The Puppeteer, 1967, Not Guilty, 1967, Dance of Life, 1981, Bad Guy, 1972, Judgment Day, 1971, Count That Day Lost, 1971, Going Up, 1971, Red, 1972, Busy, Busy, Busy, 1975, A Crime, 1977, Floored, 1979, It's the Rhinoceros Man's Life, 1983, Down Home, 1984, Gift of Tongues, 1984, Dead Center, 1984, City Desk, 1985, The Wild West: A Liberated Look, 1987, St. Patrick's Day, 1987, Frissons, 1989, I Have Seen the Future..., 1989, Out of the Frying Pan, 1990, Gone to the Dogs, 1994, Left Face, 1994, Right Face, 1994, Family Values, 1994, Dr. Hyde and Mr. Jekyll, 1994, The Bargain, 1995, The Mother, 1995, The People Store, 1995, Tomorrow the World, 1995, The Robbery, 1996, Absolutely Fabulous Fairy Tales, 1996, Fancy Bread, 1996, Be Still My Liver, 1996, Yuletide Treasure, 1996, The Hero, 1999, Homicidal Murders, 2002, The Gap, 2003, Humanoids Using Goodness, 2003, Monody, 2004, Wow!, 2005; contbr. articles to profl. jours. Office Phone: 212-228-1440.

BENEFIELD, EMILY ANNE, nurse, human services manager; d. James Henderson and Verla Jane Benefield; children: Kimberly Anne Davis, Jerry Justin Davis. Assoc., Texarakana C.C., 1971; BS in Health Care Adminstrn., Tex. A & M, 1975. RN Bd. of Nurse Examiners State of Tex., 1971, cert. case mgr., Commn. Case Mgr. Cert., 2003, legal nurse cons., Am. Legal Nurse Cons. Cert. Bd. Nursing supr. St. Michaels Hosp., Texarkana, Ark., 1971—72, Wadley Regional Med. Ctr., Texarkana, Tex., 1972—73; don New Boston Gen. Hosp., New Boston, Tex., 1973—75; nursing instr. Texarkana C.C., Texarkana, Tex., 1975—78; co-owner Jerry Davis Farms, Texarkana, Tex., 1975—2000; case mgr. Tex. Assn. Sch. Bds., Austin, Tex., 2000—04; instr. Austin C.C., Austin, Tex., 2003—; owner Legal Nurse Cons. and Case Mgmt. Svcs., Austin, Tex. Advisor Austin C.C. Case Mgmt. Adv. Bd., Austin, Tex., 2003—. Contbr. jour. article TASB Risk Mgmt. Life mem. Presbyn. Women, Texarkana, Tex., 1989; pres., life mem. Parent Tchrs. Assn., Texarkana, Tex., 1990; pres. DAR, Texarkana, Tex., 1992; treas. Pleasant Grove Band Boosters Assn., Texarkana, Tex., 1996; edn. advisor Bowie County Rep. Party, Texarkana, Tex., 1998—99. Nominee Christine Nelson Vol. of Yr. award, Texarkana Tex., 1982. Mem.: Cert. Case Mgrs. (Austin chpt. 2002—05), Am. Assn. Legal Nurse Cons. (assoc.; capital area chpt. 2004—). Presbyterian. Avocations: photography, genealogy.

BENEFIELD, JANIS WILSON, school librarian, media specialist; b. San Angelo, Tex., Apr. 17, 1947; d. Woodrow and Madolynne Bradley Wilson; m. Harry Clayton Reno, Sept. 21, 1968 (dec. Nov. 10, 1968); m. Lester Benefield, Dec. 0, 1977 (div. Nov. 0, 1981); 1 child, Bradley Lynn. BA, U. Houston, 1968; MLS, North Tex. State U., 1974. Lic. tchr. secondary english State Bd. Educator Certification, Tex., 1969, tchr. secondary french State Bd. Educator Certification, Tex., 1969, cert. profl. all-level learning resources specialist State Bd. Educator Certification, Tex., 1977. Tchr. Gabbs (Nev.) Sch., 1969—71, Mary S. Black Intermediate Sch., Battle Mountain, Nev., 1971—73; dist. libr. Dolores County Schs., Dove Creek, Colo., 1973—74; children's and young adult libr. Moore Meml. Pub. Libr., Texas City, Tex., 1974; libr. media specialist Westchester Jr. H.S., Houston, 1975—85; libr. resources and media specialist Nottingham Elem. Sch., Houston, 1985—. Freelance storyteller, Houston, 2001—. Tutor Spring Br. Ind. Sch. Dist., Houston, 2000—05; leader Tallowood Bapt. Ch., Houston, 1983—88. Named Tchr. of Yr., Nottingham Elem. Sch., 2002; grantee, Apache Corp., 2003; J. Landon Short Mini grant, Partnerships and Vol. Programs Dept., 1990, 1991, 2003, 2005. Mem.: Tex. Computer Edn. Assn., Tex. Assn. for Gifted and Talented, Tex. Libr. Assn., Pi Delta Phi (sec. 1967—68, award French Cultural Svcs. Houston 1968), Beta Phi Mu. Conservative. Southern Baptist. Avocations: travel, reading, ballet, flute, walking. Home: 14800 Memorial Drive 274 Houston TX 77079 Office: Nottingham Elementary School 570 Nottingham Oaks Trail Houston TX 77079 Office Phone: 281-560-7460.

BEN-ELI, MICHAEL URI, management consultant; b. Haifa, Israel, Mar. 23, 1943; s. Arie Lazarus Ben-Eli and Clara (Bejarano) B.-E.; m. Marcia Ann Glocester, Feb. 25, 1973 (div.); 1 child, Gabrielle Meredith. AA in Arch., Archl. Assn. Sch. of Arch., London, 1969; PhD, Brunel U. Inst. Cybernetics, Uxbridge, Eng., 1976. Rsch. assoc. to Dr. R. Buckminster Fuller, Carbondale, Ill. & Phila., 1969-73; cons. N.Y.C., 1976-82; pres. The Cybertel Cons. Group, Inc., N.Y.C., 1982—. Adj. asst. prof. Mt. Sinai Sch. Medicine, CCNY 1980-84; lectr. in field, U.S., Europe; U.S. co-chmn. systems study group Internat. Joint Comm. Great Lakes Water Level Reference; cons. Can. Ministry on Environment and other internat. orgns.; spl. advisor to dep. min. Environ. Can. tech. coop. del. to Beijing. Contbr. articles to profl. jours. Active Friends of Nat. Maritime Mus., N.Y.C., B.O.T. Nat. Maritime Mus., Haifa. Mem. Am. Soc. Cybernetics, N.Y. Acad. Sci., Internat. Soc. for System Scis. Avocations: mountain climbing, skiing, tennis.

BENENSON, JAMES, JR., manufacturer; b. Moultrie, Ga., Mar. 9, 1936; s. James and Mary (Camp) B.; m. Sharen Statler, Aug. 28, 1966; children: James, Clement. BS, MIT, 1958. With F. Eberstadt & Co., N.Y.C., 1960-65, Walker, Hart & Co., N.Y.C., 1965-68, James Benenson & Co., Inc., N.Y.C., 1968—; CEO, Vesper Corp., Newtown Square, Pa., 1978—; chmn. bd. Arrowhead Holdings Corp., Cleve., 1983—. Served with U.S. Army Chem. Corps, 1959. Woodrow Wilson scholar, 1959-60; Andover Teacher fellow, 1958-59 Mem. Hort. Soc. N.Y., N.Y. Bot. Garden (dir.), Soc. of Cincinnati, Century Assn., Racquet Club (Phila.), Buck's Harbor Yacht Club (Brooksville, Maine), N.Y. Yacht Club. Episcopalian. Office: care Vesper Corp 3400 W Chester Pike Newtown Square PA 19073-4638

BENENSON, MARK KEITH, lawyer; b. N.Y.C., Oct. 13, 1929; s. Aaron and Luba (Stein) B.; m. Letizia Pitigliani, Dec. 29, 1959; children: Alexander, Daniela. BSS., CCNY, 1951; JD, Columbia U., 1956. Bar: N.Y. 1956. Atty. Dept. Labor, Washington, 1957-58; practiced in N.Y.C., 1958—. Bd. dirs. Amnesty Internat. U.S.A., 1966-80, sec., 1966-67, chmn., 1968-71, vice chmn., 1972-73, gen. counsel, 1972-80; pres. Vanguard Found., Inc., 1962— Contbr. articles to profl. jours., mags. and newspapers. Exec. sec. Nat. Found. for Firearms Edn., 1983-91, Pres. 1991—. With U.S. Army, 1951-53. Recipient John Amber Gun Digest Writing award, 1998. Home and Office: 585 W End Ave New York NY 10024-1715

BENERIA, LOURDES, economist, educator; b. Boi, Lleida, Spain, Oct. 8, 1939; came to U.S., 1964; d. Agusti Beneria and Josepa Farre; children: Jordi, Marc. Licenciatura, U. Barcelona, Spain, 1961; MPhil, Columbia U., 1974, PhD in Econs., 1975. Coord. program on rural women ILO, Geneva, 1977-79; asst. prof. Rutgers U., New Brunswick, N.J., 1975-81, assoc. prof., 1981-86; prof. city and regional planning and women's studies Cornell U., Ithaca, NY, 1987—, dir. program on gender and global change, 1987—92, 2000—03, dir. Latin Am. studies program, 1993—97, dir. internat. studies in planning, 2003—; pres. Internat. Assn. for Feminist Econs., 2003—. Recipient Narcis Monturiol award for rsch. in the social scis., Barcelona. Office: Cornell Univ CRP W Sibley Hall Ithaca NY 14853-2148

BENES, SOLOMON, biomedical scientist, physician; b. Iasi, Romania, Mar. 28, 1925; came to U.S., 1978; s. Moritz and Cecilia (Abramovici) B.; m. Liudmila Topor, Mar. 27, 1954. MD, U Bucharest, Romania, 1952. Intern microbiology lab. Mil. Hosp., Bucharest, 1949—50, fellow microbiology lab., 1950—51, dir. clin. lab. outpatient dept., 1951—52; dir. rsch. lab. Ctr. Radiobiology Rsch., Bucharest, 1953—57, 1959—66; chief physician microbiology lab. Mil. Hosp., Bucharest, 1967—73; chief physician clin. lab. Ctr. Haematology, Bucharest, 1973—76; assoc. medicine Havard Med. Sch., Boston, 1978—81; asst. rsch. scientist, asst. prof. SUNY Downstate Med. Ctr., Bklyn., 1982—95; sr. rsch. scientist, asst. prof. SUNY Rsch. Found., Bklyn., 1995—98; ret., 1998. Author: (with others) Seminars in Infectious Diseases, 1983; contbr. articles to Sexually Transmitted Diseases, Antimicrobial Agts. and Chemotherapy, Jour. Clin. Microbiology, Proceedings of the 6th Internat. Symposium on Human Chlamydial Infections. Col. Romanian Army Med. Svc., 1946—73. Achievements include discovery that the Trachoma biovar of Chlamydia trachomatis is able to achieve intercellular propagation in cell culture and that, in a proper cell setting, this bacterium spreads from cell to cell in cell culture, contrary to what was generally believed. Home: 2421 Shellpot Dr Wilmington DE 19803-2547 Personal E-mail: lands280@cs.com.

BENESCH, WILLIAM MILTON, molecular physicist, atmospheric researcher, educator; b. Balt., Apr. 22, 1922; s. Jerome William and Blanche (Koshland) B.; m. Joan Sagner, June 1, 1946; children— Amy Joan, Sarah Elizabeth, Jane Margaret. B.A., Lehigh U., 1942; M.S., Johns Hopkins U., 1950, Ph.D., 1952. Asst. prof. U. Pitts., 1953-60; asst. prof. molecular physics U. Md., College Park, 1962-63, assoc. prof., 1964-66, prof., 1967—, prof. emeritus, 1992—, dir. Inst. Molecular Physics, 1973-76; cons. Argonne Nat. Lab., Ill., 1978-80. Contbr. numerous articles to profl. jours. Served as sgt. USAR, 1944-66. Fellow Commn. for Relief of Belgium, Liege, 1952-53, Weizmann Inst., Rehovoth, Israel, 1960-62, Johns Hopkins U., Balt., 1977— . Fellow Am. Phys. Soc., Optical Soc. Am. (assoc. editor jour. 1978-84), Washington Acad. Sci. (bd. mgrs. 1988-89, v.p. adminstrv. affairs 1989-90), Philosophical Soc. Washington; mem. Am. Geophys. Union, Soc. Applied Spectroscopy, Cosmos Club (Washington), Johns Hopkins U. Club (Balt.). Avocation: bird watching, duplicate bridge, Bronze Life master. Home: 4444 Linnean Ave NW Washington DC 20008-2317 Office: U Md Inst Phys Sci Ipst Bldg College Park MD 20742-0001

BENESTANTE, VINCENZO, writer; b. Chgo., June 16, 1945; s. Anthony Victor Benestante and Frieda Ann Dobrin; m. Adelheid Engst (div.); 1 child, Adrian; m. Sabina Trooger, Mar. 7, 1997. BA, M Performing Arts, So. Ill. U., 1968. Opera singer various theaters, Switzerland, 1968—70; actor various theaters, TV, Germany, Italy, France, 1970—98; freelance author, translator, 2002—; performance poet, 2002—. Author: (short stories) Anthologie Der Fantasie, 2000. Finalist, Miami Grand Slam Spoken Word Poetry. Mem.: Lip, Tongue and Ear Poetry Guild (officer 2003—, lectr. in drama in poetry). Avocations: scuba diving, bicycling, reading. Home and Office: 10725 SW 146th St Miami FL 33176 E-mail: genomm@earthlink.net.

BENET, LESLIE ZACHARY, pharmacologist, educator; b. Cin., May 17, 1937; s. Jonas John and Esther Racie (Hirschfeld) Benet; m. Carol Ann Levin, Sept. 8, 1960; children: Reed Michael, Gillian Vivia. AB in English, U. Mich., 1959, BS in Pharmacy, 1960, MS in Pharm. Chemistry, 1962; PhD in Pharm. Chemistry, U. Calif., San Francisco, 1965; PharmD (hon.), Uppsala U., Sweden, 1987; PhD (hon.), Leiden U., Netherlands, 1995; DSc (hon.), U. Ill., Chgo., 1997, Phila. Coll. Pharm. and Sci., 1997, L.I. U., 1999. Asst. prof. pharmacy Wash. State U., Pullman, 1965—69; asst. prof. pharmacy and pharm. chemistry U. Calif., San Francisco, 1969—71, assoc. prof., 1971—76, prof., 1976—, vice chmn. dept. pharmacy, 1973—78, chmn. dept. pharmacy, 1978—96, dir. drug studies unit, 1977—, dir. drug kinetics and dynamics ctr., 1979—98, chmn. dept. biopharm. scis., 1996—98. Mem. pharmacology study sect. NIH, Washington, 1977—81, chmn., 1979—81, mem. pharmacol. scis. rev. com., 1984—88, chmn., 1986—88; mem. generic drugs adv. com. FDA, Washington, 1990—94; mem. Sci. Bd., 1992—98; chair external rev. com. CBER, 1998, chair expert panel on individual equivalence, 1998—2000; mem. sci. adv. bd. SmithKline Beecham Pharms., 1989—92, Pharmetrix, 1989—92, Alteon, Inc., 1993—, TheraTech, Inc., 1993—96, Roche Biosci., 1998—2001, Pain Therapeutics, Inc., 1999—, UMD, Inc., 1999—, Silico Insights, Inc., 2000—, InforMedix, 2001—; chmn. bd. AvMax, Inc.; bd. dirs. OxoN Medica, Inc., InforMedix, Inc., Josman Labs., Inc., Impax Pharmas., One World Health. Assoc. editor Pharmacology and Therapeutics, 1995—2000, editor Jour. Pharmacokinetics and Biopharmaceutics, 1976—98, mem. editl. bd. The Effect of Disease States on Drug Pharmacokinetics, 1976, Pharmacology, 1979—, Pharmacy Internat., 1979—82, Pharm. Rsch., 1983—95, Pharmacokinetic Basis for Drug Treatment, 1984, Pharmacokinetics: A Modern View, 1984, ISI Atlas of Sci.: Pharmacology, 1988—89, Integration of Pharmacokinetics, Pharmacodynamics and Toxicokinetics in Rational Drug Development, 1992, Clinical Applications of Mifepristone (RU486) and Other Antiprogestins, 1993, Pharm. News, 1994—98, AAPS Jour., 1999—, Molecular Interventions, 2000—, Chemistry and Pharm. Bull., 2000—, Drug Metabolism and Pharmacokinetics, 2002—, Current Drug Metabolism, —, Giving Full Measure to Counter Measures, 2004; contbr. more than 460 articles to profl. jours. Apptd. Forum on Drug Devel. and Regulation, 1988. Named ISI Highly Cited Rschr., 2003; recipient Rsch. Achievement award in pharm. scis., Pharm. Sics. World Congress, 2004, Career Achievement award in oral drug delivery, Controlled Release Soc., 2004. Fellow: AAAS (mem.-at-large exec. com. pharm. scis. sect. 1978—81, 1991—95, chair 1996—97), Am. Assn. Pharm. Scientists (pres. 1986, treas. 1987, bd. dirs. 1988—93, Disting. Pharm. Scientist award 1989, Disting. Svc. award 1996, Wurster rsch. award in pharmaceutics 2000), Acad. Pharm. Scis. (chmn. basic pharmaceutics sect. 1976—77, mem.-at-large exec. com. 1979—83, pres. 1985—86, Rsch. Achievement award 1982); mem.: ISSX (councillor 1992—96, treas. 1998—99), AAUP, Pharm. Scis. World Congress (Rsch. Achievement award 2004), Inst. Medicine of NRC (chmn. com. accelerating rsch., devel. & acquisition med. countermeasures against biol. warfare agts. 2002—), Am. Assn. Colls. Pharmacy (bd. dirs. 1992—95, pres. 1993—94, Volwiler Rsch. Achievement award 1991), Am. Coll. Clin. Pharmacy, Drug Info. Assn., Internat. Pharm. Fedn. (bd. pharm. scis. 1988—, chair 1996—2000, Host-Madsen medal 2001), Generic Pharm. Industry Assn. (mem. blue ribbon com. on generic medicines 1990), Am. Soc. for Pharmacology and Exptl. Therapeutics, Am. Soc. Clin. Pharmacology and Exptl. Therapeutics (Rawls-Palmer award and lectureship 1995), Am. Pharm. Assn. (Higuchi Rsch. prize 2000), Am. Coll. Clin. Pharmacology (Disting. Svc. award 1988), Am. Found. for Pharm. Edn. (bd. dirs. 1987—, Disting. Svc. "Profile" award 1993), Inst. Medicine of NAS (forum on drug devel. and regulation 1988—94, chmn. com. on antiprogestins 1993, membership com. 1994—97, chmn. other health profns. sect. 1995—97, chmn. com. pharmacokinetics and drug interactions in elderly 1996—97, mem. Round Table R & D Drugs, Biologics & Med. Devices 1997—2000, bd. on health scis. policy 1999—), Sigma Xi, Phi Lambda Sigma, Rho Chi (Ann. Lecture award 1990). Home: 601 Van Ness Ave Apt 451 San Francisco CA 94102-3259 Office: U Calif San Francisco Dept Biopharm Scis 533 Parnasus Rm U68 San Francisco CA 94143-0446 Office Phone: 415-476-3853. Business E-Mail: benet@itsa.ucsf.edu.

BENEWITZ, MAURICE CHARLES, labor arbitrator, educator; b. Hartford, Conn., Nov. 16, 1923; d. Doris L. Benewitz; m. Lesley Frank Alan Benewitz. AB in Econs., Harvard U., 1947; PhD in Econs., U. Minn., 1954. From asst. prof. to prof., dept. chair Baruch Coll., N.Y.C., 1955-75; arbitrator Manhasset, N.Y., 1958—. Dir. Nat. Ctr. for the Study of Collective Bargaining in Higher Edn., N.Y.C., 1970-73. Author: Higher Education Arbitration, 1988. Mem. Am. Arbitration Assn. (panel mem.), Fed. Mediation and Conciliation Svc. (panel mem.), N.Y. State Pub. Employee Rels. Bd. (panel mem.), N.Y.C. Office Collective Bargaining (panel mem.), N.J. State Med. Bd., Nat. Acad. Arbitrators, Phi Beta Kappa. Home and Office: 261 Thompson Shore Rd Manhasset NY 11030-2240

BENEZRA, NEAL, museum director, curator; b. Oakland, Calif., Aug. 20, 1953; m. Maria Makela; 1 child, Ava. BA, U. Calif. at Berkeley, 1976; MA, Stanford U., 1981, PhD, 1983; postgrad., German Acad. Exch. Svc., 1983. Coord. Anderson Collection, Atherton, Calif., 1980-83; asst. curator Des Moines Art Ctr., 1983-84, curator, 1984-85; assoc. curator The Art Inst. Chgo., 1985-86, curator, 1987-91, asst. dir. art and pub. programs, 1996, dep. dir., Frances and Thomas Dittmer curator modern and contemporary art, 2000—02; chief curator Hirshhorn Mus. and Sculpture Garden, Smithsonian Instn., Washington, DC, 1991—96, asst. dir. art & pub. progs., 1996—99; dir. San Francisco Mus. Modern Art, 2002—. Vis. lectr. U. Ill., Urbana-Champaign, 1988; vis. assoc. prof. U. Chgo., 1990; mem. Smithsonian Coun.; art adv. bd. mem. U. Calif., San Francisco; art adv. panel IRS, Dept. Treasury. Curator exhbn./author catalogue: Robert Arneson: A Retrospective, 1986, Ed Paschke: Paintings, 1989, Affinities and Intuitions: The Gerald S. Elliott Collection of Contemporary Art, 1990, Martin Puryear, 1991, Bruce Nauman, 1993-94, Stephen Balkenhol, 1995-96. Grad. fellow Stanford U., 1978-81, McCloy fellow in German art, 1984-85. Office: San Francisco Mus Modern Art 151 Third St San Francisco CA 94103-3159*

BENFER, DAVID WILLIAM, hospital administrator; b. Toledo, Ohio, May 28, 1946; s. Wilson L. and Marjorie (Baringer) B.; m. Mary Sturner, Sept. 5, 1970; children: Emily, Matthew, Andrew. BA, Wittenberg U., 1968; MBA in Hosp. Adminstrn., Xavier U., 1970. Asst. admintrn. Med. Coll., Ohio Hosp., Toledo, 1971-76, exec. dir., CEO, 1976-81, Bon Secours Hosp., Grosse Pointe, Mich., 1982-84, Henry Ford Hosp., Detroit, 1985-92; pres., CEO, St. Joseph Med. Ctr., Joliet, Ill., 1992-99; CEO St. Raphael Healthcare System, New Haven, 1999—. Dir. Merchants and Mfrs. Bank, Stereotaxis, Inc.; fellow Berkeley Coll. Yale U., 2002—. Co-author: Issues in Health Care Management, 1982; contbg. author: Sisters of Bon Secours Centennial, 1982. Trustee, chmn. Family Svcs., Detroit and Wayne County, 1982-92; chmn. AIDS Consortium Southeastern Mich., Toledo, 1988-92l v.p. Med. Value Plan, Inc., 1986-91; chmn. S.E. Mich. Hosp. Coun.; bd. dirs. U. St. Francis, Joliet, 1993-2002; vice chmn. New Ctr. Area Coun., 1991-92; mem. Mich. Tastefest, 1996; bd. dirs., chmn. Ctr. Econ. Devel., Will County C. of C., Ill., New Haven Symphony, v.p. bd. Recipient Commendation 114th Ohio Gen Assembly, 1981, Torch of Liberty award Anti Defamation League, 2005; Berkeley Fellow, Yale U., 2003. Fellow Am. Coll. Health Care Execs. (coun. regents 1989-92, bd. govs. 1992—2000, Robert S. Hudgens award 1982, chair 1998-99); mem. Am. Hosp. Assn. (regional policy bd.), Conn. Hosp. Assn. (bd. dirs.), Cath. Health Assn. (bd. dirs.), Quinnipiack Club (New Haven), Country Club Detroit (Grosse Pointe), New Haven Country Club. Roman Catholic. Avocations: jogging, golf. Office: St Raphael Healthcare System Hosp St Raphael 659 George St New Haven CT 06511-5324

BENFIELD, ANN KOLB, lawyer; b. Reading, Pa., May 1, 1946; d. Curtis Kepler and Stella (Kolb) B. BA, George Washington U., 1969, MA, 1974; JD, U. Ky., 1983. Ky. 1983, U.S. Ct. Appeals (6th cir.) 1985, U.S. Supreme Ct. 1987; cert. mental health consumer cons./educator; cert. trained mediator. Probation officer Superior Ct. of D.C., Washington, 1973-78; jud. law clk. to chief judge U.S. Dist. Ct. (we. dist.) Ky., Louisville, 1983-86, jud. atty. to fed. sr. judge, 1989-95; trial atty. Ogden, Welsh and Newell (formerly Ogden & Robertson), Louisville, 1986-89; pvt. practice Louisville, 1995—2001; ret., 2002; pro bono practice, 2002—. Adj. prof. U. Louisville Sch. Law, 1993, pro bono legal svcs., 2001-. Mem. exec. com., bd. dirs. Ky. chpt. ACLU, 1988-89, 91—, nat. bd. dirs., 1992-94, sec., 1995-96, treas., 1996-98, mem. legal panel, 1988—; mem. Reproductive Freedom Adv. Com., 1994-2001; mem. steering com. Fellowship Reconciliation, Louisville, 1997-2002; mem. governing coun. U. Louisville Women's Ctr., 1998-2001; rape crisis advocate Ctr. for Women and Families, 1997—, domestic violence advocate, 1998-; bd. dirs., gen. counsel Depressed Self-Help Svcs., Inc., 1998-2000. Fellow: Ky. Bar Found. (bd. dirs. 1994—96, charter mem.); mem.: Louisville Bar Assn., Ky. Alliance Against Racism and Polit. Repression (life), Ky. Bar Assn. (Donated Legal Svcs. Recognition award 2000, 2001, 2003), Ky. Paso Fino Horse Assn. (sec. 2000—01), Amicus Club of ACLU (founder Ky. chpt. 2004), Phi Beta Kappa, Order of Coif. Home and Office: 50 Shrivers Corner Rd Gettysburg PA 17325 Office Phone: 502-426-2266. Personal E-mail: akbenfield@aol.com.

BENFIELD, JOHN RICHARD, surgeon, educator; b. Vienna, June 24, 1931; arrived in U.S., 1938, naturalized, 1945; s. Richard and Charlotte Lola Benfield; m. Joyce A. Cohler, Dec. 22, 1963; children: Richard L., Robert E., Nancy J. AB, Columbia U., 1952; MD, U. Chgo., 1955. Diplomate Am. Bd. Surgery, Am. Bd. Thoracic Surgery. Intern Columbia-Presbyn. Hosp., NYC, 1955-56; E.H. Andrews fellow in thoracic surgery U. Chgo., 1956-57; chief resident and instr. in surgery U. Chgo. Clinics, 1962-64, resident in surgery, 1956-57, 59-63; asst. prof. surgery U. Wis., 1964-67; asst. prof. UCLA, 1967-69, assoc. prof., 1969-73, prof., 1973-77, clin. prof., 1978-88; prof. surgery, chief cardiothoracic surgery, vice chmn. surgery U. Calif. Davis Med. Ctr., Sacramento, 1988-95, prof. surgery, chief thoracic surgery, 1995-98, prof. emeritus, 1998—; attending surgeon V.A. Martinez Med. Ctr., 1988-98; courtesy staff Kaiser Permanente Med. Ctr., Sacramento, 1988-98. James Utley prof. surgery, chmn. dept. surgery Boston U., 1977; chmn. surgery City of Hope Nat. Med. Ctr., Duarte, Calif., 1978-87; bd. dirs. Am. Bd. Thoracic Surgery, 1982-88; cons. U.S. Naval Med. Ctr., San Diego, 1968-88; mem. sr. staff VA Wadsworth Med. Ctr., LA, 1978-88. Editor Current Problems in Cancer, 1975-86; mem. editl. bd. Annals Thoracic Surgery, 1979-2001, assoc. editor, 1987-2001; mem. editl. bd. Annals Surg. Oncology, 1994-2000; contbr. articles to profl. jours., chpts. to books. Sec., trustee Univ. Synagogue, LA. Served as capt. M.C. U.S. Army, 1957-59, Korea. Grantee Life Ins. Med. Rsch., 1962-66, Am. Heart Assn., 1968-71, USPHS, 1971-92. Mem. ACS (bd. govs. 1982-88, 92-98), Am. Surg. Assn., Am. Assn. Thoracic Surgery, Am. Assn. Cancer Rsch., Am. Med. Writers Assn., Internat. Assn. Study Lung Cancer, Internat. Soc. Surgery, Calif. Med. Soc., Ctrl. Surg. Assn., LA Acad. Medicine, The Royal Soc. Medicine (Gt. Britain), The Transplantation Soc., Soc. Thoracic Surgeons (v.p. 1994-95, pres. 1995-96), Soc. Univ. Surgeons, Pacific Coast Surg. Assn. (v.p. 1995-96), Soc. Surg. Oncology, Am. Coll. Chest Physicians (pres. Calif. chpt. 1996-97), Western Thoracic Surgeons Assn. (pres. 1989-90), Internat. Surg. Soc., Thoracic Surgery Dirs. Assn. (pres. 1995-97), Thoracic Surgery Found. for Rsch. and Edn. (pres. 2003-). Office Phone: 310-794-7333. Personal E-mail: j.benfield@verizon.net.

BENFIELD, MARION WILSON, JR., law educator; b. Belwood, N.C., July 26, 1932; s. Marion Wilson and Gazzie Cleo (Martin) B.; m. Dalida Quijada, Feb. 21, 1964; children: Marion, Steve, Robin, Rosalina, Christopher, Jeanette, Antonio, Maria. AA, Gardner-Webb Coll., Boiling Springs, N.C., 1951; AB in English, U. N.C., 1953; LLB, Wake Forest U., 1959; LLM, U. Mich., 1965. Bar: N.C. 1959. Asst. dir. Inst. Govt. U. N.C., 1959-61; individual practice law Hickory, N.C., 1961-63; asst. prof. law U. Ga., 1963-65; assoc. prof. Case Western Reserve U., 1965-66, U. Ill., 1966-68, prof., 1968-88, Albert E. Jenner, Jr. prof. law, 1988-90, assoc. dean, 1980-85; disting. chair law Wake Forest U., 1990-97, adj. prof., 1997-98; vis. prof. U. Tex., 1998—. Vis., prof. U. Houston, 1976-77, Duke U., 1979, NYU, 1984, Peking U., 1985, Shenzhen U., China, 1986, Loyola U., L.A., 1995, U. Tex., 1998-2001, U. Ala., 2001; mem. Nat. Conf. of Commrs. on Uniform State Laws, 1973—. Reporter, draftsman: The Uniform Land Transactions Act and Uniform Simplification of Land Transfers Act, 1970-77, Revised Uniform Commercial Code, Article 2A, 1995-9, Article 2, 2002-03; author: Social Justice through Law-New Approaches in the Law of Contracts, 1970, (with W.H. Hawkland) Cases and Materials on Sales, 1979, 4thd edit., 2004, (with Peter Alces) Commercial Paper and Alternative Payment Systems, 1987, (with Peter Aces) Payment Systems, 1993; mem. editl. bd.: Uniform Commercial Code, 1974—, Uniform Land Transactions Act and Uniform Simplification of Land Transactions Act, 1982-93. Served with U.S. Army, 1954-56. Mem. Am. Law Inst., ABA. Home: 10 Overlook Cir New Braunfels TX 78132-4728 E-mail: mbenfield@compuvision.net.

BENFORD, GREGORY ALBERT, physicist, writer; b. Mobile, Jan. 30, 1941; s. James Alton and Mary Eloise (Nelson) Benford; m. Joan Abbe, Aug. 26, 1967; children: Alyson Rhandra, Mark Gregory. BS, U. Okla., 1963; MS, U. Calif., San Diego, 1965, PhD, 1967. Research asst. U. Calif., San Diego, 1964—67; postdoctoral fellow Lawrence (Calif.) Radiation Lab., 1967—69, research physicist, 1969—71; prof. physics U. Calif., Irvine, 1971—. Cons. in field. Author: (novels) If the Stars are Gods, 1977, In the Ocean of Night, 1977, The Stars in Shroud, 1978, Find the Changeling, 1980, Timescape, 1980 (Nebula award), Against Infinity, 1983, Across the Sea of Suns, 1984, Artifact, 1985, Heart of the Comet, 1986, In Alien Flesh, 1986, Great Sky River, 1987, Tides of Light, 1989, Beyond the Fall of Night, 1990, Chiller, 1993, Furious Gulf, 1994, Sailing Bright Eternity, 1995; author: (with Mark O Martin) A Darker Geometry, 1996; author: Foundation's Fear, 1997, Cosm, 1998, The Martian Race, Eater, 2000; author: (collections) Matter's End, 1994; editor: Far Futures, 1995; editor: (with Martin H. Greenburg) The New Hugo Winners Volume IV, 1997; editor: Nebula Awards Showcase 2000: The Year's Best SF and Fantasy Chosen by the Science Fiction and Fantasy Writers of America, 2000; editor: (with George Zebrowski) Skylife: Space Habitats in Story and Science, 2000; editor: Worlds Vast and Various, 2000, Deep Time, 1999, Cosm, 1999, Eater, 2000. Recipient Brit. Sci. Fiction award, 1981, Australian Ditmar award for internat. novel, 1981, John Campbell award for best novel, 1981, UN medal in Lit., 1993, Lord prize in Sci., 1994, Lord Found. prize, 1995; fellow Woodrow Wilson, 1963—64; grantee Office Naval Rsch., 1975—, 1982—, Army Rsch. Orgn., 1977—82, Air Force Office Sci. Rsch., 1982—, Calif. Space Office, 1984—85. Mem.: NASA Sci. Adv. Bd., Soc. Sci. Exploration, Sci. Fiction Writers Am. (Nebula award 1975, 1981), Royal Astron. Soc., Am. Phys. Soc., Phi Beta Kappa. Office: Univ California Physics Dept 4129 Frederick Reines Hall Irvine CA 92697-4575 Business E-Mail: gbenford@uci.edu.*

BENFORD, HARRY BELL, naval architect; b. Schenectady, Aug. 7, 1917; s. Frank Albert and Georgia (Rattray) B.; m. Edith Elizabeth Smallman, Apr. 26, 1941; children— Howard Lee, Frank Alfred, Robert James. BSE. in Naval Architecture and Marine Engring, U. Mich., 1940. With Newport News Shipbldg. Co., Va., 1940-48; mem. faculty U. Mich., Ann Arbor, 1948-59, 60-83, prof. naval architecture, 1959-83, prof. emeritus, 1983—, chmn. dept. naval architecture and marine engring., 1967-72. Exec. dir. maritime rsch. adv. com. NRC, 1959-60 Author 4 books, 150 tech. papers. Fellow Soc. Naval Architects and Marine Engrs. (hon. mem., pres.'s award 1957, Linnard prize 1962, Taylor medal 1976), Royal Instn. Naval Architects; mem Tau Beta Pi, Phi Kappa Phi. Office: U Mich Dept Naval Architecture Ann Arbor MI 48109-2145 E-mail: harben@engin.umich.edu.

BENFORD, ROBERT DEE, social studies educator, editor; b. Akron, Ohio, July 22, 1951; s. Robert Dee Benford, Sr. and Carolyn Sue Benford; m. Michelle Hughes Miller, Aug. 17, 1990; children: Kiri Elaine Miller, Cambra Rae Benford-Miller. BA, U. Tex., 1981, MA, 1984, PhD, 1987. CEO Benford and Assocs., Inc., Houston, 1969—85; social sci. rsch. assoc. III Hogg Found. for Mental Health U. Tex., Austin, 1986—87; prof. dept. sociology U. Nebr., Lincoln, 1987—2000; prof. So. Ill. U., Carbondale, 2000—, chair dept. sociology, 2000—03, pres. faculty senate, 2005—. Editor Jour. of Contemporary Ethnography, Thousand Oaks, Calif., 2000—04; series editor Twayne's Social Movements Past and Present, N.Y.C., 1995—99. Editor: (ency.) Compendium of Social Issues; contbr. articles to profl. jours. Exec. coun. The Drake Group, Des Moines, 1999—2001; peacekeeping coord./trainer Red River Peace Network, Austin, 1984—85; del., peace rsch. del. to Cuba Pastors for Peace, Mpls.; vol. coord. Austin Peace and Justice Coalition, 1983—84; co-founder gun free zone movement U. Nebr., 1994—96. Recipient People Who Inspire award, Black Masque chpt. Mortarboard Nat. Honor Soc., 1998, U. Grad. fellowship, U. of Tex. at Austin, 1982—85. Mem.: So. Sociol. Soc., Soc. for Study of Symbolic Interaction, Soc. for Study of Social Problems, Midwest Sociol. Soc. (pres.-elect 2004—05, pres. 2005—), Am. Sociol. Assn. (chair peace, war, and social conflict sect. 1998—99), Phi Kappa Phi, Alpha Chi, Alpha Kappa Delta (pres.Gamma chpt. 1984—85). Achievements include research in social movements, peace movements, Chinese democracy movement, environmentalism, nuclear politics, political discourse. Home: 45 Hillcrest Dr Carbondale IL 62901 Office: So Ill U 3426 Faner Hall Carbondale IL 62901-4524 Office Phone: 618-453-7610. Business E-Mail: rbenford@siu.edu.

BENGE, TIMOTHY J., music educator, conductor; b. L.A., Aug. 3, 1957; s. Robert Williams Benge and Helen Virginia Benge-Boyle, Billie Boyle (Stepfather); 1 child, Robert Kenneth Bennett-Benge. MusB, Calif. State U., 1980; MusM, U. Redlands, 1989; D of Musical Arts, U. So. Calif., 1996. Cert. tchr. Commn. Tchr. Credentialing, Calif., 1981, preliminary adminstrv. svcs. Commn. on Tchr. Credentialing - CA, 2001. Music dir., condr. So. Calif. Ctr. Music and Arts, Riverside, 1984—96; owner, prodr. Camerata Studios, Anaheim, 1988—98; exec. dir. Calif. Alliance Arts Edn., Pasadena, 1998—2001; instrumental music specialist San Diego City Schs., 2001—03; dir., instrumental music Capistrano Valley H.S., Mission Viejo, 2001—. Adjudicator Drum Corps Internat., 1985—94, Winter Guard Internat., 1984—94; dir., chmn. So. Calif. Ctr. Music and Arts, Riverside, 1990—96; dir. Calif. Arts Advocates, 2001—03; profl. musician, Calif., 1980—; cons. in field. Musician (conductor): (concerts) Five to twelve concerts annually; prodr.: (producer of cd albums) 54 CD's. Exec. dir. Calif. Alliance Arts Edn., 1998—2001; mem., bd. dir. Calif. Arts Advocates, 2001—03. Scholar, U. So. Calif., 1988—91. Mem.: Calif. Music Educators Assn. (collegiate rep. 1999—2001), So. Calif. Sch. Band and Orch. Assn., Airplane Owners and Pilots Assn., Pi Kappa Lambda. Avocation: private pilot. Office Phone: 949-364-2744.

BENGERT, W. RAYMOND, lawyer, chemical engineer; b. Kansas City, Oct. 15, 1928; s. Harry C. and Lola E. Bengert; m. Penny Ann Bengert, Dec. 27, 1970. BS in Chemistry, U. Mo., 1953, JD, 1956. Bar: Calif. 1975. Profl. baseball player, 1944—46, 1948—49; chmn. Draft Rockefeller for Pres., Denver, 1958—60; pres. Bengert Tire Chains, Denver and Kansas City, 1960—68; founder Baskets-of-Hope, San Carlos, Calif., 1968—74; pres. IGF Container Corp., San Carlos, 1972—83; atty. San Francisco, 1975—. Cons. Bengert Enterprises, La Quinta, Calif., 1998—. Patentee chem. process.

Served with USMC, 1946—48. Mem.: Calif. State Bar, Indian Ridge Country Club. Avocations: poetry, tennis. Office: PO Box 1475 Carmel CA 93921 Office Phone: 760-771-5323. Fax: 760-771-2225.

BENGSTON, BILLY AL, artist; b. Dodge City, Kans., June 7, 1934; Founder Artist Studio, Venice, Calif., 1960; aesthetic cons., co-designer Disneyland Call Ctr., Anaheim, Calif., 1998; established Pelican Club Prodns., Ltd., 1982. One-man shows include Galerie Neuendorf, Frankfurt, Germany, 1993, Rosamund Felsen Gallery, Santa Monica, Calif., 2000, Danese Gallery, N.Y.C., 2001, exhibited in group shows at Art Inst. Chgo., 1963, 1972, Sao Paolo, Brazil, 1965, Gagosian Gallery, N.Y.C., 2002, one-man shows include Whitney Mus. Am. Art, 1967—69, Biennial Exhbn., 1979, retrospective, L.A. County Mus. Art, 1968, 1988, Stedelijk van Abbemuseum, Eindhoven, The Netherlands, 1969, retrospective, Contemporary Arts Mus., Houston, 1988, Oakland (Calif.) Mus., 1988, The Contemporary Mus., Honolulu, 1988, Represented in permanent collections Mus. Modern Art, N.Y.C., Art Inst. Chgo., L.A. County Mus. Art, Whitney Mus. Am. Art, Ft. Worth Art Ctr. Mus., Guggenheim Mus., Beauborg, Paris, N.Y.C., Nat. Gallery, Washington, commd., Calif. State Office Bldg., L.A., 1990; contbr. articles to art jours. Nat. Found. Arts grantee, 1967, Ford Found. grantee Tamarind Lithography Workshop, 1968, 87; Guggenheim fellow, 1975. Home: 110 Mildred Ave Venice CA 90291-3020

BENGTSON, JANICE MARIE, music educator; b. Syracuse, N.Y., Oct. 29, 1955; d. Phillip David and Barbara Jean Post; m. Edwin Glenn Bengtson, May 28, 1986; children: Celeste, Megan. MusB in Edn., U. South Fla., 1977; MA in Ednl. Leadership, Troy (Ala.) State U., 1995. With USAF, 1977, advanced through grades to master sgt., 1990, ret., 1997; musician USAF Bands, Langley AFB, Va., 1977—97; tchr. band Newport News (Va.) Schs., 1997—98, Hampton (Va.) City Schs., 1998—99; program mgr. Ga. Tech., Atlanta, 1999—2004; tchr. band Douglasville (Ga.) County Schs., 2004—. Mem. faculty State U. West Ga., Carrollton, Ga., 2002; mem., performer Nat. Chamber Players, York County, Va., 1992—; spkr. in field; presenter in field. Musician: Tidewater Winds Nat. Symphony Winds, 1990—, Tara Winds, 1999—, (songs) Grand Serenade for an Awful Lot of Winds, 1992 (Grammy award, 1992); narrator: Storybook, 1995. Mem.: Ga. Music Educators Assn. Home: 4775 Liberty Rd Villa Rica GA 30180

BENGTSON, ROGER DEAN, physicist, department chairman; b. Wausa, Nebr., Apr. 29, 1941; s. Fridolph M. and Edith E. (Pearson) B.; m. Billie A. Spies, June 15, 1963; children— Nissa C., Hans E. BS, U. Nebr., 1962; MS, Va. Poly. Inst. and State U., 1964; PhD, U. Md., 1968. Aerospace engr. NASA-Langley Research Ctr., Hampton, Va., 1962-67; research assoc. U. Tex., Austin, 1968-70, asst. prof. physics, 1970-75, assoc. prof., 1975-81, prof., 1981—, chmn. dept., 1984-88. Mem. Am. Phys. Soc., AAAS, Sigma Xi Home: 411 Honeycomb Rdg Austin TX 78746-5324 Office: U Tex Dept Physics C-1600 Austin TX 78712

BENGTSSON, ERLING BLÖNDAL, classical cellist, educator; b. Copenhagen, Mar. 8, 1932; arrived in U.S., 1990; s. Valdemar and Sigridur (Nielsen) Bengtsson; m. Merete Bloch-Jørgensen, Oct. 19, 1958; children: Henrik Bløndal, Stefan Bløndal. Diploma, Curtis Inst. Music, Phila., 1950. Asst. tchr. cello Curtis Inst. Music, Phila., 1949—50, tchr. cello, 1950—53; prof. music Royal Danish Conservatory Music, Copenhagen, 1953—90; tchr. cello Swedish Radio's Inst. Advanced String Studies, Stockholm, 1958—78; prof. music Staatliche Hochschule für Musik, Cologne, Germany, 1978—82, U. Mich. Sch. Music, Ann Arbor, 1990—. Tchr. cello master classes, Europe and U.S., 1953—. Performer: numerous LPs and CDs, 1949—, worldwide concerts, 1950—. Named knight 1st class, Order of Dannebrog, Queen of Denmark, 1972, grand knight, Order of Falcon, Pres. Iceland, 1970, chevalier du violoncello, Ind. U. Eva Janzer Meml. Cello Ctr., 1993; recipient award of distinction, Manchester (Eng.) Internat. Cello Festival, 2001. Avocation: collecting modern Scandinavian art. Home: 1217 Westmoorland Ypsilanti MI 48197 Office: U Mich Sch Music 1100 Baits Dr Ann Arbor MI 48109 E-mail: cellist@erlingbb.com.

BENHABIB, JESS, adult education educator; b. Istanbul, Turkey, June 9, 1948; s. Jack and Nelli Benhabib; m. Madeline Jennifer Blum, May 12, 1950; children: Nicole, Michael Eric. PHD, Columbia U., 1976. Paulette Godard prof. polit. economy NYU, 1991—, dean of social scis., 1997—2000, dean of arts and sci., 1998—2000. Editor: Jour. of Econ. Theory, 1992, (book) Cycles and Chaos in Economic Equilibrium, 1992. 2d lt. Ordinance-Turkish Army, 1974, Balikesir, Turkey. Fellow: Econometric Soc. Home: #16 37 Washington Sq West New York NY 10011 Office: NYU 269 Mercer St 7th Fl New York NY 10003 Office Phone: 212-998-8971. Business E-Mail: jess.benhabib@nyu.edu.

BEN-HAIM, ZIGI, artist; b. Baghdad, Iraq, Nov. 28, 1945; came to U.S., 1970; s. Jacob and Violet (Halawe) B.-H.; m. Tsipi Inberg, July 28, 1980; 1 child, Yori Lee. Diploma, Avni Inst. Fine Arts, Tel Aviv, 1970, Calif. Coll. Arts and Crafts, 1971; MFA, San Francisco State U., 1974. Guest artist fellow Artists Union, Russia, 1992. Prin. works include sculptures and paintings Bklyn. Mus., Buscaglia-Castellani U. Mus., Ghent (Belgium) Mus., Israel Mus., Jerusalem, Malmo Mus., NYC, Jewish Mus., NYC, Tel Aviv Mus., U. Md., College Park, Westminster Bank, NYC, Chelouche Gallery, Tel Aviv, Herbert Johnson Mus., Cornell U., Ithaca, NY, Jewish Mus., NYC, Baumgartner Gallery, Washington, Art Gallery Hamilton, Ont., Can., Munro Gallerie, Hamburg, Germany, Cleve. Mus. Art, Jersey City Mus., Stux Gallery NYC, Las Vegas Art Mus, Grounds for Sculpture. N.J., Stux Gallery, N.Y.C. Recipient Achievement award Israel Ministry Culture, 1971; grantee N.Y. State Coun. on Arts, 1983, NEA, 1984, Pollock Krasner Found., 1990, 96; DAAD fellow, Berlin. Home: 94 Mercer St New York NY 10012-4425 Office Phone: 646-220-4685. Personal E-mail: zigi@zigiland.com.

BENHAM, EMILY, fundraiser; b. Reading, Pa., Feb. 6, 1959; d. Arthur William Benham Jr. and Barbara Reed Bowles; m. James R. Connors, June 9, 1984; 1 child, Joshua Benham Connors. BA, Amherst Coll., 1981. Cert. fund raising exec. Gen. mgr. Evansville (Ind.) Philharm., 1982-84; exec. dir. S.D. Symphony, Sioux Falls, 1985-87; dir. devel. Coconut Grove Playhouse, Miami, Fla., 1987-88, Fla. Orch., Tampa, 1989-93, Am. Stage, St. Petersburg, Fla., 1993-95; v.p. devel. Bayfront Health Found., St. Petersburg, 1995—. Mem. Nat. Soc. Fundraising Execs. (bd. dirs. 1995-99), Assn. Healthcare Philanthropy (cabinet mem. 1994—). Office: Bayfront Health Found 701 6th St S Saint Petersburg FL 33701-4814 E-mail: emily.benham@bayfront.org.

BENHAM, HELEN, music educator; b. N.Y.C., Dec. 4, 1941; d. Charles Mead and Dorothea Wheaton Benham; m. Samuel S. Kim, June 12, 1965; 1 child, Sonya Wheaton Kim Guardo. MusB, Oberlin Conservatory Music, 1962; BA, Oberlin Coll., 1963; MS, The Juilliard Sch., 1965; PhD, Rutgers U., 2001. Music faculty Diller-Quaile Sch. Music, N.Y.C., 1964—75, Mannes Coll. Music, N.Y.C., 1966—82, Monmouth Conservatory Music, Red Bank, NJ, 1967—; prof. music Brookdale C.C., Lincroft, NJ, 1973—. Concert artist, piano and harpsichord. Author: Piano for the Adult Beginner Books I and II, 1977. Trustee, sec. A. Louis Scarmolin Trust. Named Outstanding Young Women of Am., 1978. Mem. Music Tchrs. Nat. Assn., Nat. Guild Piano Tchrs., Am. Musicological Soc., Shore Music Educators Assn. Avocations: swimming, walking. Home: 960 Elberon Ave Long Branch NJ 07740-4709 Office: Brookdale CC Music Dept 765 Newman Springs Rd Lincroft NJ 07738-1597 Office Phone: 732-224-2065.

BENHAM, JAMES H., state official; b. Twin Falls, Idaho, July 14, 1944; s. James Henry and Matilda (Riggs) B.; m. Ann Elizabeth McIntosh, Mar. 27, 1965; 2 children. BA in Polit. Sci., Idaho State U., 1990, MPA, 1992. From police officer to chief of police Pocatello (Idaho) Police Dept., 1988-94; U.S. marshal dept. justice U.S. Dist. Idaho, Boise, 1994—. Contbr. articles to profl. jours. Bd. dirs. Nat. Criminal Justice Assn., 1992-93. Mem. Idaho Peace Officers Assn. (pres. 1986), Idaho Chief of Police Assn. (pres. 1990-91), Pocatello Police Relief Assn., Lions, Phi Kappa Phi. Methodist. Avocations: golf, fishing, hunting, gardening, exercise. Office: US Marshal for Dist Idaho 550 W Fort St # 010 Boise ID 83724-0101

BENHAM, ROBERT, state supreme court justice; m. Nell (Dodson) B.; children: Corey Brevard, Austin Tyler. BS in Polit. sci. (hon.), Tuskegee U., 1967; JD, U. Ga. Lumpkin Sch. of Law, 1970; LLM, U. Va., 1989. Judge Ga. Ct. Appeals, Ga., 1984-89; justice Supreme Ct., State of Ga., Atlanta, 1989—, presiding justice, former chief justice, 1995. Mem. adv. bd. 1st So. Bank. Chmn. Gov.'s Commn. on Drug Awareness and Prevention, State of Ga.; mem. Ga. Hist. Soc.; trustee Ga. Legal Hist. Found.; bd. dirs. Cartersville (Ga.) Devel. Authority, Cartersville-Bartow C. of C.; deacon, former Sunday Sch. supt. The Greater Mt. Olive Bapt. Ch. Recipient Ben F. Johnson, Jr. Pub. Svc. award, Ga. State Univ. Sch. Law, 2004. Mem Atlanta Bar Assn. (bd. dirs. jud. sect.), Ga. Bar Found., Lawyers Club Atlanta, Masons, Shriners, Elks. Office: Ga Supreme Ct 244 Washington St SW Rm 572 Atlanta GA 30334-9007 Fax: (404) 657-4329.

BENHAMOU, ERIC A., information technology company executive; MSEE, Stanford U.; diplome d'Ingenieur, Ecole Nationale Superieure d'Arts et Metiers, Paris; doctorate (hon.), Ben Gurion U. of Negev, Widener U., Western Govs. U., U. S.C. Project mgr., software mgr., design engr. Zilog, Inc.; v.p. Bridge Commn., 1981—87; CEO 3Com Corp., Santa Plz., Calif., 1990—2000, chmn., 1990—99, palmOne, Inc., Milpitas, Calif., 1999—, CEO, 2001—02. Bd. dirs. Smart Valley Inc., Cypress Semiconductor, Legato, Santa Clara U. Sch. Bus., New Am. Found., Intransa, Atrica, INSEAD Sch. Bus., Stanford U. Sch. Engring., Ben Gurion U. of Negev; chair Am. Electronics Assn. Nat. Info. Infrastructure Task Force; apptd. to Pres. Info. Tech. Advisory Com., 1997. Recipient Pres. Environ. and Conservation Challenge award, 1992, Fgn. Investment Jubilee award Israeli Prime Min. Benjamin Netanyahu, 1998, Ellis Island medal honor, 1998. Office: palmOne Inc 400 N McCarthy Blvd Milpitas CA 95035

BENHOFF, EDWARD SPRENG, marketing professional; b. Cleve. s. Homer E. and Helen (Spreng) B.; m. Barbara Anderson, June 28, 1958 (dec.); children: Mary Rebecca, Caroline Mae, Amy Helen; m. Jacqueline D. Chant, Aug. 21, 1993. BS, Colgate U., 1957. Claims adjuster Liberty Mutual Ins., Cleve., 1957-58, Erie, Pa., 1959—; export mgr. Hupp Corp., Cleve., 1959-69, Marus & Wimer, Cleve., 1969-70; pres. Tradecom Internat. Inc., Cleve., 1970—. Bd. dirs., Cleve., Pappas & Assoc., Cleve. Contbr. articles to profl. jours. Gov. Gyro Internat. Dist. 1, 1987-88; mem. No. Ohio Dist. Export Council U.S. Dept. Commerce, Cleve., 1987--. Sgt. USNG, 1958-62. Export Devel. award Case western Res. U. sch. Mgmt. and dept. Commerce, 1970, Exporter of the Yr., U.S. Sml. Bus. Adminstrn., 1987, Disting. Svc. award, O.F.C.A. Mem. Ohio Fgn. Commerce Assn. (v.p., pres. 1974-76, 98-99), Cleve. World Trade Assn., Worldwide D-I-Y Coun. (chmn. 1997-98), Am. Soc. Internat. Execs., Nat. Assn. Export Coun., Internat. Gyro Club (dist. I gov. 1987-88). Presbyterian. Avocations: tennis, skiing, reading, walking. Home: 2967 Country Club Ln Twinsburg OH 44087-2951 Office: Tradecom Internat Inc 32750 Solon Rd Ste 9 Solon OH 44139-2846 Office Phone: 440-248-9116. E-mail: tradecominternational@att.net, edbtrade@aol.com.

BENI, GERARDO, engineering educator, electrical engineer; b. Florence, Italy, Feb. 21, 1946; came to U.S., 1970; s. Edoardo and Tina (Bazzanti) B.; m. Susan Hackwood, May 24, 1986; children: Catherine Elizabeth, Juliet Beatrice. Laurea in Physics, U. Firenze, Florence, Italy, 1970; PhD in Physics, UCLA, 1974. Research scientist AT&T Bell Labs., Murray Hill, N.J., 1974-77, Holmdel, N.J., 1977-82, disting. mem. tech. staff, 1982-84; prof. elec. and computer engring. U. Calif., Santa Barbara, 1984—91, dir. Ctr. for Robotic Systems in Microelectronics, 1985—91, prof. elec. engring. Riverside, 1991—, dir. multimedia lab. and studio, 1991—94, chmn. elec. engring. dept., 1997—98. Dir. Multimedia Lab & Studio, 1991—94. Founder, editor: Jours. Robotic Systems, 1983 (Jour. of Yr. award 1984); editor: Recent Advances in Robotics, 1985, Vacuum Mechatronics, 1990; contbr. more than 160 articles to tech. jours.; 16 patents in field. Fellow AAAS, Am. Physics Soc. Office: U Calif-Riverside Coll Engring Riverside CA 92521-0001 E-mail: beni@ee.ucr.edu. *Produce in freedom; give in freedom; and in freedom enjoy.*

BENIEN, RUTH MARIE, lawyer; b. Norton, Kans., May 25, 1957; d. Alfred Arthur and Genevieve Irene (Kirk) B. BS in Journalism, U. Kans., 1979, JD, 1982. Bar: Kans. 1982, U.S. Dist. Ct. Kans. 1982, U.S. Ct. Appeals (10th cir.) 1985, U.S. Ct. Appeals (fed. cir.) 1996, U.S. Dist. Ct. (we. dist.) Mo. 1999. Assoc. Schnider, Shamberg & May, Chartered, Shawnee Mission, Kansas City, Kans., 1982-83, Shamberg, Johnson, Bergman & Goldman, Chartered, Merriam, Kans., Kansas City, 1984-86, ptnr., 1986-89, Shetlar, Benien et al, Kansas City, 1989-93, Benien Law Offices, Chartered, 1993—. Mem. ATLA, Nat. Employment Lawyers Assn., Kans. Bar Assn., Kans. Trial Lawyers Assn. (bd. govs. 1984—, pres. 1994-95), Wyandotte County Bar Assn. (bd. dirs. 1986-94, pres. 1993-94), U. Kans. Alumni Assn. (journalism law soc.), Assn. Women Lawyers Greater Kansas City (exec. com. 1983—, bd. dirs. 1983-94, v.p. 1984-85, pres. 1985-86), Kans. Women Attys. Assn., Jr. League of Wyandotte and Johnson County (bd. dirs. 2001-04, mem. exec. com. 2003-04), Leadership 2000, Phi Alpha Delta. Home: 334 N 17th St Kansas City KS 66102 Office: Benien Law Offices, Chtd 707 Minnesota Ste 603 Kansas City KS 66101 Office Phone: 913-621-7100.

BENIGNO, THOMAS DANIEL, lawyer; b. Queens, NY, July 29, 1954; s. John Baptiste and Ernesta Mary (Yannaco) B.; m. Maria Angelica Vasquez, Jan. 26, 1980; children: Diana Maria, Laura Michelle, John Frederick. BA with honors, Hofstra U., 1976; JD, Benjamin Cardozo Law Sch., 1979. Bar: N.Y. 1981, U.S. Dist. Ct. (so. and ea. dists.) N.Y. 1985. Atty. Legal Aid Soc., Bronx, N.Y., 1979-84; ptnr. Benigno, Cassisi & Casissi, Floral Park, N.Y., 1984-87; mng. ptnr., gen. counsel Benigno/Gurrieri Real Estate Mgmt. and Devel., Bklyn., 1984-95. Pres. Gurben Properties, Inc., Floral Park, 1987-88, Movies for Kids Inc., Valley Stream, N.Y., 1989-90; gen. counsel Our Gang Assocs. Inc. (dba Thin White Line), Cedarhurst, N.Y., 1988-90. Mem.: NY Bar Assn., Rotary Internat. (pres. Malverne chpt. 2001—04). Office: 269 Hempstead Ave Ste 2 Malverne NY 11565-1224

BENINATI, FRANCIS ANTHONY, lawyer; b. London, Nov. 23, 1947; came to U.S., 1965; s. Emanuele Santino and Maria Louisa (Stoppani) B.; m. Elizabeth Joy Kellogg, June 6, 1970; children: Elizabeth, Andrew. AB, Duke U., 1969; JD, U. Va., 1972. Bar: Ill. 1972, U.S. Dist. Ct. (no. dist.) Ill. 1972. Assoc. Roan & Grossman, Chgo., 1972-81; pvt. practice Chgo., 1981-83; ptnr. Rosenthal and Schanfield, Chgo., 1983--. Lectr. in field. Contbr. articles to profl. jours. Treas. Elmhurst (Ill.) YMCA Swim Team, 1986-87. Mem. ABA, Chgo. Bar Assn., Ill. Bar Assn., Chgo. Estate Planning Council. United Ch. of Christ. Avocations: photography, racquetball.

BENING, ANNETTE, actress; b. Topeka, May 29, 1958; m. Steven White, 1984 (div. 1991); m. Warren Beatty, March 12, 1992; children: Kathlyn Bening Beatty, Benjamin Beatty, Isabel Ashley Ira Beatty, Ella Corinne Beatty. Student, Mesa Coll.; theatre degree, San Francisco State U.; studied at, Am. Conservatory Theatre. Films include The Great Outdoors, 1988, Valmont, 1989, The Grifters, 1990 (Acad. award nomination best supporting actress 1990), Postcards from the Edge, 1990, Guilty by Suspicion, 1991, Regarding Henry, 1991, Bugsy, 1991, Love Affair, 1994, Richard III, 1995, The American President, 1995, Mars Attacks!, 1996, The Siege, 1998, American Beauty, 1999 (Acad. award nom. best actress), In Dreams, 1999, What Planet Are You From, 2000, Open Range, 2003, Being Julia, 2004 (Named Best Actress Nat. Bd. Rev. Motion Pictures 2004, Golden Globe for Best Actress, 2005); stage appearances Coastal Disturbances, 1986, (Tony award nomination 1986, Clarence Derwin award 1987, Theatre World award 1987), Spoils of War, 1988, Hedda Gabler, 1999; TV movies: Manhunt for Claude Dallas, 1986, Hostage, 1988; TV series: Liberty's Kids (voice only); TV appearances: Sesame Street, 1969, Miami Vice, 1987, Wiseguy, 1987, The Sopranos, 2004. Avocation: scuba diving. Office: Creative Artists Agy c/o Kevin Huvane 9830 Wilshire Blvd Beverly Hills CA 90212-1804

BENIOFF, MARC, Internet company executive; BS in Bus. Admin., U. of Southern Calif., 1986. With Apple Computer; founder Liberty Software; various leadership positions in sales, mktg. and prod. devel. Oracle Corp., 1996—99, sr. v.p. web/workgroup systems div., 1995—96, sr. v.p. mktg., 1996—99; founder, chmn., CEO Salesforce.com, Inc., 1999—, also bd. dir. Apptd. by Pres. George W. Bush as co-chairman President's Information Technology Advisory Com. (PITAC), 2003—; apptd. by Hawaiian Gov. Linda Lingle Citizens to Achieve Reform in Edn., 2003—; bd. dirs. Grand Central Communications, 2003—. Co-author: Compassionate Capitalism, 2004. Founder salesforce.com Found., 2000—. Named Northern Calif. Entrepreneur of Yr., Ernst & Young, 2003, Alumni Entrepreneur of Yr., U. SC Marshall Sch. Bus., 2004, Entrepreneur of Yr., SunBridge; named one of Top 10 Entrepreneurs to Watch, Fortune, 25 people responsible for turning e-business around, BusinessWeek, 20 Most Influential People in the Industry, CRM Mag., Agenda Setters, Silicon.com; recipient Promise of Peace award, Prime Min. of Israel Benjamin Netanyahu, Bridge award, HEAVEN (Helping Educate, Activate, Volunteer, and Empower via the Net). Created an on-demand hosted Customer Relationship Management (CRM) solution that would replace traditional enterprise software technology which went public in June, 2004. Office: salesforce.com 1 Market St Ste 300 San Francisco CA 94105

BENIRSCHKE, KURT, retired pathologist, educator; b. Glueckstadt, Germany, May 26, 1924; arrived in US, 1949, naturalized, 1955; s. Fritz Franz and Marie (Luebcke) B.; m. Marion Elizabeth Waldhausen, May 17, 1952; children: Stephen Kurt, Rolf Joachim, Ingrid Marie. Student, U. Hamburg, Germany, 1942, 45-48, U. Berlin, 1943, U. Wuerzburg, 1943-44; MD, U. Hamburg, 1948; DVM (hon.), U. Zürich, 2004. Resident, Teaneck, N.J., 1950-51, Peter Bent Brigham Hosp., Boston, 1951-52, Boston Lying-in-Hosp., 1952-53, Free Hosp. for Women, Boston, 1953, Children's Hosp., Boston, 1953; pathologist Boston Lying-in-Hosp., 1955-60; teaching fellow, assoc. Med. Sch. Harvard, 1954-60; prof. pathology, chmn. dept. pathology Med. Sch. Dartmouth, Hanover, N.H., 1960-70; prof. reproductive medicine and pathology U. Calif., San Diego, 1970-94; chmn. dept. pathology U. Calif. at San Diego Sch. Med., La Jolla, 1976-79; ret. U. Calif., San Diego, 1994. Dir. research San Diego Zoo, 1975-86, trustee, 1986—, pres., 1998-2000; cons. NIH, 1957-70. Served with German Army, 1942-45. Mem. Am. Soc. Pathology, Internat. Acad. Pathology, Am. Coll. Pathology, Am. Acad. Arts and Scis., Teratol. Soc., Am. Soc. Zool. Vets. Home: 8457 Prestwick Dr La Jolla CA 92037-2023 Office: Univ Calif San Diego Med Ctr 200 W Arbor Dr San Diego CA 92103-8321 Office Phone: 619-543-2618. Business E-Mail: kbenirsc@ucsd.edu.

BENISSAN, JORDAN MESSAN, music educator; b. Kinshasa, Zaire, Sept. 3, 1958; arrived in U.S., 1987; s. Jacques Barrigah and Nadou Addy Benissan; m. Andrea Tilden (div.); 1 child, Olivia Dodzi. Degree in bus., Inst. Scis. Commls., Lome, Togo, 1982; master drummer, Sch. African Drumming, Lome, 1983. Instr. U. Okla., Norman, 1986—87, Macalester Coll., St. Paul, 1997—98, St. Catherine Coll., St. Paul, 1997—98; world music tchr. Colby Coll., Waterville, Maine, 1998—. Author: Drumming Through the Spirit of My Ancestors, 1997, Beautiful Music of West Africa, 2003 (nominee Best World Music award Phoenix Mag.), (album) Let Play My Music, 2004. Home: 12 High St Waterville ME 04901 Office: Colby Coll Music Dept 4000 Mayflower Hill Waterville ME 04901 Office Phone: 207-872-9146.

BENITEZ, ARMANDO GERMAN, professional baseball player; b. Ramon Santana, Dominican Republic, Nov. 3, 1972; Pitcher Balt. Orioles, 1994—98, N.Y. Mets., N.Y.C., 1999—2003, N.Y. Yankees, N.Y.C., 2003, Seattle Mariners, 2003, Fla. Marlins, Miami, 2004—, San Francisco Giants, 2004—. Named to, Nat. League All-Star Team, 2003, 2004; recipient Nat. League Rolaids Relief award, 2001. Office: San Francisco Giants Pacific Bell Park 24 Willie Mays Plaza San Francisco CA 94107

BENITEZ, BRIGIDA, lawyer; b. Nov. 11, 1968; BS with high honors, U. Fla., 1990; JD cum laude, Boston Coll., 1993. Bar: Mass. 1993, DC 2002, U.S. Supreme Ct., U.S. Dist. Ct., DC and U.S. Ct. Appeals (4th, 6th, 7th, 8th and DC cir.). Ptnr., litig. dept., internat. arbitration dept. Wilmer, Cutler, Pickering, Hale & Dorr, LLP, Washington. Spkr. in field; mem. advisory com. Minority Corp. Counsel Assn. Contbr. articles to profl. jours.; editor (in chief): Boston Coll. Law Rev. Recipient Excellence in Legal Profession award, Mex. Am. Legal Def. and Ednl. Fund, 2004, Woman of the Year, Hispanic Bus. Mag., 2005; Nat. Hispanic Scholar. Mem.: ABA (standing com. election, law advisory commn.), Barristers, Women's Bar Assn. DC (former co-chair litigation forum), Hispanic Bar Assn. DC (pres.), Hispanic Nat. Bar Assn. (former v.p. external affairs), DC Bar (pro bono com.). Office: Wilmer Cutler Pickering Hale & Dorr LLP 1801 Pennsylvania Ave Washington DC 20006 Office Phone: 202-663-6678. Office Fax: 202-663-6363. E-mail: brigida.benitez@wilmerhale.com.*

BENITEZ, SYLVIA MARIA, artist; b. Balt., June 27, 1957; d. Eugene E. Benitez and Betty Stewart. BFA, U. Md., 1979; postgrad., Manhattan Graphics Ctr., 1992, Greenwich House Pottery, 1994-95. One-woman shows include Tompkins Squ. Libr., N.Y.C., 1982, Johns Hopkins U., 1986, Howard County C.C. Gallery, 1987, Madeira Sch. Gallery, Mc Lean, Va., 1987, Columbia (Md.) Assn. Arts, 1988, Cardinal Gallery, Annapolis, Md., 1990, Villa Julie Coll., Balt., 1991, Museo de Historia, Puerto Rico, 1997, Galeria Raices, 1997, Neuberger Mus., 1998; exhibited in group shows at Kentler Internat. Drawing Ctr., Bklyn., 1993, Artist Talk on Art, N.Y.C., 1993, Kingsborough C.C., Bklyn., 1993, 96, One Main, Bklyn., 1993, Socrates Sculpture Pk., Long Island City, N.Y., 1993, Empire Fulton Ferry Sculpture Pk., 1993, Deutche Bank, N.Y.C., Look Out Sculpture Pk., Damascus, 1994, Embarcadero Ctr., San Francisco, 1994, Metro Regional Ctr., Portland, Oreg., 1994, Transmission Gallery, Scotland, 1994, Gallery One Twenty Eight, N.Y.C., 1995, Howard County Ctr. Arts Gallery, 1995, Pier Show, Bklyn., 1995, Franklin Furnace, 1996, Whitney Mus. Am. Art, Fairfield County, 1998; murals painted at Pocomoke (Md.) H.S., 1988, Rock Creek Elem. Sch., Silver Spring, Md., 1991, Howard Career Ctr., Wilmington, Del., 1993, Steven Decatur Sch., Clinton, Md., 1993, St. Catherines of Siena Sch., Wilmington, 1994, Lefferts Homestead, Bklyn., 1994, Thurmont Mid. Sch., 1996. Avocations: foreign languages, reading. Home: 4006 Macalpine Rd Ellicott City MD 21042-5325

BENIVEGNA, VITO NICHOLAS, language educator; b. Hamden, Conn., Apr. 29, 1935; s. Frank and Louise Benivegna; m. Maria Theresa Narcisi, June 25, 1966; children: Andrea Smith, Michael. BA, Fairfield U., 1957; MA, U. Ill., 1964. Spanish tchr. West Haven (Conn.) H.S., 1958—61, North Haven (Conn.) Jr. H.S., 1961—62; grad. tchg. asst. U. Ill., Urbana, 1962—65; instr. Spanish U. Dayton, Ohio, 1965—66; grad. tchg. assoc. U. Ariz., Tucson, 1967—69; prof. Spanish Belleville (Ill.) Area Coll., 1969—98; ret. Adj. prof. Southwestern Ill. Coll., Belleville, Ill., 1998—. Avocations: volunteer work, reading, travel.

BENJAMIN, ADELAIDE WISDOM, retired lawyer, retired community volunteer and activist; b. New Orleans, Aug. 23, 1932; d. William Bell and Mary (Freeman) Wisdom; m. Edward Bernard Benjamin Jr., May 11, 1957; children: Edward Wisdom, Mary Dabney, Ann Leith, Stuart Minor. Student, Hollins Coll., 1950-52; BA in English, Newcomb Coll., 1954; JD, Tulane U., 1956; student, Loyola U., New Orleans, 1980-81; grad. extension program Sewanee Theol. Sch., U. South, 1982. Assoc. Wisdom, Stone, Pigman and Benjamin, New Orleans, 1956-58; tchr. ext. courses Sewanee Theol. Sem., 1984-88; ret., 1959. Spkr., panelist on sch. issues various local and nat. groups. Mem. Tulane Law Rev., 1954—56, compiler, editor, pub. Trinity Ch. supplemental songbook, 1980. Trustee Mary Freeman Wisdom Charitable Found., sec., 1987—92, pres., 1990—94, treas., 1994—, pres., 2000—; sec. bd. dir. YWCA, New Orleans, 1967—68, 1st v.p., 1968—69; bd. dir. Kingsley House, New Orleans, 1971—77; trustee Metairie Pk. Country Day Sch., 1971—79, sec., 1976—79; mem. adv. bd. Tulane Summer Lyric Theatre, Tulane U., 1972—, pres. adv. bd., 1977—79; pres. PTA, 1975—76; bd. dir. Children's Hosp., New Orleans, 1976—79; mem. adv. bd. Pub. Radio Sta. WWNO, 1980—; bd. dir. Parenting Ctr., 1981—; pres. E&A Charitable

Found., New Orleans, 1983—; pres. bd. New Orleans Symphony, 1984—89; mem. Loving Cup selection com. New Orleans Times Picayune, 1985; bd. dir. La. Mus. Found., New Orleans, 1989—, S.E. La. coun. Girl Scouts US, New Orleans, 1989—97, Loyola U., New Orleans, 1989—99, mem. exec. com., 1996—99, hon. bd. mem., 2003—; bd. dir. Louise S. McGehee Sch., New Orleans, 1990—97, v.p., 1991—97, hon. bd. dir., 1991; pres. New Orleans Mus. Art Fellows Forum, 1991—; mem. exec. com. La. Mus. Found., New Orleans, 1991—; bd. dir. Newcomb Children's Ctr., New Orleans, 1991—94; mem. adv. bd. dept. psychiatry La. State U. Med. Ctr., 1992—; mem. exec. bd. La. Philharm. Orch., 1992—; mem. Newcomb Dean's Coun., 1997—, pres., 2002—; bd. dir. Nat. D-Day Mus., New Orleans, 1998—2002; sec. parish coun. Trinity Episc. Ch., New Orleans, 1973—75, sec. vestry, 1975—79, active, leader Trinity Quartet, 1979—84. Recipient Weiss Brotherhood award Nat. Conf. Christians and Jews, 1986, Outstanding Philanthropist, Nat. Soc. Fundraising Exec., 1986, Volunteer Activist Award, St. Elizabeth Guild, 1986, Jr. League Sustainer award, 1987, Disting. Alumna award McGehee Sch., 1987, George Washington Honor Medal for Individual Achievement, Freedom Found. at Valley Forge, 1988, Living and Giving award Juvenile Diabetes Found. 1991, Outstanding Citizen New Orleans award La. Colonials, 1994, Jacques Yenni award Outstanding Cmty. Svc. Sch. Bus. Adminstrn. Loyola Univ., 1994, Integritas Vitae award for outstanding cmty. svc. Loyola U., 1994, Classical Arts Patron award Tribute to the Classical Arts, 1998, Big Bros./Big Sisters award for cmty. svc., New Orleans, 2004; named Goodwill Ambassador for Louisiana Gov.'s Commn. Internat. Trade, Industry and Tourism, 1987, Sweet Art, Contemporary Arts Ctr., 1988, Significant Role Model, Young Leadership Coun., 1988, Woman of Distinction S.E. La. Girl Scout Coun., 1992; named among Outstanding Alumni Class of 1954, Tulane U., 2004. Mem. ABA, LWV, La. Bar Assn., New Orleans Bar Assn., Jr. League New Orleans (exec. com. 1971-72, bd. dir. 1967-72), Ind. Women's Orgn., Com. 21, Am. Symphony Orch. League, Quarante Club (2d v.p. 1978-79), Debutante Club, Le Debut des Jeunes Filles Club, New Orleans Town Gardners (pres. 1979-80), Thomas Wolfe Soc. (life mem.). Home: 1837 Palmer Ave New Orleans LA 70118-6215

BENJAMIN, ANDRE LAUREN (DRE, ANDRÉ 3000), vocalist, actor; b. Ga., May 24, 1975; 1 child, Seven Sirius. Performer OutKast, 1992—. Singer: (albums) Southernplayalisticadillacmuzik, 1994, ATLiens, 1996, Aquemini, 1998, Stankonia, 2000 (Grammy awards: Best Rap Album, 2001, Best Rap Performance By A Duo Or Group for song "Ms Jackson", 2001), Big Boi and Dre Present...Outkast, 2001 (Grammy award: (with Killer Mike) Best Rap Performance By A Duo Or Group for song "The Whole World", 2002), Speakerboxxx/The Love Below, 2003 (Grammy awards: Album Of The Yr., 2003, Best Urban/Alternative Performance for song "Hey Ya!", 2003, Best Rap Album, 2003, MTV Video Music award Best Hip-Hop Video for song "Hey Ya!", 2004, MTV Video Music award Best Special Effects In a Video for the song "Hey Ya!", 2004, MTV Video Music award for Best Art Direction In a Video for the song "Hey Ya!", 2004, MTV Video Music award Video of Year for the song "Hey Yeah!", 2004, Am. Music Awards Favorite Album Rap/Hip-Hop, 2004); actor: (TV guest appearances) Martin, 1995, Mad TV, 2000, Saturday Night Live, 2003, The Shield, 2004; (films) Be Cool, 2005, Four Brothers, 2005. Recipient Best New Rap Group of Yr., Source awards, 1995, Favorite Band, Duo or Group-Pop or Rock, Am. Music Awards, 2004, Favorite Band, Duo or Group-Rap/Hip-Hop, 2004, Duo/Group Artist of Yr., Billboard Music Awards, 2004, Billboard 200 Duo/Group Album Artist of Yr., 2004, Hot 100 Duo/Group of Yr., 2004, R&B/Hip-Hop Duo/Group of Yr., 2004, Digital Track of Yr., 2004. Office: Arista Records Inc 1540 Broadway New York NY 10036-4074 Address: Arista Records inc 8750 Wilshire Blvd Beverly Hills CA 90211-2713*

BENJAMIN, BEZALEEL SOLOMON, architectural engineer, educator; b. Anand, India, Feb. 21, 1938; came to U.S., 1971; s. Solomon and Penninah (Ellis) B.; m. Nora Jacob David, Feb. 25, 1962; children— Ashley Bezaleel, Jennifer Elana B.E. in Civil Engring., Bombay U., India, 1957; D.I.C., Imperial Coll., London, 1958; MS in Engring., London U., 1959, PhD, 1965. Design engr. M.N. Dastur & Co., Bombay, 1961-63; postdoctoral fellow U. Surrey, Eng., 1965-66; prin. lectr. Hatfield Poly., Eng., 1966-71; asst. prof. archtl. engring. U. Kans., Lawrence, 1971-72, assoc. prof., 1972-76, prof., 1976—. Vis. Fulbright prof. Technion, Haifa, Israel, 1987-88. Author: The Analysis of Braced Domes, 1963, Structural Design with Plastics, 1969, Structures for Architects, 1975, Building Construction for Architects and Engineers, 1978, Structural Evolution: An Illustrated History, 1990, Statics, Strengths and Structures for Architects, 1992; (children's book) Susan Altencroft, 1976; (novels) Rampaging Lovers, 1988, A Nazi Among Jews, 1990, Bene Israel Tales, 1991, The Jewish Amendment, 1992, David Rahabi, 1993. Jewish. Avocation: writing. Office: U Kans Sch Architecture Lawrence KS 66045-0001 Office Phone: 785-864-4383. Business E-Mail: sben@ku.edu.

BENJAMIN, BRENT D., state supreme court justice, lawyer; b. Marietta, Ohio, July 3, 1957; m. Janice Benjamin; 5 children. BA in Political sci., Ohio State U., 1981, JD, 1984. Bar: W.Va. 1984, U.S. Fourth Circuit Ct. of Appeals, U.S. Dist. Ct. Southern W.Va., W.Va. Supreme Ct., Ky. Supreme Ct. 2001. Atty. Robinson and McElwee, Charleston, W.Va., 1983—90, ptnr., 1990—2004; justice W.Va. Supreme Ct. of Appeals, 2004—. Former treasurer W.Va. Republican Party. Mem.: ABA, Kanawha County Bar Assn., W.Va. State Bar Assn. Office: WVa Supreme Ct Appeals Capitol Complex Bldg 1 Charleston WV 25305

BENJAMIN, EDWARD BERNARD, JR., lawyer; b. New Orleans, Feb. 11, 1923; s. Edward Bernard and Blanche (Sternberger) B.; m. Adelaide Wisdom, May 11, 1957; children: Edward Wisdom, Mary Dabney, Ann Leith, Stuart Minor. BS, Yale U., 1944; JD, Tulane U., 1952. Bar: La. 1952. Practiced in, New Orleans, since 1952; ptnr. Jones, Walker, Waechter, Poitevent, Carrere & Denegre, New Orleans, 1967—. Pres. Am. Coll. Probate Counsel, 1986-87, Internat. Acad. Estate and Trust Law, 1976-78; vice chmn. bd. trustees Southwestern Legal Found., 1980-88, bd. dirs., 1988-90; chmn. bd. Starmount Co., Greensboro, N.C., 1968-88, chmn. emeritus, 1988—. Editor-in-chief Tulane U. Law Rev., 1951-52; mem. editl. bd. Cmty. Property Jour., 1974-89. Trustee Hollins Coll., 1966-87; chancellor Episcopal Diocese of La., 1984-2003, Trinity Episcopal Ch., New Orleans, 1974-92; mem. adv. bd. CCH Estate & Fin. Planning Svc., 1982-88; chmn. Salvation Army City Commd. Adv. Bd., 1965-68; pres. New Orleans Jr. C. of C., 1953. 1st lt., F.A. pilot, U.S. Army, 1943-46. Mem. Am. Coll. Tax Counsel, Am. Law Inst., ABA (sec. taxation sect. 1967-68, coun. 1976-79, coun. real property, probate and trust law sect. 1978-81), La. Bar Assn. (chmn. taxation sect. 1959-60), La. Law Inst., La. Bar Found. (trustee 1998-99), New Orleans Country Club, Southern Yacht Club, New Orleans Lawn Tennis Clu Home: 1837 Palmer Ave New Orleans LA 70118-6215 Office: Jones Walker Waechter Poitevent Carrere & Denegre 201 Saint Charles Ave Fl 51 New Orleans LA 70170-5100 Office Phone: 504-582-8114. Business E-Mail: ebenjamin@joneswalker.com.

BENJAMIN, GEORGES CURTIS, emergency physician, consultant; b. Chgo., Sept. 28, 1952; s. George and Tessie Cozie (Edwards) B.; m. Yvette Josphanie Janisse; children: Stephanie, Kali. BS, Ill. Inst. Tech., 1973; MD, U. Ill., 1978. Diplomate Am. Bd. Internal Medicine, Am. Bd. Med. Examiners. Intern and resident internal medicine Brooke Army Med. Ctr., San Antonio, 1978-81; dept. emergency medicine Madigan Army Med. Ctr., Tacoma, 1981-83; chief emergency medicine Walter Reed Army Med. Ctr., Washington, 1983-87; chair. dept. com. health & ambulatory care Dist. Columbia Gen. Hosp., Washington, 1987-90; commr. pub. health Dist. Columbia, 1990-91; health policy cons., 1992-95; emergency physician Holy Cross Cmty. Hosp., Silver Spring, Md., 1991-95; dep. sec. Pub. Health State of Md., Balt., 1995-99; sec. Dept. Health and Mental Hygiene, Balt., 1999—2002; exec. dir. APHA, 2002—. Emergency physician Patuxent Naval Air Station, Patuxent River, Md., 1989, Nisqually Clinic, Yelm, Wash., 1981-82, Allenmore Com. Hosp., Tacoma, 1981-82; house internist Greater Southeast Com. Hosp., Washington, 1985-87; clin. instr. emergency medicine, Georgetown U., 1988-95; adj. prof. Health Care Scis., 1993, asst. prof. medicine Uniformed Svcs. U. Health Scis., Bethesda, Md., 1984-87. Editl. bd. Jour. Nat. Med. Assn., 1986-93; reviewer Am. Coll. Physician Execs., 1989—, Am. Jour. Emergency Medicine, 1986-94, Mil. Medicine, 1983-87; contbr. articles to profl. jours. Bd. dirs. Hosp. Sick Children, Boarder Baby Project, Inc. Whiteman Walker Clinic Inc.; adv. bd. D.C. Commn. Pub. Health Disability and Injury Prevention Program, 1993, Montgomery County HIV/AIDS Citizens, 1992-93; bd. trustees Am. Cancer Soc.; bd. govs. Medico Chirurg. Soc. D.C.; mem. D.C. Emergency Med. Svcs. Com., 1990-91, D.C. State Health Coord. Coun., 1990-91; gov. commn. Welfare Policy State of Md., 1993. With M.C. U.S. Army, 1978-87, USAR, 1974-78. Recipient Cert. Recognition, 1993, Coun. Govs. Svc. award, 1991, Disting. Pub. Svc. award, 1991, Cert. Appreciation Best Friends of D.C., 1991, Cert. Appreciation D.C. Pub. Schs., 1991, Svc. award Medico Chirurg. Soc., 1990, Recognition award D.C.G.H. Med./Dental staff, 1990; decorated Army Commendation medal, 1983, Comdrs. award, 1981, Eisenhower Proclamation medal, 1970. Fellow ACP, Am. Coll. Emergency Physicians (Nat. Key Contact 1987-90, 92-95, gov. affairs com. 1993, D.C. chpt. v.p. 1988-90, D.C. chpt. pres. 1989-90, liaison rep. emergency nurses assn. 1992-95, nat. health policy com. Dallas 1992-93); mem. APHA, AMA, Nat. Med. Assn. (mil. and aerospace medicine sect. sec. 1983, nat. co-chmn. 1985, 86, nat. chmn. 1987, emergency medicine nat. chmn. 1990-93), Medico Chirurg. Soc. (violence task force chmn. 1992-94), Am. Coll. Physicians Execs., Assoc. State Territorial Health Ofcls. (sec./treas. 1999-2000, pres. 2001-02). Office: APHA 800 I St NW Washington DC 20001-3710 Office Phone: 202-777-2430. E-mail: georges.benjamin@apha.org.

BENJAMIN, JEFF, lawyer, pharmaceutical executive; b. Bklyn., Dec. 28, 1945; s. Haskell and Lillian (Sikofski) B.; m. Betty Gae Meckler, Mar. 21, 1971; children: Lily Meckler, Ross Meckler. BA, Cornell U., 1967; JD cum laude, NYU, 1971. Bar: N.Y. 1971, U.S. Dist. Cts. (so. and ea. dists.) N.Y. 1972. Assoc. Kronish, Lieb, Shainswit, Weiner & Hellman, N.Y.C., 1971-74; atty. Ciba-Geigy Corp., Ardsley and Tarrytown, N.Y., 1974—, counsel for regulatory affairs, 1976—, divsn. counsel, 1978—, asst. gen. counsel, 1985—, dir. legal dept., assoc. gen. counsel, 1986-89, v.p., gen. counsel, 1996-97; assoc. gen. counsel, ethics and law compliance officer Novartis Corp., N.Y.C., 1997—2001, v.p. dep. gen. counsel, ethics and law compliance officer, 2005—. Mem. adv. bd. Brennan Ctr. for Justice, 2002—; lectr. in field; mem. bd. dirs. Ethics Officer Assn., 2005—. Contbr. articles to law jours. Mem. Citizens Adv. Com., Ramapo, N.Y. With USAR, 1969—74. Mem. ABA, Antitrust Section, Litigation Section, Cornell U. Alumni Assn. (admissions amb.), Order of Coif. Home: 13 Park Ave New City NY 10956-1107 Office: Novartis Corp 608 Fifth Ave 10th Fl New York NY 10020-2305

BENJAMIN, KARL STANLEY, artist, art educator; b. Chgo., Dec. 29, 1925; s. Eustace Lincoln and Marie (Klamsteiner) B.; m. Beverly Jean Paschke, Jan. 29, 1949; children: Beth Marie, Kris Ellen, Bruce Lincoln. Student, Northwestern U., 1943, 46; BA, U. Redlands, 1949; MA, Claremont Grad. Sch., 1960. With dept. arts Pomona Coll., Claremont, Calif., 1979-97, Loren Barton Babcock Miller prof., artist-in residence, 1978-94, prof. emeritus, 1997—; prof. art Claremont Grad. Sch. Traveling exhbns. include New Talent, Am. Fedn. Arts, 1959, 4 Abstract Classicists, Los Angeles and San Francisco museums, 1959-61, West Coast Hard Edge, Inst. Contemporary Arts, London, Eng., 1960, Purist Painting, Am. Fedn. Arts, 1960-61, Geometric Abstractions in Am., Whitney Mus., 1962, Paintings of the Pacific, U.S., Japan and Australia, 1961-63, Artists Environment, West Coast, Amon Carter Mus., Houston, 1962-63, Denver annual, 1965, Survey of Contemporary Art, Speed Mus., Louisville, 1965, The Colorists, San Francisco Mus., 1965, Art Across Am, Mead Corp., 1965-67, The Responsive Eye, Mus. Modern Art, 1965-66, 30th Biennial Exhbn. Am. Painting, Corcoran Gallery, 1967, 35th Biennial Exhbn. Am. Painting, 1977, Painting and Sculpture in California: The Modern Era, San Francisco Mus. Modern Art, 1976-77, Smithsonian Nat. Collection Fine Arts, Washington, 1976-77, Los Angeles Hard Edge: The Fifties and Seventies, Los Angeles County Mus. Art, 1977, Corcoran Gallery, Washington, Cheney Cowles Mus., Spokane, 1980, Calif. State U., Bakersfield, 1982, Henry Gallery, U. Wash., 1982, U. Calif., Santa Barbara, 1984, L.A. Mcpl. Art Galleries, Barnsdall Park, 1986, Turning the Tide: Early Los Angeles Modernists, Santa Barbara Mus. Art, Oakland Mus., others, 1989-91, L.A. County Mus. Art, 1996, After Geometric Expression, L.A. Mus. Art, 2004; rep. permanent collections, Whitney Mus., L.A. County Mus. Art, San Francisco Mus. Art, Santa Barbara (Calif.) Mus. Art, Pasadena (Calif.) Art Mus., Long Beach (Calif.) Mus. Art, La Jolla (Calif.) Mus. Art, Fine Arts Gallery San Diego, U. Redlands, Mus. Modern Art, Israel, Pomona Coll., Scripps Coll., Univ. Mus., Berkeley, Calif., Wadsworth Atheneum, Nat. Collection Fine Arts, Seattle Mus. Modern Art, Newport Harbor Mus., U. N.Mex. Mus. Art, Wash. State U., L.A. Mus. Contemporary Art, Houston Mus. Contemporary Art, Balt. Mus. Art; retrospective exhbn. covering yrs. 1955-87 Calif State U. at Northridge, 1989, retrospective exhbn. 1979-94, Pomona Coll., 1994, 450 year survey Calif. art Orange County Mus. Art, Newport Beach, 1998-99, LA (Calif.) County Mus., 2004, San Diego (Calif.) Mus. Art, 2004. Served with USNR, 1943-46. Visual Arts grantee NEA, 1983, 89. Office: Pomona Coll Dept Arts 333 N College Way Dept Arts Claremont CA 91711-4429 also: Claremont Grad U Art Dept 251 E 10th St Claremont CA 91711-3913 Office Phone: 909-426-1483.

BENJAMIN, LLOYD WILLIAM, III, university president; b. Painesville, Ohio, Sept. 2, 1944; s. Lloyd William Jr. and Shirley M. (Emmett) B. BA, Emory U., 1966; PhD, U. N.C., 1973. Prof. art history East Carolina U., Little Rock, 1970-76; prof. U. Ark., Little Rock, 1976—95, dean fine arts, 1983-88, dean arts and humanities, 1988-95; v.p. acad. affairs Valdosta State U., 1995-2000; pres. Ind. State U., 2000—. Author: History Early Netherlandish Painting, 1977, Art of Designed Environments-Netherlands, 1983; co-author: Drawings from the Collection of Herbert and Dorothy Vogel, 1986; also articles. Mem. Arts and Humanities Commn., 1990-91; pres. Ark. Endowment for Humanities, 1986, Friends of KLRE/KUAR, 1990. Mem. S.E. Coll. Art Conf. (pres. 1994—), Golden Key, Phi Kappa Phi. E-mail: lwb@isugw.indstate.edu.

BENJAMIN, LORNA SMITH, psychologist; d. Lloyd Albert and Esther Smith; children: Laureen, Linda. AB, Oberlin Coll., 1955; PhD, U. Wis., 1960. NIMH fellow dept. psychiatry U. Wis., 1958-62, clin. psychology intern, 1960-64, asst. prof., 1966-71, assoc. prof., 1971-77, prof. psychiatry, 1977-88; prof. psychology U. Utah, 1988—. Adj. prof. psychiatry U. Utah, 1988-; rsch. assoc. Wis. Psychol. Inst., Madison, 1962-66. Contbr. articles to profl. jours. Mem.: APA, Soc. Psychotherapy Rsch., Phi Beta Kappa. Office: Univ Utah Dept Psychology 380 S 1530 E Salt Lake City UT 84112-8934 Office Phone: 801-581-4463. E-mail: lsb_3@msn.com. *I attribute my success to a high energy level, and to some teachers and friends who supported me in times and places women were unwelcome.*

BENJAMIN, MARTIN E., photographer, art educator; s. Grant Earl and Margaret Benjamin; m. Donna Fitzgerald, June 25, 1980. BA, U. Albany, 1971. Photographer U. Albany, 1970—73; owner, dir. Rock Shots, Schenectady, 1977—; photographer Black Star Agy., NYC, 1977—; prof. art Union Coll., Schenectady, 1979—. Adj. instr. Coll. St. Rose, Albany, 1973—79. Book, Rock Styles by Tommy Hilfiger, 2001, exhibitions include Great Modern Pictures, N.Y.C., 2001. Recipient 1st Pl. award, Time Life Corp., N.Y.C., 1974, Bronze medal, Nikon Corp., Tokyo, 1990. Avocations: gardening, fishing, golf, travel. Office: Union Coll Dept Visual Arts Schenectady NY 12308

BENJAMIN, REGINA MARCIA, physician, administrator; b. Mobile, Ala., 1956; B in chemistry, Xavier U., New Orleans, 1979; MD, U. Ala., Birmingham, 1984; MBA, Tulane U., 1991. Internship and residency Med. Ctr. of Ctrl. Ga., Macon; med. dir. nursing homes, 1990—95; founder, adminstr. Bayou La Batre (Ala.) Rural Health Clinic, Inc., 1990—; assoc. dean rural health U. South Ala. Coll. Medicine. Med. mission, Honduras, 1993. Recipient Nelson Mandela Award for Health and Human Rights, Kaiser Family Found., 1997, Nat. Caring Award, Caring Inst., 2000, President's Award, U. Ala. Birmingham, 2001. Fellow: Am. Acad. Family Physicians; mem.: Med. Assn. State of Ala. (pres. 2002—03), NAS, AMA (Women in Medicine Panel 1986—87, pres. Edn. and Rsch. Found. 1997—98). Achievements include First African Am. woman to become pres. of a state med. soc. in the US, 2002; featured in Nat. Libr. Medicine exhibit Changing the Face of Medicine honoring women physicians, 2003. Office: 318 Patrician Dr Spanish Fort AL 36527-9461

BENJAMIN, RUTH, writer; b. Tacoma, Mar. 5, 1934; d. Samuel David Turteltaub and Rebecca Shallit; m. Arthur Isaac Rosenblatt, Aug. 5, 1956; children: Paul, Judy. BA, Sarah Lawrence Coll., 1956. Circulation dept. staff The Am. Inst. Physics, N.Y.C., 1953-54; prodn. asst. Esquire, Inc., N.Y.C., 1955-56; asst. editor Hillman Periodicals, N.Y.C., 1957-58; devel. dept. staff Poets & Writers, Inc., N.Y.C., 1983-84; adminstrv. asst. RKK&G Mus. & Cultural Facilities Cons., 1995—. Author: Naked at Forty, 1984, Movie Song Catalog, 1993. Mem. The Authors Guild, Inc., The Players. Avocations: reading, theater, cabaret. Home: 1158 5th Ave New York NY 10029-6917 E-mail: jnotebook@aol.com.

BENJAMIN, THOMAS EDWARD, music educator, composer, conductor; b. Bennington, Vt., Feb. 17, 1940; s. Paul Alfred and Frances (Stern) B.; m. Elizabeth Klein, Aug. 25, 1963 (div. 1986); children: Matthew, Sarah; m. Carol Jean Russell, May 28, 1994. BA, Bard Coll., 1961; MA, Harvard U., 1963; PhD, Eastman Sch. Music, 1968. Prof. U. Houston, 1968-87; tchr. Nat. Music Camp, Interlochen, Mich., 1969-71, 77-83; prof. music theory Peabody Conservatory, Balt., 1987—. Author: The Craft of Modal Counterpoint, 1978, Counterpoint in the Style of Bach, 1986; co-author: Techniques and Materials of Tonal Music, 4th edit., 1992, Music for Analysis, 4th edit., 1996; mem. editl. bd. Jour. Music Theory Pedagogy, 1989-96; 40 published compositions. Resident fellow MacDowell Colony, 1982, 83, 96; composer grantee Meet-the-Composer, 1980, 86, 88; Composer award NEA, 1978; resident fellow Yaddo, 1978, 80, 84. Mem. ASCAP (Std. Music award 1975-97), Am. Soc. Univ. Composers, Nat. Coun. Coll. Music Soc. Avocations: gardening, sailing. Home: 4093 Fragile Sail Way Ellicott City MD 21042-5018 E-mail: tben2@comcast.net.

BENJAMIN, WILLIAM CHASE, lawyer; b. Glen Cove, N.Y., Dec. 2, 1947; AB, Princeton U., 1969; postgrad., Grad. Inst. Internat. Affairs, Geneva, 1969-70; JD, Harvard U., 1973. Bar: N.Y. 1974, U.S. Tax Ct. 1978, Mass. 1983. Assoc. Cleary, Gottlieb, Steen & Hamilton, Brussels, 1975-78, N.Y.C., 1978-82; assoc. Hale and Dorr, Boston, 1982-84, jr. ptnr., 1984-86, sr. ptnr., 1986—. Fulbright scholar, 1969-70. Mem. ABA, Internat. Bar Assn., Mass. Bar Assn., Boston Bar Assn., Internat. Fiscal Assn. Avocations: skiing, tennis, swimming, sailing. Office: Wilmer Cutler Pickering Hale and Dorr LLP 60 State St Boston MA 02109-1816 Office Phone: 617-526-6318. E-mail: william.benjamin@wilmerhale.com.

BENJAMIN, WOAN-JUE JANE, education educator, researcher; d. Hanson and Pi-Lein Cheng; m. Seldon David Benjamin, June 22, 1985; children: Sonya Donna, Sophia Dion. PhD, U. N.C., 1990; BEd, Taiwan Nat. U., 2005. Teacher Certification Ont., Can., 1992. Asst. prof. Centennial Coll., Toronto, Canada, 1992—97; assoc. prof. Mansfield U., Mansfield, Pa., 1999—. Counselor Pvt., Toronto, Ontario, Canada, 1992—97. Author: (textbook) Assessment in the K-12 Classroom - Theory and Practice, 2005. Faculty Rsch. award, Mansfield U., 2000, 2001, 2002, 2003, 2004, 2005. Mem.: Chinese Am. Ednl. R & D Assn. (assoc.), Assn. of Tchr. Educators (assoc.), Nat. Coun. on Measurement in Edn. (assoc.), Am. Edn. Rsch. Assn. (assoc.). Office: Mansfield Univ 203B Retan Ctr Mansfield PA 16933 Office Phone: 570-662-4797. E-mail: jbenjami@mnsfld.edu.

BENKARD, JAMES W. B., lawyer; b. N.Y.C., Apr. 10, 1937; s. Franklin Bartlett and Laura Derby (Dupee) B.; m. Margaret Walker Spofford, Dec. 12, 1964; children: Andrew Minturn, James Robinson, Margaret Mercer. AB, Harvard U., 1959; LLB, Columbia U., 1963. Bar: N.Y. 1963. Assoc. Davis Polk & Wardwell, N.Y.C., 1963-73, ptnr., 1973—, co-chmn. firm pro bono com. Law clk. to Hon. Charles D. Breitel, Appellate Div. First Dept. & N.Y. Ct. Appeals, 1966—67. Trustee Vassar Coll., Poughkeepsie, N.Y., Tchrs. Coll., N.Y.C., Environ. Def. Fund, N.Y.C., St. Mark's Sch., Southborough, Mass, Columbia Law Sch. Alumni Assn., Scenic Am. Mem. Am. Coll. Trial Lawyers, Knickerbocker Club, River Club (N.Y.C.), Fishers Island Country Club. Office: Davis Polk & Wardwell 450 Lexington Ave Fl 31 New York NY 10017-3982 Office Phone: 212-450-4000. Office Fax: 212-450-3800. Business E-Mail: james.benkard@dpw.com.*

BENKLER, YOCHAI, law educator; LLB, Tel-Aviv U., 1991; JD, Harvard U., 1994. Assoc. Ropes & Gray, 1994—95; law clk. to Hon. Stephen G. Breyer US Supreme Ct., 1995—96; asst. prof. NYU, 1996—99, assoc. prof., 1999—2000, prof., 2000—03; prof. law Yale U., New Haven, 2003—. Contbr. articles to law jours. Office: Yale Law Sch PO Box 208215 New Haven CT 06520 E-mail: yochai.benkler@yale.edu.

BENKOWSKI, ANN MARIE, writer; b. Marion, Ohio, Dec. 7, 1965; d. Ronald Merl and Patricia Ann (Wakely) Richie; m. Timothy Jay Benkowski; children: Corrina, Alyssa, Courtney, Thomas. Diploma, Writer's Digest Sch., Cin., 2000, diploma, 2001. Cashier Burger King, Marion, 1982—84; sec., bookkeeper Rotary Towers, Marion, 1984—85; clk., bookkeeper Western & So. Life, Marion, 1985—88; computer programmer Fullfillment Corp., Marion, 1989—95; sec., bookkeeper Northfield, Minn., 1997—. Author: (novels) Accidents Can Happen; contbr. poetry to anthologies (Editor's Choice award, 2002, Internat. Poet of Merit award, 2002, Commemorative award, 2002). Mem.: Internat. Soc. of Poets (hon.). Avocations: reading, cross stitch, crocheting, gardening. Home: 9260 310th St W Northfield MN 55057 Personal E-mail: act@ll.net.

BENMOSCHE, ROBERT H., insurance company executive; BA in Math., Alfred U., 1966. With Chase Manhattan Bank, Paine Webber, 1982, sr. v.p. mktg., 1984-86, CFO retail bus., 1986-87, dir. securities ops., 1987, exec. v.p.; exec. v.p. individual bus. dept. Met. Life Ins. Co., 1995—97, pres., CEO, 1997—98, chmn., CEO, 1998—2000, MetLife Inc., 2000—. Bd. dirs. N.Y. Philharm. Lt. U.S. Army Signal Corps, 1966-68. Mem. Life Ins. Mktg. and Rsch. Assn. (bd. trustees). Office: Met Life 1 Madison Ave New York NY 10010-3603

BENN, THEODORE ALEXANDER (ALEC BENN), writer; b. London, July 10, 1918; came to U.S., 1925, naturalized, 1933; s. Theodore and Beatrice Alice (Martin) B.; m. Ethel Borner, June 14, 1940 (div.); 1 child, Theodore A. Jr.; m. Caroline Meredith Whittingham, Dec. 31, 1959; children: Alexander W., Richard R. ScB in Engring., Brown U., 1939; postgrad., NYU, 1939-40, 83-87, Columbia U., 1946-56. Exec. Aluminum Co. Am., Edgewater, N.J., 1939-44, 46-48; writer Merrill Lynch Pierce Fenner and Smith, N.Y.C., 1948-51, McGraw Hill, N.Y.C., 1952; copy dir., v.p., creative dir. Doremus & Co., N.Y.C., 1953-64; v.p. Kudner Agy., N.Y.C., 1964-65, J.M. Mathes, N.Y.C., 1965-66, Bozell & Jacobs, N.Y.C., 1966-67; pres. Benn & MacDonough, Inc., N.Y.C., 1967-87, Short Hills, N.J., 1987-88. Columnist Money and Power, 1988; author: 27 Most Common Mistakes in Advertising, 1978, 23 Most Common Mistakes in Public Relations, 1982, Advertising Financial Products and Services, 1986, The Unseen Wall Street of 1968-1975 and Its Significance For Today, 2000; playwright: Love Game (Nat. Arts Club award 1952); Answer the Sphinx, 1952, The Comedy of Love and Power, 2002, A Tale of Tangled Love, 2003, The Comedy of Love & Power, 2004; contbr. articles to profl. jours. Lt. (s.g.) USN, 1944-46. Recipient awards for advt. Mem.: Deep Canyon Tennis Club, Racquets Club Short Hills, Univ. Club. Avocation: tennis. Home (Summer): 63 Great Oak Dr Short Hills NJ 07078-3426 Home (Winter): 73224 Bill Tilden Ln Palm Desert CA 92260 Personal E-mail: cmbenn@aol.com.

BENNER, C. JONATHAN, lawyer; b. 1948; BA in Internat. Svc., Am. Univ., 1970; JD, Georgetown Univ., 1973. Bar: DC 1973. Gen. counsel Fed. Maritime Commn., 1981—84; ptnr. Eckert Seamans Cherin & Mellott, LLC; ptnr., trans., environ. and natural resources Troutman Sanders LLP, Washington, 2001—. Mem.: DC Bar, Maritime Adminstrv. Bar Assn. Office: Troutman

Sanders LLP Ste 1000 401 Ninth St NW Washington DC 20004-2134 Office Phone: 202-274-2880. Office Fax: 202-654-5647. Business E-Mail: jonathan.benner@troutmansanders.com.

BENNER, MARY WRIGHT, freelance/self-employed conference director; b. Chgo., Aug. 4, 1956; d. Robert V.L. and Sara Helen (Beeler) W.; m. Thomas G. Benner, Aug. 8, 1987; children: Sara Eleanor, Robert Fox. BA, Conn. Coll., 1979; MBA, Columbia U., 1983. Rsch. assoc. Acad. for Contemporary Problems, Washington, 1979-81; rating specialist Standard & Poor's, N.Y.C., 1983-84; asst. adminstr. Twp. of Princeton, N.J., 1984-86; v.p. Fin. Guaranty Ins. Co., N.Y.C., 1986-99, mgr. dept. govt. affairs, 1997-99; cons., 1999—. Bd. dirs. Nat. Com. for Pub./Pvt. Partnerships, 1997-99; mem. sponsor adv. com. Women Exec. in State Gov., 1998-99; mem. steering com. Rebuild Am. Coalition, 1997-99; co-chair Uniting Citizens for Housing Affordability in Newton, 2000-04; chair out reach commn. Eliot Ch. of Newton, 2001—. Mem. Pub. Works Forum (bd. dirs. 1986-88), Assn. for Govtl. Leasing and Fin. (bd. dirs. 1991-95, treas. 1994-95), Assn. Fin. Guaranty Insurers (chmn. com. govt. affairs 1997-99), Rebuild Am. Coalition (exec. bd. dirs. 1998-88), Cape Cod Chamber Mus. Festival, (v.p., bd. dirs. 2000-03), The Conf. Bd. (program dir. 2002—), Can-Do (bd. dirs. 2005-), Mass. Literacy Project (bd. dirs. 2005-). Avocations: cooking, tennis. Home and Office: 136 Washington St Newton MA 02458-2250 Personal E-mail: mwbenner@rcn.com.

BENNER, RICHARD BYRON, philosophy educator; b. Somers Point, NJ, Dec. 6, 1936; s. Theodore Roosevelt and Carolyn Mildred (Wilkinson) B.; m. Ethel Barbara Blair, June 7, 1958 (div. Oct. 1996); children: Richard Byron Jr., Kathryn Lynn, Cheryl Susan; m. Linda Jean Foster, Dec. 24, 1996; 1 stepchild, Genevieve Lynn Fox. BA, Villanova U., 1969; MS, Fla. State U., 1972; postgrad., U. Pa., 1972-77. Clin. lab. chief Shore Meml. Hosp., Somers Point, N.J., 1961-62; med. rschr. Bryn Mawr (Pa.) Hosp., 1962-71; office mgr. O.C. Plumbers, Inc., Ocean City, N.J., 1972-79; plumbing contractor Doctor's Plumbing and Heating, Ocean City, 1979-85; hist. preservationist R.B. Benner and Son, Ocean City, 1985-93; animal care specialist Wildlife Aid, Inc., English Creek, N.J., 1993-95; instr. philosophy Atlantic Cape C.C. (formerly Atlantic C.C.), Mays Landing, NJ, 1995-99, asst. prof. philosophy and religion, 1999—. Adj. asst. prof. philosophy Ocean County Coll., Toms River, NJ, 1998—99, 2002—03; gen. edn. project task force NJ County Coll.; spkr. in field. Contbr. articles, photographs to profl. publs. Founder, pres. Ocean City Hist. Preservation Soc., 1986-90. With U.S. Army, 1958-61; vol. U.S. Dept. Interior, N.J. Divsn. Fish and Game. Recipient 1st place photo award Egg Harbor Twp., 1995, 96, cert. of recognition Exch. Club, 1991, Lindback Dist. Tchg. award, 2004. Mem. AAUP, NEA, Am. Philos. Assn., Philosophy Edn. Soc., Def. Wildlife, Environ. Def. Fund., Earth Justice Legal Def. Fund, Natural Resources Def. Coun., Mensa. Avocations: outdoor and wildlife photography, conservation. Home: 6037 Main St Mays Landing NJ 08330-1896 Office: 5100 Black Horse Pike Mays Landing NJ Office Phone: 609-343-4976. Business E-Mail: rbenner@atlantic.edu.

BENNER, RICHARD EDWARD, JR., marketing consultant, volunteer, investor; b. Jersey City, Dec. 7, 1932; s. Richard E. and Dorothy (Linstead) B.; m. Virginia Hart; children: Linda, Richard III, Christopher. BS, Lehigh U., 1954; postgrad., NYU, 1959-63. Sales exec. IBM Corp, Norwalk, Conn., 1955-58; with Avon Products, Inc., N.Y.C., 1959-78, group v.p. mktg. and internat., 1972-78; divsn. exec. v.p. Sara Lee, Kansas City, Mo., 1979-86; mktg. cons. Kansas City, 1987—. Bd. dirs. Game Hill, Inc., Weston, Mo., exec. com., chmn., bd, dirs., cons. Exec. Svc. Corp., 1993—; LINC, Local Investment commn., 21st Century Initiative; mentor Helzberg Entrepreneurial Mentoring Program, 1998—. Bd. dirs., pres. Northland Homes Partnership for the Homeless, 1988-94; active Eccumedia, 1987-89; maj. corp. com. chmn. United Way, N.Y.C., 1976; Rep. committeeman, Bergan County, 1973; mem. SCORE, 1990—, vice chmn., 1991-92; vice chair cmty. rels. Exec. Svc. Corps, 1990—, chmn., 1993-97, dir., 1997—; trustee Shepherd Ctr. North, 2000—; Stephen minister, 1998—. Named Mentor of Yr. (Kansas City), Helzberg Entrepreneuriel Mentoring Program, 1995—. Mem. Direct Selling Assn. Edn. Found. (bd. dirs. 1982-84). Clubs: Beaverkill Trout (Livingston Manor, N.Y.) (bd. dirs. 1975-78); Old Pike Country (bd. dirs. 1987-90). Lodges: Rotary (bd. dirs., Polio Plus area coord., past pres.). Lutheran. Avocations: fly fishing, investing, gardening. Home and Office: 4404 NW Normandy Ln Kansas City MO 64116-1553

BENNER, RICHARD WALTER, oil company executive, geologist, engineer; b. Dayton, Ohio, June 2, 1922; s. Frederick and Edna Marie B.; m. Parnel Gillilan, Mar. 19, 1949 (dec. Apr. 1970); m. Donna Tschappat, Nov. 24, 1978 (dec. Sept. 1995). BS in Geology, U. Mich., 1947, MS in Geology, 1948. Registered profl. engr., Colo. Photo geologist Texaco, Inc., Lewistown, Mont., 1947-48, field geologist, 1948-59, dist. geologist Denver, 1959-66, spl. projects geologist, 1966-77; v.p. Kissinger Petroleum Corp., Englewood, Colo., 1977-81, Kissinger Drilling & Exploration, Englewood, 1981-86; pres. Kissinger Exploration, Inc., Denver, 1981-86; cons. Corpus Christi, Tex., 1987—; ret., 2003. Author, co-author: Ann. Field Book Publs., Rocky Mountain Geol. Soc. and Montana Geol. Soc., 1949-77; co-author Geological Atlas of Rocky Mountain Region, Wind River Basin, Wyo., 1970, U.S. Geol. Bull., Reserves of Oil and Gas in Rocky Mountain Region, 1977. With U.S. Coast Guard, 1943-44, lt. U.S. Navy, 1944-46, ETO, PTO. Named Hon. Alumnus, William Woods U., 2002. Mem. Am. Assn. Petroleum Geologists, Sigma Gamma Upsilon (50 yr. mem.). Home and Office: 5206 Wooldridge Rd Corpus Christi TX 78413-3833

BENNET, DOUGLAS JOSEPH, JR., academic administrator; b. Orange, N.J., June 23, 1938; s. Douglas Joseph and Phoebe (Benedict) B.; m. Susanne Klejman, June 27, 1959 (div. 1995); children: Michael, James, Holly; m. Midge Bowen Ramsey, July 27, 1996. BA, Wesleyan U., Middletown, Conn., 1959; MA, U. Calif., Berkeley, 1960; PhD, Harvard, 1968. Asst. to econ. adv. AID, New Delhi, 1963—64; spl. asst. to Am. ambassador to India, 1964—66; asst. to Vice Pres. Hubert H. Humphrey, 1967—69; adminstrv. asst. to U.S. Senator Thomas Eagleton, 1969—73, to U.S. Senator Abraham Ribicoff, 1973—73; staff dir. com. budget U.S. Senate, 1974—77; asst. sec. state congressional relations, 1977—79; adminstr. AID, Washington, 1979—81; pres. Roosevelt Ctr. for Am. Policy Studies, 1981—83; pres., CEO Nat. Pub. Radio, Washington, 1983—93; asst. sec. state Internat. Orgnl. Affairs Dept. State, Washington, 1993—95; pres. Wesleyan U., Middletown, Conn., 1995—; trustee Wellesley Coll. Mem. Coun. Fgn. Rels., Cosmos Club. Democrat. Home: 269 High St Middletown CT 06457-3208 Office: Office of Pres Wesleyan U 229 High St Middletown CT 06459-3208

BENNETT, ALAN M., corporate financial executive; BS in acctg., Susquehanna U. Cert. Pub. Acct. Audit mgr. Ernst & Young; various positions Pirelli Armstrong Tire Corp.; CFO Aetna Bus. Resources Aetna Inc., 1995—97, v.p., dir. internal audit, 1997—98, v.p., corp. controller, sr. v.p., CFO. Mem. bd. dirs. Gaylord Hosp.; mem. acctg. adv. bd. U. Conn.; former trustee Conn. Policy and Econ. Coun. Mem.: Conn. Soc. Cert. Pub. Accts., Am. Inst. Cert. Pub. Accts., New Haven Lions Club (past pres.). Office: 151 Farmington Ave Hartford CT 06156*

BENNETT, ALAN R., lawyer; b. Greenwich, Conn., Apr. 12, 1948; BA with honors, Univ. Conn., 1969; JD, Columbia Univ., 1972. Bar: D.C. Atty. Office of Gen. Counsel, FDA, Washington, 1972—76; assoc. Weil Gotshal & Manges, 1976—77; spec. counsel U.S. Senate Com. Govt. Affairs, 1977—81; assoc. Kaye Scholer Fierman Hays & Handler, 1981—84, ptnr., 1985—86, Fox Weinberg Bennett, 1986—99, Bennett Turner Coleman, 1999—2002; ptnr. corp. dept. & co-leader life sciences group practice Ropes & Gray, Washington, 2002—. Harlan Fiske Stone scholar. Mem.: ABA, N.Y. State Bar Assn., D.C. Bar, Phi Beta Kappa. Office: Ropes & Gray One Metro Ctr Suite 900 700 12th St NW Washington DC 20005-3948 Office Phone: 202-508-4604. Office Fax: 202-508-4650. Business E-Mail: alan.bennett@ropesgray.com.

BENNETT, ALEXANDER ELLIOT, lawyer; b. Houston, Aug. 9, 1940; s. William Ernest and Verna Evelyn (Donelan) B.; m. Marilyn A. Bennett, June 6, 1960 (div. 1981); children: Andrew, Laura, Peter; m. Brooksley Born, Oct. 9, 1982; children: Nicholas Landau, Ariel Landau. BA, U. Mich., 1961, JD, 1963. Bar: D.C. 1964. Assoc. Arnold & Porter, Washington, 1966-70, ptnr., 1971—. Editor U. Mich. Law Rev., 1963. Mem. ABA, D.C. Bar Assn., Order of Coif. Democrat. Avocations: sailing, tennis. Home: 2319 Tracy Pl NW Washington DC 20008-1640 Office: Arnold & Porter Thurman Arnold Bldg 555 12th St NW Washington DC 20004-1206 Office Phone: 202-942-5192. Office Fax: 202-942-5999. Business E-Mail: alexander.bennett@aporter.com.

BENNETT, AMANDA, editor; m. Terence B. Foley; 2 children. Grad. cum laude, Harvard U., 1975. Auto industry reporter Wall St. Jour., Pentagon & State Dept. reporter, Beijing corr., mgmt. editor/reporter, nat. economics corr., chief Atlanta bur.; mng. editor projects The Oregonian, 1998—2001; editor, v.p. Lexington Herald-Leader, 2001—03; editor, exec. v.p. Phila. Inquirer, 2003—. Mem. Pulitzer Prize Bd., 2002—. Author: Death of the Organization Man, 1991; co-author (with Sidney Rittenberg): The Man Who Stayed Behind, 1993; co-author: (with Terence B. Foley) In Memoriam, 1998. Co-recipient Pulitzer Prize for nat. reporting, 1997. Office: Philadelphia Inquirer PO Box 8263 400 N Broad St Philadelphia PA 19101*

BENNETT, ANDREW DAVID, alcohol/drug abuse services professional; b. Bklyn., Apr. 21, 1947; s. Reginald and Thelma Bennett; m. Deborah Vitale, Aug. 12, 1984 (div. 1997). BS in Cmty. Svc. and Social Welfare, SUNY, 1977. Cert. alcohol and drug counselor Calif. Cert. Bd. Alcohol and Drug Counselors. Alcoholism counselor Cortland (N.Y.) County Mental Health Ctr., 1977—82; employee counseling rep. Hughes Aircraft Co., El Segondo, L.A., 1982—85; founder Counselor's Recovery Group, La Mesa, San Diego, 1989—91; chem. dependency counselor Broad Horizons, Ramona, San Diego, 1991—97; program dir. LaPosta Substance Abuse Ctr.-So. Indian Health Coun., Boulevard, Calif., 1997—99; counselor, trainer Phoenix House Found., Descanso, San Diego, 2001—03. Contbr. articles to profl. jours. Chmn. youth adv. subcom. Cortland County Youth Bur., 1978—80. Recipient Eagle Feather for contbns. to Native Am. Recovery, 2000. Mem.: Nat. Assn. Alcoholism and Drug Abuse Counselors. Avocations: body surfing, free diving, surf casting, jazz/Afro-Cuban percussion. Office: Aurora Behavioral Healthcare 11878 Ave of Industry San Diego CA 92128 Office Phone: 858-487-3200. E-mail: unterwiser@hotmail.com.

BENNETT, ARLIE JOYCE, clinical social worker emeritus; b. Central Lake, Mich., Nov. 22, 1921; d. Charles Herbert and Bernice Evelyn (Miller) B. Student, Alma (Mich.) Coll., 1946-48; BA, U. Mich., 1950, MSW, 1955. Bd. cert. diplomate emerita Am. Bd. Examiners in Clin. Social Work. Social worker Ypsilanti (Mich.) State Hosp., 1950-54; staff social worker Kalamazoo Child Guidance Clinic, 1955-67, chief social worker, 1967-71; clin. social worker State Tech. Inst. Rehab. Ctr., Plainwell, Mich., 1971-90; pvt. practice, Kalamazoo, 1991-92. Field instr. Mich. State U., 1959-76, Western Mich. U. Sch. Social Work, Kalanazoo, 1971-90, U. Mich., 1967-71. Author: Pie Is in the Eye of the Beholder, 1980, War and Memory, 1991; editor newsletter Late Show Connection, 1993—; also articles. Vol. record reviewer Cath. Family Svcs. Agys., Kalamazoo; bd. dirs. Youth Opportunities Unltd., Kalamazoo, 1968—. Tech. sgt. WAC, AUS, 1944-46, ETO. Mem. NASW (past chmn. and officer), AAUW (legis. chmn. Kalamazoo br. 1985-89, 93-95, pres. 1991-93, pub. policy chmn. 1999-), Mensa (local coord. 1990—), Loners Am. (pres. Mich. chpt. 1990-92, 97-98), U. Mich. Alumnae Club (past pres. and officer), Phi Kapa Phi. Avocations: poetry, writing, camping, seat weaving, upholstery. Home: 1110 W Maple St Kalamazoo MI 49008-1846

BENNETT, BETTY T., literature educator, dean, writer; b. N.J. children: Peter, Matthew. BA, Bklyn. Coll., 1962; MA, NYU, 1963, PhD, 1970. Adj. asst. prof. dept. English and comparative lit. SUNY, Stony Brook, 1970-75, asst. chmn. comparative lit., 1971-72, asst. to dean Grad. Sch., 1970-79, adj. assoc. prof., 1975-79; assoc. prof. English and humanities Pratt Inst., Bklyn., 1979-81, prof., 1981-85, dean Sch. Liberal Arts and Scis., 1979-85; dean Coll. Arts and Scis. Am. U., Washington, 1985-97, disting. prof. lit., 1997—. Fellowship reader Danforth Found., 1978-79; edn. liaison officer N.Y. State, 1977-80; co-dir. NEH Inst., 1989-90. Author: British War Poetry in the Age of Romanticism: 1793-1815, 1976, The Letters of Mary Wollstonecraft Shelley, Vol. I, 1980, The Letters of Mary Wollstonecraft Shelley, Vol. II, 1983, The Letters of Mary Wollstonecraft Shelley, Vol. III, 1988, Mary Diana Dods: A Gentleman and a Scholar, 1991, Mary Diana Dods: A Gentleman and a Scholar, paperback edit., 1994, Mary Wollstonecraft Shelley: An Introduction, 1998; editor (with Donald H. Reiman and Michael Jaye): The Evidence of the Imagination, 1978; editor: (with Charles Robinson) The Mary Shelley Reader, 1990; editor: Proserpine and Midas and Relation of the Cenci, 1992, The Selected Letters of Mary Wollstonecraft Shelley, 1995, Lives of the Great Romantics III: Mary Shelley, 1999; editor: (with Stuart Curran) Mary Shelley in Her Times, 2000; cons. editor and author gen. intro.: The Novels and Selected Works of Mary Wollstonecraft Shelley, 1996, book rev. editor: Keats-Shelley Jour., 1976—94. Keats-Shelley Assn. Am. Disting. scholar, 1992; NEH fellow, 1974-75, Henry E. Huntington Libr. fellow, 1976, Am. Coun. Learned Socs. fellow, 1977-78; Am. Philos. Soc. grant, 1980-81, NEH grant, 1984-87. Mem. MLA, Byron Assn., Keats-Shelley Assn. Am. (bd. dirs.), Soc. for Textual Scholarship (exec. com. 1993—), NYU Alumni Assn., Phi Beta Kappa (founding pres. Zeta chpt. of D.C.). Office: Am U Dept Lit Coll Arts and Scis 4400 Massachusetts Ave NW Washington DC 20016-8001 Office Phone: 202-885-1885. Business E-Mail: bbennet@american.edu.

BENNETT, BRADFORD CARL, research scientist; b. Dayton, Ohio, May 27, 1953; s. Carl Vernon and Norma June (Linkinhoker) B. BSME, U. Wis., 1975; MSME, Stanford U., 1976, PhD in ME, 1982. Staff engr. Acurex Corp., Mt. View, Calif., 1988; sr. rsch. scientist MCAT Inst., San Jose, 1988-93; dir. Somatic Learning Ctr., San Francisco, 1993—, co-coord. 1993 profl. tng. in Hanna Somatic Edn.; assoc. Novato Inst. for Somatic Rsch. and Tng., 1991—; lectr. dept. kinesiology San Francisco State U., 1995—. Contbr. articles to profl. jours. Mem. N.Am. Soc. for Psychology of Sport and Phys. Activity, Trager Inst., Cloud Hands West Tai Chi Assn. (chmn.), Tai Chi Friends Reunion (chmn. 1991-97). Office: San Francisco State U Dept Kinesiology 1600 Holloway Ave San Francisco CA 94132-1722

BENNETT, BRADLEY FREDERICK, retired military officer, science association director; b. New Milford, Conn., Aug. 29, 1911; s. Frederick Lum and Florence Kay Bradley; m. Eunice Gwendolyn Meissner (div. 1933); m. Virginia White, Dec. 22, 1956; children: Bradley Robert, Bruce Roy. MS, MIT, 1940, MS in Physics, 1953. Commd. ensign USN, 1935, advanced through grades to capt., 1983; asst. planning officer Norfolk Navy Yard, Portsmouth, Va., 1940—43; hull supt. Pearl Harbor (Hawaii) Navy Yard, 1943—47; engring. svc. officer US Naval Rsch. Labs., Washington, 1947—50, dir. adminstrn., 1960—63, dir., 1963—65; repair supt. US Fleet Repair Facility, Yokuska, Japan, 1950—51; dir. materials rsch. divsn. Bur. Ships Navy Dept., Washington, 1951—57; commdg. officer U.S. br. office Office Naval Rsch., London, 1957—60; v.p. Univ. Rsch. Assn., Washington, 1967—77. Hydropneumatic explosion rschr. USN, Washington, 1953—55. Capt. USN, 1954—65. Decorated Bronze star USN. Fellow: Royal Instn. Eng.; mem.: Philos. Soc. of Washington (pres. 1973), Brit. Royal Soc. Medicine, Am. Geophys. Union, Am. Soc. Metals, N.Y. Acad. Scis., Cosmos Club (chmn. program com. 1965—73, Washington). Achievements include research in metallurgical factors affecting cavitation damage; Rayleigh scattering of gamma rays. Avocation: ancient numismatics. Home: 750 S La Pasada Cir # 18 Green Valley AZ 85614

BENNETT, BRUCE S., publishing executive; Pub. Telegram & Gazette, Worcester, Mass. Bd. mem. Worcester Regional C. of C., Mass.; bd. dir. Worcester Regional Rsch. Bur., Worcester Bus. Develop. Corp. Office: Telegram and Gazette 20 Franklin St PO Box 15012 Worcester MA 01615-0012 Office Phone: 508-793-9200. Office Fax: 508-767-9512. E-mail: bbennett@telegram.com.

BENNETT, BRUCE W., retired construction executive, civil engineer; b. St. Joseph, Mo., Dec. 24, 1930; s. Bruce W. and Laura Louella (Clark) B.; m. Barbara Gail Haase, July 26, 1957; children: Stacy Suzanne, Bruce W. BS in Civil Engring., U. So. Calif., 1954. Project mgr. George A. Fuller & Co., Chgo., 1956-61; contract mgr. Huber, Hunt & Nichols, Indpls., 1961-70, v.p., 1970-82, exec. v.p., 1982-84, pres., 1984-95, ret., 1995. Pres. Hunt Corp., 1988-95, bd. dirs. Served to capt. USAF, 1954-57 Mem. Archimedes Circle, David Wilson Assocs., Newcomen Soc. Clubs: Indpls. Athletic, Skyline (Indpls.). Republican. Avocations: tennis, golf. Home: 437 Seville Ave Newport Beach CA 92661-1528

BENNETT, C. LEONARD, electrical engineer; b. Lowell, Mass., Oct. 5, 1939; s. C. Leonard and Ruth E. (Glow) B.; m. Patricia Ann Derival, Aug. 22, 1966; children: Craig, Dawn Marie. BS in Elec. Engring., Lowell Tech. Inst., Mass., 1961; MS, N.C. State U., Raleigh, 1964; PhD, Purdue U., 1968. Registered profl. engr., Mass. Research engr. Purdue U., 1968; mem. tech. staff Sperry Research Ctr., Sudbury, Mass., 1968-73, mgr. systems applications, 1973-83; cons. engr. Raytheon, Marlboro, Mass., 1983—2004, sr. prin. engring. fellow, 2004—; lectr. in field. Contbr. chpts. to books, articles to profl. jours.; patentee field. Chmn. Groton Fin. Com., Mass., 1970-76; treas. Groton Ctr. for the Arts, 1976-78; coach Groton Jr. Hockey, 1979-86, Groton Little League Baseball, 1981-84; mem. com. local troop Boy Scouts Am., 1983—; bd. dirs. Groton Dunstable Soccer Club, 1981-92, Nashoba Valley Youth Soccer League, 1986—; soccer referee U.S. Youth Soccer Assn., 1987—. Fellow IEEE (assoc. editor Trans. on Antennas and Propagation 1983-96); mem. Internat. Union of Radio Scis., Eta Kappa Nu, Tau Beta Pi, Phi Kappa Phi, Sigma Pi Sigma. Home: 304 Reedy Meadow Rd Groton MA 01450-1408 Office: Raytheon 1001 Boston Post Rd E Marlborough MA 01752-3789

BENNETT, CARL, retired discount department store executive; b. Greenwich, Conn., Jan. 27, 1920; s. Mayer and Rebecca (Lipsky) B.; m. Dorothy Becker, June 24, 1951; children: Marc Mitchell, Robin Cheryl Bennett Kanarek, Bruce Kenneth. Student, NYU, 1937-38. Wholesale liquor salesman, Conn., 1940-51; founder, ret. chmn. bd., chief exec. officer Caldor, Inc., Norwalk, Conn., 1951-84; ptnr. DorCal Assocs., Norwalk, Conn., 1984—. Chmn. Bi-Cultural Day Sch., Stamford, Conn., 1965-67, treas., 1967-68; bd. dirs. Stamford Hosp., nat. bd. dirs. NCCJ; mem. Am. com., internat. bd. govs. Weizmann Inst. Served with AUS, 1942-45. Recipient Amudin award outstanding work Hebrew day schs., 1965, disting. service award Prime Minister Israel, 1973; named Retailer of Yr., 1982; named to Retailers Hall of Fame, 1983 Mem. World Bus. Council (charter), Nat. Retail Mchts. Assn. (bd. dirs.) Clubs: Sailfish Point Country (Stuart, Fla.); Quaker Ridge Country (Scarsdale, N.Y.). Office: DorCal Assocs 607 Main Ave Norwalk CT 06851-1058

BENNETT, CAROL(INE) ELISE, retired reporter, actress; b. New Orleans, Dec. 27, 1938; d. Gerald Clifford Graham and Edna Doris (Toennies) Kerr; m. Ralph Decker Bennett, Jr., Feb. 27, 1966; children: Ralph Decker III, Katherine Elise. BA, U. B.C., Vancouver, Can., 1960; BLS, McGill U., Montreal, Que., Can., 1962. Libr. various locations, 1962-76; reporter TV/radio Washington-Ala. News Report, Washington, 1981-2001; ret., 2001. Actor: (plays) Girl in My Soup, 1978; (films) Prime Risk, 1984; host (TV series) Modern Maturity, 1986—88. Vol. reader Rec. for Blind, Washington, 1985—. Mem.: AAUW, AFTRA, SAG, Nat. Press Club, Soc. Profl. Journalists. Avocation: tennis. Home: 115 Southwood Ave Silver Spring MD 20901-1918

BENNETT, CHARLES ANDREW, economics professor, department chairman; b. NYC, Feb. 8, 1943; s. Joseph C. and Catherine F. (Gallagher) B.; divorced; 1 child, William C.B. BA in Econs. with honors, St. Francis Coll., Bklyn., 1965; MA in Econs., Fordham U., 1968; student, 1968. Grad. asst., tchg. fellow Fordham U., Bronx, NY, 1965-68; instr. econs. Gannon U., Erie, Pa., 1968-76, asst. prof., 1976—, dir. Ctr. for Econ. Edn., 1977—, chmn. dept. econs. and fin., 1986—97. Author: Principles of Microeconomics Manual for External Study Courses, 1977, 12th edit., 2003; mem. bd. editors Worth Pub., NYC, Harper & Row, NYC, Wadsworth Pubs., NYC, Dryden Press, NYC, McGraw Hill Pub. Co. Mem. Erie Mayor's Office Cmty. Affairs; mem. microcomputer com. Fairview (Pa.) Sch. Dist., mem. resource com. strategic planning action group, mem. tech. edn. task force; mem. steering com. Family Support Svcs., Erie; mem. task force on citizenship Pa. Dept. Edn.; mem. strategic planning com. Dahlkemper Sch. Bus. Adminstrn. Recipient award for meritorious support of free enterprise BP Oil, 1980, Leavey award for excellence in econ. edn. Freedoms Found., 1984, Internat. Paper award Joint Coun. on Econ. Edn., 1988, Com. to Excellence award in econ. edn., 1989. Mem. Pa. Coun. Econ. Edn., Nat. Fedn. Ind. Bus. (mem. adv. panel), Nat. Assn. Econ. Educators, Nat. Coun. Econ. Edn., Econ. Am., Assn. for Pvt. Enterprise Edn. Avocations: biking, swimming. Home: 5570 Sebago Dr Fairview PA 16415-2223 Office: Gannon U 109 Univ Sq Erie PA 16541 Office Phone: 814-871-7585. Business E-Mail: bennett@gannon.edu.

BENNETT, CHARLES FRANKLIN, JR., biogeographer, educator; b. Oakland, Calif., Apr. 10, 1926; s. Charles Franklin and Charlotte Louise (Normand) B.; m. Carole Ann Messenger, Nov. 30, 1947; 1 child, Ashley Lynn. PhD, UCLA, 1959. Instr. UCLA, 1959-60, asst. prof., 1960-65, assoc. prof., 1965-69, prof. biogeography, 1969—; prof. emeritus, 1993—. Cons. in field. Author: Human Influence on Zoogeography of Panama, 1968, Man and Earth's Ecosystems, 1976, Conservation of Natural Resources, 1983; contbr. articles to profl. jours. Guggenheim fellow, 1970-71. Fellow AAAS, Royal Geog. Soc.; mem. Ecol. Soc. Am., Brit. Ecol. Soc., Assn. Tropical Biology, Soc. for Conservation Biology, Fauna and Flora Preservation Soc., Am. Inst. Biol. Scis. Avocation: collecting natural history books. Home: 317 S Anita Ave Los Angeles CA 90049-3805 Office: UCLA Dept Geography 405 Hilgard Ave Los Angeles CA 90095-9000

BENNETT, CHARLES LEON, vocational and graphic arts educator; b. Salem, Oreg., Feb. 5, 1951; s. Theodore John and Cora Larena (Rowland) B.; m. Cynthia Alice Hostman, June 12, 1976 (div.); m. Lynn Marie Toland, Aug. 12, 1977 (div.); children: Mizzy Marie, Charles David.; m. Christina M. Crawford, Dec. 19, 1987 (div.); m. Iris J. Perrigo, Mar. 17, 2001. AS in Vocat. Tchr. Edn., Clackamas C.C., 1977; AS in Gen. Studies, Linn Benton C.C., 1979; BS in Gen. Studies, Ea. Oreg. State Coll., 1994. Tchr. printing Tongue Point Job Corps, Astorial, Oreg., 1979-80; tchr., chmn. dept. Portland (Oreg.) Pub. Schs., 1980—; owner, mgr. printing and pub. co. Portland, 1981-87. With AUS, 1970-72. Mem. NRA, Oreg. Vocat. Trade-Tech. Assn. (cept. chmn., pres. graphic arts divsn., Indsl. Educator of Yr. 1981-82), Oreg. Vocat. Assn. (Vocat. Tchr. of Yr. 1982-83), Graphic Arts Tech. Found., In-Plant Printing Mgmt. Assn., Internat. Graphic Arts Edn. Assn. (v.p. N.W. region VI), Oreg. Assn. Manpower Spl. Needs Pers., Oreg. Indsl. Arts Assn., Internat. Platform Assn., Nat. Assn. Quick Printers, Am. Vocat. Assn., Pacific Printing and Imaging Assn., Inplant Printing Mgmt. Assn., Portland Club Lithographers and Printing House Craftsmen. Republican. Home: 20295 S Unger Rd Beavercreek OR 97004-8884 Office: 546 NE 12th Ave Portland OR 97232-2719 Office Phone: 503-916-5100 ext 2039. Business E-Mail: cbennett@pps.k12.or.us.

BENNETT, CHARLES LEONARD, astrophysicist, educator; b. New Brunswick, NJ, Nov. 16, 1956; s. Lawrence Herman and Devora Mae (Spintman) B.; m. Renee Elizabeth Marlin, Sept. 2, 1984; 1 child, Andrew. BS in Physics & Astronomy, U. Md., 1978; PhD in Physics, MIT, 1984. Astrophysicist NASA - Goddard Space Flight Ctr. (GSFC), Greenbelt, Md., 1984—2004, head infrared astrophysics branch, 1996—2002, sr. scientist exptl. cosmology, 2002—04; prof. physics and astronomy Johns Hopkins U., Balt., 2005—. Dep. prin. investigator Differential Microwave Radiometers (DMR) instrument on Cosmic Background Explorer (COBE), leader of COBE DMR software effort NASA, 1987—96, prin. investigator Wilkinson Microwave Anisotrophy Probe (WMAP) mission, 1996—, co-investigator Legacy Archive for Microwave Background Data Analysis, 2003—. Co-editor: After the First Three Minutes, 1991, Dark Matter, 1995. Named Most Highly Cited Rschr. in space sci. worldwide, ISI, 2002, Alumus of Yr.,

Physics Dept. U. Md., 2003; recipient NASA Outstanding Performance rating, 1985, 1994, GSFC Group Achievement Award for COBE, 1988, NASA/GSFC Performance Award, 1989, NASA Group Achievement Award for COBE, 1990, NASA Exceptional Sci. Achievement Medal for COBE, 1992, GSFC Group Award for MAP Proposal, 1996, NASA/GSFC Performance Award, 1996, 1998, 2002, NASA MIDEX Group Award, 1997, NASA/GSFC Leadership Award, 1999, "Best of What's New" Award in Aviation and Space for WMAP, Popular Sci., 2001, NASA/GSFC Ctr. of Excellence Group Achievement Award for MAP, 2002, NASA/GSFC Group Achievement Award for MAP, 2002, NASA Outstanding Leadership Medal for devel. and success of WMAP, 2003, NASA Performance Award, 2003, "Breakthrough of Yr." Award for WMAP/Sloan proof of Dark Energy, Sci. Mag., 2003, NASA Group Achievement Award to WMAP Sci. Team, 2004, John C. Lindsay Meml. Award for Space Sci., NASA, 2003, NASA Exceptional Sci. Achievement Medal for WMAP, 2004, Mid Career Stellar Award, Rotary Nat. Award for Space Achievement, 2005. Fellow AAAS, Am. Phys. Soc.; mem. NAS (Henry Draper Medal, 2005), Am. Acad. Arts and Sciences, Am. Inst. Physics, Am. Astron. Soc., Internat. Astron. Union, Sigma Xi. Democrat. Jewish. Achievements include discovery of new gravitational lenses; first detection of atomic and molecular transitions; research on precise measurements of spectrum and anisotropy limits on the cosmic microwave background radiation, large radio astronomy surveys. Office: Johns Hopkins U Dept Physics & Astronomy Bloomberg 209 Baltimore MD 21218-2686*

BENNETT, CLAY, cartoonist; b. Clinton, S.C., Jan. 20, 1958; m. Cindy Procious; children: Sarah, Matt, Ben. B in Art and History, U. North Ala., 1980. Artist Pitts. Post-Gazette, Fayetteville Times, Fayetteville, NC; editl. cartoonist St. Petersburg Times, 1981—94, Christian Sci. Monitor, Boston, 1998—. Editl. cartoonist King Features Syndicate, 1994—. Named Editl. Cartoonist of Yr., Editor & Pub. Mag., 2001; recipient Nat. Headliner award, 1999, 2000, 2004, John Fischetti award, 2002, 2005, Pulitzer Prize for Editl. Cartooning, 2002. Office: Christian Sci Monitor One Norway St Boston MA 02115 E-mail: claybennett@earthlink.net.*

BENNETT, DAVE W., talent agent, consultant; s. James A. and Barbara J. Bennett. BA, Queen's U., 1988—90. V.p. The Talent Ho., NYC, 1999—, talent agt. Toronto, Canada, 1995—99. Bd. mem. KAEDEC- Travel/Tourism Panel, Kingston, Canada, 1992—95. Democrat-Npl. Avocations: travel, theater, books. Office: The Talent House 311 West 43rd St Ste 602 New York NY 10036 Business E-Mail: talenthousenyc@earthlink.net.

BENNETT, DAVID BARNES, school librarian; b. West Palm Beach, Fla., Apr. 18, 1957; s. John Emerson and Priscilla Barnes Bennett; 1 child, Michael. BA in humanities, Stetson U., 1975—79; MLS, UNC Chapel Hill, 1985—87. Systems libr. Triangle Rsch. Libraries Network, Chapel Hill, NC, 1986—89, Robert Morris U., Moon Township, Pa., 1989—. Bd. mem. Chatham Baroque, Pitts., 2001—05. Avocations: kayaking, hot air balloons, music. Home: 320 Dunlap St Pittsburgh PA 15214 Office: Robert Morris Univ 6001 University Blvd Moon Township PA 15108 Office Phone: 412-262-8474. E-mail: bennett@rmu.edu.

BENNETT, DICK, college basketball coach; b. Pitts., Apr. 20, 1943; m. Anne; children: Kathi, Amy, Tony. BS in phys. edn., Ripon Coll., 1965; MEd, UW-Stevens Point. Basketball coach West Bend (Wis.) HS, 1965-66; coach various Wis HS teams, 1966-76, UW-Stevens Point, 1976-85, UW-Green Bay, 1985-95, U. Wis., Madison, 1995—2000, Wash. St. U., Pullman, 2003—. 1st team at U. Wis. (17-15) appeared in 1996 N.I.T.; 2d team (18-10) made 2d U. Wis. appearance in N.C.A.A. tournament in 50 yrs., put together sch.'s 1st 6-game winning streak since 1951. Named WSUC Coach of Yr., 1982, 1985, NAIA Coach of Yr., 1984, NAIA Area IV Coach of Yr., 1985, Mid-Continent Coach of Yr., 1990, 1992, NABC Dist. 11 Coach of Yr., 1992, 1994, Basketball Times Midwest Coach of Yr., 1994. Achievements include 21-yr. collegiate coaching record, 395-214 (.649). Office: Bohler Athletic Complex Wash State Univ Basketball PO Box 641602 Pullman WA 99164-1602

BENNETT, DOUGLAS CARLETON, academic administrator; b. Rochester, N.Y., June 25, 1946; s. Frank Clinton Jr. and Roberta Lincoln (Evans) B.; m. Dulany Young Ogden, June 20, 1981 (div. 1993); 1 child, Thomas Baldrige; m. Ellen Trout, 1997. BA magna cum laude, Haverford Coll., 1968; M of Philosophy, Yale U., 1971, PhD, 1976. Asst. prof. dept. polit. sci. Temple U., Phila., 1976-80, assoc. prof., 1980-88, prof., assoc. dean Coll. Arts and Scis., 1988-89; provost Reed Coll., Portland, Oreg., 1989-93; exec. dir. Portland Area Libr. Sys., 1993-94; v.p. Am. Coun. Learned Socs., N.Y.C., 1994-97; pres. Earlham Coll., Richmond, Ind., 1997—. Author: Transnational Corporations v.s. the State, 1985; contbr. numerous articles and book revs. to polit. sci. jours. Mem. nat. community rels. com. Am. Friends Svc. Commn., Phila., 1982-86, mem. Latin Am. panel internat. div., 1985-89, clk. Latin Am. panel, 1988-89; bd. trustees Germantown Friends Sch., 1985-89, Friends Sem., N.Y.C., 1996-97; trustee Germantown monthly meeting Soc. of Friends Ch., 1984-89. Recipient Alumni award Haverford Coll., 1988; fellow Woodrow Wilson Internat. Ctr. for Scholars, 1980-81; fellowship grantee Am. Coun. Learned Socs./Social Sci. Rsch. Coun., 1976-77, Carnegie Endowment for Internat. Peace, 1976-77. Mem. Ctr. for Rsch. Librs. (bd. dirs. 1997—). Democrat. Avocations: reading, films. Office: Earlham Coll 801 National Rd W Richmond IN 47374-4021 E-mail: dougb@earlham.edu.

BENNETT, EDWARD HENRY, reinsurance executive; b. Glens Falls, N.Y., July 22, 1917; s. Harry and Elizabeth Chandler (Clark) B.; m. Louise Faris, Aug. 3, 1946; children: Faris Elizabeth Ramseur, Anne Louise Petronis. AB, Princeton U., 1940. With Guy Carpenter & Co., Inc., N.Y.C., 1940-51, asst. v.p., 1951-54, v.p., dir., 1954-76, vice chmn., chief adminstrv. officer, 1976-82; dir. Mitsui Sumitomo Ins. USA Inc. (formerly Mitsui Marine & Fire Ins. Co. of Am.), N.Y.C., 1987—. Bd. dirs. Bartlett Carry Club, Inc., Tupper Lake, N.Y., 1988—, Mitsui Sumitomo Ins. Co. Am., N.Y.C., 2002—. Maj. USAAF, 1942-46, lt. col. USAFR. Decorated Legion of Merit. Mem. SAR, Res. Officers Assn., Princeton Club of N.Y., Nassau Club of Princeton, The Down Town Assn. N.Y. Republican. Episcopalian. Address: 6 Heerdt Farm Ln Pound Ridge NY 10576-1616

BENNETT, EDWARD VIRDELL, JR., surgeon; b. Nashville, July 17, 1947; s. Edward Virdell and Florence Elaine (Nelson) B. BA in Biology, Fisk U., 1969; MD cum laude, Ohio State U., 1973. Fellow in surgery Johns Hopkins U., Balt., 1973—75; intern, then resident Johns Hopkins Hosp., Balt., 1973—75; resident in surgery and cardiothoracic surgery Albany (N.Y.) Med. Ctr. Hosp., 1975—80, instr. in surgery, 1976—80; asst. prof. surgery Health Ctr. U. Tex.-San Antonio, 1980—83; practice medicine specializing in cardiothoracic surgery Sayre, Pa., 1983—91; mem. staff Robert Packer Hosp., Sayre, 1983—91; mem. Guthrie Clinic, Ltd., Sayre, 1983—91; chief cardiac surgery Guthrie Clinic Ltd., Sayre, 1990—91; cardiac surgeon Albany Cardiothoracic Surgeons, P.C., 1991—, pres., 2000—; mem. staff Albany Med. Ctr. Hosp., 1991—, St. Peters Hosp., Albany, 1991—; chief cardiac surgery St. Peter's Hosp., Albany, 1997—; clin. asst. prof. Albany Med. Coll., 1991—; med. dir. cardiac surgery Champlain Valley Physicians Hosp., 2003—. Bd. dirs. St. Peter's Hosp. Prodr. med. motion picture; contbr. articles to med. jours. Mem. N.Y. State Cardiac Adv. Com., 1995—. Named one of Best Drs. in Am., 2001—, Top Surgeons in Am., 2002—. Fellow ACS, Am. Coll. Chest Physicians, Am. Coll. Cardiology; mem. Soc. Thoracic Surgeons, Upstate Soc. Thoracic Surgeons (pres. 2000—), Internat. Soc. for Heart Transplantation, Sigma Xi, Alpha Omega Alpha, Omega Psi Phi. Republican. Episcopalian. Avocations: sailing, scuba diving, skiing.

BENNETT, ELLIOTT REUBEN, band director, composer; b. San Francisco, Feb. 26, 1957; s. Claude Elliott and Mary Lavonne (Cobb) Bennett; m. Patti Ann Hancock, Sept. 27, 1980; 1 child, Matthew Elliott. BS in Music Edn., Jacksonville State U., Ala., 1979. Band dir. Fyffe HS, Ala., 1979—81, Clay County HS, Ashland, Ala., 1991—96, Carlisle Pk. Mid. Sch., Guntersville, Ala., 1996—; bandsman US Army, Tacoma, Seoul, Republic of Korea, 1981—91. Arranger Sibelius Music, 2002—. Presenter woodworking 21st Century Club Art on the Lake, Guntersville, 2001—. With U.S. Army, 1981—91. Recipient Video Prodn. award, Apple Found., Guntersville City Schs., 2004—05. Fellow: Ala. Edn. Assn., Ala. Bandmaster's Assn. Avocations: bicycling, reading, woodworking. Home: 465 Rush Cir Guntersville AL 35976 Office: Carlisle Pk Mid Sch 801 Sunset Dr Guntersville AL 35976 Office Phone: 256-582-5182. Business E-Mail: ebennett@gcboe.net.

BENNETT, SISTER ELSA MARY, retired secondary education educator; b. Muskegon, Mich., Dec. 13, 1930; d. Thomas B. and Elsa (Koelbel) B. BS, Our Lady of Lake Coll., San Antonio, 1955, MEd, 1971. Registered massage therapist, Tex.; Reiki master. Tchr. phys. edn. parochial schs., Abilene, Tex., Tulsa, San Antonio, Houston, Ennis, Tex., Alexandria, La., 1954, tchr., coach San Antonio, 1969—74, 1986—87, pub. schs., Mich., 1974—78; tchr. St. Augustine Sch., Laredo, Tex., 1978—79; adminstr., coach Our Lady of Lake U., 1979—86; phys. therapy aide Warm Springs Rehab., San Antonio, 1989—90; tchr. San Antonio Ind. Sch. Dist., 1990—2000; ret., 2000. With pub. rels. dept. San Antonio City Parks and Recreation Dept., 1987-89; masseuse, Reiki and water aerobics instr. Retirement Ctr. at Our Lady of the Lake Convent, San Antonio, 2000—. Instr. ARC, San Antonio, 1952. Mem. AAHPER and Dance, Tex. Assn. Health, Phys. Edn., Recreation and Dance. Avocations: golf, swimming, sailing, bowling, travel. Home: 2318 Town Grove Dr San Antonio TX 78238-5023

BENNETT, GARY LEE, physicist, consultant; b. Twin Falls, Idaho, Jan. 17, 1940; s. Joseph Albert and Adelaide Phillipa (Leonard) B.; m. Cleo Sue Guetschow McMurtrie, Sept. 14, 1961. AA, Boise State U., 1960; BS, U. Idaho, 1962, M of Nuclear Sci., 1966; PhD, Wash. State U., 1970. Physicist, engr. Idaho Nat. Lab., Idaho Falls, 1962-66; mgr. project Lewis Rsch. Ctr., Cleve., 1970-71; mgr. safety U.S. Atomic Energy Commn., Germantown, Md., 1971-74; br. chief U.S. Nuclear Regulatory Commn., Silver Spring, Md., 1974-79; dir. nuclear ops. U.S. Dept. Energy, Germantown, 1980-85, dep. office dir., 1985-88; program mgr. advanced technology NASA, Washington, 1988-91, deputy div. dir., 1992-94, aerospace cons., 1994—. Author: The Star Sailors, 1980, 2d edit., 2005; contbr. articles and papers to profl. jours. Served as staff sgt. ANG, 1957-63. Recipient numerous profl. and govt. awards including Dist. Alumnus award Boise State U., 1990, Silver & Gold award U. Idaho Alumni Assn., 1994, Schreiber-Spence Space Achievement award, 1996, Friend of Darwin award Nat. Ctr. Sci. Edn., 2000. Fellow AIAA (Aerospace Power Systems Award, 1995), Brit. Interplanetary Soc., Am. Phys. Soc.; mem. AAAS, Fedn. Am. Scientists, Am. Astronaut. Soc., Am. Assn. Physics Tchrs., Planetary Soc., Com. Sci. Investigation Claims Paranormal, Sci. Fictions Writers Am., Nat. Space Soc., Ams. United Seperation of Ch. and State (mem. nat. adv. bd.), Sigma Xi, Sigma Pi Sigma. Home and Office: 5000 Butte Rd Emmett ID 83617-9500

BENNETT, GENEVIEVE, artist; b. Chgo., Feb. 11, 1927; d. Joseph and Mary Sieczka; m. William A. Bennett, Jan. 31, 1953; children: William George, J. Daniel, Gordon Dean. BA, Calif. State U., Fullerton, 1974; MA, Calif. State U., Long Beach, 1978. Artist, Anaheim, Calif. Tchr. art Ebell Club Anaheim, 1985-97, Whittier and Anaheim, Calif.; lectr. N.Am. temple mound builders. One-woman shows include Calif. Poly. U., Pomona, 1995, Orange County Fair, Calif., 1995, Anaheim Mus., 1997, exhibitions include Hotel-Restaurant La Musardiere, Giverny, France, 2002, Anaheim Arts Coun. Annual Souree, 2004 (Artist Honoree). Recipient Grumbacher Gold medal, 1999, Celebrating Remarkable Women Among Us award Orange County chpt. Nat. Assn. Women Bus. Owners, 1999, Cert. Spl. Congl. Recognition, Loretta Sanchez, 1999, Beyond the Call award Anaheim (Calif.) Arts Coun. and Arts in Pub. Places, 2002. Mem. Am. Internat. Culture and Art Assn., Nat. League Am. Pen Women (state v.p. 1997-98, Am. Internat. Culture and Art Assn., Orange County br. pres. 1997-98, recipient State Women of Achievement award, 1998), Calif. State U. Art Alliance, So. Calif. Women's Caucus for Art, Orange County Fine Arts, Phi Delta Gamma (Phi chpt.). Avocations: archaeology, piano, music, travel, art meetings. Home: 2026 W Judith Ln Anaheim CA 92804-6511

BENNETT, GEORGE FREDERICK, retired investment company executive; b. Quincy, Mass., Aug. 16, 1911; s. Wallace Cherrington and Lois E. (Williams) B.; m. Helen F. Brigham, Oct. 25, 1935; children— Peter C., George Frederick, Robert B. AB cum laude, Harvard, 1933. With First Boston Corp., Boston, 1934-37, Newton, Abbe & Co., Boston, 1937-43; with State Street Research & Mgmt. Co., Boston, 1943—, partner, 1946—. Chmn. State St. Exchange Fund, Boston; pres. State St. Investment Corp., Boston, Fed. St. Fund, Inc., Boston; dir. Campbell Taggert, Inc., Dallas, Middle South Utilities, Inc., N.Y.C., N.E. Electric System, Hewlett Packard Co., Palo Alto, Calif., Fla. Power & Light Co., Miami, Ford Motor Co., Detroit, John Hancock Mut. Life Ins. Co., Boston, Hanna Mining Co., Cleve. Treas. Harvard U., Harvard-Yenching Inst.; trustee Wheaton (Ill.) Coll., Rockefeller U., Gordon Conwell Theol. Sem., Com. Econ. Devel., Washington. Mem. Pi Eta. Clubs: Harvard (Boston and N.Y.C.); Union (Boston); Links (N.Y.C.). Home: 712 Main St Hingham MA 02043-3327 Office: State Street Rsch & Mgmt Co One Financial Ctr Boston MA 02111

BENNETT, G(EORGE) KEMBLE, engineering educator; b. Jacksonville, Fla., Apr. 2, 1940; s. George K. and Murla E. (Weeks) B.; m. Jill Alison McMaster, June 5, 1982; children: Russell William, Paige E., Alison Kemly; BS in math., Fla. State U., 1962; MS in engring. math., San Jose State U., 1968; PhD in indsl. engring., Tex. Tech U., 1970. Profl. engr., Fla., Tex. Assoc. engr. Martin Co., Orlando, Fla., 1962-63; engr. Lockheed Research Labs., Palo Alto, Calif., 1963-64, sr. engr., 1964-66; asst. dir. Computer Ctr., Tex. Tech U., Lubbock, 1966-69; vis. scientist NASA Manned Spacecraft Lab., Houston, 1969-70; asst. prof. indsl. engring. Va. Poly. Inst., Blacksburg, 1970-73; prof., chmn. indsl. and mgmt. systems engring. U. South Fla., Tampa, 1973-86; pres., CEO G. Kemble Bennett & Associates, 1975-79; staff engr. Honeywell Avionics Divsn., 1984-86; prof., head indsl. engring. Tex. A&M U., College Station, 1986—91, assoc. dean engring., 1991-2002, dir. Tex. Engring. Extension Svc., 1992-2002, assoc. vice chancellor engring, 1992-2002, dir. Tex. Engring. Expt. Sta., 2002-, vice chancellor engring., 2002-, dean Dwight Look Coll. Engring., 2002-. Assoc. editor IIE Transactions; mng. editor Logistics Spectrum; contbr. articles to nat. and internat. jours. Fellow Inst. Indsl. Engineers. (Fla. West Coast Engr. of Year 1979, 82, Albert G. Hozlman Disting. Educator Award, 1996), Soc. Logistics Engineers. (bd. referees The Annals; Eccles Medal, 1997); Mem. Am. Soc. Engring. Edn., The Inst. Mgmt. Scis., Tau Beta Pi, Phi Kappa Phi. Republican. Methodist. Office: Dwight Look Coll Engring Texas A&M U 3126 TAMU College Station TX 77845-3126

BENNETT, GERALDINE EUDORA (JERRIE BENNETT), mental health services professional, nursing educator; b. Creighton, Pa., Apr. 23, 1921; d. Harry Curtin and Ellnora Mira (Guyer) Baish; m. Donald Patrick Bennett, Aug. 10, 1953 (div. 1971); children: Brent Norman, Terrance Patrick(dec.), Patricia Eileen Bennett Wilson(dec.). RN, Sewickley Valley Sch. Nursing, 1942; BS, U. Calif., 1953; MA, Kent State U., 1969. RN Pa., Calif., Mich., Ohio, Fla. Asst. supr. oper. rm. Merrit Hosp., Oakland, Calif., 1947-48; surg. asst. Robert Foote, MD, Bakersfield, Calif., 1949-51; adminstrv. asst. Permanente Found. Hosp., L.A., 1953; mem. faculty surgery, oper. rm. Queen of Angels Coll. Nursing, L.A., 1954-55; tchr. exceptional edn. Canton (Ohio) Pub. Schs., 1967-69; nurse ICU Naples (Fla.) Cmty. Hosp., 1970-71; tchr. exceptional edn., guidance counselor Collier County Schs., Naples, 1971-86; psychiat. crisis counselor David Lawrence Mental Health Ctr., Naples, 1987-96. Founder, 1st coord. Collier County Spl. Olympics, Naples, 1971—77; dir. S. Fla. dist. Spl. Olympics, Tallahassee, 1977—80; chmn. Selective Svcs. Bd., Naples, 1981—2002; capt. CAP Squadron 8, Naples, 1990—; bd. dirs. Founding First Charter Sch. Collier County, 1997—98, Gabriel Ho. for Children, 1998—99, Naples Ret. Inc., 1989—98; sr. intern adv. bd. 14th Congl. Dist., Ft. Meyers, Fla., 1990—93; mem. Lay Assn. Sisters of Charity, NJ, 2001—. With USN, 1942—45, PTO. Named Hon. U.S. Olympian, 1983. Mem.: AAUW, Navy League Coun., Am. Legion, Alpha Eta Rho, Phi Delta Kappa. Republican. Roman Catholic. Avocations: swimming, painting, volunteer work, travel. E-mail: jbdora@aol.com.

BENNETT, GRACE, publishing executive; Adminstrv. mgr. Detroit Free Press. Office: Detroit Free Press 600 W Fort St Detroit MI 48226-2706

BENNETT, HAROLD EARL, physicist, optics researcher; b. Missoula, Mont., Feb. 25, 1929; s. Edward Earl and Linda Queen (McCoy) B.; m. Jean Louise McPherson, Aug. 17, 1952 (div. Nov. 1984); m. Dorothy Jean Searles, Nov. 17, 1984; children: Jeanie Nybo, Dorothy Anne Picking. BA, U. Mont., 1951; MS, Pa. State U., 1953, PhD, 1955. Instrument-rated pilot. Grad. asst. Pa. State U., State College, 1951-55; physicist Wright Air Devel. Ctr., Dayton, Ohio, 1955-56, Naval Air Warfare Ctr. (name Naval Weapons Ctr. 1964-93), China Lake, Calif., 1956-62, rsch. physicist, 1962-95, ret., 1995, assoc. head rsch. dept. physics div., 1972-91; cons. optical physics Quoin Inc., Ridgecrest, Calif., 1995-96; pres. Bennett Optical Rsch. Inc., Ridgecrest, 1995—; chair Space Applications Com., IWV 2000 Orgn., Ridgecrest, Calif., 1996—. Co-chmn. Laser Induced Damage in Optical Materials Conf., Boulder, Colo., 1979-96. Adv. editor Optics Communications, 1969-86; contbr. over 100 articles on optics to profl. jours., chpts. to books; holder 14 patents on optical instruments and systems. Pres. Indian Wells Valley Community Concert Assn., Ridgecrest, Calif., 1974-75; sr. fellow Naval Weapons Ctr., 1990; former mem. Calif. Rep. State Ctrl. Com. Recipient LTE Thompson award Naval Weapons Ctr., 1974, Tech. Dir.'s award, 1983; Capt. Robert Dexter Conrad award Dept. Navy, 1979, Disting. Alumnus award U. Mont., 1991, Dep. Comdr.'s award for R & D, 1995, Tech. Leadership award Navy High Energy Laser Project, 1995, Navy Meritorius Civilian Svc. award, 1995, cert. of recognition for creative devel. of tech. innovation NASA, 2004. Fellow Optical Soc. Am. (assoc. editor Jour. 1968-79, bd. dirs. 1972-75), Internat. Soc. for Optical Engring. (bd. dirs. 1985-87, v.p. 1987, pres. 1988, Tech. Achievement award 1983, organizer and chair Laser Power Beaming II Conf. 1995, chair Free Electron Laser Challenges Conf. 1997, chair Free Electron Laser Challenges II 1999), Maturango Mus. (life). Republican. Achievements include development of polishing techniques for reducing scattered light from mirrors, thin film optics, laser power beaming to space and fabrication of large light weight, low expansion low scatter adaptive optic mirrors. Home: 916 N Randall St Ridgecrest CA 93555-3007 Office: 201 N Sanders St Ridgecrest CA 93555-3867 Office Phone: 760-384-1177. E-mail: bennett@bennettopticalresearch.com.

BENNETT, HARRY LOUIS, history professor; b. Ansonia, Conn., Dec. 22, 1923; s. Louis and Florence (Swole) B.; m. Claire Davis, July 2, 1949; 1 dau., Lisa Brierley. BA, Yale U., 1944, MA, 1948, PhD, 1954. Welfare investigator, Conn., 1950-51; mem. faculty Quinnipiac Coll., Hamden, Conn., 1951—, prof. history, dean coll., 1956-67, v.p. acad. affairs, 1967-69, 72-90, prof., chmn. history, 1969-72, provost, 1972-90, acting pres., 1978-79, provost emeritus, 1990, emeritus prof. history, 1992—. Sec.-treas. Conn. Conf. Community and Jr. Colls., 1955-62, v.p., 1962-64, pres., 1964-65; chmn. standing com. accreditation Conn. Council Higher Edn., 1964-65, vice chmn., 1985-86; chmn. Conn. Adv. Com. on Accreditation, 1986-88. 1st lt., inf. AUS, 1944-46, MTO. Mem. Am. Hist. Assn., Am. Cath. hist. Assn., New Eng. Hist. Assn., Orgn. Am. Historians, Assn. Study Conn. History, Conn. Hist. Soc., New Haven Colony Hist. Soc. Roman Catholic. Home: 21 Knollwood Rd North Haven CT 06473-4328

BENNETT, HENRY, publishing executive; b. N.Y. Prodn. editor, book designer U. Calif. Press, Berkeley, 1974—76; assoc. mng. editor, dir. media prodn. ctr. Curriculum R&D Group, U. Hawaii, Honolulu, 1979—81; v.p. printing divsn. Transpac Corp., Pago Pago, Am. Samoa, 1982; editor, mgr. Bishop Mus. Press, Honolulu, 1983—88; v.p. mktg. Pacific Trade Group (now Islander Group), Waipahu, Hawaii, 1988—89; pres. Ind. Resources, Honolulu, 1989—; editor Kamehameha Schs. Press, Honolulu, 1993—2001, dir., 2001—. Panelist biennium lit. grants rev. Hawaii State Found. on Culture and the Arts, Honolulu, 1997, 99, 2003; spkr., presenter in field. Charter mem. Alliance for Drama Edn., Honolulu, 1979—, bd. dirs., 2003—. Mem.: Hawaii Book Pubs. Assn. (founding mem., past pres.), Hawaii Yacht Club. Avocations: diving, sailing, first aid and emergency medicine, theater, reading. Office: Kamehameha Shcs Press 1887 Makuakane St Honolulu HI 96817

BENNETT, JACK FRANKLIN, oil industry executive; b. Macon, Ga., Jan. 17, 1924; s. Andrew Jackson and Mary Eloise (Franklin) B.; m. Shirley Elizabeth Goodwin, Sept. 17, 1949; children: Jackson Goodwin, Philip Davies, Hugh Franklin, Elizabeth Fraser. BA, Yale U., 1944; MA, Harvard U., 1949, PhD, 1951. Negotiator Joint U.S.-U.K. Export Import Agy., Berlin, Germany, 1946-47; teaching fellow finance Harvard, 1949-51; spl. asst. to adminstr. Tech. Assistance Program, U.S. Dept. State, Washington, 1951-52; economist U.S. Mut. Security Agy., Washington, 1952-53; sr. economist Presdl. Commn. on Fgn. Econ. Policy, 1954; sr. fgn. exch. analyst Exxon Corp., N.Y.C., 1955-58, dep. European fin. rep. London, 1958-60; treas. Esso. Petroleum Co., Ltd., London, 1960-61; asst. treas. Exxon Corp., N.Y.C., 1961-65, mgr. gen. econs. dept., 1965-66, mgr. coordination and planning dept., 1966-67; gen. mgr. supply dept. Exxon Co., U.S.A., Houston, 1967-69; v.p., dir. Exxon Internat., N.Y.C., 1969-71; sr. v.p. Exxon Corp., N.Y.C., 1975-89, also bd. dirs., ret., 1989. Dep. undersec. for monetary affairs U.S. Dept. Treasury, Washington, 1971-74, undersec. for monetary affairs, 1974-75. Contbr. articles to profl. jours. Trustee Com. Econ. Devel. With USNR, 1943-46. Mem. Stanwich Club (Greenwich, Conn.), York (Maine) Club, Blind Brook Club, John's Island Club (Fla.). Republican. Office: 21 Marker Way Vero Beach FL 32963 E-mail: jbnt@aol.com.

BENNETT, JAMES THOMAS, economics professor; b. Memphis, Oct. 19, 1942; m. Sara Ellen Dorman, Sept. 2, 1967. BS in Ops. Research magna cum laude, Case Inst. Tech., 1964, MS in Mgmt. Sci., 1966; PhD in Econs., Case Western Res. U., 1970; student Grad. Sch. Bus., Columbia U., 1964-65. Teaching fellow Case Inst. Tech., 1968-69; instr. bus. Cleve. State U., 1967-68; asst. prof. econs. George Washington U., Washington, 1970-75; assoc. prof. econs. George Mason U., Fairfax, Va., 1975-77, Eminent Scholar and William P. Snavely prof. polit. economy and pub. policy, 1975—. Dir. John M. Olin Inst. for Employment Practice and Policy; chmn. faculty senate George Mason U., 2002-. Co-author: The Political Economy of Federal Government Growth: 1958-1978, 1980; Better Government at Half the Price, 1981; Deregulating Labor Relations, 1981; Underground Government: The Off-Budget Public Sector, 1983; Destroying Democracy: How Government Funds Partisan Politics, 1985, Unfair Competition: The Profits of Nonprofits, 1989, Patterns of Corporate Philanthropy: Ideas, Advocacy and the Corporation, 1989, Health Research Charities: Image and Reality, 1990, Health Research Charities II: The Politics of Fear, 1991, Official Lies: How Washington Misleads Us, 1992, Unhealthy Charities: Hazardous to Your Health and Wealth, 1994, Cancer Scam: The Diversion of Federal Cancer Funds to Politics, 1998, The Food and Drink Police: America's Nanies, Busybodies, and Petty Tyrants, 1999, From Pathology to Politics: Public Health in America, 2000, Public Health Profiteering, 2001, The Future of Private Sector Unionism in the United States, 2002, Tax-Funded Politics, 2004, Information Technology and the World of Work, 2004; contbr. chpts. to books, articles to profl. jours.; editor Jour. Labor Rsch. Ford Found. scholar, 1960-64; Continental Grain Corp. fellow; McKinsey scholar; Case Inst. fellow, 1965-67; Fed. Res. Bank Cleve. fellow, 1969-70 Mem. Am. Econ. Assn., So. Econ. Assn., Pub. Choice Soc., Western Econ. Assn., Am. Statis. Assn., Phila. Soc., Mont Pelerin Soc., Phi Beta Kappa, Sigma Xi, Tau Beta Pi, Alpha Lambda Delta, Phi Theta Kappa. Office: George Mason U Dept Econs Fairfax VA 22030 Business E-Mail: jbennett@gmu.edu.

BENNETT, JANICE LYNN, publisher, educator; b. Chgo., Jan. 31, 1951; d. Harry Albert and Dorothy Marie Goodman; m. James Stephen Bennett, Oct. 6, 1973; children: Scott James, Anne Christine. BA in Graphic Design, No. Ill. U., 1973; BA in Spanish, Met. State Coll. of Denver, 1993; MA in Spanish Lit., U. Colo., 1997. Graphic artist Montgomery Ward, Chgo., 1973-74; asst. prodn. mgr., art dir. Crow Publs., Denver, 1977-80; owner, graphic artist, typographer Charter Graphics, Classic Typography, Denver, 1980-89; Spanish instr. Met. State Coll. of Denver, 1995—2000; pub., editor, author Libri de Hispania, Littleton, Colo., 2000—. Translator Denver Pub. Schs., Greenlee Elem., Denver, 1993-94; translator, interpreter World Youth Day, Denver, 1993; bilingual tchg. asst. Knapp Elem., Denver, 1990-91; freelance writer

Denver Cath. Register. Author: Guia práctica a la literatura, el análisis y la redacción, 1998; author, pub., editor: Sacred Blood, Sacred Image: The Sudarium of Oviedo, New Evidence for the Authenticity of the Shroud of Turin, 2001, 2d edit., 2005, St. Laurence and the Holy Grail: The Story of the Holy Chalice of Valencia, 2002, 2d edit., 2004. Mem. MLA, Altar and Rosary Soc. (pres. 2000-01, 2002-03), Am. Assn. of Tchrs. of Spanish and Portuguese, Pub. Mktg. Assn., Cath. Book Pub. Assn., Spanish Ctr. for Sindonology, Sigma Delta Pi, Phi Sigma Iota. Avocations: travel, photography, piano, biblical studies, drawing and painting. Office: Libri de Hispania PO Box 270262 Littleton CO 80127-0005 Home Fax: 303-973-3014. Personal E-mail: bennettjanice@mac.com.

BENNETT, JAY D., lawyer; children: Summer, Lillian, Sky. BA with honors, U. N.C., 1974; JD cum laude, Harvard U., 1977. Bar: U.S. Dist. Ct. (no. and mid. dist.) Ga., U.S. Ct. Appeals (4th, 5th, 9th and 11th cirs.), U.S. Supreme Ct. Assoc. Alston & Bird, Atlanta, 1977-83, ptnr., 1983—, and chmn., trial practice group. Morehead scholar Morehead Found. 1970-74. Mem. State Bar Ga., Atlanta Bar Assn., Lawyers Club Atlanta, Trial Attys. Am., Phi Beta Kappa. Avocations: flying, skydiving, motorcycling, fishing. Office: Alston & Bird LLP One Atlantic Ctr 1201 W Peachtree St Atlanta GA 30309-3424 Office Phone: 404-881-7643. E-mail: jbennett@alston.com.

BENNETT, JEAN LOUISE MCPHERSON, physicist, research scientist; b. Kensington, Md., May 9, 1930; d. Archibald Turner and Margaret Fitch (Willcox) McPherson; m. Harold Earl Bennett, Aug. 17, 1952 (div. Nov. 1984). BA summa cum laude, Mt. Holyoke Coll., 1951, DSc (hon.), 1992; MS, Pa. State U., 1953, PhD in Physics, 1955. Physicist Wright Air Devel. Ctr., Dayton, Ohio, 1955-56, Naval Ordnance Test Sta. (now Naval Air Warfare Ctr. Weapons Div.), China Lake, Calif., 1956-85, sr. research scientist, 1987-93, 95; vis. prof. U. Ala., Huntsville, 1986-87, Mt. Holyoke Coll., South Hadley, Mass., 1994-95; ret., 1996—. Mem. NRC Evaluation Panel Nat. Bur. Stds., Ctr. for Radiation Rsch., 1979-85, Nat. Inst. Stds. and Tech. Mfg. Engring. Lab., 1988-94, U.S. Nat. Com. for Internat. Commn. for Optics, 1984-85, 88-95; vis. scientist Inst. Optical Rsch., Royal Inst. Tech., Stockholm, Mar.-Sept., 1988, 98, 99, 2000, 01. Author: (with Lars Mattsson) Introduction to Surface Roughness and Scattering, 1989, revised 1999; author: Surface Finish and Its Measurement, 1992; contbr. sci. articles to profl. jours.; patentee in field. Recipient Tech. Achievement award Soc. Photo-Optical Instrumentation Engrs., 1983, L.T.E. Thompson award Naval Weapons Ctr., 1988, Women in Sci. and Engring. Lifetime Achievement award, 1993, Outstanding Sci. Alumni award Pa. State U., 1999; named sr. fellow Naval Weapons Ctr., 1989, Disting. Fellow, 1994. Fellow Optical Soc. Am. (v.p. 1984, pres.-elect 1985, pres. 1986, past pres. 1987, chmn. book publ. com. 1991-94, David Richardson medal 1990); mem. Am. Inst. Physics (subcom. on books 1990-94), Phi Beta Kappa, Sigma Xi, Sigma Delta Epsilon, Iota Sigma Pi, Pi Mu Epsilon, Sigma Pi Sigma. Achievements include being the first woman to receive PhD in Physics at Pa. State U., 1955; first woman pres. Optical Soc. of Am. Office: Code 4T41A0D Michelson Lab Naval Air Warfare Ctr Stop 6302 1900N Knox Rd Ridgecrest CA 93555 E-mail: jbennett@ridgenet.net.

BENNETT, JOE CLAUDE, pharmaceutical executive; b. Birmingham, Ala., Dec. 12, 1933; s. Claude and Clara Lucille (Clark) B.; m. Nancy Miller, June 17, 1958; children: Katherine Diane, Miller, Clark Barton. AB, Samford U., 1954; MD, Harvard U., 1958; DSc (hon.), U. Ala., 1992. Diplomate Am. Bd. Internal Medicine (governing bd. 1987—, cert. exam. com. for 1989, ind. com. R & D, 1988—), Am. Bd. Rheumatology, Nat. Bd. Med. Examiners. Intern Univ. Ala. Hosp., Birmingham, 1958-59, resident, 1959-60; rsch. assoc. molecuar biology NIH, Bethesda, Md., 1962-64; sr. rsch. fellow div. biology Calif. Inst. Tech., Pasadena, Calif., 1964-65; asst. prof. dept. medicine, assoc. prof. dept. microbiology, asst. dir. div. clin. immunology and rheumatology U. Ala. Med. Sch., Birmingham, 1965-70, dir. div. clin. immunology and rheumatology, 1970-83, prof., chmn. dept. microbiology, 1970-82, prof., chmn. dept. medicine, 1982-92, Spencer Prof. Med. Sci., 1992—, dir. multipurpose arthritis center, 1977-84, disting. faculty lectr., 1979; pres. U. Ala., Birmingham, 1993-96; pres., COO BioCryst Pharms., Birmingham, 1996—. Physician in chief U. Ala. Hosp.; vis. prof. U. Mo.-Columbia Sch. Medicine, 1987, U. Leiden, The Netherlands, 1988, Baylor U. Coll. Medicine, Houston, 1989, others; invited lectr. various univs., confs. including IX Pan-Am. Congress Rheumatology, Buenos Aires, 1986, U. Mo.-Columbia Sch. Medicine, 1987, Cornell Med. Sch., 1986, U. Colo., 1986; mem. sci. adv. bd. Merck Sharp & Dohme Rsch. Labs., 1987-89, Gorgas Meml. Inst. Tropical and Preventive Medicine, 1985—, others; mem. bd. health sci. policies, NIH, NAS, 1988—. Editor: Vistas in Connective Tissue Diseases, 1968; co-editor: Rheumatology and Immunology, 2d edit., 1986, Cecil Textbook of Medicine, 1988—, Cecil Essentials of Medicine; editor-in-chief Am. Jour. Medicine, 1986-97, Arthritis and Rheumatism, 1975-80; mem. editorial bd. Protein and Peptide Revs., 1980—, Current Opinion in Rheumatology, 1988—, Arthritis and Rheumatism, 1969-75; contbr. numerous articles, papers, book revs., abstracts to profl. publs. Recipient Ala. Acad. Honor award, 1987, Seale Harris award So. Med. Assn., 1987; John and Mary R. Markle Found. scholar in acad. medicine, 1965-70; recipient Rsch. Career Devel. award NIH, 1965-75; fellow Arthritis and Rheumatism Found., Harvard Med. Sch., Mass. Gen. Hosp., 1960-62 Fellow AAAS (sec. N. Med. scis. nominating com. 1989—); mem. Am. Bd. Internal Medicine (exec. com. 1992), Federated Coun. of Internatl Medicine, Assn. of Am. Med. Colls. (adv. panel on biomed. rsch. 1991-92), Inst. Medicine NAS, ACP (master 1990), Am. Assn. Immunologists, Am. Fedn. Clin. Rsch., Am. Coll. Rheumatology (pres. 1981-82, bd. dirs. planning group 1986-87), Am. Soc. Biol. Chemists, Am. Soc. Clin. Investigation, Am. Soc. Microbiology, more. Home: 3520 River Bend Rd Birmingham AL 35243-4832 Office: BioCryst Pharms 2190 Parkway Lake Dr Birmingham AL 35244-1879

BENNETT, JOEL HERBERT, construction company executive; b. Chgo., Nov. 7, 1936; m. Seraphima H. Lamb, 1999; children: Evan Alan, Julie Andrea. BSChemE, U. So. Calif., L.A., 1958, MSChemE, 1962; MBA in Ops. Rsch., UCLA, 1960. Chem. process engr. C. F. Braun & Co., Alhambra, Calif., 1960-65, with bus. devel., 1965-73; v.p. Arthur G. McKee & Co., Cleve., 1973-78, Parsons Engring. Sci., Inc., Pasadena, Calif., 1978-81; sr. v.p. Santa Fe Braun Inc., Alhambra, 1981-89; exec. v.p. The Parsons Corp., Pasadena, 1989-92, 96—; pres. Parsons Environ. Svcs. Inc., Pasadena, 1992-96, Harland Bartholomew & Assocs., 1992-95; exec. v.p. The Parsons Corp., 1995-96; sr. v.p. Parsons Brinckerhoff, Inc., N.Y.C., 1997—2004; chmn., pres. PB Power Inc., NYC, 1998—2004; chmn. PB Power, 1998—2004; chmn., pres. Parsons Brinckerhoff Internat., Inc., 2001—. Bd. dirs. Inst. Redesign Lng.; co-chair environ. mgmt. adv. bd. U.S. Dept. Energy, 1994-01. Author: (with others) Project Management, 1989. Dir. Calif. State U. L.A. Found.; mem. bd. advisors The Asian Am. Architects/Engrs. Assn. Mem. Am. Inst. Chem. Engrs., Jonathan Club (L.A.). Avocations: skiing, jogging, tennis, music. Home: 128 Outrigger Mall Marina Del Rey CA 90292-5793 Office: Parsons Brinckerhoff Inc 444 S Flower St 37th Fl Los Angeles CA 90071 Office Phone: 213-896-5671.

BENNETT, JOHN CHARLES, former engineering and construction executive; b. Dover, N.J., Jan. 23, 1925; s. John and Therese Adele (Weiss) B.; m. Betty Evelyn Koenig, June 17, 1950; children: John Lance, Stephen Gary. BS in Engring., Swarthmore Coll., 1945. Registered profl. engr., 48 states, D.C., P;R., Venezuela, Greece; registered profl. planner, N.J.; registered land surveyor, La. Field engr., supt., dist. mgr., v.p., engring. ptnr., dir. The Austin Co., N.Y.C., Cleve., Canada, 1946—79, v.p. spl. projects in Greece, Mid. East and North Africa, 1975-79; pres., CEO, Structors, Inc., Chgo., 1979-82, Advanced Tech. Sys., Fairlawn, N.J., 1982-85; chmn. bd. Scandia, Inc., Atlanta, 1979-82; owner, operator Abacus Bennett Farm, Blairstown, N.J., 1985—. Asst. sec. HUD, Washington, 1973. Pres., bd. dirs. N.J. Easter Seal Soc., Morris Plains, 1968-74, Morris County Rehab. Ctr., Morris Plains, 1971-74; bd. dirs. Morris Ctr. YMCA, Morristown, N.J., 1978-92. Lt (j.g.) USN, 1943-46. Mem. Nat. Bd. Engring. Examiners, Newcomen Soc., Loyal Order Ky. Cols., Intrepids Club, Tau Beta Pi. Home and Office: 12 Moraine Rd Morris Plains NJ 07950-2711

BENNETT, JOHN JOSEPH, electronics executive; b. Camden, NJ, Sept. 4, 1923; s. John Henry and Margaret Katherine (Bloxsum) B.; m. Dolores Florence Griffiths, June 17, 1943; children: Jill, T. Robert, T. Richard. Student, Centenary Coll., 1951-55; MBA, Mich. State U., 1961; DBA, George Washington U., 1974. Commd. 2d lt. USAAF, 1943; advanced through grades to col. USAF, officer various operational and mgmt. jobs, 1942-60; asst. comptroller Hdqrs. AFSC, Washington, 1961-66; asst. to Asst. Sec. Air Force and dep. chief staff, Personnel Hdqrs. USAF, Washington, 1967-69; ret. USAF, 1969; exec. dir. Mauchley Edn. Inst., Washington, 1969-70; pres. Sycom, Inc., Washington, 1969-70; mgr. aerospace def. practice Peat, Marwick, Mitchell & Co., Washington, 1970-74; prin. dep. asst. U.S. Sec. of Def., Washington, 1975-76, Asst. Sec. of Navy, Washington, 1976-77; dir., exec. office pres. Fed. Acquisition Inst., Washington, 1977-79; chief exec. officer ANADAC, Inc., Washington, 1979-88, chmn. bd., 1988-92, chmn. emeritus, 1992-96. Lectr. George Washington U., 1979—89; chmn. bd. dirs. TBG Reliance Corp., 1997—. Author: The Next Generation Management Systems for Systems Management, 1967, Department of Defense Systems Acquisition Management, 1974, Program Management Principles and Practices, 1994; author: (with others) Systems Concepts for Human Resources Management, 1968. Decorated Legion of Merit, D.F.C., Air medal with 4 oak leaf clusters; recipient Disting. Civilian Svc. award, 1976, Disting. Pub. Svc. award, 1977. Methodist. Home: 343 Bayshore Dr Palm Harbor FL 34683-5482 Office: TBG Reliance 405 Orange St Palm Harbor FL 34683-5449 E-mail: jbennett@wewatch.net.

BENNETT, JUDY A., music educator; b. Madison, S.D., Apr. 10, 1952; d. George Raymond and Berthein Cary Gannon; m. Jeffrey A. Bennett, June 15, 1974; children: Don Dean, Christopher Lee, Alexander Jeffrey. BS, Dakota State U., 1978. Vocal/gen. music tchr. Uinta County Sch. Dist. #1, Evanston, Wyo., 1978—92, Sch. Dist. La Crosse, Wis., 1992—96, Galena (Ill.) Pub. Schs., 1996—98, Albany (Wis.) Pub. Schs., 1998—2001; H.S. vocal music tchr. Sch. Dist. Monroe, Wis., 2001—05. Composer songs. Dir. Cmty. Choir, Evanston, 1978—86, Hazel Green, Wis., 1998; bd. dirs. Monroe Theatre Guild, 2000. Mem.: NEA, Wis. Choral Dirs. Assn. (5 Star award 2005), Monroe Edn. Assn., Wyo. Edn. Assn., Music Educators Nat. Conf. Home: 1706 23rd Ave Monroe WI 53566 Office: Monroe High School 1600 26th St Monroe WI 53566 Personal E-mail: j_bennett@charter.net. E-mail: judy.bennett@monroe.k12.wi.us.

BENNETT, KENNETH ALAN, retired biological anthropologist; b. Butler, Okla., Oct. 3, 1935; s. Kenneth Francis and Lillian Imogene (McDaniel) B.; m. Helen Lucille Maze, Sept. 6, 1959; children: Letitia Arlene, Cheri Lynn. AS, Odessa Coll., 1956; BA, U. Tex., 1961; MA, U. Ariz., 1966, PhD, 1967. Asst. prof. anthropology U. Oreg., 1967-70; assoc. prof. U. Wis., Madison, 1970-75, prof., 1975-97, ret., 1997. Forensic anthropology cons. to Wis. law enforcement agys. and Wis. state crime lab., 1970—98. Author: The Indians of Point of Pines, Arizona, 1973, Fundamentals of Biological Anthropology, 1979, Skeletal Remains from Mesa Verde National Park, 1975, A Field Guide for Human Skeletal Identification, 1987, 2nd edit., 1993; editor Yearbook of Phys. Anthropology, 1976-81; contbg. editor Social Biology, 1981-87; mem. editl. com. Ann. Revs. in Anthropology, 1987-91; editor, reviewer Human Biology, 1981-87; contbr. articles to profl. jours. Mem. Wis. Burial Sites Preservation Bd., 1988. With U.S. Army, 1956-58. NIH fellow, 1964-67 Mem. Am. Assn. Phys. Anthropologists, Am. Soc. Naturalists, Human Biology Council, Soc. for Study Evolution, Am. Acad. Forensic Scis., Soc. for Study Human Biology, Soc. Systematic Zoology, Am. Assn. Physical Anthropologists (exec. com. 1976-81), Sigma Xi. Home: 5718 Hammersley Rd Madison WI 53711-3450

BENNETT, LERONE, JR., retired magazine editor, author; b. Clarksdale, Miss., Oct. 17, 1928; s. Lerone and Alma (Reed) Bennett; m. Gloria Sylvester, July 21, 1956; children: Alma Joy, Constance, Courtney; 1 child, Lerone III. BA, Morehouse Coll., 1949, LittD (hon.), 1966; HHD (hon.), Wilberforce U., 1977; DLitt (hon.), Marquette U., 1979, Voorhees Coll., 1981, Morgan State U., 1981; LHD (hon.), U. Ill., 1980, Lincoln Coll., 1980, Dillard U., 1980; LittD (hon.), Howard U., 1982; LHD (hon.), Boston U., 1987; DLitt (hon.), Tuskegee U., 1989. Reporter Atlanta Daily World, 1949—51, city editor, 1952—53; assoc. editor Ebony mag., Chgo., 1953—58, sr. editor, 1958—87, exec. editor, 1987—2003. Vis. prof. hist. Nothwestern U., 1968—69. Author: Before the Mayflower: A History of Black America, 1619-1964, 1962, 3d edit., 1982, The Negro Mood, 1964, What Manner of Man, A Biography of Martin Luther King, Jr., 1964, Confrontation: Black and White, 1965, Black Power U.S.A., 1968, Pioneers in Protest, 1968, The Challenge of Blackness, 1972, The Shaping of Black America, 1975, Wade in the Water, 1979, Forced Into Glory: Abraham Lincoln's White Dream, 2000; contbg. author: New Negro Poets: USA, 1964, American Negro Short Stories, 1966. Trustee Columbia Coll. Recipient Patron Saints award, Soc. Midland Authors, 1965, Book of the Yr. award, Capital Press Club, 1963, AAAL Acad./Inst. lit. award, 1978. Mem.: Sigma Delta Chi, Kappa Alpha Psi, Phi Beta Kappa.

BENNETT, LINDA LOU, library director; b. Sidney, Ark., Nov. 17, 1941; d. Charles Orbra Richardson and Thelma Camilla Marchant Richardson; m. John Allan Bennett, Nov. 12, 1960; children: Dawn Denise McCoy, Tracy Lynne Royer. BS in Edn., S.E. Mo. State U., Cape Girardeau, 1968; MLS, U. Mo., 1995. Cert. tchr. Mo. Libr. staff Kent Libr. S.E. Mo. State U., Cape Girardeau, 1968—69; libr. Pattonville Sr. H.S., Bridgeton, 1969—71; instr. Festus Pub. Sch. Dist., Mo., 1971—75; edn. rsch. and devel. project Ark. Dept. of Edn., Little Rock, 1989—91; libr. dir. U. Ark C.C., Batesville, 1991—. Author: Teamwork: The Name Of The Game In Recruitment; Retention: A Game Plan, 1991. Com. mem. Rep. Party, Batesville, 1986; chairperson The Ark. State Libr. Bd., Little Rock, 2002. Mem.: ALA (assoc. cert.), Ark. Libr. Assn. (assoc.; com. mem.). Baptist. Avocations: reading, watercolor painting, travel, family activities. Home: 3120 Alice Dr Batesville AR 72501 Office: U of Ark Community Coll 2005 White Drive Batesville AR 72501

BENNETT, MARGARET AIROLA, lawyer; b. San Francisco, Calif; AB cum laude, U. Calif., Berkeley, 1972; JD, U. San Francisco and Loyola U., 1976. Bar: Ill.1976, US Dist. Ct. (no. dist.) Ill. 1977, US Ct. Appeals (7th cir.) 1983. Intern Cook County State's Atty.'s Office, Chgo., 1975-76; assoc. Dunlap, Thompson & Boyd, Ltd., Libertyville, Ill., 1977-79; ptnr. Bennett & Bennett, Ltd., Oak Brook, Ill., 1980-96; pvt. practice The Law Offices of Margaret A. Bennett, Oak Brook, Ill., 1997. Atty. rep. McDonald's Corp., Oak Brook, 1982—, County of DuPage, Wheaton, Ill., 1990-95. Counsel fo DuPage Ill. Fair and Exposition Authority, County of DuPage, 1991-95, co-chmn. next generation com.; mem. devel. coun. Good Samaritan Hosp., 1988-92. Mem. DuPage County Bar Assn. (chmn. real estate law com. 1994-95, Cert. of Appreciation 1989, Bd. Dir. award 1998, chmn. profl. responsibility com. 1996-97, chmn. family law com. 1997-98), Ill. State Bar Assn. (assembly mem., 1996-2000, Cert. of Appreciation 1990, real estate sect. counsel 1996-2002, jud evaluation com. 1998—), Womens Bar Assn. DuPage County, Evang. Health Found. (bd. sponsors 1988-92). Republican. Episcopalian. Avocations: golf, reading, skiing, travel. Office: Ste 718 1200 Hanger Rd Oak Brook IL 60523-1908

BENNETT, MARK J., state attorney general; m. Patricia Tomi Ohara. BA in polit. sci. summa cum laude, Union Coll., 1976; JD magna cum laude, Cornell U., 1979. Law clk. to Hon. Samuel P. King, Chief Judge U.S. Dist. Ct. Hawaii; asst. US atty. Washington, 1980—82, Honolulu, 1982—90; litig. ptnr. McCorriston Miller Mukai MacKinnon LLP, Honolulu, 1991—2002; pro bono spl. dep. atty. gen., spl. asst. pros. atty. Hawaii State Ct.; atty. gen. State of Hawaii, Honolulu, 2003—. Instr. criminal and civil trial advocacy Atty. Gen.'s Adv. Inst., Washington; instr. U. Hawaii Sch. Law. Recipient Spl. Achievement Award, US Atty. Gen., 1986. Republican. Office: 425 Queen St Honolulu HI 96813 Office Phone: 808-586-1500.

BENNETT, MARY See THOMPSON, DIDI CASTLE

BENNETT, MARY FRAN, librarian; b. Cannonsburg, Pa., Aug. 6, 1947; d. Donald Eugene and Frances Maisel Gumpper; m. John Edwin Bennett, Sept. 1, 1990; children: Daniel, Thomas, Jennifer Rachana. BA, Bluffton Coll., 1969; MA in L.Am. studies, La. State U., 1971, MLS, 1976. Certified Public Librarian Ohio Libr. Coun., 2001. Reference asst./outreach Lorain (Ohio) Pub. Libr., 1971—76; reference libr. Cuyahoga County Pub. Libr., Parma, Ohio, 1977—78, coord. info. and referral, 1978—86; libr. mgr. Geauga County Pub. Libr., Middlefield, Ohio, 1987—92, Chardon, Ohio, 1992—. Mem.: ALA (chmn. PLA mktg. com. 2004—, John Cotton Dana award 1999), Chardon C. of C., Ohio Libr. Coun. Avocations: therapy dog handling, photography. Office: Geauga County Pub Libr 110 E Park St Chardon OH 44024 Office Phone: 440-285-7601.

BENNETT, MICHAEL L., agricultural products executive; Chmn. Terra Industries. Office: Terra Industries Inc 600 4th St Sioux City IA 51101 Office Phone: 712-277-1340.

BENNETT, MICHAEL VANDER LAAN, neuroscience educator; b. Madison, Wis., Jan. 7, 1931; s. Martin Toscan and Cornelia (Vanderlaan) B.; m. Ruth Berman, July 19, 1963 (div. 1993); children: Nicholas Toscan, Elena Paula; m. R. Suzanne Zukin Nov. 19, 1997. BS, Yale U., 1952; DPhil, Oxford U., Eng., 1957. Research worker Coll. of Physicians and Surgeons Columbia U., N.Y.C., 1957-58, rsch. assoc., 1958-59, asst. prof. neurology, 1959-61, assoc. prof. neurology, 1961-66; co-dir. neurobiology Marine Biol. Lab., Woods Hole, Mass., 1970-74; prof. anatomy Albert Einstein Coll. Medicine, Bronx, N.Y., 1967-74, prof. neurosci., 1974—, chmn. neurosci., 1982-96, Sylvia and Robert S. Olnick Prof. of Neurosci., 1986—. Editor rev. jours.; contbr. articles to profl. jours. Hon. Pepsi Cola scholar, 1948, Rhodes scholar, 1952; Grass Fellow, 1958. Fellow AAAS; mem. NAS, Am. Physiol. Soc., Am. Soc. Cell Biology, Biophys. Soc., Soc. Neurosci., N.Y. Road Runners Club, Phi Beta Kappa. Avocations: running, skiing, scuba, science. Office: Albert Einstein Coll of Medicine Dept Of Neurosci Bronx NY 10461 Office Phone: 718-430-2536. Business E-Mail: mbennett@aecom.yu.edu.

BENNETT, NANCY EVANS, secondary school educator; b. Rochester, N.Y., May 14, 1944; d. Fank Clinton, Jr. and Roberta (Evans) Bennett; children: Karen, Lindsay. BS, Davis & Elkins Coll., 1966; MS, U. So. Calif., Brussels, 1976. Cert. tchr. N.J., Pa. Tchr. Bald Eagle (Pa.) Schs., 1966-68, John Hill Sch., Boonton, NJ, 1969, Antwerp Internat. Sch., Ekeren, Belgium, 1976, Meml. Jr. Sch., Whippany, NJ, 1976-84, Bernardsville (N.J.) Schs., 1985-93; tchr., supr. K-8 sci. Summit (N.J.) Pub. Schs., 1993-95; supr. math/sci. Hackettstown (N.J.) Pub. Schs., 1995-98; tchr. math/sci. Unity Charter Sch., NJ, 1998-99; tchr. sci. Mendham (N.J.) Boro Schs., 1999—. Presenter in field. Active East Hanover (N.J.) Sch. Bd., 1987—89. Mem.: ASCD, NSTA, NEA, N.J. Edn. Assn., N.J. Sci. Tchrs. Assn. (pres.), Am. Chem. Soc., Jr. League, Embroiderers Guild Am. (pres.). Home: 5 Cypress Cir Morristown NJ 07960-6786 Office: Mendham Boro Schs 100 Dean Rd Mendham NJ 07945

BENNETT, P. TYSON, lawyer; b. Annapolis, Md., Nov. 21, 1947; B, Towson Coll.; JD, Univ. Balt., 1971. Bar: Md. 1972. Ptnr. Reese & Carney, Columbia, Md. Adj. faculty, sch. law, disabilities law Johns Hopkins Univ. Mem.: Edn. Law Assn. (bd. dir. 1996—98, pres. 2004—05), Md. Coun. Local Sch. Bd. Attys (past pres.). Office: Reese & Carney Ste 200 Hawthorne Exec Ctr 10715 Charter Dr Columbia MD 21044-2871 Office Phone: 410-740-4600. Office Fax: 410-730-7729. Business E-Mail: ptb@reese-carney.com.

BENNETT, PAUL B., stock exchange executive; BA in econ., U. Chgo.; PhD in econ., Princeton U. Various positions Fed. Reserve Bank of NY, 1978—93, sr. v.p. rsch. group, 1994—99, sr. v.p. capital markets rsch., 1999—2001; sr. v.p. and chief economist NY Stock Exch., 2001—. Office: NY Stock Exch 11 Wall St New York NY 10005

BENNETT, PAUL FREDERICK, lawyer; b. Oakland, Calif., Sept. 12, 1949; BA with distinction, U. Calif., Berkeley, 1971, JD, 1974. Bar: Calif. 1974, U.S. Dist. Ct. (no. dist.) Calif. 1975, U.S. Ct. Appeals (9th cir.) 1975, U.S. Dist. Ct. (cen. dist.) Calif. 1976, U.S. Dist. Ct. (so. dist.) Calif. 1982, U.S. Supreme Ct. 1989. Ptnr. Gold Bennett Cera & Sidener, San Francisco, 1974—. Mem. ABA (antitrust law sect., bus. and banking sect., litigation sect. class actions and derivative suits subsect.), Nat. Assn. Securities and Comml. Law Attys., Bar Assn. San Fncisco, State Bar Calif., Bar of Supreme Ct. U.S. Office: Gold Bennett Cera & Sidener 595 Market St San Francisco CA 94105-2802 E-mail: pfb@gbcsf.com.

BENNETT, PEGGY DEE, music educator; b. Sarasota, Fla., Nov. 23, 1949; d. Virgil and Freda Blanche (Hines) Bennett; m. John Van Harlan Quick, Dec. 27, 1984. BS in Music Edn., Ball State U., 1971, MA in Music Edn., 1975; PhD in Music Edn., U. North Tex., 1981. Tchr. elem. music East Allen County Sch., Ft. Wayne, Ind., 1971—73, Ft. Wayne Cmty. Schs., 1974—78; prof. music edn. U. Tex., Arlington, 1981—96, Tex. Christian U., Ft. Worth, 1996—2000, Oberlin Coll. Conservatory, Ohio, 2001—. Adj. faculty Ind.-Purdue U, Ft. Wayne, 1975—78; mediator Cmty. Mediation Ctr., Bozeman, Mont., 2000—. Co-author: SongWorks: Singing in the Education of Children, 1997, SongWorks: Singing from Sound to Symbol, 1999; editor: SongPlay, 1999; contbr. articles to profl. jours. Named Outstanding Alumni, Ball State U., 1990, U. North Tex., 1992; recipient Chancellor's award for excellence in tchg., 1991. Mem.: Music Educators Nat. Conf. Office: Oberlin Conservatory 77 W College Oberlin OH 44074 Office Phone: 440-775-8947.

BENNETT, PETER BRIAN, medical researcher, educator; b. Portsmouth, Hampshire, Eng., June 12, 1931; s. Charles Risby and Doris Isobel (Peckham) B.; m. Margaret Camellia Rose, July 7, 1956; children: Caroline Susan, Christopher Charles BSc, U. London, 1951; PhD, U. Southampton, 1964, DSc, 1984; Dr. honoris causa, U. de la Mediterranean, France, 2001. Asst. head surg. sect. Royal Navy Physiol. Lab., Alverstoke, Eng., 1953-56, head inert gas narcosis sect., 1953-66; dep. dir., prin. sci. officer, head pressure physiology sect. Royal Naval Physiol. Lab., Alverstoke, 1968-72; head pressure physiology group Can. Def. and Civil Inst. for Environ. Rsch., Toronto, Ont., 1966-68; prof. biomed. engring. Duke U., Durham, N.C., 1972-75, assoc. prof. physiology, 1975—, prof. anesthesiology, 1972—, dir. rsch. dept. anesthesiology Med. Ctr., 1973-84, dir. Nat. Divers Alert Network, 1980—2003; dep. dir. F.G. Hall Lab. Environ. Rsch., 1973-74; co-dir. F.G. Hall Lab. Environ. Research, 1974-77, dir., 1977-88; sr. dir. Hyperbaric Ctr., 1988—. Cons. in field Author: The Aetiology of Compressed Air Intoxication and Inert Gas Narcosis, 1966; author, editor: The Physiology and Medicine of Diving and Compressed Air Work, 1969, Russian edit., 1987, 4th edit., 1993; contbr. over 200 articles to profl. jours. With RAF, 1951-53. Recipient Letter of Commendation, Pres. Ronald Reagan, 1981, Sci. award Underwater Soc. Am., 1980, Leonard Greenstone Safety award Nat. Assn. Underwater Instrs., 1985, 1st Prince Tomohito of Mikasa Japan prize, 1990, Craig Hoffman Meml. award, 1992, Dan Seap Mentor award, 1998, Ernst & Young Entrepreneur of Yr. in Life Scis. award, NC and SC, 2002, Reaching Out award Diving Equipment Mfrs., 2002. Fellow Nat. Underwater Explorers Club; mem. Undersea Med. Soc. (pres. 1975-76, mem. exec. com. 1972-75, editor jour. 1976-79, 1st Oceaneering Internat. award 1975, Albert R. Behnke award 1983), Am. Physiol. Soc., European Undersea Biomed. Soc., Russian Acad. Sci. (fgn. mem., Pavlov medal 2001), Aerospace Med. Soc., Marine Tech. Soc., Croatian Undersea and Hyperbaric Med. Soc. (hon.), Nat. Acad. Scuba Educators (Meritorious Svc. award 1997). Avocations: gardening, swimming, boating. Home: 213 Lancaster Dr Chapel Hill NC 27517-3430 Office: Duke U Med Ctr Divers Alert Network 6 W Colony Pl Durham NC 27705 Office Phone: 919-490-6161. E-mail: pbennett25@nc.rr.com.

BENNETT, PETER DUNNE, retired marketing educator; b. Mt. Pleasant, Tex., Feb. 19, 1933; s. Alvin Lowell and Jessie Lorene (Wintz) B.; m. Mary Lou Sanders, Aug. 23, 1953; children— Bonnie Kathleen, Blythe Allison BBA, U. Tex., Austin, 1955, MBA, 1961, PhD, 1965. Mktg. rep. IBM Corp., Lubbock, Tex., 1957-60; lectr. U. Tex., Austin, 1961-63; vis. researcher U. Chile, Santiago, 1963-64; prof., chmn. dept. mktg., assoc. dean, bus. Pa. State

U., University Park, 1964-97; gen. contractor State College, Pa., 1997—. Bd. dirs. Walshire Asurance; cons. and lectr. in field. Author: Consumer Behavior, 1973, Marketing, 1988, Dictionary of Marketing Terms, 1989, 2d edit. 1995; editor numerous books in field; contbr. chpts. to books. Mem. Habitat for Humanity. Served to capt. USAF, 1955-57 Named Disting. Visitor, U. Tex., 1979. Mem. Assn. Consumer Research, Am. Mktg. Assn. (v.p. mgmt. 1983-85, editor 1982-84) Democrat. Presbyterian. Avocations: golf, sailing, water-skiing, house building, wood working. E-mail: pdb1@psu.edu.

BENNETT, PHILIP, editor; b. San Francisco; m. Monica Klien-Samanez; 1 child. Grad., Harvard Univ. Reporter Lima Times, Lima, Peru; with Boston Globe, 1984—97, fgn. correspondent to metro editor, 1984—95, fgn. editor, 1995—97; stringer Washington Post, Peru, 1982—84, nat. sec. editor, 1997—99, asst. mng. editor, fgn. news, 1999—2005, mng. editor, 2005—. Office: Mng Editor Wash Post 1150 15th St NW Washington DC 20071-0002 Office Phone: 202-334-7513. Business E-Mail: bennettp@washpost.com.

BENNETT, RICHARD EDWARD, lawyer; AB, Boston Coll., 1975, JD, 1978. Bar: Mass. 1978, U.S. Dist. Ct. Mass. 1979, U.S. Ct. Appeals (1st cir.) 1979, U.S. Ct. Appeals (fed. cir.) 1989. Atty. Willcox, Pirozzolo & McCarthy, P.C., Boston, 1979—. Office: Willcox Pirozzolo & McCarthy PC 50 Federal St Boston MA 02110-2500

BENNETT, RICHARD THOMAS, lawyer; b. Birmingham, Ala., Dec. 30, 1939; s. Marie (Goodwin) B.; m. Geraldine McIntosh, Sept. 1, 1961; children: Jeff, Ty, Ashley, John. BA, Miss. Coll., Clinton, 1961; MA, Miss. Coll., 1962; JD, U. Miss., Oxford, 1965. Bar: Miss. 1965, D.C. 1991, U.S. Dist. Ct. (no. dist.) Miss. 1965, U.S. Dist. Ct. (so. dist.) Miss. 1971, U.S. Supreme Ct. 1973. From assoc. to ptnr. Henly Jones & Henley and successor firms, Jackson, Miss., 1965-80; ptnr., prin. Bennett, Lotterhos, Sulser and Wilson, P.A., Jackson, 1980—. Pres. Miss. Bankruptcy Conf., Inc., 1981-82. Pres. Clinton Ednl. Found. for Excellence, Inc., 1991-92. Capt. U.S. Army Res., 1969-76. Fellow Miss. Bar Found.; mem. FBA (pres. Miss. chpt. 1993-94, 5th cir. officer 1995-97), Miss. Bar (pres. 2000-01), Hinds County Bar Assn. (pres. 1983-84), Phi Alpha Delta, Omicron Delta Kappa. Baptist. Avocation: long-distance running. Office: Bennett Lotterhos Sulser and Wilson PA One Jackson Pl 188 E Capitol St Ste 1400 Jackson MS 39201-2133

BENNETT, ROBERT F., senator; b. Salt Lake City, 1933; s. Wallace F. Bennett; m. Joyce McKay; 6 children. BS, U. Utah, 1957. Various staff positions U.S Ho. of Reps., U.S. Senate, Washington; CEO Franklin Quest, Salt Lake City, 1984-90; senator from Utah, U.S. Senate, Washington, 1993—, chmn. agr. appropriations subcom., mem. joint econs. com., fin. instns. subcom., mem. banking, housing, urban affairs com., appropriations com., govt. affairs com., small bus. com. Mem. Rep. high tech. task force, govt. affairs com.; lobbyist various orgns., Washington; head Dept. Transp.'s Congl. Liaison. Author: Gaining Control. Chmn. Education Strategic Planning Commn. Utah State Bd. Edn. (mem. Edn. Strategic Planning Com.). Recipient Light of Learning award for Outstanding Contbns. to Utah edn., 1989; named Entrepreneur of Yr. for Rocky Mtn. region INC. magazine, 1989. Republican. Office: US Senate 431 Dirksen Senate Ofc Bldg Washington DC 20510-0001*

BENNETT, ROBERT LEROY, computer software development company executive; b. Salt Lake City, May 16, 1937; s. Edward L. and Helen (Hofheins) B.; m. Linda Lou Anderson, Aug. 25, 1961; children: Keri Lynn, Troy, Nicole, Jessica, Candice, Chelsea. *Daughter Keri Lynn, MD and board certified psychiatrist and child psychiatrist, is clinical director of pediatric psychiatry at Utah State Hospital. Keri Lynn and her husband Kurt Herrmann, have five children. Son Troy, BA 1988 BYU, MA 2002 North Eastern University,teaches and coaches high school history and volleyball, respectively, in Skokie, IL. Troy and his wife Elizabeth have four children. Daughter Nicole, BA 1991, MA 1994 BYU, teacher in the English Department at Brigham Young University. Nicole and her husband Brian Wistisen, have five children. Daughter Jessica, BS 2000 BYU, teacher and coach of high school. Jessica and her husband Travis Williams have three children . Daughter Candice, BA 2000, MPA, 2003, BYU, married to Daniel Smoot with one child.* BA, Brigham Young U., 1962; JD, UCLA, 1965. Bar: Calif. 1966, U.S. Supreme Ct. 1969. Atty., advisor CIA, Washington, 1965-70; exec. v.p., chief operating officer Mead Data Central, Inc. (now Lexis-Nexis), Washington and N.Y.C., 1970-81; assoc. Heidrick and Struggles, Inc., N.Y.C., 1982-83; pres., chief exec. officer Mirror Systems, Inc., Cambridge, Mass., 1983—93; prin. Bennett, Fisher, Giuliano and Gottsman: The Electronic Publishing Group, N.Y.C., 1993—2000. Mem.: ABA. Mem. Lds Ch. Personal E-mail: RLBLLB@earthlink.net.

BENNETT, ROBERT R., telecommunications company executive; b. Apr. 19, 1958; BA in Econ. (with Honors), Denison U.; MBA, Columbia U. With The Bank of N.Y.; v.p., dir. fin. Telecom., Inc., 1987-90; prin. fin. officer Liberty Media Corp., Englewood, Colo., 1990, exec. v.p., CFO, exec. v.p., sec. & treas., 1995—97, CFO, 1996—97, CEO, 1997—2005, pres., 1997—, also bd. dirs., mem. exec. com., 1994—. Bd. dirs. OpenTV Corp., UnitedGlobalCom, Inc., Ascent Media Group, Inc., Liberty Satellite & Technology, Inc., IAC/Interactive Corp., 2001—04, Starz Encore Group. Office: Liberty Media Corp 12300 Liberty Blvd Englewood CO 80112-7009

BENNETT, ROBERT ROYCE, engineering and management consultant; b. Spokane, Wash., May 7, 1926; s. Fred Alonzo and Rebecca Jane (Sommerville) B.; m. Margaret Stewart Keyes, Aug. 20, 1950; children: Susan Bennett Olson Nelson, Philip K., Laurie B. Mapes. BS, Calif. Inst. Tech., 1945, MS, 1947, PhD, 1949. Registered profl. engr., Oreg.; lic. surveyor, Oreg. Mem. tech. staff Hughes Aircraft, Culver City, Calif., 1949-54; v.p. TRW Systems, Redondo Beach, Calif., 1954-65; engring. mgmt. cons. Eugene, Oreg., 1965—. Contbr. articles to profl. jours.; patentee in field. Served to lt. (j.g.) USNR, 1944-54. Fellow IEEE. Republican. Presbyterian. Home and Office: 85334 S Willamette St Eugene OR 97405-9568 Business E-Mail: bennett500@prodigy.net.

BENNETT, ROBERT STEPHEN, lawyer; b. Bklyn., Aug. 2, 1939; s. F. Robert and Nancy (Walsh) Bennett; m. Ellen C. Bennett, Sept. 20, 1969; children: Catherine, Peggy, Sarah. BA, Georgetown U., 1961; LLB, Georgetown Law Ctr., 1964; post grad., U. Va. Law Sch., 1961—62; LLM, Harvard U. Law Sch., 1965. Bar: Va. 1964, DC 1965, US Supreme Ct. 1969, Mont. Law clk. to Hon. Howard F. Corcoran US Dist. Ct., DC, 1965—67; asst. US atty. Washington, 1967—70; assoc. Hogan & Hartson, Washington, 1970—75; adj. prof. George Washington U., 1975—79; spl. counsel DC Commn. on Jud. Disabilities and Tenure, 1976—82; former ptnr. Dunnells, Duvall, Bennett & Porter, Washington; legal cons. Senate Fgn. Rels. Com., 1981, 1982; spl. counsel US Senate Select Com. on Ethics, 1981—82; ptnr., civil and criminal enforcement matters and complex civil litigation, white collar crimes Skadden, Arps, Slate Meagher & Flom, LLP, Washington. Written and lectured on complex criminal and civil matters; judge Court of Arbitration for Sport. Contbr. articles to publs. Named one of 75 Best Lawyers in Washington, Washingtonian survey mag.; fellow Am. Coll. Trial Lawyers. Fellow: Am. Coll. Trial Lawyers; mem.: Def. Rsch. Inst., Va. Trial Lawyers Assn., DC Bar Assn., Va. State Bar, ABA (co-chmn. several ABA Nat. Inst. programs). Home: 1840 24th St NW Washington DC 20008-4024 Office: Skadden Arps Slate Meagher & Flom LLP 1440 New York Ave NW Ste 600 Washington DC 20005 Office Phone: 202-371-7180. Office Fax: 202-661-8205. Business E-Mail: rbennett@skadden.com.

BENNETT, ROBERT THOMAS, lawyer, accountant; b. Columbus, Ohio, Feb. 8, 1939; s. Francis Edmund and Mary Catherine (Weiland) B.; B.S., Ohio State U., 1960; J.D., Cleve. Marshall Law Sch., 1967; m. Ruth Ann Dooley, May 30, 1959; children— Robert Thomas, Rose Marie. Admitted to Ohio bar, 1967; C.P.A., Ernst and Ernst, Cleve., 1960-63; with tax assessing dept. Cuyahoga County (Ohio) Auditor's Office, Cleve., 1963-70; mem. firm Bartunek, Bennett, Garofoli and Hill, Cleve., 1975-79; mem. firm Bennett & Klonowski, Cleve., 1979-83; mem. firm Bennett & Harbarger, Cleve., 1983-88. Exec. vice chmn. Cuyahoga County Rep. Orgn., 1974-88; state chmn. Ohio Rep. Orgn., 1988—; mem. Rep. Nat. Com., 1988—; bd. dirs. Univ. Hosp. of Cleve. and S.W. Gen. Health Ctr. Republican. Roman Catholic. Mem. Citizens League Club, Capitol Hill Club (Washington). Contbr. articles to profl. publs. Home: 4800 Valley Pky Cleveland OH 44126-2847 Office: Ohio Rep Party 211 S 5th St Columbus OH 43215-5203

BENNETT, ROBERT WILLIAM, law educator; b. Chgo., Mar. 30, 1941; s. Lewis and Henrietta (Schneider) Bennett; m. Harriet Trop, Aug. 19, 1979. BA, Harvard U., 1962, LLB, 1965. Bar: Ill. 1966. Legal asst. FCC commr. Nicholas Johnson, 1966-67; atty. Chgo. Legal Aid Bur., 1967-68; asso. firm Mayer, Brown & Platt, Chgo., 1968-69; faculty Northwestern U. Sch. Law, Chgo., 1969—, prof. law, 1974—, dean, 1985-95, Nathaniel L. Nathanson prof., 2002—. Author (with LaFrance, Schroeder and Boyd): (book) Handbook on Law of the Poor, 1973; author: Talking it Through: Puzzles of American Democracy, 2003. Knox Meml. fellow, London Sch. Econs., 1965—66. Fellow: Am. Bar Found. (pres., bd. dirs.); mem.: ABA, Am. Law Inst., Chgo. Coun. Lawyers (pres. 1971—72). Home: 2130 N Racine Ave Chicago IL 60614-4002 Office: Northwestern U Sch Law 357 E Chicago Ave Chicago IL 60611-3059 Office Fax: 312-503-5950. E-mail: r-bennett@law.northwestern.edu.*

BENNETT, RODNEY DEE, music educator; b. Wichita Falls, Tex., Mar. 7, 1958; s. Vernon Clifton and Beulah Lee (Johnson) B.; m. Marilyn K. Spencer, Aug. 15, 1980; 1 child, Ronald David. MusB, B of Music Edn., Midwestern State U., 1982; MusM, Ea. N.Mex. U., 1998. All-level music cert., Tex. Field musician USMC, Camp Pendleton, Calif., 1976-78; equipment mgr. Midwestern State Univ. Band, Wichita Falls, Tex., 1978-82; dir. bands Munday (Tex.) Ind. Sch. Dist., 1983—. Pvt. music tchr., Wichita Falls, 1980—; music adjudicator Tex. Music Adjudication Assn., Pleasanton, Tex., 1991—. Named Citizen of Yr., Munday C. of C., 1993. Mem. Assn. Tex. Small Sch. Bands, Tex. Music Educators Assn. (region II band chmn. 1994—, Leadership and Achievement award 1994, 2000, Honor Condr.-Honor Band 1994, 2000), Nat. Band Assn. (Citation of Excellence 1993, 2000), Am. Sch. Band Dirs. Assn., Phi Beta Mu. Baptist. Avocations: photography, model trains, railroad history. Home: PO Box 776 Munday TX 76371-0776 Office: Munday Ind Sch Dist PO Box 300 Munday TX 76371-0300

BENNETT, RONALD THOMAS, photojournalist, federal official; b. Portland, Oreg., Nov. 6, 1944; s. E.E. Al and Donna Mae Bennett; m. Michelle Bennett; 6 children. Student, Portland State U., 1964-67; student in photojournalism, U. Wash., 1965; student pre-law and bus. mgmt, Multnomah Coll., Portland, 1963—64; BA. Lab. technician, photographer Sta. KATU-TV, Portland, 1963-65; staff photographer Oreg. Jour., Portland, 1965-68, UPI Newspictures, L.A., 1968-70; staff photojournalist UPI at White House, 1970-88; sr. photo editor The San Diego Union, 1988-89; owner, CEO Capital TV, La Jolla, Calif., 1989-97; graphic artist, illustrator, 1997—. Internat. launch svcs. mission integrator, 1997-99; instr. photojournalism Portland State U., 1967; mem. standing com. U.S. Senate Press Photographers Gallery, 1980-89, sec.-treas.; CEO, Ronald T. Bennett Photography Frameable Original Photos & Note Cards, 1995—; dir. photography HUD, Washington, 1999—. Photographer: Assassination, 1968; one-man show Lake Oswego, Oreg., 1979; group exhbns. Libr. of Congress, 1971-89; exhibited in juried art shows in Calif. and Ariz., show photography, Offtrack Gall. Mem. coun. Town of La Jolla, Calif., Assic, Vol. Buyers, chmn. Brown Goods. Recipient 1st prize World Press Photo Assn., 1969, Calif. Press Photographers, 1968, 69, Gold Seal competition, 1968, 69; nominated for Pulitzer prize, 1968, 76, 77, 78, first prize, Internatl. Exhibition of Photography, 1996-99. Mem. White House News Photographers (bd. dirs. photo exhbn. com. 1974-78, 1st prize 1976, 77, 78, 80, 84, 86, 87), Nat. Headliner Club (1st prize 1969, 78), Nat. Press Photographers Assn. (1st prize 1972), San Diego Art Guild and Colo. Art Assn., Calif. Press Photographers Assn., Rotary (staff photographer La Jolla chpt., Achievement award Am. Project 1992, 93), German Shepherd Dog Club.

BENNETT, SAUL, public relations agency executive; b. N.Y.C., Oct. 21, 1936; s. Philip and Ruth (Weinstein) Ostrove; m. Joan Marian Abrahams, Aug. 15, 1965; children: Sara (dec.), Charles, Elizabeth. BS in Journalism, Ohio U., Athens, 1957. Engaged in pub. rels., 1963—; from acct. supr. to v.p. Rowland Co., N.Y.C., 1965—74; from v.p. to sr. v.p. Robert Marston and Assocs., N.Y.C., 1974—78, exec. v.p., 1978—86, ptnr., 1979—, sr. exec. v.p., 1986—; pres. Robert Marston Mktg. Communications Inc., 1996—. Cons. in field. Author: (poems) New Fields and Other Stones, Jesus Matinees and Other Poems, 1998, Harpo Marx at Prayer, 2000. With USAR, 1958-59, 61-62. Mem. Pen Am. Ctr. E-mail: saulben@aol.com.

BENNETT, SCOTT BOYCE, retired librarian, consultant; b. Kansas City, Kans., July 22, 1939; s. Preston Theodore Bennett and Viola Louise (Scott) Mayberry; m. Carol Jean Glass, June 20, 1960; children: Beth Louise, Theodore David, Myron Richard, Kristellen Anne. AB magna cum laude, Oberlin Coll., 1960; MA in English, Ind. U., 1966, PhD in English, 1967; MS in Libr. Sci., U. Ill., 1976. Woodrow Wilson teaching intern St. Paul's Coll., Lawrenceville, Va., 1964-65; asst. prof. English U. Ill., Urbana-Champaign, 1967-74, from instr. to asst. prof. to assoc. prof. libr. adminstrn., 1974-81; asst. libr. collection mgmt. Northwestern U., Evanston, Ill., 1981-89; dir. Milton S. Eisenhower Libr. Johns Hopkins U., Balt., 1989-94; univ. libr. Yale U., New Haven, 1994-2001; project worker Coun. Ind. Colls. and Coun. on Libr. and Info. Resources, 2001—. Contbr. articles to profl. jours. Adv. panel library and archival preservation Ill. State Libr., adv. bd. Ill. State Archives; rev. panelist NEH; chair project Rsch. Librs. Group; prin. state-wide preservation planning Md. Woodrow Wilson Nat. fellow 1960-61, Ind. U. Dissertation Yr. fellow, Haskell fellow, 1966-67, U. Ill. Faculty fellow, 1969, Hon. Vis. Rsch. fellow Victorian Studies Ctr. U. Leicester, Eng., 1979, Am. Coun. Learned Socs. fellow, 1978-79. Mem. AAUP (pres., sec. Urbana-Champaign chpt. 1975-78, various other offices), Rsch. Soc. Victorian Periodicals (exec. bd. 1971-73, pres. 1977-82). Address: 711 S Race Urbana IL 61801-4132

BENNETT, SCOTT LAWRENCE, lawyer; b. N.Y.C., July 8, 1949; s. Allen J. and Rhoda Bennett. BA with high distinction, U. Mich., 1971; JD, Cornell U., 1974. Bar: NY 1975, U.S. Ct. Appeals (2d cir.) 1975, U.S. Dist. Ct. (so. and ea. dists.) N.Y. 1975, U.S. Supreme Ct. 1976. Assoc. Donovan, Leisure, Newton & Irvine, N.Y.C., 1974—79; sr. v.p., assoc. gen. counsel, sec. The McGraw-Hill Cos., Inc., N.Y.C., 1979—. Mem.: ABA, Assn. Am. Pubs. (lawyers com.), Assn. Bar City N.Y., N.Y. State Bar Assn., Phi Beta Kappa. Office: The McGraw Hill Co Inc Fl 48 1221 Avenue Of Americas New York NY 10020-1095 Business E-Mail: Scott_Bennett@Mcgraw-Hill.com.

BENNETT, SHARON KAY, music educator; b. West Jefferson, Ohio; BMus, Eastman Sch. Music, 1960, MMus, 1962. Asst. prof. U. Iowa, Iowa City, 1980-84; from asst. prof. to prof. Capital U., Columbus, Ohio, 1992—. Adj. lectr. Otterbein Coll., Westerville, Ohio, 1986-87, Capital U., 1985-92; resident colaratura Nurnberg (Germany) Opera, 1970-73, Hamburg (Germany) State Opera, 1973-76; resident guest artist Scottish Opera, Glasgow, 1976-77; presenter symposium. Author: 40 Vocalises, 1993, Class Voice Simplified, 1994. Recipient 1st place Iowa Symphony competition, 1981; named to Women of Achievement, YWCA, 1986; Rockefeller Found. grantee, N.Y.C., 1966-68; Old Gold fellow U. Iowa, Iowa City, N.Y. and Paris; Capital U. faculty devel. grantee, 1995. Mem.: Music Tchrs. Nat. Assn. (nat. cert.), Coll. Music Soc., Nat. Assn. Tchrs. of Singing, LWV of Met. Columbus (v.p. for voter svc.), Sigma Alpha Iota (sec. 1985—87). Avocations: gardening, painting.

BENNETT, SHIRLEY ANN, maintenance executive, business technologist educator; b. Buffalo, Nov. 5, 1952; d. Edward Stoklosa and Florence (Ulanowski) Valin; m. Jeffrey Michael Bennett, July 3, 1975; children: Tara, Shauna, Shira, Brett, Eric. BS in Edn., SUNY Coll. at Buffalo, Buffalo, 1974; MBA, SUNY, Buffalo, 1982. Cert. tchr., N.Y. Tchr. Niagara Falls (N.Y.) Bd. Edn., 1974-75, Kensington Bus. Inst., Buffalo, 1976-80; asst. prof. SUNY, Buffalo, 1980—. Mem. Epsilon Delta Epsilon, Iota Lambda Sigma (Alpha Lambda chpt.). Home: 76 Alran Dr Williamsville NY 14221-1409 Office: SUNY at Buffalo EOC 465 Washington St Buffalo NY 14203-1707

BENNETT, STEPHEN M., computer company executive; b. Madison, Wis., Mar. 8, 1954; BA in Fin. and Real Estate, U. Wis., 1976. Various mgmt. positions GE Appliances, GE Med. and GE Supply; v.p. of Ams. GE Elec. Distbn. and Control; pres., CEO Vendor Fin. Svcs., GE Capital e-Business; exec. v.p., CEO GE Capital subsidiary of GE Corp.; CEO, pres. Intuit, 2000—. Office: Intuit Inc 2535 Garcia Ave Mountain View CA 94043-1111*

BENNETT, STEVEN ALAN, lawyer; b. Rock Island, Ill., Jan. 15, 1953; s. Ralph O. and Anne E. B.; m. Jeanne Aring; children: Preston, Spencer, Hunter, Whitney. BA in Art History, U. Notre Dame, 1975; JD, U. Kans., 1982. Bar: Tex. 1983, Ohio 1995, U.S. Dist. Ct. (no. dist.) Tex. 1983, U.S. Ct. Appeals (5th cir.) 1983, U.S. Supreme Ct. 1995. Atty. Freytag, Marshall et al, Dallas, 1982-84, Baker, Mills & Glast, Dallas, 1984-87; ptnr. Shank, Irwin, Conant et al, Dallas, 1987-89; sr. v.p., gen. counsel Bank One, Tex., N.A., Dallas, 1989-94; sr. v.p., gen. counsel, sec. Banc One Corp., Columbus, Ohio, 1994-99; exec. v.p., chief legal officer, sec. Cardinal Health, Inc., Dublin, Ohio, 1999-2001; pvt. practice Columbus, 2001—03; sr. v.p., gen. counsel USAA Fed. Savs. Bank, San Antonio, 2003—04; exec. v.p. USAA, San Antonio, 2004—, gen. coun., 2004, sec., 2004. City councilman, Mesquite, Tex., 1984-86, mayor pro tem, 1985; trustee Meadowview Sch., Mesquite, 1985-92; chair fin. com. St. Brendan Ch., Hilliard, Ohio, 1998-2003; pres., bd. dirs. Dallas Dem. Forum, 1993-94; bd. dirs. Ohio Hunger Task Force, Columbus; trustee Woodrow Wilson Internat. Ctr. for Scholars, Washington, 1996-2002, vice-chmn., 1999-2002; bd. dirs. Capital U. Law Sch., Columbus, 1998-2003, Ctr. for Thomas More Studies, Dallas; mem., Citizens Commn. for City-County Svc. Integration, San Antonio, 2003-. Fellow Am. Bar Found., Ohio State Bar Found.; mem. ABA, Dallas Bar Assn., Ohio State Bar Assn., Columbus Bar Assn., St. Thomas More Soc. (Dallas bd. dirs. 1990-94), Am. Corp. Counsel Assn. (sec. 1999-2000, bd. dirs. 1996-2002, chair policy com. 1997-99), Phi Beta Kappa. Avocation: landscape photography. Office: Gen Counsel C3E USAA 9800 Fredericksburg Rd San Antonio TX 78288 Office Phone: 210-498-1888. Personal E-mail: sabennett@satx.rr.com.

BENNETT, THOMAS, orchestra executive; Exec. dir. S.D. Symphony Orch., Sioux Falls, 1996—. Bd. mem. Am. Symphony Orchestra League. Office: SD Symphony Orchestra Ste 116 300 N Dakota Ave Sioux Falls SD 57104-6020 E-mail: tombennett@sdsymphony.org.

BENNETT, THOMAS B., federal judge; b. Phila., Jan. 6, 1949; BS, W.Va. U., 1970, MA, 1973, JD, 1976. Bar: W. Va., 1976, Tex., 1979. Instr. econs. W.Va. U., 1971-76; law clk. hon. John R. Brown U.S. Ct. Appeals 5th Cir., 1976-77; assoc. Bowles, Rice, McDavid, Graff & Love, 1977-79, ptnr., 1980-95; judge US Bankruptcy Ct. for Northern Dist. of Alabama, Birmingham, 1995—. Office: 1800 5th Ave N Rm 128 Birmingham AL 35203-2111 Office Phone: 205-714-3880. Office Fax: 205-714-3882.

BENNETT, THOMAS LEROY, JR., clinical neuropsychology educator; b. Norwalk, Conn., Sept. 25, 1942; s. Thomas LeRoy and Gertrude Upson (Richardson) B.; m. Jacqueline Beekman, Aug. 5, 1972; children: Dean, Shannon, Brian, Laurie. BA, U. N. Mex., 1964, MS, 1966, PhD, 1968. Diplomate Am. Bd. Profl. Neuropsychology (examiner, treas. 1993-96, 2001--, pres.-elect 1995-97, pres. 1997-99), Am. Bd. Forensic Examiners, Am. Bd. Profl. Disability Cons., Am. Bd. Profl. Psychology. Asst. prof. Calif. State U., Sacramento, 1968-70; assoc. prof., then prof. psychology and physiology Colo. State U., Ft. Collins, 1970-98, coord. exptl. psychology sect., 1978-81, 92-95, prof. emeritus, 1998—; pvt. practice neuropsychology Ft. Collins, 1981—. Mem. allied health staff Poudre Valley Hosp., Ft. Collins; clin. dir. Ctr. for Neurorehab. Svcs., Ft. Collins. Author: Brain and Behavior, 1977, The Sensory World, 1978, The Psychology of Learning and Memory, 1979, Exploring the Sensory World, 1979, Introduction to Physiological Psychology, 1982, The Neuropsychology of Epilepsy, 1992, Brainwave-R: Cognitive Strategies for Brain Injury Rehabilitation, 1997, Mild Traumatic Brain Injury, 1999, Psychology Video Teaching Modules: The Brain, 2d edit., 1997, Psychology Video Teaching Modules: The Mind, 2000; also articles and book chpts.; assoc. editor Rehab. Psychology, Archives of Clinical Neuropsychology; mem. editl. bd. Cognitive Rehab., Archives Clin. Neuropsychology, Jour. Head Injury, Bull. of Nat. Acad. Neuropsychology, Neuropsychology Rev., others. Elder Timnath Presbyterian Ch. Named Outstanding Grad. Educator for Coll. Natural Scis., 1998. Fellow APA, Nat. Acad. Neuropsychology (editl. bd. Bull., bd. dirs. 1993-95, conv. chmn. 1993, 94), Am. Psychol. Soc., Am. Coll. Profl. Neuropsychology (pres. 1997-99); mem. Am. Coll. Forensic Examiners, Psychonomic Soc., Rocky Mountain Psychol. Assn., Soc. for Cognitive Rehab., Nat. Head Injury Found. (provider's coun.), Colo. Head Injury Found. (provder's coun.), Internat. Neuropsychol. Soc., Colo. Neuropsychol. Soc., Sigma Xi (named Colo. State U. Honored Scientist 1996). Home: 213 Camino Real Fort Collins CO 80524-8907 Office: Colo State U Dept Psychology Fort Collins CO 80523-0001 Office Phone: 970-493-6667. *Always look for something good in everyone you meet.*

BENNETT, TONY (ANTHONY DOMINICK BENEDETTO), entertainer; b. Astoria, N.Y., Aug. 3, 1926; s. John and Anna (Suraci) Benedetto; m. Patricia Beech, Feb. 12, 1952 (div. 1971); children: D'Andrea, Daegal; m. Sandra Grant, Dec. 29, 1971 (div. 1984); children: Joanna, Antonia. Ed., Am. Theatre Wing, N.Y.C.; MusD, U. Berkeley. Ofcl. artist Ky. Derby, 2001. Classic pop vocalist, entertainer (frequent appearances on TV, in concert); singer: (albums) Treasure Chest of Songs, 1955, Tony, 1957, Count Basie Swings, Tony Bennett Sings, 1958, Blue Velvet, 1959, To My Wonderful One, 1960, Bennett and Basie Strike Up the Band, 1961, I Left My Heart in San Francisco, 1963 (Grammy award album of the year, 1962), I Wanna Be Around, 1963, Love Story, 1971, Summer of '42, 1972, Sunrise, Sunset, 1973, 16 Most Requested Songs, 1986, The Art of Excellence, 1986, Bennett/Berlin, 1987, The Movie Song Album, 1989, Astoria, 1990, Forty Years: The Artistry of Tony Bennett, 1991, Perfectly Frank, 1992 (Grammy award best traditional vocal performance, 1992), Steppin' Out, 1993 (Grammy award, Best Traditional Pop Vocal, 1993), The Essence of Tony Bennett, 1993, In Person! With Count Basie and His Orchestra, 1994, MTV Unplugged, 1994 (Grammy award Album of the Year, Best Traditional Pop Vocal), Here's to the Ladies, 1995, Tony Bennett on Holiday, 1997, Tribute to Billie Holiday, Bennett Sings Ellington-Hot and Cool, 1999, The Ultimate Tony, 2000, Playin' With My Friends: Bennett Sings The Blues, 2001 (Grammy award best traditional pop vocal album, 2003), The Essential Tony Bennett, 2002, A Wonderful World, 2002; owner, rec. artist Improv Records; exhibitions include Butler Inst. of Am. Art, Youngstown, Ohio, 1994, Nat. Arts Club, N.Y.C.; appeared in: The Scout, 1994; appeared in (TV films) Men, Movies & Carol, 1994, The Scout, 1994, Sinatra: 80 Years My Way, 1995, (TV series) The Simpsons, 1989, Muppets Tonight, 1996, (TV spl.) Tony Bennett on Holiday: A Tribute to Billy Holiday, 1997, Analyze This, 1999, TV guest appearances The Andy Williams Show, 1966, The Jackie Gleason Show, 1969, Space Ghost Coast to Coast, 1994, Suddenly Susan, 1997; author: The Good Life: The Autobiography of Tony Bennett. Served with inf. AUS, World War II. Named to Star on Hollywood Walk of Fame; recipient Gold records for recs., Because of You, I Left My Heart in San Francisco, Best Male Vocalist award, Cash Box mag., 1951, Grammy lifetime achievement award, Salute to Greatness award Martin Luther King Ctr., Atlanta.*

BENNETT, TYRONE LAMONT, engineer, director; b. Charleston, S.C., Nov. 11, 1963; s. Janie A. Bennett-Fortune and Melvin Bennett, Everett Fortune (Stepfather); m. Gloria J. Brown, Apr. 22, 2000. B of Tech., SUNY, Utica, 1988; MS, SUNY, Stony Brook, 1997. Cert. soil mechanic NY State Dept. Transp., 1987. Asst. engr. Bklyn. Union Gas Co., 1989—90; gas turbine elec. systems, engr. Dept. Def., Navy, Norfolk, Va., 1990—93; sales engr. Quentzel Plumbing Supplies, Inc., Bklyn., 1995—98; rsch. engr. Stony Brook Univ.-Ctr. for Thermal Spray Rsch., NY, 1996—; infrastructure technologist Ctr. for Thermal Spray Rsch., Stony Brook, NY, 1999—; asst. dir., sci. & tech. entry programs Stony Brook U., Dept. Tech. and Soc., NY, 2000—. Pres., Model Student Clubs of Am. Better World JL Inst., Bklyn., 1984—90, jr.

goodwill amb., 1984—91; bd. dirs. U. Transp. Rsch. Ctr., CUNY, Manhattan, 1998—; L.I. rep. for sci. and tech. confs. LISTEP Conf. Com., Stony Brook, NY, 2000—; exec. com. Assn. for Program Adminstr. of Collegiate Sci., Inc., Bronx, 2001—; faculty mem. Nat. Sci. Found., Math, Sci., and Tech. Partnership+, 2003—08; chmn. transportation adv. com. Stony Brook U., 2003—. Author: (novels) The Eyes of Mephistopheles, The Bible is Still the Number One Best Seller; prodr.: (outreach exhibition) Opportunities in Thermal Spray Technology (Presdl. mini grant, 1999). Sci. judge N.Y. Acad. Sci., Queens, 1986—90; youth min. Bethel Temple COGIC, Far Rockaway, NY, 1980—94; ordained rev. and evangelist Universal Ch. of God, Bklyn., 1983—89. Recipient award, N.Y. Acad. Sci., 1990. Mem.: ASME (assoc. Student Competition award 1986), Robotics Internat. (corr.), Metall. Soc. of ASM (assoc.). Democrat. Achievements include design of Speed boat propeller for sonic speeds; first to Role Model for underrepresented minorities at the local, state and national levels in higher education and secondary schools; development of first lecture course of transportation at the State of New York at Stony Brook; Liason between New York State Department of Transportation and Stony Brook University's Center for Thermal Spray Research and the Department of Technology & Society; first to Certified Lobbyist for Stony Brook University and represents SBU at the Science Coalition in Washington, D.C; Black Man of Distinction and recipient of the New York Senate award 1999; research in in corrosion prevention and infrastructure technology; annual coordinator of transportation in the 21st Century Symposium. Avocations: travel, writing, sports, dining, thinking. Office: Stony Brook Univ 358 Harriman Hall Stony Brook NY 11794-3760 Office Phone: 631-632-3205. Personal E-mail: thaderx@aol.com. Business E-Mail: tyrone.bennett@stonybrook.edu.

BENNETT, VELMA JEAN, elementary school educator; b. Jacksonville, Fla., Sept. 29, 1942; d. William Bud Baily, Daniel (stepfather) and Dessie Mae (Coleman) Ray; m. Warren Carlton Bennett, May 2, 1958 (div. Apr. 1968); children: Arlene, Beverly, Carla, Doreen Bennett-Samuel, Eric, Rodney. Student, Boston State Coll., U. Mass., Boston, 1976-82, Am. Inst. for Fgn. Study, Kenya, 1980; MEd, Cambridge Coll., 1983; postgrad., Emmanuel Coll., Mass., 1995, Harvard U., 1995-96; MA of Edn. in Sch. Adminstrn., Emmanuel Coll., 2004. Tchr. middle grades St. James Ednl. Ctr., Boston, 1971-76; student tchr. William Monroe Trotter Sch., Boston, 1981; tchr. Crispus Attucks Children's Ctr., Roxbury, Mass., 1981-83; head tchr. Ellen Jackson Children's Ctr., Boston, 1983-84; tchr. grade 1 Franklin Delano Roosevelt Sch., Hyde Park, Mass., 1984-85; tchr. Henry Grew Sch., Hyde Park, 1985-87; tchr. grade 1 Ralph Waldo Emerson Sch., Roxbury, 1987-88; tchr. Hamilton Elem. Sch., Brighton, Mass., 1988-93. Chairperson, mem. parent involvement Boston Pub. Schs., 1993-97, sch. based union rep., 1994-95, sec. healthy kids program, 1994-96, faculty senate acting sec., 1996-97. Author of poetry. Active Shaklee, Roxbury, Mass., 1989-96, Peoples Bapt. Ch., Boston, 1990. Mem. Internat. Women's Writing Guild, Acad. Am. Poets, Internat. Soc. Poetry. Democrat. Baptist. Avocations: sign making, decorating, writing, grandchildren. Personal E-mail: vjbaneba@netscape.net.

BENNETT, VIRGINIA COOK, music educator, consultant; d. Leland LeRoy and Janet Roberts Cook; m. Edward James Bennett, Jan. 30, 1965; children: Susan Elizabeth, Edward James. MusB in Edn., Drake U., 1965, MusM. in Edn., 1978; PhD, U. Iowa, 1991. Instr. music and choirs Cedar Rapids (Iowa) Schs., 1965—66; instr. Newton (Iowa) Cmty. Schs., 1967—68, instr. elem. music, 1974—79; lectr. music edn. Drake U., Des Moines, 1979—80; chair music dept. and choir dir. Des Moines Area C.C., Ankeny, Iowa, 1984—97; assoc. prof. and chair, music edn. area Drake U., Des Moines, 1997—. Cons., curriculum and assessment various sch. dists., Iowa, 1998—; clinician Nebr. Music Educators State Conf., Lincoln, 2000, Ohio Music Educators State Conf., Cinn., 2000, Wis. Music Educators State Conf., Madison, 2001, N.D. Music Educators State Conf., Fargo, 2001, Minn. Music Educators State Conf., Mpls., 2001, Mich. Music Educators Ann. Conf., Ann Arbor, 2002, S.D. Music Educators Ann. Conf., Brookings, 2002, National Assn. For Music Edn. Nat. Conf., Nashville, 2002—, Mountain Lake (Va.) Symposiam on Tchg. Music Methods, Mountain Lake, Va., 2003. Contbr. articles to profl. jours. Mem. Governors Adv. Com. on Intergovernmental Affairs, Iowa, 1985—87; founding bd. mem. Newton Cmty. Edn. Found., Iowa, 1986—91; co-chair c.c. campaign United Way, Ankeny, Iowa, 1993—97; v.p. Newton Cmty. Schools Bd. Edn., Iowa, 1984, mem., 1984—91, pres., 1985—86. Mem.: Music Educators Nat. Conf., Iowa Alliance Arts Edn., Iowa Choral Dirs. Assn., Am. Choral Dirs. Assn., Iowa Music Educators Assn. (pres. 1996—98, Disting. Svc. Award 2001), Nat. Assn. Music Edn. (north ctrl. divsn. pres., nat. exec. bd. mem. 2000—02), Pi Kappa Lambda, Kappa Alpha Theta, Mu Phi Epsilon. Methodist. Avocations: reading, travel. Home: 203 Foster Dr Des Moines IA 50312 Office: Drake University 25th and University Des Moines IA 50311 Office Phone: 515-271-2823. Personal E-mail: vandjbenn@aol.com. E-mail: virginia.bennett@drake.edu.

BENNETT, WILLIAM MICHAEL, internist, educator, nephrologist; b. Chgo., May 6, 1938; s. Harry H. and Helen A. (Kaplan) B.; m. Sandra S. Silen, June 12, 1977; four children. Student, U. Mich., 1956-59; BS, Northwestern U., 1960, MD, 1963. Diplomate Am. Bd. Internal Medicine, Am. Bd. Nephrology, Am. Bd. Clin. Pharmacology. Intern U. Oreg., 1963-64; resident Northwestern U., 1964-66; practice medicine specializing in internal medicine Portland, Oreg. and; Boston; mem. staff Mass. Gen. Hosp., 1969-70; asst. prof. medicine U. Oreg. Health Scis. Center, 1970-74, asso. prof., 1974-78, prof. medicine and pharmacology, 1978-2000, ret., 2000. Author: Pharmacology and Management of Hypertension, 1994, Manual of Nephrology, 1990, Drug Therapy in Renal Failure, 1994; contbr. articles to med. jours. Served with USAF, 1967-69. Master ACP; mem. Am. Soc. Nephrology (pres. 1998-99), Transplantation Soc., Internat. Soc. Nephrology, Am. Soc. Pharmacology and Exptl. Therapeutics. Office: Legacy Good Samaritan Hosp Transplant Svcs 1040 NW 22d Ave Ste 480 Portland OR 97210 also: NW Renal Clinic 1130 NW 22d St Ste 640 Portland OR 97210 Office Phone: 503-413-6555. E-mail: bennettw@lhs.org.

BENNETT, WILLIAM RALPH, JR., physicist, researcher; b. Jersey City, Jan. 30, 1930; s. William Ralph and Viola (Schreiber) B.; m. Frances Commins, Dec. 11, 1952; children: Jean, William Robert, Nancy. AB, Princeton U., 1951; MA, PhD, Columbia U., 1957; MA (hon.), Yale U., 1965; D.Sc. (hon.), U. New Haven, 1975. Rsch. asst. physics Columbia Radiation Lab., 1952-54; mem. Pupin Cyclotron Group, 1954-57; mem. faculty Yale U., New Haven, 1957-59, 62—, prof. physics and applied sci., 1965-72, Charles Baldwin Sawyer prof. engrng. and applied sci., prof. physics, 1972-98, prof. emeritus, 1998—, fellow Berkeley Coll., 1963-81, master Silliman Coll., 1981-87, life fellow Silliman Coll., 1981—. Tech. staff Bell Telephone Labs., Murray Hill, NJ, 1959—62; cons. Tech. Rsch. Group, Melville, NY, 1962—67, Inst. Def. Analysis, Washington, 1963—70; vis. scientist Am. Inst. Physics Vis. Scientist Program, 1963—64; vis. prof. Brandeis Summer Inst. Theoretical Physics, 1969; cons. mem. bd. dirs. Laser Scis. Corp., Bethel, Conn., 1968—71; mem. adv. panels atomic physics and astrophysics Nat. Bur. Stds., 1964—69; cons. CBS Labs., Stamford, Conn., 1967—68, AVCO Corp., 1978—81, Reeves Sci. Co., New Haven, 1989—91, Oak Ridge Assn. Univs., Washington, 1991—92, MCG Internat., New Haven, 1992—93, Kahn Electronics, NY, 1998—2000, Premier Heart, 1999, U. Cin., 2000; mem. lab. adv. bd. for rsch. Naval Rsch. Adv. Com., 1968—78; guest Soviet Acad. Scis., 1967, 69, 79; rschr. gas lasers and atomic physics, gravitational physics, applications of computers to med. diagnostics. Author: Introduction to Computer Applications, 1976, Scientific and Engineering Problem Solving With the Computer, 1976, The Physics of Gas Lasers, 1977, Atomic Gas Laser Transition Data: A Critical Evaluation, 1979, Health and Low Frequency Electromagnetic Fields, 1994; editl. adv. bd. Jour. Quantum Electronics, 1965-69; guest editor Applied Optics, 1965. Recipient Western Electric Fund award for outstanding tchg. Am. Assn. Engrng. Educators, 1977, Outstanding Patent award R & D Coun. N.J., 1977, Eli Whitney Patent award Conn. Patent Lawyers Assn., 1994, DeVane medal Phi Beta Kappa, 2000; fellow Alfred P. Sloan Found., 1967, Guggenheim Found., 1967, John Fenders fellow, 1987. Fellow IEEE (life, Morris Liebmann award 1965), Am. Phys. Soc., Optical Soc. Am.; mem. Sigma Xi.

BENNETT-JOHNSON, EARNESTINE ROSE, education educator, consultant; b. New Orleans, Aug. 16, 1954; d. Henry Clay and Virginia Jacobs Bennett. BA, Dillard U., 1976; MS, Grambling State U., 1994, EdD, 1999. Cert. spl. edn. Regular tchr. Orleans Parish Sch. Bd., New Orleans, 1977—82, 1989—94, external cons., 2000—01; intelligence analyst U.S. Army, 1982—89; rsch. assoc. Ednl. Rsch. Quarterly Grambling (La.) State U., 1994—99, grad. tchg. asst., 1994—99; instr. So. U. New Orleans, 2000—, U. Phoenix, Metairie, La., 2001—. Webmistress African-Ams. in La. Higher Edn., 2001—; com. mem. La. Hist. Black Coll. & Univ. Consortium, 2001—; interium NTE/Praxis coord. So. U., New Orleans, 2002—. Author: The Influence of American Crime and Violence on College Universities and Schools, 2001; contbr. articles to profl. jours. Scholar, African Ams. in La. Higher Edn., 1997. Mem.: Assn. for the Advancement Ednl. Rsch., Nat. Assn. for African-Am. Econ. Networking Devel., Kappa Delta Pi, Phi Delta Kappa. Democrat. Mem. Lds Ch. Avocations: music, writing, surfing the net. Office: So Univ New Orleans Coll Edn 6400 Press Dr New Orleans LA 70126

BENNETT MINNERLY, DENISE PATRICIA, artist, art educator; b. Cleve., Sept. 24, 1960; d. Gordon W. and Yvonne L. (Debegasa) Bennett; m. Barry H. Minnerly, May 9, 1987; children: Sarah Anne, Gillian Catherine. BS, BA cum laude, U. Vt., Burlington, 1984. Cert. tchr. K-12. Pub. rels. profl. Royal Copenhagen, N.Y., 1985-87; art tchr. Stamford (Conn.) Schs., 1987-88, After Sch. Art Program, Darien, Conn., 1988-92, Rowayton, Conn., 1988-95. Founder, dir. Rowayton Civic Assn., 1987-2003, Darien Arts Coun., 1988. Author, illustrator: (children's book) Color Tree, 1991; author: Molly Meets Mona & Friends, 1995. Vol. Women's Crisis Ctr., Norwalk, Conn., 1982—. Avocations: tennis, paddle, running, dance. Home: 183 Highland Ave Norwalk CT 06853-1109

BENNETT-WILKES, THERESA WILLIAMS, writer, educator; b. Yakima, Wash., Jan. 1, 1950; d. Everett Pendleton Williams Sr. and Blanche Madelyn Williams; m. Willie Lee Wilkes, Nov. 7; m. Frank L. Bennett, Sept. 24, 1977 (dec. Mar. 1978); 1 child, Kamilah M. Bennett. BA in Social Studies, Bennett Coll., 1972; M in Urban Planning, U. Wash., 1978. Planner San Bernardino County, San Bernardino, Calif., 1979—84; cmty. planner 63 CES, Norton AFB, Calif., 1986—88; sr. planning officer Ipswich (Eng.) Borough Coun., 1989—92; planner II zoning City of High Point, NC, 1996—97; exec. dir. Empowerment and Enterprise Devel. Corp. Bennett Coll., Greensboro, NC, 1998—99; instr., adj. prof. Guilford Tech. C.C., Jamestown, NC, 1998—2002. Cons. in field. Author: A Taste of Theresa..., 1999. Active Greensboro Housing Coalition, 1998—99, Martin Luther King Statue Com., San Bernardino, Calif., 1981, Co. Ctrl. Com., San Bernardino, Calif., 1983—84; hon. life mem. Md. Congress Parents and Tchrs., Inc., 1996—. Named Disting. Alumna, Nat. Assn. for Equal Opportunity in Higher Edn., 1984; named one of Outstanding Young Women of Am., 1979, 1982; recipient Martin Luther King Jr. award, 1968. Mem.: Royal Town Planning Inst. (chartered). Avocations: writing, reading, travel, cultural events, music. Office: Holly Tree Publ LLP PO Box 1113 High Point NC 27261

BENNETT-WILLIAMS, SHARON K., mental health services professional, writer; b. San Antonio, Tex., May 3, 1957; d. L.E. and Essie Lee Bennett; m. Burnett M. Williams, May 31, 1996; m. Howard L. Perkins, Mar. 11, 1981 (div. Sept. 1, 1984); children: Jerrick L. Perkins, Sharena L. Perkins. BA, Sam Houston State U., 1979; BSN, U. Incarnate Word. Legal nurse Cons., Mid-West Gold LNC, 1998; lic. real estate agent Coldwell Banker Sch. Real Estate, 2004. Svc. rep. III USAA-Insurance, San Antonio; nurse 1 surg. unit Boone Med. Ctr., Columbia, Mo., 1997—98; nurse 1 med. surg. Dekalb Med. Ctr., Decatur, Ga., 1998—99; RN case mgr. TLC StaffBuilders, Atlanta, 1999—2003, Wellpoint-Blue Cross Blue Shield, Vinings, Ga., 2002—03, sr. RN health coach Atlanta, 2003—. RN peer group leader Blue Cross Blue Shield Ga., Atlanta, 2004. Author: (novels) The L.E. Bennett Story: Living the Dream, 2001; co-author Shoe Fetish: A Woman's Odyssey of Love for Her Men, 2002; author: (poem) I Never Dreamed (Editor's Choice award, 2001). Vol. Childrens Miracle Network, San Antonio, 1986—94, Spl. Olympics, 1986—94, Am. Cancer Soc., 1986—94. Avocations: painting, writing, decorating. Home: PO Box 468 Redan GA 30074 Personal E-mail: myprespective@bellsouth.net.

BENNETZEN, JEFFREY L., molecular biologist; BA in biology, U. Calif., San Diego, 1974; PhD in biochemistry, U. Wash., 1980; postdoctoral study, Wash. U., 1980—81, Stanford U., 1980—81, U. Calif., Berkeley, 1980—81. Rsch. scientist Internat. Plant Rsch. Inst., 1981—83; asst. to full prof. Purdue U., 1983—99, Umbarger prof. genetics, 1999—2003; Norman Giles Eminent Scholar chair in molecular biology and functional genetics U. Ga., 2003—. Vis. prof. U. Calif., Davis, 1998. Mem. editl. bd. Current Opinion in Plant Biology, Ency. Life Scis. Recipient McKnight Found. award, Plant Biology, 1986, Fulbright award, 1990, Faculty Rsch. award, Sigma Xi, 1995, Nehru Centenary Professorship, U. Hyderabad, 2002. Mem.: Nat. Acad. Scis. Office: U Ga C426A Life Sci Bldg Athens GA 30602 Business E-Mail: maize@uga.edu.

BENNEY, DOUGLAS MABLEY, direct marketing executive, consultant; b. Cold Spring Harbor, NY, Aug. 7, 1922; s. William Mabley and Wilhelmina (Walters) B.; m. Eugenia Sammis, Sept. 30, 1944 (div. Jan. 1980); children: William Douglas, Barbara Gates, Robert Scott; m. Barbara Mueller, July 8, 1983; stepchildren: Gregory Carmichael, Andrew Carmichael. Navy air cadet, U. N.C.-Chapel Hill, 1943, Cornell U., 1943; student in engrng., Purdue U., 1939-41; AB, Colgate U., 1946-49; postgrad., Columbia U., 1951-52. With Curtis Publs., Phila., 1950-63; editor, assoc. pub. Jack & Jill, 1960-63; mktg. mgr. edn. div. Doubleday & Co., N.Y.C., 1963-67; advt. and sales mgr. Hearst Book div., N.Y.C., 1967-68; v.p. creative svcs. Nat. Liberty Corp., Valley Forge, Pa., 1968-72; v.p. mktg. Gerber Life Ins. Co., N.Y.C., Pa., 1972-75; sr. mktg. officer Internat. Group Plans, Washington, Pa., 1975-78; v.p. mktg. Maxon Adminstrs., Inc., Irvington, N.Y., 1978-89; pres. A&B Advt., Inc., Springdale, Md., 1989—. Lt. (j.g.) AC, USN, 1943-46; PTO. Recipient award Artists Guild Delaware Valley, 1969, Direct Mail Mktg. Assn., 1965, Myasthenia Gravis Found., 1985, Profl. Ins. Mass Marketers Assn., 1992, 94, 96. Mem. Direct Mktg. Assn. Washington, Greater Washington Soc. Assn. Execs., Mt. Vernon Country Club (Alexandria, Va.). Achievements include patents for newspaper inserts, self-mailers. Avocations: woodworking, sailing, photography, scuba diving.

BENNIGHOF, JAMES MALCOLM, academic administrator; b. Balt., Aug. 29, 1957; s. Raymond Howard and Jane Paugh Bennighof; m. Dorene Parsons, June 30, 1979; children: Elspeth Anne, Samuel James. MusB, U. Richmond, 1979; MA, U. Iowa, 1981, PhD, 1984. From instr. to prof. Baylor U., Waco, Tex., 1984—2001, prof., 2001—, assoc. dean academic affairs sch. music, 2001—03, vice provost academic adminstrn., 2003—. Composer. Contbr. articles to profl. jours. Office: Baylor Univ Sch Music #97408 Waco TX 76798-7408 Office Phone: 254-710-6500.

BENNIN, BRUCE, physician; b. Chgo., Dec. 29, 1943; s. Morris David and Beatrice (Samuels) B.; married, 1971; children: Steve, Howard. BS, Bradley U., 1966; D in Medicine, Chgo. Med. Sch., 1971. Intern Michael Reese Hosp., Chgo., 1971-72; resident Cook County Hosp., Chgo., 1973-76, attending physician, 1976—; asst. clin. prof. U. Ill., Chgo., 1976—; dermatologist Deerfield Dermatology Assocs., Ill., 1976—99, Dermatology Ptnrs. of the North Shore, Northbrook, Ill., 1999—; asst prof. dermatology Rush Med. Ctr., 1999—. Cons. Highland Park (Ill.) Hosp., 1976—. Fellow Am. Acad. Dermatology; mem. AMA, Ill. Dermatol. Soc., Chgo. Dermatol. Soc. Office: Northbrook Dermatology Ptnrs of the North Shore 400 Skokie Blvd Northbrook IL 60062

BENNING, JOSEPH RAYMOND, principal; b. Streator, Ill., May 23, 1956; s. Joseph Charles and Shirley Ann (Smith) B.; m. Katherine Marie Turner, Apr. 24, 1976; children: Jennifer Nichole, Joseph Donald. BA, Augustana Coll, 1978; MS in Edn., No. Ill. U., 1988. Cert. state supr., teaching, Ill. Tchr., coach Fulton (Ill.) High Sch., 1978—79; recreation dir. Fulton Recreation Corp., 1979; tchr., coach Streator (Ill.) High Sch., 1979—80, Woodland High Sch., Streator, 1980—83; program dir. Ill. State Bd. Edn., Ottawa, 1983—85; prin. St. Mary Grade Sch., Streator, 1985—89; assoc. supt. schs. Cath. Diocese Peoria, Ill., 1989—91, supt. schs., 1991—94; prin. St. Bede Acad., Peru, Ill., 1994—99, St. Columba Sch., Ottawa, Ill., 1999—2005, Sacred Heart Sch., Lombard, Ill., 2005—. Pres. Streator Youth Football League, 1984-90; adv. bd. Streator High Sch., 1985-89; prins. adv. bd. Cath. Diocese Peoria, 1987-89. Recipient CJ McDonald award Streator Youth Football League, 1989. Mem. ASCD, Nat. Cath. Edn. Assn., Nat. Assn. Secondary Sch. Prin., Nat. Assn. Elem. Sch. Prin., Ill. Elem. Sch. Assn., Cath. Conf. Ill., KC. Roman Catholic. Avocations: sports, music. Office: Sacred Heart Sch 322 W Maple Lombard IL 60148 Office Phone: 630-629-0536. E-mail: benningjr@hotmail.com.

BENNING, MARY ETZOLD, interior designer; b. El Paso, Tex., Mar. 8, 1957; d. David Enberg and Mary (Francis) Etzold; m. George Henry Benning III, Nov. 2, 1985; children: Mary Francis, Lucy Alexander. AA, Stephens Coll., 1977, BFA, 1979. Lic. interior designer Tex. Designer Bus. Products & Svcs., Inc., El Paso, 1979-80; display designer Popular Dept. Store, El Paso, 1980-83; residential designer Reinharts Fine Furniture, El Paso, 1983-85; comml. designer Flooring Systems, Inc., El Paso, 1985-86, Charlotte's Comml. Interiors, El Paso, 1986-88; comml. interior designer N.Mex. State U., Las Cruces, 1988-94, Henry Benning Assocs., Inc., El Paso, 1994—2005. Cons. Cinch This Textile Designs, 2003—. Bd. dirs. Epilepsy El Paso, 1987-90. Mem.: AIA, Tex. Assn. Interior Designers, Am. Soc. Interior Designers, Pan Am. Soc. Am., El Paso Symphony Guild, Jr. League El Paso, Magna Carta Dames Am. (life), Colonial Dames Am. (life). Republican. Episcopalian. Avocations: reading, sewing, walking, gourmet cooking, travel. Office: 1205 Myrtle Ave El Paso TX 79901 E-mail: marycitab@sbcglobal.net.

BENNINGTON, RONALD KENT, lawyer; b. Circleville, Ohio, July 16, 1936; s. Ralph P. and Delorice (Dudley) B.; m. Barbara Schumm, June 19, 1959; children: Scott C., Amy E. BA magna cum laude, Kenyon Coll., 1958; JD summa cum laude, Ohio State U., 1961. Assoc. Black, McCuskey, Souers & Arbaugh, Canton, Ohio, 1961-65, ptnr., 1965—. Sec. Hoover Worldwide Corp., 1969-86; bd. dirs. United Hard Chrome, Inc. Bd. trustees Plain Twp., Canton, 1972-78, Malone Coll., Canton, 1982—, chmn. 1984-86, Timken Mercy Med. Ctr., Canton; adv. com. Kenyon Coll., Gambier, Ohio; mem. Leadership Canton; bd. dirs. ARC, Canton; fundraising United Way Fund Drive; trust com. Hoover Found.; ambassador Ohio Found. Ind. Colls.; steering com. Pro Football Hall of Fame, 1985—; Big Ten football ofcl., 1984—; trustee The Hoover Found., Canton, Greater Canton C. of C.; bd. assocs. Union Coll., Alliance, Ohio. Fellow Am. Bar Found., Ohio State Bar Found.; mem. ABA, Ohio Bar Assn., Stark County Bar Assn., Greater Canton C. of C. (bd. trustees), Ea. Ohio Football Ofcls. Assn. (pres. 1986—), Stark County Law Libr. Assn. (pres.). Republican. Presbyterian. Home: 3528 Darlington Rd NW Canton OH 44708-1714 Office Phone: 330-458-4220.

BENNINGTON, THOMAS FRANCIS, lawyer, county official; BA, North Ctrl. Coll., 1984; JD, DePaul U., 1987. Bar: Ill. 1987, U.S. Dist. Ct. (no. dist.) Ill. 1987. Ptnr. Chuhak & Tecson, P.C., Chgo., 1987—; commr. DuPage County, Ill. Bd., Wheaton, 1998—. Commr. DuPage Cmty. Svc. Block Grant Commn., Wheaton, 1988—88, Forest Preserve Dist. DuPage County, Wheaton, 1998—2002, DuPage Cmty. Devel. Commn., Wheaton, 1998—; bd. dirs. Ill. Prairie Trail Authority, Wheaton. Com. mem. Nat. Assn. Counties Homeland Security Task Force, Washington, 2004—; bd. mem. United Way Met. Chgo., 2004—; mem. Med. Response Corp, Wheaton; bd. mem. United Way South DuPage, Downers Grove, Ill., 2000—03; trustee North Ctrl. Coll. Bd. Trustees, Naperville, 1998—2000; bd. mem. U. Ill. Coop. Ext. Bd. (DuPage Unit), Wheaton, 2000—; asst. scoutmaster Boy Scouts Am., Downers Grove, 2005—; vol. Conservation Found., Naperville, 2000—05; active FEMA Cmty. Emergency Response Team, Darien, Ill., 2004; membership chmn. Nat. Conf. Rep. County Ofcls., Washington, 2003—05. Recipient 2003 Vol. Leadership award, United Way Met. Chgo., 2003, Pedal Power award, Chicagoland Bicycle Fedn., 2004. Mem.: ABA, DuPage Bar Assn., Chgo. Bar Assn., St. Charles Sportsmen's Club, Phi Alpha Delta (pres. 1986—87). Office: Chuhak & Tecson PC 26th Fl 30 South Wacker Dr Chicago IL 60606 Office Phone: 312-855-4317. Home Fax: 312-444-9027; Office Fax: 312-444-9027. Business E-Mail: tbennington@chuhak.com.

BENNINGTON, WILLIAM JAY, management consultant; b. Dayton, Ohio, Apr. 16, 1939; s. Jay G. and Mary Joahnn (Weisner) Kirby; m. Pamela Joan Manus, Oct. 22, 1977; children: J. Bret, J. Brad, J. Brian, J. William; 1 adopted child, Christian LeSuer. BA in Journalism, U. Dayton, 1965. Asst. city editor Dayton Jour. Herald, 1964-66; asst. pub. rels. Pickands Mather & Co., Cleve., 1966-67; dir. pub. rels. Bayless-Kerr Co., Cleve., 1967-69; mgr. corp. pub. rels. Eaton Corp., Cleve., 1969-71; v.p. communications The Allen Group, Melville, N.Y., 1971-77; dir. pub. info. ITT Corp., N.Y.C., 1977-78; sr. v.p. corp. affairs Colonial Penn Group, Phila., 1978-85; pres. SGI Communications, Inc., 1985-90, Laurel Communications, Moorestown, N.J., 1990-96, The Phoenix Partnership, Inc., Moorestown, 1995-97. Dir. pub. rels., comms. and cmty. rels. Blue Cross and Blue Shield of N.C., 1996-99, v.p. corp. comm., 1999-2000, v.p. tng. and orgnl. devel., 2000-04, pres. Bennington Enterprises, LLC, Moorestown, N.J., 2004—. Home: 201 Laurence Dr Moorestown NJ 08057-2806 Office Phone: 856-235-2952. Personal E-mail: wjbpjb@comcast.net.

BENNINK, JACK RICHARD, microbiologist, researcher; b. Corry, Pa., Feb. 18, 1953; s. Ivan Guy and Mary Lou (Hurlbert) B.; m. Cindi Sue Merkle, May 29, 1976; children: Nathanael Scott, Tara Susanne. BA, Asbury Coll., 1975; PhD, U. Pa., 1978. Staff mem. Basel (Switzerland) Inst. for Immunology, 1980-82; asst. prof., assoc. prof. Wister Inst., Phila., 1982-87; sr. investigator NIH, Bethesda, Md., 1987—. Contbr. articles to profl. jours. Recipient Pub. Health Svc. award, 1990, 94, 95, 96, 99, 2000. Mem.: Am. Soc. Virology, Am. Assn. Immunologists. Office: NIH Rm 213 Bldg 4 Bethesda MD 20892-0440 Business E-Mail: jbennink@nih.gov.

BENNION, JOHN WARREN, urban education educator; b. Salt Lake City, Nov. 25; s. M. Lynn and Katherine Bennion; m. Sylvia Lustig; children: Philip, Stanford, David, Bryan, Grant, Andrew. BS in Philosophy, English, U. Utah, 1961, MA in Edn. Adminstrn., 1962; PhD in Edn. Adminstrn., Ohio State U., 1966. Tchr. Granite High Sch., Salt Lake City, 1961-63; asst. instr. Ohio State U., Columbus, 1963-64, adminstrv. asst., 1965-66; adminstrv. intern Parma (Ohio) Sch. Dist., 1964-65; asst. supt. Elgin (Ill.) Pub. Schs., 1966-68; asst. prof. edn. adminstrn. Ind. U., Bloomington, 1968-69; supt. Brighton Cen. Schs., Rochester, N.Y., 1969-79, Bloomington (Minn.) Pub. Schs., 1979-80, Provo (Utah) Sch. Dist., 1980-85, Salt Lake City Schs., 1985-94; prof. urban edn., dir. Utah Edn. Consortium U. Utah, Salt Lake City, 1994—. Dir. Utah Urban Sch. Alliance, Salt Lake City; ednl. cons. Comprehensive Sch. Reform, Salt Lake City. Mem. ASCD, Assn. Early Childhood Edn., Am. Assn. Sch. Adminstrs. (Nat. Superintendent of Yr. award 1992, Disting. Svc. award 2002), Phi Delta Kappa, Rotary. Home: 1837 Harvard Ave Salt Lake City UT 84108-1804 Office: Utah Urban School Alliance #202 2040 Murray Holladay Rd Salt Lake City UT 84117-5122

BENNION, SCOTT DESMOND, physician; b. Casper, Wyo., July 26, 1948; s. Desmond and Wanda Bennion; m. Stephanie Dawn Bennion; children: Scott, Beau, Brandon. BS summa cum laude, U. Wyo., 1970, MS, 1972; MD, U. Utah, 1975. Diplomate Nat. Bd. Med. Examiners, Am. Bd. Internal Medicine, Am. Bd. Dermatology, Am. Bd. Dermatologic Immunology/Diagnostic and Lab. Immunology. Intern U. Rutgers Med. Sch., 1975-76, resident in internal medicine, 1976-78, chief resident dept. medicine, 1978; commd. 2d lt. U.S. Army, 1976, advanced through grades to col., 1991; resident in dermatology Fitzsimons Army Med. Sch., Denver, 1981-84, chief resident dermatology svc., 1984, chief dept. clin. investigations, 1994-96, chmn. lab. animal use and care com., 1994-96; asst. chief dermatology svc. 98th Gen. Hosp., Nuremburg, Germany, 1986, chief dept. health clinics, 1987-88; chief immunodermatology sect. dermatology svc. Fitzsimons Army MC, Aurora, Colo., 1989—96; command surgeon ARTASK, Kuwait, 1992; command surgeon joint task force Kuwait and Army Ctrl. Command-Forward, 1992; dermatology cons. to the Army Surgeon Gen.,

1996-99; chief Troop Med. Clin. Fitzsimmons Army Garrison, 1996-99. Asst. clin. prof. dept. dermatology U. Colo. Health Sci. Ctr., 1992—99, assoc. prof. clin. dermatology, 1999—; assoc. prof. clin. medicine U. Wash. Med. Ctr. Contbr. chpts. to books: Military Dermatology, 1994, Secrets of Dermatology, 1996, 2d edit., 2000, Dubois Lupus, 1997, also articles to profl. publs. Pres. Nuremburg Elem. Sch. PTSA; asst. cubmaster, cubmaster, chmn. Volksmarch com. Boy Scouts Am., 1986; pres. Foxridge Improvement Assn., 1992-01, pres., 1994-01; bd. dirs. Wyo. Make a Wish Found., 2000-; mem. Alcova Lake Area Bd., 2001-; trustee Casper Coll., 2000-, sec. to bd., 2002-04, treas. to bd., 2004-; trustee Anam Chara Hospice, Denver, 2001. Named to Order of Mil. Med. Merit, 1987; named Cubmaster of Yr. Bavaria dist. Boy Scouts Am., 1987, Businessman of Yr., Nat. Rep. Congl. Com. Bus. Adv. Coun., 2001; recipient Legion of Merit award, 1999. Fellow: ACP, Am. Acad. Dermatology (mem. govt. medicine task force 1996—2000, Colo. Dermatology Soc. rep. to adv. bd. 1997—, Wyo. Acad. Dermatology rep. to adv. bd., mem. rev. bd. to adv. bd. 2005—); mem.: Dermatology Found. Leadership Soc. (chmn. Wyo.), Ctrl. Wyo. Skin Clinic, Wyo. Acad. Dermatology (sec. 1999—2003, pres. 2003—), Soc. for Investigative Dermatology, Assn. Mil. Dermatologists (sec.-treas. 1990—96, guest editor jour. 1991, pres. 1998—99, Residents award 1984), Assn. Mil. Surgeons, Phi Kappa Phi. Avocations: skiing, diving. Home: 2800 Garden Creek Rd Casper WY 82601 Office: 2241 Farnum St Ste 204 Casper WY 82609-4108 Office Phone: 307-234-0003.

BENNIS, WARREN GAMELIEL, business administration educator; b. N.Y.C., Mar. 8, 1925; s. Philip and Rachel (Landau) B.; m. Clurie Williams, Mar. 30, 1962 (div. 1983); children: Katharine, John Leslie, Will Martin; m. Mary Jane O'Donnell, Mar. 8, 1988 (div. 1991); m. Grace Gabe, Nov. 29, 1992. AB, Antioch Coll., 1951; hon. cert. econs., London Sch. Econs., 1952; PhD, MIT, 1955; LLD, Xavier U., Cin., 1972, George Washington U., 1977; LHD (hon.), Hebrew Union Coll., 1974, Kans. State U., 1979; DSc (hon.), U. Louisville, 1977, Pacific Grad. Sch. Psychology, 1987, Gov.'s State U., 1991; LHD (hon.), Doan Coll., 1993; LLD (hon.), London (Eng.) Bus. Sch., 2004. Diplomate Am. Bd. Profl. Psychology. Asst. prof. psychology MIT, Cambridge, 1953-56, prof., 1959-67; asst. prof. psychology and bus. Boston U., 1956-59; prof. Sloan Sch. Mgmt., 1959-67; provost SUNY-Buffalo, 1967-68, v.p. acad. devel., 1968-71; pres. U. Cin., 1971-77; U.S. prof. corps. and soc. Centre d'Etudes Industrielles, Geneva, Switzerland, 1978-79; exec.-in-residence Pepperdine U., 1978-79; George Miller Disting. prof.-in-residence U. Ill., Champaign-Urbana, 1978; Disting. prof. Bus. Adminstrn. Sch. Bus., U. So. Calif., L.A., 1980-88; univ. prof., disting. prof. bus. adminstrn. U. So. Calif., L.A., 1988—. Vis. lectr. Harvard U., 1958-59, Indian Mgmt. Inst., Calcutta; vis. prof. U. Lausanne (Switzerland), 1961-62, INSEAD, France, 1983; bd. dirs. The Foothill Group. Author: Planning of Change, 4th edit., 1985, Interpersonal Dynamics, 1963, 3d and 4th edits., 1975, Personal and Organizational Change, 1965, Changing Organizations, 1966, repub. in paperback as Beyond Bureaucracy, 1974, The Temporary Society, 1968, Organization Development, 1969, American Bureaucracy, 1970, Management of Change and Conflict, 1972, The Leaning Ivory Tower, 1973, The Unconscious Conspiracy: Why Leaders Can't Lead, 1976, Essays in Interpersonal Dynamics, 1979; (with B. Nanus): Leaders, 1985, On Becoming a Leader, 1989, (with I. Mitroff) The Unreality Industry, 1989, Why Leaders Can't Lead, 1989, Leaders on Leadership, 1992, An Invented Life: Reflections on Leadership and Change, 1993, Beyond Bureaucracy, 1993, (with J. Goldsmith) Learning to Lead, 1994, (with M. Mische) Reinventing the 21st Century, 1994, Beyond Leadership, 1994, Herding Cats: Bennis on Leadership, 1996, Organizing Genius, 1997, The Temporary Society, 1998, Co-Leaders, 1999, Old Dogs, New Tricks, 1999, (with G. Heil and D. Stephens) Douglas McGregor Re-Visited, 2000; co-leaders, 1999, Managing the Dream, 2000; co-author: Geeks & Geezers, 2002, On Becoming a Leader, 2003; cons. editor Calif. Mgmt. Rev., Mgmt. Series Jossey-Bass Pubs. Mem. Pres.' White House Task Force on Sci. Policy, 1960-70; mem. FAA study task force U.S. Dept. Transp., 1975; mem. adv. com. N.Y. State Joint Legis. Com. Higher Edn., 1970-71; mem. Ohio Gov.'s Bus. and Employment Coun., 1972-74; mem. panel on alt. approaches to grad. edn. Coun. Grad. Schs. and Grad. Record-Exam Bd., 1971-73; chmn. Nat. Adv. Commn. on Higher Edn. for Police Officers, 1976-78; adv. bd. NIH, 1978-84; trustee Colo. Rocky Mountains Sch., 1978-82; bd. dirs. Am. Leadership Forum, 1984-89; mem. vis. com. for Humanities MIT, 1975-81; trustee Antioch Coll., Salk Inst.; chmn. adv. bd. Harvard U. Ctr. for Pub. Leadership. Capt. AUS, World War II. Decorated Bronze Star, Purple Heart; recipient Dow Jones award, 1987, McKinsey Fedn. award, 1967, 68. Mem. Am. Acad. Arts and Scis. (co-chmn. policy coun. 1969-71), Am. Mgmt. Assn. (dir. 1974-77), U.S. C. of C. (adv. group scholars). Office: U So Calif Sch Bus University Park Los Angeles CA 90089-0001 Office Phone: 213-740-0766.

BENNUR, MALLIKARJUNA, automotive executive; arrived in U.S., 1990; s. SiddeGowda and Parvathi Bennur. PhD, Indian Inst. Tech., Bombay, 1989; postgrad., Laval U., Que., Can., 1990, U. Toronto, 1991. Registered profl. engr. Assoc. prof. rsch. Laval U., Que., 1992—94; engring. cons. Que., 1995—97; chief engr. Group NewTech. Internat., Montreal, 1997—99; computer-aided engring. lead N&V prestige and luxury car group GM, Milford, Mich., 1999—. Contbr. articles to profl. jours. Recipient People Make Quality Happen award, GM, 2004; Indsl. Rsch. fellow, Natural Scis. and Engring. Rsch. Coun. of Can., 1996. Fellow: ASME, Soc. of Automotive Engrs. Achievements include invention of A New Full Contact Disc Brake for Automobiles. Office: GM Corp Mail Code 483-394-206 3300 GM Rd Milford MI 48380 E-mail: mbennur@gmail.com.

BENNY, SANDRA MARIE, artist; b. Cleve., 1944; m. Richard Lee Vaux, Sept. 6, 1969; 1 child, Joseph Nikolai BFA, Ohio U., 1966; MA, No. Ill. U., 1970. Adj. prof. Long Island U., C. W. Post Campus, Greenvale, NY, 1977—. One-person shows include Locust Valley (N.Y.) Gallery, 1985, The Gallery, Roslyn, N.Y., 1987, Jain Marunouchi Gallery, Soho, N.Y., 1993, 2003 others; group exhbns. include Md. Inst. Coll. Art, Balt., 1992, Thomas J. Walsh Art Gallery, Fairfield, Conn., 1993, Sally Harvey Fine Art, Aspen, Colo., 1993, many others; represented in permanent collections ARAMCO Corp., Houston, The Washington County Mus. Fine Arts, Hagerstown, Md., Arthur Anderson and Co., Huntington, N.Y. Russian Orthodox. Home and Office: 4 Lloyd Ln Huntington NY 11743-9758 Office Phone: 631-549-4341. Personal E-mail: smbennyart@hotmail.com.

BENOIT, COLLEEN CANNON, elementary school educator; b. Lake Charles, La., Apr. 13, 1966; d. James Dale and Maureen Catherine Cannon; m. John Barry Benoit, Apr. 28, 1963; children: Benjamin Charles, John Braxton, Cecilia Catherine. BS in Early Childhood Edn., McNeese State U., Lake Charles, La., 1992; MS in Ednl. Tech., McNeese State U., 2005. Elem. sch. tchr. Calcasieu Parish Sch. Sys., Lake Charles, La., 1988—; fitness instr. Christus St. Patrick - Gigi's, Lake Charles, La., 1988—. Mentor in the tchr. advancement program Milken Family Found., Lake Charles, La., 2003—. Recipient Tchr. of the Yr. award, AA Nelson Elem. Sch., 1997, 2004, 2005, Elem. Tchr. of Yr. award, Calcasieu Parish, Class Act award, KPLC-TV, 1997; fellow Artist's Fellowship Grant for Dance, State of La., 1998. Office Phone: 337-477-1775.

BENOIT, JOHN J., state official; m. Sheryl Benoit; children: Benjamin, Sarah. AA, Riverside City Coll.; BS, Calif. State U., 1978; MA in Pub. Adminstrn., U. Calif., San Bernardino, 1993. Law enforcer; state assembly mem. Dist. 64 Calif. State Assembly, 2002—. Mem. Desert Sands Unified Sch. Dist. Bd. Edn.; mem. budget com.; mem. rules com.; vice chair ins. com. Mem. United Way, 1989—. Republican. Roman Catholic. Mailing: Rm 4144 PO Box 942849 Sacramento CA 94249 Office: Ste 230 1223 University Ave Riverside CA 92507

BENOIT, LEE DAVIS, elementary school educator, consultant; d. Lee Vardaman Davis and Willie Mae Luker; children: Jonathan William, Julie Anne. BAE in Elem. Edn., U. Miss., 1971; MA in Curriculum and Tchg., Mich. State U., 1992. Cert. Nat. Bd. Profl. Tchg. Stds., tchr. Miss. 4th grade tchr. Lake Charles (La.) Sch. Dist., 1971—72; 2nd grade tchr. Newport News (Va.) Sch. Dist., 1976—77; tchr., reading coord. Cairo (Egypt) Am. Coll., 1978—95; 4th grade tchr. Oxford (Miss.) Sch. Dist., 1996—. Co-dir. U. Miss. Writing Project, 2003—, staff devel. presenter, 2001—; clin. supr. U. Miss., 1996—. Mem. Pilot Club, Oxford, Miss., 1998—2000. Mem.: Nation Coun. Tchrs. English (assoc.), Oxford-Lafayette C. of C. (assoc.), Delta Kappa Gamma (assoc.; treas. 2000—02). Avocations: travel, real estate management, estate sales/auctions, remodeling older homes, reading. Home: 405 Choctaw Dr Oxford MS 38655 Office: Oxford Elem Sch 1627 Hwy 30 E Oxford MS 38655

BENOIT, MARILYN B., psychiatrist, medical association administrator; b. Trinidad & Tobago, 1943; MD, Georgetown U., 1973; cert. Specialist Health Svcs. Adminstrn., George Washington U., 1993. Diplomate Am. Bd. Psychiatry and Neurology with subspecialty in child and adolescent psychiatry. Resident in psychiatry Georgetown U., Washington, 1973—75, resident in child psychiatry, fellow in child psychiatry, 1975—77, clin. assoc. prof. psychiatry; med. dir., exec. dir. Devereux Children's Ctr., 1993—98; pvt. practice, cons., 1998—. Part-time pvt. practice psychiatry. Fellow: Am. Acad. Child and Adolescent Psychiatry (pres. 2001—03); mem.: AMA, Am. Psychiat. Assn. Home: 43 Prospect Bay Dr W Grasonville MD 21638 Office: 1015 33d St NW Washington DC 20007 Office Phone: 202-607-3032.

BENOIT, PHILIP GROSVENOR, communications executive, educator, writer; b. Syracuse, N.Y., June 11, 1944; s. Paul Grosvenor and Doris Louise (Pond) B.; m. Candace Gail Blohm, Sept. 11, 1971; children: Kimberly Whitney, Marie Suzanne. BA, St. Lawrence U., 1966; MA, SUNY-Oswego, 1973. Asst. prof. communications SUNY-Oswego, 1971-79; dir. pub. rels. Hartwick Coll., Oneonta, N.Y., 1979-84; dir. comms. Dickinson Coll., Carlisle, Pa., 1984-96; dir. pub. affairs Middlebury Coll., Vt., 1996—2005; assoc. v.p. Coll. Comms. Franklin Marshall Coll., Lancaster, Pa., 2005—. Author: (with Carl Hausman) Do Your Own Public Relations, 1983, Radio Station Operations, 1989, Positive Public Relations, 1990, (with O'Donnell and Hausman) Announcing: Broadcast Communicating Today, 5th edit., 2003, Modern Radio Production, 6th edit., 2003. Served to capt. U.S. Army, 1966-69. Decorated Bronze Star. Avocations: photography, music. Business E-Mail: phil.benoit@landm.edu.

BENOIT, RICHARD ARMAND, lawyer, retired police chief; s. Oliver Maurice and Delina Marie Benoit; m. Elizabeth Benoit, Nov. 17, 1962; children: Karen Marie, Richard Michael. AS, Bristol Community Coll., Fall River, Mass., 1972; BS, Salve Regina U., 1975, MS, 1979; JD, So. New Eng. Sch. Law, New Bedford, 1989. Bar: Mass. 1990. Police officer New Bedford Police Dept., 1967-71, sgt., 1971-75, lt., 1975-82, capt., 1982-86, chief of police, 1986—; pvt. practice law New Bedford, 1990-97; ret., 1997; pvt. practice law, 1997—. With U.S. Army, 1959-62. Mem. ABA, Mass. Bar Assn., New Bedford Bar Assn., Bristol County Bar Assn. Avocations: swimming, golf, reading. Home: 209 Maywood St New Bedford MA 02745-5108

BENOIT, WILLIAM LYON, communication educator; b. New Castle, Ind., Mar. 17, 1953; s. Garvey and Berneice (Lyon) B.; m. Pamela Jean Gay, May 18, 1974; 1 child, Jennifer Melissa. BS, Ball State U., 1975; MA, Cen. Mich. U., 1976; PhD, Wayne State U., 1979. Vis. asst. prof. Miami U., Oxford, Ohio, 1979-80; asst. prof. Bowling Green (Ohio) State U., 1980-84; from asst. prof. to assoc. prof. U. Mo., Columbia, 1984—97, prof., 1997—. Co-dir., host Doctoral Honors Seminar on Argument, Bowling Green, 1980-81; chmn. Cen. States Rhetorical Theory and Criticism, 1987-88; mem. rsch. com. Am. Forensic Assn., 1988-89; dir. grad. studies communication dept. U. Mo., Columbia, 1989. Author: Accounts, Excuses, and Apologies, 1995; editor Jour. Comm., 2003-05; contbr. articles to profl. jours. Recipient Fedn. prize Cen. States Speech Assn., 1986. Mem. Internat. Communication Assn., Internat. Soc. History of Rhetoric, Internat. Soc. Study Argument, Speech Communication Assn. (rsch. bd. liaison 1987-89), Cen. Mo. Amateur Astronomers. Office: U Mo Dept Communication 115 Switzler St Columbia MO 65203-4154

BENOLIEL, JOEL, lawyer; b. Seattle, June 11, 1945; s. Joseph H. and Rachel (Maimon) B.; m. Maureen Alhadeff, Mar. 1971; 1 child, Joseph D. BA in Polit. Sci., U. Wash., 1967, JD, 1971. Bar: Wash., US Dist. Ct. (we. dist.) Wash., US Ct. Appeals (9th cir.), US Mil. Ct. Appeals. Assoc. atty. MacDonald, Horgue & Bayless, Seattle, 1971-73, ptnr., 1973-78; v.p., gen. counsel Jack A. Benaroya Co., Seattle, 1978-84; ptnr. Trammell Crow Co., Seattle, 1985-87, Spieker Ptnrs., Bellevue, Wash., 1987-92; sr. v.p. law and real estate, gen. counsel Price Costco, Inc. (now Costco Wholesale Corp.), Issaquah, Wash., 1992—. Bd. dir. Overlake Sch., Redmond, Wash., 1995—, Congregation Ezra Bessaroth, Seattle, 1992-95. With US Army, 1968-74. Avocations: tennis, boating, skiing, reading fiction. Office: Costco Wholesale Corp 999 Lake Dr Issaquah WA 98027-5367

BENOWITZ, JOEL, surgeon; b. Bklyn., Oct. 3, 1950; s. Albert and Miriam Benowitz; m. Joan Ellen Broder, Nov. 24, 1976; children: Lauren, Alison, Jacqueline. BA, Long Island U., 1971; MD, Autonomous U., Mex., 1975. Diplomate Am. Bd. Surgery, cert. breast ultrasound Am. Soc. Breast Surgeons. Resident, chief resident surgery Brookdale Hosp. Med. Ctr., Bklyn., 1975—81, attending surgeon, 1981—87, Long Beach (N.Y.) Med. Ctr., 1982—, dir. surgery, 2000—, chmn. med. staff, 2002—; attending surgeon S. Nassau Cmty. Hosp., 1996—, N. Shore Univ. Hosp., Syosset, NY, 1999—. Bd. trustees Congregation Beth Shalom, Long Beach, 1990—, Long Beach Med. Ctr., 2000—; clin. asst. prof. NY Coll. Osteo. Medicine, 1999—. Named Profl. of Yr., St. James of Jerusalem, Long Beach, 2002. Fellow: Am. Coll. Surgeons. Avocations: boating, travel, reading, horseback riding. Home: 978 Gerry Ave Lido Beach NY 11561 Office: 206 W Park Ave Long Beach NY 11561 Office Phone: 516-889-9100. E-mail: jbenowitz@aol.com.

BENSELER, DAVID P., foreign language educator; b. Balt., Jan. 10, 1940; s. Ernest Parr and Ellen Hood Escar (Turnbaugh) B.; m. Suzanne Shelton, May 25, 1985; children: James Declan, Derek Justin. BA, West Wash. U., 1964; MA, U. Oreg., 1966, PhD, 1971. From asst. prof. to assoc. prof. Wash. State U., 1969—77; prof., chair dept. German, Ohio State U., 1977—91; chair dept. modern langs. and lits. Case Western Res. U., 1991-98, Louis D. Beaumont U. prof. humanities, 1991-98, Emile B. de Sauzé prof. modern lang. and lit., 1998—2004, Emile B. de Sauzé prof. emeritus modern lang. and lit., 2004—. Disting. vis. prof. fgn. langs. U.S. Mil. Acad., West Point, N.Y., 1987-88, N.Mex. State U., Las Cruces, 1989; founding dir. German Studies program Case Western Reserve U. and Max Kade Ctr. for German Studies; mem. numerous coms. Case Western Res. U., U.S. Military Acad., U.S. Naval Acad., U. Akron, Ohio State U., Wash. State U., Ind. U., Emory U., U. Md., U. Cin., U. Wis., Pa. State U., U. Va., U. Mich., various others; lectr., panel mem., workshop condr., cons. in field. Compiler, editor: (with Suzanne S. Moore) Comprehensive Index to the Modern Language Journal, 1916-1996, MLJ Electronic Index, 1997—; author/editor over 50 books, bibliographies, jours.; contbr. chpts. to books and articles to profl. jours. With USN, 1957—63. Decorated Bundesverdienstkreuz I. Klasse (Germany); recipient Army Commendation medal for disting. civilian svc. U.S. Mil. Acad., 1988; Lilly Found. Faculty Renewal fellow Stanford U., 1975, Fulbright grad. fellow, 1967-68, NDEA fellow, U. Oreg., 1964-67; various other grants, fellowships, scholarships. Mem. MLA, AAUP, Am. Assn. Applied Linguistics, Am. Assn. Tchrs. of German, Am. Coun. on the Tchg. of Fgn. Langs., Am. Goethe Soc., Am. Soc. for 18th Century Studies, German Studies Assn., Lessing Soc., Soc. German-Am. Studies, Phi Sigma Iota, Sigma Kappa Phi, Delta Phi Alpha. Office Phone: 216-368-3071. Business E-Mail: david.benseler@case.edu.

BEN-SHAHAR, OMRI, law and economics educator; b. Tel-Aviv, Oct. 20, 1962; s. Chaim and Yael (Bucks) Ben-S.; m. Sarah Clarke, Jan. 28, 1993; children: Ziv, Maya. LLB, Hebrew U., Jerusalem, 1989, BA in Econs., 1990; LLM, Harvard U., 1991, PhD in Econs., 1995. Law clk. Supreme Ct. of Israel, 1989-90; sr. fellow Harvard Law Sch., 1994-95; rsch. fellow Israeli Democracy Inst., 1995—; prof. law and econs. Tel-Aviv U.; panel mem. Israel's Antitrust Ct., 1997; prof. law U. Mich. Law Sch., Ann Arbor, 1999—; founder, dir. Olin Ctr. for Law and Econs. Contbr. articles to law jours. Lt. Israeli Def. Force, 1980-84. Olin fellow in law and econs. Harvard Law Sch., 1990-94, Fulbright fellow U.S. Govt., 1990-91, Lady Davis fellow Hebrew U., 1990-91. Office: U Mich Sch Law 900 Legal Rsch 625 S State St Ann Arbor MI 48109-1215 Office Phone: 734-763-4608. Office Fax: 734-734-8309. E-mail: omri@umich.edu.*

BEN SHAUL, YOCHANAN MENASHSHEH See MISHLER, JOHN

BEN-SHIR, RYA HELEN, medical librarian; b. Ottawa, Ont., Can., 1955; came to U.S., 1981; m. Alan H. Peres, June 26, 1977. BA, McGill U., 1977, MLS, 1979. Med. libr. Jewish Rehab. Hosp., Montreal, 1979—81; mgr. health sci. resource ctr. MacNeal Hosp., Berwyn, Ill., 1981—99; mgr. intelligencentes Takeda Pharm. N.Am., Inc., Lincolnshire, Ill., 2000—. Author (software package and manual): Fast Inter-Library Loan and Statistics, 1984, 85; contbr. articles to profl. jours. Recipient Hosp. Libr. Yr. award MLA, 1989 Recipient John Cotton Dana Spl. award ALA, 1992. Office: Takeda Pharm N Am Inc 475 Half Day Rd Lincolnshire IL 60069 Office Phone: 847-383-3223. E-mail: rbenshir@tpna.com.

BENSIE, LORI ANNE, music educator; b. Garfield Hts., Ohio, Aug. 10, 1966; d. Edwin and Terryl Lynn Maulis; m. Timothy Bensie, June 20, 1992; children: Kayla, Bryan. MusB, Kent State U., 1988, MusM, 1996. Music tchr. Music on the Move, Cleve., 1988—89; music tchr. 5-8 Twinsburg City Schools, Ohio, 1989—99, music tchr. K-1, 1999—. Children's choir dir. Twinsburg Congl. Ch., Ohio, 1992—96, 1999—. Mem.: MENC. Avocation: scrapbooks. Home: 1688 W Idlewood Dr Twinsburg OH 44087 Office: Twinsburg City Schools Darrow Rd Twinsburg OH 44087

BENSINGER, DAVID AUGUST, dentist, dean; b. St. Louis, May 14, 1926; s. William and Esther (Lissner) B.; m. Myra Blass, Dec. 24, 1944 (div. June 1972); children: Judith Ann (Mrs. William Thomas Haynes), Scott David; m. Susan Cohn Hartman, May 31, 1975. BA, Washington U., 1944; DDS, St. Louis U., 1948; postgrad. health systems mgmt, Harvard U. Sch. Bus. Adminstrn., 1977. Mem. faculty, adminstrn. Sch. Dentistry Washington U., St. Louis, 1949—, assoc. prof. dept. periodontics, 1956-76, prof., 1976-90, assoc. dean, 1970-76, acting dean, 1976-83, exec. assoc. dean, 1983-87; dean Washington U. Sch. Dental Medicine, 1987-90, dean, prof. emeritus, 1990; practice dentistry, specializing in periodontics St. Louis, 1949-90; mem. staff Barnes, Jewish hosps., St. Louis; mem. deans com. VA Hosp.; mem. nat. adv. com. Dental Edn. Rev. Com., NIH, 1969-72. Cons. Scott AFB, St. Louis, 1956-62; mem. adv. coun. SBA, 1975. Editor: Jour. Greater St. Louis Dental Soc, 1963-70; asso. editor: Jour. Mo. Dental Assn, 1966-73. Mem. exec. bd. Ladue (Mo.) Sch. Sys., 1964-67; chmn. bd. counselors U. Calif. Med. Ctr., San Francisco, 1995-98; chmn. regional cabinet Wash. U., San Francisco, 1996—; elected trustee Coll. of Notre Dame, Belmont, Calif., 1998—, chmn. fin. and investment com. Lt. M.C., U.S. Army, 1948-49, capt. med. dept. USAF, 1955-56. Fellow Am. Coll. Dentists, Internat. Coll. Dentists; mem. ADA (ho. of dels.), Mo. Dental Assn. (pres. 1973-74, jud. coun.), Greater St. Louis Dental Soc. (bd. dirs. 1963-70, Svc. award 1971), Am. Acad. Peridontology, Internat. Assn. Dental Rsch., Midwest Soc. Peridontology (pres. 1972-73), Pierre Fouchard Acad., Royal Soc. Medicine (Eng.), Inst. Internat. Edn. (vice chmn. bd. dirs., chmn. exec. com. 1996-98), Washington U. Alumni Assn. (Alumnus of Yr. 1968), Univ. Club (St. Louis), St. Louis Club, Harvard Club (Boston and N.Y.C.), Omicron Kappa Upsilon. Home: 2100 Pacific Ave San Francisco CA 94115-1585

BENSINGER, PETER BENJAMIN, consulting firm executive; b. Chgo., Mar. 24, 1936; s. Benjamin Edward and Linda Elkus (Galston) B.; m. Judith S. Bensinger; children: Peter Benjamin, Jennifer Anne, Elizabeth Brooke, Virginia Brette. Grad., Phillips Exeter Acad., 1954; BA, Yale, 1958; hon. degree, San Marcos U., Peru, 1978; LLD (hon.), Dan Kook U., Seoul, Republic of Korea, 1980. Various mktg. positions Brunswick Corp., Chgo., 1958-65, new products mgr., 1966-68; gen. sales mgr. Brunswick Internat., Europe, 1965-66, spl. products mgr., 1966-68; chmn. Ill. Youth Commn., 1969-70; dir. Ill. Dept. Corrections, Chgo., 1970-73; exec. dir. Chgo. Crime Commn., 1973; adminstr. Drug Enforcement Adminstrn., Washington, 1976-81; pres. Bensinger, DuPont & Assocs., Chicago, 1982—. Chmn. Ill. Criminal Justice Info. Authority, 1991—; cons. various orgns.; del. White House Conf. on Corrections, 1971, Drug Abuse, 1988, U.S. Del. to Interpol, 1978. Pres. Lincoln Park Zool. Soc., Chgo., 1962-63; governing life mem., also mem. men's council Chgo. Art Inst.; mem. Ill. Alcoholism Adv. Council, Ill. Law Enforcement Commn., Ill. Council on Diagnosis and Evaluation Criminal Defendants, Ill. Narcotics Adv. Council; adv. com. Center for Studies in Criminal Justice, So. Ill. U., Center for Studies in Criminal Justice, U. Chgo.; vice chmn. ad hoc adv. com. U.S. Dept. Justice Nat. Inst. Corrections; mem. exec. com. Am. Bar Assn. Nat. Commn. Corrections; chmn. Ill. Task Force on Corrections, 1969; mem. bd. Fed. Prison Industries, Inc., 1973-85; bd. dirs. Jewish Fedn. Met. Chgo., Council Community Services Met. Chgo., Ill. Commn. on Children, Children's Meml. Hosp., Chgo., 1988—; bd. dirs., mem. exec. council Anti-Defamation League; regional bd. dirs. NCCJ; trustee Phillips Exeter Acad.; chmn. nat. law enforcement explorers conf. Boy Scouts Am., 1981, U.S. del. to, Interpol, 1978. Recipient Young Leadership award Jewish Fedn.-Welfare Bds. Met. Chgo., 1969, award for excellence John Howard Assn., 1972, Disting. Svc. award Govt. of Peru, 1978, U.S. Dept. of Justice award, EEO award, 1979, Disting. Svc. medal USCG, 1981, John Phillips award Phillips Exeter Acad., 1990, Lincoln medal Lincoln Acad., 1998. Mem. Am. Correctional Assn. (bd. dirs.), Assn. State Correctional Adminstrs. (sec. 1971-72, pres. 1972-73), Internat. Assn. Chiefs of Police (mem. exec. com.), Nat. Sheriffs Assn. (life), Chgo. City Club (bd. dirs.), Arts Club, Comml. Club Chgo., Yale Club (N.Y.C.), Shoreacres Club (Lake Bluff), Casino Club (Chgo.). Office: 20 N Wacker Dr Chicago IL 60606-2806

BENSINGER, STEVEN J., insurance company executive; b. N.Y.C., Jan. 12, 1955; m. Karen Bensinger; children: Kaylin, Kyle. BS, NYU, 1976. CPA, N.Y. Ptnr. Coopers & Lybrand, N.Y.C., 1976-87; exec. v.p., CFO Skandia Am. Group, N.Y.C., 1987-90, pres., COO; exec. v.p., CFO Combined Specialty Group, Inc.; treas. Am. Internat. Group, Inc., N.Y.C., 2002—05, sr. v.p., 2005, exec. v.p., 2005—, CFO, 2005—. Mem. AICPA, Brokers & Reins. Markets Assn., Reins. Assn. Am., Soc. Ins. Accts., N.Y. State Soc. CPAs, NYU Stern Sch. Bus. Alumni Assn. (bd. dirs.). Office: Am Internat Group Inc 70 Pine St New York NY 10270*

BENSMAIA, REDA, French studies educator, researcher; b. Kouba, Algeria, Oct. 15, 1944; arrived in U.S., 1979; s. Kaddour and Saleha (Benouniche) Bensmaia; m. Joelle Proust, Feb. 2, 1947 (div. June 1989); children: Sliman, Djamel; m. Maurizia Natali, Oct. 22, 1995. Licence es-lettres, Facultes des lettres, Aix-En-provence, France, 1969, MPhil, 1971; BA, Ecole Pratique, Paris, France, 1977, PhD, 1981. Asst. prof. Institut d' Etudes Politiques, Algiers, Algeria, 1973-74, U. Algiers, Algeria, 1974-76; prof. philosophy Lycée Français, San Francisco, 1979-81; assoc. prof. U. Minn., Mpls., 1981-85; dir. Paris Ctr. for Critical Studies, 1985-88; assoc. prof. U. Minn., Mpls., 1988-89; prof. U. Va., Charlottesville, 1989—91, Brown U., Providence, 1991—. Author: The Barthes Effect, 1987, The Year of Passages, 1995, Alger ou la maladie de la mémoire, 1997, Experimental Nations or the invention of the Maghreb, 2003; editor: On Gilles Deleuze, 1989; contbr. articles to profl. jours. Decorated chevalier des Palmes Academiques France; recipient award, Am. Inst. for Maghrebi Studies, 1995; grantee, NEH, 1983; EDP grantee, U. Minn., 1989. Mem.: MLA, Coun. for Internat. Ednl. Exch. (steering com., adv. bd. curriculum), Sites (adv. bd.), Lendemains (adv. bd.), Continuum (adv. bd.). Avocations: writing poetry and fiction, music, hiking. Office: Brown U Dept French Studies PO Box 1961 Providence RI 02912-1961

BENSMAN, STEPHEN J., school librarian, researcher; b. Sheboygan, Wis., Aug. 26, 1938; s. Solomon and Leah Z. Bensman; m. Miriam Roza, July 9, 1936. MLS, U. Wis., 1975, PhD in History, 1977. Fgn. law libr. U. Wis., Madison, 1975—78; libr. La. State U., Baton Rouge, 1978—. Contbr. articles to profl. jours. Specialist 6 U.S. Army, 1963. Mem.: ALA, Am .Soc. Info. Sci.

and Tech., Beta Phi Mu, Phi Beta Kappa, Phi Eta Sigma. Home: 724 Shady Lake Pky Baton Rouge LA 70810-4328 Office: LSU Librs La State Univ Baton Rouge LA 70803-3300 Office Phone: 225-578-6932. Personal E-mail: bensmans@bellsouth.net. Business E-Mail: notsjb@lsu.edu.

BENSON, AL BOWEN, III, oncologist, educator; b. Buffalo, N.Y., Dec. 23, 1950; BA, SUNY, 1972; MD, SUNY, Buffalo, 1976. Diplomate Am. Bd. Internal Medicine, cert. med. oncology Am. Bd. Internal Medicine. Intern U. Wis. Hosps., Madison, 1976—77, resident medicine, 1977—79; co-dir. medicine Nat. Pub. Health Svc., Ill., 1979—81; fellow oncology U. Wis. Hosps., Madison, 1981—84; attending physician Northwestern Meml. Hosp., Chgo., 1984—, Lakeside VA Med. Ctr., Chgo., 1984—. Prof. medicine U. Ill., 1979—81, Northwestern U., 1984—, assoc. dir. clin. investigations, 1995—. Office: Northwestern Univ 676 N St Clair Ste 850 Chicago IL 60611-2998

BENSON, ALVIN K., physicist, geophysicist, consultant, educator; b. Payson, Utah, Jan. 25, 1944; s. Carl William and Josephine Katherine (Wirthlin) B.; m. Connie Lynn Perry, June 17, 1966; children: Alauna Marie, Alisa Michelle, Alaura Dawn. BS, Brigham Young U., 1966, PhD in Physics, 1972. Cert. environmentalist; registered profl. engr., Utah. Nuc. group physicist Phillips Petroleum Co., Arco, Idaho, 1966; assoc. prof. physics Ind. U., New Albany, 1972-78, head physics dept., 1976-78; sr. rsch. geophysicist Conoco, Inc., Ponca City, Okla., 1978-81, supr. geophysical rsch., 1981-85; geophysics rsch. assoc. DuPont, Ponca City, 1985-86; prof. geophysics Brigham Young U., Provo, Utah, 1986—2001, prof. emeritus, 2001—; prof. physics Utah Valley State Coll., 2001—. Cons. Dames and Moore Engring., Salt Lake City, 1987-88, 98-99, DuPont, Ponca City, 1989-91, Kuwait U., 1991-92, Coleman Rsch., Laurel, Md., 1991, Centennial Mine, Boise, 1990-91, Certified Environ., Salt Lake City, 1991-92, EPA, Washington, 1992, Digital Exploration Ltd., East Grinstead, Eng., 1993-94, Paterson, Grant & Watson Ltd., Toronto, 1994, Ground Water Tech., Norwood, Mass., 1995, Inst. for Geology and Geotech. Engring., Lyngby, Denmark, 1995-96, Conoco, Inc., Houston, 1997, Centurion Mines, Salt Lake City, 1997, ThermoRetec, Billings, Mont., 1999, Environ. Contractors, Inc., Provo, 2000, Anadarko, Houston, 2000, Kleinfelder, Salt Lake City, 2001, Monsanto, Soda Springs, Idaho, 2002, Moxtek, Inc., Orem, Utah, 2004; developer vis. geoscientist program Brigham Young U., Utah Valley State Coll.; rsch. bd. Am. Biog. Inst., 1995; developer vis. physicist program Utah Valley State Coll. Author: Seismic Migration, 1986, Theory and Practice of Seismic Imaging, 1988, The Birth and Growth of Planet Earth, 1996; (CD-ROM) Seismic Migration, 1997; mem. editl. bd. Jour. Applied Geophysics, 2000—; contbr. over 460 articles to profl. jours. Bishop LDS Ch., New Albany, 1976-78, Stake High Coun., Tulsa, 1979-81; High Priest group leader, Orem, 2002-; active polit. adv. com. Rep. Party, Provo, 1990; polit. cons. Guatemala, 1991-92. Recipient Hon. Sci. award Bausch and Lomb, Rochester, NY, 1966, Citation of Meritorious Achievement in Geophysics, Soc. Exploration Geophysicists, 1994; Geophysics grantee Rotary, Provo, 1987, Am. Assn. Petroleum Geologists, Tulsa, 1988, Geol. Soc. Am., Boulder, Colo., 1988, Bur. of Reclamation, Washington, 1994, Nat. Pk. Svc., Washington, 1995, NSF, 1997, Dyn Corp., Boston, 1998, ThermoRetec, 1999, Dames and Moore, 1999, NSF, 2002. Mem. Am. Phys. Soc., Am. Geophys. Union, Soc. Exploration Geophysicists (referee 1980-99), Environ. and Engring. Geophys. Soc., Utah Geol. Assn., Utah Acad. Scis., Arts and Letters. Achievements include development of a stable, explicit seismic depth imaging algorithm, a residual depth imaging algorithm for seismic data, phase-shift plus variable-length transform imaging algorithm, linearized elastic wave decomposition and inversion process for seismic data, an aperture compensated migration-inversion process for seismic data, a thermoacoustic wave equation for temperature changes in human tissue, a modified self-consistent quantum field theory, algorithm to estimate dry-rock compressibility, compressional and shear wave velocities for porous fluid-filled rocks in situ, 3-D, prestack seismic imaging algorithm; research in ground penetrating radar and very low frequency electromagnet and electrical resisistivity methods, delineating hazardous materials and faulting in the subsurface, solution to the Heisenberg magnetic exchange model and to the BCS model of superconductivity and to the model of superfluidity. Home: 249 W 1100 S Orem UT 84058-6709 Office: Utah Valley State Coll Dept Physics Orem UT 84058 Office Phone: 801-863-7497. Business E-Mail: bensonal@uvsc.edu.

BENSON, CRAIG ROBERT, former governor; b. NYC, Oct. 8, 1954; m. Denise Benson; 2 children. B in Fin., Babson Coll., 1977; MBA, Syracuse U., 1979. With Teradyne Inc., Boston, 1979—81, Inetlan, Chelmsford, Mass., 1981—83; co-founder Cabletron, 1983, dir. ops., 1984—89, chmn., COO, treas., 1989—97, pres., CEO, chmn., treas., 1998—99; dir. bd. dirs. Enterasys, Rochester, NH; gov. State of N.H., Concord, 2003—05. Adj. prof. entrepreneurship Babson Coll., 2000. Republican.

BENSON, D(AVID) MICHAEL, plant pathologist; b. Dayton, Ohio, Aug. 28, 1945; s. Phillip Wayne and Edna Mae (Yowler) B.; m. Patricia D. Miller, Jan. 28, 1967; children: Julie Ann, Jeremy M., Jamie M. BS, Earlham Coll., Richmond, Ind., 1967; MS, Colo. State U., 1968, PhD, 1973. Postdoctoral fellow U. Calif., Berkeley, 1973-74; prof. plant pathology N.C. State U., Raleigh, 1974—. Editor: Phytopathology, 1988-90, Crop Prot., 1993-96, Can J. Microbiology, 1993-96, APS Press, 1998-2001; contbr. articles to profl. jours. Fellow Am. Phytopathol. Soc.; mem. Sigma Xi (v.p. 1987, Young Rschr. award 1980), Gamma Sigma Delta (treas. 1991-93, pres. 1994-95). Office: N C State Univ Dept Plant Pathology Campus Box 7629 Raleigh NC 27695-7629

BENSON, DONALD ERICK, finance company executive; b. Mpls., June 1, 1930; s. Fritz and Annie (Nordstrom) B.; children: Linda K., Nancy A., Stephen D.; m. Roberta Mann, 1992. BBA in Acctg., U. Minn., 1955. CPA, Minn. From staff to partnership Arthur Andersen & Co., Mpls., 1955-68, MEI Corp., Mpls., 1968-86; pres. MEI Diversified Inc., Mpls., 1986-94; exec. v.p. Marquette Fin. Companies, Mpls., 1992—; also bd. dirs. Bd. dirs. Mair Holdings, Inc., Minn. Twins Baseball Club, Mass. Mut. Corp. Investors, Mass. Mut. Participation Investors, Internat. Cargo Holdings, Inc., Nat. Merc. Bancorp.; dir. Swedish Coun. Am. and its Royal Round Table. Chmn. Bethel U. Found., St. Paul; past chmn. Pk. Nicollet Med. Services, Mpls.; past pres. Boys and Girls Clubs, Mpls., Minn. Mem. AICPA, Minn. CPA Soc., Mpls. Club, Interlachen Country Club.

BENSON, EDWIN WELBURN, JR., trade association executive; b. Nashville, Feb. 18, 1945; s. Edwin Welburn and Mildred B.; m. Jamie Suzanne Parks, Aug. 14, 1982; 1 child, Edwin III. BA, Vanderbilt U., 1967. V.p. The Benson Co., Nashville, 1970-78; assoc. exec. dir. Country Music Assn., Nashville, 1979-91, exec. dir., 1992—. Bd. govs. Nashville C. of C. With U.S. Army, 1967-70. Mem. Leadership Music Alumni, Leadership Nashville Alumni, The Rec. Acad., Acad. TV Arts and Scis., Am. Soc. Assn. Execs. Avocations: golf, travel, music. Office: Country Music Assn 1 Music Cir S Nashville TN 37203-4312

BENSON, ELIZABETH POLK, art specialist; b. Washington, May 13, 1924; d. Theodore Booton and Rebecca Dean (Albin) Benson. BA, Wellesley Coll., 1945; MA, Cath. U. Am., 1956. Mus. aide, curator Nat. Gallery of Art, Washington, 1946-60; curator Pre-Columbian Collection Dumbarton Oaks, Washington, 1962-79, dir. Ctr. for Pre-Columbian Studies, 1971-79; rsch. assoc. Inst. Andean Studies, Berkeley, Calif., 1980—. Lectr. Cath. U. Am., Washington, 1968—69; adj. prof. Columbia U., N.Y.C., 1973; sr. lectr. U. Tex., Austin, 1985; Andrew S. Keck disting. vis. prof. Am. U., Washington, 1987; cons. Montreal Mus. Fine Arts, 1980—84, 1990—92; mem. adv. bd. L.Am. Indian Lits. Jour., Pitts., 1989—; co-curator traveling exhbn. Birds and Beasts of Ancient L.Am., 1995—98; mem. exec. com. Peruvian Am. Rsch. Found. Author: The Maya World, 1967, 1972, 1977, The Mochica, 1972, Birds and Beasts of Ancient Latin America, 1997; co-editor: Olmec Art of Ancient Mexico, 1996, Ritual Sacrifice in Ancient Peru, 2001. Mem.: Coll. Art Assn., L.Am. Indian Lits. Assn. (v.p. 1989—), The Lit. Soc., Soc. Women Geographers (mus. com. 1994—). Home and Office: 8314 Old Seven Locks Rd Bethesda MD 20817-2005

BENSON, FRANCES GOLDSMITH, publishing executive; b. Orange, N.J., Oct. 27, 1945; BA, Wells Coll., 1967. Dir. ILR Press Cornell U., Ithaca, NY, 1982-95; editor-in-chief Cornell U. Press, Ithaca, NY, 1995—2002, editl. dir. ILR Press, 2002—. Mem. adv. bd. Ctr. Study of Working Class Life, 2002—03; mem. Rutgers U. Press Coun., 2003—. Mem. Indsl. Rels. Rsch. Assn. Business E-Mail: fgb2@cornell.edu.

BENSON, GREGORY, music educator; MusB Edn., Ctrl. Mich. U.; MusM, Bowling Green State U.; PhD, Mich. State U. Prof. and chair, dept. of music Coll. of Ea. Utah, Price, Utah, 1999—. Mem.: Utah Music Educators Assn. (editor), Nat. Band Assn. (utah state chair), Coll. Band Dirs. Nat. Assn. (secretary-treasurer, western divsn.).

BENSON, JAMES BRACKEN, lawyer; b. Bloomington, Ill., Mar. 14, 1945; s. Thomas Bracken and Ruth Mabel (Glasener) B.; m. April Lane, June 4, 1972; children: Corey L. Benson, Eric L. AB, Dartmouth Coll., 1967; JD, Harvard U., 1970. Bar: N.Y. 1971, N.J. 1985. Assoc. Strock, Strock & Lavan, N.Y.C., 1970-77; assoc., gen. counsel, corp. v.p. Automatic Data Processing, Inc., Roseland, N.J., 1977—. Office: Automatic Data Processing Inc 1 A D P Blvd Roseland NJ 07068-1786

BENSON, JAMES M., investment company executive; b. 1945; m. Marlene Benson; 2 children. BA in Econs., U. Ill., 1968; MBA, U. So. Calif., 1972. CLU. With Pacific Mut. Life Inst. Co., 1968-84; ptnr. Mgmt. Compensation Group, 1984-93; former pres., COO Equitable Life Assurance Soc. U.S., N.Y.C., former bd. dirs.; pres., CEO New Eng. Fin., Boston, 1997-98, chmn., CEO, 1998—2002; pres. individual bus. MetLife, Inc., 1999—2002; chmn., pres., and CEO Gen Am. Fin. Corp., 2002; sr. exec. v.p., pres. sales and mktg. John Hancock Fin. Svcs., Inc., 2002—; pres., CEO John Hancock Life Ins. Co., 2002—; dir. John Hancock Subs., LLC. Bd. dirs. Achilles Track Club, The Am. Coll., Christopher Reeve Found., Alliance Francaise, Hosp. for Spl. Surgery, African Wildlife Found.; founder, chmn. World T.E.A.M. Sports. Office: John Hancock Fin Svcs Inc John Hancock Pl PO Box 111 Boston MA 02117*

BENSON, JEANNE P., music educator; b. Taylorville, Ill., July 21, 1948; d. George A. Pranske and Rosetta S. Strohl; m. Wayne A. Benson, Nov. 29, 1969; 1 child, Jennifer Leigh. BS Edn., Eastern Ill. U., 1970. Vocal dir. Cissna Park Sch., Ill., 1970—72; vocal, piano instr. Kankakee Sch. Dist., Ill., 1982—. Vocal dir. New Park Singers, Kankakee, 1988—; vocal dir., mgr. Kankakee Orch. Chorus, 1986—; vocal dir. Kankakee Valley Theatre, 1978—. Mem.: Ill. Music Educators, Music Educators Nat. Conf. Office Phone: 815-933-0709.

BENSON, JIM, finance company executive; Chmn., pres., chief exec. MetLife affiliate New Eng. Fin.; pres. individual svc. MetLife; chmn., pres., CEO GenAm. Fin. Corp., 2002; interim CEO Nat. Assn. of Insurance and Financial Advisors, 2002—03. Office: 700 Market St Saint Louis MO 63101

BENSON, JOANNE E., retired lieutenant governor; b. Jan. 4, 1943; m. Robert Benson; 2 children. BS, St. Cloud State U. Mem. Minn. Senate, St. Paul, 1991-94; lt. gov. State of Minn., St. Paul, 1994-98; CEO, Minn. Bus. Acad., St. Paul, 1999—2005.

BENSON, JOHN ALEXANDER, JR., internist, educator; b. Manchester, Conn., July 23, 1921; s. John A. and Rachel (Patterson) B.; children: Peter M., John Alexander III, Susan Leigh, Jeremy P. BA, Wesleyan U., 1943; MD, Harvard Med. Sch., 1946. Diplomate Am. Bd. Internal Medicine (mem. 1969-91, sec.-treas. 1972-75, pres. 1975-91, pres. emeritus 1991—), Subsplty. Bd. Gastroenterology (mem. 1961-66, chmn. 1965-66). Intern Univ. Hosps., Cleve., 1946-47; resident Peter Bent Brigham Hosp., Boston, 1949-51; fellow Mass. Gen. Hosp., Boston, 1951-53; rsch. asst. Mayo Clinic, Rochester, Minn., 1953-54; asst. in medicine Mass. Gen. Hosp., 1954-59; instr. medicine Harvard U., 1956-59; head divsn. gastroenterology U. Oreg. Med. Sch., Portland, 1959-75, prof. medicine, 1965-93; prof. emeritus Oreg. Health & Sci. U., Portland, 1993—, interim dean Sch. Medicine, 1991—93, dean emeritus, 1993—, asst. dir. Ctr. for Ethics in Health Care, 1992—2003; prof. internal medicine U. Nebr. Coll. Medicine, Omaha, 2003—. Cons. VA Hosps., Madigan Gen. Army Hosp., John A. Hartford Found. Editorial bd.: Am. Jour. Digestive Diseases, 1966-73, The Pharos, 2000—; contbr. articles to profl. jours. Mem. Oreg. Med. Ednl. Found., 1967-73, dir., 1967-73, pres., 1969-72; bd. dirs. N.W. Ctr. for Physician-Patient Comm., 1994-99, Am. Acad. on Physician and Patient, 1994-99; bd. dirs. Found. for Med. Excellence, 1996-2003, pres., 1998-2000; trustee Oreg. Health & Sci. U. Found., 1999-2003. With USNR, 1947-49. Mem. AAS, AMA, ACP (master), Am. Gastroenterol. Assn. (sec. 1970-73, v.p. 1975-76, pres.-elect. 1976-77, pres. 1977-78), Am. Clin. and Climatol. Assn. (v.p. 1997), Am. Soc. Internal Medicine, Western Assn. Physicians, North Pacific Soc. Internal Medicine, Am. Fedn. Clin. Rsch., Federated Coun. for Internal Medicine, Am. Assn. Study Liver Disease, Western Soc. Clin. Investigation, Soc. Health and Human Values, Assn. Health Svcs. Rsch., Inst. Medicine NAS, Phi Beta Kappa, Sigma Xi, Alpha Omega Alpha. Office: 983332 Nebr Med Ctr Omaha NE 68198-3332 Office Phone: 402-559-4887. Business E-Mail: jabenson@unmc.edu.

BENSON, JOHN SCOTT, lawyer; b. Atlanta, Sept. 17, 1947; s. Lawrence Walker and Betty Lamar (Chick) B.; m. Louise Kathryn Sweet, July 22, 1984; children: Nathaniel Scott, Elisabeth Sweet. BA magna cum laude, Vanderbilt U., 1969; JD, U. Va., 1974. Bar: Fla. 1974, Colo. 1988. Assoc. Martin, Ade, Birchfield & Johnson, Jacksonville, Fla., 1974-78, ptnr., 1978-88, Kraemer, Kendall & Benson, P.C., Colorado Springs, Colo., 1988—. Bd. dirs. Associated Unit Cos., Inc., 1986-90, El Paso County Physicians Found., 2000—; adj. prof. U. Colo. Coll. Bus., Colorado Springs, 1996-98. Bd. dirs. Cerebral Palsy of Jacksonville, 1980-88, pres., 1986; mem. Fedn. Council YMCA Indian Guides, 1985-86; bd. dirs. Children's Services of Jacksonville, 1986-88, adv. bd. Grace Fellowship Ch., 2000—. Served to 1st lt. U.S. Army, 1969-71, Vietnam. Decorated Air medal; named one of Outstanding Young Men in Am., 1979. Mem. Colo. Bar Assn., El Paso County Bar Assn., Colorado Springs Estate Planning Coun., Christian Legal Soc., Christian Mgmt. Assn., Phi Beta Kappa, Phi Kappa Sigma. Republican. Avocations: sunday school teaching, camping, skiing. Office: 430 N Tejon St Ste 300 Colorado Springs CO 80903-1167 E-mail: jbenson@k2blaw.com.

BENSON, KEITH J., healthcare management educator; s. Walter and Beverly F. Benson; m. Lori Fox Fox, July 18, 1987; children: Andrew K.(dec.) children: Kyle J., Megan N., Mark R., Claire E. BS, U. Md., U. Coll., Asian Divsn., Tokyo Japan, 1987; MHA, Pa.State U., Univ. Pk., Pa., 1991; PhD, PhD, Pa. State U., Univ. Pk., Pa., 2001. Coord., MHA program Penn State U., Univ. Pk., Pa., 1991—93; asst. prof. Winthrop U., Rock Hill, SC, 1999—. Dir., health svcs. mgmt. program Winthrop U., Rock Hill, SC, 1999—. Bd. mem. SC. Rural Health Assn., Columbia, SC, 2003—. Staff sgt. USAF, 1982—89. Decorated Air Force Commn. Medal USAF. Mem.: Assn. of U. Programs in Health Adminstrn., Acad. of Mgmt. Lutheran. Office: Winthrop Univ 517 Thurmond Bldg CBA Rock Hill SC 29733 Office Phone: 803-323-4834. Business E-Mail: bensonk@winthrop.edu.

BENSON, KENNETH VICTOR, manufacturing executive, lawyer; b. New Lisbon, Wis., Aug. 2, 1929; s. Carl W. and Ottilia (Olson) B.; m. Alice May Drewry, June 23, 1951; children: Jennifer, Elizabeth, Kenneth, Jonathan, Nathan. BBA, U. Wis., 1951, JD, 1957. Bar: Wis. 1957. Sales trainee, sales corr. Marathon Corp., Menasha, Wis., 1953-54; practice law with Benson & Day, Marshfield, Wis., 1957-58; sr. v.p., dir., exec. com. Kohler Co., Wis., 1959-81; pres., mem. exec. com., dir. Vollrath Co., Sheboygan, Wis., 1982-89; ptnr. Benson, Zufelt & Donohue, Sheboygan, 1990-92. Bd. dirs. Sheboygan United Fund, 1969-75, Wis. 4-H Found., Inc., 1988-92, Sheboygan YMCA, 1971-79, sec., 1975-76, v.p., 1977-79; pres. Sheboygan Comty. Players and Civic Orch., 1967-69, bd. dirs., 1963-76; bd. dirs. Sheboygan Retirement Home, 1976-85, v.p., 1979-80, pres., 1980-81; trustee Lakeland Coll., 1978-92. With AUS, 1951-53. Mem. Home: 125 White Ash Dr Pine Knoll Shores NC 28512-6218

BENSON, KEVIN E., transportation executive; With Trizec-Hahn Corp., 1977—95, CFO, 1983—86, pres., 1986—95, CEO, 1987—95; CFO Canadian Airlines Internat., 1995—96, pres., CEO, 1996—2000; pres. Jim Pattison Group, 2000—01; pres., CEO Ins. Corp. British Columbia, 2001—02, Laidlaw Inc., 2002—03, Laidlaw Internat., Naperville, Ill., 2003—. Bd. dir. Manulife Financial, 1995—. Office: Laidlaw International Ste 400 55 Shuman Blvd Naperville IL 60563*

BENSON, LUCY WILSON, historian, consultant; b. NYC, Aug. 25, 1927; d. Willard Oliver and Helen (Peters) Wilson; m. Bruce Buzzell Benson, Mar. 30, 1950 (dec. Mar. 1990). BA, Smith Coll., 1949, MA, 1955; LHD (hon.), Wheaton Coll., 1965; LLD (hon.), U. Mass., 1969; LHD (hon.), Bucknell U., 1972; LLD (hon.), U. Md., 1972; LHD (hon.), Carleton Coll., 1973; LLD (hon.), Amherst Coll., 1974, Clark U., 1975; HHD (hon.), Springfield Coll., 1981; LHD (hon.), Bates Coll., 1982; LLD (hon.), Lafayette Coll., 1999. Mem. jr. exec. tng. program Bloomingdale's, N.Y.C., 1949-50; asst. dir. pub. rels. Smith Coll., 1950-53; rsch. asst. dept. Am. studies Amherst Coll., 1956-57; pres. Amherst LWV, Mass., 1957-61, pres. Mass., 1961-65, nat. pres., 1968-74; mem. Gov.'s cabinet and sec. human svcs. Commonwealth of Mass., 1975; mem. spl. commn. on adminstrv. rev. U.S. Ho. of Reps., Washington, 1976-77; under sec. State Security Assistance, Sci. and Tech. U.S. Dept. State, Washington, 1977-80; cons. U.S. Dept. State and SRI Internat., Washington, 1980-81; pres. Benson and Assocs., Amherst, 1981—. Vice-chair Citizen Network Fgn. Affairs; bd. dirs. Dreyfus Fund, others, Internat. Exec. Svc. Corps. Pub. adv. com. U.S. Trade Policy, 1968; mem. town meeting Amherst, 1957—74, 2000; mem. fin. com., 1960—66; mem. Gov. Mass. Spl. Com. Rev. Sunday Closing Laws, 1961, Mass. Adv. Bd. Higher Ednl. Policy, 1962—65, Gov. Mass. Com. Rev. Salaries State Employees, 1963; adv. com. racial imbalance and edn. Mass. Bd. Edn., 1964—65; Mass. adv. com. U.S. Commn. Civil Rights, 1964—73; vice-chair Mass. Adv. Coun. Edn., 1965—68; Mass. Com. Children and Youth Com. to Study Report by U.S. Children's Bur. Mass. Youth Svc. Divsn., 1967; steering com. Urban Coalition, 1968, exec. com., 1970—75, 1980—84, co-chair, 1973—75; vis. com. John F. Kennedy Sch. Govt.; trilateral commn. Coun. Fgn. Rels.; former bd. govs. Am. Nat. Red Cross, Common Cause, Women's Action Alliance; bd. govs. Internat. Ctr. Election Law and Adminstrn., 1985—87; spl. commn. Mass. Legislature Study Budgetary Powers Trustee U. Mass., 1961—62; trustee Edn. Devel. Ctr., Newton, Mass., 1967—72, Nat. Urban League, 1974—77, Brookings Instn., 1974—77, Smith Coll., 1975—80, Alfred P. Sloan Found., 1975—77, 1981—2000, Bur. Social Sci. Rsch., Inc., 1985—87; bd. dirs. Catalyst, 1972—90, Atlantic Coun. U.S., 1988—, vice-chair, 1993—2000; trustee Lafayette Coll., 1985—2000, vice-chair, 1990—2000, trustee emeritus, 2000—. Recipient Achievement award, Bur. Govt. Rsch. U. Mass., 1963, Disting. Svc. award, Boston Coll., 1965, Northfield Mt. Hermon Sch., 1976, Disting. Civil Leadership award, Tufts U., 1965, medal, Smith Coll., 1969; fellow, Radcliffe Inst., 1965—67. Mem.: ACLU, NAACP, Internat. Inst. Strategic Studies, Nat. Acad. Pub. Adminstrn., Jersey Wildlife Preservation Trust Channel Islands, E. African Wildlife Soc., Assn. Am. Indian Affairs, Urban League, UN Assn. Home and Office: 46 Sunset Ave Amherst MA 01002-2097

BENSON, MAJORIE LOUISE, retired humanities educator; b. Jackson, Tenn., Jan. 1, 1927; d. Robert and Essie Mae Hunt; children: Bruce, Bernita, Dyka, Linda Stokes. BA, Lane Coll., Jackson, Tenn., 1955; MA, Tenn. State U., Nashville; studied Revolution History, Mid. Tenn. State, Murfreesboro, 1968; studied African Am. Studies, U. Gainsville, Fla., 1986; degree (hon.), Lambuth, Jackson, 1979, Charleston, SC, 1994. Coord. E. Madison County Cmty. Assn., Jackson, 1982—, Meals on Wheels, Jackson, 1992—; supporter VFW, Jackson, 2002—. Named one of Women of Yr., E. HS Alumni Assn., Jackson, 1982—2003. Mem.: NAACP (exec. bd. 1996). Home: 160 Cotton Grove Rd Jackson TN 38305-9274

BENSON, MORGAN, energy engineer, military officer; b. Washington, Sept. 20, 1948; s. Wilmer Kersey and Virginia Cabell Benson; m. Elaine Rae Page, Oct. 26, 2000; children: Jennifer R., Jason C. Gaskill, Karen L., Matthew E. Gaskill, Erik P. Gaskill. BS, U. Del., 1972; MBA, U. Scranton, 1984. Cert. energy engr., Assn. Energy Engrs., 2000, registered profl. engr., Ky., 1974. Commd. 2d lt. U.S. Army, 1972, advanced through grades to lt. col., 1994; facilities engr. Scranton (Pa.) Army Ammunition Plant, 1979—86; chief environ. br. U.S. Army Tobyhanna (Pa.) Army Depot, 1986—88; energy mgr. HQs, US Army, Europe / 7A, Heidelberg, Germany, 1988—94; chief of utilities U.S. Army 26th Area Support Group, Heidelberg, 1994—99; project mgr. Walter Reed Army Med. Ctr., Washington, 1999—2000; installation energy mgr. U.S. Army Dugway (Utah) Proving Ground, 2000—. Ops. officer HQs, U.S. Army 21st TAACOM, Kaiserslautern, Germany, 1988—94, HQs, U.S. Army V Corps, Heidelberg, 1994—96. Assoc. editor: Encyclopedia of World War II. Lt. col. CAP, 1999—. Decorated Meritorious Svc. medal HQs, U.S. Army, Europe /7A, Army Commendation medal, 7th Oak Leaf Cluster; recipient Energy Mgmt. award, Sec. of the Army, 2002, Fed. Energy and Water Mgmt. award, Dept. of Energy, 1998, 2003. Fellow: Soc. Am. Mil. Engrs. (life; post pres. 1997—99, Silver medal 1994, Paul W. Thompson medal 1996, Regional Vice President's medal 1994); mem.: ASME, Ret. Officers Assn. (life). Avocations: military history, genealogy, travel. Office: 620A Coyote Cove Dugway UT 84022-5000 E-mail: bensonm@dpg.army.mil.

BENSON, P. GEORGE, dean, finance educator; b. Lewisburg, Pa., June 3, 1946; s. Paul Benson and Anna Louise (Stolz) McDowell; m. Jane Alison Oas, July 17, 1982; children: Jeffery George, Laura Jane, Alison Louise. BS in math., Bucknell U., 1968; postgrad., NYU, 1970-71; PhD in decision scis., U. Fla., 1977. Mgmt. analyst U.S. Army Security Agy., Arlington, Va., 1968-69; computer scientist Bell Telephone Labs., Whippany, NJ, 1969-71; prof. of decision scis. Carlson Sch. Mgmt. U. Minn., Mpls., 1977-93, head decision scis. area, 1983—88, dir. Ops. Mgmt. Ctr., 1992—93; dean Grad. Sch. Mgmt., Sch. Mgmt. at Newark, Sch. Bus. at New Brunswick Rutgers U., 1993—98; dean and Simon S. Selig, Jr. Chair of Econ. Growth, Terry Coll. Bus. U. Ga., Athens, 1998—. Judge Malcolm Baldridge Nat. Quality Award, 1997-2000, bd. overseers 2004-; bd. dirs. Nutrition 21 Inc., Purchase, NY, Univ. Ventures Inc., Newark, NJ; bd. advisors Executrack Inc., Atlanta; bd. trustees Ga. Coun. Econ. Edn.; cons. Minn. Dept. Transp., St. Paul, 1982-89, The Pillsbury Co., Mpls., 1985-87, Ga.-Pacific, Mpls., 1985, First Minn., Mpls., 1987-89, Norwest, Mpls., 1990-93, W.R. Grace, N.Y., 1991, Unisys, Mpls., 1992-94, AT&T, Mpls., 1992-93, Control Data Corp., Mpls., 1991. Author: (with James McClave) Statistics for Business and Economics, 6th edit., 1994, A First Course in Business Statistics, 6th edit., 1995; contbr. articles to profl. jours; bi-monthly columnist Ga. Trend mag. Bd. advisors Metro Atlanta C. of C.; bd. govs. Buckhead Club, Atlanta. Grantee U.S. Dept. Transp., 1988-90; fellowship Burlington No., 1982-86. Fellow Decision Scis. Inst., 2000-; Mem. Inst. Mgmt. Scis., Am. Statis., Am. Soc. for Quality Control, Soc. for Judgment and Decision Making, U. Minn. Golf Club (pres. 1991-92), Bucknell U. Golf Club, Phi Eta Sigma, Beta Gamma Sigma, Alpha Iota Delta, Sigma Chi. Avocation: golf. Office: Terry Coll Bus U Ga 335 Brooks Hall Athens GA 30602

BENSON, RICHARD, dean, photographer; Prof. Yale U. Sch. Art, 1979—, dean, 1996—. Co-author: Maritime Album, 100 Photog. & Their Stories, 1997, Lay this Laurel, 1972; author: Face of Lincoln, Work of Atget; author: (photog. by Lee Friedlander) Am. Monument; Represented in permanent collections Mus. Modern Art. Office: Office of the Dean Yale U Sch Art PO Box 208339 New Haven CT 06520*

BENSON, ROBERT CRAIG, III, business consultant; b. Waukegan, Ill., May 27, 1944; s. Robert Craig II and Leona (Pollard) B.; m. Ree Ann Christensen, June 3, 1961; children: Bradley, Barry. BA in Bus. Adminstrn. and Math., Dakota Wesleyan U., Mitchell, S.D., 1967. CPA, Cert. Mgmt. Cons. Supervising sr. Broeker Hendrickson & Co., St. Paul, 1967-70; ptnr.

Sands Benson & Weinberg, St. Paul, 1970-73; mgr. Miller, McCollom & Co., Denver, 1973-74; mng. ptnr. Benson Wells & Co., Denver, 1974-84; pres. Am. Bus. Advisors, Denver, 1984—. Lectr. Ctr. for Leadership Devel., Kiev, Ukraine, 1998—; Opperman disting. alumni lectr. Dakota Wesleyan U., 2002. Contbr. articles to profl. jours. Bd. mem., chair Denver Youth for Christ, 1975-85; elder Cherry Hills Cmty. Ch., Highlands Ranch, Colo., 1982-87; bd. mem. COMPA Food Bank, Denver, 1986-93, Global Connections Internat., 2000-2003, Project C.U.R.E., 2000-04, Dakota Wesleyan U., 2004—. Mem.: AICPA (mgmt. cons. divsn.), Inst. Mgmt. Cons., Colo. Soc. CPAs (co-chmn. profession practice bd. 1981—82). Avocations: golf, skiing, teaching about god. Office: Am Bus Advisors Inc 6635 S Dayton Ste 210 Greenwood Village CO 80111 E-mail: bob@abadvisors.com.

BENSON, ROBERT EUGENE, lawyer; b. Red Oak, Iowa, Apr. 7, 1940; s. Paul J. and Frances (Sever) B.; m. Ann Marie Lucke, July 20, 1968; children: Steven J., Robert J., Katherine A. BA, U. Iowa, 1962; LLB, U. Pa., 1965. Bar: Colo. 1965. Assoc. Holland & Hart, Denver, 1965-71, ptnr., 1971—. Adj. faculty U. Denver Coll. Law, 1992. Author: The Power of Arbitrators and Courts to Order Discovery in Arbitration, 1996, Application of the Pro Rata Liability, Comparative Negligence and Contribution Statues, 1994; co-author: How to Prepare For, Take and Use a Deposition, 5th edit., 1994; mng. editor: Colorado Construction Law, 1999, 2003, 05; contbr. articles to profl. jours. Capt. USAF, 1965-73. Mem. ABA, Colo. Bar Assn., Denver Bar Assn., Coll. Comml. Arbitrators. Avocations: golf, skiing. Home: 5454 Preserve Pky N Greenwood Village CO 80121-2185 Office: Holland & Hart LLP 555 17th St Ste 3200 Denver CO 80202-3950 Office Phone: 303-295-8234. Business E-Mail: rbenson@hollandhart.com.

BENSON, SIDNEY WILLIAM, chemistry researcher; b. N.Y.C., Sept. 26, 1918; m. Anna Bruni, 1986; 2 children. AB, Columbia Coll., 1938; A.M., PhD, Harvard U., 1941; Docteur Honoris Causa, U. Nancy, France, 1989. Rsch. asst. Gen. Electric Co., 1940; rsch. fellow Harvard U., 1941-42; instr. chemistry CCNY, 1942-43; group leader Manhattan Project Kellex Corp., 1943; asst. prof. U. So. Calif., 1943-48, assoc. prof., 1948-51, prof. chemistry, 1951-64, 76-89, distng. prof., 1986—, disting. prof. emeritus, 1989—, dir. chem. physics program, 1962-63; rsch. chemist Nat. Rsch. Coun., Divsn. 9, 1944—46; dir. dept. kinetics and thermochemistry Stanford Rsch. Inst., 1963-76; sci. dir. Hydrocarbon Rsch. Inst. U. So. Calif., 1977-90, sci. dir. emeritus, 1991—; rsch. assoc. dept. chemistry and chem. engring. Calif. Inst. Tech., 1957-58; vis. prof. UCLA, 1959, U. Ill., 1959; hon. Glidden lectr. Purdue U., 1961; vis. prof. chemistry Stanford U., 1966-70, 71, 73; mem. adv. panel phys. chemistry Nat. Bur. Standards, 1969-72, chmn., 1970-71; hon. vis. prof. U. Utah, 1971; vis. prof. U. Paris VII and XI, 1971-72, U. St. Andrews, Scotland, 1973, U. Lausanne, Switzerland, 1979. Frank Gucker lectr. U. Ind., 1984—; Brotherton prof. in phys. chemistry U. Leeds, 1984; cons. G.N. Lewis; lectr. U. Calif., Berkeley, 1989. Author: Foundations of Chemical Kinetics, 1960, rev. edit. 1982, Thermochemical Kinetics, 1968, 2d edit., 1976, Critical Survey of the Data of the Kinetics of Gas Phase Unimolecular Reactions, Reactions, 1970, Chemical Calculations, 3d edit., 1971, Atoms, Molecules and Chemical Reactions, 1972; founder, editor-in-chief Internat. Jour. Chem. Kinetics, 1967-83; mem. editl. adv. bd. Combustion Sci. and Tech., 1973-94, Oxidation Comms., 1978—, Revs. of chem. Intermediates, 1979-87, Hydrocarbon Letters, 1980-81, Jour. Phys. Chemistry, 1981-85; sci. adv. coun. Annales Medicales de Nancy, 1993—. Recipient Polanyi medal Royal Soc. Eng., 1986; faculty rsch. award U. So. Calif., 1984, Presdl. medal, 1986, Peter Kapitsa Gold Medal award Russian Acad. Natural Sci., 1997; Guggenheim fellow, 1950-51, Fulbright fellow, France, 1950-51, fellow NSF, 1957-58, 71-72; recipient citation Chem. Rev., 2000; nominated for Scientist of Yr. Internat. Biog. Ctr., Cambridge, Eng., 2002. Fellow AAAS, Am. Phys. Soc.; mem. NAS, Am. Chem. Soc. (Tolman medal 1977, Hydrocarbon Chem. award 1977, Langmuir award 1986, Orange County award 1986), Faraday Soc., Indian Acad. Sci., Phi Beta Kappa, Sigma Xi, Pi Mu Epsilon, Phi Lambda Upsilon, Phi Kappa Phi Home: 1110 N Bundy Dr Los Angeles CA 90049-1513 Office: U So Calif University Pk Mc 1661 Los Angeles CA 90089-0001

BENSON, STEVEN DONALD, marketing professional, mechanical engineer, writer; b. Longview, Wash., Oct. 11, 1953; s. Steven Hughes Benson and Donna Ruth (Johnson) McKinney; m. Patricia Joyce Krauss, Feb. 14, 1982; children: Steven William, Patricia Ann. AA in Drafting, Merit Davis, 1973; AA in Robotics, AMADA Sch., Buena Park, Calif., 1997. Precision sheet metal mechanic Ariz. Precision Sheet Metal, Phoenix, 1980-86, Neilson Mfg. Inc., Salem, Oreg., 1986—2002; co-owner Time Honored Gifts, Salem, 1988—94; pres. Advanced Sheet Metal Applications, Salem, 1986—; co-owner A-Cab Taxi and Transp. Svcs. LCC, Salem, 2000—05, Gizmo Med. Transport Inc., 2003—05, BACA Safety, 2004—05. Instr. Oreg. Advanced Tech. Consortium, Wilsonville, 1990-1994; sheet metal instr. Clackamas C.C., Oregon City, Oreg., 1997-2003; editor, pub. Precision Sheet Metal Chronicle, electronic mag., 1998—; pres. Brake Tng. & Cons; chmn. Precision Sheet Metal Cosn Author: (textbooks) Introduction to Precision Press Brake, 1991, Intermediate Press Brake, 1992, Advanced Precision Press Brake, 1994, Press Brake Technology, 1997, Lasers, Punches, PressBrakes & Shears, 2001, Darkness to Light, 2002, (software) Advanced Sheet Metal Applications (ASMA 4.0), 1982, 1990, 1992, 1996, 1997; contbr. articles to profl. jours. Sec., treas. Bike PAC of Oreg., Salem, 1988-2001, lobbyist, 1992; mem. A Brotherhood Against Totalitarian Enactments (ABATE), Oreg., Inc.; chief petitioner Statewide Initiative Petition, Oreg. (Road to Freedom award, Bike PAC of Oreg., 1992); hon. chmn. Oreg. chpt. Nat. Rep. Congl. Com., 2002. Named Businessman of Yr., NRCC, 2003; recipient Edn. award, Fabricators and Mfg. Assn. Internat., 1999, Article of the Yr. award, Croydon/FMA, 2001, Congl. Leadership award, 2002, Freedom isn't Free award, Bike PAC of Oreg., 1997, Legends of BikePac award, 2001, Reader's Choice award, TheFabricator.com, 2003, 2004. Master: Masons (worshipful master); mem.: Internat. Sheet Metal Workers (local 16), Soc. Mfg. Engrs., Fabricators and Mfrs. Assn. (adv. com. precision sheet metal 1997—, coun., vice chair 2004—05, chair 2005—). Avocations: family activities, children, politics, indian moto-cycles, british sports cars. Office: Advanced Sheet Metal Applications 398 Rose St NE Salem OR 97301-4468 Home: 2952 Doaks Ferry Rd NW Salem OR 97304 Office Phone: 503-399-7514. E-mail: steve@asmachronicle.com, sbenson37@comcast.net.

BENSON, THOMAS LUTHER, academic administrator; b. White Plains, NY, Mar. 2, 1940; s. Wilbert Ernest and Elaine Dorothy Benson; m. Eleanor Jo Rodger, June 14, 1964 (div. Dec. 1975); 1 child, Anders. BA, Augustana Coll., 1962; BD, Harvard U., 1966; PhD, MA, Johns Hopkins U., 1975. Assoc. prof. philosophy, dir. hons. program U. Md., Balt., 1969-86; v.p., provost St. Andrew's Coll., Laurinburg, N.C., 1986-94; pres. Green Mountain Coll., Poultney, Vt., 1994—2002, pres. emeritus; exec. dir. World Edn. Corps., 2003—. Contbr. Ency. Religion, 1987, Interdisplinary: Essays from the Literature, 1998; contbr. articles to profl. jours. including Issues in Integrative Studies, ASIANetwork Exch. Bd. dirs. Isle La Motte Preservation Trust, Isle La Motte, Vt., 1998—, Vt. World Trade Orgn., Burlington, Vt., 1996-2000, chmn. bd. Myanmar Found., 2002-; mem. adv. bd. Dorset (Vt.) Theatre Festival, 1999—; mem. alumni bd. dirs. Harvard Divinity Sch., 1995-98. Recipient Francis Asbury award United Meth. Bd. Higher Edn,. 1997; named Disting. Alumnus of Yr. Augustana Coll., 2001. Mem. Assn. for Integrative Studies (pres. 1983-85), ASIANetwork (adv. coun. 1993-95), Jefferson Legacy Fond. (dir. 1998—, pres. 2003-), Vt. Assn. Ind. Colls. (v.p. 1998—), Phi Beta Kappa. Lutheran. Avocations: tennis, swimming, hiking, reading, travel. Office: 225 Central Park West #618A New York NY 10024 Office Phone: 212-213-3970. Personal E-mail: tbenson@aol.com.

BENSON, WILLIAM EDWARD (BARNES), geologist; b. West Haven, Conn., May 15, 1919; s. John Edward and Lucia Purdy (Barnes) B.; m. Mary Freda Hill, July 11, 1944; children— Sharon (Mrs. J.G. Rachel), Lynn (Mrs. J.D. Walker), William Edward. BA, Yale U., 1940, MS, 1942, PhD, 1952. Geologist Conn. Geol. and Natural History Survey, 1940-42; geologist U.S. Geol. Survey, 1942-54, br. chief, 1953-54; exec. sec. divsn. earth sci. NAS/NRC, 1954-55; chief geologist Manidon Mining Inc., N.D., 1955-56; program dir., sect. head NSF, 1956-75, chief scientist earth sci. divsn., 1975-79; sci. adv. to Office of Pres., Washington, 1976-77; pvt. cons., 1980—. Vis. prof. U. Hawaii, 1980; sr. staff assoc. NAS, 1980-99; docent Smithsonian Inst., 1996-. Contbr., editor profl. jours. Served with USNR, 1944-45. Yale U. fellow, 1940-42. Fellow Geol. Soc. Am., Am. Geophys. Union, AAAS (sec. sect. E 1969-73, chmn. sect. E 1974-75); mem. Geol. Soc. Washington (v.p. 1958), Pick and Hammer Soc. (chmn. 1970-73), Phi Beta Kappa, Sigma Xi (lectr. 1980-81). Home: 7531 Parish Ln Falls Church VA 22042-3521 E-mail: bilfre@aol.com.

BENSTON, GEORGE JAMES, accountant, economist; b. N.Y.C., Mar. 18, 1932; s. William and Rose L. B.; m. Alice N. Schwartz, July 28, 1951; children: Kimberly Wayne, Randall Craig. BA, Queens Coll., 1952; MBA, NYU, 1953; PhD, U. Chgo., 1963. CPA, N.C. Acct. CPA firms, 1952-53; acctg. and tax specialist 1st Nat. Bank of Atlanta, 1956-57; asst. prof. acctg. Ga. State U., 1957-58, U. Chgo., 1962-66; assoc. prof. acctg. and fin. U. Rochester, 1961-69, prof. fin., acctg. and econs., 1969-87; Harlan prof. fin., acctg. and econs. Emory U., Atlanta, 1987—, assoc. dean faculty rsch. and ctr. devel., 1990-92, area coord. fin., 1988-90, 92-96, area coord. acctg., 1993-96. Vis. prof. U. Calif., Berkeley, Grad. Sch. Bus. Studies, London, London Sch. Econs., Hebrew U., Jerusalem; hon. vis. prof. City U. London, Oxford U.; trustee Coll. Retirement Equities Fund; Disting. Internat. Lectr. Am. Acctg. Assn., 1980. Author: Corporate Accounting Disclosure in the UK and the USA, 1976, Contemporary Cost Accounting and Control, 1970, 77, Analysis of Causes of SLA Failures, 1985, The Separation of Commercial and Investment Banking: The Glass-Steagall Act Revisited and Reconsidered, 1990, Regulating Financial Markets: A Critique and Some Proposals, 1999; assoc. editor, mem. editl. bd. Jour. Money and Credit Banking, Jour. Acctg. Pub. Policy; others; contbr. articles to profl. jours. Ford Found., U.S. Steel and Woodrow Wilson fellow, 1958-59; Olin Disting. fellow Oxford U. Mem. Shadow Fin. Regulation Com., Fin. Economists Roundtable, Am. Acctg. Assn., Am. Fin. Assn., Am. Econ. Assn., Fin. Mgmt. Assn., Phi Beta Kappa, Beta Gamma Sigma. Home: 3572 Knollwood Dr NW Atlanta GA 30305-1022 E-mail: benston@bus.emory.edu.

BENSUSSEN, GALE K., health products company executive; b. 1946; BS, U. So. Calif.; JD, Southwestern U. Sch. Law. Bar: Calif. 1979. Rep. Transatlantic Bus. Partnership; founding exec. Leiner Health Products, Carson, Calif., 1974, pres. Bd. mem. Consumer Healthcare Products Assn.; bd. dir. Ind. Colleges of Southern Calif.; spkr. in field. Office: Leiner Health Products Inc 901 E 233d St Carson CA 90745 Office Phone: 310-835-8400. Office Fax: 310-835-6615.

BENT, ALAN EDWARD, political science professor; b. Shanghai, June 22, 1939; s. Walter J. and Tamara (Rocklin) B.; m. Dawn Bickler, Aug. 13, 1977; 1 son by previous marriage, Ronald Geoffrey. BS, San. Francisco State U., 1963; MA, U. So. Calif., 1968, Claremont Grad. Sch., 1970, PhD, 1971; MBA, Xavier U., 1985. Instr. polit. sci. Chapman Coll., Orange, Calif., 1969-70; research assoc. Mcpl. Systems Research, Claremont Grad. Sch., 1970-71; asst. prof. polit. sci., assoc. dir. Inst. Govtl. Studies and Research Memphis State U., 1971-74; assoc. prof., chmn. dept. pub. adminstrn. Calif. State U., Dominguez Hills, 1974-77; prof. polit. sci. U. Cin., 1977-81, 82-92, head dept. polit. sci., 1977-81; dean Coll. Arts and Scis. U. No. Colo., Greeley, 1981-82, prof. polit. sci., 1981-82; prof. pub. adminstr. Troy State U., Europe, 1989-92. Cons. police agys., govtl. and pvt. instns. Author: Escape from Anarchy: A Strategy for Urban Survival, 1972; The Politics of Law Enforcement: Conflict and Power in Urban Communities, 1974, 2d edit., 1976; co-author: Police, Criminal Justice and the Community, 1976, Collective Bargaining in the Public Sector: Labor-Management Relations and Public Policy, 1978; co-editor, contbr. Urban Administration: Management, Politics and Change, 1976, 2d edit. 1977; contbr. articles to profl. jours.; bd. editors: Rev. Pub. Personnel Adminstrn., 1980-89, Spectrum, A Jour. of Comparative Politics and Devel., New Delhi, 1984-92. Served to capt. USAF, 1964—69. NASPAA fellow, 1981-82 Home: 1006 Oro St Laguna Beach CA 92651-3534 E-mail: rory2@cox.net.

BENT, GEORGE ROBERTS, III, dean, art historian, educator; b. Rochester, N.Y., Sept. 29, 1963; s. George Roberts and Ruth (Schoen) Bent; m. Lorriann Therese Olan, Feb. 20, 1965; children: Miles, Catalena, William. BA, Oberlin Coll., Ohio, 1985; MA, Stanford U., Calif., 1988, PhD, 1993. Asst. prof. art history Washington & Lee U., Lexington, Va., 1993—99, assoc. prof. art history, 1999—, assoc. dean, 2003—. Author: Pictures and Visions, 2005; contbr. articles to profl. jours. Vol. Montessori Ctr. for Children, Lexington, Va., 1998—99; Elder Lexington Presbyn. Ch., 2001—05. Fulbright scholar, Florence, Italy, 1990—91, 1999—2000. Home: 604 Marshall St Lexington VA 24450 Office: Washington & Lee Univ Washington Hall 25 Lexington VA 24450 Office Phone: 540-458-8748. Office Fax: 540-458-8995. E-mail: bentg@wlu.edu.

BENTEL, CAROL RUSCHE, architect; m. Paul Bentel, 1987. BArch, Washington U., St. Louis, 1979; MArch (with hons.), NC State U., 1981. Registered Mass., NY. Asst. prof. architecture Ga. Inst. Tech., 1984—85; ptnr. Bentel & Bentel, Locust Valley, NY, 1987—. Tchg. asst. NC State U., 1980—81; vis. assoc. prof. NY Inst. Tech., 1999—; juror architecture Fulbright Found., 1996—98; vis. adj. prof. City Coll. NY, 1997; lectr. in field. Recipient First prize, Mcpl. Arts Soc., 1985, Disting. Alumni award, Washington U . St. Louis, 1999; fellow, Partitions, Inc., 1980, Samuel Kress Found., 1993—94, Am. Acad. Rome, 1993—94; grantee, Fulbright-Hays, 1985—86; scholar, Washington U., 1974—79, Fulbright scholar, U. Venice, 1985—86. Fellow: AIA (nat. com. design, chair Rome conf. 2001, scholar 1977—81); mem.: NY State Assn. Archs. Office: 22 Buckram Rd Locust Valley NY 11560 Office Phone: 516-676-2880. E-mail: crb@beltelandbentel.com.

BENTEL, FREDERICK RICHARD, architect, educator; b. N.Y.C., Jan. 2, 1928; s. Carl August and Mary (Muller) B.; m. Maria L. R. Azzarone, Aug. 16, 1952 (deceased Nov. 8, 2000); children: Paul Louis, Peter Andreas, Maria Elisabeth. BArch., Pratt Inst., 1949; grad. fellow, Mass. Inst. Tech., MArch., 1950; DArch., Technische Hochschule, Graz, Austria, 1953. Registered architect, N.Y., 1956, N.J., 1960, Va., 1958, Vt., 1970, Conn., 1985, Mo., 2001, Del., 1998, Mass., 2001, profl. planner, N.J., 1967. Architect, partner Bentel & Bentel (AIA), Locust Valley, N.Y., 1957—; pres. Correlated Designs Inc., Locust Valley, 1961—; ptnr. Old Path Realty, Cobblestone Enterprises. Prof. Sch. Architecture, Pratt Inst., 1955-70; prof. Sch. Architecture, N.Y. Inst. Tech., 1969—. Author publs. in field. Founding mem. com. Locust Valley Bus. Dist. Planning; adv. bd. Oyster Planning and Hist. Preservation Commn., 1970-73; mem. Oyster Bay Hist. Preservation Commn., 1975-91; alt. APD panel N.Y. State Coun. on Arts, 1985-86, St. Joseph's Coll. Libr. Arch., L.I., chpt. AIA, 1990, St. Stephen's Ch., Warwick, N.Y., L.I. chpt. AIA, 1991, Pavilion, Old Westbury, N.Y. Fulbright scholar, 1952-53; recipient awards in field including 1st pl. commn. Islip Bay Shore downtown redevel. competition, 1976. Fellow AIA (task force for archtl. graphic stas., St. Joseph's Coll. Libr. Arch. L.I. chpt. 1990, St. Stephen's Ch., Warwick, N.Y., L.I. chpt. 1991, Pavilion, Old Westbury, N.Y., Gramercy Tavern, N.Y.C., L.I. chpt. 1996, Nat. Design award, 2003); mem. N.Y. Soc. Architects (numerous awards), Am. Italy Soc., MIT Alumni Assn. (ednl. coun.), Home: 23 Frost Creek Dr Locust Valley NY 11560-1029 Office: Bentel & Bentel Architect & Planner 22 Buckram Rd Locust Valley NY 11560-1928 Office Phone: 516-676-2880. E-mail: architecture@bentelandbentel.com.

BENTEL, PAUL LOUIS, architect, educator; m. Carol Rusche, 1987. BA in Visual Studies (magna cum laude), Harvard Coll., 1979, M in Architecture (with hons.), 1982; student, Swiss Fed. Inst. Tech., Zurich, 1981—82; PhD in History Theory, Criticism, MIT, 1992. Ptnr. Bentel & Bentel, Locust Valley, NY, 1985—; prof. history, preservation and design Columbia U., 1993—. Dir. Am. archl. design studio Swiss Fed. Inst. Tech., 1988—90; dir. hist. preservation program Columbia U., 2001—02; reviewer GSA. Mem. U.S. Internat. Commn. on Monuments and Sites. Fellow: AIA; mem.: Soc. for Preservation of L.I. Antiquities (bd. dirs.), Soc. Archl. Historians. Office: Bentel & Bentel 22 Buckram Rd Locust Valley NY 11560

BENTELE, BRIGITTE, mathematics educator; arrived in U.S., 1956; d. Max and Magda Bentele. BA, Earlham Coll., 1966; MAT, Johns Hopkins U., 1970. Computer programmer Svc. Bur. Corp., Wheaton, Md., 1966—68; tchr. math. So. High Sch., Balt., 1969—74; layout artist Read's, Inc., 1974—76; tchr. math. Brearley Sch., NYC, 1976—84, Trinity Sch., 1984—, head math. dept., 1994—. John Klingenstein fellow, Tchrs. Coll., 1982. Mem.: Math. Assn. Am., Nat. Coun. Tchrs. Math.

BENTLEY, ANTHONY MILES, lawyer; b. N.Y.C., July 16, 1945; s. Herbert A. and Dorothy Dene (Hyman) B. BA, U. Pa., 1967; JD, Fordham U., 1971. Bar: N.Y. 1971, U.S. Ct. Appeals (2d cir.) 1971, Pa. 1973, U.S. Dist. Ct. (so. and ea. dists.) N.Y. 1973, U.S. Tax Ct. 1976, U.S. Supreme Ct. 1976, U.S. Ct. Appeals (fed. cir.), 1995, U.S. Claims Ct. 1996, U.S. Dist. Ct. Ariz. 1996, U.S. Ct. Internat. Trade 1996. Assoc. Hughes Hubbard & Reed, N.Y.C., 1970, Cahill Gordan & Reindel, N.Y.C., 1971-75, Goldstein Shames Hyde, N.Y.C., 1975-76; sole practice N.Y.C., 1977—. Spl. master N.Y. County Supreme Ct., 1977—, N.Y. County Civil Ct., 1994—; arbitrator N.Y.C. Ct. N.Y. Coun. Editor Fordham Law Rev., 1970-71; founding editor Fordham Urban Law Jour., 1971. Trustee Am. Judges Found. With U.S. Army, 1963-65. Recipient Disting. Svc. award FTC, 1976, 79. Mem. ABA, Assn. of Bar of City of N.Y., Assn. Trial Lawyers Am., Pa. Bar Assn., Phila. Bar Assn., Mensa, Intertel, Am. Judges Assn. (N.Y. del.), N.Y. County Lawyers Assn., N.Y. Civil and Criminal Cts. Bar Assn. Jewish. Address: 116 W 72nd St New York NY 10023-3315

BENTLEY, CHARLES RAYMOND, geophysics educator; b. Rochester, N.Y., Dec. 23, 1929; s. Raymond and Janet Cornelia (Everest) B.; m. Marybelle Goode, July 3, 1964 (dec. Oct. 13, 2004); children: Molly Clare, Raymond Alexander. BS, Yale U., 1950; PhD, Columbia U., 1959. Rsch. geophysicist Columbia U., 1952-56; Antarctic traverse leader and seismologist Arctic Inst. N.Am., 1956-59; project assoc. U. Wis., 1959-61, asst. prof., 1961-63, assoc. prof., 1963-68, prof. geophysics, 1968-98, A.P. Crary prof. geophysics, 1987-98, prof. emeritus, 1998—. Recipient Bellingshausen-Lazarev medal for Antarctic rsch. Acad. Scis. USSR, 1971; NSF sr. postdoctoral fellow, 1968-69; NAS-USSR Acad. Sci. exch. fellow, 1977, 90 Fellow AAAS, Am. Geophys. Union, Arctic Inst. N.Am., Am. Polar Soc. (hon., bd. dirs.); mem. AAUP, Soc. Exploration Geophysicists, Internat. Glaciological Soc. (Seligman Crystal award 1990), Am. Quarternary Assn., Oceanography Soc., Am. Geol. Inst., Geol. Soc. Am., Phi Beta Kappa, Sigma Xi. Achievements include research on Antarctic glaciology and geophysics, satellite studies of geomagnetic anomalies, magnetotelluric exploration of Earth structure, satellite radar and laser altimetry, ice coring and drilling services. Home: 5618 Lake Mendota Dr Madison WI 53705-1036 Office: U Wis Geophys & Polar Rsch Ctr Weeks Hall 1215 Dayton St Madison WI 53706 Office Phone: 608-238-8873. Business E-Mail: bentley@geology.wisc.edu.

BENTLEY, CHARMAINE CLARK O'FALLON, secondary school educator; b. Austin, Dec. 15, 1954; d. Harold Roy and Maria Rafaela Bentley; m. Charles Oliver Mixon, May 4, 1980; 1 child, Charlotte Farrar Mixon. BA in Anthropology, BS in Geological Sci., U. Tex., 1977; BS in Computer Sci., SW Okla. State U., 1984, MEd in Math., 1988. DATA engr. Dresser Industries, Magcobar DATA, Oklahoma City, 1972-82; tchr. Dallas Ind. Sch. Dist., 1988—, tchr., technologist F.D. Roosevelt H.S., 1992—2003, chmn. computer sci. curriculum com., 1997-98, 2003—04. Sec. F.D. Roosevelt H.S. Site Base Decision Making com., 1999—2001; mem. SBDM com., 1999—; mem. faculty advisory com. Dallas (Tex.) Ind. Sch. Dist., 2001—, chmn. faculty advisory com., 2003—; presenter in field. Asst. troop leader Girl Scout U.S., Farmers Branch, Tex., 1992-95, Sunshine Literacy Project Coord., 1989-91; v.p. IB Parent Booster com. Clark H.S., Plano, Tex., 1995-96, sec., 1996-97; troop chmn. Boy Scout Am., Elk City, Okla., 1986-87; mem. F.D. Roosevelt H.S. Site Based Decision Com., 1998—, sec., 1998-2001. Recipient Award of Appreciation, City of Farmers Branch, 1990; scholar F.D. Roosevelt HS, 1991, 94. Mem. IEEE, Am. Assn. Petroleum Geologists, Nat. Coun. Tchrs. Math., Internat. Soc. Tech. Edn., Tex. Computer Edn. Assn., Assn. Tex. Profl. Educators, Tex. Computer Edn. Assn. Computer Sci. (computer sci. spl. interest group, area 5 rep. 2000-02, sec./treas. 2002—), Assn. Computing Machinery, Computer Sci. Tchrs. Assn. (steering com. 2003-04, bd. dirs. 2005—, chmn. membership com. 2005—). Episcopalian. Avocations: reading, woodwork, photography, gardening, pocket watches. Office Phone: 972-925-6800. Personal E-mail: charmainebentley@csta.acm.org.

BENTLEY, CLARENCE EDWARD, savings and loan association executive; b. Ranger, Tex., Oct. 9, 1921; s. Clarence Edward and Rosa Estelle (Bryant) B.; m. Gloria Gill, Oct. 9, 1943; children: Jon, Kitty, Perry (dec.). Student, McMurry U., Abilene, Tex., 1939-42. Pres. Abilene Savs. Assn., 1944-77, Southwestern Group Fin. Co., Houston, 1976-77; pres. United Savs. Assn. Tex., Houston, 1977-80, chmn. bd., 1980-85; dir., chmn. bd. Sandia Fed. Savs. & Loan, Albuquerque, 1986-89; dir. Kaneb Pipeline Partners, 1990—. Chmn. bd. dirs. United Fin. Mortgage Co., Dallas, United Fin. Group, Inc., Houston, 1980-86; bd. dirs. Kaneb Services Inc., Investors Mortgage Ins. Co., Boston; adb.bd. FNMA, 1980-81; trustee Thrift Instns. Short Term Liquidity Fund, N.Y.C., N.Y., 1982-83. Contbr. articles to profl. publns. Pres. Abilene Indsl. Found., 1970, United Fund Abilene, 1962, United Way, 1960; mem. bd. Tex. State Hosps., 1962-64; mem. Tex. Fin. Commn., 1964-76, chmn., 1971. Served with USAAF, 1942-43. Recipient Outstanding Citizen award City of Abilene, 1964, Disting. Alumnus award McMurry U., 1971, John T. Mahone award 1981. Mem. Nat. Savs. and Loan League (pres. 1970-71), Tex. Savs. and Loan League (pres. 1970-71), Assn. Thrift Holding Cos. (chmn. bd. 1985-87), Abilene C. of C. (pres. 1964). Clubs: Abilene Country (pres. 1951). Episcopalian. Home: 52 Rue Maison St Abilene TX 79605-4710 Office Phone: 325-670-9237. E-mail: cbent63@yahoo.com.

BENTLEY, DIANNE H. GLOVER, minister, consultant; BA, Drew U., 1976; MDiv, Drew Theol. Sch., 1997. LCSW HIV prevention counselor Pa. Dept. Health, 2003. Cons., trainer L.E.A.D., 2004; pastor First United Meth. Ch. of Sayre. Dir. Ministry Resource Libr., Madison, NJ, 1994—97; pres. Bridge of Penn-York Valley Churches, Sayre, 1999—2002; chair Poverty Task Group, 2000—05, Teen Pregnancy Prevention Task Force, 2002—. Mentor Prudential Youth Leadership Inst., Wyo. Ann. Conf. United Meth. Ch.; mem. Com. Status and Role Women, Pa. Recipient Edwin A. Lewis Theology award, Drew Theol. Sch., 1997, GFWC Short Story award, 1991. Mem.: Binghamton Dist. Pastors' Assn., Lambda Iota Tau. Methodist. Home: 77 Murray St Sayre PA 18840 Office: First United Meth Ch 200 W Lockhart St Sayre PA 18840

BENTLEY, DIERKS, country singer, songwriter; b. Phoenix, Nov. 20; Rschr. TNN TV; signed with Dangling Rope Records, 2001, Capitol Records, Nashville, 2002—. Singer: (albums) Don't Leave Me In Love, 2001, Dierks Bentley, 2003, Modern Day Drifter, 2005, (singles) What Was I Thinkin', 2003. Named Top New Artist, Acad. Country Music, 2003. Office: Capitol Records 3322 W End Ave Nashville TN 37203 Office Phone: 615-269-2000. E-mail: dbstreet@dierks.com.

BENTLEY, DONALD LYON, mathematics professor, statistics educator, minister; b. L.A., Calif., Apr. 25, 1935; s. Byron R. and Clara Viola (Lyon) B.; m. Anne P. Alexander, Aug. 28, 1957; children: James, Jillene, Janet. BS, Stanford U., 1956, MS, 1958, PhD, 1961; MDiv, Claremont Sch. Theology, 1998. Ordained Congregationalist minister 1998. Asst. prof. math. stats. Colo. State U., Ft. Collins, 1961-64; asst. prof. math. Pomona Coll., Claremont, Calif., 1964-67, assoc. prof., 1967-74, Burkhead prof. math., 1974—2001, ret., 2001; consulting minister Pilgrim Congl. Ch., Pomona, Calif., 1998—2005, assoc. minister, 2005—. Cons. Allergan Pharm., Irvine, Calif., 1968-80, Intermedics IntraOcular, Pasadena, Calif., 1981-86, Tokos Med. Corp., 1986-90, Cardio Genisis Corp., 1995-2000. Co-author: Linear Algebra with Differential Equations, 1973. Fellow Royal Statis. Soc., Am. Statis. Assn.; mem. Inst. Math. Stats., Nat. Assn. Congrl. Christian Chs. (chair exec. com. 1994-95, moderator-elect 2002-03, moderator 2003-04). Avocations: music, woodworking, geneaology.

BENTLEY, FRED DOUGLAS, SR., lawyer; b. Marietta, Ga, Oct. 15, 1926; s. Oscar Andrew and Ima Irene (Prather) B.; children from previous marriage: Fred Douglas, Robert Randall; m. Jane Morrill McNeel, Nov. 7, 1997. BA, Presbyn. Coll., 1949; JD, Emory U., 1948; HHD (hon.), PhD (hon.), LHD (hon.), Kennesaw State U., 2000. Bar: Ga. 1948. Sr. mem. Bentley & Dew, Marietta, 1948-51; ptnr. Bentley, Awtrey & Bartlett, Marietta, 1951-56, Edwards, Bentley, Awtrey & Parker, Marietta, 1956-75, Bentley & Schindelar, Marietta, 1975-80, Bentley, Bentley & Bentley, Marietta, 1975—. Pres. Beneficial Investment Co., Newmarket, Inc., Happy Valley, Inc., Bentley & Sons, Inc.; founder, chmn. emeritus bd. Charter Bank and Trust Co.; founder, trustee emeritus Kennesaw Coll. Mem. Ga. Ho. Reps., 1951-57, Ga. Senate, 1958; past pres. Cobb County (Ga.) C. of C.; founder, hon. curator Bentley Rare Book Galleries-Brenau U., Kennesaw State U.; mem., past chmn. Ga. Coun. Arts, 1976-89; mem. Gov.'s Fine Arts Com., 1990-92, Cummer Mus. of Art (hon. life); attache Ghana Olympic Com.; founder Cobb Emergency Svc.; fell. US Supreme Ct. Museum Acquisition Com., US Constitution Museum; Served with USN. Recipient Blue Key Cmty. Svc. award, Founder's award, 1992, Clarisse Baquell award for outstanding svc., Spl. Svc. award Kennesaw State U., Robert Cleveland award for lifetime achievement in law; named Citizen of Yr., C. of C., 1951, Leader of Tomorrow, Time mag., 1953, Vol. Citizen of Yr., Atlanta Jour./Constn., 1981, Kennesaw Hist. Soc. Man of Yr., 1996, Brenau U. Man of Yr. award, 1996, President's award Kennesaw State U., 1999, Disting. Alumna Marietta HS, Bus. Assoc. of Yr. award ABWA, 2002, The Extra Mile trphy, 2003, Disting. Alumna, Emory U. Law Sch., 2004; fellow J. Pierpont Morgan Libr., Oct. 15 Fred Bentley Day City & Coun.; Bridge named in his honor, 2000. Fellow Am. Trust Brit. Libr., Marietta Cobb Mus. Art (founder), U.S. Supreme Ct. Hist. Soc., U.S. Const. Ctr.; mem. Ga. Bar Assn., Ga. Mus. Art (bd. advisors, hon. life), Nat. PTA (hon. life), Cobb Landmarks Soc. (founder), Kennesaw Mountain Jaycees (founder), Rotary (hon. life), Georgian Club (bd. dir.). Republican. Presbyterian. Home: 1441 Beaumont Dr Kennesaw GA 30152-3201 Office: 241 Washington Ave NE Marietta GA 30060-1958

BENTLEY, JAMES LUTHER, former journalist; b. Panama City, Fla., Jan. 24, 1937; s. Thomas Pierce and Sara Pope (Woodruff) B.; m. Patricia Ann Daniel, July 30, 1965. Student Ga. Inst. Tech, Ga. State U., 1958-61, N.C. State U., 1962. Reporter Atlanta Constitution, 1958-64, asst. city editor, 1964-66, night city editor, 1966-71, city editor, 1971-79; corr. Reuters Ltd., 1967-79; dir. info. TVA, 1979; mng. editor Cox News Svc., Washington, 1979-98. Bd. dirs. Friends of Jekyll Island, Hofwyl Plantation. Served with U.S. Army, 1961-63. Mem. Rotary. Lutheran. Home: 317 Old Plantation Rd Jekyll Island GA 31527-0857 E-mail: jimbentley@bellsouth.net.

BENTLEY, JOSHUA MARK, lawyer; b. San Francisco, Feb. 27, 1965; s. John Martin and Ruth Catherine (Marshall) B.; m. Emily Elaine Blanchard, Aug. 15, 1990; children: Kaitlin Meredith, Olivia Roxanne, William Blanchard. BA, U. Calif., Santa Barbara, 1983-88; JD, U. Santa Clara, Calif., 1991. Bar: Calif. 1991, U.S. Dist. Ct. Calif. 1991. Dep. dist. atty. San Mateo County Dist. Atty.'s Office, Redwood City, Calif., 1991-93; gen. ptnr. Smith, Bentley & Hartnett, Redwood City, 1993—. Recipient Congl. Recognition, Congresswoman Anna Eshoo, 1996. Mem. ABA, Calif. State Bar. Republican. Roman Catholic. Office: 461 Laurel St San Carlos CA 94070-2413

BENTLEY, KAREN GAIL, elementary school educator; b. Salina, Kans., Oct. 21, 1956; d. John Kennedy and Merle Lynn Blundon; m. Rodney Ray Bentley, Feb. 17, 1984 (dec. Sept. 1996). MusB cum laude, U. Mo., 1978; MusM, So. Ill. U., 1981. Grad. asst. So. Ill. U., Edwardsville, 1980—81; dir. music Ind. Congrl. Ch., St. Louis, 1978—81; tchr. elem. music Western Hghts. Schs., Oklahoma City, 1981—. Bd. dirs. Civic Music, 1985—, Orch. League, 1994—; bd. rep. PTA, 1992—; cantor Christ the King Cath. Ch., 1985—95. Republican. Episcopalian. Avocations: theater, raising Great Danes. Home: 11117 Quail Creek Rd Oklahoma City OK 73120 Office: John Glenn Elem Sch 6500 S Land Oklahoma City OK 73159

BENTLEY, KENNETH CHESSAR, oral surgeon, educator; b. Montreal, Que., Can., Sept. 22, 1935; s. Albert Edwin and Lilian Beatrice (Hoare) B.; m. Jean Wadsworth, Aug. 19, 1961; children: Douglas, Margaret. DDS, McGill U., 1958, MD, CM, 1962. Intern, then resident Montreal Gen. Hosp. and Bellevue Hosp., NY, 1962-66; from asst. prof. to assoc. prof. McGill U., 1966-67, prof. dentistry, 1975-98, prof. emeritus, 1998; dean McGill U. Sch. Dentistry, 1977-87; jr. asst. dental surgeon Montreal Gen. Hosp., 1966, assoc. dental surgeon, assoc. dir. dentistry, 1968, dental surgeon-in-chief, 1970-2000. Cons. oral and maxillofacial surgery Royal Victoria Hosp.; pres. Thistle Coun. Quebec; pres., bd dirs. Griffith McConnell Residence Nursing Home. Co-author: Advanced Oral Radiographic Interpretation, 1979. Named Decorated Hospitaller, Order St. John Jerusalem; recipient Queen's Golden Jubilee medal, 2002. Fellow Am. Coll. Dentists, Internat. Coll. Dentists, Royal Coll. Dentists Can., Pierre Fauchard Acad., Academie Dentaire Du Quebec; mem. Assn. Oral and Maxillofacial Surgeons Que., Bellevue Soc. Oral Surgeons, Can. Dental Assn. (chmn. council hosp. services 1971-75, council edn. 1982-85), Can. Assn. Oral and Maxillofacial Surgeons (sec.-treas. 1970-71), Internat. Assn. Oral Surgeons, Montreal Dental Club (sec. 1968, pres.1992), Nat. Dental Exam. Bd. Can., Order Dentists Que., St. Andrew's Soc. Montreal (1st v.p.). Avocations: music, pipe organ, scottish country dancing. E-mail: kcb@total.net.

BENTLEY, LISA, publisher; married; 2 children. BA in English, U. Iowa. Acct. exec. Bozell; with SW Media Corp., Dallas, NY; sales exec. People and Life mag., L.A., NY; regional mgr. info. tech. Time mag., 1992—99; founding pub. Bus. 2.0 Mag. (formerly eCompany Now), 1999—. Office: One California St 29th Fl San Francisco CA 94111

BENTLEY, MARGARET ANN, librarian; b. Tawas City, Mich., June 13, 1956; d. Rupert A. and Joy A. (Bills) B. AB in English, Gordon Coll., 1978; MA in Libr. Sci., U. Mich., 1979. Cert. libr. Mich. Adult svcs. libr., asst. dir. Shiawassee Dist. Libr. (formerly Owosso Pub. Libr.), Owosso, Mich., 1979—. Mem.: AAUW (treas. 1984—2005), Mich. Libr. Assn., Phi Alpha Chi, Lambda Iota Tau, Beta Phi Mu. Avocations: reading, crafts, camping. Office: Shiawassee Dist Libr 502 W Main St Owosso MI 48867-2607 Office Phone: 989-725-5134. E-mail: margaret61356@yahoo.com.

BENTLEY, MARY LOU, religious organization administrator; b. Spokane, Wash., Dec. 5, 1941; d. Lawrence Francis Conway and Lois Mary Gonyea Conway; m. Donald Lawrence Bentley, Apr. 22, 1961; children: Donald Lawrence Bentley Jr., William Patrick, Mary Catherine (Cathy) Barton, Elizabeth Anne Thompson, Penelope (Penny) Susan Fitzgerald, Karen Jean Krantz. B in gen. studies, Gonzaga U., 1991. Ch. organist Fairchild AFB Cath. Chapel, Fairchild Air Force Base, Wash., 1968—72; ch. musician McClellan AFB Cath. Chapel, McClellan Air Force Base, Calif., 1973—77, Fairchild AFB Cath. Chapel, Fairchild Air Force Base, Wash., 1977—87, dir. of sacramental preparation, 1983—87; dir. of religious edn. St. Francis of Assisi Cath. Ch., Spokane, Wash., 1991, U.S. Air Force Chapel, RAF Bentwaters-Woodbridge, England, 1992; liturgy coord. St. Mary's Cath. Ch., Spokane Valley, Wash., 1994—. Mem. Spokane Diocesan Liturgical Commn., Spokane, Wash., 1994—, Diocese of Spokane Deacon Formation Com., Spokane, Wash., 2001—, Diocese of Spokane Deacon Coun., Spokane, Wash., 1984—86. Author: (mag. article) Deacon As Servant Leader. Named Family Svcs. Vol. of the Yr., U. S. Air Force Family Svcs., 1972. Cath. Avocations: travel, music, reading. Home: 4903 N Lincoln St Spokane WA 99205 Office Phone: 509-928-3210. Personal E-mail: litcoord@aol.com.

BENTLEY, RICHARD NORCROSS, regional planner, writer, educator; b. Chgo., Mar. 17, 1937; s. Richard and Phoebe Wrenn (Norcross) B.; m. Carolyn Stiglic, Sept. 10, 1977; children: Nicholas Northrup, Julia Wrenn. BA, Yale U., 1959; MFA, Norwich U., 1992. Chief project mgr. Kate Maremont Found., 1965-70, Rose Assocs., N.Y.C., 1973-75, Adv. Svcs. for Better Housing, N.Y.C., 1975-78, Mass. Dept. Community Affairs, Boston, 1978-83; chief planner Mayor's Office Housing, Boston, 1983-86; planning dir. Boston Housing Authority, 1986-87; sr. planning mgr. Pioneer Valley Planning Commn., West Springfield, Mass., 1987-88. Instr. Internat. City Mgmt. Assn., Washington, 1982-90; instr. creative writing U. Mass., 1992-2003, Cambridge Coll., 1994-2000, Mass. Coll. Liberal Arts, 1995-99, Holyoke C.C., 1997-99; instr. MFA program Vt. Coll., 1997, 99; adj. prof. Western New England Coll., 2000—, Am. Internat. Coll., 2004—. Author: Post-Freudian Dreaming, 2002; mng. editor Peregrine Mag., 1991-93. Bd. govs. Groton (Mass.) Sch., 1990-95; gov.'s appointee Mass. Mortgage Rev. Bd., 1984—; del. Dem. State Conv., Mass., 2000. Served with U.S. Army, 1960-62. Recipient Internat. Fiction award Paris Writers' Workshop, 1994. Mem.: Am. Planning Assn., Nat. Assn. Housing and Redevel. Ofcls., Assn. Yale Alumni Assembly (del. 2000—03), Soc. Mayflower Descs., Assn. Personal Historians (founding), Harvard Club (Boston), Yale Club (Conn. Valley), Amherst Yacht Club. Home: 24 N Prospect St Amherst MA 01002-2014 Office Phone: 413-781-1780. E-mail: rbentley@valinet.com.

BENTLEY, ROBERT RANDALL, lawyer; b. Marietta, Ga., Jan. 16, 1959; s. Fred D. Sr. and Sara M. (Moss) B.; m. Susan Knight, Sept. 19, 1981; children: Elisabeth, Randall Jr. BBA, U. Ga., 1981; JD, Ga. State U., 1984. Bar: Ga., 1984. Dist. mgr. Frito-Lay, Inc., Atlanta, 1981-82; ptnr. Bentley, Bentley & Bentley, Marietta, Ga., 1984—. Bd. dirs. Charter Bank & Trust Co., Marietta, vice-chmn., 2001—. Trustee Cobb Cmty. Ch.; disting. guest Internat. Olympic Com., Country of Guana, 1996; exec. bd. Walker Sch., Marietta, 1996—. Named One of Five Outstanding Young Georgians, Jr. C. of C., 1992. Mem. State Bar Ga., Cobb Bar Assn., Cobb C. of C., Leadership Cobb Alumni Assn. (pres. 1996), Phi Alpha Delta (pres. 1983). Avocations: collecting art, golf, tennis. Office: Bentley Bentley & Bentley 241 Washington Ave NE Marietta GA 30060-1958 Home: 1133 Mossy Rock Rd NW Kennesaw GA 30152-4800

BENTLEY, SELINA MILLER, music educator, director; b. Thomasville, Ga., May 27, 1959; d. Robert E. and Barbara Ann Miller; m. Alton Keith Bentley, July 31, 1999; children: Brooks Allison, Donald McCurry. BA in Music Edn., Charleston (S.C.) So. U., 1982; MA in Ednl. Leadership, State U. West Ga., 1993. Cert. tchr. Ga. Choral dir. Dougherty H.S., Albany, Ga., 1982—88, Eastbrook Mid. Sch., Dalton, Ga., 1988—89, N.W. Whitfield H.S., Tunnel Hill, Ga., 1989—2004, Westover H.S., Albany, 2004—. Judge's chmn. Miss Spirit of Ga. Scholarship Orgn., Albany, 2004. Mem.: Music Educators Nat. Conf., Ga. Music Educator's Assn. Home: 2101 Lullwater Road Albany GA 31707 Office: Westover High School 2600 Partridge Drive Albany GA 31707 Office Phone: 229-431-3320. Office Fax: 229-431-3349. Personal E-mail: millerbentley@yahoo.com. E-mail: salina.bentley@dougherty.k12.ga.us.

BENTLEY, THOMAS ROY, retired language educator, writer; b. Belfast, No. Ireland, June 5, 1931; s. Thomas and Anne (Hill) B.; m. Joan M. Williams, Dec. 24, 1955; children: Kimberley, Shannon, Carolyn. BA, U. Toronto, 1960, MA, 1966; EdB, Ont. Coll., 1961; PhD, Meml. U., Nfld., Can., 1970. Assoc. dean edn. U. B.C., Vancouver, Can., 1973-77, head lang. edn., 1978-79, acting dean edn., 1979-81, prof. lang. edn., 1983-96, prof. emeritus, 1996—. Cons. to maj. cos. on comm. and transp. issues; co-founder Internat. Lifewriting Network. Author 4 books on English comms.; editor 12 books on Can. lit.; contbr. articles to profl. jours.; broadcaster numerous programs on radio and TV. Mem. Nat. Assn. Tchrs. English (chmn. internat. assembly 1981), Assn. Profs. Emeriti, Nat. Conf. for Rsch. in English, Can. Coun. Tchrs. English (editor, bd. dirs., 1975-78), Vancouver Club. Office: 5529 University Blvd Vancouver BC Canada V6T 1K5 Business E-Mail: roy.bentley@ubc.ca.

BENTLY, DONALD EMERY, electrical engineer; b. Cleve., Oct. 18, 1924; s. Oliver E. Bently and Mary Evelyn (Conway) B.; m. Susan Lorraine Pumphrey, Sept. 1961 (div. Sept. 1982); 1 child, Christopher Paul. BSEE with distinction, U. Iowa, 1949, MSEE, 1950; DS (hon.), U. Nev., 1987. Registered profl. engr., Calif., Nev. Pres. Bently Nev. Corp., Minden, 1961-85, chief exec. officer, 1985—2002, Bently Rotor Dynamics and Research Corp., Minden, 1985—2002; also chmn. bd. dirs. Bently Nev. Corp., Minden; chief exec. officer and chmn. Nat. Tribology Svcs., Inc., 2001—. Chief exec. officer Gibson Tool Co., Carson City, Nev., 1978—; bd. dirs. Sierra Pacific Resources, 1982-83. Contbr. articles to profl. jours.; developer electronic instruments for the observation of rotating machinery, and the algorithm for rotor fluid-induced instability; inventor in field. Trustee Inst. World Politics. With USN, 1943-46, PTO. Named Inventor of Yr., State of Nev. Innovation and Tech. Coun., 1983; recipient first Decade Decade award, Vibration Inst., 1992, Myklestad award; inducted to Jr. Achievement of Northern Nev. Bus. Leaders' Hall of Fame. Mem. ASME (industry adv. bd.), Am. Petroleum Inst., St. Petersburg (Russian Fedn.) Acad. Engring., Sigma Xi, Eta Kappa Nu, Tau Beta Pi, Sigma Alpha Epsilon. Episcopalian. Avocations: skiing, hiking, biking. Office: Bently Nev Corp 1711 Orbit Way Minden NV 89423-4114

BENTON, ALLEN HAYDON, biology professor; b. Ira, N.Y., Sept. 4, 1921; s. Haydon Willey and Pearl Amelia (Diddy) B.; m. Marjorie Lois Hall, Aug. 16, 1947; children: Thomas Hall, Christopher Allen, Holly Anne. BS, Cornell U., 1948, MS, 1949, PhD, 1952. Jr. wildlife biologist U.S. Fish and Wildlife Service, 1949; asst. prof. biology SUNY-Albany, 1949-57, assoc. prof., 1957-62; prof. biology SUNY-Fredonia, 1962-73, disting. teaching prof., 1973-84, faculty exchange scholar, 1975-84, prof. emeritus, 1984—. Vis. prof. Stephen F. Austin Coll., 1957, Concord Coll., Athens, W.Va., 1969-70, U. Minn. Biol. Sta., 1970; cons. Nuclear Fuel Services Inc., Fla. Arthropod Collection, Roger Tory Peterson Inst. for the Study of Natural History. Author: (with W.E. Werner Jr.) Field Biology and Ecology, 3rd edit., 1974, Atlas of Fleas of the Eastern United States, 1980, Manual for Field Biology and Ecology, 6th edit., 1983, Wild Worlds, 1988, Light and Natural, 1992, Birding Through Life, 2004, (books of poetry) The Nature of Nature, 1976, Sonnets from Nebraska and Beyond, 1984, Slivers of Jade, 1987, Reflections on a Water Lily Pool, 2003, The Wheel of Life, 2004, A Sense of Nonsense, 2004; columnist Dunkirk (N.Y.) Evening Observer, Albany (N.Y.) Knickerbocker News, Jamestown (N.Y.) Post Jour.; freelance writer on nature and sci.; contbr. articles to profl. jours. Served with cav. U.S. Army, 1942-46. Decorated Bronze Star; grantee Research Found. SUNY, 1963, 83; NSF grantee, 1972; E.N. Huyck Found. grantee, 1976-78 Mem. Am. Ornithologists Union, Am. Soc. Mammalogists, Wilson Ornithol. Soc., Fedn. N.Y. State Bird Clubs (pres.), PTA (life), Sigma Xi, Phi Kappa Phi. Home: 292 Water St Fredonia NY 14063-2025

BENTON, ANDREW KEITH, academic administrator, lawyer; b. Hawthorne, Nev., Feb. 4, 1952; s. Darwin Keith and Nelda Lou Benton; m. Deborah Sue Strickland, June 22, 1974; children: Hailey Michelle, Christopher Andrew. BS in Am. Studies, Okla. Christian Coll., 1974; JD, Oklahoma City U., 1979. Bar: Okla. 1979, U.S. Dist. Ct. (we. dist.) Okla. (admitted to) 1982. Sole practice, Edmond, Okla., 1979-81, 83-84; ptnr. Benton & Thomason, Edmond, 1981—83; asst. v.p. Pepperdine U., Malibu, Calif., 1984—85, v.p., 1985—87, v.p. adminstrn., 1987—89, v.p. univ. affairs, 1989—91, exec. v.p., 1991—2000, pres., 2000—. Chmn. precinct, state conv. del. Okla. Reps., 1980. Mem.: Am. Coun. on Edn., Assn. of Ind. Calif. Coll. & Univ., Nat. Assn. Ind. Coll. & Univ., Okla. Bar Assn. (contbr. articles to ednl. community), ABA (chmn. subcom. emerging land use trends 1987—88, chmn. subcom. decisional trends 1988—90), Calif. Club, Jonathan Club. Republican. Mem. Ch. Of Christ. Office: Pepperdine U 24255 Pacific Coast Hwy Malibu CA 90263-0002*

BENTON, ANNIE RUTH, artist; b. Midland City, Ala., Feb. 9, 1943; d. William Ezzra and Effie (Carlile) Richards; m. Norman Spurgeon Benton, Aug. 9, 1963; children: Chandra Danise Benton Sellers, Melissa Ann Benton Mauldin. Student, Geroge C. Wallace Tech. Sch., 1994. Sec., renewal clk., underwriter, various other positions ind. ins. agys. Exhibited paintings in various exhbns. (2d and 3d pl. awards); author, editor, pub. Square News newsletter, 1990-91; composer songs, including Pressed Between the Pages. Mem. Assembly of God Ch. Avocations: sewing, clothing design, flower gardening, crafts, home decor.

BENTON, AUBURN EDGAR, lawyer; b. Colorado Springs, Colo., July 12, 1926; s. Auburn Edgar and Ella Dot (Heyer) B.; m. Stephanie Marie Jakimowitz, June 8, 1951; children: Margrit Laura, Mary Ellen. BA, Colo. Coll., 1950; LLB, Yale U., 1953. Bar: Colo. 1953, U.S. Dist. Ct. Colo. 1953, U.S. Ct. Appeals (10th cir.) 1954. Assoc. Holme Roberts & Owen LLP, Denver, 1953-57, ptnr., 1957-91, of counsel, 1992—. Mem. Bd. Edn. Denver Pub. Schs., 1961-69; mem. Colo. Commn. Higher Edn., Denver, 1975-85; mem. Colo. Bd. Ethics, Denver, 1975-98; mem. Nat. Common Cause Bd., Washington, 1975-85; dir. soc. sci. found. U. Denver. Mem. Colo. Bar Assn., Denver Bar Assn., Cactus Club (Denver), Phi Beta Kappa. Democrat. Home: 901 Race St Denver CO 80206-3735 Office: Holme Roberts & Owen LLP 1700 Lincoln St Ste 4100 Denver CO 80203-4541 Office Phone: 303-861-7000.

BENTON, DANIEL C., investment company executive; AB, Colgate U., 1980; MBA, Harvard U. Pres. Pequot; founder, chmn. CEO Andor Capital Mgmt., Stamford, Conn., 2001—. V.p of bd. Whitney Mus. Am. Art; trustee Colgate U., James B. Colgate Soc., 2001—. Mailing: c/o Whitney Mus Am Art 945 Madison Ave New York NY 10021 Office: Andor Capital Mgmt 153 East 53 St 58th Floor New York NY 10022*

BENTON, JACK MITCHELL, management consultant; b. Bakersfield, Calif., July 15, 1941; s. James Edwin and Alice Kathryn (Hawthorne) B.; m. Suzanne Wilken, June 14, 1964; children: Mitchell Brian, Andrea Katherine. BS in Acctg., Calif. State U., Chico, 1964. CPA Calif., NY. Acct. Arthur Young & Co., Los Angeles, 1964-68; chief fin. officer Newport Nat. Bank, Newport Beach, Calif., 1968-70; mng. dir. human resources Chase Manhattan Bank & Chase Manhattn Capital Markets Corp., N.Y.C., 1970-87; sr. v.p., mgr. human resources Bank Tokyo, Ltd.-N.Y. Agy. Bank Tokyo Trust Co., N.Y.C., 1987-93; mng. dir. Alec Peters Assoc., N.Y.C., 1993-95, Cromwell Ptnrs., Inc., N.Y.C., 1995-96, Ward Howell Internat., N.Y.C., 1996-98; v.p. Mitsubishi Materials U.S.A., N.Y.C., 1998-2000; v.p. gen. affairs Mitsubishi Silicon Am., Salem, Oreg., 2000—02, Sumco, U.S.A., 2002—05, mgmt. cons., 2005—. Served with USCG, 1960-61, USCGR, 1961-68. Mem. AICPA, Soc. Human Resource Mgmt., Calif. Soc. CPA, N.Y. State Soc CPA, Shek-O Country Club, Hong Kong. Home: 2328 NW Glisan St #9 Portland OR 97210 E-mail: jackbentonx@comcast.net.

BENTON, KAY MYERS, sales executive; b. Balt. d. Brenton Ellsworth and Kevera (Hauf) Myers; m. Gregory W. Lewis, June 29, 1962 (div. Sept. 1986); children: Stacy Kay French, Gregory Lawrence; m. Robert David Benton, Nov. 19, 1988. BA, U. Md. Profl. model, Washington, 1971-76; sr. mgr. Unisys, McLean, Va., 1976-86; dir. bus. devel. Planning Rsch. Corp., McLean, 1986-87, Baxter Travenol, Reston, Va., 1987-88; real estate assoc. Prudential, Potomac, Md.; dir. bus. devel. ISN Corp., 1989-91, TRW, 1991-95; global strategic sales mgr. Sun Microsys., McLean, Va., 1995—. Cons. Andersen Cons., Washington, 1988-89. Contbr. articles to profl. publs. Mem. AIAA, Am. Assn. Airport Execs., Airports Cons. Coun., Air Traffic Control Assn., Industry Adv. Coun., Washington Transp. Seminar, Md. Realtors Assn., Montgomery County Bd. Realtors, Washington Club, The City Club, Army-Navy Country Club, Congl. Country Club, Kappa Delta. Republican. Methodist. Avocations: golf, tennis, travel. Home: 8031 Cobble Creek Cir Potomac MD 20854-2732

BENTON, LEE F., lawyer; b. Springfield, Ohio, Feb. 18, 1944; AB, Oberlin Coll., 1966; JD, U. Chgo., 1969. Bar: Calif. 1970. Mng. ptnr. Cooley Godward LLP, Palo Alto, Calif. Teaching fellow Stanford Law Sch., 1969-70. Mem. Order Coif, Phi Beta Kappa. Office: Cooley Godward LLP 5 Palo Alto Sq 3000 El Camino Real Palo Alto CA 94306-2120

BENTON, MARJORIE CRAIG, federal agency administrator; m. Charles William Benton, three children. LHD, Nat. Coll. Edn., 1981, Lincoln Coll., 1982, Columbia Coll., 1983, Northwestern U., 1983; LLD (hon.), John Marshall Law Sch., 1984; D of Pub. Svc. (hon.), St. Xavier Coll., Chgo., 1987; PhD (hon.), Mundelein Coll., 1988. Pub. del. U.S. Mission to UN, 1977, del. spl. session on disarmament, 1978; mem. commn. UN Assn., 1978-79; spl. adv. UN Disarmament Commn., 1979; U.S. rep. UNICEF, 1980-83; mem. Commn. on White House Fellowships, Washington, 1993, chmn. bd. dirs., 1994—. Vice chair Pub. Media, Inc., Chgo.; bd. dirs. Royal Packaging Industries, Van Leer, The Netherlands; co-chair Am. for Strategic Arms Limitation Talks, 1977-79; U.S. Commr. Internat. Yr. of Child; mem. adv. com. Agy. Internat. Devel. Private Voluntary Orgns., 1981-82; co-chair Symphony for Survival, Chgo., 1982. Co-founder The Peace Mus., Chgo., Chgo. Found. for Women, Women's Issues Network, Chgo.; hon. chair Save the Children Fedn., N.Y.; pres. Chapin Hall Ctr. for Children U. Chgo.; chair bd. dirs. Coun. on Founds., Washington, 1994-96; mem. com. on univ. resources Harvard U., Cambridge, Mass., Internat. Humn Rights Law Inst. DePaul Coll. of Law, Chgo., Inst. Social & Econ. Policy in the Middle East, Harvard U., Middle East Policy Coun., Washington; mem. Bernard Van Leer Foundation, The Netherlands, The Van Leer Group Foundation, The Netherlands; trustee Benton Foundation, Washington, DC; del. Dem. Nat. Conv., 1972, 76, 82, 88, 92; commn. del. selection Dem. Nat. Com., 1973, 88; del. Dem. Mid-Term Conv., 1974, 78, 83; mem. procedures com. Dem. Nat. Conv., 1978; mem. Ill. Dem. Platform com., 1975; Ill. co-chair Inaugural Com., 1977; mem. rules com. Dem. Nat. Conv., 1980, 87; mem. affirmative action com. Ill. Dems., 1984; del.-at-large Dem. Nat. Conv., 1984. Recipient Oustanding Pub. Svc. award UNICEF, 1978, Alumni Svc. award Nat. Coll. Edn., 1979, Woman of Achievement award, Cleve. City Women's Club, 1980, Adlai Stevenson award, 1981, Outstanding Achievement in Cmty. Leadership award YMCA, 1982, Better Govt. Assn. award, 1983, Lincoln award Ill. Citizenx for Handgun Control, Louis Lerner Disting. Svc. award Ill. Pub. Action Coun., Leadership award Chgo. Chpt. Nat. Assn. Fundraising Execs., Woman of Achievement award, Girl Scouts of Am., Chgo., Jane Addams Internat. Women's Leadership award, 1991, Full Circle award, 1993; Co-recipient Disting. Grantmaker Award, Coun. on Founds., 2004; Midwest Women's Ctr. 10th Anniversary Honoree, 1986. Mem. Chgo. Pediat. Soc. (hon.), Am. Orthopsychiatric Assn., Arts Club Chgo., Econ. Club Chgo., River Club N.Y.

BENTON, NICHOLAS, theater producer; b. Boston, Oct. 18, 1926; s. Jay Rogers and Frances (Hill) B.; m. Kate Bigelow, June 5, 1954; children: Frances Hill, Kate, Emily Weld, Louisa Barclay. Grad., Phillips Exeter Acad., 1945; AB, Harvard U., 1951. Promotion writer Life mag., N.Y.C., 1951-55, Fortune mag., N.Y.C., 1955-56; staff writer Time Mag., N.Y.C., 1956-57; advt. promotion mgr. Archtl. Forum, N.Y.C., 1957-64; gen. promotion mgr. Time-Life Books, Alexandria, Va., 1965-68, dir. pub. rels., 1968-83, v.p., 1977-83; lectr. pub. procedures course Radcliffe Coll., 1976-82; producing dir. Am. Kaleidoscope Theatre, 1983-85; pub., editor Middlesex House Press, N.Y., 1999—. Mem. Nat. Book Awards Com., 1971; co-chmn. Nat. Book Awards Week Com., 1975-79; vice-chmn. Am. Book Awards, 1981-82. Author: A Benton Heritage, 1964, The Call of the Weld, 1999, The Seven Weld Brothers, 2004; co-producer musical Phoenix '55, 1955, Salad Days, 1958, The Golden Age, 1984, the Perfect Party, 1986, Love Letters, 1989, The Heart's a Wonder, 1990; author, dir. (play) Not So Long Ago, 1995. Pres. East 69th St. Assn., 1963-64; 1st v.p. Soc. Meml. Sloan-Kettering Cancer Ctr., 1963-64, asst. treas., 1964-66, treas., 1967-68; exec. com. Friends of the Theatre Collection, Mus. of City of N.Y., 1983-86; pres. Land Owners Assn. Indian Neck, Wareham, Mass., 1993-95; chmn. tutoring program Harvard U., NY H.S., 1991—. With AUS, 1945-46. Recipient Opera Vol. Yr., Opera Guild Internat., 2000. Mem. Pubs. Publicity Assn. (pres. 1970-71), New Eng. Historic Geneal. Soc. (trustee 1979-95, corr. sec. 1982-88, v.p. 1988-93), N.Y. Geneal. and Biog. Soc., Assn. Am. Pubs. (freedom to pub. com. 1979-82), Time-Life Alumni Soc. (bd. dirs. 1994—), Soc. of Colonial Wars (editor newsletter 2005—), Harvard Club (bd. mgrs. N.Y.C. chpt. 1971-73), Bourne Cove Yacht Club (commodore Wareham, Mass. chpt. 1988-91), N.Y. City Opera (bd. dirs. 1995-99, guild pres. 1995-99, editor Tempo newsletter 1993-00). Home and Office: 129 E 82nd St New York NY 10028-0836 Home (Summer): Indian Neck Wareham MA 02571

BENTON, NICHOLAS FREDERICK, publisher; b. Ross, Calif., Feb. 9, 1944; s. Frederick C. H. and Jeanne Emma (Brun) B.; m. Donna Carley, Apr. 15, 1979 (div. Oct. 1984); m. Janine Schollnick, Oct. 20, 1985 (div. Apr. 2000). AA, Santa Barbara City Coll., Calif., 1963; BA, Westmont Coll., 1965; MDiv cum laude, Pacific Sch. Religion, Berkeley, Calif., 1969. Reporter Santa Barbara News Press, 1961-66; dir. Christian edn. Plymouth Ch., Oakland, Calif., 1966-69; chief corr. Berkeley Barb, 1970-72; dir. advt. display Syufy Enterprises, San Francisco, 1973-76; regional dir. Exec. Intelligence Rev., Washington, 1976-87; chief Washington corr. Century News Svc., Falls Church, Va., 1987—2002, chmn., chief exec. officer, 1987—2002; owner, editor Falls Church News Press, 1991—; pres., CEO Benton Comms., Inc., 2002—. Pres. Falls Church Baseball, Inc., 1991—; clk. Emmaus Ch., 1989-92; bd. dirs. Arlington (Va.) Symphony, 1992-93, bd. dirs., mem. Falls Church Edn. Found., 2003-. Recipient Bus. of Yr. award Falls Church City Coun., 1991, Bus. Contbn. to Cmty. award, 1997, Bus. of Yr. award Fall Church City Coun., 2001, Grand Marshall Falls Church Meml. Day Parade, 2001; named to Media Honor Roll, Va. Sch. Bd., 1998. Mem. Greater Falls Church C. of C. (bd. dir. 1991—, pres. 1993-94, Pillar of Cmty. award 1993, 2003), LWV of Falls Church, mem. Falls Church City Dem. Com., Optimists Club, White House Corr. Assn., Nat. Press Club (Washington). Mem. United Ch. Christ. Office: Falls Church News Press 929 W Broad St Ste 200 Falls Church VA 22046-3121 Personal E-mail: nfbenton@aol.com. Business E-Mail: nfbenton@fcup.com.

BENTON, OBIE FOLSOM, publishing executive, writer; b. Elba, Ala., Dec. 28, 1932; s. Charlie D. and Johnnie Victoria Benton; m. Mary Rebel Bennett, July 3, 1952; 1 child, Sharon Jean. Cert. bldg. inspector So. Std. Bldg. Code Congress, 1992. CEO AAA-Writer's Inkhorn Pub., Winter Haven, Fla., 1998—, ret.; comml. bldg. insp. City of Nashville, 1987—98. Pres. Ambassador Bible Inst. Pub.: The Great Deception, Full Moon Dance, Seniorscene Mag., World To Come Mag.; author: The Book of Prophecies, The Apocalypse. Min., dir. Ch. of God, Congregation Beth-el, Auburndale, Fla., 1981—2003. Independent. Avocations: writing, landscaping, travel. Office: AAA-Writer's Inkhorn Pub PO Box 7483 Winter Haven FL 33883

BENTON, WILLIAM DUANE, federal judge; b. Springfield, Mo., Sept. 8, 1950; s. William Max and Patricia F. (Nicholson) B.; m. Sandra Snyder, Nov. 15, 1980; children: Megan Blair, William Grant. BA in Polit. Sci. summa cum laude, Northwestern U., 1972; JD, Yale U., 1975; MBA in Accounting, Memphis State U., 1979; student Inst. Jud. Adminstrn., NYU, 1992; LLD (hon.), Ctrl. Mo. State U., 1994; LLM, U. Va., 1995; LLD (hon.), Westminster Coll., 1999. Bar: Mo. 1975; CPA, Mo. Ensign USN, 1972; advanced through grades to capt., 1993; judge advocate USN, Memphis, 1975-79; chief of staff for Congressman Wendell Bailey, Washington, 1980-82; pvt. practice Jefferson City, Mo., 1983-89; dir. revenue Mo. Dept. of Revenue, Jefferson City, 1989-91; judge Mo. Supreme Ct., Jefferson City, 1991—2004, chief justice, 1997-99; judge US Ct. Appeals (8th cir.), Kansas City, Mo., 2004—. Adj. prof. Westminster Coll., 1998-, U. Mo.-Columbia Sch. Law, 1998-. Contbr. articles to profl. jours.; mng. editor Yale Law Jour., 1974-75 Chmn. Multistate Tax Commn. Washington, 1990-91; chmn. Mo. State Employees Retirement System, Jefferson City, 1989-93; regent Ctrl. Mo. State U., 1987-89; dir. Coun. for Drug Free Youth, Jefferson City, 1989-97; mem. Mo. Mil. Adv. Com., 1989-91; mem. Mo. Commn. Intergovernmental Coop., Jefferson City, 1989-91; trustee, deacon 1st Bapt. Ch., Jefferson City. Danforth fellow JFK Sch. Govt. Harvard U., 1990. Mem. AICPA (tax com. 1983—), Mo. Bar Assn. (tax com. 1975—), Mo. Soc. CPA's (tax com. 1983—), Navy League, Mil. Order of World Wars, Vietnam Vets of Am., VFW, Am. Legion, Phi Beta Kappa, Beta Gamma Sigma, Rotary. Baptist. Lt. USN, 1975-80. Capt. JAGC USNR, 1993-2002. Office: 10-20 US Courthouse 400 E 9th St Kansas City MO 64106-2605 Office Phone: 816-512-5815.

BENTSEN, KENNETH E., JR., former congressman; b. Houston, June 3, 1959; m. Tamra Bentsen; children: Louise, Meredith. BA, U. St. Thomas, Houston, 1982; M in Pub. Adminstrn., Am. U., 1985. Mem. staff Congressman Ronald D. Coleman, 1983-87; assoc. staff U.S. House Appropriations Com., 1985-87; chair Harris County Dem. Party, 1990-93; investment banker Houston, 1987-94; mem. 104th-107th Congresses from 25th Tex. dist., 1995—2003; mng. dir. Pub. Strategies Inc., Washington, 2003—. Democrat. Presbyterian. Office: Pub Strategies Inc 607 14th St NW Ste 500 Washington DC 20005

BENTSEN, KENNETH EDWARD, architect; b. Mission, Tex., Nov. 21, 1926; s. Lloyd Millard and Edna Ruth (Colbath) B.; m. Mary Dorsey Bates, Dec. 3, 1953; children: Molly Bates, Elizabeth Jean, Kenneth Edward Jr., William Lloyd. BS, U. Houston, 1951, BA, 1952. Pvt. practice architecture, prin. Kenneth Bentsen Assocs., Houston, 1958-91. Projects include Baylor Coll. Medicine, Jones and Anderson Med. Research Tower, M.D. Anderson-R. Lee Clark Clinic Bldg., West Tower, Clin. Care Ctr., Tex. Children's Hosp., Houston, Tex. Med. Ctr., Agnes Arnold Hall, Philip Hoffman Hall, U. Houston, M.D. Anderson Library, U. Houston, Pan Am. U., Grad. Sch. Bus., U. Tex, M.D. Anderson Environ. Rsch. Ctr., U. Tex, Learning Ctr., Allied Health Sci. & Nursing, U. Tex. Med. Br., Galveston, Compaq Ctr., Houston State Law Ctr., Austin, Tex., Harris County Adminstrn. Bldg., Houston, Tex. Commerce Bldg. Complex, McAllen, Tex. Bd. dirs. Tex. Children's Hosp., Cultural Trust Coun. Tex.; past bd. dirs. Tex. Commn. on the Arts, Mayor's Com. Bd. Appeals, Mus. Fine Arts, Blaffer Gallery; past mem. adv. coun. U. Tex. Sch. Architecture Pres.'s Adv. Com. Recipient numerous design awards. Mem. AIA, Tex. Soc. Architects, Houston C. of C. Office: Kenneth Bentsen FAIA 12 E Greenway Plz Ste 1100 Houston TX 77046-1201

BENTSEN, LLOYD, former government official, former senator; b. Mission, TX, Feb. 11, 1921; s. Lloyd M. and Edna Ruth (Colbath) B.; m. Beryl Ann Longino, Nov. 27, 1943; children: Lloyd M. III, Lan, Tina. JD, U. Tex., 1942. Bar: Tex. 1942. Practice law, McAllen, Tex., 1945-48; judge Hidalgo County, Tex., (hdqs. Edinburg), 1946-48; mem. 80th-83d congresses from 15th Tex. Dist.; pres. Lincoln Consol., Houston, 1955-70; U.S. Senator from Tex., 1971-93; chmn. senate fin. com.; mem. senate commerce, sci., transp. and joint com. on taxation and congl. joint econ. com.; sec. Dept. Treasury, Washington, 1993-94; ptnr. Verner, Lipfert, Bernhard, McPherson and Hand. Democratic nominee for Vice Pres. U.S., 1988. Served to maj. USAAF, 1942-45. Decorated D.F.C., Air Medal with 3 oak leaf clusters; recipient Presdl. medal of Freedom, 1999.*

BENTZ, DALE MONROE, retired librarian; b. York County, Pa., Jan. 3, 1919; s. Solomon Earl and Mary Rebecca (Wonders) B.; m. Mary Gail Menius, June 13, 1942; children: Dale Flynn, Thomas Earl, Mary Carolyn. AB, Gettysburg Coll., 1939; BSL.S., U. N.C. Chapel Hill, 1940; MS, U. Ill., 1951. With Periodicals dept. U. N.C. Library, Chapel Hill, 1940-41, Serials Dept., Duke U. Library, Durham, N.C., 1941-42; asst. librarian E. Carolina Tchrs. Coll., Greenville, N.C., 1946-48; head processing dept. U. Tenn. Library, Knoxville, 1948-53; assoc. dir. libraries U. Iowa, Iowa City, 1953-70, univ. librarian, 1970-86, univ. librarian emeritus, 1986—. Editor U. Tenn. Library Lectures, 1952; contbr. articles to profl. jours. Pres. Iowa City Bd. Edn., 1962-63 Mem. Iowa Library Assn. (pres., 1959-60), ALA (pres. resources and tech. services div. 1975-76), AAUP, Assn. Coll. and Research Libraries, Beta Phi Mu (pres. 1966-67) Clubs: Triangle (pres. 1958-59), Univ. Athletic (sec. 1979-80). Lutheran. Home: 701 Oaknoll Dr # 430 Iowa City IA 52246-5168 Personal E-mail: dalembentz@hotmail.com.

BENTZ, LAURA MARIE, secondary school educator; b. Miami, Fla., Dec. 12, 1951; d. Edward E. and Frances D. Eicher; m. Robert L. Bentz, Aug. 11, 1973; children: Brian, Marc. BS, Fla. State U., 1973; MS, Fla. Internat. U., 1980; cert. edn. specialist, Nova U., Ft. Lauderdale, Fla., 1985. Tchr. Pinellas County Schs., Fla., 1973—. Team mgr. Soccer Assn., Clearwater, Fla., Palm Harbor, Fla., 1990—2004; sec., treas. Boys Scouts Am., Clearwater, 1991—; mem. adv. com. Med. Magnet, Palm Harbor, 1996—2004; mem. cons. Heritage Meth. Ch., Clearwater, 1991—. Named Secondary Tchr. of the Yr., Assn. Careers Tech., 1987, 2004, Tchr. of the Yr., Family and Consumer Sci., 1988; named one of Top Ten Tchrs. of the Yr., Pinellas County Schs., 1989, 2004. Mem.: Pinellas County Family and Consumer Scis. Assn. (pres.), Fla. Assn. Family and Consumer Scis. (sec.), Am. Assn. Family and Consumer Scis., Phi Delta Kappa (com. chair). Avocations: water sports, travel. Home: 2872 Sea Pines Cir W Clearwater FL 33761 Office: Countryside HS 3000 SR 580 Clearwater FL 33761

BENVENISTE, JACOB, retired physicist; b. Portland, Oreg., Dec. 21, 1921; s. Nissim Aslan and Boule (Capeluto) B.; m. Lucie Almeleh, Apr. 23, 1944; children: Richard Nissim, David Mark, Daniel Stephen. BA, Reed Coll., 1943; PhD, U. Calif., Berkeley, 1952. Physicist Lawrence Livermore (Calif.) Nat. Lab., 1950-63; dir. nuclear effects subdiv. Aerospace Corp., San Bernardino, Calif., 1963-68; v.p., dir. research Physics Internat. Corp., San Leandro, Calif., 1968-72; sr. staff scientist Aerospace Corp., El Segundo, Calif., 1972-82; chief scientist Northrop Research and Tech. Ctr., Palos Verdes, Calif., 1982-88. Mem. adv. rsch. panel Def. Nuclear Agy., Washington, 1965-68; chmn. adv. tech. panel USAF, El Segundo, 1973-77. Patentee in field; contbr. articles to profl. jours. Chmn. Livermore Joint Union High Sch. Dist., 1955-63. Served with USNR, 1944-45. KERR Scholar, Reed Coll., 1941. Mem. AAAS, Am. Phys. Soc., Phi Beta Kappa, Sigma Xi. Jewish. Avocations: auto mechanics, needlepoint. Home: 4458 170th Ave SE Bellevue WA 98006-6500 E-mail: luciejack@webtv.net.

BENVENISTE, LAWRENCE, dean; 1 child, Jeffrey. BS in math., U. Calif., Irvine, 1972; PhD in math., U. Calif., Berkeley, 1975. Staff economist FRS, Wash., DC; faculty U. So. Calif., U. Rochester, U. Penn., Northwestern U.; assoc. prof. fin. Wallace E. Carroll Sch. Mgmt., Boston Coll.; US Bancorp prof. fin. Carlson Sch. Mgmt., U. Minn., Twin Cities, 1996—99, chair fin. dept., 1999—2000, assoc. dean faculty and rsch., 2000—01, interim dean, 2001, dean, prof. fin., 2001—. Bd. dirs. Rimage Corp., 2003—, Alliance Data Sys. Office: Carlson Sch Mgmt 321 19th Ave S Rm 4-300 Minneapolis MN 55455 Office Phone: 612-625-6692. Business E-Mail: lbenveniste@csom.umn.edu.

BEN-VENISTE, RICHARD, lawyer; b. N.Y.C., Jan. 3, 1943; s. Isaac and Sylvia (Schultz) B.-V. AB magna cum laude, Muhlenberg Coll., 1964, LLD (hon.), 1975; JD, Columbia U., 1967; LLM, Northwestern U., 1968. Bar: N.Y. 1968, U.S. Dist. Ct. (so. dist.) N.Y. 1968, U.S. Ct. Appeals (2nd cir.) 1969, U.S. Supreme Ct. 1974, D.C. 1975, U.S. Ct. Appeals (1st cir.) 1976, U.S. Ct. Appeals (D.C. cir.) 1982, U.S. Dist. Ct. (no. dist.) Calif. 1983, U.S. Dist. Ct. D.C. 1983. Asst. U.S. atty. (so. dist.) N.Y. U.S. Dept. Justice, 1968-73, chief, spl. prosecution sect., 1971—73, chief, Watergate Task Force, Watergate Spl. Prosecution Force, 1973-75; spl. outside counsel Senate Subcom. on Govtl. Ops., Washington, 1976-77; ptnr. Melrod, Redman & Gartlan, 1975-81, Ben-Veniste & Shernoff, 1981-90, Weil, Gotshal & Manges, Washington, 1990—2002, Mayer, Brown, Rowe & Maw LLP, Washington, 2002—. Chmn. D.C. Advisory Com. on Prison Edn. Reform, 1984-86; chief minority counsel Senate Whitewater Com., 1995-96; co-founder Trial Lawyers for Pub. Justice, 1982; presdl. appointment Mem. Interagy. Working Group (to declassify Nazi era documents), 2000—; commr., The Nat. Commn. on Terrorist Attacks Upon the U.S.(The 9-11 Commn.), 2003-04. Co-author: Stonewall, The Real Story of the Watergate Prosecution, 1977. Recipient Outstanding Pub. Svc. award Seymour Assn., 1976; named one of 75 Best Lawyers in Washington, Washingtonian Mag., 2002; Harlan Fiske Stone Scholar. Office: Mayer Brown Rowe & Maw LLP 1909 K St NW Washington DC 20006-1101 Office Phone: 202-263-3333. Office Fax: 202-263-3300. E-mail: rben-veniste@mayerbrownrowe.com.

BENVENUTTI, PETER J., lawyer; b. Gulfport, Miss., June 24, 1949; s. Peter J. and Elizabeth Cullen (Beyer) B.; m. Lise A. Pearlman, May 31, 1974; children: Anna B., Jamie E., Amalia R. AB, Harvard U., 1971; JD, U. Calif., Berkeley, 1974. Bar: Calif. 1974, U.S. Dist. Ct. (no. dist.) Calif. 1974, U.S. Dist. Ct. (ea. dist.) Calif. 1977, U.S. Dist. Ct. (ctrl. and so. dists.) Calif. 1989, U.S. Dist. Ct. Ariz. 1990, U.S. Ct. Appeals (9th cir.) 1984. Assoc. Dinkelspiel & Dinkelspiel, San Francisco, 1974-80, ptnr., 1981-88, Heller, Ehrman, White & McAuliffe, San Francisco, 1988—; mng. ptnr. San Francisco Office, 1995-97. Bd. dirs. ARC, 1981-83. Mem. ABA, Bar Assn. San Francisco (pres. Calif. bankruptcy forum 1993-94, lawyer rep. 9th Cir. Jud. Conf. 1994—). Democrat. Home: 1147 Clarendon Cres Oakland CA 94610-1807 Office: Heller Ehrman White & McAuliffe 333 Bush St San Francisco CA 94104-2806 Office Phone: 415-772-6403. Office Fax: 415-772-6268. E-mail: pbenvenutti@hewm.com.

BENYEI, CANDACE REED, psychotherapist; b. N.Y.C., Feb. 25, 1946; d. Harlow John and Jacqueline de la Valtaire (Smyth) Reed; m. Curt Christian Benyei, July 1, 1967; children: Tara Elaine, Christian Harlow. BA in Chemistry, Colo. Coll., 1967; MS in Sch. Psychology, So. Conn. State U., 1985; MS in Marriage and Family Therapy, U. Bridgeport, Conn., 1987; PhD in Clin. Psychology, Union Inst., Cin., 1988; MPS, N.Y. Theol. Sem., 1994. Lic. marriage and family therapist, Conn. Rsch. assoc. Cornell U., Ithaca, N.Y., 1967-68; rsch. asst. Yale-New Haven Hosp., 1968-70, Clairol, Inc., Stamford, Conn., 1970-71; asst. chaplain So. Conn. State U., New Haven, 1984-85; adj. prof. U. Bridgeport, 1988-89; cons. family svcs. div. Danbury (Conn.) Superior Ct., 1990-91; mgr., pres. Whimsy Brook Farm, Ltd., Redding, Conn., 1972—; dir. Inst. for Human Resources, Redding, 1985—. Lectr. So. Conn. State U., 1990—97; adj. prof. Fairfield U., 1990—97; acting exec. dir. Burning Tree, Inc., 1998—; founder, tchg. elder Congregation of the Way, 2000—; adminstr. Schulhof Animal Hosp., 1999—. Author: Called to Be Lonely: A Company of Clowns, 1984, A Cape Cod Journal, 1985, Understanding Clergy Misconduct in Religious Systems: Scapegoating, Family Secrets and the Abuse of Power, 1998, How to Get There From Here: Creating God Among Us, 2002; contbr. poetry to jours. Pres. Fairfield Coop. Ext. Coun., 1975-78; mem. Redding Bd. Edn., 1978-86; lic. lay reader Episc. Diocese Conn., 1982-91, mem. diocesan com. on spiritual direction, 1985-87; assoc. Order of Holy Cross, 1986—; mem. adv. com. Ellis Clark Regional Agri-Sci. and Tech. Ctr. Mem.: Nat. Ctr. Homeopathy, Conn. Holistic Health Assn., Conn. Assn. Marriage and Family Therapists (clin mem., approved supr.), Am. Assn. Marriage and Family Therapists (approved supr.), Conn. Psychol. Assn., Conn. Farm Bur. (bd. dirs.), Am. Quarter Horse Assn. Democrat. Avocations: photography, gardening, poetry. Office: Inst Human Resources 29 Giles Hill Rd Redding CT 06896-2511 Office Phone: 203-938-9309.

BENZ, EDWARD JOHN, SR., clinical pathologist; b. June 11, 1923; s. Henry John and Gertrude Nora (Heffernan) B.; m. Verna Marie Cuddyre, June 20, 1945; children: Edward John, Thomas James, Gregory Paul, Mary Louise. BS, U. Pitts., 1943, MD, 1946; MS, U. Minn., 1952. Intern St. Joseph's Hosp., Pitts., 1946-47; resident, fellow Mayo Found., Mayo Clinic, 1949-53; pathologist, dir. labs. St. Luke's Hosp., Bethlehem, Pa., 1953-84, v.p. med. affairs, 1984-89; med. dir. utilization rev. Sacred Heart Hosp., Allentown, Pa., 1990-98. Adj. prof. microbiology Lehigh U., Bethlehem, 1956-64; pres. Lab. Clin. Pathology, Bethlehem, 1956-88, ret., 1988; cons. Palmerton (Pa.) Hosp., Allentown (Pa.) State Hosp.; past dir. Miller Meml. Blood Bank, Bethlehem Mem. adv. com. Pa. Sec. Health on Clin. Labs., 1973-89; mem. health sci. adv. com. Lehigh U., 1973-89. Contbr. articles to profl. publs. Trustee St. Luke's Hosp., 1968-71; pres. Pa. Assn. Clin. Pathologists, 1966-67. Capt. M.C., AUS, 1947-49. Fellow Coll. Am. Pathologists (past chmn. anat. path. commn., past del. from Pa.), Am. Soc. Clin. Pathologists; mem. Internat. Acad. Pathology, Am. Assn. Pathologists and Bacteriologists, Am. Assn. Blood Banks, Am. Coll. Physician Execs., Saucon Club, Valley Country Club, Sigma Xi, Alpha Omega Alpha. Home and Office: 4011 Green Pond Rd #30 Bethlehem PA 18020

BENZ, EDWARD JOHN, JR., internist, hematologist, educator, health facility executive; b. Pitts., May 22, 1946; s. Edward John and Verna Marie (Cuddyre) B.; m. Margaret A. Vettese; children: Timothy Edward, Jennifer Kirsten. AB in Biology cum laude, Princeton U., 1968; MD magna cum laude, Harvard U., 1973. Diplomate Am. Bd. Internal Medicine, Am. Bd. Hematology. Resident Peter Bent Brigham Hosp., Boston, 1973-75; fellow pediatric hematology Children's Hosp. Med. Ctr., Boston, 1974-75; fellow adult hematology Yale U. Sch. Medicine, New Haven, 1978-79, asst. prof. internal medicine, 1979-82, assoc. prof. internal medicine, human genetics, 1982-87, prof. internal medicine, human genetics, 1987-92, chief sect. hematology, 1987-92, chmn. dean's curriculum task force, 1987-88, assoc. chmn. dept. internal medicine, 1988-92; Jack D. Myers prof., chmn. dept. medicine U. Pitts. Sch. Medicine, 1993-95; Sir William Osler prof., dir. dept. medicine Johns Hopkins U. Sch. Medicine., Balt., 1995-2000; prof. molecular biology and genetics Johns Hopkins U. Sch. of Medicine, 1995-2000; physician-in-chief Johns Hopkins Hosp., Balt., 1995-2000; pres., CEO Dana Farber Cancer Inst., Boston, 2000—; Richard & Susan Smith prof. medicine, prof. pediat. and pathology Harvard Med. Sch., Boston, 2000—. CEO Dana Farber Ptnrs. Cancer Care, Boston, 2000—; dir. Dana Farber Harvard Cancer Care, Boston, 2000—; rsch. assoc. molecular hematology Nat. Heart, Lung, Blood Inst., Bethesda, Md., 1975—78; chmn. curriculum com. Yale Sch. of Medicine, New Haven, 1985—88; prof. pro-tem, hon. vis. chief of svc. Brigham & Women's Hosp., 1997; surgeon USPHS, 1975—78; adj. prof. biol. scis. Carnegie Mellon U., 1993—95; Howard Hiatt vis. prof. Harvard Med. Sch., 1998; Clement Finch prof. U. Wash., 1998; Bulfinch vis. prof. medicine Mass. Gen. Hosp., Harvard Med. Sch., Boston, 2000; Haynes disting. vis. prof. medicine Duke U., 2000; Franz Inglefinger vis. prof. Boston U., 2001; Litchfield lectr. Oxford U., 1999; lectr. in field; mem. governing bd. Dana Farber Children's Hosp. Cancer Cure, 2000—. Author: Molecular Genetics Methods, 1987; co-editor: Hematology, Principles and Practice, 1990, 3d edit., 1999; mem. editl. bd. Blood, 1988—94, New Eng. Jour. Medicine, 2002—; assoc. editor: New Eng. Jour. Medicine; contbr. over 200 articles to profl. jours. Recipient Career Devel. award NIH, 1982, Edward Paradiso Rsch. award Cooley's Anemia Found., N.Y.C., 1985, Basil O'Connor award March of Dimes, 1980, Disting. Eagle Scout award Boy Scouts Am., 2003. Fellow: AAAS, ACP, Am. Acad. Arts and Scis., Molecular Med. Soc.; mem.: NIH (study sect. 1984—, chmn. 1993—95), Inst. Medicine, Assn. Profs. Medicine, Am. Soc. Human Genetics, Am. Clin. and Climatol. Soc., Am. Soc. Hematology (exec. coun. 1994, v.p. 1998, pres.-elect 1999, pres. 2000), Am. Fedn. Clin. Rsch., Assn. Am. Physicians, Am. Soc. Clin. Investigation (nat. coun. 1987—91, pres. 1991—92), Md. Club, Johns Hopkins Club, Princeton Elm Club, Interurban Clin. Club, Alpha Omega Alpha, Sigma Xi, Phi Beta Kappa. Office: Dana Farber Cancer Inst 44 Binney St Boston MA 02115 Office Phone: 617-632-4266. Personal E-mail: ebenz@comcast.net.

BENZ, MARILYN CHRISTINE, elementary school educator; b. Stamford, Conn., Sept. 13, 1948; d. Laurence Paul and Marjorie Helen (Scribner) Benz; m. James Sloan Nelson, June 4, 1971 (dec. Apr. 1975); 1 child, Becky. BA in Sociology, Notre Dame Coll., 1970. Social worker N.H. Divsn. Welfare, Concord, 1970-71; tutor remedial reading Title I BASK Program, Manchester, N.H., 1976-80; tchr. 4th grade Raymond (N.H.) Sch. Dist., 1980-89, tchr. 3d grade, 1989—. V.p. Lamprey River Elem. PTO, Raymond, 1983-85; mentor writing process Lamprey River Elem. Sch., 1983—; bd. dirs. Excellence in Edn. Named N.H. Tchr. of Yr., 2003. Mem. ASCD, N.H. Nat. Edn. Assn. (negotiator 1992-2002), Raymond Edn. Assn. (v.p. 2001-02). Avocations: travel, quilting, reading. Home: 49A Dale Rd Hooksett NH 03106 Office: Lamprey River Elem Sch 33 Old Manchester Rd Raymond NH 03077-2345 Office Phone: 603-895-3117. Personal E-mail: linbenz789@aol.com. Business E-Mail: lbenz@raymond.k12.nh.us.

BENZER, SEYMOUR, neuroscience educator; b. NYC, Oct. 15, 1921; s. Mayer and Eva (Naidorf) Benzer; m. Dorothy Vlosky, Jan. 10, 1942 (dec. 1978); children: Barbara Ann Benzer Freidin, Martha Jane Benzer Goldberg; m. Carol A. Miller, May 11, 1980; 1 child, Alexander Robin. BA, Bklyn. Coll., 1942; MS, Purdue U., 1943, PhD, 1947, DSc (hon.), 1968; DSc, Columbia U., 1974, Yale U., 1977, Brandeis U., 1978, CUNY, 1978, U. Paris, 1983, Rockefeller U., N.Y.C., 1993, Cold Spring Harbor Watson Sch. of Biol. Scis., 1999. Mem. faculty Purdue U., 1945—67, prof. biophysics, 1958—61, Stuart disting. prof. biology, 1961—67; prof. biology Calif. Inst. Tech., 1967—75, Boswell prof. neurosci., 1975—; biophysicist Oak Ridge Nat. Lab., 1948—49; vis. assoc. Calif. Inst. Tech., Pasadena, 1965—67. Contbr. articles to prof. jour. Recipient award of honor, Bklyn. Coll., 1956, Sigma Xi rsch. award, Purdue U., 1957, Ricketts award, U. Chgo., 1961, Gold medal, N.Y. City Coll. Chemistry Alumni Assn., 1962, Gairdner award of merit, 1964, McCoy award, Purdue U., 1965, Lasker award, 1971, T. Duckett Jones award, 1975, Prix, Leopold Mayer French Acad. Scis., 1975, Louisa Gross Horwitz award, 1976, Harvey award, Israel, 1977, Warren Triennial prize, Mass. Gen. Hosp., 1977, Dickson award, 1978, Rosenstiel award, 1986, T.H. Morgan medal, Genetics Soc. Am., 1986, Karl Spencer Lashley award, 1988, Gerard award, Soc. Neurosci., 1989, Helmerich award, 1990, Wolf Found. prize in medicine, Israel, 1991, Bristol-Myers Squibb Neurosci. award, 1992, Crafoord prize, Royal Swedish Acad. Scis., 1993, Mendel award, Brit. Genetical Soc., 1994, Alberto Feltrinelli prize, Accademia dei Lincei, Italy, 1994, Internat. prize for biology, Japan, 2000, Passano award, 2001, Neurosci. award, Acad. Sci. USA, 2001, March of Dimes prize, 2002, Pasarow award, 2002, Bower award, Franklin Inst., 2004, Internat. award, Gairdner Found., 2004, Peter Gruber Found. award, Gruber Found., 2004; Rsch. fellow, Calif. Inst. Tech., 1949—51, Fulbright rsch. fellow, Pasteur Inst., Paris, 1951—52, sr. NSF postdoctoral fellow, Cambridge, Eng., 1957—58. Fellow: Indian Acad. Sci. (hon.); mem.: AAAS, European Acad. Scis., Acad. des Sci. France (fgn. mem.), Royal Acad. Sci. Spain (fgn. mem.), Royal Soc. London (fgn. mem.), NY Acad. Sci., Harvey Soc., Am. Philos. Soc. (Lashley award 1988), Am. Acad. Arts and Sci. Home: 2075 Robin Rd San Marino CA 91108-2831

BENZLE, CURTIS MUNHALL, artist, art educator; b. Lakewood, Ohio, Apr. 20, 1949; s. Arthur George and Martha (Munhall) B; m. Suzan Scianamblo, Feb. 6, 1972 (div. 1995); children: Elliott, Kyle, Marisa; m. Sally Jo Havas, Aug. 28, 1996 (div. 1999). Student, Hillsdale Coll., 1967-69; BFA, Ohio State U., 1972; postgrad., Rochester Inst. Tech., 1973; MA, No. Ill. U., 1978. Owner, mgr. Oz Crafts, Hilton Head, S.C., 1973-76, Benzle Porcelain Co., Columbus, Ohio, 1980—, Benzle Applied Arts, Hilliard, Ohio, 1988—. Owner Creative Spirit Workshop; exec. dir. Ohio Designer Craftsmen, 1996—99; instr. U. S.C., Beaufort, 1978—79; prof., chair dept. dimensional studies Columbus Coll. Art and Design, 1982—, dir. com. art project; pres. Japan-USA Exch. Exhbn., 1988—92; bd. overseers Am. Crafts Assn., 1991—96; trustee Am. Crafts Coun., 1992—96. One-man show U. S.C., 1979, Indpls. Mus. Art, 1984, Lawrence Gallery, Portland, Oreg., 1986, Running Ridge Gallery, Santa Fe, 1986, Akasaka/Green Gallery, Tokyo, 1987, 90, Zanesville Art Ctr., 1988, Swidler Gallery, 1990, Tsukushi Gallery, Kitakyushu, Japan, 1991, del Mano Gallery, 1998, Canton (Ohio) Mus. Art, 2004-05, Sherrie Gallery, Columbus, 2004-05, also others; exhibited in numerous group shows, 1971—, including Smithsonian Instn., 1980, 83, Leeuwarden, Suntory Art Mus., Tokyo, 1984, Cermaic Nat. Everson Mus., Syracuse, 1988, Internat. Competition of Ceramics, Mino, Japan, 1989, Seto (Japan) Ceramic and Glass Ctr., 2003 21st Century Ceramics, Canzani Gallery, Columbus, Ohio, St. Joseph Gallery, Netherlands, 2004-05; represented in numerous permanent collections, including Smithsonian Instn., Everson Mus. Art, Los Angeles County Mus. Art, Cleve. Mus. Art, White House Collection Contemporary Craft. Mem. Ohio Citizens Com. for Arts, 1986—. Nat. Endowment for Arts fellow, 1980, Ohio Arts Coun. fellow, 1981, 83, 84, 86, 88, Greater Columbus Arts Coun. fellow, 1987. Mem. Am. Crafts Coun. (bd. overseers 1991-96, trustee 1992-96), Nat. Coun. on Edn. in Ceramic Art, Ohio Designer Craftsmen (bd. dirs. 1982-84, pres. 1985-87). Avocation: gardening. Business E-Mail: cbenzle@ccad.edu.

BEPKO, GERALD LEWIS, academic administrator, law educator; b. Chgo., Apr. 21, 1940; s. Lewis V. and Geraldine S. (Bernath) B.; m. Jean B. Cougnenc, Feb. 24, 1968; children: Gerald Lewis Jr., Arminda B. BS, No. Ill. U., 1962; JD, Ill. Inst. Tech.-Chgo. Kent Coll. Law, 1965; LLM, Yale U., 1972. Bar: Ill. 1965, U.S. Supreme Ct. 1968, Ind. 1973. Assoc. Ehrlich, Bundesen, Friedman & Ross, Chgo., 1965; spl. agt. FBI, 1965-69; asst. prof. law Ill. Inst. Tech.-Chgo. Kent Coll. Law, 1969-71; prof. Ind. U., Indpls., 1972-86, assoc. dean acad. affairs, 1979-81, dean, 1981-86, v.p., 1986—2002, interim pres., 2003. Vis. prof. Ind. U.-Bloomington, summers, 1976, 77, 78, 80, U. Ill., 1976—77, Ohio State U., 1978—79; cons. and reporter Fed. Jud. Ctr.; bd. dirs. First Ind. Bank/Corp., Ind. Energy Inc. & Ind. Gas Co., Inc., 1989—97, Lumina Found. for Edn., Indpls. Life Ins. Co.; mem. Conf.

Commrs. on Uniform State Laws, 1982, Permanent Editl. Bd. for the Uniform Comml. Code, 1993—; mem. Ind. Lobby Registration Commn., 1992—, vice chair, 1992—96, chair, 1996—2000. Author: (with Boshkoff) Sum and Substance of Secured Transactions, 1981; contbr. articles on comml. law to profl. jours. Indpls. Chgo. Title and Trust Co. Found. scholar 1962-65; Ford Urban law fellow, 1971-72. Fellow Am. Bar Found., Ind. State Bar, Indpls. Bar Found.; mem. ABA, Ind. State Bar Assn., Indpls. Bar Assn., Country Club Indpls., Rotary. Methodist. Office: Ind U 355 Lansing St Indianapolis IN 46202-2815

BERALL, FRANK STEWART, lawyer; b. NYC, Feb. 10, 1929; s. Louis J. and Jeannette F.; m. Christiana Johnson, July 5, 1958 (dec. July 1972); children: Erik Dustin, Elissa Alexandra; m. Jenefer M. Carey, Sept. 1, 1980. BS, Yale U., 1950, JD, 1955; LLM in Tax, NYU, 1959. Bar: N.Y. 1955, Conn. 1960; accredited estate planner. Assoc. firm Mudge, Stern, Baldwin & Todd, N.Y.C., 1955-57, Townley, Updike, Carter & Rodgers, N.Y.C., 1957-60; atty. Conn. Gen. Life Ins. Co., Bloomfield, Conn., 1960-65; atty. trust dept. Hartford Nat. Bank & Trust Co., Conn., 1965-67; assoc. Cooney & Scully, Hartford, Conn., 1968-70; ptnr. Copp & Berall, LLP and predecessors, Hartford, 1970—. Asst. in instrn. Yale U. Law Sch., 1954—55; lectr. U. Conn. Sch. Ins., 1964—72; instr. estate planning Am. Coll. Life Ins., 1968—69; v.p., sec., gen. counsel John M. Blewer, Inc., Essex, Conn., 1969—86; counsel Conn. Gov.'s Strike Force for Full Employment, 1971—72; lectr. U. Conn. Law Sch., 1972—73; counsel Conn. Gov.'s Commn. on Tax Reform, 1972—73, State Tax Commr.'s Commn., 1972—75; adj. asst. prof. grad. tax program U. Hartford, 1973—74; counsel Com. on Tax Law Clarification, 1984—88; lectr., spkr. in field. Co-author: A Practitioners Guide to the Tax Reform Act of 1969, 1970, Estate Planning and the Close Cooperation, 1970, Planning Large Estates, 1970, Revocable Inter Vivos Trusts, 1985, The Migrant Client: Tax, Community Property, and Other Considerations, 1994; sr. editor Conn. Bar Jour., 1969—, mem. editl. bd. Estate Planning mag., 1973—, Practical Tax Lawyer, 1988—, Jour. Taxation of Trusts and Estates, 1988—92, Estate Tax Planning Advisor. Bd. dirs. Bloomfield Interfaith Homes, 1967—71; adv. coun. U. Hartford Tax Inst., 1970—82; trustee Culver Ednl. Found., 1997—99; co-chmn. adv. coun. Hartford Tax Inst., 1986—94; co-chmn. Notre Dame Estate Planning Inst., 1977—. 1st lt., F.A. U.S. Army, 1951—52. Fellow: Am. Coll. Trust and Estate Counsel (Conn. chpt. chmn. 1975—81, mem. editl. bd. 1975—87, regent 1977—82); mem.: ABA, Am. Law Inst. (exec. coun. 1978—82, 2004—), Hartford County Bar Assn. (chmn. com. liaison with IRS 1972—74, com. charter and by-laws 1975), Internat. Acad. Estate and Trust Law (life), Conn. Bar Assn. (chmn. tax sect. 1969—72, exec. com. 1969—, exec. com., estates and probate sect. 1973—, vice chmn. com. on specialization 1974—77, chmn. 1984—86), Am. Coll. Tax Counsel, Culver Summer Schs. Alumni Assn. (v.p. 1975—85, bd. dirs. 1985—91, 1993—2001, pres. 1997—99), Yale Club of Harford (dir. 1998—, pres. 1999—2001, 2005—), Culver Club Ctrl. New Eng. (pres. 1996—), Tax Club of Hartford (pres. 1975—76). Office: Copp & Berall LLP 864 Wethersfield Ave Hartford CT 06114-3184 Business E-Mail: frank_berall@coppberall.com. *As a tax lawyer, I view my job as helping to keep the system going by seeing to it that my clients pay the government all it is legally entitled to receive in taxes, but no more, and doing pro bono work for the improvement of the entire federal and state tax law system.*

BERAN, CAROL LOUISE VIERTEL, English language educator; b. Bklyn., Jan. 29, 1944; d. Maurice and Olive H.B. Viertel; m. Rudolf Beran, Aug. 24, 1968; children: Rudolf, Gregory. BA, Susquehanna U., 1966; MA in Tchg., Johns Hopkins U., 1967; PhD, U. Calif., Berkeley, 1977. Tchr. English, Patapsco H.S., Dundalk, Md., 1967-68; prof. English, St. Mary's Coll., Moraga, Calif., 1977—. Author: Living Over the Abyss: Margaret Atwood's Life Before Man, 1993; contbr. articles to profl. jours. Grantee Can. Embassy, 1985-96. Mem. Assn. Can. Studies in U.S., Western Social Sci. Assn., Margaret Laurence Soc., Margaret Atwood Soc. Lutheran. Office: St Mary's Coll PO Box 4336 Moraga CA 94575-4336

BERAN, DENIS CARL, publisher; b. Apr. 14, 1935; s. Carl Earl and Jessica Mary (Bogue) B.; m. Virginia Martha Knox, Feb. 20, 1960; children: Michael Knox, Elizabeth Virginia. BA in Econs., U. Mich., 1958; postgrad. in mktg. mgmt., Harvard Bus. Sch., 1976; Internat. Strategies Program, Columbia U., 1984. With McGraw-Hill Pubs. Co., N.Y.C., 1962—, advt. sales trainee, 1962, dist. mgr. nucleonics, 1962-65; dist. mgr. Business Week, 1965-70, sales devel. mgr., 1970-72, mktg. dir., 1972-76, asst. pub., 1979, internat. pub. dir., 1980-85, v.p. Europe McGraw-Hill, 1976-79; v.p. advt. Gannett Internat., 1986-87, v.p. mktg., 1988-89. Chmn. New Canaan Am. Cancer Soc., 1973-75; dir. So. Fairfield County Am. Cancer Soc., 1972-76, 80-90, 1st v.p., 1975-76. 1st lt. USMC, 1958-61. Mem. Internat. Periodical Pubs. Assn. (exec. com.), Aircraft Owners and Pilots Assn. (v.p. 1990-2000), New Canaan Country Club, Grand Harbor Club. Republican. Roman Catholic. Home: 5550 N Harbor Village Dr Vero Beach FL 32967-7268 Office Phone: 772-794-1900. E-mail: denisberan1@peoplepc.com.

BERAN, GEORGE WESLEY, veterinary microbiology educator; b. Riceville, Iowa, May 22, 1928; s. John and Elizabeth (Buresh) B.; m. Janice Ann Van Zomeren, Dec. 21, 1954; children: Bruce, Anne, George. DVM, Iowa State U., 1954; PhD, Kans. U., 1959; LHD, Silliman U., Philippines, 1973. Diplomate Am. Coll. Vet. Preventive Medicine, Am. Coll. Epidemiology. Epidemic intelligence officer USPHS, 1954-56; asst. prof. biology Silliman U., Dumaguete City, Philippines, 1960-63, chmn. dept. agr., 1962-71, assoc. prof. microbiology, 1963-67, prof. microbiology, 1967-73; prof. vet. microbiology and preventive medicine Iowa State U., Ames, 1973-93, disting. prof. vet. microbiology, immunology-preventive med., 1993—; dir. WHO Collaborating Ctr. in Food Safety, 1994—. Cons. WHO, Belize, Ecuador, Mex., India, Laos, Malaysia, Philippines, Jamaica, Surinam, Barbados; rsch. del. USSR/Iowa State U. exch. program, Moscow, 1989-90, Latvia, 1993; rsch. cons., Taiwan, 1983, 96, 98, Hungary, 1988, 90, U. Yucatan, 1989-90, 97, 98, 2003, Ukraine, 1996, Japan, 1998; vis. lectr. Nat. Inst. Vet. Bioproducts and Pharms., Beijing, Faculty Vet. Medicine, Huazhong Agrl. U. Wuhan, Peoples Republic of China, 1988; cons. Pan Am. Health Orgn., 1979, 85, 93, 95, 96, 98, 99, 2000, 02; cons. USDA-Palestine; mem. WHO Expert Panel on Zoonoses, 1980-99; mem. expert panel on risk assessment WHO-FAO; Fulbright prof. Ahmadu Bello U., Zaria, Nigeria, 1980; mem. subcom. on drug use in animals NRC, 1993-98, mem. nat. adv. com. on microbiol. criteria for foods, 1997-99; adv. com. Wellcome Trust, 1998-99; mem. Food Safety and Inspection Svc. Task Force for Veterinarians, 1999-2000; mem. HACCP Based Inspection Models Project, 1999-2000 Editor, co-editor books on zoonoses and vet. pub. health; contbr. articles to profl. jours., chpts. to books. Active Ames Humane League, Ames chpt. Ptnrs. of Ams., UN Assn.; election supr. OSCE, Bosnia, 1998, Kosovo, 2000; mem. adv. com. Nat. Cath. Rural Life Ctr., 2001. Recipient James H. Steele award World Vet. Epidemiology Soc., 1979, Nat. Meritorious Svc. award Livestock Conservation Inst., 1989, Gold Head Cane award Am. Vet. Epidemiology Soc., 1993. Mem. AVMA (mem. coun. pub. health and regulatory vet. medicine, Internat. Svc. award 1996, Pub. Svc. award 1999), Am. Coll. Vet. Preventive Medicine (pres.), Conf. Pub. Health Veterinarians (pres.), Am. Assn. Food Hygiene Veterinarians (Outstanding Tchr. award 1978), Assn. Tchrs. Vet. Pub. Health and Preventive Medicine, Iowa Vet. Med. Assn. (chair pub. health com.), Iowa Pork Producers Assn. (pseudorables com.), Practical Farmers Iowa (Svc. to Agr. award, Sustainable Agr. Achievement award), U.S. Animal Health Assn. (com. on pseudorables, pub. health, food safety, feed safety, chair com. on feral swine), Cardinal Key, Sigma Xi, Phi Beta Delta, Phi Kappa Phi (pres.), Gamma Sigma Delta (Svc. to Agr. Merit award 1995), Phi Zeta, Alpha Zeta, Phi Eta Sigma. Home: 304 24th St Ames IA 50010-4834 Office: Coll Vet Medicine Iowa State U Rm 2280 Ames IA 50011-0001 Office Phone: 515-294-7630. Business E-Mail: gberan@iastate.edu.

BERAN, JOHN R., banker; BS in Indsl. and Sys. Engring., MS in Mgmt. Sci., U. Dayton. Exec. v.p. BancSystems Assn.; chmn., CEO Green Machine Network Corp.; sr. v.p. Electronic Payment Services Group Soc. Corp.; pres., CEO Money Access Svc.; exec. v.p., chief info. officer Comerica Inc., Detroit, 1995—. Bd. dir. WTVS Channel 56, U. Dayton; adv. com. mem. U. Dayton Sch. Engring.; bd. dir. Mich. Virtual U.; steering com. The Clearing House; exec. com. Banking Industry Tech. Secretariat. Office: Comerica Tower 500 Woodward Ave Detroit MI 48226-3416

BERANEK, KIM MARIE, music educator; b. Racine, Wisc., Mar. 13, 1962; d. Donald L. Frosland and Naomi B. Larrabee Frosland; m. David John Beranek, Dec. 20, 1985; children: Jonathan, Timothy, Samuel, Daniel. BA in Music Edn., Northwest Nazarene U., 1985; MA in Music Edn., U. Oreg., 1992. Lic. tchr. Oreg., Idaho. Music tchr. Medford (Oreg.) Sch. Dist., 1985—90, Eugene (Oreg.) Sch. Dist., 1990—91, Salem-Keizer Sch. Dist., Salem, Oreg., 1991—. Accompanist Rogue Valley Choral, 1985—90, S-KHONOR Choir, 1990—94; specialist Weather's Music Corp., Salem, 1994—; cons. Oregon Dept. Educators Music Educators, Salem, 1985—2005; coord. North by Northeast Homeschoolers, Salem, 1996—. Mentor Music Specialists, Oreg., 1985—; cert. mem. Harmony Road and Music in Me, 1995—2004; mem. music com. South Salem Nazarene Ch., 1991—, choir dir., 2002—03. Mem.: Friends of Music, Oreg. Music Educators Assn., Northwest Nazarene U. Alumni Assn., Nazarene Mission Soc., Phi Delta Lamba Hon. Soc. Republican. Nazarene. Avocations: reading, travel, homeschooling, piano, teaching. Home: 842 Maine Ave NE Keizer OR 97303-4650 Office Phone: 503-399-3311. E-mail: kimberanek@aol.com.

BERANEK, LEO LEROY, acoustical engineer, consultant; b. Solon, Iowa, Sept. 15, 1914; s. Edward Fred and Beatrice (Stahle) B.; m. Phyllis Knight, Sept. 6, 1941 (dec. Nov. 1982); children: James Knight, Thomas Haynes; m. Gabriella Sohn, Aug. 10, 1985. AB, Cornell Coll., 1936, D.Sc. (hon.), 1946; MS, Harvard U., 1937, D.Sc., 1940; D.Eng. (hon.), Worcester Poly. Inst., 1971; D.Comml. Sci. (hon.), Suffolk U., 1979; LL.D. (hon.), Emerson College, 1982; Dr. Pub. Service (hon.), Northeastern U., 1984. Instr. physics Harvard U., 1941—43, asst. prof., 1941—43; dir. Electro-Acoustics and Systems Rsch. Labs., 1941-46; assoc. prof. communications engring. MIT, 1947-58; pres., dir., chief exec. officer Bolt Beranek & Newman, Cambridge, Mass., 1953-69, dir., 1953-84, chief scientist, 1969—71; pres., chief exec. officer, dir. Boston Broadcasters, Inc., 1963-79, chmn. bd., 1980-83; pres. Am. Acad. Arts and Scis., Cambridge, 1989-94. Part-owner WCVB-TV, Boston, 1972-82; chmn. bd. Mueller-BBM GmbH, Munich, 1962-86. Author: Acoustic Measurements, 1949, 2d edit., 1986, Music, Acoustics and Architecture, 1962, Noise Reduction, 1960, Noise and Vibration Control, 1971, 2d edit., 1988, Noise and Vibration Control Engineering, 1992, Concert and Opera Halls: How They Sound, 1996, Concert Halls and Opera Houses: Music, Acoustics and Architecture, 2004. Charter mem. bd. overseers Boston Symphony Orch., 1968-80, chmn., 1977-80, trustee, 1977-87, chmn. bd. trustees, 1983-86, hon. chmn., 1987, life trustee 1994-; mem. bd. overseers Harvard U., 1984-90; mem. coun. for arts MIT, 1972—; life trustee Cornell Coll., 1998—. Guggenheim fellow, 1946-47; recipient Presdl. certificate of merit, 1948, Abe Lincoln TV award So. Bapt. Conv., 1976, Lord Rayleigh award Mex. Inst. Acoustics, 2002, Nat. Medal of Science award, 2002, Per Bruel Gold medal ASME, 2004. Fellow NAE (bd. dir, marine bd., com. pub. engring. policy, aeros. and space engring. bd.), AAAS, IEEE (chmn. profl. group audio 1950-51), Am. Phys. Soc., Am. Acad. Arts and Scis. (Scholar-Patriot Disting. Svc. award 2000), Audio Engring. Soc. (pres. 1967-68, Gold medal 1971, gov. 1966-71), Acoustical Soc. Am. (mem. coun. 1944-47, v.p. 1949-50, pres. 1954-55, Bienniel award 1944, Sabine award 1961, Gold medal 1975, Hon. mem. 1994); mem. Inst. Noise Control Engring. (charter pres. 1971-73, dir. 1973-75, 1st Disting. Noise Control Engr. 1997), Internat. Inst. Acoustics (hon. fellow 2000), Am. Inst. Archs. (hon.), Acad. Disting. Bostonians, Greater Boston C. of C. (dir. 1973-79, v.p. 1976-79, Disting. Cmty. Svc. award 1980, 83), Phi Beta Kappa, Sigma Xi, Eta Kappa Nu (eminent mem. 2000). Episcopalian. Home and Office: 975 Memorial Dr Ste 804 Cambridge MA 02138-5755

BERARDUCCI, ADRIENNE, nursing educator, researcher; d. Anthony Frank and Josephine Gertrude Berarducci. PhD, U. of South Fla., 2001, MS, 1989; BS summa cum laude, Daemen Coll., 1987. Cert. bd. cert. adult nurse practitioner, ANCC, RN N.Y. Charge nurse Sisters of Charity Hosp., Buffalo, 1976—79; staff nurse, rsch. coord. VA Med. Ctr., Buffalo, 1979—87; staff nurse Sarasota Meml. Hosp., 1988—89; nurse practitioner Sarasota Palms Hosp., 1989—90; nursing instr. U. of Tampa, Fla., 1991—92, So. Coll., Orlando, Fla., 1994—94; nurse practitioner Internal Medicine Assocs., Sarasota, 1990—95; pvt. practice nurse practitioner in internal medicine Sarasota, 1996—2001; asst. prof. U. of South Fla., Tampa, 2001—; nurse practitioner Bayview Med. Assocs., Sarasota, Fla., 2002—. Sci. cons. Alliance for Better Bone Health, Mason, Ohio, 2003—; med.-legal cons. pvt. law firms, Sarasota, 2001—; parenteral/enteral therapy cons. U.S. Ethicare Corp., Buffalo, 1983—85. Author: (clin. monograph) Osteoporosis: Clinical Issues, Detection, and Treatment Strategies, (rsch. presentation) Osteoporosis-related, health-promoting practices of primary care providers (Grad. Student Rsch. award, 1999), Development and testing of an instrument to measure women's knowledge of osteoporosis (Grad. Student Rsch. award, 2000); contbr. articles to profl. jours. Recipient Meritorious Svc. award, VA Rsch. Ctr., 1985, rsch. study grants (2), Merck & Co., Inc, 1999, rsch./ednl. grants (2), Alliance for Better Bone Health, 2001; grantee, Bur. of Health Professions, 2000—03. Mem.: ANA (assoc.), Fla. Nurses Assn. (assoc.; treas. dist. 20 2003—), Fla. Osteoporosis Bd. (assoc.; bd. dirs. 2003), Sigma Theta Tau (hon.), Phi Kappa Phi (life). Liberal. Roman Catholic. Achievements include research in osteoporosis; development of psychometric instruments for osteoporosis-related research; nationally recognized for osteoporosis and women's health research and education. Avocations: dog and cat care and training, gourmet cooking, antique and art glass collecting, antique children's literature collecting. Office: U South Florida MDC Box 22 12901 Bruce B Downs Blvd Tampa FL 33612 E-mail: aberardu@hsc.usf.edu.

BERBARY, MAURICE SHEHADEH, physician, military officer, hospital administrator, educator; b. Beirut, Jan. 14, 1923; arrived in US, 1945, naturalized, 1952; s. Shehadeh M. and Marie K. Berbary; children: Geoffrey Maurice, Laura Marie. BA, Am. U., Beirut, 1943; MD, U. Tex., Dallas, 1948; MA in Hosp. Adminstrn., Baylor U., 1970; diploma, Army Command and Gen. Staff Coll., Leavenworth, Kan., 1963, Air Force Sch. Aerospace Medicine, San Antonio, 1964, Army War Coll., Carlisle, Pa., 1969. Diplomate Am. Bd. Ob-Gyn., Am. Coll. Healthcare Execs. Intern Parkland Meml. Hosp., Dallas, 1948-49, resident in ob-gyn., gen. surgery and urology, 1949-53; resident in ob-gyn. Walter Reed Army Hosp., Washington, 1955-57; fellow in obstetric and gynecologic pathology Armed Forces Inst. Pathology, Washington, 1959-60; practice clin. medicine in ob-gyn., 1953—; capt. MC U.S. Army, 1952, advanced through grades to col., 1968, sr. flight surgeon, 1970; chief dept. ob-gyn. U.S. Army Hosp., Ft. Polk, La., 1957-59, Womack Army Hosp., Ft. Bragg, N.C., 1960-62; div. surgeon 1st. inf. div., Ft. Riley, Kans., 1963-64, 3d. Armored div., Germany, 1964-65; corps surgeon V. Corps, Germany, 1965-67, 24th Army Corps, S. Vietnam Theater of Operation, 1970; comdr., hosp. adminstr. U.S. Army Hosp., Teheran, Iran, 1954-55; comdr. 43d Hosp. Group Complex, Vietnam, 1969-70; command surgeon U.S. Armed Forces Command and U.S. Army South, U.S. C.Z., Panama, 1970-73; comdr. 5th Gen. Hosp., Stuttgart, West Germany, 1973-77, Munson Army Hosp., Ft. Leavenworth, Kans., 1977-81; sr. staff officer dept. ob-gyn William Beaumont Army Med. Ctr., Ft. Bliss, Tex., 1981-83; ret., 1983; cons. health care adminstrn. and med.-legal affairs, 1984—. Vis. lectr. ob-gyn. pathology Duke U. Med. Ctr., Durham, N.C., 1960-62; clin. instr. dept. ob-gyn. U. Kans. Coll. Medicine, Kansas City, 1963-80, advanced to clin. asst. prof., 1980—; instr. 5th Army NCO Acad., Fort Riley, Kans., 1963-64. Decorated Legion of Merit with three oak leaf clusters, Bronze Star medal, Meritorious Svc. medal, Army Commendation medal, Combat Air medal, Sr. Flight Surgeon's badge, Expert Field Med. badge. Fellow: ACS, Am. Coll. Health Care Execs., Am. Coll. Ob-Gyn.; mem.: AMA, Dallas County Med. Assn., Tex. State Med. Assn., Am. Hosp. Assn., Soc. U.S. Army Flight Surgeons, Am. Occupl. Med. Assn., Assn. Mil. Surgeons, Internat. Platform Assn., N.Y. Acad. Scis. Avocation: languages. Home and Office: 7923 Abramshire Ave Dallas TX 75231-4712 Office Phone: 214-349-1402. E-mail: utopal@aol.com, gmb1994@aol.com.

BERCH, REBECCA WHITE, state supreme court justice, lawyer; b. Phoenix, June 29, 1955; d. Robert Eugene and Janet Kay (Zimmerman) White; m. Michael Allen Berch, Mar. 9, 1981; 1 child, Jessica. BS summa cum laude, Ariz. State U., 1976, JD, 1979, MA, 1990. Bar: Ariz. 1979, U.S. Dist. Ct. Ariz., U.S. Ct. Appeals (9th cir.), U.S. Supreme Ct. Assoc., ptnr. McGroder, Tryon, Heller, Rayes & Berch, Phoenix, 1979-85; dir. legal rsch. and writing program Ariz. State U. Coll. Law, Tempe, 1986-91, 94-95; solicitor gen. State of Arizona, Phoenix, 1991-94, 1st asst. atty. gen., 1996—98; judge Ariz. Ct. Appeals, 1998—2002; justice Ariz. Supreme Ct., Phoenix, 2002—, vice chief justice, 2005—. Mem. Judicial Ethics Advisory Com., Bd. Certified Ct. Reporters, Arizona Supreme Ct. Com. on Examinations, Arizona Judicial Coll. Bd.; co-chair Arizona Appellate Practice Inst. Co-author: (Book) Introduction to Legal Method and Process, 1985, 2002, Teacher's Manual for Introduction to Legal Method and Process, 1992, 2002, Handling Complex Litigation, 1986; Bd. editors Jour. Legal Writing Inst., 1993—2002; contbr. articles to profl. jours. and newspapers. Bd. dirs. Tempe-Mesa chpt. ACLU, 1984—86, Homeless Legal Assistance Project, Phoenix, 1990—98. Recipient Outstanding Service award, Arizona Atty. General's Office, 1992, 1994, Outstanding Alumnus award, Ariz. State U. Coll. Law, 1999. Mem. Ariz. Women Lawyer's Assn. (Profl. Achievement award 2002), Ariz. State Bar Assn. Republican. Methodist. Avocations: reading, travel. Office: Ariz Supreme Ct 1501 W Washington St Phoenix AZ 85009-3831 Office Phone: 602-542-4535. Business E-Mail: Rberch@Azbar.org.

BERCHEM, ROBERT LEE, SR., lawyer; b. Milford, Conn., Aug. 17, 1941; s. Robert W. and Barbara (Maher) B.; m. Lee Contrucci, Feb. 19, 1966; children: Kerry, Robert L. Jr., Jonathan. AB, Fairfield U., 1962; LLB, Villanova U., 1965; LLM, U. Mich., 1967. Bar: Conn. 1965. Law clk. U.S. Dist. Ct., Conn., 1965-66; prin. Berchem, Moses & Devlin, P.C., Milford, 1967—. Trustee Fairfield (Conn.) U.; chmn. Milford Hist. Dist. Commn., 1976—. Mem. ABA, Conn. Bar Assn., New Haven County Bar Assn., Milford Bar Assn. Democrat. Roman Catholic. Avocations: golf, skiing. Home: 125 W River St Milford CT 06460-3420 Office: Berchem Moses & Devlin PC 75 Broad St Milford CT 06460-3331

BERCOVITCH, SACVAN, English language professional, educator; b. Montreal, Que., Can., Oct. 4, 1933; s. Alexander and Brytha (Avrutick) B.; m. Susan L. Mizruchi; children: Eytan, Alexander. BA, Sir George William Coll., 1961; MA, Claremont (Calif.) Grad. Sch., 1963, PhD, 2965; LittD (hon.), Concordia U., 1993; DHL (hon.), Claremont U., 2005. Asst. prof. English and Am. lit. Brandeis U., 1966-68; asso. prof. U. Calif., San Diego, 1968-70; prof. English and Am. Lit. Columbia U., 1970-83; Powell M. Cabot rsch. prof. Am. lit. Harvard U., 1983—. Lectr., Kyoto, Tokyo, Shanghai, Beijing, Amsterdam, Frankfurt, Konstanz, Lisbon, Jerusalem, Tel Aviv, Salzburg, Coimbra, Montreal, Rome, Budapest, Paris, Venice, Bologna, Toronto, Oxford, Berlin, Moscow, Prague, Olomouc, Ostrava, Brno, Yale U., Princeton U., U. Pa., U. Calif., Berkeley, L.A., San Diego, Irvine, Cornell U., Dartmouth Coll., Concordia Coll., Claremont Grad. Sch., many others; advisor, cons. in field. Author: Typology and Early American Literature, 1972, The American Puritan Imagination, 1974, The Puritan Origins of the American Self, 1975, The American Jeremiad, 1978, Reconstructing American Literary History, 1986, Ideology and Classic American Literature, 1986, The Office of the Scarlet Letter, 1991, The Rites of Assent: Transformations in the Symbolic Construction of America, 1992; gen. editor: Cambridge History of American Literature (8 vols.); author more than 100 essays and revs.; trans. Yiddish lit. Am. Philos. Soc. fellow, 1968-69, Guggenheim fellow, 1969-70, Am. Coun. Learned Socs. fellow, 1971-72, Nat. Humanities Inst. fellow, 1975-76, Ctr. for Advanced Study in Behavioral Scis. fellow, 1978-79, NEH fellow, 1978-79, 86-87, Woodrow Wilson Ctr. fellow, 1990-91, Time-Life fellow Huntington Libr., 1994—, Cabot fellow for achievement in humanities, Mellon Emeritus fellow, 2004—; recipient James Russell Lowell prize for scholarship, 1992, Disting. Scholar award for extraordinary lifetime contbns. in Early Am. Lit., 2003, Award for Excellency in Tchg., Jay B. Hubbell award for lifetime achievement in Am. lit. studies. Fellow Am. Acad. Arts and Scis.; mem. MLA (mem. exec. com. Am. sect. 1976-78), English Inst., Am. Studies Assn. (pres. 1982-84) Office Phone: 617-495-2511. Business E-Mail: bercovit@fas.harvard.edu.

BERCU, BARRY BERNARD, pediatric endocrinologist; b. Montreal, Aug. 10, 1944; m. Sandra Bercu, 2 children. BS, U. Md., 1965, MD, 1969. Diplomate Nat. Bd. Med. Examiners, Am. Bd. Pediatrics, Am. Bd. Pediatric Endocrinology; lic. physician, Mass., Md., Fla. Med. intern V and VI Med. Svc. Boston City Hosp., 1969—70; asst. and sr. resident pediat. Mass. Gen. Hosp., Boston, 1970—72; clin. and rsch. fellow pediatric endocrinology & metabolism Harvard Med. Sch., Boston, 1974—77; clin. and rsch. fellow endocrinology dept. internal medicine Tufts U. Med. Sch., New Eng. Med. Ctr., Boston, 1974—77; clin. assoc. Nat. Inst. Child Health and Human Devel., NIH, Bethesda, Md., 1977—79, head pediatric endocrine unit neonatal & pediatric med. br., 1979—82, head pediatric endocrine unit, pregnancy rsch. br., 1982—84; assoc. prof. pediat. Uniformed Svcs. U., Bethesda Naval Ctr., 1980—84; assoc. rsch. prof. child health and devel. George Washington U. Sch. Medicine and Health Scis., Washington, 1983—84; prof. pediat., biochemistry and molecular biology, pharmacology and therapeutics U. South Fla. Coll. Medicine, Tampa, 1984, pres. faculty coun., 1998—99. Grant reviewer various orgns.; chmn. U. IRB Com.; mem. Dir.'s Conf. on Uses and Abuses of Growth Hormone in Children, Nat. Inst. Child Health and Human Devel., NIH, 1983-; mem. med. adv. bd. Parent Coun. Growth Normality, 1985—; mem. pediatric clin. oncology group Clin. Oncology Program, 1989—, MAGIC Found., 1995—; mem. staff All Children's Hosp., St. Petersburg, 1984-, Shriner's Hosp., Tampa, 1985-, Tampa Gen. Hosp., 1986-, others; instr. online courses Bioethical Considerations in Human Subject Rsch., Therapeutic Interventions in Aging-Growth Hormone, 2004; chmn. numerous internat. and nat. symposia, 1985—. Mem. editl. bd. Jour. Clin. Endocrinology and Metabolism, 1986-89, Jour. Anti-Aging Medicine, 1998—, Internat. Jour. Integrative Medicine, 2003—, Jour. Evidence Based Integrative Medicine, 2003—, Jour. Rejuvenation Medicine, 2004—, Jour. Clin. Intervention Into Aging, 2005—; editl. manuscript reviewer Acta Endocrinologica, Am. Jour. Nutrition, Biol. Psychiatry, Biology of Reprodn., Clin. Endocrinology, Clin. Pediatrics, Endocrine Jour., Endocrine Revs., Endocrinology, European Jour. Pediatrics, Hormone and Metabolic Rsch., Jour. AMA, Jour. Clin. Endocrinology and Metabolism, Jour. Clin. Investigation, Metabolism, Advances in Pituitary Disease: Metabolic, New England Jour. Medicine, Neuroendocrine and Psychosocial Issues, 2001, others; contbr. articles to profl. jours.; patentee in field. Bd. dirs. Birth Defects Found., Fla. Bay Area chpt., 1991—, chmn. med. adv. com., 1991; mem. expert divsn. vaccine injury compensation and mem. bd. dirs. USF Divsn. Sponsored Rsch., 1994-95. Grantee NIH, NIDA, BioNebr., Eli Lilly and Co., Genentech Corp., Daniel Pharm. Corp., Serono Labs., Am. Cancer Soc. Fla., ICN Pharms., Merck & Co., Novo Nordisk, Pfizer, Pharmacia Peptides, Inc., Pharmacia & Upjohn, Wyeth-Ayerst, Alkermes, Astra Zeneca, Infimed, BioPtnrs. and LG Bioscis. Mem. AMA, Am. Acad. Pediatrics (endocrinology sect.), Am. Assn. Clin. Endocrinologists, Am. Fedn. Clin. Rsch., Am. Pediatric Soc., Am. Pituitary Assn., Endocrine Soc., Fla. Endocrine Soc., Fla. Med. Assn., Hillsborough County Med. Assn., Hillsborough County Pediatric Soc., Lawson Wilkins Soc. Pediatric Endocrinology, Soc. Pediatric Rsch., So. Soc. Pediatric Rsch., Tampa Bay Area Soc. Neurosci. Office: All Children's Hosp USF Coll Medicine 801 6th St S Saint Petersburg FL 33701-4899 Business E-Mail: bercub@allkids.org.

BERCZI, ANDREW STEPHEN, academic administrator, educator; b. Budapest, Hungary, Aug. 15, 1934; s. Stephen Andrew and Iren Maria (Bartha) B.; m. Susan Bartok, Aug. 30, 1958; children— Thomas Edgar, Peter Alexander. EE, U. Tech. Scis., Budapest, 1956; BSc, Sir George Williams U., 1961, BA, 1963; MBA, McGill U., 1965, PhD, 1972. Engr. Bell Telephone Co., Montreal, 1956-59, mem. hdqrs. staff acctg., 1959-62, supr. computer systems, 1962-65; prof. quantitative methods, chmn. dept. quantitative methods Sir George Williams U., 1965-71; dean Faculty of Commerce and Adminstrn. Concordia U., Montreal, 1971-77; dean Faculty of Grad. Studies Wilfrid Laurier U., Waterloo, Canada, 1978-87, v.p. fin. and adminstrn.,

1987-98, prof. mgmt. scis. and decisions scis., 1999—. Cons. govtl. agys., pvt. industry; lectr. U. Calif. at Berkeley, U. Va., U. Chgo., U. Waterloo. Author: Exercises in Management Science, 1968, Problems in Managerial Operations Research, Vol. I and II, 1969, The Stock Exchange - A Total System Approach, 1970; contbr. over 80 articles and papers to profl. jours. and assns. McConnell fellow, 1965-66; Canada Council fellow, 1966-67; Quebec Province scholar, 1967-68 Fellow AAAS.; mem. IEEE, Operations Research Soc. Am., Canadian Operations Research Soc., Inst. Mgmt. Scis., Assn. Systems Mgmt., Fin. Execs. Inst., Acad. of Mgmt., Am. Statis. Assn. Home: 76 McCarron Crescent Waterloo ON Canada N2L 5N1 Office: Wilfrid Laurler U 75 University Ave W Waterloo ON Canada N2L 3C5 E-mail: aberczi@wlu.ca.

BERDAHL, KELLY JOHN, music educator, secondary school educator; b. Dickinson, N.D., Dec. 1, 1967; s. Orley John and Glenna Mae Berdahl. MusB in Edn., Mont. State U., 1994. Dir. instrumental music East Bakersfield H.S., Calif., 1994—2002; dir. bands Bozeman H.S., Mont., 2002—. Guest condr. So. Mont. Invitational Band Festival, Big Timber, 2004. Home: 433 Hunters Way Bozeman MT 59718 Office: Bozeman High Sch 205 North 11th Ave Bozeman MT 59715 Office Phone: 406-522-6269. Office Fax: 406-522-6222. E-mail: kberdahl@bozeman.k12.mt.us.

BERDAHL, ROBERT MAX, history professor, former academic administrator; b. Sioux Falls, S.D., Mar. 15, 1937; s. Melvin Oliver and Mildred Alberta (Maynard) B.; m. Margaret Lucille Ogle, Aug. 30, 1958; children—Daphne Jean, Jennifer Lynne, Barbara Elizabeth. BA, Augustana Coll., 1959; MA, U. Ill., 1961; PhD, U. Minn., 1965. Asst. prof. history U. Mass., Boston, 1965—67; asst. prof. history U. Oreg., Eugene, 1967—72, assoc. prof., 1972—81, prof., 1981—86; dean U. Oreg. (Coll. Arts and Scis.), 1981—86; prof. U. Ill., 1986—93, vice chancellor academic affairs, 1986—93; prof. U. Calif., Berkeley, 1997—; pres. U. Tex., Austin, 1993—97; chancellor U. Calif., Berkeley, 1997—2004. Research asso. Inst. for Advanced Study, Princeton, 1972-73 Author: The Politics of Prussian Nobility, 1988; (with others) Klassen und Kultur, 1982; contbr. articles to profl. jours. Fulbright fellow, 1975-76; Nat. Endowment Humanities fellow, 1976-77 Mem.: Am. Acad. Arts and Scis.

BERDAN, ROBERT J., lawyer; b. Waukesha, Wis., Aug. 31, 1946; BS with honors, U. Wis., Milw., 1968, MS with honors, 1969; JD cum laude, Marquette Univ., 1975. Bar: Wis. 1975, US Ct. Appeals 7th cir. 1975. V.p., head compliance and best practices dept. Northwestern Mutual Life Ins., 1996—2000, v.p., gen. counsel, sec., 2000—. Mem.: ABA, Milw. Bar Assn., State Bar Wis., Alpha Sigma Mu. Office: Northwestern Mutual Life Ins Legal Dept 720 E Wisconsin Ave Milwaukee WI 53202

BERDON, ROBERT IRWIN, judge; b. New Haven, Dec. 24, 1929; s. Louis J. and Jean (Cohen) B.; m. Nancy Tarr, Aug. 30, 1964 (dec. Mar. 1992); 1 child, Peter A. BS, Duke U., 1951; JD, U. Conn., 1957; LLM in Jud. Process, U. Va., 1988. With Bank of Manhattan, 1953-54; pvt. practice New Haven, 1957-73; treas. State of Conn., 1971-73; judge Superior Ct., State of Conn., New Haven, 1973-91; justice Supreme Ct., State of Conn., 1991-99, ret., 1999, judge trial referee, 2000—. Adj. prof. law U. Bridgeport Sch. Law, 1986-91; lectr. in law U. Conn. Sch. of Law, 1993; assoc. fellow Saybrook Coll., Yale U., 1986—; lectr. Am. Bd. Trial Advs., 1986; mem. Conn. Bd. Pardons, 1991-92. Contbr. articles to profl. jours. Recipient Judiciary award Conn. Trial Lawyers Assn., 1976, Disting. Alumni award U. Conn., 1977, Outstanding State Trial Judge in U.S. award ATLA, 1982, Pub. Svc. award U. Conn. Sch. Law Alumni Assn., 1989, Judiciary award Conn. Bar Assn., 1991, Hartford Neighborhood Housing Coalition award, 1992, RosCossi - Koskoff Justice award Conn. Trial Lawyers Assn., 1999, Jud. Recognition award Conn. Def. Lawyers Assn., 1999, citation Conn. Bar Assn., 2000, Lifetime Achievement award New Haven County Bar Assn., 2003. Home: 226 Pleasant Point Rd Branford CT 06405-5609 Office: Superior Ct 235 Church St New Haven CT 06510

BEREDJIKLIAN, PEDRO KIRKOR, physician; BA, Haverford Coll., Haverford, Pa., 1988; MD, Columbia U., N.Y., 1992. Diplomate Am. Bd. of Orthopaedic Surgery, IL, 2000. Asst. prof. of orthopaedic surgery U. Pa. Sch. of Medicine, Phila., 1998—. Fellow: Am. Acad.of Orthopaedic Surgery. Home: PA

BEREK, PETER, language educator; b. Bklyn., June 20, 1940; s. Leo and Ida (Kantrowitz) B.; m. Ellen H. Stark, June 10, 1962; children— Rachel, Martha, Elizabeth BA, Amherst Coll., 1961; MA, Harvard U., 1963, PhD, 1967. Instr. English, Hamilton Coll., Clinton, N.Y., 1965-67; asst. prof. English, Williams Coll., Williamstown, Mass., 1967-72, assoc. prof., 1972-77, prof., 1977-90, dept. chmn., 1980-86, Morris prof. rhetoric, 1984-90, dean of coll., 1975-78, spl. asst. to pres., 1987-90; prof. English Mt. Holyoke Coll., South Hadley, Mass., 1990—, dean faculty, provost, 1990-98, interim pres., fall 1995. Cons. NEH, Washington, 1973-76, 86-87, 89. Contbr. articles to profl. jours. Woodrow Wilson Found. fellow, 1961-62; NEH fellow, 1971-72, 82-83. Mem. MLA, Shakespeare Assn. Am. Jewish. Home: 87 Woodlot Rd Amherst MA 01002-3452 Office: Mt Holyoke Coll Dept English South Hadley MA 01075 Office Phone: 413-538-2311. E-mail: pberek@mtholyoke.edu.

BERENATO, AGNUS MCGLADE, women's college basketball coach; b. Dec. 9, 1956; m. Jack Berenato; children: Theresa Marie, Andrew, Joey, Clare, Christina. Student, U. N.C., 1976-77; BA in Sociology, Mt. St. Mary's Coll., Emmitsburg, Md., 1980, DHL (hon.), 1995. Profl. basketball player Entente Senonaise, Sens, France, 1975-76; head coach Rider Coll., 1981-85; asst. coach Ga. Tech U., 1986-88, head coach women's basketball, 1988—2003, U. Pitts., 2003—. Recipient Disting. Alumni award Mt. St. Mary's Coll., 1984; named Ga. Win Coll. Coach of Yr., 2000, Divsn. I Ga. Coach of Yr., 2002, Coach WBCA All Star Challenge, 2002; Sports Ethics fellow Inst. Internat. Sports, 1996; inducted into Rider Coll. Hall of Fame, 2002. Mem. Atlanta Tip-off Club (nat. adv. bd.), Atlanta Women's Network Inc., Women's Basketball Coaches Assn., Ga. Women's Intersport Network, Atlanta Women in Sports, Naismith Hall of Fame. Office: U Pitts PO Box 7436 Pittsburgh PA 15213 Business E-Mail: aberenato@athletics.pitt.edu.

BERENATO, JOSEPH C., manufacturing executive; b. 1947; BS in Engring., U.S. Naval Acad.; MA in English, U. Va.; MBA in Fin., NYU. Various exec. mgmt. positions Mfrs. Hanover Trust Co.; v.p., CFO, treas. Ducommon Inc., L.A., 1991-95, exec. v.p., COO, 1995-96, pres., 1996—, pres., CEO, 1997—, also bd. dirs. Office: Docommun Inc 23301 Wilmington Ave Carson CA 90745

BERENBAUM, MAY ROBERTA, entomology educator; b. Trenton, N.J., July 22, 1953; BS, Yale U., 1975; PhD, Cornell U., 1980. Asst. prof. entomology U. Ill., Urbana-Champaign, 1980-85, assoc. prof. entomology, 1985-90, prof. entomology, 1990-95, head dept., 1992—, Swanlund prof. entomology, 1996—. Assoc. editor Am. Midland Naturalist, 1982-85; mem. editl. bd. Jour. Chem. Ecology, Chemoecology, Proceedings of the Nat. Acad. Scis. USA. Recipient Presdl. Young Investigator award NSF, 1984, Founder's award Entomol. Soc. Am., 1994. Mem. AAAS, NAS, Am. Philos. Soc., Am. Assn. Arts and Scis., Entomol. Soc. Am. (fellow 2002), Ecol. Soc. Am., Phytochem Soc. Am., Internat. Soc. Chem. Ecology, Sigma Xi. Achievements include research in chemical aspects of insect-plant interaction, evolutionary ecology of insects, phototoxicity of plant products, host-plant resistance. Office: U Ill Dept Entomology 286 Morrill Hall 505 S Goodwin Ave Urbana IL 61801-3707 E-mail: maybe@uiuc.edu.*

BERENDES, MARY BENEDICTA, music educator; b. N.Y.C., Nov. 28, 1927; d. Joseph Henry and Anna Catherine (Fraser) B. MusB, Marywood Univ., Scranton, Pa., 1955; MM, U. Notre Dame, 1963; MS, Marywood Univ., Scranton, Pa., 1979; PhD, U. Pitts., 1973; postgrad., The Catholic Univ. Am., Univ. Tex., Our Lady of the Lake Univ. Music specialist St. Bernadine Sch., Balt., 1948-50, St. Patrick Sch., Scranton, 1950-52, Sacred Heart Sch., Mt. Holly, N.J., 1952-57, St. Leo Sch., Ashley, Pa., 1957-58, Holy Rosary Sch., Scranton, 1958-65, Little Flower Sch., Washington, 1965-67, Saint Rosalia Sch., Pitts., 1967-70; prof. Marywood Univ., 1973—. Reviewer for Ministry and Liturgy. Editor: Masses of Cadeac, 1962. NEH grantee, 1982. Mem. AAUP, Am. Musicological Soc., Pastoral Musicians. Roman Catholic. Avocations: reading, crocheting, swimming. Home and Office: Marywood Univ Scranton PA 18509-1598 E-mail: berendes@ac.marywood.edu.

BERENDES, THERESA MARIE, mathematics educator; b. Evansville, Ind., Oct. 13, 1967; d. Frank Allen and Mary Lee Catherine Lamble; m. Joseph Edwin Berendes, June 29, 1991; children: Adam, Laura, Jack, Lance. BS, Ind. U., 1990, MEd, 2002. Math tchr. Warrick County Sch. Corp., Boonville, Ind., 1990—91, St. John Sch., Newburgh, Ind., 1992—. Pres. Resurrection Parishioners Club, 2004, bd. mem., 2005. Mem.: Assn. Supervision and Curriculum Develop., Evansville Area Reading Coun. Roman Catholic. Business E-Mail: theresab@sjbnewburgh.org.

BERENDT, JOHN LAWRENCE, writer, editor; b. Syracuse, N.Y., Dec. 5, 1939; s. Ralph Sidney and Carol (Deschere) B. AB, Harvard U., 1961. Assoc. editor Esquire mag., N.Y.C., 1961-69; sr. staff editor Holiday mag., N.Y.C., 1969; assoc. prodr. David Frost Show, N.Y.C., 1969-71; writer Dick Cavett Show, N.Y.C., 1973-75; editor N.Y. Mag., N.Y.C., 1977-79; columnist Esquire mag., N.Y.C., 1982-94. Author: Midnight in the Garden of Good and Evil, 1994 (Pulitzer prize finalist for gen. non-fiction 1995), The City of Falling Angels, 2005; contbr. articles to profl. jours Mem. PEN, Century Assn. Office: c/o William Morris Agy 1325 Ave of the Americas New York NY 10019-0002

BERENDZEN, RICHARD, astronomer, educator, author; b. Walters, Okla., Sept. 6, 1938; s. Earl Emmanuel and Florine Adora (Harrison) B.; m. Gail Anita Edgar, Nov. 26, 1964; children: Deborah Carol, Natasha Karina. BS, MIT, 1961; MA, Harvard U., 1967, PhD, 1969; LLD (hon.), W.Va. Wesleyan U., 1979; LHD (hon.), Bridgewater Coll., 1983; LLD (hon.), Kean Coll. of NJ, 1984, Seton Hall U., 1985; DS (hon.), U. Columbo, Sri Lanka, 1985; LLD (hon.), U. Charleston, 1986, U. Balt., 1990. Staff scientist Geophysics Corp. Am., 1959-64, Ling-Temco-Vought, 1961-62; lectr. Harvard U., 1964, 66; mem. staff Project Physics, 1965; mem. faculty Boston U., 1965-73, assoc. prof. astronomy, 1971-73, acting dept. chmn., 1971-72; prof. physics, dean Coll. Arts and Sci., Am. U., Washington, 1974-76; univ. provost Am. U., Washington, 1976-79, pres., 1980-90, prof., 1990—; commentator on edn. and astronomy Stat. WUSA-TV/WTOP, Washington, 1984-90; cons. NASA, 1991, 98; sr. scholar Woodrow Wilson Internat. Ctr. Scholars, 2005—. Commentator on NASA for NBC-TV, 2003; cons. space sci. bd. NAS, 1973-74, mem. panel astron. survey com., 1971-73; cons. acad. affairs Am. Coun. on Edn., 1973-74; cons. to pub. cos.; Am. specialist in Asia Am. Council Edn. and Dept. State; adv. Am. Inst. Physics, Library of Congress, Internat. Communication Agy., UNESCO, Smithsonian Instn., NSF; univ. evaluator Commn. Higher Edn. Middle States Assn. Colls. and Secondary Schs.; chmn. priorities and planning com. Assn. Am. Colls., 1978-80, chmn. pres.'s adv. com., 1977-79; program evaluator US Armed Forces Inst.; mem. rev. panel human resources NRC; lectr. USIA; host spls. on astronomy and higher edn. NBC-TV, 1976-77; organizer Space 2000 Symposium, 1999; frequent guest radio and TV shows; researcher on cosmology, history of astronomy, sci. and soc., Am. and internat. edn. Author: Education in and History of Modern Astronomy, 1972, Life Beyond Earth and the Mind of Man, 1973, Man Discovers the Galaxies, 1976, Is My Armor Straight? A Year in the Life of a University President, 1986, Come Here: A Man Overcomes the Tragic Aftermath of Childhood Sexual Abuse, 1993, Pulp Physics: Humankind in Space & Time Audio Series, 2000; founding editor Jour. Coll. Sci. Teaching; contbr. numerous articles and revs. to profl. jours. Bd. dirs. Bus. Coun. for Internat. Understanding, 1980-84, Assn. Am. Colls., 1981-83, European Inst., Group Hospitalization Med. Svc. Inc., Nat. Network for Youth, Inc., 1994-97; chmn. Com. on Fng. Students and Instl. Policy, 1981-82; chmn. Employment/Edn. Bur. Greater Washington Bd. Trade, 1989; co-chmn. AIDS project Meyer Found., 1988-90; mem. DC Com. on Pub. Schs., 1988-90; chmn. DC Commn. on Budget and Fin. Priorities, 1989-90, 94; mem. NASA Exploration Adv. Task Force, 1988-91; chmn. bd. dir. Orphan Found. Am., 1996-97; dir. NASA's DC Space Grant Consortium, 2000—. Named one of Top Young Educators Change: Mag. of Learning, 1978; recipient Mortar Bd. Faculty award, 1977, Freedoms Found. Valley Forge award, 1982, Glenn T. Seaborg award Internat. Platform Assn., 1997; fellow Com. Scientists Investigating Claims of the Paranormal, 1977-78. Fellow AAAS; mem. Internat. Astron. Union, Internat. Assn. Univ. Pres., Am. Astron. Soc., Am. Assn. U. Adminstrs., Am. Assn. for Higher Edn., Internat. Assn. Univs., NY Acad. Scis., Am. Assn. Physics Tchr., Astron. Soc. Pacific, History of Sci. Soc., Nat. Sci. Tchrs. Assn., Am. Assn. Higher Edn., Am. Conf. Acad. Deans, Washington Inst. Fgn. Affairs, Cosmos Club, Sigma Xi, Kappa Mu Epsilon, Phi Eta Sigma, Phi Kappa Phi. Home: 1300 Crystal Dr 1402 Arlington VA 22202-3234 Office: Am U Dept Physics Washington DC 20016-8058 Office Phone: 202-885-2798. Personal E-mail: rberendzen@aol.com.

BERENFELD, MARK M., chemist; b. Moscow, Aug. 14, 1940; s. Moisey I. Berenfeld and Fanya I. Prosmushkina; m. Genya Berenfeld, Oct. 9, 1971; children: Benjamin, Sonya. BS, Engring. Inst., Moscow, 1965; MS, Lomonossov U., Moscow, 1970; PhD, Karpoff Sci. Inst. Physics, Moscow, 1974. Sr. scientist Pigment and Varnishes Co., Moscow, 1971-77, Dyestuff Co., Moscow, 1977-89; R&D chemist Fabricolor, Inc., Paterson, NJ, 1991—95; sr. sci. chemist Jos. H. Lowenstein, Inc., Bklyn., 1996—2002; rsch. scientist Chem. Compounds, Inc., Newark, 2002—. Mem. Am. Chem. Soc. Home: 46 Hornblower Ave Belleville NJ 07109-2520 Personal E-mail: mberenfeld@msn.com.

BERENGER, TOM (THOMAS MICHAEL MOORE), actor; b. Chgo., May 31, 1950; m. Lisa Berenger, 1986 (div. 1997); m. Patricia Alvaran, 1997. Actor stage prodns. The Rose Tattoo, Streetcar Named Desire, End as a Man, Electra; motion pictures include Beyond the Door, 1975, The Sentinel, 1977, Looking for Mr. Goodbar, 1977, In Praise of Older Women, 1979, Butch and Sundance: The Early Days, 1979, The Dogs of War, 1981, The Big Chill, 1983, Eddie and the Cruisers, 1983, Firstborn, 1984, Fear City, 1984, Rustler's Rhapsody, 1985, Platoon, 1987 (Oscar nomination), Someone to Watch Over Me, 1987, Betrayed, 1988, Born on the Fourth of July, 1989, Major League, 1989, Love at Large, 1990, At Play in the Fields of the Lord, 1991, Sniper, 1993, Sliver, 1993, Gettysburg, 1993, Major League 2, 1994, Chasers, 1994, Last of the Dogmen, 1995, The Substitute, 1996, An Occasional Hell, 1996, The Gingerbread Man, 1998, Shadow of Doubt, 1998, One Man's Hero, 1999, Diplomatic Siege, 1999, Fear of Flying, 2000, Takedown, 2000, Cutaway, 2000, Watchtower, 2001, Training Day, 2001, The Hollywood Sign, 2001, True Blue, 2001; TV movies include Johnny We Hardly Knew Ye, 1977, Flesh and Blood, 1979, Body Language, 1995, Avenging Angel, 1995, Body Language, 1995, Rough Riders, 1997, In the Company of Spies, 1999, The Junction Boys, 2002, Capital City, 2004; TV series include One Life to Live, 1975-76, Peacemakers, 2003; TV miniseries include Detective, 2005, Into the West, 2005. Office: care CAA 9830 Wilshire Blvd Beverly Hills CA 90212-1804*

BERENS, MARK HARRY, lawyer; b. St. Paul, Aug. 4, 1928; s. Harry C. and Gertrude M. (Scherkenbach) B.; m. Barbara Jean Steichen, Nov. 20, 1954; children: Paul J., Joseph F. (dec.), John M., Stephen M., Thomas M., Michael M., Lisa B. Moran, James M., Daniel M. BS in Commerce (Acctg.) magna cum laude, U. Notre Dame, 1950, JD magna cum laude, 1951; postgrad., U. Chgo., 1951-53. Bar: Ill. 1951, D.C. 1955, U.S. Supreme Ct. 1971; CPA, Ill. Assoc. Mayer, Brown and predecessors, Chgo., 1956-61, ptnr., 1961-96; chmn., CEO Attys.' Liability Assurance Soc., Inc., Chgo., 1987-95; ptnr. Altheimer & Gray, Chgo., 1996—2003, Bell, Boyd & Lloyd LLC, Chgo., 2003—. Nat. chmn. Nat. Assn. Law Rev. Editors, 1950-51; chmn. bd. dirs. Attys.' Liability Assurance Soc. (Bermuda) Ltd., 1979-95; bd. dirs. Accts. Liability Assurance Co., 1986-2004. Editor-in-chief Notre Dame Law Rev., 1950-51; contbr. articles to profl. jours. 1st lt. JAGC U.S. Army, 1953-56. Mem. D.C. Bar Assn., Chgo. Bar Assn., Am. Law Inst., The Comml. Bar Assn. (London), Union League Club, Lawyers Club of Chgo., Met. Club, Sunset Ridge Country Club (Northbrook). Republican. Roman Catholic. Home: 1660 North Ln Northbrook IL 60062-4708 Office: Bell Boyd & Lloyd LLC 70 W Madison St Chicago IL 60602 Office Phone: 312-781-6808. Business E-Mail: mberens@bellboyd.com.

BERENS, WILLIAM JOSEPH, lawyer; b. New Ulm, Minn., Dec. 12, 1952; s. Robert J. and Lorraine M. (O'Brien) B.; m. Janet Christiansen, June 13, 1975; children: Margaret, Elizabeth, Catherine. BA, Coll. St. Thomas, 1975; JD, U. Minn., 1978. Bar: Minn. 1978. Assoc. Dorsey & Whitney, LLP, Mpls., 1978-83, ptnr., estate and trust svcs. group.; chmn., tax, estate planning group, 1984—. Adj. prof. William Mitchell Coll. of Law, St. Paul, 1981-84. Fellow: Am. Coll. Trust and Estate Counsel. Office: Dorsey & Whitney LLP 50 S 6th St Minneapolis MN 55402-1498 Office Phone: 612-340-2621. Office Fax: 612-340-2868. E-mail: berens.bill@dorsey.com.

BERENSON, GERALD SANDERS, physician; b. Bogalusa, La., Sept. 19, 1922; s. Meyer A. and Eva (Singerman) B.; m. Joan Seidenbach, Mar. 7, 1951; children— Leslie, Ann, Robert, Laurie. BS, Tulane U., 1943, MD, 1945. Intern U.S. Navy Hosp., Great Lakes, Ill., 1945-46; practice medicine specializing in cardiology New Orleans; mem. staff Charity Hosp., Hotel Dieu; instr. dept. medicine Tulane U., 1949-52, prof. epidemiology Sch. Pub. Health, 1992—; asst. prof. medicine La. State U. Med. Sch., 1954-58, assoc. prof., 1958-63, prof., 1963-92, Boyd prof., 1988-92, prof. emeritus, 1992—; prof. medicine, biochemistry and pediatrics Tulane U. Sch. Medicine, New Orleans, 1992—. Dir. Specialized Ctr. Rsch. Arteriosclerosis, New Orleans, 1972-87, Nat. Rsch. and Demonstration Ctr. in Arteriosclerosis, 1984-87, Nat. Ctr. Cardiovascular Health, Sch. Pub. Health and Tropical Medicine Tulane U., 1992—; sr. vis. physician Charity Hosp. La., New Orleans, 1948—; cons. Touro Infirmary, 1967—. Contbr. articles to profl. jours. Served with USNR, 1945-48. USPHS fellow U. Chgo., 1952-54 Mem. Am. Coll. Cardiology (gov. La. 1985-88, trustee 1988, chmn. prevention com. 1990-93), So. Soc. Clin. Investigation (pres. 1969), La. Heart Assn. (pres. 1971), New Orleans Acad. Internal Medicine (pres. 1966), Musser-Burch Soc. (pres. 1981), Soc. Geriatric Cardiology (pres. 1999-00), Sigma Xi, Alpha Omega Alpha. Home: 505 Northline St Metairie LA 70005-4435 Office: Tulane Sch Pub Health Nat Ctr Cardiovascular Health 1440 Canal St Ste 1838 New Orleans LA 70112-2750 Office Phone: 504-988-7197. E-mail: berenson@tulane.edu.

BERENTS, MACK, sociologist, researcher; BA in Sociology, Calvin Coll., 1985; MS in Sociology, U. Wis., Madison, 1988, PhD in Sociology, 1992. Project asst. Wis. Ctr. Ednl. Rsch., Madison, Wis., 1986—91, data coord., 1991—92; lectr. dept. sociology U. Wis., 1991; assoc. scientist RAND, Washington, 1992—97, social scientist, 1998—2000, sr. social scientist, 2000—02; assoc. prof. pub. policy and edn. dept. leadership, policy and orgns. Vanderbilt U., Nashville, 2002—. Adj. prof. ednl. policy and leadership U. Md., College Park, 2002; adj. sr. social scientist RAND, Washington, 2002—; dir. grad. studies dept. leadership, policy and orgns. Peabody Coll. Vanderbilt U., Nashville, 2003—; assoc. dir. Nat. Ctr. Sch. Choice U.S. Dept. Edn., 2004—; guest lectr.; presenter to profl. confs. Author: Facing the Challenges of Whole-School Reform, 2002, Challenges of Conflicting School Reforms, 2002, Examining Gaps in Mathematics Achievement, 2005; contbr. chapters to books, articles to profl. jours. Elder Midtown Fellowships, Nashville, 2004—. Mem.: Population Assn. of Americas, Am. Ednl. Rsch. Assn., Am. Sociological Assn. Avocations: reading, running, soccer, basketball, cooking. Office: Dept Leadership Policy and Orgns Peabody Coll Vanderbilt U Peabody Box 514 Nashville TN 37203-5701

BERENTSEN, KURTIS GEORGE, music educator, conductor; b. North Hollywood, Calif., Apr. 22, 1953; s. George O. and Eleanor J. (Johnson) B.; m. Jeanette M. Sacco, Aug., 1975 (div. 1977); m. Floy I. Griffiths, March 17, 1984; 1 child, Kendra Irene. MusB, Utah State U., 1975; MA in Music, U. Calif., Santa Barbara, 1986; cert. colloguy, Concordia Coll., 1996. Cert. cmty. coll. tchr., Calif., pub. tchr., Calif.; commd. minister Luth. Ch., Mo. Synod, 1996. Dir. music Hope Luth. Ch., Daly City, Calif., 1975-81; gen. mgr. Ostara Press, Inc., Daly City, Calif., 1975-78; condr. U. Calif., Santa Barbara, 1981-86; dir., condr. Santa Barbara oratorio Chorale, 1983-85; dir. music 1st Presbyn. Ch., Santa Barbara, 1983-84, Goleta (Calif.) Presbyn. Ch., 1984-85; minister music Trinity Luth. Ch., Ventura, 1985-92, Christ Luth. Ch. & Sch., Little Rock, Ark., 1992-98; dir. choral music Concordia U., Portland, Oreg., 1998—; instr. Ventura Coll., 1987-88; music dir., condr. Gold Coast Community Chorus, Ventura, 1988-92. Choir dir. Temple Beth Torah Jewish Community, Ventura, 1982-87; adj. prof. Pepperdine U., Malibu, Calif., 1988; chorus master Ventura Symphony Orch., 1987. Condr. oratorios Christus Am Oelberg, 1983, Elijah, 1984, Hymn of Praise, 1988, cantata Seven Last Words, 1979, 84, Paukenmesse, 1989, Mozart's Requiem, 1990, 2005, Requiem-Fauré, 1991, 2002, Judas Maccabaeus-Handel, 1992; soloist 15 major oratorio and opera roles, 1971-92, Nat. Anthem, L.A. Dodgers, 1989; dir. (with John Rutter) Gold Coast Community Chorus, Carnegie Hall, N.Y.C., 1991, Tribute to America, Lincoln Ctr. Concert, N.Y.C., 1991. Min. music, tchr. Christ Luth. Ch. and Sch., Little Rock, 1992—. First place winner baritone vocalist Idaho Fedn. Music Clubs, 1971, recital winner Utah Fedn. Music Clubs, 1974. Mem. Choral Condrs. Guild, Assn. Luth. Ch. Musicians, Am. Guild of English Handbell Ringers, Am. Choral Dirs. Assn., Music Educators Nat. Conf., Sigma Nu (sec., song leader 1973-75). Home and Office: 2811 NE Holman St Portland OR 97211-6067 Office Phone: 503-280-8511. E-mail: kberentsen@cu-portland.edu.

BERENZWEIG, JACK CHARLES, lawyer; b. Bklyn., Sept. 29, 1942; s. Sidney A. and Anne R. (Dubowe) B.; m. Susan J. Berenzweig, Aug. 8, 1968; children: Mindy, Andrew. B.E.E., Cornell U., 1964; JD, Am. U., 1968. Bar: Va. 1968, Ill. 1969. Examiner U.S. Pat. Off., Washington, 1964-66; pat. adviser U.S. Naval Air Systems Command, Washington, 1966-68; ptnr. Brinks, Hofer, Gilson & Lione and predecessor firm, Chgo., 1968—. Editorial staff Am. U. Law Rev., 1966-68; contbr. articles to profl. jours. Mem. ABA, Chgo. Bar Assn., Ill. State Bar Assn., Bar Assn. 7th Fed. Cir., Va. State Bar, Internat. Trademark Assn. (bd. dirs. 1983-85), Brand Names Edn. Found. (bd. dirs. 1993-2000), Meadow Club (Rolling Meadows, Ill.), Miramar Club (Naples, Fla.), Delta Theta Phi. Home: 127 W Oak St Apt A Chicago IL 60610-5422 Office: Brinks Hofer Gilson & Lione Ltd Ste 3600 455 N Cityfront Plaza Dr Chicago IL 60611-5599 Office Phone: 312-321-4212. Business E-Mail: jcb@brinkshofer.com.

BERENZWEIG, SUSAN SMITH, psychologist; b. Bklyn., Feb. 13, 1949; d. Joseph J. and Lucille Smith; m. Marc S. Berenzweig, June 28, 1970 (div. 1992); children: Adam Louis, Julie Lewis. AB, Brown U., 1971; MA, Yeshiva U., 1990, PsyD, 1992. Lic. psychologist, N.Y. Supervising psychologist Ctr. for Preventive Psychology, White Plains, N.Y., 1991—; pvt. practice Mamaroneck, N.Y., 1992—. Contbr. articles to profl. jours. Pres. Westchester Chorale, 1982—84; pres. woman's divsn. UJA, Larchmont and Mamaroneck, NY, 1984—86. Mem. Westchester County Psychol. Assn., N.Y. State Psychol. Assn., Brown U. Alumni Assn. (pres. Westchester chpt. 1992-94). Office Phone: 914-698-2368.

BERES, MARY ELIZABETH, religious organization administrator; b. Birmingham, Ala., Jan. 19, 1942; d. John Charles and Ethel (Belenyesi) Beres. BS, Siena Heights Coll., Adrian, Mich., 1969; PhD, Northwestern U., 1976. Joined Dominican Sisters, 1960. Tchr. St. Francis Xavier Sch., Medina, Ohio, 1962-64, St. Edward Sch., Detroit, 1964-67, Our Lady of Mt. Carmel Sch., Temperance, Mich., 1967-69, asst. prin., 1968-69; tchr. math. St. Ambrose H.S., Detroit, 1969-70; vis. instr. Cornell U., 1973-74; assoc. prof. orgn. behavior Temple U., Phila., 1974-84; assoc. prof. mgmt. Mercer U., Atlanta, 1984-91; founder, sr. assoc. Leadership Sys., Atlanta, 1988—, Mid-Atlantic chpt. Prioress Dominican Sisters of Adrian, Atlanta, 2004—. Mem. World Pilgrims, 2002—; bd. dirs. Aquinas Ctr. Theology, 2001—. Contbr. chpts. to books; organizer of symposia in areas of corp. leadership, orgn. change and cross-cultural comm. Bd. dir. Ctr. for Ethics and Social Policy, Phila., 1980—84, Assn. Global Bus., 1989—91; program planning com. of interdepartmental group in bus. adminstrn. U. Ctr. in Ga., 1987—91, chair, 1988—90; trustee Adrian Dominican Ind. Sch. Sys., Adrian, Mich., 1971—79; pres. bd. dirs. New Ventures Network, 1998—2001; active Atlanta Clergy and Laity Concerned, 1986—95; econ. pastoral imlementation com. Archdiocese of Atlanta, 1988—89, Atlanta Archdiocesan Planning and Devel. Coun., 1991—93; episcopal moderator women Religious Archdiocese of Atlanta, 1993—97, Atlanta Conf. Sisters, 1984—, pres., 1993—97, 2001—; vicar Consecrated Life Archdiocese of Atlanta, 2001—. Recipient Legion of Honor membership Chapel of the Four Chaplains, Phila., 1982, Disting. Tchg. award Lindback Found., 1982, Cert. for Humanity Mercer U, 1985. Mem. NAFE, Acad. of Mgmt., Dominican Sisters of Adrian, Mich. (strategic planning com. 2000-01), Faith Alliance of Met. Atlanta, 2004-. Democrat. Roman Catholic. Office: Mid-Atlantic Mission Chpt PO Box 76453 Atlanta GA 30358 Personal E-mail: mbberes@bellsouth.net.

BERESFORD, ANNETTE DIANA, researcher; b. Bethesda, Md., Feb. 26, 1958; d. Spencer Moxon and Ann Lincoln Beresford; children: Conner Crossman, Mekha Schmidt. BS summa cum laude, U. So. Miss., 1991; M Pub. Policy and Adminstrn., Jackson State U., 1997; PhD in Pub. Adminstrn., Fla. Atlantic U., 2002. Analyst Hancock Bank, Gulfport, Miss., 1985-93; program mgr., planner Bd. Trustees of State Instns. of Higher Learning, Jackson, Miss., 1993—97; fin. specialist divsn. securities and investor protection Office of Contr., West Palm Beach, Fla., 1997—2002; vis. instr. Fla. Atlantic U., Jupiter, Fla., 2002—03; rsch. assoc. Nat. White Collar Crime Ctr., Morgantown, W.Va., 2003—. Bd. dirs. Mayan Towers, Palm Beach Shores. Contbr. articles to profl. jours. Named to Am. Acad. Disting. Students, Am. Ctr. for Grad. Edn., 1996-97; Breland scholar U. So. Miss., 1990-91; Newell doctoral fellow Fla. Atlantic U., 2000-2001. Mem. Am. Soc. for Pub. Adminstrn., Pub. Adminstrn. Theory Network, Phi Kappa Phi, Pi Alpha Alpha. Office: Nat White Collar Crime Ctr 12 Roush Dr Morgantown WV 26505

BERESFORD, BRUCE, film director; b. Sydney, New South Wales, Australia, Aug. 16, 1940; s. Leslie and Lona (Warr) B.; m. Rhoisin Patricia Harrison, 1965; children: Benjamin, Cordelia, Adam; m. Virginia Patricia Mary Duigan, 1985; 1 child, Trilby. BA, Sydney U., 1961. Films officer Brit. Film Inst., London, 1965-70; film advisor Arts Council of Great Britain, London, 1967-70 Dir. films Dons Party, 1976 (Best Dir. award Australian Film Inst.), The Getting of Wisdom, 1977, Money Movers, 1978, The Club, 1980, Tender Mercies, 1981, Puberty Blues, 1982, King David, 1984, Her Alibi, 1989, Driving Miss Daisy, 1989, Mr. Johnson, 1990, The Black Robe, 1991, Rich in Love, 1992, A Good Man in Africa, 1994, Silent Fall, 1994; dir., writer: Breaker Morant, 1980, Fringe Dwellers, 1985, Crimes of the Heart, 1986, (segment) Aria, 1988; producer, dir.: The Adventures of Barry McKenzie, 1972, Barry McKenzie Holds His Own, 1974, Last Dance, 1996, Paradise Road, 1997, Sydney: A Story of a City, 1999, Double Jeopardy, 1999. Mem. Dirs. Guild U.S.A. Avocations: opera, skiing, Australian football, tennis.

BERESFORD, DOUGLAS LINCOLN, lawyer; b. Washington, June 1, 1956; s. Spencer Moxon and Ann (Lincoln) B.; m. Lori Anne Mainous, Sept. 22, 1990; children: Alexander Gould, Erik Mainous. AB cum laude, Harvard U., 1978; JD, Georgetown U., 1982. Bar: D.C. 1982, U.S. Ct. Appeals (D.C. cir.) 1984, U.S. Supreme Ct. 1986. Assoc. Morgan, Lewis & Bockius, Washington, 1982-83, Newman & Holtzinger, P.C., Washington, 1983-89, ptnr., 1989-94, Long, Aldridge & Norman, Washington, 1994-2000, Hogan & Hartson LLP, Washington, 2000—. Office: Hogan & Hartson LLP 555 13th St NW Ste 700E Washington DC 20004-1161 Office Phone: 202-637-5819. Business E-Mail: dlberesford@hhlaw.com.

BERESNEV, IGOR ALEXANDROVITCH, geophysicist; b. Moscow, July 18, 1959; s. Alexandr Fedorovitch and Lyudmila Vasilievna (Gavrilova) B.; m. Anna Svyatoslavna Dukarskaya, July 16, 1988; children: Maria, Pavel. MS, Moscow State U., 1981; PhD, Inst. Physics of the Earth, Moscow, 1986. Jr. researcher Inst. Physics of the Earth, Moscow, 1984-89, researcher, 1989—. Contbr. articles to profl. jours.; patentee in field. Mem. Acoustical Soc. Am., Am. Geophys. Union, Seismol. Soc. Am., European Geophys. Soc. Avocations: politics, pop music, cross country skiing. Home: Anadyrskiy Proezd 63-85 Moscow Russia 129336 Office: EES-4/MS D-443 Los Alamos Nat Lab Los Alamos NM 87545-0001 also: Inst Physics of Earth Bolshaya Gruzinskaya 10 123810 Moscow Russia

BEREUTER, DOUGLAS KENT, foundation administrator, former congressman; b. York, Nebr., Oct. 6, 1939; s. Rupert Wesley and Evelyn Gladys (Tonn) B.; m. Louise Meyer, June 1, 1962; children: Eric David, Kirk Daniel. BA, U. Nebr., 1961; M in City Planning, Harvard U., 1966, MPA, 1973. Urban planner HUD, San Francisco, 1965-66; dir. div. state and urban affairs Nebr. Dept. Econ. Devel., 1967-68, state planning dir., 1968-70; coord. fed.-state relations Nebr. State Govt., 1967-70, urban planning cons., 1971-78; assoc. prof. U. Nebr., 1971—73, Kansas St. Univ., 1971—78; mem. Nebr. Legislature, 1974-78, U.S. Ho. Reps. from 1st Nebr. Dist., 1979—2004, mem. fin. svcs. com., mem. internat. rels. com., vice chmn. intelligence com., mem. transp. and infrastructure com.; pres. The Asia Found., San Francisco, 2004—. Mem. Nebr. State Crime Commn., 1969-71; chmn. standing com. on urban devel. Nat. Conf. State Legislatures, 1977-78; mem. Nat. Agrl. Export Commn., 1985-86. Served as officer U.S. Army, 1963-65. Mem. Am. Planning Assn., Phi Beta Kappa, Sigma Xi. Republican. Lutheran. Office: The Asia Found PO Box 193223 San Francisco CA 94119

BEREZIN, SERGEI, professional hockey player; b. Voskresenska, Russia, Nov. 5, 1971; Mem. Toronto Maple Leafs, 1994—2001, Phoenix Coyotes, 2001—02, Montreal Canadiens, 2002, Chicago Blackhawks, 2002—03, Washington Capitals, 2003—. Mem. Russian Hockey Team, 1994. Named to NHL All-Rookie Team, 1997; recipient Silver medal, World Jr. Championships, 1991. Office: Toronto Maple Leafs Air Canada Ctr 40 Bay St Ste 300 Toronto ON Canada M5J 2X2

BEREZIN, TANYA, acting coach, educator, actress; b. Phila., Mar. 25, 1941; d. Maurice and Bettye (Shifrin) Berezin; m. Robert Leeming Thirkield, June 29, 1969 (div. June 1977); children: Lila Joy, Jonathon Schuyler; m. Mark Beers Wilson, Oct. 18, 1987. Student, Boston U., 1959—63. Co-founder Circle Repertory Co., N.Y.C., 1969, artistic dir., 1986-94, pvt. coach, studio class, seminars, 1994—; resident acting coach All My Children, One Life to Live ABC, N.Y.C., 1994-99; resident acting coach Another World NBC, N.Y.C., 1997-98; resident acting coach As the World Turns CBS, N.Y.C., 1998-99. Actor: (TV shows) St. Elsewhere, 1984, Law and Order, 1992—94, 2000—04, Crossing Jordan, 2004; (plays) Angels Fall, 1983, Moundbuilders, 1975 (Obie award), Sympathetic Magic, 1997; (films) Awakenings, 1993; prodr.: Prelude to a Kiss, Destiny of Me, Three Hotels, Baltimore Waltz. Avocation: gardening.

BERG, A. SCOTT (ANDREW SCOTT BERG), writer; b. Norwalk, Conn., 1949; Grad., Princeton U., 1971. Author: Lindbergh, 1999 (Pulitzer prize for biography 1999), Goldwyn: A Biography, Max Perkins: Editor of Genius, 1978 (Nat. Book award), Kate Remembered, 2003; (films) Making Love, 1982; co-prodr., co-writer Goldwyn, 2001. Trustee Princeton (NJ) U., 1999—2003, Libr. of Am., 1999—. Guggenheim fellow, 1982. Office: Janklow & Nesbit Assocs 445 Park Ave 13th Fl New York NY 10022

BERG, ALAN, lawyer, arbitrator; b. Scranton, Pa., June 5, 1947; s. Donald and Lucile (DeLugo) Berg; m. Rita A. Samin, June 15, 1975 (dec. Feb. 20, 2001); children: Thomas M., Matthew P., Andrew J. BA, Hartwick Coll., Oneonta, N.Y., 1969; JD, St. John's U., 1972; LLM in Labor Law, NYU, 1975. Bar: N.Y. 1973, U.S. Dist. Ct. (dists. N.Y.) 1973, U.S. Ct. Appeals 1973, U.S. Supreme Ct. 1976. Atty. N.Y. State Labor Rels. Bd., 1972—79, adminstrv. law judge, 1979—80, chief judge, 1980—84, gen. counsel, 1984—91, N.Y. State Employment Rels. Bd., 1991—2003, arbitrator, 2003—. Judge N.Y. Law Sch. Wagner Moot Ct.; advisor NYU Law Sch. student adv. program. Trustee Freeport Meml. Lib., NY, 1976—81; coach Freeport H.S. summer basketball team, 1973—; N.Y. all-star team N.Y.-Phila. basketball festival, 1985—86, 1988—97; arbitrator Better Bus. Bur. Recipient George Emma Meml. Sportsmanship award, 1986, Citizen award, Freeport Boosters Club, 1987. Mem.: Indsl. Rels. Rsch. Assn., N.Y. State Bar Assn., St. John's Law Sch. Alumni Assn. Home: 108 Delaware Ave Freeport NY 11520-1313

BERG, CHARLES G., insurance company executive; m. Casey Wiggins; 3 children. BA in Polit. Sci., Macalester Coll., St. Paul, MN, 1978; degree in law, Georgetown U. Founder, CEO Health Ptnrs., Inc.; exec. v.p. med. delivery Oxford Health Plans, Inc., 1998—2000, exec. v.p. med. delivery and tech., 2000—01, pres., COO, 2001—02, pres., CEO, 2002—. Bd. dirs. America's Health Ins. Plans. Office: Oxford Health Plans Inc 48 Monroe Turnpike Trumbull CT 06611

BERG, DANIEL, science and technology educator; b. N.Y.C., June 1, 1929; s. Jack and Hattie (Tannenbaum) B.; m. Frances Helena Ely, Aug. 18, 1956; children: Brian, Laura, Meredith. BS, CCNY, 1950; MS, Yale U., 1951, PhD, 1953; grad. execs. program, Carnegie-Mellon U., 1972. With Westinghouse Electric Corp., Pitts., 1953-77, research div. mgr., then tech. dir., 1976-77; prof. sci. and tech. Carnegie-Mellon U., 1977-83, dean Mellon Coll. Sci., 1977-81, univ. provost, 1981-83; v.p. acad. affairs, provost, Inst. prof. sci. and tech. Rensselaer Poly. Inst., Troy, N.Y., 1983-85, pres., 1985-87, Inst. prof., 1987—. Bd. dirs. Hy-Tech. Machine Co., Inc.; chmn. bd. Crystek Inc.; mem. Pa. Sci. and Engring. Found., 1975-76; mem. vis. coun. sci. and engring. CCNY, 1980-84; mem. vis. coun. Sch. Computer Sci., Carnegie-Mellon U., 1992—; mem. Yale U. Coun., 1981-85; assoc. fellow Jonathan Edwards Coll., 1982—; cons. to industry and govt. Author, editor, patentee in field. Fellow IEEE, AAAS, INFORMS, Am. Inst. Chemists, N.Y. Acad. Scis.; mem. Nat. Acad. Engring. (coun. 1985-88), Am. Chem. Soc., Cosmos Club of Washington, Rivers Club of Pitts., Phi Beta Kappa, Sigma Xi, Alpha Chi Sigma, Tau Beta Pi. Home: 12 The Crossways Troy NY 12180-7263 Office: Rensselaer Poly Inst 5015 CII Troy NY 12180-3522

BERG, DAVID HOWARD, lawyer; b. Springfield, Ohio, Mar. 4, 1942; s. Nathan Stewart Berg and Mildred (Besser) Berg-Filion; children: Geoffrey Alan, Gabriel Adam, Caitlin Hannah; m. Kathryn Page, July 10, 1994. Student, Tulane U., 1963; BA in English, U. Houston, 1964, JD, 1967. Bar: Tex. 1967, NY 1989, US Dist. Ct. (so., no. we., ea. dist. Tex., so., ea. dist. NY, we. dist. Va.), U. Ct. Appeals (2d, 4th, 5th, 8th and 11th cirs.), US Supreme Ct. 1970. Law clk. NLRB, Washington, 1967-68; ptnr. David Berg & Assocs., Houston, 1968-77, Berg & Androphy, 1977—. Mem. fed. ct. lawyers adv. com. U.S. Dist. Ct. (so. dist.) Tex.; spl. counsel commn. on lawyer discipline, Tex. State Bar, 1996—. Author, The Trial Lawyer: What It Takes to Win, 2003; contbr. articles and essays to mags. Adv. Jimmy Carter Transition Govt., Washington, 1976, Mayor Kathy Whitmire Campaign, 1980-91; patron Friends of Menil Collection, 1990-91; adv. campaign Mayor Bob Lanier, 1991; chmn. Imagine Houston, City of Houston; adv. bd. Camp for All; bd. dirs. U. Houston Law Ctr, Law Found., 1996, Houston Shakespeare Festival, 1997, Anti-Defamation League, 2002, Houston Holocaust Mus.; chmn. bd. Houston Area Water Corp., 1999-; mem. Pres. Council Tulane Univ. 2000-. Recipient 1st pl. for best feature article in a scholarly jour. Nat. Assn. Publ., 1991; Theatreworks USA Goodworks award, 2002. Fellow Internat. Acad. Trial Lawyers, Tex. Bar Found., Houston Bar Found.; mem. ATLA, State Bar Tex. (chmn. grievance com. 1984-85), NY State Bar Assn., Tex. Trial Lawyers Assn., Houston Trial Lawyers Assn., Houston Bar Assn., U. Houston Law Alumni Assn. (bd. dirs. 1992-95), Am. Bd. Trial Advocates (assoc.). Democrat. Jewish. Avocations: writing, running, fishing. Home: 16 Sunset Blvd Houston TX 77005-1838 Office: Berg & Androphy 3704 Travis St Houston TX 77002-9550 Office Phone: 713-529-5622. Office Fax: 713-529-3785. Business E-Mail: dberg@bafirm.com.

BERG, DEBRA SCHWEIGER, business owner; b. Urbana, Ill., Apr. 17, 1953; d. Jean Burtch Wright; m. Wesley Schweiger, Aug. 6, 1977 (div.); m. Paul A. Berg, Nov. 14, 2004 BA in Polit. Sci. with high distinction, U. Ill., 1975, MPA, 1979. Congl. intern, Washington, 1974; intern IRS, Washington, 1975; legis. intern Ill. Senate Appropriations Com., Springfield, 1975, budget analyst, 1975—77, Ky. Legis. Rsch. Commn., Frankfort, 1977—80; rsch. analyst Minn. Legis. Audit Commn., St. Paul, 1980—81; fin. analyst Group Health, Inc., Mpls., 1981—85; asst. to dir. global environ. policy project H.H. Humphrey Inst., Mpls., 1981; pres., owner Internat. Bus. Assocs. (U.S., Mex., Korea, Hungary, Brazil, Poland, Argentina, Indonesia), Shoreview, Minn., 1985—96; tech. writer Amdocs, Inc., 1997—2000, gcom, Inc., Champaign, Ill.; founder Power of One Pub., Champaign. Spkr. in field; Mark Victor Hansen protege Enlightened Millionaire Inst., 2005 Author: The Power of One: Heroes Forging America's Civic Reawakening from Sea to Shining Sea, 2004. Charles Merriam scholar for local govt. rsch. and writing. Mem. Nat. Assn. Women Writers, Nat. Polit. Sci. (hon.), Pi Sigma Alpha. Republican. Avocations: photography, vocal performing, gardening. Home and Office: 2909 Green Valley Ln Champaign IL 61822-6192

BERG, G. VIVIAN, artist; b. Worcester, Mass., Feb. 28, 1932; d. Emil Mauritz Mattson and Gunhild Maria Israelson; m. Kenneth George Berg, May 10, 1957; children: Donna Maria, Leah Christine. Tng. cert., Ward Sch. Airline Tng., Worcester, 1951; diploma, Worcester Sch. Bus., 1951. Sec. Ea. Airlines, N.Y.C., 1951-52; legal sec. Office of Russell W. Anderson, Worcester, 1953-61; tchr. art Auburn, 1976-2000. One woman shows include Ogunquit (Maine) Art Ctr., Shore Road Gallery, Boston, Harrison Conf. Ctr., Marlboro, Mass; group shows include Cultural Assembly Portrait Show, UN Conf. Women in Nairobi, 1985; represented in more than 450 permanent, pvt., corp. and pub. collections including Milford (Mass.) Fed. Bank, Milford Savs. Bank, 1st Svc. Bank, Pepperell, Mass., Merrimac Valley Credit Union, North Andover, Mass., Spencer Savs. Bank, Medway (Mass.) Nat. Bank, Unibank for Savs., Hoosac Savs. Bank North Adams, Mass., Medway Co-Operative Bank, Methuen (Mass.) Co-Operative Bank, Am. Eagle Credit Union, Manchester, Conn., TruNorth Fin., North Adams, N.E. Cmty. Credit Union, Haverhill, Mass., Haverhill Co-Op Bank, Falmouth Security Fed., Roslindale Co-Operative Bank, Falmouth Security Fed., Mass., Roslindale Coop., Mass., New Eng. Design Assocs., Worcester, Oxford (Mass.) Free Pub. Libr., Atlantis Gallery Worcester Mass., Shore Rd. Gallery Ogunquit Maine Mem. Am. Soc. Marine Artists, Am. Mensa Ltd., Nat. Mus. Women in the Arts. Episcopalian. Studio: 8 Inwood Rd Auburn MA 01501-1115 E-mail: gvivianberg@verizon.net.

BERG, GORDON HERCHER, banker; b. New Haven, May 14, 1937; s. John Edward and Dazma Charlotte (Hercher) B.; m. Ruth I. Gardner, Aug. 26, 1961; (div. Feb. 1985); children: Elizabeth, Deborah, Mary, Beatrice, Gordon; m. Patricia Pridham, Apr. 27, 1985. AA, Mitchell Coll.; BA, Ohio Wesleyan U., 1959; MBA, NYU, 1963; grad., Stonier Grad. Sch. Banking, 1967; MTS, Harvard U., 1988. Asst. sec. Irving Trust Co., N.Y.C., 1959-64; v.p. New England Merchants Bank, Boston, 1964-68; ptnr. The Sprague Co., Boston, 1968-70; pres., chief exec. officer Berg & Co. Inc., BMFC, Inc., Boston, 1970-84; pres. Berg & Co., Inc., Boston, 1984—. Med. ethicist. Contbr. articles to prfl. jours. Past pres., trustee emeritus Derby Acad., Hingham, Mass., 1972. Mem. Mortgage Bankers Assn. Am. (cert. mortgage banker award, 1983), Masons. Republican. Avocations: theology, precision cabinet making, offshore sailing, celestial navigation, mountain glacier climbing. Office: Berg & Co Inc 2006 Quay Villiage ct 102 Annapolis MD 21403 E-mail: berg@bergandco.com.

BERG, JANICE CAROL, elementary school educator; b. Painesville, Ohio, Feb. 18, 1953; d. Kenneth White Edds and Audrey Helen Nelson; children: Peter James, Steven Alan. BS in Elem. Edn., Slippery Rock State Coll., 1975; MEd, Slippery Rock U., 1987, cert. in early childhood edn., 1995; cert. reading specialist, Clarion U., 1994. Cert. elem. tchr. Pa. 3d grade tchr. Brookville (Pa.) Area Sch. Dist., 1975—76; 5th grade tchr. Seoul (Rep. of Korea) Fgn. Sch. Dist., 1977—78, 1st grade tchr., 1978—79; reading specialist Punxsutawney (Pa.) Area Sch. Dist., 1994, Allegheny-Clarion Valley Sch. Dist., Foxburg, Pa., 1996—. Sub. tchr. Derry Twp. Sch. Dist., Hershey, Pa., 1990; pvt. tutor, Brookville, Pa., 93. Room mother PTO, Elizabethtown, Pa., 1985; den leader, chmn. com. Boy Scouts Am., Elizabethtown, 1987—94; vacation bible sch. dir., tchr., Sunday sch. tchr., chmn. Christian edn. com. Mem.: Pa. State Edn. Assn., Seneca Reading Coun. (pres., corr. sec. 2001—02), Allegheny-Clarion Valley Edn. Assn., Keystone State Reading Assn. (mem. conf. membership com. 2002), Butler Outdoor Club (sec. 2004—05). Avocations: swimming, hiking, bicycling, reading, table tennis. Home: 404 Walnut St Emlenton PA 16373

BERG, JEFFREY SPENCER, talent agency executive; b. L.A., May 26, 1947; s. Dick Berg and Barbara Freedman; m. Denise Luria; 2 children. BA in English with honors, U. Calif., Berkeley, 1969. Vice pres., head lit. div. Creative Mgmt. Assocs., Los Angeles, 1969-75; v.p. motion picture dept. Internat. Creative Mgmt., Los Angeles, 1975-80, pres., 1980-85, chmn., chief exec. officer, 1985—. Dir. Josephson Internat., Inc., Marshall McLuhan Ctr. of Global Communication; bd. dirs. Oracle Corp., Am. Film Inst. Trustee U. Berkeley Found.; bd. govs. Music Ctr. L.A. County; pres. letters and sci. exec. bd. U. Calif. Berkeley; bd. vis. Anderson Grad. Sch. of Mgmt., UCLA. Named one of 50 Most Powerful People in Hollywood, Premiere mag., 2004—05; recipient Cavaliere Ufficiale Order of Merit, Republic of Italy, 1991. Mem. U. Calif. Berkeley Alumni Assn. Office: Internat Creative Mgmt 8942 Wilshire Blvd Beverly Hills CA 90211-1934*

BERG, JEREMY MARK, federal agency administrator, biochemist, researcher; BS in chemistry, MS in chemistry, Stanford U., 1980; PhD in chemistry, Harvard U., 1985. Visiting rsch. assoc. Charles F. Kettering Rsch Lab., Yellow Springs, Ohio, 1979; predoctoral fellow, Nat. Science Found Harvard U., Cambridge, Mass., 1980—83; Jane Coffin Childs Meml. Fund postdoctoral fellow The Johns Hopkins U. Sch. Med., Balt., 1984—86; asst. prof. chemistry The Johns Hopkins U., 1986—90, prof. chemistry, 1992—2003, co-dir., Keck Ctr. for Rational Design of Biologically Active Molecules, 2001—03; prof., dir. dept. biophysics & biophysical chemistry The Johns Hopkins U. Sch. Med., Balt., 1990—2003, dir., Markey Ctr. for Macromolecular Structure & Function, 1990—2003, dir., Inst. for Basic Biomedical Sciences, 2001—03; dir. Nat. Inst. Gen. Med. Sciences, NIH, Bethesda, Md., 2003—. Recipient Pure Chemistry award Am. Chem. Soc., 1993, Eli Lilly Biological Chemistry award Am. Chem. Soc. 1995. Office: Nat Inst of Gen Med Sciences Natcher Bldg 45 Ctr Dr Bethesda MD 20892 Office Phone: 301-594-2172.

BERG, JOHN RICHARD, chemist, former federal government executive; b. Chippewa Falls, Wis., Apr. 24, 1932; s. John and Florence Agnes (Heagle) B.; m. Virginia Marie Binet, June 16, 1956; children: John E., Thomas A., James E., Joseph M. BS in Chemistry, Coll. St. Thomas, 1954; PhD in Physical Chemistry, Iowa State U., 1961. Sr. chemist then tech mgr. 3M Co., St. Paul, 1961-82, fed. govt. mgr. Washington, 1982-86; prin. dep. asst. sec. Dept. of Energy, Washington, 1986-88, asst. sec., 1988-89; pvt. cons., 1990—. Cons. in field, 1992—; bd. dirs. Columbia Rsch. Corp. Patentee in field. Former mem. Cmty. Svcs. Program, Roseville (Minn.) Sch. Dist.; past leader, commr. Boy Scouts Am.; candidate for U.S. Congress from 4th dist. Minn.; mem. ad hoc task force Arlington County Mandatory Recycling, 1993-95, Arlington County Four Mile Run Watershed Joint Planning Commn., 1994—, Arlington C. of C., 1994—, Arlington County Environment and Energy Conservation Commsn., 1997—. Named Scouter of Yr., Boy Scouts Am., St. Paul, 1969. Mem. Am. Inst. Chemists, Am. Chem. Soc., AAAS, Phi Lambda Upsilon, Sigma Xi. Avocations: fishing, gardening, model railroading, travel. Home: 3202 N Tacoma St Arlington VA 22213-1340

BERG, JOHN TOWNSEND, physiologist, researcher; b. Mpls., July 3, 1945; s. John Wilmer and Jean Townsend Berg; m. Gemma deGuzman, Mar. 23, 1997; children: John Joseph, Melisa deGuzman. PhD, U. Hawaii at Manoa, Honolulu, 1985. Postdoctoral fellow U. Calif. San Diego, La Jolla, 1994—97; sr. rsch. fellow U. Wash., Seattle, 1998—2000; assoc. rsch. prof. U. Hawaii at Manoa, Honolulu, 2001—. Outside mem. animal use com. Oceanic Inst., Waimanalo, Hawaii, 2002—. Contbr. articles to profl. jours. Recipient Geist award, Hawaii Cmty. Found., 2001—04; Summer scholar, Pacific Health Rsch. Inst., 1983, Hawaii Heart Fellowship and Grant-in-Aide, Hawaii Heart Assn., 1985, Parker B. Francis Fellowship in Pulmonary Medicine, Parker B. Francis Found., 1988. Mem.: Am. Physiol. Soc. (life). Achievements include Demonstrated that inhibition of hypoxic pulmonary vasoconstriction prevents high altitude pulmonary edema; discovery of ginkgo biloba prevents high altitude pulmonary edema in rats; carbonic anhydrase is present in mammalian vascular smooth muscle; increased wall stress induced vascular remodeling in lung parenchyma; endotoxin prevents hyperoxic lung injury by induction of manganese superoxide dismutase. Home: 94-125 Pahu St # 29 Waipahu HI 96797 Office: Univ Hawaii at Manoa Rm 122 1951 East-West Rd Honolulu HI 96822 Office Phone: 808-956-5381. Home Fax: 808-676-2622; Office Fax: 808-956-5381. Personal E-mail: johnberg@hawaii.edu.

BERG, LAURA, Olympic athlete; b. Santa Fe Springs, Calif., Jan. 1, 1975; m. Rob Peterson. Grad., Fresno State U. Asst. softball coach Fresno State U. Mem. U.S.A. Women's Softball Team, Athens Olympics, 2004, U.S.A. Women's Softball Gold Medal Teams, ISF Work Championships, 1994, 98, 2002, Fresno State U., NCAA Championship Team, 1998, U.S.A. Women's Softball Gold Medal Team, Atlanta Olympics, 1996, U.S.A. Women's Softball Gold Medal Team, Sydney Olympics, 2000. Recipient 3-time First Team All Am., Nat. Fastpitch Coach's Assn.

BERG, LEONARD, retired neurologist, educator, researcher; b. St. Louis, July 17, 1927; s. Jacob and Sara (Kessler) B.; m. Gerry Saltzman, Mar. 25, 1948; children: Kathleen, John, Nancy. AB cum laude, Washington U., St. Louis, 1945, MD cum laude, 1949. Diplomate: Am. Bd. Psychiatry and Neurology (dir. 1978-85, pres. 1985). Intern Barnes Hosp., St. Louis, 1949-50, resident, 1950-51, Neurol. Inst., N.Y.C., 1951-53; clin. assoc. Nat. Inst. Neurol. Diseases and Blindness, NIH, 1953-55; mem. faculty Washington U. Med. Sch., 1955—98, prof. clin. neurology, 1972-89, prof. neurology, 1989-98, prof. emeritus neurology, 1998—; ret., 1998. Attending neurologist Barnes Hosp., Jewish Hosp., St. Louis; dir. Alzheimer's Disease Rsch. Ctr., Washington U., 1985-97; expert U.S. FDA, 1992-96; mem. U.S. Congress Adv. Panel on Alzheimer's Disease, 1993-96, Leonard Berg Annual Symposiums Nat. Spkrs. Co-author: Atlas of Muscle Pathology in Neuromuscular Diseases, 1956. Bd. dirs. Temple Israel, St. Louis, 1972-74, Jewish Center for Aged, 1981-98, hon. dir., 1999—. With USPHS, 1953-55. Recipient Lifetime Disting. Rsch. on Alzheimer's Disease and Related Disorders award, 7th World Alzheimer's Congress, 2000, Robert E. Schlueter Leadership award, St. Louis Met. Med. Soc., 2001, 2d Century award, Washington U. Mem. AMA, Am. Acad. Neurology, Am. Neurol. Assn. (1st v.p. 1988-89), Soc. for Neurosci., Alzheimer's Assn. (Chgo.) (bd. dirs. 1989-95, 96-98, chair med. and sci. adv. bd. 1991-95), Phi Beta Kappa, Sigma Xi, Alpha Omega Alpha. Home: 816 S Hanley Rd Apt 7D Saint Louis MO 63105-2678 Office: Washington U Alzheimer's Disease Rsch Ctr 4488 Forest Park Ave Ste 130 Saint Louis MO 63108-2212

BERG, LILLIAN DOUGLAS, chemistry educator; b. Birmingham, Ala., July 9, 1925; d. Gilbert Franklin and Mary Rachel (Griffin) Douglas; m. Joseph Wilbur Berg, Jr., June 26, 1950 (dec. Nov. 1997); children: Anne Berg Jenkins, Joseph Wilbur III, Frederick Douglas. BS in Chemistry, Birmingham So. Coll., 1946; MS in Chemistry, Emory U., 1948; AA in Music, No. Va. C.C., Annandale, 2002. Instr. chemistry Armstrong Jr. Coll., Savannah, Ga., 1948-50; rsch. asst. chemistry Pa. State U., University Park, 1950-54; instr. chemistry U. Utah, Salt Lake City, 1955-56; prof. chemistry No. Va. C.C., 1974-96, 98—. Adj. prof. No. Va. C.C., 1998—. Mem. Am. Chem. Soc., Am. Women in Sci., Am. Guild Organists, Mortar Bd. Soc., Iota Sigma Pi, Sigma Delta Epsilon, Phi Beta Kappa. Avocation: liturgical organist/conductor. Home: 124 Villa Dr Poquoson VA 23662 Office Phone: 703-573-2346.

BERG, LOUIS LESLIE, investment executive; b. Vienna, Austria, Dec. 27, 1919; s. Gustav and Hedwig (Kohn) B.; came to U.S., 1938, naturalized, 1943; student U. Vienna, 1937-38, Coll. City N.Y., 1941-43; m. Minnette

Whitman, Aug. 28, 1959; children: Sharon, Randee, Michel. Pres., Gt. Empire Corp., N.Y.C., 1946—, Bendalou Real Estate Corp., N.Y.C., 1950-60, Netherlands Securities Co., Inc., N.Y.C., 1959-62, Imported Automotive Parts, Ltd., L.I. City, N.Y.; chmn., bd. dirs. IAP Inc., Avenel, N.J., IAP West Inc., Los Angeles; bd. dirs., exec. com. Auto Internat. Assn.; advisor U.S. Congl. Adv. Bd. dir. Internat. Aviation Corp., Cosmos Industries, Kane-Miller Corp., Knickerbocker Toy Co., Inc., Vernitron Corp., Jet Aero Corp., Fidelity Am. Finance Corp., S.W. Fla. Enterprises, Sulray Inc., U.S. Airlines, Commuter Airlines, Aviation Equipment. Mem. Am. Mgmt. Assn. Club: Wings. Office: IAP Inc 26 Engelhard Ave Avenel NJ 07001-2217 also: IAP West Inc 20036 Via Baron Rancho Dominguez CA 90220

BERG, MADELAINE R., lawyer; b. Bklyn., Aug. 13, 1951; d. Gerald and Lorraine (Nodkin) B. BA, Bklyn. Coll., 1973, MFA, 1975; JD, Bklyn. Law Sch., 1980. Bar: N.Y. 1981, U.S. Dist. Ct. (so. dist.) N.Y. 1981, Pa. 1992, U.S. Dist. Ct. (ea. dist.) Pa. 1992. Spl. counsel, environ. law practice area Stroock & Stroock & Lavan LLP, N.Y.C., 1980—. Contbr. articles to profl. jours. Office: Stroock & Stroock & Lavan LLP 180 Maiden Ln New York NY 10038-4982 Office Phone: 212-806-5823. Office Fax: 212-806-6006. Business E-Mail: mberg@stroock.com.

BERG, MARTIN DAVID, lawyer; b. Akron, Nov. 6, 1942; BBA, U. Miami, 1964; JD, Columbia U., 1967. Bar: Fla. 1967, U.S. Dist. Ct. (so. dist.) Fla. 1972, U.S. Supreme Ct. 1977, U.S. Ct. Appeals (11th cir.) 1997. Atty. pvt. practice, Miami, 1970—; city atty. City of South Miami (Fla.), 1989-94. Office: 19 W Flagler St Ste 802 Miami FL 33130-4409 Office Phone: 305-371-1631.

BERG, MARY JAYLENE, pharmacy educator, researcher; b. Fargo, N.D., Nov. 7, 1950; d. Ordean Kenneth and Anna Margaret (Skramstad) B. BS in Pharmacy, N.D. State U., 1974; PharmD, U. Ky., 1978. Lic. pharmacist, N.D., Ky., Iowa. Fellow in pharmacokinetics Millard Fillmore Hosp./SUNY, Buffalo, 1978-79; asst. prof. U. Iowa, Iowa City, 1980-85, assoc. prof., 1985-95, prof., 1995—2004, prof. emeritus, 2004—; with dept. clin. rsch., clin. pharmacology/pharmacokinetics F. Hoffmann-La Roche, Ltd., Basel, Switzerland, 1992; with Office of Rsch. on Women's Health NIH, 1999. Bd. dirs. Soc. for Women's Health Rsch., 1998—2004; mem. adv. com. rsch. on women's health NIH, 1995-99, mem. task force rsch. on women's health NIH, 1997-99; mem. adv. bd. Pfizer Women's Health, 1998-2003; mem. adv. com. on pharm. scis. FDA, 1999-2002. Reviewer Cin. Pharmacy, 1984—, Epilepsia, 1987—, Annals of Pharmacotherapy, 1997—; editor: (med. symposia) Internat. Leadership Symposium, The Role of Women in Pharmacy, 1990, Women-A Force in Pharmacy Symposium, 1992, Gender Related Health Issues: An International Perspective, 1996, Global Visions of Women Pharmacists, 1998; mem. editl. adv. bd.: The Internat. Jour. of Applied and Basic Nutritional Scis., 1998—, Jour. Gender Specific Medicine, 1998—2001; mem. editl. bd. Jour. Women's Health, 2003—, XX vs XY: The Internat. Jour. of Sex Differences in the Study of Health, Disease and Aging, 2003—, Clinical Trials, 2004—; contbr. articles to numerous med., pharmacy and nutrition jours., 1998. Advisor Kappa Epsilon, Iowa City, 1980-94; pres. Mortar Bd. Alumnae, Iowa City, 1986-88. NIH grantee, 1984, Nat. Insts. on Drug Abuse grantee, 1986; recipient Career Achievement award Kappa Epsilon, 1985, Vanguard award Kappa Epsilon Merck, 1999, Master award N.D. State U., 2000; named to Iowa Women's Hall of Fame, 1999. Mem.: Leadership Internat-Women for Pharmacy (bd. dirs. 1991—2004), Fedn. Internat. Pharmaceutique (del. World Health Assembly 1992, pres. acad. sect. 2000—02), Internat. Forum of Women for Pharmacy (U.S. contact 1988—2004), Am. Pharm. Assn., Am. Epilepsy Soc., Am. Soc. Hosp. Pharmacists (chair spl. interest group clin. pharmokinetics 1987—89), Am. Assn. Pharm. Scientists, Phi Beta Delta, Kappa Epsilon, Rho Chi, Sigma Xi. Lutheran. Achievements include research in multiple doses of oral activated charcoal to clear totally absorbed drug that appears in poison control books around the world, pharmacokinetics of drug-nutrient interaction between phenytoin and folic acid, also on both national and international levels, pharmacological differences between men and women (gender analysis of medications) and among ethnic groups for prescription medicines, over-the-counter medications and alternative natural drugs, research on the interrelations among folic acid, vitamin B6, vitamin B12 and zinc in diet and without supplementation in pregnant and non-pregnant women with and without epilepsy; initiating graduate program in clinical pharmaceutical sciences at the U. Iowa College of Pharmacy. Office: U Iowa Coll of Pharmacy Iowa City IA 52242 E-mail: maryjberg@mchsi.com.

BERG, PATRICIA ELENE, molecular biologist; b. Dubuque, Iowa, Sept. 17, 1943; d. Clifford Jay and Dorothy Ruth (McKibben) Emerson; 1 child, Bridget K. Mora; m. Robert S. Weiner. SB in Math., U. Chgo., 1965; PhD in Microbiology, Ill. Inst. Tech., 1973. Postdoctoral fellow U. Chgo., 1973-78; dir. genetic engring. Bethesda Rsch. Labs., Rockville, Md., 1978-80; expert NIH, Bethesda, 1980-82, sr. staff fellow, 1982-85, Nat. Inst. Digestive Diseases and Kidney, 1985-91; assoc. prof. divsn. of pediatric hematology/oncology Sch. Medicine U. Md., Balt., 1991-98; assoc. prof. dept. biochem. and molecular biology George Washington U. Med. Sch., Washington, 1999—. Contbr. articles to profl. jours. and to NY Times, Washington Post, L.A. Times, AP, Reuters; reported on CNN, Fox, CBS, 160 TV stas., U. Chgo. scholar, 1961—65. Mem. AAAS, Am. Soc. Microbiology, Am. Soc. Hematology, Am. Assn. Cancer Rsch., Sigma Xi. Achievements include discovery of BP1, gene expressed in over 80 percent of breast cancer patients. Office: George Washington U Med Sch Dept Biochem/Molecular Biol 2300 Eye St NW Washington DC 20037-2336 Business E-Mail: bcmpeb@gwumc.edu.

BERG, PAUL, biochemist, educator; b. NYC, June 30, 1926; s. Harry and Sarah (Brodsky) Berg; m. Mildred Levy, Sept. 14, 1947; 1 child, John. BS, Pa. State U., 1948; PhD (NIH fellow 1950-52), Western Res. U., 1952; DSc (hon.) (hon.), U. Rochester, 1978, Yale U., 1978, Washington U., St. Louis, 1986, Oreg. State U., 1989, Pa. State U., 1995. Postdoctoral fellow Copenhagen (Denmark) U., 1952—53; postdoctoral fellow Sch. Medicine, Washington U., 1953—54, Am. Cancer Soc. scholar cancer research dept. microbiology sch. medicine, 1954—57, from asst. to assoc. prof. microbiology, 1955—59; prof. biochemistry Sch. Medicine, Stanford (Calif.) U., 1959—, Sam, Lulu and Jack Willson prof. biochemistry, 1970—94, Robert W. Cahill prof. cancer rsch., 1994—2000, chmn. dept. sch. medicine, 1969—74, now Cahill prof. in cancer rsch. emeritus; and dir. emeritus, Beckman Ctr. for Molecular and Genetic Med., 2000—. Dir. Stanford U. Beckman Ctr. for Molecular and Genetic Medicine, 1985—2000, Affymetrix, 1993—, Nat. Found. Biomed. Rsch., 1994—; non-resident fellow Salk Inst., 1973—83; adv. bd. NIH, NSF, MIT; vis. com. dept. biochemistry and molecular biology Harvard U.; bd. sci. advisors Jane Coffin Childs Found. Med. Rsch., 1970—80; chmn. sci. adv. com. Whitehead Inst., 1984—90; bd. sci. adv. DNAX Rsch. Inst., 1981—; internat. adv. bd. Basel Inst. Immunology; chmn. nat. adv. com. Genome Project, 1990—92. Editor: Biochem. and Biophys. Research Communications, 1959—68; editl. bd.: Molecular Biology, 1956—69; contbr. to profl. jours. Trustee Rockefeller U., 1990—92. Lt. (j.g.) USNR, 1943—46. Named Calif. Scientist of Yr., Calif. Museum Sci. and Industry, 1963, Lynen lectr., 1977, Priestly lectrs., Pa. State U., 1978, Dreyfus Disting. lectrs., Northwestern U., 1979, Lawrence Livermore Dir.'s Disting. lectr., 1983, Linus Pauling lectr., 1993; recipient Eli Lilly prize biochemistry, 1959, V.D. Mattia award, Roche Inst. Molecular Biology, 1972, Henry J. Kaiser award for excellence in teaching, 1969, Disting. Alumnus award, Pa. State U., 1972, Sarasota Med. awards for achievement and excellence, 1979, Gairdner Found. annual award, 1980, Lasker Found. award, 1980, Nobel award in chemistry, 1980, NY Acad. Sci. award, 1980, Sci. Freedom and Responsibility award, AAAS, 1982, Nat. Medal of Sci., 1983, 7th Ann. Biotechnology Heritage award, Chem. Heritage Found., 2005, numerous disting. lectureships including Harvey lectr., 1972. Fellow: AAAS; mem.: NAS, Royal Soc. (elected fgn. mem. 1992), French Acad. Sci. (elected fgn. mem. 1981), Japan Biochem. Soc. (elected fgn. mem. 1978), Internat. Soc. Molecular Biology, Am. Philos. Soc., Am. Soc. Microbiology, Am. Soc. Cell Biology (chmn. pub. policy com. 1994—), Am. Soc. Biol. Chemists (pres. 1974—75), Am. Acad. Arts and Scis., Inst. Medicine. Office: Stanford Sch Medicine Beckman Ctr B-062 Stanford CA 94305-5301 E-mail: pberg@cmgm.stanford.edu.*

BERG, ROBERT LEWIS, physician, educator; b. Spokane, Wash., Sept. 10, 1918; s. Evan and Rachel Myfanwy (Lewis) B.; m. Florence Mitcham Foster, June 18, 1943 (dec. 1985); children— Erik Christian, Astri Maren. BS, Harvard, 1940, MD, 1943. Successively intern, resident, chief med. resident Mass. Gen. Hosp., Boston, 1944-46, 50, asst. to dir. rsch. and edn., 1951-54, asst., then assoc. physician, 1951-58; Moseley travelling fellow Royal Caroline Inst., Stockholm, 1948-49; from instr. to asst. prof. medicine Harvard Med. Sch., 1951-58, Albert D. Kaiser prof., also chmn. dept. preventive, family and rehab. medicine, 1958-89; assoc. dean planning Univ. Rochester, 1982-89, assoc. prof. medicine, 1958-69, prof. medicine, 1969-89, prof. emeritus, 1989—; sr. assoc. physician Strong Meml. Hosp., 1958-69, physician, 1969-89. Acting adminstr., 1960-61; mem. NIH Epidemiology and Biometry Tng. Com., 1962-66, 67-71, chmn., 1969-70; mem. U.S. Com. Vital and Health Statistics, 1965-69, chmn., 1967-69 Author: (with M. Roy Brooks, Jr. and Miomir Savicevic) Health Care in Yugoslavia and the United States, 1976; editor: Health Status Indexes, 1973, (with Joseph S. Cassells) The Second Fifty Years: Promoting Health and Preventing Disability, 1990. Trustee Eastman Dental Center, 1971-97, chmn., 1975-79; mem. Governors commn. on domestic violence, 1982-88, Ednl. Commn. for Fgn. Med. Grads., 1983-91. Recipient George Washington Goler award, NY Pub. Health Assn., 1986, David Kaiser award, Rochester Acad. Medicine, 2002, Alumni Gold Medal, U. Rochester Sch. Medicine & Dentistry, 2002. Mem. Am. Pub. Health Assn., Assn. Tchrs. Preventive Medicine (treas. 1963-69, v.p. 1969-70, pres. 1970-72), Internat. Epidemiological Assn. Home: 45 Songbird Ln Rochester NY 14620-3174 Office: Box 644 601 Elmwood Ave Rochester NY 14642-0001 Office Phone: 585-275-3356. Business E-Mail: bob_berg@urmc.rochester.edu.

BERG, ROBERT RAYMOND, geologist, educator; b. St. Paul, May 28, 1924; s. Raymond F. and Jennie (Swanson) B.; m. Josephine Finck, Dec. 22, 1946; children: James R., (dec.), Charles R., William R. BA, U. Minn., 1948, PhD, 1951. Geologist, Calif. Co., Denver, 1951-56; cons. Berg and Wasson, Denver, 1957-66; prof. geology, head dept. Tex. A&M U., 1967—, Michel T. Halbouty prof. geology, 1982-2001, prof. emeritus, 2001—; dir. univ. research Tex. A & M U., 1972—. Cons. petroleum geology, 1959— Contbr. papers in field. Served with AUS, 1943-46. Recipient Disting. Achievement award U. Minn., 1992. Fellow Geol. Soc. Am.; mem. Am. Assn. Petroleum Geologists (disting. lectr. 1972, hon. mem. 1985, Sidney Powers Meml. award 1993, Disting. Educator award 2000), Am. Inst. Profl. Geologists (pres. 1971, hon. mem. 1988), Nat. Acad. Engring. Home: 414 Brookside Dr E Bryan TX 77801-3701 Office: Tex A&M U Dept Geology College Station TX 77843-3115

BERG, STANTON ONEAL, firearms and ballistics consultant; b. Barron, Wis., June 14, 1928; s. Thomas C. and Ellen Florence (Nedland) Silbaugh; m. June K. Rolstad, Aug. 16, 1952; children: David M., Daniel L., Susan E., Julie L. Student, U. Wis., 1949-50; LLB, LaSalle Ext. U., 1951; postgrad., U. Minn., 1960-69. Claim rep. State Farm Ins. Co., Mpls., Hibbing and Duluth, Minn., 1952—57, claim supt., 1957—70; regional mgr. State Farm Fire and Casualty Co., St. Paul, 1970—84; firearms cons. Mpls., 1961—. Bd. dirs. Am. Bd. Forensic Firearm and Tool Mark Examiners; instr. home firearms safety, Mpls., 1975—; cons. to Sporting Arms and Ammunition Mfrs. Inst., 1974-84; internat. lectr. on forensic ballistics Adv. Bd. Milton Helpern Internat. Ctr. for Forensic Scis., 1975—; mem. bd. cons. Inst. Applied Sci., Chgo., 1974—; cons. for re-exam. of ballistics evidence in Robert Kennedy assassination/Sirhan case Superior Ct. L.A., 1975; ct. expert witness in most state cts., Mil. Gen. Ct. Martial Territorial Ct. at V.I. and U.S. Dist. Cts., Supreme Ct. of Ont., Can.; mem. Nat. Forensic Ctr., 1979-98, internat. study group in forensic scis., 1985—; chmn. internat. symposiums on forensic ballistics, Edinburgh, Scotland, 1972, Zurich, 1975, Bergen, Norway, 1981, Dusseldorf, Germany, 1993. Contbg. editor: Am. Rifleman mag., 1973—84, mem. editl. bd.: Internat. Microform Jour. Legal Medicine and Forensic Scis., 1979—, Am. Jour. Forensic Medicine and Pathology, 1979—91; contbr. articles to profl. jours.; presenter: Forensic Firsts, History Channel, 2001. With U.S. Army Counter Intelligence Corp., 1948-52. Fellow Am. Acad. Forensic Sci., Am. Coll. Forensic Examiners (life, bd. cert. forensic examiner and diplomate); mem. ASTM (criminalistics subcom. 1989—, non powder guns subcom. 1990—, paintball guns and sys. subcom. 1994—), NRA, Assn. Firearms and Tool Mark Examiners (life, charter, emeritus 2004, exec. com. 1970-72, editl. com. jour., 1989-92, Disting. Mem. and Key Man award 1972, exam. and stds. com. 1975-76, Spl. Honors award 1976, nat. peer group on cert. firearms examiners 1978—, Mem. of Yr. award 2004), Forensic Sci. Soc., Internat. Assn. Forensic Scis., Internat. Assn. for Identification (life, Disting. mem., firearms subcom. sci. and practice com. 1961-74, 1986-2000, chmn. firearm subcom. 1964-66, 69-70, 91-95, lab. rsch. and techniques subcom. 1980-81, life, charter Minn. divsn.), Internat. Wound Ballistics Assn., We. Conf. Criminal and Civil Problems (sci. adv. com.), Am. Gunsmithing Assn. (life), Am. Legion (life), Army Counter-Intelligence Corp. Vets. Assn. (life), Browning Arms Collectors Assn. (life), Am. Ordnance Assn. (life), Minn. Weapons Collectors, Internat. Cartridge Collectors Assn. (life), Internat. Reference Orgn. Forensic Medicine and Scis., Internat. Assn. Bloodstain Pattern Analysts. Address: 6025 Gardena Ln NE Minneapolis MN 55432-5840 Personal E-mail: forensicb@msn.com, forensicb@aol.com.

BERG, THOMAS KENNETH, lawyer; b. Willmar, Minn., Feb. 10, 1940; s. Kenneth Q. and Esther V. (Westlund) B.; m. Margit Kathryn Larson, July 31, 1965; children: Erik, Jeffrey. BA, U. Minn., 1962, JD, 1965. Bar: Minn. 1965, U.S. Dist. Ct. Minn. 1968, U.S. Ct. Appeals (8th cir.) 1974, U.S. Supreme Ct. 1980. Atty. Dept. Navy, Washington, 1965-67; assoc. Carlsen, Greiner & Law, Mpls., 1967-79; state rep. Minn. Ho. of Reps., St. Paul, 1970-78; U.S. atty. Dept. of Justice, Mpls., 1979-81; ptnr. Popham, Haik, Schnobrich & Kaufman, Mpls., 1981-97, Hinshaw & Culbertson, Mpls., 1997—. Treas. Moe for Gov. com., 2002. Chair Gov.'s Re-election Com., St. Paul, 1984-86, Gov.'s Commn. for Drug Abuse, Mpls., 1989; U.S. Senate candidate for endorsement Dem. Farmer Labor Party, Mpls., 1994; chmn. bd. dirs. St. Paul Rehab. Ctr., 1995-97; trustee Wolf Ridge Environ. Learning Ctr., 2003—. Recipient Outstanding Narcotics Prosecution award U.S. Drug Enforcement Adminstrn., 1981. Mem. Am. Health Lawyers Assn. Office: Hinshaw & Culbertson 3100 Campbell Mithun 222 S 9th St Minneapolis MN 55402-3389

BERG, WALTER LOUIS, retired history professor; b. Tacoma, Wash., Feb. 17, 1922; s. Walter Berg and Elsie Karrenstein; m. Rosemary S. Bell (dec.); m. Eleanor R. Todd Wilson-Berg, Mar. 1, 1986; children: Karen L. Beahm, Melissa B. Mercer, Geoffrey W. BA, U. Puget Sound, 1946; MA, U. Wash., 1948, PhD, 1957. Prof. history Ctrl. Wash. U., Ellensburg, 1955—82, chmn. dept., 1965—69; ret., 1982. Fulbright prof. U. Madrid, 1961—62; vis. prof. history U. Wash., Seattle, 1963—64. Lt. USNR, 1943—46. Mem.: Am. Hist. Assn. (grad. com. 1967—69). Avocation: growing rhododendrons. Home: 1650 Agate Pass Rd NE Bainbridge Island WA 98110

BERG, WARREN STANLEY, retired bank executive; b. Lynn, Mass., Jan. 17, 1922; s. Carl W. and Gladys (Colburn) B.; m. Marjorie E. Coleman, Mar. 25, 1944; children— Peter C., Carolyn (Mrs. John Spengler), Dana S. BS, Harvard U., 1943; grad. exec. devel. program, Cornell U., 1944. Player Boston Red Sox, 1946; farm sys. coach MIT Baseball Team, 1948-50; Dir. pub. relations and sales promotion Arthur D. Little, Inc., Cambridge, Mass., 1951-65; with Shawmut Bank of Boston (N.A.), 1965-87, sr. v.p., 1969-87. Author: History of Harvard Baseball, 1964, History of Massachusetts Institute of Technology Athletics, 1950. Trustee, pres. Museum of Sci.; chmn. bd. dirs. Freedom House, Freedom Trail; pres. Freedom Trail Found.; chmn. Freedom Trail Commn.; exec. com. Wang Ctr. for Performing Arts. Served to capt. USMCR, 1943-46. Named to Harvard U. Athletic Hall of Fame (baseball). Mem. Pub. Relations Soc. Am. (presdl. citiation for meritorious service 1962), Assoc. Grantmakers of Mass. (v.p.) Clubs: Harvard (Boston), Harvard Varsity (Boston); Province Lake Country Club. Home: 635 Witchtrot Rd Sanbornville NH 03872-4224

BERG, WILLIAM JAMES, language educator, writer, translator; b. Dunkirk, N.Y., Oct. 26, 1942; s. Francis John and Adalyn Huldah (Goodwin) B.; m. Verity Anne Fry, July 2, 1966 (div. 1985); children— Jennifer Anne, Jessica Lyn; m. Laurey Kramer Martin, Feb. 1, 1986; stepchildren: Stirling Brooke Martin, Hunter Kirk Martin. Cert. pratique, Sorbonne, Paris, 1962-63; BA, Hamilton Coll., 1964; MA, Princeton U., 1966, PhD, 1969. NDEA inst. asst. Hamilton Coll., Clinton, N.Y., 1964; teaching asst. Princeton (N.J.) U., 1966; instr. French U. Wis., 1967-68, asst. prof., 1968-73, assoc. prof., 1973-79, prof., 1979—, assoc. chmn. French dept., 1974-75, 78-79, 79-80, 90-92, 99-2000, chmn. dept. French and Italian, 1982-85, 2002; dir. Acad. Yr. Abroad, Paris and N.Y.C., 1973-74. Outside examiner Swarthmore Coll., 1978, No. Ill. U., 1985, 86; outside program evaluator U. Mich., 1979; tenure reviewer Swarthmore Coll., 1982, Tulane U., 1985, Marquette U., 1992, 2000, U. Calif., Riverside, 2002; invited lectr. Rice U., 1985, U. Tenn., 1993; full prof. reviewer Georgetown U., 1984, Swarthmore Coll., 1992, U. Mich., 1994, Northwestern U., 1996, U. Colo., 1997, Va. Tech., 1999, U. Mich., 2001, NYU, 2002; U. Oklahoma, 2002. editl. bd. Summa Publs., Birmingham, Ala., 1983—; reviewer panel for travel and collections NEH, 1989. Author: (with P. Schofer and D. Rice) Poèmes, Pièces, Prose, 1973, (with G. Moskos and M. Grimaud) Saint/Oedipus. Psychocritical Approaches to Flaubert's Art, 1982, (with L. Martin) Images, 1989, The Visual Novel, 1992, (with L. Martin) Emile Zola Revisited, 1992, Gustave Flaubert, 1997, (with S. Magnan, Y. Ozzello and L. Martin-Berg) Paroles, 1999, 2d edit., 2002; author study guides on Twain's Huckleberry Finn, 1986, Tom Sawyer, 1987, (with L. Martin) Flaubert's Madame Bovary, 1989, Zola's Germinal, 1989, Maupassant's Short Stories, 1992; translator: (with P. Scott) Graphics and Graphic Information-Processing, 1981; Semiology of Graphics (design award Midwest Books Competition 1983), 1983-84; mem. editl. bd. Substance, 1971-79; contbr. articles to profl. jours. Travel grantee Am. Philos. Soc., 1969, rsch. grantee U. Wis., 1969, 75, 81-82, 86, 87; Vilas assoc., 1991-93, honors fellow, 1994—; Halverson-Bascom professorship, 1995-2000; recipient U. Wis. Chancellor's award for excellence in tchg., 1995. Mem. MLA, Am. Coun. Tchrs. of Fgn. Langs., Phi Beta Kappa. Home: 5201 Pepin Pl Madison WI 53705-4724 Office: U Wis Dept French and Italian Madison WI 53706 Office Phone: 608-262-3941. Business E-Mail: wjberg@wisc.edu.

BERGAN, EDMUND PAUL, JR., lawyer; b. N.Y.C., May 6, 1950; s. Edmund Paul and Alice (Gordon) P. B.; m. Patricia Ann Gallagher, Jan. 31, 1987; children: Annabel (dec.), Caroline. BA, Holy Cross Coll., 1971; JD, Fordham U., 1975. Bar: N.Y. 1976. Staff atty. SEC, Washington, D.C., 1975-77; v.p., assoc. gen. counsel Securities Industry Assn., N.Y.C., 1977-81; v.p., asst. gen. counsel Alliance Capital Mgmt. LP, N.Y.C., 1981-88; v.p. gen. counsel Alliance Fund Distbrs., N.Y.C., 1988-94; v.p., gen. counsel Alliance Fund Svc. Subs., N.Y.C., 1988-94; sr. v.p., gen. counsel Alliance Fund Svcs. (now Alliance Global Investor Svcs., Inc.) and Alliance Fund Distbrs. (now AllianceBernstein Rsch. and Mgmt., Inc.), N.Y.C., 1994—2003; vice chmn., CEO France Growth Fund Inc., 2004—; sr. regulatory counsel Proskauer Rose LLP, N.Y.C., 2005—. Mem. ABA (mem. fed. securities com. 1982—, investment advisers and cos. subcom. 1999—), Investment Co. Inst. (SEC rules com. 1986—2003, closed-end fund com. 1989—2003, chmn. 1992-97, various subcoms.), Assn. Bar City N.Y. (investment mgmt. com. 1999—). Republican. Roman Catholic. Avocations: historical studies, athletics. Office: Proskauer Rose LLP 1585 Broadway New York NY 10036 Office Phone: 212-969-3141. E-mail: ebergan@proskauer.com.

BERGAN, WILLIAM LUKE, lawyer; b. Auburn, N.Y., Sept. 3, 1939; s. Luke Joseph and Mary Beatrice (Twyne) B.; m. Marilyn Terese Meister, Aug. 8, 1964 (dec. May 1990); children: William Luke, Elizabeth M., Ann G.; m. Frances Maureen West, Jan. 2, 1993. BA summa cum laude, Niagara U., Niagara Falls, N.Y., 1961; JD magna cum laude, Syracuse U., 1964. Bar: N.Y. 1964, U.S. Dist. Ct. (we. dist.) N.Y. 1977, U.S. Dist. Ct. (no. dist.) N.Y. 1968, U.S. Ct. Appeals (2d cir.) 1970. Sr. ptnr. Bond, Schoeneck & King, Syracuse, 1966—. Trustee, past pres. parish coun. St. John the Evangelist Ch., Syracuse, 1993—. Capt. U.S. Army, 1964-66. Fellow Am. Bar Found., Coll. Labor and Employment Lawyers; mem. ABA, N.Y. State Bar Assn. (chmn. labor and employment law sect. 1981-82, exec. com. 1976—), Onondaga County Bar Assn., Nat. Assn. Coll. and Univ. Attys., Am. Arbitration Assn. (bd. dirs. 1984-2000), Greater Syracuse C. of C. (bd. dirs. 1992-96), Niagara U. Alumni Assn., Century Club Syracuse. Democrat. Roman Catholic. Avocation: tennis. Office Phone: 315-218-8218. E-mail: wbergan@bsk.com.

BERGÉ, CAROL, writer; b. N.Y.C., 1928; d. Albert and Molly Peppis; m. Jack Bergé, June 1955; 1 child, Peter. Asst. to pres. Pendray Public Relations, N.Y.C., 1955; disting. prof. lit. Thomas Jefferson Coll., Allendale, Mich., 1975-76; instr. adult degree program Goddard Coll., 1976; tchr. fiction and poetry U. Calif. Extension Program, Berkeley, 1976-77; assoc. prof. U. So. Miss., Hattiesburg, 1977-78; vis. prof. Honors Ctr. and English dept. U. N.Mex., 1978-79, 87; vis. lectr. Wright State U., 1979, SUNY, Albany, 1980-81; tchr. Poets and Writers, Poets in the Schs. (N.Y. State Council on Arts), 1970-72, Poets in the Schs. (Conn. Commn. Arts). Summer writing confs. Squaw Valley, Ind. U., U. Calif., Santa Cruz, 1975-1980; propr. Blue Gate Gallery of Art and Antiques, 1988-2003. Author: (fiction) The Unfolding, 1969, A Couple Called Moebius, 1972, Acts of Love: An American Novel, 1973 (N.Y. State Coun. on Arts CAPS award 1974), Timepieces, 1977, The Doppler Effect, 1979, Fierce Metronome, 1981, Secrets, Gossip & Slander, 1984, Zebras, or, Contour Lines, 1991; (poetry) The Vulnerable Island, 1964, Lumina, 1965, Poems Made of Skin, 1968, The Chambers, 1969, Circles, as in the Eye, 1969, An American Romance, 1969, From a Soft Angle: Poems About Women, 1972, The Unexpected, 1976, Rituals and Gargoyles, 1976, A Song, A Chant, 1978, Alba Genesis, 1979, Alba Nemesis, 1979, (reportage) The Vancouver Report, 1965; editor Center Mag., 1970-84, pub., 1991—; editor Miss. Rev., 1977-78, Subterraneans, 1975-76, Paper Branches, 1987, Light Years: The N.Y.C. Coffeehouse Writers and Multimedia Artists of the 1960s, 2005; contbg. editor Woodstock Rev., 1977-81, Shearsman mag., 1980-82, S.W. Profile, 1981; editor, pub. Center Press, 1970-93; pub.: Medicine Journeys (Carl Ginsburg), Coastal Lives (Miriam Sagan), 1991; co-pub.: Zebras (Carol Berge). Nat. Endowment Arts fellow, 1979-80 Mem. Authors' League, Poets and Writers, MacDowell Fellows Assn., Nat. Press Women Home: 2070 Calle Contento Santa Fe NM 87505-5406 E-mail: carolberge@earthlink.net.

BERGE, ZANE LEE, education educator, consultant; s. Mark Renn and Iva Gladys Berge; m. Nancy Biggs, Oct. 6, 1984; children: Jenna Biggs, Mark Biggs. BS, Rochester Inst. of Tech., 1977; PhD, Mich. State U., 1988. Dir. Ctr. for Tchg. and Tech., Georgetown U., Washington, 1992—95; prof. U. Md., Balt., 1995—. Dir. tng. systems grad. programs U. Md., Balt., 1995—2001. Charles A. Wedemeyer Disting. scholarship, Univ. Continuing Edn. Assn., 1999. Mem.: Assn. Mgmt., Internat. Assn. of Mgmt. (pres. divsn. of distance learning 1999—2001), Am. Ednl. Rsch. Assn. (program chair computer applications in edn. 1996—96), Assn. for Ednl. Comm. & Tech. (pres. divsn. of interactive systems and computers 1997—97), Am. Assn. for Higher Edn. Office: Univ Md 1000 Hilltop Cir Baltimore MD 21045 Office Phone: 410-455-2306. Business E-Mail: berge@umbc.edu.

BERGEN, BRUCE HARRY, lawyer; b. Newark, July 5, 1955; s. Boris and Betty Jean (Schreiber) B.; m. Jodi B. Peterson, Aug. 29, 1984; children: Stefanie, Ross. BA, Case Western Res. U., 1977; JD, Seton Hall U., 1980. Bar: N.J. 1980, U.S. Dist. Ct. N.J. 1980, N.Y. 1988, D. C. 1989. Staff atty. Union County Legal Svcs., Inc., Elizabeth, N.J., 1980-82; pvt. practice Cranford, N.J., 1982-87; assoc. Kaplowitz & Wise, Linden, N.J., 1988, ptnr., 1989-92; pvt. practice Cranford, N.J., 1992-93; assoc. Krevsky, Silber and Brown, Esquires, Elizabeth, N.J., 1993-98; ptnr. Krevsky, Silber and Bergen Esquires, Elizabeth, NJ, 1998—. Chmn. Cranford Dem. Mcpl. Com., 1983-84; mem. Union County Dem. Com., 1979—; chmn. Springfield Dem. Com., 1989—; Dem. candidate U.S. Congress 7th Dist. N.J., 1990; dem. candidate

NJ Assembly Dist. 21, 2005—. Mem. ABA, N.J. State Bar Assn., Union County Bar Assn., Rotary Club (pres. Cranford chpt. 1987-88, 2001-02). Jewish. Avocation: golf. Office: Krevsky Silber & Bergen Esquires PO Box 99 123 N Union Ave Crawford NJ 07016 Office Phone: 908-276-8855. Business E-Mail: bhb@ksb6law.com.

BERGEN, CANDICE, actress, writer, photojournalist; b. Beverly Hills, Calif., May 9, 1946; d. Edgar and Frances (Westerman) B.; m. Louis Malle, Sept. 27, 1980 (dec. 1995); 1 child, Chloe; m. Marshall Rose, June 15, 2000. Ed., U. Pa. Model during coll. Films include The Group, The Sand Pebbles, 1966, The Day the Fish Came Out, Live for Life, 1967, The Magus, 1968, Soldier Blue, The Executioner, The Adventurers, Getting Straight, 1970, The Hunting Party, Carnal Knowledge, T.R. Baskin, 1971, 11 Harrowhouse, 1974, Bite the Bullet, The Wind and the Lion, 1975, The Domino Principle, The End of the World in Our Usual Bed in a Night Full of Rain, Oliver's Story, 1978, Starting Over, 1979, Rich and Famous, 1981, Gandhi, 1982, Stick, 1985, Miss Congeniality, 2000, Sweet Home Alabama, 2002, View from the Top, 2003, The In-Laws, 2003; TV appearances include What's My Line, 1965, Coronet Blue, 1967, The Muppet Show, 1976, The Way They Were, 1981, 2010 (voice), 1984, Trying Times, 1987, Seinfeld, 1990, Images of Life: Photographs that have Changed the World, 1996, The Human Face (miniseries), 2001, Murphy Brown: TV Tales, 2002, Sex and the City, 2002, TV series: Murphy Brown, 1988-98 (Emmy award, Leading Actress in a Comedy Series, 1989, 90, 92, 94, 95), Boston Legal, 2004-; TV films Arthur the King, 1985, Murder by Reason of Insanity, 1985, Mayflower Madam, 1987, Shelley Duvall's Bedtime Stories, Vol. 7, 1993, Mary and Tim, 1996; TV miniseries Hollywood Wives, 1985, Trying Times, Moving Day; author Knockwood; photojournalist credits include articles for Life, Playboy; dramatist: (play) The Freezer (included in Best Short Plays of 1968).*

BERGEN, DORIS, psychologist, educator; b. St. Louis, Mo., Feb. 11, 1932; m. Joel S. Fink; m. James Sponseller (div.); children: Ellen Creager, Holly Andrecheck, Gail Burnett. Student, Heidelberg Coll., 1949—51; BS, Ohio State U., 1953; MA, Mich. State U., 1970, PhD, 1974. Instr., asst. prof., assoc. prof. Oakland U., Rochester, Minn., 1970—80; dean grad. sch. Wheelock Coll., Boston, 1980—84; dean grad. studies and rsch. Pittsburg State U., Pittsburg, Kans., 1984—88; prof., chair Ednl. Psychology Dept. Miami U., Oxford, Ohio, 1988—98, prof., dir. Ctr. for Human Devel., Learning and Tchg., 1998—. Assoc. dean Oakland U., Rochester, 1979—80; vis. scholar Com. Scholarly Comm. with China NAS, 1989—91; cons. Fisher-Price, Inc., 2000—; trainer Heads Up Network, 1998—99; cons. PBS TV program, Dooley and Pals, 1995—99; cons. Mayerson Found., 1994—95; cons. High/Scope, 1990—91. Author: Assessment Methods for Infants and Toddlers: Transdisciplinary Team Approaches, 1994; co-author (with J.M. Coscia): Brain Research and Childhood Education: Implications for Educators, 2001; co-author: (with R. Reid, L. Torelli) Educating and Caring for Infants and Toddlers: A Comprehensive Curriculum, 2000; editor: Play as a Learning Medium, 1974, Play as a Learning Medium, 2d printing, 1976, Play as a Learning Medium, 3d printing, 1978, Play as a Learning Medium, 4th printing, 1982, Play as a Medium for Learning and Development: A Handbook of Theory and Practice, 1988, Readings from Play as a Medium for Learning and Development, 1998; co-editor (with D. Fromberg): Play from Birth to Twelve and Beyond: Contexts, Perspectives and Meanings, 1998; co-editor:, 2005; contbr. chpts. in books, articles to profl. jours., parent brochures, book reviews, curriculum manuals, govt. booklets. Grantee Rsch. on Rescue Heroes, Fisher-Price, Inc., 2001—02, Evaluation of Dragonfly Sci. Inquiry Tng., Eisenhower Grant, 1996—99, Evaluation of Oxford/Talawanda Family Resource Ctr., Oxford/Talawanda Cmty. Svcs., 1999, Evaluation of RISE Winning Teams Early Childhood Tng., Ohio Dept. Edn., 1996—98, Evaluation of Butler County Early Intervention Tracking Program, Civitan Svc. Club, 1996—98, Instl. Devel. Grant, U.S. Dept. Edn., 1986—89, Birth through Seven: Early Intervention and Preschool Spl. Needs, U.S. Dept. Spl. Edn., 1981—84, Day Care Policy: Views of Parents and Practitioners in Mich., NSF, 1979—80. Fellow: Am. Orthopsychiatric Soc., Am. Psychol. Soc.; mem.: Nat. Assn. Early Childhood Tchr. Educators (sec. 2000—02, Found. bd. dirs.), Jean Piaget Soc., Coun. Exceptional Children (divsn. Early Childhood), Soc. Rsch. Adminstrs., Am. Evaluation Soc., Assn. for Study of Play, Nat. Assn. for Edn. Young Children (governing bd. 1996—), Soc. Rsch. in Child Devel., Am. Ednl. Rsch. Assn. (Early Childhood sect., bd. dirs. 1998—2000), Assn. Childhood Edn. Internat., Internat. Humor Soc., Phi Delta Theta, Phi Kappa Phi. Office: Miami Univ 100G McGuffey Hall Oxford OH 45056 Office Phone: 513-529-6622. Business E-Mail: bergend@mohio.edu.

BERGEN, POLLY, actress; b. Bluegrass, Tenn. d. William and Lucy (Lawhorn) Burgin; m. Freddie Fields, Feb. 13, 1956 (div. 1976); children: Kathy, Pamela, Peter. Pres. Polly Bergen Cosmetics, Polly Bergen Jewelry, Polly Bergen Shoes. Author: Fashion and Charm, 1960, Polly's Principles, 1974, I'd Love To, But What'll I Wear, 1977; author, producer for TV: Leave of Absence, 1994; Broadway plays include Champagne Complex, John Murray Andersons' Almanac, First Impression, Plaza Suite, Love Letters, Follies (Best Supporting Actress Tony and Drama Desk nominee), The Vagina Monologues, Cabaret; films include Cape Fear, Move Over Darling, Kisses for My President, At War with the Army, The Stooge, That's My Boy, The Caretakers, A Guide for the Married Man, Making Mr. Right, Cry-Baby, 1990, Dr. Jekyll and Ms. Hyde, When We Were Colored, 1994; performed in one woman shows in Las Vegas, Nev., and Reno; albums: Bergen Sings Morgan, The Party's Over, All Alone By the Telephone, Polly and Her Pop, The Four Seasons of Love, Annie Get Your Gun and Do Re Mi, My Heart Sings, Act One Sing Too; numerous TV appearances including star of The Polly Bergen Show, NBC-TV; other TV appearances include The Helen Morgan Story, 1957 (Emmy award as best actress), To Tell the Truth, The Lightning Field, The Surrogate, For Hope; miniseries include The Winds of War (Emmy nomination), 79 Park Ave, War and Remembrance, 1988 (Emmy nomination); writer, prodr. NBC movie Leave of Absence, 1994. Bd. dirs. Martha Graham Dance Ctr., The Singer Co., Soc. Singers, Calif. Abortion and Reproductive Rights Action League, Show Coalition; hon. canister campaign chairperson Cancer Care, Inc., Nat. Cancer Found.; founder Nat. Bus. Coun. for ERA; mem. Planned Parenthood Fedn., Am. Bd. Advs.; mem. nat. adv. com. NARAL, Hollywood Women's Polit. Com. Recipient Fame award Top Ten in TV, 1957-58, Troupers award Sterling Publs., 1957, Editors and Critics award Radio and TV Daily, 1958, Outstanding Working Woman award Downtown St. Louis, Inc., Golden Plate award Am. Acad. Achievement, 1969, Outstanding Mother's award Nat. Mothers' Day Com., 1984, Best Achievement in New Jewelry Design award, 1986, Cancer Care award, 1989, Woman of Achievement award LWV, 1990, Extraordinary Achievement award Nat. Women's Law Ctr., 1991, Freedom of Choice award Calif. Abortion and Reproductive Rights Action League, 1992; Polly Bergen Cardio-Pulmonary Rsch. Lab., Children's Rsch. Inst. and Hosp., Denver dedicated, 1970. Mem. AFTRA, AGVA, SAG, Actors Equity. Office: 1746 S Britain Rd Southbury CT 06488-3200 E-mail: zimzack@msn.com.

BERGEN, ROBERT LUDLUM, JR., retired materials scientist; b. Islip, N.Y., Oct. 29, 1929; s. Robert Ludlum and Alice (D'Oench) B.; m. Grace-Elizabeth Field, June 11, 1951; children: Beryl F., Alice D'Oench, Robert Ludlum III, Jennifer U. AB cum laude, Williams Coll., 1951; MS, Cornell U., 1953, PhD, 1955. Various tech. assignments Uniroyal Chem. divsn. Uniroyal, Inc., Naugatuck, Conn., 1955—68, mgr. plastics and fibers rsch. corp. R&D Wayne, NJ, 1969—72, various mgmt. assignments Uniroyal Chem. divsn. Naugatuck, 1975—75; mgr. elastomers R & D Uniroyal Chem. divsn. Uniroyal Inc., Naugatuck; group mgr. chems. and polymers R & D Uniroyal Chem. divsn. Uniroyal, Inc., Naugatuck, 1975—79, dir. corp. R & D Middlebury, Conn., 1979—81, dir., rsch., devel. and engring., Engineered Products Group, 1981—84, dir. corp. engring., 1985; adj. prof. math. U. New Haven, 1986—87; cons. Bethany, Conn., 1986—2000. Mem. adv. bd. Inst. Materials Sci., U. Conn., 1979-97; adj. prof. chemistry U. New Haven, 1964-69; chmn. Soc. Plastic Engrs., Engring. Properties, 1970-71. Author: Testing of Polymers-Stress Relaxation Tests, 1966, various publs., 1954-68. Pres. Bethany Conservation Trust, 1979-82; moderator New Haven Assn. United Ch. Christ, 1991-93; bd. dirs. Conn. conf. United Ch. Christ, 1993-97, mem. investment com., 1994-97; moderator First Ch. Christ, Bethany, 2000-04; chmn. Com. on Sr. Housing, Bethany, 2000-03. Fellow AAAS; mem. Am. Chem. Soc., Sigma Xi. Achievements include patents on improving stress cracking resistance of plastics; development of specialized impact test for plastics, of correlations between long term mech. properties of plastics and environ. stress cracking. Home and Office: 46 Bayon Dr South Hadley MA 01075-3328

BERGEN, STANLEY SILVERS, JR., retired academic administrator; b. Princeton, N.J., May 2, 1929; s. Stanley Silvers and Leah (Johnson) B.; m. Suzanne E. Miller, Nov. 16, 1965; children: Steven Richard, Victoria Elizabeth, Stuart Vaughn; children by previous marriage: Stanley Silvers III, Amy Dorle. AB, Princeton U., 1951; MD, Columbia U., 1955; hon. degrees, Bloomfield Coll., 1972, Stevens Inst., 1985; LLD (hon.), Princeton U., 1995; DSc Patterson (N.J.) State U. (hon.), 1997; DSc (hon.), Ramapo Coll. N.J., 1997, N.J. Inst. Tech., 1998; DHL (hon.), Univ. Medicine Dentistry N.J., 2002. Resident St. Luke's Hosp., N.Y.C., 1955-58, chief resident, Francis Zabriskie fellow, 1958-59, asst. chief dept. medicine, 1959-60, asst. attending physician, 1962-64; med. dir. Convalescent and Research Unit, Greenwich, Conn., 1962-64; chief medicine Cumberland Hosp., Bklyn., 1964-68; asst. dir. dept. medicine Bklyn.-Cumberland Med. Center, 1964-68, chief community medicine, 1968-70; sr. v.p. N.Y.C. Health & Hosps. Corp., 1970-71; instr. medicine Columbia, 1959-64; asso. prof. medicine Downstate Med. Sch., Bklyn., 1964-71; pres. U. Medicine and Dentistry N.J., Newark, 1971-98, founding pres. emeritus, 1998—. Prof. medicine N.J. Med. Sch., Robert Wood Johnson Med. Sch., Sch. Osteo. Medicine; prof. cmty. dentistry N.J. Dental Sch.; attending med. staff Univ. Hosp., Newark, 1971-2004, VA Hosp., East Orange, 1972-98, Robert Wood Johnson U. Hosp., 1981-98; trustee Univ. HealthCare Corp., 1993-99; chair bd. trustees Univ. Health Plans N.J., 1994-99; trustee University Heights Sci. Park, 1995-2004, chmn. bd., 1996-2004. Author articles in field. Mem. Mayor's Commn. Health and Hosps., N.Y.C., 1969-70; mem. N.J. Comprehensive Health Planning Coun., 1971-91; chmn. N.J. Commn. to Study Structure and Function N.J. Dept. Health, 1973, N.J. Abortion Commn., 1975, Adv. Coun. Grad. Edn. N.J., 1978-98; adv. com. mcpl. health svc. program R.W. Johnson, also, Nat. Conf. Mayors, 1980-85; mem. Bd. Comprehensive Health, Newark, 1976-81, treas., 1972-80; bd. dirs. Cancer Inst. N.J., 1974-98; bd. dirs. Ednl. Commn. Fgn. Med. Grads., 1982-91, sec., vice chmn., 1985-86, chmn., 1986-91; bd. dirs., mem. exec. com. Hastings Ctr. on Biomed. Ethics, 1976-, chmn. devel. com., 1980-95, mem. governance com., 1995-, chmn. elect, 1997, chmn., 1998-2004; bd. dirs., mem. exec. com. Art Center No. N.J., 1978-82; chmn. N.J. Blood Banks Task Force, 1980-90; trustee Robert Wood Johnson U. Hosp., 1985-98, exec. com. 1987-98; trustee Hackensack Med. Ctr., 1990-99, exec. com., 1992-99; bd. joint mgrs. Cancer Inst. N.J., 1991-98, trustee 1998-2002; trustee Bergen Pines County Hosp., 1994-98, exec. com. 1994-98, trustee Univ. Healthcare Corp. of N.J., 1993-97, Gilda's Club No. N.J., 1997-2000, treas., mem. exec. com., 1998-2000, Kessler Med. Rehab. Rsch. Edn. Corp., 1998-2003, Matheny Sch. and Hosp., 1998-2000, Internat. Ctr. Pub. Health Inc., 1999-2004; treas. Pres.'s Coun. N.J. Commn. Higher Edn., 1996-98; chmn. bd. trustees U. Health Plan N.J., 1997-99; chair bd. mgrs. N.J. Ctr. Biomaterials, 1997-02; bd. dirs. Blue Hill Meml. Hosp., 2000-, vice chmn. bd., 2001-04, chmn. bd. 2004—; chair strategic planning com. Eastern Maine Healthcare Sys., 2002-, nomination com., 2004-, co-chair, CEO search com., 2005-; chair bd. dirs. MedTower, 2000-04. First recipient Woodrow Wilson medal for pub. svc. leadership Gov. of N.J., 1987, Univ. medal UMDNJ, 1995. Fellow ACP, Assn. Am. Med. Colls., Am. Fedn. Clin. Rsch., Endocrine Soc., Clin. Soc. N.Y., Diabetes Assn. (v.p. 1969-70, chmn. clin. soc. 1968-69), N.Y. Acad. Scis., Am. Inst. Nutrition; mem. AMA (ho. dels. sect. on med. schs. 1978-98), Assn. Acad. Health Ctrs., Am. Diabetes Assn. (bd. dirs. N.J. affiliate), Am. Soc. Clin. Nutrition, Am. Coll. Healthcare Execs. (hon. fellow), Essex County Med. Soc., Med. Soc. N.J., Am. Hosp. Assn. (trustee 1992-94, chmn. com. grad. med. edn. 1974-76, mem. coun. profl. svcs. 1973-76, mem. governing coun. sect. met. hosps. 1984-87, com. med. edn. 1984-91, ad hoc com. on AIDS 1987-91, chmn. tech. com. biomed. ethics 1986-91, alt. del. Ho. Dels., 1991, mem. AHA regional policy bd., 1988-94, mem. internat. med. scholars program 1987-92, mem. com. to study single pathway to nat. med. licensure 1987-90, mem. com. to study clin. med. skills assessement 1988-92, trustee 1991-94, trustee regional plan commn. 1995-98), Greater Newark C. of C. (dir. 1978-84), Nat. Assn. Pub. Hosps. (trustee 1982-88), State N.J. Health Coord. Coun., Univ. Health System N.J. (trustee, exec. com. 1987-98), Univ. Hosp. Consortium (trustee 1988-92, exec. com. 1990-92), N.Y. Acad. Scis., Opera House Arts (mem. bd. advisors, 2002-, chair facilities com., 2003-, chmn. bd. 2003—). Home: 44 Greenhead Ln Stonington ME 04681 Office: U Medicine & Dentistry NJ 100 Bergen St Newark NJ 07103-2407 Personal E-mail: sasbergen@aol.com. *My career has taken many significant turns, most of which have improved my ability to lead efforts toward better and more accessible health services. I have been fortunate in the opportunity to lead a variety of activities and to express creativity through institutions and individuals. My successes are due to the extent to which this nation still rewards those willing to work hard and learn from experience, as well as to the many intelligent, compassionate mentors with whose guidance I have been blessed.*

BERGENHEIM, RICHARD C., editor; s. Robert Bergenheim. Grad., Principia Coll., Elsah, Ill., 1970; M Shakespeare Inst., Univ. Birmingham, UK. Past editor-in-chief Christian Sci. Pub. Soc., Boston; editor Christian Sci. Monitor, Boston, 2005—. Bd. dir. Christian Sci. Pub. Soc., 1988—94. Office: Christian Sci Monitor One Norway St Boston MA 02115 Office Phone: 617-450-2000. Office Fax: 617-450-7575.*

BERGENN, JAMES WALTER, lawyer; b. Bklyn., Nov. 21, 1954; s. Walter R. and V. Patricia B.; divorced: children: Kristin, Eric; m. Susan King; stepchildren: Thomas, Christopher. BA in Polit. Philosophy, Cath. U. Am., 1976; JD, Columbia U., 1979. Bar: Conn. 1979, U.S. Dist. Ct. Conn. 1979, U.S. Ct. Appeals (2d cir.) 1981. Law clk. Chief Judge U.S. Dist. Ct. Conn., Hartford, 1979-80; assoc. Shipman & Goodwin, Hartford, 1980-81, 1983-86, ptnr., 1987—; asst. defender Office of the Fed. Pub. Defender, Hartford, 1981-83. Lectr. U. Conn. Sch. Law, 1986—. Editor of daily polit. report to Pres. Carter during Carter-Mondale Reelection Campaign, 1980. Pres. Hartford Apt. Improvement Program, Inc., 1980-86; mem. Glastonbury Conservation Commn., 1985-87, Glastonbury Dem. Town Com., 1988-96, chair 1994-95; lector St. Paul's Roman Cath. Ch., 1986-96, instr., 1988-94; lector St. Patrick-St. Anthony's, 2001—. Mem. ABA, Conn. Bar Assn., Hartford County Bar Assn., Assn. Trial Lawyers Am., Conn. Trial Lawyers Assn., Nat. Assn. Criminal Def. Lawyers, Conn. Criminal Def. Lawyers Assn., Nat. Lawyers for Pub. Justice. Democrat. Roman Catholic. Avocations: basketball, skiing, reading. Home: 50 Castlewood Rd West Hartford CT 06107 Office: Shipman & Goodwin 1 Constitution Plz Hartford CT 06103-2833 E-mail: jbergenn@goodrich.com.

BERGER, ALLAN SIDNEY, psychiatrist, educator; b. N.Y.C., Nov. 26, 1931; s. Nathan and Ida (Masor) B.; m. Lois Harriet Blumfield, Dec. 27, 1953; children: Karen, Gary, Jonathan. AB magna cum laude, Syracuse U., 1951; MD, SUNY, Bklyn., 1955. Diplomate Am. Bd. Psychiatry and Neurology, 1962; additional qualification in geriatric psychiatry cert., 1991. Intern L.I. Coll. Hosp., N.Y.C., 1955-56; resident Yale U. Sch. Medicine, New Haven, 1956-58, fellow Yale Child Study Ctr., 1958-59; pvt. practice Silver Spring, Md., 1961—; asst. chief D.C. Gen. Hosp., Washington, 1961-62. Clin. prof. Georgetown U. Sch. Medicine, Washington, 1986—; cons. NIH, 1987-88; command cons. Nat. Naval Med. Ctr. Bethesda, 1990-97; mem. physician expert panel VA, 1993-96; mem. peer rev. com. on behalf of Md. Med. Licensing Bd., 1992-2003. Contbr. articles to profl. jours. Cons. Peace Corps, 1962, Hebrew Home for the Aged, Rockville, Md., 1962-72. Recipient Vicennial Medalist award Georgetown U. Sch. Medicine, 1981. Mem. AMA, Mid-Atlantic Group Psychotherapy Soc. (bd. dirs. 1977-78), Metro. Washington Soc. Adolescent Psychiatry (treas. 1979-80, pres. 1982-83), Med. and Chirurgical Faculty Md., B'nai B'rith. Republican. Avocations: tennis, swimming, gardening. Home and Office: 1302 Midwood Pl Silver Spring MD 20910-1645 Office Phone: 301-589-1443.

BERGER, ARTHUR SEYMOUR, organization executive, city official; b. NYC, Sept. 19, 1920; m. Joyce Berger. JD cum laude, NYU. Bar: NY 1949. Mcpl. atty. State of N.Y., 1963-71; pres. Survival Rsch. Found., Miami, Fla., 1981—; dir. Internat. Inst. for Study of Death, 1985—; instr. Inst. for Ret. Profls., U. Miami, 1999; instr. Lifelong Learning Soc., Fla. Atlantic U.; vice mayor City of Aventura. Instr. Acad. for Lifelong Learning, Fla. Internat. U., adj. prof., 1996-97; instr. Fla. Atlantic U. Lifelong Learning Soc., Inst. for Ret. Profls., U. Miami, Nova Southeastern U.; adj. prof. Broward Coll., 1989-94, Union Inst., 1990-92; cons. Readers Digest; former commr. City of Aventura, Fla. Author: Liberation of the Person, 1964, Aristocracy of the Dead, 1987, Lives and Letters in American Parapsychology, 1988 (outstanding acad. book list), Evidence of Life After Death: Casebook for Tough-Minded, 1988, Dying and Death in Law and Medicine, 1993, When Life Ends, 1995; co-author: The Encyclopedia of Parapsychology and Physical Research, 1991, Fear of the Unknown, 1995; co-editor: Religion and Parapsychology, 1989, Perspectives in Death and Dying, 1989, To Die or Not to Die?, 1990; mem. NYU Law Rev. Mem. Aventura (Fla.) City Commn.; mem. ethics com. Columbia Aventura Hosp. and Med. Ctr.; narrator reading program for blind Libr. of Congress. 1st lt. U.S. Army, 1942-46, 50-52. Recipient Ashby Meml. award Acad. Religion, grantee, 1985, Phys. Rsch. Found., 1984, Fla. Endowment of the Arts, 1989. Mem. DAV (life), Soc. for Sci. Exploration, Am. Soc. for Psychical Rsch., Soc. for Psychical Rsch., Parapsychol. Assn. Business E-Mail: s5rf@aol.com.

BERGER, BONNIE G., sport psychologist, educator; b. Champaign, Ill., May 20, 1941; d. Bernard G. and Mildred W. Berger; 1 child, Stephen Casher. BS, Wittenberg U., 1962; MA, Columbia U., 1965, EdD, 1972. Tchr. George Rogers Clark Jr. H.S., Springfield, Ohio, 1962-64; supr. phys. edn. Agnes Russell Elem. Sch., N.Y.C., 1964-65; asst. prof. SUNY, Geneseo, 1965-66, Dalhousie U., Halifax, N.S., Can., 1969-71, Bklyn. Coll., 1971-77, assoc. prof., 1978-82, prof., 1982-93, dir. Sport Psychology Lab., dep. chair dept. phys. edn., 1989-93; prof., assoc. dean Sch. Phys. and Health Edn. U. Wyo., Laramie, 1993-96, prof., assoc. dean Coll. Health Scis., 1996-99; prof., dir. Sch. Human Movement, Sport and Leisure Studies, Bowling Green (Ohio) State U., 1999—. Cons. in field. Author: Free Weights for Women, 1984, Foundations of Exercise Psychology, 2002; contbr. chapters to books, articles to profl. jours. Fellow Assn. for Advancement of Applied Sport Psychology (exec. bd.) Am. Acad. Kinesiology and Phys. Edn.; mem. APA, AAHPERD, Internat. Soc. Sports Psychology, N.Am. Soc. Psychology and Phy. Activity. Home: 640 Pine Valley Dr Bowling Green OH 43402 Office Phone: 419-372-7234. Business E-Mail: bberger@bgnet.bgsu.edu.

BERGER, CAROLYN, state supreme court justice; BA, U. Rochester, 1969; MA in Elementary Education, Boston U., 1971; JD, Boston U. Sch. of Law, 1976; LLD (hon.), Widener U. Sch. of Law, 1996. Bar: Del. 1976. Dep. atty. gen. Del. Dept. of Justice, 1976—79; assoc. Prickett, Ward, Burt & Sanders, Wilmington, Del., 1979, Skadden, Arps, Slate, Meagher & Flom, Wilmington, Del., 1979—84; vice chancellor Del. Ct. of Chancery, Wilmington, Del., 1984—94; justice Del. Supreme Ct., 1994—. Assoc. mem. Bd. of Bar Examiners. V.p. then pres. Milton & Hattie Kutz Home; mem. Wilmington Community Advisory Council, Junior League of Wilmington; bd. mem. Jewish Federation, Del. Region Nat. Conference of Christians & Jews. Mem.: Del. Bar Assn., Am. Bar Assn., Rodney Inn of Court, Am. Law Inst., Am. Bar Foundation. Office: Del Supreme Ct Carvel State Office Bldg 820 N French St Fl 11 Wilmington DE 19801-3509*

BERGER, DAVID, lawyer; b. Archbald, Pa., Sept. 6, 1912; s. Jonas and Anna (Raker) B.; children: Jonathan, Daniel. AB cum laude, U. Pa., 1932, LLB cum laude, 1936. Bar: Pa. 1938, D.C., N.Y. Asst. to prof. U. Pa. Law Sch., Phila., 1936-38, spl. asst. to dean; law clk. Pa. Supreme Ct., Phila., 1939-40; spl. asst. to dir. enemy alien identification program U.S. Dept. Justice, Washington, 1941-42; law clk. U.S. Ct. Appeals, 1946; pvt. practice Phila., Washington and N.Y.C.; city solicitor Phila., 1956-63; founder, chmn. Berger & Montague, P.C., Phila. Former counsel Sch. Dist. Phila.; former chmn. adv. com. Pa. Superior Ct.; mem. drafting com. fed. rules evidence U.S. Supreme Ct.; lectr. on legal subjects; David Berger chair of law for the improvement of the adminstrn. of justice established at U. Pa. Author numerous articles on law. Nat. commr. Anti-Defamation League; assoc. trustee U. Pa., mem. bd. overseers Law Sch.; presdl. appointee U.S. Holocaust Meml. Coun., 1994-2004; dir. Internat. Tennis Hall of Fame, 1995-2001; bd. dirs. ARC, Palm Beach, Fla., 1996-2002; mem. Found. for Art and Preservation in Embassies. Decorated Silver Star and Presdl. Unit Citation; named to, U. Pa. Tennis Hall of Fame, 1997. Fellow Am. Coll. Trial Lawyers, Internat. Acad. Trial Lawyers, Internat. Soc. Barristers; mem. ABA (vice-chair tort and ins. practice sect. com. on comml. torts 1988-89), Phila. Bar Assn. (pres., bd. govs., chancellor), Phila. Bar Found. (past pres.), The Athenaeum Phila., Penn Club (N.Y.C., founder), Order of Coif. Home: Elephant Walk 109 Jungle Rd Palm Beach FL 33480-4809 Office: Berger & Montague PC 1622 Locust St Philadelphia PA 19103-6305

BERGER, DAVID, history professor; b. Bklyn., June 24, 1943; s. Isaiah and Shirley (Kravitz) B.; m. Pearl Rabinowitz, June 14, 1965; children: Miriam, Yitzhak, Gedalyah. BA, Yeshiva Coll., 1964; MA, Columbia U., 1965, PhD, 1970. Ordained rabbi, 1967. Instr. Yeshiva Coll., N.Y.C., 1968-70; asst. to assoc. prof. Bklyn. Coll., 1970-80; prof. Bklyn. Coll. and the Grad. Sch., CUNY, 1980—. Author: The Jewish-Christian Debate in the High Middle Ages, 1979 (John Nicholas Brown prize 1983), The Rebbe, the Messiah, and the Scandal of Orthodox Indifference, 2001 (Samuel Belkin Lit. award, 2004), rev., 2005; co-author: Judaism's Encounter with other Cultures: Rejection or Integration?, 1997, 2d edit., 2005, Jews and Jewish Christianity, 1978; editor: History and Hate: The Dimensions of Anti-Semitism, 1986; The Legacy of Jewish Migration: 1881 and Its Impact, 1983 Bd. trustees Beth Din of Am., N.Y.C, 1995—, The Orthodox Caucus, 2003—. Recipient Bernard Revel Meml. award Yeshiva Coll. Alumni Assn., 1990. Fellow Am. Acad. for Jewish Rsch.; mem. Am. Hist. Assn., Medieval Acad. Am., Assn. for Jewish Studies (pres. 1998-2000), Internat. Assn. of Socs. for the Study of Jewish History (chair Am. sect. 1991—), Nat. Found. for Jewish Culture (vice-chair acad. adv. bd. 1996-2002, co-chair 2002—), Am. Acad. for Jewish Rsch. (exec. com. 1992—). Office: Dept History Brooklyn Coll Brooklyn NY 11210 E-mail: dberger@gc.cuny.edu.

BERGER, DIANNE GWYNNE, family life educator, consultant; b. NYC, Mar. 10, 1950; d. Harold and Mary Bell (Mott) Gwynne; m. Robert Milton Berger, Aug. 25, 1974 (dec. Nov. 2001); children: Matthew Robert Gwynne, Daniel Alan Gwynne. BS, Cornell U., 1971; MS, Drexel U., 1974; PhD, U. Pa., 1992. Cert. home econs. tchr., sexuality educator, family and consumer sci. educator and family life educator, Pa.; cert. supervision, curriculum and instrn. Tchr. family and consumer scis., health, sexuality edn. Wallingford-Swarthmore (Pa.) Sch. Dist., 1972—. Cons., Swarthmore, 1986—, Swarthmore Presbyn. Ch., 1995, Elwyn Insts., Media, Pa., 1989-91, Phila. Task Force on Sex Edn., 1991-93. Cons. Trinity Coop. Day Nursery, Swarthmore, 1980-93, Renaissance Edn. Assn., Valley Forge, Pa., 1987-94, A Better Chance, Inc., Swarthmore, 1990-91; mem. sci. bd. Adolescent Wellness and Reproductive Edn. Found. Grantee Impact, Inc., 1990, Am. Cancer Soc., 2001. Mem. NEA, Am. Assn. Family and Consumer Scis. (presenter), Soc. for Sci. Study of Sex (sec. ea. region presenter), Nat. Coun. on Family Rels., Am. Assn. Sex Educators, Counselors and Therapists (chmn. Delaware Valley sect. 1996-98). Home: 304 Dickinson Ave Swarthmore PA 19081-2001 Office Phone: 610-892-3460. E-mail: bergerdg@aol.com.

BERGER, ELEANOR, artist; b. N.Y.C., Jan. 15, 1934; d. Samuel Phillip and Lucile (Noss) B.; m. Charles Bert Weinberg, Jan. 23, 1955 (div. July 1979); children: Robert I., Nina Alice Smith. Cert. fin. arts, Cooper Union, 1957. Guest spkr. Stony Brook Mus., 1991. One-woman shows at Galleria Irlandini, Rio de Janeiro, 1968, Instituto Brazileira-Americana, Rio de Janeiro, 1968, Rahmani Gallery, Karachi, West Pakistan, 1970, Am. Consulate USIS Exhbn. Hall, Karachi, 1971, Upstairs Gallery, Huntington, N.Y., 1991, Plandome (N.Y.) Gallery, 1991, Bellemeade Gallery, Smithtown, N.Y., 1992, Gallery East, East Hampton, N.Y., 1994-95, West Harbor Gallery, Oyster Bay, N.Y., 1994, B.J. Spoke Gallery, Huntington, 1994—, Group

Shows at Gallery East, East Hampton, 1992-98, Gallery North, Setauket, N.Y., 1993—; reproduced in The Home Gallery, 1991-92; works in McGraw-Hill Inc., N.Y.C., William McGee and Co., Inc., N.Y.C., AXA Reinsurance, N.Y.C., Revlon Corp., N.Y.C., U.S. Dept. State Art Embassies Program, L.I. Mus., Stony Brook, Christopher Gallery, Stony Brook. Recipient Cert. Merit, Salmagundi Open, N.Y.C., 1990, award Excellence, Art League of L.I. 43d ann. exhbn., Heckscher Mus., Huntington, N.Y.; Represented by Gallery North, Setauket, N.Y., B.J. Spoke Gallery, Huntington, N.Y., Christopher Gallery, Stony Brook, N.Y. Jewish. Avocations: photography, music, reading, singing. Home: 23 Sterling Ln Smithtown NY 11787-4738 Office Phone: 631-265-3766.

BERGER, FRANK MILAN, biomedical researcher, research scientist, retired pharmaceutical executive; b. Pilsen, Czech Republic, June 25, 1913; came to U.S., 1947, naturalized, 1953; s. Otto and Martha (Weigner) B.; m. Bozena Jahodova, Mar. 15, 1939 (dec. Nov. 1972); children: Franklin Milan, Thomas Jan; m. A. Christine Spade, May 21, 1975. MD, U. Prague, Czechoslovakia, 1937, SUNY, 1948; D.Sc. (hon.), U. of the Scis. in Phila., 1966. Rsch. fellow physiology U. Prague, 1934-36, rsch. asst. bacteriology, 1936-38; bacteriologist Czechoslovak State Inst. Health, 1938-39; sr. resident Monsall Hosp. Infectious Diseases, Manchester, Eng., 1941-43; chief pharmacologist Brit. Drug Houses, London, 1945-47; asst. prof. pediatrics U. Rochester, 1947-49; dir. rsch. Carter-Wallace Inc., 1949-55, v.p., 1955-58; pres. Wallace Labs. div. Carter-Wallace Inc., Cranbury, N.J., 1958-73; mem. adv. coun. dept. biology Princeton U., 1961-74, lectr., prof., 1969-74; mem. sci. adv. com. Waksman Inst. Microbiology, Rutgers U., 1960-67; cons. Surgeon Gen., Walter Reed Army Med. Ctr., Washington, 1974-80; pres. Mario Negri Inst. Found. for Biomed. Rsch., Inc., 1973—; prof. psychiatry U. Louisville Med. Sch., 1974-90; hon. prof. microbiology Waksman Inst. Microbiology, Rutgers U., 1982. Chmn. Ad Hoc Study Group on Clin. and Preclin. Pharmacology, 1977-80. Fellow N.Y. Acad. Scis., Am. Coll. Neuropsychopharmacology, AAAS; mem. AMA, AAUP, Am. Pharm. Soc., Brit. Pharm. Soc., Can. Pharm. Soc., Am. Bacteriol. Soc., Soc. Exptl. Biology and Medicine, Am. Chem. Soc., Biometric Soc., Cosmos Club (Washington), Princeton Club (N.Y.C.), N.Y. Athletic Club, Sigma Xi. Achievements include inventing tranquilizer meprobamate, muscle-relaxant mephenesin, pain reliever carisoprodol, antiepileptic felbamate; also method purification penicillin. Office: 200 E 72nd St New York NY 10021-4537 Office Phone: 212-794-8520. *Concentrate on the important, rather than the urgent; try not to do what everybody else is doing; and remember that within limits of reason and decency, it is better to do what you like rather than what is expected of you.*

BERGER, FRANK STANLEY, management consultant; b. NYC; s. Ernest A. and Anna Berger; m. Judith Berger; children: Evan, Stacey. BA, Queens Coll.; MBA, NYU; postgrad., N.Y. Law Sch., IBM Edn. Center. Supr. dept. mktg. and fin. analysis Lever Bros.; v.p. fin. and adminstrn. Pacific Enterprises; mem. corp. mktg. staff Joseph E. Seagram & Sons, Inc.; from mktg. asst. to pres. Calvert Distillers; v.p., gen. sales mgr. Frankfort Distillers, exec. v.p. mktg. and fin., pres., dir.; pres. Gen. Wine & Spirits Co., N.Y.C.; pres. and dir. Seagram Distillers Co.; pres., CEO House of Seagram; dir. Joseph E. Seagram & Sons, Inc.; chmn. bd. Quadrillon Investments Inc., 1980-86; chmn. bd., pres. Viceroy Imports, Inc., 1981-86; chmn., CEO Hazel Bishop Cosmetics Inc., 1981-87; dir. Majestic PLC, 1988-89; chmn. bd. dirs., pres. CII, Inc., 1990—; chmn., pres., CEO Naturally Scientific Inc., 1996—. Trustee N.Y. Hall of Sci.; chmn. N.Y. Lunch-o-Ree Boy Scouts Am., United Jewish Appeal, Gaucho Basketball Assn., Cystic Fibrosis Soc.; exec. com. wine and spirits div. Anti-Defamation League, Pro-Am. tennis sponsor Cerebral Palsy; bd. dirs. Bronfman Found. With AUS. Mem. AIM, Nat. Assn. Chain Drug Stores, Am. Mgmt. Assn., Am. Mktg. Assn, N.Y. C. of C., Young Pres.' Orgn., Nat. Nutritional Foods Assn., Quality and Productivity Mgmt. Assn., Conf. Bd. (CEO program), Nat. Nutritional Found. Clubs: Advt. of N.Y, N.Y. Sales Execs.

BERGER, GEORGE, lawyer; b. N.Y.C., Jan. 21, 1936; BA summa cum laude, NYU, 1957, JD, 1960. Bar: N.Y. 1960, U.S. Dist. Ct. (so. dist.) N.Y. 1961, U.S. Ct. Appeals (2nd cir.) 1963, U.S. Supreme Ct. 1971, U.S. Ct. Appeals (5th cir.) 1974, U.S. Dist. Ct. (ea. dist.) N.Y. 1975, U.S. Dist. Ct. (we. dist.) 1980, U.S. Ct. Appeals (D.C. cir.) 1977, U.S. Ct. Appeals (10th cir.) 1985. Assoc. Phillips, Nizer, LLP, N.Y.C., 1960-67, ptnr., 1967—. Disting. neutral, N.Y. panel, Ctr. for Pub. Resources, 1992-93. Editor: Hazardous Waste and Toxic Torts: Law and Strategy, 1987-92. Mem. ABA, Assn. of Bar of City of N.Y. Office: Phillips Nizer LLP 666 5th Ave New York NY 10103-0001 Office Phone: 212-841-0740. E-mail: gberger@phillipsnizer.com.

BERGER, HAROLD, physicist, researcher; b. Syracuse, N.Y., Oct. 7, 1926; s. Joseph H. and Fannie A. (Stein) B.; m. Dawn Marie Beranek, Dec. 27, 1952; children: Susan, Margaret, Thomas, Joseph, Daniel. BS, Syracuse U., 1949, MS, 1951. Physicist x-ray dept. GE, Milw., 1951-59; sr. physicist Battelle Meml. Inst., Columbus, 1959-60; assoc. physicist Argonne (Ill.) Nat. Lab., 1960-70, group leader nondestructive testing, 1965-73, sr. physicist, 1970-73; nuclear physicist reactor radiation divsn. Nat. Inst. Standards and Tech. (formerly Nat. Bur. Standards), Washington, 1973-75; program mgr. nondestructive evaluation, 1975-78; chief Office Nondestructive Evaluation, 1978-81; pres. Indsl. Quality, Inc., Gaithersburg, Md., 1981—2003; sr. scientist Digitone Corp., Gaithersburg, 2003—; rsch,. assoc. Nat. Inst. Stds. and Tech., 2003—. Vis. scientist Centre d'Etudes Nucleaires, Grenoble, France, 1968-69; vis. lectr. U. Grenoble, 1968-69; pres.'s honor lectr. Non-Destructive Testing Soc., Great Britain, 1971; mem. Nat. Materials Adv. Bd. ad hoc com. on nondestructive testing, 1967-69; keynote speaker Am. Soc. Nondestructive Testing Spring Conf., Oakland, Calif., 1991, ASNT radiology topical meeting, 1993, Can. Soc. for Nondestructive Testing 30th Anniversary Conf., 1995, 4th internat. topical meeting neutron radiography Penn State U., 2001;, leader U.S. Delegation to ISO TC135 in Moscow, 1980, Ottawa, 1983; chmn. ISO Tech. Commn., subcom. 3 on acoustic methods, 1983-86; mem. adv. bd. Ctr. for Nondestructive Evaluation, Johns Hopkins U., 1998-2000. Author Neutron Radiography, 1965, Nondestructive Testing (in Understanding the Atom series), 1965; Tech. editor: Materials Evaluation, jour. of Am. Soc. Nondestructive Testing, 1969-86; editor: Practical Applications of Neutron Radiography and Gaging, 1976, Nondestructive Testing Standards— A Review, 1977, Nondestructive Testing Standards— Present and Future, 1992; Contbr. articles to profl. jours. Fellow Courtesy Johns Hopkins U. Sch. of Engring., 1986-2003. With USNR, 1944-45. Recipient spl. achievement award Nat. Inst. Standards and Tech., 1976, Silver medal Dept. Commerce, 1979. Fellow ASTM (award of merit 1988, Excellence in Symposium and Publ. Mgmt. award 1993, Briggs award com. E-7 1994, Hon. Mem. award com. E-7 1998), Am. Nuclear Soc. (Radiation Industry award 1974), Am. Soc. Nondestructuve Testing (nat. dir. 1965-68, Achievement award 1967, Mehl lectr. 1975, award for svc. as editor 1976, Gold medal award 1982, hon. mem. award 1986, keynote speaker Spring conf. 1991). Achievements include 12 patents in x-ray and optical inspection and ultrasound fields. Home: 9832 Canal Rd Gaithersburg MD 20886-5101 Office Phone: 301-330-1701.

BERGER, HAROLD, lawyer, electrical engineer; b. Archbald, Pa., June 10, 1925; s. Jonas and Anna (Raker) Berger; m. Renee Margareten, Aug. 26, 1951; children: Jill Ellen, Jonathan David. BSEE, U. Pa., 1948, JD, 1951. Bar: Pa. 1951. Practiced in, Phila.; judge Ct. of Common Pleas, Phila. County, 1971-72; chmn., moderator Internat. Aerospace Meetings Princeton U., 1965-66; chmn. Western Hemisphere Internat. Law Conf., San Jose, Costa Rica, 1967; chmn. internat. Confs. on Aerospace and Internat. Law, Coll. William and Mary; permanent mem. Jud. Conf. 3d Circuit Ct. of Appeals; mem. County Bd. Law Examiners, Phila. County, 1961-71; chmn. World Conf. Internat. Law and Aerospace, Caracas, Venezuela, Internat. Conf. on Environ. and Internat. Law, U. Pa., 1974, Internat. Confs. on Global Interdependence, Princeton U., 1975, 79; mem. Pa. State Conf. Trial Judges, 1972-80, Nat. Conf. State Trial Judges, 1972—; chmn. Pa. Com. for Independent Judiciary, 1973—. Adv. coun. Biddle Law Libr. U. Pa., 1991—2004, bd. overseers Sch. Engring. and Applied Sci., 1998—; chair Friends Biddle Law Libr., 2004—. Mem. editl. adv. bd.: Jour. Space Law, U. Miss. Sch. Law, 1973—; contbr. articles to profl. jours. Mem. We the People 200 Com. for Constn. Bicentennial, 1991; chair Friends of Biddle Law Libr. Vipa, 2004—. With Signal Corps, AUS, 1944—46. Recipient Alumnus of the Yr. award, Thomas McKean Law Club, U. Pa. Law Sch., 1965, Space award, GE, 1966, Nat. Disting. Achievement award, Tau Epsilon Rho, 1972, Spl. Pa. Jud. Conf. award, 1981, Special National Distinguished Svc. Award, Fed. Buracy, 1978. Mem.: ABA (past chmn. aerospace law com., mem. state and fed. ct. com., nat. conf. state trial judges, Spl. Presdl. Program medal 1975), Internat. Acad. Astronautics, Assn. U.S. Mems. Internat. Inst. Space Law Internat. Astronautical Fedn. (former bd. dirs.), Phila. Bar Assn. (past chmn. jud. liaison com. 1975, chmn. internat. law com. 1977), Fed. Bar Assn. (past nat. chmn. com. aerospace law, pres. Phila. chpt. 1983—84, chmn. class action and complex litig. com. 3d cir. 1990—, nat. chmn., alt. dispute resolution com. 1992—95, pres. eastern dist. Pa. chpt. 1996—2002, chair spl. bench bar liason com. eastern dist. Pa. chpt. 2001—, mem. nat. exec. coun. 1996—2002, nat. com. 1987 bi-centennial of U.S. Constn., past chmn. fed. jud. com., Presdl. award 1970, Spl. Disting. Svc. award ea. dist. chapter 2002), Inter-Am. Bar Assn. (past chmn. aerospace law com.). Office: 1622 Locust St Philadelphia PA 19103-6305

BERGER, HAROLD RICHARD, physician; b. Elizabeth, N.J., Oct. 31, 1914; s. Abraham and Frances (Herfield) B.; m. Minna Constance Wolfson, Aug. 22, 1943; children: Brian, Andrew, Alan, James. AB, Cornell U., Ithaca, N.Y.; MD, NYU Sch. Medicine. Diplomate Am. Bd. Pediatrics. Intern Elizabeth (N.J.) Gen. Hosp., 1940-41; maj. U.S. Med. Corp., 1941-46; resident in pediatrics Jersey City (N.J.) Med. Ctr., 1951-53; pvt. practice, 1946—. Mem. child health program Elizabeth Bd. of Health, Hillside Bd. of Health; sch. physician Elizabeth Bd. Edn. Recipient award Am. Bd. Pediatrics, 1954. Mem. AMA, N.J. Med. Soc., Union County Med. Soc. Avocations: golf, reading, travel. Home and Office: 987 Harding Rd Elizabeth NJ 07208-1047

BERGER, HARVEY JAMES, pharmaceutical executive, physician, educator; b. N.Y.C., June 6, 1950; s. Howard H. and Edith E. (Muskat) B.; children: Eric Michael, Mark Phillip, Nicole Elizabeth Grad., The Hotchkiss Sch., 1968; AB magna cum laude, Colgate U., 1972; MD, Yale U., 1977. Diplomate Am. Bd. Nuclear Medicine. Resident Yale-New Haven (Conn.) Hosp., 1977-81, dir. cardiovascular imaging, 1981-84; asst. prof. radiology and medicine Yale U., New Haven, 1981-83, assoc. prof., 1983-84; prof. radiology and assoc. prof. medicine Emory U., Atlanta, 1984-86; dir. Divsn. Nuclear Medicine Emory U. affiliated hosps., Atlanta, 1984-86; sr. v.p. med. affairs Centocor, Inc., Malvern, Pa., 1986—87; sr. v.p., R&D Centacor, Inc., Malvern, Pa., 1987—89; pres. R&D div., exec. v.p., med. dir. Centocor, Inc., Malvern, Pa., 1989-91; chmn., chief exec. officer, founder ARIAD Pharms., Inc., Cambridge, Mass., 1991—; chmn., CEO, founder ARIAD Gene Therapeutics, Inc., Cambridge, Mass., 1993—; chmn. ARIAD Inst. Biomed. Rsch., 1993—. Bd. dirs. Centocor Devel. Corp. I, PTC Therapeutics, Inc.; lectr. divsn. health scis. and tech. MIT, 1992-97, Harvard Med. Sch., 1992-97; adj. prof. U. Pa., Phila., 1986-92; mem. adv. study sects. Nat. Heart, Lung and Blood Inst., Washington, 1984-90; advisor Office of Dir. NIH, Washington, 1984-87; mem. panel on govt. role in civilian tech. NRC/NAS, 1989-92. Founding editor Am. Jour. of Cardiac Imaging, 1985-89; editor Nuclear Medicine Communications, 1985-88; mem. editorial bds. Investigative Radiology, 1984-88; contbr. numerous articles to profl. jours.; patentee in field. Cline Fixott award Am. Acad. Dental Radiologists, 1984, Symbol of Caring award Sarcoma Found. Am., 2005 Mem. ACP, Soc. Nuclear Medicine (com. chmn., nat. trustee, Tetalman award 1982), Am. Coll. Cardiology (editl. bd. jour. 1983-88), Am. Coll. Chest Physicians, Am. Heart Assn. (established investigator 1981, cardiovascular radiology/circulation couns.), Am. Coll. Radiology, Am. Fedn. Clin. Rsch., Assn. Univ. Radiologists (Young Investigator award 1979), N.Am. Soc. Cardiovascular Radiology, Soc. Thoracic Radiology, Soc. Exptl. Biology and Medicine, Harvard Club of Boston, Yale Club of N.Y., Phi Beta Kappa. Office: ARIAD Pharmaceuticals Inc 26 Landsdowne St Cambridge MA 02139-4216

BERGER, IVAN BENNETT, magazine editor, writer; b. July 9, 1939; s. Leynard and Celia (Berlin) B.; m. Roberta Thumim, Sept. 13, 1985 (dec. Oct. 27, 1995). Electronics and camera editor Popular Mechanics mag., N.Y.C., 1972-77; sr. editor Popular Electronics mag., N.Y.C., 1977-79; tech. editor Audio mag., N.Y.C., 1982-2000; freelance newspaper, mag. and tech. writer, 2000—. Author: The New Sound of Stereo, 1985. Mem. Am. Soc. Journalists and Authors, Internat. Motor Press Assn. Avocations: poetry, cooking, photography. Home: 459 La Grande Ave Fanwood NJ 07023-1732 Office Phone: 908-889-5818. E-mail: audioib@comcast.net.

BERGER, JEROME MORRIS, communications executive; b. Cleve., Dec. 7, 1951; s. Jack and Beatrice Berger; m. Francine Ellis, Oct. 9, 1977. BA, Boston U., 1973; MS in Journalism, Columbia U., 1976. Editor, reporter Marlboro (Mass.) Enterprise, 1977-82; reporter UP Internat., Boston, 1982-87, statehouse bur. chief, 1987-90; asst. prof. Sch Journalism Northeastern U., Boston, 1990-96; comms. dir. com. on ways and means Mass. Senate, Boston, 1996-98; comms. dir. Mass. Cultural Coun., Boston, 1998-2001; dir. media rels. Beth Israel Deaconess Med. Ctr., Boston, 2001—. Developer, cons. Nat. Polit. Awareness Test, Project Vote Smart, Boston, 1993—96. Media columnist The Middlesex News, 1996; editor-in-chief: Insuring American Health for the Year 2000, 1992; contbr. articles to profl. publs. Mem. adv. network State Fiscal Analysis Initiative, Boston, 1993-94; media cons. Graduated Income Tax Campaign, Boston, 1994. Mem. Soc. Profl. Journalists. Avocations: reading, walking. Office: 330 Brookline Ave Boston MA 02215 Personal E-mail: jfberger@theworld.com.

BERGER, JERRY ALLEN, museum director; b. Buffalo, Wyo., Oct. 8, 1943; BA in Psychology, U. Wyo., 1965, BA in Art, 1971, MA in Art History, 1972. Curator collections U. Wyo. Art Mus., Laramie, 1972-88, asst. dir., 1980-83, 87-88, acting dir., 1984-86; dir. Springfield (Mo.) Art Mus., 1988—. Office: Springfield Art Mus 1111 E Brookside Dr Springfield MO 65807-1829 Office Phone: 417-837-5700. Business E-Mail: jberger@ci.springfield.mo.us.

BERGER, JOHN PETER, writer, painter, art critic; b. London, Nov. 5, 1926; s. S.J.D. and Miriam (Branson) B. Attended, Central Sch. Art, Chelsea Sch. Art, London. Vis. fellow British Film Inst., 1990—. Began career as painter, tchr. drawing, 1948-55; exhibited works at Wildenstein Gallery, Redfern Gallery and Leicester Gallery, London; art critic Tribune, New Statesman 1951-61; scenario: (with Alain Tanner) La Salamandre, Le Milieu du Monde, Jonas (N.Y. Critics prize for best scenario of Yr. 1976), (with Timothy Neat) Play Me Something (BFI), 1989, (film scenario) Isabelle: A Story in Shots, 1998; author: Marcel Frishman, 1958, (novels) A Painter of Our Time, 1958, Permanent Red, 1960, The Foot of Clive, 1962, Corker's Freedom, 1964, The Success and Failure of Picasso, 1965, Lilac and Flag, 1990, Into Their Labours, 1991, To the Wedding, 1995, King. A Street Story, 1999, (with Patricia Macdonald) Once in Europa, 1999; (essays) Keeping a Rendezvous, 1991, (with J. Mohr) A Fortunate Man; the story of a country doctor, 1967; Art and Revolution, 1969, Moments of Cubism and Other Essays, 1969; (essays) The Sense of Sight, 1985 (pub. in Eng. as The White Bird), Photocopies, 1996, (poems) Pages of the Wound: Poems, Drawings, Photographs 1956-96, 1996, The Shape of a Pocket, 2001, John Berger Selected essays (ed. by Geoff Dyer), 2001; essays and articles include: The Look of Things, 1972, G (novel), 1972 (Booker prize 1972, James Tait Black Meml. prize 1972), Ways of Seeing, 1972, (with J. Mohr) The Seventh Man, 1975 (Union of Journalists and Writers of Paris prize for best reportage 1977), Pig Earth (fiction), 1979; About Looking, 1980; (with J. Mohr) Another Way of Telling, 1982, (with Katya Berger) Titian: Nymph and Shepherd, 1996; work for theatre (with Nella Bielski) A Question of Geography, premiere Theatre National de Marseille, 1984, Francisco Goya's Last Portrait, 1989, (with John Christie) I Send You This Cadmium Red, 2000; (non-fiction) And Our Faces, My Heart, Brief as Photos, 1984, Steps Towards a Small Theory of The Visible, 1996; Once in Europa (fiction) 1987 (award 1989); translator: (with A Bostock) Poems on the Theatre (B. Brecht), 1960, Return to My Native Land (Aime Césaire), 1969; writer (screenplay) Jonah Who Will Be 25 in the Year 2000 and others; numerous TV appearances, including: Monitor, two series for Granada TV. Served in British Army, 1944—46. Recipient George Orwell Meml. prize, 1977. Office: Quincy Mieussy 74440 Taninges France*

BERGER, LAWRENCE HOWARD, lawyer; b. Phila., May 19, 1947; s. Howard Merrill Berger and Doris Eleanor Cummins; m. Julie Mitchell Collins, Aug. 8, 1970; children: Colby Shaw, Ryan Lawrence, Lindsey Wade. BS, Mich. State U., 1969; JD, U. Va., 1972. Bar: Pa. 1972, U.S. Dist. Ct. (ea. dist.) Pa. 1973, U.S. Ct. Appeals (3d cir.) 1986. Assoc. Morgan, Lewis & Bockius LLP, Phila., 1972-79, ptnr., 1979—. Bd. dirs. US Lacrosse, 2000—, chmn., 2002—04, vice chmn., 2004—. Trustee Agnes Irwin Sch., 1984—86, Naomi Wood Charitable Trust-Woodford Mansion Mus., 1986—, Fairmount Park Coun. for Hist. Sites, 1989—95, Fairmont Park Hist. Trust, 1993—95; dir. Phila. Lacrosse Assn., 1992—2000. Recipient Frank Carr Cmty. Svc. award, 1991, Leading Bus. Lawyer award Chambers & Ptnrs, 2004, 05. Fellow Am. Bar Found.; mem. ABA (sec. com. on nonprofit corps. 1980-90), Pa. Bar Assn. (chmn. com. on uniform comml. code 1978-80), Phila. Bar Assn., Pa. Bar Inst., Banking Law Inst. (lectr. 1985), Pa. Bankers Assn. (lectr. 1980, 89), Martins Dam Club, Blue Key, Omicron Delta Kappa. Home: 360 Pond View Rd Devon PA 19333-1732 Office: Morgan Lewis & Bockius LLP 1701 Market St Philadelphia PA 19103-2903 Office Phone: 215-963-5480.

BERGER, LEV ISAAC, physicist, researcher; b. Rostov, USSR, June 23, 1929; came to U.S., 1978; s. Isaac Mark and Sara (Poltevsker) B.; m. Ninelle Rossine, July 2, 1956; 1 child, Yuri. MS in Physics, State U., Moscow, 1955; PhD in Physics, State U., Minsk, USSR, 1959; PhD in Tech. Scis., U. Steel and Alloys, Moscow, 1968. Lectr. physics U. Nonferrous Metals, Moscow, 1956-60; docent Physics U. Metallurgy, Moscow, 1960-62; prof. Poly. Inst., Moscow, 1962-77; sr. scientist New Eng. Research Ctr., Sudbury, Mass., 1979-81; lectr. physics San Diego State U., 1981-89, U. San Diego, 1989-98; pres. Calif. Inst. Electronics & Materials Sci., Hemet, 1981—. Dir. divsn. Inst. Spl. Purity Substances, Moscow, 1962-71, Introscopy Research Inst., Moscow, 1971-77. Author: Ternary Diamond-like Semiconductors, 1969, Semiconductor Materials, 1997; contbr. articles to profl. jours.; patentee in field. San Diego State U. grantee, 1983. Mem. ASTM (com. electronics, thermal measurements), Soc. for Advancement of Material and Process Engring. (exec. bd.), Am. Phys. Soc., Am. Assn. Crystal Growth, Materials Rsch. Soc., Nat. Assn. Scholars. Home: 2115 Flame Tree Way Hemet CA 92545-7803 Office: Calif Inst Electronics & Materials Sci PO Box 832 Hemet CA 92546-0832 Office Phone: 951-929-2659. Business E-Mail: info@ciems.com.

BERGER, MARVIN, medical educator; b. Bronx, N.Y., July 22, 1936; s. Jack and Hannah Berger; m. Roslynn Berger, June 26, 1965; children: David, Kenneth. BA, Ohio U., 1957; MD, Chgo. Med. Sch., 1961. Diplomate Am. Bd. Internal Medicine, Am. Bd. Cardiovasc. Disease, Am. Bd. Echocardiography. Intern Beth Israel Med. Ctr., N.Y.C., 1961-62, resident in internal medicine, 1962-64, dir. echocardiography lab., 1975—, assoc. chief cardiology, 1981—2003; fellow in cardiology Mt. Sinai Med. Ctr., N.Y.C., 1964-65; asst. prof. clin. medicine Mt. Sinai Sch. Medicine, N.Y.C., 1976-81, assoc. prof., 1982-90, assoc. prof. medicine, 1990-94; assoc. prof. Albert Einstein Coll. Medicine, Bronx, 1994—, prof. clin. medicine, 1999—. Editor: Doppler Echocardiography in Heart Disease, 1987; contbr. articles to profl. jours. Capt. U.S. Army, 1965—67. Fellow: ACP, Am. Soc. Echocardiography, Am. Coll. Cardiology, Am. Coll. Chest Physicians, N.Y. Cardiol. Soc.; mem.: AMA, Am. Heart Assn. Avocations: reading, classical music, dixieland jazz, sports. Office: Beth Israel Med Ctr 1st Ave and 16th St New York NY 10003 E-mail: mberger@bethisraelny.org.

BERGER, MAX W., lawyer; b. Bronx, NY, July 26, 1946; BBA, CCNY, 1968; JD, Columbia Univ., 1971. Bar: NY 1972, US Dist. Ct. (so. dist. NY 1973, ea. dist. NY 1975, Ariz. 1992), US Ct. Appeals (2d cir. 1973). Founding ptnr., class action litigation, securities litigation Bernstein Litowitz Berger & Grossmann LLP, NYC, 1983—. Instr. Columbia Univ. Law Sch.; lectr. Fed. Judicial Ctr., Practicing Law Inst. Editor: Columbia Survey of Human Rights Law. Trustee Baruch Coll.; mem. bd. vis. & Dean's council Columbia Univ. Law Sch. Named Trial Lawyer of the Year finalist, Trial Lawyers for Public Justice, 1997. Mem.: ABA (past chmn. Comml. Litigation sect.), Assn. Trial Lawyers Am., Fed. Bar Council, NY State Bar Assn. Office: Bernstein Litowitz Berger & Grossmann 1285 Ave of the Americas New York NY 10019 Office Phone: 212-554-1403. Office Fax: 212-554-1444. Business E-Mail: max@blbglaw.com.*

BERGER, MELVIN, allergist, immunologist; b. Phila., Mar. 7, 1950; MD, PhD in Biochemistry, Case Western Res. U., 1976. Internship, resident pediatrics Children's Hosp. Med. Ctr., Boston, 1976-78; fellow allergy & immunology Nat. Inst. Allergy & Infectious Diseases, Bethesda, Md., 1978-81; pediatrician, chief Immunology-Allergy Divsn. Rainbow Babies and Children's Hosp., Cleve., 1984—. Prof. peds. & pathology Case Western Res. U. USPHS, 1978-81, col. U.S. Army Res., 1981—. Fellow Am. Acad. Pediatrics, Am. Acad. Allergy, Asthma & Immunology. Office: Rainbow Babies Hosp Div Pediatrics/Immunology Cleveland OH 44106 E-mail: mxb12@po.cwru.edu.

BERGER, MICHAEL GARY, lawyer; b. New Haven, Apr. 16, 1946; s. Jacob and Edith (Axelrod) B.; m. Miriam Janet Haines, July 24, 1977; children: Richard, Daniel. BS, Yale Coll., 1968; JD, Columbia U., 1973. Asst. dist. atty. New York County Office of Dist. Atty., N.Y.C., 1973-76; pvt. practice, N.Y.C., 1981—. Arbitrator Am. Arbitration Assn., 1994—; mem. Criminal Justice Act Panel, N.Y.C., 1976—79; legal rep. clients in various fields including bus., medicine, profl. sports and entertainment; spkr. cmty. client and bar groups. Commentator on legal manners for Ct. TV, CNBC, Fox News, nat. and local TV programs. Mem. ABA, Fed. Bar Coun., Nat. Assn. Criminal Def. Lawyers, N.Y. State Bar Assn., Assn. of Bar of City of N.Y. Office: 250 Park Ave 20th Fl New York NY 10177-0001 E-mail: mgberger@mgberger.com.

BERGER, MILES LEE, land economist; b. Chgo., Aug. 9, 1930; s. Albert E. and Dorothy (Ginsberg) B.; m. Sally Eileen Diamond, Aug. 27, 1955; children: Albert E., Elizabeth Ann. Student, Brown U., 1948-50. Engaged in real estate and fin. svc. fields, 1950—; mng. chmn. bd. Berger Fin. Svcs. Corp., Chgo., 1950—. Chmn. bd. Mid-Am. Appraisal & Rsch. Corp., Chgo., 1959-80, also dir.; chmn. bd. Real Estate Svcs. Corp., 1969—; vice chmn. bd., trustee Heitman Fin. Ltd., 1970-98; chmn. bd. Mid Town Bank Chgo., 1974-2001; vice chmn. bd., prin. econ. cons. Columbia Nat. Bank, Chgo., 1965-96; bd. dirs. Franklin Corp., Evans Inc., Franklin Capital Corp., Innkeepers USA Trust, Universal Health Svcs., Inc., Medallion Bank; trustee Heitman Mortgage Investors, Innkeepers Am. Mem., chmn. Chgo. Plan Commn., 1980-84; cons. city Chgo. on Ill. Ctrl. Air Rights, 1967—; trustee Latin Sch. Chgo., 1967-73, treas., 1953-55, bd. dirs. Latin Sch. Found.; bd. govs. Met. Planning Coun.; bd. mgrs. James Jordan Boys Club. Mem. Am. Inst. Real Estate Appraisers, Soc. Real Estate Appraisers, Soc. Real Estate Counselors, Am. Right-of-Way Assn., Nat. Assn. Housing and Redevel. Ofcls., Nat. Tax Assn., Internat. Assn. Assessing Officers, Lambda Alpha. Jewish (trustee synagogue). Office: Berger Mgmt Svcs LLC 900 N Michigan Ave Ste 2010 Chicago IL 60611-6519 Office Phone: 312-255-0600. Personal E-mail: mberger670@aol.com.

BERGER, MIRIAM ROSKIN, creative arts therapy director, educator, therapist; b. N.Y.C., Dec. 9, 1934; d. Israel and Florence Roskin; m. Meir Berger, July 16, 1967; 1 child, Jonathan Israel. Student, Barnard Coll., 1952-53; BA, Bard Coll., 1956; postgrad., CCNY, 1956-58; Dr. Arts, NYU, 1998. Alumni dir. Bard Coll., Annandale-on-Hudson, NY, 1958-59, bd. govs., 2000—; dance therapist Manhattan Psychiatric Ctr., NYC, 1959-60; performer, educator Jean Erdman Theater of Dance, NYC, 1959-62; dir. adult program Hebrew Arts Sch., NYC, 1981; faculty Dance Notation Bur., NYC, 1974-75, 77; asst. prof. dance therapy program NYU, 1975—, acting dir. dance therapy program, 1991, dir. dance edn. program, 1993—2002; dir. creative arts therapies Bronx Psychiatric Ctr., NYC, 1970-90; faculty Pratt

Inst., 2004—05, Harkness Dance Ctr. 92nd St. Y, 2005—. Workshop leader in field; tchr., Sweden, 1981—2004, Netherlands, 1991—2002, Germany, 1993—99, Czech Republic, 1997—2005, Poland, 2000, Republic of Korea, 02, Greece, 2004—, Israel, 2004—; keynote spkr. Israel Dance Conf., 2004. Prodr. off-Broadway The Coach with the Six Insides, 1962-63; author, prodr. Non-Verbal Group Process, 1978; co-editor Am. Jour. Dance Therapy, 1991-94; led dance therapy session Senate hearing on Aging, 1992; contbr. articles to profl. jours.; editl. bd. Arts in Psychotherapy, Jour. Dance Edn., Amer. Jour. Dance Therapy. Chair Nat. Coalition of Creative Arts Therapies Assns., 2002—; bd. dirs. Theater Open Eye, 1978—82, v.p. bd. trustees, 1982—89, pres., 1989—94. Recipient NYU scholarship, 1981, Best Paper award Med Art World Congress on Arts and Medicine, 1992; inducted into Hall of Fame, Dance Libr. of Israel, 2005. Mem.: Acad. Registered Dance Therapists, Am. Dance Therapy Assn. (founder, bd. dirs. 1967—76, v.p. 1974—76, credential com. 1976, 1982, keynote speaker at nat. conf. 1991, v.p. 1992, pres. 1994—98, chmn. internat. panel 1995—, Marian Chace award 2002), Dance Libr. Israel (v.p. 1999—). Business E-Mail: miriam.berger@nyu.edu.

BERGER, MORRIS ISAIAH, humanities educator; b. N.Y.C., Aug. 5, 1928; s. Victor and Minnie (Waltzer) B.; m. Sheila B. Berger, June 12, 1957; 1 child, Jamie. BA, SUNY, Albany, 1950, MA, 1952; PhD, Columbia U., 1956. Project dir., advisor to Min. Edn. A.I.D., Somalia, 1987-90; prof., chair SUNY, Albany, 1956-2000, svc. prof., 2000—. Author: The Settlement, The Immigrant and the Public School, 1980; contbg. editor The Rev. Edn., 1977-80. Chair, bd. dirs. Capital dist. ACLU, 1971-75. Fulbright scholar, 1984; rsch. fellow SUNY Albany, 1969. Home: 222 Heritage Rd Guilderland NY 12084 E-mail: mberger@nycap.rr.com.

BERGER, PATRICIA WILSON, retired librarian; b. Washington, May 1, 1926; d. Thomas Decatur Wood and Nina Hughes; m. George Hamilton Combs Berger, May 20, 1970. BA, George Washington U., 1965; MSLS, Cath. U. Am., 1974. Asst. libr., ops. rsch. office Johns Hopkins U., Chevy Chase, Md., 1949-51, asst. ops. rsch. analyst, 1951-54; head libr. CEIR, Washington, 1954-55; chief, tech. info. and libr. svcs. Human Rels. Area Files Yale U., Washington, 1955-57; tech. info. officer, chief libr. Inst. for Def. Analyses, Washington, Arlington, Va., 1957-67; dir. tech. info. and security programs Lambda Corp., Arlington, 1967-71; chief libr. U.S. Commn. on Govt. Procurement, Washington, 1971-72; head gen. ref. br., later dep. chief libr. U.S. Patent and Trademark Office, Arlington, 1972-76; chief libr. divsn. U.S. Nat. Bur. Stds., Gaithersburg, Md., 1976-78; dir. info. resources and svcs. U.S. EPA, Washington, 1978-79; chief libr. and info. svcs. U.S. Nat. Bur. Stds., Washington, 1979-83, chief info. resources and svcs., 1983-91, dir. Office Info. Svcs., 1990-92; ret., 1992. Cons. libr., info. and security matters, 1965-95; del. 1st White House Conf. on Librs. and Info. Svc., 1979; bd. dirs. Universal Serial and Book Exch., 1983-84; chmn. Nat. Info. Std. Orgn., Am. Nat. Std. Inst., 1981-83, elected Nat. Info. Std. Orgn. fellow, 1989. Mem. editl. bd. Sci. and Tech. Librs., 1979—92; contbr. articles to profl. jours. Apptd. by Govs. of Va. to Libr. of Va. Bd., 1986-90, 90-95, vice chair, 1992-93, chair, 1993-94; bd. dirs. Va. Commn. for Reenactment of Battle First Bull Run, 1960-61; bd. dirs. Freedom to Read Found., 1988-90, 92-94; apptd. U.S. Postmaster Gen's. Commn. Lit., 1990-92. Recipient Internat. Women's Yr. award Dept. Commerce, 1976, Bronze medal, 1980, Silver medal, 1984, Outstanding Adminstrv. Mgr. award, 1985, H.W. Wilson Pub. Co. award, 1980, Disting. Svc. award U. Richmond Librs., 1989, Cert. of Recognition, Gov. State of Va., 1989, Resolution of Esteem, Va. State Libr. Bd., 1988, award Coun. Libr. and Media Technicians, 1989; named Outstanding Alumnus in Libr. and Info. Sci., Cath. U. Am., 1988, 20th Century Nat. Libr. Adv., Am. Libr. Assn./Am. Libr. Trustees Assn. Nat. Adv. Honor Roll, 2000; Cert. of appreciation Martin Luther King Jr. Fed. Holiday Commission, 1996. Mem AAAS (elected assn. fellow 1992), Spl. Librs. Assn. (exec. bd. Washington chpt. 1970-71, pres. Washington chpt. 1977, elected assn. fellow 1987), ALA (coun. 1984-88, exec. bd. 1986-90, v.p./pres.-elect 1988-89, pres. 1989-90, immediate past pres. 1990-91), D.C. Libr. Assn. (Ainsworth Rand Spofford Pres.'s award 2001), Fed. Librs. Roundtable (pres. 1982-83, Achievement award 1985), Cosmos Club, Chi Omega, Beta Phi Mu. Episcopalian. Home: 105 Queen St Alexandria VA 22314-2610 Personal E-mail: pberger@his.com.

BERGER, PAUL ERIC, artist, photographer; b. The Dalles, Oreg., Jan. 20, 1948; s. Charles Glen and Virginia (Nunez) B. BA, UCLA, 1970; M.F.A., SUNY-Buffalo, 1973. Vis. lectr. U. Ill., 1974-78; prof. art U. Wash.-Seattle, 1978—. Exhibited one-man shows of photographs, Art Inst. Chgo., 1975, Light Gallery, N.Y.C., 1977, Seattle Art Mus., 1980, Light Gallery, N.Y.C., 1982, Univ. Art Mus., Santa Barbara, Calif., 1984, Cliff Michel Gallery, 1989, Seattle Art Mus., 1990, Fuel Gallery, 1993, Galerie Lichtblick GFFK, Cologne, Germany, 1996, SOHO Photo, N.Y.C., 1999, Mus. Contemporary Photography, Chgo., 2003. NEA Photographer's fellow, 1979, NEA Visual Artist's fellow, 1986; recipient Artist's Commn., Wash. State Arts Commn., 1990. Mem. Soc. Photographic Edn., Mus. of Contemporary Photography. Office: U Wash Sch Art PO Box 353440 Seattle WA 98195-3440 E-mail: peberger@u.washington.edu.

BERGER, PEARL, library director; b. N.Y.C., Nov. 30, 1943; d. Baruch Mayer and Tova (Brandwein) Rabinowitz; m. David Berger, June 14, 1965; children: Miriam Esther, Yitzhak, Gedalyah Aaron. B in Religious Edn., Yeshiva U.; BA, Bklyn. Coll., 1965; MLS, Columbia U., 1974. Diploma tchr. Hebrew. Tchr. Hebrew & Jewish studies Yeshiva of Crown Heights, Bklyn., 1963-65; asst. libr. YIVO Inst. Jewish Rsch., N.Y.C., 1976-80; head tech. svcs. Librs. Yeshiva U., N.Y.C., 1980-81, head libr. Pollack Libr., 1981-83, head libr. main ctr. librs., 1983-85, dean librs., 1985—. V.p. Coun. Archives and Rsch. Librs. in Jewish Studies, 1984-86, pres. 1986-89. Assoc. editor: Jour. Judaica Librarianship, 1983-2004, mem. editl. bd. 2004-; first v.p. Met. Reference and Rsch. Libr. Orgn., 1996-99; contbr. articles to profl. jours.; compiler catalog Guide to Yiddish Classics on Microfiche, 1980. Recipient Benjamin Gottesman Libr. Chair Yeshiva U. Mem. ALA, Metro. Ref. Rsch. Libr. Agy. (trustee 1991—2002, sec. 1993-99, 1st v.p. 1996-99), Assn. Jewish Librs. (rsch., spl. librs. divsn., v.p. 1982-84, pres. 1984-86, voting rep. Nat. Info. Stds. Orgn. 1995-2000, v.p., pres.-elect 2000-01, pres. 2002-04). Office: Yeshiva U Dean of Libraries 500 W 185th St New York NY 10033-3299

BERGER, PHIL, musician; b. Chgo., Aug. 31, 1963; s. Sheldon and Cyrena Berger. BA in Comm., U. Iowa, Iowa City, 1985. Intern CBS, Chgo, 1986; pianist Nordstrom, Glendale, Calif., 1986—88; accompanist, performer, singer freelance, Woodland Hills, Calif., 1987—; sales mgr. Mattress Discounters, West L.A., 1999—2001. Mem. MADD; mem. and vol. performer City of Hope, Duarte, Calif., 2002—03; campaign vol. Mayor Tom Bradley. Mem.: Sierra Club, Alpha Epsilon Pi. Avocations: guitar, piano, tennis, working out. Home and Office: 6301 Glade Ave Woodland Hills CA 91367 E-mail: chitownphil@creativewc.com.

BERGER, RENEE AVA, management consultant; BA in English summa cum laude, SUNY, Buffalo, 1969, MA in Humanities/Planning, 1974; postgrad. in pub. adminstrn., George Washington U., 1977-80. Pres. TEAMWORKS, San Francisco, Washington, 1985—. Adj. prof. George Washington U., 1978-80; vis. prof. Griffith U., Australia, 1983; edn. and tng. cons. Buffalo Psychiat. Ctr., Gowanda Psychiat. Ctr., 1974-77; sr. rsch. assoc. Com. for Econ. Devel., Washington, 1978-81; dir. partnerships White House Task Force on Pvt. Sector Initiatives, 1982; cons. Aspen Inst., German Marshall Fund, Orgn. for Econ. Coop. and Devel., Paris, 1983-85. Co-author: Public-Private Partnership in American Cities: Seven Case Studies, 1982, Public-Private Partnership: An Opportunity for Urban Communities, 1981, Profiles of Excellence: Achieving Success in the Non-Profit Sector, 1991; contbr. numerous articles to profl. jours. Office: TEAMWORKS 9 Van Buren St San Francisco CA 94131-2941

BERGER, ROBERT BERTRAM, lawyer; b. N.Y.C., Sept. 1, 1924; s. Edward William and Sophie (Berkowitz) B.; m. Phyllis Ann Korona, June 14, 1947; children: Barry Robert, Mark Alan, Karen Elizabeth Berger Adametz, James Michael; m. 2d, Arlene Kidder Wills, Dec. 27, 1980; 1 stepchild, Kimberly Kidder Wills Campbell. BS, Georgetown U., 1948; JD, U. Conn., 1952. Bar: Conn. 1952, U.S. Dist. Ct. Conn. 1953, U.S. Tax Ct. 1967, U.S. Ct. Appeals (2d cir.) 1968. Sole practice law, 1952-56; ptnr. Berger & Alaimo, Enfield, Conn., 1956-82, Berger, Alaimo, Santy & McGuire, Enfield, Conn., 1982-91, Berger, Santy & McGuire, Enfield, 1991-94, Berger & Santy, Enfield, 1994—2001, Berger, Santy & Barbieri, Enfield, 2001—. Judge Probate Dist. of Enfield, 1989-94; dir. Enfield Vis. Nuses Assn., 1993-96; bd. dirs., mem. exec. com. Conn. Attys. Title Ins. Co., Rocky Hill, 1980-2003; chmn. Enfield Dem. Town Com., 1979-87, Conn. Psychiat. Security Review Bd., 1985—; bd. dirs. Catic Fin. Inc. Contbr. monthly polit. column Enfield Press, 1980-84. Pres. United Way North Ctrl. Conn., 1981-84; trustee St. Bernard's Roman Cath. Ch., 1977-90, 99-2000; trustee, exec. bd. mem. Johnson Meml. Hosp., Johnson Meml. Corp., Stafford, Conn.; bd. dirs. United Way of Capitol Area, 1981-85, United Way North Ctrl. Conn., 1977—. With USMCR, 1942-45. Decorated Purple Heart; recipient disting. svc. award Enfield Jr. C. of C., 1955, Clayton Frost award U.S. Jr. C. of C., 1959-60. Mem. ABA, Conn. Bar Assn., Hartford County Bar Assn., Enfield Lawyers Assn. (pres. 1973-74), Am. Judicature Soc., Enfield Rotary (pres. 1970-71, Paul Harris fellow 1984).

BERGER, ROBERT LEWIS, retired biophysicist; b. Omaha, Sept. 2, 1925; BS, Colo. State U., Ft. Collins, 1950; MS, Pa. State U., 1953, PhD, 1956. Instr. Park Coll., Parkville, Mo., 1950-51; postdoctoral fellow Cambridge (Eng.) U., 1956-57; asst. prof. Utah State U., Logan, 1957-60, assoc. prof., 1960-62; sr. investigator Nat. Heart Inst., Bethesda, Md., 1962-77; chief biophysics sect. Nat. Heart, Lung and Blood Inst., NIH, Bethesda, 1977-96; sr. sci. advisor Blood Rsch. Detachment Walter Reed Army Inst. Rsch., Washington, 1994—96; pvt. cons. Bethesda, 1996—; emeritus sr. investigator Walter Reed Army Inst. Rsch., 1998—. On-loan sci. exec. EEG, Inc., Las Vegas, Nev., 1959—60; vis. scientist dept. chemistry U. Calif., San Diego, 1969—71; organizer med. and biol. sect. 4th Internat. Conf. Temperature, Washington, 1971; invention devel. coord. Nat. Heart Lung Blood Inst., 1990—94. Contbr. chapters to books, articles to profl. jours.; mem. editl. bd. Jour. Biochemical and Biophysical Methods, 1982—96. Pres., CEO, fund raiser Karma House, Inc., Rockville, Md., 1974—77; bd. dirs., fund raiser Protestant Student House, Utah State U., Logan, 1958—62; adv. bd. Christian edn. United Presbyn. Ch., 1960—68. Lt. (j.g.) USCG, 1943—45, PTO. Recipient Comdrs. award for Pub. Svc., Legion of Merit Equin, 1994—96, Disting. Svc. award, Eberely Coll. of Sci. and PSH Alumni Soc., 1998. Fellow: AAAS, Am. Phys. Soc.; mem.: Am. Soc. Molecular Biology and Biochemistry, Soc. Gen. Physiology, Biophysical Soc. (chmn. discussions com. 1976—92). Democrat. Episcopalian. Achievements include invention of Berger Ball Mixer. Home: 4503 Avamere St Bethesda MD 20814-3930 Office Phone: 301-319-7692. Personal E-mail: rlberger@comcast.net.

BERGER, ROBERT MICHAEL, lawyer; b. Chgo., Jan. 29, 1942; s. David B. and Sophia (Mizock) B.; m. Joan B. Israel, Aug. 16, 1964; children: Aliza, Benjamin, David. AB, U. Mich., 1963; JD, U. Chgo., 1966. Bar: Ill. 1966, U.S. Supreme Ct. 1975. Law clk. to cir. judge Henry J. Friendly U.S. Ct. Appeals, 2d Circuit, N.Y.C., 1966-67; atty. Chgo. Legal Aid Bur. Law Reform Unit, 1967-68; mem. firm Mayer Brown Rowe & Maw, Chgo., 1968-72, ptnr., 1972-2001; adj. prof. Northwestern U. Law Sch., 1997—; exec. v.p., gen. counsel, sec. Capri Capital LP, 2001—04; sr. counsel Krasnow, Saunders & Cornblath, 2001—. Lectr. Northwestern U. Law Sch., 1973; adj. prof. grad. program in real estate law John Marshall Law Sch., 1995-97; summer inst. faculty mem. Nat. Inst. Law-Focused Edn., Chgo., 1969-74; mem. hearing bd. Ill. Supreme Ct. Atty. Disciplinary Sys., 1973-79; mem. Ill. Sec. State Adv. Com. on Revised Uniform Ltd. Partnership Act, 1984-88, mem. spl. tax adv. commn. to Ill. Dept. Ins., 1972; bd. dirs., legal counsel Consumer Fedn. Ill., 1967-71; mem. regional consumer adv. coun. coun. FTC, 1969; bd. dirs., chmn. program com. Legal Assistance Found., Chgo., 1975-78; mem. Highland Park (Ill.) Zoning Bd. Appeals, 1984-86; chmn. blue ribbon com. Cook County Recorder, 1989-92; mem. real estate adv. bd. Dai-Ichi Kangyo Bank, Chgo., 1988-93; lectr. continuing legal edn. seminars. Comment editor: U. Chgo. Law Rev, 1965-66; author: Law and the Consumer, 1969, 74; author 500 page chpt. Lending, Finance and Banking, Construction Law, 1986, 92, ann. supplements; reporter Revised Uniform Ltd. Partnership Act, 1984-88; adv. com. Restatement of the Law of Property 3d-Mortgages; contbr. articles to law jours. Pres. Am.-Israel C. of C.; trustee Am. Friends of Hebrew U.; mem. exec. com. Primo Ctr. for Women and Children; bd. dirs. Am. Friends of Hebrew U. Mem. ABA (chmn. subcom. on rev. uniform ltd. partnership act 1981-85, chmn. com. on partnerships and unincorporated bus. orgns. 1985-88), Am. Law Inst., Am. Coll. Real Estate Lawyers (bd. govs. 1995-98, nominating com., vice chmn. program com.), Chgo. Bar Assn. (bd. mgrs. 1970-72, chmn. com. on real estate fin. 1984-86, chmn. real property law com. 1987-88), Chgo. Coun. Lawyers (founder, bd. govs. 1969-71), Order of Coif, Phi Beta Kappa, Phi Kappa Phi. Office: Krasnow Saunders Cornblath LLP 500 N Dearborn St Chicago IL 60610 Office Phone: 312-832-7894. Business E-Mail: rberger@ksc-law.com.

BERGER, SANDY (SAMUEL R. BERGER), former national security advisor; b. Sharon, Conn., Oct. 28, 1945; m. Susan Harrison; children: Deborah, Sara, Alexander. AB, Cornell U., 1967; JD cum laude, Harvard U., 1971. Bar: D.C. 1971. Legis. asst. to Senator Harold E. Hughes US Senate, Washington, 1971-72; spl. asst. to Mayor John V. Lindsay City of NY, 1972; dep. dir. policy planning staff US Dept. State, Washington, 1977-80; ptnr. Hogan & Hartson LLP, Washington, 1973—77, 1981—92, internat. strategic advisor; asst. dir. nat. security Presdl. Transition Team, 1992; dep. asst. to the Pres. for nat. security affairs NSC, Washington, 1993—96, asst. to pres. for national security affairs, 1997—2000; chmn. Stonebridge Intl. LLC, Washington, 2001—; sr. advisor Lehman Brothers. Author: Dollar Harvest, 1971, (with others) Manual of Foreign Investment in the United States, 1984. Mem. ABA. Office: Stonebridge Internat Ste 300 W 555 Thirteenth St NW Washington DC 20004*

BERGER, SANFORD JASON, retired lawyer, retired securities dealer, retired real estate broker; b. Cleve., June 29, 1926; s. Sam and Ida (Solomon) Berger; m. Bertine Mae Benjamin, Aug. 6, 1950 (div. Dec. 1977); children: Bradley Alan, Bonnie Jean. BA, Case Western Res. U., 1950, JD, 1952. Bar: Ohio 52, U.S. Supreme Ct. 79, U.S. Ct. Appeals 81. Field examiner Ohio Dept. Taxation, Cleve., 1952; pvt. practice law Cleve., 1952—. Real estate cons., Cleve., 1960—; investment cons., Cleve., 1970—; lectr. The Art of Conversation and Body Lang. Contbg. author Family Evaluation in Child Custody Litigation, 1982, Child Custody Litigation, 1986, The Parental Alienation Syndrome and the Differentiation Between Fabricated and Genuine Child Sex Abuse, 1987, Family Evaluation in Child Custody Mediation, Arbitration and Litigation, 1989; copyright 10 songs:. Candidate police judge, East Cleveland, 1955; mem. Bd. Edn., Beachwood, Ohio, 1963; judge ct. common pleas Cuyahoga County, Ohio, 1986; judge Ct. Appeals, 1988, 1990, 1992, 1994; mayor Beachwood, 1967. With USMC, 1944—45, PTO. Recipient Cert. Appreciation, Phi Alpha Delta, 1969, Healer award, U.S. Supreme Ct. Chief Justice Warren Burger, 1987, Outstanding Ohio Citizen award, Ohio Gen. Assembly, 1987. Mem.: B'nai B'rith (edidtor 1968—70). Republican. Jewish. Achievements include being a successful lawyer in U.S. Supreme Ct. Case of Cleveland Bd. of Edn. vs. Loudermill, 1985; 17 appeals to Supreme Court. Avocations: poetry, writing lyrics, legal writing, drag racing, scuba diving. Office Phone: 440-461-5777. E-mail: sanlllmar@aol.com.

BERGER, SEYMOUR MAURICE, social psychologist; b. Bklyn., Jan. 7, 1928; s. Leo and Bessie Ida (Okun) Berger; m. Sara Marilyn Nappen, Sept. 7, 1952; children: Evelyn Joyce, Nancy Faith. BS, Okla. A&M Coll., 1949; MA, Columbia U., 1950; PhD, Cornell U., 1959. Instr. Trinity Coll., Hartford, Conn., 1958-59; from instr. to assoc. prof. Ind. U., Bloomington, 1959-69; prof. social psychology U. Mass., Amherst, 1969-95, prof. emeritus, 1995—, acting dean social and behavioral scis., 1991-92, dean social behavioral scis., 1992-95. Contbr. articles on social psychology to profl. jours.; mem. editorial bd. Jour. Personality and Social Psychology. Served with USNR, 1945-46; served with USAF, 1951-55. Fulbright sr. research scholar, 1975-76,83; spl. fellow NIH, 1965-66 Democrat. Jewish. Home: 459 Flat Hills Rd Amherst MA 01002-1219 E-mail: berger@psych.umass.edu.

BERGER, STEPHEN, finance company executive; b. N.Y.C., July 11, 1939; s. Saul and Paula (Rosenzweig) B.; m. Cynthia C. Wainwright, Sept. 24, 1977. BA, Brandeis U., 1959. Editor Crowell-Collier Publs., N.Y.C., 1961-62; exec. asst. to Rep. Jonathan Bingham N.Y.C., 1964-68; pres. PCM Corp., N.Y.C., 1969-73; exec. dir. N.Y. Study Commn. on N.Y.C., 1972-73; dir. Studies Commn. on Critical Choices for Americans, N.Y.C., 1973-74; commr. N.Y. Dept. Social Svcs., Albany, 1975-76; dir. N.Y. Office Planning Svcs., Albany, 1975; exec. dir. N.Y. Emergency Fin. Control Bd., N.Y.C., 1976; mem. N.Y. Bd. Social Welfare, 1977; dir. corp. devel. Oppenheimer & Co., Inc., N.Y.C., 1981-82; investment banker Odyssey Ptnrs., N.Y.C., 1983-85; chmn. U.S. Ry. Assn., Washington, 1980-87; prof. pub. adminstrn. N.Y.U., 1977-85; bd. dirs., chmn. fin. com. N.Y. Met. Transp. Authority, 1979-85; exec. dir. Port Authority, N.Y., N.J., 1985-90, Intergovtl. Policy Adv. Com. (office U.S. trade rep.), 1988-90; chmn., chief exec. officer Fin. Guaranty Ins. Co., N.Y.C., 1990-92; exec. v.p. GE Capital Corp., 1992-93; ptnr. Odyssey Ptnrs., L.P., N.Y.C., 1993—. Chmn. Odyssey Investment Ptnrs., LLC, 1997—; bd. dirs. Dayton Superior, Pro Mach Corp. Co-chair Gov.'s Com. on Scholastic Achievement; chair Gov.'s Task Force on Health Care Reform, 2003—05; trustee Brandeis U., 1994—2001. Democrat. Jewish. Office: Odyssey Investment Ptnrs 280 Park Ave Fl 38 New York NY 10017-1216 Office Phone: 212-351-7950. Business E-Mail: sberger@odysseyinvestment.com.

BERGER, THOMAS LOUIS, author; b. Cin., July 20, 1924; s. Thomas Charles and Mildred (Bubbe) Berger; m. Jeanne Redpath, June 12, 1950. BA with honors, U. Cin., 1948; postgrad., Columbia U., 1950—51; LittD (hon.), L.I.U., 1986. Librarian Rand Sch. Social Sci., N.Y.C., 1948—51; staff mem. N.Y. Times Index, 1951—52; assoc. editor Popular Sci. Monthly, 1952—53. Disting. vis. prof. Southampton Coll., 1975—76; vis. lectr. Yale U., 1981, 82; Regent's lectr. U. Calif., Davis, 1982. Author: Crazy in Berlin, 1958, Reinhart in Love, 1962, Little Big Man, 1964, Killing Time, 1967, Vital Parts, 1970, Regiment of Women, 1973, Sneaky People, 1975, Who Is Teddy Villanova?, 1977, Arthur Rex, 1978, Neighbors, 1980, Reinhart's Women, 1981, The Feud, 1983 (Pulitzer Prize nomination, 1984), Nowhere, 1985, Being Invisible, 1987, The Houseguest, 1988, Changing the Past, 1989, Orrie's Story, 1990, Meeting Evil, 1992, Robert Crews, 1994, Suspects, 1996, The Return of Little Big Man, 1999, Best Friends, 2003, Adventures of the Artificial Woman, 2004, (plays) Other People, 1970. With U.S. Army, 1943—46, ETO. Recipient Rosenthal award, Nat. Inst. Arts and Letters, 1965, Western Heritage award, 1965, Ohioana Book award, 1982; Dial fellow, 1962. Office: c/o Don Congdon Assocs 156 Fifth Ave Ste 625 New York NY 10010-7002 Office Phone: 212-645-1229. E-mail: thosberg@earthlink.net. *In my work I try to compete with that reality to which I must submit in life.*

BERGER, TOBY, electrical engineer, educator; b. Sept. 4, 1940; s. Henry and Doris L. (Goldstein) B.; m. Florence Cohen, Aug. 27, 1961; children: Elizabeth, Lawrence. BS, Yale U., 1962; MS, Harvard U., 1964, PhD, 1966. Assoc. scientist Raytheon Co., Wayland, Mass., 1962—66, sr. scientist, 1966—68, cons., 1968—75; from asst. prof. elec. engring. to prof. engring. Cornell U., Ithaca, NY, 1968—2000, Levis prof. engring., 1984—99, acting dir. Dept. Elec. Engring., 1988—, Jacobs prof. engring., 2000—. Cons. IBM, Owego, N.Y., 1975-94, Bell Labs., Murray Hill, N.J., 1987-97, TCSI, Berkeley, Calif., 1986-96; co-founder Sight Speed Tech., Berkeley, Calif., 2003—; vis. prof. ENST, Paris, 1986, Princeton U., 1989-90, Northeastern U., 1990, U. Va., 1997, 2003, Harvard U., 2004. Author: Rate-Distortion Theory, 1971, Digital Compression for Multimedia, 1998, Information Measures for Discrete Random Fields, 1998; contbr. articles to profl. jours. Fellow Guggenheim Found., 1975-76, Japan Soc. for Promotion of Sci., 1980-81, Peoples Republic of China Ednl. Ministry, 1981, Fulbright Travel fellow, 1987; recipient Shannon award, IEEE Info. Theory Soc., 2002. Fellow: IEEE (pres. info. theory group 1979, editor-in-chief Transactions on Info. Theory 1987—89, Frederick E. Terman award 1982, Leon K. Kirchmayer Grad. Tchg. award 2006); mem.: AAAS, Info. Theory Soc. of IEEE (Shannon award 2002), Am. Soc. Engring. Tech., Tau Beta Pi, Sigma Xi. Home: 422 Highland Rd Ithaca NY 14850-2216 Office: Cornell U Sch Elec & Computer Engring Ithaca NY 14853 Business E-Mail: berger@ece.cornell.edu.

BERGER, WAYNE C., retail executive; b. Nappanee, Ind. m. Judy Berger; 3 children. BA in Econs., Ind. U. Sr. systems programmer, East Coast Data Ctr. The May Dept. Stores Co., 1978, various programming and systems pos., 1978—84, regional v.p., East Coast Data Ctr., 1984—93, regional v.p., Great Lakes Data Ctr., 1993—2003, sr. v.p. info. tech. St. Louis, 2003—. Office: May Dept Stores Co 611 Olive St Saint Louis MO 63101

BERGER, WILLIAM ERNEST, newspaper publisher; b. Ferris, Ill., June 6, 1918; s. William George and Ethel (Nelson) B.; m. Jerry June Barnes, Feb. 26, 1943; children: William Edward, Barbara, John Jeffrey. Student, Carthage Coll., 1935-38. Newspaper editor and pub., Hondo, Tex., 1946-65, 81—; commr. Tex Water Rights Commn., Austin, 1965-69; pres. Assoc. Tex. Newspapers, Inc., 1957—, South Tex. Press, Inc., Hondo, 1979—. Owner Sta. KRME, Hondo, 1969—94; newspaper broker, 1980—. Treas. Medina Meml. Hosp., Hondo. 1962-64, del. Tex. Dem. Conv., 1962, 64, 66, 68, Nat. Dem. Conv., 1968. Served with AUS, 1942-46. Mem. Tex. Press Assn. (pres. 1963), South Tex. Press Assn. (pres. 1954), SAR (Patrick Henry chpt.), Headliners Club, Lions (Hondo past pres.). Methodist.

BERGER, WOLFGANG H., oceanographer, geologist; b. Erlangen, Germany; came to U.S., 1961; MS in Geology, U. Colo., 1963; PhD in Oceanography, U. Calif., San Diego, 1968. Asst. prof. Scripps Inst. Oceanography U. Calif., La Jolla, 1971-74, assoc. prof., 1974-80, prof. oceanography, 1980—; dir. Calif. Space Inst. U. Calif., San Diego, 1998—. Co-editor: Abrupt Climatic Change, 1987, Ocean Productivity, 1989, co-author: The Sea Floor, 1993. Co-chief scientist, Ocean Drilling Prog., Leg 130 (1990), Leg 175 (1997). Recipient Bigelow medal Woods Hole (Mass.) Oceanographic Inst., 1979, Huntsman medal Bedford Oceanographic Inst., Can., 1984, Humboldt award German Sci. Found., Bonn, Germany, 1986, Albert I medal, Paris, 1991, Balzan prize, 1993, Steinmann medal Geol. Vereingung, 1998, Francis P. Shepard medal, Soc. for Sedimentary Geology, 2001; Lady Davis fellow Hebrew U., 1986. Fellow AAAS, Am. Geophysical Union (Ewing medal 1988), Geol. Soc. Am.; mem. European Geophysical Soc., Academia Europaea (fgn.). Avocation: water color. Office: U Calif San Diego Scripps Inst Oceanography Dept 0244 La Jolla CA 92093-0244 Office Phone: 858-822-2545. Business E-Mail: wberger@ucsd.edu.

BERGERON, CLIFTON GEORGE, engineer, educator; b. Los Angeles, Jan. 5, 1925; s. Lewis G. and Rose C. (Dengel) B.; m. Laura H. Kaario, June 9, 1950; children— Ann Leija, Louis Kaario. BS, U. Ill., 1950, MS, 1959, PhD, 1961. Sr. ceramic engr. A. O. Smith Corp., Milw., 1950-55; staff engr. Whirlpool Corp., St. Joseph, Mich., 1955-57; research assoc. U. Ill., Champaign-Urbana, 1957-61, asst. prof., 1961-63, asso. prof., 1963-67, prof., 1967-78, head dept. ceramic engring., 1978-86, prof. emeritus, 1988—. Cons. A. O. Smith Corp., Whirlpool Corp., Ingraham Richardson, U.S. Steel Corp., Pfaudler Corp., Ferro Corp. Editor, Ann. Conf. on Glass Problems. Served in U.S. Army, 1943-46, ETO. Recipient Everitt award for tchg. excellence U. Ill., 1975; NSF grantee, 1961-82. Fellow Am. Ceramic Soc. (Outstanding Educator award 1988); mem. AAAS, Nat. Inst. Ceramic Engrs. (Friedberg lectr. 1986, Greaves-Walker award 2005), AAUP, KERAMOS, Am. Soc. Engring. Edn., Sigma Xi. Achievements include research in crystallization kinetics in glass; high temperature reactions. Home: 208 W Michigan Ave Urbana IL 61801-4944 Office: 105 S Goodwin Ave Urbana IL 61801-2901

BERGERON, EARLEEN FOURNET, actress; b. New Orleans, Aug. 7, 1938; d. Earl Joseph Fournet and Lucia (Cuccia) Wadsworth; m. James Ronald Bergeron Sr., June 17, 1961; children: Blanche Theresa, Michele Yvette, James Ronald Jr. B in Social Sci. in Theatre and Speech, Loyola U., 1960. Actor: (plays) The Secret Affairs of Mildred Wilde, 1977, The Boyfriend, 1977, The Shadow Box, 1979, California Suite, 1980, Hay Fever, 1985, Brighton Beach, 1986, Beyond Therapy, 1987, Steel Magnolias, 1988, 1989, Nunsense, 1990, Broadway Bound, 1991, The Women, 1993, Nunsense II, 1995, Stomping Grounds, 1995, 1996, Angels in America, Part I: Millenium Approaches, Part II: Perestroika, 1997, Spareribs, 1998, Come

Back Little Sheba, 1999, The Cripple of Inishmann, 2001, Ancestral Voices, 2002, Our Town, 2002, Morning's At Seven, 2004, The Aristocats, 2005, (comml.) Goodwill, 1988, Schumpert Medical Center, 1991, Cunningham and McDonald, Plastic Surgeons, 1991, JB Cable Ads, 1995, Pierre Bossier Mall, 1996; (films) Man in the Moon, 1990; (TV series) Rescue 911, 1991. Bd. dirs. Port Players, Shreveport, La.; assoc. mem. Co. Repertory Theatre, Inc., Project Shakespeare in Schs.; active Shreveport Med. Aux., 1968—97, mem. exec. bd., 1976—78; mem. Shreveport Opera Guild, 1972—97; area leader fund dr. Am. Cancer Soc., Shreveport, 1985—89. Named one of Outstanding Team Capts., United Way Fund, 1969. Mem.: Shreveport Little Theatre Guild (bd. dirs. 1985—86), Strand Theatre, Majorie Lyons Playhouse, Shreveport Little Theatre. Roman Catholic.

BERGERON, ROBERT FRANCIS, JR., (TERRY BERGERON), software engineer; b. Gloucester, Mass., Jan. 23, 1942; s. Robert Francis and Jean Ann (Francis) B.; children: Robert, Karin, Kristin; m. Marion Louise Pisarchuk, July 14, 1979; children: Steven, Tanya. ScB summa cum laude, Brown U., 1964; PhD math., MIT, 1968. Rsch. assoc. Bolt Beranek & Newman, Cambridge, Mass., 1968; instr. math MIT, Cambridge, 1969; mem. tech. staff Bell Lab., Whippany, N.J., 1969-72, supr., 1972-84; tech. mgr. AT&T Bell Lab., Warren, N.J., 1984-95; cons., sr. mgr. Cotelligent, Liberty Corner, N.J., 1996-2000; cons. Smithville, N.J., 2001—. Patentee in field; contbr. articles to profl. jours. Home and Office: 102 Southhampton Dr Smithville NJ 08205 Office Phone: 609-748-3991.

BERGERSON, DAVID RAYMOND, lawyer; b. Mpls., Nov. 23, 1939; s. Raymond Kenneth and Katherine Cecille (Langworthy) Bergerson; m. Nancy Anne Heeter, Dec. 22, 1962; children: W. Thomas C., Kirsten Finch, David Raymond. BA, Yale U., 1961; JD, U. Minn., 1964. Bar: Minn. 1964. Assoc. Fredrikson Law Firm, Mpls., 1964-67; atty. Honeywell Inc., Mpls., 1967-74, asst. gen. counsel, 1974-82, v.p., asst. gen. counsel, 1983-84, v.p., gen. counsel, 1984-92; pvt. practice law Mpls., 1992-94; v.p., sec. Telcom Sys. Svcs., Inc., Plymouth, Minn., 1994-96, dir., cons., 1996-97; v.p. bd. dirs. Hogan Bergerson, Inc., Mpls., 1997—. Mem. city coun. Minnetonka Beach, Minn., 2001—; bd. dirs. Pillsbury Neighborhood Svcs., Inc., Mpls., 1983—92. Republican. Avocations: scuba diving, bird-hunting. Home: 2303 Huntington Point Rd E Wayzata MN 55391-9740 Office: Hogan Bergerson Inc 4610 IDS Ctr Minneapolis MN 55402 Office Phone: 952-471-9664. Personal E-mail: dbergerson1@mchsi.com.

BERGESEN, ROBERT NELSON, transportation consultant; b. Phila., Pa., Nov. 1, 1937; s. Bernhard E. and Carol Pearl (Nelson) B.; m. Jean Nicol, Apr. 23, 1966; children: Susan, Jean, Jeffrey. BA, Cornell U., 1959, MBA, 1961. With Price Waterhouse and Co., NYC, 1961-63; sys. analyst Warner-Lambert, Morris Plains, NJ, 1963-66; asst. contr. C.T.I., NYC, 1970-71; contr. Flexi-Van Leasing, NYC, 1971-75; from controller to gen. mgr. Vt. Transit Co., Inc., Burlington, Vt., 1977-2000. Mem. New Eng. Bus. Assn. (bd. dir. 1993-2000). Lutheran. Home: 182 Morningside Dr Middlebury VT 05753-1074 E-mail: rbergesen@hotmail.com.

BERGESON, DONNA POTTIS, lawyer; b. Warwick, N.Y., Aug. 21, 1960; BA magna cum laude, U. S.C., 1981, JD, 1984. Bar: Ga. 1984. Ptnr., group leader, health care regulatory group Alston & Bird LLP, Atlanta. Mem. ABA, Atlanta Bar Assn., Gwinnett County Bar Assn., State Bar of Ga., Ga. Acad. Hosp. Attys., Phi Beta Kapa, Phi Eta Sigma. Office: Alston & Bird LLP 1 Atlantic Ctr 1201 W Peachtree St NW Atlanta GA 30309-3424 Office Phone: 404-881-7278. Office Fax: 404-881-7777. Business E-Mail: dbergeson@alston.com.

BERGESON, JAMES, advertising executive; Pres., COO, CEO Colle and McVoy Inc., Mpls. Pres. bd. dir. Homeward Bound Found.; bd. adv. webADTV, 2000—. Mem.: Internat. Comms. Agy. Network (pres. 1999—), Am. Assn. Advertising Agencies (nat. bd. dir.).

BERGESON, TERESA, school system administrator; b. Mass. BA in English, Emmanuel Coll., Boston, 1964; M in Counseling and Guidance, Western Mich. U., 1969; PhD in Edn., U. Wash. Tchr., sch. guidance counselor, Mass., Alaska, Wash.; exec. dir. Ctrl. Kitsap Sch. Dist., 1989-92, Wash. State Commn. on Learning, 1993-95; state supt. pub. instrn. Olympia, Wash., 1997—. V.p. Wash. Edn. Assn., 1981, pres., 1985—89. Mem.: Wash. Edn. Assn. (v.p. 1981—85, pres. 1985—89). Office: PO Box 47200 Olympia WA 98504-7200 Fax: 360-753-6712.

BERGEVIN, V. RÉAL, customer relationship management executive; b. Oshawa, Mar. 9, 1963; Bus. degree Sir Wilfrid Laurier U., 1986. With General Motors, 1984—88; with Wardair Airlines, 1988—90; with Rogers Cablesystems, 1990—92; founder John Moss Assoc., 1992—96; founder, pres. NuComm Internat., 1991—. Pub. (other) 23 Steps to an Effective Call Centre, 2000. Recipient Niagara Entrepreneur Yr. Award. Mem.: Can. Mktg. Assn., Direct Mktg. Assn. Office: NuComm Internat Corbloc Bldg 80 King St 3d Fl Saint Catharines ON Canada L2R 7G1

BERGGREN, RONALD BERNARD, surgeon, retired educator; b. S.I., N.Y., June 13, 1931; s. Bernard and Florence (Schmidt) B.; m. Mary Beth Griffith, Nov. 25, 1954; children: Karen Berggren Murray, Eric Griffith. BA, Johns Hopkins U., 1953; MD, U. Pa., 1957. Diplomate Am. Bd. Surgery, Nat. Bd. Med. Examiners, Am. Bd. Plastic Surgery (bd. dirs. 1982-88, chmn. 1987-88). Asst. instr. surgery U. Pa., 1958-62, instr., 1962-65; gen. surg. resident Hosp. U. Pa., 1958-62, resident plastic surgery, 1963-64, chief resident plastic surgery, 1964-65; sr. resident surgery Phila. Gen. Hosp., 1962-63; asst. prof. surgery Ohio State U. Sch. Medicine, 1965-68, dir. div. plastic surgery, 1965-85, assoc. prof. surgery, 1968-73, prof. surgery, 1973-86, emeritus prof. surgery, 1986—; attending staff Ohio State U. Hosps., chief of staff, 1983-85, hon. staff, 1986—. Attending staff, dir. div. plastic surgery Children's Hosp., Columbus, Ohio, 1965-90; v.p. Plastic Surgery Ednl. Found., 1984-85, pres., 1986-87; sec. Plastic Surgery Tng. Program Dirs., 1981-83, chmn., 1983-85; mem. med. adv. bd. Ohio Bur. for Children with Med. Handicaps, 1974—2004. Trustee Mid Ohio Health Planning Fedn., 1979-82, 84, PSRO, 1980-84, Scioto Valley Health Systems Agy., 1985-87; del. Coun. Med. Splty. Socs., 1982-90, dir., 1988-90. Recipient Disting. Svc. award Plastic Surgery Edn. Foun., 1990. Fellow: ACS (gov. 1996—2001, chair gov.'s com. on ambulatory surg. care); mem.: AMA, Coun. Plastic Surgical Orgn. (convenor 1996—2000), Coun. Med. Specialty Socs. (dir. 1989—90, sec. 1991—92, pres.-elect 1993, pres. 1994), Accreditation Coun. for Grad. Med. Edn. (rev. com. for plastic surgery 1983—90, mem. exec. com. 1987—90, designate chmn. 1988, chmn. 1989, mem. exec. com. 1994, chmn. 1994, institutional rev. com. 1996—2004, chair 2002—04, John C. Gienapp award 2005), Am. Soc. Maxillofacial Surgery, Am. Soc. Aesthetic Plastic Surgery (parliamentarian 1992—93), Am. Trauma Soc., Am. Burn Assn., Assn. Acad. Surgery, Am. Assn. Surgery Trauma, N.Y. Acad. Scis., Plastic Surg. Rsch. Coun. (chair 1975—76), Franklin County Med. Soc. (pres.-elect 1982—83, pres. 1983—84), Am. Assn. Plastic Surgeons (treas. 1983—85, v.p. 1988—89, pres.-elect 1989—90, pres. 1990—91), Am. Cleft Palate Assn., Ohio Valley Plastic Surg. Soc., Am. Soc. Plastic and Reconstructive Surgeons (spl. hon. citation 1995, Trustees award for spl. achievement in plastic surgery 2000), Columbus Surg. Soc., Ctrl. Surg. Soc., Alpha Kappa Kappa, Phi Kappa Psi, Sigma Xi. Office: 9787 Windale Farms Cir Galena OH 43021-9609 Personal E-mail: rbergg@aol.com.

BERGGREN, WILLIAM ALFRED, geologist, research micropaleontologist, educator; b. N.Y.C., Jan. 15, 1931; s. Wilhelm Fritjof and Lilly Maria (Skog) B.; m. Lois Albee, June 19, 1954 (div. July 1981); children: Erik, Anna Lisa, Anders, Sara Maria; m. Marie Pierre Aubry, June 19, 1982 BS, Dickinson Coll., 1952; M.Sc., U. Houston, 1957; PhD, U. Stockholm, 1960, D.Sc., 1962; doctorate (hon.), U. Utrecht, 2001, U. Athens, 2003. Research micropaleontologist Oasis Oil Co., Tripoli, Libya, 1962-65; asst. scientist Woods Hole Oceanographic Inst., Mass., 1965-68, assoc. scientist, 1968-71, sr. scientist, 1971-98, sr. scientist emeritus, 1998—; Disting. vis. prof. Rutgers U., New Brunswick, N.J., 2001—. Adj. prof. Brown U., Providence, 1968-93. Editor: Catastrophes and Earth History, 1984, Late Eocene-Early Oligocene Climatic and Biotic Change, 1992, Geochronology Time-Scales and Global Stratigraphic Correlation, 1995, Late Paleocene-Early Eocene Climate and Biotic Events, 1998; contbr. articles to sci. jours. Recipient Cushman Found. award for foraminiferal rsch., 1995, Raymond C. Moore medal in paleontology Soc. of Sedimentary Geology, 1997. Fellow Geol. Soc. Am., Geol. Soc. London (hon.); mem. NAS (Mary Clark Thompson medal 1982), Am. Assn. Petroleum Geologists, Soc. Econ. Paleontologists and Mineralogists (hon.), Paleontol. Soc. Am. (co-editor jour. 1980-84), Am. Geophys. Union. Avocation: skiing. Office: Woods Hole Oceanographic Inst 22 Water St Woods Hole MA 02543-1024

BERGGREN-MOILANEN, BONNIE LEE, education educator; b. L'Anse, Mich., June 2, 1940; d. Alvin Carl and Emma Leola (Wandell) Lydman; m. Grant Lorns Berggren, Jr., Aug. 22, 1959 (dec.); children: Grant Victor Berggren, Rex Alvin Berggren, Konnie Kay Berggren-Schneider; m. Glenn Moilanen, 2003. BA, U. Hawaii, 1961; MA, Ea. Mich. U., 1988; MA in Ednl. Adminstrn., No. Mich. U., 1991. Tchr. home econs. Baraga (Mich.) Twp. Schs., 1960-61, L'Anse Twp. Schs., 1963-65, Spencerport (N.Y.) Cen. Schs., 1979-84; presch. tchr. NCA Sch., Cmty. Action Agy., Hermansville, Mich., 1971-73; circulation supr. Spring Arbor (Mich.) Coll. Libr., 1985-87; adj. prof., supr. student tchrs. No. Mich. U., Marquette, 1989—96; co-owner, co-mgr. Menominee (Mich.) Floral, 1993-96; curriculum and tng. coord./spl. project coord. Campus Crusade for Christ, Children of The World Dept., San Clemente, Calif., 1997-2000; sr. staff Internat. Student Resources Campus Crusade for Christ, Madison, Wis., 2000—. Tchr. trainer Negaunee Pub. Schs., Negaunee, Mich., 1988—90; leader workshop Republic-Michigamme Schs., Republic, Mich., 1989—90; mem. evaluation team Marquette Pub. Schs., 1991; mem. tchr. edn. adv. coun. No. Mich. U., Marquette, 1991—96, mem. Hoppes award com., 1990—92, mem. pers. com., 1992. Libr. bd. Republic-Michigamme Schs., 1988—91; spkr. Christian Women's Club, 1989—90; bd. regents Liberty U., 1990—91; active Operation Carelift to Russia, 1997, Operation Sunrise to Africa, 2002. Fellow: Roberts Wesleyan Coll.; mem.: AAUW, DAV Aux. (life; Mich. historian 1975), AAUP, Concerned Women Am., U. Hawaii Alumni Assn., Ea. Mich U. Alumni Assn., Univ. Women No. Mich. U., Phi Delta Kappa, Phi Kappa Phi. Baptist. Avocations: reading, travel, writing, crafts. Home: HC 2 Box 772A Lanse MI 49946-9517 E-mail: bonnielb@chorus.net.

BERGHAHN, KLAUS LEO, German and Jewish studies educator; b. Duesseldorf, Germany, Aug. 5, 1937; arrived in U.S., 1967; s. Wilhelm and Anna (Bong) B.; m. Doris E. Beyer, Aug. 10, 1966; 1 child, Marcus J. Student, U. Cologne, Germany, 1957-59; Staatsexamen, U. Muenster, Germany, 1963, Dr phil, 1967. Tutor, asst. U. Muenster, 1963-67; asst. prof. German studies U. Wis., Madison, 1967-71, assoc. prof., 1971-73, prof., 1973—, chmn. German dept., 1994-97, mem. senate, 1974-78, 85-87, dir. ctr. German European studies, 1998—2005, Weinstein-Bascom prof. German and Jewish studies, 1999—2004, DAAD prof., 2004—. Vis. prof. Free U. Berlin, 1978, U. Bielefeld, Germany, 1980-81, U. Giessen, Germany, 1983, 92, U. Mich., Ann Arbor, 1984, U. Calif., Davis, 1989, Hebrew U., Jerusalem, 1993, U. London, 2005; mem. adv. bd. German Am. Art Found., Chgo., 1995-99; mem. German sect. Fulbright Commn., 1995-98; mem. adv. bd. German dept. Harvard U., 1994-95, 96-97; organizer spl. sessions, confs. and symposia, 1983—. Author: Formen der Dialogführung in Schillers klassischen Dramen, 1970, Friedrich Schiller: Vom Pathetischen und Erhabenen, 1970, Friedrich Schiller: Kallias oder über die Schönheit, 1971, Briefwechsel zwischen Schiller und Körner, 1973, Schillers Gedichte, 1980, G.E. Lessing: Hamburgische Dramaturgie, 1981, Schiller Ansichten eines Idealisten, 1986, (with Beate Pinkerneil) Am Beispiel Wilhelm Meister, 2 vols., 1980, Grenzen der Toleranz, 2000; editor: (with Reinhold Grimm) Schiller Zur Theorie und Praxis der Dramen, 1972, Wesen und Formen des Komischen im Drama, 1975, Utopian Vision Technological Innovation Poetic Imagination, 1990, (with Hans Ulrich Seeber) Literarische Utopien von Morus bis zur Gegenwart, 1983, 2d edit., 1985, (with Holub and Scherpe) Responsibility and Committment. Ethische Postulate der Kulturvermittlung. Festschrift für Jost Hermand, 1996; editor: Schiller Zur Geschichtlichkeit seines Werkes, 1976, The German-Jewish Dialogue-Reconsidered, 1996, Friedrich Schiller: Ueber die aesthetische Erzhiehung des Menschen, 2000, Goethe in German-Jewish Culture, 2001, Friedrich y Schiller: Ueber naire und sentimentalische Dichtung, 2002, Cultural Representations of the Holocaust in Germany and United States, 2002; mem. editl. bd. Monatshefte, 1975—, Mich. Germanic Studies, 1985-2000, Goethe Yearbook, 1985—, German Politics and Society, 2000—; contbr. articles and revs. to profl. jours., chpts. to books Fellow VW-Found., Germany, 1965-67, Am. Philos. Soc., 1969, 73, Inst. for Rsch. in Humanities, U. Wis., 1972, 89-94, Ctr. for Interdisciplinary Rsch., Bielefeld, 1980-81, German Acad. Exch. Svc., 1990, 99, also others; 14 summer rsch. grants U. Wis. Grad. Sch. Mem. MLA (19th and early 20th century German lit. divsn. exec. com. 1974-78, chmn. 1977, mem. 18th and early 19th century German lit. divsn. 1983-88, chmn. 1987, mem. adv. bd. MLA Profession 1997-99), Am. Assn. Tchrs. German (program and selection com. 1990), Internat. Union Germanists (program com. 1995, 2005), Lessing Soc., Schiller Soc. (medal 1984), Goethe Soc Avocations: reading, writing, music, theater, chess. Home: 2908 Oxford Rd Madison WI 53705-2220 Office: U Wis Dept German 860 Van Hise Hall 1220 Linden Dr Madison WI 53706-1525 Office Phone: 608-262-2192. Business E-Mail: klbergha@wisc.edu.

BERGHAHN, VOLKER ROLF, history professor; b. Berlin, Feb. 15, 1938; came to U.S., 1988; s. Alfred and Gisela (Henke) B.; m. Marion Ilse Koop, Dec. 29, 1969; children: Sascha, Vivian, Melvin. MA, U. N.C. Chapel Hill, 1961; PhD, U. London, 1964; Habil., U. Mannheim, 1966-69. Sr. scholar St. Anthony's Coll., Oxford, Eng., 1964-66; rsch. fellow U. Mannheim, 1966-69; lectr. U. East Anglia, Norwich, 1969-71; reader U. E. Anglia, Norwich, 1971-75; prof. U. Warwick, Coventry, 1975-88, Brown U., Providence, 1988-97, Columbia U., N.Y.C., 1998—. Author: Der Stahlhelm, 1966, Der Tirpitz Plan, 1970, Germany and the Approach of War, 1973, Modern Germany, 1982, The Americanization of West German Industry, 1945-1973, 1986, Otto A. Friedrich, 1902-1975, 1992, Imperial Germany, 19871-1914, 1995, America and the Intellectual Cold Wars in Europe, 2001, Europe in the Era of Two World Wars, 2005. Various grants and fellowships. Fellow Royal Hist. Soc.; mem. German History Soc. (pres. 1986-88), Am. Hist. Assn., German Studies Assn. Avocations: tennis, walking. Office: Columbia U Dept History New York NY 10027 Office Phone: 212-854-8604. Business E-Mail: vrb7@columbia.edu.

BERGHUIS, BRIAN, investment company executive; married. Degree, Harvard U. From analyst to mgr. Mid-Cap Growth Fund T. Rowe Price, Balt., 1985—92, mgr. Mid-Cap Growth Fund, 1992—. Office: T Rowe Price Mid Cap Growth Fund 100 East Pratt St Baltimore MD 21202

BERGIN, ALLEN ERIC, clinical psychologist, educator; b. Spokane, Wash. Aug. 4, 1934; s. Bernard F. and Vivian Selma (Kullberg) B.; m. Marian Shafer, June 4, 1955; children: David, Sue, Cyndy, Kathy, Eric, Ben, Patrick, Daniel, Michael. BS, Brigham Young U., 1956, MS, 1957; PhD, Stanford U., 1960. Diplomate Am. Bd. Profl. Psychology, 1969. Fellow U. Wis., Madison, 1960-61; prof. psychology and edn. Tchr. Coll., Columbia U., NYC, 1961-72; prof. psychology Brigham Young U., Provo, Utah, 1972-99, prof. emeritus, 1999—, dir. Values Inst., 1976-78, dir. clin. psychology, 1989-93. Assessment officer Peace Corps, Washington, 1961-66; cons. NIMH, Rockville, Md., 1969-75, 90. Co-author: Changing Frontiers in Psychotherapy, 1972, A Spiritual Strategy for Counseling and Psychotherapy, 1997, 2d edit., 2005; co-editor: Handbook of Psychotherapy, 1971, 4th edit., 1994 (citation classic 1979), Handbook of Pyschotherapy and Religious Diversity, 2000, Casebook for a Spiritual Strategy, 2004; author: Eternal Values and Personal Growth, 2002. Bishop LDS Ch., Emerson, NJ, 1970-72, Provo, 1981-84, stake pres., 1992-1995, Church Ed. Mission, San Diego, 2002-03; mem. steering com. Utah Gov.'s Conf. on Families, Salt Lake City, 1979-80. Recipient Biggs-Pine award Am. Assn. Counseling and Devel., 1986, Maeser rsch. award Brigham Young U., 1986, exemplary paper award Templeton Found., 1996, Pfister award Am. Psychiat. Assn., 1998. Republican. Avocations: world travel, writing.

BERGLEITNER, GEORGE CHARLES, JR., investment banker; b. Bklyn., July 16, 1935; s. George Charles and Marie (Preitz) B.; m. Betty Van Buren, Oct. 29, 1966; children: George Charles III, Michael John, Stephen William. BBA, St. Francis Coll., Bklyn., 1959; MBA, CCNY, 1961; PhD in Bus. Adminstrn. (hon.), Colo. State Christian Coll. Dir. instl. sales A.T. Brod & Co., N.Y.C., 1965-66; dir. instl. sales Weis, Voisin & Cannon, Inc., N.Y.C., 1966-67, C.B. Richard, Ellis & Co., N.Y.C., 1967-68; pres. Stamford (N.Y.) Fin. Co., also bd. dirs. Pres. M.J. Manchester & Co., Fashion & Time, Inc., B.J.B. Graphics, Inc., First Coinvestors, Inc., Smart Fit Foundations, Inc., Jay Co., Computer Holdings Corp., Ltd., Delhi Mfg. Corp., Delhi Industries, Delhi Mfg., Inc., Delhi Internat., Inc., Luxemborg; bd. dirs. Alpha Capital Corp., Am. Energy Mgmt. Corp., Stamford Fin., Electronic Tax Ctrs., Inc., L.I.U.G., LI Venture Capital Group, LI Venture Group, Del. County Indsl. Devel.; sponsor NY Venture Group; bd. dirs. Indsl. Devel. Agy., Delaware County, NY Chmn. Franciscan fathers Devel. Program, 1967-71; mem. Pres.'s Econ. Coun., Franciscan Spirit award, 1959-, Knight of Malta, 2001; pres. South Kortright Ctrl. Sch.; chmn. No. Catskills Econ. Devel. Coun., Econ. Devel. Coun. Stamford, Econ. Devel. Coun. Delaware County; regent St. Francis Coll.; bd. dirs. Econ. Devel. Coun., Printing Trade Sch., Cmty. Hosp. Stamford, N.Y., Stamford Econ. Devel. Coun., Delaware County Indsl. Devel. Authority County, 1999—, ECO Devel. Coun. Delaware County; sec. Delaware County Econ. Devel. Agy., 2000—; co-chair Project Strive, Albany, N.Y.; fin. com. Sacred Heart Roman Cath. Ch.; pres. Otsego Delaware Bd. Realtors, 2000; v.p. bd. dirs. Cath. Charities, 1999-2004, pres., 1999-2000, 2003-; Delaware County Indsl. Devel. sec., 2000—; pres., Stamford Rotary, 2004-. Paul Harris fellow Rotary Internat.; Internat. Rotary Benefactor; recipient St. Francis Coll. Alumni Fund award, 1965, Del. County Youth award, 1991, John F. Kennedy Meml. award, 1972, Internat. award for Svc. to Investment Commn., 1982, Youth Bur. award, 1991, St. Francis Prep Sch. Alumni Achievement award, 1993; named Stamford Citizen of Yr., 1992, Realtor of Yr., 1992, Col. Harper Grange Citizen of Yr., 1993. Mem.: Alumni Assn. St. Francis Coll., Am. Inst. Mgmt., Stamford C. of C. (pres. 1991—92), Otsego- Delaware Bd. Realtors (P.A.F. chmn., bd. dirs., pres.), Assn. Investment Bankers, Venture Assn. NJ (bd. dirs.), Conn. Venture Capital Assn., NY State Realtors Assn. (polit. action dir. 1999, trustee 2000—, bd. dirs., chmn. polit. action), CCNY Alumni Assn., Am. Legion, Cath. War Vets., Honor Legion N.Y.C. Police Dept., Univ. Club of Albany, Stamford Rotary Club (pres. 2004—), KC (4th deg.), Knights of Malta, Moose, Elks. Republican. Home: Red Rock Rd Stamford NY 12167 Office: Stamford Fin Bldg Off Bd Dirs Stamford NY 12167 Office Phone: 607-652-3311. Office Fax: 607-652-6301. Business E-Mail: dcre@wpe.com. *With all affluence, accomplishment, and success goes the responsibility of assistance; economic, social, and physical to the less fortunate of the world.*

BERGLES, ARTHUR EDWARD, mechanical engineering educator; b. NYC, Aug. 9, 1935; s. Edward H. and Victoria (Winkelmann) B.; m. Priscilla Lou Maule, June 19, 1960; children: Eric, Dwight. SB, SM, MIT, 1958, PhD, 1962; DEng (hon.), U. Porto, Portugal, 1998, Rand Afrikaans U., Johannesburg, S. Africa, 1999. Registered profl. engr., Mass. Research staff Nat. Magnet Lab., Cambridge, Mass., 1962-69; asst. prof. to assoc. prof. mech. engring. MIT, Cambridge, 1963-69, assoc. dir. heat transfer lab., 1966-69; prof. mech. engring. Ga. Inst. Tech., Atlanta, 1970-72; prof., chmn. dept. mech. engring. Iowa State U., Ames, 1972-83, prof., dir. heat transfer lab., 1983-86; Clark and Crossan prof. engring., dir. heat transfer lab. Rensselaer Poly. Inst., Troy, N.Y., 1986-97, dean of engring., 1989-92, Clark and Crossan prof. emeritus, 1997—; Glenn L. Martin Inst. prof. engring. U. Md., College Park, 1999—; sr. lectr. MIT, 1999—. Chmn. U.S. group heat transfer U.S./USSR Agreement, Washington, 1979-82; cons. to industry, mem. numerous adv. groups.; hon. prof. Beijing U. Tech. Co-author: Two-Phase Flow and Heat Transfer in the Power and Process Industries, 1981; co-editor: Two-Phase Heat Exchangers, 1988, Heat Transfer Enhancement of Heat Exchangers, 1999, others; editor: Heat Transfer in Electronic and Microelectronic Equipment, 1990; mem. editl. adv. bd. 13 jours.; contbr. numerous articles to tech. jours. Scoutmaster Boy Scout Am., Ames, 1976-84; bd. dirs. Ames Soc. for Arts, 1975-79. Recipient U.S. Sr. Scientist award Alexander von Humboldt Found., U. Hanover, Fed. Republic Germany, 1979-80, Tech. U., Munich, 1996-97, Faculty Achievement award in research Iowa State U., 1986, Nusselt-Reynolds prize Assembly Internat. Conf. on Exptl. Heat Transfer, 2001; named Anson Marston Disting. prof. engring., Iowa State U., 1981. Fellow AIAA (assoc.), ASHRAE (Edn. and Rsch. award N.E. chpt. 1993, Disting. Svc. award 1996, Anderson award 2000, Holladay award 2002), AAAS, NAE, ASME (hon. mem. 1996, v.p. 1981-85, chmn. heat transfer divsn. 1982-83, bd. govs. 1985-89, pres. 1990-91, Heat Transfer Meml. award 1979, Dedicated Svc. award 1984, Max Jakob Meml. award AIChE and ASME 1995, ASME medal 2000). Internat. Ctr. Heat and Mass Transfer (exec. com. 1984-2000, chmn. exec. com. 1996-98, Luikov medal 1998), Am. Soc. Engring. Edn. (Lamme award 1987, Centennial cert. and medal 1993), AIChE (Donald Q. Kern award 1990); mem. Soc. Automotive Engrs. (Ralph R. Teetor award 1987), Union Mech. and Elec. Engrs. and Technicians Yugoslavia (hon.), Acad. Scis. and Arts Slovenia (fgn.), Italian Nat. Acad. Scis. (fgn.), Polish Soc. Theoretical and Applied Mechanics (fgn.), Royal Acad. Engring. U.K. (fgn.), Rotary (Paul Harris fellow), Theta Chi. Republican. Lutheran. Office: Rensselaer Poly Inst Mech Aeronautical and Nuc Engring Troy NY 12180-3590 E-mail: abergles@aol.com. *My personal philosophy is to do as many things as I can, always striving for excellence and professionalism.*

BERGLUND, JOHN FINDLEY, mathematician, educator; b. Houston, Mar. 6, 1941; s. John Vernon and Dorothy Julia (Findley) B.; m. Mary Catherine Flanders, June 8, 1968; children: Catherine Jean Newhouse, Elizabeth Mary Hall, Andrew John. BA, Ohio Wesleyan U., 1962; PhD, Tulane U., 1967. Asst. prof. Wesleyan U., Middletown, Conn., 1967—71; ind. rschr. Sheffield (Eng.) U., 1970—71; vis. assoc. prof. La. State U., Baton Rouge, 1971—72; asst. prof. Va. Commonwealth U., Richmond, 1972—75, assoc. prof., 1975—82, prof., 1982—, dir. honors program, 1991—2003. Co-author: (books) Compact Semitopological Semigroups and Weakly Almost Periodic Functions, 1967, Compact Right Top. Semigroups and Generalizations of Almost Periodic, 1978, Analysis on Semigroups: Function Sp., Compactifications and Representations, 1989; contbr. articles to profl. jours. Recipient Sesquicentennial Alumnus award Ohio Wesleyan U., 1992. Mem. Nat. Collegiate Honors Coun., Am. Math. Soc., Math. Assn. Am., Nat. Coun. Tchrs. Math., Phi Beta Kappa. Home: 7716 Sweetbriar Rd Richmond VA 23229-6622 Office: Va Commonwealth U 1015 W Main St Richmond VA 23284-3010

BERGLUND, LARRY GLENN, mechanical engineer, educator; b. Mpls., Oct. 17, 1938; s. Lawrence Emil and Audrey Martina (Pearson) B.; m. Corinne Kay Swenberg; children: Bret Lawrence, Hans Nicholas. Student, St. Olaf Coll., 1956-59; BME, U. Minn., 1962, MSME, 1965; PhD, Kans. State U., 1971. Registered profl. engr., Minn. Project engr. Trane Co., LaCrosse, Wis., 1965-68; asst. prof. mech. engring. Mich. Tech. U., Houghton, 1972-75; assoc. fellow John B. Pierce Found. Lab.; lectr. Yale U., New Haven, 1975—96; prof. arch. dept. Tohoku U., Sendai, Japan, 1996—99; assoc. rsch. fellow Kimberly Clark Corp., Neenah, Wis., 1999—2000; rsch. biomed. engr. U.S. Army Rsch. Inst. Environ. Medicine, Natick, Mass., 2000—. Mem. ASHRAE (Ralph G. Nevins award 1979), ASME, Japanese. Soc. Heating Air Conditioning and Sanitation Engrs., Eta Kappa Nu, Sigma Xi, Sigma Pi Sigma, Pi Tau Sigma, Phi Kappa Phi, Pine Orchard Yacht Club. Lutheran. Achievements include research in biothermal, environmental sensory, air quality, RFR research, human thermo-physiological response modeling and simulation. Home: 156 Lakeside Dr Lebanon CT 06249-2822 Office: US-ARIEM Kansas St Natick MA 01760 Office Phone: 508-233-4833. Business E-Mail: larry.berglund@na.amedd.army.mil.

BERGLUND, ROBIN G., psychiatrist, management consultant; b. Milw., Oct. 12, 1945; s. Gunnar E. and V. June (Huebsch) B.; children: Victoria S., Christopher F.; m. Akiko Haraguchi, Oct., 2000; 1 child, Liri. BS in Biochemistry magna cum laude, Mich. State U., 1967; MBA, Harvard U., 1971; MD, Med. Univ. S.C., 1995. Engr. Eastman Kodak Co., Rochester, NY, 1967-69; v.p. The First Nat. Bank of Chgo., 1971-75, Wells Fargo Bank,

N.A., L.A., 1975-77; exec. v.p. Ponderosa Homes, Newport Beach, Calif., 1977-84; chmn., CEO Glenfed Devel. Corp., Encino, Calif., 1984-88; pres. Lowe Enterprises Northwest, Seattle, 1988-89, Met. Homes Inc., Portland, Oreg., 1989-90; pediatrician UCLA-Cedars Sinai Med. Ctr., L.A., 1995-96; psychiatrist UCLA Neuropsychiatric Inst. and Hosp., 1996-98, child psychiatrist, 1998-2000; pvt. practice child and adult psychiatry, 2000—. Bd. dirs. United Svc. Orgn., Hollywood, Calif., 1975-80, Am. Youth Soccer Orgn., Newport Beach, Calif., 1980-84, Waring Libr. Soc., Charleston, 1992-95; scoutmaster Boy Scouts of Am., San Marino, Calif., 1984-89; vol. Children's Hosp., Seattle, 1990-91. Nat. Merit and Nat. Honor Soc. scholar, Mich. State U., 1964-67. Mem. Am. Psychiat. Assn., Am. Acad. Child & Adolescent Psychiatry, Young Pres.'s Orgn., Blue Key, Phi Kappa Phi, Phi Eta Sigma, Delta Phi Epsilon, Omicron Delta Kappa. Avocations: travel, sailing. Office Phone: 818-784-4706.

BERGMAN, ARLENE, lawyer; b. NYC; BS, Adelphi U., 1974, MS, 1975; RN, CUNY, 1984; JD, Yeshiva U., 1990. Bar: NY 1991, US Dist. Ct. So. Dist. NY, US Dist. Ct. Ea. Dist. NY. Tchr. learning disabled; pvt. duty nurse; staff nurse Meml. Sloan Kettering Cancer Ctr.; joined Wilson, Elser, Moskowitz, Edelman & Dicker LLP, NYC, 1997, now ptnr. Office: Wilson Elser Moskowitz Edelman & Dicker LLP 23rd Fl 150 E 42nd St New York NY 10017-5639 Office Phone: 212-490-3000 ext. 2542. Office Fax: 212-490-3038. Business E-Mail: bergmana@wemed.com.

BERGMAN, BARBARA E., law educator; BA, Bradley U., 1973; JD, Stanford Law Sch., 1976. Bar: Calif., DC, N.Mex. Law clerk for Judge Ben C. Duniway, 9th Cir.; practiced law Wilmer, Cutler, and Pickering, DC; assoc. counsel Pres. Jimmy Carter; staff atty. Pub. Defender Svc., DC; practiced labor law Bredhoff & Kaiser; prof., evidence/trial practice, advocacy and criminal procedure U N.Mex., 1987—. Tchr. Nat. Inst. for Trial Advocacy programs, Nat. Criminal Def. Coll., Inst. for Criminal Def. Advocacy; team leader Nat. Inst. for Trial Advocacy Nat. Program, Boulder, Colo. Co-author: Every Trial Criminal Defense Resource Book, 1994, Wharton's Criminal Evidence, 15th edit.; editor: New Mexico Criminal Practice Manual, DC Criminal Jury Instructions, 4th edit.; contbr. articles to profl. jours. Recipient Richard S. Jacobson award, Roscoe Pound Found. Mem.: Nat. Assn. of Criminal Def. Lawyers (pres.-elect, has served as first v.p., second v.p., treas., sec., and bd. dir., past chair, Budget Com. and Investment Com., past co-chair, Amicus Curiae Com., Robert C. Heeney award 2000). Office: UNM Sch Law MSC11 6070 Office 3115 1 University of New Mexico Albuquerque NM 87131-0001 Address: UNM Sch Law 1117 Stanford NE Albuquerque NM 87131-0001 also: Nat Assn of Criminal Def Lawyers 1150 18th St NW Ste 950 Washington DC 20036 Office Phone: 505-277-3304. Office Fax: 505-277-4594. Business E-Mail: bergman@law.umn.edu.

BERGMAN, BRUCE E., municipal official; m.; 2 children. BA, Simpson Coll., 1970; JD, U. Houston, 1972. Clk. to Hon. M.E. Rawlings Iowa Supreme Ct., 1973-74; assoc. Williams, Hart, Lavorato & Kirtley, West Des Moines, Iowa, 1974-78, ptnr., 1978-79, Davis, Baker & Bergman, Des Moines, 1980-85, Isaacson, Clarke & Bergman, P.C., Des Moines, 1985-89; asst. city atty. City of Des Moines Legal Dept., 1989-90, solicitor, 1990-91, chief solicitor, 1991-96, corp. counsel, 1996—. Mem.: ABA, Internat. Municipal Lawyers Assn. (regional v.p. 2003—), Iowa Mcpl. Attys. Assn. (bd. dir. 1996—99, 2002—, sec., treas. 2003, v.p. 2004, pres. 2005), Polk County Bar Assn., Iowa State Bar Assn. Home: 4508 49th St Des Moines IA 50310-2970 Office: Office of the Corp Counsel City of Des Moines City Hall 400 E 1st St Des Moines IA 50309 Office Phone: 515-283-4130. E-mail: bebergman@dmgov.org.

BERGMAN, CHARLES CABE, foundation executive; b. May 1, 1933; s. Sidney Meyer and Esther Rachel (Cabe) B. AB, Harvard U., 1954. Account asst. Ketchum, MacLeod & Grove, Inc., Pitts., 1955-57; assoc. dir. devel. and alumni affairs Browne & Nichols Sch., Cambridge, Mass., 1957-59; assoc. v.p. Lavin Co., Inc., Boston and NYC, 1959-61; v.p. People to People Health Fedn., Washington, 1962-63, Inter-Am. Found. for the Arts, NYC, 1963-65; exec. v.p., treas., trustee Acad. Religion and Mental Health, NYC, 1965-72; exec. v.p., COO, dir. Inst. Religion and Health, 1972-78; sr. assoc. Jeffcoat Schoen & Morrell, 1981-82; exec. v.p., COO Pollock-Krasner Found., Inc., NYC, 1985-99, chmn. bd., CEO, 1999—. Cons. UN Ctr. on Transnat. Corps., 1979-80; dir. George Nelson & Co., N.Y.C. Cons. Adminstrv. Psychiatry Program, Yale Med. Sch., New Haven, 1971, NIMH, Argentina, 1969, Ctr. for Studies Child and Family Mental Health, NIMH, Washington, 1971; spl. adviser Pres.'s Com. on Mental Retardation, Washington, 1971, White House Conf. on Children and Youth, Washington, 1970, Maurice Falk Med. Fund, 1971; vis. lectr. U. Colo.; Presdl. fellow Aspen Inst. Humanistic Studies; mem. cultural adv. comm. N.Y.C. Dept. Cultural Affairs. Chmn. internat. coun. Am. Field Svc. Internat. Intercultural Programs; bd. dirs. The Alliance for Young Artists and Writers, Inc., NY, VSA Arts, Washington, Delfina Studios Trust, London, The Nat. Found. for Advancement in the Arts, Miami, Fla.; mem. bd. advisors Fund for Arts and Culture in Ctrl. and East Europe; bd. artistic advisors Creative Artists Network; former panelist NY State Coun. on Arts Visual Arts Program; mem. N.Y. State Coun. on Arts, 1999—; sr. advisor Foursome Investments, Ltd., London; adv. bd. Lucy Daniels Found., Raleigh, NC; mem. overseers' com. to visit Harvard U. Art Mus.; mem. NYC Cultural Affairs Adv. Com.; bd. dirs. Rubin Mus. Art. Home: 24 E 82nd St # 4C New York NY 10028-0344 Office: 863 Park Ave New York NY 10021-0342 Office Phone: 212-517-5400. Business E-Mail: cbergman@pkf.org.

BERGMAN, DONALD ARTHUR, endocrinologist, educator; b. Bklyn., Apr. 6, 1946; s. Joseph and Clara Bergman; m. Susan Menin, June 23, 1970; 1 child, Melissa. AB, Dartmouth Coll., 1967; MD, Jefferson Med. Coll., 1971. Diplomate Am. Bd. Internal Medicine, Am. Bd. Internal Medicine. Ob-gyn. resident Mt. Sinai Hosp., N.Y.C., 1971—72; med. intern NYU Hosps., N.Y.C., 1972—73; med. resident Mt. Sinai Hosp., N.Y.C., 1973—75, endocrinology fellow, 1975—77; pvt. practice N.Y.C., 1977—; asst. clin. prof. medicine Mt. Sinai Sch. Medicine, N.Y.C., 1984—97, assoc. clin. prof., 1997—2004, clin. prof., 2004—. Co-author: Mount Sinai Book of Nutrition, Clinical Practice Guidelines for Physicians-Thyroid Cancer, 2000; contbr. articles to profl. jours.; assoc. editor: Endocrine Practice, 1996—99. Bd. dirs. N.Y. Menopause Ctr., 1997—. Capt. USAR, 1971—77. Fellow: ACP, Am. Coll. Endocrinology (sec.-treas. 2000—01, trustee 2000—01, chancellor 2004—05); mem.: Endocrine Soc., Am. Assn. Clin. Endocrinologists (bd. dirs. 1993—, chair practice stds. com. 1995—97, state chpts. chair 1997—2002, sec. 1999—2000, treas. 2000—01, v.p. 2001—02, co-chmn. corp. adv. bd. 2002—03, pres.-elect 2002—03, co-chmn. ann. meeting 2003, pres. 2003—04, chair power prevention com. 2004—, pres.-elect 2005—). Office: 1199 Park Ave Apt (1f) New York NY 10128-1713

BERGMAN, EDWARD JONATHAN, lawyer, educator; b. Jersey City, Aug. 10, 1942; s. Abe and Ethel (Leitner) B.; m. Jennifer Shapiro, Feb. 1, 1969 (div.); children: Peter Jeremy, Jennifer Amy. BA, U. Pa., 1963; JD, Columbia U., 1966. Bar: N.J. 1974, U.S. Dist. Ct. N.J. 1974, U.S. Supreme Ct. 1989. Ptnr. Bergman & Barrett, Princeton, N.J., 1975—; pub. defender Princeton Borough, 1986—, Princeton Twp., 1988—; fed. mediator U.S. Dist. Ct., N.J., 1992—; mediator N.J. Superior Ct., 1995—. Lectr. Woodrow Wilson Sch., Princeton U., 1990-92, dept. politics, 2003-; affiliated faculty U. Pa. Wharton Sch. of Bus. Dept. of Legal Studies, Phila., 1995—; vis. lectr. U. Calif. at Berkeley, St. Petersburg U. Joint Mgmt. Program, Russia, 1995-99; acad. dir. negotiation workshops IGE Ltd., India, 1999-2000; cert. comml. mediator NJ Assn. Profl. Mediators. Author: (with J. Bickerman) Court-Annexed Mediation: Perspectives on Selected State & Federal Programs, 1998; contbr. articles to profl. jours. Trustee Princeton Ballet, 1984-92, Arts Coun. Princeton, 1998-2003. Mem. ABA (sec. on dispute resolution, mediation com., vice-chmn. subcom. on ct.- annexed dispute resolution, mem., sec. dispute resolution publs. bd.), N.J. Bar Assn., Mercer County Bar Assn., Princeton Bar Assn. (pres. 1986-87), Penn Basketball Club (exec. bd. 1995—), Penn Club N.Y. Avocations: wine, food, travel, sports, art and architecture. Home: 95 Wilson Rd Princeton NJ 08540-2601 Office: Bergman & Barrett PO Box 1273 Princeton NJ 08542-1273 Business E-Mail: ejb@gear3.net.

BERGMAN, GEORGE MARK, mathematician, educator; b. Bklyn., July 22, 1943; s. Lester V. and Sylvia G. (Bernstein) B.; m. Mary Frances Anderson, Dec. 26, 1981; stepsons: Jeff Elam, Michael L. Anderson; children: Clifford I. and Rebecca N. Anderson-Bergman (twins). BA, U. Calif., Berkeley, 1963; PhD, Harvard U., 1968. Asst. prof. Dept. Math. U. Calif., Berkeley, 1967-72, assoc. prof., 1972-78, prof., 1978—. Contbr. articles to profl. jours. Mem. AAUP, Am. Math. Soc. Democrat. Avocations: linguistics, folk-dancing. Office: U Calif Dept Math Berkeley CA 94720-3840

BERGMAN, HAROLD EVERETT, actor, retired lawyer, banker; b. Milw., Apr. 19, 1919; s. Harold E. Bergman and Irene Alma Schwab; m. Rosalie Grimes, July 18, 1943 (div. Mar. 1981); children: Karen, Jill, Nancy, Jane; m. Jeanne Marie Anspach, July 4, 1982 (dec. Oct. 1989); m. Mary V. Utz, Sept. 1, 2001. BS in Psychology, U. Ill., 1942; JD, U. Fla., 1950; MA in Speech, Fla. State U., 1955. Bar: Fla. 1950. Personal injury adjustor Travelers Ins. Co., Chgo., 1945—47; claims supr. Indemnity Ins. Co. N.Am., Chgo., 1947—48; sole law practice Gadsden County, Fla., 1950, 1953—56; pub. rels. dir. Tallahassee Fed. Savs. and Loan Assn., 1956—58; stockbroker A.M. Kidder & Co., Tallahassee, 1958—60; br. mgr. Security Assocs., Tallahassee, 1960—62, Halsey, Stuart & Co., Jacksonville, Fla., 1962—64, Francis I. DuPont, Miami Beach, Fla., 1964—66; pres. B-Trio Corp., Fla. and Tex., 1966—67; instl. rep. Prudential-Bache, Miami, Fla., 1967—84; profl. actor, 1973—. Lectr. in bus. law Fla. State U., Tallahassee, 1958—62. Author: The Teatro Olimpico of Vicenza, Italy, 1955; author, translator Selected Items from Der Nord-Westen Manitowoc Co., Wis., 1874-1887, 2001, Selected Items from Der Nord-Westen Manitowoc Co., Wis., 1888-1897, 2002, Selected Items from Der Nord-Westen Manitowoc Co., Wis., 1898-1901, 2003, author, translator Selected Items from Der Nord-Westen Manitowoc Co., Wis., 1902-1905, 1906-1909, 2003, 2004; actor: (plays) Plaza Suite, 1973, Catch 22, 1974, Clarence Darrow, 1977, Cyrano, 1978, The Shadow Box, 1979, Glengarry Glen Ross, 1988, Other People's Money, 1991, Broken Glass, 1994, (opera) Abduction from the Seraglio, 1978; (films) Final Countdown, 1979, Nobody's Perfekt, 1981, Harry and Son, 1983, Cocoon, 1984, Whoops, Apocalypse!, 1986, Cocoon, the Return, 1988, Somebody Has to Shoot the Picture, 1990, A Woman's Right, 1992, Radioland Murders, 1994; (TV series) Miami Vice, B.L. Stryker, Matlock, Key West, South Beach, Dawson's Creek. Staff sgt. MRTC, 1942, spl. agt. Counter Intelligence Corps, 1943—45, spl. agt. Counter Intelligence Corps, 1951—53, commd. USAR, 1947. Nominee, South Fla. Carbonell award, 1991; recipient, 1977, Bill Hindman award, 2000, Founders' award, Profl. Actors Assn. Fla., Inc., 1997. Mem.: AFTRA, SAG (Fla. coun. 1989—99, v.p. Fla. coun. 1994—98, nat. bd. 1993—99, 7th nat. v.p. 1995—97, fin. com. 1993—99, Svc. award Fla. coun. 1999), Am. Guild Musical Artists, Actors Equity Assn., Nat. Counterintelligence Corps Assn., Alpha Kappa Psi, Phi Alpha Delta. Presbyterian. Avocation: genealogy. Home: 4744 NW 49th Ct Tamarac FL 33319

BERGMAN, HERMAS JOHN (JACK BERGMAN), retired college administrator; b. May 3, 1926; s. Ruebin Eric and Esther (Schierman) Bergman; m. Jeanne Louise Culton, 1946 (div. 1961); children: Stephen, Kathleen, Marsha; m. Evelyn Alice Templeman, Apr. 6, 1963; children: Kristin, Robert. BA, Walla Walla Coll., 1948; MA, U. Puget Sound, 1963; PhD, Wash. State U., 1967. Tchr. Wash. Pub. Schs., Wenatchee and Tacoma, 1948—58, 1961—64; bus. mgr. Totem Plywood, Inc., Tacoma, 1958—61; prof. history Western Oreg. U., Monmouth, 1966—79, dean Liberal Arts and Scis., 1980—85; pres. Walla Walla Coll., College Place, Wash., 1985—90; ret., 1990. Author: The Religious Fringe; contbr. articles to profl. jours. Chmn. bd. commrs. Polk County Parks and Recreation Commn., Dallas, Oreg., 1977—80; nat. adv. coun. Am. United for Separation of Ch. and State, 1992—2001; bd. trustees Walla Walla Gen. Hosp., 1985—; chmn. bd. Internat. Children's Care Inc., Vancouver, Wash., 1981—89; bd. dirs. Walla Walla Symphony, 2003—; mem. exec. com. Oreg. Conf. Seventh-day Adventists, 1981—85; v.p. Wash. State Religious Liberty Assn. of Pacific N.W., 1991—2001; mem. exec. com. North Pacific Conf. Seventh-day Adventists, 1985—90; bd. dirs. Portland Adventist Med. Ctr., 1972—78, 1985—90, Ind. Colls. of Wash., Seattle, 1985—90, United Way of Walla Walla, 1988—91, Wash. Friends of Higher Edn., Seattle, 1985—90. Avocations: photography, geology, stamps, lapidary.

BERGMAN, JANET EISENSTEIN, food industry executive; b. N.Y., Jan. 28, 1959; d. T. Donald and Ellen (Roob) Eisenstein; m. David J. Bergman, July 14, 1985; 1 child, Jennifer Sarah. BA, Yale U., New Haven, Conn., 1981; MBA, Harvard U., Boston, 1985. Analyst asst. v.p. Putman Mgmt. Co., Boston, 1985-88; corp. v.p. Sara Lee Corp., Chgo., 1989—93, exec. dir., 1988—89, v.p., investor relations and corp. affairs, 1993—2001, sr. v.p., investor relations and corp. affairs Chgo., 2001—. Mem. Charted Finl. Analyst., Econ. Club (Chgo.). Avocations: reading, cooking.

BERGMAN, JAY, history educator; b. Youngstown, Ohio, Nov. 10, 1948; s. Moe and Hannah (Goodelman) B.; m. Julie Tina Barsel, Feb. 7, 1987; 1 child, Aaron Samuel. BA, Brandeis U., 1970; MA, Yale U., 1972, MPhil, 1973, PhD, 1977. Vis. instr. history Va. Commonwealth U., Richmond, 1978-79; vis. asst. prof. history U. Miami, Coral Gables, Fla., 1979-81; asst. prof. history Albright Coll., Reading, Pa., 1981-85, assoc. prof. history, 1985-90, Ctrl. Conn. State U., New Britain, 1990-94, prof. history, 1994—. Author: Vera Zasulich: A Biography, 1983; contbr. articles to profl. jours. Mem. Nat. Assn. Scholars. Jewish. Office: Ctrl Conn State U 1615 Stanley St New Britain CT 06053-2439 Office Phone: 860-832-2811. E-mail: bergmanj@ccsu.edu.

BERGMAN, LOWELL, television news producer; b. N.Y.C., July 24, 1945; s. Alexander Bergman and Alice (Malerman) Perlmutter; m. Sharon D. Tiller, Nov. 13, 1986; children: Jake, Josh, Muir, Shon. BA, U. Wis., 1966; MA, U. Calif., San Diego, 1968. Freelance writer, San Francisco, 1972-75; assoc. editor Rolling Stone mag., San Francisco, 1975-76; pres. staff Ctr. for Investigative Reporting, San Francisco, 1977; producer, reporter ABC News, N.Y.C., 1978-81, dir. investigations, producer, 1981-83; producer 60 Minutes CBS News, N.Y.C., 1983—96, sr. investigator, producer, 1996—99; contributor N.Y. Times; producer, corr. Frontline PBS; vis. prof. U. Calif., Berkeley. Producer: (TV show segments) Nicaragua Libre for ABC's 20/20, 1980 (Emmy award 1980), The McMartin Preschool for 60 Minutes, 1986 (Emmy award 1986); reporter Organized Crime in Arizona series, 1976 (Writers and Authors award 1976). Co-recipient Pulitzer prize public service award, 2004; recipient Alfred I. Dupont Golden Baton, 1996, 2001, Peabody Award, 1993, 2001; fellow U. Calif., San Diego, 1966—68. Office: CBS News 60 Minutes 555 W 57th St New York NY 10019-2925

BERGMAN, MARILYN KEITH, lyricist, writer; b. Bklyn. d. Albert A. and Edith (Arkin) Katz; m. Alan Bergman, Feb. 9, 1958; 1 child, Julie Rachel. BA, NYU; MusD (hon.), Berklee Coll. Music, 1995, Trinity Coll., 1997. Lyricist, collaborator (with Alan Bergman) (numerous pop, theatrical and film score songs, TV themes) Bracken's World, 1969—70, The Sandy Duncan Show, 1972, Maude, 1972—78, Good Times, 1974—79, The Nancy Walker Show, 1976, The Dumplings, 1976, Alice, 1976—82, In the Heat of the Night, 1988—94, Brooklyn Bridge, 1991—93, The Powers That Be, 1993, TV film lyrics The Hands of Time (from Brian's Song), 1971, Queen of the Stardust Ballroom, 1975 (Emmy award for best dramatic underscore and best musical material, 1975, score only), Sybil, 1976 (Emmy award for best dramatic underscore 1976, 1976), Too Many Springs (from Hollow Image), 1979, theatrical scores Something More, 1964, Ballroom, 1978 (Grammy award nominee for best cast show album, 1979), The Lady and the Clarinet, 1980, feature film songs The Marriage Go-Round, from The Marriage Go-Round, 1960, Any Wednesday, from Any Wednesday, 1966, Make Me Rainbows, from Fitzwilly, 1967, (score) In the Heat of the Night, 1967, The Windmills of Your Mind, from the Thomas Crown Affair, 1968 (Acad. award for best song, 1968, Golden Globe award best original song, 1969), His Eyes, Her Eyes, from The Thomas Crown Affair, 1968, You Must Believe in Spring, from Young Girls of Rochefort, 1968, Maybe Tomorrow, from John and Mary, 1969, Tomorrow Is My Friend, from Gaily, Gaily, 1969, There's Enough to Go Around, 1969, A Smile, A Mem'ry and an Extra Shirt, from A Man Called Gannon, 1969, Sugar in the Rain, from Stiletto, 1969, What Are You Doing the Rest of You Life?, from The Happy Ending, 1969 (Acad. award nominee for best song, 1969), I Was Born in Love With You, from Wuthering Heights, 1970, Sweet Gingerbread Man, from The Magic Garden of Stanley Sweetheart, 1970, Nobody Knows, 1970, Move, from Move, 1970, Pieces of Dreams (Little Boy Lost), from Pieces of Dreams, 1970 (Academy award nominee for best song, 1970), The Costume Ball, from Doctors' Wives, 1971, All His Children, from Sometimes a Great Notion, 1971 (Acad. award nominee for best song, 1971), Rain Falls Anywhere It Wants To, from the African Elephant, 1971, The Summer Knows, from Summer of '42, 1971 (Grammy award nominee for song of the year 1972, 1972), A Face in the Crowd, from Le Mans, 1971, Marmalade, Molasses and Honey, from The Life and Times of Judge Roy Bean, 1972 (Acad. award nominee for best song, 1972), Love's the Only Game in Town, from Pete and Tillie, 1972, Molly and Lawless John, 1972, The Way We Were, from The Way We Were, 1973 (Grammy award for song of the year, 1973, Acad. award for best song, 1973, Golden Globe award for best original song, 1974, Grammy award for best original score, 1974), Breezy's Song, from Breezy, 1973, In Every Corner of the World, from Forty Carats, 1973, Summer Wishes, Winter Dreams, from Summer Wishes, Winter Dreams, 1973, Easy Baby, from 99 and 44/100%, 1974, There'll Be Time, from Ode to Billy Joe, 1975, Evening Sun, Morning Moon, from The Yakuza, 1975, I Believe in Love, from A Star is Born, 1976 (Grammy award nomination best original score, 1977), I'm Harry, I'm Walter, from Harry and Walter Go to New York, 1976, Hello and Goodbye, from Noon to Three, 1976, Bobby Deerfield, from Bobby Deerfield, 1977, The Last Time I Felt Like This, from Same Time Next Year, 1978 (Acad. award nominee for best song, 1978), The One and Only, from The One and Only, 1978, There's Something Funny Goin' On, from ...And Justice For All, 1979, I'll Never Say Goodbye, from The Promise, 1979 (Acad. award nominee for best song, 1979), Where Do You Catch the Bus for Tomorrow, from A Change of Seasons, 1980, Ask Me No Questions, from Back Roads, 1981, How Do You Keep the Music Playing?, from Best Friends, 1982 (Acad. award nominee for best song, 1982), Think About Love, 1982, Comin' Home to You, from Author! Author!, 1982, Tootsie, from Tootsie, 1982, It Might Be You, 1982 (Acad. award nominee for best song, 1982, Grammy award nominee for best original score, 1983), If We Were in Love, from Yes, Giorgio, 1982 (Acad. award nominee for best song, 1982), Never Say Never Again, from Never Say Never again, 1983, Papa, Can You Hear Me?, from Yentl, 1983 (Academy award nomination best song, 1983), The Way He Makes Me Feel, 1983 (Acad. award nominee for best song, 1983), Will Someone Ever Look at Me That Way?, 1983 (Acad. award best original score and Grammy award nomination for best original score, 1984, Acad. award nominee for best original song, 1983), Yentl, 1983 (Acad. award for best original score, 1983), Little Boys, from The Man Who Loved Women, 1983, Something New in My Life, from Mickey and Maude, 1984, The Music of Goodbye, from Out of Africa, 1985, I Know the Feeling, from The January Man, 1989, The Girl Who Used to Be Me, from Shirley Valentine, 1989 (Acad. award nominee for best song, 1989, Golden Globe nominee for best original song, 1990, Grammy award nominee, 1990), Welcome Home, from Welcome Home, 1989, Most of All You, from Major League, 1989, Dreamland, from For the Boys, 1991, Places That Belong to You, from The Prince of Tides, 1991, It's All There, from Switch, 1991, Moonlight, from Sabrina, 1995 (Acad. award nominee for best original song, 1996, Golden Globe nominee, Grammy nominee), The Best of Friends, from Bogus, 1996, Love is Where You Are, from At First Sight, pop songs You Don't Bring Me Flowers, 1978 (Grammy award nominee for song of the year, 1978), In the Heat of the Night, The Summer Knows, Nice 'N' Easy (Grammy award nominee for song of the year, 1960), Someone in the Dark, L.A. Is My Lady, After the Rain, I Was Born in Love With You, That Face, Look Around, I Love to Dance Like They Used to Dance, What Matters Most, One Day, A Child Is Born, Sleep Warm, Sentimental Baby, Live It Up, If I Close My Eyes, Yellow Bird, Like a Lover, Where Do You Start?, On My Way to You, Ordinary Miracles (Cable Ace award and Emmy award for best original song), A Ticket to Dream (Emmy Awd. for best song), albums Never Be Afraid for Bing Crosby, The Ballad of the Blues for Jo Stafford, 1999, Barbra Streisand: The Concert (Ace nominee for writing of a spl.). Named to songwriters hall of Fame, 1980; recipient singers salute to songwriter award, Clooney Found., 1986, Aggie award, Songwriter's Guild, 1987; grantee Am. Film Inst., 1976. Mem.: ASCAP (pres., chmn. bd. dirs. 1994—). Office: ASCAP 7920 Sunset Blvd Ste 300 Los Angeles CA 90046

BERGMAN, NANCY PALM, real estate investment company executive; b. McKeesport, Pa., Dec. 3, 1938; d. Walter Vaughn and Nellie (Sullivan) Leech; m. Donald Bergman; 1 child, Tiffany Palm Taylor. Student, Mt. San Antonio Coll., 1970, UCLA, 1989-93. Corporate sec. U.S. Filter Corp., Newport Beach, Calif., 1965—. Pres. Jaguar Research Corp., L.A. and Atlanta, 1971-; owner Environ. Designs, L.A., 1976—; pres. Prosher Corp., L.A., 1978-83; now pres., dir. Futura Investments, L.A.; CEO Rescor, Inc. Author: Resident Managers Handbook. Home: 1255 Benedict Canyon Dr Beverly Hills CA 90210 also: 23540 Tapatia Rd Homeland CA 92548 Office: PO Box 15246 Beverly Hills CA 90209

BERGMAN, REńEE ROTH, music educator, pianist; b. N.Y.C., Apr. 5, 1922; d. Henry S. and Rose (Flaster) Roth; m. Reuben H. Bergman, Nov. 13, 1942; children: Roger Bergman, Richard Bergman, Robert Bergman, Randy Ritzyah Mitchell. Student, Juilliard Sch., 1931-38, BS in Piano, Edn., 1942; degree in para verbal therapy, Ursuline Coll., 1976; MA in Tchg., Manhattanville Coll., 1978. Cert. nat. music tchr., N.Y., Fla. Pvt. piano tchr., accompanist, Palm Beach County, Fla., 1940—; pvt. dance, music studio dir. New Rochelle, N.Y., 1942-46; primary supr. Temple Israel Rel Sch., New Rochelle, N.Y., 1940-76; music dir. teen summer theatre Roundabout, New Rochelle, N.Y., 1960-63; dir. summer day camp Riviera Shore Club, New Rochelle, N.Y., 1966-75; music specialist Windward Day Sch., White Plains, N.Y., 1969-75; gifted and talented, spl. edn. tchr. Columbus, Trinity, Battle Hill Schs., Wht. Plains, New Rochelle, N.Y., 1976-80; music tchr. St. Luke's Catholic Sch., Lake Worth, Fla., 1981-84, St. Mark's Catholic Sch., Boynton Beach, Fla., 1985—. Actress, playwright Onstage Little Theatre, New Rochelle, N.Y., 1950-63; pianist Palm Beach Piano Quartet, West Palm Beach, Fla., 1980-94. Fundraising performer polit. & charitable orgns., Westchester County, N.Y., 1942-72; summer mall concerts accompanist Dept. Recreation, New Rochelle, 1948-62; music chmn. city wide pub. schs. PTA, New Rochelle, 1950-60; dir., condr. sr. citizens cmty. chorus, Greenacres, Fla., 1981-91. Piano scholar Music Tchrs. Coun., New Rochelle, 1935-36. Mem. Music Teachers Nat. Assn., Fla. State Music Teachers Assn., Music Edn. League of Westchester. Avocations: golf, needlecrafts, travel. Home: 8407 Blue Cypress Dr Lake Worth FL 33467-6244

BERGMAN, RICHARD ISAAC, health information executive; b. Bklyn., Jan. 18, 1934; s. Joseph and Clara (Menchel) B.; m. Judith Hyman, June 24, 1956 (div. 1974); children: Deborah Jill, Susan Bergman Hackett; m. Victoria Smalley, June 9, 1987. SB, MIT, 1955, SM, 1956. Devel. engr. Exxon Rsch., Linden, N.J., 1956-60; mem. adj. faculty N.J. Inst. Tech., Newark, 1957-58; dir. engring. Princeton (N.J.) Chem. Rsch., 1960-67; exec. v.p. Systemedics, Inc., Princeton, 1967-80; pres. Savant Assocs., Inc., Princeton, 1980-98; exec. dir. White House Task Force on Workplace Safety and Health, Washington, 1977-78; pres. Project Masters, Inc., Princeton, 1980—. Mem. vis. com. med. dept. MIT, Cambridge, Mass., 1973-83, 86-88; Whitaker Coll., 1979-85, dir. Response Analysis Corp., Princeton, 1970-77; pres., dir. CWW, Inc., Princeton, 1998—. Contbr. articles to profl. jours.; patentee in field. Mem. AIChE (past chmn. N.J. sect.), Am. Chem. Soc., N.Y. Acad. Scis., MIT Alumni/ae Assn. (dir. 2000-03). Home: 134 Leabrook Ln Princeton NJ 08540-3622 Office: Project Masters Inc PO Box AG Princeton NJ 08542-0872 Office Phone: 609-921-0749. Personal E-mail: richard.bergman@verizon.net.

BERGMAN, ROBERT GEORGE, chemist, educator; b. Chgo., May 23, 1942; s. Joseph J. and Stella (Horowitz) Bergman; m. Wendy L. Street, June 17, 1965; children: David R., Michael S. BA in Chemistry cum laude, Carleton Coll., 1963, PhD (hon.), 1995; PhD, U. Wis., 1966. NATO fellow in chemistry Columbia U., NYC, 1966-67; Arthur Amos Noyes instr. chemistry Calif. Inst. Tech., Pasadena, 1967-69, asst. prof. chemistry, 1969-71, assoc. prof. chemistry, 1971-73, prof., 1973-77; prof. chemistry U. Calif., Berkeley, 1977—, asst. dean Coll. Chemistry, 1987-91, 96, Miller Rsch. prof., 1982-83, 93, 2003. Sherman Fairchild Disting. scholar Calif. Inst. Tech., 1984; mem. panel bioinorganic and metallobiochemistry study sect. NIH, 1977—80; cons. Union Carbide Corp., 1977—81, 1990—2001, E. I. DuPont de Nemours, 1982—85, Chevron Rsch. Co., 1983—89, Dow Chem. Co., 2001—02; disting. vis. prof. U. NC, Chapel Hill, 1999. Mem. editl. bd.: Chem. Revs., Jour. Am. Chem. Soc., Organometallics, Tetrahedron Publs., European Jour. Inorganic Chemistry; contbr. articles to profl. jours. Recipient Tchr. Scholar award, Camille and Henry Dreyfus Found., 1970—75, Excellence in Tchg. award, Calif. Inst. Tech., 1978, Merit award, NIH, 1991, E. O. Lawrence award for Chemistry, Dept. Energy, 1993, Chem. Pioneer award, Am. Inst. Chemists, 2000, Technology Transfer award, Lawrence Berkeley Nat. Lab., 2004; NIH fellow, 1964—66, Alfred P. Sloan Found. fellow, 1970—72, Guggenheim fellow, 1999. Mem.: NAS, AAAS, Am. Chem. Soc. (Organometallic Chemistry award 1986, Arthur C. Cope scholar 1987, Edward Fahs Smith award Pa. sect. 1990, Ira Remsen award Balt. sect. 1990, Arthur C. Cope award 1996, Edward Leete award 2001, James Flack Norris award 2003), Phi Beta Kappa, Phi Lambda Upsilon, Sigma Xi (Monie Ferst award 2003). Home: 501 Coventry Rd Kensington CA 94707-1316 Office: U Calif Dept Chemistry Berkeley CA 94720-0001 E-mail: bergman@cchem.berkeley.edu.

BERGMAN, RUTH CHRISTINE, elementary school educator; b. N.Y.C., Dec. 8, 1924; d. Frank Albert and Ruth Mathilda (Meyer) Bergman. B in edn., New Paltz State Tchrs. Coll., 1944; MA, Columbia U., 1954, EdD, 1965. Organist St. Andrew's Episc. Ch., New Paltz, NY, 1942—46; tchr. Walden Pub. Sch., Walden, NY, 1944—45, Poughkeepsie Pub. Sch., Poughkeepsie, NY, 1945—46, Valley Stream Pub. Schs., Valley Stream, NY, 1950; sec. Grad. Sch. of Bus., Columbia U., N.Y.C., NY, 1951—52; tchr. White Plains (N.Y.) Pub. Schs., 1953—75; instr. geography City Coll. of NY, N.Y.C., NY, 1965; ret., 1979. Author various film strips. Mem.: No. Westchester Retired Tchrs. Assn., White Plains Retired Educators Organ., Nat. Coun. for Geographic Edn., Assn. Am. Geographers, Am. Geographical Soc. Republican. Episco. Avocations: photography, piano, nursing homes. Home: 870 Long Hill Rd W PO Box 8974 Scarborough NY 10510-8974

BERGMAN, STANLEY M., health products executive; CPA. V.p. fin. and adminstrn. Henry Schein, Inc., Melville, NY, 1980-85, exec. v.p., 1985-89, chmn., CEO, pres., 1989—, bd. dir., 1982—. Office: Henry Schein Inc 135 Duryea Rd Melville NY 11747*

BERGMAN, VICTORIA BESTERMAN, small business owner, consultant; b. Covington, Ky., Aug. 22, 1944; d. John Joseph and Marion Julia (Schlueter) Besterman; m. Ralph D. Smalley, June 6, 1966 (div. Sept. 1975); m. Richard I. Bergman, June 9, 1987. BA in Polit. Sci., U. Cin., 1966, MA in Pub. Adminstrn., 1969. Adminstr., organizer state and local govt., Cin., 1966-72; project coord., planner Health Svcs., Atlantic County, N.J., 1972-73; program and budget analyst, spl. asst. to Asst. Commnr. N.J. State Govt., Trenton, 1973-77; pub. affairs officer, staff spl. reorgn. project, adminstr. U.S. Govt., EOP, Washington, 1977-81; v.p. Savant Assocs., Inc., Princeton, NJ, 1981—98. Adj. faculty in pub. adminstrn. Trenton State Coll., 1973-77; v.p. Project Masters, Inc., 1981—. Founder Princeton Cmty. Without Walls; past co-chair Princeton U. Summer Chamber Concerts Com.; founder Women's PAC of N.J., past co-chair; founder N.J. Women's Network, past trustee; mem. Princeton Twp. Zoning Bd. Adjustment, 1989—96, chair, 1995—96; mem. Regional Planning Bd. Princeton, 2000—05, chair, 2001—04, vice chair, 2004—05. Mem.: Am. Soc. Pub. Adminstrn. (past bd. dirs. sect. women in pub. adminstrn., regions I and II liaison, coun. and coms. mem. N.J. chpt., natural resources sect. environ. adminstrn. sect.), U. Cin. Alumni Assn. (Outstanding Disting. Alumna award). Avocations: reading current fiction, singing, walking, hiking. Office: Project Masters Inc PO Box AG Princeton NJ 08542-0872 Office Phone: 609-921-0749. Personal E-mail: vicky.bergman@verizon.net.

BERGMANN, ARTHUR M., writer, retired journalist, retired county official; b. N.Y., Nov. 24, 1927; s. Augustus H. Bergmann. BS in Polit. Sci. and Pub. Adminstrn., Empire State Coll., SUNY, Old Westbury, 1974; M in Pub. and Gen. Adminstrn., L.I.U., 1979. Cert. arbitrator. With N.Y. Herald Tribune, 1945-63; asst. news editor Riverhead News, 1949-50; Suffolk County (N.Y.) corr. for N.Y.C. newspapers, 1949-63; news editor Moriches (N.Y.) Tribune, 1950-51; mem. staff Newsday, 1951-71, Suffolk County polit. editor, columnist, 1965-71; chief dep. Suffolk County Exec., Hauppauge, NY, 1972-79. Chmn. Suffolk Criminal Justice Coordinating Coun., 1975-79, Arson Action Com.-Suffolk Arson Task Force, 1975-77, MTA Permanent Citizens Adv. Com., 1978-79; adv. coun. N.Y. State Crime Victims Compensation Bd., 1978-79; trustee Suffolk Acad. Medicine, 1974. Served with USAAF, 1946-47. Recipient Disting. Svc. award United Jewish Appeal, 1976; Pub. Adminstrn. award C. W. Post Coll., 1977; Disting. Svc. plaque L.I. Assn. Commerce & Industry, 1977; Exemplary Svc. award Empire State Coll., SUNY, 1981; nominated for Pulitzer prize (2). Mem. Acad. Polit. Sci., Soc. Silurians, Am. Legion, Moriches Yacht Club (past commodore, Center Moriches, N.Y.), Pi Alpha Alpha. Address: 2403 24th Way West Palm Beach FL 33407

BERGMANN, BARBARA ROSE, economics professor; b. N.Y.C., July 20, 1927; d. Martin and Nellie Berman; m. Fred H. Bergmann, July 16, 1965; children: Sarah Nellie, David Martin. BA, Cornell U., 1948; MA, Harvard U., 1955, PhD, 1959; PhD (hon.), De Montford U., 1996, Muhlenberg Coll., 2000. Economist U.S. Bur. Labor Stats., N.Y.C., 1949-53; sr. staff ecomomist, cons. Council Econ. Advisors, Washington, 1961-62; sr. staff Brookings Inst., Washington, 1963-65; sr. econ. advisor AID, Washington, 1966-67; assoc. prof. U. Md., College Park, 1965-71, prof. econs., 1971-88; disting. prof. econs. Am. U., Washington, 1988-97, prof. emeritus, 1997—. Author: (with Chinitz and Hoover) Projection of a Metropolis, 1961; (with George W. Wilson) Impact of Highway Investment on Development, 1966; (with David E. Kaun) Structural Unemployment in the U.S., 1967; (with Robert Bennett) A Microsimulated Transactions Model of the United States Economy, 1985, The Economic Emergence of Women, 1986, Saving Our Children from Poverty: What the United States Can Learn from France, 1996, In Defense of Affirmative Action, 1996, Is Social Security Broke? A Cartoon Guide to the Issues, 1999, (with Suzanne W. Helburn) America's Child Care Problem: The Way Out, 2002; mem. editl. bd. Am. Econ. Rev., 1970-73, Challenge, 1978—, Signs, 1978-85; columnist econ. affairs N.Y. Times, 1981-82. Mem. Economists for McGovern, 1977; mem. panel econ. advisors Congl. Budget Office, Washington, 1977-87; mem. price adv. com. U.S. council on Wage and Price Stability, 1979-80. Mem. AAUP (coun. 1980-83, pres. 1990-92), Am. Econ. Assn. (v.p. 1976, adv. com. to U.S. Census Bur. 1977-82), Ea. Econ. Assn. (pres. 1974), Internat. Assn. for Feminist Econs. (pres. 1999), Soc. for Advancement of Socio-Econs. (pres. 1995-96). Democrat. Home: 5430 41st Pl NW Washington DC 20015-2911 E-mail: bbergman@umd.edu, bberg@american.edu.

BERGMANN, DONALD GERALD, pharmaceutical company executive; b. Aug. 13, 1949; s. Edgar Frank and Dorothy Bertha Bergmann; m. Kathy Jeanne Dumont, Sept. 4, 1976; children: Karen Ann, Kim Jeanne. BS, Mich. State U., 1972; PhD, Ohio State U., 1978. Rschr. UCLA, 1978-81; project leader Burroughes-Wellcome Co., Kansas City, Kans., 1981-83; scientist Genentech, Inc., South San Francisco, Calif., 1983, ops. mgr., 1983-87, sr. project mgr., 1987-88; dir. biopharm. mfg. SmithKline Beecham Pharms., Phila., 1988-91, group dir. biopharm. tech. ops., 1991-95, gen. mgr. biopharms., 1995-2000; gen. mgr. global biopharms. GlaxoSmithKline Pharms., Phila., 2001—04; sr. v.p. ops. Tengion, Inc., Phila., 2005—. Contbr. articles to profl. jours. and publs. Fellow Nat. Cancer Inst., 1978-80; grantee Nat. Cancer Inst., Am. Cancer Soc. Mem.: Pharm. Rsch. and Mfrs. Am. (lectr., com. chair, steering com.), Internat. Soc. Pharm. Engring. (lectr.). Avocations: skiing, wine collecting.

BERGMANN, EUGENE B., museum executive; b. N.Y.C., June 6, 1938; s. Benno and Marjorie (Crosby) B. m. to Allison, two sons. B. Indsl. Design, Pratt Inst., 1959. Exhibit designer various comml. exhibit companies, N.Y.C., 1960-66; with Am. Mus. Natural History, 1967—2003, sr. exhibit designer, 1983—2003. Author, Excelsior, You Fathead! The Art and Enigma of Jean Shepherd, 2005, Contbr. articles to profl. jours. Served to lt. U.S. Army, 1960.

BERGMANN, PETER GEORGE, lawyer; b. N.Y.C., July 1, 1949; s. Paul and Therese (Greenfield) B.; m. Kay Kirstine Gardiner, Oct. 13, 1991. BA, NYU, 1970; JD with honors, George Washington U., 1973. Law clk to Hon. James T. Foley U.S. Dist. Ct. (no. dist.) N.Y., Albany, 1973-74; ptnr. Cadwalader Wickersham & Taft, N.Y.C., 1974—, chmn., Health Care & Not-for-Profit dept. Recipient Reverend Parks award St. Margaret's House, 1992. Mem. ABA (past chmn. Regional Forum on Health Law), N.Y. State Bar Assn., Assn. Bar City of N.Y., Fed. Bar Council, N.Y. County Lawyers Assn. (past chmn. com. health svcs.), Assn. Trial Lawyers Am., N.Y. Assn. Homes and Svcs. for Aging (gen. counsel, chmn. legal com. 1998-2000), Am. Assn. Homes for Aging (chmn. reimbursement/legal subcom.). Office: Cadwalader Wickersham & Taft LLP 1 World Fin Ctr New York NY 10281 Office Phone: 212-504-6595. Office Fax: 212-504-6666. Business E-Mail: peter.bergmann@cwt.com.

BERGMANN, WILLIAM J., personnel director; b. Dubuque, Iowa, Apr. 5, 1939; s. George John Bergmann and Martha Brehm; m. Karen Ann Kreps, Dec. 26, 1964; children: Kathleen S., John W. BA, Loras Coll., 1963; MSIR, Loyola U., Chgo., 1964. Group human resource mgr. Clow Corp., Oak Brook, Ill., 1968—78; mgr. human resources Lifetime Foam, North Lake, Ill., 1978—79; mgr. employee rels. Sara Lee Corp., Chgo., 1979—81; safety mgr. NIPSCO, Hammond, Ind., 1981—83; dir. employee rels. Am. Bakeries, N.Y.C., 1983—88; pers. dir. Stroehman Bakeries, Horsham, Pa., 1988—95; human resources dir. Perdue Farms, Milford, Del., 1995—. Mem. steering com. Project Impact, Milford United Way, Transitions; mem. Govs. Welfare Employment Com. Served with USNR, 1956—62. Mem.: Delmarva Human Resource Mgmt., Soc. Human Resource Mgmt. Avocations: golf, tennis. Home: 730 Bicentennial Blvd Dover DE 19904 Office: Perdue Farms 255 N Rehoboth Blvd Milford DE 19963 Business E-Mail: bill.bergman@perdue.com.

BERGNER, JANE COHEN, lawyer; b. Schenectady, NY, Apr. 6, 1943; d. Louis and Selma (Breslaw) Cohen; m. Alfred P. Bergner, May 30, 1968 (dec. Sept. 24, 2002); children: Lauren, Justin. AB, Vassar Coll., 1964; LLB, Columbia U., 1967. Bar: DC 1968, U.S. Dist. Ct. DC 1968, U.S. Ct. Appeals (DC cir.) 1968, U.S. Ct. Fed. Claims 1969, U.S. Ct. Appeals (fed. cir.) 1969, U.S. Tax Ct. 1979, U.S. Supreme Ct. 1992. Trial atty. tax divsn. U.S. Dept. Justice, Washington, 1967-74; assoc. Arnold & Porter, Washington, 1974-76, Rogovin, Huge & Lenzner, Washington, 1976-83; of counsel Arter & Hadden, 1983-86; ptnr. Spriggs & Hollingsworth, 1986-89, Feith & Zell, P.C., 1989-93; pvt. practice Washington, 1993—. Mem. jud. confs. U.S. Ct. Fed. Claims, U.S. Tax Ct. Author: Tax Court Practice and Court of Federal Claims Practice, West's Federal Forms, 2005; contbr. articles to profl. jours. Bd. dirs. Jewish Social Svc. Agy., Washington; former mem. cmty. adv. bd. Sta. WAMU-FM, Washington. Fellow Am. Coll. Tax Counsel; mem. ABA (sect. taxation, govt. rels. com., ct. procedure com., civil and criminal penalties com., chmn. subcom. important devels. 1991-93, chmn. regional liaison meetings com. 1993-95, sect. litig.); Vassar Coll. Class Alumnae (chair spl. gifts com. 25th reunion), DC Bar (chair taxation sect. 1985-90, chair tax audits and litig. com. 1990-93, Outstanding Sect. award 1986, Cmty. Outreach award 1993), Fed. Bar Assn., Women's Bar Assn. DC, Washington Estate Planning Coun., Women's Tax Luncheon Group, Columbia U. Law Sch. Alumni Assn., Svc. Guild Washington, Vassar Club. Office: Ste 650 1615 L St NW Washington DC 20036 Office Phone: 202-626-8215. Business E-Mail: jbergnerlaw@abanet.org.

BERGO, CONRAD HUNTER, chemistry educator; b. Evanston, Ill., Jan. 5, 1943; s. Arthur Conrad and Mary Margret (Hunter) B.; m. Nancy Wallace, Mar. 12, 1977; children: Stacey Lynn, Fred Monteabaro. BA, St. Olaf Coll., 1965; PhD, U. Minn., 1972. Asst. prof. Chieng Mai (Thailand) U., 1972-75; rsch. assoc. dept. pharmacology U. Ky., Lexington, 1975-77; asst. prof. Alliance Coll., Cambridge Springs, Pa., 1977-80; prof. East Stroudsburg (Pa.) U., 1980—. Exec. dir. Pa. State Coll. Chemistry Consortium, 1991-99; book reviewer McGraw-Hill, Freeman, Houghton Mifflin, John Wiley and West Pub. Pres. bd. dirs. Burnley Workshop, Stroudsburg, 1993-96, 99—. Recipient Cert. of Citizen Svc., Commonwealth of Pa., 1989, award Beyond War, 1990. Mem. Am. Chem. Soc., Sigma Xi. Office: East Stroudsburg Univ Chemistry Dept East Stroudsburg PA 18301

BERGONIA, RAYMOND DAVID, venture capitalist; b. Spring Valley, Ill., May 21, 1951; s. Raymond A. and Elva M. (Bernadini) B.; m. Linda Goble, Dec. 31, 1988; children: Alexandra, Andrew, Caroline, Margot. BBA, U. Notre Dame, 1973; JD, Harvard U., 1976. Bar: Ill. 1976, U.S. Dist. Ct. (no. dist.) Ill. 1976, U.S. Tax Ct. 1977; C.P.A., Ill. Assoc. Winston & Strawn, Chgo., 1976-79; legal counsel, v.p. adminstrn. Heizer Corp., Chgo., 1979-86; v.p. corp. fin. Chgo. Corp., 1986-89; exec. v.p., prin. N.Am. Bus. Devel. Co. L.L.C., Chgo., 1989—. Bd. dirs. numerous pvt. cos. Recipient Elijah Watts Sells award Am. Inst. C.P.A.s, 1973 Mem. ABA, Chgo. Bar Assn. Home: 605 Essex Rd Kenilworth IL 60043-1129 Office: NAM Bus Devel Co LLC 135 S La Salle St Chicago IL 60603-4159 Office Phone: 312-332-4950. Business E-Mail: dbergonia@northamericanfund.com.

BERGQUIST, GENE ALFRED, farmer, rancher, retired commissioner; b. Paynesville, Minn., Aug. 5, 1927; s. Albin and Viola (Heinrich) B.; m. Ann Dorothy Corwin, Aug. 2, 1958; children: Wayne A., Viola M. Grad. high sch., Rhame, N.D. Self-employed farmer-rancher, Rhame, 1948—; Slope County commr. Amidon, ND, 1982—2003; ret., 2003. Bd. dirs. Rhame, N.D. Cenex, 1970-82; bd. dirs. Harper Twp. Rhame; com. mem. Slope County Agrl. Stabilization and Conservation Svc.-USDA Commn., Amidon, 1968-84. Bd. dirs. Rhame Rural Fire Dept., 1976—, Bowman-Slope Social Svc. Bd., Bowman, N.D., 1991—, Deep Creek Twp., 1958-64, Richland Center Twp. Bd., 1952-57; elder Lyle Presbyn. Ch.; youth leader 4-H Slope County, 1950-57; mem. Bowman-Slope Revolving Loan Fund Com., 1998-2003; mem. job devel. bd. Slope and Bowman Counties, 1999—. Presbyterian. Avocations: reading, painting, fishing, riding, gardening. Office: Courthouse Amidon ND 58620

BERGQUIST, JAMES MANNING, history professor; b. Council Bluffs, Iowa, Feb. 1, 1934; s. Reuben Neil and Irene Mary (Norton) B.; m. Joan Marie Solon, May 17, 1969; children: John Norton, Charles James. BA, U. Notre Dame, 1955; MA in History, Northwestern U., 1956, PhD in History, 1966. Instr. history Coe Coll., Cedar Rapids, Iowa, 1961-63, Villanova (Pa.) U., 1963-66, asst. prof., 1966-69, assoc. prof., 1969-86, prof., 1986—2002, prof. emeritus, 2002—. Contbr. articles on Am. social history and immigration to profl. jours., chapters to books. Trustee Balch Inst. for Ethnic Studies, Phila., 1988—92, 1994—2001; mem. Pa. Task Force on Diversity in Higher Edn., 1991—94. Fellow, NEH, 1967, 1977, 1980. Mem.: AAUP (pres. Pa. divsn. 1988—90, nat. coun. 1995—2001), Ethnic Studies Assn. Phila. (pres. 1980—82), Hist. Soc. Pa., Am. Assn. State and Local History, Immigration and Ethnic History Soc. (bd. dirs. 1995—), Soc. for History of the Early Am. Republic, Orgn. Am. Historians, Am. Hist. Assn. Democrat. Roman Catholic. Avocations: swimming, travel. Home: 217 Devon Blvd Devon PA 19333-1616 Office: Villanova U History Dept Villanova PA 19085 Office Phone: 610-519-4660. Business E-Mail: james.bergquist@villanova.edu.

BERGQUIST, PETER, retired music educator; b. Sacramento, Aug. 5, 1930; s. Ed Peter and Margaret (Rogers) B.; m. Dorothy Catherine Clark, June 16, 1956; children: Carolyn, Emily (dec.). Student, Eastman Sch. Music, Rochester, N.Y., 1948-51; BS, Mannes Coll. Music, N.Y.C., 1958; MA, Columbia U., 1960, PhD, 1964. Asst. prof. Sch. Music, U. Oreg., Eugene, 1964-69, assoc. prof., 1969-73, prof., 1973-95, prof. emeritus, 1995—. Editor: Orlando di Lasso, Samtliche Werke neue Reihe, vol. 22-25, 1992—93, Orlando di Lasso: The Complete Motets, 19 vols., 1995—, Orlando di Lasso Studies, 1999; music reviewer Eugene Register Guard; contbr. articles to profl. jours. Sr. warden, jr. warden, vestryman St. Mary's Episcopal Ch., Eugene. With USAF, 1951-55. Recipient Ersted award for disting. teaching U. Oreg., 1973; Fulbright sr. rsch. awardee, 1985; Nat. Endowment for Humanities grantee, 1994-98; rsch. and travel awardee DAAD, ACLS. Mem. AAUP, Am. Musicol. Soc., Internat. Musicol. Soc., Soc. for Music Theory, Music Libr. Assn., Coll. Music Soc. Democrat. Home: 3195 Portland St Eugene OR 97405-5140 Office: Sch Music 1225 U Oreg Eugene OR 97403-1225 Business E-Mail: pbergq@uoregon.edu.

BERGQUIST, RICK, software company executive; BS in Computer Sci., Calif. Polytechnic State U.; diploma in Mgmt. Devel. Program, Harvard U. Sch. Bus. With Am. Mgmt. Sys. Inc., 1975—87; joined PeopleSoft Inc., Pleasonton, Calif., 1987, sr. v.p., 1999, chief tech. officer, 1999—. PeopleSoft Fellow award, 2002. Office: PeopleSoft Inc 4460 Hacienda Dr Pleasanton CA 94588

BERGQUIST, SANDRA LEE, medical and legal consultant, nurse; b. Carlton, Minn., Oct. 13, 1944; d. Arthur Vincent and Avis Lorene Portz; m. David Edward Bergquist, June 11, 1966; children: Rion Eric, Taun Erin. BSN, Barry U., 1966; MA in Mgmt., Central Mich. U., 1975; student U. So. Calif., 1980-82. RN, advanced RN practitioner; cert. physician asst. Commd. 2d lt. USAF, 1968, advanced through grades to lt. col., 1985; staff and charge nurse USAF, 1968-76, primary care nurse practitioner, McConnell AFB, Kans., 1976-79, officer in charge Wheeler Med. Facility, Wheeler AFB, Hawaii, 1979-83, supr. ambulatory care services, Elgin AFB, Fla., 1983-84; med.-legal cons., Pensacola, Fla., 1985—; risk mgr., quality assurance coordinator HCA-Twin Cities Hosp., Niceville, 1986-88. Bd. dirs. Elder Svcs. Okaloosa County, Fla., 1984-2003; adv. bd. Gentiva Home Health, 1990—; chair Niceville/Valparaiso Task Force on Child Abuse Prevention, Fla., 1985-88; chair home and family life com. Twin Cities Women's Club, Niceville, 1985-88; chair advancement com. Gulf Coast coun. Boy Scouts Am., 1985-87; instr. advanced and basic cardiac life support Hawaii Heart Assn. and Tripler Army Med. Ctr., 1981-83. Decorated Commendation medal with 1 oak leaf cluster, USAF Meritorious Svc. medal, Air Force Commendation medal. Mem. AACN, Am. Assn. Physician Assts., Assn. Mil. Surgeons U.S., Soc. Ret. Air Force Nurses, Soc. Air Force Physician Assts., Twin Cities Women's Club. Lutheran. Avocations: computer programming, reading, handicrafts.

BERGREN, SCOTT C., career officer; b. Mineola, N.Y. BA in Econ., Clemson U., 1970; student navigator tng., Mather AFB, Calif., 1970-71; student, Squadron Officer Sch., 1974; M in Polit. Sci., Auburn U., 1981; student, Air Command and Staff Coll., 1981, Air War Coll., 1990, Harvard U., 1996. Commd. 2d lt. USAF, 1970, advanced through grades to maj. gen., 1999, various F-4 Phantom assignments, 1971-76; air staff ops. officer programs and resources Air Staff Tng. program, Hdqs. USAF, Pentagon, Washington, 1976-77, asst. exec. officer to dep. chief staff programs/resources, 1976-77; instr., navigator and exchange officer 237th Operational Conversion Unit, RAFB Honington, Eng., 1977-80; dir. ops. force analysis div. then spl. asst. comdr. Hdqs. Tactical Air Command, Langley AFB, Va., 1981-85; comdr. 325th Tactical Tng. Wing's Aircraft Generation Squadron, Tyndall AFB, Fla., 1985-87, asst. dep. comdr. maintenance, 1985-87; dep. comdr. maintenance 33rd Tactical Fighter Wing, Eglin AFB, Fla., 1987-89; Air Univ. chair for chief staff of Air Force Maxwell AFB, Ala., 1990-91; various comdr. positions Nellis AFB, Nev., 1991-93; stationed at U.S. Ctrl. Command, MacDill AFB, Fla., 1994-96; vice comdr. San Antonio Air Logistics Ctr., Kelly AFB, Tex., 1996-97; comdr. 82d Tng. Wing, Sheppard AFB, 1997-99; dir. maintenance, dep. chief staff installations & logistics HQ/USAF, 1999-2000; comdr. Ogden Air Logistics Ctr., Hill AFB, Utah, 2000—. Decorated Silver Star, D.F.C. with silver oak leaf cluster, Purple Heart, Air medal with three silver oak leaf clusters and bronze oak leaf cluster, Small Arms Expert Marksmanship Ribbon, Rep. Vietnam Gallantry Cross with Palm, Rep. Vietnam Campaign medal. Office: Hill AFBM OO-ALC/CC 7981 Georgia St Hill AFB UT 84056-5824

BERGSON, HENRY PAUL, professional society administrator; b. Boston, Dec. 22, 1942; s. Harry, Jr. and Elizabeth (Paul) Bergson; m. Jacqueline Hope Wilson, June 11, 1966; children: Susan Elizabeth, Abigail Anne. BS, U. N.H., 1966. Various mgmt. positions Fed. Signal, Blue Island, Ill., 1970-78; dir. mktg. Tork, Mt. Vernon, N.Y., 1978-83; v.p. ops. G.C.S. Svc., Chappaqua, N.Y., 1983-85; exec. v.p. Nat. Elec. Mfrs. Reps. Assn., Armonk, N.Y., 1985-93, pres., 1994—, also bd. dirs. Bd. dirs. Elec. Industry Joint Bus. Productivity Coun. Contbr. articles to profl. jours. Chief Katonah (N.Y.) Vol. Fire Dept., 1980—84, v.p., 1984—87, pres., 1987—90, bd. dirs., 1990—, chmn. bd. dirs., 1995—; mem. Bedford Transp. Com., 1984—86; fire commr. Katonah Fire Dist., 1992—, vice chmn. bd. fire commrs., 1996—; mem. fire adv. bd. Westchester County, NY, 2001—; cmty. adv. bd. Taconic and Bedford Hills Correctional Facilities, N.Y. State Dept. Corrections; elder 1st Presbyn. Ch., Katonah, 1991—94. Capt. U.S. Army, 1967—70. Decorated Bronze Star for Valor with two oak leaf clusters, Purple Heart, Vietnam medal of Honor. Mem.: Nat. Assn. Elec. Distbrs., Nat. Assn. Elec. Mfrs. Assn. (assoc.). Republican. Avocation: collecting firematic antiques. Home: PO Box 182 Katonah NY 10536-0182 Office: NEMRA 660 White Plains Rd Fl 6 Tarrytown NY 10591-5147 Office Phone: 914-524-8650.

BERGSTEIN, DANIEL GERARD, lawyer; b. Nice, France, May 1, 1943; came to U.S., 1952; s. Max and Suzanne (Fenigstein) B.; children: Jordan, Elizabeth C. BA, CUNY, 1965; JD, Bklyn. Law Sch., 1968. Bar: N.Y. 1968, Fla. 1974. From assoc. to ptnr. Greenbaum, Wolff & Ernst, N.Y.C., 1982; ptnr. Reavis & McGrath, N.Y.C., 1982-85, Finley, Kumble, Wagner, Heine, Underberg, Manley, Myerson & Casey, N.Y.C., 1985-87, Paul, Hastings, Janofsky & Walker, N.Y.C., 1988—, chmn. telecom. practice group. Mem. ABA, French-Am. C. of C. in U.S. Office: Paul Hastings Janofsky & Walker LLP 399 Park Ave Unit 31 New York NY 10022-4618 Office Phone: 212-318-6033. Business E-Mail: danielbergstein@paulhastings.com.

BERGSTEIN, JACK MARSHALL, surgeon; b. Duluth, Minn., Apr. 21, 1955; s. Sherman and Muriel (Gilder) Bergstein; m. Amber C. Bergstein, June 15, 2002; children: Lauren, Julian stepchildren: Samara, Baye. BA in Journalism, U. Minn., 1978, MD, 1982. Diplomate Am. Bd. Surgery with added qualifications in surg. critical care; diplomate Am. Bd. Forensic Examiners, Am. Bd. Forensic Medicine. Resident surgery U. Minn., Charlotte Med. Ctr., 1982-85, 85-87; surg. critical care fellow Lincoln Med. and Mental Health Ctr., Bronx, N.Y., 1987-88; sr. attending surgeon Froedert Hosp., Milw., 1988-97; dir. trauma and surg. critical care St. Francis Med. Ctr., Peoria, 1997-99; assoc. prof. surgery U. Ill. Coll. Medicine, Peoria, 1997-99; dir. surg. critical care, assoc. dir. trauma Jon Michael Moore Trauma Ctr. W.Va. U. Hosp., Morgantown, 1999—2003; prof. surgery W.Va. Sch. Medicine, Morgantown, 1999—2003. Active staff St. Francis Hosp., Peoria, 1997—99, Warren (Pa.) Gen. Hosp., 2003—. Dir. at large Peace Studies Ctr., Milw., 1995-97; adv. bd. Peoria Safe Cmtys., 1997-99. Fellow ACS (chmn. Wis. com. on trauma 1995-97); mem. Am. Trauma Soc. (pres. Wis. 1992-97), Am. Assn. Surgery of Trauma, Ea. Assn. for the Surgery of Trauma (dir.-at-large 1999—2002, chmn. violence prevention task force, 1999—2002, vice chair violence prevention task force, 1994-99), Assn. Tchrs. Preventive Medicine, Midwest Surg. Assn., Nat. Network Violence Prevention Practitioners, Surg. Infection Soc., Am. Soc. Bariatric Surgery. Avocations: bonsai, watercolor painting, gardening. Home: Box 3300 Lindell Rd Russell PA 16345 Office: 103 W St Clair St Ste 2D Warren PA 16365 Office Phone: 814-723-2770. Personal E-mail: bergstein1@aol.com.

BERGSTEIN, JERRY MICHAEL, nephrologist; b. Cleve., June 26, 1939; s. Sol R. and Hilda (Nittscoff) B.; m. Renee M. Hillman, July 7, 1963; children: Stephanie, Michael, Jeffrey. BA, UCLA, 1961; MD, U. Minn., 1965. Diplomate Nat. Bd. Med. Examiners, Am. Bd. Pediat., Am. Bd. Pediat. Nephrology; lic. physician, Ind. Intern in pediat. U. Minn., Mpls., 1965-66, jr. pediat. resident, 1966-67, chief pediat. resident, 1969-70, postdoctoral fellow in pediat. nephrology, 1970-73; asst. prof., head pediat. nephrology UCLA, 1973-77; assoc. prof. Ind. U. Sch. Medicine, Indpls., 1977-82, head pediat. nephrology, 1977—, prof., 1982—. Mem. adv. bd. Nat. Kidney Found. Ind., 1980—; mem. adv. coun. Am. Heart Assn., 1988—. Mem. editl. bd. Child Nephrology and Urology, 1980-90, Pediat. Nephrology, 1995—; contbr. chpts. to books. Lt. comdr. USN, 1967-69. Recipient Fellowship USPHS, Washington, 1970; grantee Thrasher Fund, 1980, Amgen, 1990. Mem. Am. Soc. Nephrology, Am. Soc. Pediat. Nephrology, Am. Soc. Investigative Pathology, Soc. Exptl. Biology and Medicine. Achievements include research on the role of the fibrinolytic inhibitor plasminogen activator inhibitor-1 in the pathogenesis and outcome of the hemolytic-uremic syndrome; development of anti-tubular basement membrane antibody disease; development of radiation nephritis in bone marrow transplant patients. Office: James Whitcomb Riley Hosp for Children 702 Barnhill Dr Indianapolis IN 46202-5128 Business E-Mail: jbergste@iupui.edu.

BERGSTEIN, STANLEY FRANCIS, horse breeder, director; b. Pottsville, Pa., June 19, 1924; s. Milton Isidore and Esther Miriam (Rosenzweig) B.; m. June Carol Hanna, June 4, 1950; children: Alfred M., Lisa R. BS, Northwestern U., 1947. Writer James S. Kearns Assoc., Chgo., 1947-50, CBS TV, Chgo., 1956-57; racing sec. Sportsman's Pk., Chgo., 1957-60; exec. dir. Harness Racing Inst., Chgo., 1961-68; exec. v.p. Harness Tracks Am., Tucson, Ariz., 1961—. Pres. Am. Horse Publs., Lexington, Ky., 1969-70; trustee Hall of Fame of Trotter, Goshen, N.Y., 1980—. Editor Hoof Beats Mag., Columbus, Ohio, 1968-75; columnist Harness Horse Mag., Harrisburg, Pa., 1979-90, Times: in Harness Mag., 1990—, Daily Racing Form, 1995—. Named Horseman of Yr. Horseman and Fair World Mag., Lexington, 1971; recipient Proximity award U.S. Harness Writers, Goshen, 1978, Writers Hall of Fame award, 1986, Hall of Fame of Trotter award, 1987, Internat. award Racing Commrs., 1990, Amtote Internat. award, 1992, Disting. Svc. award U. Ariz., 2000. Mem. U.S. Trotting Assn. (v.p. publicity 1968-75). Avocation: antiquarian book and print collecting. E-mail: sfbergstein@earthlink.net.

BERGSTEN, C. FRED, economist; b. Bklyn., Apr. 23, 1941; s. Carl Alfred and Lois Halkaline (Kirk) Bergsten; m. Virginia Lee Wood, June 16, 1962; 1 child, Mark. AB, Ctrl. Meth. Coll., Fayette, Mo., 1961, LHD, 1995; MA, Fletcher Sch. Law and Diplomacy, Medford, Mass., 1962, MA in Law and Diplomacy, 1963, PhD, 1969. Internat. economist Dept. State, 1963—67; vis. fellow Council Fgn. Relations, 1967—68; asst. for internat. econ. affairs NSC, 1969—71; sr. fellow Brookings Instn., 1972—76; asst. sec. treasury internat. affairs, 1977—81; sr. assoc. Carnegie Endowment Internat. Peace, 1981; dir. Inst. Internat. Econs., 1981—. U.S. coord. U.S.-Saudi Arabia Joint Econ. Commn., 1977—81; mem. def. mgmt. bd. Task Force on Fgn. Ownership and Control, 1989—90, competitiveness policy coun., 1991—97, chmn., 1991—97; mem. panel on pub.-pvt. cooperation in civilian tech. NAS, 1990—91; mem. exec. com. Trilateral Commn., 1991—, Bretton Wood Com., 1989—, Carnegie Endowment, Nat. Commn. Am. and the New World Order, 1992, Commn. Govt. Renewal, 1992; chmn. APEC Eminent Persons Group, 1993—95; vice chmn. adv. com. on fgn. econ. policy Dept. State, 1996—. Author: The Future of the International Economic Order: An Agenda for Research, 1973, Toward a New World Trade Policy, 1975, World Politics and International Economics, 1975, Toward a New International Economic Order: Selected Papers of C. Fred Bergsten, 1972-1974, 1975, The Dilemmas of the Dollar: The Economics and Politics of United State International Monetary Policy, 1976, American Multinationals and American Interests, 1978, Managing International Economic Interdependence: Selected Papers of C. Fred Bergsten, 1975-1976, 1977, The International Economic Policy of the United States: Selected Papers of C. Fred Bergsten, 1977-1979, 1980, The World Economy in the 1980s: Selected Papers of C. Fred Bergsten, 1981, The United State in the World Economy: Selected Papers of C. Fred Bergsten, 1981-82, 1983, Bank Lending to Developing Countries: The Policy Alternatives, 1985, The United States-Japan Economic Problem, 1985, Global Economic Imbalances, 1985, Auction Quotas and United States Trade Policy, 1987, America in the World Economy: A Strategy for the 1990's, 1988, International Adjustment and Financing, 1991, Pacific Dynamism and the International Economic System, 1993, Reconcilable Differences? United States-Japan Economic Conflict, 1993, Global Economic Leadship and the Group of Seven, 1996, Whither APEC?, 1997, No More Bashing, 2002, Dollar Overvaluation and the World Economy, 2003, Dollar Adjustment: How Far? Against What?, 2004, The United States and the World Economy, 2005; mem. editl. bd.: Fgn. Affairs, 1972—77, Internat. Orgn., 1973—77, Jour. Internat. Econs., 1977—80, Fgn. Policy, 1987—. Recipient Meritorious Honor award, Dept. State, 1965, Disting. Alumnus award, Ctrl. Meth. Coll., 1975, Exceptional Svc. award, Treasury Dept., 1980, French Legion of Honor, 1987. Fellow: Chinese Acad. Social Scis. (hon.); mem.: Coun. Fgn. Rels., Am. Econ. Assn. Personal E-mail: kstewart@iie.com.

BERGSTEN, JAMES ROBERT, computer technology architect; b. N.Y.C., May 21, 1954; s. Robert Frederick and Jean Laura B.; m. Mary Elizabeth, July 20, 1980; children: Sarah Margaret, Carl Alexander. Student, Cooper Union, 1972-74. System developer NASA, N.Y.C., 1974-77; software mgr. Amdahl Corp., Sunnyvale, Calif., 1977-81; founder, pres./CEO Kolinar Corp., Santa Clara, Calif., 1981-90; v.p. engr. Andor Systems, Cupertino, Calif., 1990-94; founder, pres. ARK Rsch. Corp., San Jose, Calif., 1995—; dir. LSI Logic, Milpitas, Calif., 2000—. Bd. dirs. Ark Rsch., Kolinar, Santa Clara; owner CTHIA Prodns.; chmn., CEO Ark Storage Systems Corp., 2003—. Author: (operating system) Arts, 1995, (software) Xmenu, 1991 (ICP award 1995); co-author: (software) Kprobe, SQ Lexec, SQ Lmenu, 1995; contbr. articles to profl. jours.; patentee in field. Mem. computer adv. bd. KTEH TV, San Jose, 1985. Mem. IEEE, Assn. Computing Machinery, Audio Engrng. Soc. Avocation: composing and producing music. Home: 8 Brightwood Way Danville CA 94506 Personal E-mail: jim@thebergstens.com.

BERGSTRAESSER, PAUL, writer; b. Cleve., Sept. 2, 1967; s. Edward William and Carole (Heisel) Bergstraesser; m. Michelle Jarman, Aug. 9, 2002. BA in Philosophy, Oberlin Coll., 1989; MA in English/Creative Writing, No. Mich. U., 2000. Author: (short stories) (short story) Jimmy, 2000 (Chgo. Lit. award, 2000, Ill. Arts Coun. Lit. award, 2001).

BERGSTRESSER, PAUL RICHARD, dermatologist, educator; b. Ottawa, Kans., Aug. 24, 1941; s. Karl Samuel and May (Holmes) B.; m. Rebecca Louise Baird, Jan. 4, 1969; children: Daniel Baird, Laura Suzanne. AB, Coll. of Wooster, 1963; MD, Stanford U., 1968. Diplomate Am. Bd. Dermatology (bd. dirs. 1996-2005, v.p. 2003-05). Asst. prof. dept. dermatology U. Miami (Fla.), 1975-76; asst. prof. to prof. Southwestern Med. Ctr. U. Tex., Dallas, 1976—, chmn. dept., 1986—. Mem. dermatologic drugs adv. com., FDA, 1986-88; mem. gen. medicine study sect. GM1A, NIH, 1989-93; mem. adv. coun. Nat. Inst. Arthritis and Musculoskeletal and Skin Disease, 1999-2003. Editor Photodermatology, Photoimmunology and Photomedicine, 1990-99; contbr. numerous articles to profl. jours. Maj. U.S. Army, 1970-72. Fellow AAP, AAAS, ACP, Am. Acad. Dermatology; mem. Am. Assn. Immunologists, Assn. Am. Physicians, Soc. Investigative Dermatology (bd. dirs. 1987-92, sec.-treas. 1999-2004), Am. Assn. Tissue Banks, Am. Dermatol. Assn., Assn. Profs. Dermatology (bd. dirs. 1990-95, pres.-elect 1998-2000, pres. 2000-02). Democrat. Methodist. Avocations: choral music, running. Home: 3758 Pallos Verdas Dr Dallas TX 75229-2740 Office: U Tex Southwestern Med Ctr Dept Dermatology 5323 Harry Hines Blvd Dallas TX 75390-9069 Business E-Mail: paul.bergstresser@utsouthwestern.edu.

BERGSTROM, ALBION ANDREW, retired military officer, educator; b. Salem, Mass., Sept. 2, 1947; s. Eric Hjalmar and Helen Lawrence (Andrew) Bergstrom; m. Angela Jane Feyerabend, May 11, 1997; children: Victoria Helen, John Albion. Student, Boston U., 1965-67; BA, Colo. State U., 1969; MA, Ctrl. Mich. U., 1978; grad., Command and Gen. Staff Coll., 1982; MA, Naval War Coll., 1998. Cert. fed. ofcl. Commd. 2d lt. U.S. Army, 1969, advanced through grades to col., 1991, platoon leader, aide de camp, 1970-71, co. comdr. Ft. Hood, Tex., 1974-75; bn. exec. officer I-35 Armor, Erlangen, Germany, 1980—81; assignment officer Armor Br. U.S. Army, 1983-85, bn. comdr. 1-35 Armor, 1986-88, cols. assignment officer Pers. Command Alexandria, Va., 1988-89, chief, officer divsn. DCS pers., The Pentagon Washington, 1990-92; dep. comdr. U.S. Army Phys. Disability Agy., Washington, 1992-96; prof. jt. mil. ops., chief regional contingency planning and war fighting divsn. Naval War Coll., Newport, RI, 1996-99, prof. electives program, CDE, 2000—, prof. joint mil. ops., 2002—. Program chmn. Abrams Ch. Armor Assn., 1982—85. Del. N.H. Rep. Convs., 1966, 1968. Decorated Legion of Merit (3), Bronze Star, Purple Heart, Bronze medal, Silver medal, Order St. George; Nat. Security fellow, John F. Kennedy Sch. Govt., Harvard U., 1988—90. Mem.: VFW, 5th Inf. Divsn. Assn., Boston U. Alumni Assn., Ctrl. Mich. U. Alumni Assn., U.S. Naval Inst., Assn. U.S. Army, Armor Assn., 1st Cav. Divsn. Assn., Naval War Coll. Found., U.S. Army War Coll. Alumni Assn., Colo. State U. Alumni Assn., Order Ky. Cols., Mil. Order Purple Heart, Shriners, Masons, Am. Legion, Nat. Sojourners, Zeta Beta Tau, Phi Sigma Delta. Congregationalist. Avocations: photography, cross country skiing. Home: 19 Madison Way Portsmouth RI 02871-2249 Office Phone: 401-841-6484. E-mail: bergstra1@aol.com.

BERGT, GREGORY PAUL, chemist, consultant; b. West Point, Nebr., Nov. 20, 1948; s. Lowell Duane and Elaine Angela (Schula) B.; m. Diann Helen Stigge, May 6, 1972; children: Matthew, Lisa, Troy, Ross. BS, Nebr. Wesleyan U., 1971; postgrad., U. Minn., 1974. Chemist Wendt Labs., Belle Plaine, Minn., 1971—77, dir. sci. and regulatory affairs, 1978—87; v.p. Eudaemonic Corp., Omaha, 1987—; dir. regulatory affairs I.D. Russell Co., Longmont, Colo., 1989—95; dir. R&D Pennfield Animal Health, Omaha, 1995—. Cons. VA Hosp., Mpls., 1977. Patentee in field. Pres., St. John's Luth. Ch., Belle Plaine, 1981, Bethlehem Luth. Ch., Longmont, 1993-94; sponsoring liaison Boy Scouts Am., Belle Plaine, 1980-84; county del. Republican Party, Scott County, Minn., 1982. Recipient award Chemistry Tng. Program, NSF, 1967. Mem. Parenteral Drug Assn., Generic Pharm. Industry Assn./Animal Drug Alliance (treas., dir. Rocky Mountain Biomed. Devel. Forum 1990-95), Am. Dairy Sci. Assn., Am. Chem Soc., Am. Inst. Chemists, Am. Fedn. Ind. Pharm. Mfrs. (sec.-treas., dir. 1979—), Coun. Agrl. and Sci. Tech., Tiger Booster Club (pres. 1973-75), Rotary (pres. 1984-85). Home: 335 S 124th Cir Omaha NE 68154-2319 Office: Pennfield Animal Health 11850 Nicholas St Ste 220 Omaha NE 68154 Office Phone: 402-330-6000. Business E-Mail: pennfield-oil@juno.com.

BERGTRAUM, HENRY M., minister; b. N.Y.C., Nov. 5, 1955; s. Stanley and Bernice Natalie Bergtraum. BA, Yale U., 1977; postgrad., Yale/Union Theol. Sem., N.Y.C., 1999—. Social scis. asst. dept. polit. affairs UN Hdqrs., N.Y.C., 1978—95; resident chaplain St. John's Episcopal Hosp., N.Y.C., 1997—98; chaplain Ronald McDonald House, N.Y.C., 2000—. Elder Ch. of the Covenant, N.Y.C., 1992—. Presbyterian. Avocations: writing, poetry, swimming. Office: Ronald McDonald House 405 E 73rd St New York NY

BERGY, DEAN H., health products executive; Grad., U. Mich., Harvard PMD Program. Sr. mgr. Ernst & Young LLP; contr. Stryker, Kalamazoo, 1994—96, v.p., fin. med. divsn., 1996—98, v.p., fin., 1998—2003, v.p., CFO and sec., 2003—. Office: Stryker 2725 Fairfield Rd Kalamazoo MI 49001

BERICK, JAMES HERSCHEL, lawyer; b. Cleve., Mar. 30, 1933; s. Morris and Rebecca Alice (Gerdy) B.; m. Christine Berick; children: Michael, Daniel, Robert, Joshua. AB, Columbia U., 1955; JD, Case Western Res. U., 1958. Assoc. Burke, Haber & Berick, Cleve., 1958-60, ptnr., 1960-86, mng. ptnr., 1968-83; chmn. Berick, Pearlman & Mills Co. L.P.A., 1986-99; ptnr. Squire, Sanders & Dempsey, LLP, 2000—02, ret. ptnr., 2003—. Bd. dirs. MBNA Corp., MBNA Am. Bank, N.A., MBNA Europe Bank, Ltd., The Town and Country Trust, The Town and Country Funding Corp.; sec. A. Schulman, Inc., 1973—2003, Cleve. Browns Football Co. LLC; lectr. law Case Western Res. U., 1969—78; mem. dean's adv. coun. Case Western Res. U. Sch. Law, 1998—, Case Western Res. U. Sch. Medicine, 2004—. Founding and life trustee Rock and Roll Hall of Fame and Mus.; mem. Shaker Heights (Ohio) Bd. Edn., 1980-83; bd. visitors Columbia Coll., 1981-87, 90-96, emeritus, 2000—2004, member, 2004-; bd. dirs. Univ. Circle Inc., 1994—2004; trustee Arthritis Found. of N.E. Ohio, mem. med. and sci. com. Mem.: Soc. of Benchers, Ct. of Nisi Prius, Seagate Beach Club, Union Club (Cleve.), Shoreby Club, Order of Coif. Home: 1225 S Ocean Blvd #801 Delray Beach FL 33483 Office: Squire Sanders & Dempsey LLP 4900 Key Tower 127 Public Sq Cleveland OH 44114-1216 Office Phone: 216-479-8450. E-mail: jberick@ssd.com.

BERINGER, WILLIAM ERNST, mediator, arbitrator, lawyer, retired manufacturing executive; b. Madison, Wis., Oct. 24, 1928; s. William and Martha M. Beringer; m. Marilyn J. Walter, Aug. 4, 1984; children: Amy, Julia, Barry, Thomas, Maureen. BA summa cum laude, Lawrence Coll., 1950; JD with distinction, U. Mich., 1953. Bar: Mich. 1953, Wis. 1953, Ill. 1955. Assoc. Vedder, Price, Kaufman & Kammholz, Chgo., 1953-56; atty. law dept. Swift & Co., Chgo., 1956-71; dir. gen. law dept. Allis-Chalmers Corp., Milw., 1971-77; v.p., gen. counsel, sec. Siemens Energy & Automation, Inc., Alpharetta, 1978-94; assoc. gen. counsel Siemens Corp., 1987-94. Bd. dirs. corp. banking and bus. law sect. Wis. Bar, 1976-78; mem. antitrust and corp. policy com. U.S. C. of C., 1974-80; mem. panels Am. Arbitration Assn., Resolution Resources Corp., NASD Regulation, N.Y. Stock Exch., EEOC. Editorial bd. Mich. Law Rev, 1952-53. Bd. dirs. Hinsdale (Ill.) Community Concert Assn., 1969-71, Dupage County (Ill.) Girl Scouts U.S., 1969-71, Clarendon Hills (Ill.) Community Chest, 1968-70; vice chmn. Clarendon Hills Human Relations Commn., 1968-70; mem. Chgo. study team Nat. Commn. on Causes and Prevention Violence, 1968; chmn. MAPI Law Coun. II, 1992-94. Mem. ABA, Am. Corp. Counsel Assn. (bd. dirs. Ga. chpt. 1985-88), Atlanta Bar Assn., Lawrence U. Alumni Assn. (bd. dirs. 1998-2002), Order of Coif, Cherokee Town and Country Club, Rotary. Republican. Personal E-mail: wberinger@aol.com.

BERINSKY, ADAM JEREMIAH, political scientist, educator; b. N.Y.C., Oct. 4, 1970; s. Burton and Helene Berinsky; m. Deirdre Logan, June 9, 2002. BA, Wesleyan U., 1992; PhD, U. of Mich., 2000. Asst. prof. Princeton (N.J.) U., 1999—2003, MIT, Cambridge, 2003—04, assoc. prof., 2004—. Author: Silent Voices, 2004; contbr. articles to profl. jours. Mem.: Am. Polit. Sci. Assn. Office: MIT Dept Polit Sci 77 Mass AVe E53-459 Cambridge MA 02140 Business E-Mail: berinsky@mit.edu.

BERIO, MARINA, visual artist, photographer; b. Boston, July 30, 1966; d. Luciano and Susan (Oyama) Berio; m. Jean-Christian Bourcart, July 26, 1997; 1 child Flio Bourcart. BA, Oberlin Coll., 1988. Exhibited in group shows, John Weber Gallery, N.Y.C., 1996, Yancey Richardson Gallery, N.Y.C., 1999, Artists Space, N.Y.C., 1999, others, Represented in permanent collections Fonds Nat. d'Art Contemporain, Paris; subject of articles. Grantee Va. Ctr. for Creative Arts, 1999, Millay Colony for the Arts, 1999, MacDowell Colony, 1998-99, Aaron Siskind Found., 1998. Address: 332 Canal St Rm 5F New York NY 10013-2574

BERISFORD, JOHN L., human resources specialist; B in Polit. Sci., West Liberty Coll.; M in Indsl. Rels., W. Va. U. Various positions including several field human resources assignments Pepsi Bottling Group, Pitts., 1988—91, human resources mgr., mgr., orgn. capability, sr. labor mgr., 1991—95, dir. human resources heartland bus. unit, 1995—98, v.p. orgn. capability, head N.Am. bottling bus. Somers, NY, 1998—2001, v.p. field human resources, 2001—, v.p. human resources, 2004—. Office: Pepsi Bottling Group 1 Pepsi Way Somers NY 10589-2201 Office Phone: 914-767-6000. Office Fax: 914-767-7761.*

BERK, ALAN S., accountant; b. N.Y.C., May 11, 1934; s. Phil and Mae (Buchberg) B.; m. Barbara Binder, Dec. 18, 1960; children— Charles M., Peter M., Nancy M. BS in Econs., U. Pa., 1955; MS in Bus., Columbia U., 1956. CPA N.Y., 1960. Staff acct. Arthur Young & Co., N.Y.C., 1956-62, mgr., prin., 1962-67; sr. v.p. Avco Corp., Greenwich, Conn., 1967-75; dir. Arthur Young & Co., 1975—, ptnr., 1976—, chief fin. officer, 1979-89; nat. dir. fin., treas. Ernst & Young, 1989-92; exec. dir. Kelley, Drye & Warren, N.Y.C., 1993-94. Mem. nat. adv. group Nat. Tech. Inst. for the Deaf, Rochester, N.Y.; chmn. bd. dirs. Jewish Home for the Elderly of Fairfield County, Inc., 1997-99, vice chmn., 2002—; 1st v.p., treas. Bruce Mus., Greenwich, Conn.; mem. golf bd. Town of Greenwich, Conn.; commn. on aging Town of Greenwich. With U.S. Army, 1957. Mem. AICPA, N.Y. State Soc. CPAs, Fin. Execs. Inst., Landmark Club, Stockbridge (Mass.) Golf Club, Lake Dr. Homeowners Assn. (pres.), Stockbridge Bowl Assn. (1st v.p.). Home: 14 Cornelia Dr Greenwich CT 06830-3906

BERK, GEORGE ELLIS, cardiologist; b. N.Y.C., May 4, 1942; s. Samuel and Muriel Berkowitz; m. Noel Nelkin, Oct. 7, 1967 (div.); children: Matthew Adam, Bradley Tyler; m. Penelope Susan Smith, Apr. 25, 1998. AB, Princeton U., 1964; MD, Cornell U., 1968. Diplomate Am. Bd. Internal Medicine. Intern Cornell Cooperating Hosps., 1968—69, resident, 1969—70; cardiology fellow North Shore Univ. Hosp., 1973—75; resident Cornell Cooperating Hosps., 1972—73; pvt. practice cardiology No. Westchester Cardiology, Yorktown Heights, NY, 1975—; attending physician Westchester Med. Ctr., 1975—, No. Westchester Hosp. Ctr., 1975—. Chief divsn. cardiology No. Westchester Hosp., Mt. Kisco, NY, 1994—98; med. dir. Imaging for Life, LLC, N.Y.C. and White Plains, 1999—. Adv. bd. Free Romania Relief Fund, N.Y.C., 1992—95, Albanian Relief Assn., N.Y.C., 1992—97; bd. dirs. Westchester/Putnam divsn. Am. Heart Assn., Purchase, NY, 1981—; pres. Westchester/Putnam chpt. Am. Heart Assn., 1996—98. Maj. USAF, 1970—72. Decorated Air Force Commendation medal; recipient Congl. Proclamation, Congresswoman Nita Lowey, 2000. Fellow: Am. Coll. Cardiology (assoc.). Avocations: Oriental carpets, collecting vintage photography, art glass, pottery, running, mountain climbing. Home: 181 Hook Rd Bedford NY 10506 Office: Northern Westchester Cardiology 1888 Commerce St Yorktown Heights NY 10506 Office Phone: 914-962-4000.

BERK, GREG, lawyer; Sr. ptnr. Law Offices Greg Berk, Irvine, Calif., 1999—. Office: 5420 Trabuco Rd Ste 150 Irvine CA 92620 Business E-Mail: greg@calvisa.com.

BERK, HARLAN JOSEPH, numismatist, writer; b. Joliet, Ill., June 7, 1942; s. Sammy and Ruth (Press) B.; m. Ellen Landman, Sept. 20, 1966 (div. 1978); children: Aaron R., Shanna L.; m. Pamela Margaret Blade, June 22, 1982; 1 child, Sammy Blade. Student, U. Ill., 1960-64. Vice pres. New Star Jewelers, Joliet, 1964-85; pres. Harlan J. Berk Ltd., Joliet, 1964, Chgo. Bd. dirs. OLICON Imaging Systems, Inc., Louisville; lectr., treas. N.Y. Internat. Numis. Conv.; Am. rep. Numismatica Ars Classica, Zurich, 1990-94. Author: Roman Gold Coins, 1985, Eastern Roman Successors, 1987, Roman Gold Coins of the Medieval World 383-1453 A.D. (Robert Friedberg award 1987), Eastern Roman Successors of the Sestertius; columnist World Coin News, 1989—, What's Old (Best Fgn. Column Numismatic Literary Guild, 1989, 90, 91, 92); mem. bd. one man exhbn.3D Chgo.-Peir Walk Sculpture Exhbn., 2000-2003, sec., 2003-05. Mem. exec. com. World Heritage Mus., Champaign, Ill., 1988—; pres. Chgo. Fine Arts, 2003-; bd. advisors Loyola Univ. Chgo. Art Mus., 2005—. Mem. Internat. Assn. Profl. Numismatists (pub. rels. for Am., chmn. 2000 internat. congress Chgo.), Profl. Numismatist Guild (edn. chmn., bd. dirs., v.p., pres., immediate past pres. 2003-05, pres. 2001-2003, v.p. 1999-2001, sec. 1997-99, treas. 1995-97), Am. Numismatists Assn. (dealer liaison com., mem. editl. bd. Numismatist, advisor to authentication bd. 1975—). Democrat. Jewish. Avocations: art collecting, scuba diving, running, skiing, fishing. Office: 31 N Clark St Chicago IL 60602-2806

BERK, HAROLD, dentist, consultant, educator; b. Mpls., July 27, 1917; s. Wolf and Jennie (Sachs) B.; m. Helen Ruth Levin, Aug. 2, 1942 (dec. Mar. 2005); children: Kenneth Joel, Fredrick Matthew, Donald Allan. Student, Loras Coll., 1935—37; DDS with honors, Northwestern U., 1941; DSc (hon.), Loras Coll., 2000. Intern, resident Forsyth Dental, Boston, 1941-43; asst. chief clinic Forsyth Dental Infirmary, Boston, 1943-44, chief clinic, 1944-46; asst. clin. prof. Tufts U. Dental, Boston, 1946-50, clin. prof., 1950-90, clin. prof. emeritus, 1990—. Pres. Pulpdent Corp., Watertown, Mass., 1950-95, cons. 1995—. Pres. coun. Bradeis U., Waltham, Mass. Lt. Comdr. USPHS, 1955-57. Recipient Harold Berk Rsch. Lab award, Tufts U. Dental Alumnus Faculty award, 1996, Alumnus Merit award Northwestern U. Dentistry, 1998; Rsch. award named in his honor. Fellow Am. Coll. Dentists, Internat. Coll. Dentists, Acad. Pediat. Dentistry, Acad. Dentistry for Persons with Disabilities (founder); mem. G.V. Black Soc. (life) Fed. Dentaire Internat. (life), Am. Assn. Endodontics (life), ADA (life), Mass. Dental Soc. (life), Pierre Fauchard Acad. (life), Soc. Dentistry for Children (past pres. Mass. chpt.), Greater Boston Dental Soc. (past pres.), Internat. Assn. Dental Rsch., Sigma Xi, Omicon Kappa Upsilon. Jewish. Achievements include discovery of calcium hydroxide suspended in Aqueous methyl Cellulose, its affect on the dental Pulp-Apexification-Remineralization. Home: 369 Dudley Rd Newton Center MA 02459-2832 Office: Pulpdent Corp PO Box 780 80 Oakland St Watertown MA 02471 Office Phone: 617-926-6666. Personal E-mail: dancindoc_HB@comcast.net.

BERK, JACK EDWARD, gastroenterologist, educator; b. Phila. s. Samuel and Esther B.; m. Adeline Elizabeth Alberts, June 26, 1937; children: Philip Howard (dec.), Richard Hanna. BA, U. Pa., 1932, MSc in Medicine, 1939, DSc in Medicine, 1943; MD, Jefferson Med. Coll., 1936; postgrad., Grad. Sch. Medicine, U. Pa., 1937-38. Diplomate Am. Bd. Internal Medicine, Am. Bd. Gastroenterology. Intern Walter Reed Gen. Hosp., Washington, 1936-37; resident in medicine No. divsn. Albert Einstein Med. Ctr., Phila., 1938-39; fellow gastroenterology Grad. Hosp., U. Pa., 1939-40; Ross V. Patterson fellow physiology Jefferson Med. Coll., Phila., 1940-41; instr. gastroenterology U. Pa., 1941-46; asst. prof. medicine Sch. Medicine, Temple U., 1946-54; asst. dir. Fels Research Inst., 1946-54; assoc. prof. clin. medicine Coll. Medicine, Wayne State U., 1954-62, prof. clin. medicine, 1962-63; prof. medicine Coll. Medicine, U. Calif., Irvine, 1963-79, Disting. prof. medicine, 1979—, chmn. dept. medicine, 1963-79, head div. gastroenterology, 1963-79, asst. dean, 1979-90. Cons. VA Hosp., Long Beach, Calif., 1963-97, Cedars-Sinai Med. Ctr., 1963—, Meml. Hosp., Long Beach, 1964-97. Contbg. author: Bockus Gastroenterology, 1st and 2d edits.; assoc. editor: Bockus Gastroenterology 3d edit., 1974, editor-in-chief 4th edit., 1985, cons. editor 5th edit., 1994; editor: Developments in Digestive Diseases, Vol. 1, 1977, Vol. 2, 1979, Vol. 3, 1980; co-editor: Gastrointestinal Symptoms: Clinical Interpretation, 1991; mem. editl. bd. 13 med. jours., various times, 1959—; delivered 14 named lectureships; contbr. 200 articles to med. jours., 108 chpts. in more than 60 books. U.S. Dept. State rep. to S.Am. countries Cultural Exch. Program, 1961. Served to maj. M.C. AUS, 1941-46. Recipient Disting. Svc. award Mich. Med. Soc., 1959, Faculty Cmty. Svc. award U. Calif.-Irvine Alumni Assn., 1971, also Faculty Univ. Svc. award, 1976, Disting. Achievement award Jefferson Med. Coll. Alumni Assn., 1977, Maimonides award Maimonides Soc., 1984, Centennial award N.E. High Sch., Phila., 1990, Aldrich Disting. Univ. Svc. award U. Calif., Irvine, 1993, Bockus medal World Orgn. Gastroenterology, 1994; named Disting. Physician Nat. Found. for Ileitis and Colitis, 1980; J. Edward Berk Lectr. established U. Calif. Irvine Gastroenterology Alumni Assn., Aug., 1991, J. Edward Berk Lectr. established U. Calif. Irvine Vol. Clin. Faculty, 1991, J. Edward Berk Alumni Med. Edn. Ctr. dedicated U. Calif., Irvine, May 30, 1996. Master ACP (gov. So. Calif. region II 1976-80, Laureate award So. Calif. region 1990), Am. Coll. Gastroenterology (pres. 1975-76, Rorer award 1970, 74, 78, 79, Disting. Sci. Achievement award 1982, Clin. Achievement award 1988, Samuel Weiss award 1995); mem. AMA (chmn. sect. gastroenterology 1965-66), Am. Gastroent. Assn. (Disting. Educator award 1992), Am. Soc. Gastrointestinal Endoscopy (pres. 1958-59, Rudolf Schindler award 1966), Am. Fedn. Clin. Rsch. (chmn. Ea. sect.), Bockus Internat. Soc. Gastroenterology (pres. 1967-71), Detroit Gastroent. Soc. (pres. 1960-61), So. Calif. Soc. Gastroenterology (pres. 1967-68), L.A. Acad. Medicine (gov. 1981-84), So. Calif. Soc. Gastrointestinal Endoscopy (hon.), Orange County Acad. Medicine, Orange County Gastroenterology Soc. (founding pres.), Interam. Gastroent. Assn. (life, hon. pres. 1981—), Fgn. Med. Soc., Acad. Med. Ecuador, Peruvian and

Cuban Soc. Gastroenterology (hon.), Gastroenterology Socs. Colombia, Gastrointestinal Endoscopy Soc. Colombia, Ecuador, Venezuela and Brazilian Soc. of Gastroenterology and Nutrition, Sigma Xi, Alpha Omega Alpha. Home: 894 Ronda Sevilla Unit C Laguna Woods CA 92653-4796 E-mail: jeberk@uci.edu.

BERK, LEE ELIOT, academic administrator; m. Susan Berk. BA, Brown U., 1964; JD, Boston U., 1967. Pres. Berklee Coll. of Music, Boston, 1979—2004. Author: Legal Protection for the Creative Musician (ASCAP/Deems Taylor award, 1971). Recipient Am. Eagle award, Nat. Music Coun., 1995. Office: Berklee Coll Music Office of the President 1140 Boylston St Boston MA 02215-3631

BERK, PAUL DAVID, internist, research scientist, educator; b. Bklyn., Apr. 3, 1938; s. Charles and Helen (Goell) B.; m. Aviva Ancona, July 4, 1965 (div. Aug. 1990); children: Claire, Philip, Edward; m. Nicole Polak, 1991; 1 child, David. BA, Swarthmore Coll., 1959; cert., U. St. Andrews, Scotland, 1960; MD, Columbia U., 1964. Diplomate Am. Bd. Internal Medicine, Am. Bd. Hematology. Intern Columbia-Presbyn. Med. Ctr., N.Y.C., 1964-65, resident, 1965-66, fellow in hematology, 1969-70; clin. assoc. metabolism br. Nat. Cancer Inst., Bethesda, Md., 1966-69, sr. investigator, 1970-73; clin. asst. prof. medicine Georgetown U., Washington, 1971-75, clin. assoc. prof., 1975-77; chief sect. on diseases of the liver Nat. Inst. Arthritis, Metabolism and Digestive Diseases, NIH, Bethesda, 1973-77; prof. medicine Mt. Sinai Sch. Medicine, N.Y.C., 1977—2004, Albert and Vera List prof. medicine, 1980-89, prof. biochemistry, 1987-99, Henry and Lillian Stratton prof. molecular medicine, 1989—2004, chief divsn. hematology, 1977-89, acting chief, 1989-90, chief divsn. liver disease, 1989-01; prof. dept. medicine Columbia U. Coll. Physicians and Surgeons, N.Y.C., 2004—. Prof. biochemistry and molecular biology Mt. Sinai Sch. Medicine, 1999-2004; adj. prof. Rockefeller U., 1987-89; cons. in liver disease NIH, 1977-80, mem. adv. coun. Nat. Inst. Diabetes and Digestive and Kidney Diseases, 1990-94. Editor: (with others) Chemistry and Physiology of the Bile Pigments, 1977, Frontiers in Liver Disease, 1981, Myelofibrosis and the Biology of Connective Tissue, 1984, Hans Popper: A Tribute, 1992, Hepatic Transport and Bile Secretion, 1993, Polythemia Vera, 1994; editor-in-chief Seminars in Liver Disease, 1981-90, 96—, Hepatology, 1991-96; mem. editorial bd. Artificial Organs, 1979-92, Liver, 1980-93; contbr. articles to profl. jours. Served as sr. surgeon USPHS, 1966-69, 75-77. Recipient Merck award Columbia U., 1964; Fulbright scholar, 1959 Fellow ACP, Am. Coll. Gastroenterology; mem. Am. Liver Found. (chmn. bd. dirs. 2000-04), Am. Soc. Clin. Investigation, Assn. Am. Physicians, Am. Assn. Study of Liver Disease (councillor 1985-93, v.p. 1988, pres. 1989), Internat. Assn. Study of Liver (councillor 1988-91), Am. Soc. for Hematology, Am. Clin. and Climatological Assn., Nat. Polycthemia Vera Study Group (vice chmn. 1978-95), Soc. Exptl. Biol. Medicine (councillor 1993-96), N.Y. Soc. Study of Blood (pres. 1982-83), Sigma Xi, Phi Beta Kappa, Alpha Omega Alpha. Office: Columbia Univ Med Ctr Divsn Digestive & Liver Disease 630 W 168th St Box 83 New York NY 10032 Office Phone: 212-342-3718. Business E-Mail: pb2158@columbia.edu.

BERK, PHILIP WOOLF, journalist; b. Cape Town, South Africa, Feb. 13, 1933; arrived in U.S., 1952; s. Benjamin and Rebecca (Brenner) Berk; m. Ruth Greenberg, June 20, 1954; children: Benjamin, Alexander, Ann, Melanie. BA, UCLA, 1955; gen. secondary life tchg. credential, Calif. State U., Northridge, 1963—63; MA, Calif. State U., 1965. With The Argus Group, Johannesburg, 1974—83; pres. Hollywood Fgn. Press Assn., 1989—; internat. freelancer. Mem.: Phi Eta Sigma. Home: 6829 Mclennan Ave Van Nuys CA 91406-4530 Office: The Argus Group PO Box 1014 Johannesburg South Africa 2000*

BERKA, MARIANNE GUTHRIE, health and physical education educator; b. Queens, N.Y., Dec. 25, 1944; d. Frank Joseph and Mary (DePaul) Guthrie; m. Jerry George Berka, June 1, 1968; children: Katie, Keri. *Katie Anne Berka, daughter, graduated with a BA from Skidmore College in 1997 and a dual master's degree in Clinical Psychology and Art Therapy from Long Island University in 2001. Keri Lynn Berka, daughter, received a BA from Skidmore College in 2000, and a DVM from the University of Missouri in 2004 and practices at Center Moricaes in Long Island, New York. Jerry G. Berka, husband, graduated from Wesleyan in 1963 and Cornell Law School in 1966 and has been practicing law in Bay Shore since 1969.* BS, Ithaca Coll., 1966, MS, 1968; EdD, NYU, 1990. Tchr. Northport H.S., 1966—67; prof. health, Phys. Edn. and Recreation Nassau C.C., Garden City, NY, 1968—. Adj. assoc. prof. Hofstra U., Hempstead, NY, 1998—. Mem.: AAHPER, AAHPERD, Am. Coll. Sports Medicine (cert. health/fitness instr.), Am. Assn. Sex Educators, Counselors and Therapists (cert. sex educator), N.Y. State Assn. Health, Phys. Edn., Recreation and Dance (J.B. Nash scholarship com. 1983—2000, Nassau Zone Disting. Svc. award 1988, Nassau Zone Higher Edn. Tchr. of Yr. 2003), Assn. Women Phys. Educators N.Y. State (chpt. chmn. 1973—74, chpt. treas. 1980—84). Roman Catholic. Home: 90 Bay Way Ave Brightwaters NY 11718-2012 Office: P226 HPER Nassau Community Coll Garden City NY 11530 Office Phone: 516-572-8147. Business E-Mail: berkam@ncc.edu.

BERKE, JOSEPH H., psychotherapist; b. Newark, Jan. 17, 1939; arrived in Eng., 1965; m. Roberta Elzey (div.); children: Joshua, Deborah; m. Lisa Pickar. Degree, Columbia U., 1960; MD, Albert Einstein Coll. Medicine, 1964. Diplomate Am. Bd. Med. Examiners, lic. physician N.Y., Calif. Mixed med. intern L.I. Coll. Hosp., NY, 1964—65; rsch. fellow in psychotherapy and social scis. Phila. Assn., London, 1965—69; pvt. pratice psychotherapy London, 1965—. Dir. Arbours Housing Assn., 1970—, Arbours Crisis Ctr., 1973—, Arbours Assn., 1975—2000; lectr., supr. Arbours Tng. Program in Psychotherapy and Social Psychiatry, 1974—97; vis. lectr. internat. univs.; cons. psychotherapist Hammersmith and Fulham Assn. Mental Health, 1984—89; sec. Inst. Phenomenol. Studies, London, 1966—76; psychotherapist The Langham Clinic, London, 1965—67. Author (with Mary Barnes): Mary Barnes: Two Accounts of a Journey Through Madness, 1971, 3d rev. edit., 2002, Brit. edit., 1971, 2d rev. Brit. edit., 1990, also Finnish, Danish, Dutch, French, Norwegian, Swedish, German, Spanish, Portuguese, Japanese and Italian edits., adapted as radio prodn., stage play; author: (with Calvin C. Hernton) The Cannabis Experience: An Interpretive Study of the Effects of Marijuana and Hashish, 1974, 1976; author: Butterfly Man: Madness, Degradation & Redemption, 1977, French edit., 1980, I Haven't Had to Go Mad Here, 1979, Spanish edit., 1980, The Tyranny of Malice: Exploring the Dark Side of Character and Culture, 1988, Brit. edit., 1989, Finnish edit., 1991, Portuguese edit., 1992; editor, contbr.: Counter Culture, 1969, co-editor, contbr.: The Arbours Experience of Alternative Community Care, 1995, Even Paranoids Have Enemies: New Perspectives on Paranoia and Persecution, 1998, Beyond Madness: PsychoSocial Interventions in Madness, 2001; contbr. articles to profl. jours., chpts. to books. Fellow: Am. Bd. Med. Psychotherapists and Psychodiagnosticians (diplomate), Royal Soc. Medicine; mem.: Link Psychotherapy Ctr., Assn. Arbours Psychotherapists, U.K. Coun. Psychotherapy, Soc. Authors (London). Address: 5 Shepherd's Close London N6 5AG England

BERKEBILE, CHARLES ALAN, geology educator, hydrogeology researcher; b. Queens, N.Y., Mar. 4, 1938; s. Charles Dean and Bernice (Manlove) B.; children: Patricia Berlowe. BS, Allegheny Coll., 1960; MA, Boston U., 1961, PhD, 1964. Mem. rsch. staff MIT, Cambridge, 1963—64; asst. prof. Southampton Coll. L.I. U., NY, 1964—67, assoc. prof., dept. chair Southampton Coll., 1969—75, prof., assoc. dir. Southampton Coll., 1975—81; rsch. mineralogist Corning Glass Works, NY, 1967—69; prof., dept. chair Corpus Christi State U., Tex., 1981—91; prof., dir. Tex. A&M U., Corpus Christi, 1991—2004, prof., asst. dean, 1994-98, Regents prof., 2001—04, ret., 2004, prof. emeritus, 2005. Vis. assoc. chemist Brookhaven Nat. Lab., Upton, N.Y., 1966-67; vis. sr. rsch. geologist Princeton (N.J.) U., 1979-80. Contbr. articles to profl. jours. Mem. Regional Stormwater Master Plan Adv. Com., Corpus Christi, 1989-90, Mayor's Adv. Com. on Water Issues, Corpus Christi, 1991-92; treas., bd. dirs. Rockport (Tex.) Country Club Estates Homeowners Assn., 1991-94. Named Outstanding Educator, Koch Industries, 2001. Fellow Geol. Soc. Am.; mem. Assn. Ground Water Scientists and Engrs., Nat. Ground Water Assn., Nat. Assn. Geology Tchrs., Tex. Ground Water Assn. (hon., life, bd. dirs., v.p. ground water sci. 1994, pres. 1995-96), Corpus Christi Geol. Soc. Avocations: golf, music. Home: 314 Champions Dr Rockport TX 78382-6906 E-mail: alanb@pyramid3.net.

BERKELEY, EDMUND, JR., retired archivist, educator; b. Charlottesville, Va., Apr. 1, 1937; s. Edmund and Dorothy A. Berkeley; m. Elizabeth Makaritis, June 9, 1963; children: Maria Randolph, Edmund III. BA, U. South, 1958; MA in Am. History, U. Va., 1961. Prep. sch. tchr., 1961-63; asst. archivist Archives divsn. Va. State Libr., 1963-65; sr. asst., asst. curator Manuscripts divsn. U. Va., Charlottesville, 1965-69, univ. archivist, 1976-87, curator manuscripts, 1970-87, records adminstr., 1976-99, dir. spl. collections dept., 1987-93, sr. curator, 1994, univ. archivist, sr. assoc. dir., 1995-99, assoc. prof. Coll. Arts and Scis., 1976-99, assoc. prof. emeritus, 1999—. Cons. U. Ga. Library, George C. Marshall Library, SUNY-Stony Brook. Nat. Hist. Publs., Ashantilly Press. Editor: Autographs and Manuscripts: A Collector's Manual, 1978; author, editor articles to profl. jours. Commn. grantee Dept. Edn. Fellow Soc. Am. Archivists (coun. 1977-81); mem. Soc. Am. Architects, Mid-Atlantic Regional Archives Conf., Assn. Documentary Editing, Va. Hist. Soc. Episcopalian. Home: 2403 Bennington Rd Charlottesville VA 22901-2205 E-mail: eb2c@virginia.edu.

BERKELEY, (ED)WARD, performing arts association administrator, music educator; b. NYC; Grad, Carleton Coll., Minn., 1966. Artistic dir. Willow Cabin Theater Co.; now dir., undergrad. opera studies Juilliard Sch., NYC, 1987—; and gen. dir. Aspen Opera Theatre Ctr., Colo. Benedict Disting. Vis. Prof. of Theater Carleton Coll., 2003. Office: Aspen Opera Theatre Ctr 2 Music School Rd Aspen CO 81611 also: Opera Studies The Juilliard Sch 60 Lincoln Ctr Plz New York NY 10023-6588

BERKELHAMER, JAY ELLIS, pediatrician; b. Tuscaloosa, Ala., Apr. 8, 1942; s. Louis H. and Belle F. B.; m. Jacqueline Beth Colman, June 12, 1966; children: Beth Carolyn, Sara Kay, Adam Colman. BS, U. Mich., 1963, MD, 1967. Resident U. Chgo., 1967-70, asst. prof., 1972-78, assoc. prof., 1978-84, prof., 1984-93, assoc. chair, dir. residency program, 1986-93, assoc. dean ambulatory care, 1983-88; chair pediatrics Henry Ford Health Sys., Detroit, 1993-99. Prof. pediatrics Case Western Res. U., Cleve., 1994-99; clin. prof. pediatrics and communicable diseases U. Mich., Ann Arbor, 1994-99; sr. v.p. for med. affairs Children's Healthcare of Atlanta, 1999—; clin. prof. pediats. Emory U., Atlanta, 1999—. Lt. comdr. USPHS, 1970-72. Robert Wood Johnson Health Policy fellow NAS, Washington, 1978-79. Mem. Am. Acad. Pediatrics (pres. Ill. chpt. 1992, pres.-elect 2005), Chgo. Pediatric Soc. (pres. 1987, Archibald L. Hoyne award 1993), Ambulatory Pediatric Assn. (pres. 1986). Office: 1600 Tullie Circle Atlanta GA 30329 Office Phone: 404-785-7005. Office Fax: 404-785-7027.

BERKELHAMMER, ROBERT BRUCE, lawyer; b. Providence, Oct. 27, 1949; s. Cyril Lester and Anne Louise (Rossman) B.; m. Miriam June Finkelstein, Mar. 9, 1975; children: Jessi, Max, Abby. BA, U. Rochester, 1971; JD, Boston U., 1974. Bar: R.I. 1975, U.S. Dist. Ct. R.I. 1977, Mass. 1998, Conn. 2001. Atty. NLRB, Pitts., 1974—77; ptnr. Licht & Semonoff, Providence, 1977—97, Chace Ruttenberg & Freedman, LLP, Providence, 1997—. Pres. Jewish Family Service, Inc., Providence, 1988-91. Mem.: ABA, R.I. Jewish Hist. Assn. (pres. 2000—02), R.I. Bar Assn. Jewish. Home: 131 Laurel Ave Providence RI 02906-4622 Office: Chace Ruttenberg & Freedman LLP 1 Park Row Ste 300 Providence RI 02903-1235 Office Phone: 401-453-6400. Business E-Mail: rberkelhammer@crfllp.com.

BERKELMAN, KARL, physics professor; b. Lewiston, Maine, June 7, 1933; s. Robert George and Yvonne (Langlois) Berkelman; m. Mary Bowen Hobbie, Oct. 10, 1959; children: Thomas, James, Peter. BS, U. Rochester, N.Y., 1955; PhD, Cornell U., 1959. From asst. prof. to prof. physics Cornell U., Ithaca, N.Y., 1961—, dir. lab. nuclear studies, 1985-2000; sci. assoc. DESY, Hamburg, Fed. Republic of Germany, 1974-75, CERN, Geneva, 1967-68, 81-82, 91-92, 2000-2001. Office: Cornell U Newman Lab Ithaca NY 14853

BERKENKAMP, FRED JULIUS, management consultant; b. Alma, Wis., Oct. 19, 1925; s. Julius Henry and Elisabeth Helen Berkenkamp; m. Ruth Ethelyn Taylor; children: Linda Birch, Vicki Fitzgerald, Thomas, JoAnne. BS in Electron Engring, U. Wyo., 1948; postgrad., U. Syracuse, N.Y., 1951. Quality control mgmt. Gen. Electric Co., Syracuse, 1948-55, corporate cons. mfg. mgmt. N.Y.C., 1955-65, mgr. planning jet engines Cin., 1966-68, mgr. nuclear fuels mfg. Wilmington, N.C., 1969; corp. exec. v.p., pres. Appliance Group, Roper Corp., Kankakee, Ill., 1970-80; pres., chief exec. officer, dir. Allied Structural Steel Co. subs. MSL Industries/Alleghany Corp., Chicago Heights, Ill., 1980-83; pres. Berkenkamp & Co. Inc., mgmt. cons., 1984—; pres., CEO FMH, Inc., Newport Beach, Calif., 1988-91. Trustee Community Coll., 1974-80. Served with USNR, 1944-46. Mem. Assn. Home Appliance Mfrs. (chmn. bd. dirs.), Gas Appliance Mfrs. Assn. (dir.), Rotary, Sigma Chi. Home: 14216 W Cavalcade Dr Sun City West AZ 85375-5624

BERKENSTADT, JAMES ALLAN, lawyer; b. Chgo., June 26, 1956; s. Edward Jules and Lois Marion (Solomon) B.; m. Holly Lynn Cremer, Aug. 3, 1985; children: Rebecca, Bradley. BA, Northwestern U., 1978; JD, So. Ill. U., 1981. Bar: Ill., Wis. Litigation atty. Pollina & Phelan, Chgo., 1982-85; atty. for security dept. Chgo. Cubs Nat. League Ball Club, Chgo., 1982-84; litigation atty. Axley & Brynelson, Madison, Wis., 1986-87; v.p., corporate counsel The Wisconsin Cheeseman, Inc., Madison, 1987—. Author: Black Market Beatles: The Story Behind The Lost Recordings, 1995, Nevermind: Nirvana, 1998; prodr. The Beatles Tapes CD, 1994—, Live At The Edgewater: vol. 1 and 2 CD; historian for The Beatles, 2002—; contbr. articles to Musician mag. Bd. dirs. Cremer Charitable Found., Madison, 1989—, Alliant Energy Ctr. Bd. Dane County; Transport 20/20 Madison; historian/archivist for rock band Garbage, George Harrison. Mem. NARAS. Avocations: golf, writing. Office: The Wisconsin Cheeseman Inc 301 Broadway Dr Sun Prairie WI 53590-1799

BERKERY, ROSEMARY T., lawyer, investment company executive; b. 1953; BA magna cum laude, Coll. Mt. St. Vincent; JD, St. John's U., Jamaica, N.Y. Bar: N.Y. 1980. Atty. Shearman & Sterling, NYC, 1978—83, Merrill Lynch & Co., Inc., NYC, 1983—95, sr. v.p., assoc. gen. counsel, 1995—97, co-dir. global securities rsch. and econs. group, 1997—2000, sr. v.p., head U.S. pvt. client group mktg. and investment, 2000—01, exec. v.p., gen. counsel, 2001—. Editor: St. John's Law Rev. Office: Merrill Lynch and Co Inc 4 World Financial Ctr 32d Fl New York NY 10080*

BERKEY, DENNIS D., academic administrator; b. Wooster, Ohio, May 27, 1947; s. William Bruce and Mary Louise (Schrock) B.; m. Catherine Grooms, Aug. 24, 1974; children: Cristin, Aaron, Jessica. BA, Muskingum Coll., New Concord, Ohio, 1969; MA, Miami U., Oxford, Ohio, 1971; PhD, U. Cin., 1974. Lectr. U. Cin., 1972-73; instr. Miami U., Oxford, Ohio, 1973-74; asst. prof. math. Boston U., 1974-79, assoc. prof. math., 1979-93, prof. math., 1993—, dean Grad. Sch., 1987—2002, dean arts and scis., 1987—2002, provost, 1987—91, 1996—2004; pres. Worcester Poly. Inst., Mass., 2004—. Author: Calculus, 1983, 3d edit., 1992, Applied Calculus, 1986, 3d edit., 1994, Calculus for Management, 1986, 3d edit., 1994. Recipient Metcalf Award for Excellence in Tchg., Boston U., 1978. Mem. Am. Math. Soc., Math. Assn. Am., Soc. for Indsl. and Applied Math. Home: 1 Drury Ln Worcester MA 01609 Office: Worcester Poly Inst 100 Institute Rd Worcester MA 01609 Office Phone: 508-831-5200. Business E-Mail: dberkey@wpi.edu.

BERKHOUDT, THOMAS WALTER, director; b. Buffalo, Jan. 22, 1967; s. Herman and Ethel Berkhoudt; m. Kimberly Susan Miller, Sept. 12, 1992; children: Drew Addison, Erika. BS in Acctg., Alfred U., 1989; MBA, U. Rochester, 1994. Jr. acct. U. Rochester, NY, 1989—92, sr. acct., strong meml. hosp., 1992—94, spl. projects adminstr., dept. medicine, 1994—96, sr. cardiology adminstr., cardiology unit, 1996—2000; fin. & reporting specialist Rochester Inst. Tech., 2000—03, asst. dir. sponsored programs fin. mgmt. svcs., 2003—. Sr. assoc. Rochester Chpt. Cert. Football Officials, 2003; treas. Rochester Cardiovasc. Soc., 1996—2000. Mem.: Med. Group Mgmt. Assn. (assoc.), Am. Acad. Med. Adminstrs. (assoc.), Nat. Coun. U. Rsch. Adminstrs. (assoc.). Avocations: running, gardening, tennis, golf, travel.

BERKLAND, JAMES OMER, geologist; b. Glendale, California, July 31, 1930; m. Janice Lark Keirstead, Dec. 19, 1966; children: Krista Lynn, Jay Olin. AA, Santa Rosa Jr. Coll., 1951; BA, U. Calif., Berkeley, 1958; MS, San Jose State U., 1964; post grad., U. Calif., Davis, 1969—72. registered engring. geologist, Calif. Psychiat. tech. Sonoma State Hosp., Calif., 1951—57; with U.S. Geol. Survey, 1958—64; engring. geologist U.S. Bur. Reclamation, 1964—69, cons. geologist, 1969—72; asst. prof. Appalachian State U., Boone, NC, 1972—73; county geologist Santa Clara County, San Jose, Calif., 1973—94; ret., 1994. Mem. geology tech. adv. com., San Jose, Calif.; adj. prof. San Jose State U., Calif., 1973—75; lectr. gen. edn. conf. Sci. and Tech. Soc., 1985—89, coord. com. Calif. conv., 1978; mem. evening faculty San Jose City Coll., Calif.; mem. West Valley Legis. Com., Calif., 1979—90; lectr. ann. deposit receipt seminar San Jose Real Estate Bd., Calif., 1980—85; discoverer in field; featured spkr. Keynote Speakers, Inc.; geology tchr. Sonoma High Sch. Adult Edn., Calif., 2001—03. Contbg. numerous articles to profl. journals.; originator seismic window theory for earthquake prediction, 1974; TV and radio appearances including PBA, Frontline, Evening Mag., People are Talking, 48 Hours, Sightings, You Bet Your Life, Science Faction, Science Fiction Cable, Two on the Town, In Search of CNN News, WGN, KIRO, KSL, KIEV, KGO, KCBS, KNYV, KOA, KOGO, KVEN, KSCO, KOMO, KPFK, Two at Noon, KPFA-FM Radio, The Other Side, Northwest Afternoon, Art Bell's Coast to Coast, Town Meeting, Ron Owens Show, Laura Lee Show, Art Bell Show, Kathi Gori Show, Extra, Strange Universe; articles on work featured in OMNI, STERN, Wall St. Jour., Bergen's Tidende, San Francisco Examiner, San Francisco Chronicle, L.A. Times, Nat. Geog., Am. Health, The Astrology Ency., Old Farmers Almanac, 1991, Gilroy Dispatch, Bakersfield Californian, San Jose Mercury News, Sonoma Index Tribune, Intuition, Farmers Almanac, others; editor, pub.: SYZYGY An Earthquake Newsletter, 1990—; co-founder Quakeline. Active mem. Statue of Liberty Found., NY; treas. Creekside Pk. Pl. Homeowner's Group, Calif.; mem. various city and county adv. boards Calif.; mem. legis. com. Rt. 85 Task Force, Calif., Earthquake Watch, Calif., 1979—82, New Weather Observer, Calif., Nat. Wildlife Fedn., Calif.; mem. tech. and soc. San Jose Sch. Dist., Calif., 1980—, mem. role model program, 1995—97; mem. Sonoma Land Trust, Calif.; bd. dir. Glen Ellen Cmty. Ch., Calif., 2001—; Nat. Wildlife Fedn.; v.p. West Coast Aquatics, Calif., Creekside Pk. Pl. Swim Team, Calif.; mem. ctr. study early man East Valley WMCA, Calif.; mem. legis. com. West Valley YMCA, Calif., 1980—; mem. Found. for the Study of Cycles, Calif., invited lectr. monthly and ann. meeting.; mem. The Nature Conservancy, Calif.; charter mem. The Dolphin Inst.; docent Bouverie Nature Preserve, Calif., 1999—; mem. Jack London Found. Recipient Resolution of Commendation Santa Clara Bd. Supervisors., 1994; Dwight E. Stanford fellow, A.J. Robinson Found. Mem. Smithsonian Inst. (assoc.), Ret. Pub. Employee Assn. Calif., Alumni Assn. San Jose State U., Sons of Norway, Sonoma Hist. Soc., Jack London Reading Group, Lions Club (various offices and awards, including pres. Valley of the Moon Lions, 2002-03, Lion of Yr. Awards 1990,91,93,94). Home: 1175 Chauvet Rd # 1926 Glen Ellen CA 95442-1926 Fax: 707-935-6512. Personal E-mail: syzygyjob@aol.com.

BERKLEY, EMILY CAROLAN, lawyer; b. Richmond, Va., Mar. 2, 1950; d. Charles Garvice and Edna Gray (Berkley) Broom; m. Richard E. Bird, Sept. 6, 1969 (div. Mar. 1988); children: Jessica A. Bird, Martel J. Bird. Student, Coll. of William and Mary, 1968—70; BS in Psychology cum laude, Tufts U., 1972; JD magna cum laude, Temple U., 1977. Ptnr. Ballard Spahr Andrews & Ingersoll LLP, Phila., 1977—. Seminar panelist Pa. Bar Inst., 1992, 98-2003, 05, Practicing Law Inst., 1993-2005. Long range planning com. Performing Arts for Tredyffrin-Easttown Sch. Dist., Berwyn, Pa., 1989, chair subcom. on creativity, futures com., 1990; active United Way, 1989-91; bd. dirs. Devon-Strafford Little League, 1992-95. Fellow: Am. Bar Found. (life); mem.: ABA (bus. law sect. chair task force on exporation of Uniform Comml. Code 1995—97, vice chair internat. comml. law subcom. 1997—99, bus. law sect. liaison U.S. Sec. of State's adv. com. on pvt. internat 1997—99, vice chair legal opinions com. 2002—04, chair legal opinions 2004—, mem. uniform comml. code com., fed. regulation securities com.), N.Y. TriBar Opinion Com., Phila. Bar Assn., Pa. Bar Assn. (bus. law sect., chair legal opinion task force, chair article 9 task force, sec.), Am. Law Inst., Am. Coll. Comml. Fin. Lawyers (bd. regents 1993—2001, pres. 2000). Office: Ballard Spahr Andrews et al 1735 Market St Ste 5100 Philadelphia PA 19103-7599 Office Phone: 215-864-8611. Business E-Mail: berkley@ballardspahr.com.

BERKLEY, EUGENE BERTRAM (BERT BERKLEY), envelope company executive; b. Kansas City, Mo., May 8, 1923; s. Eugene Bertram (Bert) Berkowitz and Caroline Newman (Newburger) B.; m. Joan Meinrath, Sept. 1, 1948; children: Janet Lynn Berkley Dubrava, William (Bill) Spencer Berkley, Jane Ellen Berkley Levitt. BA, Duke U., 1948; MBA, Harvard U., 1950. Pres., CEO Tension Envelope Corp., Kansas City, Mo., 1962-88, chmn. bd., 1967—. Patentee in field. Bd. dirs. The Inst. for Ednl. Leadership Inc., Washington; trustee, chmn. U. Kansas City, 1983-85, vice chmn., 1981-83, North Campus Devel. Com., policy bd., charter mem. Univ. Assocs.; chmn. bd. dirs. Minority Supplier Coun., 1986-88, bd. dirs. Ewing Marion Kauffman Found., Ctr. for Entrepreneurial Leadership, 1991-2002; chmn. Ctr. for Bus. Innovation, 1987-89; bd. dirs. Nat. Youth Info. Network, 1997—; mem. adv. bd. Nat. Coun. Econ. Edn., 1993-95, human resources com. Heart of Am. United Way, 1983, chmn. Comprehensive Needs and Svc. Survey Com., 1971; pres. Civic Coun. of Greater Kansas City, 1967-68, charter mem., bd. dirs. 1982-83; pres. C. of C. of Greater Kansas City, 1968-69; bd. dirs. Menorah Med. Ctr. Bd., 1980-94; mem. Kitchen Cabinet, Kansas City, Mo. Sch. Dist., 1990-92; chmn. adv. com., bd. dirs. Ctr. for Workforce Preparation, U.S. C. of C., 1989-91; trustee Midwest Rsch. Inst., exec. com., 1969-72; bd. dirs. Kansas City Area Health Planning Coun., Inc., 1982-83, Nat. Minority Supplier Devel. Coun., 1989-98; chmn. bd. dirs. Human Svcs. Testing and Retng. Coun., 1983-90; active Bus. Roundtable Dept. Social Svcs. State of Mo., 1989-99; adv. bd. U. Kans. Natural History Mus., 1994-2000, Nat. Parks and Conservation Assn., 1986—; bd. dirs. Can. Cellulose Co., Vancouver, BC, 1973-80, founder, LINC, 1992; chmn. local investment commn. LINC Mo. Dept. Social Svcs., 1992-95, exec. comm., 1992—; mem. exec. com. Ctr. for Mgmt. Assistance, 1980-83; mem. Mayor's Prayer Breakfast Com., 1964-84; mem. exec. com., met. chmn. Nat. Alliance of Businessmen of Met. Kansas City, 1973; dir. family and cmty. trust State of Mo., 1999—; bd. dirs. Centerpoint for Leaders, Washington, 2001—. Decorated Bronze Star; recipient Brotherhood award NCCJ, 1968, numerous other awards, including Mr. Kansas City award C. of C. of Greater Kansas City, 1972, Disting. Svc. award Johnson County Friends of the Libr. (Johnson County, Kans.), 1982, Chancellor's medal U. Mo.-Kansas City, 1989, Disting. Svc. to State Govt. award Nat. Govs. Assn., 2000. Mem. Envelope Mfrs. Assn. (exec. com. 1960-63, 67-70, 76-79, vice chmn. exec. com. 1981-83, v.p. 1981-83, pres. 1983-85), Flexographic Tech. Assn. (bd. dirs. 1993-97), Oakwood Country Club, Homestead Country Club. Avocations: flyfishing, race walking, camping, white water rafting, backpacking. Office: Tension Envelope Corp 819 E 19th St Kansas City MO 64108-1781 Office Phone: 816-471-3800. E-mail: bertberkley@tension.com.

BERKLEY, JAMES DONALD, clergyman; b. Yakima, Wash., May 19, 1950; s. Donald William and Erma Ercile (Van Meter) B.; m. Deborah Milam, Aug. 18, 1974; children: Peter James, Mary Milam. BS, U. Wash., 1972; MDiv, Fuller Theol. Seminary, 1975, D Ministry, 1980. Intern First Presbyn. Ch., Yakima, Wash., 1971-73, Bel Air Presbyn. Ch., L.A., 1973-75; asst. pastor Community Presbyn Ch., Ventura, Calif., 1975-78; sr. pastor Dixon (Calif.) Community Ch., 1978-85; sr. assoc. editor Leadership jour. Christianity Today Inc., Carol Stream, Ill., 1985-90, editor Your Church, 1990-94; sr. assoc. pastor First Presbyn. Ch., Bellevue, Wash., 1994—2002; nat. issues ministry dir. Presbyns. for Renewal, Bellevue, 2002—. Author: Making the Most of Mistakes, 1987, Called into Crisis, 1988, The Dynamics of Church Finance, 2000, Essential Christianity, 2001; gen. editor: Preaching to Convince, 1986, Leadership Handbooks of Practical Theology, Vol. I, 1992, Vols.

II and III, 1994; editor reNEWS, 1999—. Recipient 1st place award interview Evangelical Press Assn., 1991, 92. Republican. Avocations: bagpipes, hiking, golf, films, music. Home: 304 128th Ave NE Bellevue WA 98005-3242 Office: Presbyterians for Renewal 304 128th Ave NE Bellevue WA 98005 Office Phone: 425-637-7742. E-mail: jimberkley@msn.com.

BERKLEY, MARY CORNER, neurologist; b. Balt., Apr. 6, 1926; d. Henry Evans and Eleanor (Diggs) Corner; m. Kelly McKenzie Berkley, Sept. 3, 1955 (dec. Oct. 1984); children: Henry Evans, Robert Bruce; m. Warren Frederick Gorman, May 31, 1986 (dec. Mar. 2000). AB, Bryn Mawr Coll., 1946; MD, Johns Hopkins U., 1950. Diplomate Am. Bd. Psychiatry and Neurology. Intern, resident Cin. Gen. Hosp., 1950-52; resident in medicine Strong Meml. Hosp., Rochester, N.Y., 1952-53, fellow in neurology, 1953-56; pvt. practice Rochester, 1956-58, Janesville, Wis., 1958-60; resident in neurology U. Mich. Med. Ctr., Ann Arbor, 1960-64; sr. instr. Hahnemann Med. Coll., Phila., 1965-68; pvt. practice neurology Gallipolis, Ohio, 1968-70, Mt. Vernon, Ill., 1970-76; staff neurologist VA Med. Ctr., Phoenix, 1976-95, ret., 1995. Fellow Am. Acad. Neurology; mem. Alpha Omega Alpha.

BERKLEY, PETER LEE, lawyer; b. Newark, N.J., Mar. 10, 1939; s. Irving S. and Goldie A. (Karp) B.; m. Nancy R. Margolis, Aug. 2, 1964; children: James, Alison Wagonbeld, John. BA, Williams Coll., 1960; JD, Harvard U., 1963. Bar: N.J. 1963, U.S. Dist. Ct. N.J. 1963. Assoc. Riker, Danzig, Scherer & Brown, Newark, 1963—68; ptnr. Riker, Danzig, Scherer & Hyland, Newark and Morristown, N.J., 1969-83; mng. ptnr. Riker, Danzig, Scherer, Hyland & Perretti, L.L.P., Morristown, 1984—95; ptnr. Riker, Danzig, Scherer, Hyland & Perretti, LLP, Morristown, 1996—99, of counsel, 1999—. Trustee Livingston (N.J.) Symphony Orch., 1975-89. Mem. ABA, N.J. State Bar Assn., Am. Coll. Real Estate Lawyers, Harvard Law Sch. Alumni Assn. N.J. (pres. 1980-81), Williams Coll. Alumni Assn. Ctrl. N.J. (pres. 1986-89), Phi Beta Kappa. Office: Hdqrs Plz 1 Speedwell Ave Morristown NJ 07962-1981 Office Phone: 973-451-8403. Business E-Mail: pberkley@riker.com.

BERKLEY, ROBERT CLARKSON, retired lawyer; b. Pago Pago, American Samoa, May 23, 1940; s. William Leneave and Charlotte Hamilton (Priest) B.; m. Janice Anne Wertz, Sept. 6, 1969; children: William Bradley, Meredith Anne. AB, Duke U., 1961; JD, U. Va., 1967; MS, U.S. Naval War Coll., 1977. Bar: Va. 1967, Ga. 1968, U.S. Supreme Ct. 1971, U.S. Ct. Mil. Appeals 1972, U.S. Dist. Ct. (we. dist.) Va. 1991, U.S. Bankruptcy Ct. (we. dist.) Va. 1991. Commd. ensign USN, 1961, advanced through grades to capt., 1982, ret., 1991; exec. officer Naval Legal Svc. Office, Subic Bay, The Philippines, 1977-79; fleet judge adv. Comdr. Seventh Fleet, Yokosuka, Japan, 1979-81; staff judge adv. Chief of Naval Material, Alexandria, Va., 1981-84; commanding officer Naval Legal Svc. Office, Norfolk, Va., 1984-87; dir. litigation Office of Navy Judge Adv. Gen., Alexandria, Va., 1987-89; asst. judge adv. gen. of the Navy USN, Alexandria, 1989-90; staff judge adv. Naval Air Sys. Command, Alexandria, 1990-91; ptnr. Petty, Livingston, Dawson, Devening & Richards, P.C., Lynchburg, Va., 1991-98. Del. Rep. State Conv., Richmond, Va., 1993, Rep. City Com., Lynchburg, 1993—. Decorated Navy Commendation medal Sec. of the Navy, Yokosuka, 1981, Meritorious Svc. medals Sec. of Def., 1984, 87. Mem. Va. State Bar (bd. govs. mil. law sect. 1996—), Ga. State Bar. Presbyterian. Avocations: jogging, boating.

BERKLEY, SHELLEY, congresswoman, lawyer; b. NYC, Jan. 20, 1951; m. Larry Lehrner. BA in Polit. Sci., U. Nev., 1972; JD, U. San Diego, 1976. Former in-house counsel Southwest Gas Corp.; former dep. dir. Nev. State Commerce Dept.; mem. Nev. State Assembly, 1982—84; vice chair Nev. U. and Community Coll. Sys. Bd. of Regents, 1990—98; v.p. govt. and legal affairs Sands Hotel, 1996—98; mem. U.S. Congress from 1st Nev. dist., 1999—, mem. transp. and infrastructure com., internat. affairs com., vet. affairs com. Former bd. chair Nev. Hotel and Motel Assn.; former nat. dir. Am. Hotel-Motel Assn.; former delegate White House Conference on Tourism. Bd. trustees Sunrise-Columbia Hosp. Mem.: Nev. State Bar Assn. Democrat. Office: US Ho Reps 439 Cannon Ho Office Bldg Washington DC 20515-0001 also: Dist Office 2340 Paseo Del Prado Ste D-106 Las Vegas NV 89102*

BERKLEY, STEPHEN MARK, entrepreneur, investor; b. N.J., 1944; s. Irving S. and Goldie A. Berkley; children: David, Michael. Student, London Sch. Econs., 1964-65; BA in Econs., Colgate U., 1966; MBA, Harvard U., 1968. Mgmt. cons. Boston Cons. Group, 1968, 71-73; mgr. strategic planning Potlatch Corp., 1973-77; v.p. bus. devel. Qume Corp. subs. ITT, Hayward, Calif., 1977-80, v.p., gen. mgr. memory products divs., 1980-81; v.p. mktg. Quantum Corp., Milpitas, Calif., 1981-83, chmn., CEO, 1987-92, chmn., 1992-93, 95-98; pres. Plus Devel. Corp. (Quantum subs.), 1983-87, chmn., CEO, 1987-92; pres. The Rosewood Found., 1991—. Bd. dirs. Quantum Corp., Edify Corp.; chmn. Coactive Computing Corp.; instr. bus. and econs. East Carolina U., 1969-71. Bd. dirs. Hidden Harvest, 2005—. Served to lt. USNR, 1968-71. Mem. Corp. Planners Assn. (dir.), Harvard Bus. Sch. Club No. Calif., Los Altos Golf and Country Club, The Reserve Golf Club, Phi Beta Kappa. Avocations: golf, modern art, travel.

BERKLEY, WILLIAM ROBERT, insurance holding company executive; b. Oct. 31, 1945; m. Marjorie Andepos, June 19, 1971; children: Lisa A., W. Robert Jr., Lauren E. BS, NYU, 1966; MBA, Harvard U., 1968. Founder, chmn., chief exec. officer W.R. Berkley Corp., 1967—, pres., 2000—. Officer and/or dir., chmn. Assoc. Cmty. Bancorp, Inc., Conn. Cmty. Bank, N.A., Strategic Distbn., Inc.; officer and/or dir. Atlee of Del., Inc., FLOORgraphics, Inc., Interlaken Capital, Inc. and affiliates, FFS Holdings, Inc., The First Marblehead Corp., Kiln Plc, Five Mile Capital Ptnrs., LLC. Co-chmn. Sabin Vaccine Inst.; chmn. bd. overseers Stern Sch. Bus., NYU; vice chmn. bd. trustees, exec. com. U. Conn.; vice chmn. bd. trustees, exec. com., fin. com., investment com. NYU; bd. dirs., exec. com. Georgetown U. Office: W R Berkley Corp 475 Steamboat Rd Greenwich CT 06830-6608

BERKMAN, LISA F., public health educator; PhD, U. Calif., Berkeley, 1977. Thomas D. Cabot prof. pub. policy Harvard Sch. Pub. Health, Boston, chair Dept. of Soc., Human Develop., and Health. Contbr. articles to profl. jours. Mem.: Inst. of Medicine of NAS. Achievements include research in on psychosocial influences on health outcomes. Office: Harvard Univ Kresge Bldg Rm 709 677 Huntington Ave Boston MA 02115*

BERKMAN, LOUIS, steel company executive; b. Canton, Ohio, Jan. 15, 1909; s. Hyman L. and Sarah (Galman) B.; m. Sandra Weiss, Apr. 14, 1935 (dec. Aug. 1983); children: Marshall, Donna Berkman Paul. DBA (hon.), Bethany Coll.; DBus Sci. (hon.), U. Steubenville. Pres., treas. Louis Berkman Co., Steubenville, Ohio, 1931—; pres., chmn. Parkersburg Steel Corp., W.Va., 1946—; pres., treas. Follansbee Steel Corp., W.Va., 1954—; chmn. exec. com., dir. Ampco-Pitts. Corp., Pitts., 1979—. Chmn. bd., pres. First Fin. Group, Inc., Washington, Pa.; dir. Asso. Communications Corp. Pres., trustee Louis and Sandra Berkman Found., Steubenville, 1952—, Ampco-Pitts. Found.; mem. adv. com. Ft. Steuben Area council Boy Scouts Am. Mem. Steubenville C. of C., Pitts. Symphony Soc., Oglebay Inst.; mem. B'nai B'rith. Clubs: Rotarian, Elk, Steubenville Country; Westmoreland Country (Export, Pa.); Downtown (Pitts.), Concordia (Pitts.). Office: Ampco-Pittsburgh Corp 600 Grant St Pittsburgh PA 15219 Office Phone: 740-283-3722.

BERKMAN, MICHAEL G., lawyer; b. Poland, Apr. 4, 1917; came to U.S., 1921; s. Harry and Bertha (Jay) B.; m. Marjorie Edelstein, Nov. 28, 1941; children— Laurel, William BS, U. Chgo., 1937, PhD, 1941; JD, DePaul U., 1958; LLM in Intellectual Property, John Marshall Law Sch., 1962; spl. courses, Harvard U., 1943, MIT, 1943. Bar: U.S. Patent Office 1960. Research chemist Argonne Nat. Lab., 1946-51; assoc. dir., chief chemist Colburn Labs., Chgo., 1951-59; instr. chemistry Roosevelt U., Chgo., 1946-49; patent lawyer Mann, Brown & McWilliams, Chgo., 1959-63; ptnr. Kegan, Kegan & Berkman, Chgo., 1963-84, Trexler, Bushnell, Giangiorgi & Blackstone, Chgo., 1984-91; pvt. practice law Glenview, Ill., 1991—. Chem. cons.; expert witness in patent law. Contbr. articles to profl. jours. Served to 1st lt. Signal Corps, U.S. Army, 1942-46. Mem. Am. Chem. Soc., ABA, Patent Law Assn., Chgo., Sigma Xi. Home and Office: 939 Glenview Rd Glenview IL 60025-3172 Office Phone: 847-724-6643.

BERKMAN, RICHARD LYLE, lawyer; b. Pitts., Sept. 4, 1946; s. Allen H. and Selma (Wiener) B.; m. Toni Seidl, June 7, 1998; children: Benjamin, Lisa, Daniel. AB magna cum laude, Harvard U., 1968, JD cum laude, 1973. Bar: Pa. 1973, U.S. Dist. Ct. (ea. dist.) Pa. 1973, U.S. Ct. Appeals (3d cir.) 1975, U.S. Supreme Ct. 1986. Asst. to dir. Office Emergency Preparedness Exec. Office of U.S. President, Washington, 1970; law clk. to Hon. Edward R. Becker U.S. Dist Ct., Phila., 1973-74; ptnr. Dechert LLP, Phila., 1974—. Adj. prof. Temple Law Sch. Co-author: Damming the West, 1971, Pennsylvania Evidence, 1974; contbr. articles to profl. jours. Bd. govs. Am. Jewish Com., Hebrew Union Coll.; officer, bd. dirs. Congregation Rodeph Shalom; active Salzberg Seminar on AIDS. Lt. (j.g.) USN, 1968-70. Mem. ABA, Phila. Bar Assn., Am. Law Inst. Avocations: reading, charities, sports. Office: Dechert LLP 4000 Bell Atlantic Tower 1717 Arch St Philadelphia PA 19103-2793 Office Phone: 215-994-2684. Business E-Mail: richard.berkman@dechert.com.

BERKMAN, WILLIAM ROGER, lawyer, army reserve officer; b. Chisholm, Minn., Mar. 29, 1928; s. Carl Emil and Millie (Mikkelson) B.; m. Betty Ann Klamt, Dec. 17, 1950. AB, U. Calif., Berkeley, 1950, JD, 1957. Bar: Calif. 1957, D.C. Ct. Appeals 1957, D.C. 1957. Law clk. to judge James Alger Fee, U.S. Ct. Appeals 9th cir., 1957-58; assoc. Morrison & Foerster, San Francisco, 1958-67, mem. firm, 1967-79; comdg. gen. 351st Civil Affairs Command, Mountain View, Calif., 1975-79; chief Army Res., Dept. of Army, Washington, 1979-86; mil. exec., Res. Forces Policy Bd., Office Sec. Def. Dept. of Def., Washington, 1986-92. Mng. editor: Calif. Law Rev, 1956-57. Pres. Sausalito (Calif.) Bd. Libr. Trustees, 1976-78; pres. Civil Affairs Assn., 1979-80, 93-99; bd. dirs. Army Distaff Found., 1988-92; dir. Sausalito-Marin City Sanitary Dist., pres., 2002—. Maj. gen. U.S. Army, 1979—. Decorated DSM with oak leaf cluster, Def. DSM, Def. Superior Svc. medal, S. Order of Calif., U.S. Spl. Ops. command medal U.S. Army, USN, C.G., Legion of Merit medal, Army Commendation medal; named to Hall of Fame Sr. Army Res. Comdrs. Assn.; recipient Meritorious Svc. medal, Army Outstanding Civilian Svc. medal. Mem.: ABA (chmn. standing com. on lawyers in armed svcs. 1988—91), U.S. Army Civil Affairs Corp. (hon. chief civil affairs), US Civil Affairs Corps, Res. Officers Assn., Assn. U.S. Army, State Bar Calif., Civil Affairs Assn. (hon.; pres. 1992—99, pres. emeritus 1999—), Army and Navy Club, Lions (dir. Sausalito Marin City san. dist., pres.). Home: 33 Atwood Ave Sausalito CA 94965-2245 Office Phone: 415-332-0863.

BERKOBEN, JOHN PERRI, physician; b. Lakewood, N.J., 1947; BA, Cornell U., 1969; MD, U. Pa., 1973. Intern Montefiore Hosp., Bronx, 1973-74, resident, 1974-76. Cardiology fellow Boston U. Med. Ctr., 1976-78. Mem. Am. Coll. Physicians, Am. Coll. Cardiology, N.Am. Soc. Pacing & Electrophysiology, Mass. Med. Soc. Office: Lahey-Arlington 20 Wall St Burlington MA 01803

BERKOFF, ADAM T., lawyer; b. Milwaukee, Wis., June 5, 1969; BA with honors & distinction, Univ. Wis., Madison, 1991; JD, Marquette Univ., 1994. Bar: Wis. 1994, Ill. 1994. Ptnr., chmn. Condominium & Complex Mixed-Use Devel. practice group DLA Piper Rudnick Gray Cary, Chgo. Adj. prof. DePaul Univ. Real Estate Ctr. Editor (exec.): Marquette Law Rev. Mem.: Chgo. Bar Assn. (mem. condominium subcom.), State Bar Assn. Wis., Golden Key, Iron Cross Soc. Office: DLA Piper Rudnick Gray Cary Suite 1900 203 N LaSalle St Chicago IL 60601-1293 Office Phone: 312-368-7266. Office Fax: 312-630-5331. Business E-Mail: adam.berkoff@dlapiper.com.

BERKOFF, CHARLES EDWARD, pharmaceutical and biotech consultant; b. London, Sept. 29, 1932; arrived in US, 1963, naturalized, 1975; s. Maurice and Dora (Landy) B.; children: Timothy, David, Kevin; m. Heide-Gisela Triesch, 1997. BS in Chemistry (1st class honors), U. London, 1956, DIC, 1958; PhD, Imperial Coll., U. London, 1959. Chartered chemist. Dir. GlaxoSmithKline, Phila., 1964-83; exec. v.p. ImuTech, Inc., Huntingdon Valley, Pa., 1983-84; pres., CEO Antigenics, Inc., Horsham, Pa., 1984-89; pres., chief exec. officer Creative Licensing Internat., Inc., Sarasota, Fla., 1987—, CEBRAL, Inc., 1987—. Research fellow Johns Hopkins U., Balt., 1959-60; sr. research fellow Southampton U., Eng., 1960-61; mem. Adv. Council Smithsonian Sci. Info. Exchange, Washington, 1976-82. Contbr. articles to profl. jours.; patentee numerous U.S. and fgn. patents. Monsanto Research fellow Imperial Coll. Sci. and Tech., 1956-59; Fulbright scholar, 1959-60; recipient Statue of Victory World Culture prize Centro Studi e Ricerche Delle Nazioni, 1985. Fellow Am. Chem. Soc., Royal Soc. Chemistry; mem. Am. Arbitration Assn., Entomol. Soc., Am. Inst. Chem. Engrs., Licensing Execs. Soc. Clubs: Engrs. Club of Phila. Republican. Unitarian Universalist. Avocations: writing, tennis, guitar, bridge, swimming. Office: CEBRAL Inc PO Box 5850 Sarasota FL 34277-5850 Office Phone: 941-923-3268. Personal E-mail: cebral@comcast.net.

BERKOFF, MARK ANDREW, lawyer; b. Boston, Aug. 8, 1961; s. Marshall Richard and Bebe R. B.; m. Susan Lynn Ochalek; children: Alexander, Rachel. BA with honors, U. Wis., 1983; JD, U. Chgo., 1986. Bar: Ill. 1987, U.S. Dist. Ct. (no. dist. Ill., no. dist. Ind.), U.S. Ct. Appeals (7th cir.) 1990. Ptnr. Piper Rudnick, Chgo., 1986—2004; ptnr., co-chmn. Bankruptcy & Bus. Reorganization practice group DLA Piper Rudnick Gray Cary, Chgo., 2005—. Contbr. articles to profl. jours. Vol. Am. Cancer Soc., Chgo., 1993-96; mem. & past chmn. Corp. Donations Com. Make-A-Wish Found. No. Ill.; gen counsel Bus Products Credit Assn. Mem. ABA, Chgo. Bar Assn., Turnaround Mgmt. Assn., Am. Bankruptcy Inst., Phi Beta Kappa, Phi Kappa Phi. Avocations: sports, collecting Currier & Ives prints, Numismatics. Office: DLA Piper Rudnick Gray Cary LLP 203 N LaSalle St Suite 1900 Chicago IL 60601-1293 Office Phone: 312-368-4000. Office Fax: 312-236-7516. Business E-Mail: mark.berkoff@dlapiper.com.

BERKOFF, MARSHALL RICHARD, lawyer; b. Milw., Wis., Apr. 10, 1937; s. Louis S. and Edith E. (Cohen) B.; m. Bebe R. Brandwein, June 19, 1960; children: Mark Andrew, Jonathan Hale, Adam Todd. BA, U. Wis., 1959; LLB, Harvard U., 1962. Bar: Wis. 1962, U.S. Dist. Ct. (we. and ea. dists.) Wis. 1962. Ptnr. Michael, Best & Friedrich, Milw., 1962—. Co-author: Employment Law Challenges of 1987, 1987, Labor Relations: The New Rules of the Game, 1984, The Legal Issues of Managing Difficult Employees, 1987; author/editor Currier and Ives "The New Best 50", 1991. Chmn. Charles Allis and Villa Terrace Art Mus., Milw., 1983-96; chmn. Milw. County War Meml. Corp., 1989-94, bd. dirs., 1983; chmn. bd. dirs. St. Michael Hosp., Milw., 1988-89; bd. dirs. Covenant Health Care, 1993-95. Mem. ABA (labor and employment sect., hosp. and health care law sect.), Wis. Bar Assn., (chmn. labor law sect. 1977-78), Milw. Bar Assn., Am. Hist. Print Collector Soc. (pres. 1987-90, bd. dirs. 2002—). Avocations: writing, lithographs, fishing. Office: Michael Best & Friedrich 100 E Wisconsin Ave Ste 3300 Milwaukee WI 53202-4108 Office Phone: 414-271-6560.

BERKON, MARTIN, artist; b. Bklyn., Jan. 30, 1932; s. Samuel F. and Sara (Hodes) B.; m. Eileen Phyllis Eichel, July 10, 1960. Student, Pratt Inst., 1952; BA, Bklyn. Coll., 1954; MA, NYU, 1959. Mem. adj. faculty Fairleigh Dickinson U., 1966, Nassau C.C., 1966-67; lectr. City Coll., CUNY, 1968-69; guest lectr. Middlebury Coll., 1977, Nassau C.C., 1982, St. Thomas Aquinas Coll., 1995; interviewed L.I. Art Scene TV, 1986. One-man shows include Smolin Gallery, N.Y.C., 1962, 20th Century West Gallery, N.Y.C., 1967, Soho Ctr. for Visual Artists, N.Y.C., 1974, Genesis Galleries, N.Y.C., 1978, Adelphi U., Garden City, N.Y., 1983, Blue Hill Cultural Ctr., Pearl River, N.Y., 1995, Schering Plough Corp. Gallery, Madison, N.J., 2001; exhibited in group shows at Bklyn. Mus., 1958, Silvermine (Conn.) Guild Artists, 1963, Ohio U. Gallery, 1964, Ball State U., 1965, Wesleyan Coll. at Ga., 1965, Butler Inst. Am. Art, 1965, 67, 69, Aldrich Mus. Contemporary Art, Ridgefield, Conn., 1974, 75, 82, New Britain (Conn.) Mus., 1974, Am. Fedn. Arts traveling show, 1975-77, Meadowbrook Art Gallery Oakland U., Rochester, Mich., Flint (Mich.) Inst. Art, 1974-76, Firehouse Gallery, Garden City, 1982, Barbara Walter Gallery, N.Y.C., 1982, Spaceport USA Kennedy Space Ctr., 1985, 87, NASA collection traveling exhbn. Visions of Flight, 1988-91, Vero Beach (Fla.) Mus. Art The Abstract Image, 1996, Blue Hill Cultural Ctr., Pearl River, 1997-98; represented in permanent collections Aldrich Mus. Contemporary Art, Ridgefield, Texaco Inc., White Plains, N.Y., Pepsico Inc., Somers, N.Y., Pfizer Inc., Rye Brook, N.Y.; commd. NASA, 1984, 87, NASA Gallery of Art, Kennedy Space Ctr., Vero Beach Mus. Art. Home: 503 Devries Ct Piermont NY 10968-1068 E-mail: marteil@msn.com.

BERKOW, IRA HARVEY, writer, journalist; b. Chgo., Jan. 7, 1940; s. Harold Grosswald and Shirley (Halperin) B.; m. Dolores Case, Apr. 18, 1978. BA, Miami U., Oxford, Ohio, 1963; MS in Journalism, Northwestern U., 1964. Reporter Mpls. Tribune, 1965-67; sports columnist, sports editor Newspaper Enterprise Assn., N.Y.C., 1967-76; sports columnist, feature writer N.Y. Times, N.Y.C., 1981—. Author: Oscar Robertson The Golden Year, 1971, (with Walt Frazier) Rockin' Steady, 1974 (Am. Libr. Assn. Best Books of Yr. 1975), Beyond the Dream, 1975, Maxwell Street, 1977, The DuSable Panthers, 1978, (with Rod Carew) Carew, 1979, Red: The Biography of Red Smith, 1986, The Man Who Robbed the Pierre, 1987, Pitchers Do Get Lonely and Other Sports Stories, 1988; editor: Hank Greenberg: The Story of My Life, 1989, (with Jackie Mason) How to Talk Jewish, 1991, (with Jim Kaplan) The Gospel According to Casey, 1992, To the Hoop: The Seasons of a Basketball Life, 1997, Court Vision, 2000, The Minority Quarterback, and Other Lives in Sports, 2002, Playwright: The Shakespeare of the Press Box, 2003. Recipient Page One award Newspaper Guild, Mpls., 1966, Scripps-Howard Feature award N.Y.C., 1969, N.Y. Pub. Libr. commendation, 1978, 2005, AP Sports Editors award, 1982, 93, 94, 95, 96, 2001, Disting. Achievement medal Miami U., 1988, Feature Reporting award Deadline Club, 1994, award N.Y. State Newspaper Pubs., 1990; nominee ACE awards, 1983, Edgar award, 1988; finalist Pulitzer prize for commentary, 1988, Harold Washington Profl. Achievement award Roosevelt U., 2003; named to Hall of Achievement, Northwestern U. Medill Sch. of Journalism, 1997; mem. N.Y. Times Pulitzer-Prize-Winning Team for Nat. Reporting, 2001. Mem. Baseball Writers Assn. Am., Authors Guild, PEN, Mystery Writers Am. Office: NY Times 229 W 43rd St New York NY 10036-3959 Office Phone: 212-556-7371.

BERKOWITZ, BRAD ALAN, financial analyst; b. Woodmere, NY, May 5, 1964; s. Morton Michael and Barbara Judith Berkowitz. BS in Econs., U. Pa., 1986; MBA in Fin., NYU, 1993. Investment analyst Integrated Resources, N.Y.C., 1986—89; fixed income sales Lehman Bros., N.Y.C., 1989—94; fin. cons., prin. AXA Advisors, N.Y.C., 1995—2000; stock analyst Cramer, Berkowitz, N.Y.C., 2001—. Adv. bd. mem. Smartix, Internat., N.Y.C., 2002—. Author: (Book) The 21st Century Guide to Bachelorhood, 1999, The Iran Barkley Story: The Rise and Fall of a Boxing Champion, 2001; co-author: Natural Disaster, 2001. Mem.: AFTRA, Am. Mensa. Jewish. Avocations: golf, sports, movies, theater, acting. Home: Apt 30A 1520 York Ave New York NY 10028 Office: Cramer Berkowitz 14th Fl 909 Third Ave New York NY 10022 Personal E-mail: berkathome@aol.com.

BERKOWITZ, EDWARD C., lawyer; b. Perth Amboy, NJ, Apr. 9, 1935; s. Samuel and Anna (Gluck) B.; m. Lois, Sept. 24, 1961; children: Steven, Peter. BA, Cornell U., 1956; LLB, Harvard U., 1959. Bar: N.J. 1960, D.C. 1966, Va 2003,U.S. Supreme Ct. 1964. Atty. Garretson & Levine, Perth Amboy, N.J., 1960-64; atty. advisor NLRB, Washington, 1964-66; gen. atty. Communications Satellite Corp., Washington, 1966-70; ptnr. Lane & Edson P.C., Washington, 1970-89; ptnr., of counsel Zuckerman, Spaeder, Goldstein, Taylor & Kolker, Washington, 1989-2001; of counsel Nixon Peabody LLP, Washington, 2001—03; gen. counsel Kastle Sys. Internat. LLC, 2003—. Contbr. articles to profl. jours. Mem. Cornell Univ. Coun., Ithaca, Cornell Real Estate Coun., Ithaca; mem. Potomac Appalachian Trail Club, Washington, Cornell Club of Washington. Capt. USAR, 1960-69. Democrat. Jewish. Avocations: hiking, biking, cross country skiing. Home: 3339 Legation St NW Washington DC 20015-1711 Office: Kastle Sys Internat 1501 Wilson Blvd Arlington VA 22209 Office Phone: 703-284-0337. Business E-Mail: eberkowitz@kastle.com.

BERKOWITZ, LAWRENCE M., lawyer; b. Leavenworth, Kans., Nov. 29, 1941; s. Barney and Sarah (Kramer) B.; m. Ursula Lustenberger, Sept. 2, 1969; children: Lizbeth Berkowitz, Leslie Berkowitz. BA Polit. Sci., U. Mich., 1963, JD, 1966. Bar: Mo. 1966, N. Mex. 1997, US Dist Ct. (ea., we. dist. Mo., Kans., N. Mex.), US Ct. Appeals (8th, 10th DC cir.), US Supreme Ct. Law clerk Judge John W. Oliver, U.S. Dist. Ct., we. dist. Mo., Kansas City, Mo., 1966-68; assoc., ptnr. Stinson, Mag & Fizzell, P.C., Kansas City, Mo., 1968-97; ptnr., litig. & mediation practices Berkowitz Oliver Williams Shaw & Eisenbrandt LLP, Kansas City, Mo., 1997—. Mng. ptnr. Stinson, Mag & Fizzell, Kansas City, 1991-92. Bd. dirs. Nelson Gallery Bus. Coun., Kansas City, 1989—, Downtown coun., Kansas City, 1992-93; trustee Kansas City Art Inst., 1994—. Fellow Am. Coll. Trial Lawyers, Am. Bar Found., Mo. Bar Found.; mem. ABA, Am. Judicature Soc., Kansas City Met. Bar Assn., Lawyers Assn. Kansas City, Mo. Bar Assn., Soc. Profls. Dispute Resolution. Avocations: tennis, hiking, skiing, history, reading. Office: Berkowitz Oliver Williams Shaw & Eisenbrandt Ste 500 Two Emanuel Cleaver Blvd Kansas City MO 64112 Office Phone: 816-627-0211. Office Fax: 816-561-1888. Business E-Mail: lberkowitz@bowse-law.com.*

BERKOWITZ, RICHARD LEE, obstetrician/gynecologist; b. N.Y.C., July 28, 1940; MD, NYU, 1965. Diplomate Am. Bd. Ob/gyn. Intern Kings County Hosp. Ctr., N.Y.C., 1965-66; resident in ob/gyn. N.Y. Hosp.-Cornell Med. Ctr., N.Y.C., 1968-72; staff Mt. Sinai Hosp., N.Y.C., 1982—2003; prof., chmn. ob/gyn. reproductive sci. Mt. Sinai Med. Ctr., N.Y.C., 1985—2003; staff Presbyn. Hosp., 2003—; prof. ob-gyn., dir. quality improvement Columbia U. Med. Ctr., N.Y.C., 2003—. Fellow Am. Coll. Obstetricians/Gynecologists; mem. Am. Gynecol. and Obstet. Soc., Am. Inst. Ultrasound Medicine, N.Y. Obstet. Soc., Soc. Gynecol. Investigation, Soc. Maternal-Fetal Medicine (SMFM). Office: Columbia Univ Med Ctr Dept Ob-gyn 622 W 168th St PH 16 New York NY 10032 also: 16 E 60th St New York NY 10022

BERKOWITZ, STEPHEN DAVID, sociologist, educator; b. N.Y.C., N.Y., Nov. 26, 1943; s. Bernard and Sylvia (Coplan) B.; m. Harriet Bertha Friedmann, Sept. 1, 1968 (div. Jan. 1974); m. Teresa Norma Traynor, Jan. 8, 1974; children: Shawn Daniels, Colin Daniels. AB, U. Mich., 1965, grad. study in sociology, 1965—67; PhD, Brandeis U., 1975. Tchg. fellow, asst. U. Mich., Brandeis U., 1965—68; joint rsch. fellow Edn. Devel. Ctr./Stanford Rsch. Inst., 1969—71; asst. prof. dept. social studies U. Sask., Regina, Canada, 1971—73; lectr. dept. sociology U. Toronto, 1973—75, asst. prof. dept. sociology, 1976—81; from asst. prof. to fellow New Coll., U. Toronto, 1976—81; rsch. assoc. Inst. for Quantitative Analysis of Social and Econ. Policy, U. Toronto, 1974—81; asst. prof. dept. sociology U. Vt., 1980—87; prof. dept. sociology U. Ft. Hare, Alice, South Africa, 1997—99; assoc. prof. dept. sociology U. Vt., 1987—96, prof. dept. sociology, 1996—2001, prof. emeritus sociology, 2002—; CEO Am. Protective Devices, Inc., 2002; mng. dir. Inst. for Study in South Africa, 2002—. Vis. asst. prof. dept. sociology Meml. U. Nfld., 1978; vis. scholar dept. sociology Harvard U., 1987—88; chief scientist OMNIDAT, LLC, 2001; mem. adv. com. Internat. Network for Social Network Analysis, 1977—83; mem. adv. com. on sci. and edn. Contact Can., Ottawa, 1977—80. Author: (book) Death Before Honor, 2003; author: (with R. Logan) Canada's Third Option, 1978; author: An Introduction to Structural Analysis: The Network Approach to Social Research, 1982, Models and Myths in Canadian Sociology, 1984; author: (with B. Wellman) Social Structures: A Network Approach, 2d edit., 1997; author: (with Howard Ball and Mbulelo Mzamane) Multicultural Education in Colleges and Universities: A Transdisciplinary Approach, 1998; author: (with Mbulelo Mzamane) The Mbeki Turn: South Africa After Mandela, 2002; contbr. articles to profl. and scholarly jours., chpts. to books; assoc. editor: Can. Jour. Sociology, 1980—83. Mem. program com. Chavurah, 1981—82; v.p. non-partisan com. Can. Unity Through Diversity, 1978—80; mem. adv. bd. B'Nai Brith Hillel

Found., Toronto, 1979—80. Recipient NIMH trainee and fellowship, Ctr. for Rsch. on Social Orgn., U. Mich., 1965—66, tchg. fellowship in sociology, U. Mich., 1966—67, Brandeis fellowship in sociology, 1967—68, NIMH Advanced Field Tng. fellowship, Brandeis U., 1968—69, Brandeis fellowship in sociology, 1969—70. Mem.: ASA (mem. exec. adv. bd. sect. on math. sociology 1999—, steering com. sect. on math. sociology 1997—, steering com. sect.-in-formation math. sociology 1995—97), Internat. Network for Social Network Analysis, Alpha Kappa Delta. Avocations: writing detective fiction, listening to classical music, collecting rare and out-of-print books, Go. Office: Dept Sociology 31 S Prospect St Burlington VT 05405 also: Inst for Study in South Africa PO Box 44 Underhill VT 05489

BERKOWITZ, SUZANNE TRESP, secondary school educator; b. Mattawa, Ont., Can., Apr. 5, 1960; came to U.S., 1964; d. Gunter Hermann and Emilie Anna (Imhauser) Tresp; m. Steven Berkowitz, June 11, 1983; 1 child, Andrew. BA in English, SUNY, Binghamton, 1982; MA in English, CUNY, 1993. Tchr. English, Montauk Jr. High Sch., Bklyn., 1986—; faculty Queensborough Community Coll., Bayside, N.Y., 1992-96. Avocations: swimming, gardening, working out, travel. Home: 25046 41st Dr Little Neck NY 11363-1710 Office: Montauk Jr High Sch 4200 16th Ave Brooklyn NY 11204-1002

BERKOWITZ, TERRY, artist, fine arts educator; b. Bklyn. s. Alfred David and Ruth Anna (Weisberg) B. Cert., Sch. Visual Arts, 1971; MFA, Sch. of Art Inst. Chgo., 1973. Prof. Baruch Coll. CUNY, 1996—. One-woman shows include P.S.I., Long Island City, 1978, Joseloff Gallery, Hartford (Conn.) Art Sch., 1982, Contemporary Arts Mus., Houston, 1990, Whitney Mus. Am. Art, NYC, 1992, Sculpture Ctr., NYC, 1994, Metronom, Barcelona, Spain, 1999; group exhbns. include Alternative Mus., NYC, 1990, Constrn. in Progress/Lodz, Poland, 1990, Circulo de Bellas Artes, Madrid, 1991, Cleve. Ctr. Contemporary Arts, 1996, 3 Paralelos, 3 Meridianos, Aljibe, Lanzarote, Spain, 2003, Carcel De Amor, Reina Sofia Nat. Mus. Ctr. of Art, Madrid, Spain, 2005 Fellow, MacDowell Colony, 1989, Fulbright, 1997; grantee, Jerome Found., 1990; Creative Arts in Pub. Svc. fellow, NEA, 1974—75. E-mail: artifice@pipeline.com.

BERKSON, JACOB BENJAMIN, lawyer, writer; b. Washington County, Md., Dec. 6, 1925; s. Meyer and Ida Evelyn (Berman) B.; m. Ann Goldstein, June 25, 1955 (div.); children: Daniel Jeremy, Susan Kay, James Meyer. BA, U. Va., 1947, LLB, 1949, JD, 1970; grad., US Naval Sch., Naval Justice, Newport, RI, 1952, Fed. Exec. Inst., Charlottesville, Va., 1972, USNR Midshipmen's Sch., Columbia U., NY; attended, Naval Sch. Oriental Langs. (Japanese). Bar: Md. 1949, Va. 1949, U.S. Supreme Ct. 1965, Calif. 1975. Sole practice, Hagerstown, Md., 1949-52, 54-64; ptnr. McCauley, Cooey, Berkson & Wright, Hagerstown, 1964-70; dep. gen. counsel U.S. GSA, Washington, 1970-76; pvt. practice law Hagerstown, 1976—. Instr. Law Hagerstown Bus. Coll., 1986; trial magistrate, Hagerstown and Washington County, Md., 1951-52; mem. Legis. Coun. Md., 1955-58; del. Md. Legislature, 1955-58; trial magistrate, Hagerstown, 1958-59. Recipient commendation for svc. to U.S. Naval Acad. and pub. interest Chief of Naval Personnel, 1956. Author: Shingahi Saburo and Short Stories, 1978, Comin' Home, 1993, A Canary's Tale: The Final Battle: Politics, Poisons and Pollution vs. the Environment and Public Health, 1996; case editor, co-founder Va. Law Weekly, 1948; contbr. articles to profl. jours., address to Congrl. Record. Scoutmaster local coun. Boy Scouts Am.; organizer, dir. County Youth Conservation Corps; active Big Bros.; bd. dirs. Doub's Woods County Park, Devil's Backbone County Park; assisted in establishment of C&O Canal Nat. Histo. Park, 1954-70; camp sponsor YMCA; advt. Model Youth Legis.; pres. PTA; chmn. Washington County Park Commn., 1961-66; bd. dirs. Rachel Carson Coun., Inc., Chevy Chase, Md., 1996-2003. WWII USNR V12 program line officer UVA, 1944, Commissioned Ensign, 1945, ordered to staff Comdr. Naval Base, Saipan, Marianas I., staff legal officer, 1945—46, Judge Advocate General Courts Martial, recalled, 1952, Korean War, Lt. USNR, ordered to Pusan, Korea, ordered to Comdr. Naval Forces, Far East, Yokosuka, Japan, staff legal, trial counsel, 1952—53, Defense Counsel before General Courts Martial, ordered to serve as staff legal officer to Comdr. Destroyer Divsn. 322 on Round the World Mission, 1953—54, aboard USS Healey DD 672, Navy JAG duties. Mem. ABA, Calif. Bar Assn., Va. Bar Assn., Md. Assn. County Civil Attys. (pres., award for svc. as pres. 1966), Washington County Bar Assn. (pres.), Am. Legion, Hagerstown Club, Lions (pres.), Speakers Soc., Elks, Torch Club (Hagerstown), Thomas Jefferson Soc. Alumni U. Va., Lile Law Soc U. Va. Republican. Jewish. Home and Office: 1419 Potomac Ave Hagerstown MD 21742-3315

BERKSON, JIM, ecologist, educator; b. Hagerstown, Md., Dec. 15, 1962; s. Jacob Benjamin Berkson and Ann Berkson Abrams, Irving Melvin Abrams (Stepfather); m. Ginger Diane Calzada, Aug. 27, 1995; 1 child, Torrey Caitlin. BA in Ecology, U. Calif., San Diego, 1984; MS in Zoology, U. B.C., Vancouver, Can., 1988; PhD in Biology, Mont. State U., 1996. Statis. methods analyst III, Calif. Dept. Fish and Game, Long Beach, Calif., 1988—89; biometrician Columbia River Inter-Tribal Fish Commn., Portland, Oreg., 1989—98; adj. asst. prof. dept. biology U. Oreg., Eugene, 1997; asst. prof. dept. fisheries and wildlife scis. Va. Tech. Inst., Blacksburg, 1998—2003, founder, dir. Horseshoe Crab Rsch. Ctr., 2000—03, assoc. prof. dept. fisheries and wildlife scis., 2003—, unit leader, ecologist Nat. Marine Fisheries Svc. RTR Unit, 2003—. Chmn. Coll. Natural Resources Diversity com. Va. Tech. Inst., Blacksburg, 2000—02; leader, co-founder S.E. Data Assessment and Rev. Process, Nat. Marine Fisheries Svc., Charleston, SC, 2001—02; mem. Project Kaleidoscope Faculty for 21st Century, Washington, 2001—; chmn. Atlantic States Marine Fisheries Commn. Horseshoe Crab Stock Assessment Com., Washington, 2002—; leader Population Dynamics Recruiting Program, Nat. Marine Fisheries Svc., Blacksburg, Va., 2003—; chmn. sci. and stats. com. South Atlantic Fisheries Mgmt. Coun., Charleston, SC, 2004—. Editor: (book) Incorporating Uncertainty into Fishery Models; mem. editl. bd.: Environ. Mgmt., 2003—; contbr. articles to profl. jours. Grantee, Cambrex, Inc., 2000-2005, Nat. Fish and Wildlife Found., 2001-2002, Va. Sea, 2001-2003, Nat. Wild Turkey Fedn., 2001-2005, Atlantic States Marine Fisheries Commn., 2002-2003, Nat. Marine Fisheries Svc., 2003-2007. Mem.: NSTA, Coll. of Natural Resources Faculty Assn. (pres. 2003—04), Ecol. Soc. of Am., Soc. for Conservation Biology, Am. Fisheries Soc. Achievements include development of Va. Tech's Horseshoe Crab Rsch. Ctr. which is now the largest horseshoe crab research program in the world. Avocation: travel. Office: NMFS RTR Unit at Va Tech 100 Cheatham Hall Blacksburg VA 24061 Office Phone: 540-231-5910. Business E-Mail: jberkson@vt.edu.

BERKSON, SADIE, volunteer; b. Winnipeg, Man., Can., June 18, 1913; came to U.S., 1927; d. Samuel and Minnie (Liss) Finkelstein; m. Isadore J. Berkson, Feb. 3, 1940 (dec. Oct. 1982). Exec. sec. Convenant Club, Chgo., 1929-40. Supr. blood bank ARC, WWII and Six Days War, Israel; past mem. bd. dirs. Fedn. and Jewish United Fund; charter, life bd. dirs. Louis A. Weiss Meml. Hosp., Brandeis Hadassah, B'nai B'rith, Art Inst. Chgo., Friends Chgo. Pub. Libr., Mus. Contemporary Art, Nat. ARC; chmn. 1st Women's Israel Bond Dr., 1948; a founder women's br. Brandeis divsn., Chgo.; co-chmn. 1st women's gift divsn. Jewish Combined Jewish Appeal, 1947; founder 1st spl. women's gift divsn. Crusade of Mercy, 1970; bd. overseers Ill. Inst. Tech.-Chgo.-Kent Coll. Law, 1992—, chmn. Consular Ball, 1993, 94; chmn. Rita Hayworth Ball for Alzheimer's Assn., Chgo., 1987, also bd. dirs. and co-chmn. Chgo. support group, hon. emeritus bd. dirs., 1996—. Recipient award of merit ARC, Woman of Yr. award Crusade of Mercy, 1970, Cartier Disting. Humanitarian award Alzheimer's Assn., 1992, Archtl. award for I.J. Berkson Res. Reading Room, Ill. Inst. Tech.-Chgo. Kent Coll. Law, 1992, Disting. Svc. award Ill. Inst. Tech.-Chgo.-Kent Coll. Law, 1994, honoree Chgo. Rita Hayworth Ball for Alzheimer's, 1997; established, endowed I.J. Berkson Scholarship Fund for Alzheimer's rsch., 1983; endowed I.J. Berkson Res. Reading Room, 1992; seeded, established I.J. and Sadie Berkson Scholarship Fund, Chgo.-Kent Coll. Law, 1992. Mem. Soc. Wills and Endowment for Alzheimer's Assn. (founding). Avocations: painting, golf, tennis, world travel. Home: 200 E Delaware Pl Apt 34A Chicago IL 60611-7710

BERKUS, JAMES, talent agent; Pres. United Talent Agy., Beverly Hills, Calif., chmn., 1997—. Bd. advisors IFILM Corp., Hollywood. Named one of 50 Most Powerful People in Hollywood, Premiere mag., 2004—05. Office: United Talent Agy 9560 Wilshire Blvd Fl 5 Beverly Hills CA 90212-2400 E-mail: berkusj@unitedtalent.com.*

BERL, JOSEPH M., lawyer; b. Bklyn., Oct. 1, 1942; AB, Columbia U., 1964; JD with honors, George Washington U., 1967. Bar: N.Y. 1968, D.C. 1972, U.S. Supreme Ct. 1972. Law clk. to Hon. Frank H. Myers D.C. Ct. Appeals, 1967-68; trial atty. Div. Trading and Markets, SEC, Washington, 1968-70, br. chief, 1970-71; ptnr. Fortas & Koven, Washington, 1971-83, Stroock and Stroock and Lavan, Washington, 1984-86, Baker & Hostetler, Washington, 1986-98, Powell Goldstein LLP, Washington, 1998—. Mem. ABA (mem. corp., banking and bus. law sect.), D.C. Bar. Office: Powell Goldstein LLP 3d Fl 901 New York Ave NW Washington DC 20001-4413 Office Phone: 202-624-7271. Business E-Mail: jberl@pogolaw.com.

BERLACK, EVAN RADEN, lawyer; b. NYC, Apr. 1, 1934; s. Harris and Edith Ann (Raden) B.; m. Kay Baumler, July 15, 1963 (dec. July 1986); children: Andrew E., Kenneth H.; m. Phyllis Bonanno, Oct. 14, 1989. AB magna cum laude, Harvard U., 1956, LLB, 1962. Bar: NY 1963, DC 1969. Fgn. service officer U.S. Dept. State, Washington and Paris, 1963-66, atty., adviser Office Legal Adviser Washington, 1966-68; assoc. Arent, Fox, Kintner, Plotkin & Kahn, Washington, 1968-73, ptnr., 1974; of counsel Baker Botts LLP, Washington. Co-editor: Coping with U.S. Export Controls, 1985-86, 88-2000. 1st lt. USAF, 1956-59. Mem. ABA, Am. Soc. Internat. Law, Harvard Club (N.Y.C., Washington). Clubs: Harvard (N.Y.C. and Washington). Avocations: swimming, baseball, classical music, history. Office: Baker Botts LLP 1299 Pennsylvania Ave NW Washington DC 20004 Office Phone: 202-639-7771. Office Fax: 202-585-1073. E-mail: evan.berlack@bakerbotts.com.

BERLAGE, GAI INGHAM, sociologist, researcher; b. Washington, Feb. 9, 1943; d. Paul Bowen and Grace (Artz) Ingham; m. Jan Coxe Berlage, Aug. 7, 1965; children: Jan Ingham, Cari Coxe. BA, Smith Coll., 1965; MA, So. Meth. U., 1968; PhD, NYU, 1979. Tchr. math. Piner Jr. High Sch., Sherman, Tex., 1968-69; asst. prof. sociology Iona Coll., New Rochelle, N.Y., 1971-83, assoc. prof., 1983-88, chmn. dept., 1981—90, 1996—2003, prof., 1988—. Coord. urban studies program, 1984-90, gerontology program, 1984-90, NCAA faculty athletic rep., 1996—. Author: Experience with Sociology: Social Issues in American Society, 1983, Understanding Social Issues: Sociological Fact Finding, 1987, 2d edit., 1990, 3d edit., 1993, Women in Baseball: The Forgotten History, 1994, Understanding Social Issues: Critical Thinking and Analysis, 1996, 6th edit., 2003; mem. editl. bd. Jour. Sport and Social Issues, 1990-94; contbr. articles to profl. jours. Commr. Wilton Commn. on Aging and Social Svcs., 1980-88, chmn., 1982-88; co-chmn. Wilton Task Force on Youth Coun., 1988; chmn. Wilton Task Force Com. for Outreach Program, 1981-82, Wilton Task Force on Day Care, 1983-88; mem. Wilton Task Force for Pub. Health Nursing Assn., 1981-82, Wilton Sport Coun., 1985-88; bd. dirs. Wilton Meals on Wheels, 1983-88; fellow N.Am. Faculty Network of Northeastern Univs. Ctr. for Study of Sport in Soc. Recipient Best Profl. Paper award Third Annual Cooperstown Symposium on Baseball and the Am. Cultre; named to Iona Coll. Women of Achievement, 1993. Mem. Am. Sociol. Assn., N.Am. Soc. Sociology of Sport (treas. 1992-93), Wilton Assn. for Gifted Edn. (pres. 1980-81), N.Am. Soc. for Sports History, Soc. for Am. Baseball Rsch., Women's Sport Found. (resources coun.). Office: Iona Coll Dept Sociology New Rochelle NY 10801 Office Phone: 914-633-2594. Business E-Mail: gberlage@iona.edu.

BERLAGE, JAN INGHAM, lawyer; b. Lewiston, N.Y., Nov. 17, 1969; s. Jan Coxe and Gai Elizabeth (Ingham) B. BA, Wesleyan U., 1992; postgrad., Oxford U., 1992; JD, U. Va., 1995. Law clk. to Hon. E. Stephen Derby U.S. Bankruptcy Ct. Dist. Md., Balt., 1995—96; assoc. Day, Berry & Howard, Hartford, Conn., 1996—2001, Ballard Spahr Andrews & Ingersoll, Balt., 2001—. Adj. prof. U. Md. Sch. Law, 2005—. Exec. editor Jour. Law and Politics, Charlottesville, 1994-95, mem. editl. bd., 1993-94; author: Aguilar Expression, 1990; contbr. articles to profl. jours. Deacon Avon Congl. Ch., 1997-2001; mem. Rep. Town Com., Avon, 1998-2001; mem. Avon Zoning Bd. Appeals, 1999-2001; exec. adv. bd. Heroes-Helping-Heroes, Inc., 2003—. Mem. ABA (vice chmn. young lawyers divsn. individual rights and responsibilities sect. 2001-02, chmn. 2002-03, awards judge 2005—, chmn. young lawyers divsn. bankruptcy com. 2003-05, chmn. ethics and profl. responsibility com. 2005—), Md. State Bar Assn. (chmn. young lawyers divsn. edn. com. 2003-04, membership chmn. 2004—05), Federalist Soc. (pres. U. Va. chpt. 1994-95, co-chmn. Hartford chpt. 1997-2001, bd. dirs. Chesapeake chpt. 2001—), Conn. Young Lawyers Assn. (co-chmn. comml. law and bankruptcy sect. 1997-2000, co-chmn. civil rights sect. 2000-01), N.Y. Bar Assn. (comml. law and fed. litig. sects., intellectual property subcom. 1998-2001), Jefferson Literary and Debating Soc., N.Am. Securities Adminstrn. Assn. (task force 1994), Oxford U. Legal Soc., United Oxford/Cambridge U. Club, Phi Delta Phi, Psi Upsilon, Phi Beta Kappa. Office: Ballard Spahr Andrews & Ingersoll 300 E Lombard St Baltimore MD 21202-3268 Home: 16422 J M Pearce Rd Monkton MD 21111 Office Phone: 410-528-5674. Personal E-mail: Jan_Berlage@msn.com. Business E-Mail: Berlageji@ballardspahr.com.

BERLAND, ABEL EDWARD, lawyer, real estate agent; b. Cin., Aug. 27, 1915; s. Samuel and Anne (Brod) B.; m. Meredith E. Tausig, Aug. 31, 1940; children: Michael Gardner, Richard Bruce, James Robert. JD, DePaul U., 1938, LHD, 1975. Bar: Ill. 1938. Vice chmn. Rubloff, Inc., Chgo. Real estate cons. Contbr. articles on real estate to profl. scholarly and trade jours. Life trustee, mem. acad. affairs com. DePaul U.; chmn. Civic Fedn. Chgo., 1989-90; bd. dirs. Crime Commn. Chgo.; mem. adv. bd. Salvation Army; mem. Newberry Libr. pres.'s coun. Fellow Brandeis U., 1958—; recipient Nat. Community Service award Jewish Theol. Sem. Am. Mem. Am. Chgo. Bar Assns., Nat. Assn. Realtors, Realtors Nat. Mktg. Inst. (C.C.I.M.), Am. Soc. Real Estate Counselors (pres. 1970), Pvt. Libraries Assn., Manuscript Soc., Am. Arbitration Assn. (nat. panel arbitrators), Shakespeare Soc. Am., Lex Legio, Assn. Internat. de Bibliophile, The Realty Club of Chgo. (pres. 1988), Gamma Mu, Pi Kappa Delta, Lambda Alpha, Omega Tau Rau. Clubs: Book of California; Caxton, Mid-Day, Economic, Brandeis University (founder 1949, pres. 1954), Standard (Chgo.); Grolier (N.Y.C.); Roxburghe of San Francisco; Philobiblon (Phila.). Home: 251 Sylvan Rd Glencoe IL 60022-1225 Office: 233 N Michigan Ave Ste 2200 Chicago IL 60601-5806

BERLAND, DAVID I., psychiatrist, educator; b. St. Louis, Aug. 1, 1947; s. Harry I. and Mildred (Cornblath) B.; m. Elaine Prostak, May 22, 1977; children: Katharine J., Rachel P. BA, U. Pa., 1969; MD, U. Mo., 1973. Diplomate Am. Bd. Psychiatry and Neurology. Resident psychiatry Menninger Found., Topeka, Kans., 1973-78, staff child and adolescent psychiatrist, 1978-83; dir. div. child and adolescent psychiatry St. Louis U. Med. Sch., 1983-93; with dept. adolescent psychiatry St. Luke's Hosp., Chesterfield, Mo., 1993-97; pvt. practice St. Louis, 1997—. Contbr. articles to profl. jours. Fellow Am. Acad. of Child and Adolescent Psychiatry; mem. AMA (rotating seat relative value update com. 1996-99), Soc. of Profs. of Child and Adolescent Psychiatry,. Jewish. Office: 7700 Clayton Rd Ste 103 Saint Louis MO 63117 Office Phone: 314-644-6910.

BERLAND, GRETCHEN K., medical educator, filmmaker; BA, Pomona Coll., 1986; MD, Oreg. Health and Sci. U., 1996; internship and residency, Wash. Univ. Med. Ctr. Barnes Hosp., St. Louis, 1996—99. Employed by PBS programs Nova and MacNeil/Lehrer Prodn.; asst. prof., internal med. Yale U. Sch. of Med., New Haven, 2001—. Named a MacArthur Fellow, 2004. Office: Yale Univ Med Sch-Internal Med 333 Cedar St PO Box 208025 New Haven CT 06520-8025

BERLE, PETER ADOLF AUGUSTUS, lawyer, media director; b. N.Y.C., Dec. 8, 1937; s. Adolf Augustus and Beatrice (Bishop) B.; m. Lila Sloane Wilde, May 30, 1960; children: Adolf Augustus, Mary Alice, Beatrice Lila, Robert Thomas. BA (Knox fellow), Harvard U., 1958, LLB, 1964; LLD (hon.), Hobart Smith Coll., 1977, L.I. U., 1993, So. Vt. Coll., 1996; LLB (hon.), North Adams Tchrs. Coll., 1988. Bar: N.Y. 1964, U.S. Dist. Ct. (so. and ea. dists.) N.Y. 1966, U.S. Ct. Appeals (2d cir.) 1966, U.S. Supreme Ct. 1973. Assoc. Paul, Weiss, Rifkind, Wharton & Garrison, N.Y.C., 1964-71; ptnr. Berle, Butzel & Kass, N.Y.C., 1971-76; N.Y. state commr. environ. conservation, 1976-79; ptnr. Berle, Kass & Case, 1979-85; pres., CEO (pub. Audubon mag.) Nat. Audubon Soc., 1985-95; dir., host The Environment Show N.E. Pub. Radio, 1995—2001, weekly commentator, 2001—; pres. Sky Farm Prodns. Inc., 2002—; trustee Twentieth Century Fund, Inc., 1971—, chmn., 1982-87. Tchg. fellow econs. Harvard Coll., Cambridge, Mass., 1963-64; assoc. adj. prof. Sch. Urban Affairs Hunter Coll., 1974, 84; vis. prof. environ. sci. and forestry SUNY, 1980. Author: Does the Citizen Stand a Chance, 1974. Mem. N.Y. State Assembly, 1968-74; chmn. N.Y. Gov.'s Transition Task Force on Environment, 1974-75; commr. N.Y. State Moreland Act Commn. on Nursing Homes, 1975-77; bd. dirs. Clean Sites, Inc., 1986-93; chmn. Commn. on the Adirondacks in the 21st Century, 1989-90; mem. EPA adv. group on biotech., 1989-92, EPA adv. grout air quality; mem. nat. com. environ., 1991-92, nat. commn. superfund, 1992-94; mem. joint pub. adv. com. N.Am. Commn. on Environ. Coop., 1994-2002; dir. N.Y. Ind. Sys. Operator, 1999—; adv. bd. Harvard U. Com. on Environment; mem. commn. internat. environ. law World Conservation Union; pres. Stockbridge Land Trust, 2001—. 1st lt. USAF, 1959-61. Decorated Commendation medal; named Outstanding Legislator Eagleton Inst. Politics, 1971 Mem. ABA, N.Y. State Bar Assn., Assn. of Bar of City of N.Y. (environ. law com., profl. responsibility com., energy policy com., internat. human rights com., internat. environ. law com.). Episcopalian. E-mail: pberle@audubon.org.

BERLEANT, ARNOLD, philosopher; b. Buffalo, Mar. 4, 1932; s. Bernard and Elizabeth (Barkun) B.; m. Riva Schiller, Aug. 1, 1958; children: Daniel, Andrea, Anne Nicole. Student, SUNY, Fredonia, 1949-51; MusB, Eastman Sch. Music; BM, U. Rochester, 1953, MA, 1955; PhD, SUNY, Buffalo, 1962. Teaching fellow SUNY, Buffalo, 1958-60, instr., 1960-61, lectr., 1961-62; asst. prof. philosophy C.W. Post Campus, L.I.U., 1962-65; asso. prof. C.W. Post Center, L.I.U., 1965-70, prof., 1970-92, prof. emeritus, 1992—. Bingham prof. humanities U. Louisville, 1994; vis. assoc. prof. San Diego State Coll., 1966; mem. social sci. faculty Sarah Lawrence Coll., 1966-68 Author: The Aesthetic Field, 1970, Art and Engagement, 1991, The Aesthetics of Environment, 1992, Living in the Landscape: Toward an Aesthetics of Environment, 1997, Re-thinking Aesthetics, 2004, Aesthetics and Environment, 2005; editor: Environment and the Arts, 2002; co-editor: The Aesthetics of Natural Environments, 2004; founding editor online jour. Contemporary Aesthetics, 2003; contbr. articles to profl. jours. Served with U.S. Army, 1954-56. Am. Council Learned Socs. grantee, 1972, 76 Mem. AAUP, Internat. Assn. Aesthetics (sec.-gen. 1987-95, pres. 1995-98), Am. Soc. Aesthetics (sec.-treas. 1978-88), Internat. Inst. Applied Aesthetics (Lahti, Finland), Finnish Soc. Aesthetics (hon.), Sydney Soc. Lit. and Aesthetics (hon.), French Soc. Aesthetics (mem. com. of honor), Internat. Assn. Aesthetics (hon. life). Home: PO Box 52 Castine ME 04421-0052 E-mail: ab@contempaesthetics.org.

BERLEKAMP, ELWYN RALPH, mathematics professor, entrepreneur; b. Dover, Ohio, Sept. 6, 1940; s. Waldo and Loretta Berlekamp; m. Jennifer Joan Wilson, Aug. 21, 1966; children: Persis, Bronwen, David. BSEE, MSEE, MIT, 1962, PhD in Elec. Engring., 1964. Asst. prof. U. Calif., Berkeley, 1964-66; mem. tech. staff Bell Labs., Murray Hill, N.J., 1966-71; prof. math. U. Calif., Berkeley, 1971—, assoc. chmn. of elec. engring. and computer sci. dept., 1975-77; pres. Cyclotomics, Berkeley, 1981-89, Axcom, Berkeley, 1989-90. Bd. dirs. AK Peters, Ltd.; chmn. bd. Math. Sci. Rsch. Inst., Berkeley, 1994—96, Internat. Computer Sci. Inst., Berkeley, 2000—03. Author: Key Papers in Coding Theory, 1974, Algebraic Coding Theory, 1984; co-author: Winning Ways, vols. 1 and 2, 1982, Mathematical Go, 1994, The Dots and Boxes Game, 2000; author or co-author more than 80 published articles and papers, holder 12 patents in field. Named Outstanding Young Elec. Engr., Eta Kappa Nu, 1971; fellow, Am. Assn. Advancement Sci., 2004. Fellow: IEEE (Best Rsch. Paper award 1967, Centennial medal 1984, Koji Kobayashi award 1990, Hamming award 1991), Info. Theory Soc. of IEEE (pres. 1973, Shannon award 1993); mem.: NAS, NAE, AAAS, Am. Math. Soc. (bd. govs. 1980—82), Nat. Acad. Arts and Scis. Avocation: bicycling. Home: 120 Hazel Ln Piedmont CA 94611-4033 Office: 2039 Shattuck Ave 408 Berkeley CA 94704 Office Phone: 510-849-4214.

BERLEY, DAVID RICHARD, lawyer; b. Bklyn., Apr. 9, 1942; s. Alexander and Ruth (Ginsburg) B.; m. Sharon Lee Freeman, Aug. 10, 1964 (div. 1975); children: Steven N., Barbara Robin; m. Katalin Fine, Feb. 14, 1992 (div. 2003) BS, Boston U., 1963; JD, Boston Coll., 1966. Bar: Mass. 1966, U.S. Dist. Ct. Mass. 1966, U.S. Ct. Claims 1970, Fla. 1977, U.S. Dist. Ct. (so. dist.) Fla. 1977, U.S. Tax Ct., U.S. Ct. Appeals (11th cir.). Pvt. practice, 1966-77; gen. counsel Ecnocar Internat. Inc., Miami, Fla., 1976-77; v.p., gen. counsel Emergency Med. Services Assn., Inc., Miami, 1977-79, pvt. practice, 1979-85; ptnr. Berley & Littman, PA, Miami, 1985-94; pvt. practice Miami, 1994—. Active Greater Miami Heart Assn., Jewish Fedn. Greater Miami, Bus. Vols. for Arts; past chmn. City of Miami Waterfront adv. bd., Coconut Grove Playhouse Soc. of Stars; mem. citizens' adv. bd. Sta.-WLRN Pub. Radio; mem. City of Miami Fin. Com. Mem. Mass. Bar Assn., Fla. Bar Assn. (grievance com.), Fla. Internat. Bankers Assn., Boston Coll. Law Sch. Alumni Assn., Greater Miami C. of C., Coconut Grove C. of C., Coconut Grove Playhouse Soc. Stars. Office: 848 Brickell Ave Ste 200 Miami FL 33131-2981 Address: 1415 Panther Ln Naples FL 34109 Office Phone: 305-373-8000. Business E-Mail: drberley@cs.com.

BERLIN, ALAN DANIEL, lawyer, consultant, real estate company officer; b. Bklyn., Oct. 20, 1939; s. Joseph Jacob and Rose (Smith) B.; m. Renee Wellinger, Dec. 22, 1962; children— Nicole Suzanne, Allison Leigh. BBA, CCNY, 1960; LLB, NYU, 1963, LLM, 1968. Bar: NY 1963. Assoc. Aranow, Brodsky, Bohlinger, Einhorn & Dann, N.Y.C., 1965-68; asst. counsel Gen. Electric Co., N.Y.C., 1968-70; tax counsel Norton Simon Inc., N.Y.C., 1970-77; asst. prof. Pace U. Grad. Sch. Bus., 1977-85; pres. Belco Petroleum Corp., N.Y.C., 1977-88, The Crown Group, White Plains, N.Y., 1988-95; ptnr. Aitken Irvin Berlin & Vrooman L.L.P., 1995—. Spl. cons. to UN Dept. Tech. Cooperation for Devel., 1989—, UN Ctr. for Transnat. Corps., 1990—; hon. assoc. Ctr. for Petroleum and Mineral Law and Policy, U. Dundee, Scotland, 1993—. Author monographs on fed. income tax. With U.S. Army, 1963-65. Mem. ABA, Internat. Bar Assn., N.Y. State Bar Assn., Assn. of Bar of City of N.Y., Inter-Am. Bar Assn., Assn. Internat. Petroleum Negotiators. Lodges: Masons. Office: Aitken Irvin Berlin & Vrooman LLP 2 Gannett Dr White Plains NY 10604-3403 Business E-Mail: adberlin@aibvlaw.com.

BERLIN, ANDREW MARK, advertising agency executive; Copywriter Ogilvy & Mather; co-founder, prin., mng. dir. Goodby Berlin & Silverstein, San Francisco, 1983-92; pres. DDB Needham N.Y., N.Y.C., 1992-93; chmn., CEO Berlin Wright Cameron, N.Y.C., 1993—95; founding ptnr. Fallon McElligott Berlin, N.Y.C., 1995—97, Berlin Cameron & Ptnrs., N.Y.C., 1997—2001; CEO and chief creative officer Red Cell, N.Y.C., 2001—. Recipient Agy. of the Yr. for Berlin Cameron/Red Cell, AdAge, 2003. Office: Berlin Cameron/Red Cell 1370 Broadway, 7th Fl New York NY 10018

BERLIN, FRED SAUL, psychiatrist, educator; b. Pitts., July 27, 1941; s. Sidney Danial and Pauline (Ritt) B.; m. Mary Ann Pazics, Oct. 3, 1969; children: Debra, Alison, Samantha, Ryan. BS, U. Pitts., 1964; MA, Fordham U., 1966; PhD, Dalhousie U., Halifax, N.S., Can., 1970, MD, 1974. Intern McGill U. Sch. Medicine, Jewish Gen. Hosp., Childrens Hosp., Montreal, Can., 1974-75; psychiat. resident Johns Hopkins Hosp., Balt., 1975-76; Johns Hopkins exch. resident Maudsley Hosp., London, 1977; chief resident dept. psychiatry and behavioral sci. Johns Hopkins Hosp., Balt., 1977-78; assoc. prof. dept. psychiatry and behavioral sci. Johns Hopkins U. Sch. Medicine; dir. Sexual Disorders Clinic Johns Hopkins Hosp. Attending physician Johns Hopkins Hosp., mem. house staff coun., 1976-77, mem. adv. com. house staff coun., 1977-78, mem. utilization rev. com., 1977-78, gender identity com., 1980-81; mem. Johns Hopkins U. Med. Sch. Coun., 1982-84; mem. bd.

student advisors Johns Hopkins U. Sch. Medicine, 1980—; bd. dir. Nat. Inst. for Study Prevention and Treatment Sexual Trauma. Contbr. numerous articles to profl. publs. Recipient cert. appreciation Balt. County Police, 1989, 93. Fellow Am. Psychiat. Assn.; mem. AMA, Am. Acad. Psychiatry and Law (pres. Chesapeake Bay chpt.), Md. Psychiat. Assn. (legis. com. 1989—). Avocations: amateur radio, ponds and gardens. Office Phone: 410-539-1661. Personal E-mail: berlinf@aol.com.

BERLIN, GREGORY ALAN, library director; b. Chgo., Ill., Mar. 18, 1956; s. Ernest Mario and Elaine Alfreda Helga (Lofgreen) Berlin; m. Robin Renee David, June 27, 1976; children: Mindy, Nicholas. BA, Andrews U., 1979; MLS, Ind. U., 1992. Libr. dir., tchr. Highland View Acad., Hagerstown, Md., 1979—81, Milo Adventist Acad., Days Creek, Oreg., 1982—85, Great Lakes Adventist Acad., Cidar Lake, Mich., 1987—. Author: (short stories) Guide Mag., 1982—83. Mem. So. Umpqua Land Adv. Com., Douglas County, Oreg., 1984—85. Recipient Outstanding Social Studies Student Tchr. award, Mich. Coun. on Social Svcs., 1979. Seventh Day Adventist. Home: 7249 Acad Rd Cedar Lake MI 48812 Office: Great Lakes Adventist Acad 7477 Acad Rd Cedar Lake MI 48812 Office Phone: 989-427-5181. Office Fax: 989-427-1089. E-mail: masterlibrarian@hotmail.com.

BERLIN, HOWARD RICHARD, investment company executive, retired portfolio manager; b. White Plains, N.Y., Dec. 30, 1935; s. Simon and Frances (Held) B.; m. Joy Monte Shortino, June 10, 1961; children: Howard R. Jr., Asa Ward, Carter Franklin. BS in Econs., U. Pa., 1957; postgrad., NYU, 1962-63. Security analyst Merrill Lynch, N.Y.C., 1961-69, v.p. capital markets, 1969-86; sr. portfolio mgr. Neuberger & Berman, N.Y.C., 1986—2001, prin. ptnr., mem. exec. com., 1990—2001; ret., 2001; mng. mem. The Maverick Group, LLC. Pres. Berlin Assocs. Inc. Hon. nat. campaign chmn. Uriah P. Levy Ctr., US Naval Acad.; scholarship co-chmn. Inst. Am. Indian Arts; trustee Heard Mus., Phoenix. Cmdr. USN, 1957—59. Mem. Fin. Analyst Fedn., Naval Res. Assn., Ret. Officers Assn., Boulders Club (Carefree, Ariz.). Avocations: land development, small business development. Personal E-mail: howardandjoyce@hotmail.com.

BERLIN, IRA, historian, educator; b. N.Y.C., May 27, 1941; s. Louis and Sylvia Toby (Lebwohl) B.; m. Martha L. Chait, Aug. 31, 1963; children—Lisa Jill, Richard Aaron. PhD, U. Wis., 1970. Vice pres. I.B. Alan, Inc., 1967-69; book rev. editor Wis. Mag. History, 1969; instr. U. Ill.-Chgo., 1970-72; asst. prof. history Fed. City Coll., Washington, 1972-74; prof. history U. Md., 1976—. Mem. Columbia U. Seminar, Columbia U. Econ. History Program; dir. Freedmen and So. Soc. project Nat. Archives, also mem. adv. council Author: Slaves Without Masters: Free Negros in the Antebellum South, 1975 (Book prize Nat. Hist. Soc. 1975), Freedom: Documentary History of Emancipation, Slavery and Freedom in the Era of the American Revolution (J.F. Jameson award, Am. Hist. Assn., Founders award Confederate Meml. Literary Soc., Thomas Jefferson award Soc. Historians of Fed. Govt.); Power and Culture: H.G. Gutman and the American Working Class, 1988; also articles. Recipient Distinguished Teaching award U. Wis., 1969; Younger Humanist fellow Nat. Endowment Humanities, 1971; Bi-Centennial prof. Centre de Recherche sur l'histoire des Etats-Unis, Paris, 1987; fellow Davis Ctr. Hist. Studies, Princeton U., 1975, Ctr. for Advanced Studies in the Behavioral Scis., 1989-90. Fellow Am. Acad. Arts and Scis.; mem. Am. Hist. Assn., So. Hist. Assn., Orgn. Am. Historians, Internat. Sociol. Assn. (com. on race and ethnicity) Jewish. Office: Univ Md Dept History College Park MD 20742-0001

BERLIN, KENNETH, lawyer; b. N.Y.C., July 9, 1947; s. Joseph and Helen (Cohen) B.; m. Sue Ann Keller, June 27, 1971; children: Jennifer, Theodore. BA, U. Pa., 1969; JD, Columbia U., 1973. Bar: NY 1974, DC 1982, US Ct. Appeals (DC cir.) 1981, US Ct. Appeals (7th cir.) 1984, US Ct. Appeals (6th cir.) 1987, US Dist. Ct. DC 1988. Assoc. Paul, Weiss, Rifkind et al, NYC, 1973-75, Kramer, Levin, Nessin et al, NYC, 1975-78; sect. chief, wildlife and marine resources sect., environ. and nat. resources divsn. US Dept. Justice, Washington, 1979—81; counsel legis. specialist Nat. Audubon Soc., Washington, 1981-82; ptnr. Winston & Strawn, Washington, 1982-87, Winthrop, Stimson, Putnam & Roberts, Washington, 1987-94; ptnr., environ. practice area Skadden, Arps, Slate, Meagher & Flom, LLP, Washington. Asst. editor Columbia U. Law Rev.; contbr. articles in the field. Chmn. bd. dirs. Rare Ctr. for Tropical Bird Conservation, Environ. Law Inst., Am. Bird Conservancy; bd. dirs. Defenders of Wildlife, Ctr. for Internat. Environ. Law. Mem. ABA (former vice chmn. environ. quality com. natural resources law sect., former chairperson health environ. rights com. individual rights and responsibilities sect.), Am. Ornithologists Union, Internat. Com. Environ. Law. Office: Skadden Arps Slate Meagher & Flom 1440 New York Ave NW Ste 600 Washington DC 20005 Office Phone: 202-371-7350. Office Fax: 202-661-8207. Business E-Mail: kberlin@skadden.com.

BERLIN, KENNETH DARRELL, chemistry professor, consultant, researcher; b. Quincy, Ill., June 12, 1933; s. Kenneth Marion Fischer and Mary Esther (Beckley) B.; m. Grace Frances Smith, Apr. 3, 1937; children: Grace Esther, James Darrell. BA cum laude, North Ctrl. Coll., Naperville, Ill., 1955; PhD, U. Ill., 1958. Postdoctoral fellow U. Fla., Gainesville, 1958-60; asst. prof. chemistry Okla. State U., Stillwater, 1960-63, assoc. prof., 1963-66, prof., 1966-71, Regents prof., 1971—. Spl. cons. Nat. Cancer Inst., Bethesda, Md., 1969—; cons. E.I. DuPont Co., Wilmington, Del., 1969-70, Am. Heart Assn., Oklahoma City, 1983-86, Ariz. Disease Control Commn., 1989—. Co-author: Organic Chemistry, 1972, Phosphorous Stereochem, 1977; contbr. rsch. Jour. Organic Chemistry, 1960, articles to profl. jours. Recipient Regents Disting. Tchg. award, 1998, Sigma Xi rsch. award Okla. State U., Stillwater, 1969, Okla. Chemist of Yr. award, 1977. Fellow Okla. Acad. Sci. (scientist of yr. 1976), Burlington No. Faculty Achievement award 1988, Eminent Faculty award 1998, Okla. medallion Excellence in Tchg. at Coll./Univ. Regents Disting. Rsch. award 2003); mem. Am. Chem. Soc. (sr.), Internat. Soc. Hetercyclic Chemists, Alpha Chi Sigma. Mem. Assembly Of God Ch. Office: Okla State Univ Dept Chemistry Ps I Stillwater OK 74078-0001 Office Phone: 405-744-5950. Business E-Mail: kdb@okstate.edu.

BERLIN, PATRICIA, lawyer; b. N.Y.C., Aug. 13, 1949; d. Irving and Muriel (Kashinsky) B.; m. Victor R. Goldmerstein, Sept. 22, 1974; 1 child, Blake. BA, CUNY, 1976; JD, U. Bpl., Conn., 1984. Clk. State of Conn., Middletown, 1984-85; pvt. practice Stratford, Conn., 1985—. Alt. Zoning Bd. Appeals, Easton, Conn., 1990—. Mem. ABA, Conn. Bar Assn., Greater Bpl. Bar Assn. Democrat. Jewish. Avocations: reading, exercise, travel, golf. Home: 37 Ridgeway Rd Easton CT 06612-1717 Office: Patricia Berlin Atty At Law 3288 Main St Stratford CT 06614-4800 Office Phone: 203-378-3766. Business E-Mail: pbaugust@aol.com.

BERLIN, STEVEN RITT, oil industry executive; b. Pitts., July 1, 1944; s. Sidney D. and Pauline (Ritt) B.; children: Leslie, Jessica, Loren. BBA, Duquesne U., 1967; MBA, U. Wis., 1969. Prof. U. Houston, 1970—72; various fin. positions Cities Svc. Co., Tulsa, 1973-83; v.p. fin. Citgo Petroleum, Tulsa, 1983-85, gen. mgr., 1985-86, CFO, 1986-97; prof., assoc. dean U. Tulsa, 1997-99; chief fin. officer Kaiser-Francis Oil Co., Tulsa, 1999—. Speaker various industry, profl. seminars; mem. Acctg. Edn. change Commn. Mem. bd. visitors U. Wis.; sec.-treas. Green T Club of Tulsa. Mem. AICPA, Am. Acctg. Assn., Okla. Soc. CPAs, Stanford U. Alumni Assn., Beta Gamma Sigma. Avocations: jogging, reading. Office: Kaiser-Francis Oil Co 6733 S Yale Ave Tulsa OK 74136-3302 Home: 1243 E 32d St Tulsa OK 74105 Business E-Mail: cfo@berlin.com.

BERLIND, BRUCE PETER, poet, educator; b. Bklyn., July 17, 1926; s. Peter Sydney and Mae (Miller) B.; m. Doris Lidz, 1947 (div. 1950); m. Mary Elizabeth Dirlam, 1954 (div. 1983); children: Lise, Anne, John, Paul, Alexandra; m. Jo Anne Pagano, 1985. Student, Mercersburg Acad., 1941-43; AB, Princeton U., 1947; MA, Johns Hopkins U., 1950, PhD, 1958. Instr. English Colgate U., Hamilton, N.Y., 1954-58, asst. prof., 1958-63, assoc. prof., 1963-66, prof., 1966-80, Charles A. Dana prof. English, 1980-88, prof. emeritus, 1988—, chmn. dept. English, 1967-72, 80-83; poet in residence U. Rochester, 1966. USIS lectr., Germany, 1963, with Hungarian P.E.N. Translation Program, Budapest, 1977, 79, 84, 86, 88, 91. Author: (poems) Ways of Happening, 1959, Companion Pieces, 1971; translator: (poems) Selected Poems of Agnes Nemes Nagy, 1980, Birds and Other Relations: Selected Poetry of Dezso Tandori, 1987, When You Became She by Imre Oravecz, 1994, The Journey of Barbarus by Ottó Orbán, 1997, Charon's Ferry: Fifty Poems of Gyula Illyés, 2000; assoc. editor: (poems) The Hopkins Rev., 1949-53; contbr. poems, essays, revs. to mags. 1st lt. AUS, 1945-46, 50-52. Recipient Meml. medal Hungarian PEN, 1986; Fulbright grantee, Hungary, 1983-84. Mem. PEN Am. Ctr., Poetry Soc. Am., Am. Lit. Translators Assn., AAUP (mem. council, past pres. N.Y. State Conf.) Home: PO Box 237 Hamilton NY 13346-0237 E-mail: bberlind@mail.colgate.edu.

BERLIND, ROBERT ELLIOT, artist, educator; b. NYC, Aug. 20, 1938; s. Peter Sidney Berlind and Mae (Miller) Bach; m. Dorothy Welch, June 1963 (div. 1974); 1 child, Alexey Fuller; m. Nancy Lee Hubbard, June 17, 1978 (div. 1993); 1 child, Gabriel Peter; m. Mary Lucier, June 7, 1997. BA, Columbia U., 1960; BFA, Yale U., 1962, MFA, 1963. Assoc. prof. art N.S. Coll. of Art and Design, Halifax, Can., 1974-76; prof. SUNY, Purchase, 1979—. One man exhbns.: Alexander Milliken Gallery, N.Y.C., 1981, 82, Tomasulo Gallery, Union Coll., 1983, Ruth Siegel Gallery, N.Y.C., 1984, 86, 88, 90, Gallery One, Toronto, Can., 1985, Warren Wilson Coll., Swananoa, N.C., 1986, St. Peter's Ch., N.Y.C., 1988, Delaware Valley Arts Alliance, Narrowsburg, N.Y., 1992, Tibor de Nagy Gallery, N.Y.C., 1994, 96, 98, 2001, 05, Hampshire Coll. Main Gallery, Amherst, Mass., 1995, Reynolds Gallery, Richmond, Va., 1996, Wright State U., Dayton, Ohio, 1997, Newberger Mus. Art, Purchase, N.Y., 1998; group shows: N.Y. Studio Sch., 1986, The Bronx Mus. of the Arts, 1987, Sherry French Gallery, N.Y.C., 1987, One Penn Pla., N.Y.C., 1988, Fay Gold Gallery, 1988, Art Mus. Fla. Internat. U., 1989, Meml. Art Gallery U. Rochester, 1989, Found. Mona Bismarck, Paris, 1991, Am. Acad. and Inst. Arts and Letters, 1992, Neuberger Mus., Purchase, N.Y., 1994, Maier Art Mus., Lynchburg, Va., Ringling Mus. Art, Sarasota, Fla., 2000, Locks Gallery, Phila., 2002, NAD Painting Ctr., N.Y.C., 2004, 05, Alexander Hogur Gallery, Tulsa, 2005, others. Recipient award in painting Am. Acad. Inst. Arts and Letters, 1992, Pollock-Krasner award, 1997; NEA fellow in painting, 1993. Mem. Coll. Art Assn., Internat. Assn. Art Critics, Nat. Acad. Design. Home: 215 W 20th St Apt 4W New York NY 10011-3552 Personal E-mail: berlind4@aol.com.

BERLIND, ROGER STUART, stage and film producer; b. N.Y.C., June 27, 1930; s. Peter Sydney and Mae (Miller) B.; m. Helen Polk Clark, July 7, 1962 (dec.); 1child, William Polk; m. Brook Wheeler, May 19, 1979. AB, Princeton U., 1952. Account exec. Eastman Dillon, Union Securities & Co., N.Y.C., 1956-60; gen. ptnr. Carter, Berlind & Weill, N.Y.C., 1960-65; chmn. exec. com. Cogan, Berlind, Weill & Levitt, Inc., N.Y.C., 1965-69; chief exec. officer Shearson Lehman Bros., N.Y.C., 1969-73, vice chmn. bd., 1974-75. Bd. dris. Lehman Bros. Prodr.: (films) Beyond Therapy, 1987; (plays) Rex, Music Is, Diversions and Delights, The Merchant, The 1940's Radio Hour, Passione, The Lady from Dubuque, Amadeus, Sophisticated Ladies, Lydie Breeze, Nine, All's Well that Ends Well, The Real Thing, The Rink, Joe Egg, After the Fall, Precious Sons, Big Deal, Long Day's Journey into Night, Ain't Misbehavin', Jerome Robbins' Broadway, City of Angels, Artist Descending A Staircase, Lettice and Lovage, Death and The Maiden, Guys and Dolls, Passion, Indiscretions, Hamlet, Getting Away with Murder, A Funny Thing Happened on the Way to the Forum, Skylight, Steel Pier, The Life, A View from the Bridge, The Judas Kiss, The Blue Room, Closer, Amy's View, Kiss Me Kate (Tony award, 2000), Copenhagen (Tony award, 2000), Proof (Tony award, 2001), Dance of Death, Medea, The Wild Party, Anna in the Tropics, Wonderful Town, Caroline or Change, Who's Afraid of Virginia Wolf. Hon. trustee Am. Acad. Dramatic Arts. With CIC, U.S. Army, 1952-54. Mem. League Am. Theatres and Producers (gov.), Princeton Club (N.Y.C.), Univ. Club, River Club, Century Assn.

BERLINE, JAMES H., advertising executive, public relations executive; b. Youngstown, Ohio, Aug. 6, 1946; s. James Howard and Eloise Blanche (Smith) Berline; children: Erin Michele, Jess Brandon, Quincy Blaine. BA in Econs., U. Mich., 1968; MS in Advt., U. Ill., 1971. V.p. Campbell-Ewald Co., Detroit, 1971-76; sr. v.p. Batten Barton Durstine & Osborn Inc., Troy, Mich., 1976-78, exec. v.p. Southfield, Mich., 1984-85; pres. Yaffe Berline Inc., Southfield, 1980-82; pres., CEO Berline Group, Birmingham, Mich., 1982—. Bd. dirs. Leadership Detroit Alumni; pres. MAGNET (Mktg. and Advt. Global Network). Program chmn. United Found., Detroit, 1984; mem. adv. bd. Jr. League; founder Winning Futures; trustee Detroit Sci. Ctr., 1985—, Juvenile Diabetes Found., 1994; chmn. comm. com. Leadership Detroit, 1993; bd. dirs. Make-A-Wish Found., chmn., 2001—03; trustee CATCH, mem. exec. com.; bd. dirs. Operation Able, Minds, 2003—. Mem.: Young Pres. Orgn. (chair office commn. 1994, trustee, com. chmn. Ea. Mich. chpt.), World Pres. orgn., Detroit C. of C. (mktg. com. 1987—88), Greater Detroit Alliance Bus. (bd. dirs. 1984—86), Birmingham Athletic Club (pres.), U. Mich. Grad. M Club (bd. dirs. 1986), U. Mich. Club Detroit (past bd. govs.), Adcraft Club (bd. dirs. 1980—99, pres. 1988). Avocations: squash, travel, golf. Office: 70 E Long Lake Rd Bloomfield Hills MI 48304 Office Phone: 248-593-7402.

BERLINER, ALLEN IRWIN, dermatologist; b. N.Y.C., Apr. 18, 1947; s. Joseph Benjamin and Ruth (Kaplan) B.; m. Edwina BA, Queens Coll., 1967; MD, SUNY, Buffalo, 1971. Diplomate: Am. Bd. Dermatology. Intern Nassau County Med. Ctr., East Meadow, N.Y., 1971-72; resident in dermatology Boston U. Med. Ctr., 1974-76, chief resident, 1976-77; practice medicine specializing in dermatology Norwood, Mass., 1977—; asst. clin. prof. Tufts U., 1980-90, assoc. clin. prof., 1990—; chief dermatology sect. Caritas Norwood Hosp., 1986—; assoc. staff, Tufts-New Eng. Med. Ctr. Bd. dirs. Mass. Acad. Dermatology. Served as surgeon USPHS, 1972-74. Mem. Am. Acad. Dermatology, New Eng. Dermatol. Soc., Mass. Acad. Dermatology (pres. 1994-95). Office: 95 Chapel St Norwood MA 02062-3161 Office Phone: 781-762-5858.

BERLINER, BARBARA, retired librarian, consultant; b. Bklyn., July 14, 1947; d. Robert and Mildred M. (Sklar) Morris; 1 child, Stefanie Lauren. BA in Anthropology, NYU, 1969; MLS, Columbia U., 1970. Libr. N.Y. Pub. Libr., N.Y.C., 1970-81, sr. libr., telephone reference, 1981-86, supervising libr., tele. reference, 1986-92, head libr., Mid-Manhattan sci. and bus., 1992-93; coord. NYPL Express, N.Y.C., 1993—2002. Cons. John Wright, N.Y.C., 1991; bibliographer Collier's Encyclopedia. Author: The Book of Answers, 1990. Mem. ALA, Planetary Soc. Avocations: sports, astronomy. Home: 235 Portside Dr Edgewater NJ 07020

BERLINER, HANS JACK, retired computer scientist; b. Berlin, Jan. 27, 1929; came to U.S., 1937, naturalized, 1943; s. Paul and Theodora (Lehfeld) B.; m. Araxie Yacoubian, Aug. 15, 1969 (dec.). BA, George Washington U., 1954; PhD, Carnegie Mellon U., 1975. Systems analyst U.S. Naval Rsch. Lab., 1954-58; group head systems analysis Martin Co., Denver, 1959-60; adv. systems analyst IBM, Gaithersburg, Md., 1960-69; prin. rsch. scientist Carnegie-Mellon U., Pitts., 1974-98. Mem. editorial bd. Artificial Intelligence, 1976-98, Pitman: Research Notes in Artificial Intelligence, 1984-98, Internat. Jour. Intelligent Sys., 1986, Theoretical Computer Sci., 1990. Served with AUS, 1951-53. Awarded title Internat. Grandmaster Corr. Chess, 1968; inducted into U.S. Chess Hall of Fame, 1990. Fellow Am. Assn. for Artificial Intelligence; mem. Internat. Joint Conf. Artificial Intelligence, U.S. Chess Fedn., Internat. Computer Chess Assn. Achievements include being among the leading chess players in U.S., 1950-75, N.Y. State champion, 1953, So. Open champion, 1949, U.S. Open Corr. Chess champion, 1955, 56, 59, World Corr. Chess champion, 1968-72; developed first computer program to defeat a world champion at his own game (backgammon), 1979; co-developer Hitech, first chess computer to become a U.S. Chess Fedn. sr. master; among top 0.5% of all registered tournament chess players; discovered B* tree search algorithm, 1975, SNAC method of constructing polynomial evaluation functions, 1979. Home: 4000 N Ocean Dr Apt 1903 Riviera Beach FL 33404-2849 E-mail: berliner@cs.cmu.edu.

BERLINER, HERMAN ALBERT, university provost and officer, economist, educator, dean; BA, CCNY, 1965; PhD, CUNY, 1970. Assoc. prof. econs. Hofstra U., Hempstead, N.Y., 1970-85, assoc. dean advisement, 1975-76, assoc. provost, 1976-83, dean Sch. Bus., 1980-82, 83-90, prof. econs., 1985—, provost, dean faculties, 1989-2001, Lawrence Herbert disting. prof., 1996—, provost, sr. v.p., 2001—. External Periodic Review Evaluator, Mid. States, 2003, Health and Welfare Coun., LI, NY, 1997-2005, Nassau County Assessment Improvement Commn., NY, 1999-2000. Assoc. editor Am. Economist, 1975-80, 83—. Home: 93 Plymouth Dr N Glen Head NY 11545-1126 Office: Hofstra U Office of Provost Hempstead NY 11549 Office Phone: 516-463-5402. Business E-Mail: herman.berliner@hofstra.edu.

BERLINER, PATRICIA MARY, psychologist; b. Bklyn., Mar. 14, 1946; d. Monroe and Rose (Schmidt) B. BA, St. Joseph Coll., Bklyn., 1966; MA, NYU, 1974, PhD, 1990. Joined Sisters of St. Joseph, 1966. Tchr. parochial schs., Bklyn., Queens, L.I., 1968-73; counselor Bishop Kearney High Sch., Bklyn., 1973-79; dir. religious edn. Our Lady of Guadalupe Parish, Bklyn., 1979-82; counselor Office Counseling Svcs., NYU, 1982-84; psychotherapist Mich. State U., E. Lansing, 1984-85; dir. counseling svc. St. John's Hosp., Elmhurst, N.Y., 1985-89; psychotherapist, clin. coord. New Hope Guild Ctr., Howard Beach, NY, 1989—99; co-founder/dir. Women for a New World, 1980—; pvt. practice, 1991—. Cons. Marriage Tribunal, 1991-97, Rockville Centre, N.Y., 1991—, N.Y. State Disability Determination Svc.; co-founder Elizabeth's House, 1996; mem. bd. advisors Dr. Phil Show Contbr. articles to profl. jours. Clergy sexual abuse review bd. CMSM (N.Y./N.J.); leadership team Greater N.Y. ARC. NYU grad. assistantship, 1982-84. Mem. APA (disaster crisis network, evaluator continuing edn. devel. com., Psychritiques book reviewer), N.Y. State Psychol. Assn. (disaster response network), Psychology of Religion, Psychology of Women. Roman Catholic. Home: 140 Beach 112th St Far Rockaway NY 11694-2401 Office: 101-18 104th St Ozone Park NY 11416-2636 Office Phone: 718-849-4029. E-mail: pberl@juno.com.

BERLINER, PAUL F., music professor; PhD, Wesleyan. Prof. ethnomusicology (specializes in African music, jazz, & improvisation) Northwestern U. Author: Soul of Mbira: Music & Traditions of the Shona People of Zimbabwe, 1978 (ASCAP Deems Taylor Award), Thinking in Jazz: Infinite Art of Improvisation, 1994 (Soc.Ethnomusicology's Alan Merriam Prize Outstanding Book in Musicology); contbr. articles to Ethnomusicology, Music Educators Jour., Jazz Educators' Jour. & other profl. jours. Fellow: Am. Acad. Arts & Sci. Office: Northwestern University Music Adminstration Building 711 Elgin Rd Room 19 Evanston IL 60208-1200 Office Phone: 847-491-7106. Business E-Mail: pbe256@northwestern.edu.*

BERLINER, RUTH SHIRLEY, real estate company executive; b. N.Y.C., June 20, 1928; d. Irving William and Florence (Tomback) Blum; m. Arthur Ivan Berliner, Sept. 23, 1948; children: Daniel Scott, Michael Robert, Eric Lance. BA, Empire State Coll., Westbury, N.Y., 1974; diploma, Wilsey Sch. Interior Design, Hempstead, N.Y., 1975; MBA, Adelphi U., 1980. Lic. real estate broker, N.Y. Sec. to dir. librs. NYU, N.Y.C., 1948-50; sec. Paragon Mut. Syndicates Inc., N.Y.C., 1958-72; v.p. Paragon Mut. Investors Svcs., N.Y.C., 1972-78; pres. Ruth S. Berliner, Inc., N.Y.C., 1978—. Pres. Irmed Corp., 1983—; cons. E. 59th St. Assocs., N.Y.C., 1962-70, Amrep Corp., N.Y.C., 1968-75, FKBA Assocs., N.Y.C., 1974-78; mem. stores com. Real Estate Bd. N.Y., 1984-96. V.p. NYU Dental Sch. Parents Assn., 1974-76; bd. dirs. Hadassah, Hewlett, N.Y., 1978-87; advisor Citizens for Charter Change, N.Y.C., 1987—. Mem. Nat. Assn. Realtors, Real Estate Bd. N.Y. (store com. 1984-98, econ. devel. com. 1994-99), Inwood Club, Nat. Realty Club, Williams Club, N.Y. Athletic Club. Avocations: tennis, swimming, dance, painting.

BERLINGER, NORMAN THOMAS, physician, author; b. Detroit, Sept. 16, 1944; s. Stanley Edmund and Bernice (Glinka) B.; m. Patricia Ann Cybert, June 17, 1968; 1 child, Michael. BS, U. Mich., 1966, MD, 1970; PhD, U. Minn., 1978. Diplomate Am. Bd. Otolaryngology. Intern Henry Ford Hosp., Detroit, 1970-71; resident U. Minn. Hosps., 1971-73, 77-79; assoc. scientist Sloan-Kettering Inst. for Cancer Rsch., N.Y.C., 1973-77; instr. U. Minn. Med. Sch., Mpls., 1977-79; asst. prof. Uniformed Svcs. U. Health Scis., Bethesda, Md., 1979-81; surgeon, clin. br. NIH, Bethesda, 1979-81; assoc. prof. U. Minn. Med. Sch., 1981-88; surgeon Oakdale ENT, P.A., Mpls., 1988—. Cons. FMC, Phila., 1986-88; advisor for marine mammals Minn. Zoo, Apple Valley, 1986-88. Contbr. numerous articles to textbooks, articles to profl. jours. and lay periodicals. Comdr. USNR, 1979-81. Grantee NIH, 1973-81, Am. Otological Soc., 1986-88; Nat. Cancer Inst. rsch. fellow, 1974-77. Fellow Am. Acad. Otolaryngology (Meritorious Svc. award 1987); mem. Assn. for Rsch. in Otolaryngology, Phi Rho Sigma. Avocations: piano, tennis, stamp collecting/philately. Office: 2440 Lorien St Minnetonka MN 55305-2813

BERLINGER, WARREN, actor; b. Bklyn., Aug. 31, 1937; s. Elias and Frieda (Shapkin) B.; m. Betty Lou Keim, Feb. 18, 1960. Student, Profl. Children's Sch., 1952-55, Columbia, 1958. Broadway appearances include Annie Get Your Gun, 1946, Happy Time, 1950, Take a Giant Step, 1951, Anniversary Waltz, 1955, Roomful of Roses, 1957, Blue Denim, 1958 (Theatre World award 1959), Come Blow Your Horn, 1960, Bernardine, 1953; London appearance in How to Succeed in Business Without Really Trying, 1963-64; film appearances include The Long Goodbye, Spinout, The World According to Garp, My African Adventure, Outlaw Force, Hero, 1992, Crime and Punishment, 1994, Feminine Touch, 1994, Dear God, 2000, The Great John Rexx, 2002, Time and Again, 2002, So They Call Him Sasquatch, 2002, Another Pretty Face, 2003; TV appearances on Secret Storm, 1955-57, The Funny Side, 1971-72, Touch of Grace, 1973, My African Adventure, 1986, Take Two, 1987, Agatha Christie's Death on Safari, (TV series) Shades of L.A., 1991, Picket Fences, 1993; films include Hero, That Thing You Do!, Dear God, T.O. Friends, November Conspiracy; plays include Lend Me a Tenor, 4318 Clarindon Road, 2003. Named hon. mayor of Chatsworth Calif., 1968, hon. sheriff, 1975; recipient Theatre World award, 1958.

BERLOW, ROBERT ALAN, lawyer; b. Detroit, Feb. 11, 1947; s. Henry and Shirley (Solovich) B.; m. Elizabeth Ann Goldin, Sept. 20, 1972; children: Stuart, Lisa. BA, U. Mich., 1968; JD, Wayne State U., 1971. Bar: Mich. 1971, U.S. Supreme Ct. 1978. Asst. to dean, instr. law sch. Wayne State U., Detroit, 1971-72; mem. Radner, Radner, Shefman, Bayer and Berlow, P.C., Southfield, Mich., 1972-78; gen. counsel Perry Drug Stores, Inc., Pontiac, Mich., 1978-80, gen. counsel, sec., 1980-82, v.p., gen. counsel, sec., 1982-88, sr. v.p., gen. counsel, sec., 1988-93, sr. v.p., chief adminstrn. officer, gen. counsel, sec., 1993-94, exec. v.p., gen. counsel, sec., 1994-95; sr. mem. Dykema Gossett, PLLC, Bloomfield Hills, Mich., 1995—, also chmn. retail practice group. Pres. Agy. for Jewish Edn., Metro Detroit, 1993-95, v.p., 1987-93; bd. dirs. Jewish Cmty. Ctr. Met. Detroit, 1989-2003, v.p., 1992-93, treas., 1996-97, sec., 1997-98. Mem. ABA, Mich. Bar Assn. (chair comml. leasing and mgmt. of real estate com. of real property law sect. 1993-98, chmn. real property law sect. 2001-2002). Avocations: sports, photography. Office: Dykema Gossett PLLC 39577 N Woodward Ave Bloomfield Hills MI 48304-2837 E-mail: r.berlow@dykema.com.

BERLOWITZ, LESLIE, cultural organization administrator; BA in English with honors, NYU, 165; MA in English, Columbia U., 1967. Mem. dept. English NYU, N.Y.C., 1967-96, asst. dean U. Coll. Arts and Scis., Washington Square Coll. Arts and Scis., 1969-73, dir. acad. program devel., 1973-81, asst. v.p. acad. affairs, 1981-84, assoc. v.p. acad. affairs, 1984-88, dep. v.p. acad. affairs, 1988-91, v.p. instnl. advancement, 1991-96; exec. officer Am. Acad. Arts and Scis., Cambridge, Mass., 1996—. Founder, dir. The Humanities Coun., 1977-96, Faculty Resource Network, 1985-96; nat. dir. AmeriCorps, Project SafetyNet, 1995-96. Editor: (with Denis Donoghue and Louis Menand) America in Theory, 1988, Greenwich Village: Culture and Counterculture, 1990. Bd. dirs. Mass. Inst. Psychoanalysis; panelist Boston Jewish Film Festival; exec. bd. Corp. Yaddo; active Fund for Artists' Colonies, Inc., Coun. Internat. Edn. Exch., Urban Rsch. Ctr., Am. Jewish Congress, Fedn. Jewish Philanthropies, Joseph S. Gruss Found.; panelist NEH. Recipient

Pacesetter award Tougaloo Coll., 1993. Fellow N.Y. Inst. Humanities, Am. Acad. Arts & Scis. 2004; mem. MLA, Century Assn. (N.Y.). Office: Am Acad Arts and Scis Norton's Woods 136 Irving St Cambridge MA 02138-1929 Fax: (617) 576-5055.*

BERLUSCONI, MARINA, publishing executive; b. Milan, Aug. 10, 1966; d. Silvio Berlusconi. V.p. Fininvest, 1996; chairwoman Arnoldo Mondodori Editore, 2003. Bd. dir. Mediaset S.p.A., Mediolanum S.p.A., Medusa S.p.A., 21 Investimenti S.p.A. Named one of most powerful women, Forbes mag., 2005. Mailing: via Mondadori 1 20090 Segrate Milano Italy*

BERMACK, ELAINE, speech educator; b. Jersey City, N.J., Oct. 8, 1930; d. Morris and Irene (Hendel) Dalberg; m. Eugene Bermack, Mar. 18, 1951; children: Alison, Kiri, Marla. BA, NYU, PhD, 1988; MA, Columbia U., 1969. Lic. speech and lang. pathology, lic. tchr. of the deaf, N.Y. Tchr. of speech improvement N.Y.C. Bd. of Edn., 1951-57; asst. prof. speech CUNY, 1971—, St. John's U., Queens; instr. of comm. Nassau C.C., Garden City. Chmn., CEO Presentations Plus, Manhasset Hills, N.Y., 1996—. Mem. Am. Speech and Hearing Assn. (cert. speech lang. pathology), L.I. Speech and Hearing Assn.

BERMAN, ARIANE R., artist; b. Danzig, Mar. 27, 1937; m. Mario La Rossa, 1965. B.F.A., Hunter Coll., N.Y.C., 1959; M.F.A., Yale, 1962; AAUW and Found. des Etats-Unis fellow, U. Paris, 1962-63. Juror nat. screening com. Fulbright grants, 1976-77, chmn. screening com., 1977-78. One man shows at Center Gallery, Conn., 1963, Harry Salpeter Gallery, N.Y.C., 1966, Brentano's Art Gallery, N.Y.C., 1973, Graphic Art Gallery, Tel Aviv, 1973, Galleria San Sebastianello, Rome, 1973, Eileen Kuhlik Gallery, N.Y.C., 1971, 73, Pub. Mus., Oshkosh, Wis., 1974, Wustum Mus. Fine Arts, Racine, Wis., 1974, Fontana Gallery, Pa., 1963, 71, 74, Galleria d'Arte Helioart, Rome, 1974, Munson Gallery, Conn., 1975, Ward-Nasse Gallery, N.Y.C., 1975, 77, 80, Phila. Art Alliance, 1980, Silvermine Guild Artists, Conn., 1976, Kornblee Gallery, N.Y.C., 1982, Babson Coll., Mass., 1983, Northwood Inst., Mich., 1983, Westenhook Gallery, Mass., 1984, Phoenix Gallery, N.Y.C., 1985, 87, Concordia Coll., Bronxville, N.Y., 1989, Gallery 84 Inc., N.Y.C., 1992, L'Artisanat, Mass., 1992, others; exhibited in group shows at Galerie Atrium Arits, Geneva, Switzerland, 1975, F 15 Gallery, Norway, 1974, Galeries Raymond Duncan, Paris, 1964, Asso. Am. Artists, N.Y.C., 1971, Circle Galleries Ltd., N.Y.C., 1974, Margo Feiden Galleries, N.Y.C., 1972, Gallery 500, Pa., 1973, Van Straaten Gallery, Chgo., 1974, Genesis Gallery, N.Y.C., 1978, Marymount Coll., N.Y.C., 1983, NYU, 1982, Fairleigh Dickenson U., 1982, Allentown Art Mus., Pa., 1982, numerous others; represented in permanent collections at Am. Petroleum Inst., Israel Ministry of Tourism, USIA, McGregor-Doniger, Inc., Shipley Sch., Bryn Mawr, Pa., Readers Digest, N.J. Bd. Edn., Athena Gallery, New Haven, Charles E. Ellis Coll., Newton Square, Pa., Hearst Corp., Met. Mus. Art, Phila. Mus. Art, Phila. Art Alliance, Ms. mag., Seventeen, Redbook, Feminist Press, Duke U., Newspaper Advt. Bur., Purdue U., Phila. Child Guidance Ctr., others. Recipient Yale Painting prize, 1960, Purchase award Purdue U., 1964, Stella Drabkin Meml. award, ACPS Purchase prize, 1973, Catherine Lorillard Wolfe Arts Club Gold medal, 1973, Hon. mention Hudson River Mus., 1974, Artists Equity award, 1985. Mem. Am. Color Print Soc., Nat. Assn. Women Artists, Yonkers Art Assn., Women's Caucus for Art, Met. Painters and Sculptors, Pen and Brush, League of Present Day Artists, Sheffield Art League, Silvermine Guild of Artists, Soc. Women Artists (past corr. sec.), Hunter Coll. Alumni Assn. (Hall of Fame 1974) Home: 161 W 54th St New York NY 10019-5322 Office Phone: 212-765-2030. *I use art as a means of communicating to people. My work is representational and tries to depict life in all its humor, sorrow, satiric aspects, and dream-like qualities of humanity as I see it. I particularly use color for emphasis in everything I do— paintings, graphics, plastics, and sculpture.*

BERMAN, ARTHUR LEONARD, retired state legislator; b. Chgo., May 4, 1935; s. Morris and Jean (Glast) B.; m. Barbara Dombeck; children: Adam, Marcy Padorr. BS in Commerce & Law, U. Ill., 1956; JD, Northwestern U., 1958. Bar: Ill. 1958. Atty. pvt. practice, Chgo.; ptnr. White, White & Berman, Chgo., 1958-74, Maragos, Richter, Berman, Russell & White, Chtd., 1974—81, Chatz, Berman, Maragos, Haber & Fagel, Chgo., 1981-82, Berman, Fagel, Haber, Maragos & Abrams, Chgo., 1982-86, Karlin & FLeisher, Chgo., 1986-99; cons. Chgo. Bd. Edn., 2000—. Spl. atty. Bur. Liquidations, Ill. Dept. Ins., 1962-67; spl. asst. atty. gen. Ill., 1967-68; mem. Ill. Ho. of Reps., 1969-76, Ill. Senate, 1977-99; legis. policy advisor to Chgo. Bd. Edn., 2000—. Pres. 50th Ward Young Dems., 1956-60; v.p. Cook County Young Dems., 1956-60, 50th Ward Regular Dem. Orgn., 1955-99; active 48th Ward Regular Dem. Orgn., 1967-99; exec. bd. Dem. Party, Evanston, Ill., 1973-99; bd. govs. State of Israel Bonds. Mem. ABA, Ill. Bar Assn., Chgo. Bar Assn. (bd. mgrs. 1988-89), Nat. Assn. Jewish Legislators (pres. 1987-89), U. Ill. Alumni Assn., Phi Epsilon Pi, Tau Epsilon Rho. Office: 6007 N Sheridan Rd Chicago IL 60660-3039 Personal E-mail: senatorart2000@aol.com.

BERMAN, BARRY, marketing educator; b. Bklyn., Dec. 2, 1944; s. Abraham Louis and Gussie Boyarsky B.; m. Linda Nancy Grossman, June 9, 1968; children: Glenna Laurie, Lisa Naomi. BBA, CCNY, 1966, MBA, 1968; PhD, CUNY, 1973; postgrad., Hofstra U., 1999—. Instr. mktg. Hofstra U., Hempstead, N.Y., 1967-71, asst. prof., 1971-74, assoc. prof., 1974-79, prof., 1979-80, 81—, Walter H. "Bud" Miller distin. prof. bus., 1989—, acad. dir. exec. MBA program, 1999—; assoc. prof. Rutgers U., Newark, N.J., 1980-81. Cons. State Edn. Dept. N.Y., Albany, 1971—, N.Y. Telephone Corp., N.Y.C., 1978, Singer Co., Stamford, Conn., 1985, Fortunoff's, L.I., 1990, John Wiley and Sons, N.Y.C., 1992, NCR, 1998, Savvy Sys., 1998, Kohl's, 1999, Simon Properties, 2001, Olympus Am. Melville N.Y., 2004, Duane Reade, N.Y.C., 2004 Co-author: Principles of Marketing, 1995; author: Marketing Channels, 1996. NDEA fellow; Bernard M. Baruch scholar. Mem. Am. Mktg. Assn., Am. Collegiate Retailing Assn., Acad. Mktg. Sci., So. Mktg. Assn., Beta Gamma Sigma. Avocations: photography, computers, baking. Home: 2037 Oliver Way Merrick NY 11566-5423 Office: Hofstra U Hofstra Univ 144 Weller Hl Hempstead NY 11549-0001 Office Phone: 516-463-5711. E-mail: mktbxb@hofstra.edu.

BERMAN, BERNARD MAYER, lawyer; b. Phila., May 9, 1940; s. Henry and Mildred (Ginsburg) B.; m. Mona Halpern, June 7, 1964; children: Minda, Kyle, Joshua. BA, Swarthmore (Pa.) Coll., 1962; LLB, Columbia U., 1965, JD, 1969. Bar: Pa. 1965, U.S. Dist. Ct. (ea. dist.) Pa. 1966, U.S. Ct. Appeals (3d cir.) 1966, U.S. Supreme Ct. 1969. Jud. law clk. Ct. of Common Pleas, Phila., 1965-66; pvt. practice Phila., 1965-66; pub. defender trial atty. Delaware County, 1966-77; jud. law clk. Ct. of Common Pleas, Delaware County, Pa., 1967-74; pvt. practice Delaware County, 1966-89; ptnr. Scallan, March, Berman & Hurwitz and predecessor firms, Media, Pa., 1966-88, Scallan and Berman, Media, 1988-89, Bernard M. Berman and Assocs., Media, 1989-97; mng. ptnr. Berman Asbel & Berman, 1997—2004; ptnr. Berman & Asbel, 2005—. Mem. Spl. Com. to Revise Rules of Civil Procedure, Delaware County, 1974-75; arbitrator Am. Arbitration Assn., 1968—; mediator Fee Dispute Resolution Com., Delaware County, 1997—. Mem., Guy G. DeFuria Amer. Inn of Ct., 1997—, sec. young men's com. Phila. Fedn. Jewish Agys., 1966, 67; pres. B'nai B'rith Simon Wolf Lodge, Wallingford, Pa., 1978-80, Southeastern Pa. and Del. coun., 1984-86, bd. govs. dist. 3, Phila., 1984-89. Mem. ABA, Pa. Bar Assn., Delaware County Bar Assn., Rose Valley Chorus (parliamentarian 1986-87), Phi Sigma Kappa Found. (trustee 1995-2003, investment com. 1998-2001), Phi Sigma Kappa (grand coun. 1983-91, grand pres. 1991-95, Ct. of Honor, 1995—, dir, legal com. Phi Sigma Kappa Properties, Inc., 2003—). Avocations: tennis, sailing, amateur theater, gardening, singing. Office: Berman & Asbel LLP 20 W Third St Media PA 19063-2824 E-mail: bmb@BermanLaw.com.

BERMAN, BRUCE, entertainment company executive, television producer; b. N.Y.C., Apr. 25, 1952; Grad., Calif. Inst. Arts Film Sch.; grad. magna cum laude in history, UCLA, 1975; JD, Georgetown U., 1978. Bar: Calif. 1978. Asst. to Jack Valenti Warner Bros., Burbank, Calif.; asst. to Peter Guber Casablanca Filmworks, 1979; asst. to Sean Daniel and Joel Silver Universal Pictures, 1979, v.p. prodn., 1982, Warner Bros., 1984, sr. v.p. prodn., 1988, pres. theatrical prodn., 1991-96, chmn., CEO Village Roadshow Pictures, 1998; pres. Worldwide Prodn., 1991-96. Founder Plan B Entertainment, 1996—. Office: Village Roadshow Pictures care Warner Bros Studios 3400 W Riverside Dr Ste 900 Burbank CA 91505-4639

BERMAN, BRUCE JUDSON, lawyer; b. Roslyn, N.Y., Oct. 9, 1946; s. Howard M. Berman and Soosha T. (Draizen) Hurwitz; children: Daniel H., Ann N., Andrew J., Josie A.; m. Susan Leigh Readinger, Dec. 29, 1991. BA, Williams Coll., 1968; MBA, Columbia U., 1972; JD, Boston U., 1972. Bar: Fla. 1973, U.S. Dist. Ct. (so. dist.) Fla. 1980, U.S. Dist. Ct. (mid. dist.) Fla. 1990, U.S. Ct. Appeals (5th cir.) 1980, U.S. Ct. Appeals (11th cir.) 1981, U.S. Supreme Ct. 1976. Assoc. Guggenheimer & Untermyer, N.Y.C., 1973-79; from assoc. to ptnr. Myers, Kenin, Levinson, Frank & Richards, Miami, Fla., 1979-85; ptnr. Weil, Gotshal & Manges LLP, Miami, 1985-2000, McDermott, Will & Emery LLP, Miami, 2000—. Spl. ad hoc trial com. to Dade County (Fla.) Cir. Ct., 1988—; apptd. Fla. Supreme Ct. ct. reporter cert. planning com., 1995, Supreme Ct. Com. on Std. Jury Instrns. in Civil Cases, 2000, 03, Fla. Supreme Ct. workgroup on access to pub. records, 2000. Author: Florida Civil Procedure, 1998—99, 2001—05. Mem. New World Symphony Cmty. Bd., Miami Beach, Fla., 1991-2000; bd. dirs., Daily Bread Food Bank, 2002—. Mem. Internat. Bar. Assn., Fla. Bar (civil procedure rules com. 1984-2004, chmn. 1988-90, jud. adminstrn. rules com. 1988-2002, chmn. 1993-94), Dade County Bar. Office: McDermott Will & Emery LLP 201 S Biscayne Blvd Ste 2200 Miami FL 33131 Office Phone: 305-347-6530. Business E-Mail: bberman@mwe.com.

BERMAN, CAROL, commissioner; b. Bklyn., Sept. 21, 1923; d. Hyman and Sarah (Levy) B.; m. Seymour Jerome Berman, May 19, 1944; children: Elizabeth, Charles. BA, U. Mich., 1943. Trustee Bd. Edn., Lawrence, N.Y., 1973-77; senator State of N.Y., Albany, 1978-84; spl. rep. State Divsn. for Housing, Hempstead, N.Y., 1985-86; commr. N.Y. State Commn. on Lobbying, Albany, 1988-92, N.Y. State Commn. of Elections, Albany, 1992—2005. N.Y. co-chair Nat. Jewish Dem. Coun., 1988—2005, Met. Airport Noise Mitigation Rev. Commn., 1992—; del. Dem. Nat. Conv., N.Y., 1992; vice-chair Nassau Dem. County Com., Mineola, N.Y., 1970-72. Mem. Phi Beta Kappa, Phi Kappa Phi. Jewish. Avocations: grandchildren, golf. Home: 42 Lord Ave Lawrence NY 11559-1324 Office: NY State Bd Elections 40 Steuben St Albany NY 12207 Office Phone: 518-474-8100.

BERMAN, CAROL SIEGEL, artist; b. Cleve., June 4, 1932; d. Maurice Myron and Florence (Blatt) Siegel; m. Sidney A. Berman, July 20, 1956 (dec.); children: Steven Eric, Adrian Jennifer. Student, New Orleans Acad. Art, 1949-50, Tulane U., 1951, Thomas Nelson Coll., 1969-70. Studio owner, portrait artist, tchr., Reston, Va., 1970—. Tech. illustrator No. Va., 1974—84; represented by Herndon (Va.) Old Town Gallery, 1986—87, Reston Art Gallery, 1988. One-woman shows include Herndon Old Town Gallery, 1986, 1987, Greater Reston Art Ctr., 1988, exhibited in group shows, 1987, 1988, 1989, 1990, 1994, 1995, 1996, 2003, Foundry Gallery, 1989. Recipient 1st pl. drawing award, Va. Fine Arts Festival, 1987, Best in Show award, Jewish Coun. on Aging, 1992, Art from Older Hands, 2000, Young at Art Show, 2003. Mem.: League of Reston Artists (Best in Show award 1983, 1st pl. mixed media award 1994, 1st pl. pastels 1998, Best in Show award 1999, 1st pl. pastels 1999). Democrat. Jewish.

BERMAN, CHERYL R., advertising company executive; b. Chgo. BA in Journalism, U. Ill., Urbana. Copywriter, various positions Leo Burnett Co., Chgo., 1974-99, chief creative officer, chmn. U.S. bd. dirs., 1999—. Composer advt. music for McDonald's, Hallmark, Kraft, Walt Disney World, Chgo. Bulls; songwriter/composer Remember the Magic, Celebrate the Future Hand in Hand. Named Ad Woman of Yr. Women's Advt. Club Chgo., 1997.

BERMAN, CHRIS, sportscaster; b. May 10, 1955; BA in History, Brown U., 1977. Disc jockey WERI, Westerly, R.I., 1977-78; broadcaster WNVR Radio, Waterbury, Conn., 1978-79; weekend sports anchor WVIT-TV, Hartford, Conn., 1979; NFL studio host, anchor SportsCenter, baseball commentator ESPN, 1979—, host NFL Countdown; sports commentator KFRC-Radio, San Francisco, 1986, WFAN-Radio N.Y., 1987. Host NFL GameDay, Sunday night NFL telecasts, NFL draft coverage, commentator major league baseball games, host Baseball Tonight, SportsCenter ESPN. Appeared as himself in 10 films, including Little Big League, Necessary Roughness, Eddie, The Garbage Picking Goal Kicking Philadelphia Phenomenon, Big Daddy, Second String, Even Steven, Kingpin, The Program, Celtic Pride, The Longest Yard, also TV programs, including Spin City, The Jersey, and Arli$$. Named nat. sportscaster of yr. Nat. Sportscasters and Sportswriters Assn., 1989, 90, 93, 94; named among top stars of the '90's TV Guide, 1990; winner sports Emmys for NFL GameDay, 1989, 92, 95, CableACE awards, 1989, 92, 93, 94; voted best cable sportscaster Cable Guide, 1987, 88, 90. Office: ESPN ESPN Plaza Bristol CT 06010

BERMAN, DANIEL LEWIS, lawyer; b. Washington, Dec. 14, 1934; s. Herbert A. and Ruth N. (Abramson) B.; children: Priscilla Decker, Jane, Katherine Ann, Sara Mark, Heather, Melinda. BA, Williams Coll., 1956; LLB, Columbia U., 1959. Bar: N.Y. 1960, Utah 1962, Wyo. 2004. Assoc. Chadbourne, Parke, Whiteside & Wolff, N.Y.C., 1959-60; asst. prof. law U. Utah, 1960-62; pvt. practice Salt Lake City, 1962—; sr. ptnr. Berman & Savage PC, Salt Lake City, 1981—. Vis. prof. U. Utah, 1970, 74, 77; mem. Utah Coordinating Coun. Higher Edn., 1965-68; mem. Salt Lake County Merit Coun., 1974-80; mem. nominating commn. Utah Appellate Ct., 1999—2003. Trustee Salt Lake Art Ctr., 1978-80; Dem. candidate for U.S. Senate from Utah, 1980; mem. Utah Transit Authority, 1992-97. Mem. Am. Law Inst., Salt Lake Area C. of C. (bd. govs. 1976-79). Democrat. Jewish. Office: Berman & Savage PC 50 S Main St Ste 1250 Salt Lake City UT 84144-2073 Office Phone: 801-328-2200. Personal E-mail: dlb@bermansavage.com.

BERMAN, DAVID, lawyer, poet; b. NYC, Sept. 11, 1934; s. Joseph and Sophie (Hersh) B. BA with honors, U. Fla., 1955; postgrad. Johns Hopkins U., 1955-56; JD, Harvard U., 1963. Bar: Mass. 1963. Tchg. fellow Harvard Coll., 1962-63, 66-67; law clk. to justice Mass. Supreme Ct., 1963-64; asst. atty. gen. Commonwealth of Mass., 1964-67; assoc. Zamparelli & White, 1967, ptnr., 1968-74; pvt. practice, 1974-82, 1990—; ptnr. Berman & Moren, Medford, Mass., 1982-89. Author: Future Imperfect, 1982, Slippage, 1996, Early Mandamus in Massachusetts, Massachusetts Legal History, 1998, David Berman Greatest Hits, 1965-2002, 2003. Trustee Cantata Singers, 1981—. Mem. ABA, Mass. Bar Assn., Mass. Bar Found., Middlesex Bar Assn. (Most Outstanding Trial Lawyer Appelate award, 1998), Harvard Club (Boston), Signet Soc., Confrerie de la Chaine des Rotisseurs, Ordre Mondial, Masons. Republican. Unitarian. Home: 33 Birch Hill Rd Belmont MA 02478-1729 Office: 100 George P Hassett Dr Medford MA 02155-3264 Office Phone: 781-395-7520.

BERMAN, ELLEN SUE, energy and telecommunications executive, theatre producer; Student, U. N.C., Greensboro, 1960-62, U. N.C., Chapel Hill, summer 1961, U. Calif., Berkeley, summer 1962; BA in Russian, Barnard Coll., 1964. Legis. asst. Senator Joseph Tydings, 1965-66; rsch. assoc. Washington Poverty Program United Planning Orgn., 1966-70; pres. Consumer Energy Coun. Am. Rsch. Found., Washington, 1973—. Mem. Office Tech. Assessment Residential Energy Conservation Adv. Com., 1976-77, Magnetic Fusion Adv. Com., 1986-87, Aspen Inst. Energy Policy Forum; mem. coun. for the Arts MIT, 1995—; mem. Com. on Energy and Econ. Devel. NAACP; mem. German Marshall Fund Adv. Com. on Energy Efficiency in Swedish Bldgs. Co-author: A Decade of Despair, A Compendium of Utility-Sponsored Appliance Rebate Programs, Transportation, Energy and Environment: Balancing Goals and Identifying Policies, 1995, Restructuring the Electric Utility Industry: A Consumer Perspective, 1998; author: Equity and Energy: Rising Energy Prices and the Living Standards of Lower Income Americans, 1983, Oil, Gas or .? A Guide to Saving Heating Dollars, The Consumer and Energy Impacts of Oil Exports, Operating Costs of Refrigerators/Freezers and Room Air Conditioners, If You Want to Lower Your Heating Bill, It's Time to Raise the Roof, A Comparative Analysis of Utility and Non-Utility Based Energy Services Companies, A State by State Compendium of Energy Efficiency Programs Using Oil Overchange Funds; (reports) The Consumer and Energy Impacts of Oil Exports, 1984, A Comprehensive Analysis of a Crude Oil Import Fee: Dismantling a Trojan Horse, 1982, A Comparison of Crude Oil Decontrol and Natural Gas Deregulation: An Analysis of the Impract of Immediate Decontrol of Crude Oil and Related Products on End Use Consumers, Natural Gas Deregulation: A Case of Trickle Up Economics, 1982; pub. The Quad Report, 1993—. Bd. dirs. Barnard in Washington, 1994—; bd. trustees Wider Opportunities for Women; bd. mgrs. Adas Israel Congregation, 1996—; chmn. bldgs. and gounds com. Woodley Park Towers condominium. Named Woman of the Eighties, Ladies Home Jour., 1979; grantee German Marshall Fund. Mem. Barnard Coll. Washington Alumnae Assn. (bd. dirs.), Cosmos Club (admissions com., mem. coun. arts, named one of Key Women 2004). Home: 2737 Devonshire Pl NW Washington DC 20008-3479 Office: Consumer Energy Coun Am 2000 L St NW Ste 802 Washington DC 20036-4913 Office Phone: 202-659-0404.

BERMAN, GAIL, film company executive; b. 1957; m. Bill Masters, 1980; 2 children. B in Theater, U. Md., 1978. Former exec. prodr. Comedy Channel, HBO; from v.p. TV to pres. and CEO Sandollar Prodns., 1991—97, advisor, 1997—98; founding pres. Regency TV, 1998—2000; pres. entertainment Fox Broadcasting Co., 2000—05; pres. Paramount Pictures, Hollywood, Calif., 2005—. Named one of 100 Most Powerful Women in Entertainment, Hollywood Reporter, 2003, 2004, 50 Most Powerful Women in Am Bus., Fortune Mag., 2003, Most Powerful Women, Forbes mag., 2005; recipient Lucy award, Women in Film, 2003. Office: Paramount Pictures Corp 5555 Melrose Ave Los Angeles CA 90038 Office Phone: 310-369-1000.*

BERMAN, GEOFFREY LOUIS, diversified financial services company executive; b. L.A., July 15, 1953; s. Geoffrey M. and Patricia A. (Meyer) B.; m. Autumn Joy Patton, Mar. 26, 1983; children: Arielle Louise, Michelle Elise. BA/BS in Bus. Adminstrn., U. of the Pacific, 1975; JD, Southwestern U., 1985. Loan officer Union Bank, L.A., 1975-80; adminstrv. asst. Credit Mgrs. Assn., L.A., 1980-82; asst. v.p. Mitsui Mfrs. Bank, L.A., 1982-86; asst. sec., mgr. adjustment bur. Credit Mgrs. Assn., Burbank, Calif., 1986-97; v.p. turnaround management Devel. Specialists, Inc., L.A., 1997—. Dir. Comml. Fin. Conf. Calif., L.A., 1978-80; co-chair insolvency laws com. Am. Bankruptcy Inst., Alexandria, Va., 1994—, dir., 2002—; mem. panel of mediators Ctrl. Dist. Bankruptcy Ct., L.A., 1995—; chmn. Task Force on Gen. Assignments for Benefit of Creditors, 1995-2000. Author: (manual) ABI Creditor's Com. Manual, 1995, ABI General Assignments for the Benefit of Creditors, A Practical Guide, 2000; contbg. editor Am. Bankruptcy Inst. Jour., 1996—, Fed. CT Receiver, 1999-2000; contbr. articles to profl. jours. Mem. task force City of Buena Park (Calif.) Investment Policy Rev. Com., 1995. Recipient Recognition award Fed. Bar Assn., L.A., 1986. Mem. L.A. Bankruptcy Forum, Bay Area Bankruptcy Forum, Orange County Bankruptcy Forum. Office: Devel Specialists Inc 333 S Grand Ave Ste 2010 Los Angeles CA 90071-1524 E-mail: gberman@dsi.biz.

BERMAN, GIZEL, sculptor; b. Sobrance, Slovakia, Aug. 26, 1919; came to U.S., 1946; d. Armin and Margit (Kaufman) Herskovits; m. Nicholas Berman, Dec. 23, 1941; 1 child, Margaret. Student, Uzhorod Bus. Coll., Czechoslovakia, 1935-37, Nagay Design Sch., Budapest, Hungary, 1938, Inst. Michot, Brussels, 1939. Lectr. in schs. and orgns. Survivors of the Holocaust, Seattle, 1980-90. Exhibited bronze sculptures at galleries in Seattle, Portland, Oreg. and Vancouver, B.C., Can., 1950—. Mem. Survivors of the Holocaust, Seattle, 1950—; with Herzl-Ner Tamid Conservative Congregation. Recipient Holocaust Meml. award Jewish Fedn. Greater Seattle, 1981; participant Album Internat., Geneva, 1979. Mem. Hadassah (life). Democrat. Avocations: horseback riding, skiing, tennis, hiking. Home: 10281 E Jenan Dr Scottsdale AZ 85260-5903

BERMAN, GREG, think-tank executive; BA Wesleyan Univ. Project coord. Red Hook Cmty. Justice Ctr., N.Y., 1994—96; dep. dir. Ctr. for Ct. Innovation, N.Y., 1996—2002, dir., 2002—. Contbr. articles in law jour. Mem. bd. Poets House, N.Y. Coro Fellow in Public Affairs. Office: Center for Court Innovation 520 8th Ave New York NY 10018

BERMAN, HOWARD LAWRENCE, congressman, lawyer; b. LA, Apr. 15, 1941; m. Janis Schwarz Berman. BA, UCLA, 1962, LLB, 1965. Bar: Calif. 1966. Vol. VISTA, Balt., San Francisco, 1966-67; assoc. Levy, Van Bourg & Hackler, L.A., 1967-72; mem. & majority leader Calif. State Assembly from 43d dist., 1972—82; mem. U.S. Congress from 28th Calif. dist., Washington, 1983—. Mem. jud. com., immigration and claims sub com.; ranking mem. on courts, the internet, and intellectual property subcoms.; mem. internat. rels. com., Middle East and Ctrl. Asia subcom. Pres. Calif. Fedn. Young Democrats, 1967-69 (budget com.); mem. adv. bd. Jewish Fund for Justice. Democrat. Office: US Ho Reps 2221 Rayburn Ho Office Bldg Washington DC 20515-0528 also: Dist Office 14546 Hamlin St Ste 202 Van Nuys CA 91411*

BERMAN, JEFFREY A., lawyer; b. L.A., Sept. 3, 1946; s. Dorothy Rosenthal; m. Susan C. Sturzenberger, Oct. 7, 1947. BS, Univ. of Calif., Santa Barbara, 1964—68; JD, UCLA, 1968—71. Ptnr. Proskauer Rose, L.A., Calif., 1979—97, Sidley Austin Brown and Wood, L.A., Calif., 1997—. Bd. dirs. Am. Found. For Tibetan Cultural Preservation, Glendale, Calif., 2002—05. Fellow: Coll. of Labor and Employment Lawyers; mem.: Employers Group Legal Com. (chair, amicus com. 1994—2005). Office: Sidley Austin Brown & Wood 555 West Fifth St 40th Floor Los Angeles CA 90064 Office Phone: 213-896-6655. Office Fax: 213-896-6600. E-mail: jberman@sidley.com.

BERMAN, JENNIFER R., urologist; BA in Spanish and psychology, Hollins Coll., 1986; MS in human anatomy and physiology, U. Md. Sch. Medicine, 1988; MD, Boston U. Sch. Medicine, 1992. Resident in gen. surgery U. Md., 1994, resident in urology, 1998; fellow in urology/pelvic floor reconstructive surgery David Geffen Sch. Medicine, LA, 2001; former co-dir. (with sister Laura) Network Excellence in Women's Sexual Health, 1998—2004; co-dir. women's sexual health clinic Boston U. Sch. Medicine, masters med. sci. thesis advisor, 1998, instr. urology, 2000—01; dir. female sexual medicine ctr. UCLA, 2001—; asst. prof. urology UCLA Med. Ctr., 2001—; co-host (with sister Laura) Berman & Berman, Discovery Health Channel, 2004—. Vis. prof. U. Kan. Med. Ctr., 2002, Emory U., Atlanta, 2003; lectr. in field; mem. editl. bd. Healthgate Inc., Sexual Health Capsule and Comment; mem. sci. adv. bd. Quanlilife Pharm., Cellegy Pharm., Auxillum. Co-author (with sister Laura): For Women Only: A Revolutionary Guide to Overcoming Sexual Dysfunction and Reclaiming Your Sex Life, 2001, Secrets of the Sexually Satisfied Woman, 2005; contbr. articles to profl. jour. Named Women's Health Adv. Yr., Calif. Gov. Conf. Women, 2001; recipient Rising Star Yr., Nat. Assn. Women Bus. Owners, 2002, Women of Action award, Israel Cancer Rsch. Fund, 2002, Women Who Make a Difference award, LA Bus. Jour., 2002, Outstanding Programming award, Cable Positive /TV Guide, 2003. Mem.: AMA, Am. Urological Assn., Soc. Study Impotence, Sexual Medicine Soc. N. Am., Internat. Soc. Study Women's Sexual Health. Office: Female Sexual Medicine Ctr David Geffen Sch Medicine UCLA 924 Westwood Blvd Ste 515 Los Angeles CA 90024 Office Phone: 310-794-3030. Office Fax: 310-794-2490. Business E-Mail: jberman@mednet.ucla.edu.*

BERMAN, JOEL DAVID, mathematics professor; b. Mpls., Feb. 2, 1943; s. Morris and Hilda Berman. BA, U. Minn., 1965; PhD, U. Wash., 1970. Asst. prof. U. Ill., Chgo., 1970—75, assoc. prof., 1975—82, prof., 1982—. Office: Univ of Ill at Chgo MSCS Dept 851 S Morgan St Chicago IL 60607

BERMAN, JOSHUA G., lawyer; b. Miami, July 14, 1970; BS in Govt. magna cum laude, Cornell U., 1991; JD magna cum laude, U. Mich., 1994. Bar: Ill. 1994, DC, US Dist. Ct. No. Dist. Ill. 1995, US Dist Ct. So. Dist. NY

1998, US Ct. Appeals 2nd Cir., US Ct. Appeals 7th Cir., US Ct. Appeals 9th Cir., US Supreme Ct. Law clk. to Hon. Joel M. Flaum US Ct. Appeals 7th Cir.; with Jenner & Block, Chgo.; asst. US atty. So. Dist. NY; assoc. investigative counsel Webster Commn., 2001; joined pub. integrity sect. US Dept. Justice, 2002; ptnr. Sonnenschein Nath & Rosenthal LLP, Washington, 2004—. Adj. prof. law Georgetown U., Am. U., George Washington U., The Cath. U. of Am. Mem.: ABA (nat. co-chair white collar crime subcom. pub. corruption and extortion). Office: Sonnenschein Nath & Rosenthal Ste 600, E Tower 1301 K St NW Washington DC 20005 Office Phone: 202-408-5208. Office Fax: 202-408-6399. Business E-Mail: jberman@sonnenschein.com.

BERMAN, JOSHUA MORDECAI, lawyer, manufacturing executive; b. Rochester, N.Y., Aug. 4, 1938; s. Jeremiah Joseph and Rose (Rappaport) B.; m. Ruth Freed, Mar. 17, 1996; children: Marc Ethan, Eve. BBA summa cum laude, CCNY, 1958; JD cum laude, Harvard U., 1961. Bar: Mass. 1961, N.Y. 1984. With Goodwin, Procter & Hoar, Boston, 1961-80, ptnr., 1969-80; pres. Berman Engel P.C., 1980-85; counsel Kramer, Levin, Naftalis & Frankel, 1985—. Chmn. bd. CEO Tyco Internat. Ltd., 1970—73; adviser Fidelity Investments, 1971—, Rank Group Ltd., Auckland, New Zealand, 1996—, Med. Info. Tech., Inc., 1970—. Founder, pres. Boston Children's Sch., 1965-66. Home: Alexandra La Frasse 1660 Chateau d'Oex Switzerland

BERMAN, KEITH, solicitor, lawyer; b. Liverpool, Eng., Dec. 23, 1942; came to U.S., 1980; s. Joseph and Gerty Berman; children; Chloé Jo, Jade Kara, Kate Alexis. LLB with honors, U. Liverpool, 1963. Admitted as solicitor Supreme Ct. Eng. and Wales, 1966; bar: N.Y. 1980, U.S. Dist. Ct. (so. and ea. dists.) N.Y. 1982, U.S. Ct. Internat. Trade 1992, U.S. Ct. Appeals (fed. cir.) 1992. Founding ptnr. Bermans English Solicitors, Liverpool, Manchester, 1970—, N.Y.C., 1980—. Trustee Fifth Ave Synagogue, N.Y.C., 1986—. Mem. ABA, Law Soc. Eng. and Wales, Comml. Law League Am., Internat. Bar Assn. Office: Bermans 1775 Broadway #608 New York NY 10019-1903 E-mail: 3kb@bermans.net.

BERMAN, LAURA, sex therapist; BA in anthropology, U. Vt., 1990; MA in health edn., NYU Sch. Edn., 1992; MSW, NYU, 1994, PhD in philosophy, 1997. Fellow in human sexual therapy NYU Med. Ctr., 1997; former co-dir. (with sister Jennifer) Women's Sexual Health Clinic, Boston U. Med. Ctr.; co-dir. (with sister Jennifer) Network Excellence Women's Sexual Health; clinical asst. prof. ob-gyn. and psychiatry Feinberg Sch. Medicine Northwestern U.; dir. Berman Ctr., Chgo., 2004—; co-host (with sister Jennifer) Berman & Berman: For Women Only, Discovery Health Channel, 2004—. Co-author (with sister Jennifer): For Women Only: A Revolutionary Guide to Overcoming Sexual Dysfunction and Reclaiming Your Sex Life, 2001, Secrets of the Sexually Satisfied Woman, 2005. Found. bd. mem. Soc. Sci. Study Sexuality (SSSS). Recipient Rising Star Yr., Nat. Assn. Women Bus. Owners, LA, 2002, Women Action award, Israel Cancer Rsch. Fund, 2002. Mem.: Am. Assn. Sex Educators, Counselors, and Therapists, Internat. Soc. Study Women's Sexual Health, Am. Assn. Social Workers. Office: Berman Ctr LLC 211 E Ontario Ste 800 Chicago IL 60611 Office Phone: 800-709-4709, 312-255-8088. Office Fax: 312-255-8007.*

BERMAN, LORI BETH, lawyer; b. N.Y.C., June 27, 1958; d. George Gilbert and Sara Ann (Abrams) B.; m. Jeffrey Ganeles, Nov. 26, 1983; children: Caryn Elissa, Steven Aaron. BA magna cum laude, Tufts U., 1980; JD, George Washington U., 1983; LLM, U. Miami, 2002. Assoc. Margolies, Edelstein & Scherlis, Phila., 1983-84, White and Williams, Phila., 1984-87, Brownstein Zeidman & Schomer, Washington, 1987-89; v.p. legal & compliance Pointe Savs. Bank, Boca Raton, Fla., 1990-95; dist. rep. Congressman Robert Wexler, Boca Raton, 1997-99; assoc. Belson & Lewis, Boca Raton, Fla., 2002—. Mem., Jour. Internat. Law and Econs. Mem. exec. coun. United Jewish Appeal Fedn., Washington, 1987-89, Boca Raton, 1990—, Leadership Boca, 1992. Mem. ABA, D.C. Bar Assn., Fla. Bar Assn., Boca Raton C. of C. Democrat. Jewish. Office Phone: 561-750-7600.

BERMAN, MARSHALL FOX, lawyer; b. Portsmouth, Va., Aug. 27, 1939; s. Israel and Etta (Fox) B.; m. Barbara Pressner, Aug. 29, 1965 (dec. Feb. 1993); m. Karen Orloff Kaplan, Nov. 18, 1996; children: Richard Joseph, Deborah Lynn. BA, U. Va., 1961, postgrad. in rhetoric, 1961-62; JD, Am. U., 1967; LLM in Labor Law with highest honors, George Washington U., 1970. Bar: Va. 1967, D.C. 1971, U.S. Supreme Ct. 1971. Tchr. reading pub. schs., Washington, 1965-66; staff D.C. Minimum Wage and Indsl. Safety Bd., 1966-67; atty. NLRB, Washington, 1968-71; assoc. Gall, Lane & Powell, Washington, 1971-75; ptnr. Dow, Lohnes & Albertson, Washington, 1975-91, Epstein, Becker and Green, Washington, 1992-98, Hewes, Gelband, Lambert and Dann, Washington, 1999—2000, Ruben & Aronson, Washington, 2000—; spl. master for labor and employment cases U.S. Dist. Ct. D.C., 2001—. Co-author: Aviation Drug Testing Handbook, 1989, Aviation Drug Testing Operating Manual, 1990. Mem. ABA, Fed. Bar Assn., D.C. Bar Assn., Va. Bar Assn. Office: 4800 Montgomery Lane Ste 150 Bethesda MD 20814 Home: 1555 Colonial Ter Apt 100 Arlington VA 22209-1426 Office Phone: 202-337-4808. Personal E-mail: lawfirmmberman@yahoo.com.

BERMAN, MICHAEL ALLEN, hospital administrator, pediatric cardiologist; b. Bklyn., Sept. 11, 1942; MD, SUNY, Syracuse, 1967; postgrad in pediatrics, Johns Hopkins Sch. Medicine. Pediatrics resident Johns Hopkins U. Sch. Medicine, 1967—68; fellowship in pediatric cardiology Yale U., 1970—76; pediatric cardiologist Nat. Inst. of Health; chief of clinical pediatric cardiology and dir., cardiac catheterization lab. Yale U.; joined U. Maryland, 1976; dir. pediatric cardiology, dept. pediatrics U. Maryland Sch. Medicine, 1976—84, chmn. dept. pediatrics, 1984—97; sr. v.p., chief med. officer NY Presbyterian Hosp., 1997—99, exec. v.p., dir., 1999—. Achievements include development of Berman Angiographic Catheter device, used to diagnose cardiac problems in pediatric patients. Office: NY Presbyterian Hosp Herbert Irving Pavilion 161 Fort Wash Ave 14th Fl New York NY 10032

BERMAN, MICHAEL BARRY, lawyer; b. NYC, Apr. 10, 1942; s. Mark S. and Roslyn (Roberts) B.; m. Rochelle Holland, June 7, 1969 (dec. Jan. 2002); 1 child, Michele. BA, Iowa Wesleyan U., 1964; MAT, Trenton State Coll., 1973; MA in Indsl. Rels., Rutgers U., 1977; JD, Cardozo Sch. Law, N.Y.C., 1984. Bar: N.J. 1985, D.C. 1985, U.S. Ct. Appeals (3d cir.) 1985, U.S. Ct. Appeals Vets. Claims 1999, U.S. Supreme Ct. 1989. Assoc. Jerome A. Gertner, Lakewood, N.J., 1984-86; staff atty. Ocean-Monmouth Legal Svcs., Toms River, N.J., 1986-87; assoc. Cohen, Meshulam & Cohen, Verona, N.J., 1987-89, Krieger & Ferrara, Jersey City, 1989; pvt. practice Lakewood, N.J., 1989-90; ptnr. Collins & Berman, Toms River, NJ, 1990—2001; sole practitioner Toms River, 2001—. Asst. to chmn. N.J. Pub. Employment Rels. Com., Trenton, 1973-81; gen. counsel Nat. Mus. Am. Jewish Mil. History, 1992-98, 2000--. V.p. Lakewood Cmty. Sch. Bd., 1984-87; active Lakewood Bd. Edn., 1984-87, 89, Rep. Cen. Com., Lakewood, 1987-88; pres. Lakewood Rep. Club, 1992-93; adv. bd. Ocean County Cath. Charities; pres. Congregation Ahavat Shalom, 1993-95. With U.S. Army, 1968-70. Mem. Ocean County Bar Assn., N.J. Bar Assn. (subcom. alimony support 1987), Jewish War Vets (state comdr. N.J. chpt. 1985-86, nat. com. 1985-89, nat. judge advocate 1992-98, nat. quartermaster 1996-98, nat. comdr. 1998-99), Vietnam Vets Am. (v.p. N.J. chpt. 1990-92, gen. counsel 2000--), Masons. Office: PO Box 1447 Lakewood NJ 08701 Office Phone: 732-901-7035.

BERMAN, MIRIAM NAOMI, librarian; b. Phila., May 27, 1929; d. Max Isaac and Sonia Leona (Brown) Mosevitzky; m. Aaron Arthur Berman, July 4, 1955; children: David Hirsh, Raphael Judah, Michael Jonah. BA, CUNY, 1950, MA, 1952; MLS, Pratt Inst., 1975. Lic. profl. librarian, N.Y.; lic. elem and secondary tchr., N.Y. Tchr. Crown Heights Yeshiva, Bklyn., 1950-52, Pub. Sch. 26/N.Y.C. Bd. Edn., Bklyn., 1952-64; exec. Aaron Berman Gallery, N.Y.C., 1976-77; librarian Bklyn. Pub. Library, 1977-79, Aviation High Sch., L.I., N.Y., 1979-89, Sheepshead Bay High Sch., Bklyn., 1989-96; ret., 1996. Juror Art Auction Com., N.Y.C., 1972-77. Mem. N.Y.C. Library Assn. (treas. 1985-87). Avocations: music, art, theater, ballet.

BERMAN, MONA S., actress, playwright, theater director, theater producer; b. Jersey City, 1925; d. Edward and Mary (Auster) Solomon; m. Caroll Z. Berman (dec.); children: Marcie Berman Ries, Laura Jane. BA, Beaver Coll., 1945; postgrad., Columbia U.; MFA, Boston U., 1957. Tchr. English, drama Jersey City HSs; actress indsl., stage, TV, Valley Players Holyoke, Mass.; actress Millbrook Playhouse, Mill Hall, Pa., 1991; owner, dir. Theater Sch. and Producing Co., Maplewood, NJ. Chmn. drama edn. YM-MWHA Met. N.J. Cons., Clark Ctr. Performing Arts, N.Y.C., 1965—66; instr. South Orange, Maplewood Adult Sch., 1967; artistic dir. Children's Theatre Co. Inc., Maplewood, 1968—70; cons. Whole Theater Co., City Theatre, Miami, Fla., 2000; dir. pub. rels. Co. 3 by 2. Author: (plays) Hello Joe, That Ring in the Center, The Big Show, Interim, Who Can Belong?, Sudden Changes, Without Malice, Interim 2; prodr., dir.: (plays) A Night of Stars; guest theater reviewer: El Paso Herald Post, 1980—82; mem. artistic steering com. Women's Theatre Project. Active Boston United Fund, 1955—59, chmn. Boston residential area, 1957; bd. dirs. Greater Boston Girl Scouts Am., 1956—58; active S. Fla. Theater League, City Theatre, Miami, Fla.; bd. dirs. Tufts Med. Faculty Wives, 1956—58. Mem.: Creative Alliance, Profl. Actors Assn. Fla., Actors Equity Assn., Dramatist Guild. Address: 8925 Collins Ave Miami FL 33154-3530 Personal E-mail: emessbee1@bellsouth.net.

BERMAN, NEIL SHELDON, retired chemical engineering professor; b. Milw., Sept. 21, 1933; s. Henry and Ella B.; m. Sarah Ayres, June 3, 1962; children: Jenny, Daniel. BS, U. Wis., 1955; MS, MA, U. Tex., 1961, PhD, 1962. Engr. Std. Oil Co. Calif., L.A., 1955-62; rsch. engr. E.I. DuPont Co., Wilmington, Del., 1962-64; from asst. prof. to prof. chem. engring. Ariz. State U., 1964-2000, prof. emeritus, 2000—, Grad. Coll. Disting. Rsch. prof., 1984-85; ret., 2000. Cons. air pollution, fluid dynamics; mem. Phoenix Air Quality Maintenance Area Task Force, 1976-77. Contbr. articles on fluid dynamics of polymer solutions, air pollution, thermodynamics and chem. engring. edn. to profl. jours. Served to capt. M.S.C. USAR, 1956-58. Recipient numerous grants for rsch. in fluid dynamics and air pollution. Fellow Am. Inst. Chem. Engrs. (chmn. Ariz. sect. 1978-79), AAAS, Ariz.-Nev. Acad. Sci. (corr. sec. 1981-88, pres.-elect 1988-89, pres. 1989-90); mem. ASME, Am. Chem. Soc., Am. Phys. Soc., Ariz. Coun. Engring. and Sci. Assns. (chmn. 1980-81), Soc. Rheology, Am. Soc. Engring. Edn., Am. Acad. Mechanics, Nat. Assn. State Acads. Sci. (mem.-at-large bd. dirs.), Sigma Xi, Tau Beta Pi, Phi Kappa Phi. Home: 418 E Geneva Dr Tempe AZ 85282-3731 Office: Ariz State U Dept Chem Engring Tempe AZ 85287-6006 Business E-Mail: neil.berman@asu.edu.

BERMAN, PATRICIA KARATSIS, arts specialist; b. San Francisco, Oct. 2, 1953; d. George Emanuel and Hermoine Linda (Foster) Karatsis; m. William Issachar Berman, May 15, 1979; children: Ian, Melissa, Benjamin. BS, Duke U., 1975; MA, NYU, 1977. Dir. Vorpal Gallery, N.Y.C., 1976-83; visual arts coord. East End Arts Coun., Riverhead, N.Y., 1983-89, program dir., 1989-94, exec. dir., 1994-97; dir. mem. svcs. Alliance on N.Y. State Orgns., 1997—, assoc. dir., 1999—. Cons. N. State Coun. on Arts, NYC, 1985—, Suffolk Assn. Jewish Schs., Huntington, NY, 1985; adj. lectr. dept. anthropology Bklyn. Coll., 1976-77, Drew U., 1977; adj. tech. asst. dept. instrn. Suffolk County CC, 1992-93; bd. dirs. Riverhead Bus. Improvement Dist., chair; panelist NJ State Coun. on Arts, 2005 Contbr. articles to East End Arts News; host cable arts show, 1986-87. Adminstr. L.I. Baroque Ensemble, 1996—; panelist N.J. State Coun. on the Arts, 2005—; Trustee Commack (N.Y.) Jewish Ctr., 1984—86. Mem. Duke U. Alumni (AAAC chair Suffolk County 1998-2004). Home: 22 Daisy Ln Commack NY 11725-4106 Office: Alliance NY State Arts Org PO Box 96 Mattituck NY 11952-0096 E-mail: pkbarts@aol.com.

BERMAN, PAUL JUSTIN, lawyer; b. Chgo., Jan. 7, 1951; s. Barry L. and Judith M. (Mendelsohn) B.; m. Susan Elizabeth Schonberger, June 25, 1972; children: David Benjamin, Michael Jonathan. BA, Harvard U., 1972, JD, 1975. Bar: D.C., U.S. Ct. Appeals (3rd, federal and D.C. cirs.), U.S. Supreme Ct.; reg. U.S. Patent Atty. Assoc. Covington & Burling, Washington, 1975-83, ptnr., 1983—, chmn., Intellectual Property Practice Group. Dir. Harvard Ctr. for Info. Policy Rsch., Cambridge, Mass., 1976—; intellectual property com. mem., MIT. Co-author: High and Low Politics: Information Resources for the 1980's, 1977. V.p. Temple Emanuel, Kensington, Md., 1987—. Mem. Am. Intellectual Property Law Assn. Office: Covington & Burling PO Box 7566 1201 Pennsylvania Ave NW Washington DC 20004-2401 Office Phone: 202-662-5468. Office Fax: 202-778-5468. Business E-Mail: pberman@cov.com.

BERMAN, RICHARD ANGEL, health facility administrator; b. Cin., Jan. 23, 1945; s. Isidore Alexander and Cecilia (Angel) B.; m. Jean Berman; 1 child, Joshua BBA with distinction, U. Mich., 1966, MBA with distinction, MHA, U. Mich., 1968. Spl. asst., asst. sec. health, dir. health policy Econ. Stblzn. Program, HEW, Washington, 1972-74; sr. program cons. Robert Wood Johnson Found., Princeton, N.J., 1974-77; asst. dean, assoc. hosp. dir. N.Y. Hosp.-Cornell Med. Ctr., N.Y.C., 1974-77; dir. N.Y. State Office Health Sys. Mgmt., Albany, 1977-80; commr. N.Y. State Divsn. Housing and Cmty. Renewal, 1981-83; exec. v.p. NYU Med. Ctr., N.Y.C., 1983-86; prof. health care mgmt. NYU Sch. Medicine, 1983-86; candidate for U.S. Congress 1986, 1986; spl. cons. McKinsey and Co., N.Y.C., 1987-90; v.p. Korn/Ferry Internat., N.Y.C., 1990-91; pres. N.Am. Howe-Lewis Internat., N.Y.C., 1991-92, pres., CEO, 1992-94; pres. Manhattanville Coll., Purchase, N.Y., 1995—. Cons. in field; bd. dirs. Health Ins. Plan Greater N.Y., NCAA-Divsn. III Pres.'s Coun., 2002—. Contbr. articles to profl. jours. Chmn. N.Y. State Bldg. Code Coun., 1981-83; mem. N.Y. State Housing Fin. Agy., 1981-83, N.Y. Statewide Health Coord. Coun.; adv. bd. Ctr. Hosp. Fin. and Mgmt.; bd. dirs. N.Y.C. Pub. Devel. Corp., 1985-90; mem. Prospective Payment Assessment Commn., 1989-95; exec. com. N.Y. March of Dimes Bd., 1980-95; mem. Mayor's Mgmt. Adv. Task Force, 1991-93; nat. adv. coun. Nat. Inst. for Nursing Rsch., NIH, 1991-94; trustee SUNY, 1993-95; bd. dirs. Inst. for Student Achievement, Manhasset, N.Y., 199-2001, Today's Students Tomorrow's Tchrs., Yorktown Heights, N.Y., 1998—, Westchester Med. Ctr., Valhalla, N.Y. Recipient Horace M. Kallen Disting. Cmty. Svc. award Am. Jewish Congress, 1981, Brotherhood award NCCJ, 1985, Disting. Achievement award B'nai B'rith, 1997, award of honor Westchester Holocaust Edn. Ctr., 2002. Fellow Am. Coll. Health Care Execs., N.Y. Acad. Medicine (assoc.); mem. APHA, Am. Hosp. Assn., Pub. Health Assn. N.Y., Nat. Acad. Sci. Inst. Medicine. Office Phone: 914-323-5230. Business E-Mail: bermanr@mville.edu.

BERMAN, RICHARD BRUCE, lawyer; b. Freeport, N.Y., Sept. 26, 1951; s. Nathan and Helen Dorothy (Raiden) B.; m. Laurie Michael, Nov. 2, 1985. BA in Speech Communication, Am. U., 1973; JD, U. Miami, 1976. Bar: Fla. 1976, U.S. Dist. Ct. (so. dist.) Fla. 1976, D.C. 1978. Atty. Travelers Ins. Co., Ft. Lauderdale, Fla., 1977-84; assoc. Frank & Flaster P.A., Sunrise, Fla., 1984-88, DeCasare & Salerno, Ft. Lauderdale, Fla., 1988-89; pvt. practice, 1989—. Bd. dirs. Frosch Health Care Cons., Inc., Lauderhill, Employers for Ins. Reform, 2002-04—; mem. worker's compensation rules com. Fla. Bar, 1991-94; bd. dirs. Fla. Workers Advs., 1991—, chmn. media rels. com., 2000—04. Mem. panel health care Dem. Legis. Task Force, Ft. Lauderdale, 1985-87; mem. adv. bd. Reflex Sympathetic Dystrophy Syndrome Assn. Fla., 1992—94; mem. B'nai Brith; bd. dirs. Mommy & Me Enterprises, 1997-2002. Mem. ABA, ATLA, D.C. Bar, Fla. Bar Assn., Acad. Fla. Trial Lawyers, Broward County Trial Lawyers Assn. Avocations: writing and performing music, theater, writing children's music. Office Phone: 954-741-7066. E-mail: rbberman@gate.net, rbberman@richardbberman.com.

BERMAN, RICHARD KEITH, television producer, film producer; b. N.Y.C., Dec. 25, 1945; BA in Speech, U. Wis., Madison, 1967. Dir. current programming Paramount, 1984—87. Sr. prodr. Big Blue Marble, 1977-82 (Emmy award); ind. prodr. HBO, PBS, 1982-84; prodr., writer (story): Star Trek: Generations, 1994, Star Trek: First Contact, 1996, Star Trek: IMAX, 1998, Star Trek: Insurrection, 1998; prodr., writer (story), (TV): Star Trek: Deep Space Nine-Emissary/Emissary, 1993, Star Trek: Voyager-Caretaker, 1995; supervising prodr.: Star Trek: The Next Generation-Encounter at Farpoint, 1987, -All Good Things, 1994, (series) Star Trek: The Next Generation, 1987-94, exec. prodr., 1991-94 (also co-creator with Gene Roddenberry); creator (TV series) Star Trek: Deep Space Nine/DS9, 1993-99; co-creator (TV series) Star Trek: Voyager, 1995-2001; creative cons. Star Trek: The Experience, 1998. Office: c/o Paramount Television Grp Bun Cooper 232 5555 Melrose Ave Los Angeles CA 90038-3112

BERMAN, RICHARD MILES, judge; b. N.Y.C., Sept. 11, 1943; s. Samuel and Sophie Berman; m. Emily Krasna, May 29, 1979 (div. Nov. 1983). BS, Cornell U., 1964; JD, NYU, 1967; diploma in comparative law, U. Stockholm, 1968, diploma in internat. law, 1970; MSW, Fordham U., 1996. Bar: N.Y. 1971. Assoc. Davis, Polk & Wardwell, N.Y.C., 1970-74; exec. asst. Senator Jacob K. Javits, N.Y.C., 1974-78; gen. counsel, exec. v.p., dir. Warner Cable Comm. Inc., N.Y.C., 1978-86; gen. counsel, sec. MTV Networks, Inc., N.Y.C., 1983-86; ptnr. LeBoeuf, Lamb, Greene & MacRae, N.Y.C., 1986-95; mng. ptnr. L.A., 1989-91; judge Family Ct. State of N.Y., 1995-98, U.S. Dist. Ct. (so. dist.) N.Y., 1998—. Exec. dir. N.Y. State Alliance Save Energy, Inc., N.Y.C., 1977—78; mem. N.Y.C. Child Abuse Task Force, 1995, N.Y. State Permanent Commn. Justice Children, 1996—2000; chmn. collegiality com. U.S. Dist. Ct. (so. dist.) N.Y., 2000—. Judge Valente, Clarence Palitz and Jacob Levy Found. scholar, NYU Sch. Law, 1964—67, Thord-Gray fellow, Am.-Scandinavian Found., 1967—68, Donald Frank Sussman Meml. scholar, Cornell U. Mem.: U.S. Jr. Davis Cup Squad (met. N.Y.C.). Avocations: tennis, horseback riding, house restoration. Office: US Dist Ct 40 Centre St New York NY 10007-1502

BERMAN, ROBERT L., human resources specialist; BS, U. Minn.; M in Indsl. and Labor Rels., Cornell U. Dir. human resources consumer imaging bus., dir. human resources Colo. divisn., dir. and divisional v.p. human resources global ops. Eastman Kodak Co., 1983—2002, v.p., dir. human resources, 2002—. Office: Eastman Kodak Co 343 State St Rochester NY 14650 Office Phone: 585-724-4000. Office Fax: 585-724-1089.*

BERMAN, ROBERT S., marketing consultant; b. N.Y.C., Apr. 13, 1932; s. Sydney and Beatrice (Lipman) B.; m. Eleanor Rae Greenwald, June 16, 1956 (div. 1973); children: Thomas, Eric, Terry; m. Sherry Rona Frawley, May 29, 1975 (div. 1994); m. Sharon Louise Erbe, Oct. 5, 1996. BA, Cornell U., 1953, MA, 1954; advanced mgmt. certificate, Harvard U., 1964. Vice pres. Marschalk, Inc., N.Y.C., 1962-64; exec. v.p. DeGarmo, Inc., N.Y.C., 1964-70, 1970-80; exec. v.p., gen. mgr. D'Arcy MacManus & Masius, N.Y.C., 1980-83; chmn. exec. com. Margeotes Fertitta & Weiss, 1984-88; ptnr. Ber/Cam Ptnrs., 1987-89; pres. Berman Mktg. Network, Naples, 1983—. Instr. dept. communications Parsons Sch., 1968-70, Pratt Inst., 1974-76; columnist Madison Ave. Mag., N.Y.C., 1968-72. Dir. Collier County Spl. Olympics Internat. Served to 1st lt. U.S. Army, 1954-56. Named Advt. Accountman of the Yr. N.Y. Advt. Council, 1969 Mem. Unity of Naples (bd. dirs.), The Conservancy, Civil War Roundtable N.Y., Komos Aiden Theatrical Assn., Quill and Dagger Club, Cornell Club, The Vineyards Golf Club, Naples Bath and Tennis Club. Office: 4080 Kensington High St Naples FL 34105-5666

BERMAN, RONALD CHARLES, lawyer, accountant; b. Chgo., July 7, 1949; s. Joseph and Helen Berman; m. Kristine K. Topp, May 1, 1993; children: Daniel J. Lohr, Joseph James. BBS with highest honors, U. Ill., 1971, JD with honors, 1974. Bar: Ill. 1974, Wis. 1976; CPA, Wis. Mem. tax staff Grant Thornton, Chgo., 1974-76, tax supr. Madison, Wis., 1976-78, tax mgr., 1978-81, ptnr. tax dept., 1991-94; assoc. Neider & Boucher, Madison, 1995, shareholder, 1996—. Lectr. cont. legal edn. U. Wis., 1999—. Mem. editl. adv. bd. Physician's Tax Advisor Newsletter, 1986-89, Physician's Tax and Investment Advisor, 1989-93. Scoutmaster Boy Scouts Am., Middleton, Wis., 1978—; fin. chmn. Mohawk Dist. Four Lakes Coun., Madison, 1981—85, chmn. endowment fund, 1984—92, v.p. fin., 1992—94, mem. exec. bd., 1982—, treas., 1994—96, nat. rep., 1996—2004; cubmaster Boy Scouts Am., Middleton, 2001—02, asst. cubmaster, 2002—; v.p. Scouts on Stamps Soc. Internat., 1996—2002, bd. dirs., 1986—96, Madison Pension Coun., 1986—98, pres., 1988—89. Recipient Silver Beaver award Boy Scouts Am., 1981, Middleton Good Neighbor award Middleton Good Neighbor Festival, 2000. Mem.: AICPA, ABA, Web Network Profls., Nat. Coun. Planned Giving, Wis. Planned Giving Coun., Madison Estate Coun., Ill. Bar Assn., State Bar. Wis., Wis. Inst. CPAs, Optimists, Order of Coif, Phi Alpha Delta, Phi Kappa Phi, Alpha Pi Omega. Avocations: photogrphy, stamp collecting/philately, camping. Home: 3906 Rolling Hill Dr Middleton WI 53562-1224 Office Phone: 608-661-4500. Business E-Mail: rberman@neiderboucher.com.

BERMAN, SANFORD SOLOMON, motion picture sound designer, composer, arranger, artist; b. Long Branch, N.J., Nov. 14, 1951; s. Jerome Sidney and Marion (Solomon) B. BFA, Phila. Coll. Art, 1974. Freelance sound designer, record prodr./arranger, musician/composer. Vis. prof. UCLA. Sound designer, supr. (features) Bedazzled, Scary Movie, Double Jeopardy, Analyze This, Brokedown Palace, Neil Somon's Odd Couple 2, Hard Rain, Hush, Multiplicity, Jade, Virtuosity, Wings of Courage, Bad Girls, Tombstone, Striking Distance Aladdin (Golden Reel winner, FX Editl., Oxcar nomination), Love Field, Unlawful Entry, J.F.K. (FX Editl., Brit. Acad. award, Coldeen Reel nominee), Hot Shots!, Back to the Future (The Ride), Revenge (Golden Reel nominee), Immediate Family, Oliver & Company (Golden Reel winner), The Princess Bride (Golden Reel nominee), The Seventh Sign (Golden Reel nominee), da, Big Bad John, Going Under Cover, Mac & Me, Weeds, Jaws III, Cloak & Dagger, The Stone Boy, Wolfen, Strange Invaders, That Championship Season, The Sword & The Sorcerer, History of the World Part I, Miss Lonelyhearts, Ten to Midnight, The House on Sorority Row, Evilspeak, Q, Summerspell, Suburbia, Roar, Sweet Sixteen, The Fatal Game, Radioactive Dreams, The Glory of Kahn, (short subjects) A Hard Rain, Ballet Robotique (Oscar nomination), The Wizard of Change, The Quest, A Trip to Tomorrow, Bird & The Robot, The Water Engine, Lean Machine, Wind Tunnel, Environmental Effects, New Magic, The Collector, Niagara, Lets Go!, Tour of the Universe, Runaway Train, Zargon, Deep Water Rescue, Rollercoaster, Monte Carlo Race, Alpine Highway, Toyota, Chevrolet, Jet Helicopter, Call From Space; keyboardist for James Brown "Static", 1996; creator comic effects Eat It (Grammy nomination), Like a Surgeon (Grammy nomination), New Duck (Grammy nomination); prodr., arranger, keyboardist Secret Smiles; composer (feature film scores) Screamers, Cataclysm, (comm ls.) Toyota, 1986, Celica, 1986; appeared with Bruce Springsteen, Steel, Hall & Oates, Chuck Berry, Dwayne Eddy, Jr. Walker & The All-Stars, James Brown, others. Mem. ACLU, So. Calif., 1985—, People for the Am. Way, So. Calif., 1985—, Am. Jewish Congress, 1982—. Recipient Brit. Acad. award Brit. Acad. of Film and TV Arts, Gt. Britain, 1992. Mem. Motion Picture Sound Editors (pres. 1992—, Golden Reel award 1988, 92), Acad. of Motion Picture Arts and Scis., Nat. Acad. Recording Arts and Scis., Am. Soc. Music Arrangers and Composers, Motion Picture Editors Guild. Democrat. Avocations: drawing, antique and classic automobiles, books.

BERMAN, SHARI SPRINGER, film director, scriptwriter; b. N.Y., July 1964; m. Robert Pulcini. BFA in Film, Columbia U., 1995. Author: (screenplays) Am. Splendor, 2003 (Grand Jury prize Sundance Film Festival, 2003, Critics award Cannes Film Festival, 2003, Open Palm award IFP, 2003, The New Dir.'s award Edinburgh (Scotland) Internat. Film Festival, 2003, named Best Film, Montreal's (Can.) Comedia Festival, 2003, The Critics award Deauville Film Festival, 2003); co-dir.: (films) Off The Menu: The Last Days of Chasen's, 1997 (named one of Ten Best Movies of 1998, USA Today and CNN, 1998, Best Documentary Grand Jury award Hamptons Internat. Film Festival, Spl. Jury award Locarno Internat. Film Festival, Spl. Jury award Newport Film Festival), The Young and the Dead, 2000, Hello, He Lied, 2002.

BERMAN, SHAWN L., finance educator; b. LA, July 3, 1967; s. Sorrell and Josephine Ann Berman. PhD, U. Wash., 1998. Asst. prof. Boston U., 1998—2001, Santa Clara (Calif.) U., 2001—. Contbr. chapters to books, articles to profl. jours. Vol. ACLU, Seattle, 1993—97; mem., del. to state conv. Dem. Party, Seattle, 1996—98. Recipient Beckwith award, Boston U. Graduating Class, 2000. Green Party. Home: 1206 Utah St San Francisco CA 94110 Business E-Mail: sberman@scu.edu.

BERMAN, STANLEY ZISSMAN, allergist, immunologist, educator, internist, department chairman; b. New Orleans, June 17, 1941; s. Herman Zissman and Golda (Kleinfeldt) Feir; adopted s. Leo Berman; m. Leslie Dale Miller, July 7, 1968; children: Jason Lee, Laura Elizabeth. Student, Tulane U., 1959-62; BSM, Northwestern U., Evanston, Ill., 1963; MD, Northwestern U., Chgo., 1966. Diplomate Am. Bd. Internal Medicine, Am. Bd. Allergy and Immunology. Intern Chgo. Wesley Meml. Hosp., 1966-67; med. resident Mayo Grad. Sch. Medicine, Rochester, Minn., 1969-71; fellow in allergy and immunology Scripps Clinic and Rsch. Found., La Jolla, Calif., 1971-73; chmn. allergy Lovelace Clinic now Lovelace Health Sys., Albuquerque, 1973—99, ret., 1999; clin. asst., assoc. prof. dept. medicine U. N.Mex. Sch. Medicine, Albuquerque, 1973—98, clin. prof. dept. medicine, 1998—2000; prof. U. St. Francis, Albuquerque, 2003—. Spkr. in field. Co-author, reviewer, contbr. articles to profl. jours. Lt. comdr. M.C., USNR, 1967-73, U.S. Submarine Svc., USS Nathanael Greene, 1967-69. Fellow ACP, Am. Coll. Chest Physicians, Am. Acad. Allergy, Asthma and Immunology (emeritus); mem. Am. Thoracic Soc. (pres. N.Mex. chpt. 1977-78), N.Mex. Lung Assn. (bd. dirs. 1977-78). Avocations: jogging, travel, history. Office: 7416 Vista Del Arroyo Ave NE Albuquerque NM 87109-2941

BERMAN, STEPHEN ALAN, neurologist; b. Oak Park, Ill., Mar. 15, 1948; s. Edward and Esther Ruby Berman; m. Sherry Bursztajn. BS, U. Ill., Champaign-Urbana, 1970. Diplomate Am. Bd. Psychiatry and Neurology, Am. Bd. Clinical Neurophysiology . Intern Greater Balt. Med. Ctr., 1976—77; resident in neurology Baylor Coll. Medicine, Houston, 1977—80, fellow in genetics and muscle disease, 1980—83; asst. prof. neurology U. Chgo., 1983—89, U. Tex. and MD Anderson Cancer Ctr., Houston, 1989—90; instr. neurology Harvard Med. Sch., Boston, 1990—92, asst. prof., 1992—96; prof. neurology La. State U., Shreveport, 1996—2000; prof. medicine neurology Dartmouth Med. Coll., Hanover, NH, 2000—; chief neurology White River Junction Vets. Med. Ctr., White River Junction, Vt., 2000—. Med. dir. lab. clinical neurophysiology La. State U., Shreveport, 1997—2000. Contbr. articles to profl. jours.; mem. editl. bd. E-Medicine, 1999. Med. adv. com. Multiple Sclerosis Soc., Shreveport, La., 1997—2000. Recipient Rsch. award, Clarence A. Hawkinson Meml. Fund, 1983—84, Brain Rsch. Found., 1984—87, Tchr. Investigator Devel. award, NIH, 1985—89, Physician Scientist award, Nat. Inst. Aging, 1992—96; fellow, Muscular Dystrophy Assn., 1981—83; grantee, Alzheimer Found., 1984—85, Louis Bloch Fund grant, 1984—87. Mem.: Soc. for Neurorehabilitation (cert.), Am. Acad. Neurology (quality stds. subcom., therapeutics and tech. assessment subcom. 1998), Alpha Omega Alpha (v.p. Ill. chpt. 1973—74), Phi Beta Kappa. Jewish. Office: Dartmouth Med Sch 215 N Main St White River Junction VT 05009 Office Phone: 802-295-9363 5489. Business E-Mail: stephen.berman@dartmouth.edu.

BERMAN, STEPHEN G., toy manufacturing executive; b. 1965; V.p., mng. dir. TH-Q Internat., Inc., 1991-95; co-founder, exec. v.p., sec. JAKKS Pacific Inc., Malibu, Calif., 1995-96, pres., COO, sec., dir., 1996—. Office: JAKKS Pacific Inc Ste 250 22619 Pacific Coast Hwy Malibu CA 90265-5080 Fax: (310) 317-8527.

BERMAN, STEVE WILLIAM, lawyer, author; b. Chgo., Nov. 13, 1954; s. Mert E. and Lois Ann (Eliot) B.; m. Janet S. Friend, June 18, 1979 (dec.); children: Eliot Michael, Jacob Paul, Abby Hannah; m. Katherine Weisfield Berman. BS, U. Mich., 1976; JD, U. Chgo., 1980. Bar: Ill. 1980, Wash. 1982, U.S. Dist. Ct. Ill. 1980, U.S. Ct. Appeals (7th cir.) 1980, Wash. 1982, U.S. Dist. Ct. 1982, U.S. Ct. Appeals (3d and 9th cirs.), U.S. Supreme Ct. 1986. Assoc. Jenner & Block, Chgo., 1980-82, Shidler, McBroom & Gates, Seattle, 1982-85; resident ptnr. Bernstein, Litowitz, Berger & Grossman, Seattle, 1986-89; ptnr. Betts, Patterson & Mines, Seattle, 1989-92; mng. ptnr. Hagens Berman, LLP, Seattle, 1993—. Apptd. spl. asst. atty. gen. State of Wash., 1996-98, State of Ariz., 1996-97, State of Ill., 1996-98; adj. prof. law U. Puget Sound, Tacoma, 1983-84; asst. coach Syracuse U., 1976. Author: A Tarnished Hero, 1988; contbr. articles to profl. jours. Mem. com. Juvenile Conf., Seattle, 1984; apptd. spl. counsel Wash. State Bar, 1988-93. Mem. Nat. Assocs. Securities and Comml. Attys. (bd. dirs. 1991—), Trial Lawyers for Pub. Justice, Mercle Island Boys and Girls Club (bd. dirs.). Jewish. Avocations: running, rowing, hiking, skiing. Office: Hagens & Berman 1301 5th Ave Ste 2929 Seattle WA 98101-2603

BERMAN, STEVEN ERIC, audiologist; b. Newark, N.J., July 4, 1948; s. Milton and Maxine Berman; m. Shirley Ann Sviben, May 23, 1992; children: Stacy Beth, Daniel Max. BEd, U. Miami, 1972; MA, Kean Coll., 1975; PhD, Fla. state U., 1978. Dir. spl. edn. Colquitt County Sch. Sys., Moultrie, Ga., 1975—78; dir. Audiology Med. Coll. Pa., Phila., 1978—98; v.p. Eartech Inc., Cherry Hill, NJ, 2001—. Cons. Speech Pathology Salem Home Care, Salem, NJ, 1980—; dir. Speech and Hearing Ctr. So. Ocean County Hosp., Manahawkin, NJ, 1995—; pres. Coastal Audiology, Toms River, NJ, 2002—; cons. Ga. Basket and Crate, Thomasville, 1979—81, Voorhees Pediat. Hosp., Voorhees, NJ, 1998—. Author (internat. lectr.): Vibrotactile Stimulation, 1977. Assoc. M'Kor Shalom, Voorhees, 2002. Grantee, State Ga., 1978. Mem.: Pa. Speech Lang. Hearing Assn., N.J. Speech Lang. Hearing Assn., Am. Speech Lang. Hearing Assn. (cert. audiology and speech pathology). Avocations: golf, tennis, travel. Home: 22 Nolen Cir Voorhees NJ 08043 Office: EARTECH Barclay Pavilion Rt 70 Ste 13 Cherry Hill NJ 08034

BERMAN, WALTER S., treasurer; With Am. Express, 1965—96, CFO Travel Related Svcs.; CFO, Am. Express Fin. Advisors, N.Y.C.; treas. Am. Express, IBM, 1999—2000; sr. v.p. fin. Am. Express, N.Y.C., 2001—02, exec. v.p., corp. treas., 2002—. Office: Am Express Co World Fin Ctr 200 Vesey St New York NY 10285

BERMAN, WILLIAM H., retired publishing company executive; b. Stamford, Conn., 1936; Grad., U. of Pa., 1959. Exec. v.p. Houghton Mifflin Co., Boston, retired, 1993.

BERMANI, ERIC J., musician, conductor; s. Joseph C. and Doris P. Bermani. A in Hotel Mgmt., Bay State Coll., 1993; MusB in Organ, Boston Conservatory, 1998; postgrad., St. Joseph Coll. Cert. liturgical musician Archdiocese of Boston. Dir. music, organist Trinity Episcopal Ch., Woburn, Mass., 1994—97, St. Jean-Baptiste Roman Cath. Ch., Lynn, Mass., 1995—98, St. John the Evangelist Roman Cath. Ch., Winthrop, Mass., 1997—2000; dir. liturgy/music, organist St. Catherine of Siena Roman Cath. Ch., Norwood, Mass., 2000—. Dir.: CD Hodie Christus Natus Est, 2004. Mem.: Nat. Assn. Pastoral Musicians, Organ Hist. Soc., Am. Guild Organists (mem. exec. com. Boston chpt. 2000—03), Pi Kappa Lambda. Avocations: reading, walking, theater. Office: St Catherine of Siena Parish 549 Washington St Norwood MA 02062 Office Phone: 781-762-6080 ext. 26.

BERMANN, GEORGE ALAN, law educator; b. Fall River, Mass., Dec. 2, 1945; s. Sigmund Dressler and Mae (Gordon) B.; m. Sandra Lekas, Dec. 28, 1969; children: Sloan, Suzanne, Grant. BA, Yale U., 1967, JD, 1971; LLM, Columbia U., 1975. Bar: NY 1972, US Dist. Ct. (so. dist.) NY 1980, US Dist. Ct (ea. dist.) NY 1980; US Supreme Ct., 1992. Assoc. Davis Polk & Wardwell, NYC, 1970-73; asst. prof. law Columbia U., NYC, 1975-79, assoc. prof., 1979-81, prof., 1981-93, Charles Keller Beekman prof. law, 1993—2002, Jean Monnet prof. of European Union Law, 2001—, Walter Gellhorn prof. law, 2002—; exec. dir. Columbia Summer Program, Netherlands, 1979-82; internat. comml. arbitrator Am. Arbitration Assn., NYC, 1983-88, Internat. C. of C., Paris. Vis. prof. law U. Paris and U. Rouen, France, 1981-82, Tulane U. Law Sch., 1988-89; lectr. Internat. Faculty for Teaching Comparative Law, Strasbourg, France, 1975. Bd. dirs. Columbia Jour. of Transnational Law, 1989—; contbr. chpt. to book, articles to profl. jours.; editor: Am. Jour. Comparative Law, 1976—; editor-in-chief Columbia Jour. European Law. Marshall scholar Sussex, Eng., 1967-68; Jervey fellow Parker Sch. Fgn. and Comparative Law, NYC, 1973-75. Mem. ABA, Am. Fgn. Law Assn. (bd. dirs. 1983-88, v.p. 1988—), Deutsch-Amerikanische Juristen Vereingung, German Am. Law Assn. (bd. dirs. 1979-84), Societe de Legislation Comparee Paris, Acad. internationale du droit comparé, Internat. Law Assn., Phi Beta Kappa. Home: 57 Hemlock Cir Princeton NJ 08540-5405 Office: Columbia U Sch Law Jerome L Green Hall 435 W 116th St New York NY 10027-7297 E-mail: gbermann@law.columbia.edu.*

BERMANT, GORDON, psychologist, lawyer, consultant, writer; b. L.A., Oct. 10, 1936; s. Ira George and Josephine (Wilson) B.; m. Roberta Mae Woolever, June 1958 (div. July 1975); children: Laura Diane, Daniel Bennett, Jennifer Wilson; m. Geri Lorraine Lincoln, Aug. 20, 1983. BA, UCLA, 1957; PhD, Harvard U., 1961; JD, George Mason U., 1991. Bar: Va. 1991, U.S. Ct. Appeals (4th cir.) 1991. Assoc. prof. U. Calif., Davis, 1964-69; fellow Battelle Seattle Rsch. Ctr., Seattle, 1969-76; sr. rsch. psychologist Fed. Jud. Ctr., Washington, 1976-82, dir. innovations and sys. dept., 1982-86, sr. rsch. advisor, 1986-91, dir. planning and tech., 1992-97; cons. Burke, Va., 1997—. Bd. dirs. Budd Study Ctr., N.Y.C.; Justice Web Collaboratory, Chgo.; sec., bd. dirs. Internat. Jud. Acad., Washington; lectr. U. Penn., Phila., 1994—. Author: Biological Bases of Sexual Behavior, 1974; editor: Ethics of Social Intervention, 1977, Markets and Morals, 1977, Psychology and Law, 1976. Pres. elect San Francisco, 2000-01. Grantee NSF, 1965-68, NIH, 1968-69. Fellow APA, Am. Psychol. Soc.; mem. ABA, Am. Jud. Soc., Law and Soc. Assn., Am. Bankruptcy Inst. Avocations: hiking, skiing. Office: 5603 Tilia Ct Burke VA 22015 E-mail: gordon.bermant@verizon.net.

BERMAS, STEPHEN, lawyer; b. NYC, Apr. 27, 1925; BS, Cornell U., 1949, JD, 1950; LLM, NYU, 1957. Bar: N.Y. 1950. Assoc. Wagner, Quillinan, Wagner & Tennant, NYC, 1950-51; law sec. to chief justice U.S. Dist. Ct. (so. dist.) NY, NYC, 1951-55; assoc. Gordon, Brady, Caffrey & Keller, NYC, 1955-59; ptnr. Medine & Bermas, NYC, 1959-63, Feltman & Bermas, NYC, 1964-66; sr. atty. Columbia Gas System Corp., NYC, 1966-69; asst. gen. counsel Continental Group Inc., NYC, 1970-77, assoc. gen. counsel, 1978-82; v.p., gen. counsel Continental Can Co. Inc., Norwalk, Conn., 1982-86, exec. v.p., gen. counsel, 1987-91; v.p., gen. counsel Continental Plastic Containers, Inc., 1991—2001; gen. counsel Lockwood, Kessler and Bartlett, Inc., 1998—. Instr. law Queen's Coll, NYC, 1964-68; adminstrv. law judge Office Profl. Med. Conduct NY State Dept. Health, NYC, 1993—. Mem. ABA. Office: 1 Aerial Way Syosset NY 11791-5501 Office Phone: 516-938-0600.

BERMEL, JOHN J, insurance company executive, corporate financial executive; BSc in bus. adminstrn., Georgetown U.; MBA in fin., Wharton Sch. Contr. of ins. ops. United Healthcare; contr. MetraHealth; contr. healt bus. Aetna Inc., 1997—2000, chief regional fin. officer, 2000—01, v.p., CFO, health bus. ops., 2001—. Office: Aetna Inc 151 Farmington Ave Hartford CT 06156

BERMES, EDWARD WILLIAM, JR., biochemist, educator; s. Edward William and Magdelen Bermes; m. Patricia Anne Skokan, Oct. 19, 1957; children: Kathleen Lynn Onori, Edward William Bermes,III, Mark Lawrence, Alicia Marie Joebgen, Christopher John. BS, St. Mary's Coll., 1950—54; MS, Loyola U., 1954—56, PhD, 1957—59. Asst. prof. Loyola U. Med. Ctr., 1959—69; dir. of biochemistry St. Francis Hosp., Evanston, 1961—69; assoc. prof. Loyola U. Med. Ctr., 1969—74, prof., 1975—99, prof. emeritus, 1999—. Dir. of clin. chemistry Loyola U. Med. Ctr., 1969—97, dir. of clin. lab., 1981—97, acting chmn., pathology, 1982—86, assoc. chmn. pathology, 1986—96; chmn., editl. rev. group Doody's Health Sci. Book Rev., 1993—2000. Author: (exibition) Effect of Hemolysis on Serum Chemistry Values (Gold Medal: ASCP/CAP Meeting, 1978); contbr. chapters to books; mem. editl. bd. Clin. Chem., 1981—90, Clinical and Applied Hemostasis, 1994—2002, Annals of Clinical Laboratory Science, 1978—82, 1990—2000; author: of over 100 articles published in profl. jours. including the Annals of Clinical Laboratory Science, Blood Coagulation and Fibrinolysis, British Journal of Experimental Pathology, Clinical Chemistry, et. al. Recipient Natelson award, Chgo. Sect., Am. Assoc. for Clin. Chemistry, 1976, Diploma of Honor, Assn. of Clin. Scientists, 1980, Edn. award;Outstanding Efforts in Edn. and Tng., Am. Assn. for Clin. Chemistry, 1983, Presdl. Citation, 1998, Outstanding Contributions to Clin. Chemistry award, Am. Assn. Clin. Chemistry, 2005. Fellow: Nat. Acad. of Clin. Biochemistry; mem.: Commn. on Accreditation in Clin. Chemistry (bd. dirs. 1981—), Assn. of Clin. Scientists, Am. Assn. of Pathologists, Am. Chem. Soc., Commn. on Edn. in Clin. Chemistry (pres. 1989—96), Am. Assn. for Clin. Chemistry (sec. 1978—80, mem. fin. com, exec. com., bd. dir. 1978—80, chmn., commn. on edn. and science 1985—87, Outstanding Contbns. Clin. Chemistry award 2005), Sigma Xi. Home: 1907 Sunnyside Circle Northbrook IL 60062 Office: Loyola University Medical Center 2160 So First Ave Maywood IL 60153 Personal E-mail: ebermes@sbcglobal.net. E-mail: ebermes@lumc.edu.

BERMUDES, DAVID GORDON, research scientist, educator; b. Manchester, NH, Mar. 24, 1958; s. Ralph Donald and Nancy Gail (Whitmore) Bermudes; m. Nancy Lee Coote, June 21, 1997; children: Ari Benton, Alexandra Manebur. BA, Oberlin Coll., 1982; PhD, Boston U., 1987. Adminstr. planetary biology internship NASA, Boston, 1984—85; grad. student fellow NSF, Boston, 1985—87; postdoctoral assoc. Med. Coll. Wis., Milw., 1988—91, Yale U. Sch. of Medicine, New Haven, 1991—93, assoc. rsch. scientist, 1993—95, asst. prof. medicine adj., 1996—; sr. rsch. scientist Vion Pharmaceuticals, Inc., New Haven, 1995—97, assoc. dir. of biology, 1997—99, dir. of microbiology, 1999—. Cons. Millisecond Pasteurization, LLC, New York, 1999—2002; bd. dirs. Millisecond Technologies Corp., New York. Contbr. articles to profl. jours. Univ. fellow, Boston U., 1983—84, grad. fellow, NSF, 1985—87, postdoctoral fellow, NIH, 1989, NRS award, postdoctoral fellow, 1992—93. Mem.: AAAS (assoc.), Am. Assn. Cancer Rsch. (corr.), Am. Soc. Microbiology (corr.). Achievements include patents for vectors for the diagnosis and treatment of cancer; (with John Pawelek and Brooks Low) tumor targeted salmonella with reduced virulence; patents pending for compositions and methods for tumor-targeted delivery of effector molecules; project discovery leader and head of manufacturing for development of the first tumor-targeted salmonella administered to humans; first to tumor-targeted salmonella (with John Pawelek and Brooks Low), a novel therapeutic agent for treatment of solid tumors; patents for (with John Pawelek and Brooks Low) vectors for the diagnosis and treatment of cancer. Home: 524 N Main St Wallingford CT 06492 Office: Vion Pharmaceuticals Inc 4 Science Park New Haven CT 06511 Office Phone: 203-672-4528. E-mail: dbermudes@vionpharm.com.

BERMUDEZ, EUGENIA M. See DIGNAC, GENY

BERMUDEZ, JORGE ALBERTO, bank executive; b. Gibara, Oriente, Cuba, Apr. 29, 1951; came to U.S., 1961; s. Diomedes R. and Melba (Santos) B.; m. Denise M. Pressley, Nov. 8, 1974; children: Jorge II, Andres, Elena, Antonio. BS, Tex. A&M U., 1973, MA, 1975. Teaching asst. Tex. A&M U., College Station, 1973-75; intern Fed. Intermediate Credit Bank, Houston, 1974; exec. trainee Citibank, N.Am., N.Y.C., 1975, v.p., 1981-88, head credit policy Latin Am., 1988-92, dep. group head Latin Am., 1992-93; pres. Citibank Argentina, 1993-96; divsn. head Citibank Latin Am. South, 1996—; exec. v.p., global cash mgmt. & trade Citibank, N. Am., 1998—2000; exec. v.p. Citibank e-bus., 2000—02; CEO Citibank Latin Amer., 2002—04; sr. internat. advisor Citigroup Inc., 2004—. Bd. dirs. Sienbra, Buenos Aires. Bd. dirs., treas. Norfield Children's Ctr., Weston, Conn., 1989-93; coun. mem. St. Francis of Assisi, Weston, 1991-93. Republican. Roman Catholic. Avocations: chess, walking, travel, reading, tennis. Office: Citigroup Inc 399 Park Ave New York NY 10022-4699

BERN, DORRIT J., apparel company executive; BSc in Bus., U. Wash. Mem. staff Sears, Roebuck & Co.; pres., CEO Charming Shoppes, Inc., Bensalem, Pa., 1995—, Chmn., 1997—. Bd. dirs. So. Co. Atlanta. Mem. Active Keeping Kids Warm, Bensalem, Pa. Mem.: Atlanta C. of C. (bd. dirs.). Office: Charming Shoppes Inc 450 Winks Ln Bensalem PA 19020-5993

BERN, MARC JAY, lawyer; b. Milw., June 19, 1950; s. James Ellis and Harriet (Kramer) B.; children: Lindsay, Jesse, Noah, Erica; m. Cathy Anthone; 1 child, Emma. BA with distinction, U. Wis., 1972; JD, Ill. Inst. Tech., 1975. Bar: Wis. 1975, US Dist. Ct. (ea. and we. dists.) Wis., N.Y. 1983, US Dist. Ct. (so. and ea. dists.) N.Y., US Dist. Ct. (we. dist.) N.Y. 1990, US Dist. Ct. Pa., US Dist. Ct. Ariz. Assoc. Habush, Gillick, Habush, Davis & Murphy, Milw., 1975-79; ptnr. Gillick, Murphy, Gillick, Bern & Wicht, Milw., 1979-82; assoc. Lipsig, Sullivan, Liapakis, N.Y.C., 1983-84; sr. trial assoc. Julien & Schlesinger, P.C., N.Y.C., 1984-86, Trolman & Glaser, P.C., N.Y.C., 1986-88; pvt. practice law, 1988-91; counsel Weitz & Luxembourg PC, 1992-95; sr. ptnr. Napoli, Kaiser, Bern & Assocs. LLP, 1995—, Napoli Bern LLP, 2002—. Lectr. Milw. Area Tech. Coll., 1979-80, Continuing Edn. State Bar Wis., 1978—, Melvin Belli Seminar, Am. Trial Lawyers Assn., 1982—, Hahneman Med. Coll., 1980, Practicing Law Inst., 1984—, Wis. Acad. Trial Lawyers, Madison, 1981—, NYU Sch. Continuing Edn., 1985—, Inst. Continuing Profl. Edn., 1981-82, N.Y. State Trial Lawyers Assn., 1986-88, Mealeys Seminars, 1999—, Fen-Phen, Rezulin, Methyl Tertiary Butyl Ether. Mem. Am. Trial Lawyers Assn., State Bar Wis., State Bar N.Y., Am. Judicature Soc., Am. Soc. Law and Medicine, N.Y. State Trial Lawyers Assn., Assn. Trial Lawyers Am. (ann. conv. lectr. 1991), Delta Theta Phi. Home: 65 First Neck Ln Southampton NY 11968 Office: 115 Broadway 12th Fl New York NY 10006 Office Phone: 212-267-3700. E-mail: Lawbern@aol.com, mjbern@napolibern.com.

BERN, PAULA RUTH, columnist; b. Pitts. children: Bruce, Caryn, Marshall, Samuel, Rona. BA, Pa. State U., 1956; MA, U. Pitts., 1978, PhD, 1980. Editor-in-chief Jaffe Pub. Co., L.A., 1958-63; on-air producer Sta. WQED-TV, Pitts, 1963-65; dir. univ. rels. and devel. Robert Morris U., Pitts. and Coraopolis, 1965-69, Point Park Coll., Pitts, 1969-72; pres. Bern Asocs., Inc., 1972—; CEO The Exec. TV Workshop, Pitts., 1987—. Tchr. sr. exec. seminars grad. sch. Urban and Pub. Affairs, Carnegie Mellon U., 1985-90; trustee Ptts. Ballet Theatre, Inc., 1973-95 Contb. editor New Women mag., 1988—; syndicated columnist Scripps Howard NewsSvc., Washington, 1988—; Author: Point Park College: A History, 1980; How to Work for a Woman Boss (Even if You'd Rather Not)., 1987. Bd. dirs. council for Internat. Visitors, 1975-91; Exec. Women's Council, 1980—; adv. council Internat. Poetry forum, 1979—, Pa. Comn. for Women; bd. dirs. Assn. Commns. Women, bd. dirs. Conflict Resolution Ctr. Internat., Inc., 1998—, bus. dispute resolution alliance. Recipient Am. Coun. on Edn. awad, 1982 Mem. Women in Comm., Pub. Rels. Soc. Am., Press Club Western Pa., Delta Sigma Rho, Phi Beta Kappa. Office: Scripps Howard News Svc Ste 1000 1090 Vermont Ave NW Washington DC 20005-4906 E-mail: paularbern@aol.com.

BERN, RONALD LAWRENCE, telecommunications industry executive, writer; b. Anderson, SC, Aug. 23, 1936; s. Samuel Harris and Minnie (Siegel) B.; m. Elaine Kay Lefkowitz, Dec. 25, 1960; children: Brett Alan, Melissa Lynn. BA in Journalism, U. S.C., 1958, MA in Journalism, 1961. Writer William Barton Marsh Co., NYC, 1958-59; editor, writer Univac div. Sperry Rand, NYC, 1959-60; editor, mgr. Bell Tel. Labs., NYC, 1961-63; pres. Ronald Bern Co., NYC, 1965—85, 1990—2000; corp. sr. v.p. The LVI Group, Inc., NYC, 1985-90. Cons. AT&T Co., NY, NJ, 1966-85, The LVI Group, Nico Constrn.; bd. dir. Talon Corp., The Bern Co., Inc., Healing Images Inc., Riverstone Svc., Inc. Author: An American in the Making, 1960, The Successful Salesman, 1972, The Legacy, 1975; Gone Fishin': The 100 Best Spots in New Jersey, 1998, Gone Fishin': The 100 Best Spots in New York, 1999; contbr. articles to profl. publ. Bd. dir. North Brunswick Little League, NJ, 1975-79; mem. North Brunswick Planning Commn., 1984. With US Army, 1958-59, 61-62. Fellow SC Press Assn., 1960. Mem. South Caroliniana Soc. Democrat. Jewish. Avocations: fishing, reading, travel. Home: 37 Hidden Lake Dr North Brunswick NJ 08902

BERNABE, JOSEPH MICHAEL, music educator; b. Raritan, NJ, Feb. 11, 1952; s. Joseph Peter and Esther Bernabe; m. Alice A. Giordano, July 6, 1980; children: Nicole, Michael. BA, Fairleigh Dickinson U., Madison, NJ, 1977. Band dir. Parsippany HS, NJ, 1977—, golf coach, 1982—. Pvt. instr., 1973—. Recreation mem. Rockaway Boro Recreation Com., NJ, 1994—. Mem.: USGA, MENC, Internat. Clarinet Soc. Avocations: golf, sports. Home: 31 Maplewood Dr Rockaway NJ 07866 Office: Parsippany HS 309 Baldwin Rd Parsippany NJ 07054

BERNABEI, RAYMOND, management consultant; b. New Castle, Pa., Nov. 26, 1925; s. Leo and Maria Bernabei; m. Rosella E. Taucher, May 4, 1946; children: Raymond L., Alan J., Rosemary, Leo J., Lori J. BS in Math. and Geography, Indiana U. of Pa., 1947; MEd in Ednl. Adminstrn., U. Pitts., 1950; cert. in guidance and counseling, Duquesne U., 1960; DEd, Western Res. U., 1966. Math. tchr., head basketball coach Clymer (Pa.) H.S., 1947-50; math. tchr. Tarentum (Pa.) H.S., 1950-54; dir. guidance and testing, head football coach Tarentum Sch. Dist., 1954-61; asst. jr.-sr. H.S. prin. Hampton Twp. (Pa.), 1961-63; grad. asst. Western Res. U., Cleve., 1963-64; dir. secondary edn. Mentor Pub. Schs., Ohio, 1964-65, asst. supt., 1965, supt., 1965-67; asst. exec. dir. Bucks County (Pa.) Schs., 1967-80; mgmt. cons. I.E. Banreb Assocs., Longwood, Fla. Vis. tchr. John Carroll U., Cleve., 1965, Bowling Green (Ohio) U., 1966, N.S. Summer Sch./Dalhousie U., Halifax, Can., 1967, Wis. State U., Eau Claire, 1968, U. Ala., University, 1969, 71, U. Nev., Las Vegas, 1970, 72, 93, Cleve. State U., 1970, Laurence U., Sarasota, Fla., 1971, 72, 73; adj. prof. U. Ala., 1974, 75, 76, Lehigh U., Bethlehem, Pa., 1978, 80, 81, 82, Rollins Coll., Winter Park, Fla., 1983—; presenter in field. Recipient Disting. Prof. award Nat. Acad. Sch. Execs., 1973, Recognition award Nat. Soccer Coaches Athletic Assn., 1983, Bill Jeffrey award, 1985, Honor award Nat. Soccer Coaches Assn. Am., 1991, Honor award Nat. Intercollegiate Soccer Ofcls. Assn., 1975, Disting. Svc. award Pa. State Athletic Dirs. Assn., 1987, Nellie DelCamp Excellence in Tchg. award Rollins Coll., 1995, 2002; named to Western Pa. Hall of Fame, 1977, Nat. Soccer Hall of Fame, 1978, Allegheny-Kiski Valley Hall of Fame, 1979, Nat. Assn. Intercollegiate Athletics Hall of Fame, 1994, Ind. U. Pa. Hall of Fame, 1996. Home and Office: 541 Woodview Dr Longwood FL 32779-2614

BERNACCHI, RICHARD LLOYD, lawyer; b. LA, Dec. 15, 1938; s. Bernard and Anne B. BS with honors in Commerce (Nat. Merit Found. scholar), U. Santa Clara, 1961; LL.B. with highest honors (Legion Lex scholar, Jerry Geisler Meml. scholar), U. So. Calif., 1964. Bar: Calif. 1964. Assoc. Irell and Manella, L.A., 1964-70, ptnr., 1970—; lectr. Am. Law Inst., 1972-73; lectr. data processing contracts and law U. So. Calif., L.A., 1972, 78, 81. Co-chmn. Regional Transp. Com., 1970-72; mem. adv. bd. U. So. Calif. Computer Law Inst., 1979—, Ariz. Law and Tech. Inst., 1982-86; U. Santa Clara Computer and High Tech. Law Jour., 1982-90. Author: (with Gerald H. Larsen) Data Processing Contracts and the Law, 1974, (with Frank and Statland) Bernacchi on Computer Laaw, 1986; editor-in-chief U. So. Calif. Law Rev., 1962-64; adv. bd. Computer Negotiations Report, 1983-95, Computer and Tech. Law Jour., 1984-93, Computer Law Strategist, 1984-94. Capt. AUS, 1964—66, PTO. Mem. ABA (mem. adv. com. on edn. 1973-74, chmn. subcom. taxation computer sys. of sect. sci. and tech. 1976-78), L.A. Bar Assn., Computer Law Assn. (bd. dirs. 1973-86, chmn. preconf. symposium on law and computers 1974-75, West Coast v.p. 1976-79, sr. v.p. 1979-81, pres. 1981-83, adv. bd. 1986—), Internat. Bar Assn. (co-chmn. sect. on bus. law mem. com. on internat. tech. and e-commerce law 1995-98, steering com. 1998—), Am. Fedn. Info. Processing Socs. (mem. spl. com. electronic funds transfer sys. 1974-78), Order of Coif, Scabbard and Blade, Beta Gamma Sigma, Alpha Sigma Nu. Office: Irell & Manella 1800 Avenue Of The Stars Los Angeles CA 90067-4276 Office Phone: 310-203-7503. Business E-Mail: dbernacchi@irell.com.

BERNAL, IVAN, chemist, educator; b. Barranquilla, Colombia, Mar. 28, 1931; arrived in U.S., 1949; s. Enrique and Eva (Gonzalez) Bernal; m. Constance Craytor, Nov. 30, 1957; 1 child, Susan Scott. PhD, Columbia U., 1963. Postdoctoral fellow Harvard U., Cambridge, Mass., 1963-64; asst. prof. SUNY, Stony Brook, 1964-67; chemist Brookhaven Nat. Lab., Upton, N.Y., 1967-73; prof. U. Houston, 1973—. Grants referee Counsel Sci. and Indsl. Rsch. Orgns., Pretoria, South Africa, 1986, Canberra, Australia, 1987—; vis. prof. Tech. U. Munich, 1999—2000. Author: (book) Symmetry, 1971; editor:

Elsevier Sci. Pubs., 1985—, Sterochem of Oganometallic & Inorganic Compounds, 5 vols.; contbr. articles to profl. jours. Founder, bd. dirs. Environ. Inst., U. Houston, 1989. Recipient U.S. Sr. Scientist award, Alexander von Humboldt Found., 1976, 1983, 1991; fellow, Australian Nat. U., 1983, 1986, 1992, David Sarnoff, RCA Corp., 1959—61, Soconony Mobil, Columbia U., 1962—63, Oriel Coll. Vis., Oxford U., 1992. Fellow: N.Y. Acad. Sci.; mem.: Am. Chem. Soc. (com. profl. tng. 1984—, Ann. award rsch. SE Tex. chpt. 1984), Sigma Xi. Office: U Houston Dept Chemistry Houston TX 77204-5003 E-mail: ibernal@uh.edu.

BERNAL-LABRADA, EMILIO, writer, poet, interpreter, translator; b. Havana, Cuba; came to U.S., 1956; s. Emilio Labrada Bernal and Sofia Escobar; m. Margaret Tijerina (div. Apr. 1976); children: Sophia, Hilda, Emily. Student, U. Havana. Sr. Spanish reviewer Orgn. Am. States, Washington, 1962-89; chief Office Pub. Info., N.Am. Acad. Spanish Lang., N.Y.C., 1996—. Dir. Labrada Lang. Svcs., Sterling, Va.; pres. Emilia Bernal Found., Washington, D.C.; newspaper columnist Nuestro Idioma de Cada Día, Language, Our Daily Fiesta. Author: La prensa liEbre, 2001; editor, revisor, publr. author (prologue) Emilia Bernal: su vida y su obra; author: (prologue) Arboles genealógicos de la Cuba española, 1997; contbr. Antología de El trujamán, Inst. Cervantes, 2002; bilingual columnist (website) coloquio.com. Mem. Real Acad. Española. Achievements include featured as first author in "Antología de El trujamán", Inst. Cervantes, Spain, 2002. Avocations: tennis, ping pong/table tennis, photography. Home and Office: 20864 Great Falls Forest Dr Sterling VA 20165-2428 Office Phone: 703-406-1277. E-mail: emiliolabrada@msn.com.

BERNANKE, BEN S., federal official; b. Augusta, Ga., Dec. 13, 1953; s. Philip Richard and Edna Rivy (Friedman) B.; m. Anna Friedmann, May 29, 1978; children; Joel, Alyssa. BA in econ., Harvard U., 1975; PhD in econ., MIT, 1979. Asst. prof. econ. Grad. Sch. Bus., Stanford U., 1979—83, assoc. prof. econ., 1983—85; prof. econ. and pub. affairs Princeton U., 1985—96, Howard Harrison and Gabrielle Snyder Beck prof. of econ. and pub. affairs, 1996—2002, chair, dept. econ., 1996—2002; mem. bd. govs. FRS, Washington, 2002—05; mem., chmn. Coun. Econ. Advisors, 2005—. Rsch. assoc. Nat. Bur. Econ. Rsch., Cambridge, Mass., 1982; vis. prof. MIT, Cambridge, 1983. Contbr. articles to profl. jours.; editor: Am. Econ. Rev., 2001—. Hoover Instn. fellow, 1982-83, Alfred P. Sloan Found. rsch. fellow, 1983-84. Fellow: Am. Acad. Arts and Scis., Econometric Soc. Office: Coun Econ Advisors 1800 G St NW 8th Fl Washington DC 20502

BERNANKE, HAROLD, retired physician; b. N.Y.C., Apr. 28, 1929; s. Philip and Anna (Handel) B. BA, NYU, 1950; MD, Downstate Med. Ctr., Bklyn., 1954. Diplomate Am. Bd. Internal Medicine. Intern Maimonides Hosp., Bklyn., 1954-55; resident in internal medicine VA Hosp., Bklyn., 1955-56, Beth Israel Hosp., N.Y.C., 1958-59; fellow in cardiology Yale Med. Sch.-West Haven (Conn.) VA Hosp., 1959-60; instr. cardiology Upstate Med. Sch., Syracuse, 1960-61; physician East Nassau Med. Group, 1961-62, Montefiore Hosp. Med. Group, 1962-70; pvt. practice Bronx, N.Y., 1970—. Capt., M.C., U.S. Army, 1956-58. Mem. County Med. Soc., Alpha Omega Alpha. Avocations: tennis, swimming. Office: 201 E Mosholu Pkwy N Bronx NY 10467-3612

BERNARD, ALEXANDER, protective services official; b. LA, Apr. 23, 1952; s. Louis and Hannah (Bergman) Bernard; m. Diana LoRee Winstead, Dec. 17, 1976; children: Michael Alexander, Andrew Alexander. AA magna cum laude, L.A. Valley Coll., 1976; BS summa cum laude, Calif. State U., L.A., 1989. Parking meter collector LA (Calif.) City Clk.'s Office, 1973—79; police officer LA (Calif.) Airport, LA, 1979—95, sgt. police svcs. divsn., 1995—2003; gen. mgr. Kern Law Enforcement Assn., Bakersfield, Calif., 2003—. Adv. com. Calif. Commn. Peace Officer Stds. and Tng., 1999—2004, vice chmn., 2001, chmn., 02. Contbr. articles to profl. jours. Active Boy Scouts Am. Mem.: NRA (life), Ret. Peace Officers Assn. Calif., LA Airport Peace Officers Assn. (pres. 1981—89, bd. dirs. 1992—94, pres. 1994—95), Fraternal Order Police, LA Airport Police Suprs. Assn. (v.p. 1997—98, pres. 1999—2003, v.p. 2003, bd. dirs.), Balloon Fedn. Am., So. Calif. Balloon Assn., Peace Officers Rsch. Assn. Calif. (chpt. pres. 1982—84, state bd. dirs. 1984—85, chpt. pres. 1985—87, state bd. dirs. 1987—2003, ethnic rels. com. 1993—94, exec. com. 1994—2003, sec. 1999—2003, state bd. dirs. 1987—2003), Calif. Peace Officers Assn., Labor and Employment Rsch. Assn., Law Enforcement Alliance Am. (life), Internat. Police Assn. (life), Calif. Rifle and Pistol Assn. (life), Golden Key (life), Phi Kappa Phi (life). Democrat. Avocations: travel, record collecting, hot air ballooning. Office: Kern Law Enforcement Assn 3417 Pegasus Dr PO Box 82516 Bakersfield CA 93380 E-mail: kleagm@etcrier.net.

BERNARD, ANDRÉ PHILIPPE, publishing executive, writer; b. Newton, Mass., Apr. 15, 1956; s. Albert Yves and Ethel Potts Bernard; m. Jennie F. McGregor, June 16, 1990; children: Lucia McGregor, Elizabeth Eustis. BA, Franklin and Marshall Coll., 1979. Asst. editor Viking Penguin, N.Y.C., 1985—87; exec. editor David R. Godine, Boston, 1987—89; sr. editor Simon & Schuster, N.Y.C., 1989—91, Book of Month Club, N.Y.C., 1991—93, dir. acquisitions, 1993—96; exec. editor Harvest Books/Harcourt Brace, N.Y.C., 1996—98, editor-in-chief, 1998—2001; v.p., pub. Harcourt Brace, N.Y.C., 2001—. Bd. trustees PEN, N.Y.C., 2003—, chair forums com., 2003—, chair nominating com., 2004; bd. dirs. German Book Office, N.Y.C., The Kenyon Rev.; mem. internat. freedom to publish com. Assn. Am. Publishers, N.Y.C., 1992—98. Author: Rotten Rejections: A Literary Companion, 1990, Now All We Need is a Title: Famous Book Titles and How They Got That Way, 1996, Madame Bovary C'est Moi!: The Great Characters of Literature and Where They Came From, 2003; author: (with Clifton Fadiman) Bartlett's Book of Anecdotes, 2000; author: (with Bill Henderson) The Complete Rot, 1993; contbg. editor: The American Scholar, 1998—. Bd. dirs. Mercantile Libr., N.Y.C., 1992—96. Jerusalem fellow, Jerusalem Book Fair, 2000. Mem.: Ye Buz Fuz, Miami Valley Hunt and Polo Club, Mahkeenac Boat Club, Century Assn. Office: Harcourt Brace 15 E 26th St New York NY 10010

BERNARD, ANTHONY M., retired lawyer, judge; b. Youngstown, Ohio, Nov. 28, 1918; s. Ben W. and Laura Bernard; m. Jane Cleary Bernard, June 4, 1945; children: Patricia, Kathleen, Jane Ann, Christine, Michael, Mark, Mary, Daniel. BS, Notre Dame U., 1940, LLB, 1942, JD, 1960. Cert. pilot, AMEL. Atty. Kosach-Morgante-Bernard, Youngstown, 1958-65, Kosach-Bernard-Hess, Youngstown, 1965-70, Bernard-Hess-Bailey, Youngstown, 1970-81; judge Girard (Ohio) Mcpl. Ct., 1982-94; ret., 1994. Organizer program treatment in lieu of incarceration for addicts convicted of crime. Lt. USN, 1942-46. Named Man of Yr., Alcohol Treating Orgn., 1977-81; recipient commendation Ohio State Hwy. Patrol, 1987. Mem. Am. Trial Lawyers, Ohio Acad. Trial Lawyers (Lawyers Judge 1991), Mahoning Co. Bar. Assn., Trumbull Co. Bar. Assn. Democrat. Avocations: cards, travel, tinkering, grandfathering, fishing. Home: 966 Villa Pl Girard OH 44420-2081

BERNARD, APRIL, poet, literature educator; BA, Harvard U. Former sr. editor Premiere, GQ, Vanity Fair; instr. Amherst Coll., Yale U.; prof. lit., MFA core faculty Bennington Coll., 1998—2003, assoc. dean acad. affairs Vt., 2003—. Author: (novels) Pirate Jenny, (poetry) Blackbird Bye Bye (Walt Whitman prize, Acad. Am. Poets), Psalms: Poems, 1993, Swan Electric: Poems, 2002; contbr. poems, literary essays, and articles to various publs. Guggenheim fellow, 2003. Office: Bennington Coll One College Dr Bennington VT 05201 Office Phone: 802-442-5401. E-mail: aprilbernard@earthlink.net.*

BERNARD, CATHY S., management corporation executive; b. Bronx, N.Y., Nov. 13, 1949; d Burton and Norma (Ebb) B. BBA, George Washington U., 1971, M of Pub. Adminstrn., 1978; MA, U. Miami, 1972. Cert. property mgr. Staff asst. HEW, Washington, 1970-74; evaluation specialist OEO, Washington, 1974; tchr. St. Patrick's Acad., Washington, 1975; asst. prof. No. Va. C.C., Woodbridge, 1976-78; adj. prof. Prince George's CC, 2002; staff dir. Dem. Nat. Conv., N.Y.C., 1976; pres., chief exec. officer CSB Assocs. Mgmt. Corp., Riverdale, Md., 1977—. Mem. Housing Opportunities Commn., Kensington, Md., 1979-93, chmn., 1988, vice chair, 1980, 87, chair pro tem, 1986, chair housing honor roll, 1985-88, Moderate Priced Dwelling Unit Commn.; mem. exec. coun. Inst. Real Estate Mgmt., Washington, 1982-87, cert. property mgr.; adj. prof. bus. Prince Georges C.C., 2002. Adv. coun. Suburban Hosp., Bethesda, Md., 1984-89; bd. dirs. Ivymount Sch. for Handicapped, Potomac, Md., 1984—, chmn. bd. dirs., 2003, chair property com., chair bldg. expansion project, 1999-2002; treas. Jewish Coun. on Aging, 1988; bd. dirs., chair property com. Jewish Found. for Group Homes, Rockville, Md., 1989-91; bd. dirs. Roundhouse Theatre, Wheaton, Md., 1994—, treas., 1995—; bd. dirs. McLean Sch. Md., 2001, trustee 2001—04, vice chmn., sec., site com. chair, 2002; bd. dirs. Bethesda's Imagination State, 2003—; trustee Temple Emanuel, Kensington, Md., 1994-97; candidate Md. State Legislature, 1986; pres. Cmty. Housing Res. Bd., 1985. Recipient Hughes award for property mgmt., 1980, Jewish Coun. award, 1989. Mem. Montgomery County C. of C. (bd. dirs., v.p. housing com. 1981-82), Apt. and Office Bldg. Assn. (bd. dirs., chmn. affordable housing com. 1990-99). Office: CSB Assocs Mgmt Corp PO Box 647 Riverdale MD 20738-0647

BERNARD, DAVID EDWIN, artist; b. Sheridan, Ill., Aug. 8, 1913; s. Edwin Louis and Cecile Louise Bernard; m. Vivian Lanfear Bernard, Aug. 21, 1948; 1 child, Joy Bernard Wieter. BFA, U. Ill., 1939; MFA, U. Iowa, 1949. Graphic artist K.B. Butler & Assocs., Mendota, Ill., 1941—42; instr. art Maryville Coll., Tenn., 1946—48; asst. prof., prof. Wichita State U., 1949—83, ret., 1983; artist St. Cloud, Fla., 1983. Numerous print exhbns. Mem.: Oscola Ctr. Arts, Wichita Art Mus., Soc. Am. Graphic Artists. Avocations: travel, gardening, crafts, history, sculpting, woodcarving.

BERNARD, DAVID GEORGE, retired management consultant; b. Cambridge, Mass., Oct. 30, 1921; s. Frederick and Fayetta (Smith) B.; m. Edith Barnes, Dec. 10, 1960; 1 child, Andrew; children by prior marriage: Jeffrey, Frederick, Joan, Peter. BS, Harvard U., 1943, MBA, 1947. Gen. sales mgr. Am. Can. Co., N.Y.C., 1958-61; sr. v.p. Medusa Corp., Cleve., 1961-63; v.p. Internat. Paper, N.Y.C., 1968-78, Nat. Can Corp., Chgo., 1978-81; exec. v.p. Fischbach Corp., N.Y.C., 1981-83; pres. Delta Marine Supply Corp., N.Y.C., 1983-84. Bd. dirs. Trojan Techs. Inc. Bd. dirs. S.C.A.N. Served to lt. USN, 1943-46, PTO. Mem. Newcomen Soc., Bay Head Yacht Club (N.J.). Democrat. Episcopalian. Home: 254 E 68th St Apt 27E New York NY 10021-6017

BERNARD, DONALD RAY, retired law educator; b. San Antonio, June 5, 1932; s. Horatio J. and Amber (McDonald) B.; children: Doren, Kevin, Koby; m. Elizabeth Priscilla Gilpin, 1986. Student, U. Mich., 1950-52; JD, U. Tex., 1958, BA, 1954, JD, 1958, LLM, 1964. Bar: Tex. 1958, U.S. Ct. Mil. Appeals, 1959, U.S. Supreme Ct. 1959; lic. comml. pilot. Commd. ensign U.S. Navy, 1954, advanced through grades to commdr., 1956-75, retired, 1975; briefing atty. Supreme Ct. Tex., Austin, 1958-59; asst. atty. gen. State of Tex., Austin, 1959-60; ptnr. Bernard & Bernard, Houston, 1960-80; pvt. practice law Houston, 1980-94; prof. internat. law U. St. Thomas, Houston, 1991-94; guest lectr. Sch. Bus. Mont. State U., 1995-96; mng. dir. Mental Resources LLC, 2003—. Mem. faculty S.W. Sch. Real Estate, 1968-77. Author: Origin of the Special Verdict As Now Practiced in Texas, 1964; co-author: (novel) Bullion, 1982. Bd. dirs. Nat. Kidney Found., Houston, 1960-63; chmn. Bd. Adjustment, Hedwig Village, Houston, 1972-76; bd. regents Angeles U. Found., The Philippines; chmn. of the bd. Metro Verde Devel. Corp., The Philippines; bd. dirs. Gloria Dei Luth. Ch., Endowment Found. Comdr. USN, 1950-92; ret., air show pilot Confederate Air Force, 1970-80. Mem. Lawyers Soc. Houston (pres. 1973-74), Houston Bd. Realtors, ABA, Inter-Am. Bar Assn., Tex. Bar Assn. (com. liaison Mex. legal profession), Houston Bar Assn. (chairperson emeritus internat. law sect.), Internat. Bar Assn. (del. to 1st seminar with Assn. Soviet Lawyers, Moscow, 1988), Assn. Soviet Lawyers, Lawyer-Pilot Bar Assn., Sons of the Republic of Tex., Lic. Execs. Soc., St. James's Club, Masons, Shriners, Alpha Tau Omega, Phi Delta Phi. Lutheran. Home: 14 Scenic Dr Whitehall MT 59759-9789 E-mail: donbernard@msn.com.

BERNARD, EDDIE NOLAN, oceanographer; b. Houston, Nov. 23, 1946; s. Edward Nolan and Geraldine Marie (Dempsey) B.; m. Shirley Ann Fielder, May 30, 1970; 1 child, Elizabeth Ann BS, Lamar U., 1969; MS, Tex. A&M U., 1970, PhD, 1976. Geophysicist Pan Am. Petroleum Co., 1969; rsch. asst. oceanographic rsch. Tex. A&M U., College Station, Tex., 1969-70; rschr. NOAA, 1970-73, dep. dir. pacific marine environ. lab. Seattle, 1980-82; rschr. Joint Tsunami Rsch. Effort, 1973-77; dir. Nat. Tsunami Warning Ctr., 1977-80, Pacific Marine Environ. Lab., Seattle, 1982—, chmn. Nat. Tsunami Hazard Mitigation Program, 1997—2004. Dir. NOAA hydrothermal vents program, fisheries oceanography program; exec. com. Coop. Inst. for Marine Resource Studies and adv. bd. for Coll. of Oceanic and Atmospheric Sci., Oreg. State U., 2002-; adminstrv. bd. Joint Inst. Marine and Atmospheric Rsch. U. Hawaii; mem. Washington Sea Grant Steering Com., 1987—; sci. coun. Joint Inst. for Marine Observations, Scripps Instn. of Oceanography, 1992—; exec. com. Cooperative Inst. for Arctic Rsch. U. Alaska; advisor Japan Marine Sci. and Tech. Ctr., 2000—. Editor: Tsunami Hazard: A Practical Guide for Tsunami Hazard Reduction, 1991, Developing Tsunami Resilient Communities, 2005; contbr. articles to profl. jours. Named Best of New Generation award, Esquire Mag., 1984; recipient Meritorious Presdl. Rank award, Pres. Clinton, 1993, Pres. G.W. Bush, 2002, Gold medal, US Dept. Commerce, 2004. Mem. Internat. Union of Geodesy and Geophysics (chmn. Tsunami comm. 1987-95), Am. Geophys. Union, Oceanography Soc. Office: Pacific Marine Environ Lab 7600 Sand Point Way NE Seattle WA 98115-6349 E-mail: eddie.n.nernard@noaa.gov.

BERNARD, H. RUSSELL, anthropologist, educator, editor; b. N.Y.C., June 12, 1940; s. Herman Fink and Lillian (Rosenfeld) B.; m. Carole May Phillips, Jan. 28, 1962; children: Elyssa Lynn, Sharyn Kymm. BA, CUNY, 1961; MA, PhD, U. Ill., 1968. From asst. prof. to assoc. prof. Wash. State U., Pullman, 1966-72; rsch. assoc. Scripps Inst. Oceanography, La Jolla, Calif., 1972; from assoc. prof. to prof. W.Va. U., Morgantown, 1972-79; prof. anthropology U. Fla., Gainesville, 1979—. Prof. Nat. Mus. Ethnology, Osaka, Japan, 1991, U. Cologne, 1994-95. Editor (with B.P. Pelto): (books) Technology and Social Change, 1972; editor:, 1987; editor: (with J. Salinas) The Otomí, 1978; editor: Native Ethnography, 1989, Handbook of Methods in Cultural Anthropology, 1998, (jours.) Cultural Anthropology Methods Jour., 1989—98, Field Methods, 1999—; author: (books) Research Methods in Cultural Anthropology, 1988, 1994, 2002, Social Research Methods: Qualitative and Quantitative Approaches, 2000; co-author (with W. Penn Handwerker): Data Analysis with MYSTAT, 1994; collaborator: (films) Aegean Sponger Divers (Chris Plaque award 1975), 1969—; contbr. articles to profl. jours. Recipient Alexander von Humboldt Rsch. award, 1994-95; Fulbright Rsch. scholar, 1969-70; grantee NSF, 1967—, NEH, 1976-85, Am. Philol. Soc., 1972. Mem. Soc. for Applied Anthropology (editor Human Orgn. 1976-81), Am. Anthrop. Assn. (editor-in-chief Am. Anthropologist 1981-89, Franz Boas award 2003). Business E-Mail: ufruss@ufl.edu.

BERNARD, HUGH YANCEY, JR., law educator, librarian; b. Athens, Ga., July 17, 1919; s. Hugh Yancey and Marguerite Louise (Vonderau) B. AB, U. Ga., 1941; BS in Library Sci., Columbia U., 1947; JD with honors, George Washington U., 1961. Bar: D.C. 1961, U.S. Ct. Appeals (D.C. cir.) 1962, U.S. Supreme Ct. 1969. Librarian copyright office, Library of Congress, 1947-60; law librarian George Washington U., Washington, 1960-81, asst. and assoc. prof. law, 1962-70, prof., 1970-81, prof. emeritus, 1981-; cons. law sch. history, 1981-83; cons. USAID, Kabul, Afghanistan, 1974, law libr. devel. Cath. Univ. of Am., 1975, Del. Law Sch., Wilmington, Del., 1976. With USAAF, 1942-46, USNR, 1964-69. Recipient Profl. Achievement award George Washington Law Assn., 1981. Mem. Am. Assn. Law Libraries, Law Librarians Soc. Washington, Phi Beta Kappa, Phi Alpha Delta, Kappa Delta Pi. Republican. Baptist. Lodges: Masons, K.T., Shriners, Scottish Rite. Author: The Law of Death and Disposal of the Dead, 1966, 2d ed. 1979; Public Officials, Elected and Appointed, 1968; book review editor, George Washington law Review, 1959-60; contbr. Your Complete Guide to Estate Planning, 1971. Home: 3563 S Leisure World Blvd Apt 1A Silver Spring MD 20906-1715

BERNARD, JOHN MARLEY, lawyer, educator; b. Phila., Feb. 6, 1941; s. Edward and Opal (Marley) B.; children: John Marley Jr., Kendall M., Katherine M., James M.; m. Esther L. von Laue, May 31, 1986. BA, Swarthmore Coll., 1963; LLB, Harvard U., 1967. Bar: Pa. 1967. Assoc. Montgomery McCracken Walker & Rhoads, Phila., 1967-73, ptnr., 1973-86, Ballard Spahr Andrews & Ingersoll, LLP, Phila., 1986—. Lectr. Temple U. Law Sch., Phila., 1975-95; instr. Phila. Acad. for Employee Benefits Tng., 1996-99; guest instr. U.S. Dept. Labor, Washington, 1984-96; instr. U. Pa. Wharton Sch., Phila., 1989-90; bd. dirs. PENJERDEL Employee Benefits Assn., Phila. Contbg. author: Handbook of Employee Benefits, 1989. Mem. ABA, Pa. Bar Assn. Office: Ballard Spahr Andrews & Ingersoll LLP 1735 Market St Fl 51 Philadelphia PA 19103-7599 E-mail: bernard@ballardspahr.com

BERNARD, KENNETH JAMES, mathematics professor; m. Sandra Lee Catino, Aug. 5, 1977; children: Jennifer Marie, Rebecca Noel. EdD, U. Rochester, 1978. Prof. math. Niagara (N.Y.) U., 1977—98; prof. Chowan Coll., Murfreesboro, NC, 1998—2003, chmn. Dept. Math., 1998—2003; prof. math. Va. State U., Petersburg, Va., 2003—. Author: Foundations of Mathematics. First lt. U.S. Army, 1973—75. Recipient Excellence in Tchg. award, Niagara U., 1994; grantee, GTE Tech. Focus Grant, 1997—98, Tex. Instruments, 1999, ExxonMobil Found., 2002, Va. Dept. Edn., 2005. Mem.: AAUP (assoc.; pres. chpt. 2001—03), Math. Assn. Am. (assoc.), Nat. Coun. Tchrs. Math. (assoc.). Office: Virginia State University PO Box 9068 Petersburg VA 23806 Office Phone: 804-524-5416. Office Fax: 804-524-5746. E-mail: kbernard@vsu.edu.

BERNARD, LAWRENCE B., lawyer; b. Rockville Centre, NY, June 13, 1948; BA, Cornell U., 1970; JD, Harvard U., 1973. Bar: DC 1973, US Dist. Ct, DC 1979, US Ct. Appeals (2nd cir.) 1987, US Supreme Ct. 1989, Md. 1991, US Ct. Appeals, Fed. Cir. 1992, US Dist. Ct., Md. 1992, US Ct. Appeals (4th cir.) 1994, Va. 1996, US Dist. Ct. 1997, Va. (ea. dist.) 1997. Atty. FTC, 1974—87; ptnr. Comml. Litig. and Advt. Law Depts. Venable LLP, Washington, DC. Instr. FTC-NITA Trial Advocacy and Deposition Prog., 1980—87; assoc. profl. lectr. in law George Washington U., 1989—91. Mem.: ABA, Va. Bar Assn., DC Bar Assn., Md. State Bar Assn. Office: Venable LLP 575 7th St NW Washington DC 20004 Office Phone: 202-344-4854. Office Fax: 202-344-8300. E-mail: lbbernard@venable.com.

BERNARD, LORA MARIE, journalist, public relations and development specialist; b. Indiana, Pa., Apr. 3, 1963; d. Paul George and Alwine Michelle Bernard. BS in Journalism, U. of North Tex., 1985. Reporter Ft. Worth Star Telegram, 1988—90, Galveston County Daily News, Tex., 1991—93; dep. Galveston County Sheriff's Office, Galveston, Tex., 1993—95; sr. reporter Texas City Sun, Texas City, Tex., 1999—2004; cmty. comm. officer La Marque Indep. Sch. Dist., Marque, Tex., 2004—; exec. dir. La Marque Indep. Sch. Dist. Edn. Found., Marque, Tex., 2004—. Cons., freelance writer and photographer Bernard Media Svcs. (DBA), Texas City, Tex., 1997—. 3d v.p. LWV of Galveston Area, Galveston, Tex., 2002—04. Recipient Finalist Spot News, Dallas Press Club, 2003, Finalist, Splty. Reporting/column, 2002, First Pl. Splty. Reporting, AP Mng. Editors Assn., 2003, First Pl. Investigative Reporting, 2002, First Pl. Splty. Reporting, 2002. Mem.: Nat. Schs. Pub. Rels. Assn., Kiwanis. Episcopal. Avocations: decorating, current affairs, crafts, travel. Home: 2507 Seventh Ave N Texas City TX 77590 Office: La Marque Indep Sch Dist 1727 Bayou Rd La Marque TX 77568 Office Phone: 409-938-4251 247. Personal E-mail: loramarie@sbcglobal.net. E-mail: lbernard@la-marque.isd.tenet.edu.

BERNARD, LOUIS JOSEPH, surgeon, educator; b. Laplace, La., Aug. 19, 1925; s. Edward and Jeanne (Vinet) B.; m. Lois Jeannette McDonald, Feb. 1, 1976; children: Marie Antonia, Phyllis Elaine. BA magna cum laude, Dillard U., New Orleans, 1946; MD, Meharry Med. Coll., 1950. Diplomate: Am. Bd. Surgery. Instr. surgery Sch. Medicine, Meharry Med. Coll., Nashville, 1958-59, prof., 1973-90, chmn. dept. surgery, 1973-87, dean, 1987-90, v.p. for health svcs., 1988-90; practice medicine specializing in surgery, 1959-69; mem. clin. faculty U. Okla., 1959-69, assoc. prof., vice chmn. dept. surgery, 1969-73, chmn. dept. surgery, 1973-87, disting. prof. emeritus, 1990—. Dir. Drew-Meharry Morehouse Consortium Cancer Ctr., 1990-96. Contbr. articles in field to profl. jours. Mem. Okla. State Bd. Corrections, 1968-69. With M.C. U.S. Army, 1951-53. USPHS research fellow NCI, U. Rochester, 1953-54 Fellow ACS, Southeastern Surg. Congress; mem. Soc. Surg. Oncology, Internat. Surg. Soc., Am. Assn. Cancer Edn., Alpha Omega Alpha. Democrat. Roman Catholic. Home: 156 Queens Ln Nashville TN 37218-1826

BERNARD, LOWELL FRANCIS, retired academic administrator, educator; b. Long Beach, Calif., Dec. 14, 1931; s. Francis Montgomery and Irma Viola (Phillips) B.; m. Diana Gypson, June 15, 1957; children: Deborah Diana Bernard North, Steven Lowell, Jocelyn Dawn Bernard Jablonski. BA in Microbiology, UCLA, 1955, MS in Pub. Health and Pre Medicine, 1959. Registered sanitarian, Calif. Instr. pub. health edn. UCLA, 1955-59; asst. dir. Heart and Tb Assn., Poughkeepsie, N.Y., 1959-60; instr. Dutchess Community Coll., Poughkeepsie, 1960-66; dir. edn. Cleve. Health Edn. Mus., 1966-69, exec. dir., 1969-88; adj. asst. prof. Med. Sch. Case Western Res. U., Cleve., 1969-83, adj. asst. prof. pediatrics, 1985-89, dir. Cleve. Health Edn. Project, 1989-97, adj. asst. clin. prof. family medicine, 1990-99, rsch. cons., 1997-98; ret., 1999. Adminstr. Case Western Res. U. Urban Area Health Edn. Ctr., 1991-97; internat. cons. to mus., 1969-2000; speaker, media appearances in field. Author profl. publs. Bd. dirs. Cleve. chpt. Epilepsy Found. Am., 1972-76; trustee Doan's Ctr. Inc., Retinal Vascular Found., 1984-89; mem. men's coun. Gibbs Mus.; bd. dirs. Kiawah Naturalist Conservancy. Recipient Outstanding Service to City award City of Cleve., 1972; fellow in pub. health Case Western Res. U. Med. Sch., 1985-97. Mem. WHO (cons. Internat. Union of Health Edn.), Am. Alliance for Health, Phys. Edn., Recreation and Dance, Am. Assn. Health and Med. Mus. (v.p. 1971-73, pres. 1973-75), Assn. Sci. and Tech. Ctrs. (bd. dirs. 1976-83, sec.-treas. 1978-83, program chmn. 1979), Am. Assn. Mus. (program chmn. nat. meeting 1979, mus. assessment program evaluator 1982-89, mem. mus. accreditation team 1983-89), Aesculapian Soc., Am. Pub. Health Assn., Cleve. Acad. Medicine (hon.), Am. Soc. Sex Educators, Therapists and Counselors (cert. sex educator), Mid-West Mus. Conf., Ohio Mus. Assn., Greater Cleve. Growth Assn., Kiawah-Seabrook Exch. Club. Republican. Presbyterian. Avocations: sports, travel. Home: 13102 Muir Dr NW Gig Harbor WA 98332

BERNARD, RICHARD LAWSON, retired geneticist, educator; b. Detroit, Aug. 12, 1926; s. Clarence Rolla and Ilda Gentry (Lawson) B.; m. Ruth V. Thorne, June 14, 1952 (div. 1975); children: Betty Ruth Marnell, Richard Thorne Bernard, Alice Jean Woodley, Daniel Lawson Bernard. Student, U. Mich., 1943—45, Okla. State U., 1947—48; BS, Ohio State U., 1949, MS, 1950; PhD, NC State U., 1960. Research geneticist USDA, Urbana, Ill., 1954-88; prof. plant genetics U. Ill., Champaign, 1966-92, prof. emeritus, 1992—. Served with USAF, 1945-47. Baptist.

BERNARD, RICHARD PHILLIP, lawyer; b. Chgo., May 29, 1950; s. Martin Joseph Jr. and Ruth (Hadka) B.; m. Svetlana Shoutova; children: Rachel, Benjamin, Alex. BA, Mich. State U., 1972; JD, NYU, 1976; M of Pub. Affairs, Princeton U., 1976; grad. Advanced Mgmt. Program, Harvard U., 1998. Bar: N.Y. 1977. Assoc. Milbank, Tweed, Hadley & McCloy, N.Y.C., 1976-84, ptnr., 1985-94; exec. v.p., gen. counsel New York Stock Exchange, N.Y.C., 1996—; exec. dir., resource sec. Russian Securities Commn., Moscow, 1995. Participating atty. Legal Aid Soc. Community Law Offices, N.Y.C., 1977-80; mem. internat. legal adv. com. Cairo Stock Exchange, 2001—. Mem. ABA (banking and bus. sects., com. on fed. regulation of securities). Democrat. Avocations: russia, carpentry. Office: New York Stock Exchange 11 Wall St New York NY 10005-1905

BERNARD, ROBERT WILLIAM, plastic surgeon; b. N.Y.C., Aug. 18, 1942; Student, U. Mich., 1959-60; BA in Zoology with honors, U. Vt., 1963, MD cum laude, 1967. Diplomate Am. Bd. Surgery, Am. Bd. Plastic Surgery. Intern U. Pa. Hosp., Phila., 1967-68; resident in gen. surgery NYU Med. Ctr.,

1968-72, resident in plastic surgery, 1972-74; asst. prof. plastic surgery NYU Med. Sch., 1972—86; chief plastic surgery No. Westchester Hosp., Mt. Kisco, NY, 1982-87, 96—, White Plains (NY) Hosp., 1979-86, United Hosp., Port Chester, NY, 1986-94. Author, editor: book Aesthetic Restoration of the Aging Face, 1997; editor: Aesthetic Surg. Jour., 1993—98; contbr. articles to profl. jours. Fellow: ACS; mem.: AMA (Recognition award 1983, 1984, 1986, 1988, 1990, 1992, 1995, 1998, 2001, 2004), Am. Cancer Soc., Westchester County Med. Soc., NY Regional Soc. Plastic and Reconstructive Surgery (chair sci. program com. 1984—85, pres. 1986—87, mem. exec. com. 1987—88), NY State Med. Soc. (pres. plastic surgery sect. 1983—84), Am. Soc. Aesthetic Plastic Surgery (pres. 2003—04). Office: 10 Chester Ave White Plains NY 10601-5112 also: 91 Smith Ave Mount Kisco NY 10549-2810 Office Phone: 914-761-8667.

BERNARD, STEPHEN ALAN, oncologist; b. High Point, N.C., 1947; MD, U. N.C., 1973. Diplomate Am. Bd. Internal Medicine, Am. Acad. Internal Medicine, am. Bd. Oncology. Intern Colum-Presbyn. Med. Ctr., 1973-74, resident in medicine, 1974-76; fellow in hematol. oncology Washington U. Hosps., St. Louis, 1976-78; mem. staff U. N.C. Hosp., Chapel Hill, 1981—; assoc. prof. U. N.C. Sch. Medicine, Chapel Hill, 1990—. Mem. ACP, Am. Soc. Clin. Oncology. Office: U NC Sch Medicine Cb # 7305 Chapel Hill NC 27599-0001

BERNARD, STEVEN MARTIN, lawyer; b. N.Y.C., Dec. 14, 1946; s. Louis and Osne (Rubin) B.; m. Jean Marie Castle, Feb. 15, 1969; children: Aric, Matthew, Alexandria, Jordana. BA, CCNY, 1967; JD, Bklyn. Law Sch., 1972. Bar: N.Y. 1973, Calif. 1973. Atty., sect. of fin. ICC, Washington, 1972-73; assoc. Rhodes & Sherrod, Fremont, Calif., 1973-74; ptnr. Rhodes, McKeehan & Bernard, Fremont, 1974-76, McKeehan, Bernard & Wood, Fremont, 1976-89; with Bernard & Wood, Fremont, 1989-96, Bernard, Balgley & Bonaccorsi, Newark, Calif., 1997—. Sec. G.I. Forum, Fremont, 1975; pres. Temple Beth Torah, Fremont, 1976-79. Mem. Assn. Trial Lawyers Am., N.Y. Bar Assn., Calif. Bar Assn., Washington Twp. Bar Assn. Democrat. Jewish. Avocations: sports, skiing, reading, coaching youth sports. Home: 40358 Canyon Heights Dr Fremont CA 94539-3009 Office: Bernard Balgley & Bonaccorsi 3900 Newpark Mall Fl 3 Newark CA 94560-5243 Office Phone: 510-791-1888. E-mail: sbernard@earthlink.net, stevenbernardlaw@yahoo.com.

BERNARDI, ROY A. (ROMOLO ALBERT BERNARDI), federal agency administrator; b. Syracuse, N.Y. m. Alice Bernardi; children: Dante, Bianca. AA, Onondaga C.C., 1964; B in Internat. Rels., U. Americas, Mexico City, 1966; M in Guidance and Counseling, Syracuse U., 1972. Spanish tchr. Liverpool High Sch., Syracuse, guidance counselor, 1971-73; auditor City of Syracuse, 1973-93, mayor, 1993—2001; asst. sec. community planning & devel. US Dept. H.U.D., Washington, 2001—04, dep. sec., 2004—. Bd. dirs. Eye Rsch. Found. of Ctrl. N.Y.; former trustee Leukemia Soc. of Am., Syracuse chpt.; hon. chmn. Big Brother/Big Sister Orgn., Am. Diabetes Assn. of Ctrl. N.Y.; chmn. exec. com. Syracuse Symphony. Avocations: cooking, reading. Office: US Dept HUD 451 7th St SW Rm 10100 Washington DC 20410-9000

BERNARDIN, THOMAS L., advertising executive; Grad., Hillsdale Coll. Acct. dir. McCann-Erickson, Detroit, McCann-Erickson Europe; sr. v.p., dir. internat. ops. Campbell-Mithum-Esty Advt., Southfield, Mich., 1988—90, exec. v.p., mgmt. dir., 1990—92, pres., 1992—94, Bozell/North (formerly Campbell-Mithum-Esty Advt.), 1994—97; exec. v.p., gen. mgr. Bozell, NYC, 1997, pres., CEO; pres., chief oper. officer Lowe US, NYC, 2003, pres., CEO, 2003—04; CEO Leo Burnett USA, NYC, 2004—05; pres. Leo Burnett Worldwide, NYC, 2004—05, chmn., CEO Chgo., 2005. David Rockefeller fellow, 2002. Mem.: Am. Advt. Fedn. (mem. exec. com., chair corp. mems.), Found. Fighting Blindness (trustee). Office: Leo Burnett Worldwide Inc 35 W Wacker Dr Chicago IL 60601 Office Phone: 312-220-5959. Office Fax: 312-220-3299.*

BERNARDINI, CHARLES, lawyer, alderman; BS, U. Ill., 1968, JD, 1972; LLM, John Marshall Law Sch. Legis. asst. to Spkr. Ill. Ho. of Reps., 1972-73; sr. counsel Am. Hosp. Supply Corp., 1974-81; alternate del. Dem. Nat. Conv., 1980; spl. prosecutor for election fraud Cook County, Ill., 1981-83; commr., 1986-92; mem. Gov.'s Election Reform Commn., 1985; del. Dems. Abroad Dem. Conv., 1992; alderman City of Chgo., 1993-99; ptnr. Dykema Gossett Law Firm, Chgo., 1999—. Instr. internat. law Loyoa U. Chgo., Rome campus, 1981; counsel Allstate Ins. Co., 1983-91. Mem. Chgo.-Milan Sister City Com., 1988—. Mem. Am. C. of C. in Italy (mng. dir.). Office: Dykema Gossett Law Firm 10 S Wacker Dr #2300 Chicago IL 60606-7453 E-mail: crb43@aol.com.

BERNARDINO, CARLO ROBERTO, ophthalmologist; b. Manilla, Philippines, July 15, 1971; s. Vitaliano B. and Evelina Abuel Bernardino. Student, U. Alicante, Spain, 1991—91; BA in Biology, Lehigh U., 1993; MD, Jefferson Med. Coll., 1997. Intern Crozer-Chester Med. Ctr., Upland, Pa., 1997—98; resident in ophthalmology Wills Eye Hosp., Phila., 1998—2001, chief resident, 2000—01; oculoplastics fellow Mass. Eye and Ear Infirmary, Boston, 2001—03; asst. prof. Emery U. Sch. Medicine, 2003—. Contbg. editor www.medscape.com, Hillsboro, 2000—01. Author: (book) The Clinics Atlas of Office Procedures - Essentials in Ophthalmology, 2000; contbr. articles to profl. jours. Grantee Bausch & Lomb Young Investigator Travel grant, Contact Lens Assn. of Opthamologists, 2000, 2001. Office: Mass Eye and Ear Infirmary 243 Charles St Boston MA 02114 Home: 1365 B Clifton Rd NE Atlanta GA 30332 Personal E-mail: crbernardino@hotmail.com. Business E-Mail: rob_bernardino@emergehealthcare.org.

BERNAT, JAMES LAWRENCE, neurologist, educator; b. Cin., May 23, 1947; s. Mitchell Joseph and Ruth Claire (Betagole) B.; m. Judith Elaine Lenzner, June 8, 1969; children: Deborah Eden, David Clare. BA, U. Mass., 1969; MD, Cornell U., N.Y.C., 1973. Diplomate Am. Bd. Psychiatry and Neurology. Resident in medicine Dartmouth-Hitchcock Med. Ctr., Hanover, N.H., 1973-74, resident in neurology, 1974-77, staff neurologist Lebanon, 1995—, assoc. chmn. neurology sect., 1999—2002; staff neurologist VA Med. Ctr., White River Junction, Vt., 1977-94; prof. medicine Dartmouth Med. Sch., Hanover, 1991—, asst. dean, 1995—99, dir. program in med. ethics, 1995—. Author: Neurology: Problems in Primary Care, 1987, 2d edit., 1993, Ethical Issues in Neurology, 1994, 2d edit., 2002; editor (editl. bd.): Neurocritical Care; co-editor: Palliative Care in Neurology, 2004. Bd. dirs. Vt. Ethics Network, Montpelier, 1995-2000, New Eng. Organ Bank, 1999—, Hospice V.N.H., 1999-2002; mem. Dana Alliance Brain Initiatives. Fellow ACP, Am. Acad. Neurology (chair ethics, law & humanities com. 1993-03, exec. bd. 1993-97). Office: Neurology Sect Dartmouth-Hitchcock Med Ctr Lebanon NH 03756 Office Phone: 603-650-5104. Business E-Mail: bernat@dartmouth.edu.

BERNATOWICZ, FRANK ALLEN, management consultant; b. Chgo., Nov. 3, 1954; s. Chester and Pauline (Maciula) B.; m. Kathleen Ann Carlson, Apr. 29, 1978; children: Amy Elizabeth, Laura Ann. BSEE, U. Ill., 1976; MBA in Fin., Loyola U., Chgo., 1981, postgrad. in acctg., 1982-84. Registered profl. engr., Ill.; CPA, Ill. Engr. Commonwealth Edison Co., Chgo., 1976—79, gen. engr., 1979—82, prin. engr., 1982—84; sr. cons. Brenner Group, Chgo., 1984—85; supr. Ernst & Young (formerly Ernst & Whinney), Chgo., 1985, mgr., 1985—86; sr. mgr. Ernst & Young, Chgo., 1986—88, ptnr., 1989—96; prin. J. Alix & Assoc., Chgo., 1996—99; ptnr. PricewaterhouseCoopers, Chgo., 1999—2001, BDO Seidman, Chgo., 2001—03; mng. prin. FAB Adv. Svcs., LLC, Chgo., 2003—. Spkr. in field. Mem. bd. regents Mercy Boys Home, 1990—. Mem. ABA (assoc.), AICPA, Am. Bankruptcy Inst., Ill. Soc. CPAs, Nat. Soc. Profl. Engrs., Turnaround Mgmt. Assn., Comml. Law League, Am. Bankruptcy Inst., Chgo. Soc. Clubs (Met.). Avocations: golf, racquetball, computers, investments. Home: 6543 Hillcrest Dr Burr Ridge IL 60527 Office: FAB Adv Svcs 1 E Wacker Dr Ste 3300 Chicago IL 60601 Office Phone: 630-655-3474. Business E-Mail: fab@fabadvisory.com.

BERNAU, SIMON JOHN, mathematics professor; b. Wanganui, New Zealand, June 12, 1937; came to U.S., 1969; s. Earnest Lovell and Ella Mary (Mason) B.; m. Lynley Joyce Turner, Aug. 11, 1959; children: Nicola Ann, Sally Jane. B.Sc., U. Canterbury, Christchurch, New Zealand, 1958, M.Sc., 1959; BA, Cambridge (Eng.) U., 1961, PhD, 1964. Lectr. U. Canterbury, 1964-65, sr. lectr., 1965-66; prof. math. U. Otago, Dunedin, New Zealand, 1966-69; assoc. prof. U. Tex., Austin, 1969-76, prof., 1976-85; prof., head math. dept. Southwest Mo. State U., Springfield, 1986-88; prof., chmn. dept. math. scis. U. Tex., El Paso, 1988-95; dean Coll. Sci. Calif. State Poly., Pomona, 1995—2002, prof. dept. math., 2002—. Researcher numerous publs. in field, 1964—; referee profl. jours., 1965— . Gulbenkian jr. research fellow Churchill Coll., Cambridge U., 1963-64 Mem. Am. Math. Soc. (reviewer 1965—), Math. Assn. Am., London Math. Soc. Office: Calif State Poly U Coll of Sci 3801 W Temple Ave Pomona CA 91768-2557 Home: 1322 Crown Way Paso Robles CA 93446

BERNAUER, DAVID W., retail company executive; married; three children. Grad., N.D. State U., 1967, D (hon.) of Pharmacy, 2000. Pharmacist Walgreen Co., 1967-79, dist. mgr., 1979-87, regional v.p., 1987-90, v.p., treas., 1990-92, v.p. pres. purchasing, chief info. officer, 1992-94, sr. v.p., chief info. officer, 1996-99, pres., COO, 1999—2002, pres., CEO, 2002—. Bd. dirs. Students in Free Enterprise; bd. trustees Field Mus., Chgo.; co-chmn. N.D. State U. Coll. Pharm. Devel. Fund. Recipient Dist. Alumni award, N.D. State U. Mem.: Nat. Assoc. Chain Drug Stores (exec. com., bd. dirs., treasurer). Office: Walgreen Co 200 Wilmot Rd Deerfield IL 60015

BERNBACH, JOHN LINCOLN, marketing professional; b. 1944; s. William Bernbach. Grad. polit. sci., Georgetown U. Trainee account mgmt., then v.p. account services Gilbert Advt., 1966-72; with DDB Needham Worldwide, Inc. (formerly Doyle Dane Bernbach), Paris, 1972-79, London, 1979-84, pres., chief exec. officer internat. div. N.Y.C., 1984-86, pres., 1986-93, vice chmn., 1993-94; chmn., CEO The Bernbach Group, Inc., N.Y.C., 1994—; gen. ptnr. Barnet-Bernbach-Carduner LLC, N.Y.C., 2000—03; pres., COO, NTM, Inc., N.Y.C., 2003—. Office: NTM Inc 32 E 57th St 10th Fl New York NY 10022

BERND, CLIFFORD ALBRECHT, language educator; b. Bronxville, N.Y., May 14, 1929; s. Wilhelm Ludwig and Bertha Maria (Albrecht) Bernd; m. Eline Christa Schmidt-Nickels, Dec. 29, 1972; children: Matthias Albrecht, Christian Wilhelm. BA, N.Y. Univ., 1950; MA, Univ. Md., Coll. Pk., Md., 1952; PhD, Univ. Heidelberg, Heidelberg, Germany, 1958. Instr. in German Princeton Univ., Princeton, NJ, 1958—61, asst. prof. German, 1961—64; assoc. prof. of German Univ. Calif., Davis, Calif., 1964—68, prof. of German, 1968—. Vis. prof. German Univ. Leicester, England, 1977; chair Univ. Calif., Davis, Calif., 1965—76. Author: Theodor Storm's Craft of Fiction, 1963, 1966, German Poetic Realism, 1981, Poetic Realism in Scandinavia and Central Europe, 1995, Theodor Storm. The Dano-German Poet and Writer, 2003, 2d edit., 2005. Fellow, Fritz Thyssen Found., 1971; Fulbright Rsch. Scholar, Fulbright Assn. and Found., 1968. Mem.: MLA, Grillparzer Soc. (pres. 1992—), Am. Assn. of Tchrs. of German (pres NJ chpt. 1962—64), Theodor Storm Gesellschaft, Germany (corr.). Cath. Home: 1013 Plum Ln Davis CA 95616 Office: Dept of German Univ Calif 1 Shields Ave Davis CA 95616 E-mail: cabernd@ucdavis.edu.

BERNDT, ELLEN GERMAN, lawyer; b. N.Y.C., 1953; BS, Denison U., 1975; JD, Capital U., 1984. Bar: Ohio 1984. Legal asst. Borden Chem. Inc., Columbus, Ohio, 1978-84, corp. atty., 1984-90, asst. sec., corp. atty., 1990-96, corp. sec., asst. gen. counsel, 1996—. Mem. Am. Corp. Counsel Assn., Ctrl. Ohio Corp. Counsel Assn. (pres. 1997). Office: Borden Chem Inc 180 E Broad St Columbus OH 43215-3799

BERNDT, ERNST RUDOLF, economist, educator; b. Crespo, Entre Rios, Argentina, Apr. 13, 1946; came to U.S., 1949; s. Markus William and Charlotte Marie (Zimmerman) B.; m. Martha Ann Mirly, June 10, 1967 (div. 1982); children: Jeffery, Nathan; m. Joan Margaret Curran, May 15, 1994. BA with honors, Valparaiso U., 1968; MS., U. Wis., 1971, PhD, 1972; PhD (hon.), Uppsala U., 1991. Staff economist Exec. Office of the Pres. U.S. Govt., Washington, 1971-72; asst. prof. U. (Vancouver) B.C., Can., 1973-78, assoc. prof., 1978-80; prof. applied econs. MIT, Cambridge, Mass., 1980—. Dir. program on technol. progress and productivity measurement Nat. Bur. Econ. Rsch., Cambridge; rsch. assoc. Nat. Bur. Econ. Rsch., Cambridge, 1980—; acad. affiliate Analysis Group, Inc., Belmont, Mass., 1985—. Contbr. profl. articles. Most cited economist under age 40 in 1985. Mem. Am. Econ. Assn., Econometric Soc., Conf. Rsch. in Income and Wealth. Independent. Lutheran. Office: MIT Sloan Sch of Mgmt 50 Memorial Dr # E52 452 Cambridge MA 02142-1347 E-mail: ebermdt@mit.edu.

BERNE, BRUCE J., chemistry professor; BS, Bklyn. Coll., 1961; PhD (NASA fellow, NSF fellow), U. Chgo., 1964. NATO postdoctoral fellow U. Brussels, 1964-65; asst. prof. chemistry Columbia U., N.Y.C., 1966-69, assoc. prof., 1969-72, prof., 1972—98, Higgins prof. chemistry, 1998—, chmn. dept. chemistry, 2002—. Vis. prof. U. Tel Aviv, 1972-73, Sackler Disting. lectr., 1985, Miller Inst. U. Calif., Berkeley, 1993-94; vis. scientist IBM Thomas J. Watson Rsch. Labs., Yorktown, N.Y., 1990-92, 2000—; Reilly lectr. U. Notre Dame, 1998; Davidson lectr. U. Kans., 1998; Albert K. Moscowitz lectr. U. Minn., 2000; Moses Gomberg lectr. U. Mich., 2000; Joseph Huschfelder lectr. U. Wis., Madison, 2001; Joe L. Franklin Meml. lectr. Rice U., 2003. Mem. editl. bd. Jour. Statis. Physics, 1976-79, Advances in Chem. Physics, 1984—, Jour. Phys. Chemistry, 1985-88, Jour. Chem. Physics, 1985-88, Chem. Physics Letters, 2000—; assoc. editor Phys. Rev. Letters, 2000—, Procs. of NAS, Jour. Clin. Theory and Computation. Recipient Alexander von Humboldt Found. award 1998, award in theoretical chemistry Am. Chem. Soc., 1995, Joseph O. Hirschfelder prize in theoretical chemistry U. Wis., Joel Henry Hildebrand award in theoretical and exptl. chemistry of liquids Am .Chem. Soc., 2002; Alfred P. Sloan Found. fellow, 1968-71, John Simon Guggenheim Found. fellow, 1972-73. Fellow: AAAS, Am. Acad. Arts and Scis., Am. Phys. Soc.; mem.: Nat. Acad. Scis. Office: Dept Chemistry Columbia U MC 3103 3000 Broadway New York NY 10027-6941 Office Phone: 212-854-2186. Business E-Mail: berne@chem.columbia.edu.

BERNE, STANLEY, author; b. Staten Island, New York, June 8, 1923; s. William and Irene (Daniels) B.; m. Arlene (Zekowski), May 17, 1952. BS, Rutgers Univ., 1951; MA, N.Y.Univ., 1952; post grad. fellow, La. State U., 1954-59. Cert. tchr., mentally retarded, N.Y. Tchg. fellow La. State U., Baton Rouge, 1954-59; assoc. prof. English Ea. N. Mex. U., Portales, 1960-80, rsch. assoc. prof. in English, 1980—. Chmn. of the bd. Am., Canadian Publishers, Inc., Santa Fe, N. Mex., 1980-97; bd. dir. New Arts Found., Inc., Santa Fe, N. Mex., 1990—; guest lectr. U. Ams., 1965, U. S.D., 1968; Styrian Hauptshulen Paedagogische Akademie, Graz, Austria, 1969; founder, developer first dept. for tchg. mentally retarded, Dallas Pub. Sch., 1952-53. Author: A First Book of the Neo-Narrative, 1954; Cardinals and Saints, 1958; The Dialogues, 1962; The Multiple Modern Gods and Other Stories, 1964; The Unconscious Victorious and Other Stories, 1969; The New Rubaiyat of Stanley Berne, 1973; Future Lang., 1976, The Great Am. Empire, 1981; Every Person's Little Book of P-L-U-T-O-N-I-U-M, 1992; Alphabet Soup, 1998; To Hell with Optimism!!, 1996; Gravity Drag, 1998; Swimming to Significance, 1999; At One With Birds, 2000; Empire Sweets-Or-How I Learned to Live and Love in the Greatest Empire on Earth, 2003; Legal Tender or It's All About Money!, 2003; You and Me or How to Survive in the Greatest Empire on Earth!, 2003; (inclusion in anthologies) Trace, 1965; First Person Intense, 1978; Breakthrough Fictioneers, 1979; American Writing Today, 1992; Dictionary of the Avant-Gardes, 1993; New World Writing II, 1957; The Living Underground, 1999; prodr. and co-host (with Arlene Zekowski) nine Part TV Series for PBS, Future Writing Today; The Am. Empire, a trilogy. Served in USAF, 1942-46, PTO. Decorated Medal of Philippine Liberation; World War II Victory medal; recipient four Rsch. Awards, Ea. N. Mex. U.; recipient St. John Perse Award for internat. prose, 1998. Mem. PEN, com. of small mag., editors, poets, New Eng. Small Press Assn.; Rio Grande Writers Assn.; Santa Fe Writers Coop. Avocations: painting, design, collage. Home: PO Box 4595 Santa Fe NM 87502-4595 Address: Rising Tide Press N Mex PO Box 6136 Santa Fe NM 87502-6136

BERNER, ANDREW JAY, library director, writer; b. Bronx, NY, Apr. 5, 1952; s. Bernard and Phyllis (Stern) B. BA in History cum laude, Herbert H. Lehman Coll., 1974, MA in History, 1979; MS in Libr. and Info. Sci., Pratt Inst., 1982. Tchr. NYC Bd. Edn., NY, 1979-82; asst. libr. The Univ. Club Libr., NYC, 1982-84, assoc. libr., 1984-86, acting dir., 1986-87, dir., 1987-93, dir., curator of collections, 1993—. Co-founder, dir. OPL Resources, Ltd., 1984-99. Author: Time Management in the Small Library, 1987, (with Guy St. Clair) The Best of OPL, 1990, The Best of OPL II, 1997, Time Management in Libraries and Information Services, 1999, The University Club: An Architectural Celebration, 1999, Treasures of The University Club, 1999; author, editor The Illuminator, 1990—, The Univ. Club Libr. Quar., 1984-90; editor (newsletter) The One-Person Libr., 1984-98; contbr. articles to profl. jours. Fellow Spl. Librs. Assn. (chair, chair-elect mus., arts and humanities divsn. 1990-92, pres.-elect, pres. NY chpt. 1994-96, bylaws chair, pub. rels. chair, dir. awards); mem. Century Assn., Grolier Club. Office: The Univ Club Libr 1 W 54th St New York NY 10019-5404

BERNER, FREDERIC GEORGE, JR., lawyer; b. Washington, May 7, 1943; s. Frederic George and Florence Grace (Carlton) B.; m. Lorraine Ann Ouellette, Sept. 28, 1968; children: Frederic George, III, Christina Lorraine, Jennifer Jane. BA, Middlebury Coll., 1965; MBA, Am. U., 1970; JD, George Washington U., 1973. Bar: D.C. 1973, U.S. Dist. Ct. (D.C. dist.) 1973, U.S. Ct. Appeals (D.C. cir.) 1974, U.S. Ct. Appeals (4th cir.) 1977, U.S. Ct. Appeals (11th cir.) 1984, U.S. Ct. Appeals (10th cir.) 1994, U.S. Ct. Appeals (7th cir.) 2001, U.S. Supreme Ct. 1980. Econ. intelligence officer CIA, Washington, 1965-67, 70; assoc. Sidley & Austin, Washington, 1973-80; ptnr. Sidley Austin Brown & Wood LLP, Washington, 1980—. Contbr. articles to profl. jours.; bd. editl. advisors Pub. Utilities Fortnightly, 1992-2000. Gen. counsel, bd. dirs. Washington chpt. Nat. Hemophilia Found., 1976—80. 1st lt. U.S. Army, 1967—70. Mem.: ABA, Charitable Found. of Energy Bar Assn. (bd. dirs. 2004—), Found. of Energy Law Jour. (bd. dirs. 2004—), Natural Gas Roundtable, D.C. Bar, Energy Bar Assn. (pres., bd. dirs. 2004—), Order of Coif. Republican. Presbyterian. Home: 7605 Glenbrook Rd Bethesda MD 20814-1319 Office: Sidley Austin Brown & Wood LLP 1501 K St NW Washington DC 20005 Office Phone: 202-736-8232. E-mail: fberner@sidley.com.

BERNER, LEO DE WITTE, JR., retired oceanographer; b. Pasadena, Calif., Feb. 11, 1922; s. Leo De Witte and Maude Alena (Wright) B.; m. Arvetta Jo Hankins, June 28, 1947; children: Jo Anne Berner Thomas, Ernestine Elizabeth Berner Ice. BA, Pomona Coll., 1943; MS, UCLA-Scripps Instn. Oceanography, 1952, PhD, 1957. Fishery biologist U.S. Fish and Wildlife Service, La Jolla, Calif., 1957-58; asst. research biologist Scripps Instn. Oceanography, La Jolla, 1958-60, acting curator marine invertebrates, 1960-61; vis. asst. prof. U. Oreg., Oreg. Inst. Marine Sci., 1961; asso. program dir. NSF, Washington, 1961-65; adminstrv. scientist Tex. A&M U., College Station, 1965-66, asso. prof., 1966-72; asst. dean Tex. A&M U. (Grad. Coll.), 1967-71, assoc. dean, 1971-84, dean, 1984-87, prof. oceanography, 1972-87, prof. emeritus, dean emeritus, 1987—. Vol. George Bush Presdl. Libr. Archives, 1990-2002. Served with USNR, 1943-47. Fellow AAAS; mem. Am. Soc. Limnology and Oceanography, Oceanographic Soc., Assn. Tex. Grad. Schs. (1st v.p. 1981-82, pres. 1982-83), Sigma Xi. Home: 514 Helen Greathouse Cir Midland TX 79707-6116 Personal E-mail: bunsen@cox.net.

BERNER, ROBERT FRANK, managerial statistics educator, administrator; b. Cleve., Nov. 30, 1917; s. Frank Otto and Marie (Gideon) B.; m. Ruth Harriet Levis, Nov. 6, 1943 (dec. Jan. 2005); children: Robert Frank, Mary Elizabeth, John David, Jean Harriet (dec.). BS, U. Buffalo, 1939, MBA, 1948; PhD, U. Chgo., 1961. Tchr. Palmyra (N.Y.) H.S., 1939-41; instr. stats. U. Buffalo, 1946-48, acting chmn. dept., 1948-49; asst. dean U. Buffalo (Evening Coll.), 1949-52, asst. prof. stats., 1952-63; assoc. prof. dept. mgmt. sci. SUNY, Buffalo, 1963-65, prof. mgmt. sci. and ops. analysis, 1965-81, prof. emeritus, 1981—; pres. emeritus Ctr. of SUNY, Buffalo, 1983-85; chmn. MBA program com., 1976-81. Adj. prof. internat. exec. program, 1982-90, acting dean divsn. continuing edn., 1952-55, dean, 1955-76; Fulbright prof. Robert Coll., Istanbul, Turkey, 1968-69, U. Nairobi, Kenya, 1975-76 Chmn. adult edn. com. Cmty. Welfare Coun. Buffalo and Erie County, 1962-64; bd. dirs. Creative Edn. Found., 1969-89, emeritus trustee, 1990; bd. dirs. Ch. Mission Help Western N.Y., 1990-96, sec., 1992, treas., 1993-96; mem. Rep. Coun. and Fund. Mgmt. Adv. Com., Canterbury Woods, western N.Y., 1999-2003. Capt. F.A., 10th Mountain divsn. AUS, 1941-45. Decorated Bronze Star, Silver Star; named to Creative Problem Solving Inst. Hall of Fame, 2005. Mem. AAUP, Assn. Univ. Evening Colls. (past pres.), Nat. Univ. Extension Assn., Am. Coun. Edn., Assn. Continuing Higher Edn., Am. Assn. Univ. Adminstrs., Am. Soc. Tng. Dirs. (chpt. sec. 1952-56), Equality Club (pres. 1986-87), Theta Chi, Beta Gamma Sigma, Alpha Sigma Lambda (past nat. pres.) Episcopalian (warden Calvary Ch. 1973-74, 76-77, 86-88, treas. 1996-2000, mem. commn. ministry Diocese Western N.Y. 1971, 95—, chmn. commn. on continuing edn. 1974-76, diocesan coun. 1988-91, diocese planning and vision com. 1989-92). Home: 715 Renaissance Dr Apt 113 Williamsville NY 14221-8033 E-mail: berner@buffalo.edu.

BERNER, ROBERT LEE, JR., lawyer; b. Chgo., Dec. 9, 1931; s. Robert Lee and Mary Louise (Kenney) B.; m. Sheila Marie Reynolds, Jan. 12, 1957; children: Mary, Louise, Robert, Sheila, John. AB, U. Notre Dame, 1953; LL.B., Harvard U., 1956. Bar: Ill. 1956, NY 1989. With Petit, Olin, Overmyer & Fazio, Chgo., 1957—63, Baker & McKenzie, Chgo., 1963—; ptnr., 1964—2000; sr. counsel, 2000—. Mem. vis. com. Northwestern U. Law Sch., 1981-85; mem. legal adv. com. N.Y. Stock Exch., 1995-98. Mem. vis. com. U. Chgo. Div. Sch., 1972—, chmn., 2001—; mem. legal aid com. Met. Family Svcs., Chgo., 1972—, chmn., 1991—93; mem. adv. bd. Cath. Charities, Chgo., 1971—, Loyola U., 1972—; mem. coun. Coll. Arts and Letters, U. Notre Dame, 2001—; trustee Cath. Theol. Union, Chgo., 1999—; bd. dirs. Link Unltd., Chgo., 1972—, pres., 1990—92; bd. dir. World Trade Ctr. of Chgo., 1989. Mem. ABA (chmn. bus. law sect. 1987-88), Ill. State Bar Assn., Chgo. Bar Assn., Legal Club Chgo. (pres. 1974-75), Law Club Chgo. (pres. 1991-92). Home: 932 Euclid Ave Winnetka IL 60093-1418 Office: Baker & McKenzie One Prudential Plz 130 E Randolph St Ste 3500 Chicago IL 60601-6342 Office Phone: 312-861-2890. Business E-Mail: robert.l.berner@bakernet.com.

BERNER HARRIS, CYNTHIA KAY, librarian; b. Concordia, Kans., Aug. 31, 1958; d. William Clifford and Donna Darlene (Brown) B.; m. Dwight Harris, May 1, 1999. AA, Cottey Coll., 1978; BA, U. Kans., 1980; MALS, U. Denver, 1981. System cons. Panhandle Libr. Network, Scottsbluff, Nebr., 1981-82; dir. Winfield (Kans.) Pub. Libr., 1982-84; from Westlink br. mgr. to coord. ext. svcs. Wichita (Kans.) Pub. Libr., 1984-95, coord. adminstrv. svcs., 1995—2000, dir. of librs., 2000—. Editor Propeller mag., 1995-96 (Jr. League Wichita); editor (newsletter) LWV, Wichita Met., 1993. Pres. PEO Sisterhood (chpt. IM), Wichita, 1989—90; active Jr. League Wichita; project chair STARBASE, 1997—98, dir. cmty. rels., 1998—99; trustee at large Bibliog. Ctr. for Rsch., 2001—05, exec. com., 2002—04; tech. adv. bd. City of Wichita, 2000—; fin. chair Nat. Conf. for Cmty. and Justice Walk, 2003. Mem.: ALA, Kans. Libr. Assn. (chair pub. libr. sect. 1988—89, mem. legis. com. 1997—2001, nominating com. 1998—99, mem. legis. com. 2002—), Mountain Plains Libr. Assn. (chair profl. devel. grants com. 1983—84, 1986—87, chair pub. libr. sect. 1988—89, chair intellectual freedom com. 1988—90, sec. 1996—97, mem. nominating com. 1998—2000), Pub. Libr. Assn. (dir. pub. libr. sys. sect. 1995—98, dir. pub. libr. sys. com. 1998—2001). Methodist. Home: 6418 Oneil St Wichita KS 67212-6327 Office: Wichita Pub Libr 223 Main St Wichita KS 67202 E-mail: ictbooks@yahoo.com.

BERNERS-LEE, TIMOTHY JOHN, inventor of world wide web, research scientist, writer; b. London, Eng., June 8, 1955; BA with honors, Queens Coll., Oxford U., England, 1976; DFA (hon.), Parsons Sch. Design, N.Y., 1996; DU (hon.), Essex U., 1998, So. Cross. U., 1998, Open U., 2000; DLaw (hon.), Columbia U., 2001; DSc (hon.), Southampton U., 1996, Oxford U., 2001, U. Port Elizabeth, 2001. With Plessey Telecom. Ltd., Dorset, England, 1976—78, D.G. Nash Ltd., Dorset, England, 1978—80; ind. cons. CERN, European Particle Physics Lab., Geneva, 1980; tech. design cons. Image Computer Sys. Ltd., 1981—84; fellow CERN, European Particle Physics Lab., Geneva, 1984; dir. World Wide Web Consortium MIT, Cambridge, Mass., 1994—, 3Com Founders chair & sr. rsch. scientist, Lab. Computer Sci., 1999—. Author: Weaving the Web, 1999. Co-recipient ACM Software Sys. award, 1995, Prize for Sci. and Tech. Rsch., Prince of Asturias Found., 2002; named to Order of the British Empire, 1997; recipient Young Innovator of Yr., Kilby Found., 1995, hon. Prix Ars Electronica, 1995, IEEE Koji Kobayashi Computers and Comm. award, 1997, Duddell Medal, Inst. Physics, 1997, Disting. Svc. award, Interactive Svcs. Assn., 1997, MCI Computerworld/Smithsonian award for Leadership in Innovation, 1997, Columbus prize, Internat. Comm. Inst., 1997, Charles Babbage award, 1998, Mountbatten medal, Elec. Coun., 1998, Lord Lloyd of Kilgerran prize, Found. for Sci. and Tech., 1998, Lifetime Achievement award in Tech. Excellence, PC Mag., 1998, The Eduard Rhein Tech. award, 1998, Paul Evan Peters award of ARL, Educause and CNI, 2000, Pioneer award, Elec. Freedom Found., 2000, George R. Stibitz Computer Pioneer award, Am. Computer Mus., 2000, Spl. award for Outstanding Contbn., World Television Forum, 2000, Sir Frank Whittle medal, Royal Acad. Engring., 2001, Japan prize, Sci. and Tech. Found. Japan, 2002, Albert medal, Royal Soc. for the Encouragement of Art, Manufactures and Commerce, 2002, Millennium Tech. Prize, Finnish Tech. Award Found., 2004; fellow Marconi Found., 2002; MacArthur fellowship, 1998. Fellow: British Computer Soc., Royal Soc., Instn. Elec. Engrs. (hon.); mem.: Am. Acad. Arts & Scis. Achievements include invention of the World Wide Web in 1991; knighted by Queen Elizabeth II in 2004. Office: World Wide Web Consortium MIT/200 Technology Square Cambridge MA 02139

BERNET, MICHAEL MEIR MANFRED, psychologist, writer; s. Julius YomTov Bernet and Charlotte Koenigshoefer (Stepmother); m. Sheila Siegel, Sept. 13, 1998; m. Veda Saul, Apr. 6, 1952 (div.); m. Rena Renee Frumah Rickler, Mar. 0, 1960 (div.); children: Yoram, Ilan Dov, Eytan; 1 child, Miriam Miri Arie-Nissenboim. BA, SUNY, Albany, 1978; MA, So. Conn. State U., 1980; PhD, CUNY, 1980. Asst. civil engr. various orgns., England, 1951—55, 1955—58; freelance reporter Eilat, 1958—62; editor, pub. Hashavu'a Be'Eilat, 1959—60; free-lance writer, editor, translator, reviewer NYC, 1962—70; programming writer IBM, Yorktown Heights, 1968—69; dir., trainer, facilitator Tivyon Growth Ctr., Kfar Shmaryahu, Israel, 1971—77; sch. psychologist Bd. of Edn., NYC, 1983—95; psychotherapist Inst. Somat Awareness, 1979—2000; ret. Author: (non-fiction) The Time of the Burning Sun, (non-fiction, update of earlier work) The Time of the Burning Sun: Six Days of War, Twelve Weeks of Hope; translator (and updater): (non-fiction) Between East and West: History of the Jews of North Africa; ghost writer (autobiography) Cookie; editor (and rewriter): (non-fiction) Why Viet Nam?. Presenter, mentor, discussant Internat. Assn. Jewish Geneal. Socs., 1999—2005. With Israel Def. Forces, 1948—49. Achievements include research in Style in the Perception of Affact and its Relation to Mental Health. Personal E-mail: mbernet@aol.com.

BERNET, WILLIAM, psychiatrist; b. Omaha, Nov. 25, 1941; s. Francis Herbert and Florence Anne Bernet; m. Susan Andree Scully, Jan. 28, 1978; children: Henry Gardner, Alice Caroline. MD, Harvard Med. Sch., Boston, 1967. Diplomate Am. Bd. of Forensic Psychiatry, 1987. Dir., divsn. of forensic psychiatry Vanderbilt U. Sch. of Medicine, Nashville, Tenn., 2003—. Office: Vanderbilt University School of Medicine 1601 Twenty-Third Ave South Nashville TN 37212 Office Phone: 615-327-7130. E-mail: william.bernet@vanderbilt.edu.

BERNEY, BOB, film company executive; b. Okla., 1954; m. Jeanne Reinhart; children: Sean, Liam. BA in Film, U. Tex., 1976. Mgr. Greenway Theater, Houston, Showcase Theater, Dallas; owner Inwood Theater, Dallas; founder Inwood Films; sr. v.p. mktg. and distbn. IFC Films, N.Y.C., 2000—02; ptnr. Newmarket Films, Beverly Hills, Calif., 2002—. Cons. Memento Newmarket Films. Recipient Trailblazer award, Deep Ellum Film Festival, 2003. Office: Newmarket Films 202 N Canon Dr Beverly Hills CA 90210

BERNFELD, GERALD E., editor, writer, retired nursing educator; b. New Britain, Conn., Nov. 2, 1939; s. Edward Emil Bernfeld and Helene Betty Jenosky; m. Elizabeth Linda Jack, July 11, 1964; children: Edward Gerald, Michael Christopher, Maria Helena Flaherty. AB, Thomas Edison State Coll., Trenton, NJ, 1973; diploma in nursing, 2076th USAR Sch., Wilmington, DE, 1981; diploma in Russian studies, Ind. U., Bloomington, 1961. LPN, Del., 1981, N.J., 1981, N.Y., 1981. Intelligence rsch. analyst USAF Fgn. Tech. Divsn., Dayton, Ohio, 1965—67; transl. editor, mgr. Frank C. Farnham Co., Philadelphia, Pa., 1968—72; sr. clin. info. scientist Squibb Inst., Princeton, NJ, 1972—75; clin. data mgr. E.R. Squibb and Sons, Princeton, NJ, 1976—79; clin. svcs. mgr. Wyeth-Ayerst Rsch., Radnor, Pa., 1979—84, clin. compliance mgr., 1984—95; rsch. adminstrn. mgr. Wyeth-Ayerst, Radnor, Pa., 1995—97. Chief wardmaster, chief med. instr. USAR. Contbr. articles to profl. jours. Master sgt. USAR. Mem.: Drug Info. Assn. (spkr.), Am. Translators Assn. (past chpt. v.p.), Am. Med. Writers Assn. (past chpt. v.p.). Roman Catholic. Avocations: military enthusiast, cartoonist, writing, linguistics, travel. Home: 1503 Cliff Road Wynnewood PA 19096-3530

BERNFIELD, SUSAN, playwright, performing company executive; b. Bethesda, Md., July 1, 1964; d. Merton R. and Audrey Bernfield; m. Claude M. Millman, July 13, 1991; children: Milo Robin Bernfield-Millman, Beattie John Bernfield-Millman. BA, U. Pa., 1986. Cert. actor Cir. in the Sq. Profl. Workshop, N.Y., 1990. Artistic dir. New Georges, N.Y.C., 1992—. Sec. bd. dirs. Alliance of Resident Theatres, N.Y.C., 1998—. Prodr.: (plays) 25 premiere prodns.; author: (introduction) Women Playwrights: The Best of 2002, (plays) Barking Girl, Out From Under It (Vital Theater Co.), Tracy Petunia, Nice Chair (New Georges), etc. Bd. dirs. N.Y. Women's Agenda, N.Y.C., 2003—04. Recipient OBIE award, The Village Voice, 1996; O'Neill Playwrights Conf. fellowship, Eugene O'Neill Theater Ctr., 2003. Democrat. Office: New Georges 109 W 27th St Ste 9A New York NY 10001

BERNHAGEN, DEBBIE ANNE, middle school educator; b. Agusta, Ga., Aug. 23, 1958; d. August T. and Maria C. (Obidienté) B. BS in Phys. Edn., U. S.C., 1981, Interdisciplinary MA in Phys. Edn., 1990. Cert. tchr., S.C.; nat. bd. cert. tchr. in phys. edn.; cert. water safety instr. and trainer, lifeguard tng. instr. ARC. Student trainer women's athletic dept. U. S.C., Columbia, 1979-81, grad. asst., 1981-82; fitness dir. Nautilus, Columbia, 1982-83; water safety instr. trainer phys. edn.-health, athletic dir., dept. chmn., coach Richland County Sch. Dist. 2, Columbia, 1983—; cashier, asst. bookkeeper Piggly Wiggly, Columbia, S.C., 1976-79. Pool mgr. Columbia Parks and Recreation Dept., summers 1985—, Recreation vol. Midlands Ctr., Columbia, summers 1973-74. Named Outstanding Mid. Sch. Phys. Edn. Tchr. of Yr., State of S.C., 1991, 99, Tchr. of Yr., Summit Pky., 1991, Red Cross Vol. of Yr., 1998. Mem. AAHPER and Dance, NEA, S.C. Assn. Phys. Edn., Health, Recreation and Dance, Nat. Athletic Trainers Assn., S.C. Edn. Assn. Avocations: swimming, softball, physical fitness, camping, guitar. Home: 710 Westover Rd Columbia SC 24210 Office Phone: 803-699-3580 X 3419. E-mail: dbernhag@spm.richland2.org.

BERNHAGEN, LILLIAN FLICKINGER, retired school health consultant; b. Cleve., Oct. 1, 1916; d. Norman Henry and Bertha May (Rogers) Flickinger; m. Ralph John Bernhagen, Sept. 2, 1940; children: Ralph, Janet Elizabeth Darling, Penelope Anne Braat. Student, Ohio Wesleyan U., 1934—37; BS, RN, Ohio State U., 1940, MA, 1958; postgrad., LaVerne Coll., 1972—73. Cert. health edn. specialist; cert. holistic coach Journeys of Wisdom Inst. Asst. dir. Kiwanis Health Camp for Underprivileged Children, Steubenville, Ohio, summer 1940; asst. dir. nurses Jefferson Davis Hosp., Houston, 1940-41; ARC instr. Ohio State U., 1943, 63, elem. edn. lectr., 1970, health edn. instr., 1976-77; dir. health svcs. Worthington (Ohio) City Schs., 1951-76; spl. cons. venereal disease and sex edn. Ohio Dept. Health, 1976-82; sch. health cons., 1976-98; vice chmn. medicine, edn. com. on sch. and coll. health AMA, 1976-78, chmn., 1978-80. Author: Sex Education: Understanding Growth and Social Development, 1968, What A Miracle You Are-Boys, 1968, 3d rev. edit., 1986, What A Miracle You Are-Girls, 1968, 3d rev. edit., 1986, Toward a Reverence for Life, 1971, Personality, Sexuality and Stereotyping, 1974, (with others) Growth Patterns and Sex Education: A Suggested Curriculum Guide K-12, 1967; contbr. articles to profl. jours., mags. Bd. dirs. Hearing and Speech Ctr. of Columbus and Franklin County, 1954-57, sec., 1957; mem. nat. adv. com. Nat. Ctr. for Health Edn., 1978-82; sec.-tres. Ohio Wesleyan U. Class of 38, 1968-78, 83-88; bd. dirs. V.D. Hotline Columbus and Franklin County, 1974-87, bd. expansion chmn., 1978-85, pres., 1985-86; mem. profl. adv. com. Ptnrs. Home Health Inc., 1991-97; mem. Worthington Hist. Soc., Doll Docent, 1982—; mem King Ave. United Meth. Ch., 1938—, mem. marriage counseling com., 1997-98, mem. choir, 1950—2004, pres., 1961-63, pastor/parish rels. com., 1985-88, bd. trustees, 1989-92, adminstrv. coun., 1992-98, homosexual study com., 1998-99, edn. commn., 1982-85, nominations and pers., 1992-94; treas. Franklin County Women's Golf Tournament, 1992. Recipient Centennial award Ohio State U., 1970, Outstanding Alumna award Ohio State U. Sch. Nursing, 1964, Disting. Service award Mich. Sch. Nurses Assn., 1972, hon. mention La Sertoma Internat. Woman of Yr., 1972, Alumni award of hon. Ohio Wesleyan U., 1998 Fellow Am. Sch. Health Assn. (v.p. 1974, pres. 1976, governing coun. 1973-88, chmn. health guidance in sex edn. com. 1963-67, 71-77, chmn. sr. adv. coun. 1983-89, Disting. Svc. award 1969, Howe award 1979, cert. of merit, 1985, mem. awards com. 1986-89, mem. hist. com. 1989—, constn. and bylaws com. 1997-99), APHA (chmn. com. on urban health problems 1972); mem. NEA (life, ret.), Sex Edn. and Info. Coun. of U.S., Worthington Edn. Assn. (v.p. 1961-62, Tchr. of Yr. 1972-73), Ctrl. Ohio Tchrs. Assn. (chmn. sch. health svcs. sect. 1963), Ohio State U. Women's Golf Assn. (chmn. 1973, parliamentarian 1988—), Ohio Wesleyan U. Alumni Assn. (bd. dirs., chmn. alumni recognition com. 1994-95, chmn. bylaws revision com. 1991-96, mem. orgn. com. 1994-95), Columbus Women's Dist. Golf Assn. (treas. 1985, sec. 1987, v.p. 1989, pres. 1990, adv. bd. 1991-98, parliamentarian 1996-98), Chi Omega (pres. Columbus Alumnae chpt. 1947-49, fin. adv. Ohio Wesleyan U. 1964-76, Outstanding Alumna of Yr. State of Ohio 1986), Ohio State U. Nursing Alumni Soc. (Disting. Alumni award, 2004), Pi Lambda Theta (citation award 1971, mem. program com. 1986-89, chmn. by laws revision com. 1990-2000, parliamentarian), Journeys of Wisdom, Monnett Club, Worthington Women's Club, Sigma Theta Tau, Phi Delta Kappa. Home and Office: 5916 Linworth Rd Worthington OH 43085-3357 E-mail: lfbern@aol.com.

BERNHARD, ALEXANDER ALFRED, lawyer; b. New Orleans, Sept. 20, 1936; s. John Helenus and Dora (Solosko) B.; m. Martha Ruggles, Nov. 21, 1959 (div.); children: John, Jason, Frederic; m. Joyce Harrington, Dec. 30, 1976 (div.); m. Myra Mayman, Nov. 2, 1986. BS, MIT, 1957; LLB, Harvard U., 1964. Bar: Calif. 1964, Oreg. 1965, Mass. 1966, N.H. 1991. Law clk. to judge U.S. Ct. Appeals (9th cir.), 1964-65; assoc. Johnson, Johnson & Harrang, Eugene, Oreg., 1965-66, Bingham, Dana & Gould, Boston, 1966-71, Hale and Dorr, Boston, 1971-73, jr. ptnr., 1973-75, sr. ptnr., 1975—2004, of counsel, 2005—. Trustee, bd. dirs. Mass. Eye and Ear Infirmary, chmn., 1992-96, chmn. emeritus, 1996—. Lt. (submarines) USNR, 1957-61. Mem.: ABA, Boston Bar Assn., Longwood Cricket Club, Union Boat Club. Office: Wilmer Cutler Pickering Hale and Dorr LLP 60 State St Boston MA 02109-1803 Office Phone: 617-526-6220. Business E-Mail: alexander.bernhard@wilmerhale.com.

BERNHARD, BERL, lawyer; b. N.Y.C., Sept. 7, 1929; s. Morris and Celia B.; children— Peter Berl, Robin Churchill, Andrew Morris BA in Govt. magna cum laude (Rufus Choate scholar), Dartmouth Coll., 1951, A.M., 1974; JD, Yale U., 1954; LL.D., Central Ohio State Coll., 1963. Bars: D.C., 1954, U.S. Supreme Ct., 1957. Assoc. Davis, Polk, Wardwell, Sunderland & Kiendl, N.Y.C., summer 1953; law clk. to U.S. dist. judge, 1954-56; assoc Turney & Turney, 1956-59; staff dir. U.S. Commn. on Civil Rights, 1961-63; ptnr. Hughes, Hubbard & Reed, Washington, 1972-75, Verner, Liipfert, Bernhard, McPherson and Hand and predecessor firms, 1959, 63—, chmn.; ptnr. Fed. Affairs & Legis., Govt. Affairs practices DLA Piper Rudnick Gray Cary, Washington, 2004—. Bd. dirs. UNC Inc.; gen. counsel, dir. Evening Star Newspaper Co., Washington, 1974-78, WJLA, Inc., Washington, 1976-80; staff dir. U.S. Commn. on Civil Rights, 1961-63, cons. under sec. polit. affairs Sec. State, 1963-65; adj. prof. law Georgetown U. Law Ctr., 1963-65; spl. counsel, dir. The White Ho. Conf. "To Fulfill These Rights," 1966; counsel Lawyers Com. for Civil Rights Under Law. Contbr. articles to profl. jours. Gen. counsel Dem. Senatorial Campaign Com., 1965-71; spl. counsel Dem. Nat. Com., 1965-71; staff dir. Senator Edmund S. Muskie, 1971, nat. campaign mgr., 1972; mem. D.C. Bd. Higher Edn., chmn. fin. com.; trustee Dartmouth Coll., 1974-84, Joe Davies Found., 1968-87; sr. advisor to Sec. of State, 1980-81; chmn., CEO Washington Federals, U.S. Football League; bd. dirs. Harriman Polit. Action Com., 1980-89; mem. bd. visitors Nelson A. Rockefeller Ctr. for Social Scis., 1983-90; mem. bd. overseers The Amos Tuck Sch. Bus. Adminstrn., Dartmouth Coll., 1985-90; bd. dirs. Aspen Inst., 1988—, chmn., 1991-96; trustee Fed. City Coun., 1988-92; bd. trustees Muskie Found., 1997. Recipient Arthur S. Flemming award D.C. Jr. C. of C., 1960, Ten Outstanding Young Men award U.S. Jr. C. of C., 1962 Mem. Am. Bar Assn., Bar Assn. D.C., Assn. Interstate Practitioners, Nat. Panel Arbitrators, Am. Arbitration Assn., Casque and Gauntlet, Phi Beta Kappa, Sigma Nu, Phi Delta Phi Clubs: Metropolitan (Washington); Yale (N.Y.C.). Home: 1693 Epping Farms Rd Annapolis MD 21401-6673 Office: DLA Piper Rudnick Gray Cary 1200 19th St NW Washington DC 20036-2412 Office Phone: 202-861-3839. Office Fax: 202-689-7494. Business E-Mail: berl.bernhard@dlapiper.com.*

BERNHARD, CATHERINE CLARE, lawyer; b. Houston, June 24, 1962; d. Jim and Virginia Bernhard. BA, U. Mass., 1984; JD, U. Tex., 1987. Bar: Tex. 1987, cert.: Tex. Bd. Legal Specialization (Criminal Law) 1996. Staff atty. Dallas County Criminal Dist. Courts, Dallas, 1987—90; lawyer Dallas County Pub. Defenders Office, Dallas, 1990—2002; pvt. practice Law Office of Catherine Bernhard, Red Oak, Tex., 2002—. Mem.: Nat. Assn. Criminal Def. Lawyers, Tex. Criminal Def. Lawyers Assn., Dallas County Criminal Def. Lawyers Assn. Office: Law Office of Catherine Bernhard PO Box 2817 Red Oak TX 75154 Office Phone: 972-617-5548. Home Fax: 972-617-6055; Office Fax: 972-617-6055. Business E-Mail: cbern@worldlogon.com.

BERNHARD, HERBERT ASHLEY, lawyer; b. Jersey City, Sept. 24, 1927; s. Richard C. and Amalie (Lobl) B.; m. Nancy Ellen Hirschaut, Aug. 8, 1954; children: Linda, Alison, Jordan, Melissa. Student, Mexico City Coll., 1948; BEE, N.J. Inst. Tech., 1949; MA in Math., Columbia U., 1950; JD cum laude, U. Mich., 1957. Bar: Calif. 1958, U.S. Dist. Ct. (cen. dist.) Calif. 1958, U.S. Dist. Ct. (no., ea. and so. dists.) Calif. 1963, U.S. Ct. Claims 1966, U.S. Dist. Ct. (ea. and we. dists.) Wis. 1982, U.S. Dist. Ct. (ea. and we. dists.) Ark. 1982, U.S. Dist. Ct. Nebr. 1982, U.S. Ct. Internat. Trade 1979, U.S. Tax Ct. 1969, U.S. Ct. Appeals (2d, 3d, 4th, 5th, 7th, 8th, 9th, 10th, 11th and D.C. cirs.) 1969, U.S. Supreme Ct. 1965. Research engr. Curtis-Wright Co., Caldwell, N.J., 1950-52, Boeing Aircraft Co., Cape Canaveral, Fla., 1952-55; assoc. O'Melveny & Myers, Los Angeles, 1957-62; ptnr. Greenberg, Bernhard, et al, Los Angeles, 1962-85, Jeffer, Mangels, Butler & Marmaro, Los Angeles, 1985—. Instr. math. U. Fla., Cape Canaveral, 1952-55; instr. elec. engring. U. Mich., Ann Arbor, 1955-57; referee L.A. Superior Ct., 1985—, arbitrator, 1988—, judge pro tem, 1988—; judge pro tem L.A. Mcpl. Ct., 1985—, Beverly Hills Mcpl. Ct., 1989—, Malibu Mcpl. Ct., 1994—. Contbr. articles to profl. jours. Chmn. adv. com. Skirball Mus., 1976-98; bd. overseers Hebrew Union Coll., 1976-98. With USAF, 1946-47. Recipient Disting. Achievement award N.J. Inst. Tech., 1998. Mem. Jewish Publ. Soc. (trustee 1986-96). Office: 78557 Alliance Way Palm Desert CA 92211-3069

BERNHARD, JAMES M., JR., engineering executive; m. Dana Bernhard. Grad., La. State U., 1976. Founder The Shaw Group, Inc., Baton Rouge, 1987—, CEO, 1987—, pres., 1987—2003, chmn., 1990—, La. State Dem. Party, 2005—. Mem. Pipe Fabricators Inst. Mem. Com. of 100 for State of La.; chmn. Select Coun. for Revenues and Expenditures for La.'s Future; active La. State U. Alumni Assn., Tiger Athletic Found., La. Tech. U. Found., St. George Cath. Ch. and Sch., Ducks Unltd., Krewe of Endymion; supporter United Way, Baton Rouge Area Found., St. George Cath. Ch., St. George Cath. Sch., East La. Tech. U. Named Marketer of Yr., 1994, Entrepreneur of Yr. in La., 1995, Perpetual Founder of Cath. H.S.; named one of Top Ten CEOs, Greater Baton Rouge Bus. Report, 1993; recipient Prevent Child Abuse La.'s Corp. Champions for Children award, 1997, Ernst and Young Entrepreneru of Yr. award, 2001, Ace award, La. State U. Golf Program, Tiger Athletic Found. Augie Cross Meml. Mem. of Yr. award. Mem.: Associated Building Contractors, American Welding Society, Associated Gen. Contractors. Avocations: golf, duck hunting, horseback riding, bill fishing, coaching Little League sports. Office: Shaw Group Inc 4171 Essen Ln Baton Rouge LA 70809 Office Phone: 800-747-3322, 225-932-2500. Office Fax: 225-932-2661.

BERNHARD, JEFFREY DAVID, dermatologist, educator, editor; b. Buffalo, Oct. 31, 1951; AB, Harvard Coll., 1973; MD, Harvard Med. Sch., 1978. Diplomate Am. Bd. Dermatology. Knox fellow St. John's Coll. Cambridge U., England, 1973—74; chief resident dermatology Harvard Med. Sch., Boston, 1982; fellow photomedicine Mass. Gen. Hosp., 1983; mem. faculty Med. Sch. U. Mass., Worcester, 1983—86, chief dermatology, assoc. prof. Sch. Medicine, 1986—2002, assoc. dean for admissions Med. Sch., 1989—95, prof. Med. Sch., 1992—2002, acad. chief dermatology, 2002—. Author: Itch: Mechanisms and Management of Pruritus, 1994; asst. editor Jour. Am. Acad. Dermatology, 1993-98, editor, 1998—; mem. editl. bd. Jour. European Acad. Dermatology and Venereology, Yearbook of Cancer, 1981-88, Yearbook of Dermatology, 1988-97, Internat. Jour. Dermatology, Jour. Geriat. Dermatology, 1993-97. Named J. Graham Smith, Jr., hon. lectr., 2000, Narins Meml. Lectr., 2001, Novy lectr., U. Calif., Davis, 2002, Lorincz lectr., Chgo. Derm. Soc., 2002, Luscombe lectr., Jefferson Med. Coll., 2003, Sydney Watson Smith lectr., Royal Coll. Physicians Edinburgh, 2004, Ervin Epstein lectr., Pacific Dermatol. Assn., 2004; named an hon. mem., Czech. Soc. Dermatol, 2002. Fellow: Royal Coll. Physicians (Edinburgh); mem.: Coun. Sci. Editors, European Soc. History of Dermatology, History Dermatology Soc., Quinsigamond Dermatol. Soc., New Eng. Dermatol. Soc. (pres. 1990—91), Assn. Profs. Dermatology, Czech Soc. Dermatology (hon.), Sir James Saunders Soc., Royal Soc. Medicine, Am. Dermatol. Assn., European Acad. Dermatology and Venereology, Soc. for Investigative Dermatology (bd. dirs. 1981—83), Am. Acad. Dermatology (Presdl. citation 2000), James C. White Club, Aesculapian Club Boston, Sigma Xi, Alpha Omega Alpha, Phi Beta Kappa. Office: U Mass Meml Med Ctr 55 Lake Ave N Worcester MA 01655-0002 Office Phone: 508-334-5979.

BERNHARD, LISA, news correspondent; Intern Rolling Stone mag.; asst. editor Us mag.; correspondent E!, Romance Classics, Total TV, The Cable Guide; dep. editor TV Guide; entertainment correspondent Fox News Channel, 2003—; interviewed numerous celebrities including Michael, Jackson, Ellen DeGeneres, and Paul McCartney. Guest appearances include: Today Show, The View, Access Hollywood, CBS Early Show. Office: Fox News Network LLC 1211 Avenue of the Americas New York NY 10036*

BERNHARD, SANDRA, actress, comedienne, singer; b. Flint, Mich., June 6, 1955; d. Jerome and Jeanette B., 1 child. Stand-up comedienne nightclubs, Beverly Hills, Calif., 1974-78; films include Cheech and Chong's Nice Dreams, 1981, The King of Comedy, 1983 (Nat. Soc. Film Critics award), Sesame Street Presents: Follow That Bird, 1985, Track 29, 1988, Without You I'm Nothing, 1990, Hudson Hawk, 1991, Truth or Dare, 1991, Inside Monkey Zetterland, 1993, Dallas Doll, 1994, Unzipped, 1995, Catwalk, 1995, Plump Fiction, 1996, Somewhere in the City, 1997, Lover Girl, 1997, The Apocalypse, 1997, An Alan Smithee Film: Burn Hollywood Burn, 1997, I Woke Up Early the Day I Died, 1998, Exposé, 1998, Wrongfully Accused, 1998, Dinner Rush, 2000, Playing Mona Lisa, 2000, The Third Date, 2003; also appears in Heavy Petting, 1988, Perfect, 1985, The Whoopee Boys, 1986, Casual Sex?, 1988; stage appearances (solo) Without You I'm Nothing, 1988, Giving Till It Hurts, 1992, I'm Still Here...Damn It, 1998-99; TV appearances (host) Living in America, 1990; regular guest The Richard Pryor Show, Late Night with David Letterman; TV series Instant Comedy with the Groundlings, The Hitchhiker, The Full Wax, Tales from the Crypt, Roseanne, Space Ghost Coast to Coast, The Larry Sanders Show, Clueless, Chicago Hope, Highlander, Comedy Central's The A-List, 1992-1993, Superman (voice), Ally McBeal, Hercules (voice), 1999, The Sandra Bernhard Experience (host), 2001-2002; (TV movies) Freaky Friday, 1995, The Late Shift, 1996; albums (co-author 8 songs) I'm Your Woman, 1985, Without You I'm Nothing, 1988, Excuses for Bad Behavior, Part I, 1994; books include Confessions of a Pretty Lady, 1988, Love Love Love, 1993, May I Kiss You On The Lips, Miss Sandra?, 1998. Office: Joanne Schwartz Mgmt 330 W 56 St New York NY 10019

BERNHARD, WILLIAM FRANCIS, thoracic surgeon, cardiovascular surgeon; b. Bklyn., Dec. 11, 1924; s. William and Helen (Conroy) B.; m. June Horne, Sept. 17, 1948; children: Susan, William Francis, Christine, Margaret, Catherine, John, Ann, James, Robert, Peter. BA, Williams Coll., 1946; MD, Syracuse U., 1950; MS (hon.), Harvard U., 1990. Intern Syracuse U. Hosp., 1950-51; asst. resident Children's Hosp. Med. Center, Boston, 1951-52; dir. surg. research lab. Children's Hosp., Boston, 1960—, assoc. surgeon, 1962-66; sr. assoc. in cardiovascular surgery Children's Hosp. Med. Center; asst. resident, Peter Bent Brigham Hosp, Boston, 1952-57; attending staff cardiovascular surgery, 1973—; attending staff, 1974—; resident Bellevue Hosp., Columbia div., N.Y.C., 1957-58, Columbia-Presbyn. Hosp., N.Y.C., 1959; attending surgeon thoracic and cardiovascular surgery VA Hosp., West Roxbury, Mass., 1960—; clin. assoc. surgery Harvard Med. Sch., 1962-66, asst. clin. prof. surgery, 1966-68, assoc. clin. prof. surgery, 1968-71, prof. surgery, 1971—; sr. surgeon Brigham and Woman's Hosp., Boston, 1987; prof. surgery emeritus Harvard Med. Sch., 1994. Cons. in cardiothoracic surgery Beth Israel Hosp., Boston, 1986. Ensign USNR, 1944-46. Mem. ACS., New Eng. Surg. Soc. (sr.), Am. Heart Assn., Mass. Med. Soc., Am. Assn. Thoracic and Cardiovasc. Surgery, Soc. Thoracic Surgery, Soc. Univ. Surgeons, Am. Acad. Pediatrics, New Eng. Cardiovasc. Soc., Internat. Soc. Heart Transplantation, Soc. Vascular Surgery, Am. Soc. Artificial Internal Organs, Am. Surg. Assn. Home: 58 Singletary Ln Framingham MA 01702-6161 Office: Children's Hosp 300 Longwood Ave Boston MA 02115-5737

BERNHARDT, ARTHUR DIETER, urban planner, consultant; b. Dresden, Germany; arrived in U.S., 1966; s. Rudolf B. and Charlotte (Aitz) B. Dipl. Ing., U. Tech., Munich, Fed. Republic Germany, 1965; postgrad., U. So. Calif., 1966-67; M. City Planning, MIT, 1969. Various positions constrn. cos., 1955-68; dir. Program in Industrialization of Housing Sector, MIT, Cambridge, Mass., 1969-76; pres. Program in Industrialization of Housing Sector, Cambridge, 1977-89; chief exec. officer, dir. Program in Industrialization of Housing Sector, Inc., Cambridge and N.Y.C., 1989—2001; pres. DBG Berlin, Germany and N.Y.C., 2001—. Internat. building industry cons., Cambridge, Mass., and N.Y.C., 1973—; asst. prof. MIT, 1970-76 Author books; contbr. articles to profl. jours. Mem. exec. com. Mass. Gov.'s Adv. Com. on Manufactured Housing, 1974-75; NRC del. 8th Gen. Assembly Internat. Council Bldg. Research, 1974. Fed. Republic Germany fellow, 1965, 66, 67, 68; MIT fellow, 1968, 69; MIT grantee, 1970; Fed. Republic Germany grantee, 1965; Alfred P. Sloan Found. grantee, 1970; Dept. Commerce grantee, 1972; HUD grantee, 1972, 74. Mem. Internat. Coun. Bldg. Rsch., Am. Acad. Polit. and Social Sci., Am. Planning Assn., Am. Judicature Soc. (assoc.)

BERNHARDT, HAROLD O., retired history educator; s. Christian Andreas Bernhardt and Christine Andrea Christensen; m. Marcia Ann Webter, Aug. 14, 1948; children: Debra, Andra. BS, Mich. State U., 1948; MS, U. Wis., 1951; postgrad., Northwestern U. History tchr., coach Litchfield (Mich.) H.S.,

1948—50; mus. dir., 1962—2005. Co-editor: Men, Mines & Memories: 40 Years of Sports. Founding pres. Iron County Mus., Caspian, Mich., dir.; bd. dirs. State Hist. Soc., Ann Arbor, Mich.; pres. Iron River Twp. Zoning Bd., 1967—83, Friends of Heritage Trail, Iron River Twp., 1999—; we. pres. No. Wis. Histl. Consortium, Caspian, 1985—. With U.S. Army, 1942—45, ETO. Avocations: sports, photography, travel, canoeing, camping. Home: 233 Bernhardt Td Iron River MI 49935 Office: Iron County Mus Caspian MI 49915

BERNHARDT, MARCIA BRENDA, mental health counselor; b. Jersey, N.J., Aug. 22, 1938; d. Jerome and Mitzie (Cohen) B. BA, Fairleigh Dickinson U., 1960; MA, Columbia U., 1960-63, postgrad., 1968-70, Hunter Coll., 1973-74. Nat. cert. counselor. Rsch. asst. Tchrs. Coll., Columbia U., N.Y.C., 1963-64; counselor JOIN, N.Y.C., 1965-66; project assoc. Bd. Higher Edn. N.Y., N.Y.C., 1966-68, Tchrs. Coll, Columbia U., N.Y.C., 1968-70; counselor Nassau Community Coll., Garden City, N.Y., 1970-72; rsch. scientist Div. for Youth, N.Y.C., 1972-73; rsch. assoc. Family Svc. Assn., N.Y.C., 1974-76; counselor Div. Blind Svcs., West Palm Beach, Fla., 1984-96. Sec., chairperson adv. bd. com. Lighthouse for the Blind, West Palm Beach, 1984-90. Mem. AAUW, Am. Mental Health Counselors Assn., Mental Health Counselor Assn. Greater Palm Beach County, Am. Soc. for Handicapped Children in Israel, Hadassah. Democrat. Jewish. Avocations: theater, ballet, opera, art, swimming. Home: 40 Chatham B West Palm Beach FL 33417-1807 E-mail: mbbernhardt@hotmail.com.

BERNHARDT-KABISCH, ERNEST KARL-HEINZ, English and comparative literature educator; b. Chemnitz, Germany, Nov. 15, 1934; came to U.S., 1955; s. Karl-Heinz and Brunhild Anna Bertha (Kabisch) Bernhardt; m. Eva Carolyn Dessau, Sept. 1, 1956; 1 child, Ethan Karl. *Maternal grandfather Ernst Kabisch was an officer in the German army before and during World War I, rising to a brigadier general, and a distinguished military historian. Father was an actor in Germany. Father-in-law was the well-known German-Jewish composer Paul Dessau.* BA, U. Calif., Berkeley, 1957, MA, 1959, PhD, 1962. Instr. Ind. U., Bloomington, 1962-64, asst. prof., 1964-68, assoc. prof., 1968-80, prof., 1980-99, prof. emeritus, 1999—. Dir. Living Learning Ctr., Ind. U., Bloomington, 1977-90, resident dir. Overseas Study Program, Hamburg, Germany, 1990-91, 94-95; translator. Author: Robert Southey, 1977, Begegnungen mit Erda, 1991; co-editor: Yearbook of Comparative and General Literature, 1980-90; contbr. articles and revs. to profl. jours.; translator (German) fiction radio plays, TV documentaries, essays, monographs, poetry. Mem. AAUP, Am. Comparative Lit. Assn., Modern Lang. Assn., Oesterreichischer Alpenverein, N.Am. Soc. for Study of Romanticism. Democrat. Avocations: mountain climbing, skiing, gardening, music, poetry. Home: 616 S Jordan Ave Bloomington IN 47401-5122 Office: Dept English Ind Univ Bloomington IN 47405 E-mail: bernhard@indiana.edu.

BERNHEIM, DANIEL S., lawyer; b. Phila., Dec. 17, 1954; BA, U. Pa., 1976; JD, Villanova U., 1980; LLM in trial advocacy, Temple U., 1994. Bar: Pa. 1980, US Dist. Ct., Eastern Dist. Pa. 1980, US Tax Ct. 1985, US Ct. Appeals, Third Circuit 1985. Shareholder Silverman Bernheim & Vogel, P.C. Adj. faculty mem. Temple U. Sch. Law; lectr. in field Pa. Banker's Assn., Pa. Bar Inst., Nat. Bus. Inst. Named one of Pa. Super Lawyers, Phila. Mag., 2004. Mem.: Pa. Trial Lawyers Assn., Assn. Trial Lawyers Am., ABA (mem. section on bus. law and lit.), Phila. Bar Assn. (mem. state civil judicial com. 1984—, chmn. motion ct. subcommittee). Office: Silverman Bernheim & Vogel Two Penn Ctr Plz Ste 910 Philadelphia PA 19102 Office Phone: 215-569-0000. Business E-Mail: dbernheim@sbvlaw.com.

BERNHEIMER, G. MAX, art appraiser; MA in Classical Civilization, Harvard U.; attended, Intercollegiate Ctr. for Classical Studies, Rome, Am. Sch. of Classical Studies, Athens, London Inst. Archeology. With Christie's, NYC, 1992—, specialist in ancient Greek, Roman, Etruscan, Egyptian and Near Eastern Art, sr. v.p., internat. dept. head, antiquities. Author: Glories of Ancient Greece, 2001; co-author: Ancient Glass from the Collections of Dr. Elie Borowski. Office: Christie's/NY 20 Rockefeller Plz New York NY 10020 Office Phone: 212-636-2245. Office Fax: 212-636-4926. Business E-Mail: mbernheimer@christies.com.*

BERNHEIMER, MARTIN, music critic; b. Munich, Sept. 28, 1936; came to U.S., 1940, naturalized, 1946; s. Paul Ernst and Louise (Nassauer) B.; m. Lucinda Pearson, Sept. 30, 1961 (div. Feb. 1989); children: Mark Richard, Nora Nicoll, Marina and Erika (twins); m. Linda Winer, Sept. 27, 1992. MusB with honors, Brown U., 1958; student, Munich Conservatory, 1958-59; MA in Musicology, NYU, 1961. Free-lance music critic, 1958—; contbg. critic N.Y. Herald Tribune, 1959-62; mem. music faculty NYU, 1959-62; contbg. editor Mus. Courier, 1961-64; temporary music critic N.Y. Post, 1961-65; N.Y. corr. Brit. Publ. Opera, 1962—65; L.A. corr., 1965—; corr. West Coast Brit. Opera Mag., 1965—; asst. to music editor Saturday Rev., 1962-65; mng. editor Philharmonic Hall Program, N.Y.C., 1962-65; music editor, chief critic L.A. Times, 1965-96; N.Y. corr. Brit. Publ. Opera, 1997—. Mem. faculty U. So. Calif., 1966-71, music faculty UCLA, 1969-75, Calif. Inst. Arts, 1975-82, Calif. State U., Northridge, 1978-81, Rockefeller Program for Tng. of Music Critics; mem. Pulitzer Prize Music Jury, 1984, 86, 90; L.A. corr. for Swiss publ. Opernwelt, 1984—. Contbg. author New Groves Dictionary; contbr. liner notes for recordings; appearances on radio and TV, Met. Opera Broadcasts; contbr. articles to Vanity Fair, Music Quar., The Critic, Opera News, Mus. Am., Fin. Times, London, Sidewalk N.Y. (internet), others; N.Y. corr. Fin. Times and Opera mag.; lectr., moderator, essayist on Met. Opera Broadcast. Recipient Deems Taylor award ASCAP, 1974, 78, Headliners award, 1979, Pulitzer Prize for disting. criticism, 1982, Lifetime Achievement award Svc. to Music, Calif. Assn. Profl. Music Tchrs., 1990. Mem. Nat. Opera Inst. (ind. selection com. 1980), Pi Kappa Lambda (hon.). E-mail: mbern@earthlink.net.

BERNHOLC, JERZY, physicist, educator; b. Szczecin, Poland, Feb. 12, 1952; arrived in U.S., 1978, naturalized, 1986; s. David and Irene Bernholc; m. Alissa Seligman, Aug. 1, 1982; children: Stuart, Judith. BS in Physics and Math., U. Lund, Sweden, 1973, PhD in Physics, 1977. Postdoctoral rschr. IBM Watson Rsch. Ctr., Yorktown Heights, NY, 1978-80; sr. physicist Exxon Corp. Rsch. Labs., Clinton, NJ, 1980-86; assoc. prof. physics NC State U., Raleigh, 1986-90, prof., 1990-2000, Drexel prof., 2000—; disting. vis. scientist Oak Ridge Nat. Lab., 2002—, dir. ctr. for high performance simulation, 2004—. Chmn. Electronic Structure Algorithms, Raleigh, 1992, organizing com. ann. workshops, 1992—; co-chmn. Grid, Wavelet and Multigrid Methods, Lyon, France, 1996, NATO Workshop Multiscale Methods in Chemistry, Eilat, Israel, 2000; mem. ONR Panel on Fgn. Field Offices, 1992; joint peer rev. bd. NSF Supercomputing Ctrs., 1988—91; adv. coun. NC Supercomputing Ctr., Research Triangle Park, 1990—92, Research Triangle Park, 1998—; chair NC Com. on Partnership for Advanced Computational Infrastructure, 1996—99; panel high performance computing NSF, Washington, 1992; exec. com. Nat. Computational Sci. Alliance, Urbana, Ill., 1998—2002, leader nanomaterials/electronic structure team, 1998—2002; com. of visitors NSF Supercomputing Ctrs. and Computational Infrastructure Program, 1999; program com. Internat. Conf. on Computational Physics, San Diego, 2003; chair Prog. Com. Divsn. Computational Physics of APS, 2002; mem. southeastern sect. prog. com. of APS Prog. Com. Divsn. Computational Physics, 2003; sci. adv. com. Ctr. for Nanophase Materials Scis. Oak Ridge Nat. Lab., 2002—, mem. adv. com. divsn. computer sci., 2003—; strategic planning workshop Dept. of Energy, 2003; Grand Challenges in Nanomaterials workshop NSF, 2003; mem. rev. panel materials scis. divsn. Lawrence Berkeley Labs., 2003; mem. program com. Southeast Sec. APS, 2003; mem. sci. com. 7th Internat. Conf. on Intermolecular and Magnetic Interactions in Matter, Poland, 2003, Workshop on Functional Materials, Athens, Greece, 2004, 05; chair, fellowship com. Div. Computational Physics, APS, 2004, chair com. govt. rels., 04, mem. program com., 04; mem. rev. com. Dir.'s Rsch. and Devel. Fund, 2004; mem. organizing com. Workshop on Recent Devel. in Electronic Structure Algorithms, 2004, Fall Creek Falls Workshop on High-End Computing in Sci. and Engring., Tenn., 2004; panel mem. workshop Basic Rsch. Needs Effective Solar Energy Utilization Dept. Energy, Bethesda, 2005; panel mem. Crosscutting Areas: New Tools Dept. Energy, 2005; mem. sci. com. Workshop on Functional Materials, Athens, Greece, 2005. Specialist editor materials sci.: Computer Physics Comm., 1998—. Panel mem. AIChE, 2002. Recipient Outstanding Innovation award IBM Rsch. Divsn., Yorktown Heights, 1979, Alumni Oustanding rsch. award NC State U., Raleigh, 1992, Creativity Ext. award NSF, Washington, 1996, finalist sci. category Computerworld Smithsonian, Washington, 1997. Fellow: Am. Phys. Soc. (vice-chair computational physics 2001, chmn.-elect 2002, chmn. fellowship com. 2002, chmn. 2003, mem. ad hoc com. on condensed matter physics 2003, past chair 2004, vice chmn. Rahman prize com. 2004, chmn. Rahman prize com. 2005, mem. Jesse Beams award com. southeastern sect. 2004, Jesse Beams award for outstanding rsch. Southwestern sect. 2004); mem.: Materials Rsch. Soc., Sigma Xi. Home: 2309 Byrd St Raleigh NC 27608-1411 Office: Ctr High Performance Simulation PO Box 7518 Raleigh NC 27695-7518 Office Phone: 919-515-3126.

BERNI, ROSEMARIAN RAUCH, rehabilitation and oncology nurse; b. Portland, Oreg., Sept. 30, 1925; d. George Laverne and Mabel (Rose) Rauch; m. Albert Hawthorne Berni, Oct. 25, 1947; children: George, Michael, William, Albert. Student, Oreg. State Coll., 1943-44; BS in Nursing, Univ. Oreg., 1947; M in Nursing, U. Wash., 1973. RN Wash., Oreg. Clin. nursing instr. Univ. Oreg. Sch. of Nursing, Portland; spl. duty nurse Doernbecher Hosp., Portland, Oreg., 1948; night supr. Halcyon Psychiat. Hosp., Seattle, Wash., 1962; staff nurse psychiat. nursing unit U. Wash. Hosp., Seattle, 1963, head nurse phys. medicine and rehab. nursing unit, 1964-66, asst. dir. nursing, 1966-67; dir. rehab. med. intermittent catheter team U. Hosp. and Harborview Med. Ctr., Seattle, 1973-82; rehab. clin. nurse specialist U. Wash. Med. Ctr., Seattle, 1973—. Clin. instr. U. Wash. Sch. Nursing, 1967-76, instr. dept. rehab. medicine, 1967-73; dir. nursing svc. Rehab. Nursing Unit, Dept. Rehab. Medicine, U. Wash., Seattle, 1967—; asst. prof. dept. rehab. medicine, U. Wash., 1973-78, assoc. prof. emeritus, 1981, mem. grad. sch. faculty, 1975—; dir. Rehab. Nursing Pathways in Depth, 1967—; chmn. rehab. nursing ctr., ARN 1981; presenter World Rehab. Fund, Cyprus; active on numerous hosp. and univ. coms., presenter many seminars and workshops in Wash. and nationwide. Author: (with Fordyce, Wilbert E.) Behavior Modification and the Nursing Process, 1973, 2nd edit., 1977; contbr. articles to profl. jours. and chpts. to books; producer films, audio and video presentations and course curricula. Vol. RN, Whidbey Island, Wash., 1981-2000; tutor pub. schs. Recipient Svc. award, Wash. State Health Facilities Assn., 1974, Wash. State Heart Assn., 1976, Leadership award, Rehab. Nursing Inst., 1981. Mem. ANA (coun. clin. nurse specialists), Nat. League of Nursing, Assn. of Rehab. Nurses (founding pres. Wash. chpt., nat. pres. 1980, Leadership award 1980), Assn. Women in Sci., N.Y. Acad. Sci., N.W. Neurological Rehab., Nat. Stroke Assn., Wash. State Head Injury Found., Univ. Wash. Alumni Assn., Sigma Theta Tau, Alpha Lambda Delta, Alpha Tau Delta. Home: PO Box 868 Freeland WA 98249-0868 Office: Stroke Support Group Whidbey Gen Hosp Dept Rehab Medicine Seattle WA 98195-0001

BERNICK, CAROL LAVIN, consumer products company executive; m. Howard Bernick; three children. BA, Tulane U., 1974. From mem. mktg. staff to pres. Alberto-Culver N.Am., Melrose Park, Ill., 1974—94; pres. Consumer Products Worldwide Alberto Culver, 1994—98, pres. Consumer Products N.Am., 1998—2002, chmn. bd., 2004—. Founder Friends of Prentice; mem. women's bd. Boys and Girls Clubs, Chgo.; regent Lincoln Acad. Ill.; mem. exec. com. of adv. bd. Kellogg Sch., Northwestern U.; mem. Tulane U. Bd.; bd. dirs. Northwestern Meml. Healthcare. Recipient Leadership in Bus. award YWCA Met. Chgo., 1992, award for philanthropy Harvard Club of Chgo., Disting. Alumni award Tulane U., 2003. Mem. World Pres. Orgn., Econ. Club Chgo., Exec. Club Chgo., Com. 200 Chgo. Network. Office: Alberto-Culver Co 2525 Armitage Ave Melrose Park IL 60160-1163 Office Phone: 708-450-3000. Personal E-mail: cbernick@alberto.com.

BERNICK, DAVID M., lawyer; b. San Francisco, June 16, 1954; s. Herman Charles and Joan (Schutz) B.; m. Christine A. Clougherty, Aug. 13, 1983; 1 child, Evan Daniel. BA, U. Chgo., 1974, JD, 1978; MA, Yale U., 1975. Bar: Ill. 1978. Ptnr., mem. firm com. Kirkland & Ellis, Chgo., 1984—. Mem. Comml. Club, Jud. Conf. Com., Mid-Am. Club, Phi Beta Kappa. Office: Kirkland & Ellis LLP 200 E Randolph St Fl 54 Chicago IL 60601-6636 Office Phone: 312-861-2248. Office Fax: 312-861-2200. Business E-Mail: dbernick@kirkland.com.

BERNICK, HOWARD BARRY, manufacturing executive; b. Midland, Ont., Can., Apr. 10, 1952; came to U.S., 1974, naturalized, 1976; s. Henry and Esther (Starkman) B.; m. Carol Lavin, May 30, 1976; children: Craig, Peter, Elizabeth. BA, U. Toronto, Ont., 1973. Investment banker Wood Gundy Ltd., Toronto, 1973-74, First Boston Corp., Chgo., 1974-77; dir. of profit planning Alberto Culver Co., Melrose Park, Ill., 1977-79, v.p. corp. devel., 1979-81, group v.p., chief fin. officer, 1981-85, exec. v.p., 1985-88, pres., COO, 1988-94, also bd. dirs.; pres., CEO, 1994—. Bd. dirs. AAR Corp. Mem. Cosmetic, Toiletry & Fragrance Assn., Econ. Club Chgo. Office: Alberto-Culver Co 2525 Armitage Ave Melrose Park IL 60160-1163

BERNICKER, ERIC HOWARD, oncologist; b. Elizabeth, N.J., June 25, 1964; s. Richard Paul and Leah Joan Bernicker; m. Daphne Scott Bernicker, Oct. 5, 1991; children: Lily, Carl. BA in History, Yale U., 1986; MD, Baylor U., 1990. Bd. cert. internal medicine Am. Bd. Internal Medicine, bd. cert. med. oncology Am. Bd. Internal Medicine. Med. oncologist Med. Clinic Houston, 1996—. Mem. exec. com. St. Lukes Episcopal Hosp.; mem. quality coun. Med. Clinic Houston. Mem.: ACP, Am. Soc. Clin. Oncology (presdl. appointee clin. practice com. 2000—03). Office: Med Clinic Houston 1707 Sunset Blvd Houston TX 77005

BERNIER, GEORGE MATTHEW, JR., oncologist, educator, dean; b. Portland, Maine, June 29, 1934; s. George Matthew and Lillian Theresa (Wallace) B.; m. Mary Jane Marron, June 29, 1963; children: George Matthew, III, Elizabeth Wallace. AB, Boston Coll., 1956; MD, Harvard U., 1960. Intern Univ. Hosps., Cleve., 1960-61, resident, 1961-62, 65-66, U. Fla. Hosps., Gainesville, 1964-65; fellow in biochemistry U. Fla., 1962-64; instr. Case Western Res. U., Cleve., 1966-67, asst. prof. medicine, 1967-72, assoc. prof., 1972-75, prof., 1975-78; dir. div. med. oncology Univ. Hosps., Cleve., 1974-78; prof., chmn. dept. medicine Dartmouth Med. Sch., Hanover, N.H., 1978-86, Joseph M. Huber prof. medicine, 1982-86; dean, prof. medicine U. Pitts. Sch. Medicine, U. Pitts., 1987-95; dean medicine, v.p. acad. affairs U. Tex. Med. Br., Galveston, 1995-99, v.p. edn., 1999—2001, prof. emeritus, 2001—. Contbr. articles to profl. jours. Trustee Jackson Labs., Bar Harbor, Maine, 1973—; mem. White House Commn. on Complementary and Alternative Medicine. Served to lt. col. M.C. U.S. Army, 1967-70. Leukemia Soc. Am. scholar, 1970-75 Fellow A.C.P.; mem. Am. Soc. Hematology, Am. Soc. Clin. Oncology, Am. Soc. Clin. Investigation, Am. Assn. Immunologists., Assn. Am. Physicians, Am. Clin. and Climatological Assn., Nat Bd. Med. Examiners (mem.-at-large 2000—, mem. presdl. commn. policy for complementary and alter. medicine 2000-2002). Address: 227-11 Langler Rd Newton MA 02459

BERNIKOW, PIEDAD A., lawyer; b. N.Y.C. d. Antonio and Nastia (Feliz) Fontanes; m. Jerold C. Lieberman, Aug. 5, 1979. BA, NYU, 1977; JD, Touro Coll., 1985. Bar: N.J. 1987, D.C. 1989; U.S. Dist. Ct. Fed. Dist. 1987. Law clk. Bankruptcy Ct. (so. dist.), N.Y.C., Port Authority N.Y. and N.J., N.Y.C., mgr. lease and concession dept.; assoc. Horowitz, Bross, Simins & Imperial, Secaucus, N.J., 1987-88; pvt. practice Morristown, N.J., 1987-89; asst. counsel The Howard Savs. Bank, Livingston, N.J., 1989-90; comml. arbitrator/mediator N.J.; practice ltd. to alternate dispute resolution, 1990—; mem. neutral panel FDIC, 1995—. Comml. arbitrator Arbitration Forums, Inc., Tarrytown, N.Y., 1991—; of counsel Sprout House, Inc., Chatham, N.J., 1988-89; mem. arbitration and mediation panel Golden Valley Consulting Group, 1994—; pres. Exec. Strategems; mem. adv. com. Am. Arbitrations Ctr. for Mediation; lectr. in field. Contbr. articles to profl. jours. Bd. dirs. Domestic Abuse and Rape Crisis Ctr. of Warren County, Belvedere, N.J., 1988-89. Mem. N.J. Bar Assn., D.C. Bar, Am. Arbitration Assn. (mem. panel 1985—), NASD (arbitration panel 1994—). Avocations: writing, creating and designing board games, reading, cooking. Office: PO Box 11178 Saint Paul MN 55111-0178

BERNING, ROBERT WILLIAM, librarian; b. Carroll, Iowa, Dec. 2, 1949; s. Norbert John and Marjorie Lavine (Miller) B. BSE, N.W. Mo. State U., 1972; MLS, Emporia State U., 1974. Cert. pub. libr. Iowa. Sch. libr. Mount Ayr (Iowa) Cmty. Schs., 1974-76, Wall Lake (Iowa) Cmty. Schs., 1977-79, West Point (Nebr.) Pub. Schs., 1979-81; dir. Dubuque County Libr., Farley, Iowa, 1981-82; sch. libr. HLV Cmty. Schs., Victor, Iowa, 1982-84; dir. Carlisle (Iowa) Pub. Libr., 1985—. Mem. adv. bd. State Libr. Iowa, Des Moines, 1987, 89; mem. adv. com. Ctrl. Iowa Regional Libr., Clive, 1992-94, 98—. Libr. rep. Lanning Bequest com. City of Carlisle, 1995-97, Mng. Info. for Rural Am. (MIRA), 1998; mem. com., task force Iowans Can't Wait (Enrich Iowa), State Libr. Iowa, Des Moines, 1995-96; mem. Mayor's Select Com. on Property Taxes, Des. Moines, 1998-99. Mem. ALA, KC, Iowa Libr. Assn. (govtl. affairs com. 1988-91), Iowa Small Libr. Assn. (sec. 1985-87), Carlisle Lion's Club, Carlisle C. of C. (libr. rep. 1990—), Alpha Phi Omega (life). Roman Catholic. Avocations: collecting antiques, travel, gardening. Office: Carlisle Pub Libr 135 School St PO Box S Carlisle IA 50047 Office Phone: 515-989-0909. E-mail: carlpl1@mchsi.com.

BERNKNOPF, DAVID SCOTT, journalist; b. N.Y.C., Mar. 20, 1958; s. Arthur and Dorothy Yvette (Silverstein) B.; m. Mary Helen Martin, May 19, 1990; children: Zachary, Sarah Elizabeth. BS in Journalism, Northwestern U., 1980. Exec. prodr. Cable News Network, Atlanta, 1990-98, dir. news planning, 1998-2000, v.p., dir. news planning, 2000—. Vis. prof., Hearst fellow U. Colo. Sch. Journalism and Mass Comm., Boulder, 1999; mem. journalism sch. adv. bd. Breneau U., Gainesville, Ga; editor-at-large Travel Girl Mag., 2001—; prin. Atamira Cmtys. Media Strategy Firm, 2001—. Recipient Emmy prodr. Oklahoma City Bombing, 1995, prodr. Olympic Pk. Bombing, 1996. Mem. Atlanta Press Club. Fax: 404-827-4141.

BERNMÚDEZ, CARMEN, trust company executive; b. Costa Rica, 1944; m. Thomas J. Feeney, 1986. Attended, Colegio Superior de Señprotas, Santa Monica City Coll. Bull fighter, Costa Rica, Mex. City, 1962—67; various positions TWA, 1967—85; chmn., treas. Marathon Asset Mgmt. Co., 1985—94; founder, chmn., CEO Mission Mgmt. & Trust Co., 1994—. Apptd. hon. consul of Costa Rica to US by Pres. of Costa Rica. Worked with Central Am. Free Trade Agreement (CAFTA). Recipient Woman of Enterprise, Avon, 2001, Leading Woman Entrepreneur, STAR Group (sponsored by IBM and Chase Manhattan Banking), 2001. Mem.: US Hispanic C. of C., Nat. Minority Supplier Devel. Coun., Nat. Law Ctr. for InterAmerica Free Trade. Achievements include first woman to run a Fiduciary Trust co. in US. Office: La Paloma Corp Ctr 3567 E Sunrise Dr Ste 235 Tucson AZ 85718-3203 Office Phone: 520-557-5559.

BERNOT, JANE CATHERINE, retired education educator; b. Washington, D.C., June 18, 1923; d. Cleveland Hensel and Jeffie Washington (Abel) Stauffer; m. Joseph John Bernot, June 18, 1951; children: Joseph Michael, John Cleveland. AA, George Washington UNiv., Washington, 1944; BS in Physical Edn., George Washington Univ., Washington, 1945; MA in Health Edn., N.Y. U., N.Y., 1950; PhD, The Fielding Inst., Santa Barbara, 1980. Cert. sex eductaor Am. Assn. of Sex Educators Counselours and Therapists, 1978, sex counselor Am. Assn. of Sex Educators Counselours and Therapists, 1989, First Aid, Safety Edn. Am. Red Cross. Tchr. ballroom, tap, ballet Franklin B. Walker Dance Studios, Washington, 1940—41; exercise tchr., mgr. Emile Health Club, Washington, 1942—45; physical edn. tchr. Paul Jr. H.S., Washington, 1945—46; health and physical edn. tchr. Pub. Sr. H.S., Washington, 1946—57, Bethesda Chevy Chase H.S., Chevy Chase, Md., 1957—60; prof. natural sci. Monotgomery Coll., Takoma Pk., Md., 1960—92, coach women's volleyball, 1980. Editor: (jour.) AAHPRED, 1986; contbr. articles pub. to profl. jour. Islands in crisis project Virgin Islands Assn. for Health, 1988—89. Mem.: Nat. Dance Assn., GWU Women's P.E. Alumnae Assn. (pres. 1955—65), Am. Assn. of Health Physical Edn. (life; pres. 1973—74), Am. Alliance of Health Physical Edn. Recreation and Dance (life; pres. 1963—64). Achievements include During my 50 yr. career I have devel., produced, and presented over 100 ednl. sessions at profl. meetings conventions and conf. and served on chaired on com; development of taught first water exercise credited coll. course. Avocations: jewelry making and design, writing, psychic phenomena, water exercising.

BERNS, KENNETH IRA, physician; b. Cleve., June 14, 1938; s. Charles and Delnet (Cohn) Berns; m. Laura Louise Lawless, June 26, 1964; children: Jonathan Charles, Deborah Louise. Student, Harvard U., 1956—59; AB, Johns Hopkins U., 1960, PhD, 1964, MD, 1966. Intern Johns Hopkins Hosp., 1966—67; asst. prof. microbiology Johns Hopkins U. Sch. Medicine, 1970—74, asst. prof. pediat., 1970—76, asso. prof. microbiology, 1974—76; dir. Johns Hopkins U. Sch. Medicine (Yr. I program), 1973—76; prof., chmn. dept. immunology and med. microbiology, prof. pediat. U. Fla. Coll. Medicine, Gainesville, 1976—84, dean, 1997—2002, v.p. health affairs, 2000—02; R.A. Rees Pritchett prof., chmn. dept. microbiology Cornell U. Med. Coll., 1984—97; pres. and COO Mt. Sinai Med. Ctr., N.Y.C., 2002—03; dir. U. Fla. Genetics Inst., 2003—. Howard Hughes med. investigator, 1970—75; mem. microbiology test com. Nat. Bd. Med. Examiners, 1979—82, chmn., 1983—86, mem. exec. bd., 1986—95; mem. Recombinant DNA adv. com. NIH, 1980—83, chmn., 1982—83, mem. virology study sect., 1985—89; mem. genetic biology panel NSF, 1981—84; Fogarty sr. internat. fellow virology dept. Weizmann Inst. Sci., Rehovot, Israel, 1982—83; ad hoc mem. Bd. Sci. Counselors Nat. Inst. Allergy and Infectious Diseases, 1982, permanent mem., 1992—96; del. U.S.-Japan Coop. Program on Recombinant DNA, 1981; mem. Internat. Com. Taxonomy of Viruses, 1981—98; mem. virology and microbiology adv. com. Am. Cancer Soc., 1985—89, mem. liaison com. on med. edn., 1989—92; mem. composite com. U.S. Med. Licensing Exam., 1995—98; nat. adv. coun. Nat. Ctr. Rsch. Resources, 1999—2003. Bd. trustees Johns Hopkins U., 2000—06. Served with USPHS, 1967—70. Recipient Faculty Rsch. award, Am. Cancer Soc., 1975—76, Disting. Svc. award, Nat. Bd. Med. Examiners, Disting. Svc. Mem., Assn. Am. Med. Coll.; fellow Shell Oil, 1963—64; grantee Am. Cancer Soc., 1970—72, NIH, 1970—76, 1980—, NSF, 1973—75, 1979—80; Fogarty Sr. Internat. Fellowship, 1982—83. Fellow: AAAS; mem.: NAS, Inst. Medicine of NAS, Internat. Union Microbiol. Socs. (v.p. 1990—94), Soc. Pediatric Rsch., Soc. Gen. Microbiology, Am. Soc. Virology (pres. 1988—89), Assn. Med. Sch. Microbiology Chairmen (chmn. com. pub. policy 1979, counselor 1980—83, pres. 1985), Am. Soc. Microbiology (pres. 1996—97), Am. Soc. Biol. Chemists, Am. Acad. Microbiology (bd. govs. 2003—), Alpha Omega Alpha, Sigma Xi, Phi Beta Kappa. Office: Univ Fla Miller Health Ctr PO Box 1001961 Gainesville FL 32610-0196

BERNS, PAMELA KARI, artist, publisher; b. Sturgeon Bay, Wis., Sept. 4, 1947; d. Robert Matthew and Judith B. BA, Lawrence U., 1969; MFA, U. Wis., Madison, 1971. Owner, mgr. Sta. Gallery, Ephraim, Wis., 1968—79; pub., editor Chgo. Life Mag., 1984—. One-woman shows include Francis Hardy Gallery, Ephraim, Wis., 1976; group shows include New Horizons, Chgo., 1975, Watercolor Soc., Racine, 1972-82 (2d prize 1976, 82); represented in permanent collections State of Ill. Ctr., Bergstrom-Mahler Art Ctr.; poster design Peninsula Arts Assn., Fish Creek, Wis., 1980 Mem. adv. bd. Chgo. Media Watch. Recipient V.I.P. in her Cmty. award NOW, 1977. Mem. Chgo. Artists Coalition (art dir. 1980-85). Avocations: piano, painting.

BERNS, SHELDON, lawyer; b. Cleve., Dec. 13, 1932; BBA, Ohio State U., 1958; JD, Case Western Res. U., 1960. Prin. Kahn, Kleinman, Yanowitz & Arnson Co., L.P.A., Cleve., 1960—2002; mem. Berns, Ockner & Greenberger, LLC, Beachwood, Ohio, 2002—. Councilman City of Beachwood, Ohio, 1970-77; mem. Cuyahoga County Rep. Exec. Com., 1968—, vice chmn., 1980-88. Mem. ABA, Greater Cleve Bar Assn., 8th Jud. Conf. (life), Order of Coif. Office: Berns, Ockner & Greenberger 3733 Park E Dr #200 Cleveland OH 44122-4334 Office Phone: 216-831-8838. E-mail: sberns@bernsockner.com.

BERNSEN, CORBIN, actor; b. North Hollywood, Calif., Sept. 7, 1954; s. Jeanne Cooper; m. Brenda Cooper, 1983 (div. 1987); m. Amanda Pays Nov. 19, 1988; children: Oliver, Henry, Angus Moore, Finley. BA in Theater Arts, MFA in Playwriting, UCLA. Teaching asst. UCLA. Appeared in (films) King Kong, 1976, S.O.B., 1981, Hello, Again, 1987, Bert Rigby, You're A Fool, 1989, Major League, 1989, Disorganized Crime, 1989, Shattered, 1992, Frozen Assets, 1993, Major League 2, 1994, Tales From the Hood, 1995, Menno's Mind, 1996, Kounterfeit, 1996, Bloodhounds, 1996, The Great White Hype, 1996, Circuit Breaker, 1997, An American Affair, The Misadventures of Margaret, 1998, Drop Dead, 1998, Beings, 1998, Major League: Back to the Minors, 1998, The Misadventures of Margaret, 1998, Young Hearts Unlimited, 1998, Rubbernecking, 2000, Killer Instinct, 2000, Delicate Instruments, 2000, Borderline Normal, 2000, The Tomorrow Man, 2001, Judgement, 2001, Final Payback, 2001, Dead Above Ground, 2002, I Saw Mommy Kissing Santa Claus, 2002, The Commission, 2003, The List, 2004, Death and Texas, 2004, Quiet Kill, 2004, The Naked Ape, 2005, Raging Sharks, 2005, Kiss Kiss, Bang Bang, 2005; (TV series) Ryan's Hope, 1983, 1984-85, L.A. Law, 1986-1994, A Whole New Ballgame, 1995, The Cape, 1996, The Young and the Restless, 2003, 04, General Hospital, 2004-; (TV films) Breaking Point, Danielle Steel's 'Full Circle', 1996, The Cape, 1996, The Dentist, 1996, Tidal Wave: No Escape, 1997, Loyal Opposition: Terror in the White House, 1998, Nightworld: Riddler's Moon, 1998, Recipe for Revenge, 1998, Two of Hearts, 1999, Gentle Ben, 2002, Atomic Twister, 2002, The Santa Trap, 2002, Gentle Ben 2: Danger on the Mountain, 2003, Love Comes Softly, 2003, Call Me: The Rise and Fall of Heidi Fleiss, 2004, They Are Among Us, 2004, Ordinary Miracles, 2005; assoc. prodr.: (films) The Dentist II, 1998, 3 Day Test, 2005; TV guest appearances include Star Trek: The Next Generation, 1987, Dear John, 1988, Anything But Love, 1989, Seinfeld, 1990, The Larry Sanders Show, 1992, The Nanny, 1993, Touched by an Angel, 1997, Tracey Takes On..., 1999, 7th Heaven, 1999, Nash Bridges, 1999, Jag, 1999, 2000, 02, 04, The Outer Limits, 2000, Son of the Beach, 2000, Yes, Dear, 2000, Baywatch, 2000, The West Wing, 2001, Dragnet, 2003, Just Shoot Me!, 2003, Third Watch, 2004, Cuts, 2005. Office: ABC TV Gen Hosp 4151 Prospect Ave TV Ctr Los Angeles CA 90027*

BERNSEN, HAROLD JOHN, political scientist, educator, retired military officer; b. Boston, Nov. 25, 1936; s. Harold Arthur and Solveig Bachrud (Birkrem) B.; m. Doris Ann Champion, Mar. 5, 1960. BA, Dartmouth Coll., 1958. Commd. ensign USN, 1958, advanced through grades to rear adm., 1988, comdg. officer USS LaSalle, 1980-82, comdg. officer USS Lexington Pensacola, Fla., 1983-84, dir. plans and policy, staff comdr. in chief U.S. Cen. Command Tampa, Fla., 1985-86, comdr. Mideast Force, 1986-88, dir. plans and policy staff comdr. in chief Atlantic Fleet Norfolk, 1988-91; dep., chief of staff, comdr. in chief Atlantic Fleet, 1991; ret., 1991. Spkr. on Mid. East issues. Bd. dirs. Am. Bahraini Friendship Soc.; chmn. bd. dirs. Nat. Coun. on U.S.-Arab Rels.; pres. trustees Physicians for Peace. Decorated Disting. Svc. Medal, Def. Superior Svc. Medal, Legion of Merit; Royal Norwegian Order of Merit (Norway); Order 1st Class (Bahrain). Mem.: Assn. Naval Aviation, Army Navy Country Club, Army Navy Club, N.Y. Yacht Club. Avocations: sailing, golf, cooking, gardening. E-mail: hbernsen@cox.net.

BERNSON, MARCELLA S., psychiatrist; b. N.Y.C., Aug. 24, 1952; d. Maxwell Isaac and Priscilla Edith (Zuckerman) Bernson; m. Robert A. Foster, Aug. 7, 2001. BA in Biology summa cum laude, Hofstra U., 1973; MD, Albert Einstein Coll. Medicine, 1976. Diplomate Am. Bd. Psychiatry and Neurology. Resident in psychiatry Bronx (N.Y.) Mcpl. Hosp. Ctr., 1976—79; assoc. dir. med. student edn. in psychiatry U. Medicine and Dentistry N.J.-N.J. Med. Sch., Newark, 1979—81; pvt. practice psychiatry Westfield, NJ, 1981—86; cons. psychiatrist Healthwise EAP, Elizabeth, NJ, 1985—86; staff psychiatrist Elizabeth Gen. Med. Ctr., 1985—88, 1992—95, med. chief adult ambulatory svcs. dept. psychiatry, 1986—87, asst. dir. dept. psychiatry, 1987—88; dir. tng. psychiat. svc. VA Med. Ctr., East Orange, NJ, 1988—89; med. dir. partial care Occupl. Ctr. Union County, Roselle, NJ, 1989—92; cons. psychiatrist Union County Ednl. Svcs. Commn., Westfield, 1992—95; med. dir. Richard Hall CMHC, Bridgewater, NJ, 1995—99, staff psychiatrist, 2003—; with devel. disabilities ctr. Morristown (N.J.) Meml. Hosp., 1999—2003. Instr. U. Medicine and Dentistry N.J.-N.J. Med. Sch., Newark, 1979—81, asst. prof. clin. psychiatry, 1988—89; mem. human rights com. Divsn. Devel. Disabilities, State of N.J. Mem.: N.J. Psychiat. Assn. (Union County rep. 1989—90, Morris County rep. 2000—02), Am. Psychiat. Assn. Avocation: short fiction. Office: Richard Hall CMHC 500 N Bridge St Bridgewater NJ 08807

BERNSTEIN, ARTHUR D(ONALD), lawyer, consultant; b. Chgo., Mar. 31, 1942; s. Charles M. and Edith Ann (Eisenberg) B. AB, Columbia U., 1964; JD, Stanford U., 1967. Bar: D.C. 1967, Calif. 1967, Va. 1989. Atty. adviser ICC, Washington, 1967-68; assoc. to ptnr. Galland, Kharasch, Calkins & Morse, Washington, 1968-83; of counsel Law Office of Suzette Matthews, Washington, 1983-89; ptnr. Bernstein & Matthews, Middlebrook, Va., 1989—. Pres. Dispute Resolutions, Inc., Roanoke, Va., 1993-95. Office: Bernstein & Matthews HC 32 Box 16 Middlebrook VA 24459-9507 Office Phone: 540-885-7840. Personal E-mail: adbusfans@aol.com.

BERNSTEIN, BARRY JOEL, lawyer; b. Charleston, S.C., Feb. 11, 1961; s. Charles Stanley Bernstein and Sara Blum Baumwald; m. Charlene Wilkins, May 29, 1998; children: Brandi Nichole, Alexander Nicholas. BA, U. S.C., 1983, JD, 1995; postgrad., U.S. Army Command & Gen. Staff Coll., 2001. Bar: S.C., U.S. Dist. Ct. S.C. Security mgr. Boeing, Wichita, Kans., 1986-88; pres. Security Cons., Inc., Charleston, S.C., 1988-92; law clk. Bernstein and Bernstein, P.A., Charleston, 1992-95; ptnr. Breland and Bernstein, Greenville, S.C., 1995-97; owner, pres. Bernstein Law Firm, Greenville, 1998-2000; gen. counsel Adjutant Gen. of S.C., 2000—. Dir. Homeless Animal Res. and Placement, Greenville, 1995-2000. 1st lt. U.S. Army, 1983-86, col. JAG S.C. N.G., 1978—. S.C. Nat. Guard scholar U. S.C., 1980, Helen Gullickson scholar U. S.C. Sch. of Law, 1994, Claude M. Sapp scholar; named Officer of Yr. ROA, Kans. Mem. ABA, S.C. Trial Lawyers Assn., Comml. Law League Am., Scottish Rite, Masons (past master), Phi Delta Phi (magister 1994-95, province pres. 1996-98), Zeta Beta Tau. Jewish. Home: 304 Lost Creek Columbia SC 29212 Office: Adjutant General of SC 1 National Guard Rd Columbia SC 29201-4766 Business E-Mail: bernsteinbj@sc-arng.ngb.army.mil.

BERNSTEIN, CHARLES BERNARD, lawyer; b. Chgo., June 24, 1941; s. Norman and Adele (Shore) B.; m. Roberta Luba Lesner, Aug. 7, 1968; children: Edward Charles, Louis Charles, Henry Jacob. AB, U. Chgo., 1962; JD, DePaul U., 1965. Bar: Ill. 1965, U.S. Supreme Ct. 1972. Assoc. Axelrod, Goodman & Steiner, Chgo., 1966-67, Max & Herman Chill, Chgo., 1967-74, Bellows & Assocs., Chgo., 1974-81, Marvin Sacks Ltd., Chgo., 1981; sole practice, 1981—. Basketball press dir. U. Chgo., 1967-74. Author: (with Stuart L. Cohen) Torah and Technology: The History and Genealogy of the Anixter Family, 1986; (with Neil Rosenstein) From King David to Baron David: The Genealogical Connections Between Baron Guy de Rothschild and Baroness Alix de Rothschild, 1989; The Rothschilds of Nordstetten: Their History and Genealogy, 1989; contbr. articles to mags., profl. jours. Officer Congregation Rodfei Zedek, 1979—83, 2002—04, bd. dirs., 1978—93, 2000—. Recipient Am. Jurisprudence award, 1963, My Brother's Keeper award Am. Jewish Congress, 1977, Kovod award Rodfei Zedek Men's Club, 1998; co-recipient 2d Century award Jewish Theol. Sem. Am., 1999. Mem. Chgo. Bar Assn., Ill. State Bar Assn., Chgo. Jewish Hist. Soc. (treas. 1977-79, v.p. 1979-82, dir. 1977—), Chgo. Pops Orch. Assn. (treas., exec. com. 1975-81), Am. Jewish Hist. Soc., Art Inst. of Chgo., Chgo. Hist. Soc., Jewish Geneal. Soc. (dir. 1977—), Nu Beta Epsilon, B'nai B'rith (citation meritorious svc. Dist. Grand Lodge 6 1969). Home: 5400 S Hyde Park Blvd Apt C10 Chicago IL 60615-5828 Office: 10 S LaSalle St Ste 1400 Chicago IL 60603-1080 Office Phone: 312-263-0005.

BERNSTEIN, CHARLES GERALD, lawyer; b. Balt., Dec. 29, 1939; s. Sydney Jack Bernstein and Esther (Cohen) Siegel. BA, Western Md. Coll., 1961; JD, U. Md., 1968. Bar: Md. 1968, U.S. Dist. Ct. Md. 1968, U.S. Ct. Appeals (4th cir.) 1968, U.S. Supreme Ct. 1968. Law clk. Supreme Bench, City of Balt., 1967-68; asst. state's atty. Office of State's Atty., City of Balt., 1968-70; asst. U.S. atty. Office of U.S. Atty., State of Md., Balt., 1970-72; assoc. Dickerson, Nice, Sokol & Horn, Balt., 1973-74; fed. pub. defender Fed. Pub. Defender's Office, Balt., 1974-80; ptnr. Frank, Bernstein, Conaway & Goldman, Balt., 1980-83; pvt. practice Balt., 1983-87; ptnr. Bernstein, Sakellaris & Ward, Balt., 1988—. Office: Bernstein & Skellaris 1522 World Trade Ctr Baltimore MD 21202

BERNSTEIN, DANIEL LEWIS, lawyer; b. Durham, N.C., Aug. 19, 1937; s. Edward Morris and Edith (Lewis) B.; m. Ann Lust; children: Kenneth, Margaret. AB, Amherst Coll., 1959; LLB, Harvard U., 1962. Bar: N.Y. 1962, D.C. 1976. Assoc. Law Offices of A.L. Bienstock, N.Y.C., 1962-66, Hale Russell & Gray, N.Y.C., 1966-69, ptnr., 1970-84, Reid & Priest, N.Y.C., 1984-91, mng. ptnr., 1990-91; ptnr. Mannheimer Swartling, Stockholm, Sweden, N.Y.C., 1991-93, Law Office of Daniel L. Bernstein, N.Y.C., 1994—2003; sr. v.p., gen. counsel Lantis Eyewear Corp., N.Y.C., 1996—2003; ptnr. Sussman, Sollis, Ebin, Tweedy & Wood LLP, N.Y.C., 2001—. Trustee Georges Lurcy Charitable and Ednl. Trust, N.Y.C., 1982—. Dir. The Arts and Scis. Found. U. N.C., Chapel Hill, 1994-2000; trustee The Colleen Giblin Found., Oradell, N.J., 1994—, Walnut Hill Sch., Natick, Mass., 1999—. Mem.: ABA, Bar Assn. of City of N.Y., Alumni Coun. Amherst Coll. (mem. exec. com. 2004—). Office: Sussman Sollis Ebin Tweedy & Wood LLP 8th Fl 767 Fifth Ave New York NY 10153

BERNSTEIN, DAVID WILLIAM, lawyer; b. Bklyn., Feb. 13, 1938; s. Sidney Abraham B. and Carol Elsa Silverman; m. Carol Ellen Lamberg, June 16, 1959 (div. 1977); m. Melissa Lewis, Mar. 7, 1980; children: Andrew, Donna, Lauren. BA magna cum laude, Harvard U., 1959, LLB magna cum laude, 1962. Bar: N.Y. 1962. Assoc. atty. Rogers & Wells, N.Y.C., 1962-67; ptnr. Clifford Chance Rogers & Wells, N.Y.C., 1967—, chmn. corp. dept., 1989-97. Contbr. numerous articles to Internat. Fin. Law Rev., 1996—. Bd. dirs. Internat. Preschs., 1966—. Mem. Inwood Country Club (sec. 1982-91). Republican. Jewish. Avocation: golf. Office: Clifford Chance US LLP 31 W 52d St New York NY 10019-0005 Fax: 212-878-8375. Office Phone: 212-878-8342. E-mail: david.bernstein@cliffordchance.com.

BERNSTEIN, DONALD CHESTER, brokerage house executive, lawyer; b. St. Louis, July 29, 1942; s. Michael Charles and Laura (Schmidt) B.; m. Estelle Marla Cohen, Jan. 17, 1946; children: Kimberleigh, Chad, Aaron. BSBA, Washington U., 1964, JD, 1967; LLM, U. London, 1968. Bar: Mo. 1967. V.p., counsel A.G. Edwards & Sons, Inc., St. Louis, 1969—. Mem. Mo. Bar Assn., Bar Assn. Met. St. Louis. Republican. Jewish. Home: 22 Twin Springs Ln Saint Louis MO 63124-1138 Office: A G Edwards & Sons Inc 1 N Jefferson Ave Saint Louis MO 63103-2205 Office Phone: 314-955-3777. E-mail: don.bernstein@agedwards.com.

BERNSTEIN, DONALD SCOTT, lawyer; b. Bklyn., July 11, 1953; s. Emanuel and Shirley (Smithline) B.; m. Jo Ellen Finkel, May 31, 1987; children: Daniel Emanuel, Julia Clare. BA, Princeton U., 1975; JD, U. Chgo., 1978. Bar: N.Y. 1979, U.S. Dist. Ct. (ea. and so. dists.) N.Y. 1979. Assoc. Davis Polk & Wardwell, N.Y.C., 1978-86, ptnr., 1986—, head insolvency & restructuring practice group. Panelist Practicing Law Inst., N.Y.C., 1983—, Am. Law Inst., ABA, 1991—, Am. Bankruptcy Inst., 1991—; mem. vis. com. U. Chgo. Law Sch., 1995-98, chmn., 1997-98; mem. ofcl. U.S. del. Insolvency Working Group, UN Commn. on Internat. Trade Law. Contbg. author Collier on Bankruptcy, 1996—, bd. editors, 2000—. Bd. dirs. Altro Health and Rehab. Svcs., Bronx, N.Y., 1988-90, N.Y. chpt. Am. Diabetes Assn., 1992-96; mem. exec. com. bankruptcy lawyers div. United Jewish Appeal Fedn., 1985—. Mem. ABA (bus. bankruptcy com., com. on legal opinions), Am. Coll. Bankruptcy (bd. dirs., 2001—), New York County Lawyers Assn. (bd. dirs. 1992-94), Nat. Bankruptcy Conf. (exec. com. 1996-99, chmn. 2004—), Am. Bankruptcy Inst., Assn. Bar City N.Y. (audit com. chmn. 2000—, com. on bankruptcy and corp. reorgn. 1979-83, 85-88, chmn. 1993-96, mem. tribar opinion com. 1988—, chmn. 1998—), Internat. Insolvency Inst. (bd. dirs.). Office: Davis Polk & Wardwell 450 Lexington Ave Fl 21 New York NY 10017-3982 Office Phone: 212-450-4092. Office Fax: 212-450-3092. Business E-Mail: donald.bernstein@dpw.com.

BERNSTEIN, EDWIN S., judge; b. Long Beach, NY, Aug. 15, 1930; s. Harry and Lena (Strizver) B.; children: Andrea, David. BA, U. Pa., 1952; LLB, Columbia U., 1955. Bar: NY 1955, U.S. Ct. Appeals (2d cir.) 1962, U.S. Dist. Ct. (ea. and so. dists.) NY 1962, U.S. Tax Ct. 1962, U.S. Supreme Ct. 1964, Md. 1981, DC 1982. Mem. bd. contract appeals Dept. Army, Heidelberg, Germany, 1968-72; regional counsel U.S. Navy, Quincy, Mass., 1972-73; adminstrv. law judge U.S. Dept. Labor, Washington, 1973-79, Fed. Mine Safety and Health Rev. Commn., Washington, 1979-81, U.S. Postal Svc., Washington, 1981-87, USDA, Washington, 1987-2000. Liaison rep. Administrv. Conf. of U.S., Washington, 1983-84; guest lectr. SUNY-Albany, 1978, U. Md., 1982, George Washington U., 1984. Author: U.S. Army Procurement Handbook, 1971; Establishing Federal Administrative Law Judges as an Independent Corps, 1984, also articles. Bd. dirs. Washington Hebrew Congregation, 1985-88. Recipient Meritorious Civilian Svc. award Dept. Army, 1972. Mem. ABA, Fed. Bar Assn., DC Bar Assn., Fed. Adminstr. Law Judges Conf. (pres. 1983-84), Papermill Assn. (pres. 1980-81), Masons. Avocations: golf, bridge, sailing, wines, opera. Home and Office: 5314 Angel Wing Dr Boynton Beach FL 33437 E-mail: edangel@adelphia.net.

BERNSTEIN, ELIZABETH ANN, retired executive secretary; b. London, Aug. 13, 1928; arrived in U.S., 1960; d. Eugene and Ethel (Housley) Horsfall-Ertz; m. Alvin Bernstein, Mar. 5, 1975. Sec. various firms, 1948—58, Icelandic Airlines, Reykjavik, Iceland, 1958—59; legal and med. sec. various firms, 1960—82, 1982—89; ret., 1989. Author (poetry): Tsunami, 1994, Pull of the Tides, 1998, Many Moons Rising, 2002, numerous poems. Mem.: Bay Area Poets Coalition, Calif. Fedn. Chaparral Poets (2nd prize poems 2004—05). Democrat. Avocations: reading, writing, music, gardening, travel. Mailing: PO Box 94 Paradise CA 95967-0094

BERNSTEIN, ELLEN, business owner; b. Lansberg, Germany, Oct. 14, 1946; came to U.S., 1949; d. Harry and Betty (Lokensky) Dru; m. Alan Mark Bernstein, Nov. 7, 1971; children: Gary Drew, Randy Scott. Student, Fashion Inst. of Tech., 1964-65, Heffley Queensboro Coll., 1965. master advt. specialist. With Handmacher-Vogel, N.Y.C., 1965-68; sales exec., office mgr. Lee Mar Blouses, N.Y.C., 1968-84; sales exec. Rhoda Lee Blouses, N.Y.C., 1984-85, All-Types Advt., Pomona, N.Y., 1985-87; pres., owner Accent on Promotions, Inc., Pomona, N.Y., 1987—. Mem. com. Comms. Profls. of Rockland, Children's Mus.; vol. Venture Assn. Mem. Westchester Women in Comm., Rockland County Women's Network (bd. dirs. publicity com. 1985—, pres. 1991-93), Specialty Advt. Assn. Greater N.Y. (edn. com. 1990-92, bd. dirs. 1999—, pres. 2003-2004). Avocations: art, volleyball, horseback riding, reading. Office Phone: 845-362-0994.

BERNSTEIN, ELLIOT ROY, chemistry professor; b. NYC, Apr. 14, 1941; s. Leonard H. Bernstein and Geraldine (Roman) Goldberg; m. Barbara Wyman, Dec. 19, 1965; children: Jephta, Rebecca. AB, Princeton U., 1963; PhD, Calif. Inst. Tech., 1967. Postdoctoral fellow U. Chgo., 1967—69; asst. prof. Princeton U., N.J., 1969—75; assoc. prof. Colo. State U., Ft. Collins, 1975—80, prof. chemistry, 1980—; vis. prof. Bilbao, Madrid, Saville, Spain, 2000. Cons. Los Alamos Nat. Lab., 1975—83, Philip Morris, 1984—91, Du Pont Corp., 1985—92; Third Cycle in Chemistry lectr., Switzerland, 1998. Contbr. articles to profl. jours. Fellow NSF, 1961—62, Woodrow Wilson, 1963—64, JSPS, 1996. Fellow: Am. Phys. Soc., AAAS; mem.: Am. Chem. Soc., Sigma Xi. Office Phone: 970-491-6347. Business E-Mail: erb@lamar.colostate.edu.

BERNSTEIN, GERALD WILLIAM, management consultant, researcher; b. Boston, Nov. 25, 1947; s. Alan Irwin and Anne (Fine) B.; m. Kathleen Ann Chaikin, Jan. 12, 1985. BS in Aero. Engring., Rensselaer Poly. Inst., 1969; MS in Engring., Stanford U., 1978. Transp. engr., dept. transp. State of NY, Albany, 1969-70; transp. planner Kennebec Regional Planning Com., Winslow, Maine, 1974-77; dir. transp. dept. SRI Internat., Menlo Park, Calif., 1979-95; v.p. BACK Mgmt. Svcs., San Francisco, 1995-98; mng. dir. Stanford Transp. Group, San Francisco, 1998—. Session chmn. aviation workshop NSF, 1985, 91, 99, 2002; profl. conf. chmn. Contbr. articles to profl. jours. Chmn. transp. com. Glenn Park Neighborhood Assn., San Francisco, 1982-85; dir. Balboa Terrace Neighborhood Assn., San Francisco, 1986-88; trustee Congregation Beth Israel-Judea, 1991-93. With U.S. Army, 1970-72. Recipient Cert. Appreciation City of Waterville, Maine, 1977. Mem. Am. Inst. Aeronautics and Astronautics (sr. mem.), Transp. Rsch. Bd. NRC (chmn. econs. and forecasting com.), Toastmasters Club (Menlo Park, pres. 1986). Democrat. Jewish. Avocations: flying, skiing. Office: Stanford Transp Group 236 W Portal Ave Ste 359 San Francisco CA 94127-1423 Business E-Mail: gbernstein@stg.llc.com.

BERNSTEIN, GERDA MEYER, artist; Student, Art Inst. Chgo., MFA, 1978. Founder Artists, Residents of Chgo., 1973. One woman shows include Angeleski Gallery, N.Y.C., 1960, Artists, Residents of Chgo. Gallery, 1974, 75, 78, Elmhurst (Ill.) Coll., 1979, Karl Ernst Osthaus Mus., Hagen, West Germany, 1982, A.I.R. Gallery, N.Y.C., 1985, 89, Neuer Berliner Kunstverein, 1987, Bochum (Germany) Mus., 1987, Badischer Kunstverein, Karlsruhe, Germany, 1987, Rockford (Ill.) Coll., 1991, Beacon St. Gallery, Chgo., 1993, Fassbender Gallery, Chgo., 1994, 97, Robert F. DeCaprio Art Gallery, Moraine Valley Coll., Palos Hills, Ill., 1994, Alt. Mus., N.Y.C., 1995, Alternative Mus., N.Y.C., 1995, Ellis Island Immigration Mus., N.Y.C., 1996, Fassbender Gallery, Chgo., 1997, 2000, Reicher Gallery, Lake Forest, 2001, Fassbender-Stevens Gallery, Chgo., 2003, Kuusthaus Potsdam, Germany, 2003; exhibited in group shows at Art Inst. Chgo., 1954, 55, 56, 77, 82, 89, 92, 94, Isaac Delgado Mus., New Orleans, 1954, San Francisco Mus. Art, 1955, U. Chgo., 1961, U. Wis., Madison, 1962, 93, Whitney Mus. Am. Art, N.Y.C., 1973, Carleton Coll., Northfield, Minn., 1974, Sangamon State U., Springfield, Ill., 1974, Ill. State Mus. Art, Springfield, 1976, A.I.R. Gallery, 1977, 84, 88, 1134 Gallery, Chgo., 1977, U. Mo., St. Louis, 1977, U. Ill., Urbana and Chgo., 1977, Cultural Ctr., Chgo., 1978, 81, 89, Rutgers U., New Brunswick, N.J., 1979, Columba Coll., Chgo., 1981, Print Club Phila., 1981, Midwest Mus. Am. Art, Elkhart, Ind., 1981, Purdue (Ind.) U., 1981, Mus. Contemporary Art, Chgo., 1984, No. Ill. U., DeKalb, 1984, 90, Neuer Berliner Kunstverein, 1984, Women's Interart Ctr., N.Y.C., 1985, U.N. Conf. Women, Nairobi, Kenya, 1985, Ministerio de Cultura, Madrid, 1986, Chgo. Office Fine Arts, 1989, Franklin Furnace Gallery, N.Y.C., 1991, Peace Mus., Chgo., 1993, Spertus Mus., Chgo., 1994, Minn. Mus. Am. Art, St. Paul, 1995, Southeastern Ctr. Contemporary Art, Winston-Salem, N.C., 1995-96, Ellis Island, N.Y., 1996. Active Feminist Majority, Planned Parenthood, So. Poverty Law Ctr., Amnesty Internat., Holocaust Mus. Mem. NOW. Democrat. Avocations: reading, walking, music. Home: 1728 N North Park Ave Chicago IL 60614-5710 Studio: 1060 W Adams Chicago IL 60607

BERNSTEIN, GIORA, artistic director; b. Vienna; Studied with Igor Markevitch; doctorate, Boston U. Mem. Boston Symphony; founder, dir. Boston Chamber Orch., Claremont (Calif.) Music Festival; founding music dir., condr. Colo. Music Festival. Guest condr. Liege Philharmonic, Stuttgart Philharmonic, Netherlands Chamber Orch., Tonkunstler Orch. Vienna, Berlin Symphony Orch., Basel Radio Orch., St. Gallen Symphony, San Remo Symphony, Haifa Symphony Orch., Seattle Symphony Orch., Colo. Symphony Orch. Recipient Westinghouse Debut Recital award, City of Claremont commendation, County of L.A. commendation, Calif. Fedn. of Music Club award, Nat. Fedn. of Music Club award, Coleman Chamber Music award, six ASCAP awards, Excellence in the Arts award Gov. of Colo.; Internat. Acad. at Mozarteum fellow, Salzburg, Austria; Juilliard Sch. of Music scholar, Brandeis U. scholar, Boston U. scholar. Office: Colorado Music Festival 900 Baseline Rd #100 Boulder CO 80302-4256

BERNSTEIN, H. BRUCE, lawyer; b. Omaha, Dec. 9, 1943; s. David and Muriel (Krasne) B.; m. Janice Ostroff, Aug. 27, 1967; children: Daniel J., Jill M. AB, Cornell U., 1965; JD, Harvard U., 1968. Bar: Ill. 1968, Ill. Supreme Ct. 1968, US Dist. Ct. no. dist. Ill. 1969, ea. dist. Wis. 1997, US Ct. of Appeals 7th cir. 1981, 6th cir. 1995. Ptnr. secured transactions Sidley Austin Brown & Wood LLP, Chgo., 1974—, mem. exec. com. Gen. counsel Comml. Fin. Assn. 1995-2001 Past bd. dirs. Jewish Family and Cmty. Svc. Agy. Mem. ABA, Ill. Bar Assn. (past chmn. Comml., Banking and Bankruptcy Law section), Chgo. Bar Assn. (past chmn. Uniform Comml. Code Com.), Am. Coll. Comml. Fin. Attorneys, Am. Coll. Bankruptcy, Nat. Bankruptcy Conf., Standard Club, Mid-Day Club, Northmoor Country Club, Harvard Club. Avocation: golf. Office: Sidley Austin Brown & Wood LLP 10 S Dearborn St Ste 4500 Chicago IL 60603 Office Phone: 312-853-7635. Office Fax: 312-853-7036. Business E-Mail: bbernstein@sidley.com.

BERNSTEIN, I. MELVIN, dean, materials scientist; b. NYC, Oct. 14, 1938; s. Emanuel and Helen (Wolitzer) B.; m. Katherine Sarah Russo, June 7, 1964; 1 child, Elana BS, Columbia U., 1960, MS, 1962, PhD, 1965. Postdoctoral assoc. Central Electricity Generating Bd., Berkeley, Eng., 1966-67; scientist U.S. Steel Research Lab., Monroeville, Pa., 1967-72; from asst. prof. to prof. Carnegie-Mellon U., Pitts., 1972-87, assoc. dean engring., 1978-82, prof., head dept. metall. engring and materials sci., 1982-87; provost, acad. v.p. Ill. Inst. Tech., Chgo., 1987-90, chancellor, 1990-91; v.p. arts, scis. and engring., dean faculty Tufts U., Medford, Mass., 1991-2001; provost, sr. v.p. Brandeis U., 2001—03; dir. univ. programs Dept. of Homeland Security, Washington, 2003—. Chief cons. MCL, Monroeville, 1972-82; liaison scientist Office Naval Research, London, 1977-78; mem. Nat. Materials adv. bd., 1990-96. Co-editor: Handbook of Stainless Steel, 1977, Hydrogen Effects in Metals, 1973, 76, 1981; assoc. editor Metall. Trans., 1977-82. Mem. Pitts. Dem. Com., 1971-75; bd. govs. Ben Gurion U., Israel, 1993—. Jewish. Office Phone: 202-254-5839. Personal E-mail: mel.bernstein@att.net.

BERNSTEIN, JANE, writer; b. Bklyn., June 10, 1949; d. David and Ruth (Levinson) B.; m. Paul Glynn; children: Charlotte, Rachel. BA, NYU, 1971; MFA, Columbia U., 1977. Asst. prof. creative writing Carnegie Mellon U., Pitts. Author: Departures, 1979, Seven Minutes in Heaven, 1986, (non-fiction) Loving Rachel, 1988, various short stories, screenplays, mag. articles. Fellow N.J. Council on the Arts, 1981, 86, Nat. Endowment for the Arts, 1983. Mem. Authors Guild, Writers Guild Am. East, Nat. Writers Union, PEN.

BERNSTEIN, JANE AGAR, music educator, writer; b. N.Y.C., Mar. 23, 1947; d. Samuel and Claire Bernstein; m. James Leslie Ladewig, July 28, 1977; 1 child, Lily Bernstein Ladewig. BA, CCNY, 1967; MusM, U. Mass., 1968; PhD, U. Calif., 1974. Asst. prof. Tufts U., Medford, Mass., 1976—80, assoc. prof., 1980, prof., 1987—90, chair music dept, 1988—94, Austin Fletcher prof. music. Author: Print Culture and Music in Sixteenth-Century Venice; editor: Women's Voices Across Musical Worlds; author: Music Printing in Renaissance Venice, The Scotto Press (1539-72) (Otto Kinkeldey award, 1999); editor: (musical scores) The Sixteenth-Century Chanson, (musical score) Philip Van Wilder: The Collected Works. Recipient Disting. Alumna Citation of Excellence, U. Mass., 1990; fellow, Gladys Krieble Delmas Found., 1982—83, NEH, 1987—88; grantee, Am. Philos. Soc., 1986, Am. Coun. Learned Socs., 1995; John Simon Meml. Guggenheim fellow, Guggenheim Found., 2000—01. Mem.: AAAS, Am. Acad. Arts and Scis., Am. Inst. Verdi Studies, Renaissance Soc. Am., Am. Musicological Soc. (bd. dirs. 1986—88), Phi Beta Kappa (hon.). Avocations: needlepoint, travel. Office: Tufts University Music Department Medford MA 02155

BERNSTEIN, JAY, pathologist, researcher, educator; b. NYC, May 14, 1927; s. Michael Kenneth and Frances (Kaufman) B.; m. Carol Irene Kritchman, Aug. 11, 1957; children: John Abel, Michael Kenneth. BA, Columbia U., 1948; MD, SUNY, Bklyn., 1952. Diplomate Am. Bd. Pathology. Asst. pathologist Children's Hosp. Mich., Detroit, 1956-58, assoc. pathologist, 1959, attending pathologist, 1960-62, cons. in lab. medicine, 1977—93, cons. emeritus, 1993—; attending pathologist Bronx Mcpl. Hosp. Ctr., N.Y.C., 1962-68; asst. prof. pathology Albert Einstein Coll. Medicine, Bronx, N.Y., 1962-64, assoc. prof. pathology, 1964-68; chmn. dept. anatomic pathology William Beaumont Hosp., Royal Oak, Mich., 1969-90, dir. Rsch.

Inst., 1983-98, assoc. med. dir., 1990-98, hon. consulting pathologist, 1999—; clin. prof. pathology Wayne State U. Sch. Medicine, Detroit, 1977—99. Chmn. sci. adv. bd. Nat. Kidney Found. Mich., 1986-88, nat. sci. adv. bd., 1976-82; sci. advisor Nat. Inst. Child Health, USPHS, 1976-81; profl. adv. bd. Nat. Tuberous Sclerosis Assn., 1990-93; clin. prof. health sci. Oakland U., Rochester, Mich., 1980-90; vis. prof. pathology Albert Einstein Coll. Medicine, Bronx, 1974-2001; com. on renal disease WHO; cons. pathologist Internat. Study of Kidney Diseases in Children, Lupus Study Group. Co-editor: Perspectives in Pediatric Pathology; past contbg. editor Jour. Pediatrics; past mem. editl. bd. Pediatric Nephrology; mem. editl. bd. Jour. Urologic Pathology; contbr. articles to profl. jours. With USN, 1945-46. Recipient Henry L. Barnett award Am. Acad. Pediats., 1997. Mem. AMA, Am. Soc. Investigative Pathology, Internat. Acad. Pathology (U.S.-Can. divsn.), Am. Soc. Clin. Pathologists, Soc. Pediatric Pathology (co-founder, past pres., Farber lectr. 1982, Spl. Disting. Colleague award 1987, 97), Am. Pediatric Soc., Am. Soc. Nephrology, Internat. Pediat. Nephrology Assn., Renal Pathology Soc. (past pres., Renal Pathology Founder award 1997), Am. Soc. Pediatric Nephrology (Founder's award 1999). Office Phone: 248-898-1256. E-mail: jaybernstein@earthlink.net.

BERNSTEIN, JEFFREY, conductor, composer; b. Ithaca, NY, June 9, 1967; s. Jerome and Maxine Bernstein; m. Susan Deming, Sept. 20, 1967; 1 child, Celia Deming-Bernstein. AB, Harvard Coll., 1989; MusM, Yale U. Sch. Music, 1992; PhD, U. Calif., 2001. Founding dir. LAVA (LA Vocal Artists), 2003—; dir. of choral music Occidental Coll., 1997—2005; acting assoc. dir. of choral activities Harvard U., Cambridge, Mass., 1995—96. Singer LA Master Chorale, LA, 1997—. Composer: (oratorio) Telos, (chomolungma) Choral-Orchestral. Home: 1474 Campus Rd Los Angeles CA 90042 Personal E-mail: jeffrey@lavamusic.org.

BERNSTEIN, JOSEPH, lawyer; b. New Orleans, Feb. 12, 1930; s. Eugene Julian and Lola (Schlemoff) Bernstein; m. Phyllis Maxine Askanase, Sept. 4, 1955; children: Jill, Barbara, Elizabeth R., Jonathan Joseph. BS, U. Ala., 1952; LLB, Tulane U., 1957. Bar: La. 1957. Clerk to Justice E. Howard McCaleb of La. Supreme Ct., 1957; assoc. Jones, Walker, Waechter, Poitevent, Carrere & Denegre, 1957—60, ptnr., 1960—65; pvt. practice New Orleans, 1965—. Former gen. counsel Alliance for Affordable Energy. Past pres. New Orleans chpt. March of Dimes, New Orleans Jewish Cmty. Ctr.; past nat. exec. com. Am. Jewish Com.; trustee New Orleans Symphony Soc.; past mem. adv. council New Orleans Mus. Art. 2d lt. AUS, 1952—54. Mem.: ABA, La. Bar Assn., Zeta Beta Tau, Phi Delta Phi. Republican. Jewish. Home: 708 Explanade Ave Bay Saint Louis MS 39520 Office Phone: 228-466-4423. E-mail: Joelou1@bellsouth.net.

BERNSTEIN, JOSH, dentist; Grad., U. Calif. Berkeley, U. Pacific Dental Sch. Clinical instr. Las Vegas Inst. for Advanced Dental Studies. Featured cosmetic dentist Extreme Makeover. Contbr. articles to profl. journ. Named one of Am. Top Dentists, Consumers' Rsch. Coun. of Am.; recipient Dental Practice of Yr., The Richards Report. Mem.: Calif. Dental Assn., ADA, Dental Orgn. for Conscious Sedation, Am. Acad. Cosmetic Dentistry. Office: 2317 Channing Way Berkeley CA 94702*

BERNSTEIN, KENNETH ALAN, lawyer; b. Bklyn., Oct. 11, 1956; s. Jay M. and Marjorie J. (Rosenthal) B.; m. Joy S. Smilon, Aug. 10, 1980; children: Lisa, Lauren. BA, SUNY, Binghamton, 1978; JD, Am. U., 1981. Bar: N.Y. 1982, U.S. Dist. Ct. (so. and ea. dists.) N.Y. 1982. Asst. dist. atty. N.Y. County Dist. Atty's. Office, N.Y.C., 1981-86; assoc. Law Office of Robert I. Elan/Kenneth A. Bernstein, Lake Success, N.Y., 1986-92, Torino & Singer, P.C., Mineola, NY, 1992—98; ptnr. Torino & Bernstein, P.C., Mineola, 1998—. Mem. ABA, N.Y. State Trial Lawyers Assn., N.Y. Bar Assn., Nassau County Bar Assn. Home: 309 Syosset Woodbury Rd Woodbury NY 11797-1214 Office: Torino & Bernstein PC 200 Old Country Rd Mineola NY 11501 E-mail: kenneth.bernstein@torinoandbernstein.com.

BERNSTEIN, LAWRENCE R., inorganic chemist, pharmaceutical chemist; b. L.A., Dec. 23, 1955; s. Emil O. and Eleanor R. (Mordell) B.; children: Hannah L., Aaron A. AB, Harvard U., 1977, AM, 1978; PhD, Stanford U., 1985. Tutor in geol. sci. Harvard U., Cambridge, Mass., 1977-78; exploration geologist Brit. Petroleum, San Francisco, 1979-81; geologist U.S. Geol. Survey, Menlo Park, Calif., 1982-86; sr. rsch. scientist Yaskawa Co., Mountain View, Calif., 1990-92; rsch. dir. Terrametrix, Menlo Park, Calif., 1992—. Founder, dir., cons. GeoMed, Inc., Menlo Park, 1995—. Author: Minerals of the Washington, D.C. Area, 1980; patentee in pharma. field. Fed. Jr. fellow U.S. Govt., 1973-77; John Harvard hon. scholar, 1976, 77. Mem. Mineral Soc. Am., Am. Soc. for Bone and Mineral Rsch., Am. Chem. Soc., Internat. Ctr. for Diffraction Data (chmn. subcom. 1998—, minerals editor 1992—), Phi Beta Kappa, Sigma Xi. Achievements include discovery of compounds to administer gallium and other metals orally for the treatment of cancer; discovery of promising new treatment for psoriasis and related skin diseases. Home: 285 Willow Rd Menlo Park CA 94025-2711 Office: Terrametrix 285 Willow Rd Menlo Park CA 94025-2711 Office Phone: 650-324-3344. E-mail: larry.b@earthlink.net.

BERNSTEIN, LESLIE, academic administrator, biostatistician; BA, U. Calif., 1965; MS, U. So. Calif., 1978, PhD, 1981. Rsch. assoc. dept. preventive medicine U. So. Calif., L.A., 1981-82, asst. prof. biostats./epidemiology, 1982-88, assoc. prof. biostats./epidemiology, 1988-91, prof. biostats./epidemiology, 1991—, sr. assoc. dean faculty affairs, 1996—2003, AFLAC Inc. chair in cancer rsch., 1997—, vice provost med. affairs, 2003—. Sci. dir. U. So. Calif. Cancer Surveillance program, 1988—; mem. bd. sci. counselors Nat. Cancer Inst., 2001—; mem. sci. adv. panel Calif. Gov., 1989-92; mem. sci. com. Internat. Soc. Study Esophageal Diseases, 1994—; chair adv. com. L.I. Breast Cancer Cancer Study, Columbia U., 1994-2000; chair external adv. com. Nurse's Health Study Harvard U., 1995—; sci. adv. com. Registry for Rsch. on Transplacental Carcinogenesis, U. Chgo., 1997—; external adv. com. No. Calif. Cancer Ctr., Hawaii Cancer Ctr., 1997—. Contbr. over 250 articles to profl. jours. Office: U So Calif/Norris Cancer Ctr 1441 Eastlake Ave # 4449 Los Angeles CA 90033-0804

BERNSTEIN, LESTER, editorial consultant; b. NYC, July 18, 1920; s. Isidore and Rebecca (Axelrod) B.; m. Jacqueline Lipscomb, Feb. 6, 1946; children: Lynn, Nina, Paul, Daniel. AB, Columbia U., 1940. Reporter N.Y. Times, 1940-48; writer, fgn. corr., editor Time mag., 1948-58; dir. info. NBC, 1958-60, v.p. corp. affairs, 1960-62; nat. affairs editor Newsweek, 1963-65, exec. editor, 1965-69, mng. editor, 1969-72, editor, 1979-82; editorial cons., 1982-85; v.p. corporate communications RCA Corp., 1973-79. Cons. N.Y. Internat. Festival of the Arts, 1987-92. Recipient Nat. Mag. award for gen. excellence, 1981. Mem.: Century Assn. Home (Summer): PO Box 779 Castine ME 04421-0779

BERNSTEIN, LISA E., law educator; b. 1964; BA in Economics, U. Chgo., 1986; JD cum laude, Harvard U., 1990. Bar: NY 1994. Law clk. US Dist. Ct. Dist. Mass., Boston, 1990—91; assoc. prof. law Boston U. Sch. Law, 1991—95, Georgetown U. Law Ctr., 1995—96, prof., 1996—98, U. Chgo. Law Sch., 1998—. Vis. rsch. fellow in law & economics Harvard Law Sch., 1991; vis. assoc. prof. law U. Pa. Sch. Law, 1995, Georgetown U. Law Ctr., 1994; vis. prof. U. Chgo. Law Sch., 1997, Columbia U. Sch. Law, 1998. Mem.: Am. Law & Economics Assn. (bd. mem. 1999—). Office: U Chgo Law Sch 1111 E 60th St Chicago IL 60637 Office Phone: 773-834-2881. E-mail: lbernst621@aol.com.

BERNSTEIN, MARK, information technology executive; BS in Mech. Engring., U. Colo., 1973; MBA, Coll. Notre Dame, 1991. Joined Palo Alto Rsch. Ctr. (PARC), Calif., 1979—, mgr. rsch. strategy, 1992—2000, assoc. ctr. dir., 2000—01, pres., center dir., 2001—. Office: Palo Alto Research Center 3333 Coyote Hill Rd Palo Alto CA 94304 Office Phone: 650-812-4000.

BERNSTEIN, MELVIN, provost; BS, MS, PhD, Columbia U. Formerly with U.S. Steel Fundamental Rsch. Lab.; former mem. faculty, head dept. materials sci. and engring., assoc. dean engring. Carnegie-Mellon U., Pitts.; former provost, acad. v.p., chancellor, sr. v.p. Ill. Inst. Tech.; v.p. arts, scis. and engring., dean faculty arts, scis. and engring. Tufts U., Medford, Mass., 1991—2001; provost, sr. v.p. acad. affairs Brandeis U., Waltham, Mass., 2001—03; dir. univ. programs Dept. Homeland Security, Washington, 2003—. Lectr., presenter in field; mem. Nat. Materials Adv. Bd.; tech. cons. in field. Contbr. articles to profl. jours. Bd. overseers Boston Mus. Sci.; bd. govs. Ben-Gurion U., Israel. Fellow: Am. Soc. Materials. Office: Dept Homeland Security Sci and Tech Directorate Washington DC 20528 Office Phone: 202-254-5839. E-mail: mel.bernstein@att.net.

BERNSTEIN, MERTON CLAY, law educator, arbitrator; b. NYC, Mar. 26, 1923; s. Benjamin and Ruth (Frederica (Kleeblatt)) B.; m. Joan Barbara Brodshaug, Dec. 17, 1955; children: Johanna Karin, Inga Saterlie, Matthew Curtis, Rachel Libby. BA, Oberlin Coll., 1943; LL.B., Columbia U., 1948. Bar: N.Y. 1948, U.S. Supreme Ct. 1952. Assoc. Schlesinger & Schlesinger, 1948; atty. NLRB, 1949-50, 50-51, Office of Solicitor, U.S. Dept. Labor, 1950; counsel Nat. Enforcement Commn., 1951, U.S. Senate Subcom. on Labor, 1952; legis. asst. to U.S. Sen. Wayne L. Morse, 1953-56; counsel U.S. Senate Com. on R.R. Retirement, 1957-58; spl. counsel U.S. Senate Subcom. on Labor, 1958; assoc. prof. law U. Nebr., 1958-59; lectr., sr. fellow Yale U. Law Sch., 1960-65; prof. law Ohio State U., 1965-75; Walter D. Coles prof. law Washington U., St. Louis, 1975-96, Walter D. Coles prof. emeritus, 1997—; mem. adv. com. to Sec. of Treas. on Coordination of Social Security and pvt. pension plans, 1967-68. Prin. cons. Nat. Commn. on Social Security Reform, 1982-83; vis. prof. Columbia U. Law Sch., 1967-68, Leiden U., 1975-76; mem. adv. com. rsch. U.S. Social Security Adminstrn., 1967-68, chmn., 1969-70; cons. Adminstrv. Conf. of the U.S., 1989, Dept. Labor, 1966-67, Russell Sage Found., 1967-68, NSF, 1970-71, Ctr. for the Study of Contemporary Problems, 1968-71. Author: The Future of Private Pensions, 1964, Private Dispute Settlement, 1969, (with Joan B. Bernstein) Social Security: The System That Works, 1988; contbr. articles to profl. jours. Del White Ho. Conf. Aging, 1995; mem. Bethany (Conn.) Planning and Zoning Commn., 1962—65, Ohio Retirement Study Commn., 1967—68; co-chmn. transition team for St. Louis Mayor Freeman Bosley Jr., 1993; mem. Bd. of Health, City of St. Louis, 1993—2000; pres. bd. Met. Sch. Columbus, Ohio, 1974—75; mem. Brewster (Mass.) Bd. Health, 2001—, chair, 2002—; candidate for Dem. nom. US Senate, Mo., 1991—92; bd. dirs. St. Louis Theatre Project, 1981—84. With AUS, 1943—45. Fulbright fellow, 1975-76, Elizur Wright award, 1965. Mem. ABA (sec. sect. labor rels. law 1968-69), Internat. Assn. for Labor Law and Social Security (bd. dirs. U.S. chpt. 1973-83, 88-91), Fulbright Alumni Assn. (bd. dirs. 1976-78), Indsl. Rels. Rsch. Assn., Am. Arbitration Assn. (mem. adv. com. St. Louis region 1987—), Nat. Acad. Social Ins. (founding mem., bd. dirs. 1986-91). Democrat. Jewish. E-mail: bernstein@wulaw.wustl.edu.

BERNSTEIN, MICHAEL IRWIN, lawyer; b. Bklyn., Mar. 31, 1938; s. Samuel Bernard and Fay Louise (Barotz) B.; m. Janice Esther Reisner, Sept. 2, 1961; children: Lynne, Marci, Susan. BA in Econs., U. Mich., 1959; LLB, Columbia U., 1962. Bar: N.Y. 1963, U.S. Dist. Ct. (so., west and ea. dists.) N.Y. 1963, 2001, U.S. Ct. Appeals (2d cir.) 1963, U.S. Supreme Ct. 1974. Atty. NLRB, N.Y.C., 1962-65; assoc. Nordinger, Riegelman, Benetar & Charney, N.Y.C., 1965-70; ptnr. Aranow, Brodsky, Bohlinger, Benetar & Einhorn, N.Y.C., 1971-78, Benetar, Isaacs, Bernstein & Schair, N.Y.C., 1979-89, Benetar Bernstein Schair & Stein, N.Y.C., 1989—2004, Bond, Schoeneck + King, PLlC, 2004—. Lectr. in field. Contbr. numerous articles to profl. jours. Fellow N.Y. State Bar Found; mem. ABA (chmn. fed. labor standards legis. com. 1985-88, past. chmn. subcom. on occupational health and safety, past. chmn. subcoms. on age discrimination and equal pay), N.Y. State Bar Assn. (past chmn. labor and employmeny law sect, mem. exec. com., mem. special com. yoputh outreach, mem. ad hoc com. on law sch. liasisons, past chmn com. on intake and investigation, task force of reviewing practices), N.Y.C. Bar Assn. (past chmn. com. on labor law, past chmn. spl. com. on non-legal pers.), Coll. Labor and Employment Lawyers. Home: 24 South Pl Chappaqua NY 10514-3612 Office: Bond Schoeneck + King PLLC 330 Madison Ave New York NY 10017-5001 Office Phone: 646-253-2310. Business E-Mail: mbernstein@bsk.com.

BERNSTEIN, MITCHELL HARRIS, lawyer; b. N.Y.C., Sept. 19, 1949; s. Melvin and Gladys (Weissman) B.; m. Barbara Veitch, Oct. 8, 1978; children: Jonathan, Matthew, Emily. AB, U. Pa., 1970; JD, Yale U., 1973. Bar: N.Y. 1974, U.S. Ct. Appeals (2d cir.) 1974, U.S. Dist. Ct. (so. and ea. dists.) N.Y. 1974, U.S. Ct. Appeals (5th and D.C. cirs.) 1980, U.S. Supreme Ct. 1980, D.C. 1981, U.S. Ct. Appeals (4th cir.) 1981, U.S. Dist. Ct. D.C. 1982, U.S. Ct. Appeals (3d cir.) 1985. Assoc. Breed, Abbott & Morgan, N.Y.C., 1974-77; sr. atty. U.S. EPA, Washington, 1977-81; assoc. Skadden, Arps, Slate, Meagher & Flom, Washington, 1981-83, ptnr., 1983-93; mem. Van Ness Feldman, Washington, 1994—. Bd. advisors Chem. Waste Litigation Reporter, Washington, 1985—. Mem. ABA, D.C. Bar. Assn. Office: Van Ness Feldman Ste 7 1050 Thomas Jefferson St NW Washington DC 20007-3837 Office Phone: 202-298-1820. E-mail: mhb@vnf.com.

BERNSTEIN, NADIA J., lawyer; b. Salford, Lancashire, Eng., Feb. 26, 1945; came to U.S., 1948; d. David Colin and Rose (Bolton) Cohen; m. David J. Adler, Mar. 1977 (div. 1992); m. Robert Bernstein, May, 1997. BA, CCNY, 1966; JD, NYU, 1973. Bar: N.Y. 1974, U.S. Dist. Ct. (so. and ea. dists.) N.Y. 1974, U.S. Ct. Appeals (2d cir.) 1975, U.S. Supreme Ct. 1983. Assoc. Rosenman Colin Freund Lewis & Cohen and predecessor firms, NYC, 1973-82; ptnr. Rosenman & Colin, NYC, 1983-87; v.p., gen. counsel Montefiore Med. Ctr., NYC, 1987-89, sr. v.p., gen. counsel, 1989-98; v.p., gen. counsel, corp. sec. C.R. Bard, Inc., Murray Hill, NJ, 1999—2004; prin. The NJ Bernstein Law Firm, 2004—. Mem. legal affairs com. Greater N.Y. Hosp. Assn., N.Y.C., 1987-99; mem. bioethics task force, subcoms. on patient decision making, reproductive techs. and physician-assisted suicide, commn. women's equality Am. Jewish Congress, N.Y.C., 1989-94; mem. bd. ethics Village Briarcliff Manor, N.Y., 1997-; conf. bd. Coun. Chief Legal Officers, 1999-2004; mem. N.J. Gen. Counsel's Group, 1999-2004; instl. rev. bd. Montefiore Med. Ctr., 2005—. Bd. dirs. Berkeley-in-Scarsdale (N.Y.) Assn., 1989-91. Mem.: ABA (forum on health care, law practice mgmt. com. antitrust law sect., corp. practices com. bus. law sect.), Am. Corp. Coun. Assn. (law mgmt. com. 2000—04), Advanced Med. Tech. Assn. (legal com. 2002—04), Women Bus. Leaders U.S. Health Care Industry, Exec. Women of NJ (honoree 2000), NY State Bar Assn. (exec. com. health law sect. 1996—99, co-chair in-house counsel com. health law sect.), Am. Health Lawyers Assn., Assn. Bar of City of NY. Democrat. Office: 1 Sunnyside Ct Briarcliff Manor NY 10510

BERNSTEIN, PAUL, retired academic dean; b. Phila., Pa., Jan. 19, 1927; s. Abraham and Jennie (Geek) B.; m. Irma Shuster, Apr. 10, 1949; children: Jay Ira, Lisa Beth. BS, Temple U., 1949, MEd, 1950; PhD, U. Pa., 1955. Tchr. social scis. Phila. pub. schs., 1949-55; prof. European history, chmn. social scis. dept. Lock Haven (Pa.) State Coll., 1955-64, Plattsburg (N.Y.) State U. Coll., 1964-66; dean Coll. Gen. Studies, Rochester Inst. Tech., 1966-76, dean grad. studies, 1976-92, ret., 1993. Tchr. Elderhostel, Bradenton, Fla., 1998-99. Author: (with R. Green) History of Civilization, 2d edit., 1962, Career Education and the Quality of Working Life, 1980, American Work Values, 1997, Letters to Eleanor: Voices of the Great Depression, 2004; mng. editor Lock Haven Bull., 1959-64; author articles on Swedish labor mgmt. issues capitalism and consumerism; manuscript reviewer Polity Press, 1998. Co-chmn. Citizens for Humphrey, Monroe County, N.Y., 1968. Served with AUS, 1944-47; mem. adv. bd. Rochester Bus. Hall of Fame Selection Group, 2002—. Grantee Am. Philos. Soc., 1959; Grantee Swedish Bicentennial Com., 1980 Mem. Ind. Rel. Research Assn., Assn. Gen. and Liberal Studies (exec. bd., pres. 1978-79) Clubs: Elks. Republican. Jewish. Home: 1 Linden Cv Pittsford NY 14534-4614 Business E-Mail: pxbbbu@rit.edu.

BERNSTEIN, PHYLLIS J., financial consultant; b. N.Y.C., Oct. 10, 1955; d. Stanley and Esther Bernstein; m. Robert Kuchner, Dec. 10, 1978. BBA, Hofstra U., 1977. CPA NY. Staff auditor promoted to sr. Pantasote, Greenwich, Conn., 1977—79; sr. promoted to mgr., corp. auditing RCA (now GE), N.Y.C., 1979—85; tech. mgr., personal fin. planning AICPA, N.Y.C., 1985—88, sr. tech. mgr., personal fin. planning, 1988—91, dir., personal fin. planning, 1991—2001; pres. Phyllis Bernstein Consulting, Inc, N.Y.C., 2001—. Editl. adv. bd. mem. Jour. of Accountancy, Jersey City, 2002—; editl. adv. bd. The Tax Advisor, Jersey City, 2002—; adv. bd. mem. Personal Fin. Planning Monthly, Denver, 2002—, Fee-only Client Newsletters, Jericho, NY, 1998—; founder AICPA Ctr. for Investment Adv. Services, 1998—2000; creator and dir. AICPA Personal Fin. Specialist Designation Program, New York, NY, 1985—2001, AICPA Personal Fin. Planning Membership Sect., New York, NY, 1985—2001. Author: (trade book) Financial Planning for CPAs, 2000, Investment Advisory Relationships: Managing Client Expectations in an Uncertain Market, 2002; contributor and editor: book Guide to Registering as an Investment Advisor, 1997; editor: (newsletter) The Planner, 1985—. Sec. and concours chair Jaguar Touring Club, Monclair, NJ, 1995—98; mem. Young Leadersip Cabinet United Jewish Appeal, N.Y.C., 1994—2000; bd. dirs. Jewish Fedn. of Ctrl. NJ Endowment Found., Scotch Plains, 1998—2002; chair investment com. Jewish Fedn. Ctrl. N.J., 2002. Named Top 100 Most Influential Persons in Acctg., Acctg. Today, 1997—2001, Top 10 Names to Know in PFP, 1999—2002, One of four movers, shakers and decision makers, Fin. Planning mag. Mem.: AICPA (legis. and regulation task force pers. fin. planning sect. 2001—02), NY State Soc. of CPAs (fin. planning com. 2002), Fin. Planning Orgn., All-Star Fin. Group (v.p. 2002), Jaguar Touring Club (sec. and concours chair 2000). Democrat. Avocations: skiing, travel, shopping, dining, restoring Jaguars, gardening. Office: Phyllis Bernstein Consulting Inc 7 Penn Plaza Ste 1600 New York NY 10001 Business E-Mail: phyllis@pbconsults.com.

BERNSTEIN, RICHARD ALLEN, food products executive; b. N.Y.C., June 28, 1946; s. Sidney and Ethel Helen (Shankman) Bernstein; m. Amelia Fishman, Nov. 21, 1944; children: Bradley Ross, Jennifer Anne. BA in Econs., NYU, 1968. V.p. Pease & Ellman Inc., N.Y.C., 1968-70; pres. P&E Properties Inc., N.Y.C., 1970—; chmn. Western Pub. Co. Inc., N.Y.C., 1984-96; chmn., pres., CEO Western Pub. Group Inc., N.Y.C., 1984-96; chmn. Gen. Med. Corp., Richmond, Va., 1987-93, Harris Wholesale Co., Cleve., 1988-92; chmn., pres., CEO Rabco Health Svcs., Inc., N.Y.C., 1991-93; chmn. Millbrook Distbn. Svcs., Inc., Leicester, Mass., 1997—; chmn., CEO, Rabco Luxury Holdings LLC, 1997—, Breguet LLC, 1997—, B. Manischewitz Co., 1998—. Chmn., pres., CEO Penn Corp., 1986—96; mem. adv. bd. Chase Manhattan Bank, 1985—; chmn., CEO R.A.B. Holdings, Inc., 1996—, Millbrook Distbn. Svcs., Inc., 1997—, Brequet LLC, N.Y.C., 1997—2002, Rabco Luxury Holdings LLC, N.Y.C., 1997—. Trustee Police Athletic Legaue, N.Y.C., 1982—, NYU, 1988—; bd. dirs. Big Apple Circus, Inc., 1992—98, Hosp. for Joint Diseases, N.Y.C., N.Y. State Employee Retirement Sys., N.Y.C.; mem. N.Y. State Commn. on Regulation of Lobbying, Albany, 1982—86; bd. overseers Stern Sch. Bus. NYU; candidate for comptr. City of N.Y., 1981. With U.S. Army, 1969. Fellow, Yeshiva U., 1986. Mem.: Econ. Club N.Y. Republican. Jewish. Office: RAB Holdings 444 Madison Ave Ste 601 New York NY 10022-6903 Office Phone: 212-688-4500.

BERNSTEIN, ROBERT, retired physician, federal official, retired military officer; b. N.Y.C., Feb. 20, 1920; s. Morris and Rose (Gordich) B. BA, Vanderbilt U., 1942; MD, U. Louisville, 1946. Diplomate Nat. Bd. Med. Examiners, Am. Bd. Internal Medicine. Commd. 2nd lt. U.S. Army, 1942, advanced through grades to maj. gen., 1973; intern Grasslands Hosp., Valhalla, N.Y., 1946-47; resident Walter Reed Army Med. Ctr., Washington, 1952-55, dep. comdr., 1972-73, comdg. gen., 1973-78; surgeon U.S. Mil. Assistance Command, Vietnam, 1970-72; ret., 1978; commr. for spl. health svcs. Tex. Dept. Health, Austin, 1978-80, commr. of health, 1980-91. Adj. prof. U. Tex. Health Sci. Ctr., 1982—. Contbr. articles to mil. and med. jours. Decorated D.S.M. with oak leaf cluster, Legion of Merit with two oak leaf clusters, Bronze Star with oak leaf cluster, Purple Heart. Fellow ACP; mem. Soc. Med. Consultants to Armed Forces, Internat. Soc. Internal Medicine, Phi Delta Epsilon, Phi Kappa Phi, Alpha Epsilon Pi, Alpha Omega Alpha. Home: 3805 Greystone Dr Austin TX 78731-1505 E-mail: rakgen@aol.com.

BERNSTEIN, ROBERT JAY, lawyer; b. Bklyn., July 1, 1948; s. Martin Emanuel and Vera (Muter) B.; m. Janet Rodolico, Oct. 28, 1978. BA cum laude, cert. in pub. and internat. affairs, Princeton U., 1970; JD cum laude, U. Mich., 1975. Bar: Colo. 1976, N.Y. 1977. Law clk. to judge Richard P. Matsch U.S. Dist. Ct., Denver, 1975-76; assoc. Fried, Frank, Harris, Shriver & Jacobson, N.Y.C., 1976-80, Cowan, Liebowitz & Latman, P.C., N.Y.C., 1980-82, ptnr., 1982—2004; pvt. practice N.Y., 2004—. Mem. faculty, lectr. on copyright devels. Practicing Law Inst. Program, 1986, 88, 91, New Music Sem., 1987; guest lectr. on entertainment law U. Mich., 1987, 90; lectr. copyright law and litig. Copyright Soc. U.S.A., 1985, 87. Co-author column on copyright law N.Y. Law Jour., 1987—; contbr. articles on copyright law to Billboard mag., Entertainment and Sports Lawyer mag., others. Grantee Princeton U., 1969. Mem. ABA (sec. of patent, trademark and copyright lawyers, 1980—, forum com. on entertainment and sports law Music and Personal Appearances Div., 1980—, com. internat. copyright treaties and laws 1982-84, sub-com. on People's Republic of China., lectr. copyright law, forum com. on the entertainment and sports industries 1986), Am. Intellectual Property Law Assn. (sec., bd. dirs. 1990—, chmn. copyright law com. 1988-90, moderator panel on negotiation recording contracts, 1990, lectr. current devel. copyright law ann. meeting 1989, 93), Assn. Am. Pubs. (lawyers com. 1990-96), Assn. Bar City of N.Y. (com. copyright and literary property 2004—), Copyright Soc. of the USA (v.p., pres.-elect 1998-2000, pres. 2000-02, hon. trustee 2002—). Avocations: tennis, jazz saxophone, piano, skiing, golf, romance languages. Office: The Law Office Robert J Bernstein 488 Madison Ave 9th Fl New York NY 10022 Office Phone: 212-705-4811. Personal E-mail: bjaybird@aol.com. Business E-Mail: rjb@robert-bernsteinlaw.com.

BERNSTEIN, ROBERT M., plastic surgeon; b. N.Y.C., July 13, 1952; BS in Psychology, Tulane U., New Orleans, 1973; MD, U. Medicine and Dentistry of N.J., 1978. Lic. N.Y., N.J., Calif., diplomate Nat. Bd. Med. Examiners, Am. Bd. Dermatology, Am. Bd. Hair Restoration Surgery. Resident in internal medicine U. Medicine and Dentistry of N.J., 1978—79; resident in dermatology Albert Einstein Coll. Medicine, N.Y.C., 1979—81, chief resident in dermatology, 1981—82; pvt. practice dermatology, 1982—95; pvt. practice hair restoration surgery N.Y.C., 1995—. Med. dir. New Hair Inst. Med. Group, 1996—; website content mgr. newhair.com, 1997—; asst. in clin. dermatology Coll. Physicians and Surgeons, Columbia U., N.Y.C., 1982—85, instr. clin. dermatology, 1985—90, assoc. in clin. dermatology, 1990—95, asst. clin. prof. dermatology, 1995—2000, assoc. clin. prof. dermatology, 2000—; asst. attending dermatologist Manhattan Eye, Ear and Throat Hosp., N.Y.C., 1982—2000; attending, dept. dermatology Englewood Hosp., NJ, 1982—, pharmacy and therapeutics com., NJ, 1982—88, chmn. quality assurance and compliance com., dept. dermatology, NJ, 1990—94; asst. dermatologist Presbyn. Hosp., N.Y.C., 1982—90, assoc. dermatologist, 1990—96; asst. attending dermatology svc. N.Y. Presbyn. Hosp., 1996—2000, assoc. attending dermatology svc., 2000—; examiner Am. Bd. Hair Restoration Surgery, 2000—; mem. Almay Stress Info. coun. Almay Cosmetics, N.Y.C., 1990—92, mem. Almay Health Watch Coun. adv. bd., 1992—96; evaluation com. World Hair Soc., Scientific Workshop, Orlando, Fla., 1999—2000; lectr. in field. Contbg. editor: Dermatologic Surgery, 1998—, Jour. Aesthetic Dermatology and Cosmetic Dermatologic Surgery, 1998—2000; contbr. articles, editorial reviews, book and textbook chapters; guest appearances ABC, CBS, and Fox 5 News, featured on Good Morning America, The Discovery Channel. Named Surgeon of the Month, Hair Transplant Forum Internat., The Best Doctors in NY, 2000, 2001, Top Doctors: NY Metro Area, 2001, America's Top Doctors 2001-Surgical Hair Restoration; recipient Continuing Med. Edn. award, Am. Acad. Dermatology, 1982—99, Platinum Follicle award for Outstanding Achievement in Scientific and Clin. Rsch. in Hair Restoration, Internat. Soc. of Hair Restoration

Surgery, 2001; Tulane Scholar. Fellow: Am. Acad. Dermatology; mem.: Am. Hair Loss Coun., Am. Soc. for Dermatologic Surgery, Am. Acad. Aesthetic and Restorative Surgery, World Soc. of Hair Restoration Surgeons, North Jersey Dermatologic Soc., N.Am. Acad. Cosmetic and Restorative Surgery, Internat. Soc. Hair Restoration Surgery (mem. scientific and edn. com. 1999—2001, mem. certification com. 2002, ad hoc preceptorship com. 2001), Am. . Laser Medicine and Surgery, Am. Soc. Hair Restoration Surgery, Am. Acad. Cosmetic Surgery (mem. Am. hair loss coun.), N.Am. Soc. Phlebology. Office: 125 E 63d St New York NY 10021 Address: 2150 Center Ave Fort Lee NJ 07024 Office Phone: 212-826-2400, 201-585-1115. Office Fax: 201-585-0464. Business E-Mail: contact@bernsteinmedical.com.

BERNSTEIN, SANFORD IRWIN, biology professor; b. Bklyn., June 10, 1953; s. Harold and Adele Dorothy (Kutner) B.; m. Laurel Spear, July 10, 1983. BS, SUNY, Stony Brook, 1974; PhD, Wesleyan U., 1979. Rsch. fellow U. Va., Charlottesville, 1979-82; asst. prof. biology San Diego State U., 1983-85, assoc. prof., 1985-88, prof., 1988—. Assoc. dir. Molecular Biology Inst., 1987-92, dir. 1992-95; co-dir. DNA cert. program, 1983—, chair biology dept., 1995-2000, coord. joint-doctoral program in cell and molecular biology with U. Calif. San Diego, 2000—; established investigatorship Am. Heart Assn., 1989-94; mem. grant rev. panels NIH, Am. Heart Assn. Mem. editl. bd. Devel. Biology, 1991-95; contbr. articles to profl. jours. Muscular Dystrophy Assn. fellow, 1979-82, grantee, 1984—; grantee NIH, 1983—, NSF, 1997-2000. Mem.: AAAS, Am. Physiol. Soc., Biophys. Soc., Am. Soc. Biochemistry and Molecular Biology, Am. Soc. Cell Biology, Genetics Soc. Am., Sigma Xi. Achievements include research in developmental regulation of muscle gene expression in Drosophila, muscle protein isoform function, alternative RNA splicing. Office: San Diego State U Biology Dept and Molec Bio Inst San Diego CA 92182-4614 Business E-Mail: sanford.bernstein@sdsu.edu.

BERNSTEIN, SOL, cardiologist, educator; b. West New York, N.J., Feb. 3, 1927; s. Morris Irving and Rose (Leibowitz) B.; m. Suzi Maris Sommer, Sept. 15, 1963; 1 son, Paul. AB in Bacteriology, U. So. Calif., 1952, MD, 1956. Diplomate Am. Bd. Internal Medicine. Intern Los Angeles County Hosp., 1956-57, resident, 1957-60; practice medicine specializing in cardiology L.A., 1960—; staff physician dept. medicine Los Angeles County Hosp./U. So. Calif. Med. Ctr., L.A., 1960—, chief cardiology clinics, 1964, asst. dir. dept. medicine, 1965-72, med. dir., 1974-94; med. dir. central region Los Angeles County, 1974-78; dir. Dept. Health Svcs., Los Angeles County, 1978; assoc. dean Sch. Medicine, U. So. Calif., L.A., 1986-94, assoc. prof., 1968—; med. dir. Health Rsch. Assn., L.A., 1995—2005. Cons. Crippled Childrens Svc. Calif., 1965—. Contbr. articles on cardiac surgery, cardiology, diabetes and health care planning to med. jours. Served with AUS, 1946-47, 52-53. Fellow A.C.P., Am. Coll. Cardiology; mem. Am. Acad. Phys. Execs., Am. Fedn. Clin. Research, N.Y. Acad. Sci., Los Angeles, Am. heart assns., Los Angeles Soc. Internal Medicine, Los Angeles Acad. Medicine, Sigma Xi, Phi Beta Phi, Phi Eta Sigma, Alpha Omega Alpha. Home: 4966 Ambrose Ave Los Angeles CA 90027-1756 Office: 1640 Marengo St Los Angeles CA 90033-1036 Business E-Mail: sol@hsc.usc.edu.

BERNSTEIN, STAN, federal bankruptcy judge; b. L.A., 1941; m. Jane Ellen Hirschfield; 3 children. BA, Brandeis U., 1962; MA, U. Chgo., 1964; PhD, Harvard U., 1970; JD, Rutgers U., 1973. Bar: Mich. 1974, Ohio 1974, Calif. 1985, Ariz. 1989, Mass. 1991. Mem. faculty U. Calif., Davis, 1967-70, Rutgers U., 1970-73; assoc., ptnr. Honigman, Miller, Schwartz & Cohn, Detroit, 1974-82; bankruptcy judge for Ea. Dist. Mich., U.S. Bankruptcy Ct., Detroit, 1982-84; ptnr. Gendel, Raskoff, Shapiro & Quittner, L.A., 1984-85, Dickinson, Wright, Detroit, 1985-89; shareholder Brown & Bain, Phoenix, 1989-90; ptnr. Foley, Hoag & Eliot, Boston, 1991-96; bankruptcy judge for Ea. Dist. N.Y., U.S. Bankruptcy Ct., Central Islip, 1996—. Mem.: Nat. Conf. Bankruptcy Judges. Office: US Bankruptcy Ct 290 Federal Plz Central Islip NY 11722-4437 Office Phone: 631-712-5742. Business E-Mail: stan_bernstein@nyeb.uscourts.gov.

BERNSTEIN, STANLEY JOSEPH, manufacturing executive; s. David William and Irene Mildred Bernstein; m. Cathy Ann Grey; children: Michael A., Geoffrey T. BA, Brown U., 1965; JD, U. Pa., 1968. Bar: Mass. 1968. Mgr. Am. Biltrite Inc., Chelsea, Mass., 1968-71, div. gen. mgr. Cambridge, Mass., 1971-78, v.p. corp. devel., 1978-82; exec. v.p. The Biltrite Corp., Waltham, Mass., 1983-85, chmn., chief exec. officer, 1986—, also bd. dirs. Bd. dirs. Shenzhen Biltrite-SPEC Soling Co., Ltd., Shenzhen, China, Atlanta. Life trustee Roxbury Latin Sch., West Roxbury, Mass.; trustee Brown U. Office: The Biltrite Corp PO Box 9045 51 Sawyer Rd Waltham MA 02454-9045 E-mail: stanley.bernstein@biltrite.com.

BERNSTEIN, STEVEN, librarian, writer; b. Washington; s. Philip and Miriam Bernstein. BA, George Washington U., 1977; cert., Catonsville C.C., 1994; MA, Duquesne U., 2000. Feature writer North Hills Mag., Valencia, Pa., 2000—01. Rschr. Thomas Fleming, N.Y., 1999—; cons. Ft. Pitt Mus., Pitts., 1999—2000; rschr. Pa. Hist. and Mus. Commn., 2000. Rschr.: The New Dealers War: FDR and The War Within World War II, 2001, The Illusion of Victory: America in World War I; contbr. articles to jours. and mags. Avocation: outdoor activities. Home: PO Box 83704 Gaithersburg MD 20883-0704

BERNSTEIN, STUART A., former ambassador; b. Washington, D.C., 1938; m. Wilma Bernstein; children: Brian, Adam, Alison. Leader in real estate devel., investment and mgmt. Mid-Atlantic region, Washington; U.S. amb. to Denmark US Dept. State, Copenhagen, 2001—05. Apptd. commr. Internat. Cultural and Trade Ctr., 1991; apptd. trustee John F. Kennedy Ctr. for Performing Arts, 1992—2001. Former bd. trustees Am. Univ.; former bd. dirs. Weizman Inst. of Sci. Personal E-mail: sbern11@aol.com.

BERNSTEIN, TRACY GINA, editor; b. N.Y.C., Oct. 12, 1961; d. Robert Alan and Vicki (Kanner) Bernstein; m. Eric Beldoch, Aug. 23, 1992; children: Nicholas Beldoch, Rachel Beldoch. BA, Yale U., 1983. Exec. editor New Am. Libr., N.Y.C., 2002—. Office: New American Library 375 Hudson St New York NY 10014

BERNSTEIN, WARREN J., lawyer; AB cum laude, Rutgers Coll., 1977; JD, U. Pa., 1980. Bar: NY 1981. Ptnr., co-chair Real Estate Dept. Kaye Scholer LLP, NYC. Mem.: Assn. Bar. of City NY, NY State Bar Assn. Office: Kaye Scholer LLP 425 Park Ave New York NY 10022 Office Phone: 212-836-8073. E-mail: wbernstein@kayescholer.com.

BERNSTEIN, WILLIAM JOSEPH, glass artist, educator; b. Newark, Dec. 3, 1945; s. Jacob and Rosalind (Merliss) B.; m. Katherine Schachter, July 21, 1968; children: Joshua, Alex. BFA, Phila. U. of Arts, 1968. Artist in residence Penland (N.C.) Sch. of Crafts, 1968-70; instr. Summervail Workshop, Vail, Colo., U. So. Calif., L.A., Pilchuck Glass Ctr., Stanwood, Wash., Naples (N.Y.) Mill Sch.; tchr. Bezalel Acad., Jerusalem, Israel, 1997—. One-man show Hodges Taylor Galley, Charlotte N.C., 1997; exhibited in group shows at Somerhill Gallery, Chapel Hill, N.C., Grohe Glass Gallery, Boston, Marx Gallery, Chgo., Am. Craft Mus., N.Y.C., John Michael Kohler Arts Ctr., Sheboygan, Wis., Spaso House, Moscow, U.S.S.R., The Denver Art Mus., Laguna Art Mus., Laguna Beach, Calif., Milwaukee Art Mus., J.B. Speed Art Mus., Louisville, Ky., Va. Mus. Fine Arts, Richmond, Ark. Arts Ctr. Decorative Arts Mus., Little Rock, Galerie Angela Hollings, Hameln, Germany, J&L Lobmeyr, Vienna, Austria, Galerie Rob van den Doel, The Hague, The Netherlands, Isetan Galleries, Japan; represented in permanent collections the Corning (N.Y.) Mus. of Glass, the Mint Mus. Art, Charlotte, N.C., Nat. Collection Fine Art, Washington, Greenville (S.C.) County Mus. Art, Australian Coun. for the Arts, Sidney, Morse Gallery Art, Winter Park, Fla., Ft. Lauderdale (Fla.) Mus. Arts, R.J. Reynolds Collection, Winston-Salem, N.C., Craft and Folk Mus., L.A., Glasmus., Frauenau, Germany, Ark. Art Ctr., Little Rock, Glasmus., Ebeltoft, Denmark, J&L Lobmeyr, Vienna, Austria, Asheville (N.C.) Mus. Art, Yamaha Corp., Japan, Chrysler Mus. Norfolk, Va., Newark (N.J.) Mus., Charles A. Wustan Mus. Arts, Racine, Wis. Louis Comfort Tiffany Found. grantee, 1975, NEA Master Craftsman Apprenticeship, 1976; NEA fellow, 1974, N.C. Arts Coun. fellow, 1983, masterworks fellow Creative Glass Ctr. Am., 1990. Office: 469 Hannah Branch Rd Burnsville NC 28714-7569 E-mail: wberns1141@aol.com.

BERNSTINE, DANIEL O'NEAL, law educator, academic administrator; b. Berkeley, Calif., Sept. 7, 1947; s. Annias and Emma (Jones) B.; m. Nancy Jean Tyler, July 27, 1971 (div. Mar. 1986); children: Quincy Tyler, Justin Tyler. BA, U. Calif., Berkeley, 1969; JD, Northwestern U., Chgo., 1972; LLM, U. Wis., 1975; LLD (hon.), Hanyang U., Seoul, Korea, 1999, Waseda U., Tokyo, 2003; PhD (hon.), Nizhny Novgorod Linguistics U., Russia, 2004. Bar: D.C. 1970, Wis. 1979. Prof. law Howard U. Law Sch., Washington, 1975-78, gen. counsel, interim dean, 1987-90; prof. law U. Wis. Law Sch., Madison, 1978-97, dean, 1990-97; pres. Portland (Ore.) State Univ., 1997—. Author: Wisconsin and Federal Civil Procedure, 1986. Bd. dirs. Madison Cmty. Found., 1990-94, Portland Urban League, Legacy Health Sys., Willamette United Way, 2001—04; mem. Portland Multnomah Progress Bd., 1998—, Kellogg Commn. on the Future of State and Land-Grant Univs., 1997-2000. Mem. Am. Law Inst., Portland C. of C. (bd. dirs.). Office: Portland State Univ PO Box 751 Portland OR 97207-0751 Office Phone: 503-725-4419. Business E-Mail: bernsined@pdx.edu.

BERNT, BENNO ANTHONY, entrepreneur, investor; b. Bielitz, Austria, Mar. 14, 1931; came to U.S., 1953, naturalized, 1961; s. Victor and Grete Bernt; m. Constance Smigel, June 22, 1957; children: Karin, Eric, Steve. BS in Engring. cum laude, Fed. Inst. Tech., Vienna, Austria, 1952; DCS in Bus. and Econs. cum laude, U. Econs. & Bus. Adminstrn., Vienna, 1953; MBA, Carnegie Mellon U., 1954. Fin. and mfg. exec. Chrysler Corp., 1954-59; mfg. and bus. planning exec., subs. gen. mgr. Whirlpool Corp., 1959-68; pres. Cissell Mfg. Co., Louisville, 1968-70; gen. mgr. Simonds Abrasive Co., Phila., 1970-73; v.p. fin. ESB Ray-O-Vac Corp., Phila., 1973-76, exec. v.p., dir., 1977-78; pres., CEO RAYOVAC, Madison, Wis., 1979-82; sr. v.p. fin. and planning, CFO Nat. Intergroup Inc., Pitts., 1983-87; chmn. The Griffin Group, Pitts., 1988—, Univ. Ptnrs., Inc., 1997—; interim CEO Carnegie Tech. Edn., Inc., 1998-99. Bd. dirs. Pitts. Tissue Engring. Initiative, Carnegie Sci. Ctr.; dir. tech. transfer Carnegie Mellon U., 1992—97. Chmn. adv. bd. Sch. Computer Sci. and Sch. Music Carnegie Mellon U., 1993—; bd. dirs. Pitts. Symphony, Carnegie Sci. Ctr., Pitts. Mem. Duquesne Club, Pitts. Golf Club. Office: Griffin Group Ptnrs LP 308 Schenley Rd Pittsburgh PA 15217-1173 *I believe the measure of one's true success lies in how well we are using our own potential, and how well we are serving others.*

BERNTHAL, ERIC L., lawyer; b. Syracuse, N.Y., June 21, 1946; BA, Columbia U., 1967; JD with honors, George Washington U., 1970. Bar: D.C. 1970, U.S. Supreme Ct. 1975. Law clk. to Hon. Ruggero J. Aldisert U.S. Ct. Appeals (3rd cir.), 1970-72; ptnr. Arent, Fox, Kintner, Plotkin & Kahn, Washington, 1972—86; with Latham & Watkins LLP, 1986—, now mng. ptnr., Washington office. Mem. ABA, Fed. Comm. Bar Assn., Order of the Coif. Office: Latham & Watkins Ste 1000 555 11th St NW Washington DC 20004-1304

BERNTHAL, FREDERICK MICHAEL, association executive; b. Sheridan, Wyo., Jan. 10, 1943; s. Erwin and Erna Bernthal; m. Heather A. Lancaster; 1 child, Justin. BS, Valparaiso U., 1964; PhD, U. Calif., Berkeley, 1969. Rsch. staff Yale U., New Haven, 1969-70; prof. Mich. State U., East Lansing, 1970-80; legis. asst. Senator Howard Baker, Washington, 1978-80, chief legis. asst., 1980-83; mem. U.S. Nuc. Regulatory Commn., Washington, 1983-88; asst. sec. oceans, environment, and sci. Dept. of State, Washington, 1988-90; dep. dir. NSF, Washington, 1990-94; pres. Univs. Rsch. Assn., Washington, 1994—. Bd. dirs. PPL Corp., Sci. Svc., Inc. Contbr. 45 articles to sci. jours. NATO Sr. Scientist fellow U. Copenhagen, 1977; Congl. Sci. fellow Am. Phys. Soc., 1978-79. Fellow Am. Phys Soc.; mem. AAAS, Am. Chem. Soc., Cosmos Club of Washington. Republican. Lutheran. Office: Univs Rsch Assn 1111 19th St NW Ste 400 Washington DC 20036-3627 Office Phone: 202-293-1382. E-mail: bernthal@ura.nw.dc.us.

BERNTHAL, HAROLD GEORGE, health products executive, director; b. Frankenmuth, Mich., June 11, 1928; s. Wilfred Michael and Olga Bertha (Stern) B.; m. Margaret Hrebek, Jan. 25, 1958; children: Barbara Anne, Karen Elizabeth, James Willard. BS in Chemistry, Mich. State U., 1950. Pres. Am. Hosp. Supply Corp., Evanston, Ill., 1974-85; chmn. Cobern Inc., Lake Forest, Ill., 1986—. Life trustee Northwestern Meml. Hosp., Chgo.; hon. bd. dirs. Valparaiso (Ind.) U.; former chair Wheat Ridge Ministries; former governing mem. Chgo. Symphony Orch. Served with AUS, 1950-52. Recipient Lumen Christi medal Valparaiso U., 1988. Mem. Health Industries Assn. (past pres.), Health Industry Mfr.'s Assn. (past mem. exec. com.), Pharm. Mfrs. Assn. (past chmn. med. device com., Knollwood Club, Old Elm Club, The Reserve, Bigfoot Country Club.

BERNTSON, GARY GLEN, psychiatry, psychology and pediatrics educator; b. Mpls., June 16, 1945; s. Edward Mathias and Meryle Berntson; m. Susan Berntson, July 11, 2002. BA, U. Minn., 1968, PhD, 1971. Postdoctoral fellow Rockefeller U., N.Y.C., 1971-73; asst. prof. dept. psychology Ohio State U., Columbus, 1973-77, assoc. prof., 1977-81, prof., 1981—, prof. dept. pediatrics, 1983—, prof. of psychiatry, 1988—. Affiliate scientist Yerkes Regional Primate Rsch. Ctr., Emory U., Atlanta, 1984-95; mem. initial rev. group ADAMHA, Washington, 1989-91, NIMH, Washington, 1991-93, NIH, 2004—; mem. fellowship rev. panel NSF, Washington, 1991-95. Contbr. over 150 articles to profl. jours., 20 chpts. to books; co-editor: Handbook of Psychophysiology. Fellow NSF, 1969, USPHS, 1972. Mem. Soc. for Neurosci., Soc. for Psychophysiol. Rsch.; fellow AAAS. Achievements include novel concepts of control of the autonomic nervous system and psychosomatic relations. Office: Ohio State U Dept Psychology 1885 Neil Ave Columbus OH 43210-1222 Office Phone: 614-292-1749.

BERO, MARILYN PROCINO, retired volunteer; b. Auburn, N.Y., Sept. 12, 1937; d. Jack Anthony and Mary Louise (Cefaratti) Procino; m. James Donald Bero, Feb. 10, 1962; children: Mark J., Michael A., Matthew R. BA in Elem. Edn., Marywood Coll., 1959; postgrad., Syracuse U., 1961. Tchr. Auburn (N.Y.) Sch. Sys., 1959-61; sec.-treas. Hampton Rd. Constrn. Corp., Seneca Falls, NY; ret. Adviser to jury design competition Wesleyan Chapel; bd. dirs. Seneca Falls Savs. Bank. Adv. commn. Women's Rights Nat. Hist. Park; mem. Seneca Falls Sch. Dist. Bd., 1976—85, v.p., bd. dirs., 1978, pres., 1980—83; bd. dirs. Seneca County Child Care Ctr., 1975—84, pres., 1975—79; co-chmn. bldg. fund drive Nat. Women's Hall of Fame, Inc., Seneca Falls, 1978—79, pres., 1980—83; chair Women's Invitational Art Show, 1998; bd. dirs. Alpha Day Sch., Seneca Falls, 1972—75, Happiness House, Geneva, NY, 1968—72, CAUSE, United Way, Seneca County United Way, 1986—90, Seneca Cmty. Players. Named Citizen of the Yr., Rotary, 1983; recipient Unsung Heroine award, Syracuse chpt. NOW, Cmty. Svc. award, 2005. Mem.: AAUW, Women's League Seneca Falls (pres. 1978—79). Republican. Roman Catholic. Home: Box 670 2934 Route 89 Seneca Falls NY 13148

BERO, MEG ANN, museum director, curator, educator; d. Beverly Patricia and George Harry George; m. Dan Michael Bero, Jan. 29, 1977; children: Evan Daniel, Marissa Patricia, Lindsay Tess. BS in Edn., U. Mo., 1972; MAT, Aurora (Ill.) U., 2000; student in Mus. Studies, No. Ill. U., 2005—. Art educator Batavia (Ill.) Pub. Schs., 1992—96; curator edn. Schingoethe Mus. Native Am. Cultures Aurora (Ill.) U., 1996—2000, assoc. dir., curator Schingoethe Ctr. Native Am. Cultures, 2001—, adj. faculty, 2003—. Cons. Air Classics Mus., Aurora, 2003—04; creator mus. edn. program MAIZE: Museum Artifact Inquiry Zone, 1999; lectr. in field. Exhibitions include Norris Gallery, St. Charles, Ill., 2000, Aurora U., 2004—05. Grantee, Ill. Humanities Coun., 2003—04. Mem.: Mt. Plains Mus. Assn. (presenter), Nat. Art Edn. Assn. (assoc.), Ill. State Hist. Soc. (assoc. Superior Achievement award 2003), Ill. Assn. Mus. (assoc.; presenter, Superior Achievement award 2002, 2003), Am. Assn. Mus. (assoc.), Ill. Art Edn. Assn. (assoc.; v.p. 2002—05, presenter, named Ill. Mus. Educator of Yr. 1999). Avocations: painting, antiques, gardening, reading, travel. Office: Aurora University Schingoethe Museum 347 South Gladstone Ave Aurora IL 60506-4892 Office Phone: 630-844-7844. Office Fax: 630-844-8884. E-mail: mbero@aurora.edu.

BEROLZHEIMER, KARL, lawyer; b. Chgo., Mar. 31, 1932; s. Leon J. and Rae Gloss (Lowenthal) B.; m. Diane Glick, July 10, 1954; children: Alan, Eric, Paul, Lisa. BA, U. Ill., 1953; JD, Harvard U., 1958. Bar: Ill. 1958, U.S. Ct. Appeals (7th cir.) 1964, U.S. Ct. Appeals (9th cir.) 1969, U.S. Supreme Ct. 1976. Assoc. Ross & Hardies, Chgo., 1958—66, ptnr., 1966—76; v.p. legal Centel Corp., Chgo., 1976-77, v.p., gen. counsel, 1977-82, sr. v.p., gen. counsel, 1982-88, sr. v.p., gen. counsel, sec., 1988-93; of counsel Ross & Hardies, Chgo., 1993—2003, McGuire Woods LLP, 2003—. Nat. adv. bd. Ctr. for Informatics Law, John Marshall Law Sch., Chgo., 1988-93; mem. Corp. Counsel Ctr., Northwestern U. Law Sch., 1987-93, mem. emeritus, 1993—; mem. adv. bd. Litigation Risk Mgmt. Inst., 1989-95; bd. dirs. Milton Industries, Chgo., 1973-2005, Devon Bank, Chgo., 1985—; cons. Mt. Pulaski Tel. and Elec. Co., Lincoln, Ill., 1981-86; sec., gen. counsel Consol. Water Co., Chgo., 1968-72; mem. human rels. task force Chgo. Cmty. Trust, 1988-90. Bd. dirs. The Nat. Conf. Commn. and Justice, Chgo., presiding co-chmn., 1987-90, mem. nat. exec. bd. dirs., 1988-98, chair investment com., 1991-94, nat. co-chair, 1992-95, pres., 1993-94, chair, 1995-98; exec. bd. Internat. Coun. Christians and Jews, 1996-2000, v.p., 1998-2000; bd. dirs. Evanston (Ill.) Mental Health, 1975-82, chair, 1978-80; dir. Evanston Cmty. Found., 1996-2003, vice chair, chair grants com., 1996-98, chair, 1999-2001, chair coun. advisors, 2003—; bd. dirs. Beth Emet Found., 1997; trustee Northlight Theatre, Evanston, 1992-2004, vice-chair, 1993-99; mem. coun. The Communitarian Network, 1993-96; trustee Beth Emet Synagogue, Evanston, 1985-87, 89, 2004-, sec., 1985-89; chair Capital Campaign Plan com., 1994-97; discrimination priority com. United Way, 1990-97, vice-chair, 1993; mem. assembly Parliament of the World's Religions, 1993; mem. Ill. atty. gen.'s ad hoc com. for creation of justice commn., 1994; adv. com. Ill. Justice Commn., 1995-96; adv. bd. Nat. Underground R.R. Freedom Ctr., 1997—. 1st lt. U.S. Army, 1953-55. Fellow Am. Bar Found.; mem. ABA (chair telcom. com. bus. law sect. 1982-86, dispute resolution com. 1986-90, office com. 1991-95, mem. Coalition for Justice 1993-97, bd. editors Bus. Law Today 1995-97, co-chair conflicts of interest com. 1997-2001, past chair 2001-03), Chgo. Bar Assn. (devel. of law com. 1963-77, chair 1971-73), Chgo. Coun. Lawyers. Democrat. Office: McGuire Woods LLP Ste 4100 77 W Wacker Dr Chicago IL 60601-1815 Home: 522 Church St Apt 6D Evanston IL 60201 Office Phone: 312-750-8642. Personal E-mail: dkberolz@comcast.net.

BERRA, P. BRUCE, computer science educator; b. Smiths Creek, Mich., Apr. 14, 1935; s. Mike John and Dorothy (Nelson) B.; 1 son, Marshall R. BS, U. Mich., 1958, MS, 1962; PhD, Purdue U., 1968. Sr. engr. Hughes Aircraft Corp., Culver City, Calif., 1958-60; engr., tech. advisor Bendix Corp., Ann Arbor, Mich., 1960-63; instr. U. Mich.-Dearborn, 1964-65; asst. prof. info. engring. Boston U., 1965-66; assoc. prof. Syracuse U. (N.Y.), 1968-74, 74—, prof., chmn. indsl. engring. and ops. research, 1978-82, prof. elec. and computer engring., 1982-96; dir. N.Y. State Ctr. for Advanced Tech./Software Engring., 1991-96; dir. Info. Tech. Rsch. Inst., disting. prof. info. tech. Wright State U., Dayton, Ohio, 1997-2000. Cons. IBM Corp., Bell No. Rsch., IITRI, PAR Tech., SCEEE, Singer Link, TRW, KAMAN, Opticomp. Gen. chmn., organizer Workshop on Database Machines, 1980-89. USAF Office of Sci. Research univ. resident research fellow, 1982-83 Fellow IEEE; mem. IEEE Computer Soc. (editor-in-chief CS Press 1981-83, vice chmn. publs. bd. 1984-85, governing bd. 1985-86, 89-91, disting. visitors program 1986-88, 89-91, gen. chmn. internat. conf. on data engring. 1986). E-mail: bberra@worldnet.att.net.

BERRA, YOGI (LAWRENCE PETER BERRA), former professional baseball player, coach and manager; b. St. Louis, May 12, 1925; s. Peter and Pauline (Longsoni) B.; m. Carmen Short, Jan. 26, 1949; children— Lawrence A., Timothy Thomas, Dale Anthony. PhD (hon.), Montclair State U., 1996. Profl. baseball player with NY Yankees, 1946-63, mgr., 1964, coach, 1975-84, mgr., 1984-85; coach NY Mets, 1965-72, mgr., 1972-75; coach Houston Astros, 1986-89; former v.p. Yoo-Hoo Chocolate Beverage Co. Author: (with Ed Fitzgerald) Yogi Berra: The Autobiography of a Professional Baseball Player, 1961, (with Tom Horton): It Ain't Over ..., 1989, The Yogi Book: I Really Didn't Say Everything I Said, 1998, (with Dave Kaplan) When You Come to a Fork in the Road, Take It, 2001, 10 Rings-My Championship Seasons, 2003. Served with USNR, 1943-46. Recipient Am. League Most Valuable Player award, 1951, 54, 55; elected to Baseball Hall of Fame, 1972; established Am. League record for most home runs by a catcher, lifetime: 313. Mem.: Lion, Elk, Moose. Achievements include being a mem. Am. League All-Star Team, 1949-62, mem. of record 10 World Series Championship teams, 1947, 49-53, 56, 58, 61-62; inducted into Baseball Hall of Fame, 1972. Office: Yogi Berra Mus and Learning Ctr Montclair State U 8 Quarry Rd Little Falls NJ 07424-2161

BERRA-MARFISI, ELEANORE-LUCIA, retired secondary school educator; d. Angelo A. and Mary Ann Berra; m. Dominic Marfisi, Aug. 7, 1971. BA, Albertus Magnus Coll., 1957; MA, Fairfield U., 1960; MS, So. Conn. Coll., 1969. English prof. Sacred Heart Coll., Hamden, Conn., 1960—62; English, art chair Sacred Heart Acad., Hamden, 1963—69; English prof. Forest Park Jr. Coll., St. Louis, 1971—73; English, art chair St. Mary's HS, St. Louis, 1969—80, prin., adminstr., 1981—91; ret., 1991. Bd. dirs. Shaw Cmty. Sch. Bd.; supervisory com. Marianist Schs. Author: Jewish Art in Christian Symbols, 1969, Dolci: Italian Sweets, 1981, Italian Roots, American Flowers, 1999, Sicily: Crossroads of Culture, 2002, The Hill: Its History, Its Recipes, 2003, I Remember Nonna, 2004. Bd. dirs. Young Musicians Assn., St. Louis, 2000—; bd. mem. advocate St. Louis State Hosp. Named Outstanding Adv. Bd. Mem., Shaw Sch. Bd., 1977—78. Mem.: St. Louis Italian Club, Pi Lambda Theta. Avocations: piano, flute, pottery, painting.

BERRESFORD, JOAN KELL, elementary school educator; d. James Jerome and Mary (Simon) Kell; m. William John Berresford, June 1970; children: Andrea Berresford Mulligan, Heather Anne. BSME, Mansfield U., Pa., 1969, MSME, 1976. Vocal music tchr. h.s. Athens Area Sch. Dist., Pa., 1969—72; aide for blind student BLAST Intermediate Unit, Mansfield, Pa., 1978—80; elem. music tchr. So. Tioga Sch. Dist., Mansfield, Pa., 1982—2004; supr. student tchrs. Mansfield U., 2004—05. Dir., hostess Pa. Music Educators Assn. Songfests, Mansfield, 1985—2004; clinician Pa. Music Educators Assn. Conv., Phila., 2001, Hershey, 02; guest choral dir. Pa. Music Educators Assn. at N.Y. and Pa. festivals, 1990—2004. Pres. Philantrophic Edn. Orgn., Mansfield, 1976—2004; mem. 1901 soc. Mansfield Libr., 2001—04; sec.,v.p. Mansfield Zoning Bd.; state bd. Ctrl. Diocese of Pa. Episscopal Ch. Women, Mansfield; sr. warden St. James Episcopalian Ch., Mansfield; relay com. Am. Cancer Soc. Relay for Life, Mansfield, 1994—2004. Named Tchr. of Yr., So. Tioga Sch. Dist., 1994; recipient Citation of Excellence, Pa. Music Educators Assn., 2004. Mem.: Am. Choral Dirs. Assn. (chair childrens choir 2001—05). Episcopalian. Avocations: cooking, quilting, singing, piano, volunteering. Home: 145 Wakefield Terr Mansfield PA 16933

BERRESFORD, SUSAN VAIL, philanthropic foundation executive; b. NYC, Jan. 8, 1943; d. Richard Case and Katherine Vail (Marsters) Berresford Hurd; m. David F. Stein (div.); 1 son, Jeremy Vail Stein. Student, Vassar Coll., 1961-63; BA cum laude in Am. History, Radcliffe Coll., 1965. Vol. UN Vol. Services, NYC, summer 1962; sec. to Theodore H. White, summer 1964; program officer Neighborhood Youth Corps, NYC, 1965-67; program specialist Manpower Career Devel. Agy., NYC, 1967, human resources adminstrn. specialist, 1968; freelance cons., writer Europe & US, 1968-70; program officer nat. affairs div. Ford Found., NYC, 1970-80, program officer in charge, 1980-81, v.p., 1981-95, exec. v.p., COO, 1995-96, pres., 1996—. Named one of 100 Most Powerful Women in World, Forbes mag., 2005. Office: Ford Foundation 320 East 43rd St New York NY 10017*

BERREY, ROBERT FORREST, lawyer; b. Oak Park, Ill., Dec. 7, 1939; s. Rhodes Clay and Regina (Kasprovich) B.; m. Rebecca L. Newell, Apr. 10, 1993; children from previous marriage: Adam Forrist, Ellen Catherine, Kevin Joseph. AB, Harvard U., 1962; JD, U. Chgo., 1968. Bar: Ill. 1969, Ohio 1986. Atty. Torshen, Fortes & Eiger, Chgo., 1970-75; atty. Jewel Cos., Inc., Chgo., 1975-76, sec., 1976-80, v.p., sec., gen. counsel, 1980-85; v.p., gen. counsel Tomkins (formerly Philips) Industries, Inc., 1986-91; ptnr. Chernesky, Heyman & Kress, Dayton, Ohio, 1991-98; formerly of counsel Bieser, Greer & Landis LLP, Dayton, Ohio; venture capital investments Chapel Hill, NC. With AUS, 1962-65. Mem. Governors Club, Old Chatham Golf Club. E-mail: robert@berrey.org.

BERRIDGE, GEORGE BRADFORD, retired lawyer; b. Detroit, June 9, 1928; s. William Lloyd and Marjorie (George) B.; m. Mary Lee Robinson, July 6, 1957; children: George Bradford, Elizabeth A., Mary L., Robert L. AB, U. Mich., 1950, MBA, 1953, JD, 1954. Bar: N.Y. 1954. Assoc. Chadbourne & Parke, N.Y.C., 1954-61; gen. atty., v.p. law Am. Airlines, Inc., N.Y.C., 1961-71; sr. v.p., gen. counsel Americana Hotels, Inc., N.Y.C., 1971-74, Nat. Westminster Bank U.S.A., N.Y.C., 1975-89, Nat. Westminster Bancorp, N.Y.C., 1989-93; ret., 1993. Contbr. articles to U. Mich. Law Rev. Served to lt. (j.g.) USN, 1951-53. Recipient Howard P. Coblentz prize U. Mich. Law Sch., 1954. Episcopalian. Home: 2 Circle Ave Larchmont NY 10538-4219

BERRIDGE, MARY LLOYD, photographer; BA in Arts and Ideas-Lit. & Photography, U. Mich., 1986; MFA in Photography, Yale U., 1991. Adj. instr. Concordia Coll., Bronxville, NY, 1992, Fairleigh Dickinson U., Rutherford, NJ, 1992—94, Nassau C.C., Garden City, NY, 1994—96, Sch. Visual Arts, N.Y.C., 1997; artist-in-residence, adj. instr. Coll. New Rochelle, NY, 1993; lectr. Princeton (N.J.) U., 1998—99. Exhibitions include The Ctr. for Photography, Woodstock, N.Y., 1991, Mus. Modern Art, N.Y.C., 1991, Berkshire Mus., Pittsfield, Mass., 1992, OPSIS Found., N.Y.C., 1992, Coll. New Rochelle, 1993, Midtown Y Photography Gallery, N.Y.C., 1993, Ind. Arts Gallery, Jamaica, N.Y., 1994, U. Rochester, N.Y., 1995, Blue Sky Gallery, Portland, Oreg., 1996, San Marino Mus. Photography, 1997, Robert Mann Gallery, N.Y.C., 1997, Soc. for Contemporary Photography, Kansas City, 1997—98, Mus. Fine Arts, Houston, 1997, M.H. de Young Meml. Mus., San Francisco, 1997, Cathedral of St. John the Divine, N.Y.C., 1997, Portland (Maine) Mus. Art, 1998, San Francisco Camerawork, 1998, U. Mich., Ann Arbor, 1999, Ctr. for Documentary Studies, Duke U., Durham, N.C., 1999, Pleasures and Terrors of Domestic Comfort, 1991, The Human Condition/Photography, 1995, 1996, Double Take, 1996—97, A Positive Life: Portraits of Women Living with HIV, 1997. Recipient The Ernst Haas award, Maine Photographic Workshops, 1996, The Dorothea Lange-Paul Taylor prize, Ctr. for Documentary Studies, Duke U., 1996, The Romeo Martinez Internat. award, Ministry of Culture of the Republic of San Marino, 1997; fellow Fellowship award, Soc. for Contemporary Photography, Kansas City, Mo., 1997, Artist's fellow, N.Y. Found. for the Art, 1996; John Simon Guggenheim Meml. fellow, 1997. E-mail: berridge@princeton.edu.

BERRIEUM, CHERETHA, secondary school educator, educational association administrator; b. Newark, N.J., Jan. 29, 1975; d. Sonnie Berrieum, Sr. and Corrine Berrieum; 1 child, Jordan Cory Patrick. BS, Fla. Meml. U. CEO, pres. Ednl. Support Sys. Inc, Miami Gardens, Fla., 2003—; tchr. Chancellor Charter Sch., North Lauderdale, Fla. Ednl. cons. not-for-profit orgns., Miami-Dade/ Broward County, Fla. Grantee, Fla. Dept. of Edn. Mem.: ASCD. Democrat. Office: Ednl Support Sys Inc Ste 227 99 NW 183rd St Miami FL 33169 Office Phone: 786-313-7633. Office Fax: 305-249-6208. E-mail: cheretha@edusupportonline.com.

BERRIGAN, HELEN GINGER, federal judge; b. New Rochelle, Apr. 15, 1948; m. Joseph E. Berrigan Jr. BA, U. Wis., 1969; MA, Am. U., 1971; JD, La. State U., 1977. Staff rschr. Senator Harold E. Hughes, 1971-72; legis. aide Senator Joseph E. Biden, 1972-73; asst. to mayor City of Fayette, Miss., 1973-74; law clk. La. Dept. Corrections, 1975-77; staff atty. Gov. Pardon, Parole and Rehab. Commn., 1977-78; prin. Gravel Brady & Berrigan, New Orleans, 1978-94, Berrigan, Litchfield, Schonekas, Mann & Clement, New Orleans, 1984-94; judge U.S. Dist. Ct. (ea. dist.) La., New Orleans, 1994—. Active La. Sentencing Commn., 1987. Active Com. of 21, 1989, pres., 1990-92, ACLU of La., 1989-94, Forum for Equality, 1990-94, Amistad Rsch. Ctr. Tulane U., 1990-95. Mem.: New Orleans Assn. Women Attys., La. Assn. Criminal Def. Lawyers, La. State Bar Assn. Office: US Dist Courthouse 500 Poydras St Rm C556 New Orleans LA 70130-3313*

BERRIGAN, PATRICK JOSEPH, lawyer; b. Niagara Falls, Ont., Can., Nov. 3, 1933; came to U.S., 1950; s. Thomas Joseph and Florence Cecilia (Glynn) B.; m. Shirley Mae Snyder, July 6, 1957; children: Carolyn, Deborah, Patrick Jr., Susan, Ann, Mary, James, Tara. BA in English, Holy Cross Coll., 1954; LLB, Notre Dame U., 1957. Bar: N.Y. 1958, U.S. Dist. Ct. (we. dist.) N.Y. 1960, U.S. Dist. Ct. (we. dist.) Pa. 1976, U.S. Ct. Appeals (2d cir.) 1962, U.S. Ct. Appeals (3rd cir.) 1977. Assoc. Runals, Broderick, Shoemaker, et al, Niagara Falls, N.Y., 1959-78; pvt. practice, Niagara Falls, 1978—. Spl. investigator City of Niagara Falls, 1972; spl. dist. atty. County of Niagara N.Y., Lockport, 1974-76; mem. Judicial Conf. of the State of N.Y., 1978-80; counsel N.Y. State Assembly Com. on mortgages, Albany, 1960-63; hearing officer Com. on Jud. Conduct, 1992—. Mem. Niagara U. Adv. Bd., Lewiston, N.Y., 1978-82; bd. dirs. Nat. Conf. of Christian and Jews, Niagara Falls, 1977; mem. Youth Bd., Niagara Falls, 1965-68. Sgt. U.S. Army, 1957-59; pres. Mount St. Mary's Adv. Bd., 1982—, bd. trustees, 1990-97; bd. dirs. Health System Niagara, 1997-99; trustee, v.p. Mount St. Mary's Hosp., 1999—. Mem. ABA (gen. practice sect. labor law 1991—), Niagara Falls Country Club (bd. govs.), Niagara Falls Bar Assn., Niagara County Bar Assn., N.Y. Bar Assn. Republican. Roman Catholic. Avocations: hockey player (old timers), golf. Home: 790 Thornwood Dr Lewiston NY 14092-1167 Office: PO Box 712 800 Main St Niagara Falls NY 14302-0712 Office Phone: 716-285-1535. Business E-Mail: pat.berrigan@bpg-law.com.

BERRING, ROBERT CHARLES, JR., law educator, law librarian, legal association administrator; b. Canton, Ohio, Nov. 20, 1949; s. Robert Charles and Rita Pauline (Franta) B.; m. Leslie Applegarth, May 20, 1998; children: Simon Robert, Daniel Fredrick. BA cum laude, Harvard U., 1971; JD, M.L.S., U. Calif.-Berkeley, 1974. Asst. prof. and reference librarian U. Ill. Law Sch., Champaign, 1974-76; assoc. librarian U. Tex. Law Sch., Austin, 1976-78; dep. librarian Harvard Law Sch., Cambridge, Mass., 1978-81; prof. law, law librarian U. Wash. Law Sch., Seattle, 1981-82, U. Calif., Boalt Hall Law Sch., Berkeley, 1982—, dean sch. library and info. scis., 1986-89, Walter Perry Johnson Prof. Law, 1998—, dir. law library, interim dean, 2003—04. Mem. Westlaw Adv. Bd., St. Paul, 1984-91; cons. various law firms; mem. on Legal Exch. with China, 1983—, chmn., 1991-93.; vis. prof. U. Cologne, 1993. Author: How to Find the Law, 8th edit., 1984, 9th edit., 1989, Great American Law Revs., 1985, Finding the Law, 1999; co-author: Authors Guide, 1981; editor Legal Reference Svc. Quar., 1981—; author videotape series Commando Legal Rsch., 1989. Chmn. Com. Legal Ednl. Exch. with China, 1991—93. Robinson Cox fellow U. Western Australia, 1988; named West Publishing Co. Acad. Libr. of Yr., 1994. Mem. Am. Assn. Law Libraries (pres. 1985-86), Calif. Bar Assn., ABA, ALA, Am. Law Inst. Office: U Calif Law Sch Boalt Hl Rm 345 Berkeley CA 94720-0001 Business E-Mail: berringr@law.berkeley.edu.

BERRITT, HAROLD EDWARD, lawyer; b. N.Y.C., Jan. 3, 1936; s. Philip H. and Anne L. (Rimer) B.; m. Charlotte Bayer, July 1957 (div. Nov. 1976); children: Gail J., Richard E.; m. Nancy A. Brown, Jan. 8, 1977; children: Matthew P., Alexis C. BBA, U. Mich., 1957, JD, 1960. Bar: N.Y. 1961. Assoc. Stroock & Stroock & Lavan, N.Y.C., 1961-69; ptnr. Pryor, Cashman, Sherman & Flynn, N.Y.C., 1969-95, Rubin Baum Levin Constant & Friedman, N.Y.C., 1995-97; shareholder Greenberg Traurig, Miami, 1997—. Trustee Nat. Found. for Advancement in the Arts, Miami. Mem. ABA, Fresh Meadow Country Club, Commanderie De Bordeaux. Avocations: classical music, wine, golf, tennis. Office: Greenberg Traurig 1221 Brickell Ave Miami FL 33131-3224 E-mail: berritth@gtlaw.com.

BERRUGA-FILLOY, ENRIQUE, ambassador; b. Mexico City, Sept. 15, 1959; s. Arsenio Berruga and Eulalia Filloy; m. Delia Sanchez-Cervantes, Apr. 6, 1986; children: Mercedes, Bernardo. BA, El Colegio de Mexico, Mexico City, 1982; MA, Johns Hopkins U., 1984. Lic. in internat. rels. Advisor sec. Ministry Fgn. Affairs, Mexico City, 1984-87; sec. of info. Embassy of Mex. to U.S., Washington, 1987-89; sec. for polit. affairs Embassy of Mex. to U.K., London, 1989-90; chargé d'affaires Mexican Embassy in Ireland, Dublin, 1991-92; chief of cabinet of sec. Ministry of Fgn. Affairs, Mexico City, 1993; chief of advisors of sec. Ministry Fgn. Affairs, Mexico City, 1993; gen. dir. internat. rels. Ministry of Edn., Mexico City, 1993-94; chief of advisors to min. fgn. affairs Ministry Fgn. Affairs, 1993—97; rank of Amb. of Mex., 1996; amb. of Mexico to Costa Rica, 1997-2000; CEO Mexican Inst. for Internat. Cooperation, 1999—2000; dep. min. fgn. affairs Ministry Fgn. Affairs, 2000—03; perm. Mex. rep. UN, New York, 2004—. Sec.-gen. Mexican Commn. of UNESCO, Ministry of Edn., Mexico City, 1993. Author: Destino: Los Pinos, 1982, El Martes del Silencio, 1994, Propiedad Ajena, 2000; contbr. articles to newspapers. Fulbright scholar ITT, Washington, 1982-84. Mem. Asociacion del Servicio Exterior Mexicano. Avocations: fiction writing, reading, golf, running. Office: UN Two UN Plz 28th Fl New York NY 10017 Home: 178 E 72nd St New York NY 10021 E-mail: eberruga@sre.gob.mx, enriqueberruga@hotmail.com.

BERRY, ALICE ALLEN, retired music educator; b. Bowling Green, Ky., June 23, 1946; d. Oscar Ainsworth and Dorothy (Maddox) Allen; m. Thomas Kay Berry, June 18, 1967; 1 child, Carl Thomas. B in Music Edn. cum laude, Murray State U., 1968. Cert. tchr. Ky., tchr., supr. spl. K-14 Ill. Choral music tchr. McCracken County Pub. Schs., Lone Oak, Ky., 1968—69, Cmty. Unit Sch. Dist. #186, Murphysboro, Ill., 1969—2002. Guest festival choral dir. Jefferson County Music Tchrs. Assn., Ina, Ill., 1993; guest dir. Murphysboro Voices United, 1993; adjudicator music contests Ill. Grade Sch. Music Assn., 1996—, Ill. HS Assn., 1980—; guest choral dir. So. Ill. Grade Sch. Vocal Music Festival, 1998, 2000, 02; guest festival choral dir. Miss. Valley Conf., Belleville, Ill., 2005; guest pianist Walnut St. Bapt. Ch., Carbondale, Ill., 2003. Performer (singer): (guest soloist) Quad State Festival Chorus, 1965, All State Chorus, 1964. Vol. Meals on Wheels, Jackson County Sr. Citizens, Murphysboro, 2002—, So. Ill. U. Choral Union, Carbondale, 2003—; vol. music dir. Cmty. Ecumenical Vacation Bible Sch., Lebanon, Ill., 2003—; choral dir. 1st Bapt. Ch., Murphysboro, 1974—78, 1981—2001; choir dir. United Meth. Ch., Murphysboro, 1969—70; guest choral dir. Cantata United Meth. Ch., Murphysboro, 2002. Named Unsung Hero, Sta. WSIL-TV, 1996, Class Act, 2002. Mem.: NEA (life), Jackson County retired Tchrs. Assn., Am. Choral Dirs. Assn., Ill. Music Edn. Assn. (adjudicator 1983, choral chmn. dist. 6 1988—, 25-Yr. Recognition award 1995), Music Educators Nat. Conf., Ill. Ret. Tchrs. Assn., Sigma Alpha Iota. Home: 2019 Commercial Ave Murphysboro IL 62966 Personal E-mail: atberry@midwest.net.

BERRY, ANDREW T., lawyer; b. 1940; BA cum laude, Princeton U., 1962; LLB, Harvard U., 1965. Bar: NJ 1965, NY 1981, U.S. Dist. Ct. (ea. dist. NY), U.S. Dist. Ct. (Tex.), U.S. Dist. Ct. (Colo.), U.S. Ct. Appeals (2d, 3rd, 5th, and 11th cir.), U.S. Supreme Ct. Ptnr. McCarter & English, Newark. Arbitrator U.S. Dist. Ct. (NJ Dist.), 1987—; spkr. in field. Contbr. articles to profl. jours. Bd. dirs. NJ Performing Arts Ctr., Newark Alliance; mem. risk mgmt. and ins. adv. bd. Atlantic Health Systems. Fellow: Am. Bar Found.; mem.: ABA, London Ct. Internat. Arbitration, Am. Arbitration Assn. (arbitrator, mem. comml. adv. coun. NJ), Am. Law Inst. (cons. various projects and coms.), Internat. Bar Assn., NJ State Bar Assn., Essex County Bar Assn., Assn. of the Bar City of NY. Office: McCarter & English LLP Four Gateway Ctr 100 Mulberry St Newark NJ 07102 Office Phone: 973-639-2097. Office Fax: 973-624-7070. E-mail: aberry@mccarter.com.

BERRY, ANN THACKREY, retired journalist; b. Manhattan, Kans., July 11, 1930; d. Russell Ira and Emily Ethel (Sheppeard) Thackrey; m. Hardy D. Berry, Jan. 27, 1950; children: Russell Stuart, Elizabeth Lee, John Newell. BS in Journalism, Kans. State U., 1951; postgrad., Mont. State U., 1958-59; MS in Pub. Affairs, N.C. State U., 1973. Reporter, editor Manhattan Tribune-News, 1949-52; copy editor Raleigh (N.C.) Times, 1966-67, consumer reporter, 1972-74, editorial writer, columnist, 1974-89; editorial writer The News & Observer, Raleigh, 1989—98. Co-chair Raleigh Pre-Sch., 1964-65. Recipient 1st Pl. Editorial Writing award N.C. Press Assn., 1983, 87, 91, 2d Pl. 1995, 3d Pl. Columns award, 1987. Democrat. Episcopalian. Avocations: reading, studying China, travel, art.

BERRY, BRIAN JOE LOBLEY, geographer, educator, urban planner, political economist; b. Sedgley, Stafford, Eng., Feb. 16, 1934; arrived in U.S., 1955, naturalized, 1965; s. Joe and Gwendoline Alice (Lobley) B.; m. Janet Elizabeth Shapley, Sept. 6, 1958; children: Duncan Jeffrey, Carol Anne (dec.), Diane Leigh, Karen. BSc with honors, Univ. Coll., London, 1955; MA, U. Wash., 1956, PhD, 1958; AM (hon.), Harvard U., 1976. Instr. geography, civil engrng. U. Wash., Seattle, 1957-58; asst. prof. geography U. Chgo., 1958-62, assoc. prof., 1962-65, prof., 1965-72, Irving B. Harris prof. urban geography, 1972-76, dir. Ctr. Urban Studies, chmn. dept. geography, 1974-76; Frank Backus Williams prof. urban and regional planning Harvard U., 1976-81, chmn. Ph.D. Program in Urban Planning, dir. Lab. for Computer Graphics and Spatial Analysis, fellow Inst. Internat. Devel., 1976-81, prof. sociology, 1978-81; dean H. John Heinz III Sch. of Pub. Mgmt. Carnegie-Mellon U., 1981-86, Univ. prof. urban studies and pub. policy, 1981-86; founders prof. U. Tex., Dallas, 1986-91, prof. polit. econ., 1986—, Lloyd Viel Berkner Regental prof., 1991—, chmn. Bruton Ctr. for Devel. Studies, 1988-95, dean Sch. Social Scis., 2005—. Author numerous books; contbr. articles to profl. jours. Fellow Univ. Coll., U. London, 1983; recipient Victoria medal Royal Geog. Soc., 1988, Rockefeller prize Dartmouth U., 1992; named Lord of Hastingleigh, County Kent, 2000, Vautrin Lud Laureate in Geography, 2005. Fellow AAAS, Am. Acad. Arts and Scis., Urban Land Inst., Brit. Acad. (corr.), Weimer Inst. Real Estate and Land Econs., Royal Geog. Soc., So. Regional Sci. Assn.; mem. NAS (coun. 1999-2002), Assn. Am. Geographers (hon. award 1968, pres. 1978-79, Anderson medal 1987), Am. Inst. Cert. Planners, Acad. Medicine, Engring. and Sci. Tex., Regional Sci. Assn., Inst. Brit. Geographers, Sigma Xi. Office: U Tex-Dallas Sch Social Sci Richardson TX 75083-0688 Office Phone: 972-883-2041. E-mail: brian.berry@utdallas.edu, bjlb@comcast.net.

BERRY, CAROL ANN, insurance company executive; b. Walla Walla, Wash., Sept. 8, 1950; d. Alan R. and Elizabeth A. Berry; m. Mark Brooks. BA, Wash. State U. Cert. compliance profl. Asst. mgr. L.A. reg. claims CIGNA, Santa Monica, Calif., 1981—83; reg. adminstr. Equicor, Sherman Oaks, Calif., 1983—89; dir. sys. for managed care Blue Cross of Calif., Woodland Hills, 1989—90; dir. field account svcs. Managed Health Network, L.A., 1990—93; pres. VertiHealth Adminstrs., Chatsworth, Calif., 1993—2000; cons., expert witness, 2000—01; sr. v.p. Claim Recoveries Unlimited, 2001—04, HealthLogic Sys. Corp., 2004—. Lectr. in field. Mem. Pres.'s Commn. Status of Women. Mem.: NAFE, Healthcare Execs., Health Care Administrs. Assn. (past pres. bd. dirs.), Health Fin. Mgmt. Assn., Wash. State U. Alumni Assn. Home and Office: 6155 Lockhurst Dr Woodland Hills CA 91367-1203 Office Phone: 818-340-0486. E-mail: cberry8@sbcglobal.net.

BERRY, CHARLENE HELEN, librarian, musician; b. Highland Pk., Mich., Jan. 4, 1947; d. Harold Terry and Mattie Lou (Colvin) B. BSE, Wayne U., 1964-68, MA, 1969-70, MLS, 1971-74; postgrad., Howard Sch. Broadcast Arts, 1992, Irene's Myomassology Inst., 1997; DMin, U. Sem. Ch., 1997. Ordained music minister. Libr. asst. Wayne State U., Detroit, 1970-74; libr. serials cataloger SUNY, Stony Brook, 1975-79; cataloger Madonna U., Livonia, Mich., 1980—. Organist various area chs., Detroit, 1981—, 1st Ch. of Christ, Wyandotte, Mich., 1986—; music min. Gospel Light House Ministries, Detroit, 1991—; scholar, performer, tchr. hammer dulcimer, 1986—; libr. cons. Superior Twp. (Mich.) Libr. Bd., 1989-91; host Charlene Berry's Dulcimer World, Sta. WCAR, Garden City, Mich., WALE, Providence, R.I., WLLZ 560 AM, Southfield, Mich., 1997—, Sta. WPON AM 1460, Southfield, Mich., 1997—. Composer: Dulcimer Delights, 1991, marches, waltzes, free compositions and solo symphony, 1993, Dulcimer Praise, 1993, Fruits of the Spirit, 1993; solo recs.: Traditional Dulcimer, 1989, Christmas Dulcimer, 1989, Sacred Dulcimer, 1990, Dulcimer Fun, 1991, Dulcimer Praise, 1993, Fruits of the Spirit, 1993, Dulcimer Americana, 1994; (video) Hammering the Hammer Dulcimer, 1994, Music of Light/Light and Life, 1995, Under der Linden, 1996, Joy, Peace, Healing, 1998, Hymns of Prayer and Praise, 1999. Pres. Libr. Staff Assn., SUNY, 1978-79; ch. libr. Ch. Bds. Coms., Long Island, Detroit, 1975—; bd. dirs. Livonia Symphony Soc.; performing artist Mich. Touring Arts Agy., 1994—. Recipient Performance award Silver Springs Dulciner Soc., 1988, 89, 90, Interat. Order of Merit, ASCAP; named Internat. Woman of Yr., 1992-93, Most Admired Woman of Decade. Fellow Internat. Biographical Assn. (life). Am. Biographical Inst. (Woman of Yr. 1993); mem. AAUW, ALA, NAFE, Am. Biographical Rsch. Assn. (hon. dep. gov.), Bus. and Profl. Women, Am. Soc. of Notaries, Am. Fedn. Musicians, Am. Guild Organists (bd. dirs. 1985-88), Plymouth C. of C., Luth. Ch. Musicians Guild, Order Ea. Star, Kappa Delta Pi. Home and Office: Dulcimer Evente 49614 Oak Dr Lot 67 Plymouth MI 48170-2353

BERRY, CHRIS, broadcast executive; b. Decatur, Ill., Aug. 11, 1960; s. Richard Lyman and Phyllis Lee (Phipps) B.; children: James Christopher Jr., Nicholas Andrew. BA, U. Miss., 1981. Prodr. WHBQ-TV, Memphis, 1981—82; news editor CBS Radio-KNX Newsradio, LA, 1982—86; exec. prodr. CBS Radio, Washington, 1986—87; news dir. WBBM, Chgo., 1987—96; v.p., gen. mgr. ABC News Radio, 1996—2002; pres., gen. mgr. ABC Radio, WMAL, Washington, 2002—. Profl. advisor dept. journalism U. Miss., Oxford, 1988—; mem. journalism adv. com. U. Nebr., 1995—; bd. dirs. Emergency Task Force, Washington Bd. Trade. Committeeman Nat. Freedom of Info. Ctr., Chgo., 1990-96; bd. dirs. Wreath of Hope Charity, Chgo., 1990-95; comm. chair United Way of Capital Region, 2004—. Recipient Angel award Religion in Media, L.A., 1985, George Foster Peabody award, 2001, Dupont award, 2001. Mem. Radio and TV News Dirs. Assn. (Edward R. Murrow award 1991, Freedom of Info. award 1993), Soc. Profl. Journalists, Ill. News Broadcasters Assn., Writers Guild Am., Chgo. Headline Club (bd. dirs. 1990-95, Peter Lisagor award 1990), Fairfax County C. of C. (bd. dirs. 2004—). Presbyterian. Office: ABC Radio - WMAL 4400 Jenifer St NW 4th Fl Washington DC 20015 Business E-Mail: chris.j.berry@abc.com.

BERRY, CHUCK (CHARLES EDWARD ANDERSON BERRY), musician, composer; b. St. Louis, Oct. 18, 1926; s. Henry William, Sr., and Martha Banks Berry; m. Themetta Suggs, Oct. 1948; 4 children: Darlen Ingrid, Melody Exes, Aloha Isa Lei, Charles Edward Anderson, Jr. Popular artist in rock and roll music, plays guitar, saxophone, piano; concert, TV appearances, 1955—; rec. artist Chess Records; appeared in film Go, Johnny Go, Rock, Rock, Rock, 1956, Jazz on a Summer's Day, 1960, Let the Good Times Roll, 1973; composer: Rock 'n' Roll Music; albums include: After School Sessions, 1958, One Dozen Berry's, 1958, Rockin' At The Hops, 1959-60, New Juke Box Hits, 1960, Chuck Berry, 1960, More Chuck Berry, 1960, On Stage, 1960, Twist, 1960, You Can Never Tell, 1964, Greatest Hits, 1964, 2 Great Guitars, 1964, Chuck Berry in London, 1965, Fresh Berrys, 1965, St. Louis to Liverpool, 1966, Golden Hits, 1967, At the Fillmore, 1967, Medley, 1967, In Memphis, 1967, Concerto in B Goods, 1969, Home Again, 1971, The London Sessions, 1972, Golden Decade, 1972, St. Louis to Frisco to Memphis, 1972, Let the Good Times Roll, 1973, Golden Decade, Vol. 2, 1973, Bio, 1973, Back in the U.S.A., 1973, Golden Decade, Vol. 5, 1974, I'm a Rocker, 1975, Chuck Berry 75, 1975, Motorvatin', 1976, Rockit, 1979, Chess Masters, 1983, The Chess Box, 1989, Missing Berries: Rarities, 1990, On the Blues Side, 1993, others; soundtrack Hail! Hail! Rock n' Roll, 1987; author: autobiography Chuck Berry, 1987. Recipient Grammy award for Lifetime Achievement, 1984; named to Rock and Rock Hall of Fame, 1986. Office: Berry Park 691 Buckner Rd Wentzville MO 63385-5442*

BERRY, CLARE GEBERT, real estate broker; b. Carlisle, Pa., Oct. 4, 1955; d. George Robert and Helen (Davis) Gebert; m. James Isaac Vance Berry Jr., June 16, 1977; 1 child, James Isaac Vance Berry III. BA, Auburn U., 1977. Advt. assoc., circulation mgr. The News-Gazette, Lexington, Va., 1977-79; sales and editorial asst. Ponte Vedra Recorder, Ponte Vedra Beach, Fla., 1979—81; co-founder, bus. mgr. The Sun-Times Newspaper, Jacksonville Beach, Fla., 1981-82; mgr. Arvida-Clearview Cable TV, Ponte Vedra Beach, 1982-85; broker, agt. Watson Realty Corp., Ponte Vedra Beach, Fla., 1985-90, Marsh Landing Realty, Ponte Vedra Beach, 1990-93; founder, broker, owner Berry & Co. Real Estate, Ponte Vedra Beach, 1993—. Com. chmn. The Players Championship, Ponte Vedra Beach, 1982—; dir. Marsh Landing Homeowners Assn. Bd., Ponte Vedra Beach, 1989-90; dir. Ponte Vedra Pub. Edn. Found., 1994—, N.E. Fla. Regional Planning Coun., 2000—. Recipient Realtor of Yr., Realtors' Assn., 1992, Residential Mem. of Yr., 1998. Mem. Fla. Assn. Realtors, Nat. Assn. Realtors, N.E. Fla. Builders Assn. Sales and Mktg. Coun., N.E. Fla. Assn. of Realtors (bd. dirs. 1998-00, chmn. edn. com. 2000), Ponte Vedra Rotary, Jr. League Jacksonville. Avocations: writing, promotions, aviation, music, tennis. Home: 113 Linkside Cir Ponte Vedra Beach FL 32082-2032 Office: Berry & Co Real Estate 330 Hwy A1A Ste 200 Ponte Vedra Beach FL 32082-1824 Office Phone: 904-273-4800.

BERRY, DAVID J., former financial services company executive; b. Columbus, Ohio, Apr. 14, 1944; s. Maurice Glenn Berry and Janice (Eshelman) Read; m. Janet Lynn Tewksbury, Mar. 24, 1977; children: Jeffrey James, Jennifer Jean, Jon Andrew, Amy Jo. Student, Miami U., Oxford, Ohio, 1963-64, Ohio State U., 1965-66. Registered prin. SEC. Ind. fin. svc. salesman, 1966-74; gen. agt. Sun Life Assurance Co. Can., Columbus, 1975-85; pres. Strategic Info. Svcs., Columbus, 1986-87; v.p. IDS Life Ins. Co., Mpls., 1990—; assoc. mgr. IDS Fin. Svcs. Inc., Columbus, 1988, region dir., 1989; v.p. IDS Life Ins. Co., Mpls., 1991-2000; ret., 2000. Chmn. Agy. Mgmt. Tng. Coun., Columbus, 1982-83. Bell ringer Salvation Army, Columbus, 1975-85; vol. instr. Learning Disabled Children, Columbus, 1980-83; pres. PTA, Worthington, Ohio, 1983. Fellow Life Underwriting Tng. Coun., Columbus, 1981. Mem. Nat. Assn. Securities Dealers, Gen. Agts. and Mgrs. Assn. (pres. 1979-82), Mpls. Life Underwriters Assn. Avocations: travel, various sport participation, poetry. Office: IDS Life Ins Co IDS Tower # 10 Minneapolis MN 55402-2100

BERRY, DEAN C., lawyer; b. Lumberton, NC, July 17, 1957; AB magna cum laude, AM, Harvard Univ., 1979, JD cum laude, 1982; LLM, NYU, 1990. Bar: NY 1982. Ptnr., Trusts & Estates practice & chmn. recruiting com. Coudert Bros. LLP, NYC. Editor: Harvard Law Rev., 1981—82. Mem.: ABA, Soc. Trusts & Estates Practitioners, Assn. Bar City of NY, Phi Beta Kappa. Office: Coudert Bros LLP 1114 Ave of the Americas New York NY 10036 Office Phone: 212-626-4287. Office Fax: 212-626-4120. Business E-Mail: berryd@coudert.com.

BERRY, DEAN LESTER, lawyer; b. Chgo., Jan. 20, 1935; s. Ruben W. and Leonore C. (Nelson) B.; m. Donna J. Zack, Nov. 16, 1962 (dec.); children: Megan, Thomas. BA with distinction, DePauw U., 1955; JD with distinction, U. Mich., 1960. Bar: Ohio 1961, U.S. Dist. Ct. (no. dist.) Ohio 1962. Assoc. Squire, Sanders & Dempsey L.L.P., Cleve., 1960-70, ptnr., 1970—2002, counsel, 2002—03. Lectr. various programs, Order of Coif. Author: Local Government in Michigan, 1960; contbr. articles to profl. jours.; participant in Quiz Kids radio program, 1945-47. Mem. council City of Rocky River, Ohio, 1967-71; mem. cen. com. Cuyahoga County Rep. Orgn., Ohio, 1963-75, mem. exec. com., 1969-2001. Served to 1st lt. USAF, 1955-57. Mem. Ohio State Bar Assn., Portage County Bar Assn., Greater Cleve. Bar Assn. (com. chmn. 1978), Soc. Profl. Journalists. Avocations: travel, crossword puzzles. Home: 478 Ravine Dr Aurora OH 44202-8236 Personal E-mail: dlberry@adelphia.net.

BERRY, DENNIS, newspaper publishing executive; B in Advt. and Pub. Rels., U. Ga. Pub. Atlanta Jour.-Constn.; pres., CEO Manheim Auctions, 1995—2000; pres., COO Cox Enterprises, Inc., 2000—, also bd. dirs. Bd. dirs. Cox Comm., Inc., Cox Radio, Inc.; chmn. bd. AutoTrader.com. Mem. adv. bd. Grady Coll. Journalism and Mass Comm.; bd. dirs. Atlanta Area Coun., Boy Scouts Am., Ctrl. Atlanta Progress, Advt. Coun., United Way,

Emory Bd. Visitors, Mission New Hope; mem. bd. advisors Ga. State U.; past chair bd. dirs. Better Bus. Bur. Met. Atlanta. Office: Atlanta Newspapers PO Box 4689 72 Marietta St NW Atlanta GA 30302

BERRY, ELIZABETH EMBREE, director; d. Benjamin F. and Melody J. Berry. BA in Psychology, La. Tech U., 2001, MA in Counseling & Guidance, 2003. Dir. Greek life Rhodes Coll., Memphis, 2003—. Workshop presenter Kappa Delta Sorority, Memphis, 2004—05, Chrisitan Bros. U., Memphis, 2004—05. Mem.: ACPA, NASPA, Assn. Frat. Advisors, Phi Mu (v.p. alumnae group 2005—). Office: Rhodes Coll 2000 North Pky Memphis TN 38112

BERRY, ESTER LORÉE, vocational nurse; b. St. Joseph, La., Sept. 19, 1945; d. Sim and Ruby Jordan; (div.); children: Roderick Bryant, Pamela Elaine. A degree in nursing and art, Calif. State U., 1996; diploma poet/writer, Internat. BIB Ctr. Lic. vocat. nurse. Ward clk. Santa Fe Hosp., Compton, Calif., 1969-72; supr. J.C. Penney's, Carson, Calif., 1973-80; asst. mgr. Std. Comm., Carson, 1981-84; lic. vocat. nurse, nurse King Drew Med., L.A., 1984-94; medicine nurse Martin Luther Jr. Hosp., 1996-99; poet Nobles Theatre of the Mind, Paris, London, N.Y.C., 2004—. Author: numerous poems. Named hon. mem., Vets. Am., 1999—2001, Best Poet of Yr., 2001; named to Comdrs. Club, DAV, 2002—03, Wall of Tolerance, Ala., 2004; recipient Editors Choice award, 1999—2001, Silver Internat. Poet of Merit, Bronze Commemorative medallion, Best Poet award, 2002—03, Best Poet of Yr. award, Internat. Libr. Poetry, 2004, Bronze Leader award, Comdr. Club, DAV, 2001, certificate, Profl. Women's Adv. Bd. Mem.: Profl. Women's Adv. Bd. Avocations: fishing, sewing, photography, crocheting, outdoor camping. Home: Apt P230 27-700 Landau B Cathedral City CA 92234 Address: PO Box 31226 5126 Bus Oak Cir Raleigh NC 27622

BERRY, FRED CLIFTON, JR., editor, writer; b. Neponset, Ill., May 11, 1931; s. Fred C. and Dorothy (Benedict) B.; m. Irene Semcho, Nov. 10, 1958; children: Jeffrey, Thomas BS, George Washington U., 1961; MA, Stanford U., 1967. Commd. 2d. lt. U.S. Army, 1955, advanced through grades to col. (select), 1975; editor-in-chief Air Force Mag., Washington, 1980-83; chief U.S. editor, exec. v.p. Interavia Pub. Group, Washington, 1983-86; pres. FCB Assocs., Herndon, Va., 1986—. Author: Sky Soldiers, 1987, Strike Aircraft, 1987, Chargers, 1988, Gadget Warfare, 1988, Air Cav, 1988, Inventing the Future, 1993, Inside the CIA, 1997; Milestones of the First Century of Flight, 2002, United State Army at War- 9/11 Through Iraq, 2003; co-author: CNN: War in the Gulf, 1991, Flights, 1994, Medics at War, 2005; editor: Avon Books illustrated series on near future warfare 1990, Air Traffic Control, 1990; editor Air Power History mag., 1989-91; contbr. articles to profl. jours. Trustee Air Force Hist. Found. Mem. Authors Guild Am., Nat. Press Club (Washington). Avocation: flying. Office: FCB Assocs PO Box 710654 Herndon VA 20171-0654 Office Phone: 703-608-9183. E-mail: clifb@fcbassoc.com.

BERRY, GAIL W., psychiatrist, educator; b. Kalamazoo, Mich., Nov. 7, 1939; BA, Kalamazoo Coll., 1960; MD, NYU, 1964; cert. in psychoanalysis, N.Y. Med. Coll., 1976. Lic. Am. Bd. Psychiatry and Neurology. Clin. instr. psychiatry Mt. Sinai Sch. Medicine, N.Y.C., 1969—76, asst. clin. prof. psychiatry, 1976—; tng. and supervising psychoanalyst Psychoanalytic Inst. N.Y. Med. Coll., Valhalla, NY, 1980—; assoc. attending psychiatrist Mt. Sinai Hosp., N.Y.C., 1981—. Adj. prof. psychiatry N.Y. Med. Coll., Valhalla, 1984—. Fellow: Am. Psychiat. Assn. (life; disting.); mem.: Am. Acad. Psychoanalysis (asst. editor jour. 1984—2002), Am. Acad. Psychoanalysis and Dynamic Psychiatry (consulting editor jour. 2002—). Office: 11 S 1474 Third Ave New York NY 10028

BERRY, GUY CURTIS, polymer science educator, researcher; b. Greene County, Ill., May 11, 1935; s. Charles Curtis and Wilma Francis (Wickes) B.; m. Marilyn Jane Montooth, Jan. 26, 1957; children: Susan Jane, Sandra Jean, Scott Curtis. BSCh.E., U. Mich., 1957, MS in Polymer Sci., 1958, PhD, 1960. Fellow Mellon Inst., Pitts., 1960-65, sr. fellow, 1965—90; assoc. prof. chemistry Carnegie-Mellon U., Pitts., 1966-73, prof., 1973—2002, acting dean, 1981-82, acting head dept. chemistry, 1983-84, head dept. chemistry, 1990-95, Univ. prof., 2002—. Vis. prof. U. Tokyo, 1973, Colo. State U., Ft. Collins, 1979, U. Kyoto, Japan, 1983 Editor Jour. Polymer Sci., 1988-93, Progress in Polymer Sci., 2002--; mem. editl. bd. Jour. Rheology, 1990—, Chemtracts-Macromolecular Chemistry, 1990-94; contbr. over 200 articles to sci. jour. Recipient Bingham medal Soc. of Rheology, 1990; Polymeric Materials: Sci. and Engring. fellow. Fellow Am. Phys. Soc., Polymeric Materials: Sci. and Engring.; mem. AAAS, Am. Chem. Soc. (Pitts. Chemistry prize 1994), Soc. Rheology. Office: Carnegie Mellon U Dept Chem 4400 5th Ave Pittsburgh PA 15213-2617 Office Phone: 412-268-3131. E-mail: gcberry@andrew.cmu.edu.

BERRY, HALLE MARIA, actress; b. Cleve., Aug. 14, 1966; d. Jerome and Judith (Hawkins) B.; m. David Christopher Justice, Dec. 31, 1992 (div. 1996); m. Eric Benet, Jan. 24, 2001 (div. Jan. 3, 2005). BA, Cuyahoga C.C., Cleveland, 1986. Spokeswoman, Revlon cosmetics, 1996-. Actress in films Jungle Fever, 1991, The Last Boy Scout, 1991, Strictly Business, 1991, Boomerang, 1992 (Image award nom. 1992), Father Hood, 1993, The Program, 1993, The Flintstones, 1994, Losing Isaiah, 1995, The Rich Man's Wife, 1996, Executive Decision, 1996, Race The Sun, 1996, Girl 6, 1996, B*A*P*S, 1997, Bulworth, 1998, Why Do Fools Fall in Love, 1998, Victims of Fashion, 1999, Ringside, 1999, X-Men, 2000, Swordfish, 2001, Monsters Ball, 2001 (Acad. award best actress 2002), Die Another Day, 2002, X2: X-Men United, 2003, Gothika, 2003, Catwoman, 2004, (voice) Robots, 2005; (TV movies) Solomon & Sheba, 1995, The Wedding, 1998, Oprah Winfrey Presents: Their Eyes Were Watching God, 2005; actress, exec. prodr., (TV films) Introducing Dorothy Dandridge, 1999 (Emmy award best actress 2000, Golden Globe award best actress 2000, Image award, SAG award and three NAACP Image awards 2000), exec. prodr. Lackawanna Blues, 2005; TV mini-series Queen, 1992; TV series include Living Dolls, 1989, Knots Landing, 1992; (TV appearances) Amen, 1991, A Different World, 1991 They Came From Outer Space, 1991, Martin, 1996, Frasier (voice only), 1998, The Bernie Mac Show, 2002. Named Miss Teen All-Am., 1985, Miss USA first-runner up, 1986, Miss U.S.A., 1987. First African Am. actress to win Academy award for best actress for the film Monsters Ball, 2002. Mailing: Vincent Cirrincione Assoc Ltd Ste 205 8721 Sunset Blvd West Hollywood CA 90069*

BERRY, JACOB OBADIAH, not-for-profit developer, rancher; b. LA, Aug. 14, 1954; s. Francis Oscar and Harriet Leaf Beregi. BA, Denver U., 1976. Prin., owner 120 acre farm, Newell, SD, 1979—85; ranch hand cattle ranches in western SD, 1985—96; pres. Am. Cross Found., Amarillo, Tex., 1996—. Author: Horse Creek, 1999, (screenplays) Pagan Desire, 2002. Achievements include patent for Cross design; utility patent for Cross structure. Avocations: country western dance, horseback riding. Office: American Cross Foundation PO Box 9492 Amarillo TX 79105 Office Phone: 806-374-6758. Business E-Mail: acf@americancrossfoundation.org.

BERRY, JAMES LEE, retired educator; b. Hollywood, Calif., May 19, 1939; s. Ralph (Red) Lee and Lillie Pauline (Pilkenton) B.; m. Sharon Joyce Hess, April 14, 1963; children: Jamie, Diana, Daniel. BS in Edn., Pitts. State U., 1961; MEd, Ga. Southern U., 1975; grad., Command and Gen. Staff Coll., 1978; MBA, Webster U., 1983. Advanced through grades to lt. col. U.S. Army, 1982, ret., 1982; spl. agent Dept. Defense, San Antonio, Tex., 1983-84; sr. army instr. Northeast Military Magnet, Kansas City, Mo., 1986-2000; ret., 2000. Coach shooting, weighlifting. Decorated Bronze Star, Meritorious Svc. medal with 3 oak leaf clusters, Army Commendation medal, 1 oak leaf cluster; Vietnam Cross of Gallantry. Avocations: shooting, weightlifting, painting. Home: PO Box 751 Lawrence KS 66044-0751

BERRY, JANET CLAIRE, librarian; b. Jonesboro, Ark., Dec. 1, 1948; d. Troy Berry and Olivia Rosetta (Irwin) Thompson; m. Julius Jerome Mitcham, Mar. 27, 1970 (div. 1981); m. Gary Neville Hays, Nov. 10, 1987 (div. 1989); m. Norman M. Floyd, Nov. 21, 2003 BSE, U. Cen. Ark., 1970; MLS, Vanderbilt/Peabody U., 1981. Libr./tchr. Greenbrier (Ark.) High Sch., 1970-72; employment counselor Dixie Employment Agy., Little Rock, 1973-76; sr. libr. asst. U. Ark. for Med. Sci., Little Rock, 1976-85; coord. cataloging svc. Ark. State Libr., Little Rock, 1985—. Instr. U. Ark., Little Rock, 1986-88. Editor La Docere for Am. Bus. Women's Assn. newsletter (regional top 5 award 1991, 92). Mem. West Baseline Neighborhood Assn., sec., 1997—2005; mem. Leion Hut Neighborhood Assn., sec., 1997—2005, Southwest Little Rock United for Progress, 1998—, v.p., 1999, pres., 2000—05; mem. environ. task force City of Little Rock, 1999—; bd. dirs. Friends of Ctrl. Ark. Libr. Sys., 1999—2003. Mem. ALA, Ark. Libr. Assn. (pres. 1983-84), Ark. Region Sports Car Club of Am. (editor 1988-98), Am. Bus. Women's Assn. (La Petite Roche chpt., editor 1990-92, 1992 Woman of Yr.), LWV (Pulaski county chpt.). Methodist. Avocations: road rallies, working sports car races, bird watching, caring for cats, civic meetings. Office: Ark State Libr One Capitol Mall Little Rock AR 72201

BERRY, JAYME GAYLE, music educator; b. El Paso, Feb. 28, 1958; d. James Wimberly Tooke V and Ila June Tooke; m. Keith Allen Berry, May 24, 1983; children: Jessica Love, Jonathan Keith, Melody Faith. MusB summa cum laude, McMurry U., 1980. Cert. K-12 music tchr. N.Mex., Orff. Elem. music tchr. Alamogordo (N.Mex.) Pub. Schs., 1983—. Composer: Farolitas, 1994. Worship team pianist Calvary Chapel, Alamogordo, 2000—04., Oscar Meyer grantee, 2001, Tex.-N.Mex. Power Co. grantee, 2004. Mem.: N.Mex. Music Educators Assn., Am. Orff Schulwerk Assn. (mem. at large N.Mex. chpt.), Am. Choral Dir. Assn. Republican. Protestant. Avocations: genealogy, music. Home: 1714 Buena Vista Ct Alamogordo NM 88310 Office: Buena Vista Elem 2600 19th Alamogordo NM 88310 Office Phone: 505-439-3400. E-mail: buck131@hauns.com.

BERRY, JOHN CHARLES, psychologist, academic administrator; b. Modesto, Calif., Nov. 29, 1938; s. John Wesley and Dorothy Evelyn (Harris) B.; m. Arlene Ellen Sossin, Oct. 7, 1978; children: Elise, John Jordan, Kaitlyn. AB, Stanford U., 1960; postgrad., Trinity Coll., Dublin, Ireland, 1960—61; PhD, Columbia U., 1967. Rsch. assoc. Judge Baker Guidance Ctr., Boston, 1965—66; psychology assoc. Napa State Hosp., Imola, Calif., 1966—67, staff psychologist, 1967—75, program asst., 1975—76; program dir. Met. State Hosp., Norwalk, Calif., 1976—77; asst. supt. Empire Union Sch. Dist., Modesto, 1977—93, dep. supt., 1993—. Contbg. author: Life History Research in Psychopathology, 1970. Mem.: Assn. Calif. Sch. Adminstrs., Am. Psychol. Assn., Sigma Xi. Home: 920 Eastridge Dr Modesto CA 95355-4672 Office: Empire Union Sch Dist 116 N Mcclure Rd Modesto CA 95357-1329

BERRY, JOHN CHARLES, literature educator; b. Royal Oak, Mich., Jan. 14, 1966; s. Marion Grace Cenci and Douglas Berry. A in Liberal Arts, Oakland C.C., Royal Oak, Mich., 1997; BA in English, U. Okla., 2002; MA in Creative Writing, U. of Okla., Norman Oklahoma, 2005. Writing cons. U. Okla. Writing Ctr., Norman, 2000—03; freshman composition instr. U. Okla., Norman, 2003—05; mem. English faculty Bismark State Coll., ND, 2005—. Author: (short stories) Windmill. Vol. Norman Animal Shelter, Okla., 2000. Faculty Assn. scholarship, Oakland C.C., 1995, Acad. Excellence scholarship, Oakland C.C. Bd. of Trustees, 1996, Transfer Student scholarship, Okl.a U. Coll. of Engring., 1997. Mem.: Sigma Tau Delta (life), Gamma Beta Phi. Home: 413 1/2 W Thayer Bismarck ND

BERRY, JONI INGRAM, hospice pharmacist, educator; b. Charlotte, N.C., June 6, 1953; d. James Clifford and Patricia Ann (Ebener) Ingram; div.; children: Erin Blair, Rachel Anne, James Rosser. BS in Pharmacy, U. N.C., 1976, MS in Pharmacy, 1979, D in Pharmacy, 2003. Lic. pharmacist, N.C. Resident in pharmacy Sch. Pharmacy, U. N.C., Chapel Hill, 1977-79, adj. asst. prof., 1985—; pharmacist Durham County Gen. Hosp., Durham, N.C., 1977-79; coord. clin. pharm. Wake Med. Ctr., Raleigh, N.C., 1979-80; co-dir. pharmacy edn. Wake Area Health Edn. Ctr., Raleigh, 1980-85; clin. pharmacist Hospice of Wake County, Raleigh, 1980—; co-owner Integrated Pharm. Care Systems, Inc., 1995—. Mem. editorial adv. bd. Hospice Jour., 1985-91, 94—, Jour. Pharm. Care in Pain and Symptom Mgmt., 1992—; reviewer Am. Jour. Hospice Care, 1996-98; editor pharmacy sect. notes NHO Coun. Hospice Profls.; contbr. articles to profl. jours. Troop leader Girl Scouts U.S.A., Raleigh, 1987-2004, trainer, 1989-91, mgr. svc. unit, 1990-94; Sunday sch. tchr. St. Phillips Luth. Ch., Raleigh, 1990-92, 94-95, asst. min., 1995—, choir mem. 1998-2000. Recipient Silver Pinecone award Girl Scouts U.S., 1991, Golden Rule award J.C. Penney Co., 1991. Mem.: Wake County Pharm. Assn. (sec. 1982—85), N.C. Hosp. Pharmacists (bd. dirs. 1984—86, program com. 1988—91), N.C. Pharm. Assn. (chair com. 1981—84, mem. continuing edn. com. 1986—87, Don Blanton award 1985), Am. Pain Soc., Nat. Hospice Orgn., Am. Soc. Hosp. Pharmacists, Acad. Pharmacy Practice and Mgmt. (mem.-at-large 1996, chair specialized sect. 1999—2002), Am. Pharmacist Assn. (hospice pharmacist steering com. 1990—, mem. at large Acad. Pharmacy Practice and Sci.), Nat. Coun. Hospice Profls. (pharmacy sect. leader 1998—), Rho Chi. Democrat. Avocations: gardening, weightlifting, aerobics. Office: Hospice Wake County 1300 Saint Marys St Raleigh NC 27605-1276

BERRY, JULIE MERRITT, small business development consultant; b. Macon, Ga., May 21, 1963; d. John William and Latha Virginia (Rachels) M.; m. Charles Ross Berry, Jan. 19, 1991; children: Alyson Latha, Rachel McLees, Symantha Ross. BA, Emory U., 1985; postgrad., Ga. State U., 1989-90. Contr. asst. Decatur (Ga.) Hosp., 1985-86; credit account mgr. Am. Sci. Products, div. Baxter Travenol, Stone Mountain, Ga., 1986-87; asst. area/dist. credit mgr. Sherwin Williams Co., Atlanta, 1987-89; credit adminstr. Lafarge Corp., Atlanta, 1989-91; fin. analysis mgr. Addison Corp., Atlanta, 1991-94; credit supr. Avon Products, Inc., Atlanta, 1994-95; co-owner Shandon Enterprises, Fayetteville, Ga., 1993—. Class agt. Emory Alumni Fund Bd., Atlanta, 1987-92; del. Emory Assembly III, 1990-93; rep. Emory Alumni Reunion Com., 1990. Mem. NAFE, Kappa Delta. Republican. Avocations: reading, piano, travel, cooking, volunteer work. Home: 170 Glenwood Ln Fayetteville GA 30215-8123

BERRY, KARIS JEANINE, elementary school educator, adult education educator; b. Newport News, Va., July 22, 1975; d. Isaac L. and Ann K. McDonald. BA in Elem. Edn., N.C. Ctrl. U., 1997; MA in Reading, Lang., and Literacy, The Coll. William & Mary, 2002. Tchr. Newport News (Va.) Pub. Schs., 1997—2001, adult edn. tchr., 1998—, reading specialist, 2001—. Grantee, Va. Power, 2000; scholar, Target Found., 2001. Mem.: NEA (grantee 2000), Va. State Reading Coun., Internat. Reading Assn., Tidewater Assn .N.C. Ctrl. U. Alumni Assn. (life; rec. sec. 1998—2004, chaplin 1998—2004). Democrat. Avocations: travel, piano, swimming. Home: 14 Tillerson Drive Newport News VA 23602 Office Phone: 757-591-4500. Personal E-mail: krsjmc@yahoo.com.

BERRY, KATHLEEN A., English language educator; b. L.A., Calif., June 22, 1958; d. Raymond Albert and Robin Lee Berry. BA in Linguistics, MA in Edn., U. Calif., Berkeley, 1981, credential in single subject tchg./English, 1982. Instr. English U. Calif. Ext., Berkeley, 1992—2004, tchr. trainer, 1992—2004; instr. English U. Calif., Berkeley, 1994, Contra Costa C.C., San Pablo, Calif., 1996—, Laney C.C., Oakland, Calif., 2001—; instr. Las Positas C.C., Livermore, Calif., 2004—. Cons. grammar Am. Med. Writers Assn., San Francisco, 1999—. H.s. program coord. Albany (Calif.) Adult Sch., 1984. Mem.: Tchrs. of English to Spkrs. of Other Langs. Avocations: yoga, quilting. Office: Laney C C 900 Fallon St Oakland CA 94607 E-mail: katy622@yahoo.com.

BERRY, KATHRYN-GRACE, geriatrics nurse; b. Linden, Tex., Sept. 28, 1929; d. Wright Allen and Gladys Bowden; m. Wayman Byron Berry, Jan. 6, 1947; children: Ron, James Byron, Celia Elizabeth Froehlig. Diploma in nursing, Univ. Ala., 1969. Cert. nursing Ala. Nurse, Huntsville, 1970—80; charge nurse various nursing homes, Pulaski, Tenn., 1980—85, Andmore, Ala., 1987—90; tchr. GED program Huntsville, 1990—97. Active Christians Helping Others, Ardmore, 1985—95; mem. Friends Ardmore Libr., 1990—95; pres. United Meth. Women, 1985. Avocations: oragami, reading, boating, fishing, crafts, painting. Home: 809 Stuart Ln Brentwood TN 37027-5824

BERRY, LORRAINE LEDEE, state senator; b. St. Thomas, V.I., Nov. 15, 1949; d. Joseph and Emelda Ledee; m. Richard Berry; children: Roxanne, Kurt. Attended, U. V.I. Mem. V.I. Legis., 1982—, pres., 1997-99. Mem. econ. devel., agr., consumer protection, health, govt. and operation coms.; chair fin. com. Office: Capitol Bldg PO Box 1690 St Thomas VI 00804-1690 Office Phone: 340-693-3507. E-mail: LBerry19@hotmail.com, lberry@senate.gov.vi.

BERRY, MARGARET ANNE, lawyer; b. Terre Haute, Ind., Jan. 2, 1950; d. David Warren and SHirley J. Martin; m. Howard H. Berry, Jan. 2, 1981. BA, Ind. U., Bloomington, 1973, JD, 1976. Bar: Ind. 1976; U.S. Dist. Ct. (so. dist.), Ind. 1976; U.S. Supreme Ct., 1984. Assoc. Eugene Weaver Atty., Brazil, Ind., 1976-81; sole practitioner pvt. practice, Brazil, Ind., 1981—; chief deputy prosecutor 13th Jud. Cir., Brazil, Ind., 1978-81, deputy prosecuting atty., 1977-94. Com. on character and fitness Superme Ct. Ind., Indpls., 1988—; pres. bd. dirs. YMCA Clay County, Brazil, Ind., 1992-97, I.U. Residence Hall Alumni Assn., Bloomington, Ind., 1991-93. Co-chair Capital Campaign YMCA Clay County, Brazil, Ind., 1993—; bd. mem. Preservation Assn. Clay County, Brazil, Ind., 1995—; candidate for Judge Rep. Party Clay County, Brazil, Ind., 1994. Mem. Ind. State Bar Assn., Clay County Bar Assn., Natural Athlete Strength Assn., All Natural Physique and Power Conf. Republican. Avocations: powerlifting, antique collecting, gardening. Office: 13 W National Ave Brazil IN 47834-2536

BERRY, MARION, congressman; b. Aug. 27, 1942; m. Carolyn Berry; 2 children. BS, U. Ark., 1965. Ptnr., gen. mgr. family farm, Gillett, Ark.; commr. Ark. Soil and Water Conservation Commn., 1986-94, chmn., 1992; spl. asst. to Pres. Agrl. Trade and Food Assistance, 1993; mem. U.S. Congress from 1st Ark. dist., 1997—; mem. agr. com., transp. and infrastructure com. Democrat. Avocations: hunting, fishing. Office: 2305 Rayburn HOB Washington DC 20515-0401

BERRY, MARK SEAN, music educator; s. Vernon Lyle and Judy Elaine Berry. B in Music Edn., Ohio State U., 1994; MusM in Percussion Performance, U. Mich., 1997, D of Musical Arts, 2004. State of Ohio Teaching Certificate Ohio, 1994. Percussion instr. Thomas Worthington (Ohio) H.S., Worthington, 1992—95, Marion Cadets Drum and Bugle Corps, Marion, Ohio, 1992—94, Whitehall (Ohio) H.S., Whitehall, 1991—94, Livonia (Mich.) Franklin H.S., Livonia, 1996—98; adj. prof. percussion U. Mich., Flint, 1996—97; vis. prof. percussion W.Va. U., Morgantown, 1998—99, Western Ky. U., Bowling Green, 2001—02, asst. prof. percussion, 2002—. Snare line mem. Ltd. Edit. Drum and Bugle Corps, Columbus, Ohio, 1988—89; percussionist Westerville (Ohio) Symphony Orch., 1992, Mich. Percussion Group, Ann Arbor, Mich., 1995—2001, Jackson (Mich.) Symphony Orch., 1995—97, Adrian (Mich.) Symphony Orch., 1996, Gt. Lakes Symphony Orch., Detroit, 1996, Ft. Wayne (Ind.) Philharm., Fort Wayne, Ind., 1997, W.Va. U. Faculty Laureate, Morgantown, 1998—99; timpanist Cleve. Baroque Ensemble, Novi, Mich., 1996; lead steel drummer and percussionist Panchita Steel Band, Ann Arbor, 1997—2001; drumset player Western Ky. U. Faculty Jazz Ensemble, Bowling Green, 2003—; timpanist and percussionist Bowling Green Western Symphony Orch., Ky., 2001—02; prin. timpanist Bowling Green Chamber Orch., 2001—; percussion faculty Mich. Summer Music Inst., Ann Arbor, 2001—02; mem. Ryu Sei Marimba Duo, Bowling Green, Ky., 2001—. Composer: (electro-acoustic composition) Haru No Bu-fu-u; contbr. percussion concerto; dir.: (steel band ensemble) Millenium Stage Concert, Kennedy Ctr.; musician: (recording) Coyote Dreams, Historic Works for Percussion, Soundscapes, Panchita!, Marimba Duo Playing, (marimba soloist) Westerville South Day of Percussion; contbr. Fellow, U. Mich. Sch. of Music, 1995—97, U. Mich., 1997—2001; grantee, Coun. of Postsecondary Edn., 2003, Coun. on Postsecondary Edn., 2003; scholar, Ohio State U., 1990—95. Mem.: Ky. Music Educator's Assn., Percussive Arts Soc. Office: Western Kentucky University - FAC Bldg 1 Big Red Way Bowling Green KY 42101 Business E-Mail: mark.berry@wku.edu.

BERRY, MARY FRANCES, history professor, former federal agency administrator; b. Nashville, Feb. 17, 1938; d. George Ford and Frances Southall (Wiggins) B. BA, Howard U., 1961, MA, 1962; PhD, U. Mich., 1966, JD, 1970; hon. degree, Cen. Mich. U., Howard U., U. Akron, 1977, Benedict Coll., U. Md., Grambling State U., 1979, Bethune-Cookman Coll., Clark Coll., Del. State Coll., 1980, Oberlin Coll., Langston U., 1983, Marian Coll., Haverfod Coll., 1984, Colby Coll., CUNY, 1986, DePaul U., 1987. Bar: D.C. 1972. Asst. prof. history Central Mich. U., Mt. Pleasant, 1966-68; asst. prof. Eastern Mich. U., Ypsilanti, 1968-69, assoc. prof., 1969-70, U. Md., College Park, 1969-76; acting dir. Afro-Am. studies, 1970-72, dir., 1972-74, acting chmn. div. behavioral and social scis., 1973-74, provost div. behavioral and social scis., 1973-76; prof. history, prof. law U Colo. at Boulder, 1976-80, chancellor, 1976-77; prof. history and law Howard U., Washington, 1980—87; Geraldine R. Segal prof. Am. Social Thought U. Pa., Philadelphia, 1987—; asst. sec. for edn. US Dept. Health Edn. & Welfare, Washington, 1977-80; vice chairperson U.S. Commn. on Civil Rights, Washington, 1980—82; chaiperson U.S. Commn. on Civil Rights, Washington, 1993—2004. Adj. assoc. prof. U. Mich., 1970-71; mem. com. visitors U. Mich. Law Sch., 1976-80; mem. nat. adv. panel on minority concerns Coll. Bd., 1980-84; mem. adv. bd. Feminist Press, 1980—; mem. research adv. com. Joint Ctr. for Polit. Studies, 1981—; mem. editorial adv. com. Marcus Garvey Papers, 1981—; mem. adv. bd. Inst. for Higher Edn. Law and Governance, U. Houston, 1983—. Author: Black Resistance/White Law, 1971 (rev. 1994), Military Necessity and Civil Rights Policy, 1977, Stability, Security and Continuity, Mr. Justice Burton and Decision-Making in the Supreme Court, 1945-58, 1978, (with John Blassingame) Long Memory: The Black Experience in America, 1982; Why ERA Failed, 1986, Politics of Parenthood: Child Care, Women's Rights, and the Myth of the Good Mother, 1993, The Pig Farmer's Daughter and Other Tales of American Justice, 1999, Health Care Challenge: Acknowledging Disparity, Confronting Discrimination, And Ensuring Equality, 1999, My Face Is Black Is True: Callie House and the Struggle for Ex-Slave Reparations, 2005; assoc. editor Jour. Negro History, 1974-78; contbr. articles, revs. to profl. jours. Bd. dirs. ARC, Washington, 1980—; trustee Tuskegee U., 1980—; mem. adv. bd. Project '87, 1978—; mem. council UN U., 1986— Recipient Athena (disting. alumni) award U. Mich., 1977, Roy Wilkins Civil Rights award NAACP, 1983, Image award, 1983, Allard Lowenstein award, 1984, President's award Congl. Black Caucus Found., 1985, Woman of Yr. award Nat. Capital Area YWCA, 1985, Hubert H. Humphrey Civil Rights award Leadership Conf. on Civil Rights, 1986, Rosa Parks award SCLC, Black Achievement award Ebony Mag., Woman of Yr. award Ms. Mag., 1986. Mem. ABA, Nat. Bar Assn., D.C. Bar Assn., Nat. Acad. Public Adminstrn., Orgn. Am. Historians (exec. bd. 1974-77), Assn. Study of Afro-Am. Life and History (exec. bd. 1973-76), Am. Hist. Assn. (v.p. for profession 1980-83), Am. Soc. Legal History, Coalition 100 Black Women (hon.), Delta Sigma Theta (hon.) Independent. Office: U Pa 208 College Hall Rm 216E Philadelphia PA 19104 E-mail: mfberry@sas.upenn.edu.*

BERRY, NATHAN ERNEST, ophthalmologist; b. Jackson, Tex., Apr. 1, 1971; s. Don Wayne and Patty Lynn Berry; m. Lisa Adelia Lee, July 13, 1996; children: Annalise, Ellie. BS, Abilene Christian U., 1993; MD, Tex. Tech U., 1999. Intern in internal medicine Scott & White Hosp., Temple, Tex., 1999—2000, resident in ophthalmology, 2000—03, chief resident in ophthalmology, 2002—03; pvt. practice ophthalmology Cataract and Eye Ctr. of Cleburne, Tex., 2003—. Mem. judiciary rev. bd. Abilene (Tex.) Christian U., 1992—93; presenter in field. Grantee, Broadway Ch. of Christ, Lubbock, Tex., 1989. Mem.: AMA, Christian Ophthalmology, Am. Acad. Ophthalmology, Cleburne C. of C. Republican. Mem. Ch. Of Christ. Avocations: golf, soccer, basketball, piano, guitar. Home: 2493 Glenn Ranch Dr Burleson TX 76028 Office: Cataract Eye Ctr of Cleburne Cleburne TX 76033

BERRY, PAMELA C., secondary school educator; b. Oct. 24, 1941; d. Joseph Charles and Elenor (Kucharski) B.; 1 child, Katie Julia. BA, Western Mich. U., 1965; MA, U. Mich., 1975; Edn. Specialist, Wayne State U., 1985, postgrad. Lic. profl. tchr. Tchr. East Prairie Jr. H.S., Vicksburg, Mich., 1965-66, Allen Park (Mich.) H.S., 1966—. English dept. chair, 1969-81, tchr. English, 1993—. Rsch. asst. U. Mich., Ann Arbor, 1973-75, Wayne State U., Detroit, 1981-82, dir. politics in edn., 1981-82; spl. projects dir. Allen Park Pub. Schs., 1981-92; cons. Humanistic Mgmt. Sys., Columbus, Ohio, 1981-82; mem. Internat. Yr. of the Child, Wayne State U., Detroit, 1981-82; mem. std. setting com., (task force ensuring excellent educators, 2001) Mich. Dept. Edn., Lansing, 1998, content adv. com., 1998—, mem. task force State Bd. Edn., 2002; tech. liaison Allen Park Pub. Schs.; trainer Trainers County Mentoring Program. Pres. Young Dems., 1978-82; precinct dir. Dem. Party, del., 1985—. Nominee Phoebe Apperson award, Nat. PTA, 1985, Disney Tribute to Tchrs.; recipient Disting. Tchr. of Writing, Northwood U., 2001. Mem. Nat. Coun. Tchrs. English, Mich, (nominee Disney Tribute to tchr., Mich. Tchr. Yr.), Coun. Tchrs. English, Mich. Reading Assn., Phi Delta Kappa. Avocations: golf, reading, travel, theater, writing.

BERRY, PATRICK LOWELL, chemical engineer; b. Hillsboro, Ohio, Mar. 24, 1951; s. Russell Luther and Phyllis Louise Berry; m. Verna Ann McMullen, Sept. 11, 1971; children: Sean Patrick, Brenna Kathleen. BS in Chem. Engring., Ohio State U., 1973; MS in Ops. Rsch., George Washington U., 1986. Cert. Army Acquisition Corps - Level III U.S. Army, 1992. Chem. officer US Army, Aberdeen Proving Ground, Md., 1974—78, chem. engr., 1978—86, supervisory chem. engr., 1986—. Comdr. 2d lt. USAR, 1973, 2d lt. U.S. Army, 1974—76, 1st lt. U.S. Army, 1976—78, resigned capt. USAR, 1983. Recipient US Army R&D Achievement Award, 1994, 1998, 2000, US Army Meritorious Civilian Svc. Award, 2000, US Army Achievement Medal Civilian Svc., 2004. Mem.: AIChE, Internat. Soc. for the Systems Scis., Am. Assn. for Aerosol Rsch., Inst. for Ops. Rsch. and the Mgmt. Scis., Hon. Order of the Dragon, Omega Rho. Democrat. Achievements include designing and developing the first fielded US Army Biological Detection Systems, M31, M31A1 and M31E2. Avocations: birdwatching, travel, history. Home: 3138 Aldino Rd Churchville MD 21028 Office: US Army Edgewood Chem Biol Ctr 5183 Blackhawk Rd Aberdeen Proving Ground MD 21010-5424 Office Phone: 410-436-5522. Personal E-mail: bidsberry@aol.com. Business E-Mail: patrick.berry@us.army.mil.

BERRY, PHIL HUNTER, orthopedic surgeon; b. Jackson, Miss., June 18, 1937; married; 3 children. MD, U. Miss. Sch. Medicine, 1966. Intern Parkland Meml. Hosp., Dallas, 1966—67, resident, 1967—68, 1970, Baylor Med. Ctr., 1968, Tex. Scottish Rite Hosp., 1969; orthopedic surgeon pvt. practice, Dallas. Founder Southwest Transplant Found., 1994; mem. Health and Human Svc. Adv. Com. on Organ Transplantation. Recipient Max Cole Leadership award, 1996, Freedoms Found. award, Disting. Alumni award, U. Miss. Sch. Medicine, Champions of Hope award, Nat, Kidney Found., Pioneer Hero award, Internat. Organ Replacement. Mem.: AMA (precursor Live & Then Give Organ Donor Awareness Campaign, bd. trustees, AMA Foun., Benjamin Rush award for citizenship and cmty. svc. 2000), Tex. Orthopaedic Assn. (past pres.), Tex. Soc. Sports Medicine (past pres.), Dallas County Med. Soc. (past pres.), Tex. Med. Assn. (TMA) (founder Live & Then Give Organ Donor Awareness Campaign, pres. 1997—98, mem. TMA Found. (Tex. del. to AMA Ho. Del.)). Avocations: golf, skiing, tennis. Office: Oak Cliff Orthopedia Assn 221 W Colo Blvd Dallas TX 75208-2363 Office Phone: 214-941-4243. Office Fax: 214-943-2671.

BERRY, RICHARD LEWIS, writer, magazine editor, lecturer, programmer; b. Greenwich, Conn., Nov. 6, 1946; s. John William and Dorothy May (Buck) B.; m. Eleanor von Auw, June 7, 1968. BA, U. Va., 1968; MSc, York U., Can., 1972. Rsch. asst. MacMaster U., Hamilton, Canada, 1973-74; project engr. Intraspace Internat., Toronto, 1974-75; tech. editor Astronomy mag., Milw., 1976-78, editor, 1978-82, editor-in-chief, 1982-91; editor Telescope Making mag., Milw., 1978—91; editl. dir. Earth mag., 1990-91, cons., 1992; freelance writer, programmer, lectr., 1991—; editor Cookbook Camera Newsletter, 1994-99. Mem. adv. bd. Global Network of Automatic Telescopes; com. chair Internat. Space Sta. Amateur Telescope Project, Astron. League, 2002—. Author: Build Your Own Telescope, 1985, Discover the Stars, 1987, (with others) The Star Book, 1984, Introduction to Astronomical Image Processing, 1991, AIP Image Processing Software, 1991, BatchPIX Image Processing Software, 1992, Choosing and Using a CCD Camera, 1992, The CCD Camera Cookbook, 1994, The Dobsonian Telescope: A Practical Manual for Building Large Aperture Telescopes, 1997, Handbook of Astronomical Image Processing, 2000; contbg. author: Robotic Observatories, 1989, ST6PIX Image Processing Software, 1992, CB245 Image Processing Software, 1994, Multi245 Image Compositing Software, 1995, QColor Color Synthesis Software, 1997, Astronomical Image Processing for Windows, 2000, 2d edit., 2004; editor: Telescope Optics, Design and Evaluation, 1988. Mem. adv. bd. Global Network of Automatic Telescopes; mem. Internat. Space Station Amateur Telescope com. Astron. League. Recipient Clifford-Holmes award Astronomy for Am., 1981, Dorothea Klumpke-Roberts award Astron. Soc. Pacific, 1990, Omega Centauri award Tex. Star Party, Clyde W. Tombaugh award Riverside Telescope Makers Conf., 1995, G. Bruce Blair award Western Amateur Astronomers, 1998, Leslie C. Peltier award Astron. League, 2001, Astron. League award, 2002; Asteroid 3684 Berry named in his honor by Internat. Astron. Union, 1990. Mem. Internat. Amateur Profl. Photoelec. Photometry, Internat. Dark Sky Assn., Am. Astron. Soc. Avocation: photography. E-mail: rberry@wvi.com.

BERRY, RICHARD STEPHEN, chemist; b. Denver, Apr. 9, 1931; s. Morris and Ethel (Alpert) B.; m. Carla Lamport Friedman, Sept. 4, 1955; children: Andrea, Denise, Eric. AB, Harvard U., 1952, AM, 1954, PhD, 1956. Instr. chemistry Harvard U., 1956-57, U. Mich., 1957-60; asst. prof. Yale U., 1960-64; assoc. prof. U. Chgo., 1964-67, prof., 1967—, James Franck Disting. Svc. prof., 1989—; Arthur D. Little prof. MIT, 1968; Phillips lectr. Haverford Coll., 1968; spl. advisor to dir. Argonne Nat. Lab., 2004—. Cons. Avco-Everett Rsch. Labs., 1964—83, Argonne Nat. Lab., 1976—, Oak Ridge Nat. Labs., 1978—81, Los Alamos Sci. Lab., 1975—2005, mem. adv. com. theory; vis. prof. U. Copenhagen, 1967, 79; mem. adv. panel for chemistry NSF, 1971—73; mem. rev. com. radiol. and environ. rsch. divsn. Argonne Nat. Lab., 1970—76; mem. evaluation panel measures for air quality Nat. Bur. Standards; mem. numerical data adv. bd. NRC, 1978—86, chmn., 1981—86, mem. com. strengthening linkages between math. and scis., 1997—99, mem. steering com. panel on environ. monitoring, mem. com. on atomic and molecular sci., 1984—89; com. on chem. scis NAS-NRC, 1977—79; mem. adv. panel on health of sci. and tech. enterprise, mem. adv. panel on nat. labs. Office Tech. Assessment; mem. adv. bd. Environ. Health Resource Ctr., Chgo., Inst. for Theoretical Physics, Santa Barbara, 1989—91; mem. vis. com. divsn. applied physics Harvard U., 1977—81; Hinshelwood lectr. Oxford (Eng.) U., 1980; mem. adv. panel dept. chemistry Princeton U., 1978—81; prof. associé U. Paris-Sud, 1979—80; Newton Abraham prof. Oxford U., 1986—87, Phi Beta Kappa lectr., 1989—90, Welch Symposium lectr., 1995; pres. Telluride Summer Rsch. Ctr., 1989—93; chair com. transnat. exch. sci. data Nat. Rsch. Coun., 1994—97; Frederick Kaufman lectr. U. Pitts., 1996; Sackler lectr. Tel Aviv (Israel) U., 1999; F.C. Bartell lectr. U. Mich., 1999. Author: Understanding Energy, 1988; co-author: TOSCA, The Total Social Cost of Fossil and Nuclear Power, 1979, Physical Chemistry, 1980, 2d edit., 2000, Thermodynamic Optimization of Finite Time Processes, 2000; assoc. editor: Jour. Chem. Physics, 1971-74, Accounts Chem. Rsch., 1975-90, Revs. Modern Physics, 1983-95, Phys. Rev. A, 1986-92, Phys. Rev. E, 1992-94, Phys. Chemistry Chem. Physics, 1999-2002; bd. dirs. Bull. Atomic Scientists, 1974-83; adv. editor: Resources and Energy, 1978-92; contbr. articles to profl. jours. Recipient Heyrovsky medal Czech Acad. Sci., 1997; Alfred P. Sloan fellow, 1962-66; Guggenheim fellow, 1972-73; MacArthur prize fellow, 1983; Alexander von Humboldt Stiftung prize fellow, 1993. Fellow AAAS (chmn. chemistry sect. 1993-94), Am. Phys. Soc. (coun. 1993-95, publs. oversight com. 1996-2000, panel on pub. affairs, 2001—, chmn. few-body sys. topical group 1994-95), Am. Acad. Arts and Scis. (v.p. 1987-90, 95-98), Japan Soc. for Promotion of Sci.; mem. NAS (home sec. 1999-2003, chair report rev. com. 2000-04), Am. Chem. Soc., Royal Danish Acad. Arts and Letters (fgn.), Sigma Xi (nat. lectr. 1976-77). Office: Univ Chgo Dept Chemistry 5735 S Ellis Ave Chicago IL 60637-1403 Office Phone: 773-702-7021. E-mail: berry@uchicago.edu.

BERRY, ROBERT JOHN, architect; b. Concord, Mass., Nov. 10, 1947; A in Archtl. Engring., Wentworth Inst. Tech., 1967; BArch, U. Ariz., 1971. Registered architect, Mass. Asst. prof. Wentworth Inst. Tech., Boston, 1974-81, 90-94; prin. Robert J. Berry, Architect, Boxborough, Mass., 1974—. Mem. Am. Soc. Archtl. Perspectivists (exhibitor 1986). Avocations: photography, golf, painting. Home and Office: 171 Summer Rd Boxboro MA 01719-2001

BERRY, ROBERT VAUGHAN, retired electrical manufacturing company executive; b. Newark, Mar. 24, 1933; s. Harold Silver and Elizabeth Lippincott (Vaughan) B.; m. Victoria Shaw, Mar. 8, 1958; children: Patricia E., Michael V. BA, Dartmouth Coll., 1954. With Thomas & Betts Corp., Memphis, 1957-95, dir., 1972-85, v.p. fin., 1975-83, sr. v.p., 1983-95; ret., 1995; pres. Thomas & Betts Internat., Inc., 1975. Bd. dirs. Ames Rubber Corp., Hamburg, N.J. Trustee Carrier Found. Psychiat. Hosp., Belle Mead, N.J., 1984-92. 1st lt. Airborne Corps U.S. Army, 1954-57. Mem. Baltusrol Golf Club (Springfield, N.J.), Harbour Ridge Golf Club (Stuart, Fla.), Summerlea Golf and Country Club (Montreal, Que., Can.), Mid Ocean Club (Bermuda), Royal and Ancient Golf Club of St. Andrews (Scotland), Hanover (N.H.) Country Club. Republican. *Have a little fun each day - if you wait until the end you might miss it.*

BERRY, ROBERT WORTH, lawyer, retired law educator, retired military officer; b. Ryderwood, Wash., Mar. 2, 1926; s. John Franklin and Anita Louise (Worth) Berry. BA in Polit. Sci., Wash. State U., 1950; JD, Harvard U., 1955; MA, John Jay Coll. Criminal Justice, 1981. Bar: D.C. 1956, U.S. Dist. Ct. (D.C.) 1956, U.S. Ct. of Appeals (D.C. cir.) 1957, U.S. Ct. Mil. Appeals 1957, Pa. 1961, U.S. Dist. Ct. (ea. dist.) Pa. 1961, U.S. Dist. Ct. (ctrl. dist.) Calif. 1967, U.S. Supreme Ct. 1961, Calif. 1967, U.S. Ct. Claims 1975, Colo. 1997, U.S. Dist. Ct. Colo. 1997, U.S. Ct. Appeals (10th cir.) 1997, U.S. Tax Ct. 1959. Research assoc. Harvard U., 1955-56; atty. Office Gen. Counsel U.S. Dept. Def., Washington, 1956-60; staff counsel Philco Ford Co., Phila., 1960-63; dir. Washington office Litton Industries, 1967-71; gen. counsel U.S. Dept. Army, Washington, 1971-74, civilian aide to sec. army, 1975-77; col. U.S. Army, 1978-87; prof., head dept. law U.S. Mil. Acad., West Point, N.Y., 1978-86; ret. as brig. gen. U.S. Army, 1987; mil. asst. to asst. sec. of army, Manpower and Res. Affairs Dept. of Army, 1986-87; asst. gen. counsel pub. affairs Litton Industries, Beverly Hills, Calif., 1963-67; chair Coun. of Def. Space Industries Assns., 1968; resident ptnr. Quarles and Brady, Washington, 1971-74; dir., corp. sec., treas., gen. counsel G.A. Wright, Inc., Denver, 1987-92, dir., 1987-2000; pvt. practice law Fort Bragg, Calif., 1993-96; spl. counsel Messner & Reeves LLC, Denver, 1997—2004. Bd. dirs. G.A. Wright Mktg., Inc., v.p./gen. counsel, 2001-; bd. dirs. Denver Mgmt. Svcs. Inc., v.p., gen. counsel, 2001—; foreman Mendocino County Grand Jury, 1995-96. With U.S. Army, 1944-46, 1951-53. Decorated Bronze Star, Legion of Merit, Disting. Service Medal; recipient Disting. Civilian Service medal U.S. Dept. Army, 1973, 74, Outstanding Civilian Service medal, 1977. Mem. Am. Corp. Counsel Assn. (ACCA), Calif. Bar Assn., Pa. Bar Assn., Colo. State Bar Assn., Colo. Bar Assn. (com. on admissions and legal edn.), Denver Bar Assn., Army-Navy Club, Army-Navy Country Club, Phi Beta Kappa, Phi Kappa Phi, Sigma Delta Chi, Lambda Chi Alpha. Protestant. Office Phone: 303-393-5336. E-mail: bobb@gawright.com.

BERRY, SHARON ELAINE, interior designer; b. Kansas City, Mo., May 27, 1945; d. Ralph Epping Hohmann and Ruth Justine (Sturm) Hohmann Gibson; m. Max Allen Berry, Apr. 8, 1984. Grad. high sch., Kansas City; grad, Pierce Sch. Interior Design, 1972. Designer Danie Dunn Interiors, Kansas City, 1972-76, 80-83; co-owner, operator Clift-Willard Interiors, Leawood, Kans., 1976-80; head decorating dept. Carpets by Johnson and Johnson, Overland Park, Kans., 1983-84; owner, operator Nouveau Interiors, Shawnee Mission, Kans., 1984-92; coord. Met. Orgn. To Counter Sexual Assault, Kansas City, 1994-96, mem. adv. bd. adult survivor program, 1996—; pres. Recovery Records, 1996-98; dir. funding and devel. Cypress Recovery, Inc., Olathe, Kans., 1999-2000, bd. dirs., 1998; dir. fund devel. Rick's Place Found., 2000—01; owner Wild Berry Interior Design, 2002—. Vol. Design Excellence Awards Com., Kansas City, 1982-88; designer Designers Showhouse, Kansas City, Mo., 1975-90; participant Design '81 Congress, Helsinki, 1981, Gourmet March of Dimes, 1988, 90; writer City Limits, entertainment mag., Family News mag. Editor newsletter Survivors United Reading Empowerment (S.U.R.E.); contbr. to anthology The Bridge Is Out But I Can Fly; co-writer, co-prodr. CD Who Will Save the Children; editor, writer, newsletter Cypress Recovery. Vol. exec. dir. Recovery Is For Everyone Found., Olathe, 1996; vol. dir. pub. rels. Women's Resource Network, Shawnee Mission, 2000-02; v.p. internat. tng. in comm. JoCo Club. Recipient 2 Telly awards, gold award Houston Internat. Film Festival, 2d place Kans. Film Festival, cert. of merit Internat. Film and Video competition for video Who Will Save the Children, 1995. Avocations: writing, painting, sewing, gardening. E-mail: wildberry@prodigy.net.

BERRY, STEPHEN D., psychology educator, researcher; b. Chgo., June 14, 1947; s. John Joseph and Kathlyn (Murphy) Berry; m. Cathyann Therese Baldwin, July 12, 1969; children: Kimberly, Seanna, Kevin, Scott. BA sum laude, U. Notre Dame, 1969; MA with honors, U Conn., 1972, PhD, 1976. Postdoctoral U. Calif., Irvine, 1975-79; asst. prof. Miami U., Oxford, 1979-81, assoc. prof., 1981-95, prof., 1996—. Contbr. articles to profl. jours., speaker Miami U. Speakers Bur., Oxford, Ohio, 1985—. Fellow Am. Assoc. for Advancement of Sci., 1985, Am. Psychol. Soc., 1989. Mem. AAAS, Soc. for Neurosci. (pres. Miami Valley chpt. 1987-88), Am. Psychol. Soc., Sigma Xi (pres. Miami U. chpt. 1988-89). Roman Catholic. Achievements include contbr. to neurobiology of learning and memory, investigated roles of arousal and attention in learning. Office: Miami U Psychology Dept 216 Benton Hall Oxford OH 45056

BERRY, STEPHEN L. (STEVE), writer, lawyer; b. Atlanta, Sept. 2, 1955; m. Amy Berry. BA in Polit. Sci. cum laude, Valdosta State Coll., 1977; JD, Mercer Univ., 1980. Bar: Ga. 1980. City atty., St. Mary's, Ga., 1982, 1984; judge City Ct., St. Mary's, Ga., 1982—84; atty. Camden County Bd. Edn., St. Mary's, Ga., 1987—89; now atty. private practice, St. Mary's, Ga. Author: (novels) The Amber Room, 2003 (NY Times Bestseller list, Publishers Weekly Bestseller list, USA Today Bestseller list, Booksense Bestseller list), The Romanov Prophecy, 2004 (NY Times Bestseller list, Publishers Weekly Bestseller list, USA Today Bestseller list, BookSense Bestseller list), The Third Secret, 2005 (NY Times Bestseller list, USA Today Bestseller list, BookSense Bestseller list). Mem. Camden County Bd. Edn., Ga., 1988—92, Camden County Bd. Commrs., Ga., 2003—, chmn., 2001—02. Recipient 1st Place, Ga. State Bar fiction writing contest, 2001. Mem.: State Bar Ga. Office: PO Box 5100 Saint Marys GA 31558 E-mail: steveberry@tds.net.*

BERRY, SUSAN TURNER, artist, educator; b. Middletown, Conn., May 19, 1947; d. Benjamin Franklin and Eleanor Ruth (Hastings) T.; m. Tom V. Berry; children: Cheryl Felder, Scott Bluman, Sharon Garcia. AA with honors, Broward C.C., Davie, Fla., 1985; student, Fla. Atlantic U., 1985-86; BA, Norwich U., 1988, MA, 1990; postgrad., We. Ky. U. Owner, operator Lesue's Originals Custom Dressmaking, Pembroke Pines, Fla., 1978-83; sr. tutor Norwich U., Northfield, Vt., 1991-92; info. sys. coord. Infiltrator Sys., Inc., Old Saybrook, Conn., 1992-95, Fla. Dept. Edn., Tallahassee, 1996-97; freelance artist Clinton, Maine, 1997—; pres. Visual Insights, Inc., Clinton, 1998—; instrnl specialist math Elizabethtown Cmty. Tech. Coll., 2001—, adj. prof. computers and women's studies, 2001—. Spl. edn. tutor Spaulding H.S., Barre, Vt., 1986-89; adult edn. instr., computer software trainer, 1999. Creator, graphic artist publ. Meeting the Challenge, Fla. Dept. Edn., 1996 (Spl. Svc. award 1996); book poetry illustrator, In Other Words, 2004. Sec. Law and Politics Soc., Fla. Atlantic U., Boca Raton, 1986. Mem. Phi Kappa Phi (Honor Soc. Western Ky. U.). Avocations: country walks, painting, drawing. Home: 505 Robbins Dr Vine Grove KY 40175-6083

BERRY, WES, literature educator; s. Kenneth Wayne and Linda Lou Berry. BA, Western Ky. U., 1993; MA, U. Miss., 1995, PhD, 2000. Instr. English U. Miss., Oxford, 1995—2000; asst. prof. English Rockford (Ill.) Coll., 2000—04, Western Ky. U., 2005—. Contbr. articles to profl. jours. Mem.: MLA, Assn. for Study of Lit. and Environment (exec. coun. 2004—). Independent. Avocations: hiking, canoeing, travel, reading, writing.

BERRY, WILLIAM LEE, business administration educator; b. Indpls., Dec. 24, 1935; s. George Lee and Anna Marie (Hansert) B.; m. Carol M. Berry; children: Ann Kathleen, Lee Michael, Lynn Colleen. BS, Purdue U., 1957; MS, Va. Poly. Inst., 1964; DBA, Harvard U., 1969. Mfg. trainee GE, various locations, 1957-60, supr. mfg. Salem, Va., 1960-64; from asst. prof. to assoc. prof. indsl. mgmt. Purdue U., West Lafayette, Ind., 1968-76; prof. prodn. mgmt. Ind. U., Bloomington, 1976-82; C. Maxwell Stanley prof. prodn. mgmt. U. Iowa, Iowa City, 1982-87, sr. assoc. dean Coll. Bus. Adminstrn., 1983-87, dir. Mfg. and Productivity Ctr., 1986-87; Belk prof. bus. adminstrn., chmn. ops. mgmt. area U. N.C., Chapel Hill, 1988-92; prof. bus. adminstrn. Ohio State U., 1992—, Richard Ross chair in mgmt., dir. Ctr. Excellence in Mgmt., 1995—. Vis. prof. IMD, Lausanne, Switzerland, 1987-88; cons. in field. Co-author: Operations and Logistics Management, 1972, Production Planning, Scheduling and Inventory Control: Concepts, Techniques and Systems, 1974, Master Production Scheduling: Principles and Practice, 1979, Manufacturing Planning and Control for Supply Chain Management, 1984, 5th edit., 2005, ITEC: Manufacturing Planning and Control/Manufacturing Strategy Simulation, 1992, Production and Inventory Control Integrated, 1992; contbr. articles to profl. jours. 1st Enterprise fellow Kenan Inst., 1988-90. Fellow Decision Scis. Inst. (v.p. 1983-84, sec. 1985-86, pres.-elect 1987, pres. 1988); mem. Inst. Indsl. Engrs. (v.p. 1979-81, dir., Disting. Service award 1979), Ops. Mgmt. Assn. (v.p. 1981-85, pres.-elect 1985-86, pres. 1986-87, dir., Disting. Leadership award 1987), Am. Prodn. and Inventory Control Soc., Inst. Mgmt. Sci., Ops. Research Soc. Office: Fisher Coll of Bus Ohio State U Columbus OH 43210 Office Phone: 614-292-3173.

BERRY, WILLIAM MARTIN, financial consultant; b. Chgo., June 21, 1920; s. William John and Mary Frances (Martin) B.; m. Julia McIntire Vail, Dec. 19, 1972; children: William E., Mary P., Peter D. BS, St. Mary's Univ., 1941; MA, DePaul U., 1949. Divsn. contr. Hughes Aircraft Co., Culver City, Calif., 1950-55; div. contr. TRW, Redondo Beach, Calif., 1955-58; mgr. mgmt. cons. dept. Peat, Marwick, Mitchell and Co., L.A., 1958-61; v.p. Litton Industries Inc., Beverly Hills, Calif., 1961-74; chmn., CEO NN Corp., Milw., 1974-80; chmn. Northwestern Nat. Ins. Group, 1981-84. Bd. dirs. PK Tool & Die Mfg. Co., Chgo. Bd. dirs. Columbia Hosp., Milw., 1976—, Milw. Assn. Commerce, 1976-81, Milw. Symphony Orch., 1974-81, United Performing Arts Fund., Milw., 1977-81. With U.S. Army, 1941-46. Mem. Fin. Execs. Inst., Milw. Club, Milw. Country Club, Univ. Club. Avocations: woodworking, languages. Home and Office: 13800 N Birchwood Ln Mequon WI 53097-1702

BERRY, WILLIAM WILLIS, retired utilities executive; b. Norfolk, Va., May 18, 1932; s. Joel Halbert and Julia Lee (Godwin) B.; m. Elizabeth Mangum, Aug. 23, 1958; children: Preston Blackburn, John Willis, William Godwin. BSEE, Va. Mil. Inst., 1954; MC in Commerce, U. Richmond, 1964. Registered profl. engr., Va. Engr. Gen. Electric Co., 1954-55; with Va. Power, Richmond, 1957-92, v.p. divsn. ops., then sr. v.p. comml. ops., 1976-78, exec. v.p., 1978-80, pres., COO, 1980-83, pres. CEO, 1983-85, chmn., CEO, 1985-86, Dominion Resources Inc., 1986-90, chmn. Richmond, 1990-92. Bd. dirs. New Market Corp., Richmond, 1983—2005. Chair ISO New Eng., Holyoke, Mass. Mem. Commonwealth Club, Country Club Va. Republican. Personal E-mail: wwberry@earthlink.net.

BERRYHILL, HENRY LEE, JR., retired geologist; b. Charlotte, N.C., Nov. 6, 1921; s. Henry Lee and Viola Estelle (Johnston) B.; m. Louise Randall Russell, Sept. 13, 1947; children: Stuart Randall, Keith Courtney. BS, U. N.C., 1947, MS in Geology, 1949. With U.S. Geol. Survey, 1948-86, chief publs. officer Denver, 1963-65, research marine geologist, 1965-66, chief marine geology Gulf of Mexico-Caribbean region office Corpus Christi, Tex., 1967-70; chief Office Marine Geology, Washington, 1970-73, sr. research marine geologist Corpus Christi, 1973-86; gen. cons., 1986-99; ret., 1999; Tech. adviser offshore prospecting com. ECAFE, 1972-73; Dept. Interior rep. Fed. Intragy. Com. on Marine Sci. and Engring., 1970-73; program mgr. integrated environ. assessment Outer Continental Shelf N.W. Gulf of Mexico, 1973-86; U.S. rep. marine geology panel U.S.-Japan Coop. Programs in Natural Resources, 1973-95; ret. Cons. Nat. Center for Geoscis., India, 1981-87. Author: Geology and Coal Resources of Belmont County, Ohio, 1963, Geology of the Ciales Area, Puerto Rico, 1965, Coal-Bearing Upper Pennsylvanian and Lower Permian Rocks, Washington Area, Pennsylvania, 1971, The Worldwide Search for Petroleum Offshore-A Status Report for the Quarter Century, 1947-72, 1974, Seismic Models of Late Qua ternary Facies and Structure, Northern Gulf of Mexico, 1986. Contbr. articles to sci. publs. Served with USAAF, 1942-45. Decorated DFC, Air medal with 3 oak leaf clusters; recipient Outstanding Performance award U.S. Geol. Survey, 1969, a seafloor feature of the Gulf of Mexico named Berryhill Basin in his honor, 1995. Fellow Geol. Soc. Am.; mem. Am. Assn. Petroleum Geologists (co-recipient Jules Braunstein meml. award 1987), Sierra Club (chmn. Coastal Bend group 1980-81, 86-89), Sigma Xi. Episcopalian. Home and Office: 922 Burnt Hickory Cir Marietta GA 30064 *Besides an innate enthusiasm for learning, the greatest single factor that has shaped my life has been the choice of a profession that I could pursue as if it were my hobby.True satisfaction comes from the heartfelt knowledge of work well done. No amount of praise can supplant that innermost feeling of achievement. Above all, never fear to try.*

BERRYMAN, GUY, musician; b. Fife, Scotland, Apr. 12, 1978; Student, U. Coll. London. Bassist Coldplay, 1998—. Musician: (albums) Parachutes, 2000 (Grammy award: Best Alternative Music Album, 2001), A Rush of Blood to the Head, 2002 (Grammy awards: Best Alternative Music Album, 2002, Best Rock Performance By A Duo Or Group With Vocal for song "In My Place", 2002, Grammy award: Record Of The Yr. for song "Clocks", 2003), Live 2003, 2003. Office: Capital Records 1750 North Vine St 10th Floor Hollywood CA 90028

BERRYMAN, MARY ANNE PIERCE, elementary school educator; b. Morrilton, Ark., June 4, 1937; d. Homer Rowland and Margaret (Oldham) Pierce; m. James Cleo Berryman, Aug. 5, 1961; children: James Andrew, Cathryn Anne. BA in Interior Design, U. Okla., 1959; MS in Religious Edn., Southwestern Seminary, Ft. Worth, 1961; tchr.'s cert., Ouachita Bapt. U., Aradelphia, Ark., 1970. Salesperson Ellison's Furnishings, Ft. Worth, 1961-62; interior designer J.C. Penny Co., Ft. Worth, 1962-63; tchr. Arkadelphia Pub. Schs., 1970—2003; ret., 2003. Chmn. Arkadelphia Drive for Arthritis Found., 1977. Named Tchr. Yr., Arkadelphia C. of C., 1984-85, State of Ark. Exemplary Tchr. of Econs., 1991-92. Mem. AAUW (local pres. 1976-77, chmn. Ark. state edn. found. 1977-78, lt. gov. 1985-86, gov. Ozark Dist. 1998-99, named. Disting. Gov., 2000), S.W. Reading Coun. (pres. 1978-79), Civitan (lt. gov. Ozark dist. 1989-90), Civitan (local v.p., sec., pres.), Delta Kappa Gamma, Kappa Kappa Iota (pres. 1986-88, 94-96, state bd. pos. 2), Civitan Club (local v.p., pres. 1988-89).

BERRYMAN, RICHARD BYRON, lawyer; b. Indpls., Aug. 16, 1932; s. Herbert Byron and Ruth Katherine (Mayerhoefer) B.; m. Virginia Marie Asti, June 9, 1957; children: Steven, Susan, Kenneth. BA, Carleton Coll., 1954; JD, U. Chgo., 1957. Bar: D.C. 1957. Atty. bur. of aeronautics U.S. Dept. Navy, Washington, 1957-59, atty. office gen. counsel, 1959-62; assoc. Cox, Langford & Brown, Washington, 1962-65, ptnr., 1965-68, Fried, Frank, Harris, Shriver & Jacobson, Washington, 1968-90; pvt. practice Washington, 1990—. Mem. vis. com. Law Sch. U. Chgo., 1978-82; trustee Carleton Coll., Northfield, Minn., 1982-86; dir. Pericles Inst., Washington, 1996-2000. Mem. ABA. Office: 6901 Old Gate Ln Rockville MD 20852 also: 1200 G St NW Ste 800 Washington DC 20005 Office Phone: 301-881-7397. Personal E-mail: rbbesq@aol.com.

BERRYMAN, ROBERT GLEN, finance educator, consultant; b. Freeport, Ill., Nov. 22, 1928; s. Loyd Vernon and Gladys Leone (Hicks) B.; m. Ruth Madelyn Bjorngjeld, Aug. 25, 1955; children: Peter, David, Kathryn. BSBA, Northwestern U., 1950, MBA, 1951; PhD, U. Ill., 1958. CPA, Ill., Minn. Staff auditor Deloitte & Touche, Chgo., 1951-54, mgr. Mpls., 1969-70; instr. U. Ill., Champaign, 1954-58; asst. prof. acctg. U. Minn., Mpls., 1958-61, assoc. prof., 1961-65, prof., 1965-95, dir. grad. studies in acctg., 1980-83, chmn. dept. acctg., 1963-65, 70-73, 1990-95; exec. dir. fin. Cedar Riverside Assocs., Mpls., 1974-75. Cons. in field. Mem. editl. bd. Issues in Acctg. Edn., 1995-98; contbr. articles to profl. publs. Adviser to audit com. Minn. State Colls. and Univs., 1997-2001 Recipient Horace T. Morse-Amoco All Univ. Tchg. award U. Minn., 1976, Outstanding Tchr. award Carlson Sch. Mgmt., U. Minn., Green Eyeshade award Minn. Acctg. Assn., Tchg. award U. Minn. Alumni Assn., Mpls., 1978, Leon Radde Outstanding Educator award Inst. Internal Auditors, 1988. Mem. AICPA (chmn. acctg. theory subcom. 1979-83, continuing profl. edn. exec. com. 1979-82, bd. examiners 1980-83, Disting. Achievement in Acctg. Edn. award 1999), Inst. Internal Auditors (bd. regents 1979-83, bd. govs. Twin City chpt. 1981-91, cert. internal auditor), Minn. Soc. CPA (bd. dirs. 1965-69, 78-83, first recipient and honoree R. Glen Berryman award 1976), Accountability Minn. (pres. and bd. dirs.), Am. Acctg. Assn. (Outstanding Acctg. Educator 1994, Auditing Educator 1992). Home: 1462 Brenner Ave Saint Paul MN 55113-1671 Office: Univ MN Carlson Sch of Mgmt 321 19th Ave S Minneapolis MN 55455-0438 E-mail: gberryman@csom.umn.edu.

BERS, ABRAHAM, electrical engineering and physics educator; b. Cernauti, Bukovina, Romania, May 28, 1930; came to U.S., 1949; s. Isaias and Berta (Lechter) B.; m. Anita Alden Burrage, June 17, 1966; children: Rachel, Joshua. BS with highest honors, U. Calif., Berkeley, 1953; SM, MIT, 1955, ScD, 1959. Rsch. asst. Rsch. Lab. Electronics MIT, Cambridge, Mass., 1953-58, instr. dept. elec. engring. and computer sci., 1958-59, asst. prof., 1959-63, assoc. prof., 1963-71, prof., 1971—. Dir. rsch. Ecole Polytechnique, Paris, 1979-80; vis. prof. U. Paris-Orsay, 1981-92; vis. scientist CEA-Euratom, Cadarache, France, 1995, Limeil-Valenton, France, 1995. Co-author: Waves in Anisotropic Plasmas, 1963, Physique des Plasmas, Vols. 1-2, 1994; contbr. chpts. to books, articles to profl. jours. Faculty Exch. fellow Ford Found., Tech. U. Berlin, 1966, fellow J.S. Guggenheim Meml. Found., U. Paris, 1968-69. Fellow: Am. Phys. Soc. (chmn. divsn. plasma physics 1991—92); mem.: AAAS, Univ. Fusion Assn. (pres. 1988—89), N.Y. Acad. Sci., St. Botolph Club Boston. Avocations: tennis, skiing.

BERS, DONALD MARTIN, physiology educator; b. N.Y.C., Dec. 13, 1953; s. Harold Theodore and Penny (Wall) B.; m. Kathryn Eileen Hammond, July 17, 1976; children: Brian Alexander, Rebecca Ann. BA, U. Colo., 1974; PhD, UCLA, 1978. Postdoctoral research fellow UCLA, 1978-79, asst. research physiologist, 1980-82, adj. asst. prof., 1981-87; postdoctoral research fellow Edinburgh (Scotland) U., 1979-80; asst. prof. U. Calif., Riverside, 1982-86, assoc. prof., 1986-89, prof., 1989-92, divisional dean, dir. biomed. scis. program, 1991-92; prof., chmn. dept. physiology Loyola U., Chgo., 1992—. Author: Excitation-Contraction Coupling and Cardiac Contractile Force, 1991, 2001; assoc. editor News in Physiol. Sci.; mem. editl. bd. Am. Jour. Physiology, Circulation Rsch., Jour. Pharm. and Exptl. Therapeutics, Jour. Molecular Cell Cardiology; contbr. articles to profl. jours. Bd. dirs. Am. Heart Assn., Riverside, 1985-92, pres., 1989-91. Fellow Am. Heart Assn., L.A., 1978-80, Brit.-Am., Am. Heart Assn., 1980-81; recipient New Investigator Rsch. award NIH, 1982-85, Rsch. Career Devel. award NIH, 1985-90. Fellow: Internat. Soc. Heart Rsch. (mem. coun.), Am. Heart Assn.; mem.: AAAS, Biophys. Soc. (mem. coun., mem. exec. bd.), Am. Physiol. Soc., Soc. Gen. Physiology.

BERSCHEID, ELLEN S., psychology professor, writer, researcher; b. Colfax, Wis., Oct. 11, 1936; d. Sylvan L. and Alvilde (Running) Saumer; m. Dewey Mathias Berscheid, Nov. 21, 1959. BA, U. Nev., 1959, MA, 1960; PhD, U. Minn., 1965. Market rsch. analyst Pillsbury Co., Mpls., 1960-62; asst. prof. psychology and mktg. U. Minn., Mpls., 1965-66, asst. prof. psychology, 1967-68, assoc. prof., 1969-71, prof., 1971-88, Regents' prof. psychology, 1988—. Mem. NRC Assembly Behavioral and Social Scis., 1973-77. Co-author: Interpersonal Attraction, 1969, 78, Equity: Theory and Research, 1978, Close Relationships, 1983, Psychology of Interpersonal Relationships, 2005, also numerous articles; mem. numerous editl. bds., past editorships. Recipient Disting. Scientist award Soc. Exptl. Social Psychology, 1993. Fellow APA (Donald T. Campbell award 1984, editor Contemporary Psychology Jour. 1985-91, Disting. Sci. Contbn. award 1997, Presdl. Citation 2003), Soc. Personality and Social Psychology (pres. 1985), Soc. for Psychol. Study Social Issues, Am. Acad. Arts and Scis.; mem. Internat. Soc. for the Study Personal Relationships (pres. 1990-92), Soc. Exptl. Social Psychology (exec. bd. 1971-74, 77-80, 85-89, Disting. Scientist award 1993), Gown-in-Town Club. Lutheran. Avocation: interior design. Home: 329 Park Cir Menomonie WI 54751 Office: U Minn Dept Psychology N309 Elliott Hall Minneapolis MN 55455

BERSHAD, JACK R., retired lawyer; b. Phila., May 20, 1930; m. Helen Abby (Jay), Apr. 7, 1957; children: Thomas, Daniel, Robert. BS, Temple U., 1951; JD, Harvard U., 1954; LHD, Moore Coll. Art. Bar: D.C. 1954, Pa. 1955, U.S. Supreme Ct. 1985. Mem. firm Blank Rome LLP, Phila., 1958—2002, chmn., 1991—99, chmn. emeritus, 2000—, ret., 2002. Bd. dirs. Commerce Bancorp, Inc., Commerce Bank, N.A. Former chmn. bd. mgr. and trustees Moore Coll. Art, Phila.; trustee Phila. Mus. Art, 1989—, Jewish Fedn. Greater Phila.; bd. dirs. Opera Co., Phila., 1989—, Ben-Gurion U. Negev, Am. Assocs., 1998—, chair Mid. Atlantic Region; bd. govs. Mid. East Forum, 2000—; bd. dirs., pres. Phila. Chamber Music Soc., 2004-. With U.S. Army, 1954-56. Mem. ABA, Pa. Bar Assn., D.C. Bar Assn., Phila. Bar Assn. Office: Blank Rome LLP 1 Logan Sq Fl 3 Philadelphia PA 19103-6998 Office Phone: 215-569-5511.

BERSHAD, NEIL JEREMY, electrical engineering educator; b. Bklyn., Oct. 20, 1937; BEE, Rensselaer Poly. Inst., 1958, PhD in Elec. Engring, 1962; MSEE, U. So. Calif., 1960. Mem. tech. staff Hughes Aircraft Co., Culver City, Calif., 1958—62, staff engr., 1964—69; prof. elec. engring. and computer sci. U. Calif., Irvine, 1966—94, prof. emeritus, 1994—. Contbr. more than 100 articles on communication theory, signal processing and adaptive filtering to profl. jours. 1st lt. USAF, 1962-65. Fellow IEEE (assoc. editor comm. jour., acoustics, speech and signal processing jour.). Office Phone: 949-824-6709. Business E-Mail: bershad@ece.uci.edu.

BERSI, ANN, lawyer; BA, MA, San Diego State U.; JD, Calif. Western Sch. of Law; PhD in Higher Edn. Adminstrn., U. Conn. Bar: Calif. Past mem. law firms Morris, Brignone & Pickering, Lionel, Sawyer & Collins, Las Vegas; dir. employee rels. State of Nev., 1981-83; exec. dir. State Bar Nev., 1983-89; dep. dist. atty. civil divsn. Clark County Dist. Atty.'s Office, Las Vegas. Past instr. pub. adminstrn. Pace U., N.Y.; legal counsel Clark County Sch. Dist. Bd. Trustees, Clark County Bd. Equalization; mem. State Jud. Selection Commn., 2000—. Mem. State Bar Nev. (pres. bd. govs. 1999-2000). Office: District Attorneys Office PO Box 552215 Las Vegas NV 89155-2215 Office Phone: 702-455-4761. Business E-Mail: bersia@co.clark.nv.us.

BERSIN, ALAN DOUGLAS, state agency administrator, lawyer; b. Bklyn., Oct. 15, 1946; s. Arthur and Mildred (Laikin) B.; m. Elisabeth Van Aggelen, Aug. 17, 1975 (div. Dec. 1983); 1 child, Alissa Ida; m. Lisa Foster, July 20, 1991; children, Madeleine Foster, Amalia Rose. AB magna cum laude, Harvard U., 1968; student, Oxford U., 1968-71; JD, Yale U., 1974; LLD (hon.), U. San Diego, 1994, Calif. Western Sch. Law, 1996, Thomas Jefferson Sch. Law, 2000. Bar: Calif. 1975, U.S. Dist. Ct. (ctrl. dist.) Calif. 1975, U.S. Ct. Appeals (9th cir.) 1977, Alaska 1983, U.S. Dist. Ct. Alaska 1983, U.S. Dist. Ct. Hawaii 1992, U.S. Dist. Ct. (so. dist.) Calif. 1992, U.S. Supreme Ct., 1996. Exec. asst. Bd. Police Commrs., LA, 1974-75; assoc. Munger, Tolles & Olson, LA, 1975-77, ptnr., 1978-92; spl. dep. dist. atty. Counties of Imperial and San Diego, Calif., 1993-98; supt. pub. edn. San Diego City Schs., 1998—2005; sec. edn. State of Calif., Sacramento, 2005—. Adj. prof. of law U. So. Calif. Law Ctr.; vis. prof. Sch. Law U. San Diego, 1992-93; named spl. rep. for U.S. s.w. border by U.S. Atty. Gen., 1995-98; mem. Atty Gen.'s adv. com. of U.S. Attys., 1995-98; tech. adv. panel Nat. Inst. of Justice Law Enforcement, adv. com. FCC/NTIA Pub. Safety Wireless; founder U.S./Mex. Binat. Lab. Program; chmn. bd. dirs. U.S. Border Rsch. Tech. Ctr., S.W. Border Coun.; chmn. Calif. Commn. on Tchr. Credentialing, 2000-02; mem. Nat. Bd. Profl. Tchg. Stds. Recognition, 2002; coun. visitors Calif. We. Sch. Law, 2002—; mem. bd. overseers Harvard U., 2004—. Named Rhodes scholar 1968; recipient Resolution of Merit award Mayor and City Coun. L.A., 1991, Spl. Achievement award Hispanic Urban Ctr., 1992, Peacemaker's award San Diego Mediation Assn., 1997, Morgan award San Diego LEAD, 1998, Learned Hand award, AJC, 2001, Courageous Leadership award, San Diego C. of C., 2003. Mem. Assn. Bus. Trial Lawyers (bd. govs. 1986-88), Inner City Law Ctr. (chmn. bd. dirs. 1987-90). Democrat. Jewish. Avocations: scuba diving, skiing, travel. Office: Gov's Office Office of Sec for Edn 1121 L St, Ste 600 Sacramento CA 95814 Office Phone: 916-323-0611. Office Fax: 916-323-3753.

BERSIN, RICHARD LEWIS, physicist; b. NYC, July 4, 1929; s. Maxwell Hilary and Virginia (Greenfield) B.; m. Lillian Freda Braudy, Mar. 21, 1954 (div.); children: Joshua Morris, Adam Samuel; m. Ruth Ann Hargrave, July 25, 1976; children: Jacob David Antonio, Rebekah Adeline Juana. BS in Physics, MIT, 1950; MS in Math. and Physics, Northeastern U., Boston, 1962. Physicist Tracerlab, Inc., Boston, 1950-58; divsn. mgr. Lab. for Electronics Corp., Waltham, Mass., 1958-69; pres., founder Internat. Plasma Corp., Berkeley, Calif., 1969-74; exec. v.p. Dionex Gas Plasma Sys., Hayward, Calif., 1974-79; dir. dry processing Perkin Elmer Corp., Wilton, Conn., 1979-83, dir. tech. mktg., 1983-84; pres., cons. Emergent Techs. Corp., 1985—; engring. specialist Ulvac Japan, Ltd., Chigasaki, Japan, 1989-92; sr. tech. staff mem. Ulvac Techs., Inc., Methuen, Mass., 1992—2002. Patentee in field. Mem. IEEE, Am. Vacuum Soc. Democrat. Episcopalian. Office Phone: 978-887-6959. Personal E-mail: richard.bersin@verizon.net.

BERSOFF, DONALD NEIL, lawyer, educator, psychologist; b. NYC, Mar. 1, 1939; s. Irving and Mina (Cohen) B.; children by previous marriage: David, Judith; m. Deborah Leavy, Oct. 16, 1988; 1 child, Benjamin. BS, NYU, 1958, MA, 1960, PhD, 1965; student, U. Va. Law Sch., 1973-74; JD, Yale U., 1976. Bar: Md. 1976, D.C. 1984, Pa. 1990. Asst. prof. Ohio State U.; assoc. prof. U. Ga., U. Md. Sch. Law; ptnr. Ennis, Friedman & Bersoff, Washington, 1982-88, Jenner & Block, Washington, 1988-89; coord. joint JD and PhD program in law and psychology U. Md. Sch. Law and Johns Hopkins U. Dept. Psychology., 1976-82; dir. law and psychology program Med. Coll. Pa.-Hahnemann U., Phila., 1990-2001, Villanova (Pa.) U. Law Sch., 1990-2001, prof. emeritus, 2001—. Adj. prof. Drexel U., Phila., 2001—; psycholegal cons., 2001—. Author: Learning to Teach: A Decision-Making System, 1976, Ethical Conflicts in Psychology, 1995, 3d edit., 2003, Law and Mental Health-Pennsylvania, 1999. With USAF, 1965-68. N.Y. State Regents coll. teaching fellow. Mem. ABA, APA (mem. coun. of reps. 1991-94, bd. dirs. 1994-97, chair policy and planning bd. 1999, coun. of reps. 1999-2001), Am. Psychology-Law Soc. (pres. 1980-81. Lifetime Achievement award 2002). Home: 780 College Ave Haverford PA 19041-1205 Office: Villanova Law Sch Villanova PA 19085 Office Phone: 610-649-8448. E-mail: bersoffd@law.villanova.edu.

BERSON, ANTHONY M., oncologist; b. 1958; MD, Hahnemann U., 1984. Cert. Radiation Oncology 1990. Intern, internal medicine Mount Zion Hosp., San Francisco, 1984—85; fellow Lawrence Berkeley Lab., Berkeley, Calif., 1986—87; resident radiation oncology U. Calif., San Francisco, 1985—89; assoc. prof. N.Y. Med. Coll.; chmn., radiation oncology dept. St. Vincent's Hosp.-Manhattan, 1995—. Recipient Luther Brady Radiation Oncology award, 1984, ASTRP Travel award to ESTRO Meeting, Florence, Italy, 1991. Office: St Vincent Hosp 325 W 15th St New York NY 10011 Office Phone: 212-604-6081.

BERSON, ELIOT LAWRENCE, ophthalmologist, medical educator; b. Boston, 1937; MD, Harvard U., 1962. Intern Calif. Hosp., San Francisco, 1962-63; resident in ophthalmology Barnes and McMillan Hosps., St. Louis, 1963-66; clin. assoc. ophthalmologist Nat. Inst. Neurol. Diseases and Blindness, Bethesda, Md., 1966-68; asst. Mass. Eye and Ear Infirmary, Boston, 1968-73, asst. surgeon, 1974-78, dir. Berman-Gund Lab. for Study of Retinal Degenerations, Harvard Med. Sch., 1974—, assoc. surgeon in ophthalmology, 1979-84, surgeon in ophthalmology, 1984—. Instr. Harvard U. Sch. Medicine, Boston, 1968-70, asst. prof., 1971-76, assoc. prof. ophthalmology, 1976-82, Chatlos prof. ophthalmology, 1982—. Surgeon USPHS, 1966-68. Mem. AMA, Assn. for Rsch. in Vision and Ophthalmology, Am. Acad. Ophthalmology, Am. Ophthal. Soc. Office: Berman-Gund Lab Mass Eye and Ear Infirmary 243 Charles St Boston MA 02114-3002

BERSON, JEROME ABRAHAM, chemistry professor; b. Sanford, Fla., May 10, 1924; s. Joseph and Rebecca (Bernicker) B.; m. Bella Zevitovsky, June 30, 1946; children: Ruth, David, Jonathan. BS cum laude, CCNY, 1944; MA, Columbia U., 1947; PhD, 1949. NRC postdoctoral fellow Harvard U., 1949-50; asst. chemist Hoffmann-LaRoche, Inc., Nutley, N.J., 1944; asst. prof. U. So. Calif., 1950-53, asso. prof., 1953-58, prof., 1958-63, U. Wis., 1963-69, Yale U., 1969-79, Irénée du Pont prof., 1979-92, Sterling prof., 1992-94; Sterling prof. emeritus, 1994—; dir. div. phys. sci. and engring. Yale U., 1983-90. Vis. prof. U. Calif., U. Cologne, U. Western Ont., U. Karlsruhe, U. Lausanne; Fairchild Disting. scholar Calif. Inst. Tech.; cons. Riker Labs., Goodyear Tire & Rubber Co., am. Cyanamid Co., IBM, Cord Labs., SMC Corp., B.F. Goodrich Corp., Lubrizol Corp.; mem. medicinal chemistry study sect. NIH, 1969-73; mem. adv. panel chemistry NSF, 1964-70. Author: Chemical Creativity, 1999, Chemical Discovery and the Logicians' Program, 2003; mem. editorial adv. bd.: Jour. Organic Chemistry, 1961-65, Accounts of Chemical Rsch., 1971-77, 94-96, Nouveau Journal de Chimie, 1977-85, Chem. Revs., 1980-83, Jour. Am. Chem. Soc., 1988-93; contbr. articles to profl. jours. Served with AUS, 1944-46, CBI. Recipient Alexander von Humboldt award, 1980, Townsend Harris medal Alumni Assn. CCNY, 1984, Merit award NIH, 1989, Lit. award German Chem. Industry Assn., 2000; John Simon Guggenheim fellow, 1980 Fellow Am. Acad. Arts and Scis.; mem. NAS, Am. Chem. Soc. (Calif. sect. award 1963, James Flack Norris award 1978, Nichols medal 1985, Roger Adams award 1987, Arthur C. Cope scholar 1992, Oesper award 1998, chmn. div. organic chemistry 1971), Chem. Soc. London, Phi Beta Kappa, Sigma Xi, Phi Lambda Upsilon. Home: 45 Bayberry Rd Hamden CT 06517-3401 Office: Yale U Dept Chemistry PO Box 208107 New Haven CT 06520-8107 E-mail: jerome.berson@yale.edu.

BERSTEIN, ROBERT L., investment banker; b. Cambridge, Mass., July 12, 1975; s. Irving Aaron and Suzanne Berstein. BA, Cornell U., 1997. Investment banker Merrill Lynch, San Francisco, 1997—98, N.Y.C., 1998—99; v.p. Advanta Ptnrs., N.Y.C., NY, 1999—2004; investment banker Broadview Internat. divsn. Jefferies, Waltham, Mass., 2004—05, Needham & Co., LLC, Boston, 2005—. Chmn. NY Pvt. Equity Network, NYC, 2001—04. V.p. bd. dirs. Cornell U. Assn. Class Officers, Ithaca, NY, 2000—; young alumni nat. chmn. Cornell U. Fund, Ithaca, NY, 2002—; adv. coun. entrepreneurship enterprise program Cornell U., Ithaca, 2002—. Mem.: Univ. Club NYC, Harvard Club, Cornell Club, Sigma Phi (pres. 1996—97). Office: Needham & Co LLC 1 Post Office Sq Ste 1900 Boston MA 02109 Home: 205 Walden St # 6B Cambridge MA 02140 Office Phone: 617-457-0942. Personal E-mail: berstein@gmail.com.

BERT, CHARLES WESLEY, mechanical and aerospace engineer, educator; b. Chambersburg, Pa., Nov. 11, 1929; s. Charles Wesley and Gladys Adelle (Raff) B.; m. Charlotte Elizabeth Davis (June 29, 1957); children: Charles Wesley IV, David Raff. BSME, Pa. State U., 1951, MS, 1956; PhD in Engring. Mechanics, Ohio State U., 1961. Registered profl. engr., Pa., Okla. Jr. design engr. Am. Flexible Coupling Co., State Coll., Pa., 1951-52; aero. design engr. Fairchild Aircraft div. Fairchild Engine and Airplane Corp., Hagerstown, Md., 1954-56; prin. M.E. Battelle Inst., Columbus, Ohio, 1956-61; sr. research engr., 1961-62; program dir., solid and structural mechanics research, 1962-63; cons., 1964-65; assoc. prof. U. Okla., 1963-66, prof., 1966—2004; Benjamin H. Perkinson Chair prof. engring. Sch. Aerospace and Mech. Engring., 1978—2004; George L. Cross rsch. prof. U. Okla., 1981—2004, prof. emeritus, 2004—. Instr. engring. mechanics Ohio State U., Columbus, 1959-61; dir.Sch. Aerospace and Mech. Engring. U. Okla., 1972-77, 90-95; vis. scholar U. Calif., San Diego, 1996; cons. in field; chmn. Midwestern Mechanics Conf., 1973-75; Honor lectr. Mid-Am. State Univs. Assn., 1983-84; seminar lectr. Midwest Mechanics, 1983-84; Plenary lectr. Internat. Conf. on Composite Structures, Paisley, Scotland, 1987. Mem. editl. bd. Composite Structures Jour., 1982—, Jour. Sound & Vibration, 1988—, Composites Engring., 1991-95, Mechanics of Composite Materials and Structures, 1993-2001, Applied Mechanics Revs., 1993—, Composites, 1996-98, Internat. Jour. Structural Stability and Dynamics, 2000—, Jour. of Sandwich Structures and Materials, 1997—, Mechanics of Advanced Materials and Structures, 2002-; assoc. editor: Exptl. Mechanics, 1982-87, Applied Mechanics Revs., 1984-87; contbr. chpts. to books and articles to profl. jours. 1st lt. USAF, 1952-54. Sr. Rsch. scholar U. Calif., San Diego, 1996; recipient Disting. Alumnus award Ohio State U. Coll. engring., 1985. Fellow AAAS, AIAA (nat. tech. com. structures 1969-72, chmn. Ctrl. Okla. sect. 1966-67), ASME (Cen. Okla. sect. exec. com. 1973-78, 90-95, 99-01, sec. 1990-91, region X mech. engring. dept. heads com. 1972-77, 90-95, chmn. 1975-77, 10-session symposium named in his honor 1999), Am. Soc. Composites (bd. dirs. 1996-98, Disting. Rsch. award 1999), Am. Acad. Mechs. (bd. dirs. 1978-82, pres.-elect 2001-02, pres. 2002-03), Soc. Exptl. Mechanics (monograph com. 1978-82, chmn. 1980-82, sec. Mid-Ohio sect. 1958-59, chmn. 1959-60, adv. bd. 1960-63), Soc. Engring. Sci. (bd. dirs. 1982-88); mem. NSPE, Okla. Acad. Sci., Okla. Soc. Profl. Engrs., Scabbard and Blade, Pa. State Alumni Assn. (Outstanding Engring. Alumnus award 1992), Sigma Xi, Sigma Tau, Pi Tau Sigma, Sigma Gamma Tau (Disting. Engr. award), Tau Beta Pi (Disting. Engr. award). Achievements include co-development of world's smallest pressure transducer capable of measuring both steady and fluctuating pressures; first general solution of cylindrically orthotropic plates of radially varying thickness under arbitrary body forces; origination of several minimum-weight optimal designs for multicell cylindrical pressure vessels, experimental techniques and associated data reduction equations for determining residual stresses in both flat-sheet and thick-walled cylindrical specimens of composite materials; first successful application of Kennedy-Pancu system identification method to shell structures, noninteger polynomial version of Rayleigh's method to heat conduction; first application of differential quadrature method to static structural problems, structural vibration problems and non-linear structural problems; first application of noninteger polynomial method to finite element analysis; first dynamic stability analysis of unicycles and monocycles; origination of concept of stress gages for composite materials; research on sandwich structures with bimodular facings, prediction of ply steer behavior of automobile tires, non-linear flutter of laminated composite panels; many others. Home: 2516 Butler Dr Norman OK 73069-5059 Office: U Okla Sch Aerospace and Mech Engring 865 Asp Ave Norman OK 73019-1052 *Set high yet realistic goals, put forth the extra effort to achieve them, and practice the Golden Rule.*

BERT, CLARA VIRGINIA, retired home economics educator, school system administrator; b. Quincy, Fla., Jan. 29, 1929; d. Harold C. and Ella J. (McDavid) B. BS, Fla. State U., 1950, MS, 1963, PhD, 1967. Cert. tchr., Fla.; cert. home economist; cert. pub. mgr. Tchr. Union County High Sch., Lake Butler, Fla., 1950-53, Havana High Sch., Fla., 1953-65; cons. rsch. and devel. Fla. Dept. Edn., Tallahassee, 1967-75, sect. dir. rsch. and devel., 1975-85, program dir. home econs. edn., 1985-92, program specialist resource devel., 1992-96, program specialist, spl. projects, 1996-99, program dir. grants mgmt., 1999-2000; ret., 2000. Cons. Nat. Ctr. Rsch. in Vocat. Edn., Ohio State U., 1978; field reader U.S. Dept. Edn., 1974-75. Author, editor booklets. Mem. devel. bd., mem. adv. bd. Fla. State U. Coll. Human Scis. Family Inst., 1994—; mem. nat. com. for the capital campaign Fla. State U. Found., 2002—. U.S. Office Edn. grantee, 1976, 77, 78; recipient Dean's award Coll. Human Scis., Fla. State U., 1995; named Disting Alumna Coll. Human Scis., Fla. State U., 1994. Mem. Am. Home Econs. Assn. (state treas. 1969-71), Am. Vocat. Assn., Fla. Vocat. Assn., Fla. Vocat. Home Econs. Assn., Am. Vocat. Edn. Rsch. Assn. (nat. treas. 1970-71), Nat. Coun. Family Rels., Am. Ednl. Rsch. Assn., Fla. State U. Alumni Assn. (bd. dirs. home econs. sect. 1976-81, pres.-elect 1978-79, 79-80), Havana Golf and Country Club, Fla. State U. Ctr. Club, Kappa Delta Pi, Kappa Omicron Nu (chpt. pres. 1965-66), Delta Kappa Gamma (pres. 1974-76), Sigma Kappa (pres. corp. bd. 1985-91), Phi Delta Kappa.

BERT, ELLIS LAWRENCE, retired judge; b. N.Y.C., July 11, 1927; s. Jacob Bert and Rose Borenstein; m. Allyne Sackley, Dec. 26, 1954; children: Alison, Melissa. BA, Hunter Coll., 1950; JD, Bklyn. Law Sch., 1959. Civil rights compliance specialist Social Security Adminstrn., Balt., 1967—70; regional counsel Equal Employment Opportunity Commn., Albuquerque, 1970—73, Atlanta, 1976—79, supv. trial atty., 1973—83, adminstrv. judge Dallas, 1983—87, 1992—94; ret. Probation officer Ct. Spl. Sessions, N.Y.C., 1955—61. Author short stories. Atty. Miss. summer project Lawyers Constitutional Def. Com., 1964; dir. Onondish Neighborhood Svcs., Syracuse, NY, 1966—67; asst. corp. counsel Law Dept. City of N.Y., 1961—66. With USCG, 1945—46. Mem.: Tex. Bar Assn. Democrat.

BERTAGNOLLI-COMSTOCK, AMANDA K., mathematician, educator; AS, Faulkner State Coll., 1992; BS, U. Mobile, 1994; MS, U. South Ala., 1996. Math. instr. Bishop State C.C., Mobile, Ala., 1996—2004; sr. pharm. sales rep. Glaxo Smith Kline, 2004—. Com. mem. and phys. fitness choreographer City of Daphne (Ala.) Miss Jubilee Scholarship Program, 2000—. Mem.: Math. Assn. Am. Avocations: exercising, running, ballroom dancing, reading. Office: Bishop State CC 351 N Broad St Mobile AL 36603

BERTE, NEAL RICHARD, academic administrator; b. May 7, 1940; s. Edward H. and Wenonah Maureen (Stevens) B.; m. Anne; children: Becky, Julie, Mark, Scott. BS in Polit. Sci, U. Cin., 1962, MS (Ford Found. scholar), 1963, EdD, 1966; Rockefeller Found. fellow, Union Theol. Sem., N.Y.C., 1962-63; postgrad., Garrett Theol. Sem., Evanston, Ill., 1966-67, Harvard U., 1966; LHD (hon.), U. Cin., 1993. Asst. dir. Coll. Entrance Exam. Bd., Evanston, 1966-68; exec. asst. to pres., asst. prof. Ottawa (Kans.) U., 1968-70; dean New Coll.; assoc. prof. U. Ala., 1970-74; v.p. ednl. devel., dean New Coll., 1974-76; pres. Birmingham (Ala.)-So. Coll., 1976—, chancellor, 2004—. Project dir. NSF grants, 1972; chmn. session Internat. Council on Edn. for Teaching World Assembly, Nairobi, Kenya, 1973; faculty Danforth Found. sponsored C.C. Inst., Stephens Coll., 1973; steering com. Carnegie Found. funded project Coop. Assessment of Experiential Learning, 1974-77; mem. Commn. on Ednl. Credit, Am. Council Edn., 1975-81, Danforth Found. exec. com. for Danforth Fellows Program, 1974-75; nat. adv. council for career edn. HEW, Office Edn., 1976-79; sec.-treas. So. U. Conf., 1977-80, v.p., 1984-85, pres., 1985-86; vis. scholar Inst. for Ednl. Mgmt., Harvard Grad. Sch Edn., 1990-91; co-chmn. Region 2020, Ala., 1997—; bd. dirs. Ala. Ctr. for Law and Civic Edn. Contbr. articles to edn. jours. Mem. adminstrv. bd. Canterbury United Meth. Ch., Birmingham, 1977—, univ. senate United Meth. Ch., 1986-88; chmn. Univ. United Fund campaign, 1973; bd. dirs., mem. exec. com. United Fund, Tuscaloosa, Ala., 1974-75, chmn. edn. div., 1975; chmn. sect. for pvt. ednl. insts. Jefferson-Shelby-Walker Counties United Appeal, 1977; chmn. pub. employees div. United Way campaign, 1978; v.p. Coun. for Advancement Pvt. Colls. in Ala., 1977-82, pres., 1982-83; chmn. com. to select Man of Year in Birmingham, 1977; chmn. selection com. Rhodes Scholarships for Ala., 1976-81; bd. dirs. Jefferson-Shelby Counties Lung Assn., 1978-79, Ala. Partners for Progress with Guatemala Program, 1977—, Carraway Meth. Hosp., 1977-80, Brookwood Hosp., 1982-90, Neighborhood Housing Svc., Birmingham, 1977-78, Birmingham Symphony Assn., 1976-80, 82-87, Cmty. Affairs Com., 1976-87, Operation New Birmingham, 1976-89; bd. govs. Relay House Club, Birmingham, 1983-87, Circle S Industries, Selma, Ala., 1983—, Parisian, Inc., Birmingham, 1983-88; bd. dirs. NCCJ, 1978—, Birmingham Summerfest, 1979—, March of Dimes, 1979-86, Am. Heart Assn., 1980-84, So. Rsch. Inst., 1982—, Leadership Birmingham, 1981—, Leadership Ala., 1990-93; bd. dirs., chmn. long range planning com., chmn. program for Scout Expn. Jefferson County coun. Boy Scouts Am., 1977—; exec. com. Men's Com., Birmingham Symphony Assn., 1977-84; bd. dirs. Jefferson Fed. Savs. and

Loan Assn., Birmingham, 1978-91, Birmingham Festival Arts, 1982-89, bd. advisors, 1989, trustee, 1990, pres., 1981—; chmn. Birmingham Area United Way, 1983; trustee Advent Episc. Day Sch., 1977-87, Gorgas Scholarship Found., 1976-88, New Coll.-Sarasota, U. South Fla., 1977-79; founding mem., bd. dirs. Progressive Alliance, 1986—; bd. dirs. Met. Devel. Bd., 1987-88, Greater Birmingham Conv. and Visitors Bur., 1988; commn. pub. rels. Nat. Assn. Ind. Colls and Univs., 1992-94, bd. dirs., 1994; adv. bd. pub. Edn. Found. Jefferson County Bd. Edn., 1999—; bd. dirs. Civil Rights Inst., 2000; co-chair Campaign for Restoration of Birmingham's Hist 16th St. Bapt. Ch., mem. found. bd., 2004—; chmn. steering com. McWane Cmty. Adv. Panel, 2004—; bd. dirs. U. Ala. Health Svcs. Found., 2004—; v.p. Birmingham Civil Rights Inst., 2005. Recipient Outstanding Citizens award Lawson State C.C. Coll., 1977, Outstanding Citizen award in Birmingham Erskine Ramsay Award Com., 1978, Brotherhood award NCCJ, 1984, Outstanding Svc. award Black Student Union, 1986, Outstanding Cmty. Svc. award Mortar Bd., 1986, James M. Tingle award, 1986, Disting. Svc. award, Sigma Alpha Epsilon, 1991, Medal of Honor, DAR, 1995, Leadership award Birmingham Regional Planning Commn. promoting regional cooperation, 2000, award of distinction Nat. Interfrat. Coun., 2004, Outstanding Svc. award Martin Luther King, Jr. Unity Breakfast, 2005; elected to Ala. Acad. Honor, 1979; named one of 10 Outstanding Cmty. Leaders Birmingham Post-Herald, 1984, one of Top 10 Current Leaders in Birmingham, The Birmingham News, 1990, 99, one of 10 leaders Bus. First jour., 1990, Birmingham Citizen of Yr. award for outstanding civic and cmty. svc., 1986, Outstanding Ala. Civic Leader Nat. Soc. Fund-Raising Execs., 1991, Disting. Citizen City Coun. of Birmingham, 1992, one of top ten mems. of 1997 Class of Movers and Shakers, Birmingham Bus. Jour.; named to Sigma Alpha Epsilon Leadership Sch. Hall of Fame, 1994. Mem. Am. Assn. Univ. Adminstrs. (pres. Alpha chpt. 1978-79), Greater Birmingham Area C. of C. (bd. dirs., exec. com. 1978-80, v.p. for govtl. rels., policy com. 1986, pres. 1988, chmn. exec. com. 1989), Am. Assn. Colls. (pres.'s adv. coun. 1977-78), Am. Assn. for Higher Edn. (chmn. Southeastern Regional Coun. 1973, chmn. panel on three-year degree programs 1973, program chmn. 1974, adv. bd. NEXUS Project 1974-75), Assn. for Innovation in Higher Edn. (adv. bd. 1973), Kiwanis Internat. (Disting. Pres. award 1992-93, George F. Hixon fellow 1995), Phi Beta Kappa (pres. 1975), Phi Delta Kappa. Clubs: The Redstone Club, The Jefferson Club, Downtown Birmingham Kiwanis (chmn. Ministers Day 1977, chmn. Youth-of-the-Year selection com. 1978, pres. 1992-93, Disting. Pres. award). Office: Chancellor Birmingham So Coll Box 549005 Birmingham AL 35254 E-mail: rberte@bsc.edu.

BERTELSMAN, WILLIAM ODIS, federal judge; b. Cincinnati, Ohio, Jan. 31, 1936; s. Odis William and Dorothy B.; m. Margaret Ann Martin, June 13, 1959; children: Kathy, Terri, Nancy. BA, Xavier U., 1958; JD, U. Cin., 1961. Bar: Ky. 1961, Ohio 1962. Law clk. firm Taft, Stettinius & Hollister, Cin., 1960-61; mem. firm Bertelsman & Bertelsman, Newport, Ky., 1962-79; judge U.S. Dist. Ct. (ea. dist.) Ky., Covington, 1979—, chief judge, 1991-98; instr. Coll. Law U. Cin., 1965-72; city atty., prosecutor Highland Heights, Ky., 1962-69. Adj. prof. Chase Coll. of Law, 1989—. Contbr. articles to profl. jours. Served to capt. AUS, 1963-64. Mem.: U.S. Jud. Conf. (standing com. on practice and procedure 1989—95, liaison mem. adv. com. on civil rules 1989—95, 6th cir. rep. 2004—), Ky. Bar Assn. (bd. govs. 1978—79), ABA. Republican. Roman Catholic.

BERTENSHAW, WILLIAM HOWARD, III, radio and television producer; b. NYC, Nov. 28, 1930; s. William Howard Jr. and Grace Annette (Miller) B.; m. Betty J. Underriner, July 7, 1956 (dec. Nov. 1975); children: Jane Ann, Judith Ann, Jo Ann; m. Bobbi C. Slachofsky, Dec. 16, 1984 (div. Sept. 2002). BA in Communications, Ohio Wesleyan U., 1950. Asst. mktg. editor Bus. Week mag., N.Y.C., 1953-55; radio-TV dir. Hardy Burt Assocs., N.Y.C., 1955-57; radio-TV producer Empire Broadcasting Corp., N.Y.C., 1957-60, Nat. Episcopal Ch., N.Y.C., 1960-70; producer MBS, N.Y.C., 1970-75; dir. communications Council of Chs. City of N.Y., 1975-84; exec. producer, chief exec. officer Radio & TV Roundup Prodns., N.Y.C., 1984—; producer TKR Cable TV, N.Y.C., 1987—. Guest lectr. Upsala U., East Orange, N.J., 1970-75, So. Meth. U., Dallas, 1972, Seton Hall U., South Orange, N.J., 1974, Pace U., N.Y.C., 1980, Syracuse (N.Y.) U., 1982; vice chmn. dept. communications N.J. Coun. Chs., 1986—; host People Working for People, Sta. WWOR-TV, N.Y.C., 1988-92; programmer Cable TV Network of N.J., 1985-2000; producer The Jersey Cape TV series, 1990—. Host Inner-Dimension Community Concerns, Union Eyes and Perspective on the News Sta. WOR Radio, WOR Special Report, N.Y., 1970—. Pres. Rep. Club, West Cape May, N.J., 1986-87; vice chmn. communications N.J. Coun. Chs., 1986-89; committeman Cape May County N.J. Rep. Orgn., 1987-90, Essex Coun. N.J. Rep. Orgn., 1960-85. Sgt. U.S. Army, 1951-53. Recipient Gabriel award Washington Conf., 1966-67, Radio Programming award Ohio State U., 1969, Columbus Film Festival award Ohio Coun. Chs., 1970, Radio-TV award N.J. Coun. Chs., 1983, Olive award, 1982-84, Cape award Cable TV Network NJ, 1987, Angel award Excellence in Media, Hollywood, Calif., 1999-2005. Mem. AFTRA, Delfon Recording Soc. (dir. comm. 2001—), Nat. Lima Bean Assn. (founder), Alpha Sigma Rho, South Jersey Bird Club. Clubs: Suburban Sports Car (N.J.) (v.p., co-founder 1956-61). Episcopalian. Home: 653 Sun Haven Dr Clayton NJ 08312-1955 Office Phone: 856-881-2570. E-mail: delfon@att.net, whb@att.net.

BERTERO, KAREN E., lawyer; b. Mar. 16, 1957; AB, Univ. Calif., Berkeley, 1978; JD, UCLA, 1981. Ptnr. corp. transactions and securities Gibson Dunn & Crutcher LLP, LA. Mem. exec. com. and diversity com. Gibson Dunn & Crutcher. Mem.: ABA, State Bar Calif., Order of Coif, Phi Beta Kappa. Office: Gibson Dunn & Crutcher LLP 333 S Grand Ave Los Angeles CA 90071-3197 Office Phone: 213-229-7360. Office Fax: 213-229-6360. Business E-Mail: kbertero@gibsondunn.com.

BERTHELSDORF, SIEGFRIED, retired psychiatrist; b. Shannon County, Mo., June 16, 1911; s. Richard and Amalia (Morschenko) von Berthelsdorf; m. Mildred Friederich, May 13, 1945; children: Richard, Victor, Dianne. BA, U. Oreg., 1934, MA, MD, 1939. Intern U.S. Marine Hosp., Staten Island, N.Y., 1939-40; psychiat. intern Bellevue Hosp., N.Y.C., 1940-41; psychiat. resident N.Y. State Psychiat. Hosp., N.Y.C., 1941-42; research assoc. Columbia U. Coll. Physicians and Surgeons, N.Y.C., 1942-43; asst. physician Presbyn. Hosp. and Vanderbilt Clinic, N.Y.C., 1942-51; supervising psychiatrist Manhattan (N.Y.) State Hosp., 1946-50; asst. adolescent psychiatrist Mt. Sinai Hosp., N.Y.C., 1950-52; psychiat. cons. MacLaren Sch. for Boys, Woodburn, Oreg., 1952-84, Portland (Oreg.) Pub. Schs., 1952-67; ret., 1984. Clin. prof. U. Oreg. Health Scis. Ctr., 1956—; tng. and supervising analyst Seattle Psychoanalytic Inst., 1970—. Author: Treatment of Drug Addiction in Psychoanalytic Study of the Child, Vol. 31, 1976, Ambivalence Towards Women in Chinese Characters and Its Implication for Feminism, American Imago, 1988, (with others) Psychiatrists Look at Aging, 1992. Bd. dirs., v.p. Portland Opera Assn., 1960-64, Portland Musical Co., 1987-92; bd. dirs. Portland Chamber Orch., 1964-70, 92-94, 96-97, exec., 1997-2003. Maj. USAF, 1943-46. Recipient Henry Waldo Coe award U. Oreg. Med. Sch., Portland, 1939, citation Parry Ctr. for Children, Portland, 1970, Child Advocacy award ORAPT, 1998. Fellow Am. Psychiat. Assn. (life), Am. Geriatrics Soc. (founding fellow); mem. Am. Psychoanalytic Assn. (life), Portland Psychiatrists in Pvt. Practice (charter, pres. 1958), Mental Health Assn. (bd. dirs., chmn. med. adv. com. 1952-60), Multnomah County Med. Soc. (pres.'s citation 1979), Oreg. Psychoanalytic Found. (founding mem.), Am. Rhododendron Soc. (bd. dirs., v.p. Portland chpt. 1956-58, Bronze medal and citation 1974), Am. Rhododendron Species Found. (bd. dirs. 1960-75), Phi Beta Kappa, Sigma Xi, Phi Sigma, Phi Mu Alpha. Avocations: farming, music. Home: 10880 SW Davies Rd # 1007 Portland OR 97008 Personal E-mail: SiegfriedMD@aol.com. *Life's challenge is to close the hiatus between what we are and what we aspire to be: "Edel sei der Mensch, Hilfreich und gut! --".*

BERTHELSEN, RICHARD A., lawyer; b. Racine, Wis., Sept. 14, 1944; BS, U. Wis., 1966, JD, 1969. Bar: Wis. 1969, U.S. Dist. Ct. Wis., 1969. Assoc. Murphy, Huiskamp, Stolper, Brewster & Desmond, Madison, Wis., 1969-72; gen. counsel Nat. Football League Players Assn., Washington, 1984—. Gen. counsel U.S. Football League Players Assn., Washington, 1983-86, N.Am. Soccer League Players Assn., Washington, 1982-86, Major Indoor Soccer League Players Assn., Washington, 1983-91; lectr. various legal/sports seminars. Mem. Nat. Sports Law Inst. (bd. advisors), Sports Lawyers Assn. (bd. dirs.), Wis. Bar Assn. (pres. 1997-99). Office: NFL Players' Assn 2021 L St NW Washington DC 20036

BERTHIAUME, GAYLE, elementary school educator; b. Minn. BS in edn., St. Cloud State Coll., 1969—72; M of curriculum and instrn., St. Cloud State U., 1986—94. Apple Certified Final Cut Pro HD Apple Computer, Inc., 2005, Kindergarten Endorsement Minn. Bd. of Tchg., 1972, Reading Certification Minn. Bd. of Tchg., 1972. Tchr. Milaca Pub. Schools, Milaca, Minn., 1972, Becker Pub. Schools, Minn., 1972—. Apple disting. educator Apple Computer, Inc., 2001—; tchr. quality enhancement profl. devel. consortium St. Cloud State U., 2004—, tchr. quality enhancement co-teacher, 2004—; tchr. mentor Scholastic.com, 2003—04, nat. tchr. adv. bd., 2003—; apple learning interchange editl. rev. bd. Apple Computer, Inc., 2004—; rschr. and developer Minn. Tchr. Network, 2000—; teachers as learners and leaders profl. devel. activist Edn. Minn., 2003—; presenter in field. Author: (publication) Creating Books and Movies in a Digital Classroom, (website) Kindergarten Pieces, First Grade Online. Recipient Apple Disting. Educator, Apple Computer, Inc., 2001, Internet Educator of the Yr., Classroom Connect, 2002, Apple Learning Interchange Recognized Author, Apple Computer, Inc., 2003, Becker Tchr. of the Yr., Becker Edn. Assn., 1987, 1988; Inspired Educator, Inspiration Software, 2001, Minn. Tchr. Network grant, US West and NEA, 1997. Mem.: Becker Edn. Assn. (pres. 1986—90), Edn. Minn. (amb. 2001—05), Am. Fedn. of Teachers, Nat. Edn. Assn., Nat. Coun. of Teachers of English, Internat. Reading Assn. (tech., communication and literacy com. 2005—), Internat. Soc. for Tech. in Edn., Internat. Assn. of Webmasters and Designers, Assn. of Macintosh Trainers. Avocations: travel, rosemaling, photography. Office Phone: 763-261-6330.

BERTHOT, JAKE, artist, educator; b. Niagara Falls, N.Y., Mar. 30, 1939; Student, New Sch. Social Rsch., 1960-61, Pratt Inst., 1960-62. Mem. faculty Cooper Union, 1960-62, Yale U., New Haven, 1982-90, Sch. Visual Arts, N.Y.C., 1992—. Artist in residence Dartmouth U., 1995. One-man shows include O. K. Harris Gallery, N.Y.C., 1970, 1972, 1975, Portland (Oreg.) Ctr. Visual Arts, 1973, Galerie de Gestlo, Hamburg, Germany, 1973, 1977, David McKee Gallery, N.Y.C., 1976, 1978, 1982, 1983, 1986, 1988, 1989, 1991, 1995—2004, Nina Nielsen Gallery, Boston, 1979, 1984, 1992, 1995, 1996, 2000—02, Nigel Greenwood Gallery, London, 1979, 1991, U. Calif. Berkeley, 1984, Galleri Olsson, Stockholm, 1987, 1990, 1996, Nat. Art Gallery, Washington, 1989, Cork Gallery Lincoln Ctr., N.Y.C., 1991, Jaffe-Friede and Strauss Gallery, Hanover, N.H., 1995, The Phillips Collection, Washington, 1996, Cooper Union, N.Y.C., 1999, Marist Coll., 2005, exhibited in group shows at Whitney Mus. Art, N.Y.C., 1969, McKee Gallery, 2000, 2003, Randolph-Macon Woman's Coll., 2003, Whitney Mus. Art, N.Y.C., 1972, 1974, 1978, Art Inst. Chgo., 1971, Mus. Modern Art, N.Y.C., 1977, 1981, 1983—85, Meadows Art Gallery, Dallas, 1985, others, Represented in permanent collections Australian Nat. Gallery, Balt. Mus. Art, U. Calif. Berkeley Mus., Dallas Mus. Fine Arts, Fogg Mus. Harvard U., Guggenheim Mus., Mus. Modern Art, Whitney Mus. Art, others. Named academician, Nat. Acad. Design; recipient Acad. Inst. award, Am. Acad. Arts & Letters, 1994; grantee, The Elizabeth Found., 1995—96; Guggenheim fellow, 1981. Address: Betty Cuningham Gallery 541 W 25th St New York NY

BERTIN, JOHN JOSEPH, aeronautical engineer, educator, researcher; b. Milw., Oct. 13, 1938; m. Ruth Easterbrook; children: Thomas Alexander, Randolph Scott, Elizabeth Anne, Michael Robert. BA, Rice Inst., Houston, 1960; MS, Rice U., 1962, PhD, 1966. Aerospace technologist NASA Johnson Space Ctr., Houston, 1962-66; prof. U. Tex., Austin, 1966-89; program mgr. for space initiative MTS, Sandia Nat. Labs., Albuquerque, 1989-94; vis. prof. USAF Acad., Colorado Springs, Colo., 1988-89, prof. aero. engring., 1994—2004, prof. emeritus, 2004—. Cons. McGinnis, Lochridge & Kilgore, Austin, 1978-83, Sandia Nat. Labs., Albuquerque, 1980-89, BPD Difesa e Spazio, Rome, 1980-82, NASA, 1994-96, Sci. Applications Internat. Corp., 1996; detailed to Office of Space, U.S. Dept. Energy Hdqs., 1991-92; dir. Ctr. Excellence for Hypersonic Tng. and Rsch., 1985-89; mem. sci. adv. bd. USAF, 1989-93, mem. adv. group Flight Dynamics Labs., 1989-93; tech. chmn. Space 2000 Conf., 1998-99; aerothermodynamics cons. Columbia Accident Investigation Bd., 2003; adj. prof. Rice U., 2003-; cons. Return to Fligh Shuttle Team, 2004-2005. Author: Engineering Fluid Mechanics, 1987, Hypersonic Aerothermodynamics, 1994, Aerodynamics for Engineers, 2002; contbg. author Letterwinner, 1999—; editor: Hypersonics, 1989, Advances in Hypersonics, 1992; assoc. editor Jour. Spacecraft and Rockets, 2000-01. Pres. Western Hills Little League, Austin, 1975; mem. arts subcom. NASA, 1987-91; mem. Aerospace Engring. Bd. Panel NRC, 1996-97, USAF hypersonics program rev. com., 1997-98; mem. attendance com. Rice Athletic Dept., 2002--; mem. adv. bd. Rice Owl Club, 2002--. Recipient Gen. Dynamics Tchg. award U. Tex. Coll. Engring., 1978, Tex. Exec. Tchg. award Ex-Students Assn. U. Tex., 1982, Faculty award Tau Beta Pi, 1986, award for meritorious civilian svc. Dept. Air Force, 1993, Gen. Daley award USAFA, 1996, Exemplary Civilian Svc. Award medal, 1996, F.J. Seiler Rsch. award, USAFA, 1997, Disting. Alumni award, Rice U., 2005. Fellow AIAA (dir. region IV 1983-86, Disting. Lectr., Thermophysics award 1997, publs. bd. 1998-2000, aerothermodynamic cons. Columbia accident investigation bd. 2003, Outstanding Civilian Career Svc. award 2004). Office Phone: 719-333-8464, 713-348-3617. E-mail: wiseoldowl60@pcisys.net.

BERTINI, CATHERINE ANN, former international organization official; b. Syracuse, NY, Mar. 30, 1950; d. Fulvio and Ann (Vino) B.; m. Thomas Haskell, 1988. BA, SUNY, 1971; DHL (hon.), SUNY, Cortland, 1999; DSc (hon.), McGill U., Montreal, Can., 1997; DSc, Pine Manor Coll., 2000; DHL (hon.), Am. U. Rome, 2001; D in Pub. Svc. (hon.), John Cabot U., Rome, 2001; PhD (hon.), Slovak Agrl. U., Nitra, Slovak Republic, 2001; DHL (hon.), Loyola U., 2002, U. S.C., 2003, Dakota Wesleyan U., 2003, Colgate U., 2004. Youth dir. N.Y. Rep. State Com., 1971-74; with Rep. Nat. Com., 1975-76; mgr. pub. policy Container Corp. Am., 1977-87; dir. Office Family Assistance, U.S. Dept. Health and Human Svcs., 1987-89; acting asst. sec. U.S. Dept. HHS., 1989; asst. sec. USDA, 1989-92; UN panel mem. sec. gen.'s High Level Personalities on African Devel., UN, 1992-95; exec. dir. UN World Food Programme, Rome, 1992—2002; personal humanitarian envoy UN Sec. Gen., 2002; policy maker in residence Gerald Ford Sch. Pub. Policy U. Mich., 2002; chmn. U.N. Sys. Standing Com. on Nutrition, 2002—; under-sec. gen. mgmt. U.N., 2002—05. Bd. dirs. Tupperware Corp., Orlando, 2005—. Mem. Ill. State Scholarship Comm., 1979-84; mem. Ill. Human Rights Comm., 1985-87; spl. envoy of Sec. Gen. to the Horn of Africa, 2000. Recipient Leadership in Human Svcs. award Am. Pub. Welfare Assn., 1990, Pub. Svc. award Am. Acad. Pediatrics, 1991, Leadership award Nat. Assn. WIC Dirs., 1992, Internat. Girl Guides and Girl Scouts, 2002, Chgo. Coun. Fgn. Rels., 2004, Quality of Life award Auburn U., 1994, Disting. Alumni award Nelson A. Rockefeller Coll. Pub. Affairs and Policy, 1997, Award for Excellence Assn. African Journalists, 2002, World Food Prize Laureate, 2003, Global Leadership award, 2004. Fellow Harvard U., 1986.

BERTINI, RICHARD G., orthopedist; b. Pawtucket, RI, July 27, 1932; s. Armand Arthur and Elizabeth (Kinne) Bertini; m. Lois Diane Higgins, July 29, 1961; children: Lori Diane Rolfe, Jena Elaine McNulty, Richard George Jr. AB, Wesleyan U., Middletown, Conn., 1954; MD, Albany Med. Coll., N.Y., 1958. Diplomate Am.Bd. Orthopaedic Surgery. Intern R.I. Hosp., Providence, 1956—59, resident, 1959—63; chief Orthopedic Dept. Meml. Hosp. of RI, Pawtucket, RI, 1972—90. Pres. RI Med. Soc., 1987—88; founder RI Med. Soc. Ins. Brokerage Corp., 1988. Ships physician Schooner Te Vega:Landmark Sch. Tall Ships Atlantic Crossing, 1984 Azorea-Eng., 1985. Recipient Dr. Charles L. Hill award, R.I. Med. Soc., 1996, Christians for Justice Action Nat. Award, United Ch of Christ (jointly with Lois), 1999, Chair's lifetime Achievement award, Talladega Coll. (jointly with Lois), 2003, Emeriti award, Brown U. Sch. of Medicine, Providence, R.I., 1999. Democrat. United Ch. Of Christ. Home: 60 Norton St Pawtucket RI 02860

BERTINO, FRED, advertising executive; m. Arminda Bertino; children: Niia, Tana, Eric. BA in English Lit., Boston U. V.p., creative group head Della Femina McNamee WCRS; pres., co-creative dir. Anderson Veduccio Bertino Advt.; pres., chief creative officer Hill Holliday, Boston, 1990—2001. Mem. staff Art inst. New Eng. Recipient award NY Advt. Club, NY Art Dir.'s Club, One Show, Hatch Awards, Andy Awards, New Eng. Best of Broadcasting, Commn. Arts mag., Conn. Art Dir.'s Club, Grand Effie award for Creative Effectiveness, Arhena Newspapers, Stephen Kelly Awards, Grand Clio award. Office: McMarthy Mambro Bertino 580 Harrison Ave Boston MA 02118 Office Phone: 617-670-9700. Office Fax: 617-670-9711.

BERTINO, JOSEPH ROCCO, physician, educator; b. Port Chester, N.Y., Aug. 16, 1930; s. Joseph and Madaleine (Posillipo) B.; m. Mary Patricia Hagemeyer, Sept. 29, 1956; children: Frederick, Amy Marie, Thomas Allen, Paul Phillip. Student, Cornell U., 1947-50; MD, Downstate Med. Center N.Y., 1954. USPHS Research fellow U. Wash. Sch. Medicine, Seattle, 1958-61; mem. faculty Yale U. Sch. Medicine, 1961-87, assoc. prof. pharmacology and medicine, 1964-67, prof., 1967-87, Am. Cancer Soc. prof., 1975—; head program molecular pharmacology and therapeutics Sloan Kettering Ctr., 1987—; prof. medicine and pharmacology Cornell U. Sch. Medicine, N.Y.C., 1987—. State scholar for medicine, 1950—54; disting. prof. medicine and pharmacology UMDNJ, 2002—. Contbr. articles to profl. jours. Recipient Honor medal Am. Cancer Soc., 1992. Mem. Am. Soc. for Clin. Investigation, Am. Soc. Hematology, Biol. Chemists, Pharmacology and Therapeutics. Home: 117 Sunset Hill Rd Branford CT 06405-6419 Office: 195 Little Albany St New Brunswick NJ 08901-1914 Office Phone: 732-235-8510. Business E-Mail: bertinoj@umdnj.edu.

BERTLES, JOHN FRANCIS, physician, educator; b. Spokane, Wash., June 8, 1925; s. John Francis and Henrita Swart (Brown) B.; m. Jeannette Winans, 1948 (div. 1978); children: Mark Dwight, Jacquelyn Eve, John Francis.; m. Lila De Paganne, 1981. BS, Yale U., 1945; MD, Harvard U., 1952. Diplomate Am. Bd. Internal Medicine. Intern Presbyterian Hosp., N.Y.C., 1952-53, asst. resident in medicine, 1953-55; research fellow in hematology U. Rochester and Strong Meml. Hosp., 1955-56; research fellow in immunohematology Harvard U. Med. Sch. and Mass. Gen. Hosp., Boston, 1956-58, research fellow in hematology, 1958-59; instr. in medicine Harvard U. Med. Sch. at Mass. Gen. Hosp., 1959-61; dir. hematology-oncology div. St. Luke's Hosp. Center, N.Y.C., 1962-95, asst. attending physician, 1962-64, assoc. attending physician, 1964-71, attending physician, 1971-95; dir. transfusion services St. Luke's Roosevelt Hosp. Ctr., 1981-95; sr. research asso. dept. biol. scis. Columbia U., 1970-71, asst. clin. prof. medicine, 1962-67, assoc. clin. prof., 1967-71, assoc. prof., 1971-74, prof., 1974-95, prof. emeritus of medicine, 1995—; attending physician Montefiore Med. Ctr., N.Y.C., 1995-97; clin. prof. medicine Albert Einstein Coll. Medicine, N.Y.C., 1995-97. Vis. prof. medicine Nuffield dept. clin. medicine Radcliffe Infirmary, U. Oxford, Eng., 1977-78; cons. to various govt. agys., including hematology study sect. NIH, 1972-76, 82-84, blood rsch. rev. group, 1978-82; mem. dirs. coun. N.Y. Heart Assn., 1974-90; mem. basic rsch. adv. com. Nat. Found. March of Dimes, 1977-80. Contbr. articles to profl. publs. Ensign USNR, 1945-46. Fellow ACP; mem. Am. Soc. Clin. Investigation, Am. Physiol. Soc., Am. Soc. Hematology, Am. Fedn. Clin. Rsch., Am. Chem. Soc., Alpha Omega Alpha. Office: 72 Pondfield Rd W Apt 3K Bronxville NY 10708

BERTOLAMI, CHARLES NICHOLAS, dean, dental educator, oral surgeon; b. Lorain, Ohio, Dec. 31, 1949; s. Salvatore Charles and Michela (Orlando) B.; m. Linda Silva, June 27, 1977; children: Michela, Joseph. AA, Lorain Community Coll., 1969; DDS, Ohio State U., 1974; DMedSci, Harvard U., 1979. Diplomate Am. Bd. Oral and Maxillofacial Surgery. Chief resident Mass. Gen. Hosp., Boston, 1979-80, asst. oral surgeon, 1983; asst. prof. U. Conn., 1980-83, Harvard Sch. Dental Medicine, Boston, 1983-89; assoc. prof. UCLA Sch. Dentistry, 1989-90, prof., 1990—95, chmn. sect. oral & maxillofacial surgery, 1989—95, assoc. dean faculty affairs; chief dental svcs. UCLA Med. Ctr., 1990—95; dean Sch. Dentistry U. Calif., San Francisco, 1995—. Mem. editl. bd. Jour. of Oral and Maxillofacial Surgery; contbr. articles to profl. jours. Recipient Callahan Meml. award Ohio Dental Assn., 1974; named Disting. Alumnus, Ohio State U. Coll. Dentistry, 1996, Harvard Sch. Dental Medicine, 2000; grantee USPHS, 1983-. Fellow Am. Assn. Oral and Maxillofacial Surgeons (exec. com. 1983-84), Am. Coll. Dentists, Internat. Coll. Dentists; mem. ADA, Internat. Assn. Dental Rsch. (program chmn. 1984-85), Am. Assn. Dental Rsch. (v.p. 2000-01, pres.-elect, 2001-02, pres. 2002-03). Office: UCSF Sch Dentistry 513 Parnassus Ave S-630 San Francisco CA 94143-0430

BERTOLET, RODNEY JAY, philosophy educator; b. Allentown, Pa., Mar. 22, 1949; s. Frank and Helen (Johnson) B. BA, Franklin & Marshall Coll., 1971; PhD, U. Wis., 1977. Asst. prof. philosophy Purdue U., West Lafayette, Ind., 1977-82, assoc. prof. philosophy, 1982-90, prof. philosophy, 1990—, dept. head, 1991—. Author: What Is Said, 1990. Mem. Am. Philos. Assn., Ind. Philos. Assn. (pres. 1983-84). Office: Purdue Univ Dept Philosophy 100 N University St West Lafayette IN 47907-2098 Office Phone: 765-494-4275. E-mail: bertolet@purdue.edu.

BERTOLINI, JOSEPH CLIFFORD, political scientist, educator; m. Martha Ann Yellen, Aug. 22, 1982. BA, St. Johns's U., N.Y., 1969; MA, NYU, 1972, PhD in Polit. sci., 1983. Dept. chair history and politics Kew-Forest Sch., Forest Hills, NY, 1998—2003. Adj. asst. prof. politics St. John's U., Jamaica, NY, 1978—99, NYU, N.Y.C., 1996—2001; mem. editl. adv. bd. Collegiate Press, San Diego, 1994—98. Author: The Serpent Within: Politics, Literature and American Individualism; co-author: Women Leaders in Contemporary United States Politics, New Europe at the Crossroads II; contbr. articles to profl. jours. Recipient Outstanding H.S. Tchr. award, U. Chgo., 1995. Mem.: Internat. Movement Interdisciplinary Study of Estrangement, Internat. Soc. Study European Ideas, Northeastern Polit. Sci. Assn., Am. Polit. Sci. Assn. Office: Kew-Forest School 119-17 Union Turnpike Forest Hills NY 11375 Office Phone: 718-268-4667. Business E-Mail: jbertolini@kewforest.org.

BERTOLINI, MARK T., insurance company executive; BSc in bus. adminstrn., Wayne State U.; MBA in fin., Cornell U. CEO, previously COO SelectCare, 1992—95; sr. v.p., regional segment Cigna HealthCare; exec. v.p. NYLCare Health Plans; sr. v.p., splty. products Aetna Inc., 2003—. Office: Aetna Inc 151 Farmington Ave Hartford CT 06156

BERTOLINI, ROBERT J., pharmaceutical executive; BA in Econs., Rutgers U. CPA. With Coopers & Lybrand, 1983; ptnr. PricewaterhouseCoopers, 1993—2003; exec. v.p., CFO Schering-Plough Corp., 2003—. Mem.: Am. Coll. Emergency Physicians. Office: Schering-Plough Corp 2000 Galloping Hill Rd Kenilworth NJ 07033-0530

BERTOLINO, DEAN A., lawyer; b. Nyack, NY, Nov. 7, 1968; BA, U. Ariz., 1990; JD, Harvard U., 1994. Bar: Mass. 1994, NY 1995. Assoc. Brown & Wood LLP, NYC, 1994—99; asst. gen. counsel BOC Group, Murray Hill, NJ, 1999—2001; v.p., gen. counsel Airgas, Inc., Radnor, Pa., 2001—. Mem.: ABA, Assn. of Bar City of NY. Office: Airgas Inc 259 N Radnor Chester Rd Ste 100 PO Box 6675 Radnor PA 19087-8675 Office Phone: 610-230-3070. Office Fax: 610-687-1052.

BERTOLLI, EUGENE EMIL, sculptor, consultant; b. Boston, Feb. 19, 1923; s. Adolph and Julia (Manetti) B.; m. Jean Helen Tamburine, Apr. 21, 1956; children— Eugene Robert, Lisa Marie AB cum laude, Boston Coll., 1943; postgrad., Washington and Lee U., 1944. Dir. ednl. reconditioning Madigan Convalescent Hosp., Tacoma, 1945-47; sr. v.p. design Napier Co., Meriden, Conn., 1947-85; sculptor, goldsmith Bertolli Studio, Meriden, Conn., 1947—, also cons. design and jewelry techniques, 1947—. Dir. City Savs. Bank, Meriden, Napier Co.; sculpture awards juror Am. Artists Profl. League, N.Y.C., 1993, Hudson Valley Art Assn., Inc., N.Y.C., 1984, 94. Works include bronze portrait The Outdoorsman (Am. Artists Profl. League award 1983) Mem. and officer Meriden Bd. Edn., 1958-63; pres. Meriden Pub. Libr.

Bd., 1964-86; trustee Meriden-Wallingford Hosp. Capt. AUS, World War II. Recipient internat. outstanding jewelry design award Swarowski Internat., 1968, 69, John Manship Meml. award Rockport Art Assn., 1985, Franz Denghauser Meml. award for sculpture, 1988, award for sculpture Acad. Artists Assn., 1992, 94, Paul Manship Meml. award for excellence in sculpture North Shore Arts Assn., 1992, 93, portrait sculpture award Am. Artists Profl. League, 1994, L.J. Meiselman meml. award for Artistic Excellence of Sculpture for Portrait Bust, Am. Artists Profl. League, 1996 Grand Nat. Exhbn.; inducted into Meriden Hall of Fame for achievement in field of art, 1995. Mem. Acad. Artists Assn. (gold medal for sculpture 1982-84, 88-92, Hon. award 2000), North Shore Arts Assn. (juror of awards and membership admission 1993, spl. portrait sculpture award 1980, Katharine Taylor Weems sculpture award 1989), Am. Artists Profl. League (juror of awards 1993), Hudson Valley Art Assn. (juror of awards 1994), Mfg. Jewelers and Silversmiths, Internat. Platform Assn., Meriden Art Assn. (pres. 1957-58), Guild Boston Artists, Salmagundi Club. Roman Catholic. Home: 73 Reynolds Dr Meriden CT 06450-2532

BERTOLUCCI, BERNARDO, film director; b. Parma, Italy, Mar. 16, 1941; s. Attilio and Ninetta Bertolucci; m. Clare Peploe, 1978. Attended, Rome (Italy) U. Dir.(films): The Grim Reaper, 1962, Before the Revolution, 1964 (Young Critics award Cannes Film Festival), La Via del Petrolio, 1965, His Partner, 1968, The Conformist, 1970 (Nat. Film Critics Best Dir. award), The Spider's Strategem, 1970, Last Tango in Paris, 1972, 1900, 1976, Luna, 1979, Tragedy of a Ridiculous Man, 1981, The Last Emperor (Golden Globe award for Best Dramatic Picture, 1987, Best Dir., Best Screenplay, Best Original Score, Best Editor, Best Cinematography, Best Sound, Best Prodn. Design, Art Dir., Best Costume Design, Acad. award fo, Acad. award for Best Picture of Yr., Best Dir., Best Screenplay Adaptation, Best Film honor Brit. Acad. Film and TV Arts, The Sheltering Sky, 1990, Little Buddha, 1994, Stealing Beauty, 1996, Besieged, 1998 (Globo D'Oro award for Best Film 1999; actor: (of poems). Office: care Recorded Picture Co 24 Hanway St London W1T 1UH England also: care Jeff Berg ICM 8942 Wilshire Blvd Beverly Hills CA 90211-1934

BERTONE, THOMAS LEE, management consultant; b. Pittsburg, Kans., Nov. 15, 1938; s. Anthony and Gaye Kittle Bertone; m. Ellen Reville Kniffin, Sept. 6, 1969; children: Elizabeth Reville, Katherine Logan. AB cum laude, Harvard U., 1960; MA, Stanford U., 1963; D Pub. Adminstrn., George Washington U., 1971. Budget examiner on def. U.S. Bur. Budget, Washington, 1964-67; cons., assoc. Booz Allen & Hamilton, Washington, 1967-69, 78-80; dir. budget rev. Office Fiscal Affairs, N.J. Legislature, Trenton, 1973-75, exec. dir. Office Fiscal Affairs, 1975-78; regional dir. state and local govt. cons. Coopers & Lybrand, Phila., 1980-82; dir. internat. cons. Grant Thornton, Chgo., 1986-90; pres. Thomas L. Bertone & Assocs., Pennington, N.J., 1982-86, 90—. World Bank decentralization adviser to permanent sec. Sri Lanka Ministry Local Govt., 1985-89; ADB advisor to budget dir. Budget Office, Federated States Micronesia, 1993-95; IMF budget advisor to min. fin. Palestine Authority, Gaza and West Bank, 1995; U.S. AID intergovtl. fiscal rels. advisor to prime min. and min. fin. Fedn. Bosnia Herzegovina, 1997; evaluator for U.S. Agy. Internat. Develop. fiscal reform program in Kosovo, 2003. Sr. advisor on state fin. amd mgmt. to gov. candidate State of W.Va., Charleston, 1970-72; pro bono cons. N.J. Office Mgmt. and Budget, Trenton, 1999. 2d lt. U.S. Army, 1964, Korea. Mem. ASPA, Inst. Mgmt. Cons. (cert.), Assn. Govt. Accts. (cert. govt. fin. mgr.). Democrat. Avocations: scuba diving, skiing, horseback riding, shooting and gun collecting, dogs. Home and Office: 337 Waterman Rd East Dummerston VT 05346 Office Phone: 802-387-4567. Business E-Mail: tom_bertone_ab60@post.harvard.edu.

BERTOZZI, CAROLYN R., chemistry professor; b. Boston, 1966; AB in Chemistry summa cum laude, Harvard U.; PhD, U. Calif., Berkeley, 1993. Summer intern Bell Labs, 1987; postdoc. fellow U. Calif., San Francisco, prof. chemistry Berkeley, 1996—. Contbr. articles to profl. jours. including J. Org. Chem., Chem. and Biol., Biochem. MacArthur fellow 1999—. Mem. Am. Chem. Soc. (Arthur C. Cope Scholar Award, 1999). Office: U Calif Berkeley Chemistry Dept 813A Latimer Berkeley CA 94720-0001

BERTRAM, JEAN DESALES, writer; b. Burlington, Iowa, Sept. 28; d. Val Randall and Ruth Cecilia Bertram; 1 child, Larkin Bertram-Cox Montgomery . BA, U. N.C., Greensboro, 1942; MA, U. Minn., 1951; PhD, Stanford U., 1963. Reporter Greensboro News Record, 1942-43; founder dept. pub. rels. Burlington Industries, Greensboro, 1943-49; asst. to dean edn. U. N.C., Greensboro, 1949-50; instr. U. Minn., Mpls., 1950-51; dir. radio performance Mpls. Vocat. High Sch., 1951-52; dir. Children's Theatre Touring Co., Jr. League Mpls., 1951-52; prof. theatre arts San Francisco State U., 1952-88. Cons. Wadsworth Pub. Co., Belmont, Calif., 1966; dir. Readers' Repertory, San Francisco State U., 1967-72; dir. Jean De Sales Bertram Players, San Francisco, 1971-74; founder, developer storytelling program San Francisco State U., 1971-88; cons. Scott-Foresman, Chgo., 1983; senator acad. senate San Francisco State U., 1983-84, dir. com. for lectures, arts and spl. programs, 1985-87; tax preparer, 1994. Author: (textbooks) The Oral Experience of Literature, 1967, The Actor Speaks, 4 edits., 1981-87, Tell Me a Story!, 5 edits., 1982-88; author, dir. Girl Scout Nat. Convention pageant Finding Your Own Adventure, 1955; prodr., dir., adapter, editor: (religious plays) A Symphonetic Easter Drama, 1954, The Awakening, 1954, The Vision of Isaiah, 1970, The Cherry Tree, 1971; author, dir.: (plays) American Cameos, 1976, Jeremiah The Prophet, 1999; author: (poem) Cosmorama, 1971; actress one-woman show numerous women from Shakespeare's plays, 1971-88; author: (short story) The Giraffe and the Canary, 1999; contbr. articles to profl. jours. Stanford-Wilson fellow Stanford U., 1962-63. Mem. Found. Bibl. Rsch., Acad. Am. Poets, Phi Beta Kappa (sec. Omicron of Calif. chpt. 1977-79, 83-88, pres. 1979-81, v.p. 1981-83, ofcl. del. Triennial coun. 1979, 82). Avocations: sculpturing in clay, poetry writing, photography.

BERTRAM, PHYLLIS ANN, lawyer, communications executive; b. Long Beach, Calif., July 30, 1954; d. William J. and Ruth A. Bertram. AA, Long Beach City Coll., 1975; BS in Acctg., U. So. Calif., 1977; MBA, Calif. State U., Long Beach, 1978; JD, Western State U., 1982. Bar: Calif. 1982, U.S. Dist. Ct. 1982, U.S. Ct. Appeals (9th cir.) 1982. Instr., lifeguard City of Long Beach, 1972-78; swimming, softball, volleyball and basketball sports ofcl., 1972—; mgmt. cons., 1978—; mgr. Pacific Bell, 1983—. Asst. commr. Met. Conf. Cmty. and Jr. Colls., Long Beach, 1978-84; instr. seamanship, fire sci. and bus. adminstrn. Long Beach City Coll., 1977—; instr., lectr. regulatory rels., policy, requirements; guest lectr. sports officiating camps and tng. sessions. Instr. CPR, water safety, small craft, first aid ARC, 1972—; mem. Rep. Nat. Com. Recipient resolutions Calif. Senate and Assemby, Long Beach City Coun., numerous svc. awards ARC; ednl. rsch. grantee City of Long Beach, 1972. Mem. U. So. Calif. Alumni Assn., U. So. Calif. Commerce Assocs., Assn. MBA Execs., Bay Area Career Women, (corp. sec., bd. dirs., leadership adv. coun.), So. Calif. Volleyball Ofcls. Assn., Nat. Assn. Sports Ofcls., So. Calif. Baskeball Ofcls. Assn., Women's Basketball Ofcls. Assn., Women's Swim Ofcls. Assn. (pres.), So. Calif. Softball Umpires Assn., ABA, State Bar Calif., FBA, L.A. County Bar Assn., Internat. Platform Assn., Town Hall Calif., Commonwealth Club Calif., Calif. State U. at Long Beach Alumni Assn., Seal Beach Yacht Club, Delta Theta Phi. Office: 2600 Camino Ramon Ste 2W850 San Ramon CA 94583

BERTRAM, REX ALAN, lawyer; b. Evansville, Ind., Sept. 20, 1955; s. Paul Frederick and Elaine Daisy Bertram; m. Julie Elizabeth Hummer, Oct. 5, 1996 AA, St. Louis C.C., 1978; BSBA, U. Mo., St. Louis, 1980; JD magna cum laude, St. Louis U., 1983. Bar: Mo. 1983. Assoc. Peper, Martin, Jensen, Machiel & Hetlage, St. Louis, 1983-86; atty., prin. Bertram, Peper & Hier, P.C., St. Louis, 1986—. V.p. JCR Hotel, Inc. d/b/a Ramda, Jefferson City, Mo., 1987—, Ulysses Fin., Ltd., St. Louis, 1986—. Editor-in-chief St. Louis U. Law Jour., 1982-83. Chmn. bd. dirs. Paraquad, Inc., St. Louis, 1989-92. Mem. Ch. of Christ. Office: Bertram Peper and Hier 720 Olive St Ste 617 Saint Louis MO 63101-2331 E-mail: RexBertram@bphstl.com.

BERTRAM, SUSAN, rehabilitation services professional; b. Darlington, S.C., July 7, 1945; d. Ernest and Leigh (Ogburn) Lowry; m. John David Bertram, Dec. 7, 1980. BFA, U. Ga., 1966; MS, Ga. State U., 1993. Cert. rehab. counselor, nat. cert. counselor, Ga.; lic. profl. counselor, Ga. Social work/counselor State of Ga., Atlanta, 1967—95, rehab. counselor, 1995—. Mem. Nat. Rehab. Assn., Ga. Rehab. Assn. Avocations: travel, reading, yoga.

BERTRAND, FREDERIC HOWARD, retired insurance company executive; b. Montpelier, Vt., Aug. 5, 1936; s. George Joseph and Dolores Gertrude (Mallory) B.; m. Elinor Maude Pierce, June 11, 1960; children: Kimberly Sue, Michael Scott, John Frederic (dec.). BSCE magna cum laude, Norwich U., 1958; postgrad., Georgetown U. Law Sch., 1961-63, Carnegie-Mellon U. Sch. Indsl. Adminstrn., 1967-68; JD, Coll. William and Mary, 1967; D in Bus. Mgmt. (hon.), Norwich U., 1991. Bar: Va. 1967, Vt. 1970; registered profl. engr., Vt. Engr.-adminstr. CIA, Washington, 1960-70; asst. counsel, assoc. counsel, v.p., sr. v.p., bd. dirs. Nat. Life Ins. Co., Montpelier, 1970-83, exec. v.p., chief oper. officer, 1983-85, pres., chief oper. officer, 1985-87, chmn., chief exec. officer, 1987-97, also bd. dirs. Bd. dirs., chair Chittenden Bank, Burlington, 2004—; bd. dirs. Union Mut. Fire Ins. Co., New Eng. Guaranty Ins. Co., Montpelier; bd. dirs. Cen. Vt. Pub. Svcs. Co., Rutland, 1985—, chair, 1997—; bd. dirs. Vt. Elec. Transmission Co., 1998—; bd. dirs. Catamount Energy Corp., 1995—2004, chair, 1997-2002; bd. dirs. The Home Svc. Store, Rutland, 2000—; civilian aide to Sec. of Army, Washington, 1981-93. Alderman City of Montpelier, 1974-76, pres. city coun., 1975-76, mayor, 1976-78; bd. dirs. Ctrl. Vt. Econ. Devel. Corp., 1985-98; chmn. Vt. Bus. Roundtable, 1995-97, bd. dirs., 1987-98; trustee Norwich U., Northfield, Vt., 1979-85. Recipient Outstanding Alumnus award Norwich U., 1980, Citizen of Yr. award Vt. C. of C., 1992, U.S. Army Disting. Civilian Svc. award, 1993. Mem. Am. Coun. Life Ins. (bd. dirs. 1989-94, chmn. 1993), Vt. Bar Assn., Washington County Bar Assn., Theta Chi, Epsilon Tau Sigma. Republican. Roman Catholic.

BERTRAND, JAMES C., history professor; b. Grand Jct, Colo., Mar. 14, 1947; s. John Nicholas and Mary Louise Bertrand; m. Cheryl (Cherie) Ann Nelson, Oct. 3, 1970; children: Brian, Brenda, Bradley, Brent, Brett, Brandon. AA, Mesa Jr. Coll., 1967; BA, Western State Coll., 1969; MEd, Ariz. State U., 2000. Tchr., coach Norwood/Delta Sch. Dist., Delta, Colo., 1976—83, Pagosa Springs HS, Pagosa Springs, Colo., 1983—85, Maricopa HS, Maricopa, Ariz., 1985—88, Marcus de Nira HS, Tempe HS Dist., Tempe, Ariz., 1988—91, Woodland Pk. HS, Woodland Pk., Colo., 1991—97; tchr., durriculum dir. dist. Buckeye Union Sch. Dist., Buckeye, Ariz., 1997—2001; tchr., athletic dir., soc. studies chair, coach Cripple Creek-Victor HS, Cripple Creek, Colo., 2001—. North ctrl. evaluation team Dept. Edn., Ariz., 1971. Contbr. articles various profl. jours. Sch. sponsor El Pomar, Woodland Pk., Colo., 1998—99, Colo. Close up, Cripple Creek, Colo., 2001—; dir. of summer basketball Cripple Creek HS, Cripple Creek, Colo., 2001—02; mem. Nat. Hope Found., Ariz., 1997—2001. Named Tchr. of Yr., Cripple Creek Sch. Dist., 2002—03. Mem.: Nat. State Gifted and Talented, Colo. Athletic Dirs. Assn. Independent. Cath. Avocations: reading, sports, fishing. Office: Cripple Creek HS 410 N B St Cripple Creek CO 80813 Office Phone: 719-689-2661 x19. Office Fax: 719-689-2256. E-mail: jbertrand@ccvschools.com.

BERTRAND, LUC, stock exchange executive; BA in philosophy, Univ. Ottawa, Can. Co-founder Pollit, Bertrand brokerage firm, Canada, 1985; v.p. and mng. dir. Instl. Sales Group Nat. Bank Fin., Canada; bd. dir. Montreal Stock Exch., Canada, 1992—94, mem. exec. com., 1994—96, vice chmn., 1996—97, chmn., 1998—2000, pres. and CEO, 2000—; ptnr., exec v.p., & resident dir. Deacon Capital Corp., Canada, 1993—98. Former gov. Canadian Securities Inst.; gov. Canadian Investor Protection Fund, 1996—2002; vice chmn. bd. Boston Options Exch. Group LLC; mem. bd. Internat. Fin. Ctr. Montreal, Regulatory Svc. Inc., Securities Industry Adv. Coun. Office: Bourse de Montreal Inc PO Box 61 800 Victoria Square Montreal H4Z1A9 Canada Office Phone: 514-871-2424.

BERTRAND, REBEKAH PICKETT, religious studies educator; b. Balt., Feb. 2, 1974; d. John Conn and Susan Rae Pickett; m. Jay James Bertrand, Feb. 14, 1992; children: Bethany Leigh, Kathryn Lynne. Grad., Atlantic Bapt. Bible Coll., 1997. Summer missionary Child Evangelism Fellowship, Richmond, Va., 1984—90; customer rels. cons. J. Crew Group, Inc., Lynchburg, 1990—94; bank teller First Fed. Bank, Chester, 1994; daycare dir., tchrs. aid Grace Bapt. Ch. & Sch., Petersburg, 1995; presch. tchr. Old Hundred Rd., Chester, 1995—96; dorm parent, adminstrv. asst. Atlantic Bapt. Bible Coll., 1996; missionary, tchr. Bapt. Bible Fellowship Internat., Springfield, Mo., 1998—. Avocations: music, reading, writing. Home: Forestier Ingelramstraat 34 8530 Harelbeke Belgium Office: Bapt Bible Fellowship Internat Springfield MO 65801

BERTSCH, FREDERICK CHARLES, III, finance company executive; b. Bklyn., Mar. 17, 1942; s. Frederick Charles and Norma Elizabeth (Hodgkins) B.; m. Ana Maria Carmen Natteri, Aug. 20, 1971; children— Frederick C., Ana Cecilia BA, Wesleyan U., Middletown, Conn., 1965; MBA, U. Pa., 1967. Supr. Ford Motor Co., Dearborn, Mich., 1967-69; cons. Cresap, McCormick & Paget Inc., N.Y.C., 1969-73; dir. corp. devel. IU Internat., Phila., 1973-76; v.p. corp. devel. Enterra Corp., Radnor, Pa., 1976-84, v.p. fin., chief fin. officer, 1985-86; founder F.C. Bertsch & Co., Inc., St. Davids, Pa., 1988—; v.p., CFO Gladwin Corp., Coraopolis, Pa., 1995. Pres. Radnor ABC (A Better Chance), Wayne, Pa., 1984-85, now bd. dirs Avocations: golf, fishing, gardening. Home and Office: 416 Round Hill Rd Saint Davids PA 19087-4728 E-mail: fcbertsch@fast.net.

BERTSCH, GARY KENNETH, political science professor; b. Vallejo, Calif., June 8, 1944; s. Gideon and Freda (Hepper) B.; m. Joan Elizabeth Brubacher, Feb. 29, 1964; children: Dawn, Todd, Jason. BA, Idaho State U., 1966; MA, U. Oreg., 1968, PhD, 1970. Vis. prof. U. Zagreb, Yugoslavia, 1969-70; prof. polit. sci. U. Ga., Athens, 1970—. Vis. prof. nat. security affairs Air U., Dept. Def., Maxwell AFB, Ala., 1981-82; Fulbright prof. politics U. Lancaster, Eng., 1984-85; dir. Ctr. Internat. Trade and Security, 1987—. Author numerous books, including East-West Strategic Trade and the Atlantic Alliance, 1983; Reform and Revolution in Communist Systems, 1991; editor: Engaging India, 1999, Dangerous Weapons, Desperate States, 1999, Crossroads and Conflict, 2000, also numerous articles. Recipient numerous awards for tchg. U. Ga., 1970—, profl. chair for disting. tchg., 1982—, numerous rsch. grants, 1970—. Mem. Am. Polit. Sci. Assn., Internat. Studies Assn. Home: 228 Henderson Ave Athens GA 30605-1037 Office: U Ga Dept Internat Affairs Athens GA 30602 Office Phone: 706-542-2985. Business E-Mail: gbertsch@uga.edu.

BERTSCH, PAUL M., ecologist, director; b. Oct. 28, 1956; BS in Plant sci., U. Conn., 1978; MS in Soil Chemistry, Va. Poly. Inst., 1980; PhD in Soil Phys. Chemistry-Mineralogy, U. Ky., 1983. Rsch. specialist dept. agronomy U. Ky., Lexington, 1983, asst. prof. dept. agronomy, 1984; asst. rsch. prof. divsn. biogeochemistry Savannah River Ecology Lab., Aiken, SC, 1984—89; vis. scientist applied and atomic physics Nat. Synchrotron Light Source, Brookhaven Nat. Lab., Upton, NY, 1992—93; assoc. rsch. prof. divsn. bigeochemistry Savannah River Ecology Lab., Aiken, SC, 1989—95; prof., dir. Advanced Analytical Ctr. for Environ. Scis., U. Ga., Savannah River Ecology Lab., Aiken, SC, 1995—, dir., 1999—; faculty mem. Med. U. S.C., Charleston, 2001—; affiliate facutly mem. engring. U. Ga., 2002—. Presenter in field. Contbr. articles to profl. jours. Fellow: Soil Sci. Soc. Am. (assoc. editor 1994—2001, selection com. 1999—, evaluation com., chmn. divisn. soil chemistry 2003—04, Career Achievement award 2004, Jackson award 1996), Am. Soc. Agronomy; mem.: AAAs, Internat. Soil Sci. Soc., Internat. Clay Minerals Soc., Clay Minerals Soc. (coun. 1997, awards com. 2001, v.p. 2001, program devel. com. 2004—), Am. Geophysical Union, Am. Chem. Soc., Sigma Xi, Phi Sigma, Phi Kappa Phi, Gamma Sigma Delta. Achievements include patents for in-situ groundwater remediation by selective colloid mobilization, 1998. Office: Savannah River Ecology Lab Univ Ga Drawer E Aiken SC 29808 Business E-Mail: bertsch@srel.edu.

BERTSCHY, TIMOTHY L., lawyer; b. Pekin, Ill., Nov. 12, 1952; AB magna cum laude, U. Ill., 1974; JD, George Washington U., 1977. Bar: Ill. 1977, U.S. Dist. Ct. (cen. dist.) Ill., U.S. Ct. Appeals (7th cir.) 1982, U.S. Supreme Ct. Atty. Heyl, Royster, Voelker & Allen, Peoria, Ill., 1977—84, ptnr., 1984—. Author articles in law jours. Pres. Ill. Lawyers Assistance Prog., Ill. Equal Justice Found.; past pres. Ill. Coalition Equal Justice; co-chmn. Ill. Needs Study II. Fellow Ill. State Bar Found., Am. Bar Found.; mem. ABA (ho. dels. 1995—, co-chair sect. litigation bus. torts com. 2003-, bd. gov. 2004-), Ill. State Bar Assn. (bd. gov. 1984-90, pres. 1998-99, Lincoln Legal Writing Award), Peoria County Bar Assn (chmn. Diversity Comm.,bd. mem.); Am. Judicature Soc.; Bar Assn. Cent. & So. Dist. (co-chmn. Rules & Practices); Ill. Township Attys. Assn. (pres. 1989-93, bd. dir. 1985-92 & 2002-). Office: Heyl Royster Voelker & Allen PC 124 SW Adams St Ste 600 Peoria IL 61602-1352 E-mail: tbertschy@hrva.com.

BERTUCELLI, ROBERT EDWARD, accountant, educator; b. Bklyn., Mar. 23, 1948; s. Leo and Gertrude Augusta (Roggenkamp) B.; children: Nikole, Gina; m. Loretta Strand, Jan. 7, 2005. AAS, Suffolk C.C., 1968; BS, C.W. Post Coll., 1970; MS, L.I. U., 1974. CPA, N.Y.; cert. fin. planner; chartered life underwriter. Acct. Arthur Young & Co., Westbury, N.Y., 1970-72; sr. tax. mgr. Peat Marwick Mitchell & Co., Jericho, N.Y., 1972-77; prof. acctg. and taxation C.W. Post Coll., 1977—; pvt. practice Smithtown, N.Y., 1977-83, Hauppauge, N.Y., 1989-94; ptnr. Bertucelli Barragato & Co., Smithtown, 1983-89, Bertucelli & Malaga L.L.P., Ronkonkoma, NY, 1994—. Lectr. Person Wolinsky Assocs., 1977—. Mem. St. Patrick's Sch. Bd., Smithtown, N.Y., 1982-92, pres., 1985-88, 90-92; bd. trustees, St. Charles Hosp. and Rehab. Ctr., Port Jefferson, NY, 2003—. Mem.: AICPA, Estate Planning Coun. (pres. 1996—97), Nat. Assn. Accts., N.Y. Soc. CPAs (author, lectr. 1989—, Haskins Silver medal 1972), Smithtown C. of C. (treas. 1988—90). Roman Catholic. Office Phone: 631-738-0200. E-mail: reb@taxprofs.com.

BERUBE, BRIAN A., lawyer; b. 1962; BA, Coll. Holy Cross; JD, Boston Coll. Bar: 1988. Law clk. New Hampshire Supreme Ct.; mem. corp. dept. Choate, Hall & Stewart, Boston; of counsel Cabot Corp., Boston, 1994—2003, v.p., gen. counsel, 2003—. Bd. dirs. New Eng. Legal Found. Mem.: ABA, Boston Bar Assn., Am. Corp. Counsel Assn. Office: Cabot Corp Two Seaport Ln Ste 1300 Boston MA 02210-2019 Office Phone: 617-342-6175. Office Fax: 617-342-6103.

BERVEN, NORMAN LEE, counselor, psychologist, educator; b. Des Moines, May 14, 1945; s. Arthur N. and Ruth N. (Sharp) B.; m. Estella Stone, Oct. 11, 1969; 1 child, Jennifer. BS, U. Iowa, 1967, MA, 1969; PhD, U. Wis., 1973. Lic. psychologist; cert. rehab. counselor, lic. profl. counselor. Rehab. counselor San Mateo County Mental Health Svc., San Mateo, Calif., 1969-71; rsch. assoc. Internat. Ctr. for Disabled, N.Y.C., 1973-75; asst. prof. counseling and spl. svcs. Seton Hall U., South Orange, N.J., 1975-76; asst. prof. to prof. rehab. psychology, program chair U. Wis., Madison, 1976—. Cons. to univ., govt. and pvt. non-profit programs. Editor: Rehab. Counseling Bull., 1985-92, assoc. editor, 1982-85, editorial bd., 1980-82, 92—; editorial bd. Rehab. Psychology, 1981-99, Vocat. Evaluation and Work Adjustment Jour., 1980—, Assessment in Rehab. and Exceptionality, 1992-96; co-editor: Counseling Theories and Techniques for Rehabilitation Health Professionals, 2004; contbr. articles to profl. jours., chpts. to books. Recipient Varsity Disting. Alumni award rehab. psychology program U. Wis., 1994, Disting. Alumni award grad. programs in rehab. U. Iowa, 1997; grantee U.S. Dept. Edn., 1986—, Spencer Found., 1981-82, Wis. Alumni Rsch. Found., 1979-80. Fellow APA (rehab., counseling and evaluation, measurement and stats. divsn.); mem. ACA (rsch. award 1986), Am. Rehab. Counseling Assn. (disting. profl. award 1990, rsch. award 1981, 84, 86, 92, 93, 95, 2000, 04, Disting. Career Rsch. award 1998), Nat. Rehab. Counseling Assn. (bd. dirs. N.J. chpt. 1975-76, bd. dirs. Wis. chpt. 1981-83, bd. dirs. Calif. chpt. 1971, Meritorious Svc. award Wis. chpt. 1992), Nat. Rehab. Assn. (Grad. Lit. award 1988, bd. dirs. S.W. Wis. chpt., 1980—, San Mateo chpt. 1969-71, Disting. Svc. award Wis. chpt. 1997), Assn. for Counselor Edn. and Supervision, Assn. for Assessment in Counseling and Edn., Assn. for Specialists in Group Work, Vocat. Evaluation and Work Adjustment Assn., Nat. Coun. on Rehab. Edn., Nat. Coun. Measurement Edn., NAMI (Nat. Alliance for the Mentally Ill) Wis. Home: 417 Samuel Dr Madison WI 53717-2144 Office: U Wis Madison Rehab Psychology 432 N Murray St Madison WI 53706-1407 Office Phone: 608-263-7917. Business E-Mail: nlberven@wisc.edu.

BERVIG, V. ARLEEN HAALAND, clergyperson, music teacher; b. Woden, Iowa, Sept. 29, 1925; d. Clarence Selmer and Mary (Yost) Haaland; m. Arthur Leonard Bervig, June 9, 1946 (div. Aug. 1977); children: Ronald Arthur, Gregory Dean, David Allen. Student, King's Coll., New Castle, Del., 1944-45; BA in English magna cum laude, Bemidji (Minn.) State U., 1991; student, Oxford (Eng.) U., 1991. Cert. lay pastor Lutheran Ch. Am. Chair/liaison Ch. Women United, Mpls., 1970-75, dir. ecumenical seminars, 1972-75; pres. Am. Luth. Ch. Women, Mpls., 1973-74; personnel adminstr. Charmilles/Andrews, Hopkins, Minn., 1980-81; bd. regents Oak Grove Luth. H.S., Fargo, N.D., 1980-85, campus chaplain, 1986-88; with ELCA, N.D., 1986-88; pastor First Lutheran, Akeley, Minn., 1982-85, Our Savior/Zion Parish, Federal Dam/Boy River, Minn., 1992-95, Bethlehem, Backus, Minn., 1995-96. Pres. Ministerial Assn., Park Rapids, Minn., 1984-85; mem. interdisciplinary team Hospice, St. Joseph's Hosp., Park Rapids, 1984-85; synod rep. Minn. Coun. Chs., Mpls., 1991-96; mem. Pastor's Cluster Group, 1993-95. Author: Color Coded, 1996; contbr. articles to newspapers. Mem. joint religious legis. coalition Minn. Coun. Chs., St. Paul, 1991-96; mem. Minn. Citizens Organized Acting Together, St. Paul, 1990-96; dir. Cmty. Choirs, 1980-93. Recipient grants in field. Mem. Smithsonian Assocs., Wilson Ctr. Assocs. Avocations: painting, music, writing, travel, exercise. Home: 607 W 7th St Apt 219 Park Rapids MN 56470-1387

BERWALD, HELEN DOROTHY, education educator; b. Lac Qui Parle County, Minn., Mar. 15, 1925; BA, U. Minn., 1948, BS, MA, 1951, PhD, 1962. Tchr. Robbinsdale (Minn.) High Sch., 1951-52; mem. faculty Carleton Coll., Northfield, Minn., 1952—, prof. Emeritus edn., 1987—; prof. edn. Mem. Minn. State Adv. Com., 1962-89; dir. programs in tchr. edn. Assn. Colls. Midwest; dir. Chgo. Urban Semester, Video Tape Project; mem. African Edn. Survey Team; mem. accreditation task force Am. Assn. Colls. Tchr. Edn., formerly mem. exec. com., bd. dirs.; mem. standards and process com., mem. exec. com., also chmn. appeals bd. Nat. Council Accreditation Tchr. Edn., formerly mem. coordinating bd. Pres. Minn. Assn. Colls. Tchr. Edn.; mem. Phi Beta Kappa, Pi Lambda Theta. Home: 4963 S Prairie Hill Dr Green Valley AZ 85614

BERWANGER, KATHLEEN A., secondary school educator; b. Cin., Aug. 25, 1944; d. John A. and Anna Marie (Hollarn) Pfarr; m. Robert H. Grossheim, July 30, 1966 (div. Oct. 1983); 1 child, Robert John; m. Duane L. Berwanger, June 11, 1988. BA, Edgecliff Coll., Cin., 1966; MEd, Wright State U., 1989. Cert. tchr., Ohio. Tchr. English Loveland (Ohio) City Schs., 1966-67, 72—, chair dept. English, 1995—; tchr. lang. arts St. Columban, Loveland, 1968-72. Mem. St. Columban Sch. Bd., 1969-71; active various fundraisers St. Columban Ch Named Outstanding Tchr., Denison U., 1997, Ohio U., 1997. Mem. NEA, Ohio Edn. Assn., Loveland Edn. Assn., Nat. Coun. Tchrs. English (writing judge 1994—), Ohio Coun. Tchrs. English. Avocations: reading, gardening. Home: 8187 Woodruff Rd Cincinnati OH 45255-4536

BERWICK, DONALD M., administrator; m. Ann Greenberg; children: Ben, Dan, Jessica, Rebecca. MPA summa cum laude, John F. Kennedy Sch. Govt.; MD cum laude, Harvard Med. Sch. Assoc. pediatrics Children's Hosp., Boston; cons. pediatrics Mass. Gen. Hosp.; co-founder, co-principal investigator Nat. Demonstration Project on Quality Improvement in Healthcare, 1987—91; pres., CEO Inst. Healthcare Improvement, Boston. Clinical prof. pediatrics and health care policy Harvard Med. Sch.; vice-chmn. US Preventive Services Task Force, 1990—96; mem. adv. commn. Consumer Protection & Quality in Healthcare Industry, 1997, 98. Contbr.; co-author: Curing Health Care, New Rules: Regulation, Markets and the Quality of American Health Care; editl. bd. The British Med. Jour. Ind. mem., bd.

trustees Am. Hosp. Assn., 1996—99; mem. judges panel Malcolm Baldrige Nat. Quality Award Program, 1989—91. Mem.: Nat. Acad. Sci. (mem., Inst. Medicine), Internat. Soc. Med. Decision-Making (pres.), Agency Healthcare Rsch. and Quality (chmn., nat. adv. coun.), Agency Healthcare Policy and Rsch. (chmn., Health Services Rsch. Rev. Study Sect. 1995—99). Office: Dept Health Policy and Mgmt Inst HealthCare Improvement 375 Longwood Ave 4th Floor Boston MA 02215 Office Phone: 617-754-4852. Office Fax: 617-754-4865. E-mail: dberwick@ihi.org.

BERZ, DAVID RICHARD, lawyer; b. Chgo., May 21, 1948; m. Sherry Kirschner, Sept. 5, 1970; children: Douglas, Alexander. BA, George Washington U., 1970, JD with honors, 1973. Bar: DC 1973, US Supreme Ct. 1977, NY 1985. Mng. ptnr. Weil, Gotshal & Manges, LLP, Washington, 1985—, head environmental practice. Lectr. in field; mem. Environmental Law Inst. Co-author (environmental treatise): Environmental Law in Real Estate and Business Transactions, 3 vols., 1992; contbr. articles to profl. jours.; mem. editl. bd. Chemical Waste Litigation Reporter 1986-; environmental editor Inside Litigation 1991- Bd. dirs., pres. Washington Hebrew Congregation; mem. exec. bd. Am. Jewish Com.; mem. bd. overseers Hebrew Union Coll., 2004—; mem. adv. bd. George Washington Univ. Nat. Law Ctr. Fellow Am. Bar Found.; mem. US C. of C. (mem. environ. com. 1993-), DC Bar., Fed. and ABA (Fellow (ABA), mem. environmental controls com., corp., banking and bus. law sect., vice-chmn. environmental quality control com. sect. administrv. law 1978-81), Defense Rsch. Inst. (mem., environmental law com.) Office: Weil Gotshal & Manges LLP 1501 K St NW Ste 100 Washington DC 20005-5608 Office Phone: 202-682-7190. Office Fax: 202-857-0940. Business E-Mail: david.berz@weil.com.

BERZON, MARSHA S., federal judge; b. Cin., 1945; BA, Radcliffe Coll., 1966; JD, Boalt Hall Sch. Law, 1973. Bar: Calif. 1973, D.C. 1975. Clerk Judge James Browning, 9th Cir., 1973—74, Justice William Brennan, 1974—75; atty. Woll & Mayer, Washington, 1975—77, Altshuler, Berzon, Nussbaum, Berzon & Rubin, San Francisco, 1978—2000; judge U.S. Ct. Appeals 9th Cir., 2000—. Lectr. U. Calif. Sch. Social Welfare, Berkeley, Calif., 1992, La. State U. Sch. of Law, 2003; practitioner-in-residence Cornell Sch. of Law, NY, 1994, Ind. U. Law Sch., 1998. Mem.: Fed. Bar Assn., State Bar of Calif., DC Bar Assn., Am. Law Inst., Am. Bar Found. Office: US Ct Appeals 9th Cir PO Box 193939 San Francisco CA 94119-3939

BERZOW, HAROLD STEVEN, lawyer; b. Bklyn., Oct. 22, 1946; s. Julius and Lillian (Hershkowitz) Brzozowsky; m. Lynore Kushner, Aug. 22, 1970; children: Alan, Jason, Rachel. BA, Bklyn. Coll., 1968; JD, Bklyn. Law Sch., 1971. Bar: N.Y. 1972, U.S. Dist. Ct. (so. and ea. dists.) 1973, U.S. Dist. Ct. (no. dist.) N.Y. 1998, U.S. Ct. Appeals (2d cir.) 1975, U.S. Supreme Ct. 1978. Assoc. Finkel, Nadler & Goldstein, N.Y.C., 1971-77; ptnr. Finkel, Goldstein, Berzow, Rosenbloom & Nash, LLP, N.Y.C., 1977—2004; ptnr., chmn. bus. reorganization practice group Ruskin Moscou Faltischek P.C., Uniondale, NY, 2004—. Mem. ABA, N.Y. County Bar Assn., N.Y. State Bar Assn., Am. Bankruptcy Inst. Jewish. Office: Ruskin Moscou Faltischek PC E Tower 15th Fl 190 EAB Plz Uniondale NY 11556 Office Phone: 516-663-6600. Business E-Mail: hberzow@rmfpc.com.

BE SANT, CRAIG, marketing executive; Pres. TMP Worldwide, Chgo.; dir. mktg. Monster.com, Indpls., 1998—; mgr. recruiting adv. Chgo. Tribune. Office: Chgo Tribune 435 N Michigan Ave Chicago IL 60611-4066

BESANT, LARRY XON, retired librarian, administrator, consultant; b. Centralia, Ill., Mar. 13, 1935; s. Ben Vern and Marjorie Loyce (Jarboe) B.; m. A. Jean Hofstetter, Dec. 31, 1953; children: Vicki, Lizabeth, Paul, Peter, Mary. AA, Centralia Jr. Coll., Ill., 1959; BS in Chemistry, U. Ill., Urbana, 1961, MSL.S., 1962. Asst. librarian Chem. Abstract Assn., Columbus, Ohio, 1962-68; asst. dir. U. Houston Library, 1968-71, Ohio State U. Library, Columbus, 1972-82; dir. libraries Linda Hall Library, Kansas City, Mo., 1982-85; dir. libraries Camden-Carroll Library Morehead (Ky.) State U., Ky., 1985—2004. Library cons. in field; speaker in field Contbr. numerous articles, revs. to Library Mgmt. Bull., Am. Libraries, other profl. publs. Served with USAF, 1954-57. Mem. ALA, Spl. Librs. Assn. (pres. Ky. chpt. 1996-97, 2002-2003), Ky. Libr. Assn. Democrat. Baptist. Avocations: fishing, book collecting (jack london). Home: 428 N Wilson Ave Morehead KY 40351-1172 Office: Morehead State U Camden-Carroll Libr Morehead KY 40351 Personal E-mail: l.besant@adelphia.net.

BESAW, JENNEA D., music educator, entrepreneur; b. Dallas, Tex., Aug. 10, 1974; d. Danny E and Belinda Lee Potter; m. James Michael Besaw, June 9, 2001. Legal asst. Law Offices of R.E. Luna, Dallas, 1996—97; strategic change knowledge mgmt. PriceWaterhouse Coopers, Dallas, 1997—2001; owner/pres. Little Musicmaker, Arlington, Tex., 2001—. Ednl. rep. Brook Mays Music, Ft. Worth, 2001—. Author: (web site development) littlemusicmaker.com. Mem.: Music Teacher's Nat. Assn., Am. Coll. of Musicians, Tex. Music Teacher's Assn., Nat. Guild of Piano Teachers. Achievements include development of music education program offered to preschools. Avocation: running. E-mail: jennead@attbi.com.

BESCH, EMERSON LOUIS, physiologist, educator, retired dean; b. Hammond, Ind., June 9, 1928; s. Ernest Henry and Carolyn (Dieckmann) B.; m. H. Jean Whitstine, May 28, 1955; children: Karen J., Kevin D., Kathleen L., Kristine A. BS in Biology/Chemistry, S.W. Tex. State U., 1952, MA in Biology/Chemistry, 1955; PhD in Physiology, U. Calif., Davis, 1964. Grad. instr. biology dept. S.W. Tex. State U., San Marcos, 1954-55; research asst., NIH trainee U. Calif., Davis, 1960-64, research physiologist, lectr., 1964-67; research assoc. Pacific Missile Range, USN, Point Mugu, Calif., 1960-64; from assoc. to full prof., head dept. physiology Kans. State U., Manhattan, 1967-74, from assoc. to full prof. mech. engring., 1967-74; prof. mech. engring. U. Fla., Gainesville, 1974-93; prof. physiology U. Fla. Coll. Vet. Medicine, Gainesville, 1974-93, assoc. dean, 1974-87, acting dean, 1980-81, exec. assoc. dean, 1987-88, prof. emeritus, 1993—. Served to capt. USNR. Fellow Aerospace Med. Assn. (exec. council 1985-88, profl. excellence award 1987); mem. Am. Physiology Soc., Soc. for Exptl. Biology & Medicine, Aerospace Physiologist Soc. (pres. 1984-86), Am. Soc. Heating, Refrigerating & Air Conditioning Engring. Achievements include research in environmental physiology and acceleration biology. Home: 15207 Rompel Trail Dr San Antonio TX 78232-4255 Office: U Fla Coll Vet Medicine PO Box 100144 Gainesville FL 32610-0144

BESCH, EVERETT DICKMAN, veterinarian, dean, educator; b. Hammond, Ind., May 4, 1924; s. Ernst Henry and Carolyn (Dieckmann) B.; m. Mellie Darnell Brockman, Apr. 3, 1946; children: Carolyn Darnell, Ceryl Lynn, Cynthia Lee, Charlotte Ann, Everett Dickman. D.V.M., Tex. A&M Coll., 1954; M.P.H., U. Minn., 1956; PhD, Okla. State U., 1963. Instr. U. Minn., 1954-56; asst. prof. Okla. State U., 1956-64, prof., head dept. vet. parasitology and pub. health, 1964-68; dean Sch. Vet. Medicine, La. State U., 1968-88, prof., 1988-89. Sec.-treas. Assn. Am. Vet. Med. Colls., 1973-78, sec. coun. deans, 1976-80, chmn. coun. deans, 1980-81; mem. Nat. Adv. Coun. Health Professions Edn., 1982-86; treas. Am. Vet. Med. Found., 1991-93, v.p., 1993-94, pres., 1994-95, mem., 1995-97; bd. dirs. Coun. Agrl. Sci. and Tech., 1991-95; bd. dirs., divsn. agr., Nat. Assn. State Univs. and Land Grant Colls., 1980-82, mem. commn. on vet. medicine, 1979-82; cons. U.S. Army Surgeon Gen. in Vet. Med. Edn., 1973-85; cons. in pub. health and vet. edn. NIH, WHO, Pan Am. Health Orgn., NAS, others. Contbr. articles to profl. jours., chapters to books. Served with USN, 1942-48. Mem. AVMA (ho. of dels. 1988-91, exec. bd. 1991-97, award 1999), Assn. Tchrs. Vet. Pub. Health and Preventive Medicine (pres. 1968-69), La. Vet. Med. Assn. (named Vet. of Yr. 1976, Tex. Vet. Med. Assn., Conf. Pub. Health Veterinarians (pres. 1971-72), Am. Assn. Food Hygiene Veterinarians (pres. 1976-77), Am. Assn. Vet. Parasitologists (pres. 1964-65). Achievements include research in arthropod vectors of disease, internal parasites of ruminants. Home: 1453 Ashland Dr Baton Rouge LA 70806-7838

BESCH, LORRAINE W., special education educator; b. Orange, N.J., June 27, 1948; d. Robert Woodruff and Minnie (Wrightson) B.; m. William Lee Gibson, July 10, 1982. AA in Liberal Arts, Mt. Vernon Coll., 1968; BA in Sociology, U. Colo., 1970; MA in Spl. Edn., U. Denver, 1973. Cert. handicapped thcr., N.J. Elem. resource rm. tchr. Beeville (Tex.) Ind. Sch. Dist., 1973-75; trainable mentally retarded tchr. Kings County Supt. Schs., Hanford, Calif., 1975-78; h.s. resource rm. tchr. Summit (N.J.) Bd. Edn., 1980-81, Westfield (N.J.) Bd. Edn., 1981-99, head coach field hockey, 1981-83, mem. crisis mgmt. team, 1982-87, in class support tchr. English, 1993-99. Named to Women's Inner Circle Achievement, 1996; recipient Internat. Sash of Academia, ABI, 1997. Mem. AAUW, Smithsonian Nat. Mus. Am. Indian (charter), Sky Meadows Cir. Nat. Mus. Women in Arts, CEC (learning disabilities divsn.), Westfield Edn. Assn. (del. 1983-90, tech. com. 1993-94, conf. funds com. 1994-99), Hartford Family Found. (v.p., sec. 1991-97, trustee 1997—), Wrightson-Besch Found. (sec.-treas. 1994-99, pres. 1999—), Archaeology Conservancy (life), 1892 Founders Soc., Morristown Meml. Health Found., Col. Williamsburg Burgesses, Nat. Trust Historic Preservation, N.J. Hist. Society. Avocations: travel, reading, gardening, cooking, tennis. Home: 8 Lone Oak Rd Basking Ridge NJ 07920-1613

BESCHLOSS, MICHAEL R., historian, writer, commentator; b. Chgo., Nov. 30, 1955; s. Morris and Ruth Beschloss; m. Afsaneh Mashayekhi, Oct. 20, 1991; children: Alexander, Cyrus. BA, Williams Coll., 1977; MBA, Harvard U., 1980; LHD (hon.), St. Mary's Coll., 2001; LDH, Williams Coll., 2003. Historian Smithsonian Instn., Washington, 1982—85; sr. assoc. mem. St. Anthony's Coll., U. Oxford, England, 1985—86; vis. fellow Russian Rsch. Ctr. Harvard U., Cambridge, Mass., 1986—87; fellow Annenberg Found., Washington, 1988—96. Commentator The News Hour with Jim Lehrer, PBS, Arlington, Va., 1994—; contbr. ABC News, N.Y.C., 1998—. Author: Kennedy and Roosevelt: The Uneasy Alliance, 1980, Mayday: Eisenhower, Khrushchev and the U-2 Affair, 1986, The Crisis Years: Kennedy and Khrushchev, 1991, Taking Charge: The Johnson White House Tapes, 1963-1964, 1997, Reaching for Glory: Lyndon Johnson's Secret White House Tapes, 1964-1965, 2001, The Conquerors: Roosevelt, Truman and the Destructio of Hitler's Germany, 2002; co-author (with Strobe Talbott): At the Highest Levels: The Inside Story of the End of the Cold War, 1993; editor: American Heritage: The Presidents, 2003; cinematographer:. Trustee White House Hist. Assn., Washington, 1998—, Thomas Jefferson Found., Charlottesville, Va., 1999—, Urban Inst., Washington, 1999—, Nat. Archives Found., Washington, 2000—; commr. Pres.' Commn. on White House Fellowships, Washington, 1993—96. Recipient Ambassador Book prize, English-Speaking Union of U.S., N.Y.C., 1991, Harry S. Truman Pub. Svc. award, Truman Pub. Svc. Award Commn., Independence, Mo., 2004, Order of Lincoln, Lincoln Acad. Ill., Chgo., 2004. Fellow: Soc. Am. Historians; mem.: Am. Hist. Assn., Century Assn., Cosmos Club.*

BESCHTA, ROBERT LEE, hydrologist, educator; s. Vernon Mathew Beschta and Eleanor May Armitage; m. Charlaine Kay Bicanich, June 5, 1965; children: David Allen, Julie Ann Bescha, Robert Duane. BS, Colo. State U., 1965; MS, Utah State U., 1967; PhD, U. Ariz., 1974. Cert. hydrologist Am. Inst. of Hydrology, 1990. Prof. forest hydrology Coll. of Forestry, Oreg. State U., Corvallis, 1974—99; prof. emeritus Coll. of Forestry, Oreg. State Univ., Corvallis, 1999—. Cons., Corvallis, Oreg., 1980—2004. Contbr. articles to profl. jours. Mem.: Am. Water Resources Assn. (bd. dirs. 2002—04). Office: Coll Forestry Oreg State Univ SW 30th and Jefferson Way Corvallis OR 97331 Office Phone: 543-737-4952.

BESDINE, RICHARD WILLIAM, medical educator, researcher; b. NYC, Apr. 12, 1940; s. Alan Xerus and Betty (Bronstein) Besdine; m. Judith Anne Bailey, June 22, 1963 (div. May 1980); m. Fox Welte, July 1, 1981; children: Molly Bailey Besdine, Sarah Besdine Freedman. BS cum laude, Haverford Coll., 1961; MD, U. Pa. Sch. Medicine, 1965. Diplomate in internal medicine and in infectious diseases and geriatrics Am. Bd. Internal Medicine; diplomate Nat. Bd. Med. Examiners. Intern Beth Israel Hosp. Medicine, Boston, 1965-66, asst. resident in internal medicine, 1966-67, fellow in immunology and infectious diseases, 1969-72; rsch. fellow in medicine Harvard Med. Sch., Boston, 1969-72, instr. in medicine, 1972-75, asst. prof. medicine, 1975-86, lectr. in medicine, 1986-89, co-founder, divsn. aging, developer, academics geriatrics fellowship training program; assoc. prof. medicine, cmty. medicine and healthcare U. Conn. Health Ctr. Sch. Medicine, 1986-89, dir. Travelers Ctr. on Aging, assoc. prof. family medicine, 1988-2000; prof. medicine, cmty. medicine and healthcare U. Conn. Sch. Medicine, 1990-2000, chief divsn. geriatrics, dept. medicine; dir. U. Conn. Geriatric Edu. Ctr.; from asst. to assoc. in medicine Beth Israel Hosp., 1972-75, asst. physician in medicine, 1975-82; assoc. physician in medicine Brigham and Women's Hosp. and Beth Israel Hosps., 1982-88; prof. medicine, Greer prof. geriatric medicine, dir. Ctr. Gerontology and Health Care Rsch., dir. divsn. geriat. Brown Med. Sch., 2000—; interim dean medicine and biol. scis. Brown U., 2002—. Staff internist Hebrew Rehab. Ctr. for Aged, Roslindale, Mass., 1972-86, dir. geriatric med. edn., 1981-86; attending med. staff John Dempsey Hosp., 1986—, Hebrew Home and Hosp., 1987—, McLean Home and Village, 1987—; mem. cons. med. staff Inst. Living, Newington VA Med. Ctr.; cons., presenter in field; Noble Wiley Jones lectr. U. Oreg. Health Scis. Ctr., Portland, 1980; mem. Harvard-Hastings Project on Ethical Issues in Care of Elderly, 1982-86; vis. prof. U. Toronto Sch. Medicine, 1983, Montreal (Can.) Neurol. Inst., 1984, U. Geneva, 1990, U. Mich., 1991, U. Wis., 1991, Baylor U., 1991, U. Kans. Med. Ctr., 1992, Fallon Clinic and Health Plan, 1992; chair fed. task force on geriatric edn. NIH, 1986; mem. adv. bd. John A. Hartford Found. grant Johns Hopkins U. Sch. Medicine, 1994; chmn. western delegation Seminar on Aging, Singapore, Hong Kong, Taipei and Kuala Lumpur, 1987; mem. spl. adv. group White House Conf. on Aging and Mental Health, 1980-81; mem. task force on reversible dementia in the elderly Nat. Inst. on Aging, 1978-80, cons. geriatric medicine, prin. investigator, Claude Pepper Older Americans Independence Ctr.; dir. health stds. and quality bur., chief med. officer Healthcare Fin. Adminstrn., 1995-97; sr. adv. healthy aging project, Healthcare Financing Adminstrn. Co-author: Handbook of Geriatric Care, 1982; editor: Health and Disease in Old Age, 1982, 2d edit., 1988; mem. editl. bd. Geriat. Rev. Syllabus, 1989, 93, 96, assoc. editor, 1991, 93, 96; contbr. chpts. to books and articles to profl. jours. Surgeon USPHS Nat. Ctrs. for Disease Control, 1967—69; bd. dirs. Inst. for Cmty. Rsch., Hartford, 1987—2000, New Britain Meml. Hosp., 1993, Am. Fedn. for Aging Rsch., 1993—, Am. Geriat. Soc., 1994—, pres.; bd. dirs. Alzheimers Assn., 1998; bd. trustee Am. Soc. of Cons. Pharmacists, 2000—. Royal Soc. Medicine Found. travelling fellow U. Glasgow, 1972; grantee Geriatric Edn. Ctr., 1983-91, John A. Hartford Found., 1988-94, Charles A. Dana Found., 1988-90, Conn. State Dept. on Aging, 1989-91, Travelers Rsch. Inst. on Health Promotion and Aging, 1990, Howard and Bush Found., 1990, Robert Wood Johnson Found., 1991-93, Travelers Found., 1991, 92, 94, NIH Pepper Ctr., 1996. Fellow ACP, Am. Geriat. Soc. (pres.-elect 2002, pres., 2003-04, chmn., 2004-05, Milo D. Leavitt award 1991), Gerontol. Soc. Am. (Joseph T. Freeman award 1995), Am. Soc. Aging (Pres. award 1997). Home: 33 Broadview Dr Barrington RI 02806 Office: Brown Med Sch Box G-B Providence RI 02912 E-mail: richard_besdine@brown.edu.

BESEN, STANLEY MARTIN, economist; b. Bklyn., Dec. 17, 1937; s. Moe and Sylvia (Forgang) B.; m. Marlene Dubliner, June 10, 1961; children: Roberta Ann, Elizabeth Rebecca. BBA, CCNY, 1958; MA, Yale U., 1960, PhD, 1964. Acting asst. prof. econs. U. Calif.-Santa Barbara, 1962-63; economist Inst. Def. Analyses, 1963-65; mem. faculty Rice U., Houston, 1965-80, prof. econs., 1974-79, Cline prof. econs. and fin., 1979-80; co-dir. network inquiry spl. staff FCC, 1978-80; sr. economist Rand Corp., Washington, 1980-92; v.p. CRA Internat., Washington, 1992—. Vis. Henley prof. law and bus. Columbia U., 1988—89; vis. prof. law and econs. Georgetown U. Law Ctr., 1990—91; mem. task force nat telecomms. policy making Aspen Inst. Program Comms. and Society, 1977; mem. adv. panel on intellectual property rights in an age of electronics and info. Office of Tech. Assessment, 1984—85, mem. adv. panel on comms. sys. for an info. age, 1986—88; mem. com. on internet searching and the domain name sys. The Nat. Acads. Computer Sci. and Telecomm. Bd., 2001—04; mem. bd. on earth scis. and resources, com. on licensing geographic data and svcs. NRC, 2003—04. Author: Misregulating Television: Network Dominance and the FCC, 1984, also articles; co-editor Rand Jour. Econs., 1985-88; mem. editorial bds. profl. jours. Fellow Brookings Instn., 1971-72, NSF, 1973-75 Home: 4918 Western Ave Bethesda MD 20816-1714 Office: CRA Internat 1201 F St NW Ste 700 Washington DC 20004-1204 Office Phone: 202-662-3833. Personal E-mail: sbesen@crai.com.

BESHAR, CHRISTINE, lawyer; b. Paetzig, Germany, Nov. 6, 1929; came to U.S., 1952, naturalized, 1957; d. Hans and Ruth (vonKleist-Retzow) von Wedemeyer; m. Robert P. Beshar, Dec. 20, 1953; children: Cornelia, Jacqueline, Frederica, Peter. Student, U. Hamburg, 1950-51, U. Tuebingen, 1951-52; BA, Smith Coll., 1953. Bar: N.Y. 1960, U.S. Supreme Ct. 1971. Assoc. Cravath, Swaine & Moore, N.Y.C., 1964-70, ptnr., 1971—. Bd. dirs. Catalyst for Women Inc., 1977-94; trustee Colgate U., 1978-84, Smith Coll., 1987-97; mem. state bd. Nature Conservancy, N.Y., 1993-96. Inst. Internat. Edn. fellow, 1952-53; recipient Disting. Alumnae medal Smith Coll., 1974. Fellow: Am. Coll. Probate Counsel; mem.: Fgn. Policy Assn. (bd. dirs. 1978—87), UN Assn. (bd. dirs. 1975—89), N.Y. Bar Found. (bd. dirs. 1977—2001), N.Y. State Bar Assn. (ho. of dels. 1971—80, v.p. 1979—80), Assn. Bar City N.Y. (exec. com. 1973—75, v.p. 1985—86), Am. Bar Found., Gipsy Trail Club, Cosmopolitan Club. Office: Cravath Swaine & Moore 825 8th Ave 43d Fl New York NY 10019-7475 also: Stone House Farm PO Box 533 Somers NY 10589-0533 Office Phone: 212-474-1698. Business E-Mail: cbeshar@cravath.com.

BESHAR, PETER JUSTUS, lawyer, insurance company executive; b. NYC, Nov. 20, 1961; s. Robert Peter and Christine (Wedemeyer) Beshar; m. Sarah Elizabeth Eggleston Jones, Jan. 5, 1991; children: Isabel Emma, Henry Frederick, Sophie Charlotte. BA, Yale U., 1984; JD, Harvard U., 1989. Bar: NY 1989. Law clerk to the Hon. Vincent L. Broderick, NYC, 1989-90; assoc. Simpson, Thacher & Bartlett, NYC, 1990—92; spl. asst. to the Hon. Cyrus Vance Internat. Conf. on the Former Yugoslavia, 1992-93; asst. atty. gen. Office of Atty. Gen., NYC, 1994; assoc. Gibson, Dunn & Crutcher, NYC, 1995—99, ptnr., 1999—2004; sr. v.p., gen. counsel, corp. sec. Marsh & McLennan Companies Inc., NYC, 2004—. Mem. lawyers com. Nat. Ctr. for State Courts, Williamsburg, Va., 2004—. Trustee Rye Country Day Sch. Mem. Coun. Fgn. Rels. Office: Marsh & McLennan Companies Inc 1166 Ave of the Americas New York NY 10036-2774

BESHAR, ROBERT PETER, lawyer; b. N.Y.C., Mar. 3, 1928; m. Christine von Wedemeyer, Dec. 20, 1953; children: Cornelia, Jacqueline, Frederica, Peter. AB honors with exceptional distinction, Yale U., 1950, LLB, 1953. Bar: N.Y. 1954. Asst. gen. counsel Waterfront Commn. N.Y. Harbor, 1954-55; law sec. Hon. Charles D. Breitel, Appellate div. 1st dept. N.Y. Supreme Ct., N.Y.C., 1956-58; spl. hearing officer Justice Dept., 1967-68; dep. asst. sec. Commerce; dir. Bur. Internat. Commerce; nat. export expansion coordinator Commerce Dept., Washington, 1971-72; pvt. practice, N.Y.C., 1972—2004; pres. various family enterprises, 1993—. Bd. dirs. Nat. Semicondr. Corp. (audit and dir's. affairs coms., counsel to bd. dirs. 1972-98); mem. bus. adv. panel Nat. Commn. for Rev. of Antitrust Laws, 1978-79; mem. Mcpl. Securities Rulemaking Bd., 1982-85; bd. govs. Fgn. Policy Assn., 1991-1998. Author: Current Legal Aspects of Doing Business With Sino-Soviet Nations, 1973; editor: Manhattan Auto Study, 1973. Trustee Westchester Coll. Found., 1992—; mem. Planning Bd. of Somers, 1984-97. Scholar of the House, Yale U., 1950. Mem. ABA (chmn. corp. and antitrust law com. 1982-85), N.Y. State Bar Assn., Elizabethan and Gypsy Trail Clubs, Phi Beta Kappa. Home: 120 E End Ave New York NY 10028-7552 also: PO Box 533 Somers NY 10589-0533 Office Phone: 914-276-2425. E-mail: rpbeshar@netscape.net.

BESHEAR, STEVEN LYNN, lawyer; b. Dawson Springs, Ky., Sept. 21, 1944; AB, U. Ky., Lexington, 1966, JD, 1968. Bar: N.Y. 1969, Ky. 1971. Assoc. White and Case, N.Y.C., 1968-70; later ptnr. Beshear, Meng and Green, Lexington; mem. Ky. Ho. of Reps., 1974-79; atty. gen. State of Ky., Frankfort, 1979-83, lt. gov., 1983-87; ptnr. Stites & Harbison, Lexington, 1987—. Bd. editors, Ky. Law Jour., (1967-68.). Mem. Fayette County Bar Assn., Ky. Bar Assn., ABA, Order of Coif, Phi Beta Kappa, Phi Delta Phi, Omicron Delta Kappa. Office: Stites & Harbison Ste 2300 250 W Main St Lexington KY 40507-1758 Office Phone: 859-226-2300. E-mail: sbeshear@stites.com.

BESHEARS, CHARLES DANIEL, insurance executive; b. Vandalia, Mo., Sept. 6, 1917; s. Charles D. and Anabel (Baker) B.; m. Mildred Domreis, Nov. 1941 (deceased); m. Louise Davis Clarke, Sept. 1980; children: Jacqueline, Charles, Scott (dec.), Melanie; stepchildren: Crescente, Maria-Asuncion, Hernan Errazuriz. Grad. exec. program bus. mgmt., UCLA, 1968; advanced mgmt. program, Harvard U., 1971; diplomas in property and casualty ins. and mgmt., Ins. Inst. Am.; grad., Am. Coll. Life Underwriters, 1978. CLU. With Farmers Ins. Group, L.A., 1937—79, v.p. field ops., 1966—68, v.p. charge property and casualty ops., 1968—73; pres., dir. Farmers New World Life Ins. Co., Mercer Island, Wash., 1973—79; dir. Ohio State Life Ins. Co., 1973—79, Investors Guaranty Life Ins. Co., 1973—79; cons. Chilean Ins. Industry, 1980—95; pres. Reaseguros Britania, Chile, 1999—. Bd. govs., honors. com. Internat. Ins. Soc. Inc. With USAAF, ETO, 1942-45. Mem. DAV, VFW, Am. Legion, Non-Commd. Officers Assn., Chile Club. Address: Correo Sto Domingo Clasificador 15 V Region San Antonio Chile *You can accomplish any goal you want to set for yourself, if the desire is strong enough. Are you willing to pay the price?.*

BESIER, JAMES LOUIS, pharmacist, educator; b. Waukegan, Ill., Feb. 23, 1954; s. Louis Clark and Jessie Olive Besier; m. Janice Lynn Halloran, Nov. 2, 1979; children: Matthew, Christopher, Robert. BS, U. Cin., 1977, MS, 1990; PhD, Union Inst. & U., 2004. Lic. pharmacist Ohio, Ky. Staff pharmacist Children's Hosp. Med. Ctr., Cin., 1977—89; svc. chief pediat. Strong Meml. Hosp., Rochester, NY, 1989—90; staff pharmacist U. Cin. Hosp., 1990—91; pharmacy mgr. U. Hosp., Cin., 1991—97; asst. dir. pharmacy St. Luke Hosps., Ft. Thomas, Ky., 1997—. Adj. asst. prof. Coll. Pharmacy U. Cin., 1991—2004, adj. assoc. prof. Coll. Nursing, 2004—; spkr. Glaxo Pharm. Rsch., Triangle Park, NC, 1994—97, Greater Cin. Health Coun., 2003—; lectr. Coll. Nursing, U. Cin., 1998—; adv. coun. Gateway Cmty. & Tech. Coll., Edgewood, Ky., 2002—. Contbr. articles to profl. jours. Bus. edn. cons. Jr. Achievement, Cin., 1995—99; coun. ministries Westwood-Cheviot Ch. of Christ, Cin., 2001—02. Mem.: Am. Assn. Coll. Pharmacy, Am. Soc. Health Sys. Pharmacists. Home: 914 Cedarpark Dr Cincinnati OH 45233 Office: St Luke Hosp Dept Pharmacy 85 N Grand Ave Fort Thomas KY 41075 Office Phone: 859-572-3345. E-mail: jbesier@fuse.net.

BESING, RAY GILBERT, lawyer, educator; b. Roswell, N.Mex., Sept. 14, 1934; s. Ray David and Maxine Mable (Jordan) B.; children: Christopher, Gilbert, Andrew, Paul. Student, Rice U., 1952—54; BA, Ripon Coll., 1957; postgrad., Georgetown U., 1957; JD, So. Meth. U., 1960. Bar: Tex. 1960. Ptnr. Geary, Brice, Barron, & Stahl, Dallas, 1960-74; sr. ptnr. Besing, Baker & Glast, Dallas, 1974-77; prin. Law Offices of Ray G. Besing, P.C., Dallas, 1977—96. Sr. rsch. fellow Faculty Laws U. Coll. London, 2002-03; lectr. in field, 2003—. Author: Who Broke Up AT&T?: From Ma Bell to the Internet, 2000; mng. editor So. Meth. U. Law Jour., 1959-60. Pres. Dallas Cerebral Palsy Found., 1970; trustee Ripon Coll., 1969—76; mem. Tex. Gov.'s Transition Team on Telecom., 1982; mem. exec. coun. Episc. diocese Dallas, 1969—72; bd. dirs. Dallas Symphony, 1972, Dallas Theatre Ctr., 1971, Found. for Santa Fe C.C., 2001—03, Found. for Santa Fe Concert Assn., 1998—2001. Tex. Moot Ct. champion, 1958. Mem. Tex. Bar Assn., Dallas Bar Assn., Dallas Jr. C. of C. (v.p. 1964), Sigma Chi. Democrat. Episcopalian. Office Phone: 505-988-1553. E-mail: raybesing@nets.com.

BESLEY, MORRISH ALEXANDER (TIM BESLEY), civil engineer; b. New Plymouth, New Zealand, Mar. 14, 1927; arrived in Australia, 1950; s. Hugh Morrish and Isobel (Alexander) B.; m. Nancy Marguerite Cave, Feb. 15, 1952 (dissolved 2001); children: Trevor J., Grant A., Rodney G.; m. Sarah Harrington, Aug. 11, 2001; children: Hugh I., Hannah Alice. BE in Civil Engring., U. New Zealand, 1950; B Legal Studies, Macquarrie U., Sydney,

Australia, 1984; Barrister at Law, Supreme Ct. NSW, 1985; DSc (hon.), Macquarrie U., 2002. Chartered profl. engr., Australia. Engr. Ministry of Works, New Zealand, 1950; with Snowy Mountains Hydro-Electric Authority, 1950-67; 1st asst. sec. Dept. External Territories, 1967-72; exec. mem. Fgn. Investment Review Bd., 1975-76; 1st asst. sec. Dept. of Treasury, 1973-76; sec. Commonwealth Dept. Bus. and Consumer Affairs, ACT, Australia, 1976-81; comptroller gen. Customs, 1976-81; mng. dir. Monier Ltd., Sydney, 1982-87, chmn., CEO, 1987; chmn. Monier Redland Ltd., 1988, Redland Australia, 1988-95; exec. chmn. Commonwealth Indsl. Gases Ltd., Sydney, 1988-90; chmn. The CIG Group, 1988-93, Commonwealth Banking Corp., 1988-91, Commonwealth Bank Australia, Sydney, 1991-99. Pres. Metal Trades Industry Assn., Sydney, 1989-91, nat. pres. 1990-92; chmn. Leighton Holdings Ltd., Sydney, 1990-2001. Chmn. Royal Bot. Gardens, Sydney, 1989—92; dir. O'Connell St. Assocs. Pty. Ltd., 1990—; mem. Red Shield Appeal Com., Sydney, 1987—99, Sydney Adv. Bd. The Salvation Army, 1994—99, Legacy Appeal Com., Sydney, 1988—2003; mem. mgmt. bd. Australian Grad. Sch. Mgmt., 1983—92, Chancellor Macquarie U., 1994—2001; chmn. Co-op Rsch. Ctr. for Greenhouse Gases, 2003—, Wheat Export Authority, 2005—, Australian Rsch. Coun., 2002—. Decorated mem., officer and companion, Order of Australia. Fellow Australian Acad. Tech. Sci. and Engring. (pres. 1998-2002); mem. Royal Sydney Yacht Squadron, Nat. Press Club, Union Club, Elanora Country Club, Australian Club Sydney. Home: Pvt Box 304 Cammeray NSW 2062 Australia

BESLOW, WILLIAM S., lawyer; b. Paterson, N.J., June 7, 1948; s. Harry George and Marion Gertrude (Doan) B.; m. Evelyn Z. Beslow, Dec. 20, 1970; children: Lauren Allegra, Jonathan Doan. BA, Yale U., 1969; JD, Columbia U., 1972; LLM in Taxation, NYU, 1977. Bar: N.Y. 1973, U.S. Dist. CT. (so. dist.) N.Y. 1979. Assoc. Davis, Polk & Wardwell, N.Y.C., 1972-79; sole practice N.Y.C., 1980—. Fellow: Am. Acad. Matrimonial Lawyers; mem. ABA, Assn. Bar City N.Y., N.Y. State Bar Assn. Office: Law Office William S Beslow Rockefeller Ctr 620 Fifth Ave New York NY 10020

BESS, ALAN L., pharmaceutical executive, physician; b. Phila., Oct. 14, 1954; s. Harold L. and Elaine Bess; m. Kathryn Victoria Karas, Feb. 1, 1989; 1 child, James Millon. BA, Susquehanna U., 1976; MD, Temple U., 1980. Resident Thomas Jefferson U. Hosp., Phila., 1980-82; dir. med. svcs. Abbott Labs., North Chicago, 1982-86; sect. head drug safety Hoffmann-La Roche, Nutley, N.J., 1986-94, dir. drug safety, 1994-95, v.p. pharma devel. safety, 1995-2000; v.p. clin. safety and epidemiology Novartis Pharms., East Hanover, N.J., 2000—. Mem. AMA, Am. Acad. Pharm. Physicians, Am. Coll. Clin. Pharmacology, Pharm. Rsch. and Mfrs. Assn., Drug. Info. Assn., Inst. Internat. Rsch. Avocations: martial arts, antiquities. Home: 50 Westview Rd Wayne NJ 07470-6233 Office: Novartis Pharms One Health Plz East Hanover NJ 07936 Office Phone: 862-778-5555. Business E-Mail: al.bess@pharma.novartis.com.

BESS, OLEAN, counselor, educator; b. Florence, S.C., Feb. 23, 1934; d. Yankey and Mary Jane Baker; m. Willie Bess, Sept. 13, 1953 (dec. Sept. 1988); children: Barbara, Sandra. B in Liberal Arts, Coll. New Rochelle, 1988; MDiv, N.Y. Theol. Sem., 1992; DD, United Theol. Sem., 1995. Bookkeeper Paintset Fashions, N.Y.C., 1960-71; office mgr. Rug Hold Inc., N.Y.C., 1971-92; substitute tchr. Pub. Sch. #176, Laurlton, N.Y., 1992—. Part-time counselor N.Y. Hosp. Rickers Island Jail, N.Y.C. and Elmont, N.Y., 1992—, King Harbor Nursing Home, Bronx, 1992—. Author: Mixed Felling, 1972, Poems and Things, 1973, Our World Stopped Turning and I Stepped Off, 1999. Home: 191-14 113th Rd Saint Albans NY 11412

BESS, RONALD W., advertising executive; b. Bloomington, Ill., July 9, 1946; s. Bloice Monroe and Mary (Trussel) B.; m. Teresa N. Shute, July 22, 1970; children: Daniel, Laura. BS in Mktg., U. Ill., Champaign, 1968, M, 1972. Account exec. Foote, Cone and Belding, Chgo., 1972-75; v.p. account dir. Needham, Harper and Steers, Chgo., 1975-81; sr. v.p. group account dir. DDB Needham, Chgo., 1981-87; pres. Bayer Bess Vanderwarker, Chgo., Foote, Cone & Belding, Chgo.; chmn., CEO diversified group Young Rubicam Inc., NYC, 2001—03, vice chmn, Integration and Bus. Dev., 2003; CEO Euro RSCG-Chgo, Canada, 2004—. Office: Euro RSCG 36 E Grand Ave Chicago IL 60611

BESSANT, CATHERINE POMBIER, bank executive, marketing professional; b. Jackson, Mich. m. John E. Clay; 2 children. BBA in Fin., Mktg. and Eng. Lit., U. Mich. Joined NationsBank, 1982; pres., cmty. devel. bank Bank Am. Corp. (formerly NationsBank), 1998—2000; pres., consumer real estate banking Bank Am. Corp., 1999—2000, pres., Fla. ops., 2000—01, chief mktg. exec., 2001—. Trustee Enterprise Found. Bd. dirs. Children's Theatre Charlotte, Blue Cross Blue Shield Fla., Inc. Named one of Most Powerful Women in Banking, US Banker Mag., 2003. Office: Bank Am Corp 100 N Tryon St Charlotte NC 28255

BESSER, GRETCHEN ROUS, writer, educator; b. Bklyn., Dec. 1, 1928; d. Ben and Sidonya (Menkes) Rous; m. Albert Gordon Besser, Dec. 28, 1952; children: James, Neal, Brian. BA in French with honors, Wellesley Coll., 1949; MA, Middlebury Coll., 1950; PhD, Columbia U., 1967. Instr. Fairleigh Dickinson U., Rutherford, N.J., 1955-57, Columbia U., N.Y.C., 1957-59, 63-67; asst. prof. Lehman Coll., CUNY, Bronx, 1967-70, Rutgers U., Newark, 1972-73; PhD examiner Monash U., Victoria, Australia, 1979; instr. in lit. N.J. Com. for The Humanities, New Brunswick, 1985-90; faculty mem. New Sch. U., N.Y.C., 1989—; ski columnist Recorder Pub. Co., Stirling, N.J., 1993—; instr. Distance Instrn. for Adult Learners program New Sch. U., N.Y.C., 1994—2000; instr. New Sch. Online U., 2000—. Author: Balzac's Concept of Genius, 1969, Nathalie Sarraute, 1979, The National Ski Patrol, 1983, Germaine de Staël, Revisited, 1994; contbr. World Lit. Today, 1978—, French Rev., 1973—, Ski Patrol Mag., 1978- Instr. first aid ARC, 1971-82; internat. liaison Nat. Ski Patrol, 1980-85, nat. historian, 1980—; mem. selection com. U.S. Nat. Ski Hall of Fame, 1982—, bd. dirs., 1997—; bd. dirs. Internat. Skiing History Assn., 1997-2004, Vt. Coun. on the Humanities, 2001—; pres. Wellesley Class of 1949, 2004—. Fulbright Commn. grantee, 1949-50; Wellesley scholar, 1949; recipient Ullr award Internat. Skiing History Assn., 1997. Mem. Am. Assn. Tchrs. French, Ea. Ski Writers Assn., Nat. Assn. Snowsports Journalists Am. Jewish. Avocations: opera, skiing, hiking. Home and Office: 3679 Stagecoach Rd Morrisville VT 05661 E-mail: grbesser@together.net.

BESSETTE, ANDY F., diversified financial services company executive; BS, U. Conn.; MS, U. RI. Mkg. acct. exec. Sheraton Corp., 1977—80; various positions in corp. real estate and corp. svcs. Travelers Ins., 1980—99, v.p. corp. real estate and svcs., 1999—2002; sr. v.p., chief adminstrv. officer St. Paul Co., Inc., 2002—. Office: St Paul Cos 385 Washington Saint Paul MN 55102

BESSEY, PALMER QUINTARD, surgeon; b. Glen Ridge, N.J., Aug. 14, 1944; MD, U. Vt., 1975. Diplomate Am. Bd. Surgeons, Am. Bd. Critical Care Surgery. Intern U. Ala. Hosp., Birmingham, 1975-76, resident in surgery, 1976-81; fellow metabolism and nutrition Brigham and Women's Hosp., Boston, 1981-83; assoc. dir. Burn Ctr. N.Y. Presbyterian Hosp., 2000—; prof. surgery Weill Med. Coll. Cornell U., 2000—. Mem. ACS (region chief), Assn. Acad. Surgery, Soc Univ. Surgeons, Am. Assn. Surgery Trauma, ASPEN, Soc. Critical Care Medicine, Ctrl. Surg. Assn., Am. Surg. Assn., Am. Bd. Surgery (bd. dirs.), Am. Burn Assn. (com. on trauma). Office: Dept Surgery Box 137 P-703 525 E 68th St New York NY 10021 E-mail: pqb2001@med.cornell.edu.

BESSIE, SIMON MICHAEL, publisher; b. N.Y.C., Jan. 23, 1916; s. Abraham and Ella (Brainin) B.; m. Constance Ernst, Sept. 12, 1945; children: Nicholas, Katherine; m. Cornelia Schaeffer, Dec. 21, 1968. BA magna cum laude, Harvard U., 1936. Reporter Newark Star Eagle, 1936; with rsch. dept. RKO-Radio Pictures, 1936-38; editor Market Rsch. Monthly, 1938; freelance writer Europe, Africa, 1938-39; assoc. editor, war editor, war corr. Look mag., 1940-42; editor Harper & Bros., 1946-52, gen. editor, 1952-59; co-founder Atheneum Pubs., 1959, pres., 1963-75; sr. v.p. Harper & Row, N.Y.C., 1975-81, v.p., 1988-91, also bd. dirs., 1975-87; pres. Joshuatown Pub. Assocs., Lyme, Conn., 1981—; co-pub. Cornelia and Michael Bessie Books, 1981—. Cons. editor Counterpoint Press, 1995-2002, Perseus Books Group, 1999-2002; lectr. English, Columbia U., 1953-59; dir. novel workshop New Sch., 1959-63, dir. Franklin book programs, 1963-72; chmn. vis. com. Harvard U. Press, 1972-78, bd. dirs., 1980-91; bd. dirs. Am. Book Pubs. Coun., 1964-69, Ctr. for Comm., 1981—; chmn. trade book div. Assn. Am. Pubs., 1970-72, bd. dirs., 1972-76, chmn., 1974-75, chmn. freedom to read com., 1975-78, internat. freedom to pub. com., 1975—; mem. exec. com. Ctr. for the Book, Libr. of Congress, 1979—, chmn., 1983—. Author: Jazz Journalism, 1938; contbr. numerous articles to mags. Bd. overseers vis. com. dept. history Harvard U., 1964-77; chmn. lit. panel Nat. Arts Council, 1971-74, chmn. spl. projects panel, 1974-81; chmn. bd. advisors Sta. WNET, 1979-83, trustee, 1983-96, life trustee, 1997—; chmn. book com. Alfred P. Sloan Found., 1986-91, mem. tech. book com., 1992-2001. Served as chief news bur. psychol. warfare br., 1943-44, Algiers, Sicily, Italy; chief psychol. warfare combat team 1944, So. France; dep. dir. USIS, 1944-46, France. Recipient Presdl. Medal of Freedom, 1946, Curtis Benjamin award Assn. Am. Pubs., 1986. Mem. Council Fgn. Relations, Assn. Harvard Alumni (dir. 1974-77), Phi Beta Kappa. Clubs: Century Assn. (N.Y.C.), Harvard (N.Y.C.); Federal City (Washington). Home and Office: 296 Joshuatown Rd Lyme CT 06371-3035 E-mail: mbessie@snet.net.

BESSIN, ROLF HARTWIG, retired surgeon, educator; b. Hamburg, Germany, July 5, 1939; MD, George Washington U., 1964. Diplomate Am. Bd. Surgery. Intern Balt. City Hosp., 1964-65, resident in surgery, 1965, 68-71; fellow in surgery Johns Hopkins Hosp., Balt., 1968-71; pvt. practice Morristown, N.J. Attending surgeon Morristown Meml. Hosp. Fellow ACS, Southeastern Surg. Congress; mem. Eastern Vascular Surgery, Vascular Surgery Soc. N.J.

BESSINGER, RAYMOND CARLTON, nutritionist, educator; b. Pickens, S.C., July 25, 1948; m. Renee P. Pritchett, May 18, 1991. BBA, Ga. So. U., 1970; MBA, Ga. State U., 1974, MS in Exercise Sci., 1986, MS in Nutrition, 1988; PhD, U. N.C., 1996. Dietitian Am. Dietetic Assn., 1988. Instr. Clemson U., SC, 1974—75; pers. analyst State Merit Sys., State of Ga., Atlanta, 1976—78, pers. analysis supr., 1978—80; adj. instr. Coll. St. Francis, Atlanta, 1984; asst. prof. Marywood U., Scranton, Pa., 1996—99, Winthrop U., Rock Hill, SC, 1999—2003, assoc. prof., 2003—. Author, editor: book Management and the Brain, 1983; contbr. articles to profl. jours., chapters to books. With U.S. Army, 1970—72, Vietnam. Grantee, U. Rsch. Coun., Winthrop U., 2001—04; Nutrition Rsch. fellow, Inst. Nutrition, U. N.C., 1994—95. Mem.: Coun. Undergraduate Rsch., Nat. Osteoporosis Found., SC. Dietetic Assn. (treas. and mem. of bd. of directors 2002—03), Am. Dietetic Assn. Office: Winthrop Univ 314 Life Sci Bldg Rock Hill SC 29733 Office Phone: 803-323-4553. Business E-Mail: bessingerr@winthrop.edu.

BESSIRE, MARK H.C., museum director; BA, NYU; MA in art hist., Hunter Coll.; MBA, Columbia U. Dir. Inst. Contemporary Art, Maine Coll. Art, 1998—2003, Bates Coll. Mus. Art, Lewiston, Maine, 2003—. Office: Bates Coll Mus Art Olin Arts Ctr, Rm 202 2 Andrews Rd Lewiston ME 04240-6028 E-mail: mbessire@bates.edu.

BESSMAN, SAMUEL PAUL, pediatrician, educator, biochemist; b. Newark, Feb. 3, 1921; m. Alice Neuman, July 3, 1945; children: Joel David, Ellen. Student, Coll. William and Mary, 1938-41; MD, Washington U., St. Louis, 1944. Intern, asst. resident St. Louis Children's Hosp., 1944-45; asst. prof. pediatrics George Washington U., 1947-54; dir. research Children's Hosp., Washington, 1947-54; asso. prof. pediatrics U. Md., 1954-59, prof. pediatric research, 1959-68, prof. biochemistry, 1962-68; prof., chmn. dept. pharmacology and nutrition U. So. Calif., 1968-91, prof. pediatrics, 1969-91, prof. emeritus, 1991—. Dir. research Rosewood State Hosp., Md., 1962-68, Jewish Home for Retarded Children, Washington, 1962-68 Founding editor Biochem. Medicine; mem. editorial bd. Analytical Biochemistry. Pres. First Dist. Cmty. Coun., Balt., 1965; trustee Robert Lindner Found.; pres. Molly Towell Found., Alsam Found. Served with USPHS, 1945-47. Recipient Crawford Long award U. Ga., 1963, Creative Scholar award U. So. Calif., 1978, Maimonides award Technion, 1979, Disting. Sci. Achievement award Am. Heart Assn., 1984, Inst. for Advanced Studies award Louis Pasteur Libr. and Sci. Found., 1986, Alumni Achievement award Washington U. Med. Sch., 1994. Fellow AAAS, Am. Acad. Pediat.; mem. Am. Soc. Biol. Chemists, Soc. Pediat. Rsch., Am. Inst. Nutrition, Am. Soc. Pharmacology and Exptl. Therapeutics, Sigma Xi, Alpha Omega Alpha. Achievements include introduction of EDTA treatment of lead poisoning, theoretical basis of hepatic coma, mechanism of insulin action chemistry mental retardation, genetic basis of malnutrition, artificial implantable pancreas, creatine phosphate energy shuttle. Home: 7404 Woodrow Wilson Dr Los Angeles CA 90046-1323 E-mail: bessman@usc.edu.

BESSON, LUC, film director, film producer; b. Paris, Mar. 18, 1959; m. Anne Parillaud (div.); 1 child; m. Milla Jovovich, Dec. 14, 1997 (div. 1999); m. Virginie Silla, Aug. 28, 2004; 2 children. Founder Les Films du Loup, Paris, 1982—. Works include: Le Dernier Combat, 1982, Subway, 1984, The Big Blue, 1988, La Femme Nikita, 1990, Atlantis, 1991, The Professional, 1994, The Fifth Element, 1997, Taxi, 1998, The Messenger: The Story of Joan of Arc, 1999, Taxi 2, 2000, Kiss of the Dragon, 2001, Wasabi, 2001, The Transporter, 2002, Taxi 3, 2003, Crimson Rivers 2: Angels of the Apocalypse, 2004, Banlieue 13, 2004, Unleashed, 2005, others.*

BEST, BROOKIE MANNING DUGAN, pharmacologist; d. Michael Patrick Dugan and Vicky Lynnette Manning; m. William Gainey Best, III, July 31, 1999; children: Alexander Jacob children: Noah Gainey. BS in Chemistry, U. Calif., La Jolla, Calif., 1994; PharmD, U. of Calif., San Francisco, Calif., 1999; cert., U. of Calif., La Jolla, CA, 2002; student in Advanced Studies, Clin. Rsch., U. of Calif., La Jolla, Calif., 2003—. Lic. pharmacist Bd. Pharmacy, Calif., 1999. Resident in pharmacy practice San Diego (Calif.) Med. Ctr. U. of Calif., 1999—2000, asst. clin. prof. San Francisco (Calif.) Sch. of Pharmacy, 2000—, pharmacokinetic specialist San Diego (Calif.) Med. Ctr., 2000—, rsch. fellow San Diego (Calif.) Pediat. Pharm. Rsch. Unit, 2001—04. Asst. clin. prof. San Diego (Calif.) Sch. Pharmacy and Pharm. Scis. U. Calif., 2004—; admissions interviewer San Diego (Calif.) Sch. Pharmacy and Pharm. Scis. U. of Calif., 2002—; mem. therapeutic drug monitoring com. NIH Pediatric AIDs Clin. Trials Group, 2001—02; mem., ednl. policy and academic oversight com. San Diego (Calif.) Sch. Pharmacy and Pharm. Scis. U. of Calif., 2003—, mem., residency adv. com. San Diego (Calif.) Med. Ctr., 2003—; lectr. San Diego (Calif.) Sch. Pharmacy and Pharm. Scis. U. Calif., 2003—. Reviewer: Jour. Pediats., 2000; reviewer Antimicrobial Agts. and Chemotherapy, 2003—; contbr. articles to profl. jours. Vol. pharmacist attending U. Calif. San Diego Student -Run Free Med. Clinic Project, 1999—; judge Greater San Diego (Calif.) Sci. & Engring. Fair, 2001. Recipient Baker Appreciation award, Baker Elem. Sch., San Diego Unified Sch. Dist., 1998; fellow Nat. Rsch. Svc. award, Nat. Inst. for Child Health and Human Devel., 2001—04; scholar Nat. Merit scholarship, U. of Calif., San Diego, 1990, Julian Weiss Clin. Pharmacy Rsch. scholarship, U. of Calif., San Francisco Sch. of Pharmacy, 1998. Mem.: Am. Coll. Clin. Pharmacy, Calif. Soc. Health Systems Pharmacists (co-chmn. cmty. outreach com. 2001—02), Calif. Pharm. Assn., Am. Soc. of Health Systems Pharmacists, Am. Pharm. Assn., Rho Chi. Avocations: snowboarding, water-skiing. Office: U Calif San Diego 9500 Gilman Dr MC 0657 La Jolla CA 92093-0657 E-mail: brookie@ucsd.edu.

BEST, FRANKLIN LUTHER, JR., lawyer; b. Lock Haven, Pa., Dec. 14, 1945; s. Franklin L. and Hazel M. (Yearick) B.; m. Kimberly R., May 1, 1982 BA, Yale U., 1967; JD, U. Pa., 1970; postgrad., Columbia U., 1994. Bar: Pa. 1970. Assoc. MacCoy, Evans & Lewis, Phila., 1970—74; asst. counsel Penn Mut. Life Ins. Co., Phila., 1974—77, asst. gen. counsel, 1978—84, assoc. gen. counsel, 1985—99, mng. corp. counsel, 1999—2004, mng. corp. counsel, sec., 2004—; counsel, asst. sec. Penn Ins. and Annuity Co., Phila., 1983—96, counsel, sec., 1996—. Lectr. Pa. Bar Inst., 1976-84. Author: Pennsylvania Insurance Law, 1991, 2d edit., 1998; contbr. articles to profl. jours. Bd. dirs. Ctr. City South Neighborhood Assn., 1979-80, pres., 1978-79; mem. Com. of Seventy, 1978-84; sec. Washington Sq. Assn., 1977-87; mem. 30th Ward Rep. Exec. Com., 1972-84, West Pikeland Twp. Open Spaces Com., 1987-99, chair, 1995-99, planning commn., 1994—, chair, 1996—. Mem.: ABA, Phila. Bar Assn., Internat. Claim Assn. (sec. 1995—2000, exec. com. 1979—81, 1985—88, 1995—, pres. 2002—03), Yale Club Phila. Baptist. Office: Penn Mut Life Ins Co 600 Dresher Rd Horsham PA 19044-2204 Office Phone: 215-956-7754. Business E-Mail: best.frank@pennmutual.com.

BEST, GARY THORMAN, commercial real estate broker; b. San Diego, Mar. 11, 1944; s. Roland Elmer and Mildred Mae (Thorman) B.; m. Hollyce Susan Hill, Feb. 22, 1967 (div. Mar. 1973); 1 child, Melissa Anne; m. Georgia Anne Flaherty, May 22, 1973; children: Roland Bryant, Heather Anne. AAS, Pima Community Coll., 1979. CCIM Comml. Investment Members. Sales Mohawk Data Sci. Corp, Tulsa, Okla., 1968-69; exec. v.p. Mid-Am. Mgmt. Corp., Tulsa, 1969-73; real estate sales Cragin Lang Free and Smythe, Cleve., 1973-74; land sales Coldwell Banker Comml., Tucson, 1975-80, mgr. sales Cin., 1981, resident mgr. Nashville, 1982-83, investment sales Tucson, 1984—86; v.p. Del E. Webb Realty and Mgmt. Co., Tucson, 1986-87; pres. Best Comml. Real Estate, Tucson, 1987-93; sec./treas. Best Asset Mgmt. Svc., Phoenix, 1993-98, chmn. credit rev. com., 1991-94; with Coldwell Banker Success Realty, Tucson, 1994-97; assoc. broker comml. div. Realty Exec. So. Ariz., 1997—. Regional v.p. Comml. Investment Real Estate Inst., 1992-94, cert. comml. investment mem.; pres. So. Ariz. chpt. Cert. Comml. Investment Mems., Tucson, 1990; mem. New Am. Network, Tucson, 1987-93, mem. adv. bd., 1992-93. Mem. fin. com. Symington for Gov., Tucson, 1990, Kolbe for Congress, Tucson, 1988; adv. bd. Goodwill Industries of Tucson, Tucson Unified Sch. Dist.; dir. Family Counseling Agy., 1995-01,05—, treas., 1996-98, 1st v.p., 1998-99, pres., 1999-2000; chmn. adv. bd. Casa de la Luz, Tucson, 2000-2002, found. 2003; dir. Comin' Home, 2002-05. Recipient Pres. of Yr. award Civitan Internat., Ariz. dist., Tucson, 1979. Mem. Tucson Assn. Realtors (bd. dir. 1988-91, v.p. 1992, treas. 2003, v.p., 1992, 2004, govt. affairs com. 1998-2000, pres.-elect 2005—), Ariz. Assn. Realtors (bd. dir. 1989-91, 92-94, exec. com. 1992, 2004-05, regional v.p., 2004-2005), Tucson Econ. Devel. Corp. (bd. dir., chmn. 1990), Greater Tucson Econ. Coun. (bd. dir., exec. com. 1990-93), Tucson Met. C. of C. (bd. dirs., chmn. 1993-94, Small Bus. Leader of Yr. award 1989). Avocations: travel, reading, geneology. Office: 1745 E River Rd Ste 245 Tucson AZ 85718-7634 Office Phone: 520-444-0799. E-mail: gbest11@comcast.net.

BEST, JACOB HILMER, JR., retired hotel chain executive; b. Evanston, Ill., July 21, 1937; s. Jacob Hilmer and Clara (Cornell) B.; m. Janet Patricia Donnelly, June 20, 1959; children: Jacob Hilmer III, Peter B., Julie Donnelly Best. BS in Hotel Adminstrn., Mich. State U., 1959; postgrad, Stanford U., 1979. From sales rep. to dir. of sales Sheraton Hotels, Chgo., Wash., 1960-62; asst. to owner Camelback Inn, Scottsdale, Ariz., 1963-64; from sales mgr. to exec. v.p. Marriott Hotels, 1964-84; pres. Ramada Inns, Phoenix, 1984-85; pres., CEO, Wyndham Hotels, Dallas, 1985-87, Red Lion Hotels & Inns, Vancouver, Wash., 1987-91, Omni Hotels, Hampton, N.H., 1992-96; ind. cons., 1996-98; COO Tauck Tours, Westport, Conn., 1998-99. Named charter mem. Mich. State U. Sch. of Hospitality Hall of Fame, 1995. Mem. Am. Hotel and Motel Assn. Republican. Roman Catholic. Avocations: golf, reading, fishing. Home: PO Box 56 Rancho Santa Fe CA 92067-0056 Personal E-mail: pops7217@aol.com.

BEST, JERRY LAVON, insurance consultant; b. Garrett, Ind, Feb. 1, 1952; s. William E. Best and Marie Trausch; m. Donna Smith Jean, Sept. 2, 1978 (div. July 1980); m. Susan Shelby Abdulla, Aug. 10, 1954; children: Chelsea A., Natalie P. A in Bible Studies, Grace Bible Coll., Carey, NC, 1994; B in Psychology, Nat. Christian Counseling, Sarasota, Fla., 2000. Lic. Lovesent Ministries, 2003. With WRG Enterprises, Sarasota, 1975-77; sales ins. George Washington Life, Pt. Charlotte, Fla., 1978-80; CEO, pres. Best & Assoc. Svc., Venice, Fla., 1980-90, Consumer Awareness Group, Sarasota, 1990—. Pres. Nat. Christian Consulting Assn., Sarasota, 1994-2000; mem. adv. bd. Crown Life, Inc., Sarasota, 1999-2001, Individual Med. Account Flexible Health & Accident (Bonus Concept, Annuity). Prodr.: songs Miracles Are Really True. Mem. Bus. Music Inc., Lions. Republican. Achievements include patents for Lighted Basketball Hoop; invention of Lazer Hoop. Avocations: Charismatic Jazz, songwriter, musician, & guitarist., tennis, basketball, boating, skiing. Home: 5667 Creekwood Dr Sarasota FL 34233-1510 E-mail: JBEST03@aol.com.

BEST, JUDAH, lawyer; b. NYC, Sept. 4, 1932; s. Sol and Ruth (Landau) B.; 1 child, Stephen Andrew. AB, Cornell U., 1954; LLB, Columbia U., 1959. Bar: NY 1959, DC 1961, U.S. Supreme Ct. 1963. Trial atty. Solicitor's Office, U.S. Dept. Labor, Washington, 1960-61; asst. U.S. atty. for D.C., 1961-64; assoc. to ptnr. Chapman, DiSalle & Friedman, Washington, 1964-70; ptnr. Dickstein, Shapiro & Morin, Washington, 1970-80, Steptoe & Johnson, Washington, 1980-87, Debevoise & Plimpton, Washington, 1987—2002, of counsel, 2003—04, LeBoeuf Lamb Greene MacRae LLP, Washington, 2004—. Participant trial advocacy program U. Va. Sch. Law, 1981—. Contbr. articles to profl. publs. Served with U.S. Army, 1954-56 Fellow Am. Coll. Trial Lawyers; mem. ABA (coun., litigation sect. 1977-81, chmn. subcom. on litigation 1982-84, mem. fed. regulation securities com., corp. bank and bus. law sect., pub. contracts sect., vice chmn. ABA Task Force Report on RICO 1983-85, chmn. litigation sect. 1988-89, sect. del. 1989—, mem. standing com. on fed. judiciary 1990-93, chmn. 1996-97, mem. spl. com. on governance 1993-95), Fed. Bar Assn. (commr.), DC Bar Assn., Am. Bar Found., Am. Law Inst., Cosmos Club, Washington Golf and Country Club, Smithsonian Am. Art Mus. Office: LeBoeuf Lamb Greene MacRae LLP 1875 Connecticut NW Washington DC 20009 Office Phone: 202-986-8004. Business E-Mail: jbest@LLGM.com.

BEST, LAURENCE EDWARD, lawyer; b. New Orleans, June 14, 1949; s. Kermit Roosevelt and Frances Elizabeth (Hicks) Best; m. Julie B. Guten (div.); children: Erin Lynn, Mark Edward, Kevin John; life ptnr. Kory Chatelain, Oct. 13, 2001. BS in Acctg., U. New Orleans, 1971; JD, Tulane U. Sch. Law, 1974. Bar: La. 1974, U.S. Dist. Ct., ea. dist., La. 1974, U.S. Dist. Ct., western dist., La., U.S. Dist. Ct., middle dist., La. 1974, U.S. Supreme Ct. 1979, U.S. Dist. Ct., so. dist., Tex. 1991, U.S. Dist. Ct., so. dist., Miss. 1991. Atty. Waitz & Downer, Houma, La., 1974—78, Waitz, Downer & Best, Houma, 1978—83, Hebert & Abbott, New Orleans, 1983—84; ptnr. Abbott, Webb, Best & Meeks, New Orleans, 1984—88, Abbott, Best & Meeks, New Orleans, 1988—91, Best Koeppel, New Orleans, 1991—. Invited guest U.S. Ct. Appeal (5th cir.) Jud. Conf., San Antonio, 2000. Presenter, author, panelist numerous radio shows, legal publs., meetings, TV shows. Treas. Forum for Equality, 1992-93, chair-elect and chair, 1993-95; mem. Forum for Equality/Equality Club; cmty. dir. Forum for Equality, 2001; founder, bd. mem. New Orleans Lesbian and Gay Cmty. Ctr., 1994-95; mem. adv. com. City of New Orleans Human Rels. Commn., 1994-96; mem. La. Log Cabin Reps. 2003, Human Rights Campaign Fed. Club, Svc. Members Legal Def. Network, Parents and Friends of Lesbians and Gays, donor to annual scholarship fund, 1996-; mem. Lambda Legal Def. Fund. Recipient Legal Eagle award, La. Electorate of Gays and Lesbians, 1996, award for outstanding leadership and svc. to the Lesbian and Gay Counsel, New Orleans Human Rights Campaign, 2001, Annual Acclaim award for lesbian and gay polit. activism, New Orleans Forum for Equality, 2003. Mem.: Nat. Lesbian and Gay Bar Assn., Fed. Bar Assn. New Orleans, La. Trial Lawyer Assn., La. Assn. Def.Counsel, Def. Rsch. Inst., Tex. Bar Assn., La. Bar Assn., Maritime Law Assn., U. New Orleans Alumni Assn., Tulane U. Alumni Assn. and Assoc. Club. Democrat. Avocations: reading, cooking, wine. Office: Best Koeppel 2030 St Charles Ave New Orleans LA 70130 Office Phone: 504-598-1000. Office Fax: 504-524-1024. Business E-Mail: lebest@bestkoeppel.com.

BEST, LAWRENCE C., medical products executive, manufacturing executive; From acct. to ptnr. Ernst & Young, Akron, Ohio, 1971—81, ptnr., 1981—92; fellow Securities and Exchange Commn., Washington, 1979—80;

exec. presdl. exchange The White House, Washington, 1981; sr. v.p. Boston Scientific Corp., Natick, Mass., 1992—, CFO, 1992—. Bd. dirs. Biogen, Inc. Office: Boston ScientificCorp 1 Boston Scientific Pl Natick MA 01760-1537

BEST, MARIANNE, adapted physical education educator, consultant; b. Mattoon, Ill., Mar. 6, 1947; d. James Earl and Julietta Ann (Koebele) Lucier; m. Dennis Charles Best, Aug. 12, 1972; children: Nichole Denise, Ryan Charles EArl. BS in Edn., Ea. Ill. U., 1969; MS, Ill. State U., 1988. Tchr. Mattoon (Ill.) High Sch., 1969-70; tchr., coach East Leyden High Sch., Franklin Park, Ill., 1970-72, Coal City (Ill.) High Sch., 1972-75; tchr., cons. Grundy County Spl. Edn. Coop., Morris, Ill., 1984—2002; ret. Vol. ARC, Mattoon, 1959-73, Am. Cancer Soc., Morris, 1980-84. Mem. NEA, AAH-PERD, Ill. Assn. Health, Phys. Edn., Recreation and Dance (v.p. 1992—, adv. bd. 1990—, state convention speaker 1990-91, exec. bd. 1992—, v.p. for children, adapted phys. edn. cons. 1990, 92, gov. affairs com. 1997—, state conv. planning bd. 1997—), Ill. Edn. Assn. Roman Catholic. Avocations: collecting and restoring antiques, piano, travel, children's sports. Home: 725 E Main St Morris IL 60450-2318

BEST, MELVYN EDWARD, geophysicist; b. Victoria, B.C., Can., Mar. 8, 1941; s. Herbert Best and Irene Jessie (Kelly) MacKenzie; m. Virginia Marie Pignato, July 19, 1970; children: Lisette Anne, Aaron Michael. BSc in Math. and Physics with honors, U. B.C., Vancouver, 1965, MSc in Physics, 1966; PhD in Theoretical Physics, MIT, 1970. Geophysicist mineral exploration Shell Can. Resources Ltd., Calgary, Alta., Can., 1972-77, divsn. geophysicist minerals, 1980-82, mgr. petroleum engrng. rsch., 1982-85; head non-seismic rsch. Royal Dutch Shell Exploration and Prodn. Labs., The Hague, The Netherlands, 1978-80; geophys. advisor Teknica Resource Devel. Ltd., Calgary, 1985-86; head basin analysis subdivision Atlantic Geoscience Ctr. Geol. Survey Can., Dartmouth, N.S., 1986-90, dir. Pacific Geosci. Ctr. Sidney, B.C., 1990-94, sr. rsch. scientist, 1994-97; geophys. cons. Bemex Consulting Internat., Victoria, B.C., 1997—; environ. geophys. Lockheed-Martin Corp., Edison, N.J., 2001—. Vis. lectr., rsch. assoc. dept. physics McGill U., Montreal, Que., 1970—72; mem. panel Jeanne d'Arc hydrocarbon resource assessment Can. Govt., 1987—90; mem. petroleum geology working group Office Energy R&D, 1987—92; mem. oil and gas com. Can. Nfld. Offshore Petroleum Bd., 1990—94, official Can. rep. coom. coordination joint prospecting for mineral resources in Asian offshore waters, 1992—94; sessional lectr. Sch. Earth and Ocean Scis. U. Victoria, 1995—, adj. prof. earth and ocean scis., 1998—; adj. prof. geology and geophysics U. Calgary, 1998—; part-time sr. geophysicist Lockheed Martin Corp., Edison, NJ, 2001—. Author: Resistivity Mapping and Electromagnetic Imaging, 1992; editor: (with J.B. Boniwell) A Geophysical Handbook for Geologists, 1989, (with T.P. Ng) Development and Exploitation Scale Geophysics, 1995; assoc. editor Bull. of the Can. Soc. Petroleum Engrs., 2004—. Vol. lectr. Can. Coll. Chinese Studies, Victoria, B.C., 1995-99; vol. Victoria chpt. Habitat for Humanity, 1996-97. Recipient meritorious svc. award Can. Soc. Exploration Geophysicists, Calgary, 1996. Mem. Can. Soc. Exploration Geophysicists (chmn. continuing edn. com. 1982-85, mem. tech. com. 1985 convention, assoc. editor jour. 1986-93, 95-2003, editor jour. 1993-95), Soc. Exploration Geophysicists (prodn. and devel. geophysics com. 1985-88, geophys. rsch. com. 1988—, organizer workshop 1989, instr. continuing edn. 1985-2000), Soc. Environ. and Engrng. Geophysics (assoc. editor jour. 1995-97, 2000-02, editor 1997-2000, v.p. coms. 2003-2005, gen. chmn. Symposium on Application of Geophysics to Environ. and Engrng. Problems meeting 2005-2006), Assn. Profl. Engrs., Geologists and Geophysicists Alta. (cert.), Assn. Profl. Engrs. and Geoscientists B.C. (cert.). Avocations: competitive badminton, squash, tennis, hiking, sailing. Home and Office: Bemex Cons Internat 5288 Cordova Bay Rd Victoria BC Canada V8Y 2L4 Office Phone: 250-658-0791.

BEST, PHILLIP JOHN, psychology and neuroscience educator; b. Bklyn., July 10, 1940; BS in Math., Rensselaer Poly. Inst., 1962; PhD in Psychology, Princeton U., 1965. Rsch. assoc. Brain Rsch. Lab., U. Mich., Ann Arbor, 1965-68; asst. prof. psychology U. Va., Charlottesville, 1968-72, assoc. prof. psychology and psychiatry, 1972-76, prof. psychology and behavioral medicine, 1976-88, dir. neurosci. grad. program, 1983-86; prof., chmn. dept. psychology U. New Orleans, 1988-90; prof. psychology and neurosci. Miami U., Oxford, Ohio, 1990—, chmn. dept. psychology, 1990-95. Hon. rsch. fellow cerebral functions group dept. anatomy Univ. Coll., London, 1982-83; vis. scholar Neural Sys. Lab., U. Ariz., Tucson, 1996. Cons. editor Psychobiology, 1986-98; assoc. editor Psychonomic Bull. and Rev., 1993-99, Behavioral and Cognitive Neuroscience Reviews; contbr. articles to sci. jours. Ruling elder Oxford Presbyn. Ch., 1993-96, 98-01; bd. dirs. Campus Ministry, Oxford, 1999-2005. Named Citizen of Yr., Oxford, 2004; postdoctoral fellow NSF, 1965; rsch. grantee NIH, 1969—, NSF, 1974—. Fellow Am. Psychol. Soc. (charter); mem. Soc. for Neurosci., Kiwanis Oxford (pres. 2005), Sigma Xi (Rschr. of Yr. 2002). Democrat. Achievements include research on brain mechanisms of behavior, activity of hippocamapal neurons in spatial navigation. Home: 1451 Dana Dr Oxford OH 45056-8902 Office: Miami U Psychology Dept Oxford OH 45056-1601 Fax: 513-529-2420. Office Phone: 513-529-2421. E-mail: bestpj@muohio.edu.

BEST, ROBERT MULVANE, insurance company executive; b. Newcomerstown, Ohio, May 9, 1922; s. Chester R. and Beatrice (Mulvane) B.; m. Shirley Marie Smith, Nov. 25, 1994; children: Eric, Linda, Grant. BS, Ohio State U., 1947. Agt. Bus. Men's Assurance Co. Am., Columbus, Ohio, 1946-48; mgr. group sales Security Mut. Life Ins. Co., Binghamton, N.Y., 1948-49, asst. supt. agys., 1949-51, dir. sales, 1951-53; mgr. Bus. Men's Assurance Co., Columbus, 1952-61; v.p. in charge agys. Security Mut. Life Ins. Co. N.Y., Binghamton, 1961-66, exec. v.p., 1966-69, pres., 1969—, chief exec. officer, 1972-87, chmn. bd., 1977-90; chmn., chief exec. officer Home Mut. Ins. Co., 1986-89. Mem. exec. com. Life Inst. Guaranty Copr., N.Y.C., 1980-89; mem. N.Y. Inst. bd., N.Y.; chmn. bd. trustees bus. coun. Inst. Trust. Trustee Bus. Coun. N.Y. State, Inc.; former dir. Valley Devel. Found., Binghamton; mem. coun. SUNY; bd. govs. Internat. Ins. Seminars; bd. dirs. Twin Tier Home Health Care, Inc., Binghamton; former mem. N.Y. State Bd. Regents, Am. Coun. Life Ins.; chmn. Med. Index Bur., Inc., Boston, 1989; dir. Greater Broome Cmty. Found., Inc. Lt. (j.g.) USNR, 1942-46. Mem. Am. Soc. CLUs (regional v.p. 1967-70), Am. Council Life Ins. (bd. dir.), Life Ins. Council N.Y. (bd. dir.), Broome County C. of C. (bd. dir. 1970-75, pres. 1974), Empire State C. of C. (former pres., bd. dirs.). Clubs: Binghamton City (bd. dirs. 1969-73); Oteyokwa Lake (Hallstead, Pa.) (pres. 1970-71); Econ. (N.Y.C.). Home: 41A Crestmont Rd Binghamton NY 13905-4117 Personal E-mail: sbest12@aol.com.

BEST, ROBERT WAYNE, gas transmission company executive, lawyer; b. Nappanee, Ind., Oct. 8, 1946; s. Wayne and Helen F. (Kendall) B.; m. Mary Beth Hoffman, Apr. 7, 1967; children— Stephanie, Sean, Ashley BS, Ind. State U., 1968; JD, Ind. U., 1974. Bar: Ky., Ind. Atty. Tex. Gas Transmission Corp., Owensboro, Ky., 1974-79, sr. atty., 1979-81, gen. counsel, 1981-82, v.p., gen. counsel, 1982-85, pres., chief exec. officer, 1985-89, pres., chief operating officer, 1989-1995; chmn., pres. & CEO Atmos Energy Corp., Dallas. Dir. Cardinal Fed. Savs. Bank. Bd. dirs. Leadership Owensboro, Brescia Coll., Mercy Hosp., Ky. Ind. Coll. Fund., United Way Owensboro-Daviess County; mem. exec. com. Strategies for Tomorrow; mem. Ky. Econ. Devel. Corp. Mem. ABA, Ky. Bar Assn., Ind. Bar Assn., Fed. Energy Bar Assn. Democrat. Roman Catholic. Avocations: golf, reading. Office: Atmos Energy Corp PO Box 650205 Dallas TX 75265-0205 Home: 440 Flint Point Dr Houston TX 77024-6749

BEST, SUSAN MARIE, artist, educator; b. Peoria, Ill., July 4, 1949; d. Robert H. and Shirley (Critchlow) Coyle; m. David G. Best, Sept. 12, 1970 (div. May 1987); children: Timothy, Molly, Abby, George; m. Richard J. Gualandi, Dec. 20, 1996. BPhar, U. Ill., Chgo., 1972; MA in Fine Arts, Ill. State U., Normal, 1988, MFA, 1991. Grad. pharmacist S&C Drugs, Peoria, 1972, Indian Hosp., Pine Ridge, S.D., 1974-76; instr. art Ill. State U., Normal, 1988-91, Bradley U., Peoria, 1992-93, Ill. Ctrl. Coll., Peoria, 1991-93; artist, 1970—. Gallery artist Struve Gallery, Chgo., 1991-93; active Longue Vue Mus. Art Program. Exhbn. Contemporary Art Ctr., Oleczyn, Poland. Bd. dirs. St. Thomas Sch., Peoria, 1980-83, Amateur Mus. Club, Peoria, 1982-84; bd. dirs. Peoria Art Guild, 1994—. Recipient Percent for Art award City of New Orleans, 1997, also various awards for art including 2 grants from Ill. Arts Coun. Access Program, 1995; Ill. State U. fellow, 1988-91. Mem. AAUP, AAUW, NOW, Contemporary Arts Ctr. of New Orleans, New Orleans Mus. Art, Chgo. Artists Coalition, Lakeview Art Mus., Sun Found., Planned Parenthood Assn., So. Poverty Law Ctr. Democrat. Avocations: skiing, jogging, piano. Studio: 811 Opelousas Ave New Orleans LA 70114-2429 E-mail: smbgu@earthlink.net.

BEST, WILLIAM ROBERT, internist, educator, dean; b. Chgo., July 14, 1922; s. Gordon and Marian Burton (Shapland) B.; m. Ruth Johanna Stuchlik, Sept. 2, 1944; children: Barbara Ann Best Mulch, Patricia Marian Best Williams. BS, U. Ill., l945; MD, U. Ill., Chgo., l947, MS, l951; postgrad. math. biology, U. Chgo., l964-65. Diplomate Am. Bd. Internal Medicine, Am. Bd. Hematology. From intern to fellow in hematology then to resident U. Ill. Hosp., 1947-51; asst. prof., assoc. prof. medicine U. Ill. Coll. Medicine, Chgo., 1953-67, prof., assoc. dean, 1972-81; chief Midwest Rsch. Support Ctr., VA Hosp., Hines, Ill., 1967-72, chief staff, 1981-92, sr. health svcs. rschr., 1992—; prof. medicine, assoc. dean for VA affairs Loyola U. Stritch Sch. Medicine, Maywood, Ill., 1981-92; chief staff U. Ill. Hosp., Chgo., 1976-81. Contbr. numerous articles to sci. jours. 1st lt. U.S. Army, 1951—53. Named Alumnus of Yr., U. Ill. Med. Alumni Assn., l980. Fellow ACP; mem. AMA (br. pres. 1985), Am. Statis. Assn., AAAS. Episcopalian. Avocations: sailing, computing, radio-controlled model airplanes. Home: 1712 Waverly Cir Saint Charles IL 60174-5869 Office: Midwest Ctr Health Svcs and Policy Rsch Edward Hines Jr VA Hosp Hines IL 60141 Personal E-mail: w.and.r.best@sbcglobal.net. Business E-Mail: best@research.hines.med.va.gov.

BESTEHORN, UTE WILTRUD, retired librarian; b. Cologne, Germany, Nov. 6, 1930; arrived in U.S., 1930; d. Henry Hugo and Wiltrud Lucie (Vincentz) Bestehorn. BA, U. Cin., 1954, BEd, 1955, MEd, 1958; MS in Library Sci., Western Res. U. (now Case-Western Res. U.), 1961. Tchr. Cutter Jr. HS, Cin., 1955-57; tchr., supr. libr. Felicity (Ohio) Franklin Sr. HS, 1959-60; with libr. sci. dept. Pub. Libr. Cin. and Hamilton County, 1961-78, with libr. info. desk, 1978-91; ret., 1991. Mem. textbook selection com. Felicity-Franklin Sr. HS, 1959—60; supr. health alcove sci. dept. and ann. health lectures Cin. Pub. Libr., 1972—77. Book reviewer Libr. Jour., 1972—74, author, inventor Rainbow 40 marble game, 1971, Concominium game, 1976, patentee indexed packaging and stacking device, 1973, mobile packaging and stacking device, 1974. Mem. Clifton Town Meeting, 1988—; mem. Bookfest 90 com. Pub. Libr. Cin. and Hamilton County. Recipient cert. of Merit and Appreciation, Pub. Libr. Cin., 1986. Mem.: Greater Cin. Calligraphers Guild (reviewer New Letters pub. 1986—88), Pub. Libr. Staff Assn. (exec. bd., mem. activities com. 1965, mem. welfare com. 1966, Golden Book 25 Yr. Svc. pin 1986), Cin. Chpt. Spl. LIbrs. Assn. (archivist 1963—64, editor Queen City Gazette bull. 1964—69, archivist 1965—70), Friends of Libr., Delta Phi Alpha (nat. German hon. 1951). Republican. Mem. United Ch. Of Christ. Avocations: calligraphy, painting and sketching, writing, photography, violin. Home: 3330 Morrison Ave Cincinnati OH 45220-1440

BESTERMAN, DOUGLAS, composer, orchestrator; BA in Music History and Theater, U. of Rochester, 1985. Orchestrator Broadway shows: Damn Yankees, 1994—95; Big, 1996; King David, 1997; Fosse, 1999—2001 (Tony award Best Orchestrations, 1999); The Music Man, 2000—01; The Producers, 2001— (Tony award Best Orchestrations, 2001); Seussical, 2000—01; Thoroughly Modern Millie, 2002—04 (Tony award Best Orchestrations, 2002); Dracula, The Musical, 2004—05; A Christmas Carol; Radio City Music Hall Christmas Spectacular; orchestrator off-Broadway shows: Weird Romance; Jack's Holiday; Johnny Pye and the Foolkiller; The Gifts of the Magi; Godspell; orchestrated ballet: But Not for Me; orchestrated for film/TV: Pocahontas, 1995; Cinderella, 1997; Anastasia, 1997; orchestrated for film/TV Mulan, 1998, Gepetto, 2000, South Pacific, 2001, Fosse, 2001, Chicago, 2002; arranger for vocalist: Toni Braxton; Kathy Lee Gifford; Jerry Hadley; Patti LuPone; Mandy Patinkin; Chita Rivera. Office: Local 802 AFM 320 W 48th St New York NY 10036-1302*

BESTON, ROSE MARIE, retired academic administrator; b. South Portland, Maine, Sept. 27, 1937; d. George Louis and Edith Mae (Archibald) Beattie; m. John Bernard Beston, Feb. 1, 1970 BA, St. Joseph's Coll., 1961; MA, Boston Coll., 1963; PhD, U. Pitts., 1967; cert. of advanced study, Harvard U., 1978. Mem. faculty St. Joseph's Coll., Maine, 1967-68, SUNY, Oneonta, 1968-69, S.E. Mo. State Coll., 1969-70, U. Queensland and Western Australian Inst. Tech., 1970-76, U. Hawaii, Manoa, 1976-77; assoc. acad. dean Worcester State Coll., Mass., 1978-80; dean for acad. affairs Castleton State Coll., Vt., 1980-84; pres. Nazareth Coll. Rochester, NY, 1984-98; ret., 1998. Former mem. Neylan Commn., Assn. Cath. Colls. and Univs., Pres. Network of Campus Compact. Contbr. articles to profl. jour. Mem. AAUW.

BETANCOURT, CONCHITA, music educator; b. Pinar del Rio, Cuba, Aug. 2, 1949; arrived in U.S., 1962; d. Humberto and Yolanda Betancourt; m. Jose C. Suarez, Sept. 8, 1967 (div. Sept. 1985); 1 child, Jose H. Suarez; m. Arcadio Cancio, Feb. 5, 1995. MusB, U Miami, 1976, MusM, 1992. Piano tchr. pvt. practice, Miami, Fla., 1969—2003; assistanship U Miami (Fla) Sch. of Music, 1987, 1991—92. Chairperson Nat. Guild of Piano, Miami, 1984—2003. Mem. Women Fighters for Democracy, Miami, 1997—2003, Cuban Women's Club, Miami, 1997—2003. Recipient Honor Scholarship, U Miami, Coral Gables,Fla., 1978, Music Scholarship, 1975—79. Cath. Home: 8840 S W 4 Terrace Miami FL 33174

BETANCOURT LOPEZ, ANTONIO L., association executive; b. Belen de Umbria, Colombia, Jan. 9, 1944; came to U.S., 1967; s. Angel Maria and Pastora (Lopez) B.; m. Kyoko Funayama-Kagawa, July 1, 1982; children: Kiantar, Annika, Kyboter, Isaac. Sec. gen. CAUSA Internat., N.Y.C., 1979-89; asst. to pres. New World Comms., N.Y.C., 1980-83; exec. v.p. Internat. Security Coun., Washington, 1984-90; exec. dir. Assn. for the Unity of Latin Am., Washington, 1983—, Summit Coun. for World Peace, Washington, 1981—; dep. sec. gen. Fedn. for World Peace, Washington, 1991—; pres. Young Gruppe, Inc., Washington, 1992—, News & Communication, Inc., 1993—. Pres. Group Internat. Arte, Washington, 1996—, World Inst. for Devel. and Peace, 1996—; sec.-gen. Interreligious and Internat. Fedn. for World Peace-N.Am., 2002—; chmn. exec. bd. Internat. Assn. Educators for World Peace, 2002—. Exec. editor jour. Global Affairs, 1984-90; exec. dir. conf. procs. Mem. Family Fedn. for World Peace and Unification, N.Y.C., 1996—; bd. dirs., bd. mem. Universal Ballet Acad. and Universal Ballet Found., 2004, Martin Luther King Jr. Family Life Inst., 2005, Tiempos del Mundo Found., 2005. Recipient commendation Cath. U., La Plata, Argentina, 1984, Acad. award Mexican Acad. Internat. Law, 1985, Grand Medal of Peace, Dem. People's Republic of Korea, 1996, Academician of honor U. San Andres, Chile, 2003; named hon. citizen Santo Domingo City, 1987. Mem. N.Y. Acad. Sci., Oxford Club, Korea Soc., Wilson Ctr. for Scholars. Avocations: gardening, antique collecting and restoration, hiking, fishing. Home: 6305 Queens Chapel Rd University Park MD 20782-2131 Office: Summit Coun for World Peace 3600 New York Ave NE Washington DC 20002-1947 E-mail: thirdway@widp.org.

BETENSON, GAYE BRINTON, secondary school educator; b. Salt Lake City, Utah, Aug. 4, 1953; d. Brinton Phil and Helen Rae Reese Brinton; m. Donald Blaine Betenson, June 7, 1974; children: Bryan Donald, Brandon Blaine, Amber Betenson Mann, Ashley, Michelle, Michael Phil. BA in Bus. & Edn., So. Utah State Coll. Cert. tchr. Utah, 1973. Tchr. Bingham HS, South Jordan, Utah, 1973—79, Indian Hills Mid. Sch., Sandy, Utah, 1980—81; asst. coord., competency-based testing Utah State Office Edn., Salt Lake City, 1985—89, coord., competency-based testing, 1989—94; tchr. West Jordan HS, Utah, 1997—; tchr., adult HS South Pointe HS, Sandy, 2004—. Advisor Bingham High Chpt. FBLA, South Jordan, Utah, 1973—79, advisor West Jordan HS Chpt., West Jordan, Utah, 1997—; tchr. teen mother program Valley HS, Sandy, 1976—, tchr., home and hosp., 1997. Mem.: Utah Bus. Educators Assn., UACTE. Latter-Day Saint. Avocations: sewing, quilting, embroidery. Home: 11275 Rick Cir South Jordan UT 84095-4065 Office: West Jordan HS 8136 S 2700 W West Jordan UT 84088 Office Fax: 801-256-5670. Personal E-mail: gayebetenson@msn.com. Business E-Mail: gaye.betenson@jordan.k12.ut.us.

BETHEA, LOUISE HUFFMAN, allergist; b. Jackson, Miss., Mar. 27, 1947; d. Theodore G. and Frances (Allen) Huffman; m. Henry L. Bethea, Sept. 15, 1946; children: Mary, Samuel, Sarah. BS, Miss. Coll., Clinton, 1968; MD, U. Miss., 1972. Diplomate Am. Bd. Allergy and Immunology, Am. Bd. Pediatrics. Resident pediatrics U. Miss., Jackson, 1973-75; fellow allergy & immunology U. Fla., 1977-79; pvt. practice Houston, 1983—. Instr. pediatrics U. Miss., 1975-77, U. Fla., 1979-80; active Houston Northwest Med. Ctr., 1983—; cons. in field. Fellow Am. Acad. Allergy, Asthma and Immunology, Am. Coll. Allergy, Am. Acad. Pediatrics. Republican. Episcopalian. Avocations: photography, travel, arts and crafts. Home: 92 Hollymead Dr The Woodlands TX 77381-5121 Office: 17070 Red Oak Dr Ste 107 Houston TX 77090-2615 Office Phone: 281-580-6494.

BETHEL, COLIN ANTHONY IVAN, pediatric surgeon, educator; b. Nassau, Bahamas, Mar. 8, 1962; s. Peter Ivan Bethel and Jeanette Braithwaite. BA, Harvard Coll., 1983; MD, Columbia U., 1987. Diplomate Am. Bd. Surgery. Resident in surgery Yale Sch. Medicine, New Haven, 1987-95; rsch. fellow in pediat. surgery U. Calif., San Francisco, 1990-93; resident in pediat. surgery Ohio State U./Columbus (Ohio) Children's Hosp., 1995-97. Contbr. articles to profl. jours. Recipient Rsch. award Am. Acad. Pediats., 1992, Harold Hyam Wingate Found., 1990-92. Fellow ACS (assoc., rsch. scholar 1992-93); mem. Brit. Assn. Pediat. Surgery, Yale Surg. Soc. Office: N J Med Sch 90 Bergen St Newark NJ 07103-2425

BETHEL, DENISE, art appraiser; MA, Courtland Inst. Art, U. London. Dir., photography Rare-Book Auction House, 1980—90; with Sotheby's, NYC, 1990—, sr. v.p., dir., photographs. Lectr. in field. Contbr. articles to photography jours. Office: Sotheby's 1334 York Ave New York NY 10021 Office Phone: 212-894-1149. Office Fax: 212-894-1150. Business E-Mail: denise.bethel@sothebys.com.*

BETHEL, JOANN D., computer programmer, analyst; b. Ardmore, Okla., Nov. 20, 1956; d. Dorvin and Marian (McKinney) B. Student, U. Okla., 1998—; AS in Computer Sci., AS in Math., Oklahoma City C.C., 1999. Computer operator Security Nat. Bank and Trust, Norman, Okla., 1978-84, programmer, 1984-87, programmer analyst, 1987-90, tech. svc. officer, 1990-95; programmer analyst C-TEQ, Oklahoma City, 1995-2000, v.p., 2000-2001; programmer InterCept, Inc., Oklahoma City, 2001—. Okla. Coun. Tchrs. of Math. scholar, 1996. Mem.: Golden Key Honor Soc., Tau Beta Pi, Phi Theta Kappa. Home: 3915 Bellwood Dr Norman OK 73072-3622 E-mail: JDBethel@ix.netcom.com.

BETHEL, KATHLEEN EVONNE, librarian; b. Washington, Aug. 4, 1953; d. Frederick Errington and Helen Evonne (Roy) B. BA, Elmhurst Coll., Ill., 1975; MLS, Rosary Coll., River Forest, Ill., 1977, MA Northwestern U., 1989. Receptionist Newberry Library, Chgo., 1975-77; br. and reference librarian Maywood Pub. Library, Ill., 1977-78; asst. librarian Johnson Pub. Co., Chgo., 1978-81; librarian African-Am. studies Northwestern U., Evanston, Ill., 1982—. Trustee DuSable Mus. African Am. History, Chgo. Mem. ALA, NAACP, Black Caucus of ALA, Assn. for the Study of African Am. Life and History, Inc., Caribbean Studies Assn., Toni Morrison Soc., Alpha Gamma Phi. Office: Northwestern Univ Library 1970 Campus Dr Evanston IL 60208 Office Phone: 847-491-2173.

BETHEL, MARILYN JOYCE, librarian; b. Detroit, Jan. 14, 1935; d. Thomas Agmey and Mary Helen (Lisek) Hepfner; m. Herschel Earl Bethel, June 20, 1960 (div. Mar. 1969); 1 child, Mary Joyce. BA in Edn., Fla. Atlantic U., 1974; MLS, La. State U., 1975, MEd, 1976; postgrad., Fla. Atlantic U., 1977-78. Cert. reading specialist Fla. Cons. Fla. Diagnostic and Learning Resources, Ft. Lauderdale, 1979-80; libr. Cocnut Creek (Fla.) Elem. Sch., 1980-82; cons. Fla. Coll. Bus., Pompano, 1982-84; libr. Broward County Librs., Hallandale, Fla., 1983, cataloger Ft. Lauderdale, 1983-90, br. head Deerfield, 1990-92, libr. Pompano, 1992-95, Ft. Lauderdale, 1995-2000, ret., 2000. Cons. Fla. Diagnostic and Learning Resources, 1979-80; mem. behavioral objectives writing team Broward County Spl. Edn., 1981. Advisor to periodical Biography Today, 1992—; writer newsletter Exceptional Student, 1979-80. Vol. crisis counselor Sexual Assault Treatment Ctr., Broward County, Fla., 1977-78; lectr., instr. New Covenant Ch., Pompano, 1984-87. With USAF, 1954-55. Recipient Cert. of Appreciation, Bd. County Commrs., Ft. Lauderdale, 1978. Mem. ALA (com. for cataloging for children 1989-95, liaison Freedom to Read 1979-80), Fla. Libr. Assn., Broward County Libr. Assn., Nat. Alzheimers Assn. Republican. Presbyterian. Avocations: floral arranging, snorkeling, swimming, reading. Home: 272 NE 39th Ct Deerfield Beach FL 33064-3545

BETHELL, CHARLYN, music educator; b. Great Falls, Mont., May 12, 1951; d. Hoyt Cecil and Hester Rosetta Bethell; m. Guy Urban, Jan. 17, 1987; children: Cody Bethell Urban, Amy Katherine Urban. BA cum laude, We. Washington State U., 1973, EdB cum laude, 1974; diploma, Det Judsk Musikkonservatorium, Aarkus, Denmark, 1976; cert., Kodaly Ctr. Am., 1983; EdM, Cambridge Coll., 1991. Social worker Dept. Pub. Welfare, Boston, 1976—79; studio tchr. Brookline (Mass.) Music Sch., 1978—2000; music specialist Waldorf Sch., Lexington, Mass., 1983—87, Concord (Mass.) Pub. Sch., 1987—. Founding mem. New Art Winds, Newton, Mass., 1982—89; studio tchr. oboe Phillips Acad., Audover, Mass., 1995—; faculty methodology Kodaly Music Inst., Boston, 1998—; cons. Pro-Arte Chamber Orch., Cambridge, Mass., 1995—96. Chair religious edn. com. First Parish Watertown, Mass., 2003—. Mem.: Music Educators Nat. Conf., Internat. Double Reed Soc., Boston Area Kodaly Educators (pres.). Unitarian. Avocations: travel, guitar, cooking. Home: 1034 Belmont St Watertown MA 02472 Office: Willard Sch 185 Powder Mill Rd Concord MA 01742

BETHISHOU, ASHOOR, corporate financial executive; BS in Acctg., Calif. State U., 1990; MBA in Fin., Pepperdine U., 1997. CPA. Lead auditor, cost acct. LA Dept. Water & Power, 1990—98; CFO, COO Pronounced Tech., Reseda, Calif., 1990—2000; contr., sr. mgmt. team AdvanTel, Inc., San Jose, Calif., 2000—01; v.p. fin., CFO Younan Properties, Inc., LA, 2002—03; v.p. fin. Morrison Homes, 2004—. Home: 3135 Silver Oak Ct Turlock CA 95382

BETHKE, LOUISE VIRGINIA, music educator, writer; b. Neenah, Wis., Mar. 22, 1932; d. Herbert August and Sigrid Natalie Bethke. Diploma in Theology and Music, Patten U., 1957; student, U. Calif., Berkeley, 1958—60, Holy Names U., Oakland, Calif., 1978—81. Performer (piano/organ) Christian Cathedral, Oakland, 1954—82; music instr. Patten U., Oakland, 1955—81, Music Studio in Home, Oakland, 1982—. Composer: (complete Easter cantata words and music) Behold, The Lamb of God, author numerous poems. Named Honoree For Exceptional Achievement, Leadership & Svc., Patten U. Alumni Walk of Honor, 1997; recipient Talent award for organ, Patten Conservatory Music, 1957, Achievement award trophy, 1960. Mem.: Internat. Soc. Poets (life), Music Tchrs.' Assn. Calif. (life), Alumni Assn. Patten U. (life). Avocations: reading, writing, piano, organ, harp. Office Phone: 510-535-1790. Personal E-mail: lbethke@msn.com.

BETHMANN, LAURA, artist, writer; b. Jersey City, May 5, 1953; d. John Carlton and Marie (Liso) Donnelly; m. Christian Michael Bethmann, May 7, 1977; children: Kathryn Marie, Cara Lynn. Student, Middlesex County Coll., Edison, N.J., 1971-73, Rutgers U., 1975, Univ. Coll., Syracuse, N.Y., 1978, Pratt Inst., N.Y.C., 1979, Pa. Acad. Fine Art, Phila., 1980-81. Artist, 1982—; instr. art, 1985—; lectr., demonstrator, 1994—; writer Storey Publishing, Pownal, Vt., 1994—. Judge local and regional art exhibits. Author: Nature Printing with Herbs, Fruits and Flowers, 1996 (Benjamin Franklin award Pubs. Mktg. Assn. 1997). Mem. Nature Printing Soc. Achievements include master gardener. Office: Laura Bethmann Studios 110 Locust St Tuckerton NJ 08087-2836

BETHUNE, GORDON, airline executive; married; 3 children. BS, Abilene Christian U., Dallas; AMP, Harvard U., 1992. Lic. comml. pilot, lic. airframe and power plant mechanic. V.p. engring. and maintenance Braniff and Western Airlines; sr. v.p. ops. Piedmont Airlines; v.p., gen. mgr. Renton div. Boeing Comml. Airplane Group, 1988-94; chmn., CEO Continental Airlines, Inc., Houston, 1994—. Served with USN. Named Aerospace Laureate for comml. air transport Aviation Week & Space Technology, 1996. Office: Continental Airlines Inc 1600 Smith St Houston TX 77002-7362

BETT, ROBERT SCOTT, music educator; b. Kingman, Kans., Aug. 31, 1953; s. Robert Lawrence and Juanita Maxine Bett; m. Wendy Diane Wheaton, June 1, 1979; children: Jessica Lynn, Diana Rebecca. B in music edn., U. North Colo., 1975, M in music edn., 1981. Music educator Thornton Elem., Colo., 1975—79, Baseline Jr. High, Boulder, 1979—81, West Jefferson Jr High, 1983—84, West Arvlda H S, 1984—86, Mandalay Mid. Sch., Westminister, Colo., 1986—88, Moore Mid. Sch., Arvada, Colo., 1988—2005. Mid. level rep. Music Assn. of Jefferson County, 1984—86. Mem.: Am. Sch. Band Dir. Assn., Colo. Bandmasters Assn., Music Educators Nat. Conf., Phi Beta Mu. Avocations: golf, skiing, bicycling. Home: 8800 W 81st Dr Arvada CO 80005

BETTAC, ROBERT EDWARD, lawyer; b. Ashland, Ohio, Aug. 13, 1949; s. Donald Albert and Ruth Lavina (Foos) B.; m. Suzanne Lee Shepherd, June 30, 1979; children: Jacqueline Lee, Robert Mitchell. BA in Polit. Sci., Ashland U., 1972; JD, U. Cin., 1979. Bar: U.S. Dist. Ct. (we. and so. dists.) Tex. 1983, U.S. Dist. Ct. (no. dist.) Tex. 1989, U.S. Ct. Appeals (5th and 11th cirs.) 1981, U.S. Dist. Ct. (ea. dist.) Tex. 2001. Assoc. Foster & Assocs., Inc., San Antonio, 1979-84; ptnr. Foster, Bettac & Heller, P.C., San Antonio, 1984-89, Akin Gump Strauss Hauer & Feld, San Antonio, 1989—2003. Author: (with others) Texas Practice Guide, 2d ed., 1983. Mem. Witte Mus. Coun., San Antonio, 1984—, San Antonio Public Library Found. Bd., 2003—. Home: 126 Rosemary Ave San Antonio TX 78209-3841 Office: Ogletree Deakins Nash Smoak & Stewart 112 E Pecan St Ste 2600 San Antonio TX 78205 Office Phone: 210-354-1300. E-mail: bob.bettac@odnss.com.

BETTENHAUSEN, MATTHEW ROBERT, state official, lawyer; b. Joliet, Ill., Aug. 6, 1960; s. Robert Theodore and E. Colleen Bettenhausen. BS summa cum laude in Acctg., U. Ill., 1982, JD cum laude, 1985. Bar: Ill. 1985. Assoc. Sonnenschein, Carlin, Nath & Rosenthal, Chgo., 1985; law clk. to judge Chgo., 1985-87; asst. U.S. atty. U.S. Dept. Justice, Chgo.; dep. gov. Criminal Justice and Pub. Safety State of Ill., 2000—03; dir. state & territorial coordination US Dept. Homeland Security, Washington, 2003—05; dir. Office of Homeland Security State of Calif., 2005—. Dep. chief Criminal Receiving and Gen. Crimes Sects. U.S. Attys. Office, dep. chief Organized Crime and Drug Enforcement Task Force, acting chief appeals, assoc. chief entire criminal divsn.; adj. prof. adv. trial advocacy and evidence John Marshal Law Sch., Chgo.; lectr. in field. Bd. dirs. Bicentennial of Constl. Commn., Tinley Park, Ill., 1985—. Recipient Civic award, C. of C. Tinley Park, 1985, scholarship, Nat. Inst. Trial Advocacy, 1987. Office: State Capitol Bldg Sacramento CA 95814

BETTERIDGE, FRANCES CARPENTER, retired lawyer, mediator; b. Aug. 25, 1921; d. James Dunton and Emily (Atkinson) Carpenter; m. Albert Edwin Betteridge, Feb. 5, 1949 (div. 1975); children: Anne, Albert Edwin, James, Peter. AB, Mt. Holyoke Coll., 1942; JD, N.Y. Law Sch., 1978. Bar: Conn. 1979, Ariz. 1982. Technician in charge blood banks Roosevelt Hosp. and Mountainside Hosp., N.Y.C., Montclair, N.J., 1943-49; sub. tchr. Greenwich (Conn.) H.S., 1978-79; intern and asst. to labor contracts office Town of Greenwich, 1979-80; vol. referee Pima County Juvenile Ct., Tucson, 1981-85; sole practice immigration law Tucson, 1982-87; judge Pro Tempore Pima County Justice Cts., 1988-91. Commr. Juvenile Ct., Pima County Superior Ct., Tucson, 1985-87; hearing officer Small Claims Ct., Pima County Justice Cts., Tucson, 1982; mediator Family Crisis Svc., Tucson, 1982-85. vol. referee Pima County Superior Ct., 1981-85; lectr. Tucson Mus. Art, 1994— Pres. H.S. PTA, Greenwich, 1970, PTA Coun., 1971; mem. Greenwich Bd. Edn., 1971-76, sec. 1973-76; com. chmn. LWV Tucson, 1981, bd. dirs., 1984-85; bd. dirs., sec. Let The Sun Shine Inc., Tucson, 1981—; bd. dirs. Ariz. Sr. Acad., 2003–; medicare vol. Pima Coun. on Aging, 2003—. Mem. ABA, Conn. Bar Assn., Ariz. Bar Assn., Pima County Bar Assn., Tucson Sr. Acad., Point o'Woods Club. Republican. Avocations: imports folk art from Oaxaca, Mex, travel. Home and Office: 7659 S Vivaldi Ct Tucson AZ 85747 Personal E-mail: fmotz@aol.com.

BETTI, JOHN ANSO, federal official, retired automotive executive; b. Ottawa, Ill., Jan. 6, 1931; s. Louis and Ida (Dallari) B.; m. Joan Doyle, Aug. 22, 1953; children: Diane, Denise, Donna (dec.), Joan. BSMechE, Ill. Inst. Tech., 1952; MS in Engring., Chrysler Inst. Engring., 1954. Registered profl. engr., Mich. Student engr. to asst. chief engr. Chrysler Corp., 1952-62; with Ford Motor Co., 1962-89, from exec. engr. body engring. to v.p., gen. mgr. truck ops., 1962-76; v.p. product devel. Ford of Europe, Inc., Warley, England, 1976-79, also dir.; with N.Am. Automotive Ops., Dearborn, Mich., 1979-84, v.p. powertrain and chassis ops., 1979-83, v.p. mfg. and bus. devel., 1983-84; exec. v.p. tech. affairs and operating staffs Ford Motor Co., Mich., 1985—88, bd. dirs. fin. and exec. coms., 1985—89, exec. v.p. diversified products ops. Dearborn, Mich., 1988-89; undersecretary of def., acquisition and nat. armaments dir. Dept. Def., Washington, 1989-91. Instr. Lawrence Inst. Engring., Wayne State U., Detroit, 1953-59; chmn. bd. Ford Motor Co., Caribbean Inc., 1979-84, Ensite Ltd. Can., 1979-84, Ford Aerospace corp., 1988-89, Ford Electronics and Refrigeration Corp., 1988-89; dir. collins & Aikman Corp., 1991-94; mem. dir. compensation com. Breed Tech., 1992-94, Kaysor-Roth Corp., 1993-94. Bd. dirs. Mich. Opera Theatre, 1984-87; trustee Detroit Inst. for Children, 1985-89; mem. nat. adv. com. U. Mich. Engring. Sch., 1985-89; chmn. bd. trustees GMI Engring. and Mgmt. Inst., 1985-89. Recipient Alumni Profl. Achievement award Ill. Inst. Tech., 1980; John Morse Meml. scholar. Mem. Lost Tree Club (North Palm Beach, Fla.), Jupiter Hills Club (Tequesta, Fla.), Bloomfield Hills C.C., Tau Beta Pi, Pi Tau Sigma, Alpha Sigma Phi, Beta Omega Nu. Personal E-mail: jbetti@bellsouth.net.

BETTINGHAUS, ERWIN PAUL, research scientist; b. Peoria, Ill., Oct. 28, 1930; s. Erwin Paul and Paula (Bretscher) B.; m. Carole Irma Overmier, Apr. 5, 1952; children: Karen Lee, Joyce Anne, Bruce Alan. BA, U. Ill., 1952, PhD, 1959; MA, Bradley U., 1953. Instr. Mich. State U., East Lansing, 1958-60, asst. prof., 1960-64, assoc. prof., 1964-69, prof., 1969-97, prof. emeritus, 1997—, chmn. dept. comm., 1972-76, dean Coll. Comm. Arts and Scis., 1976-96, dean emeritus, 1997—; dep. dir. AMC Cancer Rsch. Ctr., Denver, 1997—2002; sr. scientist Cooper Inst., 2002—05, assoc. v.p., 2003—05; sr. scientist Klein Buendel, Inc., 2005—. Vis. prof. U. Okla., 1970-71 Author: The Nature of Proof, 1971, Persuasive Communication, 1994. Mem. Nat. Cancer Adv. Bd., 1988-94. With U.S. Army, 1953-56. Mem. AAAS, APA, Internat. Comm. Assn. (pres. 1982), Am. Comm. Assn., Assn. for Edn. in Journalism, Assn. Comm. Adminstrn. (pres. 1991). Home: 2170 S Parfet Dr Lakewood CO 80227-1900 Office: 1667 Cole Blvd Ste 225 Golden CO 80401 Office Phone: 303-565-4341. Business E-Mail: ebettinghaus@kleinbuendel.com.

BETTIS, JEROME ABRAM, professional football player; b. Detroit, Feb. 16, 1972; Student, U. Notre Dame. Running back L.A. Rams (moved to St. Louis 1995), 1993—94, St. Louis Rams, 1995, Pitts. Steelers, 1996—. Named NFL Rookie of Yr., Sporting News, 1993; named to Pro Bowl, 1993, 1994, 1996. Avocation: bowling. Office: 3400 S Water St Pittsburgh PA 15203-2349 Mailing: PO Box 6763 Pittsburgh PA 15212*

BETTISCH, JOHANN, linguist, researcher; b. Temeschburg, Romania, July 29, 1932; arrived in Germany, 1990; s. Matthias and Maria (Kanyady) B.; m. Katharina Reitter, Oct. 21, 1959; 1 child, Edmond. Diploma in Russian langs., U. Bucharest, 1957; D in Philology, U. Timisoara, Rumania, 1988. Electrotechnician Electromontaj, Timisoara, Romania, 1952-55; fgn. lang. tchr. German and Hungarian schs. Resita, Romania, 1957-63; sch. insp. County Caras-Severin, Resita, 1963-67; dep. dir. German H.S., Resita, 1967-74; fgn. lang. lectr. Engring Inst. (now named Eftimie Murgu U.), Resita, 1974-82, pro-dean, 1982-89; owner Trans. Bur., Stuttgart, Germany, 1990. Hon. prof. Internat. Albert Schweitzer U., Geneva. Author: Breviary of Chinese Literature, 1981, 2d edit., 2001, Technical English, 1983, Russian Language for Engineers, 1986, Die Technik auf Deutsch, 1988, Grimaces Behind the Mirror, 2000; co-editor: Lang., Lit. and Folklore, 1968—78, Kaffeepause, 2001, Das verbotene Grinsen, 2001, La mintea cocosului, 2002;: Philosophische Pillen, 2002, The Cultural Doctorate in Philosophy of Linguistics, 2002, Gedankensplitter, 2003, Kurze Erzählungen, 2003, Zu Zweit um die Welt, 2003, Geschichten aus der Wirklichkeit, 2003, Zwischen Sinn und Unsinn, 2003, Kurze Erzaehlungen, 2003, Der Junge, 2003, Quarzit, 2004, Pastillen, 2004, Bilder aus dem Alltag, 2004, others, Weisse Mause im Gurkenglas, 2004; translator: E. Gherasim's Pocketphilosophy, 2000, Bilder aus dem Alltag, 2004, Weisse Mäuse im Gurkenglas, 2004; co-editor: On the Typology of Linguistical Structures, 2005, Luftschlossruinen, 2005; contbr. over 150 articles to profl. jours. With Romanian mil., 1955-57. Recipient award County Caras-Severin Nat. Inventions Saloon, 1987. Mem. NY Acad. Scis., World Writers Assn. Avocations: etymology research, esperanto, science fiction. Home and Office: Engelberg St 42 70499 Stuttgart Germany Personal E-mail: jbettisch@aol.com.

BETTISON, CYNTHIA ANN, museum director, archaeologist; b. St. Louis, Sept. 8, 1958; d. William Leslie and Barbara Ann (Yunker) B. BA in Anthropology and Biology, Pitzer Coll., 1980; MA in Anthropology, Eastern N.Mex. U., 1983; ABD in Anthropology, U. Calif., Santa Barbara, 1986, PhD in Anthropology, 1998. Cert. profl. archaeologist Archaeol. Stds. Bd., 2004. Asst. curator dept. anthropology U. Calif., Santa Barbara, 1988-89, curator dept. anthropology, 1990-91; dir. Western N.Mex. U. Mus., Silver City, 1991—. Co-dir. Western N.Mex. U. Archaeol. Field Sch., 1992, 94, 95; lectr. Western N.Mex. U., 1992, 93, adj. asst. prof. dept. social scis., 1994—; various archaeol. positions, 1981—. Contbr. articles to profl. jours. Recipient Conservation Assessment Program grant, 1994-95, NEH, 1994; Gila Nat. Forest grantee, 1992, 94, 95, Silver City Lodgers Tax Bd. grantee, 1992, Andrew Isabell Meml. Fund grantee U. Calif., 1990, SIMSE grantee, 1994-95, 95-96. Mem. AAUW, Am. Assn. Mus., Am. Anthrop. Assn., Am. Soc. Conservation Archaeology, N.Mex. Mus. Assn. (pres. 2002-04), Soc. for Am. Archaeology, Archaeol. Soc. N.Mex., N.Mex. Archaeol. Coun. (sec. 1993-94), Coun. Mus. Anthropology (sec. 1992-94), Assn. of Coll. and Univ. Mus. and Galleries (bd. dirs. 2004—, sml. mus. adminstrn. com. bd. mem.)), Mountain Plains Mus. Assn., Univ. Women's Club, Univ. Club, Optimist Club (sec. Silver City chpt. 1992), Silver City Rotary Club (v.p. 1999-2000, pres. elect 2000-2001, pres. 2001-2002, dist. 5520 asst. gov. 2002-04), Silver City Grant County C. of C., Chpt. BR PEO, Phi Kappa Phi. Office: Western NM Univ Mus 1000 W College Ave Silver City NM 88061-4158 E-mail: bettisonc@wnmu.edu.

BETTLER, JANET LOUISE BELL, foreign language educator; b. New Castle, Ind., Apr. 14, 1940; d. Richard Mahlon and Eleanor Pauline (Kelsey) Bell; m. Alan Raymond Bettler, Aug. 16, 1964 (div. Jan. 1975); 1 child, William Robert. Student, U. de Grenoble, France, 1961; BA cum laude, Hanover Coll., 1962; MAT, Ind. U., 1964; postgrad., Sorbonne, 1966. Lic. secondary tchr. in English and French, Ind. Grad. asst., dept. of French Ind. Univ., Bloomington, Ind., 1962-64; tchr. Odon (Ind.) High Sch., 1964-65; lab. sch. instr., dept. of edn. Ind. Univ., Bloomington, 1965-66; tchr., dept. chair, coord. Fgn. Lang. in Elem. Schs. Greenfield (Ind.)-Cen. High Sch., 1974—; instr., remedial English, math, algebra Ind. Vocat. Tech. Inst., Indpls., 1988-91. Mem. task force French proficiencies, spl. cons. Dept. of Edn., State of Ind., Indpls., 1986-88, French textbook reviewer, 1990, French proficiencies tester, 1990—, fogn. lang. tchr. tng. cadre, 1994—. Co-author: (learning packets) Regional French Cuisine, 1977, The Opera "Carmen", 1977, Francophone Africa, 1984. Mem. Ethnic Hoosiers, Indpls., 1991. Recipient NEH grants Ind. Univ., Bloomington, 1964, Ohio State Univ., 1977, Purdue Univ., 1980; named Presbyn. Jr. Yr. Abroad, Presbyn. Ch., Grenoble, 1960-61. Mem. NEA, Am. Assn. Tchrs. French (past sec. Ind. chpt.), Ind. State Fgn. Lang. Tchrs. Assn. (nominating com.), Classroom Tchrs. Assn. (scholarship chair), Delta Kappa Gamma (past treas. local chpt.). Presbyterian. Methodist. Avocations: playing organ, conducting student tours ot europe, french cooking. Home: 336 Longfellow Ct Greenfield IN 46140-3136 Office: Greenfield-Cen High Sch 810 N Broadway St Greenfield IN 46140-1440

BETTMAN, GARY BRUCE, National Hockey League Commissioner; b. N.Y.C., June 2, 1952; s. Howard G. and Gretel J. (Pollack) B.; m. Michelle Weiner, Aug. 24, 1975; children: Lauren, Jordan, Brittany. BS, Cornell U., 1974; JD, NYU, 1977. Bar: N.Y. 1978, N.J. 1978, U.S. Dist. Ct. (so. and ea. dists.) N.Y. 1979. Assoc. Proskauer Rose, N.Y.C., 1977-80, Gutkin, Miller et al, Milburn, N.J., 1980-81; asst. gen. counsel NBA, N.Y.C., 1981-84, v.p., gen. counsel, 1984-89, sr. v.p., gen. counsel, 1989-93; commr. NHL, N.Y.C., 1993—. Mem. N.Y. State Bar Assn., Assn. of Bar of City of N.Y. (chmn. com. on sports law), N.J. Bar Assn., Sports Lawyers Assn. (bd. dirs. 1985-93, entertainment and sports law com. 1990-93), Phi Kappa Phi. Avocations: skiing, sailing, tennis. Office: NHL 47th Flr 1251 Ave of the Americas New York NY 10020

BETTMAN, JAMES ROSS, management educator; b. Laurinburg, N.C., Sept. 15, 1943; s. Roland David and Virginia Gertrude (Hare) B.; m. Joan Carol Scribner, Dec. 16, 1967; 1 child, David James. BA, Yale U., 1965, MPhil, PhD, Yale U., 1969. Prof. mgmt. Grad. Sch. Mgmt., UCLA, 1969-82; IBM rsch. prof. Fuqua Sch. Bus., Duke U., Durham, N.C., 1982-83, Burlington Industries prof., 1983—. Author: An Information Processing Theory of Consumer Choice, 1979, The Adaptive Decision Maker, 1993, Emotional Decisions: Tradeoff Difficulty and Coping in Consumer Choice, 2001; co-editor Jour. of Consumer Rsch., 1981-87, editor monographs, 2002--; contbr. chpts. to books, articles to profl. jours. Recipient Melamed prize for bus. rsch., 2000; named ISI HIghly Cited Rschr., Econs./Bus., 2003. Fellow APA, Am. Psychol. Soc.; mem. Assn. Consumer Rsch. (bd. dirs. 1976-79, pres. 1987, fellow in consumer behavior 1992), Inst. Ops. Rsch. and Mgmt. Sci., Am. Mktg. Assn. (Harold M. Maynard award 1979, Paul D. Converse award 1992, Irwin/McGraw-Hill Disting. Mktg. Educator award 2000). Democrat. Episcopalian. Home: 213 Huntington Dr Chapel Hill NC 27514-2419 Office: Duke U Fuqua Sch of Bus Durham NC 27708-0120 Office Phone: 919-660-7851. Business E-Mail: jrb12@mail.duke.edu.

BETTMANN, MICHAEL ALFRED, physician; b. N.Y.C., Nov. 4, 1943; s. Ernst Herbert and Hilda Irene (Kallberg) B.; m. Ellen Hofheimer, Mar. 18, 1967; children: William Henry, Joanna Ellen, Robert Ernst. AB, Dartmouth Coll., 1965; MD, Albert Einstein Coll. Medicine, 1969. Diplomate Nat. Bd. Med. Examiners, Am. Bd. Radiology. Intern in pediatrics Babies and Children's Hosp., U. Hosps. of Cleve., 1969-70; resident in diagnostic radiology Harvard Med. Sch., Boston, 1972-75; staff radiologist Beth Israel Hosp., Boston, 1975-76, New England Deaconess Hosp., Boston, 1976-77; radiologist Peter Bent Brigham Hosp., Boston, 1977-88; acting dir. cardiovascular and interventional radiology Brigham-Women's Hosp. (formerly Peter Bent Brigham Hosp.), 1985-88; radiologist and chief cardiovascular imaging The Univ. Hosp., Boston City Hosp., 1988-93; dir. radiology The Univ. Hosp., 1992-93; radiologist, chief cardiovascular and intervention radiology Dartmouth-Hitchcock Med. Ctr./Mary Hitchcock Meml. Hosp., Lebanon, N.H., 1993, also dir. radiology rsch. Prof. radiology Dartmouth Med. Sch., 1993, Boston U. Sch. Medicine, 1989; vis prof. Green Lane Hosp., Auckland, New Zealand, 1986, vis. scientist MRC Clin. Rsch. Ctr., Harrow, Middlesex, U.K.; assoc. prof. radiology Harvard Med. Sch., 1984-88, asst. prof., 1980-84, Peter Bent Brigham Hosp., Harvard Med. Sch., 1980-84, instr. radiology, 1975-76, 77-79, Beth Israel Hosp., 1975-76; lab. instr. biology Dartmouth Coll., Hanover, N.H., 1963-65; vis. prof. dept. radiology, Yale U., 1983; vis. prof. Royal Perth Hosp., St. Margaret's Hosp. for Children, We. Australia, 1984, Ottawa Gen. Hosp./Ottawa-Hull Radiological Soc., 1985, Dallhousie U., Victoria Gen. Hosp Halifax, Nova Scotia, 1986; vis. prof./cardiovascular radiologist Green Lane Hosp., Auckland, New Zealand, 1986, Yale U. Med. Sch., 1988, U. Leuven, Belgium, 1988, McGill U. Med. Sch., 1990, La. State U. Med. Sch., 1992, L.I. Jewish Hosp., 1992, Yale-New Haven Med. Ctr., 1993; mem. faculty Brigham and Women's Hosp./Harvard Med. Sch., 1987, Soc. Uroradiology, Vancouver, B.C., 1990; invited lectr. in field. Editl. bd. Jour. of Interventional Radiology, 1985—, Investigative Radiology, 1990-94, Jour. of Vascular and Interventional Radiology, 1990-92, Am. Jour. of Roentgenology, 1989—; reviewer New England Jour. of Medicine, 1982—, Chest, 1983—, Radiology, 1983—, Am. Jour. of Roentgenology, Investigative Radiology, JAMA, 1988—, Circulation, 1988—; editl. adv. bd. Diagnostic Imaging, 1984-94; assoc. editor Academic Radiology, 1995—; assoc. editor, reviewer Cardiovascular and Interventional Radiology, 1982-92; contbr. numerous articles to profl. jours. Picker scholar James F. Picker Found., 1978; prin. investigator rsch. grants, 1990—. Fellow Am. Coll. Radiology (com. contrast media 1989—, mem. learning file com., 1989), Am. Heart Assn. (cardiovascular rsch. study com. 1984, program moderator 1988, 89, exec. com. coun. on cardiovascular radiology 1990—, com. scientific sessions program 1990-93, vice chair coun. on cardiovascular radiology 1993-95, chair 1995—), Soc. of Cardiovascular and Interventional (chmn. rsch. divsn., mem. ann. meeting com. 1990-93, chmn. com. on contrast agts. 1990-92, fellowship com., scientific program com., exec. com. 1991-93, mem. other coms.); mem. Assn. of Univ. Radiologists, Am. Roentgen Ray Soc., Radiol. Soc. of N.Am., New England Soc. for Cardiovascular and Interventional Radiology (pres. 1983-84, mem. faculty annual course 1986). Avocations: gardening, jogging, skiing. Office: Dartmouth-Hitchcock Med Ctr Dept Radiology 1 Medical Center Dr Dept Lebanon NH 03756-0002

BETTS, BARBARA STOKE, artist, educator; b. Arlington, Mass., Apr. 19, 1924; d. Stuart and Barbara Lillian (Johnstone) Stoke; m. James William Betts, July 28, 1951; 1 child, Barbara Susan (dec.). BA, Mt. Holyoke Coll., 1946; MA, Columbia U., 1948. Cert. tchr. NY, Calif., Hawaii. Art tchr. Walton (N.Y.) Union Schs., 1947-48, Presidio Hill Sch., San Francisco, 1949-51; freelance artist San Francisco, 1951; art tchr. Honolulu Acad. Arts, summer 1952, 59, 63, 85, spring 61, 64; libr. aide art rm. Libr. of Hawaii, Honolulu, 1959; art tchr. Hanahauoli Sch., Honolulu, 1961-62, Hawaii State Dept. Edn., Honolulu, 1958-59, 64-84; owner Ho'olaule'a Designs, Honolulu, 1973—; art editor Scrapbook Press, 2002—, Portfolio Cons. of Hawaii, 1990—. Staff artist: The Arcadian newsletter, 2000—, James W. Betts & Co.; illustrator: Cathedral Cooks, 1964, In Due Season, 1986, From Nowhere To Somewhere On A Round Trip Ticket, 2003; exhibited in Hawaii Pavilion Expo '90, Osaka, Japan, State Found. Culture and Arts, group shows since 1964, one woman shows 1991, 96, 99; represented in Arts of Paradise Gallery, Waikiki, 1990-2001, Hale Ku'ai, a Hawaiian Coop., 1998-2001; traveling exhbns. include Pacific Prints, 1991, Printmaking East/West, 1993-95, Hawaii/Wis. Watercolor Show, 1993-94. Mem. Hawaii Watercolor Soc. (newsletter editor 1986-90), Nat. League Am. Pen Women (art chmn. 1990-92, sec. 1992-94, 2000-02, nat. miniature art shows 1991, 92, 93, 95), Honolulu Printmakers (dir. 1986, 87), Assn. Hawaii Artists, scholarship aid programs, Mount Holyoke Coll., Mary Lyon Soc., Rutgers Univ., Col. Henry Rutgers Soc. Republican. Episcopalian. Avocations: art, travel, writing, photography. Home: 1434 Punahou St #1028 Honolulu HI 96822-4740 Office Phone: 808-955-7817. Personal E-mail: kimorail@aol.com.

BETTS, BERT A., retired treasurer, accountant; b. San Diego, Aug. 16, 1923; s. Bert A. and Alma (Jorgenson) B.; m. Barbara Lang; children: Terry Lou, Linda Sue, Sara Ellen, Bert Alan, Randy Wayne, LeAnn, John Chauncey, Frederick P., Roby F., Bruce H. BBA, Calif. Western U., 1950. CPA, Calif. Accountant John R. Gillette, 1946-48; ptnr. Gillette & Betts, 1949-50; pvt. accounting practice, 1951-54; ptnr. Betts & Munden, Lemon Grove, Calif., 1954-57; sr. ptnr. Bert A. Betts & Co., 1958-59; treas. State of Calif., 1959-67; prin. Bert A. Betts & Assos., 1967-77. Chief exec. officer Internat. Prodn. Assocs., 1970-87; dir. Lifetime Communities Inc.; gen. partner Sacramento Met. Airport Properties 4, Ltd., 1970-2002. Author (with Barbara Lang Betts): A Citizen Answers. Mem. Lemon Grove Sch. Bd., 1954-57; Calif. chmn. Max Baer Heart Fund; state employees chmn. Am. Cancer Sco., 1962-64, bd. dirs. county br., 1963-69, Sacramento County campaign chmn., mem. exec. com., 1965, pres. Sacramento chpt., 1967-68; sponsor All Am. B-24 Liberator Collings Found. Served as 1st lt. USAAF, 1942-45. Decorated D.F.C., Air medal with four clusters; recipient Louisville award Municipal Finance Officers Assn. U.S. and Can., 1963; honored by Calif. Mcpl. Treas.'s Assn., 1964; inductee Hoover H.S. Hall of Fame, San Diego, 1998, Grossmont Health Dist. Gallery of Honor, 2002. Mem. Nat. Assn. State Auditors, Comptrs. and Treas's Mcpl. Forum N.Y., Calif. Soc. CPAs, San Diego Squadron Air Force Assn. (past vice comdr.), Am. Legion, 2d Air Div. Assn., 8th Air Force Hist. Soc., VFW, Commemorative Air Force (col.), Native Sons. Golden West, Internat. B-24 Liberator Club, Foresters, Lemon Grove Masonic Lodge, Calif. Scholarship Fedn. (life), DFC Soc., Sigma Phi Epsilon, Beta Alpha Psi (hon.), Alpha Kappa Psi (hon.). Clubs: Eagles; Men's (Lemon Grove) (pres.), Lions (Lemon Grove) (treas.); Commonwealth. Presbyterian. Home: 441 Sandburg Dr Sacramento CA 95819-2559 also: 1830 Avenida Del Mundo Coronado CA 92118-3018 Personal E-mail: blbbabbetts@earthlink.net.

BETTS, DIANNE CONNALLY, economist, educator; b. Tyler, Tex., Sept. 23, 1948; d. William Isaac and Martine (Underwood) Connally; m. Floyd Galloway Betts Jr., Feb. 14, 1973. BA in History, So. Meth. U., 1976, MA in History, 1980; MA in Econ., U. Chgo., 1986; PhD in Econ., U. Tex., 1991. Affiliated scholar Inst. for Rsch. on Women and Gender/Stanford U., 1993—; economist, tech. analyst, fin. cons. Smith Barney, Dallas, 1994—2000; economist, fin. cons. Morgan Keegan, Dallas, 2000—. Mem. women studies coun. So. Meth. U., 1993-94, Fulbright campus interviewing com. mem. 1992-93, pub. rels. and devel. liaison dept. econ., 1990-92, faculty mentor U. honors first year mentoring program, adj. asst. prof. dept. econ. and history, 1992—, vis. asst. prof. 1990-92; faculty, Oxford, summer 1991-93, adj. instr. dept. history, 1989-90, adj. instr. dept. econ., 1985-89, tchg. asst. dept. history, spring 1980; lectr. dept. polit. economy U. Tex., Dallas, summer 1988. Author: Crisis on the Rio Grande: Poverty, Unemployment, and Economic Development on the Texas-Mexico Border, 1994, Historical Perspectives on the American Economy: Selected Reading, 1995; contbr. articles to profl. jours. Rsch. Planning grant NSF, 1992; recipient Marguereta Deschner Teaching award, 1991; Humanities and Scis. Merit scholar, 1978. Mem. Am. Econ. Assn., Am. History Assn., Econ. History Assn., Cliometric Soc., Social Sci. History Assn., N.Am. Conf. on British Studies, Nat. Coun. for Rsch. on Women (affiliate), Omicron Delta Epsilon, Phi Alpha Theta. Home: 7802 Bryn Mawr Dallas TX 75225 Office: Morgan Keegan 5956 Sherry Ln # 2002 Dallas TX 75225-6531 Office Phone: 214-365-5525. E-mail: dcbetts@airmail.net.

BETTS, EDWARD, artist; b. Yonkers, N.Y., Aug. 4, 1920; s. Harrison and Mildred (Waterbury) B.; m. Jane Burke, June 2, 1949 (dec. 1984); children: Peter, John, Wendy; m. Edis Hatch, 1986. BA, Yale U., 1942; MFA, U. Ill., 1952. From instr. to prof. art U. Ill., 1949-84, prof. emeritus, 1984—; assoc. Ctr. for Advanced Study, 1968-69. Watercolor and acrylic painter, 1937—; one-man shows include Contemporary Arts Gallery, N.Y.C., 1953, 55, John Heller Gallery, 1956, 59, Charles Feingarten Gallery, Chgo., 1954, 56-57, Midtown Galleries, N.Y.C., 1961, 65, 68, 72, 76, 89, Krannert Art Mus., U. Ill., 1970; group shows include Corcoran biennial exhbns. Contemporary Am. Painting, 1947, 51, 55, 57, 59, Met. Mus. Am. Painting Today, 1950, Bklyn. Internat. Watercolor Exhbn., 1953, 55, 61, NAD, 1953—, Audubon Artists, Am. Water Color Soc., Calif. Water Color Soc., Bklyn. Mus., 1961, Pa. Acad., 1953-54, 59, 61, Nat. Inst. Arts and Letters, 1962, Water Color USA, Springfield (Mo.) Art Mus., 1963-64, 20th Am. Drawing Ann., Norfolk Mus. Arts and Scis., 1963, Hassam Purchase Fund Exhibit, 1961, 63, Maine 100 Artists of the 20th Century, Colby Coll., 1964; represented in permanent collections Fogg Art Mus., Upjohn Pharm. Co., La Jolla Art Ctr., Indpls. Mus. Art, Stephens Coll. (Mo.), Sandoz Pharm. Co., Atlanta U., St. Lawrence U., Irving Trust Co., N.Y.C., USIA Art in Embassies Program, New Britain Mus. Am. Art, Kans. State U., Rochester (N.Y.) Meml. Art Gallery, Springfield (Mo.) Art Mus., Davenport (Iowa) Mcpl. Gallery, Ball State U., Va. Mus. Fine Arts, Butler Inst. Am. Art, Calif. Watercolor Soc., Tupperware Internat., Orlando, Fla., 1st Nat. Bank Boston, Prudential Life Ins. Co., Newark, also pvt. collections; author: Master Class in Watercolor, 1975, Creative Landscape Painting, 1978, Creative Seascape Painting, 1981, Master Class in Watermedia, 1993. "Creative Lives: Four Maine Artists", Ogunquit Museum of American Art, 1996—. Recipient 1st prize oil painting Brick Store Mus. Exhbn., Kennebunk, Maine, 1949, Arts and Artists Miss. Exhbn., Davenport, Iowa, 1950; Grumbacher award Allied Artists, 1950, Bronze medal of honor, 1956; Audubon Artists award, 1951, 72, Gold medal of honor, 1952; Pennell medal Phila. Water Color Club, 1953, award Portland Mus. Summer Art Festival, 1957, Purchase award Hassam Fund Exhbn., 1966, Winsor and Newton award Ga. Water Color Soc., 1979. Mem. NAD (2d Altman prize 1954, Benjamin Altman prize 1957, 59, 66), Am. Water Color Soc. (Silver medal of honor 1953, 59, Remmey award 1966, Cooper award 1977), Art Students League, Ogunquit Art Assn. (past pres.), Nat. Acad. Design, Am. Watercolor Soc., Century Assn. N.Y.C. Home: 2 Wonderbrook Dr Kennebunk ME 04043-6738

BETTS, GARY B., music educator; MusB, U. Del., 1978; MusM, West Chester U., 1985. Cert. tchr. music K-12 Fla. Music educator Benjamin Sch., North Palm Beach, Fla., 1991—97, St. Paul Cath. Sch., St. Petersburg, Fla., 2001—. Office Phone: 727-823-6144.

BETTS, GENE M., telecommunications industry executive; BBA, MBA, U. Kans. CPA. Various positions in audit and tax depts. Arthur Young, 1975; ptnr. Arthur Young & Co.; asst. v.p. tax dept. Sprint Corp., Overland, Kans., 1987-88, v.p., 1988-90, sr. v.p. fin. svcs. and taxes, 1990-98, sr. v.p., treas., 1998—. Office: Sprint World Hdqrs 6200 Sprint Pkwy Overland Park KS 66251

BETTS, JAMES WILLIAM, JR., financial analyst, consultant; b. Oct. 11, 1923; s. James William and Cora Anna (Banta) B.; m. Barbara Stoke, July 28, 1951; 1 child, Barbara Susan (dec.). BA, Rutgers U., 1946; postgrad., New Sch. for Social Rsch., 1948—49; MA, U. Hawaii, 1957. With Dun & Bradstreet, Inc., 1946-86, svc. cons., 1963-64, reporting and svc. mgr., 1964-65, sr. fin. analyst Honolulu, 1965-86; owner Portfolio Cons. of Hawaii, 1979—. Cons. Saybrook Point Investments, Old Saybrook, Conn., 1979—; owner James W. Betts & Co., 1996—, Scrapbook Press, 2002—. Author: From Nowhere to Somewhere on a Round Trip Ticket, 2003; contbr. articles to mags. With AUS, 1943. Mem. Am. Econ. Assn., Nat. Assn. Bus. Economists, Western Econ. Assn., Atlantic Econ. Soc., Col. Henry Rutgers Soc., Internat. Inst. Forecasters, Transp. Rsch. Forum. Republican. Episcopalian. Home and Office: 1434 Punahou St #1028 Honolulu HI 96822-4740 Office Phone: 808-955-7817. Personal E-mail: kimorail@aol.com.

BETTS, JANET GNIADEK, lawyer; b. Chgo., Oct. 16, 1954; d. Henry M. and Betty Gniadek. BS in Dental Hygiene, Loyola U., Chgo., 1976; JD, Ill. Inst. Tech., Chgo., 1979; LLM in Taxation, Depaul U., Chgo., 1982. Bar: Ariz. 1980, U.S. Dist. Ct. Ariz. 1980, U.S. Tax Ct. Ariz. 1980, U.S. Ct. Appeals (9th cir.) Ariz. 1980. Assoc. Winston & Strawn, Phoenix, 1982-84, Streich, Lang, Weeks & Cardon, Phoenix, 1984-87; in-house counsel Brooker & Wake, Tempe, Ariz., 1987; ptnr. Gust Rosenfeld, Phoenix, 1987—99; of counsel Kutak Rock LLP, Omaha, 2000—04; mem. Jennings, Strouss & Solomon PLC, Phoenix, 2004—. Bd. dirs. Arrowhead Cmty. Bank. Past pres. ctrl div. Ariz. chpt. Am. Heart Assn., Phoenix, 1992-93, past chmn. bd. dirs. Ariz. chpt., 1994—95; bd. dirs. Ariz. Osteoporosis Coalition, Area Humane Soc., 1997-2003. Recipient Volunteer of the Year award, Amer. Heart Assn. (Ariz. affiliate), 1992-94, Fund-raising Event award, 1993-94, Devel. Chmn. award, 1992-93, Dir. Recognition award, 1991-92, Amer. Heart Assn. (Ctrl. divsn.), Polit. Excellence award, Ariz. Human Society, 2000, Mem. ABA, Ariz. Bar Assn., Maricopa County Bar Assn., Am. Heart Assn., Ariz. Humane Soc. (bd. dirs. 1997-2003). Republican. Avocations: hiking, mountain bike, golf. Office: Jennings Strouss & Salmon PLC 16427 N Scottsdale Rd #300 Scottsdale AZ 85254 Office Phone: 602-262-5927, 480-663-2162. E-mail: jbetts@jsslaw.com.

BETTS, JENNIFER LEAH, secondary school educator; b. Oneonta, N.Y., June 27, 1963; d. David Sheridan and Judith (Lewis) B.; m. Mark A. Farmer, 1998. Student, U. S.C., 1982; BA, Wells Coll., Aurora, N.Y., 1985; EdM, Harvard U., 1990. Cert. social studies tchr., N.Y. Tchr. Oneonta City Sch. Dist., 1986; tchr. history Averill Park (N.Y.) Sch. Dist., 1986-89; ednl. cons., 1990—; instr. SUNY, Oneonta, 1991; tchr. history The Galloway Sch., Atlanta, 1992-97, co-dir. The Galloway Acad., 1994-97; tchr. Atlanta Girls Sch., 2000—02; prin. lower and mid. schs. The Howard Sch., Atlanta, 2002—. Cons. Atlanta Girl's Sch., 1999-2000. Author: (activity series/curriculum) United States History Notes and Activity Series, 8 vols., 1990—. Mem. AAUW, Am. Hist. Assn., Internat. Assn. Study of Cooperation in Edn., Soc. for History Edn. Office: The Howard Sch 1246 Ponce de Leon Ave Atlanta GA 30306 E-mail: jenniferbetts@mindspring.com.

BETTS, REBECCA A., lawyer; b. Memphis, Nov. 25, 1951; BA, Dickinson Coll., 1972; JD, W.Va. U., 1976. Bar: W.Va., U.S. Dist. Ct. (so. dist.) W.Va. 1976, U.S. Ct. Appeals (4th cir.) 1978, U.S. Supreme Ct. 1984. Assoc. Spilman, Thomas, Battle & Klostermeyer, Charleston, W.Va., 1976—77; asst. U.S. atty. U.S. Atty.'s Office, 1977—81, chief civil divsn., 1979—81; founding ptnr. King, Betts & Allen, Charleston, W.Va.; U.S. atty. U.S. Dist. Ct. So. Dist., W.Va., 1994—2001; ptnr. Allen Guthrie McHugh & Thomas PLLC, 2001—. Adv. com. on rules & procedures 4th Cir., 1995—2001; civil justice reform act adv. com. So. Dist. W.Va., 1991, com. for local rules and subcom. on criminal rules, 92. Mem. editl. bd.: W.Va. Law Rev. Mem.: The Legal Aid Soc. of Charleston (bd. dirs.), W.Va. State Bar (past mem. com. on legal ethics), Order of Coif. Office: Allen Guthrie McHugh & Thomas PO Box 3394 Charleston WV 25333 Office Phone: 304-345-7250. Business E-Mail: rabetts@agmtlaw.com.

BETTS, RICHARD KEVIN, political science professor; b. Easton, Pa., Aug. 15, 1947; s. John Rickards and Cecelia Agnes (Fitzpatrick) B.; m. Adela Maria Bolet, July 25, 1987; children: Elena, Michael, Diego. BA, Harvard U., 1969, MA, 1971, PhD, 1975. Lectr. in government Harvard U., Cambridge, Mass., 1975-76, vis. prof., 1985-88; rsch. assoc. Brookings Instn., Washington, 1976-81, sr. fellow, 1981-90; dir. Saltzman Inst. War and Peace Studies, Columbia U., N.Y.C., 1997—, Shifrin prof. polit. sci., 1998—2002, Saltzman prof., 2002—; dir. nat. securities studies Coun. on Fgn. Rels., 1996-2000. Mem. staff Senate Select Com. on Intelligence, Washington, 1975-76, NSC, Washington, 1977; adj. prof. Johns Hopkins U., Washington, 1978-85, 88-90; cons. CIA, 1980-91, 93-99, 2003—; dir. ctrl. intelligence Nat. Security Adv. Panel, 1993-99; mem. Nat. Commn. on Terrorism, 1999-2000; occasion lectr. Nat. War Coll., Fgn. Svcs. Inst., U.S. Mil. Acad. Author: Soldiers, Statesmen and Cold War Crises, 1977 (2d edit. 1991, Lasswell award 1979), Surprise Attack, 1982, Nuclear Blackmail and Nuclear Balance, 1987, Military Readiness, 1995; co-author: The Irony of Vietnam, 1979 (Woodrow Wilson award 1980), Nonproliferation and U.S. Foreign Policy, 1980; editor: Cruise Missiles, 1981, Conflict After the Cold War, 1994, 2d edit., 2001, Paradoxes of Strategic Intelligence, 2003. Mem. foreign policy staff Mondale Presidential Campaign, Washington, 1984; mem. Assn. for Retarded Citizens, Bergen County, N.J., 1990—. Recipient Sumner prize Harvard U., 1976, Article award Nat. Intelligence Study Ctr., Washington, 1979, 81, Disting. Scholar award Internat. Studies Assn., 2005. Mem. Internat. Inst. for Strategic Studies, Am. Polit. Sci. Assn., Internat. Studies Assn. (Disting Scholar award 2005), Soc. for Historians Am. Fgn. Rels., Consortium for Study Intelligence. Democrat. Avocation: cinema history. Home: 1199 The Strand Teaneck NJ 07666-2020 Office: Columbia U Saltzman Inst War & Peace Studies 420 W 118th St New York NY 10027-7213

BETTY, CHARLES GARRY (GARRY BETTY), Internet company executive; BChemE, Ga. Inst. Tech., 1979. Joined IBM, 1980; sr. v.p. sales, mktg. and internat. ops. Hayes Microcomputer Products, 1984-89; pres., CEO Digital Comm. Assocs., Inc., 1990—96; pres., COO Earthlink Inc., Atlanta, 1996; CEO EarthLink Inc., Atlanta, 1996—. Chmn. Ga.'s High Tech Month, 1993; bd. dirs. DBT OnLine, allAutoRepair.com., Global Payments, Inc; mem. Ga. Tech Adv. Bd.; chmn. Physician's Data Corp. Bd. dirs. Carter Center Bd. of Councilors. Named Top 40 Under 40 list in Atlanta's bus. cmty., Outstanding Young Person, Atlanta Bus. Chronicle, Disting. Alumni award, Coll. Engr. Ga. Tech, 2000, Tech. Leadership award, Los Angeles C of C, 2001. Office: EarthLink Inc 1375 Peachtree St Atlanta GA 30309

BETZ, A. LORRIS, dean, educator, pediatrician, consultant; b. LaCrosse, Wis., Feb. 9, 1947; s. Alert L. and Charlotte M. (Kopp) B.; m. Ann C. Doyle, Aug. 30, 1968; children: Jennifer A., Bryan L. BS, U. Wis., 1969, MD., PhD, 1975. Intern pediatrics U. Calif., San Francisco, 1975, resident in pediatrics, 1975-79; asst. prof. pediatrics and neurology U. Mich., Ann Arbor, 1979-83, assoc. prof. pediatrics and neurology, 1983-87, prof. pediatrics, surgery, neurology, 1987—99, dir. neurosurg. rsch., surgery, 1987—99, assoc. dean for faculty affairs, 1993-97, interim dean Med. Sch., 1997—99; dean, sr. v.p. health sci. U. Utah Med. Sch., Salt Lake City, 1999—. Cons. NIH, Bethesda, Md., 1985—. Editorial bd.: Jour. Neurochemistry, 1986-94; contbr. articles to Sci., Brain Rsch., Sci. Am., Stroke, Am. Jour. Physiology. Grantee, NIH, Univ. Mich., 1980—; named Established Investigator, Am. Heart Assn., Univ. Mich., 1981. Mem. Internat. Soc. Cerebral Blood Flow and Metabolism (bd. dirs. 1991—, sec. 1995—), Internat. Soc. Neurochemistry, Am. Physiol. Soc., Soc. for Pediatric Rsch., Am. Pediatric Soc., Phi Beta Kappa, Sigma Xi, Alpha Omega Alpha. Achievements include research in basic mechanisms that are responsible for moving nutrients and electrolytes between the blood and the brain of mammals, processes that produce brain injury following a stroke. Office: Health Sci Ctr Moran Eye Ctrs Fl 5 50 N Med Dr Salt Lake City UT 84132-0001

BETZ, HANS DIETER, theology educator; b. Lemgo, Lippe, Germany, May 21, 1931; came to U.S., 1963, naturalized, 1973; s. Ludwig and Gertrude (Vietor) B.; m. Christel Hella Wagner, Nov. 10, 1958; children: Martin, Ludwig, Arnold. Student, Kirchliche Hochschule, Bethel, Fed. Republic Germany, 1951-52, U. Mainz, Fed. Republic Germany, 1952-55, 56-58, Westminster Coll, Cambridge, Eng., 1955-56; Doctor Theologiae, U. Mainz, Fed. Republic Germany, 1957; Habilitation, U. Mainz, 1966. Pastor Evangelical Ch., Rhineland, Fed. Republic Germany, 1961-63; from asst. prof. to prof. Sch. Theology, Claremont Grad. Sch., Calif., 1963-78; prof. N.T. and early Christian lit. U. Chgo., 1978-2000, Shailer Mathews prof., 1989—; prof. emeritus; chmn. dept. N.T. and early Christian lit. U. Chgo., 1985-94. Rsch. fellow Inst. Advanced Study, Hebrew U., Jerusalem, 1999. Author, editor numerous books and articles in German and English, 1959— Recipient Humboldt Rsch. prize, 1986; Lady Davis fellow Hebrew U., Jerusalem, Israel, 1990, Sackler scholar Tel Aviv U., 1995, McCarthy scholar Pontifical Biblical Inst., Rome, 2004; NEH rsch. grantee, 1970-83, Am. Assn. Theol. Schs. grantee, 1977, 84. Mem. Soc. Bibl. Lit. (pres. 1997), Studiorum Novi Testamenti Societas (pres. 1999-2000), Chgo. Soc. Bibl. Rsch. (pres. 1983-84). Office: U Chgo 1025 E 58th St Chicago IL 60637-1509

BETZ, HARLAN D., pastor, religious studies educator; b. Belle Plaine, Iowa, Oct. 21, 1947; s. Clegg and LauraBelle Betz; m. Sharon Ann Adams; children: Joshua Christopher, Sarah Christine Loeffler. BA in Classical Greek, U. Iowa, 1970; ThM in New Testament Lit. and Exegesis, Dallas Theol. Sem., 1974; PhD in Biblical studies, Cambridge Grad. Sch., 1998. Youth pastor Irving Bible Ch., Tex., 1972—76; ch. planting pastor LeMars Bible Ch., Iowa, 1976—82; pastor Lake Ray Hubbard Bible Ch., Rockwall, Tex., 1982—92; sr. pastor First Bapt. Ch., Spencer, Iowa, 1992—98, Kingwood Bible Ch., Tex., 1998—. Bible Conf. spkr. youth and family camps in Tex., Iowa, and Colo. Spkr.: cassette albums The Creation, The Fall, The Flood, The Secrets of Samuel, Elijah the Prophet, How to Respond When Life Is Not Fair, Shipping Out and Shaping Up, Talking With Our Father, Calvary's Major Figures, How to Have a Godly Marriage, Discovering His Call, How to Walk the Walk, How to Be Spirit-Filled, How to Win in Spiritual Warfare, and others; author: Setting the Stage for Eternity. Honored by George W. Bush as a Life Member of Rep. Nat. Com. Mem.: Ambassadors for Christ in Coll. (pres.), Nat. Honor Soc., Eta Sigma Phi. Avocations: hunting, golf, tennis. Home: 2711 Grove Manor Kingwood TX 77345

BETZ, JAMES EDMOND, lawyer; b. Fort Sill, Okla., Jan. 17, 1953; s. Chalres William Betz and Shirley Marion Barrett; m. JoAnn Mary Betz, Jan. 6, 1973 (div. Apr. 1995); 1 child, Amy JoAnn Varricka; m. Linda J. Lankow April 3, 2004. BSBA with distinction, U. Minn., 1975; JD, Hamline U., 1979. Bar: Minn. 1980, U.S. Dist. Ct. Minn. 1983. Ptnr. Markve, Anne-Markve & Betz, Mpls., 1976-82, Villaume & Betz, Mpls., 1982-83; pvt. practice Mpls., 1983-88, Anoka, Minn., 2001—; ptnr. Lange, Megarry & Betz, Bloomington, Minn., 1988-89, Dunkley, Bennett, Christensen & Madigan, P.A., Mpls., 1989—2001. Tchr., instr. Minn. Legal Asst. Inst., Minnetonka, 1986-91; adj. prof. Hamline U. Sch. of Law, St. Paul, 1988-90; mem. arbitrator panel Am. Arbitration Assn., Mpls., 1988—. Author: (with others) Minnesota Cause of Action Manual, 1993. Vol. atty. Chrysalis Ctr. for Women, Mpls., 1986—; vol. Habitat for Humanity, Mpls., 1991, Spl. Olympics, St. Paul, 1987-91. Mem. ATLA, Minn. Trial Lawyers Assn., Minn. Bar Assn., 18th Dist. Bar Assn., Anoka County Bar Assn., U. Minn. Alumni Assn., Hamline U. Alumni Assn. (pres. 1989-90). Avocations: golf, hiking, camping, skiing. Office: 2140 4th Ave N Anoka MN 55303 E-mail: jbetz@jamesbetz.com.

BETZ, JOHN WELLS, research scientist; b. 1954; m. Donna Kleppe; children: Christopher Stanley, Sharon Molly, Peter John, James Michael. BSEE, U. Rochester, 1976; M in Elec. and Computer Engring., Northeastern U., 1979, PhD in Elec. and Computer Engring., 1984. Engr., engring. mgr. RCA Automated Sys., Burlington, Mass., 1976—85; mem. tech. staff, sect. leader Analytic Scis. Corp., Reading, 1985—89; fellow MITRE Corp., Bedford, 1989—. Contbr. articles to profl. jours. Home: 536 Springs Rd Bedford MA 01730 Office: MITRE Corp 202 Burlington Rd Bedford MA 01730 Office Phone: 781-271-8755.

BETZER, SUSAN ELIZABETH BEERS, physician, geriatrician; b. Evanston, Ill., Aug. 24, 1943; d. Thomas Moulding and Mary Ella (Waidner) Beers; m. Peter Robin Betzer, June 18, 1965; children: Sarah Elizabeth, Katherine Hannah. AB in Biol. Scis. magna cum, Mount Holyoke Coll., 1965; PhD in Oceanography, U. R.I., 1972; MD, U. Miami, 1978. Diplomate Am. Bd. Family Practice, Am. Bd. Geriat. Rsch. assoc. dept. marine sci. U. South Fla., St. Petersburg, 1973-74, rsch. scholar, scientist, 1975-76; resident in family practice Bayfront Med. Ctr., St. Petersburg, 1978-81; pvt. practice St. Petersburg, 1982—; clin. asst. prof. dept. family medicine U. South Fla., Tampa, 1982—. Cons. physician Fed. Employee Health Clinic, Honolulu, 1981-82. Contbr. articles to profl. jours. Adv. com. St. Petersburg H.S., 1996-2002; bd. dirs. Fla. Orch., Tampa, 1983-86, 88-, pres., 1985-86, mem. exec. com., 1988-, vice-chair bd. trustees 1996-2002, sec., 2002-, founder, chair audience devel. com., St. Petersburg, 1990-94; bd. dirs. Suncoast Ctr. Cmty. Mental Health, St. Petersburg, 1992-93; trustee Bayfront Health Found., 1996-2004, chmn., 2001-03; trustee Bayfront Health Svcs., 1992-96, vice-chair, 1993-96; vol. physician St. Petersburg Free Clinic, 1979-. Named Woman of Distinction, Suncoast coun. Girl Scouts U.S., 1994; recipient Golden Baton award, St. Petersburg Fla. Orch. Guild, 1994, Chmns. award, Fla. Orch., 1997, Svc. award, Pinellas County Med. Soc., 1999, Philanthropy Vol. of Yr., Tampa Bay chpt. Assn. Fundraising Profls., 2003, Humanitarian Physician of Yr., Tampa Bay Area, Fla. Med. Bus., 2004. Mem.: Fla. Acad. Family Physicians (Dr. of the Day, Fla. Legislature 1995, 1996), Am. Med. Women's Assn., Am. Acad. Family Physicians (Mead Johnson award 1980), Mount Holyoke Alumnae Assn. (alumnae honor rsch. com. 1988—91, alumnae devel. com. 1996—2003, pres. 2003—, Alumnae medal of honor 2000), Phi Beta Kappa. Avocations: symphony, birding, cooking, reading. Home: 1830 7th St N Saint Petersburg FL 33704-3322 Office: 461 7th Ave S Saint Petersburg FL 33701-4818

BEUCHERT, EDWARD WILLIAM, lawyer; b. NYC, Feb. 13, 1937; s. August Vincent and Anna Beuchert; m. Elizabeth Sadowsky, Aug. 5, 1961; children: Edward, Jon, Philip, Suzanne, Alexandra. BA cum laude, Fordham U., 1958; JD cum laude, Harvard U., 1961. Bar: N.Y. 1962. Assoc., then ptnr. and counsel Seward & Kissel, N.Y.C., 1963-99. Bd. dirs. Cotswold Assn., Inc., 1977-85, 1996-2002, v.p. 1979-80, 98-99, pres., 1980-82. Contbr. articles to profl. jours. Bd. dirs. Edgemont Cmty. Coun., Inc., 1984-90, sec., 1984-86, v.p., 1987-90. 1st lt. U.S. Army, 1961-63. Recipient Silver Box award, Edgemont Cmty. Coun., 1998. Republican. Roman Catholic. Home: 53 Inverness Rd Scarsdale NY 10583-3525

BEUGEN, JOAN BETH, communications company executive; b. Mar. 9, 1943; d. Leslie and Janet (Glick) Caplan; m. Sheldon Howard Beugen, July 16, 1967. BS in Speech, Northwestern U., 1965. Founder, prin., pres. The Creative Establishment, Inc., Chgo., N.Y.C., San Francisco and L.A., 1969—87; founder, pres. Cresta Comm. Inc., Chgo., 1988—. Spkr. on entrepreneurship for women. Contbr. articles to profl. jours. Trustee Mt. Sinai Hosp. Med. Ctr.; del. White House Conf. on Small Bus., 1979; bd. dirs. Chgo. Network, Chgoland Enterprise Ctr., Girl Scouts Chgo. Named Entrepreneur of Yr., Women in Bus.; recipient YWCA Leadership award, 1985. Mem.: Overseas Edn. Fund Women in Bus. Com., Nat. Women's Forum, Com. of 200, Women in Film, Chgo. Film Coun., Chgo. Audio-Visual Prodrs. Assn., Midwest Soc. Profl. Cons., Chgo. Assn. Commerce and Industry, Ill. Women's Agenda, Nat. Assn. Women Bus. Owners (pres. Chgo. bhpt. 1979), Econ. Club Chgo. Office: The Cresta Group 1050 N State St Chicago IL 60610-7829

BEUGNOT, BERNARD ANDRE HENRI, literature educator; b. Paris, July 3, 1932; s. Raoul P.H. Beugnot; m. Brigitte L'Hermite, June 11, 1960; children: Marie-Christine, Nicolas, Sophie. Student, Ecole Normale Superieure, Paris, 1954; licence, U. Sorbonne, Paris, 1955, MA, 1956, PhD, 1969; agregation, U. France, Paris, 1958. Prof. Coll. Chartres, France, 1960-62; assoc. prof. French U. Montreal, Que., Can., 1962-69, prof. French lit., 1970—, chmn. French dept., 1965-69, 85-91, prof. emeritus French dept., 1997—. Mem. editing com. Can. Coun. Humanities, Ottawa, 1970-75, 78-81; editor: J.L.G. Balzac, Entretiens, 1972, F. Ponge, Oeuvres Completes, 2 vols., 1999-2002, 20 other books and over 120 articles on 17th-century and contemporary lit.; co-author (monograph) Boileau, 1973, Manuel Bibliographie, 1982. Lt. inf. French Army, 1958-60. Recipient Prix Halphen Acad. Francaise, 1974, Prize 2000 for Humanities, ACFAS, Ordre Nat. du Merite, Govt. France, 1977, Palmes Academiques, 1988, Ordre Nat. du Québec, 2003. Fellow Royal Soc. Can. Home: 4720 Grosvenor Montreal PQ Canada H3W 2L8 Fax: 514-481-1355. E-mail: beugnotmontreal@videotron.ca.

BEUHL, ANN MARIE, school librarian; b. Watertown, Wis., Mar. 2, 1952; d. Lawrence John Vogel and Marion Ann Hackbarth; m. Mark Alan Buehl, May 26, 1973. BS in Edn., U. Wis., 1974, MLS, 1978. Dir. sch. libr. media Parkview Jr./Sr. High Sch., Orfordville, Wis., 1974—; dir. dist. libr. media Parkview Sch. Dist., 1977—. Co-chair, chair Parkview Sch. Dist. Curriculum Coord. Coun., 1995—. Mem.: ASCD, ALA, NEA, Internat. Soc. Tech. Edn., Wis. Libr. Assn., Wos. Edn. Media Assn., Wis. Edn. Assn. Democrat. Avocations: reading, gardening. Office: Parkview Jr/Sr High Sch 106 W Church St Orfordville WI 53576

BEUKEMA, JOHN FREDERICK, lawyer; b. Alpena, Mich., Jan. 30, 1947; s. Christian F. and Margaret Elizabeth (Robertson) B.; m. Cynthia Ann Parke, May 25, 1974; children: Frederick Parke, David Christian. BA, Carleton Coll., 1968; JD, U. Minn., 1971. Bar: Minn. 1971, U.S. Ct. Mil. Appeals 1974, U.S. Dist. Ct. Minn. 1975, U.S. Ct. Appeals (8th cir.) 1981, U.S. Ct. Appeals (fed. cir.) 1984, U.S. Supreme Ct. 1988, U.S. Dist. Ct. (we. dist.) Wis. 1997, U.S. Ct. Appeals (9th cir.) 1999. Assoc. Faegre & Benson, Mpls., 1971, 75-79, ptnr., 1980—. Vestryman Cathedral Ch. St. Mark, Mpls., 1983-86, 2002-05; bd. dirs. Neighborhood Involvement Program, Mpls., 1986-90, pres., 1989-90; bd. dirs. Ronald McDonald House of Twin Cities, 1991-97, sec., 1995-97. Lt. JAGC, USNR, 1972-75. Mem. ABA, Minn. State Bar Assn., Hennepin County Bar Assn. Republican. Episcopalian. E-mail: jbeukema@faegre.com.

BEUMER, RICHARD EUGENE, retired engineering executive; b. St. Louis, Feb. 26, 1938; s. Eugene Henry and C. Florence (Braun) Beumer; m. Judith Louise Rockett, June 25, 1960; children: Kathryn, Karen, Mark. BSEE, Valparaiso U., 1959. Registered profl. engr., Mo., Ill., Ariz., Md., Okla., Ohio, Ga., Va., Mich., D.C., Mass., N.Y., N.C. With Sverdrup Corp. Cos., 1959—; v.p. Sverdrup & Parcel and Assocs., St. Louis, 1974—78; sr. v.p., exec. v.p., dir. Sverdrup & Parcel Assocs., St. Louis, 1979—81; pres. Sverdrup & Parcel Assos., St. Louis, 1982—85; sr. v.p. Sverdrup Corp., 1986—88, exec. v.p., 1989—92, pres., 1993; pres., CEO Sverdup Corp., 1994—95; chmn., CEO Sverdrup Corp., 1996—99; vice chmn. Jacobs Engring. Group, Inc., 1999—2003; ret., 2003. Vice-chmn. Thrivent Fin. for Luths., Valparaiso U. Chmn. St. Louis Regional Chamber and Growth Assn., 1998—99; divsn. chmn. United Way St. Louis, 1980; bd. dirs. Downtown St. Louis, Inc., 1982—91, Jr. Achievement, St. Louis Sci. Ctr.; past chmn. Luth. Med. Ctr., St. Louis; trustee, chmn. St. Louis Luth. High Schs. Recipient Disting. Alumni award, Valparaiso U., 1983. Mem.: NSPE, Mo. Soc. Profl. Engrs., Constrn. Industry Round Table (past chmn.), Design Profls. Coalition (past chmn.), Cons. Engrs. Coun. Mo. (pres. 1980), Am. Cons. Engrs. Coun. (nat. bd. dirs. 1979—82), St. Louis Elec. Bd. (pres. 1983), The Bogey Club, Old Warson Club, The Moles. Lutheran. Personal E-mail: rebeumer@att.net.

BEUOY, DAVID LEE, lawyer; b. Chgo., Dec. 16, 1949; s. Everett Marion and Patricia L. (Brown) B.; children: Michael David, Jonathan Dean. BA, U. Ala., 1974, JD, 1977. Bar: Ala. 1977, U.S. Dist. Ct. (no. dist.) Ala., U.S. Ct. Appeals (11th cir.) 1983. Pvt. practice, Russellville, Ala., 1977-86; ptnr. Burke & Beuoy, Arab, Ala., 1986—. With USAF, 1970-72. Office: 725 N Brindlee Mountain Pkwy Arab AL 35016-1056 Office Phone: 256-586-9000.

BEUOY, JEAN, portrait artist, educator; b. Seattle, Nov. 29, 1944; d. John Burdette Pratt and Esther Mary Hasper; m. James L. Beuoy Jr., Apr. 18, 1991; children: Collette M. Pratt, Yvette Pratt. Student, Otis Art Inst., 1972-73, Calif. State U., Long Beach, 1996; BA magna cum laude, Calif. State U., Dominguez Hills, 1996. Instr. Art Inst. L.A., 1997-99, Brooks Coll., Long Beach, 1999—. Exhbns. include sculpture in marble, alabaster and wood, drawings, oil paintings, watercolors, and mixed media at Angels Gate Cultural Ctr., L.A. Art Assn. Gallery, Gallery by the Sea, San Pedro, Calif., Calif. State U., Dominguez Hills The Art Inst. L.A., Westwood Art Assn. Gallery, Joslyn Ctr. Gallery, Torrance, Calif., Tishman Plz., Westwood, Tokai Bank, Playa Del Rey, Calif., among others. Vol. art instr. Rolling Hills (Calif.) Covenant Ch., 1996-97. Mem. Torrance Fine Arts Guild. Democrat. Avocations: designing furniture, gardening. Office: 4643 W 133d St Hawthorne CA 90250

BEUSCH, JOHN ULRICH, engineer, researcher; b. Erie, Pa., Apr. 22, 1938; s. Andrew and Ruth B. Beusch; m. Donna Marie Williams, Dec. 23, 1961; children: Cheryl Susan, Laura Kristine. *Grandfather and namesake, John Ulrich Beusch, of Buchs, Switzerland had his grandfather as namesake. This tradition has been repeated on alternate generations beginning in approximately 1700. Father Andrew (Andreas) came to the USA in 1926. Daughter Cheryl, MBA Columbia University, manages high-income investments for General Motors Asset Management. She has a daughter, Rory, and a son, Alec Washecka. Daughter Laura, MBA Wharton University of Pennsylvania, is vice-president of General Electric Commercial Finance and has two sons, Alton Leroy Miles IV and Ian Andreas Miles.* BS, Rochester (NY) Inst. Tech., 1961; MBA, Boston U., 1971; PhD, MIT, Cambridge, 1965. Staff, group leader, divsn. head MIT Lincoln Lab., Lexington, 1965—. Chair Stow (Mass.) Conservation Commn., 1974—80; trustee Randell Libr. Fund, Stow, 1980—86; pres., dir. Stow Conservation Trust, 1986—. Achievements include patents in field. Avocations: aerobics, exercise, carpentry. Home: 416 Taylor Rd Stow MA 01775 Office: MIT Lincoln Lab 244 Wood St Lexington MA 02420 Office Phone: 781-981-7908. Business E-Mail: beusch@ll.mit.edu.

BEUTEL, BILL, television news anchor; Grad., Dartmouth Coll. With various radio/tv stas.; with CBS Radio, N.Y.C., ABC Inc., 1962—; anchor, reporter Channel 7 Eyewitness News at 6 and 11 PM, N.Y.C.; bur. chief ABC News, 1968. Host A.M. America, 1975. Prodr. numerous documentaries such as the fall of the Berlin Wall and the integration of East and West Germany, the rise of Hitler and the origins of WW II and the Holocaust. Office: WABC TV ABC Inc Seven Lincoln Sq New York NY 10023-5998

BEUTHER, HENRIK GEORG, astrophysicist; b. Cologne, Germany, May 10, 1971; arrived in US, 2003; s. Henning and Rosmarie Hildegard (Behrmann) Beuther; m. Christina Jurgens Beuther, June 15, 2001; 1 child, Johann Christoph Henning. Diploma in physics, U. Cologne, Germany, 1999; PhD in physics, U. Bonn, Germany, 2002. Postdoc Mars-Planck-Inst. for R., Bonn, Germany, 2002—03, Harvard-Smithsonian Ctr., Cambridge, Mass., 2003—. Contbr. articles various profl. jours. Emmy-Noether fellow, Deutsche Forschungsq., 2003. Avocations: literature, running, tennis, theater. Home: 20 Foster St Arlington MA 02474 Office: Harvard Smithsonian Ctr for Astophysicists 60 Garden St Cambridge MA 02138 Office Phone: 617-476-7647. E-mail: hbeuther@cfa.harvard.edu.

BEUTLER, ARTHUR JULIUS, manufacturing executive; b. LaCrosse, Wis., Sept. 2, 1924; s. Arthur Julius and Augusta Henrietta (Dobe) B.; m. Carolee Yvonne Crawford, Dec. 28, 1952; 1 child, Karen Elizabeth. BSEE, U. Wis., 1948, Grad. in EE, 1968. Registered profl. engr., Wis. Trainee inventor program Gen. Electric Co., Schenectady, N.Y., 1948-51, devel. engr. Milw., 1951-59, project engr., 1959-61, sr. engr., 1961-64; chief engr. Dings Magnetic Separator Co., Milw., 1964-67; pres., owner Creative Engring. Assocs., Inc., Greendale, Wis., 1967-72, 88—; v.p. mfg. Gettys Mfg. Co., Racine, Wis., 1972-79, v.p. internat., 1979-81; v.p. tech. planning div. motion control div. Gould, Inc. (formerly Gettys Mfg. Co.), Racine, 1981-88. Cons. engr. mfg. control systems, robotics. Patentee elec. controls. Served with U.S. Army, 1943-46, PTO. Mem. IEEE (sr., chpt. chmn. 1969-72), NSPE, Soc. Mfg. Engrs. (cert.), Tau Beta Pi, Eta Kappa Nu.

BEUTLER, ERNEST, physician, research scientist; b. Berlin, Sept. 30, 1928; arrived in U.S., 1936, naturalized, 1943; s. Alfred David and Kaethe (Italiener) Beutler; m. Brondelle Fleisher, June 15, 1950; children: Steven Merrill, Earl Bryan, Bruce Alan, Deborah Ann. PhB, U. Chgo., 1946, BS, 1948, MD, 1950; PhD (hon.), Tel Aviv U., Israel, 1993. Cert. Am. Bd. Internal Medicine, 1958, in Hematology 1976. Intern U. Chgo. Clinics, 1950—51, resident in medicine, 1951—53; asst. prof. U. Chgo., 1956—59; chmn. divsn. medicine City of Hope Med. Ctr., L.A., 1959—78; chmn. dept. clin. rsch. The Scripps Rsch. Inst., La Jolla, Calif., 1978—82, chmn. dept. basic and clin. rsch., 1982—89, chmn. dept. molecular and exptl. medicine, 1989—. Clin. prof. medicine U. So. Calif., 1964—79, U. Calif., San Diego, 1979—; mem. hematology study sect. NIH, 1970—74, 1989—91, nat. heart, lung, and blood adv. coun. mem., 1994—97; Spinoza chair U. Amsterdam, 1991; mem. med. adv. com. Red Cross Blood Program, 1972—78; mem. adv. com. Blood Products FDA, 1984—88; chmn. sci. adv. com. Puget Sound Blood Ctr., Seattle, 1975—81; mem. sci. adv. coun. Cystic Fibrosis Found., 1976—78; mem. sci. bd. vis. Okla. Rsch. Found., 1980—84; chmn. sickle cell disease task force Nat. Heart, Lung and Blood Inst., NIH, 1990; mem. sci. adv. bd. Burnham Inst., La Jolla, Calif., 1996—, chmn., 1998—. Author: 8 books; contbr. numerous articles in med. jours.; mem. editl. bds. profl. jours.:. 1st lt. U.S. Army, 1953—55. Recipient Gairdner award, 1975, Blundell prize, 1985, Nat. Heart, Lung, and Blood Inst. Merit award, NIH, 1987, Nat. Acad. Clin. Biochemistry Lectureship award, Kodak Instruments, 1990, Mayo Soley award, Western Soc. Clin. Investigation, 1992, 5th ann. Excellence award, Gen. Clin. Rsch. Program, 1993, City of Medicine award, 1994, Outstanding Rsch. award, Am. Soc. Clin. Pathologists, 2000, Profl. Achievement citation, U. Chgo., 2003. Mem.: NAS, Inst. Medicine, Am. Soc. Human Genetics (mem. exec. com. 1968—72), Am. Soc. Hematology (mem. exec. com. 1968—72, v.p. 1977, pres. 1979, E. Donnall Thomas Lecture and Prize 2003, Thomas Medal and Lectureship 2003, Stratton Medal 1974), Western Assn. Physicians (pres. 1989), Am. Soc. Clin. Investigation, Assn. Am. Physicians, Am. Acad. Arts and Scis. Jewish. Achievements include invention of screening tests for galactosemia and other genetic disorders; co-discovery of glucose-6-phosphate dehydrogenase deficiency; origination of X inactivation hypothesis; research in glycolipid disorders; hemochromatosis. Avocation: music. Office: The Scripps Rsch Inst 10550 N Torrey Pines Rd La Jolla CA 92037-1000 Office Phone: 858-784-8040. E-mail: beutler@scripps.edu.

BEUTLER, FREDERICK JOSEPH, information scientist; b. Berlin, Oct. 3, 1926; came to U.S., 1936, naturalized, 1943; s. Alfred David and Kaethe (Italiener) B.; m. Suzanne Armstrong, Jan. 5, 1969; children— Arthur David, Kathryn Ruth, Michael Ernest. SB, MIT, 1949, SM, 1951; PhD, Calif. Inst. Tech., 1957. Faculty U. Mich., Ann Arbor, 1957—, prof. info. and control engring., 1963-90, prof. emeritus, 1990—, chmn. computer info. and control engring., 1970-71, 77-90, chmn. grad. elect. engring. systems program, 1985-90. Vis. prof. Calif. Inst. Tech., 1967-68; vis. scholar U. Calif. at Berkeley, 1964-65 Editorial cons. Math. Rev., 1965-67, 75-88; contbr. articles to profl. jours. and books. Bd. dirs. Ann Arbor Civic Theatre, 1976-78, 91-94. With AUS, 1945-46. NSF rsch. grantee, 1971-75, 76-81, 92-94, Air Force Office Sci. Rsch. grantee, 1970-74, 75-80; NASA grantee, 1959-69. Fellow IEEE (life); mem. Soc. Indsl. and Applied Math. (coun. 1969-74, mng. editor Jour. Applied Math. 1970-75, editor 1984-90, editor Rev. 1967-70), Am. Math. Soc., U. Mich. Retirees Assn. (bd. dirs., sec.-treas. 1994—), Barton Boat Club, Racquet Club of Ann Arbor, Rotary Club of Ann Arbor. Office: Elec Engr and Comp Sci Bldg Univ Michigan Ann Arbor MI 48109-2122 Business E-Mail: fjb@umich.edu.

BEUTLER, LARRY EDWARD, psychologist, educator; b. Logan, Utah, Feb. 14, 1941; s. Edward and Beulah (Andrus) B.; children: Jana, Kelly, Ian David, Gail. BS, Utah State U., 1965, MS, 1966; PhD, U. Nebr., 1970. Diplomate Am. Bd. Clin. Psychology. Asst. prof. psychology Duke U., Ashville, N.C., 1970-71; asst. prof. Stephen F. Austin State U., Nacogdoches, Tex., 1971-73; assoc. prof. Baylor Coll. Medicine, Houston, 1973-79; prof. U. Ariz., Tucson, 1979-90, U. Calif., Santa Barbara, 1990—2002, Pacific Grad. Sch. Psychology, Stanford U., Palo Alto, Calif., 2002—. Author: Eclectic Psychotherapy, 1983; co-author: Systematic Treatment Selection, 1990, Guidelines for the Systematic Treatment of the Depressed Patient, 2000, Integrative Assessment of Adult Personality, 2003, others; editor Jour. Cons. Clin. Psychology, 1990-96; editor Jour. Clin. Psychology, 1997—2004. Fellow APA (pres. divsn. psychotherapy, 1997, pres. divsn. clin. psychology, 2002), Am. Psychol. Soc.; mem. Soc. Psychotherapy Rsch. (pres. 1986-88). Home: 2620 Piedra Verde Ct Placerville CA 95667 Office: Pacific Grad Sch Psychology 935 E Meadow Palo Alto CA 94303 Business E-Mail: lbeutler@pgsp.edu.

BEUTLER, SUZANNE A., retired secondary school educator, artist; b. Cin., Oct. 23, 1930; d. Robert and Marguerite (Pierson) Armstrong; m. Frederick J. Beutler, Jan. 5, 1969; children: Richard and Mark Ireland. BA, U. Wis., 1954; MA, U. Mich., 1966, PhD, 1974, BFA, 2000. Cert. tchr. Middle sch. tchr. Ann Arbor (Mich.) Pub. Schs. Vis. lectr. U. Mich., Ann Arbor; adj. lectr. Eastern Mich. U., Ypsilanti. Author 3 manuals with Lang. Art Projects; contbr. articles to profl. jours.; developed writing program using personal classroom experiences. Recipient Tchr. Recognition award, 1986; grantee in field. Mem. Phi Delta Kappa (Svc. Key award 1992). Home: 1717 Shadford Rd Ann Arbor MI 48104-4543 Office Phone: 734-663-4870. E-mail: sbeutler@umich.edu.

BEUTTENMULLER, RUDOLF WILLIAM, lawyer; b. St. Louis, Dec. 20, 1953; s. Paul A. and Doris R. (Henle) B.; m. Ragina Lee Winters, July 14, 1984. AB cum laude, Princeton U., 1976; JD with distinction, Duke U., 1980. Bar: Tex. 1980, U.S. Dist. Ct. (no. dist.) Tex. 1980. Assoc. Jenkens & Gilchrist, Dallas, 1980-83; ptnr. Gregory, Self & Beuttenmuller, Dallas, 1983-88, Bradley, Bradley & Beuttenmuller, Irving, Tex., 1988-93; dir. Thomas Cinclair & Beuttenmullen, Dallas, 1994—. Articles editor Duke Law Jour., Durham, 1979-80. Mem. Rep. Nat. Com., Washington, 1984. Mem. ABA, Dallas Bar Assn., Duke Law Alumni Assn., Princeton Alumni Assn. Home: 4428 Irvin Simmons Dr Dallas TX 75229-4247 Office: 5335 Spring Valley Rd Dallas TX 75254-3009 Office Phone: 972-991-2121. Business E-Mail: rudybeutt@tcblawfirm.com.

BEVAN, ROBERT LEWIS, lawyer; b. Springfield, Mo., Mar. 23, 1928; s. Gene Walter and Blanche Omega (Woods) B.; m. Ronice Diane Gartin, Jan 25, 1977; children: Matthew Gene, Lisa Ann. AB, U. Mo., 1950; LLB, U. Kansas City, 1957. Bar: Mo. 1957, D.C. 1969. Adminstrv. asst. U.S. Senator T. Hennings Jr., Washington, 1957-60; legis. asst. U.S. Senator E.V. Long, Washington, 1960-69; sr. govt. relations counsel Am. Bankers Assn., Washington, 1970-84; ptnr. Hopkins & Sutter, Washington, 1984-95; of counsel Stinson, Mag and Fizzell, Kansas City, Mo., 1995-2001. Ghost author: The Intruders, 1967; contbg. editor U.S. Banker, 1985-88. Fieldman Dem. Nat. Com., 1968. Served with U.S. Army, 1946-47, 1951-53. Mem. ABA (bus. law sect., chmn. banking law com. 1988-92, commn. on IOLTA 1997-2000, co-chmn. joint banking com. 1999-2000), Echequer Club. Avocation: art and antiques. Office: Ste 301 4545 Wornall Rd Kansas City MO 64111

BEVAN, TIM, film producer; m. Joehy Richardson, 1992 (sep. 1997); 1 child, Daisy. Formed Working Title Films (with Eric Fellner) 1982-; Prodr. films (with Sarah Radclyffe) My Beautiful Laundrette, 1986, Sammy and Rosie Get Laid, 1987, Paperhouse, 1989; Personal Svcs., 1987, For Queen and Country, 1989, Dark Obsession, 1990, The Tall Guy, 1990, Chicago Joe and the Showgirl, 1990, London Kills Me, 1992, Rubin and Ed, 1992; (with Graham Bradstreet) A World Apart, 1988, Fools of Fortune, 1990; (with Carlos Davis and Anthony Fingleton) Drop Dead Fred, 1991, (with Paul Webster and Ronna B. Wallace) Bob Roberts, 1992; (with Eric fellner) French Kiss, 1995, Moonlight & Valentino, 1995, Bean, 1997, The Matchmaker, 1997, The Borrowers, 1997,The Hi-Lo Country, 1997, Elizabeth, 1998 (BAFTA Best British Film, ALFS awd., 1999), What Rats Won't Do, 1998, Plunkett & MacLeane, 1999; For TV Tales of the City, 1993, The Borrowers, 1993, More Tales of the City, 1998, High Fidelity, 2000, Bridget Jones Diary, 2001, Captain Corelli's Mandolin, 2001, 40 Days and 40 Nights, 2002, Ali G Indahouse, 2002, About A Boy, 2002, The Guru, 2002, Johnny English, 2003, Love Actually, 2003, The Calcium Kid, 2003; exec. prodr.: The Rachel Papers, 1989, Year of the Gun, 1991, A Kiss Before Dying, 1991, Posse, 1993, Romeo is Bleeding, 1993, The Hawk, 1993, Four Weddings and a Funeral, 1994, The Hudsucker Proxy, 1994, Panther, 1995, Dead Man Walking, 1995, Loch Ness, 1995, Fargo, 1996, The Big Lebowski, 1998, Notting Hill, 1999, O Brother, Where Art Thou?, 2000, The Man Who Cried, 2000, The Man Who Wasn't There, 2001, Long Time Dead, 2002, My Little Eye, 2002, Thirteen, 2003, The Shape of Things, 2003, Ned Kelly, 2003, The Italian Job, 2003; prodr. TV: Frankie's House, 1992, Underbelly (exec.), 1992. Recipient ShowEast's Kodak award for excellence in filmmaking (with Eric Fellner), 2003.

BEVAN, WILLIAM, retired foundation executive; b. Plains, Pa., May 16, 1922; s. William and Elizabeth Merle (Jones) B.; m. Dorothy Louise Chorpening, Feb. 17, 1945; children: William III, Mark Filbert, Philip Ross. AB with honors, Franklin and Marshall Coll., 1942, ScD, 1979; MA, Duke U., 1943, PhD, 1948, LLD, 1972; ScD, Fla. Atlantic U., 1968, Emory U., 1974, U. Md., 1981, Kans. State U., 1987; DHL, So. Ill. U., 1989. Instr. psychology Duke U., 1947, William Preston Few prof. psychology, 1974-92, prof. emeritus, 1992—, provost, 1979-83; instr., then asst. prof. psychology Heidelberg Coll., Tiffin, Ohio, 1946-48; mem. faculty Emory U., 1948-59, prof. psychology, 1958-59; prof. psychology, chmn. dept. Kans. State U., 1959-62, dean arts and scis., 1962-63, v.p. acad. affairs, 1963-66; fellow Center for Advanced Study Behavioral Scis., Stanford, Calif., 1965-66; sr. postdoctoral fellow NSF, 1965-66; v.p., provost Johns Hopkins U., Balt., 1966-70, prof. psychology, 1966-74; exec. officer AAAS, 1970-74, pub. Science, 1970-74; mem. adv. bd. Univ. Coll., U. Md., 1978-86; bd. govs. Research Triangle Inst., 1979-82; v.p John D. and Catherine T. MacArthur Found., Chgo., 1983-91, ret., 1991. Mem. adv. bd. Ctr. Advanced Study U. Va., 1976-89. Editorial adv. bd.: Am. Men and Women of Sci., 12th edit, 1972, Social Sci. Citations Index, 1972-77; contbr. articles to profl. jours. Trustee Human Resources Research Orgn., 1968-88, Franklin and Marshall Coll., 1971-76, Coll. Retirement Equity Fund, 1972-90, Ctr. for Creative Leadership, 1972-79, Biosis. Info. Svc., 1974-80, Am. Psychol. Found., 1970-77, 83-89, Assn. Advancement of Psychology, 1974-78, William T. Grant Found., 1977-90, HumRRO Internat. Inc., 1985-89, Jackson Meml. Lab., 1986-90. With USNR, 1944-70. Recipient Franklin & Marshall Coll. Disting. Alumni award, 1966, Duke U. Disting. Alumni award, 1997-98; Fulbright scholar U. Oslo (Norway), 1952-53. Fellow: AAAS, APA; mem.: Am. Psychol. Soc., Soc. Exptl. Psychologists, Am. Acad. Arts and Scis., History of Sci. Soc., So. Soc. Philosophy and Psychology, Psychonomic Soc., Inst. Medicine of Nat. Acad. Sci., Cosmos Club (Washington), Sigma Xi, Phi Beta Kappa. Home: Croasdaile Village 10 Boardman Ct Durham NC 27705

BEVAN, WILLIAM ARNOLD, JR., emergency physician; b. Sault St. Marie, Mich., June 23, 1943; s. William Arnold and Syneva Lois (Martin) B.; m. Martha Lynn Peterson, Dec. 29, 1973; children: Terry Eugene, Brian William, Patrick Jon. BS, U. Minn., 1966, MD, 1970. Diplomate Am. Bd. Family Practice, Am. Bd. Emergency Medicine. Intern U. Utah, 1970—71; family practitioner Vail Mountain Med. Profl. Corp., Vail, Colo., 1972—83; emergency physician Vail Valley Emergency Physicians, 1983—; dir. Vail Valley Med. Ctr., 1990—. Dir. Vail Valley Emergency Dept., 1992—, pres. med. staff, 1977; adviser Western Eagle County Ambulance Dist., 1983—. Trustee Shattuck St. Mary's Sch., Faribault, Minn., 1977—; football coach Battle Mountain H.S., Vail, 1978—; trustee, bd. dirs. Vail Christian H.S., 1998—, football coach; Eagle Scout. Named Man of Yr. Boy Scouts Am., 1966, 77. Fellow Am. Coll. Emergency Physicians; mem. AMA, Rocky Mountain Med. Soc., Colo. Med. Soc., U. Minn. Alumni Assn. (life). Republican. Lutheran. Home: 25 Cottonwood Rd Eagle CO 81631 Office: Vail Valley Emergency Dept 181 W Meadow Dr Vail CO 81657-5058 Mailing: Box 1143 Avon CO 81620 Office Phone: 970-476-8065.

BEVAN, WILLIAM CHARLES, systems analyst; b. Cheverly, MD, Mar. 26, 1957; s. William Charles and Jean Bevan. BA Polit. Sci., George Wash. U., 1979; MS Info. and Telecom., MS Systems Mgmt., Capitol Coll., 1997; MBA, George Mason U., 1998; PhD Candidate Info. Systems, U. of Md. Balt., 2000. Bus. mgr. McGraw-Hill Publications, Washington, 1987—88; dir. of fin. Club Managers Assn. of Am., Alexandria, Va., 1990—91; aviation, biometric and intelligent sys. analyst FBI, Washington, 1991—; CEO Aviation by Bevan & Browne, North Bethesda, 1995—. Cons. Ab3, North Bethesda, 1995—. Author: (book) Around the World Under the Sea, 2002 (Toastmasters Internat. Dist. 36 Disting. Svc., 2001). Pres. FBI toastmasters Toastmasters Internat., Washington, 1999—2001; pilot CAP, Frederick, 1999—2002; divsn. gov. Toastmasters Internat., Rockville, MD., 2001—02, area gov. Washington, 2000—01. Second lt. CAP USAF, 1999—2002, Maryland. Mem.: IEEE, Am. Assn. for Artificial Intelligence, Am. Radio Relay League. Avocations: golf, scuba diving, flying, tennis, rocketry. Office: Federal Bureau of Investigation 935 Penn Ave NW Washington MD 20535 Office Phone: 202-324-3000. Office Fax: 202-324-8826. Personal E-mail: wbevan@juno.com. Business E-Mail: wbevanjr@leo.gov.

BEVELACQUA, JOSEPH JOHN, physicist, researcher; b. Waynesburg, Pa., Mar. 17, 1949; s. Frank and Lucy Ann B.; m. Terry Sanders, Sept. 4, 1971; children: Anthony, Jeffrey, Megan, Peter, Michael, Karen. BS in Physics, Calif. State Coll., 1970; postgrad., U. Maine, 1970—72; MS in Physics, Fla. State U., 1974, PhD, 1976. Diplomate Am. Bd. Health Physics; cert. radiol. shield survey engr.; cert. health physicist (comprehensive and power reactors), sr. reactor operator cert. Teaching/rsch. asst. U. Maine, 1970-72; tchg. and rsch. asst. Fla. State U., 1973-76; rsch. asst. NSF, 1975-76, rsch. assoc., 1976; nuclear engr. Bettis Atomic Power Lab., West Mifflin, Pa., 1973, sr. nuclear engr., 1976-78; ops. rsch. analyst U.S. Dept. Energy, Oak Ridge, 1978-80, chief physicist advanced laser isotope separation program, 1980-83; sr. radiol. engr. GPU Nuclear Corp. (Three Mile Island Sta.-Unit 2), Middletown, Pa., 1983-84; Three Mile Island emergency preparedness mgr. GPU Nuclear Corp., Middletown, 1984-86, mgr. TMI-2 safety rev. group, 1986-89, dir. radiol. controls TMI-2, 1989; supt. health physics Point Beach Nuclear Power Plant Wis. Electric Co., Two Rivers, 1989-95; prodn. planning mgr. Point Beach Nuclear Plant, 1995—96; pres., CEO Bevelacqua Resources, Richland, Wash., 1993—; sr. radiol. controls tech. advisor USDOE-Office River Protection, Hanford, 1996—2005, acting dir. environ. divsn., 2000. Cons. U.S. Dept. Energy Process Evaluation Bd. of Isotope Separation, Washington, 1981-82; acting asst. mgr. environ., safety, health, and quality USDOE- Office River Protection, Hanford. Author: Contemporary Health Physics: Problems and Solutions, 1995, Basic Health Physics: Problems and Solutions, 1999, 20 health physics tng. manuals pub. by Bevelacqua Resources, 3 CD-ROMS for health physics tng.; contbr. articles to profl. jours. including Physical Rev. Letters and Physics Letters. Mem. Rep. Presdl. Task Force, Nat. Rep. Senatorial Com. Recipient Outstanding Performance award, Dept. of Energy, 1982, 1996—2004, Profl. Excellence award, U. Pa., 2000; grantee, USAF, NSF, Von Humboldt fellow, U. Hamburg. Mem. Am. Nuc. Soc. (Ea. Wash. chpt.), Am. Phys. Soc., Am. Acad. Health Physics (profl. devel. com. 1992-94, chmn. 1994, nom. com. 1994-96), Health Physics Soc., Susquehanna Valley Health Physics Soc. (mem. exec. com.), N.Y. Acad. Scis., Soc. Nuc. Medicine, Nuc. Utility Coordinating Group on Emergency Preparedness Implementation, Babcock and Wilcox Owners Group on Emergency Preparedness, Profl. Reactor Operators Soc., Health Physics Soc. (Columbia chpt., placement com. 1989-92, nominating com. 1994-97), Am. Bd. Health Physics (vice chmn. comprehensive panel of examiners 1990, chmn. 1991, nat. office mem.), U.S. Golf Assn., Tri Cities Ams. Ice Hockey Booster Club, Oak Ridge Sportsman's Club, Sigma Pi Sigma. Republican. Lutheran. Achievements include research in theoretical studies of light nuclei, few nucleon transfer reactions, radiation shielding, laser isotope separation, free electron lasers, neutron nuclei; symmetry violations in nuclei, grand unification theories, quark models of nuclear forces, neutrino interactions; nuclear fuel cycle, laser fusion and gravitational collapse of stars, beta dosimetry, internal dosimetry, health effects of ionizing radiation; nuclear reactor safety, accident analysis, fusion reactor safety, health physics at fusion reactors, radon health effects and mitigation, radioactive and mixed waste management; applied health physics, internal and external dosimetry, dark matter, strange matter, symmetry violations in nuclei, cosmology, radiation effects during low earth orbit, lunar missions; planetary missions, quantum field theory, astrophysics, supersymmetry, quantum gravity, string theory, twister theory, muon colliders, neutrino dose equivalents, genetic approaches for cancer research; heavy ion cancer therapy, therapy applications using microbeams and nanotechnology; quantum chromodynamics, differential geometry, general relativity, gravitation, neutrino physics, neutrino dosimetry; special relativity, standard model of particle physics and radiation induced immune system activation. Avocations: golf, ice hockey, lacrosse. Home and Office: Bevelacqua Resources 343 Adair Dr Richland WA 99352-8563 Personal E-mail: bevelresou@aol.com.

BEVER, CHRISTOPHER THEODORE, JR., neurologist; b. Washington, Apr. 10, 1949; s. Christopher Theodore and Josephine Jordan (Morton) B.; m. Patricia Ann Thomas, Sept. 23, 1978; children: Erica Jane, Theodore Louis, Katherine Meryl. AB, Washington U., 1971; MD with Distinction in Rsch., U. Rochester, 1975. Intern U. Cin., 1975-76; resident in internal medicine Rutgers Coll. Medicine and Dentistry N.J., Piscataway, 1976-77; resident in neurology Columbia-Presbyn. Med. Ctr., N.Y.C., 1977-80; vis. fellow Coll. Physicians and Surgeons Columbia U., N.Y.C., 1979-80; rsch. assoc. NIH, Bethesda, Md., 1980-82, sr. staff fellow, 1982-84; asst. prof. dept. neurology U. Tenn. Ctr. for Health Scis., Memphis, 1984-87; asst. prof. U. Md., Balt., 1987-92, assoc. prof., 1992-98, prof., 1998—. Vis. cons. dept. neurology Nat. Naval Med. Ctr., Bethesda, 1981-84; staff neurologist VA Med. Ctr., Memphis, 1984-87, Univ. Hosp. U. Tenn., 1984-87; cons. neurologist Bapt. Meml. Hosp., Memphis, 1986-87; staff neurologist VA Med. Ctr., Balt., 1987—, U. Md. Hosp., 1987—; co-dir. Mid South Multiple Sclerosis Clinic, Memphis, 1986-87; chief neurology svc. Dept. Vets. Affairs Med. Ctr., Balt., 1990—. Contbr. articles to profl. jours. and chpts. to books; ad hoc reviewer for numerous scientific jours. Fellow U. Rochester Alumni Assn., 1972, 73, NIH, 1979-80, Scottish Rite Com. on Rsch. in Schizophrenia, 1974. Fellow Am. Acad. Neurology; mem. AAAS, Md. Acad. Neurology, Soc. for Neurosci., Internat. Soc. for Interferon Rsch., Soc. for Neurochemistry, Am. Neurol. Assn. Office: U Md Hosp Dept Neurology 22 S Greene St #N4W46 Baltimore MD 21201-1544 E-mail: christopher.bever@med.va.gov.

BEVERIDGE, ANDREW ALAN, sociologist, educator, consultant; b. Madison, Wis., Apr. 27, 1945; s. Jacob Melvin and Bonnie Belle Beveridge; m. Fredrica Rudell, Apr. 17, 1970; 1 child, Sydney Jocelyn. BA, Yale U., 1967, MPhil, PhD, Yale U., 1973. From asst. to assoc. prof. sociology Columbia U., N.Y.C., 1973—81; from assoc. prof. to prof. sociology Queens Coll. and Grad Ctr. CUNY, N.Y.C., 1981—. Demographic and census cons. N.Y. Times, Newspaper Divsn., N.Y.C., 1993—; demographic litig. cons. in redistricting, housing and jury composition cases, 1993—; monthly demographic topic columnist Gotham Gazette, N.Y.C., 2001—. Author: African Businessmen and Development in Zambia, 1979; contbg. author: New York and Los Angeles: Politics, Society and Culture, A Comparative View, 1974—; contbr. articles to profl. jours. Trustee, pres. Yonkers (N.Y.) Sch. Bd., 1986—90; founding mem., v.p. Citizens and Neighbors Organized to Protect Yonkers, 1987—92; 2d v.p. Yonkers Dem. Party, 1991. Grantee, NSF, 1976—78, 2002—05, NEH, 1984—85, Robert Wood Johnson Found., 1994—2001, Ford Found., 2000—01; ACLS fellow, 1978—79, Regional Econ. History Rsch. Ctr. fellow, Hagley Found., 1978—79. Mem.: Am. Assn. Pub. Opinion Rsch., Ea. Sociol. Soc. (v.p. 1997—98), Social Sci. History Assn., Population Assn. Am., Am. Sociol. Assn. Democrat. Achievements include social explorer mapping and visual display system; patents pending for. Avocation: bicycling. Home: 50 Merriam Ave Bronxville NY 10708 Office: Queens Coll Sociology- 233 PH 65-30 Kissena Blvd Flushing NY 11367-1597 Office Phone: 718-997-2837. Business E-Mail: andrew.beveridge@qc.cuny.edu.

BEVERIDGE, CATHY JO, lawyer; b. Columbus, Ohio, July 29, 1965; d. George Fredrick and Dorothy Mae Beveridge. BA, U. Ga., 1986; JD, Emory U., 1989. Bar: Fla. 1989, cert.: labor and employment law. Shareholder, practice group leader Fowler White Boggs Banker, Tampa, Fla., 1989—. Contbr. articles to profl. jours. Mem. Leadership Tampa, 1999—2000; chair bd. dirs. Spring Tampa Bay, 2001—02; bd. dirs. Tampa Club, 2003—04. Named Employment Law and Upcoming Individual, Chambers USA Am. Leading Lawyers for Bus., 2005; named one of The Best Lawyers, 2005; recipient Fla. Trend Legal Elite, Fla. Mem.: Fla. Bar (sec., treas. labor and employment law sect. 1999—2000, CLE chair, labor, and employment law sect. 2001—02, chair, labor and employment law sect. 2003—04), Hillsborough County Bar (chair, labor and employment law sect. 1995—96). Office: Fowler White Boggs Banker 501 E Kennedy Bld Ste 1700 Tampa FL 33602 Office Phone: 813-228-7411. Office Fax: 813-229-8313. Business E-Mail: cbeveridge@fowlerwhite.com.

BEVERIDGE, CRAWFORD, information technology executive; BS in social sci., U. Edinburgh; MS indsl. adminstrn., U. Bradford. Human resources mgmt. positions Hewlett-Packard Co., Digital Equipment Corp., Analog Devices; v.p. corp. resources Sun Microsystems, 1985—91, exec. v.p. people and places and chief human resources officer Santa Clara, Calif., 2000—; CEO Scottish Enterprise, Scotland, 1991—2000. Bd. dir. Autodesk, Memec, Scottish Equity Ptnr., Ltd. Recipient comdr., Order of British Empire, 1995. Office: Sun Microsystems Inc 4150 Network Cir Santa Clara CA 95054 Office Phone: 800-555-9786. Office Fax: 650-960-1300, 408-276-3804.

BEVERIDGE, TERRANCE JAMES, microbiology educator, researcher; b. Toronto, Ont., Can., Apr. 29, 1945; s. Fredrick Charles and Doris Elizabeth (Hooks) B.; m. Janice Elizabeth Barnett, Sept. 9, 1970; children: Braden Charles, Jennifer Bree. BS, U. Toronto, 1968, Diploma in Bacteriology, 1969, MS, 1970; PhD, U. Western Ont., 1974. Rsch. assoc. U. Western Ont., London, 1975-78; from asst. prof. to assoc. prof. U. Guelph, Ont., 1978-86, prof., 1986—, Killam prof., 1995-97, Can. rsch. chair, 2002—. Vis. prof. Zentrum für Ultrastruckturforschung, Vienna, Austria, 1984, Biozentrum, Universität der Basel, Switzerland, 1987; dir. Nat. Scis. and Engring. Rsch. Coun. of Can. (NSERC) Gueiph Regional STEM Facility, 1980—. Editor: Metal Ions and Bacteria, 1989, Advances in Bacterial Paracrystalline Surface Layers, 1993; editor Can. Jour. Microbiology, 1982-88, Jour. Bacteriology, 1988-97, Biorecovery, 1987—, Internat. Jour. of Resource and Environ. Biotech., 1994—, Microbiology, 1997—, Arch. Microbiology, 1998—. Recipient Steacie prize, Nat. Sci. and Engring. Rsch. Coun. of Can., 1984, Can. Soc. Microbiology award, 1994, Sigma Xi award, 1994, Culling medal, 2001. Fellow Royal Soc. Can. (dir. life scis. 1992-95), Am. Acad. Microbiology, Austrian Acad. Sci.; mem. Can. Soc. Microbiologists, Microscopical Soc. Can., Am. Soc. Microbiology (divsnl. award 1984), Electron Microscopic Soc. Am., Nat. Centre Excellence, Can. Bacterial Disease Network, Can. Inst. Advanced Rsch. (assoc. 1988—). Avocations: hiking, cross country skiing. Office: U Guelph Coll Biol Scis Dept of Molecular and Cellular Biology Guelph ON Canada N1G 2W1 Office Phone: 519-824-4120 53366.

BEVERLEY, BARBARA SALLY, librarian, educator; b. Melrose, Mass., July 12, 1942; d. George Edward Blomgren and Dorothy Barbara (Protzman) Blomgren Pervere; m. John Alan Beverley, Mar. 26, 1966; children: Laurel Ann, Richard John. BA, Northeastern U., 1965, MA, 1968; MLS, SUNY, Albany, 1979. Cert. pub. libr., tchr. N.Y., Mass. Instr. Northeastern U., Boston, 1965—69, Endicott Jr. Coll., Beverly, Mass., 1969—70; tchr. Ysleta Ind. Sch. Dist., El Paso, Tex., 1967; libr. cons. Schenectady, 1980—86; libr. NY Dept. of State, 1980—81, NY State Divsn. Equalization and Assessment, Albany, 1982—88; dir. libr. svcs., records mgmt. officer Empire State Devel., Albany, 1988—. Mem. adj. faculty SUNY Albany Grad. Sch. Info. Sci. and Policy, 1990-2001; del. N.Y. State Gov.'s Conf. on Librs., Albany, 1990; mem. working group Capital Region Info. Sys., Albany, 1994. Contbr. articles to profl. jours.; author: Organizing the Special Library: Why and How, 1984, Computerized Services Available with a Microcomputer and Modem, 1991. Bd. dirs. Friends of N.Y. State Libr., 1996—99. Mem. Spl. Librs. Assn. (chmn. internat. rels., Upstate N.Y. chpt. 1993—; pres. 1989-90, bd. dirs. 1988-2002), N.Y. State Interagy. Info. Group (chmn. publs. 1993-2003, trustee 1989-92, chair 1987-88, bd. dirs. 1985-2002), N.Y. State Forum for Info. Resource Mgmt, Capital Dist. Bus. Librs. (pres. 1995-2002, planning com. 2002—), Hudson-Mohawk Libr. Assn., Spl. Librs. Assn., NY Libr. Assn., Capital Dist. Libr. Coun. (trustee 2001—), Beta Phi Nu. Avocations: horseback riding, travel, reading. Office: Empire State Devel 30 S Pearl St Albany NY 12245 Business E-Mail: bbeverley@empire.state.ny.us.

BEVERLEY, CORDIA LUVONNE, gastroenterologist; b. Jamaica, W.I., Oct. 19, 1950; d. Hurdley Aston and Joyce Ruby (Baker) Beverley. BA, Hunter Coll., 1971; MD, NYU, 1975. Diplomate Am. Bd. Gastroenterology, Am. Bd. Internal Medicine. Intern Columbia U., Harlem Hosp. Ctr., N.Y.C., 1975—76, resident in medicine, 1976—78; clin. fellow divsn. gastroenterology N.Y. Hosp./Cornell U. Med. Coll., 1979—82; asst. physician Rockefeller U. Hosp., 1978—81; pvt. practice gastroenterology, 1981—. Fellow Postdoctoral fellow, Nat. Inst. Alcohol Abuse and Alcoholism, 1980—82. Mem.: Women's Med. Assn. N.Y.C. Office: 1085 Park Ave New York NY 10128-1168 Home: Apt 29E 1365 York Ave New York NY 10021-4044 Office Phone: 212-876-1886.

BEVERLEY, JANE TAYLOR, artist; b. Columbus, Ohio, July 22, 1918; d. William Worland and Elsie Mary (Blum) Taylor; m. William Elmer Halley, Aug. 7, 1941 (dec. 1971); 1 Child, Hannah Jane Halley Denbow; m. George Treadgold Beverley, June 17, 1972 (dec. Dec. 1983); 1 stepson, George T. Beverley. BS in Social Adminstrn., Ohio State U., 1939. Statistician Ohio Dept. Pub. Welfare, Columbus, 1939-41; adminstrv. asst. Legis. Digest and Review, Columbus, 1954-71; custody mediator, court investigator Court of Domestic Relations, Columbus, 1971-86; freelance artist Columbus, 1986—. V.p. Ohio Correctional and Court Services 1980-82. Author: Report Ohio Sch. Survey Commission, 1955. Pres. Nat. Women's Party Ohio, 1956-60, Women's State Com. Ohio, 1961-62; mem. Ohio Sch. Survey Commn., 1953-55; mem. bd. rev. Bexley Movie; former trustee, mem. adminstrv. coun. Bexley United Meth. Ch., 1950; active Ameriflora, 1991-92; mem. sustaining bd. I Buckeye Boy's Ranch, 1991—; mem. crew II Am. Cancer Soc.-Bexley Thrift Shop, 1989-2002; sec. Children's Hosp. Mem. AAUW (hon. life), Bexley Woman's Club (pres. 1989-90), Mt. Carmel Aux., Ladies Oriental Shrine (class pres. 1983), Childhood League Bd. II, Bexeley Art League, Ohio State U. Assn. (life), Sigma Alpha Sigma (pres. 1938-39). Republican. Avocations: sewing, reading, gardening, bridge, swimming. Home and Office: 17 Coventry LN Athens OH 45701-3718

BEVERLIN, LANA SUE, art educator; b. Nowata, Okla., Apr. 8, 1951; d. Billie Brown and Mary Ruth (Runk) Veach; m. Lany G. Beverlin, Sept. 4, 1970; children: Laran Casey, Loren Cree. AA, NCMC Jr. Coll., 1977; BS in Edn., Truman U., 1979. Leather craftsman Veach Saddlery Co., Trenton, Mo.; educator art Harrison R-IV Sch., Gilman City; instr. art NCMC Jr. Coll., Trenton; educator art Trenton R-IX Schs. Mem. art adv. bd. Scholastic Arts Mag., NYC, 1996—2004. Mem.: NEA, Mo. Art Edn., Mo. Tchrs. Assn. (local pres., sec., treas. 1980—99). Avocations: drawing, reading, walking. Office: Trenton High Sch Okla Ave Trenton MO 64683

BEVERSDORF, DAVID QUENTIN, neurologist, researcher; b. Bloomington, Ind., May 28, 1965; s. Samuel Thomas and Norma (Beeson) B. BS, Ind. U., 1987; MD, Ind. U., Indpls., 1992. Med. resident Meth. Hosp. Ind., Indpls., 1992-93; neurology resident Dartmouth-Hitchcock Med. Ctr., Lebanon, N.H., 1993-96; behavioral neurology fellow U. Fla. Coll. Medicine, Gainesville, 1996-98; asst. prof. neurology Ohio State U. Med. Ctr., Columbus, 1998—. Contbr. articles to profl. jours. including Procs. Nat. Acad. Scis., Lancet, Neurology, Psychiatry Rsch.-Neuroimaging, Jour. Neurology, Neurosurgery and Psychiatry, and Physiology and Behavior. Rsch. grant Stallone Fund, L.A., 1994, grantee Nat. Inst. on Drug Abuse, 2002, Nat. Inst. Neurol. Diseases and Stroke, 2002. Mem. Internat. Neuropsychol. Soc., Am. Acad. Neurology, Cognitive Sci. Soc., Soc. for Neurosci., Cognitive Neurosci. Soc., Phi Beta Kappa. Office: Ohio State U Med Ctr Dept Neurology 1654 Upham Dr Columbus OH 43210-1250 Office Phone: 614-293-8531. Business E-Mail: beversdorf-1@medctr.osu.edu.

BEVIER, LILLIAN RIEMER, law educator; b. Washington, 1939; m. Michael BeVier; children: Nicholas, Eric, Miranda. BA, Smith Coll., Northampton, Mass., 1961; JD, Stanford U., 1965. Bar: Calif. 1966, Va. 1979. Asst. gen. sec. Stanford (Calif.) U., 1965-66, rsch. assoc., 1966-68; assoc. Spaeth, Blase, Valentine & Klein, 1968-70; now prof. law Henry L. and Grace Doherty Charitable Found. U. Va.; assoc. prof. U. Santa Clara Law Sch. Vis. scholar Nat. Constn. Ctr., Phila., 2003. Author: Campaign Finance 'Reform' Proposals: A First Amendment Analysis, 1997, Is Free TV for Federal Candidates Constitutional, 1998. Vice-chair Legal Svc. Corp, Washington, 2003—; mem. Bd. Martha Jefferson Health Svc. Corp.; currently vice-chair Piedmont CASA, Va. Mem.: Local Govt. Atty.'s Assn. Va., Federalist Soc. (nat. Bd. Visitors), Order of Coif (commr.), Raven Soc. Office: U Va Sch Law Charlottesville VA 22901 Office Phone: 434-924-3132. E-mail: lrb5s@virginia.edu.

BE VIER, WILLIAM A., retired religious studies educator; b. Springfield, Mo., July 31, 1927; s. Charles and Erma G. (Ritter) Be V.; m Jo Ann King, Aug. 11, 1949; children: Cynthia, Shirley. BA, Drury Coll., 1950; ThM, Dallas Theol. Sem., 1955, ThD, 1958; MA, So. Meth. U., 1960; EdD, ABD, Wayne State U., 1968. With Frisco Rlwy., 1943-45, 46-51, John E. Mitchell Co., Dallas, 1952-60; instr. Dallas Theol. Sem., 1958-59; prof. Detroit Bible Coll., 1960-74, registrar, 1962-66, dean, 1964-73, exec. v.p., 1967-74, acting pres., 1967-68; prof., dean edn., v.p. for acad. affairs Northwestern Coll., Roseville, Minn., 1974-81, prof., 1981-95, prof. emeritus, 1995—. Editor The Discerner. Bd. dirs. Religion Analysis Svc., Mpls., 1979-2004, pres., 1989-2004. With USMC, 1945-46, 50-51; ret. col. Army Res. Mem. Res. Officers Assn., Ind. Fund Chs. of Am. (nat. exec. com. 1991-94, v.p. 1993-94), Huguenot Hist. Soc., Bevier-Elting Family Assn., Phi Alpha Theta. E-mail: wabjab41@juno.com.

BEVILACQUA, EDDIE, forest biometrician, statistician; b. Toronto, Ont., Canada, Oct. 20, 1961; s. Mario and Colette Bevilacqua. PhD, U. Toronto. Lic. forester Ont. Profl. Foresters' Assn. Tutor forest mgmt. U. Toronto, 1990—95; asst. prof. SUNY, Coll. Environ. Sci. and Forestry, Syracuse, NY, 1998—2004, assoc. prof., 2004—. Cons. Eddie Bevilacqua and Assocs., Newmarket, Ont., 1988—98. Recipient Edward Elsworth Johnson Undergrad. Forestry scholarship, U. Toronto, Faculty of Forestry, 1983—84, R.W. Lyons Admissions scholarship, 1980—81, B. Harper Bull Conservation Fellowship award, Met. Toronto and Region Conservation Authority, 1983, Ont. Profl. Foresters Assn. prize, U. Toronto, Faculty of Forestry, 1984, U. Toronto Open fellowship, 1997—99, Postgraduate Rsch. award, Natural Scis. and Engring. Rsch. Coun. of Can., 1985, 1995—97, Faculty of Forestry Award for Tchg. Excellence, U. Toronto, Faculty of Forestry, 1993, 1995; scholar Postgraduate Rsch. award, Natural Scis. and Engring. Rsch. Coun. of Can., 1984. Mem.: Soc. of Am. Foresters, Can. Inst. of Forestry, Ont. Profl. Foresters' Assn. Office: SUNY Coll Environ Sci and Forestry 320 Bray Hall Syracuse NY 13210 Office Phone: 315-470-6697. E-mail: ebevilacqua@esf.edu.

BEVILACQUA, LOUIS J., lawyer; b. Boston, Dec. 21, 1948; BA, Coll. Holy Cross, 1970; MBA, NYU, 1977; JD, Fordham U., 1977. Bar: N.Y. 1977. Assoc. to ptnr. Sage Gray Todd & Sims, N.Y.C.; ptnr. Cadwalader, Wickersham & Taft, N.Y.C., 1987—, chmn. Corp. Mergers & Acquisitions Dept. & mem. mgmt. com. Mem. ABA, N.Y. County Lawyers Assn. Office: Cadwalader Wickersham & Taft LLP 1 World Fin Ctr New York NY 10281 Office Phone: 212-504-6057. Office Fax: 212-504-6666. Business E-Mail: louis.bevilacqua@cwt.com.

BEVILACQUA, MAURIZIO, member of Canadian parliament; b. Sulmona, Italy, June 1, 1960; m. Elena Cesaroni; 2 children. BA, York U., Toronto. Exec. asst. Members of Provincial and Federal Parliaments, Toronto, Ottawa, Can., 1982-88; mem. parliament Ho. of Commons, Ottawa, 1988—, chmn. standing com. on fin., 1997—2002, parliamentary sec. to the min. of labour (human resources develop.), 1993—95, parliamentary sec. to the min. of employment & immigration (human resources develop.), 1993—96, sec. of state sci., rsch. and develop., 2002, sec. state internat. fin. instns., 2002—03. Opposition critic for employment: youth and disabled, assoc. opposition critic for energy, mines and resources, 1988-90; mem. standing coms. on Energy, Mines and Resources; Labour, Employment and Immigration and Human Rights and Status of Disabled Persons, 1988-90; chair of standing com. on Human Resources Devel., 1995-97; chair standing com. on fin., 1997-2002. Co-founder Vaughn Comty. of Assns. to Restore Environ. Safety; past pres. Coun. York Student Fedn.; active on many local bds. and in local assns. Office: Can Ho of Commons Rm 540 N Ctr Block Ottawa ON Canada KIA0A6

BEVINGTON, DAVID MARTIN, English literature educator; b. N.Y.C., May 13, 1931; s. Merle Mowbray and Helen (Smith) B.; m. Margaret Bronson Brown, June 4, 1953; children: Stephen, Philip, Katharine, Sarah. BA, Harvard U., 1952, MA, 1957, PhD, 1959. Instr. English Harvard U., 1959-61; asst. prof. U. Va., 1961-65, asso. prof., 1965-66, prof., 1966-67; vis. prof. U. Chgo., 1967-68, prof., 1968—. Phyllis Fay Horton disting. svc. prof. in the humanities, 1985—. Vis. prof. N.Y. U. Summer Sch., 1963, Harvard U. Summer Sch., 1967, U. Hawaii Summer Sch., 1970, Northwestern U., 1974 Author: From Mankind to Marlowe, 1962, Tudor Drama and Politics, 1968, Action is Eloquence, Shakespeare's Language of Gesture, 1984, Shakespeare, 2002; editor: Medieval Drama, 1975, The Complete Works of Shakespeare, 5th edit., 2003, The Bantam Shakespeare, 1988, English Renaissance Drama: A Norton Anthology, 2002. Served with USN, 1952-55. Guggenheim fellow, 1964-65, 81-82; sr. fellow Southeastern Inst. Medieval and Renaissance Studies, summer 1975; sr. cons. and seminar leader Folger Inst. Renaissance and Eighteenth-Century Studies, 1976-77 Mem. MLA, AAUP, Renaissance Soc. Am., Shakespeare Assn. Am. (pres. 1976-77, 95-96), Am. Acad. Arts and Scis., Am. Philos. Soc. Office: Univ Chgo English Dept 5801 S Ellis Ave Chicago IL 60637-5418 Office Phone: 773-702-9899. Business E-Mail: bevi@uchicago.edu.

BEVINGTON, EDMUND MILTON, electrical machinery manufacturing company executive; b. Nashville, Oct. 31, 1928; s. John Laurence and Mary (Halloran) B.; m. Elizabeth Anne Rickey, Sept. 8, 1951 (dec. June 1962); children: Milton, Rickey, Peter (dec.); m. Paula Maureen Lawton, Apr. 24, 1965; children: George, Mary-Laurence, Christian, Charles, Justin. Grad., Canterbury Sch., 1945; S.B. in Chem. Engring. Mass. Inst. Tech., 1949; MBA, Harvard, 1951. Plant supr. Dewey & Almy Chem. Co. (name changed to W.R. Grace Co., 1954), Cambridge, Mass., 1951-54, marketing research mgr., 1954-56; merchandising mgr. Westinghouse Electric Co., Staunton, Va., 1956-58, So. zone sales mgr. Atlanta, 1958-59; with The Trane Co., Atlanta and LaCrosse, Wis., 1959—, v.p., gen. mgr. consumer products div., 1969-70, exec. v.p., 1970-73; chmn., pres. Servidyne Systems, Inc., Atlanta, 1974—2002, Bevington & Co., Atlanta, 2002—. Bd. dirs. AAA South. Mem. corp. devel. com. MIT, 1978—, bd. dirs. MIT Corp., 1985-91; chmn. Ga. Conservancy, 1989-92, bd. dirs.; bd. dirs. Atlanta coun. Boy Scouts Am., also v.p., 1989-90, pres., 1990-92; bd. dirs. So. region Boy Scouts Am.; pres. Metro Group, 1992-97; bd. dirs. Ga. Dept. Cmty. Affairs, 1988-92; bd. dirs. Flannery O'Connor-Andalusia Found, 2002. Mem. Pres.' Cir. of NAS, MIT Alumni Assn. (v.p. 1983-85, pres. 1985-86), Ga. Alliance Sci. Edn. (founder 2004), Harvard Club, (NYC and Boston), Piedmont Driving Club (Atlanta), Tau Beta Pi, Sigma Alpha Epsilon.

BEVIS, ROBERT E., retired oil industry executive; b. N.Y.C. Attended in Bus. Adminstrn., NYU, 1936—42. Various sales positions with S.O. Co. of NJ and NY, 1937—47; various positions with Esso Std. Oil Co. S.A., 1953—54; former pres. Esso Std. Oil Co., San Juan, 1955; v.p., dir. Esso West Africa, Lagos, Nigeria, 1957—59; mktg. coord. for Africa, Mid. East, Spain and Portugal Esso Std. Mediterranean Inc., Geneva, 1961; acting div. mgr. Esso Std. Mediterranean Inc. Libya Div. of Std. (Near East), Inc., 1963; mktg. mgr. Esso Std. Near East, Tripoli, Libya, 1968-91; mgr. Exxon Co. U.S.A., Balt.; ret. Exxon Corp., 1970. Cons. NASA. Lt. Commander (Naval Aviator) USN, 1942—45, positions/special intelligence assignments with USN, 1945—53, ret. USN, 1957. Address: 310 Five Farms Ln Lutherville Timonium MD 21093

BEWKES, EUGENE GARRETT, JR., investment company executive, consultant; b. Norwood, Mass., Sept. 28, 1926; s. Eugene Garrett and Helen (Van Vlaanderen) B.; m. Marjorie Louise Klenk, Aug. 20, 1949; children: Eugene Garrett III, Jeffrey Lawrence, Robert David. BA, Colgate U., 1948; JD, Yale U., 1951; LLD, Colgate U., 1991. Bar: N.Y. 1952. With firm Chapman, Bryson, Walsh & O'Connell, N.Y.C., 1951-55; atty.-adviser also asst. Office Sec. USAF, 1955-57; with Am. Mgmt. Assn., 1957-61, gen. mgmt. div., mgr., 1959-61; gen. counsel, sec., asst. v.p. Reuben H. Donnelley Corp, 1961-67; v.p. law and adminstrn., sec. Canada Dry Corp., 1967-68; v.p. Norton Simon, Inc., N.Y.C., 1968-72, sr. v.p., 1972-73, exec. v.p., 1973-77, vice chmn. bd., 1977-81; chmn., pres., chief exec. officer Am. Bakeries Co., 1982-88; cons. Paine Webber Group, Inc., N.Y.C., 1988—2003. Chmn. emeritus bd. trustees Colgate U., Hamilton, N.Y. With USNR, 1945-46. Mem. Yale Club (N.Y.C.), Johns Island Club, Redstick Golf Club, Sankaty Club Nantucket, Phi Beta Kappa, Delta Kappa Epsilon, Phi Delta Phi. Home: PO Box 8307 Vero Beach FL 32963-8307 Office: Lightyear Capital 23d Fl 51 W 52d St New York NY 10019-6096

BEWKES, JEFFREY L., television broadcasting company executive; BA, Yale U.; MBA, Stanford U., 1977. Ops. dir. Sonoma Vineyards, Inc., Healdsburg, Calif.; acct. officer Citibank, NA, NYC; exec. v.p., CFO Home Box Office, N.Y.C., 1987—91, pres., COO, 1991—95, chmn., CEO, 1995—2002; chmn. entertainment. & networks group. Time Warner Inc., N.Y.C., 2002—. Mem. adv. coun. Yale U., Stanford U. Grad. Sch. of Bus., Am. Mus. Nat. Hist. Office: Time Warner Inc 75 Rockefeller Plz New York NY 10019*

BEWLEY, JOHN DEREK, botany researcher, educator; b. Preston, Lancashire, Eng., Dec. 11, 1943; s. Clifford and Marion (Garner) B.; m. Christine E. Nee Kite, Sept. 3, 1966; children: Alexander, Janette Louise. BSc, U. London, 1965, PhD, 1968, DSc, 1983. Asst. prof. U. Calgary, Alta., 1970-73, assoc. prof., 1973-77, prof. biology, 1977-85; prof., chmn. dept. botany U. Guelph, Ont., 1985-90, prof. botany, 1990—2005, Univ. prof. emeritus, 2005—, dir. plant biol. program, 1993-94. E.W.R. Steacie Meml. fellow in natural scis. and engring. Rsch. Coun. Can., 1979-81; recipient Career Rsch. Excellence award Sigma Xi, 1993, Disting. Biologist award Can. Coun. Univ. Chairs, 1994; named Highly Cited Author, ISI, 2002. Fellow Royal Soc. Can. (rapporteur plant biology div. 1984-85, convenor 1985-87); mem. Can. Soc. Plant Physiologists (C.D. Nelson award 1978, Gold medal 1992, sec. 1983-85, v.p. 1987-88, pres. 1988-90), Natural Scis. and Engring. Rsch. Coun. Can. (chmn. plant biology grant selection com. 1988-90), Internat. Soc. Seed Sci. (pres. 2005—). Home: 26 Waverley Dr Guelph ON Canada N1E 6C8 Office: U Guelph Axelrod Bldg Dept Molecular andCellular Biology Guelph ON Canada N1G 2W1 Office Phone: 519-824-4120 54451. E-mail: dbewley@uoguelph.ca.

BEXTERMILLER, THERESA MARIE See METZGER, THERESA

BEY, JOAN S., retired public information officer; b. Boston, Ind., Nov. 30, 1927; d. Frank J. Schoemaker and Lestra J. (Turner) Schoemaker/Kelly; m. John J. Bey, May 8, 1954 (dec. June 1968); children: Anna Marie Bey Witt, Joseph M., John C. BA, St. Mary of the Woods Coll., 1949. Reporter, food editor Indpls. Times, 1950-58; freelance pub. rels. profl., cons. Indpls., 1971-90; with pub. info. dept. Ivy Tech. State Coll., Indpls., 1983-97, ret., 1997. Recipient Vesta award Am. Meat Inst., 1952. Mem. Nat. Fedn. Press Women (writing awards 1980s, 90s), Woman's Press Club Ind. (historian 1984—2005, pres. 1982-84, Kate Milner Rabb award 1986), Soc. Ind. Pioneers, Ind. Hist. Soc. Roman Catholic.

BEYER, AARON JAY, lawyer; b. Plainfield, N.J., Mar. 26, 1946; s. Solomon and Pearl (Lieberman) B.; m. Francine Simmons, Apr. 21, 1974; 1 child, Jared Solomon. BA, Rutgers Coll., 1968; JD, Temple U., 1971. Bar: N.J. 1971, D.C. 1974, Pa. 1977, U.S. Supreme Ct. 1976. Assoc. Smith, Stratton, Wise & Heher, Princeton, N.J., 1971-74, Howrey & Simon, Washington, 1974-77, Ballard, Spahr, Andrews & Ingersoll, Phila., 1977-79; ptnr. Meltzer & Schiffrin, Phila., 1979-87, Fox, Rothschild, O'Brien & Frankel, Phila., 1987—. Bd. dirs. Jewish Nat. Fund, Phila., 1987-88, chmn. lawyers' divsn.; pres. Soc. Hill Civic Assn., Phila. 1987-89. Lefferts scholar, Rutgers U., 1966-68. Mem.: Nassau Club. Republican. Home: 632 Spruce St Philadelphia PA 19106-4114 Office: Fox Rothschild O'Brien & Frankel 2000 Market St Ste 10 Philadelphia PA 19103-3231

BEYER, BARBARA LYNN, transportation executive, consultant; b. Miami, Fla., Feb. 16, 1947; d. Morten Sternoff and Jane (Hartman) Beyer. BA, George Washington U., 1978. Supr. printing office Saudi Arabian Airlines, 1966-67; ops. coord. Modern Air Transport, Miami, 1968-70, acct. Berlin, 1970-72; rep. Johnson Internat. Airlines, Washington, 1974-75; v.p., bd. dirs. Avmark, Inc., Washington, 1975—, pres., 1989—; chmn., bd. dirs. Avmark Internat., London, 1985—; mng. dir. Avmark Asia Ltd., Singapore, 1988-89, also bd. dirs., chmn. bd. dirs. Hong Kong, 1989—; pub. Avmark Aviation Economist, London, 1986—. Mem. adv. bd. aviation bus. dept. Embry-Riddle Aero. U. Mem.: Nat. Bus. Aircraft Assn., Aviation Space Writers (internat. bd. dirs. 1986—88, award 1978), Am. C. of C., Nat. Press Club, Internat. Aviation Club, Aero Club, Fgn. Corr. Club. Avocations: reading, horseback riding, home improvement. Office: Avmark Inc 415 Church St NE Ste 203 Vienna VA 22180 Office Phone: 703-528-5610. Personal E-mail: bbeyer@avmarkinc.com.

BEYER, DONALD STERNOFF, II, former state offical; b. Trieste, Free Territory of Trieste, June 20, 1950; arrived in U.S., 1952. s. Donald Sternoff Sr. and Nancy Prew (McDonald) B.; m. Carolyn Anne (McInerney), July 15, 1972 (div.); children: Donald III, Stephanie; m. Megan (Carroll), Sept. 19, 1987; children: Clara, Grace. BA in Econ., magna cum laude, Williams Coll., 1972. Former pres., v.p. and other positions Don Beyer Volvo, Falls Ch., Va., 1974—; lt. gov. Commonwealth of Va., Richmond, 1990-98. Urban at large mem. Commonwealth Transp. Bd., Va., 1987-90; chmn. Va. Econ. Bridge Initiative, Va. Chmn. Baliles for Gov., No. Va., 1985; Paul Simon for Pres., Va., 1988; Bill Clinton for Pres., Va., 1992; mem. 11th Dist. Dem. Com., Vienna, Va., 1992; Dem. nominee Gov. of Va., 1998. Named Time Mag. Quality Dealer of Yr., Va., 1991; Dealer of Excellence Award; Grand Award for Highway Safety, Nat. Safety Fedn.; James Wheat Award for Svc. to Virginians with Disabilities; Earl Williams Leadership in Tech. Award. Mem. Land Rover Alexandria (pres. 1997); No. Va. Bus. Roundtable; No. Va. HighTech. Coun. (co-founder); Bd. mem. Youth for Tommorrow; Washington Cmty. Found.,and the Red Cross. Democrat. Episcopalian. Avocations: golf, skiing, climbing. Office: Don Beyer Volvo 1231 W Broad St Falls Church VA 22046-2167

BEYER, GERRY WAYNE, lawyer, educator; b. Sept. 12, 1956; s. O. Frank and Lorraine Hazel (Kopper) B.; m. Margaret Mary Brewer, June 17, 1983. BA summa cum laude, Ea. Mich. U., 1976; JD summa cum laude, Ohio State U., 1979; LLM, U. Ill., 1983, JSD, 1990. Bar: Ohio 1980, Ill. 1980, Tex. 1984, U.S. Ct. Mil. Appeals 1990, U.S. Supreme Ct. 1991. Assoc. Knisley, Carpenter, Wilhelm & Nein, Columbus, Ohio, 1980; instr. law U. Ill., Champaign, 1980-81; asst. prof., assoc. prof. law St. Mary's U., San Antonio, 1981-87, prof., 1987—2005; Gov. Preston E. Smith Regents prof. Sch. Law Tex. Tech. U., Lubbock, 2005—. Vis. prof. Boston Coll. Law Sch., 1992-93, U. N.Mex., 1995, So. Meth. U. Sch. Law, 1997, Santa Clara U. Sch. Law, 1999-2000; lectr. Inst. Tex. Bar Rev., Austin, 1984-88, BAR/BRI Bar Rev., Houston, 1984-90, 99—, SMH Bar Rev., Boston, 1990-95, West Bar Rev., 1996-97; adv. bd. paralegal divsn. S.W. Sch. Ct. Reporting, 1990-92. Author quar. jour. articles in Estate Planning Devels. for Tex. Profls., 1981—, Texas Wills and Estates: Cases and Materials, 1987, 91, 2000, Teaching Materials in Estate Planning, 1995, 2000, 2005, Wills, Trusts, and Estates: Examples and Explanations, 1999, 2002, 2005, West's Legal Forms- Real Estate Transactions - Residential (vols. 19 & 19A), 2002, Texas Law of Wills, 3d ed., 2002; co-author: West's Legal Forms - Real Estate Transactions (vols. 19-23), 1986, West's Texas Forms - Probate and Administration of Estates (vols. 12, 12A, 12B), 1996, Texas Law of Wills, 2d edit., 1992, ann. supplement to Tex. Will Manual, 1986-2004, Modern Dictionary for the Legal Profession, 1993, 3d edit., 2001, Wills, Trusts and Estates for Legal Assistants, 2002. Mem. ABA (vice chair significant current lit. com., probate and trust divsn. of real property, probate and trust law sect. 1990-95, vice-chair non-tax issues in drafting wills and revocable trusts 1996-99); ACTEC, ATLA, Tex. Bar Assn., Ill. State Bar Assn., Order Coif, Order Barristers, Southwest Found. for Biomed. Rsch. (animal rsch. com. 1986-91). Home: PMB 203 4414 82nd St Ste 212 Lubbock TX 79424 Office: Tex Tech Univ School Law 1802 Hartford St Lubbock TX 79409-0004 Office Phone: 806-742-3990 x302. Business E-Mail: gwb@ProfessorBeyer.com.

BEYER, KAREN HAYNES, social worker; b. Cleve., Jan. 30, 1942; BA, Ohio State U., 1965; MSW, Loyola U., Chgo., 1969; postgrad. Family Inst., Northwestern U., 1979; MPA, Roosevelt U., 1992; CBA, U. Ill., Chgo., 1995; MBA, Keller Grad. Sch. Mgmt., 2004. Lic. clin. social worker, Ill. With Cuyahoga County Divsn. Child Welfare, Cleve., 1965, Dallas County Child Welfare Unit, Dallas, 1966, Luth. Social Svsc. Ill., Chgo., 1967-73; pvt. practice psychotherapy, family mediation Schaumburg, Ill., 1975-93; therapist Family Svcs. Assn. Greater Elgin (Ill.), 1973-77, dir. prof. svcs., 1977-83; dir. HHS Village of Hoffman Estates, Ill., 1983-93; exec. dir. Larkin Ctr., Elgin, Ill., 1993-2000, Ecker Ctr., Elgin, 2000—. Mem.: NASW, Altusa, Cosmopolitan Club, Rotary. Unitarian Universalist. Achievements include defying a court order to divulge client's therapy records, which was appealed to the US Supreme Court (1996, Jaffee vs. Redmond and the Village of Hoffman Estates). The majority decision supported the protection of client privacy and resulted in stronger guarantees of confidentiality in therapy. Office: Ecker Ctr for Mental Health 1845 Grandstand Pl Elgin IL 60123

BEYER, LISA, journalist; b. Lafayette, La., 1961; BJ, U. Tex., 1983. Staff Austin American-Statesman; editor Daily Texan; sr. correspondent Asiaweek, Singapore, 1984-88; staff writer Time Internat., NYC, 1988—90, assoc. editor, World Sect., 1990—91; Jerusalem bur. chief Time Mag., 1991—2000, sr. editor, Soc. Sect. editor NYC, 2000—01, sr. editor, World Sect. editor,

2001—04, asst. mng. editor, Nation Sect. editor, 2004—. Interviewed leaders such as Yassar Arafat, Yitzhak Rabin, Benjamin Neanyahu and Ehud Barak. Office: Time Mag 1271 Avenue of the Americas New York NY 10020 Office Fax: 212-522-0023.

BEYER, MARY EDEL, primary education educator; b. Winona, Minn., July 16, 1932; d. Edmund Aloysious and Gertrude Cecilia (Knopick) Edel; m. Argene Lester Beyer, June 7, 1958 (dec. Aug. 1985); children: Jason Edel Beyer, Trudy Edel Beyer, Gerard Edel Beyer, Jeremy Edel Beyer. AS in Edn., Winona State U., 1952, BS, 1967, MS, 1978. Cert. elem. tchr., Minn. Tchr. 1st grade Dodge Ctr. (Minn.) Sch., 1952-55; tchr. 1st grade, kindergarten Dist. 857, Lewiston, Minn., 1955-63; tchr. kindergarten Dist. 861, Winona, 1968-95, Stockton (Minn.) Sch., 1966-70; tchr. Rollingstone Elem. Sch., 1970-95; owner MEME's Doll Mus. Sch. del. Minn. Edn. Effective Program, 1987-95; pres. Winona Dist. 861 Reading Com. Contbr. to Poland Today Pol-Am. Jour., 1993; celebrity reader Children's Books Reading on the mall, 1990; photographer, writer School News Winona Post, 1985-95; freelance writer. Spencer, cadet mem. USO Group, Winona, 1950-52; leader Girl Scouts-Boy Scouts, 1952-70; mem. Sweet Adelines, 1978—; sings lead Hiawatha Valley Sweet Adelines, sec. 1994-97; apptd. commr. City of Winona Hist. Preservation Commn., 1996—; soprano St. Stanislaus Kostka choir, 1996—; sec. activity coun. Sr. Citizen Friendship Ctr., 1999—; tour guide riverboats on Miss. River, Winona Port. Recipient Pres.'s award Lakeside St. Machines, Winona, 1992, Disting. Svc. award, 1993, Diamond award 4-H Club, Winona, 1995; named Master Knitter Extension Office, Winona, 1985, Ky. Belle of the Blue Grass Gov. of Ky., 1951. Mem. PTA (pres.), Minn. Reading Assn. (del. 1985-95), Polish Heritage Soc. (sec. 1967—), Am. Legion Aux., Knights Columbus (4th degree lady). County Hist. Soc. (mus. vol.), Winona Athletic Club, C. of C. (bus. edn. intern 1995). Avocations: photography, fashion modeling, music, art, doll collecting. Home: 260 W Broadway St Winona MN 55987-5224

BEYER, MORTEN STERNOFF, airlines executive; b. N.Y.C., Nov. 13, 1921; s. Otto Sternoff and Clara (Mortenson) B.; m. Jane I. Hartman, Sept. 29, 1945 (div. 1989); children: Barbara, Nancy (Mrs. James Henry Evans), James, William; m. Catherine Frick Randall, Nov. 30, 1990. BA with honors, Swarthmore Coll., 1943. Various positions Pan Am. World Airways, 1943-48; asst. to v.p. operations and maintenance Capital Airlines Inc., Washington, 1948-60; sr. v.p. operations, maintenance and sales Riddle Airlines Inc., Miami, Fla., 1960-63; dep. dir. gen., gen. mgr. Saudi Arabian Airlines, Jeddah, Saudi Arabia, 1964-67; exec. v.p. Modern Air Transport, Inc., Miami, 1967-70, pres., 1970-71, Capital Internat. Airways, Inc., Nashville, 1971-72, Phoenix Airlines Inc., Detroit, 1972-73; pres., chief exec. officer Johnson Internat. Airlines, Inc., Missoula, Mont., 1974-75; chmn. AVMARK Inc., Arlington, Va., 1975-92, AVMARK Internat. Ltd., London, 1985-92; chmn., CEO Morten Beyer & Agnew, Ind., 1992—. Cons. USAF, 1954-55, Miami, Fla., 1963-64 Editor: Internat. Aviation ORACLE and Future Aircraft Values. Democratic candidate U.S. Reps., 1956; pres. Fairfax County Young Democrats, 1956-57. Mem.: Toastmasters Internat. (pres. 1952-56). Home: 4200 Cathedral Ave Apt 1114 Washington DC 20016 Office: MBA Inc 2107 Wilson Blvd Ste 750 Arlington VA 22201-3042 Office Phone: 703-276-3200. Business E-Mail: mba@mba-consulting.com.

BEYER, RICHARD J., priest, writer; b. Burlington, Iowa, Nov. 13, 1949; s. Catherine Elizabeth and Kenneth Harold Beyer. MA, St. Paul Sem., 1981. Chaplain Ctrl. Tex. Vets. Healthcare Sys., Temple, 1993. Author: (book) Medjugorje: Day by Day, 1991, Blessed Art Thou, 1996. Mem.: Nat. Assn. Vet. Affairs Chaplains. Roman Catholic. Home: 1315 Chapelwood Dr Waco TX 76712 Office: Dept Vet Affairs Hosp 1901 Veteran's Blvd Temple TX 76504 Office Phone: 254-778-4811 ext. 4879. Office Fax: 254-771-4523. Personal E-mail: PadreBeyer@aol.com. Business E-Mail: Richard.Beyer@med.va.gov.

BEYER, SUZANNE, advertising agency executive; b. N.Y.C. d. Harry and Jennie Hillman; m. Isadore Beyer; children: Pamela Claire, Hillary Jay. Grad., Conservatory of Mus. Art, N.Y.C., 1947; student, Nassau C. C., N.Y.C., 1963-65. Singer, tchr. piano, N.Y.C., 1947-66; asst. to v.p. media dir. Robert E. Wilson, Advt., N.Y.C., 1967-72; media planner, media buyer frank J. Corbett div. BBDO Internat., N.Y.C., 1972-77, Lavey/Wolff/Swift divsn. BBDO Advt., N.Y.C., 1977-80; sr. media planner Lavey/Wolff/Swift (divn. BBDO Advt.), N.Y.C., 1980-83, media supr., 1983-94, Lyons, Lavey, Nichel, Swift, N.Y.C., 1995-96; pharm. advt. med. media cons., 1996—. Soprano Opera Assn., Nassau, N.Y., 1976-99; soprano United Choral Soc., Woodmere, L.I., 1970-99, soprano Armand Sodero Chorale, Baldwin, Long Is., 1980-86, soprano Rockville Ctr. Choral Soc., 1986—. Mem. Pharm. Advt. Coun., L.I. Advt. Club, Healthcare Bus. Women's Assn. Home: 66 Fonda Rd Rockville Centre NY 11570-2751

BEYER, SYLVIA, social psychologist; b. Unterpremstetten, Austria, Jan. 12, 1964; came to U.S., 1986; d. Roland and Rosa B. Beyer; m. Edward Matthew Bowden; children: Thoomas Edward Roland, Andreas James, Robert William. Vordiplom, U. Tuebingen, Germany, 1985; MA, U. Oreg., 1987, PhD, 1991. Vis. prof. U. Mich., Flint, 1990-91; asst. prof. U. Wis. Parkside, Kenosha, 1991-97, assoc. prof., 1997—. Contbr. articles to profl. jours. Grantee Nat. Sci. Found. Mem. Am. Psychological Soc., Soc. Personality & Social Psychology. Avocation: gardening. Office: U Wis Parkside Dept Psychology 900 Wood Rd Kenosha WI 53144-1133 Office Phone: 262-595-2353. E-mail: beyer@uwp.edu.

BEYERL, SCOTT ALAN, investment company executive; b. Ridgewood, N.J., Dec. 12, 1961; s. Stuart C. and Theresa M. Beyerl. BJ, U. Mo., 1984. Reporter/anchor/photographer WBBH-TV, Fort Myers, Fla., 1984-88; reporter/anchor WIXT-TV, Syracuse, N.Y., 1988-93; sr. writer Fidelity Investments, Boston, 1993-94, editor, 1994-95, mgr. media relations, 1995-97, dir. media relations, 1997-98, sr. dir. media relations, 1998-2001, v.p., 2001—. Mem. Syracuse Press Club (various broadcasting awards). Office: Fidelity Investments 82 Devonshire St R22A Boston MA 02109-3614 E-mail: scott.beyerl@fmr.com.

BEYERLEIN, ADOLPH LOUIS, retired chemist, educator; b. Phillipsburg, Kans., May 2, 1937; s. Fred Michael Beyerlein and Ernestine Kolb; m. Anne Mo-Yung Wong; 1 child, Irene. BS, Kans. State Coll., 1960; PhD, U. Kans., 1966. Postdoctoral fellow Rice U., Houston, 1966—67; asst. prof. Clemson U., SC, 1967—72, assoc. prof., 1972—77, prof., 1977—2001, chair chemistry dept., 1995—2001, prof. emeritus, 2001—, bldg. cons., 2002—, coord. nanotech. and health scis. rsch., 2003—. Mem. commn. grad. studies Clemson U., 1986—89, 1989—92, chmn. chemistry dept. tenure and promotion com., 1980—81, 1989—91; presentor at nat. and internat. sci. confs. Contbr. articles to numerous profl. jours. Coun. Luth. Ch., Clemson, 1996—99. Fellow Postdoctoral fellow, Welch Found., 1966—67; grantee, NSF, 1977—79, Los Alamos Nat. Lab., 1979—80, 1980—81, NSF, 1981—83, IAEA, 1985—88, SC. Energy Rsch. Devel. Ctr., 1986, EPA and Electric Power Rsch. Inst., 1988—91, Electric Power Rsch. Inst., 1992—2000, NSF, 1997—2001, Greenville Hosp. Biomedical Coop., 1999—2001. Mem.: AAAS, AIChE, Am. Soc. for Heating and Refrigeration Engrs., Am. Chem. Soc. (examinations inst. com. 1992—93), Sigma Xi, Phi Kappa Phi. Office: Clemson Univ Dept Chemistry Clemson SC 29631 Business E-Mail: albrl@clemson.edu.

BEYER-MEARS, ANNETTE, physiologist; b. Madison, Wis., May 26, 1941; d. Karl and Annette (Weiss) Beyer. BA, Vassar Coll., 1963; MS, Fairleigh Dickinson U., 1973; PhD, Coll. Medicine and Dentistry N.J., 1977. NIH fellow Cornell U. Med. Sch., 1963-65; instr. physiology Springside Sch., Phila., 1967-71; teaching asst. dept. physiology Coll. Medicine & Dentistry N.J., N.J. Med. Sch., 1974-77, NIH fellow dept. ophthalmology, 1978-80; asst. prof. dept. ophthalmology U. Medicine and Dentistry N.J., N.J. Med. Sch., Newark, 1979-85, asst. prof. dept. physiology, 1980-85, assoc. prof. dept. physiology, 1986—, assoc. prof. dept. ophthalmology, 1986—. Vis. assoc. prof. dept. ophthalmology and vision sci. U. Wis., Madison, 1995—; cons. Alcon Labs. Contbr. articles in field of diabetic lens and kidney therapy to profl. jours. Chmn. admissions No. N.J., Vassar Coll., 1974-79; mem. minister search com. St. Bartholomew Episcopal Ch., N.J., 1978, fund-raising chmn., 1978, 79; del. Episc. Diocesian Conv., 1977, 78; long range planning com. Christ Ch., Ridgewood, N.J., 1985-87, vestry, 1994-95. Recipient NIH Nat. Rsch. Svc. award, 1978-80, Found. CMDNJ Rsch. award, 1980; grantee Juvenile Diabetes Found., 1985-87, NIH, NEI grantee, 1980-95, Pfizer, Inc. grantee, 1985-89, 93—. Mem. Am. Physiol. Soc., N.Y. Acad. Scis., Soc. for Neurosci., Am. Soc. Pharmacology and Exptl. Therapeutics, Assn. for Rsch. Vision & Ophthalmology, Internat. Soc. for Eye Research, AAAS, The Royal Soc. Medicine, Internat. Diabetes Found., Am. Diabetes Assn., European Assn. Study of Diabetes, Aircraft Owners and Pilots Assn., Sigma Xi. Home: 120 Ely Pl Madison WI 53726-4015

BEYERS, WILLIAM BJORN, geography educator; b. Seattle, Mar. 24, 1940; s. William Abraham and Esther Jakobia (Svendsen) B.; m. Margaret Lyn Rice, July 28, 1968. BA, U. Wash., 1962, PhD, 1967. Asst. prof. geography U. Wash., Seattle, 1968-74, assoc. prof., 1974-82, prof., 1982—, chmn. dept. geography, 1991-95, 2005—. Mem.: Western Regional Sci. Assn., Regional Sci. Assn., Assn. Am. Geographers. Home: 7159 Beach Dr SW Seattle WA 98136-2077 Office: U Wash Dept Geography PO Box 353550 Seattle WA 98195-3550 Fax: 206-543-3313. Office Phone: 206-543-5871. E-mail: beyers@u.washington.edu.

BEYMAN, JONATHAN ERIC, investment company executive; b. Newark, Dec. 31, 1955; s. Bernard B. and Miriam (Simon) Beyman; m. Susan Elizabeth Bleckman, Aug. 23, 1981; children: Michael, Daniel, Max. BS, U. Ct., 1976; MBA, Cornell U., 1981. CPA Conn. Sr. acct. Arthur Young and Co., NYC, 1976-79; asst. v.p. Chem. Bank, 1981-84; sr. cons. Am. Mgmt. Systems, 1985; v.p. Citibank North Am. Investment Bank, 1985-86, Lehman Bros., 1986-88, sr. v.p., 1988-91, mng. dir., 1991-94, 99-00, mng. dir., chief info. officer, 2000—02, global head ops., tech. divsn., 2002—; exec. v.p., chief ops. and tech. Lehman Bros. Holdings Inc., NYC, 2002—; chief info. officer, sr. v.p. CUC Internat., Stamford, Conn., 1994-97; co-chief info. officer, exec. v.p. Cendant Corp., 1997-98; pres. Cendant Interactive, 1998-99. Bd. dirs. Depository Trust and Clearing Corp., Dice, Inc.; N.Y. adv. bd. Donors Choose Org. Mem.: AICPA. Democrat. Jewish. Avocations: bicycling, reading, carpentry. Business E-Mail: jbeyman@lehman.com.

BEYONCÉ, (BEYONCÉ GISELLE KNOWLES), singer; b. Houston, Tex., Sept. 4, 1981; d. Matthew and Tina Knowles. Mem. group Destiny's Child, Houston, 1990—. Spokesperson L'Oreal, Tommy Hilfiger for fragrance "True Star". Singer: (albums) Destiny's Child, 1998, The Writing's on the Wall, 1999 (Platinum album 7 times, Grammy awards: Best R&B Song for Say My Name, 2000, Best R&B Performance By A Duo Or Group With Vocal, 2000), Survivor, 2001 (debuted at #1 Billboard Album Chart, Platinum 3 times, Grammy award: Best R&B Performance By A Duo Or Group With Vocal, 2001), 8 Days of Christmas, 2001, Destiny Fulfilled, 2004, (solo album) Dangerously in Love, 2003 (Grammy awards: Best Female R&B Vocal Performance, 2003, Best R&B Performance By A Duo Or Group With Vocals for song The Closer I Get To You, 2003, Best R&B Song for Crazy In Love, 2003, Best Contemporary R&B Album, 2003, Best Rap/Sung Collaboration for song Crazy in Love, 2003, MTV Video Music award Best Female Video for the song Naughty Girl, 2004), Live at Wembley, 2004; actor: (films) Austin Powers in Goldmember, 2002, I Know, 2003, The Fighting Temptations, 2003; composer: (films) Romeo Must Die, Charlie's Angels, Austin Powers in Goldmember, Bad Boys II, Fighting Temptations, Bridget Jones: The Edge of Reason, Soul Plane; actor: (TV Guest Appearances) Oprah Winfrey Show, 2003, 2004, The View, 2004, 20 / 20, 2004, Top of the Pops, 2004, Saturday Night Live, 2004, 106th & Park Top 10 Live, 2005. Named Pop Songwriter of Yr., ASCAP, 2001, Best Female R&B artist, BET awards, 2004; named one of 50 Most Influential African-Americans, Ebony Mag., 2004; recipient 4 Billboard Music awards, 2000, 2 Billboard Music awards, 2001, Am. Music award, 2000, 2 Am. Music awards, 2001, MTV Music Video award, 2001, 4 World Music awards, 2001, Image award, NAACP, 2000, 2001, Sammy Davis, Jr. award, 2000, Soul Train award, 2000.

BEYRLE, JOHN R., ambassador; BA, Grand Valley State; MS, Nat. War Coll. Polit. officer US Embassy-Moscow, Russia, US Embassy-Sofia, Bulgaria, 1985—87; mem. US Delegation to the CFE Negotiations, Vienna; staff officer to Sec. State George Shultz, Sec. State James Baker; fgn. policy advisor to Senator Paul Simon; dir. for Russian, Ukrainian and Eurasian Affairs NSC, Washington, 1993—95; counselor for polit. and econ. affairs US Embassy-Prague, Czech Republic, 1997—99; dep. spl. advisor to sec. for the New Independent States US Dept. State, Washington; dep. chief of mission US Embassy-Moscow, Russia, 2002—05; US amb. to Bulgaria US Dept. State, Sofia, 2005—. Address: American Embassy Sofia Bulgaria 16 Kozyak St 1407 Sofia Bulgaria Office: American Embassy Sofia Bulgaria Dept of State 5740 Sofia Pl Washington DC 20521-5740 Office Phone: 359-2-937-5100. Office Fax: 359-2-937-5320. Business E-Mail: irc@usembassy.bg.*

BEYTAGH, FRANCIS XAVIER, JR., law educator; b. Savannah, Ga., July 11, 1935; BA magna cum laude (hon.), U. Notre Dame, 1956; JD, U. Mich., 1963. Bar: Ohio, 1964, U.S. Supreme Ct., 1967, Ind., 1972. Clk. Fuller, Seney, Henry, and Hodge, Toledo, 1961; sr. law clk. to Chief Justice Earl Warren U.S. Supreme Ct., Washington, 1963-64; assoc. Jones, Day, Cockley, and Reavis, Cleve., 1964-66; asst. to solicitor gen. U.S. Dept. Justice, Washington, 1966-70; prof. law U. Notre Dame, 1970-74, 75-76; prof., dean U. Toledo, 1976-83; Cullen prof. law U. Houston, 1984-85; prof., dean Ohio State U. Coll. Law, 1985-93, prof., 1993-97; spl. counsel Jones, Day, Reavis, and Pogue, Columbus, Ohio, 1993-96; pres., prof. Fla. Coastal Sch. Law, Jacksonville, 1997-98, prof., 1998—, founders' chair, 2000—. Vis. prof. law, U. Va., Charlottesville, 1974-75; U. Mich., 1983-84; So. Meth. U., Dallas, 1997. Editor in chief Mich. Law Rev., 1962-63; author: Supplement to Kauper's Constitutional Law: Cases and Materials, 1977; Constitutional Law: Cases and Materials, 5th edit., 1980, supplements, 1981, 82, 84; Constitutionalism in Contemporary Ireland, 1997; contbg. articles to profl. jour. Capt. USNR ret. Fulbright fellow, 1994. Fellow Am. Bar Found. (life); mem. ABA; Fla. Bar, Jacksonville Bar Assn., Order of Coif. Home: 49 Marsh Creek Rd Amelia Island FL 32034-6414 Office: Fla Coastal Sch Law 7555 Beach Blvd Jacksonville FL 32216-3000 Business E-Mail: fbeytagh@fcsl.edu.

BEZANSON, THOMAS EDWARD, lawyer; b. Hartford, Conn., Aug. 1, 1945; s. Philip Thomas and Lillian (Carlson) Bezanson; m. Janie H. Bezanson, Aug. 10, 1969; children: Philip, Jeffrey. BA, Grinnell Coll., 1967; MA, Rutgers U., 1971, JD, 1974. Bar: NY 1975, US Dist. Ct. (Ea. and So. Dists.) 1975, US Ct. Appeals (2nd Cir.) 1975, US Ct. Appeals (6th Cir.) 1980, US Supreme Ct. 1991, US Dist. Ct. (Dist. Ariz.) 1992, US Ct. Appeals (5t Cir.) 1995. Assoc. Chadbourne & Parke LLP, NYC, 1974—81, ptnr., 1981—, chmn., Products Liability Practice Group. Author: 42 poems, 1993; mgn. editor Rutgers Law Rev., 1973—74. Bd. dirs. Westchester Philharm., 1992—98, NY Lawyers Pub. Interest Inc., 1997—, Legal Aid Soc., 1999—2002, Duke U. Sch. Law, 2003—. With U.S. Army, 1967—69. Mem.: ABA, Fed. Bar Coun. (program com.), NY State Commn. on the Jury, Assn. Bar City NY. Office: Chadbourne & Parke 30 Rockefeller Plz Fl 31 New York NY 10112-0129 Office Fax: 212-541-5369. Business E-Mail: tbezanson@chadbourne.com.*

BEZKOROVAINY, ANATOLY, medical educator, biochemist; b. Riga, Latvia, Feb. 11, 1935; s. Ignatius and Olga (Solovey) Bezkorovainy; m. Marilyn Grib, June 14, 1964; children: Gregory, Alexander. BS, U. Chgo., 1956; PhD, U. Ill., 1960; JD, Ill. Inst. Tech., 1977. Bar: Ill. 1977. Rsch. assoc. Oak Ridge Nat. Lab., Tenn., 1960—61; chemist USDA, Ames, Iowa, 1961—62; mem. faculty Rush-Presbyn. St. Luke's Med. Ctr., Chgo., 1962—, asst. prof., 1962—67, assoc. prof., 1967—73, prof. biochemistry, 1973—2004, emeritus prof., 2004, assoc. chmn., dir. ednl. programs biochemistry dept., 1980—2000. Adj. prof. Dr. Scholl Coll. Podiatric Medicine, North Chicago, Ill., 2000—. Author: Basic Protein Chemistry, 1970, Biochemistry of Nonheme Iron, 1980; co-author (with Rafelson and Hayashi): Basic Biochemistry, 1980; co-author: (with Miller-Catchpole) Biochemistry and Physiology of BifidoBacteria, 1989; co-author: (with Rafelson) Concise Biochemistry, 1995; contbr. articles to profl. jours. Numerous grants, NSF, NIH, Am. Heart Assn., indsl. instns., 1962—90. Mem.: Inst. Food Technologists, Am. Chem. Soc., Am. Soc. Biol. Chemists, Am. Dairy Sci. Assn. Eastern Orthodox. Home: 4 Northbend Ln Galena IL 61036

BEZOLD, CLEMENT, futurist; b. Coral Gables, Fla., 1948; BS, Georgetown U., 1970; PhD, U. Fla., 1976. Asst. dir. Ctr. Govtl. Responsibility, Fla.; vis. scholar The Brookings Inst., 1974-77; pres. Inst. for Alternative Futures, Alexandria, Va., 1977—. Pres. Alternative Futures Assocs., 1982—; cons. to local, state, fed. govts. in U.S. and internat., WHO, major corps. including Disney, AT&T, pharm. and health care cos.; tchr. Am. U., U. Fla., Antioch U.; spkr. in field. Editor: Anticipatory Democracy (introduction by Alvin Toffler), 1978; co-author: (with R. Carlson and J. Peck) The Future of Work and Health, 1985 (Am. Health Mag. book award); co-editor: (with Erica Mayer) Future Care: Responding to the Demand for Change, 1996, The Future of Complementary and Alternative Approaches (CAAs) in US Healthcare, 1998, (with J. Frenk & S. McCarthy) 21st Century Health Care in Latin American and the Caribbean, 1998, Genomics and Society Project for UK-ESRC, 2002. Bd. dirs. World Future Soc. Office: Inst Alternative Futures 100 N Pitt St Ste 235 Alexandria VA 22314-3134 Office Phone: 703-684-5880. Business E-Mail: cbezold@altfutures.com.

BEZOS, JEFFREY PRESTON, multimedia executive; b. Albuquerque, N. Mex, Jan. 12, 1964; s. Miguel and Jacklyn Bezos; m. Mackenzie Tuttle, 1993. Degree in Elec. Engring. and Computer Sci. (summa cum laude), Princeton U., 1986. With FITEL, NY, 1986—88, Bankers Trust Co., NY, 1988-90, v.p., 1990, D.E. Shaw & Co., NY, 1990-94, sr. v.p., 1992-94; founder Amazon.com Inc., Seattle, 1994—, chmn., 1994—, pres., 1994—99, 2000—, CEO, 1996—, treas., sec., 1996—97; founder Blue Origin, Seattle, 2000—. Mem. staff FITEL, NY, 1986-88; bd. dirs., Drugstore.com, 1998- Named Person of the Year, TIME mag., 1999; named one of 40 Under 40 Richest, Fortune, 2003. Mem. Phi Beta Kappa. Live on the Internet July 16, 1995, first book sold: "Fluid Concepts & Creative Analogies: Computer Models of the Fundamental Mechanisms of Thought"; Funding Blue Origin, builders of low cost vehicles that would send passengers into space on short flights. Office: Amazon com Inc 1200 12th Ave S Ste 1200 Seattle WA 98144*

BEZOZO, KENNETH K., lawyer; b. Bklyn., Sept. 14, 1955; BA cum laude, Syracuse U., 1977; JD cum laude, Yeshiva U., Benjamin N. Cardozo Law Sch., 1980; LLM in Taxation, cum laude, NYU, 1981. Bar: NY 1981, Tex. 1981. Ptnr., tax, bus. and estate planning Haynes and Boone LLP, NYC. Spkr. in field. Mem.: NY State Bar Assn., ABA (Taxation Sect., corp. tax com.). Office: Haynes and Boone LLP 399 Park Ave New York NY 10022 Office Phone: 212-659-4999. Office Fax: 212-884-8222. Business E-Mail: kenneth.bezozo@haynesboone.com.

BHABHA, HOMI K., humanities educator, writer; b. Mumbai, India, 1949; BA, U. Bombay, 1970; M.Phil, U. Oxford, 1974, MA, 1977, D.Phil, 1990. Chester D. Tripp prof. in humanities U. Chgo.; Anne F. Rothenberg prof. English and Am. lit. Harvard U., Cambridge, 2001—; dir. Harvard Humanities Ctr., 2005—. Sr. fellow Old Dominion U.; vis. prof. Princeton U., U. Pa.; faculty fellow Sch. of Criticism and Theory Dartmouth Coll.; lectr. Richard Wright lecture series, Ctr. Black Lit. and Culture, U. Pa., 1991, Annual Interdisciplinary Lecture, Sch. Oriental and African Studies, U. London, 1995, W.E.B. Du Bois Lectures, Harvard U., 1999, Presdl. Lectr., Stanford U., 2000, Clarendon Lectures, U. London, 2001—02. Editor: Nation and Narration, 1990; author: The Location of Culture, 1993; editl. bd. mem. Critical Inquiry, October, contbr. Artforum. Fellow Radcliffe Inst., 2004—05. Office: Harvard U Humanities Ctr Barker Ctr 136 Cambridge MA 02138 Office Phone: 617-495-0739, 617-495-0730. E-mail: hbhabha@fas.harvard.edu.*

BHADRA, JAYANTA, computer scientist, electrical engineer; B in Computer Sci. and Engring. (hon.), Jadavpur U., Calcutta, 1993; M in Computer Sci. and Engring., Indian Inst. Tech., Kharagpur, India, 1994; PhD in Elec. and Computer Engring., U. Tex., 2001. Software engr. Motorola India Electronics Ltd., Bangalore, 1995—96; rsch. asst. Ga. Inst. Tech., Atlanta, 1997, U. Tex., Austin, 1997—2001; tech. lead, r&d custom tools front-end semiconductor products sect. Motorola Inc., Austin, 2001—04; tech. lead, r&d custom tools front-end Freescale Semiconductor Inc., Austin, 2004—. Recipient Silver medal, Indian Inst. Tech., 1994, Motorola Sci. and Tech. Soc., 2003; fellow, Grad. Aptitude Test Engring., 1993—94; scholar, Tex. Advanced Tech. Program Devel., 1999—2000. Mem.: IEEE. Achievements include research in modeling design constraints to avoid false results in dynamic circuit verification; elimination of gate/switch level simulations; model checking security protocols using pre-configuration; automatic validation of chip-level assertions in verifying high performance circuits; methodology for validating manufacturing test vector suites for custom designed scan-based circuits; design constraints in verifying high performance embedded dynamic circuits; program slicingg for hierarchical test generation; language formalism for verification of powerPC(TM) custom memories using compostions of abstract specifications; full chip false timing path identification; automatic formal verification of interacting finite state machines; patents pending for analysis tool for path extraction and false path identification and method thereof; research in full chip false timing-path identification; method to identify false critical paths using ATPG techniques; automatic validation test generation using extracted control models; patents pending for analysis tool for deriving correspondence between storage elements of two memory models and method thereof; research in solidarity of functional verification and manufacturing test generation using enhanced equivalence checking; hierarchical test generation approach using program slicing techniques on hardware description languages; automatic generation of high performance embedded memory models for powerPC microprocessors; genCRAM: Test-view Generation for Memories; verification of a system-on-chip using computation slicing. Office Phone: 512-996-4885.

BHADURI, RANJAN, investment management professional; b. Hamilton, Ont., Can., July 26, 1969; s. Rajat Kumar and Manjushree Bhaduri. BSc (hon.), McMaster U., Hamilton, 1991; M in Math, U. of Waterloo, Ont., 1992; PhD, U. of Hawaii at Manoa, Honolulu, 1999; MBA (co-op), McMaster U. (Exch. Program at Norwegian Sch. of Mgmt.), Hamilton and Oslo, 2001. Math. instr., prof. U. of Hawaii, Honolulu, 1992—99; affiliate East-West Ctr., Honolulu, 1997—99; fin. analyst Bank of Montreal, Toronto, 2000—00; risk analyst Scotia Markets, Toronto, 2001—02; assoc. Northwater Capital Mgmt., Toronto, 2002—. Math. cons., 1991—2001. Recipient McMaster U. Travel scholarship, 2001, grad. scholarship, U. of Waterloo, 1992, Undergrad. award, Nat. Sci. and Engring. Rsch. Coun., 1988—90; scholar, U. of Hawaii at Manoa, 1992—99. Mem.: Math. Assn. of Am., Am. Math. Soc., Am. Contract Bridge League. Achievements include research in created Chelios Rings and a new spectrum from arbitrary rings; combinatorial number theory and in the financial sector (applied mathematical finance). Office: Northwater Capital Mgmt Inc Ste 4700 BCD Pl 181 Bay St Toronto ON Canada M5J2T3 Home: 8 Park Rd Ste 2606 Toronto Canada M4W 3S5 Office Phone: 416-365-2860. Office Fax: 416-360-0671. E-mail: rbhaduri@northwatercapital.com.

BHAGAT, PHIROZ MANECK, mechanical engineer; b. Oct. 28, 1948; came to U.S., 1970; s. Maneck Phirozshaw and Khorshed Eduljee (Batliwala) B.; m. Patricia Jane Steckler, Oct. 13, 1979; children: Kay, Sarah. BTech, Indian Inst. Tech.-Bombay, 1970; MS in Engring., U. Mich., 1971, PhD, 1975. Rsch. fellow in applied mechanics Harvard U., Cambridge, Mass., 1975-77; asst. prof. engring. Columbia U., N.Y.C., 1977-81; staff engr. Exxon Mobil Rsch. & Engring. Co., Florham Park, N.J., 1981-83, sr. staff engr., 1983-2001; sr. engring. assoc. Exxon Mobil Rsch. and Engring. Co., Annandale, NJ, 2001—03; founder, prin. Internat. Strategy Engines, LLC, Westfield, NJ, 2004—. Adj. asst. prof. Columbia U., N.Y.C., 1981-84; head sci. computing group Exxon/Mobil Rsch. & Engring. Co., Florham Park, 1988-90; mng. dir. Janus Enterprise Internat., 1992-94. Author: Pattern Recognition in Industry, 2005; contbr. articles to profl. jours. K.C., Mahindra scholar, 1970, J.N. Tata scholar, 1970; Horace Rackham predoctoral fellow,

1973-74, 74-75. Mem. AIChE, ASME, N.Y. Acad. Scis., Tau Beta Pi, Sigma Xi. Achievements include research and development of neural nets and pattern recognition technology in technical and business applications, providing cutting edge data driven modeling solutions for improved operations and profitability in the financial and process industries; first to develop the application of pattern recognition technology for technical and business operations in the petroleum and chemical industry. Office: 519 Alden St Westfield NJ 07090-3040 Office Phone: 908-232-1190. Business E-Mail: pmbhagat@strategyengines.com.

BHAGAVAN, MANU BELUR, history professor; BA, Carleton Coll., 1992; MA, U. Tex., 1994, PhD, 1999. Lectr. in history U. Tex. at Austin, Austin, Tex., 1999; vis. asst. prof. history Carleton Coll. and St. Olaf Coll., Northfield, Minn., 2000; Singh vis. lectr. South Asian studies and history Yale U., New Haven, 2000—01; asst. prof. dept. history and polit. sci. Manchester Coll., North Manchester, Ind., 2001—04; asst. prof. dept. history Hunter College-CUNY, New York, NY, 2004—. Bd. trustees KSPC (Charitable) Trust, Bangalore, Karnataka, India; bd. dirs. Ind. Consortium Internat. Programs, Ind., 2001—04. Author: (monograph) Sovereign Spheres: Princes, Education and Empire in Colonial India (Oxford University Press, 2003), (essay) CounterCurrents.org, (book revs.) The Journal of Asian Studies, (book rev.) Am. Hist. Rev. Jour., Peace and Change Jour., (essays in Pakistani newspaper) The Nation, (essay in newspaper) The Kashmir Observer; contbr. articles to profl. jours.; contbr. (edited book) Understanding Contemporary India; editor: (jour.) Sagar: South Asia Graduate Research Jour.; meml. editl. adv. bd. SAGAR: A South Asia Grad. Rsch. Jour. Grantee, Ind. Network Devel. India Awareness (INDIA), 2002; Fgn. Lang. HEA Title VI fellow, U. Wis.-Madison, 1995, Title VI Fgn. Lang. and Area Studies fellow, U. Tex. at Austin, 1995-96, David Bruton Jr. U. fellow, 1997-98, Ford Found. Area Studies and Social Sci. Rsch. grant, 1994, Coca-Cola World Fund grant, Yale U., 2000-01, ICIP grant, Ind. Consortium Internat. Programs, 2002, Plowshares Peace Studies grant, Manchester Coll., 2002-03. Mem.: Assn. Asian Studies (South Asia Coun. grant 2002), Am. Hist. Assn., Phi Kappa Phi, Phi Alpha Theta. Office: Dept History Hunter Coll CUNY 695 Park Ave New York NY 10021 Office Phone: 212-772-5482. Office Fax: 212-772-5545. E-mail: manu.bhagavan@hunter.cuny.edu.

BHAGAVATH, BALASUBRAMANIAN, medical researcher; s. Mookandy and Vanaja Balasubramanian; m. Vasanthi Pillai. BS, MB, Madras Med. Coll., 1989. Ho. officer Govt. Gen. Hosp., Madras, India, 1989; med. officer (specialist) Nat. U. Hosp., Singapore, 1998—99, registrar, 2000—01; resident Med. Coll. of Ga., Augusta, 2001—; sr. ho. officer in ob/gyn Govt. Hosp. for Women and Children, Madras, India, 1990; sr. ho. officer in surgery Govt. Gen. Hosp., Madras, India, 1990—91; sr. ho. officer in anesthesia George Eliott Hosp., Nuneaton, United Kingdom, 1991—92; sr. ho. officer in ob/gyn Southmead Hosp., Bristol, United Kingdom, 1992—93; sr. sho in obstetrics Birmingham Maternity Hosp., Birmingham, United Kingdom, 1993—94; registrar in ob/gyn Glasgow Royal Infirmary, Glasgow, United Kingdom, 1994—95, Falkirk Royal Infirmary, Falkirk, United Kingdom, 1995—96; transitional yr. intern Lemuel Shattuck Hosp., Jamaica Plain, Mass., 1996—97. Sec. Soc. for the Study of Andrology and Sexology, Singapore, 2000—01. Contbr. articles to profl. jours. Com. mem. Singapore Vegetarian Soc., Singapore, 2000—01. Recipient Raja Sir Ramasamy Mudaliar Gold medal, Madras Med. Coll., 1988, Branfoot Meml. prize, 1988, Best Tchg. Resident, Berlex, 2001—02, Prof. Donald M. Sherline, MD Jr. Resident of the Yr., Med. Coll. of Ga., 2001—02; Nat. Talent Search Exam., U. Grants Commn., 1984. Mem.: Royal Coll. Obstetricians and Gynecologists, Am. Coll. Obstetrics and Gynecology (assoc.), Augusta Gynecol. and Obstet. Soc. (assoc.), Endocrine Soc. (assoc.). Avocations: travel, reading, music. Office: Med Coll of Georgia Ob-gyn 1120 15th St Augusta GA 30912

BHARADWAJ, PREM DATTA, physics professor; b. Gorakhpur, India, May 20, 1931; arrived in U.S., 1960; s. Ganga Dhar and Bhagwati Devi (Sharma) B.; m. Vidya Wati Sharma, Feb. 14, 1949; children: Rakesh Kumar, Rajnesh Kumar, Vidhu Rani Eranki, Sudha Kar. BS 1st class with merit, NREC Coll. Khurja, 1950; MS 1st class, Agra U., 1952; PhD, SUNY, Buffalo, 1964. Asst. prof. physics B.R. Coll. Agra, India, 1952—54, 1959—60; lectr. physics GPIC Tehri, Tehri Garhwal, India, 1954—56, Govt. Coll. Meerut, India, 1956—59; grad. asst. physics SUNY, Buffalo, 1960—62; from asst. prof. physics to assoc. prof. physics Niagara U., Niagara Falls, NY, 1962—66, prof. physics, 1966—, chmn. dept. physics, 1976—86. Cons. NSF, 1966-71; reviewer N.Y. State Regents Exams. in Medicine and Dentistry, 1976; co-founder India Assn. Buffalo, 1961, Hindi Samaj Greater Buffalo, 1986; summer rsch. participant NSF, La. State U., Baton Rouge, 1965; vis. prof. dept. crystallography Rosewell Park Cancer Inst., Buffalo, N.Y., 1970-71. Co-author: Intermediate Agriculture Physics and Climatology, 1954; contbr. articles to profl. jours. Pres. Sathya Sai Ctr. Buffalo, Amherst, N.Y., 1990-93, Hindi Samaj of Greater Buffalo, Amherst, 1996-97; mem. trust com. Hindu Cultural Soc. Western N.Y., 1999-2001. Recipient Rajiv Gandhi Nat. Unity award for excellence Govt. India, 1995, Hind Rattan (Jewel of India) award Govt. of India, 1995; named Internat. Man of Yr. Internat. Biog. Ctr., Cambridge, Eng., 1999. Mem. India Assn. of Buffalo (award for outstanding work in edn. and cmty. 1997), Hindi Samaj of Greater Buffalo, Am. Phys. Soc. Democrat. Hindu. Home: 100 N Parrish Dr Amherst NY 14228-1477 Office: Niagara U Physics Dept Lewiston Rd Niagara Falls NY 14109 Business E-Mail: pdb@niagara.edu.

BHARDWAJ, ANISH, neuroscientist, medical educator; b. June 3, 1960; MD, Coll. Medicine, u. Ibadan, Nigeria. Diplomate Am. Bd. Neurology and Psychiatry, lic. Md., NY State. Intern Univ. Coll. Hosp., Ibadan, Nigeria, 1984—85; med. officer Sokoto Clinic, Nigeria, 1985—86; rsch. fellow dept. neurology Mt. Sinai Sch. Medicine, NYC, 1987—89, resident in neurology, 1990—92, chief resident in neurology, 1992—93; resident in internal medicine Elmhurst Hosp., Mt. Sinai Sch. Medicine, NYC, 1989—90; neurosci. crit. care fellow Johns Hopkins U. Sch. Medicine, Balt., 1993—95, nat. stroke assn. fellow, 1994—96, instr. depts. neurology, neurol. surgery, anesthesiology and crit. care medicine, 1995—96, dir. neurosci. crit. care fellowship tng. program, 1996—, assoc. prof. neurology, neurological surgery, and anesthesiology and critical care medicine; staff attending neurosci. crit. care unit Johns Hopkins Hosp., Balt., 1995—99, asst. prof. neurology, 1998—, co-dir. neurosciences-critical care divsn., 2000—, vice-chair, inpatient svcs., dept. neurology; staff attending, dept. neurology John Hopkins Bayview Med. Ctr., Balt. Spkr. in field. Contbr. articles to profl. jours.; ad hoc reviewer: Jour. Cerebral Blood Flow and Metabolism, Crit. Care Medicine. Fellow: Am. Heart Assn. (fellow, stroke coun. 1996, hon. mention Robert G. Siekert Young Investigator award in stroke 1995, Clinician-Scientist award 1996, established Investigator award 2001); mem.: AMA, Am. Neurological Assn., Nigeria Med. Coun., Soc. for Neurosci., Nat. Stroke Assn. (Fellowship Career Devel. award 1994), Am. Acad. Neurology. Office: Johns Hopkins U Sch Medicine Dept Neurology Meyer Bldg 8-140 600 N Wolfe St Baltimore MD 21287 Office Phone: 410-955-7481. Office Fax: 410-614-7903. Business E-Mail: abhardwa@jhmi.edu.

BHARGAVA, ASHOK, retired economics professor; b. Agra, India, July 1, 1943; came to U.S., 1966; s. Mahabir Prasad and Chandra Kanti Bhargava; m. Deviyani J. Bhatt, June 11, 1970 (dec. Oct. 1999); children: Amit, Kamini. BA with honors, Delhi (India) U., 1963, MA, 1965; MS, U. Wis., 1969, PhD, 1975. Lectr. Siri Ram Coll. Commerce, Delhi, 1965-66; asst. U. Wis., Madison, 1967-70, instr. Whitewater, 1970-75, asst. prof., 1975-77, assoc. prof., 1977-80, prof., 1980—2003, chmn. dept. econs., 1981-87, 1999—2003, asst. dir. global bus. resource ctr., 1998—2003; prof. emeritus, 2003—; comptroller Feingold Senate Com., 2003—04. Cons. Wis. Exports Coop., Madison, 1988-92; dir. Ctr. for Bus. and Mgmt. Svcs., U. Wis. Whitewater, 1989-91, coord. rsch., 1989-92, dir. Ctr. for Econ. Edn. 1995-99; pres. Bhargava Assocs., Bus. and Econ. Cons. Editor: Indian Economics Studies, 1984, Studies of the Indian Economy, 1985; mem. editl. bd. Bull. Concerned Asian Scholars, 1978-2003, Issues in Internat. Bus., 1986-92; mng. editor Devel. Update, 1988—; contbr. articles to profl. publs. Bd. dirs. Indian Devel. Svc., Chgo., 1975-95, Madison Area Tech. Coll. Found., 2000-03; treas. Combat Blindness Found., Madison, 1985-2000; mem. Gov.'s Coun. on Asian Affairs, 1985-96, sec., 1988-96; bd. dirs. minority bus. devel. fund State of Wis., 1989-2003; co-chair Wis. Orgn. of Asian Ams., 1995-2000; founder Village Libr. Fund, 1995—. Mem. Assn. Indian Econ. Studies (sec.-treas. 1981-89, chmn. 1989-91), Assn. Managerial Econs. (sec. 1984-2003), Assn. Internat. Bus. Studies, Eastern Econ. Assn. (area rep. 1988-96). Avocations: squash, volunteer work. Home: 4806 Waukesha St Madison WI 53705-4845 E-mail: ashokbhargava1@yahoo.com.

BHARGAVA, MANJUL, mathematics professor, researcher; b. Canada, 1975; AB in Mathematics, Harvard U., 1996; PhD in Mathematics, Princeton U., 2001. Teaching fellow Harvard U., 1993—95; visiting lecturer US/Canada Mathcamps, 1997—98; researcher Ctr. for Comm. Rsch., Princeton, NJ, 1996, Inst. for Advanced Study; visiting lecturer Princeton U., prof. mathematics, 2003—. Fellow Clay Mathematics Inst., Cambridge, 2000—. Named one of Brilliant 10, Popular Sci. mag., 2002; recipient First prize, NY State Sci. Talent Search, 1992, Morgan prize for outstanding rsch., Am. Mathematical Soc., 1997; grantee Fellowship in Mathematics, Hertz Found., 1996—2000. Office: Princeton U Mathematics Dept Fine Hall Washington Rd Princeton NJ 08544

BHARGAVA, RAMESHWAR NATH, physicist; b. Allahabad, UP, India, Dec. 25, 1939; came to U.S., 1960; s. Gajadhar Prasad and Rupkanti Bhargava; m. Veena Bhargava, Aug. 15, 1965; children: Sidharth, Amitabh. BS, U. Allahabad, 1957, MS, 1959; PhD, Columbia U., 1966. Fellow IBM Watson Lab., Columbia U., N.Y.C., 1965-66; cons. IBM Watson Rsch. Ctr., Yorktown Heights, N.Y., 1966-67; mem. tech. staff Bell Labs, Murray Hill, N.J., 1967-70, Philips Labs, Briarcliff Manor, N.Y., 1970-78, dept. head, 1978-89, assoc. dir., 1989-93; pres. Nanocrystals Tech., Briarcliff Manor, N.Y., 1993—. Organizer symposia and internat. profl. confs.; chmn. Gordon Conf., N.H., 1977. Patentee inventor 3-D TV, Harmonics in High Temperature Superconductors, Doped nanocrystals, digital x-ray imaging. Recipient Chancellor's Gold medal U. Allahabad, 1959. Fellow IEEE, Am. Phys. Soc. Home: 5 Morningside Ct Ossining NY 10562-3003 Office: Nanocrystals Tech PO Box 820 Briarcliff Manor NY 10510-0307

BHARITKAR, SUNIL GANPAT, research scientist, data processing executive; b. Pune, India, Apr. 20, 1969; came to U.S., 1991; s. Ganpat Raoji and Saraswati Ganpat B. BE, U. Pune, India, 1990; MS, Case Western Res. U., 1995; PhD, U. So. Calif., 2001. Vis. rschr. Hitachi, Japan, 1994; mem. tech. staff Ford Motor Co., 1998-99; tech. specialist Oppenheimer, Wolff & Donnelly LLP, 2000—02, Greenberg Traurig LLP, 2002—. Pres., co-founder Audyssey Labs., Inc., 2002—. Contbr. articles to profl. jours.; patentee in field. Home: 2461 Coolidge Ave #1 Los Angeles CA 90064 Office: U So Calif Signal/Image Processing Ins 3740 McClintock Ave Los Angeles CA 90089-2564 Fax: 213-740-4651. E-mail: bharitka@sipi.usc.edu.

BHARTIA, PRAKASH, defense research management executive, researcher, educator; b. Calcutta, West Bengal, India, Jan. 6, 1944; arrived in Can., 1967, arrived in US, 2003, permanent resident, 2004; s. Benarshi Prasad and Bhagwati Devi (Chirimar) B.; m. Savitri Kanhai, Apr. 27, 1971; children: Sanjay Manish, Anil Manoj. B in Tech. with honors, Indian Inst. Tech., Bombay, 1966; MSc, U. Man., Winnipeg, Can., 1968, PhD, 1971. Assoc. prof. U. Regina, Sask., Can., 1976, asst. dean, 1975-77; def. scientist, chief R&D br. Nat. Defence, Ottawa, Ont., Can., 1977—; head navigation sect. Defence Rsch. Establishment Ottawa, 1981-85; dir. R&D air Defence Hdqrs., Govt. of Can., Ottawa, 1985-86; dir. R&D commnications and space Nat. Defence, Govt. of Can., 1986-89; dir. sonar div. Defence Rsch. Establishment Atlantic, Halifax, 1989-91; dir. radar div. Defence Rsch. Establishment Ottawa, 1991—; chief Defence Rsch. Establishment Atlantic, 1992-97; dir.-gen. Def. Rsch. Establishment, Ottawa, 1997—2003; exec. v.p. Natel Engrng. Co. Inc., Chatsworth, Calif., 2004—. Adj. prof. U. Ottawa, 1977-96, Daltech, 1997—; dir. Can. Microelectronics Centre, Kingston, 1986-88; mem. elec. engrng. grant selection com. Natural Scis. and Engrng. Rsch. Coun., Ottawa, 1990—, chmn. ind. chair evaluation com., Victoria, 1991; bd. dirs. Tradex Investment Funds, Ottawa, Canadian Ctr. Marine Communication. Author: Microstrip Antennas, 1980, Millimeter Wave Engineering and Applications, 1984, E Plane Integrated Circuits, 1987, Millimeter Wave Microstrip and Printed Circuit Antennas, 1990; author, editor: Microwave Solid State Circuit Design, 1988, Microstrip Lines and Slotlines, 1996, RF and Microwave Coupled Line Circuits, 1999, Microstrip Antenna Design Handbook, 2000; patentee in field. Mem. engrng. adv. com. Queen's U., Kingston, 1989-92, chmn. bd., 1992. Decorated Order of Canada; recipient Queen's Golden Jubilee Medal. Fellow: IEEE, Can. Acad. Engrs., Royal Soc. of Can., Instn. Elec. and Telecomm. Engrs.; mem.: India Soc. Engrs., Eng. Inst. Can. Hindu. Home: 21026 Schoenborn St Canoga Park CA 91304 Office: Natel Engring Co Inc 9340 Owensmouth Ave Chatsworth CA 91311 Office Phone: 818-734-6511. Personal E-mail: bhartiaprakash@hotmail.com. Business E-Mail: pbhartia@natelengr.com.

BHARUCHA, ASHOK J., psychiatrist; MD, Penn State Coll. of Medicine, Hershey, PA, 1988—92; Residency in Adult Psychiatry, Harvard Med. Sch., Boston, MA, 1992—96; Geriatric Psychiatry Fellowship, U. of Wash. Sch. of Medicine, Seattle, WA, 1996—97. Lic. Am. Bd. Psychiatry and Neurology ABPN, Inc., IL, 1998. Resident in adult psychiatry Harvard Med. Sch., Boston, 1992—96; geriatric psychiatry fellow U. Wash. Sch. Medicine, Seattle, 1996—97; asst. prof. of psychiatry U. of Pitts. Sch. of Medicine, Pitts., 2000—. Adj. asst. prof. Grantee Career Devel. award, Nat. Inst. on Aging, 2004—. Home: 5030 Fifth Ave 315 Pittsburgh PA 15232 Office: Wpic 3811 O'Hara St Pittsburgh PA 15213 Office Phone: 412-383-4845. Home Fax: 412-383-4846; Office Fax: 412-383-4846. Personal E-mail: bharuchaaj@msx.upmc.edu.

BHARUCHA, JAMSHED, academic administrator; b. July 24, 1956; BA, Vassar Coll.; MA in Philosophy, Yale U.; PhD in Psychology, Harvard U. Asst. prof. Dartmouth Coll., 1983—89, assoc. prof., 1989—95, prof., 1995—97, John Wentworth chair in psychol. and brain scis., 1997—2002, assoc. dean faculty for social scis., 1997—2000, dep. provost, 2000—01, dean faculty, 2001—02; provost, sr. v.p. Tufts U., Medford, Mass., 2002—, prof. psychology, 2002—. Mem. Linguistics and Cognitive Sci. program Dartmouth Coll., mem. Electro-Acoustic Music program; commentator various segments NPR; mem. adv. panel NSF; fellow Ctr. for Advanced Study in the Behavioral Scis. Stanford U. Contbr. articles to profl. jours. Fellow: Am. Inst. Indian Studies. Avocation: violin. Office: Provosts Office Tufts Univ Medford MA 02155

BHAT, BAL KRISHEN, geneticist, plant breeder; b. Srinagar, India, May 3, 1940; came to U.S. 1989; s. Justice Janki Nath and Dhanwati (Kaul) B.; m. Sarla Kaul, Sept. 23, 1966; children: Arun Bhat, Anupama Bhat. MSc, Indian Agrl. Rsch. Inst., New Delhi, 1963; PhD, I.A.R.I., New Delhi, 1967. Rsch. assoc. Rockefeller Found., New Delhi, 1967; plant breeder in charge of rsch. Birla Inst. of Sci. Rsch., Rupar, Punjab, India, 1967-68; scientist C Reg. Rsch. Lab. Coun. of Sci. and Indsl. Rsch., Srinagar, India, 1968-74, head, 1972-79, 87-89, scientist E I, 1974-79, scientist E II, 1981-85, deputy dir., 1985-89; v.p., dir. rsch. Bot. Resources, Inc., Independence, Oreg., 1989-95; cons., 1995—. Rsch. fellow U. Tasmania, Hobart, Australia, 1979-81, sr. rsch. fellow, 1981-86; cons. in field. Contbr. over 110 articles to profl. jours. Named Scientist of the Yr., Reg. Rsch. Lab., Srinagar, 1976. Fellow: Indian Soc. Genetics and Plant Breeding; mem.: Am. Botanical Coun., Coun. for Agrl. Sci. and Tech., Soc. for Advancement of Breeding Rsch. in Asia and Oceania, Crop Sci. Soc. Am., Am. Soc. Agronomy. Achievements include introduction and organization of commercial production of crops to new lands such as hops in India, pyrethrum in Australia, others; evolved a number of new cultivars in hops, pyrethrum, and medicinal and aromatic plants. E-mail: balkrishen@yahoo.com.

BHAT, YASSER M., gastroenterologist, physician, researcher; m. Sualiheen Shaw. MBBS, Kasturba Med. Coll., Mangalore, India, 1998. Diplomate Am. Bd. Internal Medicine. Internal medicine SUNY Stony Brook, East Meadow, 1999—2000, Cleve. Clinic Found., 2000—03; fellow in gastroenterology U. Pitts., 2003—04, rsch. assoc., 2004—05. Contbr. chapters to books, scientific papers. Recipient Schering-Plough award, Am. Assn. Study Liver Disease, Boston, 2004, U. Kans. award, Esophageal Motility and Reflux Evaluation meeting, New Orleans, 2005. Mem.: ACP, Am. Coll. Gastroenterology, Am. Gastroent. Assn., Am. Soc. Gastrointestinal Endoscopy, NY Acad. Scis.

BHATI, MAHENDRA (MACH) TAKASHI, artist; b. Fukuoka, Japan, Apr. 4, 1975; s. Deo Kalyan and Midori Tone Bhati. BA in Chemistry, BS in Biology, Emory U., 1996; postgrad., La. State U., School Medicine, 1997—2001, MD, 2001. Rsch. assoc. Emory Eye Inst., Atlanta, 1994-96; graphic designer Molecular Vision, 1995-96; rsch. asst. Walden Woods Rsch. Ctr., 1997; software developer IXL, 1997; vis. scholar Ctr. Advanced Visual Studies MIT, Cambridge, 1998; instr., cons. Pa. Coll. Optometry, Phila. Vol. blood drive ARC, Atlanta, 1996—97; med. asst. Martin Luther King, Jr. Health Ctr., Shreveport, La., 1999. Contbr. abstracts, photographs to profl. jours.; contrib. (publications, photography) Bullwater Review, 1994, Between 1 and 3, 1999, Jama, 1999, Liars Shot Lying, 1999, New Physician, 1999, Life of the City, 1999, The Museum of Modern Art, 1999, NYC, 1999. Vol. blood drive ARC, Atlanta, 1996—97. Recipient John W. Bick award, La. Psychiatric Medial Assn., 2001, Hon. Mention Creative Arts Contest, Am. Med. Student Assn.; fellow Howard Hughes, NSF, 1996; scholar Stipe scholar in visual arts, John Gordon Stipe Soc., 1994, dean's scholar Atlanta Coll. Art, 1996, Clin. Rsch. Scholar, dept. Neuropsychiatry, Phila. Mem.: Internat. Soc. Arts, Scis. and Tech., Am. Psychiatric Assn., AMA.

BHATIA, PETER K., editor, journalist; b. Pullman, Wash., May 22, 1953; s. Vishnu N. and Ursula Jean (Dawson) B.; m. Elizabeth M. Dahl, Sept. 27, 1981; children: Megan Jean, Jay Peter. BA, Stanford U., 1975. Polit. reporter, asst. news editor Spokesman Rev., Spokane, Wash., 1975-77; news editor Dallas Times Herald, 1980-81; asst. news editor San Francisco Examiner, 1977-80, news editor, 1981-85, dep. mng. editor/news, 1985-87; mng. editor Dallas Times Herald, 1987-88; editor York Dispatch, York, Pa., 1988-89; mng. editor The Sacramento Bee, 1989-93; exec. editor The Fresno Bee, 1993; mng. editor The Oregonian, Portland, 1993-97, exec. editor, 1997—. Pulitzer Prize juror, 1992-93, 98-99; bd. dirs. Am. Press Inst. Mem. adv. bd. Knight Ctr. Specialized Journalism U. Md.; mem. adv. bd. Murrow Sch. Communication Wash. State U.; mem. new media adv. bd. Oreg. State U.; bd. chmn. Albertina Kerr Ctrs. for Children, 2001—02, found. chair, 2004—05; chmn. bd. St. John Fisher Sch., 2000—04. Mem.: Investigative Reporters and Editors, South Asian Journalists Assn., Nat. Assn. Minority Media Execs., Asian Am. Journalists Assn., AP Mng. Editors (bd. dirs. 1991—97), Am. Soc. Newspaper Editors (bd. dirs. 1997—, treas. 2000—01, sec. 2001—02, v.p. 2002—03, pres. 2003—04), Stanford U. Alumni Assn. (bd. dirs. 1998—2001), Theta Delta Chi, Sigma Delta Chi. Office: The Oregonian 1320 SW Broadway Portland OR 97201-3499 Office Phone: 503-221-8393. Business E-Mail: pbhatia@news.oregonian.com.

BHATIA, RAJAN, engineer, physicist, researcher; arrived in U.S., 1985, permanent resident; s. Prem S. and Shakun Bhatia. Student, U. Mont., Butte, 1985—88; BS in Engring. Physics, U. Maine, Orono, 1991. Laser systems rsch. engr. Amoco Laser Co., Naperville, Ill., 1990—90, Amoco Corp. - Amoco Tech. Co., Naperville, 1990—92; laser systems tech. engr., non-linear acoustics physicist Johnson & Johnson, Claremont, Calif., 1992—95, sr. laser systems engr. Palo Alto, Calif., 1996—97; laser systems rsch. engr. Cygnus, Monroe, Wash., 1995—96; sr. rsch. scientist IRIS/IRIDEX, Sunnyvale, Calif., 1997—99, Qculight Inc., Bothell, Wash., 1999—2000; sr. mem. tech. staff Tyco Internat., Eatontown, NJ, 2001—01; prin. photonics staff engr. NIS, San Jose, Calif., 2001—. Electro-optical sys. engr. NASA, Greenbelt, Md., 1990; presenter in field. Contbr. articles to profl. jours. Scholar, U. Maine, 1988—91. Mem.: ASM Internat., Japanese Soc. Applied Physics, Internat. Soc. Optical Engring., Optical Soc. Am. Achievements include research in various diverse areas of Laser Engineering, Photonics, Electro-Optics, Biomedical Lasers, High Power Lasers, Non-Linear Optics, Fiber-Optics, Biomedical Acoustics & Ultrasound; design of various in Biomedical Lasers, High Power Lasers, Non-Linear Optics, Fiber-Optics, Biomedical Acoustics & Ultrasound. Personal E-mail: gumalaser24@mail.com.

BHATIA, REENA KOHLI, computer science educator; b. New Delhi, Aug. 8, 1970; arrived in U.S., 1999; d. Satish Kumar and Pushpa Kohli; m. Somesh Bhatia, Sept. 18, 1993; children: Shreya, Neha. BA Math., Delhi U., New Delhi, India, 1992; BS Computer Sci., Math., Tex. Women's U., Denton, 2000; AS Biology (hon.), Texarkana Coll., 1998. Cert. Tchr. Tex. Intern I.T. TWV Tech. Dept., Denton, Tex., 2000; networking tchr. Frisco ISD, Frisco, Tex., 2001—02; tchr. computer sci. Lewisville ISD. LLL, Tex., 2002—. Mem.: Tex. Assn. of Profl. Educators. Hindu. Avocation: reading. Office Phone: 972-219-6900 ext.2217. E-mail: bhatiar@llsd.net.

BHATTACHARJYA, ASHOKE SANJOY, economist, researcher; b. Shillong, India, Jan. 17, 1965; s. Arunoday and Supriya Bhattacharjya; m. Shamoli Bhattacharjya; 1 child, Amit. BA with honors, Delhi U., 1985; MA, Delhi (India) Sch. Economics, 1987; PhD, MPhil, Columbia U., 1993. Instr. NYU, N.Y.C., 1990—93; adj. asst. prof. Columbia U., N.Y.C., 1993—94; economist, corp. planning and policy Pfizer, N.Y.C., 1993—96; assoc. dir. health econs. Janssen Pharmaceutica, Titusville, NJ, 1996—97, dir.,outcomes rsch., 1997—2001; sr. dir. bus. intelligence and analytics Jannsen Pharmaceutica, Titusville, NJ, 2001—; exec. dir. health policy & econ. Johnson & Johnson, 2004—. Lectr., program for econ. policy mgmt. World Bank, Columbia U., N.Y.C., 1992—93; invited lectr. program on pharm. industry MIT, Cambridge, Mass., 1997—98; invited conf. chair/spkr. numerous profl. orgns.; jour. referee Econ. Theory, Jour. Econ. Dynamics and Control, Health Econs. Contbr. articles to profl. jours. Recipient All India Entrance Merit scholarship, Delhi U., 1982—85, Naqvi Meml. Merit scholarship, Delhi Sch. of Economics, 1986—87, President's fellowship, Columbia U., 1987—90, Standards of Leadership award, Johnson &Johnson, 1997—2002, Excellence award, Internat. Ctr. for Mental Health Policy and Econ., 2003. Mem.: Ad Hoc Pharm. Industry Working Group, Nat. Assn. Bus. Economists, Am. Econ. Assn. Home: 1 Colebrook Ct Princeton NJ 08540 Office: Janssen Pharmaceutica (Johnson&Johnson) 1125 Trenton-Harbourton Road Titusville NJ 08560 Personal E-mail: bashoke@aol.com. E-mail: abhattac@janus.jnj.com.

BHATTACHARYA, BHASWATI, preventive medicine physician; b. Calif. BA, U. Pa.; MA in pharmacology, Columbia U.; MPH in internat. health, Harvard U.; MD, Rush Med. Coll. Resident in preventive medicine Mt. Sinai Med. Ctr., NYC, with cmty. and preventive medicine dept.; pvt. practice in preventive medicine, pub. health., holistic medicine and holistic healing counseling NYC; attending physician dept. family practice and cmty. medicine Wyckoff Heights Med. Ctr., NY-Presbyn. Hosp., Bklyn., dir. rsch. dept. medicine, dir. divsn. complementary and alternative medicines; asst. prof. family practice Weill Med. Coll., Cornell U. Asian Am. health subcommittee advisor to US Senator Hillary Rodham Clinton; contbr. expert Dorland's Med. Dictionary. Founder women's health program Sakhi, NYC. Recipient Leadership award, AMA Found., 2004. Mem.: Am. Assn Physicians of Indian Origin, Am. Holistic Medicine Assn. (Nat. award 1998), S. Asian Pub. Health Assn. (bd. dir. 2004—). Office: Wyckoff Hts Med Ctr Medicine/Ob-Gyn 374 Stockholm St Brooklyn NY 11237 Office Phone: 718-907-4951. Business E-Mail: bhb9002@nyp.org.

BHATTACHARYA, SATYAJIT, research scientist; came to U.S., 1993; s. Amal and Rekha B. BS, U. Poona, Pune, Maharashtra, India, 1985, MS, 1987; diploma in Computer Sci., Indian Inst. Computer Studies, Pune, 1988; MS, U. Toronto, 1993; PhD, Calcutta U., India, 2001. Rsch. assoc. Mt. Sinai Sch. Medicine Vets. Affairs Med. Ctr., N.Y.C., 1993-94, asst. rsch. scientist, 1994-95, NYU Med. Ctr., N.Y.C., 1994-95; rsch. assoc. Amgen Inc., Thousand Oaks, Calif., 1995-96; rsch. scientist Meml. Sloan-Kettering Cancer Ctr., N.Y.C., 1996—. Inventor in field; contbr. articles to profl. jours. Coun. Sci. and Indsl. Rsch. fellow, 1991. Fellow Royal Microscopic Soc.; mem. AAAS, Am. Chem. Soc., N.Y. Acad. Scis., Histochem. Soc. (Outstanding Young Investigator award 1999), Metastasis Rsch. Sic., European Soc. Analytical and Cell Pathology (Best Oral Presentation award 2002), Internat. Soc. Quality and Diagnostic Pathology, Am. Molecular Pathology Soc.,

Harlem Children Soc. (founder, CEO, pres. 2000—), Sigma Xi (pres. Rockefeller U. chpt. 2003). Avocations: reading, writing, swimming, sports, music. Office: Meml Sloan-Kettering Cancer Ctr Dept Pathology Box 105 1275 York Ave New York NY 10021 E-mail: bhattacs@mskcc.org.

BHATTACHARYA, SYAMAL KANTI, biomedical scientist, educator; b. Calcutta, India, Feb. 13, 1949; arrived in U.S., 1974, naturalized, 1983; s. Sudhir Chandra Bhattacharya and Prabhabati Battacharya; m. Keka Karabi Ghoshal, Dec. 11, 1969; children: Sumoulindra Titu, Julie Keka, Syamal Dave. BS with honors, U. Calcutta, 1968; BA in English Lit., 1969; MS, Murray State U., 1976; AM, Washington U., St. Louis, 1978; PhD, Memphis State U., 1979. Diplomate Am. Bd. Bioanalysis; cert. profl. chemist Nat. Cert. Commn. Chemistry and Chem. Engring., lic. med. lab. dir. Tenn. Dept. Pub. Health. Instr. chemistry Netaji Shakshaytan, Calcutta, India, 1968—69; sr. instr. chemistry Bhabanath Instn., Calcutta, 1969—70; R&D chemist Swastik Household and Indsl. Products Pvt. Ltd., Bombay, 1970—74; sr. rsch. tech. Washington U. Med. Sch., St. Louis, 1976—77; rsch. assoc. U. Tenn. Med. Ctr., Memphis, 1979—80, instr. medicine, 1980—82, mem. surgery faculty, 1983—, dir. surg. rsch. labs., 1982—, founding dir. chemistry and nutrient data output lab., 1982—, instr. surgery, 1983—84, asst. prof. surgery, 1984—88, asst. prof. medicinal chemistry, 1985—91, assoc. prof. medicinal chemistry, 1991—99, prof. pharm. scis., 1999—, assoc. prof. surgery, 1988—98, prof. surgery, 1998—, assoc. prof. anatomy and neurobiology, 1988—95, prof. neurology, 1999—. Adj. prof. surgery NY Med. Coll., 1988—97; vis. prof. surgery Yale U. Sch. Med., 1985; vis. prof. pediats. U. Cin. Med. Ctr. and Cin. Children's Hosp., 1985; vis. prof. pediatric surgery Johns Hopkins U. Sch. Med., 1987; vis. prof. surgery Rush-Presbyn.-St. Luke's Med. Ctr., Chgo., 1987, NY Med. Coll., 1987—88; vis. prof. biochemistry George Washington U. Sch. Medicine, Washington, 1988, Howard U., 1989; vis. prof. surgery East Tenn. State U., 1989; vis. prof. microbiology Bose Inst., Calcutta, 1999, Calcutta, 2001; external examiner doctoral dissertation faculty scis. Jadavpur U., Calcutta, 2002—; commr. Nat. Cert. Comm. Chemistry & Chem. Engrg., Washington, 1987—; v.p. Nat. Registry in Clin. Chemistry, Washington, 1999—2000, pres., 2000—01; grant reviewer, mem. pathology-A study sect. NIH, 1993—95. Contbr. numerous publs. to biomed. and sci. jours., to nat. and internat. sci. confs.; ad hoc reviewer: for numerous sci. and profl. jours. Grantee Am. Heart Assn., 1986—87, NIH, 1988—95. Grantee Muscular Dystrophy Assn. Am., 1983—84; recipient Presdl. rsch. fellowship, Memphis State U., 1978—79, Indian Nat. scholarship, Govt. India, New Delhi, 1965—69, Govt. India scholarship, Bank of India, 1974—75, rsch. grant, U. Physician's Found., 1985—86, Varian Instrument Group of Am., 1986—99, U. Tenn. Med. Group, 1997—99, Nat. Rsch. Svc. award in medicine, NIH, 1979—81. Fellow: Am. Coll. Nutrition, Indian Chem. Soc., Am. Instn. Chemists (cert. profl. chemist 1980); mem.: ACS, AAAS, Am. Oil Chemists' Soc., Internat. Soc. Brain Rsch., Soc. Neurosci., NY Acad. Scis., Am. Soc. Molecular Biology and Biochemistry, Coll. Am. Pathologists, Am. Fedn. Clin. Rsch., Royal Soc. Chemistry (chartered chemist 1981), U. Tenn. Faculty Club (Memphis), Phi Kappa Phi, Sigma Xi. Office: U Tenn Med Ctr 956 Court Ave Ste B220 Memphis TN 38163-2814 E-mail: sbhattachary@utmem.edu.

BHATTACHARYYA, DEV, information technology executive, consultant; s. Santosh and Bela Bhattacharyya; m. Sheena Mukhopadhyay, Oct. 9, 1984; children: Rupsha, Reeshav. BS/MS, Birla Inst. Tech. and Sci., 1982. Cert. JBuilder 5 Enterprise Borland Software Corp., 1990, Visibroker C+ Borland Software Corp., 1990, Visibroker Java Borland Software Corp., 1990, C+ Builder Borland Software Corp., 1990, Java Programming Brainbench, 1997, Delphi Programming Brainbench, 1999. Prin. cons. Borland Software Corp., Princeton, NJ, 1998—2002; dir. distributed technologies Starwood Hotels and Resorts Worldwide Inc., White Plains, NY, 2002—05; v.p. tech. solutions ITC Infotech USA, Princeton, 2005—. Pres. Emryn Internat. LLC, Sparta, NJ, 2000—05. Author: (book) BPB Publications - From Delphi 2 You, 1997; contbr. technical articles in field. Mem.: IEEE, IEEE Computer Soc., Assn. Computing Machinery, Planetary Gemologists Assn., Coun. of Vedic Astrology. Achievements include development of value ERP open source; Grafx-Shop - graphics editor and publisher; Mystic Prediction Engine - astrology; FTP-Shop - FTP Client. Home: 678 Glen Rd Sparta NJ 07871 Personal E-mail: devb@ieee.org.

BHAUMIK, MANI LAL, physicist; b. Calcutta, India, Jan. 5, 1932; came to U.S., 1959, naturalized, 1968; s. Gunadhar and Lolita (Pramanik) B. BS, U. Calcutta, 1951, MS, 1953; PhD, Indian Inst. Tech., 1958, DSc (hon.), 1995. Fellow U. Calif. at Los Angeles, 1959-63; with Xerox Electro-Optical Systems, Pasadena, Calif., 1961-67, Northrop Corp. Labs., Hawthorne, Calif., 1968-71, research dir., 1971-75; mgr. Laser Tech. Lab., Northrop Research and Tech. Center, 1976-84, sr. staff scientist, 1984-86. Lectr. physics Calif. State U., Long Beach, 1967-69. Author: Code Name YOD, 2005; contbr. articles to profl. jours. Fellow Am. Phys. Soc., IEEE. Achievements include patents in field. Office: Laser Tech Lab PO Box 24050 Los Angeles CA 90024-0050 *A strong and innate belief in basic human goodness has often pulled me out of hostile circumstances where one is likely to lose faith in humanity.*

BHAVSAR, NATVAR PRAHLADJI, artist; b. Gothava, India, Apr. 7, 1934; came to U.S., 1962; s. Prahladji V. and Babu P. B.; m. Janet Brosious, Jan. 15, 1978; children: Shashin, Ajay, Rajeev. AM, Bombay State Higher Art Exam., 1958, Govt. Diploma Art, 1959; BA in Liberal Arts and English Lit, Gujarat U., Ahmedabad, India, 1960; MFA, U. Pa., 1965. Instr. in art U. R.I., 1967, 68, 69. One-man shows include Obelisk Gallery, Boston, 1968, 69, Max Hutchinson Gallery, N.Y.C., 1970, 71, 72, 74, 77, 78, in Houston, 1978, Gallery A. Sydney, Australia, 1970, Gallery Chemould, Bombay, 1970, Kenmore Gallery, Phila., 1963, 74, Kingspitcher Gallery, Pitts., 1977, Gloria Luria Gallery, Bayharbor Fl., 1978, 98, Wichita (Kans.) Art Mus., 1979, 85, Pembroke Gallery, Houston, 1985, 87; Gettler/Pall/Saper, N.Y.C., 1984, Bose-Pacia Modern Gallery, N.Y.C., 1986, ACP Viviane Ehrli Gallery, Zurich, Switzerland, 1997, Art-Garage, Zug, Switzerland, 2000, Dialectica, NY, 2000, Sundaram Tagore Gallery, 2001, 02, World Economics Forum, Davos, Switzerland, 2000 Pardo St. Croix Gallery, milan and Rome, Italy, 2003; group shows include Jewish Mus., N.Y.C., 1970, Whitney Mus. Am. Art, 1970 (2), Indpls. Mus. Art, 1970, 78, U. Sydney, 1970, Columbus (Ohio) Gallery Fine Arts, 1971, U. Rochester, 1971, Max Hutchinson Gallery, 1973, Am. Acad. Arts and Letters Art Gallery, N.Y.C., 1973, Ruth S. Schaffner Gallery, Los Angeles, 1974, Reed Coll., 1974, Rockland Ctr. for Arts, West Nyack, N.Y., 1979, Fifth Triennale, New Delhi, India, 1981, Il Sud del Mondo, L'Altra Arte Contemporanea Galleria Civica de Arte Contemporarea, Pizzo, Italy, 1991, Gloria Lurie Gallery, Bay Harbor, Fla., 1978, 92, IlSud del Mondo, L'Attra Contemporanca, Commune di Marsa, Pizzo, Italy, 1991, Angolazioni e Prospettive Della Visione, Nell'Arte Contemporanea, Centro Museografico, Palazzo S.Domenico, Taverna, Italy, 1991, Viviane Ehrli Gallery, Art Cologne (Germany) Internat., 1998, 99; represented in permanent collections Met. Mus. Art, N.Y.C., Boston Mus. Fine Arts, Guggenheim Mus., N.Y.C., Chase Manhattan Bank, N.Y.C., Wichita Art Mus. (Kans.), Herbert F. Johnson Mus. at Cornell U., Australian Nat. Gallery, Canberra, Library of Congress, M.I.T., Ulrich Mus. Art, Wichita, Lannan Found., Power Inst., Sydney, Rose Art Mus. at Brandeis U., U. Mass., Amherst, U. Del., Whitney Mus. Am. Art, N.Y.C., Worcester (Mass.) Mus., Am. express co., N.Y.C., N.B.C., N.Y.C., Olympia and York, Toronto, Readers Digest, N.Y., United Bank of Switzerland, N.Y.C.; monograph Natvar Bhavsar Painting and the Reality of Color (Irving Sandler), 1998. John D. Rockefeller III Fund fellow, 1965-66, Guggenheim Meml. Found. fellow, 1975-76. Achievements include being subject of profl. articles. Home: 131 Greene St New York NY 10012-3220

BHIDAYASIRI, ROONGROJ, neurologist, researcher; s. Mitr and Nisaratana Bhidayasiri. MD, Chulalongkorn U., Bangkok, Thailand, 1993. Diploma in Geriatric Medicine Royal Coll. of Physicians and Surgeons of Glasgow, 1998. Physician Innsbruck U. Hosp., Austria, 1994—95, Royal London U. Hosp. and Southend Hosp., London, 1995—96, U. Hospitals of Wales, Cardiff, England, 1997, U. Coll. London Hosp., 1997, U. of Oxford Hosp. Radcliffe Infirmary, England, 1998, Guy's, St. Thomas' and King's Coll. Hosps., London, 1998—99, 1998—99, U. Hosp. of Cleve., Cleveland, Ohio, 1999—2000, UCLA Med. Ctr. and Sch. of Medicine, 2000—. Bd. mem. Chulalongkorn U. Alumni of Calif., LA, 2002—. Author: (book) Neurological Differential Diagnosis, Neuroradiology Casebook, (jour. article) Am. Jour. of Ophthalmology, Annals of N.Y. Acad. of Sci., Jour. of Vestibular Rsch., Jour. of Neurology Neurosurgery Psychiatry, Annals of Oncology. Bd. mem. Thai Assn. of So. Calif., LA, 2002—03; chairperson New Wave Group, LA, 2002—03. Recipient New Millennium Investigator award, Dystonia Med. Rsch. Found., 2001—02; Lilian Schorr fellow, Parkinson's Disease Found., 2003—04. Fellow: Royal Soc. Medicine (assoc.); mem.: Movement Disorders Soc., Royal Coll. Physicians (Edinburgh) (licentiate), Royal Coll. Physicians (London) (licentiate), L.A. Coun. World Affairs (assoc.), Assn. Brit. Neurologists (assoc.), Am. Acad. Neurology (assoc.). Buddhist. Achievements include research in New treatment in dystonia using transcranial magnetic stimulation. Avocations: violin, piano, chess, squash. Office: UCLA Med Ctr and Sch of Medicine 710 Westwood Plz Los Angeles CA 90095 Business E-Mail: rbh@ucla.edu.

BHIDE, MANOHAR GOPAL, nuclear scientist, educator; b. Pune, Maharashtra, India, Nov. 9, 1935; arrived in U.S., 1994, naturalized, 2001; s. Gopal Ramchandra and Manorama Gopal Bhide; m. Meena Mohiniraj Joshi, Jan. 7, 1981; children: Unmesh, Amit, Sonia. BSc in Math., U. of Mumbai, 1954, MSc in physics, 1956, PhD, 1971. Registered profl. engr., Argonne Nat. Lab., IL., USA, 1958, cert. Atomic Energy Rsch. Establishment, Harwell, U.K., 1960; Yoga tchr. Kaivalyadham, Lonavala, Maharashtra, India, 1984. Fellow Ramnarain Ruia Coll., Mumbai, India, 1954—56; sci. officer Bhabha Atomic Rsch. Ctr., Trombay, Mumbai, India, 1956—94; adj. faculty in physics No. Va. C.C., Annandale, Va., 1997; substitute tchr. Fairfax County Pub. Schs., Va., 1998—. Exch. scientist Atomic Energy Rsch. Establishment, Harwell, Didcot, Berkshire, United Kingdom, 1958—60; affiliate Internat. Inst. of Nuc. Sci. & Engring., Argonne, Ill., 1960—62; sec. disarmament study group Govt. of India, Dept. Atomic Energy, Mumbai, 1962—67; sci. sec. XII Pugwash Conf. on Sci. & World Affairs, Udaipur, Rajasthan, India, 1964—64; Indian del. IAEA Seminar on Physics of Fast & Intermediate Reactors, Vienna, 1961—61, Second UN Conf. on Peaceful Uses of Atomic Energy, Geneva, 1958—58; adj. prof. Southeastern U., Washington, 1999—. Editor: Vidnyan Kutuhal, Marathi Mahasangh-Vidnyan; contbr. articles to profl. jours. Co-founder, treas. Marathi Vidnyan Mahasangh, 1980—82; founder, treas., sec. Madhyamumbai Marathi Vidnyan Sangh, Mumbai, India, 1971—93; co-founder, treas. Mumbai Shubham Karoti Parivar, Mumbai, 1979—88; camp leader Student Voluntary Work Camps, Turbhe, Gorkamat & Kadav, India, 1953—54; active Bhabha Atomic Rsch. Ctr. Maharashtra Mandal, Mumbai, 1970—94, Kokannagar Yuvak Mandal (Youth Club), 1965—75; vis. lectr. Shramik Vidyapeeth Ministry Non-formal Edn. Govt. India, 1973—82. Recipient V. K. Bhagawat prize, Ramnarain Ruia Coll., Mumbai, India, 1954; scholar, U. of Mumbai, India, 1952—54. Fellow: Soc. for Advancement of Electrochem. Sci. and Tech. (life; internal auditor Mumbai chpt. 1988—93); mem.: Am. Assn. Univ. Profs., Am. Nuc. Soc., Indian Nuc. Soc. (life), Nat. Assn. for Applications of Radiation and Radioactive Isotopes (life), Assn. Med. Physicists India (life), Indian Assn. for Radiation Protection (life; mem. organizing com. of ann. conf. 1990), Indian Physics Assn. (life), Sierra Club. Avocations: photography, nature walks, music, museums, yoga. Home: 8156 Larkin Lane Vienna VA 22182-5232 Personal E-mail: mhbhide@hotmail.com.

BHUIYAN, MOHAMMAD ALI, university administrator, educator, consultant; b. Dhaka, Bangladesh, Jan. 1, 1959; came to U.S., 1986; s. Nasir Uddin and Luthfunnesa (Khanam) B.; m. Shamima Amin, Aug. 28, 1986; 1 chlid, Muzaffer Ahmed. BSS, U. Dhaka, 1980; MBA, Indian Inst. Mgmt., Bangalore, 1983, Ga. State U., Atlanta, 1988; PhD, U. Fla., 1993. Sales mgr. Brit. Am. Tobacco, Dhaka, 1983-84; lectr. U. Dhaka, 1984-86; grad. rschr. U. Fla., Gainesville, 1989-93; lectr. Morris Brown Coll., Atlanta, 1989; instr. U. Fla., Gainesville, 1992-93; coord. internat. bus. Savannah (Ga.) State U., 1993-96; head dept. bus. Fort Valley (Ga.) State U., 1996-97; asst. dean, prof. Hampton (Va.) U., 1997-2000; prof., dir. OFC Venture Challenge Clark Atlanta U., Ga., 2000—. Contbr. articles to profl. jours. Bd. dirs. Better Bus. Bur., Savannah and Macon, Ga., 1994-97, Jr. Achievement, Savannah, 1994-96, ARC, Savannah, 1994-96, Am. Heart Assn., Savannah, 1994-96. Recipient Best Tchr. award Savannah State U., 1994; World Bank fellow, 1986-88. Mem. Acad. of Mgmt., Am. Econ. Assn., Bangladesh Econ. Assn. (life), Am. Assn. Higher Edn., Soc. for Advancement of Mgmt. (life), Acad. Internat. Bus., Rotary club of Savannah (bd. dirs 1995). Avocations: travel, swimming. Home: 3246 Paces Mill Rd SE Atlanta GA 30339 Office: Hampton U Sch Bus Sch Bus Hampton VA 23668

BHUSHAN, BHARAT, mechanical engineer; b. Jhinjhana, India, Sept. 30, 1949; came to U.S., 1970, naturalized, 1977; s. Narain Dass and Devi (Vati) B.; m. Sudha Bhushan, June 14, 1975; children: Ankur, Noopur. BE Mech. Engring. with honors, Birla Inst. Tech. and Sci., 1970; MSME, MIT, 1971; MS in Mechanics, U. Colo., 1973, PhD in Mech. Engring., 1976; MBA, Rensselaer Poly. Inst., 1980; DSc, U. Trondheim, Norway, 1990; D of Tech. Scis., Warsaw (Poland) U. Tech., 1996; D honoris causa, Metal Polymer Rsch. Inst., Nat. Acad. Scis. at Gomel, Belarus, 2000. Mem. rsch. staff dept. mech. engring. MIT, Cambridge, 1971-72; rsch. asst., instr. dept. mech. engring. U. Colo., Boulder, 1973-76; phys. tribology program mgr. R&D divsn. Mech. Tech. Inc., Latham, NY, 1976-80; rsch. scientist, tech. svcs. divsn. SKF Industries, Inc., King of Prussia, Pa., 1980-81; devel. engr., mgr., gen. products divsn. lab. IBM Corp., Tucson, 1981—86; rsch. staff mem., mgr. head-disk interface Almaden Rsch. Ctr., IBM Rsch. Divsn., San Jose, Calif., 1986-91; Ohio eminent scholar, Howard D. Winbigler prof. mech. engring. Ohio State U., Columbus, 1991—, dir. Nanotribology lab. info. storage, 1991—. Expert investigator Automotive Specialists, Denver, 1973-76; vis. sr. scientist dept. machine design and materials tech., Royal Norwegian Coun. for Sci. and Indsl. Rsch., U. Trondheim, 1987, USSR Acad. Sci., Moscow, Gomel, Vilnuis, Leningrad, 1989; vis. scholar dept. mech. engring., chemistry and materials sci. and mineral engring. U. Calif., Berkeley, 1989; Sony sabbatical chair prof. Sony Corp. Rsch. Ctr., Fujitsuka, Japan, 1997; guest prof. dept. physics and engring. U. Cambridge, 1999; Inst. Fine Tech., Tech. U. Vienna, 1999; sr. academic visitor, Ecole Polytechnique Federale de Lausanne, Inst. de Physique de la Matiere Complexe, Switzerland, 2003; rsch. student supr.; spkr. over 250 invited presentations, 60 keynote and plenary addresses, and internat. confs. worldwide. Author: Tribology and Mechanics of Magnetic Storage Devices, 1990, 2d edit. 1996, Mechanics and Reliability of Flexible Magnetic Media, 1992, 2d edit. 2000, Principles and Applications of Tribology, 1999, Introduction to Tribology, 2002; co-author (with B.K. Gupta) Handbook of Tribology: Materials, Coatings and Surface Treatments, 1991; mem. editl. bd. Jour. Friction and Wear of Belarus, Tribology Letters and Storage; assoc. editor Jour. Tribology, 1986-90; co-editor Proceedings on Tribology and Mechanics of Magnetic Storage Systems Symposia, 1984-90; editor Handbook of Micro/Natrotribiology, 1995, 2d edit., 1999, Modern Tribology Handbook, Vol. 1 Principles of Tribology, 2001, Vol. 2 Materials, Coatings and Industrial Applications, 2001, Springer Handbook of Nanotechnology, 2004; editor 25 books; co-editor-in-chief Microsystem Technologies: Micro- & Nanosystems and Information Storage and Processing Systems, 2002; editor-in-chief, founding editor ASME series Advances in Info. Storage Sys., 1991-93, World Scientific, 1994-99; editor-in-chief CRC Mechanics and Materials Sci. series, Jour. Info. Storage and Processing Sys., 1999-2001; contbr. over 50 handbook chpts., 500 tech. papers, 60 tech. reports, 4005 articles to profl. jours. in field. Recipient Alfred Noble prize ASCE, IEEE, ASME, AIME, Western Soc. Engrs., 1981, George Norlan award, U. Colo., 1983, Regents Disting. Svc. award, 1985, GPD Achievement award IBM Corp., 1983, Invention Achievement award, 1985, Rsch. Divsn. award for Outstanding Achievement, 1987, Outstanding Tech. Achievement award, 1990, Tech. Excellence award Am. Soc. Engrs. India, 1989, Cert. Appreciation award NASA, 1987, Lumley Rsch. award, Ohio State U., 1997, 2001, Alexander von Humboldt Rsch. prize for Sr. Scientists U. Ulm, 1998-99, U. Karlsruhe, 1998-99, Fulbright Sr. Scholar award Tech. U. Vienna, 1999, UN Sr. TOKTEN Expert award, Dehli, Bangalore, India, 1999, Max Planck Found. Rsch. award for Outstanding Fgn. Scientists Max Planck Inst. for Metals Rsch., Düsseldorf, Germany, 2002; Ford Found. fellow MIT, 1971; grantee USN, NASA, Dept. Energy, USAF, Franco-Am. Commn. for Ednl. Exch. Interfound. grantee Ecole Ctrl. Lyon, 1999. Fellow STLE, IEEE, ASME (cert. of recognition Design Engring. Conf., Henry Hess award 1980, Burt L. Newkirk award 1983, Gustus L. Larson Meml. award 1986, Tribology Divsn. Best Paper award 1989, Melville medal for Best Current Original Paper 1992, Bd. Govs. award for Valued Svcs. as Founding Chair of ISPS Divsn. 1997, Bd. Govs. award for Valued Svcs. as Chair of ISPS Divsn. 1998, Charles Russ Richards Meml. award 2000, Robert Henry Thurston Lecture award, 2004), NY Acad. Scis.; mem. NSPE, IEEE (sr.), ASEE, Soc. Tribologists and Lubrication Engrs., Am. Soc. Lubrication Engrs., Am. Acad. Mechanics, Internat. Humanists Soc., Tri-City India Assn., Internat. Acad. Engring. Russia (fgn.), Byelorussian Acad. of Engring. and Tech. (fgn.), Acad. of Triboengring. of Ukraine (fgn.), Soc. of Tribologists of Belarus (hon.), Soc. Tribologists and Lubnicetim Engr., Rotary, Sigma Xi, Tau Beta Pi, Pi Tau Sigma. Hindu. Achievements include 16 patents in field; pioneer in tribology and mechanics of magnetic storage devices; leading researcher in field of micro/nanotribology using single probe microscopy. Home: 10235 Widdington Close Powell OH 43065-9059 Office: Ohio State U 206 W 18th Ave Columbus OH 43210-1107 Office Phone: 614-292-0651. Business E-Mail: bhushan.2@osu.edu.

BHUYAN, PRAKASH K., virologist, researcher; b. N.Y.C., Apr. 29, 1969; s. Kailash C. and Durga K. Bhuyan; m. Varsha U. Gogate, Mar. 31, 1997; children: Anjalee P., Sangeetha P. MD, PHD, U. Tex. Southwestern, Dallas, 1998. Cert. internal medicine Am. Bd. Internal Medicine, 2001, infectious diseases subspecialty Am. Bd. Internal Medicine, 2005. Fellow infectious diseases U. Pa., Phila., 2001—04, attending and instr. medicine, 2004—. Contbr. articles to profl. jours. (Austrian award Outstanding Fellows in Infectious Diseases, 2004). Mem.: Infectious Disease Soc. Am. Office Phone: 215-662-3185. E-mail: bhuyan@prodigy.net.

BIAGIOLI, JOHN ALLAN, lawyer; b. Kansas City, Mar. 12, 1953; s. Mario L. and Mary F. (Schaub) B.; m. Beverly J. Arnold, June 12, 1981. BA in English, U. Mo., 1975, JD, 1980. Bar: Mo. 1980, U.S. Dist. Ct. (we. dist.) Mo. 1980. Atty. David Williams Law Office, Independence, Mo., 1980-82, pvt. practice, Independence, Mo., 1982-90; ptnr. James & Biagioli, Independence, Mo., 1990—. Active Hope House, Independence, 1990—. Mem. Kansas City Metro. Bar Assn., Eastern Jackson County Bar Assn. Avocation: sports. Office: James & Biagioli 123 W Kansas Ave Independence MO 64050-3713

BIALASIEWICZ, JAN TADEUSZ, electrical engineering educator; b. Pruszkow, Poland, June 1, 1939; came to U.S., 1985; s. Piotr Pawel and Wanda Henryka Bialasiewicz; m. Ewa Teresa Wanasz, Sept. 30, 1967; children: Luiza, Seweryn. MS in Elec. Engring., Warsaw (Poland) Tech. U., 1962; PhD in Elec. Engring., Silesian Tech. U., Gliwice, Poland, 1966; DSc in Elec. Engring., Silesian Tech. U., 1972. Registered profl. engr., Colo. Head, computer control software dept. Indsl. Inst. Automation and Measurements, Warsaw, 1969-78; assoc. prof. elec. engring. Higher Inst. Electronics, Malta, 1979-80; head, computer control software dept. Nuc. Rsch. Inst., Warsaw, 1980-85; assoc. prof. elec. engring. U. Colo., Denver, 1985—. Vis. rsch. assoc., NASA Langley Rsch. Ctr., Hampton, Va., summers, 1990, 91, NASA/ASEE fellow, 1993; cons. Nat. Renewable Energy Lab., Golden, Colo., 1994—; vis. prof., Warsaw Tech. U., 1997. Author: Wavelets and Approximations, 2000; contbr. articles to profl. jours. Pres. Rocky Mountain chpt. Kosciuszko Found., Denver, 1993—. Named Prof. Tech. Scis., Pres. Republic of Poland, 2001. Mem. IEEE, AAUP, Polish Inst. Arts and Scis. in Am. Roman Catholic. Avocations: travel, skiing, classical music. Office: U Colo at Denver CB110 PO Box 173364 Denver CO 80217 E-mail: jtbialas@carbon.cudenver.edu.

BIALKIN, KENNETH JULES, lawyer, director; b. N.Y.C., Sept. 9, 1929; s. Samuel and Lillian (Kastner) B.; m. Ann Eskind, Aug. 19, 1956; children: Lisa Beth, Johanna. AB, U. Mich., 1950; cert. of attendance, London Sch. Econ., 1952; JD, Harvard U., 1953. Bar: N.Y. 1953, U.S. Dist. Ct. (ea. dist.) N.Y. 1955, U.S. Supreme Ct. 1964, U.S. Dist. Ct. (so. dist.) N.Y. 1972, U.S. Ct. Appeals (2d cir.) 1976. Assoc. Willkie Farr & Gallagher, N.Y.C., 1953-60, ptnr., 1960-88, Skadden, Arps, Slate, Meagher & Flom, N.Y.C., 1988—. Adj. prof. law NYU, 1967-87; lectr., commentator legal and fin. symposia; mem. N.Y. Stock Exch. Legal Adv. Commn., 1983-92, 98—, chmn. internat. securities subcom., 1989-98; bd. dirs. Citigroup, Inc., 1986-2002, St. Paul Travelers Property and Casualty Co. 1986—2005, Mcpl. Assistance Corp. City of N.Y., Ltd.; mem. Adminstrv. Conf. of U.S., 1987-92; chmn. Com. on Fin. Svcs.; bd. govs. grad. faculty New Sch. U., 1992—; mem. N.Y. State Commn. on Edn. Reform. Editor: The Business Lawyer, 1980; bd. editors Corp. Governance Jour., 1992—; contbr. articles on corp., fin. investment law to profl. jours. Chmn. Conf. Pres. Major Am. Jewish Orgns., 1984-86; chmn. Am.-Israel Friendship League, 1995—; nat. chmn. Anti-Defamation League B'nai Brith, 1982-86; pres. Jewish Cmty. Rels. Coun. N.Y., 1989-92; vice-chmn., dir. Jerusalem Found., Inc., 1975—. Mem. ABA (chmn. fed. regulation securities com. 1974-79, chmn. com. to study fgn. investment in U.S. 1978-80, chmn. ad hoc com. on insider trading regulation 1988—, chmn. sect. corp. banking and bus. law 1981-82, 88), Am. Jewish Hist. Soc. (pres. 1997—03, chmn. 2003—), N.Y. State Com. on Edn reform, 2003-04, N.Y. County Lawyers Assn. (pres. 1986-88), Am. Bar Retirement Assn. (dir. 1981-84), Coun. Fgn. Rels., Harvard Club. Home: 211 Central Park W New York NY 10024-6020 Office: Skadden Arps Slate Meagher & Flom Fl 44 4 Times Sq New York NY 10036-6595 Office Phone: 212-735-2130. Business E-Mail: kbialkin@skadden.com.

BIALLER, NANCY, art appraiser; AB, Vassar Coll.; MA, MPhil, PhD in 16th & 17th Century Dutch Art, Yale U. With Sotheby's, London, 1976, head, Old Master Drawings NYC. Fullbright Fellow, Vienna, 1972. Office: Sotheby's 1334 York Ave New York NY 10021 Office Phone: 212-606-7230. Office Fax: 212-606-7107. Business E-Mail: nancy.bialler@sothebys.com.*

BIALO, KENNETH MARC, lawyer; b. NYC, Nov. 21, 1946; s. Walter and Mildred (Miller) B.; m. Katherine Ann Burghard; children: Darren Andrew, Caralyn Alyssa, Jacquelyn Anne, Matthew Joseph Geronimo, Kelsey Elizabeth Ariel. BS, U. Rochester, 1968; JD cum laude (Univ. scholar), NYU, 1971; LLM, London Sch. Econs., 1973. Bar: N.Y. 1972, U.S. Ct. Appeals (2d cir.) 1974, U.S. Ct. Appeals (fed. cir.) 1988, U.S. Supreme Ct. 1975. Law clk. Hon. L.W. Pierce U.S. Dist. Ct. (so. dist.) N.Y., 1971—72; assoc. Sullivan & Cromwell, N.Y.C., 1973—80; counsel, sr. counsel Exxon Corp., NYC, 1980—90; sr. counsel, chief litigation atty. Exxon Chem. Co., Darien, Conn., 1990—91; ptnr. Baker Botts, LLP, N.Y.C., 1992—2003, Emmett, Marvin & Martin, LLP, N.Y.C., 2003—. Lectr. Practicing Law Inst., N.Y.C., 1982, 88, N.Y. State Bar Assn., 1997; vice chmn. bd. State of N.Y. Mcpl. Bond Bank Agy., N.Y.C., 2000—, State of N.Y. Tobacco Settlement Fin. Corp., 2003—. Contbg. editor: Family Legal Guide, 1974; contbr. articles to profl. jours.; note and comment editor: NYU Law Rev.; host The Larchmont Report, WVOX, Whitney Radio Group, New Rochelle, N.Y., 1995—, co-host Larchmont Today, LMC-TV, Mamaroneck, N.Y., 1995—; co-founder, prin. contbr.: Plugged In, Rep. Party Pub. Svc. Newsletter, 1996—. Trustee Village of Larchmont, NY, 1991-2002, mayor, 2002—; mem. PLI Adv. Com. on Litig., 1994—; bd. govs., Univ. Club Larchmont, 1995-1999, pres., 1998-1999; v.p., bd. dirs. Little League, Larchmont, 1985-94, recreation com., 1987-89; treas., exec. com. L.I. Sound Watershed Intermcpl. Coun., Westchester County, NY, 2000-2002; mem. Westchester County Legis. Stormwater Adv. Com., 2001—. Mem. ABA (litig. sect. task force on client concerns 1994-95, subcom. class action, litig. sect.), N.Y. State Bar (antitrust com., fed. and comml. litig. sect., former chmn. corp. counsel com. 1989-91), Assn. of Bar of City of N.Y. (arbitration com. 1983-85), Fed. Bar Coun. (com. 2d cir. cts. 1985-87), Am. Arbitration Assn. (mem. arbitrators panel), Order of Coif. Avocations: tennis, baseball, opera, symphony. Office: Emmett Marvin & Martin LLP 120 Broadway New York NY 10271 Office Phone: 212-238-3058.

BIAN, RANDY XINDI, research scientist; m. Shiyuan Zhong, July 1, 1985; 1 child, Jessica. BS, Nanjing (China) U., 1982, MS, 1985, Iowa State U., 1993. Tchg. asst. Nanjing U., 1982-86; lectr. Nanjing Inst. Meteorology,

1987-88; rsch. asst. Iowa State U., Ames, 1989-92; scientist Pacific N.W. Nat. Lab., Richland, Wash., 1993—. Contbr. articles to profl. jours. Mem. AAAS, Am. Geophys. Union, Am. Meteorol. Soc. Avocations: hiking, swimming, chess, travel, fishing. Office: Pacific NW Nat Lab PO Box 999 Richland WA 99352-0999 Home: 1711 Greencrest Ave East Lansing MI 48823-2907

BIANCANIELLO, THOMAS, medical association administrator; s. Michael and Thelma Biancaniello; m. Patricia Navas, Apr. 23, 1992; children: Shannon Little, Dawn, Frank Little, Patrick Little, Christopher. BA, Hamilton Coll., 1970; MD, NY Med. Coll., 1975. Diplomate Cardiology Am. Bd. of Pediat., 1981, Am. Bd. of Pediat., 1979. Assoc. dean for med. affairs Sch. of Medicine at Stony Brook, Stony Brook, NY, 1993—; chief med. officer Stony Brook U. Hosp., Stony Brook, NY, 1994—; prof. of pediat. Sch. of Medicine at Stony Brook, Stony Brook, NY, 1995—. Chief, pediatric cardiology Sch. of Medicine at Stony Brook, Stony Brook, NY, 1980—. Pres. Am. Heart Assn., Suffolk Chpt., Long Island, NY, 1980—80; state bd. of dir. Am. Heart Assn., Syracuse, NY, 1990—92. Named Man of the Yr. in Medicine, Three Village Times, 1988; recipient Vol. of the Yr. award, Suffolk Chpt. Am. Heart Assn., 1989-1900. Office: Stony Brook U Sch Medicine Dept Pediat Stony Brook NY 11794-8111 Office Phone: 631-444-2725. Office Fax: 631-444-2894.

BIANCHI, CARISA, advertising company executive; Formerly with Benton & Bowles, L.A., Doyle Dane Bernbach; with Chiat/Day L.A., 1989-97; mng. dir., pres., CEO TBWA/Chiat/Day, San Francisco, 1998—2002, mng. ptnr. Playa del Rey, 2002, chief strategy officer L.A., 2002—. Office: TBWA/Chiat/Day 5353 Grosvenor Blvd Los Angeles CA 90066-6319

BIANCHI, GEORGE L., lawyer; b. Seattle, Nov. 5, 1952; s. Alfred and Anabel Bianchi; children: Nicole, Beau, Talia Starr. BS in Bus., U. Wash. 1978, Gonzaga, 1980, JD, 1981. Bar: Wash. Prosecutor King County Prosecutor's Office, Seattle, 1981—83; lawyer The Bianchi Law Firm, Seattle, 1984—. Trainer Dui Def. Skills, Seattle. Named Super Lawyer, Wash. Law & Politics, 2000, 2001, 2003, 2004, 2005; recipient DWI Specialist, The Minn. Soc. Criminal Justice, 1991, Deans Svs. award, Nat. Coll. Dui Def., 2003. Mem.: Nat. Assn. Criminal Def. Lawyers, Nat. Coll. Dui Def. (regent), Wash. Found. Criminal Justice (v.p. 1997—), Snohomish County Bar Assn., King County Bar Assn., Wash. State Bar Assn. Office: The Bianchi Law Firm 605 ThomasSt Seattle WA 98109 Office Phone: 206-728-9300. Office Fax: 206-728-9305. Business E-Mail: george@thebianchilawfirm.com.

BIANCHI, HOLLIS DOLCE, writer, artist, poet; b. Orange, NJ, June 25, 1952; d. Ovid Carlo Bianchi and Matilda Florence Dolce. AAS, Marymount U., Arlington, VA, 1978. Mem.: Nat. Mus. Women Arts. Avocations: harmonica, embroidery, reading. Home: 49 Florence Avenue Leonardo NJ 07737 Personal E-mail: dmapelli@aol.com.

BIANCHI, MARIA, critical care specialist, adult and acute care nurse practitioner, nursing administrator; b. Springfield, Mass. B of Nursing, Catherine Laboure Sch. Nursing, 1979; BSN, Fitchburg (Mass.) State Coll., 1985; PhD in nursing adminstrn., Universal U., 2005. Cert. post-anesthesia care nurse; critical care clin. specialist; expert witness, Mass., Conn. Recovery as mgmt. educator; mktg. and recruitment cons.; cons. in critical care nursing; clin. faculty Am. Internat. Coll., Springfield; adminstr. dept. spl. svcs., mgr. critical care Baystate Med. Ctr., Springfield, Mass., 1980-89; recruitment adminstrn. and sr. faculty St. Francis Med. Ctr. Sch. of Nursing, Hartford, Conn., 1989-92; grad. faculty U. Mass. Med. Ctr., Worcester, 1995-97; asst. prof. Grad. Sch. U. Mass., Amherst, 1998-99; faculty U. Mass. Sch. of Nursing, Amherst, per diem nurse practitioner dept. surgery Worcester, 1995—97, 1999—; CS/NP Mass Gen. Hosp., Boston. Pres. ProLase Medi-Spa & Clinic, Worcester and Springfield, Mass., TI Healthcare; nat. cons. critical care/post anesthesia issues; medicolegal cons.; laser med. provider; lectr. critical care and post anesthesia issues, empowerment, acute pain, holistic techniques, medicological documentation, trauma. Invited amb. del. People's for People's, Fed. Govt. Mem. AACN, Am. Soc. Post-Anesthesia Nursing (Boston chpt. editl. cons.), Soc. Critical Medicine, Mass. Gen. Hosp. Alumni Assn., Catherine Laboure Alumni Assn., Sigma Theta Tau. Achievements include research in pain, burn trauma, stress reduction, holistic methods for high risk individuals in maximum security penitentiary and critical care patients. Office: PO Box 614 Suffield CT 06078-0614 E-mail: mariatih@comcast.net.

BIANCO, ANTHONY JOSEPH, III, newswriter; b. Oceanside, Calif., May 17, 1953; s. Anthony Joseph Jr. and JoAnn (Reavill) B.; 1 child, Marissa. BA, U. Minn., 1976. Reporter Mpls. Tribune, 1977; bus. editor Willamette Week newspaper, Portland, Oreg., 1978-80; corr. Bus. Week mag., San Francisco, 1980-82, dept. editor N.Y.C., 1982-84, assoc. editor, 1984-85, sr. writer, 1985-92, 1996—. Author: Rainmaker, 1991, The Reichmanns, 1997, Ghosts of 42nd Street, 2004. Recipient media award for econ. understanding Amos Tuck Sch., Dartmouth Coll., 1979, award for feature writing Oreg. Newspaper Pubs., 1979, award for excellence in fin. writing N.Y. State Soc. CPA's, 1987, Disting. Editorial Achievement award McGraw-Hill, 1986, Nat. Bus. Book award, Can., 1997. Mem. Soc. Profl. Journalists. Home: 17 1st St Brooklyn NY 11231-5001 Office Phone: 212-512-3201.

BIBAUD, RENE, artist, performer, consultant; b. Longbranch, N.J., Nov. 21, 1969; d. Richard Charles and Mildred Ellen Bibaud. Artist performer Cirque Du Soleil, Montreal, 1996—2001; artist performer/cons. self employed, Kirkland, Wash., 2001—02. Home: 805 Warren Ave N Apt 302 Seattle WA 98109-5625 Personal E-mail: renebibaud@compuserve.com.

BIBB, DANIEL ROLAND, art restorer; b. Gadsden, Ala., June 10, 1951; s. Cassius Roland and Louise Selma B. Student, Jefferson State, 1969-70, DeKalb Coll., 1971-72. Sales cons. Macy's Antique Gallery, Atlanta, 1973; dir. Collector's Gallery, Atlanta, 1974-76, Connoisseur's Gallery, New Orleans, 1977-79; painting conservator Daniel R. Bibb Fine Painting Conservation & Restoration, Atlanta, 1980—; chief fund raiser Atlanta Rabbit Rescue. Researcher for pvt. collectors and museums, Atlanta, 1977-89; listed conservator, New Orleans Museum List of Restorers, New Orleans, 1988. Discovered a lost major painting of Philip IV of Spain; exhibited lost painting Atlanta High Mus. Art, 1980; publ. of discovered painting, High Mus. Monthly, 1980; conservator Anglo-Am. Art Mus., Baton Rouge, New Orleans Mus. Art.; owner Fabergé collection on loan to New Orleans Mus. Art, 1996; icon collection touring mus., La., Miss. and Ala., 1998—; contbr. articles to popular mags. Fund raiser Am. Heart Assn., Atlanta, 1987-88, March of Dimes, 1987-88, Atlanta Rabbit Rescue, 1984—; active High Mus. Art, Atlanta; vol. ARC Disaster Relief Team, Atlanta, 1992, Art Care Art Auction for fight against AIDS, 1992-93, chmn. Live Auction, 1993 Recipient Design award, Most Authentic Design, Patio Planters of the Vieux Carre, New Orleans, 1977. Mem. Nat. Trust for Historic Preservation. Republican. Baptist. Achievements include raising funds and pub. awareness of animal cruelty. Home and Office: Bibb Painting Restoration 807 Summit North Dr NE Atlanta GA 30324-5641

BIBBO, MARLUCE, physician, educator; b. Sao Paulo, Brazil, July 14, 1939; d. Domingos and Yolanda (Ranciaro) Bibbo. MD, U. Sao Paulo, 1963, ScD, 1968. Intern Hosps. das Clinicas, U. Sao Paulo, 1963, resident in morphology, 1964-66; instr. dept. morphology and ob-gyn. U. Sao Paulo, 1966-68, asst. prof., 1968-69; fellow in cytology U. Chgo., 1969-70, asst. prof. sect. cytology dept. ob-gyn., 1971-73, assoc. prof., 1973-77, assoc. prof. pathology, 1974-77, prof. ob-gyn. and pathology, 1978-92; assoc. dir. Cytology Lab., Approved Sch. Cytotech and Cytocybernetics, AMA-Am. Soc. Clin. Pathologists, 1970-91; dir. Cytology Lab., Phila., 1992—; prof. pathology and cell biology Thomas Jefferson U., Phila., 1992—, Warren R. Lane prof. pathology & cell biology, 1993—. Mem. rsch. com. Ill. divsn. Am. Cancer Soc., 1976-91. Contbr. numerous articles to profl. jours. Fellow Internat. Acad. Cytology (pres.-elect, v.p. 1987, pres. 1992, dep. editor Acta Cytologica, editor 1995), Am. Soc. Clin. Pathologists (coun. on cytopathology); mem. Am. Soc. Cytology (exec. com., pres. 1982-83), U.S. Acad. Pathology, Can. Acad. Pathology, Soc. Analytical Cytology, Coun. Cytopathology. Home: 250 S 9th St Philadelphia PA 19107-5734 Office: Cytology Lab Rm 260 Main Bldg 132 S 10th St Philadelphia PA 19107-5244 Office Phone: 215-955-6437. E-mail: bibbo@cytology-iac.org.

BIBBY, DOUGLAS MARTIN, mortgage association executive; b. Endicott, N.Y., Aug. 24, 1946; s. Dause Leveridge and Virginia (Martin) B.; m. Lorraine C. Creer, Sept. 6, 1969; children: Mariah, Ian. BA in Econs., Denison U., 1968; MBA, U. Tex, 1970. Sr. v.p. J. Walter Thompson Co., N.Y.C., Washington, San Juan, P.R., and Toronto, Can., 1971-82; v.p. Russell Reynolds Assocs., Inc., Washington, 1982-83; sr. v.p. adminstrn. Fed. Nat. Mortgage Assn., Washington, 1983-98; ptnr. The Fin. Group, Potomac, Md., 1999—. Bd. dirs. Martha's Table, 1985—, Arena Stage, 1992—, The Summit Fund of Washington, 1992—. Avocations: tennis, community affairs.

BIBBY, THOMAS FREDERICK ALLEN, physicist; b. Caracas, Venezuela, Feb. 17, 1955; came to U.S., 1955; s. T.F. Allen Bibby and Joan Francis Keefer; m. Yu Wang, Oct. 20, 1990; 1 child, Keefer. BS in Physics, Marlboro Coll., 1978; MSEE, U. Vt., 1982; PhD in Physics, Drexel U., 1992. Assoc. mem. tech. staff RCA Corp., Palm Beach Gardens, Fla., 1984; asst. mem. tech. staff David Sarnoff Rsch. Ctr., Princeton, N.J., 1985-90; postdoctoral fellow USN Naval Air Warfare Ctr., Warminster, Pa., 1993-95; sr. process engr. IPEC Westech, Phoenix, 1995; mgr. process R&D Integrated Prcoess Equipment Corp. Planar, Phoenix, 1996-97; mgr. strategic tech. Integrated Prcoess Equipment Corp., Phoenix, 1997-99; sr. tech. mgr. SpeedFam-Integrated Process Equipment Corp., Chandler, Ariz., 1999; sr. intellectual property engring. mgr./project mgr. ip Capital Group, Williston, Vt., 1999—2001; v.p. tech. Diffraction Ltd., Waitsfield, Vt., 2001—02; pvt. practice St. Albans, Vt., 2002—. Contbr. articles to profl. publs. Mem. IEEE, Am. Phys. Soc., Optical Soc. Am. Achievements include patents in field. Personal E-mail: tbibby@adelphia.net.

BIBEAULT, DONALD BERTRAND, investor; b. Woonsocket, RI, Nov. 14, 1941; s. George Bertrand and Renee (Herbert) B.; m. Gigi Loving, June 18, 1994 (div. June 2002); children: Zachary James, Jessica Renee, Dorothy Leigh. BSEE, U. RI, 1963; MBA, Columbia U., 1965; PhD, Golden Gate U., 1979, JD (hon.), 2000. COO Pacific States Steel, Union City, Calif., 1975-78, PLM Internat., San Francisco, 1979-81; turnaround advisor Varity Corp., 1981-82; pres., CEO Best Pipe and Steel Co., San Francisco, 1983-86; workout advisor Bank of Am., 1987-89; chmn. Am. Nat. Petrol, Houston, 1990-91; chmn., CEO Tyler Dawson Supply Co., Tulsa, 1990-91, Iron Oak Supply Co., Sacramento, 1990-93; pres. Bibeault and Assocs., Inc., San Rafael, Calif., 1976—; chmn. Bsquare Corp., Bellevue, Wash., 2003—. Trustee Golden Gate U., San Francisco, 1986-97; bd. advisors U. R.I. Bus., Kingston, 1993—; bd. overseers Columbia Grad. Sch. Bus., N.Y.C., 1994—2001; bd. visitors Golden Gate U. Law Sch., San Francisco, 2000—; CEO adviser underperforming cos., 1993—; chmn. bd. dirs. Bsquare Corp., Seattle, 2003—. Author: Corporate Turnaround, 1982 (Fortune award 1982); contbr. articles to profl. jours. Adv. bd. on trade Dept. Commerce, Washington, 1988-92. Lt. U.S. Army Combat Engrs., 1963-65. Mem. Turnaround Mgmt. Assn. (founding dir. 1987-91), Bankers Club San Francisco. Home and Office: Bibeault Assocs 1 Dooley Ct Novato CA 94945 Office Phone: 415-781-7200. E-mail: bibeault@aol.com.

BIBERAJ, BUTA, lawyer; b. Montenegro, June 25, 1964; came to U.S., 1967; d. Hisen and Ajshe Biberaj. JD, George Mason U., 1993. Bar: NY 1994, Md. 1994, Va. 1993, US Dist. Ct. (Ea. Dist.) Va. 1994, US Ct. Appeals (4th cir.) 1993, US Supreme Ct. 1997. Law clk. Alexandria (Va.) Pub. Defender's Office, 1992-93; front end mgr. Price Club, Fairfax, Va., 1987-95; mem. Biberaj & O'Reilly, P.L.C., Leesburg, Va., 1994-96; ptnr. Biberaj & Assocs. PC, Leesburg, Va., 1997—2004; pub. defender Loudoun County Pub. Defender, Va., 2000—02; ptnr. Biberaj and Snow PC, Leesburg, 2004—. Avocations: sports, reading. Office: Biberaj & Snow 7 E Market St Ste 225 Leesburg VA 20176 Office Phone: 703-779-2000. E-mail: biberaj@biberaj-snow-law.com.

BIBERMAN, LUCIEN MORTON, retired physicist; b. Phila., May 31, 1919; s. Lewis and Eva (Kerns) Biberman; m. Anne H. Wilner, Mar. 8, 1941 (dec. 1997); children: Leslie Biberman Gordon, Judith Biberman Robinson, Candace Biberman Evans; m. Virgina L. Hewitt, May 25, 2002. BS, Rensselaer Poly. Inst., 1940; postgrad., Harvard U., 1940-41, Stevens Inst., 1941-42. Phys. chemist Nairn Rsch. Labs., 1942-43; physicist in charge Mayport Magnetic Survey Area, Navy Dept., 1943-44; various positions from physicist in charge phys. measurements group to cons. Aviation Ordnance Dept. and Weapons Devel. Dept. Naval Ordnance Test Sta., 1944-57; assoc. dir. Labs. for Applied Scis. U. Chgo., 1957-63; rsch. staff rsch. and engring. support div. Inst. for Def. Analysis, Alexandria, Va., 1963-71, rsch. staff sci. and tech. div., 1972-96; emeritus, 1996—; ret., 1996. Vis. prof. dept. elec. engring. U. R.I., 1971-72; fellow Mil. Sensing Symposium, 1999. Decorated citation U.S. Army Ctr. for Night Vision and Electro Optics; recipient Andrew J. Goodpaster award, 1989. Fellow: Washington Acad. of Sci. (Disting. Career in Sci. award), Soc. Photo-optical Instrumentation Engrs. (emeritus), Soc. Info. Display (emeritus), Optical Soc. Am. (emeritus), IEEE (life), Military Sensors Symposium, Infrared Info. Symposia. Home: 3731 Glen Eagles Dr Silver Spring MD 20906 Office Phone: 301-460-2892. Personal E-mail: lucienmb@verizon.net.

BIBICOFF, HILLARY SUE, lawyer; b. Ft. Riley, Kans., June 26, 1966; d. Harvey and Jacqueline Ruth (Marks) B. BA, UCLA, 1988; JD, Loyola U., 1991. Bar: Calif. 1991, Washington 1993, Colo. 1994. Assoc. Cooper, Epstein & Hurewitz, Beverly Hills, Calif., 1991-93; dir. legal and bus. affairs Live Entertainment, Inc., Van Nuys, Calif., 1993-96; dir. theatrical bus. and legal affairs Rysher Entertainment Inc., Santa Monica, Calif., 1996, v.p. theatrical bus. and legal affairs, 1997; assoc. Greenberg Glusker Fields Claman Machtinger & Kinsella LLP, L.A., 1997-2000, ptnr., 2001—. Active Hollywood Women's Polit. Com., L.A., 1993-97; bd. govs. Loyola Law Sch., 1997—. Burns scholar Loyola Law Sch., 1988-91; recipient award Nat. Assn. Women Lawyers, 1991; named one of Top 20 Hollywood New Generation Dealmakers, L.A. Bus. Jour., 2001; named Woman of Achievement, Century City Women's Bus. Coun., 2002, So. Calif. Super Lawyer, Law & Politics and LA Mag., 2004. Mem. L.A. County Bar Assn. (bd. dirs. intellectual property sect. 1995-98), Beverly Hills Bar Assn., Calif. Bar Assn., Saxophone Club (steering com. 1995-2000). Avocations: bicycling, tennis, skiing, horseback riding. Office: Greenberg Glusker Fields Claman Machtinger & Kinsella LLP 1900 Avenue Of The Stars Fl 20 Los Angeles CA 90067-4301 Office Phone: 310-785-6823. Business E-Mail: hbibicoff@ggfirm.com.

BIBLER, JUNE A., legal nurse consultant, registered nurse; d. Charles O. and Donna M. Bibler. BA, Ohio No. U., Ada, 1974; MA, Ohio State U., 1980; Assoc. Degree, Columbus State C.C., 1994; cert. legal nurse cons., Capital U. Law Sch., Columbus, 2001—02. Cert. med. and surg. nursing, Am. Nursing Credentialing Ctr., 1996. RN Ohio State U. Hosps., Columbus, 1994—96, Orthop. and Trauma Surgeons, Columbus, 1996—2002; tchr. Cory-Rawson Pub. Schs., Rawson, Ohio, 1975—76; nursing asst., orthop. technician Riverside Meth. Hosp., Columbus, 1976—84, microsurgery technician, 1984—87, RN, 1999—2000; rsch. assoc. Ohio State U. Dept. Transplantation, Columbus, 1987—94; legal nurse cons. Roetzel and Andress, Columbus, 2002—. Scholar, Ohio State U. Hosps., 1992—94. Mem.: Am. Assn. Legal Nurse Cons. Home: 1400 Thurell Rd Columbus OH 43229 Office: Roetzel and Andress 155 E Broad St 12th Fl National City Columbus OH 43215 Office Fax: 614-463-9792. Business E-Mail: jbibler@ralaw.com.

BIBLIOWICZ, JESSICA M., financial analyst; b. 1959; d. Sanford and Joan Weill; 2 children. Grad., Cornell U. Formerly with assesment mgmt. divsn. Shearson Lehman Bros.; dir. sales and mktg. Prudential Mutual Funds, 1992—94; exec. v.p., oversees mutual funds and insured investor group Smith Barney, N.Y.C., 1994—97; pres., COO John A. Levin & Co., 1997—99; pres., CEO Nat. Financial Partners, N.Y.C., 1999—. Dir. Eaton Vance Mutual Funds, Gov. Com. Scholastic Achievement, Securities Industry Assn.; mem., hedge funds adv. group, investment com. Cornell U. Gov. Boys & Girls Club of Am.; regional chair, N.E. Region. Office: NFP 787 7th Ave, 49th Fl New York NY 10019

BIBUS, THOMAS WILLIAM, lawyer; b. Cin., July 13, 1949; s. Howard Fred and Ernestine G. Bibus; children: Thomas Bradley, William Jason, Rebecca Lynn, Barbara Ann. BA in Econs., U. Cin., 1971; JD, Chase Coll. of Law, 1976. Bar: Ohio 1976, U.S. Dist. Ct. (so. dist.) Ohio 1976. Expediter, dispatch inspector ILSCO Corp., Cin., 1971-72; mgmt. trainee trust dept. Provident Bank, Cin., 1972-73; purchasing agt. Cin. Butcher Supply Co., 1973-76; sole practice Cin., 1976—. Mem. membership adv. panel Choicecare, Cin., 1983-87, past vice chmn.; mem. Parents Without Ptnrs., Cin., 1984—2002, profl. adviser, 1998—, former membership dir.; founder, leader Coping with Separation; judge Concours d'Elegance, Arthritis Found. Mem. Ohio Bar Assn. (domestic rels. and probate com.), Butler County Bar Assn., Cheviot Westwood Bus. Assn. (v.p., bd. dirs. 1987-89), West Side Lawyers (founder), East Side Lawyers (founder), Am. Bankruptcy Law Forum, Sierra Club (Miami group, sub-chmn. family outings 1989-91), Jaguar Club of Greater Cin. (charter, registrar), West Coast Swing Soc. (charter), Westwood Concern, Cin. Citizens Police Acad. Alumni Assn., Hope Cmty. Singles Group, St. Monica St. George Singles Group. Office: 2962 Harrison Ave Cincinnati OH 45211-6724 also: 8050 Beckett Center Dr West Chester OH Office Phone: 513-662-0300.

BICE, LAWRENCE R., science educator; b. Leavenworth, Kans., Mar. 27, 1958; s. Clarence R. and Teresa A. Bice; life ptnr. Vici D. Shorter, May 27, 1997. MA in Sci. Edn., Ottawa U., 1998; MS in Sci. Edn., Mont. State U., 2001, postgrad. Various adminstrn. positions Monson Army Hosp., Ft. Leavenworth, Kans., 1978—99; sci. tchr. Leavenworth (Kans.) H.S., 1998—99, Lawrence (Kans.) Free State H.S., 1999—2001, Sedona (Ariz.) Red Rock H.S., 2001—03; fellow Ctr. Learning and Tchg. West Mont. State U., Bozeman, Mont., 2003—05. Mem.: Nat. Assn. Rsch. Sci. Tech., Am.Ednl. Rsch. Assn. Office: Mont State Univ SMRC 401 Linfield Hall Bozeman MT 59717

BICE, SCOTT HAAS, dean, law educator; b. L.A., Mar. 19, 1943; s. Fred Haas and Virginia M. (Scott) B.; m. Barbara Franks, Dec. 21, 1968. BS, U. So. Calif., 1965, JD, 1968. Bar: Calif. bar 1971. Law clk. to Chief Justice Earl Warren, 1968-69; asst. prof., assoc. prof., prof. law U. So. Calif., Los Angeles, 1969—, assoc. dean, 1971-74, dean Law Sch., 1980-2000, Carl Mason Franklin prof., 1983-2000, Robert C. Packard prof. law, 2000—; CEO Five B Investment Co., 1995—. Vis. prof. polit. sci. Calif. Inst. Tech., 1977; vis. prof. U. Va., 1978-79; bd.dirs. Western Mut. Ins. Co., Residence Mut. Ins. Co., Imagine Films Entertainment Co., Jenny Craig, Inc., Arena Pharms., Inc. Mem. editl. adv. bd. Calif. Lawyer, 1989-93; contbr. articles to law jours. Bd. dirs. L.A. Family Housing Corp., 1989-93, Stone Soup Child Care Programs, 1988—, L.A. Child Guidance Clinic, 2003-; trustee Bice Passavant Found., 2000—. Affiliated scholar Am. Bar Found., 1972-74 Fellow Am. Bar Found. (life); mem. Am. Law Inst. (life), Calif. Bar, Los Angeles County Bar Assn., Am. Law Deans Assn. (pres. 1997-99), Am. Judicature Soc., Calif. Club, Chancery Club (treas. 2001-02, sec. 2002-03, v.p. 2003-04, pres. 2004-05), Econ. Roundtable, Long Beach Yacht Club, Catalina Island Yacht Club (judge adv. 2002—). Home: 787 S San Rafael Ave Pasadena CA 91105-2326 Office: U So Calif Sch Law Los Angeles CA 90089-0071 Office Phone: 213-740-4549. Business E-Mail: sbice@law.usc.edu.

BICHSEL, HANS, physicist, consultant, researcher; b. Basel, Switzerland, Sept. 2, 1924; came to U.S., 1951; s. Paul and Anna Maria Bichsel; m. Sue O. Greenwalt, Sept. 12, 1959; children: Elizabeth Christine, Joseph Oliver. MA, PhD, U. Basel, 1951. Rsch. asst. Princeton (N.J.) U., 1951-55; rsch. assoc. Rice U., Houston, 1955-57; asst. prof. physics U. Wash., Seattle, 1957-59; affiliate prof. physics U. Wash., Seattle, 1992—; assoc. prof., prof. radiology U. Wash., Seattle, 1969-80; asst. prof., assoc. prof. physics U. So. Calif., L.A., 1959-68; assoc. prof. U. Calif., Berkeley, 1968-69. Cons. Internat. Commn. on Radiation Units, Bethesda, Md., 1970—, Los Alamos (N.Mex.) Nat. Lab., 1978-83, IAEA, Vienna, Austria, 1990—; vis. scientist Nat. Inst. Radiol., Scis., Chiba, Japan, 1991-96, U. Sherbrooke Med. Sch., Que., Can.; rschr. Relativistic Heavy Ion Collider, Brookhaven Nat. Lab., 1999—; referee Phys. Rev., Nuclear Instruments and Methods, Physics in Medicine and Biology, also others. Contbr. articles to profl. jours. Fellow Am. Phys. Soc.; mem. Swiss Phys. Soc. Home and Office: 1211 22nd Ave E Seattle WA 98112-3534 Office Phone: 206-329-2792. Personal E-mail: hbichsel@scientist.com.

BICK, JOHN ALAN, lawyer; b. N.Y.C., Feb. 22, 1958; s. Alan Henry and Marie (Jensen) Bick; m. Susan Hagoort; children: Jessica, Anna. AB, Dartmouth Coll., 1980; JD, Columbia U., 1983. Bar: NY 1984. Ptnr. Davis Polk & Wardwell, N.Y.C., 1983—. Office: Davis Polk & Wardwell 450 Lexington Ave New York NY 10017 Home: 164 Benedict Hill Rd New Canaan CT 06840 Office Phone: 212-450-4350. E-mail: bick@dpw.com.

BICK, KATHERINE LIVINGSTONE, neuroscientist, educator, medical researcher; b. Charlottetown, Can., May 3, 1932; came to U.S., 1954; d. Spurgeon Arthur and Flora Hazel (Murray) Livingstone; m. James Harry Bick, Aug. 20, 1955 (div.); children: James A., Charles L. (dec.); m. Ernst Freese, 1986 (dec. 1990). BS with honors, Acadia U., Can., 1951, MS, 1952; PhD, Brown U., 1957; DSc (hon.), Acadia U., 1990. Rsch. pathologist UCLA Med. Sch., 1959-61; asst. prof. Calif. State U., Northridge, 1961-66; lab. instr. Georgetown U., Washington, 1970-72, asst. prof., 1972-76; dep. dir. neurol. disorder program Nat. Inst. Neurol. and Communicative Disorders and Stroke, NIH, Bethesda, Md., 1976-81, acting dep. dir., 1981-83, dep. dir., 1983-87; dep. dir. extramural rsch. Office of Dir. NIH, 1987-90; sci. liaison Centro Studio Multicentrico Internazionale Sulla Demenza, Washington, 1990-95. Cons. Nat. Rsch. Coun., Italy, 1991-97, The Charles A. Dana Found., N.Y.C., 1993-98, Edn. Commn. of the States, 1996-99. Editor: Alzheimer's Disease: Senile Dementia and Related Disorders, 1978, Neurosecretion and Brain Peptides, Implications for Brain Functions and Neurol. Disease, 1981, The Early Story of Alzheimer's Disease, 1987, Alzheimer Disease, 1994, 2d edit., 1999, Alzheimer Disease: The Changing View, 2000; contbr. articles to profl. jours. Pres. Woman's Club, McLean, Va., 1968-69; bd. dirs. Fairfax County (Va.) YWCA, 1969-70; pres. Avenel Homeowner's Assn., 1998; pres. Emerson Unitarian Ch., 1964-66; mem. Bethesda Pl. Cmty. Coun., 1992-95, pres., 1993-94; mem. Dana Alliance for Brain Initiatives, 1993—; bd. dirs. Wilmington N.C. Child Advocacy Commn., 1998-2002; mem. vol. guild St. John's Mus. Art, Wilmington; chair Vol. Guild Cameron Art Mus., Wilmington, 2002-2003, Cameron Art Mus. bd.,2003—; rector St. Andrew's on the Sound Episcopal Ch., Wilmington, 2004— Recipient Can. NRC award Acadia U., 1951-52, NIH Dir.'s award, 1978, Spl. Achievement award NIH, 1981, 83, Superior Svc. award USPHS, 1986, Presdl. Rank award meritorious sr. exec., 1989, Genesis award Alzheimer's Assn., 2005; Universal Match Found. fellow Brown U., 1956-57, Fed. Exec. Inst. Leadership fellow, 1980 Fellow AAAS; mem. Am. Neurol. Assn., Internat. Brain Rsch. Orgn., World Fedn. Neurology Rsch. Group on Dementias (exec. sec. Am. region 1984-86, chmn. 1986-93), Alzheimer's Disease Internat., Soc. for Neurosci. (emeritus), Acad. of Medicine Washington, Dana Alliance for Brain Initiatives.

BICK, ROBERT STEVEN, lawyer, researcher; b. N.Y.C., Apr. 11, 1961; s. Daniel Marvin and Marilyn (Tankus) B. BBA with distinction, U. Mich., 1983, JD, 1986. Bar: Mich. 1986, U.S. Dist. Ct. (ea. dist.) Mich. 1986. Law clk. 45-B Dist. Ct. Mich., Oak Park, 1979; intern Nat. Law Ctr., Washington, 1980; summer assoc. Vandeveer, Garzia, Tonkin, Kerr, Heaphy, Moore, Sills & Poling, P.C., Detroit, 1984, Dykema Gossett, Detroit, 1985; assoc. Schlussel, Lifton, Simon, Rands, Galvin & Jackier, P.C., Southfield, Mich., 1986-88, Williams, Schaefer, Ruby & Williams, Birmingham, Mich., 1988-92, ptnr., 1992—. Intern Nat. Park Service Student Conservation Assn., Inc., Yosemite Nat. Park, 1979. Mem. ABA, Am. Arbitration Assn. (arbitrator 1991—), Fed. Bar Assn., Oakland County Bar Assn. (bus. law com. 1988—, continuing legal edn. com. 1989-91), Nat. Assn. Securities Dealers Assn., Inc.

(arbitrator 1989—), Nat. Futures Assn. (arbitrator 1990—), Golden Key Hornor Soc. (life), FMA Honor Soc. of the Fin. Mgmt. Assn. (life, U. Mich. chpt.). Democrat. Avocations: golf, skiing. Home: 31700 Briarcliff Rd Franklin MI 48025-1273 Office: Williams Williams Ruby & Plunkett PC 380 N Old Woodward Ave Ste 300 Birmingham MI 48009-5322

BICK, RODGER LEE, hematologist, researcher, oncologist, educator; b. San Francisco, May 21, 1942; s. Jack Arthur and Pauline (Jensen) B.; m. Marcella Bick, Mar. 3, 1980 (dec. Feb. 1995); children: Shauna Nicole, Michelle Leanne. MD, U. Calif., Irvine, 1970; PhD, Acad. Medicine, Bialystok, Poland, 1995. Diplomate Am. Bd. Quality Assessment, Am. Bd. Forensic Medicine in Oncology, Hematology, Thrombosis, Hemostasis and Product Liability, Internat. Bd. Thrombosis, Hemostasis & Vascular Medicine, Am. Bd. Pain Mgmt. Med. intern Kern County Gen. Hosp., UCLA, Bakersfield, Calif., 1970-71, internal medicine resident, 1971-72; fellow in hematology-med. oncology UCLA/Bay Area Hematology Oncology Med. Group, West Los Angeles, Calif., 1974-76; med. staff various hosps., Calif., 1974-77, med. staff, extensive adminstrv. and com. work Bakersfield, Calif., 1977-92; med. dir. oncology hematology Presbyn. Comprehensive Cancer Ctr., Presbyn. Hosp., Dallas, 1992-95. Staff hematologist/oncologist Bay Area Hematology Oncology Med. Group, Santa Monica, Calif., 1976-77, med. dir. Calif. Coagulation Labs., Inc., Bakersfield, 1977-92, San Joaquin Hematology Oncology Med. Group, 1977-92, Regional Cancer and Blood Disease Ctr. Kern, Bakersfield, 1986-92; asst. clin. prof. to clin. prof. medicine UCLA Ctr. Health Scis., 1976-94, assoc. prof. to prof. allied health profns. Calif. State U., Bakersfield, 1980-92, clin. prof. nursing and health scis., 1982-92; adj. assoc. prof. medicine/physiology, Wayne State U., Detroit; adj. clin. faculty Wesley Med. Ctr. and U. Kans. Med. Sch., Wichita, 1984-86; clin. prof. medicine U. Tex. Southwestern Med. Ctr., 1993—, clin. prof. pathology, 1993—; prof. hematology U. Tasmania Sch. Medicine, 1996; hematology cons. NASA; med. dir. UCLA/Kern Cancer Program, 1991-92, Ctrl. Calif. Heart Inst., 1990-92; invited spkr. and presenter in field, numerous internat. symposia and confs.; dir. numerous workshops in field. Author: Disseminated Intravascular Coagulation and Related Syndromes, 1983, Disorders of Hemostasis and Thrombosis: Principles of Clinical Practice, 1985, 2d. edit., 1992, 3d edit., 1997, Disorders of Thrombosis and Hemostasis, 2002; guest editor, contbr.: Thrombohemorrhagic Disorders Perplexing to the Hematologist Oncologist, 1992; guest editor: Laboratory Diagnosis of Hemostasis Problems, I, 1994, II, 1995, (monograph) Seminars in Thrombosis and Hemostasis, 1994, Common Bleeding and Clotting Problems for the Internist, 1994; editor-in-chief: Hematology: Princples of Clinical and Laboratory Practice, 2 vols., 1993, Paraneoplastic Syndromes, Hematology Oncology Clinics of North America, 1996; editor: Current Concepts of Thrombosis, 1998; contbr. numerous chpts. to books; author monographs and lab. manuals; contbr. over 250 articles and papers and numerous revs. to profl. jours. and conf. procs.; patentee in field; editor-in-chief Jour. Clin. and Applied Thrombosis/Hemostasis & Vascular Medicine, Thrombosis and Thrombophilia, 2003; mem. editl. bd. Am. Jour. Clin. Pathology, Internat. Jour. Haematology. Bd. dirs., exec. com. Bakersfield Symphony Orch., 1988-92. Fellow ACP, Am. Soc. Clin. Pathologists, Assn. Clin. Scientists, Am. Soc. Coagulationists, Internat. Soc. Hematology, Am. Coll. Angiology, Internat. Coll. Angiology, Nat. Acad. Clin. Biochemistry, Am. Heart Assn. (coun. on thrombosis, circulation and atherosclerosis; rsch. and grant peer rev. com. 1980-86), Am. Geriat. Soc. (founding fellow, Am. Stroke Assn., Am. Soc. Angiology; mem. AMA, AAAS, Am. Assn. Blood Banks, Am. Soc. Internal Medicine, Am. Soc. Hematology, Internat. Soc. Thrombosis and Haemostasis, Am. Assn. Study of Neoplastic Disease, Am. Assn. Clin. Rsch., Am. Cancer Soc., Internat. Assn. Study of Lung Cancer (founding mem.), Fedn. Am. Scientists, N.Y. Acad. Scis., Calif. Soc. Internal Medicine, Calif. Med. Assn., Calif. Thoracic Soc., Haematology Soc. Australia, Internat. Consensus Com. on Autithrombotic Therapy, numerous others. Lutheran. Avocations: ocean sailing, classical piano, brass musical instruments, photography, target archery, astronomy and astrophotography. Office: 10455 N Central Expy Ste 109 Dallas TX 75231-2215 E-mail: rbick@thrombosis.com.

BICKART, THEODORE ALBERT, university president emeritus; b. N.Y.C., Aug. 25, 1935; s. Theodore Roosevelt and Edna Catherine (Pink) B.; m. Carol Florence Nichols, June 14, 1958 (div. Dec. 1973); children: Karl Jeffrey, Lauren Spencer; m. Frani W. Rudolph, Aug. 14, 1982; 1 stepchild, Jennifer Anne Cumming. B Engring. Sci., Johns Hopkins U., 1957, MS, 1958, DEng, 1960; D Univ. (hon.), Dneprodzerzhinst State Tech. U, Ukraine, 1996. Asst. prof. elec. and computer engring. Syracuse (N.Y.) U., 1963-65, assoc. prof., 1965-70, prof., 1970-89, assoc. to vice chancellor for acad. affairs for computer resources devel., 1983-85, dean L.C. Smith Coll. Engring., 1984-89; prof. elec. engring., dean engring. Mich. State U., East Lansing, 1989-98; pres. Colo. Sch. Mines, Golden, 1998-2000. Vis. scholar U. Calif., Berkeley, 1977; Fulbright lectr. Kiev Poly Inst., USSR, 1981; vis. lectr. Nanjing Inst. Tech., China, 1981; hon. disting. prof. Taganrog Radio Engring. Inst., Russia, 1992—; fellow Accreditation Bd. for Engring. and Tch., Engring. Accreditation Commn., exec. com., 1998-2000; chmn. Engring. Workforce Commn., 1996-98; elected-mem. Johns Hopkins U. Soc. Scholars, 2001. Co-author: Electrical Network Theory, 1969, Linear Network Theory, 1981; contbr. numerous articles to profl. jours. Served to 1st lt. U.S. Army, 1961-63 Recipient numerous rsch. grants; Disting. Alumni award, Johns Hopkins U. Fellow IEEE (best paper awards Syracuse sect. 1969, 70, 73, 74, 77, chmn. com. on engring. accreditation activities 1996-98, chmn. accreditation policy coun. 2001-2003), Am. Soc. Engring. Edn. (v.p. 1997-99); mem. Am. Math. Soc., Assn. for Computing Machinery, Soc. for Indsl. and Applied Math., N.Y. Acad. Scis., Ukrainian Acad. Engring. Scis.), Internat. Higher Edn. Acad. Scis. (Russia), Internat. Acad. Informatics (Russia), Johns Hopkins U. Soc. Scholars., Johns Hopkins U. Alumni Assn. (Disting. Alumnus award), ABET Avocations: bicycling, hiking, gardening. Home: 541 Wyoming Cir Golden CO 80403-0900 Personal E-mail: tabickart@comcast.net. Business E-Mail: tbickart@mines.edu.

BICKEL, FLOYD GILBERT, III, investment counselor; b. St. Louis, Jan. 10, 1944; s. Floyd Gilbert and Mary Mildred (Welch) B.; m. Martha Wohler, June 11, 1966; children: Christine Carleton, Susan Marie, Katherine Anne, Jennifer Anne, Laura Elizabeth, Andrew Barrett (dec.) BS in Bus. Adminstrn., Washington U., St. Louis, 1966; MS in Commerce, St. Louis U., 1968. Rschr. Yates, Woods & Co., St. Louis, 1966-67; asst. br. mgr. E.F. Hutton & Co., Inc., St. Louis, 1967-70, v.p. dir. consulting svcs., 1980-88; asst. v.p., resident mgr. Bache & Co., Inc., St. Louis, 1970-72; pres. Donelan-Phelps Investment Advisors, Inc., St. Louis, 1972—80; v.p. Merrill Lynch & Co., St. Louis, 1988—2003; sr. v.p. Morgan Stanley, St. Louis, 2003—. Bd. dirs. Summit Mktg. Group, Huntleigh Assocs., Eagle River LLC. Mem. City of Des Peres (Mo.), Planning and Zoning Commn., 1975-76; chm. St. Louis County Bd. Equalization, 1976-79; pub. safety commr. City of Des Peres, 1977-80, mem. audit and fin. com., 1980-86; mem. State of Mo. Gov.'s Crime Commn., 1981-92; bd. dirs. Villa Duchesne Sch., 1986-92; alderman City of Huntleigh, 1998-2002, mayor, 2002—; chmn. St Louis Arch Angels. Recipient Disting. Alumni award, Washington U., 2002, Washington U. Olin Sch. Bus., 2005. Mem.: John M. Olin Bus. Sch. Washington U. Alumni Assn. (pres. 1995—96, nat. coun. 2001—), St. Louis Soc. Fin. Analysts, Investment Mgmt. Cons. Assn., Internat. Soc. Cert. Employee Benefit Specialists, St. Louis Club, John's Island Club, Eagle Springs Golf Club, Cordillera Golf Club, Beaver Creek Club, Bellerive Country Club. Republican. Roman Catholic. Home: 30 Huntleigh Woods Saint Louis MO 63131-4813 Office: Morgan Stanley 700 Corp Park Dr Saint Louis MO 63105 Office Phone: 314-889-9836. Business E-Mail: gil.bickel@morganstanley.com.

BICKEL, JAN E., music educator, vocalist; b. Goshen, Ind., Oct. 15, 1950; d. Charles Robert and Mary T. Bickel. BA in Music, St. Mary's Coll., Notre Dame, Ind., 1972; MusM in Vocal Performance, Chgo. Conservatory of Music, 1976; diploma in German lang. studies, U. Vienna, Austria, 1980; D of Musical Arts, Am. Conservatory of Music, Chgo., 1992. Dir. of vocal music St. Xavier U., Chgo., 1982—. Artistic dir. Xavier Classics at Noon Concert Series St. Xavier U., 1995—. Mezzo-soprano (CD) An Art Song Excursion, mezzo-soprano soloist A Midsummer Night's Dream, Chgo. Symphony Orch., Magnificat - Imant Raminsh, Requiem; singer: Die Fledermaus, La Cenerentola, Die Zauberflote, The Shining Brow, Rigoletto, Le Nozze di Figaro, Hänsel und Gretel, Madama Butterfly; condr. (CD) Of Wind and Voice, Christmas Around the World; author: (college textbook) Vocal Technique: A Physiological Approach for Voice Class. Finalist, Nat. Opera Assn.; recipient Hazel Post Gillette award, Nat. Fedn. Music Clubs, Excellence in Tchg. award, St. Xavier U., 1995, Excellence in Scholarship award, 2001, Tech. Integration award, 2003, Excellence in Rsch. award, 2005, Excellence in Scholarship award, 2005; scholar Found. for the Arts for Vocal Study, Three Arts Club of Chgo., 1975, 1976, 1977; rsch. and prodn. grantee, St. Xavier U., 2001, 2002, 2003, 2004. Mem.: AAUP (treas. St. Xavier chpt. 1999—2000, exec. bd. 2004—), Music Tchrs. Nat. Assn., Am. Choral Dirs. Assn., Nat. Opera Assn., Music Tchrs. Nat. Assn., Collegiate Music Educators Nat. Coun., Nat. Assn. Tchrs. of Singing (exec. bd. mem. Chgo. chpt.), Musicians Club of Women (Emma Roe award 1976). Achievements include research in applicaiton of particular vocal techniques applied to flute playing. Office: Saint Xavier U 3700 W 103rd St Chicago IL 60655 Office Phone: 773-298-3425. Office Fax: 773-779-9061. Personal E-mail: bickel@sxu.edu.

BICKEL, JOHN W., II, lawyer; b. Champaign, Ill., Sept. 9, 1948; s. John William and Virginia Bickel; children: Hannah, Molly, Sarah. BS, U.S. Mil. Acad., 1970; JD, So. Meth. U., 1976. Bar: N.Y. 1988, Tex. 1976, U.S. Ct. Appeals (5th and 11th cirs.) 1980, U.S. Supreme Ct. 1983. Assoc. Thompson & Knight, Dallas, 1980-83; ptnr. Brown, Thomas, Karger & Bickel, Dallas, 1983-84; co-mng., co-founder, ptnr. Bickel & Brewer, Dallas, 1984—; co-founding ptnr. Bickel & Brewer Storefront, PLLC, Dallas. Adv. mem. Tex. Supreme Ct. Jury Charge Task Force, 1992; mem. com. for qualified judiciary. Co-author: "Exhibits and other Evidence," Chpt. 13, Lawyers Cooperative Fed. Practice Guide. Mem. exec. bd. So. Meth. U. Sch. Law.; mem. Hiram A. Boaz Soc. So. Meth. U.; mem. Tex. Com.: A Time to Lead--The Campaign for So. Meth. U.; mem. adv. com. Southwestern Ball, 1997-2000, co-founder Future Leaders Program, Bickel & Brewer Nat. Pub. Policy Forum. Named a Tex. Super Lawyer, Tex. Monthly Mag., 2003. Fellow Tex. Bar Found., Dallas Bar Found. (sustaining life); mem. ABA, State Bar Tex. (past chmn. litigation com. of environ. and natural resource law sect.), N.Y. Bar Assn., Dallas Bar Assn., Markey/Wigmore Inns of Ct. (Chgo. chpt.), West Point Assn. Grads. (trustee 1997-2000, strategic planning com. 1997—), West Point Soc. North Tex. (bd. dirs. 1992-). Office: Bickel & Brewer 4800 Bank One Ctr 1717 Main St Ste 4800 Dallas TX 75201-4651 E-mail: jwb@bickelbrewer.com.

BICKEL, MINNETTE DUFFY, artist; b. New Bern, N.C., June 24, 1921; d. Richard Nixon and Minnette (Chapman) Duffy; m. William Croft, Jan. 3, 1947; children: Minnette B. Boesel, Susan B. Scioli. One-woman shows include, N.C., statewide portrait exhbns., (two 1st place awards), regional juried shows, (winner three internat. awards); portraits include Gen. Claude Larkin, Tyrone Power, Thomas Graham, James Beckwith, Arthur Rolander, Frederick E. Fox, Senator Jesse Helms, Rachel Carson, R. Bud Dwyer, William Genge, Allison Williams, Dennis O'Connor, Frank Cahouet, Dr. Robert Edwards, Robert Wilburn, Henry L. Hillman. Mem. Am. Soc. Portrait Artists (affiliated), Stroke of Genius Gallery, Washington Soc. Portrait Artists and Portrait Inst., Portrait Soc. Am. Republican.

BICKEL, PETER JOHN, statistician, educator; b. Bucharest, Romania, Sept. 21, 1940; arrived in U.S., 1957, naturalized, 1964; s. Eliezer and P. Madeleine (Moscovici) B.; m. Nancy Kramer, Mar. 2, 1964; children: Amanda, Stephen. AB, U. Calif., Berkeley, 1960, MA, 1961, PhD, 1963; PhD (hon.), Hebrew U. Jerusalem, 1988. Asst. prof. stats. U. Calif., Berkeley, 1964-67, assoc. prof., 1967-70, prof., 1970—, chmn. dept. stats., 1976-79, dean phys. scis., 1980-86, chmn. dept. stats., 1993-97. Vis. lectr. math. Imperial Coll., London, 1965-66; fellow J.S. Guggenheim Meml. Found., 1970-71, J.D. and Catherine T. MacArthur Found., 1984-89; NATO sr. sci. fellow, 1974; chmn. com. on applied and theoretical stats. NRC, 1998-2000, mem. bd. on math. scis., 2000—, chmn., 2000-03; chmn. sci. adv. coun. Stats. and Applied Math. Inst., NSF. Author: (with K. Doksum) Mathematical Statistics, 1976, 2d edit., 2000, (with C. Klaassen, Y. Ritov and J. Wellner) Efficient and Adaptive Estimation in Semiparametric Models, 1993; assoc. editor Annals of Math. Stats., 1968-76, 86-93, PNAS, 1996—2000, Bernouilli, 1996—, Statistica Sinica, 1996—2003; contbr. articles to profl. jours. Fellow J.D. and Catherine T. MacArthur Found., 1984-89. Fellow AAAS (chair sect. U 1996-97), Inst. Math. Stats. (pres. 1980), Am. Statis. Assn.; mem. NAS, Royal Statis. Soc., Internat. Statis. Inst., Am. Acad. Arts and Scis., Royal Netherlands Acad. Arts and Scis., Bernoulli Soc. (pres. 1990). Office: U Calif Dept Stats Evans Hall Berkeley CA 94720 Office Phone: 510-642-1381. Business E-Mail: bickel@stat.berkeley.edu.

BICKERMAN, PETER B., lawyer; b. Flushing, N.Y., May 10, 1952; s. Hylan A. and Evelyn (Apogi) B.; m. Karen D. Levesque, Sept. 5, 1981; children: Joshua M., Kalyn E. BA, Union Coll., Schenectady, 1973; JD, NYU, 1976. Bar: Maine 1977, U.S. Supreme Ct. 1981, U.S. Ct. Appeals (1st cir.) 1989, U.S. Dist. Ct. Maine 1977. Staff atty. State Maine, Dept. Atty. Gen., Augusta, 1977, asst. atty. gen., 1977-87; atty., shareholder Lipman & Katz, Augusta, 1987-95; sole practice Augusta, 1995-99; counsel Verrill & Dana, LLP, Augusta, 1999—. Adv. com. Maine Rules of Civil Procedure, 1991-99; justice action group task force on adminstrv. law, 2000—; mem. adv. com. on Vol. Lawyers Project, 1998—. Bd. dirs. Pine Tree Legal Assistance, 1998—, Maine Civil Liberties Union, 1999—. Fellow Maine Bar Found.; mem. Maine Bar Assn., Maine Trial Lawyers Assn. E-mail: pbickerman@verrilldana.com.

BICKERS, DAVID RINSEY, dermatologist, educator, department chairman, health facility administrator; b. Richmond, Va., Sept. 23, 1941; s. William McKenzie and Helen Virginia (Fitzpatrick) B.; m. Melinda-Lee Jaeger, May 30, 1970; 1 dau., McKenzie Winchester. AB, Georgetown U., 1963; MD, U. Va., 1967. Intern in medicine U. Iowa Hosps., Iowa City, 1967-68; resident in dermatology skin and cancer unit N.Y.U. Med. Center, 1970-73; NIH tng. fellow, guest investigator Rockefeller U., 1971-73, R.J. Reynolds scholar in clin. medicine, asst. prof., asso. physician, 1976-77; asst. prof. dermatology Columbia U. Coll. Physicians and Surgeons, 1973-76; asst. attending dermatologist Presbyn. Hosp., N.Y.C., 1973-76, med. dir., 1997—; prof. dermatology, chmn. dept. Case Western Res. U. Med. Sch., 1977-93, assoc. dean, 1990-93; med. dir. N.Y. Hosp., N.Y.C., 1997—. Dir. dermatology svc. U. Hosps., 1977-93, sr. v.p. med. program planning, 1977-89, chief staff, sr. v.p. med. affairs, 1990-93; dir. dermatology svc. Cleve. VA Hosp., 1977-89; mem. gen. medicine A study sect., NIH, 1980-84, chmn., 1982-84; adv. coun. Nat. Inst. Arthritis, Musculoskeletal and Skin Diseases, NIH, 1988-92; Carl Truman Nelson prof. dermatology, chmn. Dept. Coll. Physicians and Surgeons, Columbia U., 1994—; dir. dermatology svc. NY Presbyn. Hosp., 1994—. Author: (with L.C. Harber) Photosensitivity Diseases: Principles of Diagnosis and Treatment, 1981, 2d. edit., 1989, (with Hazen and Lynch) Clinical Pharmacology of Skin Disease, 1984; mem. editorial bd. Jour. Am. Acad. Dermatology, 1979-85, Physicians Drug Alert, 1982—, Today's Therapeutic Trends, 1983-2004, Photodermatology, 1983-88; assoc. editor Jour. Investigative Dermatol., 1987-97. Served as officer M.C. USAF, 1968-70. Decorated Air Force Commendation medal. Mem. Assn. Am. Physicians, Am. Soc. Clin. Investigation, Am. Soc. Pharmacology and Exptl. Therapeutics, Am. Fedn. Clin. Rsch., Am. Soc. Photobiology, Am. Acad. Dermatology (hon.), Am. Dermatol. Assn., Soc. Investigative Dermatology (bd. dirs. 1985-89, sec.-treas. 1989—, pres. 2003), Pasteur Club (Cleve.), Med. Strollers, Skin Pharmacology Soc. (sec. 1985-87, pres. 1987-89), Dermatology Found. (sec.-treas. 1984, chmn. bd. 1987-88), Bicontinental Assn. Edn. and Rsch. in Dermatology (founding mem.), German Dermatol. Soc. (hon.), Am. Univ. Beirut (bd. trustees, 1996), Austrian Dermatol. Soc. (hon.), Commanderie De Bordeaux, Confrérie des Chevaliers du Tastevin, Expert Panel Rsch. Inst. for Fragrance Materials, Am. Bd. Dermatology (bd. dirs. 1997—, pres. 2005) Office: Columbia Univ Med Ctr IP-1214 161 Fort Washington Ave New York NY 10032-3713 Business E-Mail: drb25@columbia.edu.

BICKFORD, MERIS J., lawyer, bank executive; JD, Univ. Maine, 1986. Asst. v.p. Merrill Merchants Bank, Bangor, Maine; pres. MSBA, Bangor, Maine, 2005—. Mem.: Maine State Bar Found. (bd. of gov.), Maine State Bar Assn. (past dist. 5 gov., pres.-elect 2004). Office: Merrill Merchants Bank 201 Main St PO Box 925 Bangor ME 04402-0925 Business E-Mail: mbickford@merrillmerchants.com.

BICKMEYER, ROBERT H., retired automotive executive; b. Bayside, N.Y., July 31, 1929; s. John and Ida Mae Bickmeyer; m. Phyllis Loretta Krafcsik, Nov. 14, 1981; children: Linda Ann Farrington, Robert Evans. Student, N.Y. U., 1953—54. Billing clk. Gen. Motors, N.Y.C., 1947—51, vehicle pricer, 1953, ins. claims clk., 1953—54, dealer rep., 1954—68, adminstrv. asst., 1968—78, asst. mgr. Detroit, 1978—84, supr., 1984—86; ret. Amb. cons. Gen. Motors, Detriot, 1988. Contbr. articles to newspapers. Bd. dirs. Dwarf-Giraffe Boys' League of Whitestone, NY, 1968—78, commr. baseball, 1974, commr. bowling, 1973, sec., publicist, 1967—78. Sgt. U.S. Army, 1951—53, Korea. Recipient Father O'Connell award, Dwarf-Giraffe Boys' League, 1976. Republican. Lutheran. Avocations: writing, softball, volleyball, golf, bicycling. Home: 2138 Jeffrey Dr Troy MI 48085

BICKNER, BRUCE, food products executive; b. 1943; BBA, De Pauw U., 1965; JD, U. Mich., 1968. Law clk. U.S. Dist. Ct., 1968-70; ptnr. Sidley & Austin, Chgo., 1970-75; with DeKalb (Ill.) Corp., 1975—, v.p., 1976, group v.p., 1980, exec. v.p., dir., 1980, pres., 1986-90, CEO, chmn. bd., 1988-98, DeKalb Energy Co., 1988-98, DeKalb Swine Breeders Inc.; co-pres. Monsanto Global Seed Group, Monsanto, Inc., DeKalb, 1998—, exec. v.p. agrl. sector.

BIDDICK, KATHLEEN ANNE, history professor, researcher; d. John Thomas and Antoinette Biddick. AB, Barnard Coll., 1971; PhD, U. Toronto, Canada, 1982. Prof. U. Notre Dame, Ind., 1983—2005, Temple U., Phila., 2005—. Dir. gender studies U. Notre Dame, Ind., 1995—98. Dir.: (multimedia installation) Cell; author: (scholarly monograph) The Typological Imaginary: Circumcision, Technology, History, The Shock of Medievalism, The Other Economy: Pastoral Husbandry on a Medieval Estate; dir.: (scholarly collection of essays) Archaeological Approaches to Medieval Europe. Fellow Fulbright Fellowship, Fulbright Found., 2002-03, Sr. Fellowship, Stanford Humanities Ctr., 1998-1999, Rockefeller Fellow, Rockefeller Found., 1993-94, Open Faculty Fellowship, Lilly Found., 1990-91; grantee, NSF, 1986-1988. Mem.: Medieval Acad., Am. Hist. Assn. (assoc.). Avocations: hiking, yoga, skiing. Office Phone: 215-204-6039. Business E-Mail: kathleen.biddick@temple.edu.

BIDDLE, ALBERT GEORGE WILKINSON, III, (JACK BIDDLE), venture capitalist; b. Chgo., Jan. 24, 1961; s. A.G.W. and Leah Anne (Breen) B.; m. Forée Pendleton McCauley, Apr. 21, 1990; children: A.G.W. IV, Caldwell Knight, Brooks Christopher. BA in Econs., U. Va., 1983. Assoc. Bus. Devel. Ptnrs., Austin, Tex., 1983-85; exec. asst. to CEO, Gartner Group, Stamford, Conn., 1985-86; prin. Vanguard Atlantic, N.Y.C., 1986-90; pres., CEO, Intercap Systems, Annapolis, Md., 1990-95; gen. ptnr. Novak Biddle Venture Ptnrs., McLean, Va., 1996—. Bd. dirs. Object Video, Paratek Microwave, Matrics. Mem. adv. counsel Office Naval Rsch. Mem.: Computer and Comm. Industry Assn., Annapolis Yacht Club, Chevy Chase Club. Office: Novak Biddle Venture Ptnrs Ste 1380 7501 Wisconsin Ave Bethesda MD 20814-6400 E-mail: jack@novakbiddle.com.

BIDDLE, BRUCE JESSE, social psychologist, educator; b. Ossining, N.Y., Dec. 30, 1928; s. William Wishart and Loureide Jeanette (Cobb) B.; m. Ellen Catherine Horgan; children: David Charles, William Jesse, Jennifer Loureide; m. Barbara Julianne Bank, June 19, 1976. AB in Math., Antioch Coll., Yellow Springs, Ohio, 1950; postgrad., U. N.C., 1950-51; PhD in Social Psychology, U. Mich., 1957. Asst. prof. sociology U. Ky., 1957-58; assoc. prof. edn. U. Kansas City, 1958-60; assoc. prof. psychology and sociology U. Mo., Columbia, 1960-66, prof., 1966-2000, prof. emeritus, 2000—, dir. Ctr. Rsch. in Social Behavior, 1966-96. Vis. assoc. prof. U. Queensland, Australia, 1965; vis. prof. Monash U., Australia, 1969, vis. fellow Australian Nat. U., 1977, 85, 93. Author: (with R.S. Adams) Realities of Teaching: Explorations with Videotape, 1970, (with M.J. Dunkin) The Study of Teaching, 1974, (with T.L. Good and J. Brophy) Teachers Make a Difference, 1975, Role Theory: Expectations, Identities and Behaviors, 1979, (with D.C. Berliner) The Manufactured Crisis: Myths, Fraud, and the Attack on America's Public Schools, 1995, (with L.J. Saha) The Untested Accusation: Principals, Research Knowledge, and Policy Making in Schools, 2002; editor: (with W.J. Ellena) contemporary Research on Teacher Effectiveness, 1964, (with E.J. Thomas) Role Theory: Concepts and Research, 1966, (with P.H. Rossi) The New Media: Their Impact on Education, 1966, (with D.S. Anderson) Knowledge for Policy: Improving Education Through Research, 1991, (with T.L. Good and I.F. Goodson) International Handbook of Teachers and Teaching, 1997, Social Class, Poverty, and Education, 2001. Served with U.S. Army, 1954-56. Fellow APA, Am. Psychol. Soc., Australian Psychol. Soc.; mem. Am. Ednl. Research Assn., Australian Assn. Rsch. Edn., Am. Sociol. Assn., Midwest Sociol. Soc. Home: 924 Yale Columbia MO 65203-1874 Office: U Mo Dept Psychology McAlester Hall Rm 210 Columbia MO 65211-0001 Business E-Mail: BiddleB@missouri.edu.

BIDDLE, DONALD RAY, aerospace transportation executive; b. Alton, Mo., June 30, 1936; s. Ernest Everet and Dortha Marie (McGuire) B.; m. Nancy Ann Dunham, Mar. 13, 1955; children: Jeanne Kay Northington, Mitchell Lee, Charles Alan. Student, El Dorado (Kans.) Jr. Coll., 1953-55, Pratt (Kans.) Jr. Coll., 1955-56; BSME, Washington U., St. Louis, 1961; postgrad. computer sci., Pa. State U. Ext., 1963; cert. bus. mgmt., Alexander Hamilton Inst., 1958. Design group engr. Emerson Elec. Mfg., St. Louis, 1957-61; design specialist Boeing Vertol, Springfield, Pa., 1962; cons. engr. Ewing Tech. Design, Phila., 1962-66; chief engr. rotary wing Gates Learjet, Wichita, Kans., 1967-70; dir. engring., R&D, BP Chems., Inc. Advanced Material Divsn., Stockton, Calif., 1971-93; prin. Biddle & Assocs., Consulting Engrs., Stockton, 1993—; pres., CEO, Big Valley Aviation, Inc., Stockton, 1997-98; CEO, Propulsion Technologies, Inc., Stockton, 1999—, United Propeller Technologies, Inc., Stockton, 1999—. Guest lectr. on manrated structures, devel. proprietary designs, small bus. devel. to various univs. and tech. socs. Patentee landing gear designs, inflatable rescue sys., glass retention sys., adjustable jack sys., cold weather start flourescent lamp, paper honeycomb core post-process sys. Scoutmaster, counselor, instl. rep. Boy Scouts Am., St. Ann, Mo., 1956-61; mem. Springfield Sch. Bd., 1964. Mem. ASME, ASTM, AIAA, Am. Helicopter Soc. (sec.-treas. Wichita chpt. 1969), Am. Mgmt. Assn., Exptl. Pilots Assn., Soc. for Advancement of Metals and Process Engring. Republican. Methodist. Home: 6449 Embarcadero Dr Stockton CA 95219-3800 Office: United Propeller Tech Inc 7515 C E Dixon St Stockton CA 95206-4922 Office Phone: 209-982-4000. Business E-Mail: dbiddle@UnitedPropeller.com.

BIDDLE, FLORA MILLER, art patron, museum administrator; Granddaughter of Gertrude Vanderbilt Whitney; m. Sydney; 4 children BA, Manhattanville Coll., 1978. V.p. Whitney Mus. Am. Art, NYC, 1958—77, pres., 1978-85, chair, 1985—95, hon. trustee. Author: The Whitney Women and the Museum They Made, 1999. Mem.: NYC Art Commn. (mem. 1980—90). Home: 17 E 97th St New York NY 10029 Personal E-mail: florabiddle@gmail.com.

BIDDLE, JEFF ESKEW, economist, educator; b. Charleston, W.Va., June 15, 1959; s. John William and Lucy Eskew Biddle; m. Kay Young, May 30, 1981; children: Jeff Eskew, John William, Stephen Charles. BS, W.Va. U., 1981; PhD, Duke U., 1985. Prof. econs. Mich. State U., East Lansing, Mich., 1991—. Office: Michigan State University 101 Old Botany East Lansing MI 48824 Office Phone: 517-353-7862. Business E-Mail: biddle@msu.edu.

BIDDLE, KIMBERLY SUE, primary school educator; b. Flemingsburg, Ky., Jan. 10, 1964; d. James Walter Warder and Ruby Kathleen Ackley; m. Howard Ashton Biddle, Mar. 22, 1987; children: Crystal Brooke, Kayla

Myranda. B of Elem. Edn., Morehead State U., 1993, M of Elem. Edn., 2000. Tchr. Flemingsburg Elem. Sch., Ky., 1994—. Coord. core knowledge Flemingsburg Elem. Sch., 2001—04, coord. gifted and talented dance, 1998—2002. Best Buddy grantee, Morehead State U. Mem.: ASCD, Ky. Edn. Assn. Baptist. Avocations: camping, reading.

BIDELMAN, WILLIAM PENDRY, astronomer, educator; b. L.A., Sept. 25, 1918; s. William Pendry and Dolores (De Remer) B.; m. Verna Pearl Shirk, June 19, 1940; children: Lana Louise Stone (dec. Mar. 2000), Linda Elizabeth McKinley, Billie Jean Little, Barbara Jo Talley. Student, U. N.D., 1936-37; SB, Harvard, 1940; PhD, U. Chgo., 1943. Physicist, Aberdeen Proving Ground, Md., 1943-45; instr., then asst. prof. astronomy Yerkes Obs., U. Chgo., 1945-53; asst. astronomer, then. assoc. astronomer Lick Obs., U. Calif., 1953-62; prof. U. Mich., 1962-69, U. Tex. at Austin, 1969-70, Case Western Res. U., Cleve., 1970-86, prof. emeritus, 1986—. Chmn. dept., dir. Warner and Swasey Obs., 1970-75; mem. adv. panel on astronomy NSF, 1959-62; mem. NRC adv. com. on astronomy Office Naval Rsch., 1964-67. Contbr. articles to profl. jours. Mem. Am. Astron. Soc. (councilor 1959-62, participant vis. prof. program 1961-65), Astron. Soc. Pacific (editor Publs. 1956-61), Internat. Astron. Union (commns. 29, 45, pres. 1964-67), Phi Beta Kappa. Presbyterian. Achievements include discovery of lines of mercury, krypton and xenon in stellar spectra; discovery of phosphorus stars; co-discovery of barium stars; research in spectral classification, astronomical data and observational astrophysics. Home: 3171 Chelsea Dr Cleveland Heights OH 44118-1256 Office: Case Western Res U Dept Astronomy 10900 Euclid Ave Cleveland OH 44106-7215 Office Phone: 216-368-4003. Business E-Mail: wsobs@grendel.astr.cwru.edu.

BIDEN, JOSEPH ROBINETTE, JR., senator; b. Scranton, Pa., Nov. 20, 1942; s. Joseph Robinette Sr.and Jean Finnegan Biden.; m. Jill Tracy Jacobs, June 17, 1977; children: Ashley Blazer, Joseph Robinette III, Robert Hunter. BA History and Polit. Sci., U. Del., 1965; JD, Syracuse U., 1968. Bar: Del. 1968. Practiced law, Wilmington, 1968-72; US senator from Del., 1973—; mem. Senate Jud. Com., chmn., 1987—95; mem. Senate Fgn. Relations Com., chmn., 2001, 2001—03; US Rep. to Gen. Assembly UN, 2000. Active New Castle (Del.) County Coun.; adj. prof. Widener U. Sch. Law, 1991-. Recipient Friend of Zion Tribute award, Jerusalem Fund, 1998, Spirit of Enterprise award, US C. of C., 1998, Silver medal of Appreciation, Czech Republic, 1999, Senator of the Year, Nat. Assn. Police Organizations, 2000, Charles Dick medal of Merit, DE chapter, Nat. Guard Assn. of the US, 2002, Balkan Peace award, Albanian Amer. Civic League, 2002, Rail Spike award, Delmarva Rail Passenger Assn., 2003. Democrat. Roman Catholic. Office: 201 Russell Senate Bldg Washington DC 20510-0001*

BIDERMAN, CHARLES ISRAEL, diversified financial services company executive; b. NYC, Oct. 24, 1946; m. Brenda Carol Nicholson (div.); 1 child, John Patrick; m. Cheryl Marie Johnson, Sept. 8, 1985 (div.); 1 child, Christopher Isaac. BA, Bklyn. Coll., 1967; MBA, Harvard U., 1971. Assoc. editor Barron's Fin. Weekly, 1971-73; pres. Charles Biderman & Co., N.Y.C. and Nashville, 1980-89, Market St. Devel. Corp. (formerly Nashville Mgmt. Corp.), 1976-80; pres., CEO, Trimtabs Fin. Svcs., Inc., Santa Rosa, Calif., 1990—. Fin. editor Wall St. Final, N.Y.C.; editor Market Trim Tabs. (constructed over 200 home including) Gaslite Condominiums and Lafayette Townhouses, Seaside Park, N.J., Three Pence Brooke Townhomes, Jackson, N.J., N.J. Quail Farms, Jackson. Bd. dris. Tenn. Dance Theater, 1977—80, Children & Family Cir., 1989. With USAF, 1966—67. Office: Trim Tabs Fin Svcs Inc 520 Mendocino Ave Ste 350 Santa Rosa CA 95401-5258 Office Phone: 707-525-1001.

BIDLACK, JEAN MARIE, pharmacologist, educator, medical researcher; b. Rochester, N.Y., Dec. 4, 1953; d. William Henry and Mary Louise (Naughton) Bidlack; m. Carl T. Helmers, Jr., Nov. 1, 2003. BA in Biology and Chemistry, Skidmore Coll., 1975; PhD in Biophysics, U. Rochester, 1979. Postdoctoral fellow U. Rochester, 1979-80, sr. instr. Ctr. Brain Rsch., 1980-81, asst. prof. brain rsch., 1981-87, assoc. prof. pharmacology, 1987-97, prof. pharmacology and physiology, 1997—. Cons. NSF, Washington, 1983—89, VA, Washington, 1986—88, Nat. Inst. Drug Abuse, Rockville, Md., 1987—, AIDS Study Sect., 1996—2002; mem. secretariat Internat. Narcotics Rsch. Conf., 1999, treas., 2004—. Contbr. articles to profl. jours. Recipient Sr. Sci. award, KO5 NIH, 1998—; fellow U. Rochester, 1975—79. Mem.: Internat. Narcotics Rsch. Conf. (v.p. and treas. 2004—), Soc. NeuroImmune Pharmacology (pres. 2004—05), Soc. Neurosci., Am. Soc. Pharmacology and Exptl. Therapeutics, Coll. on Problems of Drug Dependence Inc. Achievements include patents in field. Office: U Rochester/Sch Med and Dentistry Dept Pharm and Physiology 601 Elmwood Ave Rochester NY 14642-8711

BIDLACK, JERALD DEAN, manufacturing executive; b. Oakwood, Ohio, Nov. 18, 1935; s. Ansel Carol and Vivian Irene (Huff) B.; m. Ruth Heidenescher, Dec. 24, 1953; children: Jeffrey, Cynthia, Timothy, Bethann, Deborah. BSM.E., Tri-State U., 1956; postgrad., Wayne State U., 1959. Registered profl. engr., N.Y. Sr. engr. Cadillac Gage Co., Warren, Mich., 1956-63; engring. mgr. indsl. Moog Inc., East Aurora, N.Y., 1963-67, mng. dir. Boeblingen, Republic of Germany, 1967-69, pres. internat. ops. East Aurora, 1969—92; pres. Griffin Automation, Inc., West Seneca, NY, 1992—. Bd. dir. Graham Corp., Bush Industries, Inc.; trustee Keuka Coll. Patentee in field. Mem. com. Boy Scouts Am., East Aurora, 1973-76. Mem. Young Pres.'s Orgn. (chpt. chmn. 1981-82), Fluid Power Soc., Nat. Soc. Profl. Engrs., Buffalo and Erie County C. of C. Clubs: Country of Buffalo. Home: 323 Windsor Ln East Aurora NY 14052-1321 Office: Griffin Automation Inc 240 West Munster Rd West Seneca NY 14224 Office Phone: 716-674-2300. Business E-Mail: jbidla@griffinautomation.com.

BIDLACK, WAYNE ROSS, nutritional biochemist, toxicologist, food scientist; b. Waverly, NY, Aug. 12, 1944; s. Andrew L. Bidlack and Vivian Pearl Cowles Williams; m. Wei Wang. BS, Pa. State U., 1966; MS, Iowa State U., 1968; PhD, U. Calif., Davis, 1972. Postdoctoral fellow dept. pharmacology U. So. Calif., L.A., 1972-74, asst prof. sch. medicine, 1974-80, assoc. prof., 1980-92, prof., 1992—, asst. dean student affairs, 1988-91, chmn. dept. pharmacology and nutrition, 1991-92; chmn. dept. food sci. and human nutrition Iowa State U., Ames, 1992-95; dean Coll. Agr. Calif. State Poly. U., Pomona, 1995—. Assoc. editor Biochem. Medicine and Metabolic Biology, 1986-87; mem. editl. bd. Jour. Am. Coll. Nutrition, 1995—, Environ. Nutritional Interactions, 1996-2000, Toxicology, 2000—. Chmn. Greater L.A. Nutrition Coun., 1982-83, So. Calif. Inst. Food Technologists, 1988-89, Toxicology and Safety Evaluation divsn. Inst. Food Technologists, 1989-90, food sci. communicator, 1986-90; chmn. Nat. Coun. Against Health Fraud, 1983-85; mem. expert panel on foods and nurtrition, 1989-93. Recipient Outstanding Tchr. Award, U. So. Calif. Sch. Medicine, 1987-88, Meritorious Svc. award Calif. Dietetic Assn., 1990, Disting. Achievement award So. Calif. Inst. Food Technologists, 1990, Bautzer Faculty award Calif. State U., 1998; fellow Inst. Food Technologists, 1998, Wang Family award Calif. State U., 2002. Mem. Soc. Toxicology (chair awards com. food safety sect. 1993-94, chair 1994-95), Nat. Golden Key Soc. (hon.), Gamma Sigma Delta. Republican. Avocations: golf, book collecting. Office: Calif State Polytech U Coll of Agrl 3801 W Temple Ave Pomona CA 91768-2557 Business E-Mail: wrbidlack@csupomona.edu.

BIDWELL, CHARLES EDWARD, sociologist, educator; b. Chgo., Jan. 24, 1932; s. Charles Leslie and Eugenia (Campbell) B.; m. Helen Claxton Lewis, Jan. 24, 1959; 1 son, Charles Lewis. AB, U. Chgo., 1950, AM, 1953, PhD, 1956. Lectr. on sociology Harvard U., 1959-61; asst. prof. edn. U. Chgo., 1961-65, assoc. prof., 1965-70, prof. edn. and sociology, 1970-85, Reavis prof. edn. and sociology, 1985-2001, Reavis prof. emeritus edn. and sociology, 2001—, chmn. dept. edn., 1978-88, chmn. dept. sociology, 1988-94, dir. Ogburn-Stouffer Ctr., 1988-94. Author books in field; contbr. numerous articles to profl. jours.; editor Sociology of Edn., 1969-72, Am. Jour. Sociology, 1973-78, Am. Jour. Edn., 1983-88. With U.S. Army, 1957-59. Guggenheim fellow, 1971-72 Fellow AAAS; mem. Sociol. Rsch. Assn., Nat. Acad. Edn. (sec.), Phi Beta Kappa. Office: Dept Sociology 1126 East 59th St Chicago IL 60637 Office Phone: 773-702-0388. E-mail: c-bidwell@uchicago.edu.

BIDWELL, JAMES TRUMAN, JR., lawyer; b. N.Y.C., Jan. 2, 1934; s. James Truman and Mary (Kane) B.; m. Gail S. Bidwell, Mar. 6, 1965 (div.); children: Hillary Day Bidwell Mackay, Kimberley Wade, Cortney E.; m. Katherine T. O'Neil, July 15, 1988 (dec. Nov. 2003). BA, Yale U., 1956; LLB, Harvard U., 1959. Bar: N.Y. 1959. Atty. USAF, Austin, Tex., 1959-62; assoc. Donovan, Leisure, Newton & Irvine, N.Y.C., 1962-68, ptnr., 1968-84, White & Case, N.Y.C., 1984-98; sr. counsel Linklaters, N.Y.C., 1998—2003; ptnr. Thelen, Reid, Priest LLP, 2003—04, sr. counsel, 2005—. Pres. Youth Consultation Svc., 1973-78; trustee Berkeley Divinity Sch. Mem. ABA, Fed. Bar Assn., N.Y. State Bar Assn., N.Y. County Lawyers Assn. Episcopalian. Office Phone: 212-603-2378. E-mail: jtbidwell@thelenreid.com.

BIDWELL, ROGER GRAFTON SHELFORD, biologist, educator; b. Halifax, N.S., Can., June 8, 1927; came to U.S., 1965; s. Roger Edward Shelford and Mary B.; m. Shirley Mae Rachael Mason, July 1, 1950; children— Barbara, Alison, Roger, Gillian. B.Sc., Dalhousie U., 1947; BA, Queen's U., 1950, MA, 1951, PhD, 1954. Tech. officer Canadian Def. Research Bd., Kingston, Ont., 1951-56; asst. research officer Nat. Research Council, Halifax, 1956-59; assoc. prof. biology U. Toronto, Ont., 1959-65; prof. biology Case Western Res. U., Cleve., 1965-69, chmn. dept., 1966-68; prof. biology Queen's U., Kingston, Ont., Can., 1969-79, prof. emeritus, 1979—; I.W. Killam research prof. Dalhousie U., Halifax, 1980-85; sr. ptnr. Atlantic Research Assocs. Ltd., Wallace, N.S., 1980-91; exec. dir. Atlantic Inst. Biotech., Halifax, 1985-88. Vis. prof. Cornell U., 1961-63; vis. scientist Atlantic Regional Lab., NRC, Halifax, summer 1966, 76; cons. Faculty Edn., Simon Fraser U., 1966; Can. Sci. Exch. visitor to People's Republic of China, 1975, 77; participant Dark Skies Symposium; mem., co-founder scotobiology program Ecology of Night Symposium, Muskoka, Ont., 2005. Author: Plant Physiology, 1974, 79; co-editor: Plant Physiology: A Treatise, 1978-90; contbr. over 150 articles to profl. jours., chpts. to textbooks on biochem. mechanisms in plants, protein metabolism, CO2 metabolism in leaves, photosynthesis and metabolism in marine algae, global climate change; publs. on scotobiology. Active Crime Stoppers, Cumberland region, 1993-97, chmn., 1994-97; mem. several coms. Anglican Diocese N.S.; pres., chmn. bd. Pugwash Coop. Ltd., 1995-2000; warden Parish of Pugwash/River John, 1998-2002, parish treas., 2004-05; mem. diocesan coun. Diocese of N.S. and P.E.I., 1999-2001; mem. Pugwash and Area Cmty. Health Bd., 2001—. Recipient Queen Elizabeth II Silver Jubilee medal, 1977. Fellow AAAS, Royal Soc. Can.; mem. Canadian Soc. Plant Physiologists (founder, past sec.-treas., pres. 1972-73, Gold medal 1979), Biol. Council Can. (sec. 1973-76), Am. Soc. Plant Physiology. Avocations: bicycling, walking, skiing, bird watching, weaving.

BIDWILL, WILLIAM V., professional football executive; s. Charles W. and Violet Bidwill; m. Nancy Bidwill; children: William Jr., Michael, Patrick, Timothy, Nicole. Grad., Georgetown U. Co-owner St. Louis Cardinals Football Team (now Ariz. Cardinals), 1962-72, owner, 1972—, also chmn., 1972—, pres. Office: Ariz Cardinals PO Box 888 Phoenix AZ 85001-0888

BIEBEL, PAUL PHILIP, JR., lawyer; b. Chgo., Mar. 24, 1942; s. Paul Philip Sr. and Eleanor Mary (Sweeney) B.; divorced; children: Christine M., Brian E., Jennifer A., Susan E. AB, Marquette U., 1964; JD, Georgetown U., 1967. Bar: Ill. 1967, U.S. Dist. Ct. (no. dist.) Ill. 1967, U.S. Ct. Appeals (6th cir.) 1985, U.S. Supreme Ct. 1972. Asst. dean of men Loyola U., Chgo., 1967-69; asst. state's atty. Cook County State's Atty., Chgo., 1969-75, dep. state's atty., 1975-81; 1st asst. atty. gen. Ill. Atty. Gen., Chgo., 1981-85; pub. defender Cook County Pub. Defender, Chgo., 1986-88; ptnr. Winston & Strawn, Chgo., 1985-86, 88-94, Altheimer & Gray, Chgo., 1994-96; judge Cir. Ct. Cook County, Ill., 1996—. Contbr. articles to profl. publs. Mem. Fed. Bar Assn. (bd. dirs., pres. 1994-95), Cath. Lawyers Guild (bd. dirs., Cath. Lawyer of Yr. 1988), Ill. Judges Assn., Ill. Appellate Lawyers, 7th Cir. Bar Assn., Chgo. Bar Assn. (chmn. com. 1991-93), Georgetown Law Alumni Assn. (bd. dirs. 1991-96). Roman Catholic. Avocations: reading, golf. Home: 5415 N Forest Glen Ave Chicago IL 60630-1523 Office: Presiding Judge Criminal Divsn RM 101 2600 S California Ave Chicago IL 60608 Office Phone: 773-869-3160. Personal E-mail: jorich73@cs.com.

BIEBER, FREDERICK ROBERT, medical geneticist; b. Regina, Sask., Can., Feb. 9, 1950; s. Frederick John and Marjorie (Davidson) B.; m. Jane Marie McNamara, June 23, 1973. BA, SUNY, Oswego, 1972; MS, U. Rochester, 1976; PhD, Med. Coll. Va., 1981. Diplomate Am. Bd. Med. Genetics. Asst. prof. Harvard Med. Sch., Boston, 1985-91; assoc. prof. pathology Brigham Womens Hosp., Boston, 1992—. Author: The Malformed Fetus and Stillbirth, 1988; mem. editl. bd. Clin. Genetics; contbr. articles to profl. jours. Bd. dirs. Greyhound Friends, Hopkinton, Mass., 1992. Office: Brigham & Women's Hosp Dept Pathology 75 Francis St Boston MA 02115-6106

BIEBER, GREGG ALAN, school psychologist; b. Eureka, S.D., Jan. 25, 1961; s. Willis Aurthur and Joanne Lee Bieber. BS, U. S.D., 1985; MS, Iowa State U., 1990; EdS, U. S.D., 2004. Lic. Nat. Assn. for Sch. Psychologists, N.Am. Assn. for Masters in Psychology; Nat. Cert. Sch. Psychologist, Nat. Cert. Psychologist. Staff psychologist Southeastern Iowa Mental Health, Burlington, 1992—93; devel. asst. Mid-Step Svcs., Sioux City, 1994—95, psychologist, 1995—98; cons. Sioux City, 1998—2003; sch. psychologist Prairie Lakes AEA, Storm Lake, Iowa, 2003—. Bd. pres. 1st Unitarian Ch., Sioux City, 1995—96; bd. sec. SLAUUA, Storm Lake, 2004—05; coun. pres. Planned Parenthood, Sioux City, 1996—97. Recipient univ. scholarship, Phi Beta Kappa. Mem.: N.Am. Assn. for Masters in Psychology, Nat. Assn. for Sch. Psychologists. Democrat. Unitarian Universalist. Avocation: poetry. Home: Apt 7 914 E Milwaukee Ave Storm Lake IA 50588 Office Phone: 712-732-2257.

BIEBER, SANDER M., lawyer; b. L.A., 1950; AB, Princeton U., 1972; JD, Case Western Reserve U., 1976. Bar: D.C. 1976. Intern to Chief Justice U.S. Supreme Ct., 1974; atty. office of chief counsel fed. railroad adminstrn. Dept. Transp., 1976-78; ptnr. Dechert LLP (formerly Dechert Price & Rhoads), Washington, 1981—. Assoc. editor Case Western Reserve Law Review. Mem. ABA (corp. banking and bus. law sect., Mex. law com., internat. law and practice sect.), D.C. Bar Assn. Office: Dechert LLP 1775 I St NW # 9 Washington DC 20006-2402 E-mail: sander.bieber@dechert.com.

BIEBER-ROBERTS, PEGGY EILENE, communications educator, editor, journalist, researcher; b. Mobridge, S.D., Jan. 8, 1943; d. John J. and Lenora (Schlepp) Bieber; m. Phil Roberts. BS, No. State U., Aberdeen, S.D., 1966; MA, U. Wyo., 1984; PhD, U. Wash., 1990; postgrad. in Internat. Law, U. Edinburgh, Scotland, 2004—. Vol. Peace Corps, Turkey, 1966-68; tchr. secondary pub. schs., Idaho, 1968-69, Pine Ridge (S.D.) Reservation, 1969-71; co-founder Medicine Bow Post weekly newspaper, 1977; legis. reporter various weekly newspapers, Wyo., 1980-82; owner, pub. Capitol Times mag., Cheyenne, Wyo., 1982-84; pub. Skyline West Press, 1983—; lectr. pub. rels. and advt. U. Wash., Seattle, 1986-88; rsch. analyst Elway Rsch./Jay Rockey Co., Seattle, 1989-90; asst. prof. mass media U. Wyo., Laramie, 1990-96; journalism faculty comm. tech. Higher Colls. of Tech., Dubai, United Arab Emirates, 1996-98; polit. campaign mgr. Phil Roberts gubernatorial campaign, Wyo., 1998; assoc. prof. journalism and mass comms. Am. U. in Cairo, 1999—2003, assoc. prof., 2001—03, chair dept. journalism and mass comm., 2000—02; office mgr. Albany County Dem. Party, 2004. Indexer McGraw/Hill, Bedford Books, also others, 1988—94. Author, editor: hist. almanacs for various states, 1984—87; contbr. articles to profl. jours., chapters to books. Publicity chmn. Laramie County Dem. Com., Cheyenne, 1982; publicity chmn., precinct committeewoman Albany County Dems., 1999—2000. Named Stout fellow, U. Wash., 1990; recipient 1st Place award for feature writing, co-1st Place award for editorials, Wyo. Press Assn., 1982, Alumni Assn. Faculty Growth award, U. Wyo., 1994. Mem.: Internat. Assn. Media and Comm. Rsch., Assn. Ednl. Journalism and Mass Comm. Office Phone: 307-745-8205. Personal E-mail: bieberroberts@yahoo.com.

BIEBUYCK, JULIEN FRANCOIS, medical educator, medical association administrator; b. South Africa, Feb. 2, 1935; came to U.S., 1971, naturalized, 1985; s. Lucien Jean and Drix J. B.; m. Jeanette A. Sumner, May 10, 1961; children: Gavin L., Richard M., Clare E. MB, U. Capetown, 1959; DPhil, Oxford U., Eng., 1971. Diplomat Am. Bd. Anesthesiology. Nuffield scholar Oxford U., Eng., 1969-71; asst. prof. anesthesiology Harvard Med. Sch., Mass. Gen. Hosp., Boston, 1971-76; Eric A. Walker prof., chmn. dept. anesthesia Pa. State U. Coll. Medicine, Hershey, 1977-97, assoc. dean, 1991-97, sr. assoc. dean for acad. affairs, 1997—2000; Robert G. Petersdorf scholar-in-residence Assn. Am. Med. Coll., Washington, 2001—02, sr. cons. acad. mgmt. programs, 2002—. Mem. anesthetic and life support drugs adv. com. FDA, 1995-97. Mem. editorial bd. Anesthesiology, 1985-93; co-editor Current Opinion in Anaesthesiology; contbr. chpts. to books, articles to med. jours. Med. Found. fellow, 1972-76. Fellow Royal Coll. Anaesthetists (hon., London), Australian and New Zealand Coll. Anaesthetists (hon.); mem. AMA, Assn. Univ. Anesthesiologists, Am. Soc. Anesthesiologists (chair com. on rsch. 1994-97), Am. Physiol. Soc., Soc. Acad. Anesthesia Chmn. (past pres.), Coun. Acad. Socs. of Assn., Biochem. Soc. (London), Soc. Parenteral Nutrition, Soc. Neurosci., Soc. Neurosurg. Anesthesia, Pa. Med. Soc., Trinity Coll. Soc., Cosmos Club, Alpha Omega Alpha. Office Phone: 717-583-2679. E-mail: jbiebuyck@comcast.net.

BIECK, ROBERT BARTON, JR., lawyer; b. Wiesbaden, Germany, Apr. 13, 1952; s. Robert Barton and Mary-Jean (Boeck) B.; m. Julia A. Dietz, Apr. 20, 1991. BA in Polit. Sci., U. Nebr., 1974; JD with high honors, Tex. Tech. U., 1977. Bar: Tex. 1977, La. 1977, D.C. 1992, U.S. Dist. Ct. (ea. dist.) La. 1977, U.S. Dist. Ct. (mid. dist.) La. 1978, U.S. Dist. Ct. (we. dist.) La. 1979, U.S. Dist. Ct. (no. and so. dists.) Tex. 1991, U.S. Dist. Ct. D.C. (1994, U.S. Ct. Appeals (D.C. cir.) 1992, U.S. Ct. Appeals (5th and 11th cirs.) 1981, U.S. Supreme Ct. 1980. Assoc. firm Jones, Walker, Waechter, Poitevent, Carrere & Denegre, New Orleans, 1977-82, ptnr., 1982—. Chmn. profl. liability practice group, Jones, Walker, et al. Recipient West Horn Book award West Pub. Co., 1976; Fulbright and Jaworski scholar, 1976. Mem. ABA (litigation sect., bus. law sect., federal regulation of securities com.), Securities Industry Assn., Nat. Soc. Compliance Profls., New Orleans Bar Assn., La. Bankers Assn., 5th Cir. Bar Assn., Order of Coif, Phi Kappa Phi, Phi Delta Phi. Home: 5708 Annunciation St New Orleans LA 70115 Office: Jones Walker Waechter Poitevent Carrere & Denegre 201 Saint Charles Ave Ste 5200 New Orleans LA 70170-5100 Office Phone: 504-582-8202.

BIEDERMAN, BARRON ZACHARY (BARRY BIEDERMAN), advertising agency executive; b. N.Y.C. s. William and Sophye (Groll) B.; m. Susan Howard, Apr. 1, 1967; children: Rachel, David. BA with distinction, Cornell U., 1952; MS in Journalism, Columbia U, 1953; postgrad., U. London, 1954. Copy group head Mogul, Williams & Saylor, N.Y.C., 1955-59; sr. writer Lennen & Newell, N.Y.C., 1960-62; v.p., assoc. creative svcs. dir. Cunningham & Walsh, N.Y.C., 1962-64; sr. v.p. Needham, Harper & Steers, N.Y.C., 1964-84, exec. creative dir., 1964-74, mgmt. rep., 1974-79, dir., 1981-84; mng. dir. NH&S Corp. Futures, 1979-80; chmn., chief exec. officer NH&S/Issues & Images, 1981-84; chmn. Biederman & Co., Inc. (name changed to Biederman, Kelly & Shaffer, Inc. 1989), 1984—; chmn. emeritus Biederman, Kelly, Krimstein Ptnrs., 1998—2001; ret., 2001. Lectr. in field. Bd. dirs. Liberty Club, N.Y., 1983-87, Alvin Ailey Dance Theatre, N.Y., 1974. Recipient various advt. awards; Ford Found. fellow Eng., India, 1953-55 Mem. Fin. Comms. Soc. (bd. dirs. 1982-89, pres. 1986-87), Internat. Advt. Assn., Bank Mktg. Assn., Copywriters Club N.Y. (bd. dirs. 1960-64). Avocations: history, literature, music, gardening, travel. Home: 425 E 58th St Apt 17G New York NY 10022-2300

BIEDERMAN, EDWIN WILLIAMS, JR., retired geologist; b. Stamford, Conn., June 30, 1930; s. Edwin Williams and Thelma Frances (Morrow) B.; m. Margaret-Jane Bell White, Aug. 23, 1958; children: Robert, Mary, Jane, James. BA, Cornell U., 1952; PhD, Pa. State U., 1958. Cert. petroleum geologist. Project leader Cities Svc. Co., Tulsa, 1958-68, pres. staff Cranbury, N.J., 1968-72; asst. dir. Pa. Tech. Assistance program, University Park, Pa., 1972-77, sr. tech. specialist, 1980—2001; field ctr. dir. NSF Chautauqua Courses, University Park, 1977-80. Author: Atlas of Oil and Gas Reservoir Rocks From North America, 1986; contbr. articles to profl. jours.; holder 5 patents for geochem. exploration, in situ acidulation of phosphate rock, grate for vertical oil shale kiln, fire retardant foam, lightweight cement for oil wells. Petroleum officer USAF, 1952-54. Pa. State U. scholar 1956-58; am. Assn. Petroleum Geologists grantee 1957; recipient First Place award Project of Yr. Nat. Assn. Mgmt. and Tech. Assistance Ctrs., 1985. Mem. AAAS, Am. Assn. Petroleum Geologists, Soc. Econ. Paleontologists and Mineralogists, Geochem. Soc., Assn. Profl. Geol. Scientists.

BIEDRON, THEODORE JOHN, publishing executive, advertising executive; b. Evergreen Park, Ill., Nov. 30, 1946; s. Theodore John and Ione Margaret B.; m. Gloria Anne DeAngelo, Nov. 7, 1970; children: Jessica Ann, Lauren. BA in Polit. Sci., U. Ill., 1968. Recruitment advt. mgr. Chgo. Sun-Times, 1968-74; classified advt. mgr. Pioneer press, Wilmette, Ill., 1974-76, v.p. advt. and promotion, 1993-94, sr. v.p. sales and mktg., 1994-97, exec. v.p., 1997-2000. Pub. North Shore mag., 1997-2000; classified mgr., v.p. Lerner Newspapers, Chgo., 1976-79, assoc. pub., 1980-82, advt. dir., 1982-87; v.p., classified advt. mgr. Chgo. Sun-Times, 1987-92; pres. Chicagoland Pub. Co. divsn. Chgo. Tribune, 2000—. Pres. Northeastern Ill. U. Found., 1998-2002; trustee Northlight Theater, 1993-98. Home: 404 Jackson Ave Glencoe IL 60022- Office: Chicagoland Pub Co 2000 S York Rd Oak Brook IL 60523 E-mail: tbiedron@earthlink.net.

BIEGEL, ALICE MARIE, secondary school educator; b. Blue Island, Ill., Sept. 12, 1947; d. Stanley and Lottie (Matras) Burczyk; m. Peter Leo Biegel, July 27, 1974; children: Kevin, Nicole, Robbie, Ryan. BS in Edn., Chgo. State U., 1968; MS in Edn., Gov.'s State U., 1980. Cert. math. tchr., Ill., Fla. Tchr. algebra Eisenhower High Sch., Blue Island, 1969-71; tchr. algebra and computer edn. Thornton Fractional North & South High Sch., Calumet City, Ill., 1971-76; tchr. geometry, algebra, dir. compensatory edn. Booker High Sch., Sarasota, Fla., 1988-90; tchr. algebra, chmn. math dept. Laurel Mid. Sch., Osprey, Fla., 1990-95; algebra tchr. Riverview H.S., Sarasota, 1997—. Freshmen, jr. sponsor, prom sponsor, fgn. exchange sponsor; developer full yr. curriculum for measurements math course '75. Chmn. pub. rels. and grants com. Jr. League of Sarasota, 1988, 89-90; sponsor H.S. rowing team, 1991—. Recipient Tchr. Commendation award State of Ill., 1973. Mem. Nat. Coun. Tchrs. of Math., Sarasota Tchrs. of Math. Club. Roman Catholic. Avocations: scuba diving, interior decorating, boating. Home: 525 Freeling Dr Sarasota FL 34242-1019

BIEGEL, DAVID ELI, social worker, educator; b. NYC, July 3, 1946; s. Jack and Estelle (Lentin) B.; m. Margaret S. Smoot, Jan. 31, 1976 (div.); 1 child, Geoffrey S.; m. Ronna Kaplan, Oct. 26, 2003. BA, CCNY, 1967; MSW, U. Md., 1970, PhD, 1982. Field coord. United Farm Workers, AFL-CIO, Balt., 1971; exec. dir. Junction, Inc., Westminster, Md., 1971—72; dir. office planning and program devel. Cath. Charities, Balt., 1973—76; ctr. assoc., dir. neighborhood and family svcs. project U. So. Calif., Washington Pub. Affairs Ctr., 1976—80; asst. prof. social work U. Pitts., 1980—85, assoc. prof., 1985—86; Henry L. Zucker prof. social work practice Mandel Sch. Applied Social Scis., Case Western Res. U., 1987—, prof. psychiatry and sociology, 1987—, co-dir. Ctr. for Practice Innovations, 1991—97, chair doctoral program, 1998—2001. Co-dir. Cuyahoga County Cmty. Mental Health Rsch. Inst., 1994—2002; pres. Inst. for the Advancement of Social Work Rsch., 1999—2002; dir. rsch. and evaluation Ohio Substance Abuse and Mental Illness Coord. Ctr. Excellence, 2000—05; co-dir. Ctr. Substance Abuse and Mental Illness, 2002—. Co-editor: Innovations in Practice and Service Delivery with Vulnerable Populations Series, Family Caregiving Applications Series; editor Practice Concepts sect., The Gerontologist; contbr. articles to profl. jours., books; co-author: Neighborhood Networks for Humane Mental

Health Care, 1982, Community Support Systems and Mental Health: Practice, Policy and Research, 1982, Building Support Networks for the Elderly: Theory and Applications, 1984, Social Networks and Mental Health: An Annotated Bibliography, 1985, Social Support Networks: A Bibliography 1983-1987, 1989, Aging and Caregiving: Theory, Research and Policy, 1990, Family Preservation Programs: Research and Evaluation, 1991, Family Caregiving in Chronic Illness: Alzheimer's Dsiease, Cancer, Heart Disease, Mental Illness, and Stroke, 1991, Family Caregiving: A Lifespan Perspective, 1994, The Jewish Aged in the U.S. and Israel: Diversity, Programs and Services, 1994, Innovations in Practice and Service Delivery with Vulnerable Populations Across the Lifespan, 1999. Cons. Vol. VISTA, Raton, N.Mex., and Balt., 1967-70; active Big Bros. Am., Balt., 1974-77. N.Y. State Incentive scholar, 1963-64; VISTA Fellows Program fellow, 1968-70. Fellow Gerontol. Soc. Am.; mem. NASW, Acad. Cert. Social Workers, Soc. Social Work Rsch. Democrat. Jewish. Office Phone: 216-368-2308. Business E-Mail: david.biegel@case.edu.

BIEGEL, KIMBERLY ANN, communications executive, public relations officer; b. Livingston, NJ, May 7, 1977; d. Joanne Irene and Peter Wenceslas Svoboda; m. Patrick Andrew Biegel, Aug. 28, 2004. BA in Comm. & Pub. Rels., Marist Coll., 1999; M in Comm. and Info. Sci., Rutgers U., 2004. Intern US Equestrian Team, Gladstone, NJ, 1997—99; coach Marist Coll. Equestrian Team, Poughkeepsie, NY, 1999—2004; account exec. McShane Associates, Lebanon, 1999—2000, Rowland Comm., NYC, 2000—01, Edelman Pub. Rels., NYC, 2001—03; grad. asst. Ctr. Orgnl. Devel. and Leadership, New Brunswick, NJ, 2003—04; outreach, comm. mgr. Ctr. for Change and Innovation, Edinburgh, Scotland, 2005—. Named IHSA Zone 2 Region 1 Coach of Yr., Intercollegiate Horse Show Assn., 2004; fellow, Johnson & Johnson and The Ctr. for Organisational Devel. and Leadership, 2003-2004. Home: PO Box 336 Oldwick NJ 08858 Office: Ctr for Change and Innovation St Andrews House St Regent St Edinburgh EH1 3DG Scotland Office Phone: 0131 244 2064. Personal E-mail: kimbiegel@hotmail.com.

BIEGLER, DAVID W., energy executive; b. 1946; married. BS, St. Mary's U., 1968; postgrad., Harvard U., 1979. With Enserch Exploration Inc., 1966-78, petroleum engr., 1968-70, dist. petroleum engr., 1970-72, staff petroleum engr., then mgr. revenue control, 1972-74, chief engr., 1974-75, dir. engring. mktg. planning, then v.p. processing engring. mktg., 1975-77, v.p. land and mktg., 1977-78; exec. v.p. Pool Arabia, 1978-79; exec. v.p. eastern hemisphere Pool Intairdril, 1979-80; pres. Pool Well Servicing Co., 1980-84; pres. U.S. ops. Pool Co., 1984-85; pres., COO, CEO, chmn. Enserch Corp., Dallas, 1985—97; pres., COO, vice-chmn. TXU Corp. (formerly Tex. Utilities), Dallas, 1997—2001; CEO Estrella Energy, LP, Dallas, 2003—. Office: Estrella Energy LP 1700 Pacific Ste 2920 Dallas TX 75201

BIEGLER, LORENZ THEODOR, chemical engineering educator; b. Chgo., Sept. 10, 1956; s. Lorenz and Cecilie (Hoegele) B.; m. Lynne Morgan Webber, May 23, 1987; 1 child, Matthew. BS, Ill. Inst. Tech., 1977; PhD, U. Wis., 1981. Asst. prof. in chem. engring. Carnegie Mellon U., Pitts., 1981-86, assoc. prof., 1986-90, prof., 1990—, bayer prof., 1996—; scientist in residence Argonne (Ill.) Nat. Lab., 1990-91. Trustee Cache Corp., Austin, Tex., 1990—; cons. to various chem. and software cos. Contbr. more than 200 papers to profl. jours. and books. Recipient Presdl. Young Investigator award NSF, 1985, Best Paper award of 1988, 95, Computers and Chem. Engring. Jour., 1989, Alumni award Ill. Inst. Tech., 1977, ASEE McGraw award 1996; Disting. faculty visitor U. Alta., Can., 1990; Gambrinus fellow 1995. Mem. AIChE (dir. CAST 1989-92, sec./treas. 1993, Pitts. sect. chmn. 1993, chair 1999), Am. Chem. Soc., Ops. Soc. Am., Soc. Indsl. and Applied Math. Office: Carnegie Mellon U Chem Engring Dept Pittsburgh PA 15213

BIEHL, MICHAEL MELVIN, lawyer, writer; b. Milw., Feb. 24, 1951; s. Michael Melvin Biehl and Frieda Margaret (Krieg) Davis. AB, Harvard U., 1973, JD, 1976. Bar: Wis. 1976, U.S. Dist. Ct. (ea. dist.) Wis. 1976. Assoc. Foley & Lardner, Milw., 1976-84, ptnr., 1984—. Adj. prof. law Marquette U. Law Sch., 2001—. Author: Medical Staff Legal Issues, 1990, Doctored Evidence, 2002, Lawyered to Death, 2003; editor: Physician Organizations and Medical Staff, 1996. Mem. Mt. Sinai Med. Ctr. Clin. Investigations Com., Hastings Ctr.; election monitor first multi-party elections in Rep. Ga., 1990; dir. Colorlines Found. for Arts and Culture, Inc., chmn., bd. dirs. Milw. Psychiat. Hosp. and Aurora Behavioral Health Svcs. Mem. ABA, Am. Health Lawyers Assn., Am. Coll. of Med. Quality, Am. Soc. Law and Medicine. Mem. Unitarian Ch. Office: Foley & Lardner 777 E Wisconsin Ave Ste 3800 Milwaukee WI 53202-5367 Home: 908 Scherer Way Osprey FL 34229-6867 Office Phone: 414-297-5648.

BIEL, JESSICA, actress, model; b. Ely, Minn., Mar. 3, 1982; d. John and Kim Biel. Attended, Tufts U., 2000. Spokesmodel L'Oreal. Actor: (plays) Annie, Beauty and the Beast, Anything Goes, The Sound of Music; (TV series) 7th Heaven, 1996—2001; (films) Ulee's Gold, 1997, I'll Be Home for Christmas, 1998, Summer Catch, 2001, The Rules of Attraction, 2002, The Texas Chainsaw Massacre, 2003, (voice) It's a Digital World, 2004, Cellular, 2004, Blade: Trinity, 2004, Stealth, 2005.*

BIEL, LEONARD, JR., urologist; b. N.Y.C., Jan. 17, 1922; s. Leonard and Eleanor Roberta (Abrahams) B.; m. Lynn Arnstein, June 27, 1958; children: Pamela, Alix. AB, Yale U., 1943; MD, N.Y. Med. Coll., 1946. Diplomate Am. Bd. Urology. Intern Paterson (N.J.) Gen. Hosp., 1946-47; resident in surgery Flower and Fifth Ave. Hosps., N.Y.C., 1950-51, Bellevue Hosp., N.Y.C., 1951-52; resident in urology Mt. Sinai Hosp., N.Y.C., 1952-54; pvt. practice N.Y.C., 1954—. Asst. attending physician Mt. Sinai Hosp. Capt. U.S. Army, 1947-49; ETO. Fellow ACS; mem. AMA, N.Y. Acad. Medicine, N.Y. Med. Soc., N.Y. County Med. Soc., Am. Urol. Assn. Avocation: photography. Home and Office: 114 E 90th St New York NY 10128-1550 Office Phone: 212-369-7070. Personal E-mail: lbieljr@iopener.net.

BIELAWA, HERBERT WALTER, composer, music educator; b. Chgo., Feb. 2, 1930; s. Frank Joseph and Ethel Bielawa; m. Sandra Ilona Soderlund, June 26, 1960; children: Bruce, Lisa. BS MusB, U.Ill., Champaign, 1954, MusM, 1958, DMA, 1968. Prof. music San Francisco State U., 1964—92. Composer-in-residence Music Educators Nat. Conf. and Ford Found., Houston, 1964—66, Choral Artists, San Francisco, 2000, Unitarian-Universalist Ch., Berkeley, 2005; developer electronic music studio San Francisco State U.; founder Ilona Clavier Dua, Sounds New Ensemble. Composer: Sanas for Choir and Orchestra, 2002 (honors Waging Peace Project, 2002). 1st lt. Ordnance Corps U.S. Army, 1954—56. Mem.: Am. Music Ctr., Am. Composers Forum, Soc. Composers, Inc. Avocations: sound editing, woodworking, swimming.

BIELBY, LORENCE JON, lawyer; b. DeLand, Fla., Aug. 3, 1956; s. Charles Willard and Bernadine (Hofferber) B.; m. Mary Margaret Seanor, Apr. 7, 1984. BS, U. Fla., 1978; JD, Cumberland Sch. Law, 1983. Bar: Fla. 1984, U.S. Dist. Ct. (no. and mid. dists.) Fla. 1986, U.S. Ct. Appeals (11th cir.) 1986, U.S. Dist. Ct. (so. dist.) Fla. 1996. Asst. state atty. 2nd Jud. Cir., Tallahassee, 1983-86; ptnr. Greenberg, Traurig, Tallahassee, 1986—. Contbr. articles to profl. jours. Pres. Leon County chpt. MADD, Tallahassee, 1987-90. Mem. ABA, Fla. and Tallahassee Bar Assns., Fla. Acad. Trial Lawyers, Assn. Trial Lawyers Am., Tallahassee C. of C. (leadership com.). Democrat. Episcopalian. Avocations: carpentry, water sports, skiing, restoring automobiles. Home: 3112 Middlebrooks Cir Tallahassee FL 32312-2441 Office: Greenberg Traurig 101 E College Ave Ste 100 Tallahassee FL 32301-7703

BIELE, HUGH IRVING, retired lawyer; b. Bridgeport, Conn., July 28, 1942; s. Ray James and Blanche (McClellan) B.; m. Pamela Althea Johnson, Aug. 21, 1965 (div.); children: Jonathan Christopher, Melissa Lynne. BA, St. Lawrence U., Canton, N.Y., 1965; JD, U. Utah, 1968. Bar: Utah 1968, U.S. Dist. Ct. Utah 1968, Calif. 1972, U.S. Dist. Ct. Calif. 1972, U.S. Ct. Appeals (9th and 10th cirs.). Instr. San Francisco Law Sch., 1971-73; atty. United Calif. Bank, San Francisco, 1974—81; v.p., sr. counsel First Interstate Bank, L.A., 1974-81; ptnr. Biele & Stuehrmann, L.A., 1981-83; sr. ptnr. Biele, Stuehrmann & Lapinski, L.A., 1983-84; founding ptnr. Biele & Lapinski, L.A., 1985-89; ptnr. Barton, Klugman & Detting, L.A., 1989-91; ptnr., dir. comml. law and litigation Grace, Skocypec, Cosgrove & Schirm, L.A., 1992-95; ret., 1995. Bd. govs. Fin. Lawyer Conf., L.A., 1976-2000, pres. 1984-85, original developer, ptnr. Engine Co. No. 28 rehabilitation, 1978-88, ptnr. Engine Co. No. 28 Restaurant, 1988—, owner Biele Enterprises. Author screenplay: Corporate Cancer, 1989, Hedge of Thorns, 1990. Chmn. Vols. in Parole, L.A., 1979—80, 1989—90, Lawyers for Human Rights, 1988—2000, co-pres. elect, 1998, co-pres., 1999; commr. Episc. Diocese AIDS Ministry, L.A., 1988—93; bd. dirs. Cmty. Counseling Svc., L.A., 1989—99, pres., 1993—95, chmn. bd. dirs., 1995—99; bd. dirs. Casa de Rosa and the Sunshine Mission, 1997—2001, treas., 2001; bd. dirs., v.p., sec. Project New Hope, Inc., L.A., 1990—92. Decorated Army Commendation medal, Bronze Star with oak leaf cluster. Mem.: FBA, ABA, Internat. Bankers Assn. Calif., Calif. State Bar (fin. inst. com.), L.A. County Bar Assn. (internat. sect. exec. com. 1978—97, chmn. 1981—82, exec. com. comml. law and bankruptcy sect. 1986—2000, chair 1992—93), Fin. Lawyers Conf. (pres. 1986—87), Internat. Bar Assn., Hollywood Knolls Cmty. Club (bd. dirs. 2002—), St. Lawrence U. Alumni Assn. (pres. 1979—91). Republican. Episcopalian. Avocations: skiing, jogging, aerobics, travel. Home: 3478 Wonder View Dr Los Angeles CA 90068-1536 Office: 3478 Wonder View Dr Los Angeles CA 90068-1536 E-mail: hughbiele@aol.com.

BIELEFELDT, ANGELA R., environmental engineering educator; BSCE, Iowa State U., 1992; MSCE, U. Wash., 1994, PhDCE, 1996. EIT Colo., 2003. Asst. prof. U. Colo., Boulder, Colo., 1996—2003, assoc. prof., 2003—. Contbr. articles to profl. jours. Faculty adv. Engrs. Without Borders - CU, Boulder, Colo., 2003—05. Recipient Early Career Award - Environ. Divsn., Am. Soc. for Engring. Edn., 2003. Mem.: Internat. Water Assn., Water Environment Fedn., Assn. Environ. Engring. and Sci. Professors (Outstanding Tchg. Environ. Engring. & Sci. 2004). Achievements include patents for degradation of environmental toxins by a flamentous bacterium; a device and method for removal of gas contaminants through a shallow sparged bioreactor. Office: U Colo 428 Ucb Boulder CO 80309-0428 Office Phone: 303-492-8433. Office Fax: 303-492-7317. Business E-Mail: angela.bielefeldt@colorado.edu.

BIELIAUSKAS, VYTAUTAS JOSEPH, psychologist, educator; b. Plackojai, Lithuania, Nov. 1, 1920; came to U.S., 1949, naturalized, 1955; s. Antanas and Anele (Kasparaite) B.; m. Danute G. Sirvydaite, Mar. 12, 1947; children— Linas A., Diana B., Aldona O., Cornelius V. PhD in Psychology, U. Tuebingen, 1943; PsyD, Xavier U., 2005. Diplomate Clin. Psychology, Marital Family Therapy, Am. Bd. Family Psychology, Am. Bd. Family Psychology. Asst. prof. U. Munich, Germany, 1944-48; instr. King's Coll., Wilkes-Barre, Pa., 1949-50; mem. faculty Sch. Clin. and Applied Psychology, Coll. William and Mary, 1950-58, prof. psychology, 1953-58, head dept. psychology, 1951-57; assoc. prof. Xavier U., Cin., 1958-60, chmn. dept. psychology, 1959-78, prof., 1960-78, Riley prof. psychology, 1978-88, disting. prof. psychology emeritus, 1988—. Author: A Psychologist Looks at the Dealth Penalty, Social Justice Review, 1993 (7-8), 2002, Community Relations Training for Police Supervisors, 1969; CSSS for the H-T-P Drawings, 1981, Politics, Ethics and Morality, Social Justice Review, 1994 (3-4), 2003; contbr. articles to profl. jours. Pres., exec. officer Lithuanian World Cmty., 1988-92; exec. v.p. Lithuanian-Am. Cmty., Inc., 1994-2000; adviser on spl. programs Pres. of Republic of Lithuania, 1995-96. Lt. col. M.S.C., USAR, 1958-65. Recipient Ellis Island medal of honor, 1990. Fellow APA (pres. divsn. 13, 1986, Dist. Svc. award divsn. 36 1998); mem. Ohio Psychol. Assn. (pres. 1978-79, Disting. Svc. award 1980), Soc. Personality Assessment, Internat. Assn. for Study Med. Psychology and Religion (pres. 1972-75), Cin. Acad. Profl. Psychology, Psychologists Interested in Religious Issues (pres. 1971, exec. sec. 1973-75), Cath. Acad. Scis. in the U.S.A. (academician 1987—). Office: Xavier U Dept Psychology Cincinnati OH 45207 Office Phone: 513-745-3710. Personal E-mail: vbieliaus@aol.com. Business E-Mail: bieliaus@xavier.edu.

BIELORY, ABRAHAM MELVIN, lawyer, finance company executive; b. Modena, Italy, Sept. 20, 1946; came to U.S., 1948; s. Motel and Basia (Spielberg) B.; m. Beverly B. Berkowitz, Jan. 26, 1969; children: Jennifer Rebecca, Debra Elizabeth, David Ethan. BS, N.J. Inst. Tech., 1968; JD, U. Denver, 1973. Bar: N.J. 1974, U.S. Dist. Ct. N.J. 1974, U.S. Supreme Ct. 1979. Field engr. Control Data Corp., Mpls., 1968-69; assoc. Paschon & Feurey, Toms River, N.J., 1973-77, ptnr., 1978, VanSicle & Bielory, Toms River, 1978-88, Babcock, Hennes & Bielory, P.C., Bricktown and Toms River, N.J., 1989-96; owner ABEV Fin. Svc., Lakewood, 1976—; ptnr. Bielory & Hennes, PC, Bricktown, Toms River, 1996—. V.p. Lakewood Hebrew Day Sch., N.J., 1975-82, pres., 1982-86; trustee Hillel High Sch., Deal, N.J., 1983—; v.p. Congregation Sons of Israel, Lakewood, 1984-86, pres. 1986-88. Sgt. USAF, 1969-73. Fellow ABA; mem. ATLA, N.J. State Bar Assn., Trial Atty. N.J., Ocean County Bd. Realtors, Women's Coun. of Realtors (assoc.), Ocean County Bar Assn. (chmn. ins. com. 1975), Hudson County Bar Assn. (sr. citizen com. 1984), Internat. Lawyers Assn., Jewish War Vets. Republican. Home: 1422 14th St Lakewood NJ 08701-1504

BIELORY, LEONARD, allergist, immunologist, medical school administrator; b. Neptune, N.J., Nov. 17, 1954; s. Max and Bessie (Spielberg) B.; m. Marilyn Miriam Gilan, July 5, 1981; children: Brett Phillip, Barry Mark, Amy Beth BS, MS, Lehigh U., 1976; MD, N.J. Med. Sch., 1980. Intern, resident U. Md. Hosp., Balt., 1980-82; clin. assoc. NIH, Bethesda, Md., 1982-85; dir. divsn. allergy & rheumatology N.J. Med. Sch., Newark, 1985—, co-dir. immuno-ophthalmology svcs., prof. medicine, pediats. and ophthalmology, 1992—2002, dir. development & clinical rsch. dept. medicine; pres. med. staff Univ. Medicine and Dentistry N.J.-Univ. Hosp., 1993-95; pres., chmn. Univ. Physician Assocs., 1996-2000. Pres. med. staff ex-oficio mem. NIH Safety and Data Mgmt. Bd., 1993-98; bd. dirs Univ. Health Care Corp., acting med. dir., 1995-97; dir. Asthma and Allergy Rsch. Ctr., 1992—; prof. medicine, pediat. and ophthalmology, 2002—; chmn. clin. treatment study sect. NIH, 1993; prin. investigator Nat. Ctr. for Complementary and Alternative Medicine, NIH, 2002-04. Assoc. editor: Annuls of Allergy, Asthma & Immunology, 1996-2005; contbr. rsch. papers to profl. jours., chpt. to books. Bd. dirs. Congregation Israel, Springfield, N.J., 1988, pres., 1999-01; v.p. Kushner Yeshiva, pres. 2005-; bd. dirs St.John's Cmty. Svc., 2002-. Recipient Young Investigator award Am. Acad. Allergy and Immunology, 1985; Schering Corp. Travel grantee, 1985. Fellow ACP, Am. Acad. Allergy and Immunology; mem. Med. Soc. N.J. Jewish. Avocations: skiing, camping, rafting, bicycling. Office: NJ Med Sch Divsn Allergy & Rheumatology 90 Bergen St Ste 4700 Newark NJ 07103-2425 Office Phone: 973-972-2768. E-mail: bielory@umdnj.edu.

BIELUCH, WILLIAM CHARLES, judge; b. Nov. 12, 1918; AB magna cum laude, Brown U., 1939; JD, Yale U., 1942. Bar: Conn. 1942. Assoc. Covington, Burling, Rublee, Acheson & Shorb, Washington, 1942-43; ptnr. Bieluch, Barry & Ramenda and predecessors, Hartford, 1946-68; judge Cir. Ct. Conn., 1968-73, Ct. Common Pleas Conn., 1973-76, Superior Ct. Conn., 1976-85, Appellate Session, 1979-83, Appellate Ct. Conn., 1985-88; ret., 1988; judge trial referee, 1988—. Trustee emeritus S. S. Cyril and Methodius Roman Cath. Ch., Hartford; corporator St. Francis Hosp. and Med. Ctr., Hartford. Lt. (j.g.) USCG, WWII. Decorated Knight St. Gregory, Pope Paul VI, 1972; recipient Merit award Polish Legion Am. Vets., 1952, Man of Yr. award United Polish Socs., 1968, Archdiocesan medal of appreciation Archbishop John F. Whealon, 1970, Disting. Grad. award Nat. Cath. Elem. Sch., 1995. Mem. Conn. Bar Assn. (chmn. Jr. Bar Sect. 1948-49), Hartford County Bar Assn., KC, Phi Beta Kappa. Republican. Office: 95 Washington St Hartford CT 06106-4431

BIEMANN, KLAUS, chemistry professor; b. Innsbruck, Austria, Nov. 2, 1926; came to U.S., 1955, naturalized, 1965; PhD, U. Innsbruck, Austria, 1951. Postdoctoral fellow MIT, Cambridge, 1955-57, instr. in chemistry, 1957-59, asst. prof. chemistry, 1959-62, assoc. prof. chemistry, 1962-63, prof. chemistry, 1963-96, prof. emeritus, 1996—. Author: Mass Spectrometry, 1962; also rsch. publs. in mass spectrometry; assoc. editor Analytical Chemistry, 1985-89; mem. editl. bd. Organic Mass Spectrometry, 1967-75, Biomed. Mass Spectrometry, 1975-85, Fresenius Zeitschrift für Analytische Chemie, 1980-86, Mass Spectrometry Revs., 1981-98, Jour. Protein Chemistry, 1990-96, Jour. Am. Soc. Mass Spectrometry, 1990-96, Protein Sci., 1991-96. Trustee Drug Sci. Found., 1982-88. Recipient Tricentennial medal U. Innsbruck, 1970, Justin Powers award Am. Acad. Pharm. Scis., 1973, N.Y. sect. award Soc. Applied Spectroscopy, 1974, Exceptional Sci. Achievement award NASA, 1977, Fritz Pregl medal Austrian Microchem. Soc., 1977, Maurice F. Hasler award Spectroscopy Soc. Pitts., 1989, J.J. Thomson medal, 1991, P. Edman award, 1992, Assn. of Biomolecular Resource Facilities Beckman award, 1995. Fellow AAAS, Am. Acad. Arts and Scis.; mem. NAS, Am. Chem. Soc. (Field and Franklin award in mass spectrometry 1986, award in analytical chemistry 2001), Belgian Chem. Soc. (hon. mem., Gold medal 1962), Am. Soc. for Mass Spectrometry, The Protein Soc. Office: MIT Dept Chemistry Rm 18-297 Cambridge MA 02139-4307

BIEN, JOSEPH JULIUS, philosophy educator; b. Cin., May 22, 1936; s. Joseph Julius and Mary Elizabeth (Adams) B.; m. Françoise Neve, Apr. 8, 1965. BS, Xavier U., MA, 1958; DTC, U. Paris, 1968; postgrad., Laval Univ., 1958, Emory U., 1961-62, U. Edinburgh, 1962; D (hon.), Lucian Blaga U., 1999. Asst. prof. philosophy Univ. Tex., Austin, 1968-73; asso. prof. philosophy Univ. Mo., Columbia, 1973-79, prof. philosophy, 1979—, chmn. dept. philosophy, 1976-80, 81-83, 1993—99; vis. prof. Tex. A&M U., 1980, Dubrovnik Inst. Postgrad. Studies, Yugoslavia, 1983, 84, 85, 89, co-dir., 1990—; Mid-Am. States Univs. Assn. hon. lectr. in philosophy, 1985-86. Rsch. assoc. Russian and Slavic Rsch. Ctr., 1989-91; vis. prof. Lucian Blaga U., 1996, Hubei U., 1997, Wichita State U., 1998, U. Western Cape, 2000, Lille 3 U, 2002. Author: History, Revolution and Human Natue: Marx's Philosophical Anthropology, 1984; transl.: (M. Merleau-Ponty) Adventures of the Dialectic, 1973; editor: Phenomenology and the Social Sciences, A Dialogue, 1978, Political and Social Essays by Paul Ricoeur, 1974, Leviathan, 1986, Contemporary Social Thought, 1989, Ethics and Politics, 1992, Philosophical Issues and Problems, 1998. Am. Council Learned Socs. grantee, 1973; Dubrovnik Inst. Postgrad. Studies grantee, 1984; recipient U. Mo. faculty alumni award, 1998. Mem. Soc. Social and Polit. Philosophy (pres. 1979-80, 86-87, 93-94, 97-98), Ctrl. States Philos. Assn. (pres. 1978-79), Ctrl. Slavic Conf. (sec.-tres. 1977, 84), Southwestern Philosophy Soc. (pres. 1997-98). Democrat. Home: 100 W Brandon Rd Columbia MO 65203-3508 Office: Univ Mo Dept Philosophy Columbia MO 65211-0001

BIEN, PETER ADOLPH, language educator, writer; b. NYC, May 28, 1930; s. Adolph F. and Harriet (Honigsberg) B.; m. Chrysanthi Yiannakou, July 17, 1955; children: Leander, Alec, Daphne. Student, Harvard U., 1948-50; BA, Haverford Coll., 1952; MA, Columbia U., 1957, PhD, 1961; postgrad., Bristol (Eng.) U., 1958-59, Woodbrooke Coll., Eng., 1970-71. Lectr. Columbia U., N.Y.C., 1957-58, 59-61; instr. dept. English Dartmouth Coll., Hanover, N.H., 1961-62, asst. prof., 1963-65, assoc. prof., 1965-68, prof., 1969-97, Geisel prof., 1974-79, Frederick Sessions Beebe '35 prof. in art of writing, 1989-97, prof. emeritus, 1997—. Vis. prof. Harvard U., 1983, U. Melbourne, Australia, 1983, Woodbooke Coll., 1995, U. Thessaloniki, Greece, 1996, 2000, Princeton (N.J.) U., 2001, Columbia U., 2004, Brown U., 2005. Author: L.P. Hartley, 1963, Constantine Cavafy, 1964, Kazantzakis and the Linguistic Revolution in Greek Literature, 1972, Nikos Kazantzakis, 1972, Antithesis and Synthesis in the Poetry of Yannis Ritsos, 1980, Three Generations of Greek Writers, 1983, Tempted by Happiness: Kazantzakis' Post-Christian Christ, 1984, Kazantzakis: Politics of the Spirit, Nikos Kazantzakis-Novelist, 1989, Words, Wordlessness, and the Word: Quaker Silence Reconsidered, 1992, (with Darren J.N. Middleton) God's Struggler: Religion in the Works of Nikos Kazantzakis, 1996, (with Chuck Fager) In Stillness There Is Fullness: A Peacemaker's Harvest, 2000, On Retiring to Kendal (and Beyond), 2003, A Literary Excursion, 2003; co-author: Demotic Greek I, 1972, Demotic Greek II, 1982, Greek Today, 2004, A Century of Greek Poetry 1900-2000, 2004; translator: The Last Temptation of Christ, 1960, Saint Francis, 1962, Report to Greco, 1965 (all by Nikos Kazantzakis), Life in the Tomb (Stratis Myrivilis), 1977, 87, 2004; co-editor: Modern Greek Writers, 1972; assoc. editor Byzantine and Modern Greek Studies, 1975-82; assoc. editor Jour. Modern Greek Studies, 1983-89, editor, 1990-99. Trustee Kinhaven Music Sch., Weston, Vt., 1972-78, 81-84, 86-92, pres., 1988-90; trustee Pendle Hill, Wallingford, Pa., 1977-92, 94-2005, presiding clk., 1983-84, 86, Quaker in Residence, 1998; mem. corp. Haverford Coll., 1974-2001; pres. bd. trustees Hanover Monthly Meeting, Soc. of Friends, 1977-84; chair bd. overseers Kendal at Hanover, 1989-95, chair bd. dirs., 1995-96; trustee Am. Farm Sch., 1998—. Recipient E. Harris Harbison award for disting. teaching, Danforth Found., 1968, Golden Cross, St. Andrew Greek Orthodox Archdiocese Australia, 2000; Fulbright fellow, 1958, 1983, 1987. Mem. Modern Greek Studies Assn. (pres. 1982-84, 99-2002, mem. exec. com. 1968-85, 99—2005), Yale Club (N.Y.C.). Democrat. Home: 80 Lyme Rd # 171 Hanover NH 03755 Home (Summer): Terpni 207 Waddell Rd Riparius NY 12862 Office Phone: 603-643-5524. E-mail: peter.bien@dartmouth.edu.

BIENEN, HENRY SAMUEL, academic administrator, political scientist, educator; b. N.Y.C., May 5, 1939; s. Mitchell Richard and Pearl (Witty) Bienen; m. Leigh Buchanan, Apr. 28, 1961; children: Laura, Claire, Leslie. BA with honors, Cornell U., 1960; MA, U. Chgo., 1961, PhD, 1966. Ssst. prof. politics U. Chgo., 1965—66; asst. prof. politics & internat. affairs Princeton U., NJ, 1966—69, assoc. prof., 1969—72, prof., 1972—95, William Stewart Tod prof. politics and internat. affairs, 1981—85, James S. McDonnell Disting. Univ. prof., 1985, dir. Ctr. Internat. Studies, 1985—92, chair dept. politics, 1973—76, dir. African studies progrm, 1977—78, 1983—84, dir. rsch. Woodrow Wilson Sch. Pub. & Internat. Affairs, 1979—82, dean, 1992—94; pres. Northwestern U., Evanston, Ill., 1995—. Mem. exec. com. Inter-Univ. Seminar on Armed Forces and Soc., 1968—78, Chgo. Coun. Fgn. Rels.; cons. U.S. State Dept., 1972—88, Nat. Security Coun., 1978—79, World Bank, 1981—89, Hambrecht & Quist Investment Co., Boeing Corp., Econ Corp., Enserch Corp., Ford Found., Rockefeller Found., John D. and Catherine T. MacArthur Found., Franklin Inst., Frost & Sullivan, Canada Council, Family Health Care, Carnegie Corp., Hygrove Capital; mem. sr. review panel CIA, 1982—88; nat. co. dir. Movement for A New Congress, 1970—71; mem. Inst. Advanced Study, 1984—85, Ctr. Advanced Study in the Behavioral Scis., 1976—77; vis. prof. Makerere Coll., Kampala, Uganda, 1963—65, U. Coll., Nairobi, Kenya, 1968—69, U. Ibadan, 1972—73, Columbia U.; bd. dirs. Univ. Corp. for Advanced Internet Devel., 1998—2002; mem. Coun. on Fgn. Rels., Matthews Internat. Capital Mgmt., LLC, Consortium on Financing Higher Edn., John G. Shedd Aquarium, Steppenwolf Theatre, Alain Locke Charter Sch., Com. on Roles of Acad. Health Ctrs. in the 21st Century at Nat. Acad.'s Inst. of Medicine; Acad. fellow Carnegie Corp. on Internat. Devel. Program. Editor: World Politics, 1970—74, 1978—, Voices of Power: World Leaders Speak, 1995—; author: Tanzania: Party Transformation and Economic Development, 1967, The Military Intervenes: Case Studies in Political Change, 1968, Violence and Social Change, 1968, The Military and Modernization, 1970, Kenya: The Politics of Participation and Control, 1974, Armies and Parties in Africa, 1978, The Politcal Economy of Income Distribution in Nigeria, 1981, Political Conflict and Economic Change in Nigeria, 1985, Arms and the African Military Influence in Africa's International Relations, 1985, Of Time and Power: Leadership Duration in the Modern World, 1991, Power, Economics, and Security: The U.S.-Japanese Relationship, 1992. Bd. dirs. The Bear Stearns Co., Inc., Deltak Edn., Inc.; bd. govs., chair nominating & governance com., mem. exec. com. Coun. Fgn. Rels.; bd. dirs., mem. exec. com. Chgo. Coun. Fgn. Rels.; bd. trustees John G. Shedd Aquarium, Steppenwolf Theatre, Alain Locke Charter Sch.; bd. govs. exec. & nominating com. Argonne Nat. Lab.; bd. trustees JSTOR. Recipient Profl. Achievement award, U. Chgo., 2000, Acad. Leadership award, Carnegie Corp.; grantee, Rockefeller Found., 1968—69, 1972—73; Seeger fellow, 1989. Mem.: Am. Acad., Am. Polit. Sci. Assn., Civil Com. Comm. Club. Office: Northwestern U Z-130 Crown 633 Clark St Evanston IL 60208-0001 Business E-Mail: nu-president@northwestern.edu.*

BIENENSTOCK, ARTHUR IRWIN, physicist, educator, federal official; b. N.Y.C., Mar. 20, 1935; s. Leo and Lena (Senator) Bienenstock; m. Roslyn Doris Goldberg, Apr. 14, 1957; children: Eric Lawrence, Amy Elizabeth (dec.), Adam Paul. BS, Poly. Inst. Bklyn., 1955, MS, 1957; PhD, Harvard U., 1962; PhD (hon.), Poly. U., 1998. Asst. prof. Harvard U., Cambridge, Mass., 1963—67; mem. faculty Stanford (Calif.) U., 1967—, prof. applied physics, 1972—, vice provost faculty affairs, 1972—77, dir. synchrotron radiation lab., 1978—97, dir. Lab. for Advanced Materials, 2002—03, vice provost, dean rsch. and grad. policy, 2003—; assoc. dir. sci. Office of Sci. and Tech. Policy, Washington, 1997—2001. Mem. U.S. Nat. Com. Crystallography, 1983—88; mem. sci. adv. com. European Synchrotron Radiation Facility, 1988—90, 1993—96; mem. com. condensed matter and materials physics NRC, 1996—97, mem. bd. chem. scis. and techs., 2001—03. Contbr. scientific papers to profl. jours. Bd. dirs. Calif. chpt. Cystic Fibrosis Rsch. Found., 1970—73, mem. pres.'s adv. coun., 1980—82; trustee Cystic Fibrosis Found., 1982—88. Recipient Sidhu award, Pitts. Diffraction Soc., 1968, Disting. Alumnus award, Poly. Inst. N.Y., 1977; NSF fellow, 1962—63. Fellow: AAAS, Am. Phys. Soc. (gen. councilor 1993—96); mem.: Materials Rsch. Soc., Am. Crystallographic Assn. Jewish. Home: 967 Mears Ct Stanford CA 94305 Office: Bldg 10 Main Quad Stanford CA 94305-2061 Office Phone: 650-723-0977. Business E-Mail: a@slac.stanford.edu.

BIENENSTOCK, JOHN, pathologist, educator, health facility administrator; b. Budapest, Hungary, Oct. 6, 1936; s. Maurice and Anne (Horn) Bienenstock; m. Dody Sanders, Nov. 24, 1961; children: Jimson Andrew, Adam Sebastian, Robin Anne. MB, BChir, Westminster Med. Sch., London, 1960; postgrad., Harvard Med. Sch., 1964—66, SUNY, Buffalo, 1966—68; MD (hon.), U. Göteborg, Sweden, 1998; CM, Order of Canada, 2002. Fellow Harvard U. Med. Sch., Boston, 1964-66; Buswell fellow SUNY, Buffalo, 1966-68, asst. rsch. prof. medicine, 1967-68; asst. prof. medicine McMaster U., Hamilton, Ont., Can., 1968-74, assoc. dean rsch., 1972-78, prof. medicine and pathology, 1974—, chmn. dept. pathology, 1978-89, v.p. health scis., 1989-97, dean health scis., 1992-97, univ. prof., 1997—; dir. brain-body inst. St. Joseph's Healthcare, 2001. Founder AB Biol. Supply, Inc., 1977, Agritech Rsch. Inc., 1980; D. W. Harrington lectr. SUNY, Buffalo, 1986; Rayne vis. prof. U. Western Australia, Perth, 1987; cons. WHO, Geneva, 1970—; chief sci. officer Oratol Inc., 1997—99; chmn. sci. adv. bd. Internat. Med. Innovations, 1999; bd. dirs. Prometic Life Sci. Inc.; cons. various pharm. cos.; dir. Brain-Body Inst. St. Joseph's Healthcare, Hamilton. Editor: (book) Immunology of Lung, 1984, Mast Cell Differentiation, 1986, Recent Advances in Mucosal Immunology, 1987, Handbook of Mucosal Immunology, 1994, Mucosal Immunology, 1998, 3d edit., 2004; contbr. over 400 articles to profl. jours. Chmn., bd. dirs. Can. Red Cross Soc.; chmn. bd. Dundas Valley Sch. Art., 1984—86; chmn. adv. com. nat. blood svcs., 1985—90. Recipient Prukynje medal, Assn. Czechoslovak Socs., Prague, 1989, Ross A. McIntyre Gold medal, U. Nebr., Omaha, 1989, Finkelstein prize, Crohn's and Colitis Found., Can., 1996. Fellow: RCP (London), RCP (Can.), Royal Soc. Can.; mem.: Coll. Internat. Allergologicum (pres. 1998—2002), Soc. Mucosal Immunology (pres. 1990—92), Internat. Union Immunological Socs. (mem. coun.), Am. Thoracic Soc., Swiss Soc. Allergy and Immunology (hon.), Am. Soc. Clin. Investigation, Assn. Am. Physicians, Can. Soc. Immunology (pres. 1985—87). Jewish. Avocation: painting. Home: 2-31 Dundonald St Toronto ON Canada M4Y 1K3 Office: McMaster U Fac Health Scis 1200 Main St W Rm 3N26H Hamilton ON Canada L8N 3Z5

BIENENSTOCK, MARTIN J., lawyer; b. NYC, Nov. 14, 1952; s. Arthur H. and Elaine (Schulman) B. BS in Econs., U. Pa., 1974; JD cum laude, U. Mich. Law Sch., 1977. Bar: NY 1978, US Dist. Ct. (So. and Ea. Districts) NY 1978, US Dist. Ct. So. Dist. Ala. 1983, US Ct. Appeals (2nd Cir.) 1986, US Supreme Ct. 1987, US Dist. Ct., No. Dist. Tex., 1988, US Ct. Appeals (5th Cir.) 1989. Assoc. Weil, Gotshal & Manges LLP, NYC, 1977-85, ptnr., co-chair bus. fin. and restructuring dept., 1985—. Tchr. of Advanced Reorganization Harvard Law Sch. Writer (treatise) Bankruptcy Reorganization. Mem. ABA, Am. Coll. Bankrupty Lawyers, S.W. Legal Found.; fellow Am. Coll. Commercial Fin. Lawyers Jewish. Office: Weil Gotshal & Manges LLP 767 5th Ave New York NY 10153-0119 Office Phone: 212-310-8530. Office Fax: 212-310-8007. Business E-Mail: martin.bienenstock@weil.com.

BIENIAWSKI, ZDZISLAW TADEUSZ RICHARD, engineering educator, writer, consultant; b. Cracow, Poland, Oct. 1, 1936; came to U.S., 1978, naturalized; m. Elizabeth Hyslop, 1964; 3 children. Student, Gdansk (Poland) Tech. U., 1954-58; BS in Mech. Engring., U. Witwatersrand, Johannesburg, South Africa, 1961, MS in Engring. Mechanics, 1963; PhD in Rock Engring., U. Pretoria, South Africa, 1968; D in Engring. (hon.), U. Madrid, 2001. Prof. mineral engring. Pa. State U., Univ. Park, 1977—96, prof. sci., tech. & society, 1994-96, prof. emeritus, 1996—; pres. Bieniawski Design Enterprises, Prescott, Ariz., 1996—; Disting. prof. geol. engring. U. Madrid, Spain, 2001—. Vis. prof. U. Karlsruhe, Germany, 1972, Stanford U., 1985, Harvard U., 1990, Cambridge (Eng.) U., 1997; chmn. U.S. Nat. Com. on Tunneling Tech., 1984-85; U.S. rep. to Internat. Tunnel Assn., 1984-85. Author: Rock Mechanics Design in Mining and Tunneling, 1984, Strata Control in Mineral Engineering, 1987, Aiming High-A Collection of Essays, 1988, Engineering Rock Mass Classifications, 1989, A Tale of Three Continents, 1991, Design Methodology in Rock Engineering, 1992, Gaudeamus Igitur Poems, 1997, Alec's Journey, 1999; editor: Tunneling in Rock, 1974, Exploration for Rock Engineering, 1976, Milestones in Rock Engring., 1996; contbr. over 170 articles to profl. jours. Recipient Mayor's Proclamation of City of State Coll. Bieniawski Day, 1983, Rock Mechanics Rsch. award, 1984, disting. toastmaster internat. award, 1974; Bienawski Auditorium at U. Madrid Sch. Mines named in his honor, 2003. Avocations: genealogy, cosmology, foreign policy, financial planning. Home: The Ranch 3023 Sunnybrae Cir Prescott AZ 86303-5770

BIER, LOUIS HENRY GUSTAV, minister; b. Chgo., Jan. 12, 1933; s. Louis Wilfred and Ethel Lea (Laue) Bier; m. Helene Mueller, July 29, 1962; children: Richard Allen, Karen Elizabeth, Lisa Anne. BE, Chgo. Tchrs. Coll., 1954; B in Theology, Concordia Sem., 1959, MDiv in Theology, 1959; MEd, Boston State Coll., 1962; DRE, Smith Bapt. U., 1987, DD, 1986. Ordained ministry Luth. Ch., 1959; lic. social worker. Vicar Redeemer Luth. Ch., Phila., 1957, 1st Luth. Ch., Holyoke, Mass., 1957—58; pastor St. Paul's Luth. Ch., West Frankfort, Ill., 1959—61, Trinity Luth. Ch., Boston, 1961—98, emeritus, 1999—; chaplain VA New Eng. Health Care Sys., Boston, 1965—; instr. psychology Boston State Coll., 1967—81; mem. adj. faculty Holy Cross Greek Orthodox Sem., Brookline, Mass., 1998. Chaplain German Home Elderly, Boston, 1962, also trustee, clk. corp., 1971—; chaplain Arbour, Boston, 1969, West Roxbury VA Hosp., 1978—86; circuit counselor Luth. Ch. Mo. Synod; trustee Chapel Four Chaplains, Valley Forge, Pa., 2000; cons. Slavik Rsch. Inst.; mem. animal studies com. Beth Israel-Deaconess Hosp., Havard Med. Sch., 2000; bd. dirs. Interfaith Bible Readings, Inc. Mem. arboretum dist. Boston coun. Boy Scouts Am., 1976—79, life mem. Nat. Eagle Scout Assn.; mem. USO Coun. New Eng.; bd. mgrs. Sophia Snow Ho.; br. pres. A.A.L., 1982. Served lt. col. CAP, 1975—, chaplain, col. Mass. State Def. Fort. Recipient Honored Citizen award, Kennedy VFW, 1973, Cmty. Svc. award, Greater Boston Assn. Retarded Citizens, 1974, Lamb award, Luth. Coun., 1975, George Meany Youth Svc. award, AFL-CIO, 1983, Dist. Eagle Scout award, Boy Scouts Am., 1993, Citation award Recognition, Slovik Rsch. Inst., 1999, Svc. award, Concordia Seminary, Ft. Wayne, Ind., 1999; fellow Emerson, Mil. Chaplains Assn. USA, 1999, West, Boy Scouts Am., 1999. Mem.: Am. Assn. Mental Retardation (20 Year Citation 2002, Humanitarian Award 2002), Concordia Sem. (Servus Ecclesia Christi award), Mass. Chaplains Assn., German Aid Soc. Boston (trustee), Assn. Profl. Chaplains (life; cert., 25th Anniversary citation 2000), Mil. Chaplains Assn. (life; treas., v.p., pres.), Luth. Edn. Assn. (life), Vanderbilt Club. Avocations: swimming, golf, reading. Home: 169 Nahatan St Westwood MA 02090-3607

BIERBAUM, J. ARMIN, petroleum company executive, consultant; b. Oak Park, Ill., June 29, 1924; s. Armin Walter and Harriett Cornelia (Backmann) B.; m. Janith Turnbull, Apr. 17, 1948; children: Steve, Todd, Charles, Peter, Mark. BS, Northwestern U., 1945, MS, 1948. Project engr. Am. Oil Co., Ind., 1948-53; sales engr. Universal Oil Products Co., Des Plaines, Ill., 1953-56; tech. dir. Nat. Coop. Refinery Assn., McPherson, Kans., 1956-58; asst. plant mgr., treas., v.p., dir. Gen. Carbon & Chem. Corp., Robinson, Ill., 1958-61; cons. Williston, N.D., 1962-64; v.p. ops. Midland Coops., Inc., Mpls., 1964-72; sr. v.p. ops. Tosco Corp., Los Angeles, 1972-77; pres., chief exec. officer Gary Energy Co., Englewood, Colo., 1977-79, U.S. Ethanol Corp., Englewood, 1979-82; cons., 1983—. Served with USNR, 1942-45. Mem. Am. Inst. Chem. Engrs., Sigma Xi, Phi Epsilon Pi. Office: 1609 Ridgecrest Dr Loveland CO 80537-9073

BIERBAUM, JANITH MARIE, artist; b. Evanston, Ill., Jan. 14, 1927; d. Gerald Percy and Lillian (Sullivan) Turnbull; m. J. Armin Bierbaum, Apr. 17, 1948; children: Steve, Todd, Chad, Peter, Mark. BA, Northwestern U., 1948; student, Mpls. Art Inst., 1964; postgrad., St. Paul Art Inst., 1969-70. Rsch. asst. AMA, Chgo., 1948-49; tchr. Chgo. high schs., 1949-51; freelance artist Larkspur, Colo., 1951—. Exhibited in group shows at Foot Hills Art Ctr., 1985, 86, 87, Palmer Lake (Colo.) Art Assn., 1986-87, 88-89, Gov.'s Mansion, Bismarck, N.D., 1960; oil painting appeared in 1989 Women in Art Nat. calendar pub. by AAUW. Recipient 1st Place Purchase award, U. Minn., Mpls., 1966, Coors Classic award, Coors Beer, Golden, Colo., 1987. Mem.: Colo. Artist Assn. Republican. Avocations: cross country skiing, swimming, hiking. Home and Office: 1609 Ridgecrest Dr Loveland CO 80537-9073

BIERDS, LINDA LOUISE, language educator, poet; b. Wilmington, Del., Apr. 20, 1945; d. Henry Walter Bierds and Edith Patterson. BA, U. Wash., 1969, MA, 1971. Info. specialist U. Wash., Seattle, 1980-90, prof. English, 1990—. Author: The Stillness, The Dancing, 1988, Heart & Perimeter, 1991, The Ghost Trio, 1994, The Profile Makers, 1997 (Pen/West Poetry prize, 1998), The Seconds, 2001, First Hand, 2005; editor: Pacific N.W. Poetry Series. Fellow Nat. Endowment Arts, Washington, 1988, 96, Guggenheim Found., N.Y.C., 1995, John D. & Catherine T. MacArthur Found., Chgo., 1998. Mem. Poetry Soc. of Am., Acad. Am. Poets. Avocation: hiking.

BIERER, JOEL DAVID, lawyer; b. Bklyn., Mar. 14, 1949; s. Louis and Ray (Shprintzen) B.; m. Karen Keopuhiwa, Mar. 22, 1992. BA, SUNY, Cortland, 1971, MS, 1975; JD, U. San Francisco, 1980. Bar: Calif. 1981, U.S. Dist. Ct. (no. and ea. dists.) Calif. 1981. In house counsel Carpenters Trust Fund, San Francisco, 1980-82; assoc. Law Offices of John Pitkin, Sausalito, Calif., 1982-83; pvt. practice Sausalito, 1983-86, Larkspur, Calif., 1988-91; assoc. Law Offices of Silberman & Becker, Sausalito, 1986-88; pvt. practice law, 1988-91; v.p., atty. Law Offices of Katz & Bierer, Inc., Larkspur, 1991-95, Law Offices of Katz, Bierer & Brady, Larkspur, 1995-97; atty. Law Offices of Joel D. Bierer, Mill Valley, Calif., 1997—. Mem. ATLA, Consumer Attys. Calif., Marin County Bar Assn. Avocations: tennis, running, swimming, bicycling. Office: 103 E Blithedale Ave Mill Valley CA 94941-2062 E-mail: biererlaw@aol.com.

BIERI, BARAC S., electronics executive; b. Teufen, Appenzell Ausserroden, Switzerland, Nov. 11, 1970; m. Afshan Madarwala, Oct. 22, 1971; children: Silyas D., Ninyan B. Distbn. asst. Tyco Electronics (former AMP), Steinach, Switzerland, 1995—98, product mgr., 1998—2002, European product mgr., 2002—03; gen. mgr. Bircher Am. Inc., Elk Grove Village, Ill., 2003—. Capt. Pioneer, 1991—2003, Switzerland. Home: 1304 E Algonquin Rd Schaumburg IL 60173 Office Phone: 847-952-3730.

BIERIG, JACK R., lawyer, educator; b. Chgo., Apr. 10, 1947; s. Henry J. and Helga (Rothschild) B.; m. Barbara A. Winokur; children: Robert, Sarah. BA, Brandeis U., 1968; JD, Harvard U., 1972. Bar: Ill. 1972, U.S. Dist. Ct. (no. dist.) Ill. 1972, U.S. Ct. Appeals (1st-3d, 5th-11th and D.C. cirs.) 1974, U.S. Supreme Ct. 1980. Ptnr. Sidley Austin Brown & Wood, Chgo., 1972—; prof. Ill. Inst. Tech.-Chgo. Kent Coll. Law, 1974-95; lectr. law. U. Chgo. Law Sch. and Harris Sch. Pub. Policy, 2000—. Chmn. legal sect. Am. Soc. Assn. Execs., 1994-95. Contbr. articles to profl. jours. Pres. Neighborhood Justice Chgo., 1983-87; pres. Jewish Vocat. Svc., 1997-99. Mem. Ill. Assn. of Hosp. Attys. (pres. 1991), Chgo. Bar Assn. (bd. govs., 1982-84). Clubs: Standard (Chgo.). Jewish. Business E-Mail: jbierig@sidley.com.

BIERLEY, JOHN CHARLES, lawyer; b. Portsmouth, Ohio, Oct. 12, 1936; s. C. Harold and Mildred R. (Turner) B.; m. Ruth Lykes Webb, Sept. 26, 1964; 1 son, John Charles. BA, U. Fla., 1958, JD (Fla. Law Center Assn. scholar, Bigelow Meml. scholar Am. Legion), 1963. Bar: Fla. 1964, U.S. Dist. Ct. (mid. dist.) Fla., U.S. Ct. Appeals (11th cir.), U.S. Supreme Ct.; bd. cert. in internat. law. Practiced in, Tampa, 1964—; assoc. Fowler, White, Gillen, Humpkey & Trenam, Tampa, 1964-66; ptnr. Macfarlane, Ferguson, Allison & Kelly, Tampa, 1966-92, Macfarlane Ferguson & McMullen, Tampa, 1992-97, Smith Clark Delesie Bierley Mueller & Kadyk, Tampa, 1997—. Chmn. internat. law cert. com., Fla. Bar, 2002; pres. Internat. Cultural and Econ. Ctr., Inc., 1975-78; lectr. internat. studies U. South Fla., Tampa, 1964-72; adj. prof. Stetson Coll. Law, 1984; bd. dirs. Cayman Nat. Bank, Ltd., Bay Cities Bank, Caymanx Trust Co., Ltd.; chmn. Fla. Coun. Internat. Devel., 1974-75, 95-97, Fla. Gov.'s Conf. on World Trade, 1980, 85; pres. Tampa World Trade Coun., 1971-73; chmn. hurricane disaster com. ARC, 1968-71; dir. Tampa Bay Area Com. Fgn. Rels., 1971-91, chmn., 1991—; mem. Asian R & D Coun., State of Fla., 1986; trustee U. Fla. Law Ctr. Assn., 1981—; chmn. Southeast U.S./Japan Assn., 1991-93. Mem. external internat. adv. bd. U. Fla., 1992—; bd. dirs. Tampa Bay Rsch. Inst.; trustee U. Fla. Found., 1997—. Served to capt., USMCR, 1958-61. Recipient Fla. Blue Key award Fla. Hall of Fame, 1958; named Tampa Bay Internat. Bus. Person of Yr., 1990. Mem. ABA, Fla. Bar Assn. (chmn. internat. law com. 1972-74, chair bd. cert. internat. law 2002-03), Inter-Am. Bar Assn. (bd. dirs., silver medal 1983), Am. Soc. Internat. Law, Internat. Fiscal Assn., Coun. Fgn. Rels., Soc. Internat. Bus. Fellows (bd. dirs. 1987—), Internat. Bar Assn., Ye Mystic Krewe of Gasparilla, Univ. Club, Merrymakers Club, Phi Delta Phi, Kappa Sigma. Democrat. Presbyterian. Office: Smith Clark Delesie Bierley Mueller & Kadyk PO Box 2939 100 N Tampa St Ste 2120 Tampa FL 33602-5809 Office Phone: 813-226-1875.

BIERLY, EUGENE WENDELL, meteorologist, science foundation director; b. Sept. 11, 1931; m., 1953; 3 children AB, U. Pa., 1953; cert., U.S. Naval Postgrad. Sch., 1954; MS, U. Mich., 1957, PhD, 1968. Asst. dept. civil engring. meteorol. labs. U. Mich., Ann Arbor, 1956-60, asst. research meteorologist dept. engring. mechanics, 1960-63, lectr., 1961-63; meteorologist U.S. AEC, 1963-66; dir. meteorology NSF, Washington, 1966-71, coordinator global atmospheric research program, 1971-74, head office climate dynamics, 1974-75, head climate dynamics research sect., 1975-79, dir. div. atmospheric scis., 1979-92; dir. edn. and rsch. Am. Geophys. Union, 1992-98, sr. scientist, 1998—. Mem. biol., health and environ. rsch. adv. com. Dept. Energy, 1992—; chmn. adv. cons. bd. Geophys. Inst., U. Alaska, 1993—; chmn. adv. bd. U. Okla. Sch. Meteorology, 1994—; cons. Fla. State U., U. Okla., U. Ariz., Univs. Space Rsch. Assn., Soundprint Media Ctr. Cons. editor: Meteorology & Climatology, Encyclopedia Sci. and Tech., 9th edit., Yearbook Scis. and Tech., 2000, 2002. Congl. fellow, 1970-71 Fellow AAAS, Am. Meteorol. Soc. (pres. 1984, Charles Franklin Brooks award 1990, Cleveland Abbe award 2000); mem. Chinese Meteorol. Soc., Am. Geophys. Union, Sigma Xi (presdl. rank merit excellence sr. exec. svc. 1982). Home: 5806 Conway Rd Bethesda MD 20817-3414 Office: AGU Directorate Outreach and Rsch Support 2000 Florida Ave NW Washington DC 20009-1277 Office Phone: 202-777-7506. Business E-Mail: ebierly@agu.org.

BIERMAN, ARNOLD, optometrist; b. N.Y.C., May 6, 1943; s. William Leonard and Dora Bierman; m. Carol F. Bierman, Dec. 26, 1965; 1 child, Julie Elise. BS, OD, Pa. Coll., 1968. Pvt. practice, Lansdale, Pa., 1968—. Clin. instr. Pa. Coll. Optometry, Phila., 1968—72, asst. prof., 1972—79; visual cons. Montgomery County Intermediate Unit, Norristown, Pa., 1976—87; mem. eyecare quality assurance com. U.S. Healthcare, Blue Bell, Pa., 1992—99. Editor: Jour. Pa. Optometrist, 1979—81. Chmn. Jaycees Amblyopia Clinic, Lansdale, Pa., 1969—70. Mem.: Am. Optometric Assn., Pa. Optometric Assn., Am. Acad. Optometry (pres. ea. Pa. chpt. 1980—82), Beta Sigma Kappa. Achievements include expertise in remediating reading and/or learning problems in children and adults. Avocations: art, music, bowling, photography. Office: 2302 N Broad St PO Box 1369 Lansdale PA 19446-0749 Office Phone: 215-822-1343.

BIERMAN, DUANE ALLEN, music educator; b. Grand Mound, Iowa, Feb. 24, 1978; BA in Music, Wartburg Coll, 2000; MusM, U. No. Colo., 2002. Dir. instrumental music Allen County C.C., Iola, Kans., 2002—. Percussionist Iola Area Symphony Orch., 2002—04; guest conductor, percussionist Iola Mcpl. Band, 2004—. Contbr. articles to profl. jours.; composer: (brass quintet) Village of the Gypsies, 2002, (percussion) Suite for Timpani, 2003. Mem.: Internat. Assn. Jazz Educators, Nat. Assn. Music Educators, MENC, Kans. Band Masters Assn. Avocation: fishing. Office Phone: 620-365-5116 240.

BIERMAN, GEORGE WILLIAM, retired food scientist; b. Cleve., Mar. 2, 1925; s. George Henry and Esther Josephine (Johnson) B.; m. Nyo Jeanne Iserloth; children: Cynthia, Barbara, Marsha, Jill, Wendy, Mindy, G. Steven, Chris. BS, Rutgers U., 1951; PhD, MIT, 1956. Technician R & D Am. Can Co., Maywood, Ill., 1943-45, Schering Corp., Bloomfield, N.J., 1947-48; tech. dir. Friend Bros., Inc., Malden, Mass., 1951-58; v.p. Herbert V. Shuster, Inc., Boston, 1958-75, pres., Quincy, Mass., 1975-89, vice chmn. bd., 1989-95, sr. scientist, 1995-96; tech. cons. Shuster Labs. Inc., 1996—98; ret., 1998. Sgt. U.S. Army, 1945-47. Mem.: Nat. Fisheries Inst. (smoked fish com. 1968—98), Inst. Food Technologists, Assn. Smoked Fish Processors (tech. dir. 1968—98). Presbyterian. Avocations: gardening, motorcycling. Home: 19 Curwen Rd Peabody MA 01960-1205

BIERMAN, JAMES L., contract research organization executive; BA, Dickinson Coll., 1974; MBA, Cornell U., 1976. Ptnr. Arthur Andersen LLP, 1976—98; sr. v.p. corp. devel. Quintiles Transnational, Research Triangle Park, NC, 1998—2000, exec. v.p., CFO, 2000—. Spkr. in field. Contbr. articles to profl. jours. Mem.: N.C. Assn. CPAs. Office: Quintiles Transnational Riverbirch Bldg PO Box 13979 4709 Creekstone Dr Ste 200 Research Triangle Park NC 27709

BIERMAN, JAMES NORMAN, lawyer; b. St. Louis, Nov. 23, 1945; s. Norman and Margaret (Loeb) B.; m. Catherine Best, Apr. 10, 1983; 1 child, James Norman. AB magna cum laude, Washington U., 1967; JD, Harvard Law Sch., 1970. Bar: D.C. 1970, U.S. Supreme Ct. 1973. Assoc. Hogan & Hartson, Washington, 1970-72; asst. dean Harvard Law Sch., Cambridge, Mass., 1973-75; assoc. Foley & Lardner LLP, Washington, 1975-79, ptnr., 1979—, ptnr. in charge, 1985-2001, mgmt. com., 1989—98. Mem. nat. coun. Washington U. Coll. Arts and Scis., 1999—. Mng. editor Harvard Jour. Legis., 1969-70. Mem. Civil Rights Reviewing Authority HEW, Washington, 1979-80. Mem. ABA, Fed. Bar Assn., Supreme Ct. Bar, Washington Lawyers Com. for Civil Rights and Urban Affairs (co-chmn.), Phi Beta Kappa, Omicron Delta Kappa, Pi Sigma Alpha, Phi Eta Sigma, City Club (Washington). Home: 906 Peacock Station Rd Mc Lean VA 22102-1021 Office: Foley & Lardner LLP 3000 K St NW Fl 5 Washington DC 20007-5143 Office Phone: 202-672-5358. Business E-Mail: jbierman@foley.com.

BIERMAN, SANDRA, artist; b. Bklyn., N.Y., 1938; d. John Charles Riesberg and Martha Lee Blair; m. Arthur Bierman, Oct. 1, 1983; children: Cheryl, Steven, James. Represented by Contemporary S.W. Gallery, Santa Fe, 1994—, David Haslam, Boulder, Colo., 1992—, Gallery East, Loveland, Colo., 1996—, Augustine Arts, Lake Tahoe, Nev., 1997—, Bakersfield (Calif.) Mus., 2001; instr. workshop Am. Acad. Women Artists, Wickenburg, Ariz., 1997, Oil Painting with Sandra Bierman, Kauai, Hawaii, 2000. One-person shows include Contemporary S.W. Galleries, 1996, Lincoln Ctr. for the Arts, Ft. Collins, Colo., 1998, Bakersfield (Calif.) Mus. Art, 2001; group shows include C.S. Lewis Summer Inst. Show on Tour, 1994, Queens Coll. Art Gallery, Cambridge, Eng., 1994, 99th Nat. Exhbn. Nat. Arts Club, N.Y.C., 1995, 67th Grand Nat. Show, Salmagundi Club, N.Y.C., 1995, Artistes Americaines, Maison du Terroir, Genouilly, France, 1996, Colo. History Mus., 1996, Clymer Mus., Ellensburg, Wash., 1996, Desert Caballeros Mus., Wickenburg, Ariz., 1997, Colo. Gov.'s Invitational Show, Loveland (Colo.) Mus., 1997-2002, Art Expo, N.Y.C., 1998-99; works in permanent collections at City of Loveland, CSI Ltd., Cambridge, Eng., El Pomar Found., Colorado Springs, Colo., Gilford, Inc., N.Y.C., Herzog & Adams, N.Y.C., Harlow Club Hotel, Palm Springs, Calif., Loveland Mus., Telluride Gallery of Fine Art, Colo., Kaiser Permanente, Denver, Kohn Family Trust, Balt., Mfrs.-Hanover trust, N.Y.C., Mayo Women's Clinic, Scottsdale, Penrose Conf., Ctr., Colorado Springs, Philip Chamberlan Inc., Madison, Conn.; featured in Southwest Art Mag., Art Trends Mag., Mountain Living mag., Woman's Mag., Radiance mag., Sun Storm Fine Art Mag., US Art, Art World News, Art Bus. News, others. Recipient Colo. Gov.'s Purchase award, Loveland, 1988, Best of Show award Western Images, Boulder, 1993, medal of honor award Am. Artists Profl. League, N.Y.C., 1995. Mem. Am. Artists Profl. League, Bus. Coun. for the Arts N.Y.C., Nat. Mus. of Women in the Arts, Oil Painters Am., Am. Acad. Women Artists (nominating juror, exec. bd. dirs. 1997—). Office Phone: 303-447-8871. E-mail: art@sandrabierman.com.

BIERON, LOUISE T., physician, director; b. Rochester, N.Y., Sept. 26, 1935; d. Samuel and Michelina Granata; m. Joseph Francis Bieron, July 4, 1959 (div. Mar. 1987); children: Paul, Belinda, Diane, Ramona, Elaine. BA in Philosophy and English, Canisius Coll., 1984, MS in Edn., 1988. Chair United Way Canisius Coll., Buffalo, N.Y., 1977-83, student recruiter, 1979-84, acad. advisor, 1984-88; phys. cons. Phys. Internat., Buffalo, N.Y., 1988-96; collection cons. NCO Fin. Sys., Getzville, N.Y., 1998—. Mem. Amherst (N.Y.) Taxpayers Assn., 2000; v.p. Condominium Assn., 1992—. Republican. Roman Catholic. Avocations: swimming, reading.

BIERS, MARTIN HENRY, physician; b. Bklyn., Oct. 10, 1931; s. Louis and Sarah (Naidich) Bierfass; m. Elizabeth Jaros Biers, Feb. 11, 1962; children: Eric, Carl, John. BA, NYU, 1951; MD, SUNY, Bklyn., 1955. Cert. in internal medicine and hematology. Intern Kings County Hosp., Bklyn., 1955—56; med. resident Bklyn. Vets. Hosp., 1956—57, Montefiore Hosp., Bronx, NY, 1957—58; hematology resident Mt. Sinai Hosp., N.Y.C., 1958—59; pvt. practice White Plains, NY, 1961—. Attending medicine and chief emeritus hematology dept. White Plains Hosp. Capt. USAF, 1959-61. Mem. Am., N.Y. Med. Soc., Westchester Med. Soc. Office: 170 Maple Ave White Plains NY 10601-5115 Office Phone: 914-946-3553. Personal E-mail: mhbiers@aol.com.

BIERSTEDT, PETER RICHARD, entertainment industry consultant, lawyer; b. Rhinebeck, NY, Jan. 2, 1943; s. Robert Henry and Betty Bierstedt; m. Carol Lynn Akiyama, Aug. 23, 1980 (div. Oct. 1995); m. Lieschen van Straaten, Aug. 11, 2000. AB, Columbia U., 1965, JD cum laude, 1969; cert., U. Sorbonne, Paris, 1966. Bar: N.Y. 1969, Calif. 1977, U.S. Supreme Ct. 1973. Atty. with firms in, N.Y.C., 1969-74; pvt. practice cons. legal and entertainment industry, 1971, 75-76, 88—; with Avco Embassy Pictures Corp., L.A., 1977-83, v.p., gen. counsel, 1978-80, sr. v.p., 1980-83, dir., 1981-83; gen. counsel New World Entertainment (formerly New World Pictures), L.A., 1984-87, exec. v.p., 1985-87, sr. exec. v.p. Office of Chmn., 1987-88, also bd. dirs.; pres. subs. New World Prodns. and New World Advt. New World Pictures, 1985-88. Guest lectr. U. Calif., Riverside, 1976-77, U. So. Calif., 1986, 91, UCLA, 1987, 95-96; bd. dirs. New World Pictures (Australia) Ltd., FilmDallas Pictures, Inc., Cinedco, Inc. Exec. prodr. (home video series) The Comic Book Greats. Mem. Motion Picture Assn. Am. (dir. 1980-83), Acad. Motion Picture Arts and Scis. (exec. br.), LA Copyright Soc., ACLU. Democrat. Avocations: astronomy, literature, tennis, scuba diving. Office Phone: 323-465-4633. E-mail: peter@bierstedt.com.

BIERY, EVELYN HUDSON, lawyer; b. Lawton, Okla., Oct. 12, 1946; d. William Ray and Nellie Iris (Nunley) Hudson. BA in English and Latin summa cum laude, Abilene (Tex.) Christian U., 1968; JD, So. Meth. U., 1973. Bar: Tex. 1973, U.S. Dist. Ct. (we. dist.) Tex. 1975, U.S. Dist. Ct. (so. dist.) Tex. 1977, U.S. Dist. Ct. (no. dist.) Tex. 1979, U.S. Ct. Appeals (5th cir.) 1979, U.S. Ct. Appeals (11th cir.) 1981, U.S. Supreme Ct. 1981. Atty. Law Offices of Bruce Waitz, San Antonio, 1973-76; mem. LeLaurin & Adams, PC,

San Antonio, 1976-81; ptnr. Fulbright & Jaworski, San Antonio, 1982—2003, head bankruptcy, reorgn. and creditors' rights sect. Houston, 2004—. Policy com. Fulbright & Jaworski, 1996-98; spkr. on creditors' rights, bankruptcy and reorganization law; lectr. Southwestern Grad. Sch. Banking, Dallas, 1980, La. State U. Sch. Banking, 1994; presiding officer, U. Tex. Sch. of Law Bankruptcy Conf., 1976, 94, State Bar Tex. Creditors' Rights Inst., 1985, 88, State Bar Tex. Advanced Bus. Bankruptcy Law Inst., 1985, State Bar Tex. Inst. on Advising Officers, Dirs. and Ptnrs. in Troubled Bus., 1987; mem. bankruptcy adv. com. 5th cir. jud. coun., 1979-80; vice-chmn. bankruptcy com. Comml. Law League Am., 1981-83; mem. exec. bd. So. Meth. U. Sch. Law, 1983-91. Editor: Texas Collections Manual, 1978, Creditor's Rights in Texas, 2d edit., 1981; author: (with others) Collier Bankruptcy Practice Guide, 1993. Del. to U.S./Republic of China joint session on trade, investment and econ. law, Beijing, 1987; designated mem. Bankruptcy Judge Merit Screening Com. State of Tex. by Tex. State Bar Pres., 1979-82; patron McNay Mus., San Antonio; rsch. ptnr. Mind Sci. Found., San Antonio; diplomat World Affairs Coun., San Antonio. Fellow: Soc. Internat. Bus. Fellows (chair bd. dirs.), San Antonio Bar Found. (life), Tex. Bar Found. (life); mem.: San Antonio Young Lawyers Assn. (pres. 1979—80, Outstanding Young Lawyer award 1979), Tex. Assn. Bank Counsel (bd. dirs. 1988—90, 2001—04), Tex. Bar Assn. (chair bankruptcy com. 1982—83, chair corp., banking and bus. law sect. 1989—90), Am. Coll. Bankruptcy Attys. (chair bd. dirs.), Zonta (Chair Z club com. 1989—90), Plaza Club San Antonio (bd. dirs. 1982—), Order of Coif. Office: Fulbright & Jaworski LLP 1301 McKinney St Ste 5100 Houston TX 77010-3031 Office Phone: 713-651-5544. Office Fax: 713-651-5246. Business E-Mail: ebiery@fulbright.com.

BIES, SUSAN SCHMIDT, federal agency administrator; b. Buffalo, May 5, 1947; d. Louis Howard and Gladys May (Metke) Schmidt; m. John David Bies, Aug. 29, 1970; children: John Matthew, Scott Louis. BS, State U. Coll.-Buffalo, 1967; MA, Northwestern U., 1968, PhD, 1972. Banking structure economist FRS, St. Louis, 1970-72; asst. prof. econs. Wayne State U., Detroit, 1972-77; assoc. prof. Rhodes Coll., Memphis, 1977-80; tactical planning mgr. First Tenn. Nat. Corp., Memphis, 1980-81, dir. corp. devel., 1982-83, treas., 1983-84, sr. v.p., CFO, 1984-85, exec. v.p., CFO, 1985—95, exec. v.p. for risk mgmt., auditor, 1995—2001; mem. bd. govs. Fed. Reserve Sys., Washington, 2001—. Mem. fin. adv. com. City of Germantown, Tenn., 1978—, also budget com.; mem. investment adv. com. Tenn. Consol. Retirement System, Nashville, 1981-86; instr. MidSouth Sch. Banking, 1985-86; mem. Com. on Corp. Reporting, Fin. Exec. Inst.; mem. Bank Adminstrn. Inst. Pres., bd. dirs. North Germantown Homeowners Assn., 1978-83; treas. Germantown Area Soccer Assn., 1985-86; treas. Fury Soccer Club, 1988—; vice chmn. task force Com. on 21st Century, Rhodes Coll., Memphis, 1986-87; mem. exec. adv. bd. Sch. Accountancy Memphis State U.; bd. dirs. Memphis Youth Initiative, 1988, Memphis Ptnrs.; mem. BAI Acctg. and Fin. Commn., 1988—, Internat. Women's Forum Fellow Ctr. for Urban Affairs, 1968-69, Fed. Res. Bank Chgo., 1970. Mem. Am. Bankers Assn. (exec. com. 1986-88), Nat. Assn. Bus. Economists, Am. Econ. Assn., End Users of Derivatives Assn., Planning Execs. Inst., Fin. Execs. Inst., (bd. dirs. Memphis chpt. 1988—), Planning Forum (Managerial Excellence award Memphis chpt. 1986), Memphis Area C. of C. (bd. dirs. 1988—, tax com. 1988—, chair 1989—), Econ. Club Memphis (bd. dirs. 1986—, vice chmn. 1987-88, chmn. 1988-89), Omicron Delta Epsilon, Lambda Alpha. Episcopalian. Avocations: gardening, golf, soccer. Office: Fed Reserve System Bd of Gov 20th St & Constitution Ave NW Washington DC 20551

BIESEL, DAVID BARRIE, publishing executive; b. Chgo., Sept. 12, 1931; s. William James Trimble and Aileen Louise (Jacquith) B.; m. Donna Louise Scoggan, May 25, 1958 (div. 1975); children: Deborah Louise Biesel Brugger, William Warren; m. Diane Jane Stevens, Sept. 25, 1982. Student, U. Md., 1950-53. Supr. editl. dept. Fed. Electric Corp., Paramus, N.J., 1958-62; mgr. editl. dept. Am. Inst.Physics, N.Y.C., 1962-69; ref. book editor R. R. Bowker Co., N.Y.C., 1969-73; sr. editor Macmillan Pub. Co., N.Y.C., 1973-82, Elsevier Sci. Pubs., N.Y.C., 1983-84; v.p., editor-in-chief R. R. Bowker Co., N.Y.C., 1984-85; v.p., editorial dir. M. E. Sharpe, Armonk, N.Y., 1986-88; pres. St. Johann Press, Haworth, N.J., 1988—; dir. Assn. Publ. program Scarecrow Press, 1990-2000, editor Am. Sports History series. Contbr. articles to profl. jours.; author: Can You Name That Team, 1991 (named one of the best reference books 1991 Lib. Jour.). Warden All Saints Episcopal Ch., Bergenfield, NJ, 1985-89, 94-2000, vestryman, 1982-85, treas. 2000—; commn. on ministry Diocese of Newark, 2002—. With USMC, 1953-57. Mem. ALA, Soc. Am. Baseball Rsch., Profl. Football Rsch. Assn., N.Am. Soc. Sport History, Marine Meml. Assn., USMC Combat Correspondents Assn. (life), Soc. for Internat. Hockey Rsch., Marine Corps League. Home and Office: 315 Schraalenburgh Rd Haworth NJ 07641-1200 Personal E-mail: d.biesel@worldnet.att.net.

BIESELE, JOHN JULIUS, biologist, educator; b. Waco, Tex., Mar. 24, 1918; s. Rudolph Leopold and Anna Emma (Jahn) B.; m. Marguerite Calfee McAfee, July 29, 1943 (dec. 1991); children: Marguerite Anne, Diana Terry, Elizabeth Jane; m. Esther Aline Eakin, Mar. 9, 1992. BA with highest honors, U. Tex., 1939, PhD, 1942. Fellow Internat. Cancer Rsch. Found., U. Tex., 1942—43, Barnard Skin and Cancer Hosp., St. Louis, U. Pa., Phila., 1943—44, instr. zoology, 1943—44; temporary rsch. assoc. dept. genetics Carnegie Instn. of Washington, Cold Spring Harbor, 1944—46; rsch. assoc. biology dept. MIT, Cambridge, 1946—47; asst. Sloan-Kettering Inst. Cancer Rsch., 1946—47, rsch. fellow, 1947, assoc., 1947—55, head cell growth sect., divsn. exptl. chemotherapy, 1947—58, mem., 1955—58, assoc. scientist divsn., 1959—78; asst. prof. anatomy Cornell U. Med. Sch., 1950—52; assoc. prof. biology Sloan-Kettering divsn. Cornell U. Grad. Sch. Med. Scis., 1952—55, prof. biology, 1955—58; prof. zoology, mem. grad. faculty U. Tex., Austin, 1958—78, also mem. faculty Coll. Pharmacy, 1969—71, prof. edn. Coll. Pharmacy, 1973—78, prof. emeritus zoology Austin, 1978—99; prof. emeritus sect. molecular cell and developmental biol. U. Tex. Sch. Biol. Scis., Austin, 1999—. Cons. cell biology M.D. Anderson Hosp. and Tumor Inst., U. Tex., Houston, 1958-72; dir. Genetics Found., 1959-78; mem. cell biology study sect. NIH, 1958-63; Sigma Xi lectr. NYU Grad. Sch. Arts and Scis., 1957; Mendel lectr. St. Peter's Coll., Jersey City, 1958; featured spkr. on first Earth Day, Old Westbury Campus of N.Y. Inst. Tech., 1970; Mendel Club lectr. Canisius Coll., Buffalo, 1971; adv. com. rsch. etiology of cancer Am. Cancer Soc., 1961-64, pres. Travis County unit, 1966, adv. com. on pers. for rsch., 1969-73; counsellor Cancer Internat. Rsch. Coop., Inc., 1962-90; cancer rsch. tng. com. Nat. Cancer Inst., 1969-72; gen. chmn. Conf. Advancement Sci. and Math. Tchg., 1966. Author: Mitotic Poisons and the Cancer Problem, 1958; mem. editorial bd. Year Book Cancer, 1959-72; mem. editorial adv. bd. Cancer Rsch., 1960-64, assoc. editor, 1969-72; cons. editor: Am. Jour. Mental Deficiency, 1963-68; mem. editorial bd. The Jour. of Applied Nutrition, 1987-91; contbr. articles to profl. jours. Rsch. Career award NIH, 1962, 67, 72, 77 Fellow AAAS, N.Y. Acad. Scis., Tex. Acad. Scis.; mem. Am. Assn. Cancer Rsch. (dir. 1960-63), Am. Soc. Cell Biology, Am. Inst. Biol. Scis., Phi Beta Kappa, Sigma Xi (pres. Tex. chpt. 1963-64), Phi Eta Sigma, Phi Kappa Phi. Achievements include rsch. in provision of early evidence for abnormal chromosome numbers in cancer cells, for occasional excessively multiple-stranded state of cancer chromosomes; demonstration of a direct relation of chromosomal size in mammalian tissues and organs to the local metabolic activity, as evidenced by the local content of B vitamins, of differential toxicity in certain antimetabolites to cancer cells in culture. Home: 2500 Great Oaks Pky Austin TX 78756-2908

BIFULCO, FRANK, toy company executive; b. 1950; Degree, United States Military Academy; MS engring. sciences, Cornell U.; MA bus. mgmt., Central Michigan U. Sr. v.p., sales Procter & Gamble, chief mktg. officer, ICG Commerce; sr. v.p., mktg. Coca-Cola North Am.; sr. v.p., chief mktg. officer Timberland Co., 2001—03; pres., US Games Hasbro Inc., 2003—. Office: Hasbro Inc 1027 Newport Ave Pawtucket RI 02861-2500

BIGAL, MARCELO E, physician, researcher; b. Sao Paulo, Brazil, Oct. 13, 1969; s. Antonio C and Jamile I Bigal; m. Janaina M. Bigal, Nov. 18, 1995; children: Luisa, Hanna. MD, Sch. of Medicine at Ribeirao Preto, U. of Sao Paulo, 1989—94, MSc in Neurol. Scis., 2000, PhD in Neurol. Scis., 2001. Resident in neurology Sch. Medicine at Ribeirao Preto, U. Sao Paulo, 1995—99; neurology specialist Brazilian Bur. of Justice, 1999—2001, Brazilian Nat. Inst. Social Security, 1999—2001; prof. of neuro-psychology Barao de Maua U., 2000—01; chief of svc., dept. of neurology Santa Casa Hosp., 2000—01; dir. rsch. The New Eng. Ctr. for Headache, Stamford, 2001—; asst. prof. of neurology Albert Einstein Coll. of Medicine, Bronx, 2002—. Co-investigator AstraZeneca (sponsor for rsch.), Glaxo SmithKline (sponsor for rsch.); rschr. Einstein Aging Study, Bronx; primary investigator UCB Pharma (sponsor for rsch.), 2002—; co-investigator Allergan (sponsor for rsch.), 2002—. Reviewer Cephalalgia, Headache, Clin. Therapeutics, Future Drugs, CNS Drugs, Arch Neuropsiquiatr, 2002, (jour.) Neurology, assoc. editor (website) Vertibrae, Headache Currents, 2004; contbr. chapters to books, articles to profl. jours. Recipient Internat. Headache Soc. Ednl. award, 2001, Glaxosmithkline Ednl. award, 2001, Am. Headache Soc., Ortho-McNeil, 2002, Kapplan Award, Am. Headache Soc., 2004, Presentation Award, 2004; Internat. Headache Soc. fellowship, 2001. Fellow: Internat. Headache Soc.; mem.: Brazilian Headache Soc., Internat. Headache Soc. (assoc.), Am. Headache Soc. (Preventive Rsch. award 2004). Office: The Albert Einstein Coll of Medicine Rousso Building 1165 Morris Park Ave Bronx NY 10461 Office Phone: 718-430-3844. Personal E-mail: marcbigal@aol.com. E-mail: mbigal@aecom.yu.edu.

BIGAR, NICOLE MICHELINE, painter, sculptor; b. Paris, Nov. 24, 1926; came to U.S., 1940; d. Alfred and Madeleine (Weill) Weil; m. Raymond Bigar, Apr. 28, 1946; children: Philippe, Dominique. Student, Barnard Coll., 1945-49, Art Student's League, Mus. Modern Art. With Art Student's League, N.Y.C., Pub. Sch. 92, N.Y.C. One-woman shows at Phyllis Radcliff Gallery, N.Y.C., 1972, Randall Gallery, N.Y.C., 1977, Benson Gallery, Bridgehampton, N.Y., 1980, 81, 85, 86, 96, Benton Gallery, Southampton, N.Y., 1987, 88, 89, 90, 92, Athena Fine Arts Gallery, N.Y.C., 1993, 94, Pharos Gallery, N.Y.C., 1995, Harry Stendhal Gallery, 1999, Nabi Gallery, Sag Harbor, N.Y., 1999, M.O.C.A. Mus. of Contemporary Art, Washington, 1999; exhibited in group show at Benton Gallery, 1994, 95, 96, 98, 99, Music Festival of the Hamptons, 1997; represented in permanent collections at Guild Hall Mus., East Hampton, N.Y., Hecksher Mus., Huntington, N.Y., Lees Jr. Coll., Jackson, Ky., Scandinavian-Am. Found., N.Y.C., Vogue Publ., London, N.Y. Pub. Libr. (collection), Nat. Mus. of Women in the Arts (archives) V.p. Victor D'Amico Inst. Art, 1980—. Recipient Best Abstract Painting award Guild Hall. Avocations: writing, travel, working with children. Home: 1107 5th Ave New York NY 10128-0145

BIG BOI, See PATTON, ANTWAN

BIGBY, JUDYANN, medical educator; b. Jamaica, N.Y., 1951; children: Kenan, Naima. BA, Wellesley Coll., 1973; MD, Harvard U., 1978. Henry J. Kaiser fellow in gen. internal medicine Harvard Med. Sch. and Brigham and Women's Hosp., Boston; primary care internal medicine resident U. Wash. Affiliated Hosps., Seattle; assoc. prof. medicine Harvard Med. Sch., Boston, dir. Ctr. of Excellence in Women's Health, mem. faculty, 1983—; med. dir. Cmty. Health Programs Brigham and Women's Hosp., Boston, attending physician, 1983—. Mem. com. Assuring the Health of the Pub. in 21st Century, Inst. Medicine; mem. minority women's health panel of experts Office on Women's Health, Dept. HHS. Mem. bd. dirs. Boston Pub. Health Commn. Recipient Edna W. Smith Pioneer in Cmty. Health Care award, 2000. Office: Brigham and Womens Hosp Women Family and Cmty Programs 1620 Tremont St Boston MA 02120

BIGELEISEN, JACOB, chemist, educator; b. Paterson, N.J., May 2, 1919; s. Harry and Ida (Slomowitz) Bigeleisen; m. Grace Alice Simon, Oct. 21, 1945; children: David M., Ira S., Paul E. AB, NYU, 1939; MS, Wash. State U., 1941; PhD, U. Calif., Berkeley, 1943. Rsch. scientist Manhattan Dist., Columbia, 1943-45; rsch. assoc. Ohio State U., Columbus, 1945-46; fellow Enrico Fermi Inst., U. Chgo., 1946-48; sr. chemist Brookhaven Nat. Lab., Upton, N.Y., 1948-68; prof. chemistry U. Rochester, N.Y., 1968-78, chmn. dept., 1970-75; Tracy H. Harris prof. U. Rochester (Coll. Arts and Scis.), 1973-78; v.p. research, dean grad. studies SUNY, Stony Brook, 1978-80, Leading prof. chemistry, 1978-89, Disting. prof., 1989, Disting. prof. emeritus, 1989—. Vis. prof. Cornell U., 1953; NSF sr. fellow, vis. prof. Eidgen Techn. Hochschule, Switzerland, 1962—63; chmn. Assembly Math. and Phys. Scis. NRC-Nat. Acad. Scis., 1976—80. Mem. editl. bd.: Jour. Phys. Chemistry, Jour. Chem. Physics. Trustee Sayville Jewish Center, 1954—68. Recipient Gilbert N. Lewis lectr., 1963, E. O. Lawrence award, 1964, Disting. Alumnus award, Wash. State U., 1983, Meliora award, Univ. Rochester, 1978; fellow John Simon Guggenheim, 1974—75. Fellow: AAAS, Am. Acad. Arts and Sci., Am. Chem. Soc., Am. Phys. Soc. (Nuc. award 1958); mem.: Nat. Acad. Scis. (councilor 1982—85), Phi Lambda Upsilon, Sigma Xi, Phi Beta Kappa. Achievements include research in in photochemistry in rigid media, semiquinones, cryogenics, chemistry of isotopes, isotope separation, quantum statistics of gases, liquids and solids. Home: 900 N Taylor St 1817 Arlington VA 22203-1859 Office: 900 N Taylor St Apt 1809 Arlington VA 22203 Office Phone: 703-528-7828. Business E-Mail: jbigeleisen@notes.cc.sunysb.edu. *As a youth I became interested in a career in science because it offered the opportunity to test ideas and hypotheses objectively by experiment. This unique aspect of science, which differentiates it from all other branches of learning and knowledge, has been a guiding principle both in my professional and my personal life. My career has included research, teaching, administration and public service.*

BIGELOW, DANIEL JAMES, aerospace executive; b. Harrisville, Pa., Mar. 26, 1935; s. Raymond James and Hilda Irene (Graham) Bigelow; m. Elizabeth Jane Allison, Sept. 10, 1955; 1 child, Allison Jane. BFA in Art Advt., Kent (Ohio) State U., 1957; MA in Edn., La. Tech. U., 1974; MS in Polit. Sci., Auburn U., 1986; MS, Air U., 1987; postgrad., Ohio State U., 1989—. Commd. 2d lt. USAF, 1957, advanced through grades to col., 1979, ret., 1987; command pilot 167 combat missions Vietnam; air attaché to Soviet Union, 1983—85; dir. Soviet program Air War Coll. Air U., Ala., 1985—87; gen. mgr. aerospace divsn. Modern Techs. Corp., Dayton, Ohio, 1988—98, dir. programs corp. hdqrs., 1998—2001, dir. bus. svcs. corp. hdqrs., 2002—03; dir. investor rels. and corp. comm. MTC Tech., Inc., Dayton, 2003—. Designer artwork, writer text MTC Annual Reports, 2002—04; designer MTC Website, 2003—04. Author, editor: Soviet Studies, 1968—88; contbr. articles to profl. jours. Decorated Legion of Merit with one oak leaf cluster, DFC, 14 Air medals, Def. Superior medal; named Disting. alumni, East Liverpool (Ohio) HS Alumni Assn., 2004; recipient U.S. Am. Nat. award, CIA Dir. William J. Casey, 1985. Mem.: Am. Electronics Assn., Nat. Mus. US Army (founding sponsor), Wright "B" Flyer Assn., Strategic Air Command Assn., 3rd Mil. Airlift Squadron Assn., Kent State U. Alumni Assn., Nat. Investor Rels. Inst., Nat. Mil. Intelligence Assn., Nat. Def. Indsl. Assn., Electronic Engring. and Mfg. Group, Internat. Test and Evaluation Assn., Inst. Navigation, Miami Valley Mil. Affairs Assn., Def. Planning and Analysis Soc., Dayton Area Def. Contractors Assn. (pres. 1999—2000, bd. dirs.), Internat. Platform Assn., Am. Def. Preparedness Assn., Acad. Polit. Sci., Assn. U.S. Army, Nat. Aviation Hall of Fame, DFC Soc., Air Force Assn. Cmty. Ptnrs., Assn. Former Intelligence Officers, Air Force Mus. Found., Pararescue Assn., Air Rescue Assn. (chmn. reunion and symposium 2003, nat. bd. dirs., historian), Air Force Assn. (v.p. state legis. affairs 2001—02), F-86 Sabre Pilots' Assn., B-52 Stratofortress Assn., Ret. Officers' Assn., Airlift/Tanker Assn., Armed Forces Comm. and Electronics Assn., Pedro Helicopter Assn., Mil. Officer Assn. Am., Dayton Art Inst., Dayton Area C. of C. (vice-chmn. mil. and fed. affairs com. 2003—04, chmn. 2004—), Mil. Officers Assn. Am., Royal Air Force Club, Discussion Club Dayton (v.p. 1999—2000), Shriners, Assn. Old Crows, Order Daedalians (flight capt., pres. 2001—02), Order Quiet Birdmen, Anciente Order Quiet Birdmen, Scottish Rite, Masons, Blue Key. Presbyterian. Avocations: art, photography, jogging. Home: 2537 Indian Wells Trl Xenia OH 45385-9373 Office Phone: 937-252-9199. Business E-Mail: daniel.bigelow@mtctechnologies.com.

BIGELOW, DONALD NEVIUS, educational administrator, historian, consultant; b. Danbury, Conn., Aug. 19, 1918; s. Harry R. and Bessie M. (Nevius) B.; m. Louise M. Fournel, Sept. 21, 1957; 1 son, Pierre Nevius. BA cum laude, Amherst Coll., 1939, MA, 1945; PhD, Columbia U., 1950. Spl. agt. Inland Marine Ins., North Brit. and Merc. Ins. Co., N.Y.C. and Detroit, 1939-43; with U.S. Engr. Dept., Fairbanks, Alaska, 1942; instr. history Amherst Coll., 1943-45; instr. Columbia U., 1947-50, asst. prof., 1951-55; assoc. prof. Brandeis U., 1955-60; chief lang. and area ctrs. program Office Edn., HEW, Washington, 1961-64; head task force NDEA Title XI Inst. Program, 1964-65, dir. divsn. ednl. pers. tng., 1965-67, dir. divsn. program adminstrn., 1967-68, dir. divsn. coll. programs Bur. Ednl. Pers. Devel., 1968-71; dir. Northeast divsn. Nat. Ctr. for Improvement Ednl. Sys., 1972-74; spl. asst., assoc. commr. for Instl. Devel. and Internat. Edn., 1974-76; chief grad. tng. Office of Postsecondary Edn., Dept. Edn., Washington, 1976-82; sr. adminstr. The Nat. Faculty, Atlanta, 1985-88; spl. asst. to dep. asst. sec. Office of Postsecondary Edn., U.S. Dept. Edn., Washington, 1988-93, sr. exec. Ctr. Internat. Edn., 1993, program mgr. Dwight D. Eisenhower Leadership Devel. Act of 1992, 1993-96. Exec. dir. Javits Fellowship Bd., 1996-2000, spl. asst. Office Internat. Edn. & Grad. Edn. Office Higher Edn., 1998—, sr. advisor, 2002; vis. Fulbright prof. Am. civilization U.S. Ednl. Fund, India, U. Baroda, U. Lucknow, 1954-55; prof. humanities N.Y. Sch. Music, 1949-56; vis. prof. U. So. Fla., 1969; postdoctoral rsch. fellow George Washington U., 1970-71; lectr. U. Va., 1973; adj. prof. Am. U., 1975; cons. Ford Found., 1957, Carnegie Corp., 1958, U.S. Office Edn., 1959-60; moderator ABC TV series Seminar, 1953-54, PBS WGBH TV series on ethnicity, 1956-57; assoc. dir. com. lang. and area ctrs. Am. Coun. Edn., 1960-61; book reviewer Nat. Pub. Radio series Options in Education, 1976-77. Author: William Conant Church and the Army and Navy Journal, 1952, (with Joseph Axelrod) Resources for Language and Area Studies, 1960, (with Lyman Legters) Language and Area Centers, 1964, (with others) Non-Western Studies in the Liberal Arts College, 1964; editor: (with Hiram Haydn) Makers of the American Tradition Series, 4 vols., 1953-55, The Annals (The Non-Western World in Higher Education), 1964, The Liberal Arts and Teacher Education: A Confrontation, 1971, Schoolworlds '76, New Directions for Educational Policy, 1976, Democracy at Risk: "Leadership and Education", an Unpublished Report on the Eisenhower Leadership Program, 1992-96, 1999. Home: 2901 Q St NW Washington DC 20007-3089

BIGELOW, DOUGLAS C., otolaryngologist; MD, U. Minn., 1985. Cert. Otolaryngology Am. Bd. of Otolaryngology, 1990. Assoc. prof. U. Pa., Phila., 1991—. Dir. of otology, neurotology U. of Pa., Phil., dir. of cranial base surgery, 1991—. Named one of Best Doctors, Phila. Mag., 1994, 1996, 1998, 1999, 2002; recipient Honor Award, Am. Acad. of Otolaryngology, 2001. Office: Univ of Pa 3400 Spruce St Philadelphia PA 19063 Office Phone: 215-662-6970.

BIGELOW, GEORGE E., psychology and pharmacology scientist; b. Washington, Aug. 31, 1943; BS in Psychology, with honors, U. Md., College Park, 1965; PhD in Psychology, U. Minn., 1969. Dir. behavioral pharmacology unit Johns Hopkins U., Balt.; asst. prof., Dept. Psychiatry & Behavior Sci. Johns Hopkins U. Med. Sch., Balt., 1971—76, assoc. prof., 1976—89, prof., 1990—. Mem., Drug Abuse Adv. Com. FDA, 1987—93, cons., 1993—2002. Recipient Nyswander/Dole (Marie) award, Am. Methadone Treatment Assn., 1997. Fellow: Soc. Behavioral Medicine, Am. Psychology Soc., Coll. of Problems of Drug Dependence (pres. 1993—94, bd. dir. 1989—98, treas. 1995—98), APA (pres., div. psychopharmacology 1987—88, div. psycholpharmacology & substance abuse, div. experimental analysis behavior, div. health psychology); mem.: Am. Pub. Health Assn., Rsch. Soc. Alcoholism, Assn. for Advancement Behavior Therapy, Behavioral Pharmacology Soc. Office: Johns Hopkins U Behavioral Pharma Unit 5510 Nathan Shock Dr Baltimore MD 21224-6823

BIGELOW, MARGARET ELIZABETH BARR (M.E. BARR), retired botany educator; b. Elkhorn, Man., Can., Apr. 16, 1923; d. David Hunter and Mary Irene (Parr) Barr; m. Howard Elson Bigelow, June 9, 1956 (dec.). BA with honors, U. B.C., Vancouver, Can., 1950, MA, 1952; PhD, U. Mich., 1956. Rsch. attaché U. Montreal, Que., Can., 1956-57; instr. U. Mass., Amherst, 1957-65, asst. prof., 1965-71, assoc. prof., 1971-76, prof., 1976-89, prof. emeritus, 1989—. Author: Diaporthales in N.A., 1978, Prodromus to Loculoascomycetes, 1987, Prodromus to Nonlichenized Members of Class Hymenoascomycetes, 1990; contbr. articles to profl. jours. With Can. Women's Army Corps, 1942—46. Mem. Mycol. Soc. Am. (v.p. to pres. 1980-82, editor 1975-80, Disting. Mycologist Award, 1993), Brit. Mycol. Soc., Am. Inst. Biol. Sci. (gen. chmn. ann. meeting 1986). Avocations: gardening, reading. Home and Office: 9475 Inverness Rd Sidney BC Canada V8L 5G8

BIGELOW, MARTHA MITCHELL, retired historian; b. Talladega Springs, Ala., Sept. 19, 1921; children: Martha Frances, Carolyn Letitia. BA, Montevallo U., 1943; MA, U. Chgo., 1944, PhD, 1946. Assoc. prof. history Miss. Coll., Clinton, 1946-48, Memphis State U., 1948-49; Assoc. prof. history U. Miss., 1949-50; assoc. curator manuscripts Mich. Hist. Collections, U. Mich., Ann Arbor, 1954-57; prof. history Miss. Coll., 1957-71, chmn. dept. history and polit. sci., 1964-71. Dir. Bur. of History, Mich. Dept. State, 1971-90; sec. Mich. Hist. Commn., Mich. Dept. State, state historic preservation officer, 1971-90; coord. for Mich., Nat. Hist. Publs. and Recs. Commn., 1974-90. Contbr. articles to profl. publs. Fellow, Ency. Britannica, 1944—45; scholar Julius Rosenwald scholarship, 1943—44, Cleo Hearson scholarship, 1944. Mem. Am. Assn. State and Local History (v.p. 1979-80, pres. 1980-81, fellow summers 1958, 59), Orgn. Am. Historians, Nat. Assn. State Archives and Recs. Assn., So. Hist. Assn., Mich. Hist. Soc., Miss. Hist. Soc. Home: 201 Jefferson St Clinton MS 39056-4237 Office Phone: 601-924-2822. Personal E-mail: mbigelow@bellsouth.net.

BIGELOW, MICHAEL, film director, visual effects expert; BA, UCLA, 1982. With Dream Quest Images, Simi Valley, Calif., 1982—, tech. dir. comml. div., 1985-87, supr. motion control feature div., supr. visual effects. Comml. dir. Dept. Econ. Devel. Commonwealth of Va., 1988, also Leo/Burnett Advt. Agy. Works include: (commls.) Dodge Daytona Billboard, GE Achievement in Space, Black and Decker Hands (Clio award), Polaroid Worlds, Journey; (film features) The Fly, Nightmare on Elm Street III, Michael Jackson's Moonwalker (Smooth Criminal), Warlock, Predator, Short Circuit II, Nightmare on Elm Street IV: The Dream Master, Earth Girls are Easy, Real Men, The Abyss, Total Recall, Warlock, Deuce Bigelow: European Gigilo, 2005. Office: Dream Quest Images 2635 Park Center Dr Simi Valley CA 93065-6209*

BIGELOW, NICHOLAS PIERRE, physicist, researcher; b. Princeton, NJ, Dec. 26, 1958; s. Julian Himley and Mary Agnes (Milward) B.; m. Judith Anderson, July 26, 1981; children: Ian, Eric. BS in Elec. Engring. with high honors, Lehigh U., 1980, BS in Physics with high honors, 1981; MS, Cornell U., 1984, PhD, 1989. Lic. pilot. Mem. tech. staff AT&T Bell Labs., Holmdel, N.J., 1989-91; sr. rsch. assoc. dept. physics and astronomy U. Rochester, N.Y., 1991-92, asst. prof. physics, 1992-97, assoc. prof., 1997—, sr. staff scientist Lab. for Laser Energetics, 1992—, prof., 2000, Lee A. DuBridge prof. physics, prof. optics, 2001—. Rsch. assoc. Ecole Normale Supérieure, Paris, 1991-92, vis. prof., 1992-95. Mem. editl. bd. Laser Physics, Optics Letters; contbr. chpts. to books, numerous articles to profl. jours. and encys. Alfred P. Sloan Found. fellow, 1993-95; NSF grantee, 1994—; David and Lucile Packard Found. fellow, 1994—. Fellow Am. Phys. Soc., Optical Soc. Am., Tau Beta Pi Achievements include theoretical and experimental investigations the fields of quantum optics and atomic physics. Office: U Rochester Dept Physics and Astronomy Rochester NY 14627

BIGELOW, REBA SEETIN, artist; b. Lawrence, Kans., Apr. 16, 1928; d. George Jackman and Irene (Harrison) Seetin; m. Dwight Ernest Bigelow, Apr. 16, 1954; children: David Dwight, Brad Seetin. Assoc. Degree, Tacoma C.C., 1971; BA, U. Wash., 1974, 5th Yr. Degree for Tchg., 1983. Bus. dir. Capitol Truck Co., Topeka, 1946-49; ins. sec. Iowa Home Mutual Ins., Topeka, 1949-52; psycho record typist Topeka State Hosp., 1952-53; tchr. left/right brain art spl. edn. Seguin Sch., Seattle, 1980-83, Seattle Acad. Greater Achievement Sch., Seattle, 1983-85; sec., dir. Art/Not Terminal Gallery, Seattle, 1988—. Vol. art tchr. Pacific Arts Ctr., Seattle, 1986-88, Sch. for the Homeless, Seattle, 1987-89. Works exhibited at Crystal Star Gallery, 1991,

Art/Not Terminal Gallery, 1991, Adirmal Pub, 1995. Vol. Rep. Party, Seattle, 1983. Mem. Art/Not Terminal Gallery (fundraiser 1992-93), New Horizons for Learning (vol., student 1980-88). Avocations: line dancing, volunteering. Home: 7520 12th Ave NE Seattle WA 98115-4318

BIGELOW, ROBERT P., lawyer, arbitrator, mediator, journalist; b. NYC, Jan. 17, 1927; s. Robert R.L. and Doris W.S. (Bissell) B.; m. Katharine W. MacKenty Apr. 14, 1951; children: Katharine R., Robert S., Sanford W., Edward G. AB cum laude, Harvard U., 1950, JD, 1953. Bar: Mass. 1953. Law clk. Supreme Ct. Mass., 1953-54; assoc. Bingham Dana & Gould, Boston, 1954-56; atty., asst. counsel John Hancock Mut. Life Ins. Co., Boston, 1956-66; pvt. practice Woburn and Boston, Mass., 1966-86; of counsel Hennessy Kilburn Killgoar & Ronan, Boston, 1973-84; ptnr. Bigelow & Saltzberg, Woburn, 1980-86; counsel Warner & Stockpole, Boston, 1986-87; pvt. practice, 1987-91, 95-97, 2003—; counsel Bird & Bird, London, 1995-97; arbitrator, mediator, 1966—; hearing officer Mass. Bd. of Bar Overseers, 2003—. Adj. prof. Dartmouth Coll., 1982-84, Suffolk Law Sch., 1986-92; acting dir. New Eng. Law Inst., 1974-75. Author: (with Susan Nycum) Your Computer and the Law, 1975, Contracting for Computer Hardware, Software and Services, 1984-95, Computer Contracts, 1987-92; editor Law Office Econs. and Mgmt., 1969-78, Computer Law Svc., 1973-81, Computer Law and Tax Report, 1974-84, Computer Law Newsletter, 1979-87, cons. editor, 1988-91; cons. editor Bull. Computer Law Assn., 1971-97, editor, 1997-98; contbg. editor Cyberspace Lawyer, 1998—, Lawyers Competitive Edge, 1999—; mem. adv. bd. Guide to Computer Law, 1998-2001; contbr. articles to profl. jours. With U.S. Army, 1945-46, 51-64. Fellow AAAS, Brit. Computer Soc. (life, qualified arbitrator), New Zealand Computer Soc., I.S.P. Can. Info. Processing Soc., Am. Bar Found. (life), Coll. Law Practice Mgmt. (hon.), Australian Computer Soc. (sr.); mem. ABA (editor Computers and the Law 1966, 69, 81, Jurimetrics Jour. 1971-74, Bull. Law, Sci. and Tech. 1977-80, chmn. com. law relating to computers 1979-80, briefs editor Law Practice Mgmt. 1979-91, 93-96), Mass. Bar Assn. (chmn. econs. com. 1969-73, mem. com profl. ethics 1973-79, mem. coun. law practice 1981-84, chmn. bus. law sect. 1984-85), Computer Law Assn. (pres. 1977-79, dir. 1973-84, adv. bd. 1984—). Office: 22 Grove Pl #30 Winchester MA 01890-3864 Office Phone: 781-729-2334.

BIGELOW, SHARON LEE, elementary school educator; b. Chgo., Ill., Oct. 13, 1942; d. Clarence Ellsworth and Frances Lorraine Bigelow. BA in Edn., SUNY, 1964; MA in Ednl. Psychology, N.Y.U., 1965. Tchr. Union Free Sch. Dist., Pleasantville, NY, 1966—. Art dir. Chappaqua Recreation, Chappaqua, NY, 1961—64. Named a Sharon Lee Bigelow Day, Town Bd. & Mayor, 2001. Mem.: N.Y. State Tchrs. Assn., Pleasantville Tchrs. Assn. (pres., deleg.). Avocations: reading, calligraphy, travel .

BIGELOW, WILBUR CHARLES, education educator; b. Noxen, Pa., Mar. 18, 1923; s. Harry Charles and Mary Eva (Lutes) B.; m. Alyce Carlene Friedley, July 1, 1950; children: Douglas Charles, Andrew Briggs. BS, Pa. State U., 1944; MS, U. Mich., 1948, PhD, 1952. Rsch. assoc. U. Mich., Ann Arbor, 1952-55, asst. prof., 1955-59, assoc. prof., 1959-62, prof., 1962-93; prof. emeritus, 1993—. With USN, 1944-45, lt. comdr. USNR, ret. Mem. Am. Chem. Soc., Electron Microscopy Soc. Am. (pres. 1969), Microbeam Analysis Soc.

BIGG, DORT SHARON, lawyer; b. N.Y.C., July 2, 1930; s. Dort S. and Julie (Zeckendorf) B.; m. Meredith Bigg, July 2, 1981; children: Dort S., III, William, Patrick, Daniel Sullivan, Danny Small. AB, Dartmouth Coll., 1952; LLB cum laude, Boston U., 1955. Bar: Maine 1955, N.H. 1955, U.S. Supreme Ct. 1958, U.S. Dist. Ct. N.H., U.S. Dist. Ct. Maine, U.S. Ct. Appeals (1st and 5th cirs.). Atty. N.H. Office Atty. Gen., Concord, 1957-59; asst. U.S. atty. U.S. Dept. Justice, Concord, 1959; partner Wiggin & Nourie, PA, Manchester, N.H., 1959—. Chmn. N.H. Ballot Law Commn., 1976-91. Editor: (in chief) Boston U. Law Review, 1954-55; contbr. articles to jours. Named to Muzzle-Loading Hunters World Hall of Fame, Safari Club Internat., 1993. Fellow Am. Col. Trial Lawyers (state chairman), Internat. Soc. Barristers, Fedn. Ins. Counsel, N.H. Trial Lawyers Assn., N.H. Bar Assn., Manchester Bar Assn., Androscoggin County Bar Assn. Office: Wiggin & Nourie PA 20 Market St Manchester NH 03101-1931

BIGG, SUSAN JEANETTE, educational consultant; d. Edward and Jeanette W. Bigg. BA, Northwestern U., Evanston, Ill.; MPH, U. Ill., Chgo., 1978. Cert. Ednl. Planner Am. Inst. Cert. Ednl. Planners, Va., 1997. Employee trainer Northwestern U. Va. Lakeside, west side, various Va. Hosps., Chgo. and suburbs, Ill., 1980—2003; driving under influence (DUI) remedial edn. instr. Intervention Instrn., Inc., Chgo. and suburbs, Ill., 1985—2005; ednl. cons. Chgo. and suburbs, throughout US, 1985—. Counselor aeticulation bd. DePaul U., Chgo., 1992—; regional adviser Destination-U, LA, 2004—. Chair scholarship com. Ptnrs. in Edn., 4th Presbyn. Ch., Chgo., 1995—2000; trustee Lawrence Hall Youth Svcs., Chgo., 1982—; coll. adv. com. mem. Daniel Murphy Scholarship Found., Chgo., 2004—. Recipient Excellence in Edn. award, Struggling Teens, 2001—04. Mem.: Nat. Assn. Coll. Admissions Counselors, Ind. Ednl. Cons. Assn. (bd. dirs. 2002—05). Avocations: aerobics, reading, music, sports. Office: Susan J Bigg Educational Consultant 1410K W Wrightwood Ave Chicago IL 60614 Office Phone: 773-404-1699.

BIGGAR, JOHN R., utilities energy executive; B in Polit. Sci., Lycoming Coll.; JD, Syracuse U. V.p. finance PP & L Resources, Allentown, Pa., sr. v.p., CFO; exec. v.p., CFO PPL Corp., Allentown, 2001—, also bd. dirs. Bd. dirs. PPL Electric Utilities Corp.; mgr. PPL Energy Supply, LLC, PPL Transition Bond Co., LLC. Office: PP&L Resources Two North 9th St Allentown PA 18101-1179

BIGGART, NICOLE WOOLSEY, dean; m. James Biggart; 1 child, Scott. BA, Simmons Coll., 1969; MA, U. Calif., Davis, 1977; PhD, U. Calif., Berkeley, 1981. Asst. to full prof. mgmt. and sociology U. Calif., Davis, 1981—2002; Jerome J. and Elsie Suran chair in tech. mgmt. Grad. Sch. Mgmt., U. Calif., Davis, 2002—, dean, 2003—. Presenter in field; adv. bd. Sloan Found., 1999—, social sci. rsch. coun. program on corp. as social instn., 1999—. Co-author: (books) Governor Reagan, Governor Brown: Sociology of Executive Power, 1984, Enhancing Organizational Performance: Issues Evidence, Techniques, 1997, The Changing Nature of Work/Occupational Analysis, 1999; author: Charismatic Capitalism: Direct Selling Organizations in America, 1989; mem. editl bd.: Orgn. Studies, 1996—; co-editor, 2002—; mem. editl. bd.: Am. Jour. Sociology, 1990—92, Adminstrv. Sci. Quarterly, 1986—91; editor: (books) Economic Sociology: A Reader, 2001; contbr. articles, chapters to books. Mem.: Am. Sociol. Assn. (orgn., occupations, and work section coun. 1997—98, econ. sociology section organizing com. 1998—2002, chair-elect 1998—99, chair 1999—2000), Soc. Advancement Socio-Econ. (exec. coun. 1995—98), Macro Orgn. Behavior Soc. Office: Grad Sch Mgmt Univ Calif Davis One Shields Ave Davis CA 95616-8609 Office Phone: 530-752-7366. Office Fax: 530-754-5824. Business E-Mail: nwbiggart@ucdavis.edu.

BIGGERS, JONATHAN EDWARD, music educator, consultant; b. Oak Ridge, Tenn., Feb. 10, 1960; s. Robert Edward and Margaret Valentine Biggers. MusB, U. Ala., 1982, MusM, 1984; cert. perfectionnement, Conservatory of Music, Geneva, Switzerland, 1985, cert. virtuosity, 1986; DMA, Eastman Sch. Music, 1991. Dir. music 1st Meth. Ch., Fayette, Ala., 1982—84; organist Holy Trinity Anglican Ch., Geneva, 1984—87, 3d Presbyn. Ch., Rochester, NY, 1988—89, dir. music, organist, 1989—91; asst. prof. music, Link endowed chair Binghamton U., NY, 1992—2001, assoc. prof. music, Link endowed chair, artist-in-residence, 2002—, chair dept. music, 2004—. Organ cons., organ projects in various chs. U.S., Switzerland. Performer: (CD recording) Sleepers Wake! A Reger Perspective, 1994, concerts on Pipedreams, Minn. Pub. Radio program, 1982—, numerous radio broadcasts;over 150 organ concerts and master classes, throughout U.S. and Europe, 1990—, (CD recording) Bach on the Fritts!, 1995. Recipient 1st prize (unanimous), Geneva Internat. Competition, 1985, Calgary (Can.) Organ Festival Concerto Competition, 1990. Mem.: Am. Guild Organists (bd. dirs. Binghamton chpt., 2d prize nat. playing competition 1982). Office: Binghamton U Dept Music PO Box 6000/Vestal Pkwy E Binghamton NY 13902-6000 E-mail: biggers@binghamton.edu.

BIGGERT, JUDITH BORG, congresswoman, lawyer; b. Chicago, Aug. 15, 1937; d. Alvin Andrew and Marjorie Virginia (Mailler) Borg; m. Rody Patterson Biggert, Sept. 21, 1963; children: Courtney Ray, Alison Mailler, Rody Patterson, Adrienne Taylor. BA, Stanford U., 1959; JD, Northwestern U., 1963. Bar: Ill. 1963. Law clk. to presiding justice US Ct. Appeals (7th cir.), Chgo., 1963-64; sole practice Hinsdale, Ill., 1964—99; mem. Ill. Gen. Assembly, 1993—98, asst. Rep. leader, 1995—98; mem. US Congress from 13th Ill. dist., 1999—, mem. fin. svcs. com., edn. and workforce com. stds. ofcl. conduct, chmn. sci. com. subcom. on energy, mem. bipartisan working group on youth violence. Mem. bd. editors Law Rev., Northwestern U. Sch. Law, 1961-63. Pres. Hinsdale Twp. HS Dist. 86 Bd. Edn., 1983-85; pres. Jr. League Chgo., 1976-78, treas., bd. mgrs., 1966—; chmn. Hinsdale Antiques Show, 1980; pres. Oak Sch. PTA, Hinsdale, 1976-78; pres.-treas. Chgo. jr. bd. Travelers Aid Soc., 1965-70; Sunday sch. tchr. Grace Episcopal Ch., Hinsdale, 1978-80, 82-85; chair, treas., 2d v.p. bd. dirs. Vis. Nurses Assn. Chgo., 1978; bd. dirs. Salt Creek Ballet, 1990-98. Recipient Servian award Jr. aux. U. Chgo. Cancer Rsch. Foun., Woman Yr. in Govt., Politics, and Civic Affairs DuPage YWCA, 1995, Hero of the Taxpayer, Am. for Tax Reform. 2000, 02, award for pub. svc., Am. Chem. Soc., 2003, Excellence in Edn., Nat. Assn. Coll. Admission Counseling, 2002, Friend of Edn., Ill. & Nat. Edn. Assn., 2002, Outstanding Leadership to Homeless and Victims of Domestic Violence, Chgo., Pub. Sch., 2002, Disting. Achievement for Protecting and Expanding Opportunities for Children and Youth Who Are Homeless, Chgo. Coalition for the Homeless, 2002, Spirit of Enterprise award US C. of C.; named one of 100 Women Making a Difference; inductee to Hinsdale Ctrl. HS Hall Fame, 1997. Mem. ABA, Ill. Bar Assn., DuPage Bar Assn., Coalition Women Legislatures. Republican. Office: US Ho of Reps 1317 Longworth Ho Off Bl Washington DC 20515-1313 also: Dist Off 6262 S Rte 83 Ste 305 Willowbrook IL 60527 Office Phone: 202-225-3515.*

BIGGINS, J. VERONICA, bank executive; m. Franklin Biggins; children: Dawn, Kenzie. B, Spelman Coll.; M, Ga. State U.; postgrad., U. Md. Asst. br. mgr. Citizens and So. Nat. Bank, Atlanta, affirmative action officer, compliance mgr., employee relations mgr., mgr. Atlanta personnel, exec. v.p., dir. human resources. Lectr. in field. Bd. dirs., co-chmn. freedom fund dinner NAACP; bd. dirs. Atlanta chpt. Urban League; chmn. personnel com., bd. dirs. United Way; bd. dirs., chmn. student affairs com., vice chmn. fundraising Spelman Coll.; mem. governing bd., vice chmn. Zoo Atlanta Capital Campaign; mem. exec. com. Leadership Atlanta, 1983; mem. bd. visitors Grady Hosp.; mem. bd. trustees YWCA, Exodus, Inroads, Inc.; chmn. nominating com. NW Girl Scout Council; mem. Atlanta women's fund adv. com. Recipient Outstanding Performance award Inroads, Atlanta, 1986, Urban Bankers, 1987, trail blazer award Nat. Assn. Negro Bus. and Profl. Women's Clubs, Inc. Mem. Am. Bankers Assn. (chmn. human resource div.), Dogwood City Links, Chautaugua Circle. Episcopalian. Office: Citizens and So Ga Corp PO Box 4899 Atlanta GA 30302-4899

BIGGS, ALAN RICHARD, plant pathologist, educator; b. Lewisburg, Pa., June 22, 1953; s. Edgar Harold and Yvonne S. Biggs; m. Lise N. Sade, Oct. 3, 1981 (div 2005); children: Benjamin Jesse Biggs Sade, Skylar Rose Biggs Sade. BS, Pa. State U., 1976, MS, 1978, PhD, 1982. Rsch. scientist Can. Dept. Agr., Vineland, Ont., 1983-89; assoc. prof. W.Va. U., Kearneysville, 1989-95, prof., 1995—. Editor: Defense Mechanisms of Woody Plants Against Fungi, 1992, Cytology, Histology and Histochemistry of Fruit Tree Diseases, 1992; assoc. editor Phytopathology, 1986-88, Plant Disease, 1994-96; sr. editor Plant Disease, 1998-2000, editor-in-chief, 2001-2003. Recipient Lee M. Hutchins award, 1993, USDA Sec. Honor award, 2001, 2002. Mem. Am. Phytopath. Soc. (Lee M. Hutchins award 1993). Avocations: photography, bicycling, jazz guitar. Office: WVa U Tree Fruit Rsch and Edn Ctr PO Box 609 Kearneysville WV 25430-0609

BIGGS, ARTHUR EDWARD, retired chemicals executive, social services administrator; b. N.Y.C., Jan. 3, 1930; s. Arthur Edward and Pauline (Maier) B.; m. Charlotte Marion Elliott, Sept. 10, 1955; children— Arthur Edward III, William Elliott, Nancy Catherine, Andrew David BS in Acctg. and Fin. Magna cum laude, U. Md., 1951; MBA in Fin. and Prodn. with distinction, Harvard U., 1957. Mgmt. cons. McKinsey & Co., Inc., N.Y.C., 1957-62; asst. controller Mobil Oil Co., N.Y.C., 1963-66, controller, 1966-68; v.p., gen. mgr. plastics div. Mobil Chem. Co., Rochester, N.Y., 1969-73, exec. v.p. N.Y.C., 1974-82, pres., 1982-86. Chmn. bd. dirs. The Century Group, 1987-91. Vice pres. bd. dirs. Vis. Nurse Svc. N.Y., 1975-88; bd. advisers Pace U., N.Y.C., 1976-88; trustee Quinnipiac Coll., Hamden, Conn., 1982-92, chmn., 1986-90; bd. dirs. Ptnrs. in Care, N.Y.C., 1983-88, chmn., 1983-88; trustee Conn. Conf. Ind. Colls., chmn., 1987-89; trustee Harvard Sch. Bus. 1st lt., pilot USAF, 1951-55. Baker scholar Harvard U., 1957. Mem. Racquet Club Boca Raton, Woodfield Country Club (Boca Raton). Avocation: tennis.

BIGGS, BARRY HUGH, lawyer; b. Portland, Oreg., Mar. 24, 1935; s. Hugh Lawry and Elra (Ware) B.; m. Betty Lou Boehm, Aug. 25, 1957; children: Jonathan Hugh, Julianne. BS, U. Oreg., 1956; LLB, Stanford U., 1960. Bar: Wash. 1960. Assoc. Lane Powell Moss & Miller, Seattle, 1960-68; ptnr. Lane Powell Spears Lubersky, Seattle, 1969-92, of counsel, 1992—. Mem. ABA, Wash. State Bar Assn., Tacoma-Pierce County Bar Assn., Seattle Tennis Club, Vashon Island Golf & Country Club, Phi Gamma Delta. Home: 26032 Gold Beach Dr SW Vashon WA 98070-8531

BIGGS, J. O., lawyer, manufacturing executive; b. Kansas City, Mo., Feb. 17, 1925; s. John Olin and Parilee Catherine (Story) B.; m. Marilyn Frances Sweeney, Dec. 27, 1947; children— Melissa Anne, John Kevin, Brian Sweeney. AB, U. Kans., 1947, LLB, 1949. Bar: Kan. bar 1949, Mo. bar 1950, Ia. bar 1953. With legal dept. Kansas City Life Ins. Co., 1950-51; exec. asst. to industry members Regional Wage Stblzn. Bd., 1951-52; dir. labor relations Meredith Pub. Co., 1952-58; with Gustin-Bacon Mfg. Co. (merger into Certain-teed Products Corp. 1966), 1958—, v.p., asst. to pres., 1962-63, pres., chief exec. officer, 1963-66; exec. v.p. Ardmore, Pa., 1966-69; pres. Thermo-Kinetic Corp., 1969-76; mem. firm Wagner, Leek & Mullins, 1976—. Cons. in field; sr. v.p., gen. counsel Exec. Hills, Inc., Shawnee Mission, Kans., 1979—. Active Big Bros. of Tucson. Mem. Am., Mo., Kans., Johnson County bar assns., Kansas City Met. Bar Assn., Am. Mgmt. Assn., Sigma Alpha Epsilon, Phi Alpha Phi. Clubs: Skyline (Tucson), Country (Tucson); Carriage (Kansas City). Republican. Presbyterian. Home: 8743 Riggs Ln Shawnee Mission KS 66212-1281 Office: 7101 College Blvd Ste 1100 Shawnee Mission KS 66210-2078

BIGGS, JASON, actor; b. Pompton Plains, NJ, May 12, 1978; s. Gary and Angela Biggs. Student, NYU, Montclair State U. Actor: (films) Conversations With My Fahter, 1991, The Boy Who Cried Bitch, 1991, American Pie, 1999, Boys and Girls, 2000, Loser, 2000, Saving Silverman, 2001, American Pie 2, 2001, Prozac Nation, 2001, American Wedding, 2003, Jersey Girl, 2004; (TV series) Drexell's Class, 1991, As the World Turns, 1994—95; (Broadway plays) The Graduate, 2002. Office: c/o SFM 1122 S Robertson # 15 Los Angeles CA 90035

BIGGS, JEFFREY ROBERT, political scientist; b. New Castle, Pa., May 2, 1941; s. Wallace R. and Janice E. Biggs; m. Janet Allen Mathews, May 24, 1969; children: Jennifer M., Jessica E. BA, Harvard U., 1963; MA, Victoria U., Wellington, New Zealand, 1965; PhD, George Washington U., 1975. With U.S. Consulate Gen., Rio de Janeiro, 1974-78; attache U.S. Embassy, Lisbon, Portugal, 1978-81; dir., pres. bur. inter-Am. affairs Dept of State, Washington, 1981-84; deputy chief of mission Am. Embassy, La Paz, Bolivia, 1985-87; press sec. spkr. of house U.S. Ho. Reps., Washington, 1987-94; sr. advisor Office Nat. Drug Control Policy, Washington, 1995; dir. congl. fellowship program Am. Polit. Sci. Assn., Washington, 1997—. Mem. adv. bd. sr. Fulbright enhancement program, Robert Wood Johnson Health Policy Fellowship Adv. Bd./Pub. Diplomacy Coun. Co-author: Honor in the House: Speaker Tom Foley, 1999, A Congress of Fellows: Fifty Years of the American Political Science Association Congressional Fellowships Program 1953-2003, 2003; contbr. articles to profl. jours. Fulbright fellow, Wellington, New Zealand, 1964-65, Congl. fellow Am. Polit. Sci. Assn., 1984-85. Mem. Am. Polit. Sci. Assn., Diplomatic-Consular Officers Ret. Assn., Pub. Diplomacy Coun. Avocations: fly fishing, hiking, writing. Home: 6406 Kenhowe Dr Bethesda MD 20817-5446 Office: Am Polit Sci Assn 1527 New Hampshire Ave NW Washington DC 20036-1203 Business E-Mail: jbiggs@apsanet.org.

BIGGS, JOHN HERRON, retired insurance company executive; b. St. Louis, July 19, 1936; s. Peter Willis and Lillian (Herron) B.; m. Penelope Frances Parkman, June 13, 1959; 1 child, Henry. AB magna cum laude, Harvard U., 1958; PhD in Econ., Wash. U., 1983. V.p., contr. Gen. Am. Ins. Co., 1970-77; vice chancellor for adminstrn. and fin. Washington U., St. Louis, 1977-85; chmn., pres., chief exec. officer Centerre Trust Co., 1985-89; pres., COO Tchrs. Ins. and Annuity Assn./Coll. Retirement Equities Fund, 1989-93, chmn., pres., CEO, 1993—2002. Bd. dirs. Boeing Co., JPMorgan-Chase Co.; emeritus trustee, past pres. Mo. Bot. Garden; bd. trustees Emeritus Health Solutions. Dir., past chmn. Nat. Bur. Econ. Affairs; trustee Washington U.; chmn. bd. trustees J. Paul Getty Trust, Emeriti Health Svcs.; trustee Danforth Found.; past chmn. United Way N.Y.C. Fellow: Soc. of Actuaries; mem.: Coun. Fgn. Rels., St. Louis Club, Harvard Club N.Y., Sky Club, Westchester Country Club. Home: 240 E 47th St Apt 23D New York NY 10017-2137 Office: 780 3d Ave 18th Fl New York NY 10017 Office Phone: 212-838-8071. E-mail: jbiggs@tiaa-cref.org.

BIGGS, ROBERT DALE, Near Eastern studies educator; b. Pasco, Wash., June 13, 1934; s. Robert Lee and Eleonora Christina (Jensen) B. BA in Edn, Eastern Wash. Coll. Edn., 1956; PhD, Johns Hopkins U., 1962. Rsch. assoc. Oriental Inst. U. Chgo., 1963—64, asst. prof. Assyriology, 1964-67, assoc. prof. Assyriology, 1967-72, prof. Assyriology, 1972—2004, prof. emeritus, 2004—. Author: ŠÀ.ZI.GA: Ancient Mesopotamian Potency Incantations, 1967, Inscriptions from Tell Abu Salabikh, 1974, Inscriptions from al-Hiba-Lagash: The First and Second Seasons, 1976; co-author: Cuneiform Texts from Nippur, 1969, Nippur II: The North Temple and Sounding E, 1978; editor: Discoveries from Kurdish Looms, 1983; assoc. editor: Assyrian Dictionary, 1964-87; editor Jour. Near Ea. Studies, 1972—; mem. editorial bd. Assyrian Dictionary, 1995—. Fulbright scholar Univ. Toulouse, France, 1956-57; fellow Baghdad Sch., Am. Schs. Oriental Rsch., 1962-63, Am. Rsch. Inst. in Turkey, 1972, Danforth fellow, 1956-62. Mem. Am. Oriental Soc. (pres. Mid. Western br. 1978-79), Archaeol. Inst. Am. (pres. Chgo. soc. 1985-92), Brit. Sch. Archaeology Iraq. Office: U Chgo 1155 E 58th St Chicago IL 60637-1540 Office Phone: 773-702-9540. Business E-Mail: r-biggs@uchicago.edu.

BIGGS-WILLIAMS, EVELYN ANN, librarian; b. Atmore, Ala., Sept. 27, 1950; d. John Henry and Mary Evelyn (Smith) Biggs; m. Michael Robin Williams, June 14, 1986. BS, U. South Ala., 1971; MLS, Fla. State U., 1972. Libr. Escambia Acad., Canoe, Ala., 1972-73; asst. libr. Jefferson Davis C.C., Brewton, Ala., 1973-91, libr., 1991-94, head libr., 1994-97. Mem. ALA, Ala. Libr. Assn., Ala. Instnrl. Media Assn. (past pres.), Nat. Geneal. Soc., Escambia County Hist. Soc. (v.p.). Methodist. Avocations: wildflowers, genealogy, photography, piano. Office: Jefferson Davis C C 220 Alco Dr Brewton AL 36426-2716

BIGHAM, DARREL E., history educator; b. Harrisburg, Pa., Aug. 12, 1942; s. Paul D. and Ethel Bigham; m. Mary Elizabeth Hitchcock, Sept. 23, 1965; children: Matthew, Elizabeth. BA, Messiah Coll., 1964; postgrad., Harvard Div. Sch., 1964-65; PhD, U. Kans., 1970. Asst. prof. history U. So. Ind., Evansville, 1970-75, assoc. prof., 1975-81, prof., 1981—. Author: We Ask Only a Fair Trial, 1987, An Evansville Album, 1988, Towns and Villages of the Lower Ohio, 1998, Images of America: Evansville, 1998, Images of America: Evansville, The World War II Years, 2005, On Jordan's Banks: emancipation and its aftermath in the Ohio River Valley, 2005, After Slavery, 2005; contbr. articles to scholarly jours. and anthologies. Dir. Hist. So. Ind. 1986—; exec. dir. Leadership Evansville, 1976-79; chmn. Evansville Bicentennial Coun., 1974-76; bd. dirs. Evansville Mus., 1972—, treas., 1977-78, pres., 1979-81; bd. dirs. Met. Evansville Progress Commn., 1981-85, chmn., 1983-85; bd. dirs. Conrad Baker Found., 1971-85, Planned Parenthood S.W. Ind., 1978-79; trustee Evansville Vanderburgh County Pub. Libr., 1971-81; chmn. 175th Anniversary Com. City of Evansville, 1985-87; Presdl. appointee Abraham Lincoln Bicentennial Commn., 2000—. Rockefeller Bros. Theol. fellow, 1964-65, NDEA fellow, 1965-68. Mem. Soc. Ind. Archivists (dir. 1972-75, pres. 1977-79), Am. Hist. Assn., Orgn. Am. Historians (newsletter editl. bd. 2001-2003), Ind. Assn., Historians (chair hist. edn. com. 1994—, pres. 1999-2000), Ind. Hist. Soc., Vanderburgh County Hist. Soc. (pres. 1981-84, 93-96). Mem. United Ch. of Christ. Home: 8215 Kuebler Rd Evansville IN 47720-7427 Office: U So Ind Dept History Evansville IN 47712 Business E-Mail: dbigham@usi.edu.

BIGHAM, WANDA DURRETT, religious organization administrator; b. Barlow, Ky., June 19, 1935; d. Herbert Martin and Ada Florene (Baker) Durrett; m. William M. Bigham, Jr., June 7, 1958; children: William M. III, Janet Kaye, Julia Lynn. BME, Murray State U., 1956; MM, Morehead State U., 1971, MHE, 1973; EdD, U. Ky., 1978; cert., Inst. For Ednl. Mgmt. -Harvard U., 1982; LittD (hon.), Loras Coll., 1989. Dir. TRIO programs Morehead (Ky.) State U., 1972-85, assoc. dean acad. affairs, dir. instructional sys., 1982-85, acting dean grad. and spl. acad. programs, 1984-85; exec. asst. to pres. Emerson Coll., Boston, 1985, v.p. for devel., 1986; pres. Marycrest Coll., Davenport, Iowa, 1986-92, Huntingdon Coll., Montgomery, Ala., 1993—2003; asst. gen. sec. for schs., colls. and univs. The United Meth. Ch., Nashville, 2003—. Bd. dirs. NAICU, 2002-03; bd. dirs., pres. Asia-Pacific Fedn. Christian Schs.; bd. dirs. Internat. Assn. Meth.-Related Schs., Colls. and Univs., Montgomery Symphony Orch., 1993-2003, Ala. Shakespeare Festival, 1996-2003, NASCUMC, 1996-2003; exec. com., pres. Univ. Senate United Meth. Ch., Ctrl. Ala. chpt. ARC, Montgomery, 1995-2003, pres, 2001-2002; mem. Leadership Ala., 1994—; co-chair Quad Cities Vision for the Future, Davenport, 1987-92. Recipient Pres.'s award Davenport C. of C., 1988, Women of Spirit and Note award Cmty. Com. of Davenport, 1991, Hope for Humanity award Jewish Fedn. of QC, Rock Island, Ill., 1993, Women's Acad. of Honor award Ala. Bus. and Profl. Women's Found., 2004; named to Alumni Hall of Fame, Morehead State U., 1988, Disting. Alumna, Murray State Coll., 1988, Woman of Distinction award Girl Scouts South Ctrl. Ala., 2001. Mem. Am. Coun. on Edn. (mem. coun. of fellows, bd. dirs. 1994-97, fellow in higher edn. adminstrn. 1983-84), Internat. Assn. Univ. Pres., Montgomery C. of C., Com. of 100, Sigma Alpha Iota (Sword of Honor 1956), Phi Kappa Phi, Kappa Delta Pi. Office: United Meth Ch Gen Bd Higher Edn and Ministry 1001 19th Ave S PO Box 340007 Nashville TN 37203-0007 Mailing: PO Box 340007 Nashville TN 37203-0007 Office Phone: 615-340-7406. Business E-Mail: wbigham@gbhem.org.

BIGHAM, WILLIAM J., lawyer; b. Bryn Mawr, Pa., July 4, 1949; s. Robert H. and Regina B.; m. Cindy K. Elkins, Aug. 12, 1972; children: Justin K., Joel M., Meredith E. BBA with honors, Siena Coll., 1971; JD with honors, Rutgers U., 1974. Bar: N.J. 1974, D.C. 1977, U.S. Ct. Appeals (3d cir.) 1983, U.S. Supreme Ct. 1985. Jud. law clk. to Hon. Samuel D. Lenox, Jr. Chancery Divisn. Superior Ct. of N.J., Trenton, N.J., 1974-75; mng. dir., shareholder Sterns & Weinroth, Trenton, 1975—. Mem.: ABA, N.J. Bar, D.C. Bar, Mercer County Bar Assn. Roman Catholic. Office: 50 W State St Ste 1400 Trenton NJ 08607-1220 Office Phone: 609-392-2100.

BIGLAND-RITCHIE, BRENDA RACHEL, physiologist, educator, neurophysiology researcher; b. Jordans, Eng., Sept. 23, 1927; came to U.S., 1958; d. Ranulf Aggs and Dorothy Eva (Shaw) Bigland; m. J. Murdoch Ritchie, July 28, 1951; children: Alasdair John, Anne Jocelyn. BSc, U. Coll., London, 1949, PhD, 1968; DSc, London U., 1987. Med. rsch. coun. fellow U. Coll., London, 1949-51, asst. prof. physiology, 1951-53; rsch. instr. Albert Einstein Coll. Medicine, Bronx, N.Y., 1963-66; physiology lectr. Hunter Coll., Bronx,

N.Y., 1966-67; asst. prof. biology Marymount Coll., Tarrytown, N.Y., 1967-70; prof. biology and rehab. scis. Quinnipiac Coll., Hamden, Conn., 1973-94; fellow John B. Pierce Lab., New Haven, Conn., 1985-94; prof. pediatrics, lectr neurology Yale U. Sch. Medicine, New Haven, Conn., 1994—. Adj. prof. pediatrics Sch. Medicine, Yale U., 1988-94; nat. and internat. lectr.; mem. organizing com. Internat. Union Physiological Scis. Commn. for Human and Exercise Physiology, Helsinki, 1990, Glasgow, 1993. Author 17 book chpts.; contbr. more than 50 articles to profl. jours. Fellow Alexander von Humboldt Found., 1991, NIH, 1976-94, Multiple Sclerosis Found., Muscular Dystrophy Found., 1978-84, among others. Fellow Am. Coll. Sports Medicine; mem. Soc. for Neurosci., Brit. Physiol. Soc., Am. Physiol. Soc., Internat. Union of Physiol. Socs.

BIGLARI, HAMID, investment banker; s. Manouchehr and Parvin Biglari; m. Laya Khadjavi, Apr. 1, 1994; children: Roxana Sahar, Mandana Yasmine. BA, BS, Cornell U., 1978—81; MS, Princeton U., 1981—84, PhD, 1984—87. Ptnr. McKinsey & Co., NYC, 1991—2000; head of corp. strategy Citigroup, NYC, 2000—. Bd. mem. Graham Windham, NYC, 2000—02. Home: 447 East 57th St Apt 11 New York NY 10022 Office: Citigroup 388 Greenwich St 35th Flr New York NY 10013 E-mail: biglarih@citigroup.com.

BIGLER, BLADE TARL, music educator; b. Portales, N.Mex., July 28, 1976; s. Eddie and Susan Bigler. MusB Edn., U. of Okla., 1999. Band dir. Ardmore (Okla.) Band, 1999—2004, Tishomingo (Okla.) Band, 2004—. Home: 2206 Cimmaron Dr Ardmore OK 73401 Office Phone: 580-371-2322. E-mail: tishband@yahoo.com.

BIGLER, GLADE S., lawyer; b. Brigham City, Utah, Apr. 21, 1928; s. Horace J. and Marie (Schow) Bigler; m. Lois A. Bigler, Sept. 4, 1951; children: Cathy, Nadine, Elaine, Thad, Pat. BS in Zoology, U. Utah, 1950, JD, 1956. Bar: Utah 1956, U.S. Dist. Ct. Utah 1956, U.S. Ct. Appeals (10th cir.) 1956, U.S. Supreme Ct. 1970. Ins. adjuster Travelers Ins. Co., 1956—58; gen. atty. VA, Salt Lake City, 1958—60, loan guaranty atty., 1960—68, dist. counsel, 1974—98, ret., 1998. Adminstrv. law judge, 1971—74; counsel, 1974—95; ret., 1995; lectr. in field; pres. Nat. Fedn. Fed. Employees Local 990, 1961—62. Served with USN, 1950—53, served with USNR, 1953—81. Fellow: Am. Coll. Legal Medicine; mem.: Fed. Bar Assn. (pres. 1964—65), Res. Officers Assn. (pres. Salt Lake chpt. 1978—79). Mem. Lds Ch. Home: 3003 Kenwood St Salt Lake City UT 84106-3704 E-mail: glade.bigler@juno.com.

BIGLER, HAROLD EDWIN, JR., retired investment company executive; b. N.Y.C., Apr. 27, 1931; s. Harold Edwin and Elizabeth Augusta (Cutler) B.; m. Lorinda Jennings Bailey, June 21, 1980; children by previous marriage: John Stephen, Diane Elizabeth Bigler Whatley, William Campbell. AB, Brown U., 1953; MBA, Babson Inst., 1957; postgrad., Harvard U. Bus. Sch., 1975. Investment analyst Conn. Gen. Life Ins. Co., 1957-64, asst. sec., 1964, sec., 1964, 2d v.p., 1966-68; v.p. Securities Group, Hartford, 1968-81; chmn. C.G. Investment Mgmt. Co., Inc., 1975-81; pres., dir. Conn. Gen. Fund, Income Fund, Mcpl. Bond Fund, Money Market Fund, Companion Fund, Companion Income Fund, 1975-81. Chmn. Bigler Investment Mgmt. Co.; chmn. bd. Bigler Ptnrs., Inc.; gen. ptnr. Crossroads Fund, Crossroads Capital Fund; dir. Conn. Water Service, Inc., Vantage Computer Systems, Inc., various CIGNA mutual funds; chmn. investment adv. com., State of Conn., 1972-78; mem. investment com. Brown U., Providence, R.I., 1968-80; former chmn. Conn. Higher Edn. Student Loan Authority; bd. dirs. New Eng. Asset Mgmt. Co. Inc.; bd. dirs. New Eng. Monthly, Inc. Served as lt. (j.g.) USN, 1953-55. Mem. Am. Council Life Ins. (chmn. securities investment com. 1972-76), Fin. Analysts Fedn. (dir. 1974-76), N.Y. Soc. Security Analysts, Hartford Soc. Fin. Analysts (pres. 1966-67), The Hartford Club, Hartford Golf Club, The Moorings Club (Vero Beach, Fla.). Republican. Home: 14 Thicket Ln West Hartford CT 06107-1320

BIGLER, LOIS LORRAINE, mathematics educator; d. Henning and Bertha Louise (Jones) Hanson; m. Robert H Bigler; children: Heidi Bigler Cole, Wendy, Randall Ward. BA with distinction, Colo. State U., 1955—59; MEd, Tex. State U., 1998—2003. Texas Lifetime Teaching Certificate Tex. Edn. Agy., 1985. Math. tchr. Estes Pk. H.S., Colo., 1975—85, La Vernia H.S., Tex., 1985—. Tchr. of dual credit coll. algebra and precalculus St. Phillips Coll., San Antonio, 2003—; v.p. student govt. Colo. State U. Chmn. libr. bldg. com. Estes Pk. Woman's Club, 1968—69. Named Miss Leadership, AAUW, Colo. State U., 1959; named one of Twelve Pacemakers, Colo. State U., 1959; recipient Freshman Woman with Highest GPA, 1959; scholar, Boettcher Found., 1955—59. Mem.: Nat. Coun. Tchrs. Math., Estes Pk. Woman's Club, SPURS at Colo. State Univ. (pres. 1956—57), Epsilon Sigma Alpha (pres. 1968—69), Kappa Kappa Gamma (life; pres., rush chmn. 1956—58). Protestant. Avocations: travel, gardening, reading. Office: La Vernia HS 225 Fm 775 La Vernia TX 78121 Office Phone: 830-779-2181.

BIGUM, RANDALL K., retired military officer; b. Lubbock, Tex., Dec. 11, 1949; BS in Bus., Ohio State U., 1973; student pilot tng., Williams AFB, Ariz., 1973-74; student F-4 pilot tng., 71st Tactical Fighter Squadron, MacDill AFB, Fla., 1974; student, USAF Fighter Weapons Sch., Nellis AFB, Nev., 1977; student F-15 pilot tng., 58th Tactical Tng. Wing, Luke AFB, Ariz., 1979; student, Squadron Officer Sch., 1980; M in Mil. Art and Sci., Army Command and Gen. Staff Coll., 1985; student, Nat. War Coll., 1993, Syracuse U., 1996. Commd. 2d lt. USAF, 1973, advanced through grades to brig. gen., 1998, various pilot assignments, 1974-77; weapons officer 59th Tactical Fighter Squadron, Eglin AFB, Fla., 1977-79, F-15 instr. pilot, 1979-80; various positions Nellis AFB, 1980-84; air ops. staff officer advanced program office Hdqs. Tactical Air Command, Langley AFB, Va., 1985-88, dep. chief. staff for requirements, 1985-88; ops. officer then comdr. 53rd Tactical Fighter Squadron, Bitburg Air Base, Germany, 1988-91; chief fighter devel. br. Office Undersec. Air Force Acquisition, Pentagon, Washington, 1991-92; comdr. 18th Ops. Group, Kadena Air Base, Japan, 1993-95; exec. officer to dep. comdr. in chief U.S. European Command, Stuttgart-Vaihingen City, Germany, 1995-97; comdr. 4th Fighter Wing, Seymour Johnson AFB, N.C., 1997-99; dep. dir. combat weapon sys. Hdqrs. Air Combat Command, Langley AFB, Va., 1999-2000, dir. combat weapon sys., 2000; dir., strategic initiatives Lockheed Martin Missiles and Fire Control, 2001—02, v.p., strike weapons bus. Orlando, Fla., 2002—. Dir. requirements, Hdqrs. Air Combat Command, Langley AFB, Va., 2000-01. Decorated D.F.C., Legion of Merit, Air medal with three oak leaf clusters, Small Arms Expert Marksmanship Ribbon. Office: Lockheed Martin Missiles and Fire Control 5600 Sand Lake Rd MP 455 Orlando FL 32819-8907

BIGUS, LAWRENCE WEAVER, lawyer; b. Apr. 2, 1955; s. Kenneth Eli and Elma (Weaver) Bigus. BBA magna cum laude, U. Houston, 1977, JD, 1980. Bar: Mo. 1980, U.S. Dist. Ct. (we. dist.) Mo. 1980. Ptnr. Bigus & Bigus, Kansas City, Mo., 1980—96, Stinson, Morrison & Hecker LLP (and predecessors), Overland Park, Kans., 1996—. Contbr. articles to profl. jours. Pres. congregation Beth Torah; bd. trustees Hyman Hebrew Acad. Named one of Outstanding Young Men Am., 1984; recipient scholarship, Trust div. Kans. Bankers Assn., 1980. Mem.: Kansas City Bar Assn., Mo. Bar Assn., Order of Coif, Jaycees (keyman Kansas City chpt. 1983, 1984, keyman Mo. chpt. 1984), Betta Gamma Sigma, Phi Kappa Phi. Republican. Jewish. Office: Stinson, Morrison & Hecker LLP 9200 Indian Creek Pkwy #450 Overland Park KS 66210 E-mail: lbigus@stinsonmobeck.com.

BIGWOOD, ROBERT WILLIAM, lawyer; b. Fergus Falls, Minn., June 30, 1956; s. Robert M. and Barbara I. (Barr) B.; m. Gretchen K. Brink, July 8, 1978; children: Maria, Daniel, Mark. BA cum laude, U. Minn., 1977, JD, 1980. Bar: Minn. 1980, U.S. Dist. Ct. Minn. 1980. Ptnr. Pemberton Sorlie and Rufer, Fergus Falls, 1980—. Pres., Campaign chmn. Fergus Falls United Fund, 1987-88; pres., Lakeland Hospice, Inc., Fergus Falls, 1985-87. Mem. Minn. State Bar Assn., Kiwanis, Phi Kappa Phi. Republican. Methodist. Home: 618 N Ann St Fergus Falls MN 56537-1717 Office: Perberton Sorlie and Rufer 110 N Mill St Fergus Falls MN 56537-2135

BIHARY, JOYCE, federal judge; b. Detroit, Oct. 24, 1950; BA, Wellesley Coll., 1972; JD, U. Mich., 1975. Bar: Ga. 1975. Atty. Alston, Miller & Gaines, 1975-77, Rogers & Hardin, 1977-79, ptnr., 1979-87; bankruptcy judge U.S. Dist. Ct., Atlanta, 1987—. Mem. Ga. Assn. Women Lawyers, Atlanta Bar Assn., Southeastern Bankruptcy Law Inst. (adv.); fellow Am. Coll. Bankruptcy, Lawyers Found. Ga., Ga. Consortium Personal Fin. Literacy, Coalition Debtor Edn. Office: US Bankruptcy Ct US Courthouse 75 Spring St SW Atlanta GA 30303-3309

BIHLDORFF, JOHN PEARSON, hospital director; b. Boston, Aug. 3, 1945; s. Carl Birger and Martha Bowling (McCandless) B.; m. Jane Sargent Lyman, Mar. 30, 1968; children: Jennifer, Nathan, David. AB, Harvard U., 1969; MPH, Yale U., 1971. With McMaster U. Med. Ctr., Hamilton, Ont., Can., 1971-77, assoc. exec. dir., 1975-77; dir. program planning, asst. prof. divsn. med. adminstrn. Vanderbilt U. Med. Ctr. & Sch. Medicine, 1977-78; assoc. hosp. dir., COO U. Conn. Health Ctr.-John Dempsey Hosp., Farmington, 1978-81; asst. exec. dir. U. Conn. Health Ctr., 1981-82, hosp. dir., 1982-86; pres., CEO St. Luke's Health Found. and Hosp., New Bedford, Mass., 1986-91, Newton-Wellesley Hosp., Newton, Mass., 1991-2001. Chmn. bd. dirs. VHA of Mass., Inc., 1995-97; chmn. bd. dirs. VHA Healthfront, 1995-97; bd. dirs. Tufts Assocs. Health Plan, 1994-96. Home: 107 Elm St Canton MA 02021-1255

BIJUR, PETER I., retired petroleum company executive; b. NYC; m. Kjestine Anderson; children from previous marriage: Kristin Anne, Matthew Montgomery, David Barrett. BA in Polit. Sci., U. Pitts., 1964; MBA, Columbia U., 1966. Various dist. and regional sales positions Texaco, Inc., 1966—71, mgr. Buffalo sales dist., 1971—73, asst. to sr. v.p. for pub. affairs, 1973—75, staff coord. dept. strategic planning, 1975—77, asst. to exec. v.p. Buffalo sales dist., 1977—80; mgr. Rocky Mountain Refining & Mktg., 1980—81, asst. to chmn. bd., 1981—84; pres. Texaco Oil Trading and Supply Co., 1984, v.p. spl. projects, 1984—86; pres., chief exec. officer Texaco Can. Inc., Don Mills, Canada, 1987—89; chmn. Texaco Ltd., London, 1989—91; pres. Texaco Europe, 1990—92; sr. v.p. Texaco, Inc., White Plains, NY, 1992—96, vice chmn. bd., 1996, chmn. bd. dirs., CEO, 1996—2001. Adv. bd. Proudfoot Cons. Co.; strategic adv. coun. Gas Tech. Inst.; bd. dirs. Gulf Mark Offshore, Inc. Office: 1055 Washington Blvd Stamford CT 06901 Office Phone: 203-324-2242.

BIKALES, NORBERT M., chemist, science administrator; b. Berlin, Jan. 7, 1929; arrived in U.S., 1946; s. Salomon and Bertha (Bander) Bikales; m. Gerda V. Bierzonski, Apr. 28, 1951; children: Marguerite Sarlin, Edward A. BS in Chemistry, CCNY, 1951; MS in Chemistry, Polytech. U., 1956; PhD in Chemistry, Poly. U., 1961. Rsch. chemist Am. Cyanamid Co., Stamford, Conn., 1951-62; tech. dir. Gaylord Assocs., Newark, 1962-65; pres. N.M. Bikales & Co., Cons., Livingston, N.J., 1965-76; prof. chemistry, dir. continuing edn. in scis. Rutgers U., New Brunswick and Newark, N.J., 1973-79; dir. polymers program NSF, Washington, 1976-95, head Europe office Paris, 1995-98. Trustee Gordon Rsch. Conf., 1990—97, Fedn. Materials Soc., 1998—. Editor: Ency. Polymer Sci. and Tech., 1962—77; contbr. chpts. in books, articles to profl. jours. Pres. Friends of Livingston Libr., NJ, 1968—72, Livingston Symphony Orch., 1970—76; judge internat. Tech. Film '89 Festival, Pardubice, Czech Republic, 1989; v.p., sec. OSE-USA, 2000—. Recipient Twp. of Livingston award, 1976, Great Medal, City of Paris, 1985, Disting. Alumnus award, Poly. U., Bklyn., 1986, Disting. lectr. award, Soc. Polymer Sci., Tokyo, 1986, Chevalier des Palmes Académiques award, French Govt., 1993, Polish Acad. Scis., 1997, Disting. Svc. award, NSF, 1999, Lifetime Achievement award, Queens Coll., 2001. Fellow: AAAS, Am. Phys. Soc., Internat. Union Pure and Applied Chemistry (titular, sec. 1979—87, 1993—97, chmn. comm. on recycling of polymers 1993—98), N.Y. Acad. Sci. (life); mem.: Groupe Français des Polymères (sci. counselor 1994—99), Soc. Plastics Engrs. (sr.; bd. dirs. 1979—82), Polish Chem. Soc. (hon.), Am. Chem. Soc. (councilor 1987—89, chmn. polymer divsn. 1983, emeritus 2000—). Achievements include patents for materials, chemicals and chemical processes. Personal E-mail: nbikales@msn.com.

BIKEL, THEODORE, actor, singer; b. Vienna, May 2, 1924; came to U.S., 1954, naturalized, 1961; s. Josef and Miriam (Riegler) B.; m. Rita Weinberg, 1967. Student, U. London; grad., Royal Acad. Dramatic Art, London, 1948; DFA (hon.), U. Hartford, 1992; LHD, Seton Hall U., 2003. Apprentice with Habimah Theatre, Tel Aviv, 1942-44, a founder, Israel Cameri, 1944-46; theatrical prodns. include A Streetcar Named Desire, London, 1950, The Love of Four Colonels, London, 1950-52, Tonight in Samarkand, N.Y.C., 1954, The Lark, N.Y.C., 1955-56, Rope Dancers, N.Y.C., 1957-58, Sound of Music, N.Y.C., 1959-61, Fiddler on the Roof, various cities, 1968-72, 74, 77, 79, 80, 82-83, 85, 87-96, 98, 2000, 01, 02, The Rothschilds (nat. co.), 1972, Jacques Brel is Alive and Well and Living in Paris, various cities, 1974-75, The Good Doctor, various cities, 1975, Zorba, various cities, 1976, 78, Inspector Gen., N.Y.C., 1978, Threepenny Opera, Mpls., 1983, My Fair Lady, Phoenix, 1988-89, She Loves Me, various cities, 1989-90, Sholom Aleichem Lives, 1997, The Disputation, Miami, 1999, The Gathering, N.Y.C., Miami, 1999, The Chosen, Miami and N.J., 2004; opera prodns. include La Gazza Ladra, Phila., 1990, Abduction from the Seraglio, Cleve., 1992, Ariadne auf Naxos, L.A. Opera, 1992; motion pictures include African Queen, 1951; The Little Kidnappers, 1951, The Enemy Below, 1957, I Want to Live, 1958, The Defiant Ones, 1958 (Academy award nomination), Blue Angel, 1959, My Fair Lady, 1964, Sands of the Kalahari, 1965, The Russians are Coming, 1966, Sweet November, 1967, My Side of the Mountain, 1969, Darker Than Amber, 1970, The Little Ark, 1971, See You in the Morning, 1989, Shattered, 1991, My Family Treasure, 1993, Crime and Punishment, 1993, Shadow Conspiracy, 1995, Second Chances, 1997; also numerous TV appearances, 1954—; star: TV prodns. The Eternal Light, 1958, Look Up and Live, 1958-60; host-editor: TV prodn. Directions 61, 1961; weekly radio program At Home with Theodore Bikel, 1958-63; concert folk singer, 1955-, rec. artist for, Elektra and Reprise; reader books on tape including The Hope (Herman Wouk), The Glory (Herman Wouk), The Name of the Rose (Umberto Eco); Author: Folksongs and Footnotes, 1960, (autobiography) Theo, 1994, rev. edit., 2002. Mem. Nat. Coun. for Arts, 1977-82; founder arts chpt. Am. Jewish Congress, 1961-63, nat. v.p., 1963-70, chmn. governing coun., 1970-80, sr. v.p., 1980-2002; del. Democratic Nat. Conv., 1968. Recipient Emmy award, 1988, Lifetime Achievement award Nat. Found. for Jewish Culture, 1997. Mem. AFTRA, SAG, AGMA, Acad. TV Arts and Scis. (gov. 1961-65), AEA (councillor 1961-64, 1st v.p. 1964-73, pres. 1973-82, pres. emeritus 1982—), Am. Coun. Arts (bd. dirs. 1970-80), Internat. Fedn. Actors (v.p. 1981-91), Associated Actors and Artists of Am. (pres. 1989—), Acad. Motion Picture Arts and Scis., Am. Fedn. Musicians. Address: Associated Actors & Artists of Am Fl 16 165 W 46th St New York NY 10036-2501 E-mail: theoLXX@aol.com. *If I am a universalist-and I believe myself to be one-I derive my general standard of humanity from a particularist experience. For, above all and before all else, I am a Jew. That, to me, means a heightened awareness of the human condition and the sad-sweet knowledge that where we stand someone has stood before. It means a mode of living and a method of survival. Spiritually and culturally to be a Jew is to be a man on the road from Jerusalem to Jerusalem. I am an American; this is my home and my daily solace. Jerusalem, however, is my hope and my inspiration.*

BIKLE, DANIEL DAVID, research physician; b. Harrisburg, Pa., Apr. 25, 1944; s. Charles Augustus and Sarah Elizabeth (Yaukey) B.; m. Mary Elizabeth Wanner, June 20, 1965; children: Christine, Hilary. BA, Harvard U., 1965; MD, U. Pa., 1969, PhD, 1974. Diplomate Am. Bd. Internal Medicine; cert. Nat. Bd. Med. Examiners. Research intern Letterman Army Inst. Research, San Francisco, 1974-79; asst. prof. medicine U. Calif., San Francisco, 1979-86, assoc. prof. medicine, 1986-91, prof. medicine, 1991—, prof. dermatology, 1993—; co-dir. spl. diagnostic treament unit VA Med. Ctr., San Francisco, 1979—. Chmn. academic senate VA Med. Ctr., 2001—03. Editor: Assay of Calcium Regulating Hormones, 1982, Hormonal Regulation of Bone Mineral Homeostasis, 1995; contbr. articles to profl. jours., chpts. to books. Served to col. USAR, 1974-97. Research grantee NIH, 1979—, NASA, 1979—, VA, 1979—. Fellow ACP; mem. Endocrine Soc. (mem. editl. bd. 1984—), Am. Soc. Clin. Investigation, Assn. Am. Physicians (pres.-elect, pres., adv. min metal 2005—) Republican. Mem. Christian Ch. Clubs: Commonwealth of Calif., Harvard (San Francisco). Avocations: biking, skiing, tennis, sailing. Office: VA Med Ctr 4150 Clement St San Francisco CA 94121-1598

BIKLEN, STEPHEN CLINTON, retired diversified financial services company executive; b. Phila., Jan. 27, 1943; s. Paul Frederick and Anne (Chenoweth) Biklen; m. Britta Jorgensen Anderson, Oct. 21, 1989; children: Robert, Theodore. BA, Brown U., 1964; MBA, U. Pa., 1966. Auditor, acct. Coopers & Lybrand, N.Y.C., 1970-73; fin. analyst, contr. Citibank, N.Y.C., 1973-78; v.p. fin. Citibank N.Y. State, Rochester, 1978-80, bus. mgr. student loans, 1980-92, also bd. dirs.; pres., CEO, Student Loan Corp., Rochester, 1993-97, also bd. dirs.; ret., 1997. Mem. Nat. Adv. Com. Student Fin. Assistance, Washington, 1988—96; bd. dirs. Am. Student Assistance, Postsecondary Electronic Standards Coun., treas. Mem.: Consumer Bankers Assn. (chmn. edn. funding com. 1988—90, 1994—97). Avocations: golf, tennis. Personal E-mail: sbiklen@aol.com.

BIKOS, DANIEL ERNEST, meteorologist; b. Endicott, N.Y., Aug. 9, 1973; s. Ernest and Marilyn Bikos; m. Josephine Bikos, Nov. 27, 2004. BS in Meteorology, SUNY, Brockport, 1991—95; MS in Meteorology, U. Okla., Norman, 1995—98. Rsch. coord. Coop. Inst. for Rsch. in the Atmosphere, Fort Collins, Colo., 1998—. Office: CIRA / Colo State Univ 1375 Campus Delivery / Foothills Campus Fort Collins CO 80523 Office Phone: 970-491-3777. Personal E-mail: dan.bikos@alumni.ou.edu. E-mail: bikos@cira.colostate.edu.

BILAND, ALAN THOMAS, computer integrated manufacturing executive; b. Pontiac, Mich., Sept. 13, 1958; s. Alfred T. and Janice J. (Bortreger) B.; m. Martha R. Wegner, Sept. 15, 1979; children: Benjamin A., Elizabeth L. BA in Biology and Psychology, Kalamazoo Coll., 1980; MBA, U. Wis., 1990. Computer aided design/computer aided mfg. Ronningen Rsch., Vicksburg, Mich., 1980-83; sr. industry cons. Computervision, Bedford, Mass., 1981-83; mgr. CAD/CAM N.Am. J.I. Case Co., Racine, Wis., 1985-91; mgr. U.K. Info. Svcs. J.I. Case, Doncaster, England, 1991—98; v.p. & CIO Snap-On Inc., Kenosha, Wis., 1998—2001, v.p. & CIO and pres. diagnostics and info group, 2001—. Mem. Computer and Automated Systems Assn., Soc. Mfg. Engrs. Republican. Lutheran. Avocations: fishing, travel, studying german. Office: Snap-On Inc 10801 Corporate Dr Pleasant Prairie WI 53158-1603

BILANIUK, LARISSA TETIANA, neuroradiologist, educator; b. Ukraine, July 15, 1941; arrived in U.S., 1951; d. Yaroslav and Myroslava Zubal; m. Oleksa-Myron Bilaniuk, Nov. 14, 1964; children; Larissa Indira, Laada Myroslava. BA, Wayne State U., 1961, MD, 1965. Diplomate Am. Bd. Radiology, Am. Bd. Neuroradiology. Resident in radiology Hosp. of U. Pa., Phila., 1966-70; fellow Fondation Ophtalmologique, Paris, 1972; assoc. in radiology U. Pa. Sch. Medicine, Phila., 1973-74, asst. prof., 1974-79, assoc. prof., 1979-82, prof., 1982—; with Children's Hosp. of Phila., 1992—. Reviewer grants rsch. NIH, Washington, 1983—86; vis. prof. Grosshadern Clinics U. Munich, 1988; vis. prof. Inst. Med. Radiology, Kharkiv, Ukraine, 1996; lectr. in field. Co-editor: 3 radiology books; contbr. articles to profl. jours., chapters to books. Rsch. fellow, Cancer Rsch. Ctr., Heidelberg, Fed. Republic Germany, 1967—68. Fellow: Am. Coll. Radiology; mem.: Acad. Med. Sci. Ukraine (elected), Ukranian Med. Assn. N.Am., Soc. Pediatric Radiology, European Soc. Neuroradiology, Am. Soc. Neuroradiology, Radiol. Soc. N.Am., Sigma Xi. Avocations: downhill skiing, alpine hiking, glider flying, photography. Office: Childrens Hosp of Phila 324 S 34th St Philadelphia PA 19104-4345

BILANIUK, OLEKSA MYRON, physicist, researcher; b. Ukraine, Dec. 15, 1926; arrived in U.S., 1951, naturalized, 1957; s. Petro and Maria B.; m. Larissa T. Zubal, Nov. 14, 1964; children: Larissa, Laada. Student, U. Louvain, 1947—51; MS, U. Mich., 1953, MA, 1954, PhD, 1957; Dr. honoris causa (hon.), Nat. Univ. Lviv, Ukraine, 2002. Postdoctoral fellow U. Mich., 1957-58; rsch. assoc., asst. prof. U. Rochester, 1958-64; assoc. prof. physics Swarthmore (Pa.) Coll., 1964-70, prof., 1970-82, Swarthmore Centennial prof., 1982—. Vis. scientist Argentine Atomic Energy Commn., Buenos Aires, 1961-62, Institut de Physique Nucléaire, Orsay, France, spring 1980, Laboratori Nazionali di Frascati, Italy, spring 1984, U. Munich, fall 1988; vis. prof., cons. Delhi U., summer 1966, Shivaji U., Kolhapur, India, summer 1969, Faculté des Scis., Rabat, Morocco, spring 1978, Kiev U. Ukraine, spring 1994, Inst. Med. Radiology, Kharkiv, Ukraine, summer 1996; Fulbright prof. Lima, Peru, summer 1971, Kinshasa, Zaïre, fall 1975. NSF fellow Max Planck Inst., Heidelberg, Germany, 1967-68, Inst. Physique Nucléaire, Orsay, 1972; NAS exch. scientist Kiev, Ukrainian SSR, 1976. Mem. Am. Phys. Soc., Nat. Acad. Scis. Ukraine, Ukrainian Acad. Arts and Scis. in U.S. (pres. 1998-2005), Schevchenko Sci. Soc. in U.S., European Phys. Soc., Société Française de Physique, Phi Beta Kappa, Sigma Xi. Achievements include research on nuclear structure; with Deshpande and Sudarshan challenged the view that Einstein's relativity precludes the possibility of existence of particles that travel faster than light, 1962. Office: Swarthmore Coll Dept Physics Swarthmore PA 19081 E-mail: obilani1@swarthmore.edu. *The most cherished possession of humanity is its spiritual and intellectual heritage. Contributing to the enrichment of this heritage I consider to be a human's loftiest goal.*

BILAS, RICHARD A., economist; b. Passaic, NJ, Feb. 3, 1935; s. Nestor Joseph and Helen Evelyn (Smith) B.; m. Janet Lianne Harris, June 23, 1956; children: Cathy, David, Ami. AB in Math., Duke U., 1956; PhD in Econs., U. Va., 1963. Asst., then assoc. prof. U. So. Calif., L.A., 1962-67; from assoc. prof. to prof. Ga. State U., Atlanta, 1967—70; E.C. Reid prof. econs. Calif. State U., Bakersfield, 1970-87, prof. emeritus Calif., 2002—; commr. Calif. Energy Commn., Sacramento, 1987-95; Brock chair in energy econs. and policy Sarkeys Energy Ctr., Norman, Okla., 1995—96; commr. Calif. Pub. Utilities Commn., San Francisco, 1997—2002. Program on workable energy regulation bd. U. Calif., 1990—95; pres. Calif. Pub. Utilities Commn., 1998—99. Author: Microeconomics, 1967, 71, Problems in Microeconomics, 1972, Macroeconomics, 1974; mem. editl. bd. Western Econ. Assn.'s Contemporary Econ. Policy, 1990—. Active Rep. Ctrl. Com., Kern County, Calif., 1978-82; pres. bd. dirs. Mendocino Art Ctr., 2000—; treas. Cmty. Found. Mendocino County, 2003-. Nat. Def. fellow U. Va., 1959-62, Fulbright fellow to the Philippines, 1966-67; recipient Honor cert. Freedoms Found., 1977, 79. Mem. Mont Pelerin Soc., Masons, Phi Beta Kappa. Republican. Episcopalian. Avocations: golf, model trains. Home: PO Box 2466 Mendocino CA 95460-2466 Office Phone: 707-937-3913. Business E-Mail: rbilas@mcn.org.

BILBAN, FRANK J., manufacturing executive; Various financial positions Outboard Marine Corp., 1978—91; div. controller, CT Film Div. Rexene Corp., 1991—96; v.p., CFO Wedge Dia-log Inc., 1996—98; exec. v.p., CFO Alpha Holdings Inc., Dallas, 1998—2000; CFO Encore Wire Corp., McKinney, Tex., 2000—, v.p. fin., treas. & sec., 2000—. Bd. dir. Boys and Girls Club of Collin County. Office: Encore Wire Corp 1410 Millwood Rd Mc Kinney TX 75069

BILBRAY, JAMES HUBERT, retired congressman, lawyer, consultant; b. Las Vegas, Nev., May 19, 1938; s. James A. and Ann E. (Miller) B.; m. Michaelene Mercer, Jan. 1960; children: Bridget, Kevin, Erin, Shannon Student, Brigham Young U., 1957-58, U. Nev., Las Vegas, 1958-60; BA, Am. U., 1962; JD, Washington Coll. Law, 1964; D of Laws (hon.), U Nev. Las Vegas, 2001. Bar: Nev. 1965. Staff mem. Senator Howard Cannon U.S. Senate, 1960-64; dep. dist. atty. Clark County, Nev., 1965-68; mem. Lovell, Bilbray & Potter, Las Vegas, 1969-87, Nev. Senate, 1980-86, chmn. taxation com., 1983-86, chmn. interim com. on pub. broadcasting, 1983; mem. 100th-103rd Congresses from 1st Nev. dist., 1987-95; mem. fgn. affairs com., 1987-88; mem. house armed svs. com., mem. small bus. com., chmn. procurement, taxation and tourism subcom., 1989-95; ptnr. Alcalde & Fay, Arlington, Va., 1995—. Mem. subcoms. Africa, trade exports and tourism, select com. on intelligence, 1993-95; alt. mcpl. judge City of Las Vegas, 1987-89; del. North Atlantic Alliance, 1989-95; bd. visitors U.S. Mil. Acad.,

West Point, 1995-99, vice chmn., 1996-97; mem. adv. bd. Ex-Import Bank U.S., 1996-97; mem. adv. com. U.S. Nat. Security Policy, 2000-01. Bd. regents U. Nev. Sys., 1968—72; mem. Nat. Coun. State Govts. Commn. on Arts and Historic Preservation; mem. bd. visitors USAF Acad., 1991—93; mem. U.S. Nat. Security Policy Bd. Adv. Com., 2000—01, Dem. Nat. Com., 1996—; Nev. chmn. Kerry for Pres., 2004; mem. Calif.-Nev. High Speed Train Commn., 2005—, US Base Closing Commn., 2005. Named Outstanding Alumnus U. Nev., Las Vegas, 1979, Man of Yr. Am. Diabetes Assn., 1989, Man of Yr. Haddassah (Nev.), 1990 Mem. Nev. State Bar Assn., Clark County Bar Assn., U. Nev.-Las Vegas Alumni Assn. (pres. 1964-69, Humanitarian of Yr. 1984), Rotary, Phi Alpha Delta, Sigma Chi, KC. Democrat. Roman Catholic.

BILDERBACK, DONALD HEYWOOD, physicist, researcher; b. Usumbura, Burundi, Mar. 6, 1947; came to U.S., 1950; s. Allen H. and Lillian A. (Watkins) B.; m. Becky B. Belcher, Sept. 16, 1969; 1 child, Douglas H. BS in Physics, Seattle Pacific U., 1969; PhD of Physics, Purdue U., 1975. Mgr. Material Sci. X-ray Cornell U., Ithaca, N.Y., 1975-78, pres. Multiwire Labs., 1981—. Assoc. prof. Applied and Engring. Physics Cornell U., Ithaca, 1990, assoc. dir. CHESS; cons. several Synchrotron Radiation Labs., 1985—. Corr. Synchrotron Radiation News, Berkshire, U.K., 1987—; editl. bd. mem. Jour. Synchrotron Radiation, Copenhagen, 1991-2002; co-editor: (series) World Sci. Publ. Co., 1994—. Recipient award R&D Mag., 1993; co-recipient Compton award Argonne Lab., 1998. Mem. AAAS, Am. Phys. Soc., Am. Crystallographic Assn., Am. Sci. Affiliation. Republican. Achievements include developing capillary x-ray optics on a micron scale; inventor of real-time back-reflection Laue camera and the transmission x-ray mirror; developed of energy recovery linac technology for future high-brightness x-ray source. Office: Cornell Univ 281 Wilson Lab Ithaca NY 14853-8001 Office Phone: 607-255-0916. Business E-Mail: dhb2@cornell.edu.

BILDERSEE, ROBERT ALAN, lawyer; b. Albany, NY, Jan. 22, 1942; s. Max U. and Hannah (Marks) B.; m. Ellen Bernstein, June 9, 1963; 1 child, Jennifer M. BA, Columbia Coll., 1962, MA, 1964; LLB, Yale U., 1967. Assoc. Wolf Block Schorr & Solis Cohen, Phila., 1967-72; sole practice Phila., 1972-73; assoc., then ptnr. Fox Rothschild, O'Brien & Frankel, Phila., 1973-80; ptnr. Morgan Lewis & Bockius LLP, Phila., 1980-97; founding ptnr. Bildersee & Silbert, LLP, Phila., 1997—. Lectr. Temple U. Sch. Law, Phila., 1978-91; asst. in instrn. Yale U. Law Sch., New Haven, 1966; bd. dirs. ASPA Benefits Coun. Delaware Valley; mem. Northeast region and Mid-Atlantic region pension liaison coms. IRS. Author: Pension Regulation Manual, Pension Administrator's Forms and Checklists, 1987; contbg. author: Employee Benefits Handbook, 1982-98; editor: Beyond the Fringes; contbr. articles to profl. jours. Woodrow Wilson fellow, 1962. Mem. ABA, Pa. Bar Assn., Phila. Bar Assn. Avocation: wildlife photography. Office: Bildersee and Silbert LLP PO Box 599 Abington PA 19001-0599 Office Phone: 215-914-0414. E-mail: erisaplus@aol.com.

BILELLO, JOHN CHARLES, engineering educator, director; b. Bklyn., Oct. 15, 1938; s. Charles and Catherine (Buonadonna) B.; m. Mary Josephine Gloria, Aug. 1, 1959; children: Andrew Charles, Peter Angelo, Matthew Jonathan. B.E., NYU, 1960, MS, 1962; PhD, U. Ill., 1965. Sr. rsch. engr. Gen. Telephone & Electronics Lab., Bayside, N.Y., 1965-67; mem. faculty SUNY, Stony Brook, 1967-87, asst. prof., 1967-71, assoc. prof., 1971-75, prof. engring., 1975-87, dean, 1977-81; dean Sch. Engring and Computer Sci., prof. mech. engring. Calif. State U., Fullerton, 1986-89; prof. materials sci. and engring., prof. applied physics U. Mich., Ann Arbor, 1989—2004, dir. Ctr. Nanomaterials Scis., 1995—, emeritus, 2005—. Vis. rsch. assoc., Calif. Inst. Tech., Pasadena, 2003, vis. prof. Poly. of Milan, 1973-74; vis. scholar King's Coll., London U., 1983; vis. fellow NATO exchange scholar Oxford U., 1986; project dir. synchroton topography project Univ. Consortium, 1981-86; NATO vis. fellow Oxford (Eng.) U., 1998—. NATO sr. faculty fellow Enrico Fermi Center, Milan, Italy, 1973 Fellow Am. Soc. for Metals; mem. AIME, Am. Phys. Soc., Materials Rsch. Soc. Office: U Mich Dept Material Sci Engring Ann Arbor MI 48109 Office Phone: 734-764-6128.

BILELLO, JOSEPH JOHN, architecture educator, programs coordinator; b. N.Y., N.Y., June 4, 1950; s. Joseph R. and Julia R. (Gazovic) B.; m. Theresa Marie Evanko, Jan. 1, 1992; 1 child, Zoe Elizabeth. BA, U. Pa., 1972; M in arch., Washington U., 1976; PhD, U. Md., 1993. Historic architect Nat. Park Svc., Denver, 1976-79; designer Bull Field Volkman Stockwell, San Francisco, 1979-80; asst. prof. architecture King Faisal U., Damman, Saudi Arabia, 1981-82, Calif. Coll. Arts & Crafts, San Francisco, 1983-84; prin. Urban Dynamics Grove, San Francisco, 1984-87; edn. dir. AIA, Washington, 1987-95; assoc. prof., profl. programs coord. Coll. Arch. Tex. Tech U., 1995—. Contbg. editor Soc. for Coll. & U. Planning, Ann Arbor, Mich., 1994—; design cons. Joseph Bilello, Washington, 1980—; adj. prof. Cath. U., Washington, 1988-95; edn. cons. Edn. Archs. for a Sustainable Environment, Muncie, Ind., 1994—. Author: Design/Practice Education, 1995, Deciding to Build, 1993; painter. Recipient Disting. Alumni award Washington U., 1995, Creative Achievement award Assn. Collegiate Schs. Arch., 1993; fellow Am. Arch. Found., 1992. Mem. Am. Inst. Arch., Soc. Coll. Univ. Planning, Nat. Trust for Hist. Preservation. Avocations: painting, playing music, golf, skiing, hiking. Office: Tex Tech U Coll Arch Lubbock TX 79409

BILES, GLORIA C., historian, educator; d. George Graham and Lillian Oriol Crevenstene; m. Wiley Biles, June 21, 1949. BBA, U. Houston, 1947, MEd, 1957, MA, 1972; PhD, Rice U., 1979. Cert. tchr. Tex. Tchr. mid. and high sch. Houston Ind. Sch. Dist., 1957—67; lectr. U. Houston, Clear Lake, 1979—81, U. Houston, West Houston, 1979—81; adj. prof. Houston Bapt. Univ., 1984—86, asst. prof., 1986—93, assoc. prof., 1993—2002; ret., 2002. Mem. Houston Grand Opera, 1952—, Gilbert and Sullivan Soc., 1952—, Heritage Soc., 1979—, PBS, 1988—, Am. Carousel Soc., 1989—, Houston Symphony Soc., 1989—, Bush Presdl. Libr., Coll. Station, Tex., 1999—, Nat. Trust for Hist. Preservation, Mus. of Printing History, 1999—. Mem.: NEA, AAUP, Am. Hist. Assn., Phi Kappa Phi, Delta Kappa Gamma (chair coms.), Phi Alpha Theta, Phi Gamma Nu, Alpha Mu Gamma (hon.). Avocation: collecting antique carousel horses, Steuben glass and miniature animals.

BILES, JOHN ALEXANDER, pharmacologist, chemist, educator; b. Del Norte, Colo., May 4, 1923; s. John Alexander and Lillie (Willis) Biles; m. Margaret Pauline Off, June 19, 1943; children: Paula M. Murphy, M. Suzanne. BS, U. Colo., 1944, PhD (AEC fellow), 1949. Prof. pharm. chemistry Midwestern U., 1949-50; asst. prof. pharm. chemistry Ohio State U., 1950-52, U. So. Calif., L.A., 1952-53, assoc. prof., 1953-57, prof., 1957-98, disting. emeritus prof., 1999—, dean, prof. pharm. scis., 1968-94, John Stauffer dean's chair in pharmacy, 1988-94, John Biles prof., 1994—, Disting. emeritus prof., 1998—. Bd. dirs. Marion Merrell Dow; cons. Allergan Pharms., 1953—68, Region IX Bur. health Manpoer Edn., Health Resources Adminstrn., 1973, Region X, 1974, Region VI, 1975, VA Ctrl. Office Pharmacy Svcs.; mem. Nat. Adv. Coun., Edn. Health Professions, 1970—71, nat. study commn. on pharmacy, 1972—75; mem. adv. panel on pharmacy for study costs of educating profls. Nat. Acad. Scis., Inst. Medicine, 1973; mem. interdisciplinary tng. in health scis. com. Bur. Health Manpower Edn., 1972, post contrn. evaluation com., 72, health facilities survey com., 71; mem. adv. coun. Howard U. Coll. Pharmacy, 1985—90; bd. grants Am. Found. for Pharm. Edn., 1996—. Reviewer: Jour. AMA1, 1982—90. Bd. grants Am. Found. Pharm. Edn., 1996—, bd. dirs., 1999—2001, chmn. bd. grants, 1998—; elder Presbyn. Ch., Pacific Palisades, Calif., 1997—. Recipient S.C. Assocs. award for excellence in tchg., 1962; scholar Lehn and Fink, 1945. Fellow: Am. Assn. Pharm. Scientists, Acad. Pharm. Scis.; mem.: Calif. Pharm. Assn., Nat. Adv. Health Svcs. Coun. (bur. heatlh svcs. rsch. 1974), Am. Assn. Colls. Pharmacy (study commn. on pharmacy 1973—75, pres. 1990—91), Am. Cancer Soc. (mem. sci. adv. com. Los Angeles County), Am. Pharm. Assn., Phi Kappa Phi. Office: 1985 Zonal Ave Los Angeles CA 90089-0105 Office Phone: 323-442-1021. Personal E-mail: BilesJohn@aol.com, jbiles8263@charter.net.

BILEYDI, SUMER, advertising agency executive; b. Antalya, Turkey, Feb. 7, 1936; came to U.S., 1957; s. Abdurrahman M. and Neriman (Akman) B.; m. Lois E. Goode, Dec. 30, 1961; children: Can M., Sera N. BA, Mich. State U., 1961, MA, 1962. Mktg. cons. Export Promotion Ctr., Ankara, 1962; planner Gardner Advt. Agy., St. Louis, 1963-65; planning supr. Batten, Barton, Durstine & Osborn, N.Y.C., 1965-69; assoc. dir. Ketchum, Macleod & Grove, Pitts., 1969-73; sr. ptnr., dir. Carmichael Lynch, Inc., Mpls., 1974-91, sr. ptnr., 1992-98; CEO, pres. Manajans Thompson AS, Istanbul, Turkey, 1999-2001, ret., 2001. Cons. Carmichael-Lynch, Mpls., 1999-2004; cons. Leading Ind. Advt. Agy. Network, 1987-89, chmn., pres., 1989-91; CEO, pres. Global Mktg. Comm. Cons., Naples, Fla. Contbr. articles to profl. jours. Mem. Am. Mktg. Assn., Advt. Rsch. Found. Home: 4718 Navassa Ln Naples FL 34119-9554 Office Phone: 239-594-5056. E-mail: lbileydi@aol.com.

BILGER, BRUCE R., lawyer; b. Balt., Feb. 27, 1952; BA, Dartmouth Coll., 1973; MBA, JD, U. Va., 1977. Bar: Tex. 1977. Mem. Vinson & Elkins LLP, Houston, chair Energy Practice Group, co-head Bus. & Internat. Law Sect. Mem. Phi Beta Kappa. Office: Vinson & Elkins LLP 2300 First City Tower 1001 Fannin St Houston TX 77002-6760 Business E-Mail: bbilger@velaw.com.

BILGIN, AZIZE AZRA, environmental engineer, researcher; b. Tarsus, Turkey, Aug. 25, 1975; d. Ali Cevat and Gulnaz Bilgin; m. Haluk Pehlivanoglu, Oct. 5, 2002. BS, Istanbul Tech. U., Istanbul-Turkey, 1997, MS, 1999; PhD, U. Colo.-Boulder, Boulder, Colo., 2004. Postdoctoral scholar Calif. Inst. of Tech., Pasadena, Calif., 2005—; staff engr. Arcadis G&M, Denver, 2004—. Rsch. asst. U. Colo.-Boulder, Colo.; presenter in field. Contbr. articles. Fellow Future Academicians, Cukurova U., 1993-1997; grantee PhD, Higher Edn. Coun.-Turkey, 1999-2003; scholar Outstanding Students, Sabanci Corp., 1993-1997, Outstanding students, Tarsus Am. Alumni Assn., 1986-1993. Mem.: Am. Water Works Assn. (rocky mountain region). Achievements include research in In-situ remediation of acid mine drainage. Office: Calif Inst Tech 1200 Calif Blvd 138-78 Pasadena CA 91125 Office Phone: 626-395-4406. Personal E-mail: azrabilgin@yahoo.com. Business E-Mail: abilgin@caltech.edu.

BILHEIMER, MARGARET IRENE, Spanish language educator; b. Bethlehem, Pa., Jan. 22, 1948; d. John J. and Louise E. Blatnik. BA, U. Pitts., 1969; MEd, Lehigh U., 1973, EdD, 1992. Tchr. Spanish and English Bethlehem Sch. Dist.; bilingual rsch. asst. Lehigh U., Bethlehem; program dir., dir. advt. De Sales U., Center Valley, Pa.; lectr. Cedar Crest Coll., Allentown, Pa.; tchr. Spanish, reading specialist Northampton (Pa.) Area Sch. Dist. Home: 1109 W North St Bethlehem PA 18018

BILINSKY, YAROSLAV, political scientist; b. Lutsk, Ukraine, Feb. 26, 1932; s. Peter Bilinsky and Natalia (Balabaj) Bilinska; m. Wira Rusaniwskyj, Feb. 18, 1962; children: Peter Yaroslav, Sophia Vera Yaroslava, Nadia Yaroslava, Mark Paul Yaroslav. AB magna cum laude, Harvard U., 1954, postgrad. in Soviet affairs, 1956-57; PhD, Princeton U., 1958. Asso. Harvard U. Russian Research Center, 1956-58; instr. polit. sci. Douglass Coll., Rutgers U., New Brunswick, N.J., 1958-61; asst. prof. U. Del., Newark, 1961-65, assoc. prof., 1965-69, prof., 1969—2002, prof. emeritus, 2002—. Vis. instr. U. Pa., 1961; vis. prof. Columbia U., 1976 Author: The Second Soviet Republic: The Ukraine after World War II, 1964, Endgame in NATO's Enlargement: The Baltic States and Ukraine, 1999. Corr. sec. Peter and Paul Ukrainian Orthodox Ch., Wilmington, Del., 1965-66, trustee, 1967-71. Mem. Am. Assn. Advancement Slavic Studies (pres. Mid-Atlantic Slavic Conf. 1992-93), Ukrainian Acad. Arts and Scis. in U.S. (pres. 1987-90). Home: 2 Mimosa Dr Newark DE 19711-7523 Office Phone: 302-831-2355. E-mail: yby@udel.edu. *My favorite quotation is from Shakespeare: The readiness is all. I have tried to be always prepared to serve my country, my students, and my family. I am ready to live and, if it be God's will, ready to die.*

BILIRAKIS, MICHAEL, congressman, lawyer, corporate financial executive; b. Tarpon Springs, Fla., July 16, 1930; s. Emmanuel and Irene (Pikramenos) B.; m. Evelyn Miaoulis, Dec. 27, 1959; children: Emmanuel, Gus. BS in Enring., U. Pittsburgh, 1959; student, George Washington U., 1959-60; JD, U. Fla., 1963; JD (hon.), Stetson U.; hon. degree, U. Tampa. Bar: Fla. 1964; cert. coll. tchr., Fla. Atty., small businessman, Pinellas and Pasco Counties, Fla., 1968—; mem. US Congress from 9th Dist. Fla., 1983—, mem. energy & commerce com., vice chair vets. affairs com., chair health subcom. Mem. Rep. Task Force on Social Security; co-chmn. Task Force on Infant Mortality; founder, charter pres. Tarpon Springs Vol. Ambulance Service; dir. Greek Studies program U. Fla.; dir. emeritus Juvenile Diabetes and Hospice; mem. Pres.' Coun. U. Fla. Sgt. USAF, 1951-55. Named Citizen of Yr. Greater Tarpon Springs, 1972-73, Man of Yr. United Way, 1989-90. Mem. Am. Legion (comdr. 1977-79), VFW, Amvets, USAF Sgts., NCOA, Air Force Assn., Greater Tarpon Springs C. of C. (past pres., dir.), Pinellas C. of C. (gov.), West Pasco Bar Assn., Am. Judicature Soc., Fla. Bar Assn., Gator Boosters, Fla. Blue Key (hon.), Mason (33 degree), Shriner, Jester, Moose, Elks, Rotary, Eastern Star, Phi Alpha Delta, Sigma Pi. Lodges: Masons; Shriners; Moose; Tarpon Springs Rotary; Elks; Eastern Star; White Shrine of Jerusalem. Republican. Greek Orthodox. Office: US Ho of Reps 2408 Rayburn Ho Office Bldg Washington DC 20515-0909 also: Dist Office 10330 N Dale Mabry Ste 205 Tampa FL 33618*

BILKA, PAUL JOSEPH, retired physician; b. N.Y.C., Oct. 12, 1919; s. John and Josephine (Hlavaty) B.; m. Madge Ayres Mussey, Dec. 26, 1943. BS, Trinity Coll., Hartford, Conn., 1940; MD, Columbia U., 1943; MS in Medicine, U. Minn., 1950. Intern Hartford Hosp., 1944-45; fellow in internal medicine Mayo Found, Rochester, Minn., 1947-50; asst. in rheumatology Mayo Clinic, 1949-50; practice medicine specializing in rheumatology Mpls., 1950-91. Clin. prof. medicine U. Minn. Med. Sch.; cons. Mpls. VA Hosp., med. staff, 1991-. Author numerous papers in field; also producer films on rheumatology. Served to capt. M.C. AUS, 1945-47. Mem. Am. Coll. Rheumatology (master designation 1992), Nat. Soc. Clin. Rheumatology (pres. 1985-87). Clubs: Lafayette (Minnetonka, Minn.). Home: 4384 Manitou Rd Excelsior MN 55331-9445

BILL, TONY, producer, director; b. San Diego, Aug. 23, 1940; Student, Notre Dame U. Founder Bill/Phillips Prodns. (with Julia and Michael Phillips), 1971-73; ind. producer, 1973—. Bd. govs. Acad. Motion Picture Arts and Scis. Prodr.: Deadhead Miles, Steelyard Blues, 1973, The Sting, 1974, Going in Style, 1979, Hearts of the West, 1975, Harry and Walter Go to New York, 1976, Boulevard Nights, 1979; exec. producer: The Little Dragons, 1978; dir.: The Ransom of Red Chief, 1977, My Bodyguard, 1980, Six Weeks, 1982, Love Thy Neighbor, 1984, Five Corners, 1987, Crazy People, 1990, Untamed Heart, 1993, A Home of Our Own, 1993, Next Door, 1995, Beyond the Call, 1996, Oliver Twist, 1997, A Change of Snow, 1998, Harlan County War, 2000, In the Time of the Butterflies, 2001, Whitewash the Clarence Brandley Story, 2002, Last Call, 2002. Office: Barnstorm Films 73 Market St Venice CA 90291-3603

BILLAUER, BARBARA PFEFFER, lawyer, educator; b. Aug. 9, 1951; d. Harry George and Evelyn (Newman) Pfeffer. BS with honors, Cornell U., 1972; JD, Hofstra U., 1975; MA, NYU, 1982; cert. in risk scis. and pub. policy, Johns Hopkins U., 1999. Bar: N.Y. 1976, Fed. Dist. Ct. N.Y. 1977, U.S. Ct. Appeals (2d cir.) 1978, U.S. Supreme Ct. 1984. Assoc. Bower & Gardner, N.Y.C., 1974-78; sr. trial atty. Joseph W. Conklin, N.Y.C., 1978-80; assoc. dept. head Curtis, Mallet-Prevost, Colt & Mosle, N.Y.C., 1980-82; ptnr. Anderson, Russell, Kill & Olick, N.Y.C., 1982-86, Stroock & Stroock & Lavan, N.Y.C., 1986-90; ptnr., chair environ. and toxic tort practice Keck, Mahin, Cate & Koether, 1990-93; prin. Barbara P. Billauer & Assocs., Lido Beach, N.Y., 1993—. Vis. scholar Johns Hopkins U. Sch. Pub. Health, 1998-99; faculty SUNY Stony Brook Med. Sch.; adj. assoc. prof. NYU Grad. Sch., 1982-88; lectr. Rutger's U. Med. Sch.; jud. screening com. Coordinated Bar Assn., 1983-86; mem. spl panel Citywide Ct. Adminstrn. 1982-85; bd. dirs. Weizmann Inst., Am. Com. Co-author: The Lender's Guide to Environmental Law: Risk and Liability, 1993. Fellow Am. Bar Found.; mem. ABA (indoor air polution 1990-93), Met. Womens Bar Assn. (v.p. 1981-83, pres. 1983-85, chmn. bd. 1985-87), Nat. Conf. Womens Bar Assn. (bd. dirs., v.p. 1989-95), Internat. Coun. Shopping Ctrs. (environ. com.), Brit. Occupl. Hygiene Soc., Environment Toxic Torts. Home: 2867 Tilden St NW Washington DC 20008-3837 E-mail: omniscience@starpower.net.

BILLER, JOEL WILSON, lawyer, retired diplomat; b. Milw., Jan. 17, 1929; s. Saul Earl and Mildred (Wilson) B.; m. Geraldine Pollack, May 1, 1955; children— Sydney, Andrew, Charles. BA, U. Wis., 1950; JD, U. Mich., 1953; MA, Northwestern U., 1959. Bar: Wis. 1953. Atty., Milw., 1953-55; vice consul Am. consulate, Le Havre, France, 1956-58; econ. officer Am. Embassy, The Hague, Netherlands, 1959-62; internat. relations officer State Dept., Washington, 1962-66; econ. officer, asst. dir. AID mission, Quito, Ecuador, 1966-69; econ. counselor Am. embassy, Buenos Aires, 1969-71; dir. AID mission, Santiago, Chile, 1971-73; spl. asst. to undersec. state for econ. affairs Washington, 1973-74; spl. asst. to dep. sec. state, 1974; dep. asst. sec. state for comml. and spl. bilateral affairs, 1974-76; dep. asst. sec. state for transp., telecommunications and comml. affairs, after, 1976; sr. v.p. Manpower Inc., Milw., 1979-97, sr. v.p., gen. counsel, 1997-98, sr. v.p. internat. corp. affairs, 1999—; pres. Internat. Confedn. of Pvt. Employment Agys., 2004—. Mem. Am. Fgn. Service Assn. Office: Manpower Inc 5301 N Ironwood Rd PO Box 2053 Milwaukee WI 53201-2053

BILLER, JOSE, neurologist; b. Montevideo, Uruguay, Jan. 18, 1948; B in Medicine, A.V. Acevedo Inst., Montevideo, Uruguay, 1965; MD, U. de la Republica, Montevideo, Uruguay, 1974. Diplomate Am. Bd. Psychiatry and Neurology (bd. dirs. 1994—), Am. Bd. Neurology and Vascular Neurology. Intern Maciel Hosp., Montevideo, Uruguay, 1974—76, Columbus Hosp., Chgo., 1976-77; resident in neurology Henry Ford Hosp., Detroit, 1977-78, Loyola U. Hosp., Hines VA Hosp., Ill., 1978-80, chief resident neurology, 1979—80; fellow cerebral vascular diseases Bowman Gray Sch. Med., Winston Salem, NC, 1980-81, instr. neurology, 1981; asst. prof. neurology Loyola U., Chgo., 1982-84, U. Iowa Coll. Medicine, Iowa City, 1984-87, assoc. prof. neurology, 1987-90, prof. neurology, 1990-91; prof. Northwestern Sch. Medicine, Chgo., 1991-94; dir. stroke program, dir. acute stroke care unit Northwestern Meml. Hosp., Chgo., 1991-94; prof., chmn. dept. neurology Ind. U., 1994—2003; prof., assoc. chmn. dept. neurology Loyola U. Stritch Sch. Med., Chgo., 2003—, dir. neurology residency training program, 2003—05, acting chmn. dept. neurology, 2004—05, prof., chmn. dept. neurology, 2005. Prof. ad-honorem U. of the Republic Sch. of Medicine, Uruguay, 1997—; mem. editl. bd. Stroke, Stroke-Clin. Update, Neurol. Rsch.; Internat. bd. editors: CNS Drugs; cons. physician neurology svc. VA Hosp., Iowa City, 1984-91, staff physician Northwestern Meml. Hosp., Chgo., 1991-94; neurology cons. Rehab. Inst. Chgo., 1991-94; active med. staff Ind. U. Hosps., 1994-03, Loyola U. Hosp., 2003—, cons. Roudebush VA Med. Ctr., 1994-03. Author, co-author of more than 430 articles, book chpts., abstracts; 6 edited books; editor Seminars in Cerebrovascular Diseases and Stroke, Jour. Stroke and Cerebrovascular Diseases. Fellow ACP, Am. Acad. Neurology, Stroke Coun. Am. Heart Assn.; mem. AMA, N.Y. Acad. Sci., Am. Soc. for Neurology Investigation, Internat. Stroke Soc., Inter-Am. Coll. Physicians and Surgeons, Am. Neurolog. Assn., Am. Heart Assn., Argentinian Neurol. Soc. (hon.), Uruguayan Neurol. Soc. (hon.). Office: Maguire Bldg 105/2700 2160 S First Ave Maywood IL 60153 Business E-Mail: jbiller@lumc.edu.

BILLERA, LOUIS J(OSEPH), mathematics professor; b. N.Y.C., Apr. 12, 1943; s. Joseph James and Florence Ann B.; m. Jeanne Marie Kebba, June 20, 1964; children: John L., Mark A. BS, Rensselaer Poly. Inst., 1964; postgrad., Princeton U., 1964-65; MA, CUNY, 1967, PhD, 1968. Asst. prof. Cornell U., Ithaca, N.Y., 1968-73; postdoctoral fellow Hebrew Univ., Jerusalem, Israel, 1969; assoc. prof. Cornell U., Ithaca, N.Y., 1973-80, prof. math., 1980—, Rutgers U., New Brunswick, N.J., 1985-89, assoc. dir. DIMACS Ctr. Discrete Math./Theoretical Computer, 1988-89; acting dir. Ctr. for Applied Math., Cornell U., Ithaca, N.Y., 1995-96; rsch. prof. Math. Sci. Rsch. Inst., Berkeley, 1996-97. Vis. rsch. assoc. Brandeis U., Waltham, Mass., 1974-75; prof. invité CORE, U. Catholique de Louvain, Belgium, 1980; vis. prof. Mittag-Leffler Inst., Sweden, 1992, 2005. Contbr. over 65 articles to profl. jours. Fellow Ednl. Testing Svc., 1964-65, NDEA, 1965-68, NSF, 1969; recipient D.R. Fulkerson prize Am. Math. Soc. and Math. Programming Soc., 1994. Mem.: Math. Assn. Am., Am. Math. Soc. Office: Cornell U Dept Math Malott Hall Ithaca NY 14853-4201

BILLETER, ANNE MARGARET, librarian; b. Sanford, Fla., Apr. 11, 1946; d. Jack J. and Barbara (Whipple) B.; m. Robert Luis Hoolko, Nov. 25, 1972; 1 child, Steven John. BA, Rutgers U., 1968; MLS, U. N.C., 1969; PhD, U. Ill., 1979. Youth svcs. libr. Rockingham County Libr., Eden, N.C., 1969-71; rsch. assoc. Libr. Rsch. Ctr. U. Ill., Urbana, 1972-74; vis. lectr. Sch. Libr. Sci. U. So. Calif., L.A., 1975-77; children's libr. Glendale (Calif.) Pub. Libr., 1976-78; ref. libr., lectr. So. Oreg. State Coll., Ashland, 1980; head ref. svcs. Josephine County Libr., Grants Pass, Oreg., 1981-85; adult svcs. coord. Jackson County Libr., Medford, Oreg., 1985—97, mgr. collection dept., 1997—2001, mgr. children's, young adult and outreach, 2001—03, mgr. children's, young adult and south region, 2003—. Compiler: Directory of Southern Oregon Libraries, 1980. Trustee Josephine County Hist. Soc., Grants Pass, 1981-88, So. Oreg. Hist. Soc., Medford, 1992-98. Fellow U. N.C., 1969. Mem. ALA, So. Oreg. Libr. Fedn., Oreg. Libr. Assn. (v.p., pres.-elect 1993-94, pres. 1994-95), Beta Phi Mu, Phi Kappa Phi. Avocations: reading, genealogy, quilting. Home: 4999 Griffin Creek Rd Medford OR 97501-9586 Office: Jackson County Libr Svcs Ashland Libr 410 Siskiyou Blvd Ashland OR 97520 Office Phone: 541-774-6987. Business E-Mail: billeter@jcls.org.

BILLETER, ROBERT JAMES, newspaper publisher; b. Clarksburg, W.Va., Aug. 16, 1926; s. Arch and Mabel Edith (Westfall) B.; m. Eileen Billie Horvath, Apr. 14, 1972; 1 child, William Fletcher. BS, W.Va. U., 1951. Editor Pendleton Times, Franklin, W.Va., 1951-53; copy editor Herald-Dispatch, Huntington, 1953-54; reporter The Post, Morgantown, 1954-56; copy editor Sun-Telegraph, Pitts., 1956-60, Post-Gazette, Pitts., 1960-81, night city editor, 1981-85, makeup editor, 1985-91; pub. The Weston (W.Va.) Democrat, 1992—. With U.S. Army, 1945-47. Episcopalian. Avocations: wine tasting, sailing, hiking, skiing. Home: One E 4th St Weston WV 26452 Office: The Weston Democrat 306 Main Ave Weston WV 26452-2046 Business E-Mail: news@westondemocrat.com.

BILLIAS, GEORGE ATHAN, historian, educator; b. Lynn, Mass., June 26, 1919; s. Athan O. and Grace (Papadakis) B.; m. Joyce Baldwin, Dec. 28, 1948 (dec.); children: Stephen, Athan, Nancy; m. Margaret Neussendorfer, Aug. 17, 1986. BA magna cum laude, Bates Coll., 1948; MA, Columbia U., 1949, PhD, 1958. Nat. def. historian USAF, 1951-54; instr. U. Maine, 1954-57, asst. prof., 1957-59, assoc. prof., 1959-62, Clark U., Worcester, Mass., 1962-66, prof. Am. history, 1966—, Jacob and Frances Hiatt prof. history, 1983-89, Jacob and Frances Hiatt prof. emeritus, 1989—. Author: Massachusetts Land Bankers of 1740, 1959, General John Glover and His Marblehead Mariners, 1960, Elbridge Gerry: Founding Father and Republican Statesman, 1976; editor, contbr.: George Washington's Generals, 1964, Law and Authority in Colonial America: Selected Essays, 1965, The American Revolution: How Revolutionary Was It?, 1965, 4th edit., 1989, Interpretations of American History: Patterns and Perspectives, 2 vols., 1967, 7th edit., 2000, George Washington's Opponents, 1969, The Federalists: Realists or Ideologues?, 1970, American History: Retrospect and Prospect, 1971, Perspectives on Early American History, 1973, American Constitutionalism Abroad, 1990, The Republican Synthesis Revisited: Essays in Honor of George Athan Billias, 1992, George Washington's Generals and George Washington's Opponents, 1993, George Bancroft, Master Historian, 2004; contbr. numerous articles to profl. jours. With M.C., U.S. Army, 1941-46, ETO. Decorated Bronze Star; Am. Philos. Soc. grantee, 1965; Guggenheim fellow, 1961-62, Am. Coun. Learned Socs. fellow, 1968-69, NEH fellow, 1970-71, 79, 86, Huntington Libr. fellow, 1989-90. Mem.: Am. Antiquarian Soc. (honoree symposium The Republican Synthesis Revisited 1989), Mass. Hist. Soc., Am. Hist. Assn., Inst. Early Am. History and Culture (coun. 1969—72), Columbia Seminar in Early Am. History, Phi Beta Kappa. Office: Clark U Dept History Worcester MA 01610

BILLICK, BRIAN, professional football coach; b. Fairborne, Ohio, Feb. 28, 1954; m. Kim Billick; children: Aubree, Keegan. Student, Brigham Young U. Mem. Dallas Cowboys, 1977; asst. coach U. Redlands, 1977-78; grad. asst. Brigham Young U., Provo, Utah, 1978; asst. dir. pub. rels. San Francisco 49ers, 1979-80; coach receivers, tight ends, quarterbacks San Diego State U., 1981-85; offensive coord. Utah State U., 1986-88; asst. coach Stanford (Calif.) U., 1989-91; offensive coord. Minn. Vikings, 1992-98; head coach Balt. Ravens, 1999—. Earned All Western Athletic Conf. honors and honorable mention All-America in 1976 as a tight end, Brigham Young U. Achievements include being the architect of Minnesota Vikings offense that scored 556 points to break NFL record of 541 points. Office: c/o Baltimore Ravens 11001 Owings Mills Blvd Owings Mills MD 21117-2857

BILLICK, STEVEN M., emergency medical technician; m. Jean Billick; children: Carolyn, Brian. BSc in Bus. Adminstrn., John Carroll U., 1977. CPA AICPA. Acct. Deloitte & Touche, Cleve., 1977—91; v.p., controller NACCO Industries, 1991—96; sr. v.p., treas., CFO Signature Brands, 1996—98; exec. v.p. Agilysys, Inc., Mayfield Heights, Ohio, 2000—, CFO, 2000—. Office: Agilysys Inc 6065 Parkland Blvd Mayfield Heights OH 44124

BILLIG, ETEL JEWEL, theater director, actress; b. N.Y.C., Dec. 16, 1932; d. Anthony and Martha Rebecca (Klebansky) Papa; m. Steven S. Billig, Dec. 23, 1956 (dec. Aug. 1996); children: Curt Adam, Jonathan Roark. BS, NYU, 1953, MA, 1955; student, Herbert Berghof Studio, N.Y.C., 1955-56. Cert. elem. and high sch. tchr. Actress Washington Square Players, N.Y.C., 1950-55, Dukes Oak Theatre, Cooperstown, N.Y., 1955, Triple Cities Playhouse, Binghampton, N.Y., 1956, Candlelight Dinner Playhouse, Summit, Ill., 1970, 73, 77, 79, 90; mng. dir. Theatre 31, Park Forest, Ill., 1971-73; asst. mgr. Westroads Dinner Theatre, Omaha, 1973-76; mng. dir., actress Forum Theatre, 1973, 94; mng. dir., actress, producing dir. Ill. Theatre Ctr., Park Forest, 1976—; mng. dir., actress Goodman Theatre, Chgo., 1987, 95, Ct. Theatre, 1990, Wisdom Bridge Theatre, 1991; dir. drama Rich Ctrl. H.S., Olympia Fields, Ill., 1978-86. Del. League of Chgo. Theatres Russian Exchange to Soviet Union, 1989; actress Drury Lane, Oak Brook, Ill., 1989; mem. adj. faculty theatre program Prairie State Coll., 2004—05; cons. and lectr. in field. Appeared in films including the Dollmaker, Running Scared, Straight Talk, Stolen Summer; (TV series) Hawaiian Heat, Missing Persons, Untouchables. V.p. Nat. Coun. Jewish Women, Park Forest, 1968-70; sec. Community Arts Coun., Park Forest, 1984-86; pres. Southland Regional Arts Coun., 1986-92. Recipient Risk Taking award NOW, 1982; grantee Nebr. Arts Coun., 1975, Ill. Arts Coun., 1995, 96, 2000, Athena award Matteson Area C. of C., 1997, Abby Found. award, 1997; named to Park Forest Hall of Fame, 2000. Mem. AFTRA, SAG, Actors' Equity Assn., League Chgo. Theatres, Ill. Arts Coun. Theatre Panel, Prodrs. Assn. Chgo. Area Theatre (sec. 1988-89), Bus. in the Arts Coun. of C. of C. (charter), Rotary (bd. dirs. Park Forest chpt. 1988-97, sec. 2000, hall of fame 2000). Avocations: travel, antiques. Office: Ill Theatre Ctr PO Box 397 Park Forest IL 60466-0397 Office Phone: 708-481-3510. E-mail: ilthctr@bigplanet.com.

BILLIG, FREDERICK STUCKY, mechanical engineer; b. Pitts., Feb. 28, 1933; s. Thomas Clifford and Melba Helen (Stucky) B.; m. Margaret Rose Pelicano, Nov. 30, 1933; children: Linda Ann Baumler, Donna Marie Bartley, Frederick Thomas, James Richard. B of Engring., Johns Hopkins U., 1955; MS, U. Md., 1958, PhD, 1964. From assoc. engr. to group supr. Applied Physics Lab., Johns Hopkins U., Laurel, Md., 1955-77, asst. dept. supr., 1977-87, assoc. dept. supr., chief scientist, 1987-96; pres., chmn. of bd. Pyrodyne, Inc., Glenwood, Md., 1996—. Lectr. U. Md., College Park, 1965-96, Space Inst., U. Tenn., Tullahoma, 1965-99, UCLA, 1987-89, Purdue U., 1986-93, SUNY, Buffalo, 1987, Va. Poly. Inst. & State U., 1983—; lectr. hypersonics short course, Munich, London, Paris, Rome, 1988; NATO Adv. Group for Aerospace Rsch. Devel. lectr. Ramjet and Ramrocket propulsion system for missiles short course, Monterey, Calif., London, Munich, 1984; mem. consultants panel Project SQUID, Office of Naval Rsch., 1972-74; cons. propulsion directorate USAF Nat. Aerospace Plane Program; bd. dirs. Croft Leominster. Contbr. articles to profl. jours.; mem. editl. bd. Johns Hopkins APL Tech. Digest, 1981-89; patentee (with others) cooled leading edges, fuel injector pilons, high reactivity fuels for supersonic combustion ramjets, a supersonic combustion missile, translating cowl inlet with retractable propellant injection struts, protellant utilization system. Mem. Joint Army-Navy-NASA-Air Force Working Group on Combustion, 1971-74, U.S. nat. com. Internat. Airbreathing Engines Com., 1972-74, chmn., 1980-98, v.p., 1993-98; mem. hypersonic propulsion peer rev. group NASA, 1980; mem. sci. adv. bd. USAF, 1988-92, sci. adv. bd. aerospace vehicles standing panel, 1988-92. Recipient Silver medal Combustion Inst., 1970, Nat. Aerospace Plane Program Pioneer award, 1989, M. M. Bondaruck award USSR Acad. Sci. and Aviation Sport Fedn., Meritorious Civilian Svc. award Dept. Air Force, 1992, Aviation Week and Space Tech.-Aeronautics and Propulsion Laurels award, 1996; elected to Nat. Acad. of Engring., 1995, Engring. Hall of Fame U. Md., 1997. Fellow AIAA (tech. com. on airbreathing propulsion 1966-68, tech. com. on propellants and combustion 1970-72, membership chmn. coun. nat. capital sect. 1971-73, standing com. on membership 1973-84, treas. nat. capital sect. 1973-74, sec. 1974-75, standing com. on publs. 1974-82, bd. dirs. region 1 1974-81, v.p. bd. dirs. membership svcs. 1981-82, Hugh L. Dryden lectr. in rsch. 1992); mem. NAE, Combustion Inst., Md. Acad. Sci., Pi Tau Sigma, Phi Kappa Phi. Republican. Avocations: golf, fishing, hunting. Address: 15020 Rolling Hills Dr Glenwood MD 21738-9625 Office Phone: 410-489-4467. Business E-Mail: pyrodyne@comcast.net.

BILLIG, ROBERT EMANUEL, psychiatric social worker; b. N.Y.C., May 21, 1946; s. Benjamin and Pearl (Kwiat) B. BA, McKendree Coll., 1966; MS, Fort Hays (Kans.) State Coll., 1969; MSW, Marywood Coll., 1974. Diplomate Clin. Social Work Am. Bd. Examiners in Clin. Social Work; cert. hypnotherapist Nat. Bd. Hypnotherapist Examiners. Psychiat. social worker S.I. Devel. Ctr., 1974-76, Queens and Bklyn. Devel. Ctrs., 1976-79, Bellevue Psychiat. Hosp., N.Y.C., 1979-88; pvt. practice, 1988—. Adminstr. Bellevue Cmty. Support Sys., 1983-86. Mem. Acad. Cert. Social Workers, Nat. Assn. Social Workers, N.Y. State Soc. Clin. Social Work Psychotherapists, Am. Soc. Hypnotherapy, Am. Assn. Profl. Hypnotherapists, Am. Assn. Behavioral Therapists, Mensa. Jewish. Home: 10 Park Ter E New York NY 10034-1504

BILLIG, THOMAS CLIFFORD, publishing executive, marketing professional; b. Pitts., Aug. 20, 1930; s. Thomas Clifford and Melba Helen (Stocky) Billig; m. Helen Page Hine, May 14, 1951; children: Thomas Clifford, James Frederick. BSBA summa cum laude, Northwestern U., 1956. Ins. mgr., asst. dir. pers., asst. to chmn. Butler Bros. (now City Products Corp.), Chgo., 1954-59; market rsch. mgr. R.R. Donnelley & Sons, Chgo., 1959-61; pres., dir. Indsl. Fiber Glass Products Corp., Scottville and Ludington, Mich., 1962-69; cons. mass mktg. mgr. Mpls., 1969-71; v.p. Mail Mktg. Systems and Services, St. Paul and Bloomington, Minn., 1971-74; pres., chmn., chief exec. officer Billig & Assocs., Mpls. and Duluth, Minn., 1974—; pres. NIARS Corp., Duluth, 1974—85, 1995—2003, Fins and Feathers Pub. Co., Mpls., 1977-89; pres., dir. N. Coast Mktg. Corp., St. Paul, 1992—; chmn., CEO Sportsman's Mktg. Inc., Superior, Wis., Lake Elmo, Minn., 1998—. Author: Nat. Ins. Advt. Regulation Svc., 1972—; author, pub.: NAIC Model Laws, Regulations and Guidelines, 1976—83. With USNR, 1948—56. Recipient Samuel Dresner Plotkin award, Northwestern U., 1956. Mem.: Beta Gamma Sigma, Delta Mu Delta. Office: 1423 N 8th St Superior WI 54880-6664 also: 3394 Lake Elmo Ave N Box 852 Lake Elmo MN 55042-9799 E-mail: niarsi@aol.com.

BILLINGS, CHARLES EDGAR, physician; b. Boston, June 15, 1929; s. Charles Edgar and Elizabeth (Sanborn) B.; m. Lillian Elizabeth Wilson, Apr. 16, 1955; 1 dau., Lee Ellen Billings Kreinbihl. Student, Wesleyan U., 1947-49; MD, N.Y. U., 1953; M.Sc. (Link Found. fellow), Ohio State U., 1960. Diplomate: Am. Bd. Preventive Medicine. Instr. to prof. depts. preventive medicine and aviation Sch. Medicine Ohio State U., 1960-73, dir. div. environ. health Sch. Medicine, 1970-73, clin. prof. Sch. Medicine, 1973-83, prof. emeritus, 1983—; rsch. scientist indsl. and systems engring., 1992—. Med. officer NASA Ames Rsch. Ctr., Moffett Field, Calif., 1973-76; chief Aviation Safety Rsch. Office, 1976-80, asst. chief for rsch. Man-Vehicle Systems rsch. divsn., 1980-83, sr. scientist, 1983-91; chief scientist Ames Rsch. Ctr., 1991-92; cons. Beckett Aviation Corp., 1962-73; surgeon gen. U.S. Army, 1965-77, FAA, 1967-70, 75, 83; mem. NATO-AGARD Aerospace Med. Panel, 1980-86; assoc. advisor USAF Sci. Adv. Bd., 1978-90; mem. human factors adv. panel U.K. Civil Aviation Authority, 1999-2001; mem. aviation adv. bd. Ohio U., 2000-01. Contbr. chpts. to books, numerous articles in field to med. jours. Served to maj. USAF, 1955-57. Recipient Air Traffic Svc. award FAA, 1969, Walter M. Boothby rsch. award, 1972, PATCO Air Safety award, 1979, Disting. Svc. award Flight Safety Found., 1979, John A. Tamisea award, 1980, Laura Taber Barbour Air Safety medal, 1981, Outstanding Leadership medal NASA, 1981, 90, Jeffries Aerospace Med. Rsch. medal AIAA, 1986, Lovelace award NASA Soc. Flight Surgeons, 1996, Forrest and Pamela Bird award Civil Aviation Med. Assn., 2001, Henry L. Taylor Founders award Aerospace Human Factors Assn, 2002; Ames Rsch. Ctr. fellow, 1989. Fellow AIAA (assoc.), Royal Aero. Soc., Aerospace Med. Assn. (pres. 1979-80); mem. AMA, Internat. Acad. Aviation and Space Medicine. Office: 265 Baker ISE Bldg 1971 Neil Ave Columbus OH 43210-1210 Home: 411 Middleton Ave Granville OH 43023

BILLINGS, DAVID ARTHUR, music educator; b. Binghamton, NY, Aug. 9, 1955; s. Ziba Wesley and Hilda Louise Billings. BFA, Pa. State U., 1977; MM, Eastman Sch. Music, 1979, DMA, 1989. Min. of music Parkwood Presbyn. Ch., Allison Pk., Pa., 1981—2004; dir. music/organist Oakmont Presbyn. Ch., Pa., 2004—; accompanist Pitts. Concert Chorale, Pa., 1985—; adj. prof. music Duquesne U., 1981—85. Mem.: Organ Artists of Pitts. (chmn.), Am. Guild Organists (dean, Pitts. chpt.). Home: 2618 Herron Rd Allison Park PA 15101 Office: Oakmont Presbyn Ch 415 Pennsylvania Ave Oakmont PA 15139

BILLINGS, FRANKLIN SWIFT, JR., federal judge; b. Woodstock, Vt., June 5, 1922; s. Franklin S. and Gertrude (Curtis) B.; m. Pauline Gillingham, Oct. 13, 1951; children: Franklin, III, Jireh Swift, Elizabeth, Ann. S.B., Harvard U., 1943; postgrad., Yale U. law Sch., 1945; JD, U. Va., 1947. Bar: Vt. 1948, U.S. Supreme Ct., 1958. With dept. electronics Gen. Electric Co., Schenectady, N.Y., 1943; bldg. dept. Vt. Marble Co., Proctor, 1945-46; pvt. practice law Woodstock, 1948-52; mem. firm Billings & Sherburne, Woodstock, 1952-66; asst. sec. Vt. Senate, 1949-55, sec., 1957-59; sec. civil and mil. affairs State of Vt., 1959-61; exec. clk. to gov., 1955-57; judge Hartford Mcpl. Ct., 1955-63; mem. Vt. Ho. of Reps., 1961-66, chmn. jud. com., 1961, speaker of ho., 1963-66; judge Vt. Superior Ct., 1966-75, assoc. justice, 1975-83, chief justice, 1983-84; judge U.S. Dist. Ct. Vt., 1984-94, chief judge, 1988-92, sr. ct. judge, 1994—. Active, Town of Woodstock, 1948—. Served as warrant officer 1st class attached Brit. Army, 1944-45. Decorated Purple Heart; Brit. Empire medal. Mem. Vt. Bar Assn., Delta Theta Phi. Office: US Dist Ct PO Box 598 Woodstock VT 05091-0598

BILLINGS, HAROLD WAYNE, library director, editor; b. Cain City, Tex., Nov. 12, 1931; s. Harold Ross and Katie Mae (Price) B.; m. Bernice Schneider, Sept. 10, 1954; children: Brenda, Geoffrey, Carol. BA, Pan Am. Coll., 1953; MLS, U. Tex., 1957. Tchr. Pharr-San Juan-Alamo (Tex.) H.S., 1953-54; catalog libr. U. Tex., Austin, 1954-57, asst. chief catalog libr., 1957-65, chief acquisitions libr., 1965-67, asst. univ. libr., 1967-72, assoc. dir. gen. librs., 1972-77, acting dir. gen. librs., 1977-78, dir. gen. librs., 1978—2003. Sec. Tex. Bd. Libr. Examiners; mem. adv. com. Tex. Higher Edn. Coordinating Bd. Libr. Formula, 1987-92, acad. support formula adv. com., 1993-94; mem. steering com. Tex-Share Project, 1993-94; trustee Amigos Bibliographic Coun., 1980-83; chmn. Coun. Acad. Rsch. Librs., 1979-81; chmn. rsch. librs. adv. com. Online Computer Libr. Ctr. (OCLC), 1980-82, 87-88, mem. OCLC Users Coun.; bd. dirs. Ctr. Rsch. Librs., Chgo., 1989-96, Assn. Rsch. Librs., 1989-92; mem. Tex. Coun. State Univ. Librs., Assn. Rsch. Librs. Preservation Com., Collection Devel. Com., Coun. on Libr. Resources Preservation and Access Com., Coun. on Libr. Resources/Assn. Am. Pubs. Joint Working Group on Electronic Info., 1993-94; mem. adv. bd. Project Muse-Johns Hopkins U. Press, Balt., 1995-98; mem. N.Am. adv. bd. Lit. Online, 1997—; assoc. Tex. Telecomm. Policy Inst., 1996-2003; mem. coun. on libr. and info. studies area studies materials task force ACLS, 1998-99; mem. adv. coun. for Stanford U. Librs., 1998-2003; mem. steering com. Digital Libr. Fedn., 1999-2003; vis. coms. U. Tenn., U. Wyo.; project dir. numerous fed. grants. Author: Education of Librarians in Texas, 1956, Edward Dahlberg: American Ishmael of Letters, 1968, A Bibliography of Edward Dahlberg, 1972, The Leafless American, 2d edit., 1986, Magic and Hypersystems: Constructing the Information-Sharing Library, 2002, M.P. Shiel: A Biography of His Early Years, 2005; editor books in field; contbr. to jours.; mem. editl. bd. Libr. Chronicle, 1970-97 Sec., trustee Littlefield Fund for So. History, 1977-2003. Mem. ALA (Hugh C. Atkinson Meml. award 2002), Tex. Libr. Assn., Assn. Coll. Rsch. Librs. Democrat. Office: U Tex Librs PO Box P Austin TX 78713-8916 Business E-Mail: billings@mail.utexas.edu.

BILLINGS, PATRICIA JEAN, inventor; b. Clinton, Mo., Feb. 15, 1926; d. Chester Irwin and Zoe Elizabeth (Strieby) Billings; m. William Marlman, June 21, 1949; 1 child, Melanie Ann Runge. Student, Amarillo Coll., 1955. Med. rschr. on Histoplasma capsulation and TB USPHS, 1946-48; rschr. Kansas City T.B. Sanitarium, 1951; med. technologist, 1960-67; tuberculosis rschr. Kansas City County Hosp., 1967-71; rschr. Craftcote, 1971-73; pres. Geobond, 1989—, Craftcote Internat., Inc. Spkr. Simmons Coll., Boston, Fire Materials Conv., Egypt, 1988; interviewed numerous TV shows including The Unbelievable, Gordon Elliott Show, CBS This Morning, Fox 41 News, Am. Chem. Soc., Pub. TV, Boston, Dateline, 1998; inventor Geoboval Construction Material, 6 patents, featured in articles: People Magazine, Wall St. Journ., Automated Builder-internet MIT network (inventor of week). 4 patents. Mem. adv. bd. Mus. History of Women, Washington. Named Inventor of Week, MIT. Achievements include research in 20 products for use in construction field. Home: 8120 Lee Blvd Shawnee Mission KS 66206-1219

BILLINGS, THOMAS NEAL, computer and publishing executive, management consultant, entrepreneur, journalist, writer; b. Milwaukee, Wis., Mar. 2, 1931; s. Neal and Gladys Victoria (Lockard) B.; m. Barta Hope Chipman, June 12, 1954 (div. 1967); children: Bridget Ann, Bruce Neal; m. Marie Louise Farrell, Mar. 27, 1982 (dec. Jan. 2003). AB with honors, Harvard U., 1952, MBA, 1954. V.p. fin. and adminstrn. and technol. innovation Copley Newspapers Inc., LaJolla, Calif., 1957-70; group v.p., dir. tech. Harte-Hanks Comm. Inc., San Antonio, 1970-73; exec. v.p. United Media Inc., Phoenix, 1973-75; asst. to pres., dir. corp. mgmt. systems Ramada Inns, Inc., Phoenix, 1975-76; exec. dir. NRA, Washington, 1976-77; pres. Strategic Ideation Inc., N.Y.C., 1977—; chmn. Bergen-Billings Inc., N.Y.C., 1977-80; pres. The Assn. Svc. Corp., San Francisco, 1978—, Recorder Printing and Pub. Co. Inc., San Francisco, 1980-82; v.p. adminstrn. Victor Techs. Inc., Scotts Valley, Calif., 1982-84; mng. dir. Saga-Wilcox Computers Ltd., Wrexham, Wales, 1984-85; chmn. Thomas Billings & Assocs., Inc., Reno, 1978—, Intercontinental Travel Svc. Inc., Reno, 1983-88, Oberon Optical Character Recognition Ltd., Hemel-Hemstead, Eng., 1985-86. Bd. dirs. 5M Corp., San Francisco, Intercontinental Rsch. Coun., London, Corp. Comm. Coun., Alameda, Digital Broadcasting Corp., Mountain View, Calif., Lenny's Restaurants, Inc., Wichita, Kans., Tymyndr Corp., Dover, Del., Zzyzzyx Corp., Reno, Harrod's Hotel & Casino Corp., Las Vegas, Pandemonium Pictures, Inc., San Moteo, Calif., Bonanza Enterprises, Inc., Virginia City, Nev., Quillmill Ltd., London, Better Betting Systems, Inc., Alameda, Calif., Video Stream, Inc., Cupertino, Calif., ResuMaster Corp., Walnut Creek, Calif., ProcessMaster Corp., Pleasanton, Calif., Enterprise House, Alameda, Chut! Cheri's Chic Chit Choppe, S.A., Laguna Beach, Calif., Waters Equipment Co., Inc., San Francisco, Goldstein Miller and Assocs. Inc., San Bruno, Calif., Silicon World Search Group, Inc., Alameda, Calif., Knicker's Ltd., Reno; dir., CEO Insignia Software Solution Group, High Wycombe, Eng., Cupertino, Calif., 1986-89; chmn. Intercontinental News Svc. Inc., London and Alameda, Calif., 1989—; v.p. Cromer Equipment Co., Oakland, Calif., 1991-94; chmn. Newton Group of Cos., Las Vegas, 1993—, Info. Integrity Internat., Inc., Las Vegas, London, 1994—, WordMaster Corp., Reno, 1995—, GolfDoctor!Inc., Las Vegas, 1998—, First Impact Inc., Alameda, Calif., 2000—; CEO Assurant Software, Inc., Palo Alto, Calif., 2002—; editor, pub., CEO The-View-Less-Seen.com, Alameda, Calif., 2001—; adj. prof. U. Phoenix, San Jose, Calif., 1999—, Coll. San Mateo, Calif., 2000—, Monterey (Calif.) Inst. Internat. Studies, 2001—, Deep Springs Calif. Coll., 2002—; spkr. and seminar leader; co-inventor StrokSavr Software, 1994. Author: Creative Controllership, 1978, Our Credibility Crisis, 1983, Non-Euclidean Theology, 1987, Ruminations on Meta Mentality, 1990, Fixing our Broken System, 1992, Our Dissembling Society, 1997, Our Co-Dependent World, 1998, A Christmas Carol-The Musical!, 1999, All Roads Lead to Ausfardt, 2000, The View Less Seen, 2002; (series) The Ethnic Epicure, 1995—, The View Less Seen, 2000—; editor: The Vice President's Letter, 1978-92; pub. The Microcomputer Letter, 1982-94, Synthetic Hardware Update, 1987-93, Windows on Tomorrow Magazine, 1994-99; editor: Intercontinental News Svc. London and Alamedia, Calif., 1985—; theatre critic, editl. columnist The Alameda Jour., 1998—. Bd. dirs. Nat. Allergy Found., 1973—, The Wilderness Fund, 1978—, San Diego Civic Light Opera Assn., 1965-69; chief exec. San Diego 200th Anniversary Expn., 1969; founder, exec. dir. Am. Majority Party, 1993—, The Millenium Three Found., 1996—, The Remembrance Soc., 1996—, People Finders' Inc., 1996—, Corp. Comm. Counsel Inc., 1996—, Alameda Cmty. Theatre Alliance, 1998—, Alameda Repretory Theatre, 1999—; voice talent Voice Wizardry, Alameda, Calif., 1999-; bass cantor and lector St. Joseph Basilica, Alameda, Calif., 1994-; soloist with Kol Truah, Temple Israel, Almeda, 2004—. With U.S. Army, 1955-57. Recipient Walter F. Carley Meml. award, 1966, 69. Fellow U.K. Inst. Dirs.; mem. Am. Newspaper Pubs. Assn., Inst. Execs. Inc. (dir.), Inst. Newspaper Fin. Officers, West Side Tennis Club, LaJolla Country Club, Washington Athletic Club, San Francisco Press Club, Harvard Club (N.Y.C.), Elks, Sigma Delta Chi. Office: PO Drawer I Alameda CA 94501-0262 Office Phone: 510-769-2000. E-mail: himself@tnbillings.com.

BILLINGSLEY, LANCE W., lawyer; b. Buffalo, Apr. 18, 1940; m. Carolyn Gouza Billingsley, Aug. 25, 1962; children: Lance II, Brant, Ashlynn. BA, U. Md., 1961; JD, U. Buffalo, 1964; state and local, Harvard U., 1988. Pntr., assoc. Nylen & Gilmore, Riverdale, Md., 1964-75; ptnr. Meyers, Billingsley, Rodbell & Rosenbaum, P.A., Riverdale, 1975-2000, Rifkin, Livingston, Levitan, Silver, Greenbelt, Md., 2000—. Adj. prof. U. Md., U. Calif., 2003-; bd. of regents U. Sys. Md., 1995-2003, chmn. 1995-99; bd. visitors U. Md., 1990-95; vice-chmn. U. of Md. Found., 1985-2000; bd. dirs. U. Md. Med. Sys., 1995-2003; asst. atty. gen. State of Md., 1967-68; city atty. Hyattsville, Md., 1976-2003; chmn. Nat. Wildlife Visitors Ctr., 1989-94; chmn. bd. Prince George's County Econ. Devel. Corp., Landover, Md., 1983-92. Contbr. articles to numerous law publs. Chmn. Dem. State Cen. Com., 1970-74, Dem. Com. Prince George's County, 1974-80. Named One of Outstanding Young Men Am., 1975-80. Mem.: Md. Bar Assn., ABA (young lawyers exec. com. 1972—74, editl. bd. Barrister mag. 1973—75), U. Md. Alumni Assn. (bd. govs.), M Club, Terrapin Club (bd. dirs. 1983—2001, pres. 1998—99), Columbia Country Club (Chevy Chase, Md.), Omicron Delta Kappa. Avocations: skiing, backpacking. Home: 7102 College Heights Dr Hyattsville MD 20782-1154 Office: Rifkin Livingston Levitan & Silver LLC 6305 Ivy Ln Ste 500 Greenbelt MD 20770-1405 Office Phone: 301-345-7700. E-mail: lbillingsley@rlls.com.

BILLINGSLEY, SHIRLEY ANN, writer, poet; b. Center, Tex., Sept. 3, 1953; d. Leonard Waymon and Verna Mae (Moore) B.; m. Willie L. Skinner, Oct. 12, 1980; 1 child, Melinda Sue. Diploma, Coastal Coll., Bossier City, La., 1991. Author: articles, poems. Avocations: reading, writing, poetry. Home: 519 Dixon St Lufkin TX 75904-2244 E-mail: bshirle2000@yahoo.com.

BILLINGTON, BARRY E., lawyer; b. Bruceton, Tenn., June 24, 1940; s. Charles Raymond and Edith Virginia (Bowles) Billington; m. Bonnie Leslie Johnson, Oct. 16, 1971 (div. Mar. 23, 1990); children: Erin Alexis, Barry E. Jr. AB in Econs., Davidson Coll., 1964; JD, Emory U., 1968. Bar: Calif. 1969, U.S. Dist. Ct. (ctrl. dist.) Calif. 1969, Ga. 1971, U.S. Dist. Ct. (no. dist.) Ga. 1971. Assoc. Surr & Hellyer, San Bernardino, Calif., 1968-70; with Mfrs. Life Ins. Co., Atlanta, 1970-71; assoc. Carter, Ansley, Smith & McClendon, Atlanta, 1971-72; of counsel Raiford & Hills, Decatur, Ga., 1972-75; ptnr. Raiford, Hills, Billington & McKeithen, Atlanta, 1975-77; mem. Rich, Bass, Kidd, Witcher & Billington, Decatur, 1977-82; ptnr. Billington & Beasley, Decatur, 1982-83, Billington & Turner, Atlanta, 1983-85; owner Barry E. Billington & Assocs., Atlanta, 1985—. Editor: Ga. Rep. Party Newsletter, 1968. Candidate 4th dist. U.S. Ho. Reps., 1980; publicity dir. San Bernardino County Reps., 1969—70; alt. del. Rep. Ctrl. Com. Calif., 1969—70; publicity dir. San Bernardino County Ronald Reagan Com., 1970; chmn. 4th dist. Conservative Caucus, 1977—79; candidate 52d dist. Ga. Ho. Reps., 1978. With Police Corps U.S. Army, 1958—60. Mem.: ATLA, ABA (mem. litig. sect. 1969—89), Diplomat Nat. Coll. Advocacy Trial Advocacy Course, Nat. Assn. Criminal Def. Lawyers, Ga. Assn. Criminal Def. Lawyers, Ga. Trial Lawyers Assn., Decatur-DeKalb Bar Assn. (chmn. spkr.'s com. 1977—78), Atlanta Bar Assn. (mem. spkr.s com., litig., family law, criminal law sects. 1974—77). Home: 7208 Peachford Circle Atlanta GA 30338 Office: 3 Dunwoody Park Ste 103 Atlanta GA 30338-6709 Office Phone: 770-396-7286. Business E-Mail: barry@billingtonandassociates.com.

BILLINGTON, DAVID PERKINS, civil engineering educator; b. Bryn Mawr, Pa., June 1, 1927; s. Nelson and Jane Newkirk (Coolbaugh) B.; m. Phyllis Bergquist, Aug. 26, 1951; children: David Jr., Elizabeth Billington Fox, Jane Billington Flucker, Philip, Stephen, Sarah BS in Engring., Princeton U., 1950; postgrad. (Fulbright fellow), U. Louvain, Belgium, 1950-51, U. Ghent, 1951-52; DHL (hon.), Union Coll., 1990; DSc (hon.), Grinnell Coll., 1991; DEng (hon.), Notre Dame U., 1997. Registered profl. engr., N.J. Structural engr. Roberts & Schaefer Co., N.Y.C., 1952-60; assoc. prof. civil engring. Princeton U., N.J., 1960-64, prof. civil engring., 1964—, Gordon Y.S. Wu prof. engring., 1996—. A.D. White prof.-at-large Cornell U., 1987-93; cons. in field Author: Robert Maillart's Bridges, 1979 (Dexter award 1979), Thin Shell Concrete Structures, 1982, The Tower and the Bridge, 1983, Robert Maillart and the Art of Reinforced Concrete, 1990, The Innovators: The Engineering Pioneers Who Made America Modern, 1996, Robert Maillart: Builder, Designer, Artist, 1997, The Art of Structural Design: A Swiss Legacy, 2003. With USN, 1945-46. Recipient Dana award, Charles A. Dana Found., 1990, N.J. Prof. of Yr. award, Carnegie Found., 1995, Sarton medal, U. Ghent, Belgium, 1999, Sarton chair award, 1999—2000, Dir.'s award, NSF, 2003, John P. McGovern Lecture award in sci., Cosmos Club Found., 2004, Charles Zollman award, Pre-stressed & Pre-cast Concrete Inst., 2004; grantee NEH, 1969—89, NSF, 1963—83, NEA, 1977—79, NSF, 1991—94, 2001—, Walter L. Robb Sr. Engring. Edn. fellow, Nat. Acad. Engring., 2005—; vis. scholar, Phi Beta Kappa, 1984—85. Fellow Am. Acad. Arts and Scis., Am. Concrete Inst. (hon.); mem. NAE, ASCE (hon., 3 awards 1956-57, History and Heritage award 1986, George Winter award 1992), Internat. Assn. for Bridge and Structural Engring., Internat. Assn. Shell Structures (hon.), Soc. for History Tech. (Usher prize with J. Doig 1995). Republican. Episcopalian. Home: 45 Hodge Rd Princeton NJ 08540-3011 Office: Princeton U Dept Civil and Environ Engring Princeton NJ 08544-0001 Office Phone: 609-258-4606. Business E-Mail: billington@princeton.edu.

BILLINGTON, JAMES HADLEY, historian, librarian; b. Bryn Mawr, Pa., June 1, 1929; s. Nelson and Jane (Coolbaugh) B.; m. Marjorie Anne Brennan, June 22, 1957; children: Susan Billington Harper, Anne Billington Fischer, James Hadley, Jr., Thomas Keator. BA, Princeton U., 1950; PhD, Oxford U., 1953, LittD (hon.), 2002, Lafayette Coll., 1981; DLitt (hon.), U. Pitts., 1988, Duke U., 1995, William & Mary, 2005; LHD (hon.), LeMoyne Coll., 1982, RI Coll., 1982, Cath. U. Am., 1983, NYU, 1987, Va. Theol. Sem., 1990, Williams Coll., 1991, Hood Coll., 1992, U. Scranton, 1992, U. Albany, 1993, Georgetown U., 1993, Bates Coll., 1993, Am. U., 1995, Mt. Holyoke Coll., 1995, U. San Diego, 1998, Lawrence U., 1999, Washington Coll., 1999, U.

South, 1999, Quinnipiac U., 2000, Carthage Coll., 2002, St. Norbert Coll., 2003, Jewish Theol. Sem., 2005, St. Mary's Coll., 2005; HHD (hon.), Furman U., 1986, Ball State U., 1988, Russian State U. Humanities, 2001; D in Pub. Svc. (hon.), George Washington U., 1990; LLD (hon.), Dartmouth Coll., 1990, U. Notre Dame, 1995; D in Humane Scis. (hon.), U. Tblisi, 1999; EdD (hon.), Montreat Coll., 2000; MBA (hon.), Jones Internat. U., 2005. Instr. history Harvard U., Cambridge, Mass., 1957-58, fellow Russian Rsch. Ctr., 1958-59, asst. prof. history, 1958-61; assoc. prof. history Princeton U., NJ, 1962-64, prof., 1964-73; dir. Woodrow Wilson Internat. Ctr. for Scholars, Washington, 1973-87; Libr. of Congress Washington, 1987—. Chmn. Bd. Fgn. Scholarships (Fulbright program), 1971-73, mem. 1973-76; vice-chmn. Atlantic Coun.'s Working Group on the Successor Generation, 1982-86; trustee St. Alban's Sch., 1979-82; dir. Am. Assn. for Advancement of Slavic Studies, 1968-71; spl. cons. to Chase Manhattan Bank on East-West Matters, 1971-73; vis. rsch. prof. to Inst. History of Acad. Scis. of USSR in Moscow, 1966-67, U. Helsinki, 1960-61, École des Hautes Études en Sciences Sociales, Paris, 1985, 88; vis. lectr. to various univs. in Europe and Asia. Author: Mikhailovsky and Russian Populism, 1958, The Icon and the Axe: An Interpretive History of Russian Culture, 1966, (Serbian transl., 1988, Japanese transl., 2000, Russian transl., 2001), The Arts of Russia, 1970, Fire in the Minds of Men: Origins of the Revolutionary Faith, 1980, (Italian transl., 1986), Russia Transformed: Breakthrough to Hope, Moscow, August 1991, 1992, The Face of Russia, 1998 (Russian transl., 2001); writer, host: (3-part TV series) The Face of Russia, 1998; mem. adv. bd. Fgn. Affairs, 1974-92, Theology Today, 1974-84; script writer and host of Humanities Film Forum, 1973; contbr. chpts. to books, numerous articles to profl. jours. Trustee John F. Kennedy Ctr. for Performing Arts, Ctr. Theol. Inquiry, Nat. Bldg. Mus., Woodrow Wilson Internat. Ctr. for Scholars, Am. Folklife Ctr.; bd. regents Nat. Libr. Medicine. 1st lt. U.S. Army, 1953-56. McCosh faculty fellow Princeton U., Guggenheim fellow, 1960-61; Rhodes scholar, 1950-53; Fulbright rsch. prof. U. Helsinki, 1960-61; decorated Chevalier Order of Arts and Letters of France, 1985, Comdr., 1991; recipient Gwanghwa medal Republic of Korea, 1991, Woodrow Wilson award Princeton U., 1992, Russian Orthodox medal, 1994, Knight Comdr.'s Cross of Order of Merit Fed. Republic of Germany, 1995, Vologda Universal Sci. Lib. award, 1999, Pushkin medal, 1999, UCLA medal, 2000. Mem. Am. Philos. Soc., Am. Acad. Arts and Scis., Russian Acad. Scis., Cosmos Club, Phi Beta Kappa. Office: The Library of Congress 101 Independence Ave SE Washington DC 20540-0002

BILLINTON, ROY, engineering educator; b. Leeds, Eng., Sept. 14, 1935; s. Edwin and Nettie (Billinton); m. Alice Joyce McKenna, July 21, 1956; children— Leslie, Kevin, Michael, Christopher, Jeffrey. B.Sc.E.E., U. Man., 1960, M.Sc., 1963; PhD, U. Sask., 1967, D.Sc., 1975. Journeyman electrician McCaine Electric, Winnipeg, Man., Can., 1956; mem. system operation dept. and system planning dept. Man. Hydro, from 1960; asst. prof. to prof., head dept. elec. engring. U. Sask., Saskatoon, 1964—, assoc. dean, acting dean, now prof. emeritus; cons. PowerComp Assocs. Author: Power System Reliability Evaluation, 1970, (with R. J. Ringlee and A. J. Wood) Power System Reliability Calculations, 1973, (with C. Singh) System Reliability Modelling and Evaluation, 1977; (with R.N. Allan) Reliability Evaluation of Engineering Systems, 1983, Reliability Evaluation of Power Systems, 1984, (with R.N. Allan) Reliability of Large Electric Power Systems, 1988, (with R.N. Allan, L. Salvaderi) Applied Reliability Assessment in Electric Power Systems, 1990, (with W Li) Reliability Assessment of Electric Power Systems Using Monte Carlo Methods, 1994; also articles. Recipient Sir George Nelson award Engring. Inst. Can., 1965-67, Ross medal, 1972, Centennial Disting. Svc. award Can. Elect Assn., 1991; Disting. Researcher award U. Saskatchewan. Fellow IEEE (Outstanding Power Engring. Educator award 1992, McNaughton medal 1994, Third Millenium medal 2000, Outstanding Engr. Educator award 2001), Royal Soc. Can., Engring. Inst. Can., Can. Acad. Engring. Home: 3 McLean Crescent Saskatoon SK Canada S7J 2R6 Office: U Sask Dept Elec Engring Saskatoon SK Canada S7N 0W0

BILLION, JOHN JOSEPH, surgeon, retired state representative; b. Sioux Falls, S.D., Mar. 4, 1939; s. Henry Alphonse and Evelyn Margaret (Heinz) B.; div.; children: Matthew, Suzanne, John, James, Jane; m. Deborah Wagner, Mar. 22, 1980; children: Timothy, Allyson. BA, Loras Coll., 1960; MD, Stritch-Loyola U., 1964. Diplomate Am. Bd. Orthopedic Surgery. Resident orthopedics St. Francis Hosp., Peoria, Ill., 1964-69; orthopedic surgeon Sioux Falls, 1971-96; state rep. State of S.D., 1992-96. Vice-chair SD Dem. party, 1997-98; chair Minnehaha Dem. party, 2005-. Maj. USAF, 1969-71. Fellow Am. Acad. Orthopedic Surgeons. Democrat.

BILLMAN, BROOKES D., JR., law educator; b. 1949; BA, Princeton U., 1971; JD, U. Cin., 1974; LLM in Taxation, NYU, 1975. Bar: Ohio 1974, DC 1976. Atty. Howrey & Simon, Washington, 1975, Hogan & Hartson, Washington, 1976; instr. law NYU Sch. Law, 1977-78, asst. prof., 1979-81, assoc. prof., 1981-84, prof., 1984—, dir. grad. tax program, 1984—88, assoc. dean grad. divsn., 1989—94, assoc. dean planning & tech., 2002—. Office: NYU Sch Law Vanderbilt Hall Rm 430 40 Washington Sq S New York NY 10012-1099 Office Phone: 212-998-6158. E-mail: billmanb@juris.law.nyu.edu.*

BILLMAN, IRWIN EDWARD, publishing company executive; s. Herman Frank and Ruth (Dutchen) B. BS in Econs, Wharton Sch., U. Pa., 1962. Asst. controller Whelan Drug Co., 1965-66; v.p., treas. Curtis Circulation Co., Phila., 1966-71; exec. v.p., COO Penthouse Internat. Ltd. & Gen. Media Internat. Ltd., 1971—81; pres., publisher Oui Mag., N.Y.C., 1981-82; pres. Billman Media Group; ptnr. Mag. Communications Cons. Pres. Global Distribution Svcs., Inc. Mem. Periodical and Book Assn. Am. (pres. 1977-81, bd. dirs. 2004—), Am. Circulation Execs. Soc. (pres. 1998-2000), Assn. Circulation Execs. (U.K.). Home: PO Box 350 Westhampton NY 11977-0350 Office: PO Box 850 Remsenburg NY 11960-0850

BILLNITZER, BONNIE JEANNE, nurse, gerontologist; b. Mar. 7, 1935; d. George Gottfried and Sarah Edna Elizabeth (Park) Haffelder; m. Harold R. Billnitzer, Apr. 28, 1956; children: J. Stephen, David A., John Mark, Timothy P., Michael M. BA in Psychology, U. Mich., 1977; ADN, U. Toledo, Ohio, 1989; BSN, Med. Coll. Ohio, Ohio, 1992. RN, Ohio; cert. gerontol. nurse, cert. cardiovascular nurse. Adminstrv. mgr. Med. Coll. Ohio Ambulatory Care Ctr., Toledo, 1972-79; cardiovascular nurse St. Vincent Med. Ctr., Toledo, 1988-92; case mgr. The Vis. Nurse Svc., Toledo, 1992-97; pvt. practice RN case mgr. Perrysburg, Ohio. Mem. credentialing com. for RN St. Vincent Med. Ctr., Toledo, 1991-92. Recipient Logan award for Clin. and Theoretical Excellence in Nursing, U. Toledo, 1989. Mem. AAUW, ANA, Ohio Nurses Assn., Toledo Dist. Nurses Assn. (1st v.p. 1995-96), Am. Holistic Nurses Assn., Am. Assn. Critical Care Nurses, Internat. Order St. Luke the Physician. Lutheran. Avocations: music, reading, antiques, quilting. Home: 1084 Eastbrook Dr Perrysburg OH 43551-1646

BILLS, ROBERT HOWARD, political party executive; b. North Conway, NH, Jan. 13, 1944; s. Howard William and Mary Catherine (Jackson) B.; m. Donna Gail Florian; children: Emily Ida, Katherine Mary. Staff writer Weekly People Newspaper, Bklyn., 1970-74, Palo Alto, Calif., 1974-76; nat. sec. Socialist Labor Party, Sunnyvale, 1980—, mem. nat. exec. subcom., 1976-79. Office: Socialist Labor Party of Am PO Box 218 Mountain View CA 94042-0218 Business E-Mail: socialists@slp.org.

BILLUPS, CHAUNCEY, professional basketball player; b. Sept. 25, 1976; m. Piper Riley; 2 children. Student, U. Colo., 1997. Guard Boston Celtics, 1996-97, Toronto Raptors, 1997-98, Denver Nuggets, 1998-00, Minnesota Timberwolves, Minneapolis, 2000—02, Detroit Pistons, 2002—. Named NBA Finals MVP, 2004. Achievements include mem. NBA Championship Team, 2004. Avocation: music. Office: c/o Detroit PIstons Palace of Auburn Hills 2 Championship Dr Auburn Hills MI 48326

BILLUPS, NELDA JOYCE, elementary school educator; b. Kirksville, Mo., Sept. 23, 1939; d. Parley Bennett and Grace June (Cunningham) Rudy; m. Kenneth Lee Ebling, June 16, 1963 (div. 1976); 1 child, Vinton Eric; m. Donald Paul Billups, June 5, 1981; stepchildren: Donna Gonzalez, Debbie Banuche. BS in Elem. Edn., N.E. Mo. State Tchrs. Coll., 1960; MEd, Northeast Mo. State Coll., 1963. Cert. elem. tchr. 1st grade tchr. Bloomfield (Iowa) Elem. Sch., 1960-63; 2d grade tchr. Cherokee Elem. Sch., Overland Park, Kans., 1963-67, 3d grade tchr., 1968—97; ret. Adult Sunday sch. tchr. Mem. NEA, PEO, AARP Grief and Loss Support Group, Alzheimer's Support Group, NEA Shawnee Mission,Red Hat Soc. Avocations: music, flowers, church work.

BILLY, GEORGE JOHN, library director; b. Rahway, N.J., Apr. 10, 1940; s. George and Marie (Zeleznik) B.; m. Valerie Jean McGreevy, July 19, 1969; children: Margaret, Christine. BA in History, Rutgers U., 1962; MLS, Pratt Inst., 1968; MA in HIstory, Adelphi U., 1973; PhD in History, CUNY, 1982. Ref. libr. Buffalo and Erie County Pub. Libr., 1968-70; acquisitions and ref. libr. Queensborough Community Coll., Bayside, N.Y., 1970-76; reader svcs. libr. U.S. Mcht. Marine Acad. Libr., Kings Point, N.Y., 1977-84, chief libr., 1984—. Adj. prof. Palmer Sch. Libr. Info. Sci., C.W. Post/Long Island U., Greenvale, N.Y., 1983—. Author: Palmerston's Foreign Policy: 1848, 1993; compiler booklets in field. Mem. Selection com. Sch. Bd., Manhasset, 1992-94. Charles Freeman Meml. scholar, 1958-62, Buffalo and Erie County Pub. Libr. scholar, 1967-68. Mem. ALA, Assn. Coll. and Rsch. Librs., L.I. Coun. Acad. Libr. Dirs., Nassau County Libr. Assn., Beta Phi Mu. Office: US Mcht Marine Acad 300 Steamboat Rd Kings Point NY 11024-1699

BILLY, GERRY DEE, protective services official; b. Zanesville, OH, Feb. 6, 1951; s. Paul and Jean (Drake) Billy; m. Mary Lynn Bibart, June 19, 1976; children: Angela Mishonne, Paul James. AAS cum laude (hon.), Muskingum Area Tech. Coll., Zanesville, 1975; BA cum laude, Ohio Dominican Coll., 1980; M Criminal Justice, U. Ala., 1990. Detective Muskingum Sheriff Dept., Zanesville, 1974—76; agent-in-charge Tri-County Anti-Crime Program, Newark, Ohio, 1978—80; investigator Porter, Wright Law Office, Columbus, Ohio, 1978—80; instr. criminal justice law enforcement Ctrl. Ohio Tech. Coll., Newark, 1978—; sheriff Licking County, Newark, 1981—; prin. Billy & Assocs. criminal justice cons. Cons. Varasso & Assocs. Archs./Planners, Newark, 1978—. Chmn. Ohio Police Olympics, Columbus, 1976—; asst. dir. Licking County Spl. Olympics, 1980—; trustee Licking County Hist. Soc., 1982—; bd. dirs. Licking County chpt. ARC, 1983—; appt. mem. Commn. on Prison Crowding, 1984. Served as mil. police investigator AUS, 1983—. Named Outstanding Young Man of Am., US Jaycees, 1981—83, Outstanding Young Man of Licking County, Newark Area Jaycees, 1982, Outstanding Law Enforcement Officer of Ohio, 1990, Outstanding Criminal Justice Profl. of Ohio, 1990; recipient Disting. Svc. award, Newark Area Jaycees, 1980—82, Appreciation award, Ohio Spl. Olympics, 1983, cert. Accommodation, Am. Legion, 1983, Presdl. award of Honor, Granville Jaycees, 1983, Disting. Svc. award, US Jaycees, 1982, Appreciation award, Nat. Child Safety Coun., 1981, Outstanding Instr. award, Muskingum County Law Enforcement Acad., 1976. Mem.: Am. Jail Assn. (spkr. nat. conf. 1985), Am. Correctional Assn., US Dept. Justice Drug Trafficking Commn. (law enforcement coord. com.), Ohio Augo Theft Investigator's Assn., Nat. Sheriff's Assn., Buckeye State Sheriff's Assn. (tng. coord. 1982—, pres. 1994), Narcotic Assn. of Regional Coordinating Officers OH (pres. 1984—, Exec. Svc. award 1982), VFW, Hon. Order Ky. Cols., Masons. Republican. Luth. Avocations: golf, basketball, hunting, painting, design. Home: 14 Richards Rd Newark OH 43055-2159 Office: Licking County Sheriff's Dept 155 E Main St Newark OH 43055-5434 E-mail: sheriffbilly@alink.com.

BILSON, WESLEY, health products executive; b. L.A., July 25, 1933; s. George and Hattie Bilson; m. Judith Wolfe, Sept. 17, 1995; children: Meredith, Amy, Jeffrey, David, Gregory, Jessica. BA, UCLA, 1955. Asst. film editor and writer Desilu Prodns., Hollywood, Calif., 1959-62; pres. W & W Hosp. Devel. Corp., Beverly Hills, Calif., 1962-65, Diversified Health Svcs., Inc., Beverly Hills, 1965-72, Druthers Agy., Inc., Marina Del Rey, 1972-78; chmn. Delano Regional Med. Ctr., Delano, Calif., 1978—92; pres. Delmed Corp., Pacific Palisades, 1992—, Cardiac Renewal Ctrs. Am., Pacific Palisades, 1999—. Health care bus. cons., 1965—; bd. dirs. Ecoly Internat., Inc., Chatsworth, Calif.; pres. United Hosp. Assn., L.A., 1986. Advisor to pres. of Soviet Union, 1988-92; bd. dirs. Kehelat Israel, Pacific Palisades, 1998—; founding mem. Bus. Execs. Move for Vietnam Peace, Washington, 1963-72. 1st lt. USAF, 1956-59. Mem. Riviera Country Club. Jewish. Avocations: political policy issues, skiing, tennis. Office: Demed Corp 881 Alma Real Dr Pacific Palisades CA 90272

BILSTROM, JON WAYNE, lawyer; b. Chgo., Mar. 1946; m. Kathy Bilstrom. BS, U. Iowa, 1968, JD, 1974. Bar: Iowa 1974, Ill. 1974, Mo. 1991. Gen. counsel Exchange Nat. Bank, Chgo.; v.p., gen. counsel First Wis. Corp., Milw.; ptnr. Katten Muchin & Zavis, Chgo.; gen. counsel, sec. Merc. Bancorp Inc., St. Louis, 1990—99; pres., CEO The Bar Plan Mut. Ins. Co., St. Louis, 2001—02; exec. v.p. governance, regulatory rels., and legal affairs, sec. Comerica Inc., Detroit, 2003—. Served U.S. Army. Office: Comerica Inc Comerica Tower at Detroit Ctr 500 Woodward Ave MC 3391 Detroit MI 48226

BILTONEN, RODNEY LINCOLN, biochemistry educator, pharmacology educator; b. Ont., Can., Aug. 24, 1937; came to U.S., 1941; s. Frank Emil and Frances Cecilia (Castren) B.; m. Margaret Jane Kobel, Aug. 6, 1960; children— Michael Andrew, Eric Franklin AB, Harvard Coll., 1959; PhD, U. Minn., 1965. Asst. prof. Johns Hopkins U., Balt., 1966-72; assoc. prof. biochemistry and pharmacology U. Va., Charlottesville, 1972-77, prof., 1977—2003, prof. emeritus, 2003—, assoc. dean, 1979-81, assoc. provost, 1981-84. Vis. prof. Gulbenkian Inst., Portugal, 1970-71, U. Lund, Sweden, 1971, Cayetano, Lima, Peru, 1976, U. N.C., Chapel Hill, 1980, CNR, Genoa, Italy, 1993, The Technical U. Denmark, 1995; James Disting. prof. physics St. Francis Xavier U., Antigonish, N.S., 1984; cons. in field. Assoc. editor Biophys. Jour., 1991-95; mem. editl. bd. Chemistry and Physics of Lipids, 1995—; contbr. numerous articles to profl. jours. Recipient G.T. Walker award, Sigma Xi, 1965, Huffman Meml. award, Calorimetry Conf., 1989; fellow, NIH, 1965—66; grantee, NSF, 1968—99, NIH, 1970—. Fellow: Biophys. Soc. (councilor 1984—86); mem.: Am. Calorimetry Conf. (chmn. 1976—77). Office: Univ Va Dept Pharmacology 1300 Jefferson Park Ave Charlottesville VA 22908-0735 E-mail: rlb1t@virginia.edu.

BINA, MELVINA JEAN HUMPAL, elementary school educator; b. Decorah, Iowa, Nov. 21, 1948; d. Melvin John and Darlene Mae (Jirak) Humpal; m. James V. Bina, June 1, 1974. BS, Viterbo Coll., LaCrosse, Wis., 1971; MA, Ohio State U., 1988. Cert. tchr. Tchr. St. Anthony Sch., Athens, Wis., 1971-74; substitute tchr. Franklin County, Columbus, Ohio, 1974; tchr. Groveport (Ohio) Madison Local Sch. Dist., 1974—. Co-treas. PTO, Groveport Madison Local Sch. Dist., 1987-88. Franklin County Tchr. Ctr. math. grantee, Columbus, 1983. Mem. NEA, Delta Kappa Gamma (pres. 1986-88), Phi Delta Kappa. Roman Catholic. Avocations: reading, travel, collecting cookie cutters, collecting children's books. Office: Asbury Elem 5127 Harbor Blvd Columbus OH 43232-6263 Home: 2624 Steiner House Columbus OH 43219-3148

BINDEL, THOMAS HERBERT, chemistry educator; b. Augsburg, Germany, Sept. 27, 1954; s. Thomas Joseph and Ingeborg Maria Bindel; m. Rose Mary Drotar, Dec. 23, 1975; children: Aaron, Sarah, Nathaniel, Peter, Mary. BA, U. Colo., 1975, PhD, 1980. Asst. prof. U. Wis., Stevens Point, 1982—83; lectr. U. Colo., Denver, 1990—; tchr. sci. Jefferson County Schs., Arvada, 1984—. Vis. asst. prof. U. Colo., Boulder, 1980—82, 1983—84. Contbr. articles to profl. jours. Mem.: Colo. Chemistry Tchrs. Assn. (pres. 1991—92), Am. Chem. Soc. Avocations: reading, fishing, tennis, softball. Office: Pomona High Sch 8101 W Pomona Dr Arvada CO 80005 Office Phone: 303-982-0661. E-mail: tbindel@jeffco.k12.co.us.

BINDENAGEL, JAMES DALE, university executive; b. Huron, S.D, June 30, 1949; s. Gordon Dean and Patricia Jean (Williams) B.; m. Jean Kathleen Lundfelt, Dec. 26, 1971; children: Annamarie, Carl Jakob. BA, U. Ill, 1971, MPA, 1977. Officer U.S. Embassy U.S. Dept. State, Seoul, Republic of Korea, 1975—77; with U.S. Consulate, Bremen, Germany, 1977-79; econ. officer Office Ctrl. European Affairs U.S. Dept. State, Washington, 1980-83; polit. officer Am. Embassy, Bonn, Germany, 1983-86; acting dir. Can. affairs U.S. Dept. State, 1988-89; dep. chief mission Am. Embassy, Berlin, 1989-90; divsn. chief developing countries and trade orgns. U.S. Dept. State Econ. and Bus. Affairs Bur., 1991; dir. Rockwell Internat., 1991-92; dir. Office Ctrl. European Affairs U.S. Dept. State, Washington, 1992-94; dep. chief mission Am. Embassy, Bonn, Germany, 1994-96, chargé d'affaires, acting amb., 1996—97; sr. coord. New Transatlantic Agenda German Marshall Fund, 1997-98; dir. Washington Conf. on Holocaust-era Assets; amb. spl. envoy for Holocaust issues, 1999—2002; spl. negotiator Conflict Diamonds, 2002—03; v.p. Chgo. Coun. on Fgn. Rels., 2003—05, De Paul U., 2005—. Trustee Remembrance, Responsibility and Future Fund, 1999-2002, Arthur F. Burns Fellowship. Capt. USAR, 1971-74. Decorated comdrs. cross Order of Merit Germany; recipient V.P. Nat. Performance award, 1998, Disting. Honor award, U.S. State Dept., 2000, Presdl. Meritorious Svc. award, 2002. Mem.: Woodstock Bus. Conf., Coun. on Fgn. Rels., Am. Coun. on Germany, Am. Polit. Sci. Assn. (Congl. fellow 1987—88), Pi Sigma Alpha. Roman Catholic. Avocations: tennis, hiking. Home: 3740 N Lake Shore Dr Apt 4B Chicago IL 60613-4201 Office Phone: 312-362-7579. E-mail: jdbindena@depaul.edu.

BINDER, AMY FINN, public relations company executive; b. N.Y.C., June 13, 1955; d. David and Laura (Zeisler) Finn; children: Ethan Max, Adam Finn, Rebecca Eve. BA with honors, Brown U., 1977; MBA, Columbia U. Freelance photographer, N.Y.C., 1977-78; account exec. Newton & Nicolazza, Boston, 1978-79, Agnew, Carter, McCarthy, Boston, 1979-80; dir. pub. relations City of New Rochelle, N.Y., 1980-82; dir. urban communications Ruder-Finn, N.Y.C., 1982-85, v.p., 1985-86, exec. v.p., 1986-87; pres. Ruder-Finn America, N.Y.C., 1987; CEO, exec. mng. dir. RFBinder Partners, Inc. Ruder Finn Group, 2001—. Photographer: Museum without Walls, 1975, The Spirit of Man: Sculpture of Kaare Nygaard, 1975, Knife Life and Bronzes, 1977, St. Louis: Sculpture City, 1988, The Triumph of the American Spirit: Johnstown, Pennsylvania, 1989. Mem. Internat. Ctr. of Photography (mem. pres. coun.), Pres. Assn. of Am. Mgmt. Assn. Democrat. Jewish.

BINDER, DAVID FRANKLIN, lawyer, writer; b. Beaver Falls, Pa., Aug. 1, 1935; s. Walter Carl and Jessie Maivis (Bliss) Binder; m. Deana Jacqueline Pines, Dec. 25, 1971; children: April, Bret. BA, Geneva Coll., 1956; JD, Harvard U., 1959. Bar: Pa. 1960, U.S. Ct. Appeals (3d cir.) 1963, U.S. Supreme Ct. 1967. Law clk. to chief justice Pa. Supreme Ct., 1959—61; counsel Fidelity Mut. Life Ins. Co., Phila., 1964—66; ptnr. Bennett, Bricklin & Saltzburg, Phila., 1967—68; mem. Richter, Syken, Ross, and Binder, Phila., 1969—72, Raynes, McCarty, Binder, Ross and Mundy, Phila., 1972—. Mem. faculty Pa. Coll. Judiciary; judge pro tempore Phila. Common Pleas Ct., 1991—97; lectr., course planner Pa. Bar Inst.; mem. civil procedural rules com., ad hoc com., mem permanent com. evidence Supreme Ct. Pa. Author: Hearsay Handbook, 1975, ann. supplements, 4th edit., 2001, Binder on Pennsylvania Evidence, 1999, 3d edit., 2003. Recipient Disting. Alumnus award, Geneva Coll., 1981. Mem.: ATLA (lectr.), ABA, Am. Coll. Trial Lawyers, Am. Bd. Trial Advs., Pa. Trial Lawyers Assn., Phila. Bar Assn., Pa. Bar Assn., Harvard Law Sch. Assn., Union League. Home: 1412 Flat Rock Rd Narberth PA 19072-1216 Office: Raynes McCarty Binder Ross and Mundy 1845 Walnut St Ste 2000 Philadelphia PA 19103-4767 Office Phone: 215-568-6190. Business E-Mail: dfbinder@raynesmccarty.com.

BINDER, ELAINE KOTELL, associations consultant; b. Boston, Oct. 12, 1938; d. Maxwell and Florence (Blumsack) Kotell; m. Richard A. Binder, Aug. 28, 1960; children: Mark Stephen, Jonathan Stuart. AB, Radcliffe Coll., 1960; MA, U. Md., 1975. Tchr. City of Medford, Mass., 1960-62; project dir. Wider Opportunities for Women, Washington, 1971-75, Women's Equity Action League Fund, Washington, 1976-78; mng. ptnr. Binder, Elster, Mendelson, Wheeler, Bethesda, Md., 1978-80; adminstrn. dir. AAUW, Washington, 1980-85; exec. dir. B'nai B'rith Women, Washington, 1985-94. Pres. Binder Assocs., Bethesda, 1994—; prin. ptnr. Tecker Consultants, Trenton, N.J., 1994—; cons. Bethesda, 1975-76. Co-author: Careers for Peers, 1973; contbr. articles to profl. jours. Trustee Temple Shalom, Silver Spring, Md., 1974-76; pres., v.p. Montgomery County Commn. for Women, Rockville, Md., 1978-80; commr. Anti-Defamation League, N.Y., 1985—; bd. dirs. Jewish Coun. for the Aging, 1996—. Fellow Am. Soc. Assn. Execs. (bd. dirs. 1990-93, vice chmn. 1994), Greater Washington Soc. Assn. Execs. (com. chair 1989—). Democrat. Jewish. Avocations: music, art, collecting native american art and artifacts, reading. Office: Tecker Consultants 427 River View Exec Park Trenton NJ 08611 also: Binder Assocs 6704 Bradley Blvd Bethesda MD 20817-3045

BINDER, GORDON M., venture capitalist; b. St. Louis, 1935; m. Adele Binder, 1964. BS in elec. engring., Purdue U., 1957; MBA, Harvard U., 1962. Asst. to v.p. Litton Industries, 1962-64; fin. mgmt. Ford Motor Co., 1964-69; CFO Sys. Devel. Corp., 1971-81; v.p., CFO Amgen, Thousand Oaks, Calif., 1982-88, CEO, 1988-2000, chmn. bd., 1990-2000; mng. dir. Coastview Capital LLC, L.A., 2001—. Former chmn. Pharm. Rsch. and Mfrs. of Am. (PhRMA), Biotechnology Industry Assn. (BIO), MIT. Am. Cancer Soc. Found. Baker scholar Harvard U. Office: Coastview Capital LLC Ste 1850 11111 Santa Monica Blvd Los Angeles CA 90025

BINDER, HARRY J., lawyer; b. N.Y.C., Apr. 12, 1948; m. Gloria L. Binder, May 15, 1955. BBA cum laude, CCNY, 1968; JD, Cornell U., 1971. Bar: NY, U.S. Dist. Ct. (ea. and so. dists.) NY, U.S. Dist. Ct. (so. dist.) Ala., U.S. Ct. Appeals (2d and 11th cirs.), U.S. Tax Ct., U.S. Supreme Ct. Atty. Law Offices of Jack Solerwitz, Mineola, NY, 1972—73; pvt. practice Patchogue, NY, 1973—77; sr. ptnr. Binder & Binder PC, Happauge and N.Y.C., 1978—. Trustee NY State Health Commn., Smithtown, 1976—78. Mem.: ATLA, NY State Trial Lawyers Assn., NY State Bar Assn. Office: Binder & Binder PC 1500 New York Ave Huntington Station NY 11746 Business E-Mail: harry@binderandbinder.com.

BINDER, L. JAMES, retired magazine editor, journalist; b. Jackson, Mich., June 21, 1926; s. Leonard George and Ethel Cecile (Lilly) B.; m. Margery Elizabeth Rose, Sept. 6, 1950; children: Timothy James, Michael Paul, Douglas Harold. BS, Central Mich. U., 1952. Editor Wingfoot Clan, Goodyear Tire & Rubber Co., 1952-54, Wayne (Mich.) Eagle, 1954-55; news editor Pontiac (Mich.) Press, 1955-57; editor, newsman AP, 1957-60; state editor Detroit News, 1960-67; editor-in-chief Army mag., Washington, 1967-93; corr., book reviewer Nat. Observer, 1962-67; v.p publs. Assn. U.S. Army, 1992-94; ret., 1993. Author: Lemnitzer: A Soldier for His Time, 1997; editor: Front and Ctr., 1991; contbr. articles to various publs. Served with USN, 1944-46; with USAR, 1950-54. Recipient George Washington Honor medal Freedoms Found., 1975, George Washington award editorial, 1974, 76 Mem. VFW, Am. Soc. Mag. Editors, Soc. Profl. Journalists, Cosmos Club, Nat. Press Club, Detroit Press Club, Ends of Earth Club, Soc. of Midland Authors, Am. Legion, Tin Can Sailors. Methodist. Home: 12728 Inverness Way Woodbridge VA 22192-5036 Personal E-mail: ptsable@aol.com.

BINDER, MICHAEL BERNARD, dean, researcher; b. Bklyn., Mar. 19, 1943; s. Nathan Binder and Muriel Goldstein; m. Nancy Ann Kessler, May 25, 1969; 1 child, Amy Cheryl. BA, NYU, 1965; MLS, Rutgers U., 1967; PhD, U. Pitts., 1973. Libr. Def. Intelligence Agy., Arlington, Va., 1967; tchr. fellow U. Pitts., 1969—70; libr. dir. Bradford (Pa.) Campus Pitts., 1972—74, Fairleigh Dickinson U., Rutherford, NJ, 1978—85; head libr. Clinch Valley Coll., Wise, Va., 1974—78; dean librs. Western Ky. U., Bowling Green, 1985—. Co-author: Advances in Library Administration, 1983; author: Videotex and Teletext, 1985; contbr. articles to profl. jours. Bd. dirs. Barren River Imaginative Mus. Sci., Bowling Green, 2000—03. Fellow, U.S. Dept. Edn., 1968—69; N.Y. Regents scholar, N.Y. Bd. Regents, 1961—65. Mem.:

ALA (pres. N.J. chpt. ACRL divsn. 1980), Am. Soc. Info. Sci., Ky. Libr. Assn. Avocations: tennis, music, weightlifting. Office: Western Ky U 1906 College Heights Blvd Bowling Green KY 42101

BINDER, STEVEN F., publishing executive; Assoc. pub. Golf Link; sr. acct. mgr. Golf Illustrated; v.p., advt. dir. ELLE Mag.; v.p., exec. pub. Mirabella; v.p. corp. sales, regional sales dir. Hacjette Filipacchi, 1995; assoc. pub. Allure Mag., 1999—2001; sr. v.p., pub. Golf Digest Mag., 2001—. Office: PO Box 850 Wilton CT 06897-0850

BINDLEY, WILLIAM EDWARD, pharmaceutical executive; b. Terre Haute, Ind., Oct. 6, 1940; s. William F. and Gertrude (Lynch) B.; children: William Franklin, Blair Scott, Sally Ann. BS, Purdue U., 1961; grad. wholesale mgmt. program, Stanford U., 1966. Asst. treas. Controls Co. Am., Melrose Park, Ill., 1962-65; vice-chmn. E.H. Bindley & Co., Terre Haute, 1965-68; pres., chmn. bd., CEO Bindley Western Industries, Inc., Indpls., 1968—2001; CEO Priority Healthcare, Lake Mary, Fla., 1994—97, pres., 1996, now chmn. Scholl scholarship guest lectr. Loyola U., Chgo., 1982; guest lectr. Young Pres. Orgn., Palm Springs, Calif. and Dallas, 1981, 82, 84, Ctr. for Entrepreneurs, Indpls., 1983, Purdue U., West Lafayette, Inc., De Pauw U., Greencastle, Ind., disting. lectr. Georgetown U., Washington, 1989—, mem. adv. bd.; bd. dirs. Key Bank NA, Cleve., Shoe Carnival, Inc.; former owner basketball team Ind. Pacers. State dir. Bus. for Reagan-Bush, Washington and Indpls., 1980; trustee Marian Coll., Indpls., Indpls. United Way, St. Vincent Hosp., Indpls.; bd. dirs. Indpls. Entrepreneurship Acad., Nat. Entrepreneurship Found., U.S. Ski Team, chmn. fin., exec. com. mem.; mem. adv. bd. Rose Hulman Inst. Tech.; mem. pres.'s coun. Purdue U., dean's adv. bd. Named Hon. Ky. Col., 1980, Sagamore of the Wabash, Gov. Orr, State of Ind., 1989, Entrepreneur of Yr., State of Ind., 1992. Mem. Young Pres. Orgn. (area dir., chmn. 1982, award 1983), Nat. Wholesale Druggists Assn. (dir. 1981-84, Svc. award 1984), Purdue U. Alumni Assn. (life), Woodstock Club, Meridian Hills Countryn Club. Republican. Roman Catholic. Avocations: skiing, golf, tennis, boating. Office: Priority Healthcare 250 Technology Pk Lake Mary FL 32746*

BINDSCHADLER, DAVID E., mathematician, department chairman, application developer; b. Pitts., Oct. 16, 1948; s. Ernest and Madora Bindschadler; m. Valerie Yvette Verreault, May 27, 1972; children: Michael David, Kevin Richard. BS in math., Ohio State U., Columbus, 1970; MA in math., Ind. U., Bloomington, 1973, PhD in math., 1976. Asst. to assoc. prof. Wayne State U., Detroit, 1976—85; sr. systems engr. Electronic Data Sys., Troy, Mich., 1985—97, Unigraphics Solutions, Troy, 1997—99; chair math. and computer sci. dept. Lawrence Tech. U., Southfield, Mich., 1999—. Presenter at profl. conf. Am. Math. Soc., 1977—, Soc. Indsl. and Applied Math., 1977—85; CAD/CAM trainer Electronic Data Sys.; judge Grand award Computer Sci. Internat. Sci. and Engring. Fair, Detroit, 2000. Contbr. articles to profl. jours. Coach Huntington Woods Pk. and Recreation, Mich., 1985, 1989; parent sponsor, Future Problem Solvers of Am. Berkley Pub. Sch., Mich., 1990, 1993; Sunday sch. tchr. First Presbyn. Ch., Royal Oak, Mich., 1993—94. Recipient cert. of appreciation, Berkley Pub. Sch., 1987. Mem.: Soc. for Indsl. and Applied Math., Am. Math. Soc. Achievements include development of condition for symmetries of area minimizing surfaces; invention of developable surface design tool. Avocations: chess, strategy games, racquetball. Office: Lawrence Tech U 21000 West Ten Mile Rd Southfield MI 48075

BINES, HARVEY ERNEST, lawyer, educator, writer; b. Winthrop, Mass., Nov. 25, 1941; s. Carl and Lillian (Cooper) B.; m. Joan Carol Paller, Dec. 27, 1964; children: Jonathan W., Joel T., Susanne R., Benjamin E. BS, MIT, 1963; JD, U. Va., 1970. Bar: Mass 1971, Va. 1971, U.S. Dist. Ct. Mass., U.S. Dist. Ct. (ea. dist.) Va., U.S. Ct. Appeals (1st, 3d, 4th, 7th and D.C. cirs.), U.S. Supreme Ct. Law clk. to hon. John D. Butzner Jr. U.S. Ct. Appeals (4th cir.), Richmond, Va., 1970-71; asst. prof. Law Sch. U. Va., Charlottesville, 1971-74, assoc. prof. Law Sch., 1974-76; assoc. Sullivan & Worcester, Boston, 1976-79, ptnr., 1980—. Adj. prof. Boston Coll. Law Sch., Chestnut Hill, Mass., 1981-88, bd. dirs., treas. Schweitzer Fellowship, Boston. Author: Investment Management Law and Regulation, 1978, 2d edit., 2004, supplement, 2005. Lt. USNR, 1963-67. Mem.: Boston Bar Assn., Am. Law Inst. Home: 36 Clarke St Lexington MA 02421-4916 Office: Sullivan & Worcester 1 Post Office Sq Ste 2300 Boston MA 02109-2129 Office Phone: 617-338-2828. Business E-Mail: hbines@sandw.com.

BINFORD, GREGORY GLENN, lawyer; b. Canton, Ohio, Oct. 8, 1948; s. Edwin and Helen Marie B. BA, Case Western Res. U., 1970, JD, 1973. Bar: Ohio 1973. Ptnr. Guren, Merritt, Cleve., 1973-84, Benesch, Friedlander, Cleve., 1984—. Councilman, Bratenahl, Ohio. Mem. ABA, Nat. Health Lawyers Assn., Cleve. Bar Assn. (former chair health law sect.). Office: BF America Bldg 200 Public Sq Ste 2300 Cleveland OH 44114-2378

BINFORD, HENRY C, history professor; b. Berea, Ohio, May 2, 1944; s. Henry Francis and Dorothy Johnston Binford; m. Janet Cyrwus, Sept. 9, 1991; children: Charles, Evan. AB, Harvard, 1966; MA, U. Sussex, England, 1967; PhD, Harvard U., 1973. Asst. prof. Northwestern U., Evanston, Ill., 1973—79, assoc. prof., 1979—. Author: (book) The First Suburbs, 1985. Office: Northwestern U 1881 Sheridan Rd Evanston IL 60208

BINFORD, JESSE STONE, JR., chemistry professor; b. Freeport, Tex., Nov. 1, 1928; s. Jesse Stone and Eglan Lee (Bracewell) B.; m. Lolita Ramona Fritz, June 8, 1955; children: Lincoln Bracewell, Jason Jolly. BA in Chemistry, Rice U., 1950, MA in Chemistry, 1952; PhD in Phys. Chemistry, U. Utah, 1955. Instr. chemistry U. Tex., Austin, 1955-58; asst. prof. U. of the Pacific, Stockton, Calif., 1958-60, assoc. prof., 1960-61; Fulbright prof., chmn. dept. chemistry Univ. Nacional Autonoma de Honduras, Tegucigalpa, 1968-69; vis. rsch. prof. Thermochemistry Lab., U. Lund, Sweden, 1971, researcher, 1982-83; rsch. fellow Chelsea Coll., U. London, 1983; assoc. prof. U. South Fla., Tampa, 1961-72, prof., 1972—2003, emeritus prof., 2004—. Cons. Fla. consortium AID, Honduras, 1969, Exxon Prodn. Rsch. Co., Houston, 1974; chmn. State Univ. Faculty Senate Coun., Fla., 1975-76; dir. gen. chemistry program U. South Fla., 1978-82, 98-2003; vis. prof. dept. chem. engring. Rice U., 1993-94, rschr. Cox Lab. for Biomed. Engring., Inst. Bioscis. and Bioengring., 1993-94; mem. Inst. for Biomolecular Sci., U. South Fla., pres. faculty senate, 1999-2000. Author: (textbook) Foundations of Chemistry, 1977, 2nd edit., 1985; contbr. articles to profl. jours., 1956—. Active bicycle adv. com. Hillsborough County, Tampa, 1975-93, chairperson bicycle adv. com., 1990-93; faculty advisor U. South Fla. Bicycle Club, 1972-2004; coord. spl. tutoring program Danforth Found., Tampa, 1968. Grantee Petroleum Rsch. Fun, 1960-62, USPHS (NIH), 1966-68, Rsch. Corp., 1986. Mem. AAUP, AAAS, Am. Chem. Soc. (nat. and Tex. sect.), Calorimetry Conf., League of Am. Bicyclists, Golden Key, Sigma Xi, Phi Beta Kappa, Phi Lambda Upsilon, Sigma Pi Sigma, Omicron Delta Kappa. Avocations: bicycling, travel, reading. Office: U South Fla Dept Chemistry 4202 E Fowler Ave Tampa FL 33620-8000 Home: 5600 Bull Creek Rd Austin TX 78756-1010

BINFORD, ROSLYN BETH, psychologist; d. Lowell Eugene and Marybeth Binford. BA, U. Minn., 1997, MA, 2002, PhD, 2003. Psychology intern U. Chgo., Chicago, Ill., 2002—03, postdoctoral fellow, 2003—04, clin. instr., 2004—. Recipient NIMH Travel award, NIMH, 2004; scholar Waller, U. Minn., 1997; Minn. Women's Psychologists Master's scholarship, Minn. Women's Psychologists, 2002. Mem.: APA, Acad. for Eating Disorders. Office Phone: 773-834-9101.

BING, DAVID, retired professional basketball player, metal products executive; b. Washington, Nov. 29, 1943; children: Cassaundra, Bridgett, Aleisha. BA in Econ., Syracuse U., 1966. With Detroit Pistons, 1966-74, Wash. Bullets, 1975-77, Boston Celtics, 1977-78; owner, chmn., CEO, The Bing Group, Detroit, 1980—. Named Rookie of Yr., 1967, Basketball Hall of Fame, 1989, Most Valuable Player, NBA All-Star Game, 1976, Nat. Small Bus. Person of Yr., 1984, Nat. Minority Supplier of Yr., 1984; recipient Schick Achievement award, 1990. Achievements include named to First Team NBA All Star, 1968, 71, Second Team, 1974, All Rookie Team, 1967; leading scorer in Syracuse U. history; All-Star 7 times. Office: The Bing Group 11500 Oakland St Detroit MI 48211-1073

BING, STEVE, film producer; b. Mar. 31, 1965; s. Peter S. and Helen Bing; 1 child, Damien. Writer (films) Missing in Action, 1984, Missing in Action 2: The Beginning, 1985, Kangaroo Jack, 2003, (TV series) Married...With Children, 1987—97; prodr.: (films) Without Charlie, 2001, Night at the Golden Eagle, 2002, The Big Bounce, 2004; exec. prodr.: Get Carter, 2000; actor: The Dark Backward, 1991. Named one of 50 Most Powerful People in Hollywood, Premiere mag., 2005. Address: 1801 Avenue of the Stars #150 Los Angeles CA 90067*

BING, XU, artist; b. Chongqing, China, 1955; arrived in US, 1990; Grad., Central Acad. of Fine Arts, Beijing, 1981, MFA, 1987. Instructor Central Acad. of Arts, Beijing, 1988. Former dir. Chinese Artists Assn.; honorary fellow U. Wisconsin, 1990; art residency Am. Acad., Berlin, 2003—04. Exhbns. include: Modern Chinese Prints, British Mus., London, 1986, Xu Bing: A Book from the Sky, Nat. Fine Arts Mus., Beijing, 1989, Looking for Tree of Life: A Journey to Asian Contemporary Art, Mus. Modern Art, Saitama, Japan, 1992, Maos Goes Pop: China Post-1989, Mus. Contemporary Art, Sydney, 1993, Transversions, 2nd Johannesburg Biennale, Johannesburg, South Africa, 1997, Beyond the Form: The Transformation and Symbolic of Chinese Character in Arts, NY Lincoln Ctr. Cork Gallery, NYC, 1998, Crossings, Nat. Gallery of Can., Ottawa, 1998, Banner Project, MOMA, NYC, 1999, Half A Century of Chinese Woodblock Prints, Mus. Art Ein Harod, Israel, 1999, 1st Fukuoka Asian Art Triennale, Fukuoka Asian Art Mus., Japan, 1999, Concerning Truth, Gallery 400, Sch. of Art Inst. Chgo., 1999, Tobacco Project, Duke U., NC, 2000, Word Play: Contemporary Art by Xu Bing, Arthur M. Sackler Gallery, Smithsonian Instn., Wash., DC, 2001, Where Does the Dust Collect Itself?, Wales, 2001 (Artes Mundi prize), Commons Gallery, U. Hawaii, Honolulu, 2002, Living Word 2, Herbert F. Johnson Mus. Art, Cornell U., Ithaca, NY, 2002, Biennale of Sydney, Mus. Contemporary Art, Australia, 2002, Asia Pacific Triennial, Queensland Art Gallery, Brisbane, Australia, 2002, ES 2002 Tijuana: Bienal Internacional de Estandartes, Centro Cultural Tijuana, Mexico, 2002, The First Guangzhou Triennial - Reinterpretation: A Decade of Exptl. Chinese Art 1990-2000, Guang Dong Mus. Art, China, 2002, 4th Shanghai Biennale, Shanghai Art Mus., China, 2002, Book from Sky, Princeton U. Art Mus., NJ, 2003, Fukuoka Asian Art Mus., Japan, 2003, Drawing the Line: Contemporary Artists Reassess Traditional East Asian Calligraphy, Pacific Asia Mus., Pasadena, Calif., 2003, Drawing the World: Masters to Hipsters, Vancouver Art Gallery, Can., 2003, Love and/or Terror: Contemporary Book Art, U. Ariz. Mus. Art, Tucson, 2003, First Beijing Internat. Art Biennale, China Nat. Mus. Fine Arts, Beijing, 2003, Happiness, Mori Art Mus., Tokyo, 2003, Chinese Printmaking Today, Brit. Libr., London, 2003, Artes Mundi Prize Exhbn., Nat. Gallery Mus. Wales, Cardiff, 2004. Named to, Art in Am. Ann. Guide, 2004—05; recipient Youth Friends award, NYC Dept. Edn., Sch. Art League, 2005; Coca-Cola fellow, Am. Acad. Berlin, 2004. Business E-Mail: xubing@xubing.com.

BINGAMAN, JEFF, senator; b. El Paso, Tex., Oct. 3, 1943; s. Jesse and Beth (Ball) B.; m. Anne Kovacovich, Sept. 13, 1968, 1 child BA in Govt., Harvard U., 1965; JD, Stanford U., 1968. Bar: N.Mex. 1968. Asst. atty. gen., N.Mex., 1969; atty. Stephenson, Campbell & Olmsted, 1971-72; ptnr. Campbell, Bingaman & Black, Santa Fe, 1972-78; atty. gen. State of N.Mex., 1979—82; U.S. senator from N.Mex. U.S. Senate, 1983—, mem. armed svcs. com., mem. joint econ. com., mem. Senate Dem. steering and coordination com., mem. Senate Den. tech. and comm. com., ranking minority mem., mem. energy and natural resources subcom. of energy prodn. and regulation, mem. labor and human resources com. U.S. Army Reserves, 1968-74. Democrat. Meth. Home: PO Box 5775 Santa Fe NM 87502-5775 Office: US Senate 703 Hart Senate Bldg Washington DC 20510-0001*

BINGER, WILSON VALENTINE, civil engineer; b. Greenwich, N.Y., Feb. 28, 1917; s. George and Blanche (Wilson) B.; m. Barbara Ridgway, May 19, 1947 (dec. 1984); children: Wilson Valentine, Mary Blanche, Julia Ridgway; m. Jane E. Schwarz, Apr. 24, 1986. AB cum laude, Harvard, 1938, MS in Engring., 1939. Registered profl. engr., N.Y., Ohio. Soils engr. U.S. Army Engrs., Wilmington, Del., 1939-40; soils and found. engr. Gatun 3d Locks project, Panama Canal, 1940-43; soils engr., resident engr. Parsons Brinckerhoff, Hogan & MacDonald, Caracas, Venezuela, 1945-46, chief soils engr. Buenos Aires, Argentina, 1948-49; chief soils and found. sect. Isthmian Canal Studies, Panama Canal, 1946-47; chief soils and geology br. Mo. River divsn. U.S. Army Engrs., Omaha, 1947-48; v.p. Porterfield-Binger Constrn. Co., Youngstown, Ohio, 1950-52; regional mgr. Tippetts-Abbett-McCarthy-Stratton, Bogota, Colombia, 1952-56; assoc. ptnr. Tippetts-Abbett-McCarthy-Stratton, N.Y.C., 1957-61, ptnr., 1962-84; chmn., 1975-84; cons. engr., 1985—. Author papers in field. Pres., trustee Chappaqua (N.Y.) Libr., 1967-69; trustee Robert Coll., Istanbul, Turkey, 1970—, vice chmn., 1974-78, sec., 1992—; bd. dirs. Regional Plan Assn., N.Y., 1983-88; chmn. bd. deacons Congl. Ch., 1959-62, trustee, 1985-88. Recipient Disting. Citizen award Warren (Ohio) Met. Area Assn., Steinmetz award Consulting Engr. Mag., Diamond Ann. Lifetime Achievement award N.Y. Assn. Cons. Engrs. Fellow ASCE, Inst. Civil Engrs. (U.K.), Am. Cons. Engrs. Coun. (v.p. 1973-75), N.Y. Acad. Scis.; mem. NAE, Royal Acad. Engring. U.K. (fgn. mem.), Am. Inst. Cons. Engrs. (councillor 1971-73, pres. 1973), NSPE, U.S. Com. Large Dams (mem. exec. com. 1964-69, sec. 1962-78), Internat. Com. Large Dams (v.p. 1978-81), N.Y. Assn. Cons. Engrs. (v.p., dir. 1964-65), Moles, Internat. Road Fedn. (dir. 1975-82, mem. exec. com. 1975-82), Fedn. Internat. des Ingenieurs Conseils (mem. exec. com. 1976-83, treas. 1976-79, v.p. 1980-81, pres. 1981-83), Century Club, Harvard Club (N.Y.C.), Univ. Club, East India Club (London), Phi Beta Kappa. Home: 1110 Meadow Ridge Redding CT 06896

BINGHAM, CHRISTOPHER, statistics educator; b. N.Y.C., Apr. 16, 1937; s. Alfred Mitchell and Sylvia (Knox) B.; m. Carolyn Higinbotham, Sept. 23, 1967 AB, Yale U., 1958, MA, 1960, PhD, 1964. Research fellow Conn. Agrl. Expt. Sta., New Haven, 1958-64; research assoc. in math. and biology Princeton U., N.J., 1964-66; asst. prof. stats. U. Chgo., 1967-72; assoc. prof. applied stats. U. Minn., Mpls., 1972-79, prof., 1979—. Contbr. articles to profl. jours. Fellow Am. Statis. Assn., Inst. Math. Stats.; mem. Royal Statis. Soc., Biometric Soc., Soc. Indsl. and Applied Math Home: 605 Winston Ct Mendota Heights MN 55118-1039 Office: U Minn Sch Stats 313 Ford Hall 224 Church St SE Minneapolis MN 55455-0493 E-mail: kb@umn.edu.

BINGHAM, ELIZABETH ELLIOTT, librarian; b. Butler, Ala., June 29, 1948; d. James Howard and Emogene (Shamburger) Elliott; m. Clifton O. Bingham, Jr., Apr. 16, 1965 (div. Mar. 1977); 1 child, Clifton O. BS, La. State U.-Baton Rouge, 1970, MS, 1971. Reference libr. East Baton Rouge Parish Libr., 1970-74, head mid-city br., 1974-75, head adult svcs., 1975—; sec. task force White House Conf. on Librs. and Info. Svcs., 1994-97, La. Endowment for Humanities, 1995-96, v.p. 1996-97; cons. Bingham & Assocs. Contbr. articles to profl. jours. HEW fellow, 1975. Recipient YMCA Woman of Achievement, 1997. Mem. Libr. Adminstrn. and Mgmt. Assn. (sec. 1994-96), Intellectual Freedom Round Table (treas. 1995-97), Am. Library Assn. (pres. Jr. Mem. Round Table 1979-80, mem. coun. 1994—), La. Library Assn. (treas. 1979-80, recipient Mid-Career award 1983, 1st v.p./pres.-elect 1989-90, pres. 1990-91. Essae M. Culver Disting. Svc. award 1997), Southeastern Library Assn. Democrat. Presbyterian. Clubs: Altrusa Internat., Jr. League (Baton Rouge); Found. for Hist. La. E-mail: bbingham@ebr.lib.la.us. Office: 7817 N Jefferson Pl Cir 2d Fl #E Baton Rouge LA 70809-8633 Office Phone: 225-907-6189. E-mail: binghamassociate@aol.com.

BINGHAM, GEORGE WALTER CHANDLER, retired sales executive; b. Cambridge, Mass., Jan. 1, 1925; s. George Hutchins Bingham Jr. and Audrey Wellington (Wack) Bingham Suter; m. Carolyn Susan Webb, Nov. 25, 1967; 1 child, Susan Cordelia. Student, Dartmouth Coll., 1943—44, student, 1946—48; BA, Gettysburg Coll., 1950; postgrad., Columbia U., 1950—51. With CBS TV, N.Y.C., 1951—55; account exec. Gill-Perna Sta. Reps., N.Y.C., 1955—56, Walker Representation Co., N.Y.C., 1956—57; v.p., mgr. New Eng. sales Walker-Rawalt, Inc., Boston, 1957—61; pres. New Eng. Spot Sales, Inc., Boston, 1961—95; mgr. New. Eng. sales Stone Reps., 1960—70; mgr. New Eng. sales Jack Masla & Co., Boston, 1970—80, Weiss & Powell, Boston, 1983—86, Katz & Powell, Boston, 1987—95, New Eng. Spot Sales Inc., Belmont, Mass., 1995—2000; ret., 2000. Treas., co-owner So. Maine Broadcasting Corp., Sanford/York County, 1975-83, Essex Broadcasting Corp., Newburyport, Mass., 1977-83. Exec. com. Dartmouth Coll. Class of 1947; officer, dir. Camp Allen, Bedford, N.H., 1983—. With USNR, 1943-46. Mem. New Eng. Assn. Radio and TV Sta. Reps. (pres. 1963-64), Broadcasters Found., Mass. Soc. SAR, Mass. Soc. Mayflower Descs. (officer, dep. gov. 1976-87), Am. Legion (comdr. post 281 1974-76, 85-92), Boston's Advt. Post, Harvard Faculty Club, Boston Athenaeum, Kiwanis, Phi Alpha Theta, Kappa Kappa Kappa (hon.). Democrat. Episcopalian. Avocations: history, theater, cross country skiing. Home: 208 Lewis Rd Belmont MA 02478-3833

BINGHAM, GLORIA FUTRELL, retired secondary school educator; b. Pollock, La., May 15, 1933; d. A.D. and Vaudiene (Dunn) Futrell; m. Lawrence C. Bingham, Dec. 5, 1954; children: Pamela B. Lancaster, Carla D., Valerie D. BA, N.E. La. U., Monroe, 1972, M.Ed., 1985, postgrad.; student in bookkeeping, La. Bus. Coll., 1952. Cert. secondary tchr., libr.-media scis., academically gifted edn., reading, La. Tchr., librarian Ouachita Parish Schs., Monroe; coord. regular and spl. edn. Richland Parish Schs., Rayville, La., tchr. social studies and English, librarian; ret., 1992. Contbr. articles to profl. jours. Co-founder Northeast La. Susan G. Komen Found.; bd. dirs. La. Bapt. Found., Northeast La. Alzheimer's Assn., Susan G. Komen Breast Cancer Found. Named La. Mother of Yr., Am. Mothers La., 2005. Mem. Ouachita Tchrs. Assn. (past sec.-treas.), Ouachita Librarians Assn. (past. pres.), Alpha Delta Kappa (past chpt. pres., past state officer).

BINGHAM, J. PETER, electronics research executive; married; 2 children. BS in Physics cum laude, Polytechnic Inst., N.Y.; MS in Exptl. Physics, PhD in Elec. Engring., U. Md. With RCA Consumer Electronics, David Sarnoff Rsch. Ctr.; exec. v.p., tech. Thomson Consumer Electronics; v.p. engring. Philips Consumer Electronics Co., 1982-91; with Philips Rsch. Philips Electronics N.Am. Corp., 1991; pres. Philips Rsch., 1991—. Bd. dirs. Indsl. Rsch. Inst. Recipient David Sarnoff award, RCA Lab. Achievements award; Named in his honor Bingham Peak in Antarctica, Arctic Inst. of North Am. Office: 23 Brookwood Dr Briarcliff Manor NY 10510-2040

BINGHAM, JEFFREY L., government agency administrator, musician; b. Bridgeport, Conn., Oct. 1, 1952; s. John H. and Teresa A. Bingham, Wladyslaw Miszewski and Alfreda M. Wisniewski; m. Deborah A, Berlingo, June 14, 1980; 1 child, Maureen E. BA, Sacred Heart U., 1974. Govt. examiner IRS, Bridgeport, Conn., 1974—. Vol. music and hospitality Holy Family Passionist Retreat Ctr., West Hartford, Conn., 1999—2005; dir. music St. Anthony Roman Cath. Ch., Ansonia, Conn., 2002—05. Mem.: Nat. Assn. Pastoral Musicians (sec. 2002—05, treas. 2002—05). Roman Catholic. Office Phone: 203-384-5722. Personal E-mail: jeffcpsinger@snet.net.

BINGHAM, JINSIE SCOTT, broadcast company executive; b. Greencastle, Ind., Dec. 28, 1935; d. Roscoe Gibson and Alpha Edith (Robinson) Scott; m. Frank William Wokoun, Jr. (dec.); children: Douglas Scott, Richard Frank; m. Richard Innes Bingham, June 24, 1964. Student, DePauw U., Greencastle, 1952-53, Northwestern U., 1953, Coe Coll., 1953-54. Exec. sec. Ind. Young Dems., 1958-60; receptionist Ind. Ho. of Reps., Indpls., 1959; saleslady Avon Products, Greencastle, 1961-64; sales mgr. Sta. WJNZ (formerly WXTA), Greencastle, 1969-77, owner, pres., gen. mgr., 1977-94; owner Radio Greencastle, 1977—. Owner, pres. gen. mgr. Sta WJNZ, 1977-94; past ptnr. Sta. WVTL, Monticello, Ill., Sta. KBIB, Monette, Ark.; speaker DePauw U. Comm. Seminar, 1981-85; vis. lectr., 1986—. Co-author: Putnam County Indiana Land Patents, 2004. Com. chair Legis. Awareness Seminar, 1978—86; co-chair Greencastle Gaelic Festival, 1983—84; charter mem. Greencastle 2001, 1985—, Greencastle Civic League, 1984—, Greencastle Merchant's Assn., 1983—97, Cmty. Resources Com., 1982—87; charter mem., corp. sec. Main St. Greencastle, 1983—87, v.p., 1987—88, pres., 1989—90, chmn., 1990—91; v.p. United Way, 1996—97, campaign chair, 1996—97, campaign advisor, 1998—99; announcer Putnam County Fair Parade, 1977—; co-chmn. centennial com. Putnam County Courthouse, 2001—; v.p. Putnam County Mus., 2002, pres., 2003—04; tour guide Putnam County Conv. and Visitors Bur., 1998—; active Putnam County Coun. on Aging and Aged, 1999—; pres. Putnam County Hist. Soc., 1996—97, sec., 1998—; bd. dirs., v.p., sec., pres., hon. dir. Putnam County Found.; co-founder Greencastle H.S. Alumni Assn., 1995, founding chmn. scholarship fund, 1995—; active Govs. Commn. for a Drug Free Ind., 1991—; v.p. West Ctrl. Ind. Econ. Devel. Coun., 2003—; mem. Lilly Scholar Selection Com., 1998—; vice chmn. Putnam County Dem. Ctrl. Com., 2001—; bd. dirs. Putnam County Comprehensive Ctr., 1994—2000, Opportunity Housing, 1995—2002; charter mem., bd. dirs. Greencastle Devel. Ctr., 1988—89, Greencastle Cmty. Child Care Ctr., 1983—87; v.p. Greencastle Zoning Bd. Appeals, 1985—88, pres., 1988—; charter mem., bd. dirs. Greencastle Vol. Fire Dept., 1986. Sagamore of the Wabash, Ind. Gov. Evan Bayh, 1995; Limestone State Seal, 1996, Seal of City, Greencastle, 1996; named Hoosier Know It All Champion, Sta. WTTV, Indpls., 1998; named to Ind. Broadcasters Hall of Fame, 1999; named one of 53 Trailblazing Women of Ind., 1999, Outstanding Citizen Greencastle Jaycees, 1981; named to Putnam County Agr. Hall of Fame Putnam County Farm Bur., 2002; recipent Disting. Hoosier Award, conferred by Gov. Joseph Kernan, 2004 Mem. AARP (Capital City task force 2000), Nat. Soc. DAR (Centennial chmn. Washburn chpt. 2002, sec. 1994-2003, chaplain 1988-2004, chpt. regent 2003—), Broadcast Pioneers (life), Putnam County Bd. Realtors, Am. Women in Radio and TV (pres. Ind. chpt. 1979-82, Lifetime Achievement award 1996), Indpls. Network Women in Bus. (charter), Women in Comm., Inc. (bd. dirs. 1983-84, MATRIX co-chair 1984, Frances Wright award 1993), Am. Legion Aux., Nat. Assn. Broadcasters, Soc. Profl. Journalists, Ind. Broadcasters Assn. (v.p. FM 1982), Putnam County Extension Adv. Coun. (4H), Natural Resources Svc. Land Use Study Group, Greencastle Bus. and Profl. Women's Club (pres. 1975-76, 78-79, Woman of Yr. 1994), Indpls. Ad Club, Women's Press Club Ind., Indpls. Press Club, Nat. Fedn. Press Women, Ind. Dem. Editl. Assn. (sec. 1987, v.p. 1988, pres. 1990), Ind. C. of C., Greencastle C. of C. (bd. dirs. 1979-83, pres. 1982, amb. 2001—. Citizen of Yr. 1997), VFW (pres. ladies aux. 1966-68), Ind. Geneal. Soc. (bd. dirs. West Ctrl. divsn. 2005—), Milestone Care Soc., Packard Club Ind., Ind. Soc. Pioneers, Daus of 1812 (pres. Tippecanoe chpt. 1981, state v.p. 1982), Daus. of the Union, Internat. Order Job's Daus., Soc. Descendants of Valley Forge, Rotary (bd. dirs., pres. 1994-95, bull. editor 1995—, dist. conf. planner 1997, Paul Harris fellow 1998, del. world conf. 1998), Order Ea. Star, Women of Moose, Milestone Car Soc., Genealogical Soc. (bd. dirs., 2005-), Delta Theta Tau, Sigma Delta Chi. Mem. Christian Ch. (Disciples Of Christ). Office Phone: 765-653-3565. Business E-Mail: jinsie@ccrtc.com.

BINGHAM, JUNE, playwright; b. White Plains, N.Y., June 20, 1919; d. Max J.H. and Mabel (Limburg) Rossbach; m. Jonathan B. Bingham, Sept. 20, 1939 (dec. July 1986); children: Sherry B. Downes, Micki B. Esselstyn (dec. 1999), Timothy, Claudia B. Meyers; m. Robert B. Birge, Mar. 28, 1987; 1 stepchild, Robert R. Student, Vassar Coll., 1936-38; BA, Barnard Coll., 1940; LittD (hon.), Lehman Coll., 2002. Writer, editor U.S. Treasury, Washington, 1943-45; editorial asst. Washington Post, 1945-46; writer Tarrytown (N.Y.) Daily News, 1946. Author: Do Cows Have Neuroses?, Do Babies Have Worries?, Do Teenagers Have Wisdom?, Courage to Change: An Introduction to Life and Thought of Reinhold Niebuhr, 1961, Courage to Change: An Introduction to Life and Thought of Reinhold Niebuhr, paperback edit., 1992, U Thant: The Search for Peace, 1970, (plays) Triangles, 1986, Eleanor and Alice, 1996, You and the I.C.U., 1990; author: (with others) The Inside Story: Psychiatry and Everyday Life, 1953, The Pursuit of Health, 1985; author: (mus.) Squanto and Love, 1992, Young Roosevelts, 1993, The Other Lincoln, 1995, The Strange Case of Mary Lincoln, 2001; contbr. articles to nat. mags., newspapers and profl. jours. Bd. dirs. Riverdale Mental Health Assn., 1983-2005, Woodrow Wilson Found., Princeton, N.J., 1959-64, 83-89,

Lehman Coll. Found., 1983-90, Ittleson Ctr. for Childhood Rsch., 1958-90, Franklin and Eleanor Roosevelt Inst., 1992-2002; founder T.L.C.; trained liaison comforter Vol. Program of Presbyn. Hosp., N.Y.C., mem. hosp. ethics com. Named Alumna of the Yr., Rosemary Hall, 1976. Mem. Authors Guild (nominating com. 1987-90), Dramatists Guild, PEN, Cosmopolitan Club. Democrat. Avocations: tennis, golf, theater, movies, reading. Home: 5000 Independence Ave Bronx NY 10471-2804

BINGMAN, CHARLES FRANKLIN, public relations executive, educator; b. West Allis, Wis., Sept. 11, 1929; s. Clyde James and Bernice (Hengstler) B. BBA, U. Wis., 1952, MBA, 1956. Mgr. planning and control Nasa-Johnson Space Ctr., Houston, 1962-66; dep. dir. mgmt. programs Office Manned Space Flight Nat. Aero. and Space Adminstrn., Washington, 1967-71; dep. assoc. dir. orgn. mgmt. U.S. Office Mgmt. and Budget, Washington, 1971-76; dep. adminstr. Urban Mass Transp. Adminstrn. U.S. Dept. Transp., Washington, 1976-79, spl. asst. to dep. sec., 1982-83; exec. dir. Pres.'s mgmt. improvement coun. Exec. Office of The Pres., Washington, 1979-80, mgmt. advisor White House Office of Policy Devel., 1980-81; vis. prof. pub. adminstrn. dept. George Washington U., Washington, 1984-97; cons. U.S. and internat. govts., 1985—; fellow Ctr. for Study of Am. Govt., Johns Hopkins U., Washington, 1997—. Author: Japanese Government Leadership and Management, 1989, Serving Two Presidents: A History of the Bureau of the Budget, 1992, Revitalizing Federal Management, 1983; contbr. articles to profl. jours. Pres. Woodlake Towers Condo Assn., 1996—2002. Capt. U.S. Army, 1951—65. U.S. Info. Agy. grantee, 1992. Fellow Nat. Acad. Pub. Adminstrn.; mem. Sr. Execs. Assn. (pres. 1968-69, bd. dirs. 1982-85), Fed. Exec. Inst. Alumni Assn. (bd. dirs. 1983-86), William A. Jump Found. (bd. dirs. 1987—), Cosmos Club. Republican. Avocations: writing, jogging, hiking, reading. Home: 3100 S Manchester St Apt 815 Falls Church VA 22044-2716 E-mail: user7352@aol.com.

BINIENDA, JOHN J., state legislator; b. Worcester, Mass., June 22, 1947; s. Thaddeus Andrew and Mary Gertrude (O'Coin) B.; children: Julie Ann, John Joseph Jr., Jamie Thaddeus. BA, Worcester State Coll., 1970, postgrad., 1970-74. State rep. Dist. 17 Mass. Ho. of Reps., 1987—, chmn. Com. on Revenue. Mem. Ward 7 Dem. Com., 1987—; mem. South Worcester Neighbor Ctr. Mem. Worcester State Coll. Alumni Assn., Am. Legion (Main St. chpt.), Polish Naturalization Ind. Club, Polish Am. Vet. Club, K.C. (3d degree). Office Phone: 617-722-2320. Business E-Mail: Rep.JohnBinenda@house.statema.us.

BINIENDA, ZBIGNIEW KAROL, research scientist, consultant; b. Warsaw, May 13, 1951; s. Karol and Danuta Janina Binienda; m. Renata Wieslawa Wojnarowicz, June 24, 1975; children: Hubert Zbigniew, Adrianna Renata. PhD, Cornell U., Ithaca, NY, 1985—90; DVM, Agrl. U., Warsaw, Poland, 1969—75. Rsch. biologist FDA/NCTR, Jefferson, Ark., 1990—; adj. asst. prof. U. Ark. for Med. Scis., Little Rock, 1998—. Rsch. specialist Cornell U. Med. Sch., NYC, 1981—85. Contbr. articles to profl. jours. Pres. Polish-Am. Cultural Assn. Ark., Little Rock, 1993—95. Grantee, Cornell U. Bd. of Trustees, 1986—89. Mem.: Soc. for Neuroscience. Roman Catholic. Achievements include patents for radioimmunoassay of progesterone in milk. Avocations: travel, opera music, swimming. Home: 11231 Rivercrest Drive Little Rock AR 72212 Office: Nat Ctr for Toxicol Rsch/FDA 3900 NCTR Drive Jefferson AR 72079-9502 Office Phone: 870-543-7920. Home Fax: 870-543-7745; Office Fax: 870-543-7745. Personal E-mail: zbinienda@ntr.fda.gov. E-mail: zbinienda@nctr.fda.gov.

BINION, CELIOUS, retired parochial school educator; b. Carthage, Jan. 31, 1940; d. George Lewis and Ellene Steel; children from previous marriage: Vicki Pearson, Yolanda Davis. BS, Jackson State U., 1961; MA, Chgo. State U., 1981, Olivet Nazarene U., Kankakee, Ill., 2001. Tchr. Bd. Edn., Chgo., 1964—69, libr., 1970—2001; tchr. Dist. 143, Posen, Ill., 1969—70, St. Clotilde Cath. Sch., Chgo., 2001—03; ret., 2003. Counselor Ill. Young Authors, Bloomington, 1986—; sec. Connexion, Inc., Chgo., 1998—. Author: (children's book) Buffy Goes Skating, 1987, (poems) Poetry for the Soul, 2004. Drama helper vol. Washington Pk. Field House, Chgo., 1986—97; vol. Sherman Pk. Libr., Chgo., 1999—2003, Connexions, Chgo., 1999—; sec. Chgo. State's Libr. Club, 1999—2001; Sunday sch. tchr. God's House of All Nations, 1989—. Named Tchr. of the Yr., Leary Corp., 2003; grantee, Kate Maremont Assn., 1987, Kizzy Found., 2001. Mem.: Phi Beta Kappa. Avocations: reading, writing, music, tennis. Home: 7747 S King Dr Chicago IL 60691

BINKLEY, DAVID A., human resources specialist; BS, Mich. State U. Regional mgr. human resources Whirlpool Corp., Benton Harbor, Mich., 1984—86, mgr. employee rels. parts distribution ctr. LaPorte, Ind., 1986—89, dir. exec. devel. corp. human resources, 1989—92; dir. human resources Whirlpool Corp. Europe, Comerio, Italy, 1992—94; dir., human resources Whirlpool Corp. Asia, Singapore, 1994—95, v.p. human resources Greater China, 1995—96; corp. dir. mgmt. resources Whirlpool Corp., Benton Harbor, Mich., 1996—98, v.p. human resources N.Am. divisn., 1998—2001, sr. v.p. global human resources, 2001—. Office: Whirlpool Corp 2000 N M-63 Benton Harbor MI 49022-2692 Office Phone: 269-923-5000. Office Fax: 269-923-5443.*

BINKLEY, LUTHER JOHN, philosophy educator; b. Wernersville, Pa., Oct. 7, 1925; s. Harry Garfield and Jennie Theresa (Yoder) B.; m. Betty Jane Bowman, June 5, 1964. AB, Franklin and Marshall Coll., 1945; BD, Lancaster (Pa.) Theol. Sem., 1947; PhD, Harvard U., 1950. Ordained to ministry United Ch. of Christ, 1949. Instr. philosophy Franklin and Marshall Coll., Lancaster, 1949-51, asst. prof., 1951-56, assoc. prof., 1956-62, prof., 1962-91, prof. emeritus, 1991—, chmn. dept., 1962-74, dir. humanities program, 1972-74. Vis. fellow Cambridge (Eng.) U., 1959-60, Princeton (N.J.) U., 1967, 69; adj. prof. Temple U., Phila., 1965-83, Pa. State U., Harrisburg, 1975-88. Author: The Mercersburg Theology, 1953, Contemporary Ethical Theories, 1961, Conflict of Ideals: Changing Values in Western Society, 1969. Mem. Pub. Coun. for Humanities in Pa., Phila., 1975-79; mem. instnl. ethics com. Lancaster Regional Med. Ctr., 1985—; mem. instnl. rev. bd. Lancaster Gen. Hosp., 1988—, mem. cmty adv. bd. Penn State Ambulatory Rsch. Network. Recipient Disting. Coll. Tchg. award Lindback Found., 1962. Mem. AAUP (pres. Franklin and Marshall chpt. 1962-63, 50 Yr. Svc. award 2000), Am. Philos. Assn., Philos. Soc. for Study Sport (pres. 1977-78), Hershey Country Club, Lancaster Torch Club (pres. 1956-57, Silver award 1999), Phi Beta Kappa (pres. Theta chpt. Pa. 1970-71). Avocations: travel, golf, tennis, attending opera and symphony concerts, reading. Home: PO Box 473 Hershey PA 17033-0473 Office: Franklin and Marshall Coll PO Box 3003 Lancaster PA 17604-3003 Personal E-mail: ljbinkley@aol.com.

BINKLEY, MARILYN ROTHMAN, educational research administrator; b. N.Y.C., Jan. 27, 1948; d. Edgar and Mollie (Rothenberg) Rothman. BA, Bklyn. Coll., 1968; MA, Columbia U., 1971; EdD, George Washington U., 1983. Tchr. N.Y.C. Pub. Schs., 1972-77; reading splst. Internat. Sch., Geneva, 1975-77; instr. Marymount Coll. Va., Arlington, 1978-80; edn. cons. Washington, 1980-85; sr. assoc. Office Ednl. Rsch. and Improvement U.S. Dept. Edn.; edn. policy fellow Inst. Ednl. Leadership, 1987-88; sr. assoc. Nat. Ctr. Edn. Statistics, 1988—. Nat. rsch. coord. Internat. Assn. for the Evaluation of Edn. Adv., reading literacy study, 1988—95; U.S. coord. Internat. Adult Literacy Study, 1994—99; cons. Severn Sch., 1980—83, Dept. Def. Dependent Schs., 1979, Dover Sch. Singapore, 1978; dep. dir. Internat. Life Skills Study, 1998—2001; nat. project dir. OECD Program for Indicators of Student Achievement, 1998—2001; internat. co-dir. Adult Literacy and Life Skills Survey, 1998—2000; dir. item devel. Nat. Assessment of Edn. Progress, 2001—. Mem. Am. Ednl. Rsch. Assn., Am. Statistical Assn., Nat. Assn. Ind. Schs., Nat. Coun. Tchrs. English, Nat. Assn. Measurement and Evaln., Nat. Reading Conf., Internat. Assn. Evaln. of Ednl. Achievement, Internat Reading Assn., Coll. Reading Assn., Orton Soc., Assn. Supervision and Curriculum Devel., Va. Reading Assn., Md. Reading Assn., Greater Washington Reading Assn., Delta Phi Epsilon, Phi Delta Kappa. Home: 12024 Gatewater Dr Potomac MD 20854-2875 Office: US Dept Edn 1990 K St NW Washington DC 20001-2029

BINKLEY, TIMOTHY, computer graphics designer, educator; b. Balt., Sept. 14, 1943; s. Enos G. and Grace (Joy) Binkley; m. Sonya Shannon, 1993. BA in Math. with honors, U. Colo., 1965, MA in Math., 1966; PhD in Philosophy, U. Tex., 1970; postgrad. in computer sci., Courant Inst., NYU, 1979-82. Asst. prof. Notre Dame U., Ind., 1970-73; postdoctoral fellow Temple U., Phila., 1973-75; mem. faculty New Sch. for Social Rsch., N.Y.C., 1975-77; chair dept. humanities and scis. Sch. Visual Arts, N.Y.C., 1976-88, dir. computer edn., 1982—98, dir. Inst. for Computers in the Arts, 1986—98, chair MFA program in computer art, 1988—98; pres. Artware, 1996—. Co-dir. telecom. event Heinrich Hertz Centennial Celebration, Bronx, Bklyn., 1987. Author: Wittgenstein's Language, 1973; author: (with others) Reason and Violence, 1974, Culture and Art, 1976, Philosophical Perspectives on Metaphor, 1981, Philosophy Looks at the Arts, 1987; author: (software) Paint Brush, 1983, Starmaker, 1988, Symmetry Studio, 1990, GAIN Engine, 1999, Agnet Wrangler, 2000; contbr. articles to profl. jours.; exhibitions include computer installations Face to Face and Drawn to the Light in Computer and Art Exhbn., IBM Gallery Sci. and Art, N.Y.C., 1988, Ctr. Fine Arts, Miami, Fla., 1988, Represented in permanent collections Franklin Inst., Phila., Autoform in Gretta Sarfaty's retrospective exhbn. Musea Da Imagem E Do Som, Sao Paulo, Brazil, collaborative paintings with G. Sarfaty, Symmetrical Reincarnations I and II; computer art dir.: (videos) A Price for Every Progress, 1987; Pink Slip Out of Nowhere, 1988; dir.: (films) Portrait of Sean, 1972, The Seasons, One Minute of Pure Chance, 1973, Existence, Synchrony, 1974; mem. editl. adv. bd. Philosphy and Lit., 1976—85, Art & Academe, 1988—. NEH Younger Humanist fellow, 1973—74, Ford Found. fellow, 1974—75, Oldright fellow, NDEA fellow, O'Brien Rsch. grantee, 1971, NEH Grantee, 1977. Mem.: Am. Soc. Aesthetics (trustee 1981—84), Assn. Computing Machinery (bd. dirs. N.Y.C. 1987—, chair spl. interest group computer graphics 1988—), Phi Beta Kappa.

BINNEY, JAN JARRELL, publishing executive, marketing professional; b. Frankfort, Ind., Aug. 16, 1941; d. Robert and Susie (Meek) Jarrell; m. Joseph M. Binney, June 23, 1962; 1 child, Robert J. BS, Purdue U., 1962; MA, Coll. N.J., 1972. Speech-lang. pathologist pub. schs., various locations, 1962-84; pvt. practice speech pathology East Brunswick, N.J., 1982-85; pres. The Speech Bin, Inc. Pub., Vero Beach, Fla., 1984—. Editor profl. publs. Deacon Presbyn. Ch., 1985-87, elder, 1987-90; bd. dirs., chpt. chmn. ARC, Indian River Country, Fla. Fellow Am. Speech, Lang. Hearing Assn. (legis. councilor 1981-89, bd. dirs. pub. info. exch. 1987-89, com. on equality 1988-90, bd. dirs. polit. action com.), N.J. Speech, Lang. Hearing Assn. (pres. 1981-82, hon. 1984), Exch. Club Indian River (sec. 1998-99, bd. dirs. 2001-2002), Exch. Club Indian River Found. (charter, sec. 2002—), Pi Beta Phi Alumnae Club (treas.). Office: The Speech Bin Inc 1965 25th Ave Vero Beach FL 32960-3000 Office Phone: 772-770-0007. Business E-Mail: jan@speechbin.com.

BINNEY, ROBERT HARRY, bank executive; b. London, Oct. 21, 1945; s. Roy and Barbara (Poole) B.; m. Valerie Kay Greene, May 4, 1979; children: Alexandra, Christopher, Nicholas, Paul. MA in Mech. Scis., Cambridge (Eng.) U., 1967; MBA, Manchester (Eng.) Bus. Sch., 1971. Mktg. exec. Rank Xerox, Birmingham, Eng., 1967-69; with Chase Manhattan Bank, various locations, 1971-96; exec. Orion Bank, London, 1971-72; from mgr. expansion and diversification to bus. exec. Chase Manhattan Bank, N.Y.C., 1972—91, bus. exec. Europe and Mid. East for global securities svc., 1991—96; mng. dir. Europe, Mid. East, Africa worldwide securities svcs. Citibank, N.A., London, 1996—2003; with Citigroup, 1998—, mng. dir. global transaction svcs. in Europe, Mid. East, Africa London, 2003—04, mng. dir. global client devel., 2004—. Mem. Surrey County Cricket Club. Anglican. Avocations: travel, tennis, bridge. Office: Citigroup Ctr Canada Sq Canary Wharf London E14 5LB England Business E-Mail: robert.binney@citigroup.com.

BINNIAN, EMILY FAULKNER, geographer; b. Seattle, Wash., May 11, 1959; d. Samuel Shaw Binnian; m. William Garst Campbell, June 28, 1986; 1 child, James Morison Campbell. BA in Geography, Macalester Coll., 1982. Spatial analyst North Slope Borough Planning Dept., Anchorage, 1984—88; scientist Contractor to USGS EROS Alaska, 1988—. Adj. faculty Alaska Pacific U., Anchorage, 1986—86, U. Alaska, 1982—82. Home: 3231 Redoubt Ct Anchorage AK 99517 Office: SAIC at US Geological Survey 4230 University Dr Anchorage AK 99508 Office Phone: 907-786-7033. E-mail: binnian@usgs.gov.

BINNIE, BRIAN, business executive and test pilot; BS in Aerospace Engrng., MS in Fluid Mechanics, Brown U.; MS in Aeronautical Engrng., Princeton U.; grad., US Navy Test Pilot Sch., Patuxent River, Md., Naval Aviation Safety Sch., Monterey, Calif. Lic. Airline Transport Pilot. Program bus. mgr., test pilot Scaled Composites, Mojave, Calif. Flight test experience includes: Scaled's Model 318 White Knight, Scaled's Model 316 SpaceShipOne, Roton Flight Test, F/A-18 Electronic Warfare Suite Testing and Integration, F/A-18 TSSAM Weapon Launch Envelope Expansion, A-6E TSSAM Weapon Launch Envelope Expansion, F/A-18 SLAM-ER Weapon Launch Envelope Expansion, A-6E SLAM-ER Weapon Launch Envelope Expansion, F/A-18 LEX Fence Performance Map, F/A-18 ATARS Transonic Handling Evaluation, A-7E Structural Flight Test Qualification Program, F/A-18 KC-10 Wing Tip Refueling Pod Evaluation, A-7E KC-10 Wing Tip Refueling Pod Evaluation, F/A-18 F404 2nd Source (Pratt & Whitney vs GE) Engine Envelope Expansion, F/A-18 Hi-Energy Nose Strut -T/Off and Landing Eval, F/A-18 First LGB Weapon Delivery Using Self-Lasing FLIR. Mem.: Am. Inst. Aeronautics and Astronautics (pub. mem.), Soc. Exptl. Test Pilots. Achievements include completing the ROTON: Hazard Analysis / Aircrew Checklists / Normal & Emergency Procedures; conducting Flight Test / Developed Operational Flight Procedures (Tactics)/ providing Fleet Training (1 to 5 day course) for F/A-18 and AV-8B EW Suites; expanding curriculum to include Foreign Military Customers and provided in-country training to Finland, Malaysia and Italy; writing all the operational checklists and providing the Fleet Tactics Manual for the TSSAM Weapon System; planning and executing the first (and only) radar chase of the Tomahawk cruise missile to demonstrate more effective surface fleet training; preparing and briefing the Australian Air Force on new Operational Flight Software for their F/A-18 aircraft; pilot for the second record flight of Space ShipOne on October 4, 2004, which won the Ansari X prize; second person in history to earn his commercial astronaut wings as a result of historic flight on Space ShipOne. Office: Scaled Composites Inc Mojave Airport 1624 Flight Line Mojave CA 93501 Office Phone: 661-824-4541. Office Fax: 661-824-4174.*

BINNIG, GERD KARL, physicist, educator; b. July 20, 1947; m. Renate Binnig, 2003; 2 children. BA in Physics, Goethe U., Frankfurt, Germany, 1973; PhD, Goethe U., Frankfurt, Fed. Republic Germany, 1978. Rsch. staff mem. IBM Zurich Rsch. Lab., 1978—, group leader, 1984—, fellow, 1987—; with Stanford U., 1985—86; hon. prof. physics U. Munich, 1987—. Mem. rsch. team IBM's Almaden Rsch. Ctr., San Jose, 1985—86; vis. prof. Stanford U., 1987—88; mem. tech. coun. IBM Acad., 1990—; mem. adv. bd. Bild der Wissenschaft, 1990—. Author: Aus dem Nichts, 1989; mem. editl. bd.: Rev. Sci. Instruments, 1990—92. Co-recipient Nobel prize in physics, 1986; named to Nat. Inventors Hall of Fame, 1994; recipient physics prize, German Phys. Soc., 1982, Otto Klung prize, 1984, Elliot Cresson medal, Franklin Inst., 1987, Grosses Verdienstkreuz mit Stern und Schulterband des Verdienstordens, 1987, Minnie Rosen award, Ross U., 1988. Fellow: Royal Microscopical Soc. (hon.), Acad. Scis. (assoc.). Achievements include invention of Scanning Tunneling Microscope. Avocations: music, tennis, soccer, golf. Office: IBM Rsch GmbH Zurich Rsch Lab Saumerstrasse 4 Postfach Rüschlikon CH-8803 Zurich Switzerland

BINNING, BETTE FINESE (MRS. GENE HEDGCOCK BINNING), athletic association official; b. Brandon, Manitoba, Canada, Sept. 20, 1927; father is an Am. citizen. d. Henry Josiah and Beatrice Victoria (Harrop) Ames; m. Gene Hedgcock Binning, May 3, 1952; children: Gene Barton, Barbara Jo, Bradford Jay. Grad., Brandon Coll., 1944; student, Brandon U., 1944—46. Exec. sec. to mgr. Gardner Denver Co., Denver, 1950—52; mem. age. group swimming com. Amateur Athletic Union U.S., 1966—68, women's swimming com., 1968—69, age group swimming objectives subcom., 1970—71, mem. age. group swimming com., 1970—72, del. Conv., 1971—77, women's swimming com., 1972—76, del. Conv., 1979—80. Okla. state chmn. age group swimming Amateur Athletic Union, 1966-68, 70-72, chmn. women's swimming com., 1968-69, 72-79, mem. Okla. exec. bd. for all amateur sports, also registration com., 1971-79; mem. U.S. Olympic com., 1972-80; nat. dir. swimming records, 1972-81; U.S. rep. to records com. Amateur Swimming Assn. Am., 1975-83, dir. records com., 1975-83; dir., sec. records com. Union Amateur de Natacion de las Americas, 1979-83; tech. ofcl. Pan Am. Games, Mex. City, 1975, San Juan, P.R., 1979; ofcl. XXI Olympiad, Montreal, PQ, Can., 1976; mem. interim organizing com. U.S. Olympic Festival, 1986; athletic adv. dir. U.S. Olympic Festival 1989, 1987-88. Team capt. YMCA fund drives, 1966-78; mem. adv. com. Internat. Gymnastics Hall of Fame, 1996-99. Mem. Kerr Mcgee Swim Club (dir. 1968-75), Quail Creek Golf and Country Club(sports dir. women's golf assn. 2003, pres. 2005), Okla. City Ski Club, Vail Athletic Club Colo. Presbyterian. Home: 3101 Rolling Stone Rd Oklahoma City OK 73120-1841 also: Vail Internat 205 300 E Lionshead Cir Vail CO 81657-5204 Home Fax: 405-751-6906. E-mail: Bettebinning@yahoo.com.

BINNING, WILLIAM CHARLES, political science professor; b. Mar. 8, 1944; m. Maureen G. Fannon, Nov. 26, 1966; children: Patrick, Catherine. BA in Politics, St. Anselm's Coll., 1966; PhD in Govt. and Internat. Rels., U. Notre Dame, 1970. Asst. prof. polit. sci. Youngstown (Ohio) State U., 1970—77, assoc. prof., chmn. polit. sci., 1977—84, prof., 1984—. Project dir. NSF, 1978—79, grant evaluator, 1979; part-time staff mem. Office of Gov. G. Voinovich, Ohio, 1991—; arbitrator Am. Arbitration Assn., 2000—. Fellow, NDEA. Mem.: AAU, ASPA, Midwest Polit. Sci. Assn., Am. Polit. Sci. Assn. Office: Dept Polit Sci Youngstown State U 410 Wick Ave Youngstown OH 44555-0001 Business E-Mail: wcbinning@ysu.edu.

BINNS, JAMES EDWARD, retired banker; b. Alameda, Calif., Oct. 5, 1931; s. Guy Vivian and Beatrice (Jury) B.; m. Marjean Friesen, Feb. 21, 1951; children: Cheryl Jean Binns Smith, Jana Lee Binns Gualco, Lori LeAnn Binns Mauer. Student, U. Nev., 1950-51; grad., Sch. Bank Audit and Control, U. Wis., 1963, Am. Inst. Banking, 1964. With Sierra Pacific Power Co., Reno, 1948-50; with First Interstate Bank of Nev., Reno, 1951-91, asst. cashier, 1957-63, asst. to cashier, 1963-65, auditor, 1965-84, asst. v.p., 1968-75, v.p., 1975-91; Cameo Jewelry and Loan, Reno, 1992-93; instr. Am. Inst. Banking. Past chmn. internal audit com. City of Reno. Mem. Sierra Nevada Cmty. Access TV, Reno Hot August Nights. Mem. AARP (past pres. Western Nev. chpt., treas., bd. dirs., dir. weekly TV prodn. N. Nev. chpt.), Am. Inst. Banking (past pres. Sierra-Nev. chpt., past nat. assoc. coun.), Bank Adminstrn. Inst. (cert. bank auditor, charter pres. chpt., past state dir.), Data Processing Mgmt. Assn. (charter mem. Sierra-Nev. chpt., past pres.), Inst. Internal Auditors (cert. internal auditor, past charter pres. chpt.), Western Indsl. Nev., Masons, Shriners, Elks, Lakeridge Tennis Club, Reno Toastmasters (past pres.), Reno H.S. Alumni Assn. (life, 1st treas.), E. Clampus Vitus (Las Plumas Del Oro chpt.), Graeagle Tennis Club, Reno C. of C. (mem. spl. events coun., Vol. of Yr. award 2001, Outstanding Svce. award 2003). Home: 1720 Allen St Reno NV 89509-1252 *A true leader must accept all reasonable challenges being fully cognizant that his and the group's success can only be achieved through the combined efforts of all participants.*

BINNS, JANE CAMILLE, humanities educator; b. Ann Arbor, Mich., Aug. 4, 1967; d. Robert Caryl and Lenore Eloise Binns; m. Michael James Monkman, Aug. 11, 1990 (div. Apr. 4, 2002); 1 child, Cale August Monkman. BS, Ea. Mich. U., 1989; MEd, Syracuse U., 1995; MFA, Naropa U., 1999. Survey analyst, tech. writer Syracuse U., NY, 1993—97; instr. English Met. State Coll. of Denver, 2000—. Author: (short stories) Pocket Change, 2004, (manual and audio tape) Talking to the Media: A How-to for New Readers, Pocket Change - flash fiction collection, 2004; contbr. short stories to anthologies (Jack Kerouac fellowship for prose, 1998, Oakland C.C. Writer's at Work, 1999), articles to profl. publs. Process and procedures manual editor Women's Polit. Caucus, Ann Arbor, Mich., 1991—93; newsletter editor NOW, Ann Arbor, 1991—93. Avocations: swimming, playing piano, writing.

BINO, MARIAL DESOLYN, librarian, educator; b. Hurley, Wis., May 11, 1916; d. John and Mary B. BE, U. Wis., 1939, cert. Aeronautics Instr., 1942; MS in Libr. Sci., Columbia U., 1958, MA in Devel. Psychology, 1966. Cert. tchr., Wis. Tchr. elem. schs., Wis., 1940-42, 50-52; aeronautic ground instr. U. Wis., Menomonie, 1942-43, aeronautic ground instr. civil air law Eau Claire, 1943-45; tchr. math., sooc. scis. Arbor Vitae-Woodruff (Wis.) H.S., 1945-46; social worker dept. social svcs. Iron County, Hurley, 1946-50; sch. dist. libr. Hurley Sch. Dist., 1952-91. Instr. children's lit. Gogebic C.C., Ironwood, Mich., 1963; vis. lectr. U. Wis., Platteville, summer 1963. Scout leader Girl Scouts Am., Hurley, 1946-50; youth leader ARC, Hurley, 1950-52; mem. City Coun., Hurley, 1982-84. Mem. AAUW, Charles F. Menniger Soc. Avocations: travel, lecturing, reading, writing, swimming.

BINOCHE, JULIETTE, actress; b. Paris, Mar. 9, 1964; Student, Nat. Conservatory of Drama. Appearances in films include Les Nanas, La Vie de Famille, Rouge Baiser, 1985, Rendez-Vous, 1985, Mon beau-Frère a tué ma soeur, Mauvais Sang, 1986, Un tour de Manège, The Unbearable Lightness of Being, 1988, Les amants du Pont-Neuf, 1991, Wuthering Heights, 1992, Damage, 1992, Trois Couteurs: Bleu, 1993, The Horseman on the Roof, 1995, A Couch in New York, 1995, Le Hussard Sur Le Toit, 1995, The English Patient, 1996 (Academy award, 1996), Alice et Martin, 1998, Les Enfants du Siecle, 1999, La Veuve de Saint-Pierre, 2000, Chocolat, 2000, Decalage Horaire, 2002, Country of My Skull, 2004.

BINSFELD, CONNIE BERUBE, former state official; b. Munising, Mich., Apr. 18, 1924; d. Omer J. and Elsie (Constance) Berube; m. John E. Binsfeld, July 19, 1947; children: John T., Gregory, Susan, Paul, Michael. BS, Siena Heights Coll., 1945, DHL (hon.), 1977; LLD (hon.), No. Mich. U., 1998; DHL (hon.), Mich. State U., 1998, Thomas Cooley Sch. of Law, 1999; LLD (hon.), Saginaw Valley State U., 2000, Lake Superior State U., 2000; DHL (hon.), U. Notre Dame, 2000, Grand Valley State U., 2000, DHL (hon.). County commr. Leelanau County, Mich., 1970-74; mem. Mich. Ho. of Reps., 1974-82, asst. rep. leader, 1979-81; del. Nav. Conv., 1980, 88, 92; mem. Mich. Senate, 1982-90, asst. rep. leader, 1979, 81; lt. gov. State of Mich., 1990-98. Mem. adv. bd. Nat. Park Sys. Named Mich. Mother of Yr., Mich. Mothers Com., 1977; Northwestern Mich. Coll. fellow; named to Mich. Women's Hall of Fame, 1998. Mem. Nat. Coun. State Legislators, LWV, Siena Heights Coll. Alumnae Assn. Republican. Roman Catholic. E-mail: Connieltgov@mailstation.com.

BINSTOCK, ROBERT HENRY, public policy educator, writer; b. New Orleans, Dec. 6, 1935; s. Louis and Ruth (Atlas) B.; m. Martha Burns, July 27, 1979; 1 dau., Jennifer. AB, Harvard U., 1956, PhD, 1965. Lectr. Brandeis U., Waltham, Mass., 1963-65, asst. prof., 1965-69, assoc. prof., 1969-72, Stulberg Prof. law and politics, 1972-84, dir. Policy Ctr. Aging, 1979-84; prof. aging, health and soc. Case Western Res. U., Cleve., 1985—. Mem. com. on an Aging Soc. Nat. Acad. Scis., Washington, 1982-86. Author: America's Political System, 1972, 5th edit., 1991, America's Political System: Urban, State and Local, 1972, 3d edit., 1979, Feasible Planning for Social Change, 1966; editor: The Politics of the Powerless, 1971, Too Old for Health Care?, 1991, Dementia and Aging, 1992, International Perspectives on Aging: Population and Policy Changes, 1982, Handbook of Aging and the Social Sciences, 1976, 5th edit., 2001, The Future of Long Term Care, 1996, Home Care Advances: Essential Research and Policy Issues, 2000, The Lost Art of Caring: A Challenge to Health Professionals, Families, Communities and Society, 2001, The Fountain of Youth: Cultural, Scientific, and Ethical Perspectives on a Biomedical Goal, 2004. Bd. dirs. White House Task Force on Older Ams., 1967-68; chmn. adv. panel Office Tech. Assessment, U.S. Congress, 1982-84; tech. adviser, del. White House Conf. on Aging, 1971, 81; trustee Boston Biomed. Research Inst., 1971-84; mem. gov.'s adv. com. Dept. of Elder Affairs Mass., 1974-84; chair, adv. bd. Nat. Acad. on Aging, 1991-95. Recipient Haak-Lilliefors award Mich. State U., 1979, Arthur S. Flemming award Nat. Assn. State Units on Aging, 1988, Key award APHA, 1992, Am. Soc. Aging award, 1994; fellow Ford Found., 1959-69; rsch. grantee NIH,

1968-73. Fellow Gerontol. Soc. Am. (pres. 1976, Donald P. Kent award 1981, Brookdale Prize award 1983), Assn. Gerontol. in Higher Edn.; mem. APHA (chair gerontol. health sect. 1996-97). Office: Case Western Res Univ 2040 Adelbert Rd Cleveland OH 44106-4901

BINTLIFF, BARBARA ANN, law educator, library director; b. Houston, Jan. 14, 1953; d. Donald Richard and Frances Arlene (Appling) Hay; m. Byron A. Boville, Aug. 20, 1977 (div. 1992); children: Bradley, Bruce. BA, Cen. Wash. U., 1975; JD, U. Wash., 1978, MLL, 1979. Bar: Wash. 1979, U.S. Dist. Ct. (ea. dist.) Wash. 1980, Colo. 1983, U.S. Dist. Ct. Colo. 1983. Libr. Gaddis and Fox, Seattle, 1978-79; reference libr. U. Denver Law Sch., 1979-84; assoc. libr., sr. instr. Sch. Law U. Colo., Boulder, 1984-88, assoc. prof., libr. dir., 1989—2001, prof., 2001—, Nicholas Rosenbaum prof. law, 2002—. Legal cons. Nat. Ctr. Atmospheric Rsch., Environ. and Societal Impacts Group, Boulder, 1980; vis. prof. U. Wash., Seattle, 1996, chair U. Colo. Boulder, Faculty Assembly, 2003—. Co-author: Colorado Legal Resources: An Annotated Bibliography, 2004; editor: A Representative Sample of Tenure Documents for Law Librarians, 1988, 2d edit., 1994, Chapter Presidents' Handbook, 1989, Representatives Handbook, 1990, Marketing Toolkit for Academic Law Libraries, 2004; assoc. editor: Legal Reference Svcs. Quarterly, Perspectives: Teaching Legal Research and Writing; contbr. articles to profl. jours. Named Disting. Alumnus, Ctrl. Wash. U., 2000; recipient Boulder Faculty Assembly Excellence Svc. award, 2001, Calhoun Svc. award, U. Colo., 2002, Frederick Charles Hicks award, Assn. of Law Librs., 2005. Mem. Am. Assn. Law Librs. (v.p./pres.-elect 2000-01, pres. 2001-02), Am. Law Inst. (elected), Colo. Bar Assn., Colo. Assn. Law Librs. (pres. 1982), Southwestern Assn. Law Librs. (pres. 1987-88, 91-92). Episcopalian. Office: U Colo Law Libr 2405 Kittredge Loop Dr Rm 190 Boulder CO 80309-0402 Business E-Mail: barbara.bintliff@colorado.edu.

BINTLIFF, CATHY SNYDER, artist, educator; b. Atlanta, May 24, 1956; d. David Louis and Llewellyn (Marchman) Snyder; m. Warren Burnett, Jr. Bintliff, Sept. 10, 1977; children: Sage Frost, Sky Forest, Sierra Dawn. BS in Art Edn., Millersville (Pa.) State Coll., 1978; MS in Art and Cultural Mgmt., Rosemont (Pa.) Coll., 2001. Cert. instructional tchr. art K-12 Pa. Art tchr. Lower Daughin Mid. and H.S., Hummelstown, Pa., 1979—81; office mgr., bookkeeper Trainer's Restaurant, Quakertown, Pa., 1981—82; photography retail mgr. Larmon Photo, Quakerstown, 1983—85; tchr. art, co-dir. summers Montessori Acad. of Pa., Boyertown, 1989—94; art and 2d grade tchr. United Friends Sch., Quakertown, 1988—89, 1994—98; JFC camp dir. Abington Quarterly Mtg., Newtown, Pa., 1998—; allied therapist Progressions of Pottstown, Pa., 1998—2001. Cons., host for Ukranian student Sister Cities Boyertown/Bohodukiv, 2000—. Editor: Center Stage (Ctr. for the Arts) newsletter, 2000—01; sculpture, Union, 1998, banner, Martin Luther King for Unity, 1999. Vol Unity Coalition, Boyertown, 1999—; JFC oversight com. JFC Abington Quarterly Mgt., Phila., 2000—. Recipient Scholastic award, Sico Found., 1974—78. Democrat. Mem. Soc. Of Friends. Avocations: travel, sculpture, theater production. Home: 150 Himmelwright Rd Barto PA 19504

BINTZ, EDWARD E., lawyer; b. Sept. 29, 1958; BS, Fordham Univ., 1980; JD, George Washington Univ., 1984; LLM, Georgetown Univ., 1992. Bar: N.Y. 1985, D.C. 1988. Ptnr., Benefits & Employment Law Practice Group Arnold & Porter, Washington. Contbr. articles to profl. jours. Office: Arnold & Porter 555 Twelfth St NW Washington DC 20004-1206 Office Phone: 202-942-5045. Office Fax: 202-942-5999. Business E-Mail: edward.bintz@aporter.com.

BINZEN, PETER HUSTED, columnist; b. Montclair, N.J., Sept. 24, 1922; s. Frederick William and Lucy Beckwith (Husted) B.; m. Elisabeth Virginia Flower, June 12, 1951; children: Lucy Binzen Wildrick, Jennifer Binzen Cardoso, Jonathan Peter, Katherine. BA in Polit. Sci, Yale U., 1947; postgrad. (Nieman fellow), Harvard U., 1962. Reporter UP, N.Y.C., 1947, Passaic (N.J.) Herald-News, 1947-50; reporter, editor Phila. Bull., 1951-82; reporter Phila. Inquirer, 1982-87; columnist Inquirer, 1987—2005. Author: Whitetown U.S.A, 1970, (with Joseph R. Daughen) The Wreck of the Penn Central, 1971, The Cop Who Would Be King, 1977; editor: Nearly Everybody Read It, 1998. Served with U.S. Army, 1943-45. Decorated Bronze Star.

BIOLCHINI, ROBERT FREDRICK, lawyer; b. Detroit, Sept. 22, 1939; s. Alfred and Erma (Barbetti) Biolchini; m. Frances Lauinger, June 5, 1965; children: Robert F., Douglas C., Frances E., Tobin M., Thomas A., Christine M. BA, U. Notre Dame, 1962; LLB, George Washington U., 1965. Bar: Okla., Mich., 1965. Assoc. Doerner, Stuart, Saunders, Daniel, Anderson & Biolchini, Tulsa, Okla., 1968-71, ptnr., 1971-94, Stuart, Biolchini & Turner, Tulsa, 1994—. Pres., CEO Pennwell Corp.; chmn. bd. dirs., CEO, PennEnergy, Inc., Valley Nat. Bank, Ameritrust Holding Co., Bank of Jackson Hole, Old Faithful Underwriting Ltd.; mem. Lloyds of London, 1979—; bd. dirs. Bank of The Lakes. Bd. dirs. Thomas Gilcrease Mus., past pres., chmn. bd., 1977-80, dir. emeritus, 1980—; bd. dirs., sec., legal clk. Tulsa Ballet Theatre, Inc., 1976-84; trustee Monte Cassino Endowment, 1978—; pres. Monte Cassino Sch. Bd., 1970-77; chmn. Christ the King Parish Coun., 1974-75; mem. adv. coun. U. Notre Dame Law Sch., 1982-2000, trustee U. Notre Dame, 2001—; chmn. Cath. Diocese Tulsa Fund for Future, 1998—; bd. dirs. legal counsel Tulsa Area United Way, 1986—; mem. pres.'s coun. Regis Coll., 1986—; Okla. chmn. Lawyers for Bush, 2000. Capt. U.S. Army, 1965-67. Mem. Okla. Bar Assn., Mich. Bar Assn., Met. Tulsa C. of C. (bd. dirs. 1992—), Summit Club, Southern Hills Country Club, Club Ltd., Knights of Malta, Knights of the Holy Sepulchre. Roman Catholic. Home: 1744 E 29th St Tulsa OK 74114-5402 Office: First Place Tower 15 E 5th St Ste 3300 Tulsa OK 74103-4340

BIONDI, ANTHONY, municipal official; b. Norristown, Pa., Apr. 10, 1962; s. Rober B. and Sylvia (Linfante) B.; m. Fran Biondi. BA, Villanova (Pa.) U., 1985. Fin. clk. Borough of Norristown, 1986-88, asst. dir. fin., 1988-91, dir. fin., 1991-94, borough administr., 1994—. Address: 235 E Airy St Norristown PA 19401-5003

BIONDI, FRANK J., JR., entertainment company executive; b. N.Y.C., Jan. 9, 1945; s. Frank J. and Virginia (Willis) B.; m. Carol Oughton, Mar. 16, 1974; children: Anne, Jane. BA, Princeton U., 1966; MBA, Harvard U., 1968. Assoc.-corp. fin. Shearson Lehman, Inc., N.Y.C., 1970-71, Prudential Securities, N.Y.C., 1969; prin. Frank J. Biondi Jr. & Assocs., N.Y.C., 1972; dir. bus. analysis Teleprompter Corp., N.Y.C., 1972-73; asst. treas., assoc. dir. bus. affairs Children's TV Workshop, N.Y.C., 1974-78; dir. entertainment program planning HBO, N.Y.C., 1978, v.p. programming ops., 1979-82, exec. v.p. planning and adminstrn., 1982-83, pres., chief exec. officer, 1983, chmn., chief exec. officer, 1984; exec. v.p. entertainment bus. sector The Coca-Cola Co., 1985; chmn., CEO, Coca-Cola TV, 1986; pres., CEO, Viacom Inc, N.Y.C., 1987-96; chmn., CEO, Universal Studios, Inc., Universal City, Calif., 1996-98; pres. Biondi Reiss Capital Mgmt., N.Y.C., 1998—99; sr. mng. dir. WaterView Advisors LLC, Santa Monica, Calif., 1999—. Bd. dirs. Bank of N.Y., Seagram Co. Ltd., Vail Resorts, Inc., USA Network Inc, Amgen, Inc., 2002-, Hasbro Inc., 2002-. Bd. dirs. Leake-Watts Svcs., Yonkers, N.Y., 1975, Mus. TV and Radio, N.Y.C., Claremont Grad. U., Princeton U. Mem. Princeton of N.Y. Club, Edgartown Yacht Club, Game Creek Club (Vail, Colo.). Office: Waterview Advisors 2425 Olympic Blvd Ste 4050W Santa Monica CA 90404-4030

BIONDI, LAWRENCE, academic administrator, priest; b. Chgo., Dec. 15, 1938; s. Hugo and Albertina (Marchetti) B. BA, Loyola U., Chgo., 1962, Ph.L., 1964, M.Div., S.T.L., Loyola U., Chgo., 1971; MS, Georgetown U., 1966, PhD in Sociolinguistics, 1975. Ordained priest Roman Cath. Ch., 1970. Joined Soc. Jesus; asst. prof. sociolinguistics Loyola U., Chgo., 1974-79, assoc. prof., 1979-81, prof., 1982-87, dean Coll. Arts and Scis., 1980-87; pres. St. Louis U., 1987—. Mem. Joint Commn. on Accreditation of Health Care Orgs., 1998—. Author: The Italian-American Child: His Sociolinguistic Acculturation, 1975, Poland's Solidarity Movement, 1984; editor: Poland's Church-State Relations in the 1980s, 1980, Spain's Church-State Relations, 1982. Trustee Xavier U., 1981-87, Loyola Coll., Balt., 1988-94, Santa Clara U., 1988-98, Kenrick-Glennon Sem., 1988-94, St. Louis U., 1982—, Loyola U., Chgo., 1988-97; bd. dirs. Epilepsy Found. Am., 1985-95, Civic Progress, St. Louis, 1987—, Regional Commerce and Growth Assn., 1987—, Mo. Bot. Gardens, 1987—, St. Louis Zoo, 1994, St. Louis Symphony, 1994, Harry S. Truman Inst. for Nat. and Internat. Affairs, 1987—, Tenet Health Care Sys., 1998—, St. Louis Sci. Ctr., 2000—, Boys Hope Girls Hope, 1996—, St. Louis Art Mus., 1997—, Grand Ctr., St. Louis, 1987—. Mellon grantee, 1974, 75, 76, 82; Humanitarian of Yr., Arthritis Found., 1999; Leon R. Strauss Urban Pioneer award, 2001. Mem. Linguistic Soc. Am., MLA, Am. Anthrop. Assn.; Knight of Italian Order of Merit. Office: St Louis U 221 N Grand Blvd Saint Louis MO 63103-2006

BIONDI, MANFRED ANTHONY, physicist, researcher; b. Carlstadt, N.J., Mar. 5, 1924; s. Manfred Anthony and Helen Biondi; m. Elaine Theresa Leitkam, May 12, 1952; children: David Mark, George Philip BS in Physics, MIT, 1944, PhD, 1949. Research assoc. MIT, Cambridge, 1948-49; with Westinghouse Research Labs, Pitts., 1949-60, adv. physicist, 1952-57, mgr. physics dept., 1957-60; prof. physics U. Pitts., 1960-86, prof. emeritus, 1987—; also dir. Atomic Scis. Inst., 1968-79; exchange prof. U. Paris, 1976-86. Trustee Upper Atmosphere Rsch. Corp.; mem. adv. com. Army Rsch. Office, Durham, N.C., NAS, 1962-64; mem. exec. coun. Fedn. Am. Scientists, 1966-68; mem. adv. panel physics NSF, 1970-72; mem. Army basic rsch. steering com. NRC, 1985-88, chmn., 1987-88. Mem. editl. bd. Jour. Applied Physics, 1966-68. Served with USNR, 1943-46. Fellow AAAS, Am. Phys. Soc. (chmn. div. electron and atomic physics 1957, chmn. gaseous electronics conf. 1962-64, Davisson-Germer prize 1984); mem. Am. Geophys. Union, Earth and Sky (adv. bd. 1992-94). Home: 1375 Hillsdale Dr Monroeville PA 15146-4444 Office: U Pitts Dept Physics And Astro Pittsburgh PA 15260 Office Phone: 412-624-9287. Business E-Mail: biondi@pitt.edu.

BIONDI, PETER J., assemblyman; b. June 23, 1942; Dep. mayor Hillsborough Twp., 1985, mayor, 1986—93; assemblyman N.J. Gen. Assembly, 1998—; asst. rep. leader, 2002—. Mem. Hillsborough Twp. Com., 1983—84, Hillsborough Twp. Planning Bd., 1986—99, Somerset County Planning Bd., 1994—96, Somerset County Bd. Chosen Freeholders, 1994—97, dep. dir., 1995, dir., 96. Mem. Hillsborough Capital Planning Com., 1994—95; spl. commr. Joint Ins. Fund, 1996; mem. Somerset County Youth Svcs. Commn., 1996—, co-chair, 1997; mem. Indsl. Pollution Control Financing Authority, 1997. With USAR, 1961—67. Republican. Office: 1 E High St Somerville NJ 08876 E-mail: AsmBiondi@njleg.org.

BIPPUS, DAVID PAUL, manufacturing executive; b. Evansville, Ind., Nov. 29, 1949; s. James Paul and Mary Louise (Elder) B.; m. Kohnne Susann Heikens, Aug. 28, 1971; 1 child, Laura. BS, Iowa State U., 1971; MBA with honors, Boston U., 1975. Cert. CPCU. Tech. mgr. Ill. Dept. Transp., Springfield, 1976; asst. dir. planning Horace Mann Ins. Co., Springfield, 1976-79; mgr. fin. planning Hydro-Transmission div. Sundstrand Corp., Ames, Iowa, 1979-82; controller Hydraulics div. Sundstrand Corp., Rockford, Ill., 1982-84; v.p. fin., sec., treas. Suntec Industries, Inc., Rockford, 1984-89, v.p. ops., sec., treas., 1989-94; corp. controller Reliant Industries, Inc., Rock Falls, Ill., 1994, CFO, 1995-99; v.p. fin. and info. tech. Haldex Hydraulics, Co., 1999—. Instr. Lincoln Land Community Coll., Springfield, 1976-78. Bd. dirs. New Am. Theater, Rockford, 1991-97, pres., 1993-95; bd. dirs. Parents for Gifted Edn., Rockford, 1989-91; bd. dirs. Rockford Civic New Comers, 1982-85; mem. Story County Planning and Zoning Commn.; mem. ch. coun. Zion Luth. Ch., 1998-2001, pres., 2000-2001. 1st lt. U.S. Army, 1972-76. Mem. Fin. Exec. Inst. (bd. dirs. local chpt. 1989—, pres. 1993-94), Soc. of CPCU's, Nat. Assn. Accts., Am. Legion, Forest Hills Country Club. Republican. Avocations: photography, woodworking. Home: 113 Rivers Edge Dr Cherry Valley IL 61016-8802 Office: Haldex Hydraulics Co 2222 15th St Rockford IL 61104-7313

BIQUE, STEPHEN, computer scientist, educator; b. Waukegan, Ill., Apr. 1, 1959; s. Janine Ann and Neil James Bique; children: Anna-Maria Janine Eriksson-Bique, Sylvester David Eriksson-Bique, Linda Anneli Eriksson-Bique. BA, U. N.D., 1983, MS, 1985; MS, PhD, U. Joensuu, Finland, 2002. Software developer PACT Corp., Munich, 2000—01, cons., 2001; asst. prof. U. Kuopio, Finland, 2001—02; asst. prof. computer sci. U. Ala., Fairbanks, 2002—. Pres. Custom Computing Consulting Corp., Ingleside, Ill., 2001—04. Recipient Am. Fulbright award, US Govt., 1990-1991. Home: 418 Sixth Ave Apt 401 Fairbanks AK 99701 Office: Univ Ala PO Box 756660 Fairbanks AK 99775-6660 Office Phone: 907-474-1995. Business E-Mail: ffsfb@uaf.edu.

BIRBAHADUR, DINDIAL, secondary school educator; b. Albion Estate, Guyana, Oct. 28, 1944; came to the U.S., 1980; s. Pandit and Mangree Birbahadur; m. Rabby Devi Jaikaran, Feb. 23, 1969; 1 child, Devendra. BA, U. Guyana, 1971, diploma in edn., 1972; advanced diploma in ednl. studies, U. Leeds., 1976; MEd, U. V.I., 1984. Elem. tchr. Dept. Edn., Guyana, 1963-71, secondary tchr., 1971-74; math. lectr. Lilian Dewar Coll. Edn., Guyana, 1974-80; secondary math. tchr. V.I. Dept. Edn., 1980-89, master tchr., 1989—, chmn. math. dept., 1986—99, registrar/sys. analyst, 1999—. Math. lectr. U. Guyana, 1975-80; instr. U. V.I., 1981-89; math. examiner Caribbean Examination Coun., Barbados, 1978-80; statis. advisor U. V.I., 1982—; mem. Territorial Tech. Com., V.I., 1994—; state coord. for Presdl. award in elem. and secondary math. Author: Use of Objective Testing in Mathematics, 1976. Fellow Govt. of U.K., 1975; recipient Presdl. award for excellence in math. teaching Pres. of U.S., 1995. Mem. Nat. Coun. Tchrs. Math., Math. Assn. Am., V.I. Math. Tchrs. Assn., St. Croix Fedn. Tchrs., Coun. Presdl. Awardees in Math., Lions. Avocations: reading, playing chess, swimming, fishing, touring. Home: PO Box 2811 Frederiksted VI 00841-2811 Office: Arthur A Richards Jr High 20 & 21 Stoney Ground Frederiksted VI 00840 Personal E-mail: dbirbah@yahoo.com.

BIRCH, ADOLPHO A., JR., state supreme court justice; b. Washington, Sept. 22, 1932; 3 children. Attended, Lincoln U., Pa., 1950—52; BA, JD, Howard U., 1956. Bar: Tenn. 1957. Pvt. practice, Nashville, 1958—66; asst. pub. defender Davidson County, 1963—66, asst. dist. atty., 1966—69; judge Davidson County Gen. Sessions Ct., 1969—78, Tenn. Criminal Ct. (20th Jud. Dist.), 1978—87; presiding judge Trial Cts. of Davidson County, 1981—82; mem. Ct. of the Judiciary, 1983—86; former judge Tenn. Ct. Criminal Appeals; chief justice Tenn. Supreme Ct., Nashville, 1996—97, assoc. justice, 1994—. Former assoc. prof. legal medicine Meharry Medical Coll.; former law lecturer Fisk U., Tenn. State U.; assoc. prof. Nashville Sch. of Law, 1991—; disting. jurist-in-residence U. Memphis. Mem. Harvard Law Review, 1954—56. With USNR, 1956—58. Mem.: ABA, Nat. Bar Assn. Jud. Coun., Napier Lobby Bar Assn. (past pres.), Nashville Bar Assn., Tenn. Bar Assn., Nat. Bar Assn. Office: 304 Supreme Court Bldg, 401 7th Ave N Nashville TN 37219-1407*

BIRCH, GLYNN R., non-profit organization administrator; children: Courtney(dec.), Adrian, Rahmlee. Vol. speaker MADD Ctrl. Fla. Chpt., Orlando, bd. dirs., 1998, pres., 1999; nat. bd. dirs. MADD, Irving, Tex., 2000—, nat. v.p. victims issues, 2003—05, nat. pres., 2005—. Spkr. in field. First male and minority to become president of MADD. Office: MADD Nat Office 511 E John Carpenter Frwy Ste 700 Irving TX 75062*

BIRCH, IAN, editor-in-chief; Joined Emap, 1984—90; editorial dir. Heat, Emap, Closer, Emap; editor-in-chief Us, Winner Media, 1990—94; rejoined Emap, 1994—2004; gen. editor-in-chief exec Gemstar-TV Guide Internat. Inc., 2004. Mem.: British Soc. of Magazine Editor (chair). Office: Gemstar TV Guide Internat Inc 4th Floor 1211 Avenue of the Americas 28th Fl New York NY 10036 Office Phone: 212-852-7500. Office Fax: 212-852-7323.*

BIRCH, PATRICIA, choreographer, director; b. Englewood, N.J. d. Abraham S. and Mary (Levinsohn) B.; m. A. William J. Becker III; children: Jonathan Heath, Alison Becker Hurt, Peter Heath. BA, Bennington Coll. Dancer Martha Graham Co., N.Y.C., West Side Story, 1960. Choreographer, dir. (Broadway and Off-Broadway prodns. music theater and opera stage work) You're A Good Man Charlie Brown, The Me Nobody Knows, A Little Night Music, Grease, Candide, Over Here, Diamond Studs, Pacific Overtures, The Mikado, Gilda Radner, Live From New York, Zoot Suit, They're Playing Our Song, The Cradle Will Rock, Street Scene, In the Time of the Comedian Harmonists, The Happy End, Lawyers, Lovers and Lunatics, Portraits in Jazz, Really Rosie, Raggedy Ann, A Walk on the Wild Side, Elvis, The Mass, The Jumping Frog of Calaveras County, The Gershwin Gala, Club 12, Fanny Hackabout Jones, What About Luv, American Enterprise, Band in Berlin, Parade, Exactly Like You, I Sent A Letter To My Love, The Snow Queen, King Island Christmas, Like Jazz, Lawyers, Lovers and Lunatics, The Great Ostrovsky Prince Music Theatre, 2004, A Wedding, 2004, Of Thee I Sing and Let Them Eat Cake, Chicagoline Lyric Opera, 2004, The Thomasfeky Project; dir., choreographer videos The Very Thought of You, NBC Olympic Video, Better Not Tell Her, True Colors, Money Changes Everything, Frankie, It's My Party, Beat Street Strut; choreographer videos Harlem Shuffle, She Bop, Jump, concert dance Ballet for The American Ballroom Theater, Mass. Opera Co. of Boston, N.Y.C. Opera, Abstract Opera U. Ark.; dir. TV programs Dance in America, Christmas With Flicka, Celebrating Gershwin, Natalie Cole, Unforgettable, 20th Anniversary, Dancing, Natalie Cole's Untraditional Xmas; musical staging/choreographer for TV programs Saturday Night Live, The Gary Shandling Show, Good Sports, The Orchestra, Robert Klein Special, The Oscars, American Music Awards, The Grammys, The Electric Co., The Muppets, Square One, Goldie Hawn Spl., This is the Moment TV Donny Osmond, films Grease, Big, Awakenings, Sleeping With the Enemy, Billy Bathgate, Cowboy Way, Used People, the Wild Party, Roseland, Grease II, First Wives Club, The Human Stain, The Stepford Wives. Recipient 2 Emmy awards NATAS, 1988, 92, 5 Tony nominations, DGA nomination, Fred Astaire award. E-mail: patbirch@nyc.rr.com.

BIRCH, STANLEY FRANCIS, JR., federal judge; b. Langley Field, Va., Aug. 29, 1945; BA, U. Va., 1967; JD, Emory U., Atlanta, 1970, LLM in Taxation, 1976. Law clk. to Hon. Judge Sidney O. Smith Jr. U.S. Dist. Ct. (no. dist.) Ga., 1972—74; mem. firm Greer, Sartain & Carey, Gainesville, Ga., 1974—76, Deal, Birch, Jarrard & Link, Gainesville, 1976—83, Birch, Hartness & Link, Gainesville, 1983—85, Vaughan, Davis, Birch & Murphy, Atlanta, 1984—90; judge U.S. Ct. Appeals (11th cir.), Atlanta, 1990—. Lt. U.S. Army, 1970—72. Mem.: Lawyers Club Atlanta, 11th Cir. Hist. Soc., Gainesville Northeastern Bar Assn., Atlanta Bar Assn., Ga. Bar Found., State Bar Ga., Calvert Hall Alumni Assn., Emory U. Sch. Law Alumni Assn. (past pres.), U. Va. Alumni Assn., Ga. Legal History Found., Old Warhorse Lawyers Club, Theta Delta Chi. Office: US Ct Appeals 11th Cir 56 Forsyth St NW Atlanta GA 30303*

BIRCHARD, CATHERINE SUZANNE SIEH, artist; b. New Rochelle, NY, Jan. 20, 1964; d. Theodore and Eleanor Anne Becker Sieh; m. Richard Edward Birchard, Oct. 9, 1987; 1 child, Dylan. BA, Cornell U., Ithaca, N.Y., 1985. Painting, Munch (1938), 1997, exhibited in group shows at Westbeth Gallery, NYC, 1998, Gallery 402, 1998, Erector Sq. Gallery, New Haven, Conn., 1998, Silvermine Guild Galleries, New Canaan, Conn., 1998, The Macy Gallery, Valhalla, NY, 1999, The Art Club Gallery, NYC, 2000, NY Law Sch. Gallery, 2000, The Gallery on the Hudson, Irvington, NY, 2001, Pelham Arts Ctr. Gallery, Pelham, NY, 2002, Phoenix Gallery, NYC, 2002, The Arts Exch. Gallery, White Plains, NY, 2002—, 2003, The Macy Gallery, Valhalla, NY, 2003, Iona Coll. Arts Ctr., New Rochelle, NY, 2003. Recipient Juror's Selection Award, 1998, Cresson Pugh Award for Most Innovative, 1997; named Inaugural Westchester Biennial Artist, Castle Gallery, 1998. Mem. Mamaroneck Artists' Guild (bd. dir. 1998—, newsletter editor 1998-99, dir. programs 1998-2001, dir. publicity 2001-, membership juror 2001-), Orgn. Ind. Artists, Ctr. for Book Arts. Avocations: music, book collecting.

BIRCHFIELD, JOHN KERMIT, JR., lawyer; b. Roanoke, Va., Jan. 8, 1940; s. John Kermit and Christine (Luke) B.; m. Glenys Garnell, Nov. 14, 1964; 1 child, Guthrie Kathryn BS in Econs., Roanoke Coll., 1968; JD, U. Va., 1971. Bar: N.Y., 1972, U.S. Dist Ct. (so. dist.) N.Y., 1972, U.S. Ct. Appeals (2d cir.), 1972. Assoc. Shearman & Sterling, N.Y.C., 1971-81; ptnr. Holtzmann, Wise & Shepard, N.Y.C., 1981-83; sr. v.p. legal and govtl. affairs, gen. counsel Ga. Pacific Corp., Atlanta, 1983-88; mng. dir. Century Ptnrs., Atlanta, Darien, Conn., 1988—; sr. v.p., gen. counsel, corp. sec. M/A-COM, Boston, 1990-95. Chmn. and lead ind. dir. Mass. Fin. Compass Group Mutual Funds, 1998—; bd. dirs. Intermountain Industries, Inc., Mass. Fin. Offshore Funds, Displaytech, Inc., chmn., 1996—2001; former chmn. bd. dirs. Chas. P. Young Co.; chmn. bd. dirs. Dairy Mart Convenience Stores, Inc., 1999—2003. Author: How to Borrow on the Eurodollar Market, 1981, The Multinational Joint Venture, 1981. Chmn. adv. bd. Park Pride, 1986-90; bd. dirs., exec. com. Atlanta Ballet, 1984-88, chmn., 1987-88, vice chmn., 1986-87; bd. dirs. Atlanta Music Festival Assn., 1984-90, Friends Piedmont Hosp., 1985-90; bd. dirs., exec. com., treas. Assn. Am.-Indian Affairs, 1983-86; bd. dirs. High Mus. Art, 1986-91, exec. com., 1988-89; bd. visitors Emory U., 1985-88, bd. dirs. Emory U. Mus. Art and Archaeology, 1988-92; bd. dirs., chmn. collections com. Cape Ann Hist. Assn., 1993—; trustee Roanoke Coll., 1988—, Chatham Hall, 1988-94. Mem. ABA, Atlanta Bar Assn., Assn. Bar City N.Y., N.Y. State Bar Assn., Am. Law Inst., Am. Arbitration Assn., Racquet and Tennis Club, India House Club, Piedmont Driving Club, Farmington Country Club, Shendoah Club, Annisquam Yacht Club, Union Boat Club, Somerset Club. Home: Cranberry Hill 33 Way Rd Gloucester MA 01930-4315 Business E-Mail: kermitb@displaytech.com.

BIRCHFIELD, MARTHA, librarian; b. Tallahassee, Fla., July 19, 1946; d. Merrill Charles and Bessie Christine (Dyar) Futch; m. James DeMaris Birchfield, Dec. 5, 1969. BA, Fla. State U., 1967, MA, 1969, MS, 1976. Catalog libr. Fla. State U. Law Libr., Tallahassee, 1977-78, acquisitions libr., 1978-80; libr. Coun. of State Govts., Lexington, Ky., 1980; head libr. Lexington C.C., 1980—2000, prof., 2000—. Prof. Lexington C.C. Co-chair Ky. Gov.'s Conf. on Libr. and Info. Svcs., 1991; bd. dirs. Ky. Preservation. Recipient Lexington-Fayette County Hist. Preservation award, 1994. Mem. ALA, Assn. of Coll. and Rsch. Libr. (pres. Ky. chpt. 1986-87), Southeastern Libr. Assn. (chair const. com. 1988-90), Ky. Libr. Assn. (bd. dirs. 1986-87), Phi Beta Kappa (pres. Alpha of Ky. 1991-92). Democrat. Episcopalian. Avocation: architectural historic preservation. Home: 320 Linden Walk Lexington KY 40508-3020 Office: Bluegrass Cmty and Tech Coll 201 A/T Bldg Lexington KY 40506-0235 E-mail: mbirchfield@qx.net.

BIRCK, MICHAEL JOHN, telecommunications industry executive; b. Missoula, Mont., Jan. 25, 1938; s. Raymond Michael and Mildred (Johnson) B.; m. Katherine Royer, Sept. 3, 1960; children: Kevin, Joni Birck Stevenson, Christopher. BSEE, Purdue U., 1960, PhD in Engring. (hon.), 1995; MSEE, NYU, 1962. Mem. tech. staff Bell Tel. Labs., Murray Hill, N.J., 1960-66; dir. engring. Communication Apparatus Corp., Melrose Park, Ill., 1967-68, Wescom, Inc., Downers Grove, Ill., 1968-75; co-founder, chmn. Tellabs, Inc., Naperville, Ill., 1975—, CEO, 1975—2000, 2002—04. Mem. bd. dirs. Tellabs Inc., Naperville, Ill., ITW, Glenview, Ill., Molex Inc., Lisle, Ill. Patentee in field. Dir. Purdue Rsch. Found., West Lafayette, 1989—; trustee Benedictine Univ., 1988—, Purdue U., 1999-; bd. dirs. Hinsdale Hosp., 1995, Ill. Math and Sci. Acad. Fund, Aurora, Mus. Sci. and Industry, Chgo. Recipient High Tech Entrepreneur award Crain's Ill. Bus., Chgo., 1984, Outstanding Engring. Alumni award Purdue U., 1991, Outstanding Master Entrepreneur award Inc. Mag./Ernst & Young, 1995; named Outstanding Elec. Engring. Alumnus Purdue U., 1995, IEEE Ernst Weber Engring. Leadership Recognition award, 2001, 2003 Medal of Honor, Electronic Industries Alliance. Mem. Hinsdale Golf Club. Republican. Roman Catholic. Avocations: running, tennis, golf. Office: Tellabs Inc 1415 W Diehl Rd Naperville IL 60563

BIRD, BRAD, film director, writer, animator; b. Kalispell, Mont. married. With Walt Disney Co.; dir., screenwriter Warner Bros.; dir. Pixar Animation Studios, 2000—. Animator: (films) The Fox and the Hound, 1981; The Plague Dogs, 1982; dir., writer The Iron Giant, 1999; dir., writer, actor (voice) The Incredibles, 2004 (Academy award for best animated feature film of yr., 2005); writer Batteries Not Included, 1987; exec. cons.: (TV films) The Simpsons Christmas Special, 1989; dir.: Do the Bartman, 1990; dir., writer, animation prodr.: (TV series) Amazing Stories, 1985; dir., exec. cons. The Simpsons, 1989; writer, creator Family Dog, 1993; exec. cons. The Critic, 1994; King of the Hill, 1997. Office: Pixar Animation Studios 1200 Park Ave Emeryville CA 94608*

BIRD, CAROLINE, author; b. N.Y.C., Apr. 15, 1915; d. Hobart Stanley and Ida (Brattrud) B.; m. Edward A. Menuez, June 8, 1934 (div. Dec. 1945); 1 dau., Carol (Mrs. John Paul Barach); m. John Thomas Mahoney, Jan. 5, 1957 (dec. 1981); 1 son, John Thomas. Student, Vassar Coll., 1931-34; BA, U. Toledo, 1938; MA, U. Wis., 1939; LHD (hon.), Keene State Coll., 1988. Desk editor N.Y. Jour. Commerce, 1943-44; editl. rschr. Newsweek mag., N.Y.C., 1942-43, Fortune mag., N.Y.C., 1944-46; with Dudley-Anderson-Yutzy, pub. relations, N.Y.C., 1947-68; Froman Disting. prof. Russell Sage Coll., 1972-73; Mather prof. Case Western Res. U., Cleve., 1977. Author: The Invisible Scar, 1966, Born Female, 1968, rev. edit., 1970, The Crowding Syndrome, 1972, Everything a Woman Needs to Know to Get Paid What She's Worth, 1973, rev., 1982, The Case Against College, 1975, Enterprising Women, 1976, What Women Want, 1979, The Two-Paycheck Marriage, 1979, The Good Years, 1983, Second Careers, 1992, Lives of Our Own, 1995; chief writer: The Spirit of Houston, 1978; also articles in nat. mags. Mem. review bd. Dept. State, 1974. Mem. Am. Soc. Journalists and Authors, Am. Sociol. Assn. Home: 8118 Sawyer Brown Rd #B113 Nashville TN 37221-1402

BIRD, DAVID R., lawyer; b. June 7, 1949; BS, Brigham Young U., 1973, JD, 1977. Bar: Utah 1977, U.S. Ct. Appeals (10th cir.) 1978, U.S. Supreme Ct. 1987. Atty., shareholder environ., energy and natural resources dept. Parsons, Behle & Latimer, Salt Lake City. Spkr. in field. Co-author: Utah Environmental and Land Use Permits and Approval Manual, 1980, Brownfields Law and Practice, 2003, others. Bd. dirs. Utah Found.; trustee Barrick Mercer Gold Mine Found.; mem. workers compensation adv. coun. Labor Commn.; mem. environ. adv. coun. Salt Lake Valley Health Dept.; past chair legis. affairs com. Salt Lake Area C. of C. Mem.: ABA, Utah State Bar (mem. legis. affairs com. 1979—2001, chmn. water com. 1981—83, environ. law com. 1983—85, energy and natural resources sect. 1988—89, pres.-elect 2004—, jud. coun.), Utah Mfrs. Assn. (mem. legis. com., environ. com.), Utah Mining Assn. (exec. com., tax com., environment com.), Boy Scouts Am., Phi Kappa Phi. Office: Parsons Behle & Latimer One Utah Ctr 201 S Main St Ste 1800 PO Box 45898 Salt Lake City UT 84145-0898 Office Phone: 801-532-1234. Office Fax: 801-536-6111. E-mail: dbird@pblutah.com.

BIRD, DICK, sign painter; b. Mpls., July 10, 1937; s. Earl Edward and Ruth Ann (Brown) B.; m. Kathleen Susan Hilary, Jan. 24, 1959; children: Thomas Richard, Timothy Phillip, Patrick Lawrence. Owner Bird Sign Co., Mpls., 1968-92; sign shop mgr. Holiday Sta. Stores, Bloomington, Minn., 1992-97. Tchr. sign painting St. Paul Vo-Tech.; sign and graphic specialist Sign Shop, U. Minn., 1998-99. Author: Freehand Lettering, 1983, The Art of Freehand Pinstriping, 1984, How to Build a Low-Buck Streetrod, 1995. With U.S. Army, 1955-58. Mem. Minn. Street Rod Assn., Nat. Street Rod Assn. Avocations: custom cars, boat building, songwriting, dance, skiing. Home and Office: 4401 Morgan Ave N Minneapolis MN 55412-1244

BIRD, ERIN T., urologist; b. Ft. Wayne, Ind., Nov. 5, 1967; s. Donald William and Marjorie Elizabeth Bird; m. Kimberly C. Bird, Aug. 15, 1987; children: Morgan, Andrew. BS in Biology, Howard Payne U., 1989; MD, Baylor Coll. Medicine, 1993. Asst. prof. USUHS, Bethesda, Md., 2002—03, Scott & White, Tex. A&M U., Temple, 2003—. Maj. USAF, 1999—2003. Home: 1619 Mill Creek Rd Salado TX 76571 Office: Scott & White 2401 S 31st St Temple TX 76508

BIRD, FRANCIS MARION, JR., lawyer; b. Atlanta, Jan. 14, 1938; s. Francis Marion Sr. and Mary Adair (Howell) B.; m. JoAnn Galvin, Aug. 1994; children from previous marriage: Barbara, Michael. AB, Princeton U., 1959; LLB, Emory U., 1964; LLM, Harvard U., 1966. Bar: Ga. 1964, U.S. Ct. Appeals (3d cir. and 11th cir.), U.S. Dist. Cts. (no. dist. and mid. dist.) Ga. Officer USN, 1959-62; assoc. Jones Bird & Howell, Atlanta, 1964-70, ptnr., 1971-82, Alston & Bird, Atlanta, 1982-88; pvt. practice Atlanta, 1988—; ptnr. Bird & Godbey LLP, 2003—. Dir., sec. Summit Industries, Inc., 1980—. Adv. bd. mem. The Devereux Ga. Treatment Network, Kennesaw, Ga., 1989—. Mem. ABA, State Bar of Ga. (chmn. Standing Com. on Publs. 1977-78), Atlanta Bar Assn. (chmn. small firm/sole practitioner sect. 1995-96), Cobb County Bar Assn., Lawyers Club of Atlanta, Old War Horses Lawyers Club. Avocations: writing, walking. Office: Bird & Godbey 400 Colony Sq NE Ste 1750 1201 Peachtree St NE Atlanta GA 30361-6320*

BIRD, HECTOR RAMON, child psychiatrist, psychoanalyst, educator; b. San Juan, P.R., Feb. 5, 1939; s. Hector F. and Yvette (Baker) B.; m. Sandra Lopez, May 23, 1970; 1 child, Alejandra Y. BA, U. Mich., 1960; MD, Yale U., 1965; cert. in psychiatry and child psychiatry, Columbia U., 1972; cert. in psychoanalysis, W.A. White Inst., N.Y.C. Diplomate Am. Bd. Psychiatry and Neurology. Asst. dir. child psychiatry St. Luke's Hosp., N.Y.C., 1972-78; dir. tng. in child psychiatry Columbia U., N.Y.C., 1978-80, prof. clin. psychiatry, 1984—; dir. child psychiatry U. P.R. Med. Sch., San Juan, 1980-86; dep. dir. child psychiatry N.Y. State Psychiat. Inst., N.Y.C., 1986—. Contbr. articles to profl. jours. Founding dir., pres. bd. dirs. Teatro de la Opera, San Juan, 1982-86; dir. Pro-Arte Musical, San Juan, 1982-86. Lt. USN, 1966-68. Recipient Profl. Achievement award Boricua Coll., N.Y.C., 1987, Wilfred C. Hulse Meml. award N.Y. Coun. on Child and Adolescent Psychiatry, 2001. Fellow Am. Acad. Child and Adolescent Psychiatry, Am. Acad. Psychoanalysis (trustee); mem. Am. Psychopathological Assn., Soc. Rsch. in Child and Adolescent Psychopathology, William A. White Psychoanalytic Soc. Roman Catholic. Home: 321 W 78th St Apt 6A New York NY 10024-6514 Office: 145 Central Park W New York NY 10023-2004 Office Phone: 212-874-5311. Personal E-mail: hecbird@aol.com.

BIRD, L. RAYMOND, investor; b. Plainfield, NJ, Jan. 22, 1914; s. Lewis Raymond and Bessie (MacCallum) Bird; m. May Ethel Siercks, June 5, 1949. Student, NYU, 1946—47. With shipping dept. Horn & Hardart Co., 1936—46, control auditor, 1946—49, gen. supt. in commissary, 1949—51; asst. to treas. fin. and legal Lockheed Electronics Co. (formerly Stavid Engring., Inc.), 1951—55, treas., 1955—60; pres., dir. State Bank of Plainfield, NJ, 1960—62; investor, 1962—. Treas. Route Twenty Two Corp. Plainfield area committeeman Young Life Campaign, Inc.; pres. Plainfield Camp of Gideons; chmn. bd. trustees, chmn. exec. com., chmn. fin. and investments com. Barrington Coll.; mem. exec. com., treas. Christian Bus. Men's Com. of Ctrl. NJ; bd. dirs. Child Evangelism Fellowship NJ, Sudan Interior Mission; trustee Evangelistic Com. Newark and Vicinity; bd. dirs., treas. Friends in Christ. Gen. staff officer from pvt. to 1st lt. 6th Armored Divsn., AUS, 1941—45. Mem.: Plainfield Area C. of C., Am. Mgmt. Assn., Internat. Christian Leadership. Baptist. Home and Office: 527 Park Ave Quarryville PA 17566-1400

BIRD, LARRY JOE, professional athletics manager, former professional basketball coach; b. West Baden, Ind., Dec. 7, 1956; s. Joe and Georgia B; m. Dinah Mattingly Oct. 1, 1989. Student, Ind. U., 1974, Northwood Inst., West Baden, Ind., 1974; BS, Ind. State U., 1979. Player Boston Celtics, 1979-92, spl. asst. to exec. v.p., 1992-97; head coach Ind. Pacers, Indianapolis, Ind., 1997—2000; pres., basketball ops. Ind. Pacers., 2003—. Author: (with Bob Ryan) Drive, 1989; actor (film) Blue Chips, 1994. Mem. US Gold Medal team World Univ. Games, Sophia, Bulgaria, 1977; NBA championship team, 1981, 84, 86; NBA All-Star Team, 1980-88, 1990-92; gold medal Olympic basketball team (Dream Team), Barcelona, 1992; named Collegiate Player of Yr. AP, UPI and Nat. Assn. Coaches, 1978-79; Rookie of Yr. NBA, 1980; MVP NBA All-Star Game, 1982, NBA, 1984-86, NBA Playoffs, 1984, 86; named to All-NBA first-team, 1980-88; named one of 50 Greatest Players in NBA history, 1996; inducted into Basketball Hall of Fame, 1998.

BIRD, MARK DOUGLAS, magnet designer, engineering researcher; b. Roanoke, Va., Apr. 5, 1966; s. Jennings Thrall and Marianne McKenzie Bird. BS in Mechanics, Mich. State U., 1988; MSME, Stanford U., 1989, PhD in Mech. Engring., 1992. Mgr. resistive magnet program Nat. High Magnetic Field Lab., Tallahassee, 1992—, asst. scholar, scientist, 1992-96, assoc. scholar, scientist, 1996-2000, head engring. svcs., 1999—2001, scholar, scientist, 2000—, interim head engring. analysis, 2003—. Contbr. articles to profl. jours.; inventor in field. Leadership donor United Way of the Big Bend, Tallahassee, 1999—. Grad. rsch. fellow NSF, 1988-91, Sage Grad. fellow Cornell U., Ithaca, N.Y., 1988, Andrew D. White fellow, 1988. Mem. ASME (assoc.). Methodist. Avocations: bicycling, volleyball. Home: 8750 Cabin Hill Rd Tallahassee FL 32311 Office: 1800 E Paul Dirac Dr Tallahassee FL 32310-3748 Office Phone: 850-644-7789. E-mail: bird@magnet.fsu.edu.

BIRD, MARY LYNNE MILLER, professional society administrator; b. Buffalo, Feb. 25, 1934; d. Joseph William and Mildred Dorothy (Wallette) Miller; m. Thomas Edward Bird, Aug. 23, 1958; children: Matthew David, Lisa Bronwen. AB magna cum laude, Syracuse U., 1956; postgrad., Columbia U., 1956-58. Mem. rsch. staff Ctr. for Rsch. in Personality, Harvard U., Cambridge, Mass., 1959-62, Ctr. Internat. Studies, Princeton (N.J.) U., 1962-66, Inst. Internat. Social Rsch., Princeton, 1965, Sch. Internat. Affairs, Columbia U., N.Y.C., 1966-67, Coun. Fgn. Rels., N.Y.C., 1967-69, Twentieth Century Fund, N.Y.C., 1969-72; asst. to pres. World Policy Inst., N.Y.C., 1972-74; dir. devel. Fund for Peace, N.Y.C., 1974-78; dir. fellows program Exec. Council Fgn. Diplomats, N.Y.C., 1978-79; dir. devel. Engender Health, N.Y.C., 1979—83; exec. dir. Am. Geog. Soc., N.Y.C., 1983—. Cons. Fedn. Am. Scientists, Washington, 1974-75. Trustee Bel Canto Opera Co., N.Y.C., 1975—90. Maxwell Citizenship scholar Syracuse U., 1952-56. Fellow AAAS; mem. NAS (com. on geography, liaison mem. 1984-2000), Assn. Am. Geographers, Soc. Woman Geographers, Inst. for Current World Affairs (trustee), Nat. Coun. Geog. Edn., 100-Yr. Assn. N.Y., Conf. Latin Americanist Geographers, Planning Com. for Nat. Assessment on Edni. Progress in Geography, Nat. Music Theatre Network (bd. dirs.), St. David's Soc. (past pres.), Colonial Dames Am., Mid-Atlantic Club N.Y.C. (bd. dirs.), Princeton Club, Welsh Women's Club NY, Am. Soc. Assn. Execs., The Bohemians, Phi Beta Kappa, Phi Kappa Phi, Eta Pi Upsilon. Avocations: singing, sailing. Office Phone: 212-422-5456. Business E-Mail: MLBird@amergeog.org.

BIRD, PAUL S., lawyer; b. Nov. 21, 1960; BA, Yale U., 1983, JD, 1987. Bar: NY 1989, Conn. 1989, Paris 1992. Law clerk to Hon. Robert W. Sweet US Dist. Ct., So. Dist. NY, 1987—88; assoc. Debevoise & Plimpton LLP, NYC, Paris, 1988—95, ptnr. NYC, 1995—, co-head Mergers & Acquisitions Group. Mem.: ABA, Assn. Bar of City NY, Internat. Bar Assn. Office: Debevoise & Plimpton LLP 919 Third Ave New York NY 10022 Office Phone: 212-909-6435. E-mail: psbird@debevoise.com.

BIRD, ROBERT BYRON, chemical engineering educator, author; b. Bryan, Tex., Feb. 5, 1924; s. Byron and Ethel (Antrim) Bird. Student, U. Md., 1941—43; BS, U. Ill., 1947; PhD, U. Wis., 1950; postdoctoral fellow, U. Amsterdam, 1950—51; DEng (hon.), Lehigh U., 1972, Washington U., 1973, Tech. U. Delft, Holland, 1977, Colo. Sch. Mines, 1986; ScD (hon.), Clarkson U., 1980, The Technion, Israel, 1993, Tex. A&M U., 1999; D in engring. sci. (hon.), Eidgenössische Tech. Hochschule, Zürich, Switzerland, 1994; DrEngring (hon.), Kyoto (Japan) U., 1996. Asst. prof. chemistry Cornell U., 1952—53, Debye lectr., 1973, Julian C. Smith lectr., 1988; rsch. chemist DuPont Exptl. Sta., 1953; mem. faculty U. Wis., 1951—52, 1953—57, prof. chem. engring., 1957—92, C.F. Burgess distinguished prof. chem. engring., 1968—72, John D. MacArthur prof., 1982—92, Vilas research prof., 1972—92, chmn. dept., 1964—68, emeritus prof., 1992—; Burgers prof. Technische Univ. Delft, The Netherlands, 1994. Vis. prof. U. Calif., Berkeley, 1977, Univ. Catholique de Louvain, Belgium, 1994; D. L. Katz lectr. U. Mich., 1971; W. N. Lacey lectr. Calif. Inst. Tech., 1974; K. Wohl Meml. lectr. U. Del., 1977; W. K. Lewis lectr. MIT, 1982; R. H. Wilhelm lectr. Princeton U., 1991; G. N. Lewis lectr. U. Calif., Berkeley, 1993; Ascher Shapiro lectr. MIT, 1997; lectr. Lectures in Sci. Humble Oil Co., 1959, 61, 64, 66; lecture tour Am. Chem. Soc., 1958, 75, Canadian Inst. Chemistry, 1961, 65; cons. to industry, 1965—90; mem. adv. panel engring. sci. divsn. NSF, 1961—64. Author (with others): Molecular Theory of Gases and Liquids, 2d printing, 1964; author: Transport Phenomena, 64th printing, 2002, Spanish edit., 1965, Czech edit., 1966, Italian edit., 1970, Russian edit., 1974, Chinese edit., 1990, 2d English edit., 2002, Chinese translation, 2004, Een Goed Begin: A Contemporary Dutch Reader, 1963, 2d edit., 1971, Comprehending Technical Japanese, 1975, Chinese edit., 1985, Dynamics of Polymeric Liquids, Vol. 1, Fluid Mechanics, Vol. 2, Kinetic Theory, 1977, 2d edit., 1987, Japanese transl. Vol. 1, 1999, Vol. 2, 2004, Reading Dutch: Fifteen Annotated Stories from the Low Countries, 1985, Basic Technical Japanese, 1990, Technical Japanese Supplements: Polymer Science and Engineering, 1995, also numerous rsch. publs.; Am. editor (with others) Applied Sci. Rsch., 1969—86, 1989—98; mem. adv. bd.: Indsl. and Engring. Chemistry, 1970—72, mem. editl. bd.: Jour. Non-Newtonian Fluid Mechanics, 1975—; contbr. Served to 1st lt. AUS, 1943—46. Decorated Bronze Star, knight Order Orange Nassau Netherlands; recipient Curtis McGraw award, Am. Assn. Engring. Edn., 1959, Westinghouse award, 1960, Corcoran award, 1987, Centennial Medallion, 1993, Nat. Medal Sci., 1987; Fulbright fellow, Holland, 1950, Guggenheim fellow, 1958, Fulbright lectr., 1958, Japan, 1962—63, Sarajevo, Yugoslavia, 1972. Fellow: AIChE (William H. Walker award 1962, Profl. Progress award 1965, Warren K. Lewis award 1974, Founders award 1989, Inst. Lect. award 1992 1992), Am. Acad. Arts and Scis., Am. Phys. Soc.; mem.: NAE, NAS, Royal Flemish Acad. Belgium for Scis and Arts (fgn.), Royal Dutch Acad. Scis. (fgn.), Soc. Rheology, Soc. Chem. Engrs. Japan (hon.), Am. Chem. Soc. (chmn. Wis. sect. 1966, unrestricted rsch. grant Petroleum Rsch. Fund 1963), Am. Assn. Netherlandic Studies, Wis. Acad. Scis., Am. Acad. Mechanics, Arts and Letters, Sigma Tau, Omicron Delta Kappa, Phi Kappa Phi, Alpha Chi Sigma, Tau Beta Pi, Sigma Xi (v.p. Wis. sect. 1959—60), Phi Beta Kappa. Office: U Wis Dept Chem and Biol Engring 3004 Engring Hall 1415 Engineering Dr Madison WI 53706-1607 Business E-Mail: bird@engr.wisc.edu.

BIRD, SAMUEL N., judge; b. El Dorado, Ark., Jan. 19, 1940; m. LeAnne McElveen; 2 children. BS, Fla. State U., 1962; JD, U. Ark., 1970. Commd. 2d lt. USAF, 1962, advanced through ranks to capt., 1966, with Air Force Security Svc., resigned, 1967; ptnr. Williamson, Ball & Bird, Monticello, Ark., 1970-91; cir. chancery judge 10th Jud. Cir., 1991—97; assoc. judge Ark. Ct. of Appeals, Little Rock, 1997—. Pres. S.E. Ark. Legal Inst., 1974. Pres. Monticello Rotary, 1976-77. Home: 10119 Garrison Rd Little Rock AR 72223 Office Phone: 501-682-7477. Business E-Mail: sam.bird@arkansas.gov.

BIRD, SUE (SUZANNE BRIGIT BIRD), professional basketball player; b. Syosset, NY, Oct. 16, 1980; d. Herschel and Nancy Bird. Degree in comm. sci., U. Conn., 2002. Basketball player Christ the King High School, NY, U. Conn., 1998—2002; profl. basketball player Seattle Storm, WNBA, 2002—. Member USA Basketball Women's Sr. Nat. Team, 2002, 04. Named Naismith Player of Yr., 2002, AP Player of Yr., 2002, Best Female Coll. Athlete, ESPY Awards, 2002; named to Parade Mag. All-Am. first team, 1998, First Team All-WNBA, 2002, 2003, WNBA Western Conf. All-Star Team, 2002, 2003; recipient Wade Trophy, 2002, Honda Award for Women's Coll. Basketball Player of Yr., 2002. Achievements include mem.NCAA Divsn. 1 Nat. Championship Team, U. Conn., 2000, 02; mem. US Women's Basketball FIBA World Championship Gold Medal Team, 2002; Selected as the No. 1 overall pick in the 2002 WNBA Draft; mem. US Women's Basketball Team, Athens Olympics, 2004. Office: Seattle Sonics and Storm 351 Elliott Ave W Ste 500 Seattle WA 98119 Business E-Mail: StormFans@sonics-storm.com.

BIRD, THOMAS EDWARD, foreign language and literature educator; s. Harry J. and Paula W. (Boyce) B.; m. Mary Lynne Miller, Aug. 23, 1958; children: Matthew David, Lisa Bronwen. AB magna cum laude, Syracuse U., 1956; postgrad., Harvard U., 1958-59; MA, Middlebury Coll., 1960; AM, Princeton U., 1965; postgrad., Warsaw U., 1990—. Lectr., assoc. prof. Slavic langs. and lit. Queens Coll., CUNY, Flushing, 1965—; dir., co-dir. Ctr. Jewish Studies, 1996-98. Bd. dirs. Pax Romana, Benyumin Shekhter Found., Cymdeithas Madoc, St. David's Soc., St. Nicholas Soc., Soc. of Colonial Wars, chmn. Flag Svc. Com., 1997—. Gen. Soc. of the War of 1812 (pres. New York State Soc.), Soc. of Mayflower Descendants. Author: Patriarch Maximos IV, 1964; editor: Aspects of Religion in the Soviet Union, 1971, The Hard Life of Jura Odcesty, 1980, The 1863 Uprising in Byelorussia, 1980, Skovoroda: An Anthology, 1994, Zapisy; mem. editl. bd. Diakonia, Nationalities Papers, Polish Rev. Served with US Army (Military Intelligence) 1957-62. Recipient George Arents Library award, Isaiah award for interreligious dialogue, Amer. Jewish Com., 1996, Maxwell Citizenship Scholar, 1952-56, NDFL fellow, 1962-65, Woodrow Wilson Fell., 1965, Presdl. Tchg. Awd., 1991. Fellow Soc. for Values in Higher Edn., Phi Beta Kappa Soc.; mem. AAUP, MLA, SAR, Amer. Assn. for Advancement Slavic Studies, Am. Assn. Tchrs. Slavic and East European Langs., Amer Coun.Tchrs. Russian, Columbia U. Faculty Seminars, Belarusan Inst. Arts and Scis., Internat. Assn. Belarusan Studies (v.p.), Polish Inst. Arts and Scis., Russian-American Scholars Assn., Shevchenko Scientific Soc., Ukrainian Acad. Arts and Scis., Hon. Soc. Cymmrodorion, Dobro Slovo, Princeton Club N.Y., Nassau Club Princeton, Sons Am. Colonists, Colonial Order of the Acorn, Phi Beta Kappa, Phi Kappa Alpha. Office: Queens Coll CUNY Rufus King Hall 65-30 Kissena Blvd Flushing NY 11367-1597

BIRD, TOPANGA, artist, writer; d. Nora Gallagher and James Lott Ahern; m. Pierre deVise, Nov. 16, 1979 (div. June 30, 1983). BA in Comm. Arts, Columbia Coll., Chgo.; MA in Clin. Psychology, Pepperdine U., 1993—96. Exhibitions include As:If - Exploring the Intersection of Lang. and Form, Urban/Landscapes, Karen Finley/Memento Mori; editor: (newspaper) LA Bus. Jour. (Best Use of Photography, 1992, Best Spot News, 1993, 1st Pl. Editl. Writing, 1996). Dir. 46th ward city coun. office City Coun. of the City of Chgo., 1984—85, chief of staff/mcpl. code revision com., 1984—86. Mem.: Nat. Assn. of Broadcast Engineers and Technicians (hon.), Psy Chi (life). Office: Arena X7 P O Box 106 Hollywood CA 90068 E-mail: arenax7@yahoo.com.

BIRD, WENDELL RALEIGH, lawyer; s. Raleigh Milton and R. Jean Bird. BA summa cum laude, Vanderbilt U., 1975; JD, Yale U., 1978. Bar: Ga. 1978, Ala. 1980, Calif. 1981, Fla. 1982, U.S. Ct. Appeals (2d, 3d, 4th, 5th, 6th, 7th, 8th, 9th, 10th and 11th cirs.) 1979-83, U.S. Supreme Ct. 1983. Law clk. to judge U.S. Ct. Appeals (4th cir.), Durham, NC, 1978-79, U.S. Ct. Appeals (5th cir.), Birmingham, Ala., 1979-80; pvt. practice San Diego, 1980-82; atty. Parker, Johnson, Cook & Dunlevie, Atlanta, 1982-86; sr. ptnr. Bird & Loechl, LLC, Atlanta, 1986—. Adj. prof. Emory U. Law Sch., Atlanta, 1985—90; lectr. Washington Non-Profit Tax Conf., 1982—. Author: The Origin of Species Revisited, 2 vols., 1987; contbg. author: Federal and State Taxation of Exempt Organizations, 1994, CCH Federal Tax Service, 1988—; mem. bd. editors Yale U. Law Jour., 1977-78, others; contbr. articles to profl. jours. Recipient Egger prize Yale U., 1978, Vanderbilt U. award, 1972. Mem.: ABA (litigation sect., taxation sect., com. on exempt orgns., past chmn. subcom. on religious orgns., past chmn. subcom. on state and local taxes, chmn. subcom. on charitable contbns., sect. on real property probate and trust, com. charitable gifts), Am. Law Inst., Ga. Bar Assn., Fla. Bar Assn., Calif. Bar Assn., Ala. Bar Assn., Phi Beta Kappa. Republican. Avocations: science, skiing, photography, genealogy, piano, architecture. Home: 92 Blackland Rd NW Atlanta GA 30342-4420 Office: Bird & Loechl LLC 1150 Monarch Plz 3414 Peachtree Rd NE Atlanta GA 30326-1153 Office Phone: 404-264-9400.

BIRDER, DUDLEY DAMIAN, music educator; b. St. Paul, Mar. 23, 1927; s. Cecil Edward and Wanda Zana (Smith) B.; m. Mary Barany, Feb. 2, 1930; children: James P., John D., Dudley D. Jr., M. Alicia, M. Joan, M. Cresence. AB, U. Notre Dame, 1950, MusM, 1952. Assoc. prof. St. Francis Xavier U., Antogonish, N.S., Can., 1954-56; dir. music St. Marks Ch., St. Paul, 1956-58; prof. St. Norbert Coll., De Pere, Wis., 1958—; artistic dir. SNC Music Theatre, De Pere, 1962—; dir. Dudley Birder Chorale, De Pere, 1975—. Bd. dirs. Birch Creek Performance Ctr., Egg Harbor, Wis., 1997—; guest condr. Green Bay (Wis.) Symphony Orch., 1996-2005, Carnegie Hall, 1999, Mid Am. Prodns., 90, 93, 96, 97, 98. With USN, 1945-46. Roman Catholic. Avocation: golf. Home: 136 Saint Francis Dr Green Bay WI 54301-1336 Office: St Norbert Coll 100 Grant St De Pere WI 54115-2002

BIRDSALL, CHARLES KENNEDY, electrical engineer; b. N.Y.C., Nov. 19, 1925; s. Charles and Irene Birdsall; m. Betty Jean Hansen, 1949 (div. 1977); children: Elizabeth(dec.), Anne(dec.), Barbara, Thomas, John; m. Virginia Anderson, Aug. 21, 1981. BS, U. Mich., 1946, MS, 1948; PhD, Stanford U., 1951. Various microwave amplifier projects Hughes Aircraft Co., Culver City, Calif., 1951—55; leader electron physics group GE Microwave Lab., Palo Alto, Calif., 1955-59; prof. elec. engring. U. Calif., Berkeley, 1959-91, prof. Grad. Sch., 1994—. Founder Plasma Theory and Simulation Group, 1967; founder, chmn. Energy and Resources Group, ERG, 1972—74; cons. on fusion simulations Lawrence Livermore Lab. of U. Calif., 1960—86; prof. Miller Inst. Basic Rsch. in Sci., 1963—64; sr. vis. fellow U. Reading, England, 1976; rsch. assoc. Inst. Plasma Physics Nagoya (Japan) U., 1981, co-founder computational engring. sci. (CES) undergrad. program, 2000; Chevron vis. prof. energy Calif. Inst. Tech., 1982; area coord. phys. electronics/bioelectronics, 1984—86; lectr. Plasma Sch. Internat. Ctr. for Theoretical Physics, Trieste, Italy, 1985—99; joint U.S.-Japan Inst. Fusion Theory vis. prof. Inst. Plasma Physics, Nagoya U., fall 1988, spring 2002; vis. prof. Gunma U., Kiryu, Japan, 2003; Intergovtl. Personnel Act AirForce Rsch. Lab., Albuquerque, 2002—. Author: (with W.B. Bridges) Electron Dynamics of Diode Regions, 1966, (with A.B. Langdon) Plasma Physics via Computer Simulation, 1985, 91, 93, 2002, (with S. Kuhn) Bounded Plasmas, 1994. Served with USNR, 1944—46. U.S.-Japan Coop. Sci. Program grantee, 1966-67; Fulbright grantee U. Innsbruck, 1991; recipient Berkeley Citation, 1991; first recipient (with A.B. Langdon) of Dawson award for pioneering plasma simulation, 2003. Fellow IEEE (1st recipient Plasma Sci. and Applications award June 1988), AAAS, Am. Phys. Soc.; mem. Sigma Xi, Tau Beta Pi, Eta Kappa Nu. Achievements include being the co-originator many-particle plasma simulations in two and three dimensions using cloud-in-cell/particle-in-cell methods, 1966; holder 24 patents. Home: 4050 Valente Ct Lafayette CA 94549-3412 Office: U Calif EECS Dept Cory Hall Berkeley CA 94720-1770 Office Phone: 510-643-6631. Business E-Mail: birdsall@eecs.berkeley.edu.

BIRDSALL, NANCY, economist; b. Feb. 6, 1946; BA in Am. Studies, Newton Coll. of the Sacred Heart, 1967; MA in Internat. Rels., Johns Hopkins U., 1969; PhD in Econs., Yale U., 1979. Social sci. analyst Smithsonian Inst., 1972-76; economist, various policy and mgmt. positions World Bank, Washington, 1979-93; exec. v.p. Inter-Am. Devel. Bank, Washington, 1993-98; sr. assoc., dir. Econ. Reform Project Carnegie Endowment for Internat. Peace, 1998—2001; pres. Ctr. Global Devel., 2001—. Sr. adviser Rockefeller Found., 1988-89; active numerous coms. Nat. Acad. of Scis.; chair bd. dirs. Internat. Ctr. for Rsch. on Women; bd. dirs. Bd. of Population Coun., numerous others. Author numerous publs. on econ. devel. issues.

BIRDSALL, STEPHANIE E., artist; b. Atlanta, Ga., Nov. 28, 1954; d. Eugene P. and Marion D. Erwin; m. William M. Birdsall, Jan. 1, 2001; children: Christopher M., Philip Chase Norfleet, William Andrew, Marion Katherine. BA, U. Ga., 1970, Rhodes Coll., 1972; diploma in Art, City and Guilds of London Arts Sch., 1972. Artist, 1971—. Contbr. chpts. to books. Co-chair Boots and Bandannas, Durango, Colo., 1996—98. Finalist Arts for the Parks Mini 100, Nat. Pk. Acad. of Arts, 2004; named Best in Show, Bridgeport Mus. of Arts and Scis., 1978 Barnum Festival Art Show; recipient Guild Hall Etching award, London Royal Acad., 1975, Painter, Stainer's and Brusars award, City and Guilds of London Arts Sch., 1976, 1st prize in Graphics, Bridgeport Mus. of Arts and Scis., 1977 Barnum Festival Art Show, Daniel Smith award, Pastel Soc. of North Fla., 2002 National Pastel Show, Grumbacher Gold medallion, 2004 National Exhibition, 2nd pl. award, Lone Star Pastel Soc., 2003 National Pastel Exhibition, Hon. Mention, 2004 National Pastel Exhibition, Exceptional Merit award, Southeastern Pastel Soc., 2004 International Exhibition, Pastel Painters of Maine award, Pastel Painters of Cape Cod, 2004 For Pastels Only Exhibition, Award of Merit, Pastel Painters of West Coast, 2004 Membership Exhibition, 2nd pl. award, Wichita Ctr. for Arts, 2004 Pastel National, Arts for the Parks Nat. Exbhn. Hermanguiles award, 2004, Exceptional Merit award, Dagas Pastel Soc., 2004. Fellow: Pastel Soc. of Conn. (signature mem.); mem.: Fla. State Capital Permanent Collection Mus., Fla. Mus. Art and Culture, Plein Air Soc. of Fla.

(signature mem.), Collier County Arts Coun., Pastel Soc. of West Coast (assoc.), Pastel Soc. of N.Mex, (assoc.), Pastel Soc. of North Fla. (assoc.), Pastel Soc. of Colo. (assoc.), Oil Painters of Am. (assoc.), Degas Pastel Soc. (assoc.), Pastel Soc. of Am. (assoc.), Catherine Lorrilard Wolfe Art Club (assoc.), Portrait Painters of Am. (assoc.), SW Fla. Pastel Soc. (assoc.). Achievements include Museum of the Everglades Permanent Art Collection; research in Listed in Artist's Blue Book, American Artists; Published in Miller, Vincent, How Did You Paint That? 100 Ways to Paint Still Life and Florals Vol II, International Artist 2005. Office: Artist's Studio 794 Twelveth Ave S Naples FL 34102 Home: 313 N Deer Track Rd Tucson AZ 85749 Office Phone: 239-571-8895. Personal E-mail: sbirdartist@comcast.net.

BIRDSALL, WILLIAM FOREST, retired librarian; b. Farmington, Minn., Oct. 30, 1937; s. Herman Elden and Mae Elizabeth (Daugherty) B.; m. Ann Elizabeth Page, Dec. 20, 1965; children— Sarah, Stephanie, Thomas BA, U. Minn., 1955, MA, 1964; PhD, U. Wis., 1973. Reference libr. Iowa State U., Ames, 1961-63; head pub. svcs. Wis. State U., La Crosse, 1965-70; asst. dir. for pub. svcs. U. Man., Winnipeg, Canada, 1973-77, assoc. dir. for pub. svcs.ervices, 1977-81; univ. libr. Dalhousie U., Halifax, Canada, 1981-97; exec. dir. Novanet, Inc., Halifax, 1998—2002; ret., 2002. Author: Myth of the Electronic Library, 1994, Understanding Telecommunications and Public Policy, 1998; contbr. articles to libr. periodicals. Mem. Atlantic Provinces Library Assn. (pres. 1984), Man. Library Assn. (pres. 1981), Can. Library Assn. (council 1981, 84) Home: 54 Village Crescent Bedford NS Canada B4A 1J2 Office Phone: 902-835-2821. Personal E-mail: billbirdsall@accesswave.ca.

BIRDSEYE, THOMAS EARL, freelance/self-employed writer; b. Durham, N.C., July 13, 1951; s. Irving Earl and Mary Carmichael Birdseye; m. Deborah Sue Holsclaw, May 18, 1974; children: Kelsey, Amy. BA in Mass Comm., Western Ky. U., 1974, BA in Elem. Edn., 1977. Tchr. ESL, Japan, 1983—84; elem. edn. tchr. Sandpoint, Idaho, 1986—89; freelance writer Corvallis, Oreg., 1989—. Spkr. in field. Author 17 children's books. Recipient Children's Choice Book award, Internat. Reading Assn., 1989, Best of 1990, Soc. Sch. Librs. Internat., Children's Choice Book award, Internat. Reading Assn., 1995, Nebr. Golden Sower award, 1996, Wash. Children's Choice award, 1996, Mo. Show Me award, 1996, Md. Black-Eyed Susan award, 1997, Lampman award, Oreg. Libr. Assn., 1999, Storytelling World award, 2002, Oppenheim Best Book award-gold, 2002. Mem.: Author's Guild. Avocations: mountain climbing, skiing, backpacking. Home: 511 NW 12th St Corvallis OR 97330 Office Phone: 541-752-9837.

BIRDSONG, ALTA MARIE, volunteer; m. Kenneth Layne Birdsong; children: Suzanne Denise Huff, Jeffrey Layne Birdsong. BBA in Acctg. magna cum laude, U. North Tex., 1955. Cost engr. Tex. Instruments, Inc., Dallas, 1955-62; part-time acct. Atlanta, 1972—. Mem. DeKalb County Cmty. Rels. Com., 1981-93, chair, 1984-87; mem. Atlanta Regional Com. Adv. Group, 1981-88, Met. Atlanta United Way, 1985-98, resource investment vol. sch. age children; chair Sch. Age Child Care Coun., 1987-90; mem. Dekalb County Task Force on Personal Care Homes, Dekalb County Task Force on Domestic Violence; mem. steering com. for bond referendum Dekalb B. Edn.; mem. Vision 2020 Governance Stakeholders ARC, 1994-95; mem. Camp Fire Boys and Girls. Recipient John H. Collier award for Camp Fire, 1991, Luther Halsey Gulick award for Camp Fire, 1993, Frederic E. Ruccius award for Camp Fire, 1993, Mortar Bd. Alumni Achievement award, 1991, Woman of Yr. award Atlanta Alumnae Panhellenic, 1983, Women Who Have Made a Difference award DeKalb YWCA, 1985, Ember award Camp Fire, 1998, Tom Murphy State Service Good Heart Vol. award, 2002. Mem.: AAUW (rec. sec. 1982—84, mem. v.p. 1984—86, pres. elect 1986—87, divsn. pres. 1987—89, assn. nominating com. 1993—97, chair 1995—97, Atlanta chpt. pres. 2001—03, co-chair Sister-to-Sister Summit 2002, chair Woman to Woman Summit 2002, Achievement award 1999), Nat. Women's Conf., Freedoms Found. at Valley Force (sec. 1983—85, treas. 1985—87, v.p. publicity 1988—89, v.p. 1990—91, Atlanta chpt. pres. 1991—92, ea.-so. region adv. 1994—97, treas. 1999—2000, Atlanta chpt. pres. 2000—01), Atlanta Coun. Camp Fire (region fin. officer 1989—90, v.p. 1990—92, pres. 1992—94), Atlanta Alumnae Panhellenic (v.p. 1977—78, pres. 1978—79), Delta Gamma Alumnae (treas. 1972—74, Atlanta chpt. 1st v.p. 1985—87, Oxford award 1992). Home: 5241 Manhasset Cv Atlanta GA 30338-3413

BIRDSONG, GEORGE YANCY, manufacturing executive; b. Suffolk, Va., Nov. 8, 1939; s. William McLemore and Yancey (Brooking) B.; m. Sue Benton, June 10, 1961; children: Anne Cabell, David Jefferson, Charles Randolph. BA, Washington and Lee U., Lexington, Va., 1961; LLB, U. Va., 1964, diploma in basic advanced mgmt., 1968. Bar: Va. 1964. Mem. Godwin & Godwin, Suffolk, 1964-66; sec.-treas. Birdsong Peanuts divsn. Birdsong Corp., Suffolk, 1965—, exec. v.p., 1981-97, pres., 1997—99, CEO, 1999—. Bd. dirs. SunTrust Bank. Dir. Suffolk Redevel. and Housing Authority, 1966—85, chmn., 1966—83; pres. Louise Obici Meml. Hosp. Found., Suffolk, 1980—; chpt. pres. Tri-County Area Planned Parenthood, 1969—; mem. pres.'s adv. coun. Va. Wesleyan Coll., 1971—89, trustee, 1989—; mem. exec. com. Future of Hampton Roads, 1983—96; founding dir. Suffolk YMCA, 1987—91; mem adv. bd. Young Leaders Soc. of Hampton Roads, 2001—; bd. dirs. Hampton Roads United Way, 1980—84; sec., bd. dirs. Suffolk Cmty. Health Ctr., 1992—99; bd. dirs. Va. Found. Ind. Colls., 1994—. Recipient Disting. Svc. award Suffolk Jaycees, 1971, Order of the Red Triangle YMCA of South Hampton Rd., 1993, Humanitarian award Tidewater chpt. NCCJ, 1997; named 1st Citizen, Suffolk, 1997. Mem. Va. Bar Assn., Suffolk Bar Assn., Va. Mfrs. Assn. (bd. dirs. 1977-79, 87-89), Suffolk C. of C., Suffolk Sports Club, Suffolk Tennis Assn., Elks, Rotary. Methodist. Home: 608 Riverview Dr Suffolk VA 23434 Office: Birdsong Corp 612 Madison Ave Suffolk VA 23434

BIRDWELL, JAMES EDWIN, JR., retired banker; b. Chuckey, Tenn., Apr. 22, 1924; s. James Edwin and Mary Eleanor (Earnest) B.; m. Marilyn Margaretta Gibson, Dec. 20, 1949; children: James Edwin III, Amy Eleanor, Todd Gibson. AB, Tusculum Coll., 1949; MA, Vanderbilt U., 1951. Tchr., coach Doak H.S., 1948-50; field rep. 3d Nat. Bank, Nashville, 1951-52; trainee Va. Nat. Bank, 1957, v.p., from 1962; chmn., pres. 1st Am. Bank, Clinton, Tenn., 1973-84; vice chmn. 1st Am. Nat. Bank, Knoxville, Tenn., 1984-90. Bd. dirs., Coal Creek Mining & Mfg. Co., Areawide Devel. Corp. Commr. Bldgs. and Grounds Virginia Beach, Va., 1970-72; bd. dirs. Daniel Arthur Rehab. Ctr., Oak Ridge, Tenn., 1974-84, Oak Ridge Hosp., 1976-82, Meth. Med. Ctr. Found., Oak Ridge; v.p. Roane Anderson Econ. Coun., 1976-90; chmn. Clinton Port Authority, 1978—; mem. exec. com. Melton Hill Regional Indsl. Authority, Clinton, 1978-95; mem. Anderson County Tax Adv. Bd., 1978—, Indsl. Devel. Bd. Anderson County, 1978—. With USNR, 1942-46, 52-57. Decorated Air medal. Mem. Am. Bankers Assn., Tenn. Bankers Assn., Robert Morris Assocs., Bank Adminstrn. Inst., Bank Mkg. Assn., Oak Ridge Country Club, Civitans, LeConte Club. Republican. Methodist. Office: Am South Bank 245 S Main St Clinton TN 37716-3603 Personal E-mail: jjeb2jr@comcast.net.

BIRDWELL, SUSAN ELIZABETH SMITH, artist; b. Memphis, Jan. 27, 1948; d. Mark Black and Mildred Elizabeth (Tinsley) Smith; m. William DeWitt Whitten, Feb. 14, 1970 (dec. Dec. 1990); 1 child, Christopher Mark; m. Tony Lee Birdwell, May 17, 2003 BFA in Painting, Memphis State U., 1971. Counselor Tenn. Dept. Human Svcs., Memphis, 1971-74, Nashville, 1980-81; interviewer Tenn. Dept. Employment Security, Nashville, 1981-85; portrait artist, Nashville, 1980—. Works represented in pvt. collections throughout U.S.; cover designer Letters for All Seasons, 1991. Pres. Rep. Career Women, Memphis, 1976; mem. exec. com. Shelby County Rep. Com., Memphis, 1978-80, mem. steering com., 1977-80; youth counselor Belmont United Meth. Ch., Nashville, 1985—. Named Miss. Tennessee Young Rep., Young Reps., 1969. Mem. Hort. Soc. Davidson County, Portrait Soc. Am., Warner Park Garden Club, Alpha Phi. Avocations: fly fishing, writing, gourmet cooking, interior decorating, travel. Home: 418 Wears Valley RD Townsend TN 37882-3306 Studio: PO Box 496 Townsend TN 37882 Office Phone: 865-448-0241. Personal E-mail: mtnbirdstudio@aol.com.

BIRELY, WILLIAM CRAMER, investment banker; b. Thurmont, Md., Nov. 13, 1919; s. Victor Morris and Dorothy Grace (Rouzer) B.; m. Luelle Avis Langness, July 21, 1943. Student, Strayer U., 1937-38, Am. U., 1941-42. With Nat. Wildlife Assn., U.S. Govt., 1938—47; indsl. analyst War Prodn. Bd.; with Folger, Nolan, Inc., Washington, 1947-52, v.p., 1950-52; gen. partner Rouse, Brewer & Becker (now Morgan Stanley), Washington, 1952-55; exec. v.p., treas. Birely & Co., Washington, 1955-62, pres., 1962-67; also dir.; v.p. Mason & Co. (now Legg, Mason, Wood, Walker, Inc.), 1967-70; investment banker Lang & Co., Washington, 1970-85, Chapin, Davis & Co., Balt., 1985-89, Lang Div. Moors & Cabot, Inc., Alexandria, Va., 1989—. V.p., dir. Thurmont (Md.) Bank (now Bank of Am.), 1962-73; adv. bd. Farmers & Mechanics Nat. Bank (now affiliate of Mercantile Bankshares Corp, Balt.), Thurmont, 1975-76; mem. adv. council SBA, 1962-66 Mem. gen. inaugural coms. Eisenhower and Nixon, 1953, 57, Nixon and Agnew, 1968, 72, Bd. Appeals Montgomery County, 1965, Montgomery County Council, 1965-66, Reagan and Bush, 1980, 84, Bush and Quayle, 1988; treas. Young Republican Club of Montgomery County, 1947, pres., 1948; del. Md. Rep. Conv., 1952, 56, 60, apptd. on Nat. Alcohol Beverage Control Assn. Constn., Laws Com., Fed. Affairs and Legis. Com., 1966, Served with F.A. AUS, 1943-44. Recipient Gov.'s citation for outstanding service to Md. Mem. NRA (life), Am. Legion (life), Huguenot Soc. Washington (life, former v.p.), S.A.R. (life, former nat. trustee), Soc. Mayflower Descs., Soc. Colonial Wars (life), Soc. War 1812, St. Andrews Soc., Frederick County Hist. Soc. (life), Carroll County Hist. Soc. (life), Washington Hist. Socs. (life), Montgomery County Hist. Soc. (life; mem. bd. mgmt.), Bond Club, Nat. Press Club, Army and Navy Club, Izaak Walton League Am. (nat. life), U.S. Capitol Hist. Soc., (chmn. fin. com.), Assn. Childhood Edn. Internat. (chmn. fin. com.), N.Am. Blue Bird Soc. Home: PO Box 590 Olney MD 20830 Office: Lang Div Moors & Cabot Inc 1600 Prince St Ste 113 Alexandria VA 22314-2836 Office Phone: 301-924-2521.

BIRENBAUM, JONATHAN, lawyer; b. Waterbury, Conn., Sept. 12, 1953; s. Bernard and Ethel (Shiller) B. AB, Colgate U., 1975; JD, Union U., 1978. Bar: N.Y. 1979, U.S. Dist. Ct. (so. and ea. dists.) N.Y. 1979, U.S. Supreme Ct. 1984, Conn. 1996. Assoc. Mudge Rose Guthrie Alexander & Ferdon, N.Y.C., 1978-85, ptnr., 1986-95, Paul, Hastings, Janofsky & Walker LLP, 1995—, vice chmn. mgmt. - Stamford Office. Mem. ABA, Assn. of Bar of City of N.Y. Office: Paul Hastings Janofsky & Walker LLP 1055 Washington Blvd Stamford CT 06901-2216 Office Phone: 203-961-7410. Office Fax: 203-359-3031. Business E-Mail: jonathanbirenbaum@paulhastings.com.

BIRENBAUM, LEO, retired engineering educator; b. N.Y.C., Dec. 1, 1927; s. Morris and Esther (Ditman) B.; m. Mary Giurato, Feb. 17, 1961; children: Eric, Nellie, Maija. BSEE, Cooper Union, 1946; MSEE, Poly. Inst. N.Y., 1958, MS in Physics, 1974. Electronics engr. N.Y. Naval Shipyard, Bklyn., 1948-51; from rsch. asst. to assoc. prof. Poly. U. N.Y., Bklyn., 1951-93, prof. emeritus, 1993—. Sec. C95.4 com. Am. Nat. Standards Inst., N.Y.C., 1969-79. Patentee microwave devices. Served with USN, 1946-47. Mem. IEEE (sr.), Bioelectromagnetics Soc., N.Y. Acad. Scis., Sigma Xi, Tau Beta Pi. Home: 44 Mohawk Rd Yonkers NY 10710-5010 Office: Polytech U 6 Metrotech Ctr Brooklyn NY 11201-3840 Office Phone: 718-260-3319. Business E-Mail: lbirenba@duke.poly.edu.

BIRENBAUM, WILLIAM M., former university president; b. Macomb, Ill., July 18, 1923; s. Joseph and Rose (Whiteman) B.; m. Helen Bloch, Mar. 8, 1951; children: Susan, Lauren Amy, Charles. Dr. Law, U. Chgo., 1949; L.H.D., Columbia Coll., Chgo., 1970. Dean students Univ. Coll., 1955-57. Dir. research, conf. bd. Asso. Research Councils, Ford Found. project study post-doctoral internat. ednl. exchanges, 1954-55; asst. v.p. Wayne State U., 1957-61; dean New Sch. Social Research, N.Y.C., 1961-64; v.p., provost Bklyn. Center, L.I. U., 1964-67; pres. Edn. Affiliate, Bedford-Stuyvesant Devel. & Services Corp., Bklyn, 1967-68, S.I. Community Coll., 1968-76; pres. Antioch U., 1976-85. Author: Overlive: Power, Poverty and the University, 1968, Something for Everybody is Not Enough: An Educator's Search for His Education, 1971; Contbg. author: Student Personnel Work in Urban Colleges. Cons. Austrian Ministry Edn., Vienna, 1969; higher edn. adviser Republic of Zambia, 1972; cons. U. Zambia, 1972; faculty Salzburg Seminar in Am. Studies, 1976; founder Nat. Student Assn., 1946-48; chmn. Mich. Cultural Commn., 1960-61; founder, original dir. Detroit Adventure, vol. assn. cultural instns., 1958-61; bd. adv. Bklyn. Acad. Music, 1965—, Bklyn Inst. Arts and Scis; trustee Friends World Coll., Westbury, N.Y., Hasbro Childrens Found., 1985—, Lit. Vols. of N.Y.C., 1986—. Mem. Chgo. Bar Assn., Delta Sigma. Home: 108 Willow St Brooklyn NY 11201-2202

BIRGE, PATRICK MICHAEL, sculptor, art educator; b. Longmont, Colo., Mar. 15, 1970; s. Alfred Anthony and Margaret Ann Birge. BA in Fine Arts and Philosophy, U. Notre Dame (Ind.), 1992; BFA in Sculpture, U. Notre Dame, South Bend, Ind., 1994; MA in Sytematic Theol., Washington Theol. Union, Washington, D.C., 1999; MFA in Sculpture, George Washington U., Washington, D.C., 2002. Artist and dir. Reunion Studios, Washington, 1993—. Guest curator Georgetown U., Washington, 2000—01; contract art handler Smithsonian Instn., 2001; adj. instr. art No. Va. C.C., Annandale, 2003—; artist-in-residence Wesley Theol. Sem., Washington, 2004—05; lectr. in field. Exhibitions include Princeton Theol. Sem., N.J., 2000, prin. works include sculpture The Burning Bush, 1999—, St. Francis, 2005—, Tikkun Chanukiah, 2005—. Recipient Steck Meml. prize Art, George Washington U., 2000, 2001; scholar, Notre Dame Alumni Assn., Greensboro, N.C., 1988. Mem.: Coll. Art Assn. Avocations: mystical literature, movies, travel to India. Home: 1614 Manchester Ln NW Washington DC 20011 Office: No Va CC 4001 Wakefield Chapel Rd Annandale VA 22003 E-mail: reunionstudios@hotmail.com.

BIRGENEAU, ROBERT JOSEPH, academic administrator, physicist, researcher; b. Toronto, Ont., Can., Mar. 25, 1942; arrived in US, 1963; s. Peter Duffus and Isobel Theresa (Meehan) B.; m. Mary Catherine Ware, June 20, 1964; children: Michael, Catherine, Patricia, Michelle. BSc, U. Toronto, 1963; PhD in physics, Yale U., 1966. Vis. tchr. Benedict Coll., Columbia, SC, summer 1965; instr. dept. engring. and applied sci. Yale U., New Haven, 1966-67; Nat. Research Council Can. postdoctoral fellow Oxford U., England, 1967-68; mem. tech. staff Bell Labs, Murray Hill, NJ, 1968-74, research head scattering and low energy, physics dept., 1975; guest sr. physicist Brookhaven Nat. Lab., Upton, NY, 1968—; vis. scientist RisNational Lab., Roskilde, Denmark, 1971, 79; prof. physics MIT, Cambridge, 1975—2000, Cecil and Ida Green prof. physics, 1982—2000, assoc. dir. Rsch. Lab. of Electronics, 1983-86, head solid state, atomic and plasma physics, 1987-88, head dept. physics, 1988-91, dean Sch. Sci., 1991-2000; pres., prof. physics U. Toronto, 2000—04; chancellor U. Calif., Berkeley, 2004—. Cons. Bell Labs., 1977-80, IBM Rsch. Labs., Yorktown Heights, NY, 1980-83, Sandia Nat. Labs., Albuquerque, 1985-92; mem. steering com. Panel on Neutron Scattering, NAS, 1977, mem. exec. com. Major Materials Facilities Com., 1984; co-chmn. Gordon Conf. on Quantum Solids and Fluids, 1979, Gordon Conf. on Condensed Matter Physics, 1986; mem. external adv. com. physics divsn. Los Alamos Nat. Lab, 1982-86; mem. policy and adv. bd. Cornell High Energy Synchrotron Source, 1980-84, chmn., 1983-84; mem. rev. panel on neutron scattering Dept. Energy, 1980, 82, mem. Basic Energy Sciences Adv. Com., 1991-94, chair Panel on Rsch. Reactors, 1996, Panel on Synchrotron Radiation Sources & Sci., 1997; mem. materials rsch. adv. com. NSF, 1989-90; mem. adv. coun. NEC Rsch. Inst., 1995-; mem. sci. policy com. Lawrence Berkeley Nat. Lab., 1997-2000; co-chair Polaroid Sci. and Tech. Bd., 1998-2001; mem. external adv. com. physics dept., Oxford U., 2000-; chair. vis. com. ETH Domain, Switzerland, 2002. Contbr. articles to profl. jours.; assoc. editor for condensed matter physics, Physical Review Letters, 1980-83; mem. editorial bd. Physical Review B, 1987-89. Trustee Associated Universities., Inc., 1990-97, Boston Mus. Sci., 1992-2001, Brookhaven Sci. Assocs., 1997-2000, Univ. Health Network, 2000-, Royal Ontario Mus., 2000-, United Way Greater Toronto Campaign Cabinet, 2000-, Universities Rsch. Assn., Inc., 2000-; bd. governors Argonne Nat. Lab., 1992-2001; mem. physics fellow selection com. Sloan Found., 1995-2001; bd. dirs. St. Michael's Hosp., 2000-. Recipient Yale Sci. and Engring. Alumni Achievement Award, 1981, Wilbur Lucius Cross Medal, Yale U., 1986, Bertram Eugene Warren Award, Am. Crystal Assn., 1988, Magnetism Award, Internat. Union Pure and Applied Physics, 1997; 48th Richtmyer Meml. lectr. Am. Assn. Physics Tchrs., 1989, A.W. Scott lectr. Cambridge U., 2000. Fellow AAAS (exec. coun. 1992-94), Am. Phys. Soc. (Oliver E. Buckley Prize Com., 1981, 1990-01; Oliver E. Buckley Prize for Condensed Matter Physics, 1987, Julius E. Lilienfeld award 2000), Am. Acad. Arts Sci. (membership com., 1989-92), Royal Soc. London, Royal Soc. Can, Inst. Physics. Roman Catholic. Avocations: landscaping, squash, basketball. Office: U Calif Office Chancellor 200 Calif Hall Berkeley CA 94720*

BIRIBAUER, RICHARD FRANK, lawyer; b. May 30, 1950; s. Frank Anton and Mary M. (Valle) Biribauer; m. Linda Carey, Aug. 26, 1972; children: James Richard, David Tyler, Tia Renee. AB, Rutgers U., 1972; JD, Washington and Lee U., 1975. Bar: Va. 1975, DC 1976. Assoc. Law Offices of Fulton Brylawski, Washington, 1975—77; trademark counsel Johnson & Johnson, New Brunswick, NJ, 1977—83, internat. trademark counsel, 1984—91, chief trademark counsel, 1991—. Contbr. articles to Washington and Lee U. Law Rev., to Mng. Intellectual Property. Mem.: ABA, Va. State Bar Assn., DC Bar Assn., Pharm. Trademarks Group, Inter Am. Assn. Indsl. Property, Internat. Trademark Assn. Office: Johnson & Johnson One Johnson & Johnson Plz New Brunswick NJ 08933 Office Phone: 732-524-2845. Business E-Mail: rbiriba@corus.jnj.com.

BIRK, DAVID R., lawyer; BA, U. Fla., 1969; JD, Cornell U., 1972. Bar: N.Y. 1973. Ptnr., atty. Burstein & Marcus, 1977-80; assoc. atty. Jacobs, Persinger & Parker, 1974-77; sr. atty. Avnet Inc., Great Neck, N.Y., 1980-89, sr. v.p., gen. counsel, chief of staff, 1989—. 1st lt. U.S. Army, 1972-74. Mem. N.Y. State Bar (corr. law com.), Assn. of Bar of City of N.Y. (profl. discipline com.). Office: Avnet Inc 2211 S 47th St Phoenix AZ 85034-6403

BIRK, JOHN R., management consultant; b. Boston, Aug. 11, 1951; s. Harold F. and Jane Birk; m. Susan Arnold, Feb. 9, 1980; children: John R. Jr., Andrew A. BA in Econs. and English, Colgate U., 1974; Advanced Mgmt. Program, Harvard Bus. Sch., 1991. Sales rep. Procter & Gamble, N.Y.C., 1975-76, dist. field rep. White Plains, N.Y., 1976, unit mgr. Dallas, 1976-78; sales devel. mgr. Pepsi Cola Co., Purchase, N.Y., 1978-80, regional sales mgr. San Francisco, 1980-83; dir. sales and mktg. MCI Comm. Inc., Atlanta, 1983-84, v.p. sales and mktg., 1984-85; pres., bd. dirs. U.S. Telecomm Svcs. Co., Kansas City, 1985; pres. N.E. divsn. US Sprint, Purchase, 1986-87, pres. we. group San Francisco, 1987-88; exec. v.p., COO, dir. ADVO, Inc., 1988—89; pres., COO, dir. ADVO Inc., Windsor, 1989-92; pres., CEO, dir. Wright Express Corp., South Portland, Maine, 1992-94, chmn., 1994-95; pres. Ideon Group Inc. (formerly Safe Card Svcs., Inc.), Jacksonville, Fla., 1995; mgmt. cons. John R. Birk & Assocs., Ponte Vedra Beach, Fla., 1995—; operating exec. Evercore Ptnrs., 1996—. Bd. dirs. Commonwealth Telephone Enterprises, Inc., Splty. Products Insulation Inc., chmn.; fin. commr. Ctrl. Beach Fire Dist., Charlestown, RI. Bd. dirs. Prevent Blindness, Atlanta, 1984-85, United Way, White Plains, 1986-87, Westchester County Assn., 1986-87, Bay Area Coun., 1987-88, United Way Greater Portland, 1993-95, Found. for Blood Rsch., Inc., 1993-95, Colgate U. Alumni Corp., 1995-99; chmn. Colgate U. Pres. Club, 1996-99. Republican. Roman Catholic. Avocations: tennis, golf, skiing. Office Phone: 904-273-7819. E-mail: jrbirk@aol.com.

BIRK, LEE (CARL LEE BIRK), psychiatrist, educator; b. New Albany, Ind., Feb. 8, 1935; s. Glover McMurtrey and Marie Clyde (Carpenter) B.; m. Emily Perkins Gantt, June 21, 1958 (div. Jan. 1970); children: Elizabeth Waring, Alexandria Lee; m. Ann Harrison Wegner, June 15, 1973 (div. June 1990); children: Lara Blakiston, Jeffrey Lee. Student, Speed Scientific Sch., 1952-53, U. Louisville, 1953-54; BA in Zoology & Chemistry, Valparaiso U., 1956; MD, Johns Hopkins U., 1960. Intern U. Va. Hosp., Charlottesville, 1960-61; resident Harvard Med. Sch., Mass. Mental Health Ctr., Boston, 1961-62, 63-66; instr. psychiatry Harvard Med. Sch., Cambridge, Mass., 1968-69, asst. prof. psychiatry, 1969-73, asst. clin. prof. psychiatry, 1973-76, assoc. clin. prof. psychiatry, 1976—; dir. Learning Therapies, Inc., Newton, Mass., 1971-89, Concord, Mass., 1989-98, Burlington, Mass., 1998—; attending in psychiatry McLean Hosp., Belmont, Mass., 2003—. Vis. prof. Inst. Living, Hartford, Conn., 1975; Rhoads lectr. Duke U. Sch. Medicine, 1994. Author/editor: Behavior Therapy in Psychiatry, 1972, Psychoanalysis and Behavior Therapy, 1973, Biofeedback: Behavioral Medicine, 1973; mem. editorial bd. Psychotherapy & Psychosomatics, 1974—, Family Process, 1975-78, 82-83, Jour. of Marital & Family Therapy, 1983-90, Jour. of Psychotherapy Integration, 1989—. Capt. USAF, 1962-63. Mem. Am. Family Therapy Assn., Am. Coll. Psychiatrists, Am. Soc. Clin. Psychopharmacology, Soc. Exploration of Psychotherapy Integration (co-founder). Independent. Avocations: helicopter skiing, whitewater rafting/kayaking. Mailing: 8 Hart St Burlington MA 01803-1525 Office: 22 Mill St St 405 Arlington MA 02476 Office Phone: 781-643-0880. E-mail: lbirkmd@comcast.net.

BIRK, PEG J., lawyer; BA, U. Houston, 1976; JD, William Mitchell Coll. Law, 1983. Bar: Minn. 1983. Sr. corp. counsel St. Paul Companies, 1990—97; city atty. St. Paul, 1997—99; gen. counsel AM. Internat. Group, Inc., 1999, Domestic Brokerage Group; sr. v.p., gen. counsel Federated Mutual Ins. Co., Owatonna, Minn., 1999—. Bd. dirs. McKnight Found., Internat. Alliance Exec. Women; U.S. delegate Asian Pacific Econ. Corp., 2002—; bd. trustees Hamline U.; dep. Minn. Bus. Partnership. Office: Federated Mutual Ins Co 121 E Park Sq Owatonna MN 55060 Office Phone: 507-455-6915. Office Fax: 507-455-5997. E-mail: pjbirk@fedins.com.

BIRK, ROBERT EUGENE, retired internist; b. Buffalo, Jan. 7, 1926; s. Reginald H. and Florence (Diebolt) B.; m. Janet L. Davidson, June 24, 1950; children— David Eugene, James Michael, Patricia Jean, Thomas Spencer, Susan Margaret AB, Colgate U., 1948; MD, U. Rochester, 1952. Diplomate Am. Bd. Internal Medicine. Intern, resident Henry Ford Hosp., Detroit, 1952-57, chief 2d med. div., 1961-66, asst. to chmn. dept. medicine, 1965-66; practice medicine specializing in internal medicine Grosse Pointe, Mich., 1966-89; sr. active staff St. John Hosp., 1966-89, chief dept. medicine, 1967-70, dir. health edn., dir. grad. med. edn., 1975-86, exec. dir. continuing med. edn., 1975-86; dir. med. affairs St John Ambulatory Care Corp., St. John Home Care Svcs., 1980-89; v.p. clin. affairs St. John Health Corp., 1985-89. Assoc. prof. medicine Wayne State U., 1969-89 Contbr. articles to profl. jours. Mem. trustee's coun. U. Rochester, 1973-75, Med. Ctr. alumni coun., 1974-75; bd. trustees St. John Hosp., Macomb Ctr., 1986-89; corp. mem. bd. Boys Clubs Met. Detroit, 1973-89; trustee Mich. Cancer Found., 1980-89, bd. dirs., 1982-85. With U.S. Army, 1943-46. Fellow ACP, Detroit Acad. Medicine; mem. AMA, Assn. Hosp. Med. Edn. (trustee region IV 1986-87), Mich. Assn. Med. Edn. (trustee 1985-86), Am. Soc. Internal Medicine, Am. Acad. Med. Dirs., Alpha Tau Omega. Republican. Episcopalian. Home: 8 Eagle Claw Dr Hilton Head Island SC 29926-1853

BIRKELAND, BRYAN COLLIER, lawyer; b. Hibbing, Minn., May 29, 1951; s. Lionel Owen and Peggy Jean Birkeland; m. D.J. Loras, Jan. 5, 1974; children: Brett Holton, Blair Leigh, Blake Owen. Student, Washington and Jefferson Coll., 1969-70; BA with high honors, U. Tex., 1973, JD with honors, 1975. Bar: Tex. 1976. Ptnr. Jackson Walker, LLP, Dallas, 1982—. Pres., dir. Globalaw, Ltd. Grantee, Moody Found., 1971. Mem. ABA, State Bar Tex., Dallas Bar Assn., Order of Coif, Phi Beta Kappa, Phi Kappa Phi, Delta Sigma Rho, Tau Kappa Alpha. Presbyterian. Office: Jackson Walker LLP 901 Main St Ste 6000 Dallas TX 75202-3797 Office Phone: 214-953-6000. E-mail: bbirkeland@jw.com.

BIRKELBACH, ALBERT OTTMAR, retired oil industry executive; b. Oak Park, Ill., Feb. 22, 1927; s. August and Ann B.; m. Shirley M. Spandet, Aug. 21, 1948; children: J.A., Lisa M., Grace L. Birkelbach Boland, Ann C. Birkelbach. BSCh.E., U. Ill., 1949. Various engring., supervisory and mgmt. positions Globe Oil & Refining Co., Lemont, Ill., 1949-53, Anderson Prichard Oil Corp., Cyril, Okla., 1953-58, Signal Oil & Gas Co., Los Angeles, 1958-64; mng. dir. Raffinerie Belge de Petroles, Antwerp, Belgium, 1964-74; v.p. Occidental Petroleum Corp., London, Eng., 1972-74; cons. in field,

1974-75; pres. ATC Petroleum Inc., N.Y.C., 1975-81, also dir.; pres. Amorient Petroleum Corp., Laguna Niguel, Calif., 1981-84; mgmt. cons., 1984-87. Served with USCG, 1945-47. Decorated knight Order Leopold Belgium). Home: 33957 N 66th Way Scottsdale AZ 85262 Address: 33957 N 66th Way Scottsdale AZ 85262-7231

BIRKELUND, JOHN PETER, investment company executive; b. Chgo., June 23, 1930; s. George R. and Ruth (Olsen) B.; m. Constance I. Smiles, Oct. 25, 1958; children: Gwynne Tibbetts, Elizabeth Oberbeck, Constance Olivia, Diana. AB, Princeton U., 1952; doctorate (hon.), Brown U., 2002. Cons. Booz Allen & Hamilton, Chgo., 1956; v.p. Amsterdam Overseas Corp., N.Y.C., 1956-67; co-founder, chmn. New Court Securities Corp., N.Y.C., 1967-81; pres. Dillon, Read & Co., Inc., N.Y.C., 1981-86, CEO, 1986-93, chmn., 1994-97; sr. advisor UBS Warburg LLC, N.Y.C., 1998—2002; gen. ptnr. Saratoga Ptnrs., N.Y.C., Darby Overseas Ptnrs., Washington. Chmn. Polish-Am. Enterprise Fund, Polish.-Am. Freedom Found., Nat. Humanities Ctr., N.C. Chair Thomas J. Watson Inst. for Internat. Studies, Providence; trustee N.Y. Pub. Libr., N.Y.C., 1990—, Frick Collection, 2004. Lt. USNR, 1953—55. Mem. Coun. Fgn. Rels., Phi Beta Kappa (senate, 2004-), The Links Club, Univ. Club, The Blind Brook Club, Clove Valley Rod and Gun Club. Home: 510 Weed St New Canaan CT 06840-6127 Office: Saratoga Ptnrs 535 Madison Ave 4th Fl New York NY 10022

BIRKENHEAD, THOMAS BRUCE, theater producer, educator; b. NYC, Dec. 19, 1931; s. Thomas A. and Florence (Morison) B.; m. Susan Leslie Arkin, Dec. 3, 1954 (div. 1983); m. Maria Martins, May 26, 1999; children: Peter Lawrence, David Andrew, Richard James, Alison Jane, Leila Alessandra. BA, Bklyn. Coll. CUNY, 1954, MA, 1958; PhD, New Sch. Social Rsch., 1963. From lectr. to prof. econs. Bklyn. Coll. CUNY, 1957-72, prof., 1972-75; dean Sch. Social Scis., 1972-75; prof. emeritus Bklyn. Coll. CUNY, 1975—. Bus. mgr. Theatre II, Glen Cove, NY, 1970—74; mgmt. cons. Keystone Ctr. Performing Arts, 1999—. Co-mgr. Do Black Patent Leather Shoes Really Reflect Up?, Present Laughter, Master Harold and the Boys, Children of a Lesser God, Ain't Misbehavin, Brighton Beach Memoirs, Biloxi Blues, Broadway Bound, Barbara Cook in Concert, Run For Your Wife, Rumors, Lost in Yonkers, Jake's Women, Goodbye Girl; gen. mgr.: Cape Cod Melody Tent, 1969—71, Twyla Tharp on Broadway, 1980—81; gen. mgr. Joe Egg, 1985, Social Security, 1986, Long Days Journey Into Night, London and Tel Aviv, 1986, Ain't Misbehavin, N.Y.C., 1988—89, Japan, 1990, Fresh Air Taxi, 1993, Honky Tonk Highway, 1994—96, Dream a Little Dream, 1994—95, Duke and the Dutchess, 2001—; co-prodr.: 1995 Tony Award Broadcast, N.H.K. Japan, —; prodr.: High Mountain Ghost, 1996—98; sec.-treas.: Highly Ent., 1995—. Founding mem., sponsor U.S. Shooting Team, U.S. Holocaust Meml. Mus., Am. Air Mus., Eng., U.S. Naval Meml. Found., WWII Meml., U.S. Olympic Com. Named T. Bruce Birkenhead scholarship in his honor, Performing Arts Mgmt. Program Bklyn. Coll. Mem. NRA, US Naval Inst., Habitat for Humanity, Amnesty Internat., Women in Mil. Svc. for Am., Groucho Club (Eng.), World Jewish Congress, Carter Ctr., Victorian Soc., Friends of Israel Def. Force Home and Office: 353 W 44th St Apt 1A New York NY 10036-5416 E-mail: brucebirkenhead@yahoo.com.

BIRKERTS, GUNNAR, architect; b. Riga, Latvia, Jan. 17, 1925; came to U.S., 1949, naturalized, 1954; s. Peter and Meria (Shop) B.; m. Sylvia Zvirbulis, July 29, 1950; children— Sven Peter, Andra Sylvia, Erik Gunnar. Diplomingeneur Architekt, Technische Hochschule, Stuttgart, Germany, 1949; D (hon.), Riga Tech. Univ., Latvia, 1990. Designer Perkins & Will, Chgo., 1950-51, Eero Saarinen & Assos., Bloomfield Hills, Mich., 1951-55; prin. chief designer Minoru Yamasaki & Assos., Birmingham, Mich., 1955-59; pres. Gunnar Birkerts & Assos., Inc., Birmingham, 1959; asst. prof. architecture U. Mich., 1961, asso. prof., 1963-69, prof., 1969-90; Graham fellow, 1970; architect in residence Am. Acad. in Rome, 1976; 1st Lawrence J. Plym. disting. prof. architecture U. Ill., 1982; Thomas S. Monaghan architect-in-residence prof. U. Mich., Ann Arbor, 1984; Bruce Alonzo Goff prof. of creative architecture U. Okla., 1990. Prin. works include Schwartz House, Northville, Mich. (First Honor award AIA 1962, Merit award Detroit chpt. AIA 1963, Archtl. Record award 1961), Univ. Reformed Ch., Ann Arbor Mich. (award Ch. Archtl. Guild Am. 1962), Peoples Fed. Savs. & Loan Bank, Royal Oak, Mich., 1963 (Merit award Detroit chpt. AIA 1963), Fisher Adminstrv. Ctr., Detroit (award of merit Mich. Soc. Architects 1967, Merit award Detroit chpt. AIA 1967), Detroit Inst. Arts addition (25 Yr. award AIA 2002), 1300 Lafayette Apts., Detroit, Tougaloo (Miss.) Coll. (award of honor Mich. Soc. Architects 1974), Vocat.-Tech. Campus, So. Ill. U., Glen Oaks Community Coll. Campus, Centreville, Mich., Lincoln Sch., Columbus, Ind. (AIA Detroit chpt. and nat. Honor awards 1968, 70, 25 yr. award Mich. AIA), Fed. Res. Bank, Mpls. (award excellence Am. Inst. Steel Constrn. 1974, design award Am. Iron and Steel Inst. 1975), IBM Corp. Computer Center, Sterling Forest, N.Y. (honor award Detroit chpt. AIA 1973), Contemporary Arts Mus., Houston (honor award Detroit chpt. AIA 1975), Dance Instructional Facility at Purchase (award honor Mich. Soc. Architects 1977, Honor award Detroit chpt. AIA 1978), Calvary Baptist Ch., Detroit (Honor award Mich. Soc. Architects 1979, award of excellence Am. Inst. Steel Constrn. 1979), IBM Office Bldg., Southfield, Mich. (Honor award Mich. Soc. Architects 1980, energy conservation award Owens Corning Fiberglas Corp. 1977), Duluth Public Libr. (Honor award Mich. Soc. Architects 1981), Fire Sta., Corning, N.Y. (honor award Mich. Soc. Architects 1977), Corning Mus. of Glass, Law Libr. Addition, U. Mich. (award of excellence AIA and ALA 1985), U.S. Embassy bldg., Helsinki, Finland, Coll. of Law bldg., U. Iowa (Award of Honor-Mich. Soc. Architects 1987), Uris Library addition, Cornell U. (honor award Mich. Soc. Architects 1984), Dist. Office Bldg., Green Bay, Wis., Ferguson Residence, Kalamazoo, Mich. (award of honor Mich. Soc. Architects 1986), Chapel & Enbl. Facility, Camp Wildflecken, Fed. Republic Germany (Silver Castle award U.S. Army Corps. Engrs., European div. 1986), St. Peter's Luth. Ch., Columbus, Ind (award of honor Detroit chpt. AIA 1986, 90), Domino's world hdqrs., Ann Arbor, Mich. (bldg. recognition award Engring. Soc. Detroit 1987, M award for Excellence in Masonry Design Masonry Inst. Mich., 1989), Libr. Addition Conservatory Music Oberlin Coll., Ohio, Prototype Franchise Bldg. Domino's Pizza, Inc. (award of honor Mich. Soc. Architects 1989), Jackson, Mich., Cen. Libr. addition U. Calif., San Diego, Sports Svcs. Bldg. U. Mich., U.S. Embassy, Caracas, Venezuela, Libr. U. Mich., Flint (Design and Constrn. showcase '94 award), Coll. Law Ohio State U., (award of honor AIA Mich., 1995), Kemper Mus. Contemporary Art and Design, Kans. City Mo. (Lighting award, 1995), Ch. Servant, Kentwood, Mich.; exhbns. include Akron Inst. Art, 1954, Sao Paulo (Brazil) Bienniale, 1962, 40 under 40, USA-NY, Architects League, 1965, Mus. Modern Art, N.Y.C., 1971, Notre Dame U., 1973, N.Y. Mus. Modern Art, 1979, Neuberger Mus., Purchase, N.Y., 1981, Am. Acad. and Inst. Arts and Letters, N.Y.C., 1981, U. Ill., 1983, U. Md., College Park, 1985, Saginaw Art Mus., Mich., 1985, Notre Dame U., 1985, Pratt Inst., Bklyn., 1986, NYU, 1986, The Triennale, Milan, Italy, 1986, Judah L. Magnes Mus., Berkeley, Calif., 1986, Nat. Ctr. for Study of Frank Lloyd Wright, Ann Arbor, 1988, St. Peter's Cathedral, Riga, Latvia, 1989, Torino '90, Turin, Italy, 1990, The 3d Belgrade Triennial of World Architects, 1991, The Athenaeum Music and Art Libr., LaJolla, Calif., 1991, Kansas City Art Inst., 1992, Lawrence Tech. U., Southfield, Mich., 1993, Latvian Nat. Libr., 2000 (Am. Archtl. award Chgo. Atheanum), Venezia and Archtl. Bieniale, 2002. Named Young Designer of Year Akron Inst. Art, 1954, Mich. Artist of Yr. Mich. Artrain, 1993; recipient 1st prize Internat. Furniture competition, Cantu, Italy, 1955; 3d prize Internat. competition for Cultural Centre, Belgian Congo; Design award Progressive Architecture mag., 1957, 59, 61, 71; award of excellence Archtl. Record, 1968; Nat. Gold medal Tau Sigma Delta, 1971; Gold medal Detroit chpt. AIA, 1975; Gold medal Mich. Soc. Architects, 1980; Brunner Meml. prize Am. Acad. and Inst. Arts and Letters, 1981; Mich. Art award Arts Found. Mich., 1988, Disting. Prof. Assn. Collegiate Schs. Architecture, 1990; Order of Three Stars, Republic of Latvia. Fellow AIA, Graham Found., Latvian Architects Assn.; mem. Mich. Soc. Architects (Award of Honor 1989), Ch. Archtl. Guild, Hon. Order Ky. Cols. Office: 65 Grove St Apt 241 Wellesley MA 02482 Office Phone: 248-626-5661. Business E-Mail: gunnarbirk@aol.com.

BIRKESTOL, ANNABELLE MOLLIE ELSIE, retired elementary school educator; b. Stanwood, Wash., May 29, 1923; d. Ole and Ingeborg Birkestol. *The family matriarch, Anne Birkestol, and her children filed timber claims between Lake Ozette and the Pacific Ocean in Washington State. The southern tip of Lake Ozette was named Birkestol Point in their honor. The worst shipping tragedy along the North Pacific Coast occurred January 2, 1903, when the captain of the three-masted bark Prince Arthur mistook the light in the Birkestol cabin for the Tatoosh Island beacon. The captain and seventeen crew members lost their lives in the shipwreck. The bodies were buried near the cabin overlooking the Pacific. The monument is maintained by Seattle's Norwegian Commercial Club.* BA in edn., Pacific Lutheran U., 1945; grad. studies U. Wash. (hon.), 1969. Elem. tchr. Woodinville Sch., Woodinville, Wash., 1945—47, Wilson Sch., Mukilteo, Wash., 1948—54, Conway Sch., Conway, Wash., 1954—76; ret., 1976. Mem. Wash. State Edn. Assn., Olympia, Wash., 1945—76, NEA, 1945—76. Mem.: Wash. State Sch. Retirees' Assn., Am. Assn. U. Women, Nat. Women's Hist. Mus., Stanwood Area Hist. Soc. (life; pres. 1978—79), Norwegian Am. Mus. Vesterheim (life), Sons of Norway Stanwood, Pacific Lutheran U. Q Club, Frijov Lodge No. 17 Sons of Norway Stanwood. Republican. Lutheran. Avocations: opera, museums, historic preservation. Home: 4515 Norman Rd Stanwood WA 98292

BIRKHEAD, GUTHRIE SWEENEY, JR., political scientist, dean; b. Holden, Mo., Oct. 28, 1920; s. Guthrie Sweeney and Yula Donna (Glass) B.; m. Louise Gartner, Aug. 16, 1952; children— Guthrie Sweeney III, Richard Gartner, Evan Clark. AA, Jefferson City (Mo.) Jr. Coll., 1940; AB, U. Mo., 1942, A.M., 1947; MA, Princeton, 1949, PhD in Politics, 1951. Mem. faculty Syracuse U., 1950—, prof. polit. sci., 1960—, chmn. dept., 1959-62, 66-67, dir. met. studies program, 1968-73; asso. dean Maxwell Sch., 1973-77, dean, 1977-88. Also dir. pub. adminstrn. programs, 1959-62; dir. research UN Inst. Pub. Adminstrn. for Turkey and Middle East, 1955-56; cons. Pakistan Adminstrv. Staff Coll., Lahore, 1962-64, Ford Found., Pakistan, 1967-68 Co-author: River Basin Administration and the Delaware, 1960, Science and State Government in New York, 1960, Decisions in Syracuse, 1962; Editor: Administrative Problems in Pakistan, 1966, A Look to the North: Canadian Regional Experience, 1974, Education for Public Service, 1980; Contbr. articles to profl. jours. Chmn. pub. finance com. Community Renewal Plan, Syracuse, N.Y., 1970-72; exec. dir. com. local govt. and home rule N.Y. State Constl. Conv., 1967, Syracuse Charter Commn., 1972-74; mem. Nat. Com. Water Quality Policy Nat. Acad. Scis.-NRC, 1974-76; com. to review the metropolitan Washington area water supply study Nat. Acad. Engring/Nat. Research Council, 1977-84. Served with inf. AUS, 1942-46. Fellow Nat. Mcpl. League, 1952-53. Fellow Nat. Acad. Pub. Adminstrn.; mem. AAAS, Am. Soc. Pub. Adminstrn., Phi Beta Kappa, Sigma Xi. Home: 220 Lockwood Rd Syracuse NY 13214-2035 E-mail: guthrieinc@msn.com.

BIRKINBINE, JOHN, II, philatelist; b. Chestnut Hill, Pa., Mar. 29, 1930; s. Olaf Weimer and Gertrude Marie (Tyson) B.; m. Ausencia Barrera Elen, Dec. 19, 1969; children: John III, Bayani Royd. Degree, Haverford Sch., 1948. Chmn., CEO Am. Philatelic Brokerages, Tucson, 1946—. Chmn. bd. dirs. Ariz. Philatelic Rangers, Tucson, 1987—; bd. dirs. Postal History Found. Chmn. bd. 1869 Pictorial Rsch. Assn., 1969, bd. dirs., 1970-76, chmn. Baha'i Faith Adminstrv. Body, Pima County, Ariz., 1977-81, 83-91; sheriff, chmn. Santa Catalina Corral of Westerners Internat., Tucson, 1986; bd. dirs. Tucson chpt. Nordmanns-Forburdet (Norse Fedn.), 2002—. Recipient Large Gold and Spl. award Spanish Soc. Internat., San Juan, P.R., 1982, New Zealand Soc. Internat., Auckland, 1990, Large Internat. Gold award Australian Soc. Internat., Melbourne, 1984, Swedish Soc. Internat., Stockholm, 1986, Singapore Soc. Internat., 1995, U.S. Soc. Internat., San Francisco, 1997, Internat. Gold award U.S. Soc. Internat., Chgo., 1986, Bulgarian Soc. Internat., Sofia, 1989. Mem. Am. Philatelic Soc. (U.S. Champion of Champions award 1985), U.S. Philatelic Classics Soc. (disting. philatelist award 1995), Am. Philatelic Congress (McCoy award 1969, 97), Scandinavian Collectors Club, Collectors Club N.Y., Western Cover Soc. Avocations: swimming, travel, music, West U.S. historical research, Japanese antiques. Office: Am Philatelic Brokerages PO Box 36657 Tucson AZ 85740-6657 Personal E-mail: jb2nd@earthlink.net. *To look for and appreciate the good qualities in each individual, to have sympathy and empathy for their problems, and to provide exceptional service in an attempt to satisfy their needs and desires.*

BIRKLAND, THOMAS ANDREW, political scientist, consultant; b. Seattle, Sept. 19, 1961; s. James R. and Kathleen S. B.; m. Molly K. Eness, June 17, 2000. BA in Polit. Sci., U. Oreg., 1984; MA in Polit. Sci., Rutgers U., 1985; PhD in Polit. Sci., U. Wash., 1995. Rsch. analyst N.J. Dept. Transp., Trenton, 1985-87; aide to gov. Office of Gov. Thomas Kean, Trenton, 1987-88; asst. mgr. Strategic Planning N.J. Dept. Transp., Trenton, 1988-90; prof. SUNY, Albany, 1995—. Author: After Disaster, Agenda Setting, Public Policy, and Focusing Events, 1987, An Introduction to the Policy Process: Theories, Concepts, and Models of Public Policy Making, 2001. Mem. ASPA, Am. Polit. Sci. Assn., Assn. Pub. Policy Analysis and Mgmt., Earthquake Engring. Rsch. Inst. Office: SUNY Milne Hall 135 Western Ave Albany NY 12222 Fax: 518-442-5298. E-mail: birkland@albany.edu.

BIRKY, JOHN EDWARD, banker, financial consultant; b. Minier, Ill., July 16, 1934; s. John G. and Gertrude K. (Nafziger) B.; m. Susan Becker, Dec. 13, 1937; children: John Brian, Kathleen Debera. BS in Indsl. Adminstrn., U. Ill., 1957; postgrad., Ohio State U., 1957; MBA, Case Western Res. U., 1975. Cert. data processor. Asst. to mgr. Caterpillar Tractor Co., Peoria, Ill., 1957-61; cons. Sutherland Co., Peoria, 1961-63; mgr. United Research Services, San Mateo, Calif., 1963-69; dir. Case Western Res. U., Cleve., 1969-72; v.p. Fed. Res. Bank, Cleve., 1972-79; exec. v.p. Banc Systems Assn., West Lake, Ohio, 1979-83, Citizens Banking Corp., Flint, Mich., 1983-92, also chmn. auto com., mem. corp. exec. com., 1986-92; fin. planner Bonita Springs, Fla., 1992-98; fin. adviser Amex Fin. Advisors, Inc.; ind. fin. cons. Hopedale, Ill. Bd. dirs. Citizens Bank, Flint, Comml. Nat. Bank, Berwyn, Ill., Citizens Leasing Corp., Grand Rapids, Mich., Flin Inst. Music; chmn. Magicline Inc., 1989-91; speaker various profl. confs. Contbr. articles to banking jours. Mem. Rep. precinct com., Sierra Vista, Ariz., 1964-65; life mem. Pres.'s Task Force, Washington, 1980; advisor automation commn. ARC, Flint, 1987; mem. exec. bd., treas. Flint Inst. Music, 1986-88, vice chmn.; mem. Am. Bank Adminstrn. Ins.; bd. dirs. Flint Inst. Music; elder, lay pastor 1st Presbyn. Ch., Flint, 1988-91; past mem. adv. com. U. Mich., Flint, Boys Club Cleve., Cuyahoga C.C., Ashland Coll.; bd. dirs. Catalina coun. Golden Eagle Club Boy Scouts; pres. Friends of Catalina Resource Svcs. Capt. USAF, 1957-60. Mem.: Data Processing Mgmt. Assn., Am. Bankers Assn., Acacia, U. Ill. Alumni Assn. (life), Am. Legion, Tucson Alumni Club (v.p.), Saddlebrooke Country Club, Scottish Rite, Shriners, Masons. Republican. Avocations: golf, tennis, barbershop singing.

BIRLE, JAMES ROBB, investor; b. Phila., Jan. 25, 1936; s. John George and Mildred C. (Donnelly) B.; m. Mary Margaret McDaniels, Jan. 28, 1961; children— James Robb, Jr., Anne Margaret, Alexandra Lea, John George II BSM.E., Villanova U., 1958. With Gen. Electric Co., San Jose, Calif., 1958, gen. mgr. nuclear energy bus., 1969-77, v.p., gen mgr. far east business div. N.Y.C., 1977-81, v.p., gen mgr. air condition div. Louisville, 1981-82, sr. v.p., group exec. constrn. and engring. svcs. group Westport, Conn, 1982-85, sr. v.p. corp. trading ops. N.Y.C., 1985-88; ptnr. The Blackstone Group, N.Y.C., 1988-94; co-chmn., CEO Collins & Aikman Group, N.Y.C., 1988-94; chmn. Resolute Ptnrs., LLC, Village of Golf, Fla., 1994—; non-exec. chmn. Mass. Mut. Fin. Svcs. Co., 2005—. Bd. dirs. Mass. Mut. Fin. Svcs. Co. 1992-, chmn. bd. Mass Mutual Fin. Group; former mem. Transparency Internat. Former trustee Villanova U., 2005-. Republican. Avocations: tennis, golf, reading, sailing. Office: Resolute Ptnrs LLC 2 Pine Ln East Village Of Golf FL 33436 Home: 2 Pine Ln E Village Of Golf FL 33436

BIRMAN, JOSEPH LEON, physics professor; b. NYC, May 21, 1927; m. Joan Sylvia Lyttle, Feb. 22, 1950; children: Kenneth, Deborah, Carl-David. BS, CCNY, 1947; MA, Columbia U., 1950, PhD, 1952; DSc honoris causa, U. Rènnes, France, 1974. From sr. physicist to head luminescence sect. GTE Research Labs., N.Y., 1952-62; Mary Amanda Wood vis. prof. U. Pa., 1960; assoc. prof. physics NYU, 1962-64, prof., 1964-74; Henry Semat prof. physics CCNY, 1974-88; Disting. prof. physics CCNY and CUNY, 1987—. Cons. rsch. labs.; vis. prof. U. Paris VI, Ecole Normale Superieure, 1969-70, Japan Soc. for Promotion of Sci., Rsch. Inst. for Fundamental Physics, U. Kyoto, Japan, 1978, 80, Inst. Hautes Etudes Scientifiques, Bures/Yvette, France, 1976, 78, 80, 82, 86, 87-88, 91, U. Regensburg, 1983, 84, 85; vis. prof. dept. theoretical physics Oxford (Eng.) U., 1981, 84, 85, 86; Lady Davis vis. prof. Technion, Israel, 1981, 95, 1996-2005; vis. prof. Peking, Fudan, Nanking, Xian Univs., 1980, 82, 85, U. Stuttgart, 1986, U. de Paris VI, 1987-88, 91, Nankai U., 2004; Meyerhoff vis. prof. Weitzmann Inst., Rehovoth, 1988; founder, chmn. Am. coordinating com. Chinese Scholars Program, joint program of Am. Phys. Soc. and Chinese Acad. Sci./Chinese State Com. Edn., 1983-86. Author: Theoretical Physics, 1952, Handbuch der Physik, Vol. 25/2b, 1974, reprinted 1984 (Russian transl. 1978); editor: Light Scattering in Solids, 1976, 79; co-editor: Laser Optics of Condensed Matter, 1988; mem. editl. bd., cons. Springer Verlag, Plenum Press, Nova Pubs., World Sci. Press, Oxford U. Press; contbr. more than 300 articles to profl. jours. Hon. mem. US nat. bd. Human Rights in China, 1990-05, 05-. Served with USNR, 1945-46. Research grantee NSF, NRC-U.S., Army Research Office, Aerospace Research Labs., Dept. Def.; J.S. Guggenheim Meml. Found. fellow, 1980-81. Fellow Am. Phys. Soc. (com. on internat. freedom of scientists 1991-93, chmn. 1993, chair forum internat. physics 1999), AAAS (com. on sci. freedom and responsibility 1991-93, chair Wigner Prize com 2000), NY Acad. Scis. (human rights com. 1980-, chair 1993-05, gov.-at-large 1989-90, v.p. 1991-92), Com. Concerned Scientists (nat. bd. dirs.), Human Rights in China (hon. mem., nat. bd.). Office: CCNY Physics Dept 138th St And Convent Ave New York NY 10031

BIRMELIN, ROBERT, artist; b. Newark, 1933; BFA, Yale U., 1956, MFA, 1960. Tchr. Queens Coll., NYC. One-man shows include Galerie Claude Bernard, Paris, 1981, Montclair Art Mus., Montclair, NJ, 1984, Schaefer Gallery Custavus Adolphus Coll., St. Peter, Minn., 1986, Galeria Mara, Buenos Aires, 1990, Rider U. Art Gallery, Lawrenceville, NJ, 1991, Morris Mus., Morristown, NJ, 1991, Jaffe Baker Gallery, Boca Raton, Fla., 1992, Contemporary Realist Gallery, San Francisco, 1993, 1995, Ralph Greene Galllery, Albuquerque, 1994, Godwin-Ternbach Mus. Queens Coll., Flushing, NY, 1996, Jersey City Mus., Jersey City, NJ, 1997—98, Hackett-Freedman Gallery, San Francisco, 2001, others. Recipient Carnegie Prize, NAD Annual, Altman Prize, Purchase award, Am. Inst Arts and Letters, San Francisco Mus., H.G. Scheidt Meml. Prize, Pa. Acad. Art; grantee, Am. Acad. Rome, 1961—64, Nat. Inst. Arts and Letters, 1968, Louis Comfort Tiffany Found., 1973, NJ Coun. for Arts, 1980, 1988, Nat. Endowment of Arts, 1976, 1982, 1989. Address: Peter Findlay Gallery 41 E 57th St New York NY 10022*

BIRMINGHAM, KAREN LYNNE, pharmacist; BS, Wingate (N.C.) U., 1993; PharmD, Med. U. S.C., 1999. Registered pharmacist S.C. Bd. Pharmacy, Ga. Bd. Pharmacy, 1999, cert. advanced disaster life support Nat. Disaster Life Support Edn. Consortium, 2004, Adult Immunizations Am. Pharm. Assn., 2003. Rsch. specialist Med. U. S.C., Charleston, 1990—98; clin. specialist cardiac surgery/critical care N.E. Ga. Med. Ctr., Gainesville, Ga., 2001—. Adj. facultySch of Pharmacy, Mercer U. South, Atlanta, 2001—; clin. asst. prof. Coll. of Pharmacy, U. Ga., Athens, 2001—. Author: (newsletter) Ngmc Pharmacy Focus, 2001—04; contbr. articles to profl. jours. Mem.: Ga. Soc. Hosp. Pharmacists, Am. Soc. Health Sys. Pharmacists, Soc. Critical Care Medicine, Alpha Chi.

BIRMINGHAM, RICHARD GREGORY, lawyer; b. Buffalo, N.Y., Aug. 14, 1929; s. William Anthony and Laura Louise (Reimann) B.; m. Suzanne M. Cannon, May 20, 1961; children: Barbara A. McCarty, Maureen E., Gregory S. BA, U. Notre Dame, 1951; JD, SUNY, Buffalo, 1957. Bar: N.Y. 1957, Del. 1984, Pa. 1993. Law clk. to justices appellate div. N.Y. Supreme Ct. (4th dept.), Rochester, 1957-60; ptnr. Phillips, Lytle, Hitchcock, Blaine & Huber, Buffalo, 1960-84, 90-94, ret., 1994, ptnr. Wilmington, Del., 1984-90. Lt. comdr. USN, 1951-54, Korea. Mem. ABA, N.Y. State Bar Assn., Del. Bar Assn., Erie County Bar Assn., Rivermont Country Club. Republican. Roman Catholic. Office: 510 Shelli Ln Roswell GA 30075-2988 Personal E-mail: rgsb510@hotmail.com.

BIRMINGHAM, RICHARD JOSEPH, lawyer; b. Seattle, Feb. 26, 1953; s. Joseph E. and Anita (Loomis) B. BA cum laude, Wash. State U., 1975; JD, Seattle U., 1978; LLM in Taxation, Boston U., 1980. Bar: Wash. 1978, Oreg. 1981, U.S. Dist. Ct. (we. dist.) Wash. 1978, U.S. Tax Ct. 1981. Ptnr. Davis Wright Tremaine, Seattle, 1982-93; shareholder Birmingham Thorson & Barnett, P.C., Seattle, 1993—. Mem. King County Bar Employee Benefit Com., Seattle, 1986, U.S. Treasury ad hoc com. employee benefits, 1988—. Contbg. editor: Compensation and Benefits Mgmt., 1985—; contbr. articles to profl. jours. Mem. ABA (employee benefits and exec. compensation com. 1982—), Wash. State Bar Assn. (speaker 1984-86, tax sect. 1982—), Oreg. State Bar Assn. (tax sect. 1982—), Western Pension Conf. (speaker 1986), Seattle Pension Round table. Democrat. Avocations: jogging, bicycling, photography. Home: 3820 49th Ave NE Seattle WA 98105-5234 Office: Birmingham Thorson & Barnett PC 3315 Two Union Square 601 Union St Seattle WA 98101-2341 Business E-Mail: RBirmingham@BTBPC.com.

BIRMINGHAM, STEPHEN, writer; b. Hartford, Conn., May 28, 1931; s. Thomas J. and Editha (Gardner) B.; m. Janet Tillson, Jan. 5, 1951 (div.); children: Mark, Harriet, Carey. BA cum laude, Williams Coll., 1950; postgrad., Univ. Coll., Oxford (Eng.) U., 1951. Advt. copywriter Needham, Harper & Steers, Inc., 1953-67. Author: Young Mr. Keefe, 1958, Barbara Greer, 1959, The Towers of Love, 1961, Those Harper Women, 1963, Fast Start, Fast Finish, 1966, Our Crowd: The Great Jewish Families of New York, 1967, The Right People, 1968, Heart Toubles, 1968, The Grandees, 1971, The Late John Marquand, 1972, The Right Places, 1973, Real Lace, 1973, Certain People: America's Black Elite, 1977, The Golden Dream: Suburbia in the 1970's, 1978, Jacqueline Bouvier Kennedy Onassis, 1978, Life at the Dakota, 1979, California Rich, 1980, Duchess, 1981, The Grandes Dames, 1982, The Auerbach Will, 1983; The Rest of Us, 1984, The LeBaron Secret, 1986, Americas Secret Aristocracy, 1987, Shades of Fortune, 1989, The Rothman Scandal, 1991, Carriage Trade, 1993, The Wrong Kind of Money, 1997; contbr. numerous articles to numerous periodicals. Served with AUS, 1951-53. Mem. New Eng. Soc. of City of N.Y., Phi Beta Kappa. Democrat. Episcopalian. Address: 1247 Ida St Cincinnati OH 45202-1525 Office Phone: 513-241-8919.

BIRMINGHAM, THOMAS F., lawyer, former state legislator; b. Aug. 4, 1949; married; two daughters. AB in Social Studies cum laude, Harvard Coll., 1972; Rhodes Scholar, Oxford Univ., 1972—75; JD cum laude, Harvard Coll., 1978. Bar: Mass.; U.S. Dist. Ct. Mass.; 1st Cir. Ct. of Appeals; U.S. State Supreme Ct. Asst. gen. counsel Internat. Union Electrical Workers, 1978-80; assoc. atty. Flamm, Kaplan, Paven & Feinberg, 1980-83; ptnr. Flamm & Birmingham, 1984-93; mem. Mass. Senate, Boston, 1991—2002, pres., 1996—2002; ptnr. Feinberg, Charnas & Birmingham, 1994—. Faculty mem. Boston Labor Guild Sch. Indsl. Rels., 1980-85; senate chair Edn. Arts and Humanities Com., 1991-92, Ways and Means Com. State Mass., 1993-2002; mem. Steering and Policy Com. State Mass., 1993-2002. Commr. Chelsea Redevelopment Authority, 1985-88; bd. dirs. New England Higher Edn., 1991—. Harvard Coll. Academic scholar, 1969-72, U. Coll. Galway scholar, 1970, Rhodes scholar, 1972-75; Teaching fellow Harvard Coll., 1971. Mem. Mass. Bar Assn. (labor law sec. coun. mem.). E-mail: Tbirming@sen.state.ma.us.

BIRMINGHAM, WILLIAM JOSEPH, retired lawyer; b. Lynbrook, N.Y., Aug. 7, 1923; s. Daniel Joseph and Mary Elizabeth (Tighe) B.; m. Helen Elizabeth Roche, July 23, 1955; children: Deirdre, Patrick, Maureen, Kathleen, Brian. ME, Stevens Inst. Tech., 1944; MBA, Harvard U., 1948; JD, DePaul U., Chgo., 1953. Bar: Ill. 1953, U.S. Patent and Trademark Office, 1955, U.S. Dist. Ct. (no. dist.) Ill. 1960, U.S. Supreme Ct. 1961, U.S. Ct. Appeals (7th cir.) 1962, U.S. Ct. Appeals (3rd cir.) 1968, U.S. Ct. Mil. Appeals 1973, U.S. Ct. Appeals (Fed. cir.) 1982, U.S. Ct. Claims 1986; registered profl. engr., Ill., Ind. Chem. engr. Standard Oil Co. Ind., Chgo.,

1948-53; patent atty., 1953-59; assoc. Neuman, Williams, Anderson & Olson, Chgo., 1959-60, ptnr., 1961—91, Leydig, Voit & Mayer, Ltd., Chgo., 1991-93, of counsel, 1994—96; ret., 1997. Served to capt. USNR, 1942-75, ret. Mem. ABA, ASME, Fed. Cir. Bar Assn., Am. Intellectual Property Law Assn., Intellectual Property Law Assn. Chgo. Home: 233 Pine St Deerfield IL 60015-4853

BIRNBAUM, BARRY WILLIAM, special education educator; b. Chgo., Oct. 9, 1952; s. Irving and Beatrice (Factoroff) B. BS, So. Ill. U., 1974; MA, Northeastern Ill. U., 1980; EdD, Nova U., 1991. Cert. secondary spl. edn. tchr., elem. tchr., middle sch. tchr. Tchr. Wood Dale (Ill.) Sch. Dist., 1982-86, Palm Beach (Fla.) Cmty. Schs., Palm Beach County, 1985-93; program prof. Nova U., Ft. Lauderdale, Fla., 1993-95; inclusion specialist Sch. Dist. # 59, Arlington Heights, Ill., 1996-97; prin. Neumann Sch., Chgo.; ednl. svcs. adminstr. South Ctrl. Comm. Svcs., Chgo., 1997-98; prof. spl. edn. Chgo. State U., 1997-2000, Northeastern Ill. U., Chgo., 2000—. Named Fla. Tchr. of Yr., Fla. Assn. for Gifted, 1991, IBM/Tech. and Learning Tchr. of Yr., 1992, Prof. Recognized Spl. Educator in Teaching and Adminstrn., Coun. for Exceptional Children. Mem. Phi Delta Kappa. Democrat. Jewish. Avocations: theater, reading, technology. Home: 5225 W Eddy St Chicago IL 60641-3309 Office: Northeastern Ill U Classroom 402A Spl Edn 5500 N St Louis Ave Chicago IL 60625 Office Phone: 773-442-5593. E-mail: b-birnbaum@neiu.edu.

BIRNBAUM, CHARLES A., landscape architect; Pvt. practice; coord. landscape initiative Nat. Pk. Svc., 1992—. Loeb fellow Grad. Sch. Design Harvard U., 1998, instr. profl. devel. program Grad. Sch. Design; instr. Nat. Preservation Inst.; founder Cultural Landscape Found. Editor: Preserving Modern Landscape Architecture I and II, Pioneers of American Landscape Design, Design with Culture: Claiming America's Landscape Heritage. Recipient Samuel H. Kress fellow, Am. Acad. in Rome. Fellow: Am. Soc. Landscape Archs. Office: Nat Park Svc 1201 Eye St Washington DC 20005

BIRNBAUM, EDWARD LESTER, lawyer; b. Bklyn., Aug. 2, 1939; s. Isaac and Rita Birnbaum; m. Madeleine Birnbaum, Apr. 10, 1965; children: Amanda, Jordan. BA, CUNY, 1961; LLB, NYU, 1964. Bar: NY 64, US Dist. Ct. (so. and ea. dists.) NY 67, US Ct. Appeals (2d cir.) 70, US Supreme Ct. 71, US Dist. Ct. (we. dist.) NY 83. Assoc. Korkus & Korkus, NYC, 1964—66, Herzfeld & Rubin, P.C., NYC, 1967—. Lectr. field; mem. faculty NYU Sch. Continuing Edn., Law Taxation, 1987—; arbitrator small claims night ct. Contbr. articles to profl. jours. Coach Little League Baseball, Little League Basketball; pres., v.p. Village Saddle Rock Civic Assn.; chmn. bd. appeals Village Saddle Rock, candidate trustee; town counsel North Hempstead, NY; del. jud. conv. Liberal Party County Com. Mem.: ATLA, ABA, NY Bar Found., NY State Trial Lawyers Assn., Am. Arbitration Assn. (arbitrator), Nassau County Bar Assn., Queens County Bar Assn., NY County Bar Assn., NY State Bar Assn. (chmn. com. Supreme Ct., ho. dels.). Home: 70 Shelly Ln Great Neck NY 11023-1822 Office: Herzfeld & Rubin PC 40 Wall St New York NY 10005-2349 Office Phone: 212-471-8540. E-mail: ebirnbaum@herzfeld-rubin.com. *Life is to be lived with understanding and consideration for others and with understanding and consideration from others.*

BIRNBAUM, IRWIN MORTON, lawyer; b. Bklyn., July 15, 1935; s. Sol N. and Rose (Cohen) B.; m. Arlene R. Burrows, June 8, 1957; children: Bruce J., Leslie R. Birnbaum Ventura, Amy G. Birnbaum Heath. BS in Acctg., Bklyn. Coll., 1956; JD, NYU, 1961. Bar: N.Y. 1962. Budget officer Montefiore Med. Ctr., Bronx, NY, 1962-70, v.p., chief fin. officer, 1970-86; counsel Proskauer & Rose LLP, N.Y.C., 1986-89, ptnr., 1989-97; COO Yale Univ. Sch. Medicine, New Haven, 1997—2004, sr. advisor to the dean, 2004—05. Chmn. bd. irs. FFH/N.E. Ins. Com., 1998-2004, chmn.-elect FOJP Svc. Corp.; mem. exec. com. and chair fin. com. MCIC Vt., Inc.; adj. prof. Robert Wagner Sch. Pub. Svc., NYU; lectr. pub. health, health policy, adminstrn. Sch. Medicine Yale U.; corporator South County Hosp., South Kingstown, R.I.; chmn.-elect FOJP Svc. Corp Editor: Health Care Law Treatise, 1990. Trustee, treas., exec. com. Malmonides Med. Ctr., Bklyn., 1988—; sec./treas., exec. com. Hosp. Trustees N.Y. State, 1990-97; bd. dirs. Jewish Home for the Aged, New Haven Fellow N.Y. Acad. Medicine; mem. Assn. of Bar of City of N.Y. (sec. com. on medicine and law 1989-90, sec. health law com. 1995-96), Am. Acad. Hosp. Attys. (spl. com. in health care systems). Avocations: sailing, tennis, reading, travel. Home: 383 Temple St New Haven CT 06511-6801 Business E-Mail: irwin.birnbaum@yale.edu.

BIRNBAUM, JAY W., plastic surgeon; b. Bklyn. s. David and Alpha Louise Birnbaum; m. Andrez Birnbaum, Mar. 23, 1991; children: Sophie Louise, Savannah Emily. BA in Anthropology, Bklyn. Coll., 1971, BS in Chemistry, 1977; MD, Med. U. SC, 1980. Assoc. prof. surgery Mt. Sinai Sch. Medicine, N.Y.C., 1989—; chief plastic surgery Mt. Sinai Hosp., Queens, NY, 1991—. Fellow: ACS; mem.: Am. Soc. Aesthetic Plastic Surgeons, Am. Soc. Plastic Surgeons. Avocations: tennis, skiing, cooking. Office: 74 E 79t St New York NY 10029

BIRNBAUM, JEFFREY, columnist, political correspondent; BA magna cum laude, U. Pa., 1977. White House corr. Wall Street Jour.; sr. polit. corr. Time mag., 1995—97; chief mng. officer Fortune mag., Washington, DC bur., 1998—2004; polit. contbr. FOX News Channel, 1998—; columnist Washington Post, 2004—. Guest appearances Special Report with Brit Hume, FOX News Channel. Author: Showdown at Gucci Gulch, 1987 (Carey McWilliams Award, Am. Polit. Sci. Assn., 1988), The Lobbyists: How Influence Peddlers Get Their Way in Washington, 1992, Madhouse: The Private Turmoil of Working for the President, 1996, The Money Men: The Real Story of Fund-raising's Influence on Political Power in America, 2000. Recipient Aldo Beckman award for Excellence in feature writing about the presidency, 1994. Office: Washington Post 1150 15th St NW Washington DC 20071 Address: FOX News Channel 400 N Capitol St NW Ste 550 Washington DC 20001*

BIRNBAUM, LUCIA CHIAVOLA, historian, educator; b. Kansas City, Mo., Jan. 3, 1924; d. Salvatore and Kate (Cipolla) Chiavola; m. Wallace Birnbaum, Feb. 3, 1946; children: Naury, Marc, Stefan. AB, U. Calif., Berkeley, 1948, MA, 1950, PhD, 1964. Lectr. U. Calif., Berkeley, 1963-64, rsch. assoc., 1982-83, 86, 90-96; asst. prof. history San Francisco State U., 1964-69; mem. faculty Feminist Inst., Berkeley, 1981—; prof. doctoral program feminist spirituality Calif. Inst. Integral Studies, San Francisco, 1994—2000, prof., 2001—. Guest lectr. U. Sydney, Australia, 1989, U. Melbourne, Australia, 1989, U. di Padua, 1990; adj. prof. Calif. Coll. Arts and Crafts, Oakland, 1991-92. Author: La Religione e le Donne Soculo Americane, 1981, Liberazione della Donna: Feminism in Italy, 1986 (Am. Book award 1987), 1988, Black Madonnas, Feminism, Religion and Politics in Italy, 1993, 97, 2001; Dark Mother: African Origins and Godmothers, 2001, 04, Gatherer, She is Everywhere: Anthology of Womanist/Feminist Writing in Spirituality, 2004; contbr. articles to profl. jours. Recipient Am. Book award Before Columbus Found., 1987, Anniversary award San Francisco State U., 1988, Premio Internazionale di Saggistica Salvatore Valitutti, Salerno, Italy, 1998, Enheduanna award for excellence in woman-centered lit., 2002, Founding Mother award Women's Spirituality MA and PhD programs, Calif. Inst. Integral Studies, 2003, cert. scholarly advancement 6th Ann. Cheikh Anta Diop Conf., 2004; vis. scholar Grad. Theol. Union, 1983-94, 95-96, Inst. Rsch. Women and Gender, Stanford U., 1987-94, Disting. woman scholar U. Calif., Davis, 1987; named to Internat. African Am. Multicultural Hall of Fame, 1996. Mem. ACLU, PEN Am. Ctr., Orgn. Am. Historians, Am. Italian Hist. Assn. (pres. western regional chpt. 1978-82), Nat. Women's Studies Assn., Ctr. Women and Religion Grad. Theol. Union, Women's Party for Survival. Home: 349 Gravatt Dr Berkeley CA 94705-1503 Office: Calif Inst Integral Studies 1453 Mission St San Francisco CA 94103 Office Phone: 415-575-6100 ext. 466. Business E-Mail: lbirnbaum@ciis.edu. E-mail: lucia@darkmother.net. *We are living in times of great peril and extraordinary possibility. The most hopeful variable, perhaps, is that the silent of the earth--women-- have begun to speak aloud, to stop careening madness, and to turn the earth towards life.*

BIRNBAUM, NORMAN, writer, humanities educator; b. N.Y.C., July 21, 1926; s. Silas Jacob and Jean (Bermen) B.; children: Anna, Antonia. BA, Williams Coll., 1947; MA, Harvard U., 1951, PhD, 1958. Editor OWI, 1943-45; tchg. fellow Harvard U., 1948-52; tutor Adams House, 1949- 52; asst. lectr. London Sch. Econs. and Polit. Sci., U. London, 1953-55, lectr., 1955-59; fellow Nuffield (Eng.) Coll., Oxford (Eng.) U., 1959-66; vis. prof. faculty letters and human scis. U. Strasbourg, France, 1964-66; prof. grad. faculty New Sch. Social Rsch., 1966-68; prof. Amherst Coll., 1968—. Mem. Inst. Advanced Study, 1975-76; guest fellow Wissenschaftskolleg, Berlin, 1986; Mellon vis. prof. humanities Georgetown U. Law Ctr., 1979-81; prof. Georgetown U., 1981-2001, prof. emeritus, 2001— sr. scholar policy studies, 2002-; cons. NSC, Exec. Office Pres., 1978; vis. prof. Ecole des Hautes Etudes en Scis. Sociales, Paris, 1991; chair scholarly adv. bd. Internat. Inst. Peace, Vienna, 1991—. Author: Sociological Study of Ideology (1940-60), 1962; (with others) Sociology and Religion, 1968, Crisis of Industrial Society, 1969, Towards a Critical Sociology, 1971, Beyond the Crisis, 1977, Social Structure and the German Reformation, 1980, The Radical Renewal, 1988, Searching for the Light, 1993, After Progress, 2001; contbg. editor Change mag. of Higher Edn., 1970-74; mem. editl. bd. Praxis, 1986-92, The Nation, 1978—; editl. cons. Patisan Rev., 1971-83. Cons. Giovanni Agnelli Found., 1972-75; mem. Wellfleet Psychohistory Conf., 1970-; adviser UAW, Congrl. Progressive Caucus, 1996-; mem. exec. com. New Dem. Coalition, 1978-, chmn. policy adv. coun., 1980-82; mem. nat. exec. com. Dem. Socialist Organizing Com., 1973-77, nat. adv. bd., 1980-82; mem. founding editl. bd. New Left Rev., London, 1959; sec. com. sociology religion Internat. Sociol. Assn., 1959-, chmn., 1970-74; adviser Dem. Nat. Campaign, 1976, Edward M. Kennedy campaign, 1979, Cranston campaign, 1980, Jackson campaigns, 1980, 1988; adviser European Socialist Parties, 1979—; founding com. Campaign for Am. Future, 1996; Fulbright chair Univ. Bologna, 1998; visitor London Sch. of Econs., 1998, Nuffield Coll., 2001. Guggenheim fellow, 1971. Fellow: Inst. Policy Studies (sr.); mem.: Am. Sociol. Assn. (coun. 1979—82). Office: Georgetown U Law Ctr 600 New Jersey Ave NW Washington DC 20001-2075 Office Phone: 202-662-9062. E-mail: birnbaum@law.georgetown.edu. *I have always thought that one of the strongest ethical and biological forces propelling us is a concern for our children— for our own children and for the continuation of humanity. This elementary sense of care seems increasingly challenged, by doctrines of callousness and selfishness, poorly disguised as recognition of the sovereignty of the market. It is that sovereignty which threatens us as citizens, and which accounts for the outbursts of hatred and rage we know as the new ethnicity, the new fundamentalism, the new nationalism--all of them, alas,very old.*

BIRNBAUM, SHEILA L., lawyer, educator; b. 1940; BA, Hunter Coll., 1960, MA, 1962; LL.B., NYU Sch. Law, 1965. Bar: NY 1965. Legal asst. Superior Ct., NYC, 1965; assoc. Berman & Frost, NYC, 1965-70, ptnr., 1970-72; prof. Fordham U., NYC, 1972-78; prof. law NYU, NYC, 1978—84, assoc. dean, graduate divsn., 1982-84; ptnr. mass tort and insurance litigation Skadden, Arps, Slate, Meagher & Flom, LLP, NYC, 1984—. Chair NY State Adv. Com. on Civil Practice, 1981—86; adj. prof. law NYU Sch. Law, 1984—; mem. 2nd Cir. Com. on the Improvement of Civil Litigation, 1986—88, NY State Jud. Commn. on Minorities, 1988—91; exec. dir. Second Cir. Task Force for Racial, Ethnic and Gender Fairness, 1994—97; mem. jud. conf. adv. com. on rules and civil procedure US Supreme Ct., 1997—2004; chair, Commn. Fiduciary Appointments NY State Court System, 2000—; lectr. in field; mem. adv. com. to the Restatement of the Law of Product Liability and Complex Litigation Project. Author: (with Rheingold) Products Liability, Law, Practice Science, 1974; co-author: Practitioner's Guide to Litigating Insurance Coverage Actions; columnist NY Law Jour., Nat. Law Jour.; contbr. articles to profl. jours. First pres. and founding mem. Judges and Lawyers Breast Cancer Alert. Named one of 50 Most Powerful Women in Am. Bus., Fortune Mag., 100 Most Outstanding Members of the Legal Profession, Nat. Law Jour., 75 Most Influential Women in Bus., Crain's NY Bus.; named to, Hunter Coll. Hall of Fame; recipient John J. McCloy Meml. award, Fund for Modern Courts, 2003, Florence E. Allen award, NYU Sch. Law and NY Women's Bar Assn., Louis D. Brandeis award, Am. Jewish Congress, Law and Society award, NY Lawyers for the Public Interest, NYU Law Alumni award for Outstanding Achievement in the Legal Profession, George A. Katz Torch of Learning award, Milton S. Gould award for Outstanding Appellate Advocacy, Award for Achieving the Highest Standards of Professional Excellence, Touro Law Sch. Mem. NYC Bar Assn. (mem. exec. com. 1978—, jud. com. 1977), NY Women's Bar Assn. (pres. 1974-75), ABA (coun. of the sect. of torts and insurance practice 1982-86, spl. com. on the future of the legal profession 1996-97, House of Delegates 1997-98, chmn. product gen. liability, consumer land coms., Margaret Brent Women Lawyers of Achievement award), Am. Law Inst. (mem. coun. 1989-), Assn. of Bar of City of NY (exec. com. 1978—, 2nd century com. 1984-86, v.p. 1987), Phi Beta Kappa, Phi Alpha Theta, Alpha Chi Alpha. Office: Skadden Arps Slate Meagher & Flom LLP 4 Times Sq New York NY 10036 Office Phone: 212-735-2450. Office Fax: 917-777-2450. E-mail: sbirnbau@skadden.com.

BIRNBERG, JACK, financial executive; b. June 15, 1937; s. Max and Yetta (Halpern) B.; m. Louise Rothstein, June 7, 1959; children: Michael, Steven, John, Jeffrey. BS, Fairleigh Dickinson U., 1959. Acct. firm Scholtz, Simon & Miller, 1960-61; contr., officer Scott, Harvey Co., Inc., 1962-63; pres. M.A. Allan & Co., Inc., Clifton, NJ, 1963-71, dir., 1963-71; chmn. bd. Edios, Inc., 1969-77, Jack Birnberg & Assocs., Inc.; pres. NE Regional Assn. Small Bus. Investment Corp., NY, 1970—71, Internat. Equities, Ltd., Clifton, 1970-71. Chmn. bd., dir. Tappan-Zee Capital Corp., 1973-2005, exec. com. NE Region; chmn. bd. BB Energy Corp., Waldorf Auto Leasing Corp., Waldorf Group, Inc.; dir., chmn. exec. com. Ferdon Equipment Corp.; chmn. bd. dirs. Met. Fin. Corp., 1968—, AIP Risk Group, 1968—, Ascot Solutions, Inc., 1980; mem. Midwest Stock Exch., 1968-76, Phila.-Balt.-Washington Stock Exch., 1968-76; guest lectr. Fla. Atlantic U., 2000-01. Co-host radio program Off The Record, Sta. WPBR, 2001-01; radio talk show host Jack Birnberg Speaks Out, NYC, 2001-, Sta. WVNJ, 2004-. Pres. Passaic County Children's Shelter, 1967-68; bd. dirs. Birnberg Found., 1969—, Boys Club, Paterson, NJ, 1970-75, Barnert Hosp., 1971-91, Employee Retirement Benefit Assn., 1975-1985, Barnert Temple, 1976-1995; chmn. met. divsn. United Jewish Appeal, 1970; dir. greater Paterson YW-YMHA, 1970-75; pres. Daus. Miriam Home for Aged, 1995-1997, bd. mem., 1971—, bd. dirs., 1995-97; chmn. Expo 200 Barnert Temple, 1976—; trustee various corps., U.S. Bankruptcy Ct. Mem. N.E. Regional Assn. Small Bus. Investment Corps. (pres. 1985-86), Nat. Assn. Small Bus. Investment Corps. (bd. govs. 1985-93), B'nai B'rith (trustee Greater Clifton chpt. 1962-64), Preakness Hills Country Club (bd. govs. 1992-96, treas. 1994-95), Polo Club Boca Raton. Office: 201 Lower Notch Rd Little Falls NJ 07424-1802 Office Phone: 973-256-8280. E-mail: jackbirnberg@aol.com.

BIRNEY, MAURA KAY, nurse, educator; d. Lewis D. and Catherine M. Burdine; m. Nelson Dean Birney, Jan. 27, 1996; children: David Eddy Jr., Jason, Nicole. BSN, Wheeling SJ U., 2001. Cert. nat. bd. cert. career & tech. edn., Nat. Bd. Profl. Tchg. Standards, 2004; profl. vocat. edn. Ohio Dept. Edn. Diversified health occupations tchr. Belmont Harrison Vocat. Sch. Dist., St. Clairsville, Ohio, 1996—; RN Harrison Cmty. Hosp., Cadiz, Ohio, 1999—. Student advisor Skills USA Belmont Career Ctr., Ohio, 1996—; health occupations divsn. pres. Ohio Assn. Career & Tech. Edn., Columbus, 2004—. Mem.: Ohio Ednl. Assn. (assoc.; del. 1997—98). Methodist. Avocations: reading, travel. Home: 45501 Unionvale Rd Cadiz OH 43907 Office: Belmont-Harrison Vocat Sch 110 Fox-Shannon Pl Saint Clairsville OH 43950 Office Fax: 740-695-5330.

BIRNEY, ROBERT CHARLES, retired academic administrator, psychologist; b. Westmont, N.J., May 2, 1925; s. Charles Alexander and Florence (Moore) B.; m. Margaret Ann Momerak, June 18, 1949; children: Reed Charles, Ruth Elizabeth, Barbara Ann, Robert Carl. BA, Wesleyan U., 1950; MA, U. Mich., 1951, PhD, 1955. Mem. faculty Amherst (Mass.) Coll., 1954-67, prof. psychology, 1965-67; dean Sch. Social Scis. Hampshire Coll., Amherst, 1968-70, v.p., 1971-78; dir. planning Colonial Williamsburg (Va.) Found., 1978, v.p. rsch., 1979-86, sr. v.p., 1986-90; ret., 1990. Vis. prof. Ruhr U., Fed. Republic Germany, 1966-67; spl. rsch. human motivation. Editor (with Richard Teevan) Van Nostrand Insight Series, 1961-70. Lt. USAAF, 1943-46. Decorated Air medal with 3 oak leaf clusters. Fellow Am. Psychol. Assn.; mem. AAUP, New Eng. Psychol. Assn. (pres. 1975), Cosmos Club, Phi Beta Kappa, Sigma Xi. Office: Colonial Williamsburg Found S Henry St Williamsburg VA 23185

BIRNEY, WALTER LEROY, religious administrator; b. Garden City, Kans., Apr. 25, 1934; s. Claude David and Mildred Elizabeth (Ferris) B.; m. Iva Lou Mosher, June 18, 1954; children: Mickey, Scotty, Gary, Lorrie, Lindie. BA, Dallas Christian Coll., 1956. Min. First Christian Ch., Benjamin, Tex., 1954-57, Bellaire Christian Ch., San Antonio, 1957-58, Copeland (Kans.) Christian Ch., 1958-84; coord. Nat. Missionary Conv., Copeland, 1966—. Dean, promoter Ashland (Kans.) Christian Camp, 1961-84; promoter S.W. Sch. Missions, Copeland, 1973-84. Named Outstanding Alumnus Dallas Christian Coll., 1988, Named to Dallas Christian Coll. Basketball Hall of Fame, 2004. Mem. Christian Ch. Avocation: long distance running. Office: Nat Missionary Conv PO Box 11 Copeland KS 67837-0011 Office Phone: 620-668-5259. E-mail: wbirney11@aol.com.

BIRNKRANT, HENRY JOSEPH, lawyer; b. Phila., Jan. 24, 1955; s. Harry Philip and Myra Arlene (Hendler) B.; m. Lynn Rachel Goldin, Oct. 23, 1983; children: Aviva Michelle, Beth Elana. BA magna cum laude, U. Rochester, 1976; JD, Columbia U., 1979; LLM, NYU, 1983. Bar: D.C. 1979, U.S. Dist. Ct. D.C. 1980; U.S. Ct. Appeals (D.C. cir.) 1980, U.S. Tax Ct. 1984. Assoc. Bergson, Borkland, Margolis & Adler, Washington, 1979-82, Covington & Burling, Washington, 1983-88, Cole, Corette & Abrutyn, Washington, 1988-90, ptnr., 1991-96; ptnr., co-chair, tax sect. Alston & Bird LLP, Washington, 1997—. Author: (with others) Butterworth's International Taxation of Financial Instruments and Transactions, 1989; editor: Columbia Jour. Law and Social Problems, 1979; contbr. articles to profl. jours.; bd. advisors Jour. Internat. Taxation. Mem. ABA (tax section), Internat. Bar Assn., Thomson West Tax Adv. Bd., Tax Treaty Subcommittee of U.S. Council for Internat. Bus. (chair). Home: 5506 Durbin Rd Bethesda MD 20814-1012 Office: Alston & Bird LLP North Bldg 11th Fl 601 Pennsylvania Ave NW Washington DC 20004-2601 Office Fax: 202-756-3333. Business E-Mail: hbirnkrant@alston.com.

BIRNKRANT, SHERWIN MAURICE, lawyer; b. Pontiac, Mich., Dec. 20, 1927; BBA, U. Mich., 1949, MBA, 1951; JD with distinction, Wayne State U., 1954. Bar: Mich. 1955, U.S. Dist. Ct. (ea. dist.) Mich. 1960, U.S. Supreme Ct. 1960, U.S. Ct. Appeals (6th cir.) 1966. Mem. Oakland County Bd. Suprs., 1967-68, Birnkrant & Birnkrant P.C., Bloomfield Hills, Mich., 1995—; asst. atty. City of Pontiac, Mich., 1956-67, city atty., 1967-83; of counsel Schlussel, Lifton, Simon, Rands, Galvin & Jackier, Southfield, Mich., 1983-90, Sommers, Schwartz, Silver & Schwartz, Southfield, 1990-95. Mem.: ABA (Mich. chmn. pub. contract law sect. 1979—97, chmn. urban, state and local govt. law sect. 1987—88, ho. dels. 1990—93, alt. del. to ho. dels. 1993—96, vice chmn. coordinating com. model procurement code state and local 1974—), Mich. Assn. Mcpl. Attys. (pres. 1975, coun. pres. 1992—), Oakland County Bar Assn. (chmn. ethics and unauthorized practices com. 1961—62), State Bar Mich. (chmn. pub. corp. law sect. 1973—74, coun. adminstrv. law sect. 1975—76). Office: Birnkrant & Birnkrant PC 7 W Square Lake Rd Bloomfield Hills MI 48302

BIRNS, MARK THEODORE, physician; b. Bklyn., Sept. 24, 1949; s. Leon and Naomi B.; m. Ann Krieger, Aug. 15, 1976; children: Samantha Lynn, Michael Eric, Kevin Douglas. BA, Case Western Res. U., 1971; MD, Albert Einstein Coll. Medicine, 1974. Diplomate: Am. Bd. Internal Medicine, Am. Bd. Gastroenterology. Intern Bronx Mcpl. Hosp. Ctr. Albert Einstein Hosps., 1974-75, resident in medicine, 1975-77; fellow in gastroenterology U. Oreg. Health Scis. Ctr., 1977-79; asst. chief gastroenterology Walter Reed Army Med. Ctr., 1979-83; asst. prof. medicine U. Health Scis., 1980-83; emergency physician Shady Grove Adventist Hosp., part time, 1980-83, Frederick Meml. Hosp., Washington, 1980-83; practice medicine specializing in gastroenterology and endoscopic biliary surgery Rockville, Md., 1983—; active staff Shady Grove Adventist Hosp., sec. med. staff, 1986-87, chief gastroenterology sect., vice chmn. dept. medicine, 1988, 89, mem. exec. com., 1990-92, mem. laser com., 1992, 93, 94, 95, mem. OR com., 1996-97; assoc. clin. prof. medicine dept. gastroenterology Georgetown U., Washington, 1988—; active staff Suburban Hosp.; courtesy staff Montgomery Gen. Hosp. Vice chmn. Health Delivery Orgn., Mid Atlantic Med. Svcs. Health Plan, 1997-2004, peer review com., 2005-; treas., contract coord. Gastrointestinal Endoscopy Assocs., LLC, 1995—, Gastrointestinal Rsch. Assocs., LLC, 1999—. Major contbg. author: Radiology of the Liver, Biliary Tract, Pancreas and Spleen, 1987. Synagogue chair Israel Bonds Congregation B'nai Tzedek, 1994—, synagogue divsn. chair Washington, 2003—; alumni rep., mem. admissions com. Case Western Res. U., 1998—; healthcare adv. com. Eagle Bank, Md., 2000—. Served to maj. USAR. Fellow ACP, Am. Coll. Gastroenterology; mem. AMA (Physician Recognition award 1978, 81, 84, 87, 90, 93), Am. Gastroent. Assn., Am. Soc. Gastrointestinal Endoscopy (postgrad. edn. com. 1991-92), Md. Soc. Gastrointestinal Endoscopy (exec. bd.), Montgomery County Med. Soc. Home: 11413 Twining Ln Rockville MD 20854-1860 Office: 9711 Medical Center Dr Ste 308 Rockville MD 20850-3388 Office Phone: 301-251-1244.

BIRNS, NICHOLAS BOE, literature educator, editor; b. N.Y.C., May 30, 1965; s. Laurence Richard Birns and Margaret Ann Boe. AB, Columbia U., 1988; MA, NYU, 1990, PhD, 1992. Mem. faculty New Sch. U., N.Y.C., 1995—, Coll. New Rochelle, Bronx, 1996—2002. Vis. asst. prof. Western Conn. State U., Danbury, 1992-93; invited lectr. U. Stockholm, 1997-98; vis. rsch. fellow U. Newcastle, Australia, 2001. Editor: Powys Notes, 1998-2002; book rev. editor: Antipodes, 1994-2001, editor, 2001—; author: Understanding Anthony Powell, 2004; contbr. articles to profl. jours. Devel. fellow NYU, 1988-89. Mem. Guild of Scholars of Episcopal Ch. Episcopalian. Avocations: baseball, music, following current events. Home: 205 E 10th St New York NY 10003-7634 Office: New Sch U 66 W 12th St New York NY 10011-8603 E-mail: birnsn@newschool.edu.

BIRNSCHEIN, DANIEL JOHN, music educator; b. West Allis, Wis., Mar. 27, 1979; s. Mark Richard and Gladys Elizabeth Birnschein; m. Elizabeth Grace Baker, Dec. 14, 2002. BS in Music Edn., Bob Jones U., 2001, MusM in Ch. Music, 2003. Music tchr. Bapt. Coll. of Ministry and Falls Bapt. Acad., Menomonee Falls, Wis., 2003—. Trumpet player Spartanburg Symphony, S.C., 1999—2001, Anderson Symphony, S.C., 2000. Composer: (instrumental composition) Sonata for Trumpet and Piano, Fanfare for Brass Quintet, (choral composition) Psalm 97, Psalm 91, Rend Thou the Firmament, 2002, (vocal composition) Christ's Wounds. Recipient Hon. Mention, Milw. Youth Symphony Orch. Concerto Competition, 1997, 2d Place, Henry Janice Competition, 1998, 1999, MTNA Ensemble Competition, 2000. Office: Falls Baptist Academy N69 W12703 Appleton Ave Menomonee Falls WI 53051

BIRNSTIEL, CHARLES, consulting engineer; b. N.Y.C. s. Charles Conrad and Margarete (Heckel) B. BCE, NYU, 1954, MCE, 1957, EngScD, 1962. Mem. faculty NYU, Bronx, 1954-73, prof. civil engring., 1968-73, Poly Inst. N.Y., Bklyn., 1973-74; cons. structural and mech. engring. N.Y.C.; head engring. firm, 1974—; prin. assoc. Hardesty & Hanover LLP, N.Y.C. Adj. prof. civil engring. Columbia U., N.Y.C., 1989-2000. Patentee elevated rail transit guideway with noise attenuators; contbr. chpt. to book and articles to profl. jours. Fellow ASCE (State-of-the-Art paper award, Roebling award Met. sect. 2003), Instn. Civil Engrs. (U.K.); mem. Am. Railway Engring. and Maintenance of Way Assn., Internat. Assn. Bridge and Structural Engring., Structural Stability Rsch. Coun. Lutheran. Home and Office: 68-19 Fleet St Flushing NY 11375 Office Phone: 718-268-9188. Personal E-mail: cbirnstiel29@msn.com. Business E-Mail: cbirnstiel@compuserve.com.

BIRO, JAN CHARLES, physician, research scientist; b. Budapest, Hungary, July 7, 1950; s. Janos Biro and Katalin Kurucz; m. Charlotte Follin, Mar. 15, 1990; children: Josephine, Andrea. MD, Femmelweis U., 1974; PhD, Karolinska Inst., 1983; cert. in Bioinformatics, EBI, 1999. Internist Karolinska

Hosp., Stockholm, 1980—83, endocrinologist, 1983—89, Clinic Hormonal Health, Stockholm, 1985—2003; bioinformatician Homulus Found., Stockholm, 2003—, San Francisco, 2003—. Assoc. prof. Karolinska Inst., Stockholm, 1985—; CEO Sengel Clinic, Stockholm, 1990—92, MCD-AB, Stockholm, 1990—, Homulus Informatics, Stockholm, 1991—. Contbr. 70 sci. publs. in field. Founder, CEO G. Gallow fellowship, 2003. Mem.: Swedish Med. Assn., Swedish Soc. Medicine, Rotary Club. Achievements include patents in field. Avocations: horseback riding, swimming, driving, theater, travel. Office Phone: 415-777-1443.

BIRO, LASZLO, dermatologist; b. Czechoslovakia, May 31, 1929; came to U.S., 1956; s. Sandor and Margaret (Klein) B.; m. Dolores Macchiaroli, July 9, 1961; children: David, Lisa, Deborah, Michele. MD, Univ. Med. Sch., Debrecen, Hungary, 1953. Diplomate Am. Bd. Dermatology. Intern Kings County Hosp., Bklyn., 1957-58; resident Bellevue Hosp., N.Y.C., 1958-60; pvt. practice medicine specializing in dermatology N.Y.C., 1960-61, Bklyn., 1960—; emeritus dept. dermatology Bklyn. Hosp., Luth. Med. Ctr.; clin. prof. dermatology SUNY, Downstate Med. Ctr., 1971—. Contbr. articles on skin tumors to profl. jours. Fellow ACP, Am. Acad. Dermatology, N.Y. Acad. Medicine; mem. AMA, Kings County Med. Assn., Bay Ridge Med. Soc. (pres. 1987-88), N.Y. State Dermatol. Soc., Bklyn Dermatol. Soc., Internat. Soc. Tropical Dermatology, N.Y. Acad. Scis., Am. Coll. Cryosurgery (v.p. 1996), Semmelweis Sci. Soc. (pres. 1985). Office: 9921 4th Ave Brooklyn NY 11209-8347 Office Phone: 718-833-7616. Personal E-mail: laszlobiro@aol.com.

BIRO, SUSAN C., adult education educator; d. James K. Biro and Barbara J. D'Amico; life ptnr. Lisa C. Oursler, Sept. 21, 1997. EdD, Widener U., 2005. Mng. editor Slack Inc., Thorofare, Pa., 1995—2000; dir. distance learning Widener U., Chester, 2000—. Mem. Stand Up for what's Right & Just, Wilmington, 2003—. Achievements include research in Active research in higher education, distance learning, and adjunct faculty development.

BIRON, CHRISTINE ANNE, medical science educator, researcher; b. Woonsocket, R.I., Aug. 8, 1951; d. R. Bernard and Theresa Priscilla (Sauvageau) B. BS, U. Mass., 1973; PhD, U. N.C., 1980. Rsch. technician U. Mass., Amherst, 1973—75; grad. rschr. U. N.C., Chapel Hill, 1975—80; postdoctoral fellow Scripps Clinic and Rsch., La Jolla, Calif., 1980; fellow U. Mass. Med. Sch., Worcester, 1981—82, instr., 1983, asst. prof., 1984—87; vis. scientist Karolinska Inst., Stockholm, 1984; asst. prof. Sch. Medicine Brown U., Providence, 1988—90, assoc. prof., 1990—96, prof., 1996—, Esther Elizabeth Brintzenhoff prof., 1996—, chair Dept. Molecular Microbiology & Immunology, 1999—, dir. grad. program in pathobiology, 1995—99; sci. adv. bd. Trudedce Inst., 2004—. Mem. AIDS and related rsch. study sect. 3 NIH, 1991-93; mem. exptl. immunology study sect. NIH, 1993-97, immunology working group sci. rev.; co-organizer Keystone Symposium on Innate Immunity to Pathogens, 2005. Assoc. editor: Jour. Immunology, 1990—94, 2000, bd. editors: Procs. of Soc. for Exptl. Biology and Medicine, 1993—99, sect. editor: Jour. Immunology, 1995—99; editor: Jour. Nat. Immunity, 1994—98, Jour. Leukocyte Biology, 1999—2000; mem. editl. bd.: Virology, 2001—03; contbr. articles, revs. to sci. jours.; mem. adv. bd. editors: Jour. Exptl. Medicine, 2002—. Leukemia Soc. Am. fellow, 1981, Spl. fellow, 1983, scholar, 1987; grantee NIH, 1985—; rsch. grantee MacArthur Found., 1991-96. Fellow AAAS (scholar 2002—); mem. Am. Assn. Immunologists (co-chmn. symposium 1990, 94, 95, 96, 98, 99), Am. Soc. Virology, Am. Assn. Immunology (block co-chair nat. meetings 1996-99, program com. 1998-2000), Soc. Natural Immunity (co-chair program for 2001 meeting), Sigma Xi. Office: Brown U PO Box G-B618 Providence RI 02912-0001

BIRREN, JAMES EMMETT, research and development company executive; b. Chgo., Apr. 4, 1918; m. Elizabeth S., 1942; children: Barbara Ann, Jeffrey Emmett, Bruce William. Student, Wright Jr. Coll., 1938; BEd, Chgo. State U., 1941; MA, Northwestern U., 1942, PhD, 1947, ScD (hon.), 1985; postgrad., U. Chgo., 1950—51; PhD (hon.), U. Gothenberg, Sweden, 1983; LLD (hon.), St. Thomas U., Can., 1990. Tutorial fellow Northwestern U., 1941-42; rsch. asst. project for study of fatigue Office Sci. Rsch. and Devel., 1942; rsch. fellow NIH, USPHS, 1946-47; rsch. psychologist gerontology unit NIH, 1947-51; rsch. psychologist NIMH, 1951-53, chief sect. on aging, 1953-64; dir. aging program Nat. Inst. Child Health and Human Devel., Bethesda, Md., 1964-65; dir. Gerontology Ctr.; prof. psychology U. So. Calif., 1965-89, Disting. prof. emeritus, 1992—, dean Davis Sch. Gerontology, 1975-86, Brookdale Disting. scholar, 1986-90, dir. Inst. Advanced Study in Gerontology and Geriat., 1981-89; dir. Borun Ctr. Gerontol. Rsch. UCLA, 1989-93, assoc. dir. Ctr. on Aging, 1990—. Fellow Ctr. for Advanced Study in Behavioral Scis., Stanford, Calif., 1978-79; Green vis. prof. U. B.C., 1979; vis. scientist Cambridge (Eng.) U., 1960-61; Harold E. Jones meml. lectr. U. Calif., Berkeley, 1965; mem. LA County Bd. Suprs.' Com. on Aging, 1967-69; sr. fellow U. So. Calif. Urban Ecology Inst., 1968-70; mem. Dean's Coun., U. So. Calif., 1970-86; chmn. aging rev. com. Nat. Inst. Aging, 1974-75; program dir. Integration of Info. on Aging: Handbook Project, 1973-76; mem. steering com. Care of Elderly, Inst. of Medicine, 1976-77; bd. dirs. Sears Roebuck Found., 1977-80; chmn. life course prevention rsch. rev. com. NIMH, 1985-87; cons. Roche Seminars on Aging Series, 1980-82. Author: Psychology of Aging, 1964; editor: Handbook of Aging and the Individual, 1959, (with K.W. Schaie) Handbook of the Psychology of Aging, 1996, Encyclopedia of Gerontology, 1996, (with R.B. Sloane) Handbook of Mental Health and Aging, 1992; contbr. articles to books, profl. publs.; bd. collaborators: Gerontologia, 1956-89; asst. editor: Jour. Gerontology, 1956-61, assoc. editor 1961-63, editor-in-chief 1968-74, chmn. publs. com., 1975-78, adv. editl. bd., 1956-69; bd. adv. editors: Devel. Psychobiology, 1967-69; adv. editor: Jour. Human Devel., 1957-58. Mem. adv. com. and del. White House Conf. on Aging, 1995. With USNR, 1943-46; to scientist dir. USPHS Scientist Corps, 1947-65. Recipient award for rsch. on problems of aging CIBA Found., 1956, Stratton award Am. Psychopath. Assn., 1960, Sr. 65er award Dist. 65 Retail Workers and Dept. Store Union, Sr. 65er award AFL-CIO, 1962, medal for meritorious svc. USPHS, 1965, citation Am. Assn. Ret. Persons, 1970, Am. Pioneers in Aging award U. Mich., 1972, commendation for disting. contbns. to field of gerontology Mayor of LA, 1968, 74, Merit award Northwestern U. Alumni Assn., 1976, Creative Scholarship and Rsch. award U. So. Calif., 1979, Disting. Educator award Assn. Gerontology in Higher Edn., 1983, Eminent Svc. award Stovall Found., 1984, award of Distinction Am. Fedn. for Aging Rsch., 1986, Sandoz prize for rsch. on aging, 1989, Can. Assn. Gerontology award, 1990, Disting. Emeritus award U. So. Calif., 1992, Pres.'s award Am. Soc. on Aging, 1996, Disting. Career Contbn. to Gerontology award Gerontol. Soc. Am., 2002, Ollie Randall award Nat. Coun. on Aging, 2004, Hall of Fame award Am. Soc. on Aging, 2004; USPHS rsch. fellow, 1946-47. Fellow AAAS, Am. Geriat. Soc. (founding fellow Western divsn.), Am. Psychol. Assn. (Disting. Sci. Contbn. award 1968, chmn. membership com. 1969, Disting. Contbn. award Divsn. Adult Devel. and Aging 1978, pres. divsn. 1955-56, editor newsletter 1951-55), Gerontol. Soc. (pres. 1961-62, chmn. publs. com. 1974-77, award for meritorious rsch. 1966, Brookdale award 1980); mem. Am. Physiol. Soc., Internat. Assn. Gerontology (chmn. exec. com. 1966-69, chmn. program com. 1968-69), Psychonomic Soc., Western Gerontol. Soc. (dir. 1965-, pres. 1968-69), Golden Key Club, Skull and Dagger Club, Sigma Xi, Phi Kappa Phi. Office: UCLA Ctr on Aging 10945 Le Conte Ave Los Angeles CA 90024-2828

BIRREN, SUSAN J., medical educator; PhD, UCLA. Asst. prof. biology Brandeis U., Waltham, Mass. Contbr. articles to profl. jours. Mem.: Soc. for Neurosci. Achievements include research in in how embryonic precursor cells respond to local environmental cues during the development of the mammalian nervous system. Office: Brandeis Univ MS008 Dept Biology Neurosci PO Box 549110 Waltham MA 02454

BIRSTEIN, ANN, writer, educator; b. NYC, May 27, 1927; d. Bernard and Clara (Gordon) B.; m. Alfred Kazin, June 26, 1952 (div. 1982); 1 child, Cathrael. BA, Queens Coll., 1948. Lectr. The New Sch. Queens Coll., N.Y.C., 1953-54; writer-in-residence CCNY, 1960; lectr. The Writers Workshop, Iowa City, 1966, 72; lectr. Sch. Gen. Studies Columbia U., N.Y.C., 1985-87; dir., founder Writers on Writing Barnard Coll., N.Y.C., 1988—. Adj. prof. English Hofstra U., L.I., 1980, Barnard Coll., N.Y.C., 1981-93; film critic Vogue mag. Author: Star of Glass, 1950, The Troublemaker, 1955, The Sweet Birds of Gorham, 1966, Summer Situations, 1972, Dickie's List, 1973, American Children, 1980, The Rabbi on Forty-Seventh Street, 1982, The Last of the True Believers, 1988, What I Saw at the Fair, 2003; co-editor: The Works of Anne Frank; contbr. articles to numerous mags. Nat. Endowment of Arts grantee, 1983; Fulbright fellow, 1951-52. Mem. PEN (former mem. exec. bd., former chair admissions com.), Authors Guild (former mem. coun.), Phi Beta Kappa (hon.). Democrat. Jewish. Home: 1623 3rd Ave # 27jw New York NY 10128-3638 Personal E-mail: abirstein@aol.com.

BIRSTEIN, SEYMOUR JOSEPH, aerospace transportation executive; b. N.Y.C., May 1, 1927; s. Harry D. and Golde (Lenoff) B.; divorced; 1 child, Diane. BA in Chemistry, NYU, 1947; MS in Phys. Chemistry, Mont. State U., 1948; postgrad., Bklyn. Poly. Inst., 1949-50, Cornell U., 1953. Rsch. chemist Airco, Murray Hill, N.J., 1949-50; br. chief Air Force Cambridge Rsch. Labs., Bedford, Mass., 1951-76; pres. SJB Assoc., Inc., Marlborough, Mass., 1977—. Contbr. articles to profl. jours.; patentee in field. Fellow Am. Inst. Chemists; mem. Am. Chem. Soc., Am. Meteorol. Soc., Sigma Xi. E-mail: sjdbirstein@yahoo.com.

BIRTCIL, ROBERT FRANKLIN, JR., dental educator; b. Mar. 27, 1942; s. Robert Franklin and Margaret (Watson) B.; children: Lindsay Marie, Sean Robet. Student, U. Calif., 1960-62, DDS, 1967. Practice medicine specializing in dentistry, Kensington, Calif., 1970-94; faculty mem. U. Calif., Sch. Dentistry, San Francisco, 1970—, clin. prof., 1988—. Expert cons. operative dentistry, Calif. Dental Assn., Sacramento, 1980-94, expert cons. in biomaterials, 1980-94; mem. superiority of service rev. panel, Calif. Dental Service, San Francisco, 1983-94. Contbr. articles to profl. jours. Bd. dirs. Kensington Cmty. Svc. Dist., Calif., 1976-77, Kensington Property Owners Assn., 1978. Served to Rear Adm. USNR, 1970-2000, Vietnam. Decorated Legion of Merit, Bronze Star, Purple Heart. Fellow Acad. Gen. Dentistry, Acad. Dentistry Internat. (membership com. 1979-84), Internat. Coll. Dentists (counselor dist. 13 1982-98), Am. Coll. Dentists; mem. ADA, Calif. Dental Assn., Omicron Kappa Upsilon (chtp. pres. 1986), Delta Sigma Delta (chpr. grand master 1985-87). Republican. Methodist.

BIRTEL, FRANK THOMAS, mathematician, philosopher, educator; b. New Orleans, Apr. 4, 1932; s. Frank N. and Virginia B.; m. Jane Ella C. Moriarty, Sept. 16, 1964 (dec. 1986); children: Rebecca Anne, Michael Teilhard; m. Margaret S. Bishop, July 28, 1990. BS, Loyola U. South, 1952; MS, U. Notre Dame, 1953, PhD in Math., 1960. Sr. mathematician USN Nuc. Power Schs., 1955-57; instr. Conn. Coll. for Women, New London, 1956-57; lectr. Yale U., 1961-62; asst. prof. Ohio State U., 1960-62; asst. prof. math. Tulane U., 1962-64, assoc. prof., 1964-67, prof., 1967—, univ. prof., 1981—2002, spl. asst. to pres., 1975-76, dep. provost, 1976-78, acting dean Grad. Sch., 1978, acting provost, 1978, provost, dean, 1979-81, dir. program of Judeo-Christian Studies, 1982—, univ. prof. emeritus, 2002—. Vis. prof. U. Nijmegen, Netherlands, 1968—69; mem. Ochsner Found. Clin IRB, 2002—. Editl. adv. bd. Zygon: The Jour. of Sci. and Religion, 1995—. Trustee New Orleans Mus. Art, 1978-80, 83-86, St. Mary's Dominican Coll., New Orleans, 1977-86. Yale U. postdoctoral fellow, 1961-62; sr. Fulbright lectr. Eng., Scotland, Germany, Netherlands, 1968-69. Mem. Am. Math. Soc. (assoc. sec. 1977-88). Roman Catholic. Home: 1229 Cadiz St New Orleans LA 70115-3903 Office: Tulane U Dept Math New Orleans LA 70118 E-mail: ftbirtel@tulane.edu.

BISANZO, MARK THOMAS, sales executive; b. Port Chester, N.Y., Sept. 28, 1941; s. Dominic Daniel and Pauline Ann (Zak) B.; m. Mary Jane Ann Baldino, July 2, 1966; 1 child, Mark Christopher. AAS, Westchester C.C., 1963; BSME, N.Y. Inst. Tech., 1966; MBA, Fordham U., 1972. Instrument engr. Bechtel, N.Y.C., 1966-68, M.W. Kellogg, N.Y.C., 1968-70; sr. controls engr. Power Gas Corp., N.Y.C., 1970-71, Am. Electric Power, N.Y.C., 1971; sr. v.p. Control Assocs., Allendale, N.J., 1971—, 2000—. Mem. adv. bd. Fisher Controls Co., Marshalltown, Iowa, 1997—; bd. dirs. Control Assocs. Pres. Bergen Cath. H.S. Fathers' Club, Oradell, N.J., 1991-94; coach Park Ridge (N.J.) Athletic Assn., 1980-90; mem. Our Lady of Mercy Roman Cath. Ch. Noctornal Adoration Soc., Park Ridge; v.p. Middlebury Collegiate Alumni Coll. Parents Alumni Assn., 2005—. Mem. Soc. Gas Operators (v.p. 2005—), Instrument Soc. Am. (v.p. N.Y. chpt. 1984-85, v.p. 2005). Avocations: skiing, photography, travel. Home: 67 Degroff Pl Park Ridge NJ 07656-1406 Office: Control Assocs 20 Commerce Dr Allendale NJ 07401-1600 Office Phone: 201-934-9200. E-mail: mark.bisanzo@control-associates.com.

BISBEE, GERALD ELFTMAN, JR., investment company executive; b. Waterloo, Iowa, July 12, 1942; s. Gerald Elftman and Maxine Cole (Prather) Bisbee; m. Linda Elaine Ude, Aug. 22, 1970; children: Gerald Elftmann III, Katherine Elizabeth. BA, North Cen. Coll., Naperville, Ill., 1967; MBA, U. Pa., 1972; PhD, Yale U., 1975. Adminstr. Med. Ctr. Northwestern U., Chgo., 1968-70; asst. prof. Yale U., New Haven, 1974-78, assoc. dir. health svcs., 1975-78; pres. Hosp. Rsch. and Ednl. Trust, Chgo., 1978-84; v.p., shareholder Kidder, Peabody & Co., NYC, 1984-88; chmn., chief exec. officer Sequel Corp., New Canaan, Conn., 1988-89, Apache Med. Systems, Inc., Washington, 1989-97; chmn., CEO Health Mgmt. Acad., Alexandria, Va., 1998—; chmn., pres., CEO ReGen Biologics, Inc., Franklin Lakes, NJ, 1998—. Adj. prof. Northwestern U. Kellogg Sch. Mgmt., Evanston, Ill., 1979—83; mem. exec. adv. com. Weatherhead Sch. Mgmt. Health Sys. Program, Case Western Res. U., Cleve., 1984—86; mem. vis. com. Harvard U. Health Svcs., Boston, 1986—92; bd. dirs. Cerner Corp., ReGen Biologics Inc., Health Mgmt. Acad. Co-author: Musculo-Skeletal Disorders: Their Frequency of Occurrence and Their Impact on the Population of the United States, 1978, Financing of Health Care, 1979, Managing the Finances of Health Institutions, 1980; author: Multihospital Systems: Policy Issues for the Future, 1981. Mem. adv. com. Waveney Care Ctr., New Canaan, 1987. Grantee, USPHS, 1972—75. Mem.: Yale Club (NYC). Home and Office: The Bisbee Group 110 Wellesley Dr New Canaan CT 06840-3530 Personal E-mail: gbisbee@aol.com.

BISBEE, JOYCE EVELYN, retired utility company executive; b. Portage, Wis., May 15, 1941; d. Orris Dean and Helen Paulina (Golz) B. BS, U. Wis., Stout, 1963; MEd, U. N.C., 1971. Cert. family and consumer sci. Ext. home economist U. Wis., Racine, 1964-68; tchr., dept. chair Oshkosh (Wis.) Pub. Schs., 1963-64, 68-74; mgr. ednl. rels. J.C. Penney, N.Y.C., NY, 1974-78; v.p. Creamer Dickson Basford, PR, 1978-81; consumer affairs rep. Bklyn. Union, 1983-85, consumer advocate, 1986-92, mgr. consumer outreach and edn., 1992-98; dir. consumer comm. and advocacy KeySpan Corp., 1998—2003; ret., 2004. Mem. consumer affairs com. Bar Assn. City N.Y., 1993-98. Mem. adv. com. N.Y.C. 4-H Youth Program, 1985-96; active East 60s Neighborhood Assn., N.Y.C., 1993-2003. Recipient Alumni Disting. Svc. award U. Wis.-Stout, 1978. Lutheran. Avocations: craft shows, cultural performances, cats, travel. Home: 5815 American Pkwy # 101 Madison WI 53718

BISCARDI, CHESTER, composer, educator; b. Kenosha, Wis., Oct. 19, 1948; s. Chester Frank and Anne Rose (Rizzo) B. Student, Università di Bologna (Italy) and Conservatorio di Musica G. B. Martini, Bologna, 1969-70; BA in English Lit. with honors, U. Wis., 1970, MA in Italian Lit. (Ford Found. fellow), 1972, MM in Composition, 1974; MMA, Yale U., 1976, DMA, 1980. Tchg. asst. Italian U. Wis., Madison, 1970—73, tchg. asst. theory, 1973—74, ad hoc instr. Italian for reading knowledge, 1973—74; tchg. fellow Italian for singers Yale U., New Haven, 1975—76; seminar instr. Fed. Correctional Instn. Oxford U., 1978; faculty mem. music dept. Sarah Lawrence Coll., 1977—; seminar and program faculty Acad. Yr. in N.Y.C., 1984; dir. music program Sarah Lawrence Coll., 1987—, William Schuman chair music, 1995—. Vis. prof. summer program in Florence at Villa Corsi-Salviati in Sesto Fiorentino with U. Mich., 1987, 94; composer-in-residence U. Wis., 1985, The Chamber Music Conf. and Composers' Forum of the East, Bennington, Vt., 1990. Composer: Tartini, 1972, Turning, 1973, Chartres, 1973, Indovinello, 1974, orpha, 1974, Heabakès: Five Sapphic Lyrics, 1974, they had ceased to talk, 1975, Trusting Lightness, 1975, Tenzone, 1975, Music for the Duchess of Malfi, 1975, Trio, 1976, At the Still Point, 1977, Eurydice, 1978, Mestiere, 1979, Trasumanar, 1980, Di Vivere, 1981, Good-bye, My Fancy!, 1982, Music for Witch Dance, 1983, Chêz Vous, 1983, Piano Concerto, 1983, Incitation to Desire (tango), 1984, 1993, Tight-Rope, 1985, Piano Sonata, 1986, rev., 1987, Traverso, 1987, No Feeling is the Same as Before, 1988, Companion Piece (for Morton Feldman), 1989, 1991, Netori, 1990, Music for an Occasion, 1992, rev., 2003, The Gift of Life, 1990—93, Baby Song of the Four Winds, 1994, Guru, 1995, Resisting Stillness, 1996, What a Coincidence, 1997, I Wouldn't Know About That, 1997, Modern Love Songs, 1997—2002, Prayers of Steel, 1998, Now You See It, Now You Don't, 1998, The Child Comes Every Winter, 1999, Someone New, 1999, Music for NASDAQ Market Site TV, 1999, Recovering, 2000, In Time's Unfolding, 2000, At Any Given Moment, 2002, Piano Quintet, 2004. Recipient Prix de Rome, Am. Acad. in Rome, 1976-77, Aaron Copland award, 2001; Composer/Librettist grantee Nat. Endowment for Arts, 1977-78, 80-81; Composers' Conf. fellow, Johnson, Vt., 1974-75; Wis. Arts Bd. grantee, 1976; Nat. Acad. and Inst. Arts and Letters Charles E. Ives scholar, 1975-76; Guggenheim fellow, 1979-80; Mellon Found. grantee, 1979; Am. Music Ctr. grantee, 1980; McDowell Colony fellow, 1981, 84, 92, 94-95, 98, 2000, 04; Martha Baird Rockefeller Fund grant, 1982; Creative Artists Pub. Svc. Program fellow in music, 1983; Japan Found. fellow, 1989-90; N.Y. Found. for Arts Artists fellow in music composition, 1990, 98; Rockefeller Found. Bellagio Study and Conf. Ctr. residency, Lago di Como, Villa Serbelloni, Italy, 1993; Humanities residency Bogliasco Found., Villa Orbiana, Italy, 1999, 2005, Fromm Music Found. at Harvard Commn., 1999-2002. Mem. Am. Composers Alliance, Am. Acad. in Rome, Am. Music Ctr., Broadcast Music, MacDowell Colony, Century Assn., also others. Office: Sarah Lawrence Coll Music Dept Bronxville NY 10708 Home: 380 Riverside Dr 4C New York NY 10025-1819 Office Phone: 914-395-2334. Business E-Mail: biscardi@slc.edu.

BISCHEL, MARGARET DEMERITT, physician, consultant; b. Moorhead, Minn., Nov. 8, 1933; d. Connie Magnus Nystrom and Harriett Grace (Petersen) Zorner; m. Raymon DeMeritt, 1953 (div. 1958); 1 child, Gregory Raymon; m. John Bischel, 1961 (div. 1964); m. Kenneth Dean Serkes, June 7, 1974. BS, U. Oreg., Eugene, 1962; MD, U. Oreg., Portland, 1965. Diplomate Am. Bd. Internal Medicine, Nat. Bd. Med. Examiners. Resident, straight med. intern Los Angeles County/U. So. Calif. Med. Ctr., 1965-68, NIH fellow nephrology, 1968-70, asst. prof. renal medicine, 1970-74; asst. prof., instr. medicine U. So. Calif., 1968-74; instr. nephrology East L.A. City Coll., 1971-74; dir. med. edn. Luth. Gen. Hosp., Park Ridge, Ill., 1974-78, dir. nephrology sect., 1977-80, pres. med. staff, 1974-88; founding mem., med. dir., dir. med. svcs. Luth. Health Plan, Park Ridge, 1983-87; clin. assoc. prof. medicine Abraham Lincoln Sch. Medicine U. Ill., 1975-80; sr. cons. Parkside Assocs., Inc., Park Ridge, 1986-88; pvt. practice Chgo., 1974-88; physician Buenaventura Med. Clinic, Ventura, Calif., 1989-94, med. dir., 1992-94; prin. Apollo Managed Care Cons., Santa Barbara, Calif., 1988—. Trustee Luth. Health Care System, Park Ridge, 1986-90, Unified Med. Group Assn., Seal Beach, Calif., 1993-94; hon. lifetime staff mem. Luth. Gen. Hosp., Park Ridge; mem. formulary com. HealthNet, 1992-94, med. adv. com. TakeCare, 1993-94, quality assurance com. PacifiCare, 1993-94; mem. doctor's adv. network AMA, 1994-96; JCAHO advisor for behavioral health care providers. Mem. editl. adv. bd. Capitation Mgmt. Report; author 35 texts including Managing Behavioral Healthcare, 2005, The Credentialing and Privileges Manual, 2001, rev. edit., 2005, Medical Review Criteria Guidelines for Managed Care, 4th edit., 2005; editor: Med. Mgmt. Manual, Managed Care Bull.; contbr. chpts. to books and articles to profl. jours. Fellow: ACP (Calif. Gov.'s advisor 1993—95); mem.: Am. Coll. Physician Execs. Avocations: real estate, gardening. Office: Apollo Managed Care Cons 860 Ladera Ln Santa Barbara CA 93108-1626 Office Phone: 805-969-2606. Personal E-mail: mbischel@cox.net. Business E-Mail: mbischel@apollomanagedcare.com.

BISCHOF, JUSTIN HOWARD, conductor; b. Toronto, Can., Apr. 8, 1967; s. Bruce Anton Bischof and Jennifer Margaret Spence. MusB, Manhattan Sch. Music, 1990, MusM, 1992, D of Music, 1998. Dir. music Ch. of Reserrection, Porte Avenue, NY, 1995—2001; prof. music history Barnard Coll., N.Y.C., 1994—2000; prof. music Manhattan Sch. Music, 1999—; founder, condr. Madis Choral Co., 2003—. Recipient Bromspm Ragen award, Manhattan Sch. Music, 1990, Nat. Pianist prize, Am. Guild Organists, 2000. Avocations: tennis, travel. Home: 544 W 156th St #3W New York NY 10032

BISCHOFBERGER, NORBERT W., medical products company executive; b. 1956; PhD in Organic Chemistry, Eidgenossische Tech Hochschule, Zurich, Switzerland. Postdoctoral rsch. in steroid chemistry Syntex; rsch. prof. in organic chemistry and applied enzymology Harvard U.; sr. scientist DNA chemistry Genentech DNA Sythesis Group, 1986-90; dir. organic chemistry Gilead Scis. Inc., Foster City, Calif., 1990-93, v.p. organic chemistry, 1993-98, sr. v.p. R&D, 1998-2000, exec. v.p. R&D, 2000—. Office: Gilead Scis Inc 333 Lakeside Dr Foster City CA 94404 Fax: (650) 573-4800.*

BISCHOFF, DAVID CANBY, retired university dean; b. Bellefonte, Pa., May 27, 1930; s. Eugen Carl and Jean Stuart (Canby) B.; m. Patricia A. Halfacre, Aug. 15, 1954; children: Cynthia, Steven, Ingrid. BS, Pa. State U., 1952, PhD, 1958; MS, U. N.C., 1953. Asst. prof. dept. phys. edn. U. Mass., Amherst, 1957-60, asso. prof., 1960-63, prof., 1963—, asso. provost for profl. schs., 1972-79, dep. provost, 1982-84; assoc. chancellor, 1983-92; dean U. Mass. Sch. Phys. Edn., 1973-92. Vis. prof. Wesleyan U., 1968-69; bd. dirs. Bay State Games. Past pres. Amherst Community Chest, Amherst Am. Field Service; mem. Amherst Planning Bd., 1958-62; trustee The Hotchkiss Sch., 1990-96; trustee Portland (Maine) Mus. Art. Capt. USAF, ret., 1953-55. Mem. AAHPER, Nat. Coll. Phys. Edn. Assn. (past pres.) Clubs: Algonquin, Hillsboro, Anglers (N.Y.C.). Home: 46 Burbank Farm PO Box 462 Yarmouth ME 04096-0462

BISCHOFF, FREDERICK CHRISTOPHER, III, retired accountant; b. Walhalla, S.C., Oct. 1, 1941; s. Frederick Christopher and Kathleen (Kay) B. Student, Ga. Inst. Tech., 1965; BBA, Ga. State U., 1966; BS (hon.), Ohio Christian U., 1968. Market devel. mgr. Grizzard Advt., Atlanta, 1966-71; v.p. Leedy Enterprises Inc., Atlanta, 1971-72; contract adminstr. APAC-GA Inc., Atlanta, 1973-92, APAC-Carolina, Inc., 1992—2003; ret., 2003. Active Fulton County Young Reps., Atlanta, 1964-68, High Mus. of Art; mem. Ga. Marine Safety Commn., 1959-62. Mem. Palmetto Trust for Hist. Preservation, Ga. Hist. Soc., Atlanta Hist. Soc., Am. Legion, S.C. Hist. Soc., Nat. Trust for Historic Preservation, Darlington C. of C. (bd. dirs.), Florence C. of C., Kiwanis, Darlington Pilot Club Found. (bd. dirs.), Ponte Vedra Club, Darlington Country Club. Methodist. Avocations: photography, travel. Home: 502 Cashua St Darlington SC 29532-2808

BISCHOFF, KENNETH BRUCE, chemical engineer, educator; b. Chgo., Feb. 29, 1936; s. Arthur William and Evelyn Mary (Hansen) B.; m. Joyce Arlene Winterberg, June 6, 1959; children: Kathryn Ann, James Eric. BS, Ill. Inst. Tech., 1957, PhD, 1961. Asst. to assoc. prof. U. Tex., Austin, 1961-67; assoc. prof., then prof. U. Md., 1967-70; Walter R. Read prof. engring. Cornell U., 1970-76, dir. Sch. Chem. Engring., 1970-75; Unidel prof., biomed. and chem. engring. U. Del., 1976-98, emeritus, 1998—, chmn. dept. chem. engring., 1978-82. Mem. NRC Bd. on Chem. Scis. and Tech., 1984-86, various coms., 1984—; cons. Exxon Rsch. and Engring., NIH, Gen. Foods Corp., W.R. Grace Co., Koppers Co., DuPont Co. Author: (with D.M. Himmelblau) Process Analysis and Simulation, 1968, (with G.F. Froment) Chemical Reactor Analysis and Design, 1979, 2d edit., 1989; chmn., editor: (with R.L. Dedrick and E.F. Leonard) The Artificial Kidney, Process 1st. Internat. Symposium Chem. Reaction Engring., 1970, (with R.M. Koros and T.R. Keane) Process 9th Symposium, 1986; mem. editorial bd. Advances in Chemistry Series, 1973-76, 78-81, Jour. Bioengring., 1976-80, Jour. Pharmacokin. Biopharmaceutics, 1975-92, Biotech. Progress, 1987-2000, Advances in Chem. Engring., 1981-2000. Recipient Ebert prize Acad. Pharm. Scis., 1972, Founders award Chem. Indsl. Inst. Toxicology, 1992, Disting. Alumni award Ill. Inst. Tech., 1996, Profl. Achievement award, 1997; Shell Found. fellow, 1959, NSF fellow, 1960, U. Ghent fellow, 1960-61, NAE fellow. Fellow AAAS, AIChE (dir. 1972-74, chmn. food, pharm. and bioengring.

divsn. 1985, chmn. nat. program com. 1978, Profl. Progress award 1976, Food Pharm. and Bioengring. divsn. award 1982, 34th Ann. Inst. lectr. 1982, R.H. Wilhelm award 1987); mem. Am. Inst. Chem. Engr., Am. Chem. Soc., Am. Soc. Artificial Internal Organs, Engrs. Coun. for Profl. Devel. (bd. dirs. 1972-78), Coun. Chem. Rsch. (governing bd. 1981-84, chmn. 1985), Catalysis Soc., AAUP, N.Y. Acad. Scis., Sigma XI, Tau Beta Pi, Phi Lambda Upsilon, Omega Chi Epsilon, Alpha Chi Sigma. Home: PO Box 467 Rehoboth Beach DE 19971-0467

BISCHOFF, MARILYN BRETT, clinical social worker, personal life coach psychotherapist; b. Mt. Vernon, N.Y., Apr. 16, 1930; d. Arthur Cushman and Mary Kathryn (Clark) Brett; m. Walter A. Bischoff, Mar. 25, 1961; children: Holly, Robert. BA magna cum laude, CCNY, 1959; MSW, Columbia U., 1961; PhD in Social Work, Boston Coll., 1985; cert. in gerontology, U. Mass., Dartmouth, 2000. Diplomate clin. social work Am. Bd. Examiners Social Work, bd. cert. diplomate clin. social work NASW. Clin. social worker Providence Child Guidance Clinic, 1961-65, 69-73; pvt. practice clin. social worker Attleboro, Mass., 1994—, Providence, 1965-94; instr. Providence Coll., 1988-89. Personal life coach; spkr. field. Active Attleboro (Mass.) Area Mental Health Assn., 1975—94. Fellow, Columbia U., 1959—60; grantee, NIMH, 1960—61. Mem.: NASW (sec.-treas. (S.E. Mass. chpt.) 1967—68, mem. speaker's bur. (RI chpt.) 1987), RI Group Psychotherapy Soc. (chair membership com. 1985—96), Acad. Cert. Social Workers, Attleboro Ski Club, Columbia U. Alumni Assn., Phi Beta Kappa. Avocations: travel, photography, sewing. Home and Office: 10 Norfolk Row Attleboro MA 02703-1629 Office Phone: 508-222-7085. E-mail: drmarilynb@aol.com.

BISCHOFF, SUSAN ANN, newspaper editor; b. Indpls., July 31, 1951; d. Thomas Anthony and Betty Jean (Coons) Bischoff; m. Jim B. Barlow, June 20, 1975; 1 child, Samantha Lynn Barlow Martinez. BA, Ind. U., 1973. Rschr., reporter Congl. Quar., Washington, 1973-74; city desk reporter Houston Chronicle, 1974-75, bus. reporter, 1975-79, asst. bus. editor, 1979-84, bus. editor, 1984-86, asst. mng. editor, 1986-2000, dep. mng. editor, 2000—03, assoc. editor, 2003—. Houston corr. Kiplinger, Tex. Letter, Washington, 1980-85; juror Pulitzer Prizes in Journalism, 2004, 05. Mem. class policy Leadership Houston, 1992—94; mem. exec. com. Gulf Coast affiliate United Way, 1994—2002; pres. Friends of Houston Girl Scouts, 2002—; bd. dirs. Houston Chronicle Employees Fed. Credit Union, 1980—87, San Jacinto Coun. Girl Scouts US, 1997—2003, Child Adv., US Olympic Festival VII, Houston, 1985—86, Gulf Coast Mar. of Dimes Birth Defects Found., 1989—2001, YES Coll. Prep. Sch., 1999—2002, AIDS Found., Houston, 2002—; founding bd. dir. Greater Houston Women's Found.; mem. bd. visitors Anderson Cancer Ctr. U. Tex. Named Outstanding Woman in Houston Journalism, YWCA, 1989, Fabulous Femme, Greater Houston Women's Found., 1994, Woman of Distinction, Crohn's & Colitis Found., 1996; recipient Outstanding Vol. Achievement award, Gulf Coast United Way, 1995, Outstanding Media award, Nat. Soc. Fund Raising Execs., 1997, Nat. Thanks award, San Jacinto Girl Scouts, 2001, Mayborn award, Cmty. Leadership Tex. Daily Newspaper Assn., 2001, honoree, Jewish Cmty. Ctr. of Houston Children's Scholarship Ball, 2002, Strong, Smart and Bold award, Houston Girls, Inc., 2003. Mem.: Soc. News Design, Am. Assn. Sunday and Feature Editors (named to Features Hall of Fame 2003), Am. Soc. Newspaper Editors (dir.), Press Club of Houston Ednl. Found. (founding bd. dir.). Home: 2929 Buffalo Speedway # 112 Houston TX 77098 Office: Houston Chronicle 801 Texas Ave Houston TX 77002-2996 Business E-Mail: susan.bischoff@chron.com.

BISCHOFF, THERESA A., not-for-profit association executive; b. Rockville Ctr., NY, Nov. 16, 1953; d. Robert and Colette (Burke) Peters. BS in Acctg. cum laude, U. Conn., 1975; MBA, NYU, 1991. Cert. CPA, 1977. Sr. dir. acctg. svcs. NYU Med. Ctr., NYC, 1984-87, v.p. fin., 1987-93, dep. provost, exec. v.p., 1993—98, pres., 1998—2003; clin. prof. health care mgmt. NYU Sch. Medicine, NYC, 1993—2003; CEO ARC in Greater NY, NYC, 2004—. Bd. dirs. Combined Coord. Coun., 1984-03, chair, 1998-02; mem. adv. com. United Hosp. Fund, 1994-03; mem. adminstrv. bd. Coun. Tchg. Hosp., 1995-03. Mem. AAMC (chair 2002-03), Greater NY Hosp. Assn. (mem. bd. dirs. 1994-03, mem. health care exec. forum 1987—, sec. 1990-92), Healthcare Assn. NY State (trustee 1994-02), Soc. Health Svc. Adminstrs., Mut. Am. (trustee 2001-), Dov Pharm. (trustee 2003-), U. Conn. Found. Bd. Office: ARC in Greater NY 150 Amsterdam Ave New York NY 10023

BISCONTI, ANN STOUFFER, public opinion research company executive; b. Chgo., Nov. 22, 1940; d. Samuel Andrew Stouffer and Ruth Rachel McBurney; m. Raffaele Ludovico Bisconti (dec. Oct. 19, 1999); children: Alessandra Ilus Wilkes, Giulia Rachel; m. Charles William Dyke, Oct. 13, 2002. Student, Harvard U., 1958—60; BA with honors, McGill U., 1962; PhD, The Union Inst., Cin., 1978. Assoc. study dir. Nat. Commn. on Allied Health Edn., Washington, 1977—79; dir. Washington office Higher Edn. Rsch. Inst., 1979—80; ptnr. Human Resources Policy Corp., Washington, 1980; dir. Nat. Ctr. for Allied Health Leadership, Washington, 1981—83; v.p. rsch. Nuc. Energy Inst., Washington, 1983—96; pres. Bisconti Rsch., Inc., Washington, 1996—. Mem. adv. com., risk comm. program EPA, Washington, 1988; advisor tech. cooperation program in Malaysia IAEA, Vienna, 1990; mem. adv. com., risk comm. Orgn. for Econ. Cooperation and Devel., Paris, 1991. Author: College and Other Stepping Stones, 1980; co-author: Higher Education and the Disadvantaged Student, 1972, The Power of Protest, 1975, College as a Training Ground for Jobs, 1977. Pres. Congl. Award Coun., 8th Congl. Dist., Md., 1990—93; advisor long-range planning com. Town of Somerset, Chevy Chase, Md., 2002; career advisor Harvard U., Cambridge, 1996; rsch. advisor NASA Alumni League, Washington, 1998. Recipient Disting. Svc. Award, Am. Soc. Allied Health Professions (now Assn. Schs. Allied Health Profls.), 1983. Mem.: World Assn. Pub. Opinion Rsch., Am. Nuc. Soc. (bd. dirs. 1993—96, 2004—, Best Paper award 1989, Outstanding Session award 1990, 1992), Am. Assn. Pub. Opinion Rsch. Avocations: geography/travel, foreign languages, gardening.

BISEL, MARSHA MCCUNE, elementary school educator; b. Winchester, Ind., Jan. 27, 1950; d. Floyd Elder and Vista Coral (Rust) McCune; m. Ronald G. Bisel, June 20, 1971; children: Kyle, Brooke, Kam, Robin. BS in Edn. summa cum laude, Taylor U., 1972; MA in Edn., Ball State U., Muncie, Ind., 1975. Life lic. K-8 tchr., Ind. Tchr. Ridgeville (Ind.) Elem. Sch., 1972; grade level coord. Deerfield Elem. Sch., Ridgeville. Mem. civic theatre bd. Summer Performance Co., Portland, Ind., 1997-98; bd. dirs. Habitat for Humanity, 1998; with Jay County Girls Little League, Jay County Soccer, Patriot Booster Club, Ch. choir, organist, soloist. Avocations: acting, singing. Home: 6528 S Us Highway 27 Portland IN 47371-8829

BISER, LARRY, music educator, director; b. Jersey Shore, Pa., Aug. 21, 1943; s. Charles I. and Phyllis Linn Biser; m. Diane Holly Triplett, July 14, 1967; 1 child, Stacy Lynne. MusB, Westminster Choir Coll., Princeton, 1965; M in Ch. Music, Concordia U., River Forest, IL, 2002. Organist-choirmaster Bristol United Meth. Ch., Pa., 1961—65; min. music Arlington Forest United Meth. Ch., Va., 1965—67, East Congl. United Ch. of Christ, Grand Rapids, Mich., 1969; music dir. and condr. Chamber Choir of Grand Rapids, 1972—; assoc. prof. music Aquinas Coll., 1997—. Condr. (recordings) Works for Cathedral Spaces, A Christmas Spectacular; condr.: broadcast Chamber Choir of Grand Rapids and the Mormon Tabernacle Choir, 1995, Youth Chamber Choir of St. Petersburg, The Chamber Choir of Grand Rapids, and The Kapella Orchestra, 1999. Mem.: Am. Guild English Handbell Ringers, Chorus Am., Am. Choral Dirs. Assn., Am. Guild Organists (program chair regional conv. 1985, 2005). Avocations: gardening, stained glass fabrication, travel, reading, interior decorating. Home: 1110 Giddings Ave SE Grand Rapids MI 49506 Office: East Congl United Ch of Christ 1005 Giddings Ave SE Grand Rapids MI 49506 Office Phone: 616-245-0578.

BISH, DAVID LEE, mineralogist; b. Arlington, Va., Mar. 5, 1952; s. Henry L. and Rosemary M. B.; m. Karen, July 15, 1981; 1 child, Rebecca L. BS, Furman U., 1974; PhD, Pa. State U., 1977. Rsch. assoc. Harvard U., Cambridge, Mass., 1977-80; tech. staff mem. Los Alamos (N.Mex.) Nat. Lab., 1980—. Assoc. editor Am. Mineralogist, 1987-91, Clays and Clay Minerals, 1993—, Zeitschrift fur Kristallographie, 1996-99; author: Crystal Structures and Cation Sites, 1988; author, editor: Modern Powder Diffraction, 1989, Thermal Analysis in Clay Science, 1990; contbr. articles to profl. jours. Panel mem. Los Alamos Community Pride, 1985. Recipient Award for Materials Sci. Rsch. Xerox Corp., 1977. Fellow Mineralogical Soc. Am.; mem. Clay Minerals Soc. (coun. mem. 1987-90, Jackson award 1995, pres. 1998-99), Am. Geophys. Union, Internat. Assn. for Study Clay Minerals, Phi Beta Kappa. Achievements include discovery of phenomenon of anion exchange in mixed-hydroxide minerals; development of quantitative analysis by X-ray powder diffraction using the Rietveld method. Home: 790 Los Pueblos St Los Alamos NM 87544-2617 Office: Los Alamos Nat Lab Mail Stop D469 Los Alamos NM 87545-0001

BISHAR, JOHN JOSEPH, JR., utilities executive, lawyer; b. N.Y.C., Jan. 22, 1950; s. John Joseph Sr. and Mildred (Marron) B.; m. Noreen Ellen Leddy, Aug. 5, 1972; children: Kimberly, Kelly, Lauren. BA, Georgetown U., 1971; JD, Fordham U., 1974. Bar: NY 1975, U.S. Dist. Ct. (so., ea. dist. NY) 1975. Assoc. Cullen & Dykman, Garden City, NY, 1974-80; sr. v.p., gen. counsel, corp. sec. LITCO Bancorporation, 1980-87; ptnr. Cullen & Dykman, Garden City, NY, 1987—2002, mng. ptnr., 1993—2002; sr. v.p., gen. counsel Keyspan Corp., Bklyn., 2002—05, corp. sec., 2003—05, exec. v.p., gen. counsel, corp. sec., chief governance officer, 2005—. Bd. dirs. YMCA of Long Island, Huntington, N.Y., 1981—; bd. of trustees Family Life Ctr., Garden City, 1985—; gov. Cath. Sch. of St. Mary, Garden City, 1985—. Named Man of Yr. YMCA of Long Island, 1986. Mem. ABA, N.Y. State Bar Assn., Nassau County Bar Assn., N.Y. State Bankers Assn. (lawyers adv. com.), Assn. Bank Holding Co. (lawyers com.). Clubs: Cherry Valley (Garden City), Atlantic Beach (N.Y.). Republican. Roman Catholic. Avocations: sports, golf, basketball, tennis, coaching kids. Office: Keyspan Energy 21st Fl One Metro Tech Ctr Brooklyn NY 11201

BISHARA, AMIN TAWADROS, management and consulting firm executive; b. Cairo, Oct. 22, 1944; came to U.S., 1973; s. Tawadros and Fakha (Boules) B.; m. Suzi Guirguis, Aug. 27, 1977; children: James A., Robert A. BSME, Ain Shams U., Cairo, 1968; MSME, Poly. U. N.Y., 1976. Registered profl. engr., N.Y., Tex., Ill., Ariz., Pa., Fla. Field engr. Gen. Engring. Co., Cairo, 1968-71; mech. engr. Engring. Co. for Indsl. Enterprises, Cairo, 1971-73; project engr. Cosentini Assocs., N.Y.C., 1973-76; sr. engr. Ebasco Svcs., Inc., N.Y.C., 1976-79, lead engr., 1979-84; chmn., chief exec. officer PTS Tech. Svcs., Inc., Hurst, Tex., 1985-96; v.p. Metzler & Assocs., 1997-98; sr. mgr. Ernst & Young LLP, 1999—. Mem. adv. bd. Entrepreneurship Inst., Ft. Worth, 1990—. Lectr. in nuclear industry; strategic and bus. cons. Contbr. articles to profl. publs. Mem. NSPE, ASME Nuc. Air Treatment Sys. (main com.), Masons, Moslah Temple of Ft. Worth. Roman Catholic. Home: 2625 Brookridge Dr Hurst TX 76054-2761 Office Phone: 972-556-7189. Personal E-mail: amin.bishara@capgemini.com.

BISHARA, SAMIR EDWARD, orthodontist; b. Cairo, Oct. 31, 1935; s. Edward Constantin and Georgette Ibrahim (Kelela) B.; children: Dina Marie, Dorine Gabrielle, Cherine Noelle. B. Dental Surgery, Alexandria U., Egypt, 1957; diploma in orthodontics, 1967; MS, cert. in orthodontics, U. Iowa, 1970, D.D.S., 1972. Diplomate Am. Bd. Orthodontics (pres. Coll. Diplomates 1992). Practice gen. dentistry, Alexandria, 1957-68; specializing in orthodontics Iowa City, Iowa, 1970—; fellow in clin. pedontics Guggenheim Dental Clinic, N.Y.C., 1959-60; resident in oral surgery Moassat Hosp., Alexandria, 1960-61, mem. staff, 1961-68; asst. prof. dentistry U. Iowa, 1970-73, asso. prof., 1973-76, prof., 1976—. Vis. prof. Alexandria U., 1974. Contbr. articles profl. jours., chpts. in books. Fellow Am. Coll. Dentists, Internat. Coll. Dentists; mem. ADA, AAAS, World Fedn. Orthodontists (hon.), Am. Assn. Orthodontics, Internat. Dental Fedn., Internat. Assn. Dental Research, Am. Cleft Palate Assn., Assn. Egyptian Am. Scholars, Egyptian Orthodontic Soc. (hon.), Columbian Orthodontic Soc. (hon.), Greek Orthodontic Soc. (hon.), Mexican Bd. Orthodontists (hon.), Brit. Orthodontic Conf. (hon.), Omicron Kappa Upsilon, Sigma Xi Home: 1014 Penkridge Dr Iowa City IA 52246-4930 Office: U Iowa Coll Dentistry Orthodontic Dept Iowa City IA 52242

BISHER, JAMES FURMAN, journalist, writer; b. Denton, N.C., Nov. 4, 1918; s. Chisholm and Mamie (Morris) B.; m. Lynda Landon; children: Roger, James Furman Jr., Monte. Student, Furman U., 1934-36; AB in Journalism, U. N.C., 1938; Doctorate in Arts and Letters (hon.), Furman U., 1997. Editor Lumberton (N.C.) Voice, 1938-39; reporter High Point (N.C.) Enterprise, 1939-40; reporter, state editor Charlotte (N.C.) News, 1940-42, sports editor, 1946-50, Atlanta Constn., 1950-57, Atlanta Jour., 1957—; columnist The Sporting News, St. Louis; moderator weekly TV show, Football Rev., 1950-68. V.p. Bisher Hosiery Mill, Denton, N.C. Author: With A Southern Exposure, 1962, Miracle in Atlanta, 1966, Strange But True Baseball Stories, 1966, Arnold Palmer— The Golden Year, 1971, Aaron, 1974, The College Game, 1974, The Masters, 1976, The Furman Bisher Collection, 1989, Thankful, 1997, Atlanta Half-Century, 1997, Peachtree Golf Club, 2004, also numerous articles; contbr. to: anthologies including Best Sports Stories of Year, 23 times. Chmn. Ga. Christmas Seal campaign, 1961; charter mem. Atlanta-Fulton County Stadium Authority.; mem. selection com. Pro Football Hall of Fame, Coll. Football Hall of Fame, Ga.; bd. dirs. Salvation Army Boys Club, mem. adv. bd. Sarazen World Open Golf Tournament; mem. Atlanta Sports Coun. Served to lt. USNR Air Corps, 1943-46. Recipient Ga. A.P. Sports Writing award, 18 times; UPI Sports Writing award, 4 times; Turf Writing award Fla. Throughbred Breeders Assn., 1972, 75; Jake Wade award Coll. Sports Info. Dirs. Am., 1979; Sigma Delta Chi awards for best sports commentary, 1982, 93, 90; Bert McGrane award for disting. svc. to coll. football, 1982; N.C. Gov.'s award, 1986; U. N.C. Journalism Hall of Fame, 1985; named Ky. col., 1958, Sportswriter of Yr. Ga. (19 times); hon. Tar Heel, 1961; Disting. Alumnus of Yr. Furman U., 1978; Red Smith award for disting. and meritorious contbn. to art of sportswriting, 1988, Bobby Jones Sportsman of Yr. award, 1994; named to Nat. Sportscasters and Sportswriters Hall of Fame, 1989, Internat. Golf Writers Hall of Fame, 1989, Ga. Sports Hall of Fame, 1990, N.C. Sports Hall of Fame, 1995, Lifetime Achievement in Journalism award PGA in Am., 1996, Ga. Soccer Hall of Fame, 1997, Meml. Golf Journalism award, 1997; sponsor Furman Bisher Acad.-Athletic scholarship Furman U., Roger C. Bisher Scholarship Ga. Tech.; Marvin Francis award for Svc., 2001, Nat. Conf. for Cmty. and Justice award, 2001, Lincoln Werden Meml. award, N.Y. Golf Assn., 2001. Mem. Nat. Sportscasters and Sportswriters Assn. (pres. 1974-76), Football Writers Assn. Am. (pres. 1959-60), Golf Writers Assn. Am. (pres. 1992-94), Assn. Golf Writers (Europe) (life), Canongate Golf Club, Legends at Chateau Elan, Capital City Club, The European Club, Sea Island Golf Club, Gridiron Club, Chi Psi. Presbyterian. Home: 431 Lester Rd Fayetteville GA 30215-4930 Office: 72 Marietta St NW PO Box 4689 Atlanta GA 30302-4689: 21 Dunbar Creek Pte Saint Simons Island GA 31522 Office Phone: 404-526-5335. E-mail: furman@ajc.com. *My good fortune in life is not to be confused with success, whose definition yet remains vague to me. Success is some mythical goal clamored and struggled for, and whose pursuit is never-ending. One level leads to a requirement to seek another. Success, in my mind, must be related to the status of that person who achieves happiness, and yet may never have been outside his county.*

BISHOP, ALAN DOUGLAS, music educator; b. Spartanburg, S.C., Apr. 27, 1962; s. William Jack and Gwendolyn Elaine Bishop; m. Lisa Lynn Haskell, Apr. 15, 1962; children: Abby Elizabeth, Michael Alan. MusM in Edn., Valdosta (Ga.) State U., 1987. Asst. band dir. Boiling Springs (S.C.) HS, 1984—86; grad. student asst. Valdosta (Ga.) State U., 1986—87; band dir. McBee (S.C.) HS, 1987—88, Ninety Six (S.C.) HS, 1988—97, Mid. Sch. of Pacolet, SC, 1997—2002; asst. band dir. Broome HS, Spartanburg, SC, 1997. Treas. Friends of Libr. Spartanburg County Pub. Library Cowpens Br., Cowpens, SC, 2002. Mem.: S.C. Band Dirs. Assn., S.C. Music Educator's Assn. (corr.), Music Educator's Nat. Conf. (corr.). Baptist. Avocation: music. Home: 108 Paula Court Cowpens SC 29330 Office: Cowpens Middle School 150 Foster Street Cowpens SC 29330 Personal E-mail: a-lbishop@juno.com. E-mail: abisho@spa3.k12.sc.us.

BISHOP, ALFRED CHILTON, JR., lawyer; b. Alexandria, Va., Oct. 3, 1942; s. Alfred Chilton and Margaret (Marshall) B.; divorced; 1 son, Alfred Chilton III; m. 2d Catherine Ann Keppel, May 17, 1980. BA with distinction, U. Va., 1965, LLB, 1969; LLM in Taxation, Georgetown U., 1974. Bar: NY 1970, U.S. Ct. Appeals (2d cir.), 1970, U.S. Tax Ct. 1971, U.S. Ct. Claims 1971, D.C. 1977. Assoc. Shearman and Sterling, NYC, 1969-70; assoc. trial atty., Office of Chief Counsel IRS, Washington, 1970-74, sr. trial atty., 1974-80, sr. technician reviewer, 1980-81, br. chief, 1981— . Recipient Am. Jurisprudence award 1968. Mem. DC Bar Assn., Sr. Exec. Svc. Candidate Network (v.p. 1980-81, pres. 1981-82, dir. 1983), Sr. Exec. Assn., Phi Delta Phi. Episcopalian. Home: 7523 Thistledown Trl Fairfax Station VA 22039-2207 Office Phone: 202-622-8483. E-mail: abishop7@cox.net.

BISHOP, BRUCE TAYLOR, lawyer; b. Hartford, Conn., Sept. 13, 1951; s. Robert Wright Sr. and Barbara (Taylor) B.; m. Sarah M. Bishop, Aug. 31, 1974; children: Elizabeth, Margaret. BA in Polit. Sci., Old Dominion U., 1973; JD, U. Va., Charlottesville, 1976. Bar: Va. 1977, U.S. Supreme Ct., Va. 1976, U.S. Dist. Ct. (ea. dist.) Va., U.S. Dist. Ct. (we. dist.) Va., U.S. Ct. Appeals (4th cir.); diplomate Am. Bd. Trial Advocates. Law clk. to chief judge U.S. Dist. Ct. (ea. dist.) Va., 1976-77; assoc. Willcox & Savage, P.C., Norfolk, Va., 1977-82, ptnr., 1983—. Bd. dirs. Nautical Adventures, Inc., Norfolk FestEvents, Ltd., 1981—, pres., 1982-85; pres. Va. OpSail 2000 Found.; mem. bd. visitors Old Dominion U., 1972-83, sec., 1979-81, chmn., mem. various coms.; speaker in field. Treas. Norfolk Reps., 1978-82, also mem. numerous coms.; bd. dirs., chmn. regional Key Club campaign United Way South Hampton Roads; chmn., co-chmn. United Negro Coll. Fund, 1981, Four Cities United Way Campaign; trustee Va. Stage Co., 1982; pres. Community Promotion Corp.; commr. Norfolk Redevel. and Housing Authority, chmn., 2000-02; pres. ODU Ednl. Found., 2003—; active numerous other community orgns. Named Outstanding Young Man, Norfolk Jaycees; recipient Disting. Alumni award Old Dominion U., Dominion Vol. of Yr. award, 1993. Mem. ABA (mem. various sects.), Fed. Bar Assn. (pres. Tidewater chpt. 1980-81), Am. Bd. Trial Advocates, Va. Assn. Def. Lawyers, Va. Bar Assn., Va. Trial Lawyers Assn., Norfolk-Portsmouth Bar Assn., Def. Rsch. Inst., Internat. Assn. Def. Counsel (nat. trial acad. faculty 1997), Assn. Def. Attys., Def. Rsch. Inst., Old Dominion U. Alumni Assn. (bd. dirs. 1978-83), Old Dominion U. Ednl. Found. (bd. dirs. 1987—, sec. 2000-02, pres. 2003—), Norfolk C. of C. (chmn. downtown devel. com. 1980-81), James Kent Am. Inn of Ct. (master). Avocations: basketball, tennis, gardening. Office: Willcox & Savage PC One Commercial Place Norfolk VA 23510 Office Phone: 757-628-5573. Business E-Mail: bbishop@wilsav.com.

BISHOP, BUDD HARRIS, retired museum director; b. Canton, Ga., Nov. 1, 1936; s. James M. and Mary E. (Ponder) B.; m. Julia Crowder, Nov. 30, 1968. AB, Shorter Coll., Rome, Ga., 1958; M.F.A., U. Ga., 1960; student, Arts Adminstrn. Inst. Harvard, 1970. Instr. art Ensworth Sch., Nashville, 1961-63; dir. creative services Transit Advt. Assn., N.Y.C., 1964-66; dir. Hunter Mus. of Art, Chattanooga, 1966-76, Columbus (Ohio) Mus. Art, 1976-87, Samuel P. Harn Mus. Art, U. Fla., Gainesville, 1987-98, dir. emeritus. Vis. lectr. Vanderbilt U., 1962; past pres. bd. Intermuseum Conservation Lab., Oberlin, Ohio Past trustee Fla. Arts Celebration, Gainesville; mem. Gainesville Art in Pub. Places Trust; mem. faculty Ctr. for Arts and Pub. Policy; bd. dirs. Fla. Assn. Mus. Found., Inc.; mem. nat. adv. bd. Philharm. Ctr. for Arts, Naples, Fla.; trustee Hist. Rugby, Inc., Tenn.; bd. dirs. Cordell Hull Mus. and Bhplace; pres. Livingston-Overton County C. of C. Recipient gov.'s award Tenn. Art Commn., 1971, 73, Alumni Arts achievement award Shorter Coll., 1979, arts leadership award Columbus Day, 1986, Person of Yr. award in arts Gainesville Sun, 1995, Lifetime Achievement Mus. Svc. award Fla. Assn. Mus., 1997. Mem. Am. Assn. Museums, Assn. Art Mus. Dirs. (past trustee), Southeastern Museums Conf. (James R. Short award 1998), Fla. Art Mus. Dirs. Assn. (Lifetime Achievement award 1998). Office Phone: 931-823-1106.

BISHOP, C. DIANE, state agency administrator, educator; b. Elmhurst, Ill., Nov. 23, 1943; d. Louis William and Constance Oleta (Mears) B. BS in Maths., U. Ariz., 1965, MS in Maths., MEd in Secondary Edn., 1972. Lic. secondary educator. Tchr. math. Tucson Unified Sch. Dist., 1966-86, mem. curriculum council, 1985-86, mem. maths. curriculum task teams, 1983-86; state supt. of pub. instrn. State of Ariz., 1987-95, gov.'s policy advisor for edn., 1995-97, dir. gov.'s office workforce devel. policy, 1996-2000; asst. dep. dir. Ariz. Dept. Commerce, 1997-2000; exec. dir. Gov.'s Strategic Partnership for Econ. Devel., 1997—2002; pres. The Vandegrift Inst., 2000—; exec. dir. Maricopa Health Found., 2002—; mem. bd. dirs. Ariz. Bioindustry, 1997—, sec., 2000—. Mem. assoc. faculty Pima C.C., Tucson, 1974-84; adj. lectr. U. Ariz., 1983, 85; mem. math. scis. edn. bd. NRC, 1987-90, mem. new standards project governing bd., 1991; dir. adv. bd. sci. and engring. ednl. panel, NSF; mem. adv. bd. for arts edn. Nat. Endowment for Arts. Active Ariz. State Bd. Edn., 1984-95, chmn. quality edn. commn., 1986-87, chmn. tchr. crt. subcom., 1984-95, mem. outcomes based edn. adv. com., 1986-87, liaison bd. dirs. essential skills subcom., 1985-87, gifted edn. com. liaison, 1985-87; mem. Ariz. State Bd. Regents, 1987-95, com. on preparing for U. Ariz., 1983, HS task force, 1984-85, bd. Ariz. State Community Coll., 1987-95, Ariz. Joint Legis. Com. on Revenues and Expenditures, 1989, Ariz. Joint Legis. Com. on Goals for Ednl. Excellence, 1987-89, Gov.'s Task Force on Ednl. Reform, 1991, Ariz. Bd. Regents Commn. on Higher Edn., 1992, governing bd. Phoenix Union HS Dist., 2005—, Great Hearts Prep. (bd. acad. dirs., 2005-), Friends of Animal Care & Control (bd. dirs., 2005-), corp. bd. dirs. Great Hearts Preparatory Acad.; gov. bd. mem. Phoenix Union H.S. Dist., 2005-; bd. dir. Friends of Animal Care and Control. Woodrow Wilson fellow Princeton U., summer 1984; recipient Presdl. Award for Excellence in Teaching of Maths., 1983, Ariz. Citation of Merit, 1984, Maths. Teaching award Nat. Sci. Research Soc., 1984, Distinction in Edn. award Flinn Found., 1986; named Maths. Tchr. of Yr. Ariz. Council of Engring. and Sci. Assns., 1984, named One of Top Ten Most Influential Persons in Ariz. in Field of Tech., 1998. Mem. AAUW, NEA, Nat. Coun. Tchrs. Math., Coun. Chief State Sch. Officers, Women Execs. in State Govt. (bd. dirs. 1993), Ariz. Assn. Tchrs. Math., Women Maths. Edn., Math. Assn. Am., Ednl. Commn. of the States (steering com.), Nat. Endowment Arts (adv. bd. for arts edn.), Nat. Forum Excellence Edn., Nat. Honors Workshop, Ariz. Bioindustry Assn. (bd. dirs. 1997—, sec. 2000—), Phi Delta Kappa. Republican.

BISHOP, CHARLES EDWIN, academic administrator, economist, educator; b. Campobello, S.C., June 8, 1921; s. Fred and Hattie Bess (Wall) B.; m. Lee N., June 1, 2002; children from a previous marriage: Susan Ann, Mary Catherine, Charles Edwin. BS, Berea Coll., 1946; MS, U. Ky., 1948; PhD (Farm Found. fellow 1948-49), U. Chgo., 1952. Research asst. agrl. econs. U. Ky., 1947-48; research assoc. econs. U. Chgo., 1949-50; mem. faculty N.C. State U., 1950-70, prof. agrl. econs., 1956-70, head dept. agrl. econs., 1957-65, head dept. econs., 1965-66, William N. Reynolds Disting. prof., 1957-70; v.p. U. N.C., Chapel Hill, 1966-70; exec. dir. Agrl. Policy Inst., 1960-66; chancellor U. Md., College Park, 1970-74; pres. U. Ark., Fayetteville, 1974-80, U. Houston System, 1980-86. Vis. prof. Grad. Sch. Bus., U. Va., 1961-63; cons. Universidad Agraria, Lima, Peru, 1961-65; mem. Nat. Com. Agrl. Policy, Nat. Planning Assn., 1958-70; agrl. bd. Nat. Acad. Scis., 1963-68; sci. adv. com. to sec. agr., 1962-68; mem. Nat. Manpower Adv. Com., 1962-68; exec. dir. Pres. Johnson's Nat. Adv. Com. on Rural Poverty, 1966-67; mem. food adv. com. Pres. Nixon's Cost of Living Council, 1972; mem. Pres. Carter's adv. com. White House Conf. on Balanced Nat. Growth and Econ. Devel., 1978 Co-author: Introduction to Agricultural Economic Analysis, 1958. Mem. com. on vet. med. edn. So. Regional Edn. Bd., 1974; trustee Farm Found., 1968-78; bd. dirs. Winthrop Rockefeller Found., 1975-78, Resources for the Future, 1976-90, chmn., 1987-90; co-chmn. bd. Nat. Rural Ctr., 1975-79; mem. N.C. Rural Econ. Devel. Ctr., 1986-96, chmn., 1991-96; mem. Pres. Carter's Commn. on Agenda for Eighties, 1980; bd. dirs. Houston Industries, 1984-92. Sr. fellow M.D.C., 1991-2000. Fellow Am. Agrl. Econ. Assn. (pres. 1967-68); mem. Internat. Assn. Agrl. Econs., Commn. on Cen. European Econ. Devel., Alpha Zeta, Phi Kappa Phi, Gamma Sigma Delta.

BISHOP, CHARLES JOSEPH, manufacturing executive; b. Gary, Ind., June 22, 1941; s. Charles K. and Angela (Marich) Yelusich; m. Yvonne M. Stazinski, June 8, 1963; children: Stephen, Scott. BS, Purdue U., 1963; PhD, U. Wash., 1969. Mgr. advanced energy systems Boeing Co., Seattle, 1969-77; mgr. systems devel. Solar Energy Research Inst., Denver, 1977-81; v.p. tech. A.O. Smith Corp., Milw., 1981—. Mem. adv. bd. S.W. Wis. Rsch. Ctr., Milw., 1987; bd. dirs. Indsl. Rsch. Inst., 1989-92, v.p., 1993, pres. 1995-96. Contbr. articles to profl. jours. Treas. Cedarburg Comty. Scholarship Com., Wis., 1985-91; mem. indsl. liaison coun. U. Wis., Milw., 1985—, U. Wis. Coll. Engring., Madison, 1990-95; mem. Gov.'s Coun. on Sci. and Tech., 1992-94; mem. nat. coun. Alverno Coll. Recipient Cert. Recognition NASA, 1975. Mem.: Milw. Athletic Club. Republican. Roman Catholic. Avocations: fishing, travel, golf. Office: A O Smith Corp-Corp Tech 12100 W Park Pl Milwaukee WI 53224-3029

BISHOP, DAVID FULTON, library administrator; b. NYC, Nov. 23, 1937; s. Donald McLean and Clara (Zelley) B.; m. Nancy Driscoll, May 15, 1959; children: Karen McLean, Michael David. MusB, U. Rochester, 1959, postgrad., 1959-60; MS in Library Sci., Cath. U. Am., 1964; postgrad., U. Md., 1967-73. Head serials dept. U. Md. Libraries, College Park, 1967-69, coordinator tech. services, 1969-70, head systems, 1970-73; head cataloger U. Chgo. Libraries, 1973-75, asst. dir. tech. services, 1975-79; dir. libraries U. Ga., Athens, 1979-87; prof., univ. librarian U. Ill., Urbana, 1987-92; univ. libr. Northwestern U., Evanston, Ill., 1992—. Trustee Ednl. Comms. (EDUCOM), Washington, 1988-94; bd. dirs. Ctr. for Rsch. Librs., 1992-99; vice-chmn. bd. dirs. 1996-97, chmn. bd. dirs., 1997-98; bd. dirs. North Suburban Libr. System, 2000—, treas. bd. dirs., 2003—. Mem. ALA, INFORMA (steering com. 1989-93), Assn. Coll. and Rsch. Librs., Coun. on Libr. Resources (proposal rev. com. 1991-95), Coalition for Networked Info. (steering com. 1992-98). Home: 2518 Indian Ridge Dr Glenview IL 60026-1032 Office: Northwestern U Librs Evanston IL 60201 E-mail: dbishop@northwestern.edu.

BISHOP, ELIZABETH ANN, customs analyst; b. Indpls., Sept. 13, 1979; d. James Donald and Jamie Sue Romans; m. Ross Alexander Bishop, Jan. 27, 1982; children: Ross Alexander Jr., Brianna Elizabeth Jackson, Autumn Makenzy Jackson. Student in bus. and human resources, UCLA, 2000—02; student in bus., Ind. U., Indpls., 1996—2005. Paralegal, exec. asst. Thomson, Indpls., 1998—2002, buyer, 2002—04, customs analyst, 2004—. Bd. dirs. Ind. Sudden Infant Death Syndrome Ctr., Indpls. Mem. Ind. SIDS Ctr., Indianapolis, Ind., 2002—05. Mem.: Nat. Assn. Fgn. Trade Zones (licentiate). Office: Thomson 10330 N Meridian St Indianapolis IN 46290 Office Phone: 317-390-2367. Home Fax: 317-587-9088; Office Fax: 317-587-9088. Personal E-mail: elizabeth.bishop@thomson.net.

BISHOP, ELIZABETH SHREVE, psychologist; b. Ann Arbor, Mich., Nov. 18, 1951; d. William Warner Jr. and Mary Fairfax (Shreve) B. AB, U. Mich., 1972; MA, Ohio State U., 1973, PhD, 1976. Lic. psychologist Mich. Psychologist Franklin County Program for the Mentally Retarded, Columbus, Ohio, 1974, WC Mental Health, Willmar, Minn., 1977-83; chief psychologist Battle Creek (Mich.) Child Guidance Ctr., 1981; dir. psychometrics Meridian Profl. Psychol. Cons., East Lansing, Mich., 1983-92; pres. Arbor Psychol. Cons., Ann Arbor, 1991—. Trainer Girl Scouts U.S.A., 1993—, troop leader, 1968—69, 1973—74, 1980—82, 1984—86; deacon 1st Congl. Ch., 1996—2000, 2002—. Assoc. Univ. London Inst. Edn., 1976. Mem. APA, AAUW, LWV (Willmar v.p. 1979-81), Mich. Psychol. Assn., Mich. Women Psychologists (treas. 2002-), Coun. for Exceptional Children (local pres. 1977-78), Internat. Coun. Psychologists (bd. dirs. 1999-2002), Internat. Sch. Psychology Assn. Avocations: reading, travel, birdwatching, photography, music. Home: 1612 Morton Ave Ann Arbor MI 48104-4441 Office: Arbor Psychol Cons 1565 Eastover Pl Ann Arbor MI 48104-6316 Office Phone: 734-741-8844. Personal E-mail: arborpsych@sbcglobal.net.

BISHOP, GENE HERBERT, corporate financial executive; b. Forest, Miss., May 3, 1930; s. Herbert Eugene and Lavonne (Little) B.; m. Kathy S. Bishop, May 27, 1983. BBA, U. Miss., Oxford, 1952. With First Nat. Bank, Dallas, 1954-69, sr. v.p., chmn. sr. loan com., 1963-68, exec. v.p., 1968-69; pres., dir. SBIC subs. First Dallas Capital Corp.; pres. Lomas & Nettleton Fin. Corp., Dallas, 1969-75, Lomas & Nettleton Mortgage Investors, Dallas, 1969-75; chmn., CEO Merc. Nat. Bank, Dallas, 1975-81, MCorp., Dallas, 1975-90; vice-chmn., CFO Lomas Fin. Corp., 1990-91; pres., COO Lomas Mortgage USA, Dallas, 1990-91; chmn., CEO Life Ptnrs. Group, Inc., Dallas, 1991-94, also bd. dirs. Bd. dirs. First Acceptance Corp.; adv. dir. Tolleson Wealth Mgmt. Bd. dirs. State Fair Tex., Dallas; trustee Children's Med. Ctr., Dallas Meth. Hosps. Found.; mem. Dallas Citizens Coun. 1st lt. USAF, 1952-54. Mem. Terpsichorean Club, Idlewild Club, Brook Hollow Golf Club, Eldorado Country Club, Vintage Club, Dallas Country Club. Methodist. Office: 5500 Preston Rd Ste 250 Dallas TX 75205-2699

BISHOP, GEORGE FRANKLIN, political scientist, educator; b. New Haven, July 26, 1942; s. George Elwood and Mary Bridget (Trant) B.; m. Pama Mitchell, July 15, 1995; 1 child, Kristina. BS in Psychology, Mich. State U., 1966, MA, 1969, PhD, 1973. Instr. multidisciplinary social sci. program Mich. State U., East Lansing, 1972-73; asst. prof. dept. sociology and anthropology U. Notre Dame, Ind., 1973-75; dir. Greater Cin. Survey, 1981-95; rsch. assoc. behavioral sci. lab U. Cin., 1975-77, sr. rsch. assoc. Inst. for Policy Rsch., 1981-93, dir. behavioral scis. lab., 1994-95, assoc. prof. polit. sci., 1982-87, prof., 1987—, dir. grad. cert. program in pub. opinion and survey rsch., 1999—; dir. Internet Pub. Opinion Lab. Univ. Cin., 2000—. Assoc. dir. Ohio Poll, 1981-95; guest prof. Zentrum für Umfragen, Methoden und Analysen, Mannheim, Germany, 1985, 90, 92; fellow Ctr. for Study of Dem. Citizenship, Dept. Polit. Sci., U. Cin., 1992-99, fellow Inst. for Data Scis., 1996-98; summer inst. faculty Survey Rsch. Ctr., Inst. for Social Rsch., U. Mich., summer 1993; sr. cons. Burke Mktg. Rsch., Inc., Cin., 1996-98. Author: The Illusion of Public Opinion, 2005; sr. editor The Presdl. Debates: Media, Electoral and Policy Perspectives, 1978; sr. author various articles in profl. jours.; mem. editl. bd. Pub. Opinion Quar., 1987-90, Free Inquiry, 1999—; mem. editl. adv. bd. Pub. Perspective, 2000—03. Served with U.S. Army N.G., 1960-63. NSF grantee, 1977-84. Mem. AAUP (Maita Levine Svc. award 2002), Midwest Assn. Pub. Opinion Rsch. (pres. 1977-78, Mapor fellow Disting. Scholarship in pub. opinion rsch. 1994), Am. Assn. Pub. Opinion Rsch., Am. Polit. Sci. Assn., World Assn. Pub. Opinion Rsch. (treas. 1983-85). Home: 825 Dunore Rd Cincinnati OH 45220-1416 Office: U Cin Cincinnati OH 45221-0001 Business E-Mail: george.bishop@uc.edu.

BISHOP, KATHRYN ELIZABETH, film company executive, writer, realtor; b. Seattle, July 7, 1945; d. Wesley Thomas Bishop and Muriel (Robert) Leisher; divorced; 1 child, Zachary. BA, Wartburg Coll., 1966. Voice over talent Chgo. Bd. Edn. Radio Network, 1960-62; prodn. asst. Sta. CBS-TV, WBBM-TV, Chgo., 1961-63; disk jockey, engr., writer Sta. KWAR-FM, Waverly, Iowa, 1964-65; assoc. producer Bing Crosby Prodns. Inc., Chgo., 1966-69; producer Sedelmaier Films, Chgo., 1969-73; v.p., head prodn. Wakeford/Orloff Inc., L.A., 1977-78; founder, owner Stiles-Bishop Prodns. Inc., L.A., 1974—; co-founder, exec. prodr. The Colman Group Inc., L.A., 1982-87; co-founder, co-owner Rapport Films, Inc., Hollywood, Calif., 1987-92; feature film prodr., 1992—. Co-author: (screenplay) Millionaire's Club; screenwriter: Cinnamon Bear. Mem. TV Acad. Arts and Scis., Dirs. Guild Am. Avocations: pottery, sailing, skiing. Office: Stiles-Bishop Prodns Inc 12652 Killion St Valley Village CA 91607-1535 Office Phone: 818-423-1503. E-mail: kbishop@simple.net.

BISHOP, KIM IRENE, pharmaceutical consultant, psychopharmacologist; b. Williamsport, Pa., Nov. 12, 1960; arrived in Switzerland, 1996; d. Harold Dane and Irene (Pelletier) B. BA, Franklin and Marshall Coll., 1982; MS, Villanova (Pa.) U., 1986; PhD, U. London, 1995; DipPM, U. Basel, 2001. Coord. clin. rsch. Scheie Eye Inst. U. Pa., Phila., 1984-88; sr. clin. rsch. assoc. Allergan Pharms., Irvine, Calif., 1988-90; cons. Clin. Trials Rsch. Ltd., Maidenhead, Eng., 1994; sr. drug safety scientist Ciba Geigy, Basel, Switzerland, 1996-97; global projects liaison mgr. Novartis, Basel, Switzerland, 1997-99; founder, prin. cons. Global Pharma Cons., Basel, 1999—, cons. clin. devel. and psychopharm. svcs. Contbr. articles to profl. jours. Alumni regional amb. Villanova U. Overseas rsch. scholar Brit. com. for Vice Chancellors and Prins., London, 1991-94; European Behavioral Pharmacology Soc. scholar, 1994; scholar Brit. Assn. Psychopharmacology Bursary, Eng., 1993, 94. Mem. APA, INS, ECNP, Am. Acad. Neurology, Drug Info. Assn., Royal Soc. Medicine. Avocations: skiing, scuba diving, dance, horseback riding, bicycling. Office Phone: 570-546-7833. E-mail: kib@globalpharmaconsultancy.com, gpc@balcab.ch.

BISHOP, LEO KENNETH, clergyman, educator; b. Britton, Okla., Oct. 11, 1911; s. Luther and Edith (Scovill) B.; m. Pauline T. Shamburg, Sept. 15, 1935; 1 dau., Linda Paulette. AB, Phillips U., 1932, LHD, 1958; MA, Columbia U., 1944; MBA, U. Chgo., 1957; LittD, Kansas City Coll. Osteopathy and Surgery, 1964. Assoc. min. Univ. Place Ch., Oklahoma City, 1932-35; min. First Ch., Paducah, Ky., 1935-41, Ctrl. Ch., Des Moines, 1941-45; dir. St. Louis office NCCJ, 1945-48, v.p., dir. ctrl. divsn. Chgo., 1949-63; dir. pub. affairs People-to-People, Kansas City, Mo., 1963-66; v.p. Chgo. Coll. Osteopathy, 1966-72; pres. Bishop Enterprises, Colorado Springs, Colo., 1972—, also lectr. Contbr. religious and ednl. jours.; Developed: radio series Storm Warning; TV series The Other Guy, 1954. Cons. Cmty. Social Planning Coun., Mayor's Race Rels. Com., YMCA, St. Louis; Am. del. Conf. World Brotherhood, Paris, 1950; bd. dirs. Am. Heritage Found. Recipient Paducah Jr. C. of C. Most Useful Citizen award, 1937, Disting. Svc. award Dore Miller Found., 1958, Freedom Found. of Valley Forge award, 1961; named Chicagoan of Year, 1960. Mem.: Rotary, Union League, Winter Night. Home and Office: Montara Meadows A342 3150 E Tropicana Ave Las Vegas NV 89121

BISHOP, MICHAEL, writer; Writer-in-residence LaGrange Coll., 1997—. Author: A Funeral for the Eyes of Fire, 1975, And Strange at Ecbatan the Trees, 1976, A Little Knowledge, 1977, Stolen Faces, 1977, Catacomb Years, 1979, Transfigurations, 1979, Eyes of Fire, 1980, No Enemy But Time, 1982 (Nebula award), Blooded on Arachne, 1982, Who Made Stevie Crye?, 1984, One Winter in Eden, 1984, Ancient of Days, 1985, Close Encounters with the Deity, 1986, Philip K. Dick is Dead, Alas, 1987, Unicorn Mountain, 1988 (Mythopoeic Fantasy awrd for best novel, 1988), Emphatically Not SF, Almost, 1990, Count Geiger's Blues, 1992, Brittle Innings, 1994 (Locus award for best fantasy novel, 1994), At The City Limits of Fate, 1996, Blue Kansas Sky, 2000, Brighten to Incandescence: 17 Short Stories, 2003; author: (with Ian Watson) (novels) Under Heaven's Bridge, 1981; author: (collection of poems) Time Pieces, 2000; co-author (with Paul Di Filippo under penname Philip Lawson): Would It Kill You to Smile?, 1998, Muskrat Courage, 2000; editor: 3 Nebula award anthologies (Nebula awards 23, 1988, Nebula awards 24, 1990, Nebula awards 25, 1991), (anthology) Light Years and Dark, 1984 (Locus award Best Anthology, 1984); co-editor (with Ian Watson): Changes, 1983. Home and Office: PO Box 646 Pine Mountain GA 31822-0646 E-mail: mlbishop@juno.com.

BISHOP, MICHAEL D., emergency physician; b. Anna, Ill., Feb. 10, 1945; m. Mary Susan Wilkens, Dec. 28, 1965; children: Amy Elizabeth, Amanda Marie. AB, GreenvilleColl., 1967; MD, U. Ill., 1971. Diplomate Am. Bd. Emergency Medicine (oral examiner 1980—, dir. 1988-96, mem. exec. com. 1990-95, mem. several bd. coms., sec.-treas. 1991-92, pres.-elect 1992-93, pres. 1993-94). Intern Meth. Hosp. Dallas, 1971-72; emergency physician Bloomington (Ind.) Hosp., 1972—, Morgan County Meml. Hosp., Martinsville, Ind., 1978—, Fayette Meml. Hosp., Connersville, Ind., 1989—, Jackson County Meml. Hosp., Seymour, Ind., 1989—; gen. dir. Immediate Care Ctrs. in Ind., various cities, 1981—; clin. assoc. prof. med. scis. Ind. U., Bloomington, 1980—; pres., CEO Unity Physician Group P.C., Bloomington, Ind., 1971—. Bd. trustee, Sunday sch. tchr. Ellettsville (Ind.) Christian Ch.; bd. dirs. Peoples State Bank, Ellettsville; bd. dirs., sec. Ellettsville Bancshares, Ellettsville Elem. Sch. Bldg. Corp. Fellow Am. Coll. Emergency Physicians (charter, pres. Ind. chpt. 1979-80, nat. councillor 1976-81, 83, mem. nat. multi-hosp./multi-state blue ribbon task force 1981, mem. nat. ins. com. 1976-77, mem. coun. long-range planning com. 1981-82, mem. coun. steering com. 1983-85, chmn. medicare task force 1984-86, chmn. task force on physician payment reform 1986-88, mem. govt. affairs com. 1983-88, 89-93, chmn. 1984-87, 89-93, mem. nat. emergency medicine polit. action com. bd. trustees 1984-88, 89-93, chmn. 1987, 89-93, mem. fin. com. 1987-93, James D. Mills Outstanding Contbn. to Emergency Medicine award 1990, mem. awards com. 1991-93, mem. reimbursement com. 1992—, dir. 1995—, lectr. in field), AHA (mem. Ind. affil. faculty, ACLS), Am. Coll. Physician Execs., Soc. Acad. Emergency Medicine, Christian Med. Dental Soc., Ind. State Med. Assn., Med. Group Mgmt. Assn., Owen Monroe County Med. Soc. Office: Unity Physician Group PC 1155 W 3rd St Bloomington IN 47404-5016

BISHOP, OLIVER RICHARD, retired state official; b. El Dorado, Kans., Dec. 5, 1928; s. Oliver Harrison and Hazel May (Garabrandt) B.; m. Fuyo Oyake, Aug. 14, 1959; children: Lisa Naomi, Rachel Eri. BS in Pub. Adminstrn. magna cum laude, U. So. Calif., 1963; MS in Econs cum laude, U. S.D., 1971. Cert. planner, office automation profl., assisted housing mgr. Commd. 2d lt. USAF, 1956, advanced through grades to maj., 1966, ret., 1971; city mgr. City of Slater, Mo., 1971-73, City of Highland, Ill., 1973-76, City of Napoleon, Ohio, 1976-77; village mgr. Village of Westmont, Ill., 1977-85; revenue and fiscal advisor State of Ill., Chgo., 1985-99. Planning cons. Bishop's Cons. Services, Westmont, Ill., 1985—. Precinct committeeman Rep. Ctrl. com., Dupage County, Ill., 1987-88; candidate for County Bd. Dupage County Dist. 3, 1988; com. chmn. Westmont Planning Commn., 1986-95, 97-2004; bd. dirs. T.E.A.C.H., Inc., I-Care, Inc. Mem.: Inst. Cert Planners, Am. Planning Assn., Intertel, Mensa, Shriners, Masons, Elks, Omicron Delta Epsilon (pres. Lambda chpt.), Pi Sigma Alpha. Avocations: stamp collecting/philately, photography. Personal E-mail: obishop@aol.com.

BISHOP, PAUL LESLIE, civil and environmental engineering educator, environmental engineering consultant; b. Hyannis, Mass., Nov. 27, 1945; s. Paul Leslie and Victoria (Caisse) B.; m. Pamela Joan Neher, Mar. 30, 1949; children: Andrew Paul, Amanda Marie. BSCE, Northeastern U., 1968; MS in Environ. Engring., Purdue U., 1970, PhD, 1972. Registered profl. engr., N.H.; diplomate Am. Acad. Environ. Engrs. Environ. engr. Metcalf & Eddy, Inc., Boston, 1968; sanitarian Tippecanoe County, Ind., 1971-72; asst. prof. U. N.H., Durham, 1972-76, assoc. prof., chmn. dept. civil engring., 1976-82, prof. civil engring., 1982-87; environ. engring. cons. Durham, 1972-88; William Thomas prof., head dept. civil and environ. engring. U. Cin., 1988-93, Schneider prof. environ. engring., 1993—, assoc. dean engring. for rsch., 2000—, prof. environ. health, 2004—. Vis. prof. Heriot-Watt U., Scotland, 1980, Tech. U. Denmark, Lyngby, 1986-87. Author: Marine Pollution and Its Control, 1983, Pollution Prevention: Fundamentals and Practice, 2000; co-author: Stabilization/Solidification, 1994, Biofilms in Wastewater Treatment, An Interdisciplinary Approach; contbr. articles to profl. jours.; patentee in field. Bd. dirs. N.H. Solid Waste Mgmt. Bd., 1981-87, Lee Zoning Bd. Adjustment, N.H., 1981-86; chmn. Lee Planning Bd., 1975-80; mem. Durham/U. N.H. Sewer Policy Com., 1979-87, Gov.'s Task Force Waste Minimization, Ohio, 1989-92; mem. planning adv. com. Anderson Twp., Ohio, 1991-97, devel. adv. com., 1998-99. Faculty fellow ASTM, 1984; Grantee, NSF, EPA, NOAA, NIH, others. Mem. ASCE, Internat. Water Assn., Am. Acad. Environ. Engrs., Water Environ. Fedn., Assn. Environ. Engring. Profs. (pres. 1992-93), Sigma Xi. Democrat. Roman Catholic. Avocations: woodworking, reading, hiking. Business E-Mail: Paul.Bishop@uc.edu.

BISHOP, PENNY A, education educator, researcher; EdD, U. of Vt., 1995—98, MEd, 1994—95. Asst. prof. U. of Vt., Burlington, Vt., 2001—. Dir., mid. level tchr. edn. U. of Vt., Burlington, 2001—. Author: (book) The Power of Two: Partner Teams in Action. Treas. Vt. Assn. of Mid. Level Edn., 1998—2005. Office Phone: 802-656-3356.

BISHOP, REX L., management educator, department chairman; b. Findlay, Ohio; m. Audrey Whitlock Bishop; children: Jennifer Marie, Jason Edward. BA, Bowling Green State U., 1968, MEd, 1972; postgrad., Va. Poly. Inst. and State U., 1979. Camp dir. Youth Conservation Corps/Nat. Park Svc.; Upward Bound instr. Mary Washington Coll.; dir. coop. edn., acting dir. extended learning, acting divsn. chairperson arts, sci. and nursing, prof. bus. mgmt. and mktg. Germanna C.C., Locust Grove, Va., 1972—85; chair bus., econ., and legal studies Coll. So. Md., LaPlata, 1985—. Pres. Ea. Coun. Bus. Schs. and Programs; chair Assoc. Degree Commn. Assn. Collegiate Bus. Schs. and Programs, mem. at large, bd. dirs.; bd. dirs. Human Resources Assn. So. Md.; presenter in field. Contbr. articles to profl. jours. Chair edn. com. C. of C.; pres. Charles County Scholarship Fund, Inc.; chair Senatorial Scholarship Com.; bus. liaison King George Vocat. Adv. Coun.; unit commr. Boy Scouts Am.; v.p. King George Little League; bd. mem. King George Express AAU Basketball; dist. rep. King George Recreational League Football. Recipient Bus. Edn. Partnership award, Md. Bds. Edn. Assn. Office: Coll So Md PO Box 910 8730 Mitchell Rd La Plata MD 20646-0910 Office Phone: 301-934-7518. E-mail: rex.bishop@csmd.edu.

BISHOP, RICHARD WOODROW, lawyer, writer; b. Wayland, Mass., July 16, 1916; s. Warren Langmard and Edna Florella (Felch) Bishop; m. Ida Finch, Sept. 17, 1938; children: Richard L., Gregory F., Jill Rubalcaba. LLB, Boston U., 1938. Bar: Mass. 1938, Fed. 1940, U.S. Supreme Ct. 1946. Ptnr. Bishop, Ahern & Michienzi, Medford, Mass., 1938—87, of counsel, 1987—. Author: Stepping Stones to Flight, 1954, From Kite to Kitty Hawk, 1956, Prima Facie Case 4 vols., 1957—. Vestry and clk. Grace Episcopal Ch., Medford; pres. Medford (Mass.) C. of C., 1965; trustee and clk. Lawrence Meml. Hosp.; trustee Hallmark Health, Melrose. Capt. JAG U.S. Army, 1945—46. Mem.: Rotary (pres. Medford chpt. 1967). Republican. Episcopalian. Avocations: photography, stamp collecting/philately. Office: Bishop, Ahern & Michienzi 1 Shipyard Way Medford MA 02155 Home: Apt 5K 5 Stonehill Dr Stoneham MA 02180 Office Phone: 781-396-0055. E-mail: richard.w.bishop@aol.com.

BISHOP, ROB, congressman; b. Kaysville, UT, July 13, 1951; m. Jeralynn Hansen; 5 children. BA, U. Utah. Chmn. Utah State Rep. Party, 1997—2002; mem. U.S. Ho. Reps. from 1st Utah dist., 2003—. Republican. Office: 124 Cannon Ho Office Bldg Washington DC 20515-4401

BISHOP, ROBERT CALVIN, pharmaceutical company executive; b. L.A., Jan. 13, 1943; s. Harold Eames and Mary Frances (Allen) B.; m. Susan Elizabeth Ogden, Nov. 18, 1966; children: John Ogden, James Allen, Bryan Hutchings. AB in Psychology, U. So. Calif., 1966, PhD in Biochemistry, 1976; MBA, U. Miami, 1981. Rsch. assoc. Hyland Labs., Glendale, Calif., 1966-69; cons. L.A., 1970-75; program mgr. Am. Hosp. Supply Corp., Glendale, 1976-78, rsch. dir. Dade div. Miami, Fla., 1978-81, v.p. Evanston, Ill., 1981-85; pres. Allergan Med. Optics, Irvine, Calif., 1986-88; sr. v.p. Allergan Inc., Irvine, 1989; pres. Allergan Pharmaceuticals, Irvine, 1989-91, Allergan Therapeutics Group, 1991-92; pres., CEO, dir. AutoImmune, Inc., Pasadena, Calif., 1992—. Bd. dirs. MFS/Sun Life Series Trust & Compass Accts., Caliper Life Scis. Inc., Optobionics Corp., Millipore Corp. Contbr. articles to profl. jours.; patentee in field. Bd. dirs. Eye Bank Assn. Am., Washington, 1988-90, Amyotropic Lateral Sclerosis Assn., LA, 1984-87. With USAR, 1963—69. Mem. Annandale Golf Club (Pasadena, Calif.). Republican. Presbyterian. Avocation: golf. Home: 1199 Madia St Pasadena CA 91103-1961 Office: AutoImmune Inc 1199 Madia St Pasadena CA 91103

BISHOP, ROBERT LYLE, economist, educator; b. St. Louis, June 4, 1916; s. Lyle Austin and Helen (Craden) B.; m. Joan Frances Fiss, Sept. 12, 1942 (dec.). AB, Harvard, 1937, MA, 1942, PhD, 1949; postgrad., Princeton, 1938-39. Instr. econs. Harvard, 1939-42; mem. faculty Mass. Inst. Tech., 1942—, successively instr., asst. prof., assoc. prof., 1942-57, prof. econs., 1957-86, prof. econs. emeritus, 1986—, head dept. econs. and social sci., 1958-65; dean Sch. Humanities and Social Scis., 1964-73. Vis. lectr. Harvard; vis. prof. Brandeis U. Mem. Am. Econ. Assn., Econometric Soc., Am. Acad. Arts and Scis., Phi Beta Kappa. Home: 27 Amherst Rd Wellesley MA 02482-6611

BISHOP, ROBERT R., computer company executive; BS in Math. Physics with honors, U. Adelaide; MS, NYU. Sr. exec. Digital Equip. Corp., 1968—82, Apollo Computer, Inc., 1982—86; pres. world trade corp. Silicon Graphics, Inc., 1986—95, non-executive chmn. bd., world trade corp., 1996—99, chmn., COO, 1995—, chmn. bd. dir., CEO, 1999—. Internat. adv. panel Multimedia Super Corridor, Malaysia; invited prof. Swiss Fed. Inst. Tech., Lausanne; adj. prof. Stockholm Sch. Econs.; lectr. U. St. Gallen, Wirtschafts Tech.; spkr. in field. Mem.: Govs. World Econ. Forum Info-.Techs., World Intellectual Property Orgn., Industry Adv. Commn., Swiss Acad. Engring. Scis. Office: Silicon Graphics Inc 1500 Crittenden Ln Mountain View CA 94043-2776 Office Phone: 650-960-1980. Office Fax: 650-961-0595.

BISHOP, SANFORD DIXON, JR., congressman, lawyer; b. Mobile, Ala., Feb. 4, 1947; s. Sanford and Minnie Bishop; m. Vivian Creighton. BA in Polit. Sci., Morehouse Coll., 1968; JD, Emory U., 1971. Ptnr. Bishop & Buckner, P.C., Columbus, Ga., 1972—92; mem. Ga. Ho. of Reps. from 94th Dist., 1977—90, Ga. State Senate, 1991—92, U.S. Congress from 2d Ga. Dist., 1993—, mem. appropriations com. Del. Dem. Nat. Conv. 1980, 84, 88. Named Man of the Yr. Men's Progressive Club Columbus, Ga., 1977, Black Georgian of the Yr., 1983, Most Influential Black Men in Ga.; recipient Outstanding Legis. award Ga. NOW, 1983-84, Legis. Svc. award, Ga. Mcpl. Assn., 1984, 86, Friend of the Children award Child Adv. Coalition, Disting. Eagle Scout award; Earl Warren fellow, 1971-72. Mem. ABA, Nat. Bar Assn., Ga. Bar Assn., Ala. Bar Assn., Am. Judicature Soc., Shriners, Masons (32 degree), Phi Delta Phi, Pi Sigma Alpha, Kappa Alpha Psi, Sigma Pi Phi. Democrat. Baptist. Office: US Ho of Reps 2429 Rayburn Ho Office Bldg Washington DC 20515-1002 also: Dist Office Albany Towers 235 W Roosevelt Ave Ste 216 Albany GA 31701-2374*

BISHOP, SID GLENWOOD, union official; b. Gladehill, Va., Nov. 11, 1923; s. Clarence Glenwood and Lillian Helen (Onks) B.; m. Patrice Frances Collier, Nov. 14, 2004. Grad., U.S. Naval Trade Sch., 1942; cert. in labor rels., Concord Coll., Athens, W.Va., 1961. Telegraph operator Virginian R.R., 1946-47, C & O R.R., 1947-62; local chmn. Order R.R. Telegraphers, 1960-62; gen. chmn. C & O-Virginian R.R.'s, 1962-68; 2d v.p. Transp-Communication Employees Union, St. Louis, 1968-69; v.p. transp. com. divsn. Brotherhood Ry. and Airline Clks., Rockville, Md., 1969-73, asst. internat. v.p., 1973—. Mem. subcom. Labor Rsch. Adv. Coun., Dept. Labor, 1975, mem. com. on productivity, tech., growth Bur. Labor Statistics, 1975-77. With USN, 1941-46. Mem. AFL-CIO, Can. Labor Congress, Hunting Hills Homeowners Assn., VFW, Chantilly Nat. Golf and Country Club, Elks, Masons, K.T., Shriners. Home and Office: 676 NE 28th Ave Okeechobee FL 34972-3323 Business E-Mail: bishlite@strato.net.

BISHOP, SIDNEY WILLARD, lawyer; b. Denver, Oct. 28, 1926; s. Sidney W. and Helen (Marihugh) B.; m. Betty Lou Dolan, May 10, 1947; children: Linda, Thomas, Nancy, Joan, Ann, Mary, Elizabeth, Sidney Willard III, Jane. BS, Regis U., Denver, 1949; JD, U. Denver, 1950. Bar: Colo. 1950, Calif. 1958. With January & Yegge, Denver, 1949-50; dep. dist. atty. Cheyenne County, Colo., 1951-56; pvt. practice Cheyenne Wells, Colo., 1950-56; with Prudential Ins. Co. Am., LA, 1956-61, 64-68, asst. counsel law dept., 1958-61, asst. gen. solicitor, 1964-66, dir. govt. rels., 1966-68; gen. counsel Am. Ins. Assn., NYC, 1968-70; with firm Svenson & Garvin, Van Nuys, Calif., 1970-73; sr. v.p., gen. counsel Beneficial Std. Life Ins. Co., 1973-91; of counsel Adams, Duque, LA, 1991-96, Beckman, Davis, Smith & Ruddy, LA, 1996—. Confidential asst. to postmaster gen. U.S., 1961, asst. postmaster gen. bur. facilities, 1962-63, dep. postmaster gen., 1963-64. So. Calif. vice chmn. Statewide Water Devel. Com., 1959-60. Served with USNR, 1944-46. Office: 11355 W Olympic Blvd Ste 300 Los Angeles CA 90064-1614

BISHOP, STEPHEN GRAY, physicist; b. York, Pa., Jan. 26, 1939; s. John Schwartz and Carrie (Gray) B.; m. Helene Barbara Evenson, July 6, 1963; children: Hans Stephen, Lars Michael. BA in Physics with honors, Gettysburg

Coll., 1960; PhD in Physics, Brown U., 1965. Postdoctoral rsch. assoc. physics Brown U., 1965-66; NAS-NRC postdoctoral rsch. assoc. Naval Rsch. Lab., Washington, 1966-68, rsch. physicist, supr., 1968-80, head semiconductor br., 1980-89; dir. Engring. Rsch. Ctr. Compound Semiconductor Electronics and Microelectronics Lab. U. Ill., Urbana-Champaign, 1989-2000, prof. elec. and computer engring., 1989—, dir. Ctr. Optoelectronics Sci. and Techs., 1994-98, assoc. v.p. for tech. and econ. devel., 2001—04. With Max Planck Inst. fur Festkorperforschung, Stuttgart, West Germany, 1973-74; mem. navy com. Amorphous Semiconductor Tech. Rev., 1974, navy inter-lab. com. on pers. adminstrn., 1985; rsch. scientist Royal Signals and Radar Establishment, Great Malvern, U.K., 1978-79; adj. prof. physics SUNY, Buffalo, 1984—, U. Utah, 1986—; mem. tech. rev. com. Joint Svcs. Electronics program, 1980-89, tech. adv. com. Ctr. for Compound Semiconductor Microelectronics, U. Ill., Urbana-Champaign; mem. ONR Univ. Rsch. Initiative Rev. Panel, 1986, external rev. panel Ctr. for Electronic and Electro-Optic Materials, SUNY, Buffalo, 1988; mem. NSF Site Visit Rev. Panel for materials rsch. lab., U. Ill., NSF panel on light wave technology, 1988, NSF panel on interface of optical devices and systems, 1989; vis. com. Sherman Fairchild Ctr. for Solid State Studies, Lehigh U., 1991—; mem. Nat. Adv. Com., URI-ARO Ctr. for High-Frequency Microelectronics, U. Mich., 1993; edit. bd. Semiconductor Sci. and Tech., Inst. of Physics, 1992. Editor: (with others) Optical Effects in Amorphous Semiconductors, 1984, Proceedings of the MRS Symposium on the Microscopic Identification of Electronic Defects in Semiconductors, 1985; author: (with others) Deep Centers in Semiconductors, 1985, Gallium Arsenide Technology, 1990; contbr. more than 200 articles to profl. jours. Patentee in field. Trustee Gettysburg Coll., 1992—. Recipient Disting. Alumni award Gettysburg Coll., 1990. Felow Am. Phys. Soc., AAAS, Optical Soc. Am.; mem. IEEE, Lasers and Electronics Soc., Materials Rsch. Soc., Phi Beta Kappa, Sigma Pi Sigma, Sigma Xi (Pure Sci. award 1977), Tau Beta Pi (UIUC Chapt., Eminent Engr. award 1993). Office: Coordinated Scis Lab 1308 W Main St Urbana IL 61801-2307 E-mail: sgbishop@uiuc.edu.

BISHOP, STEPHEN LEWIS, music educator; b. Campbellsville, Ky., June 21, 1982; s. Charles E. and Paula F. Bishop; m. Christina Michelle Milby, June 2, 2001; 1 child, Madison Noelle. MusB in Music Edn. cum laude, Campbellsville U., Ky., 2004. Music dir. Aetna Grove Baptist Ch., Summersville, Ky., 2002—; asst. dir. bands Taylor County Schs., Campbellsville, 2004—. Recipient Profl. Leadership award, Music Educators Nat. Conf., 2004. Republican. Baptist. Avocations: fishing, guitar, travel, basketball. Home: 894 Woodhill Rd Campbellsville KY 42718 Office: Taylor County High Sch 300 Ingram Ave Campbellsville KY 42718

BISHOP, SUE MARQUIS (INA SUE MARQUIS BISHOP), retired dean; b. Charleston, W.Va., Sept. 30, 1939; d. Harold Edwin and Ina Mabel (Walkup) Marquis; m. Randal Young Bishop, Feb. 27, 1960; children: Jon Marquis, Heather Suzanne. RN, Norton Infirmary Sch. Nursing, 1960; BSN, Murray State U., 1963; MSN, Ind. U., 1967, PhD, 1983. RN, Ky., Ind., Fla., N.C. Ind. staff nurse psychiatry Norton Infirmary, Louisville, 1960-61; head nurse obstetrics, nursing supr. Murray (Ky.) Gen. Hosp., 1961-62; primary care nurse, crisis counselor infirmary Murray State U., 1962-63; staff nurse, clin. instr. Madison (Ind.) State Hosp., 1963-65; instr. through assoc. prof. Ind. U. Sch. Nursing, Indpls., 1967-89, developer child/adolescent psychiat., mental health nursing program, 1982-83, chairperson grad. dept., 1983-89; prof., asst. dean Coll. of Nursing U. South Fla., Tampa, 1989-91; dean Coll. Nursing U. N.C., Charlotte, 1992-95, dean Coll. of Nursing and Health Professions, 1995—2004, dean Coll. Health and Human Svcs., 2002—04, dean emerita, 2004—; ret., 2004. Pvt. practice marital and family therapy, 1975-89; cons. in field. Founding editor-in-chief Jour. of Child and Adolescent Psychiatric and Mental Health Nursing, 1987-91; contbr. articles to profl. jours. Bd. dirs. Carolinas blood svcs. region ARC, 1997-2002, chmn. bd. dirs., 2000—. NIMH trainee Ind. U., 1965-67, USPHS profl. nurse trainee Ind. U., 1977-78; recipient Youth Advocacy award Ind. Advs. for Child Psychiat. Nursing, 1987, Disting. Svc. award Ind. U. Sch. Nursing Alumni Assn., 1989, Nat. Youth Advocacy award Advs. for Child Psychiat. Nursing, 1990, Disting. Alumni award Ind. U. sch. Edn., 2000. Fellow Am. Acad. Nursing; mem. ANA, Psychiat. Mental Health Nursing Coun., Soc. for Edn. and Rsch. in Psychiat. Mental Health Nursing (pres. 1988-90), Am. Assn. Marital and Family Therapy, So. Nursing Rsch. Soc., So. Piedmont Alzheimer's Assn. (bd. dirs. 1999-2000), New South Hospice of Charlotte and Lincoln County (bd. dirs. 1995—2004, chair 2002-04), Sigma Theta Tau.

BISHOP, TILMAN MALCOLM, retired state legislator; b. Colorado Springs, Jan. 1, 1933; m. Pat Bishop, 1952; 1 son, Barry Alan. BA, MA, U. No. Colo. Adminstr., dir. student svcs. Mesa State Coll., Grand Junction, Colo., 1962-94; mem., pres. pro tem Colo. Senate, 1971-99, ret., 1999. Bd. dirs. Rocky Mountain Pub. Broadcasting TV, Colo. Duck Stamp Commn. Mem. World series com. Nat. Jr. Coll. Baseball; elected commr. Mesa County, 2002—; trustee El Pomar Found.; mem selection com. Colo. Sports Hall of Fame. With U.S. Army. Mem. Elks, Lions. Republican. Methodist. Avocations: fishing, small game hunting. Home: 2255 Piazza Way Grand Junction CO 81506 E-mail: tilmanmb@bresnan.net.

BISHOP, TIMOTHY H., congressman; b. Southhampton, NY, June 1, 1950; m. Kathryn Bishop; children: Molly, Meghan. AB, Holy Cross Coll.; MPA, Long Island Univ., 1981. Provost L.I. U., Southampton, N.Y.; mem. U.S. Ho. Reps. from 1st N.Y. dist., 2003—. Democrat. Office: 1133 Longworth Ho Office Bldg Washington DC 20515-3201*

BISHOP, WILLIAM PETER, science administrator, management consultant, rancher; b. Lakewood, Ohio, Jan. 18, 1940; s. William Hall and Ethel Laverle (Evans) B.; m. Sarah Gilbert, Sept. 1, 1963. BA in Chemistry with honors (Nat. Merit scholar), Coll. Wooster, Ohio, 1962; PhD (NDEA fellow), Ohio State U., 1967. Resident research assoc. Ohio State U., 1967-69; mem. staff Sandia Labs., Albuquerque, 1969-75; head nuclear waste program NRC, Washington, 1975-78; dep. dir. environ. observation div. NASA, 1978-81, dep. dir. life scis. div., 1981-83; dep. asst. adminstr. satellites NOAA, 1983-85, acting asst. adminstr. satellites and info. services, 1985-87; v.p. SAIC, Washington, 1987-89; v.p. for rsch. Desert Rsch. Inst., Las Vegas, Nev., 1989-94; assigned to U.S. Dept. of Energy, 1995-99; pres. B-plus, Inc., Paonia, Colo., 1999—. Mem. Nat. Acad. Com. Earth Studies, 1989-91, Task Group on Priorities in Space Rsch., 1990-94; chair Adv. Commn. on Geoscis. NSF, 1994-97. Author articles in field. Trustee Keystone (Colo.) Ctr., 1986-95, Nev. Devel. Authority, 1989-95, Univ. Corp. for Atmospheric Rsch., 1991-97; bd. dirs. Opportunities Industrialization Ctrs., Albuquerque, 1974-75, Cave Rsch. Found., 1967-74; dir. Western Slope Environ. Resources Coun., 200-04. Recipient Meritorious Service award NRC, 1977; Spaceship Earth award NASA, 1981; Meritorious Service award U.S. Dept. Commerce, 1985, Spl. Act or Svc. awrad, U.S. Dept. Energy, 1999. Fellow Nat. Speleological Soc. (conservation editor bull. 1974-78), Am. Astron. Soc. (v.p. tech. 1987-88); mem. AAAS, Am. Geophys. Union, AIAA, Am. Meteorol. Soc., Am. Nuc. Soc., Sigma Xi, Phi Lambda Upsilon.

BISHOP, WILLIAM WADE, advertising executive; b. Mt. Vernon, N.Y., Apr. 17, 1939; s. Kenneth Farrington and Dorothea (Renz) B.; m. Jacqueline Kenton, May 21, 1966; children: William Jr., Christopher. BA, Ohio Wesleyan U., 1961. Account exec. Ogilvy & Mather, Grey, BBDO, N.Y.C., 1964-72; v.p. Ted Bates, N.Y.C., 1972-74; category mgr. Gen. Foods Corp., White Plains, NY, 1974-79; mng. dir. Mktg. Corp. Am., Westport, Conn., 1979-80; exec. v.p. MCA Advt., N.Y.C., 1980-84, pres., CEO, 1984-86, MCA Comm. Group, 1986-89; pres. Ally & Gargano, N.Y.C., 1986-89; chmn., CEO CHC Advt., 1989-92; CEO CHC Advt. and M.E.D. Comm., 1992—; pres., CEO Ryan Direct, Westport, 1992-94; dir. South Beach Beverages, 1995—; chmn., CEO Sierra Comm. Group, 1995-2001; COO South Beach Beverage Co., 1999-2001. Owner LI Lizards, Lacrosse; ptnr. Blue Buffalo Co., 2002, B Group, 2001—. Served with USMC, 1962-68. Mem. Salem Golf Club. Republican. Congregationalist. Avocations: lacrosse, golf. Office: B Group 444 Danbury Rd Wilton CT 06897-4065 Business E-Mail: wbishop@bluebuffalocompany.com.

BISHOP-GRAHAM, BARBARA, secondary school educator, journalist; b. Angwin, Calif., Apr. 22, 1941; d. Will Francis and Esther Clara (Blissérd) Bishop; children: Gregory Mark, Steven Bishop. BA in Journalism, BA in English, BA in Art History, BFA in Painting and Drawing, U. Hawaii, 1975; nat. cert. in journalism, Kans. State U., 1994; MA in Tech. Curriculum & Instrn., Calif. State U., Sacramento, 1999. Cert. tchr., Hawaii. Photography instr., art tchr. Hawaii Sch. for Girls, Honolulu, 1974-76; substitute tchr. English State Dept. Edn., Oahu, 1977-78; English and grammar instr. Hawaii Sch. for Bus., Honolulu, 1979-80; media dir., exec. asst., historian Oriental Treasures and Points West, Honolulu, 1981-82; legal asst. Goodsill, Anderson, Quinn, Honolulu, 1983-84; lang. arts and photography tchr. Lodi (Calif.) H.S., 1984-88, writing and lang. arts tchr., 1988-93, creative writing tchr., 1989-99, journalism adviser, 1993-95, lang. arts tchr., 1993—, Brit. lit. tchr., 1995—2001, tchr. rhetoric and European lit., 2001—03. Mem. curriculum coun. Lodi Unified Sch. Dist., 1989-92, 97-2000; liaison to PTSA Lodi H.S., 1991-92, mentor tchr., 1991-94; student literary mag. advisor Lodi H.S., 1989—. Sportswriter Oakland Tribune, 1957-60, Author Three Poems, 1998; contbr. articles to profl. publs. Fundraiser chmn. Big Bros. of Am., San Francisco, 1967; media dir. Clements (Calif.) Cmty. Cares, 1985-89. Recipient Edn. Contbn. award Masons 1988-92, 20th Century Achievement award Am. Biographical Inst., 1999; grantee Nat. Endowment of Arts, rsch. Japanese Lit. 1989; social rschr. grantee Brazil, U. So. Calif. grantee, 1992; grantee S. Joaquin County Office Edn., 1996-97; champion Hawaii State barrel racing, 1980. Mem. NEA, Calif. Tchrs. Assn. (Calif. state tchrs. coun. rep. 1996-97), Lodi Edn. Assn. (conf. fund chair 1989-97). Republican. Seventh-Day Adventist. Avocations: writing, dressage riding, growing roses. Office: Lodi HS 3 S Pacific Ave Lodi CA 95242-3020

BISHOPRIC, KARL, investment banker, real estate company executive, advertising executive; b. Greensboro, N.C., Jan. 5, 1925; s. James Robert Karl and Frances (Farrell) B.; m. Rose Anne Straub, Mar. 4, 1944 (div. Jan. 1972); children: Robert Lewis, James Nelson (dec.), Bruce Graham; m. Carmen Deruth Dunlop, May 26, 1973; stepchildren: Jannette Marie Eyles, Kathryn Ruth Engelhardt. BA, U. N.C., 1945. With Houck & Co., Roanoke, Miami, Va., Fla., 1946-54, pres. Miami, Fla., 1948-54, Bishopric-Green-Fielden, Inc., Miami, N.Y.C., 1954-68, chmn. bd., 1968-73, Lando-Bishopric, Inc., 1973-74; chmn., dir. Advt. & Marketing Internat. Network, Inc., 1972-74; pres. Miami Nat. Bank, 1974-75; assoc. Oscar E. Dooly Assos., Inc., 1974-76; prin. 1st Equity Corp. of Fla., 1976-2000; pres. 1st Equity Properties, Inc., 1976-2000; v.p., dir. Fundamental Mgmt. Corp., 1986-89; pres. Swiss Atlantic Corp., 1999-2000; prin. William R. Hough & Co., Miami, 2001—04; fin. cons. RBC Dain Rauscher, 2004, Adcock Fin. Group, Tampa, Fla., 2005—. Pres. United Fund Dade County, 1967-68, trustee, 1963-; chmn. Port Action Com., 1969-71; bd. dirs. Community TV Found. S. Fla., 1965-67, v.p., 1969-72; mem. citizens bd. U. Miami, 1968-, pres. citizens bd., 1982-83, trustee, 1983-85; bd. dirs. Econ. Soc. S. Fla., 1969-73, Urban Coalition Greater Miami, 1968-72, Fla. Philharmonic Orchestra Found., 1992-98, Miami Lighthouse for the Blind, 1993-2004, chmn. fin. com., 1994-98; bd. dirs. Urban League Greater Miami, 1956-65, pres., 1956-60; chmn. budget leaders conf. United Funds and Community Councils Am., 1968; trustee Lowe Art Mus., 1973-86. Served to lt. (j.g.) USNR, 1944-46. Recipient Printer's Ink Silver medal. Mem. Greater Miami C. of C. (dir. 1971-74, trustee 1976—2003), Alpha Delta Sigma, Beta Theta Pi. Home: 600 Biltmore Way Coral Gables FL 33134-7541 Office: Adcock Fin Group 311 W Fletcher Ave Tampa FL 33612 Office Phone: 305-446-0356. Business E-Mail: karlbishopric@bellsouth.net.

BISIGNANO, FRANK, diversified financial services company executive; Sr. v.p. Shearson Lehman Bros., 1986—90; exec. v.p., chief consumer lending officer First Fidelity Bancorporation, 1990—94; with Smith Barney, 1994—2000; sr. exec. v.p., chief administrv. officer, Global Corp. and Investment Banking Group Citgroup, Inc., N.Y.C., 2000—. Bd. dirs. Depository Trust & Clearning Corp., The Options Clearing Corp., Euroclear. Office: Citigroup Inc 399 Park Ave New York NY 10043

BISKUPIC, STEVEN M., prosecutor, lawyer; b. Mar. 1961; BA, JD, Marquette U. Asst. U.S. atty. ea. dist. Wis. US Dept. Justice, 1989—2002, U.S. atty. ea. dist. Wis., 2002—. Office: 530 Fed Bldg 517 E Wisconsin Ave Milwaukee WI 53202

BISMUTH, PIERRE, artist; b. Paris, 1963; Writer (screenplays) Eternal Sunshine of the Spotless Mind, 2004 (Acad. Award for best original screenplay, 2005); exhibitions include (solo), FRAC Languedoc Roussillion, Montpellier, 1995, Lisson Gallery, London, 1996, Palais de Beaux Arts, Brussels, 1997, Kunsthalle, Vienna, 1997, Witte de With Mus., Rotterdam, 1997, Galerie Yvon Lambert, Paris, 1998, The Showroom, London, 1998, Galerie Jan Mot, Brussels, 2000, 2003, Kunsthalle Basel, 2001, Dvir Gallery, Tel Aviv, 2001, Centre d'art Contemporain de Bretigny, 2001, Sprengel Mus., Hannover, 2002, Christine Konig Galerie, Vienna, 2004, Art Basel, 2004, Galeria Sonia Rosso, Milan, 2004, Erna Hecey Gallery, Luxembourg, Cosmic Gallery, Paris, exhibitions include (group), 49th Venice Biennale, 2001, Manifesta 4, Frankfurt, 2002, Stedelijk Mus., Amsterdam, Casino, Luxembourg, MAMCO, Geneva, Musee d'Art Moderne de la Ville de Paris. Office: c/o Focus Features 100 Universal City Plz Universal City CA 91608*

BISPING, BRUCE HENRY, photojournalist; b. St. Louis, Apr. 27, 1953; s. Harry and Marian B.; m. Joan M. Berg, Sept. 29, 1984; children: Erin Elizabeth Giovanna, Trevor Thomas. B.J., U. Mo., Columbia, 1975. Summer intern Cleve. Press, 1974, The Virginian/Pilot-Ledger Star, Norfolk, 1975; staff photojournalist Mpls. Tribune, 1975-82, Mpls. Star and Tribune, 1982—. Freelance photographer Black Star Pub. Co., N.Y.C., 1975—, Sporting News, St. Louis, Business Week, Time, U.S. News World Report, Newsweek, Am. Illustrated, N.Y. Times, Los Angeles Times, other nat. and local publs.; past mem. faculty Mo. Photojournalism Workshop. Mem. Nat. Press Photographers Assn. (assoc. dir. Region 5 1981-82, dir. Region 5 1983-86, rep. to exec. com. 1984, Nat. Newspaper Photographer of Year award 1976, Regional Newspaper Photographer of Year award 1977, citation for dedication to profession 1985), Twin Cities News Photographers Assn. (pres. 1979-80), Profl. Assn. Diving Instrs. (open water instr. rating), Oldsmobile Club of Am. (bd. dirs. Minn. Club, news editor). Office: Mpls Tribune 6020 View Ln Edina MN 55436-1827 Office Phone: 612-673-7205. E-mail: bruceb65@citilink.com.

BISSELL, BRENT JOHN, advertising and direct marketing executive; b. Dearborn, Mich., July 10, 1950; s. Ernest Ross and Virginia Jane (Pete) B.; m. Libby Schulak, Dec. 4, 1971; children: John, Sarah, Elizabeth, Daniel. BA, U. Toledo, 1971. Pres. Bissell Advt., Inc., Toledo, 1975—78; creative dir. Stark Bros. Nurseries & Orchards Co., Louisiana, Mo., 1979—80; divisional gen. mgr. Consumer Pub. Co., Canton, Ohio, 1980—82; mng. dir. D'Arcy Direct Mktg., Bloomfield Hills, Mich., 1982—85; v.p., mng. dir. Bozell Direct, Chgo., 1985—87; sr. v.p., gen. mgr. McCann-Erickson Direct, Troy, Mich., 1989—93; pres. Direct Target One, Minnetonka, Minn., 1993—. Lectr. in field; instr., bd. advisors Direct Mktg. Assn. Contbg. author: Direct Marketing Handbook, 2d edit., 1991, Next Step in Database Marketing: Consumer Guided Marketing, 1996. Mem. comms. bd. Nat. Assn. Congl. Chs., 1990—93. Fellow: Fellow Internat. Soc. of Strategic Mktg. (sr.; charter); mem.: SAR, Mayflower Descs., Masons. Home and Office: 2924 Creek Ln Minnetonka MN 55305-2988 Office Phone: 612-419-3869. Personal E-mail: bjbissell@msn.com.

BISSELL, EUGENE V.N., gas industry executive; Sr. v.p., sales, mktg. AmeriGas Propane, pres., CEO, dir., 2000; now pres., CEO AmeriGas Ptnrs. LP (subs. UGI Corp.). Office: AmeriGas Ptnrs LP 460 Gulph Rd King Of Prussia PA 19406 Office Phone: 610-337-7000. Office Fax: 610-992-3259.*

BISSELL, GEORGE ARTHUR, architect; b. L.A., Jan. 31, 1927; s. George Arthur and Ruby Zoe (Moore) B.; m. Laurene Conlon, Nov. 21, 1947; children: Teresa Ann, Thomas Conlon, William George, Robert Anthony, Mary Catherine. BArch, U. So. Calif., 1953. Registered architect, Calif. Ptnr. Bissell Co., Covina, Calif., 1953-57, Bissell & Durquette, A.I.A., Pasadena, Calif., 1957-61; owner George Bissell, A.I.A., Laguna Beach, Calif., 1961-65; ptnr. Riley & Bissell, A.I.A., Newport Beach, Calif., 1965-72; pres. Bissell/August, Inc., Newport Beach, 1972-83, Bissell Architects, Inc., Newport Beach, 1983—. Bd. dirs. Newport Ctr. Assn., 1973-78, Lido Isle Community Assn., Newport Beach, 1985-87, Hamilton Cove Assn., 1991-92. With U.S. Mcht. Marine, 1944-46. Fellow AIA (pres. Orange County chpt. 1975, Calif. coun. 1978, nat. bd. dirs. 1980-83, Progressive Arch. award 1974, Nat. AIA Honor award 1978, 98, Merit award Calif. Coun. 1988, AIA Calif. Coun. Lifetime Achievement award 2000); mem. Newport Harbor Yacht Club, Lido Isle Yacht Club. Avocations: sailing, skiing, travel. Home: 108 Via Havre Newport Beach CA 92663-4905 also: Yacht Banshee Newport Beach CA 92663 Office: Bissell Architects 3422 Via Lido Newport Beach CA 92663 Office Phone: 949-675-9901. E-mail: Bisarch@aol.com.

BISSELL, JAMES DOUGAL, III, motion picture production designer; b. Charleston, SC, Aug. 6, 1951; s. James Dougal Sr. and Elizabeth McPherson (Jones) B.; m. Teresa Ann Atkinson, June 1, 1974 (div. Sept. 1987); m. Martha Wynne Snetsinger, Oct. 22, 1995; children: James Dougal, Alexander Wynne, Elizabeth Wynne. BFA in Theatre, U. N.C., 1973. Art dir. various TV movies, L.A., 1976-81; prodn. designer E.T. The Extra-Terrestrial, L.A., 1981, Twilight Zone-The Movie, L.A., 1982, The Falcon and The Snowman, Mexico City, 1983-84; prodn. designer, 2d unit dir. The Boy Who Could Fly, Vancouver, Canada, 1985, Harry and the Hendersons, L.A., 1986; prodn. designer Someone to Watch Over Me, L.A. and N.Y.C., 1986-87, Twins, L.A. and Santa Fe, 1988—. Visual cons. St. Elmo's Fire, Hollywood, 1984; title co-designer Amazing Stories, Hollywood, 1985; art dir. The Last Starfighter, Hollywood, 1983; prodn. designer, 2nd unit dir. Always, L.A., Libby Mt., Epharata, Wash., 1989; prodn. designer Arachnophobia, Venezuela, Cambria, Calif., L.A. Prodn. designer Rocketeer, 1990, The Pickle, N.Y.C. and L.A., Dennis the Menace, Chgo., 1992, Blue Chips, L.A., Chgo., New Orleans, 1993, Jumanji, Vancouver, New Eng., 1994-95, Tin Cup, Tucson, Houston, 1995, My Fellow Americans, L.A., Asheville, N.C., The Sixth Day, 1999, Cats and Dogs, 2000, Confessions of a Dangerous Mind, 2002, Hollywood Homicide, L.A., 2002; visual cons., 2d unit dir. 50 First Dates, L.A., 2003, Ring II, L.A., 2004, Good Night and Good Luck, L.A., 2005. Mem.: Acad. Motion Picture Arts and Scis., Dir.'s Guild Am., Art Dir.'s Guild (v.p.).

BISSELL, JOHN W., retired judge; b. Exeter, N.H., June 7, 1940; s. H. Hamilton and Sarah W. B.; m. Caroline M.; July 15, 1967; children— Megan L., Katharine W. AB, Princeton U., 1962; LLB, U. Va., 1965. Law clk. U.S. Dist. Ct., N.J., 1965-66; assoc. Pitney, Hardin & Kipp, Newark and Morristown, N.J., 1966-69, ptnr., 1972-78; asst. U.S. atty. N.J., 1969-71; judge Essex County, N.J., 1978-81, N.J. Superior Ct., 1981-82, U.S. Dist. Ct. N.J., Trenton and Newark, 1983—, chief judge, ret., 2001. Office: US Dist Ct Federal Square PO Box 999 Newark NJ 07101-0999

BISSELL, MINA J., research laboratory administrator, biochemist; b. Tehran, Iran, May 14, 1940; Student, Bryn Mawr Coll., 1959-61; AB in Chemistry cum laude, Radcliff Coll., Cambridge, Mass., 1963; MA in Bacteriology and Biochemistry, Harvard U., Cambridge, Mass., 1965, PhD in Microbiology-Molecular Genetics, 1969. Milton rsch. fellow, 1969-70; Am. Cancer Soc. rsch. fellow, 1970-72; staff biochemist Lawrence Berkeley Nat. Lab. U. Calif., Berkeley, 1972-76, mem. sr. staff, 1976—, co-dir. div. biology and medicine Lab. Cell Biology, 1980—, dir. divsn., 1988-92, coord. life scis., 1989-91, assoc. lab. dir. bioscience, 1989, dir. life scis. divsn. Lawrence Berkeley Nat. Lab., 1992—, mem. faculty dept. comparative biochemistry, 1979—. Vis. prof. Kettering Inst., U. Cin. Med. Schs., 1986-88; disting. vis. scientist Queensland Inst. Med. Rsch., Brisbane, Australia, 1982; mem. coun. Gordon Rsch. Conf., 1991-94; George P. Peacock lectr. pathology U. Tex., Dallas, 1992; Dean's lectr. Mt. Sinai Med. Sch., N.Y.C., 1993; presenter numerous lectures, condr. symposia; keynote spkr. Gordon Conf. on Proteoglycans, 1994, others. Mem. editl. bd. and sect. editor In Vitro Cell and Devel. Biology Rapid Comm., 1986—; mem. editl. bd. Jour. Cellular Biochemistry, 1990-92; assoc. editor In Vitro Cellular and Devel. Biology, 1990—, Molecular and Cellular Differentiation, 1992—, Molecular Carcinogensis, 1993-97, Devel. Biology, 1993—, Cancer Rsch., 1994—, Breast Jour., 1994—; contbr. numerous articles to sci. jours. Recipient 1st Joseph Sadusk award for breast cancer rsch., 1985, Ernest Orlando Lawrence award Dept. Energy, 1996, Krakower award in Pathology, 2003, Discovery Health Channel Med. Honors, 2004; Fogarty sr. fellow NIH, Imperial Can. Rsch. Fund Labs., London, 1983-84, Guggenheim fellow, 1992-93,; honored by Susan G. Komen Breast Cancer Found. Fellow AAAS; mem. Am. Soc. for Cell Biology (mem. coun. 1989-91, Women in Cell Biology Career Recognition award 1993, pres. 1997), Internat. Soc. Differentiation (bd. dirs. 1990-96). The pioneer in postulating, and then proving that the extracellular matrix (ECM), the mass of fibrous and globular proteins that surrounds cells performs a critical role in dictating a tissue's organization and function. In 1981, Dr. Bissell formulated the concept of a "dynamic reciprocity." This communication scheme between the nucleus, the cells and their microenvironment suggests that signals are sent into the cell through ECM receptors which attach to the cell's outer skeleton and convey important information to the nucleus and the chromosomes. Office: Lawrence Berkeley Nat Lab Div Life Scis 1 Cyclotron Rd Ms 83 101 Berkeley CA 94720-8260 Business E-Mail: mjbissell@lbl.gov.

BISSELL, PHIL (CHARLES P. BISSELL), cartoonist; b. Worcester, Mass., Feb. 1, 1926; s. Ralph Kenneth and Dorothy Earle (Pennell) B.; m. Beverly Barrows, Sept. 17, 1948; children: Steven Barrows, Christopher William. Student, Sch. Practical Art, Boston, 1946-48; hon. degree, Art Instrn. Sch., Mpls., 1971. Theatrical and editl. sports cartoonist Christian Sci. Monitor, 1949-53; sports cartoonist Boston Globe, 1953-65; sports and editl. cartoonist Worcester Telegram and Evening Gazette, 1967-75; sports cartoonist Boston Herald, 1975-77; editl. cartoonist Lowell (Mass.) Sun, 1980-87; illustrator, cartoonist Cartoon Corner Syndicate, Rockport, Mass., 2004. Cons. D.C. Graphics, Lexington, Mass., 1987—; originator football helmet logo New England Patriots, 1960; portrait artist City of Lowell Bridge Plaque, 1982. Represented in permanent collections Basketball Hall Fame, Springfield, Mass., Football Hall of Fame, Canton, Ohio, Baseball Hall of Fame, Cooperstown, N.Y., Internat. Swimming Hall of Fame, Ft. Lauderdale, Fla., Dwight D. Eisenhower Meml. Libr., Abilene, Kans.; cartoonist: (book) Sportspot, 1978, World Ency. of Cartooning, 1980, Tall Tales from Tall Ships, 1992. Recipient N.Am. Racing Assn. award, 1958, Scarlet Quill award Boston U., 1976, Hockey award Mass. Bay Chiefs, 1981. Mem. Baseball Writers Assn. Am., Rockport Art Assn. Home and Office: 19 Landmark Ln Rockport MA 01966-1262 *Humor and laughter can hold mankind together, and if you can share it with your fellow-man, I feel it's a successful day's work!.*

BISSETTE, WINSTON LOUIS, JR., lawyer, mayor; b. Statesville, NC, Sept. 18, 1943; s. Winston Louis III, Thomas Anderson. BA, Wake Forest U., 1965; JD, U. N.C., Chapel Hill, 1968; MBA, U. Va., 1970. Bar: N.C. 1968. Asst. v.p. Wachovia Bank & Trust Co., Winston-Salem, N.C., 1970-74; v.p., treas. Western Carolina Bank, Asheville, N.C., 1974-76; ptnr. McGuire, Wood & Bissette, P.A., Asheville, 1976—. Co-chmn. I-26 corridor Assn., 1987—; chmn. West NC Devel. Assn., 1995—98; regional adv. coun. HUD, 1986—90; mem. Gov.'s Task Force on Urban Transp., 1986, Yr. of the Mtns. Commn., 1995—97; chmn. Asheville Sports Com., 1991—97, Buncombe County Econ. Devel. Commn., 1997—2003, NC Arboretum Soc., 2003—, Grove Arcade Pub. Market Found., 2002—, Asheville Cmty. Betterment Found., 1992—; mayor City of Asheville, 1985—89, city coun., 1983—89; bd. trustees Wake Forest U., 1996—, Western Carolina U., 1995—2003; chmn. Advantage Asheville, 1996—, Grove Arcade Pub. Mkt. Found., 1992—; bd. dirs. Mission-St. Joseph's Health Sys., Inc., 1996—99, Mercy Svcs. Corp., NC Arboretum Found., AB Tech. Coll. Found., Western Carolina U. Found., Asheville Merchants Corp., 2002—, Western Carolina Industries, 2002—, Inst. at Biltmore, 2002—, Blue Ridge Pkwy. Found.; vice-chmn. Inst. Biltmore, 2002—, Met. Sewerage Dist. Buncombe County. Mem. ABA, N.C. Bar Assn., Asheville Area C. of C. (pres. 1991-92), Wake Forest U. Alumni

Assn. (pres. 1992-93), Bald Head Island Club, Biltmore Forest Country Club. Republican. Presbyterian. Avocations: golf, running. Home: 321 Old Toll Rd Asheville NC 28804-3716 Office: McGuire Wood & Bissette PA 48 Patton Ave PO Box 3180 Asheville NC 28802-3180 Office Phone: 828-254-8800. Business E-Mail: lbissette@mwbavl.com.

BISSINGER, FREDERICK LEWIS, retired manufacturing executive; b. N.Y.C., Jan. 11, 1911; s. Jacob Frederick and Rosel (Ensslin) B.; m. Julia E. Stork, Aug. 4, 1935 (dec. Dec. 1989); children: Frederick Louis, Elizabeth Julia; m. Barbara S. Simmonds, Dec. 4, 1993. ME, Stevens Inst. Tech., 1933, MS in Chemistry, 1936, DEng (hon.), 1973; JD, Fordham U., 1938. Bar: D.C. 1937, N.Y. 1939, Ohio 1943, U.S. Supreme Ct. 1943. Instr. chemistry Stevens Inst. Tech., Hoboken, N.J., 1933-36; assoc. Pennie, Davis, Marvin & Edmonds, N.Y.C., 1936-42; counsel, bus. cons. Pennie, Davis, Marvin & Edmonds (name now Pennie & Edmonds), N.Y.C., 1976—; with Indsl. Rayon Corp., Cleve., 1942-61, v.p. charge rsch., 1948-57, group v.p. mktg. and rsch., 1957-59, v.p., gen. mgr., 1959-60, pres., chief exec. officer, 1960-61; group v.p. Midland-Ross Corp., Cleve., 1961-62; v.p., dir., mem. exec. com. Stauffer Chem. Co., N.Y.C., 1962-65; v.p. Allied Chem. Corp., N.Y.C., 1965-66, exec. v.p., 1966-69, pres., chief oper. officer, 1969-74, vice chmn., 1974-76, also bd. dirs. Bd. dirs. Selas Corp. Am. Chmn. emeritus bd. trustees Steven Inst. Tech.; trustee emeritus Fordham U.; mem. N.Y. State Econ. Devel. Bd., 1975. Mem. AAAS, Am. Chem. Soc., Soc. of Chem. Industry (Am. sect.), Societe de Chimie Industrielle, Chemists Club, Sky Club, Sakonnet Golf Club, Met. Club. Home: 9 W Irving St Chevy Chase MD 20815-4218

BISSLER, RICHARD THOMAS, mortician; b. Ravenna, Ohio, Nov. 23, 1953; s. Richard Samuel and Ruth Marion (Cowan) B.; m. Jane H. Vair, Aug. 23, 1975; children: Stephanie Ann (Shawn) Arden, Carlie Jane. BS in Mortuary Sci., U. Minn., 1976; grad., Nat. Found. Funeral Svc. Mgmt., 1983. Lic. funeral dir. and embalmer Ohio; cert. crematory operator Cremation Assn. N.Am. Funeral svc. asst. Bissler & Sons Funeral Home, Kent, Ohio, 1970-74, mortician, 1976—, corp. sec., 1983-86, corp. sec.-treas., 1986-88, pres., 1988—. Bd. dirs. Home Savs. Bank, Kent; bd. dirs., treas. NSM Ins. Co. Ltd., 1997—2001. Trustee Kent Free Libr., 1986—, trustee St. Patrick's Sch. Endowment Fund, 1994—, Nat. Selected Morticians Ins. Trust, 1995-2001; bd. dirs. Selected Ind. Funeral Homes, 2003—, sec.-treas, 2005—; past bd. dirs., pres. Portage County A.C.S., Kent; past treas. NEO-SIDS Found., Akron, Ohio; mem. adult edn. adv. com. Kent City Schs.; steering com. Portage County Hospice; devel. com. United Christian Ministries, 1996-98; mem. Vision 2000 com. City of Kent; mem. Kent Bus. and Edn. adv. com.; bd. dirs. Portage Area Regional Transit Authority, 2002—. Recipient Disting. Svc. award Kent Jaycees, 1986. Mem. Nat. Funeral Dirs. Assn., Ohio Embalmers Assn., Ohio Funeral Dirs. Assn., Selected Ind. Funeral Homes (meeting chair 1989), Funeral Ethics Assn., Kent Area C. of C. (dir. 1985-89, Outstanding Bus. Person award 1992), Order of the Golden Rule, Kent Rotary (dir. 1991-93, pres. 1995-96), KC. Republican. Roman Catholic. Avocations: golf, photography, travel. Office: Bissler & Sons Funeral Home 628 W Main St Kent OH 44240-2212 E-mail: rbissler@bisslerandson.com.

BISSON, ROGER, middle school educator; b. Biddeford, Maine, Oct. 16, 1944; s. Napoleon and Simonne (Desrochers) B.; m. Janet Elizabeth Gerace, Aug. 9, 1969. BA in Biology, St. Michael's Coll., Winooski, Vt., 1969; MEd in Adminstrn. and Planning, U. Vt., 1991; tech. edn. cert., Lyndon State Coll., 1991. Cert. sci. tchr. grades 7-12, tech. edn. tchr. grades 7-12, prin. grades K-12, sci. and tech. edn. middle grades 5-8, mid. level endorsement Vt. Dept. Edn., 2001. 5th and 7th grade tchr. Sacred Heart Sch., Sharon, Mass., 1964-66; algebra I, French I and II and Latin I tchr. Notre Dame H.S., Fitchburg, Mass., 1966-68; 7th and 9th grade sci. tchr. Meml. Jr. and Sr. H.S., Bellingham, Mass., 1968-79; sci. and tech. edn. instr. grades 6, 7, 8 Folsom Sch., South Hero, Vt., 1979—2002, 8th grade sch.-to-work instr., 1992—2002; 8th grade sci. tchr. Albert D. Lawton Sch., Essex Junction, Vt., 2002—. Mem. info. tech. com. Grand Isle Supervisory Dist., North Hero, Vt., 1985-2002; tech. edn. cons. Alburg (Vt.) Elem. Sch., 1992-2002; sch.-to-work lead tchr. New Am. Sch.-Folsom, South Hero, 1992-2002, sci. lead tchr., 1994-2002; mem. tchr./bus. internship program Vt. Math. Coalition, Montpelier, summer 1994; initiator Electronic Portfolio Project 6, 7, 8, 1994-2002, Student/Bus. Internship Program, 1994—2002; tech. cons. Burlington Sch. Sys., 1996; presenter Nat. Edn. Computing Conf., Boston, spring 1994, Vt. Fest '94, Fairlee, Vt., fall 1994, Sch.-to-Work Initiative Conf., Burlington, summer 1996, Regional Edn. Television Network Conf., Burlington, fall 1997, Vt. Fest '98 Info. Tech. Conf.; presenter in field. Contbr. articles to profl. jours. Initiator Grand Isle County Networking Initiative, Grand Isle County, Vt., 1991, Grand Isle County Peer Coaching Program, Grand Isle County, 1991. Recipient Sch.-to-Work Initiative Gov.'s Office, 1995, award Lake Champlain Regional C. of C., 1996, Vocat. Edn. award Grand Isle Rotary Club, 1998; co-recipient IBM Test Flight 1991 award, Essex Junction, Vt., 1992. Mem. ASCD, NEA, NSTA, Vt. Edn. Assn., Vt. Sci. Tchrs. Assn., Vt. Tech. Edn. Assn., Grand Isle Supervisory Union (bldg rep., negotiator, grievance com., past pres.), Vt. State Tech. Coun., Vt. Inst. Sci., Math. and Tech., Vt. Info. Tech. Assn. for Avancement of Learning. Roman Catholic. Avocations: woodworking, furniture refinishing, carpentry, computer technology, fine dining. Office: Albert D Lawton Intermediate Sch 104 Maple St Essex Junction VT 05452 Office Phone: 802-872-3362. E-mail: rbisson@ejhs.k12.vt.us.

BISSON, THOMAS NOEL, history professor; b. N.Y.C., Mar. 30, 1931; s. T(homas) A(rthur) Bisson and Faith Williams Bisson; m. Margaretta Carroll Webb, Aug. 18, 1962; children: Noel, Susan. AB, Haverford Coll., 1953; MA, Princeton U., 1955, PhD, 1958; AM (hon.), Harvard U., 1987; doctor honoris causa (hon.), U. Autonoma de Barcelona, 1991. Instr. history Amherst (Mass.) Coll., 1957—60; asst. prof. history Brown U., Providence, 1960—65; assoc. prof. history Swarthmore (Pa.) Coll., 1965—67, U. Calif., Berkeley, 1967—69, prof. history, 1969—87, Harvard U., Cambridge, Mass., 1987—, Henry Charles Lea prof. medieval history, 1989—. Author: Assemblies and Representation in Languedoc in the Thirteenth Century, 1964, Conservation of Coinage: Monetary Exploitation and its Restraint in France, Catalonia and Aragon (c. AD 1000 - c. 1225), 1979, Fiscal Accounts of Catalonia under the Early Count-Kings (1151-1213), 2 vols., 1984 (Haskins medal, 1988), Medieval France and Her Pyrenean Neighbours: Studies in Early Institutional History, 1989, The Medieval Crown of Aragon: A Short History, 1986, Cultures of Power: Lordship, Status, and Process in Twelfth-Century Europe, 1991, Tormented Voices: Power, Crisis and Humanity in Rural Catalonia, 1140-1200, 1998; contbr. articles to profl. jours. Fellow, John Simon Guggenheim Meml. Found., 1964, NEH, 1975, ACLS, 1979. Fellow: Royal Hist. Soc. (London), Am. Acad. Arts and Scis., Brit. Acad. (corr.), Royal Hist. Soc. (corr.); mem.: Am. Philos. Soc., Inst. d'Estudis Catalans (Barcelona) (corr.), Reial Acad. Bones Lletres (corr.), Internat. Commn. for History of Representation and Parliamentary Instns. (v.p. 1980—), Medieval Acad. Am. (pres. 1994—95). Avocations: classical music, piano. Office: Harvard U Dept History Cambridge MA 02138

BISSOON, CATHY, lawyer; b. NYC; married; 2 children. BA in polit. sci. summa cum laude, Alfred U., NY, 1990; JD, Harvard U., 1993; exec. leadership program, The Wharton Sch., U. Pa., 2004. Bar: Pa. 1993, US Dist. Ct. We. Dist. Pa. 1993, Supreme Ct. Pa. 1994, US Ct. Appeals 4th Cir. 1995, US Ct. Appeals 3rd Cir. 1997, US Ct. Appeals 6th Cir. 2001. Law clk. to Hon. Gary L. Lancaster US Dist. Ct. We. Dist. Pa., 1994; joined Reed Smith LLP, Pitts., 1993, ptnr., 2001—, dir. diversity, 2001—, former head employment group. Bd. mem. Girl Scouts Trillium Coun., Pitts. Zoo & PPG Aquarium. Named a Nat. Hispanic Scholar, Alfred U., Harvard U. Mem.: Pitts. Met. Area Hisp. C. of C., Hispanic Nat. Bar Assn. Office: Reed Smith LLP 435 Sixth Ave Pittsburgh PA 15219 Office Phone: 412-288-3268. Office Fax: 412-288-3063. Business E-Mail: cbissoon@reedsmith.com.

BISTRIAN, BRUCE RYAN, internist, educator; b. Southampton, N.Y., Oct. 22, 1939; s. Peter and Mary Laura (Ryan) B.; m. Eleanor Alice Dix, Sept. 3, 1964; children: Tennille Ryan, Jordan Brooke, Britton Perry. BA, NYU, 1961; MD, Cornell U., 1965; MPH, Johns Hopkins U., 1971; PhD, MIT, 1975; AM (hon.), Harvard U., 1990. Diplomate in internal medicine and critical care medicine Am. Bd. Internal Medicine. Intern Cornell U., N.Y.C., 1965-66; metabolism fellow U. Vt., Burlington, 1968-69, resident in medicine, 1969-70; from asst. clin. prof. to assoc. prof. Harvard U. Sch. Medicine, Boston, 1975-90, prof. medicine, 1990—. Clin. assoc. physician rsch. resources divsn. NIH, 1975-78; lectr. MIT, 1981-84. Mem. editl. bd. Jour. Parenteral and Enteral Nutrition, Harvard Health Letter, Women's Health Watch, Critical Care Medicine; contbr. more than 400 sci. articles to profl. publ. Capt. U.S. Army, 1966-68. Recipient Goldberger award in clin. nutrition AMA, 2004; grantee Nat. Inst. Gen. Med. Scis., 1977-80, Nat. Inst. Arthritis, Metabolism and Digestive Disease, 1979-83, Nat. Inst. Arthritis, Diabetes, Digestive and Kidney Diseases, 1985-95, Nat. Cancer Inst., 1984-87. Fellow: ACP, Am. Soc. Nutritional Scis.; mem.: Inst. Medicine (com. on military nutrition rsch. 2001—), Fedn. Am. Socs. for Exptl. Biologists (bd. dirs. 2001—05), Mass. Med. Soc., Soc. Critical Care Medicine, Am. Soc. Parenteral and Enteral Nutrition (pres. 1989—90), Am. Soc. Clin. Nutrition (sec. 1993—96, v.p.-elect 1998, v.p. 1999, pres. 2000), Fedn. Am. Soc. Exptl. Biologists (pres.-elect 2004—). Presbyterian. Achievements include more than 40 patents in field. Subspecialties: Nutrition (medicine); Biochemistry (medicine). Current work: protein calorie malnutrition; total parenteral nutrition; nutrition and infection. Home: Argilla Rd Ipswich MA 01938 Office: Beth Israel Deaconess Med Ctr 1 Deaconess Rd Boston MA 02215-5321 Business E-Mail: bbistria@bidmc.harvard.edu.

BITHELL, THOMAS CHARLES, human resources specialist, insurance consultant; b. Pocatello, Idaho, Oct. 21, 1946; s. Walter Charles and Nondus (Hoge) Bithell; m. Irene Lindsay, Nov. 12, 1947; children: Susan N., Thomas L., Steven H., Cathrin S., Lindsay A., Samuel H., U. Idaho, 1969; BS in Bus., Fairleigh Dickinson U., 1977. Owner Bithell Produce & Foods Co., Moscow, Idaho, 1965-67; dist. sales mgr. Produce Supply Co., Spokane, Wash., 1967-69; personnel dir. George A. Fuller div. Northrop Corp., N.Y.C., 1975-77, Taubman Co., Inc., Southfield, Mich., 1977-80, v.p., personnel Troy, Mich., 1980-84, sr. v.p. human resources and adminstrn. Bloomfield Hills, Mich., 1984-98; pres. Tb brand, LLC, Bloomfield Hills, 1998—, Human Asset Strategies, Bloomfield Hills, 1998—. Cons. in field. Bishop LDS Ch., Bloomfield Hills, 1986-90, pres. Bloomfield Hills stake, 1994—. Capt. AUS, 1969-75. Mem. Am. Compensation Assn., Detroit Area Personnel Mgmt. Assn., Am. Mgmt. Assn., Soc. Human Resource Mgmt., Beta Thea Pi., Elks. Republican. Avocation: scuba diving. Office: 5049 Mohr Valley Ln Bloomfield Hills MI 48304 Home: 6966 Killarney Dr Troy MI 48098-2189 E-mail: TBithell@HAssets.com.

BITMAN, CLARA, writer, educator; b. Montevideo, Uruguay, Sept. 29, 1935; d. David and Hela Seniak Bitman; children: Sergio Gabriel Voda, Laura Alejandra Voda. Dir., art sch. Taller Urutí, Buenos Aires, 1973—83; dir., seminars for tchrs. Inés Moreno Inst., Buenos Aires, 1980—90, Essarp Ctr., Buenos Aires, 1984—91; lectr. Bank State College Edn., N.Y.C., 1994; Spanish tchr. B.B. Montessory Sch., Staten Island, NY, 1995—. Author: (book) El Girasol Gigante, 1998, numerous childrens books and TV programs. Vol. Ayuda Ya Inc., 1999—2003. Recipient Illustrated Poetry award, Argentinian Soc. Writers, 1980, Children's Theater Prize of Yr., Argentinian Soc. Authors, 1983. Achievements include put on stage six plays in many South Am. countries. E-mail: claser@juno.com.

BITNER, JOHN HOWARD, lawyer; b. Indpls., Feb. 27, 1940; s. Harry M. Jr. and Jeanne B. (Eshelman) B.; m. Vicki Ann D'Ianni, 1961; children: Kerry, Holly, Robin. AB in English and History, Northwestern U., 1961; JD cum laude, Columbia U., 1964. Bar: Ill. 1964. Assoc. Bell, Boyd & Lloyd LLC, Chgo., 1964-71, ptnr., 1972-99, chair corp. and secs. dept., 1988-99, vice chmn. firm, 1992-99, mem., 2000—. Contbr. articles to profl. jours.; editor Columbia Law Rev. Mem. St. Gregory Episcopal Sch. Bd.; mem. bd. visitors Columbia Law Sch, tutor, GED students at Jobs for Youth Mem. ABA, Ill. Bar Assn., Chgo. Bar Assn., Union League, Mid-Day Club, Glen View Club, Lawyers Club, Delta Upsilon, Phi Delta Phi. Episcopalian. Avocations: tennis, reading, chess, golf. Home: 2329 Lincolnwood Dr Evanston IL 60201-2048 Office: Bell Boyd & Lloyd LLC 70 W Madison St Chicago IL 60602 Fax: (312) 827-8048. E-mail: jbitner@bellboyd.com.

BITNER, JOHN WILLIAM, banker; b. Jersey Shore, Pa., July 6, 1948; s. John W. and Gertrude Elizabeth Bitner; m. Joy Lin. BS in Econs., Lebanon Valley Coll., Annville, Pa., 1970; MBA, Boston Coll., Chestnut Hill, Mass., 1983. V.p. Commonwealth Bank, Williamsport, Pa., 1970-78, Neworld Bank, Boston, 1978-81; fixed income mgr. Digital Equipment Co., Maynard, Mass., 1981-84; sr. v.p. Ea. Bank, Boston, 1984—. Author: Successful Bank Asset/Liability Management, 1992; contbr. articles to profl. jours.; guest Wake Up Call, CNBC TV, NBC Nightly News, NECN News, WBZ Radio. Mem.: Am. Bankers Assn. (mem. econ. coun.), Boston Econ. Club.

BITNEY, WOODROW WILSON, lawyer; b. Shell Lake, Wis., May 26, 1917; s. Earl Howard and Florence Ellen (Wood) B.; m. Irene Marie Hoey, Mar. 1, 1940; children— Judith, James, Mary Jane, Jacqueline, Thomas, Patricia, Michael. B.B.A. in Acctg., U. Wis., 1950, J.D., 1951. Mem. Douglas Omernick & Bitney, Spooner, Wis., 1951-66; sole practice, Spooner, 1966-82; pres. Bitney Law Firm, Ltd., Spooner, 1982—, also dir.; family ct. commr. Washburn County (Wis.), 1978-82. Served with Combat Engrs. U.S. Army, 1939-46. Mem. Inter County Bar Assn. (pres. 1955-56, sec. 1954-55, dir. 1957-58). Republican. Roman Catholic. Clubs: Lions, K.C. Office: 225 Walnut St Spooner WI 54801-1322

BITONDO, DOMENIC, engineering executive; b. Welland, Ont., Can., June 7, 1925; came to U.S., 1950, naturalized, 1956; s. Vito Leonard and Vita Maria (Gallipoli) B.; m. Delphine May Dicola, June 11, 1949; children— Michael, Annamarie, David, Marisa. BS, U. Toronto, 1947, MS, 1948, PhD, 1950. Aerodynamist, Aerophysics div. N.Am. Aviation Co., Downey, Calif., 1950-51; project engr. to chief of aerodynamics Aerophysics Devel. Corp., Santa Barbara, 1951-59; staff engr. Northrop Corp., Hawthorne, Calif., 1959-60; head test planning and analysis TRW Systems, Inc., El Segundo, Calif., 1960-61; dept. head aeromechanics dept. Systems Research and Planning div., founder, dir. Advanced Ballistic Reentry Systems Program (ABRES) Aerospace Corp., El Segundo, 1961-63; dir. engring. Aerospace Systems div. Bendix Corp., Ann Arbor, Mich., 1963-69; engring. mgr. Apollo lunar sci. expts., 1966; dir., gen. mgr. Bendix Research Labs., Southfield, Mich., 1969-79; exec. dir. research and devel. Bendix Corp., Southfield, Mich., 1979—81; pres. Bitondo Assocs. Inc., Ann Arbor, 1981—. Gordon N. Patterson lectr. U. Toronto, 1976; trustee Central Solar Energy and Research Corp., Detroit, 1978-80; dir. Continental Controls Corp., San Diego.; Def. Research Bd. Can. asst., 1948, NRC asst., 1947 Contbr. tech. articles to profl. jours. Mem. AIAA, NRC (mem. com. on mgmt. tech.), NAS (mem. task force to Indonesia in methodology of tech. planning), Mich. Energy Resource Rsch. Assn. (trustee 1978), Nat. Mgmt. Assn. (Gold Knight award), Indsl. Rsch. Inst. (emeritus). Office: 5 Manchester Ct Ann Arbor MI 48104-6562 Office Phone: 734-971-4637. Personal E-mail: deldombitondo@aol.com.

BITRAN, JACOB DAVID, internist; b. Thessaloniki, Greece, Sept. 23, 1947; arrived in U.S., 1952; s. David Jacob and Martha (Faratzl) Bitran; m. Linda Sue Androw, Dec. 26, 1970; children: Lauren, Dina. BS, U. Ill., Chgo., 1968, MD, 1971. Diplomate Am. Bd. Internal Medicine, Am. Bd. Med. Oncology, Am. Bd. Hematology. Intern in medicine Michael Reese Med. Ctr., Chgo., 1971-72, resident in internal medicine, 1973-75, clin. asst. prof. medicine, 1977-81, clin. assoc. prof., 1981-84; resident in pathology Rush Presbyn. St. Luke's Med. Ctr., Chgo., 1972-73; fellow in hematology/oncology U. Chgo., 1975-77, assoc. prof., 1984-88, prof., 1988-91; dir. divsn. hematology/oncology Luth. Gen. Hosp., Park Ridge, Ill., 1991—; prof. medicine U. Ill., Chgo., 1996-98. Mem. sci. adv. bd. Lederle Labs., Wayne, NJ, 1986—89. Editor: Lung Cancer, 1988. Fellow: ACP, Am. Coll. Chest Physicians; mem.: Am. Soc. Clin. Oncology (program chmn. 1990—91), Am. Assn. Cancer Rsch. (program chmn. 1988—89). Democrat. Achievements include development of usable chemotherapy regimen for non small cell lung cancer that has been in clinical use since 1976; research in dose intensive chemotherapy in breast cancer. Avocations: tennis, rowing. Office: Lutheran General Hospital 1700 Luther Ln Park Ridge IL 60068-1270 Office Phone: 847-268-8200. Business E-Mail: jbitran@oncmed.net.

BITSBERGER, TIMOTHY S., federal agency administrator; BA, Yale U., 1981; MBA, Harvard U., 1985. Trader Drexel Burnahm Lambert, NYC, 1985—89; sr. trading mgr., v.p. NationsBanc Capital Markets, NYC, 1989—98; sr. v.p. investments Solomon Smith Barney, NYC, 1999—2001; treasury dep. asst. sec. fed. fin. US Dept Treasury, Washington, 2001—04, asst. sec. fin. markets, 2004—. Cons. J.F. Lehman & Co., NYC, 1999. Office: Dept Treasury 1500 Pennsylvania Ave NW Rm 2334 Washington DC 20220 Office Phone: 202-622-1715. Office Fax: 202-622-0265.*

BITTENBENDER, BRAD JAMES, environmental engineer; b. Kalamazoo, Dec. 4, 1948; s. Don J. and Thelma Lu (Bacon) B.; m. Patricia Stahl Hubbell, June, 1992. BS, Western Mich. U., 1972; Cert. Hazardous Material Mgmt., U. Calif., Irvine, 1987; Cert. Environ. Auditing, Calif. State U., Long Beach, 1992. Cert. safety profl. of the Ams.; cert. hazardous materials mgr. Supr. mfg. Am. Cyanamid, Kalamazoo, 1973-77, Productol Chem. div. Ferro Corp., Santa Fe Springs, Calif., 1977-79, environ. adminstr., 1979-80; sr. environ. engr. Ferro Corp., Los Angeles, 1980-87; mgr. environ. safety and indsl. hygiene dept. Composites divsn. Ferro Corp., Los Angeles, 1988-91, Structural Polymer Systems, Inc., Montedison, Calif., 1991-95; dir. environ. safety and health dept. Culver City (Calif.) Composites Corp., 1996-98; mgr. safety, health and environ. dept. Cytec Fiberite-Calif. Divsn., L.A., 1998-99; sr. safety specialist Gen. Electric Aircraft Engines/IDC, Lynn, Mass., 2000—. Bd. dirs., mem. adv. bd. safety and health extension program U. Calif. Irvine, 1985-91. Bd. dirs. adv. com. hazardous materials Community Right to Know, Culver City, Calif., 1987-91; mem. Calif. Mus. Found., L.A., 1985-90, Mus. Contemporary Art, L.A., 1985-2000; founding sponsor Challenger Ctr.; mem. R.I. Driving Club, 1999—. Mem. Am. Inst. Chem. Engrs., Nat. Assn. Environ. Mgmt., Acad. Cert. Hazardous Materials Mgrs., Suppliers of Advanced Composites Materials Assn. (mem. environ. health and safety com. 1989-92), Am. Indsl. Hygiene Assn., Am. Soc. Safety Engrs., Nat. Fire Protection Assn., Beta Beta Beta. Republican. Presbyterian. Avocations: breeding morgan horses, skiing, distance running, reading, equestrian carriage driving. Home: 215 Everett St Wrentham MA 02093-1105 E-mail: bradbittenbender@yahoo.com.

BITTERMAN, MARY GAYLE FOLEY, foundation executive; b. San Jose, Calif, May 29, 1944; d. John Dennis and Zoe (Hames) Foley; m. Morton Edward Bitterman, June 26, 1967; 1 child Sarah Fleming. BA, Santa Clara U., 1966; MA, Bryn Mawr Coll., 1969, PhD, 1971. Exec. dir. Hawaii Pub. Broadcasting, Honolulu, 1974-79; dir. Voice Am., Washington, 1980-81, Dept. Commerce, Honolulu, 1981-83, E.-W. Ctr. Inst. Culture, Comm., 1984-88; cons. pvt. practice, 1989-93; pres., CEO KQED, Inc., San Francisco, 1993—2002, The James Irvine Found., 2002—03; Dir. Osher Lifelong Learning Inst., 2003; pres. The Bernard Osher Found., 2004—. Bd. dir. Bank of Hawaii, Honolulu, Honolulu, 1984—; vice chmn. TIDE 2000, Tokyo, 1984—93; bd. dir. McKesson Corp., San Francisco, 1995—99; trustee Am.'s Pub. TV Stas., 1997—2002; bd. dir. Bernard Osher Found.; bd. dirs. Barclays Global Investors, Bay Area Econ. Forum; bd. dir. PBS, chmn.; adv. coun. mem. Stanford Inst. Econ. Policy Rsch. Prodr.: (film) China Visit, 1978; contbr. numerous articles on internat. telecomms. to various pubs. Bd. dirs. United Way, Honolulu, 1986—93; chmn. Kuakini Health System, 1991—94; trustee Santa Clara U. Recipient Candle of Understanding award Bonneville (Utah) Internat. Corp., 1985; named hon. mem. Nat. Fedn. Press Women, 1986; Doctor of Humane Letters (honoris causa), Dominican Coll. of San Rafael, 1999; Doctor of Public Svc. (honoris causa), Santa Clara U., 2003. Mem.: Pacific Forum, CSIS (bd. gov.), Commonwealth Club Calif. (bd. dir.), Nat. Acad. Pub. Admin. (fellow). Office: One Ferry Bldg Ste 255 San Francisco CA 94111 Address: 229 Kaalawai Pl Honolulu HI 96816-4435 Office Phone: 415-677-5946. Business E-Mail: mbitterman@osherfoundation.org.

BITTERMAN, MORTON EDWARD, psychologist, educator; b. NYC, Jan. 19, 1921; s. Harry Michael and Stella (Weiss) B.; m. Mary Gayle Foley, June 26, 1967; children— Sarah Fleming, Joan, Ann BA, NYU, 1941; MA, Columbia U., 1942; PhD, Cornell U., 1945. Asst. prof. Cornell U., Ithaca, N.Y., 1945-50; assoc. prof. U. Tex., Austin, 1950-55; mem. Inst. for Advanced Study, Princeton, N.J., 1955-57; prof. Bryn Mawr Coll., Pa., 1957-70, U. Hawaii, Honolulu, 1970—; dir. Békésy Lab. Neurobiology, Honolulu, 1991—2000. Author: (with others) Animal Learning, 1979; editor: Evolution of Brain and Behavior in Vertebrates, 1976; co-editor: Am. Jour. Psychology, 1955-73; cons. editor Jour. Animal Learning and Behavior, 1973-76, 85-88, Jour. Comparative Psychology, 1988-92. Recipient Humboldt prize Alexander von Humboldt Found., Bonn, W.Ger., 1981; Fulbright grantee; grantee NSF, Office Naval Research, NIMH, Air Force Office Sci. Research, Deutsche Forschungsgemeinschaft. Fellow Soc. Exptl. Psychologists (Warren medal 1997, E.R. Hilgard award 2004), Am. Psychol. Assn. (D. O. Hebb award 2001), AAAS; mem. Psychonomic Soc. Home: 229 Kaalawai Pl Honolulu HI 96816-4435 Office: Univ Hawaii Bekesy Lab of Neurobiology 1993 E West Rd Honolulu HI 96822-2321 Office Phone: 808-956-6987. Business E-Mail: jeffb@pbrc.hawaii.edu.

BITTERWOLF, THOMAS EDWIN, chemistry educator; b. New Orleans, Jan. 19, 1947; s. Alvin John and Naomi Mae (Hendrix) B.; m. Caroline Elizabeth Means, May 25, 1968; children: Heidi Elizabeth, Katharine Naomi. BS, Centenary Coll., 1968; PhD, W.Va. U., 1976. Commd. ensign USN, 1973, advanced through grades to comdr., 1987; instr. Naval Nuclear Power Sch., Orlando, Fla., 1973-77, U.S. Naval Acad., Annapolis, Md., 1977-82; resigned USN, 1982; asst. prof. U.S. Naval Acad., Annapolis, Md., 1982-85, assoc. prof., 1985-88; assoc. prof. chemistry U. Idaho, Moscow, 1988-91, prof. chemistry, dir. teaching enhancement, 1991-96, assoc. dean coll. letters scis., 1996-98; exit stds. commr. Idaho High Schs., 1998—. Contbr. articles to refereed jours. Mem. AAAS, Am. Chem. Soc., Royal Soc. Chemistry, Sigma Xi. Methodist. Avocation: theater. Home: PO Box 8188 Moscow ID 83843-0688 Office: U Idaho Dept Chemistry Moscow ID 83844-0001

BITTING, WILLIAM M., lawyer; b. Santa Monica, Calif., Apr. 17, 1939; AB, UCLA, 1962, JD, 1965. Exec. v.p., gen counsel Pabst Brewing Co., San Antonio, chmn., CEO, 1998—2000; former CEO, co-chmn., gen. counsel S&P Co., Mill Valley, Calif.; sr. ptnr Hill Farrer & Burrill LLP, Los Angeles, Calif. Office: Hill Farrer & Burrill LLP 300 S Grand Ave 37th Fl Los Angeles CA 90071 Business E-Mail: wbitting@hillfarrer.com.

BITTINGER, CYNTHIA DOUGLAS, foundation executive; BA in Govt., Wheaton Coll., 1968; MA, Columbia U., 1970. Social studies tchr. Ridgewood (N.J.) High Sch., 1970-73; govtl. mgr. Mayor's N.Y.C. Office for Aging, 1974-76; owner, mgr. gift shop Princeton, N.J., 1978-87; exec. dir. Calvin Coolidge Meml. Found., Inc., Plymouth, Vt., 1990—. Instr. history C.C. of Vt., White River Junction, 1992—94. Commentator Vt. Pub. Radio, 2003—. Address: Calvin Coolidge Mem Found Box 97 Plymouth VT 05056

BITTNER, BARBARA JANE, management consultant; m. William R. Haushalter, Sept. 1, 1979; children: Laura B., Vanessa B. BS in Hotels, Restaurants and Instns., Pa. State U., 1969; MBA in Fin., U. Pitts., 1979. Mgmt. trainee Army and Air Force Exch. Svc., Plattsburgh, N.Y., 1969-71; food and beverage mgr. San Jeronimo Hotel, San Juan, P.R., 1971-74, Elangeni Hotel, Durban, Republic South Africa, 1974-75, Princess Hotels, Acapulco, Mex., 1975-76; conf. dir. U. Pitts., 1976-78; fin. analyst J&L Steel Corp., Pitts., 1979-83; pres. Profl. Cons. Assocs., Pitts., 1983-99; bus. analyst Wilhelm & Kruse, 1999—2002. Vol. instr. PHA, Pitts., 1990—91. Mem. Nat. Assn. Women Bus. Owners, Pa. Hotel and Restaurant Soc., Western Pa. Restaurant Assn. (assoc.), Legatus, Mt. Alvernia Athletic Assn. (pres 1998-2001). Office: Profl Cons Assocs 7078 Bennington Woods Dr Pittsburgh PA 15237-6374

BITTNER, PEG JUNE MARGARET, insurance auditor; b. Homestead, Pa., Aug. 30, 1952; d. John Adam Bittner and Martha June Myers. A in Acctg., Cmty. Coll., Pitts., 1982; degree in med. adminstrn., Duff's Bus. Sch., Pitts., 1994. Cert. managed health profl. Bookkeeper V&M Mfg., Pitts., 1972; asst. contr. J. Edward Connelly Assocs., Pitts., 1972—89; contractor acctg. Kelly Svcs., Pitts., 1989—91; bill collector Med. Bur., Pitts., 1991—95; auditor Highmark Blue Cross, Pitts., 1995—. Vol. Summer Nat. Sr. Olympics, 2005; participant YMCA's 150th Ann. Video Celebration. Mem.: Looney Tune Bowling League. Avocations: bowling, gardening, writing, fitness training.

BITTSON, ELIZABETH RINGHAM, artist; b. Dallas, Aug. 28, 1952; d. Rodger Falk and Helen (Gavin) Ringham; m. Linwood Hursel Gray, Dec. 28, 1974 (dec. Nov. 1982); m. Andrew George Bittson, Apr. 25, 1987. BFA, Stephens Coll., 1974. Drafting technician Gulf Oil Corp., New Orleans, 1974-75; free-lance artist for various clothing stores New Orleans, Houston, 1976-78; tech. illustrator Petroleum Learning Programs, Ltd., Houston, 1978-82; owner Beth Gray, Comml. Artist, Houston, 1980-86, By Beth, 1986—. Artist, calligrapher: (cookbooks) Beginnings..., 1980, A Collection of Soups, Salads and Breads, 1981, A Collection of Entrees and Vegetables, 1982. Vol. artist for spl. events Houston Symphony League, 1982—, Performing Arts Ctr. North Houston, 1987, Jr. Svc. League North Houston. Mem. AAUW, Stephens Coll. Alumnae Assn., Houston (provisional 1985-86), Olde Oaks Women's (publicity chmn. 1980-81, Houston). Roman Catholic. Home and Office: 2205 Tangley St Houston TX 77005-2607

BITZER, DONALD LESTER, electrical engineer, educator, retired lab administrator; b. East St. Louis, Ill., Jan. 1, 1934; s. Jess L. and Marjorie (Look) B.; m. Maryann Drost, July 2, 1955; 1 son, David. BS, U. Ill., 1955, MS, 1956, PhD, 1960; PhD (hon.), MacMurray Coll. Mem. faculty U. Ill.-Urbana, 1955—, asst. prof., 1960-63, assoc. prof., 1963-67, prof. elec. engring., 1967—, dir. Computer-Based Edn. Research Lab., 1967-89; disting. prof. rsch. N.C. State U., 1989—. Cons. in field. Contbr. articles to profl. jours.; pioneer PLATO-large computer-based edn. system; co-inventor plasma display panel. Recipient Indsl. Rsch. 100 award, 1966, Bobby Connelly Meml. award Miami Valley Computer Assn., 1973, Recognition award Soc. for Info. Display, 1979, Edn. award Am. Fedn. Info. Processing Socs., 1989, Elec. Engring. Disting. Alumni award U. Ill., 1992, Emmy award NATAS, 2002; named laureate Lincoln Acad of Ill., 1982; Internat. Engring. Consortium fellow, 1994. Fellow AAAS, IEEE, Assn. Devel. Computer-Based Instrnl. Sys., Internat. Engring. Consortium; mem. NAE (Vladimir K. Zworykin award), Data Processing Mgmt. Assn. (Computer Sci. Man of Yr. award), Am. Soc. Engring. Edn. (Chester Carlson award), Nat. Acad. Engring. Home: 104 Christofle Ln Cary NC 27511-6473 Office: NC State U Dept Computer Sci PO Box 8206 Raleigh NC 27695-0001

BIVENS, CAROLYN VESPER, former advertising executive, golf association commissioner-elect; m. Bill Bivens. Various sales and mktg. positions Xerox Corp., Dallas, Washington; with USA Today, 1982—2000, dir. nat. sales, v.p. nat. circulation sales Arlington, Va., 1985—91, sr. v.p., assoc. pub., 1991—2000; mng. dir. Western Region Initiative Media, 2000—01; pres., COO Initiative Media North Am., LA, 2001—05; commr.-elect Ladies Profl. Golf Assn., Daytona Beach, Fla., 2005. Chmn. bd. govs. Children's Miracle Network; bd. dirs. Ad Coun., Nat. Steppenwolf Theatre. Named one of Most Powerful Women in TV, Electronics Media mag., 2002. Mem.: Am. Assn. Advt. Agencies (mem. Media Policy Com.), Congressional Country Club. Achievements include first female commissioner in the 55 year history of the Ladies Professional Golf Association. Avocation: golf. Office: Ladies Profl Golf Assn 100 International Golf Drive Daytona Beach FL 32124-1092 Office Phone: 323-370-8000, 386-274-6200. Office Fax: 386-274-1099. E-mail: carolyn.bivens@us.initiative.com.*

BIVENS, GORDON ELLSWORTH, economist, educator; b. Nevada, Iowa, Feb. 5, 1927; s. Clarence E. and Hazel Bivens; m. Muriel Katherine Collier, Feb. 14, 1953; children: Dale Mark, Carol Sue, Bruce Alan, Paul Wayne. BS, Iowa State U., 1950, MS, 1953, PhD, 1957. Instr., asst. prof., assoc. prof. Iowa State U., 1954-62; assoc. prof., prof. econs., founding dir. Center for Consumer Affairs, U. Wis.-Milw., 1962-68; consumption economist Consumer and Food Econs. Research div. Agrl. Research Service, Dept. Agr., 1967-68; prof. family econs. and agrl. econs. U. Mo. at Columbia, 1968-76; prof. dept. family environment Iowa State U., 1976-90, head dept., 1976-80, interim assoc. dean for rsch. and grad. edn. Coll. Family and Consumer Scis., 1989-90, Mary B. Welch disting. prof. family and consumer scis., 1983—, prof. emeritus, 1989—; facilitator Alternatives to Violence workshops in prisons, 2003—. Vis. scholar Inst. Behavioral Sci., U. Colo., Boulder, 1974-75; Mem. Consumer Task Force, White House Conf. on Food, Nutrition and Health, 1969; cons. Pres.'s Com. on Consumer Interests, Office Econ. Opportunity, Glick & Lorwin, John Wiley & Sons. Founding editor: Jour. Consumer Affairs, 1967-74. Trustee Am. Home Econs. Assn. Found.; chmn. bd. govs. Center for the Family. Served with USMCR, 1945-46. Mem. Am. Econ. Assn., Am. Family and Consumer Scis., Am. Agrl. Econ. Assn., Am. Assn. for Consumer Research, Am. Council on Consumer Interests (past pres.), Tau Kappa Epsilon, Phi Kappa Phi, Alpha Zeta, Gamma Sigma Delta, Omicron Nu., Soc. Friends. Home: 802 Robin Glen Indianola IA 50125-1080 E-mail: bivans@gbronline.com.

BIVENS, MITCHEL LEE, school system administrator, minister; s. Willie Fred and Elvira Bivens; m. Etta Faye Collier, Apr. 15, 1979; children: Devara Anita Richardson, Donovan Bernard, Charles Frederick, Anthony James, Ann Marie. AA, U. Md., 1990, B in Mgmt., 1994; M in Adminstrv. Supr. and Leadership, State U. West Ga., 2004. Police identification tech. Fulton County Police Dept., Atlanta, 1995—97; paraprofessional Birney Elem. Sch., Marietta, Ga., 1997—2000, tchr., 2000—04, adminstr. asst., 2004—. Bd. mem. Young Adult Guidance Ctr., Atlanta, 1997—2003. Rev. Crown of Life Bapt. Ch., Powder Springs, Ga., 2004. Served in U.S. Army, 1972—77, adminstrv. supr. 3d Infantry Divsn. U.S. Army, 1977—79, adminstrv. supr. 7th Adjutant Gen. Co. U.S. Army, 1979—80, adminstrv. supr. 7th Eng. Brigade U.S. Army, 1980—83, Germany, instr./adminstrv. supr. Tulane U. U.S. Army, 1983—87, drill sgt. 277th Quartermaster Battalion U.S. Army, 1987—89, detachment sgt. Hdqrs. and Hdqrs. Co. U.S. Army, 1989—92, Germany, first sgt. 369th Adjutant Co. U.S. Army, 1992—93. Mem.: ASCD, Profl. Assn. Ga. Educators (bldg. coord. 2000—05), Pi Lambda Theta. Baptist. Avocations: reading, gardening, travel, cooking, baking. Home: 2551 Hencley Cir Marietta GA 30008-5682 Office Phone: 678-842-6824.

BIX, HERBERT PHILIP, historian, educator; b. Boston, Sept. 21, 1938; s. James and Francis (Shapiro) B.; m. Toshie Watanabe, 1961; children: Mark, Deborah, Meriam. BA, U. Mass., Amherst, 1960; MA, Harvard U., 1968, PhD, 1972. With U. Mass., Boston, 1970-77, Hosei U., Tokyo, 1978-88; prof., grad. sch. social sci. Hitotsubashi U., Japan; prof., history, sociology SUNY, Binghamton, 1988—, and vice chair, dir., grad. studies; assoc. in rsch. E.O. Reischauer Inst. for Japanese Studies, Harvard U., Cambridge, Mass., 1992. Author: Peasant Protest in Japan 1590-1884, 1986, Hirohito and the Making of Modern Japan, 2000 (Pulitzer Prize in gen. nonfiction, 2001, Nat. Book Critics Circle award, 2001); translator: The Japanese Monarchy; contbr. articles to profl. jours., books and newspapers. Lt. (j.g.) USNR, 1962-64, Japan. Nat. Def. Fgn. Langs. fellow U.S. Govt., 1965-69, Fulbright-Hayes Postdoctoral fellow, 1977-78; recipient Rsch. Grant award U.S.-Japan Edn. Commn., 1992-93. Mem. Assn. Asian Studies, Hist. Sci. Soc. (Japan). Office: Divsn Rsch PO Box 6000 Binghamton NY 13902 Office Phone: 607-777-3417. Business E-Mail: hbix@binghamton.edu.*

BIXBY, FRANK LYMAN, lawyer; b. New Richmond, Wis., May 25, 1928; s. Frank H. and Esther (Otteson) B.; m. Katharine Spence, July 7, 1951; children— Paul, Thomas, Edward, Janet. AB, Harvard U., 1950; LLB, U. Wis., 1953. Bar: Ill. 1953, Wis. 1953, Fla. 1974. Ptnr. firm Sidley Austin Brown & Wood, Chgo., 1963—97, sr. counsel, 1998—. Editor-in-chief Wis. Law Rev, 1952-53; mem. editorial bd. Chgo. Reporter, 1973-89. Trustee MacMurray Coll., Jacksonville, Ill., 1973-85; bd. dirs. Chgo. Urban League, 1962—, v.p., 1972-86, gen. counsel, 1972—, chmn. 1986-89; bd. dirs. Community Renewal Soc., 1973-86, Voices for Ill. Children, 1987-90; chmn. trustees Unitarian Ch., Evanston, Ill., 1962-63; bd. dirs. Spencer Found., 1967-2001, chmn. 1975-90; mem. dist. 202 bd. edn. Evanston Twp. High Sch., 1975-81, pres., 1977-79. Recipient Man of Year award Chgo. Urban League, 1974 Mem. ABA, Ill. Bar Assn., Chgo. Bar Assn., Chgo. Coun. Lawyers, Chgo. Coun. Fgn. Rels., Order of Coif, Harvard Club (pres. 1964-65), Mid-Day Club., Phi Beta Kappa. Home: 505 N Lake Shore Dr Apt 4607 Chicago IL 60611-3409 Office: Sidley Austin Brown & Wood 10 S Dearborn St Chicago IL 60603-2000 Office Phone: 312-853-7429. Business E-Mail: fbixby@sidley.com. E-mail: kfbixby@yahoo.com.

BIXLER, JOHN MOURER, lawyer; b. Washington, Oct. 14, 1927; s. John S. and Elsie (Mourer) B.; m. Miriam Calhoun, Aug. 16, 1952; children: Allyson Sue Switzer, Stephen J., Mary Lynn Frye. BS, U. Pa., 1949; LLB, Harvard U., 1954. Bar: D.C. 1954, Md. 1960. Staff mem. Charles S. Rockey & Co. CPAs, Phila., 1949-51; assoc. Miller & Chevalier, Washington, 1954-61; mem. Miller & Chevalier, Chartered, Washington, 1962-98; ptnr. Ross, Marsh & Foster, Washington, 1998—. Lectr. local estate planning couns. Am. Law Inst. ABA, NYU Inst. Fed. Taxation. Trustee D.C. Legal Aid Soc., Washington, 1975-92, U. Pa., Phila., 1975-80; trustee Concord-St. Andrew's United Meth. Ch., Bethesda, Md., chair 1975-90, treas., 1990-2001, 2003—; v.p. Meth. Home of D.C., 1982—; trustee Miller and Chevalier Charitable Found., Washington, 1969—, pres., 1969-94. Recipient Joseph Wharton award Wharton Sch. Club of Washington, 1982. Fellow Am. Bar Found.; mem. ABA (tax sect. coun. 1979-82), The Met. Club of City of Washington, Lawyers Club, The Barristers, Am. Coll. Trust and Estate Counsel (regent 1987-94, D.C. state chmn. 1983-87, Washington rep. 1987-2002), Am. Coll. Tax Coun., Confrerie des Chevaliers du Tastevin (grand chambellan hon., commanderie d'Amerique, treas. sous-commanderie de Washington). Republican. Methodist. Avocations: gardening, travel. Home: 5304 Moorland Ln Bethesda MD 20814-1334 Office: Ross Marsh & Foster 2001 L St NW Ste 400 Washington DC 20036-4946 Business E-Mail: jbixler@rossmarshfoster.com.

BIZER, MARC, literature educator; b. Ann Arbor, Mich., Feb. 28, 1960; s. Lawrence Stanley and Linda Susan Bizer. BA Comparative Lit., Brown U., 1982; Maitrise de lettres modernes, U. Paris, Sorbonne, 1985, Licence de lettres modernes, 1983; PhD Romance Langs. & Lits., Princeton U., 1993. Instr. U. Tex., Austin, 1992—93; asst. prof. French U. Tex., Austin, 1993—2001, assoc. prof. French lit., 2001—. Author: (book) La Poesie au Miroir: imitation et conscience de soi dans la poesie latine de la Pleiade, 1995, Les Lettres romaines de Du Bellay: Les Regrets et la tradition epistolaire, 2001. Sabbatical Fellowship, Am. Philos. Soc., 2002—, Fulbright-Hayes Sr. Rsch. Fellowship, U.S. Info. Agy., 1996—97. Office: U Tex Dept French & Italian Austin TX 78712-1197 Business E-Mail: mbizer@mail.utexas.edu.

BIZIOU, PETER, cinematographer; Cinematographer: (films) Bugsy Malone, 1978, Monty Python's Life of Brian, 1979, Time Bandits, 1981, Pink Floyd-The Wall, 1982, Another Country, 1984 (Cannes award best artistic contbn.), 9 1/2 Weeks, 1986, A World Apart, 1988, Mississippi Burning, 1988 (Academy award best cinematography 1988, British Acad. award 1989, award British Soc. Cinematographers 1989), Rosencrantz and Guildenstern Are Dead, 1991, City of Joy, 1992, Damage, 1992, In the Name of the Father, 1993, Road to Wellville, 1994, Richard III, 1995, The Truman Show, 1998, Unfaithful, 2001, Ladies in Lavender, 2003, Festival Express, 2004, Derailed, 2005. Office Phone: 44 0207 437 2055.

BIZON, EMMA DJAFAR, management consultant; b. Atlanta, July 22, 1958; d. H. and Aminah Djafar; m. Lawrence Walter Bizon, May 24, 1994; 1 child, Rimagene. BSc in City & Regional Planning cum laude, Bandung Inst. Tech., Indonesia, 1985; MBA, Harvard U., 1994. Planner, Indonesia, 1983—86; asst. dir. Investment Bd., Indonesia; team leader Amre, Inc., Livonia, Mich., 1994—97; cons. to fast food restaurants Mich., 1997—98. Avocations: sports, music, cooking, writing. Home: 10909 Melbourne Ct Allen Park MI 48101

BIZUB, JOHANNA CATHERINE, law librarian; b. Denville, NJ, Apr. 13, 1957; d. Stephen Bernard and Elizabeth Mary (Grizzle) B.; m. Scott Jeffrey Smith, 1992. BS in Criminal Justice, U. Dayton, 1979; MLS, Rutgers U., 1984. Law libr. Morris County (NJ) Law Libr., 1981-83, Clapp & Eisenberg, Newark, 1984-86; dir. libr. Sills Cummis, 1986-94; libr. dir. Montville (NJ) Twp. Pub. Libr., 1994-97; libr. dir. law dept. Prudential Ins. Co. Am., Newark, 1997—. Mem. ALA, NJ Law Librs. Assn. (treas. 1987-89, v.p./pres.-elect 1989-90, 99-2000, pres. 1990-91, 2000-01, past pres. 1991-92, 2001-02), Am. Assn. Law Librs. (pvt. law librs. SIS, vice chair 1992-93, chair 1993-94, chair awards com. 1992-93, 2005—), NJ Libr. Assn., Assoc. Libr. of Morris County (v.p. 1995, pres. 1996, treas. 1997-2001), Spl. Libr. Assn. NJ (treas. 1990-92), Am. Legion Aux. (treas. Rockden unit 175 1983-93). Democrat. Roman Catholic. Home: 11 Elm St Rockaway NJ 07866-3108 Office: Prudential Ins Co Am 22 Plz 751 Broad St Newark NJ 07102-3714 Business E-Mail: jbizub@prudential.com.

BIZZELL YARBROUGH, CINDY LEE, school counselor; b. Griffin, Ga., June 20, 1951; d. William Emerson and Senora Elizabeth (Henderson) B.; m. Randy Yarbrough (dec. July 1999); m. Cary W. Martin, July 9, 2001; 1 child, Delana Michelle. Student, North Ga. Coll., 1969-70; BA in Elem. Edn., MS in Behavior Disorders, West Ga. Coll., 1993; MS in Learning Disabilities, MS in Counseling and Ednl. Psychology, 1993. K-12 reading, math., sci. and elem. edn. tchr. Pike County Schs., Zebulon, Ga., 1972—; tchr., counselor of emotionally disturbed Pike County Elem. Sch., 1973—; tchr. of emotionally disturbed and behavior disorders Pike County H.S., 1993—; crisis counselor McIntosh Trail Mental Health Mental Retardation, 1994; counselor Pike County Primary Sch., 1999, Morningstar Family Svcs., 2001. Owner, operator NAHRA Ctr., 1984-93; cons. Alcoholics Anonymous, Griffin, 1982—, Pike County Coun. on Child Abuse, 1990—; lectr., presenter in field. Author: Hippotherapy for the Emotionally Disturbed, 1988; contbr. articles to profl. publs. Leader, instr. Girl Scouts U.S., Meansville, Ga., 1969-90; co-coord. Ga. Spl. Olympics, Pike County, 1980—; pres. Internat. Reading Assn., Griffin, 1978; asst. leader 4H, 1992-93; substitute Sunday sch. tchr. local Meth. Ch. Recipient Sci. award Ford Found., 1966; named Res. Champion Open Jumper, Dixieland Show Cir., 1989. Mem. N.Am. Handicapped Riders Assn. (presenter), Profl. Assn. Ga. Educators. Democrat. Avocations: horseback riding, showing hunter jumpers. Home: 250 Silver Dollar Rd Barnesville GA 30204 Office: Pike County Schs Hwy 19 Zebulon GA 30295

BIZZI, EMILIO, neurophysiologist, educator; b. Rome, Feb. 22, 1933; arrived in U.S., 1963, naturalized, 1982; s. Vittorio and Anna (Galeazzi) Bizzi; m. Jane Stockton Shaw, Aug. 9, 1941. MD summa cum laude with highest honors, U. Rome, 1958. Postdoctoral trainee Inst. Med. Pathology, U. Siena, Italy, 1958-60; postdoctoral trainee Inst. Physiology, U. Pisa, Italy, 1960-63; rsch. assoc. neurophysiol. lab., dept. zoology Washington U., St. Louis, 1963-64; vis. assoc. sect. physiology, lab. clin. sci. NIMH, Bethesda, Md., 1964-66; rsch. assoc. dept. psychology MIT, Cambridge, 1966-67, lectr. dept. psychology, 1967-68, assoc. prof. neurophysiology, 1969-72, prof., 1972-80, Eugene McDermott prof. brain scis. and human behavior, 1980—2002, inst. prof., 2002—, dir. Whitaker Coll., 1983-88, chmn. dept. Brain and Cognitive Scis., 1986-97. Contbr. chapters to books, articles and abstracts to profl. jours.; mem. editl. bd.: Brain Theory Newsletter, 1980—, Jour. Motor Behavior, 1981—, Jour. Neurobiology, 1981—. Recipient Alden Spencer award, Columbia U. Coll. Physicians and Surgeons, 1978, Hermann von Hlmholtz award, 1992; fellow Found. Rsch. Psychiatry, 1978—. Mem.: NAS, Am. Acad. Clin. Neurophysiol., Acad. dei Lincei, Am. Acad. Arts and Scis., Internat. Brain Rsch. Orgn. Office: MIT Dept Brain & Cognitive Scis Cambridge MA 02139-4307

BJERKAAS, CARLTON LEE, information technology executive; b. Fergus Falls, Minn., Apr. 17, 1948; s. Jay Oscar and Anna Marie (Bangert) Bjerkaas; children: Kristopher Scott, Eric Stefan, Todd Philip. BS, U. N.D., 1970; MS, MIT, 1977; MPA, Auburn U., Montgomery, Ala., 1983. Commd. 2d lt. USAF, 1970, advanced through grades to col., 1992; forecaster Weather Detachment, Homestead AFB, Fla., 1971-73; flight examiner Weather Reconnaissance Squadron, Andersen AFB, 1973—75; radar rsch. meteorologist A.F. Geophysics Lab., Hanscom AFB, Mass., 1976-82; chief support br. operational requirements & testing Hdqrs. Mil. Airlift Command, Scott AFB, Ill., 1983-85; chief aerospace environ. requirements Hdqrs. A.F. Systems Command, Andrews AFB, Md., 1985-87; comdr. Weather Detachment, Lajes Field, Azores, Portugal, 1987-89; asst. chief of staff Hdqrs. Air Weather Svc., Scott AFB, 1989-91, dir. resource mgmt., 1991-92, dir. program mgmt., integration, 1992-94; dir. sys. and comm., 1994-95; dir. tech., plans and programs, 1995—; sr. scientist Hdqrs. Air Weather Svc., Scott AFB, Ill., 1995-96; divsn. mgr. Sci. Applications Internat. Corp., O'Fallon, Ill., 1996—2001, ops. mgr., 2001—05, v.p. ops., 2005—. Contbr. articles to profl. jours. Mem. Sch. Dist. Com., Lajes Field Azores, 1987; chmn. Sch. Bd., Lajes Field Azores, 1988—89; coach, referee youth sports, O'Fallon, 1989—; com. chmn. Boy Scouts Am., O'Fallon, 1991—92. Fellow: Am. Meteorol. Soc.; mem.: ASPA, AAAW, Air Lift and Tanker Assn., Air Weather Assn., Acad. Polit. Sci., N.Y. Acad. Scis., Rotary, Sigma Xi, Phi Beta Kappa, Pi Alpha Alpha, Phi Eta Sigma. Methodist. Avocations: computers, soccer coaching, boy scouts. Office: Science Applications Intl Corp 731 Lakepointe Centre Dr O Fallon IL 62269-3073

BJERREGAARD, PREBEN, cardiologist, educator; b. Hansted, Denmark, Feb. 6, 1942; arrived in U.S., 1989; s. Emil Robin and Karen Bjerregaard; m. Ria Skovholm Knudsen, June 4, 1965; children: Torsten, Dorte, Jens. MD, U. Aarhus, Denmark, 1969, DMSc, 1983. Diplomate in Cardiology Denmark, 1978. Cardiology fellow U. Okla., Oklahoma City, 1972—74; rsch. fellow U. Aarhus, Denmark, 1977—81, lectr., 1981—83, Aarhus Amtssygehus, Denmark, 1983—84; asst. prof., medicine Aarhus Kommune Hosp., Denmark, 1984—88; cons. cardiologist Ibn Al Bitar Hosp., Baghdad, Iraq, 1988—89; prof., medicine St. Louis U. Hosp., 1989—. Bd. mem. IRB, St. Louis U., 1990—2003. Author: Electrocardiographic Atlas, 1981; co-editor: Cardiac Repolarization, 2003. 2d lt. Denmark Navy, 1970—71, Frederikshavn, Denmark. Achievements include discovery of a new disease called Short QT-Syndrome in 1999. Avocations: jazz, boating, Iraq history. Home: 9242 Clayton Rd Saint Louis MO 63124 Office: Saint Louis Univ Hosp 3635 Vista at Grand Saint Louis MO 63110 Office Phone: 314-577-8895. Business E-Mail: bjerregp@slu.edu.

BJONTEGARD, ARTHUR MARTIN, JR., foundation executive; b. Lynn, Mass., Mar. 23, 1938; s. Arthur M. and Irma W. (Cook) B.; m. Wilma Joy Golding, Oct. 15, 1966; children— Arthur M., Karla Kristin BA, Duke U., 1959; JD, U. Va., 1962; postgrad., Stonier Grad. Sch. Banking, Rutgers U., 1966; grad. advanced mgmt. program, Harvard U. Sch. Bus., 1974. Bar: N.J. 1962, S.C. 1967. Bank examiner U.S. Treasury Dept., Richmond, Va., 1962-66; trust officer S.C. Nat. Bank, Columbia, 1966-74, sr. v.p., 1974-81; pres. S.C. Nat. Corp., Columbia, 1981-84, vice-chmn., 1984-92; pres. Ind. Colls. and Univs. of S.C. Inc., 1992—. Commr. Columbia Housing Authority, 1995—. Pres. United Way of the Midlands, Columbia, 1984-85, S.C., 1986-87, Univ. Assocs., Columbia, 1984-85, Friday Luncheon Club, Columbia, 1984, Spring Valley Ednl. Found., 1986—, Ctrl. Carolina Community Found., 1990-96; chmn. Columbia Community Resl. Coun., 1984, Fedn. of the Blind, 1992—. Named Vol. of Yr., Urban League, Columbia, 1984; recipient Order of Palmetto award, S.C. Gov., 1992. Mem. S.C. Bar Assn., Palmetto Soc., Thomas Jefferson Soc., S.C. C. of C., Forest Lake County Club, Palmetto Club, Spring Valley Country Club. Episcopalian. Avocations: tennis, swimming, sports. Office: Ind Colls and Univs of SC PO Box 12007 Columbia SC 29211-2007

BJORK, CHRISTOPHER BRIAN, education educator; b. Stanford, Calif., Dec. 19, 1962; s. Fredrik T. and Nancy C. Bjork; m. Etsuko Sekihara, Jan. 23, 1963; children: Kai Henry, Cory Sanae. BA, Wesleyan U., 1985, MA, 1986; PhD, Stanford U., 2000. Tchg. credential Calif. Tchr. Nishimachi Internat. Sch., Tokyo, 1991—95; rsch. asst. Carnegie Found. for the Advancement of Tchg., Menlo Park, Calif., 1998—2000; asst. prof. Colgate U., Hamilton, NY, 2000—02, Vassar Coll., Poughkeepsie, NY, 2002—. Vis. scholar U. of Tokyo, 2003. Editor: (book) Education and Training in Japan; contbr. articles to profl. jours. Recipient Postdoctoral fellowship, Japan Soc. for the Promotion of Sci., 2003, Rsch. fellowship, Nat. Security Edn. Program, 1997—98; scholar, The Fulbright Orgn., 1997—98. Mem.: Am. Ednl. Rschrs. Assn., Assn. for Asian Studies, Comparative and Internat. Edn. Soc. (awards com. 1997—2004). Office: Vassar Coll 124 Raymond Ave Poughkeepsie NY 12604 E-mail: chbjork@vassar.edu.

BJORK, GORDON CARL, economist, educator; b. Seattle, Dec. 15, 1935; s. Gordon E. and Florence E. (Bloomberg) B.; m. Susan Jill Serman, Dec. 29, 1960; children: Katharine, Rebecca, Susannah, Anders. AB, Dartmouth Coll., 1957; BA (hon.), Oxford U., 1959, MA, 1963; PhD, U. Wash., 1963. Lectr. econs. U. B.C., Vancouver, Can., 1962-63; asst. prof. econs. Carleton U., Ottawa, Ont., 1963-64; assoc. prof. econs. Columbia U., N.Y.C., 1964-68; pres. Linfield Coll., McMinnville, Oreg., 1968-74; prof. econs. Oreg. State U., Corvallis, 1974-75; Lovelace prof. econs. Claremont McKenna Coll., Claremont Grad. Sch., Calif., 1975—. Henry Walker disting. vis. prof. bus. enterprise U. Hawaii, 1985-86; vis. prof. econs. Nottingham (Eng.) U., 1990; mem. nat. adv. com. on environ. policy and tech. EPA. Author: Private Enterprise and Public Interest: The Development of American Capitalism, 1969, Life, Liberty and Property: The Economics and Politics of Land Use Planning and Environmental Control, 1980, Stagnation and Growth in the American Economy, 1985, The Way It Worked and Why It Won't: Structural Change and the Slowdown of U.S. Economic Growth, 1999. Lt. USCGR, 1960-68. Rhodes scholar, 1957; Battelle Inst. fellow, 1975 Mem. Phi Beta Kappa Republican. United Ch. of Christ. Home: 4609 Vista Buena Rd Santa Barbara CA 93110-1945 Office: Claremont McKenna Coll Dept Econs Claremont CA 91711 E-mail: gbjork@mckenna.edu. *An educator teaches by what he is and what he does. My objective, as a teacher, is to mold the values and conceptual framework of the next generation.*

BJÖRK, (BJÖRK GUDMUNDSDOTTIR), singer, composer; b. Reykjavik, Iceland, Nov. 21, 1965; d. Gudmundur and Hildur; m. Thor Eldon, 1986 (div. 1988); Sindri, Isadora. Rec. artist solo album at age 11; performer with several bands; formed theatrical/rock ensemble KUKL, 1980s; rec. artist with The Sugarcubes: (albums) Life's Too Good, 1986, Here Today, Tomorrow, Next Week, 1989; solo artist: (albums) Debut, 1993, Post, 1995, Telegram, 1997, Homogenic, 1997, Selmasongs: Dancer in the Dark, 2000, Vespertine, 2001, Family Tree, 2002, Greatest Hits, 2002, Medulla, 2004; actor: (films) Juniper Tree, 1990, Dancer in the Dark, 2000 (Best Actress, Cannes Film Festival). Office: Electra Records 75 Rockefeller Plz New York NY 10019-6908

BJORKHOLM, JOHN ERNST, retired physicist; b. Milw., Mar. 22, 1939; s. Jack W. and Marion B. (Anderson) Bjorkholm; m. Mary J. Durbin, June 20, 1964; children: Kristin E., Laura J. BSE in Engring. Physics highest honors, Princeton U., 1961; MS, Stanford U., 1962, PhD in Applied Physics, 1966. Mem. tech. staff Electronics Rsch. Lab. AT&T Bell Labs., Holmdel, NJ, 1966-83, disting. mem. tech. staff, 1983-94, cons. applied physics, 1994-96; prin. scientist Components Rsch., Intel Corp., Santa Clara, Calif., 1996—2002; ret., 2002. Contbr. articles to profl. jours. Chmn. Gordon Rsch. Conf. Nonlinear Optics and Lasers, 1977; comptr. Conf. Lasers and Electro-Optics, 1989—91; trustee Princeton U., 1991—95. NSF fellow, 1961—62, Howard Hughes fellow, 1962—65. Fellow: Optical Soc. Am. (dir.-at-large 1988—90, mem. fin. and investment com. 1988—91, mem. exec. com. 1990, treas. 1992—96), Am. Phys. Soc.; mem.: NRC (mem. com. atomic, molecular and optical sci. 1988—91), IEEE (sr.). Achievements include patents in field. Home: 408 Cabonia Ct Pleasanton CA 94566-5201

BJORNCRANTZ, LESLIE BENTON, librarian; b. Jersey City, Mar. 1, 1945; d. David and Jeanne (Proctor) Benton; m. Carl Eduard Bjorncrantz, Aug. 31, 1968; 1 child, William. BA, Wellesley Coll., 1967; MLS, Columbia U., 1968. Rsch. libr. Alderman Libr. U. Va., Charlottesville, 1968-70; reference libr. Northwestern U. Libr., Evanston, Ill., 1974-78, curriculum libr.,

1970—, edn. bibliographer, 1974—, psychology bibliographer, 1989—, core libr., 1989-97, mgmt. bibliographer, 1997—. Mem. libr. adv. bd. APA, 2004—. Co-editor: (book) Curriculum Material Center Collection Policy, 1984, Guide for the Development & Management of Test Collections, 1985. Bd. dir. Internat. Visitors Ctr., Chgo., 1973-76; class rep., fund raiser class of 1967, Wellesley (Mass.) Coll., 1987-92. Scholar, Wellesley Coll., 1967. Mem. ALA, APA (libr. adv. bd. 2004—), Assn. Coll. & Rsch. Librs. (sec. 1977-79, 85-87, chair curriculum materials com. 1984-85), Am. Bus. Libr. Dirs. Avocations: reading, travel, food and wine. Home: 2146 Forestview Rd Evanston IL 60201-2057 Office: Northwestern U Libr 1970 Campus Dr Evanston IL 60208-0821 Office Phone: 847-491-7602. E-mail: l-bjorncrantz@northwestern.edu.

BJORNSON, EDITH CAMERON, foundation administrator, communications consultant; b. Orlando, Fla., Sept. 12, 1937; d. Hilliard Francis and Edith Muriel (McBride) Cameron; m. Carroll N. Bjornson, Jan. 11, 1963; children: Lisa Carol, Karl Cameron (dec.). BA, U. Fla., Gainesville, 1953, MA, 1956; profl. cert., Ecole de Cuisine LaVerenne, Paris, 1983. Copywriter Sta. WGGG, Gainesville, Fla., 1953—54; exec. asst. Actors' Studio, N.Y.C., 1956—58; prodn. asst. Omnibus, N.Y.C., 1958—59; assoc. prodr. Robert Saudek Assocs., N.Y.C., 1958—60, ABC News Adlai Stevenson Reports, N.Y.C., 1960; asst. gen. mgr. Sta. WNDT-TV, N.Y.C., 1960—63; co-prodr. The Open Mind, N.Y.C., 1963—69; dir. local programming Telepromter, Inc., N.Y.C., 1979—80; corp. v.p. programming Westinghouse Broadcasting and Cable, N.Y.C., 1980—83; cons. Sta. WNYC-TV, N.Y.C., 1984—86; v.p., sr. program officer The Markle Found., N.Y.C., 1986—98. Working group Carter Commn. on Radio and TV, Atlanta, 1992—96; strategic planning bd. Conn. Pub. TV; chmn. N.Y. New Media Assn., N.Y.C., 2002; bd. dirs. Conn. Pub. TV and Radio, 1999—, bd. advisor to Culture Connect, 2003—; exec. dir. Fulfilling the Promise project on digital comm. Century Found. and Carnegie Corp., 1999—2001; sr. advisor, Morningside Ventures Columbia U., 1999—2001; project dir., website designer Fulfilling the Promise The Century Found. Carnegie Corp., 1999—2001; website editor Digital Promise Project, 2002—03; project dir., website designer The Open Mind Digital Archive Project, Columbia Tchrs. Coll., 2002—; sr. advisor Fathom.com Columbia U., 1999—2001; sr. advisor video oral history project Healthcare Chaplaincy, 2002—; dir. oral history project The Healthcare Chaplaincy, 2003—; prin. Recorded Oral Histories, LLC; sr. cons. Liberty Concepts LLC; cons. in field. Project advisor: (computer software) Voyager Co., 1993, SimHealth, 1994, (Internet software, multi-player online games) ReInventing America, 1995, President '96; contbr. articles to profl. jours. Vice chmn. bd. dirs. HealthCare Chaplaincy, N.Y.C., 1989-96; bd. dirs. Pro-Natura USA, N.Y.C., 1995-99; life trustee Health Care Chaplaincy, N.Y.C., 1997. Recipient Emmy award Acad. TV. Arts and Scis., 1960. Mem. Internat. Assn. Culinary Profls., Night Kitchen (computer software developers bd. dirs. 1996-98), Mortar Board, Delta Gamma. Republican. Avocation: cooking. Home: 34 E Lyon Farm Dr Greenwich CT 06831-4349 Office Phone: 212-481-3949.

BJORNSRUD, MARLENE, professional athletics manager; Tennis coach Grand Canyon U., Phoenix, 1979, asst. athletic dir., sr. women's adminstr.; dir. of athletics Santa Clara U.; gen. mgr. San Jose Cyber Rays Women's United Soccer Assn., San Jose, Calif. Founder Bay Area Women's Sports Initiative, San Jose, Calif., 2005—. Recipient Nat. Coach of Yr., NAIA, 1981.

BLACHER, RICHARD STANLEY, psychiatrist; b. N.Y.C., May 24, 1924; s. Charles and Bernardine (Zolotorofe) B.; m. Sara-Lee Rudolph, July 4, 1960 (dec. 1970); 1 child, Lisa; m. Marjory May Popky, Oct. 27, 1985. BA, Brown U., 1945; MD, U. Rochester, 1948; cert. in psychoanalysis, N.Y. Psychoanalytic Inst., 1963. Diplomate Am. Bd. Psychiatry and Neurology. Clin. asst. attending psychiatrist Mt. Sinai Hosp., N.Y.C., 1955-66, assoc. attending psychiatrist, 1966-74; assoc. clin. prof. Mt. Sinai Sch. Medicine, N.Y.C., 1967-74; clin. prof. Tufts U. Sch. Medicine, Boston, 1974-85, prof. psychiatry, 1985—, lectr. in surgery, 1977—. Psychiatry lectr. Boston U. Sch. Medicine, 1995—; bd. dirs. Internat. Consortium for Study of Neurol. and Psychol. Reactions to Cardiac Surgery, 1980—. Editor: The Psychological Experience of Surgery, 1987; editl. bd. Found. of Thanatology, N.Y.C., 1988—, Wiley Series in Psychiatry, N.Y.C., 1987—; contbr. over 50 articles to profl. jours. Pres. Tenafly (N.J.) Nature Ctr. Assn., 1972; mem. steering com. Greater Boston Physicians for Social Responsibility, Cambridge, Mass., 1983-92; trustee Boston Civic Symphony Orch., 1993—. Fellow Am. Psychiat. Assn. (life); mem. Am. Psychoanalytic Assn., Internat. Psychoanalytic Assn., Am. Psychosomatic Soc., Am. Coll. Psychoanalysts, N.Y. Psychoanalytic Soc., Boston Psychoanalytic Soc. Avocations: birding, natural history. Home and Office: 50 Plainfield St Newton MA 02468-1618 Office Phone: 617-965-2399. E-mail: RBLACHER@MASSMED.ORG.

BLACHLY, BEVERLY JEAN (BJ), retired vocational and insurance consultant; b. Portland, Oreg., Oct. 6, 1933; d. Arnold G. and Verna A. (Wilkenson) Manson; m. Paul H. Blachly, Oct. 16, 1956 (dec. July 1977); children: Kathryn, Cynthia, Brian, David, Jefery. Diploma in Nursing, Emanuel Hosp., Portland, 1954; Pub.Health Cert., Simmons Coll., 1960; BSN, Tex. Christian U., Ft. Worth, 1961; MS, U. Oreg., 1967; degree in parnish nursing, Concordia Coll., 2001. RN, Oreg.; CCM, Parish Nurse. Pediatric head nurse, maternal asst. USPHS, Ft. DeFiance, Ariz., 1955-56; rsch. asst. cardiovascular divsn. U. Oreg. Med. Sch. Hosps. and Clinics, Portland, 1962-65; pub. health nurse maternal-child care project Oreg. State Bd. Health, 1964-65; rsch. asst. dept. psychiatry U. Oreg. Med. Sch. Hosps. and Clinics, Portland, 1965-77; sr. nurse coord. Intracorp, Portland, 1977-95; Cigna dedicated supr. Intracorp/Cigna, Portland, 1991-95; ret., 1997; pvt. practice rehab. cons. Portland, 1997—2000; camp nurse Multnomah County Outdoor Sch. Program, 2001—03; asst. dir. nursing svc. Sr. Retirement Facility, 2002—03; ret., 2004. Part-time contract RN Oreg. Dept. Human Svcs., 2004—05; pvt. duty home care, 2005—. Patentee in field; contbr. articles to profl. jours. Recipient Achievement award N.W. Specialist award Intracorp, 1982-83, Recognition Disting. Med.-Vocat. Svc. Rehab., Nat. Disting. Svc. Registry, 1987. Mem. Assn. Rehab. Nurses (past pres., ednl. com. and program chair, legis. com.), Holistic Nursing Assn., City Club. Avocations: hiking, sewing, reading. Home: 3348 NW Skyline Blvd Portland OR 97229-3817

BLACHLY, JACK LEE, lawyer; b. Dallas, Mar. 8, 1942; s. Emery Lee and Thelma Jo (Budd) B.; m. Lucy Largent Rain, Jan. 15, 1972; 1 son, Michael Talbot. BBA, So. Meth. U., 1965, JD, 1968. Bar: Tex. 1968, U.S. Ct. Appeals (5th cir.) 1969, U.S. Supreme Ct. 1975, U.S. Tax Ct. 1977. Trust officer First Nat. Bank in Dallas, 1968-70; ptnr. firm Reese & Blachly, Dallas, 1970-71; assoc. firm Rain Harrell Emery Young & Doke, Dallas, 1971-76; staff atty. Sabine Corp., Dallas, 1976-77, mgr. legal dept., 1977-80, v.p., gen. counsel, 1980-89; asst. gen. counsel Pacific Enterprises Oil Co. USA (merger Sabine Corp. and Pacific Enterprise Oil Co. USA), Dallas, 1989-90; pvt. practice Dallas, 1990—. Mem.: Dallas Bar Assn., Tex. Bar Assn., Dallas Gun Club. Baptist. Office: 4409 Benton Elm Dr Plano TX 75024

BLACK, ALLEN DECATUR, lawyer; b. Pitts., July 27, 1942; s. Gerald Richard and Amy Elizabeth (Haymaker) B. AB, Princeton U., 1963; LLB magna cum laude, U. Pa., 1966. Bar: D.C. 1967, Pa. 1971, U.S. Supreme Ct. 1975. Law clk. to Hon. John Minor Wisdom, New Orleans, 1966-67; trial atty. Dept. Justice, 1967-68; asst. prof. law U. N.D., Grand Forks, 1971; practice comml. and antitrust litigation law Fine, Kaplan & Black, Phila., 1975—. Lectr. in law Rutgers U., 1972-77, Temple U., 1978, U. Pa., 1985. Chmn. Bucks County Airport Authority, 1999—. Served with JAGC USN, 1968-71. Fellow Am. Coll. Trial Lawyers; mem. Am. Law Inst. (2d v.p. 2004—), Pa. Bar Assn., Phila. Bar Assn. Republican. Episcopalian. Office: 1835 Market St Philadelphia PA 19103

BLACK, BARBARA ANN, publisher; b. Eureka, Calif., Dec. 11, 1928; d. William Marion and Letitia (Brunia) Black; m. Vinson Brown, June 18, 1950 (dec Dec. 1991); children: Tamara Pinn, Roxana Hodges, Keven Brown. BA, Western State Coll., Gunnison, Colo., 1950. Cert. tchr., Colo. Editor/proofreader Naturegraph Pubs., Los Altos, Calif., 1950-53, co-owner, mgr. San Martin, Calif., 1953-60, Healdsburg, Calif., 1960-76, owner/mgr. Happy Camp, Calif., 1976—. Author: Barns of Yesteryear, 1993; co-author: Sierra Nevada Wildlife, 1996, The Californian Wildlife Region, 1999; pub. over 100 titles on natural history and Native American subjects. Mem. Am. Booksellers Assn. Baha'i Faith. Avocations: gardening, backpacking, animal training. Home: PO Box 1045 3633 Indian Creek Rd Happy Camp CA 96039-9706 Office: Naturegraph Publishers Inc 3543 Indian Creek Rd Happy Camp CA 96039-9706 Office Phone: 800-390-5353, 530-493-5353.

BLACK, BARBARA ARONSTEIN, legal history educator; b. Bklyn., May 6, 1933; d. Robert and Minnie (Polenberg) A.; m. Charles L. Black, Jr., Apr. 11, 1954; children— Gavin B., David A., Robin E. BA, Bklyn. Coll., 1953; LLB, Columbia U., 1955; MPhil, Yale U., 1970, PhD, 1975; LLD (hon.), N.Y. Law Sch., 1986, Marymount Manhattan Coll., 1986, Vt. Law Sch., 1987, Coll. of New Rochelle, 1987, Smith Coll., 1988, Bklyn. Coll., 1988, York U., Toronto, Can., 1990, Georgetown U., 1991. Assoc. in law Columbia U. Law Sch., NYC, 1955-56; lectr. history Yale U., New Haven, 1974-76, asst. prof. history, 1976-79, assoc. prof. law, 1979-84; George Welwood Murray prof. legal history Columbia U. Law Sch., NYC, 1984—, dean faculty of law, 1986-91. Editor Columbia Law Rev., 1953-55. Active N.Y. State Ethics Commn., 1992-95. Recipient Fed. Bar Assn. prize Columbia Law Sch., 1955 Mem. Am. Soc. Legal History (pres. 1986-90), Am. Acad. Arts and Scis., Am. Philos. Soc., Mass. Hist. Soc., Supreme Ct. Hist. Soc., Selden Soc., Century Assn. Office: Columbia U Sch Law 435 W 116th St New York NY 10027-7201 Office Phone: 212-854-5735. Business E-Mail: BAB@law.columbia.edu.

BLACK, BOYD CARSON, small business owner; b. Spencer, Nebr., Mar. 31, 1926; s. Royal Mitchel and Gladys Emma (Carlson) B.; m. Margaret Ann Prchal, June 26, 1948; children: Barton, Cheryl, Brian, Roger, Eric. Student, Wayne State Coll. Boiler maker various firms, 1947-56; owner, operator Blacco Splicing and Rigging Loft, Newark, Ohio, 1956—. Seminar instr. Am. Recreational Equipment, Greenville, N.C., 1979-88; tng. insp. Ohio State Agrl. Insps., Columbus, 1980-82; instr. safety seminars on lift equipment, Ohio, 1980—. Patentee in field. Mem. Heath City (Ohio) Charter Commn., 1963-64; chmn. Heath Zoning Bd. Appeals, 1963-98; del. Ohio Leadership Initiative, Yugoslavia, USSR, Poland, Hungary, 1990. With USN, 1943-46, PTO. Named Small Bus. Person of Yr., 1985. Mem. Am. Subcontractors Assn., Newark C. of C., Moundbuilders Babe Ruth Assn. (bd. dirs.), Am. Legion, Masons, USN Armed Guard Vets. Methodist. Avocations: fishing, camping, antique collecting, history. Home: 140 Claren Dr Newark OH 43056-1276

BLACK, BRUCE D., judge; b. Detroit, July 27, 1947; BA, Albion Coll., 1969; JD, U. Mich., 1971. Pvt. law practice, N.Mex., 1972—91; judge N.Mex. Ct. Appeals, 1991-96, US Dist. Ct. N.Mex., 1996—. Office: US Dist Ct New Mexico 333 Lomas Blvd NW Albuquerque NM 87102-2272 Office Phone: 505-348-2260. Office Fax: 505-348-2265.

BLACK, CAROLE, broadcast executive; b. Cin. BA in English lit., Ohio State U. With Procter & Gamble, Cin.; account supr., sr. v.p., mgmt. rep. DDB Needham, Chgo., 1983—86; v.p. worldwide mktg. home video Walt Disney Co., 1986—88, sr. v.p. mktg., TV, 1988—94; pres., gen. mgr. NBC 4, L.A., 1994—99; pres., CEO Lifetime Entertainment Svcs., 1999—. Named one of 100 Most Powerful Women in Entertainment, Hollywood Reporter, 2004; recipient CTAM Hall of Fame Award, 2000, Nat. Breast Cancer Coalition Leadership Award, 2000, Muse Award, NY Women in Film & Television, 2000, Impact Award, Nat. Hispanic Media Coalition, 2001, Women Who Change the World Award, NY Women in Communications, 2002, Matrix Award, 2002. Office: Lifetime Entertainment Svcs 309 W 49th St New York NY 10019-7404*

BLACK, CAROLYN REBECCA, music educator; b. Fayetteville, N.Y., May 6, 1945; d. Henry Andrew Black Sr. and Madeline Jackson Black; m. Arthur Jerome Hightower Sr., Dec. 28, 2002; m. Thomas Benjamin Berrien (div.); children: Dawn Berrien, Jenelle Berrien, Todd Berrien. MusB, U. N.C., 1968; MA, Columbia U., 1976. Music tchr. Mt. Vernon (N.Y.) Pub. Sch., 1968—75; choral music tchr. Ossining (N.Y.) H.S., 1975—2002. Choral dir., organist St. Matthews United Meth. Ch., Ossining, 1977—85, St. Paul's on the Hill Episcopal Ch., Ossining, 1989—, NY Acad. of Tchg. and Learning, 1997. Bd. dirs. Ossining Children's Ctr., Ossining, 2004—. Named Tchr. of Yr., Ossining Parents, Tchrs. and Students, 1991, Nat. Honor Soc., Astra chpt., 1996. Mem.: N.Y. State Sch. Music Assn. (h.s. music chair 2002—), N.Y. State Tchrs. Theatre Edn. Assn. (nomination chair), Music Educators Nat. Conf. Episcopalian. Avocations: gardening, reading. Home: M9 Kissam Rd Peekskill NY 10566

BLACK, CATHLEEN PRUNTY, publishing executive; b. Chgo., Apr. 26, 1944; d. James Hamilton and Margaret (Harrington) Black; m. Thomas E. Harvey; children: Alison, Duffy. BA, Trinity Coll., 1966. Advt. sales rep. Holiday mag., N.Y.C., 1966-69, Travel & Leisure mag., N.Y.C., 1969-70, New York mag., 1970-72; advt. dir. Ms. mag., 1972-75, assoc. pub., 1975-77, New York mag., 1977-79, pub., 1979-83; pres. USA Today, 1983, pub., 1984-91; exec. v.p. mktg. Gannett Co., Inc., 1985—91, also bd. dirs.; pres., CEO Newspaper Assn. Am., Reston, Va., 1992-95; pres. Hearst Mags., N.Y.C., NY, 1996—. Bd. dirs. iVillage, Coca-Cola Co., 1990—91, 1993—, IBM, 1995—. Trustee U. Notre Dame. Named Pub. Exec. of Yr., Advt. Age, 2000; named one of Most Powerful Women in Am. Bus., Fortune mag., 100 Most Influential Bus. Leaders, Crain's N.Y. Bus., 2002, 100 Most Powerful Women in World, Forbes mag., 2005; recipient Muriel Fox Award for Comm. Leadership Toward a Just Soc., NOW, 2000, Stephen P. Duggan Award, Inst. Internat. Edn., 2002. Mem.: Coun. on Fgn. Rels., Advt. Coun. (bd. mem.). Office: Hearst Mags 959 8th Ave New York NY 10019-3795*

BLACK, CLANTON CANDLER, JR., biochemistry professor, researcher; b. Tampa, Fla., Nov. 27, 1931; s. Clanton Candler Black and Cora (Winfred) Eady B.; m. Betty Louise Dantzler, Apr. 10, 1952; children— Marjorie Kay, Clanton Candler III, Julia Renee BSA., U. Fla., 1953, MSA., 1957, PhD, 1960. NIH postdoctoral fellow Cornell U., Ithaca, N.Y., 1960-62; C. F. Kettering Found. fellow Kettering Research Lab., Antioch Coll., Yellow Springs, Ohio, 1962-63, staff scientist, asst. prof., 1963-67; prof. biochemistry U. Ga., Athens, 1967—, disting. rsch. prof. biochemistry/molecular biology, 1982—. Fulbright-Hays scholar to USSR, 1976; cons. plant biochemistry, physiology Internat. Atomic Energy Agy. Nat. Agr. U., Lima, Peru, 1981—. Editor: CO2 Metabolism and Plant Productivity, 1976, Net Carbon Dioxide Assimilation in Higher Plants, 1972, Handbook of Biosolar Resources, Vol. IA, IB, 1982. Served to cpl. U.S. Army, 1953-55 Recipient Merit award Bot. Soc. Am., 1981, Alex Laurie award Am. Soc. Hort. Sci., 1984; Fulbright scholar, 1976, 98-99. Fellow AAAS; mem. Am. Soc. Plant Physiology (sec.-treas., v.p., pres. 1975-79), Am. Soc. Biol. Chemists, Russian Soc. Plant Physiology (hon.), Sigma Xi, Phi Kappa Phi, Phi Sigma, Gamma Sigma Delta. Baptist. Office: U Ga Dept Biochem and Molecular Bio Life Scis Bldg Athens GA 30602 Office Phone: 706-542-1334. Business E-Mail: ccblack@bmb.uga.edu.

BLACK, CLIFFORD MERWYN, academic administrator, sociologist, educator; b. Lafayette, Ohio, Mar. 6, 1942; s. Richard Allen and Ivaloo Mae (Mosher) B.; m. Angelica Hernandez; children: Jonathan Andrew, Marisela, Jose Angel, Carlos Alberto. BA, Adrian Coll., 1963; MDiv, Meth. Theol. Sch., 1966; PhD, Northwestern U., 1972. Cert. clin. sociologist; lic. profl. counselor. Asst. prof. Wilberforce (Ohio) U., 1973-74, The Ohio State U., Mansfield, 1974-78; instr. U. North Tex., Denton, 1978-79, asst. prof., 1979-83, sociology program dir., 1982-83, assoc. prof., 1983-89, chair Ctr. for Pub. Svc., 1984-86, chair dept. sociology, 1986-87, assoc. dean Sch. Cmty. Svc., 1986-88, 91-92, acting dean Sch. Cmty. Svc., 1988-90, prof., 1989-92, Tex. A&M Internat. U., Laredo, 1989-92, dean Sch. Edn. and Arts and Scis., 1992-94, dean Coll. of Arts and Humanities, 1994-96, 96-2001, Webb Co. Tex. Planning Coun., 1996-2001, Webb Co. Tex. Drug Planning Com., 1996-2001, Webb Co. Tex. Jail Case Mgmt. Supervision, 1998-2001, Webb Co. Drug Ct. Supervising Com., 1998-2001; prin. investigator US Dept. Justice/Webb Co. Tex., Laredo, Tex., 1996—2001, 3d Party Payment Com.; adminstrv. cons. Webb County Sheriff's Dept., 2005—; dir. Internat. Justice Ctr., 1996—2002; pres. CJUS Rsch. and Program Cons. Internat. Inc., 2002—; adminstrv. coord. Webb County Sheriff's Dept., 2005—. Cons. Denton County Sheriff's Dept., Denton, 1984-89; mem. state coordinating bd. com. on Two Yr. Coll. Curriculum, 1986-89. Author: (book) Alternative Sentencing: Electronically Monitored Correction Supervision, 1992; contbg. editor for Clin. Sociology Newsletter, 1983-84; mem. editorial bd. Sociol. Practice, 1984-89; contbr. numerous articles to profl. jours. Pres. Sam Houston Elem. PTA, Denton, 1985-86; trustee Denton Ind. Sch. Dist., 1986-89; mem. United Way Bd., Laredo, 1994-95; active St. Martin de Porres Cath. Ch. Recipient U.S. Dept. Justice award for Rsch. Prgms. for Elimination of Illegal Drugs. Mem. Nat. Clin. Sociology Assn. (v.p. 1984-86, certification bd. mem. 1984-90, nat. certifier 1985-92, nat. program chair for ann. meeting 1984-85), Clin. Sociology Assn. Tex. (pres. 1982-84), Nat. Sociol. Practice Assn. (exec. bd. 1990-91), Nat. Sociol. Practice Assn. (certification bd. 1990-91), Am. Sociol. Assn. (sect bd. 1981-84, sociol. practice sect. sec./treas. 1981-84), Southwestern Sociol. Assn. (chair com. on professions 1983-86), Am. Criminology Soc., Acad. Criminal Justice Scis. Avocations: field archaeology, walking, reading, writing, drawing. Home and Office: 8506 Callow Ct Laredo TX 78045-1983

BLACK, COBEY, journalist; b. Washington, June 15; d. Elwood Alexander and Margaret (Beall) Cobey; m. Edwin F. Black; children: Star, Christopher, Noel, Nicholas, Brian, Bruce. BA, Wellesley Coll., 1944; postgrad., U. Hawaii. Exec. sec. to Irene, designer Metro-Goldwyn-Mayer, 1944; actress Fed. Republic Germany, 1945-46; women's editor Washington Daily News, 1947-50; columnist Honolulu Star Bull., 1954-65, Honolulu Advertiser, 1969-85. Cons. HEW, Peace Corps; bd. dirs. Pacific and Asian Affairs Coun., Honolulu Com. on Fgn. Rels., Soc. Asian Art of Hawaii, Honolulu Media Coun.; pres. Black & Black, Inc. Author: Birth of A Princess, 1962, Iolani Luahine, 1986, Hawaii Scandal, 2002; travel editor Bangkok World, 1968-69; publicist CBS-TV series Hawaii Five-O, 1978. Mem. Hawaii State Commn. on Status of Women, 1978-86. Mem. Nat. Press Club, Nat. Soc. Colonial Dames, Lady of Dumbarton, Royal Bangkok Sports Club, Outrigger Canoe Club, Waialae Country Club, Garden Club of Honolulu. Democrat. Episcopalian. Office: Black & Black Inc 3081 La Pietra Cir Honolulu HI 96815-4736

BLACK, COFER (J. COFER BLACK), former federal official; b. Stamford, Conn. BA in Internat. Relations, MA in Internat. Relations, U. So. Calif. With CIA, 1974—2002, task force chief near East, South Asia divsn., 1995, deputy chief Latin Am. divsn., 1998—99, dir. Counterterrorist Ctr., 1999—2001; coord. US Off. Counterterrorism US Dept. State, Washington, 2002—04; vice chmn. Blackwater USA, Moyock, NC, 2005—. Recipient Distinguished Intelligence medal, George H. Bush medal for excellence, Exceptional Collector award, 1994. Office: Blackwater USA PO Box 1029 Moyock NC 27958

BLACK, LORD CONRAD MOFFAT, former publishing corporate executive; b. Montreal, Aug. 25, 1944; s. George Montegu and Jean Elizabeth (Riley) B.; m. Barbara J.E. Amiel. BA, Carleton U., 1965; LLL, Laval U., 1970; MA in History, McGill U., 1973; LLD (hon.), St. Francis Xavier U., 1979, McMaster U., 1979; LittD (hon.), U. Windsor, 1979; LLD (hon.), Carleton U., 1989. Chmn., co-owner Ea. Twps. Pub. Co., Ltd., Knowlton, Que., 1966—; pres., chmn. exec. com. Argus Corp. Ltd., 1978-79, chmn. bd., chmn. exec. com. Toronto, 1979—, CEO, 1985; chmn. The Ravelston Corp. Ltd., 1978, Hollinger, Inc., 1985, CEO, 1987; chmn., CEO Telegraph Group Ltd., 1987—2004; chmn. Hollinger Internat. Inc., 1987—2003, non-exec. chmn., 2003—04. Chmn. bd. Nat. Interest, Washington, Coun. Fgn. Rels. Author: Duplessis, 1977, reprinted as Render Unto Caesar, 1998, A Life in Progress, 1993, Franklin Delano Roosevelt: Champion of Freedom, 2003. Patron Malcolm Muggeridge Foun. Decorated officer Order of Can.; apptd. to Privy Coun. of Can., 1992, House of Lords, U.K., 2001. Mem. Hudson Inst., Ctr. Policy Studies (U.K.), Trilateral Commn. (UK), Americas Soc. (chmn.'s coun.), Internat. Inst. for Strategic Studies, Toronto Club, York Club, Toronto Golf Club, Granite Club, Univ. Club (Montreal), Mt. Royal Club (Montreal), Century Club (NYC), Everglades Club, Beach Club (Palm Beach), Athenaeum, Beefsteak, Whites (London), Garrick (London). Office: Hollinger Inc 10 Toronto St Toronto ON Canada M5C 2B7 also: Telegraph Group Ltd Canary Wharf, 1 Canada Sq London E14 5DT England also: Hollinger Internat 712 5th Ave New York NY 10019-4108

BLACK, CREED C., JR., lawyer; b. Nashville, Mar. 2, 1951; BA magna cum laude, Yale U., 1973; JD cum laude, U. Pa., 1976. Bar: Pa. 1976, U.S. Supreme Ct. 1989. Law clk. to Hon. Herbert A. Fogel U.S. Dist. Ct. (ea. dist.) Pa., 1976-77; trial atty. criminal divsn. U.S. Dept. Justice, Washington, 1977-78; spl. asst. to U.S. atty. ea. dist. Va., 1978; mem. organized crime and racketeering sect. Cleve. Strike Force, 1978-80, Phila. Strike Force, 1980-82; atty. Ballard Spahr Andrews & Ingersoll, Phila., 1982-96; pvt. practice Phila., 1996—. Mem. ABA, Fed. Bar Assn., Phila. Bar Assn., Nat. Assn. Criminal Def. Lawyers, Order of Coif. Office: 1700 Market St Ste 2632 Philadelphia PA 19103-3903 Office Phone: 215-564-4060. E-mail: ccb@creedblack.com.

BLACK, CREED CARTER, newspaper executive; b. Harlan, Ky., July 15, 1925; s. Creed Carter and Mary (Cole) B.; m. Mary C. Davis, Dec. 28, 1947 (div. 1976); children: Creed Carter, Steven D., Douglas S.; m. Elsa Goss, Dec. 9, 1977; 1 child, Michelle. BS with highest distinction and honors in Polit. Sci., Northwestern U., 1949; MA, U. Chgo., 1952; LLD (hon.), Davidson Coll., 1991; LHD (hon.), Ctr. Coll., 1996. Reporter Paducah (Ky.) Sun-Democrat, 1942-43, 46; editor Daily Northwestern, 1947; copy editor Chgo. Sun-Times, 1949, Chgo. Herald-Am., 1950; editl. writer Nashville Tennessean, 1950-57, exec. editor, 1957-59; v.p., exec. editor Savannah (Ga.) Morning News and Savannah Evening Press, 1959-60, Wilmington (Del.) Morning News and Evening Jour., 1960-64; mng. editor Chgo. Daily News, 1964-68, exec. editor, 1968-69; asst. sec. for legislation HEW, 1969-70; editor Phila. Inquirer, 1970-77; chmn., pub. Lexington (Ky.) Herald-Leader, 1977-88; pres., trustee Knight Found., Miami, Fla., 1988-98. With 100th Inf. divsn. AUS, WWII, ETO. Decorated Bronze Star; recipient Northwestern U. Alumni medal, 1973 Mem. Newspaper Assn. of Am., So. Newspaper Pubs. Assn. (pres. 1987—), Am. Soc. Newspaper Editors (pres. 1983), Nat. Conf. Editl. Writers (pres. 1962), Riviera Country Club, Kappa Tau Alpha, Lambda Chi Alpha. Methodist. Home: 11044 SW 77th Court Cir Miami FL 33156-3766

BLACK, DAVID, writer, educator; b. Boston, Apr. 21, 1945; s. Henry Arnold and Zelda Edith (Hodosh) B.; m. Deborah Hughes Keehn, June 22, 1968 (div. 1994); children: Susannah Haden, Tobiah Samuel McKee; m. Barbara Weisberg, June 20, 1996. BA cum laude, Amherst Coll., 1967; MFA, Columbia U., 1971. Free-lance writer, 1971—; writer-in-residence Mt. Holyoke Coll., South Hadley, Mass., 1982-86. Scholar-in-residence Kirkland House Mt. Holyoke Coll., Harvard U.; guest lectr. Tisch Sch. of the Arts. Author: Like Father, 1978 (Notable Book of Yr. N.Y. Times, 1978, One of 7 Best Novels of Yr. Washington Post), Minds, 1982, Peep Show, 1986, An Impossible Life, 1998; (non-fiction) Ekstasy, 1975, The King of Fifth Avenue (Notable Book of Yr. N.Y. Times AP, N.Y. Mag. 1981), Murder at the Met, 1984, Medicine Man, 1985, The Plague Years, 1986 (Nat. Mag. award reporting, Nat. Assn. Sci. Writers award); (play) An Impossible Life, 1998; (screenplay) The Confession, 1999 (Winner Writers Guild Best TV Movie of Yr., Adaptation 1999), (teleplay) Final Jeopardy; contbr. articles and stories to Harper's, The Atlantic, N.Y. Times Mag., others; story editor Hill Street Blues; prodr. Miami Vice; supervising prodr. H.E.L.P., Gidgon Oliver, Law and Order (Golden Globe nominee 1992, Edgar nominee 1992, 99, Emmy nominee 1992, 98, ABA Certificate of Merit 1998); co-creator, supervising prodr.: The Nasty Boys; co-creator, exec. prodr.: Under Fire, The Good Policeman, The Cosby Mysteries, co-exec. prodr.: Sidney Lumet's 100 Centre Street, 1999-2002; exec. prodr.: CSI-Miami, 2003; creator, exec. prodr. Copshop, 2004, Kojak, 2005, Law and Order Trial by Jury, 2005; cons. prodr. Richard Dreyfuss, The Education of Max Bickford, 2002, Monk, 2002; contbg. editor Rolling Stone, 1986-89. Recipient Atlantic Firsts award Atlantic Monthly, 1973, Playboy's Best Article of Yr. award Playboy Mag.,

1979, Nat. Assn. Sci. Writers award, 1985, hon. mention for Best Essay of Yr., 1986, Giorgi award, Cert. Merit for excellence in writing, 1998; grantee Nat. Endowment Arts, 1979. Mem. SAG, Mystery Writers Am. (former bd. dirs.), PEN, Internat. Assn. Mystery Writers, Authors Guild, Writers Guild East, Williams Club, Century Assn., Players, Explorer's Club, Columbia Club. Jewish/Unitarian.

BLACK, DAVID LUTHER, writer, consultant; b. Plainview, Tex., Apr. 3, 1934; s. Mac Truman and Wilman (Bailey) B.; m. Gloria Loyola, Mar. 31, 1984; 1 son by previous marriage, David Roger. AB, Baylor U., 1954; postgrad., U. Tex.-Austin, 1959-80. With S.W. Rsch. Inst., San Antonio; asst. to pres., dir. spl. programs, chief of party U.S. Agy. for Devel. Projects in Low Cost Housing Irrigation, Tanzania, Botswana, Colombia, 1980-84; dep. dir. regional program for sci. and tech. devel. OAS, Washington, 1984-87, advisor to sec. gen. for external affairs, 1987-96; chief of mission, U.S. rep. Interam. Inst. Cooperation on Agr., 1987-96; sr. rsch. fellow Coun. on Hemispheric Affairs, Washington, 1996—. Cons. to UNIDO, UNESCO, UNEP; advisor to Univ. in Chile Obtaining Projects with USAID Nat. Rsch. Coun., 1992—. Contbr. articles to profl. jours. on sci., Latin Am. affairs and culture. Extensive devel. experience in Latin Am., Africa, Caribbean; pres. OAS Fed. Staff Credit Union, 1989-92, v.p. 1992-96; pres. San Antonio Chamber Music Soc., 1973-76; active Cmty. Guidance Ctr. Recipient Centennial award for sci. and tech. ASME, 1980. Mem. Am. Soc. Metals (chmn. Latin Am. divsn. 1974-84), U.S. Assn. UN (bd. dirs.), Soc. Internat. Devel., U.S. Club of Rome, Nat. Press Club. Home: 3595 Poinciana Ave Coconut Grove FL 33133-6526 E-mail: davidb4799@aol.com.

BLACK, DAVID WAYNE, lawyer; b. Tulsa, May 2, 1962; s. Lenial F. and Saundra Kay (Crutchfield) B. BBA, Baylor U., 1984, JD, 1986. Bar: Tex. 1986, D.C. 1987. Dir. Geary, Porter & West, Dallas, 1986—95; exec. v.p., gen. counsel Affiliated Computer Services, Inc., 1995—2000; exec. v.p., gen. counsel, corp. sec. BearingPoint, Inc., McLean, Va., 2000—. Mem. ABA (chair young lawyer's divsn. real property law com. 1989-91, mem. corp., banking and bus. law com. 1986—, mem. exec. com. young lawyers divsn. bus. law com. 1988-91, vice chair exec. com. 1986-89, young lawyers divsn. liaison to ABA real property, probate and trust law sect. 1989-91), Dallas Bar Assn. (civic affairs com. 1986-89), Tex. Young Lawyers' Assn. (pub. com. 1987-89), Delta Theta Phi. Republican. Avocations: golf, skiing, scuba diving, travel. Office: BearingPoint Inc 1676 Internat Dr Mc Lean VA 22102-4842

BLACK, EDWARD G., lawyer; BA with honors, Brown Univ., 1986; JD, Univ. Calif., Berkeley, 1989. Bar: Mass. 1997. Law clk. Judge D. Lowell Jensen, US Dist. Ct. (no. Calif.); ptnr. corp. dept. & co-head Fish & Neave IP group Ropes & Gray, Boston. Mem.: Boston Bar Assn. (past co-chmn. Intellectual Property com.). Office: Ropes & Gray 1 International Pl Boston MA 02110-2624 Office Phone: 617-951-7984. Office Fax: 617-951-7050. Business E-Mail: edward.black@ropesgray.com.

BLACK, GARY WILLIAM, industrial engineer; b. Altoona, Pa., Sept. 3, 1960; s. Thomas L. and Joanne M. Black; m. Elena S. Vengrzhinovskaya, Feb. 14, 1998. MS, U. Tenn., Knoxville, 1998; PhD, U. Ala., Huntsville, 2001; BS, Pa. State U., 1985. Indsl. engr. Raytheon Co., Andover, Mass., 1985—87, Bristol, Tenn., 1988—94, Siemens Energy & Automation, Johnson City, Tenn., 1995—2002; mfg. engr. def. divsn. Internat. Signal & Control, Lancaster, Pa., 1987—88; asst. prof. Tenn. Technol. U., Cookeville, 2002—. Mem.: Inst. Ops. Rsch. and Mgmt. Sci., Inst. Indsl. Engineers, Alpha Pi Mu. Home: 935 Franklin Ct Cookeville TN 38506 Business E-Mail: gblack@tntech.edu.

BLACK, HENRY RICHARD, physician; b. N.Y.C., June 1, 1942; s. David Robert and Beatrice (Morris) Black; m. Benita L. Daniels, Apr. 19, 2002; children: Matthew, Dana. AB, Columbia U., 1963; MD, NYU, 1967. Diplomate Am. Bd. Internal Medicine, cert. hypertension specialist Am. Soc. Hypertension, 2001. Intern Johns Hopkins Hosp., Balt., 1967—68, resident in internal medicine, 1970—71; resident Yale-New Haven Hosp., 1971—72, chief resident in internal medicine, 1974—75; fellow Yale U., New Haven, 1972—74, practice medicine specializing in internal medicine and hypertension, 1975—92; asst. prof. Yale U. Med. Sch., New Haven, 1975—79, assoc. prof., 1979—88, prof., 1988—92, dir. hypertension svcs., 1975—92; Charles J. and Margaret Roberts prof., chmn. dept. preventive medicine, prof. internal medicine Rush U. Med. Ctr., Chgo., 1992—, assoc. v.p. rsch., assoc. dean rsch., 2000—. Bd. dirs. Am. Heart Assn., Conn., 1985—; fellow Coun. on Hypertension. Contbr. articles to profl. jours. With USPHS, 1968—70. Fellow: ACP, Am. Soc. Hypertension (exec. com. 1991—96, exec. coun. 2002—), Am. Heart Assn. (coun. epidemiology & prevention, fellow coun. on nutrition), Internat. Soc. Hypertension; mem.: Am. Soc. Preventive Cardiology (pres. 1994—95), Columbia Coll. Alumni Assn. (bd. dirs. 1983—87, v.p., acad. affairs 1986—87), Am. Fedn. Clin. Rsch. Jewish. Office: Rush Univ Med Ctr 1700 W Van Buren Chicago IL 60612 Home: 750 N Rush St Chicago IL 60611

BLACK, HILLEL MOSES, publisher; b. N.Y.C., Apr. 8, 1929; s. Isidore and Ida (Feldstein) B. BA, U. Chgo., 1949, M.English and Fgn. Langs., 1952. Copy boy N.Y. Times, N.Y.C., 1952-53; reporter AP, Pitts., Newark and Phila., 1954-58; freelance writer N.Y.C., 1959-65; editor Saturday Evening Post, N.Y.C., 1966-67; sr. editor William Morrow & Co., N.Y.C., 1967-77, editor-in-chief, 1977-82; pub. gen. books div. Macmillan Pub. Co., N.Y.C., 1983-87; pub. Richardson, Steirman & Black, N.Y.C., 1987-88; pres. Birch Lane Press, 1989-99; editorial dir. Carol Pub. Group, N.Y.C., 1989-99; exec. editor Sourcebooks, Naperville, Ill., 2000—. Author: The Watch Dogs of Wall Street, Buy Now, Pay Later, The American Schoolbook. Mem. Century Assn., Pubs. Club. Office: Sourcebooks 955 Connecticut Ave Ste 5303 Bridgeport CT 06607-1297 E-mail: hillwen@aol.com.

BLACK, JACK, actor; b. Santa Monica, Calif., Aug. 28, 1969; Student, UCLA. Actor: (films) Bob Roberts, 1992, The Never Ending Story III, 1994, Dead Man Walking, 1995, Bio-Dome, 1996, The Cable Guy, 1996, The Fan, 1996, Mars Attacks!, 1996, The Jackal, 1997, Bongwater, 1998, Enemy of the State, 1998, Cradle Will Rock, 1999, High Fidelity, 2000, Saving Silverman, 2001, Shallow Hal, 2001, Orange County, 2002, (voice) Ice Age, 2002, The School of Rock, 2003 (nominated Golden Globe for Best Performance by an Actor in a Motion Picture-Musical or Comedy, 2003), Envy, 2004, Anchorman: The Legend of Ron Burgundy, 2004, Shark Tale (voice only), 2004; (TV series) The Innocent, 1994, Mr. Show, 1995, Heat Vision and Jack, 1999, Tenacious D, 1999, (voice) Crank Yankers, 2002; singer, songwriter with Tenacious D: albums Tenacious D, 2001, Complete Masterworks, 2003.

BLACK, JACKIE JOHN, artist; d. Lloyd and Dorine Turnbow; children: Cody R. Simonsen, Derek C. Simonsen. Student, U.Utah, Salt Lake City, 1969—72. Graphic artist, art dir. Corker Sullivan Advt. Agy., Spokane, Wash., 1978—82, Coons, Corker, Sullivan Advt. Agy., Spokane, Wash., 1982—83; graphic artist, sr. art dir. Clark White and Associates, Spokane, Wash., 1983—86; freelance graphic artist Jackie Black Art, Bellingham, Wash., 1986—92, fine artist / painter Mukilteo, Wash., 1992—. Art instr. Jackie Black Art, Mukilteo, Wash., 1986—. One-woman shows include Vanilla Beans Coffee Shop, Mukilteo, 2001, exhibitions include Artist Assn. for Univ. Women, 1996—99, Snohomish Arts Coun., 1999—2000, Powell Street Gallery, San Francisco, 2001—03, Gallery Carla, 2003—05, Jezebel Gallery, Santa Fe, 2003—05, Thomas Moxley Gallery, Santa Fe, N.Mex., Agora Gallery, N.Y.C., 2005—, children's book, My Favorite Holidays. Office: Jackie Black Art 11013 55th Ave W Mukilteo WA 98275 E-mail: jackieblackjohn@verizon.net.

BLACK, JAMES ISAAC (JIB), III, lawyer; b. Lakeland, Fla., Oct. 26, 1951; s. James Isaac Jr. and Juanita (Feemster) B.; m. Vikki Harrison, June 15, 1973; children: Jennifer Leigh, Katharine Ann, Stephanie Marie. BA, U. Fla., 1973; JD, Harvard U., 1976. Bar: Fla. 1976, NY 1977, US Tax Ct. 1984. Assoc. Sullivan & Cromwell, NYC, 1976-84, ptnr., 1984—, and mng. ptnr. estates and personal practice group, 1995—. Mem. ABA, NY State Bar Assn. (persons under disability com. trusts and estates law sect. 1984-90), Assn. of Bar of City of N.Y. (sec. 1980-81, trusts estates and surrogates ct. com. 1980-83), Scarsdale Golf Club (past pres.), bd. dir. Alpha Tau Omega Found., Flagler Found., New Choral Soc. of Ctrl. Westchester and Sheridan Arts Found. Office: Sullivan & Cromwell LLP 125 Broad St Fl 28 New York NY 10004-2489 Office Phone: 212-558-3948. Office Fax: 212-558-3588. E-mail: blackj@sullcrom.com.

BLACK, JAMES ROBERT, industrial engineer; b. Davenort, Iowa, Feb. 17, 1948; s. Robert James and Anne Louise (Johnson) B.; m. Mary Ann O'Malley, June 5, 1971; 1 child, Robert Joseph. BS in Indsl. Engring., Iowa State U., 1970, MS, 1971; MBA, U. Chgo., 1976. Indsl. engr. Inland Steel Co., East Chicago, Ind., 1971-76, sr. indsl. engr., 1976-77; indsl. engring. supr. Clark Equipment Co., Jackson, Mich., 1977-78; indsl. engring. mgr. Harrison plant Graphic Sys. divsn. Rockwell Internat., Rockford, Ill., 1978-83; corp.supr. adminstrv. work mgmt. Kohler Co., Wis., 1983-87; mgr. mgf. svcs. Frigidaire Co.-Wet Products, Jefferson, Iowa, 1987—89, assembly ops. mgr., 1989—91, Kaizen facilitator Webster City, Iowa, 1991—93, paint process mgr., 1993, plant engring. mgr., 1993-95; sr. project mgr. Ctr. for Indsl. Rsch. and Svc., Iowa State U., 1995—; pres. James R. Black & Assocs., 1997—. Co-leader, guest lectr. Am. Mgmt. Assn., 1979-80; mem. adv. coun. Iowa State U. Ctr. Indsl. Rsch. and Svc., 1992-94; mem. planing com. Iowa conf. Mfg., 1991-93, chmn., 1993. Contbr. articles to profl. jours. Cons. project bus. divsn. Jr. Achievement, 1980; pack com. chmn., com. chmn. Boy Scouts Am., 1980—83, den leader, 1982—83, asst. scoutmaster, 1983—84, scoutmaster, 1984—88, dist. vice-chmn., 1984—86, dist. boy scouting chmn., 1986—88, unit commr., 2000—, dist. mem.-at-large, 2000—01, asst. dist. commr., 2001, dist. vice-chmn., 2000—01, dist. commr., 2002—04, asst. coun. commr., 2004—; asst. soccer coach, 1981—83; coach, 1984—85; mem. bd. dirs. Habitat for Humanity, exec. com., 2003—, chair ptnr. family rels. com., 2003, pres., 2004—. Fisher Governor scholar, 1968-69, Maytag scholar, 1969-70; recipient Woodbadge Boy Scouts Am., 1986, Dist. award of Merit, 2003, Silver Beaver, 2005. Mem.: Kohler Engring. and Tech. Orgn. (program chmn. 1986, chmn. 1987), Mainstream Living and Story County Devel. Ctr. (phonathon co-chmn. 1993—95, bd. dirs. 1994—2001, treas. 1995—97, v.p. 1997—99, pres. 1999—2001), Assn. for Mfg. Excellence, Am. Soc. for Quality, Inst. Indsl. Engrs. (sr.; treas. 1979—80, pres. 1980—81, bd. dirs. 1989—91, v.p. 1991—92), Rotary Internat. (web page chmn. 2001—, bd. dirs. 2005), Epsilon Sigma Phi, Alpha Phi Omega (univ. advisor 2000—02), Beta Gamma Sigma, Psi Chi, Gamma Epsilon Sigma, Tau Beta Pi, Phi Kappa Phi. Home: 3416 Valley View Rd Ames IA 50014-4613 Office: CIRAS/Iowa State U Coll Engring 2272 Howe Hl Ste 2620 Ames IA 50011-0001 Office Phone: 515-294-1507. Business E-Mail: jimblack@ciras.iastate.edu.

BLACK, JAPPIE KING, education educator, artist; d. Cecil N. and Jappie Bryant King; m. Richard W. Black. BFA, R.I. Sch. of Design, 1974; MFA, Syracuse (N.Y.) U., 1992. Faculty mem. R.I. Coll., Providence, C.W. Univ. of Rochester (N.Y.), 1978—87; artist in residence Oleans County (N.Y.) Arts Coun., 1987—89; asst. prof. Syracuse (N.Y.) U., 1996—98; faculty mem. Rochester (N.Y.) Inst. of Tech., 2000; asst. prof. Kean U., Union, NJ, 2001—. One-woman shows include Bent Not Broken, 2001, Phoenix Gallery, N.Y.C., 2004, exhibitions include Elements Unearthed Four Sculptors, 2003 (Individual Artist Grant, 01), Elements, Two Installations, 2000, The Way We Are (Bill Havens Meml. award, 2001). Recipient award, Cooperstown Art Assn., 1998, Best Sculpture/Finger Lakes Show, Meml. Art Gallery, 1991; grantee Cmty. Grant, Arts Coun. of Rochester, 1999, Cmty. Arts Grant, 1999; scholar Merit award and Assistantship, Syracuse U., 1991; S.O.S. grant, Arts Coun. of Rochester, 1994, 2004. Mem.: Tempo, Coll. Art Assn., Weavers' Guild of Rochester, Surface Design Assn., Rochester Comtemporary. Home: 5067 Lake Rd S Brockport NY 14420-9706 Office: Kean Univ 1000 Morris Ave Union NJ 07083-0411 Office Phone: 908-737-7441. Personal E-mail: kingblack@aol.com. E-mail: jblack@kean.edu.

BLACK, JEFFREY P., manufacturing executive; s. Lennox K. Black. B in Criminal Justice, Old Dominion U., 1983. Former head automotive and indsl. groups Teleflex, Plymouth Meeting, Pa., pres., 2000—, CEO, 2002—, also bd. dirs. Recipient Disting. Alumni award, Old Dominion U., 2001. Office: Teleflex 155 S Limerick Rd Royersford PA 19468

BLACK, JERRY BERNARD, lawyer; b. Bklyn., Sept. 16, 1940; s. Paul A. and Esther (Rosenberg) B.; m. Joyce Fenmore, Nov. 29, 1975; children: Abigail B., Andrew S. AB, Harvard U., 1962, LLB, 1965. Bar: N.Y. 1966, U.S. Supreme Ct. 1976. Assoc. Cravath, Swaine & Moore, N.Y.C., 1966-77; asst. sec., sr. counsel Revlon, Inc., N.Y.C., 1978-83; v.p., dep. gen. counsel Hertz Corp., N.Y.C., 1984-86; ptnr. Hill, Betts & Nash, N.Y.C., 1987-90, Wilson, Elser, Moskowitz, Edelman & Dicker, LLP, N.Y.C., 1990—. Mem. ABA (loan documentation subcom. of comml. fin. svcs. com. 1995), Assn. of Bar of City of N.Y. (com. inter-Am. affairs 1973-75), N.Y. State Bar Assn. Home: 149 E 73rd St New York NY 10021-3592 Office: Wilson Elser Moskowitz Edelman & Dicker LLP 150 E 42nd St New York NY 10017-5612 E-mail: blackj@wemed.com.

BLACK, KEITH LANIER, neurosurgeon, educator; b. Tuskegee, Ala., Sept. 13, 1957; m. Carol J. Bennett; children: Teal Etoile, Keith Quinten. BS in Biomed. Sci. with distinction, U. Mich., 1978, MD with distinction, 1981. Lic. MD, Mich., Calif.; diplomate Am. Bd. Med. Examiners, Am. Bd. Neurol. Surgery. Intern U. Mich. Med. Ctr., Ann Arbor, 1981—82, resident, 1982—87; head neuro-oncology UCLA Med. Ctr., 1988, asst. prof., 1987—91, assoc. prof., 1991—94, prof., 1994—97, Ruth and Raymond Stotter chair dept. surgery, 1992; dir. neurosurgery Cedars-Sinai Med. Ctr., 1997—; dir. Maxine Dunitz Neurological Inst., 1997—. Bd. sci. counselors Nat. Inst. Neurol. Disorder and Stroke, NIH, 1994-; ris. prof. Howard U., Washington, 1986, Taiwan U., 1993, U. Mich., Ann Arbor, 1995, lect., presenter in field. Editor, reciever and contbr. to profl. jours.; contbr. chpts to books. Recipient Dwyer award for excellence in cancer rsch., 1990, LEVI Human Rights award in medicine, 1994, Medal Honor, Charles R. Drew U. Medicine and Sci., 1995, Pres. Medal Honor, Charles M. Drew Med. Soc., 1998; grantee Nat. Cancer Inst., 1993-96, NIH, 1994-99, Robert Wood Johnson Found., 1990, Alkermes Inc., 1994-96, others; Shering scholar ACS, 1985. Mem. AMA, AAAS, Am. Assn. Neurol. Surgeons (various coms.), AMA, Brain Rsch. Inst. UCLA (adv. com.), Jonsson Comprehensive Cancer Ctr., Calif. Assn. Neurol. Surgeons, Congress of Neurol. Surgeons(various coms.), Neurosurgical Soc. Am., N. Am. Skull Base Soc. (founding mem., various coms.), Soc. Neuroscience, So. Calif. Neurosurgical Soc., S.W. Oncology Group. Achievements include patented method for selective opening of abnormal brain tissue capillaries.

BLACK, KENNETH, JR., retired insurance company executive; b. Norfolk, Va., Jan. 30, 1925; s. Kenneth and Margaret Virginia (Wolf) B.; m. Mabel Llewellyn Folger, Sept. 20, 1948; children— Kenneth III, Kathryn Anne Shoji. AB, U. N.C., 1948, MS, 1951; PhD, U. Pa., 1953. Ptnr. Colonial Ins. Agy., Chapel Hill, N.C., 1948-50; instr. U. Pa., 1952-53; chmn. ins. dept. Ga. State U., 1953-69, Regents' prof. ins., 1959-92, C.V. Starr prof. internat. ins., 1984-92, Regent's prof. emeritus, 1992—, dean Coll. Bus. Adminstrn., 1969-84, dean emeritus Coll. Bus. Adminstrn., 1992—; pres., CEO Internat. Ins. Soc., Inc., 1988-92, vice chmn., bd. dirs., 1992—2001. Author (with Huebner): Property Insurance, 1957, Life Insurance, 1958, 1964, 1969, 1972, 1979, 1982; author: (with Russell) (books) Human Behavior and Life Insurance, 1963, 1993; author: Human Behavior and Property and Liability Insurance, 1964; author: (with Keir and Surrey) Cases in Life Insurance, 1965; author: (with Huebner and Webb) Property and Liability Insurance, 1968, 1996; author: (with Huebner and Cline), 1968, 1976, 1982; author: (with Skipper) Life Insurance, 1987, 1994; author: (with Russell) (books) Human Behavior in Business, 1972, Understanding and Influencing Human Behavior, 1981; author: (with Skipper) Life and Health Insurance, 2000; editor: (jour.) Jour. Soc. Fin. Svc. Profls., 1959—2001, (ins. series) Prentice Hall, Inc., 1959—. Vice chmn. Pres.'s Commn. R.R. Retirement, 1971-73; trustee Village of St. Joseph, 1969-80; exec. dir., trustee Ednl. Found., Inc., 1969-96. Served with USN, 1944-46. Recipient Solomon S. Huebner gold medal, Am. Coll., 1985, Laureate Ins. Hall Fame, 1993, Order of the Golden Fleece, UNC, 1948, John Newton Russell Meml. award, 1999, Round Table of N.Y. Lifetime Achievement award, 2001. Mem. Am. Risk and Ins. Assn. (pres. 1964), Phi Beta Kappa, Beta Gamma Sigma, Omicron Delta Kappa, Alpha Kappa Psi. Roman Catholic. Home: 1762 Nancy Creek Blf NW Atlanta GA 30327-1912 Office Phone: 404-651-4200.

BLACK, KENNETH W., JR., retail executive; b. Aug. 13, 1959; m. Shandra Black; 2 children. BBA, MS in Acctg., Appalachian State U. CPA. Sr. mgr., fin. instns. and retail cos. Deloitte & Touche, LLP, 1983—86; v.p., corp. controller Lowe's Cos., Inc., Wilkesboro, NC, 1997—99, sr. v.p., chief acctg. officer, 1999—. Office: Lowes Cos Inc 1000 Lowes Blvd Mooresville NC 28117

BLACK, LAWRENCE, librarian; b. Bronx, NY, May 28, 1940; s. Reuben and Florence (Kuhnberg) B.; m. Linda Perlis, Dec. 8, 1968; 1 child, David. BA, Long Island U., 1963; MLS, Pratt Inst., 1965; MA in Edn., NYU, 1973; cert. in Advanced Librarianship, Columbia U., 1981. Libr. U.S. VA Hosp., Northport, NY, 1965-66; libr. assoc. NYU Librs. Gen. U. Libr., N.Y.C., 1967-68; libr. N.Y. State Inst. for Basic Rsch. in Devel. Disabilities, Staten Island, 1968—. Mem. adv. com. of librs. Med. Libr. Ctr. of N.Y., N.Y.C., 1969—2003; compiler of bibliographies, 1975-. Trustee Temple Emanu-El, Staten Island, N.Y., 1989—, founder, coord. book club 1999—. Scholarship N.Y. Libr. Club, N.Y.C., 1965; recipient Small award NYU Dept Hebrew Culture, 1969. Mem. Govt. Agy. Librs. N.Y. State, Med. Libr. Assn. N.Y., N.J. chpt., N.Y. Libr. Club., Spl. Librs. Assn., Medical Libr. Assn. (institutional rep.), Met. NY Libr. Council (institutional rep.) Democrat. Jewish. Avocation: history. Office: NY St Inst Basic Rsch Devel Disabilities 1050 Forest Hill Rd Staten Island NY 10314-6356

BLACK, LEON DAVID, private investment company executive; s. Eli Black; m. Debra Ressler; 4 children. AB in philosophy, Dartmouth Coll., 1973; MBA, Harvard U., 1975. With Drexel Burnham Lambert Inc., NYC, 1977—90, joined as assoc., fin. dept., 1977, head mergers and acquisitions, 1985—90, co-head corp. fin. dept.; co-founder The Apollo orgn. (includes Apollo Mgmt. LP, Apollo Advisors LP, Apollo Real Estate Advisors LP), 1990—. Bd. dirs. Vail Resorts Inc., Sequa Corp., United Rentals Inc., Allied Waste Industries Inc., 2000—, AMC Entertainment Inc., 2001—, Sirius Satellite Radio Inc., 2001—, Wyndham Internat. Inc. Trustee Mus. of Modern Art, Mt. Sinai Hosp., Lincoln Ctr. for Performing Arts, Met. Mus. of Art, Prep for Prep, The Jewish Mus., Cardozo Sch. of Law, The Asia Soc., Spence Sch., The Vail Valley Found. Named one of Top 200 Collectors, ARTnews Mag., 2004. Avocation: Collecting Old Masters, Impressionist, Modern and Contemporary Art, and Chinese Sculpture. Office: Apollo Advisors 2 Manhattanville Rd Purchase NY 10577*

BLACK, LISA HARTMAN, actress, singer; b. Houston, June 01; m. Clint Black, Oct. 20, 1991. Grad., High Sch. Performing Arts, Houston. TV series: Tabitha, 1977-78, High Performance, 1983, Knots Landing, 1982-86, 2000 Malibu Rd., 1993; TV Movies: Murder at the World Series, 1977, Where the Ladies go, 1980, Gridlock (also released as The Great American Traffic Jam), 1980, Beverly Hills Cowgirl Blues, 1985, Roses Are for the Rich, 1987, Full Exposure: The Sex Tapes Scandal, 1989, The Operation, 1990, The Take, USA, 1990, Fire! Trapped on the 37th Floor, 1991, Not of This World, 1991, Red Wind, 1991, The Return of Elliot Ness, 1991, Without a Kiss Goodbye, 1993, Search for Grace, 1994, Someone Else's Child, 1995, Have You Seen My Son?, 1996, Out of Nowhere, 1997, Still Holding On: The Legend of Cadillac Jack, 1998; TV mini-series: Jacqueline Susann's Valley of the Dolls, 1981, Judith Krantz's Dazzle, 1995; films: Deadly Blessing, 1981, Where the Boys Are, 1984, also recorded Hold On I'm Comin', 1979, Til My Heart Stops, 1988; prodr. Have You Seen My Son?, 1996; TV guest appearances include Police Woman, 1974, Vega$, 1978, On Stage America, 1984, The Hitchhiker, 1983, Matlock, 1986.

BLACK, LISA ZAHN, elementary school educator; b. Kansas City, Mo., Oct. 1, 1958; d. F. George and Sue (Scott) Z.; children: Whitney, Rebecca. BA, Kansas City U., 1980; MS, U. Kans., 1982. Mid. sch. tchr. Kans. State Sch. for Deaf, Olathe, 1981-88, tchr., 1983-88; 4th grade tchr. Briarwood Elem. Sch., Olathe, 1988—97, Black Bob Elem. Sch., 1998—. Portfolio cons. Emporia State U., 1994—; instr. U. Kans., 1992-94; ednl. cons. Soc. Devel. Edn., 2000—. Author: Coloring Your World With Learning, 1995, The Best of Good Apple, 1995, Munchable Math, 2000, Connecting Math and Literature, 2002; contbr. articles to profl. jours. Bd. dirs. Paul Mesner Puppets, Kansas City, Mo., 1993—, com. chmn., exec. com. BOTAR, Kansas City, 1980—; chmn. Am. Royal BBQ Contest; bd. dirs. Midwest Ear Inst., Kansas City, 1988—. Recipient Presdl. award for Excellence in Tchg. Math. Office of Pres. U.S., 1994, Excellence in Tchg. Math. award Kans. Med. Soc., 1993; Christa McAuliffe fellow, 2002; named to Kan. Tchr. Hall of Fame, 2002, Mid-Am. Edn. Hall of Fame, 2003. Mem. NSTA, Nat. Supervisors of Tchrs. of Math., Nat. Coun. of Tchrs. of Math., Soc. Presdl. Awardees, Coun. Presdl. Awards for Math., Delta Kappa. Presbyterian. Avocations: bicycling, hiking, needlepoint, backpacking. Home: 5213 W 84th Ter Shawnee Mission KS 66207-1716 Office Phone: 913-780-7310. Personal E-mail: lisazblack@yahoo.com.

BLACK, LORI ANNETTE, academic administrator; b. Tiffin, Ohio, Feb. 11, 1967; d. Marlin Jacob and Mary Jane (Gosche) B. BS, Ohio State U., 1989; MA, Calif. State U., Bakersfield, 2000. Tchr. English and speech Calvert H.S., Tiffin, 1989-96; tchr. English and speech, volleyball coach Lakota H.S., Kansas, Ohio, 1996-98; tng. coord. AFSA Data Corp., 1998-2000; regional program coord. U. Calif., Merced, 2000—. Advisor Sr. Class Calvert H.S., Tiffin, 1989-90, cheerleaders, 1989-91, Nat. Honor Soc., 1994-96; volleyball coach, 1989-98, musical and play dir. 1990-94. Named Tchr. of Month, Student Coun., Calvert H.S., 1992, 94. Mem. Ohio State U. Alumni Assn. Roman Catholic. Avocations: sports, music, reading. Office: Univ Calif Merced Ctr 2000 K St 3rd Flr Ste 300 Bakersfield CA 93301 Home: 20244 N 31st Ave Apt 2134 Phoenix AZ 85027-0303 E-mail: lablack11@yahoo.com.

BLACK, LOUIS ENGLEMAN, lawyer; b. Washington, Aug. 5, 1943; s. Fischer Sheffey and Elizabeth (Zemp) B.; m. Cecelia Whidden, Sept. 5, 1966; 1 child, Kerrison Todd. BA, NYU, 1968, JD, 1971, LLM in Taxation, 1978. Bar: N.Y. 1972. Assoc. Carter, Ledyard & Milburn, N.Y.C., 1972-79; ptnr. Van Ginkel & Benjamin, N.Y.C., 1979-83; of counsel Zimet, Haines, Moss & Friedman, N.Y.C., 1983-84, DeForest & Duer, N.Y.C., 1984-86, ptnr., 1986—2001, Black & Assocs., 2002—; mng. dir. Aleutian Capital Ptnrs., LLC, N.Y.C., 2004—. Vice-chmn. bd. dirs. MacMillan Ring-Free Oil Co., Inc., 1986-87; chmn. bd. Lee's Gourmet Farms, Inc., 1993-97, United Compressor, LLC, 2002—, Kingdom Techs., LLC, 2002—. Editor: NYU Jour. Internat. Law and Politics, 1970-71; author: Partnership Buy/Sell Agreements, 1977. Mem. ABA, N.Y. State Bar Assn. Home: 220 E 65th St Apt 24M New York NY 10021-6629 Office: Black & Associates Ste 6710 350 5th Ave New York NY 10118-6710 Office Phone: 917-656-6263. Business E-Mail: lblack@blackesq.com.

BLACK, MARILYN HAMMER, non-profit organization executive; b. Sioux City, Iowa, Apr. 25, 1923; d. Franklin Wilfred and Ruth Marie (Gray) Hammer; m. Albert Scott Black; children: Barbara Black Miller, William Scott, Patricia Black Thompson. BA, U. Without Walls, 1975; MS, U. Houston-Clear Lake, 1980; PhD in Philosophy, Summit U., New Orleans, 1998. Dir. religious edn. St. Francis Episcopal Ch., Houston, 1968-72; program dir. NCCJ, Houston, 1972-80; exec. dir. Support Ctr. Houston, 1982-86; dir. C.G. Jung Edn. Ctr., Houston, 1987-91. Mem. mission coun. St. Francis Episcopal Ch., Houston, 1982. Mem. ASTD, Non-Profit Mgmt. Assn., Nat. Soc. Fund Raising Execs. (bd. dirs. 1982). Home: 2929 W Holcombe Blvd Apt 346 Houston TX 77025-1540

BLACK, MARSHA C., environmental scientist; BS in Comprehensive Sci., Converse Coll.; PhD in Ecology, U. Tenn. Acad. & postdoctoral rsch. U. Joensuu, Finland; asst. prof. zoology Okla. State U., Stillwater, Okla., 1990—94; assoc. prof. environ. health scis. Coll. Agrl. and Environ. Scis. U. Ga., Athens, Ga., 1994—. Reviewer (for several environ. toxicology pub.); mem. editl. bd.: Environ. Toxicol. Chemistry, 2000—02. Mem.: Soc. Environ. Toxicology and Chemistry (bd. dirs.). Office: Univ Ga 148 Environ Health Bldg Athens GA 30602 Business E-Mail: mblack@uga.edu.

BLACK, MARSHA JEAN, art educator, writer; b. Petersburg, Ind., Mar. 26, 1947; d. Orace Wayne and Norma Jean (Decker) Willis; m. Richard Lee Black, Aug. 6, 1966; 1 child, William Richard. BA, St. Mary's of the Woods, 1977; MSc, Ind. U., 1981. Art tchr. St. Mary's Sch., Greensburg, Ind., 1974—98; writer. Art decorator asst. Wesleyan Ch., Greensburg, 1997—2001; project dir. Children's Mus., 1994, Stuart Lowery Dir., 96; project dir. Ind. State Mus., 1996. Co-author (Michelle Mcauliffe): Busy Teacher's Guide Art Lessons-Grade 1-3, Busy Teacher Guide Art lessons-Grade 3-5, Art and Artists Through the Centuries. Avocations: painting, drawing, reading, writing, cooking. Home: 803 West 7th St Greensburg IN 47240

BLACK, PAGE MORTON, civic worker, vocalist, musician; b. Chgo. d. Alexander and Rose Morton; m. William Black, Mar. 27, 1962. Student, Chgo. Mus. Coll. Singer, pianist Pierre Hotel, N.Y.C., Warwick Hotel, One Fifth Ave. Sherry Netherland Hotel; singer radio show and comml. Chock Full O'Nuts Corp.; rec. artist Atlantic Records, Den Records. Co-founder Page and William Black Post-Grad. Sch. Medicine, Mt. Sinai Med. Sch., 1965—; chmn. mem. exec. bd. Parkinsons' Disease Found., Columbia U. Med. Ctr.; mem. nat. vis. coun. Columbia U. Health Scis. Faculties; hon. chmn. Chock Full O' Nuts Corp., 1983—90; active Columbia Presbyn. Health Scis. Adv. Coun.; founding mem. ASPCA; mem. neurosci. com. Neurol. Inst. of N.Y. at Columbia Presbyn. Med. Ctr., Columbia Presbyn. Med. Ctr. Mem. neuroscience com. Columbia Presbyn. Health Sci. Adv. Coun. Recipient Ann. award, Parkinsons' Disease Found., 1987, Police Athletic League, 1992, Manhattan Mag. award, 1992, Lifetime Achievement award, Parkinson's Disease Found., 1997, Disting. Svc. award, 2005, Dean's award for Disting. Svc., Columbia U. Coll. Physicians & Surgeons, 1998. Home: Premium Pt New Rochelle NY 10801

BLACK, PERCY, psychology professor; b. Montreal, Que., Can., Jan. 6, 1922; s. Ovido and Rose (Vasilevsky) B.; m. Virginia Arne, June 21, 1951; children— Deborah, David, Elizabeth, Jonathan BS, Sir George Williams Coll., Montreal, 1944; MSc, McGill U., 1946; PhD, Harvard U., 1954. Instr. in social scis. U. Ky., 1948-49; rsch. asst. in race rels. U. Chgo., 1950-51; rsch. assoc. in child psychology U. Minn., 1949-50; asst. prof. psychology U. N.B., Fredericton, 1951-53; vis. scholar Univ. Coll., London, 1953-54; dir. rsch. Social Attitude Survey, Yonkers, NY, 1955-67; prof. emeritus in psychology Pace U., Pleasantville, NY, 1967—. Adj. prof. psychology U. Vt., 2000—. Contbr. author: Societies Around the World, 2 vols., 1953; author: The Mystique of Modern Monarchy, 1953; contbr. articles to profl. jours. Fellow AAAS; mem. APA, Am. Psychol. Soc., B'nai B'rith. Home: 2763 Lower Rd Barre VT 05641 E-mail: pblack@sover.net.

BLACK, PERRY, neurological surgeon, educator; b. Montreal, Oct. 2, 1930; came to U.S., 1959, naturalized 1979; s. Ovido and Rose (Vasilevsky) B.; children: Daniel Ovid, Julie Miriam, Amy Rose. BSc, McGill U., Montreal, 1951, MD, CM, 1956. Intern, then asst. resident in medicine and gen. surgery Jewish Gen. Hosp., Montreal, 1956-58; asst. resident in neurology Montreal Neurol. Inst., 1958-59; resident in neurosurgery Johns Hopkins Hosp., Balt., 1959-63, neurosurgeon, 1964-79; NIH fellow in physiology Johns Hopkins U. Sch. Medicine, 1961-62, instr. neurol. surgery, 1964-67, asst. prof., 1967-69, assoc. prof., 1969-79, asst. prof. psychiatry, 1967-70, assoc. prof., 1970-79; prof. Hahnemann U. Sch. Medicine, Phila., 1979-94, chmn. dept. neurosurgery, dir. pain treatment program, 1979-94, dir. brain tumor program, 1983-94; prof. neurosurgery Med. Coll. Pa. and Hahnemann U., 1994—, dir. malignant brain tumor program, 1995—. Dir. neurosurgery in the brain Tumor Ctr., Med. Coll. Pa. and Hahnemann U., Phila.; dir. child head injury project dept. neurol. surgery Johns Hopkins Hosp., 1963-79; dir. lab. neurol. scis., chmn. ctrl. rsch. authority Friends Med. Sci. Rsch. Ctr., Balt., 1972-79, hon. dir., 1979—; mem. neurology study sect. NIH, 1973-77; coun. neurosurg. rep. Johns Hopkins Med. Sch., 1977-78, coun. vice chmn., 1978-79. Editor: Drugs and the Brain, 1969, Physiological Correlates of Emotion, 1970, Brain Dysfunction in Children: Etiology, Diagnosis, and Management, 1981; contbr. articles to profl. jours. Bd. dirs. Epilepsy Assn. Central Md., 1966-77, chmn. profl. adv. bd., 1973-75; mem. com. of fifty Epilepsy Found. Am., 1970-76, state coordinator for Md., 1973-76 Recipient Residents Paper award So. Neurosurg. Soc., 1963, Volvo award World Fedn. of Neurosurgical Socs., 1985. Mem. AAAS, Congress Neurol. Surgeons (chmn. sci. and edn. com. 1969-72, chmn. sci. program com. 1971-72, editor newsletter 1972-75, mem. exec. com. 1972-75, mem. nominating com. 1975-77, chmn. internat. com. 1975-81, assoc. editor jour. 1976-82, editor jour. internat. neurosurgery 1976-87, Disting. Svc. award 1977), AMA, AAUP, Am. Assn. Neurol. Surgeons (Harvey Cushing Soc., mem. subcom. on continuing edn. 1974-78), Am. Pain Soc., Soc. Neurol. Surgeons, Am. Soc. Stereotactic and Functional Neurosurgery, Soc. for Neurosci., Rsch. Soc. Neurol. Surgeons, Am. Epilepsy Soc., Am. Neurol. Assn., Internat. Assn. for Study of Pain, Philadelphia County Med. Soc., Phila. Neurol. Soc. (2nd v.p. 1982-83), Pa. Neurosurg. Soc. (mem. coun. 1989—, sec., treas. 1990, pres. 1992), Mid-Atlantic Neurosurg. Soc. Office: Hahnemann Univ Hosp Dept Neurosurgery Broad & Vine Mail Stop 455 Philadelphia PA 19130-1192

BLACK, PETE, retired state legislator, educator; b. Ansbach, Germany, Sept. 16, 1946; came to U.S., 1948; s. Howard and Kadi (Fietz) B.; m. Ronda Williams, July 12, 1970; 1 child, Darin. BS, Idaho State U., 1975, MEd, 1998. Cert. elem. tchr. Tchr. Pocatello (Idaho) Sch. Dist., 1975—; mem. Idaho Ho. Reps., Boise, 1983-96, asst. minority leader, 1987-96; tech. tng. specialist Sch. Dist. 25, 1996—, info. officer, 2003—. Mem. edn. tech. coun.; mem. adv. coun. chpt. II ESEA. Bd. dirs. Arts for Idaho; mem. State Libr. Bd. With USNR, 1964. Mem. NEA, Idaho Edn. Assn. (bd. dirs.), Idaho Libr. Assn., Idaho State U. Alumni Bd., Idaho Pers. Commn. Democrat. Home: 2249 Cassia St Pocatello ID 83201-2059 Office: Idaho House of Reps Statehouse Mail Boise ID 83720-0001 Office Phone: 208-235-3257. E-mail: blackcat1@cableone.net.

BLACK, PETER RUSSELL, historian; b. Boston, Dec. 29, 1950; s. Sidney James and Adelaide (Aronoff) Black; m. Mary Elise Mattson, May 19, 1950; children: Aaron William, Laura Elizabeth. BA, U. Wis., 1972; MA, Columbia U., 1973, PhD, 1981. Staff historian Office Spl. Investigations, Washington, 1978—86, chief historian, 1986—97; sr. historian U.S. Holocaust Meml. Mus., Washington, 1997—. Adj. prof. George Mason U., Fairfax, Va., 1990—2002. Author: Ernst Kattenbrunner: Ideological Soldier of the Third Reich, 1984. Mem. spl. edn. adv. com., Arlington, Va., 1997—98; mem. exec. com. Conf. Group on Ctrl. European History, 2004. Mem.: German Studies Assn., Am. Hist. Assn.

BLACK, RECCA MARCELE, elementary school educator; b. Marion, Ind., Feb. 4, 1964; d. Charles Lee and Jerry Ann Barbour. BA in Elem. Edn., Marion Coll., 1987, MEd; postgrad., Ind. Wesleyan U. Tchr. Marion (Ind.) Community Schs.; food svc. worker Marion Coll. Baldwin Food Svc.; casual clerk, cashier, sec. U.S. Post Office; audio-visual asst. VA Med. Ctr. Reporter Marion Newspaper. Contbr. numerous articles to profl. jours. Bd. dirs. YWCA. Recipient Freshman scholar, Shugar scholar. Mem.: NEA, AAUW (bd. dirs.).

BLACK, RICHARD BRUCE, corporate executive, consultant; b. Dallas, July 25, 1933; s. James Ernest and Minerva (Braden) B.; m. Heather Bilandic; children: Kathryn Braden, Paula Anne (dec.), Erica Lynn. BS in Engring., Tex. A&M U., 1954; MBA, Harvard U., 1958; PhD (hon.), Beloit Coll., 1997. With Vulcan Materials Co., Birmingham, Ala., 1958—62; v.p. fin. Warner Electric Brake & Clutch Co., Beloit, Wis., 1962—67, dir., 1973-85; pres. automotive group, exec. v.p. corp. Maremont Corp., Chgo., 1967-72, pres. corp., COO, 1972-76, pres., chmn., CEO, 1976-79; pres., CEO, dir. Alusuisse of Am., Inc., N.Y.C., 1979-81; chmn., CEO, dir. AM Internat., Inc., Chgo., 1981-82; owner R. Black & Assocs., 1983—; chmn. ECRM, Boston, 1983—2002, pres., CEO, 2002—; gen. ptnr. KBA Ptnrs., LP, 1988-98, OpNet Ptnrs., LP, 2000—; pres. Oak Tech., Inc., Sunnyvale, Calif., 1998—99, vice chmn., 1999—2003, dir., 1988—2003. Bd. dirs. GSI Group, Inc., chmn. 2005-; bd. dirs. ECRM, Inc., Applied Optoelectronics, Inc., Alliance Fiber Optics Products, Inc., Altigen Comms., Inc., Benedetto Gartland, Inc., Trex Enterprises, Inc.; lectr. econs. Beloit (Wis.) Coll., 1964-67. Author: (with Jack Pierson) Linear Polyethylene-Propylene: Problems and Opportunities, 1958. Trustee Beloit Coll., Am. Indian Coll. Fund., Teton Sci. Sch., Bard Coll. Ctr. for Curatorial Studies, Inst. for Advanced Study, Princeton, N.J., Snake River Conservancy Found.; trustee, nat. chmn. Inroads, Inc., 1973-77. 1st lt. USAF, 1954-56. Recipient Flame of Hope Lifetime Achievement award, Am. Indian Coll. Fund, 1998, Inroads Lifetime Achievement award, 1979. Mem. Am. Alpine Club, Harvard Club (N.Y.C.). Office: ECRM Inc 554 Clark Rd Tewksbury MA 01876 Office Phone: 978-851-0207. Business E-Mail: r_black@ecrm.com.

BLACK, RITA ANN, communications executive; b. Newark, Sept. 2, 1950; d. Henry and Mary (Solomon) Black; m. David Joseph Franus, Dec. 30, 1973. BA in English, U. Rochester, 1972; MA in Journalism, Columbia U., 1975. Accredited bus. communicator. Sr. editor Book Prodn. Industry mag., New Canaan, Conn., 1972-74, 75-76; mgr. publs. AAUP, N.Y.C., 1976-78; sr. comm. specialist Ciba-Geigy Corp., Ardsley, N.Y., 1978-80, mgr. internal comm., 1980-84; exec. speechwriter IBM Corp., Armonk, N.Y., 1984-86, sr. info. rep., 1986-88, program mgr. U.S. media rels., 1988-90, program mgr. corp. media rels., 1990-91, sr. program adminstr. corp. image advt., 1991-92; nat. mktg. mgr. Deloitte & Touche LLP, Wilton, Conn., 1993-98, dir. mktg. and advt., 1999—2001. Mem.: Internat. Assn. Bus. Communicators (dir. 1982—84, Gold Quill 1983, 1984, Dist. I award of excellence 1982), Pub. Rels. Soc. Am. (Bronze Anvil award 1996), Phi Beta Kappa.

BLACK, ROBERT ALLEN, lawyer; b. Ocala, Fla., Aug. 15, 1954; s. Allen Harrison and Rose Marie (Dupree) B. BA, U. Tex., El Paso, 1977; JD summa cum laude, Tex. Tech U., 1980. Bar: Tex. 1980, U.S. Ct. Appeals (5th and 11th cirs.) 1980, U.S. Supreme Ct. 1985. Ptnr. Mehaffy & Weber, Beaumont, Tex., 1980—, mng. ptnr., 1998—. Dir. State Bar Tex., 2004-2007. Case note editor Tex. Tech Law Rev., 1979-80; editor Jefferson County Bar Jour., 1991-93. Pres. Humane Soc. S.E. Tex., Beaumont, 1983-89; bd. dirs. YMCA, Beaumont, 1985-87, Beaumont Cmty. Players, 1989-91; host TV show Pets on Parade, Beaumont, 1986-87; mem. Beaumont City Planning and Zoning Commn., 1987-90; mem. Beaumont Hist. Landmark Commn., 1989-90. Named one of Outstanding Young Men of Am., Jaycees, 1982, Super Lawyer, Tex. Monthly, 2004, 2005. Fellow: Tex. Bar Found. (chair Dist. 3 nominating com.); mem.: ABA, Am. Bar Assn. Found., Am. Contract Bridge League (pres. unit 201 1991—93, bd. govs. 1992—96, pres. 1994—96), Tex. Bar Assn. (bd. dirs. 2004—), Jefferson County Bar Assn. (treas. 1994—95, pres.-elect 1996—97, pres. 1997—98). Democrat. Avocations: book collecting, tennis, history. Home: 601 22nd St Beaumont TX 77706-4915 Office: Mehaffy & Weber 2615 Calder St Ste 800 Beaumont TX 77702-1993 Business E-Mail: BobBlack@mehaffyweber.com.

BLACK, ROBERT COLEMAN, judge, lawyer; b. Greenville, Ala., July 3, 1934; s. James Monroe and Mabel (Coleman) B.; m. Carolyn Musselwhite, Dec. 20, 1960; children: Elizabeth Anne, Robert C., Carolyn Jane. BS in Commerce and Bus. Adminstrn, U. Ala., 1960, LL.B., 1961. Bar: Ala. 1961. Law clk. to justice Ala. Supreme Ct., 1961-62; partner firm Hill, Hill, Carter, Flanco, Cole & Black, Montgomery, Ala., 1968—, spl. asst. atty. gen. Ala., 1969—; judge Circuit Ct., 1979—. Prof. law Jones Law Sch., Montgomery; instr. bus. law U. Ala. at Montgomery, Auburn U.; lectr. continuing legal edn. Ala. Bar Assn.; faculty Ala. Jud. Coll. City chmn. March of Dimes, 1966; bd. dirs. Montgomery YMCA, St. James Parrish Sch.; trustee Ala. Indsl. Sch. Served with USMCR, 1954-57. Mem. Ala. Bar Assn., Montgomery County Bar Assn. (chmn. exec. com. 1969-70, pres. 1971), Phi Delta Phi, Beta Gamma Sigma. Office: 425 S Perry St Montgomery AL 36104-4235

BLACK, ROBERT DURWARD, television producer; b. Flint, Mich., June 6, 1952; s. Joseph Perrin and Lois Jane (Hamilton) Black. BA, Wheaton Coll., 1974; cert. bus. adminstrn., U. Ill., Chgo., 1991. Sr. account exec. NCR Corp., 1982—84; contr. Bob Horsley's, Inc., 1974—82, v.p., gen. mgr., 1984—87; pres., prodr. weekly ecumenical TV broadcast 30 Good Minutes, 1987—. Prodr.: (documentaries) Peace Like a River (Bronze plaque Columbus Internat. Film Festival, 1994). Mem. bd. govs. Religion Comm. Coun., 2001—05. Office: Chgo Sunday Evening Club 200 N Michigan Ave Chicago IL 60601-5909

BLACK, ROBERT FREDERICK, retired gas industry executive; b. Mansfield, Ohio, Jan. 9, 1920; s. Judson Ammi and Pauline (Remy) B.; m. Conita Fay McCoslin, June 25, 1944; children: Ronald Gregory, Peggy Lynn. Student, Miami U., Oxford, Ohio, 1946-47. Asst. mgr. Warner Bros. Theatres, Mansfield, 1935-42; asst. treas. Red Arrow Freight Lines, Inc., Houston, 1947-56; contr., sec. Cactus Petroleum Inc., Houston, 1956-62; project contr. Del E. Webb Corp., Clear Lake City, Tex., 1962-65; treas. Mitchell Energy & Devel. Corp., The Woodlands, Tex., 1965-82. Choir dir. New Song United Meth. Ch., 2005. With USAAC, 1942-46, CBI. Named to Honorable Order of Ky. Colonels. Mem. Fin. Execs. Inst. (life, past bd. dirs. Houston chpt.), CBI Vets Assn., DeMolay Alumni Assn., Burma Star Assn., Masons (life, grand organist Grand Lodge of Ariz. 1997-98). Republican. Home: 10628 W Saratoga Cir Sun City AZ 85351 E-mail: cfbrfb@cox.net.

BLACK, ROBERT L., JR., retired judge; b. Dec. 11, 1917; s. Robert L. and Anna M. (Smith) B.; m. Helen Chatfield, July 27, 1946; children: William C., Stephen L., Luther F. AB, Yale U., 1939; LLB, Harvard U., 1942. Bar: Ohio 1946, U.S. Ct. Appeals (6th cir.) 1947, U.S. Supreme Ct. 1955. Pvt. practice, Cin., 1946-53; ptnr. Graydon, Head & Ritchey, Cin., 1953-72; judge Ct. Common Pleas, Cin., 1973-77, Ct. Appeals, Cin., 1977-89, vis. and assigned judge, 1989-92. Mem. jury instrns. com. Ohio Jud. Conf. 1973-2004, chmn. 1986-92. Contbr. articles on law to profl. jours. Councilman Village Indian Hill (Ohio), 1953-65, mayor, 1959-65; mem. standing com. Diocese of So. Ohio, Episcopal Ch., 1958-64, lay del. to gen. assembly, 1966, 69; vestryman, warden Indian Hill Episcopal Ch.; chmn. Cin. Human Rels. Commn., 1967-70. Served to Capt. U.S. Army, 1942-45. Decorated Bronze Star. Mem. Cin. Bar Assn., Ohio Bar Assn., ABA, Am. Judicature Soc., Nat. Legal Aid and Defender Assn., Phi Beta Kappa, Queen City Club, Camargo Club, Commonwealth (Cin.) Club. Republican. Episcopalian. Home: 5900 Drake Rd Cincinnati OH 45243-3306 E-mail: bopblack@cinci.rr.com.

BLACK, ROBERT LINCOLN, pediatrician, educator; b. LA, Aug. 25, 1930; s. Harold Alfred and Kathryn (Stone) Black; m. Jean Wilmott McGuire, June 27, 1953; children: Donald J., Douglas L., Margaret S. AB, Stanford (Calif.) U., 1952, MD, 1955. Diplomate Am. Bd. Pediat. Intern Kings County Hosp., Bklyn., 1955—56; resident and fellow Stanford U. Hosp., 1958—62; practice medicine specializing in pediat. Monterey, Calif., 1962—. Clin. prof. Stanford U., 1962—; cons. Calif. Dept. Health, Sacramento, 1962—; mem. Calif. State Maternal, Child, Adolescent Health Bd., 1984—93. Author (with others): California Health Plan for Children, 1979. Mem. Monterey Peninsula Unified Sch. Bd., 1965—73, pres., 1968—70; mem. Mid-Coast Health Sys. Agy., Salinas, Calif., 1975—80, pres., 1979—80; bd. dirs. Lucile Packard Found. for Child Health, 2000—, Lyceum of Monterey Peninsula, 1963—, Carmel Bach Festival, Calif., 1972—81. With USAF, 1956—58. Fellow: Am. Acad. Pediat. (Child Advocacy award sr. sect. 2002); mem.: Physicians for Social Responsibility, Monterey County Med. Soc., Calif. Med. Assn., Inst. Medicine of NAS. Democrat. Home: 976 Mesa Rd Monterey CA 93940-4612 Office: 920 Cass St Monterey CA 93940-4507 Office Phone: 831-372-5841.

BLACK, ROBERT PERRY, bank executive; b. Hickman, Ky., Dec. 21, 1927; s. Burwell Perry and Veola (Moore) B.; m. Mary Rives Ogilvie, Oct. 27, 1951; children: Patty Rives, Robert Perry. BA, U. Va., 1950, MA, 1951, PhD, 1955. Research assoc. Fed. Res. Bank, Richmond, Va., 1954-55, assoc. economist, 1956-58, economist, 1958-60, asst. v.p., 1960-62, v.p., 1962-68, 1st v.p., 1968-73, pres., 1973-92. Part time instr. U. Va., 1953—54; asst. prof. U. Tenn., 1955—56; lectr. U. Va., 1956—57; J. Boone Aiken vis. prof. banking Francis Marion Coll., Florence, SC, 1991; mem. Gov.'s Adv. Bd. Revenue Estimates, 1976—92, Va. Econ. Recovery Commn., 1991—92; mem. adv. bd. Health Corp. Va., 1981—93; mem. bd. govs. Capital Area Assy., 1989—93, mem. exec. com., 1989—93; bd. dirs. Media Gen. Corp., 1993—2001, Winchester Evening Star, Inc., Rockingham Publ. Co., T. Rowe Price's Fixed Income Mutual Funds, 1993—98. Contbr. articles to profl. jours. Past dir. Ctrl. Richmond Assn.; former trustee Collegiate Schs., past chmn.; chmn. Main to the James Devel. Com., 1971-73; adv. coun. Robert E. Lee coun. Boy Scouts Am., 1977-78; bd. dirs. Retreat Hosp., 1988-98; past pres. United Way Greater Richmond; bd. dirs., mem. exec. com., treas., chmn. fin. com. Downtown Devel. Unltd., 1975-86; chmn. adv. com. Ctr. Banking Edn., Va. Union U., 1977-79; trustee E. Angus Powell Endowment for Am. Enterprise, 1980-88, Acad. for Econ. Edn., 1990-94; mem. adv. bd. Ctr. for Advanced Studies, U. Va., 1986-94; mem. Forum Club, 1987—; bd. dirs. Va. United Meth. Homes, Inc., 1990-94, v.p., 1991-92, chmn., 1992-94; mem. Gov.'s Com. on Def. Conv. and Econ. Adjustment, 1992-94; dir. Va. Biotech. Rsch. Park, 1992-94. With AUS, 1946-47. Recipient George Washington Honor medal award Freedoms Found., Valley Forge, 1978, Brotherhood citation NCCJ, 1991, J. Curtis Hall award for outstanding svc. Va. Coun. Econ. Edn., Outstanding Svc. award Ctrl. Richmond Assn., 1991, Silver Hope award Ctr. Va. chpt. Nat. Multiple Sclerosis Soc., 1992, Disting. Citizen award Robert E. Lee coun. Boy Scouts Am., 1993, Robert P. Black Rsch. Professorship in Econs. at U. Va. established by friends, 1993. Mem. Va. Inter-Govt. Inst. (bd. dirs. 1986-93), Country Club Va. (bd. dirs. 1980-85, 88, v.p. 1981-83, pres. 1983-85), The Commonwealth Club, Kinloch Golf Club, Raven Soc., Phi Beta Kappa (past pres. Richmond chpt.), Beta Gamma Sigma, Alpha Kappa Psi, Kappa Alpha. Methodist. Home: 2133 Cedarfield Ln Richmond VA 23233-1937

BLACK, RONNIE DELANE, religious organization administrator, mayor; b. Poplar Bluff, Mo., Oct. 26, 1947; s. Clyde Olen and Leona Christine Black; m. Sandra Elaine Hulett, Aug. 27, 1966; 1 child, Stephanie. BA, Oakland City (Ind.) Coll., 1969; M Div, So. Bapt. Theol. Sem., 1972. Ordained to ministry Gen. Assn. of Gen. Bapts., 1967. Pastor Gen. Bapt. Ch., Fort Branch, Ind., 1972-78; stewardship dir. Gen. Bapt. Hdqrs., Poplar Bluff, Mo., 1978-97, exec. dir., 1997—; councilman City of Poplar Bluff, 1985-97, mayor, 1990-92, 95-96. Mem. Gen. Bapt. Ch. Office: Gen Bapts 100 Stinson Dr Poplar Bluff MO 63901-8736

BLACK, ROY, lawyer; b. NYC, Feb. 17, 1945; s. Richard and Minna (Bennett) B. BA, U. Miami, Fla., 1967, JD, 1970. Bar: Fla. 1970. Sr. asst. pub. defender Dade County, Miami, 1971-76; ptnr. Roy E. Black, P.A., Miami, 1976-79, Black and Furci, P.A., Miami, 1979-93, Black & Seiden, Miami, 1993-96, Black, Srebnick & Kornspan, Miami, 1996—2002, Black Srebnick Kornspan & Stumpf, Miami, 2002—. Legal analyst NBC, 2003—; mng. ptnr. NBC Realty TV Show "The Law Firm". Author: Black's Law: A Criminal Lawyer Reveals his Strategies in Four Cliffhanger Cases, 1999. Fundraising events sponsor Bay Point Sch., Miami. Recipient Nelson Potyner award ACLU, 1982, Criminal Justice award Dade County Bar Assn., 1991, U. Miami William R. Butler Cmty. Svc. award, 2005. Fellow: Am. Coll. Trial Lawyers; mem.: ABA, NACDL (life), Eugene Spellman Inns of Ct., Dade County Bar Assn., Internat. Acad. Trial Lawyers, Fla. Assn. Criminal Def. Lawyers, Fla. Bar Assn. Office: Black Srebnick Kornspan & Stumpf PA 201 S Biscayne Blvd Ste 1300 Miami FL 33131-4311 Office Phone: 305-371-6421. E-mail: rblack@royblack.com.

BLACK, SCOTT M., diversified financial services company executive; b. Portland, Maine; BS in Applied Math., Econ., Johns Hopkins Univ., 1968; MBA in Finance, Harvard Univ. Worked in finance Joseph E. Seagram then Xerox, 1972—75; various positions to head, corp. develop. Merrill Lynch, 1975—77; portfolio mgr. William O'Neil Co., Calif., 1977; mgr. Delphi Value Fund; founder, pres. Delphi Mgmt. Inc., Boston, 1980—. Adv. bd. Portland Mus. Art, Mus. Fine Arts, Boston, John F. Kennedy Sch. Govt, Harvard Univ., Boston, Johns Hopkins Univ., Northeastern Univ. With U.S. Army. Named one of Top 200 Collectors, ARTnews Mag., 2004. Avocation: Collecting impressionist and modern art. Office: Delphi Mgmt Inc 50 Rowes Wharf Boston MA 02110 Office Phone: 617-330-1025.*

BLACK, SHANE, screenwriter; b. Pitts., Dec. 16, 1961; s. Paul and Patricia Ann B. Screenwriter: Lethal Weapon, 1987, The Monster Squad, 1987, Lethal Weapon 2, 1989, Lethal Weapon 3, 1992, Last Action Hero, 1993, Leathal Weapon 4, 1998; screenwriter, prodr.: The Last Boy Scout, 1991 (exec. prodr.), The Long Kiss Goodnight, 1996, AWOL, 1999 (exec. prodr.); screenwriter, dir.: Kiss Kiss, Bang Bang, 2005; actor: (films) Predator, 1987, Dead Heat, 1988, RoboCop 3, 1993, Night Realm, 1994, As Good as It Gets, 1997, We, the Screenwriter, 2002, The Boy Scout, 2002. Office: David Geffen Co 9130 W Sunset Blvd West Hollywood CA 90069-3110 also: Endeavor 350 S Beverly Dr Beverly Hills CA 90212-4811*

BLACK, SHIRLEY TEMPLE (MRS. CHARLES A. BLACK), former ambassador, former actress; b. Santa Monica, Calif., Apr. 23, 1928; d. George Francis and Gertrude Temple; m. John Agar, Jr., Sept. 19, 1945 (div. 1949); 1 dau., Linda Susan; m. Charles A. Black, Dec. 16, 1950; children: Charles Alden, Lori Alden. Ed. under pvt. tutelage; grad., Westlake Sch. Girls, 1945. Rep. to 24th Gen. Assembly UN, N.Y.C., 1969-70; amb. to Ghana Accra, 1974-76; chief of protocol White House, Washington, 1976-77; amb. to Czechoslovakia Prague, 1989-92. Mem. U.S. Delegation on African Refugee Problems, Geneva, 1981; mem. public adv. com. UN Conf. on Law of the Sea; dep. chmn. U.S. del. UN Conf. on Human Environment, Stockholm, 1970-72; spl. asst. to chmn. Pres.'s Coun. on Environ. Quality, 1972-74; del. treaty on environment USSR-USA Joint Commn., Moscow, 1972; mem. U.S. Commn. for UNESCO, 1973; hon. U.S. Fgn. Svc. officer. Began film career at age 3 1/2; first full-length film was Stand Up and Cheer; other films included Little Miss Marker, Baby Take a Bow, Bright Eyes, Our Little Girl, The Little Colonel, Curly Top, The Littlest Rebel, Captain January, Poor Little Rich Girl, Dimples, Stowaway, Wee Willie Winkie, Heidi, Rebecca of Sunnybrook Farm, Little Miss Broadway, Just Around the Corner, The Little Princess, Susannah of the Mounties, The Blue Bird, Kathleen, Miss Annie Rooney, Since You Went Away, Kiss and Tell, 1945, That Hagen Girl, War Party, The Bachelor and the Bobby-Soxer, Honeymoon, 1947; narrator, actress: TV series Shirley Temple Storybook, NBC, 1958, Shirley Temple Show, NBC, 1960; author: Child Star: An Autobiography, 1988. Dir. Bank of Calif.; dir. Fireman's Fund Ins. Co., BANCAL Tri-State Corp., Walt Disney, Del Monte Corp.; Mem. Calif. Adv. Hosp. Council, 1969, San Francisco Health Facilities Planning Assn., 1965-69; Republican candidate for U.S. Ho. of Reps. from Calif., 1967; bd. dirs. Nat. Wildlife Fedn., Nat. Multiple Sclerosis Soc., UN Assn. U.S.A.; bd. dirs. exec. com. Internat. Fedn. Multiple Sclerosis Socs. Appointed col. on staff of Gov. Ross of Idaho, 1935; commd. col. Hawaiian N.G.; hon. col. 108th Rgt. N.G. Ill.; dame Order Knights Malta, Paris, 1968; recipient Ceres medal FAO, Rome, 1975, numerous other state decorations; Kennedy Center Honoree, 1998. Mem. World Affairs Coun. No. Calif. (dir.), Coun. Fgn. Rels., Nat. Com. for U.S./China Rels. Clubs: Commonwealth of Calif.*

BLACK, STEPHEN FRANKLIN, lawyer; b. N.Y.C., Nov. 28, 1944; s. Theodore Russel Black and Zelma Carmel Bernstein; m. Laurie N. Bromberg, June 25, 1967 (div. Oct. 1988); children: Hilary F., Jane S., Katharine L.; m. Anne M. Richmond, Oct. 14, 1989. AB magna cum laude, Harvard U., 1965; JD magna cum laude, U. Mich., 1968; MLitt, Oxford (Eng.) U., 1970. Bar: DC 1969. Ptnr. Wilmer, Cutler & Pickering, Washington, 1970—2001. Author: Internal Corporate Investigations, 1985, Der Zivilprozess in Den Vereinigten Staaten, 1986, Complying with Foreign Corrupt Practices Act, 1997, (play) Candlefire, 2003; contbr. articles to profl. jours. Trustee

Shakespeare Theatre, Washington, 2001—; bd. dirs. Am. Soc. Legal History, 1979—82, English Speaking Union, Washington, 2004—. Marshall scholar, 1970. Mem.: Cosmos Club (Washington). Home: 1605 22nd St NW Washington DC 20008-1921

BLACK, SUSAN HARRELL, federal judge; b. Valdosta, Ga., Oct. 20, 1943; d. William H. and Ruth Elizabeth (Phillips) Harrell; m. Louis Eckert Black, Dec. 28, 1966. BA, Fla. State U., 1965; JD, U. Fla., 1967; LLM, U. Va., 1984. Bar: Fla. 1967. Atty. U.S. Army Corps of Engrs., Jacksonville, Fla., 1968—69; asst. state atty. Gen. Counsel's Office, Jacksonville, 1969—72; judge County Ct. of Duval County, Fla., 1973—75; judge 4th Jud. Cir. Ct. of Fla., 1975—79; judge U.S. Dist. Ct. (mid. dist.) Fla., Jacksonville, 1979—90, chief judge, 1990—92; judge U.S. Ct. Appeals (11th cir.) Fla., Jacksonville, 1992—. Faculty Fed. Jud. Ctr.; mem. U.S. Jud. Conf. Com. onInns of Ct., 1984—87; trustee Am. Inns Ct. Found., 1985—91; pres. US Dist. Judge's Assn (11th Cir.), 1987—88; mem. Jud. Improvements Com., 1987—90, Com. on Court Admin. and Case Mgmt., 1990—92, Jud. Conference Com. on Fed.-State Jurisdiction, 1998—2004. Trustee emeritus Law Sch. U. Fla.; past pres. Chester Bedell Inn of Ct. Mem.: Jacksonville Bar Assn., Fla. Bar Assn. Presbyterian.

BLACK, TANYA WARD, counselor; b. St. Louis, Jan. 11, 1946; d. Herbert Ward, Sr. and Margaret Ward; m. Hollis M. Black III, Mar. 7, 1970; 1 child, Aubretia. BA in Fgn. Langs., Wheaton Coll., 1968; MA in Behavioral Sci., So. Ill. U., 1976; MEd in Counseling, Ala. A&M U., 1990. Lic. profl. counselor, nat. cert. counselor, cert. clin. mental health counselor, supr. of LPC interns. Multicultural tchr. Chgo., St. Louis, 1966—70; asst. dept. psychology So. Ill. U., 1971—76; tchr. Spanish and counselor Westminster Acad., Huntsville, Ala., 1980—84; tchr., advisor young adults, 1985—; lic. profl. counselor Trinity Counseling Ctr., Huntsville, 1992—2001, pvt. practice, Huntsville, 2001—. Presenter in field. Divorce recovery workshops for adults and children, 1991—; cons. infertility and pregnancy loss Huntsville, 1995—. Mem.: Am. Assn. Christian Counselors, Am. Counseling Assn. Avocations: backpacking, swimming, music. Office: Bob Wallace Med Bldg Ste B 101 Bob Wallace Ave Huntsville AL 35801

BLACK, THOMAS DONALD, retired religious organization administrator; b. Mercer, Pa., Feb. 7, 1920; s. Harry Alexander and Bessie (Gilkey) B.; m. Frances Anna Greenan, Mar. 1, 1923; children: David Alan, Donald Francis, Joseph Harry, Timothy John (dec.). BA, Grove City Coll., 1942, DD, 1955; MDiv, Pitts.-Xenia Theol. Sch., 1945; MST, Temple U., 1954. Ordained to ministry United Presbyn. Ch. N.Am., 1945. Founding pastor Creston Hills United Presbyn. Ch., Oklahoma City, 1945-50; pastor Blvd. United Presbyn. Ch., Phila., 1950-54, Am. Ch. in London, 1973-76; exec. sec. United Presbyn. Bd. Fgn. Mission, Phila., 1954-58; assoc. gen. sec. Commn. on Ecumenical Mission and Relations United Presbyn. Ch.-U.S.A., N.Y.C., 1958-70, gen. sec. Commn. on Ecumenical Mission and Relations, 1970-72, assoc. gen. dir. Program Agy., 1977-84; exec. dir. Gen. Assembly Council Presbyn. Ch. (USA), N.Y.C. and Atlanta, 1985-87; acting assoc. gen. sec. Nat. Coun. Chs. in U.S.A., 1989-90; interim dir. U.S. Office World Coun. Chs., N.Y.C., 1991-92. Chmn. bd. dirs. Christian Lit. Fund, Geneva, 1964-69, Ravemcco, Lit-Lit, N.Y.C., 1962-66. Author: Merging Mission and Unity, 1986; contbr. articles and pamphlets to mission and ch. publs. Interim assoc. Riverside Ch., 1992-93; pastoral assoc. Abington Presbyn. Ch., 1994-98. Presbyterian. Home: 1515 The Fairway Apt 617 Jenkintown PA 19046 *We want to be appreciated for what we are, but uncertain of being accepted, we try to justify our lives by what we have accomplished. God accepts us for what we are.*

BLACK, TIMOTHY LEE, physician; b. Toccoa, Ga., Oct. 9, 1948; s. Robert N. and Kathryn A. (Harner) B.; m. Melinda Girdley, Sept. 28, 1985. BS, Wheaton Coll., 1971; MD, U. Tenn., 1979. Diplomate Am. Bd. Surgery. Intern, then resident in gen. surgery U. Tenn., 1979-84; fellow in pediatric surgery LeBonheur Children's Hosp., Memphis, Tenn., 1984-86; pediatric surgeon Pediatric Surg. Assn. of Ft. Worth, 1986—. Contbr. articles to profl. jours. Fellow ACS; mem. AMA, Am. Acad. Pediatrics, Am. Pediatric Surgery Assn., Ft. Worth Pediatric Soc. Office: Pediatric Surg Assn Ft Worth Ste 210 901 7th Ave Fort Worth TX 76104-2724 Office Phone: 817-336-7881. Business E-Mail: tblack@coochildren.org.

BLACK, VICTORIA LYNN, writer, artist; b. Whittier, Calif., Nov. 23, 1943; d. Raymond Witty and Dorothy Ada (Burnett) Davenport; m. Bruce Robert Black, Aug. 30, 1997; m. Richard Dee Bandlow, Sept. 16, 1961 (dec. Dec. 2, 1972); children: Lisa Lynn Bandlow Dobbins, Lincoln Dee Bandlow. Model/actress Dale Garrick Agy., Beverly Hills, Calif., 1959—78, Bronson of Calif., L.A., 1968—79; prodn. asst./casting Pub. Svc. Co., Irvine, Calif., 1979—80; theatrical agt. William Carroll Agy., Burbank, Calif., 1980—83; office mgr. Greenline, L.A., 1984—86, Napier, L.A., 1986—88, Shah Safari, L.A., 1988—93; writer, artist L.A. Author poetry, short stories, articles; artist paintings and drawings, exhibited in group shows at Verdugo Hills Art Assn., Montrose, Calif., 1999—2004, Glendale (Calif.) Coll., 1986—2002, ERA Castle, La Canada, Calif., 2004, Pasadena (Calif.) Libr., 2002, Jamboree-Art Show, Pasadena, 2003—04. Named Miss Palm Springs, 1960, Miss North Shore Beach, 1961, Miss Ma-Ha-Ya Lani, 1961, Miss Typical Teen, 1961. Mem.: Utah State Poetry Soc., W.Va. Poetry Soc., Poetry Soc. Okla., Mo. State Poetry Soc., Fla. State Poets Assn., Calif. State Poetry Soc., Ariz. State Poetry Soc., Verdugo Hills Art Assn., Alpha Gamma Sigma (life). Avocations: long walks, reading, collecting, museums and art shows. Home: PO Box 959 Sugarloaf CA 92386

BLACK, WILFORD REX, JR., retired state legislator; b. Salt Lake City, Jan. 31, 1920; s. Wilford Rex and Elsie Isabell (King) B.; m. Helen Shirley Frazer; children: Susan, Janet, Cindy, Joy, Peggy, Vanna, Gayle, Rex. Student pub. schs., Utah. Locomotive engr. Rio Grande R.R., 1941-81; mem. Utah Senate, Salt Lake City, 1972-96, spkr. 3d House, 1975-76, majority whip, 1977-78, minority leader, 1981-90. Sec. Utah State Legis. Bd., United Transp.; chmn. bd. Rail Operators Credit Union, 1958—87. Mission pres. Rose Park Stake Mormon Ch. Rose Park Stake Mormon Ch.; high priest group leader Rose Park 9th Ward, 1980—83, 10th Ward, 1996—99; mem. Rose Park Stake High Coun., 1957—63. Served with USAR, 1942—45. Recipient various awards r.r. and legis. activities . Democrat. Office: 826 N 1300 W Salt Lake City UT 84116-3877

BLACK, WILLIAM B., JR., federal agency administrator; b. N.Mex. m. Iris Black; 3 children. BA in Polit. Sci., U. Md., 1971; postgrad., George Washington U., 1978—79, Nat. War Coll., Ft. McNair, Wash., 1979. Operational linguist/analyst Nat. Security Agy., Ft. George, Md., 1959—75, chief office of customer rels. and support to mil. ops., 1975—78, chief ops. maj. field installation, 1979—82, dep. chief, 1982—84, chief, 1984—86, chief office of collection mgmt., 1986—87, assoc. dep. dir. ops./mil. support, 1987—89, chief NSA/CSS rep. Europe office, 1989—92, chief of ops. analysis Group A, 1992—96, spl. asst. to dir. info. warfare, 1996—97, dep. dir., 2000—, acting dir., 2005; asst. v.p., dir. info. ops. Sci. Applications Internat. Corp./Info. Ops. Advanced Technologies and Solutions Group, 1997—2000. With U.S. Army, 1956—59. Recipient Exceptional Civilian Svc. award, U.S. Govt., 1986, 1997, Nat. Intelligence Disting. Svc. medal, 1996, Meritorious Civilian Svc. award, Sec. of Def., 1992, Sr. Exec. Svc. Presdl. Rank award, 1984, Meritorious Civilian Svc. award, Sec. of Def., 1974. Office: Nat Security Agy Central Security Svc 9800 Savage Rd Fort George G Meade MD 20755-6000*

BLACK, WILLIAM REA, lawyer; b. N.Y.C., Nov. 4, 1952; s. Thomas Howard and Dorothy Chambers (Dailey) B.; m. Kathleen Jane Owen, June 24, 1978; children: William Ryan, Jonathan Wesley. BSBA, U. Denver, 1978, MBA, 1981; JD, Western State U., Fullerton, Calif., 1987. Bar: Calif., U.S. Ct. Appeals (fed. cir.), U.S. Dist. Ct.; lic. real estate broker; lic. pvt. investigator. Bus. mgr. Deere & Co., Moline, Ill., 1979-85; dir. Mgmt. Resource Svc. Co., Chgo., 1985-86; sr. v.p. Geneva Corp., Irvine, Calif., 1986-91; pvt. practice Newport Beach, Calif., 1991-92; gen. counsel Sunclipse, Inc., 1992—97; spl. counsel Amcor, Ltd., 1992—97; dir. gen. Amcor de Mex., S.A. de C.V., 1993—97; secretario KHL de Mex. S.A. de C.V., 1995—97; v.p., gen. counsel LL Knickerbocker Co., 1997-99; CEO Kuroi Kiku Corp., Kuroi Ryu Corp., First Reconnaissance Co., 1997—; v.p., gen. counsel Thales N. Am., 1999—. Adv. bd. mem. Internat. Govt. Contractor. Mng. editor Western State U. Law Rev., Fullerton, 1984-87. Instr. Pai Lum Kung Fu Karate, Hartford, Conn., 1970-75, U.S. Judo Assn., Denver, 1975-80, United Studios Kenpo, L.A., 1995—. Recipient Am. Jurisprudence award Bancroft-Whitney Co., 1984, 85, 86; Pres.'s scholar full acad. merit scholarship, 1983. Mem. ABA, Am. Soc. Appraisers, Inst. Bus. Appraisers, Assn. Productivity Specialists, Am. Employment Law Coun., Profls. in Human Resources Assn., Am. Mgmt. Assn., Orange County Bar Assn., L.A. County Bar Assn., Orgn. Fgn. Investment, Mu Kappa Tau. Avocations: karate (2d degree black belt), Judo, skiing, scuba, golf. Office: 675 N Washington St Ste 400 Alexandria VA 22314 Business E-Mail: william.black@us.thalesgroup.com.

BLACKADAR, ALFRED KIMBALL, meteorologist, educator; b. Newburyport, Mass., July 6, 1920; s. Walter Lloyd and Harriett (White) B.; m. Beatrice J. Fenner, Mar. 23, 1946; children: Bruce Evan, Russell Lloyd, Thomas Alan. AB, Princeton U., 1942; PhD, NYU, 1950. From instr. to asso. prof. NYU, 1946-56; lectr. climatology Columbia U., 1953-55; mem. faculty Pa. State U., 1956—, prof. meteorology, 1961—, prof. emeritus, 1985—, head dept., 1967-81. Mem. exec. com. Univ. Corp. Atmospheric Rsch., 1965-68; mem. exec. com. divsn. earth scis. NRC, 1966-69; mem. Internat. Commn. on Dynamical Meteorology, 1978-94, chair working group A, 1978-85; vis. prof. Christian-Albrechts U., Kiel, Germany, 1985-95. Editor: Meteorological Research Revs., 1957; exec. editor: Weatherwise, 1981-95. Sec. Univ. Christian Assn., 1964-68. Served to maj. USAAF, 1942-46. Recipient Sr. Scientist award Alexander von Humboldt Found., 1973 Fellow AAAS, Am. Meteorol. Soc. (sec. 1965-69, pres. 1971-72, editor monographs, Charles F. Brooks award 1969, Cleveland Abbe award 1986, award for outstanding contbns. to the advance of applied meteorology 2002, chmn. publs. commn. 1978-84, chair com. on awards 1989-90), Am. Geophys. Union, Deutsche Meteorologische Gesellschaft (fgn. mem.), North Plainfield (N.J.) Hall of Fame. Baptist. Office: Pa State U 503 Walker Bldg University Park PA 16802-5013 Home: 330 Lions Hill Rd #w221 State College PA 16803 Office Phone: 814-865-0478.

BLACKALL, GEORGE FRANCIS, psychologist; b. Stamford, Conn., Sept. 13, 1959; s. Joseph and Eileen Blackall; m. Colleen Schuster. BS, Okla. State U., 1981; MBA, U. Conn., 1985; D of Psychology, Widener U., Pa., 1995. Lic. Psychologist Pa., 1996. Pediat. psychologist Phila. Child Guidance Ctr., 1995—97; dir. psychol. svcs. Pain Mgmt. Ctr., Milton S. Hershey Med. Ctr., Hershey, 1997—; pediatric psychologist Divsn. of Oncology, Milton S. Hershey Med. Ctr.; dir. of student devel. Penn State U. Coll. of Medicine; assoc. prof. of pediat., humanities and neural & behavioral scics. Penn State Coll. of Medicine. Author: (book review) Contemporary Psychology; contbr. chapters to books. Mem.: APA, Assn. of Am. Med. Colls. Office: Penn State Univ Coll Medicine 500 University Dr Hershey PA 17033 Business E-Mail: gblackall@psu.edu.

BLACKBOURN, DAVID GORDON, history professor; b. Spilsby, England, Nov. 1, 1949; s. Harry and Pamela Jean (Youngman) B.; m. Deborah Frances Langton; 2 children. BA with honors, Cambridge U., England, 1970, PhD, 1976. Lectr. Queen Mary Coll., U. London, 1976-79, Birkbeck Coll., U. London, 1985-89, prof. history, 1989-92, Harvard U., Cambridge, Mass., 1992-97, Coolidge prof. history, 1997—. Vis. Kratter prof. history Stanford (Calif.) U., 1989-90; guest lectr. U.S., England, Italy, Yugoslavia, Germany, 1976—; ann. lectr. German Hist. Inst., London, 1998; Malcolm Wynn lectr. Stetson U., Fla., 2002; hist. cons. Channel 4 TV (U.K.), History Channel (U.S.); mem. adv. com. Edmund Spruash Meml. Trust, 2002—. Author: Class, Religion and Local Politics in Wilhelmine Germany, 1980, (with G. Eley) The Peculiarities of German history, 1984, Populists and Patricians: Esssays in Modern German History, 1987; co-editor: (with R.J. Evans) The German Bourgeoisie, 1991, Marpingen: Apparitions of the Virgin Mary in Bismarckian Germany, 1993 (Am. Hist. Assn. prize best book), The Long Nineteenth Century: A History of Germany, 1780-1918, 1998, 2d edit., 2003, The Conquest of Nature: Water and the Making of the Modern German Landscape, 2006; mem. editl. bd. Past and Present, 1988—; numerous appearances on Brit. Broadcasting Sys., 1977—; contbr. articles to profl. jours. Gov. Goodrich Sch., London, 1983—86. Rsch. fellow Jesus Coll., Cambridge, 1973-76, Inst. European History, Mainz, Germany, 1974-75, Alexander von Humboldt Found. fellow, 1984-85, John Simon Guggenheim Meml. Found. fellow, 1994-95, Walter Channing Cabot fellow Harvard, 2004; German Acad. Exch. grantee, 1977. Fellow: Royal Hist. Soc.; mem.: Friends of the German Hist. Inst. Washington (bd. mem.), Am. Hist. Assn. (com. on honorary foreign membership 2001—, pres. conf. group on ctrl. European history 2003), German History Soc. (sec. 1979—81, com. 1981—86), Inst. European History Mainz (adv. bd. 1995—), German Hist. Inst. London (acad. adv. bd. 1983—92). Avocations: writing, reading, jazz, politics, classical music. Office Phone: 617-495-4303 x228. Business E-Mail: dgblackb@fas.harvard.edu.

BLACKBURN, ALEXANDER LAMBERT, author, English literature educator; b. Durham, N.C., Sept. 6, 1929; s. William Maxwell and Elizabeth Cheney (Bayne) B.; m. Jane Allison, 1957 (div. 1974); children: David Alexander, Philip William Rhodes; m. Inés Dölz, Oct. 14, 1975. BA, Yale U., 1951; MA, U. N.C., 1956; PhD, Cambridge (Eng.) U., 1963. Instr. Hampden-Sydney (Va.) Coll., 1960-61, U. Pa., Phila., 1963-65; lectr. U. Md., RAF, Upper Heyford, England, 1967-73; prof. English U. Colo., Colorado Springs, 1973-95; prof. emeritus, 1996—. Author: The Cold War of Kitty Pentecost, 1979, The Myth of the Picaro, 1979, A Sunrise Brighter Still: The Visionary Novels of Frank Waters, 1991, Suddenly a Mortal Splendor, 1995, (essays) Creative Spirit: Toward a Better World, 2001, (memoir) Meeting the Professor: Growing Up in the William Blackburn Family, 2004; editor: The Interior Country: Stories of the Modern West, 1987, Higher Elevations: Stories from the West, A Writers' Forum Anthology, 1993; editor-in-chief Writers' Forum, vols. 1-21, 1974—95. 1st lt. U.S. Army, 1951—53. Recipient Internat. PeaceWriting Award for Fiction, Ctr. for Peace, Justice and Ecology, 2003, Chancellor's award U. Colo., 1994, Faculty Book award, 1993, Am. Acad. Poets award, 1959, Frank Waters award for excellence in lit. Friends of the Pikes Peak Libr. Dist., Colorado Springs, 2005. Mem. Authors Guild, Colo. Authors League, Western Lit. Assn., PEN West. Avocation: watercolor. Home: 6030 Twin Rock Ct Colorado Springs CO 80918-3239 Personal E-mail: idb99@yahoo.com.

BLACKBURN, DESMOND K, principal; b. Mt. Vernon, NY, Jan. 24, 1974; s. Desmond and Diana M Blackburn; m. Kelli S Smith, June 28, 1997; children: Dean Q, Grant A. BS, U. of Fla., 1992—96; MS, Nova Southeastern U., 1999—2000. Professional Educator's Certificate Fla. Dept. of Edn., 1998. Math tchr. Plantation H.S., Plantation, Fla., 1996—2000; asst. prin. Sunrise Mid. Sch., Ft. Lauderdale, Fla., 2000—03; prin. Ramblewood Mid. Sch., Coral Springs, Fla., 2003—. Pres. D & G Solutions Inc., Weston, Fla., 2004—. Mem.: Fla. Assn. of Sch. Administrators (life), Nat. Mid. Sch. Assn. (life), Nat. Assn. of Secondary Sch. Principals (life), Am. Ednl. Rsch. Assn. (life), McDonald Lodge #70 (life). Democrat-Npl. Episcopal. Avocations: golf, reading, music. Home: 1041 Daisy Lane Weston FL 33327 Office: Ramblewood Middle Sch 8505 W Atlantic Blvd Coral Springs FL 33071 Office Phone: 754-322-4345. Office Fax: 754-322-4385. E-mail: desmondblackburn@browardschools.com.

BLACKBURN, ELIZABETH HELEN, molecular biologist; b. Hobart, Australia, Nov. 26, 1948; 1 child. BSc in BioChemistry, U. Melbourne, Australia, 1970, MSc in BioChemistry, 1972; PhD in Molecular Biology, Cambridge (Eng.) U., 1975; post Date in Molecular and Cellular Biology, Yale U., New Haven, Conn., 1977; DSc (hon.), Yale U., 1991. Fellow in biology Yale U., New Haven, 1975-77; fellow in biochemistry U. Calif., San Francisco, 1977-78, asst. prof., dept. molecular biology Berkeley, 1978—83, prof., dept. molecular biology, 1983—86, 1986—90, chair dept. microbiology and immunology San Francisco, 1993-99, prof., depts. biochemistry and biophysics, and microbiology and immunology, 1990—. Contbr. articles, scientific papers. Recipient Eli Lilly award in microbiology, 1988, NAS award in molecular biology, 1990, le Grand Prix Charles-Leopold Mayer, 1998, Calif. Scientist of Year award, 1999, Harvey prize, 1999, AAMC Baxter award, 1999, Novartis-Drew award for Biomedical Sci., 1999, Feodor Lynen award, 2000, AACR-G.H.A. Clowes Memorial award, 2000, Dickson prize in Medicine, 2000, Am. Cancer Soc. Medal of Honor, 2000, AACR-Pezcoller Found. award for Cancer Rsch., 2001, Alfred P. Sloan Jr. prize, GM Cancer Rsch. Found., 2001 Fellow: Royal Soc. London, AAAS; mem.: NAS (fgn. assoc. 1993), Inst. Medicine, Am. Soc. Cell Biology (pres. 1998, Australian prize 1998, Gairdner prize 1998, Passano award 1999, Rosensteil award 1999, Keio prize 1999, E.B. Wilson medal 2001). Office: U Calif Biochem and Biophys Box 2200 San Francisco CA 94143-2200 Business E-Mail: telomer@itsa.ucsf.edu.

BLACKBURN, HENRY WEBSTER, JR., retired epidemiologist; b. Miami, Fla., Mar. 22, 1925; s. Henry Webster and Mary Frances (Smith) B.; m. Nelly Paula Trocme, Jan. 10, 1951 (div. 1984); children: John Keith, Katherine Ann, Heidi Elizabeth; m. Stacy Richardson, Sept. 1, 1991. Student, Fla. So. Coll., Lakeland, 1942—43; BS, U. Miami, 1947; MD, Tulane U., 1948, DSc (hon.), 1999; MS, U. Minn., 1957; Dr honoris causa, U. Kuopio, Finland, 1988. Intern Chgo. Wesley Meml. Hosp., 1948-49; resident in medicine Am. Hosp. Paris, 1949-50; med. officer in charge USPHS, Austria, Fed. Republic Germany, 1950-53; med. fellow U. Minn., Mpls., 1953-56; ret. Divsn. Epidemiology, 1996; med. dir. Mut. Svc. Ins. Co., St. Paul, 1956; asst. prof. physiol. hygiene U. Minn., 1958-61, assoc. prof., 1961-68, prof., 1968—, lectr. medicine, 1956—, dir. lab. physiol. hygiene Sch. Pub. Health, 1972—, prof. medicine, 1972—, chmn. divsn. epidemiology, 1983-90, Mayo prof. pub. health, 1990-96. Vis. prof. U. Geneva, 1970; mem. adv. coun. Nat. Heart, Lung and Blood Inst., 1989-93; mem. com. on diet and health NRC, 1986-89; Ancel Keys lectr., 1991; mem. food adv. com. FDA, 1995-2000; Mayo chair in pub. health, 1988. Author: Cardiovascular Survey Methods, 1968, On the Trail of Heart Attacks in Seven Countries, 1995, "P.K." Irreverent Memoirs of a Preacher's Kid, 1999, If It Isn't Fun...Memoir of a Different Sort of Medical Life, Vol. I, 2001, Vol. 2, 2004; mem. editl. bd. numerous jours.; contbr. articles to profl. jours. Lt. (j.g.) USNR, 1942-50, capt. USPHS inactive res. Recipient Thomas Francis award in epidemiology, 1975, Naylor Dana award in preventive medicine, 1976, Louis Bishop award in cardiology, 1979, Gold Heart award Am. Heart Assn., 1990, Rsch. Achievement award Am. Heart Assn., 1992. Fellow APHA, Am. Coll. Cardiology, Am. Epidemiol. Soc.; mem. AAAS (chmn. med. sect.), Belgian Royal Acad. Medicine, Am. Heart Assn. (dir. 1971-74), Internat. Soc. Cardiology (coun. epidemiology 1971-74, chmn. 1986-91), Internat. Epidemiol. Soc., Alpha Omega Alpha, Phi Kappa Phi, Delta Omega. Office: U Minn Divsn Epidemiology 1300 S 2d St Minneapolis MN 55454-1075 Office Phone: 612-626-9396. Business E-Mail: blackburn@epi.umn.edu.

BLACKBURN, JAMES B., III, lawyer; b. Pitts., Nov. 16, 1946; s. James B. Jr. and Ethel Louise (Herrod) B.; m. Cynthia Jan Coote, Aug. 10, 1974; children: Sarah Louise, James B. IV, Natalie Alice. BA, Princeton U., 1969; MPA, N.C. State U., 1974; JD, Duke U., 1980. Bar: N.C. 1980. Staff atty. Gen. Rsch. Divsn, N.C. Gen. Assembly, Raleigh, 1980-84; gen. counsel N.C. Assn. County Commrs., Raleigh, 1984—. Sgt. U.S. Army, 1970-72. Mem. Internat. Mcpl. Lawyers Assn., N.C. Bar Assn. Home: 801 Kings Mill Rd Chapel Hill NC 27517 Office: NC Assn County Commrs PO Box 1488 Raleigh NC 27602-1488 Office Phone: 919-715-2893. Business E-Mail: jim.blackburn@ncacc.org.

BLACKBURN, JOHN D., insurance company executive; BA, W Ill. Univ.; MA, Univ. Ill., Springfield, 1979. CLU. Agent through sr. v.p. mktg. Country Ins. & Fin. Services, Bloomington, Ill., 1982—2001, CEO, 2001—. Chmn. Cotton States Ins., Holyoke Mutual Ins. Co., Middlesex Mutual Assurance Co., MSI Preferred Ins. Co. Office: Country Insurance 1701 N Towanda Ave Bloomington IL 61702*

BLACKBURN, JOHN LESLIE, small business owner; b. Malta Bend, Mo., Dec. 21, 1924; s. Clarence Oliver and Vivian (Mitchener) B.; m. Gloria Bullington, June 10, 1950; 1 child, Holly. BS, Mo. Valley Coll., 1950; MEd, U. Colo., 1952; PhD, Fla. State U., 1969. Counselor to men Fla. State U., Tallahassee, 1952-56; from asst. dean of men to dean student devel. U. Ala., Tuscaloosa, 1956-69, v.p. devel., 1978-90; vice chancellor student affairs U. Denver, 1969-74, vice chancellor univ. resources, 1974-78; pres. Blackburn Ednl. Techs., Tuscaloosa, 1990—; gen. sec. Am. Assn. of U. Administrators, Tuscaloosa, Ala., 1993-97; interim dir. Challenge 21, Tuscaloosa, 1998-99. Mem. Model City Mayor's Adv., Denver, 1970-73, Nat. Adv. Coun. on Extension and Continuing Edn., Washington, 1976-78; cons. to sec. HEW, Washington, 1976; mem. Ala. Commn. on Aging, 2000—; mem. Gov.'s Task Force on Devel. of Economically Distressed Counties, 2000-01. Contbr.: Pieces of Eight, 1978. Sgt. AUS, 1943-46, CBI. The Blackburn Inst. was created in his honor by U. Ala., 1995, John L. Blackburn Exemplary award in his honor by AAUA, 1991. Mem. AAUA (pres. 1977-79), Am. Coun. on Edn. (acad. affairs commn. 1970-73), Nat. Assn. Student Pers. Adminstrn. (pres. 1973-74), Nat. Inst. Rsch. and Devel. (founder 1974). Home: 1601 St Andrews Dr Tuscaloosa AL 35406-2058 Office: Blackburn Ednl Techs PO Box 2615 Tuscaloosa AL 35403-2615 E-mail: johnblackburn1@hotmail.com.

BLACKBURN, JOHN OLIVER, economist, consultant; b. Miami, Fla., Sept. 13, 1929; s. Elmer E. and Proxie (Hughes) B.; m. Jeanne Elise Miles, Nov. 29, 1957; children: Katherine Elise, John Parkinson, David Laurence. AB, Duke U., 1951; postgrad., U. Miami, 1951-52; PhD, U. Fla., 1959. CPA, Fla. From asst. prof. econs. to prof. Duke U., 1959-81, provost, 1970-71, chancellor, 1971-76; asst. prof. bus. adminstrn. Am. U., Beirut, 1961-62. Vis. prof. Davidson Coll., 1983. Author: The Renewable Energy Alternative, 1987, Solar Florida: A Sustainable Energy Future, 1993. Bd. dirs. U.S. Found. of Univ. of the Valley of Guatemala, Orlando Philharm. Orch., Fla. With USNR, 1952—55. Mem. Archs., Designers and Planners for Social Responsibility, Phi Beta Kappa. Democrat. Mem. United Ch. of Christ. Home: 221 Shell Pt E Maitland FL 32751-5843 E-mail: j.o.blackburn@att.net.

BLACKBURN, JOY MARTIN, retired librarian; b. Marietta, Ohio, Oct. 28, 1925; d. Jonathan George and Helen Joy (Smith) Martin; m. Paul Edward Blackburn, Dec. 18, 1948 (dec. Dec. 1996); children: Paul Conrow, Amy Joy. BA, Ohio Wesleyan U., 1947; MA, U. Minn, 1948. Student counselor Ohio State U., Columbus, 1948—54; editor/libr. Jones & Laughlin Steel Co., Pitts., 1955—57; rsch. libr. Tech. Mktg. Assn., Concord, Mass., 1964—66; mgr. corp. libr. Washington Nat. Ins., Evanston, Ill., 1966—85; systems libr. Luth. Gen. Hosp., Park Ridge, Ill., 1986—88; info. specialist C. Berger & Co., Carol Stream, Ill., 1989—93; ret., 1993. Rschr./editor U. Pitts. Med. Sch., 1959. Author: J&L Rsch. Bull., 1955—57. Vol. Chgo. Bot. Garden Libr., Glencoe, Ill., 1997—99, U. Va. Health Sys. Mktg. and Cmty. Outreach, 2002—, U. Va. Alderman Libr., 2002—, Va. Found. Humanities, 2004—. Mem.: U. Va. Libr. Assocs. (bd. dirs. 2001—, 2004—), Cook County Hort. Soc. (hon.), Phi Beta Kappa. Avocations: history, photography, Arctic art, culture, travel.

BLACKBURN, MARSHA, congresswoman; b. Laurel, Miss., June 6, 1952; married; 2 children. BS, Miss. St. Univ., 1973. Retail mktg.; senator Tenn. State Senate, Nashville, 1998—2002; mem. U.S. Ho. of Reps. from 7th Tenn. dist., 2003—. Del. Am. Coun. Young Polit. Leaders, S.E. Asia, 1993; appointed by Gov. Don Sundquist exec. dir. Tenn. Film, Entertainment and Music Commn., 1995; chmn. Gov.'s Prayer Breakfast, 1996; bd. dirs. Benton Hall Sch., Nashville Symphony Guild, Arthritis Found., Nashville Zoo Friends; appointed Econ. Coun. on Women, 1999. Mem. Nat. Acad. Rec. Arts and Scis., Country Music Assn., Rotary, C. of C. Republican. Office: 509 Cannon Ho Office Bldg Washington DC 20515-4305 E-mail: sen.marsha.blackburn@legislature.state.tn.u.*

BLACKBURN, MICHAEL DALE, lawyer, educator; b. Mt. Pleasant, Utah, June 28, 1951; m. Celia W. Blackburn, Aug. 21, 1973; children: Lauren, Alison, Erin, Andrew, Megan. BS in Acctg., U. Utah, 1973; JD, Stanford U.,

1978. Bar: Utah 1978, U.S. Tax Ct. 1980; CPA, Utah. Acct. John F. Forbes & Co., San Francisco, 1973-76; pvt. practice acctg. San Jose, Calif., 1976-78; ptnr. Snow, Christensen & Martineau, Salt Lake City, 1978-93, Blackburn & Stoll, LC, Salt Lake City, 1993—. Prof. taxation U. Utah, Salt Lake City, 2001—; trustee Hansen Planetarium Found., Salt Lake City, 1980—; presenter in field. Contbr. articles to profl. jours. Planned giving com. Primary Children's Hosp., Salt Lake City, 1987-89. Fellow Am. Coll. Trust and Estate Coun.; mem. AICPA (Outstanding Instr. 1988, 98), ABA, Utah State Bar Assn. (chmn. estate planning sect. 1988-89, chmn. task force multidisciplinary practice 2001-2003), Utah Assn. CPAs (pres. 2001, CPA of Yr. 1997). Office: Blackburn & Stoll LC 257 E 200 S Ste 800 Salt Lake City UT 84111

BLACKBURN, RICHARD WALLACE, retired lawyer; b. Detroit, Mich., Apr. 21, 1942; s. Wallace Manders and E. Jean (Beetham) B.; m. Dede Frances Reid, Aug. 29, 1964; children: David Thomas, Jeffrey Manders, Megan Louise. Student, Baldwin-Wallace Coll., 1960-62; AB, Mich. State U., 1964; JD, George Washington U., 1967; grad. advanced mgmt. program, Harvard Bus. Sch., 1988. Labor atty. Chesapeake & Potomac Tele. Co., Washington, 1967-70; gen. corp. atty. Chesapeake & Potomac Telephone Co., Richmond, Va., 1970-74; regulatory atty. AT&T, NYC, 1974-76; gen. atty. New Eng. Tele. Co., Boston, 1976-81, v.p., gen. counsel, 1981—91; sr. positions NYNEX World Wide Svc. Group, 1991; pres. and group exec. NYNEX Worldwide Comm., 1995—96; exec. v.p., gen. counsel, sec. Duke Energy Corp., Charlotte, NC, 1997—2004, chief adminstrv. officer, 2003—04; ret., 2003. Dir. New Eng. Legal Found., 1988; mem. Concord (Mass.) Zoning Bd. Appeals, chmn., 1984, 87; trustee Mass. Eye and Ear Infirmary. Mem. Fed. Communications Bar Assn., Am. Bar Assn., Newcomen Soc. N.Am., Boston Bar Assn. Republican. Episcopalian.

BLACKBURN, ROBERT PARKER, lawyer; b. Tacoma, Sept. 24, 1956; s. John Griffin and Dorothy Joan (Parker) B. BS with honors, Case Western Res. U., 1978; JD, Am. U., 1981. Bar: D.C. 1982, Calif. 1987, US Patent and Trademark Office 1981. Atty. Banner, Birch, McKie and Beckett, Washington, 1981-84; asst. patent counsel Agrigenetics Research Corp., Boulder, Colo., 1984-86; atty. Ciotti and Murashige, Menlo Park, Calif., 1986-87; ptnr. Irell & Manella, Menlo Park, 1987-89; dir. intellectual property Chiron Corp., Emeryville, Calif., 1989-91, v.p., chief patent counsel, 1991—2005; pvt. practice Berkeley, Calif., 2005—. Disting. scholar Berkeley Ctr. for Law and Tech., U. Calif. Berkeley Sch. Law, 2001—. Mem. AAAS, ABA, Am. Chemical Soc., Am. Intellectual Property Law Assn. (biotech. task force mem., chem. practice com., biotechnology subcom. mem.). Office: 2930 Domingo Ave #209 Berkeley CA 94705 Office Phone: 510-898-5000.

BLACKBURN, ROYCE FRANKLIN, vocalist, educator; b. Tyler, Tex., Aug. 9, 1961; s. William Royce Blackburn and Sara Pauline Moseley; m. Amy Louise Pinkerton, Aug. 12, 2000. B in Music Edn., U. Tex., Arlington, 1984; MusM, U. N. Tex., 1990; Mus D, Ind. U., 2005. Instr. voice McMurry U., Abilene, Tex., 1990—92; choral dir. Calvary Bapt. Ch., Evansville, Ind., 1993—95; artist in residence Indpls. Opera, 1995—96; asst. prof. U. N.D., Grand Forks, 1999—. Singer: (Operas) various orgns., 1990—. Mem.: Nat. Assn. Tchrs. Singing (pres. N.D. chpt. 2003—), Coll. Music Soc., Pi Kappa Lambda.

BLACKBURN, SADIE GWIN ALLEN, conservation executive; b. San Angelo, Tex., Oct. 14, 1924; d. Harvey Hicks Allen and Helen (Harris) Weaver; m. Edward Albert Blackburn Jr., Feb. 25, 1946; children: Edward III, Catherine Ledyard, Robert Allen. BA, Rice U., 1945, MA, 1975. Bookkeeper, trust dept. State Nat. Bank, Houston; tchr. elem. sch. Galveston, Tex.; mng. ptnr. Storey Creek Partnership, Houston, 1969—; dir. spl. projects San Jacinto State Park; dir. master plan State Hist. Park. Lectr. in landscape design history; spkr. in field. Co-author: Houston's Forgotten Heritage, 1822-1914, 1991; contbr. articles to gardening publs. Newsheet chmn. Jr. League, Galveston, 1950-53, art chmn., Houston Jr. League, 1957-58, chmn. garden/design com., 1991-93, mental health study com., 1959-61, 2d v.p., 1962-63, provisional chmn., 1962-63, interview chmn., 1963-64; adv. bd. Bayou Bend Gardens chmn. Mus. Fine Arts, 1973-74, Bayou Bend adv. com., 1987-89; v.p. Mental Health Assn., 1957-62, Botanic Garden Houston, 2005—; asst. treas. Child Guidance Assn., 1962-65; mem. Rice U. Hist. Commn., 1974-75; pres. River Oaks Garden Club, Houston, 1975-76; mem. adv. com. Bayou Bend Gardens, 1991—; active Buffalo Bayou Partnership, Houston Nature Conservancy, 1993, Friends of Herman Park, 1994, Meml. Park Adv., 1995, Scenic Houston Bd., 1999. Named Scenic Visionary, Scenic Houston, 2003; recipient Sweet Briar Disting. Alumna award, 1991, award, Friends of Herman Park, 2003. Mem. Garden Club Am. (zone chmn. 1977-79, founders fund vice chmn. 1979-80, dir. 1980-82, rec. sec. 1982-84, v.p. 1984-86, archive co-chmn. 1986-87, 1st v.p. 1987-89, pres. 1989-91, Achievement medal 2002), Nat. Wildflower Rsch. Ctr. (bd. dirs.), Nat. Parks and Conservation Assn. Bd. (v.p. 1995-97, sec. 1997-99), San Jacinto Mus. History (pres. bd. 1975-77, bd. dirs.), Pi Beta Phi (Carolyn Herman Lichtenberg Crest award for disting. alumnae achievement 1998). Republican. Episcopalian. Avocations: gardening, fishing, hunting, bridge, golf. Home: 1030 Potomac Houston TX 77057-1916

BLACKBURN, WILLIAM STANLEY, lawyer; b. Nashville, Nov. 7, 1951; s. William Hodge and Margaret Virginia (Ware) B.; m. Laura Ross Wilson, July 23, 1983; children: William, Margaret. BS in Economics, Auburn U., 1973; JD, U.Va., 1976. Assoc. Kilpatrick & Cody (now Kilpatrick Stockton, LLP), Atlanta, 1976—82, ptnr., 1982—. Co-chair Bus. Transactions Group, 1996—2001; mem. bus. law sect. State Bar Ga., sect. sec., 1998, sect. vice chair, 99, sect. chair, 2000, mem. legal opinions com., 1991—, chair, 1992—98, younger lawyers sect. long range planning com., 1979—80, pub. com., 1979—80, credit union com., 1980—81. Notes Editor Va. Law Review, 1975-76, mem. editorial bd., 1974-75. Sec. Boys and Girls Clubs of Metro Atlanta, Inc., 1984—, mng. bd. dirs., 1982—, mem. exec. com., 1984—; chmn. legal divsn. Fulton County, Am. Heart Assn., 1981; mem. Leadership Atlanta, 1983-84; sec. Young Men's Round Table, High Mus. Art, 1984-85, pres., 1985-86, mem., 1983-86; group chmn. United Way Atlanta, 1984, account exec.; bd. dirs. Japan-Am. Soc. Ga., 1986-90. Fellow: Am. Coll. Investment Counsel; mem.: ABA (young lawyers sect. banking law subcom. 1980—81, com. legal opinions 1992—, sect. bus. law), Cobb County C. of C. (internat. bus. coun. 1984—89), Can. Am. Soc. Atlanta (bd. dirs. 1998—2001), Atlanta Bar Assn. (cts. com. 1982—83, co-chmn. joint task force mcpl. ct. City of Atlanta 1982—83, law day com. 1984), Piedmont Diving Club, Lawyers Club Atlanta, Omicron Delta Epsilon, Phi Eta Sigma, Omicron Delta Kappa, Phi Kappa Phi, Order of Coif. Avocation: golf. Home: 2595 Habersham Rd NW Atlanta GA 30305-3557 Office: Kilpatrick Stockton LLP 1100 Peachtree St NE Ste 2800 Atlanta GA 30309-4530 Office Phone: 404-815-6400. Business E-Mail: sblackburn@kilpatrickstockton.com.

BLACKBURN, WYATT DOUGLAS, insurance executive; b. July 6, 1954; s. Wyatt W. and Marjorie C. (Wyre) B.; m. Deborah L. Garland, Feb. 28, 1987; children: Wyatt Woodrow, Taylor Lynne. BBA, West Tex. State U., 1976. Staff acct. Harvey, Messenger & Co. CPAs, Amarillo, 1974-77; audit mgr. Martin W. Cohen & Co. CPAs, Dallas, 1977-78, sr. v.p. adminstrv. ops., 1978-88, sr. v.p., CFO, 1988-94, sr. v.p., COO, 1995-97; exec. v.p., COO State Nat. Cos., Ft. Worth, 1997—. Bd. dirs. State & County Mut. Fire Ins. Co., State Nat. Ins. Co., State Nat. Specialty Ins. Co., Tex. Mem. AICPA, Tex. Soc. CPAs, Omicron Delta Epsilon. Home: 1028 Diamond Blvd Southlake TX 76092-6208 Office: State Nat Cos 8200 Anderson Blvd Fort Worth TX 76120-3620 Office Phone: 817-265-2000. Business E-Mail: wblackburn@statenational.com.

BLACKER, HELEN VIRGINIA, business manager, engineer; b. Boulder, Colo., Aug. 4, 1925; d. John Decatur and Anna Frost (Gloyd) Means; m. Leo Merrill Blacker, Nov. 11, 1954. BS in Aero. Engring., U. Colo., 1950. Engr. Bur. of Reclamation, Yuma, Ariz., 1950-52, Geol. Survey, Denver, 1952-60; phys. scientist Nat. Bur. of Standards, Nat. Oceanic and Atmposphere Adminstrn., Boulder, 1960-80; mgr. Means Rentals, Boulder, 1966—. Active Boulder Forum of Rep. Women 1982-87, bd. dirs. 1983-87, pres. 1984-85; active Blue Ribbon Com., Erie, Colo., 1986-1988; mem. Concerned Citizens of Erie, 1989—1992, Jefferson County Rep. Women's Club, 1987—, Boulder Rep. Women's Club, 1987—; pres. Means Corp. Avocation: volunteer. Home: 1076 8th St Boulder CO 80302-7106 Office Phone: 303-442-0330.

BLACKETER, JAMES RICHARD, artist; b. Laguna Beach, Calif., Sept. 24, 1931; s. Cleo Toby and Ida Hattie (Renter) B.; children: Susan Elizabeth Glover, Mary Jane Kelsey; m. Frances Kay Smith, July 18, 1997. Owner Blacketer Sign Co., Laguna Beach, 1950-53; designer/art dir. Fed. Sign and Signal Corp., Santa Ana, Calif., 1953-73; owner The Studio Antiques, Laguna Beach, 1973-95. Exhibited in group shows at Showcase 21, L.A., 1959, The Studio Gallery, Laguna Beach, Ferguson Gallery, La Jolla, Long Beach Art Mus., Porth Gallery, Laguna Beach, Pasadena Art Mus., Los Angeles County Fair, Laguna Beach Art Festival, Fresno Art Mus., Ebell Club, L.A., Wells Gallery, Laguna Beach, Oreg. Bay Mus. Maritime Exhbn., others; represented in permanent collections at Norton Simon Art Mus., Laguna Beach Art Assn., South Coast Med. Ctr. Bd. dirs. festival of Arts, Laguna Beach, 1965-66. Recipient Nat. Award for Outdoor Advertising, Nat. Elec. Sign Assn., 1970, 71, 72, Nat. Award for Design, Nat. Interscholastic Art Assn., Pitts., 1950, Pa. Award for poster design Am. Legion, State of Calif., 1946; winner various painting awards, 1950—. Mem. Laguna Beach Art Assn. (art dir. 1968-69, bd. dirs. 1969-70), Am. Soc. Marine Artist. Avocations: antique and art collecting, antique automobiles, designing historical home interiors. Address: PO Box 386 Depoe Bay OR 97341

BLACKETT, PIERS R., pediatrician; s. Felicity M. and Rupert H. Blackett. MB, U. Cape Town, South Africa, 1960, Ch B, 1967. Lic. physician South African Med. Assoc, 1967, N.Y., 1975, Okla., 1975, cert. pediat. Am. Acad. Pediat., 1975, pediatric endocrinology Am. Acad. Pediat., 1978. Assoc. prof. pediat. U. Okla., Oklahoma City, 1995—. Contbr. scientific papers. Mem. Governor's Taskforce on Child Health, Oklahoma City, 2000—. Grantee, NIH, 2004—. Mem.: Am. Diabetes Assn. (corr.). Achievements include research in lipid rsch. and pediatric endocrinology. Office: OU Children's Hosp 940 NE 13th St Oklahoma City OK 73104 Office Phone: 405-271-6764. Office Fax: 405-271-3093.

BLACKFORD, DEBRA ANN, diagnostic medical sonographer, echocardiographer; b. Monticello, N.Y., Dec. 14, 1965; d. Leo Emanuel and Anna Margaret Freaney; m. Steven Fraser, May 5, 1984 (div. Dec. 2001); children: Alyssa Lynne Fraser, Darren Tyler Fraser, Kaylen Ann; m. Richard Blackford, Apr. 8, 2004. Cert. ultrasound vascular tech. echocardiography, Ultrasound Diagnostic Sch., 1995. RDMS (OB, ABD, BR) RVT ARDMS. Lead ultrasound technologist and echocardiographer Wallkill Radiology/Mid Rockland Image Ptnrs., Middletown, NY, 1995—2001; part-time ultrasound technologist Catskill Regional Med. Ctr., Harris, NY, 1995—2001, ultrasound technologist, 2001—; part-time echocardiographer Sullivan Internal Med. Group, Monticello, 2002—. Active Monticello Fire Dept. Aux., 1984, Benevolent & Protective Order of Elks #1544, Monticello, 2002. Mem.: Soc. Diagnostic Med. Sonographers, Am. Inst. Ultrasound in Medicine. Avocations: boating, winemaking, bowling, travel. Office: Catskill Regional Med Ctr 68 Harris Bushville Rd Harris NY 12742 Office Phone: 845-794-7897.

BLACKFORD, JOHN, magazine editor; b. Norfolk, Va., Feb. 8, 1944; s. Frank Robertson and Polly (Baldwin) Blackford; m. Anne Little; children: David, Jacob. BA, U. N.C., Chapel Hill, 1967; postgrad., Temple U., 1978. Book editor Rodale Press, Emmaus, Pa., 1978—82; editor Software Retailing, Dover, NJ, 1983—84, Computer Dealer, Dover, 1984—86; exec. editor Personal Computing, Hasbrouck Heights, NJ, 1986—91; editor Computer Shopper, 1991—95, editor-in-chief, 1995—. Co-author: Build Your Harvest Kitchen, 1982. Recipient Jesse H. Neal award for best feature article Computer Dealer mag., 1984. Mem.: Appalachian Train Conf., Nature Conservancy, Computer Press Assn. Avocations: landscape photography, hiking, old-time country music, science fiction, internet surfing. Office: Computer Shopper/Ziff Davis 28 E 28th St New York NY 10016-7930

BLACKFORD, ROBERT NEWTON, lawyer, director; b. Cin., Feb. 5, 1937; s. Robert Criley and Virginia Pendleton (Yowell) B.; m. Margaret Ann Williams, July 22, 1961; children: William Pendleton, John Whitner. BSBA, U. Fla., 1960; JD, Emory U., 1968. Bar: Fla. 1968, Ga. 1968. Mem., dir. Maguire, Voorhis & Wells, P.A., Orlando, Fla., 1972-98, sec., treas., 1972-95; ptnr. Holland & Knight LLP, Orlando, 1998—2001. Dir. Hughes Supply, Inc., Orlando, 1970—, sec., 1972-96, asst. sec., 1996-98; dir., sec. Princeton Fin. Corp., 1987-94. Mem. Orlando Mcpl. Planning Bd., 1969-75, Orlando Downtown Devel. Bd., 1972-77, chmn., 1975-77, bd. dirs. Crime Commn., Inc., 1985-88; mem. Orange County's Refuse Disposal Citizens Coordination Com., 1988-90, Orange County Solid Waste Adv. Bd., 1992-96; mem. neighborhood concerns com. Orlando Naval Tng. Ctr. Base Closing Commn., 1994-96; trustee Chelsey G. Magruder Found., Inc., 1981—, pres., 1982-85, 92-94, 2000-02, sec./treas., 1998-2000; trustee Orlando Mus. Art, 1980-82, 85-91, pres. 1985-86, chmn. bd., 1986-87, v.p. 1989-91; ruling elder First Presbyn. Ch., Orlando, 1989-2003, tchr., 1970-2000; bd. dirs. Univ. Club Orlando, 1994-97, sec., 1994-96; active The Cathedral Ch. of St. Luke, 2004—. Mem. Fla. Bar Assn., Ga. Bar Assn., Orlando Area C. of C. (pres. 1980, chmn. bd. dirs. 1981), Orange County Hist. Soc. (bd. dirs. 1980-83), Country Club Orlando, Rotary Club Orlando (pres. 1991-92). Democrat. Home: 2931 Nela Ave Orlando FL 32809-6178 E-mail: rblackf398@aol.com.

BLACKHAM, ANN ROSEMARY (MRS. J. W. BLACKHAM), realtor; b. N.Y.C., June 16, 1927; d. Frederick Alfred and Letitia L. (Stolfe) DeCain; m. James W. Blackham Jr., Aug. 18, 1951; children: Ann C., James W. III. AB, St. Mary of the Springs Coll. (now Ohio Dominican U.), 1949; postgrad., Ohio State U., 1950. Mgr. br. store Filene & Sons, Winchester, Mass., 1950—52; broker Porter Co. Real Estate, Winchester, 1961—66; sales mgr. James T. Trefrey, Inc., Winchester, 1966—68; pres., founder Ann Blackham & Co. Inc. Realtors, Winchester, 1968—2001; v.p. Coldwell Banker, Winchester, 2001—. Bd. econ. advisors to Gov., 1969-74; participant White House Conf. on Internat. Cooperation, 1965; mem. Presdl. Task Force on Women's Rights and Responsibilities, 1969; exec. coun. Mass. Civil Def., 1965-69; chmn. Gov.'s Commn. on Status of Women, 1971-75; regional dir. Interstate Assn. Commn. on Status of Women, 1971-74; mem. Gov. Task Force on Mass. Economy, 1972; mem. Gov.'s Jud. Selection Com., 1972, Mass. Emergency Fin. Bd., 1974-75; bd. registration Real Estate Brokers and Salesman Commonwealth of Mass., 1991—, chmn. 1994—. Bd. visitors Ohio Dominican U., 1995—, nat. fund raising chair, 1998-99; corporator, trustee Charlestown Savs. Bank, 1974-84; corporator Winchester Hosp., 1983—, chair fund raising emergency room; bd. dirs. Winchester Hosp. Found., 1996—; mem. Winchester 350th Anniversary Commn.; design rev. commn. Town of Winchester, 1981-2003; bd. dirs. Phoenix Found., 1980-90, Bay State Health Care, Mass. Taxpayers Found., Speech and Hearing Found., Baystate Health Mgmt., Realty Guild Inc., v.p. 1995-96, bd. dirs. 1996-99, pres. 1997-98; regional selection panel White House Fellows, 1973-74; com. on women in svc. U.S. Dept. Def., 1977-80; 2d v.p. Doric Dames, 1971-74, founding mem., 1969; dep. chmn. Mass. Rep. State Com., 1965-66; sec. Mass. Rep. State Conv., 1970, del., 1960, 62, 64, 66, 70, 72, 74, 78, 90, 98, 2002; state vice-chmn. Mass. Rep. Fin. Com., 1970; alt. del.-at-large Rep. Nat. Conv., 1968, 72, del., 1980, 84, 88, 92, 96; Rep. State Committeewoman, 1996—; pres. Mass. Fedn. Rep. Women, 1964-69; v.p. Nat. Fedn. Rep. Women, 1965-79; pres. Scholarship Found., 1976-78, Mass. Fedn. Women's Clubs; alumnae liaison The Beaumont Sch. for Girls; mem. Women for Romney, 2002; mem. Gov. Romney Inaugural Com.; mem. com. Bush Reelection, 2004 Recipient Pub. Svc. award Commonwealth of Mass., 1978, Merit award Rep. Party, 1969, Pub. Affairs award Mass. Fedn. Women's Clubs, 1975; named Civic Leader of Yr. Mass. Broadcasters, 1962, Banker and Tradesman Leader Making a Difference, 1999; recipient Bus. Owner of Yr. award New England Women Bus. Owners, 1995, Disting. Alumnae award Ohio Dominican Coll., 1999, Disting. Service Citation Town of Winchester, 2003 Mem. Greater Boston Real Estate Bd. (hon., bd. dirs.), Eastern Middlesex Bd. Realtors (life mem. multi-million dollar club), Mass. Assn. Realtors (bd. dirs.), Nat. Assn. Realtors (women's coun.), Brokers Inst. (cert.), Coun. Realtors (cert., pres. 1983-84), Winchester C. of C. (bd. dirs.), Greater Boston C. of C., Nat. Assn. Women Bus. Owners, ENKA Soc. (treas. 2001—04), Rotary Internat., Tequesta Fla. Country Club, Capitol Hill Club, Ponte Vedra Club, Winchester Boat Club, Winchester Country Club, Wychmere Harbor Club, Womens City Club, Winton Club (sec., bd. dirs.), Hyannis Yacht Club. Office: Coldwell Banker 3 Church St Winchester MA 01890-2903 Business E-Mail: ann.blackham@nemoves.com.

BLACKLEDGE, DAVID WILLIAM, retired academic administrator; b. Cin., Mar. 10, 1930; s. William Clinton and Helen Louise (Van Curen) B.; m. Diana Marjorie Wiley, June 5, 1953; children: David Noel, William Dean, Alan Keith, Naomi Karen. BS, Purdue U., 1953; MA, Rutgers U., 1965; grad., Nat. War Coll., 1975. Commd. 2d lt. U.S. Army, 1953, advanced through grades to col., 1974; asst. prof. mil. sci. Rutgers U., New Brunswick, N.J., 1961-64; instr. Am. history U. Md.-Far East Divsn., Bangkok, 1967-68; dir. nat. security studies U.S. Army War Coll., Carlisle, Pa., 1978-83; dir. fin. aid Pa. State U. Dickinson Sch. Law, Carlisle, 1983—84, dir. admissions and fin. aid, 1984-94, exec. asst. to the dean, 1994-2000; ret., 2000. Co-compiler: Blackledges in America: A Genealogy of Blackledge/Blacklidge Descendants with Roots in the USA, 2002. Bd. dirs. Carlisle area United Way, 1983-86, Sarah Todd Retirement Home, Carlisle, 1989-95. Decorated Legion of Merit with oak leaf cluster. Mem. Rotary.

BLACKLEY, CHERYL ANN, freelance/self-employed music educator, musician; b. Woods Cross, Utah, June 8, 1960; d. LeGrande and Patricia Green Blackley. MusB in Secondary Edn., BS in Secondary Edn., Utah State U., 1988. Sole propr./owner and dir. S & D Music Studio, Woods Cross, 1988—; freelance musician on clarinets, saxophones, oboe/english horn & bassoon No. Utah area, 1988—. Prin. clarinet Utah State U. Alumni Band, Logan, 1984—; orch. mgr. Westminster Chamber Orch., Salt Lake City, 1992—94; founding exec. bd. mem., orch. mgr. Intermountain Chamber Orch., Salt Lake City, 1994—96; orch. mem.-reeds Utah Musical Theatre, Ogden, 1994—, orch. mgr., 1999—, asst. music dir., 2004, assoc. music dir., condr., 2005—. Composer: (orchestral works) The Mist, 1993—94, (clarinet solo) 2257 (Utah Best of Category Instrumental Composer's Guild Composition Contest, 1999), (songs) Trio No. 1 for Flute, Oboe & Clarinet (1st pl. Tchr. Composition Competition Utah Music Tchrs. Assn., 1997, 3rd pl. music for children category Composer's Guild Composition Contest, 1995), Gently Raise the Sacred Strain, arr. for Mixed Woodwind Trio (award of merit instrumental divsn. LDS Ch. Music Competition, 1996). Mem.: Utah Music Tchrs. Assn., Music Tchrs. Nat. Assn., Utah Music Educators Assn., Music Educators Nat. Conf., Golden Key, Phi Kappa Phi. Mem. Lds Ch. Avocations: reading, gardening, off-road desert racing, cooking, baking. Home: 1985 S 800 W Woods Cross UT 84087 Office: S & D Music Studio 796 W 2000 S Woods Cross UT 84087 Office Phone: 801-292-8707. Business E-Mail: sdmusic@netzero.net.

BLACKLEY, DANIEL JOHN, theater educator, theater director; b. Arlington Heights, Ill., Jan. 27, 1967; s. Terrence John and Karen Ray Blackley; m. Jodi Baldel, July 22, 1995. BA in Theater Arts, Calif. State U., Long Beach, 1990; MA in Theatrer Arts, Calif. State U., L.A., 1999. Cert. profl. clear single subject tchg. credential Calif. Tchr. English Rialto (Calif.) H.S., 1993—94; drama tchr. Montclair (Calif.) H.S., 1994—99; theater instr. El Toro H.S., Lake Forest, Calif., 1999—. Mem. Digital H.S., Lake Forest, Calif., 1999—2001; founding mem. Celebration of the Arts El Toro Fine Arts Dept., Lake Forest, 2003—, dept. chair, 2002—04. Author: (plays) Surf's Up!, A Case of Indigestion. Vol. comty. puppet theater Fun with Chalk, Mission Viejo, Calif., 2000; vol. beautification project Ho. of Ruth, Calif., 1997. Recipient Bright Idea award, Norcostco Theatre Co., 2002; grantee, Fun with Chalk, 2000, 2003. Mem.: Puppeteers of Am., Internat. Thespian Soc. (sponsor 1999—2004), Theatre Comm. Group. Office: El Toro H S 25255 Toledo Way Lake Forest CA 92630 Personal E-mail: godot67@yahoo.com.

BLACKLIDGE, RAYMOND MARK, lawyer; b. Ft. Belvoir, Va., May 17, 1960; s. Martin H. and Carol Ann (Fiarito) B.; m. Karen Marie Tennis, June 19, 1982; children: Robert Mark, Jonathon Michael, Sara Kathryn. BA, So. Ill. U., 1982; JD, John Marshall Law Sch., 1985. Bar: Ill. 1986, U.S. Dist. Ct. (no. dist.) Ill. 1986. Sole practice, West Chgo., Ill., 1986—87; ptnr., corp. sec. Grief, Bus & Blacklidge, P.C., Ill., 1987-92; sole practice West Chgo., 1992—2002, Tampa, Fla., 2002—. Bd. dirs., sr. v.p., gen. counsel, sec. The Jerger Co., Inc., Mobile Homeowners Ins. Agys., Inc., Jerger & Sons, Inc.; bd. dirs., gen. counsel, sec. Mobile USA Ins. Co., Inc., Mobile United Property & Casualty Ins. Co., Inc.; bd. dirs., sr. v.p., gen. counsel, sec., treas. MHIA Premium Fin. Co.; dir., sr. v.p., sec., treas. Mobile Adjustment Co., Inc.; arbitrator 18th Jud. Cir.; reg. lobbyist, Fla., 1994—; of counsel Edward J. Boltz, Christopher C. Benfante and David E. Caddigan, 1993-94; regional mgr. and counsel Alliance of Am. Insurers, 1992-96; title ins. agent Atty.'s Title Ins. Fund, 1994—; treas. USF Delta Chi Housing Corp., 2002—. Editor-in-chief Marshall Opinion, 1985. Pres., bd. dirs. West Chicago Clean and Proud, Inc.; bd. dirs. West Chicago R.R. Days, Inc., 1988-94; alderman City of West Chicago, 1989-94; Rep. precinct committeeman Winfield Twp. Precinct, DuPage County, 1991-94; Scoutmaster, BSA, Troop 148. St. Mark Parish, West Chgo., 1999—. Mem. Fla. Ins. Coun. (bd. dirs. 1996—), Alliance Am. Insurers (mem. govt. affairs com., alliance so. regional advisory com.), Gavel Soc., Columbian Club (v.p.), KC (trustee West Chicago 1985—, Knight of Yr. award 1987); Woodmen of the World (pres. Lodge 37, Tampa, 2001-02). Republican. Roman Catholic. Avocations: travel, religious studies, family, sports, roller blading. Office: Ste 300 8875 Hidden River Pkwy Tampa FL 33637 E-mail: rblackga@aol.com.

BLACKLOW, ROBERT STANLEY, internist, educator; b. Cambridge, Mass., June 24, 1934; s. Leo Alfred and Clara Edna (Cumenes) Blacklow; m. Winifred Young, Dec. 7, 1958; children: Stephen Charles, Kenneth Lawrence, David Alan. AB summa cum laude, Harvard U., 1955, MD cum laude, 1959; DSc (hon.), Kent State U., 1998; DMed. (hon.), U. Pecs, Hungary, 2001. Intern Peter Bent Brigham Hosp., Boston, 1959-60, resident, 1960-61, 63-64, 67-68; instr. Harvard U., 1967-70, asst. prof. medicine, 1970-76, assoc. prof., 1976-78, asst. to dean faculty of medicine, 1969-73, assoc. dean, 1973-78; prof. internal medicine Rush Med. Coll., 1978-85, dean, 1978-81; v.p. for med. affairs Rush-Presbyn.-St. Luke's Med. Center, Chgo., 1978-81; prof. medicine Jefferson Med. Coll., Phila., 1985-92, sr. assoc. dean, 1985-92; pres., dean Northeastern Ohio Univs. Coll. Medicine, 1992—2002, prof. cmty. medicine, prof. medicine, 1992—, pres., dean emeritus, 2002—; sr. scholar health policy Assn. Acad. Health Ctrs., Washington, 2002—; spl. cons. to dir. Nat. Inst. Alcohol Abuse and Alcoholism, 2003—; vis. prof. social medicine Harvard Med. Sch., 2005—. Mem. sci. adv. com. Nat. Fund Med. Edn., 1981—84, Nat. Cancer Inst., 1986—95; bd. dirs. Nat. Resident Matching Program, 1993—, pres.-elect, 1994—95, pres., 1995—96, treas., 1998—99, 2001—03, pres.-elect, 1999—2000, pres., 2000—01. Editor: (book) Signs and Symptoms, 1971, Signs and Symptoms, 6th edit., 1983; mem. editl. bd. Jour. Med. Humanities, 1997—. Trustee Chestnut Hill Sch., Newton, Mass., 1970—79, Belmont (Mass.) Hill Sch., 1973—79, Chgo. chpt. ARC, 1979, Greater Akron (Ohio) Musical Assn., 1993—2002, mem. exec. com., 1998—2002; dir. Akron Regional Devel. Bd., 1998—2003; mem. Ill. health svc. corps task force Ill. Dept. Pub. Health, 1980; corporator Belmont Hill Sch., 1978—. With USPHS, 1961—63. Sr. scholar, Assn. Acad. Health Ctrs., 2002—. Fellow: ACP, Chgo. Soc. Internal Medicine, Inst. medicine Chgo.; mem.: AAAS, Assn. Acad. Health Ctrs., Assn. Am. Med. Colls., NY Acad. Sci., Rowfant Club, Literary Club (Chgo.), Harvard Club (Boston, NYC, Chgo) (Chgo. bd. dir.), Longwood Cricket Club (Boston), Harvard Musical Assn., Badminton & Tennis Club (Boston), Cliff Dwellers Club (Chgo.), Franklin Inn (Phila.), Twin Lakes Country Club, Alpha Omega Alpha, Sigma Xi, Phi Beta Kappa. Home: 16 Birchwood Ln Lincoln MA 01773 Office: Northeastern Ohio Univs Coll Medicine 4209 State Rte 44 PO Box 95 Rootstown OH 44272-0095

BLACKMAN, CLINT CUNNINGHAM, III, lawyer; b. Albany, Ga., Sept. 24, 1955; s. Clint Cunningham Jr. and Shriley H. Blackman; m. Judy Cocke. BBA, Baylor U., 1978; grad. degree in comml. banking, Am. Bankers Assn., 1991; JD, Tex. Wesleyan U., 1994. Bar: Tex. 1994, U.S. Dist. Ct. (no. dist.) Tex. 1994, U.S. Ct. Appeals (5th cir.) 1995. Staff aide for Sen. Lloyd Bentsen U.S. Senate, Washington, 1979; corp. officer Blackman & Assoc., Longview,

Tex., 1980-86; bank officer Banc Tex. Dallas N.A., 1987-89; v.p. First City Bank N.A., Dallas, 1989-90; sr. asst. mgr. Wallace Assn. (RTC), Dallas, 1991-93; pvt. practice law Dallas, 1994—. Editor: Loan Wolf Negotiation Manual, 1993. Pres. Monticello Crossroads Homeowners Assn., Dallas, 1988-92. Mem. ABA, Dallas Bar Assn. Office: 5910 N Central Expy Ste 1380 Dallas TX 75206-5126 Fax: 214-265-7626.

BLACKMAN, JEFFREY WILLIAM, lawyer; b. L.A., Oct. 24, 1948; s. Ralph Leonard and Judith Esther (Glantz) B. BA, U. Ariz., 1970, JD, 1976. Bar: Ariz. 1976, U.S. Dist. Ct. Ariz. 1977, U.S. Ct. Appeals (9th cir.) 1980, U.S. Supreme Ct. 1980, U.S. Dist. Ct. (no. dist.) Calif. 1988. Pvt. practice, Oracle, Ariz., 1977-85; assoc. various law firms, Phoenix, Tucson, 1986-87; pvt. practice Tucson, 1988—. Participant March for the Animals, Washington, 1990, 96. 2d lt. ROTC, U.S. Army. Recipient Cert. of Appreciation, Ctr. for Environ. Protecton of the Whale Protection Fund, 1984, UNICEF, Defenders of Wildlife, Nat. Humane Edn. Soc., ASPCA, Humane Soc. of U.S., Tiger Haven, Wine Diploma, San Francisco Wine Inst. Wine Adv. Bd., 1964, Cert. of Appreciation for Service in Israel during the Gulf War, Nation of Israel; named Ptnr. for Life, Cal Farley's Boy Ranch, Amarillo, Tex., 1982. Mem. State Bar Ariz., Pima County Bar Assn., Mensa, Alliance Francaise, Animal Legal Def. Fund. Avocations: rock drummer, tennis, desert hiking, gardening, animal welfare. Office: PO Box 41624 Tucson AZ 85717-1624 Office Phone: 520-320-5155.

BLACKMAN, JOHN CALHOUN, IV, lawyer; b. Monroe, La., Dec. 13, 1944; s. John Calhoun Blackman III and Marie (Collens) Bernstein; m. Judy Swayze, Apr. 19, 1986; children: Carrie Marie, Caroline Frances, Mary Winston. BA, La. State U., 1966, JD, 1969. Bar: La. 1969, U.S. Ct. Appeals (5th cir.) 1969, U.S. Tax Ct. 1972, U.S. Supreme Ct. 1976. Ptnr. Hudson, Potts & Bernstein, Monroe, 1969-79, Blackman, Arnold & Pettway, Monroe, 1979-88, Jones, Walker, Waechter, Poitevent, Carrere & Denegre, Baton Rouge, 1988—. Adj. prof. law La. State U., Baton Rouge, 1990-93; mem. com. of 100 econ. devel., 1993—; mem. trust code com. La. State Law Inst., 1982—. Mem. La. State U. Found.; mem. adv. commn. Estate Planning and Adminstrn. Cert., 1994—99, chmn., 1998—99. Fellow Am. Bar Found., Am. Coll. Trusts and Estates Counsel (bus. planning com.), Am. Coll. Tax Counsel; mem. ABA (litigation task force, employee benefits com., taxation sect.), La. Bar Assn. (cert. tax specialist, cert. estate planning and adminstrn. specialist, chmn. taxation sect. 1976-77, chmn. liaison com. with dist. dir. IRS 1981-82, liaison com. with regional commrs. office), Estate Planning Coun. N.E. La. (pres. 1975-76), NASD (arbitrator). Republican. Episcopalian. Office: Jones Walker et al 8555 United Plaza Blvd Fl 5 Baton Rouge LA 70809 Office Phone: 225-248-2070. Business E-Mail: jblackman@joneswalker.com. E-mail: jcbandjsb@bellsouth.net.

BLACKMAN, KENNETH ROBERT, lawyer; b. Providence, May 19, 1941; s. Edward and Beatrice (Wolf) B.; m. Meryl June Rosenthal, June 7, 1964; children: Michael, Susan, Kevin. AB, Brown U., 1962; LLB, MBA, Columbia U., 1965. Bar: N.Y. 1966. Law clk. to U.S. Dist. Judge, 1965—66; ptnr. Fried, Frank, Harris, Shriver & Jacobson, LLP, N.Y.C., 1966—. Mem.: ABA, N.Y. Bar Assn., Assn. Bar City of N.Y., Phi Beta Kappa, Beta Gamma Sigma. Office: Fried Frank Harris Shriver & Jacobson LLP 1 New York Plz Fl 22 New York NY 10004-1980 Office Phone: 212-859-8000. Business E-Mail: blackke@friedfrank.com.

BLACKMAN, LEE L., lawyer; b. Phila., Aug. 28, 1950; s. Harold H. and Mary Elizabeth Blackman; m. Kathryn M. Forte, Oct. 5, 1979; 1 child, Shane Forte. BA, U. So. Calif., 1973, JD, 1975. Bar: Calif. 1975, U.S. Dist. Ct. (ctrl. dist.) Calif. 1975, U.S. Ct. Appeals (9th cir) Calif. 1977, U.S. Supreme Ct. 1980, U.S. Dist. Ct. (ea. dist.) Calif. 1984, U.S. Dist. Ct. (no. dist.) Calif. 1988. Atty. Kadison, Pfaelzer, Woodard, Quinn & Rossi, L.A., 1975-81, assoc., ptnr., 1981-87; ptnr. McDermott, Will & Emery, L.A., 1987-2000. Arbitrator L.A. Superior Ct., 1986-90; judge pro tem Superior Ct. State of Calif., 1986-92; speaker in field. Mem. editl. adv. bd. Airport Noise Report, 1989-99; article editor ABA Health Litig. Reporter, 1996-97. Mem. State Bar of Calif., Legion Lex Inn of Ct. (master bencher 1989-2000). Office: 1562 Granvia Altamira Palos Verdes Estates CA 90274 E-mail: llblackman1@cox.net.

BLACKMAN, SUE ANNE BATEY, economics researcher; b. Hamilton AFB, Calif., June 21, 1948; d. Wayman C. and Lela M. (Fasgold) Batey; m. Martin R. Blackman, Apr. 7, 1977; 1 child, Emily Batey Blackman. BA in Polit. Sci., U. Colo., 1970. Econs. rsch. aide dept. econs. Princeton (N.J.) U., 1972-79, econs. rsch. asst. dept. econs., 1979-86, sr. rsch. asst. dept. econs., 1987—. Author: (with W.J. Baumol and E.N. Wolff) Productivity and American Leadership: The Long View, 1989, (with Baumol) Perfect Markets and Easy Virtue, 1991; contbr. articles to profl. jours. Office: Princeton U Dept Econs 101 Fisher Hall Princeton NJ 08544-1021 Business E-Mail: sabb@princeton.edu.

BLACKMAR, CHARLES BLAKEY, state supreme court justice; b. Kansas City, Mo., Apr. 19, 1922; s. Charles Maxwell and Eleanor (Blakey) B.; m. Ellen Day Bonnifield, July 18, 1943 (dec. 1983); children: Charles A. (dec.), Thomas J., Lucy E. Blackmar Alpaugh, Elizabeth S., George B.; m. Jeanne Stephens Lee, Oct. 5, 1984. AB summa cum laude, Princeton U., 1942; JD, U. Mich., 1948; LLD (hon.), St. Louis U., 1991. Bar: Mo. 1948. Pvt. practice law, Kansas City; ptnr. Swanson, Midgley and predecessors, 1952-66; profl. lectr. U. Mo. at Kansas City, 1949-58; prof. law St. Louis U., 1966-82, prof. emeritus; judge Supreme Ct. Mo., 1982—92, chief justice, 1989-91, sr. status, 1992; spl. asst. atty. gen. Mo., 1969-77; labor arbitrator, active sr. judge, 1992—. Chmn. Fair Pub. Accommodations Commn. Kansas City, 1964-66; mem. Commn. Human Rels. Kansas City, 1965-66. Author: (with Volz and others) Missouri Practice, 1953, West's Federal Practice Manual, 1957, 71, (with Devitt) Federal Jury Practice and Instructions, 1970, 3d edit., 1977, (with Devitt, Wolff and O'Malley) 4th edit., 1988-92; contbr. numerous articles on probate and corp. law to profl. publs. Mem. Jackson County Rep. Com., 1952-58; mem. Mo. Rep. Com., 1956-58. 1st lt., inf. AUS, 1943-46. Decorated Silver Star, Purple Heart. Mem. Am. Law Inst., Nat. Acad. Arbitrators, Mo. Bar (spl. lectr. insts.), Disciples Peace Fellowship, Scribes (pres. 1986-87), Order of Coif, Phi Beta Kappa. Mem. Christian Ch. (Disciples Of Christ). Home (Winter): 2 Seaside Ln Apt 402 Belleair FL 33756-1989 Home (Summer): 612 Hotels Rd Jefferson City MO 65109 Office Phone: 573-893-2481. Personal E-mail: bcbb543@aol.com.

BLACKMER, DONALD LAURENCE MORTON, political scientist; b. Boston, July 6, 1929; s. Alan Rogers and Josephine (Bedford) B.; m. Joan Dexter, Aug. 25, 1951; children: Stephen, Alexander, Katherine. AB magna cum laude, Harvard U., 1952, AM, 1956, PhD, 1967. Sheldon traveling fellow Harvard U., 1952-53; exec. asst. to dir. Ctr. for Internat. Studies, MIT, Cambridge, 1956-61, asst. dir., 1961-68, lectr., 1960-61, asst. prof. polit. sci., 1961-67, assoc. prof., 1967-73, prof., 1973-95; prof. emeritus, 1995—; assoc. dean Sch. Humanities and Social Sci., 1973-81; dir. Program in Sci., Tech. and Soc., 1977-81, head dept. polit. sci., 1981-88. Research assoc. West European studies Harvard U., 1973— Author: Unity in Diversity: Italian Communism and the Communist World, 1967, (with Annie Kriegel) The International Role of the Communist Parties of Italy and France, 1975; co-author, editor: (with Max F. Millikan) The Emerging Nations: Their Growth and United States Policy, 1961, (with Sidney Tarrow) Communism in Italy and France, 1975; The MIT Center for International Studies: The Founding Years 1951-1969, 2002. With U.S. Army, 1953-55. Home: 266 Main St Concord MA 01742-4942 Office: MIT E53-373 Cambridge MA 02139

BLACKMON, DAVID W., education educator; m. Gay S. Blackmon, Dec. 20, 1970; children: Rachel B. Reyes, Rebekah B. Steen. AA, North Greenville Coll., Tigerville, 1966; BS, Carson-Newman Coll., Jefferson City, Tenn., 1969; MEd, U. S.C., 1973, PhD, 2000. Cert. elem./secondary prin. S.C. Tchr. and adminstr. Lancaster County Sch. Dist., SC, 1970—2000; assoc. prof. tchr. edn. Coker Coll., Hartsville, SC, 2001—. Active First Presbyn. Ch., Hartsville, SC, 2003; trustee North Greenville Coll., Tigerville, SC, 1983—88; pres. Carson-Newman Coll. Alumni Assn., Jefferson City, Tenn., 1994—95. With U.S. Army, 1969—70. Mem.: S.C. Assn. Colls. Tchr. Edn. (treas. 2003—, pres. elect 2005—06), Nat. Assn. Elem. Sch. Prins., Nat. Assn. Secondary Sch. Prins., Am. Ednl. Rsch. Assn., S.C. Assn. Sch. Adminstrs., Rotary Internat. (bd. dirs. 1994—2002), Phi Delta Kappa. Office: Coker Coll 300 E College Ave Hartsville SC 29550 Office Phone: 843-383-8131. Office Fax: 843-383-8135. E-mail: dblackmon@coker.edu.

BLACKMORE, JAMES HERRALL, clergyman, educator, author; b. Warsaw, N.C., Feb. 15, 1916; s. Willie Richard and Martha Janie (Sansbury) B.; m. Ruth May Lillick, Jan. 26, 1945; children: Julia, John. BA cum laude, Wake Forest Coll., 1937; BD, Colgate Rochester Div. Sch., 1940; postgrad., Duke U., 1940-41, U. Iowa, 1949; PhD, U. Edinburgh, 1951; postgrad., Princeton U. Inst. Theology, 1975. Ordained to ministry Bapt. Ch., 1940. Dir. religious edn. Parsells Ave. Bapt. ch., Rochester, N.Y., 1938-40; pastor King (N.C.) Bapt. Ch., 1941-43, Masonboro Bapt. ch., Wilmington, N.C., 1947-49, First Bapt. Ch., Spring Hope, N.C., 1951-61; dir. pub. rels. Southeastern Bapt. Theol. Sem., Wake Forest, N.C., 1963-69, dir. publs., spl. instr., 1969-83, prof. assoc. div. studies, 1983-84. Editor Outlook, 1963-84; vis. prof. Southeastern Bapt. Theol. Sem., 1985-96; interim min. Trinity Bapt. Ch., Bitburg-Metterich, West Germany, 1984; study tour with Dr. B. Elmo Scoggin, Israel, 1976; active archaeol. excavations, Tel-Areor, Tel-Dan, Israel, 1981. Author: The Cullom Lantern, A Biography of W.R. Cullom, 1963, A Preacher's Temptations, 1966, A reticule, A Collection of Short Stories and Essays, 1969, Sermons at Warsaw, 1975, Conversations About Jesus, 1977, The Wayfarer, 1977, A Flight of Sparrows, 1978, Sermons at Masonboro, 1978, Biblical Orientation, 1981, Sermons at Spring Hope, 1983, Second Acts, 1984, The A.C. Reid Legacy, 1988, Reflections on the Temptations of Christ, 1992, others; contbr. articles to religious and learned jours., also to encys. Sec. bd. dirs. Bibl. Recorder, 1959-62; chmn. hist. com. Bapt. State Con., N.C. 1970-72. Served to maj. chaplain AUS, 1943-46. Scholarship in his honor est. Southeastern Bapt. Theol. Sem., 1984; named hon. citizen King, N.C., 1993. Mem. Bapt. Pub. Rels. Assn., Lions, Kappa Delta Alpha, Chi Eta Tau. Home: 103 W Pollock St Warsaw NC 28398-1334

BLACKNER, BOYD ATKINS, architect; b. Salt Lake City, Aug. 29, 1933; s. Lester Armond and Anna B.; m. Elizabeth Ann Castleton, June 4, 1955; children: Catherine Blackner Philpot, David, Elizabeth, Genevieve Blackner Tayler. B.Arch., B.F.A., U. Utah, 1956. Registered architect, Fla., Utah, Wyo. Asst. landscape architect Nat. Park Service, Mt. Rainier, Wash., 1956; job capt. Cannon, Smith & Gustavson, Salt Lake City, 1957, Hellmuth, Obata & Kassabaum, St. Louis, 1958-59, Caudill, Rowlett & Scott, Houston, 1959-60; project architect Victor A. Lundy, Sarasota, Fla., N.Y.C., 1960-63; pvt. practice architecture Salt Lake City, 1963—. Lectr. Salt Lake C.C., 1995; adv. coun., vis. juror, critic U. Utah Grad. Sch. Architecture, 1983-99; grad. program dept. landscape architecture and environ. planning Utah State U., 1977-92; region 8 adv. panel archtl. and engring. svcs. GSA, 1977-78; spkr. in field. Featured in (book) Sarasota School of Architecture, 1995; mem. editorial adv. bd.: Symposia mag, 1977-83; contbr. articles to mags. Vice-chmn. Utah Advanced Gift Heart Fund drive, 1964; co-chmn archtl. div. United Fund drive, 1964; mem. Salt Lake City Walls Com., 1976-77, Salt Lake City Council for Arts, 1977-78, Utah Gov.'s Adv. Com. Low Income Housing, Utah Rev. Panel Emergency Energy Conservation Programs; adv. bd. Utah Citizens for Arts, Utah Soc. Autistic Children; dinner exec. com. Nat. Jewish Hosp., Nat. Asthma Ctr., Denver, 1983; bd. dirs. Utah State Divsn. History, Utah State Hist. Soc., 1989-97, U. Utah Med. Ctr. Found., 1998-2002; mem. Gov.'s Strategic Initiatives for History Task Force, 1991. Recipient Danforth Honor award, 1951, also numerous AIA awards including regional design awards for U. Utah Library Fountain, 1970, Westminster Coll. Fountain Plaza, 1972, Nat. award for Kearns/Daynes/Alley Annex, 1978, Western Mountain Region Hist. award of merit for Daynes/Kearns/Alley Annex, 1977, Am. Assn. Sch. Adminstrs. Exhibit award for Wilson Elementary Sch. Green River, Wyo., 1974, Award merit Producers' Council, Inc., 1978, award Nat. Lincoln Arc Welding Found., 1978, Urban Design award 3d Ann. Program, 1979, award of honor We. Mountain Region for HUD Low Income Housing Project, Salt Lake City Housing Authority, 1988, ACI award for Seven Canyon's Fountain, Liberty Park, Salt Lake City, 1994, Cmty. Svc award Salt Lake Found., 1995, Brownstone Bldg. Hist. Renovation award Salt Lake City Downtown Alliance Award Program, 1996, Honors in Arts award Salt Lake Area C. of C., 1997, Disting. Alumnus award U. Utah Founders Day Award Ceremony, 1997, people of vision award Prevent Blindness Utah, 1998, others. Fellow AIA (bd. dirs. Utah chpt. 1968, 71, sec. 1972-73, chmn. regional conf. 1974, pres. 1975-76; chmn. jury for Wyo. chpt. design awards program 1974, regional rep. to housing com., nat. honor award jury 1979, recorder nat. conv. 1982, mem. honor awards jury Western Mountain region 2000-02); mem. Salt Lake Area C. of C. (v.p. 1980-81, chmn. bd. 1982-83), U. Utah Alumni Assn. (bd. dirs. 1987-90), Salt Lake Swim and Tennis Club, Alta Club (bd. dirs. 1985-89, sec. 1991-92, pres. 1994-95), Rotary (treas. Salt Lake City club 1976-77, pres. 1979-80, v.p. 1987, pres. found. 1990-92). Home: 1235 E 200 S #401 Salt Lake City UT 84102

BLACKSHEAR, A. T., JR., lawyer; b. Dallas, July 5, 1942; s. A. T. and Janie Louise (Florey) Blackshear; m. Stuart Davis Blackshear. BBA cum laude, Baylor U., 1964, JD cum laude, 1968. CPA Tex.; bar: Tex. 1968, U.S. Ct. Appeals (5th cir.) 1970, U.S. Tax Ct. 1970. Acct. Arthur Andersen & Co., Dallas, 1964-66; assoc. Fulbright & Jaworski, Houston, 1969-75, ptnr., 1975—2004, chmn. exec. com., 1992—2002, of counsel, 2005—. Bd. dirs. Tex. Med. Ctr., Inc. Trustee Baylor Coll. Medicine; bd. dirs. Sam Houston Area coun. Boy Scouts Am.; bd. dirs. Spiritual Leadership Inst. Mem.: Houston Bar Assn., State Bar Tex., Houston Country Club, Coronado Club, Houston Ctr. Club. Baptist. Office: Fulbright & Jaworski 1301 Mckinney St Fl 51 Houston TX 77010-3031

BLACKSHEAR, BRUNETTA, elementary school educator; d. Clifford and Virgia Stallworth; m. Michael R. Blackshear, Aug. 8, 1981; children: Rayna, Jordyn. BA, Concordia U., 1980. Tchr. 4th grade Our Lady Of The Holy Cross, St. Louis, 1991—95; educator Normandy Sch. Dist., St. Louis, 1995—. Mem. choir St. Matthews Luth. Ch., St. Louis, 1982. Recipient Tchr. of Year Extra Mile award, Normandy Sch. Dist., Apple For Tchr. award, Iota Lambda. Mem.: NEA (assoc.). Democrat. Lutheran. Avocations: travel, shopping, collecting angels. Office: Normandy School District 3255 Lucas Hunt Road Saint Louis MO 63121 Office Phone: 314-493-0700. Personal E-mail: blckshr@aol.com.

BLACKSON, BENJAMIN F(RANKLIN), clinical social worker; b. Newark, Del., Nov. 4, 1933; s. Benjamin Franklin and Lulu Etta (Taylor) B.; m. Sirletta Fordelma Belcher; children: Benita, Barbara. BS, Coll. N.J., 1972; MSW, MBA, Rutgers U., 1975; MSW advanced cert., U. Pa.; D of Human Service, The Fielding Inst., 1988. Bd. cert. diplomate in clin. social work; cert. social work. Commd. USAF, 1952, air traffic contr., D, multi engine pilot; clin. social worker USAFR, ret., 1993; with Blackson Enterprises, Bordentown, NJ, 1969-81; CEO B.E. Inc., Bordentown, 1975—. Vice-chmn. Bordentown Recreation Com., 1973. Fellow Am. Orthopsychiat. Assn.; mem. Acad. Cert. Clin. Social Worker, Nat. Assn. Social Workers (clin. chmn. N.J. 1978-80), Nat. Fedn. Socs. for Clin. Social Work, Am. Assn. Sex Edn. Counselors and Therapists. Fax: 609 298 1973. Office Phone: 609-298-4065. E-mail: blacks0n@cs.com.

BLACKSTOCK, JAMES FIELDING, lawyer; b. L.A., Sept. 19, 1947; s. James Carne and Justine Fielding (Gibson) B.; m. Kathleen Ann Weigand, Dec. 12, 1969; children: Kristin Marie, James Fielding. AB, U. So. Calif., 1969, JD, 1976. Bar: Calif. 1976, Tenn. 1994, U.S. Dist. Ct. (ctrl. dist.) Calif. 1977, U.S. Supreme Ct. 1980. Assoc. Hill Farrer Burrill, L.A., 1976-80, Zobrist, Garner, Garrett, L.A., 1980-83; ptnr. Zobrist & Vienna, L.A., 1983; v.p., gen. counsel Tatum Petroleum, La Habra, Calif., 1983; atty. Thorpe, Sullivan, Workman & Thorpe, L.A., 1984; ptnr. Sullivan, Workman & Dee, L.A., 1985-91; prin. James F. Blackstock, PLC, L.A., 1992-93; v.p., gen. counsel Nat. Auto/Truckstops, Inc., Nashville, 1993-97, Cracker Barrel Old Country Store, Inc., Lebanon, Tenn., 1997-98; sr. v.p., gen. counsel CBRL Group, Inc., Lebanon, Tenn., 1998—2005. Pres. Commerce Assocs., U. So. Calif., 1990-93. Mem. Town Hall, L.A., 1980-90; bd. dirs. Tenn. Valley region ARC, 2002-04, Nashville chpt., 2004-05. Served to lt. USN, 1969-73; capt. USNR (ret.). Mem. ABA, Tenn. Bar Assn., Nashville Bar Assn., U. So. Calif. Alumni Assn. (bd. govs. 1990-92), Pasadena Tournament of Roses Assn., Saddle and Sirloin Club, Rancheros Visitadores. Republican. Roman Catholic. Home: 533 Turtle Creek Dr Brentwood TN 37027-5632 Office: 305 Hartman Dr Lebanon TN 37087-2519 Office Phone: 615-500-5173. E-mail: jim.blackstock@comcast.net.

BLACKSTOCK, JERRY B., lawyer; b. Monticello, Ga., Mar. 9, 1945; s. J.B. and Eugenia (Jones) B.; m. Margaret Owen, June 10, 1967; children: Towner Anson, Michael Owen, Kendrick. BA, Davidson Coll., 1966; JD, U. Ga., 1969. Bar: Ga. 1969, U.S. Ct. Appeals (5th cir.) 1970, U.S. Supreme Ct. 1978, U.S. Ct. Appeals (11th cir.) 1981, U.S. Ct. Appeals (fed. cir.) 1984. With Powell, Goldstein, Frazer & Murphy, Atlanta, 1969—2002; chair Atlanta litigation team Hunton & Williams, LLP, 2002—. Adj. prof. law Emory U., Atlanta, 1975-81; mem. adv. bd. Jour. Intellectual Property Law, U. Ga. Sch. Law, 1992-2005; chair Ga. Jud. Qualifications Commn., 1994-2002. Author: Georgia Appellate Practice Handbook, 1977, Preparation of a Lawsuit for Trial, Pre-Trial Practice, Appellate Practice, 1980; (with others) Georgia Lawyers Basic Practice Handbook, 2d edit. Pres. parents coun. Trinity Sch. Inc., 1981-82; pres. parents club Woodward Acad. Lower Sch., 1986-88, bd. dirs., treas., Woodward Acad. Upper Sch., 1988-91, v.p., 1991-92, pres., 1992-94; chmn. Ga. Athlete Agt. Regulatory Commn., 1989-2000; chmn. bd. dirs. Pastoral Counseling Svc. Atlanta; chmn. bd. visitors U. Ga. Sch. Law, 2001-04; bd. trustees Ga. Legal History Found., 1990-93; mem. Leadership Ga., 1980; mem. Leadership Atlanta, 1990, exec. com., 1991-92; chair bd. trustees Riverside Mil. Acad., 1996—. Recipient Tradition of Excellence award for Def. Lawyer of Yr., State Bar Ga., 2002. Fellow Am. Bar Found., Am. Coll. Trial Lawyers, Internat. Acad. Trial Lawyers, Ga. Bar Assn. (editor-in-chief jour. 1984-85, bd. govs. 1982-98, exec. com. 1990-95, intellectual property law, tech. law and gen. practice and trial sects.), Ga. Bar Found.; mem. ATLA (intellectual property litig. com.), ABA (intellectual property, sci. and tech., tort and ins. practice and litig. sects.), So. Trial Lawyers Assn., Ga. Trial Lawyers Assn., Atlanta Bar Assn. (editor-in-chief Atlanta Lawyer 1972-73), Am. Law Inst., Atlanta Legal Aid Soc. (adv. bd. 1979-86), Atlanta Lawyers Club, Ga. Def. Lawyers Assn. (bd. dirs. 1989-91, dir. Trial Acad. 1987), Am. Bd. Trial Advs. (diplomate, bd. dirs. 1990—, state exec. com. 1985—), Am. Arbitration Assn. (arbitrator, comml. and constrn. panels, Ga.-Ala. adv. com. for large complex cases), Licensing Execs. Soc., Internat., Am. Intellectual Property Law Assn., Computer Law Assn., Davidson Coll. Atlanta Alumni Assn. (pres. 1982-83), Bleckley Am. Inn of Ct. (master of the bench), Commerce Club, Old War Horse Lawyers Club, Cherokee Town and Country Club, 191 Club. Methodist. Avocation: running. Home: 3364 Chatham Rd NW Atlanta GA 30305-1140 Office: Hunton & Williams LLP 4100 Bank of Am Plz 600 Peachtree St Atlanta GA 30308 Office Phone: 404-888-4298. Business E-Mail: jblackstock@hunton.com.

BLACKSTOCK, VIRGINIA HARRIETT, artist; b. St. Louis; d. Charles William Valentine and Ruth (Winn) Arnott; m. Ross Holcomb Blackstock, June 13, 1953; children: Susan, Kathleen, Julianne, Brian. BS, Mo. U., 1950; MA, U. Wis., 1952. Cert. tchr. Mo. Tchr. Ctrl. Mo. State U., U. of the South, Tenn., We. State Coll., Colo. Instr. watermedia painting and drawing workshops; judge, juror for art exhbns. Exhibited in 46 one person shows; group shows in Watercolor Soc. Exhbns. include Ala., Ariz., Colo., Kans., Ky., Mont., N.Mex., La., R.I., Okla., Pa., Utah, Wash., Wyo., Midwest, and San Diego Nat. Watercolor Soc., Rocky Mountain Nat. Exhbn., Nat. Watercolor Soc., Audubon Artists, Inc., N.Y., Allied Artists of Am., Adirondacks Nat., Red River Watercolor Soc., Springville Mus. of Art, C.M. Russell Mus. Auction; paintings in books include Creative Watercolor A Step-by-Step Guide, Beckwith, The Artistic Touch I and III, Unwin, Abstracts in Watercolor, Schlemm, Exploring Color (rev. edit.), Leland; commissions include cover of Ouray Summer Guide, '94, poster for the Ouray (Colo.) Chamber Music Festival (17' by 40'), cover painting, Valley Chronicle, Paonia, Colo., mural for the city of Delta, Colo. Quick draw artist at several fund raising auctions for non-profit orgns. Winner Am. Artist Mag. Preserving Our Nat. Resources Contest, 1990, hon. mention Artist's Mag. Mem. Colo. Watercolor Soc. (signature), N.Mex. Watercolor Soc. (signature), Pa. Watercolor Soc. (signature), Mont. Watercolor Soc. (signature), Western Colo. Watercolor Soc. (signature, exhbn. chair 1991, 92, 93, 98), La. Watercolor Soc. (signature), San Diego Watercolor Soc. (signature), Audubon Artists (signature), Kans. Watercolor Soc. (signature) Episcopalian. Avocations: skiing, biking, hiking, photography, gardening. Home: 31045 L Rd Hotchkiss CO 81419-9409 Office Phone: 970-872-4045. E-mail: ruthhb@tds.net.

BLACKTON, CHARLES S(TUART), history educator; b. N.Y.C., Oct. 27, 1913; s. James Stuart and Paula Hunt (Hilburn) B.; m. Mary Jane Porri, Aug. 16, 1938 (dec. Aug. 1975); children: John Stuart, Susan Porri Blackton Tallman; m. Margaret Rosalind Hando (Baroness Delacourt-Smith), Dec. 21, 1978. BA, UCLA, 1936, MA, 1937, PhD, 1939. Teaching fellow UCLA, 1937-39; asst. prof. Adams State Coll., Colo., 1939-42; from instr. to assoc. prof. history Colgate U., Hamilton, N.Y., 1946-57, prof., 1957-74, Russell Colgate prof., 1974-82, Russell Colgate prof. emeritus, 1982—, dir. social scis. div., 1961-70. Mem. nat. selection com. Inst. Internat. Edn., 1954-56, chmn. India, Australia and Japan coms., 1956-58, mem. selection com. for Australia, 1983; cons., referee Nat. Endowment for the Humanities, 1975-81 Contbr. articles to profl. jours. Served as lt. USNR, 1943-46. Recipient award in Pacific History Am. Hist. Soc., 1940; grantee Social Sci. Research Council, 1951; Fulbright grantee, 1952-53; Fulbright lectr., 1963-64; vis. fellow U. Sri Lanka, 1971, 74, 78 Home: 24 Framers Ct Lane End Bucks H14 3LL England E-mail: peter.stetson@nrc.gc.ca.

BLACKWELDER, BRENT FRANCIS, environmentalist; b. Buffalo, Jan. 4, 1943; s. Francis Winfield and Evelyn Hellen B.; m. Teresa Ann Stotzer, Apr. 5, 1975; children: Matthew, Laura. AB summa cum laude, Duke U., 1964; MA in Math., Yale U., 1966; PhD in Philosophy, U. Md., 1975. Chmn. math. dept. Philander Smith Coll., Little Rock, 1966-68; founder Environ. Policy Ctr., Washington, 1972; chmn., founder Am. Rivers, Washington, 1973-85; founder, staff mem. Environ. Policy Inst., Washington, 1974—; v.p. Friends of the Earth, Washington, 1989-94, pres., 1994—. Bd. mem. 20/20 Vision, Washington, 1990—, Am. Rivers, Washington, 1973-93. Author: Water Conservation, 1982, Bankrolling Successes I, 1988, II, 1995. Pres. Plan Takoma, Takoma Park, Washington, 1977-83; bd. mem. League Conservation Voters, 1980-97, chmn., 1981-91. Grad. fellow NSF, 1964, Woodrow Wilson fellow, 1964; recipient Disting. Alumni award U. Md., 2001, one of Best Stewards of Enriron., Vanity Fair Mag., 2005 Episcopalian. Avocations: canoeing, golf, piano, magic, squash. Home: 3517 Rodman St NW Washington DC 20008-3118 Office: Friends of the Earth 1717 Massachusetts Ave NW Washington DC 20036 Office Phone: 202-783-7400.

BLACKWELL, F. ORIS, environmental scientist, educator; b. Feb. 27, 1925; s. Floyd Weaver and Mary Olive Blackwell; m. Eleanor Louise Edwards, May 5, 1951; children: Susan, Betsy, Mary Ruth, Stephen. BS in Bacteriology and Pub. Health, Wash. State U., Pullman, 1950; MS in Bacteriology and Pub. Health, U. Mass., 1954; MPH in Environ. Health Adminstrn., U. Calif., Berkeley, 1965, DPh in Health Adminstrn., 1967. Rsch. scientist Calif. Gen. sanitarian Benton-Franklin Dist. Health Dept., Pasco, Wash., 1950—53; health and sanitation advisor USAID Program, Peshawar, Pakistan, 1954—56, sr. sanitation advisor Dacca, 1957—59; asst. prof., acting chair dept. environ. health S.P.H. Am. U. Beirut, 1967—71; assoc. prof. environ. health Rutgers U., New Brunswick, NJ, 1967—71; assoc. prof. environ. health Sch. Medicine U. Vt., 1971—74; prof. environ. health East Carolina U., Greenville, NC, 1974—82; prof., chair dept. environ. health sci. Ea. Ky. U., Richmond, 1982—90; ret., 1990. Mem. gov. coun. USPHA, Washington, 1984—88; mem. various site visits accreditation Nat. Coun. Environ. Curriculum, Ind. State U., Ferris State U., others, 1977—78; curriculum cons. dept. bacteriology Wash. State U., Pullman, 1977; cons. water supply devel. USAID-MetaMetrics Inc., Sri Lanka, 1980; leader pub. health del. People to People Program to People's Republic of China, 1987.

Editor: (book revision) Health and Safety in the School Environment, 1978. Apptd. Citizen's Task Force on Chem. Weapons Disposal, Ky., 1984—90. With USNR, 1943—46. Named a Ky. Col., Gov. W. Wilkerson, 1988; recipient Walter Mangold award, Nat. Environ. Assn., 1989. Mem.: Am. Acad. Sanitarians (bd. dirs. 1972—77, bd. cert. diplomate, Laureate diplomate 1977), Nat. Enivron. Health Assn. (life; pres. 1975—77). Democrat. Quaker. Avocations: gardening, nature studies, conservation. Home: 305 Azalea Dr Washington NC 27889 E-mail: orisbl@peoplepc.com.

BLACKWELL, GARY E., minister, educator; b. Carbondale, Ill., Dec. 5, 1949; s. LaRue Henry and Lora Louise Blackwell; m. Linda M. Larner, Aug. 18, 1972; children: Amanda Michelle Stauter, Bronwyn Nicole Swartz, Meagan Elizabeth, Garreth Carrington. BA, So. Ill. U., Carbondale, 1971, MusM, 1978; student, So. Bapt. Theol. Sem., Louisville, Kentucky, 1982—84; MDiv, New Orleans Bapt. Theol. Sem., 1995, ThM, 2000, student, 2003—. Min. music and youth First Bapt. Ch., Titusville, Fla., 1978—80, min. music and edn. Lynn Haven, Fla., 1980—82, min. music and discipleship Lebanon, Mo., 1988—92; min. music and edn. Melrose Bapt. Ch., Roanoke, Va., 1984—88; min. music and youth Arlington Heights Bapt. Ch., 1995—95; assoc. pastor Riverside Bapt. Ch., Pascagoula, Miss., 1992—95; dir., lectr. bibl. studies William Carey Coll. on the Coast, Gulfport, Miss., 2000—; assoc. pastor Broadmoor Bapt. Ch., Pascagoula, 2002—. Dir. Bapt. Student Union, William Carey Coll., Gulfport, Miss., 2000—, lectr. biblical studies, 2000—. Mem. Habitat for Humanity, Harrision County, Miss., 2005—. Mem.: Bapt. Assn. Philosophy Tchrs., Phi Mu Alpha Sinfonia (treas. 1969—71). Southern Baptist. Avocations: golf, woodworking, restoration of antiques. Office: William Carey Coll on the Coast 1856 Beach Dr Gulfport MS 39507 Office Phone: 228-897-7215. Office Fax: 228-897-7131. E-mail: gary.blackwell@wmcarey.edu.

BLACKWELL, J. KENNETH (JOHN KENNETH BLACKWELL), state official; b. Feb. 28, 1948; m. Rosa Blackwell; children: Kimberly, Rahshann, Kristin. BS, Xavier U., Cin., 1970, MEd, 1971. Cert. govt. fin. mgr. Treas. State of Ohio, Columbus, 1994-98, sec. of state, 1999—. Mem. city coun., City of Cin., 1977-89, vice mayor, 1977-78, 85-86, mayor, 1979-80; vice-chmn. Cin. Employees Retirement Sys. Fund., 1988; dep. undersec. U.S. Dept. HUD, 1989-90; mem. Nat. Commn. Econ. Growth and Tax Reform, 1995; participant Nat. Summit on Retirement Income Savings, 1998; ptnr. Bituminex Co., 1978-82; coord. urban affairs, Xavier U., 1971-74, asst. prof. edn., 1974-77, assoc. prof., 1977-91, dir. cmty. rels., 1975-79, assoc. v.p., 1979-91; assoc. prof. U. cin., 1993; chmn. bd. adv. trustees Govt. Investment Found., Inc., 1999; ambassador U.N. Human Rights Commn., 1992-93; adv. bd. John M. Ashbrook Ctr. Pub. Affairs Ashland U., 1997; Children's Ednl. Opportunity Am. Found., 1999; bd. dirs. Black Alliance for Edn. Options; pres. Nat. Electronic Commerce Coord. Coun., 2002; bd.dir. Nat. Coun. UN, Internat. League Human Rights, nat. Coun. Lawyer's Com. for Human Rights, Pub. Tech., Inc., Internat. City Mgmt. Assn./Ret. Corp., Internat. Rep. Inst.; mem. Fed. Election Commn. adv. panel, 1999; bd. trustees Am. Coun. Young Polit. Leaders, 1995' treas. State of Ohio, 1994-99; sec. State of Ohio, 1999—; mem. Coun. Fgn. Rels. Contbr. articles to profl. jours. Mem. The Jerusalem com., 1981, Harvard Policy Group on Network-Enabled Svcs. and Givt.; co-chmn. Hamilton County Reagan-Bush campaign, Ohi, 1984; mem. exec. com. Nat. Conf. Rep. Mayors; co-chmn. Blacks for Bush campaign, Ohio, 1988; mem. adv. coun. Ohio victims of Crime, 1989; bd. dirs. Internat. Rep. Inst., 1993, Campaign Finance Inst., Physicians for Human Rights, Congressional Human Rights Found.; nat. chmn. Steve Forbes for Pres. campaign, 1999; bd. dirs. Wilberforce U., 1989; chmn. Cin. Riverfront Classic and Jamboree, 2000-01; mem. exec. bd. Youth Voter Corps, 2001; mem. nat. bd. visitors Mazza Collection, U. Findlay, 1999; hon. co-chair Meml. to Our Lost Children, 1995; trustee Grant/Riverside Hosps., 1996, Wilmington Coll., 1996; v.p. Nat. Electronic Commerce Coordinating Coun., 2001, 02; mem. bd. advisors John M. Ashbrook Ctr. Pub. Affairs, Ashland U., 1997; exec. bd. Youth Voter Corps., 2001; fellow Nat. Acad. of Pub. Adminstrn.; mem. nat. adv. bd. Princeton Review, Youth for Christ, Jewish Inst. for NAt. Security Affairs; adv. coun. Employee Welfare and Pension Plan U.S. Dept. of Labor. Fellow Harvard U., 1987, The Aspen Inst., 1984, Salzburg Seminar, Austria, 1988, Heritage Found., 1992, The Ditchley Found., 1993; scholar Urban Morgan Inst. Human Rights, 1993; recipient Disting. Alumnus award Xavier U., 1992, Superior Honor award U.S. Dept. State, 1993, Peace of City award Cin. Jewish Cmty. Rels. Coun., 1994, Family of Yr. award Nat. Coun. Negro Women, 1994, Advocacy award U.S. Small Bus. Adminstrn., 1995, Martin Luther King Dream Keeper award, 1996, Veritas award Albertus Magnus Coll., 1998, Thomas A. Van Meter scholar award Ashbrook Ctr., 1997, Pub. Svc. award NAACP, 1996, John M. Ashbrook award American Conservative Union and Ashbrook Ctr. Pub. Affairs, 2004; named one of Top 25 Pub. Sector Leaders, Govt. Tech. Mag., 2002. Mem. Nat. Govt. Fin. Officers Assn. (excellence award 1999), Nat. Assn. State Treasurers, Nat. Assn. State Auditors, Comptrs. and Treasurers (exec. com. 1995-99, Pres. award, 1996), Nat. Taxpayers Union, Nat. Assn. of Secs. of State (v.p. midwest region 2001), Nat. Assn. Securities Profls., Internat. City Mgmt. Assn. (bd. dirs. 1999), Federalist Soc., Econ. club of Columbus, Sigma Pi Phi. Republican. Office: State of Ohio Sec of State 180 E Broad St 16th Fl Columbus OH 43215 Office Phone: 614-466-2655. Business E-Mail: blackwell@sos.state.oh.us.

BLACKWELL, JOHN, science educator; b. Oughtibridge, Sheffield, Eng., Jan. 15, 1942; came to U.S., 1967; s. Leonard and Vera (Brook) B.; m. Susan Margaret Crawshaw, Aug. 5, 1965; children: Martin Jonathan, Helen Elizabeth. BSc in Chemistry, U. Leeds, Eng., 1963, PhD in Biophysics, 1967. Postdoctoral fellow SUNY-Syracuse Coll. Forestry, 1967-69; vis. asst. prof. Case Western Res. U., Cleve., 1969-70, asst. prof., 1970-74, assoc. prof., 1974-77, prof. macromolecular sci., 1977—; chmn. dept., 1985-95; F. Alex Nason prof., 1991-2000; Leonard Case Jr. prof., 2001—. Vis. prof. Kennedy Inst. Rheumatology, London, 1975, Centre National de Recherche Scientifique, Grenoble, France, 1977, U. Frieburg, Fed. Republic Germany, 1982; chmn. Gordon Conf. on Liquid Crystalline Polymers, 1992; cons. in field. Author: (with A.G. Walton) Biopolymers, 1973; mem. editorial bd. Macromolecules, 1989-92; adv. bd. Jour. Macromolecular Sci.-Physics, 1986—; internat. adv. bd. Acta Polymerica, 1992—; contbr. articles to profl. jours. Recipient award for disting. achievement Fiber Soc., 1981, Sr. Scientist award Alexander von Humboldt Found., Max Planck Inst. for Polymer Rsch., Mainz, Fed. Republic Germany, 1991, Rsch. Career Devel. award, 1973-77. Fellow Am. Phys. Soc. (exec. com. divsn. high polymer physics 1986-90, vice chmn. 1987-88, chmn. 1988-89); mem. Am. Chem. Soc. (chmn. cellulose divsn. 1999, Anselm Payen award 1999, divsn. councillor 2000-03), Am. Crystallography Soc. (chmn. fiber diffraction spl. interest group 1993-94), Biophys. Soc. (chmn. biopolymer subgroup 1975-76), Fiber Soc. Episcopalian. Home: 12614 Cedar Rd Cleveland Heights OH 44106-3220 Office: Case Western Res U Dept Macromolecular Sci Cleveland OH 44106-7202 Office Phone: 216-368-6370. Business E-Mail: john.blackwell@case.edu.

BLACKWELL, JOHN ADRIAN, JR., computer company executive; b. Tulsa, Okla., Aug. 1, 1940; s. John Adrian and Daisy Edith (Webb) B. MusB, Westminster Choir Coll., 1962, MusM, 1963. Minister of music 1st Presbyn. Ch., Warren, Ohio, 1963-68, Oklahoma City, 1968-79; artistic dir. Okla. Choral Assn., Oklahoma City, 1980-82; pres. Okla. Digital Technologies Inc., Oklahoma City, 1987-92; ptnr. JJ Enterprises (now Megabyn Assocs., Inc.), pres., owner Oklahoma City, 1992—; program mgr. S. Systems Corp., Oklahoma City, 1995-98. Cons. Union Oil Co. Calif., Oklahoma City, 1989-98; conductor Warren (Ohio) Symphony Orch., 1965-68; choral dir. NBC-TV Stars and Stripes Shows, Oklahoma City, 1975-76. Commd. ch. worker Presbyn. Ch. in the U.S.A., 1965. Recipient Paul Harris award Rotary Found., 1993. Mem. Rotary Internat. (pres. NW Oklahoma City chpt. 2001-02). Office: Megabyn Assocs 2413 NW 112th Ter Oklahoma City OK 73120-7202 Office Phone: 405-751-1392. Personal E-mail: jbmegabyn@aol.com. Business E-Mail: jblackwell@megabyn.com.

BLACKWELL, KIM LOIS, veterinarian, biomedical engineer; b. East Orange, N.J., Aug. 17, 1959; d. Charles Israel and Sharon Jones (Schwartzberg) Tiplitz; m. Mont Marlin Blackwell, Aug. 17, 1982. BS in Biomed. Engring., Boston U., 1981; VMD, U. Pa., 1986, MS in Systems Engring., 1987, PhD in Bioengring., 1988. Assoc. vet. Radbill Animal Hosp., Phila., 1986-87; rsch. scientist Environ. Rsch. Inst. Mich., Arlington, Va., 1988—. Contbr. articles to prfl. jours., 1987-93; co-inventor, patentee dynamically stable assoc. learning neuron circuit and neural network. Trustee scholar Boston U., 1977-81, Case scholar Boston U., 1980; NIH Vet. Med. Scientist Tng. Program fellow, 1981-87. Mem. Soc. for Neurosci. Democrat. Jewish. Avocations: skiing, sewing, playing piano, bicycling. Office: Environ Rsch Inst of Mich 1101 Wilson Blvd Ste 1100 Arlington VA 22209-2248

BLACKWELL, LINDA JANE, elementary school educator; b. Lawrenceburg, Ind., Mar. 28, 1938; d. Thomas Sutton and Nancy Olive Hamill; m. William J. Blackwell, Sept. 21, 1963 (dec. Aug. 1998); 1 child, William Lea. Student, Ind. U., 1956-60; BA in Anthropology, Calif. State U., 1973, MA in Anthropology, 1975. Cert. elem. tchr. Elem. sch. tchr. Park Forest (Ill.) Unified Sch. Dist., 1960-62, Torrance (Calif.) Unified Sch. Dist., 1962-64; curatorial asst., photo archivist S.W. Mus., L.A., 1975-82; elem. sch. tchr. L.A. Unified Sch. Dist., 1982—2001. Mem.: AAUW (pres. chpt. 1983—84), Phi Mu (pres. Glendale Alum chpt. 1996—2002), Delta Kappa Gamma (pres. 1998—2000). Avocation: travel. Home: 765 Prospect Dr Glendale CA 91205-3424

BLACKWELL, MICHAEL SIDNEY, broker, financial services executive; b. Ft. Bragg, N.C., June 14, 1957; s. Cedric Lee Jr. and Susan Olivia (Womack) B.; m. Janet Marie Thomas, Apr. 29, 1986; children: Sydney Marie, Catherine Leigh. Student, La. State U., 1981; BS Mktg., LaSalle U., 1993, MBA, 1994. Cert. fund specialist; registered fin. cons. From sales mgr. to nat. mktg. dir. various corps., 1977-92; v.p. Alliance Fin. Svcs., Atlanta, 1992-95, also bd. dirs., 1992-95; pres. United Securities Alliance, Atlanta, 1992-95, also bd. dirs., 1992-95; sr. v.p., spl. cons. to chmn. World Mktg. Alliance, Inc., Norcross, Ga., 1995—; mng. dir. WMA Consumer Svcs. Inc., Norcross, 1995—. Adj. faculty mem. Kent Coll., Mandeville, La., LaSalle U.; bd. dirs. 10X, Inc., Shreveport, La., Legacy, Inc., Baton Rouge. Mem. Internat. Assn. Fin. Planning, Nat. Eagle Scout Assn., Inst. Cert. Fund Specialists, Internat. Assn. Registered Fin. Cons. Republican. Baptist. Avocations: family, golf. Office: World Mktg Alliance Ste 400 400 Perimeter Ctr Terraces Atlanta GA 30346

BLACKWELL, PAUL EUGENE, SR., army officer; b. York, S.C., Aug. 19, 1941; s. Paul Webb and Ruby Mae (Hartness) B.; m. Janet Gail Glenn, June 23, 1963; 1 child, Paul Eugene Jr. BS, Clemson (S.C.) U., 1963, MS, 1965, postgrad., 1970-72, LLD, 1992. Commd. 1st lt. U.S. Army, 1963, advanced through grades to lt. gen., 1994, comdr. 1st Bn., 4th inf., 3d inf. divsn. Aschaffenburg, W. Ger., 1980-82, ops. officer 9th Inf. Div. Ft. Lewis, Wash., 1983-85, chief staff 9th Inf. Div., 1985-86, comdr. 1st Brigade, 9th Inf. Div., 1986-88, dep. dir. ops. Nat. Mil. Command Ctr., Joint Staff Washington, 1988-89; asst. div. comdr. 3d Armored Div., Germany, 1989-91; comdg. gen. 2d Armored Div., Garlstedt, Germany, 1991-92; comdr. 24th Inf. Div., Ft. Stewart, Ga., 1992-94; dep. chief staff ops. Dept. Army, Washington, 1994-96; v.p. integrated command ctrl. and comm. Raytheon Co., 2000—. Def. cons., 1996—. Ruling elder Presbyn. Ch., Puyallup, Wash., 1985—88, Beth Shiloh Presbyn. Ch., 1998—2001, clerk of session, 1999—2001, supt., 1997—99. Decorated DSM with oak leaf cluster, Silver Star with oak leaf cluster, Legion of Merit with oak leaf cluster, Bronze Star with V device with eight oak leaf clusters, Purple Heart, Air medal, Army Commendation medal with V device and three oak leaf clusters, others. Mem. 82d Airborne Div. Assn., 9th Inf. Div. Assn. (pres. 1986-88), Marine Corps Assn., Assn. of U.S. Army, Tiger Brotherhood (hon.), Am. Ordnance Assn., Octofoil Assn., 3d Armored Div. Assn., 2d Armored Div. Assn., 24th Inf. Div. Assn., Assn. U.S. Army, DAV, Masons, Shriners, Ft. Stewart Skeet Club, Phi Kappa Phi, Gamma Sigma Delta, Alpha Zeta, Alpha Tau Alpha. Avocations: hunting, skeet shooting, running. Home: 650 N Shiloh Rd York SC 29745-8378 Personal E-mail: peblackwell@raytheon.com.

BLACKWELL, RAYMOND ANTHONY, JR., singer, music educator; b. Wilmington, Del., Dec. 30, 1962; s. Raymond Anthony Blackwell and Lorraine Frances Husbands. MusB, U. Del., 1992; MusM, Binghamton (N.Y.) U., 1994. Resident artist Tri Cities Opera, Binghamton, NY, 1992—99; mem. faculty Carnegie Mellon U., Pitts., 2003—. Singer: Tri Cities Opera, Opera at Florham, Pitts. (Pa.) Opera, Opera Theater Pitts., Pitts. (Pa.) Symphony, Johnstown Symphony, Met. Opera Auditions, (albums) La Muerte de Colon. Mem.: Pi Kappa Lambda. Home: 1080 Evergreen Dr Pittsburgh PA 15232 Office: Carnegie Mellon Univ 5000 Forbes Ave Pittsburgh PA 15213

BLACKWELL, SAVANNAH ROSE, journalist; b. Austin, June 3, 1969; d. Michael George Hauty and Rose Ann Blackwell. BA with honors, U. Va., 1991; MS with honors, Columbia U., 1992. Reporter Daily News, N.Y.C., 1992, Phila. Inquirer, 1993-94, Tallahassee (Fla.) Dem., 1994-95, Valley Times, Pleasanton, Calif., 1996, San Francisco Bay Guardian, 1996—2004; exec. editor SFProgressive.com, 2004—; panelist SF Newshour, 1998—. Recipient 1st place Peninsula Press Club, 1997; 3d place Nat. Newspapers Assn., 1997, hon. mention, 1997; 2d place Calif. Newspapers Pubs. Assn., 1998, 1st place Calif. Newspaper Publishers Assn., 2003, Nat. Newspaper Assn., 2003, Press Club East Bay, 199; Pulitzer Traveling fellow, 1992-93. Mem. Soc. Profl. Journalists (1st place 1999), Investigative Reporters & Editors (Freedom of Info. award 2000). Avocations: archeaology, piano, painting. Home: 330 Parnassus Ave Apt 102 San Francisco CA 94117-3735 Office Phone: 415-902-0507.

BLACKWELL, TODD V., human resources specialist; BA in Edn., NC State U. Various positions including team leader, ops. team leader, store team leader, dist. human resources mgr., dist. team leader, regional v.p., sr. v.p. Mervyn's (a former subsidiary of Target Corp.), 1986—2000; sr. v.p. human resources Target Corp., Mpls., 2000—03, exec. v.p. human resources, assets protection, COO AMC world-wide sourcing co., 2003—. Chmn. Associated. Merchandising Corp. Bd. dirs. Kids Fitness for Life. Mem.: Omega Psi Phi. Office: Target Corp 1000 Nicoillet Mall Minneapolis MN 55403 Office Phone: 612-304-6073. Office Fax: 612-696-3731.*

BLACKWELL, VICKIE JAN, small business owner; b. Rockford, Ill., July 8, 1951; d. Robert Ellsworth and Grace (Baxter) Borcherts; m. James H. Wright, Dec. 19, 1970 (div. May 1984); children: Theresa Lynn, Jon and Jeffrey (twins). ADN, Rock Valley Coll., Rockford, 1972; student, St. Louis U.; BSN with highest honors, Purdue U., Ft. Wayne, 1983; student, Calif. Coll. Health Profls., 1997—98; MSNS, Regis U. RN, Ill., Ind., Calif. Team leader Belleville (Ill.) Meml. Hosp., 1972-80; charge nurse, head nurse Luth. Hosp. and VA Hosp., Ft. Wayne, Ind., 1980-83; ins. agt. Combined Ins. Co., Chgo., 1984; dir. nursing, adminstr. Heritage Manor North, Ft. Wayne, 1985-86, Butler (Ind.) Health Care, 1986-88; minister of music Calvary Chapel/Calvary Temple, Ft. Wayne, 1988-89; adminstr., dir. nursing Community Care Ctr., Inc., Huntington, Ind., 1989-90; adminstr., dir. nursing, supr. home health care Hooper Holmes, Inc., Orange County, Calif., 1990-92; pres., owner Continuing Edn. U. Calif. Developer home health agy., continuing edn. unit provider, Calif. Mem. Calif. Assn. Home Health Agys., NAFE, Faces Internat. L.A., Purdue Alumni Club. Avocations: gymnastics, pianist, composer. Office Phone: 815-325-7638. E-mail: lordlove@sbcglobal.net.

BLACKWELL, WILLIAM ERNEST, broadcast executive; b. Rocky Mount, N.C., Apr. 1, 1932; s. Rosser I. and Ellen W. (Wilkinson) Blackwell; m. Elizabeth Levitan Blackwell, Mar. 22, 1973. BS, Davidson Coll., 1954; MBA, U. N.C., 1958. Security analyst Jefferson Standard Life Ins. Co., Greensboro, NC, 1958—66, asst. treas., 1966—69, 2d v.p., 1969—81; v.p. corp. devel. Jefferson-Pilot Corp., Greensboro, 1981—83, sr. v.p. corp. devel., 1983—85, exec. v.p., 1986; pres. Jefferson-Pilot Comm. Co., 1991—97, OmniVest Svcs., 1998—. Served in U.S. Army, 1954—56. Mem.: Nat. Assn. Life Underwriters, N.C. Soc. Fin. Analysts, Inst. Chartered Fin. Analysts. Office: OmniVest Svcs PO Box 3384 Greensboro NC 27402-3384

BLACKWILL, ROBERT D., former federal agency administrator; b. Kellogg, ID, Aug. 8, 1939; m. Wera Hildebrand; 5 children. BA, Witchita St. U., 1962. Volunteer Peace Corps, Malawi, 1964—66; polit. counselor Am. Embassy US Dept. State, Tel Aviv, 1978—79; dir. West European affairs Nat. Security Coun. Nat. Security Coun., 1979—81; prin. dep. asst. sec. of state for polit.-mil. affairs US Dept. State, 1981—82, dep. asst. sec. of state for European affairs, 1982—83; assoc. dean Harvard U. John F. Kennedy Sch. Govt., 1983—85; spl. asst. for Nat. Security Affairs to President George Bush Exec. Office of the Pres., 1989—90; Belfer lectr. internat. security Harvard U. John F. Kennedy Sch. Govt.; U.S. amb. to India US Dept. State, 2001—03; dep. asst. to the Pres. & coord. for strategic planning Nat. Security Coun., 2003—04; pres. Barbour Griffith & Rogers Internat., Washington, 2004—. Editor: Arms Control and the US-Russian Relationship, 1996; co-editor: Conventional Arms Control and East-West Security, 1989, A Primer for the Nuclear Age, 1990; co-editor: (with Albert Carnesale) New Nuclear Nations, 1993; co-editor: (with Sergei Karaganov) Damage Limitation or Crisis? Russia and the Outside World, 1994; co-editor: (with Rodric Braithwaite and Akihiko Tananka) Engaging Russia, 1995; co-editor: (with Michael Sturmer) Allies Divided: Transatlantic Policies for the Greater Middle East, 1997; co-editor: (with Paul Dibb) America's Asian Alliances, 2000; contbr. articles to profl. jours. Recipient Comdrs. Cross of the Order of Merit, Fed. Republic of Germany. Office: Barbour Griffith & Rogers LLC 10th Fl 1275 Pennsylavania Ave NW Washington DC 20004

BLACK WOLF, TRISTAN See MACAVERY, TRISTAN

BLACKWOOD, KRISTA LANG, art director; b. Pensacola, Fla., July 8, 1970; d. Glenna Cameron and Robert Gary Lang; m. Kendrick George Blackwood, Feb. 5, 1993; 1 child, Cameron Dean. MusB in edn., Tex. Christian U., 1988—92; MusM in voice, U. of Kans., 1998—2001, MusM, 2000—02, D of musical arts, 2000—03. Founder/voice tchr./vocal coach Krista Lang Blackwood Studio, Kans. City, Mo., 1992—; tchr. Wichita Falls Ind. Sch. Dist., Tex., 1993—94; dir. of music Wheeler Meml. Presbyn., Omaha, 1995—98; dir. of choirs St. Andrew's Episcopal Ch., 2001; founder/artistic dir. Octarium, Kans. City, Mo., 2001—. Singer: (opera) Little Women, 2000, Kansas City Chorale, 2001—03, (musical theatre) Fiddler on the Roof - Hodel, 1992, Nunsense, 1993—94, Nebr. Choral Arts Soc., 1995—98, Soli Deo Gloria Cantorum, 1996—98, (musical theatre) A Little Night Music - Sondheim, 2001, (opera role) Xerxes - Xerxes, 1998, Gianni Schicchi, 2001, Rape of Lucretia - Lucretia, 2002, Cosi Fan Tutte - Dorabella, 2002. Recipient Invited to Perform Four Concerts at Nat. Conv., Am. Choral Directors Assn., 2005. Mem.: Tex. Music Educators Assn., Am. Choral Dirs. Assn., Alpha Lambda Delta, Mortar Bd., Pi Kappa Lambda (life), Mu Phi Epsilon (life; v.p. 1991—92). Avocations: travel, home restoration, reading. Office: Octarium 5930 Brookside Blvd Kansas City MO 64113 Office Phone: 816-729-6516. Personal E-mail: krista@octarium.org.

BLADEN, EDWIN MARK, judge, lawyer; b. Detroit, Feb. 2, 1939; s. Philip and Ruth Sara (Millstein) B.; m. Paula Dee Maskin, Sept. 2, 1962; children: Philip, Sara, Jeffrey. BA, Wayne State U., 1962, JD, 1965. Asst. atty. gen. State of Mich., Lansing, 1965-86; mng. atty. Moran & Bladen, Lansing, 1987-93; pvt. practice, East Lansing, Mich., 1994-97; adminstrv. law judge USCG, 1997—2003, Dept. Homeland Security, 2003—. Author: Consumer Law of Michigan, 1978. Mem. Dem. Polit. Reform Comm., Mich., 1968. With U.S. Army Security, 1957-60, Korea. Recipient Alexander Freeman scholarship Wayne State U., Detroit, 1962-65. Mem. State Bar Mich. (chmn. anti-trust sect., treas./sec. 1990-94), Nat. Assn. Fraud Units (pres. 1985-86). Office: 3448 Jackson Fed Bldg 915 2nd Ave Seattle WA 98174-1009

BLADER, JOSEPH CHARLES, psychologist, researcher; b. N.Y.C., June 11, 1960; s. Henry and Bernice Blader; m. Marie Elaine LeBlanc, Aug. 4, 1990; children: Allison R, David J. BS, Tufts U., 1981; MA, Queen's U., Ont., 1983, PhD, 1987; MSc, Albert Einstein Coll. Medicine, 2004. Lic. psychologist N.Y., 1989. Sr. psychologist Schneider Children's Hosp., L.I. Jewish Med. Ctr., New Hyde Park, NY, 1988—96; asst. prof. psychiatry N.Y. U. Sch. Medicine, N.Y.C., 1996—2000; sr. rsch. scientist L.I. Jewish Med. Ctr., North Shore, L.I. Rsch. Inst., New Hyde Park, NY, 2000—03; asst prof. psychiatry SUNY Sch. Medicine, Stony Brook, 2003—. Recipient New Investigator award, NIMH, 2001; fellow R. S. MacLaughlin fellow, Queen's U., 1983—87; grantee, NIH, 1997—, Young Investigator Award, Nat. Alliance for Rsch. on Schizophrenia and Depression, 2001—04. Mem.: APA. Achievements include research in children's sleep patterns; outcomes of children hospitalized with psychiatric illnesses; bases of aggression and behavioral dyscontrol in children; clinical trials for children with psychiatric illness. Avocations: hiking, woodworking, running, cycling. Office: Stony Brook State Univ NY Dept Psychiatry Putnam Hall Stony Brook NY 11794-8790 Office Phone: 631-632-8675. Office Fax: 631-632-8953. E-mail: joseph.blader@stonybrook.edu.

BLADES, G(ENE) GRANVILLE, accountant; b. Easton, Md., Nov. 17, 1967; s. Gene William and Jean (Wise) B. BA, Washington Coll., Chestertown, Md., 1986; PhD, Catholic U., Washington, 1990; JD, U. Md., 1994. CPA. Instr. Chesapeake Coll., Wye Mills, Md., 1990-93; ptnr. Kent & Blades, Denton, Md., 1994-95; pvt. practice Easton, 1995-98; pvt. practice, CPA Trappe, Md., 1998—. Legal counsel Trappe (Md.) Vol. Fire Dept., 1995-98; dir. Choptank-Talbot Agr. Corp. Easton, 1997—; cons. Blades Design, LLC, Trappe, 1994-98; v.p. Wise-Blades Farm Group, 1999—; pres. Trappe Acctg. Svcs., 2000—; v.p. Trappe Outreach Coun. Inc., 2000—; dep. to Gen. Conv. of Episc. Ch., 2000—. Author: Politics of Sectional Avoidance, 1990, Brief History of White Marsh Parish, 1997, The Kings of France, 2004; editor The Epistle, 1995. Treas. Habitat for Humanity Talbot Co., Easton, 1997-99; dir. Talbot Co. Humane Soc., Easton, 1996-99, Cmty. of the Ascension, 2001; sec. Old White Marsh Cemetery Corp., Trappe, 1997—. Mem. ABA, AICPA, Am. Hist. Assn., Md. Assn. CPA's, Assn. Clin. Pastoral Edu., Md. Soc. Accts., Md. Hist. Soc., New Eng. Geneal. Soc. Republican. Episcopal. Avocations: photography, travel. Home: 2814 Ocean Gtwy Trappe MD 21673-1764

BLAGDON, JANET CLAIRE, elementary school educator; b. Medford, Mass., Dec. 13, 1939; d. Harry Mainwaring and Anstias Marian (Considine) B. BS in Edn., State Coll. Boston, 1961; MS in Art Edn., Mass. Coll. Art, 1973. Cert. tchr. elem., art, English, Mass. Elem. tchr. Jenkins Sch., Scituate, Mass., 1961-63, Hatherly Sch., 1963-66; tchr. art Scituate Jr. H.S., 1966-69; elem. tchr. Obregon Sch., Pico Rivera, Calif., 1969-70, Kingsbury, Phillips, Bates Schs., Wellesley, Mass., 1970—2002. Artist: many paintings entered in juried shows, published prints, Classic Collection of Fine Arts, 1992; paintings in pvt. collections in Fla., Calif., NC, Ga., others. Recipient numerous art awards from various groups including Bristol Art Mus., South Shore Art Ctr., Plymouth Art Guild, Duxbury Art Ctr. Mem. NEA, Mass. Tchrs. Assn., Wellesley Tchrs. Assn., Copley Soc. (John Singleton Copley award 1984), South Shore Art Ctr., North River Arts Assn. Avocations: art, painting. Home: 54 Emerson Rd Needham MA 02492-2829

BLAGOJEVICH, ROD R., governor, former congressman; b. Chgo., Dec. 10, 1956; s. Rade and Millie (Govedarica) Blagojevich; m. Patti Blagojevich; children: Amy, Annie. BA in History, Northwestern U., 1979; JD, Pepperdine U., 1983. Past pvt. practice law, Chgo.; past asst. state atty. Cook County, Ill.; mem. Ill. Ho. of Reps., 1992—96, U.S. Congress from 5th Ill. dist., 1997—2002; mem. govt. reform and armed svcs. coms.; gov. State of Ill., 2003—. Democrat. Office: Office of the Governor 207 State House Springfield IL 62706 also: 100 W Randolph Ste 16-100 Chicago IL 60601

BLAHA, VERLE DENNIS, consumer products company executive, electrical engineer; b. Detroit, Nov. 21, 1929; s. Maurice Lee and Clarice Annette Blaha; m. LuVeral Alma Blaha, Aug. 11, 1956; children: Bryan Jay, Lynn Renee Blaha Melchior. BS in Bus., U. Minn., 1966, MBA, 1969. Field supr. Aero. Radio Inc., Washington, 1952-56; mgr. quality assurance Gen. Mills Electronics, Mpls., 1956-63; sr. v.p. Litton Microwave Cooking, Mpls., 1963-82; v.p., gen. mgr. Holaday Industries Inc., Eden Prairie, Minn., 1982-86; pres. Celsion Corp., Columbia, Md., 1986-91, New Opportunities

Ltd., North Oaks, Minn., 1984—, Thumper Pond Golf Course, Thumper Pond, Inc., Ottertail, Minn., 1998—, Thumper Pond Svcs., Inc., Ottertail Aggregate, Inc., Happy Acres Inc., 2004—. Lectr. on investments, U. St. Thomas, 1982-86. With USN, 1947-50, PTO. Fellow Internat. Microwave Power (chmn. bd. dirs. 1976-82). Republican. Lutheran. Avocations: hunting, fishing, building wildlife habitat. Office: New Opportunities Ltd 14 Sunset Ln North Oaks MN 55127-6454 Office Phone: 218-367-2431. E-mail: verle77@aol.com.

BLAHD, WILLIAM HENRY, physician, nuclear medicine physician; b. Cleve., May 11, 1921; s. Moses and Rae (Lichtenstader) B.; m. Miriam Weiss, Jan. 29, 1971; children— Andrea Margery, William Henry, Karen Ruth. Student, Western Res. U., 1939-40, U. Ariz., 1940-42; MD, Tulane U., 1945. Diplomate Am. Bd. Nuclear Medicine (chmn. 1982, v.p. 1986-97, exec. dir. 1998-2003), Am. Bd. Internal Medicine (bd. govs. 1981). Resident in pathology and internal medicine VA Wadsworth Med. Center, 1948-52, ward officer metabolic research ward, 1951-52, asst. chief radioisotope service, 1952-56, chief nuclear medicine dept. L.A., 1956-97, dir. nuclear medicine dept., 1997—; exec. dir. Am. Bd. Nuclear Medicine, L.A. Prof. dept. medicine U. Calif., Los Angeles; mem. ACGME residency rev. com. for nuclear medicine, 1979-97, chmn., 1991-97; mem. Joint Rev. Com. on Ednl. Programs in Nuclear Medicine Tech., 1986-93; mem. subcom. on naturally occurring and accelerator produced radioactive materials Com. on Interagency Radiation Rsch. and Policy Coordination, 1988-92; cons. nuclear medicine; mem. adv. com. on human uses radioisotopes Calif. Dept. Health Svcs.; mem. HEW Interagy. Task Force on Ionizing Radiation, 1978; dir. nuclear medicine Mt. Sinai Hosp., L.A., 1955-76, Valley Presbyn. Med. Ctr., Van Nuys, Calif., 1959-85, St. Joseph Hosp. Med. Ctr., Burbank, Calif., 1958-83. Author 3 textbooks on nuclear medicine. Contbr. numerous articles to med. jours. Served with U.S. Army, 1946-48. Grantee Muscular Dystrophy Assn. Am., 1965-69, Nat. Cancer Inst., 1973-76; recipient Lifetime Achievement award Wadsworth Physicians and Surgeons Alumni Assn., 2000, William H. Oldendorl Lifetime Achievement award West L.A. Med. Ctr., 2000. Fellow ACP, Am. Coll. Nuclear Physicians (bd. regents 1974-80); mem. AMA, Soc. Nuc. Medicine (trustee 1966-74, pres. 1977-78, Disting. Scientist award No./So. Calif. chpts. 1975, Disting. Sci. award We. Regional chpts. 1995, Disting. Pub. Svc. Career award Fed. Exec. Bd. L.A. 1998, Presdl. Disting. Svc. award 2000, 02), Health Physics Soc. (pres. So. Calif. chpt. 1964-66), Calif. Med. Assn. (sci. bd. 1975-81, chmn. adv. bd. nuclear medicine 1976-84), Am. Bd. Med. Spltys., COCERT, Soc. Exptl. Biology and Medicine, Los Angeles County, Calif. Med. Assns., We. Assn. Physicians, Am. Fedn. Clin. Rsch., Nat. Assn. VA Chiefs Nuclear Medicine (pres. 1985-87), We. Soc. Clin. Rsch., Alpha Omega Alpha. Office: Nuclear Med Dept VA Greater LA Healthcare 691/W115 11301 Wilshire Blvd Los Angeles CA 90073

BLAHNIK, JOHN G., electronics executive; BS, U. Wis.; MBA, U. Chgo. Various fin. pos. in product cost, capital appropriations and product programs GM, Detroit, 1978—81; mgr. overseas fin. analysis GM Treas.'s Office, N.Y.C., 1981, mgr. capital analysis, fin. staff, 1982, mgr. corp. financing, 1982—84, dir. cash resources mgmt. and fgn. exch., 1984, dir. fgn. exch. and internat. cash mgmt., 1984; treas. GM do Brasil, Brazil, 1984—87, gen. asst. comptroller, 1987, comptroller, 1988; exec. dir. GM L.Am. Ops., 1991—94; pres. Banco GM, 1991—94; dir. fin., Lansing (Mich.) Automotive Divsn. GM, 1994; sr. v.p., CFO Delco Electronics Corp., Troy, Mich., 1995, exec. dir. fin., 1996—98, treas., 1998—, v.p., 1998—2004, v.p. treasury, mergers, acquisitions, 2004—. Office: World Hdqrs Delphi Corp 5725 Delphi Dr Troy MI 48098-2815

BLAHUT, RICHARD EDWARD, electrical and computer engineering educator; b. Orange, N.J., June 9, 1937; s. Edward John and Julia Anna (Chamer) B.; m. Barbara Ann Krachenfels, Aug. 30, 1958; children: Gregory, Kenneth, Janice, Jeffrey. BS in Elec. Engring., MIT, 1960; MS in Physics, Stevens Inst. Tech., Hoboken, N.J., 1964; PhD in Elec. Engring., Cornell U., 1972. Engr. Kearfott (GPI), Little Falls, N.J., 1960-64, IBM, Owego, N.Y., 1964-94; courtesy prof. elec. engring. Cornell U., 1974-94; Henry Magnuski prof. and dept. head elec. and computer engring. U. Ill., Urbana, 1994—, adj. prof. elec. engring., 1986-94. Sys. cons. Ioptics Corp., Bellevue, Wash., 1994-99. Author: Theory and Practice of Error Control Codes, 1983, Fast Algorithms for Digital Signal Processing, 1985, Principles and Practice of Information Theory, 1987, Digital Transmission of Information, 1990, Algebraic codes for Data Transmission, 2003, Theory of Remote Image Formation, 2005. IBM fellow, 1980. Fellow IEEE (pres. info. theory group 1982, editor Transactions on Info. theory, Alexander Graham Bell award 1998), NAE. Republican. Roman Catholic. Home: 1502 BridgePoint Ln Champaign IL 61822-9272 Office: U Ill Dept of Elect and Computer Engring Urbana IL 61801 E-mail: blahut@uiuc.edu.

BLAIN, CHARLOTTE MARIE, internist, educator; b. Meadeville, Pa., July 18, 1941; d. Frank Andrew and Valerie Marie (Serafin) Blain; m. John G. Hamby, June 12, 1971 (dec. May 1976); 1 child, Charles J. Hamby. Student, Coll. of St. Francis, 1958—60, DePaul U., 1960—61; MD, U. Ill., Chgo., 1965. Diplomate Am. Bd. Family Practic, Am. Bd. Internal Medicine. Intern, resident U. Ill. Hosps., 1967—70; fellow in infectious diseases U. Ill., 1968—69; pvt. practice specializing in internal medicine and family practice Elmhurst, Ill., 1969—. Instr. U. Ill. Hosp., 1969—70; asst. prof. Loyola U., 1970—71; mem. staff Elmhurst Meml. Hosp., 1970—; clin. asst. prof. Chgo. Med. Sch., 1978—95, U. Ill. Med. Sch., 1995—, Rush Med. Coll., 1997—. Contbr. articles to profl. jours., chapters to books. Bd. dirs., v.p. Elmhurst Art Mus. Fellow: ACP, Am. Acad. Family Practice; mem.: AMA, DuPage Med. Soc., Am. Profl. Practice Assn., Am. Soc. Internal Medicine, Univ. Club (Chgo.). Roman Catholic. Avocations: Hapki Do (Black Belt), Tae-Kwan-Do (Black Belt), skiing. Home: 320 Cottage Hill Ave Elmhurst IL 60126-3302 Office: 135 Cottage Hill Ave Elmhurst IL 60126-3330 Office Phone: 630-832-6633. Business E-Mail: cblain@cmbyclinic.com.

BLAIN, PETER CHARLES, lawyer; b. Milw., Nov. 15, 1949; s. Emile Octave and Mary Catherine (Usalis) B.; m. Katherine Stauber, June 12, 1971; children: Thomas Peter, Timothy Charles, Katherine Elizabeth, Peter James. BS, Wis. State U., Stevens Point, 1971; JD, Georgetown U., 1978. Bar: Wis. 1978. Budget analyst VA, Washington, D.C., 1974-78; atty. Reinhart, Boerner, Van Deuren S.C. and predecessor firms, Milw., 1978—. Chmn. Wis. State Bar Insolvency Sect., 1995-97; lectr. U. Wis., Milw., 1984—. Contbr. articles to profl. jours. Active Open Space Com. Mequon, Wis. 2d Lt. U.S. Army, 1972-74 Mem. Am. Coll. Bankruptcy, Milw. Bar Bankruptcy Sect. (prog. chmn. 1984-85, sect. chmn. 1986-87, co-chair bankruptcy sect. bench/bar com. 1998—), EDWI (bankruptcy local rules com. 2002—, bd. dirs. 2002—). Democrat. Roman Catholic. Avocation: reading. Office: Reinhart Boerner Van Deuren 1000 N Water St Ste 1800 Milwaukee WI 53202-6650 Office Phone: 414-298-8129. Business E-Mail: pblain@reinhartlaw.com.

BLAINE, DAVID, magician; b. Brooklyn, NY, Apr. 4, 1973; Performed in TV spl. (also exec. prodr.) David Blaine: Street Magic, 1996, David Blaine: Magic Man, 1998, David Blaine: Frozen in Time, 2000, David Blaine: Fearless, 2002, David Blaine: Vertigo, 2002, David Blaine: Above the Below, 2003; guest performances include TV programs Rosie O'Donnel Show, Late Night with Conan O'Brien; author (book) Mysterious Stranger, 2002. Office: Creative Artists Agy 9830 Wilshire Blvd Beverly Hills CA 90212*

BLAINE, DAVIS ROBERT, valuation consultant, investment banker; b. Gary, Ind., Oct. 30, 1943; s. Jack Davis and Virginia Sue (Mintzer) B.; m. Karen Ellen Levenson, Dec. 28, 1981; children: Davis Justin, Tristan D., Brittara K., Whitney K. BA, Dartmouth Coll., 1965; MBA, U. Mich., 1969. Founder, sr. v.p. Am. Valuation Cons., Chgo., 1971-78, chmn. bd., 1978; exec. v.p. Valuation Rsch., Chgo., 1978-80, pres. L.A., 1980-83; sr. v.p. Arthur D. Little Valuation, Inc., Woodland Hills, Calif., 1983-87; owner, chmn. bd. Olesen, 1989-92; founder, mng. ptnr. Profls. Network Group, 1988—. Founder, chmn. bd. The Mentor Group Inc., L.A., 1981-; founder, pres. ICS Corp., Chgo., 1976-82, v.p. bd., 1982-87. Served to lt. (j.g.) USNR, 1966-68. Mem.: Beta Theta Pi. Office Phone: 818-991-4150, 818-597-3559. Business E-Mail: dblaine@thementorgrp.com.

BLAIR, ANDREW LANE, JR., lawyer, educator; b. Oct. 10, 1946; s. Andrew Lane and Catherine (Shaffer) B.; m. Catherine Lynn Kessler, June 21, 1969; children: Christopher Lane, Robert Brook. BA, Washington & Lee U., 1968; JD, U. Denver, 1972. Bar: Colo. 1972, U.S. Dist. Ct. Colo. 1972, U.S. Ct. Appeals (10th cir.) 1972. Assoc. Dawson, Nagel, Sherman & Howard, Denver, 1972-78; mem. Sherman & Howard LLC, Denver, 1978. Lectr. U. Denver Law Sch., 1980-83, U. Colo., Colorado Springs, 1984, U. Colo. Law Sch., Boulder, 1991. Author: Uniform Commercial Code sects. for Colorado Methods of Practice, 1982; contbr. articles to profl. jours. Mem. ABA, Colo. Bar Assn. Democrat. Methodist. Home: 1111 Humboldt St Denver CO 80218-3123 Office: Sherman & Howard 633 17th St Ste 2900 Denver CO 80202-3665 E-mail: ablair@sah.com.

BLAIR, ANN, historian; BA, Harvard U., 1984; MPhil, U. Cambridge, 1985; MA, Princeton U., 1987, PhD, 1990. Instr. U. Calif., Irvine, 1992—96; prof. history Harvard U., 1996—. Contbr. articles numerous publ. Fellow Postdoc. fellow, NSF-NATO, 1990—91, NEH, 1996, MacArthur Found. fellow, 2002. Office: Harvard U Robinson 216 Cambridge MA 02138*

BLAIR, BEN, real estate company executive; JD, Washburn U., 1965. Chmn. Coldwell Banker Griffith & Blair Realtors, Topeka. Mem. bd. regents Washburn U., Kirkville, Mo.; trustee Washburn Endowment Assn., 1993—, past chmn. endowment bd. Office: Coldwell Banker Griffith & Blair 2222 SW 29th St Topeka KS 66611

BLAIR, BONNIE KATHLEEN, former professional speedskater, former Olympic athlete; b. Cornwall, N.Y., Mar. 18, 1964; d. Charlie and Eleanor Blair; m. David Cruikshank; 1 child, Grant B. Cruikshank Student, Mont. Tech. Univ. Mem. U.S. Olympic Team, Sarajevo, Yugoslavia, 1984; Gold medalist, 500m Speedskating, Bronze medalist 1,000m Calgary Olympic Games, 1988; Gold medalist, 500m Speedskating Albertville Olympic Games, 1992, Gold medalist, 1000m Speedskating, 1992; Gold medalist, 500m Speedskating Lillehammer Olympic Games, 1994, Gold medalist, 1000m Speedskating, 1994; pro tour speedskater, 1994-95; ret. from competitive speedskating, 1995; motivational speaker, 1995—. ABC sports commentator; motivational spkr.; founder Bonnie Blair Charitable Fund; active fundraiser Am. Brain Tumor Assn. Author: Bonnie Blair: A Winning Edge. Recipient James E. Sullivan award for Outstanding U.S. amateur athlete, 1993, Sportwoman of the Year, Sports Illustrated, 1994; named Female Athlete of Yr., AP, 1994; inducted into Nat. Speedskating Hall of Fame, Internat. Women's Sports Hall of Fame, US Olympic Hall of Fame. Achievements include 1st American woman in any sport to win gold medals in consecutive Winter Olympics; 1st American speedskater to win a gold medal in more than one Olympics. Most decorated female Olympian of all time -- five gold medals, six total. Office: Octagon Mgmt Ste 300 2 Union St Portland ME 04101*

BLAIR, BRUCE G., think-tank executive; b. Creston, Iowa, Nov. 16, 1947; BS, U. Ill., 1970; MS, Yale U., 1977, PhD, 1984. Project dir. Congl. Office Tech. Assessment, 1982-85; project leader Cornell U., Am. Acad. Arts and Scis., 1985-87; rschr. Brookings Inst., Washington, 1987-2000; pres., fgn. policy analyst Ctr. for Def. Info., Washington, 2000—. Vis. prof. Yale U.; vis. lectr. Princeton U. Author: Strategic Command and Control: Redefining the Nuclear Threat, 1985, The Logic of Accidental Nuclear War, 1993, Global Zero Alert for Nuclear Forces, 1995; contbg. author: The Nuclear Turning Point: A Blueprint for Deep Cuts and De-Alerting of Nuclear Weapons, 1999; co-editor: (with K. Gottfried) Crisis Stability and Nuclear War, 1988; contbr. chpts. to books and articles to profl. jours. With USAF. MacArthur Found. Prize fellow, 1999. Office: Ctr for Def Info 1779 Massachusetts Ave NW Washington DC 20036-2109

BLAIR, BRYCE, real estate company executive; BS in Civil Engring. magna cum laude, U. N.H.; MBA, Harvard U. Ptnr. Trammell Crow Residential, 1985—93; sr. v.p. devel., acquisitions and constrn. AvalonBay Cmtys., Inc., Alexandria, Va., COO, 1999—, pres., 2000—, CEO, 2001—, chmn. bd., 2002—. Mem.: Nat. Assn. Real Estate Investment Trusts (bd. govs.), Real Estate Roundtable, Nat. Multi Housing Coun., Urban Land Inst. Office: AvalonBay Communities Inc Ste 300 2900 Eisenhower Ave Alexandria VA 22314

BLAIR, DAVID CLARK, information scientist, educator; b. Salem, Oreg., May 23, 1947; s. Jay William and Jessica Blakney Blair; m. Barbara Kerekes, Oct. 3, 1978; children: Alain Kerekes, Christopher Kerekes. BA, Whitman Coll., 1968; PhD, U. Calif., 1976. Author: Language and Representation in Information Retrieval (named Best Info. Sci. Book of the Yr., 1991). Recipient Worldtech Technology award, Control Data Corp., 1984, Annual Quest for Tech. award, Inst. Sci. and Tech., 1983. Mem.: Am. Soc. Info. Sci. and Tech. (mem. editl. bd. 1989—, named Outstanding Internat. Rschr. of Yr. 1999, Best Refereed Paper of Yr. 1980). Office: Stephen M Ross School of Business The Univ of Michigan Ann Arbor MI 48109-1234 Office Phone: 734-763-5935. Home Fax: 734-936-0279; Office Fax: 734-936-0279. E-mail: dcblair@umich.edu.

BLAIR, DIKE, sculptor, painter; b. New Castle, Pa., 1952; Attended, Skowhegan Sch. Painting & Sculpture, Maine, 1974; B, U. Colo., 1975; attended, Whitney Mus. Ind. Study Program, NY, 1976; MFA, Sch. Art Inst. Chgo., 1977. One-man shows include, Nancy Lurie Gallery, Chgo., 1980, Stefanotti Gallery, NY, 1981, Serra Di Felice, NY, 1983, Christminster Gallery, NY, 1986, Baskerville + Watson, NY, 1986, Cash/Newhouse, NY, 1987, Galerie Hubert Winter, Vienna, Austria, 1987, Carl Solway Gallery, Cin., 1988, 121 Gallery, Antwerp, Belgium, 1988, Koury Wingate Gallery, NY, 1989, Ealan Wingate Gallery, NY, 1991, Donna Beam Gallery, Las Vegas, 1993, Daniel Newburg Gallery, NY, 1994, Galerie Hubert Winter, Vienna, Austria, 1995, Charleston Heights Art Ctr., Las Vegas, 1998, Feature, Inc., NY, 1998, 2001, NY Works on Paper, LA, 2001, Whitney Biennial Am. Art, Whitney Mus. Am. Art, 2004. Mailing: 235 E 11th St New York NY 10003 E-mail: dblair2@nyc.rr.com.

BLAIR, DONALD W., shoe manufacturing company executive; b. West Chester, Pa., Apr. 4, 1958; BS in Econ., U. Pa., 1980, MBA, 1981. CPA, N.Y. Sr. acct. Deloitte Haskins & Sells, 1981-84; sr. fin. analyst PepsiCo, Inc., 1984-85; mgr. fin. planning Pepsi-Cola USA, 1985-86, group mgr., bus. planning, 1986-88; fin. dir. Pepsi-Cola New England, 1988-90, Pepsi-Cola Japan, Tokyo, 1990-92; v.p., fin. Pepsi-Cola Asia, Hong Kong, 1992-96; v.p., planning PepsiCo, Pizza Hut divsn., 1996-97; sr. v.p., fin. The Pepsi Bottling Group Inc., 1997-99; v.p., CFO Nike Inc., Beaverton, Oreg., 1999—. Office: Nike Inc 1 Bowerman Dr Beaverton OR 97005-6453

BLAIR, EDWARD MCCORMICK, investment banker; b. Chgo., July 18, 1915; s. William McCormick and Helen Haddock (Bowen) B.; m. Elizabeth Graham Iglehart, June 28, 1941; children: Edward McCormick, Francis Iglehart. Grad., Groton Sch., 1934; BA, Yale U., 1938; MBA, Harvard U., 1940. With William Blair & Co., Chgo., 1946—, ptnr., 1950-61, mng. ptnr., 1961-77, sr. ptnr., 1977—. Bd. dirs. George M. Pullman Ednl. Found.; life trustee Coll. of Atlantic, Bar Harbor, Maine; life trustee U. Chgo., Rush-Presbyn.-St. Luke's Med. Ctr., Chgo., Art Inst. Chgo. Lt. comdr. USNR, 1941-46. Home: PO Box 186 Sheridan Rd Lake Bluff IL 60044 Office: William Blair & Co 222 W Adams St Chicago IL 60606-5307

BLAIR, FRED EDWARD, social services administrator; b. Huntington, W.Va., Oct. 6, 1933; s. Fred E. and Pearl Amy (King) B.; m. Lois Ann Thomas, Aug. 16, 1958; children: Lesli Winifred, Annlyn Paige, Carter Thomas. BBA, Marshall U., 1955; MA, U. Iowa, 1965. Cert. healthcare exec. Adminstrv. asst. Jefferson Med. Coll. Hosp., Phila., 1964-66; asst. adminstr. Barberton (Ohio) Citizen Hosp., 1966-67; sr. asst. adminstrn. U. Ala. Hosp. and Clinics, 1967-68; exec. dir. Ohio Valley Med. Ctr., Wheeling, W.Va., 1969-83; pres. Ohio Valley Health Svcs. and Edn. Corp., 1983-86; pres., chief exec. officer United Care Inc. (formerly Peoples Community Hosp. Authority), Wayne, Mich., 1986-90; pres. Blair Ltd., Inc., 1991—. Instr. health services mgmt. U. Ala., Birmingham; dir. W.Va. Hosp. Service, Inc. (Blue Cross); preceptor health adminstrn. George Washington U., Med. Coll. Va. Bd. dirs. W.Va. Health Systems Agy., treas., 1978; bd. dirs. W.Va. Heart Assn., Wheeling Country Day Sch.; mem. exec. com. W.Va. Regional Med. Program; elder Vance Meml. Presbyn. Ch.; elder Mt. Pleasant (S.C.) Presbyn. Ch. Fellow Am. Coll. Healthcare Adminstrs.; mem. Am. Coll. Healthcare Execs., Am. Hosp. Assn., W.Va. Hosp. Assn., Nat. League Nursing, Am. Assn. Mental Health Adminstrs., Am. Pub. Health Assn., Mich. Hosp. Assn. (legis. and pub. policy com., svc. corp. com., HAPAC team, com. on govt. relations), S.E. Mich. Health Council (vice chair com. on health facilities planning, trustee), SAR, Rotary.

BLAIR, GREGORY JOSEPH, artist, art educator; b. Edmonton, Alberta, Canada, Mar. 1, 1977; s. Barry Eugene and Sandra Anne Blair; m. Sara Ann Christensen, Nov. 6, 1977. MFA, U. ND, 2004; BFA, U. Lethbridge, 2001. Exhibitions include Man and Nature Photography Exhibition, Arts Quest Festival, Earthworks Now International Biennial, Discovering the Native Landscapes of the Mid Atlantic, Parallel 48, Northern Exposure, 6 x 6 Miniature Exhibition, Site Unseen, North Dakota Arts and Humanities Summit Student Art Exhibition. Recipient Best of Show, ND Arts Humanities Summit Student Art Exhbn., 2004; scholar Emma Prepiora Meml. Scholarship, U. ND, 2003—04, Mavourneen Anderson Fine Arts Scholarship, 2003—04, Ethel Harriet & Stella Haugan Art Scholarship, 2003—04, Neil C. MacDonald Scholarship, 2003, George S. Varsari Award Excellence in Sculpture, U. Lethbridge, 2001. Mem.: ND Mus. Art, Coll. Art Assn. Avocations: reading, music, camping. Personal E-mail: gregblair23@hotmail.com.com. E-mail: gregblair23@hotmail.com.

BLAIR, GUY, music educator; b. Fort Dodge, Iowa, Dec. 1, 1946; s. Donald F and Marjorie A Blair; m. Jane A Blair, June 16, 1969; children: Brenna J Dooley, Lindsy M. BA music edn., Ctrl. Coll., 1965—69; MA in music edn., Drake U., 1970—72. Dir. of bands Pella Cmty. H.S., Iowa, 1973—; interim dir. of bands Ctrl. Coll., Pella, 1982—83. Exec. dir. Iowa Music Educators Assn., Iowa, 1995—2001; pres. Iowa Bandmasters Assn., 1984—85; chair Iowa Alliance for Arts Edn., 1985—87; state pres. Internat. Assn. of Jazz Educators, Iowa. Fin. councillor Peace Luth. Ch., Pella, Iowa, 2004—. Recipient Disting. Svc. award, Iowa Music Educators, 2000, Hall of Fame, Pella C. of C., 2005. Mem.: Iowa Bandmasters Assn. (pres. 1983—84, Karl King award 1991), Iowa Music Educators (Disting. Svc. award 2000). Home: 1211 Big Rock Rd Pella IA 50219 Office: Pella Cmty HS 212 E University Pella IA 50219 Office Phone: 641-628-3870. Office Fax: 641-628-7402. Personal E-mail: dfb@iowatelecom.net. E-mail: pchsgfb@pella.k12.ia.us.

BLAIR, HARRY WALLACE, political science educator, consultant; b. Washington, Mar. 25, 1938; s. James Newell and Greta (Flintermann) B.; m. Barbara Ann Shailor, Dec. 26, 1981; 1 child, Emily Rebecca. AB in History, Cornell U., 1960; MA in Polit. Sci., Duke U., 1966, PhD in Polit. Sci., 1970. Instr. polit. sci. Colgate U., 1968-70; asst. prof. polit. sci. Bucknell U., Lewisburg, Pa., 1970-77, assoc. prof., 1977-83, prof., 1983—2000, chair dept., 1982—85, 1988—90, prof. emeritus, 2000—, chair dept., 1997—98; assoc. chair dept. Yale U., 2004—. Vis. fellow Ctr. for Internat. Studies, Cornell U., 1972-73, vis. assoc. prof. rural sociology and rsch. assoc., spring-summer 1979, vis. assoc. prof., 1980-81, vis. prof. rural sociology, fall 1987; rsch. assoc. So. Asian Inst., Sch. Internat. Affairs, Columbia U., spring-summer 1974; social analyst Bur. Sci. and Tech., Office of Rural Devel., U.S. Agy. for Internat. Devel., 1981-82, sr. social sci. analyst Ctr. for Devel. Info. and Evaluation, 1992-94, sr. democracy advisor Bur. for Policy and Program Coord., Ctr. for Devel. Info. and Evaluation, 1995, 96-97; vis. fellow Sch. Forestry and Environ. Studies, Yale U., spring-summer 1986, sr. rsch. scholar, lectr. polit. sci., 2001—; sr. democracy advisor global bur. Ctr. Democracy and Governance, Agy. Internat. Devel., 1998-2001. Contbr. articles to books and profl. jours. Lt. U.S. Army, 1961-63. Home: 58 Quarry Dock Rd Branford CT 06405-4654

BLAIR, JAMES PEASE, retired freelance photographer; b. Phila., Apr. 14, 1931; s. Jacob Jackson and Dorothy Flagg (Pease) B.; m. Patricia Carol Wohlgemuth, Aug. 13, 1964 (dec. Nov. 2000); children: Matthew Ward, David Alexander; m. Elise de Vries-Ostroff, May 4, 2002. BS, Ill. Inst. Tech., 1954. Reporter, film photographer Sta. WIIC-TV, Pitts., 1958-59; freelance photojournalist, 1959-62, 94—; staff photographer Nat. Geog. Soc., Washington, 1962-94; ret., 1994. Instr. Rochester Inst. Tech., 1978, Internat. Ctr. of Photography, N.Y.C., 1992, Maine Photog. Workshops, 1988-2004, disting. vis. prof. U. Mo., 1992. Photographer: Listen With The Eye, 1964, As We Live And Breathe, 1971, Our Threatened Inheritance, 1984, Wooden Fences, 1997; one-man shows in, Pitts., 1962, New Haven, 1977, Teheran, 1975, St. Louis, 1990, Washington Cosmos Club, 2000. Lt. (j.g.) USN, 1954-56. Poynter fellow Yale U., 1977; recipient Overseas Press Club Best Photog. Reporting from Abroad award, 1977 Mem. White House News Photographers Assn., Am. Soc. Picture Profls., Nat. Press Photographers Assn., Cosmos Club. Home: 5116 Lowell Ln NW Washington DC 20016-2608 also: 27 Washington St Middlebury VT 05753

BLAIR, JOHN, technology consultant; b. Budapest, Hungary, Dec. 5, 1929; came to U.S., 1950, naturalized, 1955; s. Eugene I. and Helen (Benedek) B.; m. Constance Smith Drown, Sept. 10, 1955; children: David E., Jennifer C. BS, MS, ScD, MIT. With Pacific Semiconductors/Ramo-Wooldridge, Culver City, Calif., 1955—57; elec. engring. faculty MIT, 1957-66; dir. corp. rsch. Raytheon Co., Lexington, Mass., 1966-94; pres. JBX Techs., Inc., Wayland, Mass., 1994—. Mem. energy R&D and nat. progress The White House, 1961; mem. Army Sci. Bd., Dept. Army, Washington, 1978-84, 86-90, 97-2005; rep. Indsl. Rsch. Inst., 1977-94, emeritus, 1994—; mem. adv. bd. Coll. Engring., U. Ill., Urbana, 1986-2004; mem. dean's adv. coun. Coll. Engring., U. Mass., Amherst, 1978-94; mem. vis. com. Sch. Elec. Engring. and Computer Sci., Poly. U., Bklyn., 1991-98; mem. adv. bd. Ctr. for Intelligent Controls, MIT-Harvard U.-Brown U., 1987-94; mem. industry and univ. govt. com. U. Calif., Berkeley, 1970-74, chmn., 1974; mem. vis. com. on elec. engring. and computer sci. MIT, 1970-73, mem. vis. com. on ocean engring., 1991-95, lectr. ocean engring., 1995-98; external rev. com. Materials Sci., Los Alamos Nat. Lab., 1995-99, chmn., 1999; adv. com. Ctr. for Engring. Sci. Advanced Rsch., Oak Ridge Nat. Lab., 1996-2002; advisor Idaho Nat. Engring. and Environ. Lab., 1998-2001; mem. coun. on energy engring. rsch. Dept. Energy, 1999-2002. State industry adv. coun. MIT Sea Grant Coll. Program, 1970—; mem. Nat. Sea Grant Rev. Panel, NOAA, Dept. Commerce, 1979-85. Recipient citations Sec. of Army, 1991, Sec. Def., 2001, Basic Energy Scis. Dept. Energy, 2001; Ford Found. fellow, 1960-61. Mem. Cosmos Club. Home: 25 Moore Rd Wayland MA 01778-1417

BLAIR, KATHIE LYNN, social worker; b. Oakland, Calif., Sept. 29, 1951; d. Robert Leon Webb and Patricia Jean (Taylor) Peterson; m. Terry Wayne Blair, Dec. 29, 1970 (div. 1972); 1 child, Anthony DeVault-Blair. Eligibility worker Dept. Social Services, San Jose, Calif., 1974-76; adult and family svcs. worker State of Oreg., Portland, 1977-90. Guest speaker welfare advocacy groups, Portland, 1987. Translator: Diary of Fannie Burkhart, 1991; contbr. articles to profl. jours.; developer word game for children. Mem. ACLU, AARP, Nat. Geog. Soc., A Brotherhood Against Totalitarian Enactments, Oreg. State Pub. Interest Rsch. Group, Nat. Headache Found., Clan Chattan Assn., Portland Highland Games Assn., Nature Conservancy, Nat. Wildlife Fedn., Harley Owners Group, Ladies of Harley, Sierra Club, Wilderness Soc., Defenders of Wildlife. Democrat. Avocations: history, women's studies, writing, photography, motorcycles. E-mail: goodfoot0929@yahoo.com.

BLAIR, M. WAYNE, lawyer; b. Spokane, Washington, Oct. 17, 1942; BS in Elec. Engr., U. Washington, 1965, JD, 1968. Bar: Wash. 1968. Mem. Wash. State Bd. for Jud. Adminstrn., 1995-2000. With USAF, 1968-72. Recipient

Helen M. Geisness award, 1987, President's award, 1990. Mem. ABA (Ho. of Dels. 1988-91), Am. Judicature Soc., Washington State Bar Assn. (bd. govs. 1991-94, pres. 1998-99, Lifetime Service award, 2004), Seattle-King County Bar Assn. (trustee 1981-83, pres. 1987-88). Office: 5500 Bank of America Twr 701 5th Ave Seattle WA 98105-7097

BLAIR, MARGARET MENDENHALL, economist, consultant, law educator; b. Bartlesville, Okla., Nov. 8, 1950; d. Harold Leroy and Mary Winifred (Simmons) Mendenhall; m. Forrest Randall Blair, May 29, 1971 (div. Sept. 1979); m. Roger Lisle Conner, June 22, 1991; 1 child, Elizabeth LeeAnn Conner. BA, U. Okla., 1973; postgrad., Harvard U., 1982-83; MA, MPhil, PhD, Yale U., 1989. Reporter Houston Chronicle, 1973-75; reporter, bur. mgr. Fairchild Publ., Houston, 1975-77; corr. Bus. Week, Houston, 1977-79, bur. chief, 1979-82; economist Fed. Res. Bank N.Y., NYC, 1985; rsch. asst. Yale U., New Haven, 1985-86, lectr., 1986-87; rsch. assoc. Brookings Instn., Washington, 1987-94, sr. fellow, 1995-99; dir. Brookings Project on Corps. and Human Capital, 1996-99; co-dir. Brookings Project on Intangible Sources of Value, 1998-2001; rsch. dir., vis. prof. Sloan-GULC project bus. inst. Georgetown U. Law Ctr., 2000—04; prof. law Vanderbilt U., Nashville, 2004—. Adj. faculty U. Md. Coll. Bus. and Mgmt., 1993—94; vis. prof. Georgetown U. Law Ctr., 1996—2004; steering com., rapporteur Woodstock Seminar Series on Bus. Ethics, Washington, 1989—90; subcoun. on capital allocation Competitiveness Policy Coun., 1993—96; rapporteur Salzburg (Austria) Seminar on Internat. Fin. Markets, 1989; steering com. time horizons project Coun. on Competitiveness, Washington, 1990; mem. Task Force on Restructuring America's Labor Market Instns., MIT/Sloan Sch. Mgmt., 1997—2001, World Econ. Forum Corp. Performance Coun., 1999—2003; non-resident sr. fellow Brookings Instn., 2000—04; bd. advisors George Washington U. Sloan Program on Bus. and Soc., 1998—2002; bd. dirs. Sonic Corp.; trustee Woodstock Theol. Ctr., 2001—04. Author: The Deal Decade Handbook, 1993, Ownership and Control: Rethinking Corporate Governance for the Twenty-first Century, 1995; co-author: Unseen Wealth: Report of the Brookings Task Force on Intangibles, 2001; editor: The Deal Decade: What Takeovers and Leveraged Buyouts Mean for Corporate Governance, 1993, Wealth Creation and Wealth Sharing: A Colloquium on Corporate Governance and Investments in Human Capital, 1996, Employees and Corporate Governance, 1999, The New Relationship Human Capital in the American Corporation, 2000; contbr. articles to profl. jours. Vol. Big Sisters Washington Met. Area, 1989-92; organizer neighborhood watch group, Washington, 1990; mem. bd. advisors Ctr. for Cmty. Interest, 1993-98; mem. bd. dir. Christ Edn. Rock Spring United Ch. Christ, 2000-03; mem. Arlington County Adv. Coun. Instrn., 1999-2003. Univ. fellow Yale U., 1983-86, Leo Model fellow Brookings Instn., 1987-88; rsch. grantee Boston U. Mfrs. Roundtable, 1990, Columbia U. Instnl. Investor Project, 1994, Alfred P. Sloan Found., 1995, 96, 98, 99. Mem.: ABA (assoc.), Am. Law Econs. Assn., Am. Econ. Assn. Avocations: ballet, religious studies, cooking. Office: Vanderbilt Univ Law Sch 131 21st St S Nashville TN 37203-1181

BLAIR, MARK ERIK, psychiatrist; b. Denver, Colo., Aug. 12, 1974; s. Joseph Wayne Blair and Linda Roberts. BA in chemistry, biology, psychology, Anderson U., 1996; MD, Ind. U. Sch. of Medicine, 2000. Lic. MD Ohio; cert. bd. cert. psychiatry Wright State U. Dept. Psychiatry, 2004. Physician, psychiatrist Mental Health Mgmt., Columbus, Ohio, 2000—, State of Ohio, Dept. Corrections, Columbus, 2003—, Unison Behavioral Health Group, Toledo, 2003—04. Cpt. USAF, 1997—2003. Mem.: AMA, Physicians for Social Responsibility, Am. Psychiatric Assn. Democrat. Avocations: tennis, sports card collecting. Home: 51 Buttles Ave Columbus OH 43215 E-mail: markeblairmd@aol.com.

BLAIR, MAUDINE, psychotherapist, communications executive, management consultant; d. Eugene Goode and Della Wright Blair. MA, U. Ga., Athens, 1964; PhD, Fla. State U., Tallahassee, 1969. Diplomate Am. Psychotherapy Assn.; CGP Nat. registry of Group Psychotherapists, cert. transactional analyst, lic. psychotherapist Fla., cert. relationship specialist. Assoc. dir. of counseling and pers. svcs. Fla. State U., Tallahassee, 1964—67; dir. and founder Blair's Counseling Svc., Tallahassee, 1970—, Blair's Counseling Satellite Ctr., Tifton, Ga., 1971—92, Tenn. Comm. & Mgmt. Inst., Townsend, Tenn., 1980—89, Blair's Lodge, Townsend, Tenn., 1981—89; founder, pres. Fla. Comm. & Mgmt. Inst., Tallahassee, 1972—; founder, co-dir. CEU Studies, LLC, Tallahassee, 2005—. Co-editor: Transactional Analysis Rsch. Index vol. I, 1976, Transactional Analysis Rsch. Index vol. II, 1979; contbr. articles to profl. jours. Fellow: Am. Orthopsychiatric Assn.; mem.: Fla. Assn. Marriage and Family Therapy (clin. mem.), Internat. Transactional Analysis (clin. mem.), Am. Psychol. Assn. (life), Am. Assn. Marriage and Family Therapy (life; clin. mem.), Am. Psychotherapy Assn. (diplomate), Am. Group Psychotherapy Assn. (clin. mem.). Avocations: reading, travel, writing. Office: Blair's Counseling Svc PO Box 12697 Tallahassee FL 32317 also: CEU Studies LLC PO Box 12337 Tallahassee FL 32317 Office Phone: 850-297-2190, 850-580-2600. E-mail: BlairCare@att.net, CEUStudios@att.net.

BLAIR, MICHAEL WALTER, lawyer; b. Balt., July 22, 1955; s. Joseph E. and Mary Christine (Hathaway) B.; m. Edith Baily Moore, Sept. 9, 1978; children: Edith Baily, Katherine Hathaway, Michael Walter Jr. BA, Yale U., 1977; JD, U. Chgo., 1981. Bar: N.Y. 1982. Assoc. Debevoise & Plimpton LLP, NYC, 1981-89, ptnr., 1989—, chair Corp. Dept. Bd. dirs. N.Y. Legal Aid Soc., 1992—. Mem. Country Club of Fairfield. Office: Debevoise & Plimpton LLP 919 Third Ave New York NY 10022 Office Phone: 212-909-6775. E-mail: mwblair@debevoise.com.

BLAIR, PHYLLIS E., artist; b. N.Y.C., Oct. 5, 1922; d. Franz Joseph and Marian Jane (Burke) Emmerich; m. Thomas Slingluff Blair, Sept., 17, 1946 (dec. May, 2003); children: Joan Dix, George Dike, Hadden Slingluff. Student, Skidmore Coll., 1940-42, Art Students League, 1945, Westminster Coll., 1970-72, Bennington Coll., 1989. Asst. art dept. Skidmore Coll., Saratoga Springs, N.Y., 1940-42; art illustrator & engring. draftsman GE, Schenectady, N.Y., 1942-44, Bell Labs., N.Y.C., 1944-46; elem tchr. Clinton, Tenn., 1946-47. One-woman shows include Hoyt Inst. Fine Arts, New Castle, Pa., 1971, 93, Butler Inst. Am. Art, Youngstown, Ohio, 1982, Westminster Coll., New Wilmington, Pa., 1983, Butler Inst. Am. Art, Salem, Ohio, 1994, Cornell Mus., Delray Beach, Fla., 2004-05. Art curator Human Svcs. Ctr., New Castle, 1968-89, Jameson Health Sys., 1978-99, Jameson Care Ctr., Jameson Retirement Pl., 1978-99, Jameson Rehab Ctr., 1978-99, Almira Home, New Castle, 1990-99, Lawrence County Children and Youth Svcs., 2000, The Soup Kitchen, Boynton Beach, Fla., 2000; founding mem. Nat. Mus. of Women in the Arts, Washington, D.C. Recipient Benjamin Rush award Pa. Med. Soc., 1991. Mem. Hoyt Inst. Fine Arts (chair art com. & permanent collection 1967-99, trustee, 1967-99, Blair Sculpture Walkway named in her honor 1996), Am. Heart Assn. (Disting. Svc. award Lawrence County chpt. 1978). Avocations: golf, painting, sculpting. Home (Summer): 1611 Cold Spring Rd Williamstown MA 01267-2771

BLAIR, ROBERT ALLEN, lawyer; b. Suffolk, Va., June 25, 1946; s. Thomas Francis and Ossie Blair; m. Linda Britt, Dec. 27, 1970; children: Robert Allen II, Thomas Edward. BA in Math., Coll. William and Mary, 1968; JD, U. Va., 1973. Bar: Va. 1974, U.S. Dist. Ct. Mass. 1974, U.S. Ct. Appeals (D.C. cir.) 1976, U.S. Dist. Ct. D.C. 1980. Assoc. Goodwin, Procter & Hoar, Boston, 1973-74, Surrey & Morse, Washington, 1974-78, ptnr., 1979-81; mng. ptnr. Anderson, Hibey & Blair, Washington, 1981-95; ptnr., chair govt. practice group Manatt, Phelps & Phillips, 1995-99; co-chmn., gen. counsel GlobalOptions, LLC, Washington, 1998-99; pres. The Blair Law Firm P.C., Washington, 1999—. Chmn. nat. adv. bd. IPG Photonics Corp., 1999—, vice chmn. bd. dirs., 2000—; trustee Winkler Family Trust, 1996—. Mem. editorial bd. Law Rev. U. Va., 1971-73. Chmn. bd. Inst. on Terrorism and Subnat. Conflict, Washington, 1982-95; co-counsel Citizens for Dem. Alternatives in 1980, Washington, 1979-81; mem. adv. panel on fgn. policy, def. and arms control Dem. Nat. Com., Washington, 1982-85; mem. drafting team for fgn. policy, def. and arms control issue workshop Dem. Nat. Conf., Phila., 1982, mem. bus. coun., 1988-90, 94—, mng. trustee, 1994-95; mem. Senate Dem. Roundtable, Washington, 1983-2000; mem. Senate Dem. Leadership Circle, Washington, 1983-2000; vice chmn. Potomac Group, Washington, 1983-84, chmn., 1984-85; mem. adv. council Dem. Platform Com., Washington, 1984; spl. counsel 1984 Dem. Nat. Conv., San Francisco, 1984; spl. counsel to nat. fin. chmn. Dem. Nat. Com., Washington, 1984-85, mem. fin. bd. dirs., 1983-85, 88; mem. Nat. Dem. Club, Senate Dem. Majority Trust, 1992-99; vice chmn. Washington Fgn. Affairs Soc., 1984-87; mem. Gov.'s Econ. Adv. Council, Va., 1986-94; commr. Va. Port Authority, Commonwealth Va., 1991-96, vice chmn. finance/planning com., 1992-94, chmn., 1994-96; chmn. S Corp. Assn., Washington 1996-2000, chmn. emeritus, 2000—, chmn. reform project, 1993-96; advisory bd. Thomas Jefferson Program Pub. Policy, 1996—, chmn. devel. com., 1999—; bd. dirs. Everybody Wins, 1997-2000; mem. bd. of vis. William and Mary, 2004—. Named to Outstanding Young Men Am., U.S. Jaycees, 1976; recipient Alumni Medallion award William and Mary Coll., 2005 Mem.: ABA. Home: 4936 Rodman St NW Washington DC 20016-3239

BLAIR, SAMUEL RAY, lawyer; b. Aurora, Ill., June 19, 1941; s. Donald R. and Jeanette E. (Quirin) B.; m. Jean Jordan, Nov. 25, 1964 (div. 1977); children: Alissa Lynn Motzfeldt, Jason Jordan. BA, U. Denver, 1963; JD, Lewis & Clark Coll., 1969. Bar: Oreg. 1969, Hawaii 1990. Assoc. Hershizer, Mitchell et al, Portland, Oreg., 1970-73; pvt. practice law Salem, Oreg., 1973—, Koloa, Hawaii, 1990—. Adj. prof. law Willamette U., Salem, 1985—. Mem. Marion County Bar Assn. (pres. 1985), Oreg. State Bar Assn., Kauai Bar Assn., Hawaii Bar Assn., Hawaii Def. Counsel Assn., Hawaii Trial Lawyers Assn., Assn. Trial Lawyers Am., Hospice, Million Dollar Advocates Forum. Avocations: travel, reading, trekking, martial arts (aikido). Office: 2360 Kiahuna Plantation Dr Koloa HI 96756-9713

BLAIR, SHERRY ANN, psychotherapist, educator; b. Belleville, N.J., Dec. 17, 1961; d. Edward Joseph Blair and Barbara Ann Ingham; 1 child, Michael Joseph. BA, Rutgers U., 1997; MSSW, Columbia U., 2000; postgrad., North Ctrl. U., Prescott, Ariz., 2003—. LCSW NJ. Transitional housing & fin. coord. Manavi, Inc, Union, NJ, 1998—99; social worker, psychotherapist Women's Counseling & Psychol. Svcs., Verona, NJ, 2000—01; social worker, therapist Delta T-Group, Iselin, NJ, 2000—02; psychotherapist, social worker Assocs. in Counseling, Tng. & Psychol. Svcs., Clifton, NJ, 2000—; case mgr., family violence clinician Women Rising, Inc., Jersey City, 2001; dir., adminstr. Horizon Behavioral Health Care, Prospect Park, NJ, 2001—. Corp. cons., dir. Starbound, Inc., Lanoka Harbor, NJ, 2000—; bus. cons. Synergy Life Coaching & Psychotherapy Svcs., Montclair, NJ, 2000—; adj. prof. Women's Studies Program Rutgers U., Newark, 2000—; organizer confs., workshops in field; exec. inspirational dir. Innovative Specialists Inspirational Svcs. Crisis responder-World Trade Ctr. Crisis Care Network-Delta T Group, Iselin, 2001; field organizer NASW-PACE N.J. Chpt., Hamilton, 2002. Recipient Beth Niemi award for work for women's studies, Rutgers U. Women's Studies Program, 1997; grantee Office on Women's Health, HHS, 1997. Mem.: NASW (clin. social work supr.), EMDR Inst., Internat. Critical Incident Stress Found., Am. Acad. Experts in Traumatic Stress (bd. cert. expert, diplomate), So. Poverty Law Ctr., Columbia U. Sch. Social Work Alumni Assn., Amnesty Internat., Phi Beta Kappa, Psi Chi. Office: Horizon Behavioral Health Care 316 N 6th St Prospect Park NJ 07508 Office Phone: 973-746-0333. E-mail: sherryblair@comcast.net.

BLAIR, SYLVIA H., computer systems project engineer, small business owner; BS in Physics, Lamar U., 1976. Computer resources project engr. on F-16 and F-22 fighter aircraft Ft. Worth divsn. Gen. Dynamics, 1979—89. Session chmn., tutorials chmn. AIAA/IEEE Digital Avionic Systems Conf., 1983—86; conf. chmn., tech. program chmn. AIAA Aerospace Engring. Conf. and Show, L.A., 1983—85; chmn. AIAA Digital Avionic Tech. Com., 1987—89. Min. Higher Way Ministries, Grapevine, Tex., 1995. Recipient Navy Superior Pub. Svc. medal, U.S. Sec. of the Navy, 1988. Avocations: writing, reading, fishing, travel. Office: Ambassador Consulting PO Box 3338 Grapevine TX 76099 Office Phone: 972-304-5580. E-mail: ambassadorconsulting@earthlink.net.

BLAIR, THOMAS DELANO, museum administrator; b. Plum Branch, S.C., Apr. 8, 1946; s. Richard and Evangeline B.; m. Frances V. Veney, 1973; children: Jayson T., Todd J. BS in Bus. Adminstrn., S.C. State Coll., 1967; MBA, U. Md., 1978. CPA, Md., Cert. Internal Auditor. Asst. bank examiner FDIC, Balt., 1967, 71; auditor U.S. Army Audit Agy., Linthicum Hghts., Md., 1971-72, Dept. Defense, Arlington, Va., 1973-74; supr. mgmt. analyst U.S. Gen. Acctg. Office, Washington, 1974-79; dir. office of inspector gen. Johnson Space Ctr. NASA Goddard Space Flight Ctr., Houston, Washington, Greenbelt, Md., 1979-84; regional mgr. Office of Inspector Gen., U.S. Dept. Vet. Affairs, Atlanta, 1984-90; inspector gen. Smithsonian Instn., Washington, 1990—. Office: Smithsonian Instn 750 9th St NW Washington DC 20560-0905 E-mail: tblair@oig.si.edu.

BLAIR, VIRGINIA DEVOTO, music educator; b. Santa Rosa, Calif., Sept. 26, 1950; d. Albert Gugliamo and Thelma Helen Devoto; m. Ted Leroy Blair, June 15, 1974; children: Eric Tobias, Rebecca Christine. AA, Santa Rosa Jr. Coll., 1970; BA, Calif. State, 1973. Music tchr. San Juan Unified Sch. Dist., Sacramento, 1976; tchr. asst. Sacramento (Calif.) Montessori, 1976—79; music tchr. Concordia Montessori Sch., Concord, Calif., 1990—2004; pvt. music tchr. self-employed, Concord, 1990—. Violinist Santa Rosa Symphony, Santa Rosa, Calif., 1967—70, Sacramento Symphony, Sacramento, 1971—74. Finalist 2nd place winner, Press Democrat Etude Contest, 1967; recipient 1st place winner, 1968; scholarship, Calif. State, 1970. Mem.: Nat. Piano Guild. Avocations: gardening, scrapbooks, jogging, reading, informal piano and violin performing. Home: 4129 Cheshire Dr Concord CA 94521 Office Phone: 925-408-6115. Office Fax: 925-459-0995. E-mail: gdb564@yahoo.com.

BLAIR, WILLIAM F., elementary school educator; b. Centralia, Wash., Sept. 1, 1950; s. George H. Blair and Edythe J. Hail; m. Denise L. Boman, Sept. 10, 1971; children: Sara N., Mindy F. BA in Edn., Seattle Pacific U., 1972; MEd, U. Portland, 1990. 1st gr. tchr. Chehalis Sch. Dist., Wash., 1972—75, Centralia Sch. Dist., Wash., 1975—78; early childhood educator (k-2) Chehalis Sch. Dist., Wash., 1978—. Early childhood presenter, 1995—. Coun. mem. St. John Luth. Ch., ELCA, Chehalis, Wash., 1976—2005. Recipient Christa McCauliffe Award for Excellence in Edn., State of Wash., 1995. Mem.: NEA. Home: 736 NW Ohio Chehalis WA 98532 Office: Cascade Elem Sch 89 SW Third St Chehalis WA 98532 Office Phone: 360-807-7215. Personal E-mail: dbblair71@msn.com.

BLAIR, WILLIAM GRANGER, retired reporter; b. Chgo., Nov. 17, 1925; s. William Mitchell and Martha (Granger) B.; m. Sue Cunningham, Apr. 19, 1952 (div.); children: Robert, Bruce (dec.), Laura; m. Ellen Lopin, Sept. 29, 1970. AB in English cum laude, Princeton U., 1950. Reporter Kansas City (Mo.) Star, 1950-52; mem. staff N.Y. Times, 1953-90. Fgn. corr., Paris, 1956-62, London, 1965-67, bur. chief, Jerusalem, 1962-65, mgr. employee communications, 1968, mgr. pub. relations, 1969-70, dir. pub. relations, 1970-73, broadcast corr., 1973-79, met. reporter, 1980-90. Served with USMCR, 1943-46, PTO. Mem. reporting team whose news coverage of regional flood helped to earn Pulitzer award for The Kansas City Star, 1952; corr. in France and Algeria when N.Y. Times won 1st Pulitzer prize awarded specifically to a fgn. news staff for internat. reporting, 1958. Mem. Ivy Club. Home: 425 E 58th St New York NY 10022 Personal E-mail: wblair@nyc.rr.com.

BLAIR, WILLIAM MCCORMICK, JR., lawyer; b. Chgo., Oct. 24, 1916; s. William McCormick and Helen (Bowen) B.; m. Catherine Gerlach, Sept. 9, 1961; 1 son, William McCormick III (dec.). AB, Stanford U., 1940; LL.B., U. Va., 1947. Bar: Ill. 1947, D.C. 1972. Assoc. firm Wilson & McIlvaine, Chgo., 1947-50; adminstrv. asst. to Gov. Adlai E. Stevenson of Ill., 1950-52; ptnr. firm Stevenson, Rifkind & Wirtz, Chgo., 1955-61, Paul, Weiss, Rifkind, Wharton & Garrison, N.Y.C., 1957-61; U.S. ambassador to Denmark, 1961-64, to Philippines, 1964-67; gen. dir. John F. Kennedy Ctr., 1968-72; ptnr. firm Surrey & Morse, Washington, 1978-84, of counsel, 1984-86. Bd. dirs. Am.-Scandinavian Found., N.Y.C.; v.p. bd. dirs. Albert and Mary Lasker Found., N.Y.C., 1968-98. Capt. USAAF, 1942-46. Decorated Bronze Star U.S.; officer Order of Crown, Belgium; Order of Sikatuna, Philippines; comdr. cross Order of Dannebrog 1st class, Denmark). Mem. Am. Coun. Ambs. (vice chmn., pres. 1985-89), River Club (N.Y.C.), Phi Delta Phi. Address: 2510 Foxhall Rd NW Washington DC 20007-1123 also: 435 E 52nd St New York NY 10022

BLAIS, ROGER NATHANIEL, physics professor, academic administrator; b. Duluth, Minn., Oct. 3, 1944; s. Eusebe Joseph and Edith Seldina (Anderson) B.; m. Mary Louise Leclerc, Aug. 2, 1971; children: Christopher Edward, Laura Louise. BA in Physics and French Lit., U. Minn., 1966; PhD in Physics, U. Okla., 1971; cert. in computer programming, Tulsa Jr. Coll., 1981; cert. in bus., UCLA, 1986. Registered profl. engr., Okla. Instr. physics Westark C.C., Ft. Smith, Ark., 1971-72; asst. prof. physics and geophys. scis Old Dominion U., Norfolk, Va., 1972-77; asst. prof. engring. physics U. Tulsa, 1977-81, assoc. prof., 1981-98, prof., 1998—; assoc. dir. Tulsa U. Artificial Lift Projects, 1983—98, chmn. physics, 1986-88, vice-provost, 1989-92, provost, v.p. acad. affairs, 1998—. Contbr. articles to profl. jours. Active Leadership Okla., 2002—03; mem. Leadership Okla. XVI, 2003; bd. dirs. Light Opera Okla., 2003—, Hillcrest Splty. Hosps., 2003—. Fellow Instrumentation Sys. and Automation Soc. (dir. test measurement divsn. 1995-97, v.p. automation and tech. dept. 2003-04); mem. AAAS, AAUP, NSPE, Am. Phys. Soc., Am. Geophys. Union, Soc. Petroleum Engrs., Am. Assn. Physics Tchrs., Am. Soc. Engring. Edn., N.Y. Acad. Scis., Iron Wedge Soc., Phi Beta Kappa, Sigma Xi, Sigma Pi Sigma, Tau Beta Pi, Phi Kappa Phi. Home: 5348 E 30th Pl Tulsa OK 74114-6314 Office: U Tulsa Office of Provost 600 S College Ave Tulsa OK 74104-3139 Office Phone: 918-631-2554. Personal E-mail: rblais71@cox.net. Business E-Mail: roger-blais@utulsa.edu.

BLAISE, CLARK LEE, writer, educator; b. Fargo, N.D., Apr. 10, 1940; s. Léo Roméo Blais and Anne Marion Vanstone; m. Bharati Mukherjee, Sept. 19, 1963; children: Bart Anand, Bernard Sudhir. BA, Denison U., 1961, D (hon.), 1979; MFA, U. Iowa, 1964; Doctorate (hon.), McGill U., 2004. Prof. Concordia U., Montreal, Que., Can., 1966-78, York U., Toronto, Ont., Can., 1978-80, Skidmore Coll., Saratoga Springs, N.Y., 1980-84; vis. prof. Emory U., Atlanta, 1984-85, U. Calif., Berkeley, 1998-2000; adj. prof. Columbia U., N.Y.C., 1986-89, NYU, N.Y.C., 1986-89; prof., dir. internat. writing U. Iowa, Iowa City, 1990-98, Southampton Coll., L.I. U., 2002—05. Book reviewer, lectr., presenter workshops in field. Author: A North American Education, 1973, Tribal Justice, 1974, Days and Nights in Calcutta, 1977, Lunar Attractions, 1979, Lusts, 1982, Resident Alien, 1985, The Sorrow the the Terror, 1987, Man and His World, 1992, I Had a Father: a post-modern autobiography, 1993, Here, There and Everywhere: Modern Canadian, Australian, American and Post Modernist Theory, 1994, If I Were Me, 1997, New and Selected Stories (4 vols.), 2000-2004, Time-Lord, 2001; contbr. stories, essays to over 90 anthologies. Recipient award NEA, Guggenheim Found., Can. Coun., St. Lawrence award, Great Lakes Colls. award, Books in Can. First Novel award, Book of Yr. award Can. Booksellers, 1995, Pearson prize, 2002. Avocation: languages. Home: 130 Rivoli St San Francisco CA 94117 Fax: (415) 759-9810. E-mail: clarquito@aol.com.

BLAKE, ALLEN H., bank executive; b. Chgo., 1942; Student, Washington U., 1964, student, 1965. Joined First Bank, Inc., St. Louis, 1984—, sr. v.p., CFO, 1984—99, COO, 1998—2003, pres., 1999—, CFO, 2001—05, CEO St. Louis, 2003—. Office: First Banks Inc 135 N Meramec Ave Saint Louis MO 63105 Office Phone: 314-854-4600.*

BLAKE, BUD (JULIAN WATSON), cartoonist; b. Nutley, N.J., Feb. 13, 1918; s. George Wilbur and Hazel (Metcalfe) B.; m. Doris Gaskill, Jan. 4, 1941; children: Julian G., Mariana. Student, Nat. Acad. Design, 1935-36. Sketch artist, art dir., exec. art dir. Kudner Agy., N.Y.C., 1937-43, 46-54. Cartoonist: Ever Happen To You, syndicated by King Features; also free lance cartooning for various mags. and ads, 1954-65; cartoonist: syndicated comic strip Tiger, 1965—; Paperback cartoon books include Tiger, Tiger Turns On; others. Served with inf. AUS, 1943-46. Mem. Nat. Cartoonists Soc. (Best Humor Strip award 1971, 78, 2000), Newspaper Features Coun. Home and Office: PO Box 146 Damariscotta ME 04543-0146

BLAKE, CATHERINE C., judge; b. Boston, July 27, 1950; d. John Ballard and Jean Place (Adams) B. BA magna cum laude, Radcliffe Coll., 1972; JD cum laude, Harvard Law Sch., 1975. Bar: Mass. 1975, Md. Ct. Appeals 1977, U.S. Ct. Appeals (4th cir.) 1977, U.S. Dist. Ct. Md. 1977, D.C. 1979. Assoc. Palmer & Dodge, Boston, 1975-77; asst. U.S. atty. Dist. of Md., Balt., 1977-83, first asst. U.S. atty., 1983-85, 86-87, U.S. atty. (court-appointed), 1985-86; U.S. magistrate judge U.S. Dist. Ct. Md., Balt., 1987-95, U.S. dist. ct. judge, 1995—. Mem.: FBA, Fed. Judges' Assn., Nat. Assn. of Women Judges, Md. Bar Assn., Bar Assn. Baltimore City. Office: US Courthouse 101 W Lombard St Ste 7310 Baltimore MD 21201-2639

BLAKE, D. STEVEN, lawyer; b. Saginaw, Mich., June 2, 1940; BA, Mich. State U., 1963; JD, U. Calif., Davis, 1971. Bar: Calif. 1972. Sr. ptnr. Downey Brand LLP, Sacramento, 1971—. Adj. prof. law U. Pacific, 1998-2000. Co-author: California Real Estate Finance and Construction Law, 1995. Mem. ABA (bus. law sect.), Am. Arbitration Assn. (arbitrator), State Bar Calif. (co-chair corp. com., sect., fin. instns. com., bus. law sect., panelist, presenter numerous seminars Calif. State Bar Continuing Edn. Bar 1981-91, co-chair corps. com. bus. law sect. 1997), Yolo County Bar Assn. Office: Downey Brand LLP 555 Capitol Mall Ste 1050 Sacramento CA 95814-4601 Office Phone: 916-444-1000.

BLAKE, DAVID GORDON, lawyer; b. Bryn Mawr, Pa., July 27, 1946; s. Alton David and Eleanore (Lavery) Gordon; m. Barbara Clemens Trimble, Aug. 7, 1976; children: Chad G., Scott B. BA, Tulane U., 1969; JD, Temple U., 1973. Bar: Pa. 1973, U.S. Supreme Ct. 1979. Ptnr. Cramp, D'Iorio, McConchie & Forbes, Media, Pa., 1973-96, Beatty, Cramp, Kauffman and Lincke, Media, 1996—2002, Beatty Lincke, Media, 2002—. Solicitor Radnor Twp., Pa., 2000—. Editor Del. County Legal Jour., 1980. Pres. Responsible Living Ltd., Media, 1980-81; bd. dirs. Fox Valley Community Assn., Glen Mills, Pa., 1984-86; mem. Rep. com., Radnor Twp., Pa., 1988-2000; v.p. Ithan PTO, 1989-90; pres. Radnor Soccer Club, 1989-96; treas. Radnor-Wayne Little League, 1989; mem. Nat. Rep. Presdl. Task Force. Named Man of Yr. Wayne area Jaycees, 1976. Mem. Del. County Bar Assn. (bd. dirs. 1986-88, 98-2000), Guy de Furia Am. Inns of Ct. Avocations: reading, coaching, teaching. Home: 23 Oakmont Pl Media PA 19063-1923 Office: Beatty Lincke PO Box 901 Media PA 19063-0901 Business E-Mail: DBlake@beattylincke.com.

BLAKE, DOUGLAS MUNRO, music educator, lyricist, musicologist; b. Quincy, Ill., Sept. 24, 1955; s. Earl Clement Jr. and Elizabeth (Van Horne) Blake; m. Sandra Sue Schutt-Stejskal (div.); 1 child, Jarrett Ethan 1 stepchild, Seth Stejskal. Student, Oakton C.C., Morton Grove, Ill., 1974—75. Ind. guitar tchr., Ill., 1975—; guitar tchr. Wilmette (Ill.) Park Dist., 1976—78, Old Town Sch. Folk Music, Chgo., 1983—84, Olsen's Musicland, Palatine, Ill., 1984—91; music tchr. Ridgeville Park Dist., Evanston, Ill., 1992; guitar tchr. Waukegan (Ill.) Park Dist., 1998—, Great Lake Music, Mundelein, Ill., 1998—. Musicologist; performer WLUW, WBEZ, ECTV TCI. Musician CDs; author: musical instruction books, transcriptions, arrangements, poetry chapbooks, humor, autobiography. Subject of radio and TV documentaries. Mem.: BMI. Avocations: pool, frisbee, walking, graphic art, learning Spanish. Office: Blake 'n' Blue PO Box 713 Wilmette IL 60091

BLAKE, FRANCIS STANTON, retail executive, lawyer; b. Boston, July 30, 1949; s. George Baty and Rosemary (Shaw) B.; m. Anne McChristian, Jan. 1, 1977; children: Francis S., Margaret D. BA, Harvard U., 1971; JD, Columbia U., 1976. Bar: D.C. 1978. Law clk. to presiding justice, Washington, 1976-77, 1977-78; assoc. Leva, Hawes, Symington, Washington, 1978-81; dep. counsel Vice Pres. George Bush, Washington, 1981-83; ptnr. Swidler

& Berlin, Washington, 1983-85; gen. counsel EPA, Washington, 1985—88; v.p., gen. counsel GE Power Systems, Schenectady, NY, 1991—95, v.p., bus. devel. & alliances, 1995—98, v.p., bus. devel., 1998—2000; sr. v.p., corp. bus. devel. Gen. Electric Co., 2000—01; exec. v.p., bus. devel. & corp. ops. The Home Depot Inc., 2002—; dep. sec. U.S. Dept. Energy, Washington. Mem. bd. dirs. The Southern Co., 2004- Republican. Episcopalian. Office: The Home Depot Inc 2455 Paces Ferry Rd NW Atlanta GA 30339-4024

BLAKE, GEORGE ROWLAND, soil scientist, educator, environmental scientist, researcher; b. Provo, Utah, Mar. 14, 1918; s. Samuel Henry and Annie Matilda (Bevan) B.; m. Kathryn M. Sumsion, Feb. 26, 1941; children: Carla Paul (dec.), Rowland, Lorraine Blake Phillips, Henry; m. Helen M. Patten, May 25, 1985. BA, Brigham Young U., 1943; PhD, Ohio State U., 1949. Missionary LDS Ch., Germany, 1937-39; with FBI, Washington, 1941-42; research fellow, teaching asst. Ohio State U., Columbus, 1946-49; asst. prof., asst. research specialist Rutgers U., New Brunswick, N.J., 1949-55; assoc. prof. dept. soil sci. U. Minn., St. Paul, 1955-60, prof., 1960-84, prof. emeritus, 1984—, dir. Water Resources Research Ctr., 1979-84. NSF sr. postdoctoral fellow, Braunschweig, Fed. Republic of Germany, 1962-63; Fulbright guest prof. U. Hohenheim, Fed. Republic of Germany, 1970-71; Ford Found. cons., Chile, 1967; guest prof. U. Keszthely, Hungary, 1974, U. Warsaw, Poland, 1981; USAID cons., Morocco, 1979-88; adj. prof. Institut Agronomique et Veterinaire Hassan II Rabat Morocco, 1982-88; guest prof. Humboldt U., Berlin, German Dem. Republic, 1986; Benson Inst. cons., Guatemala, 1990, 94. Contbr. articles to profl. jours. Pub. affairs vol. LDS Ch., Frankfurt, Germany, 1996-97. Recipient Georgicon award U. Keszthely, 1974, Müncheberg Plaque Acad. of Sci., German Dem. Republic., Spl. Emeritus Recognition award Brigham Young U. Emeritus Assn., 1996. Fellow Am. Soc. Agronomy, Soil Sci. Soc. Am.; mem. Internat. Soc. Soil Sci., Soil Sci. Soc. Am., Soil Conservation Soc. Am., Sigma Xi, Gamma Sigma Delta, Omicron Delta Kappa Home: 2215 N 1400 E Provo UT 84604-2103 E-mail: grblake@gohomenet.net.

BLAKE, GERALD RUTHERFORD, retired banker; b. Knoxville, Tenn., Apr. 2, 1939; s. Roy Carl and Katherine Marie (Rutherford) B.; m. Jeanne Avonne Jones, May 11, 1962; children: Robert Alan, Douglas Mark. Student, U. Tenn., 1957-58, Sch. Bank Adminstrn., U. Wis., 1971-73. With Miller's. Inc., Knoxville, 1959—62, First Tenn. Bank, Knoxville, 1963—, eastern regional bldg. mgr., 1973—. Vice-chmn. planning com. Knoxville United Way, 1973—; pres. Ramsey Cmty. Club, 1966-67, Ramsey Elem. Sch. PTO, 1976-80; bd. dirs. Planned Parenthood Assn., 1976-77. Mem. Am. Inst. Banking, Bank Adminstrn. Inst. (pres., dir. Smoky Mountain chpt. 1976-77, state dir. 1977-79, 2d vice-chmn. Tenn. Title XX com.) Baptist. Home: 5233 Straw Plains Pike Knoxville TN 37914-6340 Office: 800 S Gay St Knoxville TN 37929-9729 *I always seem to be caught between the old and the new-in the middle of change from one accepted method or life-style to the new method or life-style, which has yet to be fully accepted. Perhaps everyone in every age is at the same situation. The time is upon us and the need is clear for a return to individualism and self-reliance, and a return to basic moral and religious principles. In doing so, one may just find the answers to most of life's problems.*

BLAKE, JAMES RILEY, professional tennis player; b. Yonkers, NY, Dec. 28, 1979; Student, Harvard U., 1998—99. Pro tennis player ATP Tour, 1999—; model IMG Models, 2002—. Mem. U.S. Davis Cup Team, 2001—03. Achievements include 2 career singles titles, 5 doubles titles. Office: c/o ATP Tour 201 ATP Boulevard Ponte Vedra Beach FL 32082*

BLAKE, JEFF, professional football player; b. Daytona Beach, Fla., Dec. 4, 1970; s. Emory Blake. Student, East Carolina U. With N.Y. Jets, 1992-93; quarterback Cin. Bengals, 1994-2000, New Orleans Saints, 2000—01, Baltimore Ravens, 2002, Arizona Cardinals, 2002—04, Philadelphia Eagles, 2004—. Selected to Pro Bowl, 1995. Home: 11513 Warbler Ledge Austin TX 78738-6007

BLAKE, JEREMY, artist; b. 1971; BFA, Sch. Art Inst. Chgo., 1993; MFA, Cal-Arts, 1995. One-man shows include One Hit Wonder, Work on Paper Inc., LA, 1999, Bungalow 8, Contemporary Arts Ctr., Cin., 2000, Angel Dust, XYZ, Toronto, Can., 2001, Mus. Contemporary Art, San Diego, 2002, Am. Mus. Moving Image, Astoria, NY, 2003, The 59th Minute: Video Art, Time Sq. Astrovision, NYC, 2003, Autumn Almanac, Feigen Contemporary, NY, 2003, Sister, LA, 2004, Galerie Ghislaine Hussenot, Paris, 2004, Centro de Arte Caja de Burgos, Spain, 2004, exhibited in group shows at Heaven's in the Backseat of My Cadillac, Name Gallery, Chgo., 1995, History of Glamour, Works on Paper Inc., LA, 1998, Fifteen, Lobby Gallery, Deutshe Bank, NY, 1999, Maximal Minimal, Feigen Contemporary, NY, 2000, Whitney Biennial Am. Art, Whitney Mus. Am. Art, 2000, 2002, 2004, BitStreams, 2001, Looking at Am., Yale U. Art Gallery, New Haven, Conn., 2002, Animations, Kunst-Werke, Berlin, 2003, Breathtaking, Art Inst. Boston, Lesley U., 2004, One Channel Only, Atrium Gallery, U. Conn. Sch. Fine Arts, 2004, Floor to Ceiling/Wall to Wall, Wadsworth Atheneum Mus. Art, Hartford, Conn., 2004. Recipient Interactive Design Rev. Medal, I.D. Mag., 1999, 79th ann. Directors Club Award for Broadcast Design & Animation, 2000; NY Found. Arts Fellowship, 1999. Mailing: c/o Feigen Contemporary Gallery 535 West 20th St New York NY 10011*

BLAKE, JOHN EDWARD, retired car rental company executive; b. Chgo., Aug. 9, 1933; s. Edward Aloysius and Laura (Schlichter) B.; m. Joan Patricia Kautz, Aug. 28, 1965; children: Kathryn, John, Amy. LLB, De Paul U., 1959. Bar: Ill. 1960. Supr. property U.S. Gypsum, Chgo., 1960-66; real estate rep. Ford Motor Co., Dearborn, Mich., 1966-68; mgr. real estate Roadway Express, Akron, Ohio, 1968-70; dir. properties Hertz Corp., N.Y.C., 1970-76, staff v.p., 1976-84, v.p., 1984-87, sr. v.p. Park Ridge, N.J., 1987-96; ret., 1996. Mem. bd. trustees Cath. Community Svcs., Archdiocese of Newark. Mem. Am. Assn. Airport Execs. (assoc.), Internat. Assn. Corp. Real Estate Execs. (chmn. bd. dirs. 1993-95, chmn. bd. trustees 1995-98, sr. advisor 1998-01). E-mail: jeblake00@yahoo.com. *With age hopefully comes wisdom and an ability to live within one's limitations while nurturing one's talents.*

BLAKE, JONATHAN DEWEY, lawyer; b. Long Branch, N.J., June 14, 1938; s. Edgar Bond and Haven (Johnstone) B.; m. Prudence Anne Rowsell, Dec. 22, 1964 (div. June 1977); children: Juliet Haven, Deborah Anne, Susanna Rowsell; m. Elizabeth L. Shriver, Dec. 9, 1977; children: Jonathan Shriver-Blake, Molly Shriver-Blake. BA magna cum laude, Yale U., 1960, LLB cum laude, 1964; BA, MA, Oxford U., Eng., 1962. Bar: D.C. 1965, U.S. Supreme Ct. 1973, U.S. Dist. Ct. D.C. 1965, U.S. Dist. Ct. Md. 1985, U.S. Ct. Appeals (D.C. cir.) 1965, U.S. Ct. Appeals (2d cir.) 1973. Assoc. Covington & Burling, Washington, 1964-72, ptnr., 1972—, chmn. mgmt. com., 1996—2002. Tchr. Howard U., Washington, 1965-70, U. Va., Charlottesville, 1965-70. Contbr. articles to profl. jours. Pres. Great Falls Citizens Assn., Va., 1967-68; exec. com., bd. dirs. Deerfield Acad, Mass., 1980-85. Rhodes scholar, 1960; recipient Gordon Brown prize, 1959. Mem. ABA (chair internat. telecomm. com. 1993-2000), Fed. Comm. Bar Assn. (pres. 1980-85). Home: 4926 Hillbrook Ln NW Washington DC 20016-3208 Office: Covington & Burling 1201 Pennsylvania Ave NW Washington DC 20004-7566 Office Phone: 202-662-5506. E-mail: jblake@cov.com.

BLAKE, KING CHARLES, humanities educator, writer; s. Spencer Wimple (Stepfather) and Mary Madelene Allen-Wimple; life ptnr. David Gordon. AA, St. Paul's Coll., 1975; BA, Concordia U., 1978; MDiv, Luth. Theol. Sem., 1993; MA, Loyola Coll., 2004. Advisor to pastors Faith Ch., Balt., 1996—2004; individual support counselor Athelas Inst., Inc., Columbia, 2000—04; outreach coord. Luth. U. Ministry, 2003—. Contbr. short stories, poems. Comm. specialist Thrivent Fin., Appleton, Wis., 2002. Mem.: Dr. Cleo Johnson's Fellowship Love Concert Choir (assoc.; chaplain, advisor, songster, comm. specialist 2003). Lutheran. Avocations: music, art, planning and organizing community events, assisting the unfortunate, reading. Personal E-mail: bltmrking@aol.com.

BLAKE, PETER, state agency administrator; BA, MS, Va. Commonwealth U. Assoc. dir. State Coun. of Higher Edn. for Va.; staff House Appropriations Com., Va. Gen. Assembly; dep. sec. edn. State of Va., Richmond, 2002—05, sec. edn., 2005—. Office: Sec Edn Patrick Henry Bldg 1111 E Broad St, 4th Fl Richmond VA 23219 Office Phone: 804-786-1151. Office Fax: 804-371-0154. E-mail: SOE-CS@governor.virginia.gov.*

BLAKE, RENÉE, broadcast executive; b. Yonkers, NY; BA, Goddard Coll., 1973. Announcer, prodr. Sta. WCBQ-AM, Oxford, NC, 1974, Sta. WANV-AM, Waynesboro, Va., 1974; talk show host, anchor Sta. WEEZ-AM, Chester, Pa., 1974—75; reporter, anchor Sta. WWDB-FM, Phila., 1975, Sta. WMMR-FM, Phila., 1975—78; programming spl. projects Drake Chenault Enterprises, LA, 1978—79; copywriter S.M. Newmark & Assoc., LA, 1980—81; reporter, pub. affairs dir. Sta. WHLY-FM, Orlando, Fla., 1981—83; news dir. Sta. WJYO-FM, Orlando, Fla., 1983—86; program dir. Sta. WKXL-AM/FM, Concord, NH, 1986-91, Sta. KXCI-FM, Tucson, 1991—93; programmer Jerrold Comm., Concord, Tucson, 1990—94; reporter, anchor Metro Networks, Phoenix, 1995—97, news bur. chief Albuquerque, 1997—2003; owner, CEO Media IQ, Albuquerque, 1996—; continuing news dir. Sta. KUNM-FM, 2003—. Interviewer, spkr. in field. Co-editor: Westside Rapper, 1970; columnist: The Drummer, 1976-77, Steppin' Out Magazine, 1983-86; creator, prodr. Music Zone Snowbank, 1988-89 (Golden Mike Merit NH Assn. Broadcasters 1988), This Island Earth, 1990 (Best of the Best 1st Place Golden Mike NH Assn. Broadcasters 1990), NH Veterans' Memorial Wall and Scholarship Committee, 1988-90 (1st Place Golden Mike NH Assn. Broadcasters 1989), Send Our Support Day, 1990; affiliate prodr. Human Rights Now, 1989 (1st Place Golden Mike NH Assn. Broadcasters 1989); contbr. articles to profl. jours. Recipient AP First Place Newscast for Kunu, 2003, In Depth Coverage award, N.Mex. Broadcasters Assn. Div., 2004. Avocations: animal rights, alternative health care, writing, social justice, voiceovers. Office: Media IQ 174 Calle Loma Parda NW Albuquerque NM 87120-3477 E-mail: renee_blake@yahoo.com.

BLAKE, RICHARD E., sculptor, art educator; b. Phila., Feb. 24, 1943; s. Richard Blake and Marjorie Williams Blake; m. Nancy Rae Mata; children: Krystin Alexis, Brélan Kinzingér, Mia Mata. BFA, Temple U., 1967. Asst. prof. art West Chester (Pa.) U., 1975-98, prof. art, 1998—. Guest lectr. Phila. Coll. Art, 1971-74; drawing instr. Hussian Sch. Art, Phila., 1981-94; vis. lectr. Am. U., Washington, 1994. One-person shows include Fresno (Calif.) Mus. Art, 1999; exhibited in group shows Am. U., Watkins Gallery, Washington, 1995, Nat. Acad. Design, N.Y.C., 1996, Mid-Atlantic Art Exhbn., Norfolk, Va., 1997, Nat. Sculpture Soc., N.Y., 1997, 2000, Fine Arts Inst., Calif., 1997, Nat. Acad. Mus., N.Y., 1998. Recipient Meiselman award Nat. Acad. Mus., 1998, Merit award 10th Ann. Internat. Exhbn. Opus X, 1997, Profile award Manhattan Arts Internat., 1997, Bertelsen award Nat. Acad. Mus., 1996, Merit award Hoyt Nat. Exhbn., 1997, 1st prize 69th Ann. Juried Exhbn., 1996. Mem. Nat. Sculpture Soc. (Alex Ettl award 1996), N.Am. Sculpture Soc. (Cavanaugh award 1995). Home: 255 Harristown Rd Kinzers PA 17535

BLAKE, ROBERT PHILIP, human services administrator, music therapist; b. Indpls., Dec. 19, 1950; s. Robert Cameron and Marian Elsie (Barkman) B.; m. Marva Lynn Basye, July 13, 1971 (div. Feb. 1983); 1 child, Heidi Kai; m. Lois Ann Bleifus, Nov. 20, 1983 (div. Mar. 1996); children: Stephanie Fawn, Robert Joseph; m. Susan Christine Seebode, July 25, 1998; 1 child, Joshua Rey. AA, Cabrillo Coll., 1971; BA, Ind. U., 1973; MA, Goddard Coll., 1979; PhD, Walden U., 1996. Registered music therapist, 1979; cert. therapeutic recreation specialist, 1979; lic. mental health profl., Wash., 1988—. Music therapist Meth. Hosp., Indpls., 1973-76; recreation therapist VA Med. Ctr., Seattle, 1979-80, Fairfax Hosp., Kirkland, Wash., 1979-80; clin. program dir. Peninsula Community Mental Health Ctr., Port Angeles, Wash., 1980-94; exec. dir. Alaska Ctr. for Children and Adults, Fairbanks, 1995-99. Student performer, composer Up With People, Tucson, 1967-70; founder, dir. People Helping People, Indpls., 1974-77, The Logos Musical, Port Angeles, 1987-95; 1st exec. dir. Wash. Assn. County Designated Mental Health Profls., Seattle, 1981-82; involuntary treatment coord., Clallam County, Wash., 1983-94; presenter internat. workshops Assn. Care of Children in Hosps., Nat. Welfare Ministeries, Am. Pers. Guidance Assn., 1974-79; exec. dir. The Logos Corp., 1987-95. Author: (book) Gut Reaction: Music Therapy, 1979, Milestones: The History of Logos, 1990, Building Toward the Year 2000: You Can't Buy It, You Have to Build It, 1991—; composer, producer (album) Reaching Out, 1977, (cassette) Touch the Intrinsic, 1989, Winds of Change, 1991; Ind. Health Careers Gov.'s award, 1974. Treas. Arctic Alliance, 1996-98, v.p., 1998; chmn. Alaska-Cmty. Partnerships for Access, Solutions and Success, 1997-98. Am. Humanist Educators Assn. Div. grantee, 1989. Mem. Up With People Internat. Alumni (rep. cast C-1968-69), Fairbanks Sunriser's Rotary Club (internat. youth exch. dir.). Democrat. Baptist. Avocations: recording studio, exotic birds and animals, music camp, timber farm, international performing group director. Office: Alaska Ctr for Children and Adults 1020 Barnette St Fairbanks AK 99701-4502 E-mail: dr_blake@mosquitonet.com.

BLAKE, STEWART PRESTLEY, retired ice cream company executive; b. Jersey City, Nov. 26, 1914; s. Herbert P. and Ethel (Stewart) B.; m. Helen Davis, Nov. 16, 1982; children by previous marriage: Nancy Blake Yanakakis, Benson Prestley. Student, Trinity Coll., 1934-35, LL.D., 1976; PhD, Western New Eng. Coll., 1980, Springfield Coll., 1982; PhD (hon.), Path Bay Coll., 1993, Quinnipiac Coll., 1993. Co-founder Friendly Ice Cream Corp., 1935, chmn., to 1979. Past chmn. bd. trustees Bay Path Coll., Longmeadow, Mass. Mem.: Colony (Springfield), Longmeadow Country, Sailfish Point Yacht (Stuart). Home: 700 Hall Hill Rd Somers CT 06071-1058 E-mail: hephenblok@aol.com.

BLAKE-INADA, LOUIS MICHAEL, cardiologist, researcher; b. Osaka, Japan, June 4, 1956; came to U.S., 1959; s. Edward Kneeland, Sr. and Setsuko (Inada) Blake. BA in Biochemistry and Molecular Biology, U. Calif., Santa Barbara, 1979; MD, Case Western Res. U., 1983. Diplomate in internal medicine and cardiovasc. diseases; Am. Bd. Internal Medicine; diplomate Am. Bd. Nuc. Medicine. Intern in gen. surgery Letterman Army Med. Ctr., San Francisco, 1983-84; resident in internal medicine Sch. Medicine Stanford U., Calif., 1988-90, resident in nuc. medicine, 1990-92, chief resident in nuc. medicine, 1991-92; fellow in cardiology Calif. Pacific Med. Ctr., San Francisco, 1992-93; fellow in cardiology, cardiac imaging U. Calif., San Francisco, 1993-95; fellow in invasive cardiology U. N.Mex. Health Sci. Ctr., 1997-98; asst. prof. medicine (cardiology), asst. prof. radiology U. Nev. Sch. of Medicine, Reno, 1998-2000; dir. echocardiography lab. Sierra Nevada VA Med. Ctr., Reno, 1999-2000; dir. nuclear cardiology Sierra Nevada Med. Ctr., Reno, 1999-2000; staff cardiologist Swedish Heart Inst., Seattle, 2000—, med. dir. Jiang Nuc. Medicine Lab. Med. dir. Swedish Cardiology Lab., Swedish Heart Inst., Seattle, 2005—. Contbr. articles to med. jours. including Am. Jour. Radiology, Jour. Nuc. Medicine, others; contbr. editor Jour. Am. Coll. Cardiology, 1993-95. Capt. U.S. Army, 1979-88. Recipient Evelyn Neizer srch. fellow, Stanford U., 1992. Fellow ACP, Am. Coll. Angiology, Am. Coll. Cardiology; mem. Am. Coll. Nuc. Physicians, Am. Heart Assn. (coun. on cardiovascular radiology), Am. Heart Assn. (coun. on vascular biology, coun. on cardiovascular and critical care medicine 1999—. coun. on vascular and molecular biology 1999—), Soc. Nuc. Medicine, Assn. Military Surgeons of the U.S., Stanford U. Alumni (life). Home: PO Box 1805 Edmonds WA 98020 Office: Swedish Med Ctr Seattle WA 98122

BLAKELY, ALLISON, history professor; b. Clinton, Ala., Mar. 31, 1940; s. Ed Walton and Alice Blakely; m. Shirley Ann Reynolds, July 5, 1968; children: Shantel, Andrei. Student, Oreg. State Coll., Corvallis, 1958-60; BA, U. Oreg., 1962; MA, U. Calif., Berkeley, 1964, PhD, 1971. Instr. history Stanford (Calif.) U., 1970-71; asst. prof. history Howard U., Washington, 1971-77, assoc. prof. history, 1977-87, assoc. dean Coll. Liberal Arts, 1989-90, dir. honors program, Coll. Liberal Arts, 1990-93, prof. history, 1987-2001, Boston U., 2001—. Reader and test devel. cons., Ednl. Testing Svc., Princeton, N.J., 1974-2001; fellowship selection panelist, Am. Coun. Learned Socs., 2001, NEH, 1979-80, chair fellowship selection panel, Ford Found., N.Y.C., 1992-94; world history nat. stds. rev. panelist, Coun. Basic Edn., Washington, 1995-96. Author: Russia and the Negro: Blacks in Russian History and Thought, 1986 (Am. Book award, 1988), Blacks in the Dutch World: The Evolution of Racial Imagery in a Modern Society, 1994; contbr. articles to profl. jours., chpts. to books. Mem. Dem. Nat. Com., Washington, 1982—; pub. mem. Fgn. Svc. Selection Bd., U.S. State Dept., 1995. Mem. Am. Hist. Assn. (nom. com. 1999—, chmn. com. on minority historians 1993-97), World History Assn., Am. Assn. Advancement of Slavic Studies, U.S. Fgn. Svc. Pub. Mems. Assn. (bd. dirs.), Phi Beta Kappa Soc. (sen. at large 1993—). Democrat. Unitarian Universalist. Avocations: music, swimming, tai chi. Home: 1 Sunnyside Rd Silver Spring MD 20910 Office: Boston U 226 Bay State Rd Boston MA 02215 E-mail: ablakely@bu.edu.

BLAKELY, EDWARD JAMES, economics professor; b. San Bernardino, Calif., Apr. 21, 1938; s. Edward Blakely and Josephine Elizabeth (Carter) Proctor; m. Maaike C. Vander Sleesen, July 1, 1971; children: Pieta C., Brette D. BA, U. Calif., Riverside, 1960; MA, U. Calif., Berkeley, 1964; MBA, Pasadena Nazerene Coll., 1967; EdD in Edn. and Mgmt., UCLA, 1971. Mgr. Pacific Telephone Co., Pasadena, Calif., 1960-65; exec. dir. Western Community Action Tng., Los Angeles, 1965-69; spl. asst. U.S. Dept. State, Washington, 1969-71; asst. chancellor, assoc. prof. U. Pitts., 1971-74; assoc. dean and prof. applied econs. and behavioral scis. U. Calif., Davis, 1974-77, asst. v.p. Berkeley, 1977-85, prof., chmn. dept. city and regional planning, 1985—2004; dean Milano Sch. Mgmt. and Urban Policy New Sch. U., N.Y.C., 2004—. Expert advisor Orgn. Econ. Cooperation and Devel., asst. to Mayor Elihu Harris, City of Oakland. Author: Rural Communities in Advanced Industrial Society, Community Development Research, Taking Local Development Initiative, Planning Local Economic Development SAGE, 1988, Separate Societies: Poverty and Inequality in U.S. Cities (Paul Davidoff award 1993), 1992, Fortress America: Gated Communities in the U.S., 1998. Chmn. fin. com. Pvt. Industry Council of Oakland (Calif.), 1978-85; vice chmn. Ecole Bilingue Sch., Berkeley, 1982-85, chmn., 1988—; chmn. bd. Royce Sch., Oakland, Calif., 1988—; sec., treas. Econ. Devel. Corp., Oakland, 1983; expert advisor Orgn. Econ. Corp. and Devel., Paris, 1986; apptd. to pres. trust Pres. Bill Clinton, 1997—; mayoral candidate City of Oakland, Calif., 1998. Served to 1st lt. USAF, 1961-63. Named 125th Anniversary Prof., U. Calif. at Riverside Berkeley Campus, 1992; named to, Athlete Hall of Fame, U. Calif. Riverside Alumni Press, 1992, Pres. Trust by Pres. Bill Clinton, 1997; recipient San Francisco Found. award, 1991, Paul Davidoff award, 1993, Rsch. award, Cmty. Devel. Soc., 2002; fellow, German Acad. Exch., 1984, Urban Studies Australian Inst. Urban St., 1985, John Simon Guggenheim fellow, 1995—96; scholar Fulbright St. scholar, Internat. Exch. Scholars, 1986. Fellow Nat. Acad. Pub. Adminstrn.; mem. Cmty. Devel. Soc. (bd. dirs. 1980-84, svc. award 1983, disting. svc. award 1990), Calif. Local Econ. Devel. (standing com. 1980-81), Am. Planning Assn. (accreditation com.), Am. Assn. Collegiate Schs. of Planning, Nat. Assn. State and Land Grant Colls. (exec. com. 1987), Phi Delta Kappa, Lambda Alpha. Clubs: Rueful Order. Home: 31 Myagah Rd Mosman NSW 2088 Australia Office: Sch of Architecture U Sydney Sydney 2066 Australia

BLAKELY, GEORGE CURTIS, II, artist; b. Long Beach, Calif., Apr. 7, 1951; s. Curtis William and Etta Inez B. BS in Bus., Calif. State U., 1974, MA in Art Design, 1976; MFA in Art Design, Tyler Sch. Art Temple, 1978. Prof. art Fla. State U., Tallahassee, 1978—. Curator Fla. State U., Tallahassee, 1987—; bd. dirs. 621 Gallery. One-man shows include San Francisco Mus. Modern Art, 1980, 621 Gallery, Tallahassee, 1990, Sheppard Gallery, Reno, 1994; group exhibits include De Cordosa, Boston, Montgomery Mus. Fine Art, Ala., Mus. Fine Art, St. Petersburg, Fla., Ctr. for Fine Art, Miami. Individual Artist grant Fine Arts Coun., Tallahassee, 1979, 86, 95, NEA grant, 1979, 88. Mem. Soc. for Photograhic Edn. (regional chmn. 1983-85). Avocations: canoeing, cross country skiing, ultra light long distant hiking, gardening, biking. Home: 304 E Bradford Rd Tallahassee FL 32303-4804 Office: Fla State U 221 FAB Tallahassee FL 32306

BLAKELY, JANE MCCARTHY, secondary school educator; b. N.Y.C., Jan. 29, 1948; d. Roscoe Albert and Daisy Caroline (Marshall) McCarthy; m. Harold Richard Blakely, Sept. 26, 1970; children: Taryn Anne, Pamela Jane. BA, Upsala Coll., 1970; M of Ednl. Leadership, Adminstrn., William Paterson Coll., 1994; EdS, Seton Hall U., 2003. Tchr. history Westwood (N.J.) High Sch., 1970-77, Ridgewood (N.J.) High Sch., 1984—, area supr. English and social studies, 1998—. Field cons. N.J. Coun. on Econ. Edn., Ridgewood and Trenton, 1985—; adj. prof. MAT Program WilliamPaterson Coll., Wayne, N.J., 2003, 04, 05. Recipient Gov.'s Award for Excellence in Teaching N.J. Senate/House, 1989; Pew Grantee Joint Coun. on Econ. Edn., 1987, 88, 90. Mem. NEA, N.J. Coun. on Social Studies, Nat. Coun. on Social Studies, Nat. Coun. Tchrs. English, Nat. Coun. History Edn., Ridgewood Adminstr. Assn., Phi Delta Kappa, Pi Lambda Theta, Kappa Delta Pi. Democrat. Avocation: reading. Home: 11 Burnham Pl Fair Lawn NJ 07410-3623 Office: Ridgewood High Sch 627 E Ridgewood Ave Ridgewood NJ 07450-3394 Office Phone: 201-670-2624. Business E-Mail: jblakely@ridgewood.k-12.nj.us.

BLAKELY, WILLIAM D., lawyer; b. Darien, Wis., Oct. 15, 1945; BA, Univ. Wis., Madison, 1968; JD, Univ. Detroit, 1977. Bar: Mich. 1977, DC 1980, Va. 1984, US Dist. Ct. (DC, Va. dist.), US Ct. Appeals (4th cir.). Atty. civil div. torts branch, US Dept. of Justice, 1977—82; ptnr., co-chmn. Aviation Litigation practice group, head No. Va. Litigation group DLA Piper Rudnick Gray Cary, Reston, Va. Editor (in chief): Univ. Detroit Law Rev. Served to Lt. Col. pilot, naval aviation, & JAG Corps USMC. Recipient Spurgeon award, Boy Scouts of Am. Mem.: ABA, Million Dollar Advocates Forum, Am. Inst. Aeronautics & Astronautics, USMC Ret. Officers Assn. Office: DLA Piper Rudnick Gray Cary Suite 400 1775 Wiehle Ave Reston VA 20190-5159 Office Phone: 703-773-4261. Office Fax: 703-773-5059. Business E-Mail: william.blakely@dlapiper.com.

BLAKEMAN, ROBYN L., advertising executive, educator; b. Omaha, Sept. 26, 1958; d. Harold Raymond and Gayle Marie Blakeman. BSc, U. Nebr., 1980; MLA, So. Meth. U., 1996. Art dir. Ad Agy., Dallas, 1984—88; instr. Art Sch., Dallas, 1987—88; asst. prof. advertising, graphic art So. Meth. U., Dallas, 1997—98; asst. prof. West Va. U., Morgantown, 1998—. Chair advt. program W. Va. U., Morgnatown, 1999—, coord. student affairs and curriculum, 1998—. Named Journalism Prof. of Yr., Perely Isaac Reed Sch. Journalism, 2000—01. Mem.: Kappa Tau Alpha. Office: West Va Univ PO Box 6010 Morgantown WV 26506

BLAKEMORE, KARIN JANE, obstetrician, geneticist; b. Stockholm, Nov. 10, 1953; d. William S. and Elaine Claire (Hoover) B.; 1 child, Joseph William. BA, U. Pa., 1975; MD, Med. Coll. Toledo, 1978. Diplomate Am. Bd. Med. Genetics, Am. Bd. Ob-gyn. Resident in ob-gyn. NYU, N.Y.C., 1978-82; fellow in clin. genetics Yale U., New Haven, 1982-85; fellow in maternal-fetal medicine Washington U., St. Louis, 1985-87; asst. prof. ob-gyn. Johns Hopkins U., Balt., 1987-93, assoc. prof. ob-gyn., 1992—. Dir. Prenatal Genetics Johns Hopkins U., Balt., 1992—, dir. Maternal-Fetal Medicine, 1994—. Author chpts. to books; guest editor Obstetrics and Gynecology Clinics of N.Am., 1993. Fellow Am. Coll. Ob-gyn., Am. Coll. Med. Genetics; mem. AMA, Am. Inst. Ultrasound and Medicine, Am. Soc. Human Genetics, Internat. Soc. Ultrasound in Medicine, Soc. for Maternal-Fetal Medicine, Soc. for Gynecol. Investigation, Am. Gynecol. and Obstet. Soc. Office: Johns Hopkins Hosp Ob/Gyn Houck 228 600 N Wolfe St Baltimore MD 21287-0005

BLAKENEY, ALLAN EMRYS, Canadian government official, lawyer, educator; b. Bridgewater, N.S., Can., Sept. 7, 1925; s. John Cline and Bertha (Davies) B.; m. Mary Elizabeth Schwartz, 1950 (dec. 1957); m. Anne Louise Gorham, May 1959; children: Barbara, Hugh, David, Margaret. BA, Dalhousie U., 1945, LLB, 1947, LLD (hon.); BA, Oxford U., 1949, MA, 1955; DCL (hon.), Mount Allison U.; LLD (hon.), York U., Toronto, U. Western Ont., London, 1991, U. Regina, 1993, U. Sask., 1995. Bar: N.S. 1950, Sask. 1951. Queen's counsel, 1961; sec. to govt. fin. office Govt. Sask., Canada, 1950-55; chmn. Sask. Securities Commn., 1955-58; ptnr. Davidson, Davidson & Blakeney, Regina, 1958-60, Griffin, Blakeney, Beke, Koskie & Lueck, Regina, 1964-70; premier of Sask., 1971-82; mem. Sask. Legislature, 1960-88; prof. Osgoode Hall Law Sch. York U., 1988—90; prof. U. Sask.,

1990—. Leader of the opposition Sask. Legislature, 1970-71, 82-87; min. of edn., Sask., 1960-61, provincial treas., 1961-62, min. pub. health, 1962-64; mem. Royal Commn. on Aborginal Peoples, 1991-93. Decorated Officer Order of Can., Sask. Order of Merit; Rhodes scholar, Oxford U., 1948—49. Fellow Royal Soc. Can. Home: 1752 Prince of Wales Ave Saskatoon SK Canada S7K 3E5 Office: U Sask Coll Law 15 Campus Dr Saskatoon SK Canada S7N 5A6 Office Phone: 306-966-5881. Business E-Mail: blakeney@duke.usask.ca.

BLAKENEY, BARBARA A., public health service officer; BS, MS, U. Mass.; diploma, Worcester City Hosp. Sch. of Nursing. Primary care nurse practitioner Amherst Med. Assoc., Amherst, Mass., Boston City Hosp., Boston; prin. pub. health nurse for homeless svcs., addiction svcs. Dept. Health and Hosp., Divsn. Pub. Health, Boston; currently dir. health svcs. for homeless Boston Pub. Health Comm. Recipient Pearl McIver Pub. Health Nurse award, Am. Nurses Assn., Theta Alpha Cptr. Ann Kibirck Nursing Leadership award, Sigma Theta Tau. Mem.: Am. Nurses Assn. (pres. 2002—). Office: Boston Pub Health Commn 1010 Mass Ave Boston MA 02118 Address: 600 Md Ave SW Ste 100 W Washington DC 20024

BLAKENEY, MARGARET ELIZABETH FLEMING, counselor, educator; b. McComb, Miss., Jan. 23, 1961; d. Hiram Lee and Lucy Joe Ann (Curran) F.; m. Ray Edward Blakeney, May 26, 1984; children: Matthew, Lacey. MEd, Miss. Coll., 1985, Ednl. Specialist degree in counseling, 2002. Tchr. Crystal Springs (Miss.) Elem., 1983—2002; acad. educator, counselor Crystal Springs H.S., Miss., 2002—. Tchr. children's ministry New Zion Bapt. Ch. Southern Baptist. Avocations: travel, ocean, mountains, painting, reading. Home: 3055 Millsaps Rd Crystal Springs MS 39059 Office: Copiah County Schs 254 Gallatin St Hazlehurst MS 39083 E-mail: magsb47@hotmail.com.

BLAKE RAMOS, DEBRA BARBARA, writer; b. Bklyn., June 17, 1959; d. Rebecca Simmons and Jack Blake; m. Manuel Joseph Ramos, Apr. 2, 1957; children: Michael Young, Shameeka Shontele Ramos, Sarah Barbara Ramos, Abraham Joseph Ramos. Bus. degree, N.Y. Bus. Sch., 1981. Telephone technician, 1983; sec. Queensboro Correctional Facility, Queens, NY, 1984; writer, 1980—2003, 2003. Author (artist): (book) A New Birth Of Poetry (Editor's Choice award, 2001), Let Them Cry (Editor's Choice award, 2002), (CD) Serenity and Passion, 2000, Let Them Cry, 2002; songwriter Hill Top Record, 2001—03; contbr. articles to profl. jours. Mem.: Internat. Soc. Of Poets (hon. Internat. Poet of Merit award 2001).

BLAKESLEE, EDWARD EATON, lawyer, insurance company executive; b. N.Y.C., July 23, 1921; s. Edward Eaton and Ada Rainbow (Harris) B.; m. Janice Callaghan, Mar. 19, 1944; children— Edward, David. LLB cum laude, NYU, 1947, LLM in Taxation, 1957; grad. exec. program in bus. adminstrn., Columbia U., 1966. Bar: N.Y. 1947. Atty. Mut. Life Ins. Co. N.Y., 1947-69, 2d v.p., gen. solicitor, 1969-73, v.p., gen. solicitor, 1973, gen. counsel, 1974-85; gen. counsel, bd. dirs. Am. Life Ins. Co. of N.Y., 1986-88; mng. dir., chief exec. officer Sargasso Mut. Ins. Co., Ltd., Hamilton, Bermuda, 1986-93, also bd. dirs. Pres. Securities Investors Indemnification Co., Ltd., Hamilton, Bermuda, 1989-90; spl. counsel Rosenman & Colin, 1990-92; of counsel Shea & Gould, 1992-94, Werner & Kennedy, 1994-99; assessor Ins. Marketplace Stds. Assn., 1997—; cons. Nat. Exec. Svc. Corps, 2001—. With AC U.S. Army, 1942—46. Mem. ABA, N.Y. State Bar Assn., Assn. Bar City of N.Y., Assn. Life Ins. Counsel, NYU Alumni Fedn. (pres. 1981-83, dir. emeritus), Fellows Am. Bar Found. (life mem.), NYU Law Alumni Assn., Univ. Club. Home: 495 Birchtree Rd Oradell NJ 07649-1303 Personal E-mail: edwardb743@aol.com.

BLAKESLEE, WESLEY DANIEL, lawyer, consultant; s. Daniel Leo and Ann Blakeslee; m. Georgia Carroll Croft, July 28, 1973; children: Jaime Kiersten, Christopher Justin, Shaun Michael. BS, Pa. State U., 1969; JD, U. Md.-Balt., 1976. Bar: Md. 1976, U.S. Dist. Ct. Md. 1977, U.S. Tax Ct. 1984. Sys. analyst NASA, Greenbelt, Md., 1969-76; assoc. Semmes, Bowen & Semmes, Balt., 1976-78; pvt. practice Dulany & Davis, Westminster, Md., 1978-83; prin. Wesley D. Blakeslee, P.C., Westminster, 1984—2000; of counsel Blakeslee & Wallace PC, Westminster, 2000—. Assoc. Gen. Couns.; lectr. Johns Hopkins Univ., 1999—, lectr., dir. computer devel. U. Md. Law Sch., Balt., 1984-89; dir. Union Nat. Bank, 1988-2000. Co-author, editor: Maryland District Court Practice, 1981, rev. 1983; author: Understanding Computers, 1984, 3d edit., 2003, Fair Use in Academia Today, 2003; co-author: UCITA, 2000. Bd. govs. Md. Law Sch. Fund, Balt., 1982—90. Mem. ABA, Fed. Bar Assn. (treas. Balt. chpt. 1984-90), Md. Bar Assn. (young lawyers sect. coun. 1982-84, Outstanding Svc. award 1984, litigation sect. coun. 1982-2001, chmn. 1995), Carroll County Bar Assn. (treas. 1984), Nat. Assn. Coll. and Univ. Attys. (co-chmn. intellectual property sect. 2000-01), Order of Coif, Delta Theta Phi. Roman Catholic. Home: 980 Hook Rd Westminster MD 21157-7335 Office: Johns Hopkins U 113 Garland Hall 3400 N Charles St Baltimore MD 21218 Office Phone: 410-516-8128. Business E-Mail: starman@jhu.edu.

BLAKESLEY, WAYNE LAVERE, JR., retired production engineer; b. Goshen, Ind., Mar. 26, 1926; s. Wayne L. Blakesley Sr. and Thelma (Brown) Cobb. Test engr. Bendix Missile Div., Mishawaka, Ind., 1952-53, engring. tech., 1955-59; field engr. RCA Service Co., Camden, N.J., 1953-55; design engr. Crown Internat., Elkhart, Ind., 1959-72, prodn. engr., 1978—95; pres. Blakesley Electronics, Syracuse, Ind., 1972-78; ret. Inventor, designer automated system for radio stas., printed circuit bd. prototyping system, printed circuit bd. multilayer overlay; designer multi-unit electronic learning lab. Mem. So. Mfg. Engrs. (sr. mem. Robotics Internat. div.), Mensa, Intertel. Avocation: public speaking. Home: PO Box 53 Syracuse IN 46567-0053

BLAKEY, G. ROBERT (GEORGE ROBERT BLAKEY), law educator; b. Burlington, NC, Jan. 7, 1936; BA, U. Notre Dame, 1957; JD, 1960. Bar: NC 1960, DC 1960. Spl atty. Organized Crime and racketeering sect. US Dept. Justice, 1960—64; asst. prof. U. Notre Dame, Ind., 1964—67; prof., 1967—74, 1980—; chief counsel Subcom. on Criminal Laws and Procedures, US Senate, 1969—74; prof. Cornell U., Ithaca, NY, 1974—80; chief counsel Select House Com. on Assassinations, 1977—79; spl. cons. Pres. Commn. for Law Enforcement and Adminstrn. of Justice, 1966—67. Author: (novels) Develop. of Law of Gambling, 1978. Mem.: Nat. Commn. for Rev. of Fed. and State Law Relating to Wiretapping and Electronic Surveillance (mem. 1974—76), Nat. Commn. on Rev. of Policy toward Gambling (mem. 1974—76), Nat. Commn. on Reform of Fed. Penal Law (mem. 1968). Office: U Notre Dame Sch Law Notre Dame IN 46556

BLAKEY, MARION C., federal agency administrator; b. Gadsden, Ala., Mar. 26, 1948; B Internatl Studies, Mary Washington Coll., U. Va.; postgrad., Johns Hopkins U. With Dept. Commerce, Dept. Dept. Edn., NEH, Dept. Transp.; prin. Blakey & Assocs., Washington, 1993—2001; adminstr. Dept. Transp.'s Nat. Hwy. Traffic Safety Adminstrn., 1992—93; chmn. Nat. Transp. Safety Bd., 2001—02; adminstr. FAA, 2002—. Office: FAA 800 Independence Ave SW Washington DC 20591-0004

BLALOCK, ANN BONAR, evaluation researcher; b. Parkersburg, W.Va., Apr. 16, 1928; d. Harry and Fay (Conley) Bonar; m. Hubert Blalock, Jr., 1951 (dec. 1991); children: Susan Blalock Lyon, Kathleen Blalock McCarrell, James W.; m. Gerhard E. Lenski, 1996. AB, Oberlin Coll., 1950; MA, U. N.C., 1954; MSW, U. Wash., 1978. Pvt. cons. Admiralty Inlet Consulting, Hansville, Wash. Cons. OECD, Paris, 1990, European Commn., Brussels, 1995. Sr. author: Introduction to Social Research, 2d edit., 1982; editor, reviewer: Evaluation Forum, 1986-97, Evaluating Social Programs, 1990; co-editor: Methodology in Social Research, 1968; contbr. articles to profl. jours. Past pres. bd. dirs. Cmty. Mental Health Clin.; mem. Gov.'s Task Force on Accountability in Govt. Recipient Rsch. award, Partnership for Employment and Tng. Careers. Mem. NASW (past pres. Wash. State chpt.), Am. Eval. Assn. (past com. chair). Home: PO Box 409 Hansville WA 98340-0409

BLALOCK, CAROL DOUGLASS, psychologist, educator; d. Allan Martin and Mary Louise Douglass; m. Harvey Anthony Blalock, Aug. 27, 1976; children: Jeanne, Patricia, Elizabeth. BEd, U. S.D., 1968; MEd in Edn., EdS in Counseling, U. Fla., 1976, PhD in Curriculum and Instrn., 1980; postgrad., U. Md., 1980—81. Nat. cert. sch. psychologist Fla., 1990, lic. sch. psychologist Fla., 1990. Tchr. Metcalf Elem., Gainesville, Fla., 1968, Gainesville (Fla.) H.S., 1969; coord. environ. edn. Sante Fe C.C., Gainesville, 1974—78, adj. faculty, 1974—78; grad. rsch. fellow U. Fla., rsch. assoc., 1979; chmn. sci. dept. Oak Hall Prep. Sch., Gainesville, Fla., 1981—84; guidance counselor Trenton (Fla.) HS, 1984—87; psychologist Marion County Schs., Ocala, Fla., 1987—; adj. faculty U. South Fla., Tampa, 1990. Author: (chpt.) A Futures Perspective on Instructional Design, 1980; co-author: (conf. summary) Computer Conf. on the Future, 1979, (chpt.) Learning Networks: The Next Step, 1981. Aux. officer Gainesville (Fla.) Police Dept., 1985—95; mem. Holy Faith Cath. Ch., Gainesville, Fla., 1976. Mem.: Fla. Assn. Sch. Psychologists, Nat. Assn. Sch. Psychologists, APA, Phi Delta Kappa. Republican. Roman Catholic. Avocations: grandchildren, travel, music, art. Office: Marion County Sch Bd Ste 5 1517 SE 30th Ave Ocala FL 34471 Office Phone: 352-671-6869.

BLALOCK, LOUISE, librarian, public administrator; b. Neptune, New Jersey, Jan. 25, 1934; BS, TCNJ, 1955; MLS, SUNY, Albany, 1971; M in Pub. Adminstrn., NYU, 1987. Acting dir. Empire State Coll., N.Y., 1972; instr. sch. library sci. SUNY, Albany, 1973-74; coordinator children's services East Providence (R.I.) Pub. Library, 1974-77; regional coordinator Island Interrelated Library System, 1977-79; dir. Barrington Pub. Library, 1979-81, New Canaan (Conn.) Library, 1981—92; chief libr. Hartford (Conn.) Pub. Libr., 1994—. Chairperson State Library Standards Task Force, 1984; active Notable Books Council, 1988, Conn. Inter-Agy. Library Planning Com., 1982-86, White House Conf. Libraries and Info. Services. 1979, Recipient Outstanding Libr. award, Conn. Libr. Assn., 1999, Libr. of Yr., Libr. Jour., 2001, Nat. Award Libr. Svc., IMLS, 2002. Mem. ALA, Am. Soc. Pub. Adminstrn., Conn. Library Assn., Fairfield Adminstrs. Group (pres. 1987), New Eng. Library Assn. (exec. bd. 1975-77), R.I. Library Assn. (pres. 1979-80).

BLALOCK, SHERRILL, investment advisor; b. Newport News, Va., June 9, 1945; d. David Graham and Martha Lee (Bennett) B.; m. Jonathan L. Smith, Oct. 27, 1985; 1 child, Graham C.G. BA, Smith Coll., 1967. Chartered fin. analyst. Investment broker Legg Mason & Co., Washington, 1968-77, Blyth Eastman Dillon, Washington, 1977-80; portfolio mgr., mng. dir. Mitchell Hutchins, N.Y.C., 1980-88; gen. ptnr., portfolio mgr. Weiss Peck & Greer, N.Y.C., 1988-95; gen. ptnr. Delphi Asset Mgmt., N.Y.C., 1995-98; founder, mng. mem. Chesapeake Asset Mgmt., N.Y.C., 1998—. Chair investment com., trustee Diocese of NY of Episcopal Ch., 2001—; trustee, vice chmn. bd. trustees, chair investment com. Estate and Property of Diocese Conv. of N.Y., 1996—2002; trustee Cathedral of St. John the Divine, 1998—, chair investment com., 1999—. Mem. Washington Soc. Investment Analysts, Inst. Chartered Fin. Analysts. Office: Chesapeake Asset Mgmt 1 Rockefeller Plz Rm 1210 New York NY 10020-2002 Office Phone: 212-218-4040.

BLALOCK, THOMAS SULLIVAN, JR., military officer; b. Winston-Salem, NC, Nov. 5, 1963; s. Thomas Sullivan and Elizabeth Weir Blalock; m. Lisa Gardner Blalock, Aug. 4, 1964. BA, Wake Forest U., 1986. Dir., squadron weapons, tactics and tng. 43rd Electronic Combat Squadron, Davis-Monthan AFB, Ariz., 1998—99; dir., wing C-130 weapons and tactics 355th Ops. Support Squadron, Davis-Monthan AFB, Ariz., 1999—2001; asst. ops. officer 41st Electronic Combat Squadron, Davis-Monthan AFB, Ariz., 2001—02, 755 Ops. Support Squadron, Davis-Monthan AFB, Ariz., 2002—03; dep. chief, spl. tech. ops. Air Combat Command, Langley AFB, Va., 2003—, chief, non-lethal SEAD (suppression enemy air def.), 2003—. Chief, electronic warfare plans Combined Air Ops. Ctr., Prince Sultan AB, Saudi Arabia, 2002—03. Maj. USAF, 1988—2005. Decorated Aerial Achievement medal US Ctrl. Command, Air Force Commendation medal 355th Wing, Commendation medal USN, Air Medal US Air Forces Europe, Air Force Commendation medal 355th Wing, Def. Meritorious Svc. Medal US Ctrl. Command; named Directorate of Ops. Action Officer of Yr., Dir. of Air and Space Ops., Air Combat Command, 2005; recipient Outstanding Grad. award, USAF Weapons Sch., 1998. Mem.: Assn. Old Crows (Joint Svc. award 2004), Alpha Phi Omega (life). Independent. Avocations: golf, sports. Home: 112 Cattail Br Hudgins VA 23076 Office: Hdqs Air Combat Command 205 Dodd Blvd Ste 101 Langley Afb VA 23665 Personal E-mail: thomas.blalock@langley.af.mil.

BLAMER, STEVEN W., advertising executive; b. Whittier, Calif., Apr. 19, 1956; m. Linda Blamer; 2 children. Grad., Ariz. State U., 1979. With FCB, Chgo., 1979—81, LA, 1984—87, DDV Needham, 1981—84; dir. new bus, exec. v.p., dir. client svcs. Grey L.A., 1989—97; mng. dir., exec. v.p. Grey LA, Grey Worldwide, 1997—98; CEO Grey London, Grey Worldwide, 1998—2000; pres., CEO Grey Worldwide NY, Grey Worldwide, 2000—03, Grey Worldwide North Am., NYC, 2003—. Poast bd. dirs. Jr. Achievement. Mem.: Am. Assn. Advt. Agys. (bd. dirs.). Office: Grey Worldwide N Am 777 3d Ave New York NY 10017

BLAN, OLLIE LIONEL, JR., retired lawyer; b. Ft. Smith, Ark., May 22, 1931; s. Ollie Lionel and Eva Ocie (Cross) B.; m. Allen Conner Gillon, Aug. 19, 1960; children: Bradford Lionel, Elizabeth Ann, Cynthia Gillon. AA, Ft. Smith Jr. Coll., 1951; LL.B., U. Ark., 1954. Bar: Ark. 1954, Ala. 1959, U.S. Dist. Ct. (no. dist.) Ala. 1959, U.S. Dist.Ct. (mid. and so. dist.) Ala. 1960, U.S. Ct. Appeals (5th cir.) 1960, U.S. Ct. Appeals (11th cir.) 1982, U.S. Supreme Ct. 1991. Rsch. analyst Ark. Legis. Coun., 1954-55; law clk. to judge U.S. Dist. Ct. (no. dist.) Ala., Birmingham, 1959-60; assoc. Spain, Gillon & Young, Birmingham, Ala., 1960-64; ptnr. Spain & Gillon and predecessor firms, Birmingham, Ala., 1965-2001; tchr. Am. Inst. Banking, 1965-68; ret., 2001. Spkr. Ala. Inst. Continuing Edn., 1978—2001. Contbr. articles to legal jours. Treas. Jefferson County Hist. Assn., 1972-81, vice chmn., 1981-86, chmn., 1986-93; mem. Jefferson County Rep. Exec. Com., 1973-76; mem. Briarwood Sch. Bd., Birmingham, 1982-86; chmn. Here's Life Birmingham, 1986-88. Capt. USMCR, 1955-58, ret. Mem. ABA, Am. Bd. Trial Advocates, Ark. Bar Assn., Ala. Bar Assn. (com. on admissions and legal edn. 1971-74, com. jud. office 1972-76, com. ins. programs, bd. bar commrs. 1987-92, chmn. task force om. on disciplinary rules and enforcement 2001-03), Birmingham Bar Assn. (exec. com. 1986-89), Ala. Def. Lawyers Assn. (v.p. 1983-84, 91-93, bd. dirs. 1988-91, sec.-treas. 1993-94, pres. elect. 1994-95, pres. 1995-96), Am. Coun. Life Ins., Internat. Assn. Def. Counsel (chmn. accident, health and life ins. com. 1987-90), Def. Rsch. Inst. (Ala. state rep. 1996-99, Louis B. Potter profl. svc. award 2000). Baptist. Home: 2100 English Village Ln Birmingham AL 35223-1729 E-mail: olblan@bellsouth.net. *My desire has been to achieve the highest standard in whatever area of life I am thrust, guided by principles of ethics and Christianity.*

BLANC, MAUREEN, public relations executive; Founder (with Simone Otus) Blanc & Otus Pub. Rels., Inc., San Francisco, 1985. Office: Blanc and Otus 303 2nd St Ste 800 San Francisco CA 94107-1327

BLANC, ROGER DAVID, lawyer; b. N.Y.C., Dec. 26, 1945; s. Robert Smith and Ara Jeanne (Ponchelet) B.; m. June Chunchin Ku, Sept. 17, 1972; children: David Jung-Wei, Gregory Jung-Lee, Cynthia Jung-Lin. BA, Yale U., 1967; JD, Columbia U., 1970. Bar: N.Y. 1971. Ptnr. Willkie Farr & Gallagher, N.Y.C. Lectr. various profl. orgns. Contbr. articles to profl. jours. Dir. Yale Alumni Schs. Com. Westchester, 1994—. Mem.: Assn. Bar City NY, Univ. Club (NYC). Office: Willkie Farr & Gallagher 787 Seventh Ave New York NY 10019-6099 Office Phone: 212-728-8206. E-mail: rblanc@willkie.com.

BLANCH, PAUL BRADFORD, biomedical engineer, researcher; b. Boston, Mar. 25, 1949; s. Euan True and Ethel Elizabeth Blanch; m. Laurel Ann McNamara, Aug. 18, 1980; children: David Paul, Kathryn Rogers Hazzard, Kimberly Bradford; m. Lorrie Rogers Wilkes, July 21, 1971 (div. Nov. 1, 1977). AA, U. Chgo., 1976; BA, Colby Coll., 1972. Registered respiratory therapist Nat. Bd. Respiratory Care, 1977, lic. Fla. Dept. Health Divsn. Med. Quality Assurance, 1990. Technologist Carney Hosp., Dorchester, Mass., 1972—73; staff therapist Seton Hosp., Waterville, Maine, 1973—74; staff therapist Shands Hosp U. Fla., Gainesville, Fla., 1974—75; supr. blood gas and stat chemistry lab. Shands Hosp. U. of Fla., Gainesville, Fla., 1975—80, respiratory equipment specialist Shands Hosp., 1980—, courtesy asst. anesthesiology Dept. of Anesthesiology Coll. Medicine, 1995—; v.p. engring. and R&D Airon Corp., Melbourne, Fla., 1997—. Mem. FSRC (Fla. Soc. for Respiratory Care), St. Petersburg, Fla., 1990—, Nat. Bd. Respiratory Care, Dallas, 1977—; cons. VersaMed Inc, Trenton, NJ, 1999—2001, Allied Med., St. Louis, 1992—97; instr. Santa Fe C.C., Gainesville, 1974—90. Co-author: Mechanical Ventilators, in Clinical Applications of Ventilatory Support, 1990, Respiratory Care in Atlas of Anesthesia: Critical Care, vol. 1, 2000, Tracheal Pressure Ventilator Control in Innovations in Mechanical Ventilation, 2000, Mechanical Ventilators in Respiratory Care - A Guide to Clinical Practice, 1991, Mechanical Ventilation in Critical Care, 2d edit., 1992, Mechanical Ventilators in Neonatal and Pediatric Respiratory Care, 2d edit., 1993, Mechanical Ventilation in Critical Care, 3d edit., 1996; mem. editl. bd.: Respiratory Care Jour., 1993—; contbr. articles to profl. jours. Coach Babe Ruth Baseball Program, Alachua, Fla., 1993—97. Recipient Literary award, Am. Respiratory Care Found., 1992, 1994, 1997, 1999; grantee, Am. Coll. Chest Physicians, 1994. Independent. Episcopalian. Achievements include design of mechanical ventilator for use during transportation of patients; pNeuton ventilator for use in an magnetic resonance imaging environment or during transportation of patients; patents in field; patents pending for. Home: 15214 NW 94th Ave Alachua FL 32615 Office: Shands Hospital at the Univ of Florida 1600 SW Archer Road Gainesville FL 32610 Office Phone: 352-265-0078. Home Fax: 352-338-9891; Office Fax: 352-338-9891. Personal E-mail: blancpb@shands.ufl.edu.

BLANCH, ROBERT JAMES, JR., lawyer; s. Robert James and Marjorie Alice Blanch; m. Carol Joy Dorman, Sept. 30, 1995; children: Tyler Evan, Alessia Rene. AB in Econs., Coll. of Holy Cross, Worcester, Mass., 1984; BSEE, Northeastern U., 1986, MSEE, 1989; JD, Boston U., 1994. Bar: Ill. 1994, U.S. Dist. Ct. (no. dist.) Ill. 1994, U.S. Patent and Trademark Office 1994, Mass. 1995, U.S. Dist. Ct. Mass. 1995, D.C. 1996, Calif. 1997, U.S. Dist. Ct. (no. dist.) Calif. 1997, US Ct. Appeals (fed. cir.) 2004. Asst. staff scientist M.I.T. Lincoln Lab., Lexington, Mass., 1987—90; assoc. Fish & Richardson, Boston, 1995—96, Brobeck Phleger & Harrison, Palo Alto, Calif., 1996—99, Orrick Herrington & Sutcliffe, Menlo Park, Calif., 2000—01; ptnr. McDermott Will & Emery, Palo Alto, 2001—. Mem. editl. staff: Am. Jour. Law and Medicine. Mem.: ABA, Tau Beta Pi, Phi Beta Kappa. Office: McDermott Will & Emery LLP 3150 Porter Dr Palo Alto CA 94304-1212 Office Phone: 650-813-5133. Office Fax: 650-813-5100. Business E-Mail: rblanch@mwe.com.

BLANCHARD, BRUCE, civil engineer, federal official; b. Ft. Stotsenburg, Philippines, Dec. 26, 1932; s. Wendell and Marcella (Palmer) B.; m. Mary Josie Cain, July 31, 1992; children: Wendell, Laura, Renee. SB in Civil Engring., MIT, 1957, SM in Civil Engring., 1964; honor. grad., Commd. and Gen. Staff Course, Ft. Leavenworth, Kans., 1980. Tchg. and rsch. asst. MIT, 1957-59, asst. lacrosse coach, 1958-59, 64; hydraulic engr. Bur. Reclamation, Dept. Interior, Denver, 1959-60, 60-61; water resources planning engr. Phoenix, 1961-66; sr. staff specialist Water Resources Coun., Washington, 1966-69; environ. specialist Office of Sec. Dept. Interior, Washington, 1970-71; dir. Office Environ. Project Rev., Washington, 1971-89; dep. dir. U.S. Fish and Wildlife Svc., Dept. of Interior, Washington, 1989-97; spl. asst. for tribal self-governance Office of Sec. of Interior, 1997—2004; asst. to dep. asst. sec. Mgmt. Office Asst. Sec. Indian Affairs Dept. Interior, Washington, 2004—05, dir. India affairs planning and policy analysis, 2005—. Editor: The Nation's Water Resources, 1968. With U.S. Army, 1951-53, 60; col. Md. N.G., 1967-85; lt. Ariz. N.G., 1961-66. Decorated Army Commendation medal, Army Meritorious Svc. medal, Army Achievement medal; recipient Commendation medal State of Md., 1976, 78, 79, Meritorious Svc. medal State of Md., 1983, Meritorious Svc. medal Dept. Interior, 1985, Disting. Svc. medal, 1999. Fellow: AAAS; mem.: ASCE, Sr. Execs. Assn., Am. Soc. Pub. Adminstrn., U.S. Armor Assn., Soc. Am. Mil. Engrs., N.G. Assn. U.S., Am. Water Resources Assn., Am. Geophys. Union, MIT Alumni Assn. (bd. dirs. 2001—03), Explorers Club (Washington group treas. 1997—), MIT Club of Washington (bd. dirs. 1997—, v.p. 1998—99, pres. 1999—2000), Phi Gamma Delta (Disting. Fiji award). Home: 80 Observatory Cir NW Washington DC 20008-3611 Office: Interior Bldg Ms4140 Washington DC 20240-0001 Business E-Mail: bruce_blanchard@alum.mit.edu.

BLANCHARD, CHARLES ALAN, lawyer, retired state senator; b. San Diego, Apr. 14, 1959; s. David Dean and Janet (Laxson) B.; m. Allison Major, 2001. BS, Lewis & Clark Coll., 1981; M of Pub. Policy, JD, Harvard U., 1985. Bar: Ariz. 1987, U.S. Dist. Ct. Ariz. 1988, U.S. Ct. Appeals (D.C. cir.) 1988, U.S. Ct. Appeals (9th cir.) 1988, U.S. Supreme Ct. 1994. Law clk. to hon. Harry T. Edwards, Washington, 1985-86; law clk. to hon. Sandra Day O'Connor U.S. Supreme Ct., Washington, 1986-87; assoc. ind. counsel Ind. Counsel James McKay, Washington, 1987-88; atty. Brown & Bain, P.A., Phoenix, 1988-97; state senator State of Ariz., Phoenix, 1991-95; dir. Office of Legal Counsel Office of Nat. Drug Control Policy, Washington, 1997-99; gen. counsel U.S. Army, 1999-2001; ptnr. Brown & Bain PA, Phoenix, 2001—04, Perkins Coie Brown & Bain PA, Phoenix, 2004—. Adj. prof. Ariz. State U. Coll. Law, 1996, 2003—; chmn. Senate Judiciary Com., Phoenix, 1991-93; Dem. candidate U.S. Congress, 1994; dir. homeland security State of Ariz., 2003; mem. regulatory rev. coun., Gov., 2004—. Contbr. articles to profl. jours. Bd. dirs. Luth. Vol. Corps., Washington, 1986-88, Florence (Ariz.) Immigrant and Refugee Rights Project, 1990-97, 2001-, Homeless Legal Assistance Project, Phoenix, 1992-97, Tempe Comty. Action Agy., 1994-97, ABA Com. on Immigration Law, 1996-98, ABA Com. on Substance Abuse, 1998-02, Childrens Action Alliance, Phoenix, 2005—, Ariz. Found. for Legal Svc. and Edn., 2005—; state committeeman Ariz. Dem. Party, Phoenix, 1991-97, 2005—; chmn. Ariz. Dem. Leadership Coun., Inc., 1992-97. Recipient Disting. Svc. award Ariz. Atty. Gen., 1992, Disting. Civilian Svc. award U.S. Army, 2001; Toll fellowship Coun. of State Govts., 1991; named Disting. Young Alumni Lewis and Clark Coll., 1987. Mem. ABA. Home: 1814 Palmcroft Dr NE Phoenix AZ 85007 Office: PO Box 400 Phoenix AZ 85001-0400 Office Phone: 602-351-8000. E-mail: cblanchard@perkinscoie.com.

BLANCHARD, DANIEL G., cardiologist; b. Mnpls., Mar. 13, 1959; s. Robert and Jeannine Blanchard; m. Jennifer Neely, Apr. 20, 2002; 1 child, Jeanette; 1 child, Rachel. MD, U. Calif. San Diego Sch. of Medicine, 1985; BS, Calif. State U., 1980. Cert. Am. Bd. of Internal Medicine, 1988, Subspecialty in Cardiology Am. Bd. of Internal Medicine, 1991, Am. Bd. of Internal Medicine, 2002. Dir. cardiac noninvasive labs. U. Calif. San Diego Med. Ctr., 1994—; prof. of medicine U. Calif. San Diego Sch. of Medicine, 2003—; chief of cardiology Thornton Hosp, U. Calif. San Diego Med. Ctr., 2002—. Author: (sci. articles, book chpts.) Cardiologic Medical Literature. Fellowship, Am. Coll. of Cardiology, 1994, Am. Heart Assn., 2000. Achievements include research in noninvasive cardiac imaging, transesophageal echocardiography. Office: Univ Calif San Diego Cardiology 9350 Campus Point Dr #0975 La Jolla CA 92037

BLANCHARD, DAVID LAWRENCE, aerospace executive, real estate developer, management consultant; b. Taulbee, Ky., Feb. 13, 1931; s. Charles Lorraine and Gwyndolyn (Johnson) B.; m. Allene Irma Horne, June 28, 1958; children: Leslie Ruth, David Lawrence Jr. AB in Religion, Ind. Wesleyan U., 1953; MS in Physics, U. Louisville, 1959; PhD in Applied Physics, Cath. U. Am., 1971. Instr. U. Louisville, 1955-57, Ind. Wesleyan U., 1957-58; rschr. Naval Ordnance Lab., White Oak, Md., 1958-64; aerospace rschr., engr. NASA Goddard Space Flight Ctr., Greenbelt, Md., 1964-71, supr., mgr., 1971-79, sr. exec., 1979-81; staff cons., dir. rsch. Ford Aerospace Corp., Houston and Detroit, 1981-84; chief engr. Ford Aerospace, Houston, 1984-85, dir., exec. dir. space programs Seabrook, Md., 1985-90; pres. Loral AeroSys, Seabrook, Md., 1990-96, Lockheed Martin Space Mission Systems, 1996-97;

founder, prin. COGENT-LLC., Kennewick, Wash., 1997—; prin., sec., treas. BBS Assocs. LLC, Kensington, Md., 1981—. NASA rsch. fellow Eidgenossische Technische Hochschule, Zurich, Switzerland, 1974-75; rsch. advisor NRC, Greenbelt, Md., 1979-80; mem. pres.'s adv. coun. Ind. Wesleyan U., 1998—; mentor for small start up businesses Dingman Sch. Entrepreneurship, 1997—; mem. ind. rev. team on space infrared telescope facility NASA, 1998—. Patentee fuze arming device. Chmn., charter mem. bus. and industry steering com. DuVal Aerospace Magnet Sch., Prince Georges County Schs. Seabrook, 1989-92, mem. bus. and industry adv. com. on sci. and tech., 1989-91; charter mem. bd. Opportunity Skyway, 1990-97; trustee, chmn. fin. com. Houghton Coll., N.Y., 1987-96, trustee, 1997-2004, gen. chmn. $45 million capital campaign, 1999-2004; charter mem., bd. trustees Md. Space Bus. Roundtable, 1989-97, pres., 1991-93; bd. visitors U. Md. Univ. Coll., 1994-2001, U. Md. Found., 1996-2001; charter mem., bd. trustees World Hope Internat., 1996—; bd. dirs. Willard J. Houghton Found., 1987-2004, chair bd., 1997-2004; bd. advisors Nanticoke Homes, 2000-02, Innovative Concepts, Inc., 1999—; chair pres. adv. coun. excellence Ind. Wesleyan U., 2000—. With U.S. Army and USAR, 1957-64. Recipient Exceptional Svc. award NASA, 1968, Exceptional Performance award, 1973. Fellow Washington Acad. Scis., AIAA (assoc.); mem. Sigma Xi, Sigma Pi Sigma. Lutheran. Achievements include research in gravity-gradient stabilization experiment on 1500 foot antenna array in low earth orbit.

BLANCHARD, GEORGE SAMUEL, retired army officer; b. Washington, Apr. 3, 1920; s. George S. and Elizabeth (Blanchard) B.; m. Beth Howard, June 9, 1944; children: Kate E. (Mrs. Ronald Hausner), Marylou C. (Mrs. John Hennessey), Deborah E. (Mrs. Eberhard Roell), Blythe H. (Mrs. Charles Watkins). Student, Am. U., 1938—40; BS, U.S. Mil. Acad., 1944; MS, Syracuse U., 1948; grad. Advanced Mgmt. Program, Harvard Bus. Sch., 1966. Commd. 2d lt. AUS, 1944, advanced through grades to gen., 1975; served as co. comdr. and staff officer Europe, 1944-47; adviser, 1955—56; with 82d Airborne Div., 1958-60, 1961-62; with ADC 1st divsn., c/s 1st Corps, 1966-68; comdr. 82d Airborne div. Ft. Bragg, N.C., 1970-72; mem. Pentagon staff, 1962-66, 68-70; comdg. gen. VII Corps U.S. Army Europe, 1973-75; comdr. in chief U.S. Army Europe, 1975—79; ret., 1979. Past pres. World USO, Gen. Analysis, Inc.; bd. dirs. Atlantic Coun. U.S. Contbr. to Ency. Brit. Vice chmn. Literacy Coun. Moore County. Decorated D.S.M. with 3 oak leaf clusters, Silver Star with oak leaf cluster, D.F.C., Bronze Star with oak leaf cluster. Mem. Assn. U.S. Army, Ret. Officers Assn. (past pres.), VFW, U.S. Soc. French Legion of Honor, Nat. Mil. Families Assn. Episcopalian.

BLANCHARD, GERALD J., music educator, conductor, singer; b. Phila., Sept. 22, 1967; s. Jerome Golden and Lavanda Louise Earl. BS in Music Edn., West Chester U., 1995; MusM, Ctrl. Mich. U., 2000; postgrad., Mich. State U., 2000—04. Mem. voice faculty, opera dir. U. Michigan-Flint, 2000—04; dir. vocal activities Kellogg C.C., Battle Creek, Mich., 2004—. Mem. voice faculty Adrian (Mich.) Coll., 1999—2000. Opera singer: CD With A Song In My Heart (2004 Young Artist Award, 2004); dir.: (opera) An Operatic Montage; singer: (choral work) Requiem Mass in D minor by Mozart. Recipient Nat. Singers Auditions award, U. Memphis/Opera Memphis, 2000; King Chavez Parks Future Faculty award, Ctrl. Mich. U. and State of Mich., 1999—2000, King/Chavez/Parks fellow, Mich. State U. and State of Mich., 2000—04, Grad. Tchg. fellow and ALANA award, Mich. State U. Sch. of Music and Grad. Sch., 2000—04. Mem.: ACDA (assoc.), Nat. Assn. Tchrs. of Singing (assoc.), MSVMA (assoc.). Office: Kellogg CC 450 North Ave Battle Creek MI 49017 Office Phone: 269-965-3931. Personal E-mail: blanchardg@kellogg.edu.

BLANCHARD, JAMES HUBERT, finance company executive; b. Augusta, Ga., July 22, 1941; BBA, U. Ga., 1963, LLB, 1965. With Page Scranon Harris McGlanney and Chapman, 1964-70; with Columbus Bank and Trust Co., 1970—; with Synovus Fin. Corp., Columbus, Ga., 1972—, CEO, 1971—2005, now chmn. bd., 2005—. Chmn. exec. com., bd. dirs. TSYS; bd. dirs. Columbus Bank and Trust Co., BellSouth Corp., W.C. Bradley Co., Sea Island Co. Trustee Columbus State U. Found.; Emory Com. Robert T. Jones, Jr. Scholarship; Carter Center Board of Councilors mem.; bd. visitors Morehouse Sch. Med.; mem. Trust for Public Land Chattahoochee River Land Protection Campaign Com.; bd. councilors Carter Ctr.; bd. visitors, mem. Advisory Com. Ga. Partnership Excellence in Education; bd. curators Ga. Historical Society. 1st Lt. and Finance Officer U.S. Army, 1965—67. Mem.: Ga. C. of C. (dir.), Ga. Rsch. Alliance (dir., past chmn.), Ga. Dept. Econ. Develop. (past chmn.), Banker Information Technol. Secretariat (dir., former chmn.), Financial Services Roundtable (dir.), Am. Bankers Assn. (dir.). Office: Synovus Fin Corp 901 Front Ave Columbus GA 31901-2722*

BLANCHARD, JAMES JOHNSTON, ambassador, retired governor; b. Detroit, Aug. 8, 1942; m. Janet Eifert; 1 son, Jay. BA, Mich. State U., Lansing, 1964; MBA, Mich. State U., 1965; JD, U. Minn., 1967; JD (hon.), Mich. State U., U. Mich., 1985, Wayne State U., 1985, Oakland U., 1984, Alma Coll., 1987, Grand Valley State U., 1988. Bar: Mich. 1968, DC 2000, US Dist. Ct. (ea. & we. dist. Mich.), US Ct Appeals (6th cir.), US Supreme Ct. Legal aid elections bur. Office Sec. State, State of Mich., 1968-69; asst. atty. gen. State of Mich., 1969-74, adminstrv. asst. to atty. gen., 1970-71, asst. dep. atty. gen., 1971-72; mem. Congress from 18th Mich. Dist., 1974-82; gov. State of Mich., 1983-91; ptnr. Verner, Liipfert, Bernhard, McPherson & Hand, Washington, 1991—93; U.S. amb. to Canada, 1993-96; ptnr. Verner, Liipfert, Bernhard, McPherson & Hand, Washington, 1996—2002; ptnr. Energy, Fed. Affairs & legis., Govt. Affairs practices DLA Piper Rudnick Gray Cary, Washington, 2002—. Former mem. Pres.'s Commn. on Holocaust, Nat. Govs. Assn. Exec. Com.; former chmn. Dem. Nat. Platform Com., Dem. Govs. Assn.; bd. drs. Ctr. for the Great Lakes; founding mem. Dem. Leadership Coun. Mem. Oakland County exec. club Mich. State U.; bd. advisors Ctr. for Policy Research. Recipient Outstanding Achievement award U. Minn., 1983-84, Tree of Life award Jewish Nat. Fund., 1984, supporter of entrepreneurship award Inc. mag., 1991, Disting. alumni award Mich. State U., 1991, Fgn. Affairs award for pub. svc., 1996; named one of Outstanding Young Men Am., U.S. Jaycees, 1978, a Michiganian of Yr. Detroit News mag., 1980. Mem. Assn. Asst. Attys. Gen., Ferndale Jaycees, State Bar Mich., Am. Bar Assn., LWV, Nat. Gov's. Assn. (chmn. legal affairs com. 1987, mem. finance com., human resources com.), Dem. Gov's. Assn. (chmn., 1988), U. Minn. Law Sch. Alumni Club, Mich. State Alumni Assn., Delta Tau Alumni Assn., U. Detroit Titan Club. Democrat. Office: DLA Piper Rudnick Gray Cary 1200 19th St NW Washington DC 20036-2412 Office Phone: 202-861-6415. Office Fax: 202-689-8565. Business E-Mail: james.blanchard@dlapiper.com.

BLANCHARD, KIMBERLY STAGGERS, lawyer, educator; b. Ann Arbor, Mich., May 17, 1954; d. Theodore R. and Bette Lee (Clark) Staggers; m. John Sears Blanchard, May 31, 1980; children: Charles Stuart, Virginia Greene. BA, Dartmouth Coll., 1976; MS, U. Wis., 1978; JD, NYU, 1981. Bar: N.Y. 1982. Assoc. Paul, Weiss, Rifkind, Wharton & Garrison, N.Y.C., 1981-83, Haythe & Curley, N.Y.C., 1983-89, ptnr., Weil, Gotshal & Manges LLP. Adj. prof. NYU Sch. Continuing Edn., 1982-88. Pres. Pelham Pub. Libr. Mem. ABA, N.Y. State Bar Assn. (exec. com. tax sect. 1996-, second vice chair). Clubs: Pelham Country (Pelham Manor, N.Y.). Democrat. Avocation: golf. Office: Weil, Gothshal & Manges LLP 767 Fifth Avenue New York NY 10153

BLANCHARD, LEONARD ALBERT, writer, consultant, educator; b. New Britain, Conn., July 30, 1947; s. Albert Edward and Sophie Marian (Lemanski) B.; children: Sarah Maddin Henniger, Henry Wyche Hunter. BA in English cum laude, Washington & Lee U., 1969; MA, Emory U., 1974, PhD, 1975. Instr. English, coach Oak Ridge (N.C.) Mil. Inst., 1969-71, St. Mark's Sch., Dallas, 1974-75; instr. English El Centro Coll., Dallas, 1975-79; writer, developer, liaison Southland Corp., Dallas, 1979-87; dir. devel. Franchise Group Internat., Little Rock, 1987-88; cons. Len Blanchard, Bradenton, Fla., 1988—. V.p. human resources Harken Internat., Bedford, Tex., 1989—90; mgmt. cons. Tropical Breeze Inn, Sarasota, 1996—99; instr. English Manatee C.C., Bradenton, Fla., 1999—. Author: An American Passion, 2001, numerous poems. Mem.: Acad. Am. Poets, Musical Heritage Soc., Amnesty Internat., Smithsonian Assn. Democrat. Avocations: swimming, hiking, classical music. Office: Manatee CC Dept English 5840 26th St W Bradenton FL 34207-3522 Business E-Mail: blanchl@mccfl.edu.

BLANCHARD, MARYANN N., state legislator; b. N.J., Oct. 12, 1942; d. Joseph Charles and Mary (Longo) Navatta; m. Raymond P. Blanchard, 1967; children: Mary Beth, Catherine Anne, Daniel, Frances Elizabeth. BA, St. Joseph's Coll., 1966. Mem. Rockingham County Dist. 26 N.H. Ho. of Reps., Concord, 1982-90, mem. dist. 33, 1996-2000, ranking minority mem., mem. resources, recreation and devel. com., mem. fin. com., 2000—05. Trustee Strawberry Banke, 1993-96, Portsmouth Pub. Libr., 1981-83; commr. Portsmouth Police Commn., 1991-96; mem. adv. coun. Coop-Ext., Rockingham, 1992-93; mem. Portsmouth Hosp. Guild; leader Swiftwater coun. Girl Scouts USA, 1978-82; mem. Portsmouth PTA; mem. Atlantic States Marine Fisheries Commn., 2001—. Mem. LWV (past pres., bd. dirs. 1967-71), Soc. Protection N.H. Forests, Audubon Soc., Parents Music Club. Roman Catholic. Office Phone: 603-271-2136.

BLANCHARD, OLIVIER JEAN, economics educator; b. Amiens, France, Dec. 27, 1948; s. Jacques and Anne B.; m. Noelle F. Blanchard, 1973; children: Marie, Serena, Giulia. PhD, MIT, Cambridge, Mass., 1977. Asst. prof. Harvard U., Cambridge, Mass., 1977-82; assoc. prof. MIT, 1983-85, prof., 1985—, chair, 1997—. Author: Lectures in Macroeconomics, 1989, Macroeconomics, 1997-02; co-editor: Qtrly Jour. of Econ., Harvard U., 1979-98. V.p. Am. Econ. Assn., 1995-96. Fellow Econometric Soc.; mem. AAAS. Office: Dept Economics MIT 50 Memorial Dr Cambridge MA 02142-1347

BLANCHARD, PAUL, academic administrator, educator; b. Flint, Mich., Apr. 5, 1943; s. Floyd E. and Loretta G. Blanchard; m. Elizabeth L. Brandt, June 18, 1966 (div. Feb. 19, 2003); children: Jaclyn(dec.), Brian; m. Mary M. Donigan, Apr. 12, 2003; children: Geoffrey, Brian. BA in Social Sci., U. Mich., Flint, 1965; MA in Polit. Sci., So. Ill. U., Carbondale, 1968; PhD in Polit. Sci., U. Ky., Lexington, 1973. Social studies tchr. Beecher H.S., Flint, Mich., 1965—67; prof. polit. sci. Ea. Ky. U., Richmond, 1970—99, dir. Ctr. for Ky. History and Politics, 1999—2003, exec. dir. govt. rels., 2004—; edn. program specialist S.C. Dept. Edn., Columbia, 1975—76; legis. liaison Ky. Atty. Gen.'s Office, Frankfort, 1985—86. Cons. Nat. Sch. Bds. Assn., Washington, 1976—78, Ky. Dept. Edn., Frankfort, 1985—86; state coord. Nat. Bicentennial Project, 1986—88. Contbr. chapters to books, articles to profl. jours.; talk show host Ea. Ky. U. Television, Richmond, 1982—92., Nat. Def. Edn. Act fellow, 1968—70. Democrat. Methodist. Avocations: walking, reading, tennis, golf. Office: Eastern Ky Univ Coates Box 111 CPO Box 41A 521 Lancaster Ave Richmond KY 40475-3102 Business E-Mail: paul.blanchard@eku.edu.

BLANCHARD, RICHARD FREDERICK, construction executive; b. Orange, N.J., Feb. 8, 1933; s. William F. and Dorothy Dew (Wright) B.; m. Jill Isles, Nov. 23, 1985. BA, Dartmouth Coll., 1955; MBA, Harvard U., 1957. Apprentice Wm. Blanchard Co., Newark, 1958-62, estimator, 1962-65, project mgr. Springfield, NJ, 1965-72, pres., 1972—2004, vice chmn., 2004—. V.p. Newark Mus., 1986—. With U.S. Army, 1957-58. Mem. Bldg. Contractors Assn. N.J. (trustee 1986—2003), N.J. State C. of C. (bd. dirs. 1980-88). Presbyterian. Avocations: mountain climbing, skiing.

BLANCHARD, TOWNSEND EUGENE, retired service companies executive; b. Du Quoin, Ill., Jan. 30, 1931; s. Townsend and Anna Belle (Jackson) B.; m. Norma Louise Barr, Dec. 18, 1960; children: John Barr, Susan Melody, Jayne Ann Blanchard Reishus, Stephen Eugene. BS, U. Ill., 1952; MBA, Harvard U., 1957. Cons. Ill. Sch. Bond Svc., Monticello, 1958-62; co-founder, treas., chief fin. officer Americana Nursing Ctrs., Monticello, 1962-75; v.p. fin., treas., CFO, chief of staff Cenco, Inc., Chgo., 1975-79; sr. v.p., CFO DynCorp., Reston, Va., 1979-97. Chmn. Employee Stock Ownership Plan DynCorp, 1997—2003. Elder Presbyn. Ch.; bd. dirs. Combined Health Appeal, 1986-96; bd. advisors Cameron Glen Care Facility, 1989-92. Lt. USNR, 1952-55. Decorated Spl. Commendation letter. Mem. Fin. Execs. Inst. (chpt. pres. 1988-89, nat. v.p. and bd. dirs. 1991-94), U. Ill. Alumni Club, Harvard U. Bus. Sch. Club, Harvard Club Washington, Am. Legion, Delta Sigma Phi (trustee nat. found. 1988-89, pres. nat. found. 1988-89, Harvey W. Herbert award 1975, Mr. Delta Sig award 1988).

BLANCHARD PORTLAND, KIMBERLY, psychologist, consultant; d. Wayne Everitt and Sandra Sargent Blanchard; m. Eric Peter Portland, Aug. 24, 2002; 1 child, Alexander James Portland. PhD, Rutgers U., 1994—99. Psychologist NY, 2001. Rsch. assoc. Nat. Ctr. on Addiction and Substance Abuse at Columbia U., New York, NY, 2001—; asst. prof. Mt. Sinai Sch. of Medicine, New York, NY, 1999—2001. Psychologist Pvt. Practice, NYC, 2001—. Tng. fellowship, Nat. Inst. of Alcoholism and Alcohol Abuse, 1997—99. Mem.: Assn. for the Advancement of Behavior Therapy. Office: CASA at Columbia Univ 633 Third Ave New York NY 10017 Office Phone: 212-841-5236. Home Fax: 212-956-8020; Office Fax: 212-956-8020. Personal E-mail: kblancha@casacolumbia.org.

BLANCHET, BERTRAND, archbishop; b. Montmagny, Que., Can., Sept. 19, 1932; s. Louis and Alberta (Nicole) B. BA, Coll. Ste-Anne-de-la Pocatiere, 1952; LTh, Laval U., 1956, DSc, 1975. Ordained priest Roman Cath. Ch., 1956, consecrated bishop 1973. Tchr. biology Coll. and Coll. d'Enseignement Gen. et Profl., La Pocatiere, 1963-73; bishop of Gaspe, Canada, 1973-92; archbishop of Rimouski, Canada, 1992—. Mem. Chevaliers de Colomb, Rimouski. Roman Catholic. Address: CP 730 34 Eveche Ouest Rimouski PQ Canada G5L 7C7 Office Phone: 418-723-3320. E-mail: bblanchet@globetrotter.net.

BLANCHET, JEANNE ELLENE MAXANT, artist, educator, performer; b. Chgo., Sept. 25, 1944; d. William H. and L. Barbara (Martin) Maxant; m. Yasuo Shimizu, Apr. 28, 1969 (div. 1973); m. William B. Blanchet, Aug. 21, 1981 (dec. May 1993). BA summa cum laude, Northwestern U., 1966; MFA, Tokyo U., 1971; MA, Ariz. State U., 1978; postgrad., Ill. State U., 1979-80; PhD, Greenwich U., 1991. Instr. Tsuda U., Kodaira, Japan, 1970-71; free-lance visual, performing artist various cities, U.S., 1973—; artist in residence YMCA of the Rockies, Estes Park, Colo., 1976-81 summers; prof. fine arts Rio Salado Coll., Surprise, Ariz., 1976-91. Lectr. Ariz. State U. West, Sun City, 1985-93; evaluator several arts couns. including Ariz. Humanities Coun., 1993, Ariz. Humanities Coun. Scholar's SPkrs. Bur., 1998—; Prescott Melodrama ragtime pianist, 1993, 94; artist with Performing Arts for Youth, 1994—. Selected for regional, state, nat. juried art shows, 1975—, mus. and gallery one-woman shows of computer art, 1988—; author: Original Songs and Verse of the Old (And New) West, 1987, A Song in My Heart, 1988, Reflections, 1989, The Mummy Story, 1990; contbr. articles to newspapers, profl. jours. Founding mem. Del Webb Hosp. Woodrow Wilson fellow, 1966; ADA B.C. Welsh scholar, 1980; recipient numerous art, music awards, 1970—, major computer art awards in regional, nat., and internat. shows, 1990—. Mem. Nat. League Am. Pen Women (sec. chpt. 1987, v.p. 1988, pres. 1990-92, pres. Colo. chpt. 1996-97), Ariz. Press Women (numerous awards in original graphics and writing 1980s, 90s), Nat. Fedn. Press Women, Northwestern U.'s John Evans Club, Henry W. Rogers Soc., P.E.O. (rec. sec. chpt. BV 1998—), Phi Beta Kappa. Avocations: computers, ragtime piano, hiking, parapsychology, duplicate bridge (life master). Home and Office: 10330 W Thunderbird Blvd # C-311 Sun City AZ 85351 *To live is to think, to create.*

BLANCHETT, CATE (CATHERINE ELISE BLANCHETT), actress; b. Melbourne, Victoria, Australia, May 14, 1969; d. Robert and June Blanchett; m. Andrew Upton, Dec. 29, 1997; children: Dashiell John, Roman Robert. Grad., Nat. Inst. Dramatic Art, Australia, 1992. Performed with Sydney Theatre Co., Belvoir St. Theatre Co. Appeared in theatre productions including Top Girls, Kafka Dances (Newcomer Award, Sydney Theatre Critics Circle, 1993), Oleanna (Rosemont Best Actress Award, 1993), Hamlet, 1995, Sweet Phoebe, The Tempest, The Blind Giant is Dancing; actress (films) Police Rescue, 1994, Parklands, 1996, Paradise Road, 1997, Thank God He Met Lizzie, 1997 (Australian Film Inst. Award for best actress in a supporting role, 1997), Oscar and Lucinda, 1997, Elizabeth, 1998 (Golden Globe for best actress-drama, 1999, Acad. Award nomination for best actress, 1999), The Talented Mr. Ripley, 1999, An Ideal Husband, 1999, Pushing Tin, 1999, The Man Who Cried, 2000, The Gift, 2000, Bandits, 2001, Charlotte Gray, 2001, The Shipping News, 2001, The Lord of the Rings: The Fellowship of the Ring, 2001, Heaven, 2002, The Lord of the Rings: The Two Towers, 2002, Veronica Guerin, 2003, Coffee and Cigarettes, 2003, The Missing, 2003, The Lord of the Rings: The Return of the King, 2003 (Screen Actors Guild Award for outstanding performance by a cast in a motion picture, 2004), The Life Aquatic with Steve Zissou, 2004, The Aviator, 2004 (Acad. Award for best actress in a supporting role, 2005, Screen Actors Guild Award for best actress in a supporting role, 2005); (TV miniseries) Heartland, 1994, Bordertown, 1995; actor, producer (films) Bangers, 1999. Office: Creative Artists Agy c/o Hylda Queally 9830 Wilshire Blvd Beverly Hills CA 90212*

BLANCHETTE, OLIVA, philosophy educator; b. Berlin, N.H., May 6, 1929; s. Delphis and Odelia (Morneau) B.; m. Dorothy M. Kennedy, May 25, 1975; children: Nicole Elizabeth, Frances Kathleen. AB in Philosophy, Boston Coll., 1953, MA, 1958; Licentiate in Philosophy, Coll. St. Albert de Louvain, Belgium, 1954; Licentiate in Sacred Theology, Weston Coll., 1961; PhD in Philosophy, U. Laval, Que., Can., 1966. Prof. Latin, Greek and English Boston Coll. High Sch., 1954-57; instr. philosophy Boston Coll., 1964-65, asst. prof., 1965-67, assoc. prof., 1967-74, prof., 1974—; dean Sch. of Philosophy, 1968-73. Dir. Inst. for Social Thought. Author: Initiative in History: A Christian-Marxist Exchange, 1967, For a Fundamental Social Ethic: A Philosophy of Social Change, 1973, The Perfection of the Universe According to Aquinas: A Teleological Cosmology, 1992, Philosophy of Being: A Reconstructive Essay in Metaphysics, 2003; contbr. articles on philosophy of history, metaphysics, philosophy of religion, and social ethics to scholarly jours. Mem. Hegel Soc. Am., Metaphys. Soc. Am., Internat. Soc. Metaphys. Home: 28 Florence St Natick MA 01760-2121 Office: Dept Philosophy Boston Coll Chestnut Hill MA 02467

BLANCHFIELD, FRANCIS J., JR., lawyer; b. Chgo., Sept. 19, 1945; BA, Coll. of Holy Cross, 1967; JD, NYU, 1970, LLM in Tax., 1974. Bar: NJ 1970, NY 1974, Ga. 1976, NC 1981, US Supreme Ct., US Tax Ct., US Ct. of Fed. Claims, 5th and 11th Courts of Appeal, ea. dist. NC. Law clk. Judge Samuel Allcorn Jr., Superior Ct. (Chancery Divsn.), Newark, 1970—71; ptnr. Hull, Towill, Norman, Barrett & Johnson, Augusta, Ga., 1973—76; spl. asst. to asst. atty. gen., tax divsn. Dept. of Justice, Washington, 1977—79, dep. asst. atty. gen., appeals, settlements and legis., tax divsn., 1979—80; shareholder Johnson and Blanchfield, Charlotte, NC, 1981—88, Blanchfield & Moore PA, Charlotte, NC, 1988—89; ptnr., practice area leader for tax Smith Helms Mulliss & Moore, Charlotte, Greensboro, Raleigh and Washington, 1989—92; shareholder Blanchfield Cordle & Moore PA, Charlotte, NC, 1992—98; ptnr. Mayer, Brown, Rowe & Maw LLP, Charlotte, 1998—, ptnr.-in-charge, Charlotte office, 1998—2004. 1st lt., instr., criminal and military law mil. police sch. U.S. Army, 1971—73, Fort Gordon, Ga. Recipient US Atty. Gen. Medal, 1980. Fellow: Am. Coll. of Tax Counsel; mem.: ABA, Fed. Bar Assn., NC Bar Assn., Charlotte Tax Roundtable. Office: Mayer Brown Rowe & Maw LLP Ste 3800 214 N Tryon St Charlotte NC 28202 Office Phone: 704-444-3510. Office Fax: 704-377-2033. Business E-Mail: fblanchfield@mayerbrownrowe.com.

BLANCK, RONALD RAY, health science university administrator, internist, military officer; b. Lancaster, Pa., Oct. 8, 1941; s. Harvey Ray and Mildred Katherine (Smith) B.; m. Donna Rae Ault, Sept. 17, 1971; children: Jennifer, Susan. BS, Juniata Coll., 1963; DO, Phila. Coll. Osteo. Medicine, 1967; DSc in Osteopathy (hon.), New Eng. Coll. Osteo. Medicine, 1982; LLD (hon.), Phila. Coll. Osteo. Medicine, 1991. Diplomate Am. Bd. Internal Medicine. Intern Lancaster Osteo. Hosp., 1967-68; resident in internal medicine Walter Reed Army Gen. Med. Ctr., 1970-73; commd. capt. U.S. Army, 1968, advanced through grades to lt. gen., 1996, ret., 2000, gen. med. officer, 1968-69, Ft. Myer, Va., 1969-70; asst. chief gen. med. svc. Walter Reed Army Med. Ctr., Washington, 1973-74, asst. chief dept. medicine, 1974-76; asst. dean student affairs Sch. Medicine Uniformed Svcs. U., Bethesda, Md., 1976-79; chief dept. medicine Brooke Army Med. Ctr., San Antonio, Tex., 1979-82; chief med. corps career activities office Army Med. Dept. Pers. Support Act, Washington, 1982-85; comdr. U.S. Army Hosp., Berlin, 1986-88, Army Regional Med. Ctr., Frankfurt, Germany, 1988-90; dir. prof. svcs., chief med. corps affairs Office of Surgeon Gen., Fall Church, Va., 1990-92; comdr. Walter Reed Army Med. Ctr., Washington, 1992-96; surgeon gen., comdr. MECOM U.S. Army, Falls Church, Va., 1996-2000; pres. U. North Tex. Health Sci. Ctr., Ft. Worth, 2000—. Asst. prof. clin. medicine Georgetown U., Washington, 1972—78; clin. instr. medicine Howard U., Washington, 1975—77; assoc. prof. medicine USUHS, Bethesda, 1976—; clin. prof. medicine U. Tex., San Antonio, 1979—80, San Antonio, 1980—82; disting. prof. mil. medicine USUHS, Bethesda, Md., 1998—. Guest editor Osteopathic Annals, 1981; mem. editorial adv. bd. History of Medicine in Vietnam, 1981. Advisor bd. regents Uniformed Svcs. U. Health Scis., Bethesda, 1992; bd. dirs. Nat. Med. Vets. Soc., Chgo., 1993; bd. regents Potomac Inst. for Policy Studies, 2000; bd. dirs. Annapolis Ctr., 2002. Decorated DSM, Bronze Star, Legion of Merit, Def. Superior Svc. medal; recipient Founder's award Tex. Coll. Osteo. Medicine, 1991. Master ACP (gov.); mem. AMA (alt. del.), Am. Osteo. Assn., Assn. Mil. Surgeons U.S. (John Shaw Billings award 1976), Berlin Internat. Med. Soc., Assn. Mil. Osteo. Physicians and Surgeons, Soc. Med. Cons. Armed Forces (assoc.), Nat. Bd. Med. Examiners. Episcopalian. Avocations: reading, jogging. Office: U North Tex Health Sci Ctr 3500 Camp Bowie Blvd Fort Worth TX 76107-2699

BLANCO, KATHLEEN BABINEAUX, governor; b. New Iberia, La., Dec. 15, 1942; m. Raymond S. Blanco, Aug. 8, 1964; 6 children. BS in Bus. Edn., U. La.at Lafayette, 1964. Tchr. Breaux Bridge High Sch.; with La. State Legis. Dist. 45, 1984-88, mem. house edn. com., mem. house transp., hwys., and pub. works com., Pub. Svc. Commn., La., 1988-94, chair, 1993-95; lt. gov. State of La., 1995—2003, gov., 2004—. Democrat. Catholic. Achievements include being first woman gov. of La. Office: Office of Gov PO Box 94004 Baton Rouge LA 70804-9004

BLANCO, LAURA, interior designer; b. Havana, Cuba, July 3, 1956; came to U.S., 1960; d. Lauro and Marina (Mardones) B.; m. Robert F. Shainheit, 1988. Studied landscape design, NY Botanical Gardens, 2000—03; studied interior design, NY Sch. Interior Design, 2002—04. Asst. box office treas., press agt. Zev Bufman Entertainment, Inc., Orlando, St. Petersburg, Fla., 1978-83; press agt. Kool Jazz Festival and Heritage Fair, Orlando, 1982; producer La. World Exposition Inc., New Orleans, 1983-84, Festival Ventures, Inc., Miami, Fla., 1985-86; producer/dir. hispanic events Festival Prodns., Inc., NYC, 1986-87; pres. Blanco Shainheit Prodns., Blanco Shainheit Music, NYC, 1988—99; ptnr. unanimo, 1992—99; pres. Laura Blanco Interiors, NYC, 2004—. Prodr. (short film) The Summer of My Dreams, 1994, La Ciudad, 1995, (feature film, award winner Havana Film Festival, 1998), Perdida, 1998. Bd. dirs. Artists Community Fed. Credit Union, 1988-90; bd. mem. Off World Theatre, 2003-05. Mem. ASCAP, Am. Latin Music Assn. Office Phone: 212-876-0053. E-mail: info@laurablanco.com.

BLANCO, MARIA ALEJANDRA, educational consultant, researcher; b. Buenos Aires, Sept. 21, 1971; d. Jose Blanco and Alba Concepcion Bruno de Blanco. BS in Kindergarten and Presch. Edn., El Salvador U., 1993, BS in Psychopedagody, 1997; EdM, Harvard U., 2001. Kindergarten and presch. bilingual tchr. Balmoral Coll., Buenos Aires, 1991—97; fellow in neuropsychopedagogy Dr. Garraham Nat. Children's Hosp., Buenos Aires, 1997—2000, psychopedagogist, mem. interdisciplinary health clinics dept., 1997—2002; ednl. cons., rschr. office ednl. devel. Austral U. Sch. Biomed. Scis., Buenos Aires, 1998—2002; ednl. cons., rschr. for faculty devel. office of ednl. devel. Harvard Med. Sch., Cambridge, Mass., 2002—; tchg. fellow in qualitative and quantitative ednl. rsch. courses learning and tchg., critical exploration in the classroom course Harvard Grad. Sch. Edn., Cambridge, 2002—. Author: Epidemiology of Learning Disabilities (Nat. Govt. award

Forum of Exemplary Students, 1998). Vol. cmty. work Roman Cath. Ch., Buenos Aires, 1984—2002. Grantee Fulbright/Nat. Ministry Edn., 2002. Mem.: Assn. Am. Ednl. Rsch. Personal E-mail: blancoma@gse.harvard.edu.

BLANCO, RAMIRO, dental educator; b. Barranquilla, Columbia; s. Cristobal Blanco and Cruz Parra; children: Maribel, Morella P, Claudia X, Andy. DMD, Zulia U., 1970; M in periodontics, Boston U., 1978. Asst. prof. Boston U., 1985; prof. Universidad de Oriente S of Med., Bolivar, 1983—85; asst. clin. prof. Boston U., 1985—2004; asst. to program dir. Dept. of Periodontics, Harvard U. Dental Sch., 2004—; pvt. practice, 1988—. Dir. dept. of dentistry Uyapar Hosp., 1983—89. Lt. Colombia Army, 1966—68. Mem.: ADA, Mass. Dental Soc., Am. Acad. Periodontology, Dental Assn. of Venezuela (pres. 1983—85). Democrat. Cath. Avocations: deep sea fishing, travel, reading. Home: Ballardvale Crossing Bldg 5 Unit A Andover MA 01810 Office: Ramiro Blanco, DMD 100 Amesbury ST Derry NH 03038 Personal E-mail: rblancodmd@verizon.net.

BLANCO MENDOZA, HERMINIO, former Mexican government official; b. Chihuahua, Mex., July 25, 1950; married; 2 children. BA in Econs., Monterrey Inst. Tech., Mex., 1971; student, U. Colo., 1971-72; MA, PhD in Econs., U. Chgo., 1978. Rsch. asst. U. Chgo., 1975-78; sr. advisor, Ministry of Fin. Govt. Mex., 1978-80; prof. econs. Rice U., Houston, 1980-85; visiting prof. Coll. Mex., 1980; researcher MIT, 1981; sr. advisor to Pres. of Mex. Govt. Mex., 1985—88, undersec. for Internat. Trade Negotiations and Foreign Trade, Ministry of Commerce and Indsl. Develop., undersec. of foreign trade, 1988—90, dep. coord., Foreign Trade Commn. of the PRIs Inst. for Econ. and Polit. Studies, 1990, chief negotiator, North Am. Free Trade Agreement, 1990—93, undersec., Internat. Trade Negotiations, 1993—94, former sec. of commerce and indsl. develop. Rschr. MIT, 1981; chmn. Prodor SC (Programas de Desarrollo Regional Sustentable, Mex.

BLAND, ANNIE RUTH (ANN BLAND), nursing educator; b. Bennett, N.C., Oct. 14, 1949; d. John Wesley and Mary Ida (Caviness) Brown; m. Chester Wayne Bland; 1 child, John Wayne; stepchildren: Jason Tyler, Adam Mathew. BSN, East Carolina U., Greenville, N.C., 1971; MSN, U. N.C., 1978; PhD in Nursing Sci., U. S.C., 2003. RN, N.C.; cert. clin. specialist in adult psychiat./mental health nursing. Staff nurse VA Med. Ctr., Durham, N.C., 1974-75, 77-80; psychiat. clin. instr. Duke U. Med. Ctr., Durham, 1980-82, asst. head nurse, 1982-90, staff nurse, 1993—99; psychiat. clin. nurse specialist John Umstead Hosp., Butner, N.C., 1990-93; psychiat. lead nursing instr. Alamance C.C., Graham, N.C., 1994-96; clin. instr. U. N.C., Chapel Hill, 1999—2000, nurse recruiter dala collector, 2000—03, asst. prof. Sch. Nursing, Greensboro, 2003—04; assoc. prof. BSN and grad. nursing dept. Ea. Ky. U., Richmond, 2005—. Asst. Sunday sch. tchr. Mt. Hermon Bapt. Ch., Durham, 1994, 96, 99-2000. Capt. USNR, 1971-97, ret. 1997. Recipient award for nursing excellence Great 100 Orgn., Raleigh, N.C., 1991, Letter of Appreciation Am. Heart Assn., Chapel Hill, 1992. Mem. ANA, N.C. Nurses Assn. (sec. dist. 11, 1981), Assn. Mil Surgeons U.S., U. N.C. Chapel Hill Alumni Assn. and Sch. Nursing, East Carolina U. Alumni Assn. and Sch. Nursing, Res. Officers Assn. Baptist. Avocations: tennis, swimming, waterskiing, skiing. Home: 509 Paso Fino Dr Richmond KY 40475-8662 Office: Coll Health Scis 208 Rowlett Bldg 521 Lancaster AVe Richmond KY 40475-3102

BLAND, DEBORAH SHAFFER, nurse; b. Tampa, Fla., Jan. 20, 1954; d. Frank Solomon and Mary Louise (Swann) Shaffer; children: Danny, Dionne. LPN, Suwanee-Hamilton Nursing Sch., Live Oak, Fla., 1984; student, Hillsborough CC, 1992—. LPN, Fla. Author: Skippy Goes to Ybor Square, 1998, Danny's Journey, 2004. Active Ladies Auxillary Post #10208, Vet. of Fgn. Wars of U.S., Salt Springs,Fla.; mem. First Bapt. Ch., Salt Springs; founder of A Journey in Poetry, 2003, Ocala Nat. Forest- Salt Springs newsletter, 2003. Mem.: Brick City Ctr. for the Arts, Fla. State Poets Assn. Avocations: writing, painting, photography, gardening, guitar.

BLAND, FREDERICK AVES, architect; b. Galveston, Tex., Dec. 21, 1945; s. David and Florence (Aves) B.; m. Morley Anne Thomson, Dec. 21, 1968; 1 child, Chloe Thomson. BA, Yale U., 1968, MArch, 1972. Registered architect, N.Y., Conn., Fla., Va., NJ, Md., Ky. Assoc. Beyer Blinder Belle, Architects & Planners, N.Y.C., 1974-77, dir. design, 1977-79, ptnr., 1979—2004, mng. ptnr., 2004—. Chief architect Yale Archeol. project Royal Abbey St. Denis, Paris, 1970-80. V.p. Bklyn. Heights Assn., 1981-86, pres., 1992-94; panel mem. N.Y. State Coun. Arts, 1985-86; exec. com. Friends of Edn., Mus. Modern Art, 1992-00; trustee Bklyn. Bot. Garden, 1993—, chmn. horticulture com., 1996-03, exec. com., 1996—, vice-chmn., 1999—; trustee Bklyn. Hist. Soc., 1998, 04, The Evergreens Cemetery, 1998—; v.p. N.Y. Found. Architecture, 1998, pres., 1999; mem. vestry Trinity Ch. Wall St., 2004—. Mem. AIA (nat. com. on design, coll. of fellows, jury of fellows 1995-97), Am. Inst. Cert. Planners, Mcpl. Art Soc. NY, Yale Arch. Sch. Dean's Coun., Heights Casino Club (bd. govs. 1981-87, pres. 1987-90), Rembrandt Club (pres. 2001-03), Yale Club (N.Y.C.). Democrat. Episcopalian. Home: 26 Pierrepont St Brooklyn NY 11201-7209 also: Wallace Rd Branford CT 06405 Office: Beyer Blinder Belle Architects 41 E 11th St New York NY 10003-4673 Office Phone: 212-777-7800.

BLAND, GILBERT TYRONE, food service executive; b. Fredericksburg, Va., Mar. 10, 1955; s. Robert Edward and Ruth Elizabeth (Bumbry) B.; children: Robert David, Allison Michelle, Elizabeth Caroline. BS, James Madison U., 1977; MBA, Atlanta U., 1979. Banking officer Continential Ill. Bank, Chgo., 1979-83; v.p. Independence Bank, Chgo., 1983-85; pres. Tymark Enterprises Inc., Norfolk, Va., 1985—; chmn. The Tycorp Group, Norfolk, Va., 1995—; owner, franchisee Burger King, No. Va., 1985—, Pizza Hut, Va. and Greensboro, N.C., 1995—. Pres. Burger King Minority Franchise Assn., Miami, Fla., 1988-92; bd. dirs. Nat. Franchise Assn., Miami, 1988-92, Burger King Diversity Action Coun., 1992-96 (charter mem.), S.E. Region Internat. Pizza Hut Franchise Holders Assn., 1996-98; marketing adv. com. Burger King, 1992-98; State of Va. Small Bus. Financing Authority, Richmond, 1990—. Chmn., exec. com., bd. advisors Old Dominion Univ. Sch. Bus., Norfolk, 1990, Va. Marine Sci. Mus. Found., Virginia Beach, 1991; trustee James Madison U. Found., 1992; bd. dirs. Hampton U. Bus. Adv. Ctr., Greater Norfolk Corp., Senatra Hosp. Norfolk, Chamber Group Plans, Inc., Norfolk State U. Athletic Found.; exec. bd. Tidewater Coun. Boy Scouts of Am. Recipient James W. Mclamore Outstanding Svc. Leadership award Burger King Franchise Assn., 1992, Community Svc. award Alpha Kappa Alpha, 1990, Norfolk Community Hosp., 1991; Burger King Endowed scholar James Madison U., 2992. Mem. Beta Gamma Sigma. Baptist. Avocations: biking, chess, swimming. Office: Tymark Enterprises Inc 223 E City Hall Ave Ste 401 Norfolk VA 23510-1716

BLAND, JAMES THEODORE, JR., lawyer; b. Memphis, June 16, 1950; s. James Theodore and Martha Frances (Downen) B.; m. Pattie L. Martin, Apr. 12, 1974. BBA magna cum laude, Memphis State U., 1972, JD, 1974. Bar: Tenn. 1975, U.S. Dist. Ct. (we. dist.) Tenn. 1976, U.S. Tax Ct. 1976, U.S. Supreme Ct. 1983, U.S. Ct. Claims 1987; cert. Estate Planning specialist. Estate tax atty. IRS, Memphis, 1974-76; atty. Armstrong, Allen, Braden, Goodman, McBride & Prewitt, Memphis, 1976-91; prin. James T. Bland, Jr. and Assocs., Memphis, 1991—. Instr. in taxation, bus. law State Tchr.'s Inst., Memphis, 1975-83; bd. dirs. Thomas W. Briggs Found., Memphis. Fellow Am. Coll. Trust and Estate Counsel, Tenn. Bar Found., Memphis and Shelby County Bar Found. (pres. 1991-93); mem. ABA (legis. initiatives com., taxation sect., specialization in estate planning real property, probate and trust sect., Achievement award 1983, 85), Fed. Bar Assn. (pres. 1987-88, nat. coun. 1979—, bd. dirs. young lawyers divsn. 1979-84, pres. Memphis mid south chpt. 1979-80), Tenn. Bar Assn. (chmn. tax sect. 1984-85, bd. govs. 1984-85, 89-90, 90-91), Tenn. Young Lawyers Conf. (pres. 1985), Memphis Bar Assn. (bd. dirs. 1990-91), Tenn. Soc. CPA's. Republican. Methodist. Office: PO Box 25345 Christiansted VI 00824 E-mail: blandjr@uipowernet.net.

BLAND, JOHN LLOYD, lawyer; b. Wichita Falls, Tex., Sept. 20, 1944; Student, Vanderbilt U.; BA, U. Tex., 1967, JD with honors, 1969. Bar: Tex. 1969. Mem. Bracewell & Giuliani, LLP, Houston, 1969—. Mem. State Bar Tex., Houston Bar Assn., Phi Delta Phi. Office: Bracewell & Giuliani LLP 2300 S Tower Pennzoil Pl 711 Louisiana St Houston TX 77002-2781 Office Phone: 713-221-1310. Business E-Mail: jbland@bracewellgiuliani.com.

BLAND, PAMELA JUNE, special education educator; b. Chgo., Ill., Oct. 12, 1947; d. Arnold Richard Johnsen and June Florence Meisenhelder Johnsen; m. William Lawrence Bland, Jan. 24, 1970; children: Eric, Todd. BS, No. Ill. U., 1969; MEd, Nat. Louis U., 1996. Lead tchr. Keeler Sch. Multiply Handicapped, Aurora, Ill., 1975—78, substitute tchr., 1979—83; case mgr. Kennedy Rehab. Ctr., 1983—86; lead tchr. DeKalb County Spl. Edn. Assn., Cortland, 1986—88, Batavia Pub. Schs. Dist. 101, 1989—94, Maywood Pub. Schs. Dist. 89, Maywood, 1994—; partime faculty early childhood spl. edn. Morton C.C., Cicero, 2003—. Mem. St. Mark's Child Care Adv. Bd., Aurora, 1990—93; presenter in field. Actor: (of poems). Mem. Fox Valley Festival Chorus, Aurora, 1970—90, Naperville Chorus, 1990—; mem., Highland dancer Tunes of Glory Pipe Band, Batavia, 1980—84; high sch. youth leader St. Mark;s Luth. Ch., Aurora, 1990—98. Recipient Editors Choice award, Nat. Libr. Poetry, 1995. Mem.: ASCD, NEA, Nat. Assn. Edn. Young Children, Maywood Edn. Assn. Lutheran. Avocations: travel, camping, boating, genealogy, history. Office: Dist 89 Roosevelt Sch Maywood Pub Schs 1925 S 15th Broadview IL 60155

BLAND, ROBERT S., insurance company executive; BS in Mktg., U. Colo. Pres. Security Funding Corp.; founder Quotesmith Corp., Darien, Ill., 1984—; chmn., pres., CEO Quotesmith.com, Inc. Bd. dir. Seton Acad., Right To Life Com. Office: Quotesmith com Inc 8205 S Cass Ave Darien IL 60561

BLANDA, SANDI, artist; b. NY, Jan. 30, 1949; m. Robert S. Blanda, Feb. 24, 1973; children: Jaime, Elyse. BA, Queens Coll., 1971. Folk artist, Great Neck, NY, 1983—. Designer sea shell mosaics in octagonal mahogany cases Sailor's Valentine; spkr. in field; instr. workshops in field. Exhibitions include Sailor's Valentine Gallery, Nantucket, Mass., 1984—99, Margaret Woodbury Strong Mus., Rochester, NY, 1988, Quester Gallery, Greenwich and Stonington, Conn., 1994—2005, Bailey-Matthews Shell Mus., Sanibel, Fla., 1996—2005, Christina Gallery, Martha's Vineyard, Mass., 1997—2005, Hoorn-Ashby Gallery, NYC and Nantucket, 1999—2005, Virtual Mus. Can., 2004—05. Recipient numerous 1st and 2nd prizes for folk art Sanibel Shell Fair, 1990-2004. Home: 18 Oxford Blvd Great Neck NY 11023-2239 Personal E-mail: sgblanda@aol.com.

BLANDER, MILTON, chemist; b. Bklyn., Nov. 1, 1927; s. Benjamin and Yetta (Schwartzman) B.; children: Benjamin, Alice, Kathryn, Daniel, Joshua. BS, CUNY, 1950; PhD, Yale U., 1953. Rsch. assoc. Cornell U., Ithaca, N.Y., 1953-55; chemist Oak Ridge (Tenn.) Nat. Lab., 1955-62; chemist, group leader Rockwell Internat. Sci. Ctr., Thousand Oaks, Calif., 1962-71; sr. chemist, group leader Argonne (Ill.) Nat. Lab., 1971-97; founder Quest Rsch., South Holland, Ill., 1995—. Recipient Materials Rsch. award U.S. Dept. Energy, 1984, Alexander von Humboldt award. Fellow AAAS, Meteoritical Soc.; mem. Metall. Soc., Am. Chem. Soc., Electrochem. Soc. (Max Bredig award 1987), Norwegian Acad. Tech. Scis. E-mail: mblander2@aol.com.

BLANDFORD, ROGER DAVID, astronomy educator; b. Grantham, Eng., Aug. 28, 1949; s. Jack George and Janet Margaret (Evans) B.; m. Elizabeth Kellett, Aug. 5, 1972; children: Jonathan, Edward. BA, Magdalene Coll., Cambridge U., 1970; MA, PhD, Cambridge U., 1974. Rsch. fellow St. John's Coll., Cambridge U., 1973-76; asst. prof. astronomy Calif. Inst. Tech., Pasadena, 1976-79, prof., 1979-89, Richard Chace Tolman prof. theoretical astrophysics, 1989—; mem. Inst. Advanced Study, Princeton, 1974-75; Pehong and Adele Chen prof. particle astrophysics and cosmology Stanford (Calif.) U., 2003—, dir. Kvali Inst. for Particle Astrophysics and Cosmology, 2003—. Contbr. articles to profl. publs. W.B.R. King scholar, 1967-70; Charles Kingsley Bye fellow, 1972-73; Alfred P. Sloan research fellow, 1980, Guggenheim fellow, 1988—. Fellow Royal Soc., Royal Astron. Soc. (Eddington medal 1999), Cambridge Philos. Soc.; mem. NAS, Am. Astron. Soc. (Warner prize 1982, Heineman prize 1998), Am. Acad. Arts and Scis., Northland Acad. Scis. Office: PO Box 20450 MS29 Stanford CA 94309 Home: 820 Monte Rosa Dr Menlo Park CA 94025-6723 Office Phone: 650-926-2600. Business E-Mail: rdb3@stanford.edu.

BLANE, HOWARD THOMAS, alcohol/drug abuse services professional, researcher; b. De Land, Fla., May 10, 1926; s. Chesley Thomas and Olive Henrietta (Van Heest) B.; children: Benjamin, Eva. BA cum laude, Harvard U., 1950; MA, Clark U., 1951, PhD, 1957. Instr. Harvard Med. Sch., Cambridge, Mass., 1957-66, asst. clin. prof., 1966-70; assoc. prof. U. Pitts., 1970-72, prof., 1972-86; rsch. prof. SUNY, Buffalo, 1986—; dir. Rsch. Inst. Addictions, Buffalo, 1986-96. Cons. Nat. Inst. on Alcohol Abuse and Alcoholism, Washington, 1970-98; v.p. Health Edn. Found., Washington, 1975—; bd. dirs. Rsch. Found. for Mental Hygiene, Albany, N.Y., 1986-96; principal investigator numerous grants. Author: The Personality of the Alcoholic, 1968; editor: Frontiers of Alcoholism, 1970, Youth, Alcoholism and Social Policy, 1979, Psychological Theories of Drinking and Alcoholism, 1987, 2nd edit., 1999. Bd. dirs. Jellinek Meml. Fund, Toronto, 1995—. Clark U. scholar, Worcester, Mass., 1950-51. Fellow APA, Am. Psychol. Soc.; mem. APHA, AAAS, Rsch. Soc. on Alcoholism. Office: Rsch Inst on Addictions 150 Lenell Rd #204 Fort Myers Beach FL 33931-5722 Office Phone: 716-852-0858. E-mail: blaneonfmb@msn.com.

BLANK, A(NDREW) RUSSELL, lawyer; b. Bklyn., June 13, 1945; s. Lawrence and Joan B.; children: Adam, Marisa. Student, U. N.C., 1963-64; BA, U. Fla., 1966; postgrad., Law Sch., 1966-68; JD, U. Miami, 1970. Bar: Ga. 1971, Fla. 1970; cert. civil trial advocate Nat. Bd. Trial Advocacy. Law asst. Dist. Ct. Judge, Atlanta, 1970-72; ptnr. A. Russell Blank & Assocs., PC, Atlanta, 1985—. Contbr. articles to profl. jours. Pub. adv. com. Atlanta Regional Commn., 1972-74. Recipient Merit award Ga. Bar Assn., 1981. Mem. ABA, ATLA, Atlanta Bar Assn., Ga. Bar Assn. (Merit award 1981), Ga. Trial Lawyers Assn. (officer), Lawyers Club Atlanta, Fla. Bar Assn., Am. Bd. Trial Advocates (advocate, bd. dirs. 2000—, pres. Ga. chpt., southeastern design v.p., 2004-05, pres. elect Southeastern regional divsn.), Xenix Soc. (bd. dirs.). Office: 230 Peachtree St NW Ste 2600 Atlanta GA 30303-1516 Office Phone: 404-553-7400. Business E-Mail: rblank@counsellor.com.

BLANK, ARTHUR M., professional sports team executive, retired home and lumber retail chain executive; b. Queens, NY, 1942; BS, Babson Coll., LLD (hon.), 1998. Acct. Arthur Young & Co., N.Y.C., 1963-67; with Daylin Inc., Los Angeles, 1967-74; v.p., treas. Handy Dan Home Improvement Ctrs. Inc., Los Angeles, 1974-78; co-founder Home Depot Inc., Atlanta, 1978, pres., COO, 1978—97, pres., CEO, 1997—2000, co-chmn., 2000—01; chmn. Arthur M. Blank Family Found., 1995—; chmn., pres., CEO AMB Group LLC, 2001—; owner, CEO Atlanta Falcons Football Club, 2002—. Bd. dir. Cox Enterprises, Staples Inc.; disting. exec. in residence Goizueta Bus. Sch., Emory Univ., 2001. Trustee Carter Ctr., Emory Univ., Cooper Inst.; bd. mem. NC Outward Bound Sch. Co-recipient Ga. Philanthropist of the Year, Nat. Soc. Fundraising Exec., 2000, Abe Goldstein Human Rels. award, Anti-Defamation League, 2001; named Ga. Most Respected CEO, Ga. Trend mag., 2001, 2003; named to Acad. Disting. Entrepreneurs, Babson Coll., 1995, Bus. Hall of Fame, Junior Achievement Atlanta, 2001, Ga. State Univ., 2002; recipient Brotherhood / Sisterhood award, Nat. Conf. of Christians & Jews, 1994. Mem.: Commerce Club. Office: Atlanta Falcons 4400 Falcon Pkwy Flowery Branch GA 30542*

BLANK, EUGENE, pediatrician, radiologist, educator; b. Balt., May 8, 1924; s. Maurice Blank and Fannie Edith Jacob; m. Esther Honikberg, June 22, 1958; children: Lisa, Anne, Linda. BA, Johns Hopkins U., 1948, MD, 1954. Diplomate Am. Bd. Pediat., Am. Bd. Radiology. Prof. emeritus in pediats. and radiology Oreg. Health Scis. U., Portland, 1991—. Author: Pediatric Images Casebook of Differential Diagnosis, 1997. 2d lt. USMC, 1942—45, South Pacific. Democrat. Avocation: writing. Home: 4940 SW Humphrey Park Rd Portland OR 97221

BLANK, LETA SONDRA, health and long term care insurance specialist; d. Newton B. and Molly Lerner Stenberg; m. Howard A. Blank. BA, CUNY; MBA, Marymount U.; Cert. of Design, Phila. Inst. Design. Fin. counselor U. Md. Corp. Extension Svc., Derwood, 1992-94; program dir. Sr. Health Ins. Asst. program U. Md., Derwood, 1994—. With Consortium Washington SHIP coords., 1996—. Contbr. (book) How to Retire Happy, 2000; contbr. Washington Post; featured and quoted in mags. Bd. assoc. Nat. Rehab. Hosp., Washington, 1994—; active Medicare beneficiary adv. bd., 1995—; program coord. Curb Abuse in Medicare/Medicaid, Md. Dept. Aging, 1996—. Mem. Delta Epsilon Sigma. Avocations: painting, golf, dance. Home: 8801 Mayberry Ct Potomac MD 20854 Office: U Md CES 18410 Muncaster Rd Derwood MD 20855 E-mail: lblank@erols.com.

BLANK, MARION SUE, psychologist, educator; b. N.Y.C., Dec. 20, 1933; d. Morris David and Tillie Jean (Sherman) Hersch; m. Martin Blank, July 3, 1955; children: Donna, Jonathan, Ari. BA, CCNY, 1955, MS in Edn, 1956; PhD, Cambridge (Eng.) U., 1961. Asst. prof. Albert Einstein Coll. Medicine, 1965-70, asso. prof., 1970-73; prof. dept. psychiatry Rutgers Med. Sch., Piscataway, N.J., 1973-83; mem. adj. faculty dept. psychiatry Columbia Coll. Physicians and Surgeons, N.Y.C., 1980—83, co-dir., devel. neuropsychiatry program, 2004—; pres. Darj on Learning, Inc., 2001—; co-dir. Devel. Neuropsychiatry Program, Columbia U., N.Y.C., 2004—. Dir. reading disabilities rsch. inst., pvt. practice, cons., 1983—; Nat. Tour lectr. Speech Pathology Assn. Australia, 1996. Author: Teaching Learning in the Preschool - A Dialogue Approach, Preschool Language Assessment Instrument, 1978, (with Rose and Berlin) The Language of Learning, 1978, Sentence Master, 1990-96, (with Berlin) A Parent's Guide to Educational Software, 1991, (with Marquis and Klimovitch) Directing School Discourse, 1994, Directing Early Discourse with Marquis and Klimovitch, 1995, The Reading Remedy, 2005. Pinsent-Darwin fellow, 1960; recipient award of commendation N.J. Speech and Hearing Assn., 1979, Spl. Edn. award Software Pubs. Am., 1990, N.J., USPHS Career Devel. award, 1965-73; named N.J. nominee Kleffner Lifetime Svc. award Am. Speech Lang. Hearing Assn., 1994, 95. Fellow APA; mem. Assn. for Children with Learning Disabilities. Home: 157 Columbus Dr Tenafly NJ 07670-1635 Office Phone: 201-567-0790. Personal E-mail: msblank@optonline.net. Business E-Mail: msb5@columbia.edu. *It is heartening, albeit at times difficult, to live in a period of revolutionary change for women.*

BLANK, MATTHEW C., broadcast company executive; m. Susan McGuirk; children: Meredith, Gordon. Degree, U. Pa.; MBA, Baruch Coll. Past sr. v.p. consumer mktg. Home Box Office; exec. v.p. mktg. Showtime Networks, Inc. (Showtime, The Movie Channel, Fliz, Showtime Extreme, Showtime en Español, Showtime Event TV), N.Y.C., 1981-91, pres., COO, 1991—, past CEO, also chmn. bd. dirs., bd. dirs., mem. exec. com. Sundance Ch. Bd. dirs. Comedy Central, Phoenix Pictures; chmn., CEO Showtime Network, Inc. Trustee Rheedlen Ctrs. Children and Families; bd. dirs. Walter Kaitz Found.; mem. exec. com. Cable Positive, active Nat. Minorities in Cable. Recipient Vanguard award for mktg., 1991, Chmn.'s award Cable TV and Mktg., 1991, Friends of Children award Rheedlen Ctrs. Children and Families, 1996, 1991, Chmn.'s award Cable TV and Mktg., 1991, Friends of Children award, Rheedlen Ctrs. Children and Families, 1996, Fairness award, Gay and Lesbian Alliance Against Defamation, 1997. Mem.: Pub. Edn. Needs Civic Involvement in Lng., Nat. Cable TV Assn. (bd. dirs.), Nat. Acad. Cable Programming (bd. govs.), NCCJ (mem. exec. bd. dirs). Office: care Showtime Networks 1633 Broadway New York NY 10019-6708

BLANK, STEVEN A., energy executive; B in History, SUNY; M in Internat. Bus., Columbia U. V.p. fin., treas. Ultramar Diamond Shamrock Corp., 1996—2002; chief acctg. officer, CFO Valero GP, LLC, San Antonio, 1999—2002, sr. v.p., CFO, 2002—. Office: Valero Corp Hqtrs One Valero Pl San Antonio TX 78212-3186 Office Phone: 210-370-2000.*

BLANKE, HENRY H., JR., retired theater educator; b. Geneva, Nebr., May 15, 1931; s. Henry H. Blanke, Sr. and Fern L. Cruse; m. Phyllis Anne Chard, June 30, 1957; children: Gregory W., Annette LaRae Blanke Hinrichs. BA, Doane Coll., 1953; postgrad., Kans. State U., 1954; MA, U. Nebr., 1958; postgrad., Ind. U., 1961—63. Tchr. English and speech Superior H.S., Nebr., 1953—57; assoc. prof. Tarkio Coll., Mo., 1959—61; instr. speech and theatre Ind. U., Bloomington, 1961—63; assoc. prof. theatre arts Nebr. Wesleyan U., Lincoln, 1958—59, 1963—99, dir. theatre arts, 1963—93; ret., 1999. Founder, artistic dir. Brownville (Nebr.) Village Theatre, 1967—99; designer Nebr. Wesleyan Elder Speech-Theatre Art Ctr., 1981. Actor: (various plays), 1949—2005; dir.: (various plays, musicals, operas), 1953—2002. Chmn. Nebr. Centennial Playwriting Com. Named Outstanding Alumni, Hixon-Lied Coll. Fine Arts, 2000; recipient Eyes on Nebr. award, Nebr. Optometric Assn., 1972, Nebr. Govs. Arts award, Nebr. Gov. J. J. Exon, 1979, Kersenbrock Humanitarian award, Doane Coll., 1993, Lincoln Mayor's Arts award, Lincoln Nebr. Arts Coun., 2001, Play Directing award, Kennedy Ctr./Am. Coll. Theatre Festival, 1986, 1987, 1994, 1998, Kennedy Ctr. Medallion of Excellence award, 1999. Mem.: Nat. Collegiate Players, Theta Alpha Phi, Alpha Psi Omega, Phi Kappa Phi. Democrat. Presbyterian. Home: 2221 N 61st St Lincoln NE 68505

BLANKENBAKER, ZARINA, adult education educator, consultant; d. M Ali Din and Saira Bakash; m. John Ford Blankenbaker; children: Lauren Sarah, Ryan Ford. BSc in secondary edn., Ind. U., 1980—83, MA in applied linguistics, 1983—84; postgrad., Summer Inst. Intercultural Communication, Portland, Oreg., Nat. Inst. Leadership Devel.; PhD in Higher Edn., Univ. N. Tex. Cert. tchg. State of Tex., 1989. Esol instr. Army Cmty. Svc., Lawton, Okla., 1985—86; fin. counselor Army Cmty. Services, Killeen, Tex., 1986—90; adj. instr. Ctrl. Tex. Coll., Killeen, 1989—90; adj. faculty/lab tutor/academic advisor Richland Coll., Dallas, 1993—97, faculty, 1997—. Bd. mem. Tex TESOL V, Dallas, 1997—99, newsletter editor, 1997—99; com. chair Tex TESOL State Conf., Dallas, 1998; pres. elect, program chair state conf. Tex TESOL V, 2005; sec. Richland Coll. Faculty Assn., Dallas, 2000—02. Mem.: Am. Assn. Women in Cmty. Colls., Assn. of Grad. Students in Higher Edn., Phi Kappa Phi. Office: Richland College 12800 Abrams Rd Dallas TX 75243-2199 E-mail: zblankenbaker@dcccd.edu.

BLANKENBURG, JULIE J., librarian; b. Madison, Wis., Dec. 22, 1956; d. Henry A. and Marjorie L. Blankenburg; m. Wayne I. Zimmerman. BA in Theatre, U. Wis., 1979, MA in LS, 1980. Asst. libr. USDA Forest Products Lab. Libr., Madison, 1988-93, libr., 1994—. Mem.: ALA, Theatre Libr. Assn., Wis. Libr. Assn., Spl. Librs. Assn. Office: USDA Forest Svc Forest Products Lab Libr One Gifford Pinchot Dr Madison WI 53726-2398 Office Phone: 608-231-9491.

BLANKENSHIP, DON L., energy executive; b. W. Va., 1950; B in Acctg., Marshall Univ. With Keebler and Flowers Industries, 1972—82; joined A.T. Massey Coal (now Massey Energy), 1982—, chmn., pres., CEO, 1992—2000, Massey Energy Co., 2000—. Bd. dir. Bluesprings Coal Co., Maxann Coal Co., Pikco Mining Co., Tall Timber Coal Co., Blackberry Creek Coal Co., Big Bottom Coal Co., Allburn Coal Co., Rawl Sales & Processing Co.; bd. dir., pres. Snowball Ptnrs., Ziebold Sapphire Ptnrs. Bd. dir. US C. of C. Named Disting. Alumni, Marshall Univ., 1999; named to Tug Valley Mining Inst. Hall of Fame, 1999, Am. Inst. CPA Bus. & Industry Hall of Fame, 2002. Office: Massey Energy 4 N Fourth St PO Box 26765 Richmond VA 23261 Office Phone: 804-788-1800. Office Fax: 804-788-1870.*

BLANKENSHIP, EDWARD G., architect; b. Martin, Tenn., June 22, 1943; BArch, Columbia U., 1966, MSc in Arch., 1967; MLitt in Arch., Cambridge (Eng.) U., 1971. Sr. v.p. Landrum & Brown, Inc., Chgo. Home: 238 Park Crest Newport Beach CA 92657

BLANKENSHIP, J. RICHARD, former ambassador; b. Troy, Ala. married. Diploma, Fla. State U. Former ptnr., dir. Capital South Group, Jacksonville, Fla.; former pres., CFO St. John's Capital; former mcpl. and govt. financing officer Raymond James and Assocs., St. Petersburg, Fla.; former acct. Peat, Marwick, and Mitchell, Jacksonville; former ptnr. J. Richard Blankenship & co.; U.S. amb. to The Bahamas US Dept. State, 2001—03; former acct. Price Waterhouse & Co., Tampa, Fla. Apptd. mem. State of Fla. Transp. Outreach Program; mem. Fla. Joint Task Force Evaluation Team.

BLANKENSHIP, JIM COLEGROVE, cardiologist; s. John Harnly and Marian (Colgrove) Blankenship; m. Mary Stark, June 9, 1984; children: Leah Shikany, Bart James, Peter Stark. MD, Cornell U., 1980. Diplomate in internal medicine and interventional cardiology Am. Bd. Internal Medicine. With Marshfield (Wis.) Clinic, 1987—89; dir. Catheterization Lab., Geisinger Med. Ctr., Danville, Pa., 1997—; prof. medicine Jefferson Med. Coll., Phila., 1989—. Office: Geisinger Med Ctr 100 N Academy Dr Danville PA 17822 Office Phone: 570-271-8067.

BLANKENSHIP, ROY, conservator, artist, writer; b. Phila., Nov. 26, 1943; m. Lynn Ann Wilkers, Apr. 6, 1968 (div. May 1993); children: Troy Insley, Beth Lynn; m. Lois Showalter, Apr. 1, 2000. BAAS Arts and Sci., U Del., 1973. Art restoration apprentice/asst. Salter Studio, Arden, Del., 1966—72; art conservation student apprentice Winterthur (Del.) Mus., 1968—72; painting conservation asst. Ted Segal Studio Phila. Mus. Art, 1969—70; painting restoration asst./apprentice Twistback Conservation Ctr., Oxford, Pa., 1970—72; gen. mgr., layout design artist The Little Giant Shopper, Newark, Del., 1970—72; art tchr. Marbrook Elem., Wilmington, Del., 1971—72; part-time art tchr. Ursuline Acad., Wilmington, 1971—72; art history and studio art tchr. Brandywine H.S., Wilmington, 1972—73; curator, exhbn. coord. Morris Libr., U. Del., Newark, 1972—73; painting conservator-in-residence Carspecken-Scott Gallery, Wilmington, 1972—78; founder Blankenship Painting and Conservation Studio, Wilmington, 1975—81; dir., owner Blankenship Conservation Ctr., Wilmington, 1981—; founder Blankenship's mail order bus., 1985—. Profl. fine art painting conservationist IIC, 1972; instr. art history U. Del., Newark, 1972; lectr., cons. in field, 1973—; curator, lectr. Albert Babb Insley retrospective exhbn. (traveling), 1984—85, Nardin Fine Arts, Ltd., Cross River, NY, 1988; organizer, guest curator, lectr. The McKissick Mus., U. S.C., Columbia, 1995; collections and chief painting conservator Boggs Fed. Bldg., Wilmington, Del., 1973—; curator Hastings Gallery, New Canaan, Conn., 1987; painting collections cons., restorer Del. Art Mus., Wilmington, Del., 1972—83; personal collections cons. to Ernest Dodge, dir. Peabody-Essex Mus., Salem, Mass., 1973—85; fellow, rsch. scientist AIC, Wash., DC, 1973—; conservators in pvt. practice Am. Inst. Cons., 1975—; chief painting conservator NEHGS, Boston, 1996—. Columnist Collecting (Gannett Papers), 1975—85; author, compiler, designer, pub.: The Delicate Palette of Albert Insley, 1982; editor: The Life and Times of Frank G. Speck (1881-1950), 1992; one-man shows include Atlas Chem. Emporium (photography), Wilmington, 1970, Swarthmore Coll., Pa., 1960, Bicentennial Retrospective exhbn., Wilmington Libr., Lou Polack Gallery, Rockport, Mass., 1978, 1983, Nancy Richardson Art and Antique Gallery, Essex, Conn., 1981, R.M. Worth Antiques and Fine Art, Chadds Ford, Pa., 2000, 2000, exhibited in group shows at Grand Opera Ho. and Del. Art Mus., Wilmington, Del., 1968, Del. Art Mus. Ceramics Retro., 1970, 1973, Chester County (Pa.) Art Assn., 2002, Hagley Mus., Wilmington, 2000, Rockport Contbg. Members Show, 2001, Main Hall, Kendal at Longwood, Pa., 2001, North Shore Ann. Exhbn., 1972—, Oil Painters of Am., 2002, one-man shows include R.M. Worth Antiques and Fine Art, Pa., 2000, exhbn. with wife, Main Hall, Kendal at Longwood, 2001, Wilmington Libr., Del., 2002, Sawyer Free Libr., Gloucester, Mass., 2002, Crosslands, Kennett Sq., Pa., 2003. Founder, organizer, head chairperson 1st Ann. Arden Ctr. Antiques Show and Sale, 1977; founder Blankenship Conservation Ctr., Wilmington, 1973—; organizer, co-chair 1st F.G. Speck Seminar, U. Pa., Phila., 1986. With USN, 1962—66, with USN, 1962—66. Mem.: NSAA, Am Artists Prof. League (Salmagundi Club), Am. Soc. Marine Artists, Soc. Del. Artists, Chester County Artist Assn. Address: PO Box 7221 Wilmington DE 19803

BLANKENSHIP, TRENT, school system administrator, educator; married; 3 children. BS in sci. Edn., U. Wyo., 1986, MA in Ednl. Adminstrn., 1991, PhD in Leadership and Human Devel., 1995. Chemistry tchr. Riverton H.S., Wyo.; chemistry and physics tchr. Heidelburg H.S. Dept. of Defense, Germany; asst. prin. Sheridan Jr. H.S., Sheridan County, Wyo.; prin. DuBois H.S. and Middle Sch., Wyo.; supt. Fremont Sch. District, DuBois, Wyo., Carbon County Sch. Dist., Rawlins; state supt. pub. instrn. State of Wyo., Cheyenne, 2003—. Mem. Wyo. CAS Policy Com. Mem. adv. bd. U. Wyo. Coll. Edn.; mem. Gov.'s Substance Abuse Com. Office: Wyo Dept Edn Hathaway Bldg 2300 Capitol Ave 2d Fl Cheyenne WY 82002-0050 Home: 3302 Hales Ranch Rd Cheyenne WY 82007-1823 E-mail: champion4children@yahoo.com.

BLANKENSTEIN, ELIZABETH M., director, educator; b. Dorchester, Mass., Feb. 16, 1958; d. Frederick F. and Elizabeth A. MacQueen; m. Ronald G. Blankenstein, May 3, 1998; 1 child, Heather L. BA, Westfield State Coll., 1980; MS, U. Bridgeport, 1983. Cert. career and tech. edn. adminstr. N.H., 2004, faculty instr. Intel, 2003. Learner services coord. Coll. Lifelong Learning, North Country Region, NH, 1985—97; dir. of the office of grad. and evening admissions and asst. dean Rivier Coll., Nashua, NH, 1997—98; dir. office grad. admissions and continuing edn. Notre Dame Coll., Manchester, NH, 1998—99; implementation specialist Jenzabar, Inc., Harrisonburg, Va., 1999—2002; dir. vocat. planning and accountability N.H. Cmty. Tech. Coll. Sys., Concord, 2002—05; assoc. v.p. acad. affairs N.H. Tech. Inst., Concord, 2005—. Faculty Granite State Coll., Manchester, NH, 1985—; cons. Office Grad. Studies Plymouth (N.H.) State U., 1989—97. Mem. adv. bd. Kennett H.S. Mktg. Program, Conway, NH, 1992—93; elected mem. Town of Madison Planning Bd., NH, 1992—97, chair, 1993—95; mem. Rte. 16 corridor study team NH Dept. Transp., Concord, 1996—97; mem. supr. adminstrv. unit 9 and 13 Sch. to Work Com., Conway, NH, 1996—97; eucharistic min. St. Elizabeth Seton Parish, Bedford, NH, 2002—; mem. Vis. Nurse Svcs. No. Carroll County, NH, 1986—88, Mt. Wash. Valley Econ. Coun., Conway, NH, 1995—97; mem. cmty. adv. bd. Internat. Paper Corp., Madison and Freedom Operations, NH, 1996—97. Fellow, Rotary Internat., 1992. Mem.: Assn. Continuing Higher Edn. (region I exceptional program com. chair 1997—), Nat. Tech Prep Network, Nat. Assn. State Dirs. Career and Tech. Edn. Consortium (assoc.). Independent. Roman Catholic. Avocations: painting, ballroom dancing. Home: 101 Crestview Rd Manchester NH 03104 Office: NH Tech Inst 31 College Dr Concord NH 03301 Office Phone: 603-271-1754.

BLANKFEIN, LLOYD C., investment company executive; b. Bronx, NY, Sept. 20, 1954; m. Laura Blankfein; 3 children. BA, Harvard U., 1975; JD, Harvard Law Sch., 1978. Corp. tax lawyer Donovan, Leisure, Newton & Irvine; joined J. Aron & Co. Currency and Commodities Divsn. The Goldman Sachs Group, N.Y.C., 1982, co-head, J. Aron currency and commodities divsn., 1994—97, co-head fixed income, currency and commodities divsn., 1997—2004, vice chmn., 2002—04, pres., COO, 2004—. Former mem. fgn. exch. com. Fed. Res. Bank, NY. Former dir. Futures Industry Assn.; co-chair fin. aid task force Harvard U., mem. exec. com. on univ. resources. Office: The Goldman Sachs Group 85 Broad St New York NY 10004

BLANKFEIN, ROBERT J., retired neurologist; b. Nov. 5, 1931; BA, Yale U., New Haven, Conn., 1954; MD, N.Y. Med. Coll., 1958. Diplomate in Neurology Am. Bd. of Neurology and Psychiatry, 1971. BxVAH resident in neurology, 1960—63; clin. asst. prof. neurology N.Y. Med. Coll., 1971-74, clin. assoc. prof. neurology, 1975—; attending neurologist Met. Hosp., N.Y., 1986—, N.Y. Hosp. Med. Ctr. Queens, 1979-95; fed. examiner in neurology U.S. Dept. Labor, 1992—. Coord. jour. club for neurology residents, N.Y. Med. Coll., 1971-89; presenter in field Mem. editl. bd. Hospital Physician, cons. editor; contbr. articles to profl. jours. Fellow, Am. Acad. Neurology, NY Acad. Medicine, Royal Soc. of Medicine, Neurophysiology fellow, EEG Hosp. U. Penn, 1963—65. Fellow ACP, Stroke Coun Office: 501 E 87 St Apt 5F New York NY 10128 E-mail: robertblankfein@verizon.net.

BLANKFIELD, BRYAN J., lawyer, automotive executive; BS, Drake U.; JD, Northwestern U. In-house legal counsel and cons. Waste Management, Inc., 1990—2002, assoc. gen. counsel, asst. sec., 1995—2002, v.p., 1998—2002; v.p., gen. counsel, sec. Oshkosh Truck Corp., Wis., 2002—. Office: Oshkosh Truck Corp 2307 Oregon St PO Box 2566 Oshkosh WI 54903 Office Phone: 920-235-9151.

BLANKFORT, LOWELL ARNOLD, newspaper publisher; b. NYC, Apr. 29, 1926; s. Herbert and Gertrude (Butler) B.; m. April Pemberton; 1 child, Jonathan. BA in History and Polit. Sci., Rutgers U., 1946. Reporter, copy editor LI (NY) Star-Jour., 1947—49; columnist London Daily Mail, Paris, 1949—50; copy editor The Stars & Stripes, Darmstadt, Germany, 1950—51, Wall St. Jour., NYC, 1951; bus., labor editor Cowles Mags., NYC, 1951—53; pub. Pacifica (Calif.) Tribune, 1954—59; freelance writer Europe, Asia, 1959—61; co-pub., editor Chula Vista (Calif.) Star-News, 1961—78; co-owner Paradise (Calif.) Post, 1977—2003. Co-owner Monte Vista (Colo.) Jour., Ctr. (Colo.) Post-Dispatch, Del Norte (Colo.) Prospector, 1978—93, Plainview (Minn.) News, St. Charles (Minn.) Press, Lewiston (Minn.) Jour., 1980—98, Summit (Colo.) Sentinel, New Richmond (Wis.) News, 1981—87, Yuba City Valley Herald, 1982—85, TV Views, Monterey, Calif., 1982—87, Summit County Jour., 1982—87, Alpine (Calif.) Sun, 1987—93, Bassica Mag., 1998—, Fingerstyle Guitar Mag., 1999. *Mr. Blankfort has received many awards including Best Editorials in California, non-dailies; 1st or 2nd place seven consecutive years, California Newspaper Publishers Association; Best Editorial in the United States, National Newspapers Association; Best Editorial U. S. suburban newspapers. Suburban Publishers Newspapers of America; Headliner of the Year, San Diego Press Club; John Swett Award, California Education Association; and Citizen of the Year, Sweetwater Education Association. Special Media Award, National Conference of Christians and Jews. Mr. Blankfort is a widely traveled writer. He has interviewed many heads of state including Fidel Castro in Cuba, Li Peng and Li Xiannin in China, and Benezir Bhutto in Pakistan.* Columnist, contbr. articles on fgn. affairs to newspapers. Active Calif. Dem. Ctrl. Com., 1963; bd. dirs. Mus. Photographic Arts, San Diego, 2003—04. Named Citizen of Yr., Sweetwater Edn. Assn., Outstanding Layman of Yr., 1966, Citizen of Yr., City of Chula Vista, 1976, Headliner of Yr., San Diego Press Club, 1980; recipient Best Editl. in Calif., non-dailies, 1st or 2d place seven consecutive yrs., Calif. Newspaper Pub. Assn., Best Editl. in US, Nat. Newspaper Assn., Best Editl. US Suburban Newspapers, Suburban Pubs. Newspapers Am., John Swett award, Calif. Edn. Assn., Spl. Media award for articles on S.Am., Nat. Conference Christians and Jews. Mem.: ACLU (pres. San Diego chpt. 1970—71), Soc. Profl. Journalists, Calif. Newspaper Pubs. Assn., East Meets West Found. (nat. v.p. 1992—98), World Federalist Assn. (pres. San Diego chpt. 1984—86, nat. bd. 1992—2000), UN Assn. (pres. San Diego chpt. 1991—93, nat. coun. 1992—97, nat. bd. 1997—2001, nat. coun. 2002—04), Internat. Ctr. Devel. Policy (nat. bd. 1985—90), Ctr. Internat. Policy (bd. dirs. 1991—), World Affairs Coun. San Diego (pres. 1996—99, dir.), Inst. of the Ams. (assoc.; internat. coun. 1994—). Achievements include interviewing many heads of state including Fidel Castro in Cuba, Li Peng and Li Ziannin in China, Benazir Bhutto in Pakistan, Kim Dae Jung in Korea, Paul Kagame in Rwanda. Home: 4008 Old Orchard Ln Bonita CA 91902-2337 Office: Ste C25 310 3rd Ave Chula Vista CA 91910-3970 Office Phone: 619-422-3667.

BLANTON, EDWARD LEE, JR., lawyer; b. nr. Hope Mills, N.C., Oct. 31, 1931; s. Edward Lee and Margaret M. (Bullard) B.; m. Cathleen Estelle Edwards, Aug. 13, 1960; children: Edward Lee III, Cathleen Estelle, Margaret Ellyn. BS, Davidson Coll., 1953; MA, Vanderbilt U., 1954; LLB, U. Md., 1960. Bar: Md. 1960. Tchr. math. Balt. City schs., 1956-59; law clk. to judge Washington, 1960-62; assoc. Cross & Shriver, Balt., 1962—65; ptnr., mgr. Maxwell Hughes & Blanton, 1965—68; ptnr. Adelberg, Rudow & Blanton, 1969-72, Blanton & McCleary, 1973-93; asst. atty. gen. State Md., Balt., 1965-68. Chmn. subcom. drafting revision Md. election laws Md. Legis. Coun., 1966-67; chmn. subcom. drafting revision Md. income tax laws Hughes Commn., 1966-67. Bd. dirs. United Christian Citizens, 1971-92, pres., 1974-75; pres. Ctrl. Balt. Ecumenical Sch. Christian Edn., 1971-74, Hist. Long Green Valley, Inc., 1980-86, Long Green Valley Assn., 1979-89; dir. Ctr. for Prevention of Child Abuse, 1991-96; mem. State Rep. Ctrl. Com., 1982-86; mem. citizens adv. com. Charles H. Hickey Sch., 1983-91, chmn., 1987-91; mem. Ctrl. Towson Com. Christian Businessmen, Balt. Coun. Fgn. Affairs; v.p., dir. Long Green Valley Conservancy, Inc., 1995-98; trustee com. Presbyn. Ch., Balt., St. James Acad., Monkton, Md., 1989-95, Egenton Home, Balt.; Rep. nominee for Atty. Gen. of Md., 1990. 1st lt. AUS, 1954-56; capt. Md. N.G., 1957-62. Mem. Nat. Lawyers Assn., Bar Assn. Balt. County, Newcomen Soc. N.Am., Christian Legal Soc., Center Club, Masons, Delta Theta Phi. Presbyterian (elder). Home: Avondell Glen Arm MD 21057 Office: 305 W Chesapeake Ave Baltimore MD 21204-4255 E-mail: eblantonjr@msn.com.

BLANTON, FAYE WESTER, legislative official; b. Tallahassee, Nov. 9, 1946; m. Edwin F. "Ed" Blanton; children: Wade, Doug, Laurel McDaniel. Staff asst. govtl. efficiency com. Fla. Senate, Tallahassee, asst. to dir. mgmt. staff, asst. sec., sec., 1996—. Advisor, counselor Girls State, Boys State, YMCA Youth Legislature, Silver-Haired Legislature; pres. PTO Leon County Sch. Dist., mem. adv. bd. Mem. Am. Soc. Legis. Clks. and Secs. (exec. com., past assoc. v.p., mem. exec. and nominating com., chair, vice-chair, mem. various coms.) Baptist. Avocations: gardening, walking, reading. Home: 610 Summerbrooke Dr Tallahassee FL 32312 Office: Fla Senate 404 S Monroe St Tallahassee FL 32399-1100 Fax: 850-487-5174. E-mail: blanton.faye@flsenate.gov.

BLANTON, HOOVER CLARENCE, lawyer; b. Green Sea, S.C., Oct. 13, 1925; s. Clarence Leo and Margaret (Hoover) B.; m. Cecilia Lopez, July 31, 1949; children: Lawson Hoover, Michael Lopez. JD, U. S.C., 1953. Bar: S.C. 1953. Ordained deacon, Bapt. Ch. Assoc. Whaley & McCutchen, Columbia, SC, 1953—66; ptnr. McCutchen, Blanton, Johnson and Barnette LLP, Columbia, 1967—. Dir. Legal Aid Service Agy., Columbia, chmn. bd., 1972-73. Gen. counsel S.C. Rep. Conv., 1962; del. Rep. State Conv., 1962, 64, 66, 68, 70, 74; bd. dirs. Midlands Cmty. Action Agy., Columbia, vice chmn., 1972-73; bd. dirs. Wildewood Sch., 1976-78; mem. Gov.'s Legal Svcs. Adv. Coun., 1976-77, Commn. on Continuing Legal Edn. for Judiciary, 1977-84, Commn. on Continuing Lawyer Competence, 1988-92, Commn. on Continuing Legal Edn. and Specialization, 1992-2000, sec. 1995, chmn., 1996-99. Mem. ABA. S.C. Bar (ho. of dels. 1975-76, chmn. fee disputes bd. 1977-81), Richland County Bar Assn. (pres. 1980), Def. Trial Attys. (state chmn. 1971-77, 80-95, exec. coun. 1977-80), Am. Bd. Trial Advs. (pres. S.C. chpts. 1989, Trial Lawyer of Yr. 2001), Toastmasters Club (pres. 1959), Palmetto Club, Phi Delta Phi. Home: 3655 Deerfield Dr Columbia SC 29204-3730 Office: 1414 Lady St Columbia SC 29201-3304

BLANTON, JACK SAWTELLE, oil company executive; b. Shreveport, La., Dec. 7, 1927; s. William Neal and Louise (Wynn) B.; m. Laura Lee Scurlock, Aug. 20, 1949; children: Elizabeth Louise Blanton Wareing, Jack Sawtelle Jr., Eddy Scurlock. BA, U. Tex., 1947, LLB, 1950. Bar: Tex. 1950. With Scurlock Oil Co., Houston, 1950-88, v.p., 1956-58, pres., 1958-83, chmn. bd., 1983-88; pres. Eddy Refining Co., Houston, 1988—. Chmn. bd. trustees Houston Endowment, Inc.; pres. Eddy Refining Co.; bd. dirs. Pogo Producing Co., Burlington No. Santa Fe, Inc. Past chmn. bd. trustees St. Luke's United Meth. Ch., Houston; past chmn. bd. regents U. Tex. System, 1985-89; past vice chmn., bd. dirs. Meth. Hosp., Houston. Mem. Nat. Petroleum Coun., Mid-Continent Oil and Gas Assn. (past pres.) Houston C. of C. (life), Sons Republic of Tex. (past pres. San Jacinto chpt.), Sam Houston Meml. Assn., Nat. Tennis Assn., U.S. Lawn Tennis Assn., Tex. Ind. Oil Producers and Refiners, Ex-Students Assn. U. Tex. (past pres.), Greater Houston Partnership (chmn. 1985-86), Delta Kappa Epsilon, Phi Delta Phi, Phi Alpha Delta. Clubs: Houston (Houston) (past pres.), River Oaks Country (Houston); El Dorado Country (Palm Springs, Calif.). also: Houston Endowment Inc 600 Travis St Ste 6400 Houston TX 77002-3000

BLANTON, JOHN ARTHUR, architect, writer; b. Houston, Jan. 1, 1928; s. Arthur Alva and Caroline (Jeter) Blanton; m. Marietta Louise Newton, Apr. 10, 1954 (dec. 1976); children: Jill Blanton Milne, Lynette Blanton Rowe(dec.), Elena Diane. BA, Rice U., 1948, BS in Architecture, 1949. With Richard J. Neutra, L.A., 1950-64; pvt. practice Manhattan Beach, Calif., 1964—. Lectr. UCLA Ext., 1967—76, 1985. Columnist: Easy Reader newspaper, 1994—96; contbr. articles to profl. jours. City commr. Bd. Bldg. Code Appeals, Manhattan Beach; chmn. Zoning Adjustment Bd., 1990, Planning Commn., 1993—99. With Signal Corps U.S. Army, 1951—53. Recipient local and nat. awards (published internationally). Mem.: AIA (contbr. book revs. to jour. 1972—76). Office: John Blanton AIA Architect 1456 12th St # 4 Manhattan Beach CA 90266-6187 Office Phone: 310-546-1200.

BLANTON, LEWIS M., federal judge; b. Cape Girardeau, Mo., Mar. 5, 1934; AB, St. Louis U., 1958, MA, 1962; JD, U. Mo., 1965. Bar: Mo. Atty. Thompson, Walther & Shewmaker, St. Louis, 1965-69, Blanton, Rice & Sickal, Sikeston, Mo., 1969-71, Robison & Blanton, Sikeston, 1971-78; assoc. judge Cir. Ct. of Scott County, Mo., 1979-91; magistrate judge U.S. Dist. Ct. (ea. dist.) Mo., Cape Girardeau, 1991—. Contbr. articles to profl. jours. Mem. ABA, Mo. Bar, Scott County Bar Assn., Cape Girardeau County Bar Assn., Bar Assn. Met. St. Louis, Fed. Magistrate Judges Assn. Office: 111 US Courthouse 339 Broadway St Cape Girardeau MO 63701-7330

BLANTON, MADGE BRANTLEY, family practice nurse practitioner; b. Candor, N.C., Oct. 19, 1934; d. Paul Adam Brantley and Donnie Mae Campbell; m. Robert G. Blanton, June 28, 1952; children: Robert N., John A., Angela B. Student, Fla. State U., 1978. Cert. notary public S.C., N.C. Tech. rep. Herring RX Drugs, Myrtle Beach, SC, 1959—62; processor Western Union, Myrtle Beach, 1959—62; asst. mgr. Army AF Exch. Svs. Svc. Sta., Myrtle Beach, 1962—79; mgr. collections Fed. Credit Union, Myrtle Beach AFB, SC, 1972—93; pvt. duty nurse Forest City, NC, 1998—. Cons. credit com. F.C.U., Myrtle Beach AFB, SC, 1979—82; nurse aid Shelby Hosp., NC, 1949—51. Contbr. poetry to anthologies. Mem.: VFW, Am. Legion. Avocation: travel. Home: 301 Pleasant Ridge Church RD Shelby NC 28152-9027

BLANTON, PATRICIA LOUISE, periodontal surgeon; b. Clarksville, Tex., July 9, 1941; d. Ben E. and Mildred L. (Russell) B. BS, Baylor U., 1964, PhD, 1967, DDS, 1974, cert., 1975. Diplomate Am. Bd. Oral Medicine. Tchg. asst. Baylor Coll. of Dentistry, Dallas, 1963-67, asst. prof., 1967-70, spl. instr., 1970-73, assoc. prof., 1974-76; resident periodontics VA Hosp., Dallas, 1975; prof. Baylor Coll. of Dentistry, Dallas, 1976-85, Baylor U. Grad. Sch., Dallas, 1976—; prof., chmn. Baylor Coll. of Dentistry, Dallas, 1983-85, prof. emeritus, 1994—, disting. alumni, 2005. Cons. VA Hosp., Dallas, 1979-82; adj. prof. Baylor Coll. of Dentistry, Dallas, 1985—; cons. Commn. on Dental Accreditation and Coun. of Dental Edn., 1981—; v.p. State Anatomical Bd., Tex., 1983-85; mem. ADA-AADS Liaison Com., 1983—; chmn. Nat. Insts. Health, Oral Biology and Medicine Study Sect. II, 1985-86. Author: Periodontics for the G.P., 1977, Current Therapy in Dentistry, 1980, An Atlas of the Human Skull, 1980 (1st place honors 1981). Invited participant Am. Coun. on Edn., Austin, 1984; mem. liaison com. Dallas County Dental Soc.-Am. Cancer Soc., Dallas, 1976-78; bd. dirs. Dallas Dental Health Programs, 1992-93, S.W. Med. Found., 1992-93; bd. devel. Hardin-Simmons U., 1995—. Named one of Outstanding Young Women in Am., 1976; named Disting. Alumna, Baylor Coll. Dentistry, 2005. Fellow Am. Coll. Dentists (pres. Tex. sect. 2003-04), Internat. Coll. Dentists; mem. ADA (alt. del., pres. 2002-2003), Tex. Dental Assn. (bd. dirs. 1995-97, v.p., pres.-elect 2003, pres. 2003—), Am. Assn. Anatomists, Am. Acad. Periodontology, Am. Acad. Oral Medicine, Am. Acad. Osseointegration, Tex. Soc. Periodontists (pres. 1998-99), S.W. Soc. Periodontology (pres. 1999-00), Dallas County Dental Soc. (pres. 1992-93), Xi Psi Phi, Omicron Kappa Upsilon (pres. 1992-93). Avocations: reading, travel. Office: 4514 Cole Ave Ste 902 Dallas TX 75205-4172 Office Phone: 214-552-7901.

BLANTON, VALLYE J., elementary school educator; b. Valdosta, Ga., Sept. 4, 1953; d. Louie Sloan and Tomie Jean (Roberts) B. BS in edn., U. Ga., 1975; MEd, Valdosta State Coll., 1977, cert., 1977-79. Tchr. Lowndes County Sch. System, Valdosta, Ga., 1975-89; assessment specialist Coastal Plains Regional Assessment Ctr., Valdosta, Ga., 1989-90; tchr. Lowndes County Sch. System, Lake Park, Ga., 1990—. Bd. dirs. Ga. Partnership for Excellence in Edn., Atlanta, 1994—; tchr. adv. com. Southeastern Regional Vision for Edn., Greensboro, N.C., 1994—; editorial bd. Tchr. Learning Resource Ctr., Dayton, Ohio, 1994—; scholarship selection com. U.S. Space & Rocket Ctr., Huntsville, Ala., 1994—. Bd. dirs. Valdosta Jr. Svc. League, 1985—, Valdosta State U. Alumni Bd., 1993—, U. Ga. Booster Club, 1982—. Named Ga. Tchr. of Yr. Ga. Dept. Edn., 1994; recipient Milken Nat. Educator award Milken Family Found., 1994. Mem. Ga Assn. Educators (profl. devel. chmn. 1975-94), Profl. Assn. Ga. Educators, Ga. Coun. Tchrs. Math., Nat. State Tchrs. of Yr. Orgn., Kappa Delta Pi, Phi Delta Kappa. Baptist. Avocations: reading, walking, volunteer work. Home: 2832 Fawnwood Cir Valdosta GA 31602-4105 Office: Lake Park Elem PO Box 869 Lake Park GA 31636-0869

BLANTON, W. C., lawyer; b. LaRue County, Ky., Apr. 13, 1946; s. Crawford and Lillian (Phelps) B. BS in Math., BA in Social Sci., Mich. State U., 1968; MEd, U. Vt., 1970; JD, U. Mich., 1975. Bar: Ind. 1975, U.S. Dist. Ct. (no. and so. dists.) Ind. 1975, U.S. Ct. Appeals (7th cir.) 1977, (8th cir.) 1996, Minn. 1996, U.S. Dist. Ct. Minn. 1996, U.S. Dist. Ct. Wisc. (we. dist.) 1996. Residence hall dir. U. Wis., Madison, 1970-72; assoc. Ice Miller Donadio & Ryan, Indpls., 1975-81, ptnr., 1982-94, Popham, Haik, Schnobrich & Kaufman, Ltd., 1995-97, Oppenheimer Wolff & Donnelly LLP, Mpls., 1997—. Mem. ABA. Democrat. Avocations: skiing, travel, bridge. Office: Oppenheimer Wolff & Donnelly LLP 3300 Plaza VII 45 S 7th St Ste 3400 Minneapolis MN 55402-1609 E-mail: wblanton@oppenheimer.com.

BLASCHKE, LAWRENCE RAYMOND, electronic security services professional; b. Elgin, Ill., Feb. 24, 1950; s. Raymond Otto and Margaret Irma (Palm) B.; m. Diane Charlotte Hartwell, Apr. 12, 1974 (dec. 1986); children: Matthew Robert, Bryan Raymond; m. Karen Juliann Larson, Feb. 14, 1987 (dec. Aug. 1993); m. Terry Leigh, July 29, 1995. AS, William Rainey Harper Coll., 1973; student, Valparaiso U., 1974—; B of Scouting, U. Scouting, 1992, M of Scouting, 1993, D of Scouting, 1995. Cert. power engr., Ind.; registered elec. maintenance Am. Coun. on Edn. Audio visual technician multi-media systems William Rainey Harper Coll., Palatine, Ill., 1970-71; jr. engr., then assoc. engr. No. Ind. Pub. Svc. Co., Hobart, 1974-79, dist. engr., 1979-84, project engr., 1984-87, Gary, 1987-92, project engr. level III Merrillville, 1992-93, spl. projects engr. level III, 1994, project leader product strategic planning, 1994-96; dispatcher power sys. and utility svcs. dept. mgmt. supr. Bethlehem Steel Corp., Burns Harbor Divsn., Chesterton, Ind., 1996—2003; customer svc. rep. Cedar Lake (Ind.) br. Grand Rapids Sash & Door, 2003—04; core comml. sales rep. Valparaiso (Ind.) br. ADT Security Svcs. Inc. (divsn. Tyco Internat.), 2004—. Co-owner, pres. TL Spectrum, Valparaiso, 2001—. Chmn. bd. social ministry Immanuel Luth. Ch., Valparaiso, 1983-84, sec. bd. evangelism, 1981-83, asst. Sunday sch. supt., 1984-85; cubmaster Boy Scouts Am., Valparaiso area, 1984-88, merit badge counselor, 1992—, asst. scoutmaster, 1992-95, com. mem., 1992-95, co-chmn. Dunes Moraine dist. advancement com. for Boy Scouts and adult leaders, 1996-97, chmn. advancement com. for scouts and adult leaders, 1996-97, mem. bd. rev., 1995-97; supervisory com. No. Ind. Fed. Credit Union, 1996-99, chmn., 1987-88, 90-96; treas. Montessori Sch. Porter County, 1981-83; bldgs. and grounds co-supt., 1983-84; sec.-treas. Quality Devel., Inc., 1990-93; active Nat. Arbor Day Found., 1992-99; jr. varsity adult leader Awana Club, Christ Cmty. Ch., Hobart, Ind., welcome team, usher, 1992-98; pres. Hobart Pub. Svc. Club, 1979-81; active Project Teach, 1992-96; loaned exec. Lake Area United Way, 2003-04. Recipient Edward A. Filene award Ind. Credit Union League and Credit Union Nat. Assn., Inc., 1991, Man of Yr. award Am. Biog. Inst., 1995. Mem. IEEE (power soc. chmn. Calumet sect. 2002—), IEEE-Stds. Assn., Assn. Energy Engrs., Nat Parks and Conservation Assn., Wilderness Soc., Consumers Union (life), Ind. Sheriffs Assn. (assoc.), Smithsonian Instn., Am. Biog. Inst. Rsch. Assn. (dep. gov.), Nat. Trust Hist. Preservation, Handyman Club Am. (life, adv. coun. 2005),

Alpha Phi Omega (pres. 1973-74). Republican. Avocations: computers, stereo audio equipment and recording, woodworking, electronics. Home: 396 W Southfield Ln Valparaiso IN 46385-9633 Office: 1151 Southpoint Cir Ste E Valparaiso IN 46385 Office Phone: 219-548-6101. E-mail: lrbtlb@yahoo.com.

BLASE, ANTHONY IDOMENEUS, retired electronics executive, writer, poet; b. Chgo., July 30, 1929; s. Nicholas George and Tousa Marie Blase; m. Aspacia Mary Manos, Aug. 31, 1952; children: Mary Kadie Burgner, Nicolette Stephane Young. BSBA, Loyola U., Chgo., 1955. Lic. gen. ins. broker Ill.; real estate broker Ill. Contr. Universal Wire and Cable Co., Chgo., 1958—64; v.p., contr. Rockola Mfg. Corp., Chgo., 1964—78; exec. v.p., treas. Wells-Gardner Electronics, Chgo., 1978—88, also bd. dirs. Author: Contemplating Forms, 1989, In Search of Alexander, 1990, Thus the Gods Taught Man, 1991, On Moral Purpose, 1992, Byzantium, 1992, Religious Paradigm?, 1993, Vessels Without Dimension, 1994, The Ultimate Comprehension, 1995, The History of Western Philosophy, 1996, The Universal Will, 1997, Historical Essays, 1998, Embracing the Universe, 1998, But Grain of Sand, 1999, The Etaireia, 1999, Uncompromising Nature, 2000, As I Understand Aristotle, 2000, Hellenism in the Post Classical World, 2001, Idomenian Ethics, 2002, From Acorn to Oak--Princip to Ground Zero, 2003, The Unlosable Wager, 2003, Unscripted Shadows, 2004, The Ideal Concept, 2004, Eternal Recurrence, 2004, Of Cardinal Virtues, 2004, Criterion of Truth, 2005, Analogous to Man, 2005, The Glow of Words in all their Prism, 2005, Philosophic Edicts, 2005;: Of Laurels Bright, 2005;: Of Laurels Bright, 2005. Cpl. U.S. Army, 1948—50. Avocation: world travel. Home: 3011 Applegate Ln Glenview IL 60025 Personal E-mail: tekanis5@aol.com.

BLASE, NANCY GROSS, librarian; b. New Rochelle, N.Y. d. Albert Philip and Elsie Wise (May) Gross; m. Barrie Wayne Blase, June 19, 1966 (div.); m. Charles M. Goldstein, July 25, 1999; 1 child, Eric Wayne. BA in Biology, Marietta (Ohio) Coll., 1964; MLS, U. Ill., 1965. Info. scientist brain info. svc. Biomed. Libr., UCLA, 1965-66; libr. Health Sci. Libr., U. Wash., Seattle, 1966-68, Medlars search analyst, 1970-72, coord. Medline, 1972-79, head Natural Scis. Libr., 1979—. Mem. libr. adv. com. Elizabeth C. Miller Libr., Ctr. for Urban Horticulture, Seattle, 1986-90. Contbr. articles to profl. jours. Mem. Bet Chaverim, Seattle, pres., 1998—2000. NSF fellow interdept. tng. program for sci. info. specialists U. Ill., 1964-65. Mem.: Internat. Tng. in Comm. (pres. Pacific N.W. region 1994—95), Am. Soc. Info. Sci. (pres. personal computer spl. interest group 1993—94, chair constn. and bylaws com. 1994—97, chair med. informatics spl. interest group 1998—99, rsch. grantee Pacific N.W. chpt. 1984—85), Phi Beta Kappa (pres. U. Wash. chpt. 1993—97, pres. Puget Sound Assn. 2001—03, mem. com. on chpts. 2002—). Avocations: walking, reading. Home: 10751 Durland Ave NE Seattle WA 98125-6945 Office: U Wash Natural Scis Libr Box 352900 Seattle WA 98195-2900 Personal E-mail: nancy@blases.org. Business E-Mail: nblase@u.washington.edu.

BLASER, MARTIN JACK, medical educator, researcher; b. NYC, Dec. 18, 1948; s. Frederick S. and Irene J. Blaser; m. Ronna W. Blaser, Sept. 3, 1979; children: Daniel, Genia, Simone. BA, U. Pa., 1969; MD, NYU, 1973. Cert. Nat. Bd. Med. Examiners. Intern in medicine U. Colo., Denver, 1973-74, resident in medicine, 1974-77, fellow in infectious diseases, 1977-79, from asst. prof. medicine to assoc. prof. medicine, 1981-89; Epidemic Intelligence Svc. officer Ctrs. for Disease Control, Atlanta, 1979-81; Scoville prof. Vanderbilt U., Nashville, 1989-2000; Frederick H. King prof. and chmn. dept. medicine NYU, N.Y.C., 2000—, prof. dept. microbiology, 2000—. Chair bacteriology study sect. NIH, Bethesda, 1994; guest investigator Rockefeller U., N.Y.C., 1987-88; invited prof. Inst. Pasteur, Paris, 1991, 92, 94, 96; v.p. Enteric Rsch. Lab., Inc., NY, 1988—; bd. sci. counselors, Nat. Cancer Inst., 2005-; spkr. in field. Editor: (book) Infections of the GI Tract, 1995, 2003; holder 22 U.S. patents for bacterial products. Recipient Young Investigator award West Soc. Clin. Investigation, 1989. Master ACP; fellow Infectious Disease Soc. Am. (councillor 1993-96, v.p. 2003, pres.-elect 2004, Squibb award 1992), Am. Epidemiol. Soc., Am. Acad. Microbiology; mem. Am. Bd. Internal Medicine (mem. subsplty. bd. infectious disease 1996-2002), Assn. Am. Physicians, Am. Soc. Clin. Investigation, Am. Clin. Climat Assn., Interurban Club. Avocations: hiking, Go. Office: Bellevue A606 Adminstrn NYU Sch Medicine 550 1st Ave New York NY 10016 Office Phone: 212-263-6394. E-mail: martin.blaser@med.nyu.edu.

BLASI, ALBERTO, Romance languages educator, writer; b. Buenos Aires, Jan. 21, 1931; s. Alberto B. and Emma (Raffo) B. Diploma en Letras, U. Buenos Aires, 1957, Licenciado en Letras, 1965; D. Letras, U. La Plata, 1976; postgrad. (fellow), U. Iowa, 1975. Sr. lectr. U. Buenos Aires, 1965-69; prof. U. Rosario, Argentina, 1969-73; vis. writer U. Iowa, 1974-75; assoc. prof. Spanish Bklyn. Coll., CUNY, 1975-79, prof. modern langs, 1979—; prof. Spanish CUNY Grad. Sch., 1979—. Author: Los Fundadores, 1962, Introducción a Lucio López, 1965, La tarea del cuento en Fin de Siglo, 1968, Güiraldes y Larbaud: Una amistad creadora, 1970, Manuel Podestá, 1982, La luna del cazador, 2002; editor: La gran aldea, 1965, Fin de Siglo, 1968, Essays on Lucio Victorio Mansilla, 1981, Movimientos literarios del siglo XX en Iberoamérica: Teoría y práctica, 1982, Don Segundo Sombra, 1983, 2d edit., 1996; contbr. articles to profl. jours. Recipient French Govt. award, Bourse de Marque, 1972, Argentine Writers Soc. Book award, 1960, CUNY rsch. award, 1980—83, 1999—2000, Argentine Found. for the Arts award, 1966, 1969, Municipality of Buenos Aires Book award, 1967. Mem. PEN Club Internat., Internat. Assn. Hispanists, Internat. Comparative Lit. Assn. Office: Brooklyn Coll Dept Modern Languages Brooklyn NY 11210

BLASI, VINCENT A., law educator; b. 1943; BA, Northwestern U, 1964; JD, U Chgo., 1967. Bar: Tex. 1968. Asst. prof. U. Tex., Austin, Tex., 1967—69; vis. asst. prof. Stanford U, 1969—70; assoc. prof. U Mich., Ann Arbor, Mich., 1970—72, prof., 1972; vis. prof. U Calif., Berkeley, Calif., 1978—79; faculty mem. Columbia U., NYC, 1983—, Corliss Lamont prof. civil liberties; Massee prof. law U. Va., 1998—2003, James Madison Disting. Prof. Law, 2003—. Author: An Empirical and Legal Analysis, 1972; editor: The Burger Court: The Counter-Revolution that Wasn't, 1983, Law and Liberalism in the 1980s, 1991, Milton's Areopagitica and the Modern First Amendment, 1996, Free Speech and Good Character, 1999, School Vouchers and Religious Liberty, 2002. Fellow: Am. Acad. Arts & Sci.; mem.: Order of Coif, Phi beta Kappa. Office: Columbia Law Sch 435 W 116th St New York NY 10027-7297 also: U Va Sch Law 580 Massie Rd Charlottesville VA 22903 Office Phone: 434-924-7359. E-mail: blasi@law.columbia.edu, vab7b@virginia.edu.

BLASICK, JAMES DAVID, finance educator; b. Alton, Ill., May 8, 1958; s. Henry John and Mary Nelle Blasick; m. Patricia Diane Mills, July 11, 1999; 1 child, Thomas Dewitt. BSc, Lambuth U., Jackson, Tenn., 1980; MBA, Sam Houston State U., 1990. Ops. mgr. Europe, Africa, Mid. East Tex. Instruments, 1980—88; instr. Sam Houston State U., Huntsville, Tex., 1988—94, U. Colo., 1994—98; assoc. dean edn. outreach Bethel Coll., McKenzie, Tenn., 1998—2001, chair divsn. social sci., 2002—05, acad. dean, 2005—. Contbr. articles to profl. jours. Home: 431 Sanders Bluff Rd Three Way TN 38343 Office: Bethel Coll 325 Cherry Ave Mc Kenzie TN 38201 Office Phone: 731-352-4235. Business E-Mail: blasickj@bethel-college.edu.

BLASIER, COLE, political scientist; s. Stewart Parnell and Helen (Cole) B.; m. Martha Hiett; children: Peter Cole, Martha Hamilton. AB, U. Ill., 1947; postgrad., U. Mex., 1947; AM, cert. Russian Inst., Columbia U., 1950, PhD in Polit. Sci., 1955. Career fgn. svc. officer U.S. Dept. State, Belgrade, Yugoslavia, 1951-54, Bonn, Federal Republic of Germany, 1954-57, Washington, 1957-60, Moscow, 1958; exec. asst. to pres., sec. bd. trustees Colgate U., Hamilton, NY, 1960—63; prof. polit. sci. U. Pitts., 1964-88; chief hispanic div. Libr. Congress, Washington, 1988-93; sr. rsch. assoc. North-South Ctr. U. Miami, Coral Gables, Fla., 1993-95. Dir. ctr. Latin Am. studies U. Pitts., 1964-74; adv. bd. Handbook Latin Am. Studies, 1972-88; exchange scholar Polish Inst. Internat. Affairs, Warsaw, Poland, 1978, Inst. Latin Am., Moscow, 1979; U.S. chmn. U.S./USSR Exch. in Latin Am. Studies, 1980-86; mgmt. cons. project to revive ancient libr., Alexandria, Egypt, 1993; Far Ea. State U., Vladivostok, Russia, 1999; adj. prof. Georgetown U., 1993-94; field work in Russia and Germany, 1996-2000; cons. in field. Author: The Hovering Giant, U.S. Responses to Revolutionary Change in Latin America, 1976, rev., 1985, The Giant's Rival, The USSR and Latin America, 1983, rev., 1987, Cuba in the World, 1979, The End of the Soviet-Cuban Partnership, Cuba After the Cold War, 1993, Russia's Institute of Europe, 1996, Electing Putin Po-Tartarski, 2000, Soviet Impact on Latin America, 2002; editor U. Pitts. Press Latin Am. series, 1968-91. Pres. UN Assn. Pitts., 1985. Lt. (j.g.) USNR, PTO, 1943-46. Fellow Rotary Santiago Chile 1947-48, Kennan Inst. Woodrow Wilson Ctr., 1978, Fulbright, Buenos Aires, Argentina, 1986, Heinz Endowment, 1988; Rockefeller Found. grantee, Cali, Colombia, 1963-64; decorated Knighthood of Isabel la Catolica (Spain), 1993. Mem. Lat. Am. Studies Assn. (pres. 1986-87), Am. Polit. Sci. Assn., Am. Fgn. Svc. Assn., Diplomatic and Consular Officers Ret., Washington Inst. for Fgn. Affairs, Cosmos Club. Home: 10450 Lottsford Rd #5009 Mitchellville MD 20721

BLASING, MUTLU KONUK, English language educator; b. Istanbul, Turkey, June 27, 1944; arrived in U.S., 1963; d. Mustafa Celal Konuk and Muzeyyen (Uzun) Dursunoglu; m. Randolph Charles Blasing, Aug. 21, 1965; 1 child, John Konuk. Student, Carleton Coll., 1963-65; BA, Coll. William and Mary, 1969; PhD, Brown U., 1974. Lectr. English U. Mass., Mass., 1974-76; asst. prof. Pomona Coll., Claremont, Calif., 1977-79, Brown U., 1979-83, assoc. prof., 1983-88, prof., 1988—. Dir. Copper Beech Press, Providence. Author: The Art of Life, 1977, American Poetry: The Rhetoric of Its Forms, 1987, Politics and Form in Postmodern Poetry, 1995; translator: Human Landscapes (N. Hikmet), 1982, Epic of Sheik Bedreddin (N. Hikmet), 1975, Things I Didn't Know I Loved, (N. Hikmet), 1975, Rubaiyat (N.Hikmet), 1985, Selected Poetry (N. Hikmet), 1986, Poems of Nazim Hikmet, 1994, Human Landscapes from my Country (N. Hikmet), 2002, Poems of Nazim Hikmet, 2002. Fellow, U. Mass., 1974—76. Office: Brown U English Dept PO Box 1852 Providence RI 02912-1852 Office Phone: 401-863-3744. Business E-Mail: mutlu_blasing@brown.edu.

BLASINGAME, DAVID THOMAS, academic administrator; b. Dermott, Ark., July 7, 1947; s. Ruel Esker and Novella (Mhoon) B.; widowed; 1 child, Joshua Scott. AB, Washington U., 1969, MBA, 1971. Mgmt. assoc. U.S. Postal Svc., Washington, 1971; assoc. dir. alumni rels. Washington U., St. Louis, 1974-76, dir. devel. sch. bus., 1976-85, exec. dir. alumni and devel. programs, 1985, asst. vice chancellor, 1985-87, assoc. vice chancellor, 1987-90, vice chancellor alumni and devel. programs, 1990—2005, exec. vice chancellor, 2005—. Cons. Mercantile Library, St. Louis, 1983-84; cons. in field. Coach Mancester Athletic Assn., St. Louis, 1976-85; bd. dirs. Gifted Resource Council, St. Louis, 1985—. Served to 1st lt. U.S. Army, 1971-73. Mem. Council Advancement of Secondary Edn., William Greenleaf Eliot Soc., Kappa Sigma Alumni Assn. Republican. Avocation: golf. Home: 825 Minarca Dr Saint Louis MO 63131-2029 Office: Washington U Vice Chancellor One Brookings Dr Saint Louis MO 63130 E-mail: david_blasingame@ais.wvstl.edu.

BLASINSKI, CLARE MARIE, librarian; b. Milw., Jan. 10, 1950; d. Henry Michael and Gertrude Julia (Bucholz) B. BS, U. Wis., Milw., 1974, MLS, 1979; MBA, Marquette U., 1990. Libr. Milw. Pub. Libr., 1983—. Recipient S.E. Asian Young Adult Literacy grant, LSCA, 1991—. Mem. Am. Libr. Assn., Am. Mktg. Assn., Am. Soc. Info. Sci., Shih Tzu Club of Southeastern Wis. (v.p. and webmaster), Beta Phi Mu. Roman Catholic. Avocations: hiking, breeding and exhibiting dogs. Home: 3162 S Brisbane Ave Milwaukee WI 53207-2606 Office: Milw Pub Libr 814 W Wisconsin Ave Milwaukee WI 53233-2309

BLASIOTTI, ROBERT VINCENT, accountant, consultant; b. Phila., Nov. 15, 1949; s. Vincent Mario Blasiotti and Hilda (Romani) Greer; m. Katheryn Phyllis Ombres, Dec. 15, 1973 (div. Apr. 1982); m. Gilda Maria Cipriani, June 17, 1988; children: Gabriella, Robert Jr. BS, Pa. State U., 1971, MBA, 1973. CPA, Pa. Jr. acct. Goldenberg, Rosenthal & Co., Phila., 1971-73, sr. acct., 1973-75; mgr. acctg. Gross & Co., Jenkintown, Pa., 1975-77; owner Blasiotti & Co. CPAs, West Chester, Pa., 1977—. CPA, advisor Big Bros. Chester County, West Chester, 1985—; cons. Presdl. Adv. Coun., 1984; fin. advisor Exton Sq. Mall Merchants Assn., 1978-89; bd. advisors Med-Trans, Inc., 1982-84. Mem. Big Bros.-Big Sisters Chester County, 1978—; trustee Rep. Presdl. Task Force, 1982—; mem. coun. St. Maximilian Kolby Ch., 1994-97; bd. advisors Our Lady's Missionaries of Eucharist, 1999—; treas. Boy Scouts Am. Pack 153, 1999-2002; Pa. chmn. Congressional Bus. Adv. Coun., 2003—. Served from 2d lt. to capt. U.S. Army, 1971-79. Mem. C. of C., Jaycees (chmn. 1980-84), Italian Social Club (fin. sec. 1992-96), KC (treas. 1994, dep. grand knight 1995, grand knight 1996, trustee 1997-99), Lions (treas. 1980-81), Men of Malvern. Roman Catholic. Avocations: stamp collecting/philately, numismatology, golf, horticulture, fishing. Office: Blasiotti & Co CPAs 882 S Matlack St Ste 208 West Chester PA 19382

BLASKEWICZ, NANCY JANE, elementary school educator; b. Pitts., Feb. 16, 1949; d. Walter Michael and Pauline Katherine Onopa; m. Gene Stanley Blaskewicz, Aug. 21, 1971; children: Julie, Michael. BS in Edn., Duquesne U., 1971, M in Reading, 1974. Tchr. Pitts. Cath. Schs., 1971—74, Keystone Oakes Sch. Dist., 1974—76, Wilmington Area Sch. Dist., 1976—. Past pres. govt. rels. Lawrence County Reading Coun., New Castle, Pa., 1976—; program chair PDK, New Wilmington, 2002—. Mem. Neshannock Lioness, New Castle, 1978—, pres.; mem. ABWA, 1976—, sec., 2004—05. Named Woman of Yr., Neshannock Lioness, 2005. Roman Catholic. Avocations: gardening, reading. Home: 187 Catalina Dr New Castle PA 16105

BLASS, DAVID MARK, psychiatrist, consultant, geriatrics services professional, researcher; b. Phila., Mar. 5, 1969; s. Elliott and Lorraine Blass; m. Malka Blass. BA, Johns Hopkins U., 1990; degree in Rabbinic Studies, Rabbi Isaac Elchanan Theol. Sem., New York, NY, 1996; MD, U. Md., 1996. Lic. psychiatrist Md., 2002; ordained rabbi N.Y., 1996. Asst. prof. psychiatry and behavioral scis. Sch. Medicine Johns Hopkins U., Balt., 2002—. Dir. Frontotemporal Dementia Clinic Sch. Medicine Johns Hopkins U., 2004—. Fellow: Phi Beta Kappa; mem.: AMA, Md. Psychiat. Assn., Am. Psychiat. Assn. Jewish. Office Phone: 410-955-6736.

BLASS, JOHN PAUL, medical educator, biochemist; b. Vienna, Feb. 21, 1937; arrived in U.S., 1938; s. Gustaf and Jolan (Wirth) B.; m. Birgit Annelise Knudsen, Dec. 20, 1960; children: Charles, Lisa. AB summa cum laude, Harvard U., 1958; PhD, U. London, 1960; MD, Columbia U., 1965. Postdoctoral fellow Am. Cancer Soc., Columbia U., 1962-63; intern Mass. Gen. Hosp., Boston, 1965-66, resident in medicine, 1966-67; research assoc. Nat. Heart and Lung Inst., Bethesda, Md., 1967-70; asst. prof. psychiatry and biol. chemistry UCLA, 1970-76, assoc. prof., 1976-78; mem. staff UCLA Hosps. Clinics, 1970-78; Winifred Masterson Burke prof. neurology, prof. medicine Cornell U. Med. Center, 1978—2005, prof. emeritus, 2005—. Attending neurologist N.Y. Hosp.; mem. NBS-1 rev. com. NIH, 1981-84; councilor Nat. Inst. Aging, 1986-89; chmn. Nat. Adv. Panel on Alzheimers's Disease U.S. Congress, 1987-91, mem., 1993-96. Jour. Neurochemistry, 1981—86, Neurochem. Rsch., 1984—86, Neurochem. Pathology, Neurobiol. Aging, Jour. Neurol. Sci., 1990—2000, Jour. Molecular Neurosci., 1999—, assoc. editor Jour. Am. Geriatric Soc., 1982—87, Age, 1993—95; Yearbook of Neurology and Neurosurgery, 1992—; co-editor: Caring for Alzheimer's Patients, 1990—, Familial Alzheimer's Disease, 1989—, Treatment of Alzheimer's Disease, 1989—, Principles of Geriatrics and Gerontology, 2d edit., 1990—, Principles of Geriatrics and Gerontology, 3d edit., 1994—, Principles of Geriatrics and Gerontology, 4th edit., 1998—; contbr. articles to profl. jours. Mem. sci. adv. bd. Will Rogers Inst., 1981-97, Allied Signal Aging Award Com., 1993-95. Served as asst. surgeon USPHS, 1967-70. Marshall scholar, 1958-60. Mem. Soc. Neurosci. (chmn. social issues com.), Biochem. Soc., Am. Soc. Biol. Chemists, Am. Soc. Neurochemistry (council, chmn. public policy com.), Internat. Soc. Neurochemistry (council, chmn. clin. com.), Am. Soc. Clin. Investigation, Am. Geriatrics Soc., Am. Fedn. Aging Rsch. (v.p., chmn. research com. 1982-87, pres. 1994-96), Assn. Alzheimers and Related Disease (sci. adv. bd. 1982-86), Am. Chem. Soc., Phi Beta Kappa, Sigma Xi, Alpha Omega Alpha. Jewish. Office: Burke Med Rsch Inst 785 Mamaroneck Ave White Plains NY 10605-2523 Home: 93 Mercer St Apt 3E New York NY 10012 Office Phone: 914-597-2351. Personal E-mail: jpblass@yahoo.com. Business E-Mail: jpblass@mail.med.cornell.edu.

BLASS, WALTER PAUL, management consultant, educator; b. Dinslaken, Germany, Mar. 31, 1930; s. Richard B. and Malvi (Rosenblatt) B.; m. Janice L. Minott, Apr. 2, 1954; children: Kathryn, Christopher, Gregory. BA, Swarthmore Coll., 1951; postgrad., Princeton U., 1951-52; MA, Columbia U., 1953. Asst. Laos and Cambodia desk officer ICA, Wash., 1957—58; gen. mgr. R.B. Blass Co., Deal, NJ, 1958—61; economist AT&T, N.Y.C., 1961—65; country dir. Peace Corps., Afghanistan, 1966—68; asst. v.p. revenue requirement studies NY Telephone Co., N.Y.C., 1968—70; dir. corp. planning AT&T, 1970—82, dir. strategic planning, 1982—85; ret., 1985—. Pres., Strategic Plans, Unltd., Warren, N.J., 1985—. Exec. Fellow-in-Residence Martino Grad. Sch. Bus. Adminstrn., Fordham U., N.Y.C., 1986-90; cons. McKinsey & Co., Telecom. Authority Ireland, McDonnell Douglas, Heller Fin., Inc.; lectr. in field; vis. prof. U. Grenoble, France, 1988, Ecole Superieure de Commerce, Chambery and Grenoble, France, 1989—; trustee Guilford Coll., 1975—, chmn. planning com., 1992-99, vice chmn. acad. affairs com., 1999—. Co-author: The Strategic Planning Handbook, 1982, Handbook of Strategic Planning, 1986. Lt., j.g., USNR, 1953-56, Woodrow Wilson Found., sr. fell., 1974-85. Mem., NY Acad. Scis., Soc. Values in Higher Edn. (dir. 1983-86, 2005—), Am. Econ. Assn., Nat. Assn. Bus. Economists, The Planning Forum (bd. dirs. 1972), Royal Econ. Soc. Home and Office: 6 Casale Dr Warren NJ 07059-6703 Office Phone: 908-647-5769.

BLASSBERG, FRANCI J., lawyer; b. Sept. 28, 1953; BA, Cornell U., 1975, JD magna cum laude, 1977. Bar: NY 1978. Ptnr., co-head Private Equity Group, mem. Mgmt. Com. Debevoise & Plimpton LLP, NYC. Editor-in-chief Debevoise & Plimpton Private Equity Report; co-editor: The Debevoise & Plimpton European Private Equity Handbook, 2004. Bd. trustees Cornell U., NY City Ballet, New Sch. U. Office: Debevoise & Plimpton LLP 919 Third Ave New York NY 10022 Office Phone: 212-909-6531. Business E-Mail: fjblassberg@debevoise.com.

BLASSINGAME, RONALD JAY, social worker; b. NYC, Apr. 20, 1948; s. Samuel and Johnnie Mae Blassingame; m. Stephanie Moore, Oct. 21, 1981 (div. Sept. 1984); m. Hope Villanueva, Aug. 30, 1985; children; Aram, Nadirah, Willie, Samuel. BSW cum laude, SUNY, Buffalo, 1971; EdM in Adult Edn., Kans. State U., 1977; MS in Human Svcs., Boston U., 1983; PhD in Sociology, Columbia State U., 1997. Social worker Wis. Children's Treatment Ctr., Madison, 1972-73; asst. dir. youth svcs. Buffalo Urban League, 1973-75; social worker alcohol & drug prevention & control program Dept. of Army, Ft. Riley, Kans., 1975-76, Germany, 1976-78; adj. lectr. Ctrl. Tex. Coll./Overseas, Stuttgart, Germany, 1977-78; supr. group homes St. Barnabas Group Homes, N.Y.C., 1979-81; dir. spl. programs Inst. for Career and Life Planning Phelps-Stokes Sch., Bklyn., 1979-81; tchg. trainer Peace Corp., Monrovia, Liberia, 1981-83; instnl. supr. ESL and cultural orientation program Internat. Cath. Migration Commn., Morong, Philippines, 1984-90; project dir. Amerisian residential program Mohawk Valley Resource Ctr. for Refugees, Utica, n.Y., 1990-92; correction counselor Cape Vincent Correctional Facility N.Y. State Dept. Correctional Svcs., 1993-96, correction counselor Taconic Correctional Facility, 1996-98; alcohol and substance abuse treatment program coord. Watertown (NY) Correctional Facility, 1998—2003; asylum officer US Dept. Homeland Security INS, Miami, Fla., 2003—. Cons. Philippine Culture Commn. Svc. Corp., Manila, 1987-88, Voice of Am., Washington, 1980-81; mem. working group Non Govtl. Com. of UNICEF, N.Y.C., 1994-97; cons. in field. Mentor N.Y. State Mentoring Program, Thousand Island Ctrl. Sch. Dist., Cape Vincent, 1993-97; spl. asst. Family Ct. of State of N.Y., 1998—. With U.S. Army, 1975-78. Recipient Cert. of Appreciation from Pres. Ronald Reagan for dedicated Peace Corps svc., Cert. of Recognition from Sec. of Def. W.S. Cohen for mil. svc. during Cold War. Mem. Am. Sociol. Assn., World Futurist Soc., Nat. Peace Corps Assn., Am. Studies Assn. of the Philippines (v.p. Bataan chpt. 1986-90), Southern Poverty. Avocations: reading, cooking, sailing. Home: 601 Merrick St Clayton NY 13624-1309

BLASZCZYK, REGINA LEE, historian, writer; b. Lawrence, Mass., Sept. 24, 1955; d. Leon and Nellie Blaszczyk; m. Edward L. O'Neill. BA, Marlboro (Vt.) Coll., 1978; MA, George Washington U., 1987, U. Del., 1990, PhD, 1995. Curator Smithsonian Nat. Mus. Am. History, Washington, 1978—89; prof. Am. studies Boston U., 1995—2002; dir. Beckman Ctr. for History of Chemistry Chem. Heritage Found., Phila., 2002—03; sr. rsch. assoc. Hagley Mus. & Libr., Wilmington, Del., 2004—. Cons., sr. scholar Chem. Heritage Found., Phila., 2003—; vis. scholar U. Pa., Phila., 2004—. Author: Imagining Consumers: Design and Innovation from Wedgwood to Corning, 2000 (Hagley prize for best book in bus. history, 2000, Choice Outstanding Acad. Title); editor: Partners in Innovation: Science Education and the Science Workforce, 2005. Vis. scholar, Charles Warren Ctr. for Studies in Am. History Harvard U., 1999—2001, sr. fellow, Lemelson Ctr. for History of Invention and Innovation, Smithsonian Instn., 2000—01, Sidney Edelstein fellow, Chem. Heritage Found., 2002—03, Spencer Baird Resident scholar, Smithsonian Cooper Hewitt Nat. Design Mus. and Smithsonian Instn. Librs., 2002. Mem.: Bus. History Conf. (trustee 1997—2001). Home: 815 Bainbridge St Philadelphia PA 19147 Business E-Mail: reginab@hagley.org.

BLASZCZYNSKI, ANDRE BOGUSLAW, economist, educator; b. Krakow, Poland, Feb. 12, 1952; came to U.S., 1962; s. Zdzislaw and Halina Blaszczynski; m. Elizabeth Blaszczynski, Sept. 21, 1974; 1 child, Christopher. BA in Econs., U. Conn., 1975, MA in Econs., 1983; MBA, Rensselaer Poly. Inst., 1980. Rsch. assoc. The Futures Group, Glastonbury, Conn., 1977-78; ops. mgmt. cons. Brook Internat. Corp., Montvale, N.J., 1978-79; instr. Morse Sch. of Bus., Hartford, Conn., 1980-81; asst. prof. Ctrl. Conn. State U., New Britain, Conn., 1981-86; instr. Tunxis C.C., Farmington, Conn., 1987-94, asst. prof., 1994-98, assoc. prof., chair dept. bus., 1998-2000; program dir., lectr. Polish Am. Bus. Sch., Krakow, 1990-91; cons. devel. program UN, Krakow, 1991; acting dean of learning Gateway C.C., New Haven, 2000—. Co-founder, moderator Conf. of Solidarity Support Orgns., 1983-90. Author: Slownik Pojec Ekonomicznych, 1993. Pres. Conn. divsn. Polish Am. Congress, Hartford, 1993-99; pres., founding mem. Polish Am. Found. Conn., New Britain, 1996—; pres. Fedn. Polish Ams., Washington, 2000—. Recipient Order of Merit Pres. of Republic of Poland, 1999. Republican. Roman Catholic. E-mail: AndreBB@home.com, gw_andre@commnet.edu.

BLATT, GREGORY R., lawyer; BA, Colgate U.; JD, Columbia. Asoc. Wachtell, Lipton, Rosen & Katz; assoc. Grubman, Indursky & Schindler; exec. v.p.-bus. affairs, gen. counsel, sec. Martha Stewart Living Omnimedia Inc.; sr. v.p., gen. counsel, sec. InterActive Corp., 2003—. Office: InterActive Corp 152 W 57th St, 42nd Floor New York NY 10019

BLATT, LAWRENCE M., pharmaceutical company executive; b. Chgo., Aug. 11, 1961; s. Harvey M. and Serane A. B.; m. Elyse Anne Salven, Apr. 20, 1990; children: Zachary, Zoe. BS in Microciology, Ind. u., 1983; MBA, Calif. State U., 1988; D of Pub. Health Adminstrn., U. LaVerne, 1996. Rsch. biologist Monsanto, St. Louis, 1983-84; dir. interferon rsch. Amgen, Thousand Oaks, Calif., 1984-96; v.p., devel. corp. officer Nat. Genetics Inst., L.A., 1996-98; v.p. rsch., corp. officer Ribozyme Pharms., Inc., Boulder, Colo., 1998—. Adj. prof. Scripps Clinic, La Jolla, 1998-2001; sr. rsch. scientist Huntington Hosp. Liver Ctr., Pasadens, Calif., 1996—. Contbr. articles to profl. jours. Rsch. grantee Norris Found., 1999. Mem. Internat. Soc. for Interferon and Cytolane Rsch., Am. Chem. Soc., Am. Soc. Microbiology. Home: 10 Shore View Ave San Francisco CA 94121-1629 Fax: 303-449-6995. E-mail: blattl@rpi.com.

BLATT, RICHARD LEE, lawyer; b. Oak Park, Ill., May 24, 1940; s. B. Lee Gray and Madelyn Gertrude (Bentley) B.; m. Carol Milner Jenkinson, May 21, 1965 (div. Dec. 1984); children: Christopher Andrew Lee, Katherine Lee, Susannah Lee; m. Carolyn Elizabeth LeBlanc, Jan. 31, 1987; 1 child, Jennifer

Lee DeNux Blatt. BA, U. Ill., 1962; JD, U. Mich., 1965. Bar: Ill. 1968, U.S. Dist. Ct. (no. dist.) Ill. 1968, U.S. Ct. Appeals (7th cir.) 1968, U.S. Supreme Ct. 1974, U.S. Dist. Ct. (so. dist.) Ill. 1977, U.S. Ct. Appeals (4th cir.) 1987, N.Y. 1989, U.S. Ct. Appeals (3rd cir.) 1990, U.S. Dist. Ct. (ea. and so. dists.) N.Y. 1998. Assoc. Peterson, Lowry, Rall, Barber & Ross, Chgo., 1968-75; ptnr. Peterson, Ross, Schloeb & Seidel, Chgo., 1975-91, Peterson & Ross, Chgo., 1991-94; sr. ptnr. Blatt, Hammesfahr & Eaton, Chgo., 1994-2000; sr. mem. Cozen & O'Connor, 2000—. Rep. Disting. Neutral Ctr. Pub. Resources Inst. for Dispute Resolution; regulation bd. arbitrators NASD. Author: (with Robert G. Schloerb, Robert W. Hammesfahr, Lori S. Nugent) Punitive Damages: A Guide to the Insurability of Punitive Damages in the United States and Its Territories, 1988; (with Robert W. Hammesfahr and Lori S. Nugent) Punitive Damges: A State-by-State Guide to Law and Practice, 1991, 4th edit., 2005, (in Japanese 1995); co-author: At Risk-Internet and E-Commerce Insurance and Reinsurance Legal Issues, 2000, At Risk-Version 2-The Definitive Guide to Legal Issues of Insurance and Reinsurance of Internet, E-commerce and Cyber Perils, 2002. Capt. inf. USAR, 1965—67, Korea. Fellow Chartered Inst. Arbitrators; mem. ABA (litigation sect., dispute resolution sect.), NSSAR (Ft. Dearborn chpt.), Ill. State Bar Assn., Chgo. Internat. Dispute Resolution Assn. (planning com.), Soc. Mayflower Desc. State Ill., N.Y. State Bar Assn., Chgo. Bar Assn. (alternative dispute resolution com.), Chgo. Club, Pi Kappa Alpha Ednl. Found. (trustee), Phi Beta Kappa, Phi Kappa Phi. Home: 1415 N Dearborn Pkwy Chicago IL 60610-1559 Office: Cozen & O'Connor 222 S Riverside Plz Ste 1500 Chicago IL 60606-6000 Office Phone: 312-382-3100. Office Fax: 312-382-8910. Personal E-mail: rblatt@earthlink.net. Business E-Mail: rblatt@cozen.com.

BLATT, SIDNEY JULES, psychology professor, psychoanalyst, investigator; b. Phila., Oct. 15, 1928; s. Harry and Fannie (Feld) Blatt; m. Ethel Shames, Feb. 1, 1951; children: Susan, Judith, David. BS, Pa. State U., 1950, MS, 1952; PhD, U. Chgo., 1957; postgrad., Western New Eng. Inst. for Psychoanalysis, 1972. Postdoctoral fellow Neuropsychiat. Inst. of U. Ill. Med. Ctr., Psychiat. and Psychosomatic Inst. of Michael Reese Hosp., 1957—59; instr. Univ. Coll. U. Chgo., 1959-60; mem. faculty Yale U., New Haven, 1960—, prof. psychology and psychiatry, 1974—; mem. faculty Western New Eng. Inst. for Psychoanalysis, 1975—. Sigmund Freud prof. psychoanalysis; Ayala and Sam Zacks prof. art history Hebrew U., 1988—89; Fulbright sr. rsch. fellow, 1988—89; mem. Rsch. Fellowship Rev. Panel NIMH, 1966—69, mem. Psychology Tng. Rev. Panel, 1969—74; vis. prof. Univ. Coll., London, 1999—2003, Cath. U. Leuven, 2003. Author: Experiences of Depression: Theoretical, Research and Clinical Perspectives, 2004; co-author (with J. Allison and C. Zimet): Interpretation of Psychological Tests, 1968, Interpretation of Psychological Tests, 2d edit., 1988; co-author: (with C.M. Wild) Schizophrenia: A Developmental Analysis, 1976; co-author: (with E.S. Blatt) Continuity and Change in Art: The Development of Modes of Representation, 1984; co-author: (with R.Q. Ford) Therapeutic Change: An Object Relations Perspective, 1994; editor (with D. Diamond): Attachment Research and Psychoanalysis, vols. I-III, 1999—2003; co-editor (with Z.V. Segal): The Self in Emotional Distress, 1993; co-editor: (with J. Corveleyn, P. Luyten) The Theory and Treatment of Depression: Towards a Dynamic Interaction Model. Named Disting. Practitioner of Psychology, Nat. Acad. Practice, 1983; recipient Disting. Contbns. to Rsch. award, Assn. Med. Sch. Profs. Psychology and APA Divsn. Psychoanalysis, 2000, Founders' Disting. Tchg. prize, We. New Eng. Psychoanalytic Soc., 2001, Hans H. Strupp Disting. Contbns. to Psychoanalysis award, 2000, Bruno Klopfer and Marguerite R. Hertz awards for dist. contbns. to psychol. assessment, Internat. Psychoanalytic Assn., Disting. Sci. Contbns. award, APA Divsn. Clin. Psychology, 2004; fellow Found. Fund Rsch. in Psychiatry, 1961—64. Mem.: AAUP, AAAS, APA, Soc. Personality Assessment (pres. 1984—86), Am. Psychoanalytic Assn. (Outstanding Sci. Paper prize 2000). Office: Yale Univ 300 George St Ste 901 New Haven CT 06511 Office Phone: 203-785-2090. Business E-Mail: sidney.blatt@yale.edu.

BLATTER, FRANK EDWARD, travel company executive; b. Denver, Jan. 9, 1939; s. Anthony John and Irene Marie (Tobin) B.; m. Barbara E. Drieth, Sept. 6, 1959; children: Dean Robert, Lisa Kay Faircloth, Paul Kelly. BS, Regis U., Denver, 1961; grad., Colo. Sch. Banking, 1966, Sch. Bank Adminstrn., 1973. CPA, Colo. Acct. McMahon, Maddox & Rodriguez (C.P.A.s), Denver, 1960-63, United Bank Denver, 1963-65; with United Banks Colo., Inc., Denver, 1965-86; pres. Cath. Cmty. Svcs., Denver, 1987, Premiere Travel and Cruises, Denver, 1988—. Mem. nat. adv. coun. and devel. com., chmn. ann. funds coun. Regis U.; chmn. adv. coun. Camp Santa Maria; crusade chmn. Am. Cancer Soc., Denver. Mem. AICPA, Tax Execs. Inst. (past pres. Denver), Colo. Soc. CPAs, Fin. Execs. Inst. (dir.), Bank Adminstrn. Inst. (dir.), Arrowhead Golf Club. Roman Catholic. Office: 3900 S Wadsworth Blvd Ste 475 Denver CO 80235-2207

BLATTMACHR, JONATHAN GEORGE, lawyer; b. Warner Robins AFB, Ga., Apr. 7, 1945; s. George Gustav and Janet Elizabeth (Tice) B.; m. Betsy Eloise Masters, Aug. 15, 1970; children: Jonathan, Jeffrey. AB, Bucknell U., 1967; JD cum laude, Columbia U., 1970. Bar: N.Y. 1973, U.S. Dist. Ct. (so. and ea. dists.) N.Y. 1973, U.S. Tax Ct. 1983, Calif. 1987, Alaska 1988, U.S. Ct. Appeals (9th cir.) 1989, U.S. Supreme Ct. 1989. Assoc. Simpson Thacher & Bartlett, N.Y.C., 1970-77; ptnr. & chmn. trusts & estates dept. Milbank, Tweed, Hadley & McCloy, N.Y.C., 1977—. Lectr. law Columbia U. Sch. Law, 1979-90; adj. prof. law NYU Sch. Law, 1983, 87; former mem. adv. bd. NYU Inst. on Fed. Taxation; former regent, fellow, former chairperson estate & gift tax com. Am. Coll. Trusts & Estates Counsel; mem. L.I. Tax and Estate Planning Coun.; mem. fin. and estate planning bd. CCH Inc.; bd. dirs. N.Y. State Bar Found. Author: Wealth Preservation and Protection for Closely-Held Buisness Owners (And Others), 1993, and others; co-author: Carryover Basis Under the 1976 Tax Reform Act, 1977, Income Taxation of Estates and Trusts; co-developer (computerized document assembly) Wealth Transfer Planning; former editor The Chase Rev., Probate Notes. Chair N.Y. Iola Fund. Capt. USAR, 1970-72. Decorated Army Commendation medal. Academician, Internat. Acad. Estate & Trust Law; fellow, Am. Bar Found.; fellow & bd. mem. N.Y. Bar Found.; mem. ABA (former chairperson com. on marital deduction-estate planning real property probate and trust law sect., former chairperson com. on generation-skipping transfer taxation, real property, probate & trust law sect.), N.Y. State Bar Assn. (former chairperson trusts & estates law sect., chairperson interest on lawyer account adv. com., former chairperson surrogate's cts. com. trusts & estates law sect.), Assn. of Bar of City of N.Y. Office: Milbank Tweed Hadley & McCloy 1 Chase Manhattan Plz Fl 47 New York NY 10005-1413 Office Phone: 212-530-5000. Office Fax: 212-822-5066. Business E-Mail: jblattmachr@milbank.com.

BLATTNER, ROBERT A., lawyer; b. Lima, Ohio, July 9, 1934; s. Simon James and Estelle Leila (Aarons) B.; m. Judith Reinfeld, Feb. 5, 1964 (div. July 1980); children: Wendy Lynn, Lauren Jill; m. Eileen Savransky, Dec. 18, 1983 BA, Northwestern U., 1956; LLB, Case Western Reserve U., 1959. Bar: Ohio 1959, Ill. 1965, U.S. Supreme Ct. 1984. Assoc. Hribar & Conway, Euclid, Ohio, 1960-62, Ulmer & Berne, Cleve., 1962-65; exec. dir. Ohio State Legal Svcs., Columbus, Ohio, 1965-67; gen. counsel, dir. real estate Sawyer Bus. Colls., Evanston, 1967-72; assoc. Guren Merritt Feibel Sogg & Cohen, Cleve., 1972-75, ptnr., 1975-84, Benesch, Friedlander, Coplan & Aronoff, Cleve., 1984-93; shareholder Kaufman & Cumberland Co., LPA, Cleve., 1994—2000; pvt. practice Chagrin Falls, Ohio, 2001—. Author: Consumer Affairs, 1973, The Construction Loan Process, 1979, Real Estate Financing, 1978, Acquisition, Development and Financing of a Commercial Complex-A Case Study, 1982; contbr. articles to profl. jours. Pres. Am. Jewish Com., Cleve., 1980-82, officer, 1976-80, chmn. adv. com., 1998—; v.p. Criminal Justice Coord. Com., Cleve., 1980-84, Cleve. Play House, bd. dirs., 1978—, pres., 1992-94, chmn., 1994-96, v.p., 1996—. Recipient Max Freedman Young Leadership award, Cleve., 1974. Mem. ABA, Ohio State Bar Assn., Cleve. Bar Assn. (chmn. real estate com. 1978-79, chmn. real estate law insts. 1979, 82, 87). Jewish. Avocations: tennis, golf, classical music, reading. Office: 30799 Pinetree Rd #415 Cleveland OH 44124-5903

BLATTNER, WILLIAM ALBERT, physician, epidemiology researcher; b. St. Louis, Oct. 16, 1943; s. Russell John and Marian Edith (Koeneke) B.; m. Diane Mach, Dec. 27, 1974; chidlren: Michael and Mary (twins), John, Matthew, Timothy. AB, Wash. U., 1966, MD, 1970. Diplomate Am. Bd. Internal Medicine, Am. Bd. Med. Oncology. Intern Strong Meml. Hosp., N.Y.C., 1970-71, asst. resident internal medicine, 1971-72; assoc. resident, asst. chief resident Sloan-Kettering Meml. Hosp., N.Y.C., 1972-73; staff assoc. Nat. Cancer Inst., Bethesda, Md., 1973-75, clin. investigator, 1975-76, sr. clin. investigator, 1976-81, chief family studies sect., 1981-87, chief viral epidemiology sect., 1987-91, founding chief viral epidemiology br., 1991—95; co-founder, assoc. dir. Inst. Human Virology, U. Md., Balt., 1996—, dir. Epidemiology and Prevention Divsn. Chmn. Balt. City Commn. on HIV/AIDS Prevention and Treatment; elected mem. adv. bd. Internat. AIDS Soc., Washington, 1989; participant 5th annual Russell J. Blattner lecture Tex. Children's Hosp., 1984. Editor: Human Retrovirology HTLV, 1990; co-editor-in-chief: Jour. AIDS, 1987—. Recipient Commendation medal USPHS, 1982, Meritorious Svc. medal, 1988, John Snow Award, Am. Health Assn., 2002. Mem. AAAS, Am. Assn. for Cancer Rsch., Am. Fedn. for Clin. Rsch., Am. Soc. Clin. Oncology, Am. Coll. Epidemiology, Internat. AIDS Soc., Phi Beta Kappa, Alpha Omega Alpha. Office: U Md Inst Human Virology 725 W Lombard St Baltimore MD 21201

BLATZ, KATHLEEN ANNE, state supreme court justice; BA summa cum laude, U. Notre Dame, 1976; MSW, U. Minn., 1978, JD cum laude, 1984; LHD (hon.), Hamline U., 1999. Psychiat. social worker, 1979—81; mem. Minn. Ho. of Reps., St. Paul, 1979—93, chmn. crime and family law, fin. instns. and ins. coms., 1985—86; judge Dist. Ct., Henne Pin County, 1993—96; justice Minn. Supreme Ct., 1996—98, chief justice, 1998—. Asst. minority leader Minn. House of Reps., 1987—90, 1993; dir. employee assistance prog. Fairview Community Hospital, 1979—81; assoc. atty. Popham, Haik, Schnobrich & Kaufman, 1984—88; asst. county atty. Hennepin County Attorney's Office, 1992—93; mem. Health and Human Services Com., Rules and Legislative Administration Com., Judiciary, Gen. Legislation Veterans Affairs and Elections Com., Taxes Com.; chair Nat. Ctr. for State Cts. Rsch. Advisory Council; mem. Conference of Chief Justices. Trustee Fairview Southdale Hospital; former mem. Children's Defense Fund Advisory Council, Governor's Task Force on Fetal Alcohol Syndrome; former vice-chair Minn. Supreme Ct. Foster Care and Permanency Task Force; former bd. mem. Big Brothers Big Sisters of Greater Minneapolis. Recipient Women in State Govt. "A Minn. Treasure" award, 27th Annual Women & Bus. Conference Career Achiev. award, 1999, Minn. Women Lawyers Myra Bradwell award, 2002, Minn. Council of Child Caring Agencies Disting. Service award, 2004. Mem.: Minn. State Bar Assn. Office: 305 Minn Judicial Ctr 25 Rev Martin Luther King Jr Blvd Saint Paul MN 55155

BLAU, BARRY, marketing professional, financial consultant; b. N.Y.C., Oct. 4, 1927; s. Emanuel B. and Henrietta Marsha (Moses) B.; m. Eileen Diane Lefkowitz, Aug. 28, 1948; children: Shawn, Peter, Emily, Juliet. With Huber Hoge & Sons, N.Y.C., 1952-57, Sullivan, Stauffer, Caldwell & Bayles, 1958-67, O&M Direct Response, 1968-77; founder Blau Mktg. Techs. Group, 1978-98. Mem. Birchwood Country Club. Jewish. Office: Bayberry Assocs No 4 LLC 9 Bayberry Ridge Rd Westport CT 06880-1713

BLAU, FRANCINE DEE, economics educator; b. N.Y.C., Aug. 29, 1946; d. Harold Raymond and Sylvia (Goldberg) B.; m. Richard Weisskoff, Aug. 1969 (div. 1972); m. Lawrence Max Kahn, Jan. 1, 1979; children: Daniel Blau Kahn, Lisa Blau Kahn. BS, Cornell U., 1966; AM, Harvard U., 1969, PhD, 1975. Vis. lectr. Yale U., New Haven, 1971; instr. econs. Trinity Coll., Hartford, Conn., 1971-74; research assoc. Ctr. for Human Resource Research, Ohio State U., Columbus, 1974-75; asst. prof. econs. and labor and indsl. relations U. Ill., Urbana, 1975-78, assoc. prof., 1978-83, prof., 1983-94; Frances Perkins prof. indsl. and labor rels. Cornell U., 1994—. Cons. law firms, 1979, 81-83, EEOC, 1981-85, U.S. Commn. on Civil Rights, 1976, 20th Century Fund Task Force on Working Women, 1970-71; mem. Nat. Acad. Scis. Panel on Technology and Women's Employment, 1984-86; mem. Nat. Acad. Scis. Panel on Pay Equity Rsch., 1985-89; rsch. assoc. Nat. Bur. Econ. Rsch., Cambridge, Mass., 1988—; vis. scholar Russell Sage Found., 1999-2000. Author: Equal Pay in the Office, 1977, (with Marianne Ferber) The Economics of Women, Men and Work, 1986, 2d edit., 1992, (with Marianne Ferber and Anne Winkler) The Economics of Women, Men and Work, 3rd edit., 1998; editor Jour. Labor Econs., 1992-95; assoc. editor Jour. Econ. Perspectives, 1994—; mem. editorial bd. Social Sci. Quar., 1978-94, Signs: Jour. Women in Culture and Soc., 1979—, Women and Work, 1984—, Indsl. Rels., 1989-97; bd. editors Am. Econ. Rev., 1998—; editor (with Ronald Ehrenberg) Gender and Family Issues in the Workplace, 1997; contbr. articles to profl. jours. Recipient Burligton Northern faculty achievement award, 1993; Harvard U. fellow, 1966-68; U.S. Dept. Labor grantee, 1977-80. Mem. Am. Econ. Assn. (v.p. 1993), Indsl. Rels. Rsch. Assn. (exec. bd. 1987-89, pres. 1997), Midwest Econ. Assn. (v.p. 1983-84, pres. 1991-92, exec. com. 1990-93), Population Assn. Am. Office: Cornell U Sch Indsl & Labor Rels Ithaca NY 14853-3901

BLAU, HARVEY RONALD, lawyer; b. N.Y.C., Nov. 14, 1935; s. David and Rose (Kuchinsky) B.; m. Arlene Joan Garrett, Mar. 21, 1964; children: Stephanie Elizabeth Kramer, Melissa Karen, Victoria Gayle. AB, NYU, 1957, LLM, 1965; JD, Columbia U., 1961. Bar: N.Y. 1961. Practiced in, NY, 1961—2002; law sec. to U.S. Dist. Judge Cooper So. Dist. N.Y., 1962—63; asst. U.S. atty. So. Dist. N.Y., 1963—66; CEO Griffon Corp., 1982—. Chmn. Griffon Corp., Aeroflex Corp.; trustee Mt. Sinai Hosp., N.Y. Mayor Village of Old Westbury. Served to capt. JAGC, AUS, 1958-66. Mem. Assn. Bar City of N.Y., Bar Assn. of Nassau County. Home: 125 Wheatley Rd Old Westbury NY 11568-1210 Office: Griffon Corp 100 Jericho Quadrangle Jericho NY 11753-2708

BLAU, HELEN MARGARET, pharmacology educator; b. London, May 8, 1948; (parents Am. citizens); d. George E. and Gertrude Blau; m. David Spiegel, July 25, 1976; children: Daniel Spiegel, Julia Spiegel. BA in Biology, U. York (Eng.), 1969; MA in Biology, Harvard U., 1970, PhD in Biology, 1975; Doctorate (hon.), U. Nijmegen, Netherlands, 2003. Predoctoral fellow dept. biology Harvard U., Cambridge, Mass., 1969-75; postdoctoral fellow div. med. genetics, dept. biochemistry and biophysics U. Calif., San Francisco, 1975-78; asst. prof. dept. pharmacology Stanford (Calif.) U., 1978-86, assoc. prof. dept. pharmacology, 1986-91, prof. dept. molecular pharmacology, 1991—99, prof. dept. microbiology and immunology, 2002—, chair dept. molecular pharmacology, 1997—2001, dir. gene therapy tech., 1997—, Donald E. and Delia B. Baxter prof., 1999—, dir. Baxter Lab. in Genetic Pharmacology, 2002—. Rolf-Sammet-Fonds vis. prof., U. Frankfurt, 2003; plenary talk on stem cells, Academic des Sci. della France at Pontifical Acad., the Vatican, Modern Biotech. Symposium, 2003; co-chmn. various profl. meetings; spkr. in field. Mem. editorial bd. 14 jours. including Jour. Cell Biology, Somatic Cell Molecular Genetics and Exptl. Cell Rsch., Molecular and Cellular Biology, Genes to Cells, Molecular Therapy; contbr. articles to profl. jours. Mem. ad hoc molecular cytology study sect. NIH, 1987-88; mem. five-yr. planning com genetics and teratology br. NICHHD/NIH, 1989. Recipient Rsch. Career Devel. award NIH, 1984-89, SmithKline & Beecham award, 1989-91, Women in Cell Biology Career Recognition award, 1992, Excellence in Sci. award FASEB, 1999, McKnight Endowment Fund for Neurosci. award, 2001; Mellon Found. faculty fellow, 1979-80, William H. Hume faculty scholar, 1981-84; grantee NIH, NSF, Ellison Med. Found., Muscular Dystrophy Assn., March of Dimes, 1978—; Yvette Mayent-Rothschild fellow for vis. profs. Inst. Curie, Paris, 1995. Fellow AAAS, Havard Overseers; mem. NAS (del. to China 1991), Internat. Soc. Differentiation (pres. 2002-04), Am. Soc. for Cell Biology (nominating com. 1985-86, program com. 1990), Soc. for Devel. Biology (pres. 1994-95), Inst. Medicine Nat. Acad. Scis., Am. Soc. Gene Therapy (bd. dirs. 1999-2002). Avocations: skiing, swimming, hiking, music, theater. Office: Stanford U Sch Medicine 269 Campus Dr CCSR 4215 Stanford CA 94305-5175 Fax: (650) 736-0080. E-mail: hblau@stanford.edu.

BLAU, JOHN, retired social worker; b. N.Y.C., Jan. 31, 1934; s. Alex Englander and Edith (Bachman) B. BBA, U. Ga., 1957; cert. of. supervision, Fordham U., 1971; MSW, Hunter Coll., 1974. Field supr. divsn. vol. and proprietary homes N.Y.C. Human Resource Adminstrn., 1962-95; ret. Former mem. N.Y.C. Interagy., Task Force on Mental Health; mem. N.Y. Found. for Sr. Citizens, N.Y. State Ombudsman Program; rschr. on adult and family home industry, homeless men and women, alternate levels of care. Former dist. leader Dem. Party 65th Assembly Dist. Part B, 1987-91; cmty. advisor N.Y. Found. for Sr. Citizens, ombudsman program long term care; co-chmn. NYCERS coalition of ret. N.Y.C. employees; chmn. Social Svc. ad-hoc com. Served with Intelligence Corps, U.S. Army, 1957-59, 61-62. Mem. Disabled Am. Vets. Assn., Acad. Cert. Social Workers, Nat. Assn. Social Workers, E 79th St. Block Assn., Nat. Alumni Assn. U. Ga., Alumni Assn. Fordham U., Alumni Assn. Hunter Coll. Home and Office: 440 E 77th St New York NY 10021-2316 Office Phone: 212-249-0429.

BLAU, MONTE, retired radiology educator; b. N.Y.C., June 17, 1926; s. Samuel and Rose (Cohen) B.; m. Guitta Drimer, June 30, 1946; children: Saul, Hannah. BS in Chemistry, Poly. Inst. Bklyn., 1948; PhD in Phys. Chemistry, U. Wis., 1952. Rsch. chemist Geochronometric Lab., Yale U., 1952-53; with div. neoplastic diseases Montefiore Hosp., N.Y.C., 1953-54; cancer rsch. scientist Roswell Park Meml. Inst., Buffalo, 1954-75; prof., chmn. dept. nuclear medicine SUNY, Buffalo, 1975-83; vis. prof. radiology Harvard Med. Sch., Boston, 1983-90. Mem. USP adv. panel on radiopharms.; chmn. med. adv. com. N.Y. State bur. Radiol. Health; chmn. med. isotopes adv. com. Los Alamos Nat. Lab. Mem. editorial bd. Jour. Nuclear Medicine. With USN, 1944-46. Mem. Soc. Nuclear Medicine (v.p. 1964, pres. 1972), Am. Chem. Soc., Am. Assn. Physicists in Medicine. Home: PO Box 605 South Wellfleet MA 02663-0605

BLAUFOX, MORTON DONALD, hypertension specialist, educator, nuclear medicine physician; b. N.Y.C., July 19, 1934; s. Emanuel and Elizabeth (Rosenblum) B.; m. Paulette Goldberg, Dec. 20, 1958; children: Laurie Beth, Ellen Ruth, Andrew David. Student, Harvard U., 1952-55; MD, SUNY, 1959; PhD, U. Minn., 1964. Diplomate Am. Bd. Internal Medicine, Am. Bd. Nuc. Medicine (bd. dirs. 1985-91). Intern Jewish Hosp. of Bklyn., N.Y.C., 1959-60; fellow in medicine Mayo Found. Med. Edn. and Rsch., Rochester, Minn., 1960-64; advanced rsch. fellow Am. Heart Assn., 1964-66; rsch. fellow in medicine Harvard Med. Sch., Boston, 1964-66; asst. in medicine and radiology Peter Bent Brigham Hosp., Boston, 1964-66; asst. prof. radiology, also assoc. in medicine Albert Einstein Coll. Medicine, Bronx, NY, 1966-71, dir. sect. nuc. medicine, 1966-76, dir. unified dept., 1976-82, chmn. unified dept., 1982—, assoc. dir. clin. rsch. ctr., 1968-72, assoc. prof. radiology, 1971-76, prof. radiology, 1976—, assoc. prof. medicine, 1972-78, prof. medicine, 1978—; asst. attending physician Bronx Mcpl. Hosp. Ctr., 1966-71, assoc. attending, 1972, attending physician, 1972—; dir. divsn. nuc. medicine Montefiore Med. Ctr., 1976-82, chmn. dept. nuc. medicine, 1982—. Cons. kidney disease control program USPHS, 1967-72; mem. adminstrv. coun. nuc. medicine VA, 1972-73; mem. panel on radiopharms. U.S. Pharmacopeia, 1970-76; mem. hypertension adv. com. N.Y.C. Dept. Health, 1975-76; mem. Am. Bd. Nuc. Medicine, 1984-90; treas. exec. com., 1987-89, chmn., 1990; mem. clin. trials rev. com. Nat. Heart, Lung and Blood Inst., 1988-92, reviewer ready rsch., 1992—; mem. subcom. on non-pharmacologic therapy of Joint Nat. Com. on Detection Evaluation and Treatment of High Blood Pressure, 1991-92; mem. Brookhaven Linac Isotope Producer Users' adv. com. Brookhaven Nat. Lab., 1992-96; mem. internat. liaison com. World Fedn. Nuc. Medicine and Biology, 1992-94; active Coun. Cardiovasc. Radiology, hon.lifetime prof. medicine Shanxi U. Med. Sch., China, 1997. Editor (with others): Seminars in Nuclear Medicine, 1970—; editor: Evaluation of Renal Function and Disease with Radionuclides, 1972—, 2d edit., 1989—, Procs. Internat. Symposium, 1972—, 1975—, 1980—, 1987—, 1990—, PDR for Nuclear Medicine and Radiology, 1971—80, Unilateral Renal Function Studies, 1978; editor: (with others) Secondary Hypertension: Current Diagnosis and Management, 1981; editor: Non-Pharmacologic Therapy of Hypertension, 1987, Newer Diagnostic Methods in Nephrology and Urology, 1986; editl. bd.: Radionuclides in Nephrology, 1980, Jour. Nuclear Medicine, 1973—81, Nephron, Uroradiology, 1978—, Nuclear Medicine Comm., 1979—, Jour. Nuclear Medicine and Allied Sci., 1982, Renal Failure, 1985—89, Am. Jour. Hypertension, 1987—, Current Hypertension Reviews, 2004—; editl. bd. Current Med. Imaging Reviews, 2004, editor-in-chief, 2005; assoc. editor: Garnet's Pediatrics, 1972—, sect. editor for diagnostics and techniques: Current Opinions in Nephrology and Hypertension, 1992—96, contbr.: The Merck Manual, 14th, 15th and 16th edits., 1982—91, Merck Manual Medical Information Home Edit., 1997; co-author: Blood Pressure Measurement: An Illustrated History, 1998; contbr. articles to profl. jours.; author: An Ear to the Chest: An Illustrated History of the Evaluation of the Stethoscope, 2002. Recipient Edward Nobel Found. award, 1963, Albert Lasker pub. health svc. award, 1980, Lifetime Achievement award Internat. Soc. Radionuclides in Nephro Urology, 2001. Fellow ACP, Am. Nephrology Soc., Am. Coll. Nuc. Physicians, Coun. on High Blood Pressure Rsch., Coun. Cardiovasc. Radiology, N.Y. Acad. Medicine (libr. com. 1985—, chmn. sect. on nuc. medicine 1993-95, chmn. ad hoc com. artifact collection, chmn. history of medicine adv. com. 1995—); mem. AMA, Am. Heart Assn., Am. Physiol. Soc., Am. Fedn. Clin. Rsch., Am. Soc. Hypertension (membership com.), Soc. Nuc. Medicine (pres. Greater N.Y. chpt. 1975-76, chmn. acad. coun. 1976-77, exec. and sci. coms., chmn. publ. com. 1979-82, trustee, Berson-Yalow award 1989), Ind. Soc. Nuc. Medicine, Internat. Soc. Nephrology, Internat. Hypertension Soc., Coun. on High Blood Pressure Rsch. (med. adv. bd.), N.Y. Med. Soc., Am. Nephrology Soc., Med. Collectors Assn. (pres. 1983-2004), Swiss Soc. Nuc. Medicine (hon., corr.), Sigma Xi, Nat. Atomic Mus. Achievements include research on hypertension, renal function and evaluation of renal function with radioisotopes, renal blood flow and renin secretion. Home: 101 Drake Smith Woods Ln Rye NY 10580-4316 Office: Montefiore Med Park 1695A Eastchester Rd Bronx NY 10461-2374 Office Phone: 718-405-8454. E-mail: blaufox@aecom.yu.edu. *My life has been directed toward the acquisition, clarification and dissemination of knowledge in the health sciences. The use of such goals to help train young people embarking on a career, with honesty and integrity, has been a particularly rewarding experience.*

BLAUSTEIN, ALFRED (AL) H., art educator, artist; b. N.Y.C., Jan. 23, 1924; s. Sydney and Sophie (Silbersher) Blaustein; m. Lotte Heilbrunn Blaustein, May 5, 1949; 1 child, Marc D. Grad., Cooper Union Art Sch., 1948. Fine arts instr. Albright Art Sch., Buffalo, 1949—52, Skowhegan Sch., Skowhegan, Maine, 1950—59, Pratt Inst., Brooklyn, NY, 1959—68; vis. prof. Yale U., New Haven, 1959—62; prof. fine arts Pratt Inst., Bklyn., 1968—2004. One-man shows include Nordness Gallery, N.Y.C., 1959, 1961, 1963, U. Nebr., 1961, Phila. Art Alliance, 1962, Laeubli Gallery, Zurich, 1962, Phila. Print Club, 1964, Franklin Seiden Gallery, Detroit, 1965, Albany Art Inst., 1965, Randolph-Macon Coll., 1967, Troup Gallery, Dallas, 1968, U. Mo., 1983, one-man shows include retrospective shows Pratt Inst., N.Y.C., 1993, 1994, one-man shows include retrospective, 2004, one-man shows include, 1998, exhibited in group shows at Metro. Mus. of Art, Pa. Acad., Carnegie Internat., Albright-Knox Gallery, Mus. of Fine Arts, Boston, Am. Acad. in Rome, Nat. Acad. of Design, Landmark Gallery, NY, Kent State U., Represented in permanent collections Whitney Mus., Metro. Mus. Art, Libr. of Congress, Chgo. Art Inst., Syracuse U., Washington U., U. Mass., Purdue U., Smithsonian Inst. Pfc USAF. Recipient Eyre medal for Graphics, Pa. Acad., 1959; Rome fellowship, Am. Acad. in Rome, 1954—57, fellowships in painting and printmaking, John Simon Guggenheim Found., 1958—61, grant, Am. Acad. Arts and Letters, 1958, Artist-in-Residence fellowship, Ford Found., 1965. Avocation: bicycling. Home: 141 E 17 St New York NY 10003

BLAVAT, JERRY (GERALD JOSEPH BLAVAT), television personality, actor; b. Phila., July 3, 1940; s. Louis Blavat and Lucille Capuano; children: Kathi, Geraldine, Stacy, Deserie. Grad. high sch., Phila. Dancer Bandstand TV show, Phila., 1953-55; record promoter Cameo/Parkway Records, Phila., 1956-59; road mgr., mgr. various rock and roll groups including Danny and the Juniors, also Don Rickles, 1957-59; night club performer, live radio show host various clubs, radio stas., Phila., 1959-62; disc jockey radio stations including WCAU, WFIL, WCAM, WPGR, WSSJ, WTKU, WVLT, WPEN, WPAZ, WPEN, Phila., Del. Valley, 1962—; program dir. Geator Gold Radio Network, Pa. Del., Md., N.J., 1989—. Owner night club Memories, Margate, N.J., 1972—; mem. nominating com. Rock & Roll Hall of Fame, Phila., 1988—; host live radio show on geatorgold.net, 1999—. TV appearances include The Monkees, Mod Squad, Joey Bishop Show, Tonight Show, Mike Douglas Show, Pat Boone Show, Merv Griffin Show; movie appearances include Baby, It's You, 1983, Desperately Seeking Susan, 1985, Cookie, 1989; producer, host TV shows Discophonic Scene, 1965-66, Jerry Blavat Show, 1966-70, On the Air with the Geator, 1991—, Backstage with Blavat, 1992—; co-prodr. Rock Rhythm and Doo Wop series PBS, 1999--; prodr. Legends of Rock, Legends of Soul, Legends of Harmony at Kimmel Regional Performing Arts Ctr., Phila.; prodr. over 30 record albums of collections/anthologies; rec. artist 5 pop singles; contbr. articles, biographies, liner notes to profl. jours., programs and record albums. Bd. dirs., performer Hero Scholarship Fund, Phila., 1963-70; bd. dirs. Police Athletic League, Phila., 1966-70; fundraiser numerous schs., chs., founds., and pub. TV. Recipient U.S. Congl. Horizon award, 2002; inductee Phila. Rock & Roll Hall of Fame, 1986, installed in permanent exhibit Rock and Roll Hall of Fame, Mus. of Radio and Records, 1998, Phila. Music Alliance Walk of Fame, 1993, Broadcast Pioneers of Phila., 2002. Mem. AFTRA, SAG, Am. Guild Variety Artists, Nat. Music Found. (adv. bd. 1989—). Avocations: horseback riding, bicycling, native american history, fitness. Office: Celebrity Showcase PO Box 25010 Philadelphia PA 19147-0210 Office Phone: 215-923-0550. E-mail: geatorgold@yahoo.com.

BLAYDES, JUNE LOUISE, volunteer; b. Indpls., June 16, 1929; d. Charles Edwin Chalfin and Freda Viola Huls (Stinger) Comer; m. Louis Justus Schulz, Feb. 7, 1948 (dec. May 1974); children: Louis K., Judy A Schulz, Larry L.; m. Fred Blaydes, Apr. 9, 1976. Grad. H.S., Indpls. Realtor Louis Schulz Co., Indpls., 1961-71; pres., owner Floral Concepts Co., Indpls., 1981-90. Pres. Christian Mothers PTA, Christ the King Sch., Indpls., 1955-63; vol. St. Vincent's Hosp., Indpls., 1974-76, Indpls. Speech and Hearing Ctr., Inpls., 1979-84; choir mem. Christ the King Ch., Inpls., 1994-96; bd. dirs. Coburn Place Safe Haven, Indpls., 1996—. Named Vol. of the Month, WMYS (1430) Radio, Indpls., 1997. Mem. Riviera Club, Women of the Moose. Republican. Roman Catholic. Avocations: family activities, travel, mall walkers group, euchre club, bridge club. Home: 6727 Limerick Ct Indianapolis IN 46250-4415

BLAYDES, SOPHIA BOYATZIES, English language educator; b. Rochester, N.Y., Oct. 16, 1933; d. James George and Helene (Bougdanos) Boyatzies; m. David Fairchild Blaydes, June 4, 1961; children: Stephanie Anne, Jeffrey Glenn. BA, U. Rochester, 1955; MA, Ind. U., 1958, PhD, 1962. Teaching asst. English Ind. U., 1955-62; instr. to asst. prof. Am. Thought and Lang. dept. Mich. State U., 1962-65; instr. to prof. English W.Va. U., Morgantown, 1966-99, chair faculty senate, 1990-91, coord. program for sr. and retired faculty, 1994—; pres. Carolinas Symposium for British Studies, 1990-91. Co-dir. Lit. Discussion Group for Sr. Citizens, 1978—; mem. faculty Elderhostel, 1985, 87, 88, 90, 94; mem. ctrl. exec. com. Folger Inst., 1992-99; chair faculty senate, bd. advisors W.Va. U., 1990-91, rep. to adv. coun. to bd. trustees, 1993-99; state del. to the 1995 White House Conf. on Aging; bd. trustees Univ. Sys., 1998-99, Women in Sci. and Health, Robert C. Byrd Health Scis. Ctr., 2004-. Author: Christopher Smart as a Poet of His Time: A Re-Appraisal, 1966, (with others) Sir William Davenant, 1981, Sir William Davenant: An Annotated Bibliography, 1986; editor: (with others) Selected Papers from the W.Va. Shakespeare and Renaissance Association, 1976, The Literary Discussion Group, 1982, 85; contbr. chpts. to books, articles to profl. jours., encys., dictionaries, bibliographies. Mem. cen. exec. com. Folger Inst., 1992-99. Recipient Disting. Manuscript award Mich. State U., 1965, Gerontology Ctr. award, 1983; named Disting. West Virginian, W.Va. Gov., 1995; grantee W.Va. Found., 1973, W.Va. Humanities, 1980; W.Va. U. Senate rsch. grantee, 1984, 89; Folger fellow, 1981, Folger grantee, 1988, 91; recipient Sigma Tau Delta Outstanding Tchg. award, 1996. Mem. Am. Soc. 18th Century Studies, MLA, W.Va. Assn. Coll. English Tchrs. (pres. 1977), Shakespeare and Renaissance Soc. W.Va. (chmn. 1978, 84), Carolinas Symposium on Brit. Studies (chair program 1989, pres. 1990, conf. chair 1993), Women in Sci. and Health (WISH), W. Va. U. Health Scis. Ctr. Home: 652 Bellaire Dr Morgantown WV 26505-2421 Office: W Va U PO Box 6296 Morgantown WV 26506-6296

BLAYLOCK, JAMES CARL, clergyman, librarian; b. Guntown, Miss., Jan. 27, 1938; s. Carl Houston and Katie Lee (Pugh) B.; m. Jo Ann Enlow, May 3, 1962; children: Jacquelyn Ann, John Thomas. AA, Southeastern Bapt. Coll., Laurel, Miss., 1962; BTh, N.Am. Theol. Sem., Jacksonville, Tex., 1964; BA, U. Tex., Tyler, 1976; MRE, Bapt. Missionary Sem., Jacksonville, 1977; MSLS, Tex A&M U., 1980. Ordained to ministry Bapt. Ch., 1962. Pastor Mt. Pleasant Ch., Bedias, Tex., 1962-64, Buena Vista Ch., Timpson, Tex., 1964-70, 1st Bapt. Ch., Maydelle, Tex., 1970-86, Corinth Ch., Jacksonville, Tex., 1986—; asst. dir. Bapt. News Svc., Jacksonville, 1969-88, dir., 1988-99; asst. editor Directory and Handbook of Bapt. Missionary Assn., Jacksonville, 1969-88, editor, 1988-99; libr. Bapt. Missionary Assn. Theol. Sem., Jacksonville, 1972—. Editor Mt. Olive Evangel, 1965-70; author: History of 1st Bapt. Ch. Maydelle, Tex., 1986, Buena Vista Bapt. Ch., 1986, Glimpses from the Past, 2003. Mem. Am. Theol. Libr. Assn., ALA, Tex. Libr. Assn. Baptist. Home: 625 W Kickapoo St Jacksonville TX 75766-4621 Office: Bapt Missionary Assn Theol Sem 1530 E Pine St Jacksonville TX 75766-5407 Office Phone: 903-586-2501.

BLAZEJOWSKI, CAROL A., professional sports team executive, retired professional basketball player; b. Elizabeth, NJ, Sept. 29, 1956; Grad., Montclair State Coll., 1978. Player Montclair State U., 1974—78, Allentown Crestettes, Pa., 1978—80, NJ Gems, 1980-81; dir. licensing NBA, 1990—95, dir. women's basketball programs, 1995—96; dir. basketball devel. WNBA, 1996—97; promotional rep. Adidas; v.p., gen. mgr. NY Liberty WNBA, 1997—2000, sr. v.p., gen. mgr., 2000—. Named Kodak All-Am., Montclair State Coll., 1976—78, Converse Women's Player Yr., 1977, Women's Basketball Player Yr., 1978; named to Naismith Basketball Hall Fame, 1994, NJ Sports Hall Fame, 1995; recipient Wade Trophy, 1978. Achievements include All-Am. selection, 1976, 77, 78; single season and career women's basketball scoring records, 1976; mem. World Univ. Gold Medal team, Mexico City, 1979; Pan Am. Silver medal team, 1979; leading scorer Women's Basketball League, 1980-81. Office: New York Liberty 2 Penn Plz New York NY 10121-0101 also: c/o Basketball Hall of Fame PO Box 179 Springfield MA 01101-0179

BLAZEK-WHITE, DORIS, lawyer; b. Easton, Md., Nov. 17, 1943; d. George W. and Nola M. (Buterbaugh) Defibaugh; m. Thacher W. White; children: Christine T., Justine M. BA, Goucher Coll., 1965; JD, Georgetown U., 1968. Bar: DC 1969, VI 1969, Md. 1978, registered: US Ct. Appeals (3rd cir.) 1969, US Ct. Appeals (DC cir.) 1971. Gen. practice with Judge Warren H. Young, St. Croix, 1968-70; assoc. Covington & Burling, Washington, 1970-76, ptnr., 1976—, chmn. Estates & Trust Practice Group. Mem.: ABA (tax sect.), DC Superior Ct. (adv. com., probate and fiduciary rules), Washington DC Estate Planning Coun., Am. Coll. Trust & Estate Counsel. Office: Covington & Burling 1201 Pennsylvania Ave NW Washington DC 20004 Office Phone: 202-662-5490. Office Fax: 202-778-5490. Business E-Mail: dblazek-white@cov.com.

BLAZER, DAN GERMAN, II, psychiatrist, epidemiologist; b. Nashville, Feb. 23, 1944; s. Dan German and Mary Elizabeth (Owsley) Blazer; m. Sherrill Walls, Aug. 19, 1966; children: Dan German III, Natasha Leigh. BA, Vanderbilt U., 1965; MD, U. Tenn., 1969; MPH, U. N.C., 1979, PhD, 1980. Diplomate Am. Bd. Psychiatry and Neurology. Fellow Montefiore Hosp. and Med. Ctr., N.Y.C., 1975—76; asst. prof., assoc. prof., then prof. psychiatry Duke U. Med. Ctr., Durham, NC, 1976—, J.P. Gibbons prof. psychiatry, 1990—, interim chair of psychiatry, 1990—93, prof. cmty. and family medicine, 1986—; dean of med. edn. Duke U., 1992—99. Chair, bd. dirs. Am. Geriat. Soc., NY, 1983; bd. dirs. ret. persons svcs. Am. Assn. Ret. Persons, Alexandria, Va., 1987—92; pres. Psychiat. Rsch. Soc., Salt Lake City, 1988; chmn. epidemiology and disease control study sect. NIH, Bethesda, Md., 1988—. Author: Life is Worth Living, 1987, Depression in Late Life, 1993, Freud vs. God, 1998, Introduction to Clinical Research in Psychiatry, 1998. Named Outstanding Alumnus, U. Tenn. Coll. Medicine, 2003; recipient Rsch. Career Devel. award, NIMH, 1977, Alex Haley award, East Tenn. Bapt. Hosp., Knoxville, 1986, Disting. Svc. award, U. N.C. Sch. Pub. Health, Chapel Hill, 1989, Milo Leavitt award, Am. Geriat. Soc., 1997, Rema LaPouse award, APHA, 2001. Fellow: Am. Psychopathol. Assn., Gerontol. Soc. Am. (Klecmeier award 2005), So. Psychiat. Assn., Am. Coll. Psychiatrists (Geriatric Psychiatry Rsch. award 2003), Am. Psychiat. Assn.; mem.: Am. Assn. Geriatric Psychiatry (pres. 2005), Inst. of Medicine NAS. Democrat. Avocations: hiking, reading. Office: Duke U Med Ctr PO Box 3003 Durham NC 27715-3003 Business E-Mail: blaze001@mc.duke.edu.

BLAZER, RANDOLPH C., diversified financial services company executive; b. 1950; Degree, Western Md. Coll.; MBA, U. Ky. Fin. cons. KPMG LLP, Washington, 1977—91, ptnr.-in-charge fed. svcs. consulting practice, 1991—97; mem. exec. team BearingPoint, Inc., 1997—2000, co-CEO, 1999—2000, bd. dirs., 1999—, CEO, 2000—, chmn. bd. dirs., 2001—. Office: BearingPoint Inc 1676 International Dr Mc Lean VA 22102

BLAZEY, MARK LEE, management consultant; b. Canadaigua, NY, Nov. 14, 1948; s. Everett J. and Ann (Marrer) B.; m. Karen S. Davison, May 8, 1950; children: Elizabeth, Mark. BA, Syracuse (NY) U., 1970; MS in Edn., SUNY, Albany, 1976, MS in Psychology and Stats., EdD, SUNY, Albany, 1978; SMG cert., Harvard U., 1984. Cert. tchr., chief sch. officer and adminstr., NY. Tchr., cons. Syracuse City Schs., 1971-76; lectr. SUNY, Albany, 1976-78; higher edn. cons. NY State Edn. Dept., Albany, 1976-78; policy analyst Office of Edn. HEW, Washington, 1978-80; sr. policy analyst Office Sec. U.S. Dept. Edn., Washington, 1980-81, dir. policy, 1981-83, dir. ops., 1983-85; prof. Rochester (NY) Inst. Tech., 1985-86, dir., assoc. dean, 1986-88, dean, 1988-92. Bd. dirs. RIT Rsch. Corp.; pres. Quantum Performance Group, Inc.; sr. examiner Malcolm Balbrige Nat. Quality award, 1995-99; founding mem., lead judge Excelsior award, NY Gov.'s exec. com., 1991-99, presiding judge Aruba Nat. Quality award, 1995-98; lead judge Vt. Quality Award, 1991-2000; judge Wis. Forward Quality award, 2000—, Del. Quality award, 2002—. Author: Insights to Performance Excellence, 1996-2004. Bd. dirs. Horton Child Care Ctr., Rochester, 1985-89; mem. Geva Angels Repertory Theater, 1985—; bd. dirs. Finger Lakes Region Edn. Ctr. for Econ. Devel., 1990-92. Recipient Frandson award for Lit., 1993, Quality Champion award State Quality Award Network, 1995. Mem. Am. Soc. for Quality (cert. quality auditor). Avocations: wood sculpture, skiing, golf, sailing. Office: 5050 Rushmore Rd Palmyra NY 14522-9414 E-mail: blazey@quantumperformance.com, QPG1@aol.com.

BLAZICH, FRANK ARTHUR, horticulturist, educator, researcher; b. N.Y.C. s. John Anthony and Mary Blazich; m. Joan April Wooden, July 10, 1976; children: Joan, Frank. AAS, SUNY, Farmingdale, 1969; BS, U. Vt., 1971, MS, 1973; PhD, Pa. State U., 1977. Grad. rsch. fellow U. Vt., Burlington, 1971—73; grad. asst. Pa. State U., University Park, 1973—77; rsch. scientist Hampton Roads Agrl. Experiment Sta., Virginia Beach, Va., 1977—78; asst. prof. N.C. State U., Raleigh, 1978—81, assoc. prof., 1981—86, prof., 1986—. Advisor Hort. Rsch. Inst., 1996—2002. Contbr. articles more than 475 articles to sci. and popular jours.; mem. editl. bd. Jour. Environ. Horitculture, 1985—2002. Vol. N.C. Mus. Natural Scis., 1982—. Served with U.S. Army, 1965—67. Recipient Porter Heneger award for horticultural rsch., So. Nursery Assn., 1990, Norman J. Coleman award, Am. Assn. Nurserymen, 1996. Mem.: Am. Soc. Hort. Sci. (assoc. editor jour. 1989—93, sci. editor 1999—2001, Outstanding Grad. Educator award 1977, Disting. Achievement award for nursery crops 1992), Am. Hort. Soc. (L.M. Ware Disting. Tchr. aard 2005). Avocations: hunting, fishing, antiques. Office: NC State U Raleigh NC 27695-7609

BLAZINA, JANICE FAY, pathologist; d. Joseph and Cordelia Evelyn B. BS, Youngstown State U., 1975; MD, Ohio State U., 1978. Diplomate Am. Bd. Pathology. Resident in anat. and clin. pathology U. Ala. Med. Ctr., Birmingham, 1978-82; assoc. pathologist various hosps., Bryan, Tex., 1982-83, High Plains Bapt. Hosp., Amarillo, Tex., 1983-84; fellow in blood banking Baylor U. Med. Ctr., Dallas, 1984-85; asst. prof. dept. pathology Ohio State U., Columbus, 1985-93, asst. prof. Sch. Allied Med. Professions, 1987-93. Asst. dir. transfusion svc. Ohio State U. Hosp., 1985-89, assoc. dir., 1989-90, dir., 1990-93, med. dir. histocompatibility, paternity, apheresis and phlebotomy svcs., 1987-93, divsn. med. tech., 1987-93; asst. med. dir. Carter Blood Ctr., Ft. Worth, 1993-95, med. dir., 1995-96. Contbr. articles to profl. publs. Bremer Found. grantee, 1987. Mem. AMA, Am. Soc. Apheresis, Am. Soc. Histocompatibility and Immunogenetics, Am. Assn. Blood Banks (insp. 1987—), Ohio Assn. Blood Banks (trustee 1990-93, sec. 1992-93), Assn. Women Sci. Cen. Ohio (v.p. 1989-90, pres. 1990-91), Nat. Alliance Mentally Ill Tarrant County (sec. 2003). Mem. Church of Christ. Avocations: gardening, cats, African violets. Personal E-mail: jbandjc@peoplepc.com.

BLAZING, MICHAEL AUGUST, internist; b. 1961; MD, U. Calif., San Francisco, 1987. Postdoctoral fellow Duke U. Med. Ctr., now asst. prof. medicine, 1991—. Recipient Clinician-Scientist award Am. Heart Assn., 1995-96. Home: 2113 Carriage Way Chapel Hill NC 27517-9466 Office: Duke U Med Ctr Dept Cardiology Rm 7403 PO Box 3126 Durham NC 27710-0001*

BLAZY, LOUIS JOSEPH, III, federal agency administrator; b. Ft. Beloir, Va., Apr. 2, 1952; s. Louis Joseph Blazy Jr. and Dorothy Virginia Blazy; m. Suzan Mary Rife-Blazy, June 1, 1975; children: Damian Louis, Christopher Michael. BA, George Mason U., 1979, MA, 1981; PhD, U. Md., 1985; MBA, George Washington U., 2002. Engr. Amry Rsch. Inst., Alexandria, Va., 1980—83; computer scientist CIA, McLean, 1983—93; dir,. U.S. Dept. Agrl., Washington, 1993—98; dir. IUTV NASA, AMES, Fairmont, W.Va., 1998—2003; dep. asst. sec. U.S. Dept. Housing & Urban Devel., Washington, 2003—05; astl dir. FBI, 2005—. Prof. U. Md., College Park, 1985—; pres. Intelligent Sys. Applications, Fairfax, Va., 1993—96. With USN, 1970—71. Mem.: AAAS, Internat. Soc. Sys. Engring., Psi Chi, Sigma Chi, Beta Gamma Sigma. Avocation: collecting Japanese wood block prints. Office: FBI 935 Pennsylvania Ave NW Washington DC 20535

BLAZZARD, NORSE NOVAR, lawyer; b. St. Johns, Ariz., July 8, 1937; s. Howard N. and Viola (Greer) B.; m. Mary Elizabeth Jecker, June 15, 1958; children: Howard Norse, Mary Catherine; m. Judith A. Hasenauer, July 2, 1977. AB, Stanford U., 1959; JD, U. Calif., Hastings, 1962. Bar: Calif. 1963, U.S. Dist. Ct. (no. dist.) Calif. 1966, Conn. 1974, U.S. Dist. Ct. Conn. 1975, U.S. Supreme Ct. 1975, U.S. Ct. Appeals (D.C. cir.) 1977, U.S. Ct. Appeals (2d cir.) 1978, Fla. 1993; CLU. Counsel Calif. Western Life Ins. Co., Sacramento, 1966-70; sr. v.p., gen. counsel NARE Life Svc. Co., Palo Alto, calif., 1970-74; pres. Blazzard, Grodd & Hasenauer, P.C., Westport, Conn., 1974—. Chmn. ins. products task force Fin. Products Stds. Bd., 1988-89; chmn. Nat. Assn. Variable Annuities, 1994. Bd. govs. Norwalk Symphony, 1979. Capt. JAGC, U.S. Army, 1962-66. Inductee Variable Annuity Hall of Fame, 1998. Mem. ABA, FBA, Calif. Bar Assn., Fla. Bar Assn., D.C. Bar Assn. Republican. Mem. Lds Ch. E-mail: norse.blazzard@bghpc.com.

BLEAKLEY, PETER KIMBERLEY, lawyer; b. Franklin, Pa., Aug. 19, 1936; s. Rollin R and Marion (St James) Bleakley; m. Mary B DeRosa; children: Jennifer A, Sarah A, Nicholas D. BA, U. Va., 1958, LL.B., 1962. Bar: Va 1962, DC 1966, US Ct Appeals (2d cir), US Ct Appeals (3d cir), US Ct Appeals (5th cir), US Ct Appeals (6th cir), US Ct Appeals (7th cir), US Ct Appeals (8th cir), US Ct Appeals (9th cir), US Ct Appeals (DC cir), US Supreme Ct, US Ct Appeals (fed cir). Trial atty. Fed. Trade Commn., Washington, 1962-66; trial atty. Dept. Justice, Washington, 1966; assoc. Arnold & Porter, Washington, 1966-70, ptnr., 1971—. Fellow: Am Col Trial Lawyers; mem.: ABA. Democrat. Avocations: tennis, skiing, bicycling, golf. Home: 3103 Hawthorne St NW Washington DC 20008-3540 Office: Arnold & Porter 555 12th St NW Washington DC 20004-1206 E-mail: peter_bleakley@aporter.com.

BLECHER, MAXWELL M., lawyer; b. Chgo., May 27, 1933; Degree, DePaul Univ.; LLB, Univ. So. Calif., 1955. Mem. Blecher & Collins P.C., Los Angeles. Mem. Nat. Commn. for Review of Antitrust Laws & Procedures, 1978—79. Contbr. articles to profl. jour. Fellow: Am. Bd. Trial Advocates, Am. Coll. Trial Lawyers; mem.: State Bar Calif., ABA (chmn. Private Antitrust Litigation Com. 1974—76, mem. Council 1976—77), Am. Judicature Soc., Assn. Bus. Trial Lawyers, Chancery Club, Com. Support Antitrust Laws, Fed. Bar Assn., L.A. County Bar Assn. Office: Blecher & Collins PC 20th Floor 611 W Sixth St Los Angeles CA 90017 Office Fax: 213-622-4222.

BLECHMAN, MARLENE SANDRA, music educator; b. Chgo., Oct. 17, 1931; d. David Gilbert and Sylvia (Singer) G.; M. Marvin Blechman, Mar. 11, 1951; children: Joel, Sanford. BA, Northeastern Ill. U., 1972, MA, 1984. Piano tchr. Highland Park and Deerfield (Ill.) High Schs., 1982-87; pvt. piano tchr. Highland Park, 1957-91. Author (with others) Syllabus Exam., 1978. Mem. Ill. State Music Tchrs'. Assn., Northshore Music Tchrs'. Assn., Nat. Guild of Piano Tchrs., Soc. of Am. Musicians, Northshore Musicians Club, City of Hope Club. Avocation: bridge. Home: 1125 Lake Cook Rd Apt 208E Northbrook IL 60062-1553

BLECHMAN, R. O., artist, filmmaker; b. Bklyn., Oct. 1, 1930; s. Samuel and Mae Blechman; m. Moisha Kubinyi, Mar. 3, 1960; children: Nicholas, Max. BA, Oberlin Coll., 1952. Freelance illustrator, N.Y.C., 1953—; freelance producer, designer animated films, 1975—; pres. R.O. Blechman, Inc., N.Y.C., 1978—, The Ink Tank, N.Y.C., 1979—. Author, illustrator: The Juggler of Our Lady, 1952, Onion Soup, 1963, Behind the Lines, an autobiography and anthology, 1980, The Life of Saint Nicholas, 1996, The Book of Jonah, 1997; exhibited one-man shows, Gallery Delpire, Paris, 1968, Graham Gallery, N.Y.C., 1978, ITC Gallery, 1981, Galerie Bartsch & Chariau, Munich, 1982, 92, 2000; represented in permanent collections, Mus. Modern Art, N.Y.C., Chase Manhattan Bank; executed murals, Mus. Natural History, U.S. Pavilion Expo '67, Folger Shakespeare Library.; films include The Juggler of Our Lady, 1958, Abraham and Isaac, 1971, Exercise, 1974, Simple Gifts, 1978, No Room at the Inn, 1978 (Clio award 1968, 69, 73), L'Histoire du Soldat, 1984 (Emmy award 1984); retrospective Mus. Modern Art, N.Y.C., N.Y., 2003. Trustee Swann found.; bd. dirs. The Olana Partnership. Mem. Alliance Graphique Internat., Am. Inst. Graphic Arts, Graphic Artists Guild. Home and Office: 205 Tompkins RD Ancram NY 12502-5351 Business E-Mail: ro@roblechman.com.

BLECHNER, MARK JACOB, psychologist, educator; b. N.Y.C., Nov. 6, 1950; BA, U. Chgo., 1972; MS, Yale U., 1975, PhD, 1977; cert. in psychoanalysis, William Alanson White Inst., 1983. Trainee in clin. psychology NIMH, 1973-76; rsch. assoc. Haskins Lab., New Haven, 1974-77; pvt. practice clin. psychology, N.Y.C., 1977—. Asst. clin. prof. psychology dept. psychiatry Columbia Coll. Physicians and Surgeons, 1981-94; dir., HIV-Clini. Svcs., tng. analyst, supr., dir. curriculum William Alanson White Inst., 1984—, Manhattan Inst. for Psychoanalysis, 1985-90; asst. clin. prof. psychology postdoctoral program in psychoanalysis NYU, 1995—. Author: The Dream Frontier; editor Hope and Mortality; contbr. articles to profl. jours. Mem. AAAS, APA, N.Y. Acad. Scis., Sigma Xi. Address: 145 Central Park W New York NY 10023-2004 Office Phone: 212-595-4648. E-mail: mblechner@psychoanalysis.net.

BLECK, PHYLLIS CLAIRE, surgeon, musician; b. Oak Park, Ill., Mar. 10, 1936; d. William Fred and Mildred A. (Jones) B. BS, U. Ill., 1958; MM, Northwestern U., 1968; DMA, U. So. Calif., 1970; postgrad., Autonoma U., Guadalajara, Mex., 1973-76; MD, Rush Med. Coll., 1979; MS in Surgery, U. Ill., 1983. Diplomate Am. Bd. Surgery, Am. Bd. Thoracic Surgery. Prin. trumpet Fla. Symphony Orch., 1960—66, Orch. Sinfonica Nat. de Peru, 1965; instr. Thornton Jr. Coll., 1966—68; lectr. U. So. Calif., 1969—73; asst. prof. Whittier Coll., 1973; intern Rush Presbyn. St. Luke's Med. Ctr., Chgo., 1979—80, resident, asst. in gen. surgery, 1980—82, instr. gen. surgery, 1982—84; resident in cardiothoracic surgery U. Medicine and Dentistry N.J., 1984—87; pvt. practice medicine specializing cardiothoracic surgery Aurora, Ill., 1987—; asst. prof. Rush U., 1996—. Editor: Mozart Divertimento for Winds; rsch. on vascular ischemia. Fellow ACS, Am. Coll. Chest Physicians, Ill. Thoracic Surg. Soc., Ill. Surg. Soc.; mem. AAAS, Soc. Thoracic Surgeons, Internat. Coll. Surgeons (pres. U.S. sect. 2004-05), Chgo. Surg. Soc., Kappa Delta Pi, Pi Kappa Lambda, Sigma Alpha Iota. Office: 120 Spalding Dr Ste 308 Naperville IL 60540 Office Phone: 630-904-0124. Personal E-mail: p.bleck@worldnet.att.net.

BLECKLEY, JEANETTE A., lawyer; b. Columbia, SC, Feb. 2, 1943; d. Thomas Marcus and Amanda Elizabeth (Cobb) B.; m. Nathan G. Pearce, Dec. 3, 1967 (div. 1979); 1 child, Angelique Nicole Pearce. AA, Young Harris (Ga.) Coll., 1963; student, American River Coll., Sacramento, 1966—67; JD, Lincoln U., Sacramento, 1974; JD (hon.), U. No. Calif., 2002. Bar: Calif., U.S. Dist. Ct. (3d dist.) Calif.; cert. tchr., Calif. Gen. office staff Procter & Gamble, Atlanta, 1962-64; contract negotiator, adminstr., purchasing agt., pub. rels. Am. Cable Elec. Supply, Inc., Sacramento, 1965-74; engring. asst. R&D,s. Ban Electronics, Sacramento, 1970; pvt. practice Sacramento, 1974—; prof. U. No. Calif., 2000—. Contbr. articles to Reflections; author, writer, composer album Willows, Wisps and Wishes, 1994. Mem. Calif. Bar Assn., Sacramento Bar Assn., Calif. Women Lawyers, Sacramento Valley Legal Svcs., Weave, Sigma Beta Sigma. Avocations: music, antique cars, writing, dance, football. Office: 2501 Darwin St Sacramento CA 95821-5509

BLEDEL, ALEXIS (KIMBERLY ALEXIS BLEDEL), actress; b. Houston, Sept. 16, 1981; d. Martin and Nanette Biedel, Martin and Nanette. Attended, Page Parkes Ctr. of Modeling and Acting; studied Film, NYU Tisch Sch., NYC, 1999—2000. Actor: (TV series) Gilmore Girls, 2000—; (films) Rushmore, 1998, Tuck Everlasting, 2002, DysEnchanted, 2004, Bride & Prejudice, 2004, The Orphan King, 2005, Sin City, 2005, The Sisterhood of the Traveling Pants, 2005; guest appearances The Late Late Show with Craig Kilborn, 2003, Late Show with David Letterman, 2005, The View, 2005. Named one of 25 Hottest Stars under 25, Teen People mag., 2002; recipient Family Friendly Forum Award, best actress in a drama, 2002. First language Spanish. Office: 17 Little West 12TH St #333 New York NY 10014-1311

BLEDSOE, DREW, professional football player; b. Ellensburg, Wash., Feb. 14, 1972; s. Mac and Barbara Bledsoe; m. Maura Bledsoe; children: Stuart, John, Henry, Healy. Student, Wash. State U. Quarterback New Eng. Patriots, 1993—2002, Buffalo Bills, 2002—04, Dallas Cowboys, 2005—. Internat. chmn. Children's Miracle Network; co-founder with wife Drew Bledsoe Found., 1999—; sponsor Parenting with Dignity, 1996—; established Albert-"Stu" Bledsoe Endowed Football Scholarship. Named to Pro Bowl, 1994, 1996, 1997, 2000. Achievements include holding NFL single season record for most passes attempted (691), 1994; single game record for most passes completed (45); led NFL in total passing yards (4,555), 1994; led NFL in completions 1994, 1996. Office: Dallas Cowboys 1 Cowboys Pkwy Irving TX 75063*

BLEHER, FRAUKE MARIA, mathematician, educator; b. Poughkeepsie, NY, May 26, 1968; d. Hartmut and Barbara Bleher. MS, U. Stuttgart, Germany, 1993, PhD, 1995. Postdoctoral rschr. U. Pa., 1996—98; asst. prof. So. Ill. U., Carbondale, 1998—2000, U. Iowa, Iowa City, 2000—03, assoc. prof., 2003—. Contbr. articles to profl. jours. Grantee, NSF, 2003—; Young Investigator grantee, Nat. Security Agy., 2001—03. Mem.: Deutsche Mathematiker-Vereinigung, Math. Assn. Am., European Math. Soc., Am. Math. Soc. Business E-Mail: frauke-bleher@uiowa.edu.

BLEIBERG, LEON WILLIAM, surgeon, podiatrist; b. Bklyn., June 9, 1932; s. Paul Pincus and Helen (Epstein) B.; m. Beth Daigle, June 7, 1970; children: Kristina Noel, Kelley Lynn, Kimberly Ann, Paul Joseph. Student, L.A. City Coll., 1950-51, U. So. Calif., 1951, Case Western Res. U., 1951-53; DSc with honors, Temple U., 1955; D in Podiatric Medicine, Pa. Sch. Podiatric Medicine, 1965; PhD, U. Beverly Hills, 1970. Served rotating internship various hosps., Phila., 1954—55; resident Bella Vista Hosp., Montebello, La., 1956—58; surg. podiatrist So. Calif. Podiatry Group, Westchester, Calif., 1956—75; health care economist, rschr. Drs. Home Health Care Svcs., 1976—; chmn. bd. Unltd. Healthcare, Metro Manila, Philippines; v.p. pub. rels. Bilbao Wellness Found., Upland, Calif.; CEO Med. Trianon, Newbury Park, Calif.; dir. biomechanics dept. Anti-Aging and Rejuvenation Clinic, Torrance, Calif.; CFO mktg. and devel. Immigration Ctr. for Law and Justice. Podiatric cons. U. So. Calif. Athletic Dept., Morningside and Inglewood (Calif.) High Schs., Royal Navy Assn., Long Beach (Calif.) Naval Sta.; exec. cons. Thomas Med. Group, Pomona, Calif., 1995, Cardiotel, Van Nuys, Calif., 1995; lectr. in field; healthcare affiliate Internat. divsn. CARE/ASIA, 1987; pres. Medica, Totalcare, Cine-Medics Corp., Strategic World-Wide Health Care Svcs.; exec. dir. Internat. Health Trust; developer Health Banking Program; adminstr. Orthotic Concepts, 1993; prof. health care econs. and med. rehab. Global U., Ontario, Calif., chmn. dept. health care econs., chmn. dept. biomechanics and phys. rehab.; CEO Integrated Wellness Ctrs., The Med. Trianon Found.; exec. dir. The Med. Trianon; exec. dir. wellness divsn. Crown Golden Eagles; mem. nat. leadership Temple U., Phila.; CEO Global Health Share 2000; bd. dirs. Filipino Vets. Found. Prodr. (films) The Gun Hawk, 1963, Terrified, Day of the Nightmare; contbr. articles to profl. jours. Hon. Sheriff Westchester 1962-64; commd. mem. Rep. Senatorial Inner Circle, 1984-86; co-chmn. health reform com. United We Stand Am., Thousand Oaks, Calif.; mem. exec. coun. State of Calif., United We Stand Am.; active 1st Security and Safety, Westlake Village, Calif., 1993—; lt. comdr. med. svcs. corps Brit.-Am. Sea Cadet Corps, 1984—; track coach Westlake High Sch., Westlake Village; exec. sec. Nat. Coalition Parents for Anti-Drug/Violence Corp., Inc. L.A. World Affairs Coun.; county inspector U.S. Election Com., Calif.; bd. dirs. Power Search Unltd. Ministries, Philippines and US; U.S. coord. Luntiang Pilipinas (Philippine Ecology Program); mem. bd. dirs. Philippine Vets. Found.; mem. Agouna C. of C., Oak Park C. of C., Las Virgenes C. of C. With USN, 1955-56 Recipient Medal of Merit, U.S. Presdl. Task Force, Grand award Top Personalities mag., 1999. Mem. Filipino Vets. Found. (bd. dirs.), Philippine Hosp. Assn. (Cert. of Appreciation 1964, trophy for Outstanding Svc. 1979), Calif. Podiatry Assn. (hon.), Am. Podiatric Med. Assn. (hon.), Acad. TV Arts and Scis., Royal Soc. Health (Eng.), We. Foot Surgery Assn., Am. Coll. Foot Surgeons, Am. Coll. Podiatric Sports Medicine, Internat. Coll. Preventive Medicine, Hollywood Comedy Club, Sts. and Sinners Club, Westchester C. of C. (hon. sheriff), Las Vegas C. of C., Hals Und Beinbruch Ski Club, Beach Cities Ski Club, Orange County Stamp Club, Las Virgenes Track Club, Masons, Shriners, Scottish Rite. Home and Office: 55 N Wendy Dr Newbury Park CA 91320-4351 Office Phone: 805-499-6900. Personal E-mail: medicaltrianon@verizon.net.

BLEICH, J. DAVID, law educator, rabbi; BA, Bklyn Coll., 1960; grad. fellow, Kollel Yeshiva Chofetz, Chaim of Radun, N.Y.C., 1958-62; MA, Columbia U., 1968; PhD, NYU, 1974. Ordained rabbi, 1957. Instr. dept. philosophy Hunter Coll., Bklyn., 1962-69; asst. prof. philosophy Stern Coll. for Women, 1972-78; vis. assoc. prof. law Benjamin Cardozo Sch. of Law, N.Y.C., 1979-83, assoc. prof. law, 1983-86, prof. of law, 1986—. Instr. Rutgers U., 1962-63, Bar Ilan U. dept. philosophy, summer, 1970; adj. prof. U. Haifa, Israel, 1974-75; assoc. prof. Yeshiva U., 1978-79, Herbert and Florence Tenzer prof. of Jewish law and ethics, 1981—; vis. Gruss prof. Talmudic Civil Law, U. Pa., 1991-93; prof. Talmud Rabbi Isaac Eichanan Theol. Sem., 1969—, dir. Inst. for Advanced Study of Jurisprudence and Family Law, 1987—; chmn. Jewish Law sect. Assn. Am. Law Schs.; mem. N.Y. State Task Force on Life and the Law, 1984—, exec. com. Acad. for Jewish Philosophy, 1980—; cons. HEW, ethnic heritage programs, 1975-76; lectr. in field. Author: Providence in the Philosophy of Gesonides, 1973, Contemporary Halakhic Problems, Vol. I, 1977, Judaism and Healing, 1980, 2d edit., 2002, Birkas ha-Chammah, 1980, Contemporary Halakhic Problems, Vol. II, 1983, Vol. III, 1989, Vol. IV, 1995, Vol. V, 2005, Time of Death in Jewish Law, 1991, Be-Netivot ha-Halakhah, Vol. I, 1996, Vol. II, 1998, Vol. III, 2000; editor: (with Fred Rosner) Jewish Bioethics: A Reader, 1979, With Perfect Faith: Foundations of Jewish Belief, 1983, Bioethical Dilemmas vol. I, 1998, vol. II, 2005; contbr. articles to Ha-Ma'ayan, Ha Ne'eman, Or Ha-Mizrah, Ha-Pardes, Moriah, Shanah ha Shanah, Tehumin, Jewish Observer, Tradition, Jewish Life, Sh'ma, Judaism, Jewish Quarterly Rev., others. Chmn. com. on med. ethics, Fedn. Jewish Philantrophies, 1973-77, mem. com. on rsch. and publication, Hosp. for Joint Diseases and Med. Ctr., 1975, bioethics com. Met. Hosp., 1984— Woodrow Wilson Nat. fellow, 1960-61, N.Y. Regents Coll. Tchg. fellow, 1960-61, Nat. Found. for Jewish Culture scholar, 1961-62, Hastings Inst. for Scs., Ethics and Life Scis. fellow, 1974-75, Irving M. Bunim Meml. award, 1981; named fellow Acad. Jewish Philosophy, 1980, vis. scholar Oxford Ctr. for Postgrad. Hebrew Studies, 1980. Mem. Assn. Am. Law Schs. (chmn. Jewish law sect. 1991-94), Union of Orthodox Rabbis U.S. and Can., Union of Orthodox Jewish Congregations of Am., Rabbinical Coun. Am. (mem. exec. bd.), Rabbinical Alliance of Am. (chmn. law com. 1971-75, v.p. 1973-75). Home: 400 E 77th St New York NY 10021-2303 Office: B N Cardozo Sch Law 55 5th Ave New York NY 10003-4301 Office Phone: 212-790-0294.

BLEICH, JEFFREY LAURENCE, lawyer, educator; b. Neubreuke, Germany, May 17, 1961; came to U.S., 1964; s. Charles Allen Bleich and Linda Sue Caplan; m. Rebecca Lee Pratt, Aug. 12, 1984; children: Jacob, Matthew, Abigail. BA in Polit. Sci., Amherst Coll., 1983; MA in Pub. Policy, Harvard U., 1986; JD, U. Calif., Berkeley, 1989. Bar: Calif. 1989, D.C. 1990, U.S. Ct. Appeals (D.C. cir.) 1990, U.S. Dist. Ct. (no. dist.) Calif. 1992, U.S. Ct. Appeals (4th cir.) 1993, U.S. Supreme Ct. 1993, U.S. Ct. Appeals (9th cir.) 1994. Law clk. U.S. Ct. Appeals, Washington, 1989-90, U.S. Supreme Ct., Washington, 1990-91; legal asst. Iran-U.S. Claims Tribunal, The Hague, 1991-92; ptnr. Munger, Tolles & Olson LLP, San Francisco, 1992—. Adj. prof. U. Calif., Berkeley, 1993—. Editor-in-chief Calif. Law Rev., Nat. Debt; columnist San Francisco Atty. Dir. White Ho. Youth Violence Initiative, 1999-2000, trustee, Calif. State U., gov., State Bar. Calif. Recipient James Madison award Soc. Profl. Journalists, 1998. Mem. ABA (amicus curiae com., top 100 lawyers in Calif., 2004, Pro Bono Publico award 1996), Bar Assn. San Francisco (pres.), Lawyers' Com. Civil Rights of San Francisco Bay Area (co-chair), Lawyers Com. Human Rights (bd. dirs. 1998—), Legal Aid Soc. (bd. dirs. 1998—), Barristers Club San Francisco (pres.), Am. Law Inst. Democrat. Avocations: short story writer, tennis, kayaking, camping. Office: Munger Tolles & Olson 560 Mission St Fl 27 San Francisco CA 94105 Office Phone: 415-512-4000. Business E-Mail: jeff.bleich@mto.com.

BLEICHER, MICHAEL NATHANIEL, mathematics professor; b. Cleve., Oct. 2, 1935; s. David B. and Rachel (Faigin) B.; m. Betty Isack, June 4, 1957; children: Helene, Laurence, Benjamin; m. E. Jeanne Smith, Dec. 31, 1980; stepchildren: Kathryn, Robert, Zaka. BS, Calif. Inst. Tech., 1957; MS, Tulane U., 1959, PhD, 1961; doctorate degree, U. Warsaw, 1961. Teaching and research asst. Tulane U., 1957-60; fellow U. Warsaw, Poland, 1960-61; NSF fellow U. Calif., Berkeley, 1961-62; mem. faculty U. Wis., Madison, 1962—93, dept. chmn., 1972-74, prof. dept. math., 1968—93, prof. emeritus, 1993—; chief adv. and liaison U.S. Dept. Energy, 1979-81. Assigned to coll. preparatory studies Inst. of Tech. Mara, Shah Alam, Selangor, Malaysia, 1987-90; founder Wis. Emerging Scholars program; chair Dept. Math. Sci. Clark Atlanta U., 1998-05.; prof. Kennesaw State U., 2005—. Author: (with A. Beck, D. Crowe) Excursions into Mathematics, 1968; co-translator: A. Mathematical Guidebook for Technologists and Engineers, 1962. Mem. Dem. Nat. Com., 1972-79; chmn. Dem. Party Wis., 1977-79. Recipient Regents award of distinction, U. Wis., 1973. Mem. Am. Math. Soc., Math. Assn. Am., Polish Math. Soc. Democrat. Jewish. Achievements include research on length and size of denominators of Egyption fractions, least length subdivision of a region into cells of a given area. Office Phone: 770-423-6103. Business E-Mail: bleicher@math.wisc.edu.

BLEICHER, SAMUEL ABRAM, lawyer, retired government agency administrator; b. Omaha, June 21, 1942; s. David Bernard and Rachael (Faigin) Bleicher; m. Beatrice Koretsky, June 16, 1965 (dec. Nov. 12, 1995); children: Leo, Zena; m. Emily Blair Chewning, May 17, 1997 (div. 2002). BA, Northwestern U., 1963; JD, Harvard U., 1966. Bar: Mich. 1966, Ohio 1972, D.C. 1979, Va. 1989, Md. 1991. Prof. law U. Toledo Coll. Law, 1966-76; dep. dir. for regulation and enforcement Ohio EPA, 1972-75; issues generalist Carter-Mondale Presdl. Campaign, Atlanta, 1976; policy analyst Carter-Mondale Transition Planning Group, Washington, 1976-77; spl. asst. to adminstr. NOAA Dept. Commerce, Washington, 1977, dir. Office Ocean Mgmt., 1977-78, dep. asst. adminstr., 1978-80, dep. gen. counsel, 1980-81; of counsel Blank, Rome, Comisky & McCauley, Washington, 1981-85; ptnr. Frank, Bernstein, Conaway & Goldman, Tysons Corner, Va., 1985-90; prin. Miles & Stockbridge P.C., Washington, 1990—2001; legis. affairs asst. Overseas Bldg. Ops. Bur., U.S. Dept. State, 2001—03, New Initiatives Divsn. dir., 2003—. Democrat. Jewish. E-mail: sambleicher@comcast.net.

BLEICHER, SHELDON JOSEPH, endocrinologist, medical educator; b. N.Y.C., Apr. 9, 1931; s. Max and Fannie (Klieger) B.; m. Diane D. Cole, Aug., 1990; children from previous marriages: Erick Max, Phillip Thaddeus Samuel, Deborah Ann Cote, Sandra Lynn Gable, Jodie Lisa Cole. AB, NYU, 1951; MS, Western Ill. U., 1952; MD, SUNY Downstate Med. Center, Bklyn., 1956. Intern L.I. Jewish Hosp. Ctr., New Hyde Park, N.Y., 1956-57; resident Boston City Hosp., 1959-60; chief rsch. fellow in medicine Harvard-Thorndike Meml. Lab., Boston, 1962-63; chief metabolic research unit Jewish Hosp. Med. Center, Bklyn., 1963-67, chief div. endocrinology and metabolism, 1967-77; pvt. practice specializing in endocrinology and diabetes Woodbury, 1990—2004; prof. medicine SUNY Downstate Med. Center, 1975—2004; chmn. dept. internal medicine The Bklyn. Hosp. Ctr., 1978—90. Cons. IAEA, Vienna, 1966—90; mem. attending staff North Shore Univ. Hosp. at Syosset, North Shore Univ. Hosp. at Plainview, North Shore Univ. Hosp. at Manhasset. Mem. editl. bd. Diabetes in News, Practical Diabetes; contbr. articles to profl. jours. Vice pres. Locust Valley Central Sch. Bd., 1981-82, pres., 1982-85. Served to capt. M.C., USNR, 1957-92, ret. NIH fellow, 1960-63; NIH research career devel. award, 1970-75; recipient Torch of Liberty award Anti-Defamation League of B'nai Brith, 1982 . Fellow: ACP, Am. Coll. Endocrinology; mem.: AMA, Juvenile Diabetes Found. Internat., Internat. Diabetes Fedn., Am. Coll. Endocrinologists, Am. Assn. Clin. Endocrinologists, Endocrine Soc., Bklyn. Soc. Internal Medicine (treas. 1983—85, sec. 1985—87, pres. 1987—89), N.Y. State Soc. Internal Medicine (state bd. dirs., treas. Bklyn. chpt., chmn. continuing edn. com.), L.I. Diabetes Assn. (pres. 1978—81), N.Y. Diabetes Assn. (bd. dirs. 1965—93, pres. 1976—78), Am. Diabetes Assn. (bd. dirs. 1979—85, nat. com. quality care Achievement award 1986, 1990, Provider Recognition award), Am. Soc. Internal Medicine, Nassau County Med. Soc., N.Y. State Soc. Medicine, Sagamore Yacht Club (fleet surgeon 1983—86). Jewish. Office: 165 Froehlich Farm Blvd Woodbury NY 11797-2906 E-mail: SJBleich@comcast.net.

BLEIDT, BARRY ANTHONY, pharmacy educator; b. South Charleston, W.Va., Mar. 29, 1951; s. Robert Anthony and Mary Frances (Gash) B.; 1 child, Brittany Alice. B in Gen. Studies, BS in Pharmacy, U. Ky., 1974; PhD, U. Fla., 1982; PharmD, Xavier U., 1994. Registered pharmacist, Fla., Calif., Ga., W.Va., Tex. Pres. Health Resources Cons., 1979—; asst. prof. pharmacy Northeastern U., Boston, 1983—86, U. Houston, 1986—89; assoc. prof. pharmacy adminstrn. Xavier U., 1989—94; med. info. scientist Astra/Merck Group, 1994—95; clin. coord., dir. postgrad. profl. edn. sch. pharmacy Hampton U., 1995—2002; prof., chair social and adminstrv. scis. dept. Loma Linda U. Sch. Pharmacy, 2002—05, assoc. dean acad. affairs, 2002—05; assoc. dean acad. affairs Coll. Pharmacy Tex. A&M U., Kingsville, 2005—. Faculty dir. Practicing Pharmacists Inst., Boston, 1983-86. Author, editor: Clinical Research in Pharmaceutical Development; contbr. articles to profl. jours.; guest editor Jour. Pharm. Mktg. and Mgmt., 1988; mem. editl. bd. Clin. Rsch. Reg. Affairs, 1983—, editor, 1999. Recipient Local Assn. Pres. of Yr., Va. Pharm. Assn., 2001. Mem.: APHA (leadership award 1999), Nat. Pharm. Assn. (James Tyson award 2001), Am. Soc. Health-Sys. Pharmacists, Am. Assn. Colls. Pharmacy (parliamentarian 1983—), Fla. Blue Key, Nat. Eagle Scout Assn., U. Fla. Hall of Fame, Phi Lambda Sigma, Omicron Delta Kappa, Rho Chi, Sigma Xi. Avocations: music, travel, ethnic restaurants, cinema. Home and Office: PO Box 3037 Kingsville TX 78363-8330 Office Phone: 757-593-7245, 361-593-4533. E-mail: bbleidt@aol.com, barry.bleidt@tamuki.edu.

BLEIER, MICHAEL E., lawyer; b. N.Y.C., Mar. 23, 1942; BA, U. Tulsa, 1962; JD, Georgetown U., 1965. Bar: Pa, D.C. Atty. Office of Gen. Counsel, Bd. Govs. Fed. Reserve System, 1971-78, sr. counsel, 1979-81, asst. gen. counsel, 1981-82; mng. counsel Mellon Bank Corp., Pitts., 1982-88; asst. gen. counsel Mellon Fin. Corp., Pitts., 1989-91, dep. gen. counsel, 1991-92, gen. counsel, exec. v.p., 1992—, sr. mgmt. com. Contbr. articles to profl. jours. Mem. Am. Bankers Assn. (vice chmn. bank counsel com. 1996-98), Lawyers Coun. Fin. Svcs. Roundtable (chmn. 1993-98). Office: Mellon Financial Corporation 1 Mellon Ctr Fl 19 Pittsburgh PA 15258-0001 Office Phone: 412-234-1537. Business E-Mail: bleier.me@mellon.com.

BLEIFELD, STANLEY, sculptor; b. Bklyn., Aug. 28, 1924; s. Benjamin and Rose (Molshatsky) B.; m. Naomi Kaplan Ruby, Sept. 5, 1949; children: Becky Paula, Emily Harriet. BFA, BSEd, Temple U., 1949, MFA, 1950; D of Fine Arts (hon.), Lyme Acad. Fine Arts, Conn., 1997. Fellow Tyler Sch. Fine Arts, Temple U., 1967—. One-person shows Peridot Gallery, N.Y.C., 1963, 65, 68, Fairfield (Conn.) U., 1967, FAR Gallery, N.Y.C., 1971, 73, 77, New Britain Mus. Art (Conn.), 1974, Kenmore Gallery, Phila., 1967, Franz Bader Gallery, Washington, 1987, 91; exhibited in group shows Internat. Art Festival, Newport, R.I., 1964, Am. Fedn. Arts, 1966, 67, Conn. Commn. on Arts, 1972, Parrish Art Mus., Southampton, N.Y., 1968, others; represented in permanent collections Mus. of City of N.Y., Fairfield (Conn.) U., New Britain Mus. Art, Tampa Bay Art Ctr., Fla., Temple U., Phila., Westmoreland Mus., Pa., Pa. State Mus., U. Edinburg (Scotland), L.B. Johnson Libr., Tex.; executed relief sculptures The Prophets, Vatican Pavilion, N.Y. Worlds Fair, 1964-65, Magic Carpet, Kokomo Pub. Libr., 1970, Family of Acrobats, Civic Ctr., Orlando, Fla., 1973, Alberta Family, Century Gardens, Calgary, Can., 1981, Father McGivney Meml. KC Internat. Hdqrs., New Haven, 1982, Christopher Columbus, 8'n KC Mus. of States, New Haven, 2000; sculptor U.S. Navy Meml., Washington, 1982—, Jacksonville, Fla., 1988, Great Lakes, Ill., 1997, San Diego, Calif., 1998, Henry C. Singleton, Sr. Monument, Key West, Fla., 1994, Marine Relief, Brookgreen Gardens, S.C., 1996, Life Size Pitcher and Catcher Baseball Hall of Fame, Cooperstown, N.Y., 2000, Lone Sailor, Vista Point Golden Gate Bridge, San Francisco, 2000, Homecoming, Norfolk, Va., 2000; designer Medal of Liberty ACLU, 1984; dir. Bleifeld Sculpture Group, New Canaan, Conn., 1966—; instr. Silvermine Guild Art, New Canaan, Conn., 1963-66, asst. prof. art Western Conn. State Coll., New Haven, 1953-55. Served with USNR, 1944-46. Recipient Shikler award, Nat. Acad. Design, 1977, Agopoff prize for Classical Sculpture, 2001, Meiselman prize, 1997, 1998, Internat prize for sculpture, Pietrasanta Versilia in the World, XI edit., 2001; fellow Tiffany, 1967. Fellow: Nat. Sculpture Soc. (pres. 1991—93, chmn. editl. bd. Sculpture Rev., treas. 1994, John Gregory award 1964, Bronze medal 1970, Proskauer award 1977, Hexter award 1990, Henry Hering award 1990, Silver medal 1991, Bronze medal 1994, Chilmark award 1994, Hexter award 1998, Henry Hering award 2000); mem.: NAD (accademician coun. 2001—, corr. sec. 2001—), N.Am. Sculpture Soc., Century Assn., Fedn. Internationale de la Medialle, Portrait Soc. Am. (adv. bd. 2000—, Agopoff prize 2001). Jewish. Avocation: tennis. Home: 27 Spring Valley Rd Weston CT 06883-1546*

BLEIFUSS, JOEL, journalist; Freelance journalist, Spain, 1986; features writer Fulton Sun, Mo.; dir., Peace Studies Program U. Mo., 1979—81; reporter, columnist & editor In These Times mag, 1986—. Office: In These Times 2040 Milwaukee Ave Chicago IL 60647 E-mail: jbleifuss@inthesetimes.com.*

BLEIFUSS, KAREN K, technologist, educator; d. John William and Betty Lorraine Dunski; m. Dennis C Bleifuss, Aug. 30, 1975. BS in med. tech., U. of Wis., 1977; MA in edn., Marian Coll., 1996. Med. technologist Cons. Physicians in Pathology, Beaver Dam, Wis., 1977—91; tchr. Moraine Pk. Tech. Coll., West Bend, 1983—91, Wayland Acad., Beaver Dam, 1991—. Mem. bd. trustees Wayland Acad., 2002—. Sec./treas. Horicon C. of C., Wis., 1983—87. Mem.: Rotary Club of Horicon. Home: W3887 Decora Rd Horicon WI 53032 Office: Wayland Acad 101 N University Ave Beaver Dam WI 53916 Office Phone: 920-885-3373 223.

BLEIL, LESLIE A., librarian; b. Lansing, Mich., Sept. 7, 1958; d. Robert E. and Barbara J. Sechler; m. Gordon R. Bleil; 1 child, Katherine A. BA, Mich. State U., 1980; MLS, Western Mich. U., Kalamazoo, 1982. Librarian Western Mich. U., Kalamazoo, 1985—92, Mich. Maritime Mus., South Haven, Mich., 1995—. Book reviewer Libr. Jour., N.Y.C., 1986-90; contbr. to books: Technical Services Today and Tomorrow, 1990, Read More About It, 1990. Mem. Kalamazoo Acad. Medicine Aux., 1990-95. Mem. Mich. Libr. Assn., Mich. Acad. Sci., Arts and Letters. Avocations: dressage, needlecrafts, gardening, reading. Home: 6472 107th Ave South Haven MI 49090-9369 Office: 91 Michigan Ave South Haven MI 49090 Office Phone: 269-637-9156. E-mail: library@michiganmaritimemuseum.org.

BLEILER, CHARLES ARTHUR, lawyer; b. Boston, Mar. 16, 1945; s. Charles Edward and Grace Rita Bleiler; m. Joyce Ann Kohlmyer, Oct. 6, 1972; children: Charles Edward. BS, Tufts U., 1967; JD, U. San Diego, 1973. BAr: Calif. 1973, U.S. Dist. Ct. (so. dist.) Calif. 1973. Commd. ensign U.S. Navy, 1967, advanced through grades to lt. comdr., resigned, 1978; ptnr. Williams, Clodig & Bleiler, San Diego, 1974-85, Bleiler & Reiter, San Diego, 1985-91, Malowney, Chialtas & Bleiler, San Diego, 1991-93; pres. Charles A. Bleiler A.P.C., San Diego, 1987—. Lectr. San Diego Trial Lawyers Assn., 1982. Bd. dirs. Rancho Santa Fe (Calif.) Cmty. Ctr., 1990-94, pres., 1993-94, bd. dirs. 2001-; mem. San Dieguito Soccer Bd., Encinitas, Calif., 1991-92; bd. dirs. Torrey Pines H.S. Found., Del Mar, Calif., 1996-98, pres., 1997-98; founding mem., lector Nativity Ch., Rancho Santa Fe; fundraiser for charitable orgns.; bd. dirs. Rancho Santa Fe Little League, 1989-92. Mem. ATLA, Calif. State Bar, San Diego County Bar Assn., Optimist Club (charter pres. Kearny Mesa club 1987-89). Republican. Roman Catholic. Avocations: sailing, horseback riding, skiing, coaching youth baseball and soccer. Home: PO Box 1653 Rancho Santa Fe CA 92067-1653 Office: 12770 High Bluff Dr Ste 380 San Diego CA 92130-2060 E-mail: bleiler@worldnet.att.net.

BLEILER, EVERETT FRANKLIN, writer, publishing company executive; b. Boston, Apr. 30, 1920; s. Joseph Eugene and Rose Caroline (Mayor) B.; m. Ellen Haas, May 12, 1956; children: Richard, John, Constance, Dorothy. AB cum laude, Harvard U., 1942; MA, U. Chgo., 1951; Diploma, U. Leiden, The Netherlands, 1952. Freelance writer, 1952-55; advt. mgr. Dover Publs., N.Y.C., 1955-60, mng. dir., 1960-65, exec. v.p., 1965-78; editorial cons. Charles Scribners Sons, N.Y.C., 1978-83. Author more than 60 books including The Checklist of Fantastic Literature, 1948, Essential Japanese Grammar, 1963, Best Tales of Hoffmann, 1967, Mother Goose's Melodies, 1970, Eight Dime Novels of the Victorian Period, 1974, Wagner, The Wehrwolf by G. W. M. Reynolds, 1975, Seventeenth Century Floral Engravings of Emanuel Sweerts, 1976, Richmond, Exploits of a Bow Street Runner, 1976, (under name Liberte E. LeVert) Prophecies and Enigmas of Nostradamus, 1979; A Treasury of Victorian Detective Stories, 1979, A Treasury of Victorian Ghost Stories, 1981, Science Fiction Writers, 1982, The Guide to Supernatural Fiction, 1983, Supernatural Fiction Writers, 1985, Science-Fiction: The Early Years, 1991, Science-Fiction: The Gernsback Years, 1998, Alice and the Snark, 2002, others; co-author: (with Wendell C. Bennett) Northwest Argentine Archeology, 1948, (with Guy Stern) Essential German Grammar, 1961. Sgt. U.S. Army, 1942-46. Recipient World Fantasy award World Fantasy Com., Providence, 1978, World Fantasy award (lifetime), London, 1988, Pilgrim award Sci. Fiction Rsch. Assn., 1984, Pres.'s award World Sci. Fiction Assn., 1986, Locus award for best non-fiction book, 1992, Living Legend award Internat. Horror Guild, 2004; named to N.J. Literary Hall of Fame, 1979; knight comdr. Order of Star, Realm of Redonda; Fulbright fellow, 1952. Democrat. Home: 4076 Interlaken Beach Rd Interlaken NY 14847-9632

BLEIWEISS, SHELL J., lawyer; b. Chgo., Mar. 7, 1950; s. Ben and Berte (Melin) B.; m. Patricia Lynn Heck, Dec. 19, 1970 (div. 1976); m. Jo Ellen Rosencrans, May 21, 1985; children: Michael Lawrence, Lowell Rosencrans. BA, So. Ill. U., 1971, MS, 1974; JD, Northwestern U., 1982. Bar: Ill. 1982, U.S. Dist. Ct. (no. dist.) Ill. 1982. Wildlife ecologist Jack McCormick & Assoc., Devon, Pa., 1973-76; project mgr. Betz Converse Murdoch, Plymouth Meeting, Pa., 1976-78; cons. McGraw Hill Publ., N.Y.C., 1978-79; assoc. Sidley & Austin, Chgo., 1981-85, Coffield, Ungaretti, Harris & Slavin, Chgo., 1985-88; ptnr. McDermott, Will & Emery, Chgo., 1988-97; atty. pvt. practice, 1998—. Environ. advisor Roland Burris for Atty. Gen. Campaign, Ill., 1986. NSF fellow, 1970. Mem. ABA (former chair environ. ADR com.), Chgo. Bar Assn. Office: 321 S Plymouth Ct Ste 1200 Chicago IL 60604-3996 E-mail: sbleiweiss@shell-bleiweiss.com.

BLENCOWE, PAUL SHERWOOD, lawyer, private investor; b. Amityville, N.Y., Feb. 10, 1953; s. Frederick Arthur and Dorothy Jeanne (Ballenger) Blencowe; m. Mary Frances Faulk, Apr. 11, 1992; children: Kristin Amanda, Alison Michelle, Caitlin Emily. BA with honors, U. Wis., 1975; MBA, U. Pa., 1976; JD, Stanford U., 1979. Bar: Tex. 1979, Calif. 1989. Assoc. Fulbright & Jaworski, Houston, 1979-86, London, 1986-87, ptnr., 1988-89, Fulbright & Jaworski L.L.P., L.A., 1989-2000, of counsel, 2000—. Editor: China's Quest for Independence: Policy Evolution in the 1970s, 1980; editor-in-chief Stanford Jour. of Internat. Law, 1978-79; contbr. articles on U.S. securities and corp. law to profl. jours. Mem. The Calif. Club, Phi Beta Kappa, Phi Kappa Phi, Beta Theta Pi. Office: Fulbright & Jaworski LLP 555 S Flower St Fl41 Los Angeles CA 90071 Office Phone: 213-892-9332. Business E-Mail: pblencowe@fulbright.com.

BLENDELL, ELIZABETH A., lawyer; BA, Mt. Holyoke Coll., 1972; JD, Boston Coll., 1980. Bar: Calif. 1980. With Latham & Watkins, L.A., 1980—, ptnr., 1988—. Mem. faculty Practising Law Inst., 1990—. Mem.: ABA, Calif. Bar Assn. Office: Latham and Watkins LLC 633 W Fifth St Ste 4000 Los Angeles CA 90071

BLENDON, ROBERT JAY, health policy educator; b. Dec. 19, 1942; s. Edward and Theresa Blendon; m. Marie C. McCormick, Dec. 31, 1977. BA, Marietta (Ohio) Coll., 1964; MBA, U. Chgo., 1966; MPH, Johns Hopkins U., 1967, DSc, 1969. Fellow Ind. U. Med. Ctr., Indpls., 1965—66; instr. dept. med. care and hosps. Johns Hopkins U. Sch. Hygiene and Pub. Health, Balt., 1969—70, asst. to assoc. dean for health care programs Sch. Medicine, 1969—70, asst. prof. dept. med. care and hosps., 1970—71; asst. dir. planning and devel. Office of Health Care Programs, Johns Hopkins Med. Instns., Balt., 1970—71; spl. asst. for health affairs to dep. undersec. for policy coordination HEW, Washington, 1971—72, spl. asst. for policy devel. to asst. sec. to health and sci. affairs, 1971—72; sr. v.p. Robert Wood Johnson Found., Princeton, NJ, 1987; prof. health policy and polit. analysis Harvard U. Sch. Pub. Health and Kennedy Sch. of Govt., Boston, 1987—; dep. dir. health policy Harvard U. Vis. lectr. Princeton U., 1972—87; sr. policy analyst com. on health svcs. industry Cost of Living Coun., Washington, 1971. Mem. editl. bd.: Jour. of Am. Med. Assn., 1992—. Mem.: Inst. Medicine NAS, Council Fgn. Rels. Home: 478 Quinobequin Rd Newton MA 02468-2127 Office: Harvard U Sch Pub Health 677 Huntington Ave Boston MA 02115-6028 Office Phone: 617-432-4502. Business E-Mail: rblendon@hdph.harvard.edu.

BLENKO, WALTER JOHN, JR., lawyer; b. Pitts., June 15, 1926; s. Walter J. and Ardis Leah (Jones) B.; m. Joy Kinneman, Apr. 9, 1949; children: John W., Andrew W. BS, Carnegie-Mellon U., 1950; JD, U. Pitts., 1953. Bar: Pa. 1954. Pvt. practice law, Pitts., 1954—; ptnr. Eckert, Seamans, Cherin & Mellott, Pitts., 1984-93, of counsel, 1993—. Mem. adv. bd. dept. mech. engring. Carnegie-Mellon U., 1992—2000. Active Churchill Vol. Fire Co.,

1970-82; charter and hon. mem. Wilkinsburg Emergency Med. Svc.; sec. Hampton Twp. Zoning Hearing Bd., 1991-92, vice-chmn., 1993; mem. Hampton Twp. Sch. Bd., 1993-97, pres. 1996; mem. Allegheny County Parks adv. bd., 2000-02; trustee, v.p. Classic Car Club Am. Mus., 2005-; bd. dirs. Gateway to the Arts. With U.S. Army, 1944-46, ETO. Decorated Bronze Star, Combat Inf. badge; recipient Disting. Svc. award Carnegie-Mellon U. Alumni Assn., 1993, Recognition award Carnegie Mellon U. Andrew Carnegie Soc., 2002. Fellow Am. Coll. Trial Lawyers, Allegheny County Bar Found.; mem. ASME, Pa. Bar Assn., Allegheny County Bar Assn., Assn. Bar of City of N.Y., Pitts. Intellectual Property Law Assn. (pres. 1977-78), Engrs. Soc. Western Pa., Carnegie-Mellon U. Alumni Assn. (exec. bd. 1996-2001, exec. com. 1997-2001), Duquesne Club, Princeton Club (N.Y.), Rolls-Royce Owners Club (bd. dirs. 1982-84, v.p. publs. 1984-87, treas. 1987-89). Avocation: old cars. Home: 4073 Middle Rd Allison Park PA 15101-1207 Office: Eckert Seamans Cherin & Mellott 600 Grant St Pittsburgh PA 15219-2702

BLÊSÊDELL, PATRICIA ROSS, elementary school educator; b. Wayne, W.Va., Feb. 22, 1946; d. Robert Charles Ross and Myrtella June Ramey; m. John Pershing Blêsêdell, Jr., Dec. 27, 1964; children: John III, Jason. EdB, Ohio U., Athens, 1981; EdM, Coll. Mt. St. Joseph, Cin., 1986. Repair switchboard tech. Chillicothe Tel. Co., Ohio, 1965—73; educator Huntington Local Schs., 1982—. Named Educator of Yr., Huntington Local Schs., 1991—92. Mem.: NEA, Ross County Edn. Assn., Ohio Edn. Assn., Delta Kappa Gamma. Avocation: travel. Office: Huntington Local Schs 188 Huntsman Rd Chillicothe OH 45601-9379

BLESSEN, KAREN ALYCE, freelance/self-employed journalist, artist; b. Columbus, Nebr. BFA, U. Nebr., 1973. Freelance illustrator, 1973-86; designer Dallas Morning News, 1986-89, freelance illustrator, designer, 1989—; owner, illustrator Karen Blessen Illustration, Dallas, 1989—; artist Times Square Bus. Improvement Dist., N.Y.C., 1994—. Illustrator Be An Angel, 1994, contbr. (art and articles) Dallas Morning News; commd. by Absolute to represent Tex. in Absolute Statehood series. Recipient Pulizer Prize for explanatory journalism, 1989, awards, N.Y. Art Dirs. Club, Soc. Newspaper Design, Dallas Press Club. Home and Office: Karen Blessen Illustration 6327 Vickery Blvd Dallas TX 75214-3348 E-mail: kblessen@aol.com.

BLESSINGER, KELLY DIANE, librarian; b. Lapeer, Mich., Nov. 8, 1976; d. Kenneth Walter and Beverly Ruth Blessinger. BA Earth Sci., Ea. Mich. U., Ypsilanti, Mich., 1998; MA Libr. and Info. Sci., U. S.C., Columbia, S.C., 1999. Reference libr. La. State U., Baton Rouge, La., 1999—. Faculty senate La. State U., Baton Rouge, 2001—02; chair, reference grants com. La. State U. Libraries, Baton Rouge, 2004—; chair, faculty senate standing com. La. State U., Baton Rouge, 2001—03. Presenter La. Libr. Asssn., SOLINET Ann. Conf.; contbr. articles pub. to profl. jour., chapters to books. Mem.: La. Libr. Assn., SLA (chair, gis awareness grant com. 2001—03, pres. So. Miss. chptr. 2004—, sec. Geography and Map Sect. 2004—, presenter, webpage adminstr., Co-Principal Investigator, SLA Endowment Funds Grant 2001—03). D-Liberal. Avocations: travel, music, cooking, art, exercise. Office: La State Univ 141 Middleton Libr Baton Rouge LA 70803 Office Phone: 225-578-8538.

BLESSING-MOORE, JOANN CATHERINE, allergist, pulmonologist; b. Tacoma, Wash., Sept. 21, 1946; d. Harold R. and Mildred (Benson) Blessing; m. Robert Chester Moore; 1 child, Ahna. BA in Chemistry, Syracuse U., 1968; MD, SUNY, Syracuse, 1972. Diplomate Am. Bd. Pediatrics, Am. Bd. Allergy Immunology, Am. Bd. Pediatric Pulmonology. Pediatric intern, then resident Stanford U. Sch. Medicine, Palo Alto, Calif., 1972-75, allergy pulmonology fellow, 1975-77; co-dir. pediatric allergy pulmonology dept. Stanford U. Children's Hosp., Palo Alto, Calif., 1977-84; clin. asst. prof. dept. OIC Stanford U. Sch. Medicine, Palo Alto, Calif., 1977-84, co-dir. pediatric pulmonology lab., 1977-84; clin. asst. prof. dept. immunology Stanford U. Hosp., 1984—; allergist Palo Alto Med. Clinic, 1984-90; pvt. practice allergy immunology-pediatric-pulmonary Palo Alto, San Mateo, Calif., 1990—. Dir. ednl. program for children with asthma Camp Wheeze, Palo Alto, 1975-90; cons. FDA, Allergy Pulmonary Adv. Bd., 1992-97; cons. in field. Author handbooks, camp program manuals; co-editor jour. supplements; mem. edit. bd. Allergy jours.; contbr. articles to sci. publs. Fellow Am. Acad. Allery, Asthma, Immunology (various offices 1980—, joint task force parameters of care asthma and allergy 1989—, Outstanding fellow 1998, Women in Allergy award 2000), Am. Coll. Chest Physicians (com. mem. 1980—), Am. Coll. of Asthma, Allergy and Immunology (mem. regent com. 1995-98); mem. Am. Thoracic Soc., Am. Lung Assn., No. Calif. Allergy Found. (bd. dirs., pres.), Peninsula Women's Assn., Santa Clara and San Mateo County Med. Soc. (bd. dirs. 1999-2004), Chi Omega. Republican. Presbyterian. Avocations: music, sailing, skiing, horseback riding, scuba diving. Office: 780 Welch Rd Ste 204 Palo Alto CA 94304-1518 also: Stanford Univ Hosp Dept Immunology Palo Alto CA 94304 Office Phone: 650-688-8480. E-mail: j_blessingmoore@hotmail.com.

BLETHEN, SANDRA LEE, pediatric endocrinologist; b. San Mateo, Calif., May 16, 1942; d. Howard Albion and Laura Katherine (Wolf) B.; m. Fred I. Chasalow, Nov. 26, 1966. BS in Biochemistry, U. Chgo., 1961; PhD in Biochemistry, U. Calif., Berkeley, 1965; MD, Yeshiva U., 1975. Diplomate Am. Bd. Pediat. Fellow biochemistry Brandeis U., Waltham, Mass., 1965-68; instr. biochemistry U. Calif., San Diego, 1968-69; asst. prof. San Francisco State U., 1969-71; resident in pediat. Columbia Presbyn. Med. Ctr., N.Y.C., 1975-77; fellow pediatric endocrinology U. N.C., Chapel Hill, 1977-79; asst. prof. pediatrics Washington U., St. Louis, 1979-84; assoc. prof. pediat. SUNY, Stony Brook, 1985-96; assoc. attending pediatrician L.I. Jewish Med. Ctr., New Hyde Park, NY, 1984-90; attending pediatrician Univ. Hosp., Stony Brook, 1991-96; cons. Genentech, Inc., South San Francisco, Calif., 1985-96, sr. endocrinologist, 1996—99, assoc. dir. product experience, 1997-2000, sr. clin. scientist, 1999—2002; v.p. med. affairs metabolic endocrinology Serono, Inc., Rockland, Md., 2002—. Cons. Diagnostic Systems Labs., Webster, Tex., 1989-96. Mem. editl. bd. Steroids, 1990—, Jour. of Endocrinology and Metabolism, 1995-98; contbr. more than 90 articles to profl. jours. Predoctoral fellow NSF, 1961-63, Postdoctoral fellow USPHS, 1965-67. Mem. Am. Pediatric Soc. (program com. 1994), Endocrine Soc., Lawson Wilkens Pediatric Endocrine Soc. (membership chair 1994-95), Soc. for Pediatric Rsch., Phi Beta Kappa, Alpha Omega Alpha. Avocation: sailing. Office: Serono Inc 1 Tech Pl Rockland MA 02370 Office Phone: 781-681-2433. Personal E-mail: sandra.blethen@serono.com.

BLETHYN, BRENDA ANNE, actress; b. Ramsgate, Kent, England, Feb. 20, 1946; m. Alan James Blethyn (div.). LittD (hon.), Kent U., 1999. Actress Royal Nat. Theater, U.K., 1975-89. Appeared in films, including The Witches, 1990, A River Runs Through It, 1992, Secrets & Lies (Best Actress award Cannes Film Festival, 1996, Golden Globe award, Acad. award nominee, Best Actress winner Brit. Acad. award), Music From Another Room, 1998, In the Winter Dark, 1998, Girls Night, 1998, Little Voice (Acad. award nominee), 1998, Saving Grace, 2000, Yellow Bird, 2001, Daddy and Them, 2001, Sonny, 2002, (voice) The Wild Thornberrys Movie, 2002, Plots with a View, 2002, The Sleeping Dictionary, 2003, Blizzard, 2003, Beyond the Sea, 2004, A Way of Life, 2004; television includes Outside Edge (Best Comedy Actress award British Comedy Awards, 1994), Grown-Ups, 1980, King Lear, 1982, Death of an Expert Witness, 1983, Chance in a Million, 1984, The Labours of Erica, 1989-90, The Buddha of Suburbia, 1993, Outside Edge, 1994-96, The Bullion Boys, 1993, RKO 281, 1999, Between the Sheets, 2003, Belonging, 2004; Broadway shows include Absent Friends (Outstanding New Talent award Theater World Awards, 1991). Office: ICM 8942 Wilshire Blvd Beverly Hills CA 90211-1934

BLEUSTEIN, JEFFREY L., motorcycle company executive; b. 1939; BS in Mech. Engring., Cornell U.; MS in Engring. Mechanics, PhD in Engring. Mechanics, Columbia U. Assoc. prof. engring. & applied sciences. Yale U., 1966—71; mem., ctrl tech. staff AMF, Inc., 1971; with Harley-Davidson Motor Inc., Milw., 1975—, pres., Trihawk, Inc., 1984—85, v.p. parts and accessories divsn., 1985—88, exec. v.p., 1990—93, pres., 1997—98, CEO, 1997—2005, chmn., 1998—; pres., COO Harley-Davidson Motor Co., 1993—97. Mem. bd. dirs. Harley Davidson Inc., 1996—, Brunswick Corp., 1997—, The Kohler Corp., 2003—; mem. Pres. Coun. on 21st Century Workplace US Dept. Labor, 2002—03. Mem. bd. dirs. Greater Milw. Com., Milw. Jewish Fedn., Milw. Florentine Opera, Med. Coll Wis.; regent emeritus Milw. Sch. Engring. Office: Harley Davidson Inc 3700 W Juneau Ave Milwaukee WI 53208

BLEVEANS, JOHN, lawyer; b. Danville, Ill., Mar. 29, 1938; s. Edward Harold and Angelita (Robinson) B.; m. Luanna Harrison Burdick, Aug. 17, 1962; children: Lincoln Edward, Melanie Catherine. BA, Trinity U., 1960; LLB, U. Tex., 1965. Bar: Tex. 1965, D.C. 1967, U.S. Supreme Ct. 1969, Ill. 1971. Mem. gen. counsel's office Acacia Mut. Life Ins. Co., Washington, 1967-68; trial and appellate atty., civil rights div. U.S. Dept. Justice, Washington, 1966-67, 69-70; exec. dir. Washington Lawyers' Com., Civil Rights Under Law, 1970-71; chief counsel Lawyers' Com., Civil Rights Under Law, Cairo, Ill., 1971-72; assoc. Mayer, Brown & Platt, Chgo., 1972-74, ptnr., 1974-83, 91-92; sr. v.p., assoc., gen. counsel Continental Ill. Nat. Bank and Trust Co. of Chgo., 1983-89; dep. gen. counsel Continental Bank N.A., Chgo., 1989-91; ptnr. Mayer, Brown & Platt, Chgo., 1991-92; of counsel Arthur Andersen & Co., Chgo., 1992-95, Hong Kong, 1996-97, Sydney, Australia, 1995-96. Tour guide Tri State Travel, Galena, Ill., 2002—; pres. Hanover Ambulance, Inc., 2000. Alderman City of Evanston, Ill., 1981-89; chmn. Evanston Zoning Bd. Appeals, 1991-92; vol. Hanover Ambulance, 1999—. Capt. USNR ret. Mem. Tex. Bar Assn., D.C. Bar Assn., Nat. Ski Patrol, Law Club Chgo. Home: 8634 Fisher Rd Hanover IL 61041-9561 E-mail: luannab@netexpress.net.

BLEVINS, CHARLES RUSSELL, publishing executive; b. Kittaning, Pa., Apr. 6, 1942; s. Clarence Ray and Elizabeth Sarah (Warren) B.; m. Gale Watkins Crittenden, Dec. 16, 1967; children: Charles Jr., Rush. BS, Ind. U., 1964. Asst. prodn. exec. Wall St. Jour., Cleve., D.C. and Princeton, 1964-71, Gannett Co. Inc., El Paso Agy., El Paso, Tex., 1971-76; prodn. exec. Rockford Newspapers, Rockland, Ill., 1976-77; corp. prodn. dir. Gannett Corp. Hdqrs., Rochester, N.Y., 1977-79, v.p., prodn. Arlington, Va., 1979-89; CEO Blevins Harding Group, Vienna, Va., 1989-98; pres., CEO Chuck Blevins & Assocs., Vienna, 1998—. Speaker European Printing Conf., Newspaper Quality Meeting Conf.; chmn. Conf. Quality-Newspaper Assn., Conf. Research & Engring. Council, Chgo., Rsch. and Engring. Coun. Com. Graphic Arts Techs. Standards Unit Loading. Creator quality standards, operating procedures USA Today, 1981-86. Judge RIT/USA Today Quality Cup for Individuals and Teams, 1992-2000; chmn. long range planning com. Vanderbilt Country Club. Mem. Am. Newspaper Pub. Assn. (tech. com. 1985-89, officer internat. newspaper group 1989—), Rsch. and Engring. Coun. of Graphic Arts (v.p. 1985-94), Rochester Inst. Tech. Coun., W.Va. Inst. Tech. Adv. Coun., Inca Fiej Rsch. Assn. (press com. 1984-89), Vanderbilt Country Club (chmn. long range planning com.). Office: Chuck Blevins & Assocs 8396 Northhampton Naples FL 34120 Office Phone: 239-348-9933. Business E-Mail: chuckblevins@chuckblevins.com.

BLEVINS, DALE GLENN, agronomy educator; b. Ozark, Mo., Aug. 29, 1943; s. Vernon Henry and Edna Gertrude Blevins; 1 child, Jeremy. BS in Chemistry, S.W. Mo. State U., 1965; MS in Soils, U. Mo., 1967; PhD in Plant Physiology, U. Ky., 1972. Postdoctoral fellow botany dept. Oreg. State U., Corvallis, Oreg., 1972-74; asst. prof. botany U. Md., College Park, 1974-78; assoc. prof. agronomy dept. U. Mo., Columbia, 1978-86, prof., 1986—. Mem. Am. Soc. Plant Physiology, Am. Soc. Agronomy, Crop Sci. Soc. Am. Office: Univ Mo Divsn Plant Scis 1-31 Agriculture Building Columbia MO 65211-7140

BLEVINS, DANNY KEITH, science educator, astronomer; s. Danny Eugene and Phyllis Jean (Wells) Blevins; m. Ida G. Trudy Butcher, Aug. 2, 1986; children: Tracy Danielle, Daniel Trevor, Danni Morgan. Tech. diploma in electronics, Mayo State Vocat. Tech. Sch., Paintsville, Ky., 1980—82; AA, Prestonsburg CC, Ky., 1983, AS, 1984; BA in Social Sci., Morehead State U., Ky., 1986, cert., 2001. Cert. lifetime radio telephone operator FCC. Tchr. Porter Elem. Sch., Hager Hill, Ky., 1986—92, Johnson County Mid. Sch., Paintsville, Ky., 1992—98, Highland Elem. Sch., Staffordsville, Ky., 1998—2001, Johnson County Alternative Sch., Hager Hill, 2001—05. Astronomer The Starguides, Staffordsville, Ky., 1998—, East Ky. Sci. Ctr., Prestonsburg, 2003—. Staff author: Soc. newsletter The Bankmule, 1984—. Mem.: Coal Miners Mus. (chmn. of bd.), Johnson Co. Edn. Assn., Van Lear Ky. Hist. Soc., Inc. (pres., chmn.). Independent. Avocations: reading, astronomy, local historical research. Office: Johnson County Alternative Sch Kentucky Rt 321 S Hagerhill KY 41222 Office Phone: 606-789-2077. Business E-Mail: dblevins@johnson.k12.ky.us.

BLEVINS, ERNEST EVERETT, genealogist, researcher, historian; b. Spartanburg, S.C., Nov. 16, 1968; s. Maurice Everett Blevins and Anne Soule Lapham; m. Lisa Ann Schlosser, Dec. 30, 1975; children: Savannah Gayle, Avery Everett(dec.), Ana Grace. *Known maternal ancestors include Mayflower pilgrims: John Alden, Isaac Allerton, William Bradford, William Brewster, Peter Browne, John Howland, William and Priscilla Mullins, Thomas Rogers, Henry Samson, George Soule, John Tilley, Richard Warren; 1732 Georgia Trustee: John LaRoche; Colonial Governors: Robert Gibes (SC); Revolutionary War ancestor: William Hasell Gibbes (SC); War Between the States: Col. John Peyre Thomas (CS-SC), Joseph Eddings LaRoche (CS-SC). Known paternal ancestors include Mayflower Pilgrim Richard Warren; colonial governor, Roger Williams (RI); Revolutionary War ancestors: Richard and John Sayles (RI); War Between the States: James Meek (CS-Missouri), Allen Blevins (US-Tenn.), Steven Harris Barnes (US-RI).* BA in Studio Art, BS in Anthropology, Coll. Charleston, S.C., 1987—92; MFA in Hist. Preservation, Savannah Coll. Art and Design, Ga., 2001. Asst. prodn. manger, stagehand Charleston Symphony Orch., SC, 1989—99, prodn. mgr., 1996; stagehand Savannah Symphony Orch., Ga., 1995—99; archtl. conservator Liollio Architecture, Charleston, SC, 1997—98; owner Blevins Hist. Rsch., Villa Rica, Ga., 1997—; guest lectr., hist. preservation Coll. Charleston, SC, 1998; hist. preservation planner, housing specialist, E. Tenn. Devel. Dist., Knoxville, 1999—2000; historian, assoc. transp. planner Ga. Dept. Transp., Atlanta, 2000—01. Bd. dirs. Warehouse Teen Ctr., Spartanburg, SC, 1986—87; chmn. Villa Rica Hist. Preservation Com., Ga., 2003. Actor: (films) Gods and Generals, The Hunley, An American Tempest, Close to Danger; contbr. articles to profl. jours. Vol. Bill Workman for Congress, Spartanburg, SC, 1986. 2nd lt. S.C. State Guard, 1998—99, Charleston. Recipient Ray A. Croc Citizenship Award, McDonald's Corp., Spartanburg H.S., 1987. Mem.: S.C. Hist. Soc., Am. Planning Assn., Am. Hist. Assn., New Eng. Hist. & Geneal. Soc., Nat. Coun. on Pub. History, Ga. Trust for Hist. Preservation, Assn. for State and Local History, Assn. Profl. Genealogists (scribe, Ga. chpt. 2004—05), Nat. Trust for Hist. Preservation, E. Tenn. Hist. Soc., Ga. Hist. Soc., Friends of the Hunley, Sons of Union Veterans of the Civil War, Alden Kindred Am. (assoc. Genealogist's Award for Complete Documentation 2004), SAR (assoc.; historian 2005), Sons of Confederate Vetrans (life), Soc. of Mayflower Descendants (life; asst. dep. gov., S.C. historian 1995—96), Alpha Phi Omega (life; v.p., adminstrn., alumni sec., historian 1988—98). Conservative. Avocations: genealogy, travel, writing, music, history. Home: 110 Evergreen Way Villa Rica GA 30180 Office: Blevins Hist Rsch 110 Evergreen Way Villa Rica GA 30180 Office Phone: 770-456-1876. Personal E-mail: blevins@alumni.cofc.edu. E-mail: blevins@cchat.com.

BLEVINS, JAMES RAY, lawyer, insurance company claims executive; b. Jefferson, N.C., Mar. 20, 1949; s. Oscar Ray and Helen Marie (Clark) B.; m. Patricia Fay Faltermann, Dec. 27, 1970; children: Jennifer Renee, James Ray Jr. BA, Wake Forest U., 1971, JD, 1978; MS in Edn., U. So. Calif., 1975. Bar: N.C. 1978, S.C. 1993; registered profl. adjuster. Claims atty. Integon Ins. Co., Winston-Salem, N.C., 1979-80, field claims mgr., asst. v.p., 1980-85; Mid-Atlantic regional claims mgr. Amerisure Ins. Co., Charlotte, 1985-90; v.p., claims mgr. Sedgwick James of the Carolinas, Columbia, S.C., 1990-92; pvt. practice claims cons. and lawyer Columbia, 1992-94; litigation mgr. Seibels Bruce Ins. Co., Columbia, S.C., 1994-98; dir. spl. claims Burlington (N.C.) Ins. Co., 1998—. Del. N.C. Dem. Conv., Raleigh, 1976, S.C. Dem. Conv., Columbia, 1996. 1st lt. U.S. Army, 1971-75, capt. N.C. Army Nat. Guard, 1975-87, lt. col. judge adv. USAR, 1987-97. Mem. ABA, N.C. Bar Assn., S.C. Bar Assn. Democrat. Presbyterian. Avocation: reading. Home: 9190 Hwy 194N Lansing NC 28643 Office: 238 International Rd Burlington NC 27215-5177

BLEVINS, KENT, religious studies educator; s. Frederick Zane and Eunice Blevins; m. Deborah Crone; children: Nicholas, Jessica, Timothy. BA, Wake Forest U., 1975; MDiv, So. Bapt. Theol. Sem., 1978, PhD, 1982. Lectr. Portuguese Bapt. Theol. Sem., Queluz, Portugal, 1984—91; asst. prof. Bapt. Theol. Sem., Rüschlikon, Switzerland, 1991—94, assoc. prof., 1994—95, Internat. Bapt. Theol. Sem., Prague, Czech Republic, 1995—98, Gardner-Webb U., Boiling Springs, NC, 1998—2004, prof., 2004—.

BLEVINS, SANDRA LEE COWAN, mathematics educator; b. Morristown, Tenn., Apr. 15, 1941; d. Thomas Ewing and Anna Marie (Russ) Cowan; m. Raymond Dean Blevins, Aug. 11, 1962; children— Raymond Dean, Robert Lee, Lisa Dawn, Mary Vee. B.S., East Tenn. State U., 1962, Ed.D., 1979; M.Math., U. Tenn., 1970. Cert. tchr., supr., prin., Tenn. Tchr., Va. High Sch., Bristol, 1962-64, Overton High Sch., Memphis, 1965-66, East Tenn. State U. High Sch., Johnson City, 1974-75, Happy Valley High Sch., Elizabethton, Tenn., 1978-79; adminstrv. asst. dept. ob-gyn East Tenn. State U. Coll. Medicine, Johnson City, 1980-82; tchr. math. Daniel Boone High Sch., Gray, Tenn., 1982— . East Tenn. State U. scholar, 1959-62; NSF fellow, 1969-70, doctoral fellow, 1976-79. Mem. Nat. Council Tchrs. of Math., Athean Lit. Soc. (life), Women of Coll. Medicine, Johnson City Christian Women's Club, Nat. Assn. Female Execs., NEA, Tenn. Edn. Assn. Sunday Sch. tchr. Central Bapt. Ch., Johnson City, also vacation Bible sch. prin., circle pres.; pres. Univ. Sch. PTA, 1974-75. Club: Altrusa (v.p. 1985-86). Avocations: reading; sewing; singing; piano; travel. Home: 1401 Buffalo St Johnson City TN 37604-7301

BLEVINS, STANLEY NANCE, minister, educator; b. Comanche, Tex., Oct. 2, 1938; s. A.J. and Ruby Blevins; m. Betty Jo Westfall, Apr. 17, 1960; children: Ronald, Kristi Dean. BA, Hardin-Simmons U., 1961; MDiv, Southwestern Bapt. Theol. Sem., 1964, D of Ministry, 1982. Sr. pastor First Bapt. Ch., Lueders, Tex., 1964—66, Jackson Ave. Bapt. Ch., Lovington, N.Mex., 1966—69, Oakwood Bapt. Ch., Lubbock, Tex., 1969—79, Ctrl. Bapt. Ch., Bryan, Tex., 1979—86, Highland Bapt. Ch., Lubbock, 1986—. Adj. prof. Wayland Bapt. U., Lubbock, 2000—; trustee Hardin-Simmons U., Abilene, Tex., 1988—97, bd. of devel., 1998—; exec. bd. Bapt. Gen. Conv. of Tex., Dallas, 1972—79, 1981—86. Contbr. articles to profl. jours. Recipient Disting. Alumnus award, Logsdon Sch. of Theology Hardin-Simmons U., 1999. Mem.: Aircraft Owners & Pilots Assn., Colo. R.R. Hist. Found., Rocky Mountain R.R. Club. Avocations: narrow gauge railroad history, photography, writing. Home: PO Box 93777 Lubbock TX 79493-3777 Office: Highland Baptist Ch 4316 34th St Lubbock TX 79410 Office Phone: 806-795-6453.

BLEVINS, STEVEN W., chiropractor; b. Davenport, Iowa, Mar. 24, 1963; s. Dwayne Blevins and Nance D. Jakubowski; m. Amy L. Lorenzen, Oct. 5, 1985 (div. June 1994); children: Cara, Kurt; m. Meg Dolan, Sept. 27, 1997. BS, Regent's Coll., 1997; D of Chiropractic, Palmer Coll. Chiropractic, Davenport, 1988. Diplomate Am. Acad. Pain Mgmt. Clinic assoc. Westside Family Healthcare, Indpls., 1988-90; owner Lebanon (Ind.) Chiropractic Clinic, 1990-95; clinic assoc. Georgetown Family Chiropractic, Indpls., 1995-96; night shift ops. non-commd. officer in charge 21 Theater Area Army Command, Kaiserslautern, Germany, 1996-97; chiropractic physician Spinal Rehab. of Am., Naperville, Ill., 1997-98; owner Blevins Chiropractic Clinic, Cary, Ill., 1998—. Mem. med. staff World Gymnastics Championships, Indpls., 1991. 1st sgt. U.S. Army, 1996-97. Recipient 3 commendation medals, 2 achievement medals U.S. Army, 1987-97, Silver Marksmanship medal, 1996. Master Masons (pres. Lodge # 221 1987-88, Kaaba Temple Shrine, Davenport York Rite Bodies, Scottish Rite Bodies); fellow Internat. Acad. Med. Acupuncture; mem. Jaycees (treas. Cary Grove chpt. 1999-2000, pres. 2000-01, region dir. 2002, one of 10 Outstanding Young Persons, Ill. chpt. 2000), Christian Chiropractic Assn., Ill. Chiropractic Assn., Palmer Internat. Alumni Assn. (life), Am. Legion, AmVets (life), Cary-Grove C. of C., Chi Rho Theta (life). Avocations: bowling, shooting sports. Office: Blevins Chiropractic 652 NW Hwy Cary IL 60013 Fax: (847) 639-4473.

BLEVINS, THOMAS E., college administrator, educator; b. Welch, W.Va., Mar. 8, 1949; s. Casper Claude and Bessie Oliv (Shumate) B.; m. Brenda Louise Mabry Lamastus, Mar. 27, 1971 (div. Oct. 1980); children: Tracy, James, Matthew; m. Betty Ruth Rader, May 23, 1992. BS, Bluefield (W.Va.) State Coll., 1971; MA, Marshall U., 1973; CAGS, Va. Tech. U., 1980, EdD, 1986. Cert. tchr., W.Va. Tchr., asst. prin. Elkhorn Jr. H.S., Powhatan, W.Va., 1971-74; tchr., media ctr. dir. Northfork (W.Va.) H.S., 1974-77; coord. audiovisual svcs. Bluefield State Coll., 1977-84, dir. instrnl. tech., 1984—, dir. tchr. edn., 1990-96, prof. edn. and English, 1988—, dir. ctr. for extended learning and acad. computing, 1996—, chief tech. officer, interim pres., 2002—, dean Virtual Coll. and Tech., 2003. Mem. adv. panel W.Va. Humanities Found., Charleston, 1978—81; mem. tech. implementation planning team State Coll. and Univ. Sys. W.Va., Charleston, 1995—96, spl. asst. to the chancellors for tech.; sr. tech. officer Gov.'s Office of Tech., State of W.Va., 1999—; dir. W.Va. Satellite Network, 2000—; dir. W.Va. Virtual Learning Network W.Va. Higher Edn. Policy Commn., 2003, dir. instrn. tech. planning and coord., 04; peer cons./reviewer Higher Learning Commn. of the North Ctrl. Assn. Recipient Edgar Dale award W.Va. Ednl. Media Assn./Assn. Ednl. Comms. and Tech., 1984. Mem. Assn. for Ednl. Comms. and Tech. (cert. com., accreditation com.), W.Va. Ednl. Media Assn. (pres. 1982-84), W.Va. C.C. Assn. (bd. dirs. 1995—), W.Va. Satellite Network, Higher Learning Commn. North Ctrl. Assn. (mem. peer reviewer corps), W.Va. Higher Edn. Instrnl. TV Consortium, Nat. Coun. for Accreditation of Tchr. Edn. (chmn. bd. examiners 1998—), Rotary of Bluefield (chair Rotoract and Rotary Info. 1995—), Elks. Democrat. Avocations: woodworking, reading, swimming. Home: 2339 Verdun Hts Bluefield WV 24701-4727 Office: Bluefield State Coll 219 Rock St Bluefield WV 24701-2100 E-mail: tblevins@bluefieldstate.edu.

BLEVINS, WILLIAM EDWARD, management consultant; b. Boissevan, Va., Oct. 18, 1927; s. Howard Muncey and Elsie Jane (Wire) B.; m. Mary Hester Jenkins, Aug. 25, 1951; children— Jeffrey Alexander, Jennifer Lynn, Bradley Edward. AB, Marshall Coll., 1951; MPA, CCNY, 1960. Personnel mgr. Equitable Life, N.Y.C., 1951-66; asst. v.p., dir. mgmt. devel. Nat. Bank Detroit, 1966-69, v.p., dir. personnel, 1969-74, sr. v.p., dir. personnel, 1974-91; exec. v.p., dir. human resources NBD Bancorp, Inc., Detroit, 1980-92; pres. WEB Communications Co., Detroit, 1993—2004. Bd. dirs. Lancaster Health Found. Trustee Bon Secour Hosp., Grosse Pointe, Mich., 1975-84; chmn. St. John Sr. Cmty., 1995-2004, St. John Health Sr. Svcs., 2000-04; bd. dirs. Oxford Inst., 1987-89, bd. dirs. Holy Cross Hosp., 1996-98; mem. corp. adv. bd. Am. Heart Assn., 1995-98; trustee Frances Rhodes, M.D. Meml. Found., 1999-2004; bd. dirs. Mich. Diabetes Assn., 1982-86, Mich. Soc. for Mental Health, 1984-87, Lancaster Heart Found., 2005—. Recipient Outstanding Alumnus award Marshall U., 1976, Hall of Fame award Lambda Chi Alpha, 1996. Mem. Am. Bankers Assn. (bd. dirs. 1974-75), Am. Inst. Banking (bd. dirs., bd. regents, chmn. 1983-90), Am. Soc. Employers (bd. dirs. 1970-94, treas. 1970-90, vice chmn. 1991-92, chmn. 1992-94), Alpha Bank Pers Group (founder, chmn. 1972-74, 86), Mich. Pers. Indsl. Rels. Group (chmn. 1980-92), Bank Adminstr. Inst. (human resources commn. 1983-88), Detroit Athletic Club, Country Club Detroit. Republican. Office: 611 Willow Valley Willow Street PA 17584-9647 Personal E-mail: webmjb@comcast.net. *How lucky I am to live in the USA. It offers a fine education to those who want it; meaningful jobs to those who prepare and strive, a wonderful place for romance, an ideal place to raise a family. I have been truly blessed with lots of help along the way.*

BLEWETT, DAVID LAMBERT, English literature educator; b. Calgary, Alta., Can., Dec. 18, 1940; s. John and Sydnay Catherine (Cole) B. BA with honors, U. Man., Winnipeg, 1962, MA, 1963; PhD, U. Toronto, Ont., Can., 1971. Lectr. McMaster U., Hamilton, Ont., Can., 1969-71, asst. prof., 1971-77, assoc. prof., 1977-84, prof., 1984—2003, prof. emeritus, 2003—. Author: DeFoe's Art of Fiction, 1979, The Illustration of Robinson Crusoe: 1719-1920, 1995, Japanese trans., 1998; editor: Roxana, 1982, Amelia, 1987, Moll Flanders, 1989, Roderick Random, 1995, Passion and Virtue; Essays on the Novels of Samuel Richardson, 2001; editor Eighteenth-Century Fiction, 1988—2003. Grantee Social Scis. and Humanities Rsch. Coun. Can., 1989-90, 96-99. Mem. Am. Soc. for Eighteenth-Century Studies, Can. Assn. for Eighteenth-Century Studies, Can. Assn. Univ. Tchrs., Internat. Assn. U. Profs. of English, Royal Soc. Lit., Reform Club, McMaster U. Faculty Assn. (pres. 1992-93). Avocations: travel, music. Home: 390 Wellesley St E # 16 Toronto ON Canada M4X 1H6 E-mail: blewett@mcmaster.ca.

BLEWETT, ROBERT NOALL, retired lawyer; b. Stockton, Calif., July 12, 1915; s. Stephen Noall and Bess Errol (Simard) B.; m. Virginia Weston, Mar. 30, 1940; children: Richard Weston Blewett (dec.), Carolyn Blewett Lawrence. LLB, Stanford U., 1936, JD, 1939. Bar: Calif. 1939. Dep. dist. atty. San Joaquin County, 1942-46; practice law Stockton, 1946-98; ptnr., pres. Blewett & Allen-Garibaldi, Inc., Stockton, 1971-98, ret., 1998. Chmn. San Joaquin County chpt. ARC, 1947-49; v.p. Goodwill Industries, 1967-68; vice chmn. Stockton Sister City Commn., 1969-70; adv. bd. bus. adminstrn. dept. U. Pacific; trustee San Joaquin Pioneer and Haggin Galleries. Fellow Am. Coll. Estate and Trust Counsel, Am. Bar Found.; mem. ABA, Am. Judicature Soc., Am. Law Inst., State Bar Calif. (mem. exec. com. on conf. of dels. 1969-72, vice chmn. 1971-72), Calif. Heritage Coun., Order of the Coif, Rotary (pres. 1987-88), Yosemite Club, San Francisco Banker's Club, Masons, Shriners, Delta Theta Phi, Theta Xi. Republican.

BLEWITT, THOMAS MICHAEL, chief federal magistrate judge; b. Pittston, Pa., Nov. 20, 1949; m. Evelyn Bubser; three children. BA, U. Scranton, 1972; MPA, Marywood Coll., 1979; JD, Temple U., 1983. Bar: Pa. 1983. Spl. investigator Pa. Bur. Consumer Protection, Harrisburg, 1972-80; assoc. Law Office Marshall E. Anders, Stroudsburg, Pa., 1983-84; asst. dist. atty. Lackawanna County, Scranton, Pa., 1984-86; asst. fed. pub. defender for mid. dist. Pa. Office Fed. Pub. Defender, Scranton, 1986-92; assoc. Lenahan & Dempsey, Scranton, 1988-89; magistrate judge for mid. dist. Pa., U.S. Magistrate Ct., Scranton, 1992—; chief magistrate judge Mid. Dist. Ct. Pa., 2002—. Office: US Magistrate Ct 217 Fed Bldg PO Box 443 235 N Washington Ave Scranton PA 18501-0443

BLEY, CARLA BORG, composer; b. Oakland, Calif., May 11, 1938; d. Emil Carl and Arlene (Anderson) Borg; m. Paul Bley, Jan. 27, 1959 (div. Sept. 1967); m. Michael Mantler, Sept. 29, 1967 (div. 1992); 1 dau., Karen. Student public schs., Oakland. Mem. adv. bd. Jazz Composers Orch. Assn. Freelance jazz composer, 1956—, pianist, Jazz Composers Orch., N.Y.C., 1964—, European concert tours, Jazz Realities, 1965-66; founder, WATT, 1973—, toured Europe with Jack Bruce Band, 1975; leader, Carla Bley Band, touring, U.S. and Europe, 1977—; composed, recorded: A Genuine Tong Funeral, 1967, (with Charlie Haden) Liberation Music Orch., 1969; opera Escalator Over the Hill, 1970-71 (Oscar du Disque de Jazz 1973), Tropic Appetites, 1973; composed: chamber orch. 3/4, 1974-75; film score Mortelle Randonnèe, 1983; recorded: Dinner Music, 1976, The Carla Bley Band: European Tour, 1977, Musique Macanique, 1979, (with Nick Mason) Fictitious Sports, 1980, Social Studies, 1980, Carla Bley Live!, 1981, Heavy Heart, 1984, I Hate to Sing, 1985, Night Glo, 1985, Sexted, 1987, Duets, 1988, Fleur Carnivor, 1989, The Very Big Carla Bley Band, 1991, Go Together, 1993, Big Band Theory, 1993, Songs with Legs, 1995, Goes to Church, 1996, Fancy Chamber Music, 1998, Are We There Yet?, 1999, 4x4, 2000, Looking for America, 2003, The Lost Chords, 2004. Named winner internat. jazz critics poll Down Beat mag., 1966, 71, 72, 78, 79, 80, 83, 84; Best Composer of Yr., Down Beat Readers' Poll, 1984, composer/arranger of yr., 1985-92; Guggenheim fellow, 1972; Cultural Coun. Found. grantee, 1971, 79; Nat. Endowment for the Arts grantee, 1973, Oscar du Disque de Jazz (for Escalator Over the Hill) 1973; named Best in Field Jazz Times critics poll, 1990, Best Arranger, Downbeat Critics Poll, 1993, 94, Best Arranger, Downbeat Readers' Poll, 1994; recipient Prix Jazz Moderne from Academie du Jazz for The very Big Carla Bley Band album, 1992. Office: Watt Works PO Box 67 Willow NY 12495-0067 E-mail: watt@ulster.net.

BLEY, JOHN L., financial executive; BA in Econs. and Polit. Sci., Pacific Lutheran U., 1980; JD, MBA Willamette U., 1985. Atty. Graham & Dunn, 1985—88; dep. supr. banking Wash. State Div. Banking, 1988—91, supr. banking, 1991—93; dir. Wash. State Dept. Fin. Instns., Olympia, 1993—2002; CEO Integra Advisors, Seattle, 2002—. Office: Integra Advisors LLC 2801 Alaskan Way Ste 300 Seattle WA 98121-1128

BLEZNICK, DONALD WILLIAM, Romance languages educator; b. N.Y.C., Dec. 24, 1924; s. Louis and Gertrude (Kleinman) B.; m. Rozlyn Burakoff, June 15, 1952; children— Jordan, Susan. BA, CCNY, 1946; MA, U. Nacional de Mex., 1948; PhD, Columbia U., 1954. Instr. romance langs. Ohio State U., 1949-55; prof. Pa. State U., 1955-67, U. Cin., 1967—, head dept., 1967-72. Vis. prof. Hebrew U., Jerusalem, 1974. Bibliographer, MLA Internat. Bibliography, 1966-81; rev. editor Hispania, 1965-73, editor-in-chief, 1974-83, editor's adv. coun., 1984—, El Ensayo Espanol del Siglo Veinte, 1964, Historia del Ensayo Espanol, 1964, Duelo en el Paraiso (Goytisolo), 1967, Madrugada (Buero Vallejo), 1969, (with W.T. Pattison) Representative Spanish Authors, 1971, Quevedo, 1972, Variaciones interpretativas en torno a la nueva narrativa hispanoamericana, 1972, Directions of Literary Criticism in the Seventies, 1972, Sourcebook for Hispanic Literature and Language, 1974, 3d expanded edit., 1995, Homenaje a Luis Leal, 1978, Studies on Don Quixote and other Cervantine Works, 1984, Critical Edition of La Diana (Jorge Montemayor), 1990, The Thought of Contemporary Spanish Essayists, 1993, Studies in Honor of Donald W. Bleznick, 1995; translator (from Spanish and Portuguese) Identity in Dispersion: Selected Memoirs from Latin American Jews, 2000, History of the University of Cincinnati Faculty Council on Jewish Affairs, 2004; founder, exec. editor Cin. Romance Rev., 1982-88; field editor: Twayne Spanish Literature Series, 1981—; contbr. articles to profl. jours., Ency. Americana. With US Army CIC, 1946-47. Decorated Knight's Cross Order Civil Merit (Spain); Am. Philos. Soc. rsch. grantee, 1964; Downer fellow CCNY, 1947-48; U. Cin. Taft rsch. and publ. grantee, 1972, 75, 78, 83, 88, 89, 92; named 1 of 15 outstanding scholars in Spanish lit. in Cuadernos Salmantinos de Filosofia, Salamanca, Spain, 1977; recipient Rieveschl award for excellence in rsch. U. Cin., 1980, award Hispania, U. So. Calif., 1983; fellow U. Cin. Grad. Sch., 1984. Mem. AAUP, Am. Assn. Tchrs. Spanish and Portuguese (exec. com. 1975—, award 1984, v.p. 1992, pres. 1993, Honored for Outstanding Career 1995, disting. svc. award 1997), MLA, Los Ensayistas (adv. bd. 1976—), Comediantes, Midwest Modern Lang. Assn., Conf. Editors of Learned Jours. (exec. com. 1978-79), Celestinesca, Cervantes Soc. Am., Phi Beta Kappa (pres. Delta chpt. of Ohio 1971-72, 86-87), Sigma Delta Pi (state dir. Ohio 1968-74, Order of Don Quijote 1970, v.p. Midwest 1975-83, Jose Martel award 1980, hon. pres. 1998), Phi Sigma Iota, Kappa Delta Pi. Home: 2444 Madison Rd Apt 1806 Cincinnati OH 45208-1255 Office: U Cin Dept Romance Langs Cincinnati OH 45221-0001 E-mail: donald.bleznick@uc.edu.

BLICKENSTAFF, CHANNING BLOUNT, retired language educator; b. Lafayette, Ind., Oct. 8, 1934; s. Earl Metzger and Barbara Mary Blickenstaff; m. Janet Frazier, Dec. 23, 1956; children: Marianne, Barbara Irene Doppelfeld. BS, Purdue U., 1956, MSEd, 1961, PhD, 1965. Asst. dept. head Purdue U., West Lafayette, Ind., 1964—71, asst. dean, 1971—79, exec. asst. dean, 1979—84; ret., 1984. Cons. West Lafayette Pub. Schools, 1969. Composer: numerous choral anthems; contbr. articles to profl. jours. Vol. Lafayette Vol. Bur., Lafayette, Ind., 1973—2005. Specialist 4th class U.S. Army, 1956—58, Korea. Recipient Excellence in Cmty. Svc. Award, Lafayette Vol. Bur., 2004. Mem.: ASCAP, Am. Choral Directors Assn. Christian (Disciples Of Christ). Avocations: reading, music performance. Home: 1700 Lindberg Road Apt 313 West Lafayette IN 47906

BLICKWEDE, DONALD JOHNSON, retired metal products executive; b. Detroit, July 20, 1920; s. Frederic H. and Laura L. (Johnson) B.; m. Meredith Lloyd, Aug. 23, 1943; children: Karen (Mrs. Kimball J. Knowlton), Jon Frederic. BS, Wayne U., 1943; postgrad., Stevens Inst. Tech., 1943-45; ScD, Mass. Inst. Tech., 1948; postgrad., Harvard, 1969. Metallurgist Curtiss Wright Corp., 1943-45; head high temperature alloys br. Naval Research Lab., 1948-50; rsch. engr. Bethlehem Steel Corp., Pa., 1950-52, div. head, 1952-63, v.p., 1964-82. Campbell Meml. lectr. Am. Metal Congress, 1968, William Park Woodside Meml. lectr., 1969, Zay Zeffries Meml. lectr., 1970; Andrews Meml. lectr. Porcelain Enamel Inst., 1972. Pres. Ea. Shore Art Ctr., Ala., 1990; leader Hazardous Abandoned Mine Finders, Green Valley, Ariz. Fellow Am. Soc. Metals (hon., pres. 1983); mem. AIME, Am. Acad. Engring., Am. Iron and Steel Inst. (chmn. gen. rsch. com. 1971-73), Indsl. Rsch. Inst. (pres. 1975), Iron and Steel Inst. Japan (hon., Yukawa Meml. lectr. 1984). Home: 3 Surrey Run Pl The Woodlands TX 77384 Office Phone: 936-321-8692.

BLICKWEDEHL, JOHN ROBERT, music educator; b. Syracuse, NY, Oct. 10, 1979; s. Robert and Patricia Blickwedehl; m. Jennifer Boschetti, June 23, 2001. B in Music Edn., Oberlin (Ohio) Conservatory, 2001; M in Music Edn., SUNY, Fredonia, 2005. Teaching Certification NY State Edn. Dept., 2001. Asst. condr. No. Ohio Youth Orch., Oberlin, 1999—2001; visual caption head Spirit of Am. Field Band, Orleans, Mass., 1999—2001; band dir. West Seneca (NY) West Sr. H.S., 2001—; brass caption head Empire Statesmen Drum and Bugle Corps, Rochester, NY, 2004—. Dir. West Seneca West Marching Band, 2001—. Musician: (principal trumpet) Future Teachers of America Honor Band. Theodore Presser scholar, Oberlin Conservatory, 2000. Mem.: NY State Band Dirs. Assn., Music Educators Nat. Conf., Phi Kappa Lambda (hon.; Oberlin Theta chpt.). Achievements include 2004 Drum Corps Associates World Champion - Empire Statesmen Drum and Bugle Corps; 1999 5th Place Drum Corps International - Glassmen Drum and Bugle Corps. Avocations: the west wing, playing with my golden retriever, playing trumpet, sketching and painting. Office: West Seneca W Sr HS 3330 Seneca St West Seneca NY 14224 Office Phone: 716-677-3350 4354. E-mail: blick@westseneca.wnyric.org.

BLIESNER, JAMES DOUGLAS, municipal/county official, consultant; b. Milw., Mar. 19, 1945; s. Milton Carl and Dorothy (St. George) B.; m. Phyllis Jean Byrd, June 15, 1966 (div. 1985); children: Tris, Cara. BA in Philosophy, Ea. Nazarene Coll., 1968; MA in Social Ethics, Andover, Newton Theol. Sch., 1973; postgrad., Boston U., 1969-70; student, N.Y. Studio Sch./Decordoua, Mus. Sch., Milw. Tech. Art Sch. Exec. dir. San Diego Youth and Community Svcs., 1974-78; cons., analyst San Diego Housing Commn., 1979-84; dir. San Diego City-County Reinvestment Task Force, 1984—. Bd. dirs. Calif. Cmty. Reinvestment Corp.; vice chmn. Calif. Reinvestment Com., 1989-91; founder, chmn. City Heights Cmty. Devel. Corp., San Diego, 1980-89; fin. com. chair Mid-City Revitalization Com., San Diego, 1988; founder San Diego Capital Collaborative; founding bd. dirs. Neighborhood Nat. Bank; instr. San Diego State U. Author monographs, 1979; visual arts exhbns. include San Diego Arts Inst., Soc. Western Artists, Santa Barbara Contemporary Arts Forum, Calif. Coun. for Humanities; films exhibited in Centro Cultural, Tijuana, Mex.; exhibited in group shows in Venice, Paris, Jerusalem, Mex., Eng., China; internat. invitee Habana Bienale. Coun. appointee City of San Diego Com. on Reapportionment, 1990, Com. on Growth and Devel., San Diego, 1989; gov. appointee Gov.'s Office of Neighborhoods, Calif., 1987; mem. City Heights Redevel. Project Com., San Diego, 1992; pres. San Diego Housing Consortium; bd. dirs. Advocates for Social Justice; com. appointee S.D. Cmty. Found.; internat. juror Shanghai Pub. Sculpture Competition. U.S.-Mex. Fund for Culture grantee, 2000, 02; recipient Award of Honor, Am. Planning Assn., 1987, Spl. Project award, 1987, Merit award, 1989, Lifetime Achievement award Non-Profit Fedn. San Diego, Outstanding Achievement award Calif. Reinvestment Commn., 1999; named Citizen of Yr. Mid-City C. of C., 1986, award Calif. Coun. Humanities, Nat. Leadership award Nat. Cmty. Reinvestment Com., 2000. Mem.: S.D. Artists Guild. Methodist. Avocation: visual arts. Home: 4106 Manzanita Dr San Diego CA 92105-4508 Office: City County Reinvestment Task Force 625 Broadway Ste 110 San Diego CA 92101 E-mail: jdbarte@sbcglobal.net.

BLIGE, MARY JANE, recording artist; b. Yonkers, N.Y., Jan. 11, 1971; d. Cora Blige. Albums include: What's the 411?, 1992, (double platinum award), My Life, 1994 (debuted at top of Billboard's R&B album chart), Mary Jane, 1995, Share My World, 1997, Mary, 1999, The Tour, 1999, No More Drama, 2001, Dance For Me, 2002, Love & Life, 2003; recordings include I'll Do For You, 1991, (duet) Changes, One Night Stand, Whenever I Say Your Name (with Sting), 2003 (Grammy award for Best Pop Collaboration With Vocals 2003). Recipient Soul Train Music award, 1993, N.Y. Music award, NAACP Image award. Office: MCA Records 1755 Broadway Fl 8 New York NY 10019-3743

BLILEY, THOMAS JEROME, JR., former congressman; b. Chesterfield County, Va., Jan. 28, 1932; s. Thomas J. and Carolyn F. Bliley; m. Mary Virginia Kelley, June 22, 1957; children: Mary Vaughan, Thomas Jerome III. BA, Georgetown U., 1952. Pres. Joseph W. Bliley Funeral Home, 1972-80; mem. U.S. Congress from 7th Va. dist., Washington, 1981-2001; former ranking minority mem. D.C. com.; former chmn. House Commerce Com.; sr. adv. govt. rels. and pub. policy Collier Shannon & Scott, Washington, 2001—. Vice-mayor Richmond City Council, 1968-70, mayor, 1970-77; past bd. dirs. Nat. League Cities; past pres. Va. Mcpl. League Past bd. dirs. Crippled Children's Hosp.; past bd. dirs. St. Mary's Hosp.; bd. visitors Va. Commonwealth U.; bd. govs. Va. Home for Boys. Served with USN. Republican. Roman Catholic. Office: Collier Shannon & Scott Washington harbour, Ste 400 3050 K St NW Ste 400 Washington DC 20007-5108*

BLIM, RICHARD DON, retired pediatrician, health facility administrator; b. Kansas City, Mo., Nov. 8, 1927; s. Miles G. and Latha Mae (Daniels) Blim; m. Myrle Rae Blim, Apr. 12, 1952; children: Richard David, Carol Rae, John Miles. BA, U. Kans., 1949, MD, 1953. Diplomate Am. Bd. Pediat. Intern U. Kans., 1953—54, resident in pediat., 1954—56; practice medicine specializing in pediat.; pres. Pediatric Assocs., Kansas City, Mo., 1956—89; dir. med. affairs St. Lukes Hosp., Kansas City, 1989—99. Peter T. Bohan lectr. U. Kans., Kansas City, 1978; Max Seham lectr. U. Minn., Mpls., 1982; mem. editl. bd. Mo. Medicine, 1978—92, Pediatric Annals, 1982—92, Pediatric News, 1983—92, Health Care Mgmt. Rev.; mem. VHA Phys. Leadership Coun. Bd. dirs. Marillac Spl. Sch. for Children, 1976—79. Served to sgt. U.S. Army, 1946—48, PTO. Named Outstanding Med. Alumnus, U. Kans. Sch. Medicine, 1978; recipient Clifford G. Grulee award, 1984, Katherine Berry Richard MD award, Children Mercy Hosp., 1997. Fellow: Am. Acad. Pediat. (chmn. Mo. chpt. 1964—67, exec. bd. 1973—80, pres. 1980—81); mem.: AMA, Coun. Med. Spltys. Soc. (rep., exec. bd. 1974—80), Met. Med. Soc. (merit award 1996), Mo. Med. Assn., S.W. Pediatric Assn. (pres. Kansas City 1963), Jackson County Med. Soc. (pres. 1973), Inst. Medicine NAS, Kans. U. Med. Alumni (pres. 1973), Loch Lloyd Club, Alpha Omega Alpha. Republican. Presbyterian. Home: 100 W 172d St Belton MO 64012 Personal E-mail: rdonblimmd@earthlink.net.

BLINDER, ALAN STUART, economist, educator; b. Bklyn., Oct. 14, 1945; s. Morris and Shirley (Rothberg) Blinder; m. Madeline D. Schwartz, July 9, 1967; children: Scott, William. AB, Princeton U., 1967; MSc, London Sch. Econs., 1968; PhD, MIT, 1971. Instr. fin. Rider Coll., Trenton, NJ, 1968—69; instr. econs. Boston State Coll., 1969; asst. prof. econs. Princeton U., 1971—76, assoc. prof., 1976—79, prof., 1979—82, Gordon S. Rentschler Meml. prof. econs., 1982—, chmn. dept. econs., 1988—90, mem. coun. econ. advisers, 1993—94; vice chmn. bd. governors Fed. Res. Bd., Washington, 1994—96. Author: Hard Heads, Soft Hearts: Tough Minded Economics for a Just Society, 1987, Central Banking in Theory and Practice, 1998, The Quiet Revolution: Central Banking Goes Modern, 2004; co-author (with C. Goodhart, P. Hildebrand, D. Lipton, and C. Wyplosz): How Do Central Banks Talk?, 2001; co-author: (with W. Baumol and E. Wolff) Downsizing in America: Reality, Causes, and Consequences, 2003; contbr. articles to profl. jours. such as Jour. Pub. Econs. Recipient W.S. Woytinsky award, 1981. Office: Dept of Econ Princeton Univ 105 Fisher Hall Princeton NJ 08544

BLINDER, ALBERT ALLAN, judge; b. N.Y.C., Nov. 27, 1925; s. William and Sarah (Gold) B.; m. Meredith Zaretzki, Nov. 16, 1961 (dec.); 1 child, Adam Z.; m. Joan Goodman, Jan. 20, 1985 (dec.). AB, NYU, 1944, postgrad., 1944-45; JD, Harvard U., 1948. Bar: N.Y. 1949, U.S. Dist. Ct. (so. dist.) N.Y. 1953, U.S. Ct. Appeals (2d cir.) 1953, U.S. Supreme Ct. 1967. Asst. U.S. atty. for so. dist. N.Y., 1950-53; asst. counsel N.Y.C. Bd. High Edn., 1953-54; asst. dist. atty. County of Bronx, N.Y., 1954-60; ptnr. Saxe, Bacon & O'Shea, N.Y.C., 1960-64, Blinder, Steinhaus & Hochhauser, N.Y.C., 1965-73; judge N.Y. State Ct. Claims, 1973-96; jud. hearing officer N.Y. State Supreme Ct., 1996—. Rsch. counsel N.Y. Commn. on Law of Estates, 1965; assoc. counsel N.Y. Commn. Revision of Penal Law, 1966-70; asst. counsel N.Y. Commn. on Eminent Domain, 1970-73; rsch. asst. N.Y. Commn. State Ct. System, 1971-73. Assoc. editor Am. Criminal Law Quar., 1968-70, mem. adv. bd., 1969-70. Mem.: ABA, Am. Judges Assn., N.Y. County Lawyers Assn., Assn. Bar City N.Y., N.Y. State Bar Assn., Internat. Bar Assn. Office: 115 Broadway Fl 15 New York NY 10006-1604 Office Phone: 212-577-2800. Personal E-mail: ABLINDER@aol.com.

BLINDER, MARTIN S., management consultant, art dealer; b. Bklyn., Nov. 18, 1946; s. Meyer and Lillian (Stein) Blinder; m. Janet Weiss, Dec. 10, 1983. BBA, Adelphi U., 1968. Acct. exec. Bruns, Nordeman & Co., N.Y.C., 1968-69; v.p. Blinder, Robinson & Co., Westbury, NY, 1969-73; treas. BHB Prodns., L.A., 1973-76; pres. Martin Lawrence Ltd. Edits., Van Nuys, Calif., 1976-94, chmn., 1986-94, bd. dirs., 1994—; dir. AZ/NY Gallery, Scottsdale, Ariz., 2000—. Pres., dir. Corp. Art Inc., Visual Artists Mgmt. Corp., Art Consultants Inc.; pres., owner, founder MSB Fine Art, Phoenix, 1994—; lectr. bus. symposia. Contbr. articles to mags. and newspapers; appeared on TV and radio. Mem. Dem. Nat. Com., benefit com. AIDS project, L.A., 1988; bd. dirs. Very Spl. Arts, 1989—; chmn. visual arts Internat. Very Spl. Arts Festival, 1989; patron Guggenheim Mus., N.Y.C., Mus. Modern Art, N.Y.C., L.A. County Mus. Art, L.A. Mus. Contemporary Art (hon. founder), Whitney Mus. Am. Art, Palm Springs Mus. Art, Hirschorn Mus., Washington, Skirball Mus., L.A., Diabetes Found. of City of Hope, B'nai B'rith Anti-Defamation League, 1999, Very Spl. Arts, Scottsdale (Ariz.) Ctr. for the Arts, Scottsdale Mus. Contemporary Art (lectr. on Keith Haring); mem. Citizens for Common Sense; bd. dirs., pres. Rsch. Found. for Crohns Disease; mem. benefit com. Art Against AIDS, 1989; co-chair artists com. for Don't Bungle the Jungle Companions of Arts and Nature, 1989; prin. sponsor, ann. fundraiser AIDS Project, L.A., 1990. Recipient resolution of commendation L.A. City Coun., 1983, State of Calif. resolution for contbn. to arts in Calif., 1983, Merit award Republic Haiti for contbn. to arts, 1985, U.S. Senate commendations, 1983, County of L.A. Bd. Suprs. resolution for contbn. to arts in So. Calif., 1983, Gov. of R.I. resolution for contbns. to arts, 1985, commendation County of L.A.-Supr. Ed Edelman, 1991, commendation for contbns. to the arts and the healing arts City of L.A., 1991, commendation for contbns. to arts and philanthropy Mayor David Dinkins, N.Y.C., 1992; Nov. 18, 1985 declared Martin S. Blinder Day in L.A. in his honor by Mayor Tom Bradley, spl. award San Diego Youth and Cmty. Svcs., Bruin Bear award for establishing Blinder Rsch. Found., UCLA Sch. Medicine, 1994. Mem. Fine Art Pub.'s Assn. (bd. dirs. 1990-94), Med. Art Assn. at UCLA. Office: MSB Fine Art PO Box H82013 Scottsdale AZ 85251

BLINDER, SEYMOUR MICHAEL, chemistry professor, physics professor, researcher; b. N.Y.C., Mar. 11, 1932; s. Morris and Ida (Styszynskaya) B.; m. Frances Ellen Bryant, July 8, 1978; children: Michael Ian, Stephen Earl, Matthew Bryant, Amy Rebecca, Sarah Jane. AB, Cornell U., 1953; MA, Harvard U., 1955, PhD, 1958. Sr. physicist Applied Physics Lab., Johns Hopkins U., 1958-61; asst. prof. chemistry Carnegie Inst. Tech., 1961-62; vis. prof. Harvard U., 1962-63; prof. chemistry and physics U. Mich., 1963—96, prof. emeritus, 1996—. Author: Advanced Physical Chemistry, 1969, Foundations of Quantum Dynamics, 1974, Introduction to Quantum Mechanics in Chemistry, Materials Science and Biology, 2004; Mem. bd. editors: Jour. Am. Chem. Soc., 1978-80; contbr. research articles to profl. jours. Guggenheim fellow, 1965-66; NSF sr. postdoctoral fellow, 1970-71 Mem. AAAS, Am. Phys. Soc., Philos. Soc. Washington, Phi Beta Kappa. Home: 1240 Ferdon Rd Ann Arbor MI 48104-3635 Office: U Mich Dept Chemistry Ann Arbor MI 48109-1055 Business E-Mail: sblinder@umich.edu.

BLINKEN, DONALD, ambassador, investment banker, brokerage house executive; b. N.Y.C., Nov. 11, 1925; s. Maurice Henry and Ethel (Horowitz) B.; m. Vera Evans, Oct. 15, 1975; 1 child, Antony John. BA magna cum laude, Harvard U., 1947. Cons. Marks & Spencer, Ltd., London, 1950-51; pres. Exchange Trading Corp., N.Y.C., 1952-53; v.p. Stein's Stores, Inc., N.Y.C., 1953-58, E.M. Warburg & Co., Inc., 1961-72; sr. v.p., chmn. exec. com. E.M. Warburg, Pincus & Co., Inc., N.Y.C., 1970-81, mng. dir., 1981-86, dir., 1987-94; U.S. amb. Budapest, Hungary, 1994-97; dir. Ion Track Instruments, Inc., 2000—02. Author: Wool Tariffs and American Policy, 1948; chmn. publ. com. Commentary, 1984-87. Pres. Bklyn. Acad. Music, 1971—76, Mark Rothko Found., 1976—88; mem. trustees' coun. Nat. Gallery Art, 1984—94; trustee SUNY, 1976—2000, chmn. bd., 1978—90; bd. dirs. N.Y. Philharmonic Soc., 1986—94, vice chmn., 1989—94; mem. U.S. 2d Circuit Nominating Panel, 1979; trustee Manville Personal Injury Settlement Trust, 1986—91, N.Y. Pub. Libr., 1990—94; dir. Inst. Internat. Edn., 1990—94, hon. trustee, 1999—; trustee Isamu Noguchi Found., 1987—94; bd. overseers Nelson Rockefeller Inst. Govt., 1985—94; chancellor Internat. Coun. Ctrl. European U., 1998—2001; trustee Ctrl. European U., 2001—; mem. adv. bd. Sch. Internat. and Pub. Affairs, Columbia U., 1998—; mem. exec. com. Citizens Democracy Corps, 1999—; hon. bd. dirs. N.Y. Philharm. Soc., 1999—; hon. trustee Inst. Internat. Edn., 1999—; sec.-gen. World Fedn. UN Assns., 2000—04. With USAAF, 1944—45. Mem. Century Assn. Club, River Club (N.Y.C.), Coun. Fgn. Rels., Coun. Am. Ambs. Home: 435 E 52nd St New York NY 10022-6445 Office: 466 Lexington Ave New York NY 10017-3140 Office Phone: 212-878-0835.

BLINKEN, ROBERT JAMES, manufacturing and communications company executive; b. N.Y.C., Apr. 18, 1929; s. Maurice Henry and Ethel (Horowitz) B.; m. Jeanne Pagnucco, Mar. 5, 1955 (div. Jan. 1967); children: Robert James, Rachel; m. Allison Matsner, Dec. 14, 1967; children: Anna, Ingrid. Grad., Horace Mann Sch., N.Y.C., 1946; BA cum laude, Harvard U., 1950. Pres. Teleprinter Corp., Paramus, N.J., 1953-61; v.p. Mite Corp., New Haven, 1961-63, pres., 1963-75, chmn., 1975-85, Comm. Network Enhancement, Mountainside, NJ, 1986—2004. Trustee Albright Inst. Archeol. Rsch., N.Y. Blood Ctr. Served to 1st lt. USAF, 1950-53. Office: 230 Park Ave Fl 26 New York NY 10169-2699

BLINN, JOHN ROBERT, secondary school educator; b. Apr. 8, 1946; BS in Journalism, Bowling Green U., 1968, BS in Edn., 1970; MA in Journalism, Ohio State U., 1969; PhD in Mass Comm., Ohio U., 1982. Tchr. English, journalism Toledo (Ohio) Pub. Schs.; publs. advisor, 1970—. Address: 1423 Devonshire St Bowling Green OH 43402 E-mail: johnrblinn@yahoo.com.

BLISS, CHARLES MICHAEL, gastroenterologist; b. Mineola, N.Y., June 18, 1936; BA, Amherst Coll., 1958; MD, Boston U., 1963. Diplomate Am. Bd. Internal Medicine. Intern Boston City Hosp., 1963—64, resident in medicine, 1965, resident, 1970, gastroenterologist, 1970—; resident in medicine U. Colo. Med. Ctr., Denver, 1967—68; fellow in gastoenterology Boston U., 1968—70, assoc. prof. medicine; gastroenterologist Univ. Hosp., Boston, 1970—. Cons. Jewish Meml. Hosp. Recipient Disting. Clinician award, Am. Gastroent. Assn., 2001. Office: Boston Med Ctr Hosp 88 E Newton St Boston MA 02118 E-mail: michael.bliss@bmc.org.

BLISS, DONALD TIFFANY, JR., lawyer; b. Norwalk, Conn., Nov. 24, 1941; s. Donald Tiffany and Marina (Popova) B.; m. Nancy Arnold, Sept. 14, 1974; children: Evan Hale, Bion Northam. JD, Harvard U., 1966. Bar: N.Y. 1969, D.C. 1971, U.S. Dist. Ct. D.C. 1975, U.S. Ct. Appeals (D.C. cir.) 1971, 84, U.S. Supreme Ct. 1975. Atty. Peace Corps, 1966-67; legis. counsel Congress of Micronesia, 1968; cons. judiciary, American Samoa, 1968; assoc. firm LeBoeuf, Lamb, Leiby & McCrae, N.Y.C., 1969; asst. to sec. HEW, 1969-72; spl. asst. to adminstr. EPA, 1972-73; exec. sec. AID, 1973-74; dep. gen. counsel U.S. Dept. Transp., 1975-77, acting. gen. counsel, 1976-77;

chair, transp. practice group firm O'Melveny & Myers LLP, Washington, 1979—. Mem. Maritime Adv. Com., 1984-85; pres. Harvard Law Sch. Assn. D.C., 1985-86; chmn. transp. sect. FBA, 1987-90; mem. interior task force Grace Commn.; nat. pres. The Ripon Soc. Author: The Law of Airline Customer Relations: Stability, Security, Safety and Service, 2002, Drug Testing and Federal Employees: Lessons from the Transportation Experience, 1988, Economic Deregulation and Safety: Are The Compatible, 1989, A Challenge to the U.S. Aviation Leadership: Launching the New Era of Global Aviation, 1991, Supreme Court Preemption Analysis: Differentiating the Hamiltonians and Jeffersonians, 1993; play The Return of Halley's Comet, 2002. Trustee Studio Theatre, Arts for the Aging, Inc., pres. exec. com., 2003-. Recipient spl. citation HEW, 1972, 73, Pres.'s Cert. Exec. Mgmt., 1973, Superior Achievement award Dept. Transp., 1976. Mem. ABA (chmn. air and space law forum 1997-99), DC Bar Assn. (co-chmn. sect. adminstrv. law and agy. practice 1988-90), Chevy Chase Club. Home: 6732 Newbold Dr Bethesda MD 20817-2223 Office: O'Melveny & Myers LLP 555 13th St NW Ste 500W Washington DC 20004-1159 Office Phone: 202-383-5331. Business E-Mail: dbliss@omm.com.

BLISS, MARY JANE, elementary school educator; b. Ravenna, Ohio, Oct. 23, 1947; d. Curtis J. Tuckerman and Ellen LaRue McMullen; m. Clifford Riggs Bliss, Aug. 24, 1968; children: Wende M. Campbell, Jennifer J. Ellis, Elizabeth H. Sadowski. BS in Edn., Kent State U., 1969, MS in Edn., 1991, ABD in Curriculum and Instrn., 2001. Cert. tchr. Ohio. Tchr. Brimfield Co-op Nursery, Kent, Ohio, 1975—76, Tots Learning Ctr., Ravenna, Ohio, 1980—81, Streetsboro Co-op Nursery, Ohio, 1981—84, Ravenna City Schs., Ohio, 1985—, literacy specialist, 2000—04; instr., cons. Kent State U., Ohio, 1998—. Mem. editl. review bd.: Ohio Resource Ctr., 2003—. Singer Ravenna Cmty. Choir, Ohio, 1980—2004; organist Lake Brady United Meth. Ch., Kent, Ohio, 1963—. Grantee, Martha Holden Jennings, 1998, 2001. Mem.: Internat. Reading Assn. (Ohio Coun. sec. 1999—2003, editl. review bd. 2002—), Phi Delta Kappa. Avocations: reading, needlecrafts, music. Office: Willyard Elem 680 Summit Rd Ravenna OH 44266

BLISS, RICK WAYNE, engineer; b. Rupert, Idaho, Apr. 7, 1953; s. Delford Victor Bliss and Naomia Katherine Olenslager; m. Colleen Taggart, July 27, 1985; children: Richard Halley, Christopher Taggart. BS in Physics, U. Utah, 1975, MS in Mech. Engring., 1976. Registered profl. engr., Utah. Tech. specialist Hercules, Inc., Magna, Utah, 1976—95; sr. engr. ATK, Magna, 1995—. Contbr. articles to profl. jours. Chair Bluffdale City Parks Com., 1991—93; founding mem., chair South Valley Jordan River Pkwy., 1993—; chair, pres. Found. for the Provo/Jordan River Pkwy., Salt Lake City, 1996—2000. Recipient Svc. award, Lions, Bluffdale, 1993, Recognition award, Bluffdale City, 2000. Mem.: AIAA. Achievements include development of advanced constitutive model that has been incorporated in LLNL's Nikead; advanced micromechanics model for composite kimina; quater math. Home: 1945 Rock Hollow Rd Bluffdale UT 84065

BLISS, ROBERT HARMS, lawyer; b. Paris, Tex., Nov. 20, 1940; s. Jack Edward and Ruth Eugenia (Harms) B.; m. Juliee Dixie Fuselier, Dec. 29, 1964; 1 child, Katherine Elaine. BA, U. Colo., 1964; JD, U. Tex., 1967. Bar: Tex. 1967; cert. civil trial specialist, mediator-arbitrator, spl. master. Since practiced in, Dallas; assoc. Johnson, Bromberg, Leeds & Riggs, 1967-72; ptnr. Bliss, Danner & Bishop, 1972-74; individual practice, 1974; pres. Bliss & Hughes, P.C., Dallas, 1978-88; pvt. practice Robert Harms Bliss P.C., 1988-98; ptnr. Glast, Phillips & Murray, PC, 1998—2002; pvt. practice, 2002—. Mem. faculty advanced real estate law State Bar Tex., 1985, 92-93, 95, 97, 99, 2000, 02; mem. faculty CLE series So. Meth. U. Sch. Law, Dallas, 1989, 92, 94, 97, 98, 99, 2000, mem. faculty The Leasing Inst., 2004-05; mem. faculty Mortgage Lending Inst., U. Tex. Sch. Law, 1994, 97, 98, 99, 2000, mem. faculty advanced real estate drafting course, 1995, 2000-04, course dir., 2002. Contbr. articles to profl. jours. Bd. dirs. Dallas Symphony Orch. Guild, Dallas Classic Guitar Soc.; mem. Gov.'s Task Force on Immigration, 1983-84, Tex. Real Estate Commn., 1983-87; adv. bd. Tex. Real Estate Rsch. Ctr., Tex. A&M U., 1985-87; ch. atty. Episcopal Diocese Dallas. Mem. Am. Coll. Real Estate Lawyers, State Bar Tex. (past chair real estate, probate and trust sect.), Dallas Bar Assn. (past chmn. real property sect.), Tex. Coll. Real Estate Attys., Assn. Atty.-Mediators (pres. North Tex. chpt.), U. Tex. Tchg. Quiz-Masters Assn., Phi Delta Phi. Home: 29 Ashton Ct Dallas TX 75230-1977 Office: PO Box 12825 Dallas TX 75225 Office Phone: 214-521-0190.

BLISS, SUSAN PEARL, music educator, writer; b. Levittown, NY, Mar. 15, 1954; d. Aaron and Henrietta Finger; m. Christopher William Bliss, June 15, 1986; children: Danielle, Gregory. Student, Eastman Sch. Music, 1972—73, Manhattan Sch. Music, 1975—78; BA, SUNY, Stony Brook, 1976; MA, U. So. Calif., 1980; PhD, UCLA, 1986. Cert. music tchr. Calif. Assoc. faculty Irvine (Calif.) Valley Coll., Scripps Coll., Claremont, Calif., 1989—90, Saddleback Coll., Mission Viejo, Calif., 1996—. Editor: Windplayer Mag., 2001—02; contbr. articles to profl. jours., popular mags. Mem.: Calif. Tchrs. Assn., Faculty Assn. Calif. CC. Home and Office: 24101 Gowrami Bay Monarch Beach CA 92629 Office: Saddleback Coll fine Arts Divsn 28000 Marguerite Pkwy Mission Viejo CA 92692-3635

BLISSETT, WILLIAM FRANK, English literature educator; b. East End, Sask., Can., Oct. 11, 1921; s. Ralph Richardson and Gladys (Jones) B. BA, U. B.C., 1943; MA, U. Toronto, 1946, PhD, 1950. Lectr dept. English U. Toronto, 1946-50, prof. English, 1965-87, prof. emeritus, 1987; assoc. prof. dept. English U. Sask., 1950-57, prof., 1957-60; prof., head dept. English Huron Coll., London, Ont., 1960-65. Author: The Long Conversation, 1981; editor: Editing Illustrated Books, 1980; editor U. Toronto Quar., 1965-76; adv. bd.: Ency. of Shakespeare and Music, 1991, Chesterton Rev., 1984—; co-editor: Spenser Ency., 1982-90; joint editor: A Celebration of Ben Jonson, 1974; subject of book: Craft and Tradition: Essays in Honour of William Blissett, 1990. Huron Coll. hon. fellow, 1966; Royal Soc. Can. fellow, 1979 Mem. Internat. Assn. Univ. Profs. English, David Jones Soc. Anglican.

BLISSMAN, BETH, director; b. Greensburg, Pa., Nov. 8, 1963; d. Bill and Peg Blissman. B in Archtl. Engring., Pa. State U., 1986; MA in Theology and Pastoral Ministry, LaSalle U., Phila., 1991; PhD in Religious and Theol. Studies, U. Denver, 2000. Project mgr. Lighting Design Collaborative, Phila., 1986—87; dir. Mesa State Newman Ctr. Mesa State Coll., Grand Junction, Colo., 1989—92; tchg. asst. U. Denver, 1994—98, interim dir. svc. learning program, 1998—99, adj. faculty, 1999—2000; dir. Ctr. for Svc. and Learning Oberlin (Ohio) Coll., 2000—. Cons. Minn. Campus Compact, Mpls., 2003—03. Liason higher edn. Santuario Sisterfarm, Welfare, Tex., 2002—05. Faculty fellow, U. Denver, 2000. Mem.: Am. Acad. Religion (co-chair religion and ecology group 2003—05). Progressive. Roman Catholic. Avocations: organic gardening, permaculture, singing, inspirational speaking, ecosocial transformation. Office: Oberlin College 68 S Professor St Oberlin OH 44074 Office Phone: 440-775-8055. Office Fax: 440-775-8754.

BLITMAN, HOWARD NORTON, construction company executive; b. N.Y.C., Dec. 9, 1926; s. Charles H. and Anna (Palestine) B.; m. Maureen Lefcort-Winter, 1975. CE, Rensselaer Poly. Inst., 1950; MA, New Sch. Social Research, 1973. Registered profl. engr., N.Y., N.J., Conn., Mass., S.C. Field engr. Drier Structural Steel Co., N.Y., 1950-51; design engr. Blitman & Tischler, N.Y.C., 1952-60; project engr. Blitman Constrn. Corp., N.Y.C., 1960-61, coordinator, 1961-62, exec. v.p., 1962-69, pres., 1969-81; pres., dir. Blitman Bldg. Corp., 1981—. Mem. housing com. State Constnl. Conv., 1968; mem. N.Y.C. Commn. Investigation Water Main Breaks; chmn. adv. bd. to dept. civil engring. Rensselaer Poly. Inst., 1999—. Mem. sch. bd. Mt. Pleasant Cottage Sch., Union Free Sch. Dist., Pleasantville, N.Y.; pres., bd. dirs. Jewish Child Care Assn. N.Y.; v.p. bd. dirs. Beth Israel Med. Ctr.; mem. coun. Rensselaer Poly. Inst.; chmn. archtl. rev. bd. Town of Scarsdale, N.Y., trustee 1989-93; trustee Village of Scarsdale, 1989, dep. mayor, 1992—; mem. Planning Bd. Scarsdale, 1994—, chmn., 1998—; trustee Rensselaer Poly. Inst., 2004. 2d lt. Chem. Corps AUS, 1944-47; 1st lt., 1951-53. Recipient Norman Tishman Human Rels. award, 1967, Albert DeMers medal, Rensselaer Poly. Inst. Fellow: NSPE (chmn. profl. engrs. in constrn., pres. 1997, chmn. 1996—97, nat. treas. 1999—2001, pres.-elect 2001—02, pres. 2002—03); mem.: ASME, ASCE, N.Y. State Soc. Profl. Engrs. (pres. 1978, pres. N.Y. chpt. 1974—75), Harmonie Club (N.Y.C.), Masons (N.Y.C.). Home: 3 Elmdorf Dr Scarsdale NY 10583-4203 Office Phone: 918-244-8600.

BLITZ, NELSON, JR., entrepreneur; m. Catherine Woodard; children: Perri, Allison. Pres. Nelson Air Device Corp., Maspeth, NY, Nelson Acquisition Corp., Rye, NY. Named one of Top 200 Collectors, ARTnews Mag., 2004. Avocation: Collecting Viennese furniture, prints and works on paper, especially Munch, Picasso, Kirchner and Johns. Office: Nelson Air Device Corp 46-28 54th Ave Maspeth NY 11378 also: Nelson Acquisition Corp 10 Pine Island Rd Rye NY 10580*

BLITZ, PEGGY SANDERFUR, corporate travel management company official; b. Pitts., Apr. 12, 1940; d. Charles I. and Rebecca Polk (McBride) Wallace; m. Clark L. Blitz, Aug. 25, 1962 (div. Apr. 1974); children: Danette L., Jonathan D. BS, Ball State U., 1962; postgrad., No. Ill. U., 1976-77. Cert. speech therapist, spl. edn. tchr. Tchr. mentally retarded Anderson (Ind.) Pub. Schs., 1962-64; speech therapist Elgin (Ill.) Pub. Schs., 1964-66; pvt. practice speech therapy Elgin, 1966-68; tchr. mentally retarded Easter Seal Rehab. Ctr., Elgin, 1968-77; account exec. Whitehall Hotel, Chgo., 1977-79; regional mgr. IVI Travel Inc., Milw., 1979-85, sr. v.p. Dallas, 1985-88; pres. Travelmasters, Inc., Chgo., 1988-91; staff devel. Kemper Securities, Inc., Chgo., 1991-92; pres. Travel Mgmt. Cons., St. John, V.I., 1991—; property mgr. Short-Term Vacation Rentals, 1992—; exec. asst. Caneel Bay Resort, St. John, V.I., 1999—. Presbyterian. Home and Office: PO Box 8333 Cruz Bay VI 00831-8333 Office Phone: 340-776-6111. Business E-Mail: pblitz@rosewoodhotels.com.

BLITZ, STEPHEN M., lawyer; b. N.Y.C., July 29, 1941; s. Leo and Dorothy B.; m. Ellen Sue Mintzer, Sept. 23, 1962; children: Catherine Denise, Thomas Joseph. BA, Columbia U., 1962, BS, 1963; LLB, Stanford U., 1966; MS in Acctg., U. Colo., 2001. Bar: Calif. 1967, U.S. Dist. Ct. (ctrl. dist.) Calif. 1967, Colo. 1996, Wis. 2004. Law clk. to judge U.S. Dist. Ct. (ctrl. dist.) Calif., 1966-67; ptnr. Gibson, Dunn & Crutcher, L.A., 1967-96, Denver, 1996-2001; of counsel Fleishman & Shapiro, Denver, 2001—. Adj. prof. law U. West L.A. Sch. Law, 1978-80, dir. Pub. Counsel, 1981-83, 94-96. Bd. dirs. Colo. Preservation, Inc., 1999—. Mem. ABA, L.A. County Bar Assn. (exec. com. 1986-96, chmn. 1994-95, real property sect.), Colo. Bar Assn., Denver Bar Assn., Order of Coif, Beta Gamma Sigma. Office: Fleishman & Shapiro PC 1600 Broadway Ste 2600 Denver CO 80202-4926 Office Phone: 303-861-1000.

BLITZER, ANDREW, otolaryngologist, educator, research scientist, writer; b. Apr. 25, 1946; s. Martin Hollander and Lyrene Iris (Lave) Blitzer; m. Patricia Volk, Dec. 21, 1969; children: Peter Morgen, Polly Volk. BA, Adelphi U., 1967; DDS, Columbia U. Sch. of Dental and Oral Surgery, 1970; MD, Mt. Sinai Sch. Medicine, 1973. Diplomate Am. Bd. Otolaryngology. Resident in gen. surgery Beth Israel Hosp., NYC, 1973—74; resident in otolaryngology Mt. Sinai Hosp., NYC, 1974—77; asst. prof. otolaryngology Coll. Phys. & Surg. Columbia U., NYC, 1977—82, assoc. prof. otolaryngology and oral surgery, 1982—84, prof. clin. otolaryngology and oral surgery, 1984—, prof. clin. otolaryngology in neurology, 1993—95; prof. clin. otolaryngology Coll. Physicians and Surgeons, Columbia U., acting chmn. dept. otolaryngology NYC, 1991—94; vice chmn. dept. otolaryngology Columbia U., NYC, 1983—91; dir. divsn. head and neck surgery Columbia-Presbyn. Med. Ctr., NYC, 1980—94, dir. multidiscipline head and neck tumor bd., dir. residency edn., 1978—94; acting dir. Otolaryngology Svc. Presbyterian Hosp.; lectr. dept. otolaryngology Mt. Sinai Sch. Medicine, NYC, 1977—; sr. attending otolaryngologist and dir. NY Ctr. for Voice and Swallowing Disorders St. Luke's/Roosevelt Med. Ctr., 1994—. Dir. NY Ctr. for Clin. Rsch.; cons., mem. spl. senses and lang. study sect. NIH. Co-author several books, author several textbooks; assoc. editor: Otolaryngology-Head and Neck Surgery; co-author: The Laryngoscope, Jour. Otolaryngology, Jour. Rhinology; contbr. chapters to books, articles to profl. jours. Recipient award for excellence, Am. Assn. Orthodontists, 1970, Tchr.-Investigator award, Nat. Inst. Neurol. Communicative Disorders and Strokes, 1978—83, Maxwell Abramson Meml. award, Excellence in Resident Teaching, 1993, James A. Newcomb award, Am. Laryngological Assn. Fellow: ACS, Am. Broncho-esophagological Assn., Am. Acad. Otolaryngology-Head and Neck Surgery (bd. dirs. 2002—, Honor award, Disting. Svc. award 1996), Am. Laryngol., Rhinol., and Otol. Soc., Am. Laryngol. Assn. (James Newcomb award 1998), Am. Acad. Facial Plastic and Reconstructive Surgery, Am. Soc. Head and Neck Surgery, N.Y. Acad. Medicine. Achievements include being a pioneer and leading authority in the use of Botox for conditions with excessive muscle function, muscle pain, tremor & muscle spasm, including spasmodic dysphonia and facial lines & wrinkles; established the field of neurolaryngology and has one of the seven fellowship programs in the country; developed new surgical techniques for the rehabilitation the paralyzed vocal cord; world leader in the management of voice and swallowing disorders, nasal and sinus surgery, laser surgery, management of facial lines and wrinkels, and head and neck surgery. Avocations: running, skiing, photography, fly fishing. Office: 425 W 59th St 10th Fl New York NY 10019-1104 Office Phone: 212-262-4444. Office Fax: 212-523-6364.

BLITZER, WOLF, news correspondent; b. Buffalo, Mar. 22, 1948; m. Lynn Greenfield; 1 child, Elana. BA in History, SUNY, Buffalo; MA in Internat. Rels., Johns Hopkins U. of Advanced Internat. Studies, Washington, DC; doctorate (hon.), King's Coll., Wilkes-Barre, Pa., Gannon Univ., Erie, Pa., Quinnipiac Coll., New Haven, Conn., SUNY, Buffalo. With Reuters New Agy., Tel Aviv, 1971—73; Washington corr. Jerusalem Post, 1973—89; mil. affairs corr. at the Pentagon CNN, Washington, 1990-92, sr. White House corr., 1992-99, host Late Edition, 1998—, sr. anchor, The World Today, 1999—, anchor, Wolf Blitzer Report, 2000—, anchor, America Votes 2004. Author: Between Washington & Jerusalem: A Reporter's Notebook, 1985, Territory of Lies, 1989 (most notable book of 1989, NY Times); contbr. articles to profl. publs. Recipient Emmy for Coverage of Oklahoma City bombing, 1996, Best in the Bus. award Am. Journalism Rev., 1994, Disting. Alumnus award Johns Hopkins U. Alumni Assn., 1999, Lowell Thomas Broadcast Journalism award for outstanding contbns. to broadcast journalism, Internat. Platform Assn., 1999, Hubert H. Humphrey First Amendment Freedoms prize, Anti-Defamation League, 2002, Ernie Pyle Journalism award for excellence in military reporting, Am. Veteran awards, 2002, Daniel Pearl award, Chgo. Press Veterans Assn., 2003; co-recipient Golden CableACE for coverage of the Persian Gulf War, Nat. Acad. of Cable Programming. Jewish. Achievements include coverage of many key events that have shaped the international political landscape and has interviewed some of recent history's most notable figures. Office: Cable Network News 820 1st St NE Washington DC 20002-4243 E-mail: wolf@cnn.com.*

BLIVAISS, DAVID HARVEY, lawyer, accountant; b. Chgo., May 4, 1949; s. Dr. Ben B. and Helen F. (Friedman) B.; m. Karen N. Rosenberg, Aug. 20, 1972; children: Jeffrey E., Sara Gray, Amanda R. BSBA in Acctg., Roosevelt U., 1971; JD, Loyola U., 1974. Bar: Ill. 1974, NJ 1991; CPA Ill. 1975, NY 1984, NJ 1990. Various positions Arthur Andersen & Co., Chgo., 1974-83, ptnr. NYC, 1983-91, Eisner LLP, NYC, 1991—. Mem. AICPA, NYSSCPA, ABA, Wall Street Tax Assn. Office: Eisner LLP 750 3rd Ave New York NY 10017 Office Phone: 212-891-4038. Business E-Mail: dblivaiss@eisnerllp.com.

BLIWISE, LESTER MARTIN, lawyer; b. Phila., Dec. 22, 1945; s. Sanford and Mollie (Cohen) B.; m. Ilene Estelle Hisiger, June 23, 1968; children: Matthew Scott, Howard Michael. BA, Rutgers U., 1967; JD, Bklyn. Law Sch., 1970. Bar: N.Y. 1971, U.S. Dist. Ct. (no. dist.) N.Y. 1971, U.S. Dist. Ct. (so. dist.) N.Y. 1975. Law asst. appellate div. 3d dept. N.Y. State Supreme Ct., Albany, 1970-71, law sec. appellate div. 3d dept., 1971-72; assoc. Burstein and Marcus, White Plains, N.Y., 1972-73, Trubin Sillcocks Edelman & Knapp, N.Y.C., 1973-78, ptnr., 1978-84, Milgrim Thomajan Jacobs & Lee, N.Y.C., 1984-85, Curtis, Mallet-Prevost, Colt & Mosie, N.Y.C., 1985-87, Schulte Roth & Zabel, LLP, N.Y.C., 1987-97, LeBoeuf, Lamb, Greene & MacRae LLP, N.Y.C., 1997—. Mem. coun. advisors Ticor Title Ins. Co., N.Y.C., 1990—. Contbr. chpts. in books Real Estate Titles, 1984, rev., 1988, 2d edit., 1994, rev. edit., 1998, Foreign Investment in the U.S., 1989, rev. 1990, 92; notes editor Bklyn. Law Rev., 1969-70. Mem. planning bd. Town of Mamaroneck, N.Y., 1984-88. Mem. N.Y. Sate Bar Assn. (del. to Ho. of dels., 1992-94, chair real estate financing and liens com., real property law sect. 1980-88, 98—, chair real property law sect. 1991-92, sec. 1988-89, 2d vice chair 1989-90, 1st vice chair 1990-91), Am. Coll. Real Estate Lawyers. Home: 155 Franklin St New York NY 10013-2936 Office: LeBoeuf Lamb Greene & MacRae LLP 125 W 55th St New York NY 10019-5369

BLIX, HANS MARTIN, retired government and international agency official; b. Uppsala, Sweden, June 28, 1928; s. Gunnar and Hertha (Wiberg) B.; m. Eva Kettis, Mar. 17, 1962; children: Marten, Goran. LL.B., U. Uppsala, 1951; PhD, Cambridge U., 1959; LL.D., Stockholm U., 1960. Assoc. prof. U. Stockholm, 1960; legal adviser Ministry Fgn. Affairs, Stockholm, 1963-76, under sec. of state in charge of internat. devel. coop., 1976-78, 79-81; minister fgn. affairs Sweden, 1978-79; dir. gen. Internat. Atomic Energy Agy., Vienna, 1981-97; exec. chmn. UN Monitoring, Verification and Inspection Commn., 2000—03. Mem. Swedish Del. UN Gen. Assembly, N.Y., 1961-81, Swedish Del. Conf. Disarmament, Geneva, 1962-78; chair Assembly States Mems. Chernobyl Shelter Fund, 1998—, Weapons of Mass Destruction Commn., 2004-. Author: Treaty Making Power, 1959, Statsmyndigheternas Internationella Forbindelser, 1964, Sovereignty, Aggression and Neutrality, 1970, The Treaty Maker's Handbook, 1974, Disarming Iraq, 2004. Mem. Inst. de Droit Internat. E-mail: hans.blix@comhem.se.

BLIXT, CHARLES A., tobacco company executive; b. Rockford, Ill., Aug. 18, 1951; m. Leslie Blixt; children: Allison, Katherine. BS, U. Ill., 1974, JD, 1977. Litigation atty. Foster, Swift, Collins and Coey, P.C., Lansing, Mich., Overholser, Ray, Flannery and Glick Ltd., Libertyville; atty. Fiat-Allis Constrn. Machinery Inc., 1979-81, Caterpillar Tractor Co., 1981-85; assoc. counsel R. J. Reynolds Tobacco Co., Winston-Salem, NC, 1985-87, counsel-litigation, 1987-89, staff v.p., asst. gen. counsel, 1994-95, v.p., asst. gen. counsel, 1995, sr. v.p., gen. counsel, 1995—99, exec. v.p., gen. counsel, 1999—. Bd. dirs Salem Coll. & Acad., Wake Forest U. Sch. Law, Targacept Inc., NC Tech. Concepts & Design Inc. Office: RJ Reynolds Tobacco Co 401 N Main St Winston Salem NC 27101-3804

BLIZARD, CHRISTIE LYNN, art educator, artist; b. Indpls., Dec. 24, 1978; d. Norman and Susan Blizard. BFA, Ind. U., Indpls., Ind., 2001; MFA, Ga. State U., 2005. Instr. drawing Fine Art Program Belvoir Ter., Lenox, Mass., 2005; tchr. Ga. State U., Atlanta, 2002—. Adv. grad. budget Art Student Union Ga. State U., Atlanta, 2002—04, vis. artist, coord., pres. Art Student Union, 2003—04, co-dir. cage space. New American Paintings South Edition, vol. 58, exhibitions include Whitney Mus. Am. Art., Newark, N.J., Traveling Western RV Biennial Art Show, 2005, Limner Gallery, N.Y., N.Y., 2003, Violence Against Women, Women Against Violence, Berkley and San Francisco, Calif., Documentation WomanMade Gallery, Chgo., Ill., Ernest G. Welch Sch. Art and Design, one-woman shows include EyeDrum Gallery, Atlanta, Ga. Recipient award, Nat. Conf. Tchrs. English, 1997, Herron Gen. award, Herron Sch. Art and Design, 1997, Herron Anniversary Painting award, 2000, Women in Leadership award, Ind. U., 2000, Mildred Darby Menz award, Herron Sch. of Art and Design, 2002; fellow, Ga. State U., 2002—05; Joseph van Sickle scholarship, Herron Sch. Art and Design, 1999—2000, Fehnel Travel scholarship, 2001, Bd. Regents scholar, Ga. State U., 2002. Mem.: Art Student Union (pres. 2002—04), Women's Caucus for the Arts (assoc.), Ind. Women Artists (assoc.), Coll. Art Assn. (assoc.). Home: 4660 Northeastern Blvd Columbus IN 47203 Personal E-mail: pearl888_9@hotmail.com.

BLIZARD, SUSAN KENNEDY, biology professor; b. Omaha, Apr. 21, 1949; d. George L. and Bernice E.A. Kennedy; m. John S. Blizard, Mar. 8, 1980. BS in Zoology, U. Nebr., Lincoln, 1972, MS in Zoology, 1974; MBA in Mgmt., Golden Gate U., 1985; ArtsD in Biology, Idaho State U., 1994. Rsch. technician Eppley Cancer Inst., U. Nebr. Med. Ctr., Omaha, 1975-80; rsch. technician U. Calif., Davis, 1980-82; adj. prof. biology C.C. So. Nev., North Las Vegas, 1983-88, prof., 1990—, chmn. sci. dept., 1996—99, chmn. biology dept., 1999—2001, interim dean of sci. and math., 2002—03, prof. biology, 2003—. Fellow Idaho State U., 1988-90. Avocation: reading mystery novels. Office: CC So Nev Biol Scis Dept H3C 3200 E Cheyenne Ave North Las Vegas NV 89030-4228 Office Phone: 702-651-3140. E-mail: sue_blizard@ccsn.nevada.edu.

BLIZNAKOV, MILKA TCHERNEVA, architect, educator; b. Varna, Bulgaria, Sept. 20, 1927; came to U.S., 1961, naturalized, 1966; d. Ivan Dimitrov and Maria Kesarova (Khorozova) Tchernev; m. Emile G. Bliznakov, Oct. 23, 1954 (div. Apr., 1974). Architect-engr. diploma, State Tech. U., Sofia, 1951; PhD, Engring.-Structural Inst., Sofia, 1959; PhD in Architecture, Columbia U., 1971. Sr. researcher Ministry Heavy Industry, Sofia, 1950-53; pvt. practice architecture Sofia, 1954-59; assoc. architect Noel Combrisson, Paris, 1959-61; designer Perkins & Will Partnership, White Plains, N.Y., 1963-67; project architect Lathrop Douglass, N.Y.C., 1967-71; assoc. prof. architecture and planning Sch. Architecture, U. Tex., Austin, 1972-74; prof. Coll. Architecture, Va. Poly. Inst. and State U., Blacksburg, 1974-98, prof. emerita, 1998—; prin. Blacksburg, 1975—. Bd. dirs. founder Internat. Archives Women in Architecture, Va. Poly. Inst. and State U., The Parthena award, 1994. Prin. works include Speedwell Ave. Urban Renewal, Morristown, N.J., 1967—69, Wilmington (Del.) Urban Renewal, 1968—70, Springfield (Ill.) Ctrl. Area Devel., 1969—71, Arlington County (Va.) Redevel., 1975—77; author (with others): Utopia e Modernitá, 1989, Reshaping Russian Archtecture, 1990, Russian Housing in the Modern Age, 1993, Nietzsche and Soviet Culture, 1994, New Perspectives on Russian and Soviet Artistic Culture, 1994, The Eastern Dada Orbit: Russia, Georgia, Ukraine, Central Europe, 1996, Signs of Times, Culture and the Emblems of Apocalypse, 1998, Women Architects in Eastern Europe: The Contributions of the Bulgarians, 1997, International Archive of Women in Architecture, 1997; author: (with others) 5th edit., 2003; author: (with others) Encyclopedia of Eastern Europe, 2000, Centropa, 2001; author: (with others) 2d edit., 2003; author: (with others) Women Architects in Japan, 2002, Housing in Russia: 20th Century, 2002; author: (with others) Encyclopedia of Twentieth Century Architecture, 2003. William Kinne scholar, 1970, vis. scholar Inst. Advanced Russian Studies, The Wilson Ctr. of Smithsonian Instn., 1988; NEA grantee, 1973-74, Am. Beautiful Found. grantee, 1973, Internat. Rsch. and Exch. Bd. grantee, 1984-93; Fulbright Hays rsch. fellow, 1983-84, 91; recipient Parthena award, 1994. Mem. Internat. Archive Women in Architecture (founder, chair bd. dirs.), Am. Assn. Tchrs. Slavic and East European Langs., Soc. Archtl. Historians, Nat. Trust Hist. Preservation, Am. Assn. Advancement of Slavic Studies, Assn. Collegiate Schs. of Planning, Inst. Modern Russian Culture (chairperson architecture, co-founder, dir.), Bulgarian Studies Assn., Assn. Collegiate Schs. of Architecture. Home: 2813 Tall Oaks Dr Blacksburg VA 24060-8109 Office: Va Poly Inst and State U Coll Architecture Blacksburg VA 24061 Business E-Mail: mbliznak@vt.edu.

BLIZZARD, ALAN, artist; b. Boston, Mar. 25, 1939; s. Thomas and Elizabeth B. BFA, Mass. Coll. Art; MA, U. Ariz.; MFA, U. Iowa, 1963. Instr. in art U. Iowa; vis. asst. prof. art Albion Coll., U. Okla.; assoc. prof. UCLA; now prof. painting Scripps Coll. and; Claremont Grad. Sch. Represented in permanent collections Bklyn. Mus., Met. Mus. Art, N.Y.C., Art Inst. Chgo., Denver Art Mus., La Jolla (Calif.) Mus. Art, Ashland U., Columbia U., McGeorge Sch. Law, Pomona Coll., Sacramento State U., Pitzer Coll., Fluor Corp., Kouri Capital Corp., N.Y.C. Office: Scripps Coll Art Dept Claremont CA 91711

BLOBEL, GÜNTER, cell biologist, educator; b. Waltersdorf, Silesia, Germany, May 21, 1936; MD, U. Tübingen, Germany, 1960; PhD in Oncology, U. Wis., 1967. Intern, Germany, 1960-62; fellow lab. cellular biology Rockefeller U., 1967-69, asst. prof. cell biology NYC, 1969-73, assoc. prof., 1973-76, prof., 1976—; investigator Howard Hughes Med. Inst., 1986—. Founder, pres. Friends of Dresden, Inc. Contbr. articles to profl.

jours. and chpts. to books. Recipient Gairdner Found. award, 1982, Warburg medal German Biochem. Soc., 1983, Wilson medal Am. Soc. Cell Biology, 1986, U.D. Mattia award Roche Inst. Molecular Biology, 1986, Louisa Gross Horwitz prize Columbia U., 1987, Waterford Biomedical Sci. award, 1989, Albert Lasker Basic Med. Rsch. award, 1993, King Faisal internat. prize for sci., 1996, Mayor's award for Excellence in Sci. and Tech., 1997, Massry Prize, 1999, Nobel Prize for Medicine, 1999, Ellis Island Medal of Honor, 2000. Mem. Nat. Acad. Scis. (U.S. Steel award in molecular biology 1978, Richard Lounsbery award 1983), Am. Acad. Arts and Scis., Japan Biochem. Soc. (hon.), Am. Soc. Cell Biology (pres. 1990), German Soc. Cell Biology (hon.), Am. Philos. Soc., European Molecular Biol. ORgn. (assoc.). Office: Rockefeller U Cell Biology Lab 66th and York Ave New York NY 10021-6339

BLOCH, DONALD MARTIN, lawyer; b. Lynn, Mass., May 16, 1939; s. Meyer James and Bertha (Berman) B.; m. Ellen Ann Green, June 18, 1961; children: Andrew Louis, Linda Phyllis, David Michael. BA, Bowdoin Coll., 1960; LLB, Harvard U., 1963. Bar: Mass. 1963, U.S. Dist. Ct. Mass. 1974. Assoc. Lane, Altman & Owens LLP, Boston, 1966-71; ptnr. Lane, Altman & Owens LLP, Boston, 1972-2001; of counsel Posternak, Blankstein & Lund, LLP, Boston, 2001—. Mem. Framingham (Mass.) Town Meeting, 1970-95, Town Charter Commn., Framingham, 1978-79, Town Finance Com., 2002—; bd. dirs. South Middlesex Assn. for Retarded, Framingham, 1980-86, Metrowest Mental Health Assn., Framingham, 1983-95, Mary Morse Healthcare Inc., 1997—, vice chair, 2000-01, chair, 2001—; mem. Mass. Adv. Com. to U.S. Civil Rights Commn., 1991-93. Capt. U.S. Army, 1963-65. Named one of Outstanding Citizens, Greater Framingham Jewish Fedn., 1983. Mem. Bowdoin Club Boston (officer, bd. dirs.), Phi Beta Kappa. Republican. Office: Posternak Blankstein & Lund LLP 800 Boylston St Boston MA 02199 Office Phone: 617-973-6169. Business E-Mail: dbloch@pbl.com. E-mail: donmbloch@aol.com.

BLOCH, ERICH, retired electrical engineer, science foundation director; b. Sulzburg, Germany, Jan. 9, 1925; arrived in U.S., 1948, naturalized, 1952; s. Joseph and Tony Bloch; m. Renee Stern, Mar. 4, 1948; 1 child, Rebecca Bloch Rosen. Student, Fed. Poly. Inst., Zurich, Switzerland, 1945—48; BSEE, U. Buffalo, 1952; hon. degrees, U. Mass., George Washington U., Colo. Sch. Mines, SUNY Buffalo, U. Rochester, Oberlin Coll., U. Notre Dame, Ohio State U.; hon. degree, Rensselaer Poly. Inst., 1989, Washington Coll., 1989, CUNY, N.Y.C., 1991, Poly. U., Bklyn., N.Y., 1993, St. Thomas Aquinas Coll. With IBM, 1952—75, v.p. gen. mgr. East Fishkill, NY, 1975—80, v.p. tech. personnel devel. Armonk, NY, 1980—84; mem. com. computers in automated mfg. NRC, 1980—84; dir. NSF, Washington, 1984—90; fellow Coun. on Competitiveness, 1990—; prin. Washington Adv. Group, 1998—; mem. Pres.'s Coun. of Advisors for Sci. and Tech., 2001—. Past vis. disting. prof. George Mason U. Patentee in field. Recipient U.S. medal of tech., 1985, Computer World/Smithsonian award for innovation, 1991, Swedish Royal Order of the Polar Star, Robert Noyce award, Semiconductor Industry Assn., 1999, Eugene Merchant Mfg. medal, ASME and Soc. Mfg. Engrs., Vanevar Bush award, Nat. Sci. Bd., 2002, Fellow award, Computer History Mus., 2004. Fellow: AAAS, IEEE (Founder's award 1990, Computer Pioneer award 1993, 1994); mem.: NAE (Arthur M. Bueche award 1997), Japan Acad. Engring., Royal Swedish Acad. Engring. Scis., Am. Soc. Engring. Edn., Am. Soc. Mfg. Engrs. (hon.). Office Phone: 202-682-0164. Business E-Mail: ebloch@theadvisorygroup.com.

BLOCH, FRANK SAMUEL, law educator; b. Jan. 16, 1945; s. Felix Jacob and Lore Clara (Misch) B.; m. Melissa Roth, Mar. 12, 1972; children: Julia Devi, Sara Shanti. BA, Brandeis U., 1966, MA, 1971, PhD, 1978; JD, Columbia U., 1969. Bar: Calif. 1970, Tenn. 1980, U.S. Dist. Ct. (no. dist.) Calif. 1971, U.S. Ct. Appeals (7th cir.) 1976, U.S. Dist. Ct. (mid. dist.) Tenn. 1980, U.S. Ct. Appeals (6th cir.) 1983. Assoc. atty. Calif. Rural Legal Assistance, Madera, Calif., 1971-72, directing atty., 1972-73; lectr. in law, clin. fellow U. Chgo., 1974-79; assoc. prof. law Vanderbilt U., Nashville, 1979-86, prof., 1986—, dir. clin. edn., 1979-2001. Pres. Legal Svcs. of Mid. Tenn., Inc., 1991-92, 95-96; cons. Adminstrv. Conf. of U.S., 1988-93, Internat. Social Security Assn., 1993-2000, Social Security Adv. Bd., 2001-02. Author: Disability Determination, 1992, Bloch on Social Security Disability, 2004; editor: Who Returns to Work and Why?, 2001; contbr. articles to profl. jours. Rsch. fellow, Internat. Social Security Assn., 1992—93, Fulbright grantee, 1986. Mem.: ABA, Nat. Acad. Social Ins. Democrat. Jewish. Office: Vanderbilt Univ Law Sch 131 21st Ave S Nashville TN 37203-1181 Office Phone: 615-322-4901.

BLOCH, HENRY WOLLMAN, diversified financial services company executive; b. Kansas City, Mo., July 30, 1922; s. Leon Edwin and Hortense Bienenstok; m. Marion Ruth Helzberg, June 16, 1951; children: Robert, Thomas M., Mary Jo, Elizabeth Ann. BS, U. Mich., 1944; D of Bus. Adminstrn. (hon.), Avila Coll., Kansas City, Mo., 1977, U. Mo., Kansas City, 1989; LLD (hon.), N.H. Coll., 1983, William Jewell Coll., Liberty, Mo., 1990, Kansas City Art Inst., 1999. Ptnr. United Bus. Co., 1946-55; hon. chmn., past CEO H & R Block, Inc., Kansas City, 1955—, also dir. Bd. dirs. Commerce Bancshares, Inc., Kansas City, CompuServe, Inc., Valentine Radford Advt.; past chmn. Midwest Rsch. Inst. Past bd. dirs. Menorah Med. Ctr.; bd. dirs., past pres. Menorah Med. Ctr. Found.; former mem. pres.'s adv. coun. Kansas City Philharmonic Assn.; chmn., dir. H & R Block Found.; past pres. of trustees U. Kansas City, Nelson-Atkins Mus. Art, trustee, dir., past chmn. bus. coun.; past bd. dirs. Jewish Fedn. and Coun. Greater Kansas City; dir., past pres. Civic Coun. Greater Kansas City; gen. chmn. United Negro Colls. Fund, 1986; bd. dirs. St. Luke's Hosp. Found., Internat. Rels. Coun., Kansas City Cmty. Found.; former mem. bd. dirs. Coun. of Fellows of Nelson Gallery Found., Am. Jewish Com.; former mem. bd. govs. Kansas City Mus. History and Sci.; bd. dirs. Midwest Rsch. Inst., vice chmn.; bd. dirs. Kansas City Symphony, past dir.; bd. dirs. Greater Kansas City Community Found.; gen. chmn. Heart of Am. United Way Exec. Com., 1978; past met. chmn. Nat. Alliance Businessmen; former mem. bd. regents Rockhurst Coll.; former mem. bd. chancellor's assocs. U. Kans. at Lawrence; former mem. bd. dirs. Harry S. Truman Good Neighbor Award Found.; bd. dirs. Internat. Rels. Coun.; bd. dirs., v.p. Kansas City Area Health Planning Coun.; past pres. Found. for a Greater Kansas City; dir. Mid-Am. Coalition on Health Care, St; Luke's Found.; trustee Jr. Achievement of Mid-Am.; vice chmn. corp. fund Kennedy Ctr. 1st lt. USAAF, 1943-45. Decorated Air medal with 3 oak leaf clusters; named Mktg. Man of Yr. Sales and Mktg. Execs. Club, 1971, Chief Exec. Officer of Yr. for svc. industry Fin. World, 1976, Mainstreeter of Decade, 1988, Entrepreneur of Yr., 1986; recipient Disting. Exec. award Boy Scouts Am., 1977, Salesman of Yr. Kansas City Advt. Club, 1978, Civic Svc. award Hyman Brand Hebrew Acad., 1980, Golden Plate award Am. Acad. Achievement, 1980, Chancellor's medal U. Mo.-Kansas City, 1980, Pres.'s trophy Kansas City Jaycees, 1980, W.F. Yates medal for disting. svc. in civic affairs William Jewell Coll., 1981, bronze award for svc. industry Wall Street Transcript, 1981, Disting. Missourian award NCCJ, 1982, Lester A. Milgram Humanitarian award, 1983, Hall of Fame award Internat. Franchise Assn., 1983; named to Bus. Leader Hall of Fame Jr. Achievement, 1980; honoree Sales and Mktg. Execs. Internat. Acad. of Achievement, 1991. Mem. Greater Kansas City C. of C. (past pres.), C. of C. Greater Kansas City (Mr. Kansas City award 1978), Acad. Squires, Golden Key Nat. Honor Soc. (hon.), Oakwood Country Club, River Club, Carriage Club, Kansas City Country Club. Jewish. Office: H&R Block Inc 4400 Main St Kansas City MO 64111-1812

BLOCH, JULIA CHANG, adult education educator; b. Mar. 2, 1942; came to U.S., 1951, naturalized, 1962; d. Fu-yun and Eva (Yeh) Chang; m. Stuart Marshall Bloch, Dec. 21, 1968. BA, U. Calif., Berkley, 1964; MA, Harvard U., 1967, postgrad. in Mgmt., 1987; DHL (hon.), Northeastern U., Boston, 1986. Vol. Peace Corps, Sabah, Malaysia, 1964-66; tng. officer East Asia and Pacific region, Washington, 1967-68, evaluation officer, 1968-70; mem. minority staff U.S. Senate Select Com. on Nutrition and Human Needs, Washington, 1971-76, chief minority counsel, 1976-77; dep. dir. Office of African Affairs U.S. Internat. Comm. Agy., Washington, 1977-80; fellow Inst. Politics Harvard U., Cambridge, Mass., 1980; asst. adminstr. Bur. for Food For Peace and Voluntary Assistance AID, Washington, 1981-87; asst. adminstr. Bur. for Asia and Near East, 1987-88; assoc. U.S.-Japan Rels. Program, Ctr. for Internat. Affairs Harvard U., Cambridge, Mass., 1988-89; amb. Kingdom of Nepal, 1989-93; group exec., v.p. Bank Am., San Francisco, 1993-96; pres. The U.S.-Japan Found., 1996-98; dir. Am. West Airlines, 1994-98, Penn Mut. Life Ins., 1997; prof. Am. studies Beida U., Beijing, 1998; amb. in residence U. Md., 2000—. Pres. U.S.-China Edn. Trust; trustee Eisenhower Exch. Fellowship, 1995-97, Nat. Com. U.S. China Rels., 1998—; U.S. Senate rep. World Conf. on Internat. Women's Yr., Mex., 1975; advisor U.S. Del. to Food and Agr. orgn. Conf., Rome, 1975; rep. Am. Coun. Young Polit. Leaders, Peoples Republic China, 1977; charter mem. Sr. Exec. Svc., 1979; head U.S. del. Biennial Session World Food Programme, Rome, 1981-86, Devel. Assistance Com. Meeting on Non-Govtl. Orgns., Paris, 1985, Intergovtl. Group on Indonesia, The Hague, Netherlands, 1987, World Bank Consultative Group Meeting, Paris, 1987, mem. exec. women in govt., 1988-93, mem. coun. fgn. rels., 1991—; vis. prof. internat. rels. Peking U., 1998—; Starr sr. fellow U.S. China Rels. Fudan U., Shanghai, adj. prof. Author: A U.S.-Japan Aid Alliance, 1991; co-author: Chinese Home Cooking, 1986. Exec. bd. mem. Internat. Ctr. for Rsch. on Women, 1974-81; mem. adv. bd. Women's Campaign Fund, 1976-78; mem. nat. adv. coun. Experiment in Internat. Living, 1981-83; mem. U.S. Nat. Com. for Pacific Econ. Cooperation, 1984—, Nat. Presdl. Debate Forum, 1987-92; bd. trustees Atlantic counsel, 2004-; mem. presdl. adv. couns. Peace Corps, 1988-89; mem. com. to visit art mus. Harvard U., 1989; founder Women Fgn. Policy Group; mem. Am. Refugee Com. Bd., 1993; mem. Am. Himalayna Found. Bd., 1994; commr. Asian Art Mus., San Francisco, 1994; trustee, bus. leadership cir., 1994—; bd. trustees Coun. Am. Ambs., 2003-; chmn. bd. dirs. F.Y. Chang Found. Hon Fulbright fellow, 1996, Woodrow Wilson fellow, 2000-; recipient Hubert Humphrey award for internat. svc., 1979, Humanitarian Svc. award AID, 1987, Leader for Peace award Peace Corps, 1987, Asian Am. Leadership award, 1989, Brotherhood/Sisterhood award NCCJ, 1996; named Outstanding Woman of Color, Nat. Inst. for Women of Color, 1982, Woman of Distinction, Nat. Conf. for Coll. Women Student Leaders and Women of Achievement, 1987, Disting. Pub. Svc. award Nat. Assn. Profl. Asian Pacific Am. Women, 1989; Ford Found. Study fellow for internat. devel. Harvard U., 1966, Paul Harris award Rotary, 1992, Award of Honor Narcotic Enforcement Assn., 1992. Mem. Orgn. Cinese Am. Women (founder, chair 1977—, bd. dirs., Woman of Yr. 1987), Asia Soc. (pres. coun. 1989, trustee, 1994), Am. Studies Ctr. (vice-chair), Prytannean Honor Soc., Coun. Fgn. Rels., Mortar Bd., Cosmos Club. Republican. Avocations: ceramics, gourmet cooking, collecting art. Office Phone: 202-884-8533. E-mail: jcbloch@aol.com.

BLOCH, KURT JULIUS, physician; b. Germany, Oct. 17, 1929; s. Max and Mathilde B.; m. Margot Bendit, June 25, 1953; children: Kenneth D., Donald B. BS, CCNY, 1951; MD, NYU, 1955. Diplomate Am. Bd. Internal Medicine, Am. Bd. Allergy and Immunology, subspecialties Rheumatology, Diagnostic Lab. Immunology. Intern, asst. resident Bellevue Hosp., N.Y.C., 1955-57; resident in medicine Mass. Gen. Hosp., Boston, 1960-61, physician, 1974—2003, sr. physician, 2003—, chief clin. immunology and allergy units, 1976—2000, chief clin. immunology unit, dir. clin. immunology lab., 2000—02; instr. medicine Harvard Med. Sch., Boston, 1965-68, asst. prof., 1968-70, assoc. prof., 1970-74, prof., 1974—2003, prof. emeritus, 2003—. Sr. investigator Arthritis Found., 1964-69 Contbr. articles to profl. jours. With USPHS, 1957-60. Mem. Am. Soc. Clin. Investigation, Am. Assn. Physicians. Achievements include research on the biologic functions of antibodies, mechanisms of inflammation of the intestine, the immunobiology of sensorineural hearing loss, and the clinical significance of antibodies to heat shock proteins. Office: Mass Gen Hosp Cardiovascular Rsch Ctr Boston MA 02114 Business E-Mail: kbloch@partners.org.

BLOCH, LUCIENNE S., writer; b. Antwerp, Belgium, Dec. 11, 1937; d. Jacques and Jana (Beller) Schupf; m. Claude Bloch, Aug. 22, 1961; children: Philippe, Claire, Justine. BA, Wellesley Coll., 1959. Author: (novels) On the Great - Circle Route, 1979, Finders Keepers, 1992; columnist; author short stories. Fellow in fiction N.Y. Found. for the Arts, 1989, resident fellow Yaddo, Saratoga, N.Y., 1984; winner PEN Syndicated Fiction Contest, 1986. Mem. PEN Am. Ctr., Authors Guild.

BLOCH, PAUL, public relations executive; b. Bklyn., July 17, 1939; s. Edwin Lionel and Antoinette (Greenberg) B. B.B. Polit. Sci., UCLA, 1962. Publicist Rogers & Cowan, Beverly Hills, Calif., 1962-70, v.p., 1970-75, sr. v.p., ptnr., 1975-83, exec. v.p., sr. ptnr., 1983—, also vice chmn., co-chmn. Asst. Am. Cancer Soc., United Way, Am. Diabetes Assn., UNICEF, 1975—; adv. council Orange County Sheriff's Dept., 1980—. Served with U.S. Army, 1957. Recipient Les Mason award Publicity Guild Am., 1991. Mem. Publicists Guild of Am. (award for publicity campaign for Brian's Song 1972), Country Music Assn. Office: Rogers & Cowan 1888 Century Park E Fl 5 Los Angeles CA 90067-1702 *I wouldn't trade my life for the world.*

BLOCH, PETER CONRAD, economist, educator; b. N.Y.C., June 8, 1944; s. Konrad Emil and Lore (Teutsch) B.; m. Marianne Nieman; children: Benjamin, Emilie. AB, Harvard U., 1967; MA, Johns Hopkins U., 1969; PhD, U. Calif., Berkeley, 1974. Maitre asst. assoc. U. Dakar, Senegal, 1974-76; vis. assoc. prof. Fletcher Sch. of Law and Diplomacy, Tufts U., Medford, Mass., 1977-80; asst. prof. Grinnell (Iowa) Coll., 1980-83; sr. scientist Land Tenure Ctr., U. Wis., Madison, 1984—, vis. asst. prof. dept. econ., 1983-85, faculty assoc. dept. forest ecology, 1999—. Pres. Terra Inst., Ltd., Mt. Horeb, Wis., 1994-97; cons. Swedish Govt., Stockholm, 1989-98, U.S. Agy. Internat. Devel., Washington, 1975—, World Bank, Washington, 1985—. Contbr. articles to profl. publs. and chpts. to books. Grantee British Know How Fund, Lincoln Inst. Land Policy, U.S. Agy. Internat. Devel., World Bank. Mem. Assn. Recherches et Etudes sur le Foncier en Atrique. Avocations: gardening, travel. Home: 21 Foxboro Cir Madison WI 53717-1201 Office: U Wis Land Tenure Ctr 1357 University Ave Madison WI 53715-1054 E-mail: pcbloch@facstaff.wisc.edu.

BLOCH, RICHARD, physician; b. Hamburg, Germany, Aug. 5, 1948; s. Leon and Helena (Wozniak) B.; 1 child, Andrew R. BA, Ind. U., 1970, MD, 1973. Diplomate Am. Bd. Internal Medicine, Am. Bd. Internal Medicine Nephrology. Intern in internal medicine Indpls. U. Hosps., 1973-74, resident in internal medicine, 1974-76, clin. fellow in nephrology, 1976-77, rsch. fellow in nephrology, 1977-78; mem. Arnett Clin., Lafayette, Ind., 1978-87, Nephrology and Internal Medicine, Indpls., 1987-99. Med. dir. dialysis St. Elizabeth Hosp., Lafayette, 1979-87; med. dir. inpatient dialysis, Meth. Hosp., Indpls., 1994-2002. Patentee in field; contbr. articles to profl. jours. Mem. Am. Coll. Physicians, Am. Soc. Nephrology, Renal Physician Assn. Office: Nephrology and Internal Med #355 1801 Senate Blvd Ste 355 Indianapolis IN 46202-1296

BLOCH, RICHARD ISAAC, labor arbitrator; b. East Orange, N.J., June 15, 1943; s. Jacques Henry and Hannah (Levi) B.; m. Susan Low, July 11, 1966; children: Rebecca Low, Michael Low. AB, Dartmouth Coll., 1965; JD, U. Mich., 1968, MBA, 1974. Bar: Mich. 1969, D.C. bar 1975. Asso. firm Seyfarth, Shaw Fairweather & Geraldson, Chgo., 1968; lectr. U. Mich. Grad. Sch. Bus. Adminstrn., 1969-71; asst. prof. law U. Detroit, 1971-75; prin. Richard I. Bloch, P.C. (labor arbitrator), Washington, 1969—. Vis. prof. law Wayne State U., 1974, George Washington U., 1983; adj. prof. Am. U., 1978, Georgetown U. Law Ctr., 1989-90; chmn. fgn. svc. grievance bd. Dept. State, 1977-80; chief umpire United Mine Workers and Bituminous Coal Operators Assn., 1980-81; arbitrator Maj. League Baseball, 1983-85, Nat. Hockey League, Electric Boat Co., Metal Trades Coun., Nat. Football League; permanent arbitrator Alcoa and United Steelworkers Am. Author: Arbitration of Discipline Cases, 1979, Labor Agreement in Arbitration, 1983, Interest Arbitration, 1986; contbr. articles to profl. jours. Mem. Dartmouth Coll. Alumni Council, 1974-77. Mem. ABA, Mich. Bar Assn., D.C. Bar Assn., Indsl. Rels. Rsch. Assn., Nat. Acad. Arbitrators (bd. govs., pres.-elect 2001, pres. 2002-). Home and Office: 4335 Cathedral Ave NW Washington DC 20016-3560 Office Phone: 202-686-1140. E-mail: bloch@aol.com.

BLOCH, STUART MARSHALL, lawyer; b. Detroit, Nov. 5, 1942; s. A. Howard and Pauline Betty (Rappaport) B.; m. Julia Chang, Dec. 21, 1968. AB, U. Miami, 1964; LLB, Harvard U., 1967. Bar: Mich. 1968, D.C. 1968. Ptnr. Ingersoll and Bloch, Washington, 1972—; chmn. Real Estate Reporter, Ltd., Washington, 1978—. Author: A Periodical Guide to FIRREA, 1989, The Workout Game, 1987, 90, The Liability Game, 1988; editor State Digest of Land Sales, 1977—, D.C. Real Estate Reporter, 1979—; fellow Salzburg Seminar, 1988. Chmn. Land Devel. Inst., Washington, 1974—; trustee Arena Stage, 1983, Black Student Fund, Washington, 1983; major gifts chmn. Harvard U. Law Sch., 1983; 25th reunion chmn. U. Miami, 1989; pres. Internat. Found. for Timesharing, 1983; mem. corp. Northeastern U., Boston, 1983; mem. bd. individual vol. svc. Jewish Nat. Fund, 1994. Recipient spl. citation Am. Land Devel. Assn., 1980; citation D.C. City Coun., 1982, Jewish Nat. Fund Tree of Life award, 1991. Mem. ABA, D.C. Bar Assn., Mich. Bar Assn., Univ. Club (Washington). Office Phone: 202-744-6947.

BLOCH, SUSAN LOW, law educator; b. N.Y.C. d. Ernest and Ruth Low; m. Richard I. Bloch; children: Rebecca, Michael. BA in Math., Smith Coll., 1966; MA in Math., U. Mich., MA in Computer Sci., PhC, 1972, JD, 1975. Bar: D.C. 1975. Law clk. to chief judge U.S. Ct. Appeals, Washington, 1975-76; law clk. to assoc. justice Marshall U.S. Supreme Ct., Washington, 1976-77; assoc. Wilmer, Cutler & Pickering, Washington, 1978-82; prof. Georgetown U. Law Ctr., Washington, 1983—. Legal analyst for impeachment procs. CBS, 1998; impeachment expert U.S. Ho. of Reps. Jud. Com., 1998. Author: Supreme Court Politics: The Institution and Its Procedures, 1994; contbr. Constl. Commentary, Duke Law Jour., Mich. Law Rev., Am. U. Law Rev., Wis. Law Rev., Law and Contemporary Problems, Georgetown Law Rev., St. Louis U. Law Jour., ABA Jour., Supreme Ct. Preview, Voice of Am., Supreme Ct. Hist. Soc. Yearbook, 1987, Supreme Ct. Hist. Soc. Yearbook, 1992, Oxford Companion to the Supreme Ct. of the United States, 1992, Biology, Culture and Law, 1993. Active Common Cause, Women's Legal Def. Fund. Recipient Smith Coll. medal, 2005. Mem. ABA, Am. Bar Found., Am. Law Inst., D.C. Bar (Bicentennial of Constn., mem. ethics com., jud. evaluation com.), D.C. Cir. Judicial Conf. (prog. chair 1993, 96), U. Mich. Com. Visitors, 1982—, Inst. Pub. Representation (bd. dirs.), Order of Coif, Phi Beta Kappa, Sigma Xi. Home: 4335 Cathedral Ave NW Washington DC 20016-3560 Office: Georgetown U Law Ctr 600 New Jersey Ave NW Washington DC 20001-2075 Office Phone: 202-662-9063. Business E-Mail: bloch@law.georgetown.edu.

BLOCK, ALLAN JAMES, communications executive; b. Oct. 1, 1954; s. Paul Jr. and Marjorie (McNab) B. BA, U. Pa., 1977. Coord. electronic tech. planning Toledo Blade Co., 1981-83, dir. electronic planning, 1984-85; dir. mktg. Buckeye Cablevision Inc., Toledo, 1985-87; v.p. cablevision and TV Blade Communications, Inc., Toledo, 1987-88, exec. v.p., 1989; co-CEO Blade Comm., Inc., Toledo, 1989—; vice-chmn. bd. Block Comm., Inc. (formerly known as Blade Comm., Inc.), Toledo, 1990—2001, mng. dir., prin. exec. officer, 2002—04, chmn. bd., prin. exec. officer, 2005—. Bd. dirs. Toledo Blade Co., P.G. Pub. Co., Buckeye Cablevision Inc. Bd. dirs. C-SPAN, Med. Coll. Ohio, 1991-2000, Nat. Cable TV Coop., Inc., 2000-03, Am. Cable Assn., 2002—. Mem. Toledo Club, Met. Club (N.Y.C.), Penn Club (N.Y.C.), Downtown Assn. (N.Y.C.), Duquesne Club (Pitts.), Inverness Club. Home: 235 14th St Toledo OH 43624-1401 Office: Block Comm Inc 541 N Superior St Toledo OH 43660-1000 Office Phone: 419-724-6035. Business E-Mail: ABlock@blockcommunications.com.

BLOCK, ALVIN GILBERT, publishing executive; b. Moline, Ill., Sept. 15, 1946; s. Sylvan Emory Block and Pauline (Kutten) Salzman; m. Sarah Cannon Michael, June 17, 1977 (div. 1984); m. Ellen Marie Chapman, Jan. 19, 1992; children: Will Chapman Block, Thomas Chapman Block BA, Bradley U., 1968. Editl. asst. Playboy mag., Chgo., 1970; exec. Salzman & Co., Davenport, Iowa, 1971-74; editor Ketchum (Idaho) Tomorrow, 1975-77; reporter Idaho Statesman, Ketchum, 1978-80; freelance writer, Sacramento, 1980-82; mng. editor Calif. Jour., Sacramento, 1983-94, editor, columnist, 1995-2000, 2004—, editor-in-chief news and publs., 2000—03, pub., 2003. Commentator Sta. KXPR-FM, Sacramento, 1985—88; co-editor Calif. Polit. Almanac; editor Calif. Govt. and Politics Annual, 1995—; v.p., editor-in-chief State Net, 1996—2003; vis. scholar Inst. Govt. Studies, U. Calif., Calif., 2004—. Councilman City of Ketchum, 1979. With U.S. Army, 1969-74. Recipient award for column Idaho Newspaper Assn., 1975, Soc. Profl. Journalists, 1995. Avocations: baseball, military history, railroading, writing. Home: 1133 Marian Way Sacramento CA 95818-3718 Office Phone: 916-552-7001. E-mail: agb@californiajournal.org, AG_Block@sbcglobal.net.

BLOCK, AMANDA ROTH, artist; b. Louisville, Feb. 20, 1912; d. Albert Solomon and Helen (Bernheim) Roth; m. Gordon J. Wolfe, June 16, 1931 (div. 1947); 1 child, Joseph G. Wolf; m. Maurice Block, Jr., July 15, 1949. Student, Smith Coll., 1930-31, U. Cin., 1933, Art Acad. Cin., 1933-40; BFA, Ind. U.-Purdue U., Indpls., 1960. Instr. Herron Sch. Art, Ind. U. Purdue U., Indpls., 1969-73; instr. lithography Indpls. Art Ctr., 1974. Adv. bd. Indpls. Art League Found., 1979-81. One-woman shows, 1444 Gallery, Indpls., 1962, Sheldon Swope Art Gallery, Terre Haute, Ind., 1963, 73, Park Avenue Gallery, Indpls., 1964, Harriet Crane Gallery, Cin., 1965, Talbot Gallery, Indpls., 1967, Merida Gallery, Louisville, 1967, Herron Mus. Art, Indpls., 1969, Editions Ltd. Gallery, Indpls., 1972, 79, Franklin (Ind.) Coll., 1973, Tucson Mus. Sch., 1977, Indpls. Art League, 1992; two-woman shows, Jason Gallery, N.Y.C., 1964, Orange County Coll., Middletown, N.Y., 1964, Washington Gallery, Frankfort, Ind., 1975, Edits. Ltd. Gallery, Indpls., 1983; exhibited in group shows, Chgo. Art Inst., 1941, Butler Inst. Am. Art, Youngstown, Ohio, Burr Gallery, N.Y.C., Hanover Coll., Wabash, Ind., De Pauw U., Soc. Am. Graphic Artists AAA Gallery, Purdue U., Istan Gallery, Tokyo, Phila. Print Club, Pa. Acad. Fine Arts, 1969, Imprint Gallery, San Francisco, 1972, Van Straaten Gallery, Chgo., 1973, McNay Inst., San Antonio, 1972, Pratt Graphics, N.Y.C., 1976, Ind. State Mus., 1976, Indpls. Mus. Art, 1977, Tucson Mus. Art, 1978, internat. traveling exhbn., Soc. Am. Graphic Artists, 1974-75, traveling exhbn., 1977, 78; represented in permanent collections, Continental Ill. Bank, Chgo., De Pauw U., Ind. State Coll., Terre Haute, Ind., Med. Soc., Indpls., Sheldon Swope Art Gallery, Stevens Coll., Boston Public Library, USIA, Lafayette (Ind.) Art Center, Lippman Assos., architects, Indpls., J.B. Speed Mus., Louisville, IBM Bldg., Indpls., Phila Mus. Art, Bklyn. Mus., Cin. Art Mus., N.Y. Public Library, Columbua U. Gallery, N.Y.C., Biodynamics Inc., Indpls., Fidelity Bank, Carmel, Ind., Tuscon Mus. Art, Indpsl. Mus. Art, Indianapolis Art Ctr. Retrospective Print and Drawing Exhib., 1992. Recipient award Ben and Beatrice Goldstein Found., N.Y.C., 1971. Mem. Soc. Am. Graphic Artists. Jewish. E-mail: minblock@cs.com.

BLOCK, ARTHUR R., communications executive, lawyer; BS in Econs., BA, U. Pa., 1975; JD, U. Mich., 1978. Ptnr. Corp. Dept. Wolf, Block, Schorr and Solis-Cohen, 1978—89; atty. Comcast Corp., Phila., 1989—; v.p., sr. dep. gen. counsel Comcast Holdings, Phila., 1994—2000; gen. counsel Comcast Corp., 2000—, sr. v.p., 2002—, sec., 2002—. Bd. mgrs. Moore Coll. of Art & Design, Phila.; site bd. City Yr. Greater Phila. Office: Comcast Corp 1500 Market St Philadelphia PA 19102

BLOCK, BARBARA ANN, biology professor; b. Springfield, Mass., Apr. 25, 1958; d. Merrill and Myra (Winograd) B. BA, U. Vt., 1980; PhD, Duke U., 1986. Postdoctoral fellow U. Pa., Phila., 1986-88; asst. prof. organismal biology U. Chgo., 1988-93; asst. prof. biol. sci. Stanford U., 1993-97, assoc. prof., 1997—. Contbr. articles to profl. jours. Recipient Presdl. Young Investigator award NSF, 1989; MacArthur fellow, 1996, Pew Conservation fellow, 1997. Mem. AAAS, Am. Soc. Zoologists, Biophys. Soc. Democrat.

BLOCK, BILL, film company executive; Student, Columbia U. Talent agent Internat. Creative Mgmt., 1984—88, talent agent, head West Coast ops., 1992—97; pres. Artisan Entertainment, Santa Monica, Calif., 1997—2003; partner, COO prodn. group Initial Entertainment Group, 2004—. Founder InterTalent Agy., 1988 (merged with Internat. Creative Mgmt. 1992).

BLOCK, CARYN S., composer; b. NYC, Mar. 26, 1953; d. William E. and Phyllis F. Block; m. John S. Kalamon, July 5, 1992. MusB in composition, Manhattan Sch. of Music, 1978; MusM in composition, Juilliard Sch., 1983; MusD in composition, Peabody Conservatory of Johns Hopkins U., 1997. Music dir., flutist Encore Chamber Players, Phila., 1987—2001; lectr. in music Coll. General Studies U. Pa., 1986, 1998—99; tchg. asst. music theory Peabody Conservatory of Music, 1993—95; music hist. faculty West Chester U. Sch. of Music, 1999; composer various solo, orch., chamber, choral, vocal, electronic/computer, dance, film and theatre music. Recipient Alexander Gretchaninoff Composition prize, The Juilliard Sch., 1982, Alexander Gretchaninoff prize in composition, 1983, Ada Arens Morawetz award in composition, Peabody Conservatory of Music, 1995, Standards Composition awards, ASCAP, 2000—04; fellow, Peabody Conservatory, 1993—95; grantee, Meet the Composer, 1976, 2000. Home: 81 W Sproul Rd Springfield PA 19064 also: 5133 Craigs View Pipersville PA 18947 Personal E-mail: caryn.block@alum.julliard.edu.

BLOCK, DAVID L., solar engineering executive; b. Davenport, Iowa, July 10, 1939; married, 1961; 2 children. BSCE, U. Iowa, 1962; MS, Va. Polytechnic Inst., 1964, PhD in Engring. Mechanical, 1966. Engr. NASA Langley Rsch. Ctr., 1962-66; staff engr. Martin Marietta Corp., 1966-68; dir. Fla. Solar Energy Ctr., 1977—. Fla. rep. Southern Solar Energy Ctr., 1977—, Solar Energy Task Force Nat. Govt. Conf., 1977—; assoc. dean engring. Fla. Tech. U., 1968-77. Mem. Internat. Solar Energy Soc., Am. Soc. Testing & Materials, Nat. Soc. Profl. Engrs., Am. Soc. Engring. Edn. Achievements include research in solar air conditioning systems, energy policy, solar energy standards and certification and marketing of energy systems. Office: Fla Solar Energy Ctr 1679 Clearlake Rd Cocoa FL 32922-5703

BLOCK, DENNIS JEFFREY, lawyer; b. Bronx, N.Y., Sept. 1, 1942; s. Martin and Betty (Berger) B.; m. Lauren Elizabeth Troupin, Nov. 27, 1967; children: Robert, Tracy, Meredith. BA, U. Buffalo, 1964; LLB, Bklyn. Law Sch., 1967. Bar: N.Y. 1968, U.S. Dist. Ct. (ea. dist.) N.Y., U.S. Dist. Ct. (so. dist.) N.Y., U.S. Ct. Appeals (2d, 3d, 5th, 6th, 7th, 8th, 9th, 10th and 11th cirs.), U.S. Supreme Ct. Br. chief SEC, N.Y.C., 1967-72; assoc. Weil, Gotshal & Manges, L.L.P., N.Y.C., 1972-74, ptnr., 1974-98, Cadwalader, Wickersham & Taft, LLP, N.Y.C., 1998—. Co-author: The Business Judgment Rule: Fiduciary Duties of Corporate Directors and Officers, Law & Business, Inc., 1987, 5th edit., 1998; co-editor: The Corporate Counselor's Desk Book, 1982, 5th edit., 1999; contbr. articles to profl. jours. Chmn. major gifts lawyers div., United Jewish Appeal Fedn., 1987-89, chmn. lawyers div., 1989-91. Mem. ABA (coun. litigation sect., com. on corp. laws sect. bus. law), Assn. of Bar of City of N.Y., Am. Law Inst. Office: Cadwalader Wickersham & Taft LLP Ste 32-106 One World Finl Ctr New York NY 10281 Office Phone: 212-504-5555. Business E-Mail: dennis.block@cwt.com.

BLOCK, DIANA R., art gallery director; b. Dallas, Tex., Feb. 4, 1942; d. Russell Vivan Rogers Jr. and Helen Olivia (Bishop) Rogers; m. Richard Daniel Mauldin, June 24, 1985; children: Rembert Mauldin, Rebecca Mauldin, Olivia Mauldin, Chris Mauldin, Catherine Mauldin. BA, So. Meth. U., 1963. Dir. DW Gallery, Dallas, 1980—88, Unt Art Gallery, Denton, Tex., 1989—. Office: U N Tex PO Box 305100 Denton TX 76203-5100 Office Phone: 940-565-4005. Office Fax: 940-565-4717. E-mail: block@unt.edu.

BLOCK, ELISE R., psychiatrist; b. Phila. BA in Psychology, U. Pa., Phila., 1978; MD, Temple U., 1982. Diplomate Am. Bd. Psychiatry and Neurology. Resident in psychiatry UCLA-NPI, L.A., 1983—86, asst. clin. prof., 1986—; pvt. practice, psychiatry L.A., 1986—. Mem. faculty UCLA Divsn. Family Medicine, 1986—89. Mem.: So. Calif. Psychiat. Soc., Am. Psychiatric Assn., Phi Beta Kappa, Alpha Omega Alpha. Office: 12011 San Vicente Blvd Los Angeles CA 90049

BLOCK, EMIL NATHANIEL, JR., retired air force officer; b. Newark, Ohio, Oct. 3, 1930; s. Emil Nathaniel and Louise Jeanette (Palmer) B.; m. Marian Lou Davis, June 9, 1956; children: Eric, Emil Darin. BS, U.S. Naval Acad., 1956; MSE in Instrumentation, MSE in Aero. and Astronautical Engring, U. Mich., 1961; MS in Bus. Adminstrn, George Washington U., 1966. Commd. 2d lt. U.S. Air Force, 1956, advanced through grades to maj. gen., 1979; spl. asst. for B-1 matters, dep. chief staff for research and devel. Hdqrs. USAF, Washington, 1976-78; chief of staff mil. airlift command, dir. Air Force C-X task force, Scott AFB, Ill., 1978-80; dir. plans Hdqrs. USAF, Pentagon, Washington, 1980-81; pres. Blime, Inc., 1981—. Decorated D.S.M. (2), Legion of Merit (3), D.F.C., Bronze Star, Meritorious Service medal (2), Air medal (5); Jimmy Doolittle fellow, 1978 Mem. Air Force Assn. E-mail: blime@cox.net.

BLOCK, FRANCESCA LIA, writer; b. Hollywood, Calif., Dec. 3, 1962; d. Irving Alexander and Gilda Rona (Klein) B.; m. Chris Schuette; children: Jasmine Angelina Schuette, Samuel Alexander Schuette. BA in English Lit., U. Calif., Berkeley, 1986. Author: Weetzie Bat, 1989 (ALA Best Book award, 1989), Witch Baby, 1991 (Sch. Libr. Jour. Best Book award), Cherokee Bat and the Goat Guys, 1992 (ALA Best Book award, N.Y. Times Book Rev. Notable Book), Ecstasia, 1993, Missing Angel Juan, 1993 (ALA Best Book award, 1993), Primavera, 1994, The Hanged Man, 1994, Baby Be Bop, 1995 (Pub.'s Weekly Best Book award, 1995, ALA Best Book award, 1995), Girl Goddess # 9, 1996, Dangerous Angels, 1998 (L.A. Times Rev. Best Seller), I Was a Teenage Fairy, 1998; author: (with Hillary Carlip) Zine Scene, 1998, Violet and Claire, 1999 (L.A. Times Rev. Best Seller), The Rose and the Beast, 2000 (L.A. Times Rev. Best Seller, Pub.'s Weekly Best Book award, 2000), Nymph, 2000, Echo, 2002; author: Guarding the Moon, 2003 (L.A. Times Rev. Best Seller, 2003), Wasteland, 2003, Goat Girls, 2004, Beautiful Boys, 2004;: Necklace of Kisses, 2005, Psyche in a Dress, 2005, various translations into French, Italian, German, Japanese, Czech, Danish, Finnish and Norwegian. Recipient Margaret A. Edwards Lifetime Achievement award, ALA, 2005. Mem. Phi Beta Kappa. Democrat. Jewish. Office: c/o Lydia Wills Paradigm Agy New York NY 10019-5206

BLOCK, ISAAC EDWARD, professional society administrator; b. Phila., Aug. 8, 1924; s. Louis Emanuel and Stella Florence (Goodman) B.; m. Marline Beryl Lewin, June 16, 1957; children: Nancy Anne, Kathie Sue, Stephen Edward BS in Physics, Haverford Coll., 1944; MA in Math., Harvard U., 1947, PhD in Math., 1952. Math. cons. Philco Corp., Phila., 1951-54; mgr. computer ctr. Burroughs Corp., Phila., 1954-59; mgr. engring. computer ctr. Univac div. Sperry Rand Corp., Phila., 1959-61, mgr. applied math. systems Blue Bell, Pa., 1961-64; tech. advisor Auerbach Corp., Phila., 1964-65; mgr. Auerbach Info. Inc., Phila., 1965-67, v.p., gen. mgr., 1967-72; v.p., dir. product planning and devel. Auerbach Pub. Inc., Phila., 1972-76; mng. dir. Soc. for Indsl. and Applied Math., Phila., 1976-94, cons., 1994—. Sec./founder, 1951-53, chmn. pubs. com., 1954-63, v.p., 1964-74, council, 1957-65, trustee, 1971-75, chmn. bd. trustees, 1974-75; lectr. Computation Lab, Wayne State U., summers 1954-55 Served with USNR, 1944-45 Fellow AAAS; mem. SIAM, Am. Math. Soc., Phi Beta Kappa, Sigma Xi. Avocations: photography, music. Home: 7904 Cobden Rd Glenside PA 19038-7255 Personal E-mail: ieblock@hotmail.com.

BLOCK, JOHN ROBINSON, newspaper publisher; b. Toledo, Oct. 1, 1954; s. Paul Jr. and Marjorie Jane (McNab) B.; m. Susan Lynn Jones, July 20, 2002. BA, Yale U., 1977. Reporter AP, Miami, Fla., 1977-78, N.Y.C., 1978-80; Washington corr. The Toledo Blade, 1980-82, European corr. London, 1982-83, Sunday editor, 1983-85, asst. mng. editor, 1985-87, exec. editor, 1987-89; co-pub., editor-in-chief The Blade, Toledo, 1989—2001; co-pub. Pitts. Post-Gazette, 1989—2001, editor-in-chief, 1993—, pub., 2001—, The Black and Pitts Post-Gazette, 2001; v.p., bd. dirs. P.G. Pub. Co., Pitts. Exec. v.p., bd. dirs. Block comms., Inc., Toledo. Chmn. City Mgr.'s Hist. Preservation Com., Toledo, 1983-85; chmn. airport com. Toledo-Lucas County Port Authority, 1994-97. Mem. Am. Soc. Newspaper Editors, Soc. Profl. Journalists, Internat. Press Inst., Nat. Press Club (Washington), Yale Club (NYC), Belmont Country Club (Perrysburg, Ohio), Grolier Club (NYC), Duquesne Club (Pitts.), Athletic Club (Columbus, Ohio), Rockwell Springs Trout Club (Castalia, Ohio). Office: The Blade 541 N Superior St Toledo OH 43697-0921 also: Pitts Post-Gazette 34 Blvd Of The Allies Pittsburgh PA 15222-1204

BLOCK, JOSEPH G., lawyer; b. Johnstown, Pa. BA with high honors, U. Mich., 1969; JD, Harvard U., 1972. Bar: Pa. 1972, DC 1977, Calif. 1981. Trial atty. Defender Assn. of Phila., 1972—76; gen. counsel to minority Permanent Sub-com. on Investigations, Govtl. Affairs Com., US Senate, 1977—79, chief counsel to minority, 1979—81; atty. Law Offices of Barry Tarlow, LA, 1981—84; trial atty. Environ. Crimes Sect., Environment and Natural Resources Div., Dept. Justice, 1985—91, asst. chief, 1987—88, chief, 1988—91; atty. EPA, 1991; spl. asst. criminal enforcement Office of Enforcement, 1991; ptnr. Environ. and Corp. Defense Depts. Venable LLP, Washington, DC. Mem. Prin., Trade and Environ. Policy Adv. Com. US Trade Rep. and EPA, 1994—. Contbr. articles to profl. jours. Master: Edward Bennett Williams Inn of Ct.; mem.: ABA (vice chair Environ. Crimes Com. 1988—), Am. Law Inst. (co-chair Annual Conf. on Environ. Crimes). Office: Venable LLP 575 7th St NW Washington DC 20004 Office Phone: 202-344-4878. Office Fax: 202-344-8300. E-mail: jgblock@venable.com.

BLOCK, JULES RICHARD, retired psychology professor, academic administrator; b. N.Y.C., Nov. 23, 1930; s. Jules Irving and Elizabeth (Shinkle) B.; m. Elizabeth Ehrenstein, Dec. 21, 1952 (div. Nov. 1978); m. Patricia Clark, Feb. 29, 1980; children— Cheryl, Janet. BA, Hofstra Coll., 1952; PhD, N.Y. U., 1962. Lectr. Hofstra U., Hempstead, N.Y., 1956-60, instr., 1960-62, asst. prof., 1962-66, assoc. prof., 1966-70, prof., 1970-79, chmn. dept. psychology, 1968-78, exec. dir. research and resource devel., 1976-85, asst. to pres. for info. systems, 1985-87, v.p. planning and liaison, 1987—2001; ret., 2002. Rsch. asst. Human Resources Rsch. and Tng. Inst., Albertson, N.Y., 1957-59, rsch. assoc., 1959-61, dir. rsch., 1961-71; pres. Instrumental Psychol. Methods, Hempstead, Inst. for Rsch. and Evaluation, Hempstead; v.p. Y&B Assocs., Hempstead, 1983-98, pres., 1998—. Contbr. articles to profl. jours. Mem. Nassau County Youth Bd., 1968-70; Exec. dir. Initial Teaching Alphabet Found., 1965-72. Served with USNR, 1952-56. Recipient award for outstanding research in rehab. Nat. Rehab. Council, 1969 Mem. Am. Psychol. Assn. Home: 33 Primrose Ln Hempstead NY 11550-4633

BLOCK, KAREN JOYCE, lawyer; b. LA, Calif., May 8, 1960; d. Sam and Marian (Resnikoff) B. BA in Polit. Sci., Calif. State U., Northridge, 1983; JD, Southwestern U., 1986. Bar: Calif. 1986. Dep. dist. atty. City of Ventura, Calif., 1986—. Mem. ABA, Calif. Dist. Atty. Assn., Ventura County Barristers (v.p. 1988—, pres. 1989-90), Ventura County Bar Assn., Kiwanis (v.p. local chpt. 1988-89, pres. 1989-91). Avocations: biking, reading.

BLOCK, LAWRENCE, writer; b. Buffalo, June 24, 1938; s. Arthur Jerome and Lenore Harriet (Nathan) B.; m. Loretta Kallett, Mar. 10, 1960 (div. 1973); children: Amy Jo Block Reichel, Jill Diana, Alison Elspeth; m. Lynne Wood, Oct. 2, 1983. Student, Antioch Coll., 1955-59. Editor Scott Meredith Lit. Agy., N.Y.C., 1957-58; editor Whitman Pub. Co., Racine, Wis., 1964-66; free lance writer, 1957—. Pres., seminar leader Write for Your Life, N.Y.C. and Ft. Myers Beach, Fla., 1983-88; instr. Hofstra U., Hempstead, N.Y., 1981 Author: (novels) Mona, 1961, Death Pulls a Doublecross, 1962, The Girl With the Long Green Heart, 1965, The Thief Who Couldn't Sleep, 1966, The Cancelled Czech, 1966, Deadly Honeymoon, 1967, Tanner's Twelve Swingers, 1967, Two for Tanner, 1968, Tanner's Tiger, 1968, Here Comes A Hero, 1968, After the First Death, 1969, The Specialists, 1969, Such Men are Dangerous, 1969, Me Tanner, You Jane, 1970, No Score, 1970, Ronald Rabbit Is A Dirty Old Man, 1971, Chip Harrison Scores Again, 1971, Five Little Rich Girls, 1976, The Topless Tulip Caper, 1975, The Sins of the Fathers, 1976, In the Midst of Death, 1976, Time to Murder and Create, 1977, Burglars Can't be Choosers, 1977, The Burglar in the Closet, 1978, The Burglar Who Liked to Quote Kipling (Nero Wolfe award), 1979, Ariel, 1980, The Burglar Who Studied Spinoza, 1980, A Stab in the Dark, 1981, Eight Million Ways to Die, 1982, The Burglar Who Painted Like Mondrian, 1983, When the Sacred Ginmill Closes (Japanese Maltese Falcon award), 1986, Random Walk, 1988, Out on the Cutting Edge, 1989, A Ticket to the Boneyard, 1990, A Dance at the Slaughterhouse, 1991, A Walk Among the Tombstones, 1992, The Devil Knows You're Dead, 1993, The Burglar Who Traded Ted Williams, 1994 (German Marlowe award), A Long Line of Dead Men, 1994, The Burglar Who Thought He Was Bogart, 1995, Even the Wicket, 1997, The Burglar in the Library, 1997, Hit Man, 1998, Tanner on Ice, 1998, Everybody Dies, 1998, The Burglar in the Rye, 1999, Hit List, 2000, Hope to Die, 2001, Small Town, 2003, The Burglar on the Prowl, 2004, All the Flowers Are Dying, 2005; (nonfiction) Writing the Novel From Plot to Print, 1979, Telling Lies for Fun and Profit, 1981, Write for Your Life, 1985, Spider, Spin Me a Web, 1988; (with Delbert Ray Krause) Swiss Shooting Talers and Medals, 1965; (with Cheryl Morrison) Real Food Places, 1981; (with Harold King) Code of Arms, 1981, (with Ernie Bulow) After Hours, 1994; (short story collections) Sometimes They Bite (trophy 813 Societe of France), 1983, Like A Lamb to Slaughter, 1984, Some Days You Get The Bear, 1993, Ehrengraf for the Defense, 1994, One Night Stands, 1999, The Lost Cases of Ed London, 2001, Enough Rope, 2002, (anthologies) Death Cruise, 1999, Master's Choice, 1999, Opening Shots, 2000, Master's Choice 2, 2000, Speaking of Lust, 2000, Speaking of Greed, 2001, Opening Shots 2, 2002, Blood on Their Hands, 2003; contbg. editor Writer's Digest, 1976-90; contbr. stories to various mags. including Cosmopolitan, Playboy, GQ, Am. Heritage, mystery mags; exec. story cons. ESPN series, Tilt!, 2005-. Named Suspense Writer of Yr., Romantic Times, 1984, Grand Maitre du Roman Noir, Calibre 38, 1996. Fellow Flat Earth Soc. of Can. (U.S. plenipotentiary 1971—), Va. Ctr. for the Creative Arts; mem. Mystery Writers Am. (pres. 2000, Edgar Allan Poe award 1985, 92, 94, 98, Grand Master award 1994), Pvt. Eye Writers Am. (pres. 1984, Shamus award 1983, 85, 96, Life Achievement award 2002), Internat. Assn. Crime Writers, Internat. Narcotics Enforcement Officers Assn., Internat. Assn. for Study of Organized Crime, Crime Writers Can., Crime Writers Assn. (U.K., Cartier Diamond Dagger Life Achievement award 2004), Crime Writers of Norway. E-mail: LB@lawrenceblock.com.

BLOCK, LAWRENCE J., federal judge; b. NYC, Mar. 15, 1951; BA magna cum laude, N.Y. Univ., 1973; JD, John Marshall Law Sch., Chgo., 1981. Law clk. to Hon. Roger J. Miner U.S. Dist. Ct. (No. dist) N.Y., 1981—82; assoc. Skadden Arps Slate Meagher & Flom, N.Y., 1983—86; atty., Comml. Litigation br. US Dept. Justice, 1986, sr. atty. adv., Office Legal Policy & Policy Devel., 1987—90; dep. asst. gen. counsel legal policy US Dept. Energy, 1990—94; sr. counsel Senate Jud. Com., Washington, 1994—2002; judge US Ct. Fed. Claims, Washington, 2002—. Adj. prof. George Mason Univ. Sch. Law, 1990—91. Contbr. articles in law jour. Office: US Ct Fed Claims Suite 708 717 Madison Pl NW Washington DC 20005 Office Phone: 202-357-6508.

BLOCK, MELVIN AUGUST, surgeon, educator; b. Evansville, Ind., July 2, 1921; s. August William and Alma (Klutey) B.; m. Marcia Jean Jacobs, May 28, 1955; children: Deborah Ann, Christopher Reed. BS, Ind. U., 1942, MD, 1944; PhD, U. Minn., 1953. Intern Ind. U. Med. Center, 1945; resident Mayo Clinic, Rochester, Minn., 1948—54; chmn. dept. surgery Henry Ford Hosp., Detroit, 1975—79, Scripps Clinic Med. Group, La Jolla, Calif., 1980—87; clin. prof. surgery U. Mich. Med. Sch., 1970—80, U. Calif., San Diego Med. Sch., 1980—93. Contbr. articles to profl. jours. Served to capt. M.C. AUS, 1945-47. Fellow Royal Coll. Surgeons Can.; mem. ACS (past gov.), Am., Central, Western (past pres.) surg. assns., Am. Thyroid Assn., Am. Gastroenterology Assn., Soc. Surg. Alimentary Tract, Soc. Head and Neck Surgeons, Soc. Internationale de Chirurgie, AMA, Calif., San Diego County med. socs., Acad. Surg. Detroit (past pres.), Detroit Surg. Soc. (past pres.), Internat. Assn. Endocrine Surgeons, Am. Assn. Endocrine Surgeons, Sigma Xi, Alpha Omega Alpha. Home: 4575 Excalibur Way San Diego CA 92122-1513 Office: Scripps Clinic Med Group 10666 N Torrey Pines Rd La Jolla CA 92037-1027 *Time is our most valuable possession. It is limited qualitatively and quantitatively. This realization should be implied in most actions.*

BLOCK, MICHAEL KENT, economics and law educator, former public policy association executive, former government official, consultant; b. N.Y.C., Apr. 2, 1942; s. Philip and Roslyn (Klein) B.; m. Carole Arline Polansky, Aug. 30, 1964 (div.); children: Robert Justin, Tamara Nicole; m. Olga Vyborna, Dec. 1, 1996. AB, Stanford U., 1964, A.M., 1969, PhD, 1972. Research analyst Bank of Am., San Francisco, 1965-66; research assoc. Planning Assocs., San Francisco, 1966-67; asst. prof. econs. U. Santa Clara, 1969-72; asst. prof. econs. dept. ops. research and adminstrv. sci. Naval Postgrad. Sch., Monterey, Calif., 1972-74, assoc. prof., 1974-76; research fellow Hoover Instn., Stanford U., 1975-76, sr. research fellow, 1976-87; dir. Center for Econometric Studies of Justice System, 1977-81; ptnr. Block & Nold, Cons., Palo Alto, Calif., 1980-81; assoc. prof. mgmt., econs. and law U. Ariz., Tucson, 1982-85, prof. econs. and law, 1989—; mem. U.S. Sentencing Commn., Washington, 1985-89; exec. v.p. Cybernomics, Tucson, 1991—2002; pres. Goldwater Inst. for Pub. Policy, Phoenix, 1992—2002; sr. policy adviser State of Ariz. Gov. Symington, 1996-97. Chair Basis Sch. Bd., 1998—; mem. Ariz. Residential Utility Consumer Bd., 1995-96, chmn. Ariz. Constl. Def. Coun., 1994-97, Ariz. Juvenile Justice Adv. Coun., 1996-97; seminar dir. Econ. Devel. Inst./World Bank, 1992-95; cons. in field. Author: (with H.G. Demmert) Workbook and Programmed Guide to Economics, 1974, 77, 80, (with James M. Clabault) A Legal and Economic Analysis of Criminal Antitrust Indictments:, 1955-80; contbr. articles to profl. publs. Fellow NSF, 1965, Stanford U. Fellow Progress and Freedom Found.; mem. Am. Econ. Assn., Phi Beta Kappa. Office: U Ariz Econ Dept McClelland Hl Rm 401 Tucson AZ 85721-0001

BLOCK, NEAL JAY, lawyer; b. Chgo., Oct. 4, 1942; s. William Emmanual and Dorothy (Harrison) Block; m. Frances Keer, Apr. 19, 1970; children: Jessica, Andrew. BS, U. Ill., 1964; JD, U. Chgo., 1967. Bar: Ill. 1967, U.S. Dist. Ct. (no. dist.) Ill. 1967, U.S. Ct. Appeals (3d and 6th cirs.) 1968, U.S. Claims Ct. 1990, U.S. Ct. Appeals (fed. cir.) 1991. Atty., advisor U.S. Tax Ct., Washington, 1967-69; assoc. Baker & McKenzie, Chgo., 1969-74, ptnr., 1974—, client credit dir., 1989—2002. Adj. prof. law Kent Law Sch., Ill. Inst. Tech., Chgo., 1986—90. Mem.: AICPA (honorable mention award 1964), ABA, Ill. Soc. CPAs (silver medal 1964, Leading Ill. Atty. 1997), Ill. State Bar Assn., Chgo. Bar Assn. (chmn. fed. tax com. 1983—84). Office: Baker & McKenzie 1 Prudential Pla 130 E Randolph St Ste 3500 Chicago IL 60601-6342

BLOCK, NED, philosopher, educator; b. Chgo., Aug. 22, 1942; s. Eli William and Blanche (Rabinowitz) Block; m. Susan Carey, May 17, 1970; 1 child, Eliza. SB in Physics and Philosophy, MIT, 1964; postgrad., Oxford (Eng.) U., 1964-66; PhD, Harvard U., 1971. Asst. prof. philosophy MIT, Cambridge, Mass., 1971-77, assoc. prof., 1977-83, prof., 1983-96, chair dept. philosophy, 1989-95, chair press cognitive rev. bd., 1992—95; prof. NYU, N.Y.C., 1996—. Mem. faculty NEH Inst., 1981, 93; grant reviewer NSF, Can. Coun.; vis. rschr. Ecole Poly., Paris, 1995—96; vis. prof. Harvard U., 2002—03. Adv. editor: Contemporary Psychology; mem. editl. bd. Cognition, Cognition and Brain Theory, Cognitive Sci., mem. adv. editl. bd. Lang. and Cognitive Processes, Mind and Lang. Philos. Studies, mem. bd. editl. advisors Behavioral and Brain Scis.; contbr. articles to profl. jours. Named one of 10 Best, Philosphers' Ann., 1983, 1990, 1995, 2002; fellow, Old Dominion Found., 1973—74, Sloan Found., 1980—81; grantee, U.S. Nat. Com. Internat. Union History and Philosophy Sci., 1979, 1983, NEH, 1979—82, NSF, 1985—86, 1988—90, Am. Coun. Learned Socs., 1988—89; Postdoctoral fellow, NIH, 1970—71, Sr. fellow, Ctr. Study Lang. and Info., Stanford U., 1984—85, fellow, Am. Acad. Arts Scis., 2004—. Mem.: Assn. Sci. Study Consciousness (pres. 2003—). Home: 37 Washington Sq W New York NY 10011-9181 Office: NYU Dept Philosophy Main Bldg 100 Washington Sq E New York NY 10003-6688 E-mail: ned.block@nyu.edu.*

BLOCK, NORMAN LOUIS, oncologist, educator; b. NYC, Aug. 31, 1938; s. Abraham Harold and Rose (Bodatsky) B.; m. Carolyn Lee Peck, May 12, 1967; children: Joseph, David, Adam, Nathaniel, Jessica. BA, NYU, 1959, MD, 1963. Diplomate Am. Bd. Urology. Intern Baylor U. Med. Ctr., Dallas, 1963-64, resident in surgery, 1966—67; resident in urology NYU Med. Ctr., N.Y.C., 1967—71; fellow in urologic oncology Meml. Sloan Kettering Cancer Ctr., N.Y.C., NY, 1971-72; attending physician Miami VA Med. Ctr., 1972-96, Jackson Meml. Hosp., Fla., 1972—; chief urology VA Med. Ctr., 1975—85; assoc. prof. urology U. Miami, 1976-82, prof. urology, 1982—, prof. biomed. engring., 1982—, L. Austin Weeks prof., 1982—, prof. oncology, 1985—. Editl. reviewer 6 jours. Contbr. numerous articles to profl. jours., including Cancer Jour. Urology, Jour. Urology, Jour. Surg. Oncology. Capt. U.S. Army, 1964-66. Recipient numerous awards, fellowships, lectureships. Mem. AMA, ACS, AAAS, Internat. Urology Soc., Internat. Soc. for Artificial Organs, Am. Fertility Soc., Am. Urol. Assn. (Southeastern sect.), Am. Soc. for Artificial Internal Organs, Am. Assn. Lab. Animal Sci. (Fla. divsn.), Southeastern Cancer Rsch. Assn., Soc. Surg. Oncology, Soc. Univ. Urologists, Southeastern Coop. Oncology Group, Soc. Govt. Svc. Urologists, So. Med. Assn., Confedn. Am. Urologists, Soc. Urologic Oncology, Colombian Urol. Soc., Fla. Med. Assn., Fla. Urologic Assn., Greater Miami Urologic Soc., Dade County Med. Soc., Bellevue Urologic Alumni Assn. Republican. Jewish. Achievements include holder six patents; research in new treatment for prostate cancer; development of new diagnostic test for bladder cancer; applied a new model for prostate cancer in animals; development of an artificial bladder, ureter, urethra sphincter. Avocation: wildlife photography. Office: U Miami Sch Medicine Dept Urology M 814 PO Box 16960 Miami FL 33101-6960 Office Phone: 305-243-6518. Business E-Mail: nblock@med.miami.edu.

BLOCK, PHILIP DEE, III, retired investment company executive; b. Chgo., Feb. 14, 1937; married; 2 children. BS in Indsl. Adminstrn. with high honors, Yale U., 1958. Trainee and engr. Inland Steel Co., Chgo., 1958-60, raw materials coordinator, 1961-65, gen. mgr. purchases, 1966-72, gen. mgr. corp. planning, 1973-76, v.p. materials and services, 1977-79, v.p. purchases, 1980-85; sr. v.p. Capital Guardian Trust Co., Chgo., 1986—2004; ret., 2004. Trustee Chgo. Hist. Soc., Shedd Aquarium Soc.; aluimni trustee Latin Sch. of Chgo., 2005—; bd. dirs. Children's Meml. Hosp. With USAFR, 1959—64. Home: 1430 N Lake Shore Dr Chicago IL 60610-6682

BLOCK, RICHARD L., sociologist, criminologist, educator; b. Cin., July 4, 1944; s. Mandell Jerold Block and Marian Abrams; m. Carolyn Rebecca Britt, June 30, 1966; children: Daniel, Devora. Prof. sociology and criminology Loyola U., Chgo., 1969—. Cons. Nat. Inst. Justice, Washington, 1980—, Chgo. Police Dept., 1985—, UN. Vienna, Austria, 1993-94. Fulbright Hayes fellow, 1978, 85-86. Mem.: Homicide Rsch. Working Group (founder), Phi Beta Kappa. Avocations: canoeing, photography. Office: Loyola U Chgo Dept Sociology 6525 N Sheridan Rd Chicago IL 60626 Office Phone: 773-508-3454. E-mail: rblock@luc.edu.

BLOCK, ROBERT CHARLES, nuclear engineering educator; b. Newark, Feb. 11, 1929; s. George and Sue (Ehrenkranz) B.; m. Rita Adler, June 28, 1952; children: Keith, Robin. BSEE, Newark Coll. Engring., 1950; MA in Physics, Columbia U., 1953; PhD in Nuc. Physics, Duke U., 1956. Elec. engr. Nat. Union Radio Corp., West Orange, NJ, 1950-51, Bendix Aviation Co., Teterboro, NJ, 1951; physicist Oak Ridge Nat. Lab., 1955-66; prof. nuc. engring. and sci. Rensselaer Poly. Inst., 1966-96, head dept. nuc. engring. and engring. physics, 1987-93, assoc. dean engring. for acad. and student affairs, 1993-96, prof. emeritus, 1997—; founder, v.p., treas. Becker, Block & Harris Inc., 1981-92. Vis. scientist Atomic Energy Rsch. Establishment, Harwell, Eng., 1962-63, Am. Inst. Physics, 1961-67; vis. prof. Kyoto (Japan) U., 1973-74; vis. physicist Brookhaven Nat. Lab., 1975, mem. vis. com. nuc. energy dept., 1982-86; cons. GE, 1968-79; cons., mem. nuc. cross sect. adv. com. AEC, 1969-72; mem. U.S. Nuc. Data Com., 1972-74, Cross Sect. Evaluation and Working Group (exec. com. 1974-2003), NRC panel on low and medium energy neutrons, 1977; dir. Gaerttner Linac Lab., 1976—; vis. faculty Sandia Nat. Lab., 1986; mem. adv. com. West Point Mil. Acad., 2004—; mem. nuc. program adv. com. Los Alamos Nat. Lab., 2004—; mem. faculty senate Rensselaer Polytech. Inst., 2003-2005. Co-author chpt. in books. Recipient Glenn Murphy award Am. Soc. Engring. Edn., 1991,

William H. Wiley Disting. Faculty award Rensselaer Poly. Inst., 1995; Japanese Ministry Edn. rsch. grantee, 1973-74. Fellow Am. Nuc.r Soc.; mem. AAAS, AAUP, IEEE, Am. Phys. Soc., Sigma Xi, Sigma Pi Sigma, Phi Beta Tau, Tau Beta Pi. Achievements include research on neutron physics, radiation effects in electronics, and radiation applications. Home: 114 3rd St Troy NY 12180 Office: Rensselaer Poly Inst Gaerttner LINAC Lab 110 8th St Troy NY 12180-3590 Office Phone: 518-276-6404. Business E-Mail: blockr@rpi.edu.

BLOCK, STANLEY HOYT, pediatrician, allergist; b. N.Y.C., Oct. 28, 1943; s. Julius and Zilla Augustus (Freidman) B. BA, U. Chgo., 1963; MD, Yale U., 1966. Diplomate Am. Bd. Pediatrics, Am. Bd. Allergy and Immunology. Intern Children's Hosp. of Phila., 1966-67; resident Babies Hosp., Columbia Presbyn. Med. Ctr., N.Y.C., 1967-69; pediatrician, allergist pvt. practice Lynn and Lowell, 1971-77; med. dir. Providence (R.I.) Cmty. Health Ctrs., Inc., 1977—. Major U.S. Army, 1969-71. Recipient Tchg. award in pediatrics R.I. Hosp. House Officers Assn., 1982, Dr. Charles L. Hill award for Pub. Svc., R.I. Med. Soc., 1995, Cmty. Partnership award Brown U. Howard R. Swearer Ctr., 1999, Disting. Tchr. award Brown U., 2000, Bert Jaffe award, R.I. Pub. Health Assn., 2002. Fellow Am. Acad. Pediatrics, Am. Acad. Allergy, Asthma and Immunology, R.I. Soc. of Allergy (former pres., sec.); mem. R.I. Med. Soc. Avocations: hiking, cross country skiing. Office: Providence Cmty Health Ctrs Inc 375 Allens Ave Providence RI 02905-5010 Business E-Mail: sblockmd@providencechc.org.

BLOCK, WILLIAM K., JR., media executive; b. New Haven, Nov. 28, 1944; s. William and Maxine (Horton) B.; m. Carol Pauline Zurheide, Aug. 1, 1970; children: Diana, Nancy, Katherine. BA, Trinity Coll., Hartford, Conn., 1967; JD, Washington and Lee U., 1972. Staff mem. Red Bank (N.J.) Register and Toledo Blade, 1972-77; advtg. mgr. Red Bank (N.J.) Register, Shrewsbury, NJ, 1977-79, sales mgr., 1979-80, pub., 1980-82; dir. ops. Toledo Blade Co., 1983-84, v.p. ops., 1984-86, v.p., gen. mgr., 1986-87, pres., 1987—, co-pub., 1990—, Pitts. Post Gazette, 1990—; v.p. Block Com., Inc., Toledo, 1987-88, pres., 1989—2001, chmn., 2002—. V.p. Toledo Sesquicentennial Commn., 1986-87; pres. Inland Press Assn., 1998-99; bd. dirs. Toledo Symphony, St. Luke's Hosp., Ohio Hist. Soc.; pres. Read for Literacy, Inc., 1989-2001; campaign chmn. United Way of Greater Toledo, 2003. With U.S. Army, Vietnam, 1968-70. Mem. Toledo Country Club, Toledo Club. Avocations: reading, travel, fishing. Office: Block Communications Inc 541 N Superior St Toledo OH 43660-0001

BLOCK, WILLIAM KENNETH, lawyer; b. N.Y.C., Oct. 23, 1950; s. Louis and Catherine Veronica (Kerr) B. BA, Colgate U., 1973; JD, Union U., Albany, N.Y., 1976. Bar: N.Y. 1977. Gen. counsel N.Y.C. Tax Commn., 1978-81; asst. commn. fin. N.Y.C. Dept. Fin., 1981-84, dep. commr. fin., 1984-89; assoc. Schwartz, Weiss, Steckler & Hoffman, P.C., N.Y.C., 1989-91; pvt. practice, William K. Block, P.C., N.Y.C., 1992—. Adj. lectr. real estate NYU, 1992—. Contbr. articles to profl. jours. Mem. ABA, Internat. Assn. Assessing Officers (chmn. met. jurisdiction coun. 1987-88, presdl. citation 1986, McCareen award 1988), N.Y. State Assessors Assn., N.Y. State Bar Assn., New York County Bar Assn. (com. on City of N.Y., real property com., govt. counsel com.), Real Estate Tax Rev. Bar Assn. (dir. 1995—), Assn. Bar City of N.Y. (com. on tax certiorari), Real Estate Tax Bd. N.Y. (com. on taxation). Democrat. Roman Catholic. Home: 115 E 34th St Apt 20K New York NY 10016-4631 Office: 295 Madison Ave Fl 38 New York NY 10017-6304 E-mail: Williamkblock@aol.com.

BLOCK, ZENAS, retired management consultant, educator; b. NYC, Dec. 7, 1916; s. Joshua and Celia (Kaplow) B.; m. Lillian Bialek, June 12, 1938 (dec. 1985); children: Richard, Karen Block Chase Graubard, Margaret Block Walker; m. Janet Andre, Aug. 13, 1988. BS, CCNY, 1938; postgrad., Bklyn. Poly. Inst., 1939-41. Chemist Clairol Inc., N.Y.C., 1938-39; chief chemist Am. Dietaids Co., Yonkers, N.Y., 1938-48; dir. labs. DCA Food Industries, N.Y.C., 1948-55, v.p. rsch., 1955-60, pres. bakery divsn., 1960-64, group v.p., 1964-71, exec. v.p., 1971-77, vice chmn. bd., 1977-79, also bd. dirs. Chmn. bd. dirs. Nisshin DCA Foods Inc., Tokyo, 1975-79, DCA Industries Ltd., Eng., 1976-79; founder, pres. Haystack Cable Vision Inc., Lakeville, Conn., 1978-80, v.p. and treas., 1980-82; adj. prof. Grad. Sch. Bus. Adminstrn., U. Conn., 1979-81; clin. prof. NYU, 1984-94, adj. prof. entrepreneurship grad. divsn. Stern Schs. Bus., NYU, 1995-2001, entrepreneur-in-residence Stern Sch. Bus., 1999-2000, founder, assoc. dir. Ctr. for Entrepreneurial Studies, 1984-89; adj. prof. mgmt. Lally Sch. Mgmt., Rensselaer Poly. Inst., 1991-92, 97-98, vis. prof., 1996-97, curriculum cons., 1997-99; founder Salisbury Sch. Ednl. Enrichment Fund, 2001— Author: It's All on the Label, 1981; (with I.C. MacMillan) Corporate Venturing: Creating New Businesses Within the Firm, 1993; mem. editl. bd. Jour. Bus. Venturing; contbr. articles to acad. and profl. jours.; patentee food processing field. Bd. dirs. N.Y.C. Mission Soc., 1983-87, Salisbury Family Svcs., 1983-87; trustee Salisbury Assoc., 1992-95; mem. bd. fin. Town of Salisbury, 1996—; mem. bd. govs. Sharon Hosp., 2002—. Home and Office: PO Box 530 Salisbury CT 06068-0530

BLODGETT, FORREST CLINTON, economics professor; b. Oregon City, Oreg., Oct. 6, 1927; s. Clinton Alexander and Mabel (Wells) B.; m. Beverley Janice Buchholz, Dec. 21, 1946 (dec. Dec. 2000); children: Cherine Eiline Klein, Candis Melis, Clinton George; m. Ilene E. Jensen Anderson, Jan. 12, 2002. BS, U. Omaha, 1961; MA, U. Mo., 1969; PhD, Portland State U., 1979. Joined C.E. U.S. Army, 1946, commd. 2d lt., 1946, advanced through grades to lt. col., 1965, ret., 1968, engring. assignments, 1947-49, 1950-53, 1955-56, 1958-60, 1963, staff engr. 2d Army Air Def. Region Richards-Gebaur AFB, Mo., 1964-66; base engr. Def. Atomic Support Agy., Sandia Base, N.Mex., 1966-68; bus. mgr., trustee, asst. prof. econs. Linfield Coll., McMinnville, Oreg., 1968-73, assoc. prof., 1973-83, prof., 1983-90, emeritus prof. econs., 1990—; pres. Blodgett Enterprises, Inc., 1983-85; founder, dir. Valley Community Bank, 1980-86, vice chmn. bd. dirs., 1985-86. Commr., Housing Authority of Yamhill County (Oreg.), chmn., 1980-83; mem. Yamhill County Econ. Devel. Com., 1978-83; bd. dirs. Yamhill County Found., 1983-91, Oreg. Internat. Coun., 1995—. Decorated Army Commendation medal with oak leaf cluster; recipient Joint Service Commendation medal, Dept. of Def. Mem. Soc. Am. Mil. Engrs. (pres. Albuquerque post 1968), Am. Econ. Assn., Nat. Ret. Officers Assn., Res. Officers Assn. (pres. Marion chpt. 1976), SAR (pres. Oreg. soc. 1985-86, v.p. gen. Nat. Soc. 1991-93), Pi Sigma Epsilon, Pi Gamma Mu, Omicron Delta Epsilon (Pacific NW regional dir. 1978-88), Rotary (pres. McMinnville 1983-84). Republican. Episcopalian. Home: 1153 NE Multnomah Dr Fairview OR 97024-3783

BLODGETT, FRANK CALEB, retired food company executive; b. Janesville, Wis., Apr. 22, 1927; s. Frank Caleb Pickard and Dorothy (Korst) B.; m. Jean Ellen Fountain, June 23, 1951; children: Caleb J., Barbara F., David K. Grad., Beloit Coll., 1950; postgrad., Advanced Mgmt. Program, Harvard U., 1969. 1st v.p., dir. Frank H. Blodgett Inc., Janesville, 1947-61, pres., dir., 1961-62; with Gen. Mills Inc., Mpls., 1961-92, v.p., dir. mktg., 1967-69, gen. mgr., v.p., 1969-73, group v.p., 1973-76, exec. v.p., 1976-80, vice chmn., 1981-92, chief fin. and adminstrv. officer, 1985-92, dir., 1980-92; ret., 1992. Bd. dirs. Medtronic, Inc., Reliastar Fin. Corp. and subs., Northwestern Nat. Life Ins. Co., HealthSpan Health Sys. Corp.; dir. Waldorf Corp., 1993—. Trustee Gen. Mills Found., 1980-92, Washburn Child Guidance Ctr., 1972-75, Beloit Coll., 1976—, Nutrition Found., 1980-84; bd. dirs. Cereal Inst., 1970-76, chmn., 1973-74; bd. dirs. Abbott Northwestern Hosp. With USN, 1944-46, PTO. Recipient Disting. Svc. citation Beloit Coll., 1990. Mem. Millers Nat. Fedn., Young Millers Orgn. (past pres.), U.S. C. of C. (bd. dirs. 1982-88), Greater Mpls. C. of C. (bd. dirs. 1975-76), Phi Kappa Psi (trustee alumni bd. Beloit 1961-62), Phi Eta Sigma. Home: 688 Hillside Dr Wayzata MN 55391-9643

BLODGETT, HARRIET, language educator; b. N.Y.C., Sept. 4, 1932; d. Morris and Fannie (Cohen) Horowitz; m. William Edward Blodgett, Sept. 4, 1955; 1 child, Bruce. BA, Queens Coll., 1954; MA, U. Chgo., 1956; PhD, U. Calif., Davis, 1968. Lectr. in English and comparative lit. U. Calif., Davis, 1973-85, 86-87, lectr. in English Irvine, 1985-86; lectr. in English, humanities and women's studies Calif. State U., Sacramento, 1982-87; lectr. Calif. State U. Stanislaus, Turlock, 1989-92, asst. prof., then assoc. prof., 1992-98, prof., 1998—2005, prof. emerita, 2005. Lectr. Stanford U., U. Calif. Santa Cruz, 1988; vis. scholar Inst. for Rsch. on Women and Gender, Stanford U., 1983, affil., 1984-92. Author: Patterns of Reality: Elizabeth Bowen's Novels, 1975, Centuries of Female Days: Englishwomen's Private Diaries, 1988; editor, compiler Capacious Hold-All: An Anthology, 1991; essayist, article writer, contbr. South-Atlantic Quar., Critique, N.Y. Times Book Rev., Internat. Fiction Rev., 19th-Century Prose, James Joyce Quar., others. Mem. Phi Beta Kappa, Phi Kappa Phi. Avocations: painting, gardening, reading. Home: 781 Mulberry Ln Davis CA 95616-3430 Office: Calif State U Stanislaus English Dept 801 W Monte Vista Ave Turlock CA 95382-0256

BLODGETT, TODD ALAN, publishing executive, marketing professional, consultant; b. Iowa City, Sept. 10, 1960; s. Gary Burl and Sandy Jean (Hodgson) B.; m. Linda Marie Reuber. BA in Journalism, Drake U., 1983. Fin. dir. Senator Roger W. Jepsen Re-election Com., Des Moines, 1983-84; staff asst. Reagan-Bush Inaugural Com., Inc., Washington, 1984-85; editorial asst. White House Staff News Summary, Washington, 1985-86; acct. exec. J.L. Whitehead & Assoc., Washington, 1986-87; domestic policy advisor Bush-Quayle '88 Com., Washington, 1987-88; sr. policy advisor analyst Rep. Nat. Com., Washington, 1989-90. Campaign advisor Blodgett for Iowa Legislature campaign, Mason City, Iowa, 1992-98, also re-election advisor; CEO Donor List Inc. Contbr. editor American Conservative, 1991—; assoc. pub. Slick Times Mag., 1993-96; exec. editor Firearms & Preparedness Mag., 1996-98; contbr. articles to popular mags.; regularly nterviewed on Am. politics on BBC. Mem. The Conservative Network, Washington, 1985—; sustaining mem. Rep. Ctrl. Com. of Iowa, Des Moines, 1983; mem. Lincoln Club of Iowa, Des Moines, 1988—. Mem. NRA (life), Ducks Unltd., Reagan Appointees Alumni Assn. (mem.), Kennedy-Warren Residents Assn. (pres. 1989-92), Univ. Club of Washington, D.C., Sigma Alpha Epsilon. Republican. Presbyterian. Avocations: hunting, snow and water skiing, coin collecting/numismatics, gun collecting, skeet shooting. Office: 8239 The Midway Annandale VA 22003-3716 Fax: (202) 319-9867.

BLODGETT, WARREN TERRELL, public affairs educator; b. Ranger, Tex., Sept. 15, 1923; s. William Serle Sr. and Alice Louise (Furman) B.; m. Dorothy Jean Chapin, Mar. 7, 1946; children: Robert Harold, William Arthur, Katherine Ann. BA, Baylor U., 1943; MS Pub. Adminstrn., Syracuse U., 1947. Research assoc. U. Tex., Austin, 1947-50, assoc. dir. policy rsch inst., 1982-90, Mike Hogg prof. urban mgmt., 1982-95, Mike Hogg prof. emeritus in urban mgmt., 1995—; personnel dir. City of Austin, 1950-52, adminstrv. asst. to city mgr., 1952-55, asst. city mgr., 1955-60; city mgr. City of Waco, Tex., 1960-63, City of Garland, Tex., 1963-64; adminstrv. asst. to gov. State of Tex., Austin, 1964-69; prin. in charge govt. cons. Peat, Marwick and Mitchell, Austin, 1969-82. Cons. Tex. Dept. Water Resources, Austin, 1984-86, Legis. Audit Com., Austin, 1984-85; Tex. Com. Economy and Efficiency in Govt., Austin, 1985-87, Tex. Office of Speaker, Austin, 1985-87. Chmn. bd. Tex. Mcpl. Retirement System, 1961-62. Served to 1st lt. U.S. Army, 1943-46. Mem. Nat. Acad. Pub. Adminstrn., Internat. City Mgmt. Assn. (fund for profession 1986-89, chmn. Found. 1980-84), Internat. City-County Mgmt. Assn. ((Disting. Svc. award 1993), Nat. Civic League (hon. life dir. 1989, chmn. 1986-87, vice chmn. 1987-88), Austin Area Urban League (treas. 1985-87). Democrat. Mem. Christian Ch. Avocation: tennis. Home and Office: 1801 Lavaca St Austin TX 78701-1341 Office Phone: 512-474-7612. Personal E-mail: blodgett@mail.utexas.edu.

BLOEDE, VICTOR CARL, lawyer, consultant, director; b. Woodwardville, Md., July 17, 1917; s. Carl Schon and Eleanor (Eck) B.; m. Ellen Louise Miller, May 9, 1947; children: Karl Abbott, Pamela Elena. AB, Dartmouth Coll., 1940; JD cum laude, U. Md., Balt., 1950; LLM in Pub. Law, Georgetown U., 1967. Bar: Md. 1950, Fed. Hawaii 1958, U.S. Supreme Ct. 1971. Pvt. practice, Balt., 1950-64; mem. Goldman & Bloede, Balt., 1959-64; counsel Seven-Up Bottling Co., Balt., 1958-64; dep. atty. gen. Pacific Trust Ter., Honolulu, 1952-53; asst. solicitor for ters. Office of Solicitor, U.S. Dept. Interior, Washington, 1953-54; atty. U.S. Justice, Honolulu, 1955-58; assoc. gen. counsel Dept. Navy, Washington, 1960-61, 63-64; spl. legal cons. Md. Legislature, Legis. Coun., 1963-64, 66-67; assoc. prof. U. Hawaii, 1961-63, dir. property mgmt., 1964-67; house counsel, dir. contracts and grants U. Hawaii Sys., 1967-82; house counsel U. Hawaii Rsch. Corp., 1970-82; legal counsel Law of Sea Inst., 1978-82; legal cons. Rsch. Corp. and grad. rsch. divsn. U. Hawaii, 1982—92; spl. legal cons. 1st Unitarian Ch. Honolulu, 1992—. Spl. counsel to Holifield Congl. Commn. on Govt. Procurement, 1970—73. Author: Hawaii Legislative Manual, 1962, Maori Affairs, New Zealand, 1964, Oceanographic Research Vessel Operations, and Liabilities, 1972, Hawaiian Archipelago, Legal Effects of a 200 Mile Territorial Sea, 1973, Copyright-Guidelines to the 1976 Act, 1977, Forms Manual, Inventions: Policy, Law and Procedure, 1982; writer, contbr. Coll. Law Digest and other publs. on legis. and pub. law. Mem. Gov.'s Task Force Hawaii and The Sea, 1969, Citizens Housing Com. Balt., 1952-64; bd. govs. Balt. Cmty. YMCA, 1954-64; bd. dirs. U. Hawaii Press, 1964-66, Coll. Housing Found., 1968-80; apptd. to internat. rev. commn. Can.-France Hawaii Telescope Corp., 1973-82, chmn., 1973, 82; co-founder, incorporator First Unitarian Ch. Honolulu. Served to lt. comdr. USNR, 1942-45, PTO. Grantee ocean law studies, NSF and NOAA, 1970—80. Mem.: ABA, Fed. Bar Assn., Am. Soc. Internat. Law, Nat. Assn. Univ. Attys. (founder & 1st chmn. patents & copyrights sect. 1974—76), Balt. Bar Assn. Home: 635 Onaha St Honolulu HI 96816-4918

BLOEDEL, JEANNE HELEN, sign language educator, artist; b. Coos Bay, Oreg., Apr. 29, 1956; d. Paul Richard and Helen Alvina Bloedel. AA, Seattle Ctrl. CC, 1976; BS, Western Oreg. U., Monmouth, 1980, MS, 1982. Tchr. continuing certification. Mem. Am. Sign Lang. Adv. Bd., Auburn, Wash., 1994. Lutheran. Avocations: graphic composition, designing, sewing. Office Phone: 253-931-4880. Business E-Mail: jbloedel@auburn.wednet.edu.

BLOEMBERGEN, NICOLAAS, physicist, researcher; b. Dordrecht, Netherlands, Mar. 11, 1920; arrived in U.S., 1952, naturalized, 1958; s. Auke and Sophia M. (Quint) Bloembergen; m. Huberta D. Brink, June 26, 1950; children: Antonia, Brink, Juliana. BA, Utrecht U., 1941, MA, 1943; PhD, Leiden U., 1948; MA (hon.), Harvard U., 1951, LHD (hon.), 2000; DSc (hon.), Laval U., 1987, U. Conn., 1988, U. Hartford, 1991, Moscow State U., 1997; LHD (hon.), U. Mass., Lowell, 1994, U. Ctrl. Fla., 1996, N.C. State U., 1998. Tchg. asst. Utrecht U., 1942—45; rsch. fellow Leiden U., 1948; mem. Soc. Fellows Harvard U., 1949—51, assoc. prof., 1951—57, Gordon McKay prof. applied physics, 1957—, Rumford prof. physics, 1974, Gerhard Gade univ. prof., 1980, prof. emeritus, 1990; prof. optics U. Ariz., 2001—. Vis. prof. U. Paris, 1957, U. Calif., 1965, Coll. de France, Paris, 1980, U. Ariz., 2001—; Lorentz guest prof. U. Leiden, 1973; Raman vis. prof., Bangalore, India, 79; Fairchild Disting. scholar Calif. Inst. Tech., 1984; hon. prof. Fudan U., Shanghai; Disting. vis. prof. CREOL U. Ctrl. Fla., 1995. Author: Nuclear Magnetic Relaxation, 1948, Nonlinear Optics, 1965, Enconters in Magnetic Resonance, 1996, Encounters in Nonlinear Optics, 1996; contbr. articles to profl. jours. Recipient Stuart Ballantine medal, Franklin Inst., 1961, Half Moon trophy, Netherlands Club N.Y., 1972, Nat. Medal of Sci., 1975, Lorentz medal, Royal Dutch Acad., 1978, Frederic Ives medal, Optical Soc. Am., 1979, von Humboldt sr. scientist award, Munich, 1980, Nobel prize in Physics, 1981, Dirac medal, U. New South Wales, Australia, 1983, Medal of Honor, Inst. Elec. and Electronic Engrs., 1983, Von Humboldt Sr. Scientist award, 1987, von Humboldt medal, Munich, 1989, Byvoet medal, U. Utrecht, 2001, Russell Varian prize, Euromar, 2005; fellow Guggenheim, 1957. Fellow: IEEE (Morris Liebmann award 1959), Am. Acad. Arts and Scis., Am. Phys. Soc. (Buckley prize for solid state physics 1958); mem.: NAE, Norwegian Soc. Scis. and Letters (fgn.), Paris Acad. Scis. (fgn. assoc.), Koninklyke Nederlandse Akademie von Wetenschappen (corr.), Indian Acad. Scis. (hon.), Optical Soc. Am. (hon.), Deutsche Akademie der Naturforscher Leopoldina, Am. Philos. Soc., Nat. Royal Dutch Acads. Scis. Office: Optical Scis Ctr Univ Ariz 1630 E Univ Blvd Tucson AZ 85721 Business E-Mail: nbloembergen@optics.arizona.edu.

BLOEMSMA, MARCO PAUL, investor; b. Heemstede, The Netherlands, July 20, 1924; s. Philippus and Wilhelmina Geertruida (Bonebakker) Bloemsma; m. Mieke Harten, Sept. 23, 1955; children: Marco Reinier, Barbara Patricia, Michiel Alexander. LLM, Leyden U., 1948. Lawyer firm van der Feltz, Voûte & Riechelmann, 1948—49; assoc., then ptnr. Blackstone, Rueb & van Boeschoten, 1951—72; pres. C. Harten Holding B.V., The Hague, 1972—85; positions formerly held include chmn. KTI-Group; chmn. ten Doesschate-groups; chmn. Euroma Holding; dir., pres., chmn. Patino-group; chmn. Lips United-group, ICL Nederland B.V., Auto-Palace group, Bloemsma Holding B.V., Nebim Handelmaatschappy B.V.; bd. dirs. Mobil Chemie B.V., Ambac B.V., Lockheed Europe N.V., Vulcaansoord N.V., Merck Sharp en Dohme Nederland N.V., Rockwool Lapinus B.V., Svenska Metallverken/Granges Nederland B.V., Winthrop Europe N.V., Packard Instruments Europe N.V., Foster Grant Europe N.V., Anchor Found. (Verolme), Mijnbouwkundige Werken, Bank Itec. Author nat. reports on fiscal and corp. subjects. Served with Dutch Naval Reserve, 1949—51. Hon. Ky. col. since 1962. Mem.: Cercle Litteraire (Lausanne), Cercle Interalliée (Paris). Home: 5 Ave de Crousaz 1010 Lausanne Switzerland E-mail: mpbloemsma@bluewin.ch.

BLOHM, ROBERT, investment banker, economist, statistician; s. William Hewitt and Irene Chmielowska Blohm; children: Eric, Francis. BA in Philosophy and math., MBA, McGill U., Montreal, Que., Can., 1981; MA in Econ., Columbia U., 1997. Product mgr. corp. mktg. Banque Nationale du Can., Montreal, 1978—81; treasury officer Merc. Bank of Can., Citicorp, N.Y.C., 1981—83; account mgr. corp. lending Toronto (Ont., Can.) Dominion Bank, 1983—85; sr. rep. corp. and govt. fin. Daiwa Securities Co. Ltd., Tokyo, 1985—86; v.p., corp. and govt. fin. Yamaichi Securities Co. Ltd., Tokyo, 1986—87; gen. mgr., Euroissuance CIBC Wood Gundy, Toronto, 1987—88; Can. rep., Peers and Co. Long-Term Credit Bank of Japan, Tokyo, 1988—93; pvt. practice investment banker, economist, statistician Hamilton, NJ, 1997—. Co-author: NERC Joint Inadvertent Interchange Taskforce Whitepaper, 2002; contbr. articles to profl. jours. press (Bus. Adv. Coun., Rep. Congl. Com., Gold Medal, 2003). Mem. registered ballot body and frequency taskforce N.Am. Electric Reliability Coun. (NERC), Princeton, 1997—; mem. inadvertent interchange payback taskforce N.Am. Energy Stds. Bd., Houston, 2003—. Mem.: Columbia Club, NYC, Montreal Amateur Athletic Assn. Roman Catholic. Achievements include recycled Japan's 1980s capital surplus by arranging internat. bond and share financing of Canadian governments, corporations, banks, & utilities, and first Japan bond issue by African Development Bank; averted Quebec's separation from Canada by disproving its economic feasibility in financial media; coined the term the internet economy in 1996 Wall Street Journal op-ed; development and financing of electricity markets and reliability standards. Avocations: writing, photography, travel, swimming, sailing. Address: 3 Dover Rd Hamilton NJ 08620-1903 Personal E-mail: rb112@columbia.edu.

BLOM, CAROL BARNES, music educator; b. Wilmington, Del., Jan. 9, 1944; d. Russell Bates and Elizabeth Raughley Barnes; m. Kenneth Gordon Blom, Apr. 19, 1969; children: Amy Virginia, Rebecca Carol (Blom) Carle. MusB, Muskingum Coll., 1965; MFA, Ohio U., 1968. Cert. tchr. N.Y. Dir. jr. H.S. band Catskill (N.Y.) Ctrl. Sch., 1965—71; dir. secondary strings South Glens Falls (N.Y.) Ctrl. Sch., 1989—2002. Cons. Nat. Edn. Svcs., Amherst, Mass., 2001—, Ednl. Testing Svcs., Princeton, NJ, 2001—. Mem.: Music Educator Nat. Conf., Am. Assn. String Tchrs., Sigma Alpha Iota (life). Home: 1072 N Creek Rd Porter Corners NY 12859

BLOM, DANIEL CHARLES, lawyer, investor, retired insurance company executive; b. Portland, Oreg., Dec. 13, 1919; s. Charles D. and Anna (Reiner) B.; m. Ellen Lavon Stewart, June 28, 1952; children: Daniel Stewart (dec.), Nicole Jan Heath. BA magna cum laude, U. Wash., 1941, postgrad., 1941-42; JD, Harvard U., 1948; postgrad., U. Paris, 1954-55. Bar: Wash. 1949, U.S. Supreme Ct. 1970. Tchg. fellow speech U. Wash., 1941—42; law clk. to justice Supreme Ct. Wash., 1948—49; since practiced in Seattle; assoc. Graves, Kizer & Graves, 1949—51; gen. counsel Northwestern Life Ins. Co., 1952—54; ptnr. Case & Blom, 1952—54; assoc., ptnr., of counsel Ryan, Swanson & Cleveland, 1956—; exec. v.p., gen. counsel Family Life Ins. Co., 1964—85, spl. counsel, 1985—91. Vice chmn. Wash. Bd. Bar Examiners, 1970-72, chmn., 1972-75; mem. industry adv. com. Nat. Assn. Ins. Commrs., 1966-68; pres. Wash. Ins. Coun., 1971-73, gen. counsel, 1975-78; mediator Arbitration Forums, Inc. Editor Wash. State Bar Jour., 1951-52; assoc. editor The Brief, 1975-76; author: Life Insurance Law of the State of Washington, 1980, Banking and Insurance, Deregulatory Cross-Currents, 1985, Hostile Insurance Company Takeovers: New Frontier of the Law, 1990, Administrative Finality Under the Washington Insurance Code, 1991, Business and Professionalism, 1994, The Civility Problem, 1995, Technics and the Civilization of Law Practice, 1997, Varieties of Regulatory Experience, 1998, Legislative Review of Administrative Rules in the State of Washington; A Light that Failed?, 2003. Chmn. jury selection Wash. Gov.'s Writer's Day Awards, 1976; bd. dirs. Crisis Clinic; trustee Bush Sch., 1971-79, v.p., 1976-77; trustee, v.p. Frye Mus., Seattle, 1976-82, World Affairs Coun. Seattle, 1972-94, Friends of Seattle Pub. Libr., 1982-87; bd. visitors U. Wash. Libr., 1988-92, Friends of U. Wash. Libr., bd. dirs., 1991-95, pres., 1991-92. 2d lt. AUS, 1942-45, PTO. Decorated Bronze Star; Rhodes scholarship finalist, 1949. Fellow: Am. Bar Found.; mem.: ABA (vice chmn. com. on life ins. law, sect. tort and ins. pratice 1971—76, chmn. 1976—78, sect. program chmn. 1978—79, mem. coun. 1979—83, chmn. pub. rels. com. 1981—83, chmn. com. on profl. independence of the lawyer 1984—85, chmn. com. on scope and correlation 1985—86, policy coord. tort and ins. practice sect. 1986—90, del. ABA to Union Internat. des Avocats 1986—91, chmn. com. on handbook and bylaws 1987—88, chmn. hist. com. 1991—94), Fedn. Regulatory Counsel (dir. 1995—97, 2002—04), Found. UIA (coun. 1990—97), Am. Arbitration Assn., Am. Coun. Life Ins. (legis. com. 1982—85), Assn. Life Ins. Counsel, Am. Judicature Soc., N.Am. Found. for Internat. Legal Practice (pres. 1987—89, dir. 1987—95, chmn. 1990—95), Union Internat. des Avocats (v.p. 1987—92), Seattle Bar Assn., Wash. Bar Assn. (chmn. legal edn. liaison com. 1977—78, award of merit 1975), Harvard Assn. Seattle and Western Wash. (trustee 1976—77), Harvard Law Sch. Assn., Rainier Club, Tau Kappa Alpha, Phi Beta Kappa. Home: 100 Ward St # 602-3 Seattle WA 98109-5613 Office: Ryan Swanson & Cleveland 1201 3rd Ave Ste 3400 Seattle WA 98101-3034 Office Phone: 206-654-2280. Personal E-mail: blomdc@msn.com.

BLOMBERG, SUSAN RUTH, training executive, consultant, author; b. Troy, N.Y., Apr. 23, 1941; d. Philip J. and Marion (Burke) Beckman; m. Harvey Blomberg; children— Michael, Jonathan. B.S. in Edn., SUNY-Plattsburg, 1963. Cert. tchr., N.Y.; cert. tng. instr. Author, educator Nat. Textbook Co., Skokie, Ill., Stamford Bd. Edn. (Conn.), 1970-78; sales and mktg. dir., v.p., ptnr. B/D Assocs., Stamford, 1978-81; dir. mktg., v.p., owner Self Paced Learning Ctr., Stamford, 1981-84; pres., owner the Tng. Connection, Stamford, 1986—; tchr. Bayshore/Brook Ave. Sch., Bayshore, N.Y., 1963-65; dir. and creator Creative Playtime ednl. sch., Stamford, 1969-70; writing cons. Stillmeadow Sch., Stamford, 1972-74; cons., inservice instr. seminars and workshops, Stamford Bd. Edn., 1974-77. Author ednl. series: Let's Create: Think and Write, 1978; lectr., author program Basic Skills in English and Creative Writing for Teachers, 1977; author Creative Writing Activity Cards, 1975. Recipient Excellence award New Eng. Tng. and Employment Coun. and Nat. Alliance of Bus., Exemplary award U.S. Dept. Labor. Mem. Internat. Reading Assn., Southwestern Area Commerce and Industry Assn., Am. Soc. Tng. and Devel. (So. Conn. br.).

BLOME, ROBERT ARTHUR, retired surgeon; b. Iowa City, June 13, 1931; s. Glenn C. and Laura (Bolle) B.; m. Louann M. Nochtels, Mar. 25, 1958 (div. 1982); children: Elizabeth Ann, Jennifer Lynn, Lori Lynn; m. Dixie V. Kyoush, Apr. 26, 1984. BA, Grinnel Coll., 1952; MD, State U. Iowa, 1955. Diplomate Am. Bd. Surgeons. Intern Emanuel Hosp., Portland, Oreg., 1955-56; resident U. Iowa Hosp., Iowa City, 1956-60, staff physician, 1960-61; practice medicine specializiing in general and thoracic surgery Nampa, Idaho, 1963-94; ret., 1994. Pres. med. staff, chief surgery Mercy Hosp., Nampa. Contbr. articles to profl. jours. Chmn. Nampa chpt. ARC; bd.

dirs. United Way, Nampa. Capt. USAF 1961-63. Mem. Idaho State Med. Soc., SW Dist. Med. Soc. (sec., pres.), Nampa Aquatic Club (pres.), Kiwanis (bd. dirs. Nampa club). Republican. Methodist. Avocations: skiing, photography, kayaking. Office: Med Ctr Physicians 215 E Hawaii Ave Nampa ID 83686-6011

BLOMGREN, BRUCE HOLMES, real estate developer, marina developer, consultant; b. Evanston, Ill., Dec. 27, 1945; s. Charles Edwin and Jane Rebecca (Holmes) B.; m. Dawn Lewis, July, 1988; children: Tracy, Kirk, Chad, Rainey. BA in Speech, Monmouth Coll., 1969. V.p., program dir. Prairieland Broadcasters, Monmouth, 1966-70; asst. press sec. Gov. of Ill. Richard Ogilvie, Springfield, 1970-73; press sec. Gov. of Mo. Christopher Bond, 1973-77; advance staff Pres. Gerald Ford, Washington, 1976; dir. mktg. Arvida Corp., Boca Raton, Fla., 1977-79; pres., CEO Brandy Group, Inc., Boca Raton, 1979-92, Brandy Marine, Inc., 1998—; pres. Nat. Marina's, Inc., 1988-90, LCP/Brandy Marinas, Inc., 1989-91, Brandy Marinas, Inc., West Palm Beach, Fla., 1990-93, Manistee (Mich.) Village Ptnrs., Harbor Village Properties, Inc., Manistee, 1995-97, Lady Yacht Charters Fla. LLC, 2002—04; exec. v.p. Brandy Group Assocs., Inc., 1989-93; mktg. exec. for new product nat. campaign Liggett Tobacco Co., 1993; dir. mktg. programs El Cid Mega Resort, Mazatlan, Mexico, 1993-94; motivational spkr., affil. W. Edwards Deming Inst. of Miami, Boone, NC, 1994-95; mng. dir. Gynn Assocs., Tampa, Fla., 1997-98. Mem. Recreational Devel. Coun. of Urban Land Inst., moderator Washington, 1985, Miami, 1984, St. Thomas, V.I., 1985; exec. v.p. Northstar Fin., Inc., 1988-90; lead moderator customer svc. program S.E. Build Co., 1997—; marina acquisitions and mgmt. cons. JMB Realty, Ptnrs., Walton St. Capital, LLC Chgo., Marine Transp. Strategy Club Resorts, Dallas, Marina Devel. Acquisitions St. Joe Corp., Jacksonville, Fla.; pres. Lady Yacht Charters Fla. LLC; lectr., spkr. in field. Author: (with others) Developing with Recreational Amentites Golf, Tennis, Skiing, Marinas. Pres. Fla. Homebuilders Polit. Action Com., Boca Raton, 1978; mem. pub. affairs com. to Gov. Bob Graham, Fla., 1982-86; organizer charity boat race Handicapped Children's Fund, Sarasota, Fla., 1985-87; bd. advisors West Shore C.C. Capt. USCG, 1979—. Mem. Nat. Spkrs. Assn., West Mich. Tourist Assn. (bd. dirs. 1995-98), Manistee Area C. of C. (bd. dirs. 1996-97), Profl. Assn. Diving Instrs., Bird Key Yacht Club (Sarasota, Fla., dir. youth sailing), Sarasota Radio Controlled Squadron (chmn. edn. com.). Republican. Presbyterian. Office: PO Box 2016 Sarasota FL 34230-2016 Office Phone: 941-360-1015. Business E-Mail: bblomgren@brandymarine.com.

BLOMQUIST, DAVID WELS, journalist; b. Detroit, June 16, 1956; s. August Wels and Sally Lou (Ball) B. AB, U. Mich., 1976; AM, Harvard U., 1978. Tchg. fellow Harvard U., Cambridge, 1978-82, asst. sr. tutor, 1981-82; supervising sect. editor CBS Inc., N.Y.C., 1982-84; staff writer The Record of Hackensack, N.J., 1984-86, state polit. corr., 1986-89, chief polit. writer, 1990-92, chief Trenton bur., 1992-94; dir. The Record Poll, Hackensack, 1992-99, dir. online devel., 1998-99; dir. new media Detroit Free Press, 1999—2001, sr. editor tech. and rsch., 2002—. Author: Elections and the Mass Media, 1982; contbr. articles to profl. jours. Mem. Am. Polit. Sci. Assn. (edn. com. 1984-86), N.J. Legis. Corrs. Club (pres. 1992), Harvard Club of N.Y., Nat. Press Club Washington. Avocations: music, ballet. Office: Detroit Free Press 600 W Fort St Detroit MI 48226-2706 E-mail: blomquist@freepress.com.

BLOMQUIST, PRESTON HOWARD, ophthalmologist; b. Austin, Tex., Aug. 13, 1960; s. Gilbert Victor and Betty Jean Blomquist; m. Mary Denise Dobias, Mar. 31, 1960; children: Brooke Amanda, Kara Elyse. BSc in Engring., U. Tex., 1982; MD, U. Tex. Southwestern Med. Sch., Dallas, 1986. Diplomate Am. Bd. of Ophthalmology. Chief eye svcs. Permanente Med. Assn. of Tex., Dallas, 1993—94, assoc. med. dir. quality resource mgmt., 1996—97, physician dir. orgnl. performance and improvement, 1995—96; asst. prof. U. Tex. Southwestern Med. Ctr., Dallas, 1998—2004, assoc. prof., 2004—. Ophthalmology residency program dir. U. of Tex. Southwestern Med. Ctr., Dallas, 2002—. Recipient Ho Din, Southwestern Med. Found., 1986. Fellow: Am. Acad. Ophthalmology; mem.: Assn. for Rsch. in Vision and Ophthalmology, Assn. Univ. Profs. Ophthalmology (assoc.), Am. Soc. Cataract and Refractive Surgeons. Office: Univ Tex Southwestern Med 5323 Harry Hines Blvd Dallas TX 75390-9057 Office Phone: 214-648-2020.

BLOMSTRAND, DOREEN KATHRYN, retired physician assistant; b. Superior, Wis., Sept. 25, 1929; d. Wesley Lawrence and Ann Kathryn (Okerstrom) Wright; m. Fritz Joseph Blomstrand, 1948 (dec. Dec. 26, 1982); children: Cynthia Dawn Reynolds, Heidi Jo Thomas, Jace Wright(dec.). Physician Asst. Program, U. of Wash., Seattle; Cmty. Health Adv. Program, Yakima Valley C.C., Wash. Physician Assistant MEDEX NW, U. of WA, 1985, Pa. Bd. Cert. Nat. Commn. on Cert. of Physician Assistants Bd., 1986, cert. EMT Ctrl. Wash. U., 1978; Tng. the trainer-qualified to teach others Ministry Tng. Ctrs., Oreg., 1997; Community Health Advocate Yakima Valley C.C., Wash., 1983, Cambodian Lang. study SE Asian Summer Study Intst. of Lang., U. of Hawaii, 1988. Full-time faculty MEDEX NW, U. of Wash., Seattle, 1990—2000; ret., still part-time faculty MEDEX NW, Sch. of Medicine, U. of Wash., Seattle, 2000—. Physician asst., health edn. coord. CAMA Svcs., United Nations Border Relief Ops., Thailand, 1986—90. Contbr. articles (Awarded second pl. in nonfiction articles, 2002). Ministry team, small group leader, mentor Eastside Foursquare Ch., Bothell, Wash., 1992—2003; vol. supplies and time with orphans Chang Mai, Thailand, 1998; vol. at distbn. ctr. for Russian immigrants Christian Friend's of Israel, Jerusalem, 1999; short-term vol. work with the poor IMPACT, Ensenada, Mexico, 1999; short term med. mission Project Mercy, Yetebon, Ethiopia, 2000; vol. Northshore Sr. Ctr., Bothell, Wash., 2000—03, Kirkland Sr. Ctr., Wash., 2001—03; short term vol. team Eastside Foursquare Ch., Metro Manila, Philippines, 2002. Recipient Humanitarian Svc. award, MEDEX NW Alumni Assn., 2003. Mem.: Fellowship of Christian Physician Assts., U. of Wash. Retirement Assn., Wash. Acad. of Physician Assts. (past bd. mem., student affairs chair 1995—2000), MEDEX NW Alumni Assn. (life; bd. mem. 1996—2003), Writer's Info. Network, NW Christian Writers Assn. Avocations: short-term international missions, writing, teaching, reading, tap dancing. Office: MEDEXNorthwest U of Wash 4311 11th Ave NE Ste 200 Seattle WA 98105 Personal E-mail: dblomstrand@earthlink.net. E-mail: doreenb@u.washington.edu.

BLOND, STUART RICHARD, magazine editor; b. L.A., Sept. 1, 1953; s. Elmer George and Anne G. Blond; m. Stella Pyrtek, July 28, 1986. BA in Art, Calif. State U., 1977. V.p. advt. Packard Automobile Classics, Fords, N.J., 1988-97; sales Packard Industries, Boonton, N.J., 1989—. Editor newsletter The Cormorant News Bull., 1988-2004; editor mag. The Packard Cormorant, 2004—. Home and Office: 84 Hoy Ave Fords NJ 08863-1938 E-mail: stuartrblond@earthlink.net.

BLONDIN, C. J., trade association administrator; b. Paterson, N.J., May 13, 1930; s. Joseph and Margaret (DeMarco) Blondin; m. Barbara Helen Barker, May 28, 1955; children: Jacqueline, Chris, Elizabeth, Barbara, David, Jennifer. BS in Engring., U.S. Coast Guard Acad., 1955; JD, George Washington U., 1962. Bar: DC 1962, U.S. Supreme Ct. 1966, appointed mil.judge: 1971. Dir. internat. affairs Nat. Marine Fisheries Svc./Nat. Oceanic & Atmospheric Adminstrn. Dept. Commerce, Washington, 1972—79, dep. asst. adminstr., 1979—86; commr. Internat. Atlantic Ocean Commn. and Internat. North Pacific Commn. Dept. Commerce, Washington, 1980—90; judge U.S.-USSR Maritime Claims Ct., Washington, Moscow, 1982—91; sr. trade assoc. U.S. Dept. Commerce, Washington, 1986—88, dep. asst. sec. internat., 1988—94; pres. Internat. Trade Assocs., Northern Neck, Va., 1994—. US rep. Internat. Pension Commn., Wahington, Ottawa, Can., 1984—93; vice chmn. Monitor Internat. Bd., Washington, 1989—2000; cons. internat. and maritime affairs US and Europe, 1994—. Editor (bus. editor): George Washington U. Law Rev., 1961—62; contbr. articles on internat. and maritime law to profl. jours. Dist. chmn. Boy Scouts Am., Nat. Capitol Area and Va., 1988—92; parliamentarian 1st Rep. Congl. Dist. Va., 1995—2000; chmn. Northumberland County Rep. Com., Va., 2001—04. Commdr. USN, 1948—73, Korea. Recipient Meritorious Svc. medal, U.S. President, 1973, Silver medal, Sec. of Commerce, 1984, Sec. of State, 1989. Mem.: Christian Men's Assn., Am. Legion (vice commander 2000—03), Mil. Officers Assn. Am. (chpt. pres. 1995—98). Republican. Roman Catholic. Avocations: boating, camping, golf, hiking, sailing.

BLONDIN, JOAN, nephrologist educator; b. Beaumont, Tex., Nov. 28, 1936; d. Joseph Albert and Ona Mae (Williamson) B. BS, La. Tech U., 1959; MNS, Cornell U., 1961; MD, La. State U., 1969. Diplomate Am. Bd. Internal Medicine. Instr. U. Ala., Tuscaloosa, 1961-62; rsch. assoc. Cornell U., Ithaca, N.Y., 1962-63; asst. specialist La. State U., Baton Rouge, 1963-65; intern Barnes Hosp., St. Louis, 1969-70, resident, 1970-72; fellow Washington U., St. Louis, 1972-74, asst. prof., 1974-78; ptnr. Nephrology Cons., Monroe, La., 1978-2000. Assoc. prof. La. State U. Sch. Medicine, Shreveport, 1978-98; adj. prof. human ecology La. Tech. U., 1988; prof. medicine La. State U. Health Scis. Ctr., 2000—; active staff St. Francis Med. Ctr., 1978-2001, North Monroe Cmty. Hosp., 1984-2000; adj. prof. Coll. Pharmacy, Northeast La. U., 1996. Contbr. articles to profl. jours. Bd. dirs. Central Bank; mem. adv. bd. Bank One; bd. trustees Nat. Kidney Found. of La., 1988-97; mem. La. Bd. Regents, 1989-94, chmn., 1992; med. dir. North La. Dialysis Ctr., 1992-97, Ruston Kidney Ctr. Fellow La. Cancer Society, 1966, NIH, 1968; recipient Disting. Svc. award La. Dietetic Assn., 1998. Mem. AAAS, ACP, End Stage Renal Disease (chmn. quality consensus com. 1994-96), Internat. Soc. Nephrology, Am. Soc. Internal Medicine, Am. Soc. Nephrology (bd. adv. 2003—), Am. Soc. Tropical Medicine and Hygiene, Am. Soc. Parenteral and Enteral Nutrition, Am. Heart Assn. (coun. on hypertension), Renal Physicians Assn. (bd. dirs., fin. com. 1991-94, chmn. quality care com.), NY Acad. Scis., La. Med. Soc. (del. 1988-2001), Ouachita Med. Soc. (pres.-elect 1998-99, pres. 1999-2000, immediate past pres., exec. com. 2000), Sigma Xi, Alpha Omega Alpha, Phi Kappa Phi, Omicron Nu. Republican. Episcopalian. Avocations: music, needlepoint, reading. Home: 5516 Bent Tree Dr Shreveport LA 71115-9564 Office: LSU HSC Shreveport LA E-mail: jblond@lsuhsc.edu.

BLONDIN-ANDREW, ETHEL D., Canadian government official; b. Tulita, N.W.T., Can., Mar. 25, 1951; d. Cecilia Modeste, adopted d. Joseph and Marie Therese Blondin; children: Troy Zanl, Tanya, Timothy Townsend. BEd, U. Alta., 1974, LLD, 2001. Tchr. Tuktoyaktuk, Ft. Franklin, Ft. Providence, 1974-81; tchr. lang. spl. dept. edn. Yellowknife, 1981-84, asst. dep. min., culture & comm., 1986—88; tchr. U. Calgary & Arctic Coll., 1983; mgr., then acting dir. Pub. Svc. Commn., Canada, 1984-86; sec. state tng. and youth Can., 1993-97, sec. state children and youth, 1997—. Mem. bd. dirs. Arctic Inst. N.Am., Nat. Steering Ctr., Aboriginal Lang. Policy Dvel.; chair Indigenous Lang. Devel. Rev. Ctr. Recipient Culture and Heritage Preservation award MLA, 1987, Hilroy Scholar award R.C. Hill Char. Found., 1982. Liberal. Roman Catholic. Office: Human Resources Devel Canada Pl du Portage 2 Phase IV 140 Promenade du Portage12fl Hull PQ Canada K1A 0J9 also: Ste # 102 51 02-50 Ave Yellowknife NT Canada X1A 3S8 also: House of Commons Ottawa K1A 0A6 Canada

BLONZ, EDWARD ROBERT, nutritionist, biochemist; b. Chgo., Nov. 17, 1949; s. Robert Blonz and Ruth Stella Eisner; m. Karen Leslie Fisher, June 27, 1982; 1 child, Joshua Aaron. BA, U. of Wis., 1971; MS, U. of Calif., Davis, 1977, PhD, 1984. Sea grant rsch. fellow U. of Calif., Davis, 1975—77, rsch. asst., vis. lectr., 1977—84; asst. prof. U. of Minn., St. Paul, 1984—87; adminstrv. project mgr. USDA Western Human Nutrition Rsch. Ctr., San Francisco, 1987—90; sci. dir. / dir. of nutrition More.com, San Francisco, 1998—2000; prin. Edward R. Blonz Cons. (formerly Nutrition Resource), Kensington, Calif., 1990—; syndicated columnist United Media, N.Y.C., 1993—. Author: (scientific text) Controversies in Nutrition: Obesity and Fad Diets, (book) The Really Simple No Nonsense Nutrition Guide, Your Personal Nutritionist: Fiber and Fat, Your Personal Nutritionist: Antioxidants, Your Personal Nutritionist: Food Additives, Your Personal Nutritionist: Calcium and other Minerals, Power Nutrition, The Nutrition Doctors A to Z Food Counter. Food adv. com. dietary supplements U.S. FDA, Washington, 2003—. Recipient Sci. Writing award, James Beard Found., 1995; grantee Rsch. grantee, Sigma Xi, 1975. Fellow: Am. Coll. of Nutrition (cert.); mem.: N.Y. Acad. of Scis, Inst. of Food Technologists, Internat. Assn. of Culinary Profls., Am. Soc. of Journalists and Authors, Nat. Assn. of Sci. Writers, Assn. of Food Journalists, Soc. for Nutrition Edn., APHA, Sigma Xi. Office Phone: 510-525-6925. Personal E-mail: er@blonz.com.

BLOOD, PEGGY A., academic administrator; b. Pine Bluff, Ark., Feb. 8, 1947; m. Lawrence A. Davis, May 31, 1975; children: Lauren A., Pawnee A., Zelana P. BS, U. Ark., Pine Bluff, 1969; MFA, U. Ark., 1971; PhD, Union Inst., Cin., 1986; MA, Holy Names Coll., 1987. Art dir. Office Econ. Opportunity, Altheimer, Ark., 1969; acting. dept. chair, asst. prof. art Univ. Ark., Pine Bluff, 1971-74; activity coord. Good Samaritan Home, Oakland, Calif., 1978-80; art instr. Chabot C.C., Hayward, Calif., 1980-81, Solano C.C., Suisun, Calif., 1980-90; prin. Palma Ceia Christian Elem. Sch., Hayward, Calif., 1983-84; curriculum chmn., instr. Calif. IMPACT, Oakland, 1985-87; ctr. dir. Chapman U., Fairfield, Calif., 1988-97; prof. fine arts Savannah (Ga.) State U., 1998—, head divsn. fine arts, 1998—. Presenter in field; cons. in field. One-woman shows include Chapman Unvi, Fairfield, Calif., AAUW, Oakland, Calif., Fort Mason, San Francisco, Calif., Hospic Savannah, Ga., CinQue Gallery, N.Y.C., and otherss, exhibitions include Univ. of Mobile, Ala., Horizon Art Festival, Martinex, Ga. (Selected Best of Show and First Prize), 2001—02, No. Calif. Women Art Festival, exhibitions include Seattle Ann. State Exhbn., Univ. Wash. Festival Show, Seattle, and many more; author: Apples are Blue, 2004, Fostering Creativity in the Challenged Student, Color Transformation, Knowledge Based Curriculum; contbr. articles to profl. jour. Sch. bd. trustee Benicia (Calif.) Unified Sch. Dist., 1989-93; bd. mem. Nat. Inst. Art & Disabilities, Richmond, Calif., 1988-90, Girl Scouts Am., Solano County, Calif., 1995-96; legis. dist. action com. mem. Omega Boys and Girls Club, Oakland, Calif. Recipient Ledalle Morehead scholarship, U. Ark., Pine Bluff, 1968, Disting. Prof. award Savannah State U, 2004-05; scholar Fulbright Sr. Splt. Candidate award, 2002—; named first Afro-Am. grad. MFA in Art, U. Ark., Fayetteville, 1971, Outstanding Bay Area Artist, Oakland (Calif.) Arts, 1985; numerous grants. Mem.: LWV (bd. dirs. 1980—82), AAUW, Willie B. Adkins Coll. Bound Program, Southeastern Art Assn., Nat. Art Edn. Assn., Coll. Arts Assn. Am., Artist Alliance of Assorted Black Colls. and Univs., Ga. Art Assn., Rotary, Alpha Kappa Alpha (1st Prize art award 1982—83). Roman Catholic. Achievements include traveled extensively thoughout Europe, Asia, and Africa. Office Phone: 912-356-2506. Business E-Mail: bloodp@savstate.edu.

BLOODGOOD-ABRAMS, JANE MARIE, artist; b. Queens, NY, Jan. 7, 1963; d. Clarence and Sheila Getty Bloodgood; m. Paul H. Abrams, June 13, 1992; children: Erica, Fiona. BS in Studio Art, Coll. of St. Rose, Albany, NY, 1985; MFA, SUNY, New Paltz, 1985. Exhibitions include Biennial, NY State Mus., Albany, 1999, Sacred Visions, Payerbach, Austria, 2000, Florence Biennale, Italy, 2001. Bd. mem. U.U. Congregation of the Catskills, Kingston, NY, 1999—2002. Recipient Mem. of the Year, Ulster County Arts Coun., 2000; grantee spl. opportunity stipend, NYS Found. Arts, 1998, Lewis Vogelstein Foundn., 2002. Mem.: Pastel Soc. Am. (signature mem. 1999—), Nat. Assn. of Women Artists (juried mem. 2002—), Catharine Lorillard Wolfe Art Club (juried mem. 2002—). Democrat. Unitarian Universalist.

BLOODWORTH, ALBERT WILLIAM FRANKLIN, lawyer; b. Atlanta, Sept. 23, 1935; s. James Morgan Bartow and Elizabeth Westfield (Dimmock) B.; m. Elizabeth Howell, Nov. 24, 1967; 1 child, Elizabeth Howell. AB in History and French, Davidson Coll., 1957; JD magna cum laude with 1st honors, U. Ga., 1963. Bar: Ga. 1962, U.S. Supreme Ct. 1971. Asst. dir. alumni and pub. relations Davidson Coll., N.C., 1959-60; assoc. Hansell & Post, Atlanta, 1963-68, ptnr., 1969-84, Bloodworth & Nix, Atlanta, 1984-95, Bloodworth & McSwain, Atlanta, 1996—2003; pvt. practice Atlanta, 2003—. Counsel organized crime com. Met. Atlanta Commn. on Crime, 1965-67; asst. sec., counsel Met. Found. Atlanta, 1968-76. Bd. dirs. Atlanta Presbytery, 1974-78; trustee Synod of S.E., Presbyn. Ch. in U.S.A., Augusta, Ga., 1982-87; trustee Big Canoe Chapel, Ga., 1983-86, 88-91, chmn. bd. trustees, 1985-86, 90-91; mem. pres.'s adv. coun. Presbyn. Homes, 1989—; mem. president's adv. coun. Thornwell Home and Sch. for Children, 1998—. elder North Ave Presbyn. Ch., Atlanta. 1st lt. Intelligence Corps, USAR, 1957-59. Recipient Jessie Dan MacDougal Scholarship award U. Ga. Found., 1963, Outstanding Student Leadership award Student Bar Assn., U. Ga., 1963. Fellow Am. Coll. Trust and Estate Counsel; mem. ABA, State Bar Ga., Atlanta Bar Assn., Atlanta Estate Planning Coun., North Atlanta Estate Planning Coun., Capital City Club, Lawyers Club, Sphinx Club, Gridiron Club, Phi Beta Kappa, Phi Kappa Phi, Omicron Delta Kappa, Alpha Tau Omega (pres. chpt. 1957), Phi Delta Phi (grad. of yr. 1963, pres. chpt. 1963). Republican. Presbyterian. Home: 3784 Club Dr NE Atlanta GA 30319-1108 Office: 706 Monarch Plz 3414 Peachtree Rd NE Atlanta GA 30326-1153 Office Phone: 404-231-9331. Office Fax: 404-231-9330. Personal E-mail: awfb@bellsouth.net.

BLOODWORTH, GLADYS LEON, elementary school educator; b. Natchitoches, La., July 9, 1946; d. Rudolph and Mary (LeRoy) Leon; m. John Edward Bloodworth, Aug. 14, 1971; children: John, Jeremy. BA, Southern U., Baton Rouge, 1968; MA, Calif. State U., Dominguez Hills, 1989. Nat. bd. cert. tchr. mid. childhood generalist NBCT/MC, 2001. Lang. arts tchr. grades 6-10 Natchitoches Parish Schs.; categorical program adviser L.A. Unified Schs., mentor tchr., 1999—, coord. gifted coord., 1988. Named Outstanding Math Tchr., 1987-88. Mem. NEA, United Tchrs. L.A., Calif. Tchrs. Assn., Women in Ednl. Leadership, Kappa Kappa Iota. Methodist.

BLOODWORTH, VELDA JEAN, librarian, educator; b. Campobello, SC, June 28, 1929; d. Lloyd Ernest and Nora Frances (McNeal) Burke; m. Clifford Burton Bloodworth, Aug. 14, 1949; children: Jill Henderson, Jackie Herschberger. BA, So. Coll., Collegedale, Tenn., 1967; MS, Fla. State U., 1968; MAT, Rollins Coll., 1979. Cert. tchr., Fla. Libr. Forest Lake Acad., Apopka, Fla., 1968-74, Rollins Coll., Winter Park, Fla., 1974—99, assoc. prof. emerita; ret., 1999. Cons. libr. Forest Lake Acad., Apopka, 1987-88. Editor, curator: (catalog for art mus. exhibit) Jessie B. Rittenhouse Poetry Collection, 1984. Mem. Fla. Libr. Assn., Beta Phi Mu. Home: 3162 Holliday Ave Apopka FL 32703-6634 Office: Rollins Coll Olin Libr 1000 Holt Ave Winter Park FL 32789-4499

BLOODWORTH, WILLIAM ANDREW, JR., academic administrator; b. San Antonio, Sept. 9, 1942; s. William Andrew Sr. and Ellan Oma (Gatliff) B.; m. Julia Ann Rankin, Nov. 27, 1964; children: Nicole, Paul William. BS, Tex. Luth. Coll., 1964; MA, Lamar U., 1967; PhD, U. Tex., 1972; grad., Harvard Inst. Ednl. Mgmt., 1989. Tchr. Boerne (Tex.) and Port Neches (Tex.) pub. schs., 1964-67; asst. instr. U. Tex., Austin, 1969-72; asst. prof. English E. Carolina U., Greenville, N.C., 1972-77, assoc. prof., 1977-82, prof., 1982-90, chmn. English dept., 1982-88, acting vice chancellor for acad. affairs, 1987-89; provost, v.p. for acad. affairs Cen. Mo. State U., Warrensburg, 1990-93; pres. Augusta (Ga.) State U., 1993—. Author: Upton Sinclair, 1977, Max Brand, 1993; contbr. articles to profl. publs., chpts. to books. Mem. Am. Assn. Higher Edn., Rotary, Phi Kappa Phi (chpt. pres. 1989-90), Phi Delta Kappa. Avocations: running, writing. Home: 819 Kamel Cir Augusta GA 30909-2709 Office: Augusta State U Office of the Pres Augusta GA 30904-2200

BLOOM, ALEXANDER, history professor, writer; b. L.A. s. Erwin and Vivian Bloom; children: Stefan, Zachary. AB, U. Calif., Santa Cruz, 1968; MA, Boston Coll., 1972, PhD, 1979. History prof. Wheaton Coll., Norton, Mass., 1978—. Lectr. Fullbright Commn., Rome, 2002. Author: Prodigal Sons, 1986; editor: Takin' It to the Streets, 1995, Long Time Gone, 2002. Democrat. Home: 144 Foster St Brighton MA 02135 Office: History Dept Wheaton Coll Norton MA 02766

BLOOM, ALFRED HOWARD, academic administrator, educator; b. N.Y.C., Feb. 27, 1946; s. Alfred H and Martha (Berrol) Bloom; m. Margaret Hennigan, Aug. 22, 1971. BA, Princeton U., 1967; PhD, Harvard U., 1974. Asst., assoc. prof. Swarthmore Coll., Pa., 1974—86, assoc. provost, 1985—86, pres., 1991—; dean of faculty, v.p. acad. affairs Pitzer Coll., Claremont, Calif., 1986—90, exec. v.p., 1990—91. Author: The Linguistic Shaping of Thought, 1981; contbr. articles to profl. jours. Fellow, Fulbright-Hays, 1968; grantee, SSRC, 1978, 1981, NEH, 1975, 1986. Mem.: Assn. Asian Studies. Avocations: study of languages and cultures, intercultural gastronomy. Office: Swarthmore Coll Office of Pres 500 College Ave Swarthmore PA 19081-1306 E-mail: abloom1@swarthmore.edu.

BLOOM, BARBARA L., dean; d. Carl S. and Karen A. (Ryder) Bloom; m. Cliff A. Maier, July 20, 2003. BA, Grove City Coll., Pa., 1990; MEd, Kutztown U. of Pa., 1998. Spl. events Easter Seals, Butler, Pa., 1994—96; fund raiser Big Brothers/Big Sisters, York, 1996; cmty. svc. coord. Berks Coun. on Higher Edn., Reading, Pa., 1996—98; cmty. dir. U. Redlands, Redlands, Calif., 1998—2000; resident dir. Santa Clara U., 2000—03; dean of student life Cogswell College, Sunnyvale, Calif., 2004—. Vol. Humane Soc., Santa Clara, Calif., 2004; mem. funding com. United Way, Redlands, 1999. Mem.: WACE, ACPA, NASPA.

BLOOM, BARRY MALCOLM, research and development company executive, consultant; b. Roxbury, Mass., Aug. 12, 1928; s. Morris and Ann (Levine) B.; m. Joan Martha Ensign, June 27, 1956; children: Catherine, Brian, Joanna. SB, MIT, 1948, PhD, 1951, postgrad., 1967; LHD (hon.), Conn. Coll., 1992. Rsch. chemist Pfizer, Inc., Groton, Conn., 1952-63, dir. medicinal chems. and rsch., 1963-71, pres. ctrl. rsch. divsn., 1971-90, v.p. rsch., 1971-90, bd. dirs., 1973—93, corp. mgmt. com., 1984-93, sr. v.p. R & D, 1990-92, exec. v.p. R & D, 1992-93; cons. pvt. practice, 1993—2004. Bd. dirs. Congl. Commn. on Fed. Drug Approval Process, PMA Commn. on Drugs for Rare Diseases; cons. U.S. Congress Office Tech. Assessment, 1976-77; mem. Conn. Tech. Adv. Bd., 1985-90. Mem. editl. bd. Ann. Reports in Medicinal Chemistry, 1968-70; patentee in field. NRC postdoctoral fellow U. Wis., 1952; Poly. Inst. Tech. fellow N.Y.C., 1980; recipient Spl. Achievement award CT Innovations, Inc., 1997. Mem. Am. Chem. Soc. (chmn. divsn. medicinal chemistry 1967), Conn. Acad. Sci. and Engring., Pharm. Mfrs. Assn. (chmn. R & D sect. 1976). Home and Office: Mackintosh Rd Lyme CT 06371

BLOOM, BARRY R., dean; BS in Biology, Amherst Coll., DSc (hon.), 1990; MA, Harvard U.; PhD in Immunology, Rockefeller U., 1963. Joined faculty Albert Einstein Coll. Medicine, 1964, named prof., 1973, chmn. dept. microbiology and immunology, 1978—90, Weinstock Prof. of Microbiology and Immunology; dean faculty Harvard Sch. of Pub. Health, Cambridge, Mass., 1998—, Joan L. and Julius H. Jacobson Prof. of Pub. Health. Cons. White House, 1977—78; investigator Howard Hughes Inst., 1990—98; mem. Global Adv. Com. on Health Rsch. WHO; chair emeritus Internat. Vaccine Inst.; mem. sci. adv. bd. Ellison Med. Found., Wellcome Trust Ctr. for Human Genetics; mem. external adv. bd. Earth Inst., Columbia U.; mem. UN Devel. Programme: Millennium Devel. Goals Working Group on Tuberculosis. Contbr. articles to profl. jours. Co-recipient Award in Immunology, Novartis, 1998; recipient Award for Disting. Rsch. in Infectious Diseases, Bristol-Myers Squibb, 1991, John Enders Award, Infectious Diseases Soc. Am., 1994, Robert Koch Gold medal for lifetime rsch. in infectious diseases, Robert Koch Found., Bonn, Germany, 1999. Fellow Am. Acad. Arts and Scis.; mem. NAS, Inst. Medicine, Am. Assn. Immunologists (pres., 1984) Office: Sch Pub Health Harvard U Kresge Bldg Rm 1005 677 Huntington Ave Boston MA 02115

BLOOM, CLAIRE, actress; b. London, Feb. 15, 1931; d. Edward Max and Elizabeth (Grew) B.; m. Rod Steiger, Sept. 19, 1959 (div. Jan. 1969); 1 child, Anna Justine; m. Philip Roth, Apr. 29, 1990 (div. Mar. 1995). Student, Badminton Sch., Bristol, Eng., Fern Hill Manor, New Milton, Eng., Guildhall Sch. Music and Drama, London. Disting. vis. prof. Hunter Coll., N.Y.C., 1989-90. Appeared as Ophelia, Stratford-Upon-Avon, 1948; plays include Ring Around the Moon, London, 1949-51, Romeo and Juliet, also as Juliet in Old Vic tour of U.S.; film roles in Limelight, Richard III, 1956, Alexander the Great, 1956, The Brothers Karamazov, 1958, Look Back in Anger, 1958, The Brothers Grimm, 1962, The Chapman Report, 1962, The Haunting, 1963,

80,000 Suspects, 1963, Alta Infidelita, 1963, Il Maestro di Vigeevano, 1963, The Outrage, 1964, The Spy Who Came in from the Cold, 1965, The Illustrated Man, 1969, Three into Two Won't Go, 1969, A Severed Head, 1971, A Doll's House, 1973, Islands in the Stream, 1976, Clash of the Titans, 1981, Always, 1984, Sammy and Rosie, 1987, Crimes and Misdemeanors, 1989, Daylight, 1995, The Book Eve, 2002, Imagining Argentina, 2002, Daniel and the Superdogs, 2003; Broadway prodns. include Rashomon, 1959; other theatre appearances include Duel of Angels, London, 1958, Altona, Royal Court Theatre, London, 1960, Ivanov, London, 1964, A Doll's House, Hedda Gabler, 1971, Vivat! Vivat Regina!, 1972; N.Y. appearance The Innocents, 1976; London appearances A Doll's House, 1973, A Streetcar Named Desire, 1974, Rosmersholm, 1977, The Cherry Orchard, 1981, These are Women, 1982-83, When We Dead Awaken, 1990, Daughters, Wives and Mothers, 1991, Silenced Voices, 1992, Women in Love, 1993, The Cherry Orchard, 1994, Long Days Journey into Night, 1996, Electra, 1998, Conversations After a Burial, 2000, A Little Night Music, 2001, A Little Night Music NYCO, 2003, Whistling Psyche, 2004; many roles Brit. and U.S. TV including In Praise of Love, 1975, A Legacy, 1975, Henry VIII, 1979, Hamlet, 1979, The Ghost Writer, 1983, Cymbeline, 1983, King John, 1983, Brideshead Revisited, 1981, Shadowlands, 1984, Time and the Conways, 1985, miniseries Queenie, 1987, Anastasia, 1987, Shadow in the Sun, 1988, The Camomile Lawn, 1991, The Mirror Crack'd, 1992, Remember, 1993, Village Affairs, 1994, Family Money, 1996, When the Dead Man Heard, 1997, The Lady in Question, 1999, Law and Order, 2003; author: Limelight and After, 1982, Leaving A Doll's House, 1996. Recipient Evening Standard award, London, 1974, Brit. Film and TV award, London, 1984; nominee Tony award, 1998, 99. Office: Marion Rosenberg Agy 1345 N Hayworth Ave Ste 104 Los Angeles CA 90046 Home: 622 3rd Ave FL 7 New York NY 10017-0723

BLOOM, DAVID ANDREW, communications operations director; s. Joel Barnett and Mavis June Bloom. BSCS, Strayer U., 1993—95. Dir. of telecom. Internat. Data Products Corp., Gaithersburg, Md., 1995—99; v.p. and chief tech. officer F-Square Comm., Damascus, Md., 1999—2000; v.p. telecom. Facilities PLUS, Inc., Gaithersburg, Md., 2000—04; dir. of ops., telephony Info Systems, Inc., Wilmington, Del., 2004—. Dir. Harp and Shamrock Soc., Gaithersburg, Md., 1999—2005. Mem.: Internat. Alliance of Avaya Users (assoc.), Building Industry Cons. Svc. Internat. (assoc.). Non-Partisan. Avocation: ballroom dancing. Office: Info Systems Inc 590 Century Blvd Wilmington DE 19808 Office Phone: 302-993-4493.

BLOOM, DAVID I., lawyer; b. Washington, Mar. 27, 1954; AB magna cum laude, Brown U., 1975; JD, Yale U., 1978. Bar: D.C. 1978, U.S. Dist. Ct. (D.C. dist.) 1978, U.S. Ct. Appeals (D.C. cir.) 1979, U.S. Ct. Appeals (5th cir.) 1983, U.S. Ct. Appeals (7th cir.) 1984. With Mayer, Brown, Rowe & Maw LLP (formerly Mayer, Brown & Platt), Washington, 1978—; ptnr. Mayer, Brown, Rowe & Maw LLP, Washington, 1985—. And chmn., tech. com. Asst. and articles editor: Energy Law Jour., 1984-99. Mem. ABA, Am. Gas Assn. (mem. legal sect. mng. com. 1990-92), Fed. Energy Bar Assn., D.C. Bar. Office: Mayer Brown Rowe & Maw LLP 1909 K St NW Washington DC 20006-1101

BLOOM, EDWARD (TED), research and development company executive; BBA magna cum laude, MBA cum laude, Boston U. Joined Internat. Data Group, Boston, 1967, mailroom clk., asst. to v.p. mktg., credit mgr., 1973—, asst. to v.p. fin., acctg. mgr., v.p., corp. contr., treas., CFO, 2002—. Bd. mem. Kobren Insight Funds, Medirges, Inc. Bd. mem. Temple Beth Elohim, Wellesley Gentleman's Soc. Office: Internat Data Group One Exeter Plaza 15th Fl Boston MA 02116

BLOOM, EUGENE CHARLES, gastroenterologist, educator; b. Tupelo, Miss., June 3, 1933; s. Robert Harold and Anna Esther (Kronick) B.; m. Joan Ellen Margoles, July 22, 1956; children: Marjorie Wynne Bloom Albert, Stacey Bloom Schlafstein, Robin Bloom Wolf. Student, Emory U., 1951—55, U. Fla., 1955—56; MD, U. Miami, 1960. Diplomate Am. Bd. Internal Medicine. Intern Cook County Hosp., Chgo., 1960—61; resident in internal medicine Jackson Meml. Hosp., Miami, Fla., 1961—63; resident in gastroent. Coral Gables VA Hosp., 1963—64; rsch. fellow dept. medicine, divsn. gastroent. U. Miami Sch. Medicine, 1964—65, rsch. scientist, 1964—66, instr. medicine, 1964—74, clin. asst. prof. medicine, 1974—; gen. practice medicine Miami, 1966—96. Mem. staff Bapt. Hosp. Miami, sec.-treas. med. staff, 1979-80, chief of staff, 1980-82; acting chief of staff Oakland Park VA Med. Ctr., 1998-99; med. cons. Social Security Adminstrn., 1996—. Contbr. articles to profl. jours. Bd. dirs. Jewish Vocat. Svc.; active Greater Miami Jewish Fedn., chmn. physicians divsn., 1979-80. Capt. M.C., U.S. Army, 1963-67, Vietnam. Recipient Disting. Alumnus award, U. Miami Sch. Medicine, 1998, Cmty. Tchr. award, Fla. chpt. ACP, 1999. Mem. AMA, AAAS, Am. Acad. Sci., Am. Coll. Gastroenterology, Am. Soc. Gastroent. Endoscopy, U. Miami Med. Alumni Assn. (chmn. Dade County chpt. 1972-75, nat. pres. 1975-77, v.p. pub. rels. 1987-89, v.p. 1987-90), Gen. Alumni U. Miami (bd. dirs. 1973-77, v.p. 1988-95, bd. overseers 1988—, sec. 1990, v.p. 1991), Fla. Gastroent. Soc., Greater Miami Jewish Fedn., Alpha Omega Alpha, Omicron Delta Kappa. Democrat.

BLOOM, FLOYD ELLIOTT, internist, research scientist; b. Mpls., Oct. 8, 1936; s. Jack Aaron and Frieda (Shochman) B.; m. D'Nell Bingham, Aug. 30, 1956 (dec. May 1973); children: Fl'Nell, Evan Russell; m. Jody Patricia Corey, Aug. 9, 1980. AB cum laude, So. Meth. U., 1956; MD cum laude, Washington U., St. Louis, 1960; DSc (hon.), So. Meth. U., 1983, Hahnemann U., 1985, U. Rochester, 1985, Mt. Sinai U. Med. Sch., 1996, Thomas Jefferson U., 1997, Washington U., 1998; DSc (hon.), Kellogg Sch., Scripps Rsch. Inst., 2005. Intern Barnes Hosp., St. Louis, 1960-61, resident internal medicine, 1961-62; research asso. NIMH, Washington, 1962-64; fellow depts. pharmacology, psychiatry and anatomy Yale Sch. Medicine, 1964-66, asst. prof., 1966-67, asso. prof., 1968; chief lab. neuropharmacology NIMH, Washington, 1968-75, acting dir. div. spl. mental health, 1973-75; commd. officer USPHS, 1974-75; dir. Arthur Vining Davis Center for Behavorial Neurobiology; prof. Salk Inst., La Jolla, Calif., 1975-83; dir. div. preclin. neurosci. and endocrinology The Scripps Rsch. Inst., La Jolla, 1983-89, chmn. dept. neuropharmacology, 1989—2005, prof. emeritus, 2005—; editor in chief Science Magazine, 1995-2000; chief exec. officer Neurome, Inc., 2000—02, chmn. bd., 2000—; editor in chief Brain Rsch., 2000—. Mem. Commn. on Alcoholism, 1980—81, Nat. Adv. Mental Health Coun., 1976—80; chmn. scientific adv. bd. Pharmavene, Inc., 1994—98; bd. dirs. Alkermes, Inc.; chmn. sci. adv. bd. Advancis Corp. Author: (with others) Biochemical Basis of Neuropharmacology, 1971, 8th edit., 2002, (with Lazerson and Hofstadter) Brain, Mind and Behavior, 1984, (with Lazerson) 2d edit., 1988, (with C.A. Nelson) 3d edit., 2000, (with W. Young and Y. Kim) Brain browser, 1989; editor: Peptides: Integrators of Cell and Tissue Function, 1980, Progress in Brain Research, vol. 199, 1994, vol. 100, 1997, (with D.J. Kupfer) Neuro-Psychopharmacology: The Fourth Generation of Progress, 1994, Handbook of Chemical Neruoanatomy, 1997, The Primate Nervous System, 1997, vol. II, 1998, vol. III, 1999, (with Beal and Kupfer) The Dana Guide to Brain Health, 2003; co-editor: Regulatory Peptides, 1979-90, (with M. Randolph) Funding Health Sciences Research, 1990; assoc. editor: Biological Psychiatry, 1993-95; editor-in-chief Science, 1995-2000, Brain Rsch., 2000—. Trustee Washington U., St. Louis, 1998—, chmn. nat. med. coun., 2000—. Recipient A. Cressy Morrison award N.Y. Acad. Scis., 1971, A.E. Bennett award for basic rsch. Soc. Biol. Psychiatry, 1971, Arthur A. Fleming award Science mag., 1973, Mathilde Solowey award, 1973, Biol. Sci. award Washington Acad. Scis., 1975, Alumni Achievement citation Washington U., 1980, McAlpin Rsch. Achievement award Mental Health Assn., 1980, Lectr.'s medal College de France, 1979, Steven Beering medal, 1985, Janssen award World Psychiat. Assn., 1989, Passerow Found. award, 1990, Herman von Helmholtz award, 1991, Pythagora award, 1994, Presdl. award Soc. for Neurosci., 1995, Golgi prize U. Brescia, 1996, Meritorious Achievement award Coun. Biology Editors, 1999, Gold medal Soc. Biol. Psychiatry, 1997, Disting. Svc. award Am. Psychiat. Assn., 2000, Thomas William Salmon medal, NY Acad. Medicine for Psychiatry and Mental Hygiene, 2004, Walsh McDermott medal, Inst. Medicine, 2004, Dedmar Coll. Disting. Grad. award, South Methodist U., 2005; Disting. fellow Am. Psychiat. Assn., 1986; named scientist of the yr. Achievement Rewards for Coll. Scientists, 1996. Fellow AAAS (bd. dirs. 1986-90, pres.-elect 2001, pres. 2002, chmn. bd. dirs. 2003), Am. Coll. Neuropsychopharmacology (mem. coun. 1976-78, chmn. program com. 1987, pres. 1988-89, Hoch award 1998); mem. NAS (chmn. sect. neurobiology 1979-83, co-chair reports rev. com. 2004—), Inst. Medicine (mem. coun. 1986-89, 93-95), Am. Philos. Soc. (chmn. Lashley award com. 2001—), Am. Acad. Arts and Scis., Soc. Neurosci. (sec. 1973-74, pres. 1976, chmn. publs. com. 1999—2002), Am. Soc. Pharmacology and Exptl. Therapeutics, Am. Soc. Cell Biology, Am. Physiol. Soc., Am. Assn. Anatomists, Rsch. Soc. Alcoholism (chmn. program com. 1985-87, pres.-elect 1989-91, pres. 1991-93), Swedish Acad. Sci. (fgn. assoc. 1989). Home: 628 Pacific View Dr San Diego CA 92109-1768 Office: The Scripps Rsch Inst 10550 N Torrey Pines Rd La Jolla CA 92037-1000 Office Phone: 858-677-0466. Business E-Mail: fbloom@neurome.com.

BLOOM, FRANCES VIRGINIA, retired music educator; b. Chgo., Oct. 31, 1911; d. Joseph and Bertha (Walker) Bloom. Student, coll. night sch. With ins. co.; stenographer, sec. L.A. County; newspaper columnist Glendale News Press, others; music tchr. violin, piano, guitar. Author: Grace Notes mag. Grantee grantee, Hilton Hotel, others. Mem.: Calif. Music Tchrs.' Assn.

BLOOM, GARY L., database company executive; BS in Computer Sci., Calif. Poly. State U., San Luis Obispo. Various tech. positions IBM Corp., Chevron Corp.; various positions Oracle Corp., Redwood Shores, Calif., 1986—2000, v.p. mainframe and integration tech. divsn., 1992—96, v.p. massively parallel computing divsn., 1992—96, sr. v.p. product and platform techs. divsn., 1996—97, sr. v.p. worldwide alliances and techs. divsn., 1997, sr. v.p. sys. products divsn., 1997—98, exec. v.p. systems product, 1998—99, exec. v.p., 1999—2000; mem. bd. dir., pres., CEO Veritas Software Corp., Mountain View, Calif., 2000—, chmn. bd. dis., 2002—, also mem. exec. mgmt. com., mgmt. com., product devel. mgmt. com. Serves on President's Cabinet Calif. Polytechnic State U., San Luis Obispo. Office: Vertas Software Corp 350 Ellis St Mountain View CA 94043 Office Phone: 650-527-8000.

BLOOM, HAROLD, humanities educator, writer; b. NYC, July 11, 1930; s. William and Paula (Lev) B.; m. Jeanne Gould, May 8, 1958; children: Daniel Jacob, David Moses. BA, Cornell U., 1951; PhD, Yale U., 1955; LHD, Boston Coll., 1973, Yeshiva U., 1976, U. Bologna, 1997, St. Michael's Coll., 1998, U. Rome, 1999, U. Coimbra, 2001, U. Mass at Dartmouth, 2002. Mem. faculty Yale U., 1955—, prof. English, 1965-77, DeVane prof. humanities, 1974-77, prof. humanities, 1977—, Sterling prof. humanities, 1983—. Vis. prof. Hebrew U., Jerusalem, 1959, Breadloaf Summer Sch., 1965-66, Soc. for Humanities, Cornell U., 1968-69; vis. Univ. prof. New Sch. Social Rsch., NYC, 1982-84; Charles Eliot Norton prof. of poetry Harvard U., 1987-88; Berg prof. Eng., NYU, 1988—2004. Author: Shelley's Mythmaking, 1959, The Visionary Company, 1961, Blake's Apocalypse, 1963, Commentary on Blake, 1965, Yeats, 1970, The Ringers in the Tower, 1971, The Anxiety of Influence, 1973, Wallace Stevens: The Poems of Our Climate, 1977, A Map of Misreading, 1975, Kabbalah and Criticism, 1975, Poetry and Repression, 1976, Figures of Capable Imagination, 1976, The Flight to Lucifer: A Gnostic Fantasy, 1979, Agon: Towards a Theory of Revisionism, 1981, The Breaking of the Vessels, 1981, The Strong Light of the Canonical, 1987, Freud: Transference and Authority, 1988, Poetics of Influence: New and Selected Criticism, 1988, Ruin the Sacred Truths, 1988, The Book of J, 1990, The Am. Religion, 1992, The Western Canon, 1994, Omens of Millennium, 1996, Shakespeare: The Invention of the Human, 1998, How to Read and Why, 1999, Stories and Poems for Extremely Intelligent Children of all Ages, 2000, Genius, 2002, Hamlet: Poem Unlimited, 2003, Best Poems of the English Language: Chaucer to Hart Crane, 2004, Where Shall Wisdom Be Found?, 2004, The Names Divine: Jesus and Yahweh, 2005; editor Chelsea House Modern Critical Views and Interpretations, 1984—. Recipient John Addison Porter prize Yale U., 1955; Newton Arvin award, 1967; Melville Cane award Poetry Soc. Am., 1970; Zabel prize Am. Inst. Arts and Letters, 1982, Christian Gauss prize Phi Beta Kappa, 1989, Internat. prize Catalonia, 2002; Reyes Internat. Prize, Mexico, 2003, Hans Christian Andersen prize of Denmark, 2005; Guggenheim fellow, 1962; Fulbright fellow, 1955; MacArthur prize fellow, 1985. Mem. Am. Acad. Arts and Letters (Gold medal 1999), Am. Philos. Soc. Home: 179 Linden St New Haven CT 06511-2407 E-mail: harold.bloom@gels.com. *Most instances of religion are mere manifestations of religiosity, which is endemic in our nation, where nine of ten say that God loves them. Spinoza observed that we should love God without expecting that God would love us in return.*

BLOOM, HYMAN (CHAIN MELAMED), artist; b. Brunoviski, Latvia, Mar. 29, 1913; came to U.S., 1920; parents Joseph Melamed and Anna Solomed; m. Nina Bohlen, 1954 (div. 1961); m. Stella Caralis, 1978. Ed., West End Community Center, Boston.; studied under, Harold K. Zimmerman, Danman Waldo Ross. Instr. Wellesley (Mass.) Coll., 1949-51, Harvard U., Cambridge, Mass., 1951-53. One-man shows, Stuart Gallery, Boston, 1945, Inst. Contemporary Art, Boston, Whitney Mus. Art, N.Y.C., 1945, 54, 68, Albright Knox Art Gallery, Buffalo, 1954, Wadsworth Atheneum, 1957, U. Conn. Mus. Art, 1969, Terry Dintenfass Gallery, 1972, 75, retrospective, Paul Mus., U. N.H., 1992, U. N.H. Mus., 1992, Bateo Coll. Mus., 2001, Nat. Acad. Design, 2002, others; exhbns. include Butler Inst. Am. Art, 1972, Esther Robles Gallery, Brentwood Park, 1976, Ind. U. Mus., Bloomington, 1977, Ind. Mus. Art, 1977-78, Inst. Contemporary Art, Boston, 1979, others; represented in permanent collections, Hirshorn Mus., Washington, Mus. Modern Art, N.Y.C., Whitney Mus. Art, Harvard U., Kalamazoo Inst. Arts, Mich., Minn. Mus. Art, St. Paul, Mus. Fine Arts, Boston, Jewish Mus., N.Y.C., Bloom Found., The Pan Orient Arts Mus. Fellow, Ford Found.; Guggenheim fellow. Mem.: Nat. Acad. Design, Am. Acad. Arts and Letters. Office Phone: 603-886-1710.

BLOOM, JACK SANDLER, investment banker; b. Boston, Mar. 20, 1957; s. Joseph and Inez (Sandler) B.; m. Jennifer Kingson, May 14, 1964; 1 child, Valerie. BA, Harvard U., 1979; MBA, MIT Sloan Sch., 1983. V.p. Allied Ventures, N.Y.C., 1983-85, Kaufman & Co., Boston, 1985-88; pres. Alpha Capital Corp., N.Y.C., 1988—; mng. dir. corp. fin. Commonwealth Assocs., 1994-95; pres. Auto Am., 1996—. Office: Alpha Capital Corp 950 3rd Ave Ste 2600 New York NY 10022-2705

BLOOM, JANE MAGINNIS, emergency physician; b. Ithaca, N.Y., June 22, 1924; d. Ernest Victor and Miriam Rebecca (Mansfield) M.; m. William Lee Bloom, Mar. 31, 1944; children: David Lee, Jan Christopher, Carolyn Wells, Eric Paul, Joseph William, Robert Carl, Mary Catherine, Thomas Mark, Patrick Martin (dec.), Arthur Emerson. BS, U. Mich., 1968, MD, 1974. Bd. cert. Am. Bd. Internal Medicine, Am. Bd. Emergency Medicine. Rotating intern Wayne County Gen. Hosp., Eloise, Mich., 1974-75; resident in internal medicine St. Mary's Hosp., Rochester, NY, 1975-77; emergency physician Emergency Physicians Med. Group, Ann Arbor, 1986—2003. Fellow: Am. Coll. Emergency Physicians (life); mem.: AMA, Mich. State Med. Soc., Am. Coll. Physicians, Am. Med. Womens Assn., Am. Assn. Women Emergency Physicians, Washtenaw County Med. Soc. Avocations: bird watching, planting trees, classical music, walking. Home and Office: 537 Elm St Ann Arbor MI 48104-2515 Office Phone: 734-761-2435.

BLOOM, JANET K., audio-visual specialist, poet; b. Tucson, Ariz. d. Benson and Christina Affeld (Johnson) Bloom. BA, Bennington Coll.; MFA, Goddard Coll. Assoc. editor Holiday Mag., NYC, 1964—65; editl. asst. Arch. Record, NYC, 1970—72; assoc. editor Arch. Forum, NYC, 1972—73. Presenter, lectr. in field. Author: Soul Progressions: Harmoniously Releasing Ourselves From What Got Into Us, 2005. Poetry workshop dir. St. Clements Ch., NYC, 1977—81. Artist Tchg. fellow, CETA, 1979—80. Mem.: Nat. Writers Union, Internat. Imagery Assn. Office: Image Grove PO Box 173 Lake Peekskill NY 10537

BLOOM, JERRY R., lawyer; b. Phila., Pa. s. Harry and Leatrice Bloom. BA, George Wash. U., 1974, MA, 1976; JD, U. Miami Sch. Law, 1980. Bar: Fla. 1981, D.C. 1981, N.Y. 1984, Calif. 1988. Assoc. Chadbourne & Parke, N.Y.C., 1982—87; ptnr. Morrison & Foerster, L.A., 1987—98, White & Case, LLP, L.A., 1998—; chair energy sector White & Case; advisor, counsel Calif. Cogeneration Coun. Energy advisor Forbes Radio Channel, Am. Airlines, 2003. Author: (article) World Generation: Making Sense of the Turmoil in the Industry, 2003; radio, TV appearances Week In Review, Adelphia Comm. Named to Super Lawyers, So. Calif. Super Lawyers, 2004, 2005; recipient Top Tier I status, Chambers USA, 2003, 2004. Office: White & Case 633 W Fifth St Ste 1900 Los Angeles CA 90071 Office Phone: 213-620-7707. Office Fax: 213-687-9758. Business E-Mail: jbloom@whitecase.com.

BLOOM, JOEL S., academic administrator; BA, CUNY; MA, PhD, Columbia U. Tchr., sch. adminstr. N.Y.C. Pub. Schs.; dir. rsch., instr. Columbia U. Tchrs. Coll., NY; mgr. N.E. Ednl. Improvement Ctr. U.S. Dept. Edn.; asst. commr. divsn. gen. acad. edn. N.J. Dept. Edn., 1984—90; v.p. acad. affairs N.J. Inst. Tech., Newark, 1990—, dean Albert Doman Honors Coll., 1997—. Chair N.J. Coll. Bound Adv. Bd., Greater Newark Consortium Bd. for Pre-Coll. Edn.; mem. N.J. Bd. for Cmtys. and Schs., N.J. Pres. Coun. Task Force on Transfer and Mission Differentiation; bd. mem. Phila. Alliance for Minority Participation, N.J. Assn. Ptnrs. in Edn. Office: Office of the VP NJ Inst Tech Newark NJ 07102

BLOOM, JOSEPH D., medical educator, psychiatrist; MD, Albert Einstein Coll. Medicine. Diplomate in psychiatry and in forensic psychiatry Am. Bd. Psychiatry and Neurology. Intern Mt. Zion Hosp. and Med. Ctr., San Francisco; resident in psychiatry Harvard U.; chief psychiat. resident Southard Clinic Mass. Mental Health Ctr.; chief mental health unit Alaska Native Health Svc. USPHS; pvt. practice Anchorage; dir. cmty. psychiatry tng. program Oreg. Health Sci. U., Portland, 1977, chmn. dept. psychiatry, 1986-94, interim dean Sch. Medicine, 1993-94, dean Sch. Medicine, 1994-2001. Office: Oreg Health Scis U Sch Medicine 3181 SW Sam Jackson Park Rd Portland OR 97201-3011 Office Phone: 503-494-6689. E-mail: bloomj@ohsu.edu.

BLOOM, LAWRENCE STEPHEN, retired clothing company executive; b. New Rochelle, N.Y., Apr. 30, 1930; s. Hyman and Eleanor (Bursch) B.; m. Mary Ann Hendricks, Aug. 15, 1959; children: Mark, Julie. BS in Commerce and Fin, Bucknell U., Lewisburg, Pa., 1952. Trainee Gimbels, N.Y.C., to 1954; with Warnaco Inc., 1954-90; former chmn. Warnaco Men's Knitwear (Puritan, Thane and Hathaway Knitwear), Altoona, Pa. Bd. dirs. Woolknit Assocs., Nat. Sportwear and Outerwear Assocs.; chpt. chair Svc. Corps of Retired Execs. Served with AUS, 1952-54. Home: 340 Deer Run Rd Hollidaysburg PA 16648-3110 E-mail: blooml@msn.com.

BLOOM, LEE HURLEY, lawyer, consultant, retired consumer products company executive; b. NYC, June 21, 1919; s. Harry and Harriet (Bresel) B.; m. Mary Louise Tolan, Dec. 15, 1945; children: Daniel, Louise, Douglas. BS, MIT, 1940; LL.B., Harvard U., 1943. Bar: Mass. 1947, N.Y. 1951. Atty. legal div. Lever Bros. Co., N.Y.C., 1947-67, v.p., sec., gen. counsel, 1968-70, adminstrv. v.p., dir., 1970-82; pres. Unilever U.S., Inc., 1978-82, vice chmn., 1982-83. Donald L. Wilson prof., Grinnell Coll., Iowa, 1986. Chmn. bd. Larchmont (N.Y.) chpt. ARC, 1961—63; mem. Mamaroneck Planning Bd., 1959—69, Mamaroneck Town Bd., 1969—85, dep. supr., 1982—83; coord. N.Y. State Sch. and Bus. Alliance for Yonkers Pub. Schs., 1987—93; chmn. Ctr. for Performing Arts Lehman Coll., 1987—93, Sheldrake Environ. Ctr., 1995—2003; mem. Town of Mamaroneck (N.Y.) Rep. Com., 1957—69. Served to lt. comdr. USNR, 1941—46. Mem. Soap and Detergent Assn. (dir. 1971-83, vice chmn. 1978-79, chmn. 1980-82), Assn. Pvt. Enterprise Edn. (exec. com. 1985-93), Internat. C. of C. (trustee U.S. coun. 1978-86, exec. com. 1980-86, vice chmn. 1982-85, sr. trustee 1987—), UN Assn. U.S.A. (pres. so. N.Y. state divsn. 1989-93). Home and Office: 22 Myrtle Blvd Larchmont NY 10538-1823 E-mail: leehbloom@aol.com.

BLOOM, LISA READ, lawyer; b. Phila., Sept. 20, 1961; d. Peyton Huddleston Bray and Gloria Allred; children: Sarah Wong Bloom, Samuel Bloom Wong. BA, UCLA, 1983; JD, Yale U., 1986. Bar: N.Y., 1987, Calif., 1992; U.S. Dist. Ct. (so. and ea. dists.) N.Y., 1987, U.S. Dist. Ct. (cen. dist.) Calif. 1992. Assoc. Meister, Leventhal & Slade, N.Y.C., 1986-87, Robinson, Silverman, Pearce, Aronsohn & Berman, N.Y.C., 1987-91, Allred, Maroko & Goldberg, L.A., 1992—2001; co-host Closing Arguments Court TV, 2001—03, co-anchor Trial Heat, 2003—. Spkr. in field. Numerous TV and radio appearances. Recipient Cert. of Merit, Courage to Tell Found., Calif., 1993. Office: Court TV Network LLC 600 Third Ave New York NY 10016

BLOOM, MARK DAVID, lawyer; b. Phila., Sept. 25, 1953; s. Sheperd and Muriel Esther (Wallner) B.; m. Annette Rodriguez, July 17, 1982; children: Sara Michelle, Stefan Jacob. BA in Polit. Sci., Yale U., 1975; JD, U. Md., 1979. Bar: Md. 1979, D.C. 1980, Fla. 1980, U.S. Dist. Ct. Md. 1980, U.S. Ct. Appeals (4th cir.) 1980, U.S. Dist. Ct. (so. dist.) Fla. 1981, U.S. Ct. Appeals (5th and 11th cirs.) 1981, U.S. Dist. Ct. (mid. dist.) Fla. 1986. Law clk. U.S. Dist. Ct. Md., Balt., 1979-80; assoc. Greenberg, Traurig, Askew, Hoffman, Lipoff, Rosen & Quentel, Miami, Fla., 1980-86; shareholder, nat. co-chair reorganization, bankruptcy, restructuring dept. Greenberg, Traurig LLP (formerly Greenberg Traurig Hoffman, Lipoff, Rosen & Quentel, P.A.), Miami, 1986—. Lectr., author on bankruptcy and reorgn. for ALI-ABA, Norton Bankruptcy Law Inst., Exec. Enterprises, Fla. Bar Assn. Mem. Bankruptcy Bar Assn. (bd. dirs. So. Dist. Fla. 1986-87, officer 1987-90). Democrat. Jewish. Avocations: swimming, travel, wine. Office: Greenberg Traurig LLP 1221 Brickell Ave Miami FL 33131-3224 Office Phone: 305-579-0537. Office Fax: 305-579-0717. Business E-Mail: bloomm@gtlaw.com.

BLOOM, MYER, physicist, researcher; b. Montreal, Que., Can., Dec. 7, 1928; s. Israel and Leah (Ram) B.; m. Margaret Holmes, May 29, 1954; children— David, Margot. B.Sc., McGill U., 1949, M.Sc., 1950; PhD, U. Ill., 1954; D (hon.), Tech. U. Denmark, 1994; DSc (hon.), U. B.C., 2000. Research fellow U. Leiden, 1954-56; faculty U. B.C., Vancouver, 1956—, assoc. prof., 1960-63, prof. physics, 1963-93; D (hon.) Concordia U., 1995. Recipient Steacie prize, 1967, Jacob Biely prize, 1968, Gold medal Can. Assn. Physicists, 1973, Sci. Coun. of B.C. Chmn.'s award for career achievement, 1992, Izaak Walton Killam Meml. prize in natural sci., 1995; Alfred P. Sloan fellow, 1961-65; John Simon Guggenheim fellow, 1964-65; Izaak Walton Killam Meml. scholar, 1978-79. Fellow Royal Soc. Can., Am. Phys. Soc., Can. Inst. for Advanced Rsch. Achievements include research in structure and molecular motion in biological and model membranes, nuclear magnetic resonance. Home: 804-2233 Allison Rd Vancouver BC Canada V6T 1T7 Business E-Mail: bloom@physics.ubc.ca.

BLOOM, ORLANDO, actor; b. Canterbury, England, Jan. 13, 1977; s. Harry Bloom and Sonia Copeland-Bloom. Attended, Nat. Youth Theatre London, British Am. Drama Acad.; grad., Guildhall Sch. Music and Drama, 1996—99. Actor: (films) Wilde, 1997, The Lord of the Rings: The Fellowship of the Rings, 2001 (Empire award for best debut, 2001, Best Breakthrough Star award MTV Movie Awards, 2002), Black Hawk Down, 2001, The Lord of the Rings: The Two Towers, 2002, Ned Kelly, 2003, Pirates of the Caribbean: The Curse of the Black Pearl, 2003, The Lord of the Rings: The Return of the King, 2003, Troy, 2004, Kingdom of Heaven, 2005; actor, co-prodr. (films) Haven, 2004; actor: (TV series) Midsomer Murders; (plays) Casualty, London's Burning, Twelfth Night, Uncle Vanya, Little Me, Peer Gynt. Mailing: c/o ICM Oxford House 76 Oxford St London W1D 1BS England*

BLOOM, SHERMAN, retired pathology educator, photographer; b. Bklyn., Jan. 26, 1934; s. Philip and Sadie (Kaplan) B.; m. Miriam Fishman, Feb. 11, 1960; children: Naomi, Stephanie. BA, NYU, 1955, MD, 1960. Diplomate Am. Bd. Anat. Pathology. Intern in medicine Kings County Hosp., Bklyn., 1960-61; fellow in exptl. pathology, resident in anatomic and clin. pathology NYU Med. Ctr. and Bellevue Hosp., N.Y.C., 1961-65; instr. pathology NYU Sch. Medicine, 1965-66; asst. prof. U. Utah Coll. Medicine, Salt Lake City,

1966-70, assoc. prof., 1970-72, U. South Fla. Coll. Medicine, Tampa, 1973-76, prof. pathology, 1976-77, George Washington U. Coll. Medicine, Washington, 1977-88; prof., chmn. dept. pathology U. Miss. Med. Ctr., Jackson, 1988-2000, prof. emeritus, 2000—, ret., 1999; pres. PhotoTov Fine Arts, 2004. Cons. Sci. Rev., NIH; mem. cardiovascular study sect. NSF, FDA; dir. coun. on cardiovascular and geriatric health Amer Coll. Nutrition, 1998-01; bd. dirs. Scientists Ctr. Animal Welfare, pres. elect, 1987, pres., 1988. Mem. editl. bd. Jour. Am. Coll. Nutrition, 1982, Am. Jour. Cardiovascular Pathology, 1985; assoc. editor Cardiovascular Pathology, 1990; fine art photo pub. Jour. Miss. State Med. Assn.; contbr. numerous articles to profl. publs. Del. Utah State Dem. Party, 1968. NIH fellow, 1962; Dilthey Found. fellow, 1982. Fellow Am. Coll. Nutrition; mem. Internat. Acad. Pathologists, Am. Physiol. Soc., Am. Assn. Pathologists, Internat. Soc. Heart Research, Soc. Cardiovascular Pathology (pres. 1986-87), Photograph Soc. Am. Jewish. Home: 4433 Wedgewood St Jackson MS 39211-6219 Personal E-mail: shermanbloom@earthlink.net.

BLOOM, STEPHEN C., music educator; s. Laurence and Elaine Bloom. MusB in Edn., Ithaca Coll., 1990; MusM in Edn., Ind. U., 1998. Cert. tchr., K-9 Music Mass. Dept. Edn., 2003, tchr., Grades 5-12 Music Mass. Dept. Edn., 2003. Music dir. Monson Jr.-Sr. H.S., Mass., 1990—93; assoc. instr. music edn. Ind. U., Bloomington, 1993—95; music tchr., drug & alcohol awareness tchr. Brown Mid. Sch., Newton, Mass., 1996—96; music dir. Lynnfield Mid. Sch., 1996—. Music dir.-mid. sch. musical theater prodns. Lynnfield Mid. Sch., 1998—, music dir.-mid. sch. pioneer singers treble choir, 1998—, music dir.- mid. sch. jazz band, 1997—; summer conducting seminar Ithaca Coll., 1992, 2002; camp counselor Drumlin Farm, Mass. Audubon Soc., Lincoln, 1989—93; lectr. Lynnfield Pub. Libr., 1998—2003, Lincoln Pub. Libr., 1998—98. Singer chorus pro musica, boston, ma, tanglewood festival chorus; composer/arranger (original compositions and arrangements), conductor (moses, an inter-racial gospel opera) The Ten Commandments. Iola Taylor Music Edn. scholar, Ithaca Coll., 1988. Mem.: Music Educators Nat. Conf., Mass. Music Educators Assn., Am. Coaster Enthusiasts, Chorus Pro Musica, Pi Kappa Lambda. Independent. Office: Lynnfield Pub Schs 505 Main St Lynnfield MA 01940 Office Phone: 781-334-5810 37100.

BLOOM, WILLIAM MILLARD, furnace design engineer; b. New Kensington, Pa., Aug. 10, 1925; s. William Lewis and Natalie Tillbrook (McMillan) B.; m. Judith Ann Callen, May 23, 1953; children: Kimberly Ann, Stacey Ellen. BA, Geneva Coll., 1951; BSME, Carnegie Inst. Tech., 1951. Registered profl. engr., Pa. Fuel engr. maintenance dept. Brackenridge (Pa.) Plant, Allegheny Ludlum Steel, 1951-56; fuel engr. gen. engring. divsn. Allegheny Ludlum Steel Corp., Brackenridge, 1956-59, sr. engr. furnaces and fuels, gen. engring. divsn., 1959-61; chief engr. furnaces and fuels gen. engring. divsn. Allegheny Ludlum Industries, Pitts., 1961-71; asst. to v.p. engring. spl. assignments Allegheny Ludlum Steel Corp., Brackenridge, 1971-81, mgr. furnace design engring., mfg. engring. Pitts., 1981-92; pvt. practice cons. indsl. furnaces Pitts., 1992—. Cons. Alloy Rods Corp., Hanover, Pa., 1989, Timet Corp., Henderson, Nev., Toronto, Ohio, IPM Corp., Ridgeway, Pa., Columbus, Ohio, Tube Turn Corp., Louisville, True Temper, Geneva, Ohio, Arnold Engring., Chgo., Altech, Dunkirk, N.Y., Posco, Korea, Kuhlman Electric, Lexington, Ky., 1961-92. With U.S. Army, 1944—46, ETO. Mem. NSPE, Assn. Iron and Steel Engrs. (life, bd. dirs., chmn. combustion com., AISE-KELLY award 1st pl. 1979), 70th Divsn. Assn. (life), Theta Xi (life). Republican. Methodist. Achievements include patents for Bar Furnace Seals, Annealing Apparatus, Coil Quench, Conveyor Roll, Tunnel Furnace, Annealing Furnace, Steel Scrap Preheater, Apparatus Scrap Preheater, Roll Turner/Remover, Jet Heat Reucperator, Replaceable Ladle Heater Seals, High Temp Fan Plug, Hot Strip Mill Cover Heat Retention; developed high temperature hydrogen anneal tunnel furnace for grain oriented silicon steels that significantly lowered watt losses/pound to develop class of steel, jet heat recuperators that reduce continous anneal furnaces fuel input by 50% and increases production 50%. Home: 1522 King John Dr Pittsburgh PA 15237-1590

BLOOMBERG, BRETA CHAPMAN, music educator; b. Clay Center, Kans. d. Wayne and Margaret Bloomberg. B in Music Edn., U. Kans., 1977; MusM, Kans. State U., 1982. Orch. tchr. Ponca City (Okla.) Pub. Sch., 1978—80; orch. and elem. music tchr. Clay County Pub. Sch., Clay Center, Kans., 1985—90; elem. music tchr. Manhattan (Kans.) Pub. Sch., 1990—99; orch. dir. Topeka (Kans.) Pub. Sch., 1999—. Double bassist Topeka Symphony, 1998—; pvt. music tchr.; owner antique business Margaret B's. Conductor: Youth Philharmonic, Topeka Symphony Soc., 1998—. Mem. Topeka/Shawnee County Landmarks Commn., 1998—; cmty. action coun. rep. Highland Pk., Topeka, 2005; dir. music Highland Pk. United Meth. Ch., 2003—; tennis official Big 12 Conf. and other USTA events. Recipient Mid. Level Orch. Tchr. of Yr., N.E. Kans. Music Educators, 2003. Mem.: DAR, Rotary. Methodist. Avocations: golf, antiques, cross stitch, reading, historic preservation. Home: 2844 SE Kentucky Topeka KS 66605 Office: Topeka High Sch 800 SW 10th Topeka KS 66612

BLOOMBERG, LAWRENCE S., security firm executive, art appraiser; b. Montreal, Que., Can., May 28, 1942; s. Sol and Sylvia Bloomberg; m. Frances Bloomberg; children: Debra, Bonnie, Jonathon. B of Commerce, Sir George Williams U., 1963; MBA, McGill U., 1965; LLD (hon.), Concordia U., 1996. Chartered fin analyst. Various mgmt. positions including head of rsch., v.p., dir. Instnl. Equity Sales, Nesbitt, Thomson and Co. Ltd., 1965-76; v.p., dir. Instnl. Equity Sales, Nesbitt Thomson and Co., 1975-79; founding mem. 1st Marathon Securities, Ltd., 1979; pres., CEO, dir. 1st Marathon Inc., 1984-99; adv. Nat. Bank Fin., Inc., 1999—. Past mem. Young Pres.'s Orgn.; past mem. bd. govs. Toronto Stock Exch.; founding mem. Concordia's Faculty of Commerce and Admininstrn. Bus. Adv. Com.; bd. dirs. Nat. Bank Can.; founding dir., bd. dirs. MARS. Chmn. Mt. Sinai Hosp., Baycrest Ctr. for Geriatric Care; dir. Simon Wiesenthal Ctr., Inc.; co-chmn. toronto's 1994 United Jewish Appeal/Operation Exodus Campaign; active United Way campaigns; past gov. Jr. Achievement of Can.; mem. Rector's Cir., Concordia U., founding mem. Faculty of Commerce and Adminstrn. Bus. Adv. Com.; past bd. dirs. Toronto Internat. Film Festival Group, Royal Ont. Mus. Found.; mem. Can. Inst. Internat. Affairs; former bd. dirs. Toronto Stock Exch.; former mem. Bus. Coun. on Nat. Issues, C.D. Howe Inst., Investment Dealers Assn. Can., CDN Coun. of Chief Exec. Recipient Human Rels. award Can. Coun. Christians and Jews, Outstanding Vol. Award Assn. Profl. Fundraisers, 2003. Mem. XPO, World Pres.'s Orgn., Rector's Cir. of Concordia U. Avocations: running, golf. Office: Nat Bank Financial 130 King St W Toronto ON Canada M5X 1J9

BLOOMBERG, MARY BETH, public affairs executive; b. Boston, Sept. 6, 1947; d. Edward Theodore and Ida Tina (Bram) B. BA, Colo. Coll., 1969; MEd, U. Va., 1972. Head resource tchr. Albemarle County Schs., Charlottesville, Va., 1972-76; records mgr. DAON Corp., Newport Beach, Calif., 1976-78; office mgr. Baker for Pres., Washington, 1979-80; adminstrn. dir. Nat. Rep. Senatorial Com., Washington, 1980-81; exec. asst. Senator Paula Hawkins, Washington, 1981; spl. asst. White House Conf. on Aging, Washington, 1981-82; dep. dir. U.S. Agy. for Internat. Devel., Washington, 1982-83; sr. spl. asst. to sec. Dept. Health and Human Service, Washington, 1983-86; sr. v.p. Reese Communications Co., Arlington, Va., 1987-91; sr. v.p., group mgr. Burson-Marsteller, Washington, 1991-92; prin. Direct Impact Co., Alexandria, Va., 1993—. Chmn. steering com. Found. Election Law Edn., Alexandria, 1986-87; mem. steering com. Dole Found., Washington, 1986-95; mem. ops. 50th Am. Pres. Inaugural, Washington, 1984. Mem. exec. com. Lombardi Meml. Tournament, Washington, 1984-92; bd. dirs. Vincent T. Lombardi Found., Washington, 1986-91; mem. benefit com. CARE, Washington, 1986-88; mem. Jr. League of Washington, 1983—; vice chmn. The Pres.'s Dinner, Washington, 1987-98. Mem. Women in Govt. Relations, Fed. of Rep. Women, Phi Theta Kappa. Republican. Avocations: tennis, reading, travel.

BLOOMBERG, MICHAEL RUBENS, mayor; b. Medford, Mass., Feb. 14, 1942; divorced; 2 children. Graduate, Johns Hopkins U., 1964; MBA, Harvard U., 1966. Processing clerk Salomon Brothers, 1966, gen. ptnr. sys. devel. N.Y.C.; pres. founder Bloomberg L.P., N.Y.C., 1981—, pres., CEO; pub. Bloomberg Business News, N.Y.C.; gen. mgr. Bloomberg Television, Bloomberg Radio, Sta. WBBR-AM 1130, N.Y.C.; pub. Bloomberg Mag./Bloomberg Personal Mag., Princeton, N.J., Bloomberg Personal, Skillman, N.J.; mayor N.Y.C., 2002—. Author: (autobiography) Bloomberg by Bloomberg, 1997. Chmn. bd. trustees Johns Hopkins U.; trustee Big Apple Circus, Ctrl. Park Conservancy, Met. Mus. Art, H.S. Econs. And Fin., Inst. Advanced Study, Lincoln Ctr. Performing Arts, Jewish Mus., N.Y. Police and Fire Widows' and Childrens' Fund, Spence Sch., Prep for Prep, S.L.E. Found., U.S. Ski Team Ednl. Found., Serpentine Gallery, London. Mem. U.S. C. of C. (trustee). Office: City Hall 52 Chambers St New York NY 10007-1222

BLOOMBERG, STU, television producer; B, Georgetown U.; MA in Cinema, U. Southern Calif. Chmn. ABC Entertainment, co-chmn., 1997—2002; prodr. & program developer Disney/Touchstone, 2002—. Co-chmn. ACB Entertainment TV Group. Office: Touchstone Television Productions 500 S Buena Vista St Burbank CA 91521

BLOOMENSTEIN, RICHARD B., plastic surgeon; b. N.Y.C., Oct. 29, 1934; s. Nelson S. Bloomenstein and Lucille A. Biermann; m. Susan J. Bloomenstein, Apr. 2, 1961; children: Laura, Ellen. BA, Columbia U., 1955; MD, SUNY, Bklyn., 1959. Diplomate Am. Bd. Plastic Surgery. Pvt. practice, Englewood, NJ, 1967—. Attending physician Englewood Hosp. and Med. Ctr., 1970, chief plastic surgery dept., 1970—78, surg. dir. wound healing ctr., 2003—; attending physician Valley Hosp., Ridgewood, NJ, 1980—. Author: One Day Plastic Surgery, 1984; contbr. articles to profl. jours. Vol. surgeon Heal the Children Englewood Hosp. and Med. Ctr., 1980—85. Capt. USAF, 1962—64. Fellow, SUNY Coll. Medicine, 1958, SUNY and Kings County Hosp., 1961. Fellow: ACS; mem.: NJ Soc. Plastic Surgeons, Am. Soc. Plastic Surgeons (resident prize award 1970). Office: 177 N Dean St Englewood NJ 07631 Office Phone: 201-569-2244. E-mail: rvloomenstein@msn.com.

BLOOMER, HAROLD FRANKLIN, JR., retired lawyer; b. NYC, Nov. 4, 1933; s. Harold Franklin and Allene (Cress) B.; m. Mary Jane Lloyd, July 16, 1955 (div. June 1976); children: Sarah Allene, Margaret Gail, Leslie Lloyd; m. Freya Donald, Nov. 30, 1985; children: Katharine Roma, Alice Donald. AB, Amherst Coll., 1956; LLB, Columbia U., 1967. Bar: Conn. 1967, N.Y. 1968, U.S. Dist. Ct. Conn. 1968, U.S. Dist. Ct. (so. and ea. dists.) N.Y. 1974, U.S. Ct. Appeals (2d cir.) 1974. Assoc. Debevoise, Plimpton, Lyons & Gates, N.Y.C., 1967-77; counsel Burlington, Underwood & Lord, Jeddah, Saudi Arabia, 1977-78; chief internat. counsel Saudi Rsch. & Devel. Corp., London, 1978-80; counsel Morgan, Lewis & Bockius LLP, London and N.Y.C., 1980-81, ptnr., 1981-2000. Adj. prof. Pepperdine U. Sch. Law, London, 1985. Trustee San. Products Trust, Riverside, Conn., 1965—74; trip leader Adventure Cycling Assn., Missoula, Mont., 2000; mem. Conn. com. East Coast Greenway, 2001—; co-chmn. bd. Coastal Corridor Transp. Investment Area, State of Conn., 2001—; chmn. Greenwich (Conn.) Safe Cycling, 1999—; pres. Calf Island Conservancy, Inc., Greenwich, 2004—; mem. Rep. Town Meeting, Greenwich, Conn., 1964—74, 1992—, chmn. pub. works com., 1971—74, chmn. land use com., 1998—; mem. Rep. Town Com., Greenwich, Conn., 1973—74. Lt. j.g. USNR, 1957—60. Kent scholar Columbia U., 1965-66, Stone scholar Columbia U., 1966-67. Mem. Am. Arbitration Assn. (panel of arbitrators 1990—), Riverside Yacht Club. Republican. Episcopalian. Avocations: sailing, canoeing, skiing, biking, running.

BLOOMER, WILLIAM DAVID, radiologist, oncologist, educator; b. Aug. 19, 1944; s. Ward LaVern and Vera Catherine (Rochefort) B.; m. Lauren S. Taslitz, Aug. 10, 1986; children: Whitney Dana, Brian Andrew, Gregory Stewart. AB, U. Pa., 1966; MD, Jefferson Med. Coll., Phila., 1970. Diplomate Am. Bd. Radiology, Am. Bd. Nuclear Medicine. Intern Univ. Hosps., Cleve., 1970-71; clin. fellow in radiation therapy Harvard U. Med. Sch., Boston, 1971-74, instr., 1974-76, asst. prof., 1976-80, assoc. prof., 1980-83; rsch. mem. Harvard MIT Divsn. Health Scis. and Tech., Boston, 1978-83; mem. sr. common room Lowell House Harvard Coll., Boston, 1983-87; dir. radiotherapy, radiotherapist-in-chief Mt. Sinai Hosp., N.Y.C., 1983-87; prof., chmn. dept. radiation oncology U. Pitts. Sch. Medicine, 1987-92; dir. Joint Radiation Oncology Ctr., 1987-92; dir. radiation oncology Presbyn. U. Hosp., Magee-Women's Hosp., Shadyside Hosp., 1987-92; assoc. dir. Pitts. Cancer Inst., 1987-92; pres. U. Radiotherapy Assocs., Inc., 1989-92; sr. lectr. engring. in medicine Carnegie Mellon U., 1989-92; chmn. radiation medicine Evanston Northwestern Healthcare, 1992—. Prof. radiology Northwestern U. Med. Sch., 1992—, pres. Radiation Medicine Inst., 1992—; dir. radiation oncology svcs. Condell Med. Ctr., 2004—. Contbr. articles to profl. jours. Mem. AAAS, Am. Coll. Radiology, Am. Soc. Therapeutic Radiologists, Soc. Nuclear Medicine, Radiation Rsch. Soc., Am. Assn. Cancer Rsch., Am. Soc. Clin. Oncology, Am. Coll. Radiation Oncology (Gold medal 1998). Office: Evanston Northwestern Healthcare 2650 Ridge Ave Evanston IL 60201-1718

BLOOMFIELD, CLARA DERBER, oncologist, educator, medical institute administrator; b. Flushing, L.I., N.Y., May 15, 1942; d. Milton and Zelda (Trenner) Derber; m. Victor A. Bloomfield, June 11, 1962 (div. 1983); m. Albert de la Chapelle, Jan. 1, 1984. Student, U. Wis., 1959-62; BA, San Diego State U., 1963; MD, U. Chgo., 1968. Diplomate Am. Bd. Internal Medicine, Nat. Bd. Med. Examiners. Intern in medicine U. Chgo. Hosps. and Clinics, 1968-69, resident internal medicine, 1969-70, U. Minn., Mpls., 1970-71, med. oncology fellow, 1971-73, chief resident in medicine, Jan.-June, 1972, instr., 1972-73, asst. prof. medicine, 1973-76, assoc. prof., 1976-80, prof. medicine div. oncology, 1980-89, dir. fellowship program med. concology, 1987—89, mem. univ. senate, 1986-89, mem. all univ. Commn. on Women, 1988-89; prof. medicine, chief div. oncology SUNY, Buffalo, 1989—97; head dept. medicine Roswell Pk. Cancer Inst., Buffalo, 1989—97; William G. Pace III prof. cancer research Ohio State U. Coll. Med. & Pub. Health, 1997—, dir., div. hematology & oncology, dept. Internal Medicine, 1997—. Mem. Kettering selection com. GM Cancer Rsch. Found., 1986-87; cons. Office Tech. Assessment, U.S. Congress, 1988; participant, chair various coms. Internat. Human Gene Mapping Workshops, Helsinki, Finland, 1985, France, 1987, Internat. Workshops Chromosomes in Leukemia, Lund, Sweden, 1980, Chgo., 1982, Tokyo, 1984, London, 1987, Buffalo, 1991; mem. nat. and sci. adv. bds. NIH, 1977—, mem. bd. sci. counselors divsn. cancer treatment, 1991—, organizer Internat. Hodgkins Disease Symposium, 1981; bd. dirs. cancer and leukemia group B, 1982—, mem. other coms., 1973— sponsored clin. trial groups, Nat. Cancer Inst., cons. S.W. oncology group; mem. nat. and sci. adv. bd. Don and Sybil Harrington Cancer Ctr., Amarillo, Tex., 1979—, Med. Coll. Pa., 1988—; bd. trustees Berlex Oncology Found., 1992—; vis. prof. dept. medicine W.Va. U., 1973, U. Ariz., Tucson, 1979, U. Fla., Gainesville, 1979, Emory U., Atlanta, 1980, U. Chgo., 1982, George Washington U., Washington, 1982, U. Tex., San Antonio, 1982, Brown U., Providence, 1982, Mayo Clinic, Rochester, Minn., 1982, U. Zurich, Switzerland, 1983, U. P.R., 1984, U. Witwatersand, S. Africa, 1984, Nihon U., Tokyo, 1984, Leukemia Soc. Mass., 1991; frequent invited speaker, guest lectr. symposia, workshops, continuing edn. courses, seminars, med. congresses, univs. in U.S., Europe, S. Am., Scandinavia, Eng., Japan, Republic of South Africa, New Zealand. Author: (with others) Recent Advances in Bone Marrow Transplantation, Vol. VII, 1983, New Prespectives in Human Lymphoma, 1984, Neoplastic Diseases of the Blood, 1985, Current Therapy in Hematology/Oncology 1984-85, 1985, Medical Genetics: Past, Present, Future, 1985, Directions in Oncology, Vol. 1, 1985, Medical Oncology, Basic Principles and Clinical Management of Cancer, 1985, Tumor Aneuploidy, 1985, Malignant Lymphomas and Hodgkins Disease: Experimental and Therapeutic Advances, 1985, Current Therapy in Internal Medicine, 1987, Genetic Maps, Vol. 4, 1987; contbr. over 250 articles, abstracts to profl. jours.; editor ann. Adult Leukemia series in Cancer Treatment and Rsch., 1979-85; cons. editor Leukemia and Lymphoma Yearbook of Cancer, 1980—; assoc. editor Cancer Rsch., 1981-88, editor, 91, Leukemia Rsch., 1984-87, Leukemia, 1987-89; mem. editorial bd. Jour. Clin. Oncology, 1983-88, Cancer Genetics and Cytogenetics, 1983-87, Directions in Oncology, 1984-86, Cancer Rsch. Bull., 1984-85, Med. and Pediatric Oncology, 1987—, Blood, 1988—, Annals of Medicine, 1989—, Seminars in Oncology, 1989—; editorial bd. Am. Jour. Hematology, 1985, assoc. editor, 1988—; reviewer 23 med. jours. Recipient Nat. Bd. award Med. Coll. Pa., 1981, Past State Pres.' Bus. and Profl. Women award U. Tex. System Cancer Ctr., M.D. Anderson Hosp. and Tumor Clinic, Houston, 1987, Joseph H. Burchenal Clinical Rsch. award, Am. Assn. Cancer Rsch., 2004; prin. or co-prin. investigator 8 grants, NIH, 1975—, also ACS, 1980-84, Minn. State Spl. Coleman Leukemia Rsch. Fund, 1981-89, Coleman Leukemia Rsch. Fund Endowment, 1981—, Baltzar W.A. von Platen Found., 1984-85, Genentech/Hoffman -LaRoche, 1988—. Mem. ACP, AAAS, Am. Assn. Cancer Rsch., Am. Soc. Hematology, Am. Soc. Clin. Oncology (bd. dirs. 1991—), Am. Fedn. Clin. Rsch., Cen. Soc. Clin. Rsch., N.Y. Acad. Scis., Inst. Medicine, Internat. Assn. Comparative Rsch. Leukemia and Related Diseases, Med. Soc. Finland (external mem.), Phi Beta Kappa, Alpha Omega Alpha, Sigma Delta Epsilon. Office: Comprehensive Cancer Ctr 320 W 10th Ave Columbus OH 43210

BLOOMFIELD, DAVID CHARLES, lawyer, educator, not-for-profit public executive; b. N.Y.C., Feb. 19, 1952; BA, Brandeis U., 1975; JD, Columbia U., 1984; MPA, Princeton U., 1984. Bar: N.Y. 1984, D.C. 1985; cert. primary and elem. tchr., Mass.; cert. prin./supr., N.J.; cert. supt. N.Y. Tchr. New Lincoln Sch., N.Y.C., 1975-79; analyst Advocates for Children of N.Y., Queens, N.Y., 1979-80; law clk. to Judge Robert L. Carter U.S. Dist. Ct. (so. dist. N.Y.), N.Y.C., 1984-85; assoc. Hogan & Hartson, Washington, 1985-86; atty. N.Y.C. Law Dept., 1986-89; adminstr. N.Y.C. Bd. Edn., Bklyn., 1989-90, gen. counsel, 1990-91; gen. counsel, sr. edn. advisor Manhattan Borough Pres., N.Y.C., 1991-94; exec. dir. Partnership for Effective Edn. Mgmt., N.Y.C., 1994-96; adj. asst. prof. Tchrs. Coll. Columbia U., N.Y.C., 1996—98; assoc. prof. Bklyn. Coll., CUNY, 1999—. Head edn. leadership program Bklyn. Coll., 2001; v.p. N.Y. Citywide Coun. on High Schs., 2004—. Author: African Ethnicity, 1976, Attendance Improvement Programs in N.Y.C. Schools, 1979, Children First: NYC School Governance Legislation, 1993, Strategic Management of NYC Schools, 1997, 2d edit., 2003, Technology Based Peer Education, 1999, Technology-Based Peer Education, 1999, Church/State Separation, 2001, No Child Left Behind Act, 2003, No Child Left Behind, 2003, High School Reform, 2005, Legal Issues in the Classroom, 2005; contbr. chpts. to books and articles to profl. jours. Recipient Paul Robeson prize Columbia U., N.Y.C., 1982, Harlan Fiske Stone scholar, 1982, Princeton (N.J.) U. fellow, 1982, African-Am. Inst. fellow, N.Y.C., 1976. Office Phone: 718-951-5608. Personal E-mail: david11201@nyct.net. Business E-Mail: davidb@brooklyn.cuny.edu.

BLOOMFIELD, LINCOLN PALMER, former federal agemcy administrator; b. Boston, July 7, 1920; m. Irirangi Pamela Coates, 1948; children: Pamela, Lincoln, Diana. SB, Harvard U., 1941, MPA, 1952, PhD, 1956. With US Dept. State, Washington, 1946-57, spl. asst. to asst. sec., 1952-57; sr. staff ctr. for internat. studies MIT, Cambridge, 1957—, prof. polit. sci., 1963-91, prof. emeritus, 1991—; dir. global issues NSC, Washington, 1979-80; asst. sec. for polit. mil. affairs US Dept. State, Washington, 2001—05, spl. rep. of the pres. & sec. state for mine action, 2001—05. Mem. Presdl. Commn. on 25th Anniversary of UN, 1970-71; vis. prof. Grad. Inst. Advanced Internat. Studies, Geneva, 1965, 72, 77, 79, Salzburg Seminar faculty, 1982, 86, 92, 95, moderator State Dept. seminar on fgn. policy and global issues, 1992-99; disting. vis. lectr. State Dept. Fgn. Svc. Inst., 1995. Host Christian Sci. Monitor TV program Fifty Years Ago Today, 1989—92, moderator EcoForum TV series, 1997—99; author: Evolution or Revolution?, 1957, The UN and U.S. Foreign Policy, rev. edit., 1967, In Search of American Foreign Policy, 1974, The Foreign Policy Process: A Modern Primer, 1982, co-author; editor: International Military Forces, 1964, Kruschchev and the Arms Race, 1966, Outer Space: Prospects for Man and Society, rev. edit., 1968, Controlling Small Wars, 1969, The Management of Global Disorder, 1987, Prospects for Peacemaking, 1987, Managing International Conflict, 1997. Bd. dirs. Unitarian-Universalist Assn., 1958-64, World Affairs Council of Boston, World Peace Found., Nat. Def. U., 1984-89, Can. Inst. Internat. Peace and Security, 1989-92. Lt. USNR, 1942-46. Recipient Chase prize Harvard U., 1956, EDUCOM prize Disting. Software, 1988, New Eng. Emmy award, 1992; Littauer fellow, 1952; Rockefeller fellow, 1954, 75. Fellow World Acad. Art and Sci. (elected); mem. Coun. on Fgn. Rels. Achievements include research on foreign policy, international organizations, political gaming, conflict-minimizing and policy planning strategies and systems.

BLOOMFIELD, LOUIS AUB, physicist, researcher; b. Boston, Oct. 11, 1956; s. Daniel Kermit and Frances (Aub) B.; m. Karen Shatkin, Aug. 28, 1983; children: Elana, Aaron. BA in Physics, Amherst Coll., 1979; PhD in Physics, Stanford U., 1983. Postdoctoral physicist AT&T Bell Labs., Murray Hill, NJ, 1983-85; asst. prof. U. Va., Charlottesville, Va., 1985-91, assoc. prof., 1991-96, prof, 1996—. Author: (Book) How Things Work: The Physics of Everyday Life. Recipient Alumni Tchr. award U. Va., 1992, Pres.'s Rsch. prize, 1994; named Presdl. Young Investigator NSF, 1986, Young Investigator Office of Naval Rsch., 1988, Va. Outstanding Faculty award, 1998; Alfred P. Sloan fellow, 1989. Fellow Am. Phys. Soc. (Apker award 1980, Pegram medal 2001). Jewish. Office: Univ of Va Dept Physics PO Box 400714 Charlottesville VA 22904-4714 Office Phone: 434-924-6595. E-mail: bloomfield@virginia.edu.

BLOOMFIELD, MAXWELL HERRON, III, retired history professor, retired law professor; b. Galveston, Tex., Aug. 17, 1931; s. Maxwell Herron and Violet Clemons (Turner) B.; m. Helen Lorraine Anderson, Sept. 11, 1965. BA, Rice U., 1952; LLB, Harvard U., 1957; PhD in History, Tulane U., 1962. Bar: Tex. 1957. Lectr. Tulane U., 1961-62; instr. Ohio State U., 1962-66; asst. prof. history Cath. U. Am., Washington, 1966-68, assoc. prof., 1968-74, prof., 1974—98, chmn. dept. history, 1977-80, prof. law, 1985-98, prof. emeritus, 1998—. Vis. prof. U. Va., 1973. Author: Alarms and Diversions: The American Mind Through American Magazines, 1967, American Lawyers in a Changing Society, 1776-1876, 1976, (with John McWilliams and Carl Smith) Law and American Literature, 1983, Peaceful Revolution: Constitutional Change and American Culture from Progressivism to the New Deal, 2000; mem. editl. bd. Md. Hist. Mag., 1974-75, Capitol Studies, 1979-80, Legal Studies Forum, 1985-96. With U.S. Army, 1952-54. Am. Bar Found. fellow, 1968-69, Project '87 fellow, 1981; ABA grantee, 1979-80. Mem. State Bar Tex., Am. Soc. Legal History, Am. Hist. Assn., Am. Cath. Hist. Assn., Orgn. Am. Historians, Phi Beta Kappa. Democrat. Roman Catholic. Home: 4 Legas Dr Galveston TX 77551-1568

BLOOMFIELD, SARA J., museum director; BA in English Lit., Northwestern Univ.; MA in Education. V.p. Cleveland Financial Group; dep. dir. for ops. U.S. Holocaust Meml. Coun., Washington, 1986—88, exec. dir., 1988—94; assoc. dir. for mus. programs U.S. Holocaust Memorial Museum, Washington, 1994—98, acting dir., 1998—99, dir., 1999—. Established the first Learning Disability Program for the Shaker Heights City School System. Recipient of the Young Leadership award from the American Jewish Com., 1986, Jan Karski award from the Anti-Defamation League, Washington Chap. Bd. mem, Women's Political Caucus, the Cleveland City Club and the American Jewish Com. Office: US Holocaust Meml Mus 100 Raoul Wallenberg Pl SW Washington DC 20024-2126

BLOOMFIELD, SUZANNE, artist; b. Cleve., June 23, 1934; d. Norman and Francis Latin; m. Nathaniel Bloomfield, June 17, 1956; children: Miriam, Andrew, Rachel. BSED, Ohio U., 1955; MEd, U. Ariz., 1975. Exhibited in group shows at Cleve. Mus. Art, 1950, U. Ariz., 1968, 72, No. Ariz. U., 1968, Walker Art Inst., N.Y.C., 1976, Ford Found., 1976, Fordham U., 1976, New Sch. Social Rsch., 1976, Ariz. Invitational, Flagstaff, 1980, Ohio U., 1981, U. S.D., 1981, U. Innsbruck, Austria, 1982, Iowa State U., 1983, Idaho State U., 1984, Grove Gallery U. Calif. San Diego, 1985, SUNY, Alfred, 1986, UN World Conf. on Women, Nairobi, Kenya, 1987, Pa. State U., 1987, U. Portland, 1987, Nat. Assn. Women Artists, N.Y.C., 1988, San Francisco Women Artists Gallery, 1990, Nat. Mus. Women in the Arts, Washington, 1990, City of Tucson, 1992-94, Ariz. State Capitol, 1994, Global Focus United Nations Fourth World Conf. on Women, Beijing, China, 1995, Galeria Berta Armas, Ensenada, Mex., 1997, Mus. Art, L.A., 1997, Coll. Bus. and Pub. Adminstrn. U. Ariz., 1998, Nat. Assn. Women Artists Printmaking USA Tour, 1998-2000, U. Ala., 2003, U. Tex. A&M, 2004.

BLOOMGARDEN, KATHY FINN, public relations executive; b. N.Y.C., June 9, 1949; d. David and Laura (Zeisler) Finn; m. Zachary Bloomgarden; children: Rachel, Keith, Matthew. BA, Brown U., 1970; MA, PhD, Columbia U.; cert., East Asian Inst. Pres. Rsch. & Forecasts, N.Y.C.; pres., dir. Ruder-Finn, Inc., N.Y.C., 1988—98, pres., 1998—, co-CEO, 2001—. Mem. comm. com. Brown U. Mem. comms. com. Brown U., Providence. Recipient PR Industry's All-Star award. Mem.: Women's Forum, Fgn. Policy Assn., Coun. Fgn. Rels., Am. Mgmt. Assn. (bd. dirs.), Pub. Rels. Soc. Am. Jewish. Office: Ruder Finn 301 E 57th St New York NY 10022-2900

BLOOMINGDALE, LEWIS MORGAN, retired psychiatrist; s. Lewis Morgan Bloomingdale and Irma Asiel; m. Eileen Grace Crutchlow, July 25, 1947; 1 child, Kerry Lewis. BS with honors, Yale U., 1940, B Chem. Engring., 1941; MD magna cum laude, Harvard U., 1950. Diplomate Am. Bd. Psychiatry and Neurology, lic. physician N.Y., Conn., Mass.; qualified examiner N.Y. Chem. engr. Am. Cyanamide, Wallingford, Conn., 1941—42, Manhattan Project, N.Y.C., 1942—43; clin. assoc. prof. N.Y. Med. Coll., Valhalla, 1972—98; faculty assoc. Coll. Med. Spltys., Fla. North Gulf U., Ft. Myers, 2001—02; pvt. practice child and forensic psychiatry, 1955—97. Psychiat. cons. Yonkers (N.Y.) Family Svc., 1957—65; spl. psychiat. cons. Child Protective Svcs. of Westchester County, NY, 1989—97; founder, pres. Profl. Group for Rsch. in Attention and Related Disorders; mem. adv. bd. Mental Health Dept., Westchester County, NY, 1957, 60; advisor on mental health U.S. Congressman Ottinger, Westchester County, 1965; mem., chair several coms. Westchester Med. Soc., 1955—97; pres. Westchester Psychiat. Soc., 1968—69; founder, 1st pres. Westchester Soc. Sex Edn.; cofounder Assn. Adolescent Psychiatry (merged with Assn. Child Psychiat.). Editor: Attention Deficit Disorder, 4 vols., 1983—88; co-editor: Attention Deficit Disorder, 2 vols., 1988; contbr. articles to profl. jours. With AUS, 1943—45. Fellow: Am. Psychiat. Assn. (disting. life); mem.: Am. Assn. Law and Psychiatry, World Psychiat. Assn., N.Y. Acad. Scis., Nat. Acad. Neuropsychology, Internat. Neuropsychology Soc., Mt. Vernon Bar Assn. (hon.), N.Y. Med. and Psychiat. Socs., Mental Health Soc. Westchester, Mass. Med. and Psychiat. Socs., Am. Acad. Child and Adolescent Psychiatry, Alpha Omega Alpha, Sigma Xi, Phi Beta Kappa. Avocations: tennis, travel photography, neurosciences. Home: 20 Longwood Dr Apt 378 Westwood MA 02090 Home Fax: 781-329-2444. Personal E-mail: bloomp@yahoo.com.

BLOOMQUIST, KENNETH GENE, music educator, director; b. Boone, Iowa, Dec. 29, 1931; s. Carl Arvid and Alma Florence (Lindahl) B.; m. Carole Ann Murphy, Feb. 14, 1954; children: Leslie Ann, Laurie Kathleen, Daniel John. BS in Music Edn., U. Ill., 1953, MusM, 1957. Band dir. Urbana (Ill.) Pub. Schs., 1956-57; band dir., supr. music Taylorville (Ill.) Pub. Schs., 1957-58; asst. band dir., trumpet tchr. U. Kans., Lawrence, 1958-68, dir. bands, 1968-70, Mich. State U., East Lansing, 1970-78, 88-93, dir. Sch. Music, 1978-88; dir. bands, 1988-93; dir. bands emeritus Mich. State U., East Lansing, 1993. Guest band condr., U.S., Europe, Asia, 1968—; condr. fgn. tours, 1964, 75, 76, 78, 85, 92, 95, 98, 2001, 04; cons. adjudicator of music, U.S., Europe, Mex., Taiwan, Indonesia, Japan, Thailand, Korea, Czech Republic. Contbr. articles to profl. jours., others. Pres. Music Boosters Okemos (Mich.) Pub. Schs., 1970—72, Northport (Mich.) Cmty. Arts Ctr., 2001—03; bd. dirs. Lansing Symphony Orch., 1978—84, Okemos Cmty. Ch., 1984—87, Traverse Symphony Orch., 2003—. Sgt. U.S. Army, 1953—55. Recipient Alumni award U. Ill., 1966. Mem. Nat. Band Assn. (nat. pres. 1980-82), Am. Band Masters Assn. (nat. pres. 1995-96), Coll. Band Dirs. Assn., Music Educators Nat. Conf., Nat. Bd. Assn. Acad. Winds and Percussion Arts (Hall of Fame for Disting. Band Condrs., NBA Hall of Fame, Midwest Clinic medal of honor), Phi Mu Alpha. Avocations: golf, bridge, tennis, travel, reading. Personal E-mail: kbloomqui@earthlink.net.

BLOOMQUIST, RODNEY GORDON, geologist; b. Aberdeen, Wash., Feb. 3, 1943; s. Verner A. and Margaret E. (Olson) B.; m. Linda L. Lee, Dec. 19, 1964 (div. July 1968); m. Bente Brisson Jørgensen, Aug. 4, 1977; 1 child, Kira Brisson. BS in Geology, Portland State U., 1966; MS in Geology, U. Stockholm, 1970, PhD in Geochemistry, 1977. Rschr. U. Stockholm, 1974-77; asst. prof. Oreg. Inst. Tech., Klamath Falls, 1978-80; geologist Wash. State Energy Office, Olympia, 1980-96; chief scientist Wash. State U., Olympia, 1996—2003, dir. CHP Application Ctr., 2003—, dir. Ctr. Distributed Generation and Thermal Distbn., 2004—. Author: Regulatory Guide to Geothermics, 1991; mem. editl. bd. Geothermics, 1985-88; contbr. articles to profl. jours. Smitts fellow, Sweden, 1974, Royal Rsch. fellow, Sweden, 1975-77; rsch. grantee U. Stockholm, 1975-77. Mem.: N.Am. Dist. Heating and Cooling Inst. (bd. dirs. 1988—92), Internat. Geothermal Assn. (chmn. edn. com. 1988—2004, bd. dirs. 1990—2001, 2004—), Internat. Dist. Energy Assn. (western sect. bd. dirs. 1990—, bd. dirs. 1994—97, chmn. com. govt. rels. 1997—2002, bd. dirs. 2001—04), Geothermal Resources Coun. (pres. Pacific N.W. sect. 1982—85, bd. dirs. 1985—92, pres. 1989, bd. dirs. 2001—04), Am. Blade Smith Soc. (bd. dirs. 1989—2002). Democrat. Lutheran. Avocations: skiing, backpacking, fishing, hunting. Office: Wash State Univ 925 Plum St SE Olympia WA 98501-1529 Office Phone: 360-956-2016. Business E-Mail: bloomquistr@energy.wsu.edu.

BLOOSTON, ROSELEE, cultural organization administrator, writer; b. Washington, Sept. 29, 1952; d. Arthur and Leone Isaacs Blooston; m. Jerry Michael Mosier, Sept. 9, 1983; 1 child, Oliver Blooston Mosier. BA in Drama, Vassar Coll., 1973; MFA in Theater, Trinity U., 1975. Drama instr. Smithsonian Instn., Washington, 1976; acting instr. U. Tex., Austin, 1976—79; faculty New Sch. for Social Rsch., N.Y.C., 1982—83; master tchr., dir. Paper Mill Playhouse, Millburn, NJ, 1991—96; dir., tchg. artist N.J. Performing Arts Ctr., Newark, 1997; adj. faculty Montclair (N.J.) State U., 1992—2000; founder, dir. Tunnel Vision Writers' Project, Inc., Montclair, 1998—2005. Cons. Job Performance Seminars, Bklyn., 1984—89; dir., playwriting coord. The Gathering/Whole Theater, Montclair, 1988—89; head speech dept. Action Theater Conservatory, Clifton, NJ, 1995—97. Author short stories; prodr.: 5 plays. Mem. edn. com. Montclair Editors and Writers, 2001—; mem. pub. programs com. Montclair Art Mus., 2001—04; mem. Montclair Arts Council Steering Com., 2004. Recipient Greer Garson Theater Arts award, Dallas Theater Ctr., 1974. Mem.: Internat. Womens Writers Guild, Dramatists Guild, Actors Equity Assn., Phi Beta Kappa.

BLOS, JOAN W., writer, critic, educator; b. N.Y.C., Dec. 9, 1928; m. Peter Blos, Jr., 1953; 2 children, 1 deceased. BA, Vassar Coll., 1950; MA, CCNY, 1956; DHL (hon.), Bank St. Coll. Edn., 2001. Asso. publs. div., mem. tchr. edn. faculty Bank St. Coll. Edn., N.Y.C., 1958-70; lectr. Sch. Edn., U. Mich., Ann Arbor, 1972-80; U.S. editor Children's Literature in Education, 1976-81. Author: "It's Spring!" She Said, 1968, (with Betty Miles) Just Think!, 1971, A Gathering of Days: A New England Girl's Journal, 1830-32, 1979 (Newbery medal ALA, Am. Book award 1980, Best Book of Yr., Sch. Libr. Jour.), Martin's Hats, 1984, Brothers of the Heart: A Story of the Old Northwest, 1837-38, 1985, Old Henry, 1987 (Honor book Boston Globe Horn Book award 1991), Lottie's Circus, 1989, The Grandpa Days, 1989, One Very Best Valentine's Day, 1990, The Heroine of the Titanic, 1991, A Seed, A Flower, A Minute, An Hour, 1992, Brooklyn Doesn't Rhyme, 1994, The Days Before Now, 1994, Hungry Little Boy, 1995, Hello, Shoes (Best Book award Bank St. Coll. Edn. 1999). Office Phone: 212-473-5400.

BLOSE, MAURICE LESTER, history educator; b. Lewistown, Pa., May 10, 1946; s. Maurice Lester and Helen Ann (Stewart) Blose; m. Chiquita Flo Blose, Aug. 25, 1969; children: Matthew, Michael, Nicholas. BS in hist., Shippensburg State U. Hist. tchr. Warwick Schs., Lititz, Pa. Hist. club adv., sr. class adv., model United Nations adv. Warwick Schs., Lititz, Pa. Mem.: NEA, Pa. State Edn. Assn. Democrat. Avocations: wrestling, baseball, Va. Tech. football. Home: 43 S Broad St 3 Lititz PA 17543 Office Phone: 717-626-3700. Office Fax: 717-626-6199. E-mail: 5xm52@aol.com.

BLOSER, DIETER, radiologist; b. Yugoslavia, Aug. 17, 1944; came to U.S., 1947, naturalized, 1954; s. Peter and Eva Helen Bloser; A.B., Princeton U., 1966; M.D., Case Western Res. U., 1970; m. Deborah Pierce Forbes, Nov. 25, 1967; children— Peter Forbes, Timothy Philip. Intern dept. medicine U. Hosps. of Cleve., 1970-71, resident in radiology, 1971-72, 74-76, chief resident, 1975-76; practice medicine specializing in radiology, Parma, Ohio, 1976—; mem. staff Parma Community Gen. Hosp., 1976—, chief nuclear medicine, 1977—, chief radiology, 1984—; pres. Parma Radiologic Assocs, Inc., 1990—. Gen. Hosp. Bd. dirs. Cleve. chpt. Juvenile Diabetes Found., 1986-90; active Am. Diabetes Assn., 1985—; trustee Case Western Reserve U. Sch. Med Alumni Assn., 1985-89. Served to lt. comdr. USN, 1972-74. Diplomate Am. Bd. Radiology. Mem. Am. Coll. Radiology, Radiol. Soc. N. Am., Ohio Radiol. Soc., Cleve. Radiol. Soc. (pres.-elect 1986-87, pres. 1987-88), Am. Inst. Ultrasound in Medicine, Cleve. Acad. Medicine, AMA, Ohio Med. Assn., Princeton Alumni Assn. (schs. com.), Phi Beta Kappa, Alpha Omega Alpha. Lutheran. Home: 18185 Windswept Cir Chagrin Falls OH 44023-2439 Office: 18185 Windswept Cir Chagrin Falls OH 44023-2439

BLOSSER, HENRY GABRIEL, physicist; b. Harrisonburg, Va., Mar. 16, 1928; s. Emanuel and Leona (Branum) B.; m. Priscilla May Beard, June 30, 1951 (div. Oct. 1972); children: William Henry, Stephan Emanuel, Gabe Fawley, Mary Margaret; m. Mary Margaret Gray, Mar. 16, 1973 (dec. Jan. 1995); m. Amy June Conley, May 11, 1995 (div. Feb. 1997); m. Lois Pearlena Lynch, Oct. 17, 1998. BS, U. Va., 1951, MS, 1952, PhD, 1954. Physicist Oak Ridge (Tenn.) Nat. Lab., 1954-56, group leader, 1956-58; assoc. prof. physics Mich. State U., East Lansing, 1958-61, prof., 1961-90, Univ. Disting. prof., 1990—, dir. Cyclotron Lab., 1961-89. Cons. Harper Hosp., Detroit, 1983—, Ion Beam Applications, Belgium, 1996—, others; adj. prof. radiation oncology Wayne State U., Detroit, 1996—. Bd. dirs. Midwest Univs. Rsch. Assocs., 1960-63. With USNR, 1946-48. Predoctoral fellow NSF, 1953-54, sr. postdoctoral fellow, 1966-67; Guggenheim fellow, 1973-74. Fellow Am. Phys. Soc. (Bonner prize 1992); mem. Sigma Xi, Phi Beta Kappa, Kappa Alpha. Home: 2350 Emerald Forest Cir East Lansing MI 48823-7200 Office: Mich State U Nat Cyclotron East Lansing MI 48824-1321 Business E-Mail: blosser@nscl.msu.edu.

BLOSSMAN, ALFRED RHODY, JR., banker; b. Madisonville, La., Oct. 21, 1931; s. Alfred Rhody and Mabel (Perrin) Blossman; m. Royanne Elaire Hurd, Dec. 28, 1957; children: Alfred Rhody III, Roy Edward, Gary Bennett, Christopher Hurd, David Quintin, John Eric. AB in Gen. Bus., La. State U., 1955. Pres. Blossman Hydratane Gas, Inc., Covington, La., 1963—67; chmn. First Nat. Corp., First Nat. Bank, Covington, 1968—84; pres., CEO First Nat. Bank, 1980—84, Parish Nat. Bank, Covington, 1986—, also chmn. bd. dirs. Capt. USAF, 1956—58. Mem.: Phi Delta Theta. Republican. Roman Catholic. Home: 10 Blossman Ln Covington LA 70433-4707 Office: 503 Norriego Dr Destin FL 32541 E-mail: fredb@parishnational.com. *My formula for life is shaped by the moral and ethical guidelines of my religious faith and my own personal code of ethics. Thank God, strong self discipline has made that possible, as well as channelling my enthusiasm for whatever role I have played; being it business, or hobby; educational, military service, parent or grandparent, in a positive direction.*

BLOSSOM, BEVERLY, choreographer, educator; b. Chgo., Aug. 28, 1926; d. Theodore and Florence (Pfeiffer) Schmidt; m. Roberts Blossom, 1966 (div.); 1 child, Michael. BA, Roosevelt U., 1950; MA, Sarah Lawrence, 1953. Dancer Alwin Nikolais Co., N.Y.C., 1952-62; instr. Adelphi U., L.I., N.Y., 1964-66; prof. dance dept. U. Ill., Urbana, 1967-90. Choreographer Festival Theatre, Krannert Ctr., Urbana, Radio Show, 1985, Quick-Step, 1985, Heartbeat, 1985, Interlude from Veranda, 1985; choreographer: Rehearsal for a Class Act, 1983, You Are Still With Me, Fred, 1983, Dad's Ties, 1983, Ordinary Heartbreak, 1984, Egg, 1984, Weatherwatch, 1986, Potpourri, 1986, Eye of the Beholder, 1986, Russian Tea Room, 1986, Entitled, 1987, Grass Widow, 1987, Inch, 1987, Castles in Spain, 1988, Swansong, 1989, ...Exit, 1990, The Cloak, 1990, Onward, 1991, Shards, 1993, Dead Monkey, 1996, Cynicism, 1996, Cello Lessons, 2003, others. Choreography grantee Nat. Endowment for the Arts, 1986, 87, 88, 89, 90, 92, 93, 94, 95, Ill. Arts Coun. Choreography grantee, 1980, 81, 82; recipient Bessie award, 1993. Mem.: Am. Guild of Musical Artists (cert.), Screen Actors Guild (cert.), Union of Profl. Employees (cert.). Office Phone: 847-573-8759.

BLOSTEIN, MICHAEL DAVID, music educator; b. Troy, NY, Dec. 16, 1973; s. David Frank and Robin June Blostein; m. Alyssa Danielle Wagner, June 29, 2002. MusM in Composition, U. Ariz., 1999; MusB in Music Edn., SUNY, Potsdam, 1996. Ptnr. Stop 13 Music, Troy, 2001—; music instr. Averill Pk. H.S., Averill Park, NY, 2000—. Composer: (classical music) Impression #1, Impression #2, Seven, Nebulous. Master: Masons; mem.: ASCAP (composer, pub. 2000—02), Music Educators Nat. Conf., Am. Music Ctr. (composer 2000—02). Avocations: woodworking, art. Office: Averill Park High School 146 Gettle Road Averill Park NY 12018 Home: 600 5th Avenue Troy NY 12182 Personal E-mail: mblostein@hotmail.com.

BLOTNER, JOSEPH LEO, English language educator; b. Plainfield, N.J., June 21, 1923; s. Joseph and Johanna Angela (Slattery) B.; m. Yvonne Wright, Aug. 24, 1946 (dec. 1990); children: Tracy Willoughby, Pamela Stover, Nancy Niehoff; m. Martha C. Allen, Jan. 2, 1993. BA, Drew U., 1947; MA, Northwestern U., 1947; PhD, U. Pa., 1951. Asst. dir. research services RCA Labs., Princeton, N.J., 1949-53; instr. English U. Idaho, 1953-55; asst. prof., assoc. prof. English U. Va., 1955-68; prof. English U. N.C., Chapel Hill, 1968-71, U. Mich., Ann Arbor, 1971-93, emeritus, 1993—. Vis. prof. English Trinity Coll., Hartford, Conn., 1962; William Faulkner lectr. U. Miss., 1977; vis. prof. English U. Ariz., 1982, U. Rome, 1984; cons. Ency. Brit. Ednl. Corp., Tomorrow Entertainment Inc., Center for Study So. Culture, Miss. ETV Authority. Author: The Political Novel, 1955, (with F.L. Gwynn) The Fiction of J.D. Salinger, 1959, Faulkner in the University, 1959, William Faulkner's Library: A Catalogue, 1964, The Modern American Political Novel: 1900-1960, 1966, Faulkner: A Biography, 2 vols, 1974, 1-vol. rev., 1984, Selected Letters of William Faulkner, 1977, Uncollected Stories of William Faulkner, 1979, (with Noel Polk) William Faulkner: Novels 1930-35, 1985; William Faulkner's Manuscripts: Soldier's Pay, 1987, Flags in the Dust (2 vols.), 1987, Light in August (2 vols.), 1987, Short Stories, 1987; (with Noel Polk) William Faulkner: Novels, 1936-40, 1990, William Faulkner: Novels, 1942-54, 1994, Contemporary Authors Autobiography Series, No. 25, 1996; Robert Penn Warren: A Biography, 1997, An Expected Life, 2005; mem. editorial bd. So. Humanities Rev, Mich. Quar. Rev., Faulkner Jour., Faulkner Concordance. Served to 2d lt. USAAF, 1943-45, ETO. Decorated Air medal with Battle Star; Fulbright lectr. Am. lit. U. Copenhagen, 1958-59, 63-64; Guggenheim fellow, 1965, 68, NEH fellow U. Tchrs., 1990; State Dept. grantee Europe, 1975; Rockefeller Found. research scholar, 1979; Officier de L'Ordre des Arts et des Lettres, Legion d'Honneur, Rep. of France, 1997. Sr. fellow Mich. Soc. Fellows; mem. MLA (chmn. Am. lit. sect. 1981), Phi Beta Kappa, Sigma Phi, Omicron Delta Kappa. Democrat. Home: 108 Bedford Pl Charlottesville VA 22903-4622

BLOTNER, NORMAN DAVID, lawyer, real estate broker, corporate financial executive; b. Boston, Dec. 6, 1918; s. Leon and Sarah B.; m. Helen I. Whitman (dec.), Aug. 13, 1954; 1 son, James B. McClain (dec.). AB, Harvard U., 1940, JD, 1947. Bar: N.Y. 1948. Mem. firm Spiro, Felstiner, Prager & Treeger, N.Y.C., 1947-52; with Lane Bryant Inc., N.Y.C., 1953-82, sr. v.p., gen. counsel, sec., dir., 1968-82, ret., 1982. Bd. dirs. Better Bus. Bur. Met. N.Y., until 1982. Lt. comdr. USNR, 1941—46. Named Lacrosse All-am., 1940. Mem. Assn. of Bar of City of N.Y., Harvard Varsity Club, New Rochelle Tennis Club. Republican. Home: 140 Overlook Rd New Rochelle NY 10804-4139

BLOTTNER, MYRA ANN, retired elementary school educator; b. Albuquerque, Dec. 31, 1935; d. John Edgar and Hazel Christine (Bloomgren) Manton; m. Frederick Gwynn Blottner, Dec. 28, 1957; children: Laura Christine, Cheryl Ann. BS, U. N.Mex., 1957, MA, 1992. Cert. elem. tchr., spl. edn. tchr., tchr. of gifted. Tchr. 6th grade Redwood City (Calif.) Pub. Schs., 1959—61, Albuquerque Pub. Schs., 1957—58, tchr. 5th grade, 1986—98, tchr. gifted, 1976—86, 1991—2000, sci. cons., 1990—2000; ret., 2000. Tchg. cons. sr. block U. N.Mex. students . Albuquerque Pub. Schs., 1988—91; lectr. Albuquerque Mus. Art and History, 2000, lectr. coord., 2002—03, dir. Sculpture Garden docents, 2002—; tutor in field; pvt. piano tchr., 1958—. Lectr., tour guide, v.p. vol. assn. N.Mex. Mus. Natural History, 1989; mem. coun. Diocese of Rio Grande, 1986-90; active Jr. League Albuquerque, 1995-2003. Named N.Mex. Sci. Tchr. of the Yr., N.Mex. Mus. Natural History, 1990; Tchr. Enhancement Program fellow U. N.Mex., 1991. Mem.: PEO (chpt. pres. 2005—), AAUW (pres. Albuquerque br. 1973—75), Alpha Delta Pi (pres. 1966, v.p. 1990—91). Republican. Episcopalian. Avocations: aerobics, handbell choir, bridge, gardening (master). Home: 12601 Trillium Trl NE Albuquerque NM 87111-8080

BLOUIN, FRANCIS XAVIER, JR., history professor; b. Belmont, Mass., July 29, 1946; s. Francis X. and Margaret (Cronin) B.; m. Joy Alexander; children: Benjamin, Tiffany. AB, U. Notre Dame, 1967; MA, U. Minn., 1969, PhD, 1978. Asst. dir. Bentley Library U. Mich., Ann Arbor, 1974-75, assoc. archivist Bentley Library, 1975-81, dir. Bentley Library, 1981—, asst. prof. history and library sci., 1979-83, assoc. prof., 1983-89, prof., 1989—. Author: The Boston Region..., 1980, Vatican Archives: An Inventory and Guide to Historical Documentation of the Holy See, 1998; editor Intellectual Life on Michigan Frontier, 1985, Archival Implications Machine..., 1980. Trustee Much. Student Found., 1986-91; dir. Am. Friends of Vatican Libr., 1981—, Coun. on Libr. and Info. Resources, 2001—. Fellow Soc. Am. Archivist (mem. governing council 1985-88); mem. Am. Hist. Assn., Hist. Soc. Mich. (trustee 1982-88, pres. 1987-88), Assn. Records Mgrs. and Adminstrs., Internat. Council on Archives. Office: U Mich Bentley Hist Libr 1150 Beal Ave Ann Arbor MI 48109-2113 E-mail: fblouin@umich.edu.

BLOUNT, BENROE WAYNE, physician; b. Augusta, Ga., Feb. 8, 1950; s. Benroe and Loreen Moellering B.; m. Merry Teresa Van Dam, Feb. 14, 1974 Dec. May 8, 1974); m. Young Hui Cho, Nov. 23, 1976; children: Teresa Jana, Daniel Paul. BS, U.S. Mil. Acad., 1972; MA, U. Calif., Berkeley, 1975; MD, U. Miami, 1983; MPH, U. Wash., 1990. Commd. 2d lt. U.S. Army, 1972, advanced through grades to lt. col., 1990, ret., 1994; intern, resident DeWitt Army Hosp., Alexandria, Va., 1983-86; divsn. chief, dept. vice-chair Emory Sch. Medicine, Atlanta, 1994-99; chair dept. family medicine U. Tenn., Memphis, 1999—2002; prof. Emory U., 2002—; chief family practice Kaiser, S.E., 2002—04. Contbr. articles to profl. jours., chpts. to books. Named one of Outstanding Young Men of Am., Nat. Jaycees; recipient Chmn. of Joint Chief of Staff award for Excellence in Mil. Medicine, 1993, Best Dr. in Am., 2000, 2001, 2002. Independent. Avocation: church. Office Phone: 770-452-3368.

BLOUNT, DANIEL J., lumber company executive; BS, U. Ill., Urbana; MBA, St. Ambrose U. Sr. v.p. fin. Montgomery Elevator Co., 1989-97; joined Riverwood Internat. Corp., Atlanta, 1998, v.p., CFO, 1999—2003; sr. v.p. integration Graphic Packaging Corp., Atlanta, 2003—. Office: Graphic Packaging Corp 814 Livingston Court Marietta GA 30067

BLOUNT, DAVID LAURENCE, lawyer; b. Columbia, Mo., July 14, 1954; s. Don H. and Carol (Middleton) B.; m. Laurie Susan Lucker, Dec. 30, 1978 (dec. 1980); m. Paula Lynn Abrams, Oct. 8, 1982; children: Madeline Avram, Justine Ariel. BS, Coll. William and Mary, 1975; JD, Lewis and Clark Coll., 1980. Bar: Oreg. 1980, Wash. 2002, U.S. Dist. Ct. Oreg. 1982, U.S. Ct. Appeals (9th cir.) 1987. Assoc. U.S. EPA, Washington, 1980-82, Clackamas County Dist. Atty.'s Office, Oregon City, Oreg., 1983, Acker, Underwood & Smith, Portland, Oreg., 1983-85; ptnr. Adler & Blount, Portland, 1985-89, Landye, Bennett & Blumstein LLP, 1989—. Contbr. articles to profl. jours. Bd. dirs. Burnside Projects for Homeless, Portland, 1983-85. Mem. ABA (environ. and natural resources sect.), Fed. Bar Assn., Oreg. State Bar. Assn. (environ. law sect. 1986-89, chair 1989, state of Oreg. environ. cleanup adv. com., 1989—, chair 1991), Multnomah Bar Assn., Oreg. Trial Lawyers Assn., Assn. Trial Lawyers Am., Multnomah Athletic Club. Democrat. Avocations: travel, hiking, skiing, basketball. Office Phone: 503-224-4100. Business E-Mail: dblount@landye-bennett.com.

BLOUNT, JAMES ROBERT, military career officer; b. Columbus, Ohio, Dec. 13, 1958; s. Robert and Beatrice Louise Blount; m. Kelle Ann Bush, Jan. 2, 1978; children: Daniel O., Natalie M. AA in Criminal Justice, Rollins Coll., 1980; BA in Bus. Adminstrn. and Acctg., Nat. U., 1984; ministerial cert. studies, Berean Coll., 1988; MA in Nat. Security Affairs, Naval Postgrad. Sch., 1991; MBA, U. Ctrl. Okla., 2003. Commd. ensign USN, 1985, advanced through grades to lt. comdr., 1995—, mine countermeasures officer USS Leader Charleston, S.C., 1985-87, exec. asst., navigator, legal officer USS Pensacola Little Creek, Va., 1987-89, combat cargo officer, weapons officer USS Racine Long Beach, Calif., 1992-93, 1st lt. USS Durham San Diego, 1993, ops. officer, comdr. mine countermeasure squadron one Ingleside, Tex., 1994-95; instr., co. officer, tng. officer, facilities mgr. U.S. Naval Acad., Annapolis, Md., 1995-98; comdg. officer Mil. Entrance Processing Sta., Oklahoma City, 1999—; CO Mil. Entrance Procesing Sta., 1999—2001, ret., 2001; police officer Norman, Okla., 2002. Youth leader various chs., Seaside, Calif., Rockport, Tex., Annapolis; martial arts instr. various recreation ctrs., Charleston, Monterey, Calif., Long Beach. Cpl. USMC, 1977-78, sgt. USMC, 1981-84; with USN, 1979-81. Mem. Fed. Exec. Bd. Avocations: martial arts, weightlifting, running, scuba diving. Home: 14302 1st St Santa Fe TX 77517-4152 E-mail: okccdr@usa.com.

BLOUNT, KATRINA H., elementary school educator; b. Ft. Gaines, Ga., Jan. 10, 1958; d. James Clanton hardwick and Jewel Wesson Hardwick; m. Jerry Blount, Dec. 6, 2002; children: Lindsey Smith, Audrey Michelle Smith. BS in Elem. Edn., Troy U., 1998. Tchr. Henry County Sch. Sys., Abbeville, Ala., 1999—2001, gifted tchr., 2001—. Tchr. rep. Henry County Gifted Edn. Advisory Bd., 2003. Mem.: Gamma Beta Phi, Kappa Beta Phi.

BLOUNT, KEVIN LEONARD, accountant, law administrator, actor, musician; b. Birmingham, Ala., Aug. 27, 1954; s. Walker C. Sr. and Lyniece C. and B. BS in Mktg., Long Beach State, 1977; MBA in Taxation, Golden Gate U., 1980; JD, U. Calif., San Francisco, 1984. CPA. Life ins. agt. State of Calif., Sacramento; announcer, producer Radio Station, L.A., Calif. Radio announcer, ind. prodr. cable radio sta. Author: 10 Pitfalls of Job Employment, 1990, How to Negotiate an Employment Contract with Your Employer, 1990. Mem. Nat. Soc. MBA Execs., Nat. Assn. Pub. Accts., Screen Actors Guild, AFTRA, Musicians Union. Office: 19726 Colima Rd # 11 La Puente CA 91748-3210 Office Phone: 626-293-8235.

BLOUNT, MICHAEL EUGENE, lawyer; b. Camden, NJ, July 9, 1949; s. Floyd Eugene and Dorothy Alice (Geyer) Durham; m. Janice Lynn Brown, Aug. 22, 1969; children: Kirsten Marie, Gretchen Elizabeth. BA, U. Tex., 1971; JD, U. Houston, 1974. Bar: Tex. 1974, Ill. 1980, D.C. 1981, U.S. Ct. Appeals (D.C. cir.) 1978, U.S. Ct. Mil. Appeals 1975, U.S. Supreme Ct. 1977. Atty. advisor Office of Gen. Counsel SEC, Washington, 1977-78, legal asst. to chmn., 1978-79; assoc. Gardner, Carton & Douglas, Chgo., 1980-84; ptnr. Arnstein, Gluck, Lehr, Barron & Milligan, Chgo., 1984-86, Seyfarth Shaw LLP, Chgo., 1987—. Lt. JAGC USN, 1974—77. Mem.: ABA (fed. regulation of securities com.), Chgo. Bar Assn., Order of Barons, Assn. SEC Alumni, Univ. Club (Chgo.), Phi Alpha Delta (chpt. treas. 1973). Home: 1711 Galloway Dr Inverness IL 60010-5737 Office: Seyfarth Shaw LLP 55 E Monroe St Ste 4200 Chicago IL 60603-5863 Office Phone: 312-269-8962. E-mail: mblount@seyfarth.com.

BLOUNT, ROBERT HADDOCK, management consultant, retired military officer; b. Miami, Fla., Dec. 8, 1922; s. Uriel and Aleve Sadie (Haddock) B.; m. Jeannette Mae Barclay, May 13, 1951 (dec. 1998); children: Barbara Mae, Jennifer. B.E.E., MIT, 1947; MS in Systems Engring, George Washington U., 1970; student, Naval War Coll., 1958-59. Commd. ensign USNR, 1946; transferred to U.S. Navy, 1947, advanced through grades to rear adm., 1973; comdr. submarines, service in MTO, PTO, Scotland, Panama; chief staff, aide to comdr. Submarine Flotilla 6, 1970-72; comdr. Naval Sta., Naval Base Charleston, S.C., 1972-73; comdr. U.S. Naval Forces, So. Command; also comdt. 15th Naval Dist. Ft. Amador, C.Z., 1973-75; dir. undersea and strategic warfare div. Office Chief Naval Ops. Washington, 1975-77; dep. dir. research, devel., test and evaluation OPNAV, 1977-78; comdr. Operational Test and Evaluation Force, 1978-82, ret., 1982; pvt. industry cons., 1986-90;

ret. Va. Ops. div. EDO Corp., 1990. Pres. C.Z. coun. Boy Scouts Am., 1974. Decorated D.S.M., Meritorious Service medal with star, Navy Expeditionary medal; recipient Scroll of Honor Navy League, 1974 Mem. Naval Submarine League, U.S. Naval Inst., Norfolk Yacht and Country Club, Rotary. Address: 1516 Blanford Cir Norfolk VA 23505-1706 Personal E-mail: rhblount@aol.com.

BLOUNT, ROBERT SHELLEY, III, museum director; b. Savannah, Ga., Aug. 14, 1946; s. Robert Shelley Blount Jr. and Lorraine Miller Blount; m. Andrea Gale Hardy, Aug. 25, 1968. B of Design, U. Fla., 1969; MA, Fla. State U., 1993. Creative dir. Cinegraphics Media Group, Gainesville, Fla., 1969—73; mus. adminstr. Fla. Mus. Natural History, 1973—87; exec. dir. Fla. Agrl. Mus., Tallahassee, 1987—93, Ga. Music Hall Fame, Macon, 1993—2000; pres., CEO Martin County Hist. Soc., Stuart, Fla., 2000—02, Tampa Bay History Ctr., Tampa, 2002—. Prin. Blount & Co., Gainesville, 1973—87; dir. Macon CVB, 1993—2000. Author: Spirits of Turpentine, 1993, (screenplays) Will to Win, 1987, Gospel Blues, 1995. Mem. River Walk Planners, Tampa, 2005—, Cultural Arts Execs., 2002—; bd. dirs. Douglass Theater, Macon, 1996—2000. Named Art Dir. of Yr., Nat. Assn. Campus Activities, 1982, 1986; recipient Judges award Excellence, Fla. Pub. Rels. Assn., 1982. Mem.: Am. Assn. State & Local History, Am. Assn. Mus., Music Mus. Alliance (founding dir., v.p. 1998—). Avocations: fishing, boating, bicycling. Office: Tampa Bay History Ctr PO Box 948 Tampa FL 33601

BLOUNT, STANLEY FREEMAN, marketing educator; b. Detroit, June 12, 1929; s. Harry Alfred and Thelma (Freeman) B.; m. Constance Parker, Aug. 30, 1957; children— Jeffrey Parker, Lori Maria. BA, Wayne State U., 1952, MA, 1959; PhD, Northwestern U., 1962. Account exec. Jam Handy Corp., Detroit, 1952-54; marketing mgr. Chrysler Corp., Detroit, 1954-58; instr. Northwestern U., 1961-62; asst. prof. U. Ill., 1962-63; assoc. prof. Kent State U., 1963-67; prof., dept. chmn. State U. N.Y. at Albany, 1967—, chmn. ednl. policies council, 1970—. Disting. vis. prof. U. of Americas, Mexico, 1966; dir. Femtec Inc.; exec. dir. U. Albany Found. Chmn. sub-com. legis. affairs N.Y. State affiliate Am. Heart Assn., 1974-99 . Served with AUS, 1946-48. Named Outstanding Faculty Mem. Kent State U., 1964 Mem. Sigma Xi, Gamma Theta Upsilon. Clubs: Essayons, Audubon, Phalanx. Achievements include research on environment analysis and preception, digitized land use mapping, land use and resource mgmt. Home: 11 Pheasant Ln Delmar NY 12054-4109 Office: SUNY at Albany Sch Business Albany NY 12222-0001

BLOUNT, SUSAN L., insurance company executive, lawyer; b. Pitts., July 8, 1957; d. Eugene Irving and Mary Jane Thomas (Langeluttig) B.; m. Richard A. Bard, Aug. 20, 1977; children: Sean, Abigail, Nathaniel. Student, U. Chgo., 1974-76; BA, U. Tex., 1978, JD, 1981. Assoc. Kirkland & Ellis, Chgo., 1981-85; asst. gen. counsel Prudential Residential Svcs. Co., Newark, N.J., 1989-95; staff legal positions Prudential, Newark, 1985-89, v.p., corp. sec., 1995—2004, v.p., chief investment counsel, 2004—05, v.p., gen. counsel, 2005—. Mem. NJ Commn. on Higher Edn.; bd. trustees Montclair State U., 1996—, St. James Cmty. Devel. Corp., Newark, 1997—; participant Leadership Am., 1996; mem. vestry St. Paul's Ch., Chatham, N.J., 1997—. Mem. Am. Soc. Corp. Secs. Office: Prudential Ins Co Am 751 Broad St 21st Fl Newark NJ 07102-3714

BLOUNT, WINTON MALCOLM, III, investment executive; b. Albany, Ga., Dec. 14, 1943; s. Winton Malcolm Jr. and Mary Katherine (Archibald) B.; m. Riley Sikes; children: Sikes, McLeod, Winton Malcolm IV, K. Stuart, William, Judkins. Student, U. Ala., 1962-63; BA, U. South, 1966; MBA, U. Pa., 1968. With Blount Bros. Corp., Montgomery, Ala., 1968-73, project mgr., 1972-73; with Mercury Constrn. Corp., Montgomery, 1973-77, pres., 1975-77; chief exec. officer, chmn. bd. Benjamin F. Shaw Co., Wilmington, Del., 1977-80; pres., chief operating officer Blount Internat., Ltd., Montgomery, 1980-83, pres., chief exec. officer, 1983-85, chmn., chief exec. officer, 1985-87; sr. v.p. Blount Inc., 1985-87, vice chmn., 1987-89; chmn., chief exec. officer Winton Blount III & Assocs., 1989—. Chmn., CEO Wright Plastics Co., 1989-2001, Cobb Pontiac-Cadillac & Royal Motor Co., 1990-2000, Blount-Strange Ford, Lincoln, Mercury, 1991-2000, Blount-Pittman and Assoc., 2004—. Fin. com. Ala. Rep. Com., 1980-82, chmn., 1999-01; bd. dirs. So. Rsch. Inst., 1995-99, Montgomery YMCA, Episcopal High Sch., 1988-89, 95-2001, Ala. Pub. Affairs Rsch. Coun., 1979-83, Bus. Coun. Ala.; active Tukabatchee Area coun. Boy Scouts Am., 1980-83; bd. visitors U. Ala. Coll. Commerce and Bus. Adminstrn., 1983-88; mem. bd. control Com. of 100; bd. dirs. Leadership Ala., 1989-93, 95-98, chmn. bd., 1997-98, Ala. Coun. Econ. Edn. Mem. Chief Execs. Orgn., World Pres.'s Orgn.), Montgomery C. of C. (dir. 1981-88), Del. C. of C. (dir. 1979-80), NAM (dir. 1982-85). Episcopalian. Office: 1919 South Hull Street, PO Box 230039 Montgomery AL 36123-0039

BLOUT, ELKAN ROGERS, retired biological chemistry professor, retired dean; b. NYC, July 2, 1919; s. Eugene and Lillian B. Blout; m. Joan E. Dreyfus, Aug. 27, 1939; children: James E., Susan, William L.; m. Gail A. Ferris, Mar. 29, 1985; 1 child, Darya L.M. AB, Princeton U., 1939; PhD, Columbia U., 1942; AM (hon.), Harvard U., 1962; DSc (hon.), Loyola U., 1976. With Polaroid Corp., Cambridge, Mass., 1943—62, successively rsch. chemist, assoc. dir. rsch., 1948—58, v.p., gen. mgr. rsch., 1958—62; rsch. assoc. Harvard U., Cambridge, 1950—52, 1958—60, lectr. on biophysics, 1960—62, prof. biol. chemistry, 1962—90, Edward S. Harkness prof. biol. chemistry, 1964—90, Edward S. Harkness prof. emeritus, 1990—, head dept. biol. chemistry, 1965—69; dean for acad. affairs Harvard Sch. Pub. Health, 1978—89, chmn. dep. environ. sci. and physiology, 1986—88, dir. divsn. biol. scis., prof., 1987—91, prof. emeritus, 1991—. Rsch. assoc. Children's Hosp. Med. Ctr., Boston, 1950—52, cons. chemistry, 1952—89; mem. conseil de surveillance Compagnie Financière du Scribe, 1975—81; trustee Bay Biochem. Rsch., Inc., 1973—83; mem. exec. com. divsn. chemistry and chem. tech. NRC, 1972—74, mem. assembly of math. and phys. scis., 1979—82; mem. sci. adv. com. Ctr. for Blood Rsch., Inc., 1972—92, emeritus trustee, 1992—, also mem. bd. dirs.; mem. rsch. adv. com. Children's Hosp. Med. Ctr., 1976—80, 1984—90, chmn., 1987—90; mem. vis. com. dept. chemistry Carnegie-Mellon U., 1968—72; bd. visitors Faculty Health Scis. SUNY, Buffalo, 1968—70; overseer Boston Mus. Sci.; trustee Boston Biomed. Rsch. Inst., 1990—, v.p., 1990—94; bd. govs. Weizmann Inst. Sci., Rehovot, Israel, 1978—90, gov. emeritus, 1990—; bd. dirs. Nat. Health Rsch. Found., ESA, Inc.; bd. dirs., sec.-treas. Nat. Acads. Corp.; gen. ptnr. Gosnold Investment Fund Ltd. Partnership, 1985—95; bd. dirs., investment mgr. Auburn Capital Corp., 1985—; sci. advisor Affymax Rsch. Inst., 1988—92; sr. sci. advisor FDA, 1991—99; mem. sr. adv. bd. The Ency. of Molecular Biology, 1991; mem. coun. visitors Marine Biol. Lab., 1992—; pres., trustee Inst. for Internat. Vaccine Devel., 1997—. Mem. adv. bd.: Jour. Polymer Sci., 1956—62, mem. editl. bd.: Biopolymers, 1963—85, hon. founding editor:, 1985—, mem. editl. bd.: Am. Chem. Soc. Monograph Series, 1965—72, Internat. Jour. Peptide and Protein Rsch., 1978—89, mem. editl. adv. bd.: Macromolecules, 1967—70, Jour. Am. Chem. Soc., 1978—82; contbr. articles to profl. jours. Recipient Princeton Class of 1939 Achievement award, 1970, Nat. Med. Sci. award, 1990, John Phillips award, Phillips Exeter Acad., 1998, Prof. Emeritus award for merit, Harvard Sch. of Pub. Health, 2000; fellow NRC, 1942—43. Fellow: AAAS (fin. com. 1977—84, com. on investments 1984—2001, chmn. budget com. 1988—92, treas. 1992—98), Optical Soc. Am., N.Y. Acad. Arts and Scis. (past pres. New Eng. sect.); mem.: NAS (adv. com. USSR and Eastern Europe 1979—84, treas. 1980—92, mem. com. sci. engring. and pub. policy 1992—95, treas. emeritus 1992—, audit com. 1994—2000), Fedn. Am. Socs. Exptl. Biology (investments adv. com. 1981—85), Internat. Orgn. Chem. Scis. in Devel. (coun. 1981—2005, chmn. fin. com. 1982—2005, v.p. 1982—2005, treas. 1985—2005, bd. dirs. 1985—2005), Commn. on Phys. Scis., Math., and Resources of NRC, Biophys. Soc., Am. Soc. Biol. Chemists (fin. com. 1973—82), Am. Chem. Soc. (nat. councillor 1958—61, Ralph F. Hirschmann award 1991), Russian Acad. Scis. (fgn.), Inst. Medicine. Achievements include patents in field. Home: 1010 Memorial Dr Cambridge MA 02138-4859

BLOW, GEORGE, lawyer; b. Chgo., Oct. 4, 1928; s. George Waller and Katharine Rowland (Cooke) B.; m. Sarah Wendel Kuhn, Nov. 4, 1957; children: Mary Allmand Blow Prevost, George Rowland, Wendel Matthiessen. AB cum laude, Harvard U., 1950; JD, U. Va., 1953. Bar: Va. 1953, D.C. 1954, U.S. Ct. Appeals (D.C. cir.) 1954, U.S. Ct. Mil. Appeals, 1955, U.S. Supreme Ct. 1956, U.S. Ct. Appeals (4th cir.) 1961, U.S. Ct. Appeals (fed. cir.) 1982. Assoc. Covington & Burling, Washington, 1953-63; ptnr. Patton, Boggs & Blow, Washington, 1963-93. Mem. adv. coun. Internat. Human Rights Law Group, Washington, 1988-98. Mem. Com. of 100 on Fed. City, Washington, 1984—2004, trustee, 1985-87; mem. Washington Inst. Fgn. Affairs, 1976—, bd. dirs., 1976-98; bd. dirs. Sheridan-Kalorama Hist. Assn., Washington, 1987-89. Mem. D.C. Bar, Va. State Bar, Soc. of Cincinnati in State of Va., Soc. Colonial Wars, Met. Club Washington, Order of Coif, Phi Delta Phi.

BLOWE, ARNETHIA, religious studies educator; b. Sussex County, Va., Aug. 4, 1924; d. Reverend Willie Green and Mary Lue Blowe. BS, Va. State Coll., Ettrick, 1947. Asst. dir. Christian edn. Am. Bapt. Conv. USA, 1962; cert. home econs. tchr. Va. State Dept. of Edn., 1947, tchr. K-8 N.J. Dept. of Edn., 1962, Storyteller Maplewood Adult Sch., 1991. Storyteller N.J. Storyteller's Guild, Montclair, NJ, 1990—, Nat. Black Storytellers Assn., Baltimore, Md., 1992—. Elem. tchr. Newark Pub. Sch. Sys., 1968—91. Performer: (storytelling) Black History Presentations (Black History Cert. of Appreciation, Elizabeth Urban League, 2002). Pres. Congress of Christian Edn. New Hope Missionary Bapt. Assn. Inc, Newark, 2000—. Recipient Cert. of Appreciation, Middlesex Ctrl. Bapt. Assn. N.J., 1993, award, Nat. Coun. Negro Women, 2003. Mem.: NAACP (life; exec. bd. mem. 1998—2002). Home: 930 Flora St Elizabeth NJ 07201

BLUE, CATHERINE ANNE, lawyer; b. Boston, Feb. 17, 1957; d. James Daniel and Angela Devina (Savini) Mahoney; m. Donald Sherwood Blue, 1980 (dec. 2001); children: Mairead Catherine, Edward Pierce. BA, Stonehill Coll., 1977; JD, Coll. William and Mary, 1980. Bar: Pa. 1980, N.Y. 1999; Mass. 2000. Atty. Aluminum Co. Am., Pitts., 1980-83, Pa. Dept. Revenue, Harrisburg, 1983-85, State Workmen's Ins. Fund, Pitts., 1985-87, Met. Pitts. Pub. Broadcasting (now QED Comm. Inc.), 1987-91, gen. counsel, 1991-95; regional gen. counsel ctrl. region AT&T Wireless Svcs., Paramus, N.J., 1995-97, dir. N.E. region, 1997-98, chief counsel land use, 1998-2000, v.p. land and comml. transactions, 2000—05; chief counsel land use Cingular Wireless, Paramus, 2005—. Mem. Pa. Bar Assn., Mass. Bar Assn. Democrat. Home: 44 Holiday Ct River Vale NJ 07675 Office: Cingular Wireless 15 E Midland Ave Paramus NJ 07652-2926 Office Phone: 201-576-2640.

BLUE, JOHN RONALD (J. RONALD BLUE), evangelical mission executive; b. Milw., Sept. 4, 1935; s. Earl R. and Wretha J. (Teater) B.; m. Elizabeth F. Wood, Sept. 7, 1962; children: Elisa, Laurie, David. BA, U. Nebr., 1957; cert. contact lens fitter, Ohio State U., 1960; ThM, Dallas Theol. Sem., 1965; PhD, U. Tex., Arlington, 1983. Contact lens fitter Ohio State U., Columbus, 1960-61; field dir. Ctrl. Am. Mission, 1965—75; dept. chmn. Dallas Theol. Sem., 1975-92; pres. CAM Internat., Dallas, 1992-2000; coord. Spanish-lang. Doctor Minsitries program Dallas Theol. Seminary, 2001—. Mem. adv. bd. Proclamation, Inc., Dallas, 1992—, Art Yohner Mission Ministries Info., Bradenton, Fla., 1998—, Christar, Reading, Pa., 1999—; mem. edit. bd. Evang. Missions Quar. Contbg. author: Walvoord: A Tribute, 1982, Bible Knowledge Commentary, 1983, 85, Essays in Honor of J.D. Pentecost, 1986, Devotions for Kindred Spirits, 1995, Basic Theology Applied, 1996; author: Evangelism and Missions, 2001. Lt. USN, 1957-59. Mem. Pi Epsilon Pi, Theta Xi. Republican. Avocation: travel. Home: 3504 Halifax Dr Arlington TX 76013-1909 Office: Dallas Theol Seminary 3909 Swiss Ave Dallas TX 75204 Business E-Mail: rblue@dts.edu.

BLUE, JOSEPH EDWARD, physicist; b. Quitman, Miss., Sept. 29, 1936; s. Edward Lee and Allie Belle (Corley) B.; m. Neva Rosetta Deal, Apr. 14, 1962; children: Tracy Marie, Gina Lynn. BS in Physics, Miss. State U., 1961; MS in Engring. Sci., Fla. State U., 1966; PhD in Mech. Engring., U. Tex., 1971. Physicist Navy Mine Def. Lab., Panama City, Fla., 1961-68; rsch. sci. engr. U. Tex., Austin, 1968-71; rsch. physicist Naval Rsch. Lab., Orlando, Fla., 1971-73, Meas br. head, 1973-81, supt., 1981-96; pres. Leviathan Legacy Inc., Orlando, Fla., 1996—. Author: (with others) Benchmark Papers in U/W Acoust, 1975; contbr. articles to Jour. Acoustical Soc. Am. Fellow Acoustical Soc. Am. Democrat. Methodist. Achievements include patents for low frequency acoustic source, color sonar display, time internal to pulse height converter, device for alerting manatees to danger from boats, method of alerting sea cows of the danger of approaching motor vessels; research in resonant scattering, parametric depth sounder using water's nonlinearity, substantial sound pressure from tow-powered sources, and manatee hearing, collision of whales and ships. Office: Leviathan Legacy Inc 3313 Northglen Dr Orlando FL 32806-6338 E-mail: joeblue@earthlink.net.

BLUE, MONTE LYNN, college president; b. Ft. Worth, Feb. 25, 1945; s. Bert Leonard and Mary Lee (Cooper) B.; m. Sheryl Doris O'Connor, July 1, 1966; children: Michelle Denea, Laura Lynn. BA, North Tex. State U., 1967, MA, 1972; EdD, U. Houston, 1979. Illustrator Gen. Dynamics, Ft. Worth, 1967-71; instr. advt. art, Cen. Campus San Jacinto Jr. Coll., Pasadena, Tex., 1971-74, dist. dir., instr. media, 1975-79, dean student services, South Campus, 1979-81, dean student services, Cen. Campus, 1981-83, pres., 1983—. Bd. dirs. Deer Park Ednl. Found., 1996—; bd. dirs. Southeast Econ. Devel. Coun., 1995—, chmn. bd., 1997-98; moderator Bd. of Southmore Med. Ctr.; consumer credit counselor svc. bd. dirs., 1999-2000; spkr. numerous presentations to various comty., civic and profl. groups. Contbr. articles to profl. jours.; speaker numerous presentations to various community, civic and profl. groups. Vice chmn. bd. dirs. San Jacinto YMCA, Pasadena, 1986-87, chmn., 1987-88. Named Outstanding Alumni, Ft. Worth Ind. Sch. Dist., 1984. Mem.: Tex. Pub. Cmty. Jr. Coll. Assn., Assn. Tex. Colls. and Univs., Nat. Orgn. on Legal Problems in Edn., Am. Assn. Higher Edn., Am. Assn. Cmty. Jr. Colls., LaPorte/Bayshore C. of C. (bd. dirs. 1987—89, pres. 1989), Rotary (local pres. 1986—87), Phi Theta Kappa (hon. mem. Mu Omicron Chpt., Hall of Honor 1985). Republican. Baptist. Avocation: painting. Office: San Jacinto Coll Cen 8060 Spencer Hwy Pasadena TX 77505 Office Phone: 281-542-2000.

BLUEFARB, SAM, retired humanities educator; s. Lewis Bluefarb and Millie Engel. AA, L.A. City Coll., 1949; BA, UCLA, 1951; MA, U. So. Calif., 1961; PhD, U. N.Mex., Albuquerque, 1967. Libr. Calif. State Libr., Sacramento, 1954—55, San Bernardino Pub. Libr., Calif., 1955—57; English tchr. San Pedro H.S., Calif., 1957—62; assoc. prof., English L.A. Harbor Coll., Wilmington, 1958—79; English instr. UCLA Ext., 1972. Author: (short stories) The Dubious Benefits of Nostalgia, 2003, (novels) Reunion, 1998. Pfc. U.S. Army, 1941—45. Mem.: Jewish War Veterans U.S., Hemingway Soc., Nat. Assn. Scholars. Republican. Jewish. Avocations: writing, photography. Home: PO Box 4122 Diamond Bar CA 91765

BLUEFARB, SAMUEL MITCHELL, retired physician; b. St. Louis, Oct. 15, 1912; s. Sol and Pauline (Brown) B.; m. Grace Parsons, Jan. 1, 1944; 1 son, Richard Alan; m. Leah Rose Vendig Pollock, Jan. 24, 1968; children: Fred, Nancy Pollock. BS, U. Ill., 1936; MD, 1937. Diplomate Am. Bd. Dermatology and Syphilology. Intern Cook County Hosp., Chgo., 1937-38; resident Bellevue Hosp., N.Y.C., 1939-41; practice medicine specializing in dermatology, 1941-78; sr. attending dermatologist, chmn. dept. Cook County Hosp., 1952-58; attending dermatologist VA Lakeside Hosp., 1954-78; sr. attending staff Chgo. Wesley Meml. Hosp., Passavant Hosp. Prof., chmn. dept. dermatology Northwestern U. Med. Sch., 1962-78; prof. dermatology U. South Fla., 1985-88; chmn. dept. dermatology Bay Pines VA Hosp., Fla., 1984-87. Author books and articles. Fellow Am. Acad. Dermatology and Syphilology (dir. 1969), ACP; mem. AMA, Ill. Med. Soc. (past pres. dermatol. sect.), Chgo. Med. Soc., Soc. Investigative Dermatology, Chgo. Dermatol. soc. (past pres.)., Am. Dermatol. Assn., Noah Worcester Dermatology Soc. Home: Kenwood of Lakeview 3101 Sheridan Rd Chicago IL 60657

BLUESTEIN, BARBARA ANN, librarian; b. Pitts., Feb. 3, 1952; d. Griffith and Mary Jane (Thompson) Ray; m. Michael Richard Bluestein, Aug. 26, 1973; children: Matthew Alan, Jeremy Micah. BS in Edn., Miami U., Oxford, Ohio, 1974; MEd, Xavier U., 1977. Permanent tchg. cert. ednl. media grades 7-12, Ohio. Libr. Princeton H.S., Cin., 1974-89, head libr., 1989—. Mem. adv. bd. InfOhio Oh! Teach, 2000-01. Den leader pack 72 Boy Scouts Am., Cin., 1990-95, merit badge counselor, 1992—2003, sch. night coord., 1994-97. Named Key Leader Boy Scouts Am.-Dan Beard Coun., Cin., 1994; recipient Meritorious Svc. award Boy Scouts Am.-Dan Beard Coun., Cin., 1995, Dist. Award of Merit, 1997; Jennings scholar, 1986-87. Mem. DAR, Cin. Area Sch. Librs. Assn. (treas. 2003-05), Reviewers Young Adult Lit. (v.p. 1997-99, pres. 1999-2001). Avocations: reading, swimming, waterskiing. Home: 3249 Braewood Dr Cincinnati OH 45241-3184 Office: Princeton HS 11080 Chester Rd Cincinnati OH 45246-3802

BLUESTEIN, EDWIN A., JR., lawyer; b. Hearne, Tex., Oct. 16, 1930; s. Edwin A. and Frances Grace (Ely) B.; m. Marsha Kay Meredith, Dec. 21, 1957; children: Boyd, Leslie. BBA, U. Tex., 1952, JD, 1958. Bar: Tex. 1957, U.S. Ct. Appeals (5th cir.) 1960, U.S. Dist. Ct. (so. dist.)Tex. 1959, U.S. Dist. Ct. (ea. dist.)Tex. 1965, U.S. Supreme Ct. 1967, U.S. Ct. Appeals (11th cir.) 1982. Law clk. U.S. Dist. Ct., Houston, 1958-59; assoc. Fulbright & Jaworski, Houston, 1959-65, participating atty., 1965-71, ptnr., 1971-97, head admiralty dept., 1984-93, sr. ptnr., 1990-97, of counsel, 1998—. Mem. permanent adv. bd. Tulane Admiralty Law Inst., New Orleans, 1983-2001; mem. planning com. Houston Marine Ins. Seminar, 1970-76; lectr. profl. seminars Assoc. editor: American Maritime Cases; contbr. articles to profl. jours. Mem. Tex. Coastal Mgmt. Adv. Com., Austin, 1975—78; chair Morgan's Point Beach Preservation Restoration Assn., 2001—03; bd. dirs. Barbour's Cut Seafarers Ctr., 1992—2004, Houston Internat. Seafarers Ctr., 1993—2003. Served with U.S. Army, 1952—54. Recipient Yachtsman of Yr. award Houston Yacht Club, 1978; Eagle Scout, Boy Scouts Am., 1944. Mem. Tex. Bar Found., Maritime Law Assn. U.S. (mem. exec. com. 1980-83), Houston Maritime Arbitrators Assn. (dir., sec.-treas. 1999-2005), Houston Mariners Club (pres. 1970), Southeastern Admiralty Law Inst. (dir. 1983-85, Houston C. of C. (chmn. ports and waterways com. 1978-79), Propeller Club U.S., Theta Xi (chpt. pres. 1952). Clubs: Houston Yacht (commodore 1979-80). Methodist. Home: 603 Bayridge Rd Morgan's Point TX 77571-3512 Office: Fulbright & Jaworski 1301 Mckinney St Houston TX 77010-3031

BLUESTEIN, HOWARD BRUCE, meteorology educator; b. Chelsea, Mass., Oct. 8, 1948; BSEE, MIT, 1971, MSEE, MS in Meteorology, MIT, 1972, PhD in Meteorology, 1976. Asst. prof. meteorology U. Okla., Norman, 1979-83, assoc. prof., 1983-90, prof., 1990—, George Lynn Cross rsch. prof., 2004—. Vis. asst. prof. meteorology U. Okla., Norman, 1976-79. Author: Synoptic-Dynamic Meteorology in Midlatitudes, Vol. I, 1992, Vol. II, 1993, Tornado Alley, 1999. Named Okla. Prof. of Yr., Coun. Advancement and Support of Edn., 1989. Fellow Am. Meteorol. Soc. (chair severe local storms com. 1993-95, recipient Louis J. Battan Author's award, 2001, Tchg. Excellence award, 2004). Avocations: photography, folkdancing. Office: U Okla Sch Meteorology 100 E Boyd St Rm 1310 Norman OK 73019-1015 Office Phone: 405-325-6561. E-mail: hblue@ou.edu.

BLUESTEIN, VENUS WELLER, retired psychologist, educator; b. Milw., July 16, 1933; d. Richard T. and Hazel (Beard) Weller; m. Marvin Bluestein, Mar. 7, 1954. BS, U. Cin., 1956, MEd, 1959, EdD, 1966. Diplomate Am. Bd. Profl. Psychology. Psychologist-in-tng. Longview State Hosp., Cin., 1956-58; sch. psychologist Cin. Pub. Schs., 1958-65; asst. prof. psychology U. Cin., 1965-70, assoc. prof., 1970-79, prof., 1979-93, prof. emerita, 1993—, dir. sch. psychology program, 1965-70, co-dir. sch. psychology program, 1970-75, dir. undergrad. studies, 1976-91, dir. undergrad. advising, 1991-93. Cons. child psychologist. Sec., U.S. exec. com. rsch. Children's Internat. Summer Villages, 1964—68; chmn. Ohio Interuniv. Coun. Sch. Psychology, 1967. Editor Ohio Psychologist, 1961-68, co-editor, 1972-79; contbr. articles to profl. publs. Vol. Hamilton County Parks, 1982—, vol. naturalist, 1995—; vol. educator Cin. Zoo, 1982— Recipient George B. Barbour award, 1985, 20 Yrs. of Svc. award Cin. Zoo, 2002, Hamilton County Parks Dist., 2002. Mem. AAUP, APA, Nat. Assn. School Psychologists, Ohio Psychol. Assn. (citation 1972, Disting. Svc. award 1968), Southwestern Ohio Sch. Psychol. Assn., Cin. Psychol. Assn. (sec. 1961-62), Sch. Psychologists Ohio, Forum for Death Edn. and Counseling, Kappa Delta Pi, Sigma Delta Pi, Psi Chi (award for outstanding mentor 1985, award for outstanding contbns. to undergrad. psychology students 1994). Avocations: horseback riding, wildlife photography. Office: U Cin Dept Psychology Ml 376 Cincinnati OH 45221-0001

BLUFORD, GUION STEWART, JR., engineering company executive; b. Phila., Nov. 22, 1942; s. Guion Stewart and Harriet Lolita (Brice) B.; m. Linda M. Tull, Apr. 7, 1964; children: Guion Stewart, James Trevor. BS in Aerospace Engring., Pa. State U., 1964; grad., Squadron Officers Sch., 1971; MS in Aerospace Engring., Air Force Inst. Tech., 1974, PhD in Aerospace Engring., 1978; D.Sc. hon., Fla. A&M U., 1983; MBA, U. Houston, 1987; DSc (hon.), Tex. So. U., Va. State U., Morgan State U., Stevens Inst. Tech., Tuskegee U., Bowie (Md.) State Coll., Thomas Jefferson U., Chgo. State U., Georgian Ct. Coll., Drexel U., Kent State U., Ctrl State U. Commd. 2d lt. U.S. Air Force, 1965, advanced through grades to col., 1993, F-4C fighter pilot 12 Tactical Fighter Wing Cam Ranh Bay, Vietnam, 1966-67, T-38 instr. pilot 3630 Flying Tng. Wing Sheppard AFB, Wichita Falls, Tex., 1967-72; chief aerodynamics and airframe br. Air Force Flight Dynamics Lab., Wright-Patterson AFB, Dayton, Ohio, 1975-78; NASA astronaut Johnson Space Ctr., Houston, 1978-93; ret., 1993; v.p., gen. mgr. div. engring. svcs. NYMA Inc., Greenbelt, Md., 1993-97; v.p., gen. mgr. aerospace sector Fed. Data Corp., Bethesda, Md., 1997—2000; v.p. microgravity R&D ops. Northrup Grumman Info. Tech., Herndon, Va., 2000—02; pres. The Aerospace Tech. Group, 2002—. Decorated Air medal with 9 oak leaf clusters, Def. Superior Svc. medal, Legion of Merit, Air Force Commendation medal, Air Force Meritorious Svc. medal; named Black Engr. of Yr., 1991; named to Internat. Space Hall of Fame, 1997; recipient Mervin E. Gross award Air Force Inst. Tech., 1974, Disting. Nat. Scientist award Nat. Soc. Black Engrs., 1979, Group Achievement award, NASA, 1980, 1981, 1989, 2003, Nat. Intelligence medal of achievement, 1993, Space Flight medal, 1983, 1985, 1991, 1992, Def. Meritorious Svc. medal, 1989, 1992, 1993, NASA Disting. Svc. medal, 1994, NASA Exceptional Svc. medal, 1992, Disting. Alumni award, Pa. State U. Alumni Assn., 1983, Pa. Disting. Svc. medal, 1984, Disting. Alumni award, Air Force Inst. Tech., 2002, Univ. Houston, 2003. Fellow: AIAA (bd. dirs.); mem.: ENSCO (bd. dirs.), U.S. Space Found. (bd. dirs.), Aerospace Corp. (trustee), Nat. Rsch. Coun. Aeronautics and Space Engring. Bd., Omicron Delta Kappa, Tau Beta Pi. Christian Scientist. Office: The Aerospace Tech Group PO Box 549 North Olmsted OH 44070-0549 Personal E-mail: gsbluford@adelphia.net.

BLUH, BONNIE, scriptwriter, actress; b. NYC, Mar. 29; d. Morris and Mary (Steinberg) B.; children: Craig, Kenn, Brian. Cons. Lincoln Repertory Theater, N.Y.C., 1962; dir. improvisational theater East Brunswick (N.J.) Jr. H.S., 1965; creative drama tchr., Phila., 1968-71; Emmy judge, 1989—; mentor Young Writers Inst., West Hartford, Conn., 1995—; lectr. in field. Author: Woman to Woman, 1974, Banana, 1976, The Old Speak Out, 1979, The Eleanor Roosevelt Girls, 1999, (plays) N, My Name is Nicki, 1962, Light a Candle for Charlie, 1964, Lifetime Policy, 1975, The Day God Died, 1992; co-editor: Broadway's Fabulous Fifties, 2002; actor: Many Wonder, 1989, Jesus Christ is Alive, 1990, One Woman Show, 1991, and assorted TV roles. Recipient Best Actor award Festival Short Films, N.Y., 1990. Mem. AFTRA, Authors Guild, New Dramatists (alumna exec. com.), Dramatists Guild. Jewish. Home: 55 Bethune St New York NY 10014-2010 Personal E-mail: bbluh@aol.com.

BLUHER, GREGORY, computer scientist, mathematician; b. Odessa, Ukraine, May 9, 1960; arrived in U.S., 1979; s. Froim and Alla (Shvetz) Blyukher; m. Antonia Rose Wilson, May 25, 1986; children: Andrew Emmanuel, Julia Elizabeth, Sarah Elena. MA in Math. with honors, Johns Hopkins U., 1983; PhD in Math., Princeton U., 1988; MS in Computer Sci., UCLA, 1992. Asst. prof. The Coll. of N.J., Trenton, 1987-88, Whittier (Calif.)

Coll., 1988-89; programmer The Software Toolworks, L.A., 1989-90; rschr. computer sci. dept. UCLA, 1990-92; staff programmer IBM, San Jose, 1992-93; project leader ORACLE, Redwood City, Calif., 1993-95; computer specialist Social Security Adminstrn., Balt., 1995-96; sr. computer scientist Dept. of Def., Washington, 1996-2001; IT Apps. team leader EPA, Washington, 2001—. Translator: Introduction to the Classical Theory of Abelian Functions, 1990. Interviewer alumni coun. Johns Hopkins U., Balt., 1985-89. IBM scholar, 1983. Mem. IEEE-Computer Soc. (cert. software devel. profl. 2003), Assn. Computing Machinery, Project Mgmt. Inst. (project mgmt. profl. 2004), Phi Beta Kappa. Home: PO Box 252 Simpsonville MD 21150-0252 E-mail: gbluher@computer.org.

BLUHM, BARBARA JEAN, communications agency executive; b. Chgo., Mar. 5, 1925; d. Maurice L. and Clara (Miller) B. Student Coll. William and Mary, 1943-45; BS, U. Wis., 1947. Exec. tng. program Carson Pirie Scott & Co., Chgo., 1947-52; home economist Lever Bros. Co., Chgo., 1952-57; field rep. The Merchandising Group, Chgo., 1957-62, v.p. N.Y.C., 1962-82, pres., 1982-87, chmn., 1987-90. Publicity chmn. James Lenox House Assn., N.Y.C., 1980—90; vol. Venice Little Theatre; active Coll. Club of Venice, Venice Art League, Venice Symphony, Venice Opera Guild, Friends of the Venice Libr. Mem. Venice Yacht Club, Venice Hist. Preservation League. Republican. Presbyterian. Home: 1470 Colony Pl Venice FL 34292-1550 E-mail: bbluhm@iopener.net.

BLUHM, NEIL GARY, real estate company executive; b. 1938; married. BS, U. Ill.; JD, Northwestern U. CPA Ill.; bar: Ill. Ptnr. firm Mayer, Brown & Platt, Chgo., 1962-70; pres. JMB Realty Corp., Chgo., from 1970; pres., trustee JMB Realty Trust, Chgo., 1972—. Bd. dir. Chgo. Cares Inc., Urban Shopping Ctrs. Inc., 1993—2000, Northwestern U., Alzheimer's Disease & Related Disorders Assn., Whitney Mus. Am. Art; bd. trustees Art Inst. Chgo. Mem.: Bar State Ill., Real Estate Roundtable, Standard Club, Chgo. Club. Office: Urban Shopping Ctrs Inc 132 E Delaware Ste Ste 6501 Chicago IL 60611 also: JMB Realty Corporation 900 N Michigan Ave Fl 19 Chicago IL 60611-1542*

BLUHM, WILLIAM THEODORE, political scientist, educator; b. Newark, Oct. 13, 1923; s. Frederick Theodore and Charlotte Catherine (Walz) B.; m. Eleanor Elizabeth Kearns, Apr. 22, 1950; children: Catherine Elizabeth, Susanna Marie, Andrew Edward Frederick. BA, Brown U., 1948; MA, Tufts U., 1949; PhD, U. Chgo., 1957. Instr. polit. sci. U. Rochester, 1952-53, asst. prof., 1957-63, assoc. prof., 1963-67, prof., 1967-92, prof. emeritus, 1993—; instr. polit. sci. Brown U., 1953-57. Cons. C.H. Beck Verlag, Munich, 1966-70. Author: Theories of the Political System, 1965, Building an Austrian Nation: The Political Integration of a Western State, 1973, Ideologies and Attitudes, 1974, Force or Freedom?: The Paradox in Modern Political Thought, 1984; co-author: The World of the Policy Analyst, 1990, 3d edit. 2002; editor: The Paradigm Problem in Political Science, 1982; contbr. articles profl. jours. Served with Signal Corps AUS, 1943-46. Decorated Bronze Star Medal; U. Rochester rsch. grantee, 1963-64, 68-69; Fulbright rsch. fellow Austria, 1965-66; NSF summer grantee, 1967, 68; U. Rochester Bridging fellow, 1980-81; Nat. Endowment Humanities grantee, 1976. Mem. Am. Polit. Sci. Assn., Sigma Nu. Democrat. Roman Catholic. Office: U Rochester Dept Polit Sci Rochester NY 14627 Office Phone: 585-275-5184. Business E-Mail: bluh@mail.rochester.edu.

BLUITT, KAREN, information technology executive; b. N.Y.C., Oct. 25, 1957; d. James Bertrand and Beatrice (Kaufman) B.; m. Kenneth Mark Curry, Nov. 24, 1979 (div. Dec. 1991). BS, Fordham U., 1979; MBA, Calif. State Poly. U., 1982; postgrad., George Mason U., 1994-98; PhD, Kennedy Western U., 2000. Software engr. Hughes Aircraft Co., Fullerton, Calif., 1979-81; microprocessor engr. Beckman Instruments Co., Fullerton, 1981-82, Singer Co., Glendale, Calif., 1982-83; sr. software engr. Sanders Assoc., Nashua, N.H., 1983-85; software project mgr. GTE Corp., Billerica, Mass., 1985-86; sr. software engr. Wang Labs., Lowell, Mass., 1986-87; project task leader Vanguard Rsch., Lexington, Mass., 1987-88; program mgr. Applied Rsch. & Engring., Bedford, Mass., 1989-91, Sparta, McLean, Va., 1992-93; prin. software engr. Sci. Applications Internat., Arlington, Va., 1993-94; tech. mgr. CACI, Arlington, 1994, Booz-Allen & Hamilton, Vienna, Va., 1995, MRJ Tech. Solutions, Inc., Fairfax, Va., 1996-97, Softek Systems, Inc., Fairfax, 1998—2001; pres. QSCI, Ashburn, Va., 2001—. 1st lt. U.S. Army, 1979-88. Scholar Gov. N.Y. Scholarship Com., 1975-79, Beta Gamma Sigma, 1978—. Mem. IEEE, AAUW, Am. Women in Sci., Am. Brokers Network, Assn. Computing Machinery, Soc. Women Engrs., Wash. Soc. of Engrs.

BLUM, ARTHUR, social worker, educator; b. Cleve., May 25, 1926; s. Rebecca (Pivowar) Blum; m. Lenore Sharrie Secord, Dec. 26, 1954; children: Alex, Joel. AB, Western Res. U., 1950, MS in Social Adminstrn., 1952, DSW, 1960. Group worker Cleve. Jewish Community Ctr., 1952, Cleve. Child Guidance Ctr., 1954-58; project dir. Case Western Res. U., Cleve., 1958-60, prof. social work, 1960—, Grace Longwell Coyle chair, 1987—; prof. Smith Coll., Northampton, Mass., 1961-63. Cons. Bellefaire Regional Treatment Ctr., Cleve., 1962-85, City of East Cleve., 1967-70, Jewish Welfare Fedn., Cleve., 1968-72, Fedn. Cmty. Plannning, Cleve., 1976-78, others; vis. prof. Tel Aviv U., 1971-72, 79-80. Editor: Healing Through Living, 1971, Aging and Care Giving, 1990, Innovations in Practice and Service Delivery, 1999; contbr. numerous articles to profl. jours. Sgt. U.S. Army, 1945-46, with Med. Svcs. Corp, 1952-54. Recipient Outstanding Alumnus award Case Western Res. U., 1968. Mem. AAUP, Nat. Assn. Social Workers, Coun. Social Work Edn., Assn. Group Workers. Democrat. Jewish. Avocations: camping, sailing, racquetball, gardening. Office: Case Western Res U Sch Applied Social Scis Univ Circle Cleveland OH 44106

BLUM, BARBARA DAVIS, investor; b. Hutchinson, Kans. d. Roy C. and Jo (McKinnon) Davis; children: Devin, Hunter, Ragan, Davis. BA, Fla. State U., 1960, MSW, 1961. Founder, ptnr. Mid-Suffolk Ctr. for Psychotherapy, Hauppage, L.I., N.Y., 1965-67; v.p. Restaurant Assocs. Ga., Inc., Atlanta, 1967-75; dep. adminstr. U.S. EPA, Washington, 1977-81; mem. Pres.'s Interagy. Coordinating Coun.; chair, pres., CEO Abigail Adams Nat. Bancorp and Adams Nat. Bank, Washington, 1983-98; CEO BDB Investment Partnership, 1998—; chair Main St. Bank, 2003—. Chair U.S./Japan Environ. Agreement, 1977—81; head 1st U.S. Environ. Del. to China, 1978; chmn. Environ. Policy Inst., 1981—84; sr. advisor UN Environ. Program, 1981—84; pres. UN Univ. Peace, 1986—89; chair emeritus Ctr. for Policy Alternatives; trustee Fed. City Coun., 1988—99; nat. adv. bd. U.S. SBA, 1993—2001; chmn. D.C. Econ. Devel. Fin. Corp., 1986—2002. Del. UN Mid Decade Conf. on Women, 1980; Presdl. appointee trustee and treas. Inst. for Am. Indian Art; founder, chmn. Leadership Washington, 1989; trustee, treas. Southeastern U.; trustee, chmn. investment com. D.C. Retirement Bd.; dep. dir. Carter-Mondale U.S. Presdl. campaign, 1976; dir. Carter-Mondale Transition Team, Washington, 1976—77; panelist Clinton-Gore Econ. Conf., Little Rock and Atlanta; bd. dirs., chmn. performance com. Kaiser Found. Health Plan Mid Atlantic, 1989—2004; bd. dirs., chair compensation com. Kaiser Found. Health Plan, Inc., 2001—05; bd. dirs., chair exec. com. Kaiser Found. Hosp., 2001—05; bd. dirs. Stimpson Ctr. Decorated commdr.'s cross Order of Merit W. Ger.; recipient Disting. Svc. award Federally Employed Women, Spl. Conservation award Nat. Wildlife Fedn., Orgn. of Yr. award Ga. Wildlife Fedn., 1974, Disting. Svc. award Americans for Indian Opportunity; named Bus. Woman of Yr. Nat. Assn. Bus. Women, Leukemia Soc., Assn. Women Contractors. Mem. Washington Women's Forum, Internat. Women's Forum, Cosmos Club. Democrat. Personal E-mail: bdavisblum@verizon.net.

BLUM, BETTY ANN, footwear company executive; Student, Vanderbilt U. Various positions Zayre Dept. Store, Framingham, Mass., 1970-75; divsn. pres. Mootsie Tootsies, pres. Jones N.Y., exec. v.p. Maxwell Shoe Co., Hyde Park, Mass., 1976-88, exec. v.p., 1988—. Mem. bd. women's study group Brandeis U., 1998. Trustee Dana Farber Cancer Inst., 1998; dir. 210 Internat. Found., 1991.

BLUM, BRADLEY D., former food service executive; BA, Denison U., Ohio, 1976; MA, Northwestern U., 1978. Mktg. asst. Betty Crocker General Mills, 1978, v.p. mktg. Cereal Ptnrs. Worldwide, 1990—94; sr. v.p. mktg. then pres. Olive Garden N.Am., 1994—96; exec. v.p., mem. bd. of dirs., vice chmn. Darden Restaurants Inc., 1997—2002; CEO Burger King, Corp., 2003—04. Chmn. Economic Devel. Bd., City of Winter Park, Fla. Bd. trustees Atlantic Ctr. for Arts, Fla.; adv. bd. Sun Trust Bank. Recipient Operator of the Year, Multi-Unit Foodservice, 2000. Avocations: skiing, tennis, race car driving.

BLUM, EDWARD HOWARD, investment banker; b. Washington, Jan. 1, 1940; s. Irwin Ellis and Esther (Wolff) Blum; m. Marlene H. Witman, June 8, 1965; children: Daniel Joseph, Matthew Alan. BS, Carnegie-Mellon U., 1961; MS, Princeton U., 1963, PhD, 1965. Asst. prof. Princeton (N.J.) U., 1965-67; sr. scientist, project leader, dir. rsch., v.p. Rand Corp., N.Y.C. and Santa Monica, Calif., 1967-76; dir. advanced tech. U.S. Dept. Energy, Washington, 1976-80; v.p., exec. dir. Merrill Lynch Capital Markets, Washington and N.Y.C., 1980-86; pres., CEO, vice-chmn. bd. Md. Nat. Investment Banking Co., Greenbelt, 1986-89; pres., CEO Blum & Co., Inc., Reston, Va., 1989—; CEO OG Co., Inc., Houston, Tex., 1991—. Mem. adv. bd. Solar Energy Rsch. Inst., Denver, 1983—90; bd. dirs. Fed. Pvt. Sector Partnership. Editor: Jour. Urban Analysis, 1970—77; contbr. articles to profl. jours. Chmn. Fairfax (Va.) County Info. Tech. Adv. Com., 2000—; trustee U. Detroit, 1970—79. Recipient award, Inst. Mgmt. Sci., 1974, Ops. Rsch. award, NATO, 1976. Home: 2417 Luckett Ave Vienna VA 22180-6818 Office: Blum & Co Inc 322 11800 Sunrise Valley Dr Reston VA 20191-5302 Office Phone: 703-860-3736. Business E-Mail: eblum@blumandco.com.

BLUM, EVA TANSKY, lawyer; b. Pitts., July 29, 1949; d. Harry and Jeanette N. Tansky; 1 child. BA, U. Pitts., 1970, JD, 1973. Bar: Pa. 1973. Atty. U.S. Dept. Commerce, Washington, 1973-76, U.S. Air, Washington, 1976-77; sr. v.p., dir. cmty. devel. PNC Fin. Group, Pitts., 1990—, chair PNC Found., 2002—, dir. PNC Grow Up Great, 2003—. Mem. com. Pitts. Health and Welfare Planning Assn., 1985-89; bd. dirs. Family Health Coun., Pitts., 1987-94, Forbes Health Found., 1992-96, WQED, Pitts., 1994—, U. Pitts. Alumni Assn., 1992-98, 2000—, The Ellis Sch., 1996-2002; bd. dirs., sec. ARC Western Pa. chpt. 1992-94; trustee Am. Jewish Com., Pitts., 1977—. Mem. ABA, Pa. Bar Assn., Allegheny County Bar Assn. Office: PNC Fin Svcs Group One PNC Plaza 249 5th Ave Pittsburgh PA 15222-2709 Office Phone: 412-762-2748. Business E-Mail: eva.blum@pnc.com.

BLUM, GARY BERNARD, lawyer; b. Brighton, Eng., Feb. 1, 1946; came to U.S., 1947; s. Peter and Alice (Fenchel) B.; m. Marsha Weinberg, Sept. 9, 1973; children: Annette, Jesse, Alyce. BA, U. Colo., 1968, JD, 1971. Bar: Colo. 1971, U.S. Dist. Ct. Colo. 1971, U.S. Ct. Appeals (10th cir.) 1971, U.S. Supreme Ct. 1985. Dep. pub. defender State of Colo., Denver, 1971-74, asst. atty. gen., 1975-78; shareholder Long & Jaudon P.C., Denver, 1978—2001; dir. Silver & DeBoskey P.C., 2001—. Lectr. law U. Colo.; mem. grievance com. Colo. Supreme Ct., 1988-93, mem. civil justice com.; mem. com. on lawyer conduct Fed. Ctr., 1995—, chair, 2000—; mem. Faculty Fed. of Advocates, bd. dirs. 2001—. Mem. ATLA, Colo. Bar Assn. (chmn. ethics com. 1985—), Denver Bar Assn., Colo. Def. Lawyers Assn., Am. Bd. Trial Advocates, Am. Health Lawyers Assn., Am. Arbitration Assn. Democrat. Jewish. Avocations: jogging, reading, skiing, tennis. Office: Silver and DeBoskey 1801 York St Denver CO 80206

BLUM, GERALD HENRY, retired retail executive; b. San Francisco, 1926; s. Abe and Mildred (Loewenthal) B.; children: Shelley, Todd, Ryan, Derek. AB, Stanford U., 1950. Mdse. trainee Emporium, San Francisco, 1950-51; with Gottschalks Inc. (formerly E. Gottschalk & Co., Inc.), Fresno, Calif., 1951-98, v.p., 1954-63, exec. v.p., 1963-82, pres. and vice chmn., 1982-94, ret., 1995, bd. dirs. Bd. dirs. Fresno Conv. Bur., 1954—, pres., 1985-87; bd. dirs. BBB, Fresno, 1954-77, Blue Cross, Calif. 1972-85; chmn. C.A.R.E., Fresno County, 1957—, Eagle Scout Awards Banquet, 1993, Calif. State U. Bus. Coun., Fresno, 1997-98; adv. com. Fresno County Arts Ctr., 1982-85, bd. dirs., 1958-66, v.p. 1961, 88-94; mem. Area VII Calif. Vocat. Edn. Com., 1972-75, Mayor's Bi-Racial Com., 1968-69; founding v.p. Jr. Achievement, Fresno County, 1957-63; bd. dirs. Fresno Boys Club, 1958-62, Ctrl. Calif. Employers Coun., 1956-62, treas. 1958; bd. dirs. Fresno Philharm. Orch., 1954-58, Salvation Army, Fresno, 1956-67, Youth Edn. Svc., 1956-57, Fresno County Taxpayers Assn., 1954, San Joaquin Valley Econ. Edn. Project, 1953; bd. dirs., bus. adv. coun. Fresno City Coll., 1955-57; trustee Valley Children's Hosp., 1955-57, United Crusade, Fresno, 1952-62; adv. bd. Liberty Mut. Ins. Co., 1990-2001. Recipient Disting. Svc. award Fresno Jaycees, 1959; winner World's Championship Domino Tournament, 1969, 86, 88. Mem. Nat. Retail Fedn. (dir. 1978-94), Calif. Retailers Assn. (dir. 1964-94), Fresno C. of C. (dir. county, city 1955-57, Boss of Yr., Jr. C. of C. 1980), Retail Mmgt. Inst., U. Santa Clara (dir. 1986-98), Nat. Secs. Assn. (Boss of Yr. 1978), Fresno County Stanford U. Alumni Assn. (pres. 1952), Pres. Club of Calif. State U., Rotary (v.p. Fresno club 1962), Univ. Sequoia Sunnyside Club, Downtown Club (Fresno, pres. 1978).

BLUM, JACOB JOSEPH, physiologist, educator; b. Bklyn., Oct. 3, 1926; s. Paul and Anna (Brown) B.; m. Ruth Marsey, June 3, 1960; children: Mark, Douglas, Lisa, Laura. BA, NYU, 1947; MS, U. Chgo., 1950, PhD, 1952. Mem. staff Naval Med. Rsch. Inst., Bethesda, Md., 1953-56; chief biophysics sect. gerontology br. NIH, Balt., 1958-62; prof. physiology Duke U., Durham, NC, 1962—, James B. Duke prof., 1980-97, James B. Duke prof. emeritus, 1997—. With AUS, 1945-46. Merck postdoctoral fellow, 1952, Guggenheim fellow, 1969, Fogarty sr. internat. fellow, 1992. Mem. Am. Physiol. Soc., Soc. Protozoologists (pres. 1991). Home: 16 Stoneridge Cir Durham NC 27705 Office Phone: 919-684-6937. Business E-Mail: j.blum@cellbio.duke.edu.

BLUM, JOAN KURLEY, fundraising executive; b. Palm Beach, Fla., July 27, 1926; d. Nenad Daniel and Eva (Milos) Kurley; m. Robert C. Blum, Apr. 15, 1967 (dec. Apr. 2001); children: Christopher Alexander, Martha Jane, Louisa Joan. BA, U. Wash., 1948. Cert. fund raising exec. U.S. dir. Inst. Mediterranean Studies, Berkeley, Calif., 1962-65; devel. officer U. Calif., Berkeley, 1965-67; pres. Blum Assocs., Fund-Raising Cons., San Anselmo, Calif., 1967-92; ptnr. Philmark Australia, 1980—2001; pres. The Blums of San Francisco, 1992-2001, ret., 2001. Mem. faculty U. Calif. Extension, Inst. Fund Raising, S.W. Inst. Fund-Raising U. Tex., U. San Francisco, U.K. Vol. Movement Group, London, Australasian Inst. Fund Raising. Contbr. numerous articles to profl. jours. Recipient Golden Addy award Am. Advt. Fedn., Silver Mailbox award Direct Mail Mktg. Assn., Best Ann. Giving Time-Life award, others; decorated commdr. Sovereign Order St. Stanislas. Mem. Nat. Soc. Fund-Raising Execs. (dir.), Nat. Assn. of Hosp. Devel., Women Emerging, Rotary (San Francisco), Fund Raising Inst. (Australia), Tahoe Yacht Club. Office: 202 Evergreen Dr Kentfield CA 94904-2708

BLUM, JOHN CURTIS, agricultural economist; b. Terryville, Conn., July 5, 1915; s. John A. and Marion D. (Curtis) B.; m. Mable L. Brooks, Oct. 21, 1939; children— Joanne M. Blum Kraft, John Curtis, Nancy J. BS, U. Conn., 1937, MS, 1939; postgrad., U. Wis., 1941, Dept. Agr. Grad. Sch., 1946; student, Indsl. Coll. Armed Forces, 1965-66. With Dept. Agr., 1939-75; asst. dir. dairy div. Agrl. Marketing Service, 1960-61, dir. div., 1961-63; economist Office of Adminstr., 1963-64, asst. dept. adminstr., 1964-67, dep. adminstr., 1967-74, asso. adminstr., 1974-75; economist E.A. Jaenke & Assos., Inc., Washington, 1975-83. Violinist Fairfax County (Va.) Symphony Orch., 1957-95, bd. dir., 1957-70, pres., 1959-61, treas., 1965-67; violinist McLean (Va.) Symphony, 1995—, Reston (Va.) Chamber Orch., 1998—; dist. dir. North Va. dist. PTA, 1961-63; treas. Va. Congress Parents and Tchrs., 1963-65, regional v.p., 1965-67, chmn. extension com. 1967-69, budget chmn., 1969-71, bd. mgrs., 1961-71. Lt. (j.g.) USNR, 1944-46, PTO. Mem. Am. Agr. Econ. Assn., Grange. Home: Apt 1310 20510 Falcons Landing Cir Sterling VA 20165-7596

BLUM, JOHN MORTON, historian, educator; b. NYC, Apr. 29, 1921; s. Morton Gustave and Edna (LeVino) B.; m. Pamela Louise Zink, June 28, 1944; children: Pamela, Ann, Thomas Tyler. AB, Harvard U., 1943, MA, 1947, PhD, 1950, LLD (hon.), 1980; MA, Cambridge (Eng.) U., 1963; DHL (hon.), Trinity Coll., 1970; LLD (hon.), Colgate U., 1978. Research assoc., then asst. prof. history, assoc. prof. M.I.T., 1948-57; prof. history Yale U., 1957-91, ret., 1991; Pitt prof. Cambridge U., 1963-64; Harmsworth prof. Oxford U., 1976-77. Author: Joe Tumulty and the Wilson Era, 1951, The Republican Roosevelt, 1954, Woodrow Wilson and the Politics of Morality, 1956, From the Morgenthau Diaries, Vol. I, 1959, Vol. II, 1965, Vol. III, 1967, Yesterday's Children, 1959, The Promise of America, 1966, Roosevelt and Morgenthau, 1970, V Was for Victory, 1976, The Progressive Presidents, 1980, Years of Discord, 1991, Liberty Justice Order, 1993, A Life with History, 2004, An Old Blue Corpse, 2005; assoc. editor: (with Elting E. Morison) Letters of Theodore Roosevelt (8 vols.), 1951-54; editor: The National Experience, 1963, The Price of Vision, 1973; Public Philosopher, 1985. Trustee Buckingham Sch., 1954-56, Hotchkiss Sch., 1964-70; mem. Andover Alumni Council, 1957-60. Served from ensign to lt. USNR, 1943-46. Harvard U. fellow, 1970-79. Mem. Am. Acad. Arts and Scis., Mass. Hist. Soc., Century Assn., Phi Beta Kappa. Home: 313 St Ronan St New Haven CT 06511-2327

BLUM, JOSEPH R., secondary school educator, emergency nurse practitioner; b. Bucyrus, Ohio, Aug. 12, 1949; s. Raymond A. and Alice C. Blum; m. Sandrea A. Piernik, Nov. 27, 1971; children: Amy C. Blum Schnipke, Joseph F. BS in Edn., U. Dayton, 1971; LPN, William Beaumont Army Hosp., 1972; MA in Edn., Ashland Coll., 1988. Lic. practical nurse, Ohio. Tchr. Buckeye Ctrl. Schs., New Washington, Ohio, 1973—; emergency rm. nurse St. Elizabeth Hosp., Dayton, Ohio, 1973; med. surg. nurse Willard (Ohio) Hosp., 1974; emergency rm. nurse Galion (Ohio) Cmty. Hosp., 1975—. Co-author: Dutch Town, Your Days in History, 1974. Councilman New Washington Village Coun., 1975—; mem. ctrl. com. Dem. Party, Bucyrus, Ohio, 1982—. With U.S. Army, 1971—77. Named Ohio Educator of Yr., Ohio Am. Legion, 1996; recipient Individual Achievement award, Ohio Assn. Hist. Socs., 1990, Outstanding Tchr. Am. History award, Ohio DAR, 1994. Mem.: KC, New Washington Hist. Soc. (pres.), Am. Legion. Roman Catholic. Avocations: collecting antique bottles, collecting old bricks. Home: 217 N Center St New Washington OH 44854 Office: Buckeye Ctrl HS 306 Kibler St New Washington OH 44854

BLUM, LENORE, mathematician, computer scientist, educator; m. Manuel Blum; 1 child, Avrim. PhD, MIT, 1968; LLD Mills Coll. (hon.), 1999. Postdoctoral fellow, lectr. U. Calif., Berkeley, 1968—73; faculty mem. Mills Coll., 1974—99; prof. computer sci. Carnegie Mellon U., Pitts., 1999—. Vis. prof. math. and computer sci. City U. Hong Kong, 1996—98; vis. prof. CUNY, 1985—86; vis. scientist TJ Watson Rsch. Ctr. IBM, 1987; spkr. in field. Author (with F. Cucker, M. Shub, S. Smale): Complexity and Real Computation, 1997; contbr. articles to profl. jours. Recipient Career Advancement award, NSF, 1983. Mem.: AAAS (chair math. sect. 1998—99), Am. Math. Soc. (pres., coun. 1990—92), Math/Sci. Network, Assn. for Women in Math. (pres. 1975—78), Math. Scis. Rsch. Inst. (co-dir. 1975—81), Internat. Computer Sci. Inst. Office: Dept Computer Sci Wean 4105 Carnegie Mellon Univ Pittsburgh PA 15213-3891

BLUM, MELVIN, chemical company executive, researcher; b. N.Y.C., Jan. 8, 1936; s. Paul Henry and Dora (Schneiderman) B.; m. Paula Linda Weiss, July 11, 1969; 1 child, Lara Joyce. BS, Columbia U., 1957, MA, 1959; PhD, Duke U., 1964, Burlington Inst., 1970. Pres. Atomergic Chemetals Corp., Farmingdale, NY, 1963—2004, Burlington Sci. Corp., Farmingdale, 1974—2004; v.p. Am. Roland Chem. Co., S.I., N.Y., 1984—. Author: Handbook of Rare Elements, Encyclopedia of Chemical Technology, Strategic Metal Investments, (mag.) DMSO Reporter. Capt. USAFR, 1959-65. Mem. Am. Chem. Soc., Am. Soc. Metals, Am. Nuclear Soc., Am. Inst. Physics, N.Y. Acad. Scis., Chemists Club. Home: 1385 Lyon Pl Wantagh NY 11793-2919 E-mail: mblum@optonline.net.

BLUM, RICHARD HOSMER ADAMS, foundation administrator, educator; b. Ft. Wayne, Ind., Oct. 7, 1927; s. Hosmer and Imogene (Heino) B. AB with honors magna cum laude, San Jose State Coll., 1948; PhD, Stanford U., 1951. Research dir. Calif. Med. Assn., San Francisco, 1956-58, San Mateo County (Calif.) Mental Health Service, San Mateo, 1958-60; lectr. Sch. Criminology, U. Calif., Berkeley, 1960-62; mem. faculty Stanford (Calif.) U., 1962-78, prof. dept. psychology, 1970-75, prof. dept. gynecology and obstetrics, 1982-97; mem. faculty Stanford (Calif.) U. Law Sch., 1975-78; chmn. bd. Am. Lives Endowment, Portola Valley, Calif., 1979—. Chmn. Intern. Rsch. Group on Drug Legis. and Programs, Geneva, 1969-78; pres. Bio-Behavioral Rsch. Group, Inc., Palo Alto, 1964-87; owner, operator Shingle Mill Ranch, 1964—; vis. fellow Wolfson Coll. U. Cambridge, 1984; vis. prof. social and polit. sci. U. Cambridge, 1997-98; dir. ethics program World Jurist Assn./World Peace Through Law Ctr., Washington, 2000—; dep. chmn. Commn. for the World Equity Ct.; prof. St. Josephs of Arimanthea Theol. Sem., Berkeley, Calif., China U. Polit. Sci. and Law, Beijing; guest prof. Northeastern U., Changchun, Dalian U., China; exec. dir. Knightsbridge Castle Found. Trustee Palace Mus. of the Last Emperor Puye, Manchuria, China; exec. dir. Knights Bridge Castle Found. With U.S. Army, 1951-53, Korea. Fellow APHA, AAAS, APA, Am. Psychol. Soc., Am. Sociol. Assn., Soc. Advanced Legal Studies (hon., life); mem. Archaeol. Inst. Am., Sigma Xi, Cosmos Club, Athenaeum Club, San Francisco Univ. Club. Unitarian Universalist. Home and Office: PO Box 620482 Woodside CA 94062-0482 Office Phone: 650-529-1282.

BLUM, RICKY S., electrical engineering, computer science educator; b. Phila., Apr. 10, 1959; s. Albert and Caire C. (Peterson) B.; m. Karen Louise, Aug. 19, 1989; children: Karleigh Jean, Kyle James. BSEE, Penn State U., 1984; MSEE, U. Pa., 1987, PhD in Elec. Engring., 1991. Elec. engr. IBM Fed. Systems, Owego, N.Y., 1983; communication and signal processing systems engr. GE Aerospace, Valley Forge, Pa., 1984-91; prof. elec. engring., computer sci. Lehigh U., Bethlehem, Pa., 1991—. Session chmn. for conf. Allerton Conf. and Comm., U. Ill., Conf. on Info. Scis., Princeton (N.J.) U. Contbr. articles to profl. jours., including IEEE Transactions on Info. Theory, Signal Processing, IEEE Transactions on Aerospace and Elec., Jour. Acoustical Soc. Am.; contbr. over 50 papers to jours., conf. Reviewer Jour. of Franklin Inst., Phila., 1994-95. Named Evan Pugh scholar Penn State U., 1983, 84; recipient GE PhD fellowship, 1987-91, NSF Rsch. Initiation award NSF, 1992-96, Young Investigator award Office of Naval Rsch., 1997. Mem. IEEE (sr., assoc. editor IEEE Comm. Letters, tech. reviewer for IEEE transactions 1987-94, mem. signal processing for comm. tech. com. IEEE Signal Processing Soc., mem. IEEE Lehigh Valley exec. com. 1991-95, Lehigh Valley student activities chair 1991-95, IEEE Lehigh Valley Signal Processing chpt. chmn. 1995—), Outstanding Coll. Students Am., Sigma Xi, Eta Kappa Nu (Outstanding Young Engr. 1983). Achievements include patents on Feature Extraction Processor; rsch. on analytical treatment of distributed detection with dependent observations; rsch. on info. theory. Office: Lehigh U EECS Dept 19 Memorial Dr W Bethlehem PA 18015-3006

BLUM, ROBERT M., lawyer; b. NY, July 12, 1954; BS cum laude, Northwestern U., 1975; JD, Duke U., 1978. Bar: Calif. 1978, US Dist. Ct. (No. Dist.) Calif., US Dist. Ct. (Ea. Dist.) Calif., US Dist. Ct. (So. Dist.) Calif. Ptnr. Thelen, Marrin, Johnson & Bridges, San Francisco; gen. counsel Thelen Reid & Priest LLP, San Francisco. Article & notes editor Adminstrv. Law Issue, Duke Law Jour., 1977—78; contbr. articles to profl. jours., chapters to books. Office: Thelen Reid & Priest LLP 101 Second St Ste 1800 San Francisco CA 94105-3601 Office Phone: 415-369-7277. Office Fax: 415-371-1211. Business E-Mail: rblum@thelenreid.com.

BLUM, ROBERT WILLIAM, pediatrician, researcher; b. N.Y.C., Feb. 23, 1948; s. Morris and Gladys Sylvan (Barasch) B.; m. Lynn Ann Tarrow, Mar. 3, 1973; children: Alexander, Jamie, Amanda. BA, Lafayette Coll., 1969; MD, Howard U., 1973; MPH, U. Minn., 1977, PhD, 1978. Diplomate Am. Bd. Pediat. From instr. to asst. prof. U. Minn. Sch. Pub. Health, Mpls., 1977-81;

assoc. prof. dept. pediat. U. Minn., Mpls., 1981-90, prof. dept. pediat., 1990—. Dir. divsn. gen. pediat. & adolescent health U. Minn., Mpls., 1978—; exec. bd. Alan Guttmacher Inst., N.Y.C., 1989-95, 97—; cons. in field. Editor: Adolescent Health Care, 1982, Chronic Illness & Disabiities in Childhood & Adolescence, 1984. Organizer, chmn. Health Futures I, Daytona Beach, Fla., 1986; chmn. Consortium on Children Youth & Families, Mpls., 1994-97. Bush Leadership fellow U. Minn., 1977-78; McKelvey Disting. scholar Lafayette Coll., 1971-73. Fellow Am. Acad. Pediat., Soc. for Adolescent Medicine (pres. 1992-93, Outstanding Achievement 1993); mem. APHA, Am. Pediat. Soc. Avocations: skiing, biking, cooking. Office: PO Box 721 420 Delaware St SE Minneapolis MN 55455-0374

BLUM, SAMUEL, retired research scientist; b. Aug. 1920; BS Chemistry, Rutgers U., 1942, PhD Phys. Chemistry, 1950; cert. meterology, weather forecasting, UCLA. Ret. rsch. scientist IBM Watson Rsch. Ctr., 1990. Active alumni work Rutgers U. Mem. U.S. Navy. Recipient Nat. Inventors Hall of Fame, 2002. Achievements include invention of Far Ultraviolet Surgical and Dental Procedures. Avocations: travel, gardening.

BLUM, STEVEN (H. STEVEN BLUM), career military officer; BA in History, U. Balt., 1968; MS in Social Sci., Morgan State Coll., 1973; grad., Army War Coll., 1989. Joined Army Nat. Guard, 1971, advanced through grades to lt. gen., 2003; bn. comdr. hdqrs. 1st Bn., 115th Inf., 29th Inf. Divsn. Md. Army Nat. Guard, 1985—87, exec. officer hdqrs. 3rd Brigade, 29th Inf. Divsn., 1987—88, ops. and tng. officer hdqrs. State Area Command, 1988—89, dir. plans, ops. and tng. hdqrs., 1989—92, comdr. 3rd Brigade, 29th Inf. Divsn., 1992—95, asst. divsn. comdr. 29th Inf. Divsn., 1996—99; commdg. gen. 29th Inf. Divsn. Va. Army Nat. Guard, 1999—2002; commdg. gen. Multi Nat. Divsn. SFOR-10, Operation Joint Force Bosnia-Herzegovina, 2001—02; chief of staff U.S. No. Command, Peterson AFB, Colo., 2002—03; chief Nat. Guard Bur., Arlington, Va., 2003—. Decorated Legion of Merit, Army Meritorious Svc. medal, Army Commendation medal, Army Achievement medal, Army Res. Component Achievement medal, Nat. Def. Svc. medal, Army Forces Expeditionary medal, Armed Forces Res. medal, Army Svc. ribbon, NATO medal. Office: Nat Guard Bur 1411 Jefferson Davis Hwy Arlington VA 22202-3231

BLUM, TERRY C., dean; b. Bklyn., Dec. 25, 1953; m. Paul M. Roman; children: Luke, Faith Elisabeth. BA in sociology with honors, Bklyn. Coll., 1976; MA, Columbia U., 1978, MPhil, 1980, PhD, 1982. Asst. prof. orgnl. behavior and human resource mgmt. Sch. Mgmt., Ga. Inst. Tech., 1986—88, assoc. prof. orgnl. behavior and human resource mgmt., 1988—92; prof. DuPree Coll. Mgmt., Ga. Inst. Tech., 1992—; dir. Ctr. Entrepreneurship and New Venture Devel., DuPree Coll. Mgmt., Ga. Inst. Tech., 1996—2000; Tedd Munchak chairholder in entrepreneurship DuPree Coll. Mgmt., Ga. Inst. Tech., 1996—, dean, 1999—. Mem. Prevention and Epidemiology Initial Review Group Nat. Inst. Alcohol Abuse and Alcoholism, 1988—92; mem. cmty. prevention and control study section NIH, 1997—2000. Assoc. editor: Am. Jour. Health Promotion, 1988—96, editl. bd. mem.: Social Forces, 1990—93, Alcohol, Health & Rsch. World, 1998—2001; editor: Orgns. and Occupations Divsn. Newsletter, 1993—94; manuscript reviewer: numerous jour. in field; contbr. articles. Grantee, Nat. Inst. Alcohol Abuse and Alcoholism, 1982, 1983, 1987, 1988, Nat. Inst. Drug Abuse, 1991, 1999, NIH, 1993, 1994, Coleman Found., 1999; special opportunities grant, Whitaker Found., 1998. Office: Ga Inst Tech DuPree Coll Mgmt 800 W Peachtree St NW Atlanta GA 30332-0520 Office Phone: 404-894-4924. Office Fax: 404-894-6030. Business E-Mail: terry.blum@mgt.gatech.edu.

BLUM, WILLIAM GEORGE, hematologist, clinical researcher educator; b. Lynn, Mass., Dec. 16, 1970; m. Kristie Ann Uber, May 21, 2001. BS, U. Notre Dame, 1993; MD, Med. Coll. Ga., Augusta, 1997. Cert. in hematology and med. oncology Nat. Bd. Med. Examiners, in internal medicine Nat. Bd. Med. Examiners. Asst. prof. medicine Ohio State U., Columbus, 2003—. Office: Ohio State Univ B310 Starling Loving 320 W 10th Ave Columbus OH 43210 Office Phone: 614-293-9808.

BLUMBERG, AVROM AARON, physical chemistry professor; b. Albany, N.Y., Mar. 3, 1928; s. Samuel and Lillian Ann (Smith) B.; m. Eleanor Leah Simon, Aug. 5, 1955 (dec. Sept. 1967); 1 child, David Martin; m. Judith Anne Kohlhagen, Mar. 9, 1969; children: Susan Margaret, Jonathan Samuel. BS in Chemistry, Rensselaer Poly. Inst., 1949; PhD in Phys. Chemistry, Yale U., 1953. Fellow glass sci. Mellon Inst., Pitts., 1953-59, fellow polymer sci., 1959-63; from asst. to assoc. prof. phys. chemistry DePaul U., Chgo., 1963-75, prof., 1975—, head div. natural scis. and math., 1966-82, chmn. dept. chemistry, 1986-92. Vis. lectr. chemistry dept. U. Pitts., 1957-58; cons. in field. Author: Form and Function, 1972; contbr. articles to profl. jours. Participant scientists and speakers program Mus. Sci. and Industry, Chgo., 1985—; Dem. precinct capt., Evanston, Ill., 1970-78. Mem. Am. Chem. Soc. (speakers program Chgo. sect. 1983—), Royal Soc. Chem. London, Arms Control Assn., Sigma Xi. Jewish. Avocations: music, reading, art, travel, cooking. Home: 1240 S State St Chicago IL 60605-2405 Office: DePaul U Dept Chemistry 2320 N Kenmore Ave Chicago IL 60614-3210 Office Phone: 773-325-7345. Business E-Mail: ablumber@depaul.edu.

BLUMBERG, BARBARA MARILYN, history educator, writer; b. Bronx, NY, Oct. 27, 1936; d. Albert A. and Yvette (Beneck) Schneck; m. Paul Marvin Blumberg, Aug. 25, 1955 (div. 1973); 1 child, Ira Joseph; m. Alan L. Krumholz, Apr. 12, 1974; 1 child, Mark Reuben. AB in History, U. Calif., Berkeley, 1958, MA in History, 1962; PhD in History, Columbia U., 1974. Prof. history Adelphi U., Garden City, NY, 1967-68, Queens Coll., Flushing, NY, 1968-75, Pace U., NYC, 1971—; chair Dept. of Social Scis., 1991-94. Author: The New Deal and the Unemployed: The View from NYC, 1979; Celebrating the Immigrant: An Administrative History of the Statue of Liberty National Monument, 1952-82, 1985, A National Park Emerges: The Statue as Park and Museum in Liberty: The French- American Statue in Art and History, 1986, Student Guide to the Enduring Vision: A History of the American People, 1990; co-editor NYC: Readings in History, Literature, and Culture, 1982, World Wars and Cold War, 1919-1987: Readings in Foreign and Domestic Policy, 2002, contbr. articles to profl. jours. Mem. Am. Hist. Assn., Orgn. Am. Historians, Phi Beta Kappa. Office: Pace U Pace Plz New York NY 10038 Office Phone: 212-346-1459. Business E-Mail: bblumberg@pace.edu.

BLUMBERG, BARUCH SAMUEL, academic administrator, research scientist; b. NYC, July 28, 1925; s. Meyer and Ida (Simonoff) B.; m. Jean Liebesman, Apr. 4, 1954; children: Anne, George, Jane, Noah. BS, Union Coll., Schenectady, NY, 1946; MD, Columbia U., 1951; PhD, Oxford (Eng.) U., 1957; 20 hon. doctoral degrees. Intern, then resident Columbia divsn. Bellevue Hosp., NYC, 1951—53; fellow in medicine Columbia-Presbyn. Med. Ctr., NYC, 1953—55; chief geog. medicine and genetics sect. NIH, Bethesda, Md., 1957—64; assoc. dir. clin. rsch. Fox Chase Cancer Ctr., Phila., 1964—86, v.p. population oncology, 1986—89, Fox Chase disting. scientist, 1989—, sr. advisor to pres., 1989—; univ. prof. medicine and anthropology U. Pa., 1977—; master Balliol Coll., Oxford, England, 1989—94; dir. NASA Astrobiology Inst., Moffett Field, Calif., 1999—2002; sr. adv. to the adminstr. NASA Hdqs., Washington, 2000—01; disting. scientist NASA Fundamental Space Biology, 2003—04. George Eastman vis. prof. Oxford U., 1983—84; Raman vis. prof. Indian Inst. Scis., Bangalore, India, 1986; Ashland vis. prof. U. Ky., Lexington, 1986—87; disting. vis. prof. Nat. U. Singapore, 1992; vis. prof. U. Otago, Dunedin, New Zealand, 1994; James W. McLaughlin vis. prof. U. Tex.; vis. prof. dept. medicine Stanford U. Med. Ctr.; sr. advisor to pres. Fox Chase Cancer Ctr., 1989—; fellow Ctr. Advanced Study Behavioral Scis. Stanford U., Larry Lokey disting. vis. prof. human biology. Contbr. articles to profl. jours. Lt. USNR, 1943—46. Recipient Albion O. Berstein, M.D. award Med. Soc. State of N.Y., 1969, Grand Sci. award Phi Lambda Kappa, 1972, Ann. award Eastern Pa. br. Am. Soc. Microbiology, 1972, Passano award Williams & Wilkens Co., 1974, Modern Medicine Disting. Achievement award, 1975, Internat. award Gairdner Found., 1975, Karl Landsteiner Meml. award Am. Assn. Blood Banks, 1975, Nobel prize in physiology or medicine, 1976, Scopus award Am. Friends of Hebrew U., 1977, Strittmatter award Philadelphia County Med. Soc., 1980, Disting. Svc. award Pa. Med. Soc., 1982, Zubrow award Pa. Hosp., 1986, Achievement award Sammy Davis Jr. Nat. Liver Inst., 1987, John P. McGovern award Am. Med. Writers Assn., 1988, Gov.'s Award in the Scis. Commonwealth of Pa., 1989, John Blundell award Brit. Blood Transfusion Soc., 1989, Gold Medal award Can. Liver Found. and Can. Assn. Study of Liver, 1990, Showa Emperor Meml. award Japan, 1994, Outstanding Leadership medal NASA, 2002, Lifetime Achievement award Am. Liver Found., 2005; named to Nat. Inventor Hall of Fame, 1993. Fellow ACP, Royal Coll. Physicians; mem. NAS, AAAS, Inst. Medicine NAS, Am. Acad. Arts and Scis., Assn. Am. Physicians, Am. Soc. Human Genetics, Am. Philos. Soc. (pres. 2005), Explorers Club NY, Athenaeum (London). Office: Fox Chase Cancer Ctr 333 Cottman Ave Philadelphia PA 19111 Business E-Mail: baruch.blumberg@fccc.edu.

BLUMBERG, DAVID, colon and rectal surgeon; MD, Downstate Med. Sch., Bklyn., 1988. Asst. prof. of surgery U. of Pitts. Sch. of Medicine, Pitts., 1999—. Fellow: ACS, Am. Soc. Colon And Rectal Surgeons; mem.: Assn. of Cancer Rsch., Am. Soc. of Clin. Oncology (assoc.), Assn. for Acad. Surgery. Achievements include developing a novel gene therapy to enhance radiation in shrinkage of rectal cancer; research in adenoviral gene transfer of the human inducible nitric oxide synthase gene enhances the radiation response of human colorectal cancer associated with alterations in tumor vascularity. Office Phone: 412-692-2962.

BLUMBERG, EDWARD ROBERT, lawyer; b. Phila., Feb. 15, 1951; BA in Psychology, U. Ga., 1972; JD, Coll. William and Mary, 1975. Bar: Fla., 1975, U.S. Dist. Ct. Fla. 1975, U.S. Ct. Appeals, 1975, U.S. Supreme Ct. 1979. Assoc. Knight, Peters, Hoeveler & Pickle, Miami, Fla., 1976-77; ptnr. Deutsch & Blumberg, P.A., Miami, 1978—. Adj. prof. U. Miami Sch. Paralegal Studies. Author: Proof of Negligence, Mathew Bender Florida Torts, 1988. Mem. ABA (ho. of dels. 1996-2002), ATLA, Dade County Bar Assn., Fla. State Bar (bd. govs., pres.-elect 1996-97, pres. 1997-98), Acad. Fla. Trial Lawyers, Nat. Bd. Trial Advocacy (cert. civil trial adv.), Fla. Bar Found. (bd. dirs. 1996-99, bd. govs. 1996-99), Bankers Club (chmn. bd. govs. 2003-05). Office: Deutsch & Blumberg PA 100 Biscayne Blvd Fl 28 Miami FL 33132-2304 Office Phone: 305-358-6329.

BLUMBERG, GERALD, lawyer; b. N.Y.C., July 25, 1911; s. Saul and Amelia (Abramowitz) B.; m. Rhoda Shapiro, Jan. 7, 1945; children: Lawrence, Rena, Alice, Leda. AB cum laude, Cornell U., 1931; JD cum laude, Harvard, 1934. Bar: Mass. 1934, N.Y. 1934. Pvt. practice, N.Y, 1934—; mem. firm Gerald & Lawrence Blumberg LLP. Instr. econs. Cornell U., 1931; mem. Harvard Legal Aid Bur., 1934. Bd. dirs., v.p., exec. com. Am. Com. Weizmann Inst. Sci.; internat. bd. govs. Weizmann Inst. Sci., 1982— . Mem. ABA, N.Y. State, Westchester, Yorktown bar assns., Phi Beta Kappa, Phi Kappa Phi. Home: 1305 Baptist Church Rd Yorktown Heights NY 10598-5810 Office: Gerald & Lawrence Blumberg LLP 521 5th Ave New York NY 10175-0003 Office Phone: 212-697-5550.

BLUMBERG, GRACE GANZ, lawyer, educator; b. NYC, Feb. 16, 1940; d. Samuel and Beatrice (Finkelstein) Ganz; m. Donald R. Blumberg, Sept. 9, 1959; 1 child, Rachel. BA cum laude, U. Colo., 1960; JD summa cum laude, SUNY, 1971; LLM, Harvard U., 1974. Bar: N.Y. 1971, Calif. 1989. Confidential law clk. Appellate Divsn., Supreme Ct., 4th Dept., Rochester, NY, 1971-72; tchg. fellow Harvard Law Sch., Cambridge, Mass., 1972-74; prof. law SUNY, Buffalo, 1974-81, UCLA, 1981—. Reporter Am. Law Inst., Prins. of the Law of Family Dissolution, 2002. Author: Community Property in California, 1987, Community Property in California, rev. edit., 1999, 2003, Blumberg's California Family Code Annotated; contbr. articles to profl. jours. Office: UCLA Sch Law Box 951476 Los Angeles CA 90095-1476

BLUMBERG, JOEL MYRON, cardiologist; b. N.Y.C., Oct. 17, 1940; s. Howard Godfrey and Lily Ruth (Goldberg) B.; B.A., DePauw U., 1962; M.D., N.Y. U., 1966; m. Judith Ellen Green, Aug. 23, 1964; children: Amy, Hillary, Michelle. Intern, N.Y. U.-Bellevue Med. Center, N.Y.C., 1966-67, resident in internal medicine, 1969-71; fellow in cardiology Cornell U.-N.Y. Hosp., 1971-73; pvt. practice internal medicine and cardiology, Greenwich, Conn., 1973—; attending staff Greenwich Hosp., 1973—, coronary care cons., 1973—; physician to out-patients N.Y. Hosp., 1973-77; clin. instr. Cornell U. Med. Coll., 1971-77; clin. asst. prof. Yale Sch. Medicine, 1975—; lectr. in preventive cardiology to civic groups; bd. visitors DePauw U., bd. incorporators Greenwich Hosp. Diplomate Am. Bd. Internal Medicine. Fellow A.C.P., Am. Coll. Cardiology, Am. Coll. Chest Physicians, Am. Heart Assn. (council on clin. cardiology)selected best doctors in Am., 2002, best doctors in N.Y., 2002, best doctors in Conn., 2002, Excellence in teaching award, 2002; mem. Am. Soc. Internal Medicine, N.Y. Heart Assn., Greenwich, Fairfield County, Conn. State med. socs. Club: B'nai B'rith (Stamford, Conn.). Contbr. articles to profl. jours. Home: 59 Old Stone Bridge Rd Cos Cob CT 06807-1511 Office: 2 1/2 Deerfield Dr Greenwich CT 06831-5335

BLUMBERG, MARK STUART, public health service officer, researcher; b. N.Y.C., Nov. 16, 1924; s. Sydney N. and Mollie (Leshrowitz) B.; m. Luba Monasevitch, 1952; children: Bart David, Eve Luise; m. 2d Elizabeth R. Conner, 1974. Student, Johns Hopkins U., 1942-43, Harvard U., 1943-44, DMD, 1948, MD, 1950, student Sch. Public Health, 1955. Intern, children's med. service Bellevue Hosp., N.Y.C., 1950-51; ops. analyst Johns Hopkins U. Ops. Research Office, Chevy Chase, Md., 1951-54; exchange analyst Army Ops. Research Group (U.K.), West Byfleet, Eng., 1953-54; staff Occupational Health Program, USPHS, Washington, 1954-56; asso. ops. analyst to dir. health econs. program Stanford (Calif.) Research Inst., 1956-66; asst. to v.p. adminstrn. to dir. health planning, office of the pres. U. Calif., Berkeley, 1966-70; corp. planning advisor to dir. spl. studies Kaiser Found. Health Plan, Inc., Oakland, Calif., 1970-94; dir. Kaiser Found. Health Plan of Conn., Hartford, 1982-94, Kaiser Found. Health Plan Mass., 1987-94; cons. risk adjusted measures Oakland, 1994—; co-founder, v.p. R&D TruRisk LLC, 1998—. Various times cons. Pan Am. Health Orgn., Calif. State Dept. Mental Hygiene, Carnegie Commn. on Higher Edn., various agys. HHS. Contbr. writings to profl. publs. Vol. Grenfell Med. Mission, Harrington Harbour, Que., Can., summer 1948; mem. tech. adv. com. AB 524 State of Calif., 1992—. Served with USNR, 1943-45; with USPHS, 1954-56. Mem. Ops. Research Soc. Am. (past mem. council, Health Applications sect.), Hosp. Mgmt. Systems Soc. (charter), Inst. of Medicine of Nat. Acad. Scis. Office Phone: 510-601-9536.

BLUMBERG, MICHAEL ZANGWILL, allergist; b. Phila., July 29, 1945; s. Jerome Blumberg and Vivian Rose (Liebman) Steiger; m. Barbara Sue Gurman, June 9, 1973; children: Jessica Lynn, Jason Mark. AB, Brandeis U., 1967; MD, Jefferson Med. Coll., 1971; MSHA., Va. Commonwealty U., 1998. Diplomate Am Bd Pediatrics, Am Bd Allergy and Immunology. Intern, resident N.Y. Hosp., Cornell U. Med. Ctr., 1971-73; fellow in allergy and immunology Nat. Jewish Hosp.-U. Colo. Med. Ctr., 1973-75; chief allergy sect. major Scott Air Force Base, Ill., 1975-77; physician-ptnr. Va. Adult and Pediat. Allergy and Asthma, Richmond, 1977—, mng. ptnr., 1998—; assoc. clin. prof. pediatrics Med. Coll. Va., Richmond, 1977—2002, 2000—; chief of allergy Children's Hosp. of Richmond, 1987-2000; ptnr. Clin. Rsch., Richmond, 1998—. Med advisor Sanofi-Adventec, Astra Zeneca, Glaxo SmithKline, Merck. Contbr. articles and abstracts to profl jours; contbg. editor: Review in Allergy, 1978; mem ed bd: Jour Asthma, 1996—. Mem exec comt, pres, bd dirs, chmn Beth Shalom Home Va, Richmond, 1987—95; bd dirs Jewish Community Ctr, Richmond, 1984—87; bd dirs endowment fund, mem budget comt Jewish Fedn; pres. Richmond Jewish Found., 2002. Fellow: Am Acad Pediatrics, Col Chest Physicians, Am Col Allergy, Asthma and Immunology (pub. rels.com.); mem.: Allergy and Asthma Soc. Va. (pres. 2002—04), Am Thoracic Soc, Am Acad Allergy, Asthma and Immunology (managed care com.), Am Col Allergy Sports Med (practice standards com. 1994—95), Friends of Brandeis Athletics, Masons, Phi Kappa Phi. Jewish. Avocations: American history, aerobic exercise. Office: Va Adult & Pediat Allergy and Asthma 7605 Forest Ave Ste 103 Richmond VA 23229-4936 Home: 149 W Square Court Richmond VA 23233-6159 Office Phone: 804-285-8415. E-mail: mshadoc@comcast.net, mblumberg@vaallergy.com.

BLUMBERG, NEIL, hematologist, educator; b. N.Y.C., June 14, 1948; s. Abraham Samuel and Mildred Blumberg; m. Joanna Mary Heal, May 2, 1981; children: David Anthony Heal, Lawrence Eric Heal. BS, Yale U., 1970, MD, 1975. Cert. Am. Bd. Pathology. Dir. clin. labs. and transfusion medicine, prof. pathology and lab. medicine U. Rochester Med. Ctr., NY, 1980—. Fellow: Am. Coll. Pathologists. Achievements include first to in collaboration with Dr. Joanna Heal and other colleagues redefined the boundaries and clinical importance of transfusion immunology and the role of the ABO blood group system in transfusion. Office: Univ Rochester Med Ctr 601 Elmwood Ave Box 608 Rochester NY 14642 Office Phone: 585-275-3189. Business E-Mail: neil_blumberg@urmc.rochester.edu.

BLUMBERG, PHILIP FLAYDERMAN, real estate developer; b. Miami, Fla., Nov. 10, 1957; s. David and Lee (Dickens) B.; m. Lina Esther Waingortin, Apr. 13, 1986; children: David, Peter, Douglas. BBA, U. N.C., 1979; MBA, Harvard U., 1983. Pres. Am. Ventures Corp., Miami, Fla., 1979—; mng. ptnr. Banyan Reach ltd., Cutler Ridge, Fla., 1979; pres. Realdata Info. Systems, Inc., Miami, 1984, Am. Ventures Realty Corp., Miami, 1985, Am. Ventures Realty Investors, Miami, 1990. Chmn. exam. com. Profl. Savs. Bank, Coral Gables, Fla., 1985-87. Trustee Colony Performing Arts Theatre, Miami Beach, Fla., 1985; mem. U. Miami Venture Coun., Coral Gables, 1984; co-chmn. Japan-Miami Bus. Coun., 1987-94; trustee Beacon Coun., 1988—, bd. dirs. 1997—; bd. dirs. Downtown Devel. Authority, City of Miami, 1988-94, exec. com., 1992—, chmn. transp. com., 1988—; bd. dirs. Dade County Task Force on Empowerment & Enterprise Zones, 1993-99, Brickell Area Assn., 1988—; mem. bd. trustees Temple Israel, 1989-93; chmn. Orange Bowl Spl. Events Com., 1993—; adv. coun. Orange Bowl Com., 1994—; chmn. Olympic Soccer Organizing Com., South Fla., 1993-96; bd. dirs. Dade County Transit 2020 Coalition, 1993—; mem. Tampa Bay Partnership, 1995—; mem. State of Fla. Wages Coalition for Dade and Monroe Counties, 1997-98, Joint Edn. Partnership Bd. Dirs., 1997—; bd. trustees U. Miami, 2001—. Mem. Japan-Am. Soc. South Fla. (bd. dirs. 1988-89), Japan Soc. South Fla. (bd. dirs. 1990-94), Fla. C. of C. (bd. dirs. 1997—), Greater Miami C. of C. (bd. govs. 1992—, exec. com. vice chmn. for bus. and industry/econ. devel. 1994-97), Greater Miami Fgn. Trade Zone (bd. dirs. 1996—, chmn. welfare reform task force 1996-99, chmn. internat. econ. group 1997-98, chmn. 2000—), Miami Dade Cmty. Coll. Found. (bd. dirs. 1998—), Miami-Dade County Empowerment Zone Task Force, Cmty. Partnership for Homeless Inc. (bd. dirs. 2000—). Home: 10440 Lakeside Dr Coral Gables FL 33156-3414 Office: Am Ventures Corp 255 Alhambra Cir Ste 1100 Coral Gables FL 33134-7400

BLUMBERG, PHILLIP IRVIN, law educator; b. Balt., Sept. 6, 1919; s. Hyman and Bess (Simons) B.; m. Janet Helen Mitchell, Nov. 17, 1945 (dec. 1976); children: William A.M., Peter M., Elizabeth B., Bruce M.; m. Ellen Ash Peters, Sept. 16, 1979. AB, Harvard U., 1939, JD, 1942; LLD (hon.), U. Conn., 1994. Bar: N.Y. 1942, Mass. 1970. Assoc. Willkie, Owen, Otis, Farr & Gallagher, N.Y.C., 1942—43, Szold, Brandwen, Meyers and Blumberg, N.Y.C., 1946—66; ptnr., 1949—66; pres., CEO United Ventures Inc., 1962—67; pres., CEO, trustee Federated Devel. Co., N.Y.C., 1966—68, chmn. fin. com., 1968—73; prof. law Boston U., 1966—74; dean U. Conn. Sch. Law, Hartford, 1974—84, prof. law, 1984—89, dean, prof. law emeritus, 1989—. Bd. dirs. Verde Exploration Ltd.; legal adv. com. to bd. dirs. N.Y. Stock Exch., 1989-93; adv. com. on transnat. corps. U.S. Dept. State, 1976-79; advisor corp. governance project, restatement of suretyship and restatement of agy. Am. Law Inst.; vis. lectr. U. Brabant, Tilburg, Netherlands, 1985, U. Internat. Bus. and Econs., Beijing, 1989, U. Sydney, 1992, Jagiellonian U., Cracow, Poland, 1992. Author: Corporate Responsibility in a Changing Society, 1972, The Megacorporation in American Society, 1975, The Law of Corporate Groups: Procedure, 1983, The Law of Corporate Groups: Bankruptcy, 1985, The Law of Corporate Groups: Substantive Common Law, 1987, The Law of Corporate Groups: General Statutory Law, 1989, The Law of Corporate Groups: Specific Statutory Law, 1992, The Multinational Challenge to Corporation Law, 1993, The Law of Corporate Groups: State Statutory Law, 1995, The Law of Corporate Groups: Enterprise Liability, 1998, Blumberg on Corporate Groups, 2d edit., 2005; mem. edit. bd. Harvard Law Rev., 1940-42, treas., 1941-42; contbr. articles to profl. jours. Trustee Black Rock Forest Preserve, Inc.; trustee emeritus Conn. Bar Found. Capt. USAAF, 1943-46, ETO, maj. USAF JAGD Res. 1946-55. Decorated Bronze Star. Mem. ABA, Conn. Bar Assn., Am. Law Inst., Hartford Club, Harvard Club (Boston), Army & Navy Club (Washington), Phi Beta Kappa, Delta Upsilon. Home: 791 Prospect Ave Apt B-5 Hartford CT 06105-4224 Office: U Conn Sch Law 65 Elizabeth St Hartford CT 06105-2290 Office Phone: 860-570-5192. Business E-Mail: pblumber@law.uconn.edu.

BLUME, FRED, lawyer; b. Phila., Mar. 14, 1941; married; three children. BS, Temple U., 1963; LLB, U. Penn. Law Sch., 1966. Bar: Pa. 1966, Fla. 1975, NY 1994. Law clerk to Judge D. Donald Jamieson Ct. of Common Pleas; assoc. Blank Rome LLP, Phila., 1967—72, ptnr., 1972—, adminstrv. ptnr., 1996—2002, co-chmn., 2000—02, COO, 2001—02, ptnr., privately held and emerging cos. group, mng. ptnr. & CEO, 2003—. Mem. Inst. of Law & Econ. U. Penn. Law Sch.; bd. dirs. Nati. Museum Am. Jewish History, Greater Phila. Film Office; bd. visitors Temple U. Fox Sch. of Bus. & Mgmt. Mem.: ABA (bus. section), NY Bar Assn., Fla. Bar Assn., Pa. Bar Assn., Phila. Bar Assn. Office: Blank Rome LLP One Logan Sq Philadelphia PA 19103-6998 Office Phone: 215-569-5512. Office Fax: 215-832-5512. Business E-Mail: blume@BlankRome.com.

BLUME, GINGER (ELAINE BLUME), psychologist; b. Lock Haven, Pa., Apr. 8, 1948; d. Martin Luther and Virginia Ruth (Rudy) B. BA, U. Fla., 1970, MA, 1975, PhD, 1979. Predoctoral intern in psychology VA Hosp., West Haven, Conn., 1976-77; postdoctoral intern in psychology Elmcrest Psychiat. Inst., Portland, Conn., 1977-78; pvt. practice clin. psychology Dr. Ginger E. Blume and Assocs., Middletown, Conn., 1978—. Assoc. Harrison Assocs., Inc., Cons., Berkeley, Calif.; co-owner, program dir. PMT Assocs. Inc.; co-owner/trainer TeamMasters; mem. affiliated faculty New Eng. Type Inst.; mem. adj. psychology faculty Middlesex C.C., Antioch Grad. Sch., Keene, N.H.; bd. dirs. Gilead House, halfway facility, SAFE, sexual assault clinic, Family Resource Ctr.; developer Doc-U-Chart; cons. in field. Host daily AM radio talk show, 1996-2000; monthly columnist on psychology Middletown Press, 1996—; co-author 3 workbooks on managing violence. Recipient 1st 2d, and 3d prize adults, Patton Writing Contest, 2003, President's award, CPA, 2003, 2002, 2004. Fellow APA (bus. of practice network, rep. for state of Conn. 1997-2003), mem. ASTD, Conn. Psychol. Assn. (chmn. mktg., Disting. Contbn. in Media award 1996), Orthopsychiatry Assn., Internat. Imagery Assn., AAUW (chmn. edn. found. program), Soroptimists, Exch. Club, Phi Kappa Phi, Kappa Delta. Achievements include being world's youngest twin engine female pilot at age 17. Home: 77 Oak Ridge Dr Haddam CT 06438-1053 Office: 300 Plz Middlesex 2d Fl Middletown CT 06457-5153 Office Phone: 860-346-6020 1. E-mail: gblumeasso@aol.com.

BLUME, JAMES BERYL, investment advisor; b. NYC, Apr. 9, 1941; s. Philip Franklin Blume and Mary Kirschman Asch; m. Kathryn Weil Frank, Jan. 20, 1984; 1 child, Zachary Thomas Philip. BA, Williams Coll., Williamstown, Mass., 1963; MBA, Harvard U., Boston, 1966; M. Psychology, The Wright Inst., Berkeley, Calif., 1983, PhD in Psychology, 1986. Security analyst Faulkner, Dawkins & Sullivan, N.Y.C., 1966-68; sr. v.p. Faulkner, Dawkins & Sullivan Securities, Inc., N.Y.C., 1968-73; ptnr. Omega Properties, N.Y.C., 1973-74; exec.v.p. Arthur M. Fischer, Inc., N.Y.C., 1974-77; pvt. practice psychotherapist Berkeley, Calif., 1985—91; fin. cons., 1987—93; pres. Blume Capital Mgmt., Inc., Berkeley, 1987—. Bd. dirs. Ploughshares Fund. Bd. dirs. ACLU No. Calif., San Francisco, 1988—94, 2004—, treas., 1993—94; bd. dirs. East Bay Clinic Psychotherapy, Oakland, Calif., 1981—85, Marin Psychotherapy Inst., Mill Valley, Calif., 1986—87; trustee Wright Inst., 1981—85. Mem.: Williams Club (bd. govs. 1968—72), Berkeley Tennis Club. Democrat. Jewish. Avocations: tennis, politics. Office: 1708 Shattuck Ave Berkeley CA 94709-1700 Office Phone: 510-549-3534. Business E-Mail: jbb@blumecapital.com.

BLUME, JUDY, author; b. Elizabeth, N.J., Feb. 12, 1938; d. Rudolph and Esther (Rosenfeld) Sussman; m. John M. Blume, Aug. 15, 1959 (div. Jan. 1975); children: Randy Lee, Lawrence Andrew; m. George Cooper, June 6, 1987; 1 stepchild, Amanda. BA in Edn., NYU, 1960; LHD (hon.), Kean Coll., 1987, Endicott Coll., 1995. Author: (fiction) including The One in the Middle is the Green Kangaroo, 1969, Iggie's House, 1970, Are You There God? It's Me, Margaret (selected as outstanding children's book 1970), Freckle Juice, 1971, Then Again, Maybe I Won't, 1971, It's Not the End of the World, 1972, Tales of a 4th Grade Nothing, 1972, Otherwise Known as Sheila the Great, 1972, Deenie, 1973, Blubber, 1974, Forever, 1975, Starring Sally J. Freedman as Herself, 1977, Superfudge, 1980, Tiger Eyes, 1981, The Pain and the Great One, 1984, Just As Long As We're Together, 1987, Fudge-A-Mania, 1990, Here's to You, Rachel Robinson, 1993, Double Fudge, 2002 others; (adult novels) Wifey, 1977, Smart Women, 1984, Summer Sisters, 1998; (other writings) Letters to Judy: What Kids Wish They Could Tell You, 1986; exec. producer (25 min. film) Otherwise Known As Sheila The Great, Barr Films, 1988. Founder, trustee The Kids Fund, 1981. Recipient Carl Sandburg Freedom to Read award Chgo. Pub. Libr., 1984, The Civil Liberties award ACLU, 1986, John Rock award Ctr. for Population Options, 1986, Margaret A. Edwards for lifetime achievement ALA, 1996, medal for disting. contbn. to Am. letters, Nat. Book Found., 2004; numerous Children's Choice award, U.S.A., Europe, Australia. Mem. Authors Guild (bd. dirs.), Nat. Coalition Against Censorship (adv. bd.), Soc. Children's Book Writers (bd. dirs.). Jewish. Office: c/o William Morris Agy 1325 Ave of Ams New York NY 10019*

BLUME, LAWRENCE DAYTON, lawyer; b. Kansas City, Mo., July 7, 1948; s. Dayton G. and Meredith L. B. BA, U. Ariz., 1970; JD, U. Mo., 1974. Bar: Mo. 1974, D.C. 1989, U.S. Dist. Ct. (we. dist.) Mo. 1974, U.S. Ct. Appeals (fed. cir.) 1984, U.S. Supreme Ct. 1978, U.S. Tax Ct. 1980, U.S. Ct. Internat. Trade 1981, N.Y. 1996. Ptnr. Swanson, Midgley, Gangwere, Clarke & Kitchin, Kansas City, 1974-80; prin. Miller & Blume, P.C., Washington, 1980-89; ptnr. Graham & James, Washington, 1989-2000, D.C. mng. ptnr., 1992-94; N.Y. mng. ptnr. Graham & James LLP, N.Y.C., 1994-98, firm chmn., 1998-2000; prin. Greenberg Traurig LLP, N.Y.C., 2000—. Lectr. Nat. Assn. Fgn. Trade Zones, Washington, 1981—, Am. Assn. Exporters and Importers, N.Y.C., 1984—, various colls., univs. and trade groups, 1980—; prin. instr. Seminar on Internat. Bus. Transactions and Litigation Techniques. Mem.: ABA, Order of Barristers, Customs and Internat. Bar Assn., Licensing Execs. Soc. Internat., Am.-Intellectual Property Law Assn., Am. Assn. Exporters and Importers, Internat. Trade Bar Assn., Inter-Am. Bar Assn. (sr.), Nat. Dem. Club. Democrat. Office: Greenberg Traurig 885 Third Ave Ste 2100 New York NY 10022 E-mail: bluml@gtlaw.com.

BLUME, MARSHALL EDWARD, finance educator; b. Chgo., Mar. 31, 1941; s. Marshall Edward Blume and Helen Corliss (Frank) Gilbert; m. Loretta Ryan, June 25, 1966; children: Christopher, Caroline, Catherine. SB, Trinity Coll., Hartford, Conn., 1963; MBA, U. Chgo., 1965, PhD, 1968; MA (hon.), U. Pa., 1970. Lectr. applied math. Grad. Sch. Bus., U. Chgo., 1966, instr. bus. fin. and applied math., 1967; lectr. fin. U. Pa., Phila., 1967, asst. prof., 1968-70, assoc. prof., 1970-74, prof., 1974-78, Howard Butcher prof., 1978—, chmn. dept., 1982-86, assoc. dir. Rodney White Ctr., 1978-86; prin. Prudent Mgmt. Assocs., 1982—; dir. Rodney White Ctr., 1986—. Mem. U.S. Compt. Gen. adv. bd. on Oct. 1987 stock market crash, 1987-88; prof. fin. European Inst., Brussels, 1975-76, New U. Lisbon, Portugal, 1982; vis. prof. Stockholm Sch., spring 1976, U. Brussels, 1975. Author: Mutual Funds and Other Institutional Investors, 1970, The Changing Role of the Individual Investor, 1978, The Structure and Reform of the U.S. Tax System, 1985, Revolution on Wall Street: The Rise and Fall of the New York Stock Exchange, 1993; editor: Encyclopedia of Investments, 1982, The Complete Guide to Investment Opportunities, 1984; assoc. editor Jour. Fin. and Quantitative Analysis, 1967-76, Jour. Fin. Econs., 1976-81, Jour. of Portfolio Mgmt., 1985—; mng. editor Jour. Fin., 1977-80, assoc. editor, 1985-88, Jour. of Fin. Income, 1990—. Contbr. articles to profl. publs. Trustee Trinity Coll., Hartford, Conn., 1980-86, Rosemont (Pa.) Sch., 1991—; commr. Bi-Partisan Commn. on Pa. Pension Fund Investments, 1989-93. Mem. Am. Fin. Assn. (officer 1977-80), Am. Econs. Assn., Fin. Economist Roundtable, Corinthian Yacht Club Phila., New Castle (Del.) Sailing Club, NASD (chmn. econ. adv. bd. 1998), NASDAQ Ednl. Found. (dir. 2000-2001), Measey Found. (mgr. 1997—, acad. adv. coun. 2004-), Shadow Regulatory Commn. Home: 204 Woodstock Rd Villanova PA 19085-1419 Office: U Penn Rodney L White Ctr Fin Rsch 3250 Steinberg Hall Philadelphia PA 19104

BLUME, MARTIN, physicist; b. Bklyn., Jan. 13, 1932; s. Julius and Frances (Cohen) B.; m. Sheila Bierman, June 12, 1955; children— Frederick, Janet. AB, Princeton U., 1954; A.M., Harvard U., 1956, PhD, 1960. Fulbright rsch. fellow Tokyo U., 1959-60; rsch. assoc. Atomic Energy Rsch. Establishment, Harwell, Eng., 1960-62; with Brookhaven Nat. Lab., Upton, N.Y., 1962—, sr. physicist, 1970—, head solid state physics, dep. chmn. physics dept., 1975-79, assoc. dir., 1981-84, dep. dir., 1984-96; editor-in-chief Am. Phys. Soc., Ridge, N.Y., 1997—. NSF grantee, 1973-78; recipient E.O. Lawrence award Dept. of Energy, 1981, A.H. Compton award, 2003, Meritorious Achievement award Coun. Sci. Editions, 2005 Fellow Am. Acad. Arts and Scis., Am. Phys. Soc., AAAS, N.Y. Acad. Scis.; mem. Phi Beta Kappa, Sigma Xi. Home: 284 Greene Ave Sayville NY 11782-3003 Office: Am Phys Soc 1 Rsch Rd Ridge NY 11961 also: Brookhaven Nat Lab Physics Dept Bldg 510 Upton NY 11973 Business E-Mail: blume@aps.org.

BLUME, PETER FREDERICK, museum director; b. Syracuse, N.Y., June 5, 1946; s. Edward Frederick and Charlotte (Murray) B.; m. Karolyn Waller Vreeland, Oct. 4, 1980 (div. 1998); 1 child, Susanna. BFA, Syracuse U., 1967, postgrad., 1972-73, Attingham Summer Sch., Eng., 1976, Mus. Mgmt. Inst., Berkeley, Calif., 1986. Curator Allentown (Pa.) Art Mus., 1974-84, dir., 1984—2002, Ball State U. Mus. Art, Ind., 2003—. Mem. museums panel Pa. Council on Arts, Harrisburg, 1983-87. Author exhbn. catalogs. Mem. Hist. Archtl. Rev. Bd., Allentown, 1978-83; mem. Old Allentown Preservation Assn., 1977—. Served with U.S. Army, 1967-73. Rockefeller Found. fellow Met. Mus. Art, N.Y.C., 1973-74. Mem. Rotary. Home: 2600 Fern Brook Way Muncie IN 47304 Office Phone: 765-285-3373. Business E-Mail: pfblume@bsu.edu.

BLUMENAUER, EARL, congressman; b. Portland, Oreg., Aug. 16, 1948; m. Margaret Kirkpatrick; 2 children. BA, Lewis and Clark Coll., 1970, JD, 1976. Asst. to pres. Portland State U., 1971-73; mem. Oreg. Ho. of Reps., 1973-79, Multnomah County Bd. Commrs., Portland, 1979-87; commr. Portland City Coun., 1987-96; congressman 3d Dist. U.S. Congress Oreg., 1996—; mem. transp. and infrastructure com., internat. rels. com. Recipient Nat. Bldg. Mus. Apgar Award, 2000, Am. Planning Assn. Legislator of the Year; fellow German Marshall, 1995. Democrat. Avocations: bicycling, running. Office: US House of Reps 2446 Rayburn HOB Washington DC 20515-3703 also: 729 NE Oregon St Ste 115 Portland OR 97232*

BLUMENCRANZ, PETER WILLIAM, surgeon; b. N.Y.C., Mar. 8, 1946; s. Bernard and Evelyn (Guttman) B.; m. Ann Frances Garfes, June 6, 1970; children: Brett, Lisa, Jennifer, Deborah, Todd. BA, U. Pa., 1966; MD, Cornell U., 1970. Diplomate Am. Bd. Surgery. Resident in surgery N.Y. Hosp.-Cornell U. Med. Ctr., N.Y.C., 1970-76; fellow in surg. oncology Meml. Hosp.-Sloan Kettering Cancer Ctr., N.Y.C., 1976-77; surgeon Diagnostic Clinic, Largo, Fla., 1977-79, Fla. Surg. Assocs., Clearwater, Fla., 1980-95; pres. Surg. Assocs. West Fla., Clearwater, 1995—. Bd. dirs. Morton Plant Mease Health Care, Dunedin, Fla., 1992—98, 2005—, Fla. Surg. Soc., 1998—; trustee Morton Plant Hosp., Clearwater, Fla., 1992—98, 2005—; med. dir. Moffitt Morton Plant Cancer Care, Tampa, Fla., 2001—. Trustee Shorecrest Prep. Sch., St. Petersburg, Fla., 1982-88. Lt. comdr. USN, 1972-74. Fellow Soc. Surg. Oncology, Am. Coll. Surgeons, Southeastern Surg. Congress; mem. AMA, Am. Soc. Breast Diseases, Fla. Soc. Clinical Oncology, Fla. Med. Assn., Am. Soc. Breast Surgeons, State Fla. Cancer Coun. Avocations: tennis, running. Office: Surg Assocs West Fla 303 Pinellas St Clearwater FL 33756-3354

BLUMENFELD, CHARLES RABAN, lawyer; b. Seattle, May 24, 1944; s. Irwin S. and Freda I. (Raban) B.; m. Karla Axell; children: David, Lisa. BA, U. Wash., JD, 1969. Bar: Wash. 1969, U.S. Dist. Ct. (we. dist.) Wash. 1969, U.S. Ct. Appeals (9th cir.) 1975, U.S. Supreme Ct. 1979, U.S. Dist. Ct. D.C. 1981, U.S. Ct. Appeals (D.C. cir.) 1981. Legis. counsel U.S. Senator Henry M. Jackson, Washington, 1969-72; ptnr. Bogle & Gates, Seattle, 1973-99, PerkinsCoie, Seattle, 1999—. Mem. ABA (sect. natural resources, energy and environment). Office: PerkinsCoie 1201 3rd Ave Fl 48 Seattle WA 98101-3029 Office Phone: 206-359-6364. Business E-Mail: cblumenfeld@perkinscoie.com.

BLUMENFELD, HAL, neurologist, educator; BA in Bioelectrical Engring., Harvard U., 1984; PhD in Physiology & Cellular Biophysics, Columbia U., 1990, MD, 1992. Cert. Am. Bd. Psychiatry & Neurology, 1998, Am. Bd. Clin. Neurophysiology, 2001. Internal medicine intern Columbia Presbyn. Med. Ctr., NYC, 1992—93; neurology resident Mass. Gen. Hosp., Boston, 1993—96; epilepsy fellow Yale U. Sch. Medicine, New Haven, 1996—98, assoc. rsch. scientist dept. neurology, 1998—2000, asst. prof. neurology & neurobiology, dir. med. studies in clin. neuroscience. Jr. Investigator Travel Fellowship, NIH, 2000. Mem.: AAAS, Soc. Neuroscience, Am. Epilepsy Soc. (Young Investigator Award 1999), Am. Clin. Neurophysiology Soc., Am. Acad. Neurology (Dreifuss-Penry Epilepsy Award 2005). Office: Yale U Sch Medicine Dept Neurology PO Box 208018 New Haven CT 06520-8018 Office Phone: 203-785-3865. Office Fax: 203-737-2538. Business E-Mail: hal.blumenfeld@yale.edu.*

BLUMENFIELD, MICHAEL, psychiatrist, educator; b. Bklyn., N.Y., June 14, 1938; s. Abner and Clara (Hott) Blumenfield; m. Susan Groner, June 24, 1962; children: Jay, Robert, Sharon. BA, U. Rochester, N.Y., 1960; MD, SUNY, Bklyn., 1964. Diplomate Am. Bd. Psychiatry and Neurology, 1971. Intern San Francisco Gen. Hosp., 1964—65; psychiatry resident King County Hosp., Bklyn., 1965—68, fellow psychomatic medicine, 1970—71; from asst. prof. to assoc. prof. SUNY Downstate Med Coll., 1971—80; dir. med. edn., dir. consultation-liaison divsn. with psychiatry, prof. psychiatry Westchester Med. Ctr. N.Y. Med. Coll., Valahalla, NY, 1980—. Editor: (Book) Supervision in Psychiatry, 1982; author: Pschological Cases of Burn and Trauma Patients, 1992, Consultations/Liason with Psychiatry, 2003. Recipient Cmty. Leadership award, Mental Health Assn., Westchester, N.Y., 1983, award, Soc. for Liason Psychiatry, 2004. Fellow: Acad. Psychosomatic Medicine, Am. Coll. Psychiatry, Am. Psychiat. Assn. (disting. life). Jewish. Office: 16 Donellan Rd Scarsdale NY 10583 Office Phone: 914-442-5035. Office Fax: 914-472-4756.

BLUMENGARTEN, JERRY, educational consultant; b. Bklyn., Feb. 14, 1948; s. Nathan and Jeanne G Blumengarten; m. Gail Rachel Weiner, Aug. 7, 1977; children: Neil J, Shira F. BA, U. Pitts., 1968; MA, Hunter Coll., CUNY, 1974. Lead tchr. NYC Bd. Edn., Bklyn., 1969—2001; writer, ednl. cons. Culver Co., Inc., Larkspur, Calif., 1979—. Chairperson Nat. Coun. Social Studies, Washington, 1977—78. Author: (educational booklet) The Safest You Can Be, Planning for Your Work Future. Libr. trustee Bellmore Meml. Libr., Bellmore, NY, 1992—96; cmty. curriculum advisor Mashpee (Mass.) Pub. Schools, 2002—05; charter commr. Mashpee Charter Commn., 2003—04; publicity chairperson Mashpee Civic Assn., 2004—05. With USAR, 1969—75, Ft. Tilden, NY. Recipient Outstanding Young Men of Am. award, U.S. Jaycees, 1979. Jewish. Home: 9240 SE La Creek Ct Hobe Sound FL 33455 Personal E-mail: lib218@yahoo.com.

BLUMENTHAL, CAROL, lawyer; b. Oakland, Calif., Feb. 19, 1951; m. Lloyd T. Shanley III, Jan. 25, 1982. AB, Bryn Mawr Coll., 1973; postgrad., Yale U., 1973-74; JD, Georgetown U., 1980. Bar: D.C. 1981, U.S. Dist. Ct. D.C. 1981, U.S. Ct. Appeals 1981, U.S. Ct. Internat. Trade 1982, U.S. Supreme Ct. 1984, W.Va. 1987, U.S. Supreme Ct. Appeals W.Va. 1987, U.S. Dist. Ct. (so. dist.) W.Va. 1987, U.S. Dist. Ct. Md. 1989. Prin. ptnr. Blumenthal & Shanley, Washington, 1982—. Arbitrator D.C. Bar, 1990—, mentor pro bono program, 1998—. Contbr. articles to profl. jours. Office: Blumenthal & Shanley Ste 301 1700 17th St NW Ste 301 Washington DC 20009-2419

BLUMENTHAL, DAVID, health policy expert; b. N.Y.C., Aug. 31, 1948; s. Martin and Jane (Rosenstock) B.; m. ellen G. Blumenthal, Aug. 9, 1970; children: Daniel, Karen. BA, Harvard U., 1970, MD, 1975; MPP, Kennedy Sch. Govt., Boston, 1975. Mem. profl. staff subcom. on health U.S. Senate, Washington, 1977-79; exec. dir. ctr. for health policy Kennedy Sch. Govt., Cambridge, Mass., 1980-87; sr. v.p. Brigham & Women's Hosp., Boston, 1987-91; chief health policy rsch. unit Mass. Gen. Hosp., Boston, 1991—; assoc. prof. Harvard Med. Sch., Boston. Mem. editorial bd. New Eng. Jour. Medicine, Boston, 1995—. Contbr. over 100 articles to profl. jours. Chmn. Mass. Peer Rev. Orgn., Waltham, 1997—. Office: Health Policy R&D Unit Med Practices Eval Ctr 50 Staniford St Boston MA 02114-2517

BLUMENTHAL, HERMAN THEODORE, retired pathologist; b. N.Y.C., Apr. 8, 1913; s. Samuel and Jennie (Price) B.; m. Eleonore Gottlieb, Aug. 18, 1940 (dec. 1972); children: Daniels S., Frederic A.; m. Margaret B. Phillips, May 29, 1974; children: Edward P., Shana P. BS, Rutgers U., 1934; MS, U. Pa., 1936; PhD, Washington U., St. Louis, 1938, MD, 1942. Resident in pathology Jewish Hosp., St. Louis, 1942-43; dir. labs of various hosps., 1945-65; asso. prof. pathology St. Louis U., 1947-52, adj. prof. community medicine, 1975—; mem. faculty Washington U., 1965—, research prof. gerontology, 1965—; dir. Midwest Med. Lab., 1965-82. Author: (with J.G. Probstein) Pancreatitis— A Clinical-Pathological Correlation, 1954; Editor: Cowdry's Arteriosclerosis— A Survey of the Problem, 2d edit, 1967, Medical Aspects of Gerontology, 1962, Interdisciplinary Topics in Gerontology, Vols. 1-8, 1968-71, Handbook of Diseases of Aging, 1981, Dilman's Elevational Hypothalmic Mechanisms in Aging and Disease, 1981; Contbr. articles on aging, transplanation, endocrinology, cancer, pathology to profl. jours.; editor Handbook of Diseases of Aging, 1983. Served to maj. M.C. AUS, 1942-45. Mem. Soc. Exptl. Biology and Medicine, Am. Heart Assn., Am. Diabetes Assn., Am. Assn. Cancer Research, Soc. Pathologists and Bacteriologists, Am. Soc. Exptl. Pathology, Gerontol. Soc., AAUP, Sigma Xi. Home: 6203 Washington Ave Saint Louis MO 63130-4847

BLUMENTHAL, JANE LEONARDI, librarian; d. William F. and Gwenlyn M. Banks; m. Don Michael Blumenthal. MSLS, Cath. U. Am.; BA, Coll. William and Mary. Asst. libr. Georgetown U. Med. Ctr., Wash., 1990—95, assoc. libr., 1995—96, med. ctr. libr., 1996—2000; asst. dean knowledge mgmt. Georgetown U. Sch. Medicine, Wash., 2000—; cataloger Sci. Libr., NCI-Frederick Cancer Rsch. Facility, 1980—82, tech. svcs. libr., 1982—84, asst. mgr., 1984—85; libr. dir. AMA Wash. Office, 1985—90. Chpt. assembly dir. Am. Soc. Info. Sci., 1990—92; regional adv. com. Nat. Network Librs. Medicine, Southeastern/Atlantic Region, Baltimore, 2002—. Mem.: Acad. Health Info. Profls. (disting.), Assn. Acad. Health Scis. Librs. (bd. dirs. 2002—05), Med. Libr. Assn. (sr. assoc. editor bulletin 1994—96, mem. editl. bd. bulletin 1996—99, chair leadership & mgmt. sect. 2004—05), Wildlife Rescue League, SPCA of No. Va. Office: Georgetown U Med Ctr Box 571420 Washington DC 22057-1420 Office Phone: 202-687-1187.

BLUMENTHAL, KAREN, newspaper executive; Bus. editor Dallas Morning News, 1992-94; dep. bur. chief Dallas bur. The Wall St. Jour., 1994-96, bur. chief Dallas bur., 1996—2004; sr. editor WSJ Reports, 2004—. Author: Six Days in October: The Stock Market Crash of 1929, 2002, Let Me Play, 2005. Office: The Wall St Jour 1201 Elm St Ste 5050 Dallas TX 75270-2141

BLUMENTHAL, MICHAEL CHARLES, writer, educator; b. Vineland, N.J., Mar. 8, 1949; s. Julius Ernst and Betty Blumenthal; m. Cynthia Mae Curtner, Oct. 2, 1982 (div. May 1984); m. Isabelle Germaine Leconte, Dec. 2, 1989; 1 child, Noah Gabriel. BA, SUNY, Binghamton, 1969; JD, Cornell U., 1974. Assoc. prof. English Harvard U., Cambridge, Mass., 1983-88, dir. creative writing, 1988-92; sr. Fulbright prof. Eotvos Lorand U., Budapest, Hungary, 1992-95; vis. prof. U. Haifa, Israel, 1996-97; vis. writer S.W. Tex. State U., San Marcos, 1997-98; disting. vis. poet Wichita (Kans.) State U., 1999. Sr. Fulbright prof., Free Univ. Berlin, 1999-2000; disting. vis. poet Santa Clara U., 2001; writer, editor Time-Life Books, Alexandria, Va., 1977-80; spl. asst. to chmn. NEH, Washington, 1980-81; prodr., dir. West German TV, Washington, 1981-83; Bingham poet-in-residence U. Louisville, 1982; sr. editor Cen. European U. Press, Budapest, 1988-92. Author: Laps, 1984 (Juniper prize 1994), The Wages of Goodness, 1992, Weinstock Among the Dying, 1993 (Ribelow prize 1994), When History Enters the House, 1998, Dusty Angel, 1999, God Loves Me, And So Did He: A Memoir, 2001. Bd. dirs. Ptnrs. in Edn., Austin, Tex., 1998—, MacDowell Colony, Peterborough, N.H., 1985-88; trustee Am. U. Ctr. Aix-en-Provence, France, 1992—. NEA fellow, 1984, Ingram-Merrill fellow, 1985, Guggenheim fellow, 1988-89, Fulbright fellow, 1992-95. Mem. Internat. PEN, Acad. Am. Poets (Peter I. B. Lavan award 1986), Poets and Writers, N.Y. Bar Assn. Avocations: skiing, swimming, hiking, language study, translation. Home: 3309 Merrie Lynn Ave Austin TX 78722-1608 E-mail: mcblume@attglobal.net.

BLUMENTHAL, RICHARD, state attorney general; m. Cynthia Blumenthal; 4 children. BA, Harvard Coll.; JD, Yale U., 1973. Law clk. Justice Harry A. Blackmun, 1974—75; U.S. atty. State of Conn., 1977—81, former rep., 1984—87, senator, 1987—90, state atty. gen., 1990—. Sgt. USMC, Res. Democrat. Office: Atty Gen Office PO Box 120 Hartford CT 06141-0120 Office Phone: 860-808-5318.

BLUMENTHAL, RONNIE, lawyer; b. Passaic, N.J., Nov. 27, 1944; d. Paul and Marga (Stern) B. BA, George Washington U., 1966, JD, 1969. Bar: D.C. 1969. Gen. atty. EEOC, Washington, 1969-71, spl. asst. to commr., acting chmn., 1971-78, sr. atty., 1978-82, dir. spl. svcs. staff, 1982-85, dir. compliance programs, 1985-91, acting dir. Office of Communications-Legis. Affairs, 1991-92; spl. asst. U.S. atty. Dept. Justice, Washington, 1992, dir. Office Fed. Ops., 1992-99, mediator, 1999—. Legis. fellow U.S. Senate, 1982; chmn. Performance Review Bd., Exec. Resources Bd; lectr., cons. in field. Mem. ABA, D.C. Bar Assn., Fed. Bar Assn., Exec. Women in Govt., Womens Bar Assn., Soc. Profls. in Dispute Resolution. Home: 853 Vanderbilt Beach Rd # 327 Naples FL 34108-8746 Office Phone: 202-297-1191. Personal E-mail: ronnieblum@aol.com.

BLUMENTHAL, SUSAN JANE, psychiatrist, educator, public health official; m. Edward John Markey. BA, Reed Coll., 1971; MD, U. Tenn., 1976; MPA, Harvard U., 1982; PhD (hon.), Trinity Coll., 1996, Ben Gurion U., 2005; DSc (hon.), Pine Manor Coll., 1998. Diplomate Am. Bd. Psychiatry and Neurology. Intern. Stanford U. Sch. Medicine, 1976-77, residency and fellowship, 1977-80; fellow NIMH, 1980-81, assoc. dir. Psychiatry Tng. Rev., head suicide rsch. unit and coord. of project depression, 1982-85, chief behavioral medicine program, 1985-93, chief behavioral and basic prevention rsch. br., 1991-93; clin. asst. prof. Tufts Med. Ctr., 1981-82; clin. asst. prof. psychiatry George Washington Sch. Medicine, 1982-86; clin. assoc. prof. psychiatry Georgetown Sch. Medicine, 1986-91, clin. prof. psychiatry Washington, 1991—; first dep. asst. sec. women's health HHS, Washington, 1993—97, asst. surgeon gen., 1996—2005, sr. med. and e-health advisor, 2002—05, sr. sci. advisor, 2002—05, sr. med. advisor Office of Global Health Affairs, 2003—05; clin. prof. psychiatry Tufts Sch. Medicine, 1995—; assoc. v.p. for health affairs George Washington U. Med. Ctr., 1998; pres. Global Health Inst., Washington, 2005—. Vis. prof. ob-gyn. George Washington U. Med. Ctr., 1998-99; disting. vis. prof. women's studies Brandeis U., 1999—; vis. prof. Stanford U., 2004-; hon. prof. Ben Gurion U. Sch. Medicine, 2004—; chair NIH Coord. Com. on Health and Behavior, 1991-94; co-chair NIH Reunion Task Force, 1992-94; chair fed. coord. com. breast cancer, fed. coord. com. women's health and the environ., co-chair nat. breast cancer action plan, coord. com. women's health issues and domestic violence, HHS, 1994-98; mem. Pres.'s Interagy. Coun. on Women; sr. advisor for pub. health White House Coun. on Youth Violence, 2000-02, sr. advisor on pub. health and sci. to the sec., USDA, 2000-02; vis. fellow Harvard U. Sch. Govt., 2004—; pres. Global Health Inst., 2005— Editor: Suicide Over the Life Cycle, 1989, Premenstrual Syndrome, 1985; mem. editl. bds.: Jour. Women's Health, Depression, health columnist: Elle Mag., Ladies Home Jour., U.S. News and World Report; contbr. articles to sci. jours. Mem. Nat. Commn. on Sleep Disorders Rsch., workgroup on mental health Pres. Task Force on Health Care Reform; U.S. rep. global commn. on Women's Health WHO; trustee Meridian Internat. Ctr., 2005—, Save the Children, Acad. Achievement, Hadassah HMO. Capt. USPHS, 1992-94, rear adm., 1994—. Recipient Outstanding Svc. medal, 1989, Commendation medal, 1990, Meritorious Svc. medal, USPHS, 1992, Sec.'s Honor award for Domestic Violence, 1996, Asst. Sec. for Health's award for Breast Cancer, 1996, Am. Med. Writers award, 1996, Gretchen Poston award, The Nat. Race for the Cure, 1996, Founder's award, 1996, Pub. Svc. award, Nat. Alliance for the Mentally Ill, 1996, Surgeon Gen.'s Exemplary Svc. medal, 1997, Gracie award, Assn. Women Radio and TV Profls., 1997, Inspiration Leader award, Pa. Diabetes Assn., 1997, Spl. Assignment Svc. medal, 1998, 2002, Women of Distinction award, Nat. Assn. Women in Higher Edn., 1998, Woman of Valor award, United Jewish Fedn., 1999, Mosaic award, Komen Found., 2000, Founder's award, 2000, Feminist First award for Health, Feminist Majority, 2000, Congl. award, 2001, Congl. citation, 2002, Achievement medal, 2002, Women's Ctr. Leadership award, 2003, Leadership award, Save the Children, 2004, Nat. Breast Cancer Awareness Pub. Svcs. Leadership award, 2004, Disting. Svc. award, Spirit of Life Found., 2004, Presdl. Sacher Medallion, Brandeis U., 2005; fellow, Harvard U. Sch. Govt., 2004. Mem. AMA, Am. Psychiat. Assn. (cons. Joint Coun. on Pub. Affairs, Francis Braceland award for pub. svc. 1998), Am. Coll. Psychiatrists, Am. Med. Women's Assn. (past chair com. on publicity and pub. rels., Pres.'s citation, 1996), Congl. Club, Nat. Assn. Bus. and Profl. Women (Magnificent Seven award 1996), Internat. Club, Internat. Women's Forum, Am. Suicide Found. (past bd. dirs. Washington divsn., pres.), Starlight Found. (past chmn. sci. adv. bd.). Office: Global Health Inst Ste 810 1133 Connecticut Ave Washington DC 20036 Personal E-mail: drsusanjb@aol.com.

BLUMENTHAL, WILLIAM, lawyer; b. White Plains, N.Y., Nov. 4, 1955; s. Louis and Mary (Meyer) B.; m. Marjory Susan Spodick, Dec. 30, 1979; 1 child, Deborah Louise. AB, MA, Brown U., 1977; JD, Harvard U., 1980. Bar: D.C. 1980, U.S. Dist. Ct. D.C. 1986. Cons. Policy & Mgmt. Assocs., Inc., Boston, 1977-80; teaching fellow Harvard U., Cambridge, Mass., 1978-80; assoc. Jones, Day, Reavis & Pogue, Washington, 1980-83, Sutherland, Asbill & Brennan, Washington, 1983-87, ptnr., 1988-93, Kelley Drye & Warren, Washington, 1993-95, King & Spalding LLP, Washington, 1995—2005; gen. counsel Fed. Trade Commn., 2005—. Editor Horizontal Mergers: Law and Policy, 1986; contbr. to book: The Merger Review Process, 1995, Mergers & Acquisitions Handbook, 1986. Harvey A. Baker fellow Brown U., 1977. Mem. ABA (chmn. Clayton Act com. 1992-94, chmn. monograph com. 1989-92, vice chmn. antitrust sect. 1997-98, internat. officer antitrust sect. 2003—). Business E-Mail: wblumenthal@ftc.gov.

BLUMER, CRAIG ALAN, psychologist; b. Bismarck, N.D., July 1957; s. Boyd A. and Evelyn Blumer; m. Barbara J. Holzer, Dec. 23, 1989; children: Angela Diener, Elizabeth Diener, John Diener, Natalie. BA, U. S.D., Vermillion, 1975—78; PhD, Ohio U., Athens, 1978—84. Lic. psychologist Wis., 1986. Psychologist Wis. Resource Ctr., Oshkosh, 1986—96, Oshkosh Correctional Instn., Wis., 1996—. Contbr. articles to profl. jours. Mid-week elem. children's program Algoma Blvd. United Meth. Ch., Oshkosh, Wis., 1995—2005. Mem.: APA, Christian Assn. for Psychol. Studies, Nat. Register Health Svc. Providers in Psychology, Wis. Psychol. Assn. Methodist. Achievements include development of a prison-based co-occurring disorders treatment program. Office: Oshkosh Correctional Instn 1730 W Snell Rd Oshkosh WI 54903 Office Phone: 920-231-4010. Office Fax: 920-236-2626. E-mail: craig.blumer@doc.state.wi.us.

BLUMER, FREDERICK ELWIN, retired philosophy educator; b. Glencoe, Okla., Sept. 16, 1933; s. Edward H. and Eva Marie (Forbes) B.; m. Ann Louise Anderson, June 9, 1956; children— Frederick Edward, William Robert. BA, Millsaps Coll., 1955; BD, Emory U., 1958, PhD, 1962; postgrad., Georg August U., Goettingen, Germany, 1960-61. Ordained to ministry United Meth. Ch., 1962; chaplain, instr. philosophy and religion Nebr. Wesleyan U., Lincoln, 1962-63, asst. prof., 1963-65, assoc. prof., 1965-67, prof., 1967-76, v.p. acad. affairs, 1967-70, provost, v.p. acad. affairs, 1970-76; pres. Lycoming Coll., Williamsport, Pa., 1976-89; Moll prof. faith and life Baldwin-Wallace Coll., Berea, Ohio, 1989-99, prof. emeritus, 1999—. Dean, dir. Graz (Austria) Ctr., 1972-73; mem. univ. senate United Meth. Ch., 1980-88, 93-97, pres., 1980-88, chmn. Commn. on Theol. Edn.; exec. com. Commn. Ind. Colls. and Univs. Pa., 1978-81, treas., 1988-89. Editor: Nebr. Wesleyan Univ. Press, 1967-76; Contbr. articles to profl. jours. Dir. edn. Lincoln United Way, 1971; bd. dirs. N.E. Lincoln YMCA, 1968-71, Lincoln Symphony Orch., 1971-76, Williamsport/Lycoming United Way, 1976-83; bd. mgrs. Williamsport Hosp., 1982-89; chmn. Found. Ind. Colls. Pa., 1987-88; bd. dirs. Pine Street Found., 1982-86, Lycoming Found., 1985-89. Recipient Pres.'s award Nebr. Wesleyan U., 1966; Cokesbury fellow, Dempster fellow, Rockefeller doctoral fellow Emory U. Mem. Nat. Assn. Schs., Colls., Univs. of United Meth. Ch. (pres. 1987-89), Williamsport-Lycoming C. of C. (dir., exec. com. 1976-85), Phi Kappa Phi, Pi Gamma Mu, Theta Phi, Omicron Delta Kappa. Republican. Home: 20798 Burgandy Dr Strongsville OH 44149-5602

BLUMKIN, LINDA RUTH, lawyer; b. Aug. 25, 1944; d. Louis and Edith (Fortus) Blumkin. AB cum laude, Barnard Coll., 1964; LLB cum laude, Harvard U., 1967, LLM, 1973. Bar: N.Y. 1968, U.S. Dist. Ct. (so. dist.) N.Y. 1969, U.S. Ct. Appeals (2nd cir.) 1969, U.S. Supreme Ct. 1982. Assoc. Fried, Frank, Harris, Shriver & Jacobson, N.Y.C., 1967—71, ptnr., 1979—. Lectr. Boston U., 1971, asst. prof. mgmt., 1972—73; assoc. Breed, Abbott & Morgan, N.Y.C., 1973—77; asst. dir. Bur. Competition, Fed. Trade Commn., 1977—79. Mem.: ABA, N.Y.C. Bar Assn. Office: Fried Frank Harris Shriver & Jacobson 1 New York Plz Fl 24 New York NY 10004-1901 Office Phone: 212-859-8085. Business E-Mail: linda.blumkin@friedfrank.com.

BLUMROSEN, ALFRED WILLIAM, law educator; b. Detroit, Dec. 14, 1928; s. Sol and Frances (Netzorg) B.; m. Ruth L. Gerber, July 3, 1952; children: Steven Marshall, Alexander Bernet. BA, U. Mich., 1950, JD, 1953. Bar: Mich. 1953, N.J. 1961, N.Y. 1981. Solo practice, Detroit, 1953-55; mem. faculty Rutgers Law Sch., Newark, 1955—, prof., 1961—, acting dean, 1974-75, Herbert J. Hannoch scholar, 1984, Thomas A. Cowan prof., 1986—. Dir. fed.-state rels., chief conciliations U.S. EOOC, 1965-67, cons. to chmn., 1977-79; advisor U.S. Dept. Justice, HUD, 1968-72, U.S. Dept. Labor, 1995-96; of counsel Kaye, Scholer, Fierman, Hays & Handler, N.Y.C., 1979-82; dir. Ford Found. intentional discrimination project Rutgers U., Law Sch., 1998—. Author: Black Employment and the Law, 1971, Modern Law: The Law Transmission System and Equal Employment Opportunity, 1993; author: (with Ruth Blumrosen) The Realities of Intentional Job Discrimination in Metropolitan America, 1999, Slave Nation: How Slavery United the Colonies and Sparked the American Revolution, 2005; contbr. articles to profl. jours. Fulbright scholar, South Africa, 1993, Rockefeller Inst. Resident scholar Bellagio Conf. Ctr., 1995. Mem. ABA (Ross essay prize 1983), Internat. Soc. for Labor Law and Social Security, Indsl. Relations Rsch. Assn., Order of Coif. Office: Rutgers U Sch Law 123 Washington St Newark NJ 07102-3026 Office Phone: 917-670-8878.

BLUMSTEIN, ALFRED, urban and public affairs educator; b. NYC, June 3, 1930; m. Dolores Reguera, Jan. 26, 1958; children: Lisa, Ellen, Diane. BS in Engring. Physics, Cornell U., 1951, PhD in Ops. Rsch., 1960; MS in Stats., U. Buffalo, 1954; JD (hon.), John Jay Coll., 1996. Prin. ops. analyst Cornell Aero. Lab., Buffalo, 1951-61; rsch. staff Inst. Def. Analyses, Arlington, Va., 1961-69; dir. sci. and tech. task force Pres.'s Commn. Law Enforcement and Adminstrn. Justice, Washington, 1966-67; J. Erik Jonsson Univ. prof. urban sys. and ops. rsch. H. John Heinz III Sch. Pub. Policy and Mgmt. Carnegie-Mellon U., Pitts., 1969—, dean, 1986-93, dir. Nat. Consortium on Violence Rsch., 1996—. Overseas fellow Churchill Coll. Cambridge U., 1983—; chmn. various panels NRC Com. Rsch. Law Enforcement and Adminstrn. Justice, 1982-86, chmn. com., 1980-83; mem. NRC Commn. Behavioral and Social Scis. and Edn., 1994-2000. Mem. editl. bd. Ops. Rsch. Letters, Jour. Rsch. in Crime and Delinquency, Evaluation Rev., Jour. Criminal Justice, Sci. Commn. of Internat. Soc. of Criminology, 1985-91, others; co-editor Cambridge Criminology Series; contbr. articles to profl. jours. Chmn. Pa. Commn. Crime and Delinquency, Harrisburg, 1979-90; mem. Pa. Commn. on Sentencing, 1986-96; bd. dirs. Police Found., 1990-96; nat. adv. com. Inst. Rsch. on Poverty at U. Wis., 1989-94; trustee Jewish Healthcare Found., 2001-. Fellow AAAS, Am. Soc. Criminology (pres. 1991-92, Sutherland award 1987); mem. NAE, Ops. Rsch. Soc. Am. (pres. 1977-78, Kimball medal 1985, Pres.'s award 1993, Morse lectr. 2004-), Am. Statis. Assn., Inst. Ops. Rsch. and Mgmt. Scis. (pres. 1996), Law and Soc. Assn., Inst. Mgmt. Scis. (pres. 1987-88), Internat. Fedn. Operational Rsch. Socs. (v.p. N.Am. 1992-94), Consortium of Social Sci. Assn. (pres. 1999-), Cosmos Club, Omega Rho (hon.). Home: 1455 Wightman St Pittsburgh PA 15217-1260 Office: Carnegie-Mellon U H John Heinz III Sch Pub Policy Mgmt Pittsburgh PA 15213 Office Phone: 412-268-8269. Business E-Mail: ab0q@andrew.cmu.edu.

BLUMSTEIN, JAMES FRANKLIN, law educator, lawyer, consultant; b. Bklyn., Apr. 24, 1945; s. David and Rita (Sondheim) B.; m. Andree Kahn, June 25, 1971 BA in Econs., Yale U., 1966, MA in Econs., LLB, 1970. Bar: Tenn. 1970, U.S. Ct. Appeals (6th cir.) 1970, U.S. Dist. Ct. (mid. dist.) Tenn. 1971, U.S. Supreme Ct. 1974, N.Y. 1985. Instr. econs. New Haven Coll., 1967-68; pre-law adviser office of dean Yale U., New Haven, 1968-69, sr. pre-law adviser office of dean, 1969-70, asst. in instrn. law shc., 1969-70; asst. prof. law Vanderbilt U., Nashville, 1970-73, assoc. prof., 1973-76, prof., 1976-99, spl. advisor to chancellor for acad. affairs, 1984-85, Centennial prof., 1999—2003, Univ. prof. constl. law and health law and policy, 2003—, chair faculty senate, 2001—02, univ. prof., 2003—. Assoc. dir. Vanderbilt Urban and Regional Devel. Ctr., 1970-72, dir. ctr., 1972-74; sr. rsch. assoc. Vanderbilt Inst. for Pub. Policy Studies, 1976-85, sr. fellow, 1985—, dir. health policy ctr., 1995—; Commonwealth Fund fellow, vis. assoc. prof. law and policy scis. law sch. Duke U. and Inst. of Policy Scis. and Pub. Affairs, 1974-75; adj. prof. health law med. sch. Dartmouth U., scholar-in-residence intermittently, 1976-78; John M. Olin vis. prof. Sch. Law, U. Pa., 1989; elected mem. Inst. Medicine NAS, 1990—; cons. law, health policy, civil and voting rights, land use, state taxation, torts; lectr. in field. Editor: (with Eddie J. Martin) The Urban Scene in the Seventies, 1974, (with Benjamin Walter) Growing Metropolis: Aspects of Development in Nashville, 1975, (with Lester Salamon) Growth Policy in the Eighties (Law and Contemporary Problems Symposium), 1979; (with Frank A. Sloan and James M. Perrin) Uncompensated Hospital Care: Rights and Responsibilities, 1986, (with Frank A. Sloan and James M. Perrin) Cost, Quality, and Access in Health Care: New Roles for Health Planning in a Competitive Environment, 1988; (with Frank A. Sloan) Organ Transplantation Policy: Issues and Prospects, 1989, (with Frank A. Sloan) Antitrust and Health Care Policy (Law and Contemporary Problems Symposium), 1989, (with Clark C. Havighurst and Troyen A. Brennan) Health Care Law and Policy, 1998, bd. Jour. Health Politics, Policy and Law, 1981-01; mem. adv. bd. NF IB Legal Found., 2003-; mem. pub.'s adv. bd. Nashville Banner, 1982-98; contbr. articles to profl. jours., op-ed articles to newspapers. Mem. Health Econs. Task Force, Middle Tenn. Health Sys. Agy., 1979; mem. Nashville Mayor's Commn. on Crime, 1981; chmn. Yale Alumni Schs. Com. Middle Tenn., 1983—; sec. Martin Luther King Jr. Holiday Com., State of Tenn., 1985—87; mem. Tenn. Gov.'s Task Force Medicaid, 1992—94; active Inst. Medicine Com. on Adequacy of Nursing Staffing, 1994—96; chmn. Tenn. adv. com. U.S. Commn. on Civil Rights, 1985—91, mem., 1991—97; bd. dirs. Alive Hosp., 2005—, St. Thomas Health Scis. Found.; mem. adv. bd. LWV, 1979—80; bd. dirs. Jewish Fedn. Nashville and Middle Tenn., 1981—90, mem. exec. com., 1988—90, chmn. cmty. rels. com., 1980—82, chmn. campus com., 1987—89; chmn. task force cost containment and med. malpractice Rand Corp., 1991—92; mem. adv. panel Office Tech. Assessment study of defensive medicine and use of med. tech., 1991—94; mem. adv. com. on The Records of Congress, 1997—99; cons. Leadership Nashville, 1977—, Tenn. Motor Vehicle Commn., 1986—87, Leadership Music, 1979—2002, Tenncare Reform Project, Office Gov. Phil Bredesen, 2004—; panelist Am. Arbitration Assn., 1977—2002. Bates Jr. fellow, 1968-69; grantee Ford Found./Rockefeller Found. Population Program, 1970-73, Health Policy grantee HCA Found., 1986-90; grantee State Justice Inst., 1991—2000, Robert Wood Johnson Found., 1994—2000; named One of Outstanding Young Men in Am., 1971; recipient award Univ. Rsch. Coun., 1971-72, 73-74, 79-80, 94-95, Earl Sutherland prize achievement in rsch. Vanderbilt U., 1992, Paul J. Hartman award Outstanding Prof., 1982. Mem. ABA (sec. sect. legal edn. and admissions to bar 1982-83, chmn. subcom. on state and local taxation com. on corp. law and taxation sect. on corp., banking and bus. law 1983—, mem. accreditation com. sect. legal edn. and admissions to bar 1983-89, mem. com. on state and local taxation sect. on taxation 1983—), NAS (inst. of medicine), Assn. Am. Law Schs. (chmn. law, medicine and health care sect. 1987-88, mem. exec. com. 1988-92, 2d vice chmn. sect. local govt. law 1976-78, mem. sect. coun. 1980-86), Tenn. Bar Assn. (Pres.'s award 2004), N.Y. State Bar Assn., Nashville Bar Assn. (Liberty Bell award 1987), Assn. Yale Alumni (del.), Yale U. Law Sch. Alumni Assn. (exec. com. 1985-88), Univ. Club (Nashville). Home: 2113 Hampton Ave Nashville TN 37215-1401 Office: Vanderbilt U Sch Law 21st Ave S Nashville TN 37240-0001

BLUNCK, TEDDE, lawyer, engineer, engineering company executive; b. Milw., Aug. 19, 1946; s. George C. Blunck and Pauline L. Hillebran Murphy; m. Quita R. Lininger, June 27, 1965 (div. June 1984); children: Kelle M. Blunck Gliem, Kenneth M. Blunck (dec.); m. Cathy A. Terrell, May 26, 1988; 1 child, Richard T. Antoine. BSCE, Iowa State U., 1970; JD magna cum laude, Tex. Wesleyan U., 1995. Bar: Tex. 1995, D.C. 1998, U.S. Dist. Ct. (no. dist.) Tex. 1996, U.S. Supreme Ct. 2002; lic. profl. engr., lic. profl. land surveyor. Project engr. Shive Hattery & Assocs., Iowa City, 1976-77; county engr. Madison County, Winterset, Iowa, 1977-83; head dept. transp. Veenstra & Kimm Inc., West Des Moines, Iowa, 1983-84; v.p. Huitt-Zollars, Inc., Dallas, 1984-89; project leader Parsons Brinckerhoff Quade & Douglas, Inc., Tempe, Ariz., 1989-90; asst. to project dir. PB/MK Team, waxahachie, Tex., 1990-95; legal asst. Ford Yungblut White & Salazar, P.C., Dallas, 1995-96; sr. constrn. mgr. Parsons Brinckerhoff Constrn. Svcs., Inc., Ft. Worth, 1996-97, v.p., asst. sec., mgr. legal svcs. Herndon, Va., 1997—2002; sr. assoc. counsel Parsons Brinckeihoff Quade & Douglas, Inc, 2002—. County engr. Taylor County, Bedford, Iowa, 1973-76; dir. pub. works City of Charles City, Iowa, 1970-73. Bd. dirs. Cmty. and Econ. Devel. Corp., Duncanville, Tex., 1996-97; mem. City Coun., City of Sharpsburg, Iowa, 1976. Republican. Roman Catholic. Home: 5212 Lincolnshire Court Dallas TX 75287-5427 Office: Parsons Brinckerhoff Quade & Douglas Inc 2777 Stemoions Freeway Ste 1520 Dallas TX 75207 Office Phone: 214-678-1196. Business E-Mail: blunckt@pbworld.com.

BLUNDELL, WILLIAM RICHARD CHARLES, retired electric company executive; b. Montreal, Apr. 13, 1927; s. Richard C. and Did Aileen (Payne) B.; m. Monique Audet, Mar. 20, 1959; children: Richard, Emily, Michelle, Louise. BSc, U. Toronto, 1949. Registered profl. engr., Ont. Sales engr. Can. Gen. Electric Co., Toronto, 1949-51, travelling auditor, 1951, various fin. positions, 1951-66, treas., 1966-68, v.p.-fin., 1968-70, v.p., exec. consumer div., 1970-72, v.p., exec. apparatus div. Lachine, Que., 1972-79; pres., CEO, Camco Inc., Weston, Ont., 1979-83; pres., COO, Can. Gen. Electric Co. Ltd., Toronto, 1983-84; chmn., CEO Gen. Electric Can. Inc., Toronto, 1985-90; ret., 1991. Chmn. Mfrs. Life Ins. Co., 1994—98, chmn. pub. sector pension investment bd., 2000—03; vice chair Can. Inst. for Advanced Rsch., 1998—2003; bd. dirs. CableServ, Inc., Metallic Ventures Gold Inc. Decorated officer Order of Can.; recipient Engring. Alumni medal U. Toronto, 1990. Home: 29 Rothmere Dr North York ON Canada M4N IV3 E-mail: bill_blundell@rogers.com.

BLUNT, JOYCE OMEGA, special education educator; d. Herbert and Rosemary Blunt. BA, So. U. New Orleans, 1978; MA, Xavier U., 1982; postgrad., Southeastern U., 1986. Chair, black history, grade, student coun. advisor Harahan, La., 1998—2004; mem. spl. edn. adv. coun. Jefferson Parish, Harvey, 1995—. Parent tchr. rep. Harahan, 1998—2003, dollars for scholars, 1998—2004. Named Outstanding Young Educator, Metairie Jaycees, 1994, Walmart Tchr. Yr., 2002, Reading Tchr. Yr., La. Reading Coun., Jefferson, 2002. Mem.: Nat. Assn. Univ. Women (edn. chair), Jefferson Fed. Tchrs. Union (mem.-at-large 1986—). Baptist. Avocations: travel, shopping. Home: 7924 Macon St Metairie LA 70003

BLUNT, MATT (MATTHEW ROY BLUNT), governor, former state official; b. Strafford, Missouri, Nov. 20, 1970; s. Roy Blunt; m. Melanie Blunt, Mar. 1997; 1 child, William Branch. BA in History, US Naval Acad., Annapolis, Md., 1993. Mem. Mo. Gen. Assembly, 1999—2001; sec. state State of Mo., Jefferson City, 2001—05, gov., 2005—. USN, 1993—98, lt. comdr. USNR, 1998—, engring. officer, USS JACK WILLIAMS, navigator, adminstrv. officer, USS PETERSON. Decorated achievement award USN, US Marine Corps, Humanitarian Svc. Medal. Mem.: Mo. Farm Bureau, Am. Legion, State Historical Soc. Mo. Republican. Baptist. Achievements include serving in Operation Support Democracy in Haiti and southern England and in support of Operation Enduring Freedom while in the USN. Office: Office of Gov Mo Capitol Bldg Rm 216 Jefferson City MO 65101 also: PO Box 720 Jefferson City MO 65102 Office Phone: 573-751-3222. Business E-Mail: mogov@mail.state.mo.us.

BLUNT, ROY D., congressman; b. Niangua, Mo., Jan. 10, 1950; s. Leroy and Neva (Letterman) B.; m. Roseann Blunt (div. 2003), children: Matthew Roy, Amy Roseann, Andrew Benjamin.; m. Abigail Perlman, 2003. BA in History, S.W. Bapt. U., 1970; MA in History & Govt., S.W. Mo. State U., 1972. Tchr. Marshfield (Mo.) High Sch., 1970-73; instr. Drury Coll., Springfield, Mo., 1973-82; clk. Greene County, Springfield, 1973-85; sec. of state State of Mo., Jefferson City, 1985-93; pres. Southwest Bapt. U., 1993-96; mem. 105th-108th Congresses from 7th Mo. dist., 1997—; chief dep. Ho. majority whip 106th-107th Congress, 1999—2002; Ho. majority whip 108th Congress, 2002—. Mem. Fed. Election Commn. Adv. Panel; del. Atlantic Treaty Assn. Conf., 1987; mem. Congressional Com. on Commerce, 1999—2004, Internat. Rels., 1997-98, 2004-, Ho. Reps. Steering Com., 1997-; del. Nat. Hist. Publs. and Records Commn., 1997—; mem. ho. appropriations com., 1999. Co-author: Missouri Election Procedures: A Layman's Guide, 1977, Jobs Without People: The Coming Crisis for Missouri's Workforce, 1989; Voting Rights Guide for the Handicapped Bd. dirs. Ctr. for Democracy; mem. Mo. Mental Health Advocacy Coun., 1998-99; mem. exec. bd. Am. Coun. of Young Polit. Leaders, 1998-99; chmn. Mo. Housing Devel. Commn., Kansas City, 1981, Rep. State Conv., Springfield, 1980; chmn. Gov.'s Adv. Coun. on Literacy; co-chmn. Mo. Opportunity 2000 Commn., 1985-87; Rep. candidate for lt. gov. of Mo., 1980; active local ARC, Muscular Dystrophy Assn., others. Named One of 10 Outstanding Young Americans U.S. Jaycees, 1986, Springfield's Outstanding Young Man Jaycees, 1980, Mo.'s Outstanding Young Civic Leader, 1981, Mo. Republican of the Yr. 2002; Recipient Disting. Mem. of Congress award, Am. Wire Producers Assn., 2002, Health Leadership award Am. Assn. of Nurse Anesthetists, 2003 Mem. Nat. Assn. Secs. of State (chmn. voter registration and edn. com., sec., v.p. 1990). Am. Coun. Young Polit. Leaders. Lodges: Kiwanis, Masons. Republican. Baptist. Office: US Ho of Reps 217 Cannon Ho Office Bldg Washington DC 20515-0001 also: Whip's Office H-329 The Capitol Washington DC 20515 E-mail: blunt@mail.house.gov.*

BLUNT, SHANNON DAVID, electrical engineer, researcher; b. Memphis, Oct. 20, 1975; s. Larry Wayne and Teresa Marlene Blunt; m. Paulette Marie Preisinger, Aug. 15, 1998; 1 child, Nicholas Paul. BSEE, U. Mo., 1999, MSEE, 2000, PhD in Elec. Engring., 2002. Electronics engr. US Naval Rsch. Lab., Washington, 2002—05; asst. prof. U. Kans., Lawrence, 2005. Contbr. articles to profl. jours. (Naval Rsch. Lab. Alan Berman Rsch. Publ. award, 2005). Mem.: IEEE. Achievements include research in adaptive radar pulse compression; patents pending for adaptive radar pulse compression; robust radar space-time adaptive processing; adaptive STAP detector; detector for slow-moving targets in sea clutter.

BLUTH, B. J. (ELIZABETH JEAN CATHERINE BLUTH), sociologist, aerospace technologist; b. Phila., Dec. 5, 1934; d. Robert Thomas and Catherine Cecelia (Boxman) Gowland; m. Thomas Del Bluth, Aug. 20, 1960 (dec. Aug. 6, 1980); children: Robert Thomas, Richard Del. BA in Sociology (Washington semster fellow), Bucknell U., 1953; MA, Fordham U., 1960; PhD, UCLA, 1970. Teaching fellow in methods of social research Fordham U., 1957-58; reading instr. St. Margaret's High Sch., Tappahannock, Va., 1958-59; instr. history, civics and English, Rosary High Sch., San Diego, 1959-60; successively instr., asst. prof. sociology Immaculate Heart Coll., Los Angeles, 1960-65; prof. sociology Calif. State U., Northridge, 1965-87; grantee NASA Ames Research Ctr., Moffett Field, Calif., 1982-83; grantee space sta. program NASA, Washington, 1983-87, aerospace technologist system engring. div. space sta. program office Reston, Va., 1987-90, spl. asst. to dep. program dir. space sta. freedom program and ops., 1990-94, spl. tech. asst. to dir. edn. divsn., mgr. edn. evaluation Washington, 1994—, program mgr. on-line edn. evaluation program, 1994—. Cons. Immaculate Heart Cmty., L.A., 1967-69; engring. rsch. NASA Space Sta. design Boeing Aerospace Co., 1982-83; mem. Presdl. Citizens Adv. com. on Space, Coun. Nat. Space Policy, Nat. Tech. Com. on Soc. & Tech., UN team on relevance of space activities to econ. and social devel.; professor emeritus Calif. State U., 1987—; computational scis. and informatics inst. dir.'s search com. George Mason U., 1992-93. Editor: (with others) Search for Identity Reader, vol. I and II, 1973, (with S.R. McNeal) Update on Space, vol. I, 1961, Parson's General Theory of Action, 1982, Space Station Habitability Report, 1983, Soviet Space Station Analog, 1983, Space Station Human Productivity Study NASA, 1986, Russian Mir Space Station Analog, 1993, Marching with Sharpe, 2001; contbr. articles to profl. jours. Recipient Alpha Omega faculty awards, 1966, 1974. Fellow Am. Astronautical Soc.; mem. AIAA (chpt. award for outstanding program 1980), Am. Sociol. Assn., L5 Soc., Brit. Interplanetary Soc., Inst. Social Sci. Study of Space (acad. adv. bd.), Space Studies Inst., Internat. Acad. Astronautics (com. on space econs. and benefits), Phi Beta Kappa. Republican. Office Phone: 202-358-1527. E-mail: bjb@patriot.net, bbluth@nasa.gov. *To seed the universe with intelligence you must: never give up, no matter how little progress you see day-to-day for it's the "big picture" where the changes show up; always concentrate on the practical, no matter how enticing theories appear; never forget that ideas and systems and institutions are nothing more than ideas, and ideas can change—that is the true vehicle to freedom. Always reach beyond the horizon, knowing that horizons have no limit save that of our imagination.*

BLY, CARL ANTHONY, retired music educator; b. Carbondale, Pa., Mar. 20, 1946; s. Musin Jackson and Jeanette Rose Bly; m. Randi Jean Shoremount, June 15, 1974; children: Gretchen Elizabeth, Heidi Marie. MusB in Edn., Shenandoah Conservatory of Music, 1967; MA in Conducting, George Mason U., 1987. Collegiate Professional License State Bd. of Edn., 1971. Band dir. John Randolph Tucker HS, Richmond, Va., 1971—76, Lake Braddock Secondary Sch., Fairfax County, Va., 1976—88; band dir. and dept. chair Centreville (Va.) HS, 1988—2001. Com. mem. Nat. Fedn. of HS's, Indpls., 1984—88. Musician and conductor: concert Mid-West Band and Orchestra Clinic, Bands of America's Nat. Concert Band Festival; dir.: (marching band performance) Marching Bands of America's Grand National Championship. With U.S. Army, 1966—68, Viet Nam. Recipient Presdl. Citation, Va. Governor's Sch., 1994, 1996, 1997, Citation of Excellence, Nat. Band Assn., 1998, 1999, Presdl. Citation, Va. Governor's Sch., 2001, Citation of Excellence, Nat. Band Assn., 2001; fellow Conducting fellow, Am. Symphony Orch. League, 1975—77. Mem.: Va. Band & Orch. Dirs. Assn. (pres. 1984—86, bd. dirs. 1982—), Va. Music Educators Assn., Music Educators Nat. Conf., Circus Fans Am., Circus Model Builders Assn., Circus Hist. Soc., Phi Beta Mu (pres. 1993—98). Home: 6008 Rockton Ct Centreville VA 20121-3080 Office: Same Personal E-mail: carl.bly@verizon.net.

BLY, CHARLES ALBERT, nuclear engineer, research scientist; b. Winchester, Va., Jan. 11, 1952; s. Theodore and Nancy Irma (Fisher) B.; m. April Marie Monnen, July 24, 1976. BS in Nuclear Engring., U. Va., 1978, MS in Nuclear Engring., 1983; student, Nat. Acad. Nuclear Tng., 1992-93; postgrad. in nuclear engring., U. Va., 1994—, cardiovasc. rsch. tng., 1999—. Nuclear reactor operator Nuclear Reactor Facility of the U. Va., Charlottesville, 1977-80, sr. reactor operator, 1980-83, rsch. engr., 1981-83; vis. engr. Brit. Nuclear Fuel Ltd. Springfields Works, Preston Lancashire, England, 1983; nuclear engr. Comml. Nuclear Fuel div. Westinghouse Electric, Pitts., 1983-92, Beaver Valley Power Sta. Duquesne Light Co., Shippingport, Pa., 1992-94; lead prof. Oak Ridge (Tenn.) Nat. Lab. Am. Tech. Inst., 1994-95; nuclear reactor staff Nuclear Reactor Facility of U. Va., Charlottesville, 1995-99; staff U. Va. Health Svcs. Cardiovasc. Gene Therapy Lab., Charlottesville, 1999—. Contbr. numerous articles to profl. jours. Candidate Shenandoah County (Va.) Bd. of Supervisor, 1975; mem. Ad Hoc Com. to Prevent Extension of I-66 Hwy. Through George Washington Nat. Forest, Strasburg, Va., 1979, Ad Hoc Com. to Preserve the Pitts. Aviary, 1991. Mem. ASME, IEEE, ASTM, AAAS, Am. Nuc. Soc., Am. Phys. Soc., ASM Internat., Assn. Energy Engrs., The Engring. Soc., Profl. Engr.'s Soc., Fedn. Am. Scientists, Engr.'s Soc. Western Pa., N.Y. Acad. Scis., Internat. Platform Assn. Democrat. Lutheran. Achievements include invention of fusion and hybrid fission/fusion nuclear fuel rod, combined cycle steam turbine, gas turbine nuclear power plants, neutron flux driven cold fusion in palladium; discovery of neutrino-driven nucleon fission chain reactions/nucleon decay chain reactions; discovery of graviton-driven fermion fission chain reactions; development of Bohr model of nucleons; development of Bohr model of gravitation; development of a generalized Bode's Law; development of a fundamental subatomic particle rest mass correlation. Home: 777 Mountainwood Rd Apt D Charlottesville VA 22903-6507

BLY, JAMES CHARLES, JR., finance company executive; b. Kane, Pa., Jan. 24, 1952; s. James Charles Bly Sr. and Dorothy Hau Bly Smith; m. Laurie Ann Ramadon, June 6, 1987; children: Alana W., Bridget R., James C. III, Chase N. BA, St. Bonaventure U., 1973. CLU, cert. mergers and acquisitions. Mgmt. trainee Conn. Gen. Life, Washington, 1974-76; rep. CIGNA Fin. Svcs., McLean, Va., 1976-79; mng. exec. Integrated Resources Equity Corp., N.Y.C., 1980-82; pres. Source Capital, Ltd., Pitts., 1982—; chmn., CEO Source Cos., LLC, 1998—. Mem. adv. bd. John J. Kirlin, Inc., Rockville, Md., 1980—, Royal Bank of Can., Global Fin. Svcs. Network, 1991—97; bd. dirs. Holgate Toy Co., Draper Holdings Bus. Trust, Bus. Growth Alliance, LLC. Mem.: Nat. Charitable Initiative, Alliance of Merger and Acquisition Advisors, Nat. Assn. Securities Dealers, Assn. Corp. Growth, Soc. Fin. Svcs. Profls., Allegheny Country Club, Edgeworth Club, The Stonedale Guns, Duquesne Club. Republican. Avocations: music, automobiles, history, travel, golf. Home: Spanish Tract Rd Sewickley PA 15143 Office: Source Cos LLC Ste 300 1606 Carmody Ct Sewickley PA 15143 Office Phone: 724-933-6600. Personal E-mail: soucapltd@aol.com.

BLY, ROBERT, poet; b. Madison, Minn., Dec. 23, 1926; s. Jacob Thomas and Alice (Aws) B.; m. Carolyn McLean, June 24, 1955 (div. 1979); children: Mary, Bridget, Noah Matthew Jacob, Micah John Padma.; m. Ruth Ray, June 27, 1980. Student, St. Olaf Coll., 1946-47; AB, Harvard, 1950; MA, U. Iowa, 1956. Editor, pub. Fifties Press (became Sixties, Seventies, Eighties, now Nineties), Madison, 1958—. Co-chmn. Am. Writers vs. Vietnam War, 1966—Author: (poems) Silence in the Snowy Fields, 1962, (with William Duffy and James Wright) The Lion's Tail and Eyes: Poems Written Out of Laziness and Silence, 1962, The Light Around the Body, 1967 (Nat. Book award 1968), Chrysanthemums, 1967, Ducks, 1968, The Morning Glory, 1969, The Teeth Mother Naked at Last, 1971, (with William E. Stafford and William Matthews) Poems for Tennessee, 1971, Christmas Eve Service at Midnight at Sr. Michael's, 1972, Water Under the Earth, 1972, The Dead Seal Near McClure's Beach, 1973, Sleepers Joining Hands, 1973, Jumping Out of Bed, 1973, The Hockey Poem, 1974, Point Reyes Poems, 1974, Old Man Rubbing His Eyes, 1975, The Loon, 1977, This Body is Made of Camphor and Gopherwood, 1977, Visiting Emily Dickinson's Grave and Other Poems, 1979, This Tree Will Be Here for a Thousand Years, 1979, The Man in The Black Coat Turns, 1981, Finding an Old Ant Mansion, 1981, Four Ramages, 1983, The Whole Moisty Night, 1983, Out of the Rolling Ocean, 1984, Mirabai Versions, 1984, In the Month of May, 1985, A Love of Minute

Particulars, 1985, Selected Poems, 1986 (LA Times Poetry award nominee 1986), Loving a Woman in Two Worlds, 1987, The Moon on a Fencepost, 1988, The Apple Found in the Plowing, 1989, What Have I Ever Lost By Dying?, 1992, Meditations on the Insatiable Soul, 1994, Morning Poems, 1997, Eating the Honey of Words: New and Selected Poems, 1999, The Winged Energy of Delight, 2004, My Sentence was a Thousand Years of Joy, 2005; (non-fiction) A Broadsheet Against the New York Times Book Review, 1961, Talking All Morning: Collected Conversations and Interviews, 1980, The Eight Stages of Translation, 1983, The Pillow and the Key, 1987, A Little Book on the Human Shadow, 1988, American Poetry: Wildness and Domesticity, 1990, Iron John: A Book About Men, 1990, Remembering James Wright, 1991, The Sibling Society, 1996, (with Marion Woodman) The Maiden King, 1998; editor: The Sea and the Honeycomb, 1966, A Poetry Reading Against the Viet Nam War, 1967, Forty Poems Touching Upon Recent History, 1970, Leaping Poetry, 1975, News of the Universe, 1980, Ten Love Poems, 1981, The Fifties and the Sixties, 10 vols., 1982, The Winged Life: The Poetic Voice of Henry David Thoreau, 1986, The Rag and Bone Shop of the Heart: Poems for Men, 1992, The Darkness Around Us is Deep: Selected Poems of William Stafford, 1993, The Soul Is Here for Its Own Joy, 1995; editor, The Best American Poetry, 1999; translator (from Swedish) The Story of Gösta Berling (Selma Lagerlöf), 1962, I Do Best Alone at Night (Gunnar Ekelöf), 1968, Twenty Poems of Tomas Tranströmer), 1972, Night Vision (Tomas Tranströmer), 1972, Friends, You Drank Some Darkness: Three Swedish Poets, Matinson, Ekelöf and Tranströmer, 1975, (from Norwegian) Knut Hamsun Hunger, 1967, Twenty Poems of Rolf Jacobsen, 1977, Twenty Poems of Olav H. Hauge, 1987, (from German) Twenty Poems of Georg Trakl, 1961, Selected Poems of Rainer Maria Rilke, 1980, (from Spanish) Twenty Poems of Cesar Vallejo, 1963, Forty Poems of Juan Ramon Jimenez, 1967, Twenty Poems of Pablo Neruda, 1967, Lorca and Jímenez: Selected Poems, 1973, Time Alone: Selected Poems of Antonio Machado, 1983, (with Lewis Hyde) (from Spanish) Twenty Poems of Vicente Aleixandre, 1977, (from Spanish), (prose) The Eight Stages of Translation, 1983, A Little Book on the Human Shadow, 1986, American Poetry: Wildness and Domesticity, 1990, Remembering James Wright, 1991, (from French) Ten Poems of Francis Ponge, 1990, Ten Poems of Robert Bly Inspired by the Poems of Francis Ponge, 1990, (from Rajasthani) Mirabai Versions, 1993, (from Hindi and English) The Kabir Book: 44 of the Ecstatic Poems of Kabir, 1977, The Lightning Shouls Have Fallen on Ghalib: Selected Poems of Ghalib (with Sunil Dutta), 1999. Served with USNR, 1944-45. Recipient award Nat. Inst. Arts and Letters, Nat. Book award in poetry, 1968; Fulbright grantee, 1956-57; Amy Lowell fellow, 1964-65; Guggenheim fellow, 1965-66, 72-73; Rockefeller Found. fellow, 1967 Mem. Am. Acad. Arts and Letters. Address: 1904 Girard Ave S Minneapolis MN 55403-2945*

BLYAKHMAN, YEFIM MOISEI, chemist, researcher; b. Leningrad, Russia, Dec. 11, 1937; came to U.S., 1986; s. Moisei Isaak Blyakhman and Anna S. (Itzkov) Lohs; m. Irina A. Teverovskaya, Mar. 25, 1958; 1 child, Alexander. M in Chem. Engring., Leningrad Inst. Tech., 1960, PhD in Polymer Chemistry, 1965. Chem. engr. R&D Prodn., Leningrad, 1960-64; group leader Assn. Plast-Polymer, Leningrad, 1965-71, lab. dir., 1972-84; staff scientist Ciba-Geigy, Ardsley, N.Y., 1987-92; sr. staff scientist Ciba Specialty Chemicals, Brewster, N.Y., 1993—. Adv. bd. Org. Sci. Tech. Advancement, Leningrad, 1965-81; scientific technological counsel Plast-polymer R&D and Prodn., Leningrad, 1972-78. Contbr. 154 articles to books and profl. jours.; contbr. article to Polymer Encyclopedia, 1977. Recipient 3 Gold medals Govt. Russia, Moscow, 1968, 72, 73. Mem. Am. Chem. Soc., Soc. Advancement Materials Process Engrs. Achievements include 197 patents in the area of thermoset polymers chemistry and tech. New routes to materials having high thermal stability, mechanical strength, and corrosion resistance for structural composites, adhesives coatings, electrical and electronic. Designer of numerous inventions from 1961-98 with 3 gold medals awarded in 1965, 67, 71. Home: Apt 2L 4705 Henry Hudson Pkwy Bronx NY 10471-3231 Office: Ciba Specialty Chemicals 281 Fields Ln Brewster NY 10509-2624 Office Phone: 914-785-3104.

BLYN, GEORGE, economics educator; b. N.Y.C., May 2, 1919; s. Philip and Rose (Faiby) B.; m. Charlotte Lilly; children: Stefany, Roslyn, Corliann. BA, U. Pa., 1951, MA, 1953, PhD, 1961. Chmn. econs. dept. Rutgers U., Camden, N.J., 1962-71, 77-79, 83-89, prof. emeritus, 1989—. Contbg. author: Nutritional Adequacy of Punjab and Haryana Cultivator Families, 1980, Walt Whitman and Labor, 1984, Income Distribution Among Haryans and Punjab Cultivators, 1983, Green Revolution Revisited, 1983; author: Agricultural Trends in India, 1966. Sgt. U.S. Army, 1943-46, ETO. Named Sr. Faculty Rsch. Fellow, Am. Inst. Indian Studies, 1965-66, 1979; recipient George Harrison Fellowship, U. Pa., 1952-53. Mem. Am. Econs. Assn., Assn. Am. Geographers, Assn. Indian Econ. Studies, Del. Valley Geographers Assn. (exec. com. 1970-89) Avocations: acting, singing, running. Home: 511 Winding Way Merion Station PA 19066-1118 Office: Rutgers U Dept Econs Camden NJ 08102

BLYNN, GUY MARC, lawyer; b. Bklyn., May 26, 1945; s. S. Jerry and Viola T. Vogel Blynn; children: Daniel Scott, Harlan Sterling, Aaron Seth. BS in Econs. cum laude, U. Pa., Wharton Sch. of Fin. Commerce, 1967; JD cum laude, Harvard U., 1970. Bar: N.C., N.Y., U.S. Ct. of Appeals for Fed. Cir., U.S. Ct. of Appeals for the 2d Cir., U.S. Dist. Cts. for the Middle Dist. of N.C., Southern and Eastern Dist. N.Y. Assoc. Kaye, Scholer, Fierman, Hays & Handler, N.Y.C., 1970-78; assoc. counsel R.J. Reynolds Industries Inc., Winston Salem, N.C., 1978-79; sr. counsel RJR Nabisco Inc., Winston Salem, N.C., 1979-86; dep. gen. counsel R.J. Reynolds Tobacco Co., Winston Salem, N.C., 1986-1989, v.p., dep. gen. counsel, sec., 1989—. Lectr. Wake Forest U. Sch. of Law, 1980-93; cons. Dept. Commerce, 1987-90. Contbr. articles to profl. jours. Chmn. Brand Names Edn. Found., 1988-94; bd. dirs. N.C. Vol. Lawyers for the Arts, 1985-91, pres., 1987-91; bd. dirs. Urban League Winston-Salem. Mem. ABA, Am. Arbitration Assn. (panel of arbitrators 1975-95), Carolina Patent Trademark & Copyright Law Assn. (v.p. 1979-80, pres. 1980-81), Am. Intellectul Property Law Assn. (chmn. taxation and fin. matters com. 1991-92), Am. Bar Assn. Forum Com. on Entertainment And Sports Industries, Assn. of Bar of City Of N.Y. (chmn. com. on trademarks and unfair competition 1975-78, subcommittee on patent and trademark office practice 1976-77), Anti-Defamation League (N.C. regional adv. bd. 1987—, chmn. elect 1991-93, chmn. 1993—, vice chmn. 1990-91), U.S. Trademark Assn. (bd. dirs. 1982-90, v.p. 1984-85, exec. v.p. 1985-86, pres., chmn. 1986-87). Home: PO Box 20383 Winston Salem NC 27120-0383 Office: R J Reynolds Tobacco Co 401 N Main St Winston Salem NC 27101-3804

BLYTH, MYRNA GREENSTEIN, publishing executive; b. N.Y.C., Mar. 22, 1939; d. Benjamin and Betty (Austin) Greenstein; m. Jeffrey Blyth, Nov. 25, 1962; children: Jonathan, Graham. BA, Bennington (Vt.) Coll., 1960. Sr. editor Datebook mag., N.Y.C., 1960-62, Ingenue mag., N.Y.C., 1963-68; book editor Family Health mag., 1968-71; book and fiction editor, then assoc. editor Family Circle mag., N.Y.C., 1972-78, exec. editor, 1978-81; editor-in-chief Ladies' Home Jour., 1981—2002, pub. dir., sr. v.p., 1987—2002, editor-in-chief, pub. dir., More Mag., 1998—2002, v.p., editl. dir., 2002—03; with new product devel. Meredith Corp., 2002—03; freelance writer. Mem. Pres.' commn. White House Fellows, 2002—; mem. adv. com. for ORIWH, NIH. Author: Cousin Suzanne, 1975, For Better and For Worse, 1978, Spin Sisters, 2004; columnist: Nat. Rev. Online, NY Sun; contbr. articles to New Yorker mag., New York mag., Redbook mag., Cosmopolitan mag., Readers Digest. Del. White House Conf. on Aging; mem. nat. adv. bd. Susan G. Komen Breast Cancer Found.; mem. adv. com. ORWH at NIH; mem. Pres.'s Commn on White House Fellows. Recipient Headliner award Women in Comms., Inc., 1992, Human Rels. award, Am. Jewish Com.'s Pub. Divsn., 1992, Henry Johnson Fisher award, 1999. Mem.: Women's Forum, Women's Media Group, N.Y. Women in Comm., Inc. (past pres., Amb. of Excellence, Matrix award 1988), Am. Soc. Mag. Editors, Overseas Press Club (bd. govs.), Authors League.

BOADLE-BIBER, MARGARET CLARE, physiologist, educator; b. Melbourne, Australia, Jan. 18, 1943; arrived in U.S., 1967; d. Campbell Dean and Constance Ellen (Browne) Boadle; m. Thomas Ulrich Leonard Biber, Oct. 8, 1969; 1 child, Eric Gustav Nicholas Biber. BS, U. Coll. London, 1964; DPhil, Oxford (Eng.) U., 1967. Rsch. assoc. pharm. dept. Yale U. Sch. Medicine, New Haven, 1968-69, instr. pharm. dept., 1969-71, asst. prof. pharm. dept., 1971-75; assoc. prof. physiology dept. Va. Commonwealth U., Richmond, 1975-87, prof., 1987—, interim chair, 1991-93, chair, 1993—. Contbr. articles to profl. jours. Mem.: Soc. Neuroscience, Am. Soc. Pharm. and Exptl. Therapeutics, Am. Soc. Neurochemistry. Office: Va Commonwealth U 1101 E Marshall St Richmond VA 23298-0551 Office Phone: 804-828-9756. Business E-Mail: mcbiber@vcu.edu, mbiber@mail2.vcu.edu.

BOAKES, NORMA J., mathematics professor; b. Atlantic City, Feb. 8, 1971; d. Betty J. and Norman P. Corson; m. Keith Wuertz, June 30, 1995 (div. Jan. 5, 2005); children: Matthew Benjamin, Ean Bryce. BA in Math., Glassboro State Coll., NJ, 1993; MA in Subject Matter Tchg. Math., Rowan U., NJ, 2000; D in Curriculum, Instrn., and Tech. Edn., Temple U., Pa., 2001—. Secondary Math. Tchr. Cert. NJ, 1993. H.s. math. instr. Greater Egg Harbor Regional H.S. Dist., Absecon, NJ, 1994—95, Mays Landing, NJ, 1995—2001; instr. Richard Stockton Coll. NJ. Office Tchr. Edn., Pomona, NJ, 2002—05. Recipient Resolution of Recognition, Twp. of Hamilton, Atlantic County, NJ, 1999, Disting. Secondary Sch. Tchr. Nomination, Princeton U., 1999, Internat. Space Week award, Spaceweek Internat., 1999; Consortium grant, NJ. Bus., Industry, and Sci. Edn., 1999, 2000, Classroom grant, McDonald's Corp., 1999, 2000. Mem.: Phi Delta Kappa (assoc.), Am. Edn. Rsch. Assn. (assoc.), Assn. of Math. Tchrs. NJ. (assoc.), Nat. Coun. of Tchrs. Math. (assoc.). Achievements include research in Self Efficacy Beliefs of Pre Service Elementary Science Teacher; development of Undergraduate level mathematics content courses for pre-service elementary school teachers. Home: 3713 Starlight Cir Mays Landing NJ 08330 Office: Richard Stockton Coll NJ Office of Teacher Education PO Box 195 Pomona NJ 08240-0195 Office Phone: 609-652-4668. Office Fax: 609-748-5528. Personal E-mail: nboakes@mayslanding.com. Business E-Mail: norma.boakes@stockton.edu.

BOAL, DEAN, retired arts center administrator, educator; b. Longmont, Colo., Oct. 20, 1931; s. Elmer C. and L. Mildred (Snodgrass) B.; m. Ellen Christine TeSelle, Aug. 23, 1957; children: Brett, Jed. B.Music, B.Music Edn., U. Colo., 1953; M.Music, Ind. U., 1956; D. Musical Arts, U. Colo., 1959. Mem. faculty Hastings (Nebr.) Coll., 1958-60; head piano dept. Bradley U., Peoria, Ill., 1960-66; dean, pianist Peabody Conservatory, Balt., 1966-70; prof. piano, chair music SUNY, Fredonia, 1970-73; pres. St. Louis Conservatory, 1973-76; dir. radio sta. KWMU, St. Louis, 1976-78; v.p., gen. mgr. Sta. WETA-FM, Washington, 1978-83; dir. arts and performance programs Nat. Pub. Radio, Washington, 1982-89; pres. Interlochen (Mich.) Ctr. for the Arts, 1989-95; pres. emeritus, 1995—. Author: Concepts and Skills for the Piano, Book I, 1969, Book II, 1970, Interlochen: A Home for The Arts, 1998; contbr. articles to profl. jours. Mem. adv. bd U. Colo. Coll. Music, 1987-2000; trustee Alma Coll., 1992-95; bd. dirs., chmn. Peak Assn. of the Arts, 1998-2000. Served with U.S. Army, 1953-55. Woodrow Wilson teaching fellow, 1983-89; recipient Disting. Alumnus award in Profl. Music Univ. Colo., 1987. Mem. Eastern Public Radio Network (chmn. 1979-82), Coll. Music Soc., Pi Kappa Lambda, Mu Phi Epsilon, Phi Mu Alpha. Presbyterian.

BOAL, ELLIS, lawyer; b. Evanston, Ill., Sept. 27, 1944; s. Stewart and Susan (Ballard) B.; m. Marilyn Hendrick Morehead, Aug. 11, 1979. AB, Bowdoin Coll., 1966; JD, Wayne State U., 1972. Bar: Mich. 1973, U.S. Dist. Ct. (ea. dist.) Mich. 1973, U.S. Ct. Appeals (D.C. and 6th cirs.) 1978, U.S. Ct. Appeals (1st cir.) 1981, U.S. Ct. Appeals (7th cir.) 1993. Sole practice, Detroit, 1974—. Author: Teamster Rank and File Legal Rights Handbook, rev. edit., 1984; co-producer CD "500 Days", 1996. Mem. Nat. Lawyers Guild, Belle Isle Runners, Phi Beta Kappa. Socialist. Office: 925 Ford Bldg Detroit MI 48226-3988

BOAL, LYNDALL ELIZABETH, social worker; b. London, Feb. 19, 1936; came to U.S., 1953; d. George Woodall and Mary Barbara (Pearce) Cadbury; m. R. Bradlee Boal Aug. 29, 1959 (div. Sept. 1983); children: Jennifer, Peter. BA with honors, Swarthmore (Pa.) Coll., 1957; MS, Simmons Coll., Boston, 1959. Cert. sch. social worker, N.Y.; lic. social worker, Mass. Social worker Beth Israel Hosp., Boston, 1959-60, Mt. Sinai Hosp., N.Y.C., 1960-61, Meml. Sloan-Kettering Hosp., N.Y.C., 1961-63; cons. Dist. Nursing Svc., Mt. Kisco, N.Y., 1964-65; exec. dir. Planned Parenthood, Mt. Kisco, N.Y., 1965-68; dir. social worker No. Westchester Hosp., Mt. Kisco, N.Y., 1968-78; social worker Fox lane High Sch., Bedford Schs, 1978-81; chmn. com. on handicapped Bedford (N.Y.) Schs., 1981-86; social worker Chappaqua (N.Y.) Sch., 1988—; instr. Fordham U. Sch. Social Svcs., 1994—2003. Bd. dirs. No. Westchester Guidance Ctr., Mt. Kisco, 2003-05; pres. Soc. Hosp. Social Work Dirs., Westchester, N.Y., 1976-78; mem. adv. bd. Mercy Coll. Social Work Program, 1997—, Concordia Coll. Social Work Program, 2001—; v.p. Westchester Children's Assn., 1999-2004; mem. N.Y. State Bd. for Social Work, 2004—. Chmn. Narcotics Guidance Coun., Bedford, 1972-75; No. Westchester Coun. Equality pres., Bedford, 1984-86; bd. dirs. Sherrill House, Boston, 1986-88; Dem. committeeman, Bedford, 1983-86. Mem. NASW (sec. N.Y. state chpt. 1993-95, pres. N.Y. State chpt. 1996-98, chair state pers. com. 1993-94, pres. Westchester divsn. 1969-71, 91-92, Merit Svc. award Westchester divsn. 1993, sch. social work sect. steering com. 1994-96), N.Y. State Sch. Social Workers Assn., Kappa Delta Pi. Democrat. Mem. Soc. Of Friends. Avocations: skiing, travel, spending time with family. Home: 508 Millwood Rd Mount Kisco NY 10549-3700 Office: Chappaqua Schs Off of Sch Social Worker Chappaqua NY 10514 Office Phone: 914-238-6170 X 237.

BOALER, JO, education educator; BSc in Psychology, U. Liverpool, Eng., 1985; MA in Math. Edn., London U., 1991, PhD in Math. Edn., 1996. Tchr. secondary sch. math., Camden, London, 1986—89; dep. dir. math. assessment project King's Coll., London U., 1989—93, lectr., rschr. on math. edn., 1993—98; assoc. prof. Stanford (Calif.) U., 2000—. Mem. Math. Edn. Study Panel; bd. dirs. Gender and Edn. jour. Mem.: Internat. Orgn. for Women in Math. Edn. Office: Stanford U Sch Edn 485 Lasuen Mall Stanford CA 94305-3096*

BOALS, TIMOTHY JAY, bilingual educator; b. Indpls., Dec. 18, 1960; s. Robert E. and Else V. (Kayse) B.; m. Christine Mathias, May 5, 1990; 1 child, Kenneth Alan. BA in Modern Langs., Wabash Coll., 1983; MA in Spanish, U. Va., 1986. Spanish instr. U. Va., Charlottesville, 1983-86; Spanish tchr. Foxcroft Sch., Middleburg, Va., 1987-89; vis. instr. Wabash Coll., Crawfordsville, Ind., 1989-90; lang. minority cons., title VII coord. Ind. Dept. Edn., Indpls., 1990—. Editor newsletter Lang. Minority News, 1990—. Mem. ASCD, Nat. Assn. for Bilingual Edn., Ind. Tchrs. of English to Speakers of Other Langs. Avocations: reading, hiking, guitar, tennis, soccer. Home: 1011 Gaslight Dr Sun Prairie WI 53590-3439 Office: Ind Dept Edn 229 State House Indianapolis IN 46204

BOAMAH-WIAFE, DANIEL, geographer, researcher; s. Daniel Kwabena Boamah and Elizabeth Akosua Adutwumwah; m. Lydia Lydia Ampomah, Sept. 11, 1949; children: Michael Yaw, Daniel Kwabena Jr. PhD, U. of Wis., 1978. Cert. tchr.'s A cert. Ghana Edn. Svc. Assoc. prof. U. Nebr., Omaha, 1986—; prof. geography and Black studies Calif. State U., Chico, 1991—92. Dir. Black studies Calif. State U., Chico, 1991—92. Contbr. Encyclopedia of the Great Plains. Independent. Methodist. Avocations: travel, research and writing, amateur photographer. Office: U Nebr 60th and Dodge Omaha NE 68182-0041 Office Phone: 402-554-2412.

BOARD, JOSEPH BRECKINRIDGE, JR., political scientist, educator; b. Princeton, Ind., Mar. 5, 1931; s. Joseph Breckinridge and Rachel Eleanor (Unthank) B.; children from previous marriage: Ian Robert, Annika Caroline, Amanda Anne; m. Mary Squire, Jan. 1, 1998. AB with highest honors, Ind. U., 1953, JD, 1958, PhD, 1962; BA (Rhodes scholar 1953-55), Oxford (Eng.) U., 1955, MA, 1961; PhD (hon.), Umea U., Sweden, 1973. Tchg. fellow govt. Ind. U., 1955-58, lectr. govt., 1958; asst. prof. polit. sci. Elmira Coll., 1959-61; assoc. prof. polit. sci., chmn. dept. Cornell Coll., 1961-64; prof. polit. sci., chmn. dept. Union Coll., Schenectady, 1964—, Robert Porter Patterson prof. govt., 1973—, chmn. faculty, 1983-85; pres. Paralegals-Plus Assocs., Inc., 1986—. Acad. visitor London Sch. Econs. and Polit. Sci., 1972-73; adj. prof. Albany Law Sch., 1974—; lectr. Green Mountain Acd. Lifelong Learning; scholar-in-residence Sch. Law Ind. U., 1999—; acting prof., chmn. dept. polit. sci. U. Umea, 1979; vis. prof. U. Paris (Sorbonne), 1987; mem. Rhodes Scholarship Selection Com. Nebr., 1961-62, Iowa, 1963-64, N.Y., 1991, 92; mem. regional selection com. for Woodrow Wilson Fellowships, 1966—; mem. exec. coun. Iowa Conf. Polit. Scientists, 1963-65; spl. adv. coll. and univ. affairs Young Citizens for Johnson, 1964; cons. Nat. Endowment Humanities, 1968, N.Y. State Dept. Edn., 1968; mem. polit. sci. adv. com. Fulbright-Hays Program, 1969-73; assoc., adv. com. for Western Europe Coun. for Internat. Exchange of Scholars; chmn. Scandinavian peer rev. com. Linkages Project; mem. U.S. Com. on NATO Fellowships; cons., co-host Nobel Prize broadcast Nat. Pub. Radio, 1976; vis. fellow Oriel Coll., Oxford, 1994—; acad. assoc. The Atlantic Coun.; chair bd. advisors Transnat. Rsch. Project on Effects of European Unification. Author: The Government and Politics of Sweden, 1970. Mem. bd. advisors Schenectady Salvation Army; trustee, treas. Schnectady County C.C.; trustee, patron Oriel Coll. (Oxford U.), Devel. Trust, 1991—; pres. bd. trustees Martha Canfield Libr., Arlington, Vt.; vestry mem. Zion Episcopal Ch., Manchester, Vt.; bd. dirs. Vt. Coun. on World Affairs Fulbright lectr. Sweden, 1968-69; Ctrl. Am. fellow Assoc. Colls. Midwest, 1962, NDEA fellow, Portuguese, 1963, Acad. Law Sch. Alumni fellow Ind. U.; recipient Disting. Svc. award SUNY Bd. Trustees Cmty. Colls., 1997. Mem. AAUP, Am. Assn. Rhodes Scholars, Am. Polit. Sci. Assn., Ind. Bar, Am. Arbitration Assn., Am-Scandinavian Found. (com. on fellowships 1981-), Northeastern Polit. Sci. Assn. (exec. Coun. 1972), Soc. for Advancement Scandinavian Studies (exec. coun. 1972), United Oxford and Cambridge U. Club (London), Soc. Letters (Lund U.), Acacia, Phi Beta Kappa. Democrat. Episcopalian. Home: 3740 Rt 313 W Arlington VT 05250-8998 Office: Union Coll Political Sci Dept Schenectady NY 12308 E-mail: boardj@sover.net.

BOARDMAN, CONNIE, former mayor, biologist, educator; BS, MS, Calif. State U., Long Beach. Prof. biology Cerriots C.C., Norwalk. Mem. econ. devel. com. Huntington Beach (Calif.) City Coun., mem. intergovernmental com., mem. animal care svcs. com., mem. comm. com.; alt. mem. Orange County Sanitation Dist.; coun. liaison Allied Arts Bd., Environ. Bd., Mobile Home Adv. Bd., Oakview Task Force, Sister City Assn.; mem. city coun. City of Huntington Beach, 2000—, mayor, 2002—03. Office: City of Huntington Beach 2000 Main St Huntington Beach CA 92648

BOARDMAN, D. DIXON (DENNIE DIXON BOARDMAN), investment banker; b. Nov. 7, 1945; s. T. Dennie Boardman and Vivian Dixon; m. Pauline Munn Baker (div. 1999); children: Serena Pauline, Samantha Vivian; m. Princess Arriana Hohenlohe, June 30, 2001. Student, McGill U. Sr. v.p. Kidder, Peabody; mem. chairman's coun. UBS PaineWebber; founder Optima Group, 1988—; mng. gen. ptnr. Optima Fund Mgmt., NYC, mng. dir. Bermuda. Dir. Fla. Crystals Corp.; adv. bd. J.C. Bamford Excavators, England; frequent lectr. in field. Trustee The Game Conservancy Trust; past chmn. Special Projects Com. Meml. Sloan Kettering Cancer Ctr., mem. Pres.'s Coun. Mem.: Deepdale Golf Club (pres.). Office: Optima Fund Mgmt 10 E 53rd St 29th fl New York NY 10022 also: Optima Fund Mgmt 73 Front St Hamilton HM12 Bermuda Office Phone: 212-484-3000. Office Fax: 212-484-3001.

BOARDMAN, DAVID, newspaper editor; m. Barbara Winslow; children: Emily, Madeline. BS in Journalism, Northwestern U., 1979; M in Comm., U. Wash., 1983. Copy editor Football Weekly, Chgo., 1977-79; reporter Anacortes (Wash.) American, 1979-80, Skagit Valley Herald, Mt. Vernon, Wash., 1980-81; reporter, copy editor The News Tribune, Tacoma, 1981-83; copy editor The Seattle Times, 1983, editor, reporter, 1984, nat. editor, 1984-86, local news editor, 1986-87, asst. city editor, 1987-90, regional editor, 1990-96, metro. editor, 1997—, asst. mng. editor, 1997—2003, mgn. editor, 2003—. Vis. faculty Poynter Inst. Media Studies, St. Petersburg, Fla. Recipient Goldsmith Prize in Investigative Reporting JFK Sch. Govt. Harvard U., 1993, Worth Bingham prize, 1993, Investigative Reporters and Editors award, 1993, AP Mng. Editors Pub. Svc. award, 1992, 1st place nat. reporting Pulitzer Prize, 1990, lead editor Pulitzer Prize in investigative reporting, 1997; finalist Pulitzer Prize, 1993, 98, 99, 2002, 03; juror Pulitzer Prizes, 1999-2000; fellow Japan-IBCC fellowship Ctr. Fgn. Journalists, 1995. Office: The Seattle Times PO Box 70 1120 John St Seattle WA 98109-5321 E-mail: dboardman@seattletimes.com.

BOARDMAN, EDNA, retired library media specialist, educator; b. Frazer, Mont., Jan. 22, 1935; d. Karl and Christina (Zweigle) Schieve; foster parents Emil and Ella Berg; m. Harold D. Boardman, June 1, 1959 (dec. 1985); children: Chase H., Mary E. BS, Minot State U., 1958. Cert. media specialist. English tchr. Garrison (N.D.) H.S., 1958-60, Rugby (N.D.) H.S., 1968-70, libr. media specialist, 1970-76, Magic City Campus Minot (N.D.) H.S., 1976-98; ret. Author: Censorship: The Problem that Won't Go Away, 1992, All Things Decently and in Order: And Other Writing on a Germans from Russia Heritage, 1997; contbr. articles to profl. jours. Bd. dirs. Germans from Russia Heritage Soc., Bismarck, N.D., 1990—; active Vincent United Meth. Ch., Minot, 1976—, Minot Commn. on Status of Women, 1980-82. Mem. NEA, N.D. Libr. Assn. (sect. pres. 1986-89), Sch. Libr. Media Assn. Avocations: writing, needlecrafts, photography, travel, reading. Home: 1914 N 16th St Apt 1 Bismarck ND 58501-2029

BOARDMAN, ELIZABETH DRAKE, computer security professional; b. Columbus, Ohio, Oct. 14, 1955; d. Jack Martin and Marilyn Hawk Boardman; children: Melissa Grimsley, Stephanie Grimsley. BS Bus. Adminstrn., Ohio State U., 1977; BS in Computer sci., We. Ill. U., 2003; MS in Computer Engring. and Info. Assurance, Iowa State U., 2005, MS in Info. Assurance and Computer Engring., 2006. Officer (lt., unrestricted line) U.S. Navy, Various, 1977—85; sr. computer software analyst Analysis & Tech., North Stonington, Conn., 1985—88; database adminstr. We. Ill. U., Macomb, Ill., 2000—02; tchg. asst. computer sci. Iowa State U., Ames, 2003; info. security specialist Boeing, 2005—. Mem., bd. of dirs. Girl Scouts Shining Trail Coun., Burlington, Iowa, 1995—99; fin. com. Trinity United Meth. Ch., Keokuk, Iowa, 2000—02; blue & gold officer U.S. Naval Acad., Annapolis, Md., 1992—94; vol. Girl Scouts of U.S.A., various, 1990—99; life mem. Girl Scouts. CDR (Intelligence) USNR, 1985—2004. Named Iowa Cmty. Hero Olympic Torch Bearer, Iowa Com. for Olympic Torch Run, 1996. Mem.: AAUW, Western Ill. Alumni Assn., Mil. Officers Assn. Am., The Ohio State U. Alumni Assn., Naval Res. Assn., Phi Kappa Phi, Upsilon Pi Epsilon, Chi Omega. Protestant. Avocations: volunteer work, computers, travel. Personal E-mail: nontradmisc@msn.com.

BOARDMAN, EUNICE, retired music educator; b. Cordova, Ill., Jan. 27, 1926; d. George Hollister and Anna Bryson (Feaster) Boardman. B. Mus. Edn., Cornell Coll., 1947; M. Mus. Edn., Columbia U., 1951; Ed.D., U. Ill., 1963; DFA (hon.), Cornell Coll., 1995. Tchr. music pub. schs., Iowa, 1947-55; prof. music edn. Wichita State U., Kans., 1955-72; vis. prof. mus. edn. Normal State U., Ill., 1972-74, Roosevelt U., Chgo., 1974-75; prof. mus. edn. U. Wis., Madison, 1975-89, dir. Sch. Music, 1980-89; prof. music, dir. grad. program in music edn. U. Ill., Urbana, 1989-98; ret. Author: Musical Growth in Elementary School, 1963, 6th rev. edit., 1996, Exploring Music, 1966, 3d rev. edit., 1975, The Music Book, 1980, 2d rev. edit., 1984, Holt Music, 1987; editor: Dimensions of Musical Thinking, 1989, Dimensions of Musical Thinking: A Different Kind of Music, 2002, Up the Mississippi: A Journey of the Blues, 2002. Named to MENC Hall of Fame, 2004. Mem. Soc. Music Tchr. Edn. (chmn. 1984-86), Music Educators Nat. Conf. Avocations: reading, antiques.

BOARDMAN, HAROLD FREDERICK, JR., lawyer, retired corporate financial executive; b. Darby, Pa., Nov. 23, 1939; s. Harold Frederick and Juanita (Sorzano) B.; m. Martha Eltie, May 23, 1987; children: Kimberly, Leslie, Ashley, Kyle BS, Trinity Coll., Hartford, Conn., 1961; JD with honors, George Washington U., 1964; grad. advanced mgmt. program, Duke U., 1988. Bar: D.C. 1964, Hawaii 1971, N.J. 1974, U.S. Dist. Ct. D.C. 1965, U.S. Ct. Appeals (D.C. cir.) 1965, U.S. Ct. Mil. Appeals 1965, U.S. Supreme Ct. 1969.

Gen. atty. Fed. Home Loan Bank Bd., Washington, 1964-66; atty. Hoffmann-LaRoche, Inc., Nutley, N.J., 1966, with, 1973-94, sec., 1979-94, assoc. gen. counsel, 1981-88, v.p., gen. counsel, bd. dirs., exec. com., 1989—94; of counsel Crummy, Del Deo, Dolan, Griffinger & Vecchione, Newark, 1995-96; exec. v.p., gen. counsel, bd. dirs. Rhone-Poulenc Inc., Princeton, NJ, 1996—97; sr. v.p., gen. counsel, bd. dirs., exec. com Rhone Poulenc Rorer, Collegeville, Pa., 1998-99; sr. v.p.-legal Aventis Pharms., 1999-2000, retired, 2000; of counsel Gibbons, Del Deo, Dolan, Griffinger & Vecchione, Newark, 2001—. Bd. suprs. Hideaway Taxing Dist., 2004—; bd. dirs.m sec. Hideaway Beach Assn., 2004—. Capt. JAGC USAF, 1966—73. Mem.: Pharm. Mfrs. Assn. (exec. com. law sect. 1991—94), D.C. Bar Assn., Hawaii Bar Assn., N.J. Bar Assn. Episcopalian. Avocations: golf, boating. Home: 680 Waterside Dr Marco Island FL 34145 Home (Summer): 25 Walnut Rd Ocean City NJ 08226

BOARDMAN, JOHN MICHAEL, mathematician, educator; b. Manchester, Eng., Feb. 13, 1938; arrived in U.S., 1969, naturalized, 1973; s. William Edgar and Carrie (Brown) B.; m. Jacqueline O'Brien Schulman, 1967 (div. 1977); children: Susan, Andrew. BA, Trinity Coll., Cambridge U., 1961, PhD, 1965. Vis. lectr. U. Chgo., 1966-67; asst. lectr. U. Warwick, England, 1967-68; assoc. prof. Johns Hopkins U., Balt., 1969-72, prof., 1972—. Author: Singularities of Differentiable Maps, 1967, (with R.M. Vogt) Homotopy Invariant Algebraic Structures on Topological Spaces, 1973, Modular Representations on the Homology of Powers of Real Projective Space, 1993; (with D.C. Johnson and W.S. Wilson) Unstable Operations on Generalized Cohomology, 1995, Conditionally Convergent Spectral Sequences, 1999. Served with RAF, 1956-58. Sci. Rsch. Coun. fellow, 1964-66; NSF grantee, 1970-88. Mem. Am. Math. Soc. Mem. Soc. Of Friends. Home: 6217 Northwood Dr Baltimore MD 21212-2802 Office: Johns Hopkins U Dept Math 3400 N Charles St Baltimore MD 21218-2686

BOARDMAN, JOSEPH H., federal agency administrator; b. Dec. 1948; m. Joanne Boardman; children: Joe Jr., Emily, Philip. BS, Cornell U.; MS in Mgmt. Sci., SUNY, Binghamton. Mgr. Rome Transp., Rome Parking Authority; commr. pub. transp. Broome County, NY, 1981—88; CEO Progressive Transp. Svcs., Inc., Elmira, NY; dep. commr. NY State Dept. Transp., 1995, asst. commr. Office Pub. Transp., acting commr., 1997, commr., 1997—2005; adminstr. Fed. Railroad Adminstrn., Washington, DC, 2005—. With USAF, 1966—69. Mem.: Am. Pub. Transit Assn., NY Pub. Transit Assn. (pres. 1987—89). Office: Fed Railroad Adminstrn 1120 Vermont Ave NW, 7th Fl Washington DC 20590 Office Phone: 202-493-6014. Office Fax: 202-493-6009.*

BOARDMAN, JOSEPH P., healthcare professional, music educator; s. Robert Lawrence Boardman Sr. and Dolores Boardman; children: Eric, Andrew. BS in Music Edn., William Paterson Coll., 1985; M in Music Performance, SUNY, Stony Brook, 1987. Pvt. music instr., Huntington Station, 1980—; adminstr. AHRC Suffolk, Bohemia, 1990—94; music tchr. Half Hollow Hills Sch. Dist., Dix Hills., 1997—2002, L.I. Luth. Jr./Sr. H.S., Brookville, 2002—. Freelance musician, 1980—; marching band instr. JFK Plainview-Old Bethany H.S., NY, 2000—; svc. coord. supr. United Cerebral Palsy Suffolk, Hauppauge, NY, 1993—; trainer Office of Mental Retardation and Devel. Disabilities, Huppauge, NY, 2003—. Mem.: Huntington Arts Coun., Suffolk County Music Educators Assn., Am. Fedn. Musicians. Avocation: carpentry. Home: 203 W Pulaski Rd Huntington Station NY 11746 Office: United Cerebral Palsy Suffolk 250 Mercas Blvd Hauppauge NY 11788

BOARDMAN, ROBERT A., retired lawyer; b. 1947; BA, Muskingum Coll., 1969; JD, Case Western Reserve U., 1972. Bar: Ohio 1972, Colo. 1976. Assoc. atty. Roetzel & Andress, 1972-75, atty., 1975-83; asst. gen. coun., sec. Manville Corp., Denver, 1983-87, v.p., sec., 1988-90; sr. v.p., gen. coun. Navistar Internat. Corp., Chgo., 1990—2004, ret., 2004. Office: Navistar Internat Corp 4201 Winfield Rd Warrenville IL 60555 Business E-Mail: robert.boardman@nav-international.com.

BOARDMAN, SEYMOUR, artist; b. Bklyn., Dec. 29, 1921; s. Joseph and Bessie (Warren) B. BSS, CCNY, 1942; postgrad., Ecole des Beaux-Arts, Paris, 1946-47, Atelier Fernand Leger, 1948, Art Students League, N.Y.C., 1949-50, Ecole de la Grande Chaumiere, 1950-51. One-man shows, Galerie Mai, Paris, 1951, Martha Jackson Gallery, N.Y.C., 1955, 56, Stephen Radich Gallery, N.Y.C., 1960-61, 62, A.M. Sachs Gallery, N.Y.C., 1965, 67, 68, Dorsky Gallery, N.Y.C., 1972, Aaron Berman Gallery, N.Y.C., 1978, Anita Shapolsky Gallery, N.Y.C., 1987, 91, Anderson Gallery, Buffalo, 1994; group shows include, Carnegie Internat., Pitts., 1955, Whitney Mus. Am. Art, 1955, 61, 67, Nebr. Art Assn., 1956, Kunsthalle, Basel, Switzerland, 1964, Santa Barbara Art Mus., 1964, Albright-Knox Gallery, Buffalo, 1967, Cornell U., 1971, Anita Shapolsky Gallery, N.Y.C., 1986, David Anderson Gallery, Buffalo, 1991-92; represented in permanent collections, Whitney Mus. Am. Art, Guggenheim Mus., Walker Art Ctr., Mpls., Santa Barbara Mus. Art, NYU. Served with USAAF, 1942-46. Longview Found. grantee, 1963; Guggenheim Found. fellow, 1972-73; Adolph and Esther Gottlieb Found. grantee, 1979, 83; Pollock-Krasner Found. grantee, 1985-86, 91, 98, 2001, 2003. Address: 234 W 27th St New York NY 10001-5901 Office Phone: 212-255-3897.

BOARDMAN, SHELBY J., academic administrator; 2 children. BA in Geology with honors, Miami U., Ohio, 1966; MS in Econ. Geology, U. Mich., 1969, PhD in Petrology, 1971. Mem. geology dept. Carleton Coll., Northfield, Minn., 1971—, Charles L. Denison prof. geology, geology dept. chair, 1977—83, assoc. dean, 1994—98, acting dean, 1997, dean, 2002—. Vis. scholar/rsch. assoc. U. Glasgow, Scotland, U. Kans., U. Ariz.; assoc. dir. Associated Colls. Midwest Geology in the Rockies Program, 1978, dir., 80, Keck Geology Consortium Project, Colo., 1988, faculty mem., Colo., 99; pres. geology coun. Coun. on Undergrad. Rsch., 1987—89. Editor: (volume of essays) Revolution in the Earth Sciences; contbr. articles to profl. jours. Fellow: Geol. Soc. Am.; mem.: AAAS, Am. Mineral. Soc., Am. Geophysical Union, Nat. Assn. Geoscience Tchrs., Sigma Xi. Office: Carleton Coll Dean of the Coll One North College St Northfield MN 55057

BOARMAN, PATRICK MADIGAN, economics and business administration educator, public official; b. Buffalo, 1922; m. Shi Chun (Shane) Hu, Dec. 18, 1988; m. Katrin Schumacher, Dec. 12, 1953 (div. 1980); children: Thomas, Christopher, Jesse, Barbara. AB, Fordham U., 1943; MS, Columbia U., 1946; PhD in Econs., Grad. Inst. Internat. Studies, U. Geneva, 1965. Asst. to advt. mgr. Doubleday, N.Y.C., 1944-45; fgn. corr. CBS, Geneva, 1946-48; dir. office cultural affairs Nat. Catholic Welfare Conf., Bonn, W. Germany, 1951-55; asst. prof. econs. U. Wis.-Milw., 1956-62; assoc. prof. Bucknell U., Lewisburg, Pa., 1962-67; prof. L.I.U., Greenvale, N.Y., 1967-72; prof. internat. econs., dir. rsch. Ctr. Internat. Bus., Pepperdine U., L.A., 1972-75; prof. econs. Nat. U., San Diego, 1979-93, prof. emeritus, 1993; mgr. econ. research div. employee relations and mgmt. devel. Gen. Electric Co., N.Y.C., 1964-65; mgr. econ. reports div. econ. analysis AT&T, 1969; sr. economist cons. World Trade Inst., N.Y.C., 1971; pres. Patrick M. Boarman Assocs., Internat. Bus. Cons., 1975—. Dir. rsch. Ho. Rep. Conf., Ho. of Reps., Washington, 1967-68; spl. cons. to Sec. Treasury, Washington, 1970; cons. Econ. Stblzn. Bd., Washington, 1971-72; guest lectr. U. Chgo., 1957, 64; Disting. vis. lectr. Denison U., 1959; vis. prof. econs. U. Geneva, 1965-66; supr. 3rd dist. San Diego County, Calif., 1983-85. Author: Union Monopolies and Antitrust Restraints, 1963, Germany's Economic Dilemma-Inflation and the Balance of Payments, 1964; editor: (with Hans Schollhammer) Multinational Corporations and Governments, 1975, Trade with China, 1974, (with David G. Tuerck) World Monetary Disorder, 1976; author monographs; author, contbr. numerous articles to profl. and popular jours. Served with U.S. Army, 1943. Decorated Disting. Service Cross, Order of Merit W. Germany; Fulbright fellow U. Amsterdam, 1949-50; Ford Found. fellow in econs. U. Mich., 1958; Gen. Electric Found fellow U. Va., 1965 Home: 6421 Caminito Estrellado San Diego CA 92120-3022 Personal E-mail: patboarman@hotmail.com. *To learn more and more until the end of my days about this wonderful world I inhabit has been my goal, and even passion, from the beginning. I could live 50 lives, and still not have time enough to do all the reading, writing, exploring and loving I want to do. True wealth is what is in one's head and heart and my stock of it is beyond counting.*

BOARTFIELD, ERNEST WILLIAM, music educator; b. Montgomery, Ala., Jan. 17, 1973; s. Ernest G. and Rebecca Blakey Boartfield. MusB in edn., Troy State U., 1997, MusM in edn., 1999. Cert. Instrumental Music k-12 Ala. State Dept. of Edn., 1997. Band dir. McIntyre Jr. H.S., Montgomery, Ala., 1997—98, Kendrick H.S., Columbus, Ga., 1998—99; asst. band dir. Prattville Jr. H.S., Prattville, Ala., 2000—01; band dir. Isabella H.S., Maplesville, Ala., 2001—04; band dir., asst. band dir. Millbrook Jr H.S., Stanhope Elmore H.S., Millbrook, Ala. Sec. Nat. H.S. Band Dirs. Assn., Columbus, Ga., 2005—; cons. Nat. H.S. Band Dir. Hall of Fame, Columbus, Ga., 2005—. Paul Yoder scholarship for outstanding svc., Troy State U. Music Dept., 1997. Mem.: Ala. Band Masters Assn., Music Educators Nat. Conf., Phi Mu Alpha, Kappa Kappa Psi. Achievements include tour manager for the Muscogee Troupers, Columbus, Ga. at the 1997 Presidential Inaugural Parade, Washington, D.C. Home: 817 Cottage Ln Prattville AL 36067 Office: Stanhope Elmore HS 4300 Main St Millbrook AL 36054 Office Phone: 334-285-7342.

BOARTS, LAIRD SPEER, retired insurance company executive; b. Whiteburg, Pa., Apr. 29, 1908; s. Howard M. and Elsie Grace Boarts; widowed. Grad. h.s. Agy. mgr. State Farm Ins. Co., Bloomington, Ill., 1939-73; bd. dirs. Apollo (Pa.) Trust Co., 1949-95. Bd. dirs. Pitts. Life Ins. Underwriters Assn.; tchr. life ins. program. Pres. Apollo Area Hist. Soc., 1970-77; sec. Apollo C. of C. With USN, 1945. Mem. Apollo C. of C. (organizer), Masons, Lions Republican. Presbyterian. Avocations: golf, softball, horse shoes, church and civic work.

BOAS, FRANK, retired lawyer; b. Amsterdam, North Holland, The Netherlands, July 22, 1930; arrived in U.S., 1940; s. Maurits and Sophie (Brandel) Boas; m. Edith Louise Bruce, June 30, 1981 (dec. July 1992); m. Jean Scripps, Aug. 6, 1993 (div. Dec. 2000). *Father, Maurits Boas, was a pioneer for the International Business Machines Corporation in Europe. He brought the Hollerith Punched Card System, first used in the United States for the 1890 census, to Holland and Belgium after World War I and he founded the IBM organizations in those countries.* AB cum laude, Harvard U., 1951, JD, 1954. Bar: U.S. Dist. Ct. DC 1955, U.S. Ct. Appeals (DC cir.) 1955, U.S. Supreme Ct. 1958. Atty. Office of the Legal Adviser U.S. State Dept., Washington, 1957-59; pvt. practice Brussels and London, 1959-79; of counsel Patton, Boggs & Blow, Washington, 1975-80; pres. Frank Boas Found., Inc., Cambridge, Mass., 1980—2005. Mem. U.S. delegation UN Conf. Law of Sea, Geneva, 1958, 1960; hon. sec. Am. C. of C., Belgium, 1966—78; bd. dirs. Found. European Orgn. Rsch. and Treatment Cancer, Brussels, 1978—87, Paul-Henri Spaak Found., Brussels, 1981—, East-West Ctr. Found., Honolulu, 1990—2001, Law of Sea Inst., Honolulu, 1992—97, Pacific Forum CSIS, Honolulu, 1996—, Honolulu Acad. Arts, 1997—, U. Hawaii Found., 2000—; vice chmn. Commn. Ednl. Exch., Brussels, 1980—87; mem. vis. com. Harvard Law Sch., 1987—91, Ctr. Internat. Affairs, 1988—2005. With U.S. Army, 1955—57. Decorated officer Order of Leopold II Belgium, comdr. Order of Merit Luxembourg, comdr. Order of Crown, comdr. Order of Leopold Belgium; recipient Tribute of Appreciation award, U.S. State Dept., 1981, Harvard Alumni Assn. award, 1996, Resolution of Appreciation, Hawaii Ho. Reps., 2002, Nat. Jefferson award for Outstanding Pub. Svc., 2004, Hawaii award, Am. Bd. Trial Advocates, 2005; fellow, Hawaii Pacific U., 2004. Mem.: PTO, ABA, Honlulu Social Sci. Assn., Honolulu Com. Fgn. Rels., Pacific and Asian Affairs Coun. (pres. 1998—2004), Fed. DC Bar Assn., Am. and Common Market Club (Brussels pres. 1981—85), Travellers Club (London), Pacific, Outrigger Canoe Clubs (Honolulu). Home: 4463 Aukai Ave Honolulu HI 96816-4858

BOAST, MOLLY SHRYER, lawyer; b. Cin., Apr. 10, 1948; d. Davis Maxwell Shryer and Mary Stratton (Bowlby) Baird; m. Thomas Hansen Boast, Sept. 4, 1971; 1 child, Emma Alice. BA with gen. honors, Coll. William & Mary, 1970; MS in Journalism, Columbia U., 1971, JD, 1979. Bar: N.Y. 1980, U.S. Dist. Ct. (so. dist.) N.Y., U.S. Dist. Ct. (ea. dist.) N.Y., U.S. Ct. Appeals (1st cir.), U.S. Ct. Appeals (2d cir.), U.S. Ct. Appeals (3d cir.), U.S. Supreme Ct. Teaching asst. Columbia U. Grad. Sch. Journalism, NYC, 1971-72; writer, pub. rels. George Jr. Republic, Dryden, NY, 1973-76; assoc. Le Boeuf, Lamb, Leiby & MacRae, NYC, 1979-87, ptnr., mem. exec. com., chmn. litigation dept., 1988; sr. dep. dir. to dir. Bur. of Competition, FTC, 1999—2001; ptnr., mem. litig. dept. Debevoise & Plimpton LLP, NYC, 2001—. Sec., bd. dirs. N.Y. Lawyers for the Pub. Interest, N.Y.C., 1989—; bd. dirs. Vols. Legal Svc., Inc., N.Y.C. Named Harlan Fiske Stone scholar Columbia U. Sch. Law, N.Y.C., 1979; recipient Jane Marks Murphy prize Columbia U. Sch. Law, N.Y.C., 1979. Mem. ABA (chair ins. industry com. antitrust sect. 1992-95, coun. 1995—, editl. vice-chmn. Antitrust Law Jour. 1990-92), Fed. Bar Coun. (chair com. on second cir. cts. 1990—, v.p. 1991-94, trustee 1995—), Mortar Bd. Avocations: bicycling, swimming, gardening, reading, music. Office: Debevoise & Plimpton LLP 919 Third Ave New York NY 10022 Office Phone: 212-909-1069. Fax: 212-909-6836. E-mail: msboast@debevoise.com.

BOAT, RONALD ALLEN, food products executive, television producer; b. Dayton, Ohio, Nov. 16, 1947; s. Robert Mallory and Elvetta June (Smith) B. Student, Naval Acad./Army Sch. Music, Norfolk, Va., 1968-69, Ariz. State U., 1966-68. Pres. Prodn. Svcs., Phoenix, 1968—, Greek Specialties Corp., Phoenix, 1980-94; v.p. Am. Baby Boomers, San Diego, 1984-93; co-founder, v.p. Internat. Food Network, San Diego, 1985-90; founder, pres. AMC Food Svcs. Corp., 1991-94; pres. The Natural Light Co., 1994-96. Ind. prodr. Intel, HealthSouth, Johnson & Johnson, Smith & Nephew, Honeywell, Best Western, Sperry, City of Phoenix, 1985—, Phoenix Health Plan, B.P.I., Maricopa Refining Co., P.A.R. Techs., Profitmax, Cycle-Masters, Framatome, PMH Found., Gunsite Acad., Club Med, Medidas, Cable One, Troon, Tri-Star, Toyota, Ekco, Coldwell Banker, NovaCare, KareMor Internat., Iassis Healthcare, John C. Lincoln Hosps., Crowne Plaza Hotels, Hartford Ins., Swift Trucking, Rural Metro, Opus, Aaron Rents, Orme Sch., Continental Homes, Phoenix Suns, Arkitekton, Huber, Hunt & Nichols, Korea Data Sys., Stantec, Stanley Consulting, Ramada Inns, Saudi Arabian Air Force, U.S. Geol. Survey, Coleman-Fleetwood, Hunt/CSSS, Atronic, Carvin Guitars, Primus Pharm., Boys & Girls Clubs, Rockridge TEchs.; mem. Lund Team Real Estate Adv. Bd., 1991—95; founder, pres. Group AMC, Inc.; ind. prodr. MGM Grand. With U.S. Army, 1968—71. Named Outstanding sales rep. Club Am., Dallas, 1972-73, Top Distbr. Club Am., Dallas, 1973; recipient Top Restaurant award Am. Heart Assn., Phoenix, 1988, Best of Phoenix restaurant award, 1991. Mem. Am. Radio Relay League, Internat. Platform Assn., Phi Mu Alpha Sinfonia. Republican. Avocations: music, travel, amateur radio. Office: P S A PO Box 327 Cave Creek AZ 85327- Office Phone: 800-284-3678. Business E-Mail: ronb@psavideo.com. E-mail: psa.ronb@psavideo.com.

BOAT, THOMAS FREDERICK, pediatrician, researcher, pulmonologist, educator; b. Pella, Iowa, Sept. 7, 1939; s. Bert Reuben and Anne Marie (Schoenbohm) B.; m. Barbara Mary Walling, June. 9, 1962; children: Sarah Elizabeth, Mary Barbara, Anne Christine. BA, Cen. Coll., Pella, 1961; MS, U. Iowa, 1965, MD, 1966. Diplomate Am. Bd. Pediat., Am. Bd. Pediat. Pulmonology. Resident in pediat. U. Minn., Mpls., 1966-68; clin. assoc. NIH, Bethesda, Md., 1968-70; fellow in pediat. pulmonology Case Western Res. U., Cleve., 1970-72, instr. pediat., 1972-73, asst. prof., 1973-76, assoc. prof., 1976-81, prof., 1981-82; prof., chmn. dept. pediat. U. N.C., Chapel Hill, 1982-93; chmn. dept. pediat. U. Cin. Sch. Medicine, 1993—; dir. Cin. Children's Hosp. Rsch. Found., 1993—. Prin. investigator Pediat. Pulmonary Specialized Ctr. Rsch., NIH, 1991-93; chmn. Am. Bd. Pediat., 1994. Editor Current Opinions in Pediat., 1990-93; mem. editl. bd. Lung Rsch. jour. Bd. dirs. Ronald McDonald House, Chapel Hill, 1985-88, Cystic Fibrosis Found., chmn. rsch. devel. program, 1983—. Lt. comdr. USPHS, 1968-70. Fellow: Am. Acad. Pediat.; mem.: Inst. of Medicine, Assn. Med. Sch. Dept. Chairs (pres.-elect 1994—97, pres. 1997—99), Am. Thoracic Soc. (chmn. pediat. assembly 1983—84), Am. Pediat. Soc. (pres. 2000—01). Office: Children's Hosp Med Ctr 3333 Burnet Ave SEC D6 Cincinnati OH 45229-3039 Office Phone: 513-636-4588. E-mail: thomas.boat@cchmc.org.

BOAZ, DAVID DOUGLAS, foundation executive; b. Mayfield, Ky., Aug. 29, 1953; s. Seth Thomas Jr. and Martha Elizabeth (Pruitt) B. BA, Vanderbilt U., 1975. Exec. dir. Young Am.'s Found., Sterling, Va., 1975-76; editor New Guard Mag., Sterling, Va., 1976-78; exec. dir. Coun. for a Competitive Economy, Washington, 1978-80; research dir. Clark for Pres. Com., Washington, 1980; v.p. Cato Inst., Washington, 1981-89, exec. v.p., 1989—. Bd. dirs. Ctr. for Ind. Thought, NYC, Women's Freedom Network; bd. regents Congl. Schs. Va., 1991-2003. Author: Libertarianism: A Primer, 1997; co-editor: Beyond the Status Quo, 1985, An American Vision, 1989, Market Liberalism: A Paradigm for the 21st Century, 1993, Cato Handbook for Congress, 2001; editor: Left, Right and Babyboom, 1986, Assessing the Reagan Years, 1988, The Crisis in Drug Prohibition, 1990, Liberating Schools: Education in the Inner City, 1991, The Libertarian Reader, 1997, Toward Liberty, 2002; contbr. Encyclopedia Brittanica, also books and newspapers. Office: Cato Inst 1000 Massachusetts Ave NW Washington DC 20001-5400

BOAZ, STEPHEN SCOTT, lawyer; b. Waukegan, Ill., Nov. 7, 1948; s. Cecil Perry Jr. and Isabel Smith (Simpson) B.; m. Karen Joyce Huelskamp, Sept. 14, 1985. BA, Okla. State U., 1971; M of Criminal Justice Adminstrn., Okla. City U., 1976; JD, U. Okla., 1983. Bar: Okla. 1984, U.S. Dist. Ct. (no., ea. and we. dists.) Okla. 1984, U.S. Ct. Appeals (10th cir.) 1989; cert. mediator for U.S. Dist. Ct. (we. dist.) Okla., Okla. County Dist. Ct., Western Dist. Fed. Ct.; cert. arbitrator; cert. mediator U.S. Postal Svc. Redress Program, EEOC. Police officer Stillwater (Okla.) Police Services, 1971-77; bus. mgr. Shaw's Gulf, Inc., Stillwater, 1977-81; assoc. Holloway, Dobson, Hudson & Bachman Holloway, Dobson, Hudson & Bachman, Oklahoma City, 1984-85; ptnr. Durbin, Larimore & Bialick, Oklahoma City, 1985-92; mng. atty., ptnr. Oklahoma City office Paulk, Moles & Boaz, P.C., 1992-94; pres. Boaz & Assocs., P.C., 1995—; adminstrv. law judge Okla. Dept. of Mental Health and Substance Abuse Svcs., 2004—. Instr. Oklahoma City U., 1992-94. Mem. ABA (ADR sect. 1996—, law practice mgmt. sect. 1999—), Okla. Bar Assn. (tort law com. 1990-92, ADR com. 1996—, solo and small firm com. 1999—), Okla. County Bar Assn. (ADR com. 1995—, bd. govs. 1987, membership com. 1988-89, alternative dispute resolution com. 1990-91), Okla. Acad. Mediators and Arbitrators, Assn. Atty.-Mediators (charter; pres. 2001), Fraternal Order Police (chmn. collective bargaining com. 1973-75), Rotary (sec. 1979-80, pres.-elect 1980-81). Republican. Roman Catholic. Avocation: coaching youth sports. Office: Boaz & Assocs 3613 NW 56th St Ste 300 Oklahoma City OK 73112-4520 Office Phone: 405-946-3232.

BOBAK, MARK T., lawyer; b. 1959; JD cum laude, St. Louis U. Sch. Law, 1984. With Anheuser-Busch Cos., St. Louis, 1992—96, v.p., dep. gen. counsel, 1996—2000, v.p., corp. human resources, 2000—04, group v.p., chief legal officer, 2004—. Bd. mem. US C. of C., Americans for Transp. Mobility. Office: Anheuser-Busch Cos One Busch Pl Saint Louis MO 63118

BOBANGO, JOHN ALLEN, lawyer; b. Bremerton, Wash., July 11, 1955; s. Charles John and Myrtie Bonita Bobango; m. Lisa Walker, July 31, 1982; children: Allen, Mary Lauren. BA, Ark. State U., 1978; JD, U. Memphis, 1983; LLM, U. Fla., 1984. Bar: Tenn. 1983, Ark. 1984, Fla. 1986. With Black Bobango & Morgan, Memphis, 1994—99, Farris Matthews Branan Bobango Hellen & Dunlap, PLC, Memphis, 2000—. Bd. dirs. Street Ministries, Memphis, 2003—; city councilman Memphis City Coun., 1996—99; chmn. City of Memphis, Shelby County, 2000—; mem. Meth. Found., 2005—; bd. dirs. Riverfront Devel. Corp. Redevelopment Agy., Memphis, 2004—. Mem.: Econ. Club Memphis (bd. mem.), Pi Kappa Alpha Internat. (gen. counsel to supreme coun. 2004—). Republican. Meth. Office: Farris Matthews Branan BobangoHellen & Dunlap 1100 Ridgeway Loop Ste 400 Memphis TN 38120 Office Phone: 901-259-7120. Office Fax: 901-259-7180.

BOBB, HAROLD DANIEL, chiropractor, consultant; b. Moline, Ill., Nov. 22, 1952; s. Harold Daniel and Clarice (Engholm) B.; m. Elizabeth Jean Lackey, Feb. 14, 1971 (div. Mar. 1974); m. Elzita Lemaster, Nov. 30, 1979; 1 child, Andrea; stepchildren: Kevin, Christopher. As, Black Hawk Coll., Moline, 1972; D Chiropractic, Palmer Coll., Davenport, Iowa, 1976; postgrad., Upper Iowa U., 1976-78. Diplomate chiropractic. Clinic dir. Bobb Chiropractic Ctr. P.C., Silvis, Ill., 1977—. Cons. Health Data Devel., Los Angeles, 1983—. Author: The Case Formula, 1987; contbr. articles to profl. jours. Bd. dirs. Silvis Sch. Dist. 34, 1982-86; alumni bd. dirs. Black Hawk Coll, 1987—. Mem. Ill. Prairie State Chiropractic Assn. (treas. 1980-82), Am. Chiropractic Assn., Nat. Acad. Sci., Optimist. Avocations: computers, camping, photography. Office: Bobb Chiropractic Ctr PC 813 1st Ave Silvis IL 61282-1079

BOBBITT, JAMES LYLE, computer programmer, systems analyst; s. Kenneth L. Bobbitt and MARY (deceased 1989 L Bobbitt/ Zanetti; 1 child, Nancy Jean Tone. B in Computer Science, Mercer U., 1992; Master's, Hofstra U., 1999. Owner, adminstr. Svc. PLUS/CWW, Seattle, 1990—, Global-Tek Svcs., Seattle, 2003—04.

BOBBITT, JOHN MAXWELL, surgeon, medical educator; b. Jan. 20, 1927; MD, U. Mich., 1952. Intern, then resident in surgery U. Mich., Ann Arbor, 1952-57; clin. assoc. prof. surgery Med. Sch. Marshall U., Huntington, W.Va., 1972-80. Contbr. numerous articles on nautical rsch. to popular publs., 1985—. Elected to W.Va. Ho. Dels., 1966, 68. Home: 69 Queens Ct Newport News VA 23606-2034

BOBBITT, JUANITA CRAWFORD, international organization executive; b. N.Y.C., Sept. 4, 1938; d. Philip Theodore and Lillian Beatrice (Nelson) Crawford; 1 child, Edmund Michael. BA in Romance Lang., CUNY, Bklyn., 1959; MA in Econ., NYU, 1982; MPA, Harvard U., 1984. Pub. adminstrn. officer UN, N.Y.C., 1974-84, econ. affairs officer, 1984-92, sr. pub. adminstrn. officer, 1992-97, head gender adv. svcs. unit, 1998, internat. devel. cons., 1999—. Contbr. articles to profl. jours. Exec. com. St. George's Cmty. Devel. Corp., Bklyn., 1994-99; rep. provincial coun. Episcopal Ch., 1993-96. Mem.: ASPA (exec. com., sect. internat. comparative adminstrn.), Tri-State J.F. Kennedy Alumni Assn. (exec. com. 1987—), Harvard Club (admissions com. 2001—03, program com. 2002—04), Delta Sigma Theta (pres. Bklyn. chpt. 1966—68, nat. projects com. 1973—74, chair internat. com. 1993—99, nat. social action commn. 2002—). Episcopalian. Avocations: reading, walking, dance, arts.

BOBBITT, LEROY, lawyer; b. Jackson, Miss., Nov. 1, 1943; s. Leroy and Susie (Catchings) B.; m. Andrea Marie James, Sept. 18, 1965; children: Dawn, Antoinette. BA, Mich. State U., 1966; JD, Stanford U., 1969. Bar: Calif. 1969, N.Y. 1970. Atty. East Palo Alto (Calif.) Legal Aid, 1969-70; assoc. Paul, Weiss, Rifkind, Wharton & Garrison, N.Y.C., 1970-74, Loeb and Loeb, L.A., 1974—96, ptnr. dept. entertainment; ptnr. Bobbitt & Roberts, Santa Monica, Calif. Mem. Friends of NAACP Legal Def. Fund, L.A., 1991—; bd. advisors Operation Hope, L.A., 1992—. Named one of Am.'s Top Black Attys., Black Enterprise mag., 2003. Mem. ABA, Nat. Bar Assn., Langston Bar Assn., Black Entertainment and Sports Lawyers Assn. (pres., bd. dirs. 1991-94). Democrat. Avocation: golf. Office: Bobbit & Roberts 6100 Ctr Dr Ste 910 Los Angeles CA 90045 Office Phone: 310-645-4100. Business E-Mail: lbobbitt@bobroblaw.com.

BOBBITT, PHILIP CHASE, law educator, writer; b. Temple, Tex., July 22, 1948; s. Oscar Price and Rebekah Luruth (Johnson) B.; m. Selden Anne Wallace (div. 1990). AB, Princeton U., 1971; JD, Yale U., 1975; PhD, Oxford U., 1983, MA, 1984. Bar: Tex. 1977, U.S. Supreme Ct. 1989. Law clk. to Judge Henry Friendly U.S. Ct. Appeals (2d cir.), 1975-76; asst. prof. law U. Tex., Austin, 1976-79, prof., 1979—, A.W. Walker chair in law, 1996—. Assoc. counsel to Pres. U.S. for intelligence and internat. security, 1980-81; legal counsel U.S. Senate Select Com. on Secret Mil. Assistance to Iran and

Nicaraguan Opposition, 1987-88; counselor on internat. law U.S. Dept. of State, 1990-93; dir. for intelligence NSC, 1997-98, sr. dir. critical infrastructure, 1998-99, sr. dir. strategic planning, 1999; mem. faculty Salzburg Seminar, 1987; vis. fellow Internat. Inst. Strategic Studies, 1981-82; jr. rsch. fellow Nuffield Coll., Oxford U., 1982-84, rsch. fellow, 1984-85, Anderson sr. rsch. fellow, 1985-91, mem. modern history faculty, 1984-91; guest scholar Woodrow Wilson Ctr. for Internat. Scholars, 1994; sr. rsch. fellow war studies King's Coll./U. London, 1994-97. Author: Democracy and Deterrence, 1988; (with Guido Calabresi) Tragic Choices, 1979, Constitutional Fate, 1982; (with Lawrence Freedman and Gregory Treverton) Nuclear Strategy, 1988, Constitutional Interpretation., 1991, The Shield of Achilles: War, Peace and the Course of History, 2002. Trustee Princeton U. Mem. Am. Law Inst., Internat. Inst. Strategic Studies (London), Austin Coun. Fgn. Affairs (pres. 1983—), Coun. Fgn. Rels. (N.Y.C.), Adminstrv. Conf. U.S. (spl. com. on ethics in govt.), Pacific Coun. on Internat. Policy, Nat. Infrastructure Assurance Coun., Tex. Philos. Soc., Met. Club (Washington), Yale Club, Century Assn., The Brook, Knickerbocker Club (N.Y.C.), Beefsteak Club (London), Phi Beta Kappa, Am. Acad. Art & Scis. (fellow 2004-). Democrat. Baptist. Office: U Tex Law Sch 727 E 26th St Austin TX 78705-3224*

BOBCO, WILLIAM DAVID, JR., consulting engineering company executive; s. William David and Eleanor Josephine (Dvojack) B.; m. Donna Domenica DiFrancesca, Sept. 13, 1969; 1 child, Christina Marie. BS in Engring., U. Ill., Chgo., 1969; MBA in Prodn. Mgmt., U. Chgo., 1983. Prodn. mgr. Am. Can Co., Maywood, Ill., 1972-73; with Footlik & Assocs., Evanston, Ill., 1973—, exec. v.p., 1986—. Mem. indsl. adv. bd. U. Ill. Coll. Engring., Chgo., 1992-2004, chmn. alumni devel. com., 1991-95, mem. dean selection com., 1994, com. mem. 40th Anniversary Chgo. Campus, 2004. Vol. Art Inst. Chgo., 1983—84, Animal Care League, Oak Park, Ill., 2000—02; facilities and grounds com. St. Giles Parish, 1995—97, co-chair, 1997—2001, chmn., 2001—, treas. golf com., 2000—, chmn. golf com., 2002—, chmn. golf scholarship com., 1999—, lions leap com., 1998—2001, steering com. capitol campaign, 2002, mem. fin. com., 2003—; Eucharistic Minister St. Giles Ch., 2000—, bus. mgr. selection com., 2004. Capt. Ordnance Corp. U.S. Army, 1969—72, W. Germany, Vietnam. Mem. ASME, bd. dirs. Chgo. sect. 1984-2001, newsletter editor 1987-98, vice chmn. 1991, chmn. Chgo. sect. 1992-94, region VI rep. to A World in Motion K-12 tng. program (SAE, co-sponsor 1993), Engring. Alumni Assn. U. Ill. Chgo. (pres. 1984-88, bd. dirs. 1975-99), U. Ill. Alumni Assn. (bd. dirs. 1985-91, nominating com. 1991, Loyalty award 1988, Constituent Leadership award 1991, Disting. Svc. award 1994). Independent. Roman Catholic. Avocations: travel, art, music. Office: Footlik & Assocs 2521 Gross Point Rd Evanston IL 60201-4993 Office Phone: 847-328-5644. Personal E-mail: wocbobjr@comcast.net.

BOBEK, NICOLE, professional figure skater; b. Chgo., Aug. 23, 1977; Competitive history includes: mem. of 1st place team Hershey's Kisses Challenge, 1997, placed 13th in World Championships, 1997, 3rd in Nat. Sr., 1997, 2nd (team) U.S. Postal Svc. Challenge, 1996, 3rd (team) Hershey's Kisses Challenge, 1996, 10th place Centennial on Ice, 1996, 1st place Starlight Challenge, 1995, 3rd in World Championships, 1995, 1st in Nat. Sr., 1995, 2d place, World Pro Championship, 2000, 3d place, Canadian Open, 2001, numerous others. Champions on Ice Tour, 2000-. Avocations: dance, drawing, poetry, modeling, designing clothes. Office: USFSA 20 1st St Colorado Springs CO 80906-3624

BOBER, JOANNE L., lawyer; b. NYC, Dec. 14, 1952; BA, Wash. U., 1974; JD, Georgetown U., 1980. Bar: Tex. 1980. Assoc. Moore & Peterson, 1980—82, Jones, Day, Reavis & Pogue, NYC, 1983—88, ptnr., 1989—96; sr. v.p., gen. counsel, sec. Gen. Signal Corp., Stamford, Conn., 1997—99; sr. v.p., gen. coun. Chubb Corp., Warren, NJ, 1999—2005; sr. v.p., gen. counsel, sec. J.C. Penney Corp. Inc., Plano, Tex., 2005—. Mem.: ABA, Tex. Bar Assn., Phi Beta Kappa. Office: JC Penney Corp Inc 6501 Legacy Dr Plano TX 75024

BOBER, LAWRENCE HAROLD, retired banker; b. NYC, Mar. 29, 1924; s. Michael N. and Julia (Verschleiser) B.; m. Natalie S. Birnbaum, Aug. 27, 1950; children: Stephen, Marc, Elizabeth. BS, NYU, 1949; postgrad., Grad. Sch. Bus. Adminstrn., 1949-50. With Hanover Bank (now Chase Bank), 1941-87, asst. sec., 1950-52, asst. treas., 1953-55, asst. v.p., 1955-60, v.p., 1960-71, sr. v.p. (North Am. div.-II), 1971-87. Bd. dirs. Fab Industries, Inc. Dir., past chm. The Renesselaerville Inst.; past vice chmn., bd. fellows Brandeis U.; past pres. Congregation Emanuel of Westchester; past pres. Cobblefield Homeowners Assn. White Plains, NY. 1st lt. USAAF, 1942-45. Decorated D.F.C. with two oak leaf clusters, Air medal with three oak leaf clusters; recipient Human Relations award Am. Jewish Com., 1968, Community Service award Nat. Jewish Hosp. and Research Center, 1980, Community Service award Am. Jewish Congress, 1988. Home: 7 Westfield Ln White Plains NY 10605-5459

BOBERG, DOROTHY KURTH, author; b. Lincoln, Nebr., Mar. 17, 1930; d. Herman R. and Regina E. Kurth; m. John Elliott Boberg, Sept. 17, 1951; 1 child, Mark. BA, U. Nebr., 1951; postgrad., Calif. State U., Northridge, 1959-62, U. So. Calif., 1981. Libr. Nebr. Legis. Coun., Lincoln, 1952; child welfare worker L.A. County, 1953-57, 67-68; rsch. assoc. Nuclear Facilities/Radiation Monitoring in Calif. Another Mother for Peace, Beverly Hills, Calif., 1975; exec. v.p. So. Calif. divsn. UN Assn., L.A., 1977-78. Author: Evolution and Reason Beyond Darwin, 1993; editor Nebraska Blue Book. Resolutions chair L.A. County Dem. Cen. Com.; chair UN Internat. Solar Exhibition, L.A., 1978, Mayor's Lifeline Com., Earthquake Prediction Task Force; pres. Northridge Civic Assn., 1971-73; founding bd. mem. Northridge East Neighborhood Coun., 2004; bd. dirs. Alliance for Democracy, 2004-05. Recipient Achievement award Nebr. Sec. State, 1993, Admiral, Nebr. Navy/Gov. State Nebr., 1993. Mem. AAAS, Soc. Study Evolution, AAUW (pres. San Fernando Valley Br. 1966-67), Phi Beta Kappa, Psi Chi, Alpha Kappa Delta. Home: 10912 Nestle Ave Northridge CA 91326-2849

BOBERG, WAYNE D., lawyer; b. Vincennes, Ind., Sept. 28, 1952; s. Richard W. and Merom D. (Duke) B.; m. Nancy E. Messel, Sept. 11, 1971. Student, Kans. State U., 1970-73; BS in Bus. with distinction, Ind. U., 1975, JD magna cum laude, 1978. Bar: Ill. 1978, U.S. Dist. Ct. (no. dist.) Ill. 1978. Assoc. to ptnr. Winston & Strawn, Chgo., 1978—. Bd. dirs. Nat. Entrepreneurs Found., Bloomington, Ind., 1982—; mem. bd. trustees Chgo. Symphony Orch. Mem. ABA, Chgo. Bar Assn., Chgo. Athletic Assn. Office: Winston & Strawn 35 W Wacker Dr Ste 4200 Chicago IL 60601-9703 Office Fax: 312-558-5700. E-mail: wboberg@winston.com.

BOBIC, MICHAEL P., political scientist, educator; b. Binghampton, N.Y., Mar. 22, 1963; s. Robert J. and Jane P. Bobic; m. Jennifer L. Bobic. AA, Appalachian Bible Coll., 1982; BA, Berea Coll., 1985; MA, U. Tenn., 1992, PhD, 1996. Tchg. asst. U. Tenn., Knoxville, 1990—93; adj. faculty Roane (Tenn.) State C.C., 1993—94, So. Ill. U., Carbondale, 1995—96; assoc. prof. Emmanuel Coll., Franklin Springs, Ga., 1998—, chair pre-law dept. Adj. faculty E. Tenn. State, Johnson City, 1991—93; typist Galbreath Chem. Labs., Knoxville, 1992—93. Contbr. articles to profl. jours. Mem.: KC, Phi Kappa Phi, Pi Sigma Alpha. Avocations: fencing, magic. Office: Emmanuel Coll 181 Springs St Franklin Springs GA 30639

BOBINS, NORMAN R., banker; Vice chmn. Exch. Nat. Bank Chgo., 1969-90; formerly vice chmn. LaSalle Nat. Bank, Chgo.; now pres., ceo LaSalle Nat Bank (now LaSalle Bank, N.A.), Chgo., 1990—. Bd. trustees Art Inst. Chgo. Office: LaSalle Bank NA 135 S La Salle St Fl 3 Chicago IL 60603-4404

BOBINSKI, GEORGE SYLVAN, librarian, educator; b. Cleve., Oct. 24, 1929; s. Sylvan and Eugenia (Sarbiewski) B.; m. Mary Lillian Form, Feb. 20, 1953; children-George Sylvan, Mary Anne. BA, Case Western Res. U., 1951, MS in Libr. Sci., 1952; MA, U. Mich., 1961, PhD, 1966. Rsch. asst. Bus Info. Bur., Cleve. Pub. Libr., 1954-55; asst. dir. Royal Oak (Mich.) Pub. Libr., 1955-59; dir. librs. State U. Coll. at Cortland, N.Y., 1960-67; prof., asst. dean Sch. Libr. Sci. U. Ky., 1967-70; prof. SUNY, Buffalo, 1970—2001, dean Sch. Info. and Libr. Studies, 1970-99, prof. emeritus, 2002—. Fulbright-Hays lectr. in libr. sci. U. Warsaw, Poland, 1977; trustee Western N.Y. Libr. Rsch. Coun., 1971-87, pres., 1972, 82; vis. scholar Jagiellonian U., Krakow, Poland, 1992, 97. Author: A Brief History of the Libraries of Western Reserve University, 1826-1952, 1955, Carnegie Libraries, Their History and Impact on American Public Library Development, 1969, Dictionary of American Library Biography, 1978, also articles. Mem. N.Y. Gov.'s Commn. on Librs., 1990—. With AUS, 1952-54. Recipient Meritorious Svc. medal Jagellonian U., Krakow, Poland, 1997. Mem. ALA (mem. pub. com., mem. coun.), N.Y. Libr. Assn., Assn. Am. Libr. Schs. (chmn. coun. of deans 1985-86) Home: 69 Little Robin Rd Buffalo NY 14228-1125 Office: SUNY Buffalo Sch Informatics Baldy Hall Buffalo NY 14260 Office Phone: 716-645-2412. E-mail: bobinski@buffalo.edu.

BOBINSKI, MARY FORM, library director; b. Rochester, N.Y., Aug. 29, 1928; d. George H. and Lydia Mendenhall (Richards) Form; m. George S. Bobinski, Feb. 20, 1953; children: George S. Jr., Mary Anne. BA, U. Rochester, 1951; MS, Case Western Res. U., 1952. Children's work dir. Royal Oak (Mich.) Pub. Libr., 1952-53, 55-59; supr. sch. librs. Ft. Bragg, N.C., 1953-54; lectr. Coll. Libr. Sci. U. Ky., 1968-70; dir. Amherst (N.Y) Pub. Librs., 1973—. Producer, host weekly TV show Library Limelight. Mem. governing bd. Musicalfare Theatre, 2000—. Mem. N.Y. Libr. Assn. (pres. pub. libr. sect. 1978-79). Pub. Libr. Dirs. Assn. N.Y. State (pres. 1985-86), Beta Phi Mu. Home: 69 Little Robin Rd Amherst NY 14228-1125 Office: Amherst Pub Libr 350 John James Audubon Pky Amherst NY 14228-1142 Office Phone: 716-668-4919. Business E-Mail: bobinskim@buffalolib.org.

BOBIS, DANIEL HAROLD, lawyer; b. N.Y.C., May 1, 1918; s. Morris N. and Sarah C. Bobis; m. Selma Linder, May 15, 1960 (dec. Mar. 26, 2003); children: Jodee E. Bobis Verbow, Stacee M. Bobis Miccio. LLB, St. Lawrence U., 1939; BS, Columbia U., 1947. Bar: N.Y. 1949, U.S. Patent and Trademark Office 1950, U.S. Supreme Ct. 1961, U.S. Ct. Appeals (3d cir.) 1963, N.J. 1964, U.S. Dist. Ct. N.J. 1964, U.S. Ct. Appeals (fed. cir.) 1982. Patent atty. Worthington Corp. (name now Studebaker-Worthington Corp.), Harrison, NJ, 1946-1952, patent counsel, until 1969; mem. firm Popper, Bain, Bobis, Gilfillan & Rhoades, Newark, 1969-74, Popper & Bobis, Newark, 1974-79, Popper, Bobis & Jackson, Newark, 1979-88; of counsel Lerner, David, Littenberg, Krumholz & Mentlik, Westfield, NJ, 1988—. Founder Ann. Outstanding Patent Award N.J. Coun. R & D, 1966; former instr. intellectual property matters and causes Horizon Sch. Paralegal Tng., Linden, NJ. Capt. pilot AC U.S. Army, ETO. Decorated Air medal with one silver and 2 bronze oak leaf clusters, Purple Heart. Mem.: ABA (chmn., mem. intellectual property coms.), N.J. Patent Law Assn. (pres. 1966, chmn., mem. intellectual property coms.), N.J. Bar Assn. (chmn., mem. intellectual property coms.). Home: 30 Burnham Ct Scotch Plains NJ 07076-3129 Office: Lerner David Littenberg Krumholz & Mentlik 600 South Ave W Ste 300 Westfield NJ 07090-1497 Office Phone: 908-654-5000. Business E-Mail: dbobis@ldlkm.com.

BOBISUD, LARRY EUGENE, mathematics professor; b. Midvale, Idaho, Mar. 16, 1940; s. Walter and Ida V. (Bitner) B.; m. Helen M. Meyer, June 15, 1963. BS, Coll. of Ida., 1961; MA, U. N.M., 1963, PhD, 1966. Vis. mem. Courant Inst. Math. Scis. NYU, N.Y.C., 1966-67; prof. math. U. Idaho, Moscow, 1967—2002, prof. emeritus, 2002—. Contbr. articles to profl. jours. Mem. Am. Math. Soc. Home: 860 N Eisenhower St Moscow ID 83843-9581 Office: Univ Idaho Dept Math Moscow ID 83844-1103 E-mail: bobisud@uidaho.edu.

BOBO, LAWRENCE D., sociologist; b. Nashville, Feb. 18, 1958; married. BA in sociology, Loyola Marymount U., 1979, DHL (hon.), 2001; MA in sociology, U. Mich., 1981, PhD in sociology, 1984; MA (hon.), Harvard U., 1997. With sociology dept. U. Wis., Madison, 1984—90, UCLA, 1990—97; with Harvard U., 1997—, Norman Tishman and Charles M. Diker prof. sociology and African Am. studies, 2001—. Bd. mem. Am. Inst. Rsch., Roper Ctr., Ctr. Comparative Study Race and Ethnicity, Stanford U., Inst. Govt. and Pub. Affairs, U. Ill. Founding co-editor Dubois Review: Social Sci. Rsch. Race; co-author: Racial Attitudes in America: Trends and Interpretations, 1997; sr. editor Prismatic Metropolis: Inequality in LA, 2000; co-editor: Racialized Politics: The Debate on Racism in America, 2000, Urban Inequality: Evidence from Four Cites, 2001. Mem.: Nat. Acad. Scis. Office: Harvard U Dept Sociology 1370 William James Hall 33 Kirkland St Cambridge MA 02138 Business E-Mail: bobo@wjh.harvard.edu.

BOBOC, MARIUS, education educator; b. Constanta, Romania, Aug. 31, 1967; s. Nicolae and Marcela Boboc. MA in Edn., Roosevelt U., 1997; EdD, U. No. Iowa, 2002. Progam asst. U. No. Iowa, Cedar Falls, 2001—02; asst. prof. Cleve. State U., 2002—. Asst. prof. Ovidius U., Constanta, Romania, 1997—99. Grantee, Roosevelt U., 1995—96; scholar, 1996—97; John J. Kamerick fellow, U. No. Iowa, 2001—02, C.A. & Katherine Bemler Edn. scholar, 2000—01, 2001—02, John S. Latta Endowed Doctoral scholar, 2001—02. Mem.: ASCD, Am. Assn. Colleges Tchr. Edn., Am. Assn. Higher Edn., Am. Ednl. Rsch. Assn. Office: Cleveland State University 2121 Euclid Ave Cleveland OH 44115

BOBRINSKOY, CHARLES KELLOGG, investment banker; b. Chgo., Aug. 7, 1959; s. George V. and Elizabeth (Shaw) B.; m. Mary Anne Kane, May 11, 1985; children: Gregory, Amy, Nicholas, Michael, Alexander. AB, Duke U., 1981; MBA, U. Chgo., 1983. Assoc. Salomon Bros. Inc., N.Y.C., 1983-86, v.p. Chgo., 1986-89, dir. fin., 1989-94; mng. dir. Citigroup Global Mkts. (formerly Salomon Bros. Inc.), 1994—. Bd. dirs., Envirolyne Industries, Oak Brook, Ill., 1989—. Bd. dirs. Juvenile Protection assn., Chgo., 1991—, LaRabida Hosp., 1992—. Mem. North Shore Country Club, Chgo. Club. Republican. Office: Citigroup Capital Mkts 8700 Sears Tower Chicago IL 60606

BOBROFF, HAROLD, lawyer; b. Bronx, N.Y., Apr. 29, 1920; s. Max and Mary (Platofsky) B.; m. Marion Hemendinger, Nov. 25, 1945; children: Caren Spital, Fredric Jon. BBA, City U. N.Y., 1947; JD, N.Y. Law Sch., N.Y.C., 1951. Bar: N.Y. State 1952. Ptnr. Bobroff & Olonoff (C.P.A.s), 1949-51, 52; auditor U.S. Army Audit Agy., N.Y.C., 1951-89; ptnr. Bobroff, Olonoff & Scharf, Attys., N.Y.C.; chief dep. county atty. Nassau County, N.Y., 1962-63; chief counsel joint legis. com. on ins. N.Y. State Legislature, 1965-67; pvt. practice Woodmere, N.Y., 1989—. Chief counsel com. on intergovt. relations N.Y. State Constl. Conv., 1967 Fin. sec. Nassau County Dem. Com., 1973; former chmn. bd. Trustees Nassau Community Coll.; former pres., trustee Temple Sinai of L.I.; former v.p. N.Y. Fedn. Reform Synagogues; former trustee UHAC; former comdr. Jewish War Vets Post. Served with AUS, 1942-45. Decorated Bronze Star medal with oak leaf cluster, Presdl. Unit citation with oak leaf cluster; Belgium Fouraggere; Honored by United Jewish Appeal Fedn. Mem. B'nai B'rith. Lodges: Masons. Home: Aot 3047 2701 Pickett Rd Durham NC 27705

BOBROW, SUSAN LUKIN, lawyer; b. Cleve., Jan. 18, 1941; d. Adolph and Yetta (Babkow) Lukin; m. Martin J. Bolhower, Nov. 28, 1986 (div. Dec. 1988); children from previous marriage: Elizabeth Bobrow Pressler, Erica, David. Student, Antioch Coll., Yellow Springs, Ohio, 1958-61; BA, Antioch Coll., L.A., 1975; JD, Southwestern U., L.A., 1979. Bar: Calif. 1980. Pvt. practice, Beverly Hills, Calif., 1983-88; assoc. Schulman & Miller, Beverly Hills, 1988-89; staff counsel Fair Polit. Practices Commn., Sacramento, 1990-96; sr. counsel Calif. State Lottery, Sacramento, 1996-98; asst. gen. counsel Employment Tng. Panel, Sacramento, 1998—2003, acting. gen. counsel, 2004—. Panel for paternity defense L.A. Superior Ct., 1984. Exhibited paintings at Death and Trasnfiguration Show, Phantom Galleries, Sacramento, 1994; exhibited photography U. Calif.-Davis Women's Art Collaborative, Phantom Galleries, Sacramento, 1997, Camera Arts, Sacramento, 1998, Viewpoint Gallery Exhibit, Sacramento, 1998, Nimbus Winery, 2005. Bd. dirs. San Fernando Valley Friends of Homeless Women and Children, North Hollywood, Calif., 1985-88, Jewish Family Svcs., 1997; mem. adv. bd. Project Home, Sacramento Interfaith Svc. Coun., 1990-91; v.p. cmty. affairs B'nai Israel Sisterhood, Sacramento, 1991-93; bd. dirs. Sacramento Jewish Family Svcs., 1997-98; broadcast vol. Access News, Assn. for Blind, Sacramento, 2004-2005. Recipient commendation Bd. Govs. State Bar of Calif., 1984. Mem. Inst. Noetic Scis., Sacramento Inst. Noetic Scis. (steering coun. 1994), Los Angeles County Bar Assn. (Barristers com. on adminstrn. of justice 1985), Sacramento County Bar Assn. (com. on profl. responsibility 1993-94, alt. del. to state bar conv. 1991), Sacramento Valley Photog. Arts Ctr. Democrat. Office: Employment Tng Panel 1100 J St Sacramento CA 95814-2827

BOBROWSKI, LEONARD STEPHEN, music educator, director; b. St. Louis, Nov. 21, 1956; s. Leonard Stephen and Sophie Josephine Bobrowski. BA, St. Louis (Mo.) U., 1979. Organist St. Sebastian Cath. Ch., St. Louis, 1968—85, dir. music, 1986—2005, Blessed Teresa Calcutta Cath. Ch., Ferguson, Mo., 2005—. Organist St. Casimir Cath. Ch., St. Louis, 1976—86; tchr. music St. Sebastian Sch., St. Louis, 1978—2003; music specialist Our Lady of Holy Cross Sch., St. Louis, 2003—04, St. Charles Borromeo Sch., St. Charles, Mo., 2004—. Composer: To You, O Lord, 1991, Psal for the Assumption Vigil, 1995, Psalm for the Feast of the Assumption, 1995, Responsorial Psalm for the Passlon Sunday, 1995, I am the Holy Vine, 1998, Allelula! The Strife Is Oer, 1998, In Bethlehem's Stable, 2000, It Came Upon the Midnight Clear, 1998. Recipient Composition Contest award, Am. Guild Organists, 1979, Cardinal Rigali Svc. award, Archdiocese St. Louis, 2004. Mem.: Nat. Cath. Educators Assn., Choristers Guild, Nat. Assn. Pastoral Musicians, Phi Beta Kappa. Roman Catholic. Avocations: theater, swimming, reading. Home: 1801 Lanecourt Saint Louis MO 63136 Office: St Charles Borrmeo School 431 Decatur Saint Charles MO 63301

BOBROWSKI, PAULA ELAINE, finance educator; b. Eugene, Oreg., Feb. 21, 1952; d. Robert James and Mary Ann Brewer; m. Paul M. Bobrowski; children: Leanne Harper, Nicholas. BSN, U. Oreg. Health Sci. Ctr., Portland, 1980; MBA, U. Oreg., Eugene, 1988; PhD, Syracuse U., 1996. Surg. nurse, cons. Am. Med. Internat., Riyadh, Saudi Arabia, 1982-95; surg. nurse Sacred Heart Hosp., Eugene, 1985-88, mgr. market rsch., 1988-90; tchg. assoc. Syracuse (N.Y.) U., 1990-94, rsch. assoc., 1994-95; Fulbright rsch. fellow Fulbright Commn., Tokyo, 1995-96; assoc. prof. mktg. SUNY, Oswego, 1996—. Adult edn. instr. St. Therese, Syracuse, 1997-99. Co-author: Gateway to Business, 2000; contbr. articles to profl. jours. Recipient Best paper award Am. Soc. Bus. and Behavioral Scis., 1999; grantee SUNY, Oswego, 1999, Syracuse U., 1995, DOE grantee, 2002—. Mem. CNY Fulbright Assn. (v.p. 1999), Am. Mktg. Assn. (faculty advisor), Inst. Ops. and Mgmt. Scis., 1996-99., Phi Beta Sigma (pres. 2001—). Avocations: international travel, reading, exercise. Home: 1820 Euclid Ave Syracuse NY 13224-1906 Office: SUNY Oswego Sch Bus 115 Swetman Hall Oswego NY 13126-3531

BOBROWSKY, WILLIAM JOSEPH, research scientist; b. N. Massarequa, NY, Mar. 5, 1968; s. Martin and Aldene Lundquist Bobrowsky. BA, Boston U., 1990, MA, 1992; MS, U. Mich., 2001. Tchr., coach Keene HS, Keene, NH, 1992—99; rsch. asst. U. Mich., Ann Arbor, Mich., 1999—2005.

BOBRUFF, CAROLE MARKS, radio producer, radio personality; b. N.Y.C., Nov. 11, 1935; d. Morris Frank and Harriet (Lehman) Marks; m. Jerome Bobruff, June 20, 1954 (div. 1986). Student, Quinnipac Coll., 1954-55, U. N.C., 1955-56; AS, U. New Haven, 1981; BS in Human Services, N.H. Coll., 1982. Founder, dir. Tyndall Air Force Daycare Ctr., Panama City, Fla., 1957-60; med. asst. Digestive Disease Assocs., New London, Conn., 1974-82; program coord. Pre-Trial Release Program, Norwich, New London, Conn., 1982-84; case mgr., counselor residential criminal justice program Cochegan House, Montville, Conn., 1984-85; exec. dir. Ret. Sr. Vol. Program So. New London County, 1984-91; producer, host nat. radio program A Touch of Grey, Groton, Conn., 1990-97; prodr., host Senior Focus Talk Am. Radio Network, Groton, Conn., 1997—; CEO Focus Commn. Treas. Dir. Vols. in Agys., New London, 1986—, Conn. RSVP Dirs., 1987; bd. dirs. Cochegan House, Widowed Persons Service, Waterford, Conn. Editor: Senior Citizens Guide to Discounts and Services, 1988; editor, author: RSVP Newsletter, 1984—; columnist: The Day, 1987. Pres. women's aux. New London County Med. Assn., 1986-87; bd. dirs. League Women Voters, New London, HOSPICE, New London, Am. Cancer Soc. New London County. Recipient Proclamation Community award Town of Waterford, 1989, Community Service award The Connection, Inc., 1987. Mem. Women's Network New London County, Children and Family Services, Pub. Relations Network, Nat. Assn. Female Execs., Brandeis U. Jewish. Home: 3 Pondside Ct Mystic CT 06355-3124 Office: 3 Pondside Ct Mystic CT 06355 Fax: 860-572-8239. E-mail: carole@atouchofgrey.com.

BOBZIEN, DAVID P., lawyer; b. 1946; BA in Polit. Sci., Coll. Holy Cross, 1968; JD, U. Va., 1971; LLM, George Washington U. Former judge advocate gen. U.S. Army; pvt. practice; with office profl. responsibility Justice Dept.; county atty. Fairfax, Va., 1993—. Chmn. goals commn. Fairfax County, mem. planning commn.; mem. exec. com. continuing legal edn. Va. Law Found.; bd. dirs., past pres. Fairfax Bar Found. Mem.: Local Govt. Attys. Va. (past pres.), Va. State Bar (pres.-elect 2003—04, past chmn. local govt. sect., mem. exec. com., mem. budget and fin. com., pres. 2004—). Office: 12000 Government Ctr Pkwy Fairfax VA 22035-0065

BOCCHINO, FRANCES LUCIA, retired oil company official; b. Bronx, N.Y., July 5, 1944; d. Pasquale and Mary Ruth (Lacerenza) B. Grad. high sch., Bklyn., 1962. Various positions Texaco Inc., N.Y.C., 1965-86, sr. analyst exec. dept. Harrison, N.Y., 1987-90, transfer agt., 1990-95; comms., 1995—. Active Whitestone (N.Y.) Taxpayers Assn. Mem. Corp. Transfer Agts. Assn. Republican. Roman Catholic. Home: 15-15 150th St Whitestone NY 11357-2530

BOCCIA, BARBARA, lawyer; b. Bklyn., Dec. 16, 1957; d. Daniel and Marie Boccia. BS with honors, U. Tenn., 1980; JD, U. of the Pacific, 1983; MBA with honors, San Francisco State U., 2004. Bar: Calif. 1983, D.C, 1983. Litigation lawyer, ptnr. Mullen & Filippi, San Francisco, 1983-86; litigation lawyer Jones, Brown, Clifford & McDevitt, San Francisco, 1987-88; litigation lawyer, mng. lawyer Crymes, Hardie & Heer, San Francisco, 1988-89; pvt. practice Daly City, Calif., 1989-92; sr. trial atty., supervising atty. Akin & Carmody, San Francisco, 1992-94; prin. Law Office of Barbara Boccia, Inc., Daly City, Calif., 1994—2004. Arbitrator, corp. cons., writer, educator, speaker in field. Vol. Hotline and Spks. Bur., San Francisco AIDS Found., 1987-90; mem. founding bd. dirs. Northeast Ark. Regional AIDS Network; HIV instr. ARC, 1991. Named One of Outstanding Young Women in Am., 1980. Mem. San Francisco Bar Assn., Indsl. Claims Assn., Ins. Edn. Assn., Queen's Bench, Italian Welfare Agy., Beta Gamma Sigma Honor Soc. Avocations: jogging, basketball, aerobics, writing, being a mom. Office: PO Box 2210 Daly City CA 94017-2210 E-mail: bboc@mindspring.com.

BOCEA, MARIAN, mathematician; arrived in U.S., 1999; s. Firu and Elena Bocea; m. Cristina Mariana Popovici, Sept. 21, 2000. MSc, U. Craiova, Romania, 1997, PhD, 2000; MSc, Carnegie Mellon U., 2000, PhD, 2004. Rsch. asst. U. Craiova, 1996—99; stdt. asst. Carnegie Mellon U., Pitts., 1999—2003, rsch. asst., 2003—04; burgess asst. prof. U. Utah, Salt Lake City, 2004—07. Contbr. articles to profl. jours. Grantee Math. Challenges of the 21st. Century, UCLA, Am. Math. Soc., 2000, Progress in Partial Differential Equations, ICMS, Edinburgh, European Commn. (FrameworkV), 2001; Doctoral fellow, Ministry Nat. Edn., Romania, 1996—99, TEMPUS fellow, European Commn., 1997, World Bank fellow, Nat. Coun. Sci. Rsch., Romania, 1999. Mem.: Soc. for Indsl. and Applied Math. (Student Travel award 2002), Am. Math. Soc. Achievements include research in Partial Differential Equations, Calculus of Variations, Continuum Mechanics. Office: Carnegie Mellon Univ Dept Math Pittsburgh PA 15213 E-mail: mbocea@andrew.cmu.edu.

BOCHCO, STEVEN, screenwriter, television producer; b. NYC, Dec. 16, 1943; s. Rudolph and Mimi B.; m. Barbara Bosson, 1969 (div. 1997; 2 children; m. Dayna Kalins Aug. 12, 2000. BA, Carnegie Tech. (now

Carnegie-Mellon U.), 1996. Scriptwriter, editor, prodr. Universal Studios, L.A., 1966-78; writer, prodr. MTM Enterprises, Studio City, 1978-85, Twentieth Century Fox, L.A., 1985-87; chmn. CEO Steven Bocho Prodns., L.A., 1987—. Writer: (films) (with Michael Cimino and Deric Washburn) Silent Running, 1972, (TV series) Ironside, 1967-75, Columbo, 1971-78, McMillan and Wife, 1971-76, Griff, 1973-74, Delvecchio, 1976-77, McMillan, 1977, Turnabout, 1979, (TV films) (with Harold Clements) The Counterfeit Killer, 1968, Double Indemnity, 1973, Uneasy Lies the Crown, 1990; writer, prodr.: (TV series) Bay City Blues, 1983-84, Griff, 1973-74, (TV mini series) Over There, 2005; (TV films) The Invisible Man, 1975, Richie Brockelman: Missing Twenty-four Hours, 1976, Lieutenant Schuster's Wife, 1972, Columbo: Uneasy Lies the Crown, 1990; writer, exec. prodr.: (TV series) Paris, 1979-80, (TV films) Vampire, 1979, prodr: (TV series) Capitol Critters, 1992, The Byrds of Paradise, 1994; co-creator, exec. prodr., writer: (TV series) Hill Street Blues, 1981-86 (Emmy award best drama series 1981, 82, 83, 84, Emmy award best writing in drama series 1981, 82, Golden Globe award best drama series 1982, 83), L.A. Law, 1986-87 (Emmy award best drama series 1987, 89, Emmy award best writing in drama series 1987, Golden Gobe award best drama series 1987, 88), Hooperman, 1987-89, Doogie Howser, M.D., 1989-93, Cop Rock, 1990, Civil Wars, 1991-93, NYPD Blue, 1993—2005 (Golden Globe award best drama series 1994, Outstanding Drama Series Emmy award, 1995), Murder One 1995-96, Total Security, 1997, Philly, 2001; exec. prodr.: (TV series) Public Morals, 1996, Brooklyn South, 1997-98, City of Angels, 2000. Office: Steven Bocho Productions 10201 W Pico Blvd Los Angeles CA 90064-2606*

BOCHERT, LINDA H., lawyer; b. East Orange, N.J., May 13, 1949; BA, U. Wis., 1971, MS, 1973, JD, 1974. Bar: Wis. 1974. Dir. environ. protection unit Wis. Atty. Gen. Office, 1978-80; exec. asst. to the secy. Wis. Dept. Natural Resources, 1980-91; ptnr. Michael, Best & Friedrich, Madison, Wis., 1991—. Mem. ABA, Wis. State Bar Assn. Office: Michael Best & Friedrich PO Box 1806 Firstar Plaza 1 S Pinckney St Madison WI 53701-1806 Office Phone: 608-283-2271. Business E-Mail: lhbochert@michaelbest.com.

BOCHICCHIO, KIM, literature and language educator; d. Marianne Rosar; m. James Bochicchio, Sept. 15, 1960; children: James Robert, Robert Joseph. B in Secondary Edn. English, U. Scranton, 2003; M in Edn., Wilkes U., Pa., 2005. Secondary Edn. English Pa., 2003. Dir. of cmty. edn. North Pocono Sch. Dist., Moscow, Pa., 1999—; secondary english tchr. Dunmore H.S., Pa., 2003—. Judge of sci. competition Pa. Jr. Acad. Sci., Scranton, Pa., 2003. Recipient Edn. grant, Skills in Scranton, 2004—05. Mem.: Nat. Coun. Tchrs. English, Peckville Bus. and Profl. Women (corr. sec. 2005—). Avocations: reading, writing. Office: Dunmore Sch Dist 300 W Warren St Dunmore PA 18512 Office Phone: 570-343-2110. Personal E-mail: bochicchiok2@netscape.net.

BOCHNER, BRUCE SCOTT, immunologist, educator; BA in Natural Scis. with honors, Johns Hopkins U., 1978; MD with honors, U. Ill., Chgo., 1982. Diplomate Am. Bd. Internal Medicine, Am. Bd. Allergy and Immunology. Intern, then resident in internal medicine U. Ill. Hosps., Chgo., 1982-85; fellow in clin. immunology Johns Hopkins U., Balt., 1985-88, instr. in medicine, 1988-89, asst. prof., 1989-94, assoc. prof., 1994—98, prof., 1999—, dir., Divsn. of Allergy and Clin. Immunology, 2003. Assoc. editor, mem. editl. bd. Jour. Allergy and Clin. Immunology, 1993—; reviewer various jours.; contbr. more than 165 articles to profl. jours. NIH grantee, 1989-; recipient Developing Investigator award Burroughs Wellcome Fund, 1992. Mem. Am. Assn. Immunology, Am. Acad. Asthma Allergy and Immunology (Charles Reed lectureship 1993, 2004), Am. Soc. Clin. Investigation, Alpha Omega Alpha. Office: Johns Hopkins Asthma and Allegy Ctr 5501 Hopkins Bayview Cir Baltimore MD 21224-6821

BOCHNER, MEL, artist; b. Pitts., 1940; B.F.A., Carnegie Inst. Tech., 1962. Former instr. Sch. Visual Arts, N.Y.C. One-man shows Galerie Heiner Friedrich, Munich, Galerie Konrad Fischer, Dusseldorf, Germany, Ace Gallery, Los Angeles, 1969, Galleria Sperone, Torino, Italy, 1970, Galleria Toselli, Milan, Italy, 1970, Mus. Modern Art, N.Y.C., 1971, Galerie Sonnabend, Paris, 1972, 73, 74, 78, Sonnabend Gallery, N.Y.C., 1972, 73, 76, 80, 82, 83, Lisson Gallery, London, 1972, Univ. Art Mus., Berkeley, Calif., 1974, Balt. Mus. Art, 1976, Bernier Gallery, Athens, 1977, Gallerie Schema, Milan and Florence, Italy, 1978, Galerie Art in Progress, Dusseldorf, Germany, 1979, Daniel Weinberg Gallery, San Francisco, 1981, Centre Internat. de Creation Artistique, 1982, Abbaye de Senanque, Gordes, France, 1982, Yarlow Salzman Gallery, Toronto, 1983, Daniel Weinberg Gallery, San Francisco, 1983, Pace Editions, N.Y.C., 1983, Santa Barbara Contemporary Arts Forum, 2003, Walker Art Ctr., Mpls., 2003, Galerie Grimm/Rosenfeld, Munich, 2003, Hammer Mus., L.A., 2004; group shows include Finch Coll. Mus. Art, 1967, Paula Cooper Gallery, N.Y.C., 1968, Seattle Art Mus., 1969, Mus. Modern Art, N.Y.C., 1970, Museo Civico D'Arte Moderna, Turin, Italy, 1970, Gallery Nachet St. Stephen, Innsbruck, 1971, Spoleto Festival, Itlay, 1972, Documenta V. Kassel, Germany, 1972, Sonnabend Gallery, N.Y.C., 1972, 77, 81, Kunstmuseum, Basel, Switzerland, 1972, Fogg Mus., Harvard U., Cambridge, Mass., 1973, Seattle Art Mus., Seattle, 1973, Whitney Mus. Am. Art, N.Y.C., 1973, Princeton Art Mus., 1974, Art Inst. Chgo., 1974, Mus. Modern Art, N.Y.C., 1975, Am. Drawings' Mus., Leverkusen, 1975, Art Gallery Ont., 1975, Mus. Modern Art, N.Y.C., 1976, Chgo. Art Inst., 1976, Fort Worth Mus., 1976, Detroit Inst. Art, 1976, Whitney Mus. Am. Art, N.Y.C., 1977, 83, Mus. Contemporary Art, Chgo., 1977, Phila. Mus. Art, 1978, Leo Castelli Gallery, 1978, Whitney Mus. Am. Art, N.Y.C., 1979, Palazzo Reale, Milan, Italy, 1979, W Centre Georges Pomipdou, Beauborg, Paris, 1979, MIT, 1980, Beaubourg Centre Nationale d'Art et de Culture, 1981-82, Centre Georges Pompidou, 1981-82, Chgo. Art Inst., 1982, Yale U. Art Gallery, 1982, Janet Steinberg Gallery, Sonnabend Gallery; invited exhibitor 2004 Biennial Exhbn., Whitneys Mus. Am. Art, N.Y., 2004; represented in permanent collections Los Angeles County Mus., Mus. Nat. d'Art Moderne, Paris, Whitney Mus. Am. Art; film Walking a Straight Line Through Grand Central Station, 1965, N.Y.C. Windows, 1965, Dorothea in Fifteen Positions Stasis, 1970; contbr. articles to profl. jours. Recipient Acad.-Inst. award for art, 1990. Office: care Sonnabend Gallery 420 W Broadway New York NY 10012-3764*

BOCHY, BRUCE, professional sports team manager, coach; b. Landes de Boussac, France, Apr. 16, 1955; m. Kim B.; children: Greg, Brett. Coach San Diego Padres, 1993-94, mgr., 1994—. Named Am. League Mgr. of Yr., 1996. Office: San Diego Padres PO Box 2000 San Diego CA 92112-2000*

BOCIAN, PETE, corporate financial executive; BA, Mich. State U., M in Acctg., 1982. Various mgmt. positions NCR Corp., Dayton, Ohio, 1983—2002, CFO, v.p. retail solutions divsn., 1999—2002, CFO retail and fin. group, 2002—03, v.p., fin., CFO, 2003—. Office: NCR Corp 1700 S Patterson Blvd Dayton OH 45479

BOCK, ANGELA MARIE, librarian; b. Cape Girardeau, Mo., Mar. 12, 1939; d. Byron Ford and Bonnie Marie (Farquhar) Dormeyer; m. Ralph Garland Bock, June 24, 1961; children: Julie Anne, Karen Lynnette Bock. BSEd., U. Mo., 1961. Cert. libr. K-12, Mo. Libr. Pattonville Sch. Dist., St. Louis County, Mo., 1961-62, Orchard Farm Sch. Dist., St. Charles, Mo., 1971—2003, dept. chmn., 1985—2003, chmn. North Ctrl. Accreditation Commn., 1985-87; sub. tchr., 2004—. Com. mem. Mo. Sch. Libr. Evaluation, Jefferson City, 1984; mem. evaluation team for Bayless Sch. Dist. and N.W. Sch. Dist., North Ctrl. Accreditation Commn., Mo., 1980, 85, mem. dist. prof. devel. com., 1996-97, dist. tech. com., 1996-2003. Sponsor Youth in Govt., St. Charles, 1981—; libr. 1st United Meth. Ch., St. Charles, 1969-74, dir. Vacation Ch. Sch., 1967-68. Recipient Svc. award YMCA, St. Charles, 1988. Mem. Mo. Sch. Librs., Mo. Assn. Ednl. Tech., St. Louis Suburban Librs., St. Louis Area Sch. Libr. Suprs. (sec. 1992—), Phi Delta Kappa (historian 1989-90), Delta Delta Delta (group pres. 1963-68), Kappa Epsilon Alpha, Sigma Epsilon Sigma, Pi Lambda Theta. Republican. Avocations: european travel, reading. Home: 5 Sussex Ct Saint Charles MO 63301-1114

BOCK, BROOKS FREDERICK, emergency physician; b. Orange, N.J., Sept. 19, 1943; MD, Wayne State U., 1969. Intern Detroit Gen. Hosp., 1969-70; resident in surgery Wayne State U., 1970-71, resident in urology, 1971-73, prof., chmn. dept. emergency medicine, 1985—; specialist-in-chief emergency medicine Detroit Med. Ctr.; pvt. practice. Mem. Am. Bd. Emergency Medicine, 1995—2004, pres., 2002—03. Mem. AMA, Am. Coll. Emergency Physicians, Mich. State Med. Soc., Wayne County Med. Soc. Home: 5764 Bloomfield Glens West Bloomfield MI 48322-2501 Office: 3990 John R Detroit MI 48201-2445

BOCK, RUSSELL SAMUEL, writer; b. Spokane, Wash., Nov. 24, 1905; s. Alva and Elizabeth (Mellinger) B.; m. Suzanne Ray, Feb. 26, 1970; children: Beverly A. Bock Wunderlich, James Russell. BBA, U. Wash., 1929. Part-time instr. U. So. Calif., UCLA, 1942-50; with Ernst & Ernst, CPAs, Los Angeles, 1938, ptnr., 1951-69; cons. Ernst & Young, 1969—. Author: Guidebook to California Taxes, annually, 1950—, Taxes of Hawaii, annually, 1964—; also numerous articles. Dir., treas. Cmty. TV So. Calif., 1964-74; dir., v.p. treas., So. Calif. Symphony-Hollywood Bowl Assn., 1964-70; bd. dirs. Claremont McKenna Coll., 1964-70, Cmty. Arts Music Assn., 1974-76, 78-84, Santa Barbara Symphony Assn., 1976-78, Santa Barbara Boys and Girls Club, 1980-93, UCSB Affiliates, 1983-85, Santa Barbara Civic Light Opera, 1995-97. Mem. Am. Inst. C.P.A.s (council 1953-57, trial bd. 1955-58, v.p. 1959-60), Calif. Soc. C.P.A.s (past pres.), Los Angeles C. of C. (dir. 1957-65, v.p. 1963), Sigma Phi Epsilon, Beta Alpha Psi, Beta Gamma Sigma. Clubs: Birnam Wood Golf, Santa Barbara Yacht. Office: 300 Hot Springs Rd Apt 190 Santa Barbara CA 93108-2069

BOCK, WALTER JOSEPH, zoology educator; b. N.Y.C., Nov. 20, 1933; s. Paul and Anne (Kalsch) B.; m. Katharine Lippitt, June 29, 1957; children: Katharine Rose, Susan Ruth, Walter David. BS, Cornell U., 1955; MA, Harvard U., 1957, PhD, 1959. NSF postdoctoral fellow Universität Frankfurt Main, 1959-61; asst. prof. dept. zoology U. Ill., 1961-64, assoc. prof., 1964-65; asst. prof. dept. biol. scis. Columbia U., 1965-66, assoc. prof., 1966-73, prof., 1973—. Rsch. assoc. Am. Mus Natural History, 1965—. Author: (with J.J. Morony and J. Farrand) Reference List of the Birds of the World, 1975; Contbr. articles to profl. jours. Pres. Tenafly (N.J.) Nature Ctr., 1977-80; permanent sec. Internat. Ornithol. Com., 1986-98; pres. 23d Internat. Ornithol. Congress, 2002; v.p. Internat. Congress Zoology, 2004. NSF grantee, 1962-79 Mem. Am. Ornithologists Union (Coues award 1975), Am. Soc. Zoologists, Am. Soc. Naturalists (treas. 1978-80), Soc. Study Evolution, Soc. Systematic Biology, AAAS, Brit. Ornithologists Union (corres. mem.), Deutschen Ornithologen-Gesellschaft (hon.) Home: 114 Hudson Ave Tenafly NJ 07670-1004 Office: Columbia U Dept Biological Scis New York NY 10027 Office Phone: 212-854-4487. Business E-Mail: wb4@columbia.edu. *Humans are not independent of the earth's environment in which they live and of their evolutionary history. As a scholar, I hope to learn about evolutionary and ecological mechanisms; as a teacher I hope to pass this knowledge on to others; and as a person I hope to preserve and enjoy the beauty of nature that exists about us.*

BOCKER, HANS JURGEN, editor-in-chief, consultant, finance educator; b. Thuringia, Germany, July 13, 1939; s. Hans Alfred and Liselotte (Böttcher) B.; m. Megan Elizabeth Sutton, Jan. 4, 1960; children: Adrian Alexander, Chloe April. MS in Engring., Tech. Univ., Darmstadt, 1964; MBA, Tech. Univ., Munich, 1968; Dr. Commerce, Univ. S. Africa, Pretoria, 1978. Cert. mech. engr., mgmt. prof., editor. Lectr. Univ. S. Africa, Pretoria, 1968-72, sr. lectr., 1972-78; pvt. practice indsl. and economic cons. various internat. companies and govts., 4 continents, 1969-86; assoc. prof. Wilfrid Laurier U., Waterloo, Ont., Can., 1978-84, Western Ill. U., 1984-86; editor-in-chief Finanz und Wirtschaft (Finance and Economy), London, 1986-91, Zollikerberg, B.C., Switzerland, 1992—; prof. EBS, London, 1986-91, Internat. Sch. Mgmt., 1993—. Front-page columnist for Finanz und Wirtschaft; permanent vis. prof. bus. schs.; work with Treuhand Anstalt, Berlin; presenter in field; pres. Internat. Sch. Mgmt., Dortmund, 1993—; cons. to Internet Initial Pub. Offerings; chmn. bd. numerous cos. Author: books, study guides, case studies, interviews with famous personalities. Sometime TV and radio performer. Grantee Volkswagen Found. W. Germany 1964-66, many rsch. grants. Mem. Inst. Mgmt. Sci, Am. Inst. Decision Scis., Acad. Mgmt., Canadian Purchasing Assn., Swiss Fedn. Journalists, Inst. Corp. Orgn. and Comm. Switzerland (pres.), British Assn. Fgn. Journalists, Surrey Country and Tennis Club, Rotary Internat. Avocation: classical pianist. Office: Postfach 188 CH-8125 Zollikerberg Switzerland

BOCKIAN, JAMES BERNARD, computer systems executive, writer; b. Jersey City, Sept. 16, 1941; s. Abraham and Evelyn (Skner) B.; m. Donna M. Hastings; children: Vivian Shifra, Adrian Adena, Lillian Tova. BA, Columbia U., 1963; MPA, U. Mich., 1965; MA, Yale U., 1967. Vice-consul, fgn. svc. officer Dept. State, Washington, 1967—71; sr. systems analyst J.C. Penney Co., N.Y.C., 1971—77; mgr. systems svcs., head dept. systems projects McDonnell Douglas Automation Co., Florham Park, NJ, 1977—86; prin. JBBA (James B. Bockian & Assocs., Inc.), Morristown, NJ, 1976—. V.p. MIS Thomas Cook, Inc., 1986-90, exec. cons. to Thomas Cook Group; cons. AT&T, major banks and brokerages in project mgmt. systems design and devel., 1997-2001; lectr. in field; cons. in sys. validation to the pharm. industry. Author: Management Manual for Systems Development Projects, 1979, Project Management for Systems Development, 1981, AT&T User Guide to Information Systems Development, 1980; contbr. articles to profl. jours. Mem. Internat. Soc. Pharm. Engrs., AAAS, N.Y. Acad. Scis., Internat. Assn. Cybernetics, Yale Club (N.Y.C.). Home: 280 James St Morristown NJ 07960 Office: 280 James St Morristown NJ 07960-6410 Office Phone: 973-292-9494. Personal E-mail: jimbockian@optonline.net.

BOCKOVEN, JERRY N., psychologist, educator; b. Lincoln, Nebr., Sept. 30, 1954; s. Louise Ferebee; m. Dorothy Bockoven, Dec. 22, 1975; children: Michael, Katie. PhD, U. Oreg., 1988. Lic. Psychologist Nebr., 1988. Exec. dir. Samarutan Counseling Ctr., Lincoln, Nebr., 1993—2000; chair, psychology dept. Nebr. Wesleyan U., 2000—. Clin. psychologist Lincoln Regional Ctr., Lincoln, Nebr., 1990—93. Mem.: Nebr. Psychol. Assn. (academic affairs chair 2003). American Baptist. Achievements include Alumni Award from Sioux Falls College, Sioux Falls, SD. Avocations: musical performance, magic. Office: Nebraska Wesleyan Univ 5000 Saint Paul Ave Lincoln NE 68504-2796 Office Phone: 402-465-2433. Personal E-mail: jnb@nebrwesleyan.edu.

BOCKSERMAN, ROBERT JULIAN, chemist; b. St. Louis, Dec. 20, 1929; s. Max Louis and Bertha Anna (Kremen) B.; m. Clarice K. Kreisman, June 9, 1957; children: Michael Jay, Joyce Ellen, Carol Beth. BSc, U. Mo., 1952; postgrad., Far East Intelligence Sch, Tokyo, 1954; MSc, U. Mo., 1955. Chemist Sealtest Corp., Peoria, Ill., 1955-56; prodn. mgr. Allan Drug Co., St. Louis, 1957-59; rsch. chemist Monsanto Co., St. Louis, 1960-65, purchasing agt. Sauget, Ill., 1966-67; founder, pres. Pharma-Tech Industries, Inc., Union, Mo., 1967-84; tech. dir. Overlock-Howe Consulting Group, St. Louis, 1984-85; founder, pres. Conatech Consulting Group, Creve Coeur, Mo., 1985—. Sec., mem. industry packaging adv. com. Sch. of Engring. U. Mo., Rolla, 1979—, adj. prof. dept. food sci./nutrition, Columbia, adj. prof. dept. engring. mgmt., Rolla, vis. lectr., Clayton, Northwestern U., Evanston, Ill.; vol. tutor Ladue Sch. Dist.; tutor Parkway Sch. Dist., St. Louis, Clayton (Mo.) Sch. Dist.; tech. cons. Creve Coeur Fire Protection Dist.; cons. HAZMAT Team St. Louis County; mentor U. Mo. Dept. Food Sci. and Nutrition; tech. cons. hazardous products EPA, CPSC. Tech. reviewer Jour. Inst. of Packaging Profls., Jour. Packaging Tech., Mo. Waste Control Scholarship Grants and Research, Medical Device and Diagnostic Industry Jour., Medical Plastics and Biomaterials Publication.; mem. editl. adv. bd. The Forensic Examiner; panelist (Help Desk column) Medical Device and Diagnostic Industry mag., The Forensic Examiner; contbg. author: Packaging Forensics - Package Failure in the Courts. Mem. Mo. Waste Control Coalition; mem. stormwater engring. com. City of Creve Coeur, Mo., also mem. recycling and environ. com.; tech. cons. Hazmat Team, St. Louis County, Mo.; nat. mem. Libr. Congress, Mo. Hist. Soc. With U.S. Army, 1952-54, Korea. Small Bus. Innovation rsch. grantee. Mem. ASTM, Am. Coll. Forensic Examiners, Cons. Packaging Engring. Coun., Inst. Packaging Profls. (cert. packaging profl.), Am. Technion Soc., Inst. Food Technologists Arrangements (St. Louis), Nat. Forensic Ctr., Teltech Resource Network, Am. Chem. Soc., Am. Plastics Coun., Mo. Acad. Scis., N.Y. Acad. Sci., Acad. Sci. St. Louis, Assn. Cons. Chemists and Chem. Engrs., Am. Nutraceutical Assn., Nat. Dir. Expert Witnessess, Rotary Internat., Wash. U. Century Club, Juvenile Diabetes Rsch. Found., Sigma Xi. Achievements include research on toxicological effects of additives from packaging materials upon foodstuffs, on biological and photo degradation of polymers, on technology of form/fill/seal packaging engineering, new sterilization technologies for medical devices and pharmaceuticals, barrier properties of polymer films, toxicology of chemical dusts and fumes, and food irradiation effects on humans neurotoxicity of organic solvents. Home: 54 Morwood Ln Creve Coeur MO 63141-7621 Office: Conatech Cons Group 501 N Lindbergh Blvd Creve Coeur MO 63141-7844 Office Phone: 314-995-9767. Business E-Mail: rjbockserman@conatech.com.

BOCKSTEIN, HERBERT, lawyer; b. NYC, Jan. 27, 1943; s. Stanley Joseph and Sylvia (Tannenbaum) B.; m. Bonnie Sue Ritt, Sept. 2, 1967 (div.); children: Andrew, Jana; m. Nadine Bernstein, June 27, 1988. BA, NYU, 1963, JD cum laude, 1971; MBA, Cornell U., Ithaca, NY, 1966. Bar: NY 1972, Mo. 1979. Assoc. Stroock & Stroock & Lavan, NYC, 1971-78, Stolar, Heitzmann & Eder, St. Louis, 1978-80, Finley, Kumble, Wagner, Heine, Underberg, Manley & Casey, NYC, 1980-83; ptnr. Finley, Kumble, NYC, 1983-87, Myerson & Kuhn, NYC, 1988-89, Ashinoff, Ross & Korff, NYC, 1989-90, Newman Tannenbaum, NYC, 1990—96, Blank Rome LLP, NYC, 1996—. Mem.: N.Y. State Bar Assn., Estate Planning Coun. N.Y.C., Order of Coif. Avocations: tennis, golf. Home: 70 Garth Rd Apt 3C Scarsdale NY 10583 Office: Blank Rome LLP 405 Lexington Ave New York NY 10174-0002 Office Phone: 212-885-5312. Business E-Mail: hbockstein@blankrome.com.

BOCKSTRUCK, LLOYD DEWITT, librarian; b. Vandalia, Ill., May 26, 1945; s. Harry Earl and Olive Elsie (Blankenship) B. AB cum laude, Greenville (Ill.) Coll., 1967; MA, So. Ill. U., 1969; MS, U. Ill., 1973; student, Samford U., 1973. Teaching asst. So. Ill. U., Carbondale, 1967—69; tchr. Mombasa (Kenya) Bapt. High Sch., 1969—71; teaching asst. U. Ill., Urbana, 1972—73; libr. Dallas Pub. Libr., 1973—. Instr. Inst. Genealogy and Hist. Rsch., Samford U., Birmingham, Ala., 1973—; instr. Sch. Continuing Edn., So. Meth. U., Dallas, 1974-91; instr. Geneal. Inst. of Mid-Am., U. Ill., Springfield, 1994—; columnist Dallas Morning News, 1991—. Author: Virginia's Colonial Soldiers, 1988, Genealogical Research in Texas, 1992, Revolutionary War Bounty Land Grants Awarded by State Governments, 1996, Family Tree Weekly Newspaper Columns from the Dallas Morning News, 1001-1996, 1999, Naval Pensioners of the United States, 1800-1851, 2002, Denizations and Naturalizations in the British Colonies in America, 1607-1775, 2005; contbr. articles to profl. jours. Recipient Scholarship Key award Phi Alpha Theta, 1967, History award DAR, 1989, Profl. award for hist. preservation Dallas County Hist. Commn., 1992, Filby prize for Genealogical Librarianship, 1999, Lifetime Achievement award N.E. Tex. Libr. Sys., 2003; Nat. Geneal. Soc. fellow, 1992; Gold Good Citizenship award, SAR, 2005. Mem. ALA (life), SAR (libr. gen. 1981-83), SCW (dep. gov. gen. 2000), Soc. of the Cincinnati, Jamestowne Soc., Order of Ams. of Armorial Ancestry (genealogist gen. 1993-99), Order of Founders and Patriots of Am. (genealogist gen. 1986-2000), Dallas Geneal. Soc. (dir. 1979—). Republican. Avocation: genealogy. Home: 3955 Buena Vista St Apt C Dallas TX 75204-1667 Office: Dallas Pub Libr 1515 Young St Dallas TX 75201-5499 Office Phone: 214-670-1406.

BOCOBO-BALUNSAT, DALISAY, librarian, journalist; b. Metro Manila, Philippines, Jan. 22, 1926; d. Jorge Bocobo; m. Anthony Anton Balunsat. PhB, U. Philippines, 1950. Faculty mem. Adamson U., Manila, 1950—53; corr., columnist Philippine-Am. press, 1953—; ref. libr. San Francisco Pub. Libr., 1958—84. Founder, dir. Philippine-Am. Cultural Celebration, San Francisco, 1973—, Filipino Artists, Writers and Performers, 1973—. Recipient Woman Warrior award, Pacific Asian Am. Women, John Cotton Dana Nat. Libr. award, ALA, 1975, U.S. Bicentennial award, Filipino Arts Fiesta, 1976, Salutes to Asian-Am., mayor, bd. suprs. San Francisco and Calif. Legislatures, 2002, Outstanding Cmty. Svc. award, San Francisco Bd. of Supr. and Legis., 2004, Cert. of Honor, City and County of San Francisco, 2004. Mem.: Phillipine-Am. Press Corr., Filipino Artists, Writers, Performers, ALA (Dana Nat. Libr. award 1975). Avocation: reading, writing, travel, movies, TV. Office: Filipino Artists Writers and Performers 1437 19th Ave San Francisco CA 94122

BOCOCK, SCOTT GREGORY, historian; b. Hammond, Ind., Sept. 26, 1967; s. Carman Robert and Mary Ann Bocock. B in Gen. Studies, Ind. U. N.W., Gary, 1993. Hist. interpreter, groundskeeper Buckley Homestead Lake County Pk., Lowell, Ind., 1990; pres. Cedar Lake (Ind.) Hist. Assn., 1993—95; historian Town of Cedar Lake, 1994—2001, City of Westminster, Colo., 2001—; Ind. rm. page Gary (Ind.) Pub. Libr., 1999—2000. Vol. Cedar Lake Hist. Assn., 1989—2001, Adams County Hist. Soc., Brighton, Colo., 2002. Recipient cert. for contbn., Cedar Lake Hist. Assn., Lake of Red Cedars Mus., Ind., 1992, plaque, Cedar Lake Town Coun., 2001; scholar Cornelius O'Brien Confs. on Historic Preservation, Ind U., 1990—91. Mem.: Nat. Trust for Historic Preservation, Orgn. Am. Historians, Am. Assn. State and Local History. Achievements include helping in development of Lake of Red Cedars Museum; listing Old Monon Park Dancing Pavilion in Cedar Lake on the National Register of Historic Places. Avocations: reading, writing, antiques, preserving artifacts, genealogy. Home: 13206 Parish Ave Cedar Lake IN 46303-2608

BODANSKY, DAVID, physicist, researcher; b. N.Y.C., Mar. 10, 1924; s. Aaron and Marie (Syrkin) B.; m. Beverly Ferne Bronstein, Sept. 7, 1952; children: Joel N., Daniel M. BS, Harvard U., 1943, MA, 1948, PhD, 1950. Instr. physics Columbia U., N.Y.C., 1950-52, assoc., 1952-54; mem. faculty U. Wash., Seattle, 1954—, assoc. prof. physics, 1958-63, prof., 1963-93, prof. emeritus, 1993—, chmn. dept., 1976-84. Co-author: (with Fred H. Schmidt) The Energy Controversy: The Fight over Nuclear Power, 1976, (with others) Indoor Radon and Its Hazards, 1987, Nuclear Energy: Principles, Practices, and Prospects, 1996, 2d edit., 2004; editl. bd.: Rev. Sci. Instruments, 1967-69. With Signal Corps AUS, 1943-46. Sloan Research fellow, 1959-63; Guggenheim fellow, 1966-67, 74-75 Fellow Am. Phys. Soc. (chair Panel on Pub. Affairs 1995), AAAS; mem. Am. Assn. Physics Tchrs., Am. Nuc. Soc., Health Physics Soc., Phi Beta Kappa. Achievements include research in nuclear physics, nuclear astrophysics and energy policy. Office: U Wash Dept Physics Seattle WA 98195-1560 Business E-Mail: bodansky@phys.washington.edu.

BODANSZKY, MIKLOS, chemist, educator; b. Budapest, Hungary, May 21, 1915; came to U.S., 1957, naturalized, 1964; s. Lajos and Maria (Friedner) B.; m. Agnes A. Vadasz, Apr. 21, 1950; 1 child, Eva. Diploma in chem. engring, Tech. U. Budapest, 1939, DSc, 1949. Sr. lectr. Tech. U. Budapest, 1950-56; research assoc. Cornell U. Med. Coll., 1957-59; sr. research assoc. Squibb Inst. Med. Research, New Brunswick, N.J., 1959-66; prof. chemistry and biochemistry Case Western Res. U., Cleve., 1966-83, Charles Frederic Mabery prof. research in chemistry, 1978-83, prof. emeritus, 1983—. Author: Peptide Synthesis, 1966, 2d edit., 1976, Principles of Peptide Syntheses, 1984, 2d edit, 1993, The Practice of Peptide Synthesis, 1984, 2d edit., 1994, Greek transl., 1984, Indonesian transl., 1998, Peptide Chemistry, 1988, 2d edit., 1993, The World of Peptides, 1991; editorial bd. Jour. Antibiotics, 1971-87, Internat. Jour. Peptide Protein Rsch., 1978-89. Recipient Pierce award, 1977; Morley medal, 1978; A. von Humboldt award, 1979 Mem. Am. Chem. Soc., Am. Soc. Biol. Chemistry, Hungarian Acad. Scis. (fgn.). Achievements include research in Nitrophenyl ester method of peptide synthesis, 1954; first synthesis gastrointestinal hormone secretin, 1966; synthesis vasoactive intestinal peptide, 1973.

BODDIE, DON O'MAR, recording industry executive; b. St. Louis, Mo., Nov. 22, 1944; s. George Palmer and Lucille (Owens) Johnson-Boddie; m. Martha Lee Brown, Oct. 11, 1970 (div. Dec. 1979); children: Don O'Mar, Anthony, Shawn, Shellie; m. Paula R. Smith, 1991; children: Courtney, George, Kyle. BS in Bus. Mgmt., BS in Mgmt., Tarkio Coll., 1988, St. Louis

Music Inst., 1968; MA in Tchg., Webster U., 2002. Cert. cross categorical K-12, Mo. Rec. artist Bamboo Records, St. Louis, 1966-70; producer, writer Puzzletown Prodns., St. Louis, 1970-77, James Earl World Prodns., East St. Louis, Ill. and, Memphis, 1975-79, Hi Records, Memphis, 1975-79, Motown Records, Los Angeles, 1976-78; owner, prodr., writer, artist Chrome Records, St. Louis, 1978—. Cons. Archway Studios, St. Louis, 1970-85, Music Assocs. in Mo. Corp, Jefferson City, Mo., 1978—, JD Mgmt., St. Louis, 1978—; v.p. Scorpio Prodns., Pine Lawn, Mo., 1980-82, music prodr., 1980-84. Producer: Lets Be Lovers, 1985 (Heritage award), The Legend, 1986 (Heritage award); rec. artist Can't Stop the Fire, 1987 (Heritage award), New Thing Between Us (charted Top 5 on Midwest Survey 1990, 91), True Love (charted Top 5 on Midwest Survey, 1990, 91); host, presenter Gateway Music Awards Ceremony, 1991; headliner for Cigarettes/Salem Spirit Festival, 1985; featured performer Shock Wave Music TV Show, Friends of the Black Music Soc. Gateway Awards Lacledes Landing, 1991. Mem. entertainment com. to elect Irene Smith, St. Louis, 1982, Music Assocs. Mo. (pres. 1986—), St. Louis Bd. Edn. State Mo., 1991, Chpt. 1 reading tchr. (basic skills), 1995, secondary edn. gen. edn. devel. (ABE), sr. master tchr., Adult Basic Edn., 1997, 98, music dir., Clay Cmty. Edn. Ctr.; chpt. 1 reading tchr. St. Louis Pub. Sch. Dist., 1991—, vocal music tchr., 1996—, instrumental music tchr., 1996—, spl. edn. cross categorical tchr., 1998—. Recipient Named New R&B Rec. Artist of Yr. Gateway Music award, 1990, 91, citation for exceptional performance in edn. of children with spl. needs St. Louis Pub. Sch. Dist., 2002 Democrat. Roman Catholic. Avocations: basketball, martial arts. Office: Pierre Toussaint L'Ouverture Accelerated Mid Sch 3021 Hickory St Saint Louis MO 63118 E-mail: player112244@yahoo.com.

BODDIGER, GEORGE CYRUS, insurance corporate executive, consultant; b. Polo, Ill., July 5, 1917; s. George E. and Bertha Belle (Billig) B.; m. Wilma Helen Ray, May 23, 1943; children: Nancy Boddiger Estrada, Jean Boddiger Johnstone, Kathryn Boddiger Jones. BS, U. Ill., 1939; MBA with distinction, Harvard U., 1943. Various positions Mut. of Omaha, Omaha, 1952-59; pres., dir. Pacific Fidelity Life Ins. Co., Los Angeles, 1959-71, Equitable Life Ins. Co., Washington, 1971-82; vice chmn., dir. Gulf United Corp., Jacksonville, Fla., 1982-84. Bd. dirs. Premier Parking Corp.; adv. bd. DCG Corp. Author: Getting People To Work Together Effectively (A Practical Guide to First Line Supervision), 2000. Mem. U. Ill. Found., Pres.'s Coun.; trustee, sec. Nat. Capital chpt. Nat. Multiple Sclerosis Soc., 1976-2004; pres. Multiple Sclerosis Internat. Fedn., 1983-85, pres. emeritus; elder Potomac Presbyn. Ch. With AUS, 1943-46. Recipient Norman Cohn Hope award Nat. Multiple Sclerosis Soc., Bess Goodman Humanitarian award, Lifetime Achievement award Internat. Fedn. Multiple Sclerosis Socs. Fellow Life Mgmt. Inst.; mem. Am. Coll. Life Underwriters, Harvard Bus. Sch. Club Washington (chmn., dir.), Sigma Alpha Epsilon. Clubs: Congressional Country (Bethesda, Md.); Met. (Washington). Office: 333 Russell Ave Apt 201 Gaithersburg MD 20877-2842 Office Phone: 301-216-5163.

BODDY, GEORGE WILLIAM, educational administrator; b. Sioux City, Iowa, Mar. 7, 1945; s. William George and Kathryn Marcella (Wells) B.; m. Linda Lou Barrett, Aug. 26, 1967; children: Heidi, Heath. BS, S.D. State U., 1968, MEd, 1970; PhD, U. Nebr., 1985. Cert. secondary tchr. Nebr. HS counselor Elkhorn Pub. Schs., Nebr., 1970—77; coord. spl. tng. Met. Tech. Cmty. Coll., Omaha, 1977—80; dir. program devel. U. Nebr.-Omaha, 1980—83, dir. conf. and cmty. program, 1983—. Served with USNG, 1980—. Mem.: Am. Soc. Tng. and Devel. (pres. 1981—82, Outstanding Mem. 1982). Lutheran. Home: 611 Pacific St Elkhorn NE 68022-1345 Office: U Nebr Coll Continuing Studies Omaha NE 68022

BODE, BARBARA, Internet entrepreneur, foundation executive, freelance/self-employed writer; b. Evanston, Ill. d. Carl and Margaret Emilie (Lutze) B. BA magna cum laude, MA, U. Md.; scholar, Ludwig-Maximillians-Universitat, Munich; English Speaking Union scholar, U. London; Bundesrepublik scholar, Goethe Institut, Lubeck, W. Ger.; postgrad. NDEA fellow, UCLA. Woodrow Wilson teaching intern N.C. Central U., Durham; pres. Children's Found., Washington, 1970-86, Council on Founds., 1986-89; v.p. Coun. Better Bus. Bur., 1990-95; exec. dir. Coun. Bettter Bus. Bur. Found., 1990-95; founder Campaigns Online, Washington, 1998-2000; bd. mem. Children's Found., Washington, 1986—; founder CashCares.com., 2000—03. Bd. dirs. Children's Found., Rainbow TV Works, Disability Rights, 1974-99, Edn. and Def. Fund Partnership, 1993-2001, Women's Campaign Fund, 1984-88; founding mem. Women of Washington, 1992—, Leadership Washington, class of 1994, 94—; trustee The Richmond Found., 1978-99. Woodrow Wilson Nat. Found. fellow, 1963-64. Episcopalian. Office: BodeCorp 2400 Sixteenth St NW Ste 504 Washington DC 20009 Home: 725 15th St NW Ste 505 Washington DC 20005-2109 E-mail: bb@cashcares.com.

BODE, DAVID ALLEN, music educator; b. Columbus, July 30, 1969; s. Robert Conrad and Joetta Louise Bode; m. Launa Kay Hill, Dec. 27, 1997; children: Collin, Madison. B in Music Edn., Ohio State U., 1992, MA in Music Edn., 2001. Cert. profl. tchr. Ohio. Instrumental music tchr. Columbus Diocese, 1992—95, Amanda-Clearcreek Local Sch., Ohio, 1995—96, Lancaster (Ohio) City Sch., 1996—. Avocations: boating, fly fishing. Office: Lancaster High Sch Stanbery Freshman Campus 315 E Mulberry St Lancaster OH 43130

BODEMER, ANDREW L, music educator; b. Corning, NY, May 5, 1979; s. Guy L and Susan L Bodemer. BM, SUNY Fredonia, 1997—2000; MM, U. of Conn., 2002—04. Music Education K-12 NY, 2000. Instrumental music tchr. 4-6 Eden Ctrl. Sch. Dist., Eden, NY, 2000—01; instrumental music tchr. 7-12 Cairo-Durham Ctrl. Sch. Dist., Cairo, NY, 2001—02; instrumental music tchr. 4-5 Clarence Ctrl. Sch. Dist., Clarence, NY, 2002—. Laura B. Ross Meml. scholarship, Fredonia Coll. Found., 1998, Found. Freshman scholarship, 1997, Luverne Winkler Meml. scholarship, 1999, 2000. Mem.: NBA, ECMEA, MENC/NYSSMA. D-Liberal. Home: 951 New Rd Amherst NY 14228 Office: Clarence Ctr Elementary Sch 9600 Clarence Center Rd Clarence Center NY 14032 Office Phone: 716-407-9150. Personal E-mail: abodemer@adelphia.net.

BODEN, GUENTHER, endocrinologist; b. Ludwigshafen, Germany, Jan. 8, 1935; came to U.S., 1965; s. Alwin and Irma (Godelman) B.; m. Irene Ulrike Dingeldein, Dec. 12, 1970; children: Karin, Stephanie, Eric, Dirk. MS, Heidelberg U., Germany, 1956; MD, Munich U., 1959. Intern City Hosp. Hamburg, Germany, 1960-62; rsch. fellow in biochemistry U. Tübingen, Germany, 1963-65; rsch. fellow in medicine P.B. Brigham Hosp., Boston, 1965-67; resident physician Rochester (N.Y.) Gen. Hosp., 1967-70; rsch. prof. biochemistry Temple U. Sch. Medicine, Phila., 1986—, prof. medicine, 1977—2000, Laura H. Carnell prof. of medicine, 2000—. Chief div. endocrinology/metab. Temple U. Sch. Medicine, Phila., 1987—, dir. gen. clin. rsch. ctr., 1989—. Mem. editl. bd. Jour. Clin. Endocrine Metabolism, 1985-88, Clin. Diabetes, 1995—, Am. Jour. Physiology, 1998—; assoc. editor, Diabetes, 2001—; contbr. articles to profl. jours. Rsch. grantee NIH, 1973—, Am. Diabetes Assn., 1985—; recipient Rochester N.Y. Diabetes award Rochester Acad. Medicine, 1970, Novartis Long Standing Achievement award in Diabetes, 2005. Fellow ACP; mem. Am. Diabetes Assn., Am. Soc. Clin. Investigation, Am. Endocrin Soc. Office: Temple Univ Hosp 3401 N Broad St Philadelphia PA 19140-5189 Office Phone: 215-707-8984. Business E-Mail: bodengh@tuhs.temple.edu.

BODEN, MARK EMMANUAL, investment company executive, investment advisor; b. Creston, Iowa, Dec. 11, 1948; s. Clarke Emmanual and Millie Mae (Derauf) Boden; m. Henryka E. Lampert-Boden, Dec. 28, 1985; children: Derrick Emmanual, Bryan Walter, Matthew Charles, David Burnell Milliken. BS, Iowa State U., Ames, Iowa, 1971; MDiv, Luther Theol. Sem., St. Paul, Minn., 1975—80. Ordained Am. Evang. Luth. Ch., 1980, cert. chaplaincy assoc. Hennepin County Ct. Svcs.; registered series 7 Nat. Assn. of Securities Dealers, series 63 Nat. Assn. Of Securities Dealers, options prin. Nat. Assn. Of Securities Dealers, investment advisor Nat. Assn. Of Securities Dealers, 1995, cert. supervisory securities mgmt. Nat. Assn. Of Securities Dealers, sr. advisor Nat. Assn. Of Cert. Sr. Advisors. Asst. faculty mem. Iowa State U., Ames, 1970—73; 4-H and youth dir. USDA, Waterloo, Iowa, 1973—75; youth pastor Calvary Luth. Ch., Mpls., 1977—80; chaplain, Hennepin county ct. services Hennepin County Ct. Services, Mpls., 1982; min. Am. Evang. Luth. Ch., San Mateo, Calif., 1981—83; fin. cons. investments Merrill Lynch, Des Moines, 1983—87, Shearson Lehman Hutton, Boston, 1987—91; br. mgr. investments Paine Webber, North Andover, 1991—93; 1st v.p. investments Prudential Securities, Boston, 1993—95, Morgan Stanley Dean Witter, Boston, 1995—97; assoc. v.p. Albany Fin. Group, Boston, 1997—99; pres., chief investment officer Boston Internat. Pvt. Client Group, 1999—. Vol. Hamilton-Wenham Sports Alliance, Mass., 1999—2004; vol. asst. wrestling coach Hamilton-Wenham Wrestling, Hamilton, Mass., 1996—2004; dir., haunted ln. Blueberry Ln. Assn., Hamilton, Mass., 1996—2004; ch. bd. Clifton Luth. Ch., Marblehead, Mass., 1991—95; fin. adv. bd. New Eng. Synod, AELC, Boston, 1995—97; advisor MBA intern program, 1985—2002. Recipient Letters of Commendation, Intern Supervision Behavioral Goal Setting, 2001. Mem.: Nat. Assn. Of Underwater Instr. (instr. 1969—72). Independent. Lutheran. Achievements include development of non-profit fundraising models; quail and pheasant husbandry; collegiate and H.S. wrestling tng. Avocations: scuba diving, flying, sailing, tennis, wrestling. Office: Boston Internat Pvt Client Grp Ste 1100 28 State St Boston MA 02109 Office Phone: 617-573-5054. Home Fax: 617-573-5090. Personal E-mail: meb@bipcg.com.

BODENBERG, LYNN ALAN, language educator; b. Greensburg, Ind., Jan. 5, 1953; s. Fred T. and Elizabeth F. (Hoyer) Bodenberg; m. Judith Ann Davis, Aug. 3, 1974; children: Jennifer L., Rachel K., Scott M. AA, Harrisburg Area CC, Pa., 1972; BS, Mansfield State Coll., Pa., 1974; MA, Kutztown U., Pa., 1987. Life ins. agent Met. Life, Pottsville, Pa., 1979—81; English tchr. Pottsville Area HS, 1981—, head tchr. English dept., 2003—; composition prof. Pa. State U., Schuylkill Haven, 1995—97. Vice chmn. Child Evangelism Fellowship, Schuykill Haven, 1991—94, chmn., 2005—; pres. Gideons Internat., Pottsville, 2000—02; mem.-at-large Grace E.C. Sunday Sch. Bd., Schuykill Haven, Pa., 2005. Sgt. USAR, 1974—77. Avocations: community theater, woodcarving, woodworking, gardening. Office: 16th St and Elk Ave Pottsville PA Office Phone: 570-621-2962. E-mail: bodie2@verizon.net.

BODENHAMER, DAVID JACKSON, historian, educator; b. Macon, Ga., May 4, 1947; s. David Jackson and Mary Elizabeth (Cox) B.; m. Penny Jo McClelland, Dec. 27, 1988. BA, Carson-Newman Coll., 1969; MA, U. Ala., 1970; PhD, Ind. U., 1976. Asst. prof., then assoc. prof. U. So. Miss., Hattiesburg, 1976-84, prof., asst. v.p. acad. affairs, 1985-88; dir. Polis Ctr. Ind. U., Indpls., 1989—. Head N.Am. team, exec. com. Electronic Cultural Atlas Initiative, 1997—. Author: Pursuit of Justice, 1986, Fair Trial, 1991; editor: Encyclopedia of Indianapolis, 1994; co-editor: Ambivalent Legacy, 1984, Bill of Rights in Modern America, 1992, History of Indiana Law, 2005; editor-in-chief Indiana Online: An Electronic Encyclopedia. Chmn. bd. dirs. South Miss. Community Action Agy., Hattiesburg, 1978-82; bd. dirs. Pine Belt Family YMCA, Hattiesburg, 1982-86; steering com. Regional Ctr. Plan, Indpls, 1989-92; mem. steering com. New Ind. State Mus. Task Force, 1998—, regional ctr. plan, 2002. With U.S. Army, 1970-72. Mem. Am. Soc. Legal History, Orgn. Am. Historians. Office: Polis Ctr Ste 100 1200 Waterway Blvd Indianapolis IN 46202-5140 Office Phone: 317-274-2455. E-mail: intu100@iupui.edu.

BODENHEIMER, GEORGE, broadcast executive; b. Meriden, Conn., May 6, 1958; m. Ann Bodenheimer, Aug. 4, 1984; 3 children. BA in economics, Denison U., 1980. With adminstrv. dept. ESPN Inc., Bristol, Conn., 1981—82, mktg. rep. south ctrl. region Tex., 1982—85, mktg. rep. ctrl. region, 1985, nat. accounts mgr. Rocky Mountain region, 1985—88, dir. affiliate sales and mktg. ea. divsn., 1988—89, v.p. affiliate sales and mktg. ea. divsn. Bristol, Conn., 1989—91, v.p. nat. affiliate sales, 1991—92, v.p. affiliate sales and mktg., 1992—93, sr. v.p. affiliate sales and mktg., 1993—95, sr. v.p. sales and mktg., 1995—96, exec. v.p. sales and mktg., 1996—98, pres. domestic ops., 1998—99, pres., 1999—, ABC Sports, 2003—; co-chair Media Networks divsn. Walt Disney Co., 2004—. Bd. mem. Cable & Telecom. Assoc. for Mktg., Cable TV Advt. Bur., Cable in the Classroom. Office: ESPN Inc Espn Plz Bristol CT 06010-1099 also: ABC Sports 47 W 66th St New York NY 10023

BODENSTEINER, LISA M., utilities executive, lawyer; BS Bus. Adminstrn. & Acctg., U. Nev., 1985; JD, Santa Clara U., 1989. Assoc. Thelen, Reid & Priest, 1994—96; assoc. counsel Calpine Corp., 1996—99, v.p., gen. counsel, 1999—2001, sr. v.p., gen. counsel, 2001—02, asst. sec., exec. v.p., gen. counsel, 2002—. Office: Calpine 50 W San Fernando St 5th Fl San Jose CA 95113

BODEY, BELA, immunologist, pathologist, oncologist; b. Sofia, Bulgaria, Jan. 18, 1949; came to U.S., 1985, naturalized, 1994; s. Joseph and Rossitza (Derebeeva) B.; m. Victoria Psenko, Aug. 29, 1979; children; Bela Jr., Vivian. MD, Med. Acad., Sofia, 1973; PhD in Immuno-Biology, Inst. Morphology, Bulgarian Acad. Sci., Sofia, 1977. Lic. physician, exptl. pathologist, embryologist, immuno-morphologist, thymologist, exptl. oncologist. Asst. prof. Semmelweis Med. U., Budapest, 1977-80; prof. Inst. Hematology, Budapest, 1980-83; rsch. assoc. Tufts U., Boston, 1985; rsch. fellow immuno-pathology Mass. Gen. Hosp./Harvard U., Boston, 1986; rsch. fellow Childrens Hosp. L.A., 1987-90, rsch. scientist, 1991-92; asst. prof. rsch. pathology, Sch. of Medicine Univ. Southern Calif., 1992—, prof. pathology Sch. Medicine, 1995—. Vis. prof. Alexander von Humboldt Found., Ulm, Fed. Republic Germany, 1984. Mem. Am. Assn. Cancer Rsch., Am. and Can. Acad. Pathology, French Soc. Cell Biology, French Soc. Electronmicroscopy, Internat. Soc. Exptl. Hematology, Internat. Soc. Comparative Oncology, N.Y. Acad. Scis., Free Masons. Roman Catholic. Avocations: travel, swimming, dance. Home: 8000 Canby Ave Reseda CA 91335-1378 Office: Childrens Hosp Los Angeles 4650 W Sunset Blvd Los Angeles CA 90027-6062 Office Phone: 818-886-1082. Personal E-mail: bodey18@aol.com.

BODEY, GERALD PAUL, retired medical educator; b. Hazelton, Pa, May 22, 1934; s. Allen Zartman and Marie Frances (Smith) B.; m. Nancy Louise Wiegner, Aug. 25, 1956; children: Robin Gayle Sparwasser, Gerald Paul Jr., Sharon Dawn Brantley. AB magna cum laude, Lafayette Coll., 1956; MD, Johns Hopkins U., 1960. Diplomate Nat. Bd. Med. Examiners, Am. Bd. Internal Medicine, Am. Bd. Infectious Diseases, Am. Bd. Oncology. Intern Johns Hopkins U., Balt., 1960-61, resident, 1961-62; clin. assoc. Nat. Cancer Inst., Bethesda, Md., 1962-65; resident U. Wash., Seattle, 1965-66; internist to prof. medicine U. Tex./M.D. Anderson Cancer Ctr., Houston, 1975—95, emeritus prof. medicine, 1995—, ret., 2004. Prof. internal medicine and pharmacology Univ. Tex. Health Sci. Ctr. Med. Sch., 1976—2004; clin. prof. Univ. Tex. Health Sci. Ctr. Dental Sch., 1977—95; adj. prof. microbiology, immunology and medicine Baylor Coll. of Medicine, Houston, 1975—99; mem. lunar quartine ops. team Apollo 11-14, Manned Spacecraft Ctr., NASA, joint commn. accreditation healthcare orgns. Hospitalwide Indicators Task Force, 1987—89. Mem. editl. bd. Acad. Internat. Jour. of Oncology; contbr. over 1000 articles to profl. jour. Dir. Korean Collaborative Program, 1985-95; past trustee Med. Benevolence Found. Nat. AIDS Prevention Inst.; past bd. dir. Christian Coalition Reconciliation; scholar Leukemia Soc. of Am., 1969-74. Recipient Am. Chem. Soc. prize, 1956, Merck award, 1956, Robert B. Youngman Greek prize Lafayette Coll., 1956, Eugene Yourassowsky award U. Libre de Bruxelles, Belgium, 1995; Henry Strong Denison fellow Johns Hopkins Sch. Medicine, Balt., 1958-60; scholar Leukemia Soc. Am., 1969-74. Fellow ACP, Am. Coll. Chest Physicians, Am. Coll. Clin. Pharmacology, Royal Coll. Medicine, Royal Soc. Promotion Health; mem. AMA, Am. Soc. Clin. Oncology, Infectious Diseases Soc. Am., Am. Soc. Clin. Pharmacology and Therapeutics, Am. Soc. Hematology, Am. Soc. Microbiol., Am. Sci. Affiliation, Internat. Soc. Complexity, Info. and Design, Christian Med. Soc., Tex. Med. Assn., Houston Acad. Medicine, Academia Peruana de Cirugia (hon.), Mediterranean Med. Soc. (hon.), Le Soc. Peruana Cancerologia (hon.), La Costarricensa Oncologie (hon.), Soc. Brasileira Cancerologia (hon.), Phi Beta Kappa, Sigma Xi. Methodist. Office: U Tex MDACC Box 402 1515 Holcombe Blvd Houston TX 77030-4009 Business E-Mail: gbodey@mdanderson.org.

BODEY, RICHARD ALLEN, minister, educator; b. Hazelton, Pa., Nov. 27, 1930; s. Allen Zartman and Marie (Smith) B.; m. Ruth Lois Price, 1955; children: Bronnlyn Beth Spindler, Richard Allen Jr. Student, Muhlenberg Coll., 1948—49; AB, Lafayette Coll, 1952; MDiv, Princeton Theol. Sem., 1955; postgrad., U. Toronto, 1961, Gannon Coll., 1963-64, Winona Lake Sch. Theology, 1963; ThM, Westminster Theol Sem., 1972; DMin, Trinity Evang. Div. Sch., 1984, Seabury-We. Theol. Sem., 1985. Lic. student preacher Evang. Congl. Ch, 1948-52; ordained to ministry Presbyn. Ch. U.S.A., 1955. Student pastor Zion Welsh Presbyn. Ch., Wind Gap, Pa., 1951; student supply pastor Italian Presbyn. Ch., Roseto, Pa., 1951; student pastor Westminster Presbyn. Ch., Allentown, Pa., 1952—55; pastor Marshall Meml. Presby. Ch., Lebanon, Ill., 1955—56; instr. Bible McKendree Coll., Lebanon, 1956; pastor 3d Presbyn. Ch., North Tonawanda, NY, 1956—62; instr. Buffalo Bible Inst., 1961; pastor 1st Presbyn. Ch., Corry, Pa., 1962—64, Dales Meml. United Presbyn. Ch., Phila., 1964—66; asst. prof. Westminster Presbyn. Ch., Jackson, Miss., 1966; founding prof. preaching, chmn. Practical Theol. Dept. Reformed Theol. Sem., Jackson, Miss., 1966—73; interim pastor 1st Presbyn. Ch., Hazlehurst, Miss., 1967—68; stated supply pastor Presbyn. Ch., Union Church, Miss., 1970—73, supply pastor Fayette, Miss., 1970—73; head of staff 1st Assoc. Reformed Presby. Ch., Gastonia, NC, 1973—79; chaplain Civitan, 1975; founder, dir. Gastonia Sch. Bibl. Studies, 1978—79; assoc. prof. practical theol. Trinity Evang. Div. Sch., Deerfield, Ill., 1979—87, prof., 1987—95. Dir. continuing edn. Trinity Evang. Div. Sch., 1982-87, DMin coord. and examiner, 1989-96; instr. preaching Moody Bible Inst. Corr. Sch., Chgo., 1982-86; vis. instr. Westminster Theol. Sem., Phila., 1987, 88; lectr., 1990; cons. in continuing edn., 1990-91; DMin examiner, 1994-96, 2002-03; instr. North Chgo. Theol. Inst., 1991-94; vis. faculty Columbia (S.C.) Internat. U. and Sem., 1991; seminar leader Nat. Conf. on Preaching, 1990-94; Bible conf. and retreat spkr. Author: You Can Live Without Fear of Death, 1980; editor, contbr. Good News for All Seasons: 26 Sermons for Special Days, 1987, (Korean edit., 1990), Inside the Sermon: Thirteen Preachers Discuss Their Methods of Preparing Messages, 1990, The Voice from the Cross: Seven Sermons on the Last Words of Our Lord, 1990, 2d edit., 2000, If I Had Only One Sermon to Preach, 1994; editor: Voices Trinity Evang. Div. Sch., 1980-88, Trinity Book Bull., 1989-94, The Lamb of God (Sermans by Clarence Edward Macartney), 1994; co-editor: Come to the Banquet, 1998; contbr. Ministers Manual, 1974, 82, Zondervan Pictorial Bible Ency., 1975, Baker Ency. of Bible, 1988, Handbook of Contemporary Preaching, 1993, The Complete Library of Christian Worship, 1996, Ministry to the Aging, 2005; co-editor, contbr.: Revelation Revealed Day by Day, 2001; contbr. articles and revs. to profl. jours. Chmn. Here's Life Metrolina, Gastonia Area, 1976; founding bd. chmn. Gaston Evang. Assn., 1978-79; bd. dirs. Gaston Christian Sch., 1978-79; chmn. planning com. Evang. Affirmations, 1989; chaplain Civitan, 1974. Recipient Porter Bible prize Lafayette Coll., 1950, David Fowler Atkins Jr. prize, 1952, Gastonia Evang. Assn. award, 1979. Mem. Am. Acad. Ministry (charter, adv. bd. mem.). Avocations: travel, collecting miniature cathedral and church models, collecting christian art and artifacts, music. *To me life's highest meaning and deepest satisfaction lie in a personal relationship with Jesus Christ my Saviour and Lord. My supreme aim and motive are to honor Him in everything I do. I can think of no worthier pursuit, no more challenging goal, for anyone in any age.*

BODI, SONIA ELLEN, library director, educator; b. Chgo., June 24, 1940; d. Franz Frithiof and Elsa (Noren) Bergquist; m. Peter Phillip Bodi, July 30, 1966; 1 child, Eric Christopher; stepchildren: Glenn Peter, John Jeffrey. Student, U. Edinburgh (Scotland), 1960-61; BA, Augustana Coll., Rock Island, Ill., 1962; MA Libr. Sci., Rosary Coll., 1977; MA, Northwestern U., 1986. Tchr. English and history Gemini Jr. H.S., Niles, Ill., 1962-64, Nagoya (Japan) Internat. Sch., 1964-65; tchr. English, Old Orchard Jr. H.S., Skokie, Ill., 1965-67; reference libr. Wilmette (Ill.) Pub. Libr., 1977-79, Kendall Coll., Evanston, Ill., 1979-81; head reference and instructional libr. North Park U., Chgo., 1981—, asst. prof. bibliography, 1985-87, assoc. prof., 1988-92, prof., 1992—, chmn. divsn. humanities, 1988-99, interim libr. dir., 1996-98, libr. dir., 1998—2005; instr. Dominican U. Grad. Sch. Libr. and Info. Sci., River Forest, Ill., 2004—. Contbr. articles to profl. jours. Pres. PTA, Lincolnwood, Ill., 1977—79; active Bd. Edn., Lincolnwood, 1980—91, sec., 1981—84, pres., 1984—87, LIBRAS, 2001—02; chair Ill. Coop. Collection Mgmt. Program, 2002—03; elder First Presbyn. Ch. of Evanston, 1989—, Stephen ministry leader, 1992—98; bd. dirs. Chgo. Libr. Sys., 1999—2004, Ill. Libr. Computer Sys. Orgn., 2003—05. Mem. Ill. Libr. Assn., ALA, Am. Assn. Coll. and Rsch. Librs., Beta Phi Mu. Democrat. Avocations: reading, bicycling, opera, music, piano. Home: 6710 N Trumbull Ave Lincolnwood IL 60712-3740 Office: Dominican U 7900 Divsn River Forest IL 60305 Business E-Mail: sbodi@northpark.edu.

BODIAN, NAT G., publishing and marketing consultant, author, lecturer, lexicographer, historian; b. Newark, Feb. 12, 1921; s. Louis and Fannie (Gabot) B.; m. Ruth Naiman, June 28, 1947; children: Mark, Lester. Student, Essex Jr. Coll., CCNY; grad., New Sch. for Social Research, 1947. Mgr. sales and promotion Baker & Taylor Co., Hillside, N.J., 1958-60; advt. promotion mgr. Rider Pub. Co., Hayden Book Co., N.Y.C., 1960-62; mktg., promotion mgr. Am. Elsevier Pub. Co., N.Y.C., 1963-71; mktg. dir. Transaction Books Rutgers U., New Brunswick, N.J., 1971-72, Crane Russak & Co., N.Y.C., 1972-76; mktg. mgr. John Wiley & Sons., Inc. (Wiley-Sci-Tech. div.), N.Y.C., 1976-88. Guest lectr. Boston U., NYU, CUNY, Fairleigh Dickinson U., UCLA; WWII So. Atlantic correspondent Ynak Mag.; editor various military base publs. Author: Book Marketing Handbook, Vol. 1, 1980, Vol. 2, 1983, How to Get the Most Out of Your Mailing Lists, 1982, Copywriter's Handbook, 1984, Encyclopedia of Mailing List Terminology and Techniques, 1986, Beyond Lead Generation: Merchandising Through Card Packs, 1986, The Publishers Direct Mail Handbook, 1987, Publishing Desk Reference: A Comprehensive Dictionary of Book and Jour. Marketing and Bookselling Practices and Techniques, 1988, How to Choose a Winning Title: A Guide for Writers, Editors and Publishers, 1988, NTC's Dictionary of Direct Mail and Mailing List Terminology and Techniques, 1990, Direct Marketing Rules of Thumb: 1000 Practical and Profitable Ideas, 1995, Portuguese updates edit., 1999, The Joy of Publishing: Fascinating Facts and Historic Origins About Books and Authors, Editors and Publishers, Bookmaking and Bookselling, 1996; contbr. to Trade Book Marketing, 1983, Book Publishing Career Directory, 1990, Internat. Ency. of Internat. Book Publishing, 1995, Book Marketing and Promotion: A Practical Handbook for Publishers in Developing Countries, 1999; Contributions in Various Conference Proceedings; columnist: COSMEP pub. newsletter, 1988-95; contbt. editor Against the Grain, Scholarly Pub. Today; contbr. articles and book revs. for nat. and internat. profl. jours. and trade publs. Found. mem., sec. N.J. News Writers Assn., 1941. Served with USAAF, 1942-45, YANK Field Corr., 1943-45. Nominee AAP Curtis Benjamin award, 1984 and Pub. Hall of Fame, 1986; recipient Author's Citation, N.J. Writers Conf., 1986, 87, 89. Home: 5 Henley Ave Cranford NJ 07016-1922 Personal E-mail: natbodian@aol.com.

BODIN, KATE, dean; BFA, Boston U.; MEd in Arts & Learning, Endicott Coll. Dean of faculty Montserrat Coll. of Art, Beverly, Mass., 1992—. Chairperson Gloucester Com. for Arts (mayoral appointment). Office: Montserrate College of Art PO Box 26 23 Essex St Beverly MA 01915 Office Phone: 978-921-2356 103. Office Fax: 978-921-2361. Business E-Mail: ktbodin@montserrat.edu.*

BODINE, CHRIS W., retail executive; V.p. bus. devel. CVS Pharmacy, Inc., 1997—98, sr. v.p. health care svcs., 1998—2000, v.p. merchandising, 2000—02; exec. v.p. merchandising and mktg. CVS Pharmacy, Inc. and CVS Corp., 2002—. Office: CVS Corp Corp Hdqrs 1 CVS Dr Woonsocket RI 02895

BODINE, GEOFF, race car driver; b. Chemung, N.Y., Apr. 18, 1949; children: Matthew, Barry. Profl. race car driver NASCAR, 1979—; owner, driver, 1993—. Named Rookie of Yr., NASCAR, 1982, winner, Daytona 500, 1986, Internat. Race of Champions, 1987, Holly Farms 400, 1989, Hanes 500, 1990, AC Spark Plug 500, 1990, Goody's 500, 1990, 1992, Mello Yello 500, 1991, Tyson/Holly Farms 400, 1992, Save art 300, 1993, Miller 500, 1994,

Goodwrench 400, 1994, Tyson 400, 1994, Winston Select, 1994, The Bud at the Glen, 1996; named one of 50 Greatest Drivers, NASCAR; recipient Busch Pole award, 1996. Office: c/o NASCAR PO Box 2875 Daytona Beach FL 32120-2875*

BODINE, JOSEPH IRA, lawyer; b. Greeley, Colo., June 4, 1950; s. Olen Doyle Sr. and Muriel Joy Roberts; m. LeAnne Marie Kontz, Dec. 14, 1973; children: Sabrina, Jared, Adam. BA, U. S.C., 1980; MPA, Golden Gate U., 1986; JD, Brigham Young U., 1995. Bar: Utah 1995, U.S. Dist. Ct. Utah 1995, Colo. 1996, U.S. Dist. Ct. Colo. 1996. Enlisted USAF, 1968, advanced through grades capt., 1981, ret., 1992; pvt. practice law, 1996—. Mem. transp. adv. com. City Greeley, 1997-99, chair budget adv. com., 1997-99, budget adv. com. City Greeley, 1998-2002, chair 1999-2000 Decorated Air Force Commendation medal Hdqrs. Tactical Air Command, 1988, Air Force Achievement medal Hdqrs. Tactical Warfare Ctr., 1990, Meritorious Svc. medal Hdqrs. Tactical Warfare Ctr., 1992. Mem. ABA, Colo. Bar Assn. (co-chair law edn. com. 1998-99, chair 1999-2000), Weld County Bar Assn. (pres. 2003-04), Am. Legion. Avocation: umpiring high school baseball. Office: 912 8th Ave Greeley CO 80631-1112 Office Phone: 970-304-0570.

BODINE, WILLIS RAMSEY, JR., music educator, organist; b. Austin, Tex., Nov. 15, 1935; s. Willis Ramsey and Freda Serena (Buchan) B.; m. Anna Schoff Hartung, Mar. 9, 1957; children: Elizabeth Ramsey, Catherine Lynn. MusB, U. Tex., 1957, MusM, 1960; postgrad., Nortwestdeutsche Musikakademie, Lippe-Detmold, Germany, 1957-59. Instr. in music and univ. organist U. Fla., Gainesville, 1959, asst. prof., 1962, assoc. prof., 1967, prof., 1976—2003, grad. program advisor for performance, 1993-99, prof. emeritus, 2003—. Cons. in organ design chs. in Fla., N.C. and Tex., 1962—; mus. dir. The Willis Bodine Chorale, 1987—; mem faculty Montreat and Westminster Confs. on Worship and Music, 1985—; recitals throughout Southeast, Europe, N.Y.C., 1958—. Composer: Sixth Communion Service, The Hymnal 1940 Supplement, 1960, 76. Chmn. Gainesville Cultural Commn., 1980-82. Named Fulbright Scholar, Nordwestdeutsche Musikakadamie, Fed. Republic of Germany, 1957-59, Musician of Yr., Found. for the Promotion of Music, Gainesville, 1988; recipient Disting. Faculty award Fla. Blue Key, 2002. Mem. Am. Guild of Organists (regional coord. for edn.). Democrat. Episcopalian. Avocations: architecture, genealogy. Home: 3838 SW 4th Pl Gainesville FL 32607-2713

BODKIN, HENRY GRATTAN, JR., lawyer; b. L.A., Dec. 8, 1921; s. Henry Grattan and Ruth May (Wallis) B.; m. Mary Louise Davis, June 28, 1943; children: Maureen L. Dixon, Sheila L. McCarthy, Timothy Grattan. BS cum laude, Loyola Marymount U., Los Angeles, 1943, JD, 1948. Bar: Calif. 1948. Pvt. practice, Los Angeles, 1948-51, 53-95; ptnr. Bodkin, McCarthy, Sargent & Smith (predecessor firms), L.A.; of counsel Sullivan, Workman & Dee, L.A., 1995—. Mem. L.A. Bd. Water and Power Commrs., 1972-74, pres., 1973-74; regent Marymount Coll., 1962-67; trustee Loyola-Marymount U., 1973-91, vice chmn., 1985-86. With USNR, 1943-45, 51-53. Fellow Am. Coll. Trial Lawyers; mem. Calif. State Bar (mem. exec. com. conf. of dels. 1968-70, vice chmn. 1969-70), California Club, Chancery Club (pres. 1990-96), Riviera Tennis Club, Tuna Club, Phi Delta Phi. Republican. Roman Catholic. Home: 956 Linda Flora Dr Los Angeles CA 90049-1631 Office: Sullivan Workman & Dee 800 S Figueroa St Fl 12 Los Angeles CA 90017-2521 Office Phone: 213-624-5544. E-mail: bodkin01@cs.com.

BODKIN, RUBY PATE, real estate broker, educator; b. Frostproof, Fla., Mar. 11, 1926; d. James Henry and Lucy Beatrice (Latham) P.; m. Lawrence Edward Bodkin Sr., Jan. 15, 1949; children: Karen Bodkin Snead, Cinda, Lawrence Jr. BA, Fla. State U., 1948; MA, U. Fla., 1972. Lic. real estate broker Fla. Banker Barnett Bank, Avon Park, Fla., 1943-44, Lewis State Bank, Tallahassee, 1944-49; ins. underwriter Hunt Ins. Agy., Tallahassee, 1949-51; tchr. Duval County Sch. Bd., Jacksonville, Fla., 1952-77; pvt. practice realty Jacksonville, 1976—; tchr. Nassau County Sch. Bd., Jacksonville, 1978-83; sec., treas., v.p. Bodkin Corp., R&D/Inventions, Jacksonville, 1983—; assoc. Brooke Shields Innovative Designer Products, Inc., Kendall Park, NJ, 1988-92. Author: 100 Teacher Chosen Recipes, 1976, Bodkin Bridge Course for Beginners, 1996, Class Conscious, 1999, (autobiography) Grandma Bodkin, 2000, Essay on Death, 2003; author numerous poems. Mem. Jacksonville Symphony Guild, 1985—, Southside Bapt. Ch. Recipient 25 Yr. Svc. award Duval County Sch. Bd., 1976, Tchr. of Yr. award Bryceville Sch., 1981. Mem. Am. Contract Bridge League, Nat. Realtors Assn., Southside Jr. Woman's Club, Garden Club Sweetbriar (bd. dirs.), Riverside Woman's Club Jacksonville (fin. dir. 1991-92, 3rd v.p. social dir. WCOJ, 1992-99), UDC (Martha Reid chpt. #19), Fla. Edn. Assn. (pers. problems com. 1958), Duval County Classrooms Tchrs. (v.p. membership 1957), Woman's Club Jacksonville Bridge Group, Fla. Ret. Tchrs. Assn., Fla. Realtors Assn., N.E. Fla. Realtors Assn., Jacksonville Geneal. Soc. (practicing genealogist, family historian 1986—), Friday Musicale of Jacksonville, San Jose Golf Country Club, Jacksonville Sch. Bridge. Baptist. Avocations: reading, writing, genealogy, photography, club bridge. Home: 1149 Molokai Rd Jacksonville FL 32216-3273 Office: Bodkin Jewelers & Appraisers PO Box 16482 Jacksonville FL 32245-6482 Personal E-mail: larubodkin@aol.com. *Ruby Pate Bodkin, geneaologist and honored teacher (1955-83) has traced her Pate and Bodkin ancestors back to England and Ireland. Son Lawrence (Larry) Bodkin, Jr., 40, MEd, Fla. State U., Tallahasse, is currently a prosperous owner and CEO of his own founded company, Bodkin Management and Consulting (New Directions for Associations). Daughter Karen, 53, wed C.T. Snead III in 1976, grandson (by adoption) of U.S. congressman, senator Carl Vinson of Milledgeville, Ga. Ruby's husband of 56 years, Larry Bodkin, Sr. has more than 25 US patents on his own inventions. Also, he has written many timely essays on varied subjects which he has for sale on website. He works daily at his job appraising fine jewelry for the public for their insurance purposes since he was duly certified by The American Gem Soc. years ago and enjoys the work still at age 78.*

BODLEY, HARLEY RYAN, JR., sportswriter, announcer; b. Dover, Del., Nov. 24, 1936; s. Harley Ryan and Mildred Olivia (Carver) B.; m. Patricia Jean Hall, Dec. 4, 1981 BA, U. Del., 1959; postgrad., Am. U., 1960. Sports editor Del. State News, Dover, 1959-60; sports dir. Radio WDOV, Dover, 1958-62; sports writer News-Jour. Papers, Wilmington, Del., 1960-63, night sports editor, 1963-67, asst. sports editor, 1967-71, sports editor, 1971-82; baseball editor USA Today, Washington, 1982—. Discussion leader Am. Press Inst., Reston, Va., 1967—76; TV host Sta. WHYY-TV, Wilmington, 1967—74; columnist The Sporting News, St. Louis, 1978—83; commentator NBC-TV Baseball: An Inside Look, 1987, USA Today Radio Report, 1987—89, USA Today: The TV Show, 1988—89; commentator and host Baseball Sunday United Syndications Radio Network, 1988—90; baseball analyst CNN, 1989—91; commentator CBS Radio Network baseball pregame, 1990—97, Comcast Sports Net, 2000—. Author: I Learned To Fly, So Can You, 1967; The Team That Wouldn't Die, 1981, Countdown to Cobb, 1985; writer Best Sports Stories, 1967-71, 1977-79, 1982, 1985 Flight safety counselor FAA, Phila., 1968-72. Served as sgt. U.S. Army N.G. 1956-64. Named Sportswriter of Yr., Nat. Sportscasters and Sportswriters Assn., 1961, 63, 65, 67-70, 73-75, 78-79; recipient Best of Gannett award Gannett Co., Inc., 1981, Mark Twain award AP, 1980, 25th Year award Baseball Commr., 1983, USA Today All-Star award, 2000, 01; inducted Del. Baseball Hall of Fame, 2002, Del. Sports Hall of Fame, 2004. Mem. AP Sports Editors (pres. 1981-82, Best Sports Story award 1981, 1st place award 1982), Baseball Writers Assn. Am. (Phila. chpt. chmn. 1977-78), Wilmington Sportswriters and Broadcasters (pres. 1963 sec-treas. 1965-83), Sigma Delta Chi (Top Sports award 1982) Clubs: Wilmington Country; Northeast Yacht. Episcopalian. Avocations: golf, pilot, boating. Address: care Athletes & Artists 421 7th Ave New York NY 10001-2002 Business E-Mail: hbodley@usatoday.com.

BODMAN, SAMUEL WRIGHT, III, secretary of energy, former specialty chemicals and materials company executive; b. Chgo., Nov. 26, 1938; s. Samuel W. Jr. and Lina (Lindsay) B.; m. M. Diane Barber, July 31, 1997; children: Elizabeth L., Andrew M., Sarah H. BS in Chemical Engring., Cornell U., 1961; ScD, MIT, 1964. Tech. dir. Am. R & D, Boston, 1964-70; prof. MIT, Cambridge, Mass., 1964-70; v.p. Fidelity Venture Assn., Boston, 1970-74; pres. Fidelity Venture Assocs., 1974-77; chmn. Fidelity Venture Assn., 1977; pres. Fidelity Mgmt. & Rsch. Co., Boston, 1976-86; pres., COO FMR Corp., 1982-86; exec. v.p., dir. Fidelity Group Mut. Funds, 1980-86; pres., COO Cabot Corp., Boston, 1987-88, chmn., CEO, also bd. dirs., 1988—2001; dep. sec. US Dept. Commerce, Washington, 2001—04, US Dept. Treasury, 2004—05; sec. US Dept. Energy, Washington, 2005—. Bd. dirs. Westvaco, Inc., N.Y.C., John Hancock Fin. Svcs., Thermo Electron Corp., Houston, Security Capital Group Inc. Trustee, mem. exec. com. MIT, Cambridge; trustee Isabella Stewart Gardner Mus., Boston, New England Aquarium, Boston. Episcopalian. Office: US Dept Energy Forrestal Bldg 1000 Independence Ave SW Washington DC 20585*

BODNAR, ANDREW G., pharmaceutical executive; Former assoc. chief internal medicine, acting chief cardiology, dir. internal medicine residency program Mass. Gen. Hosp., Boston; former pres. oncology/immunology and worldwide strategic bus. devel. for pharm. group Bristol-Myers Squibb, v.p. med. and external affairs, sr. v.p. strategy, 2002—. Office: Bristol-Myers Squibb Co 345 Park Ave New York NY 10154-0037

BODNAR, PETER O., lawyer; b. Queens, NY, Mar. 19, 1945; s. John and Edith (Schultz) B. BA in Govt., NYU, 1966; JD, Fordham U., 1970. Bar: N.Y. 1971, U.S. Dist. Ct. (so. dist.) N.Y. 1973. Confidential law sec. to Hon. Evans V. Brewster Family Ct. and County Ct. Westchester County, N.Y., 1970-73; pvt. practice White Plains, N.Y., 1973-77; ptnr. Bodnar & Greene, P.C., White Plains, N.Y., 1977-80, Bender & Bodnar, White Plains, N.Y., 1980-98; prin. Law Offices of Peter O. Bodnar, White Plains, N.Y., 1998-99, Bodnar & Milone LLP, White Plains, N.Y., 1999—; mng. mem. Organica USA II LLC, 2004—. Pres., CEO P.A.J. Am. Ltd./The Olo Corp., 1990—97; CEO Organica, USA, Inc., 1998—; supervisory bd. Korte-Organica RT, Budapest, Hungary, 2001—; lectr. Pace U. Sch. Law Women's Justice Ctr., 2001—; mem. supervisory bd. Vertis Environ. Fin., KFT, Budapest, Hungary, 2002—; lectr. Appellate Divsn. 2d Dept. Law Guardian Program, 2003—; chair Com. for Children's Right to Counsel, 2003—. Trustee Village of Ossining, N.Y., 1975-77. Fellow: Am. Acad. Matrimonial Lawyers; mem.: ABA (family law sect.), Westchester County Bar Assn. (family law sect., exec. com. 1992—, chair 2000—02), N.Y. State Bar Assn. (family law sect., exec. com. 2000—, lectr. custody and visitation 2003—). Office: 140 Grand St White Plains NY 10601-4831 Office Phone: 914-997-2500. Personal E-mail: usorganica@aol.com.

BODNAR, RICHARD, psychology educator; b. N.Y.C., Feb. 21, 1946; s. Julius J. and Irene A. (Monette) B.; m. Carol B. Greenman, July 4, 1981; children: Benjamin, Nicholas. BA, Manhattan Coll., 1967; MA, CCNY, 1973; PhD, CUNY, 1976. Postdoctoral fellow N.Y. State Psychiat. Inst., N.Y.C., 1976-78, rsch. scientist, 1978-79; asst. prof. Queens Coll., CUNY, N.Y.C., 1979-82, assoc. prof., 1982-85, prof., 1986—; dept. chmn., 1998—. Adj. prof. pharmacology Mt. Sinai Sch. Medicine, N.Y.C., 1991—. Contbr. more than 220 sci. articles and abstracts to profl. jours. Capt. USAF, 1967-71, Vietnam. Recipient NSF grant, 1999—. Mem. Soc. for Neurosci., Am. Psychol. Soc. (charter), AAAS. Achievements include research on role of opioid systems in ingestive behavior and analgesia, role of stress in analgesic processes, roles of gender and aging in opioid function. Office: CUNY Queens Coll Dept Psychology Flushing NY 11367

BODNER, DONALD ROGER, urologist, medical educator; b. Indpls., Aug. 31, 1953; s. Robert Stewart and Elizabeth (Wolf) B.; m. Linda Joy Abrams, Oct. 5, 1985; children: Robert, Daniel, Richard. BS, Trinity Coll., Hartford, Conn., 1975; MD, Ind. U., Indpls., 1979. Resident in urology Case Western Res. U., Cleve., 1979-84, instr. urology, 1984-85, asst. prof., 1985-92, assoc. prof., 1992—99, prof., 1999—. Section editor (urology) Jour. Spinal Cord Medicine, 1994—; guest editor: Urologic Clinical Procedures - Spinal Cord Injury, 1993. Mem. Am. Urologic Soc., Internat. Med. Soc. Paraplegia, Am. Paraplegia Soc. (pres. 1993-95). Office: Case Western Res Univ Dept Urology 11100 Euclid Ave Cleveland OH 44106-1736

BODNER, JOHN, JR., lawyer; b. Dover, N.J., May 4, 1927; s. John and Anna (Kushman) B.; m. Anne Potter; children: John Edward, Brit-Marie, Anne Kristin, Peter Andrew. Student, Cornell U., 1946-50; JD, Northwestern U., 1953; MLA, Johns Hopkins U., 1969. Bar: D.C. 1954. Bigelow teaching fellow U. Chgo. Law Sch., 1953-54; atty. Dept. Justice, Washington, 1954-56; assoc. Howrey & Simon, Washington, 1956-64; ptnr. Howrey Simon Arnold & White and predecessor, Washington, 1964—. Law lectr. various univs. With U.S. Army, 1945-46. Mem. ABA, FBA, D.C. Bar Assn., Met. Club. Roman Catholic. Home: 4707 Reservoir Rd NW Washington DC 20007-1906 Office: Howrey Simon Arnold & White 1299 Pennsylvania Ave NW Washington DC 20004-2420 Office Phone: 202-383-6899. E-mail: bodnerj@howrey.com.

BODNER, RANDALL WAYNE, lawyer; b. Danville, Ky., May 24, 1959; s. Jack Kenneth Elsie Marie (Elmore) B.; m. Elizabeth Hendrik Evans, May 31, 1986. AB summa cum laude, Dartmouth Coll., 1981; JD magna cum laude, Harvard U., 1985. Bar: Mass. 1987, U.S. Dist. Ct. Mass. 1987, U.S. Ct. Appeals (1st crct.) 1987, U.S. Ct. Appeals (2d crct.) 1991. Law clk. to Hon. Ellsworth A. Van Graafeiland U.S. Ct. Appeals (2d cir.), N.Y.C. and Rochester, N.Y., 1985-86; assoc. Ropes & Gray, Boston, 1986-90; asst. U.S. atty. criminal div. so. dist. N.Y. U.S. Dept. Justice, N.Y.C., 1990—95; ptnr. litigation dept. Ropes & Gray, Boston, 1995, head securities and corp. litigation practice group. Mem. ABA, Mass. Bar Assn., Phi Beta Kappa. Avocations: sailing, squash, golf. Office: Ropes & Gray 1 International Pl Boston MA 02110-2624 Office Phone: 617-951-7776. Office Fax: 617-951-7050. Business E-Mail: randall.bodner@ropesgray.com.

BODNEY, DAVID JEREMY, lawyer; b. Kansas City, Mo., July 15, 1954; s. Daniel F. and Retha (Silby) B.; m. Sarah Hughes; children: Christian Steven, Anna Claire, Daniel Martin. BA cum laude, Yale U., 1976; MA in Fgn. Affairs, JD, U. Va., 1979. Bar: Ariz. 1979, U.S. Dist Ct. Ariz. 1980, U.S. Ct. Appeals (9th cir.) 1980, U.S. Supreme Ct. 1983. Legis. asst., speechwriter U.S. Senator John V. Tunney, Washington, 1975-76; sr. editor Va. Jour. of Internat. Law, 1978-79; assoc. Brown and Bain PA, Phoenix, 1979-85, ptnr., 1985-90; gen. counsel New Times, Inc., Phoenix, 1990-92; ptnr. Steptoe & Johnson, LLP, Phoenix, 1992—, mng. ptnr., 2002—03. Vis. prof. Ariz. State U., Tempe, 1985, 94—. Co-author: Libel Defense Resource Center: 50-State Survey, 1982—. Bd. dirs. Ariz. Ctr. for Law in the Pub. Interest, Phoenix, 1983-90, pres., 1989-90; chmn. Yale Alumni Schs. Com., Phoenix, 1984-87; vice chmn. City of Phoenix Solicitation Bd., 1986-88, chmn., 1988-89; bd. dirs. Children's Action Alliance, 1995—, chmn., 2003—, chmn.; adv. panel on Civil Liberties to White House Commn. on Aviation Safety and Security, 1997; bd. dirs. Ariz. region Anti-Defamation League, 2001—, v.p., 2004—; adv. coun. dir. Ariz. Ctr. Pub. Policy Recipient Cert. Merit, ABA. Mem. ABA (forum com. on communication law 1984—, concerned correspondents network com. 1979—), Ariz. Bar Assn. Clubs: Yale (bd. dirs. Phoenix club 1979—), Ariz. Acad., Maricopa County Bar Assn. Democrat. Office: Steptoe & Johnson Collier Ctr 201 E Washington St 1600 Phoenix AZ 85004 Office Phone: 602-257-5212. Office Fax: 602-257-5299. Business E-Mail: dbodney@steptoe.com.

BODOFF, JOSEPH SAMUEL UBERMAN, lawyer; b. Bryn Mawr, Nov. 2, 1952; s. Bernard David and Ruth Irma (Uberman) B. BS, Pa. State U., 1974; JD, Villanova U., 1977. Bar: Pa. 1977, U.S. Dist. Ct. (ea. dist.) Pa. 1979, U.S. Ct. Appeals (3d cir.) 1980, U.S. Supreme Ct. 1988, Mass. 1987, U.S. Dist. Ct. Mass. 1988, U.S. Ct. Appeals (1st cir.) 1988, R.I. 1998, U.S. Dist. Ct. R.I. 1999. Jud. law clk. Phila. County Ct. of Common Pleas, 1977—79; assoc. Pincus, Verlin, Hahn & Reich, Phila., 1979—86; ptnr. Kaye, Fialkow, Richmond & Rothstein, Boston, 1986—91, Gaston & Snow, Boston, 1991, Warner & Stackpole, Boston, 1991—94, Hinckley, Allen & Snyder, Boston, 1994—98, Shechtman & Halperin, Boston, 1998—2000, Bodoff & Assocs., Boston, 2000—03, Bodoff & Slavitt LLP, Boston, 2003—. Dir. Am. Bankruptcy Inst., Alexandria, Va., 1995—2003, mem. exec. com., 2000—03; dir. Am. Bd. Certification, Alexandria; co-chair ABI Unsecured Trade Creditor Com., Alexandria, 1993—98, ABI Creditors' Com. Manual Task Force, 1993—94; chair ABI Task Force on Preferences, 1995—97; exec. editor ABI World, 2002—; chair NACM Bankruptcy and Insolvency Group, Portland, 1998—. Author: Cramdown: The Ultimate Chapter 11 Threat, 1992, (with others) Bankruptcy Business Acquisitions, 1998; contbr. articles to profl. publs. Mem. Mus. Coun. of Mus. of Fine Arts, Boston, 1997—99. Mem. ABA, Am. Bankruptcy Inst. (dir. 1995-2003, exec. com. 2000-2003), Am. Bd. of Certification (dir. 1996-2000), Boston Bar Assn., Nat. Assn of Credit Mgmt. Avocations: skiing, tennis, wine collecting, piano. Home: 64 Forest St Chestnut Hill MA 02467-2930 Office: Bodoff & Slavitt LLP 225 Friend St Boston MA 02114 Office Phone: 617-742-7300. Business E-Mail: jbodoff@bodoffslavitt.com.

BODOW, WAYNE R., defender; b. Bklyn., Apr. 25, 1943; s. Charles G. and Rosalind L. B.; m. Alice Turski, Aug. 29, 1971 (div. Dec. 1977); 1 child, Amy Ellen; m. Linda S. Taylor, Dec. 16, 1988 (div. Oct. 1994); 1 child, Elana Sara; m. Lillian Stienmann, June 7, 1998. BA, Rockford Coll., 1965. Bar: N.Y. 1975, U.S. Dist. Ct. (no. and we. dists.) N.Y. 1975; cert. in consumer bankruptcy law Am. Bankruptcy Bd. Cert. Pvt. practice. Mem. alternate dispute resolution panel U.S. Bankruptcy Ct. No. Dist N.Y., 1999—, lectr. in field. Contbr. articles to profl. jours. Mem. Nat. Coun. Exchangors, Nat. Assn. Consumer Bankruptcy Attys. (founder, lobbyist), Nat. Assn. Chpt. 13 Trustees (assoc.), Nat. Assn. Consumer Advocates, Am. Bankruptcy Inst., Onondaga County Bar Assn. (chmn. consumer law sect., lectr.), Ctrl. N.Y. Bankruptcy Bar Assn., Coalition Medicaid Advs. We. N.Y., Turnaround Mgmt. Assn. Office: 1925 Park St Ste 1 Syracuse NY 13208-1080 Fax: 315-422-9113. E-mail: wbodow@choiceonemail.com.

BODSWORTH, FRED, writer, ecologist; b. Port Burwell, Ont., Can., Oct. 11, 1918; s. Arthur John and Viola B.; m. Margaret Neville Banner, July 8, 1944; children: Barbara (Mrs. Edward Welch), Nancy (Mrs. Richard Hannah), Neville. Student pub. schs., Port Burwell. Reporter St. Thomas (Ont.) Times-Jour., 1940-43; reporter, editor Toronto (Ont.) Daily Star, 1943-46; staff writer, editor Maclean's Mag., Toronto, 1947-56; novelist, 1956—. Organizer, leader numerous natural history tours Author: Last of the Curlews, 1954, 2d edit., 1995, The Strange One, 1960, The Mating Call, 1961, The Atonement of Ashley Morden, 1964, The Sparrow's Fall, 1967 (also pub. in Eng., fgn. translations), The Pacific Coast, Illustrated Natural History of Canada series, 1970; (with others) Wilderness Canada, 1970; editor: Illustrated Natural History of Canada series, 1980-81. Bd. dirs. Natural Sci. of Can., 1980-88; hon. bd. dirs. Long Point Bird Obs., 1970—; chmn. bd. trustees James L. Baillie Meml. Fund for ornithol. field research, 1975-88. Mem. Fedn. Ont. Naturalists (hon. life, pres. 1964-66), Internat. PEN, Writers Union of Can. Clubs: Ornithological, Field Naturalists (past pres.), Brodie (Toronto), Writer's Tust of Can. (Lifetime Achiev. award, 2003). E-mail: fbodsworth@sympatico.ca.

BODVARSSON, ORN BODVAR, economist, educator; b. Reykjavik, Iceland, Sept. 8, 1958; arrived in U.S., 1964; s. Gunnar and Tove Bodvarsson; m. Mary Christina Bodvarsson, June 26, 1999; children: Gunnar John, Hans Peter. BS, Oreg. State U., 1979, MS, 1981; PhD, Simon Fraser U., Vancouver, B.C., Can., 1986. Vis. instr. econs. We. Wash. U., Bellingham, 1983—84, Whitman Coll., Walla Walla, Wash., 1984—85; vis. asst. prof. U. Mont., Missoula, 1986—87, Ball State U., Muncie, Ind., 1987—88; from asst. prof. to assoc. prof. St. Cloud State U., 1988—97, prof., 1997—. Cons. economist, St. Cloud, 1995—2000; vis. prof. U. Nebr., Lincoln, 2001—05. Contbr. articles to profl. jours. Named Outstanding Educator of the Year, U. Nebr., 2003—04. Mem.: Minn. Econ. Assn. (pres. 2000—01), Western Social Sci. Assn. (pres. 2000—01). Democrat. Avocations: classical piano, bicycling, cooking, outdoor activities, stock investments. Home: 2412 Field Ct Saint Cloud MN 56301 Office: Dept Econs St Cloud U Saint Cloud MN 56301 Office Phone: 320-308-2225. E-mail: obbodvarsson@stcloudstate.edu.

BODWELL, LORI, lawyer; b. Oct. 1966; AB, Bowdoin Coll., 1988; JD, Boston Coll., 1991. Bar: Alaska 1992, Maine 1993, Mass. 1992, Dist. of Alaska (US Dist. Ct.) 1994, 9th Air 1995. Mem.: Tananeu Valley Bar Assoc., Nat. Assoc. of Criminal Def. Lawyers, Alaska Bar Assn. (pres. 2002—03). Address: 712 8th Ave Fairbanks AK 99701

BOE, DAVID STEPHEN, musician, educator, dean; b. Duluth, Minn., Mar. 11, 1936; s. Egbert Thomas and Beatrice Ella (Steen) Boe; m. Sigrid North, July 23, 1961; children: Stephen, Eric. BA, St. Olaf Coll., Northfield, Minn., 1958; M.Mus., Syracuse U., 1960. Asst. prof. music U. Ga., 1961-62; mem. faculty Oberlin (Ohio) Coll. Conservatory Music, 1962—, prof. organ and harpsichord, 1976—, dean, 1976-90; organ recitalist U.S. and Europe, 1962—. Mem. advanced placement music com. Coll. Entrance Exam. Bd., 1980—83; vis. prof. Fla. State U., 1991, U. Notre Dame, 1991—92. Trustee Westfield Ctr., 2000—; chmn. scholarship com. Presser Found., 2002—; dir. music, organist First Luth. Ch., Lorain, Ohio, 1962—2002. Scholar Fulbright, Germany, 1960—61. Mem.: Nat. Assn. Schs. Music (trustee, sec. 1981—87), Phi Beta Kappa, Pi Kappa Lambda (nat. pres. 1986—90). Business E-Mail: david.boe@oberlin.edu.

BOE, MYRON TIMOTHY, lawyer; b. New Orleans, Oct. 30, 1948; s. Myron Roger and Elaine (Tracy) B. BA, U. Ark., 1970, JD, 1973; LLM in Labor, So. Methodist U., 1976. Bar: Ark. 1974, Tenn. 1977, U.S. Ct. Appeals (4th, 5th, 6th, 7th, 8th, 9th, l0th, 11th cirs.) 1978, U.S. Supreme Ct. 1978. City atty. City of Pine Bluff, Ark., 1974-75; sec.-treas. Ark. City Atty. Assn., 1975; sr. ptnr. Rose Law Firm, Little Rock, 1980—. Author: Handling the Title VII Case Practical Tips for the Employer, 1980. Served to 2d lt. USAR, 1972-73. Recipient Florentino-Ramirez Internat. Law award, 1975; Named one of The Best Lawyers in Am., Ark. Leading Employment Lawyer. Fellow Coll. Labor and Employment Lawyers, Inc., Ark. Bar Found. (bd. dirs.), Ark. Bd. Legal Specialization (sec. 1982-85, chmn. 1985-89, labor, employment discrimination, civil rights).; mem. ABA (labor sect. 1974—, employment law com. 1974—), ARC of Ark. (bd. dirs., v.p.), Ark. Bar Assn. (sec., chmn. labor sect. 1978-81, ho. of dels. 1979-82, Golden Gavel award 1983, bd. dirs., v.p., pres.), Def. Rsch. Inst. (employment law com. 1982—), Am. Employment Law Coun. (charter), Ark. Assn. Def. Counsel. Office: Rose Law Firm 120 E 4th St Little Rock AR 72201-2893

BOECKMAN, ROBERT KENNETH, JR., chemistry professor, organic chemistry researcher; b. Pasadena, Calif., Aug. 26, 1944; s. Robert Kenneth Sr. and Orletta Christine (Brinck) B.; m. Mary Helen Delton, June 19, 1976 BS, Carnegie Inst. Tech., 1966; PhD, Brandeis U., 1971. NIH fellow Columbia U., N.Y.C., 1970-72; from asst. prof. to prof. chemistry Wayne State U., Detroit, 1972-79; prof. chemistry U. Rochester, NY, 1980—, chmn. Dept. Chemistry, 2003—. Cons. Eastman Kodak, 1986—, Ricerca Inc., Painesville, Ohio, 1983-2001, Novartis Pharma AG, Basel, Switzerland, 1981—, Procter & Gamble Pharm., Cin., 1988—, Aventis, SA, 1992-99, 2001-03, Emisphere Technologies, Hawthorne, N.Y., 1999—; bd. dirs. Organic Syntheses, Pet Pride of N.Y., Inc.; v.p. Organic Syntheses, Inc., 2002—. Mem. editl. bd. Organic Syntheses, 1988-96; mem. editl. adv. bd. Can. Jour. Chemistry, 2000—03; assoc. editor Jour. Organic Chemistry, 1997—; contbr. articles to profl. jours. Recipient Career Devel. award NIH, 1976-81, award for acad. achievement Probus Club, 1979, Von Humboldt Rsch. prize for sr. scientists, 1992-93; fellow A.P. Sloan Found., 1976-80; Marshal Gates scholar, 1996-2001; Marshall Gates Jr. Prof., 2002— Fellow Japanese Soc. for Promotion Sci.; mem. Am. Chem. Soc. (chmn. organic chemistry divsn. 2001, past chair 2002), Royal Soc. Chemistry, Deutscher Chemiker Gesellschaft, Oakhill Country Club Rochester, Sigma Xi. Republican. Roman Catholic. Avocations: golf, basketball. Office: U Rochester Hutchinson Hall Dept of Chemistry Rochester NY 14627 Office Phone: 716-275-4229. Business E-Mail: rkb@rkbmac.chem.rochester.edu.

BOECKMANN, ALAN L., engineering and construction management company executive; BS in elec. engrng., U. Ariz. Joined Fluor Corp., 1974, engr.; pres., CEO Fluor Daniel; pres. Fluor Daniel's Energy & Chem. group; pres., COO Fluor Corp., 2001—02, chmn. bd., CEO, 2002—. Dir. Burlington

Northern Santa Fe, Am. Petroleum Inst., Bus. Coun. Internat. Understanding, Nat. Petroleum Coun. Dir. Orange County Performing Arts Ctr., Hearing & Speech Found.; mem. Bus. Roundtable; chmn. engring. & constrn. governors, World Econ. Forum; mem. adv. council Univ. Ariz. Coll. Engring. & Mines. Office: Flour Corp One Enterprise Dr Aliso Viejo CA 92656*

BOEDECKER, WILLARD ROGER, postsecondary education administrator; b. Chgo., Ill., Aug. 15, 1924; s. Willard Sherman and Virginia Elizabeth Boedecker; m. Peggy June Gunn, Dec. 19, 1986; children: Willard Roger, Kevin Boyd, Douglas Mark. BA, Long Beach State Coll., 1957, MA, 1959; DPA, Laurance U., 1986. Prof. Moorpark (Calif.) Coll., 1967—71, dean, 1971—82, pres., 1991—92; v.p. Oxnard (Calif.) Coll., 1982—88, pres., 1988—89, v.p., 1989—91. Pres. Shelter Cove Utility Dist., Calif., 1996—; curator programs Cape Meadcino Lighthouse, Shelter Cove, Calif., 2000—. Corp. U.S. Army, 1952—54, France. Democrat. Home: 424 Humboldt Loop Whitethorn CA 95589

BOEDER, THOMAS L., lawyer; b. St. Cloud, Minn., Jan. 10, 1944; s. Oscar Morris and Eleanor (Gile) B.; m. Carol-Leigh Coombs, Apr. 6, 1968. BA magna cum laude, Yale U., 1965, LLB, 1968. Bar: Wash. 1970, U.S. Dist. Ct. (We. Dist.) Wash. 1970, U.S. Dist. Ct. (Ea. Dist.) Wash. 1972, U.S. Ct. Appeals (9th Cir.) 1970, U.S. Supreme Ct. 1974, U.S. Ct. Appeals (D.C. Cir.) 1975, U.S. Ct. Appeals (10th Cir.) 1993. Litigation atty. Wash. State Atty. Gen., Seattle, 1970-72, antitrust div. head, 1972-76, chief, consumer protection and antitrust, 1976-78, also sr. asst. atty. gen. and criminal enforcement, 1979-81; ptnr., Litig. Practice Area Perkins Coie LLP, Seattle, 1981—. Served with U.S. Army, 1968-70, Vietnam. Mem. ABA (antitrust sect.), Wash. State Bar Assn. (antitrust sect.), Phi Beta Kappa. Lutheran. Office: Perkins Coie LLP 1201 3rd Ave Fl 40 Seattle WA 98101-3029 Office Phone: 206-359-8416. Office Fax: 206-359-9000. Business E-Mail: tboeder@perkinscoie.com.

BOEDIGHEIMER, ROBERT DAVID, lawyer; b. Mpls., Nov. 13, 1962; s. David Eugene and Phyllis Kay (Bylander) B.; m. Wendi Suzanne Lusk. BA in Philosophy, Polit. Sci. and Speech Comm. with distinction, U. Minn., 1985, JD, 1988. Bar: Minn. 1990, U.S. Dist. Ct. Minn. 1990. Law clk. to Hon. Lynn C. Olson, Anoka, Minn., 1989-90; assoc. Adams & Cesario, P.A., Bloomington, Minn., 1990-95; ptnr. McCloud & Boedigheimer, Bloomington, Minn., 1995—. Mem. ABA (litig. sect.), Minn. State Bar Assn., Minn. Trial Lawyers Assn., Nat. Employers Lawyers Assn., Wash. County Bar Assn., Dakota County Bar Assn., Nat. Bd. Trial Advocacy (cert. civil trial specialist). Republican. Roman Catholic. Avocations: racquetball, golf, weight training, skiing, watercolor painting. Office: McCloud & Boedigheimer 5001 W 80th St Ste 201 Bloomington MN 55437-1110 E-mail: RDB@Boedigheimerlaw.com.

BOEHEIM, JIM, college basketball coach; b. Lyons, N.Y., Y, Nov. 17, 1944; BA in Social Sci., Syracuse U., 1966, M in Social Sci. Full-time asst. basketball coach Syracuse (N.Y.) U., 1972-76, head basketball coach, 1976—. Mem. coaching staff U.S. basketball team Goodwill Games, Seattle, 1991 (silver medal), World Championships, Argentina (bronze medal), World Univ. Games, 1989. Hon. chmn. Kidney Found.; active orgns. Multiple Sclerosis, Cystic Fibrosis, Children's Miracle Network, Make-A-Wish, Pioneer Ctr. for Blind and Disabled, Lighthouse, People in Wheelchairs, Easter Seals, Spl. Olympics. Named Dist. II Coach of Yr., Nat. Assn. Basketball Coaches nine times, U.S. Basketball Writers Assn., 1979, 80, 91; named Big East Conf. Coach of Yr., 1984, 91 and 2000; Basketball court at the Carrier Dome named "Jim Boeheim Court" 2002. Achievements include Coached Syracuse to NCAA Championship, 2003; Coached Syracuse to 12 "Sweet 16" appearances and three NCAA championship games. Office: Syracuse Univ Basketball Dept Manley Field House Syracuse NY 13244-0001

BOEHLERT, SHERWOOD LOUIS, congressman; b. Utica, N.Y., Sept. 28, 1936; s. Sherwood John and Elizabeth Monica (Champoux) B.; divorced; children: Mark C. Brooks, Tracy Boehlert Suk, Leslie; m. Marianne Willey Phillips, July 10, 1976; 1 stepchild, Laura Brooke Drahzal. BS in Pub. Relation, Utica Coll., Syracuse U., 1961. Mgr. pub. relations Wyandotte Chems. Corp., Mich., 1961-64; chief of staff Rep. Alexander Pirnie, Washington, 1964-73, Rep. Donald J. Mitchell, 1973-79; exec. Oneida County, 1979-82; mem. U.S. Congress from 24th N.Y. dist. (formerly 23rd), Washington, 1983—; mem. permanent select com. on intelligence, transp. and infrastructure com., select com. on homeland security; mem. sci. com., 1983—, chmn., 2001—. Del. NATO parliamentary assembly; mem. N.E.-Midwest Congl. Coalition; co-chmn. N.E. Agr.; chmn. Fire Svcs. Caucus, Minor League Baseball Caucus. Author: Telling the Congressman's Story The Voice of Government, 1968. Bd. dirs. Utica Coll. Found. Served with U.S. Army, 1956-58. Named One of the 50 Most Effective Lawmakers in Washington D.C., Congressional Quarterly, 1999. Mem.: Rotary. Republican. Office: Ho of Reps 2246 Rayburn Ho Office Bldg Washington DC 20515 also: Alexander Pirnie Fed Bldg Rm 200 10 Broad St Utica NY 13501-1233*

BOEHLKE, FREDERICK JOHN, history professor; b. Phila. s. Frederick John and Freda Riess Boehlke. BA, U. Pa., 1948, MA, 1951; BDiv, Ea. Bapt. Theol. Sem., Wynnewood, Pa., 1952; PhD, U. Pa., 1958. Asst. prof. history Judson Coll., Marion, Ala., 1955—58, assoc. prof. history, 1958—63, prof. history, 1963—67, Ea. U., St. Davids, Pa., 1967—97, dean acad. programs, registrar, 1975—79, prof. emeritus, archivist, 1997—. Author: Pierre de Thomas, Scholar, Diplomat and Crusader, 1966, From Generation to Generation, 1996, The First 50 Years of Eastern University, 2003. Mem.: Am. Bapt. Hist. Soc., Bapt. History and Heritage Soc., So. Hist. Assn., Am. Hist. Assn. Republican. Southern Baptist. Avocations: philately, numismatics, birdwatching. Home: 103 Fennerton Rd Paoli PA 19301 Office: Eastern Univ 1300 Eagle Rd Wayne PA 19087 Office Phone: 610-341-5875. E-mail: fboehlke@eastern.edu.

BOEHLKE, WILLIAM FREDRICK, public relations executive, consultant; b. Chgo., Dec. 16, 1946; s. William Fredrick and Cynthia Charlotte (Blackmore) B.; m. Christine Ann Chervenak, July 19, 1969. Student, Wharton Sch. Bus., Phila., 1965-69. Pres. and CEO Data Solve Corp., Chgo., 1981-84, Lati Corp. Inc., San Francisco, 1985-89; CEO Phase Two Strategies Inc., San Francisco, 1989—. Mem. Santa Rosa Golf & Country Club, Home House (London), Penn Club N.Y. E-mail: william_boehlke@p2pr.com.

BOEHM, BARRY WILLIAM, computer science educator; b. Santa Monica, Calif., May 16, 1935; s. Edward G. and Kathryn G. (Kane) B.; m. Sharla Perrine, July 1, 1961; children: Romney Ann, Tenley Lynn. BA, Harvard U., 1957; PhD, UCLA, 1964; ScD (hon.), U. Mass., 2000. Programmer, analyst Gen. Dynamics, San Diego, 1955-59; head infosci. dept. Rand Corp., Santa Monica, 1959-73; chief scientist TRW Def. Sys. Group, Redondo Beach, Calif., 1973-89; dir. infosci. and tech. office Def. Advanced Rsch. Agy. Dept. Def., Arlington, Va., 1989-92, dir. software and computer tech. office, dir. def. rsch. and engring., 1992; TRW prof. software engring., dir. Ctr. for Software Engring. U. So. Calif., L.A., 1992—. Co-chmn. Fed. Coordinating Coun. Sci., Engring. and Tech. High Performance Computing WG, Washington, 1989-91; chmn. DOD Software Tech. Plan WG, Arlington, 1990-92, NASA G & C/Infosystems Adv. Com., Washington, 1973-76; guest lectr. USSR Acad. Sci., 1970; chmn. bd. visitors Carnegie Mellon U. Software Engring. Inst., 1997—; chmn. USAF-Sci. Adv. Bd. Info. Tech. Panel, 1994-97, Army/DARPA Future Combat Systems Software Steering Com., 2001—. Author: ROCKET, 1964, Software Engineering Economics, 1981; co-author: Characteristics of Software Quality, 1978, Software Risk Management, 1989, Software Cost Estimation with COCOMO II, 2000, Balancing Agility and Discipline, 2004; co-editor: Planning Community Information Utilities, 1972, Foundations of Empirical Software Engineering, 2005, Value-Based Software Engineering, 2005. Recipient Warnier prize Soc. Software Analysts, 1984, Freiman award Internat. Soc. Parametric Analysts, 1988, Award for Excellence Office of Sec. of Def., 1992. Fellow Internat. Coun. on Sys. Engring., Assn. for Computing Machinery (Disting. Rsch. award in Software Engring. 1997), NAE, AIAA (chair TC computers 1968-70, Info. Sys. award 1979), IEEE (gov. bd. computer sci. 1981-82, 86-87, H.D. Mills award 2000). Office: U So Calif Computer Sci Dept Los Angeles CA 90089-0781 E-mail: boehm@sunset.usc.edu.

BOEHM, EDWARD GORDON, JR., college administrator, educator; b. Washington, Jan. 30, 1942; s. Edward and Catherine (Murray) B.; m. Regina Ellen Evans, June 25, 1966; children: Evan Arnold, Andrew Edward. BS in Edn., Frostburg State U., 1964; MEd, The Am. U., 1970, D of Higher Edn., 1977. Dir. univ. devel., dean for student devel., assoc. dean/dir. admissions, instr. Coll. Arts & Scis. The Am. U., Washington, 1968-79; assoc. vice chancellor acad. affairs, asst. prof. edn., dean admissions Tex. Christian U., Ft. Worth, 1979-89; sr. v.p., asst. prof. Coll. Edn., exec. dir. Found. Marshall U., Huntington, W.Va., 1989-95; pres. Keystone Coll., La Plume, Pa., 1995—. Mem. adv. coun. Tandy Tech. Scholars, Ft. Worth, 1989-99; trustee, mem. com. The Coll. Bd., N.Y.C., 1987-91. Contbr. book chpt.: Student Services and the Law, 1988; contbr. articles to profl. jours. Bd. dirs., v.p. Boys & Girls Club, Huntington, 1989-95, Tri-State coun. Boy Scouts Am., Huntington, 1989-95; bd. dirs., pres. United Way River Cities, Huntington, 1989-95; bd. dirs. Leadership W. Va., Charleston, 1992-95, Leadership Tri-State, Ironton, Ohio, 1991-95; mem. scholastic evaluation panel Am.'s Jr. Miss, 1995-2005; bd. dirs. Tyler Hosp., 1995-2001, Waverly Cmty. House, 1996-2000; mem. Leadership Wilkes-Barre Exec. Program, Class of '96, Leadership Lackawanna Exec. Program, Class of '96, N.E. Regional Cancer Inst. Adv. Bd.; pres. bd. dirs. Pa. Assn. of Nonprofit Orgns., 1998; mem. nonprofit adv. bd. Nonprofit Resource Ctr., U. Scranton, 1998—; mem. Pa. Soc., 1997—, Team Pa. Amb., 1999—; life mem. Lackawanna Indsl. Fund Enterprises, 1999—; mem. task force Healthy N.E. Pa. Intiative, 1999-2001; bd. govs. Scranton Area Found., 2002—; bd. dir. PACU, 2003—, Pa. Campus Compact, 2003—; commr. Middle States Commn. on Higher Edn., 2005—. Named W.Va. Outstanding Fundraising Exec., Nat. Soc. Fundraising Execs., 1993, Citizen of Yr., Herald Dispatch, 1993, Disting. West Virginian, 1995; recipient Cir. of Excellence in Fundraising award Coun. for Advancement and Support of Edn., 1993, Nat. Tchr.'s award Radio Shack Adv. Coun., 2000; John Deaver Drinko Acad. fellow Marshall U. Mem. Huntington C. of C., Lawrence County C. of C., Greenup County C. of C., Engrs. Club Huntington, Huntington Rotary Club (bd. dirs. 1989-95). Avocations: tennis, soccer, history, golf, hiking. Home: 29 College Ave La Plume PA 18440 Office: Keystone Coll One College Green La Plume PA 18440-0200 Office Phone: 570-945-8500. Business E-Mail: Edward.Boehm@keystone.edu.

BOEHM, ERIC HARTZELL, information technology executive; b. Hof, Germany, July 15, 1918; came to U.S., 1934, naturalized, 1940; s. Karl and Bertha (Oppenheimer) Boehm; m. Inge Pauli, June 5, 1948 (dec.); children: Beatrice(dec.), Ronald James, Evelyn(dec.), Steven David. BA, Wooster (Ohio) Coll., 1940, Litt.D. (hon.), 1973; MA, Fletcher Sch. Law and Diplomacy, 1942; PhD, Yale U., 1951. With Dept. Air Force, 1951-58; chmn., CEO BoehmGroup.com; bd. dirs. ABC-CLIO, Santa Barbara, Calif., 1960—; pres. Internat. Sch. of Info. Mgmt., 1987-94. Chmn. bd. dirs. Internat. Acad. at Santa Barbara, 1970—2003; pub. Environ. Studies Inst., 1971—2003, Info. Inst., 1980—2003; cons. on bibliography, info. sys. Author: We Survived, 1949, 83; microfilm Policy-making of the Nazi Government, 1969; editor Historical Abstracts, 1955-83, cons., 1983; editor America: History and Life, 1964-83, cons., 1983; editor Bibliographies on International Relations and World Affairs, an Annotated Directory, 1965, Blueprint for Bibliography, a System for Social Sciences and Humanities, 1965, Clio Bibliography Series, 1973; co-editor Historical Periodicals, 1961, 2d edit., 1983-85; pub. Advanced Bibliography of Contents: Political Science, 1969, ART Bibliographies: Modern, 1972, Environ. Periodicals Bibliography, 1972; bd. advisors Info. Strategy, The Exec.'s Jour., 1984; contbr. articles to profl. jours. Bd. dirs. UN Assn., Santa Barbara, 1973-77, Santa Barbara's Adv. Bd. Internat. Relationships (Sister Cities), 1974, Friends of Public Library, Friends of U. Calif. at Santa Barbara Library; mem. affiliates bd. U. Calif.-Santa Barbara; vice chmn. New Directions Found., 1984-88; adv. bd. Nuclear Age Peace Found., 1985; chmn. BoehmGroup.com, 2003—. With USAAF, 1942-46. Recipient Disting. Alumnus award Wooster Coll., 1990. Mem. AAAS, Am. Soc. Info. Sci., Assn. Bibliography in History (v.p. 1986, pres. 1987), Calif. Library Soc., Nat. Trust Historic Preservation, Santa Barbara Com. Fgn. Rels., Am. Friends of Wilton Park, Santa Barbara C. of C. (dir. 1980-84), Univ. Club, Rotary, Phi Beta Kappa. Home and Office: 800 E Micheltorena St Santa Barbara CA 93103-2220 Office Phone: 805-965-9889. Personal E-mail: eboehm1918@aol.com.

BOEHM, FELIX HANS, physicist, researcher; b. Basel, Switzerland, June 9, 1924; came to U.S., 1952, naturalized, 1964; s. Hans G. and Marquerite (Philippi) B.; m. Ruth Sommerhalder, Nov. 26, 1956; children: Marcus F., Claude N. MS, Inst. Tech., Zurich, 1948, PhD, 1951. Research assoc. Inst. Tech., Zurich, Switzerland, 1949-52; Boese fellow Columbia U., 1952-53; faculty Calif. Inst. Tech., Pasadena, 1953—, prof. physics, 1961—, William L. Valentine prof., 1985-94, William L. Valentine prof. emeritus, 1995—; Sloan fellow, 1962-64; NSF sr. fellow Niels Bohr Inst., Copenhagen, 1965-66, CERN, Geneva, 1971-72, Laue-Langevin Inst., 1980. Recipient Humboldt award, 1980, 84. Fellow Am. Phys. Soc. (Tom W. Bonner prize 1995); mem. Nat. Acad. Sics. Achievements include research on nuclear physics, nuclear beta decay, neutrino physics, atomic physics, muonic and pionic atoms, parity and time-reversal. Home: 2510 N Altadena Dr Altadena CA 91001-2836 Office: Calif Inst Tech Mail Code 161 33 Pasadena CA 91125-0001 E-mail: boehm@caltech.edu.

BOEHM, JOHN C., JR., lawyer; BA, Univ. Va., 1976; JD, Univ. Tex., 1984. Bar: Tex. 1984. Fgn. svc. officer US Dept. of State, 1977—82; ptnr. Fulbright & Jaworski LLP, Austin, 1983—, now ptnr., head, tech. and emerging companies dept. Mem.: ABA, Travis County Bar Assn., State Bar of Tex., Nat. Assn. Bond Lawyers, Order of Coif, Phi Beta Kappa. Office: Fulbright & Jaworski LLP Ste 2400 600 Congress Ave Austin TX 78701-3271 Office Phone: 512-474-5201. Office Fax: 512-536-4598. Business E-Mail: jboehm@fulbright.com.

BOEHM, KENNETH, legal association administrator; 1 child, Christine. Talk show host Sta. WWDB-AM-FM, Phila.; prosecutor; adminstrv. asst. to Congressman Christopher Smith; legis. dir. Howard Jarvis' Am. Tax Reduction Movement; chmn. Nat. Legal Policy and Ctr., Falls Church, Va., 1991—. Counsel to bd. dirs. Legal Svcs. Corp. Office: Nat Legal and Policy Ctr 107 Park Washington Ct Falls Church VA 22046 Office Phone: 703-237-1970.

BOEHM, STEVEN BRUCE, lawyer; b. N.Y.C., May 22, 1954; s. Henry and Irene (Jonas) B. BA, Rutgers U., New Brunswick, N.J., 1975; JD, Rutgers U., Newark, 1978. Bar: N.J., 1978, D.C., 1982, U.S. Dist. Ct. N.J., U.S. Dist. Ct., D.C. Enforcement atty. SEC, Washington, 1978-81, atty. office gen. counsel, 1982, counsel to the commr., 1982-83; assoc. Sutherland Asbill & Brennan, LLP, Washington, 1983-87, ptnr., 1988—. Philip J. Levin scholar Rutgers U., 1975-78. Mem. ABA (corp., banking and bus. law com.), D.C. Bar Assn., Phi Beta Kappa, Pi Sigma Alpha. Office: Sutherland Asbill & Brennan LLP 1275 Pennsylvania Ave NW Washington DC 20004-2415 Business E-Mail: steven.boehm@sablaw.com.

BOEHM, THEODORE REED, state supreme court justice; b. Evanston, Ill., Sept. 12, 1938; s. Hans George and Frances (Reed) B.; children from previous marriage: Elisabeth, Jennifer, Sarah, Macy; m. Margaret Stitt Harris, Jan. 27, 1985. AB summa cum laude, Brown U., 1960; JD magna cum laude, Harvard U., 1963. Bar: D.C. 1964, Ind. 1964, U.S. Supreme Ct. 1975. Law clk. to Chief Justice Warren, Justices Reed and Burton, U.S. Supreme Ct., Washington, 1963-64; assoc. Baker & Daniels, Indpls., 1965-70, ptnr., 1970-88, 95-96, mng. ptnr., 1980-87; gen. counsel major appljances GE, Louisville, 1988-89; v.p., gen. counsel GE Aircraft Engines, Cin., 1989-91; dep. gen. counsel Eli Lilly & Co., 1991-95; justice Ind. Supreme Ct., Indpls., 1996—. Pres. Ind. Sports Corp., 1980-88; chmn. organizing com. 1987 Pan Am. Games, Indpls.; chmn. Indpls. Cultural Devel. Commn., 2001-; chair nominating and governance com. U.S. Olympic Com., 2004-. Mem. ABA, Am. Law Inst., Ind. Bar Assn., Indpls. Bar Assn. Office: Ind Supreme Ct State House Rm 324 Indianapolis IN 46204-2728 Office Phone: 317-232-2547. E-mail: tboehm@courts.state.in.us.

BOEHMER, RICHARD A., lawyer; b. St. Louis, June 26, 1951; BA, Harvey Mudd Coll. and U. So. Calif., 1973; JD, Loyola U., L.A., 1976. Bar: Calif. 1976. With O'Melveny & Myers, L.A. Recipient Acad. scholarship Loyola U. Sch. Law, 1974, 75. Mem. ABA, L.A. County Bar Assn., Phi Beta Kappa, Phi Kappa Phi. Office: O'Melveny & Myers 400 S Hope St Los Angeles CA 90071-2899

BOEHNE, EDWARD GEORGE, banker; b. Evansville, Ind., May 15, 1940; s. Edward John and Lucy Naomi (Strieter) Boehne; m. Patricia Graffis, Jan. 24, 1960; 1 child, Lisa Elena. BS, Ind. U., 1962, MBA, 1963, MA, 1967, PhD in Econs, 1968; LLD (hon.), Widener U., 1989, U. Del., 2001, U. So. Ind., 2002, Holy Family U., 2004. Economist Fed. Res. Bank, Phila., 1968—70, rsch. officer, economist, 1970—71, v.p., dir. rsch., 1971—73, sr. v.p., 1973—81, pres., 1981—2000. Tchr. Bradley U., 1963—65, Ind. U., 1965—67, Temple U., 1969—70; bd. dirs. Haverford Trust, 2000—, AAA Mid-Atlantic Co., 2000—, Beneficial Savs. Bank, 2000—, Toll Bros., 2000—, PennMut. Life Ins. Co., 2001—. Chmn. Pa. Hosp., 1993-97; chmn. University City Sci. Ctr., 1998-99. Recipient Lieber award Ind. U., 1967, Gov.'s citation for outstanding svc. to Pa., 1978, Whitney Young Leadership award 1986, Stephen Girard award, 1987. Office: 313 Devon State Rd Devon PA 19333-1411 Fax: 610-687-4748. E-mail: egboehne@msn.com.

BOEHNEN, DANIEL A., lawyer; b. Mitchell, S.D., Aug. 5, 1950; s. Lloyd and Mary Elizabeth (Buche) B.; m. Joan Bensing, May 22, 1976; children: Christopher, Lindsey. BS in Chem. Engring. cum laude, Notre Dame U., 1973; JD, Cornell U., 1976. Bar: Ill, U.S. Dist. Ct. (no. dist.) Ill., U.S. Ct. Appeals (7th and fed. cirs.), U.S. Supreme Ct. Atty. Allegretti, Newitt, Witcoff & McAndrews Ltd., Chgo., 1976—, assoc., 1982—; ptnr., exec. officer Allegretti & Witcoff, Ltd., Chgo., 1986—, bd. dirs., 1993—95; founder, mng. ptnr. McDonnell Boehnen Hulbert & Berghoff, LLP, Chgo., 1996—. Commr. Northbrook Planning Commn., 1993—. Named one of Top IP Lawyers in Ill., Cain's Chgo. Bus., Super Lawyers for IP Litigation, Chgo. Mag. Mem. ABA, AIPLA, Cornell Law Assn. Chg. (chmn.), Fed. Cir. Bar Assn. (bd. dirs.), Assn. Patent Law Firms (pres., bd. dirs.), Leading Lawyers Network (Ill., founding mem.). Avocations: skiing, photography, scuba diving. Office: McDonnell Boehnen Hulbert & Berghoff LLP 300 S Wacker Dr Chicago IL 60606-6709 Office Phone: 312-913-0001. Business E-Mail: boehnen@mbhb.com.

BOEHNEN, DAVID LEO, food service executive, lawyer; b. Mitchell, S.D., Dec. 3, 1946; s. Lloyd L. Boehnen and Mary Elizabeth (Buche) Roby; m. Shari A. Bauhs, Aug. 9, 1969; children: Lesley, Michelle, Heather. AB, U. Notre Dame, 1968; JD with honors, Cornell U., 1971. Bar: Minn. 1971. Assoc. Dorsey & Whitney, Mpls., 1971—76, ptnr., 1977—89; sr. v.p. law and external rels. Supervalu Inc., Mpls., 1991—97, exec. v.p., 1997—. Vis. prof. law Cornell U. Law Sch., Ithaca, NY, 1982. Mem. adv. coun. on arts and letters U. Notre Dame, 1993—; mem. adv. coun. Cornell U. Law Sch., 1983—92, chmn. coun., 1986—90; bd. dirs. Mpls. Art Inst., Guthrie Theatre. Mem.: Spring Hill Golf Club, Minikahda Club (Mpls.). Roman Cath. Office Phone: 612-828-4151. E-mail: david.boehnen@supervalu.com.

BOEHNER, JOHN A., congressman; b. Reading, Ohio, Nov. 17, 1949; m. Deborah Gunlack, 1973; children: Lindsay M., Tricia A. BS, Xavier U., 1977. Pres. Nucite Sales, Inc.; mem. Ohio Ho. of Reps., 1984-90, U.S. Congress from 8th Ohio dist., Washington, 1991—; chmn. edn. and workforce com., mem. agr. com., oversight com. Exec. mem. Nat. Rep. Congl. Com.; chmn. Ho. Rep. Conf. Com. Active Ohio Farm Bur. Mem. KC, Cin., Dayton, Middletown C. of C. Republican. Roman Catholic. Office: US Ho of Reps 1011 Longworth Bldg Washington DC 20515-3508 also: District Office 8200 Beckett Park Drive, #202 Hamilton OH 45011*

BOEHR, DIANE LINDA, librarian; b. N.Y.C., Oct. 8, 1950; d. Alvin and Elsie (Glickstein) Plotkin; m. Danny Arthur Boehr, Aug. 22, 1970 (dec. Apr. 17, 2002); children: Michelle Beth, Joshua David. BS, CCNY, 1971; MLS, U. Md., 1983. Libr. svcs. cons. Costabile Assocs., Bethesda, Md., 1983—98; cataloging sect. Nat. Libr. Medicine, Bethesda, 1998—2005, head cataloging, 2005—. Adj. prof. U. Md., College Park, 1994— Active B'nai Israel Congregation, Rockville, 1979—; pres. Washington chpt. Asthma and Allergy Found. Am., 1978-80. Mem. ALA, Beta Phi Mu. Office: Nat Libr Medicine 8600 Rockville Pike Bethesda MD 20914 Office Phone: 301-435-7059.

BOEKE, JEF DANIEL, molecular biology educator, geneticist; b. Albany, N.Y., Feb. 15, 1954; s. Daniël and Elisabeth (Muller) B.; m. Susanne Utzschneider, July 24, 1979; children: Caroline Elizabeth, Emily Ann, Annabel Clair. AB summa cum laude, Bowdoin Coll., 1976; student, McGill U., Montreal, Que., 1974-75; PhD in Molecular Biology, Rockefeller U., 1982. Postdoctoral fellow Whitehead Inst. MIT, Cambridge, Mass., 1982-85; asst. prof. molecular biology Johns Hopkins U. Sch. Med., Balt., 1986-90, assoc. prof., 1990-95, prof., 1995—2002, founder, dir. High Throughput Biology Ctr., 2002—. Organizer Mid Atlantic Yeast Meeting, Balt., 1992; co-organizer Keystone Meeting Transposition and Side-specific Recombination, 1994. Mem. editl. bd. Genome Rsch.; contbr. articles to profl. jours. including Science, Ibis, Virology, Jour. Molecular Biology, Gene, Jour. Bacteriol, Cell, Molecular Cellular Biology, Nature, Genetics, Yeast, Meths. Enzymology. Recipient award Mellon Found., 1986, faculty rsch. award Am. Cancer Soc., 1990—; James Bowdoin scholar, 1972-76, Searle scholar, 1986-89; Thomas J. Watson fellow, 1976-77, Rockefeller U. fellow, 1978-82, Helen Hay Whitney fellow, 1982-85; rsch. grantee NIH, 1986—, Human Frontier Sci. Program, 1991-94. Mem. AAAS, Am. Soc. Microbiology (editorial bd. Molecular and Cellular Biology 1989—), Genetics Soc. Am., Phi Beta Kappa. Achievements include demonstration that retrotransposons move to new sites in DNA via an RNA intermediate using a retrovirus-like mechanism; development of system for in vitro transposition; identification of host factors important for transposition, and of reverse transcriptase activity in human L1 transposon; research in molecular genetics of yeasts, mechanism of tranposition of yeast mobile genetic element Ty1, and human L1 element. Office: Johns Hopkins U Sch Med High Throughput Biology Ctr 733 N Broadway Baltimore MD 21205-2105 Office Phone: 410-955-0398. Personal E-mail: doctorbee54@yahoo.com.

BOEKELHEIDE, VIRGIL CARL, chemistry educator; b. Cheslea, S.D., July 28, 1919; s. Charles F. and Eleonor (Toennies) B.; m. Caroline Barrett, Apr. 7, 1924; children: Karl, Anne, Erich. AB magna cum laude, U. Minn., Mpls., 1939, PhD, 1943. Instr. U. Ill., Urbana, 1943-46; asst. prof. to prof. U. Rochester, 1946-60; prof. dept. chemistry U. Oreg., Eugene, 1960—. Contbr. articles to profl. jours. Recipient Disting. Achievement award U. Minn., 1967; recipient Alexander von Humboldt award W.Ger. Govt., 1974, 82, Centenary Lectureship Royal Soc. G.B., 1983, Coover award Iowa State U., 1981; Disting. scholar designate U.S.-China Acad. Sci., 1981; Fulbright Disting. prof. Yugoslavia, 1972 Mem. NAS, Pharm. Soc. Japan (hon.). Home: 2017 Elk Ave Eugene OR 97403-1788 Office: U Oreg Dept Chemistry Eugene OR 97403

BOELTER, DAVID MICHAEL, art educator; b. Iowa, Mar. 20, 1972; s. Gene LaVerne and Victoria Ruth Boelter; m. Jamii Renae Clasborne, July 24, 2004. BA, Buena Vista U., Storm Lake, Iowa, 1997; MA, U. Iowa, Iowa City, 1999, MFA, 2000. Tchrs. asst. U. Iowa, Iowa City, 1998—2000; asst. prof. art Buena Vista U., Storm Lake, Iowa, 2001—. Recipient Outstanding student achievement in contemporary sculpture, Internat. Sculpture Ctr., Hamilton, N.J. Home: 304 Geneseo St Storm Lake IA 50588 Office: Buena Vista Univ 610 W 4th St Storm Lake IA 50588 Office Phone: 712-749-2201. E-mail: boelter@bvu.edu.

BOELTER, PHILIP FLOYD, real estate company officer, construction executive; b. Independence, Iowa, Mar. 25, 1943; s. Floyd Joseph and Eileen R. (Wilson) B.; m. Linda Lee Franck, June 7, 1964; children: Carrie Lynn, John Philip. BS in Indsl. Engring., Iowa State U., 1965; JD, U. Iowa, 1968. Ptnr. Dorsey & Whitney, Mpls., 1968—2002; exec. v.p., chief oper. officer Kraus-Anderson Cos., Inc., Mpls., 2002—. Trustee Gustavus Adolphus Coll., 1996-2005; bd. dir. Jr. Achievement of the Upper Midwest, 2003-04. Mem. Mpls. Athletic Club (treas. 1992, sec. 1993, v.p. 1994, pres. 1995). Lutheran. Avocations: landscape gardening, skiing, golf, reading, volleyball. Office: Kraus-Anderson 525 S 8th St Minneapolis MN 55404 Office Phone: 612-335-2704. E-mail: pboelter@k-a-c.com.

BOENNING, HENRY DORR, JR., investment banker; b. Phila., Oct. 16, 1914; s. Henry Dorr and Clara Virginia (Smith) B.; m. Clare Huston Miller, Feb. 18, 1946; m. Sara Ann Perkins, Aug. 19, 1964. BS, U. Pa., 1935; postgrad., Harvard Bus. Sch., 1935-37. Partner Boenning & Co., Phila., 1946-70; v.p. Boenning & Scattergood, Inc., 1970—. Served from 2d lt. to maj. AUS, 1939-46. Mem. Phi Gamma Delta. Home: 936 Rock Creek Rd Bryn Mawr PA 19010-1923 Office: 4 Tower Bridge 200 Barr Harbor Dr Fl 3D West Conshohocken PA 19428-2977

BOENTGEN, MARTHA MATHILDE, artist, small business owner, educator; b. Astoria, Oreg., May 19, 1920; d. Carl and Ada Marguerite (Hoars) B.; m. Robert M. Trask, Apr. 23, 1942 (dec. Apr. 1944); m. Arthur Miller, Nov. 7, 1947 (div. Jan. 1960); children: Anna M. Miller Haskell, Jed B., Jan W. BA, U. Oreg., 1947, MA, 1956. Instr. Lower Columbia Coll., Longview, Wash., 1960-79, dept. head, 1970-79, dir. overseas study, 1971-79; cons. Pavillion Gallery, Portland, Oreg., 1979-82; owner, mgr. Lower Columbia River Fine Arts, Skamokawa, Wash. Instr. Clatsop Coll., Astoria, Oreg., 1985—. One-woman shows, 1992—. Mem. Wash. State Arts Commn., Olympia, 1967-70. Mem. Portland Art Assn., Nature Conservancy, Skamokawa Art Assn., West Side Water Works, U. Oreg. Alumni Assn., Sierra Club, Phi Beta Kappa. Republican. Episcopalian. Avocation: historic building restoration. Office: Lower Columbia River Fine Arts PO Box 8 Skamokawa WA 98647-0008

BOER, F. PETER, chemical company executive; b. 1940; AB, Princeton U., 1961; PhD, Harvard U., 1965. With Tex Div. Lab. Dow Chem. Co., 1965-78, dir; v.p., mgr. R & D Am. Can Co., 1978-83; v.p., pres. rsch. div., corp. tech. group W.R. Grace & Co., from 1983, sr. v.p., until 1989, exec. v.p., until 1995; pres., CEO, Tiger Scientific Inc., 1995—. Bd dirs. Nova Corp., ENSCO, Inc., Rhodes Techs. Inc., Sci. Protein Labs.; adj. prof. Sch. Mgmt. and chem. engring. Yale U.; mem. evaluation com. for nat. medals of tech. Dept. Commerce, 1990-97. Author: Valuation of Technology, 1999, The Real Options Solution, 2002, Technology Valuation Solutions, 2004. Mem. Nat. Acad. Engring. Office: Tiger Scientific Inc 47 Country Rd S Village Of Golf FL 33436-5615 E-mail: fpboer@concentric.net.

BOER, RALF REINHARD, lawyer; b. Berlin, Oct. 31, 1948; came to U.S., 1965; s. Karl Wolfgang Boer and Ingeborg (Krause) Serafin; m. Kathleen Marie Steinmetz, Jan. 5, 1974; children: Jessica, Charles, Alexander. BA cum laude, U. Wis., Milw., 1971; JD magna cum laude, U. Wis., Madison, 1974. Bar: Wis. 1974, U.S. Dist. Ct. (ea. dist.) Wis. 1974. Ptnr. Foley & Lardner, Milw., 1974—, ptnr.-Berlin office, 1975—76, mng. ptnr. Milw., 1992—, chmn. of firm, CEO, chmn. mgmt. com. Bd. dirs. Fiskars, Helsinki, Finland, Dyno, Hayward, Wis.; bd. dirs. internat. transactions sect. Wis. State Bar, 1987—. Author: German Labor-Management Relations Act, 1976. Bd. dirs. Internat. Inst. Wis., Milw., 1985-89; bd. dirs., adv. coun. U. Wis.-Milw. Internat. Bus. Ctr., 1987—. Mem. ABA, Wis. Bar Assn., Milw. Bar Assn. Fluent in german. Office: Foley & Lardner LLP 777 E Wisconsin Ave Ste 3800 Milwaukee WI 53202-5367 Office Phone: 414-297-5609. Business E-Mail: rboer@foley.com.

BOERSEMA, DAVID BRIAN, philosopher, educator; b. Ft. Monroe, Va., Dec. 23, 1951; s. Munroe Eskel and Waneeta Diana (Wren) B. BA, Hope Coll., Holland, Mich., 1973; MA, Mich. State U., 1978, PhD, 1985. Instr. Jackson (Mich.) C.C., 1977-78, Mich. State U., East Lansing, 1979-82, Delta Coll., Midland, Mich., 1982-84; asst. prof. Pacific U., Forest Grove, Oreg., 1985-91, assoc. prof., 1991-97, prof. philosophy, 1997—, Douglas C. Strain prof. of natural philosophy, chair, 1990—, Disting. U. prof., 2003—. Contbr. articles to profl. jours. Recipient S.S. Johnson award for tchg. Pacific U., 1994, Arthur and Lois Graves award Pomona Coll., 1994; J.J. Malone Faculty fellow Nat. Coun. on U.S.-Arab Relations, 1992, Hewlett fellow Pacific U., 2000; George F. Baker scholar, 1972. Mem. AAAS, History of Sci. Soc., Philosophy of Sci. Soc., Sigma Xi. Office: Pacific Univ 2043 College Way Forest Grove OR 97116-1797 Office Phone: 503-352-2150. Business E-Mail: boersema@pacificu.edu.

BOERSMA, LAWRENCE ALLAN (LARRY ALLAN), animal welfare administrator, photographer; b. London, Ont., Can., Apr. 24, 1932; s. Harry Albert and Valerie Kathryn (DeCordova) B.; m. Nancy Noble Jones, Aug. 16, 1952 (div. 1962) children: Juliana Jaye, Dirk John; m. June Elaine Schiefer McKim, Nov. 22, 1962; children: Kenneth Thomas McKim, Mark Rennie McKim. BA, U. Nebr., Omaha, 1953, MS, 1955; PhD, Sussex U., 1972; postgrad., U. Oxford (Eng.), 1996; ScD (hon.), U. Calif., Berkeley, 2005. Journalism tchr. Tech. H.S., Omaha, 1953-55; dir. pub. rels., chair journalism dept. Adams State Coll., Alamosa, Colo., 1955-59; advt. sales analyst, advt. salesman Better Homes and Gardens, Des Moines, NYC, 1959-63; advt. account exec. This Week Mag., NYC, 1963-66; eastern sales dir., mktg. dir. Ladies' Home Jour., NYC, 1966-75; v.p. assoc. pub., v.p. pub. Saturday Evening Post and The Country Gentleman, NYC, 1975; v.p., dir. mktg. and advt. sales Photo World Mag., NYC, 1975-77; advt. mgr. LaJolla (Calif.) Light, 1977-80; owner, photographer Allan/The Animal Photographers, San Diego, Sarasota, 1980—; pres., CEO The Photographic Inst. Internat., 1982-86; dir. cmty. rels. San Diego Humane Soc./Soc. for Prevention Cruelty to Animals, 1985-94; assoc. exec. dir. The Ctr. for Humane Edn. for So. Calif., 1994-98; owner Animal Art, San Diego, 1999—, Sarasota, Calif., 1999—. Adj. asst. prof. Grad. Sch. Bus., Pace U., NYC, 1964-65; adj. instr. NY Inst. Advt., 1974-77, others; adj. prof. Sch. Bus. Mesa Coll., San Diego, 1981-84, City Coll., San Diego, 1982-86, Winona Internat. Sch. Profl. Photography, Des Plaines, Ill., 1984-87, U. Calif., San Diego, 1985; adj. prof. Coll. Bus. Adminstrn. U. LaVerne, San Diego, 1985; tchr. Winona Internat. Sch. Profl. Photography, Photog. Inst. Internat., San Diego Natural History Mus., U. Calif. San Diego, Adams State Coll. of Colo.; pres., CEO United Animal Welfare Found., San Diego, 1992-94; chmn., CEO Internat. Dolphin Project, 1995; spkr. in field. Author: Strange Events at the House on Pk. Avenue: A Jack and Jimmy Mystery, 1996; (as Larry Allan) Creative Canine Photography, 2004, Keep Wild Animals inOUr Lives!, 2005; co-author: One Day in the Life of a Little Cougar, 2001, One Day in the Life of a Coyote Pup, 2001; photographer: (as Larry Allan) Wildcats of North Am. book series, 1998, Wild Canines of North America book series, 2000, Show Biz Tricks for Birds, 2001, El Lince, El Lince Rojo, El Puma El Coyote, El Lobo, Los Zorros, 2002; contbr. photography and articles to mags.; photographer calendars, books, and greeting cards; photographer: (motion picture) The Truth About Cats and Dogs; exhbns.: Sierra Club, Art Photo Expo, LA, 1999, others; permanent collections include Sierra Club. Spokesperson Coalition for Pet Population Control, San Diego, 1990, 93, Com. Against Proposition C-Pound Animals for Med. Rsch., San Diego, 1990; spokesperson Spay-Neuter Action Project, 1991, steering com., 1991, bd. dir., 1992-93; evaluation subcom. County San Diego Dept. Animal Control Adv. Com.; founder, chair Feral Cat Coalition San Diego County, 1992-93, clinic vol., 2001-04, bd. dirs. 2003-04; chair World Record Feral Cat Fix-athon, 2004, chmn, CEO Preserve Our Wildlife Orgn., 2005—; Calif. State Humane Officer; vol. in pub. info. San Diego/Imperial Counties chpt. ARC, 1993-2002, chpt. centennial com., 1996-97; pub. info. officers San Diego County Emergency Svc. Orgn., 1993-95; vol. photographer Calif. Wolf Ctr., 1999-2002; others; bd. dirs. Escondido Humane Soc. Found., 1994-99. Finalist Internat. Photographer of Yr., Brit. Mus. Nat. History, 2003; recipient Belding award, Advt. Club LA, 1986, 1988, Excellence award, Communication Arts Mag., 1987, Gold award, One Show, 1989, 1st Pl. Mobius Advt. award, US Festivals Assn., 1991, Gold Mercury award, Internat. Acad. Comm. Arts & Sci., 1991, Merit award, PR Club San Diego, 1994, Commendation for disting. humanitarian pub. svc., San Diego County Bd. Supr., 1994, Spl. Commendation for love and concern for all animals, San Diego City Coun., 1994, Third Pl., Outdoor Photo of Yr., Calif., 2002, Gold award, Cmty. Arts Group San Diego, 1986, Best in show, Gold award, 1988. Fellow Royal Photog. Soc. Gt. Britain, Profl. Photographers Am. (Master of Photography award 1985, Photog. Craftsman award 1986), Profl. Photographers of Calif.; mem. PRSA (chmn. So. Tier NY chpt. 1971-72), Soc. Animal Welfare Adminstr., Nat. Soc. Fund Raising Exec. (cert., bd. dir. 1988-89, treas. San Diego chpt. 1990-91, mem. nat. faculty 1992-93), Shriners (pres. Al Bahr chpt., Businessmen's Club), Masons, Sierra Club (Ansel Adams award 2005), The Wilderness Soc., Doris Day Animal League, Defenders of Wildlife, Am. Indian Edn. Fedn., Native Am. Rights Fund. Republican. Presbyterian. Home: 4238 65th Terr E Sarasota FL 34243 Business E-Mail: allananimalphoto@coverusa.com.

BOERSMA, P. DEE, marine biologist, educator; b. Mt. Pleasant, Mich., Nov. 1, 1946; d. Henry W. and Vivian (Anspach) B. BS, Ctrl. Mich. U., 1969; PhD, Ohio State U., 1974; DSc (hon.), Ctrl. Mich. U., 2003. From asst. prof. Inst. Environ. Studies to prof. U. Wash., Seattle, 1974—88, prof. zoology, 1988—, assoc. dir., 1987-93, acting dir., 1990-91, adj. prof. women's studies, 1993—2003, prof. biology, prof. womens studies, 2003—, Wadsworth chmn. conservation sci., 2005—; mem. sci. adv. com. for outer continental shelf Environ. Studies Program, Dept. Interior, 1980-83; prin. investigator Magellanic Penguin Project Wildlife Cons. Soc., 1982—. Evans vis. fellow U. Otago, New Zealand, 1995, Pew fellow in marine conservation, 1997-2000; naturalist Lindblad Expdns., 2001-04. Assoc. editor Ecological Applications, 1998-2001; exec. editor Conservation in Practice, 2000—; contbr. articles to profl. jours. Mem. adv. U.S. del. to UN Status Women Commn., N.Y.C., 1973, UN World Status Women Commn., N.Y.C., 1973, UN World Population Conf., Romania, 1974; mem. Gov. Lowry's Task Force on Wildlife, 1993; sci. adv. EcoBios, 1985-95; bd. dirs. Zero Population Growth, 1975-82, Washington Nature Conservancy, 1995-98; adv. bd. Walt Disney World Animal Kingdom, 1993—, Island press, 1999—, Compass, 2000—,; bd. dirs. Peregine Fund, 1995—, Bullitt Found., 1996-2000, Islandwood, 2001—; mem. scholar diplomatic program Dept. State, 1977. Recipient Outstanding Alumni award Ctrl. Mich. U., 1978, Matrix award Women in Comm., 1983; named to Kellogg Nat. Leadership Program, 1982-85; recipient Top 100 Outsiders of Yr. award Outside Mag., 1987, Outstanding Centennial Alumni award Ctrl. Mich. U., 1993; sci. fellow The Wildlife Conservation Soc., 1982—, Aldo Leopold Leadership fellow, 2000-01. Fellow AAAS, Am Ornithol. Union (regional rep. Pacific seabird group 1981-85); mem. AAAS, Ecol. Soc. Am., Wilson Ornithol. Soc., Cooper Ornithol. Soc., Soc. Am. Naturalists, Soc. for Conservation Biology (bd. govs. 1991-94, pres-elect 1995-97, pres. 1997-99, past pres. 1999-2001), Internat. Union for Biol. Scis. (mem. U.S. nat. com. 2001—), Gopher Brokers Club (pres. Seattle chpt. 1982-83). Office: U Wash Dept Biology PO Box 351800 Seattle WA 98195-1800 E-mail: boersma@u.washington.edu.

BOES, LAWRENCE WILLIAM, lawyer; b. Bklyn., Aug. 3, 1935; s. Lawrence and Lissi (Schaefer) B.; m. Joan Mary Elward, Oct. 2, 1965; children: Lawrence, Siobhan, Thomas. AB, Columbia Coll., 1961; JD, Columbia U., 1964. Bar: N.Y. 1965, U.S. Dist. Ct. (ea. dist.) N.Y. 1968, U.S. Dist. Ct. (so. dist.) N.Y. 1968, U.S. Ct. Appeals (2d cir.) 1971, U.S. Ct. Appeals (8th cir.) 1974, U.S. Supreme Ct. 1974, U.S. Ct. Appeals (9th cir.) 1982, U.S. Ct. Appeals (3d cir.) 1988. Law clk. to judge U.S. Ct. Appeals (2d cir.), 1964-65; assoc. Reavis & McGrath, N.Y.C., 1965-70, ptnr., 1970-88, Fulbright & Jaworski L.L.P., N.Y.C., 1989-00, ret. ptnr., 2001—; atty. Law Office of Lawrence W. Boes, 2001—. Revs. editor Columbia Law Rev., 1963-64. Mem. code rev. commn. Village of Westbury, N.Y., 1983—, chmn., 1991—; trustee Westbury (N.Y.) Meml. Pub. Libr., 2002—. Cpl. U.S. Army, 1958—60. Pulitzer scholar N.Y.C. Bd. Edn., 1954; nat. scholar Columbia U., 1962. Mem. ABA, N.Y. State Bar Assn. (com. on stds. of atty. conduct 1999-2002), Bar Assn. Nassau County (chair 1998-00, profl. ethics com.), Univ. Glee Club N.Y.C., Rotary (pres. 2004-05). Avocations: gardening, baseball, glee club singing. Office: Law Office Lawrence W Boes 256 Asbury Ave E Westbury NY 11590-2423 Office Phone: 516-997-2996. E-mail: larrywboes@aol.com.

BOESCH, DIANE HARRIET, retired elementary school educator; b. Erie, Pa., July 3, 1942; d. William Jacob and Dorothy Gertrude (Call) B. BS, Edinboro (Pa.) State U., 1964; MA, Kent (Ohio) State U., 1968; postgrad., So. Ill. U., Carbondale, 1969, CUNY, 1972, Norwalk State Tech. Coll., 1979, Northeastern U., Boston, 1982, Fla. State U., 1988. Tchr. math. Iroquois Area Sch. Dist., Erie, 1964-67; grad. asst. Kent State U., 1967-68; tchr., writer Comprehensive Sch. Math. Project, Carbondale, Ill., 1968-70; tchr. math. Weston (Conn.) Pub. Schs., 1970-2000, dept. chmn. math., 1989-2000; math edn. cons., 2000—. Dir. Weston Tchr. Ctr., 1983-84; condr. workshops on math. and writing, Conn., 1970—. Contbr. articles to profl. publs. Vol. nat. elections, Erie, 1960, West Haven, Conn., 1972. Recipient Celebration of Excellence award Conn. State Dept. Edn., 1988, Presdl. award NSF, 1990. Fellow Conn. Acad. for Edn. in Math. and Sci.; mem. NEA, Nat. Coun. Tchrs. Math., Conn. Educator Talent Pool, Conn. Edn. Assn., Weston Tchr. Assn., Coun. Presdl. Awardees in Math., Pi Mu Epsilon, Kappa Delta Pi. Republican. Lutheran. Avocations: genealogy, writing, music, reading, atlanta braves baseball. E-mail: dhb703@aol.com.

BOESCH, FRANCIS THEODORE, electrical engineer, educator; b. NYC, Sept. 28, 1936; s. Victor and Margaret (Wright) B. BS, Poly. Inst. N.Y., 1957, MS, 1960, PhD, 1963. Instr., then asst. prof. elec. engring. Poly. Inst. N.Y., 1957-63; mem. mil. research staff Bell Telephone Labs., 1963-68, mem. research staff, 1969-79; prof. elec. engring. and computer sci., dept. head Stevens Inst. Tech., Hoboken, N.J., 1979-88, dean of faculty, 1988-93, prof. elec. engring., 1993—. McKay prof. elec. engring. and computer sci. U. Calif., Berkeley, 1968-69. Author: Large-Scale Networks, 1976; editor-in-chief: Networks, 1970-81; editor: Graph Theory, 1978-81; contbr. articles to profl. jours. Vice pres. Fair Haven (N.J.) Little League, 1974; scoutmaster Fair Haven council Boy Scouts Am., 1973-78, dist. commnr. Monmouth council, 1978-80. Fellow IEEE, N.Y. Acad. Scis.; mem. Assn. Computing Machinery, Am. Math. Soc., Sigma Xi, Eta Kappa Nu. Home: 16-02 Everett Ter Fair Lawn NJ 07410-2410 Office: Stevens Inst Tech Castle Point Sta Hoboken NJ 07030 Business E-Mail: fboesch@aol.com.

BOESE, GIL KARYLE, cultural organization executive; b. Chgo., June 24, 1937; s. Carl H. and Winifred A. Boese; m. Lillian R. Boese; children: Ann Carroll, Peter Austin, Sara Elisabeth. BA, Carthage (Ill.) Coll., 1959; MS, No. Ill. U., 1965; PhD; NIMH trainee 1970, Johns Hopkins U., 1973. Instr. biology Thornton Community Coll., Harvey, Ill., 1965-67; asst. prof. biology Elmhurst (Ill.) Coll., 1967-69; dep. dir. Chgo. Zool. Park, Brookfield, Ill., 1971-80; dir. Milw. County Zool. Gardens, Milw., 1980-89; pres. Zool. Soc. Milw. County, Milw., 1989—, Found. for Wildlife Conservation, 1993—. Tech. cons. Belize Zoo and Tropical Edn. Ctr.; founder Birds without Borders Aves Sin Frontera internat. dir., mgr. Runaway Creek Nature Preescree, Belize program; dir. Miller Brewery Friends of the Field. Bd. dirs. Dian Fossey Gorilla Found., chmn. 1998-99, internat. coordinating com., pres., 1997—; bd. dirs. Lewa Conservancy Kenya; improvement assn. bd. dirs. Pewaukee Lake, Wis. Fellow Royal Geog. Soc., Am. Assn. Zool. Parks and Aquariums (bd. dirs.); mem. Hemmingway Soc., Adventurers Club. Office: Zool Soc Milw County 10005 W Bluemound Rd Milwaukee WI 53226-4346 E-mail: boese@zoosociety.org.

BOESE, SANDRA JEAN, publishing executive; b. Ely, Minn., July 31, 1940; d. John Frank and Millie Jean (Prebeg) Simonick; m. Lee Robert Boese Sr., June 15, 1963; children: Lee Robert Jr., Joy Karin. BA in Speech and Elem. Edn., Marquette U., 1962. Elem. tchr., 1962-67; pub., editor Classroom Connections, Inc., Merced and Sacramento, 1988—, also chmn. bd. Pres. Calif. State Bd. Edn., Sacramento, 1984-86; exec. dir. Teen Talk Radio Show, 1994—. Trustee Merced City Sch. Dist., 1975-83; commr. Calif. Post-Secondary Edn. Commn., Sacramento, 1983; bd. dirs. Far-West Lab., San Francisco, 1984, The Achievement Coun., San Francisco, 1985. Recipient Commendation of Exempary Svc. award Calif. State Senate, 1983, Cert. of Appreciation, Calif. State Dept. Edn., 1983; named Woman of Distinction Soroptimist Internat., 1987. Mem. AAUW (Woman of Distintion 1986), Calif. Sch. Bds. Assn. (bd. dirs. del. assembly, 1978-81, chmn. conf. 1979-80, founder chmn. polit. action com. 1982-83, Outstanding Svc. award 1982, Spl. Recognition 1986), Merced City C. of C. (pres. 1985-86, Athena award 1988), Nat. Assn. State Bds. Edn. (bd. dirs. 1984-86), Assn. Marquette U. Women (Mary Neville Bielefeld award 1986). Republican. Roman Catholic. Avocations: painting, decorating, wardrobe design, jogging. Office: PO Box 2208 Merced CA 95344

BOESEN, STEPHEN BERNARD, II, military officer; b. Lexington, Ky., June 10, 1969; s. Lavina K. Boesen; m. Anne E. Hickerson, Jan. 6, 1996; children: Zachery T., Allyson K., Benjamin G. Student in Airborne Sch., U.S. Army, 1988; degree in Criminology, U. No. Iowa, 1992; student in Infantry Officer Tng., U.S. Army, 1992, student in Bradley Fighting Vehicle Leadership, 1996. Cert. slingload inspector Ft Lee, Va., U.S. Army, 2002, combat lifesaver U.S. Army, 1993. Commd. lt. U.S. Army, 1987, advanced through grades to maj., 2002, co. exec. officer HQ Camp Casey, Republic of Korea, 1993—94, leader rifle platoon Fort Myer, Va., 1994—95, exec. officer rifle co., 1995—96, asst. ops. officer Fort Carson, Colo., 1996—98; comdr. rifle co. 1st Bn., 8th Inf. Rgt., Fort Carson, Colo., 1998—99, hdqs. co. comdr., 1999—2000; ops. officer U.S. Army, 2001—. Youth rep. St Edwards Cath. Ch., Waterloo, Iowa, 1986—87. Decorated Disting. Mil. Grad. U.S. Army Res. Officer's Tng. Corps, Army Res. Compoents Achievement medal U.S. Army, Army Svc. ribbon, Korean Def. Svc. medal, Overseas Svc. ribbon, Army Commendation, Army Achievement Medal, Meritorious Achievement medal, Global War on Terrorism Svc. medal, Global War on Terrorism Expeditionary medal, Armed Forces Res. Medal with M Device. Mem.: Nat. Infantryman's Assn., 1st Iowa Nat. Inf. Assn. (sec. 2004—05), Assn. U.S. Army (pres. 1990—91), Iowa N.G. Officer's Assn. (area pres. 2004—05), Boy Scouts Am. (star scout 1981—84, den leader 2002—03, asst. den leader 2004—05). Avocations: running, weightlifting, hiking, camping, athletics. Office: HQ 2nd Brigade Combat Team 700 Snedden Drive Boone IA 50036 Office Phone: 515-727-3802.

BOESZ, CHRISTINE C., science foundation administrator; b. Bridgeton, N.J., May 26, 1944; d. Stanley Marion and Cecilia Marie (Cantillon) Clark; m. Daniel Lester Boesz, June 26, 1965. AB, Douglass Coll., New Brunswick, N.J., 1966; MS, Rutgers U., 1967; DPH, U. Mich., 1997. Asst. prof. Math. Valdosta (Ga.) State Coll., 1967-69; statistical analyst Alamo Area Coun. Govts., San Antonio, 1969-71, Bexar County Med. Found., San Antonio, 1971-74, exec. dir., 1974-78; dep. dir. compliance office HMO U.S. Govt., Rockville, Md., 1978-86; sr. program and policy analyst Prepaid Health Care Health Care Financing Adminstrn., Washington, 1986-87, dir. compliance divsn. Prepaid Health Care, 1987-92, dir. ops. Office of Managed Care, 1992-95; v.p. govt. programs NYLCare Health Plans, N.Y.C., 1995—98; insp. gen. Nat. Sci. Found., 2000—; head regulatory accountability Aetna US Healthcare (AUSHC), 1998—99. Faculty preceptor George Washington U., 1995. Contrb. chpts. to books, articles to profl. jours. Pres. Scientists Cliffs Assn., Pt. Republic, Md., 1985-86. Recipient Pew Meml. Trust fellowship U. Mich., 1990-92. Mem. AAUW, APHA, Am. Statis. Assn., Nat. Assn. Managed Care Regulators (pres. 1985-86, sec. 1981-84, Lifetime Achievement award 1994), Zonta. Avocations: reading, travel. Office: Nat Sci Found 4201 Wilson Blvd Arlington VA 22230

BOETTCHER, ROBERT WALTER, civil engineer; b. Gooding, Idaho, Apr. 3, 1931; s. Walter Alfred and Katherine Benedicta (Hansen) B.; m. Margeurite Patricia Warner, Oct. 1, 1960; children: Eric, Edwin, Vanessa. BSCE, Wash. State U., Pullman, 1953. Civil engr. U.S. Bur. of Reclamation, Bismarck, N.D., 1955-56; materials engr. Joseph K. Knoerle & Assocs., Chgo., 1956-59; project engr. Knoerle, Bender, Stone & Assocs., Chgo., 1959-62, project mgr., 1962-73, assoc., 1973-76; sr. assoc. Envirodyne Engrs. Inc., Chgo., 1976—; chief civil engr. O'Hare Assocs., Chgo., 1981-92, MESA Joint Venture, 1992-93; sr. assoc. AOR Joint Venture, Chgo., 1993, Consoer Townsend Envirodyne Engrs., Inc., Chgo., 1994—. With U.S. Army, 1953-55. Mem. ASCE, NSPE, Ill. Soc. Profl. Engrs. Home: 1047 Dell Rd Northbrook IL 60062-3911

BOETTGER, NANCY J., state legislator; b. Chgo., May 1, 1943; m. H. David Boettger; 4 children. BS, Iowa State U., 1965; BA, Buena Vista Coll., 1982. Owner farm, 1965—; spl. edn. tchr., 1965-66; tchr. jr. H.S., 1982-86; dir. edn. Myrtoe Meml. Hosp., 1986-99; mem. Iowa Senate from 41st dist., 1994—2004, asst. majority leader, 1996—2004. Mem. Midwest Legis. Coun., 1996-2000. Mem. First Bapt. Ch., People Who Care; former bd. dirs. Harlan Cmty. Libr.; former mem. dean's adv. bd. Iowa State U. Ext. Mem. PEO, Am. Legis. Exchange Coun., Midwest Coun. State Govts. (chair health and human svcs. 1997-99), Coun. State Govts. (mem. drug task force 1998), Iowa Coun. Internat. Understanding Bd., Shelby County Found. for Edn. (former exec. dir.), Farm Bur., Pork Prodrs. Republican. Home: 926 Ironwood Rd Harlan IA 51537-5308 Office: State Capitol Dist 41 3 9th And Grand Des Moines IA 50319-0001 E-mail: nancy_boettger@legis.state.ia.us.

BOETTICHER, HELENE, retired lawyer; b. Syracuse, N.Y., Mar. 26, 1920; d. Ford and Emily (Bennett) Zogg; m. William Donald Boetticher, Oct. 18, 1958 (dec. July 1990); children: John, Amy, Sally. BA, U. Wis., 1941, LLB, 1943. Bar: Wis., Ill. Atty. NLRB, Chgo., 1951—57, OSHA Rev., Washington, 1972—73, Dept. Labor, 1973—95, counsel for litigation, 1978—95; ret. Contbr. articles to profl. jours. Democrat. Episcopalian. Avocation: travel. Home: 15204 Carrolton Rd Rockville MD 20853 Office Phone: 301-929-1297. Personal E-mail: hzb3099@att.net.

BOETTNER, DAISIE DAWSON, military officer, mechanical engineering educator; b. St. Louis, Mo., Jan. 16, 1959; d. Raymond Turner and Isabel Crichlow Wheeler; m. Brian Lee Boettner, Sept. 10, 1982 (div. Dec. 6, 2001); children: Sarah Leigh, Elizabeth Ann. BS, U.S. Mil. Acad., West Point, N.Y., 1981; MSE in Mech. Engring., U. of Mich., 1991; PhD, The Ohio State U., 2001. Registered profl. engr., Va., 2005. With U.S. Army, 1981—, advanced through grades to col., 1981—2003; comdr. 89th Ordnance Co., Bremerhaven, Germany, 1983—85; logistics officer 24th Inf. Divsn. (Mech.), Ft. Stewart, Ga., 1986—89; instr., asst. prof. U.S. Mil. Acad., West Point, NY, 1991—94, assoc. prof., 2001—; support ops. officer 524th Corps. Support Bn., Schofield Barracks, Hawaii, 1995—96; chief, ammunition plans U.S. Army Pacific, Ft. Shafter, Hawaii, 1996—98. Dir., aero-thermo group U.S. Mil. Acad., West Point, NY, 2001—03, dir., mech. engring. program, 2003—. Author: (jour. articles) ASME Jour. for Energy Resources Tech., (chpt. in edited volume) Artificial Intelligence in Engring. Design Vol. I: Design Representation and Models of Routine Design. Decorated Army Commendation medal U.S. Army, Army Achievement medal, Meritorious Svc. medal. Mem.: Soc. of Women Engrs., Am. Soc. of Mech. Engrs., Delta Kappa Gamma, Phi Kappa Phi. Avocations: running, sewing, cooking. Office: Dept Civil and Mech Engring US Mi Acad West Point NY 10996

BOEVE, DALE E., manufacturing executive; BS in Bus., Grand Valley State U., Allendale, Mich., 1979. Purchasing mgr. G.F. Office Furniture Sys., Inc., Gallatin, Tenn., 1983—85, plant mgr., 1988—90; materials mgr. Corry Hiebert (divsn. HON Industries), Lewisburg, NC, 1985—88; gen. mgr. Kruger Internat., Tupelo, Miss., 1990—95; v.p. ops. Mayline Co., Sheboygan, Wis., 1995—2000; v.p., gen. mgr. and dir. Koken Mfg., Inc., St. Louis, 2000; gen. mgr. Falcon Industries, 2001—03; dir. ops. Mohon Internat., Paris, Tenn., 2004—. With USMC. Address: 495 Sunnyside Dr Paris TN 38242

BOEWE, CHARLES ERNST, historian, educator; b. West Salem, Ill., Mar. 11, 1924; s. Fred E. and Susie E. (Wolters) Boewe; m. Mary Scurrah, June 17, 1950; children: Abigail Burnett, Emily Oliver. AB, Syracuse U., 1947, MA, 1949; PhD, U. Wis., 1955. Instr. Syracuse (N.Y.) U., Syracuse, 1949—51, Lehigh U., Bethlehem, Pa., 1955—56; asst. prof. U. Pa., Phila., 1958—64; dir. US Edntl. Found., Karachi, Pakistan, 1964—67, US Commn. for Cultural Exch., Tehran, Iran, 1967—70, Am. Studies Rsch. Ctr., Hyderabad, India,

1970—71, US Ednl. Found., New Delhi, 1971—73, Islamabad, Pakistan, 1973—80; adj. rsch. prof. Transylvania U., Lexington, Ky., 1980—85; rsch. assoc. Filson Club History Soc., Louisville, 1985—92; editor Papers of C.S. Rafinesque, Fearrington village, NC, 1992—. Adv. com. Am. Studies Rsch. Ctr., Hyderabad, India, 1980—89; treas. Am. Inst. Pakistan Studies, 1981—85; cons. in field. Contbr. articles to profl. jours.; author: Prairie Albion: An English Settlement in Pioneer Illinois, 1962, 2d edit., 1999, Profiles of Rafinesque, 2003; editor: The World or Instability, 1956, Fitzpatrick's Rafinesque, 1982, John D. Clifford's Indian Antiquities, 2000, C. S. Rafinesque Anthology, 2005. Rsch. assoc. Am. Philos. Soc., Phila., 1958—64; exec. sec. Am. Studies Assn., Phila., 1962—64; hist. manuscripts com. Acad. Natural Scis., Phila., 1963—64. With U.S. Army, 1943—46. Fellow, U. Pa., 1956—58; grantee, Am. Philos. Soc., Sicily, 1959, US Info. Agy., Egypt, 1980, Nat. Hist. Publ. and Records Commn., 1980—88. Achievements include discovery of letters and manuscripts of C.S. Rafinesque. Home: 320 Fearrington Post Pittsboro NC 27312-8560

BOFF, KENNETH RICHARD, engineering research psychologist; b. N.Y.C., Aug. 17, 1947; s. Victor and Ann (Yunko) B.; m. Judith Marion Schoer, Aug. 2, 1969 (dec. Apr. 1997); children: Cory Asher, Kyra Melissa; m. Jacque Aelanda Coppler, Aug. 20, 1999. BA, CUNY, 1969, MA, 1972; MPhil, Columbia U., 1975, PhD, 1978. Research scientist Human Resources Lab., Wright Patterson AFB, Ohio, 1977-80; sr. scientist Armstrong Aerospace Med. Rsch. Lab. (now Airforce Rsch. Lab.), Wright Patterson AFB, Ohio, 1980—, dir. design tech., 1980-91, dir. human engring. div., 1991-97; chief scientist, human effectiveness directorate Air Force Rsch. Lab., 1997—; Edenfield Exec.-in-Residence Sch. Ind. & Sys. Engrg. Georgia Inst. Tech., 2002—03. Project custodian Internat. Air. Standard Coordination Com., Washington, 1984; chmn. com. Tri-Service Human Factors Tech. Adv. Group, Washington, 1984—; chair human factors com. NATO Adv. Group Aerospace R&D, Paris, 1992—; chair human sys. tech. panel Dept. Def., 1994-97; U.S. coord. NATO Rsch. and Tech. Orgn. Human Factors, 1997—. Editor: Handbook of Perception and Human Performance, 1986, Human Engineering Data Compendium, 1988, System Design: Behavioral Perspectives on designers, Tools and Organizations, 1987; contbr. articles to profl. jours. Travel grantee Rank Prize Found., Cambridge, Eng., 1984; named Air Force Scientist of the Quarter, 1989; recipient Patent award for rap-com display tech., 1989, Human Factors Soc. award for best publ., 1989. Mem. IEEE, Human Factors Soc., Am. Psychol. Assn. (div. 21 engring. psychology). Avocations: computers, photography. Office: Armstrong Lab Human Engring Divsn Wright Patterson Afb OH 45433 Office Phone: 513-255-6327. Business E-Mail: ken.boff@wpafb.af.mil.

BOGAARD, JONATHAN HARVEY, lawyer; b. Humboldt, Iowa, Mar. 25, 1957; m. Milena B. Vujovich, Nov. 26, 1983; children: Joseph Daniel, Jonathan Thomas. BBA in Acctg., U. Iowa, 1978, MA in Acctg., JD, U. Iowa, 1981. Bar: Ill. 1981, Iowa 1981, U.S. Dist. Ct. (no. dist.) Ill. 1981, U.S. Tax Ct. 1983, U.S. Ct. Appeals (7th cir.) 1999. Assoc. McDermott, Will & Emery, Chgo., 1981—86, ptnr., 1986—91, Vedder Price, Chgo., 1991—. Bd. dirs. North Suburban YMCA, Northbrook, Ill., 1997—2002. Office: Vedder Price 222 N LaSalle Ste 2600 Chicago IL 60601-1003 Office Phone: 312-609-7651. Business E-Mail: jbogaard@vedderprice.com.

BOGAARD, WILLIAM JOSEPH, mayor, lawyer, educator; b. Sioux City, Iowa, Jan. 18, 1938; s. Joseph and Irene Marie (Hensing) B.; m. Claire Marie Whalen, Jan. 28, 1961; children: Michele, Jeannine, Joseph, Matthew. BS, Loyola Marymount U., L.A., 1959; JD with honors, U. Mich., 1965. Bar: Calif. 1966, U.S. Dist. Ct. (ctrl. dist.) Calif. 1966. Ptnr. Agnew, Miller & Carlson, L.A., 1970-82; exec. v.p., gen. counsel First Interstate Bancorp, L.A., 1982-96; vis. prof. securities regulation and banking Mich. Law Sch., Ann Arbor, 1996-97; lectr. securities regulation and corps. U. So. Calif. Law Sch., L.A., 1997—; mayor Pasadena, Calif., 1999—. Mem. Calif. Commn. on Jud. Nominees Evaluation, 1997-99. Mem. city coun., mayor City of Pasadena, Calif., 1978-86. Capt. USAF, 1959-62. Mem. Calif. State Bar, Los Angeles County Bar Assn. (Corp. Counsel of Yr. award 1988). Avocations: jogging, french and spanish languages, hiking. Office: 100 N Garfield Ave Pasadena CA 91101-1726 Office Phone: 626-799-2016. Personal E-mail: w_j_b@msn.com. Business E-Mail: bbogaard@ci.pasadena.ca.us.

BOGAN, ELIZABETH CHAPIN, economist, educator; b. Morristown, N.J., Aug. 22, 1944; d. Daryl Muscott and Tirzah (Walker) Chapin; m. Thomas Rockwood Bogan, June 5, 1965; children: Nathaniel Rockwood, Andrew Allerton. AB, Wellesley Coll., 1966; MA, U. N.H., 1967; PhD, Columbia U., 1971. Mem. faculty Fairleigh Dickinson U., Madison, N.J., 1971-92, prof. econs., 1982-92, chmn. merit scholarship com., 1981-82; reviewer univ. press Fairleigh Dickinson U., Madison, N.J.; mem. faculty Princeton (N.J.) U., sr. lectr. in econs., 1992—. Vis. prof. Princeton U., 1991. Author articles and macroecons. text Recipient Outstanding Tchr. award Fairleigh Dickinson U., 1979, 86, 87, Richard Quandt award for tchg. econs. Princeton U., 1997, 2005; NSF fellow, Pres'. fellow, Earhart fellow Columbia U., 1968-71. Mem. AAUP, Am. Econ. Assn., Ea. Econ. Assn., Atlantic Econ. Soc. Clubs: Wellesley, Beacon Hill. Congregationalist. Home: 41 Windermere Ter Short Hills NJ 07078-2254 Office: Princeton U 109 Fisher Pl Princeton NJ 08540

BOGAN, MARY FLAIR, stockbroker; b. Providence, July 9, 1948; d. Ralph A.L. and Mary (Dyer) B. BA, Vassar Coll., 1969. Actress Trinity Sq. Repertory Co., R.I., Gretna Playhouse, Pa., Skylight Comic Opera, Milw., Cin. Playhouse, Playmakers' Repertory, N.C.; mem. nat. co. No Sex, Please, We're Brit.; also TV commls., 1970-77; acct. exec. E.F. Hutton & Co., Inc., Providence, 1977-86; act. v.p. Paine Webber, 1986-97; v.p. investments Prudential Securities, Providence, 1997—2003, Wachovia Securities, 2003—; econ. reporter Sta. WPRI-TV, 1982-85, Sta. WJAR-TV, 1987—. Recipient Century Club award, 1980, 81, 82, 83, 85, Blue Chip Sales award, 1983, 85, Pacesetter Sales award, 1986-90; named Woman of Yr. Profl. Bus. and Rep. Women's Assn. Mem. Univ. Club, Brown Faculty. Home: 18 Cooke St Providence RI 02906-2023 Office: Wachovia Securities 900 Fleet Ctr 50 Kennedy Plz Providence RI 02903-2393

BOGARD, CAROLE CHRISTINE, soprano; b. Cin. d. Harold and Helen Christina (Whittlesey) Geistweit; m. Charles Paine Fisher, Dec. 30, 1966; children: Christine, Pamela. Student, San Francisco State U. Debuts include: Despina in Cosi fan Tutte (Mozart), San Francisco, 1965, Poppea in Coronation of Poppea (Monteverdi), Netherlands Opera, 1971; other appearances include, Boston Opera, N.E.T., orchs. Boston, Madrid, Minn., Phila., Pitts., San Francisco, summer festivals, Mostly Mozart, N.Y., Tanglewood, Carmel, Aston Magna, Gt. Barrington, Mass., appeared in concerts throughout Europe and with Smithsonian Chamber Players, 1976-; recorded numerous albums including 1st rec. of songs of John Duke for his 80th birthday, 1979, recital of Groupe des Six; premiered songs of Dominic Argento in, Holland, 1978, songs of Richard Cumming (in collaboration with Donald Gramm); regular participant rec. and scholarly projects, Smithsonian Instn.; judge regional auditions, Boston; tchr., with emphasis on technique as taught in last Century; recs. have been re-issued on CDs during the 1990s including Baroque Cantatas and Arias, Mozart C minor Mass, Mozart Coronation Mass., 2 CD collection American Songs, 2000; female lead 3 CD Handel opera Tamerlano, 2002. Mem. Sigma Alpha Iota Home: 161 Belknap Rd Framingham MA 01701-3886 *In my career, I've stuck to old-fashioned principles - trying to use my talent according to the standards which place singing technique on a level with the most taxing instruments. I sing for sincere acclaim and demand for my talent and my music, avoiding repertoire which would abuse my voice. I have refrained from pushing myself through "arranged" magazine articles about my hobbies and insipid appearances on TV talk shows. I have done my best rather than my most - by choice.*

BOGARD, DONALD DALE, planetary geochemist; b. Washington County, Ark., Feb. 6, 1940; s. James A. and Genevieve Bogard. BS, U. Ark., 1962, MS, 1964, PhD, 1966. Rsch. fellow Calif. Inst. Tech., Pasadena, 1966-68; sr. staff scientist NASA, Johnson Space Ctr., Houston, 1968—. Antarctic meteorite curator NASA, 1978-84; discipline scientist NASA Planetary Program, 1984-92. Contbr. over 100 sci. articles to rsch. jours. Fellow Meteoritical Soc. (sec. 1980-86); mem. Am. Geophys. Union. Office: NASA Johnson Space Ctr Mail Code SN2 Houston TX 77058

BOGARD, LAWRENCE JOSEPH, lawyer; b. Champaign, Ill., July 12, 1952; s. Morris Ray and Norma Jean (Shingleton) B.; m. Rebecca Lynn Jackson, May 6, 1978 (div. 2003); children: Caitlyn Elizabeth, Peter Jackson. AB, Vassar Coll., Poughkeepsie, N.Y., 1974; JD, Georgetown U., 1977. Bar: D.C. 1977. Atty. U.S. Customs Svc., Washington, 1977-80; assoc. Cladouhos & Brashares, Washington, 1980-84; atty. U.S. Dept. Commerce, Washington, 1984; ptnr. Rose, Schmidt, Hasley & Disalle, Washington, 1984-88, McKenna & Cuneo, Washington, 1988-98, Neville Peterson LLP, Washington, 1998—. Faculty Practicing Law Inst., 1984, 92; mem. U.S.-Can. Free Trade Agreement Ch. 19 Dispute Resolution Roster, 1991-94, panelist, 1992, panel chair 1993; mem. NAFTA Dispute Resolution Roster, 1994—, panel chair, 2001. Author: (with others) Commerce Speaks on Antidumping, 1984, Treatment of Non-Market Economies Under U.S. Antidumping and Countervailing Duty Law: A Petitioner's Perspective, 1992, (with others) Transnational Contracts, 2000—; supervisory editor Customs Law and Administration, 1998—. Mem. ABA, D.C. Bar Assn., Ct. Internat. Trade Bar Assn. Office: Neville Peterson LLP 1900 M St NW Ste 850 Washington DC 20036 Office Phone: 202-861-2959. Business E-Mail: lbogard@npwdc.com.

BOGARDUS, CARL ROBERT, JR., radiologist, educator; b. Hyden, Ky., June 26, 1933; s. Carl Robert and Jeannette Wanda (Eversole) B.; m. Norma Gail Shields, June 24, 1956; children: Carl Robert III, Cynthia Gail. BA, Hanover Coll., 1955; MD, U. Louisville, 1959. Diplomate: Am. Bd. Radiology, Am. Bd. Nuc. Medicine. Intern Penrose Cancer Hosp., Colorado Springs, Colo., 1959-60, resident, 1960-63; prof. U. Okla. Med. Ctr., 1963—, mem. staff, 1963—. Cons. Okla. hosps.; pres. Cancer Care Network, Inc.; pres. Bogardus Med. Sys. Inc. Author: Practical Applied Physics of Radiology and Nuclear Medicine, 1969; contbg. author: Benign and Malignant Tumors of the Bladder, 1971, Radiation Biology for the Physician, 1973; contbr. articles to profl. jours. Fellow Am. Coll. Radiology (bd. chancellors, sec.-treas. 1987-91, pres. 1991-92); mem. Okla. Soc. Nuc. Medicine (charter pres. 1966), Am. Soc. Therapeutic Radiology (nat. sec. 1968-70, treas. 1987-88, pres. 1989-90), S.W. Regions Soc. Nuc. Medicine, Okla. Radiol. Soc. (treas. 1970, pres. 1974-75, counselor to Am. Coll. Radiology 1976-85), Okla. County Radiol. Soc. (pres. 1974). Home: 3224 Lamp Post Ln Oklahoma City OK 73120-5621 Office: U Okla Med Ctr 825 NE 101st Oklahoma City OK 73104 Office Phone: 405-917-0500, 405-271-3577. Business E-Mail: drcrb@cancercare.net.

BOGART, JEFFREY B., lawyer, educator; b. N.Y.C., July 18, 1947; s. Robert and Corinee Bogart; m. Christine C. Bogart; children: Jaclyn, Courtney, Noah, Alexis, John Davis. BS, Bradley U., 1969; JD, U. Toledo, 1972. Bar: N.Y. 1972, Ga. 1976. Asst. dist. atty., NY, 1973—76; asst. U.S. atty. Atlanta, 1976—77; spl. prosecutor State Bar Ga., 1977—79, 1985—87. Instr. Emory Law Sch., NITA, 1985—2002, ICLE. Contbr. articles to legal jours. Mem.: ABA (white collar crime com. 1988—91), Ga. Trial Lawyers Assn. (chmn. family law 2000—01), Nat. Assn. Criminal Def. Lawyers (sentencing com.), State Bar Ga. (bench and bar com. 1982—83, 1990—92), Atlanta Bar Assn. (instr. issues and devels. in family law 1991, chmn. family law sect. 1987—88), Lawyers Club Atlanta. Office: Bogart & Bogart PC Ste 175 6640 Powers Ferry Rd Atlanta GA 30339

BOGART, JOHN H., lawyer; s. Tudor M. and Luise E. Bogart; m. Carola M. Mone. BA, U. Calif., Santa Cruz, 1978; JD, Stanford Law Sch., 1993; PhD, U. of Ill., 1985. Bar: Calif. 1993, US Supreme Ct. 2001, US Dist. Ct. So. Dist. Calif. 1993, US Dist. Ct. Ctrl. Dist. Calif. 1994, US Dist. Ct. Ea. Dist. Calif. (U.S District Court) 1994, US Ct. Appeals Ninth Circuit 1995, US Dist. Ct. Dist. Ariz. 1996, Utah 1998, US Dist. Ct. Dist. Utah 1998, US Ct. Appeals Tenth Circuit 1998. Asst. prof. of philosophy NY U., NYC, 1985—86; asst. prof. philosophy Stanford U., Calif., 1986—87; asst. prof. of philosophy U. Calif., Davis, Calif., 1987—88; asst. prof. philosophy Ariz. State U., Tempe, Ariz., 1988—89; asst. prof. of philosophy Sch. of Philosophy, USC, LA, 1989—90; adj. prof. Loyola Sch. of Law, 1995—98; assoc. Heller, Ehrman, White & McAuliffe, 1994—98; shareholder Bendinger, Crockett, Peterson, Greenwood & Casey, Salt Lake City, 2001—. Contbr. articles to profl. jours. Mem. Land Use Appeals Bd., Salt Lake City, 2002—, Repetory Dance Theater, 2000—. Fellow Mellon Post-Graduate fellow, Mellon Found., 1985-86, 1989-90. Mem.: Inns of Ct. Avocations: hiking, philosophy, training kaiken. Office: Bendinger Crockett Peterson Greenwood 170 South Main Ste 400 Salt Lake City UT 84101 Office Phone: 801-533-8383. Office Fax: 801-531-1486. E-mail: jhb@bendinger-crockett.com.

BOGATIN, MARC, lawyer; b. N.Y.C., July 22, 1956; s. Murray and Beverlee (Iglarsh) B.; m. Pamela Beth Tishman, Apr. 13, 1991; children: Jacob Murray, Joshua Harry. BA, Columbia U., 1978; JD, Cardozo Sch. Law, 1981. Bar: N.Y. 1982, U.S. Dist. Ct. (so. dist.) N.Y. 1982, U.S. Dist. Ct. (ea. dist.) N.Y. 1982, U.S. Dist. Ct. (no. dist.) N.Y. 1984, U.S. Ct. Appeals (2d cir.) 1984, U.S. Ct. Appeals (1st cir.) 1986, U.S. Ct. Appeals (6th cir.) 1987. Assoc. Stanley S. Arkin, P.C., N.Y.C., 1981—86, ptnr., 1986—89; pvt. practice Marc Bogatin, N.Y.C., 1990—. Mem. N.Y. County Lawyers Assn. Office: 52 Duane St 7th Fl New York NY 10007-1295 Office Phone: 212-406-9065.

BOGDANICH, WALT, journalist; b. Chgo., Oct. 10, 1950; s. Walter and Helen (Chabraja) B.; m. Stephanie Saul; 1 child, Nicholas Walter. BS in Polit. Sci., U. Wis., 1975; MA in Journalism, Ohio State U., 1976. Reporter, editor Compass (daily newspaper), Hammond, Ind., 1974-75; reporter Dayton (Ohio) Daily News, 1977, Cleve. Press, 1977-79, Plain Dealer, Cleve., 1980-84, Wall St. Jour., NYC, 1984-88, Washington, 1989-93; TV news prodr. Day One, ABC-TV, NYC, 1993; investigative prodr., 60 Minutes CBS, NYC; investigative editor, bus. and fin. desk NY Times, NYC, 2001—. Recipient George Polk award L.I. Univ., 1980, Polk award for nat reporting, 2005, Overseas Press Club award, 2003, Pulitzer prize for newspaper series, 1988, for nat. reporting, 2005; Gerald Loeb award. Mem. Investigative Reporters and Editors (bd. dirs. 1988-89). Office: Newsroom NY Times 229 W 43rd New York NY 10036*

BOGDANOFF, STEWART RONALD, physical education educator, coach; b. London, Aug. 16, 1940; came to U.S., 1945; s. David and Muriel (Kirby) B.; m. Eileen Dolan, Aug. 27, 1993; children: Suelyn, Jennifer, Andrew. BS, King's Coll., Briarcliff Manor, N.Y., 1963; MA, NYU, 1965, profl. degree, 1970; postgrad., Harvard U., 1988-91. Cert. in health and phys. edn., sch. adminstrn./supervision, N.Y. Tchr. health and phys. edn. Lakeland Ctrl. Sch. Dist., Shrub Oak, N.Y., 1965-96, head tchr. Thomas Jefferson Elem. Sch., 1984-96, acting prin. Thomas Jefferson Elem. Sch., 1985-86, basketball, cross country and gymnastics coach, 1964-96; ednl. cons., spkr. in field, 1996—. Writer syllabi; developer programs; author handbooks; presenter in field. Mem. N.Y. State PTA. Recipient NY State Tchr. of Yr. award State Edn. Dept., 1983, Disting. Cmty. Svc. award Yorktown Jaycees, 1983, Disting. Cmty. Svc. award Am. Heart Assn., 1983, Disting. Cmty. Svc. award Muscular Dystrophy Assn., 1983, Point of Light award, 1992, Westchester Vol. of Yr. and J.C. Penney Golden Rule award United Way, 1995, Spl. Olympics Worldwide Games Commemorative Coin, 1996, Am. medal honor, Internat. Biog. Ctr., Am. Biog. Inst., 2003, NY State Tchr Yr., Pres. Reagan, 1998; named to Nat. Tchrs. Hall of Fame, 1993, Briarcliff HS Hall of Disting. Alumni, 1995; named one of 50 Most Influential People in Westchester County in 20th Century, Gannett Jour. News, 2000; honoree as NY State Tchr. of Yr., Pres. Reagan, 1983, Pres. Clinton, 1993; named to Nat. Tchr. Hall Fame., Pres. Clinton. Mem. AAHPERD (Founders 2000 award 1995), ASCD, Nat. Assn. for Sport and Phys. Edn. (Project Inspiration award 1992), Internat. Platform Assn., N.Y. State Assn. for Health, Phys. Edn., Recreation and Dance, Phi Delta Kappa, Kappa Delta Pi (Outstanding Svc. to Society award 1983). Democrat. Avocations: golf, tennis, baseball memorabilia collecting. Home: 588A Heritage Hls Somers NY 10589-1908 Office: 3636 Gomer St Yorktown Heights NY 10598-2000 E-mail: stub@bestweb.net.

BOGDANOVICH, ALEXANDER, manufacturing executive; b. Riga, Latvia, June 28, 1950; arrived in U.S., 1991; s. Eugene and Valentina Bogdanovich; m. Elena Goryunova, Sept. 21, 1989 (div. May 28, 1991). MS, Latvian State U., 1972; cand. of sci., Latvian Acad. Sci., 1975, D of Engring., 1998; DSc, Kazan State U., 1987. Sr. rsch. fellow Inst. Polymer Mechanics, Riga, 1978—86, dep. dir., 1986—89, acting dir., 1988; rsch. dep. dir. Engring. and Tech. Ctr., Riga, 1990—91; vis. rsch. prof. N.C. State U., Raleigh, 1991—95; sr. rsch. scientist Ad Tech Systems Rsch., Inc., Dayton, Ohio, 1995—98; v.p. R&D 3Tex, Inc., Cary, NC, 1998—. Presenter in field. Author: Nonlinear Dynamic Problems of Composite Cylindrical Shells, 1993, Mechanics of Textile and Laminated Composites, 1996; contbr. articles to profl. jours.; mem. editl. bd. Composites Part B jour., 1992—, Mechanics of Composite Materials jour., 1988—, patentee in field. Recipient Friedrich Tsander award, Latvian Acad. Scis., 1987. Mem.: ASME, AIAA (sr.). Avocations: tennis, track and field, classical music, Russian literature. Home: 605 Knightsborough Way Apex NC 27502 Office: 3Tex Inc 109 MacKenan Dr Cary NC 27511 Business E-Mail: bogdanovicha@3tex.com.

BOGDANOVICH, PETER, film director, writer, producer, actor; b. Kingston, N.Y., July 30, 1939; s. Borislav and Herma (Robinson) B.; m. Polly Platt, 1962 (div. 1970); children: Antonia, Alexandra; m. L.B. Straten, 1988. Owner The Holly Moon Co., Inc., L.A., 1992—. Actor Am. Shakespeare Festival, Stratford, Conn., 1956, N.Y. Shakespeare Festival, 1958, (TV episode) Northern Exposure, 1993, Cybill, 1995, The Sopranos, 1999-, (films) Mr. Jealousy, 1997, Highball, 1997, Fifty-Four, 1998, Coming Soon, 1999, The Shoe Store, 1999, Claire Makes It Big, 1999, Rated X, 2000, The Independent, 2000, (TV miniseries) Bella Mafia, 1997; dir., producer off-Broadway plays: The Big Knife, 1959, Camino Real, Ten Little Indians, Rocket to the Moon, 1961, Once in a Lifetime, 1964; film feature-writer for Esquire, N.Y. Times, Village Voice, Cahiers du Cinema, L.A. Times, N.Y. Mag., Vogue, Variety, others, 1961—; films: The Wild Angels (2d unit dir., co-writer, actor), 1966; Targets (dir., co-writer, producer, actor), 1968, The Last Picture Show (dir., co-writer, N.Y. Film Critics award, Brit. Acad. award 1971), 1971, Directed by John Ford (dir., writer, interviewer), 1971, What's Up, Doc? (dir., co-writer, producer, Writer's Guild Am. award 1972), 1972, Paper Moon (dir., producer, Silver Shell, Mar del Plata, Spain), 1973, Daisy Miller (dir., producer, Best Dir. Brussels Festival 1974), 1974, At Long Last Love (dir., writer, producer), 1975, Nickelodeon (dir., co-writer), 1976, Saint Jack (dir., co-writer, actor, Pasinetti award, Critics prize Venice Festival 1979), 1979, They All Laughed (dir., writer), 1981, Mask (dir.), 1985, Illegally Yours (dir., producer), 1988, Texasville (dir., producer, writer), 1990, Noises Off (dir., exec. producer), 1992, The Thing Called Love (dir.), 1993; dir. (TV films) Blessed Assurance, 1997, Rescuers: Stories of Courage: Two Women, 1997, Naked City: A Killer Christmas, 1998, A Saintly Switch, 1999; author: The Cinema of Orson Welles, 1961, The Cinema of Howard Hawks, 1962, The Cinema of Alfred Hitchcock, 1963, John Ford, 1968, Fritz Lang in America, 1969, Allen Dwan: The Last Pioneer, 1971, Pieces of Time: Peter Bogdanovich on the Movies, 1973, enlarged, 1985, The Killing of the Unicorn: Dorothy Stratten: 1960-80, 1984, (with Orson Welles) This Is Orson Welles, 1992; editor: A Year and a Day Engagement Calendar, 1991—; co-dir., writer, interviewer: The Great Professional: Howard Hawks, 1967; weekly network commentator CBS This Morning, 1987-89; dir. (TV series episode) Fallen Angels, 1995, Painted Word, 1995. Mem. Dirs. Guild of Am., Writers Guild of Am., Acad. Motion Picture Arts and Scis. Address: care Martin Baum and Rick Nicita CAA 9830 Wilshire Blvd Beverly Hills CA 90212-1804*

BOGDEN, DANIEL G., prosecutor; Grad., Ashland U.; JD, U. Toledo. Dep. dist. atty. Washoe County, 1987—90; asst. U.S. atty. dist. Nev. U.S. Dept. Justice, 1990—2001, U.S. atty. dist. Nev., 2001—. Office: Lloyd George Fed Bldg 333 S Las Vegas Blvd Las Vegas NV 89101

BOGDONOFF, MAURICE LAMBERT, physician; b. Chgo., May 11, 1926; s. Harry A. and Mary Ivy (Grogan) B.; m. Diana Edith Rauschkolb, June 29, 1956; children: Vivian, Gregory, Audrey. BS, Tufts U., 1948; MD, Yale U., 1952. Intern U. Ill. Rsch. and Edn. Hosp., Chgo., 1952-53; resident in internal medicine Boston City Hosp., 1953-54; resident in radiology Columbia-Presbyn. Med. Ctr., N.Y., 1955-57; asst. prof. to assoc. prof. radiology to prof. U. Ill., Chgo., 1958-69; attending radiologist Rush-Presbyn.-St. Luke's Med. Ctr., Chgo., pres. med. staff, 1975-77; prof. radiology and medicine Rush Med. Coll., Chgo., 1970-88, 1969-88, prof. emeritus, 1988—. Cons. Argonne (Ill.) Nat. Lab., 1963-88; cons., health dir. Canal Zone Panama, 1973-80; vis. lectr. nuclear power engring. Maine Maritime Acad., 1989. Contbr. articles to profl. jours. Pres. Wheaton (Ill.) Dist. 36 Sch. Bd.,1964-67; bd. visitors Coll. of DuPage Radio and TV Sys., Glen Ellyn, Ill., 1987-94. With USN, 1944-46. Fellow Am. Coll. Radiology, Inst. Medicine, also others; mem. Chgo. Lit. Club. Republican. Avocations: boating, astronomy, classics. Home: 203 W Willow Ave Wheaton IL 60187-5238

BOGDONOFF, MORTON DAVID, internist, educator; b. N.Y.C., Dec. 8, 1925; s. M. Myron and Minnie (Alpher) B.; m. Jano Segal, July 1, 1951 (div. 1971); children— Reid, Ladd, Jesse, Drue; m. Mary Patton Welt, May 9, 1975. MD, Cornell U., 1948. Diplomate: Nat. Bd. Med. Examiners, Am. Bd. Internal Medicine. Intern, jr. asst. resident, sr. asst. resident dept. medicine N.Y. Hosp., N.Y.C., 1948-50; sr. asst. surgeon USPHS, Nat. Heart Inst., Johns Hopkins U., Balt., 1950-52; sr. asst. resident dept. medicine Duke Hosp., 1952-53, Eli Lilly Research fellow div. endocrinology and metabolism, 1953-54, chief resident dept. medicine, 1954-55; attending physician, chief metabolic div. Durham VA Hosp., 1955-56, cons., 1959-62; asso. prof. clin. medicine Med. Sch. U. Miami, 1956-57; assoc. dept. medicine Duke U., 1955-56, asst. prof. medicine, 1957-59, asso. prof., 1959-62, prof. med., 1962-69, asst. dean grad. med. edn., 1967-69; prof., chmn. dept. internal medicine U. Ill., Chgo., 1970-75; prof. medicine to prof. emeritus Med. Coll. Cornell U., 1975-95, 95—. Cons. Ft. Bragg Hosp., 1959-62, VA Hosps., Fayetteville, Durham, West-Side, Chgo.; mem. study sect. health svcs. rsch. NIH, 1966-70, Commonwealth Fund, 1985-94, Cath. Med. Ctr., 1990-94, Nat. Med. Fellowships, 1987-2002. Editor: Clin. Rsch., 1959—64; chief editor Archives of Internal Medicine, 1967—77, New Developments in Medicine, 1986—90; sci. editor: Drug Therapy, 1978—94; contbr. articles to profl. jours. Fellow Center Advanced Study Behavioral Scis., Stanford, 1977-78 Fellow A.C.P.; mem. Am. Fedn. Clin. Research (past pres.), Am., So., Central socs. clin. investigation, Assn. Am. Physicians, AAAS (chmn. Sect. N 1981-82), Endocrine Soc., Psychosomatic Soc. (past nat. councillor), Soc. Exptl. Biology and Medicine, AMA, Harvey Soc., Alpha Omega Alpha. Office: NY Hosp/Cornell Med Ctr 525 E 68th St New York NY 10021-4885

BOGEN, ANDREW E., lawyer; b. LA, Aug. 23, 1941; s. David and Edith B.; m. Deborah Bogen, Oct. 10, 1970; children: Elizabeth, Michael. BA, Pomona Coll., Claremont, Calif., 1963; LLB, Harvard U, 1966. Bar: Calif. 1966. Assoc. Gibson, Dunn & Crutcher, LA, 1966-73, ptnr. corp. transactions and securities, 1973—. Mem. exec. com. Gibson Dunn & Crutcher, 1991—. Trustee Exceptional Children's Found., LA, 1976-89, Weingart Found., 1999—; bd. dirs. St. Anne's 1990— (chmn.). Office: Gibson Dunn & Crutcher 333 S Grand Ave Ste 4400 Los Angeles CA 90071-3197 Office Phone: 213-229-7000. Office Fax: 213-229-7520. Business E-Mail: abogen@gibsondunn.com.

BOGEN, ANDREW SETH, lawyer; b. Sept. 2, 1956; m. Triss Shimony, June 10, 2002; 1 child, Ezra. Degree, Emory U., 1978; JD with honors, George Washington U. Law Sch., 1984. Bar: NY 1985. Ptnr. Harris Beach, LLP Bus. Trans., Health Regulatory and Corp. Svcs. Group, Arent Fox Health and Corp. Practice Groups, 2005. Worked with publicly-held corps., closely-held cos., start-up cos. and ventures, bus. healthcare industry. Mem.: NY Bar Assn. Bar City NY. Home: 40 W 77th St Apt 7E New York NY 10024 Office: Arent Fox PLLC 1675 Broadway New York NY 10019 Office Phone: 212-484-3947. Office Fax: 212-484-3990. Business E-Mail: bogen.andrew@arentfox.com.

BOGEN, MARK ALAN, accountant; b. Bklyn., May 23, 1956; s. Jacob and Saundra (Lapidus) B.; m. Maria Angela Dipippo, Nov. 25, 1995; children: Angela, Sarah, Laura. BS in Mgmt., SUNY, Buffalo, 1977. CPA. Staff acct. SUNY Downstate, Bklyn., 1977-81, Brookdale Med. Ctr., Bklyn., 1981; sr. mgr. Pannell Kerr Forster, N.Y.C., 1981-89, DeLoitte & Touche, N.Y.C., 1989-91; v.p., CFO Preferred Health Network, Bklyn., 1991-96; prin. Nat. Capital Group, Lake Success, NY, 1996—97; pres. Bogen Cons. Group, Mineola, N.Y., 1997—. Mem. AICPA, Healthcare Financial Mgmt. Assn. (Follmer award 1994, Reeves award 2001), Am. Assn. Bakruptcy Inst., N.Y. State Soc. CPAs, Empire State Assn. PAs, Assn. Cert. Frand Auditors (assoc.) Republican. Jewish. Avocations: golf, music. Home: 2 Elkland Rd Melville NY 11747 Office: 33 Willis Ave Ste 100 Mineola NY 11501 E-mail: Bogengroup@aol.com.

BOGEN, PAUL LOGASA, II, computer technician, researcher; b. San Antonio, Jan. 12, 1982; s. John Dean and Pamela Ann Bogen; m. Andorrea Liana Castro, Sept. 19, 2004. BS, Tex. A&M U., 2004. Project mgmt. and software engring. intern Intel Corp., Chandler, Ariz., 2003—03; undergrad. rsch. asst., linux systems adminstr. Ctr. for the Study of Digital Librs., College Station, Tex., 2003—. Lechner scholarship, Tex. A&M U., 2000-2004, Engring. Scholars Program scholarship, 2000, Coll. of Engring. scholarship, 2001-2003, Helms Study Abroad scholarship, 2002, Pres.'s scholar, 2002. Mem.: Tex. A&M Computing Soc. (v.p. internal affairs 2000—03, pres. 2003), SIGWEB, SIGCHI (student listserv adminstr. 2003—04), Assn. of Computing Machinery. Independent. Lutheran. Achievements include research in Dynamically Growing Hypertext Collections. HT'04; Incorporating Physical and Digital Artifacts into Growing Personal Collections. ECDL'04; design of Change-ABLE Tracking and Reporting Tool for Intel Corporation; development of CADRE Tool for Intel Corporation. Avocations: digital music creation, reading, writing, dogs, travel. Office: Texas A&M Univ Ctr Study of Digital Librs College Station TX 77841 Business E-Mail: plb@tamu.edu.

BOGENSCHUTZ, J. DAVID, lawyer; b. Covington, Ky., May 15, 1944; s. John Francis and Virginia Margaret (Dugan) B.; m. Mary H. McCleary, Oct. 24, 1981; children: Kathleen, Emily. BA, Miami U., Oxford, Ohio, 1966; JD, U. Cin., 1969. Bar: Ohio 1969, U.S. Dist. Ct. (so. dist.) Ohio 1970, U.S. Ct. Appeals (6th cir.) 1971, Fla. 1971, U.S. Dist. Ct. (so. dist.) Fla. 1972, U.S. Ct. Appeals (5th cir.) 1980, U.S. Dist. Ct. (mid. dist.) Fla. 1981, U.S. Ct. Appeals (4th and 11th cirs.) 1981, U.S. Dist. Ct. (ea. dist.) Wis. 1989, U.S. Ct. Appeals (3d cir.) 1999. Instr. Criminal Justice Inst. Nova U., 1977; instr. Broward County Criminal Justice Inst., 1972; asst. solicitor County of Broward, 1971, chief asst. state's atty., 1974-77; ptnr. Bogenschutz & Dutko, P.A., Ft. Lauderdale, Fla. Mem. Gov.'s Com. on Criminal Justice Standards and Goals, 1975-76; mem. bench bar liaison com. U.S. Dist. Ct. (so. dist.) Fla., 1985—, Stephen Booher Inn of Ct. Mem. ATLA, NACDL, Broward County Bar Assn. (criminal law sect. chmn. 1980-81, exec. com. 1981-86, sec., treas. 1985-86), Ohio Bar Assn., Fla. Bar Assn. (criminal law sect., grievance com. 17th jud. cir. 1982-84), Fed. Bar Assn., Greene County Bar Assn., Fla. Pros. Atty.'s Assn., Nat. Dist. Atty.'s Assn., Nat. Assn. Criminal Def. Attys. Democrat. Roman Catholic. Office: Bogenschutz & Dutko PA 600 S Andrews Ave Ste 500 Fort Lauderdale FL 33301-2851

BOGER, DAN CALVIN, economics professor, consultant; b. Salisbury, N.C., July 9, 1946; s. Brady Cashwell and Gertrude Virginia (Hamilton) Boger; m. Gail Lorraine Zivna, June 23, 1973; children: Gretchen Zivna, Gregory Zivna. BS in Mgmt. Sci., U. Rochester, 1968; MS in Mgmt. Sci., Naval Postgrad. Sch., Monterey, Calif., 1969; MA in Stats., U. Calif., Berkeley, 1977, PhD in Econs., 1979. Cert. cost analyst, profl. estimator. Rsch. asst. U. Calif., Berkeley, 1975-79; asst. prof. econs. Naval Postgrad. Sch., Monterey, Calif., 1979-85, assoc. prof., 1985-92, prof., 1992—, chmn. dept. command, control and comm., 1995—2001, chmn. dept. computer sci., 1997—2001, chmn. dept. info. warfare, 1997—2001, dean divsn. computer and info. scis. and ops., 1997—2001, founding chmn. dept. info. scis., 2002—. Cons. econs. and statis. legal matters CSX Corp., others, 1977—; bd. dirs. Evan-Moor Corp. Assoc. editor: Logistics and Transp. Rev., 1981—85, Jour. Cost Analysis, 1989—92; mem. editl. rev. bd. Jour. Transp. Rsch. Forum, 1987—91; contbr. articles to profl. jours. Lt. USN, 1968—75. Flood fellow, Dept. Econs. U. Calif., Berkeley, 1975—76, Dissertaion Rsch. grantee, A.P. Sloan Found., 1978—79. Mem.: IEEE, Inst. Ops. Rsch. and Mgmt. Sci. (sec.-treas. mil. aplications soc. 1987—91), Econometric Soc., Am. Statis. Assn., Am. Econ. Assn., Internat. Coun. Sys. Engring., Sigma Xi. Home: 27 Cramden Dr Monterey CA 93940-4145 Office: Naval Postgrad Sch Code IS Monterey CA 93943

BOGEY, BRIAN ALLEN, secondary school educator, music educator, director; b. Jamestown, N.Y., July 15, 1947; s. Martin W. and Elaine M. Bogey; m. Sandra Kae Nelson, Sept. 16, 1978; children: Kristin Dee, Kathryn Emily, Jonathan Douglas. AA, Jamestown (N.Y.) C.C., 1967; MusB in Edn., SUNY, Fredonia, 1969, MusM in Edn., 1972. Tchr. vocal music Ripley (N.Y.) Ctrl. Sch., 1969—71, Mayville (N.Y.) Ctrl. Sch., 1969—72, Jefferson Jr. H.S., Jamestown, 1972—82; dir. choral activities Jamestown (N.Y.) H.S., 1982—2003, a cappella choir dir. emeritus, 2003—; minister music Jamestown (N.Y.) Zion Govt. Ch., 2003—. Organist Jamestown First Bapt. Ch., 1965—2003, choir dir., 1965—71; dir. choral Jamestown Choral Soc., 2003—; organist, choirmaster First Luth. Ch., 1971—2003. Bd. dirs. Jamestown (N.Y.) Concert Assn., 2003—. Recipient Tchr. of Yr. award, Mayville (N.Y.) Ctr. Sch., 1972, Disting. Alumnus award, Jamestown (N.Y.) C.C., 2003. Mem.: NEA, Am. Guild Organists (dean Chautauqua chpt. 1972—76), Chautauqua County Music Tchrs. Assn. (pres. 1988), N.Y. State Ednl. Assn. Democrat. Lutheran. Avocations: travel, reading, music, visiting churches. Home: 10 Mercury Lane Jamestown NY 14701

BOGG, RICHARD ALLAN, sociologist, educator; b. Grosse Pointe, Mich., May 31, 1934; s. Sydney Elmer and Dorothy Marie B. BBA, U. Mich., 1956, PhD, 1971; postgrad., U. Exeter, England, 1957—58; MHA, Washington U., St. Louis, 1960. Asst. adminstr. Port Huron (Mich.) Hosp., 1960-62; rsch. assoc. U. Mich. Sch. Pub. Health, 1965-69; asst. prof. dept. cmty. medicine Faculty Medicine U. Alta., Edmonton, Can., 1969-72; asst. prof. dept. sociology Ball State U., Muncie, Ind., 1972-77, assoc. prof., 1977—; assoc. editor Deviant Behavior, 1992—. Contbr. papers to profl. confs., encys. and jours. USPHS trainee, 1962-65; vol. Planned Parenthood of Delaware County. Mich. Ho. of Reps. spl. rsch. grantee, 1968. Mem. Am. Sociol. Assn., ACLU. Office: Dept Sociology Ball State U Muncie IN 47306-0530 Office Phone: 765-285-5977. Business E-Mail: rbogg@gw.bsu.edu.

BOGGAN, MATTHEW K., principal; b. Kilmichael, Miss., Feb. 14, 1969; s. Jerry Leon and Mary Olene (Clark) Boggan. BA, U. Miss.; MS, Miss. State U.; EdD, Nova Southeastern U., Ft. Lauderdale, Fla. Physical edn. tchr. State Miss. Dept., Oxford, 1991—93, spl. edn. tchr. Oxford, Starkville, Miss., 1993—99; asst. prin. Meridian Pub. Schs., Minn., 1999—2001; dean students Plane Tex. Ind. Sch. Dist., 2001—02; prin. Choctaw County Schs., Ackerman, Miss., 2002—; prof. Miss. State U., Starkville, 2004—, U. Miss., Oxford, Miss., 2004—. Grantee, Create for Miss., 2003; Computer Tech. grant, State Miss., 2004. Mem.: Coun. Exceptional Children, Miss. Assn. Sch. Adminstrs., Miss. Profl. Educators. Home: PO Box 22 Weir MS 39772 Office: Wier ATT Ctr 100 School Houst St Weir MS 39772

BOGGIA, EUGENE STEPHEN, lawyer; b. Glen Cove, N.Y., Nov. 12, 1946; s. Eugene and Elena Ebbie (Albertelli) B.; m. Suzanne McDonough, Sept. 18, 1982; children: Thomas, Catherine. AB, Georgetown U., 1968; JD, NYU, 1973. Asst. dist. atty. Office of the Dist. Atty., Phila., 1973-88; ptnr. Taylor and Taylor, Phila., 1988-92; claims adminstr., asst. gen. counsel Sch. Dist. of Phila., 1992—. Settlement master, judge pro tem Ct. of Common Pleas, Phila., 1992—. With USN, 1969-71; Vietnam. Mem. Serra Internat. (dist. 28 gov. 1985-86, Phila. chpt. pres. 1980-81, 98-2000, Serran of the Yr. 1989). Democrat. Roman Catholic. Avocations: history, playing piano, golf. Office: Sch Dist of Phila 440 N Broad St 3d Fl Philadelphia PA 19130-4015 E-mail: eboggia@phila.k12.pa.us.

BOGGS, BETH CLEMENS, lawyer; b. Dubuque, Iowa, July 28, 1967; d. Theodore Alan and Mary Ann (Fleckenstein) Clemens; m. T. Darin Boggs, Mar. 9, 1991. BA, Govs. State U., 1987; JD, So. Ill. U., 1991. Bar: Ill. 1991, Mo. 1992, U.S. Dist. Ct. (so. dist.) Ill. 1991, U.S. Dist. Ct. (ea. dist.) Mo. 1992, U.S. Dist. Ct. (we. dist.) Mo. 2002, U.S. Dist. Ct. (cen. dist.) Ill. 1997. Clk. R. Courtney Hughes & Assocs., Carbondale, Ill., 1990-91; lawyer Sandberg Phoenix & von Gontard, St. Louis, 1991-93; assoc. LaTourette, Schlueter & Byrne, St. Louis, 1993-95; mng. ptnr. Landau, Omahana & Kopka, P.C., St. Louis, 1995-99; mng. and founding ptnr. Boggs, Backer & Bates, LLC, St. Louis, 1999—. Adj. faculty Webster U., 1995—. Editor student articles So. Ill. U. Law Jour., 1991; contbr. articles to profl. jours. Mem. Young Lawyers divsn. of ABA (vice chair corp. counsel com. 1991-92, editor Corp. Counsel Newsletter 1991-92), Bus. Women St. Louis, Women Lawyers Assn., Lawyers Assn. St. Louis, Def. Rsch. inst., Mo. Orgn. Def. Lawyers. Avocations: tennis, softball, golf. Office: BBB 7912 Bonhomme Ave Ste 400 Saint Louis MO 63105-3512 E-mail: bbblawyers@aol.com.

BOGGS, CATHERINE J., lawyer; b. Denver, 1954; BA, U. Denver, 1976; MS, Mich. State U., 1977; JD, U. Denver, 1981. Bar: Colo. 1982, Oreg. 1991, Calif. 1993. Atty. Sherman & Howard, 1982—90, Stoel Rives, 1991—93, Baker & McKenzie, Chgo., 1993—. Trustee Rocky Mountain Mineral Law Found., 2001—. Mem.: ABA, Soc. Mining, Metallurgy and Exploration, Soc. Mining, Oreg. State Bar Assn., Colo. Bar Assn., Calif. State Bar Assn. Office: Baker & McKenzie One Prudential Plz 130 East Randolph Dr Chicago IL 60601 Office Phone: 312-861-8000.

BOGGS, DANNY JULIAN, federal judge; b. Havana, Cuba, Oct. 23, 1944; s. Robert Lilburn and Yolanda (Pereda) Boggs; m. Judith Susan Solow, Dec. 23, 1967; children: Rebecca, David, Jonathan. AB cum laude, Harvard Coll., Cambridge, Mass., 1965; JD, U. Chgo., 1968; LLD (hon.), U. Detroit Mercy, 1994. Dep. commr. Ky. Dept. Econ. Security, 1969—70; legal counsel, adminstrv. asst. Gov. Ky., 1970—71; legis. counsel to Rep. legislators Ky. Gen. Assembly, 1972; asst. to solicitor gen. U.S. Dept. Justice, Washington, 1973—75; asst. to chmn. FPC, Washington, 1975—77; dep. minority counsel Senate Energy Com., Washington, 1977—79; of counsel Bushnell, Gage, et al., Washington, 1979—80; spl. asst. to Pres. The White House, Washington, 1981—83; dep. sec. U.S. Dept. Energy, Washington, 1983—86; judge U.S. Ct. Appeals (6th cir.), Cin., 1986—, chief judge, 2003—. Mem. adv. com. on appellate rules Jud. Conf. U.S., 1991—94, com. on automation and tech., 1994—2000. Mem. vis. com. U. Chgo. Law Sch., 1984—87, 1999—2002; trustee Lexington Sch., 1999—2005; del. Rep. Nat. Conv., 1972; staff dir. energy subcom. Rep. Platform Com., 1980. Mem.: ABA (chair appellate judges conf. 2001—02), Mont Pelerin Soc., Ky. Bar Assn., Phila. Soc., Phi Delta Phi, Order of Coif. Office: US Ct Appeals US Courthouse 601 W Broadway Ste 220 Louisville KY 40202-2227

BOGGS, GEORGE ROBERT, academic administrator; b. Conneaut, Ohio, Sept. 4, 1944; s. George Robert and Mary (Mullen) B.; m. Ann Holladay, Aug. 8, 1969; children: Kevin Dale, Ian Asher, Micah Benjamin. BS in Chemistry, Ohio State U., 1966; MA in Chemistry, U. Calif., Santa Barbara, 1968; postgrad. in ednl. adminstrn., natural scis., and edn., Calif. State U., 1969-72; PhD in Ednl. Adminstrn., U. Tex., 1984. Cert. std. tchg. specialization in jr. coll., C.C. supr., C.C. chief adminstrv. officer. Instr. chemistry Butte Coll., Oroville, Calif., 1968-85, divsn. chmn. nat. sci. and allied health, 1972-81, assoc. dean of instrn., 1981-85; pres., supt. Palomar C.C. Dist., San Marcos, Calif., 1985-2000; pres. Am. Assn. C.C.s, Washington, 2000—. Spkr. SCCCIRA, Calif., 1985; adj. instr. Austin (Tex.) C.C., 1982; guest lectr. Calif. State U., Chico, 1970, 83, 84, panelist, 1975; tchg. asst. U. Calif., Santa Barbara, 1966-68, Ohio State U., 1965-66; mem. numerous coms. for colls. and univs., Calif., 1968—; cons. U. Calif., Berkeley, 1995-2000, U. Wis., Madison, 1997-2000, Pellissippi State Tech. Coll., 1995, El Camino Coll., 1994, U. Hawaii C.C., 1994, Dept. Nat. Edn., Rep. South Africa, 1993, San Joaquin Delta C.C. Dist., 1986, Marin C.C. Dist., 1985; mem. Accrediting Bd. for Engring. and Tech., 2002—. Contbr. articles to profl. jours.; cons. editl. adv. bd. Jour. Applied Rsch. in the C.C., 1993-2000; mem. editl. bd. C.C. Rev., 1997-2000. Presenter Nat. Conf. Teaching Excellence and Conf. of Pres.'s, 1983, 93, 95, presenter, mem. coordinating com., 1984, chmn. steering com., 1985; presenter Profl. and Orgl. Devel. Network, 1984; ad hoc com. CPEC/FIPSE/Chancellor's Office, 1984; mem. steering com. Learning Assessment Retention Com., 1983-85, pres.-elect 1985-86; mem. instl. research design team No. Calif. Higher Edn. Council, 1984, mission charrette writing team, 1985. Named a scholar Gen., Ohio State U., 1963; named hon. elder, Nat. Coun. on Black Am. Affairs, 1993; named to San Diego Hall of Success, 1988; recipient Scholastic R, 1962, Nat, Honor Soc., 1962, Stanley A. Mahr Cmty. Svc. award, San Marcos Coun. C. of C., 1994, Cert. Achievement, Leadership Excellence and Cmty. Svc., Congress of U.S. Ho. Reps., 1994, Pacific Region CEO award, Assn. C. C. Trustees, Victoria, B.C., Can., 1993, Recognition award, Nat. Coun. for Rsch. and Planning Mgmt., 1997, Harry Buttimer Disting. Adminstr. award, Assn. Calif. C.C. Trustees, 1994, Dr. George R. Boggs Day proclaimed Jan. 14, in Vista, Calif., 1994, PBS O'Banion prize for tchg. and learning, 2001, Leadership award, Nat. Inst. Staff and Orgnl. Devel., 2004, Paul Elsner Internat. Excellence in Leadership award, 2004; Richardson fellow, 1982—83. Mem. NSF (adv. com. to directorate for edn. and human resources 1995-97, evaluator 1992, 93, 98), Nat. Rsch. Coun. (undergrad. sci. edn. com. 1993-95, chmn. subcom. tchg. and learning 1993-95), Assn. Calif. Coll. Tutorial and Learning Assistance (presenter 1984), Calif. Assn. C.C. (conf. presenter 1984, com. on rsch. 1985—), Assn. Calif. C.C. Adminstrs. (commn. membership devel. 1985), C.C. League Calif. (bd. dirs. 1990-92, presenter confs. 1990-98), Faculty Assn. Calif. C.C., Calif. C.C. Chief Exec. Officers' Assn, San Diego and Imperial Counties C.C. Assn., Am. Assn. Cmty. and Jr. Colls. (presenter 1989, 90, 91, 94, 95, bd. dirs. 1990-95, fed. rels. com. 1990-91, 94-95, chair elect 1993—, chair bd. dirs. 1993-94, exec. com. 1993-95, chair bd. nominating com. 1994-95), So. Calif. C.C. Chief Exec. Officers Assn. (sec., treas. 1990-2000), Phi Kappa Phi, Upsilon Pi Upsilon (pres. 1965-66), Phi Rho Pi, Rotary (pres. Durham club 1980-81, dist. sec. Calif., 1983-84, various other offices and com. positions held locally and nationally). Home: 2301 N St NW Apt 616 Washington DC 20037-1138 Office: Am Assn CCs 1 Dupont Cir NW Ste 410 Washington DC 20036 Office Phone: 202-728-0200 ext. 235. Business E-Mail: gboggs@aacc.nche.edu.

BOGGS, GEORGE TRENHOLM, lawyer; b. Charleston, SC, Apr. 17, 1947; s. Edwin and Laura (Blair) Boggs; m. Emilie Louise von Thelen, Sept. 6, 1975; children: George T. Jr., Blair M. AB, Princeton U., 1969; JD, U. Va., 1974. Bar: Va. 1974, DC 1975. Tchr. Taft Sch., Watertown, Conn., 1969—71; mem. Dickstein Shapiro Morin and Oshinsky LLP, Washington, 1974—, ptnr., 1980—. Editor (with John M. Paxman): The United Nations: A Reassessment, 1973. Mem.: ABA, Va. Bar Assn., Internat. Bar Assn. Republican. Episcopalian. Office: Dickstein Shapiro Morin & Oshinsky LLP 2101 L St NW Washington DC 20037-1526 Office Phone: 202-828-2203.

BOGGS, JACK AARON, banker, mayor, municipal government official; b. Easley, S.C., July 4, 1935; s. Walter Benston and Bessie Mae (Jones) B.; m. Isabel Thomas Brown, July 7, 1965; children— James Benston, Renee Chaplin, Edward Cunningham, Donn Lester. BS in Bus. Econs, U. S.C., 1964; grad., Sch. Banking, U. Wis., 1974. Chartered bank auditor certified internal auditor. Sec.-treas. Cedarpoint Farms Corp., Columbia, S.C., 1963-67; auditor S.C. Nat. Bank, Columbia, 1967-76; pres. S.C. Automated Clearing House Assn., 1976—2005, pres. emeritus, 2005—; sec., treas. Arcadia Publs., 2002—. Mem. 5th dist. ops. adv. com. Fed. Res. Bank of Richmond, 1997-99; instr. S.C. Bankers Sch., 1972-80; sec., treas. Five Star Pubs., 1986-88, Law Offices E.C. Boggs, PA, 2004—; bd. dirs. NACHA, Inc., 1989-2000; vice chmn. ACH Exec. Dirs. Group, 1989-90, chmn., 1991-93. Mem. town coun., Town of Arcadia Lakes, S.C., 1977-85, mayor, 1985-89, chief of police, 1990-91; treas. S.C. Fedn. Older Ams., 1982-84. With USNR, 1952-60, Air N.G., 1960-63. Mem. Inst. Internal Auditors (bd. govs. 1971-74, pres. 1973-74, internat. rsch. com. 1972-75, internat. membership com. 1976), Bank Admisntrn. Inst. (1st award 1972), S.C. Ducks Unltd. (treas. 1984-92, 98-2002, state chmn. 1992-94), Explorers Club, Sigma Delta Pi, Chi Psi. Democrat. Unitarian Universalist. Home: 804 Arcadia Lakes Dr Columbia SC 29206-1321 Office: SC Automated Clearing House Assn PO Box 1787 Columbia SC 29202-1787

BOGGS, JAMES ERNEST, chemistry professor; b. Cleve., June 9, 1921; s. Ernest Beckett and Emily (Reid) B.; m. Ruth Ann Rogers, June 22, 1948 (dec. 2002); children: Carol, Ann, Lynne. AB, Oberlin Coll., 1943; MS in Chemistry, U. Mich., 1944, PhD, 1953. Rsch. chemist Manhattan Dist. Project, Linde Air Products, Tonawanda, N.Y., 1944-46; asst. prof. dept. chemistry Eastern Mich. U., Ypsilanti, 1949-52; instr. U. Mich. at Ann Arbor, 1952-53; mem. faculty dept. chemistry U. Tex., Austin, 1953—, assoc. prof., 1958-66, prof., 1966-98; emeritus prof., 1998—; asst. dean Grad. Sch. U. Tex., Austin, 1958-67, dir. Center for Structural Studies, 1969-79, acting dir. Inst. Theoretical Chemistry, 1979-81. Program officer for theoretical and computational chemistry NSF, 1991-94; founder, organizer series Austin Symposia on Molecular Structure, 1966—; chmn. subcom. on theoretical chemistry Internat. Union Pure and Applied Chemistry, 1995-01; internat. lectr. in field. Mem. editl. bd. Jour. Molecular Structure; contbr. over 290 articles to profl. jours. Mem. Am. Chem. Soc., Am. Phys. Soc., Nat. Acad. Scis. (India), Phi Beta Kappa, Sigma Xi, Phi Lambda Upsilon, Gamma Alpha. Achievements include research in structural chemistry, microwave spectroscopy, quantum chemistry. Office: U Tex Dept Chemistry 1 University Sta A5300 Austin TX 78712 Office Phone: 512-471-7525. Business E-Mail: james.boggs@mail.utexas.edu.

BOGGS, JOSEPH DODRIDGE, pediatric pathologist, educator; b. Bellefontaine, Ohio, Dec. 31, 1921; s. Walter C. and Birdella Z. (Coons) B.; m. Donna Lee Shoemaker, June 12, 1964; 1 son, Joseph Dodridge. AB, Ohio U., 1941, Litt.D., 1966; MD, Jefferson Med. Coll., 1945. Intern Jefferson Med. Coll. Hosp., Phila., 1945-46; resident Peter Bent Brigham Hosp., Boston, 1946-48, asso. pathologist, 1947-51; instr. pathology Harvard Med. Sch., Boston, 1948-51; with Children's Meml. Hosp., Chgo., 1951—, dir. labs., 1951—; prof. pathology Northwestern U., Chgo., 1952-92, prof. emeritus, 1992—; dir. BSP Ins. Co., Phoenix. Contbr. articles to profl. jours. Mem. med. adv. bd. Ill. Dept. Corrections, Springfield, 1971-77; bd. dirs. Blood Systems Inc., Phoenix, 1972-94, Community Hosp., Evanston, Ill., 1958-61, Lorretto Hosp., Chgo., 1971-72; chmn. Chgo. Regional Blood Program, 1978-80; bd. dirs. Ben Venue Labs., 1985—. Capt. M.C., U.S. Army, 1948-51. Mem. Am. Soc. Study of Liver Disease, N.Y. Acad. Scis., Midwest Soc. Pediatric Research, Inst. Medicine, Ill. Soc. Pathologists (pres. 1965), Ill. Assn. Blood Banks (pres. 1969-70) Office: 1448 N Lake Shore Dr Chicago IL 60610-6655 Office Phone: 312-944-7975. Office Fax: 312-488-1873.

BOGGS, NORMAN JIM W., school counselor; b. Abilene, Tex. s. Norman Justus and Claudine Faith Boggs; m. Tanya Dee Boggs, Feb. 14, 2004; children: Michelle Leigh, Jared C. stepchildren: Brianna L., Shayla, Coleton. BS, Abilene (Tex.) Christian U., 1984; MEd, Hardin-Simmons U., 1987, Abilene (Tex.) Christian U., 1992; EdD, Tex. Tech. U., 2004. Tchr. Abilene (Tex.) Ind. Sch. Dist., 1985—88, counselor, 1988—2004; adj. prof. Hardin-Simmons U., Abilene, 2003—. Adj. prof. Cisco Jr. Coll., Abilene, 1993—99. Musician Abilene (Tex.) Cmty. Band, 1997—2004. Scholar, Tex. PTA, 1997; Dr. Lois Martin Endowed scholar, 1987. Mem.: Viktor Frankl Ins.t Logotherapy, Big Country Counseling Assn. (treas. 1988—90), Kappa Delta Pi, Phi Delta Kappa (v.p. 1990—92). Republican. Baptist. Avocations: motorcycling, playing trombone, writing, chess, skeet shooting. Home: 1200 Larned Lane Abilene TX 79602 Office: Abilene ISD 842 N Mockingbird Lane Abilene TX 79603

BOGGS, PAULA ELAINE, lawyer; b. Washington, May 2, 1959; d. Nathaniel Boggs Jr. and Janice C. (Anderson) Barber. BA, Johns Hopkins U., 1981; JD, U. Calif., Berkeley, 1984. Bar: Pa. 1986, D.C. 1988, Wash. 1992, U.S. Dist. Ct. (we. dist.) Wash. 1988, U.S. Ct. appeals (9th cir.) 1990, U.S. Ct. Appeals (D.C. and fed. cirs.) 1995. Sr. law clk. Office of Army Gen. Counsel, Arlington, Va., 1984-85; spl. asst. Office of Dep. Under Sec. of the Army, Arlington, 1985-86; staff atty. White House Iran-Contra legal task force, Washington, 1987-88; asst. U.S. atty. we. dist. U.S. Atty.'s Office, Seattle, 1988-93; staff dir. adv. bd. investigative capability dept. def. Dept. Def., Arlington, 1994; ptnr. Preston Gates & Ellis, Seattle, 1995—97; v.p. legal Dell Computer Corp., 1997—2002; exec. v.p., gen. counsel, sec. Starbucks, Seattle, 2002—. Mem. faculty Nat. Inst. for Trial Advocacy, 1995; adj. prof. law U. Wash., Seattle, 1993. Vol. instr. presdl. classroom for young Ams., Washington, 1991; bd. dirs. ctrl. dist. YMCA, Seattle, 1991-93, Greater Seattle YMCA, 1995—; nat. chair Johns Hopkins U. Second Decade Soc., Balt., 1995-96. With U.S. Army, 1981-88. Recipient Sec. Def. award for Excellence William J. Perry, 1994; Presdl. svc. badge Pres. Ronald Reagan, 1988; Def. Meritorious Svc. award, 1987, Spl. Achievement award Dept. Justice, 1990, 91. Mem. ABA (ho. of dels., litigation sect. co-chair bus. torts com., bus. crimes com., criminal justice sect. white collar crimes com., standing com. on constn. and bylaws), Nat. Bar Assn., Wash. State Bar Assn. (corrections com.), King County Bar Assn., Fed. Bar Assn., Wash. Women Lawyers (bd. dirs. 1991-93), Loren Miller Bar Assn. Avocations: running, bicycling, reading. Office: Starbucks 2401 Utah Ave S PO Box 34067 Seattle WA 98134

BOGGS, RALPH STUART, retired lawyer; b. Toledo, June 6, 1917; s. Nolan and Sarah (MacPhie) B.; m. Mary Frances Sharp Wiggins, Sept. 7, 1940; children: Sally Ann Boggs Bashore, William S., Robert A. AB, Denison U., 1939; LL.B., U. Mich., 1942. Bar: Ohio 1942, U.S. Supreme Ct. 1960. Spl. agt. FBI, 1942-45; practiced in Toledo, 1946-99; ptnr. Boggs, Boggs & Boggs (P.A.), 1946-87; of counsel Eastman and Smith, 1987-98; ret. Mem. Maumee Bd. Edn., 1953-69, Maumee Recreation Com., 1954-69; life mem. Toledo adv. com. Salvation Army, pres., 1981-83; pres. Maumee Men's Rep. Club, 1947-48; former chmn. bd. trustees Presbytery of Maumee, Inc.; trustee, sec. Masonic Toledo Trust, 1986-97; trustee Stranahan Theatre Trust, 1997—, sec., 1997-98; asst. sec. Otis Avery Browning Masonic Meml. Fund, 1987-97. Named to Toledo H.S. Athletes Hall of Fame, 1995. Mem. ABA, Ex-FBI Agts. Soc., Ohio Bar Assn., Lucas County Bar Assn., Toledo Bar Assn., Masons (33 degree), Shriners, Heather Downs Country Club (Toledo) (past pres., dir.), Sigma Chi (life). Presbyterian (elder). Home: 401 B St Ste 2000 San Diego CA 92101-4240 *Education, preparation and perseverance are essential to attaining success.*

BOGGS, STEVEN EUGENE, real estate broker, lawyer; b. Santa Monica, Calif., Apr. 28, 1947; s. Eugene W. and Annie (Happe) B. BA in Econ., U. Calif., Santa Barbara, 1969; D of Chiropractic summa cum laude, Cleveland Chiropractic, LA, 1974; PhD in Fin. Planning, Columbia Pacific U., 1986; JD in Law, U. So. Calif., 1990. Bar: Calif. 1990, U.S. Dist. Ct. (cen. dist.) Calif. 1990, Hawaii 1991, U.S. Ct. Appeals (9th cir.), Colo. 1999; CFP; lic. chiropractor Hawaii, Calif.; lic. radiography X-ray supr. and operator; real estate broker, Colo. Faculty mem. Cleveland Chiropractic Coll., 1972-74; pres. clinic dir. Hawaii Chiropratic Clinic, Inc., Aiea, 1974-87; pvt. practice Honolulu, 1991-99; mem. faculty Hawaii Pacific U., 1997-99; broker, dir. REO/asset mgmt. team (bank foreclosures) Coldwell Banker Walker & Co., 2000—02, RE/MAX Properties, Inc., 2002—. Cons. in field; seminar presenter, 1990—. Contbr. articles to profl. jours. Recipient Cert. Appreciation, State of Hawaii, 1981—84. Fellow Internat. Coll. of Chiropractic; mem. ABA, Am. Trial Lawyers Assn., Consumer Lawyers of Hawaii, Am. Chrioppractic Assn., Hawaii State Chiropractic Assn. (pres. 1978, 85, 86, v.p. 1977, sec. 1979-84, treas. 1976, other coms., Valuable Svc. award 1984, Cert. Appreciation 1986, Cert. Achievement 1986, Chiropractor of Yr. 1986, Outstanding Achievement award 1991), Consumer Lawyers of Hawaii (bd. dirs.). Republican. Avocations: bicycling, car racing (Formula Atlantic Race Car Champion 2003, 04). Office: 19050 Archers Dr Monument CO 80132-2807 Personal E-mail: steve@steveboggs.com. Business E-Mail: boggs@pcisys.net.

BOGGS, THOMAS HALE, JR., lawyer, director; b. New Orleans, Sept. 18, 1940; s. Thomas Hale and Corinne (Claiborne) B.; m. Mary Barbara Denechaud, Dec. 27, 1960; children— Hale, Elizabeth, Douglas. AB,

Georgetown U., 1961, LL.B., 1965. Bar: D.C. 1965, U.S. Ct. Appeals 1966, U.S. Supreme Ct. 1971. Economist Joint Econ. Com., U.S. Congress, 1961-65; spl. asst. to dir. Office Emergency Planning, 1965-66; ptnr. Patton Boggs LLP, Washington, 1966—, chmn. exec. com. Presdl. Commn. on Exec. Exch., 1979-81; Presdl. del. Independence of Solomon Islands, 1978, Trade Mission to People's Republic of China, 1979. Co-author: Private Trade Barriers in the Atlantic Community, 1964, Corporate Political Activity, 1984. Dem. candidate for U.S. Ho. of Reps. 8th Dist. Md., 1970; mem. Charter Commn., Dem. Nat. Com., 1973; trustee Fed. City Coun., Chesapeake Bay Trust, Univ. Md. Found.; dir. The Keystone Ctr., Congl. Award Found., Suburban Mortgage Assn., 1-800-CONTACTS. Mem. Am. Judicature Soc., ABA (com. chmn.), Am. Maritime, Fed. Bar Assns., Delta Theta Phi. Home: 6 E Kirke St Chevy Chase MD 20815-4217 Office: Patton Boggs LLP 2550 M St NW Ste 500 Washington DC 20037-1350 Office Phone: 202-457-6040. Office Fax: 202-457-6315. Business E-Mail: tboggs@pattonboggs.com.*

BOGGS, THOMAS HALL, JR., lawyer; b. Selma, Ala., Feb. 9, 1940; s. Thomas and Agnes Wilmothe (Cooper) B.; m. Alice Ann Southern, Nov. 13, 1983; children: Thomas Hall III, Judy Lynn, Benjamin Cooper. BS, Livingston U., 1964; JD, U. Ala., 1969. Bar: Ala. 1969; U.S. dist. Ct. (no. dist.) Ala., 1969; U.S. Ct. Appeals (5th cir.). Legal assoc. Lloyd & Dinning, Demopolis, Ala., 1969-71; ptnr. Lloyd, Dinning, Boggs & Dinning, Demopolis, 1971—. Bd. dirs. First Bank of Linden, Ala. Pres. Jaycees, Demopolis, 1971; coun. mem., pres. Demopolis City Coun., 1976-84. Col. U.S. Army, USNG, 1957-92. Named to Outstanding Young Men of Am., Nat. Jaycees, 1972, Disting. Alumnus, Livingston U., 1988, OCS Hall of Fame, U.S. Infantry Sch., Ft. Benning, Ga., 1989. Mem. Kiwanis (pres. Demopolis club 1974), 17th Jud. Bar Assn. (pres. 1973), Am. Legion, Phi Kappa Phi. Presbyterian. Avocations: speaking, writing, gardening, running, hunting, cattle farming. Office: Lloyd Dinning Boggs Dinning PO Box 740 Demopolis AL 36732 Office Phone: 334-289-0556. E-mail: tboggs@ldlcc.com.

BOGGS, WADE ANTHONY, retired professional baseball player; b. Omaha, June 15, 1958; m. Deborah Bertercelli; children: Meagann, Brett. Student, Hillsborough C.C., Fla. Baseball player Boston Red Sox, 1976-92, N.Y. Yankees, 1992-97, Tampa Bay Devils, 1997—99. Founder The Wade Boggs Foundation for Youth Athletics. Named to Am. League All-Star game, 1985—96; recipient Am. League Gold Glove Award, 1994—95. Achievements include mem. World Series Champion N.Y. Yankees, 1996; led Am. League in Batting Average (.361), 1983, (.368), 1985, (.357), 1986, (.363), 1987, (.366), 1988; led Am. League in Runs (128), 1988, (113), 1989; led Am. League in Hits (240), 1985; attained 3,000 career hits by hitting a home run, 1999; elected to Baseball Hall of Fame, 2005.*

BOGGS, WILLENE GRAYTHEN, property manager, oil and gas broker, consultant; b. Vancouver, Wash., Mar. 10, 1939; d. William Louis and Zorah (Williams) Graythen; m. Ray Buck Glasgow, Feb. 8, 1964 (div. June 1969); m. Harry Maurice Boggs, May 23, 1993. BA in History, Centenary Coll., 1975; postgrad., La. State Law Sch., 1984, S.E. La. U., 1989. Tchr., educator St. Tam Parish Sch. Bd., Lacombe, La., 1964-65; abstractor St. Tam Parish Legal News, Covington, La., 1965-66, Kansas City Title Ins. Co., New Orleans, 1966-69, Lawyers Title Ins. Corp., New Orleans, 1975-77, Frawley, Wogan, Miller & Co., New Orleans, 1977-79; owner, mgr. Idea House and Sweet Home Antiques, Metairie, La., 1973-76; owner, mgr., abstractor, oil and gas broker Willene Glasgow & Assocs., Metairie, 1969-73, owner, mgr., abstractor Covington, La., 1979-93; pres. WCV Mgmt., Inc., Nashville, 1993-94, Charlotte, N.C., 1997—; asst. to art dir. Bascom-Louise Gallery, Highlands, N.C., 1996. Legal asst. Poyner & Sprull, LLP, Charlotte, 1998. Author: Decoupage and Related Crafts, 1972; contbg. writer Times-Picayune, New Orleans, 1989, LAD News, 1998-99. Bd. dirs. Air, Water and Earth Inst., Covington, 1989; bd. dirs., pres. Pontchartrain Area Recycling Coun., Inc., Covington, 1989, 90, 91, 92, 93; mem. Citizens Adv. Com. on Solid Waste, 1988, 89, 90, 91, 92; coord. Pontchartrain Area Recycling Conv., 1988; fund raiser March of Dimes, Am. Cancer Soc., Arthritis Found., others, 1986—; pres. Mount Lori Home Owners Assn., Highlands, N.C., 1998-99. Named hon. sec. state State of La., 1987. Mem. AAUW (conf. chmn. 1988-89, 92-93, chmn. Ednl. Found. 1989-91, Mem. of Yr. award Covington-Mandeville br. 1989, v.p. membership 1991-93), Petroleum Landman's Assn., Covington C. of C. (legis. chmn. 1988—, Mem. of Yr. award 1988), Art League of Highlands (membership chmn. 1996, publicity chmn. 1997), Highlands-Cashiers Garden Club (v.p. 1997), Metrolina Paralegal Assn., N.C. Bar Assn. Legal Asst. Divsn. Avocations: fine arts, arts and crafts, restoring antique furniture, collecting antique toys. Home and Office: 8358 Christmas Ct Charlotte NC 28216-0707

BOGH, RUSSELL, state official; b. San Bernardino; m. Sheri Bogh; 3 children. BA in Bus. Econs., Calif. State U., San Bernardino. Mgr. bus. devel. Bogh Constrn.; candidate Dist. 65 Calif. State Assembly, 2000, state assembly mem. Dist. 65, 2001—. Vice-chair utilites and commerce; mem. transp., Ins., Ins. com. Republican. Mailing: Rm 4098 PO Box 942849 Sacramento CA 94249-0001 Office: 34932 Yucaipa Blvd Yucaipa CA 92399

BOGHAERT, ERWIN R., oncologist, researcher; b. Ghent, Belgium, Feb. 19, 1956; 2 children. M.D., M.S. Molecular Biology, State U. Ghent, 1984. Gen. practitioner, Belgium, 1982—84; rsch. asst. State U. Ghent, 1982—84, asst. assoc. rschr., 1984—87; vis. scholar U. Ky., 1988—91, rsch. asst. prof., 1991—97; prin. scientist oncology rsch. Wyeth, Pearl River, NY, 1997—. Grantee, Belgisch Werk Tegen Cancer, 1986, prin. investigator, Am. Cancer Soc., 1993, co-investigator, NIH, 1994; rsch. fellowship, NATO, 1988. Mem.: AAAS. Achievements include design of model for quantitative evaluation in vivo. Design method to evaluate the influence of cell-cell adhesion and proliferation on quantitative evaluation of invasion in vitro; Demonstrate the role of N-CAM in inhibition of proliferation of glial cells. Home: 93 Ludlam Rd Monroe NY 10950 Office: Wyeth 401 N Middletown Rd Pearl River NY 10965 Personal E-mail: tommelei@optonline.net.

BOGHAIRI, ANOUSHIRAVAN, cardiologist; b. Tehran, Iran, Aug. 5, 1944; arrived in US, 1973; s. Mahmood and Aghdass Boghairi; m. Azam Rashid, May 5, 1978; children: Salina, Cyrus. Grad. Tehran U., 1970. Diplomate Am. Bd. Internal Medicine, Am. Bd. Cardiovasc. Disease. Rotating intern Emam Khomeini Hosp., Tehran, 1968—70, St. John's Riverside Hosp., Yonkers, NY, 1973—74; resident in internal medicine Mt. Sinai Hosp., Hartford, Conn., 1974—75, Jersey City (N.J.) Med. Ctr., 1975—76; fellow in cardiology Jersey City Med. Ctr., 1976—77, Cleve. Clinic, 1977—78, Creighton U. Cardiac Ctr., Omaha, 1978—79, instr. medicine, 1978—79; attending cardiologist Alvarado Hosp. Med. Ctr., San Diego, 1979—80; pvt. practice La Mesa, Calif., 1980—. Former tchr. SHARP Family Physicians Residency Program; bd. govs. Grossmont Hosp. Found., La Mesa, 2002; asst. prof. medicine U. Calif., San Diego. Lt. med. corps. Iranian Army, 1971—73. Fellow: Am. Coll. Cardiology. Avocations: piano, exercise, santoor. Office: Bldg 1 Ste 115 5565 Grossmont Ctr Dr La Mesa CA 91942

BOGHANI, ASHOK BALVANTRAI, entrepreneur, management consultant; b. Bombay, Aug. 8, 1949; came to U.S., 1970; s. Balvantrai Pranlal and Charusheela (Kapadia) B.; m. Meera Kapadia, May 30, 1977; children: Ami, Amar. B of Tech., Indian Inst. Tech., Bombay, 1970; MS, MIT, 1971, M in Mech. Engring., 1973, ScD, 1974. Staff engr. Foster-Miller, Waltham, Mass., 1974-77, project mgr., 1977-79; sr. cons. Arthur D. Little, Inc., Cambridge, Mass., 1979-90, dir., 1990-2000, v.p., 1994-2000, leader N.Am. transp. and automotive practice, 1998-2000; founder, v.p. bus. devel. IntellectExchange-.com, 2000—03; mng. ptnr. FutureAct, LLC, 2003—; dir. Monitor Techs., Monitor Group, 2004—. Mem. transp. hazmat com. Transp. Rsch. Bd., Washington, 1987-94; mem. Benefits, Evaluation and Assessment com., Intelligent Vehicle Hwy. Systems Am., Washington, 1992-96. Contbr. articles to profl. jours. Recipient cert. of recognition NASA, 1976, 78. Mem. ASME, Soc. Automotive Engrs., Indus Entrepreneurs-Atlantic (charter mem.), Democrat. Avocations: photography, travel, hiking, music. Home: 3 Sawmill Rd Acton MA 01720-5835 Office Phone: 617-252-3180. Business E-Mail: ABoghani@alum.mit.edu.

BOGHOLTZ, WILLIAM E., minister; b. L.A., Mar. 25, 1959; s. Wilhelm E. and Elizabeth F. (Caulfield) B.; children: Rebekah Ann, Matthew James; m. Maria M. Sanchez, Sept. 25, 1998. BA, Wagner Coll., 1981; MDiv, Luth. Theol. Sem., 1985; DMin, Grad. Theol. Found., Donaldson, Ind., 1999. Ordained to ministry Luth. Ch. in Am., 1985. Intern/vicar Bethel Luth. Ch., Auburn, Mass., 1983-84; pastor Holy Trinity Luth. Ch., York Springs, Pa., 1985-88, Atonement Luth. Ch., S.I., N.Y., 1989-91, Our Saviour Luth. Ch., S.I., 1991—; coord./host pastor S.I. Liberian Refugee Ministry, 1997—, Adj. instr. Wagner Coll., S.I., 1993-97; mem. Christian edn. com. and parish life commn. Ctrl. Pa. synod Luth. Ch. in Am., 1986-87; mem. bishop's com. for ecumenical affairs Lower Susquehanna synod Evang. Luth. Ch. in Am., 1988, stewardship com. Metro N.Y. synod, 1990-92; tchr. religion Trinity Luth. Sch., S.I., 1990-94, 97-98; convenor, mem. S.I. Luth. Ministerium, 1989-91; chairperson Adams County Migrant Ministry, Gettysburg, Pa., 1986-88; chmn. adv. bd. Luth. Cmty. Svc., N.Y.C., 1989-94; bd. dirs. Luth. Social Svcs., N.Y.C., 1991-2000, chmn. bd. dirs., 1996-2000, sec., 1992-96; bd. dirs. Luth. Family and Cmty. Svcs., N.Y.C., 1992-2001, sec., 1994-2001. Editor, pub. booklet Churches of Oakwood/Richmondton, S.I., 1990; mem. editl. bd. Bride of Christ, 1993-96. Bd. dirs. United Way Adams County, 1985-87. Mem. Ecumenical Soc. Blessed Virgin Mary, Luth. Liturgical Renewal, S.I. Clergy Assn. (treas. 1990-91). Office: Our Saviour Luth Ch 549 Bard Ave Staten Island NY 10310-3015

BOGHOSIAN, VARUJAN YEGAN, sculptor, educator; b. New Britain, Conn., June 26, 1926; s. Mesrop and Baidzar (Saylandzian) B.; m. Marilyn Cummins, Sept. 1, 1953; 1 dau., Heidi. Student, Conn. Tchrs. Coll., 1946-48, Vesper George Sch. Art, 1948-50; B.F.A., Yale U., 19—, M.F.A., 1959; MA (hon.), Brown U., 1965, Dartmouth Coll., 1969. Instr. art U. Fla., 1958-59, Pratt Inst., 1961, Yale U., 1962-64; asst. prof. art Cooper Union Coll., 1959-64; asso. prof. Brown U., 1964-68; artist-in-residence Dartmouth Coll., 1968, prof. art, 1968—, George Frederick Jewett prof. art, 1983—; sculptor in residence Am. Acad. in Rome, 1966-67, 75. Artist woodcut portfolios Orpheus, 1951, The River Styx, 1971; numerous one-man shows including Stable Gallery, N.Y.C., 1963, 64, 65, 66, Cordier and Ekstrom, N.Y.C., 1969, 71, 73, 75, 77-80, 82, 84, 87-89, Berry Hill Galleries, 1997, 99, Arts Club of Chgo., 1970, Claude Bernard Gallery, N.Y.C., 1991, Norton Gallery Art, Palm Beach, Fla., 1993, Washburn Gallery, N.Y.C., 2004; group shows include Obelisk Gallery, Rome, 1953, Mus. Modern Art, N.Y.C., 1956, Hanover Gallery, London, 1966, retrospective Hood Mus., Hanover, N.H., 1989; represented in numerous permanent collections including, Mus. Modern Art, N.Y.C., Whitney Mus. Am. Art, N.Y.C., Met. Mus. N.Y.C., Addison Gallery Am. Art, Andover, Mass., Worcester Art Mus., Phoenix Art Mus. Chmn. bd. MacDowell Colony. With USN, 1944-46. Recipient award Nat. Inst. Arts and Letters, 1972; Fulbright grantee, Italy, 1953; U.S. Dept. State specialists grantee, 1961; fellow Howard Found., 1966, John Simon Guggenheim Found. fellow, 1985 Mem. NAD, Am. Acad. Arts and Letters (St. Botolph award 1991), Century Assn. (N.Y.C.), St. Botolph Club (Boston). Clubs: Century (N.Y.C.). Office: Darmouth Coll HB 6081 Visual Studies Office Hanover NH 03755 Office Phone: 603-646-2285.

BOGIE, LANA CECIL, librarian; d. Matt Cecil, Jr. and Ruth Cecil; m. Garnett Coleman Bogie, June 7, 1969; children: Jennifer LeAnn, Emily Hicklen, Amy DeAnn Rogers. BS in Music Edn., Trevecca Nazarene Coll., 1975, postgrad. cert. in English, 1985; MLIS, Trevecca Nazarene U., 2002. English and reading tchr. Maplewood H.S.-Metro Nashville Schs., Nashville, 1985—92; mid. sch. music tchr. Carter Lawrence Sch.-Metro Nashville Schs., Nashville, 1992—2000; elem. music tchr. J.E. Moss Elem. Sch.-Metro Nashville Schs., Nashville, 2000—03; elem. libr. info. specialist Granbery Elem. Sch.-Metro Nashville Schs., Nashville, 2003—. Asst. choir dir. Trevecca Cmty. Ch. of the Nazarene, Nashville, 1998—. Choir mem. Trevecca Cmty. Ch. of the Nazarene, Nashville. Grantee, Met. Nashville Schs. Mem.: NEA, Metro Nashville Ednl. Assn. Nazarene. Avocations: walking, reading.

BOGIS, NANA EILEEN, librarian; b. Phila., Feb. 4, 1938; d. Herman B. and Rose L. Bogis. BA, Temple U., 1960; MLS, Drexel U., 1966. Cataloger Bucks County Libr., Doylestown, Pa., 1966-68; head cataloger Montgomery County Libr., Norristown, Pa., 1968-69; dir. Mt. Holly (N.J.) Pub. Libr., 1970-74, Monroe Twp. Pub. Libr., Williamstown, N.J., 1974—. Adj. prof. Drexel U., Phila., 1967-69; cons. CBG Video Circuit, Williamstown, 1985—. Mem. ALA, Am. Film Inst., N.J. Libr. Assn. Avocations: cinema, theater, opera, travel. Home: 222 Church St Apt 2B Philadelphia PA 19106-4522 E-mail: nbogis@buyrite.com.

BOGLE, JOHN CLIFTON, investment company executive; b. Montclair, NJ, May 8, 1929; s. William Yates, Jr. and Josephine (Hipkins) B.; m. Eve Sherrerd, Sept. 22, 1956; children: Barbara, Jean, John Clifton, Nancy, Sandra, Andrew. AB magna cum laude, Princeton U., 1951; LHD (hon.), Widener U., 1997, U. Rochester, 2000; HHD (hon.), Albright Coll.; LLD (hon.), U. Del., Susquehanna U., 2001; LLD, New School U., 2001; LLD (hon.), Immaculata U., 2005, Drexel U., 2003, Pa. State U., 2004, Immaculata U., 2005, Princeton U., 2005. With Wellington Mgmt. Co., Phila., 1951-74, asst. to pres., 1954-62, sec., adminstrv. v.p., 1962-66, exec. v.p., 1966-67, pres., CEO, 1967-74; founder, CEO, chmn. Vanguard Group Investment Cos., Valley Forge, Pa., 1974-96; sr. chmn. Vanguard Group, Valley Forge, 1996-99; pres. Bogle Fin. Makerts Rsch. Ctr., Valley Forge, 2000—. Kaufman vis. prof. NYU, 1999-2000; former exec. com. CGU; former chmn. corp. objectives com. Mead Corp.; bd. dirs. Instinet Corp. Author: Bogle on Mutual Funds: New Perspectives for the Intelligent Investor, 1993, Common Sense on Mutual Funds: New Imperatives for the Intelligent Investor, 1999, John Bogle on Investing: The First 50 Years, 2000, Character Counts, 2002, The Battle for the Soul of Capitalism, 2005; subject of biography: John Bogle and the Vanguard Experiment: One Man's Quest to Transform the Mutual Fund Industry, by Robert Slater, 1996; numerous articles to profl. jours., chpts. to books. Former chmn. bd. trustees Blair Acad.; chmn. bd. dirs. Nat. Constn. Ctr.; past adv. coun. econs. dept. Princeton U.; past bd. dirs. Independence Standards Bd., Am. Indian Coll. Fund. Recipient Woodrow Wilson medal Princeton U., 1999; named One of Four Investment Giants of the 20th Century Fortune mag., 1999, One of Worlds Most Powerful Influential People Time mag., 2004. Fellow AAAS, Am. Philos. Soc.; mem. Nat. Assn. Securities Dealers (investment cos. com. 1967-74, long-range planning com. 1973-74), Investment Co. Inst. (gov. 1969-81, chmn. 1969-70), Securities and Exch. Commn. (market oversight and fin. svcs. adv. com.), Merion Cricket Club (Haverford), Merion Golf (Ardmore). Office: Vanguard Group PO Box 2600 Valley Forge PA 19482-2600 Office Phone: 610-669-6081.

BOGOLUB, DAVID LOUIS, physician; b. Elgin, Illinois, Sept. 27, 1958; s. Harry and Evelyn B.; m. Nancy Bogolub, Aug. 22, 1982 (dec. 1996); children: Rachel Elizabeth, Beth Leah. BA, U. Ill., 1979; D, Chgo. Coll. Osteo. Medicine, 1995. Diplomate Am. Osteo. Bd. Emergency Medicine. Paramedic, paramedic-in-charge Chgo. Fire Dept., 1981—91; resident EM-CARE Chgo. Coll. Osteo. Medicine, 1995—99; physician St. Bernard Hosp., Chgo., 1999—2000, Norwegian Am. Hosp., Chgo., 2000—03; adv. Bethany Hosp., Chgo., 1997—99, 2001—. Gen. instr. weapons of mass destruction U.S. Ctr. for Domestic Preparedness, U.S. Dept. Homeland Security; adj. instr. curriclum developer Acad. Counterterrorism Edn., Nat. Ctr. Biomed. Rsch. and Tng. La. State U.; curriculum developer, lectr., instr. Acad. Counterrorism Edn. Nat. Ctr. for Biomed. Rsch. and Tng., La. State U., 2003-; cons. Health Watchers Chgo., Ltd., 1985—. Mem. Am. Osteo. Assn., Am. Coll. Emergency Physicians, Am. Coll. Osteo. Emergency Physicians, Am. Coll. Osteo. Family Physicians, Ill. Coll. Emergency Physicians (com. emergency med. svc.), Com. Domestic Preparedness. Avocations: wine, cooking, camping. Home: 3836 N Tripp Ave Chicago IL 60641-3011 E-mail: davidbogolub@hotmail.com.

BOGOSIAN, ERIC, actor, writer; b. Boston, Apr. 24, 1953; s. Henry and Edwina B.; m. JoAnne Bonney, Oct. 1980. Student, U. Chgo., 1971-73; BA, Oberlin Coll., 1976. Founder, dir. The Kitchen, N.Y.C. Actor, writer: (theatre, off-broadway debut) Men Inside, 1982, Voices of America, 1982, (dir., design supr.) FunHouse, 1983, Drinking in America (Drama Desk award for outstanding solo performance 1986), 1986, Talk Radio, 1987, Sex, Drugs, Rock & Roll, 1990, Pounding Nails in the Floor with My Forehead, 1994, SubUrbia, 1994, Griller, 1998, Wake Up and Smell the Coffee, 2000; actor (films) (Cinemax spl.) Drinking in America, 1986, Talk Radio, 1988, Sex, Drugs, Rock & Roll, 1991, Dolores Claiborne, 1995, Under Siege 2, 1995, The Substance of Fire, 1996, Deconstructing Harry, 1997, Office Killer, 1997, Gossip, 1999; TV show appearances: The Twilight Zone, Miami Vice, Law & Order, Larry Sanders Show, Beggars and Choosers; TV movie appearances: The Caine Mutiny Court Martial, 1988, Witchhunt, 1994, A Bright and Shining Lie, 1998, Blonde, 2001; author: Sex, Drugs, Rock & Roll, 1990, Pounding Nails in the Floor with my Forehead, 1994, Notes from Underground, 1993, Wasted Beauty, 2005; (play and film) subUrbia, 1994, Essential Bogosian, 1994, Mall, 2000; author, creator (with Steven Spielberg) (TV series) High Incident, 1996, (voice) Arabian Knight, 1995, (voice) Beavis and Butthead do America, 1996. Recipient Obie, 1986, 90, 94, Drama Critics Circle award; grantee Nat. Endowment for Arts, Berlin Film Fest Silver Bear award, 1988. Mem. SAG, AFTRA, Writer's Guild, Actor's Equity.*

BOGREN, HUGO GUNNAR, radiology educator; b. Jönköping, Sweden, Jan. 9, 1933; came to U.S., 1970; s. Gunnar Hugo and Signe Victoria (Holmström) B.; m. Elisabeth Faxén, Nov. 1, 1956 (div. 1976); children: Cecilia, Niclas, Joakim; m. Gunilla Lady Whitmore, July 2, 1988. MD, U. Göteborg, Sweden, 1958, PhD, 1964. Diplomate Swedish Bd. Radiology. Resident, fellow U. Göteborg, 1958-64, asst. to assoc. prof. radiology, 1964-69; from assoc. prof. to prof. radiology and internal medicine U. Calif. Davis, Sacramento, 1972—. Vis. assoc. prof. U. San Francisco, 1970-71; vis. prof. U. Kiel, Fed. Republic Germany, 1980, cardiac magnetic resonance unit Royal Brompton Hosp. and Imperial Coll., London, 1986-87, 93-94, 2002-03; participant in med. aid fact finding mission, Bangladesh, 1992. Contbr. numerous articles to profl. jours., chpts. to books. Sr. Internat. Fogarty fellow NIH, London, 1986-87. Fellow Am. Heart Assn., Radiol. Soc., N.Am. Soc. Cardiac Imaging, Assn. Univ. Radiologists, Soc. Thoracic Radiology, Internat. Soc. Magnetic Resonance, Soc. Cardiovasc. Magnetic Resonance, Swedish Assn. Med. Radiology; mem. Royal Gothenburg Sailing Club Sweden (hon.), Swedish Cruising Club, Rotary (del.). Lutheran. Avocations: ocean sailing, skiing, classical music. Office: U Calif Davis Med Ctr Div Diagnostic Radiology 4860 Y St Ste 3100 Sacramento CA 95817-2307 Office Phone: 916-734-6535. Personal E-mail: hugobogren@aol.com. Business E-Mail: hugo.bogren@ucdmc.ucdavis.edu.

BOGUCKI, PETER IGNATIUS, archaeologist; b. Phila., Mar. 11, 1954; s. Alfred and Jadwiga (Kulpinska) B.; m. Virginia Creeden, Dec. 10, 1978; children: Caroline, Marianna. BA, U. Pa., 1974; MA, Harvard U., 1977, PhD, 1981. Lectr. in anthropology U. Mass., Boston, 1982-83; dir. studies Forbes Coll. Princeton (N.J.) U., 1983-94, asst. dean sch. engring. and applied sci., 1994-2000, assoc. dean. sch. engring. & applied sci., 2000—. Lectr. Archaeol. Inst. Am., 1990-91; Munro lectr. U. Edinburgh, 2005 Author: Early Neolithic Subsistence and Settlement in the Polish Lowlands, 1982, Forest Farmers and Stockherders: Early Agriculture and its Consequences in North-Central Europe, 1988, The Origins of Human Society, 1999; editor: Case Studies in European Prehistory, 1993, co-editor Ancient Europe 8000 B.C. to A.D. 1000: An Encyclopedia of the Barbarian World, 2004; mem. editl. adv. bd. Environ. Archaeology Jour., Jour. of Field Archaeology; Cambridge Manuals in Archaeology; contbr. articles to profl. jours. Grantee Nat. Geographic Soc., 1989, 90. Mem. Am. Soc. Engring. Edn., European Assn. Archaeologists, Assn. for Environ. Archaeology, Sigma Xi. Office: Princeton U Sch Engring Applied Sci Princeton NJ 08544-5263

BOGUE, ALLAN GEORGE, historian, educator; b. London, Ont., Can., May 12, 1921; married; 3 children. BA, U. Western Ont., 1943, MA, 1946; PhD, Cornell U., 1951; LL.D., U. Western Ont., 1973; D.Fil (hon.), U. Uppsala, 1977. Lectr. econs. and history, asst. librarian U. Western Ont., 1949-52; from asst. prof. to prof. history U. Iowa, 1952-64, chmn. dept., 1959-63; prof. history U. Wis.-Madison, 1964-68, chmn. dept., 1972-73, Frederick Jackson Turner prof. history, 1968-91. Mem. hist. adv. com. Math. Soc. Sci. Bd., 1965-71; Scandinavian-Am. Found. Thord-Gray lectr., 1968; mem. Council Inter-Univ. Consortium Polit. Research, 1971-73, 89-91; vis. prof. history Harvard U., 1972; dir. Social Sci. Research Council, 1973-76 Author: Money at Interest, 1955, From Prairie to Corn Belt, 1963, Frederick Jackson Turner: Strange Roads Going Down, 1998, The Earnest Men, 1981, Clio and the Bitch Goddess, Quantification in American Political History, 1983, The Congressman's Civil War, 1989, The Farm on the North Talbot Road, 2001; co-author, editor: The West of the American People, 1970, co-author, contbr.: The Dimensions of Quantitative Research in History, 1972; co-editor, contbr.: American Political Behavior: Historical Essays and Readings, 1974; co-editor: The University of Wisconsin: One Hundred and Twenty Five Years, 1975, The Jeffersonian Dream: Studies in the History of American Law Land Policy and Development, 1996. Lt. Can. Army, 1943-45. Social Sci. Rsch. Coun. fellow, 1955, 66, Guggenheim fellow, 1970, H.E. Huntington Libr. fellow, 1991, 93, Sherman Fairchild Disting. fellow Calif. Inst. Tech., 1975, Ctr. for Advanced Study in the Behavioral Scis. fellow, 1985, NEH fellow, 1985. Fellow Agr. Hist. Soc. (pres. 1963-64); mem. Orgn. Am. Historians (pres. 1982-83), Am. Hist. Assn., Econ. Hist. Assn. (pres. 1981-82), Social Sci. Hist. Assn. (pres. 1977-78), Western Hist. Assn. (hon. life). Office: 1914 Vilas Ave Madison WI 53711 Office Phone: 608-255-5643. Business E-Mail: agbogue@wisc.edu.

BOGUNOVIC, OIVERA J., psychiatrist, health facility administrator; b. Belgrade, Serbia, Yugoslavia, May 7, 1967; arrived in U.S., 1996; d. Jovan and Ljubinka Bogunovic; m. Jorge Sotelo, Aug. 8, 1999; 1 child, Emily Mamcu Sotelo. MD, U. Belgrade, 1992. Diplomate Am. Bd. Psychiatry and Neurology. Intern in medicine U. Hosp. Belgrade, 1992—93; resident in psychiatry Healt Svc. Ctr. SUNY, Bklyn., 1996—2000; fellow in geriatric psychiatry NYU Med. Ctr., N.Y.C., 2000—01; fellow in addiction psychiatry Mass. Gen. Hosp., Boston, McLean Hosp., Boston, 2001—02; clin. instr. Health Sci. Ctr. SUNY, Bklyn., 1996—2000, NYU, N.Y.C., 2000—01, Harvard Med. Sch., 2001—02; attending psychiatrist TLC Health Network, Irving, NY, 2002—, med. dir. behavioral unit, 2003—; clin. asst. prof. SUNY, Buffalo, 2003. Presenter in field. Contbr. articles to profl. jours.; co-editor: Psychiatric Svcs.; reviewer: Clin. Drug Investigation, 2002—, Am. Jour. Addictions, 2003—, Psychiat. Svcs., 2004—. Co-recipient Rsch. fund, Astra Zeneca; recipient 1st prize, Bklyn. Psychiatry Soc. Residents' Sci. Session, 1998, award for Excellence in Precepting, D'Youville Coll., 2004; Alcohol Med. scholar, 2004. Mem.: AMA, Am. Assn. Geriatric Psychiatry, Am. Assn. Addiction Psychiatry, Am. Psychiatry Assn., Sigma Xi. Home: 100 N Lake Dr #10 Orchard Park NY 14127 Office: TLC Health Network 845 Rt 5820 Orchard Park NY 14127

BOGUS, CARL THOMAS, law educator; b. Fall River, Mass., May 14, 1948; s. Isidore E. and Carolyn (Dashoff) B.; m. Dale Shepard, Sept. 5, 1970 (div. 1987); children: Elizabeth Carol, Ian Troy; m. Cynthia J. Giles, Nov. 5, 1988; 1 child, Zoe Churchill. AB, Syracuse U., 1970, JD, 1972. Bar: Pa. 1973, U.S. Dist. Ct. (ea. dist.) Pa. 1973, U.S. Dist. Ct. Appeals (3d cir.) 1976, U.S. Supreme Ct. 1977. Assoc. Steinberg, Greenstein, Gorelick & Price, Phila., 1973-79, ptnr., 1979-83; assoc. Mesirov, Gelman, Jaffe, Cramer & Jamieson, Phila., 1983-84, ptnr., 1985-91; assoc. prof. Roger Williams U. Sch. Law, Bristol, RI, 1996—2002, prof., 2002—. Vis. prof. Rutgers U. Sch. Law, Camden, 1992—96; mem. bd. visitors Coll. Law, Syracuse (N.Y.) U., 1976—2001; mem. Nat. adv. panel Violence Policy Ctr., 1993—. Author: Why Lawsuits Are Good for America: Disciplined Democracy, Big Business and the Common Law, 2001; editor: The Second Amendment in Law and History, 2001; contbr. articles to profl. jours. Bd. dirs. Handgun Control, Inc., 1987-89, bd. govs., 1992-93; bd. dirs. Ctr. to Prevent Handgun Violence, 1989-92, Lawyers Alliance for Nuclear Arms Control, 1987-89; mem. state governing bd. Common Cause R.I., 1999-2001. Recipient Common Cause Pub. Svc. award, RI, 2002. Mem. ABA (Ross Essay award 1991), Syracuse Law Coll. Assn. (exec. sec. 1979-83, 2d v.p. 1983-85). Democrat. Mem. Soc. Of Friends. Office: Roger William U Sch Law 10 Metacom Ave Bristol RI 02809-5103 Office Phone: 401-254-4617. Business E-Mail: cbogus@law.rwu.edu.

BOGUSKY, ALEX, advertising executive; Art dir. Crispin and Porter Advertising, Miami, Fla., 1987—92, creative dir., 1992—97; ptnr., exec. creative dir. Crispin and Porter Advertising (now Crispin Porter & Bogusky), Miami, Fla., 1997—. Judge Andy Awards, 2005. Work featured in NY Times, Wall Street Journal, USA Today, Newsweek, TIME, Adweek, Brandweek, Advertising Age, and Creativity. Nominee Rave award in Business, WIRED, 2005; named to Am. Advertising Federation's Hall of Achievement, 2002. Office: Crispin Porter & Bogusky LLC 3390 Mary St Ste 300 Miami FL 33133 Office Phone: 305-859-2070.*

BOGUT, ANDREW, professional basketball player; b. Melbourne, Australia, Nov. 28, 1984; Attended Univ. Utah, 2003—05. Center Milwaukee Bucks, 2005—. Starting Center Australian Olympic Basketball Team, 2004. Named Player Week (5 times), Mountain West Conf., 2004, Player Yr., 2004, Nat. Player Yr., Basketball Times, 2005, ESPN; named to All-Tournament Team, Great Alaska Shootout, 2004, First-Team All District 13, NABC, 2004, Mountain West Conf., 2004. Office: Milwaukee Bucks 1001 N Fourth St Milwaukee WI 53203*

BOGUTZ, JEROME EDWIN, lawyer, educator; b. Bridgeton, N.J., June 7, 1935; s. Charles and Gertrude (Lahn) B.; m. Helene Carole Ross, Nov. 20, 1960; children: Marc Lahn, Tami Lynne BS in Fin., Pa. State U., 1957; JD, Villanova U., 1962. Bar: Pa., U.S. Dist. Ct. (ea. dist.) Pa., U.S. Ct. Appeals (3d cir.), U.S. Supreme Ct. Assoc. Dash & Levy, Phila., 1962—63, Abrahams & Loewenstein, Phila., 1963—64; dep. dir., chief of litigation Community Legal Svcs., Phila., 1964—68, dir., 1968—78; emeritus, 1978—; pvt. practice law Phila., 1968—71; ptnr. Bogutz & Mazer, Phila., 1971—81, Fox Rothschild O'Brien & Frankel, Phila., 1981—98; judge Pro Tem Phila. Ct. Common Pleas, 1992—; ptnr. Christie, Pabarue, Mortensen & Young, P.C., Phila., 1998—. Adj. clin. prof. law Villanova (Pa.) U., 1969-72, lectr., 1987—, bd. consultors Law Sch., 1983—; pres. Internat. Mobile Machines, Phila., 1980-81, Interdigital Comm., 1980-81, also bd. dirs. ABA-JAD Lawyers Conf., 1987-92, mem. exec. coun., 1986-92, vice chmn., 1987-88, chmn., 1989-90, chmn. nominating com., 1989-90, mem. long range planning com., 1989-90; mem. adv. bd. Pa. Med. Profl. Liability Catastrophe Loss Fund, 2000—04; bd. dirs. Jefferson Park Hosp., Phila. Bd. dirs. Am. Friends of Hebrew U., 1988-93, chmn. exec. com., 1991-93, pres., 1993-95, chmn. bd. 1995-98, chair steering com., pres. Pa. Futures Commn. on Justice in the 21st Century, 1993—, chmn. of bd., 1993-97. With USAR, 1956-60. Fellow Am. Bar Found. (life), Pa. Bar Found. (life, pres. 1986-88, bd. dirs. 1983—, lifetime dir. 1991—), Am. Judicature Soc. (life, bd. dirs. 1990—); mem. ABA (ho. of dels. 1980-84, 86-96, credentials and admissions com. 1987-88, nominating com. 1992, 93, chair ABA/JAD bench bar com., vice chmn. lawyer's conf. 1987-89, chair 1988-90, co-chair mid-yr. meeting com. 1987-88, planning com., conf. sect. officers, 1988-90, bd. mem. consortium on legal svcs. and pub. 1987-91, mem. disaster relief task force, bd. dirs., commr., chmn. ABA Commn. on Advt. 1988-91, adv. coun. ABA Commn. Responsibility 1999—), Pa. Bar Assn. (pres. 1985-86, bd. dirs. 1983-90, chair Governance Com., 1996-98), Phila. Bar Found. (pres. 1981), Phila. Bar Assn. (v.p. 1978, pres.-elect 1979, chancellor 1980, sec. 1975-78, trustee 1979—), Pa. Bar Trust (life mem., chmn. 1993-2001, chmn. emeritus 2001—), Pa. House of Dels. (life; chair governance com. 1996-98), Nat. Met. Bar Leaders (founder, pres. 1979-82, pres. emeritus 1983—), Nat. Conf. Bar Pres. (exec. coun. 1981-84), Phila. C. of C. (bd. dirs. 1980-83). Republican. Jewish. Avocations: golf, sailing. Office: Christie Pabarue Mortensen & Young 1880 JFK Blvd Fl 10 Philadelphia PA 19103-7424 Home: 110 S Somerset Ave Ventnor City NJ 08406 Office Phone: 215-587-1692. Business E-Mail: jebogutz@cmpy.com.

BOGY, DAVID B(EAUREGARD), mechanical engineering educator; b. Wabbaseka, Ark., June 4, 1936; s. Jesse C. and Dorothy (Duff) B.; m. Patricia Lynn Pizzitola, Mar. 28, 1961; children: Susan, Rebecca. BS, Rice U., 1959, MS, 1961; PhD, Brown U., 1966. Mech. engr. Shell Devel. Co., Houston, 1961-63; asst. prof. mech. engring. U. Calif., Berkeley, 1967-70, assoc. prof., 1970-75, prof., 1975—, chmn. dept. mech. engring., 1991-99, founder, dir. computer mechanics lab., William S. Floyd, Jr. Disting. prof., 1993—. Cons. IBM Rsch., 1972-83 Contbr. some 300 articles to profl. jours. Served with C.E. U.S. Army, 1961-62. Fellow ASME, IEEE; mem. NAE. Achievements include research in static and dynamic elasticity, fluid jets and mechanics of computer disk files and printers. Home: 8531 Buckingham Dr El Cerrito CA 94530-2533 Office: U Calif 6103 Etcheverry Hall Berkeley CA 94720-1740

BOHAKEL, CHARLES ANTHONY, history professor, researcher; s. Charles Richard and Josephine Kathryn Bohakel. AA, Diablo Valley Coll., Concord, Calif., 1964; BA, San Francisco State U., 1966; MA, Holy Names Coll., Oakland, Calif., 1976. History instr. Brentwood (Calif.) Sch. Dist., 1967—81, Antioch (Calif.) Sch. Dist., 1981—2000, Los Medanos Coll., Pittsburg, Calif., 1982—. Edn. dir. Antioch Hist. Soc., 1998—2005, dir. rsch., 2001—05; pres. East Diablo Hist. Soc., Antioch, 2001—05. Author: History of Empire Mine, Indians of Contra Costa County, 1977, Historic Tales of East Contra Costa County. Recipient Nat. Schoolmen medal, Freedoms Found., 1977. Mem.: Conf. Calif. Hist. Socs., Am. Hist. Assn., Calif. Hist. Soc. (Galland award 1990). Democrat. Roman Catholic. Avocations: photography, freelance writing, botany, nature studies. Office: Los Medanos Coll 2700 E Leland Rd Pittsburg CA 94563 Office Phone: 925-439-2181 ext. 832. E-mail: cbohakel@losmedanos.edu.

BOHAM, KENNETH ARNOLD, academic administrator; b. Lake Forest, Ill., Mar. 27, 1955; s. Ora Conard Boham Jr. and Gertrude (Hughes) Outland; m. Betty Drew Crowder, June 9, 1984; children: Stephen Drew, Chelsea Hughes. BS, East Carolina U., Greenville, N.C., 1973-77; MEd, N.C. State U., 1982, EdD, 1988. Edn. specialist N.C. Dept. Correction, Raleigh, 1977-78; Northampton County continuing edn. coord. Halifax C.C., Weldon, N.C., 1978-82; dean extension and community svcs. Wake Tech. C.C., Raleigh, 1984-87, assoc. v.p. continuing edn., 1987-89, v.p. continuing edn., 1989-95; interim pres. Mayland C.C., 1994; pres. Caldwell C.C. and Tech. Inst., Hudson, N.C., 1995—. Mem. N.C. C.C. Adult Educators Assn. (treas. 1987-88, bd. dirs. 1988-91, pres. elect 1991-92, pres. 1992-93). Avocations: travel, reading, crafts, golf. Office: Caldwell CC and Tech Inst 2855 Hickory Blvd Hudson NC 28638-2672

BOHAN, GLORIA, travel company executive; BA, Marymount Manhattan Coll., LLD with hon., 2003. With Forbes Mag.; pres. Omega World Travel, Fairfax, Va., 1972—. Bd. dirs. Am. Bus. Conf., Greater Washington Bd. Trade, Va. C. of C. With Race for the Cure, Suited for Change, Leukemia Lymphoma Soc., Salvation Army; bd. mem. Fairfax County Edn. Found, Enterprising Women Mag, C. of C., Va. Found. Independent Coll. Recipient Woman Yr., Network Entrepreneurial Women, 1990, Entrepreneurial Visionary award, 2003; named Businesswoman of Yr., Office Depot, 2004; named to Enterprising Women of Yr. Hall Fame, 2005. Mem. Nat. Assn. Women Bus. Owners, Am. Soc. Travel Agts. (Travel Agt. of Yr. award 2004), Soc. Govt. Travel Profls. (pres. 1986-87). Office: Omega World Travel Inc 3102 Omega Office Park Fairfax VA 22031-2400 Fax: 703-350-8880. Office Phone: 703-359-0200. E-mail: gbohan@owt.net.

BOHAN, THOMAS LYNCH, physicist, lawyer; b. Terre Haute, Ind., Feb. 12, 1938; s. Richard Timothy and Anna Elizabeth (Lynch) Bohan; m. Linda Ann Sian, Nov. 26, 1960 (div. Dec. 1981); children: Richard Michael, Cecilia Anne, John Charles; m. Rhonda Beth Berg, July 4, 1987. BS in Physics, U. Chgo., 1960; MS in Physics, U. Ill., 1964, PhD in Physics, 1968; JD, Franklin Pierce Law Ctr., 1980. Bar: Maine 1980, Mass. 1980, U.S. Dist. Ct. Maine 1980, U.S. Patent Office 1980, U.S. Ct. Appeals (1st cir.) 1992, U.S. Ct. Appeals (2nd cir.) 1994, U.S. Supreme Ct. 1996. Rsch. assoc. U. Ill., Urbana, 1968—69; asst. prof. physics Bowdoin Coll., Brunswick, Maine, 1969—76; assoc. Sunenblick, Fontaine and Reben, Portland, Maine, 1980—82; ptnr. Med. and Tech. Cons. (now MTC Forensics), Portland, 1982—86, sole propr., 1986—; propr. Thomas L. Bohan & Assoc., Portland, 1985—2001, Bohan Mathers, Portland, 2002, of counsel, 2003—. Mem. Forensic Scientific Accreditation Bd., 2005—; edit. bd. Jour. Forensic Scis., 2005—. Editor (with A. Damask): Forensic Accident Investigation: Motor Vehicles-1, 1995; editor: Forensic Accident Investigation: Motor Vehicles-2, 1997; contbr. articles to profl. jours.; mem. editl. bd.: Jour. Forensic Scis., 2005—. Chmn. Community Devel. Com., Brunswick, 1976—78; organizer, treas., pres. Peaks Island Land Preserve, Inc., 1994—97. Fellow, Tex. Instruments, 1965; Rsch. grantee, Am. Heart Assn., 1970—76, The Rsch. Corp., 1972—74, NSF/NATO, 1967, Fulbright scholar, Peru, 1972—73. Fellow: Am. Acad. Forensic Sci. (chair engrng. sci. sect. 1997—98, bd. dirs. 1999—2005, exec. com. bd. dirs. 2000—05, v.p. 2005—); mem.: AAAS, Forensic Specialties Accreditation Bd. (bd. dirs. 2005—), Internat. Inst. Forensic Engring. Scis. (bd. dirs. 2005—), Maine Patent Practitioners Group, Maine Trial Lawyers Assn., Cumberland County Bar Assn., Am. Phys. Soc., Sigma Xi. Office: MTC Forensics 54 Pleasant Ave Peaks Island ME 04108-1188 also: Bohan Mathers PO Box 17707 Portland ME 04112-8707 Office Phone: 207-773-3132, 207-766-5184. Business E-Mail: tbohan2@maine.rr.com, tlb@mtcforensics.com, tlb@bohanmathers.com.

BOHANAN, DAVID JOHN, management consultant; b. Utica, NY, Dec. 13, 1946; s. Clifton Ralph and Florence Susan Bohanan; m. Judith Ann Petrocci, July 31, 1977; children: Luke, Jacob. BFA in Ceramics and Painting, Alfred U., 1968; BS in Commerce, U. Md., 1979; MBA in Mgmt., Boston U., 1981. Pub. R&R in the Med Mediterranean Pubs. Srl., Vicenza, Italy, 1974-81; pvt. practice fin. cons. Jersey City, 1981-86; bus. cons. S&B Practice Mgmt. Assocs., Greenbrook, N.J., 1986—; fin. planner Fin. Found., Inc., Greenbrook, N.J., 1986-98. Rep. Nathan & Lewis Securities, Inc., N.Y.C., 1982-93, Cadaret, Grant & Co., Syracuse, N.Y., 1994-2000, Nat. Planning Corp., 2001—. Capt. F.A., U.S. Army, 1968-74. Decorated Bronze Star with oak leaf cluster. Republican. Home: 10 Saw Mill Rd Lebanon NJ 08833-4618 Office: S&B Practice Mgmt Assocs 314 Us Highway 22 Green Brook NJ 08812-1700 E-mail: dave@bohanan.com.

BOHANNAN, LILLIAN MURIEL, elementary school educator; d. Frederick Bryant and Margaret Kathleen Elwell; m. Jesse Earl Bohannan, Dec. 15, 1979; m. Doyle Wheat, Jan. 22, 1966 (div.); children: Donna Rose Matthews, Melvin Ray Wheat, Steven Earl, Sharon Renee Kincaid. BA, Calif. Bapt. U., 1966; D in Christian Ministries, Salt Lake Bapt. Coll., 1998. Cert. tchr. Calif., 1966, Nev., 1967, Tex., 1975. Tchr. Humboldt County Sch. Dist., Winnemucca, Nev., 1966—67, Jurupa Unified Sch. Dist., Rubidoux, Calif., 1967—75, Big Spring Ind. Sch. Dist., Tex., 1975—81; prin. Sand Springs Christian Sch., Big Spring, Tex., 1982—83; supr./prin. Hillcrest Christian Sch., Big Spring, Tex., 1983—89; adminstr. Maranatha Bapt. Acad., Big Spring, Tex., 1989—. GED instr. Howard Coll., Big Spring, Tex., 1975—90; computer cons. Maranatha Bapt. Acad., Big Spring, Tex., 1999—; computer instr. Sr. Citizen's Ctr., Big Spring, Tex., 2000—02. Author: (short story collection) Let God's Creation Speak, (novel: historical christian romance) Beatrice Snell Smith, (short story collection ii) Let God's Critters Speak. Ch. leader East Side Bapt. Ch., Big Spring, Tex., 1990—2004. Mem.: Friends of Libr. Republican. Baptist. Avocation: writer of children's stories. Personal E-mail: lesslillys@crcom.net.

BOHANNAN, PAUL JAMES, anthropologist, retired dean, writer; b. Lincoln, Nebr., Mar. 5, 1920; s. Hillory and Hazel (Truex) B.; m. Laura Marie Smith, May 15, 1943 (div. 1975); 1 child, Denis Michael; m. Adelyse D'Arcy, Feb. 28, 1981. BA, U. Ariz., 1947; B.Sc., Oxford U., Eng., 1949, DPhil, 1951. Lectr. social anthropology Oxford (Eng.) U., 1951-56; asst. prof. anthropology Princeton (N.J.) U., 1956-59; prof. Northwestern U., Evanston, Ill., 1959-75, U. Calif., Santa Barbara, 1976-82; prof., dean social scis. and communications U. So. Calif., Los Angeles, 1982-87, prof. emeritus, 1987—. Author: Justice and Judgement, 1957, Africa and Africans, 1964, 4th edit., 1995, Divorce and After, 1970, We, the Alien, 1991, How Culture Works, 1995. Served to capt. U.S. Army, 1941-45. Decorated Legion of Merit; Rhodes scholar. Mem. Am. Anthrop. Assn. (pres. 1979-80), Am. Ethnol. Soc. (dir. 1963-66), African Studies Assn. (pres. 1963-64), Social Sci. Research Council (dir. 1962-64) Personal E-mail: paulboh@aol.com.

BOHANNON, CAMILLE, news anchor; b. Las Vegas, N.Mex., May 30, 1946; d. George W. Skora and Lillian Marie Guffey; m. James E. Bohannon, Sept. 26, 1970 (div. July 1987). BA, N.Mex. Highlands U., 1968. News anchor, asst. program dir. Clear Sight Cable TV, Las Vegas, 1967-68; classical music announcer Sta. WETA Radio, Washington, 1970-72; news anchor Sta. WTOP Radio, Washington, 1975-77, Sta. WRC Radio, Washington, 1977-80, WCFL Radio Chgo., 1980-83, UPI Radio Network, N.Y.C., 1983-84, Sta. WRC Radio, Washington, 1984-87, NBC/Mut. Radio Nets, Washington, 1987-92, AP Radio Network, Washington, 1992—. Ch. and choir mem. Covenant United Meth. Ch., Gaithersburg, Md., 1984—; mem. Gaithersburg Cmty. Chorus, 2000—. Recipient Best Newscast award Ill. AP Broadcasters, 1983, Outstanding Pub. Svc. Program award Chesapeake AP Broadcasters, 1987, Outstanding Spot News Reporting award, 1977. Mem. Soc. Profl. Journalists, Am. Women in Radio and TV (established multicoll. chpt. coll. students in broadcasting 1978-80). Methodist. Avocations: biking, sports viewing, reading, dogs. Office: AP Radio Network 1825 K St NW Washington DC 20006

BOHANNON, PAUL M., lawyer; b. Cushing, Okla., May 20, 1950; s. Marvin J. and Marscia (Hughes) Bohannon; m. Cynthia J. James, June 1, 1974; 1 child, Brenton. BA, Okla. State U., 1972; JD, So. Meth. U., 1975. Bar: Tex. 1975, N. Mex. 1976, admitted to practice: US Ct. Appeals (5th Cir.) 1975, US Ct. Appeals (10th Cir.) 1975, US Dist. Ct. (N. Mex.) 1976, US Dist. Ct. (We. Dist.) Tex. 1983, US Dist. Ct. (No. Dist.) Tex. 1983, US Dist. Ct. (So. Dist.) Tex., US Supreme Ct. Ptnr. Hinkle, Cox, Eaton, Coffield & Hensley, Roswell, N.Mex., 1975—83, Midland, Tex., 1983; ptnr., Environ. Practice Group Andrews Kurth LLP, The Woodlands, Tex. Mem.: State Bar N.Mex., N.Mex. Oil & Gas Assn. (founding chmn. environ. affairs com. 1988—91), State Bar Tex. (environ. law com.), Am. Arbitration Assn. (panel arbitrators), Am. Mgmt. Assn., ABA (water quality com. 1980, Environ. Law Sect.), Delta Theta Phi, Order of Coif. Democrat. Episcopalian. Office: Andrews Kurth LLP 10001 Woodloch Forest Dr Ste 200 The Woodlands TX 77380 Office Phone: 713-220-4193. Office Fax: 713-238-7180. Business E-Mail: pbohannon@andrewskurth.com.

BOHANNON, SARAH VIRGINIA, personnel professional; b. Roanoke, Va., Mar. 1, 1947; AA in Bus. Adminstrn. Mgmt., Nat. Bus. Coll., 1983. Pers. appointment clk. IRS, Richmond, Va., 1983—84; pers. technician Commonwealth of Va., Richmond, Va., 1985—97, pers. asst., 1997—98, pers. technician, 1999—2000, pers. adminstrv. specialist dept. human resource mgmt., 2001—02; human resources rep. City of Richmond, 2004. Mem. Am. Biog. Inst. (life, dep. gov. 1991, mem. women's inner circle of achievement 1991). Home: 2220 Clarke St Richmond VA 23228-6049

BOHANON, KATHLEEN SUE, neonatologist, educator; b. Mpls., 1951; BA summa cum laude, U. Minn., 1973, MD, 1977. Diplomate Am. Bd. Pediat., Am. Bd. Neonatal-Perinatal Medicine. Commd. 2d lt. USAF, 1973, advanced through grades to col., 1995; resident in pediats. Case Western Res. U., Cleve., 1977-80; gen. pediatrician USAF, 1980-85; fellow in neonatology Wilford Hall Med. Ctr., San Antonio, 1985-87; neonatologist, dir. neonatal ICU USAF Med. Ctr., Wright-Patterson AFB, Ohio, 1987-95, chmn. dept. pediat., 1995-98, chief med. staff, 1998-2000; ret., 2000; locum tenens neonatologist, 2001—03; staff neonatologist St. Mary's Hosp. and Med. Ctr., Grand Junction, Colo., 2004—. Asst. clin. prof. pediat. U. N.D. Sch. Medicine, Grand Forks, 1981-82; assoc. Wright State U. Sch. Medicine, Dayton, Ohio, 1987-2000, Uniformed Svc. U. Health Scis., Washington, 1988-2000; mem. com. Infant Bio-Ethics Com., Dayton, 1990-2000. Mem. Am. Acad. Pediat. Home: PO Box 6459 Colorado Springs CO 80934-6459

BOHARY, JAMES, artist; b. Bklyn., 1940; Visiting artist Parsons School of Fine Art, NYC, 1976; artist in residence Harry Lundeberg School of Seamanship, 1977; visiting artist Parsons School of Fine Art, Graduate School, NYC, 1980, New York Studio School, 1982, Parsons School of Fine Arts, Graduate School, NYC, 1982—83; adjunt lecturer Queens College, 1990; visiting artist Vermont Studio Center, 1991; artist in residence Dartmouth College, 1998; visiting artist, asst. prof., Painting SUNY, Purchase College, Purchase, NY, 1998; visting artist Vermont Studio Center, 1998; visiting artist Nova Scotia College of Art and Design, 1999; visiting assoc. prof. Dartmouth College, 2003—04. One-man shows include Hunter Mus., Chattanooga, Tenn., 1976, Benson Gallery, Bridgehampton, NY, 1977, Landmark Gallery, NYC, 1980, Allan Stone Gallery, 1984, 1986, Joan Prats Gallery, 1985, 1987, 1989, 1993, 1996, John Guggenheim Gallery, 1986, Elizabeth Harris Gallery, NYC, 1994, 1998, 2001, James Baird Gallery, St. John's NL Can., 2002, 2004, others, exhibited in group shows at NY Studio Sch., NYC, 1971, St. Peter's Gallery, 1972, Brata Gallery, 1972, 1973, Leo Castelli Gallery, 1976, Rensselaer Polytechnic Inst., Troy, NY, 1980, Gruenebaum Gallery, NYC, 1982, Am. Acad. and Inst. Arts and Letters, 1982, 1983, 1985, Galeria Joan Prats, Barcelona, Spain, 1984, 1986, Johnson Mus. Art Cornell U., Ithaca, NY, 1987, Phila. Mus. Art Gallery, Pa., 1988, Kouros Gallery, NYC, 1989, 1990, Benton Gallery, Southhampton, NY, 1992, Elizabeth Harris Gallery, NYC, 1993, 1995, 1999, Neuberger Mus. Art, Purchase, NY, 1998, U. Art Mus. SUNY, Binghamton, NY, 2000, Kaoshiung Mus. Fine Arts, Taiwan, 2001, J. Johnson Gallery, Jacksonville Beach, Fla., 2002, James Baird Gallery, St. John's NL, Can., 2003, Roberson Mus., Bighamton, NY, 2004, Nat. Acad. Desgin Mus., NYC, 2004, others, Represented in permanent collections Weatherspoon Art Ctr., Greensboro, NC, Valparaiso U. Mus. Art, Ind., Tyler Art Ctr., Oswego, NY, State U., Austin, Tex., Oppenheimer and Co., Seattle, North Bay Art Ctr., Can., Chem. Bank, NYC, Greenville Art Ctr., SC, Ind. U. Art Mus., Bloomington, others. Grantee, Nat. Endowment for Arts, 1983. Mem.: Nat. Acad. Design (Edwin Palmer Meml. Prize 1996, 2003). Address: c/o James Baird Gallery 221 Duckworth St St Johns Neufoundland Canada A1C 1G7*

BOHLE, SUE, public relations executive; b. Austin, Minn., June 23, 1943; d. Harold Raymond and Mary Theresa (Swanson) Hastings; m. John Bernard Bohle, June 22, 1974; children: Jason John, Christine K. BS in Journalism, Northwestern U., 1965, MS in Journalism, 1969. Tchr. pub. high schs, Englewood, Colo., 1965-68; account exec. Burson-Marsteller Pub. Relations, Los Angeles, 1969-73; v.p., mgr. pub. relations J. Walter Thompson Co., Los Angeles, 1973-79; founder, pres. The Bohle Company, L.A., 1979—; pres., CEO The Bohle Co., L.A.; former exec. v.p. Ketchum Pub. Rels., L.A. Free-lance writer, instr. communications Calif. State U. at Fullerton, 1972-73; instr. writing Los Angeles City Coll., 1975-76; lectr. U. So. Calif., 1979—. Contbr. articles to profl. jours. Dir. pub. rels. L.A. Jr. Ballet, 1971-72; pres. Panhellenic Advisers Coun., UCLA, 1972-73; mem. adv. bd. L.A. Valley Coll., 1974-75, Coll. Communications Pepperdine U., 1981-85, Sch. Journalism U. So. Calif., 1987-95, Calif. State U., Long Beach, 1988-93; bd. visitors Medill Sch. Journalism Northwestern U., 1984—. Recipient Alumni Svc. award Northwestern U., 1995; Univ. scholar, 1961-64, Panhellenic scholar, 1964-65; named to Hall of Achievement, Medill Sch. Journalism, 1997, charter mem. Hall of Fame; named to 50 Top Women in PR, PR Week, mag., 2001. Fellow Pub. Rels. Soc. Am. (bd. dirs. L.A. chpt. 1981-90, v.p. 1983, pres. 1989, del. nat. assembly 1980, 94, 95, 96, co-chmn. long-range strategic com. 1990, pres.'s adv. coun. 1991, exec. com. Counselors Acad. 1984-86, sec.-treas. 1990, chmn. 1992, sec. Coll. Fellows 1993, vice chair 1994, chmn. 1995, Silver Anvil award 1994); mem. Worldcom PR Network (bd. dirs. 2002—), World Com., Women in Comm., Shi-ai, Delta Zeta (editor The Lamp 1966-68, Woman of Yr. award 1993), Kappa Alpha Tau. Office: 1900 Avenue of the Stars # 200 Los Angeles CA 90067-4301 Office Phone: 310-785-0515 ext. 223. E-mail: sue@bohle.com.

BOHLENDER, HUGH DARROW, lawyer; b. Sacramento, Oct. 27, 1951; s. Hugh S. and Dorothy Elrene (Darrow) B.; m. Eliese Susanna Wagenseil, June 9, 1973 (div. Feb. 1982); children: Philip Edward, Karen Leslie; m. Ingrid Elizabeth Rieck, Dec. 27, 1997. BS, U.S. Mil. Acad., 1973; MA, Northwestern U., 1982, JD, 1986, postgrad. Bar: Ill. 1986, U.S. Dist. Ct. (no dist.) Ill. 1986. Commd. 2d lt. U.S. Army, 1975, advanced through grades to capt., 1977, resigned, 1981; lectr. Northwestern U., Evanston, Ill., 1984—85; assoc. Lord Bissell & Brook, Chgo., 1986—90; of counsel Allstate Ins. Co., 1990—. Dir. Ala. Ins. Guaranty Assn., 1992-93. Vice chmn. Northbrook (Ill.) Evang. Covenant Ch., 1988-91. Maj. USAR, 1986-93; ret. Mem. ABA, Ill. Bar Assn. Republican. Avocations: running, bicycling, camping, photography, computers. Office: Allstate Ins Co Allstate Plz N Northbrook IL 60062

BOHLINGER, JOHN C., lieutenant governor, former state legislator; b. Bozeman, Mont., Apr. 21, 1936; s. John and Aileen Bohlinger; m. Bette J. Bohlinger; 6 children. BA, U. Mont., 1959. Owner women's apparel store, 1961-92; mem. Mon. Ho. Reps. Dist. 14 & 94, 1993—98, Mont. State Senate, Dist. 7, Helena, 1998—2004; mem. local govt. com., pub. health, welfare and safety com.; mem. taxation com., vice chair ethics com.; lt. gov. State of Mont., 2005—. Past pres., chmn. bd. Yellowstone Arts Ctr.; bd. dirs. Billings Symphony Soc., St. Vincent de Paul Soc., Mont. State U. Billings Found., Yellowstone Treatment Ctr. Served with USMC, 1954-61. Mem. Billings Rotary Cub. Republican. Roman Catholic. Office: Office Lt Gov Capitol Station Rm 207 Helena MT 59620 Office Phone: 406-444-5665.

BOHM, HENRY VICTOR, physicist; b. Vienna, July 16, 1929; came to U.S., 1941, naturalized, 1946; s. Victor Charles and Gertrude (Rie) B.; m. Lucy Margaret Coons, Sept. 2, 1950 (dec. Oct. 2003); children: Victoria Rie, Jeffrey Ernst Thompson. AB, Harvard U., 1950; MS, U. Ill., 1951; PhD, Brown U., 1958. Jr. physicist GE, 1951, 53-54; teaching, research asst. Brown U., 1954-58, research assoc., summer 1958; staff mem. Arthur D. Little, Inc., Cambridge, Mass., 1958-59; asso. prof. physics dept. Wayne State U., Detroit, 1959-64, acting chmn. physics dept., 1962-63, prof., 1964-93, prof. emeritus Detroit, 1993—, v.p. for grad. studies and research, 1968-71, v.p. for spl. projects, 1971-72, provost, 1972-75, on leave, 1978-83, interim dean Coll. Liberal Arts, 1984-86; pres. Argonne Univs. Assn., 1978-83. Vis. prof. Cornell U., 1966-67, U. Lancaster, Eng., summer 1967, Purdue U., winter, 1977, Rensselaer Poly. Inst., winter 1992; cons.-examiner commn. on instns. higher edn. N. Central Assn. Colls. and Schs., 1971-80, mem. commn., 1974-78 Bd. dirs. Center for Research Libraries, Chgo, 1970-75, chmn., 1973; bd. overseers Lewis Coll., Ill. Inst. Tech., 1980-83. Ltjg. USNR, 1951—53. Fellow Am. Phys. Soc. Home: 39732 Eagle Trace Dr Northville MI 48167

BOHM, RICHARD D., lawyer; b. Apr. 8, 1953; BA, Stanford U., 1975; JD, Harvard U., 1978. Assoc. Debevoise & Plimpton LLP, NYC, 1978—86, ptnr., 1986—, co-head Media & Tech. and Private Equity Groups, mem. Mergers & Acquisitions and Securities Groups. Mem.: ABA, Assn. Bar City NY. Office: Debevoise & Plimpton LLP 919 Third Ave New York NY 10022 Office Phone: 212-909-6226. E-mail: rdbohm@debevoise.com.

BOHMAN, RAYNARD FREDERICK, JR., transportation executive, consultant, professional society administrator; b. Boston, July 31, 1933; s. Raynard Frederick Bohman Sr. and Theresa Dorothea Conlon; m. Douglas Ann Watson Boutin, Sept. 24, 1955; children: David John, Jack Duncan, Andrew Mackenzie. BS in Econs., U. Pa., 1955. Pres. Nat. Furniture Traffic Conf., Gardner, 1962-95, Bohman Indsl. Traffic Consultants, Gardner, Mass., 1965—; mng. dir. Internat. Furniture Transp. and Logistics Coun., Gardner, 2000—. Transp. cons. Toy Industry Assn., N.Y.C., 1955—, Nat. Sch. Supply and Equipment Assn., Silver Spring, Md., 1968—, Outdoor Power Equipment Inst., Alexandria, Va., 1970—, Craft and Hobby Assn., Elmwood Park, N.J., 1970—, others. Author: Guide to Freight Classification, 1968; editor: (manual) Furniture Packaging, 1955—, Bohman Traffic News Summary newsletter, 1972—, other newsletters; lead columnist Reed's Logistics Mgmt. mag., 1987—. 1st lt. U.S. Army, 1955-63. Recipient Order of Anthony Wayne, Valley Forge Mil. Acad., Wayne, Pa., 1951, award Nat. Def. Transp. Assn., Washington, 1955; named Transp. Columnist of Yr., Transp. Claim Prevention Coun., Northport, N.Y., 1995, Transp. Cons. of Yr., Transp. Consumer Protection Coun., Huntington, N.Y., 1999. Mem.: Eastward Ho! Country Club (bd. govs. 1968—74). Republican. Episcopalian. Avocations: travel, golf, stamp collecting/philately. Home and Office: 27 Bay Ln Chatham MA 02633 Office Phone: 508-945-2272.

BOHME, DIETHARD KURT, chemistry professor; b. Boston, June 20, 1941; s. Kurt F. and Maria (Kiesel) B. B.Sc., McGill U., 1962, PhD, 1965. Asst. prof. dept. chemistry York U., Toronto, 1970-74, assoc. prof., 1974-77, prof. chemistry, 1977—, disting. rsch. prof. chemistry, 1994—, dir. grad. program in chemistry, 1979-85, chmn. dept. chemistry, 1985—90, 2000—03, Can. rsch. chair in phys. chemistry tier 1, 2001; mem. chemistry grant selection com. Nat. Scis. and Engring. Rsch. Coun. of Can., Ottawa, 1983-86. Contbr. articles to profl. jours. NAS-NRC postdoctoral rsch. assoc., 1965-67; A.P. Sloan fellow, 1974, sr. scientist vis. fellow U. Warwick, Eng., 1978, Killam rsch. fellow, 1991-93; recipient Rutherford Meml. medal in chemistry Royal Soc. Can., 1981, A.v. Humboldt rsch. award, 1990, 99, John C. Polanyi award in Phys. and Theoretical Chemistry, 1998, Fred P. Lossing award in mass spectrometry Can. Soc. for Mass Spectrometry, 2002. Fellow Royal Soc. Can., Chem. Inst. Can. (phys. chemistry divsn. exec. 1980-83, Noranda lectr. in phys. chemistry 1983); mem. Am. Soc. Mass Spectrometry, Am. Chem. Soc. Home: 38 Alberta Dr Concord ON Canada L4K 4X5 Office: York U Dept Chemistry 4700 Keele St Toronto ON Canada M3J 1P3 Office Phone: 416-736-2100 ext 66188. E-mail: dkbohme@yorku.ca.

BOHMONT, DALE WENDELL, agricultural consultant; b. Wheatland, Wyo., June 7, 1922; s. J.E. and Mary (Armann) B.; m. Marilyn J. Horn, Mar. 7, 1969; children: Dennis E., Craig W. BS, U. Wyo., 1948, MS, 1950; PhD, U. Nebr., 1952; MPA, Harvard U., 1959. Registered investment adv., SEC. Pub. sch. tchr., Rock River, Wyo., 1941-42; from rsch. asst. to head plant scis. U. Wyo., 1946-60; assoc. dir. expt. sta. Colo. State U., 1961-63; dean, dir. agr. U. Nev., Reno, 1963-82, dean, dir. emeritus, 1982—; pres. Bohmont Cons. Inc., 1982—; mem. Brucheum Group, Waynesboro, Va., 1984; chief cons. Zygro Corp., 1999. Cons. Devel. & Resources Corp., N.Y.C., 1968—, Fredriksen, Kamine & Assocs., Sacramento, 1976, Nev. Agrl. Found., 1986—; pres. Enide Corp., Reno, 1974-80, Thermal Dynamics Internat., 1983-87, Cryabis, Inc., Reno, 1993-95; co-chmn. rsch. planning West Divsn. Agr. Expt. Stas., 1975; mem. exec. com., coun. adminstrv. heads agr. Nat. Assn. State Univ. Land Grant Colls., 1975. Author: Golden Years of Agriculture in Nevada, 1989; contbr. articles to profl. jours.; mem. editl. bd.: Crops and Soils, 1962-. Pres. Dale W. and Marilyn Horn Found., 1998—. Served with USAAF, 1942-45. Fellow AAAS, Agronomy Soc.; mem. Western Soc. Weed Scis. (hon.), Western Crop Sci. Soc. (pres. 1962-63), Nat. Expt. Sta. Dirs. Assn. (chmn. 1967-68), Am. Range Mgmt. Soc., Farm House (dir. 1962-), Weed Soc. Am. (hon.), Sigma Xi, Gamma Sigma Delta (pres. 1964-66), Alpha Zeta, Alpha Tau Alpha, Phi Kappa Phi., Lions (v.p. 1985-86, pres. 1986-87, bd. dirs. 1985-). Home: 525 Court St Reno NV 89501 Personal E-mail: bohconslt@aol.com. *There is nothing that has been done that could not have been done better; therefore, there is always room for improvement and always room at the top.*

BOHN, CHARLOTTE GALITZ, retired real estate executive; b. Chgo, Aug. 7, 1930; d. Chester Charles and Sarah Madelyn (McCarthy) B; m. Robert Allan Galitz, Nov. 25, 1955; children: Charles Robert, Thomas Allan, Madelyn Clare, (div. Sept. 1965). Student, Northwestern U., 1955, City Coll., Chgo., 1989. Lic. real estate salesperson, N.C. Lab. tech. Kraft Foods Rsch. Lab., Glenview, Ill., 1950-56; researcher data processing control Kemper Ins. Co., Chgo., 1967-70; jr. acct. Tractor Supply Co., Chgo., 1970-75; real estate salesman MGM Realty Co., Chgo., 1975-81, 85-88, Prime Realty, 1989-98; broker Bohn Real Estate Agy, Raleigh, NC, 1981-85; founder, pres. Pvt. Rsch., Chgo., 1985; ret., 1998. Researcher zoning map City of Raleigh, 1980-81; bd. dir. Off-Campus Writers Workshop. Contbr. various rsch. projects and sci. proposals. Vol. Chgo. Boys' Club; treas. churchwomen of St. Mary's, Crystal Lake, Ill.; vol. lifeguard Easter Seal Soc.-Multiple Sclerosis, Raleigh, 1983-84, PTA, 1967-77; bd. dir. Off-Campus Writer's Workshop; chair grammar sch. 50th reunion, 1994; scholarship judge Mensa, Chgo., 1995, 96, 99; nominating com., Chgo. Cath. U. Club, 2003. Recipient Adviser Emblem of Merit award Jr. Achievement, 1955. Mem. AAAS, Smithsonian Inst. (assoc.), Nat. Trust Hist. Preservation, Raleigh C. of C., Jaycee Aux. (restaurant mgr.), Chgo. N. Side Realty Bd., Nat. Geog. Soc., Wilson Ctr. Assn., Mensa (nominating), Am. Assn. Ret. Persons, Irish Am. Heritage Ctr., Libr. Congress (assoc. charter), Chgo. Cath. U. Club, Nominated, 2003-2004. Roman Catholic. Avocations: textiles, sports, antiques, music, poetry. Home and Office: Private Rsch 6126 W Roscoe St Chicago IL 60634-4145

BOHN, DENNIS ALLEN, electrical engineer, executive; b. Oct. 5, 1942; s. Raymond Virgil and Iris Elouise (Johnson) Bohn; m. Patricia Tolle, Aug. 12, 1986; 1 child, Kira Michelle. BSEE with honors, U. Calif., Berkeley, 1972, MSEE with honors, 1974. Engring. technician GE Co., San Leandro, Calif., 1964—72; R & D engr. Hewlett-Packard Co., Santa Clara, Calif., 1973; application engr. Nat. Semicondr. Corp., Santa Clara, 1974—76; engring. mgr. Phase Linear Corp., Lynnwood, Wash., 1976—82; v.p. R & D, ptnr. Rane Corp., Mukilteo, Wash., 1982—; founder Toleco Systems, Kingston, Wash., 1980. Editor: We Are Not Just Daffodils, 1975; contbr. poetry to Reason mag.; tech. editor Audio Handbook, 1976; contbr. articles to tech. jours.; columnist Polyphony mag., 1981—83. Suicide and crisis ctr. vol., Berkeley, 1972—74, Santa Clara, 1974—76. Served with USAF, 1960—64. Recipient Am. Spirit Honor medal, USAF, 1961, Math. Achievement award, Chem. Rubber Co., 1962—63. Mem.: IEEE, Audio Engring. Soc., Tau Beta Pi. Achievements include patents in field of 3. Office: Rane Corp 10802 47th Ave W Mukilteo WA 98275-5098 Business E-Mail: dennisb@rane.com.

BOHN, HENNING, economist, educator; b. Frankfurt, Germany, Aug. 10, 1960; came to the U.S., 1982; s. Lothar and Marianne Bohn; m. Oda Bittel, Aug. 20, 1983; children: Timon, Samantha, Christopher, Angelina, Eliana. PhD, Stanford U., 1986. Asst. prof. fin. U. Pa., Phila., 1986-92; assoc. prof. econs. U. Calif., Santa Barbara, 1992-96, prof. econs., 1996—. Contbr. articles to profl. jours. Mem. Am. Econs. Assn., Econometrics Soc. Avocation: travel. Office: U Calif Dept Econs Santa Barbara CA 93106 E-mail: bohn@econ.ucsb.edu.

BOHN, JAMES MATTHEW, video editor, educator; b. Manitowoc, Wis., Mar. 7, 1970; s. Lawrence Lee and Mary Ellen Bohn. BMus, U. Wis., 1992; MMus, U. Ill., 1993, PhD in Mus. Arts, 1997. Coord., labs. and web. svcs. Ill. State U., Normal, 1997—99; vis. lectr. U. Mass., Dartmouth, 1999—2004. Guest artist 7-11 Festival, Urbana, Ill., 2001, Most Significant Bytes, Alliance, Ohio, 2002. Composer: Hardguy for Trumpet and Tape, 2001, How Was It We Were Caught?, 2001, tOiZe for 3 Toy Pianos and Tape, 2002, (DVD) All fOMENgs, 2003. Mem.: ASCAP, Am. Composers Forum, Soc. Composers Inc. Avocations: home improvement, videography, computer-assisted composition. Office Phone: 508-999-2308. E-mail: jbohn@bohnmedia.com.

BOHN, MARSHA J., anthropologist, researcher; d. David M. and Evelyn H. Kipley; m. Fred Bohn, Feb. 7, 1970; children: Jeffrey, Marcus, Rochelle. AA, Saddleback Coll., Mission Viejo, Calif., 1993; student, Oxford (England) U., 1993; BS in Social Anthropology, London Sch. Econs. and Polit. Sci., 1996; MA in Med. Anthropology, Sch. Oriental and African Studies, London, 1998; postgrad., Ariz. State U., 2002—. Exec. asst. Nichols Inst. Diagnostics, San Juan Capistrano, Calif., 1989—92, Airparks Internat., San Juan Capistrano; rsch. cons. Capital Oil & Gas Ltd., London. Fellow: Am. Anthrop. Assn., Royal Anthrop. Soc.; mem.: Wellcome Inst., Med. Anthropology Assn., Alumni Assn. Sch. Oriental and African Studies, Alumni Assn. London Sch. Econs. and Polit. Sci., Alumni Assn. Saddleback Coll., Mus. Mankind, London, Honor Soc. Saddleback Coll., Alpha Gamma Sigma. Personal E-mail: marshabohn-alumni@lse.ac.uk.

BOHN, RALPH CARL, educational consultant; b. Detroit, Feb. 19, 1930; s. Carl and Bertha (Abrams) B.; m. Adella Stanul, Sept. 2, 1950 (dec.); children: Cheryl Ann, Jeffrey Ralph; m. JoAnn Olvera Butler, Feb. 19, 1977 (div. 1990); stepchildren: Kathryn J., Kimberly J., Gregory E.; m. Mariko Tajima, Jan. 27, 1991; 1 child, Thomas Carl; 1 stepchild, Daichi Tajima. BS, Wayne State U., 1951, EdM, 1954, EdD, 1957. Instr. part-time Wayne State U., 1954-55, summer 1956; faculty San Jose (Calif.) State U., 1955-92, prof. div. tech., 1961-92, chmn. dept. indsl. studies, 1960-69, assoc. dean ednl. svc., 1968-70, dean continuing edn., 1970-92, prof. emeritus, 1992—; cons. Calif. State U. Sys., 1992—; cons. quality edn. sys. USAF, 1992-2000; dir. nat. program on non-collegiate sponsored instrn. Calif. State Univ. Sys., 1995—2000, Calif. State U. Inst., 1997—99; pres. Univ. Cons., 1994—. Guest faculty Colo. State Coll., 1963, Ariz. State U., 1966, U. P.R., 1967, 74, So. Ill. U., 1970, Oreg. State U., 1971, Utah State U., 1973, Va. Poly. Inst. & State U., 1973, U. Idaho, 1978; cons. U.S. Office Edn., 1965-70, Calif. Pub. Schs., 1960, Nat. Assessment Ednl. Progress, 1968-79, ednl. div. Philco-Ford Corp., 1970-73, Am. Inst. Rsch., 1969-83, Far West Labs for Ednl. Rsch. Devel., 1971-86; adv. bd. Ctr. for Vocat. and Tech. Edn., Ohio State U., 1968-74; dir. project Vocat. Edn. Act, 1965-67, NDEA, 1967, 68; co-dir. Project Edn. Profession Devel. Act, 1969, 70; mem. commn. coll. and univ. contracts Western Assn. Schs. and Colls, 1976-78, chmn. spl. com. on off-campus instrn. and continuing edn., 1978-88; chmn. continuing edn. accreditation visit U. Santa Clara, 1976; chmn. accreditation team Nellis AFB, Nev., 1992, 2002, U. Nev., Las Vegas, 2000, Nat. U., 2000, Oreg. State U., 2001, Golden Gate U., 2001; chmn. accreditation team to Yokusaka Naval Sta., Japan, 2000, Atsugi Naval Air Facility, Japan, 2000, Yokota Air Base, Japan, 2000, Camp Pendleton Marine Corps Base, 2001, Naval Air Sta., Lamoore, 2002, Dyess AFB, 2003, Twentynine Palms Marine Corps. Base, Calif., 2003, eArmyU web-based degree programs U.S. Army, Washington, 2004, Camp Zama, Army, Tokyo, 2004, Iwakuni Marine Corps Air Sta., Japan, 2005, Osan AFB, Korea, 2005, Junsan AFB, Korea, 2005, Scott AFB, Ill., 2005, Offutt AFB, Nebr., 2005, others; sr. cons. Global Partnership Devel. Calif. State U. Sys., 2000-03. Author: (with G.H. Silvius) Organizing Course Materials for Industrial Education, 1961, Planning and Organizing Instruction, 1976; (with A. MacDonald) Power-Mechanics of Energy Control, 1970, 2d edit., 1983, The McKnight Power Experimenter, 1970, Power and Energy Technology, 1989, Energy Technology: Power and Transportation, 1992; (with others) Basic Industrial Arts and Power Mechanics, 1978, Technology and Society: Interfaces with Industrial Arts, 1980, Fundamentals of Safety Education, 3d edit., 1981, Energy, Power and Transportation Technology, 1986; (with A. MacDonald) Energy Technology, Power and Transportation, 1991; editor (with Ralph Norman) Graduate Study in Industrial Arts, 1961; indsl. arts editor Am. Vocat. Jour., 1963-66; editor Jour. Indsl. Tchr. Edn., 1962-64. Lt. (j.g.) USCGR, 1951-53, capt. Res. ret. Recipient award Am. Legion, 1945; Wayne State U. scholar, 1953. Mem. NEA, Nat. Assn. Indsl. Tech. (bd. accreditation), Am. Indsl. Arts. Assn. (pres. 1967-68, Ship's citation 1971), Am. Coun. Indsl. Art Tchrs. Edn. (pres. 1964-66, Man of Yr. award 1967), Nat. Univ. Continuing Edn. Assn. (chair accreditation com. 1988-91), Nat. Assn. Indsl. Tchr. Educators (past v.p.), Calif. Indsl. Edn. Assn. (State Ship's citation 1971), Am. Drive Edn. Assn., Nat. Fluid Power Soc., Am. Vocat. Assn. (svc. awards 1966, 67), N.Am. Assn. for Summer Sessions (v.p. western region 1976-78), Luth. Acad. Scholarship, Calif. Employees Assn. (pres. San Jose State Coll. chpt. 1966-67), Western Assn. Summer Session Adminstrs. (newsletter editor 1970-73, pres. 1974-75), Calif. C. of C. (edn. com 1969-77), Industry-Edn. Coun. Calif. (bd. dirs. 1974-80), Sci. and Human Values, Inc. (bd. dirs. 1974-2003, chmn. bd. 1976-2002), Tahoe Tavern (bd. dirs. 1987-91, chmn. bd. 1988-90), Seascape Lagoon Homeowners Assn. (bd. dirs. 1988-95, chmn. 1989-95), Nat. Gold Key Honors Soc. (hon. life). Home and Office: 713 Clubhouse Dr Aptos CA 95003-5431 Personal E-mail: rmbohn@cruzio.com.

BOHN, ROBERT G., transportation company executive; Dir. ops. European automotive group Johnson Controls; v.p. ops. Oshkosh (Wis.) Truck Corp., 1992—94, pres., COO, 1994-97, pres., CEO, 1997—, chmn. bd., 2000—. Bd. dir. Graco Inc. Office: Oshkosh Truck Corp 2307 Oregon St Oshkosh WI 54902*

BOHN, ROBERT HERBERT, lawyer; b. Austin, Tex., Sept. 2, 1935; s. Herbert and Alice B.; m. Gay P. Maloy, June 4, 1957; children: Rebecca Shoemaker, Katherine Bernat, Robert H., Jr. BBA, U. Tex., 1957, LLB, 1963. Bar: Tex. 1963, Calif. 1965. Ptnr. Boccardo Law Firm, San Jose, Calif., 1965-87, Alexander & Bohn, San Jose, 1987-91; Bohn, Bennion & Niland, 1992-97; Bohn & Bohn, 1998—. Spkr. Calif. Continuing Edn. of Bar; judge pro tem Superior Ct. of Calif., San Jose, 1975-96. Mem. ATLA, Am. Coll. Master Barristers and Advs., Consumer Attys. Calif., Am. Bd. Trial Advocates, Santa Clara County Bar Assn., Calif. State Bar Assn., Santa Clara County Trial Lawyers Assn. (pres. 1999, Trial Lawyer of Yr. 2000), Trial Lawyers Pub. Justice, Roscoe Pound Found., Million Dollar Advocates Forum, Silicon Valley Capital Club, Commonwealth Club, Texas Cowboys Assn., Phi Gamma Delta. Office: 152 N 3rd St Ste 200 San Jose CA 95112-5515 E-mail: bbohn@bohnlaw.com.

BOHNEN, MICHAEL J., lawyer; b. Buffalo, 1947; m. Joyce B. Oppenheim, 1969; children: Sharon, Deborah. BA, Harvard U., 1968, JD, 1972. Bar: Mass. 1972. Assoc. Nutter, McClennen & Fish, LLP, Boston, 1972-80, ptnr., 1980—. Lectr. Boston U. Law Sch., 1981—2001. Co-author: Mass. Corporate Forms, 1990-2004. Pres. Solomon Schechter Day Sch., Newton, 1980—82; chmn. Jewish Coun. for Pub. Affairs, 2002—04; trustee United Jewish Cmtys., 1999—2005; pres. Jewish Cmty. Rels. Coun., Boston, 1991—93; chmn. Combined Jewish Philanthropies, 1993—95, Gann Acad., 1995—. Mem. Boston Bar Assn. (chmn. corp. law com. 1997-99). Home: 60 Nathan Rd Newton MA 02459-1105 Office: Nutter McClennen & Fish LLP World Trade Center West Boston MA 02210

BOHO, DAN L., lawyer; b. Chgo., Sept. 18, 1952; s. Lawrence M. and Genevieve A. (Zurek) Boho; m. Sheri L. Krisco, Sept. 10, 1977; children: Courtney, Ashely. BA, Loyola U., Chgo., 1974, JD, 1977. Bar: Ill. 1977, Fed. Trial Bar 1977. Sr. ptnr., group leader litig. group Hinshaw & Culbertson, Chgo., 1977—. Fellow: Am. Coll. Trial Lawyers; mem.: Chgo. Trial Lawyers Club (past pres.), Ill. Bar Assn. (past del. assembly), Advs. Soc., Ill. Def. Coun., Def. Rsch. Inst., Ill. Soc. Trial Lawyers (past bd. dirs.), Fedn. Ins. and Corp. Counsel (chmn. comml. law sect.), BOMA Chgo., Japan Am. Soc. (bd. dirs.), Polish Am. Assn. (past chmn. bd. dirs.), Heartland Alliance (bd. dirs.), Phi Alpha Delta (past pres. Webster chpt.). Avocations: travel, tennis, skiing. Office Phone: 312-704-3453. Business E-Mail: dboho@hinshawlaw.com.

BOHORQUEZ, FERNANDO AUGUSTO, surgeon; b. Bogota, Colombia, July 17, 1945; came to U.S., 1972; s. Saul and Graciela (Mahecha) B.; m. Olga Martinez, June 21, 1969; children: Fernando Jr., Alex, Mauricio, Michael. MD, U. Colombia, Bogota, 1970. Diplomate Am. Bd. Surgery. Intern Montfort Hosp., Villavicencio, Colombia, 1970-71; mem. staff St. Rafael Hosp., Ibague, Colombia, 1971-72; intern Community Hosp., Roanoke, Va., 1972-73; resident in gen. surgery St. Joseph Hosp., Towson, Md., 1973-78; mem. staff Provident Hosp., Balt., 1978-80; pvt. practice Balt., 1980—. Chmn. nutritional support com. St. Joseph Hosp., Towson, 1986—, mem. surg, attending staff; mem. surg, attending staff Franklin Sq. Hosps., Balt. Mem. ACS, Balt. County Med. Assn. (bd. dirs. 1990-91), Am. Soc. Parenteral and Enteral Nutrition, U.S.A. Colombian Med. Assn. Office: 7600 Osler Dr Ste 302 Towson MD 21204-7621 Office Phone: 410-296-3847. Personal E-mail: fbohorquez@comcast.net.

BOHRER, BRIAN E., music educator; b. Rochester, NY, Nov. 4, 1977; s. Edward R and Linda B Bohrer; m. Melissa N Merritt, Aug. 11, 2002; 1 child, Charles Shaun. BM in Music Edn. and Performance, Ithaca Coll., 1999; MM in Performance and Lit., Eastman Sch. Music, Rochester, NY, 2002. Cert. in music edn. NY, 2003. Tchr. Rush-Henrietta Ctrl. Sch. Dist., Henrietta, NY, 2001—. Ch. musician Asbury First United Meth. Ch., Rochester, NY, 2000—05. Mem.: NYSSMA. Methodist. Home: 239 Spencer Road Rochester NY 14609 Personal E-mail: tenorbri@hotmail.com.

BOHRMAN, DAVID ELLIS, television news producer; b. Hollywood, Calif., Apr. 30, 1954; s. Stanford Mervyn and Ardelle Joyce (Coleman) B.; m. Catherine Marie Leuchs, June 9, 1976; children— Amber Catherine, Harrison Zerr. B.A. in French, Stanford U., 1976, B.S. in Phys. Sci., 1976; M.S. in Journalism, Columbia U., 1978. Producer KNXT, CBS, Los Angeles, 1978-80; field producer ABC News Nightline, N.Y.C., 1980-81, sr. producer, 1981-82; sr. producer ABC World News Tonight, 1982-84, ABC Polit. Broadcasts and Spl. Events, 1984-88, exec. prodr. ABC News Interactive, 1988-91, creator, exec. prodr. World News Now, 1991-93, combined unit World News Now, World News This Morning, Good Morning America News, 1992-93; exec. prodr. spl. events NBC News, 1993—97, v.p. and exec. in charge of "Moneyline with Lou Dobbs" CNNfn, 1998-99, exec. v.p. CNNfn, 1999, CEO, Pseudo Programs, 2000-01, sr. exec. prodr. "NewsNight with Aaron Brown" CNN, 2001-2004, v.p. news and prodn./Washington Bur. Chief CNN, 2004- . Patentee in field. Recipient Emmy award Nat. Acad. TV Arts and Sci., 1982, 87, 92, 94. Golden Mike awards Radio TV News Assn., 1979, Los Angeles Press Club award, 1979, Valley Press Club award, Nat. Assn. Working Women award, 1979, Dupont, Peabody, Polk awards for Nightline, Mac World Superstacks award, 1989, 90, Mac User award, 1991, Christopher award, Arthur Ashe award, 1995. Avocation: computers.

BOHRNSTEDT, GEORGE WILLIAM, educational researcher; b. Arcadia, Wis., Sept. 28, 1938; s. Russell Gail and Agnes (Brecht) B.; m. Josephine Orlanda, Aug. 11, 1962 (div. 1973); children— Elizabeth (dec.), Brian, Matthew; m. Jennifer Lou Cain, Sept. 28, 1980; 1 child, Kassandra Student, Winona State Coll., 1956-58; BS, U. Wis., 1960, MA, 1963, PhD, 1966. Research assoc. U. Wis., Madison, 1966-69; assoc. prof. Mpls., 1969-73, chmn. dept. sociology, 1970-73; prof. Ind. U., Bloomington, 1973-88, chmn. dept. sociology, 1982-86, dir. Inst. Social Research, 1974-79; sr. v.p., dir. Am. Inst. for Rsch., Palo Alto, Calif., 1988-96, sr. v.p. for rsch., 1996—. Author: (with others) Statistics for Social Data Analysis, 3d edit., 1994; Basic Social Statistics, 1991; editor: Sociological Methodology, 1970; editor Sociol. Methods and Rsch., 1971-79, 84-87, Social Psychology Quar., 1980-82. Served to U.S. Army, 1962 Fellow NSF, 1963, NIMH, 1964-66, Ctr. for Advanced Studies in Behavioral Scis., 1986-87; Found. for Child Devel. Belding scholar, 1976-77 Mem. Am. Sociol. Assn., Psychometric Soc., Soc. Exptl. Social Psychologists Avocation: jazz. Office: Am Insts Rsch Behavioral Scis John C Flanagan Rsch Ctr 1791 Arastradero Rd Palo Alto CA 94304-1337 Home: 94 Clavel Ct Palm Desert CA 92260

BOHY, RIC, writer, commentator; b. Detroit, Sept. 8, 1951; s. Raymond Robert Bohy, Patty Jean Bohy; m. JoAnn DiMaggio; children: Nathan, Jordan. BA, U. Mich., 1973. Editor Hour Detroit mag., Royal Oak, Mich., 1997—2005; editl. dir. Hour Media L.L.C., Royal Oak, 2000—05; editor Metro Times, Detroit, 2005—. Commentator, editl. writer WDIV-TV, Detroit, 1994—2005. Home: 1614 Fairview Apt A Royal Oak MI 48073 Office: Metro Times 733 St Antoine St Detroit MI 48226 Office Phone: 313-202-8014. Office Fax: 313-961-6598. Business E-Mail: rbohy@metrotimes.com. E-mail: wordsdeeds@earthlink.net.

BOICE, CRAIG KENDALL, management consultant; b. Portland, Oreg., June 25, 1952; s. Charles A. and Audrey (Larson) B.; m. Jacinta E. Remedios, Nov. 21, 1979. BA summa cum laude, Beloit Coll., 1973; MA, Yale U., 1974, MPhil, 1976, M in Pub. and Pvt. Mgmt., 1979. Instr. fellow philosophy Yale U., New Haven, 1978-79; economist Overseas Pvt. Investment Corp., Washington, 1978; sr. cons. Coopers and Lybrand, Washington and London, 1979-81; v.p. ops. Internat. Licensing Network, NYC, 1981-82; pres., chmn., CEO Boice Dunham Group, NYC, 1983—. Adj. asst. prof. NYU, 1984-99. Cons. Lake Placid (NY) Olympic Organizing Com., 1979, New Haven Homesteading Program, 1979; chmn. edn. com. Automated Meter Reading Mem. Am. Mktg. Assn., Assn. Energy Engrs., Automated Meter Reading Assn., Computer and Automated Sys. Assn., Soc. Mfg. Engrs., Internat. Assn. Energy Econ., World Future Soc. Democrat. Office: Boice Dunham Group 30 W 13th St Apt 3C New York NY 10011-7988 E-mail: bdgbusdevl@msn.com.

BOICE, FRED, academic administrator; B in Econs., Occidental Coll.; postgrad., U. Ariz. Head Boice Fin. Co.; chmn. bd. dirs. Caseworks Mfg. Inc.; mem. Ariz. Bd. Regents, Phoenix. Past pres. Jr. Achievement; past chmn. Tucson Airport Authority, Tucson Med. Ctr., U. Ariz. Found.; mem. Tucson Met. C. of C.; bd. dirs. Cmty. Found. So. Ariz.; past pres. Ariz. Cattlegrowers' Assn. Office: Ariz Bd Regents Ste 230 2020 N Central Ave Phoenix AZ 85004

BOICE, JUDITH LYNETTE, physician, writer, educator; b. Toledo, Mar. 20, 1962; d. William Vincent and Martha Hibbert Boice; children: Vincent Boice-Washburn, Sebastian Boice-Washburn. BA, Oberlin Coll., 1984; D in Naturopathic Medicine, Nat. Coll. Naturopathic Medicine, 1994; M in Acupuncture and Oriental Medicine, Oreg. Coll. Oriental Medicine, 1996. Cert. naturopathic physician Oreg. Bd. Naturopathic Examiners, lic. acupuncturist Oreg. State Med. Bd., acupuncturist Colo. Staff physician Portland (Oreg.) Addictions Acupuncture Ctr., 1995—96; staff physician, lectr. Transitions for Health, Portland, 1996—98; pvt. practice Columbia River Wellness Ctr., Portland, Oreg., 1996—97, Portland, 1998—2000, Ancient Arts Healing Therapies, Montrose, Colo., 2001—02, Seven Winds Inst., Montrose, 2002—. Spkr., trainer U.S. Forest Svc., Portland, 1995; spkr. Nat. Wellness Inst., Stevens Point, WIS., 1997—2000, Ind. Pharmacy Alliance of Am., Inc, N.Y.C., 1998. Author: (book) At One With All Life: A Personal Journey in Gaian Communities, 1990, The Art of Daily Activism, 1992, The Pocket Guide to Naturopathic Medicine, 1996, "But My Doctor Never Told Me That!": Secrets for creating lifelong health, 1999; editor: Mother Earth: Through the Eyes of Women Photographers and Writers, 1992, Mother Earth Postcard Book, 1993, Mother Earth: Through the Eyes of Women Photographers and Writers, revised edition, 2002. Grantee, Mellon Found., 1984; scholar Vorheiss, U. Cin., 1980-81. Mem.: Nat. Coun. Cert. Acupuncture and Oriental Medicine (cert. acupuncture), Nat. Writers Union, Am. Assn. Naturopathic Physicians, Phi Beta Kappa. Avocations: gardening, photography, hiking, swimming, qigong. Home and Office: 1008 W Oak Grove Rd Montrose CO 81401 Office Phone: 970-252-0985. Personal E-mail: drjudith@drjudithboice.com. E-mail: wellnessdoc@earthlink.net.

BOICU, MIHAI, computer scientist, educator; b. Romania, 1970; m. Cristina E. Boicu. PhD in Info. Technology, George Mason U., 2002. Rsch. asst. prof. computer science, assoc. dir. Learning Ctr. George Mason U., Fairfax, Va., 2002—. Recipient Deployed Application award, Am. Assn. Artificial Intelligence, 2002, Centennial Coin of U.S. Army War Coll., Gen. Robert Ivany, 2002, cert. appreciation, U.S. Army War Coll., 2001, 2002, 2003. Christian Orthodox. Office: George Mason Univ CS Dept 4400 Univ Dr MSN 4A5 Fairfax VA 22030 Business E-Mail: mboicu@gmu.edu.

BOIES, DAVID, lawyer; b. Sycamore, Ill., Mar. 11, 1941; Attended, U. Redlands; BS, Northwestern U., 1964; JD, Yale U. Law Sch., 1966; LLM, NYU, 1967; LLD, U. Redlands, 2000. Chief counsel, staff dir. Senate Antitrust Subcom., 1978, Sen. Judiciary Com., 1979; assoc. Cravath, Swaine & Moore, N.Y., 1966—72, ptnr., 1973—77, 1980—97; mng. partner Boies, Schiller, & Flexner, Armonk, NY, 1997—. Counsel FDIC, 1991—93; spl. trust counsel U.S. Dept. Justice; lead council Al Gore's presidential campaign, Florida recount, 2000. Author: Public Control of Business, 1977, Courting Justice: From New York Yankees v. Major League Baseball to Bush v. Gore, 1997-2000, 2004. Named Lawyer of the Year, National Law Journal, 1999—2000. Mem. ABA, N.Y. State Bar Assn., Assn. of Bar of City of N.Y; Phi Betta Kappa Office: Boies Schiller & Flexner LLP 333 Main St Armonk NY 10504 E-mail: dboies@bsfllp.com.

BOIES, WILBER H., lawyer; b. Bloomington, Ill., Mar. 15, 1944; s. W. H. and Martha Jane (Hutchison) B.; m. Victoria Joan Steinitz, Sept. 17, 1966; children: Andrew Charles, Carolyn Ursula. AB, Brown U., 1965; JD, U. Chgo., 1968. Bar: Ill. 1968, U.S. Dist. Ct. (no. dist.) Ill. 1968, U.S. Dist. Ct. (ea. dist.) Wis. 1973, U.S. Ct. Appeals (7th cir.) 1974, U.S. Ct. Appeals (5th cir.) 1975, U.S. Ct. Appeals (3d cir.) 1977, U.S. Supreme Ct. 1978, U.S. Ct. Appeals (8th cir.) 1994, U.S. Ct. Appeals (9th cir.) 1995. Assoc. Altheimer & Gray, Chgo., 1968-71; ptnr. McDermott, Will & Emery, Chgo., 1971—. Contbr. articles to profl. jours. Active CPR Inst. for Dispute Resolution. Mem. ABA, Am. Bar Found., Bar Assn. 7th Fed. Cir., Chgo. Bar Assn. (chmn. class litigation com. 1991-92), Chgo. Coun. Lawyers, Lawyers Club Chgo., Met. Club, Chgo. Bar Found.(dir.). Office: McDermott Will & Emery 227 W Monroe St Ste 4400 Chicago IL 60606-5096 Office Phone: 312-984-7686. E-mail: bboies@mwe.com.

BOIME, ALBERT ISAAC, art historian, educator; b. St. Louis, Mar. 17, 1933; s. Max and Dorothy (Rubin) B.; m. Myra Block, June 23, 1964; children: Robert, Eric. AB, UCLA, 1961; MA, Columbia U., 1963, PhD, 1968. Instr. social history of art Columbia U., 1966-67; assoc. prof. SUNY, Stony Brook, 1967-72, prof., chmn. dept. Binghamton, 1972-74, prof., 1974-78; prof. social history of art UCLA, 1978—. Art historian in residence Coll. Creative Studies, U. Calif.-Santa Barbara, 1973; judge NEH, Washington, 1975; mem. adv. council N.Y. Acad. Art, N.Y.C., 1981-. Author: The Academy and French Painting in the 19th Century, 1971, Thomas Couture and the Eclectic Vision, 1981, the Social History of Modern Art: Vol. 1: Art in an Age of Revolution, 1987, Hollow Icons: The Politics of Sculpture in Nineteenth Century France, 1987, Vincent Van Gogh: Sternennacht, 1989, The Art of Exclusion: Representing Blacks in the Nineteenth Century, 1990, The Social History of Modern Art Vol. 2: Art in an Age of Bonapartism, 1990, The Magisterial Gaze: Manifest Destiny and American Landscape Painting (ca. 1830-1865), 1991, The Art of the Macchia and the Risorgimento, 1993, The Odyssey of Jan Stussey in Black and White, 1995, Art and the French Commune, 1995, Violence and Utopia: The Work of Jerome Boime, 1996, The Unveiling of the National Icons: A Plea for Patriotic Iconoclasm in a Nationalist Era, 1998 (Gustavus Myers Outstanding Book award 1999), Art in an Age of Counterrevolution, 1815-1848, 2004. Served with AUS, 1955-58. Am. Council Learned Socs. fellow, 1970-71; Guggenheim fellow, 1974-75, 84-85; Regents fellow Smithsonian Institution, 1989-90. Mem. Coll. Art Assn., Soc. Fellows Am. Acad. at Rome Office: UCLA Dept Art 405 Hilgard Ave Los Angeles CA 90095-9000 Business E-Mail: boime@humnet.ucla.edu. *I am grateful for this opportunity to join with my listing the memory of my dear brother, Jerome Philip Boime, whose rare, provocative mind inspired me with the sheer joy of intellectual pursuit. Whatever present success I may have, I owe to my capacity to thoroughly enjoy my work, to exult in ideas and the unboundedness of scholarly activity, and to commit this love to my developing engagement with political, philosophical and social issues.*

BOIRE, RON, retail executive; MBA, Columbia U., London Bus. Sch. Former pres. Sony Personal Mobile Products subs. Sony Corp., former pres. Sony Electronics Consumer Sales Co., former mem. ops. com., consumer bus. coun.; exec. v.p., gen. merchandise mgr. Best Buy Co., Inc., 2003—. Active United Way. Recipient S. David Feir Internat. Humanitarian award, Anti-Defamation League, 2002.

BOIS, YVE-ALAIN, art educator, curator; b. Constantine, Algeria, Apr. 16, 1952; Baccalaureat Philosophie, Toulouse, 1969; License de Lettres Modernes, Universite Paris, 1973; PhD, Ecole des Hautes Etudes en Sci. Sociales, 1977. Prof. hist. art Johns Hopkins U., 1989—91; Joseph Pulitzer Jr. Prof. Modern Art Dept. Fine Arts, Harvard U., 1991; prof. Sch. Hist. Studies, Inst. for Adv. Study, Princeton U., 2005—. Co-curator De Stijl and French Architecture in the 1920's, Institut Francais d'Architecture, 1985, Piet Mondrian Retrospective, The Hague, Nat. Gallery Art, Mus. Modern Art, 1995, L'Informe, mode d'emploi, Centre Georges Pompidou, 1996, curator Matisse and Picasso: A Gentle Rivalry, Kimbell Art Mus., 1999, Ellsworth Kelly: Early Drawings, Fogg Art Mus., High Mus., Arts Inst. Chgo., Kunstmuseum, 1999—2000. Office: Inst for Advanced Study Princton U Einstein Dr Princeton NJ 08540*

BOISE, AUDREY LORRAINE, retired special education educator; b. Hackensack, N.J., Feb. 12, 1933; d. Paul George and Lillian Rose (Goedecker) B. BA, Wellesley (Mass.) Coll., 1955; MA, Fairleigh Dickinson U., 1977. Cert. tchr. K-8, learning disabilities, supervision. Tchr. Township of Berkeley Heights, N.J., 1958-67; learning cons. Borough of New Providence, N.J., 1978-82, 86-00, ret., 2000; learning cons. Scotch Plains/Fanwood, N.J., 1984-86; instr. Fairleigh Dickinson U., Madison, N.J., 1975-78. Several other short-term tchg. positions; supr. student tchrs., 1968, 1975-78, 2000-02; lectr. on fgn. countries and areas of U.S.; part-time travel agt. Life mem. Rep. Nat. Com. (Pres. Club 2003-06); mem. Nat. Rep. Senatorial Com., Washington, Rep. Presdl. Task Force, Washington, Rep. Congl. com., Washington, N.J. State Rep. Com., Trenton, Nat. Fedn. Rep. Women, Washington; attended presdl. inauguration, 2005 Recipient Rep. of Yr. Gold medal, Nat. Rep. Com., 2002, 2003. Mem. NEA, AAUW, N.J. Assn. Learning Cons., Assn. for Children with Learning Disabilities, N.J. Edn. Assn., Internat. Platform Assn., Fortnightly Club, Hist. Soc. Summit, Canoe Brook Country Club Methodist. Avocations: travel, photography.

BOISSEAU, RICHARD ROBERT, lawyer; b. Phila., Sept. 6, 1944; s. Robert Bartholomew and Anne Cecilia (Tierney) B.; m. Jo-Ann Elizabeth Tompkins, Jan. 20, 1970; children: Richard Andrew, Thomas, Kristen. BS cum laude, Drexel U., 1968; JD cum laude, Temple U., 1974. Bar: Ga. 1974, U.S. Dist. Ct. (no. dist.) Ga. 1974, U.S. Ct. Appeals (4th cir.) 1980, U.S. Ct. Appeals (11th cir.) 1981, U.S. Supreme Ct. 1984, U.S. Ct. Appeals (9th cir.) 1986. Ptnr. Kilpatrick Stockton LLP, Atlanta, 1974—. Contbg. author: How Arbitration Works, 1987, 93, 97, 2003; contbr. articles to profl. jours. Bd. dirs. Vis. Nurse Health Sys., Atlanta, 1976—. Mem. Ga. Bar Assn., Atlanta Bar Assn. Republican. Roman Catholic. Avocations: golf, running. Office: Kilpatrick Stockton LLP 1100 Peachtree St NE Ste 2800 Atlanta GA 30309-4530 Office Phone: 404-815-6317. Business E-Mail: rboisseau@kilpatrickstockton.com.

BOISVERT, WILLIAM ANDREW, nutritional biochemist, researcher; b. Seoul, May 7, 1962; came to U.S., 1980; s. Robert Andrew and Jung Sup (Song) B. BS in Biochemistry, U. Oreg., 1985; PhD in Nutritional Biochemistry, Tufts U., 1992. Rsch. asst. Tufts U., Boston, 1986-87, rsch. assoc., 1991-93; postdoctoral fellow Cardiovascular Rsch. Inst. U. Calif., San Francisco, 1993-94; rsch. scientist The Scripps Rsch. Inst., 1994—. Contbr. articles to sci. jours. Recipient community svc. award Elderly Soc. Jocotenango, Guatemala, 1990; scholar Nutrasweet, Inc., 1986; rsch. grantee USDA, 1988. Mem. Sigma Xi. Achievements include synthesis of several novel heterocyclic organic compounds that may have anti-malarial activity; determination of nutritional requirement of vitamin B2 (riboflavin) in the elderly population. Office: Scripps Rsch Inst Dept Immunology IMM-17 10666 N Torrey Pines Rd La Jolla CA 92037-1027

BOITANO, BRIAN, Olympic athlete; b. Mountain View, Calif., Oct. 22, 1963; Competitive in amateur ice-skating events, 1978—88; Bronze medallist World Figure Skating Championships, 1985; Gold medallist U.S. Nat. Figure Skating Championships, 1985, World Figure Skating Championships, 1986, Silver medallist, 1987; Gold medallist U.S. Nat. Figure Skating Championships, 1988, World Figure Skating Championships, 1988; Silver medallist U.S. Nat. Figure Skating Championships, 1994; U.S. Olympics 6th place, 1994; U.S. Olympic Figure Skating Gold medallist, 1988. Owner White Canvas Prodns. Author (with Suzanne Harper): Boitano's Edge: Inside the Real World of Figure Skating, 1997; performer: (TV films) Carmen on Ice, 1990 (Emmy award, 1990); featured on cover: Sports Illustrated. Named Role Model of the Yr., Profl. Skaters' Cooperative, 1998; named to U.S. Figure Skating Hall of Fame, 1996, World Figure Skating Hall of Fame, 1996; recipient Gustav Lussi award, Profl. Skaters Assn., 1999.

BOIVIN, MICHAEL J., psychologist, educator, researcher; b. Detroit, July 28, 1955; s. Joseph R. Boivin and Huguette M. Maclean; m. Grace R. Abell, Apr. 19, 1953; children: Monique D., Daniel R., Marjorie J., Matthew I. BA, Spring Arbor Coll., 1976; MPH, U. Mich., 1993; MA, PhD, Western Mich. U., 1980. Prof. psychology Spring Arbor (Mich.) Coll., 1978—96, Ind. Wesleyan U., Marion, 1996—. Adj. rsch. investigator psychiatry U. Mich., Ann Arbor, 1991—. Contbr. articles to profl. jours. Sch. bd. The King's Acad., Marion, 2001—02; head ofcl. Marion InLine Hockey Assn., 1998—2003. Recipient Outstanding Paper in Humility Theology award, John Templeton Found., 1993; fellow Fulbright Rsch. award, U.S. State Dept., 1990—91, 1993—94; scholar Kellogg Found. Leaders in Pub. Health, Kellogg Found., 1991—93; Summer Rsch. fellow, West African Rsch. Assn., 1997, Rsch. fellow, 1997, Templeton/Oxford fellow, John Templeton Found., Coun. Christian Colls. and Univs., 1999—2001. Mem.: Nat. Acad. Neuropsychology, Am. Psychol. Soc. Achievements include first to neuropsychological effects of early cerebral malaria; neuropsychology of pediatric HIV, cognitive effects of intestinal parasite treatment; research in health interventions and neuropsychological development of children in the tropics. Office: Indiana Wesleyan Univ 4201 S Washington St Marion IN 46953 Office Phone: 765-677-2992. Personal E-mail: mjboivin1@hotmail.com. Business E-Mail: michael.boivin@indwes.edu.

BOJIC, VELJKO PETAR, lawyer, writer; b. Kolasin, Montenegro, Sept. 25, 1931; arrived in U.S., 1966; s. Petar and Kata Kujovic Bojic. Degree, Univ. Law, Zagreb, Yugoslavia, 1957. Ptnr. law firm, Zagreb, 1957—63; painter Artcraft Studio, L.A.; bldg. and constrn. supr. Calif. Author: (poetry) Izgnanik, 1988, 17-57, 1991, Strune sa Lumera, 1993, Zubor mjeseceve vode, 1996, Za krovovima iznad zvljezda, 1997, Dama u belim rukavicama, 1994, Crveni klobuk, 1994, Neoteta, 1998, Tajna svadha boginje Selene, 1999, (stories) Sudbine, 1997, (plays) Mat u raju, 1994, Drame, 1995, Kosorici, 1999, Tragicni optimist, 1999, Trickling of the Moon's Water and Five Other Dramas, (poetry anthology) Orpheus in the Underworld, 2000. Recipient Rastko Petrovic lit. award, Hdqs. Exile and Assn. Writers, Belgrade, Serbia Montenegro, 2000—. Mailing: 9958 Cedar Ln El Monte CA 91731

BOJSZA, JOAN E., elementary school educator; b. Orange, N.J., Jan. 3, 1949; d. Stephen William and Josephine Rosemary (Sulpy) Horkay; m. Walter Joseph Bojsza, June 20, 1970; children: Elizabeth Joy, Katherine Anne. BS in Early Childhood Edn., U. Md., 1971. Cert. elem. edn. and nursery tchr. N.J. Preschool tchr. Woodyard Rd. Ctr., Clinton, Md., 1971—72, YWCA-Ridgeview Ctr., West Orange, NJ, 1982—91; 2d grade tchr. St. Bernard Sch., Riverdale, Md., 1972—73; title I tchr. Rockaway (N.J.) Twp. Schs., 1973—74, 4th grade tchr., 1974—75; 1st grade tchr. St. Thomas More Sch., Fairfield, NJ, 1975—77; kindergarten tchr. Newton St. Sch., Newark, 1991—99, Quitman St. Sch., Newark, 1999—2002, pre-kindergarten tchr., 2002—03, kindergarten tchr., 2003—. Project, new beginnings tchr. Summer Inst., Newark, 1998; presenter in field. Contbr. chpt. to book. Mem. coun., PTA officer, pres. various, West Orange, 1986—99; PTA officer pres. West Orange HS, 1995—98; comitteewoman West Orange Dems., 1991—96; mem. Democratic County Com. Recipient Outstanding Leaders award, Girl Scouts U.S., 1990. Mem.: Nat. Assn. Edn. Young Children, Comer Whole Sch. Reform Model (chairperson mem. parent/staff com. 2000—01), Newark Early Childhood Educators Assn. (v.p. 1993—2001, sec., newsletter editor), Essex Hudson Assn. Edn. Young Children (corr. sec. 2001—, v.p. programs 2004—), Kappa Delta Pi. Avocations: gardening, singing, crafts. Home: 25 Harvard Ter West Orange NJ 07052

BOK, DEREK, law educator, former university president; b. Bryn Mawr, Pa., Mar. 22, 1930; s. Curtis and Margaret (Plummer) B.; m. Sissela Ann Myrdal, May 7, 1955; children: Hilary Margaret, Victoria, Tomas Jeremy. BA, Stanford U., 1951; JD, Harvard U., 1954; MA, George Washington U., 1958. Fulbright scholar, Paris, 1954-55; faculty Harvard U. Law Sch., Cambridge, Mass., 1958—, prof., 1961—, dean, 1968-71; pres. Harvard U., Cambridge, 1971-91, 300th anniversary univ. prof., 1991—. Editor: (with Archibald Cox) Cases and Materials on Labor Law, 1962; author: (with John T. Dunlop) Labor and the American Community, 1970, Beyond the Ivory Tower: Social Responsibilities of the Modern University, 1982, Higher Learning, 1986, Universities and the Future of America, 1990, The Cost of Talent, 1993, (with William G. Bowen) The Shape of the River, 1998, The Trouble with Government, 2001, Universities in the Marketplace, 2003; contbr.: In the Public Interest, 1980, The State of the Nation, 1997, Universities in the Marketplace, 2003. Bd. dirs., nat. chmn. Common Cause, 1999—; chmn. bd. overseers Cts. Inst. Music, 1997-2002; chmn. bd. Spencer Found., 2002-; faculty chmn. Hauser Ctr. for Non-Profit Orgs., 2002-. Fellow Ctr. for Advanced Studies in the Behavioral Scis., 1991-92. Fellow Am. Acad. Arts and Scis., mem. Nat. Acad. Edn., Phi Beta Kappa, Am. Philosophical Soc. Office: Harvard U JFK Sch of Govt Cambridge MA 02138

BOK, JOAN TOLAND, utilities executive; b. Grand Rapids, Mich., Dec. 31, 1929; d. Don Prentiss Weaver and Mary Emily Toland; m. John Fairfield Bok, July 15, 1955; children: Alexander Toland, Geoffrey Robbins. AB, Radcliffe Coll., 1951; JD, Harvard U., 1955. Bar: Mass. 1955. Assoc. Ropes & Gray, Boston, 1955-61; pvt. practice Boston, 1961-68; atty. New England Electric Sys., Westborough, Mass., 1968-73, asst. to pres., 1973-77, v.p., sec., 1977-79, vice-chair, 1979-84, pres., CEO, 1988-89, chair, 1984-98, chair emeritus, 1998—. Past pres. bd. overseers Harvard U.; bd. dirs. Boston Adult Literacy Fund, Nat. Osteoporosis Found., Vt. Hist. Soc., Woods Hole (Mass.) Oceanog. Inst. Fellow Am. Bar Found.; mem. Boston Bar Assn., Am. Acad. Arts and Scis., Phi Beta Kappa. Unitarian Universalist. Home: 53 Pinckney St Boston MA 02114-4801 Office: 25 Research Dr Westborough MA 01582-0001

BOK, JOHN FAIRFIELD, retired lawyer; b. Boston, Aug. 30, 1930; AB magna cum laude, Harvard U., 1952, LLB magna cum laude, 1955. Bar: Mass. 1955, N.Y. 1982, Pa. 1984. Assoc. firm Ropes & Gray, Boston, 1957-62, 64-69; counsel to devel. adminstr. Boston Redevelopment Authority, 1962-64; ptnr. firm Csaplar & Bok, Boston, 1969-90, Gaston & Snow, Boston, 1990-91; of counsel Foley, Hoag & Eliot, Boston, 1991-2000. Instr. law Boston Coll. Law Sch., part-time 1974-75; lectr. Practicing Law Inst., 1974, New Eng. Law Inst., 1973 Editor Harvard Law Rev., 1954-55. Pres. Cambridge St. Cmty. Devel. Corp., 1972-75, Citizens Housing and Planning Assn., 1968-70, Met. Cultural Alliance, 1973-75, Beacon Hill Civic Assn., 1959-61, Beacon Hill Nursery Sch., 1964-65, Peddock's Island Trust, 1982-85, Mus. Wharf, 1989-94, Boston Ballet, 1991-94, Peter Faneuil Devel. Group, Inc., 1992—, Mass. Hort. Soc., 1995-98; v.p. The Cmty. Builders, Inc., 1969-97, pres. or chmn., 1998—; chmn. Boston Children's Mus., 1976-78, Mass. Housing Partnership, 1985-92, Social Policy Rsch. Group Inc., 1985-92, Boston Mcpl. Rsch. Bur., 1979-81, bd. dirs. and/or officer Boston Neighborhood Housing Svcs., 1974-76, Boston Waterfront Devel. Corp., 1970-85, Archtl. Conservation Trust for Mass., 1978-92, Wheelock Coll., 1980-95, Strawberry Banke, Inc., 1981-86, Met. Boston Housing Partnership, Inc., 1984-95, Cambridge Coll., 1984-95, Boston Housing Authority monitoring com., 1984-90, The Boston Harbor Assn., 1984-92, Back Bay Assn., 1988-92, Hist. Mass., 1989—, African Am. Meeting House, 1993—; mem. Boston Archives and Records Advt. Comm., 1988-95, Cmty. Music Ctr., 1995—, Island Alliance, 1995—, Light Boston!, 1995—. Fulbright-Hays scholar, 1976 Mem. ABA, Mass. Bar Assn., Boston Bar Assn. (chmn. land use com. 1971-74), Phi Beta Kappa. Home: 53 Pinckney St Boston MA 02114-4801

BOK, SISSELA, philosopher, writer; b. Stockholm, Dec. 2, 1934; d. Gunnar and Alva (Reimer) Myrdal; m. Derek Bok, May 7, 1955; children— Hilary, Victoria, Tomas BA, George Washington U., 1957, MA, 1958, LHD (hon.), 1986; PhD, Harvard U., 1970; LLD (hon.), Mt. Holyoke Coll., 1985; LHD (hon.), Clark U., 1988, U. Mass., 1991, Georgetown U., 1992. Lectr. Simmons Coll., Boston, 1971-72; lectr. Harvard-MIT Div. Health Scis. and Tech., Cambridge, 1975-82, Harvard U., Cambridge, 1982-84; assoc. prof. philosophy Brandeis U., Waltham, Mass., 1985-89, prof. philosophy, 1989-92; fellow Ctr. for Advanced Study, Stanford, Calif., 1991-92; Disting. fellow Harvard Ctr. Population and Devel. Studies, Cambridge, Mass., 1993—. Mem. ethics adv. bd. HEW, 1977-80; bd. dirs. Population Coun., 1971-77; mem. Pulitzer Prize Bd., 1988-97, chmn., 1996-97. Author: Lying: Moral Choice in Public and Private Life, 1978 (Melcher award, George Orwell award), Secrets: On the Ethics of Concealment and Revelation, 1982, Alva: Ett kvinnoliv, 1987, A Strategy for Peace, 1989, Alva Myrdal: A Daughter's Memoir, 1991 (Melcher award), Common Values, 1996, Mayhem: Violence as Public Entertainment, 1998; mem. editl. bd. Ethics, 1980-85, Criminal Justice Ethics, 1980—, Contention, 1990-96, Common Knowledge, 1991—, (with others) Euthanasia and Physician-Assisted Suicide, 1998. Bd. dirs. Inst. for Philosophy and Religion, Boston U.; mem. Pulitzer Prize Bd., 1989-97. Recipient Abram L. Sachar Silver medallion Brandeis U., 1985, Radcliffe Coll. Grad. Soc. medal, 1993, Barnard Coll. medal of distinction, 1995, centennial medal Harvard Grad. Sch. Arts & Scis., 1998. Fellow Hastings Ctr. (dir. 1976-84, 94-97); mem. Am. Philos. Assn.

BOKEMPER, SUE R., music educator; b. Sai City, Iowa, Feb. 11, 1962; d. Keith Leroy and Evelyn Mae Scott; m. Myron (Bo) Benjamin Bokemper, Jr., Feb. 2, 1985; children: Jessica, Erin, Daniel. AA, Rose State Coll., Midwest City, Okla., 1996; BS in Edn., U. Ctrl. Okla., 1998. Music educator Moore (Okla.) Pub. Schs., 1998—. Musician: Mid-Am. Prodns., 2004, Branson (Mo.) Live!, 2005. Music ministry, handbells Bitburg (Germany) AFB Chapel, 1988—94; music ministry Hillcrest UMC, Oklahoma City, 1996—98. Recipient Top Performance Ensemble, Music in Pks., Arlington, Tex., 2002. Mem.: Okla. Choral Dirs. Assn., Am. Choral Dirs. Assn., PEO. Roman Catholic. Avocations: running, bicycling, travel. Office: Highland E Jr HS 1200 S 4th St Moore OK 73160

BOKEN, VIJENDRA KUMAR, meteorologist, educator; b. Village-Mahavarh, Near Ghaziabad, Uttar Pradesh, India; arrived in U.S., 1999; s. Bhullar Singh and Shanti Devi; m. Sangeeta Boken. BTech in Agrl. Engring., G.B. Pant U., Pantnagar, India, 1983; MEngring in Agrl. Engring., Asian Inst. TEch., Bangkok, 1985; MEngring. in Water Resources Engring., U. Jodhpur, India, 1993; PhD, U. Man., Winnipeg, Canada, 1999. Asst. prof. U. N.D., Grand Forks, ND, 1999—2000, Tex. State U., San Marcos, Tex., 2000—01; postdoctoral rsch. assoc. U. Ga., Griffin, Ga., 2001—04; asst. prof. U. Miss., University, Miss., 2004—. Editor: Monitoring and Predicting Agricultural Drought: A Global Study, 2005. Grantee, NOAA NESDIS, U.S. Govt., 2002, NASA U. Space Grant Consortium, 2003, World Meteorol. Orgn., 2004. Mem.: Internat. Geog. Union, Am. Geophys. Union, Am. Soc. Photogrammetry and Remote Sensing. Achievements include research in drought monitoring using satellite data. Office: Univ Mississippi Geoinform Center Dept Geology and Geological Engieering University MS 38677 Personal E-mail: vkboken@hotmail.com. E-mail: vkboken@olemiss.edu.

BOKUNIEWICZ, HENRY JOSEPH, oceanography educator; b. Chgo., July 29, 1949; s. Henry Joseph and Alice Rose (Weber) B.; m. Linda Joan Sedey, Aug. 14, 1971; 1 child, Roxanna. BA, U. Ill., 1971; MPhil, Yale U., 1973, PhD, 1976. Assoc. prof. SUNY, Stony Brook, 1982-87, assoc. dean edn., 1992-98; dir. L.I. Groundwater Resource Inst., Stony Brook, 1993—; prof. oceanography SUNY, Stony Brook, 1991—. Environ. cons. Great Lakes Dock and Dredge/Amboy Aggregates, Oakbrook, Ill. and Amboy, N.J., 1985-99, Port Authority N.Y., N.Y.C., 1998-99, U.S. Army CE, N.Y.C., 1998-99. Rsch. grantee Suffolk County Water Authority, 1993-94, N.Y. State, 1997-99, U.S. Army C.E., 1997-99, NRC, 1996-98. Mem. Internat. Coun. Sci. Unions (mem. working group 1998-99), Internat. Geosphere Biosphere Program (mem. working group 1998-99), Internat. Coun. for Exploration of Seas (mem. working group 1986-99). Roman Catholic. Home: 14 Keats Pl Greenlawn NY 11740-2606 Office: Marine Scis Rsch Ctr Suny Stony Brook NY 11794-0001 E-mail: hbokuniewicz@notes.cc.sunysb.edu.

BOLAN, RICHARD STUART, urban planner, educator, researcher; b. Salem, Mass., Dec. 11, 1927; s. Robert Stuart and Mildred Elizabeth (Fay) B.; m. Elizabeth Ann Murphy, Sept. 4, 1954 (dec. 1977); 1 child, Geoffrey Stuart; m. Margaret Mary Altschul, Mar. 30, 1978 (div. May 1983); m. Nancy Jane Johnston, Dec. 19, 1987. B of Engring., Yale U., 1954; M of City and Regional Planning, MIT, 1956; PhD, NYU, 1974. Planner Providence Redevel. Authority, 1956-57, Planning and Renewal Assocs., Cambridge, Mass., 1957-58; prin. planner Boston City Planning Bd., 1958-60; dir. renewal planning Boston Redevel. Authority, 1960-62; dir. planning Boston Regional Transp. Study, 1962-64; asst. to dir. Joint Ctr. for Urban Studies of MIT and Harvard, Cambridge, 1964-67; prof. Boston Coll., Chestnut Hill, Mass., 1967-85; prof. urban planning U. Minn., Mpls., 1985-98, prof. emeritus, 1998—. Editor: Planning Metropolitan Boston, 1967; co-author: Urban Planning and Politics, 1975, Poland's Path to Sustainable Development: 1989-93, 1994; co-editor workshop procs., 1991; contbr. articles to profl. jours. Vol. United Way, Mpls., 1986-98; bd. dirs. Minn. Jobs with Peace, Mpls., 1989-96. Sgt. USAF, 1945-47, 50-51. Mem.: Assn. Collegiate Schs. of Planning (sec.-treas. 1989—93), Am. Inst. Cert. Planners, Am. Planning Assn. Democrat. Unitarian Universalist. Home: 2833 E Lake Of The Isles Pky Minneapolis MN 55408-1055 Office: U Minn Humphrey Inst Pub Affairs Minneapolis MN 55455 Office Phone: 612-625-0128. Business E-Mail: dbolan@hhh.umn.edu.

BOLAN, THOMAS ANTHONY, lawyer; b. Lynn, Mass., May 30, 1924; s. Thomas J. and Margaret (Cremin) B.; m. Marie T. Gerst, Nov. 25, 1950; children: Sean, Douglas, Mary, Jacqueline, William. BA summa cum laude, St. John's U., 1952, LLB summa cum laude, 1950, LLD (hon.), 1985. Bar: N.Y. 1951. Assoc. Burroughs & Brown, N.Y.C., 1951-53; asst. U.S. atty. Dept. Justice, N.Y.C., 1953-57; assoc. Roy M. Cohn, N.Y.C., 1957-59; with Saxe, Bacon & Bolan, N.Y.C., 1960-71, counsel, 1972-87; ptnr. Bolan, Lang, Biancone, Tiffenberg, PC, N.Y.C., 1987-89; pres. Thomas A. Bolan, PC, N.Y.C., 1989-01. Lectr. law St. John's U., 1957-61; pres., chmn. bd. 5th Ave. Coach Lines, N.Y.C., 1967-68, Championship Sports, Inc., N.Y.C., 1961—; treas., exec. dir. Feature Sports, Inc., 1959-61; chmn. bd. Merc. Nat. Bank, Chgo., 1967-68, Gateway Nat. Bank, Chgo., 1966-67; sec. Balt. Paint and Chem. Corp., N.Y.C., 1966-68, TelePro Industries Inc., N.Y.C., 1966-68; sec., dir. B.S.F. Co., N.Y.C., 1966-68, Defiance Industries, N.Y.C., 1966-68; v.p. Am. Steel and Pump Corp., N.Y.C., 1966-68, WRNJ Assocs., Atlantic City, 1961-68, Harrisburg Broadcasting Co., Palmyra, Pa., 1966-68; sec., treas., dir. Berwick Broadcasting Corp., Reading, Pa., 1967-68; dir. Overseas Pvt. Investment Corp., 1982-86. Bd. editors Nat. Law Jour., 1983-90; contbr. articles to profl. jours. Co-chmn. N.Y. Reagan Fin. Com., 1980, N.Y. Reagan-Bush Campaign Com., 1984; founder law chmn. Conservative Party, N.Y. State, 1962—; chmn. E. Side Conservative Club, N.Y.C., 1973-99; v.p. Crusade for Am., Rockville Ctr., N.Y., 1957-62; bd. regents St. Francis Coll., Bklyn., 1968—; treas. Ednl. Reviewer, 1960—; pres. Cambria Heights (N.Y.) Parish Coun., 1968-70; pres., dir. Pro Ecclesia Found., 1972-73; trustee Cambria Heights Boys Club Assn., 1968-72, St. John's U., 1987-98, emeritus, 1999—; v.p., dir. Heiser Found., 1955-73; mem. Com. to Restore Internal Security, 1979-96; mem. Coun. for Nat. Policy, 1983—, Internat. Policy Forum, 1988—; mem. Am. Coun. on Germany, 1983—, U.S. Commn. for UNESCO, 1983-85; bd. visitors Eureka Coll., 1983—, Inst. for Italian Heritage & Culture St. John's U., 1992—; nat. adv. coun. Actors Youth Fund, 1982—; mem. U.S. Senator Alfonse D'Amato's Jud. Screening Com., 1980-98; chmn., bd. dirs. Global Leadership Inst., 1986—; pres., trustee Nat. Rev. Inst., 1992—, Found. for Study of Nat. Civic and Internat. Affairs, 1993—; dir. Narnia Catechetical and Cultural Ctr., Inc., 1991-99, Am. Friends of James Joyce, 1998—; mem. N.Y. State Vets. Adv. Coun., 1989-91. With USAF, 1943-45. Decorated Air medal with 5 oak leaf clusters; recipient Medal of Honor the 52d Assn., 1981, Bella V. Dodd Meml award N.Y. County Conservative Party, 1981, Ann award Bronx County Conservative Party, 1984, Charles Edison award Conservative Party N.Y. State, 1987, Disting. Svc. award Nat. Cath. War Vets, 1985, Celtic Cross award, 1997, Cross for Conspicuous Svc. State of N.Y. 1989, Ann. Heritage award Bklyn.-Queens Conservative Party, 1991, Madison award St. John's U. Sch. Law, 1991, Annual award Nat. Traditionalist Caucus, 1994, Pietas medal St. John's U., 1997. Mem. Cath. Lawyers Guild, Internat. Assn. Jurists, Am. African Affairs Assn. (sec., bd. dirs. 1975—), Cath. War Vets. (Queens County judge adv. 1965—, nat. judge adv. 1984—, Svc. award Queens County chpt. 1968, 77, 90, elected to nat. order St. Sebastian 1981), Ret. Officers Assn. (Knickerbocker chpt.), Eight Air Force Hist. Soc., Knights of Malta. Office: 521 5th Ave Fl 10 New York NY 10175-1099

BOLAND, CHRISTOPHER THOMAS, II, lawyer; b. Scranton, Pa., June 10, 1915; s. Patrick J. and Sarah (Jennings) B.; m. Nora Cusick, Jan. 23, 1943; m. Cornelia Bingham, Mar. 1, 1980. BSS cum laude, Georgetown U., 1937; LL.B., Harvard, 1940. Staff dir. Spl. Senate Com. on Atomic Energy, 1945—47; staff dir., counsel Joint Senate-House Com. on Atomic Energy, 1947; pvt. practice Washington, 1947—; sr. ptnr. Gallagher Boland & Meiburger, Washington, 1955—93, sr. counsel, 1994—. Utility specialist Dept. Energy. Served to lt. col., intelligence USAAF, 1941-45. Mem. ABA, D.C. Bar Assn., Fed. Energy Bar Assn. (pres. 1970), Congressional Country Club (pres. 1974), Harvard Club (Washington), Burning Tree Club (Bethesda,

Md.), Rehoboth Beach (Del.) Country Club. Home: 5309 Cardinal Ct Spring Hill Bethesda MD 20816 Office: 818 18th St NW Ste 800 Washington DC 20006 Office Phone: 202-289-7200. Business E-Mail: cboland@gbmdc.com.

BOLAND, JANET LANG, judge; b. Kitchener, Ont., Can., Dec. 6, 1924; d. George William and Miriam Janet (Geraghty) Lang; m. John Brown Boland, Oct. 1, 1949; children: Michael, Christopher, Nicholas; m. Taylor Statten, Oct. 27, 2001. BA, Waterloo Coll., 1946; law degree, Osgoode Hall, 1950; hon. doctorate of law, Sir Wilfred Laurier U. Bar: Ont. 1976, named Queen's counsel 1965. Mem. firm White, Bristol, Beck & Phipps, Toronto, Ont., 1959-69; partner firm Lang Michener, Toronto, 1969-72; county ct. judge Toronto, 1972-76; judge Supreme Ct. of Ont., Toronto, 1976—, Fed. Appeals Bd., 1989. Co-chmn. Penal Reform for Women Joint Com., 1956-58 Mem. Pension Appeal Bd. Mem. Jr. League Toronto (hon. pres.), Can. Women's Sr. Golf Assn. (past pres.). Roman Catholic. Office: 1605 - 33 Harbour Sq Toronto ON Canada M5J 2G2

BOLAND, JOHN KEVIN, bishop; b. Monkstown, Ireland, Apr. 25, 1935; Attended, Catholic Univ., Washington, 1962—64; Master's, Fordham Univ., 1989. Ordained priest Roman Cath. Ch. 1959. Ordained priest, 1959; rector Cathedral of St. John the Baptist, Savannah, Ga., 1970—72; pastor Blessed Sacrament parish, Savannah, Ga., 1972—83, St. Anne parish, Columbus, Ga., 1983—95; vice chancellor Diocese of Savannah, 1965—68, vicar gen., 1973—95, personnel adv., 1976—95, chancellor, 1978—83, bishop, 1995—. Office: Catholic Pastoral Center 601 E Liberty St Savannah GA 31401-5196*

BOLANOS, MICHAEL TEMPLETON, new media executive; b. Denville, N.J., Jan. 29, 1965; s. Henry and Jean Mary (Chardi) B. Mng. dir. Bell and Barter Theater/Arts Ctr., Rockaway, N.J., 1981-83; pres. The Musicom Corp., N.Y.C., 1981—, U.S./Soviet Exch. Initiative, 1985-86; ptnr. Hart-Bolanos and Assocs., N.Y.C., 1987-88; pres. Global Programming Inc., N.Y.C., Tokyo, 1990-93; pres., CEO Entertainment Drive, N.Y.C., 1995—; sr. v.p. One World Networks, N.Y.C. & L.A., 2000—02; CEO Home Luxury, Inc., 2002—. Artistic coord. U.S./Soviet Exch. Initiative; mem. bd. Friends of Am. Theatre Wing, 1991—92; cons.,NHK-TV, Tokyo, Fujisankei Group, Osaka, Japan, 1989—91, Compuserve, Columbus, Ohio, 1993—94; lectr. Yale U.; exec. prodn. advisor Eisenhower Inst., 2001—; exec. prodr. Ofcl. Cindy Crawford website, Ofcl. Britney Spears website, NewYorkPix.com, Ofcl. Richard Simmons website; pres., CEO www.edrive.com, 2004—. Creator/reporter (Kidcast) KAMR-TV, Amarillo, Tex., 1975—76, co-creator/patentee (eDrive) Movie Viewer, 1994, creator Entertainment Drive on Compuserve, 1994, eDrive Japan on NiftyServe, 1997, (official website) www.cindy.com, 1998, www.britneyspears.com, (websites) StarClubs.com, NewYorkPix.com, 2001, www.richardsimmons.com, 2005, creator, patentee My Computer Box, 2004. Artist coord. Rally for Soviet Jewry, Coalition to Free Soviet Jews, 1987; exec. prodr. on-line coverage of telethon Muscular Dystrophy Assn., 1994-95, exec. prodr. on-line chat Artists' Rights Found., 1995; bd. dirs. U. Metaphys. Studies. Recipient Cyber 60 award N.Y. Mag., 1995, CyberStar award Virtual City Mag., 1996. Mem. The Japan Soc. (concert prodr. 1987), Am. Acad. Children's Entertainment (bd. outside advisors), Actor's Fund Am. (Inner Cir.), Internet Content Coalition, Young Entrepreneurs Assn., N.Y. New Media Assn., Sales and Mktg. Execs. N.Y., Assn. for Interactive Media, U. Metaphysical Studies. Achievements include creator/patentee My Computer Box, 2004. Avocations: acting, singing, travel, japanese language and art. Office: Entertainment Drive 2545 East Sunrise Blvd #207 Fort Lauderdale FL 33304

BOLAR, AMY LEIGH, music educator; b. Maysville, Ky., Nov. 17, 1972; d. Kenneth Allen and Cheryl Ann (Bierley) Souder; m. Keith Alan Bolar, Oct. 7, 1995. BA, Transylvania U., 1995; MA, Morehead State U., 2000. Cert. Nat. Bd. of Profl. Tchg. Standards, 2003. Music tchr. Flemingsburg (Ky.) Elem., 1995—. Edn. coord. Am. Guild English Handbell Ringers, 1998; component mgr. Flemingsburg Elem. Revision Com., 2001—. Dir. Flemingsburg Bicentennial Band, 1999; article writer Flemingsburg Elem., 1999—2000; accompanist local churches, Flemingsburg, 1995—. Recipient Golden Apple Recipient, 1999. Mem.: Music Educators Nat. Conf., Ky. Choral Dirs. Assn., Ky. Music Educators Assn., Chi Omega. Avocations: cats, candlemaking, stamp collecting/philately, music. Home: 149 Mt Gilead Rd Flemingsburg KY 41041 Office: Flemingsburg Elem 245 W Water St Flemingsburg KY 41041

BOLAS, GERALD DOUGLAS, museum director, art historian, educator; b. Los Angeles, Nov. 1, 1949; s. Norman Theodore and Elizabeth Louise (Douglas) B.; children: Ellen Claire, John David. BA, U. Calif., Santa Barbara, 1972, MA, 1975; PhD, CUNY, 1998. Tchg. asst. U. Calif., Santa Barbara, 1973-74; NEH mus. intern Yale U. Art Gallery, New Haven, 1975-76, asst. to dir., 1976-77; dir. Washington U. Gallery of Art, St. Louis, 1977-88, Portland Art Mus., Oreg., 1988-92, Ackland Art Mus., U. N.C., Chapel Hill, 1994—. Adj. prof. art history Washington U., 1982-88, U. N.C., Chapel Hill, 1994—; advisor Mo. Arts Coun., St. Louis, 1981-82; field reviewer Inst. Mus. Svcs., Washington, 1980-83; panelist NEA, 1989, NEH, 1990, 95, N.C. Arts Coun., 1995; bd. dirs. Asian Art Soc. of Washington U., 1983-88; mem. No. Calif. adv. com. Archives of Am. Art; active Lake Oswego Arts Commn., 1993-94. Author: Illustrated Checklist of Washington University Collection, 1981; contbr. to books: Ketav: Flesh and Word in Israeli Art, 1996, Paris in Japan: The Japanese Encounter with European Painting, 1987; also contbr. articles to other publs.; numerous catalog forewords. Organizer numerous exhbns. Fellow Winterthur Mus., 1993, Smithsonian Instn., 1993. Mem. Coll. Art Assn., Assn. Art Mus. Dirs. Office: U NC Ackland Art Mus Campus Box 3400 Chapel Hill NC 27599-0001 E-mail: gdbolas@unc.edu.

BOLASH, ROBERT BENJAMIN, biomedical researcher; b. Bethlehem, Pa., June 22, 1981; s. John A. and Susan (Roberts) Bolash. BS summa cum laude, Wagner Coll., 2003. Fulbright fellow, Fulbright U. student scholar Universitaet Witten/Herdecke, Witten, Germany, 2003—04; med. student U. Miami Sch. Medicine, 2004—. N.Y.C. Health Dept. rsch. trainee fellow Albert Einstein Coll. Medicine, Bronx, N.Y., 2000—01; rsch. intern St. Luke's Hosp., Bethlehem, 2000—02; tutor biology, chemistry, physics, anthropology,and study skills Wagner Coll. Peer Tutoring Ctr., Staten Island, N.Y., 2000—03; peer composition and writing tutor Wagner Coll. Writing Ctr., Staten Island, N.Y., 2000—03; summer rsch. fellow U. Pitts. Sch. Medicine, 2001; rsch. intern Staten Island U. Hosp. Multiple Sclerosis Ctr., 2001; summer rsch. fellow Harvard Med. Sch., Boston, 2002, Stanford U. Sch. Medicine, Palo Alto, Calif., 2003. Author: (peer-reviewed article) Jour. HealthCare Quality, (abstract) Jour. Metro. Area Coun. Univ. Biologists: In Vivo; presenter (lecture) Curing Diabetes with Gene Therapy: Successes and Opportunities, (conf. presentation) Ubiquitination of Clathrin-Coated Vesicle Associated Proteins, (retreat presentation) Transferrin Receptor-2 and its Trafficking, (nat. conf. presentation) Writing as the Center of the First Year College Experience. Mem.: Omicron Delta Kappa Nat. Leadership Honor Soc., Beta Beta Beta Honor Soc. Home: 1535 Thompson Ave Bethlehem PA 18017

BOLCH, CARL EDWARD, JR., petroleum company executive, lawyer; b. St. Louis, Feb. 28, 1943; s. Carl Edward and Juanita (Newton) Bolch; m. Susan Bass; children: Carl, Allison, Natalie, Melanie, Jordan. BS in Econs, U. Pa., 1964; JD, Duke U., 1967. Cert. Fla., 1967. CEO, chmn. bd. dirs. RaceTrac Petroleum,Inc., Atlanta, 1967—. Edition editor Close Corporations, 1967. Mem.: Nat. Assn. Convenience Stores (bd. dirs. 1994—), Soc. Ind. Gasoline Marketers (pres. 1987—89), Fla. Bar Assn., ABA. Office: RaceTrac Petroleum Inc PO Box 105035 Atlanta GA 30348-5035 also: RaceTrac Petroleum Inc 300 Technology Ct Smyrna GA 30082

BOLCHAZY, LADISLAUS JOSEPH, publishing company executive; b. Michalovce, Slovakia, June 7, 1937; AA in Classics, Divine Word Coll. and Sem., Conesus, N.Y., 1960; BA in Philosophy, St. Joseph's Coll. and Sem., Yonkers, N.Y., 1963; MA in Classics, NYU, 1967; PhD in Classics, SUNY, Albany, 1973. Permanent cert. Latin tchr., N.Y. Tchr. Latin and English, Sacred Heart High Sch., Yonkers, 1962-65; instr. Siena Coll., Loudonville, N.Y., 1966-67; asst. prof. La Salette Coll. and Sem., Altamont, N.Y., 1971-75; vis. asst. prof. Millersville (Pa.) State Coll., 1975-76, Loyola U., Chgo., 1976-77, adj. prof., 1979—; owner, mgr. U.S. Graphics, Chgo.-Scan Typographers, Inc., 1985—; pres. Bolchazy-Carducci Pubs., Inc., Wauconda, Ill., 1978—. Organizer seminar APA, 1975; condr. NEH summer inst. on Sophocles and Thucydides, Cornell U., 1976, on ancient history U. Mich., Ann Arbor, 1977; host Myth Is Truth, Sta. WLUC, Loyola U., 1977, Sta. WRRG, Triton Coll., 1978. Author: Hospitality in Early Rome, 1977, reprinted as Hospitality in Antiquity, 1994, A Concordance to the "Utopia" of St. Thomas More, 1978, The Coin-Inscriptions and Epigraphical Abbreviations of Imperial Rome, 1978, (with others) A Concordance to Ausonius, 1982; co-editor: The Ancient World, 1978—, The Classical Bulletin, 1988—; contbr. articles to profl. jours. Pres. Slovak-Am. Internat. Cultural Found., Inc., 1998. Teaching fellow SUNY, 1967-71; rsch. grantee Loyola U., 1977. Home: 698 Golf Ln Barrington IL 60010-7329 Office: Bolchazy Carducci Pub Inc 1000 Brown St Ste 101 Wauconda IL 60084-3120

BOLDEN, ALJERNON JOHN, dentist, public health official; b. Richmond, Va., Apr. 25, 1951; s. Charles and Eunice Virginia (Hunter) Miller; m. Jacquelyn Anderson Bolden, Aug. 14, 1982; 1 dau., Janee' Tharese. B.A., Boston U., 1973; D.M.D., Tufts U., 1976; M.P.H., Harvard U., 1980. Cons., research assoc. Newark Beth Israel Hosp., 1976-77; pvt. practice dentistry, East Orange, N.J., 1977-78; dental dir. Whittier Street Health Ctr., Boston, 1977-81, Fulton County Health Dept., Atlanta, 1981—, pres. Nat. Dental Assn.; field cons. Mexican Health Care Council, Mexico City, 1980; mem. adv. com. Mass. Minority Council on Alcoholism, Boston, 1980-81; cons., lectr. Action for Boston Community Council, 1980-81; mem. health service adv. com. Head Start, Atlanta, 1982-83. Contbr. articles to profl. jours. Vice pres. J.H. Lockett Choir, College Park, Ga., 1982; mem. Friendship Chorale, 1983; mem. New Temple Singers, St. Paul A.M.E. Ch., Cambridge, Mass., 1975-81. Recipient J. Stoke award Fulton County Health Dept., 1983. Mem. ADA, Am. Pub. Health Assn., Ga. Dental Assn., Mass. Pub. Health Assn., Alpha Omega, Omega Psi Phi. Office: Nat Dental Assn 3517 16th St NW Washington DC 20010*

BOLDEN, CHARLES F., JR., astronaut, career officer; b. Columbia, S.C., Aug. 19, 1946; m. Alexis Walker; children: Anthony Che, Kelly.l. BS, U.S. Naval Acad., 1968; MS in Sys. Mgmt., U. So. Calif., 1977; grad., U.S. Naval Test Pilot Sch., Patuxent River, Md., 1979; PhD Science (hon.), U. S.C., 1984; DHL (hon.), Winthrop Coll., 1986, Johnson C. Smith Univ., 1990. Commd. 2nd lt. USMC, 1968, advanced through grades to brig. gen., 1997, naval aviator, 1970, pilot, stationed at VMA (AW)-533 Nam Phong, Thailand, 1972-73, marine corps officer selection, recruiting officer L.A., 1973-75, various assignments at Marine Corps Air Sta. El Toro, Calif., 1975-78; test pilot, stationed at Sys. Engring. and Strike Aircraft Test Director Naval Air Test Ctr., ordnance test pilot in A-6E, EA-6B and A-7C/E aircraft; astronaut NASA, 1980, pilot on Space Shuttle Columbia, 1986, pilot of Space Shuttle Discovery, 1990, mission comdr. of Space Shuttle Atlantis, 1992, mission comdr. of Space Shuttle Discovery, 1994, asst. dep. adminstr., 1992-94; dep. comdr. midshipmen Naval Acad., Annapolis, Md., 1994; asst. wing comdr. 3rd Marine Aircraft Wing, Miramar, Calif., 1995-97; dep. comdg. gen. IMEF Force Marine Forces Pacific, 1997-98; comdg. gen. IMEF (FWD) Operation Desert Thunder, Kuwait, 1998; dep. comdr., Yokota Air Base U.S. Forces, Japan, 1998—. Decorated Disting. Flying Cross, Defense Superior Svc. medal, Defense Meritorious Svc. medal, Air medal the Strike/Flight medal (8th), NASA Outstanding Leadership medal 1992, NASA Exceptional Svc. medals 1989, 91; recipient U. So. Calif. Alumni award of Merit, 1989. Mem. Omega Psi Phi. Achievements include a veteran of four space flights. He has logged over 680 hours in space. In the space shuttle Columbia mission the crew deployed the SATCOM KU satellite and conducted experiments in astrophysics and materials processing. In that mission they conducted a successful night landing at Edwards Air Force Base. He was the pilot for the space shuttle Discovery mission in which the crew deployed the Hubble Space Telescope. Mr. Bolden was the commander for the Space shuttle Atlantis it was the first Spacelab mission. One of the experiments on that mission was an artificial beam of electrons that was used to stimulate a man-made auroral discharge. For the Space shuttle Discover he was commander again for what was the first joint US/Russian Space shuttle mission. Address: Hqrs Marine Corps Divsn Pub Affairs Washington DC 20380-0001 Office: NASA 300 E St SW Washington DC 20001-2712

BOLDEN, KRISTIN ELIZABETH, secondary school educator; b. Marietta, Ohio, May 17, 1939; d. Howard Alfred Spindler and Thelma Kathryn (Totman) Spindler Williamson; m. Norman William Holt II, June 2, 1959 (div. Feb. 1966) m. James William Bolden, Oct. 8, 1966; children: James William, Bruce Douglas, Cynthia Sue. B.S. in Edn., Ohio No. U., 1961. Cert. elem. and secondary tchr., Ohio. Tchr. Spanish, Ohio No. U., Ada, 1961; tchr. Ada Elem. Sch., 1961-62; tchr. Spanish and English, Warren High Sch., Vincent, Ohio, 1962-99; mem. Southeastern Ohio Fgn. Lang. Alliance, 1983-99. Vol. tutor Hispanics Groveland Elem. Sch., 2002-2005. Ret. and sr. vol. program Lake & Sumter County (sponsored by Mid-Fla. Cmty. Svcs., Inc.). Jennings scholar, 1973-74. Mem. Delta Kappa Gamma. Republican. Presbyterian. Avocations: bridge, piano, singing, aquacise. Home: 4524 Glen Coe St Leesburg FL 34748-7583

BOLDEN, MARION A., superintendent; b. Apr. 28, 1946; 2 children. BA in Math Edn., Montclair State U., 1968, MA in Tchg., 1982. Tchr. math. Barringer H.S., Newark, 1968—82; dir. Office of Math., Newark Schs., 1989—96, assoc. supt. tchg. and learning, interim supt. for high schs., 1996—99, supt., 1999—. Avocations: antiques, collecting black memorabilia. Office: Newark Pub Schs 2 Cedar St Newark NJ 07102 Business E-Mail: mbolden@nps.k12.nj.us.

BOLDOVITCH, GERRI, art educator; d. Joseph and Esther Boldovitch. AA, Miami Dade C.C., 1971; BA, Fla. Atlantic U., 1971—73; MS, St. Thomas U., 1980. Cert. profl. educator in art edn. K-12, prof. educator in specific learning disabilities K-12, profl. educator in varying exceptional edn. K-12, endorsement ESOL, educator English to spkrs. of other langs. Art instr. grades 10-12 Miami Norland Sr. H.S., Dade County Pub. Schs., Miami, 1973—74; art instr. K-6 Oak Grove Elem., Miami, 1974—78, Bay Harbor Elem., 1977—84; art instr. K-5 Greynolds Park Elem., Miami, 1984—87, Ojus Elem., Miami, 1987—89, North Beach Elem., Miami, 1989—91, Highland Oaks Elem., North Miami, 1991—94, Madie Ives Elem., Miami, 1994—2000, Hibiscus Elem., Miami, 1977—; art instr. k-5 Hubert O. Sibley Elem., Miami, Fla., 2003—. Mem. PTA, Dade County Pub. Schs., Miami, 1977—2000; participant South Fla. State Cmty. Safe Sch. Summit, Ft. Lauderdale, Fla., 1998. Etchings exhibited in London, sculpture exhibited in Mexico City, crafts exhibited in Can. Founding mem. Nat. Campaign for Tolerance; mem. Friends of the Everglades, Miami, 2003; contbr. United Way, Miami, 1973—2002. Named to Wall of Tolerance, Civil Rights Meml. Ctr., Montgomery, 2005. Mem.: PTA, NEA, Nat. Art Edn. Assn., United Tchrs. of Dade County. Avocations: theater, music, reading, art-related activities.

BOLDREY, EDWIN EASTLAND, retinal surgeon, educator; b. San Francisco, Dec. 8, 1941; s. Edwin Barkley and Helen Burns (Eastland) B.; m. Catherine Rose Oliphant, Oct. 20, 1973; children: Jennifer Elizabeth, Melissa Jeanne. BA with honors, De Pauw U., 1963; MD, Northwestern U., Chgo., 1967. Diplomate Am. Bd. Ophthalmology. Rotating intern U. Wash., Seattle, 1967-68; resident in gen. surgery U. Minn., Mpls., 1968-69; resident in ophthalmology U. Calif., San Francisco, 1971-74; Heed Found. fellow in retinal and vitreous surgery Washington U., St. Louis, 1974-75; mem. staff dept. ophthalmology Palo Alto (Calif.) Med. Clinic, 1975-91; dept. chmn., 1989-91; pvt. practice, San Jose, Mountain View, Calif., 1991—. Clin. instr. Stanford (Calif.) U. Med. Sch., 1975-79, asst. clin. prof., 1979-87, assoc. clin. prof., 1987—; cons. VA Hosp., Palo Alto, Calif., 1976—; vice chmn. dept. ophthalmology Good Samaritan Hosp., San Jose, 1993-95, chmn., 1995-97. Contbr. articles to med. jours., chpt. to book. Lt. comdr. M.C., USNR, 1969-71. Recipient Asbury award dept. ophthalmology U. Calif., San Francisco, 1973. Fellow: ACS, Am. Acad. Ophthalmology (honor award 1989); mem.: AMA, Cordes Eye Soc. (pres. 1995—96), Western Retina Study Club (charter, exec. sec.-treas. 1983—95), Peninsula Eye Soc. (pres. 1987—88), Am. Soc. Retinal Surgeons (charter), Retina Soc., also others. Avocations: skiing, hiking, travel. Office: No Calif Retina Vitreous Assocs Inc 2512 Samaritan Ct Ste A San Jose CA 95124-4002

BOLDT, HEINZ, aerospace engineer; b. July 12, 1923; s. August and Marie (Hamann) B.; m. Christa Friebel, Mar. 25, 1965; children: Pierre, Manon. Diploma in engring., Technische Universität, Berlin, 1951; student, Wirtschaftsakademie, Berlin, 1953—57. Tech. dir. Borsig AG, Berlin, 1951-66; mem. exec. bd. dor prodn., dir. Messerschmitt-Werke Flugzeug-Union Sud, München-Augsburg, Germany, 1967-70; exec. bd. prodn., gen. proxi Klöckner_Humboldt-Deutz, Köln, Germany, 1970-72; mem. exec. bd. for devel., constrn. and prodn. FAHR AG, Gottmadingen, Germany, 1970-72; pres. VDI-Bodenseebezirksverein, Friedrichshafen, Germany, 1971-76; mem. exec. bd. Dornier GmbH, Munich, 1972-77; pres. Deutsche Indistrieanlagen Gesellschaft mbH, Berlin, 1978-82; rep. Machinoexport. Holder over 100 patents in field. Served with German Army Air Force, 1942-45. Recipient Ring for Honour VDI-Ehrenring, 1962. Mem. Am. C. of C., Club der Luftfahrt. Home: Golfclub The Oaks 280 Saratoga Ct Osprey FL 34229-9386 also: Pullach 6a 83059 Kolbermoor Germany E-mail: heinzboldt@verizon.net.

BOLDT, JEFFREY P., embryologist, researcher; b. Buffalo, Dec. 16, 1955; s. Joseph G. and Mary J. Boldt; m. Ann L. Happ, Sept. 28, 1991; children: Amanda C., Alyssa C. PhD of Anatomical Scis., SUNY-Buffalo, 1983. Cert. High complexity lab. dir. Am. Bd. Bioanalysis, 1994. Sci. dir. CryoEggs Internat., Phoenix, 2004—05, Assisted Fertility Svcs., Indpls., 1997—. Mem.: Am. Soc. for Reproductive Medicine. Home: 13987 Springmill Ponds Circle Carmel IN 46032 Office: Assisted Fertility Services 8040 Clearvista Parkway Suite 510 Indianapolis IN 46256 Office Phone: 317-621-2497. Office Fax: 317-621-7285. E-mail: jboldt@ecommunity.com.

BOLDT, MICHAEL HERBERT, lawyer; b. Detroit, Oct. 11, 1950; s. Herbert M. and Mary Therese (Fitzgerald) B.; m. Margaret E. Clarke, May 25, 1974; children: Timothy (dec.), Matthew. Student, U. Detroit, 1968-70; BA, Wayne State U., 1972; JD, U. Mich., 1975. Bar: Ind. 1975, U.S. Dist. Ct. (so. dist.) Ind. 1975, U.S. Ct. Appeals (7th cir.) 1979, U.S. Supreme Ct. 1980, U.S. Ct. Appeals (D.C. cir.) 1983. Assoc. Ice Miller, Indpls., 1975-81, ptnr., 1982—. Bd. dirs. Brooke's Place for Grieving Young People, Inc. Contbr. articles to profl. jours. Mem. Ind. State Bar Assn., Indpls. Bar Assn., Highland Golf and Country Club (bd. dirs.). Office: Ice Miller Box 82001 1 American Sq Indianapolis IN 46282-0002 Office Phone: 317-236-2327. Business E-Mail: Michael.Boldt@icemiller.com.

BOLDT, OSCAR CHARLES, construction company executive; b. Appleton, Wis., Apr. 20, 1924; s. Oscar John and Dorothy A. (Bartmann) B.; m. Patricia Hamar, July 9, 1949; children: Charles, Thomas, Margaret. BSCE, U. Wis., 1948; hon. degree, Ripon Coll., 2001; hon. degrees (hon.), Lawrence U., 2003. Pres. O.J. Boldt Constrn. Co., Appleton, 1950-79, CEO, chmn. bd. dirs., 1979-84; chmn. bd. dirs. The Boldt Group Inc., Appleton, 1984—; sec. W.S. Patterson Co., 1963-89. Trustee Lawrence U., 1981—; emeritus bd. dirs. M&I Bank, L.A., 2002 Chmn. bd. dirs. Cmty. Found. for Fox Valley Region, 1991-93; pres. Appleton YMCA, 1955-57, Appleton Meml. Hosp., 1975-76; bd. dirs. United Health Wis., 1990-99; co-chmn. fund drive Fox Cities United Way, 1994. 2d lt. USAAF, 1943-45. Named to Paper Industry Internat. Hall of Fame, 2000, Wis. Bus. Hall of Fame, 2003, Jr. Achievement Hall of Fame, 2003, Appleton H.S. Hall of Fame, 1999; recipient Disting. Svc. award, Appleton Jaycees, 1960, Disting. Engr. award, U. Wis., 1985, Walter Rugland Cmty. Svc. award, 1988, Master Entrepreneur award, Ernst and Young, 1991, Renaissance award, 1991, Regent's award, St. Olaf's Coll., 1993, Exec. of Yr. award, N.E. Wis.'s Sales and Mktg. Mag., 1994, Disting. Alumni award, U. Wis. Alumni Assn., 1999, Disting. Contractor award, ASCE, 2000, Wis. Assoc. Gen. Contractor Horizon award, 2003, Walter A. Nushert, Sr. Constructor award, 2005; Paul Harris fellow, 1979. Mem. Appleton Area C. of C. (pres. 1967), Appleton Rotary (pres. 1975-76, Vocat. Svc. award 1977, Paul Harris fellow), Riverview Country Club (pres. 1968-69). Republican. Presbyterian. Home: 1715 Reid Dr Appleton WI 54914-5175 Office: The Boldt Group Inc PO Box 373 2525 N Roemer Rd Appleton WI 54911-8623 Office Phone: 920-225-6100. Business E-Mail: oscar.boldt@boldt.com.

BOLDT, WILLIAM GREGORY, academic administrator, consultant; b. Berkeley, Calif., Apr. 22, 1948; s. Alvin M. and Lucille Frances (Keefe) B.; m. Genene Lee Hutchins, Feb. 2, 1974; children: Kim, Kristin, Ryan. BS, U. Oreg., 1971, MS, 1975, EdD, 1980. Asst. prof. Oreg. State U., Corvallis, 1971-76, assoc. prof., 1980-86; asst. prof. U. Oreg., Eugene, 1976-80; dist. dir. Cornell U., Ithaca, N.Y., 1986-89, asst. dean coll. agriculture and life scis., 1989—; pres. Creative Mktg. Assocs., Ithaca, 1984; v.p. for univ. advancement Calif. Polytechnic State U., San Luis Obispo, Calif.; vice chancellor for univ. advancement U. Calif. Riverside, 2004—. Chair Cornell U. Mktg. Com., 1987-90, Oreg. State U. Mktg. Com., 1983-86. Author: Creative Marketing for Higher Education, 1990, Strategic Marketing for Higher Education, 1992, Marketing Your College, 1992, Fund Raising for Higher Education, 1992; editor Jour. of Extension, 1990. Pack master Cub Scouts Am., Cayuga Heights, Ithaca, 1991; trustee Tompkins County Libr., Ithaca, 1992. Recipient Outstanding Profl. award Oreg. Therapeutic Recreation Soc., 1980, Disting. Svc. award Nat. Assn. 4-H Agents, 1985, Excellence award SUNY, 1992. Mem. Epsilon Sigma Phi (Superior Performance award 1991, Nat. Mktg. Chair 1992). Office: Vice Chancellor Univ Adv Univ Calif Riverside 900 Univ Ave Riverside CA 92521

BOLDUC, DIANE EILEEN MARY BUCHHOLZ, psychotherapist; b. Elizabeth, N.J., May 1, 1953; d. Howard Robert and Barbara Ann (Bowen) Buchholz; m. David Vianney Buchholz Bolduc, May 21, 1977; children: Elizabeth, Katharine. BA cum laude in Psychology, U. N.H., 1975, MEd Counseling, 1976. Lic. clin. mental health counselor. Counselor, asst. supr., social worker III Divsn. Children & Youth Svcs., Manchester/Salem, NH, 1978—88; supr. Child Health Svcs., Manchester, NH, 1987—88; program coord. N.H. Task Force on Child Abuse & Neglect, Concord, 1988—91; dir. youth & family svcs. Luth. Social Svcs. New England, Concord, NH, 1992—94; home/sch. coord. Raymond Schs., NH, 1994—96; counselor Pelham H.S., NH, 1996—. Mem.: ACA, Am. Mental Health Counselors Assn., N.H. Sch. Counselors Assn., N.H. Mental Health Counselors Assn. (treas. 2001—), Women*Spirit*Song. Home: 189 Ray St Manchester NH 03104

BOLDUC, ERNEST JOSEPH, association management consultant, not-for-profit developer, consultant; b. Lawrence, Mass., June 11, 1924; s. Ernest Joseph and Ernestine (Mercier) B.; m. Grace Gaydis, June 23, 1945; children: Philip, Richard, Stephen. BS in M.E, Northeastern U., 1948. Cert. Assn. Exec. Market devel. rep. Kawneer Co., Boston and N.Y.C., 1950-55; market devel. rep. Kaiser Aluminum, N.Y.C., 1955-58; exec. sec. Com. Tool Steel Producers Am. Iron and Steel Inst., N.Y.C., 1958-66; exec. dir. Nat. Council Paper Industry for Air and Stream Improvement, N.Y.C., 1966-83; prin. EJB Assocs., Armonk, N.Y., 1983—. Lectr. in assn. mgmt., meeting planning; coord. program USAID for Mongolian C. of C. trade devel. delegation touring U.S., 1993; cons. to U.S. Dept. Commerce in Albania on assn. mgmt. project, 1995; cons. to World Environment Ctr. projects, Slovakia, Rumania, Bulgaria, Ukraine; cons. USAID-PEM Project, Haiti, 1998. Author: Curtain Wall Do's and Don'ts, 1955, Planning the Successful Meeting, 1959, The Art of Budgeting For Associations, 1980, The Three P's of Running Meetings, 1990; editor Tool Steel Trends, 1961-66. Vol. exec. Internat. Exec. Svc. Corps in Botswana, 1990, in Bulgaria, 1992; trustee No. Castle Hist. Soc., 1990-92; cons. to USAID Mission in Ghana, Africa on assn. mgmt. project, 1992; vol. advisor on assn. mgmt. related projects in Bulgaria for Citizens Democracy Corp in Bulgaria, 1995, Tblisi, Georgia, 1999; vol. speaker Am. Cancer Soc. on prostate cancer, 1998—; vol. advisor ACDI, VOCA and Ctr. for Internat. Pvt. Enterprise, 2001, Romania. Decorated Air medal with 3 oak leaf clusters; recipient Man of Yr. award N.Y. Producers Coun., 1955, W. Erwin Story citation Northeastern U., 1991, Vol. Recognition award Am. Cancer Soc., 1998. Mem. Am. Soc. Assn. Execs. (life; awards com. 1978-80, internat. com.

1992), N.Y. Soc. Assn. Execs. (life; dir. 1979-80, chmn. govt. rels. com. 1979-81, presdl. citation 1987, Disting. Svc. award 1993), Meeting Planners Internat. (bd. dirs. N.Y. chpt. 1979-80), Am. Arbitration Assn. (panel arbitrators). Office: 2 Sunrise Pl Armonk NY 10504-1444 Office Phone: 914-273-4697. Personal E-mail: ejbolduc@aol.com.

BOLDUC, MARTIN, research scientist; s. Richard Bolduc and Denise Fournier; 1 child, Pierre-Olivier. PhD Physics, U. Que., Montreal, 2003. Rsch. asst. SUNY - Coll. of Nanoscale Sci., Albany, NY, 2003—. Fellow Nserc Bp, 2004-2006, Rsch. Found. of SUNY, 2003-2006. Achievements include invention of magnetic silicon. Home: 67 Hillcrest Albany NY 12203 Office: SUNY - Coll Nanoscale Sci 255 Fuller Rd Albany NY Office Phone: 518-956-7018.

BOLEN, DAVID BENJAMIN, ambassador; b. Dec. 23, 1923; m. Betty Gayden; children: Cynthia, Myra, David. BS, MS, U. Colo., 1950; MPA, Harvard U., 1960; student, Nat. War Coll. Joined Fgn. Service, 1950; adminstrv. asst. Monrovia, Liberia, 1950-52; econ. asst. Karachi, Pakistan, 1952-55; detailed internat. economist Dept. Commerce, Washington, 1955-56, State Dept., 1957-58; desk officer for Afghanistan, 1958-59; detailed advanced econ. studies Harvard, 1959-60; econ. officer Accra, Ghana, 1960-62; staff asst. Washington, 1962-64; officer-in-charge Nigerian affairs, 1964-66; detailed Nat. War Coll., 1966-67; econ. and comml. officer, econ. counselor Bonn, Germany, 1967-72; econ.-comml. counselor Belgrade, 1972-74; ambassador to Botswana, Lesotho, Swaziland, 1974-76; dep. asst. sec. state for African affairs U.S. Dept. State, Washington, 1976-77; ambassador to German Democratic Republic, 1977-80; assoc. dir. internat. affairs E.I. duPont de Nemours & Co., Inc., Wilmington, Del., 1981-89, cons., 1989-94. Author (collection): Bolen Papers Repository, Hoover Archives, Stanford U.; contbg. editor: World Economic Problems and Policies, 1965. Mem. preliminary investigatory com. Del. Ct. on the Judiciary, 1990-92; mem. polit. sci. vis. com. MIT, 1983-88; trustee U. Del., 1983-92; bd. dirs. Med. Ctr. Del., Del. Coun. Econ. Edn., U.S. Coun. on Internat. Bus., 1981-89, Internat. Mgmt. Devel. Inst., 1981-89, Pacific Basin Trade and Econ. Coun., 1981-89, U.S.-USSR Trade and Econ. Coun., 1981-89, U.S.-German Dem. Republic Trade and Econ. Coun., 1981-89, Coun. Fgn. Rels., U.S.-Yugoslav Econ. Coun., 1986-90, U. Colo. Found., Inc., 1990-96; mem. U. Colo. Bus. Dean's Adv. Coun., 1992-98; dir. Denver Com. on Fgn. Rels., 1994-99; mem. U.S. Olympic track and field team, 1948; advisor Berlin Sculpture Fund, 1997—. Recipient Robert Russell Meml. award, 1948; Norlin Disting. Alumni award U. Colo., 1969; named to Hall of Honor, 1969, Alumni of Century, 1976; recipient Disting. Service award U. Colo., 1983; inducted U. Colo. Athletic Hall of Fame, 2000. Mem. Am. Coun. on Germany (chmn. Denver chpt. 1995-99), Nat. War Coll. Alumni Assn., Fgn. Serv. Assn., Wilmington World Affairs Coun. (dir. 1981-92), Internat. Amateur Athletic Assn., Wilmington Club, U. Colo. Alumni Assn., Harvard Alumni Assn.

BOLEN, M. CHRISTOPHER, lawyer; b. Ft. Worth, Tex., Dec. 26, 1958; BS in Engring. Mgmt. summa cum laude, So. Methodist U., 1981, MBA, JD, So. Methodist U., 1985. Bar: Tex. 1985, NC 1988. Mem. Womble Carlyle Sandridge & Rice PLLC, Durham, NC, co-chair intellectual property practice group. Mem.: Internat. Trademark Assn., Licensing Executives Soc., NC Technologies Assn. (bd. dirs.), NC Bar Assn. Office: Womble Carlyle Sandridge & Rice PLLC PO Box 13069 Research Triangle Park NC 27709 Office Phone: 919-484-2391. Office Fax: 919-484-2089. Business E-Mail: cbolen@wcsr.com.

BOLEN, MAX CARLTON, retired physics professor; b. Waynetown, Ind., Sept. 23, 1919; s. Forrest Blanchard and Grace Artimeci (Wilkinson) B.; m. Lois Kathleen Larkins, May 1, 1942; children: Ronald Lee, Roger Kent. AB, Wabash Coll., 1941; cert. of meterology, U. Chgo., 1943; MS, Purdue U., 1950; PhD, Tex. A&M U., 1961. Math/physics tchr. Wingate (Ind.) High Sch., 1941-42; asst. prof., prof., chmn. physics dept. Millikin U., Decatur, Ill., 1948-59; TV weatherman Decatur, Ill., 1953-55; vis. asst. prof. Tex. A&M U., College Station, 1957-58, Robert A. Welch rsch. fellow, 1958-59; assoc. prof., chmn. physics dept. Trinity U., San Antonio, 1959-63; rsch. physicist S.W. Rsch. Inst., San Antonio, 1963; assoc. prof. physics Oklahoma City U., 1963-65; prof. physics, chmn. dept. U. Tex., El Paso, 1965-69, coord. sci. edn., 1969-87, prof. emeritus physics, 1987—. Cons. in physics S.W. Rsch. Inst., San Antonio, 1962-63; advisor to exec. com. Insights Sci. Mus., El Paso, 1970—. Co-author: Challenges to Science-Physical Science, 1973, revision, 1979; contbr. articles to profl. jours. Chmn. sch. devel. div. United Way of El Paso, 1971-74; mem. Indiana Christian Youth Coun., 1938-41; exec. coun. regional planning conf., Lake Geneva, Wis., 1940; deacon, elder, trustee Presbyn. Ch. USA, Decatur, Il., San Antonio, El Paso, Tex., children's bible discussion leader, 2000-04, asst. class adminstr., 2003—; mem. Internat. Bible Study Fellowship, 1999-2000. 1st lt. U.S. Army 1942-46. Fellow AAAS, Tex. Acad. Sci.; mem. Am. Meteorol. Soc., Am. Inst. Physics, Am. Assn. Physics Tchr., Am. Phys. Soc. (membership com. div. high polymer physics 1960), Nat. Sci. Tchrs. Assn. (life), Sci. Tchr. Assn. Tex. (hon. life mem., B.T. Slater award 1986), Sigma Pi Sigma. Republican. Presbyterian. Avocations: travel, camping, reading, golf. Home: 6225 Westwind Dr El Paso TX 79912-3831

BOLENDER, JAMES HENRY, retired tire and rubber manufacturing executive; b. New Boston, Ohio, Nov. 26, 1937; s. James Harold and Lucille Virgie Bolender; m. Nancy Jo Paull, Feb. 3, 1970; 1 child, Shawn O. BS, Ohio U., 1959. Contr. Firestone Tire and Rubber Co., Valencia, Venezuela, 1971-73, Bethune, France, 1973-76, mgr. corp. acctg. Akron, Ohio, 1976-80, asst. contr., 1980-81, group v.p. fin., 1981-82, v.p., contr., 1982-88, internat. sr. v.p., 1988-91; v.p., CFO Jetstream Power Internat. Inc., Holmesville, Ohio, 1992-98. Trustee Akron Urban League and Community Ctr., 1979-81, Akron Svc. Ctr., 1982-86, Akron Gen. Med. Ctr., 1986-87.

BOLES, DAVID LAVELLE, lawyer; b. Tulia, Tex., May 22, 1937; s. Jerry Hoytt and Irma Ruth (Walker) B.; m. Kerstin Gunilla Stenrudh, May 25, 1959 (div. 1984); children— David LaVelle Jr., Kerstin Regina Boles Davenport, William Gail-Holger. Student North Tex. U., 1955-57; B.S., Trinity U., 1959; J.D., U. Tex., 1963. Bar: Tex. 1963. Asst. atty. gen. Tex., Austin, 1963-67; sole practice, Denton, Tex., 1967-69; house counsel, corp. officer Sam P. Wallace Co., Inc., Dallas, 1969-73, adminstrv. mgr. contracts, labor, indsl. rels., ins., 1973-85, house counsel, corp. officer MMR/Wallace Group, Inc. and subs., 1985-90; pvt. practice, 1990-2002. Deacon Presbyn. Ch., Austin, Denton, 1963-74, elder, Taos, N.Mex., 1999—. Mem. Tex. Bar Assn., Denton County Bar Assn., Trinity Alumni Assn. (pres. 1965), Denton C. of C. Home and Office: HC 71 Box 100A Taos NM 87571-9501

BOLES, DONALD MICHAEL, lawyer; b. N.Y.C., Nov. 30, 1951; s. Oreste George and Rosina Constance (D'Angelo) B.; m. Patricia G. Stachnick, Dec. 28, 1973; children: Jennifer Anne, Christopher Michael. Student, Fairleigh-Dickinson U., 1972-73; BEE, JD, U. Dayton, 1976. Bar: Pa. 1979, U.S. Patent and Trademark Office 1980, N.Y. 1986, N.J. 1987, U.S. Dist. Ct. N.J. 1987, U.S. Dist. Ct. (ea. dist.) N.Y. 1987, U.S. Dist. Ct. (so. dist.) N.Y. 1988. Patent atty. Westinghouse Electric Co., Pitts., 1980-82, AMP, Inc., Harrisburg, Pa., 1982-85, Ostrolenk, Faber et al, N.Y.C., 1985-86, Weingram & Zall, Maywood, N.J., 1987-89; atty. IBM, East Fishkill, N.Y., 1989-92; sr. atty. Siemens Corp., 1992-97; sr. v.p. intellectual property, chief patent strategist Interdigital Comm. Corp., King of Prussia, Pa., 1997—. Adj. instr. L.I. U., West Point, Sparkill, N.Y., 1987-95. With USMC, 1970-71 Mem. Pa. Bar Assn., Am. Intellectual Property Law Assn. Office: InterDigital Comm Corp 781 Third Ave King Of Prussia PA 19406-1409 Office Phone: 610-878-7865. E-mail: donald.boles@interdigital.com, donald_boles@yahoo.com.

BOLES, ERIC PAUL, staffing company executive; b. Albany, Ky., July 10, 1965; s. Don Howard and Doris L. (Claborn) B.; m. Tabitha Hope Appleby, Oct. 22, 1992 (div. Aug. 1995). AA in Computer Sci., U. Ky., 1990; Real Estate Cert., Cumberland Real Estate Acad., N.C., 1986; cert. paralegal, So. Career Inst., 1989; BS in Computer Sci., Am. Inst. Computer Sci., 1997. Cert. network engr. Network suport splst. Long John Silvers, Lexington, Ky., 1990-92; network engr. Pomeroy Computer Resources, Lexington, 1992-95; MIS mgr. Studio Plus Hotels, Lexington, 1995-97; v.p. Alliance Staffing, Lexington, 1997-98; owner, pres. Techsource Inc., Lexington, 1998—; co-owner Consig4u, 1999—. With U.S. Army, 1983-85. Mem. Soc. Human Resources, Lexington (Ky.) C. of C., Masons, Disabled Am. Vets. Home and Office: 813 NW 99th Ave Fort Lauderdale FL 33324-1138

BOLES, RICHARD GREGORY, clinical geneticist, researcher; b. Pasadena, Calif., Apr. 8, 1961; s. Richard Eugene and Dorothy Mae (Martolio) B.; children: Scott, Philip, Henry. BS in Biochemistry magna cum laude, U. Ariz., 1983; MD, UCLA, 1987. Diplomate Am. Bd. Pediatrics, Am. Bd. Med. Genetics. Pediatric intern, resident Harbor-UCLA Med. Ctr., Torrance, Calif., 1987-90; fellow in genetics Yale U., New Haven, 1991-93; asst. prof. pediatrics Sch. Medicine U. So. Calif., L.A., 1993—2004, assoc. prof. pediats. Sch. Medicine, 2004—; attending physician Children's Hosp. of L.A., 1993—, dir. prenatal diagnosis ctr., 1997-99. Mem. sci. adv. bd. United Mitochondria Disease Found., 1996—; mem. profl. adv. bd. Cyclic Vomiting Syndrome Assn. U.S.A./Can., 1998—. English lang. editor Micro Structure Bull., Uppsala, Sweden, 1994-99; contbr. more than 50 articles to sci. jours. Grantee United Mitochondrial Disease Found., 1997, NIH, 2000-03. Mem. Soc. Inherited Metabolic Disease, Am. Soc. Human Genetics, Phi Beta Kappa. Achievements include ongoing research projects in mitochondrial genetics, especially regarding testing modalities; research in mitochondrial disease and cycling vomiting syndrome. Office: Children's Hosp LA Box 90 4650 W Sunset Blvd Los Angeles CA 90027-6062 Office Phone: 323-669-2178. Business E-Mail: rboles@chla.usc.edu.

BOLES, ROGER, otolaryngologist; b. Oakland, California, Jan. 13, 1928; s. Albert and Julia B.; m. Marianna (Reeves), June 16, 1956; children: Martin Reeves, Melissa. BA, Stanford U., 1949; post grad., Denver U., 1950—52; MD, George Washington U., 1956. Diplomate Am. Bd. Otolaryngology, Am. Bd. Med. Splty. Intern Fitzsimmons Army Hosp., Denver, 1956—57; asst. resident through sr. clin. instr. Mich. U. Hosp., Ann Arbor, 1959—63, faculty dept. otorhinoloaryngology, 1963—74, prof., 1973—74; prof., chmn. otolaryngology U. Calif. Sch. Medicine, San Francisco, 1974—98; pres. med. staff U. Calif., San Francisco, 1982—83, prof. emeritus otolargyngology, 1998, ret., 1998. Cons. for otolaryngology to Surgeon Gen., USAF, 1975-85; mem. staff San Francisco Gen. Hosp., 1984—, Childrens Hosp. San Francisco (bd. dir. 1987-91); cons. in otolaryngology Va. Hosp., Ann Arbor, Wayne County Hosp., Eloise, Mich., So. Mich. Prison, Jackson Fed. Penitentiary, Milan, Mich., 1963-74, Letterman Gen. Hosp., Presidio of San Francisco, U.S. Naval Hosp., Oakland, Calif., 1974-93, Kaiser Hosp., Oakland, 1975, Va. Hosp., San Francisco; bd. dir. Council Med. Splty. Socs., 1981-82, sec., 1982-83; bd. dir. Am. Acad. Otolaryngology Head and Neck Surgery, 1981-88, coord. for continuing med. edn., 1980-83, pres., 1987; mem. Accreditation Coun. for Continuing Med. Edn., 1986-92, chmn., 1990; chmn. PEPP com., 1988-89, 90, vice chmn., 1989, residency rev. com. for otolaryngology; Marshall Hale Hosp., San Francisco, 1975-83, bd. dir., 1983-87; mem. Am. Bd. Med. Splty., 1984-89, exec. com., 1988-89; vis. prof. various universities; participant in conferences, conventions, workshops, seminars, inst. Contbg. chapters. to books, numerous reviews, articles, and abstracts to profl. lit. Served in MC, AUS., 1956-59. Fellow ACS (chmn. adv. coun. for otolaryngology 1977-80, adv. com. for continuing med. edn. 1982-83), Am. Laryngol. Soc.; mem. AMA (ho. del. 1975-82, bd. editors archives otolaryngology 1975-85, mem. reference com. on ins. and med. svc. 1978, adv. com. for continuing med. edn. 1981-87), AOA Hon. Med. Soc., Am. Acad. Opthalmology and Otolaryngology (assoc. sec. com. on continuing edn. 1974-80, chmn. manuals editorial com. 1977-80, mem. at large exec. com. div. otolaryngology 1977-78, mem. interspecialty cooperation com. coun. of med. splty. soc. 1986-88), Am. Acad. Facial Plastic and Reconstructive Surgery (co-chmn. standards com. 1977-80, med. edn. com. 1979-81—), Soc. Univ. Otolaryngologists (sec. treas. 1973-80, chmn. com. on under grad. curriculum 1969-74, mem. exec. council 1968-79, pres. 1978), Council Acad. Soc., Assn. Am. Med. Coll., Assn. Acad. Dept. Otolaryngology (vice chmn. sub-com. Nat. Cancer Inst. liaison com. 1977-81, chmn. edn. nominating com. 1978-79), Am. Bronco-Esophagological Assn. (mem. coun. 1981-82), Am. Bd. Otolaryngology(bd. dir. 1974-91, exec. com. 1981-88, mem. various committees 1974-91, chmn. ad hoc com. for nomination process for membership on bd. dir. 1976-77, pres. 1986-88), Am. Council Otolaryngology (mem. sub-com. on hearing 1976-80, rsch. adv. com. 1977-81, pres. 1978-79), Am. Laryngol., Rhinological and Otolaryn. Soc. (mem. editl. bd. transactions 1978-88, mem. coun. 1982-88, pres. 1986-87, historian 1994—), Am. Soc. Neck and Head Surgery, Otosclerosis Study Group, Am. Tinnitus Assn. (sci. adv. bd. 1978-81), Pacific Coast Oto-Opthal. Soc., Soc. Med. Cons. to Armed Forces, Calif. Med. Assn. (program co-chmn. sect. on allergy and otolaryngology, neurology and otolaryngology 1977-78, chmn. adv. council of otolaryngology 1979-80), Calif. Otolaryn. Soc. (pres. 1978-80), U. Calif. San Francisco Sch. Medicine Alumni Faculty Assn. (pres. 1978-79), Am. Otological Soc., Am. Laryngol. Assn. (coun. 1983-84), San Francisco Med. Soc. (bd. dir. 1983-90, treas. 1989-90), Royal Coll. Surgeons in Ireland (hon.), U. Mich. Med. Ctr. Alumni Assn. (bd. gov. 1983), Gold Headed Cane Soc. (hon.), U. Calif. San Francisco Sch. Medicine. Home: PO Box 620203 Woodside CA 94062-0203 Office: Univ Calif San Francisco Dept Otolaryngology 400 Parnassus Ave # A-717 San Francisco CA 94143

BOLEY, BRUNO ADRIAN, engineering educator; b. Gorizia, Italy, May 13, 1924; came to U.S., 1939, naturalized, 1945; s. Orville F. and Rita (Luzzatto) Bolaffio; m. Sara R. Kaufman, May 12, 1949 (dec. Sept. 1983); children: Jacqueline Boley Acquaviva, Daniel L. B.C.E., CCNY, 1943, D.Sc. hon., 1982; M. in Aero. Engring., Poly. Inst. Bklyn., 1945, D.Sc. in Aero. Engring., 1946. Asst. dir. structural research, aero. engring. dept. Poly. Inst. Bklyn., 1943-48; engring. specialist Goodyear Aircraft Corp., 1948-50; assoc. prof. aero. engring. Ohio State U., 1950-52; assoc. prof. civil engring. Columbia U., 1952-58, prof., 1958-68, dir. postdoctoral preceptor program, 1962-68; Joseph P. Ripley prof. engring., chmn. theoretical and applied mechanics Cornell U., Ithaca, N.Y., 1968-72; dean Technol. Inst., Walter P. Murphy prof. Northwestern U., Evanston, Ill., 1973-86, dean, prof. emeritus, 1986—; prof. civil engring. and engring. mechanics Columbia U., N.Y.C., 1987—. Mem. adv. com. George Washington U., Princeton U., Yale U., Cornell U., FAMU/FSU Inst. Engring., Duke U., Lehigh U., Nat. Cheng Kung U., Republic of China, Istanbul Tech. U., Rowan Coll. N.J.; mem. sci. adv. coun. Internat. Ctr. for Mech. Sics., Udine, Italy, 1980—, Istanbul Tech. U.; chmn. Midwest Program for Minorities in Engring., 1975-82; bd. govs. Argonne Nat. Lab., 1983-86; bd. advisors Who's Who in Sci. and Engring. Author: Theory of Thermal Stresses, 1960, High Temperature Structures and Materials, 1964, Thermoinelasticity, 1970, Crossfire in Professional Education, 1976; also articles, numerous tech. papers; editor-in-chief: Mechanics Research Communications; bd. editors Jour. Thermal Stresses, Bull. Mech. Engring. Edn., Internat. Jour. Computers and Structures, Internat. Jour. Engring. Sci., Internat. Jour. Fracture Mechanics, Internat. Jour. Mechs. and Control, Internat. Jour. Mech. Engring. Scis., Internat. Jour. Solids and Structures, Jour. Applied Mechanics, Jour. Structural Mechanics Software, Letters in Applied and Engring. Sci., Nuclear Engring. and Design. Recipient Disting. Alumnus award Poly. Inst. N.Y., 1974, Townsend Harris medal, 1981, commendation Ill. Ho. of Reps., 1986, Theodore von Karman medal ASCE, 1991, Outstanding Scholar award Sigma Xi, 1996, Lagrange Lectr. award Accademia Nazionale dei Lincei, Rome, 1996; NATO fellow, 1964-65, NSF fellow, 1965, Japan Soc. Promotion of Sci. Rsch. fellow, 1987. Fellow AIAA, AAAS, Am. Acad. Mechanics (pres. 1974, Disting. Svc. medal 1987), Am. Soc. Engring. Edn.; mem. ASME (hon., exec. com., pres. applied mechanics divsn. 1975, bd. govs. 1984-86, Worcester Reed Warner medal 1991, Daniel C. Drucker medal 2001), NAE (life, chmn. task force engring. edn. 1979-80, edn. adv. bd. 1982-86, editl. bd. The Bridge 1986-90, membership com. 1984-88, awards com. 1993-95, chair 1996), Soc. Engring. Scis. (pres. 1975, Disting. Svc. medal 1987, life), Assn. Chairmen Depts. Mechanics (founder, pres. 1970-72), Internat. Assn. Structural Mechanics in Reactor Tech. (chmn. 1977, adv.-gen. 1979—), Thermal Stress Congress (advisor-gen. 1997), Internat. Union Theoretical and Applied Mechanics (sec. Congress com. 1976-96, bur. 1988-96, treas. 1992-96, personal mem. Gen. Assembly 1980—, treas. 1992—), Am. Soc. Engring. Edn. (project bd. 1987, Centennial award 1993), N.Y. Acad. Scis. (Outstanding Educator of Am. 1971), U.S. Nat. Com. Theoretical and Applied Mechanics (chmn. 1975-79, personal mem. Gen. Assembly 1980—), Ill. Coun. Energy Rsch. and Devel. (chmn. 1979-84), Engring. Found. (conf. com. 1986-88). Home: 310 W 106th St New York NY 10025-3429

BOLGER, DOREEN, museum director; BA, Bucknell U., 1971; MA, U. Del., 1973; PhD, CUNY, 1983. Mem. curatorial staff Am. Wing Met. Mus. Art, N.Y.C., 1976—88, curator Am. painting and sculpture, 1989; curator painting and sculpture Amon Ctr. Mus., Ft. Worth, 1989-94; dir. RISD Mus., Providence, 1994-98, Balt. Mus. Art, 1998—. Panelist NEA, NEH; field reviewer Inst. for Mus. and Libr. Svcs.; curator women artists exhbn. for Govt. House, Annapolis, Md.; Ailsa Mellon Bruce vis. sr. fellow Ctr. for Advanced Study in the Visual Arts Nat. Gallery of Art; lectr. in field. Bd. dirs. several orgns. Chester Dale fellow Met. Mus. Art; grantee NEH, Met. Mus. Art Office: Balt Mus Art 10 Art Museum Dr Baltimore MD 21218-3898

BOLGER, DORITA YVONNE FERGUSON, librarian; b. Sharon, Pa., Apr. 18, 1951; d. Harold Edward Ferguson and Pauline May McQueen Ferguson; m. Terrence James Bolger, Sept. 24, 1977; children: Sarah Catherine Pauline, Matthew Terrence. BA, Pa. State U., 1973; MLS, Clarion U., 1978. English tchr. Greenville (Pa.) Area Schs., 1974—75; libr. asst. Pa. State U., Sharon, 1975—81; ref. libr. Westminster Coll., New Wilmington, Pa., 1981—. Mem. industry review bd. Sage Pubs., Inc., Thousand Oaks, Calif., 2001—; book rev. editor, contbr. Jour. Interlibr. Loan, Document Delivery & Electronic Access Haworth Press, Binghampton, NY, 1999—. Co-author: (novels) Church and Social Action, 1990. Founding mem., chair Mercer County (Pa.) Commn. for Women, 1989—93. Mem.: ALA. Office: Westminster Coll McGill Libr 319 S Market St New Wilmington PA 16172 Office Phone: 724-946-7330.

BOLGER, ROBERT J., lawyer; b. Phila., Apr. 25, 1955; BA with highest distinction, U. Va., JD, 1982. Bar: Md. 1982, US Dist. Ct., Md., DC 1998, US Tax Ct. Ptnr. Bus. and Mergers & Acquisitions Depts. Venable LLP, Washington, DC, Balt. Lectr. in field. Mem. Inner Cir. Michael D. Dingman Ctr. for Entrepreneurship, U. Md. Mem.: ABA (mem. Tax and Bus. Sect.), Balt. Assn. Tax Counsel, Md. State Bar Assn., Bar Assn. Balt. City, Fed. Comm. Bar Assn., Phi Beta Kappa. Office: Venable LLP 575 7th St NW Washington DC 20004 also: 1800 Mercantile Bank & Trust Bldg 2 Hopkins Plaza Baltimore MD 21201 Office Phone: 202-344-4902, 410-244-7724. Office Fax: 202-344-8300, 410-244-7742. E-mail: rjbolger@venable.com.

BOLGER, ROBERT JOSEPH, retired trade association executive; b. Phila., Aug. 9, 1922; s. Harold Stephen and Edna (Adams) B.; m. Helen Siegfried, May 22, 1954; children: Robert, Mary T., Cynthia A., Ann M., Catherine B., David A. BS, Villanova U., 1943; postgrad., Northwestern U., 1945-46, U. Pa., 1946-47, U. Geneva, 1948-49; DS in Pharmacy (hon.), Mass. Coll. Pharmacy, 1983. Salesman Container Corp., Phila., 1947; supr. sales Kraft Food Co., Phila., 1949-52; overseas mgr., dir. retail rels. Smith, Kline Beckman Corp., Phila., 1952-62; asst. to exec. v.p. Nat. Assn. Chain Drug Stores, Inc., Arlington, Va., 1962-67, pres., 1967-87; ret., 1987. Founder, developer Robert J. Bolger Assocs., 1988—; bd. dirs. Barr Labs., Pomona, NY, Am. Pharm. Inst., Washington, Am. Found. Pharm. Edn., Nat. Drug Trade Conf., pres., 1974—82. Co-author: Chain Drug Retailing, 1980. Bd. dirs. Nat. Coun. on Patient Info. and Edn.; hon. bd. dirs. Nat. Assn. Chain Drug Stores Inc.; Nacos Edn. Fedn. Lt. comdr. USNR, 1943—46, PTO. Decorated Air medal; named Man of Yr. Cosmetic and Toiletry sect. United Jewish Appeal, 1972, Chain Exec. of Yr., Chain Drug Rev., 1979; recipient Torch of Learning award Am. Friends of Hebrew U., 1987, Chain Drug Rev. Bd. Lifetime Achievement award, 1988, Robert B. Begley award for contbns. to chain drug industry, 1988. Mem. Am. Pharm. Assn., Com. of 100, U.S. C. of C., Cen. Coun. Nat. Retail Assns. (chmn.), Am. Retail Fedn. (bd. dirs.), Nat. Assn. Cmty. Pharmacists, Joint Commn. Pharmacy Practitioners, Pharmacists Against Drug Abuse (bd. dirs. 1986—), Am. Soc. Assn. Execs. (life), Nat. Assn. Execs. Club (bd. dirs.), Am. Druggist Bd. Advisers, Key Exec. Industry Coun., Alexandria Chief Execs., Belle Haven Country Club. Home and Office: 7705 Maid Marian Ct Alexandria VA 22306-2718 Office Phone: 703-660-8473. Office Fax: 703-660-8473. Personal E-mail: helenbolger@cox.net.

BOLGER, T(HOMAS) MICHAEL, lawyer; b. Minocqua, Wis., Dec. 23, 1939; s. Patrick Edward and Mary Frances (McConville) Bolger; m. Virginia Kay Empey, Aug. 24, 1968; children: John, Jennifer. BA, Marquette U., 1961; MA, PhL, St. Louis U., 1966; JD, Northwestern U., 1971. Bar: Wis. 1971. Mem. firm Quarles & Brady, Milw., 1971—, ptnr., 1978—; pres., CEO Med. Coll. Wis., 1990—. Instr. philosophy Marquette U., Milw., 1967—68. Editor: Northwestern Jour. Criminal Law, 1970—71; contbr. articles to profl. jours. Bd. dirs. Kearney Negro Welfare Found., 1974—, Milw. Repertory Theatre, 1977—, Milw. Ballet Found., Inc., 1981—; vice chmn. United Performing Arts Fund drive, 1976—77; pres. Artreach, Inc., 1979—, Milw. Repertory Theatre, 1980—, Milw. Sci. Edn. Consortium, 1994—; pres. bd. trustees Highland Cmty. Sch., 1976—, Milw. Ballet, 1987—; pres. bd. dirs. Hickory Hollow, 1978—; trustee, sec. U. Wis.-Milw. Found., 1976—; bd. dirs. Permanent Diaconate Program Milw. Archdiocese, 1977—, chmn. ednl. found., 1987—. Named Alumnus of Yr., Marquette U., 1986; recipient Spirit of Milw. award, 1986. Mem.: ABA, Assn. Acad. Health Ctrs. (bd. dirs., chair-elect 1995—), Fed. Bar Assn., Wis. Bar Assn., Milw. Bar Assn., Marquette U. Alumni Assn. (pres. 1982—84), Town, Univ. Club, Milw. Country Club, Phi Sigma Tau, Alpha Sigma Nu. Home: 137 E White Oak Way Thiensville WI 53092-6266 Office: 8701 Watertown Plank Rd Milwaukee WI 53226 E-mail: tbolger@mcw.edu.

BOLIAN, GEORGE CLEMENT, health care executive, physician; b. New Orleans, May 24, 1930; s. George William and Effie (McQuaid) B.; m. Patricia Ruth Green, July 27, 1957 (div. 1984); children— Mark Geoffrey, Gregory Wayne; m. Patricia Ann Morrison, Mar. 26, 1984; children— Joshua Sean, Zachary Ryan. BA, U. Chgo., 1950, Harvard U., 1952; MD, Tulane U., 1957. Diplomate Am. Bd. Psychiatry and Neurology. Intern Nassau County Med. Ctr., East Meadow, N.Y., 1957-58; resident psychiatry and child psychiatry U. Cin., 1958-62; instr., asst. prof. U. Wash., Seattle, 1965-70; dir. dept. psychiatry Children's Orthopaedic Hosp. and Med. Ctr., Seattle, 1968-70; assoc. prof. U. Hawaii, Honolulu, 1970-86; dir. community mental health ctr. Queen's Med. Ctr., Honolulu, 1971-83, sr. v.p., 1976-83, pres., 1983-86; practice medicine, Nashville, 1986-87; assoc. prof., acting dir. child and adolescent psychiatry Vanderbilt U., Nashville, 1987-89, dir. resident edn., 1988-93; vice chmn. dept. psychiatry, 1988—; chmn. Med. Sch. Acad. Programs Vanderbilt U., Nashville, 1993—; med. dir. The Psychiat. Hosp. Vanderbilt, Nashville, 1999—. Contbr. numerous articles to profl. jours. Served to capt. U.S. Army, 1962-65 Fellow Am. Psychiat. Assn. (life), Am. Acad. Child Psychiatry, Am. Orthopsychiat. Assn. (life); mem. AMA. Home: 6002 Hickory Valley Rd Nashville TN 37205-1306

BOLICK, RYAN, lobbyist, consultant; b. Lenoir, NC; BSBA, Appalchian State U., Boone, NC, 1997—2001. Cons. BearingPoint, Charlotte, NC, 2002—, Arthur Andersen LLP, Charlotte, NC, 2001—02; lobbyist U. of NC, Washington, 2001—01; ptnr. 33 W Consulting, Charlotte, NC, 2004—. Mem. - chancellor search com. Appalachian State U., 2003—04; vol. Jr. Achievement of Am., Charlotte, 2002—04; polit. advisor Ken Moore for NC Senate, Lenoir, 2003—03; dir. Appalachian State U. Mecklenburg County Alumni Assn., 2003—04. Mem.: Appalachian State U. Alumni Assn. R-Conservative. United Methodist. Avocations: golf, travel, politics, civic involvement, weightlifting. Home: 6844 Rothchild Drive Charlotte NC 28270 Personal E-mail: ryanbolick@hotmail.com.

BOLIN, BERT RICHARD JOHANNES, atmospheric physicist, meteorologist, researcher; b. Nyköping, Sweden, May 15, 1925; s. Richard and Karin Lovisa (Johansson) B.; m. Ulla Karin Frykstrand, June 7, 1952 (div. 1979); children: Dan, Karina, Göran. BS, U. Uppsala, 1946; MS, U. Stockholm, 1949, PhD in Meteorology, 1956. Assoc. prof. U. Stockholm, 1956-61, prof.,

1961-90; sci. dir. European Space Rsch. Orgn., Paris, 1965-67; dir. Internat. Meteorol. Inst., 1961-91; scientific advisor to Swedish Prime min./vice prime min. Stockholm, 1986-91. Chmn. joint orgn. com. GARP WMO, Geneva, 1967-71; vice chmn. Swedish Natural Sci. Rsch. Coun., 1977-80; chmn. intergovtl. panel on climate change WMO/UNEP, Geneva, 1988-97. Contbr. articles to profl. jours. Recipient OMI prize World Met. Orgn., 1981, Tyler prize U. So. Calif., 1988, Grüne Rosette Köber Stiftung, 1990, Milkankovic medal European Geophys. Soc., 1993, Blue Planet prize Asahi Glass Found., 1995, Environ. prize U. Lund, 1995, Swedish Royal medal, size 12, 1997, award for sci. co-op AAAS, 1998, Climate Protection award EPA US, 1998, Global Environ. Leadership award GEF, World Bank, 1999, Zayed prize United Arab Emirates, 2004. Mem.: Indian Acad. Sci., Norwegian Acad. Sci., Academia Nazionale delle Scienze Italy, U.S. Nat. Acad. Scis., Russian Acad. Scis., Swedish Acad. Engring. Scis., Royal Swedish Acad. Scis. (Arrhenius gold medal 2000). Mem. Social Dem. Party. Avocations: choir singing, outdoor life. Home: S Åsvägen 51 18452 Österskär Sweden E-mail: bolin.bert@telia.com.

BOLIN, DANIEL PAUL, music educator; b. Indpls., Apr. 11, 1948; s. Gillespie Green and Myrtle Genell (Runner) B.; m. Marilyn Jo McBride Rader, Aug. 8, 1970 (div. Mar. 1984); children: John William, Douglas Patrick; m. Jane Ann Crecelius, Oct. 29, 1987. BM, Butler U., 1970, MM, 1975, secondary adminstrn. cert., 1981; postgrad., U. Mich., summer 1976; EdD, Ind. U., 1988. Cert. music tchr., secondary sch. adminstr., supt., Ind. Band dir., gen. music orch. dir., asst. band dir. Wood H.S., Indpls., 1970-72; orch. dir., asst. band dir. Manual H.S., Indpls., 1972-73, band dir., 1973-74; band dir., chmn. fine arts dept. Lebanon (Ind.) H.S., 1974-77; band and choir dir., chmn. music dept. Southport H.S., Indpls., 1977-83, asst. prin., 1983-87; dir. secondary edn. Met. Sch. Dist. Perry Twp., Indpls., 1987-89, dir. pers. and student svcs., 1989-91, interim supt., 1992-93, asst. supt., 1991-95; prof., chair music dept. Butler U., Indpls., 1995—2001, assoc. prof. of music, 2001—. Facilitator I.U. Project LEAD, 1988-89; chmn. ISSMA Contest Manual Revision Com., 1982; sec. ISMA-NISBOVA Merger Com., 1978-81; bd. dirs. ISSMA, 1981-84; dir. BallState U. Mid-Am. Music Clinic, 1982, 83; mem. staff Ind. U. Music Clinic, 1974; co-owner global Ednl. Tours; chmn. Indpls. All-City H.S. Band, 1974; music dir. Eli Lilly Co., 1974; guest condr. Anthaneum Orch., 1974, Ctrl. Ind. Youth Wind Ensemble, 1980, Ind. All Region Jr. High Band, 1981; marching band com. ISMA, 1975, mem. music selection com., 1978; mem. camp staff Purdue U. Band Camp, 1981; co-founder, co-dir. Gt. Lake Music Camps, Inc., 1981—; coord. Ind. State Band, Orch. and Choir Finals, 1985-88; guest condr., host U.S. Army Field Band, 1986, 88, 89, 93, 95, 97, 99, 2001, 2003U.S. Marine Band, 1989, 94, 99; guest condr. USAF Band of the Rockies. Conferee White House Conf. for Drug-Free Am., 1987-88; mem. program bd. Young Audiences of Ind., 1992—, bd. dirs., 1994—, chmn. bd., 1996—; coord. awards ceremonies X Pan-Am. Games, 1987; v.p. bd. dirs. Indpls. Chamber Orch., 1997. Performance scholar Butler U. Mem. Am. Sch. Band Dirs. Assn. (Stanbury award 1979), Am. Assn. Sch. Adminstrs., Music Educators Nat. Conf., Ind. Music Educators Assn., Ind. Assn. for Supervision and Curriculum Devel., Ind. Assn. Pub. Sch. Supts. (charter), Ind. All-State Music Festivals Assn. (bd. dirs. 1978-81, facilities coord. 1979-80, sec. 1980-81), Ind. State Sch. Music Assn., Ind. Sch. Music Assn., Northern Ind. Sch. Band, Orchestra, & Vocal Assn., Phi Delta Kappa, Pi Lambda Theta, Phi Kappa Lambda, Phi Mu Alpha, Kappa Kappa Psi. Avocations: music, travel, historical readings. Office: Butler U Coll Fine Arts 4600 Sunset Ave Indianapolis IN 46208-3487 E-mail: dpbolin@aol.com.

BOLIN, HENRY ROBERT, retired engineer; b. N.Y.C., Nov. 24, 1926; s. Henry Otto John and Bertha (Cserkits) B.; m. Hermina Mildred Franck, Nov. 6, 1954; children: Nancy Jeanne, Robert Henry. BS in Physics, Columbia U., 1965. Jr. engr. IBM, Burlington, Vt., 1965-66, assoc. engr., 1966-68, sr. assoc. engr., 1968-72, staff engr., 1972-87, adv. engr. East Fishkill, N.Y., 1987-91; ret., 1991. Radiol. monitor Def. Preparedness Agy./FEMA St. of Vt., 1977-83. Sgt. USAF, 1948—52. Mem. IEEE, Am. Vacuum Soc., Soc. for Indsl. Archaelogy, Steamship Hist. Soc., Nat. Railway Hist. Soc., Pa. R.R. Tech. and Hist. Soc., Nat. Model RR Soc. Independent. Lutheran. Home: 13 Old Farm Rd Jericho VT 05465-2502 Personal E-mail: hrbolin@surfglobabl.net.

BOLIN, MICHAEL F., state supreme court justice; b. Jefferson County, Ala. m. Rosemary Bolin; 1 child. BS in Bus. Admin. (hon.), Samford U., 1970; JD, Cumberland Sch. of Law, 1973. Atty. pvt. practice, Birmingham, Ala., 1973—88; probate judge Jefferson County, Ala., 1988—2003; justice Ala. Supreme Ct., 2005—. Former chmn. Education and Adoption Com.; former mem. Children's Code Com., Probate Procedures Com., Adoption Com., Paternity Com. Ala Law Inst.; chief election official Jefferson County; chmn. Ala. Electronic Voting Com.; mem. Governor's Commn. on Consolidation, Efficiency, and Funding, Jefferson County Republican Exec. Com. and Steering Com.; campaign coordinator Senator Jeff Sessions, 2002; county party chmn. Jefferson County Republican Party, 2003; mem. Jefferson County Republican Assembly. Mem.: Mid-Ala. Republican Club, Ala. Probate Judges Assn. (pres., sec., treasurer, v.p., pres.). Office: Ala Supreme Ct 300 Dexter Aven Montgomery AL 36104*

BOLIN, RICHARD LUDDINGTON, industrial specialist, consultant; b. Burlington, Vt., May 13, 1923; s. Axel Birger and Eva Madora (Luddington) B.; m. Jeanne Marie Brown, Dec. 18, 1948; children: Richard Luddington, Jr., Douglas, Judith, Barbara, Elizabeth. BSChemE, Tex. A&M U., 1947; MSChemE, MIT, 1950; Diploma Advanced Mgmt. Program, Harvard U., 1969. Jr. rsch. engr. Humble Oil & Refining Co., Baytown, Tex., 1947-49; staff mem. Arthur D. Little, Inc., Cambridge, Mass., 1950-56, Caribbean office mgr. San Juan, 1957-61; gen. mgr. Arthur D. Little de Mex., Mexico City, 1961-72; pres. Internat. Parks, Inc., Flagstaff, Ariz., 1973-94, chmn., 1995—. Bd. dirs. Parque Indsl. de Nogales, Nogales, Sonora, Mex.; founder, dir. Flafstaff Inst., 1976, dir. World Econ. Processing Zones Assn., 1985-2003, dir. emeritus, 2003, adv. bd. Lowell Obs., Flagstaff, 1993-94, Astrogeology Mus. Preservation, Flagstaff, 1998-02 With U.S. Army, 1942—46. Mem.: Univ. Club of Mex. Office: PO Box 986 Flagstaff AZ 86002-0986 Office Phone: 928-779-0052. Personal E-mail: bolinflag@aol.com.

BOLINDER, SCOTT W., publishing company executive; b. 1951; m. Jill Bolinder; children: Jamie, Jesse, Anna. BA in Literature, Wheaton Coll., 1973; MSW, U. Ill., 1975. Adv. sales Huebner Pub. Co., 1979-80; pub. dir. Campus Life Mag., 1980-81, exec. v.p., 1981-82; sr. v.p. Christianity Today Inc., Carol Stream, Ill., 1982-89; v.p., pub. Zondervan Pub. House, Grand Rapids, Mich., 1989—. Bd. dirs. Edn. Assistance Ltd.; active Thornapple Evang. Covenant Ch., Grand Rapids. Capt. US Army, 1975-79. Mem. Acad. Cert. Social Workers. Avocations: music, reading, tennis, biking, Moroccan cooking. Office: Zondervan Pub House 5300 Patterson Ave SE Grand Rapids MI 49512-9512

BOLING, EDWARD JOSEPH, retired academic administrator; b. Sevier County, Tenn., Feb. 19, 1922; s. Sam R. and Nerissa (Clark) B.; m. Carolyn Pierce, Aug. 8, 1950; children: Mark Edward, Brian Marshall, Steven Clark. BS in Accounting, U. Tenn., 1948, MS in Stats., 1950; EdD in Ednl. Adminstrn, Vanderbilt U., 1961; LLD (hon.), U. Richmond, 1984. With Wilby-Kinsey Theatre Corp., Knoxville, Tenn., 1940-41, Aluminum Co. Am., 1941-42; instr. statistics U. Tenn., 1948-50; research statistician Carbide & Carbon Chem. Corp., Oak Ridge, 1950; supr. source and fissionable materials accounting Carbide & Carbon Chem. Corp. (K-25 plant), 1951-54; budget dir. Tenn., 1955-59; commr. finance and adminstrn., 1959-61; v.p. U. Tenn., 1961-70, pres., 1970-88, pres. emeritus, 1988—, univ. prof., 1988-92. Mem. So. Regional Edn. Bd., 1957-61, 70-81, 83-90, 92-96, mem. exec. com., 1974-75, 79-81, vice chmn., 1986-88; mem. Edn. Commn. of States, 1970-82; trustee, chmn. Am. Coll. Testing Program, 1983-85; dir. emeritus Allied Signal Corp., CSX, N.A. Philips, United Foods, Home Fed. Bank. Author: (with D. A. Gardiner) Forecasting University Enrollment, 1952, Methods of Objectifying The Allocation of Tax Funds to Tennessee State Colleges, 1961. Mem. Nat. Govs. Conf. Good Will Tour to Brazil and Argentina, 1960; Mem. com. on taxation Am. Council on Edn. Served with AUS, 1943-46, ETO. Mem. Am. Statis. Assn., Assn. Higher Edn., Nat. Assn. Land-Grant Colls. (com. on financing higher edn.), Am. Coll. Pub. Rels. Assn. (trustee chmn. com. taxation and philanthropy), Am. Coun. on Edn., Knoxville C. of C. (bd. dirs., chmn. bd. 1989-91), Tenn. Resource Valley (dir., chmn. bd. 1991-92, chmn. supr. com. 1992-02, chmn. 21st century jobs initiative), Am. Legion, Phi Kappa Phi (Scholarship award 1947), Beta Gamma Sigma (charter pres. Alpha chpt. 1948), Phi Delta Kappa, Omicron Delta Kappa, Beta Alpha Psi. Democrat. Office: U Tenn System Andy Holt Towers Ste 731 Knoxville TN 37996-0001

BOLING, JOSEPH EDWARD, numismatist, retired military officer; b. San Antonio, Oct. 17, 1942; s. Jack Leroy and Judy Alice B.; m. Helen-Louise Phelps, June 11, 1964 (div. 1984, m. 2005); children: L. Margaret, David A., Evan J. BS in Metallurgy, MIT, 1964; MBA, U. Wash., 1973; grad., Japanese Nat. Def. Coll., 1984. Commd. 2d lt. U.S. Army, 1964, advanced through grades to col., 1987; dep. chief staff computer architecture U.S. Army, Europe, 1989-92; asst. dep. dir. Worldwide Mil. Command Control System Def. Communications Agy., Reston, Va., 1985-89; retired U.S. Army, 1992. Author: (with others) WWII Military Currency, 1978, WWII Remembered History in Your Hands, A Numismatic Study, 1995, (also editor) Paper Money of the 20th Century: Japan Vol. 1 1979, Japan Vol. 2, 1988. Fellow Am. Numismatic Soc. (life, East Asian coinage com. 1985—); mem. Internat. Bank Note Soc. (life, pres. 1986-90, treas. 1993—, Gold medal for svc. 2001), Am. Numismatic Assn. (life, chief judge 1991-93, 95—, dir. judges' familiarization-cert. seminar 1986—, summer seminar instr. 1999—, medal of merit 1991, Howland Wood award 1995, Glenn Smedley award 2000, Farran Zerbe Meml. Disting. Svc. award 2005), Pacific N.W. Numismatic Assn. (life, sec. 1994-96, sec.-treas. 1996—, Bob Everett Meml. award 2005), Numismatic Lit. Guild, Assn. U.S. Army. Republican. Avocations: Japanese numismatics, theater. Address: PO Box 4718 Federal Way WA 98063-4718 Office Phone: 253-839-5199. Personal E-mail: joeboling@aol.com.

BOLING, MARK EDWARD, music educator; b. Nashville, Dec. 3, 1954; s. Edward J. and Carolyn (Pierce) B.; m. Anita Frances Hayman, Nov. 23, 1978; children: Jessica Leigh, Michael Edward. MusB, Berklee Coll. Music, Boston, 1981; M Music Theory, U. Tenn., 1984. Adj. music faculty U. Tenn., Knoxville, 1981-86, U. N.C., Asheville, 1984-87; performing jazz musician Knoxville, 1986-88; mem. music faculty U. Tenn., Knoxville, 1986—, asst. prof. music, 1989—, assoc. prof. music, 1993—, coord. jazz studies, 1998—. Cons. Apple Computer, Nashville, 1988-94. Author: The Jazz Theory Workbook, 1990; author computer software Elements of the Jazz Language, 1991, Curriculum for Aural Training, 1994, Creative Comping Concept for Jazz Guitar, 2004; composer/arranger/prodr. music Learning Co. fgn. lang. software products, 1994-98; artist (CD) Evidence, Mark Boling Trio, 2000, TuNe Me, Mark Boling, 2004. Jazz arts scholar Banff Ctr. for the Arts, Alta., Can., 1987. Mem. Pi Kappa Lambda. Office: U Tenn Dept Music 1741 Volunteer Blvd Knoxville TN 37916-3715 Office Phone: 865-974-3615. Business E-Mail: mboling@utk.edu.

BOLINO, AUGUST CONSTANTINO, economics professor; b. Boston, Sept. 30, 1922; s. Nicholas and Rose (Capozzi) B.; m. Thora Johnson, Sept. 15, 1951; children: Bradlee, Douglas, Jacquelyn, Gregory. BBA, U. Mich., 1948, MBA, 1949; postgrad., U. Wash., 1950-52; PhD in Economics, St. Louis U., 1957. Instr. Statistics U. Wash., Seattle, 1950-51; instr. Bus. and Econ. Idaho State U., Pocatello, 1952-55; from asst. to assoc. prof. Econs. St. Louis U., 1955-62; chief div. econ. analysis of automation, Office Manpower Automation and Tng. U.S. Dept. Labor, Washington, 1962-66; assoc. prof. Cath. U., Washington, 1966-69, prof., 1970—. Lectr. U. Md., College Park, 1963, 70-76; adj. prof. econs. Am. U., Washington, 1964-66; dir. evaluation of manpower devel. and utilization of programs br., U.S. Dept. Health, Edn., and Welfare, 1964-66; asst. to U.S. Commr. of Edn., 1964-66; cons. in field. Author: The Development of the American Economy, 1961, Manpower and the City, 1969, Career Education: Contributions to Economic Growth, 1973, The Ellis Island Source Book, 1985, The Watchmakers of Massachusetts, 1987, A Century of Human Capital by Education and Training, 1989, Thomas Angel, American, 2001, Brother Brigham's Trial, 2002; contbr. articles to profl. jours. V.p. rsch. Ellis Island Restoration Commn., 1978—. Lt. USAF, 1942-45, ETO. Rsch. fellow U. Mich., 1949; Ford Found. grant U. Minn., 1957, Rsch. grantee Am. Philosophical Soc., 1969, US Manpower Adminstrn., 1971-72, DC Cmty. Humanities Coun., 1983. Mem. Alpha Kappa Psi (disting. service award 1949, 60). Democrat. Roman Catholic. Avocation: coin and watch collecting. Home: 8515 2nd Ave Silver Spring MD 20910-3465 Office: 309 McMahon Hall Cardinal Sta Washington DC 20064 Office Phone: 202-319-5236.

BOLIVAR ZAPATA, FRANCISCO, biochemist; b. Mexico City, Mar. 7, 1948; s. Jose and Carmen (Zapata) B.; children: Francisco, Paulina, Jose. Degree in chemistry, Nat. Autonomous U. Mex., Mexico City, 1971, M Biochemistry, 1973, PhD in Biochemistry, 1975; D Honoris Causa, U. Lieje, Belgium, 1994. Assoc. rschr. Nat. Autonomous U. Mex., 1973—, full rschr. level I, 1977-83, full rschr. level III, 1983—, chmn. molecular biology dept., 1980—, dir. genetic engring. ctr., 1982—, dir. biotech. inst. Cuernacava, Mexico, 191-99, chief investigator biotech inst. Cuernavaca, Mexico, 1999—. Editor jour. Gene, 1982—; contbr. more than 120 articles to profl. jours. Recipient Manuel Noriega prize in Sci. OAS, 1988, Nat. U Prize, 1990, Prince of Asturias prize in sci. Govt. of Spain, 1991, Nat. Prize in Sci. Pres. of Mex., 1992, TWAS prize in Biology, 1997. Mem. Am. Soc. Microbiology, Academia Investigacion Cientifica, Mex. Colegio Nacional, Academia Mexicana de Ciencias (pres. 1998—). Office: UNAM Inst Biotech PO Box 510-3 Cuernavaca 62271 Mexico also: Academia Maxicana de Ciencias Ave San Jeronimo 260 Jardines del Pedregal DF 04500 Mexico

BOLL, CHARLES RAYMOND, engine company executive; b. Columbus, Ind., Mar. 29, 1920; s. Charles Raymond and Hestella (Snyder) B.; m. Mary Genevieve Lortz, Nov. 6, 1943; children: Charles Raymond III, Cynthia Ann. BS in Elec. Engring, Purdue U., 1941. With Cummins Engine Co., Inc., Columbus, 1941-89, sales engr., 1941-42, asst. regional mgr. Cleve., 1947, mgr. engine sales, 1948-52, gen. sales mgr., 1953-55, v.p. sales, 1955-60, exec. v.p. mktg., 1960-64, pres. Internat. div., 1965-66, exec. v.p., 1966-85, also bd. dirs., 1956-88, dir. emeritus, 1988—. 1st lt., Signal Corps, AUS, 1943-46. Named Outstanding Elec. Engr., Purdue U., 1992. Mem. Soc. Automotive Engrs. Home: 2940 Washington St Columbus IN 47201-2946

BOLLAG, JEAN-MARC, soil biochemistry educator, consultant; b. Basel, Switzerland, Feb. 19, 1935; came to U.S., 1965; naturalized, 1975; s. Marcel and Renee (Levy) B.; m. Brigitte Gertrud Baumgartner, Apr. 26, 1960; children: Daniel, Gideon, Roni, Judith. PhD, U. Basel, 1959. Grad. rsch. asst. Bot. Inst. U. Basel, 1956-59; postdoctoral rsch. asoc. Weizmann Inst. Sci., Rehovot, Israel, 1963-65, Cornell U., Ithaca, NY, 1965-67; asst. prof. soil microbiology Pa. State U., University Park, 1967-71, assoc. prof., 1971-77, prof., 1977—2002, prof. emeritus, 2002—. Vis. sci. CIBA-Geigy, Basel, 1975-76; dir. Ctr. for Bioremediation and Detoxification; cons. to fed. agys., chem. cos. Co-editor Soil Biochemistry Series; contbr. numerous articles in environ. microbiology and microbial control of soil pollution to profl. publs. Recipient badge of merit Polish Min. Agr., 1977, rsch. award Gamma Sigma Delta, 1982; Julius Baer fellow Weizmann Inst. Sci., 1963-65. Fellow Soil Sci. Soc., Am. Soc. Agronomy (environ. quality rsch. award 1995), Am. Acad. Microbiology; mem. AAAS, Internat. Soc. Soil Sci., Internat. Humic Substances Soc. Democrat. Home: 368 Bradley Ave State College PA 16801-6322 Office: Penn State Ctr for Bioremediation & Detox 129 Land Water Research University Park PA 16802-4900 E-mail: jmbollag@psu.edu.

BOLLAG, WENDY BOLLINGER, medical educator; b. Pitts., May 17, 1962; d. Joseph Martin and Carolyn (Cope) Bollinger; m. Roni Jaakow Bollag, June 7, 1986; children, Katherine Amanda, Anna Elizabeth. BS, Pa. State U., 1984; MS, MPhil, Yale U., 1987, PhD, 1990. Coord., lectr. physiology course Yale Physician Assoc. Program, New Haven, 1987-90, Norwalk Hosp./Yale Physician Assoc. Surg. Residency Program, New Haven, 1987-90; postdoctoral rsch. assoc. Hoffmann-La Roche, Nutley, N.J., 1991-92; asst. prof. biology Seton Hall U., South Orange, N.J., 1992-93; from assoc. prof. medicine to prof. Med. Coll. Ga., Augusta, 1993—, prof. Contbr. articles to profl. jours., chpt. to book. NSF predoctoral fellow, 1984-87. Mem. Soc. Investigative Dermatology, Endoctrine Soc., Sigma Xi. Avocations: horseback riding, gardening, reading. Office: Med Coll Ga 1120 15th St Augusta GA 30912-0006

BOLLAPRAGADA, RAMESH, information scientist, educator; s. Rajarao and Mangatayaru Dulla Bollapragada; m. Rama Bollapragada, Nov. 24, 1997. BEE, India, 1988, MS Control Systems, Engring., 1989; MBA, Carnegie Mellon U., Pitts., 1993, PhD, 1996. Sr. engr., Bangalore, India, 1989—91; mem. rsch. staff IBM, T.J. Watson Rsch. Ctr., Yorktown Heights, NY, 1994; mem. tech. staff Bell Labs, Lucent Technologies, Holmdel, NJ, 1996—2002; prof. Coll. of Bus., San Francisco State U., 2002—. Vis. prof. Adminstrv. Staff Coll. of India, Bella Vista Campus, Hyderabad, India, 2003, Hyderabad, 04, Ops. Rsch. Dept., Politecnico Di Torino, Italy, 2004, Sch. Computer Sci., Software Rsch. Inst., Carnegie Mellon U., Pitts., 2005. Author: (exhibition (conference) INFORMS Conference in Atlanta (Wagner Prize Award presentation, 2003); contbr. articles to profl. jours, numerous exhibits for scientific conferences. Recipient Advanced Technologies Excellence award, Bell Labs, Lucent Technologies; William Laramie Mellon fellow, Carnegie Mellon U., 1991—96. Achievements include patents pending for methods and apparatus for analyzing and designing various network configuration scenarios. Office Phone: 1-415-338-7487. Personal E-mail: rbollapragada@yahoo.com.

BOLLE, DONALD MARTIN, retired engineering educator; b. Amsterdam, The Netherlands, Mar. 30, 1933; came to U.S., 1955, naturalized, 1961; s. Maarten C. and Petronella (Kramer) B.; m. Barbara June Girton, Nov. 29, 1957; children— Alan Martin, Thomas Raymond, John Kenneth, Cornelis Adrianus. BS, Durham U., Eng., 1954; PhD, Purdue U., 1961; MA (hon.), Brown U., 1966. Asst. prof. elec. engring. Purdue U., 1961-62; NSF postdoctoral fellow dept. applied math. and theoretical physics Cambridge (Eng.) U., 1962-63; asst. prof. engring. Brown U., 1963-66, asso. prof., 1966-70, prof., 1970-80; Chandler-Weaver chair elec. engring. Lehigh U., Bethlehem, Pa., 1980-81; dean Lehigh U. (Coll. Engring. and Applied Sci.), 1981-88; interim vice provost info. resources Lehigh U., 1999-2000; sr. v.p. acad. affairs Poly. U., Bklyn., 1988-91, prof., 1991-99, v.p. adminstrn., 1995-96. Richard Merton vis. prof. Technische Hochschule, Braunschweig, Germany, 1967; cons. in field. Fellow IEEE, AAAS, IEE (U.K.). Home: 6448 Eichler Cir Coopersburg PA 18036-1382

BOLLEN, SHARON KESTERSON, artist, educator; b. Cin., Apr. 27, 1946; d. Marc J. and Regina (Mills) Kesterson; m. Jerry H. Bollen, June 22, 1968; children: Heather, Christopher. BA in Art, Coll. of Mt. St. Joseph, Cin., 1968; MA in Art Edn., U. Cin., 1970, EdD in Art Edn., 1980. Tchr. art Marian H.S., Cin., 1968-77; prof. art Coll. of Mount St. Joseph, Cin., 1977—. Fabric surface design art works in juried and invitational regional and nat. exhbns.; book reviewer Nat. Art Edn. Assn. Women's Caucus newsletter, 1985—. Recipient Alumni Appreciation award Coll. of Mount St. Joseph, 1993, Disting. Teaching award, 1981. Mem. Nat. Art Edn. Assn. (Student Chpt. Sponsor award 1994, Outstanding Ohio Art Educator of Yr. 1990, Western Region Higher Edn. Art Educator of Yr. 2001), Ohio Art Edn. Assn. (Outstanding Art Educator 1988, Higher Edn. Art Educator of Yr. 2000), Nat. Surface Design Assn., Am. Crafts Coun., Nat. Mus. for Women in the Arts (charter), Georgia O'Keeffe Mus. Roman Catholic. Home: 1138 Cryer Ave Cincinnati OH 45208-2803 Office: Coll of Mount St Joseph Art Dept 5701 Delhi Rd Cincinnati OH 45233-1670

BOLLENBACH, STEPHEN FRASIER, hotel executive; b. Los Angeles, July 14, 1942; s. Walter and Betty (Mason) B.; m. Suzanne Weimer, Apr. 13, 1963 (div. Dec. 1969); m. Barbara May Christeson, Dec. 31, 1970; children: Christopher, Keat. BS in Fin., UCLA, 1965; MBA, Calif. State U., 1968. CFO D.K. Ludwig Group, N.Y.C., 1977-80; chmn., CEO S.W. Savs. & Loan, Phoenix, 1980-82; sr. v.p. fin., treas. Marriott Corp., Washington, 1982-86; sr. v.p., CFO, dir. Holiday Corp., Memphis, 1986-90, Promus Cos., Memphis, 1990; exec. v.p., CFO Marriott Corp., Washington, 1992-93; pres., CEO Host Marriott Corp., Washington, 1993-95; sr. exec. v.p., CFO Walt Disney Co., Burbank, Calif., 1995-96; pres. Hilton Hotels Corp., Beverly Hills, Calif., 1996—2004, CEO, 1996—, co-chmn., 2004—. Bd. dirs. Carr Realty Corp., Washington, Mid-Am. Apt. Cmtys., Inc., Memphis, Am. West Airlines, Phoenix, Catellus Corp, Time Warner, Hilton Group PLC; mem. adv. bd. CFO Mag., Boston. Office: Hilton Hotels Corporation PO Box 5567 Beverly Hills CA 90209-5567

BOLLENDORF, ROBERT FREDRICK, retired education educator, psychologist; b. Kenosha, Wis., Sept. 11, 1946; s. Fred John Bollendorf and Lucile Zeyen; m. Linda Rae Rutcosky; children: Becky Anne Meixensperger, Bryan Robert. BA, St. Joseph's Coll., 1965—68; MS, Southern Ill. U., 1970; EdD, No. Ill. U., 1976. Clinical Psychologist State of Ill., 1977. Counselor Ill. Dept. of Corrections, Geneva, Ill., 1970—71; human services prof. Coll. of DuPage, Glen Ellyn, Ill., 1971—. Author: (novels) Sober Spring, 1988, Flight of the Loon, 1992. Pres. Lisle H.S. Boosters, Ill., 1993—95. Named Tchr. of Yr., Coll. DuPage, 1987; grant, Fund for Post Secondary Edn., 1985—87. Mem.: Am. Counseling Assn. Roman Catholic. Achievements include Grant. Avocations: swimming, bicycling, running, skiing. Office: College of DuPage Fawell Glen Ellyn IL 60137 Personal E-mail: rbollendorf@aol.com.

BOLLES, CHARLES AVERY, librarian; b. Pine Island, Minn., Aug. 10, 1940; s. Arthur Marston and Clarice Ione (Figy) B.; m. Marjorie Elaine Hancock, May 17, 1964; children: Jason Brice, Justin Brian. BA, U. Minn., 1962, MA in Libr. Sci., 1963, PhD in Libr. Sci., 1975. Catalog and serials librarian U. Iowa, Iowa City, 1964-67; asst. prof. Emporia (Kans.) State U., 1970-76, dir. Sch. Libr. Sci., 1978-80; dir. libr. devel. divsn. Kans. State Libr., 1976-78; state librarian State of Idaho, Boise, 1980—. Mem. ALA, Chief Officers State Libr. Agys., Western Coun. State Librs. (chmn. 1985-86, 98-99), Pacific N.W. Libr. Assn. (pres. 1990-91), Idaho Libr. Assn. Office: Idaho State Libr 325 W State St Boise ID 83702-6014

BOLLES, RONALD KENT, music educator; b. El Paso, Dec. 29, 1948; s. Robert Benjamin and Audrey Nadine (Hawkins) B.; m. Terri Sue Alburger Aka Reina Marie, Apr. 7, 1979; children: Gina Marie, Heather Michelle. BA in Music, San Diego State U., 1971, MEd, 1975. Cert. secondary life tchr. Tchr. Castle Pk. Jr. High Sch., Chula Vista, Calif., 1972-74; dir. choir Pacific Beach United Meth., San Diego, 1973-75, All Hallows Cath. Ch., La Jolla, Calif., 1978-79, First Christian Ch., Chula Vista, 1980-87; tchr. Bonita Vista Jr. High Sch., Chula Vista, 1974—99, Bonita Vista Sr. High Sch., Chula Vista, 1974—; with New Hope Cmty. Ch., Chula Vista, 2000—. Dist. vocal music chmn. Sweetwater Union High Sch. Dist., Chula Vista, 1980-86; site div. chmn. Bonita Vista High Sch., 1975-77; founder, dir. South Bay Cmty. Chorale, 2000—; facilitator Chula Vista Sch. Creative and Performing Arts, 1999—, vocal music festival adjudicator, 2000—; founder, dir. "New Song" worship-leading choir, 2002-. Dir. high sch. show choir "The Music Machine," 1976-99; author (with Reina Marie) Preparing an Awesome Musical Theater Audition, 1983. Named Tchr. Yr. San Diego County, 1987, Bonita Vista High Sch., Chula Vista, 1983; recipient Alumnus of Yr. award San Diego State U. Sch. of Edn., 1989; named Citizen of Yr. Bonita Kiwanis, 1990. Mem. San Diego City/County Music Educators (hon., pres. 1983-88), Music Educators Nat. Conf., Calif. Music Educators Assn., Am. Choral Dirs. Assn., So. Calif. Vocal Assn. Avocations: gardening, music, biking, movies, computers. Office: Chula Vista High Sch 820 4th Ave Chula Vista CA 91911 E-mail: directoron@yahoo.com.

BOLLEY, ANDREA, artist; d. Hildo and Laura Bolley. BFA, U. Windsor, 1975. Tchr. Activity Ctr. Art Gallery Ont., 1979, 80, Arts Sake, Toronto, 1982. One-woman shows include IDA Gallery York U., 1976, Art Gallery Brant, 1977, Pollock Gallery, Toronto, 1977-78, 80, Agnes Etherington Art Ctr., Kingston, 1981, Gallery One, Toronto, 1984-86, Klonaridis Gallery, Toronto, 1989-91, Upper Can. Brewing Co., 1993, Studio Show, 1994-2000, 02, Masterworks Found., Bermuda, 2004, Thames Art Gallery, Ont., 2004; group exhbns. include Grapestake Gallery, San Francisco, 1980, Alta. Coll. Art, Calgary, 1980, Art Gallery Ont., 1981, Art Gallery Hamilton, 1981, Gallery

One, 1984-86, Triangle N.Y., 1985, 91, Klonaridis Gallery, 1988, John Schweitzer Gallery, Montreal, 1989, Mississauga Civic Ctr. Art Gallery, 1990, Magnum Books, Ottawa, 1991, Bennington Coll., Vt., 1991, Upper Can. Brewing Co., 1992, Robert Kidd Gallery, Birmingham, Mich., 1999, Group of Ten Corkin-Shopland, Toronto, Can., 2003, McGill U., Montreal, 2003, Guild Hall, London, 2004, Masterworks, London, 2004, others; represented in permanent collections Can. Coun. Art Bank, Art Gallery Windsor, Labatt's Can. Ltd., Citicorp Ltd., Can., Can. Imperial Bank Commerce, Max Factor Ltd., Chatelaine Mag., J.E. Seagram Ltd., McGill Club, Imperial Oil, Citibank Can., Toronto-Dominion Bank, Casey House, Am. Express, Guaranty Trust, Abitibi Paper, Triangle, Toronto Sund, Arthur Gelgoot and Assoc., Premiere Mag., Bells & Whistles, and various pvt. collections. Grantee Ont. Arts Coun., 1975, 76, 78, 79, 84, 85, Can. Coun., 1976, 80; recipient Ont. Soc. Artists Purchase award J.E. Seagram and Son Ltd., 1980. Office: 132 Jarvis St Toronto ON Canada M5B 2B5 Office Phone: 416-955-0660.

BOLLING, AMY L., federal agency administrator; b. Alexandria, Va., May 13, 1971; d. Larry W. and Sarah Bolling. AS in Gen. studies, No. Va. C.C., 2003; BA in English, George Mason U., 2002. With U.S. Dept. Commerce, Arlington, Va., 1994—. Contbr. poems to lit. publs., articles to The Vince Capital Area Newspapers. Newsletter writer River Towers Condo. Assn., Alexandria, 2003—; newsletter editor, writer Faith United Meth. Ch., Alexandria, 2003—, mem. assessibility com., 2003—, mem. pastor/lay leadership com., 2003—. Recipient Editor's Choice Award, Nat. Libr. Poetry, 1993. Republican. United Methodist. Avocations: writing, reading, crocheting, music, caring for the elderly.

BOLLING, LANDRUM RYMER, retired academic administrator, writer, consultant; b. Parksville, Tenn., Nov. 13, 1913; s. Landrum Austin and Carrie Mae (Rymer) B.; m. Frances Morgan, July 6, 1936; children: Roger Landrum (dec.), Brian Austin, David Morgan, Rebecca Lucy, Daniel Wade, Sarah Middleton. BA, U. Tenn., 1933; MA, U. Chgo., 1938; LLD, Valparaiso U., Wabash Coll., Oberlin Coll., Alderson-Broadus Coll., Beloit Coll., Rose-Hulman Poly. Inst., Haverford Coll., Waseda U., Japan, Ind. State U., Ea. Nazarene Coll., Denison U., Campbell Coll., Ind. U.; LHD, Anderson Coll., Ind. Tech. Coll., Earlham Coll. Adminstrv. asst. personnel div. TVA; also housing mgr. Town of Norris, editor Norris News, 1933-36; freelance writer, 1936-37; instr. polit. sci. Brown U., 1938-40; assisted in orgn. Cmty. Svc., Inc., Yellow Springs, Ohio; editor, pub. Yellow Springs News, 1940-41; from instr. to assoc. prof. polit. sci. Beloit Coll., 1942-46; war corr. Mediterranean Theater, 1944-45; fgn. corr. Berlin and Central Europe, 1946-48; prof. polit. sci. Earlham Coll., 1948-58, gen. sec., 1955-58, pres., 1958-73; from exec. v.p. to pres. Lilly Endowment, 1973-77, pres., 1975-77; chmn. Council on Founds., 1978-81; research prof. of diplomacy Georgetown U., Washington, 1981-83; pres. The Ecumenical Inst. (Tantur), Jerusalem, 1983-89; dir.-at-large Mercy Corps, Washington, 1989—. Journalistic, editorial assignments, N.Y., Europe, 1949, 52-53; sr. fellow Ctr. for Internat. Policy, 1991—; sr. advisor Conflict Mgmt. Group, 1992—. Author: City Manager Government in Dayton, 1940; co-author: (Settel et al) This is Germany, 1950, Search for Peace in the Middle East, 1970; editor: Reporters Under Fire, 1985; contbr.: Private Diplomacy with the Soviet Union, 1987, Conflict Resolution: Track II Diplomacy, 1987. Mem. Gov. of Ind. Comm. on Post High Sch. Edn., 1968; mem. Pres.'s Commn. on 25th Anniv. UN, 1970; chmn. Internat. Quaker Working Party on Middle East Peace, 1968; mem. Am. del. Soviet-Am. Talks, Dartmouth Conf., 1974, 76, 78, 79; life mem. bd. dirs. Earlham Coll., Richmond, Ind.; bd. dirs. Haverford (Pa.) Coll., 1980-85, Youth for Understanding, Friendship Force; co-sec. DeBurght Conf. on East/West Dialogue on Human Rights, 1988—. Recipient Founder's Day medal U. Tenn. Knoxville, 1997, Peacemaker/Peace Builder award Nat. Peace Found., 2000. Mem. Assn. Am. Colls. (bd. dirs.), Gt. Lakes Colls. Assn. (chmn. bd. dirs. 1962-64), Ind. Conf. Higher Edn. (pres. 1961-62), Council Fgn. Rels., Cosmos Club, Century Club. Mem. Soc. Of Friends. also: Mercy Corps Ste 707 1730 Rhode Island Ave NW Washington DC 20036-3101 Home: 2851 Marrie Harris Rd PO Box 67 Centerville IN 47330 Office Phone: 202-463-7383. E-mail: landrum@mercycorpsdc.org.

BOLLINGER, JUDITH ANN, art educator, language educator; b. Elk City, Okla., Oct. 1, 1961; d. Robert Jack Lookingbill and Judith Cleon Van Orsdol; m. Claud Edward Bollinger, May 22, 1980; children: Jason C., Jacy L. BA in edn., SW Okla. State U., 1983. Cert. tchg. Okla State. English tchr. Carter Pub. Sch., Carter, Okla., 1984—86; art, English tchr. Sayre Jr. High, Sayre, Okla., 1988—90; thcr. Western Tech. Ctr., Burns Flat, Okla., 1988—89; art, English tchr. Merritt HS, Elk City, Okla., 1990—. Meth. Avocation: reading. Office: Merritt HS Rt 4 Box 7195 Elk City OK 73644

BOLLINGER, LEE CARROLL, academic administrator, law educator; b. Santa Rosa, CA, 1946; m. Jean Magnano Bollinger; children: Lee, Carey. BS, U. Oreg., 1968; JD, Columbia U., 1971. Law clk. to Judge Wilfred Feinberg U.S. Ct. Appeals (2nd cir.), 1971—72; law clk. to Chief Justice Warren Burger U.S. Supreme Ct., 1972—73; asst. prof. law U. Mich., 1973—76, assoc. prof., 1976—78, prof., 1978—94, dean, 1987—94, pres., prof. law, 1997—2002; provost, prof. govt. Dartmouth Coll., 1994—96; pres., prof. law Columbia Univ., 2002—. Rsch. assoc. Clare Hall, Cambridge U., 1983. Co-author (with Jackson): Contract Law in Modern Society, 1980; author: The Tolerant Society: Freedom of Speech and Extremist Speech in America, 1986, Images of a Free Press, 1991; co-editor (with Geoffrey Stone): (essay collection) Eternally Vigilant: Free Speech in the Modern Era, 2001. Bd. dirs. Gerald R. Ford Found., Royal Shakespeare Co. Recipient Medal Excellence, Columbia Law Sch. Assn., 2002, Nat. Humanitarian award, Nat. Conf. Cmty. and Justice; fellow, Am. Rockefeller Humanities. Fellow: Am. Acad. Arts and Scis., Clare Hall, Cambridge U. (hon.); mem.: Inst. Internat. Edn. Office: Columbia University 2960 Broadway New York NY 10027-6902 also: 535 W 116th St 202 Low Library Mail Code 4309 New York NY 10027*

BOLLINGER, LORI, economist; PhD, U. of Pa., 1991; MA in Law and Diplomacy, Fletcher Sch., Medford, Mass., 1985; MSc, U. of York, Eng., 1984. Sr. economist Futures Group, Glastonbury, Conn., 1997—. Contbr. articles to profl. jours. Recipient postdoctoral fellowship, Population Coun., 1992—93, doctoral fellowship, NIH, 1988—90, internat. fellowship, Rotary Club, 1982—83. Mem.: Population Assn. of Am. Office: Futures Group 80 Glastonbury Blvd Glastonbury CT 06033 Office Phone: 860-633-3501.

BOLLINGER, MICHAEL, artistic director; b. St. Louis, July 1, 1954; s. Rollie Bollinger and Blanche (Bush) Easley; m. Stephanie McClain-Bollinger; children: Tanner Michael, Allison Jeanette. Student, Webster U., 1972-73, U. Mo., 1973-74, U. Mo., St. Louis, 1974-75; BFA, Webster U., 1978. Producing dir., founder Mainstage Theatre, Lake of the Ozarks, Mo., 1978-84; artistic producing dir. Arrow Rock (Mo.) Lyceum Theatre, 1980—2004; exec. dir. Suffolk (Va.) Ctr. for Cultural Arts, 2005—. Dir. Lyceum Airwaves Theatre, 1985-88; guest instr. acting Mo. Baptist Coll., St. Louis, Stephens Coll., Columbia, Mo. Valley Coll., Marshall, mem. theatre adv. panel Mo. Arts Coun., St. Louis, 1987-90; co-prodr. Mo. State Theatre Conf., St. Louis; mem. citizens adv. bd. KBIA-PBS Radio; adv. com. InterAct; Teen to Teen Theatre, Columbia, 1992-93; adjudicator Am. Coll. Theatre Fest, Ruston, La., 1992, Tenn. Arts Commn. Artist Fellowship, Nashville, 1994, Am. Coll. Theatre, 1997. Prodr., dir., actor: nearly 200 plays and musicals, including 6 world premieres and numerous Mo. premieres. Facilities chmn. cultural planning com. Columbia Com. on the Arts, 1993—95; adjudicator Prelude Awards, Indpls., 1993, 1996, Am. Assn. Cmty. Theatre Festival Adjudication, Ill., 1997; judge Mo. State Show Choir Festival, 2003. Recipient Mo. Arts award Mo. Arts Coun., 1983, 94, Outstanding Young Men of Am. award U.S. Jaycees, 1983. Mem. Actors Equity Assn. Liberal. Avocations: photography, outdoor activities, travel, animals. Office: Suffolk Ctr Cultural Arts PO Box 0147 Suffolk VA 23439-0147 Office Phone: 757-923-0003.

BOLLINGER, RALPH RANDAL, surgeon, researcher; b. Dearborn, Mich., Oct. 3, 1944; s. Ralph Perry and Edith Delores (Algren) B.; m. Monika Irmgard Koch, May 1, 1965; children: Christine Laura, Mark Randal. BS in Biology, Tulane U., 1966, MD, MS in Biochemistry, Tulane U., 1970; PhD in Immunology, Duke U., 1977, MBA with cert. in Health Svc. Mgmt., 1997. Diplomate Am. Bd. Surgery. Stress physiology rsch. physician USAF Sch. of Aerospace Medicine, Brooks AFB, Tex., 1972-74; postdoctoral fellow, instr. in surgery, dept. immunology Duke U., Durham, N.C., 1974-76; resident in surgery Duke U. Med. Ctr., Durham, 1970-72, 1977—79, chief resident in surgery, 1979-80, asst. prof. surgery, 1980-86, asst. prof. immunology, 1981-86, assoc. prof. immunology, 1986—95, assoc. prof. surgery, 1986-91, prof. surgery, 1991—, prof. immunology, 1995—, chief of surg. transplantation, 1983—99, chief gen. surgery, 1994—2003, vice chair surgery, 2004—. Vice councillor United Network for Organ Sharing, Richmond, Va., 1986-88, councillor, 1989-91, v.p., 1991-92, pres., 1992-93; sec. Southeastern Organ Procurement Found., Richmond, 1988-89, v.p., 1989-90, pres., 1990-91; v.p. Carolina Organ Procurement Agy., Greenville, N.C., 1985-87, pres., 1987-89; trustee N.C. Kidney Found., Chapel Hill, 1983-90; pres. elect Durham-Orange County Med. Soc. 2004, pres. 2005. Contbr. numerous articles to profl. jours.; editor: Transplant Management, 1988; mem. editl. bd. Am. Surgeon, 1988, Jour. Surg. Rsch., 1993—, Jour. ACS, 1996, Graft, 1998, Jour. Investigative Surgery, 2001. Com. chmn. Troop 408, Boy Scouts Am., Durham, N.C., 1982-89; mem. staff/parish rels. com. Duke Meml. Meth. Ch., Durham, 1985-87, chmn., 2003-2004, admin. bd., 2004-, coun. on ministries, 1983-85. Maj. USAF, 1972—74. Recipient La. Pathology Soc. award Tulane U., 1979, Golden Apple award Duke U., 1984, 89. Fellow ACS; mem. Aerospace Med. Assn. (environ. sci. award 1978), Am. Soc. Transplant Surgeons (membership com. 1988, councillor 1989-93), Soc. Univ. Surgeons, Transplantation Soc., Am. Surg. Assn., N.C. Assn. Biomed. Rsch. (sec. 2001-2003, vice chmn. 2003-05, v.p. 2003-), Durham-Orange County Med. Soc. (v.p. 2004, pres. 2005). Republican. Avocations: scuba diving, gardening, white water canoeing. Home: 1120 Infinity Rd Durham NC 27712-9765 Office: Duke U Med Ctr PO Box 2910 Durham NC 27710-2910 Office Phone: 919-681-3880. Business E-Mail: bolli001@mc.duke.edu.

BOLLINGER, SHARON LOUGHLIN, history professor; d. Edward Francis and Helen Huff Loughlin; m. Jerald Allen Bollinger, Sept. 15, 1956 (div. May 17, 1974); children: Michael Allen, Lori Ann, Beth Mary, Rebecca Jane Parker; m. James Warren Nichols, July 1, 2000. AA, Palomar Coll., San Marcos, Calif., 1972; BA, MA, U. San Diego, 1976. Field historian U. Wyo., Laramie, 1980—81; adminstr. hist. programs State of Wyo., Cheyenne, 1981—92; prof. history Laramie County C.C., Cheyenne, 1993—95, El Paso (Tex.) C.C., 1995—. Founding mem., bd. dirs. Wyo. Archtl. Heritage Found., Laramie, 1980—81; mem. subcom. survey and registration Nat. Conf. State Hist. Preservation Officers, Washington, 1981—85; founding mem., bd. dirs. Wyo. Hist. Preservation Assn., Cheyenne, 1983—85; mem. Wyo. Coun. on Humanities, Laramie, 1986—91, Mormon Pioneer Nat. Hist. Trail Adv. Coun., Washington, 1986—89, Nez Perce Nat. Hist. Trail Adv. Coun., Washington, 1987—89; com. mem. Nat. Hist. Trails Ctr., Washington, 1994—95; founding mem., bd. of directors El Paso Preservation Alliance, 1996—99; creator, co-prodr. (TV series) Footprints and Footnotes, El Paso C.C., 1997—98. Contbr. articles to profl. jours. Mem. territorial penitentiary planning com. City of Laramie, 1984—86; mem. com. Laramie County Tourism Bd., Cheyenne, 1987—89; founding mem., adv. coun. mem. Wyo. Against Homelessness, Cheyenne, 1990—92; founding mem. adv. coun. Wyo. Citizen Coalition for Children and Families, Cheyenne, 1987—89; precinct com. woman Laramie County Dem. Party, Cheyenne, 1994—95; bd. dirs., coord. com. Women in Hist. Profession, Washington, 1981—83; bd. dirs. Preservation Action!, Washington, 1981—85, Cheyenne YMCA, 1987—89, El Paso (Tex.) Equality Day Coalition, 1998—2001. Recipient Hist. Rsch. award, Escondido Bicentennial Commn., 1975; grantee, Ariz. Coun. Humanities, 1977—79, Wyo. Coun. Humanities, 1980—85; Rockfeller fellow, NEH, 1978, Wyo. Hist. Preservation grantee, Wyo. Coun. Arts, 1982, Wyo.'s First Ladies grantee, Mountain Bell Found., 1989—90. Mem.: LWV (bd. dirs., sec. 1987—91), Western History Assn., Am. Assn. Women in C.C., Am. Soc. for Pub. Adminstrn. (nat. coun. mem. 1990—92). Office: El Paso C C 919 Hunter El Paso TX 79915 Office Phone: 915-831-2293. Personal E-mail: sharonathistory@aol.com. E-mail: sharonb@epcc.edu.

BOLLMAN, MARK BROOKS, JR., communications executive; b. Meriden, Conn., Aug. 24, 1925; s. Mark B. and Esther (Stevens) B.; m. Barbara Ann Smith, July 8, 1928; children— Mark Brooks, III, Richard N., Steven A. AB, Princeton U., 1949; MBA, Harvard U., 1951. Sr. v.p. Benton & Bowles Inc., N.Y.C., 1968-70; exec. v.p. Diners Club Inc., N.Y.C., 1970-72; corp. v.p. Magnavox Co., N.Y.C., 1972-75; pres. McDonald & Little Inc., Atlanta, 1975-77; sr. v.p., sr. ptnr., dir. N.W. Ayer and Ptnrs., N.Y.C., 1977-95; pres. M & B Communications, 1978—. Served with AUS, 1944-46. Decorated Purple Heart. Mem.: Clinton (Conn.); Stanwich (Greenwich, Conn.). Republican. Episcopalian. Home: 20 Rockwood Ln Greenwich CT 06830-3815

BOLLS, IMOGENE LAMB, English language educator, poet; b. Manhattan, Kans., Sept. 25, 1938; d. Don Q. and Helen Letson (Keithley) Lamb; m. Nathan J. Bolls, Jr., Nov. 24, 1962; 1 child, Laurel Helen. BA, Kans. State U., 1960; MA, U. Utah, 1962. Instr. French Kans. State U., Manhattan, 1959-60; instr. English U. Utah, Salt Lake City, 1960-62; instr. to prof. Wittenberg U., Springfield, Ohio, 1963—. Poet-in-residence, dir. journalism program Wittenberg U.; tchg. poet Antioch Writers' Workshop Antioch Coll., summers, 1992—93; intensive seminar poet Antioch Writers' Workshop Antioch Coll., summer, 1994; poetry tchr. Ohio Poet-in-the-Schs. program, 1972—82; poetry instr. acad. camp; state and nat. poetry judge. Author: (poetry) Glass Walker, 1983, Earthbound, 1989, Advice for the Climb, 1999, works represented in anthologies; contbr. more than 600 poems to mags. Recipient Individual Artist award Ohio Arts Coun., 1982, 90, Poetry prize S.D. Rev., 1983, Poetry award Kans. Quarterly, 1985, Ohioana Poetry award Ohioana Libr. Assn., 1995; finalist Vassar Miller Prize in Poetry, 1994; grantee Ireland, 1986, France, 1990, Am. Southwest. Mem. Acad. Am. Poets (assoc.), Poetry Soc. Am., Women in Comm. Avocations: Native American cultures, hiking, photography, music, travel. Address: PO Box 2917 Taos NM 87571

BOLLWAGE, J. CHRISTIAN, mayor; b. Elizabeth, N.J., Dec. 7, 1954; s. Frank and Jeanne (Hasson) B.; m. Nancy; 1 child. BA in Econs., Kean Coll., 1981, M in Pub. Adminstrn., 1989. Cert. in local planning and zoning continuing edn., Rutgers U. Sr. inward documentation clk. Sea-Land Svc. Inc., 1978-79; revenue receivables clk. Puerto Rico Marine Mgmt. Inc., 1979-80; traffic coord. Kerr Steamship Inc., 1980-85; sales & mktg. A&J Trading Corp., 1985-92; adj. prof. pub. adminstrn. Kean Coll., Union, N.J., 1989-92; mem. planning bd. Elizabeth, N.J., 1983-87; mem. city coun., 1983-92; mem. Urban Enterprise Zone Commn., Elizabeth, 1984-92; mayor City of Elizabeth, 1993—. Pres. exec. bd. N.J. State League of Municipalities, 2003—. Recipient N.J. Assn. Advancement of Mentally Handicapped award. Mem. U.S. Conf. of Mayors, Knights of Columbus, Ancient Order of Hibernians, Pi Alpha Alpha. Democrat. Roman Catholic. Home: 1113 Coolidge Rd Elizabeth NJ 07208-1005 Office: City Hall 50 Winfield Scott Plz Elizabeth NJ 07201-2462*

BOLOCOFSKY, DAVID N., lawyer, psychologist, educator; b. Hartford, Conn., Sept. 29, 1947; s. Samuel and Olga Bolocofsky; m. Debra Stein, June 25, 1994; children: Vincent, Daniel, Charly. BA, Clark U., 1969; MS, Nova U., 1974, PhD, 1975; JD, U. Denver, 1988. Bar: Colo. 1988; cert. sch. psychologist, Colo. Tchr. high sch. Univ. Sch., Ft. Lauderdale, Fla., 1972-73; ednl. coord. Living and Learning Ctr., Ft. Lauderdale, 1972-75; asst. prof. U. No. Colo., Greeley, 1975-79, assoc. prof., 1979-90, dir. sch. psychology program, 1979-82; assoc. Robert T. Hinds Jr. & Assocs., Littleton, Colo., 1988-93; hearing officer State of Colo., 1991—2002; pres. David N. Bolocofsky, P.C., Denver, 1993—. Psychol. cons. Clin. Assocs., Englewood, Colo., 1978—. Author: Enhancing Personal Adjustment, 1986, (chpts. in books) Children and Obesity, 1987, Obtaining and Utilizing a Custody Evaluation, 1989; contbr. numerous articles to profl. jours. Mem. Douglas-Elbert Bar Assn., Arapahoe Bar Assn., Colo. Soc. Sch. Psychologists (bd. dirs. 1978-96, treas. 1993-96), Interdisciplinary Commn. on Child Custody (pro bono com. 1988-93), Colo. Bar Assn. (family law sect., sec. juvenile law sect. 1990-92), Colo. Soc. Behavioral Analysis Therapy (treas. 1990-96), Arapmhc (bd. dirs. 1993-2001, bd. pres. 1995-97). Avocations: sailing, golf, skiing. Home: 9848 E Maplewood Cir Englewood CO 80111-5401 Office: 5575 DTC Pkwy Ste 370 Englewood CO 80111 Office Phone: 303-694-2220.

BOLOGNESI, DANI PAUL, virologist, educator; b. Forgaria, Italy, Mar. 19, 1941; s. Carlo and Marina (Iem) B.; m. Sarah Sampson, Aug. 1, 1964; children: James, Michael. BS, Rensselaer Poly. Inst., 1963, MS, 1965; PhD in Virology, Duke U., 1967. Rsch. assoc. dept. surgery Duke U., 1967-68; NIH postdoctoral fellow Max-Planck Institut für Virusforschung, Tübingen, Fed. Republic Germany, 1968-71; asst. prof. surgery, microbiology and immunology Duke U., Durham, N.C., 1971-72, assoc. prof. surgery, assoc. prof. microbiology and immunology, 1972-77, prof. surgery, prof. microbiology and immunology, 1977-84, James B. Duke prof. exptl. surgery, 1984—, dir. AIDS Ctr. for Rsch., 1989—; CEO Trimeris Corp., Durham, N.C., 1998—. Cons., mem. med. and sci. adv. com. Leukemia Soc. Am.; mem. NIH Virology Study Sect.; mem. Bd. Sci. Counselors, chmn. subcom. on AIDS Editor AIDS Research and Human Retroviruses, 1987—; mem. editorial bd.: Cancer Research, 1978—, Virology, 1978— . Mem. Sigma Xi. Office: Trimeris Corp Ste 300 3518 Westgate Dr Durham NC 27707-2553

BOLOMEY, ROGER HENRY, sculptor; b. Torrington, Conn., Oct. 19, 1918; s. Henry Albert and Ida (Vurlod) B.; m. Alice Susanne Ryser, June 11, 1948; children: Florence Susanne, Yvonne Marguerite. Student, Acad. Fine Arts, Florence, Italy, 1947, U. Lausanne, Switzerland, 1947-48, Calif. Coll. Arts and Crafts, Oakland, 1948-50. Prof. Herbert H. Lehman Coll., CUNY, 1968-75; prof., chmn. dept. art Calif. State U. at Fresno, 1975-83; painter, 1948-60; sculptor, 1960—. Mem. adv. bd. Mus. No. Ariz. Art Inst., Flagstaff, 1976-78, Nat. Sculpture Conf., U. Kans., Lawrence, 1971-80 Chosen to execute 2 large sculptures for state office bldg., Albany, N.Y., 1967, sculpture for, new Nassau County Supreme Ct. Bldg., 1968, Lehman High Sch., Bronx, N.Y., 1969, Eastridge Mall, San Jose, Cal., 1970, N.Y. State Office Bldg., Hauppauge, N.Y., 1973, others.; one-man shows including, Bolles Gallery, San Francisco, 1960, Royal Marks Gallery, N.Y.C., 1964, 65, numerous group exhbns., 1960—, including, 66th Arm. Exhbn., Chgo. Art Inst., 1962, Salon de Mai, Paris (France) Mus. Art, 1963, 64, Whitney Mus., 1964, Larry Aldrich Mus., Ridgefield, Conn., 1964, Carnegie Inst. Internat. Exhbn., 1964, Whitney Mus., 1964, 66, Highlights, 1964-65, Larry Aldrich Mus., 1965, Quatrieme Expn. Suisse de Sculpture, Bienne, Switzerland, 1966, Amerikanische Kunst aus Schweizer Besitz, St. Gallen, Switzerland, 1966, Contemporary Am. Painting and Sculpture, U. Ill. at Urbana, 1967; represented permanent collections, Mus. Modern Art, San Francisco Mus. Modern Art, Whitney Mus., Slädlische Kunsthalle, Mannheim, W.Ger., Larry Aldrich Mus., Bundy Art Gallery, Waitsfield, Vt., San Francisco Art Inst., Oakland Mus., Los Angeles County Mus., U. Calif. Mus. Art, Berkeley, Chase Manhattan Bank, N.Y.C., also numerous pvt. collections; curator: Forgotten Dimension. Recipient 1st prize, commn. for large mural San Jose (Calif.) State Coll. competition, 1962, 1st prize, purchase award Bundy Art Gallery competition, 1963, Sculpture prize 84th Ann. competition San Francisco Art Inst., 1965 Hon. fellow Royal Acad. Fine Arts (Hague, Netherlands); mem. San Francisco Art Inst., Am. Fedn. Arts. Achievements include being the first to use polyurethane from its fluid form as a medium of art. Address: 6968 Sweetwater Ct Boulder CO 80301-3836 Personal E-mail: bolomey3@comcast.net. *My ultimate goal is to live a fully creative life with the hope that what I do and the way I live will stimulate others to do the same.*

BOLOOKI, HOOSHANG, cardiac surgeon; b. Langeh, Iran, Mar. 28, 1937; came to U.S., 1960, naturalized, 1976; s. Hossein and Fatima (Arjomand) B.; m. C. Joanne McDonald, Aug. 30, 1975; children: Hooshang Michael, Cyrus William, Andrew John. BS cum laude, Alborz Coll., Tehran, 1954; MD, Tehran U., 1960. Intern, resident in surgery Kings County Hosp.; asst. instr. SUNY Med. Center, Bklyn., 1961-67; resident in thoracic and cardiovascular surgery Jackson Meml. Hosp. and U. Miami Sch. Medicine, 1967-69; faculty U. Miami (Fla.) Med. Sch., 1969-77, prof. surgery, 1977—; attending surgeon, dir. adult cardiac surgery Jackson Meml. Hosp., 1969—; dir. cardiopulmonary transplant program U. Miami Jackson Meml. Hosp., 1986-98. Cons. VA Hosp., Miami, 1977-90; mem. adv. panel cardiovascular surgery Ethicon Inc., Davis & Geck Co., Inc., 1974-1995; hon. prof. U. Marón Sch. Medicine, Argentina. Author: Clinical Application of Intra-Aortic Balloon Pump, 1976, 3d edit., 1998, Medical Examination Review, Thoracic Surgery, 2d edit., 1972, 3d edit. Vol. 18, 1981, Cardiovascular Surgery, Vol. 38, 1981; contbr. articles to profl. jours. Recipient Rsch. Career Devel. award NIH, 1972-77, grantee, 1972-75; recipient Grand award U. Tex. Med. Br., 1968, Masterpiece award Transplant Found. South Fla., 1996, Achievement award Iranian-Am. Med. Assn., 1999, award for outstanding svc. 2000, award for contbn. to cardiovasc. surgery Onassis Cardiac Surgery Ctr., 2000, Achievement award Onassis Surg. Found., 2000. Fellow ACS, Royal Coll. Surgeons Can., Am. Coll. Cardiology, Am. Coll. Chest Physicians; mem. AMA (cert. merit), Am. Surg. Assn., Am. Assn. Thoracic Surgery, Soc. Univ. Surgeons, Am. Heart Assn., Fla. Heart Assn. (cert. of merit), Fla. Thoracic Soc., Soc. for Thoracic Surgeons, So. Thoracic Surg. Assn. (membership com. 1985-87, chmn. 1989, v.p. 1991), Soc. Internat. de Chirugie, Internat. Cardiovascular Soc., Soc. Vascular Surgery, Internat. Soc. Heart & Lung Transplantation, Soc. Acad. Surgeons, David Park Racquet Club, Ski Club. Republican. Moslem. Office: U Miami Sch Med Thoracic Cardio Surgery R-114 Miami FL 33101 Office Phone: 305-585-5271. Business E-Mail: hbolooki@med.miami.edu.

BOL'SHAKOV, ALEXANDER, physicist; b. Leningrad, USSR, Aug. 28, 1957; s. Anatoly and Louise (Satsuk) B.; m. Elena Kuznetsova, Feb. 16, 1980 (div. 1989); children: Svetlana, Dmitry. MS, Leningrad State U., 1978, PhD, 1989. From postgrad. asst. to sr. rsch. worker Leningrad (USSR) State U., 1980-92; leader rsch. group St. Petersburg (Russia) State U., 1991-93; rsch. assoc. U. Mass., Amherst, 1993—. Govt. scholarship holder U. Oslo, Norway, 1992-93. Patentee in field; contbr. numerous articles to profl. jours. Office: Univ Mass PO Box 34510 Amherst MA 01003-4510

BOLSTER, ARCHIE MILBURN, retired foreign service officer; b. Ames, Iowa, Apr. 9, 1933; s. Horace Goodwin and Ella Schimpf B.; m. Ann Dorcas Matthews, Mar. 22, 1959; children: Christopher, Matthew, Amy. BA in Internat. Rels., U. Va., 1955; MA in Pub. Policy and Adminstrn., U. Wis., 1972. Commd. fgn. svc. officer Dept. State, 1958; assigned Phnom Penh, Cambodia, 1959-60, Tabriz, Iran, 1961-63, Tehran, Iran, 1964-66, 74-76, Bur. Intelligence and Rsch., 1966-68, Office Fuels and Energy, 1969-71; consul gen. Antwerp, Belgium, 1978-81; dep. dir. Divsn. Office Security Assistance and Sales, 1981-83; dep. chief Aviation Negotiations Divsn., 1983-84; spl. projects officer Bur. Refugee Programs, 1984-86. Freedom of Info. Act reviewer, 1984-94, 97-2003, sr. reviewer, 2003-; mem. White House Counsel's Iran-Contra Task Force, 1987-90; mem. staff U.S.-Iran Claims Tribunal, The Hague, Netherlands, 1994-96. Chmn. editl. bd. Fgn. Svc. Jour., 1971. Pres. Williamsburg Civic Assn., Arlington, Va., 1969-70. Served with USNR, 1955-58. Mem. Am. Fgn. Svc. Assn., Assn. Part-Time Profls. (bd. dirs., v.p. 1989-91). Home: 2738 N Lexington St Arlington VA 22207-1437

BOLSTER, ARTHUR STANLEY, JR., history professor; b. Bismarck, N.D., Jan. 30, 1922; s. Arthur S. and Gertrude (Pierce) B.; m. Elizabeth Barker Winkfield, Oct. 8, 1949; children: Stephen Clark, Gregory Pierce. AB, Dartmouth, 1943; MA, Harvard, 1947, PhD, 1954. Tchr. history Grosse Pointe (Mich.) High Sch., 1952-57, Pelham (N.Y.) High Sch., 1957-59; mem. faculty Harvard U., Cambridge, Mass., 1959—, prof. edn., 1967-82, prof. emeritus, 1982—. Author: James Freeman Clarke, Disciple to Advancing Truth, 1954. Served to lt. USNR, 1943-46. Mem. New Eng. History Tchrs. Assn. (pres. 1968-69, Kidger award 1970), Phi Beta Kappa. Mem. United Ch. of Christ (deacon). Home: 587 Lacosta Cir Lake Worth FL 33467-2662 Office: Harvard U Grad Sch Edn Longfellow Hall Cambridge MA 02138

BOLSTER, JACQUELINE NEBEN (MRS. JOHN A. BOLSTER), communications consultant; b. Woodhaven, N.Y. d. Ernest William Benedict and Emily Claire (Guck) Neben; m. John A. Bolster, May 8, 1954. Studied, Pratt Inst., Columbia U. Promotion mgr. Photoplay mag., 1949—53; merchandising mgr. McCall's, N.Y.C., 1953—64; dir. promotion and merchandising

Harper's Bazaar, 1964—71; dir. advt. and promotion Elizabeth Arden Salons, 1971—76; dir. creative svcs. Elizabeth Arden, Inc., 1976—78; dir. comm. Elizabeth Arden Salons, 1978—87; comm. cons., 1987—. Recipient Art Dir.'s award, 1961, 1966. Mem.: Fashion Execs. Roundtable, Fashion Group, Advt. Women N.Y. (life), Women's Nat. Rep. Club (life). Episcopalian. Home and Office: 8531 88th St Woodhaven NY 11421-1308 also: Halsey Neck Ln Southampton NY 11968 Office Phone: 718-849-0975.

BOLSTERLI, MARGARET JONES, language educator, farmer; b. Watson, Ark., May 10, 1931; d. Grover Clevel and Zena (Cason) Jones; m. Mark Bolsterli, Dec. 30, 1953 (div. Dec. 1964); children: Eric, David. BA with honors, U. Ark., 1952; MA, Washington U., St. Louis, 1953; PhD, U. Minn., 1967. Asst. prof. Augsburg Coll., Mpls., 1967-68; prof. English, U. Ark., Fayetteville, 1968-93, prof. emeritus, 1993—, dir. Ctr. for Ark. and Regional Studies, 1984-87. Fulbright lectr., Portugal, 1986; vis. rsch. fellow Yale U., 1997-98; bd. dirs. Ark. Humanities Coun., 1992-94. Author: The Early Community at Bedford Park, 1977, Vinegar Pie and Chicken Bread, 1982, Born in the Delta, 1991, A Remembrance of Eden, 1993; contbr. articles and stories to Jour. Modern Lit., So. Quar., others. NEH Younger Humanist grantee, 1970-71; Ark. Endowment for Humanities grantee, 1980, 81 Mem. MLA (pres. women's caucus), South Cen. MLA. Democrat. E-mail: mbolster@alltel.net.

BOLT, DAWN MARIA, financial planner; b. Bklyn., June 12, 1949; d. Gulick Arthur B. and Georgette Helen (Werner) Bolt-Wiggs; widowed; children: Robert B. Williams, Wesley A. Williams. BA, Bklyn. Coll., 1971. Cert. fin. planner; chartered fin. analyst. Fin. analyst Blyth Eastman Dillon, N.Y.C., 1971—77; rating agy. analyst Fitch Investors Svc., N.Y.C., 1977—78; bank analyst Merrill Lynch, N.Y.C., 1978—80; fin. analyst Moodys Investors Svc., N.Y.C., 1980—86; real estate sales agt. J.R. Silvers Realty, N.Y.C., 1987—95, Coldwell Banker Hunt Kennedy, N.Y.C., 1995—98; pvt. practice fin. planning and coaching, 1998—. Avocations: bowling, tennis, skiing, reading, coaching. E-mail: jodiedawn49@hotmail.com.

BOLT, EUNICE MILDRED DEVRIES, artist; b. Clifton, N.J., Oct. 31, 1926; d. Lambert H. and Cora DeVries; m. Maurice L. Bolt (dec. Nov. 1989); children: Macyn Bolt, Tamsen Bolt, Valerie Bolt Wegner. Grad., Pratt Inst. Art & Design, Bklyn., 1949; BA, Calvin Coll., 1952; MA, Western Mich. U., 1973. Book illustrator Fideler Pubs., Grand Rapids, Mich., 1952-53, Zondervan Pub. Co., Grand Rapids, Mich., 1953-56; prof. Calvin Coll., Grand Rapids, Mich., 1962-67, Grand Rapids C.C., 1968-91. Internat. art study tours coord. and guide, 1978—; fine art exhbn. juror, 1987—; lectr. art history, 1991—, presenter watercolor workshops, 1991—; artist-in-residence, 1995—. Exhibited in group shows at Grand Rapids Art Mus., Kalamazoo Inst. Art, U. Mich. Schlusser Gallery, Pitts. Ctr. for the Arts, Westmoreland Mus. Art, Detroit Inst. Art. Home and Studio: 2481 Autumn Ash Dr Grand Rapids MI 49512

BOLTEN, JOSHUA BREWSTER, federal official; b. Washington, Aug. 16, 1954; BA with distinction, Princeton Univ. Woodrow Wilsonn Sch. of Pub. and Internat. Affairs, 1976; JD, Stanford Law Sch., 1980. Editor Stanford Law Review, 1980; law clk. to Hon. Thelton Henderson US Dist. Ct., San Francisco, 1980; pvt. practice Bolten, O'Melveny & Myers, 1980—85; Internat. Trade Counsel US Senate Fin. Com., 1985—89; gen. coun. US Trade Rep., 1989—92; dep. asst. to the Pres. for legis. affairs The White House, Washington, 1992—93; tchr., internat. trade Yale Law Sch., 1993; exec. dir., legal & govt. affairs Goldman Sachs Internat., London, 1994—99; Policy dir. Bush-Cheny pres. campaign, 1999—2000; asst. to pres. & dep. chief of staff for policy The White House, Washington, 2001—03; dir. Office Mgmt. & Budget, Washington, 2003—. Office: Executive Office of the Pres Office of Mgmt and Budget 725 17th St NW Washington DC 20503*

BOLTON, BETTY J., medical/surgical nurse, poet; b. Lusedale, Miss., Sept. 2, 1952; d. Saul Jones and Mary Hurley Fairley; m. Joe N. Bolton, July 28, 1968; children: Terry, Benilda, Timiki; 1 child, Joe Jones. AAS, Miss. Gulf Coast Jr. Coll., 1986; postgrad., Coastal Tng., Pascagoula, Miss., 1989. Libr. ref. aide Pascagoula Libr., Miss., 1986—89; program specialist I Salvation Army Domestic Violence Women, Pascagoula, Miss., 1986—90; owner B&J Vending, Moss Point, Miss., 1990—92; home health nurse Profl. Home Health, Biloxi, Miss., 1992—97; supr. South Miss. Regional Ctr., Long Beach, Miss., 1997—99; pvt. duty nurse Jackson County and South Miss., 2000—03. Author (poetry): Best Poems of 2002, 2002 (Editors Choice award, 2002), Across the Abyss, 2002 (Editors Choice award, 2002), Best Poems of 2003, 2003 (Editors Choice award, 2003). Recipient Pres. award, Iliad Press, 2003. Mem.: Ri Rsch., Acad. Am. Poets, Internat. Soc. Poets. Ch. Of Christ. Avocations: arts and crafts, sewing, walking, creative cooking, poetry. Home: 3809 Jeffery Dr Moss Point MS 39562 E-mail: joebet51@bellsouth.net.

BOLTON, CALVIN, music educator; s. Donald and Modenia Bolton; m. Ann Peeling; children: Daniel, David. MA, MusM, Ohio State U., 1984; BA in Music, Limestone Coll., 1988; D of Musical Arts, U. N.C. at Greensboro, 1991. Dir. bands Rutherford County Schs., Forest City, NC, 1984—88; grad. tchg. assoc. Ohio State U., Columbus, 1981—84, U. N.C., Greensboro, 1988—91; vis. asst. prof. U. Mont., Missoula, 1991—92; dir. band Dist. 7 Schs., Spartanburg, SC, 1993—99; assoc. prof. music North Greenville Coll., Tigerville, SC, 1999—2003; music assoc., orch. dir., instrumental music coord. First Bapt. North Spartanburg, Spartanburg, SC, 1999—2003; music assoc. 1st Bapt. Ch., North Spartanburg, SC, 2003—. Interim dir. orch. First Bapt. North, Spartanburg, SC, 2002; timpanist Charlotte Philharm. Orch., Charlotte, NC. Author: The Ludwig Drummer,Vol. 1, 1999 (Who's Who Among America's Teachers, 2002), The Ludwig Drummer,Vol.2, 2002. Mem.: Music Educators Nat. Conf., Nat. Assn. Coll. Wind and Percussion Instrs., Percussive Arts Soc. Baptist. Avocation: fishing. Home: 117 Harvest Ln Boiling Springs SC 29316 Office: First Bapt North Spartanburg 8740 Asheville Hwy Spartanburg SC 29316-4999

BOLTON, JOHN ROBERT, ambassador, former federal agency administrator; b. Balt., Nov. 20, 1948; s. Edward Jackson and Virginia (Godfrey) B.; m. Gretchen Louise Brainerd, Jan. 1986; 1 child, Jennifer Sarah. BA summa cum laude, Yale U., 1970, JD, 1974. Bar: D.C. 1975, U.S. Dist. Ct. D.C. 1975, U.S. Ct. Appeals (D.C. cir.) 1975, U.S. Ct. Appeals (4th cir.) 1977, U.S. Ct. Appeals (3d cir.) 1978, U.S. Supreme Ct. 1978, U.S. Ct. Appeals (5th and 11th cirs.) 1981, U.S. Ct. Appeals (10th cir.) 1983, U.S. Ct. Appeals (1st, 6th, 7th, 8th and 9th cirs.) 1988, U.S. Ct. Appeals (2d cir.) 1989. Assoc. Covington & Burling, Washington, 1974-81, ptnr., 1983-85; legal cons. The White House, Washington, 1981; gen. counsel US Agy. for Internat. Devel., Washington, 1981-82, asst. adminstr. for program & policy coord., 1982-83; exec. dir. com. on resolutions Rep. Nat. Com., Washington, 1983-84; asst. atty. gen. legis. affairs U.S. Dept. Justice, Washington, 1985-88, asst. atty. gen. civil divsn., 1988-89; asst. sec. internat. orgn. affairs bur. U.S. Dept. State, Washington, 1989-93; ptnr. Lerner, Reed, Bolton & McManus (and predecessor firms), Washington, 1993-99; of counsel Kutak Rock LLP, Washington, 1999-2001; under sec. (arms control & internat. security affairs) US Dept. State, Washington, 2001—05; permanent U.S. rep. UN, NYC, 2005—. Sr. fellow, Manhattan Inst., 1993, adj. prof. George Mason U. Law Sch., 1994-96; pres. Nat. Policy Forum, Washington, 1995-96; sr. v.p. Am. Enterprise Inst., Washington, 1997-2001, commr. US Commn. on Internat. Religious Freedom, 1999-2001; mem. bd. dirs., Project for a New Am. Century, 1989-2001, Subcommittee on Internat. Law, Federalist Soc., 1999-2001 Contbr. articles to profl. jours. Served in US Army Nat. Guard, 1970—74 USAR, 1974—76. Recipient Tree of Life award, No. & So. New England Regions of Hadassah, 1990, Disting. Svc. award, US Dept. State, Edmund J. Randolph award, US Dept. Justice, 1998 Mem. Phi Beta Kappa, Pi Sigma Alpha. Republican. Lutheran. Office: UN 799 United Nations Plz 11th Fl New York NY 10017

BOLTON, KENNETH ALBERT, management consultant; b. Mar. 6, 1941; s. Albert and Myrtle (Nelting) B.; m. Maryanne Lavelle; 1 child, Katharine. BS in Indsl. Engring., Pa. State U., 1978. Registered profl. engr., Calif. With GE, Allentown, Pa., 1961-63, system mgr. Phila., 1963-72; mgr. MCS Mgmt. Internat., Washington, 1972-80, Coopers & Lybrand, Phila., 1980-82; dir. cons. Worden & Risberg, Phila., 1982-83; v.p. mktg. Laminated, Inc., Hatfield, Pa., 1983-86; pres. Mgmt. Internat., Phila., 1986-90, Wm. P. Bolton, Inc., Phila., 1990—. Contbr. articles to profl. jours. Advisor Jr. Achievement, Media, Pa., 1970; mem. adv. bd. Salvation Army. Mem. NSPE, Am. Arbitration Assn. (panel of arbitrators), Phila. C. of C. (bd. dirs. 1975, lobbyist small bus. coun. 1978), Union League Phila., St. George's Club Bermuda. Republican. Avocations: golf, computers, antiques. Home: 5900 Atlantic Ave Ventnor City NJ 08406-2862 Office: Mgmt Internat 100 S Dorset Ave Ventnor City NJ 08406-2834

BOLTON, ROBIN JEAN, artist, painter; b. Americus, Ga., Sept. 13, 1943; d. Charles Robert and Sara Maude (Sumerford) Ricketson; m. Robert Emory Bolton III, Aug. 20, 1966; 1 child, Robin Jean. BFA, U. Ga., 1972. Graphic artist Shea/Rustin Pub., Atlanta, 1966-67, Davison's Dept. Store, Atlanta, 1967, Stein Printing Co., Atlanta, 1968, Naylor Assocs., East Point, Ga., 1968, Tucker Wayne & Co., Atlanta, 1968-70, Graphique Ltd., Chgo., 1970-72, Nan Miller Gallery, Rochester, N.Y., 1985—. Instr. Comml. Art Supply, Syracuse, N.Y., pvt. studio Bridgport, N.Y., Liverpool, N.Y.; label designer Persimmon Creek Vineyards, Ga. One-woman shows include The Frog & Peach Gallery, Clayton, Ga., 1997-2000, 2002, Nan Miller Gallery Rochester, N.Y., 2002, Gallery One, San Francisco, Ga. State Botanical Gardens, 2005, Home Expressions Design Ctr., Alpharetha, Ga., 2005; exhibited in group shows at Everson Mus. Art, Syracuse, 1976, The Jacob K. Javits Fed. Bldg., N.Y.C., 1986, Islip (N.Y.) Art Mus., 1989, Kirkpatrick Art Ctr., Oklahoma City, 1989, Nat. Assn. Women Artists Centennial Exhbn., 1989, Wyoming Sem. Juried Regional Exhibit, Kingston, Pa., 1996, U. Ga. State Heritage Botanical Gardens, The Alice Callaway Bldg., 2004; permanent collections include the IBM Collection, State of Ga., State Capitol of Ga., Ga. Commn. on Women/Dept. of Labor Bldg. Atlanta, Talullah Falls Sch., Federated Hall, Talullah Falls, Ga., Farash Coop., Rochester, N.Y.; designer labels for The Persimmon Creek Vineyards Recipient Cooperstown Nat. 1st prize Cooperstown (N.Y.) Art Assn., 1975, Henry Mallory Meml. award, 1978, Arena '76 1st prize, Binghamton, N.Y., 1976, Grand prize Best of Show, Liverpool State Open, 1976, Liquitex-Binney & Smith award for outstanding achievement in field of art, Moravia Coll., Bethlehem, Pa., 1996; named Hon. Youth Art Month Artist, State of Ga., 2001. Mem. Nat. Assn. Women Artists, Liverpool Arts and Crafts Guild, DAR, UDC. Methodist. Avocations: golf, gardening, reading. Home: 4720 Sharron Point Ct Alpharetta GA 30004-3908 Office Phone: 770-521-1547. Personal E-mail: bbolton1@bellsouth.net.

BOLTON, ROGER, insurance company executive; m. Lynne Bolton; 3 children. BA in Journalism, Ohio State U., 1972. Newspaper reporter, Marion, Ohio; press sec. and staff dir. U.S. Congressman Clarence J. Brown; dir. speechwriting Reagan-Bus re-election Campaign, 1984; asst. U.S. trade rep. for pub. affairs Exec. Office of the Pres.; spl. asst. to pres. Reagan; asst. sec. of the treasury for pub. affairs, 1989; dir. of corp. media rels., dir. of commn. for the IBM server and software groups IBM, 1991—95; sr. v.p., commn. Aetna Inc., 1995—. Mem. exec. coun. Aetna Inc.; chmn. Aetna's Coun. for Org. Effectiveness; mem. bd. dirs. Aetna Found., Aetna Polit. Action Com.; mem. Aetna Pub. Policy Com.; treas. Arthur W. Page Soc.; mem. Pub. Rels. Seminar Com. Office: Aetna Inc 151 Farmington Ave Hartford CT 06156

BOLTON, ROGER EDWIN, economist, educator; b. Dover, Pa., Nov. 23, 1938; s. Oscar Jacob and Edna Irene (Hughes) B.; m. Julia Carolyn Gooden, June 27, 1964; children: Christopher, Jonathan. AB, Franklin and Marshall Coll., 1959; PhD, Harvard U., 1964. Instr. Harvard U., Cambridge, Mass., 1964-66; asst. prof. econs. Williams Coll., Williamstown, Mass., 1966-69, assoc. prof., 1969-74, prof., 1974—2003, William R. Kenan Jr. prof., 1992-93, Edward Dorr Griffin prof., 1986-92, chmn. dept., 1975-76, 79-81, dir. Ctr. Humanities and Social Scis., 1985-87, chair faculty steering com., 1991-92, William Brough prof., 1994—2003, prof. emeritus, 2003—; rsch. assoc. Ctr. for Environ. Studies, 2003—. Vis. prof. Wellesley Coll., 1977, U. Pa., 1981-82; George A. Miller vis. prof. U. Ill., 1988; disting. vis. prof. U. Wis., Madison, 1989; vis. prof. Clark U., 1993; mem. assoc. staff Brookings Instn., 1965-68; sr. economist Curran Assocs., 1973-75; rsch. assoc. Joint Ctr. for Urban Studies, 1979-81; mem. com. on place-based decisionmaking NRC, 2000-02. Author: Defense Purchases and Regional Growth, 1966; co-author: Regional Diversity, 1981; editor: Defense and Disarmament, 1966; co-editor Internat. Regional Sci. Rev., 1985-89 (mem. editl. bd.); mem. editl. bd. Annals Regional Sci., Can. Jour. Regional Sci., Growth and Change; mem. editorial bd., book rev. editor Jour. Regional Sci.; also numerous articles. Mem. Berkshire County Regional Planning Commn., Mass., 1980-81, 82-88, clk., 1983-85, vice-chmn., 1985-87; mem. Williamstown Planning Bd., 1983-86, chmn., 1985-86; bd. dirs. No. Berkshire Indsl. Park and Devel. Corp., chmn., 1986-88; mem. Hoosic River Watershed Assn., 2003—, treas. 2004—. Recipient Outstanding Contbn. to Planning award Berkshire County Regional Planning Commn., 1989; Woodrow Wilson fellow, 1959-60, Danforth fellow, 1959-64. Mem. Am. Econ. Assn., Regional Sci. Assn. (councillor 1988-91), Regional Studies Assn., Assn. Am. Geographers, Western Regional Sci. Assn. (bd. dirs. 2003-). Home: 30 Grandview Dr Williamstown MA 01267-2528 Office: Williams Coll Dept Econs Fernald House Williamstown MA Office Phone: 413-597-2393. Business E-Mail: roger.e.bolton@williams.edu.

BOLTON-HOLIFIELD, ALICE RUTH, professional basketball player; b. Lucedale, Miss., May 25, 1967; d. Linwood and Leola Bolton; m. Mark Holifield. B of Exercise Physiology, Auburn U., 1989. Basketball player C.A. Faenza, Italy, 1993, Erreti Faenza, Italy, 1994—95, Sacramento Monarchs, 1997—2001; mem. 1996 & 2000 US Olympic Team (Gold Medal Winner). Mem. U.S.A. Women's Nat. Basketball Team; launched clothing line Runwear. Lead singer: Antidum Tarantula. 1st lt. USAR. Named USA Basketball's Female Athlete of Yr., 1991, 1st Am. woman to play profl. basketball in Hungary and Sweden, 1990—91; named to, NCAA 1989 Mideast Region All-Tournament Team, 1988, 1989, NCAA Final Four All Tournament Team honors, 1988, SEC-All Academic Team, 1988, 1989, All-SEC second team, 1989; recipient gold medal, U.S. Olympic Festival, 1986, World Univ. Games, 1991, World Championship Qualifying Team FIBA World Championship, 1993, 1994 Goodwill Games, 1994, Bronze medal, World Championship, 1994; earned SEC All-Tournament Team honors, 1988, All-WNBA 1st team, 1999, named first ever WNBA player of week, 1997, mem. gold medal winning Olympic team, Atlanta, 1996, mem., U.S. Basketball Women's Nat. Team, 1995—96.

BOLTWOOD, RUSSELL LEWIS, lawyer, telecommunications industry executive; b. St. Louis, Apr. 15, 1963; s. Chester McBride and Joan Mary (Schnable) B. AB, U. Calif., Berkeley, 1986; JD, Golden Gate U., 1993. Assoc. atty. Davis, Reno & Courtney, San Francisco, 1993—96; corp. HR, risk mgr. Fritz Companies, Inc., San Francisco, 1996—97; gen. counsel, chief human resources officer UTStarcom, Inc., Alameda, Calif., 1997—. Vol. United Way, Oakland, 1987—. Mem. Am. Mensa, Commonwealth Club Calif., Toastmasters Internat. Avocations: music, backpacking, creative writing, composition of music. Home: 560 Elysian Fields Dr Oakland CA 94605-5010 Office: UTStarcom 1275 Harbor Bay Parkway Alameda CA 94502 Office Phone: 510-846-8800.

BOLTZ, CAROL HOFMANN, retired school system reading specialist; b. Warren, Pa., Oct. 26, 1934; d. James Ray and Romayne Elizabeth (Lesser) Barrett; m. John Thomas Hofmann, July 18, 1959 (div. June 1980); children: Paul Barrett Hofmann, Lynn Hofmann Waterfield; m. James Boltz, Jan. 10, 1981; 1 child, David James. MusB, Oberlin Coll., 1956; MS in Edn., SUNY, Fredonia, 1981. Cert. elem. edn. and reading tchr. Chapel organist Vassar Coll., Poughkeepsie, NY, 1956—59; dir. music Lafayette Ave. Presbyn. Ch., Buffalo, 1959—64; pvt. tchr. specializing in organ and piano, 1959—; organist 1st United Meth. Ch., Fredonia, 1967—89; organ instr. SUNY, Fredonia, 1970—71; reading tutor Fredonia Migrant Program, 1975—79; reading specialist Dunkirk Schs., Dunkirk, 1980—94; ret., 1994. Organ recitalist Founder Organ Vesper Recital Series, Fredonia, 1970-90, mem-.steering com. Rockefeller Arts Ctr., SUNY, 1998-2002; mem. exec. bd. Fredonia Chamber Players, 1986-2001; bd. dirs. Friends of Barker Libr., 2001—; vol. staff 1891 Fredonia Opera House, 1994—; coord. sponsored chairs We. N.Y. Chamber Orch., 2001— Recipient Elder Salute, Fredonia Kiwanis, 1997, Cmty. Svc. award, Chautauqua County C. of C., 2000, Hometown Hero award, DFT Comm., 2003, Footprints award, No. Chautauqua Cmty. Found., 2005. Mem. Am. Guild Organists, Internat. Reading Assn., Dunkirk Tchr.'s Assn., Fredonia Preservation Soc., Oberlin Alumni Assn. (pres. Buffalo chpt. 1960-62), Fredonia Shakespeare Club, Phi Delta Kappa, Sigma Alpha Iota, Pi Kappa Lambda. Republican. Avocations: reading, gardening, travel.

BOLTZ, DAVID, IV, music educator, musician; b. Lebanon, Pa., Oct. 1, 1949; s. David Leroy and Joyce Juanita Boltz; m. Suzanne Martin, May 21, 1977; children: Andrea Sue, Lewis Matthew. BS in Music Edn., Lebanon Valley Coll., 1972; MusM in Applied Trumpet, Cath. U. Am., 1975. Elem. band tchr. Greencastle-Antrin Sch. Dist., Pa., 1972—73; commd. lt. USAF, 1973, advanced through grades to sgt., 1985, trumpeter Washington, 1973—93, ret., 1993; instrumental music tchr. Fairfax County (Va.) Public Sch., 1993—. Pres. Fairlington United Meth., Alexandria, Va., 1978—. Mem.: Va. Music Educator's Assn. Methodist. Avocations: model railroading, birdwatching. Home: 6901 Stoneybrooke Ln Alexandria VA 22306 Office: Longfellow Mid Sch 2000 Westmoreland St Falls Church VA 22043

BOLTZ, GERALD EDMUND, lawyer; b. Dennison, Ohio, June 1, 1931; s. Harold E. and Margaret Eve (Hecky) B.; m. Janet Ruth Scott, Sept. 19, 1959; children: Gretchen Boltz Fields, Eric Scott, Jill Marie. BA, Ohio N. U., 1953, JD, 1955. Bar: Ohio 1955, U.S. Supreme Ct. 1964, Calif. 1978, U.S. Dist. Ct. (cen. dist.) Calif. 1978. Asst. atty. gen. State of Ohio, 1958; atty. spl. investigations unit SEC, 1959-60, legal asst. to commr., 1960-61, sr. trial and spl. counsel Denver, 1961-66, regional adminstr. Ft. Worth, 1967-71, L.A., 1972-78; ptnr. Fine, Perzik& Friedman, L.A., 1979-83; mng. ptnr. Rogers & Wells, L.A., 1983-92; ptnr. Bryan Cave, L.A., 1992—. Co-author: Securities Law Techniques. Served with U.S. Army, 1955-57. Mem. ABA, Fed. Bar Assn., L.A. Bar Assn., Ohio Bar Assn., Calif. Bar Assn., Bel Air Bay Club. Presbyterian (elder). Avocations: sailing, piano. Home: 1105 Centinela Ave Santa Monica CA 90403-2316 Office: Bryan Cave 120 Broadway Ste 300 Santa Monica CA 90401-2386 Personal E-mail: geboltz@adelphia.net. E-mail: geboltz@bryancave.com.

BOLY, LILLIAN BYRONELL, retired secondary English educator; b. St. Louis, Feb. 25, 1929; d. Joseph Robert and Mary Pearl (Park) B. BS in Edn., S.E. Mo. State U., 1956; MA in Edn., Washington U., St. Louis, 1964, postgrad., U. Oreg. Cert. in elem. edn., secondary English and social studies. Tchr. in one-rm. schs., Butler County, Mo., 1945-48; tchr. 3d and 4th grades Naylor (Mo.) Sch. Dist., 1949-54; tchr. 4th grade Sch. Dist. of Riverview Gardens, St. Louis, 1954-63, tchr. English, 1963-90, also sponsor Future Tchrs. Am. and Spectrum lit. publ. Mem. NEA, Nat. Coun. Tchrs. English, Mo. Assn. Tchrs. English, Greater St. Louis Tchrs. English (pres., bd. dirs.), Riverview Gardens NEA (conv. del., treas., pres.), Phi Delta Kappa (sec. St. Louis chpt. 1992-94, 2001-03, 2004—. program v.p. 2003-04)

BOMAN, MARC ALLEN, lawyer; b. Cleve., Sept. 4, 1948; s. David S. and Shirley T. (Freier) B.; m. Leah Eilenberg, June 10, 1984; children: Autumn, Heidi, Jane, David. Student, Purdue U., 1966-68; BA, Case Western Res. U., 1971, JD, 1974. Bar: Ohio 1974, Wash. 1978, D.C. 1978, U.S. Dist. Ct. (we. dist.) Wash. 1980, U.S. Ct. Appeals (9th cir.), U.S. Dist. Ct. (ea. dist.) Wash. 1985, U.S. Ct. Appeals (fed. cir.) 1986. Atty.-advisor Office of Gen. Counsel U.S. Gen. Acctg. Office, Washington, 1974-78; dep. prosecuting atty. Office of Prosecuting Atty., King County, Wash., 1978-81; assoc. Perkins Coie, Seattle, 1981-86, ptnr., 1986—. Spl. ind. dep. prosecutor ethics investigation of county execs., 1994; mem. Seattle Ethics and Elections Commn., 1995-98; spkr. in field, spl. ind. prosecutor to Met. King Cty. State v. Ridgway capital murder case, 2002. Bd. dirs. Perkins Coie Cmty. Svcs. Fellowship, 1987-97, co-chmn., 1994-97; former bd. dirs. Totem coun. Girl Scouts U.S., Seattle Day Ctr. for Adults, Madrona Neighborhood Coun.; trustee Herzl-Ner Tamid Congregation, 1987-98, pres., 1994-96; mem. Leadership Tomorrow, United Way King County-Seattle C. of C., 1987-88; trustee King County Bar Found., 1995-2000, v.p., 1997-98, pres., 1998-99. Recipient Pres.'s award King County Bar Assn., 1999; Mayoral proclamation declaring Marc Boman Day named in honor of contbn. to citizens of Seattle, 1998. Mem. Seattle King Bar Assn. (trustee 1986-89, chmn. divsn. young lawyers 1984-85), Wash. State Bar Assn. (co-chair Blue Ribbon Panel on Criminal Def. 2003-04). Office: Perkins Coie 1201 3rd Ave Fl 40 Seattle WA 98101-3029

BOMAR, LAURA BETH, music educator; b. Atlanta, Ga., Feb. 24, 1965; d. Alvie Troy and Mary Elizabeth Elliott; m. Robert Linton Bomar, June 27, 1987; 1 child, Sarah Beth. AA, Brewton-Parker Coll., 1985; BA, Tift Coll., 1987; MusM, Ga. State U., 1993. Music tchr. Butts County Schools, Jackson, Ga., 1987—. Team leader North Mulberry Elem. Sch., Jackson, Ga., 1999—, sch. coun. mem., 2003—. Mem.: Music Educators Nat. Conf., PA of Ga. Educators (bldg. rep. 2001—). Protestant. Avocations: hiking, camping, biking, reading. Office: North Mulberry Elem Sch 820 N Mulberry St Jackson GA 30233

BOMBACI, NANCY MARGARET, literature educator; b. Hartford, Conn., Mar. 25, 1963; d. Lucian and Anna Ferro Bombaci. BA, Trinity Coll., 1985, MA, 1990; PhD, Fordham U., 2000. Vis. instr. Fordham U., Bronx, NY, 1998—99, vis. asst. prof., 2000—01, St. Joseph Coll., West Hartford, Conn., 1999—2000; adj. lectr. Capital Cmty. and Tech. Coll., Hartford, 2001—03; asst. prof. writing and lit. Mitchell Coll., New London, Conn., 2003—. Author: Freaks in Late Modernist American Culture: Nathanael West, Djuna Barnes, Tod Browning and Carson McCullers, 2005. Presdl. scholar, Fordham U., 1993—97, Sr. Tchg. fellow, 1996—97. Mem.: MLA. Office: Mitchell Coll 437 Pequot Ave New London CT 06320 Office Phone: 860-701-7747. Personal E-mail: n.bomba@prodigy.net. Business E-Mail: bombaci_n@mitchell.edu.

BOMBARD, AMY LYNN, music educator; b. Akron, Ohio, Apr. 8, 1973; d. William Dennis and Ruth Ellen Pitt; m. Charles Robin Bombard, Dec. 27, 1996; 1 child, Noelle Joy. BA in Piano Performance, Pensacola (Fla.) Christian Coll., 1995, MS in Music Edn., 1997; postgrad., U. Iowa, 2001—. Grad. asst. Pensacola Christian Coll., 1995—97, prof., 1997—. Mem.: Music Tchrs. Nat. Assn., Music Educators Nat. Conf. Home: 5955 Saint Alban Rd Pensacola FL 32503-7924

BOMBARDELLI, FABIAN ALEJANDRO, hydraulic engineer, researcher; b. La Plata, Buenos Aires, Argentina, May 12, 1966; s. Reynaldo Julio Bombardelli and Nidia Ethel Michelini. Bachiller, Colegio Nacional Rafael Hernández of La Plata, La Plata, Buenos Aires, Argentina, 1983; Master in Numerical Simulation and Control, U. Buenos Aires, 1999; PhD in Civil and Environ. Engring., U. Ill., 2004. Undergrad. asst. Bur. of Pub. Rds., Buenos Aires Province, La Plata, Argentina, 1989—91; rsch. engr. Nat. Inst. for Water, Ezeiza, Argentina, 1991—98; rsch. asst. dept. civil and environ. engring. U. Ill., Urbana, Ill., 1999—2003; asst. prof. dept. civil and environ. engring. U. Calif., Davis, 2004—. Cons., Buenos Aires, 1997—98; v.p. and coord. Environ. Inst., Ctr. of Engrs. of Buenos Aires Province, La Plata, Buenos Aires, Argentina, 1994—98. Contbr. articles to profl. jours. Counselor Argentine Cmty. at Urbana-Champaign, Urbana, Ill., 2002—03. Named Outstanding Rschr., Nat. Inst. for Water, Argentina, 1994; recipient Glenn and Helen Stout award, Dept. of Civil and Environ. Engring., U. of Ill. at Urbana-Champaign, 2001. Mem.: Internat. Assn. Hydraulic Rsch., Internat. Water Resources Assn., Phi Kappa Phi. Office: Univ Calif Davis Dept Civil and Environ Engring One Shields Ave Davis CA 95616 Office Phone: 530-752-0949. E-mail: fabombardelli@ucdavis.edu.

BOMBARDIERI, MERLE ANN, psychotherapist; b. Atlanta, Mar. 16, 1949; d. Sol and Sadie (Drucker) Malkoff; m. Rocco Anthony Bombardieri, Jr., Aug. 22, 1971; children: Marcella, Vanessa. B.A. in Psychology, Mich.

State U., 1971; M.S.W., San Diego State U., 1976. Cert. clin. social workers, Mass., clin. hypnosis Am. Soc. Clin. Hypnosis; Diplomate Nat. Assn. Social Workers, Am. Bd. Examiners in Clin. Social Work. Crisis intervention worker and trainer Listening Ear, East Lansing, Mich., 1969-71; tchr. English as 2d lang. Instituto Brasil Estados Unidos, Rio de Janeiro, 1971-73; supr. infant unit Married Student Day Care Ctr., Mich. State U., East Lansing, 1973-74; psychotherapist/family life educator Family Svc. Assocs., San Diego, 1975-77; psychotherapist Dade Wallace Mental Health Ctr., Nashville, 1977-78; psychotherapist/workshop leader Met. Beaverbrook Mental Health Ctr., Waltham, Mass., 1980-81; pvt. practice psychotherapy, Acton-Belmont, Mass., 1982—; clin. dir. Resolve, Inc., infertility orgn., Belmont, 1982-84; clin. cons., 1984—; cons. HealthData Internat., Westport, Conn., 1983—, Open Door Soc., Newton, Mass., 1983—, First Day Film Corp., 1985—, Mass. Dept. Social Svcs., 1987; sec. Boston Fertility Soc., 1995, others; psychology seminar leader; radio and TV appearances. Author: The Baby Decision, 1981, (cassettes) Your Mind's Own Medicine, 1998; founder, editor, pub. Wellspring newsletter; contbr. articles to profl. and med. jours. N.Y. State Regents scholar, 1967; NIMH trainee, 1970. Mem. Acad. Cert. Social Workers, Phi Beta Kappa, Phi Kappa Phi. Home: 4 Broadview Rd Acton MA 01720-4202 Office: 33 Bedford St Lexington MA 02420-4319

BOMBERGER, RUSSELL BRANSON, lawyer, writer; b. Lebanon, Pa., May 1, 1934; s. John Mark and Viola (Aurentz) B.; divorced; children— Ann Elizabeth, Jane Carmel. BS, Temple U., 1955; MA, U. Iowa, 1956, MA, 1961, PhD, 1962; MS, U. So. Calif., 1960; LLB, JD, LaSalle U.; grad., U.S. Marine Corps Command and Staff Coll., 1987, U.S. Naval War Coll., 1991. Bar: Calif. 1970, U.S. Supreme Ct. 1975. Mem. editorial staff Phila. Inquirer, 1952-54; lectr. U. Iowa, 1955-57, U. So. Calif., 1957-58; asst. prof. U.S. Naval Postgrad. Sch., Monterey, Calif., 1958-62, assoc. prof., 1963-75, prof., 1975-89, prof. emeritus, 1989—; practice law, 1970—. Freelance writer, 1952—, communications cons., 1963—; safety cons. internat. program U. So. Calif. Inst. Safety and Systems Mgmt., 1983—; cons. Internat. Ctr. for Aviation Safety, Lisbon, 1984—; vis. fellow, Oxford U. Author: (novel) The Alternate Candidate, (broadcast series) The World of Ideas, (motion picture) Strokes and Stamps, (stage play) Closely Held; abstracter-editor: Internat. Transactional Analysis Assn. Capt. USNR, 1966-94. Decorated Meritorious Civilian Svc. medal, 1989; Am. Psychol. Found. fellow Columbia U., 1954-55, CBS fellow U. So. Calif., 1957-58, Keith fellow, Oxford U., 2004. Office: PO Box 8741 Monterey CA 93943-8741 E-mail: rbbomber@excite.com, rbbomber@lawyer.com.

BOMBIERI, ENRICO, mathematician, educator; b. Milan, Nov. 26, 1940; came to U.S., 1977; naturalized 1995; s. Carlo and Luisa (Cambi) B.; m. Susan Russell, Jan. 21, 1967, d 1999; 1 child, Donata. Grad., Trinity Coll., Cambridge; PhD, U. Milan, 1963. Prof. math. U. Cagliari, Italy, 1965, U. Pisa, Italy, 1966-74, Scuola Normale Superiore, Pisa, 1974, Inst. Advanced Study, Princeton, N.J., 1977—. Recipient Fields medal Internat. Math. Union, Vancouver, Can., 1974. Mem. Am. Acad. Arts and Scis., Nat. Acad. Sci., French Acad. Scis., Acad. Nazionale Delle Scienze Italy, Acad. Nazionale dei Lincei (nat. mem.), Swedish Royal Acad. Office: Inst Advanced Study Sch Mathematics Simonyi Hall 213 Einstein Dr Princeton NJ 08540

BOMBINO, ANGELA ROSE, administrative assistant; d. Frank Paul and Civitina Frances (Salipante) Bombino. BA in Mgmt., Boston Coll. Paralegal Certificate: Estates and Trusts Bentley Coll., Mass., Paralegal Certificate: Estate and Inheritance Taxation Bentley Coll., Mass., Paralegal Certificate: Corporations Bentley Coll., Mass., Paralegal Certificate: Fundamentals of Pension Administration Bentley Coll., Mass., Notary Public Commonwealth of Mass. Exec. asst. law dept. and corp. secretary's office New Eng. Fin., Boston, 1980—96; exec. asst. corp. planning and devel. MetLife (formerly New Eng. Fin.), Boston, 1996—98, exec. asst. integration mgmt., 1998—2000, bus. cons. strategic mgmt. group, 2000—01; staff asst. trustees office Tufts U., Medford, Mass., 2003—. Bd. mem. Mass. Youth Leadership Found. (affiliation of Hugh O'Brian Youth Found.), Boston, 1984—86, Somerville (Mass.) Pub. Safety Commn., 1990—2000. Treas. The Taylor Com. (Ward Alderman), Somerville, 1980. Roman Catholic. Avocations: piano, music, golf, languages. Office: Tufts University Ballou Hall Medford MA 02155 Office Phone: 617-627-3320. Business E-Mail: angela.bombino@tufts.edu.

BOMHAN, RUTH WALKER, social studies educator; b. Wilmington, N.C, Dec. 17, 1955; d. Robert Henry and Edna (Barritt) Walker; m. Kenneth Earl Bomhan (div.); 1 child, Kenneth Earl Jr. BA, U. N.C., Wilmington, 1984. Cert. tchr. social studies. Tchr. New Hanover H.S., Wilmington, 1984-85, Hoggard Night Sch., Wilmington, 1985-88, Lakeside H.S., Wilmington, 1988-2000, Roland-Grise Mid. Sch., Wilmington, 2000—. Mem. Smithsonian Instn., Civil War Trust, Nat. Geog. Soc., Mus. of Confederacy, World War II Meml., N.C. Coun. Social Studies, Libr. Congress, Nat. Trust Historic Preservation, Friends of Nat. Park Gettysburg, N.C. Assn. Educators, Nat. Honor soc. Polit. Sci., Colonial Williamsburg Found. Avocations: bowling, lapidary, reading, travel, martial arts. Office: Roland-Grise Mid Sch 4412 Lake Ave Wilmington NC 28403

BOMMIREDDY, RAMIREDDY, immunologist, researcher; arrived in U.S., 1998; s. Ankireddy and Lingamma Bommireddy; m. Swarooparani Ramalingam, Dec. 17, 1999; children: Sudeep children: Sreekar. BSc, Sri Subbaaraya & Narayana Coll., Narasaraopet, India, 1988; MSc, U. Hyderabad, India, 1990; PhD, Indian Inst. Sci., Bangalore, India, 1997. Jr. rsch. fellow Indian Inst. Sci., Bangalore, 1990—92, sr. rsch. fellow, 1992—96, rsch. assoc., 1996—98; postdoctoral fellow U. Cin., 1998—2002, rsch. scientist, 2003—. Exec. mem. students' coun. U. Hyderabad, 1989—90; gen. sec. Telugu Cultural Assn., Bangalore, 1993—94; mem. India Student Assn., Cin., 1998—99. Contbr. articles to profl. jours. U. Merit scholar, U. Hyderabad, 1988—90, rsch. fellow, U. Grants Commn., Govt. India, 1990—95, rsch. associateship, Dept. Biotechnology, Govt. India, 1995—98, postdoctoral fellow, NIH, 1998—2003. Mem.: Am. Assn. Immunologists (assoc.). Achievements include research in TGFbeta1 as a therapeutic target for autoimmune diseases such as diabetes, arthritis and multiple sclerosis. Avocations: chess, travel. Home: 2920 Scioto St #1000 Cincinnati OH 45219 Office: University of Cincinnati 231 Albert Sabin Way Cincinnati OH 45267 Office Phone: 513-558-0089. Personal E-mail: bommireddy66@yahoo.com. Business E-Mail: bommirr@ucmail.uc.edu.

BOMSE, STEPHEN V., lawyer; b. LA, Dec. 18, 1944; AB, Stanford U., 1964; LLB, Yale U., 1967. Bar: Calif. 1967. Assoc. Heller, Ehrman, White & McAuliffe, San Francisco, 1967—72, ptnr., 1972—, co-chair Antitrust & Trade Regulation Practice Group. Vis. prof. law Stanford U., 1988-89; rep. 9th Cir. Jud. Conf., 1980-82; gen. counsel No. Calif. ACLU, 1980—. Fellow: Am. Bar Found.; mem.: Assn. Bus. Trial Lawyers of No. Calif. (pres. 1994—95), Bar Assn. Calif., State Bar Calif., ABA, Am. Law Inst. Office: Heller Ehrman 333 Bush St San Francisco CA 94104-2878 Office Phone: 415-772-6142. Office Fax: 415-772-6268. E-mail: sbomse@hewm.com.

BONA, FREDERICK EMIL, public relations executive; b. Union City, N.J., Mar. 3, 1939; s. Henry C. and Clementina A. Bona; m. Doris L. Hurlbert, May 27, 1961; children: Lauri Paporello, Dawn Rizzo, Christine Cabana, F.A. (Rick). BS in Mktg., Fairleigh Dickinson U., 1962. Press rels. rep. W.R. Grace & Co., N.Y.C., 1962, mgr. press rels., 1970, dir. press rels., 1980, v.p. corp. communications div., 1983, dep. group exec., 1985, v.p., 1987-94; prin. The Dilenschneider Group, Inc., N.Y.C., 1994-95, LS Comms., Inc., N.Y.C., 1995—. Dep. comms. mgr. Pres.'s Pvt. Sector Survey on Cost Control (Grace Commn.), Washington, 1982-85. Mem. Overseas Press Club (bd. govs. 1988-91, 94-97), Pub. Rels. Soc. N.Y. Roman Catholic. Office: LS Communications Inc 17 Devon Rd Boonton NJ 07005-9305

BONA, JERRY LLOYD, mathematician, educator; b. Little Rock, Feb. 5, 1945; s. Louis Eugene and Mary Eva (Kane) B.; m. Pamela Anne Ross, Dec. 23, 1966; children: Rachael Elizabeth, Jennifer Dani'el. BS in Applied Math. and Computer Sci., Washington U., St. Louis, 1966; PhD in Math., Harvard U., 1971. Rsch. fellow U. Essex, Colchester, Eng., 1970-72; L. E. Dickson instr. U. Chgo., 1972-73, from asst. prof. to assoc. prof. to prof., 1973-86; prof. Pa. State U., University Park, 1986-90, Raymond Shibley prof., 1990-95, acting chmn., 1990-91, chmn., 1991-95; CAM prof. math. and physics U. Tex., Austin, 1995—2002; prof., chmn. U. Ill., Chgo., 2002—. Rsch. fellow dept. math. Harvard U. 1970, 73; U.K. Sci. and Engring. Rsch. Coun. sr. vis. fellow Fluid Mechanics Rsch. Inst., U. Essex, 1973, 74, 75, 77, 78; vis. rsch. assoc. Brookhaven Nat. Lab., 1976, 77; NAS exch. visitor to Poland, 1977; vis. prof. Centro Brasileiro Pesquisas Fisicas, Rio de Janeiro, 1980, Math. Rsch. Ctr., 1980-81, U. Brasilia, 1982, Lab. Anvendt Matematisk Fysik, Danish Tech. Sch., 1982, Inst. Math. and its Applications, U. Minn., 1985, 88, 90, 91, 2001; rsch. prof. Applied Rsch. Lab., Pa. State U., 1986-95; prof. invité U. Paris-Sud, Ctr. d'Orsay, 1982, 86-89, 92, 2001, 03, l'Inst. Nat. Sci. Rsch.-Oceanology, U. Que., 1982-87, Ecole Normale Superieure de Cachan, 1990-91, dir. rsch. CNRS, 1995, U. Bordeaux, 1995, 2001, 03, 05; invited prof. Inst. Pure and Applied Math., Rio de Janeiro, 1991-93, 99, 2000, 02, Acad. Sinica, Beijing, 1991, 96, 99, Math. Scis. Rsch. Inst., Berkeley, Calif., 1994, U. de Paris Nord, Math. Lab. Villetaneuse, 1993, 95, 99, 2005, U. Oxford, 1995, TATA Inst., Bangalore, 1999, 2001, 03-04, Inst. Sci. de la Mer, U. Que., 1999-2004, vis. adj. prof., 2004-; coll. coun.U. Chgo., 1981-84; task force on undergrad. edn. Pa. State U., 1989-91, hon. degree recipient recommendation com., 1994-95; sci. adv. com. basic rsch. math. scis. U.S. Army Rsch. Office, 1979-82, review com. divsn. math. and computer sci. Argonne Nat. Lab., 1984-90, chmn., 1985-89; rev. panel, site visit team NSF Sci. and Tech. Ctrs., 1988; mem. NATO postdoctoral fellowships rev. panel, 1991; mem. ABET evaluating team, 1992; chmn. proposal rev. panel Dept. Energy, 1993; co-dir. Math. Edn. Reform Network, 1993—2004; vis. com. dept. math. U. Ill., Chgo., 1993, MIT, 1993-97, CUNY Bklyn. Coll., 1994, U. NC, 1996, Howard U., 1999, Fla. State U., 2000, U. Okla., 2004, U. Tenn., 2005, Ill. U., 2005, Purdue U.-Indpls., 2005; forum post secondary edn. Math. Scis. Edn. Bd., 1994-2004; chmn. nat. vis. com. NY Collab. for Excellence in Tchr. Prep. in Math., Sci., Tech., 1996-2000; spkr., lectr. in field. Mem. editl. bd. SIAM Jour. Math. Anal., 1979—2005, editor-in-chief, 1987-92, 30 others; contbr. articles to profl. jours. Grantee W. M. Keck Found., 1989, NSF, 1972—; NSF grad. fellow Harvard U., 1966-70; Woodrow Wilson fellow Harvard U., 1966-67. Fellow AAAS (nat. com. chair 1994-97, nat. elected office 2001—); mem. Soc. for Indsl. and Applied Math. (com. mng. editors 1987-92, com. on coms. and appts. 1988-95, vis. lectr. 1992—, rep. to AAAS sect. com. on math. 1994-97, nat. com. chair 1987-92, Am. Math. Soc. (nat. com. chair 1989-96, 99—, com. to select Steele prize winner 1984-87, adv. com. on newsletter on collegiate math. edn. 1987-88, bd. judges for Nat. Sci. and Engring. Fair 1990, 1991, chmn. liaison com. AAAS 1990-92, com. on edn. 1992-96, chmn. subcom. grad. and postdoctoral edn. 1993-95, univ. lectr. series com. 1994—, chmn., 1999—, nomination com. 1995-97, chmn. nomination com. 1995-96, com. on coms. 1998-2002, chmn. 1998-2002), Math. Assn. Am. (com. on undergrad. program in math. 1987-91, subcom. on major in math. scis. 1989-90, subcom. on calculus reform and 1st 2 yrs. 1989-91, rep. to AAAS sect. com. on math. 1993-96, program of cons. 1994—2004), Tau Beta Pi. Achievements include setting up a fluid mechanics lab in math. depts.; helping to organize interdisciplinary programs in science, engineering, economics, finance, computer science and mathematics. Home: 360 E Randolph St Apt 3903 Chicago IL 60601 Office: U Ill Chgo Math Stat and Computer Sci Dept Chicago IL 60607 Office Phone: 312-996-3044. Business E-Mail: bona@math.uic.edu.

BONACORSI, MARY CATHERINE, lawyer; b. Henderson, Ky., Apr. 24, 1949; d. Harry E. and Johanna M. (Kelly) Mack; m. Louis F. Bonacorsi, Apr. 23, 1971; children: Anna, Kathryn, Louis. BA in Math., Washington U., St. Louis, 1971; JD, Washington U., 1977. Bar: Mo. 1977, Ill. 1981, U.S. Dist. Ct. (ea. dist.) Mo., U.S. Dist. Ct. (so. dist.) Ill., U.S. Ct. Appeals (8th cir.), U.S. Supreme Ct. 1995. Ptnr. Thompson Coburn, St. Louis, 1977—. Chairperson fed. practice com. eastern dist., St. Louis, 1987—, eight cir. jud. conf. com., St. Louis, 1987—. Fellow Am. Bar Found.; mem. ABA, ATLA, Mo. Bar Assn., Met. St. Louis Bar Assn., Am. Bd. Trial Advocates (assoc.), Order of Coif. Office: Thompson Coburn Firstar Plz Ste 3100 Saint Louis MO 63101 Office Phone: 314-552-6014. E-mail: mbonacorsi@thompsoncoburn.com.

BONAGURA, VINCENT R., pediatrician, educator, researcher; b. N.Y.C., N.Y., Mar. 30, 1949; s. Vincent P. and Vivian M. Bonagura; m. Barbara Ann Liskin, June 3, 1962 (dec. Apr. 1994); children: Elizabeth, Vivi, Rebecca, Amy. BA, Columbia U., 1971, MD, 1975. Diplomate Am. Bd. Pediatrics, Am. Bd. Allergy and Immunology (bd. dir. 1999—), Bd. Diagnostic Lab. Immunology. Intern Babies Hosp.-Columbia-Presbyn. Med. Ctr., N.Y.C., 1975-76, resident in pediat., 1976-78; asst. prof. pediatrics Columbia U., N.Y.C., 1981-82, asst. prof. pediatrics and microbiology, 1982-85; chief divsn. allergy, immunology, rheumatology Schneider Children's Hosp./L.I. Jewish Med. Ctr., 1985-99; assoc. prof. pediatrics Albert Einstein Coll. Medicine, Bronx, N.Y., 1989-94, assoc. prof. pediatrics, microbiology and immunology, 1991-94, prof., 1994—; dir. divsn. allergy/immunology North Shore/L.I. Jewish Health Care Sys., 1999—. Adj. asst. prof. microbiology Columbia U.; dir. Am. Bd. Allergy and Immunology, 2000—; appointee allergy and immunology RRC ACGME, 2001—. Contbr. articles to profl. jours. Fellow Am. Acad. Allergy and Immunology (tng. dirs. exec. com., residency rev. com., 2002-); mem. Am. Assn. Immunology, Soc. for Pediatric Rsch., Am. Coll. Rheumatology, Am. Acad. Pediatrics, Alpha Omega Alpha. Avocations: tennis, music, gardening. Office: LI Jewish Med Ctr Dept Pediatrics Schneider Children's Hosp New Hyde Park NY 11040 Office Phone: 516-465-5359. E-mail: bonagura@lij.edu.

BONAPART, ALAN DAVID, lawyer; b. San Francisco, Aug. 4, 1930; s. Benjamin and Rose B.; m. Helen Sennett, Aug. 20, 1955; children: Paul S., Andrew D. AB with honors, U. Calif., Berkeley, 1951, JD, 1954. Bar: Calif. 1955, U.S. Tax Ct. 1965, U.S. Supreme Ct. 1971. Assoc. Bancroft & McAlister (formerly Bancroft, Avery & McAlister), San Francisco, 1959-62; ptnr. Bancroft & McAlister, San Francisco, 1962-93, Bancroft & McAlister, A Profl. Corp., 1993-99, Bancroft & McAlister LLP, 1999—. Past trustee Bancroft and McAlister Found.; mem. adv. com. Heckerling Estate Planning Inst., U. Miami, Fla., 1974-87, 92—, mem. faculty, 1974, 91-2000; past dir. Myrtle V. Fitchen Charitable Trust. Mem. ABA, Am. Coll. Trust and Estate Counsel, Bar Assn. San Francisco, State Bar Calif. (cert. in estate planning, probate and trust law Bd. Legal Specialization 1991). Office: Bancroft & McAlister LLP Ste 120 300 Drake's Landing Rd Greenbrae CA 94904-3123 Office Phone: 415-464-8855 301. Business E-Mail: abonapart@bamlaw.com.

BONAPARTE, WILLIAM, communications company executive; b. Chgo., Dec. 11, 1942; Degree in Elec. Engring., Milw. Sch. of Engring., 1976. PBX installation foreman Ill. Bell Telephones Co., Chgo., 1971-73, KCX foreman, 1973-75, equipment cable engr., 1975-76, mgr. personnel, supt. PBX installation, 1978-81, wire chief, mgr. bus. services, 1981—84; area mgr. then area staff mgr., Chgo. S. Services AT&T, 1984—86; CEO, pres. Bonaparte Connection, Inc., 1986—91, Bonaparte Corp., 1991—2005, chmn., CEO, 2005—. Office: Bonaparte Corp 1455 S Michigan Ave Chicago IL 60605

BONAR, DANIEL DONALD, mathematics professor; b. Murraysville, W.Va., July 7, 1938; s. Nelson Edward and Ada Polk Bonar; m. Martha Dolores Baker, Aug. 8, 1966; 1 child, Mary Martha. BSChemE, W.Va. U., 1960, MS in Math., 1961; PhD in Math., Ohio State U., 1968. Instr. Denison U., Granville, Ohio, 1965-66, asst. prof., 1966-68, 69-71, assoc. prof., 1971-77, prof., 1977—, George R. Stibitz disting. prof. math. and computer sci., 1995, chair dept. math and computer sci., 1971-77, 96-97; asst. prof. Wayne State U., Detroit, 1968-69. Vis. asst. prof. Ohio State U., Columbus, 1968. Author: On Annular Functions, 1971; contbr. articles to profl. jours. Active Granville Sch. Bd., 1973-79, pres., 1979; active Licking County Joint Vocat. Sch. Bd., Newark, Ohio, 1974-79, Granville Devel. Bd., 1974-79, Granville Found., 1996—. Inducted into W.Va. U. Chem. Engring. Dist. Alumni Acad., 1999. Mem. Nat. Coun. Tchrs. Math., Math. Assn. Am. Democrat. Methodist. Avocations: checkers, puzzles, local history buff, farming, travel. Home: 237 W Elm St Granville OH 43023-1106 Office: Dept Math and Computer Sci Denison Univ Granville OH 43023 Office Phone: 740-587-6407. E-mail: bonar@denison.edu.

BONATO, LEO, economist; b. Vicenza, Italy, Oct. 15, 1957; s. Bonaventura Bonata and Maria Grazia (Casali) Bonato; m. Laura Valli, Dec. 20, 1959; children: Sara, Anna, Giacomo. Laurea in econs., U. Modena, Italy, 1983; MA in Econs., Boston U., 1987. From economist to project mgr. CLES, Rome, 1981—89; rsch. asst., tchg. asst. Boston U., 1985—87; mgr., macroecons. unit, rsch. dept. Banca Commerciale Italiana, Milan, 1989—95; mgr., econ. issues, econ. dept. Res. Bank New Zealand, Wellington, 1995—99; sr. economist IMF, Washington, 2000—. Contbr. articles to profl. jours. Scholar, RUI Found., 1985, Einaudi Found., 1986. Mem.: Italian Stats. Soc., New Zealand Econ. Assn., European Econ. Assn., Am. Econ. Assn. Avocations: travel, music, books, outdoors. Home: 4445 Q St NW Washington DC 20007 Office: IMF 700 19th St NW Washington DC 20431 Office Phone: 202-673-6712. Office Fax: 202-589-6712. E-mail: lbonato@imf.org.

BONAVENTURA, CELIA JEAN, biochemist, researcher; b. Silver City, N.Mex., June 19, 1941; d. Rolan James and Ruth (Hale) Taylor; m. Joseph Bonaventura, Aug. 20, 1960; children: Marina Celeste, Michelle Celia. BA, San Diego State U., 1964; PhD, U. Tex., 1968. Rsch. assoc. Duke U. Med. Ctr., Beaufort, N.C., 1972-75, asst. med. rsch. prof., 1975-84, assoc. prof., 1984-90, prof., 1990—; co-dir. Duke U. Marine Biomed. Ctr., Beaufort, 1978—. Mem. Gov.'s Task Force on Aquaculture, 1987-88. Mem. editorial bd. Hemoglobin, 1977-89; contbr. over 100 articles on structure, function and assembly of respiratory proteins to profl. jours. Mem. adv. bd. Vocat. Edn. Program, Carteret County, N.C., 1990—. Rsch. grantee NIH, NSF, Office of Naval Rsch., Nat. Oceanography and Atmospheric Adminstrn., others, 1972—. Mem. AAAS, Am. Chem. Soc., Biophys. Soc. (chmn. human rights com. 1990—). Achievements include development of new concepts in the allosteric control of respiratory proteins; establishment of Marine Biomedical Center to explore the relationships between the marine environment and the human species; research in protein engineering. Office: Duke U Marine Lab Pivers Island Beaufort NC 28516

BONAZZI, ELAINE CLAIRE, mezzo soprano; b. Endicott, N.Y. d. John Dante and Zina (Rossi) B.; m. Jerome Ashe Carrington, Sept. 21, 1963; 1 child, Christopher. BM (George Eastman scholar), Eastman Sch. Music. Currently artist-in-residence SUNY, Stonybrook; pvt. voice studio N.Y.C. Past faculty Peabody Conservatory; vis. prof. Eastman Sch. Music, Rochester, N.Y., 1979; judge nat. and internat. competitions. Debuts, Santa Fe Opera, 1958, Opera Soc. Washington, 1960, N.Y.C. Opera, 1965, Opera Internacional, Mexico City, Mexico, 1966, Metropolitan Opera at the Forum, 1973, Europe, West Berlin Festival opera, 1961, Spoleto (Italy) Festival, 1974, Castel Franco Festival Venetian Music, Venice, Italy, 1975, Berlin Bach Festival, 1976, Pks. Radio TV Difusion, 1980—; Netherlands Opera, 1978, Minn. Opera, 1985, Artpark Festival, 1987, Opera Theater of St. Louis, 1988, New Orleans Opera, 1988, Paris, 1979, Spoleto-Charleston Festival, 1981, Edmonton Opera Can., 1990, New Orleans Opera, 1990, Winnipeg Opera, 1993, Edmonton Opera, 1992; frequent Libr. of Congress concerts; title role in Pique Dame, Washington Opera, 1989, in Vanessa, Opera Theatre of St. Louis, 1988, Carlson's Midnight Angel, Opera Theatre of St. Louis, 1993, Glimmerglass Opera La Calisto, 1995; lead N.Y.C. Opera; soloist N.Y. Philharmonic, Phila. Orch., Boston Symphony, Cleve. Orch., Canadian Broadcasting Corp., PBS NET Opera Theatre, NBC, ABC, CBS TV networks, recs. on, Candide, Columbia, Vanguard, CRI, Folkways, Vox, Grenadilla, Pro Arte and Nonesuch Records; albums include The Art of Elaine Bonazzi, 2005, Bridge Records; over 40 world premiers of major works by leading composers with major orchs. and opera cos. Named 1 of 6 honored alumni 50th Anniversary Year, Eastman Sch. Music, 1971, Trustees Council U. Rochester, 1976, Recital in honor of 75th Anniversary of Eastman Sch. of Music, 1996; formerly William Matheus Sullivan grantee; recipient Concert Artists Guild award, 1960; more operatic premiers than any other living Am. singer. Mem. Mu Phi Epsilon. Achievements include being chosen by Stravinsky, Hindemith, Menotti, Chavez, Rorem, Thomson, Argento, Pasatieri, Diamond, Elliott Carter for premieres of their works, master classes Europe and U.S. *In performing great music one tries to be honest as well as inventive-in communicating emotion. And one tries to remain true to the intentions of the composer. It can be a frustrating task requiring infinite patience and infinite care, but what joy for the performer when at last he can touch the heart of the listener.*

BONCHER, AUSTIN J., music educator, director; b. De Pere, Wis., Apr. 2, 1941; m. Judith A. Boncher, Aug. 20, 1941; children: Michael, Amy. MusM, Ind. U. Music tchr. Menaska Pub. Schs., Appleton (Wis.) Pub. Schs., dir. Music Dept., dir. Fine Arts, ret. Founder Appleton (Wis.) Boys Choir, White Heron Chorale; dir. Trinity Luth. Ch. Music. Recipient Renaissance award, Thrivant Fin., 1992, Paul Harris award, Rotary, 1998. Avocations: camping, hiking, travel, reading. Home: 803 S Pierce Ave Appleton WI 54914-5418

BONCHER, MARY, talent agent; b. Green Bay, Wis. d. Anthony Peter and Bernice Mary (Lannoye) Williams; m. Joseph Phillip Boncher, Jan. 7, 1967; children: Yvette, Noelle. Diploma, Rosemary Bischoff Sch. Modeling, Milw., 1965. Dir. Mary Boncher Model Agy. & Sch. Ltd., Bloomington and St. Charles, Ill., 1970—76, Mary Boncher Model Agy. Ltd., St. Charles, 1976—84, Mary Boncher Model Mgmt. Ltd., Chgo., 1985-91; ptnr. ARIA Model & Talent Mgmt. Ltd., Chgo., 1992—2001; sec., treas.; owner, mem., v.p., sec. ARIA Model & Talent Mgmt. LLC, Chgo., 2001—03; cons. Ford Models, 2003—04; ret., 2004. Fashion reporter TV and radio Men's Fashion Assn., N.Y.C., 1975—80, Eleanor Lambert's Am. Designer, NY Fashion Press, N.Y.C., 1975—80; fashion corr. Green Bay Daily News, 1975—76. Lector Cath. mass, 1983-90, 92—; registered lobbyist, Ill.; mem. Rep. Nat. com., 1994-98. Mem. Am. Security Coun. (nat. adv. bd.), Ams. for Responsible TV and Radio, Ill. Creative Cmty. (pres. 1996-99), Washington Morgan Garage Condo Assn. (bd. dir. 2002—), Acorn Lofts Condo Assn. (bd. dirs. 2002-04). Republican. Roman Catholic.

BOND, ALISON MARY, literary agent; b. Wallington, England, Jan. 2, 1935; arrived in U.S., 1960, naturalized, 1977; d. Cyril Edgar Bond and Ivy Dorothy Wood; m. Evan L. Schwartz, Apr. 23, 1988. BA in Modern Langs. with honors, U. London, 1957. Editor Chas. Scribner Sons, N.Y.C., 1967—68; sr. editor Holt, Rinehart & Winston, 1968—73, Praeger Pubs., 1975—76; prin. owner, agt. Alison Bond, Ltd., 1977—. Trustee Sag Harbor Hist. Soc., NY, 1991—; mem. com. McGovern Campaign, N.Y.C., 1972. Mem.: Women's Media Group. Avocations: tennis, travel, reading, opera. Office: Alison Bond Ltd 155 W 72d St New York NY 10023 Office Phone: 212-874-2850.

BOND, ALMA HALBERT, psychoanalyst, author; b. Phila., Feb. 6, 1923; BA in Psychology (with honors), Temple U., 1944; MA in Psychology, NYU, 1951; PhD in Devel. Psychology, Columbia U., 1961. Diplomate Am. Bd. Psychotherapy. Pvt. practice psychoanalysis pvt. practice, N.Y.C., 1953-91; tng. analyst Inst. Psychoanalytic Tng. and Rsch., N.Y.C., 1963—. Author: Who Killed Virginia Woolf, A Psychobiography, 1989, 2000, (with Lucy Freeman) America's First Woman Warrior: The Courage of Deborah Sampson, 1992, Dream Portrait, 1992, Is There Life After Analysis?, 1993, On Becoming a Grandparent, 1994, Profiles of Key West, 1996, the Autobiography of Maria Callas, a Novel, 1998, 2000, I Married Dr. Jekyll and Woke Up Mrs. Hyde, or What Happens to Love, 2000, Tales of Psychology: Short Stories to Make You Wise, 2002; sr. writer CAYO mag.; contbr. Key West Citizen, Solaris Hill, Tropic Keys, Time Out, Remember. Lt. USN, 1944—46. Recipient Honors in Psychology Temple U., 1944, Winner Am. Literary Press Contest, 1993, Runner up First Novel Contest, 1995, Hemingway award, Fla. State awards for fine writing. Mem.: Inst. for Psychoanalytic Tng. and Rsch., Internat. Psychoanalytic Assn., APA. Home and Office: 345 S End Ave Apt 3J New York NY 10280-1064 Office Phone: 212-786-3230. E-mail: almahb@aol.com.

BOND, CHARLES, lawyer, writer; s. Jay D. and Jennie Bond; m. Katherine Russell. AB, Duke U., 1971; JD, U. Calif., San Francisco, Calif., 1974. Atty. Hassard Bonnington, San Francisco, 1974—79, Bond Curtis, Berkeley, Calif., 1979—. Gen. counsel Ctr. Practical Health Reform, Jacksonville, Fla., 1999—. Avocations: musician, poet, writing.

BOND, CHRISTOPHER SAMUEL (KIT BOND), senator, lawyer; b. St. Louis, Mar. 6, 1939; s. Arthur D. and Elizabeth (Green) B.; 1 child, Samuel Reid. BA with honors, Princeton U., 1960; LLB, U. Va., 1963. Bar: Mo. 1963, U.S. Supreme Ct. 1967. Law clk. to presiding chief justice U.S. Ct. of Appeals (5th cir.), Atlanta, 1963-64; assoc. Covington & Burling, Washington, 1965-67; pvt. practice law Mexico, Mo., 1968; asst. atty. gen., chief counsel consumer protection div. State of Mo., 1969-70, gov., 1973-77, 81-85; auditor, 1971-73; ptnr. Gage & Tucker, Kansas City, 1985-87; U.S. senator from Mo., 1987—; chmn. small bus. com. 104th Congress. Mem. appropriations com., 1991—, chmn. subcom. on VA, HUD and ind. appropriations agys., 1991—, subcom. on def., 1993—, subcom. on fgn. ops., 1999—, subcom. on transp., 1995—; budget com., 1989—, environment and pub. works com., 1995—, subcom. on drinking water, fisheries and wildlife, 1995—; chmn. small bus. com., senate Rep. policy com.; pres. Gt. Plains Legal Found., Kansas City, Mo., 1977-80; chmn. Rep. Gov.'s Assn., Midwestern Gov.'s Conf., chmn. con. on econ. and community devel., 1981-83, chmn. con. on energy and environment, 1983-84. Republican. Presbyn. Office: US Senate 274 Russell Senate Bldg Washington DC 20510-0001*

BOND, DENNIS EARL, auditor; b. Kansas City, Kans., Dec. 12, 1950; s. Earl Lloyd and Carrie Irene (Law) B.; m. Karla Jo Kennamer, July 28, 1979; children: Holly, Ryan, Blake. BS, Abilene Christian U., 1972. Sr. auditor Laventhol & Horwath, CPA, Dallas, 1972-73; sr. acct. Kruchten & Magnuson, CPA, Ft. Collins, Colo., 1973-74; advanced sr. auditor Blue Cross Blue Shield Kansas City, Mo., 1974-81; audit supr. Blue Cross Blue Shield Mo., Kansas City, Mo., 1981-84, br. mgr., 1984-90, unit mgr. St. Louis, Mo., 1990-92; mgr. Blue Cross Blue Shield Miss., St. Louis, 1992—. Mem. Healthcare Fin. Mgmt. Assn. (advanced). Republican. Mem. Ch. of Christ. Avocations: golf, boating, water-skiing. Home: 430 Lantana Ln Saint Peters MO 63376-5309 Office: Blue Cross Blue Shield Miss Ste 350 13545 Barrett Parkway Dr Ballwin MO 63021-5896

BOND, ENRIQUETA CARTER, science administrator; b. Buenos Aires, May 22, 1939; d. James Prescott and Harriette Mortley (Bovard) Carter; m. Langhorne Bond, Aug. 26, 1962; children: Langhorne Carter, Prescott McCook. BA in Zoology and Physiology, Wellesley Coll., 1961; MA in Biology and Genetics, U. Va., 1963; PhD in Molecular Biology and Biochem. Genetics, Georgetown U., 1969. Asst. prof., acting chmn. biology Chatham Coll., Pitts., 1970-73; asst. prof., dept. exec. dept. med. scis. So. Ill. U., Springfield, 1974-78; staff officer Nat. Acad. Scis., Inst. of Medicine, Washington, 1979-80, divsn. dir., 1981-88, exec. officer, 1989-94; pres. Burroughs Wellcome Fund, Durham, NC, 1994—. Bd. regents Nat. Libr. Medicine, Bethesda, Md., 1996—; bd. sci. counselors Nat. Ctr. Infectious Disease Control and Prevention, Atlanta, 1997—; bd. mem. health sci. policy Inst. Medicine, Washington, 1994-97, Nat. Academies' Com. on Sci., Engring., and Pub. Policy Contbr. articles to profl. jours. Bd. dirs. NC Biotech Ctr., Research Triangle Park, NC, 1995—, pres., 1998; bd. dirs. Rsch. Triangle Found., 1996—; mem. leadership coun. Rsch. America!, Alexandria, Va., 1996—. Recipient Profl. Staff award Nat. Acad. Sci., 1985. Mem. AAAS, APHA, Inst. Medicine (mem. coun. 1999—), Am. Soc. Microbiology, Soc. for Advancement of Women's Health Rsch. (sec. bd. dirs. 1995—), Sigma Xi. Episcopalian. Avocations: needlepoint, reading. Office: Burroughs Wellcome Fund PO Box 13901 Research Triangle Park NC 27709-3901

BOND, FRANCES TORINO, academic administrator, consultant; b. Balt., Jan. 8, 1939; d. Michael Torino and Josephine Baccacchione; widowed; children: William, Michael, Geoffrey, James. BS, Towson State U., 1955, MEd, 1963; PhD, U. Md., 1973. Faculty Towson (Md.) State U., 1962-74, chairperson early childhood, 1975-81, assoc. dean, 1982-94; assoc. dir. Fellows Program Peace Corps, Washington, 1994—99; spl. asst. to U.S. Sec. of Edn., 1999—2001; dir. profl. devel. PBS Ready to Learn, Alexandria, Va., 2001—. Creator, host, writer (video series) First Steps, 1987—; co-author (booklet) Reading to Your Child, 1985. Democrat. Roman Catholic. Office: PBS 1320 Braddock Pl Alexandria VA 22314 Home: 1201 Braddock PL Apt 215 Alexandria VA 22314-1669

BOND, GEORGE CLEMENT, anthropologist, educator; b. Knoxville, Tenn., Nov. 16, 1936; s. J. Max and Ruth Elizabeth (Clement) B.; m. Alison Murray, Sept. 21, 1940; children: Matthew, Rebecca, Jonathan, Sarah. BA, Boston U., 1959; MA, London Sch. Econs., 1962, PhD, 1968. Lectr. U. East Anglia, Norwich, Eng., 1966-68; asst. prof. Columbia U., N.Y.C., 1968-74, assoc. prof. Tchrs. Coll., 1974-80, prof., 1980—, dir. Inst. African Studies, 1989—99, dir. Ctr. for African Edn., 2003—. Author: Politics of Change in a Zambia Community, 1976; editor: African Christianity, 1979, Social Stratification and Education, 1981, The Social Construction of the Past, 1994, AIDS in Africa and the Caribbean, 1997, Contested Teurains and Constructed Categories, 2002, Witchcraft Dialogues, 2003; contbr. articles to scholarly publs. Home: 229 Larch Ave Teaneck NJ 07666-2345 Office: Columbia U Teacher College Dept Internat and Transcultural Studies Box 10 Anthropology/Edn New York NY 10027-7213 Office Phone: 212-678-3311. E-mail: gcb1@columbia.edu, bond@exchange.tc.columbia.edu.

BOND, JAMES MAX, JR., architect, academic administrator; b. Louisville, July 17, 1935; s. James Max and Ruth (Clement) B.; m. Jean Davis Carey, Oct. 11, 1961; children: Carey Julian, Ruth Marion. BA magna cum laude, Harvard U., 1955, MArch., 1958; DHL (hon.), N.J. Inst. Tech., 1993. Registered architect, N.Y., 1963. Archtl. apprentice various offices, Paris, N.Y.C., 1959-64; arch. Ghana Nat. Constrn. Corp., Accra, Ghana, 1964-65; instr. U. Sci. and Tech., Kumasi, Ghana, 1965-67; exec. dir. Architect's Renewal Commn., N.Y.C., 1967-68; asst. prof. to prof. and chmn.Grad. Sch. Architecture and Planning Columbia U., N.Y.C., 1970-85; prof., dean Sch. Architecture and Environ. Studies CCNY, 1985-92; ptnr. Bond, Ryder and Assocs., N.Y.C., 1969-90, Davis Brody Bond, LLP, N.Y.C., 1990—. Favrot chair Taubman Sch. Arch. U. Mich., 1999, vis. prof., 2003. Prin. works include Bolgatanga Libr. bldg., Ghana, Schomburg Ctr., N.Y., Studio Mus., Harlem, N.Y.C., Martin Luther King Jr. Ctr. and Tomb, Atlanta, Birmingham Civil Rights Museum; firm selected assoc. arch., World Trade Ctr. Memorial site. Commr. City Planning Commn., N.Y.C., 1980-87; bd. dirs. Mcpl. Arts Soc., N.Y.C., 1986; mem. N.Y. Bldg. Congress, 2002—; bd. dirs. Regional Plan Assn., 2003— Fulbright grantee, 1958. Fellow AIA (Harry B. Rutkins Meml. award for svc. to profession 1983, Whitney M. Young Jr. Citation award 1987); mem. Am. Acad. Arts and Scis., Nat. Orgn. Minority Architects, Phi Beta Kappa. Democrat. Home: 800 Riverside Dr Apt 5E New York NY 10032 Office: Davis Brody Bond LLP 315 Hudson St New York NY 10013-1009 Office Phone: 212-633-4781. Business E-Mail: mbond@davisbrody.com.

BOND, JILL KAWA, lawyer; b. Buffalo, N.Y., Nov. 29, 1961; d. Stanley and Harriett Stiegler Kawa; m. Keith N. Bond, July 26, 1986; children: Jonathan, Christine, Andrew. BA, Canisius Coll., 1982; JD, SUNY, Buffalo, 1985. Bar: N.Y. 1986. Assoc. Hurwitz & Fine, PC, Buffalo, 1985-88; corp. counsel Rich Products, Buffalo, 1988-99, dep. gen. counsel, 1999—. Bd. dirs. Clarkson Ctr., Buffalo, 1996-2000, Sister to Sister, 2001-02, Aquarium of Niagara, 2001-04; mem. Leadership Buffalo, 1996—; mem. adv. coun. United Way of Erie County, Emerging Leader Soc. Named to 40 Under 40, Bus. First, Buffalo, 1996. Mem. Women's Bar Assn. State N.Y. (dir. western N.Y. chpt. 1996-99), Erie County Bar Assn. (mem. labor com. 1996—), Niagara Frontier Corp. Counsel Assn. (dir., sec. 1992—). Office: Rich Products Corp 1150 Niagara St Buffalo NY 14213-1797 Home: 70 Briarhill Rd Buffalo NY 14221-1809

BOND, JOHN RICHARD, astrophysicist; b. Toronto, Ont., Can., May 15, 1950; MS, Calif. Inst. Tech., 1975, PhD, 1979. Rsch. scientist Kellogg Radiation Lab., Calif. Inst. Tech., Pasadena, 1977-78; postdoctoral fellow U. Calif., Berkeley, 1978-81; rsch. fellow Inst. Astronomy, Cambridge, Eng., 1982-83; asst. prof. Stanford (Calif.) U., 1981-85; assoc. prof. Stanford U./CITA, Stanford, Toronto, 1985-87; prof. Canadian Inst. Theoretical Astrophysics (CITA), Toronto, 1987—, acting dir., 1990-91, 94-95, dir., 1996—. Assoc., fellow Can. Inst. for Adv. Rsch., Toronto, 1985-86, 86—. Contbr. over 180 articles to profl. jours. Richard P. Feynman fellow, 1974-75; Sloan Found. Rsch. fellow, 1985-89; E.W.R. Steacie fellow, 1989-91, Steacie prize, NRC, 1989, others; recipient C.S. Beals award Can. Astron. Soc., 1996, CAP/CRM prize in Theoretical Math. and Physics, 1998, AAS/APS Heineman prize, 2002, NSERC award of excellence, 2003, Office of the Order of Can Fellow: Inst. Physics, Am. Phys. Soc., Royal Soc. Can., Royal Soc. London; mem.: Am. Acad. Arts and Scis. (hon. fgn.), Can. Astron. Soc., Internat. Astron. Union, Am. Astron. Soc., Order Can. (officer). Achievements include cosmological research on the nature of the dark matter that accounts for over 90% of the mass of the universe and on the origin and evolution of galaxies and other cosmic structures. Office: Can Inst Theoretical Astro 60 George St Toronto ON Canada M5S 3H8 Business E-Mail: bond@cita.utoronto.ca.

BOND, JON ROY, political science professor; b. Chickasha, Okla., Dec. 30, 1946; s. Henry Lee and Othelle (Payne) B.; m. Patricia Anne Garner (div. Apr. 1989); 1 child, Lynn Elizabeth Bond; m. Wanda Karon Martin Frazier, July 11, 1992; children: Mika Karon Frazier, Monika Kara Frazier. BA, Okla. State U., 1969, MA, 1973; PhD, U. Ill., 1978. Prof. polit. sci. Tex. A&M U., 1976—. Co-author: President in the Legislative Arena, 1990, Promise and Performance of American Democracy, 2001; co-editor: Jour. Politics, 1993-97, Polarized Politics: Congress and the President in a Partisan Era, 2000; contbr. articles to profl. jours. Precinct chair Brazos County Democratic Party, College Station, 1984-87. Mem. Am. Polit. Sci. Assn., Midwest Polit. Sci. Assn. (exec. coun. 1992-95), Southern Polit. Sci. Assn. (mem. exec. coun. 2000-2001, v.p.-elect 2002. v.p. 2003, pres.-elect 2005-2006), Pi Sigma Alpha (exec. coun. 1994-98, pres.-elect 2005-2007). Democrat. Methodist. Home: 1412 Frost St College Station TX 77845-5630 Office: Tex A&M U Dept Polit Sci 4348 TAMU College Station TX 77843-4348 Office Phone: 979-845-4246. E-mail: jonbond@polisci.tamu.edu.

BOND, JULIAN, civil rights association executive; b. Nashville, Jan. 14, 1940; s. Horace Mann and Julia Agnes (Washington) B.; m. Pamela S. Horowitz, Mar. 17, 1990; children by previous marriage: Phyllis Jane, Horace Mann, Michael, Jeffrey, Julia. BA, Morehouse Coll., 1971; LLD (hon.), Dalhousie U., 1969, U. Bridgeport, 1969, Wesleyan U., Conn., 1969, U. Oreg., 1969, Syracuse U., 1970, Eastern Mich. U., 1971, Tuskegee Inst., 1971, Howard U., 1971, Morgan State U., 1971, Wilberforce U., 1971, Patterson State Coll., 1972; LLD (hon.), N.H. Coll., 1973, Detroit Inst. Tech., 1973; DCL (hon.), Lincoln (Pa.) U., 1970, Bates Coll., 1998, Northeastern U., 1999, Edward Waters Coll., 1995, Gonzaga Sch. Law, 1997, Calif. State U., Monterey Bay, 1998, Washington U., 2000; LLD (hon.), Audrey Cohen Coll., New York, 2001, Williams Coll., 2005. A founder Com. Appeal for Human Rights, 1960, exec. sec., 1961; a founder Student Nonviolent Coordinating Com., 1960, communications dir., 1961-66; reporter, feature writer Atlanta Inquirer, 1960-61, mng. editor, 1963; mem. Ga. Ho. of Reps., from Fulton County, 1965-75, Ga. State Senate, 1975-87. Vis. prof. history and politics Drexel U., 1988-89; Pappas fellow U. Pa., 1989; vis. prof. Harvard U., fall 1989, 91; prof. U. Va., fall 1990, 1993—, Am. U., 1991—, Williams Coll., fall 1992. So. corr. Reporting Racial Equality Wars; narrator Parts 1 and 2, Eyes on the Prize. Mem. adv. bd. Harvard Bus. Sch., Initiative on Social Enterprise; bd. dirs. So. Conf. Edn. Fund, So. Poverty Law Ctr., Coun. for Liveable World; pres. emeritus So. Poverty Law Ctr.; chmn. bd. dirs. NAACP, 1998—; chmn. Premier Auto Group Diversity Coun.

BOND, KARLA JO, elementary school educator; b. Abilene, Tex., Oct. 11, 1951; d. David Lipscomb and Elizabeth Rosalie (Henthorn) Kennamer; m. Dennis Earl Bond, July 28, 1979; children: Ryan Jeffrey, Blake Justin. BS in Edn., Abilene Christian U., 1972; MA, Maryville U., 1994. Tchr. Abilene (Tex.) Christian Campus Sch., 1972-73, LaMarque (Tex.) Pub. Schs., 1973-78, Kansas City (Kans.) Unified Sch. Dist. 500, 1979-90, Ft. Zumwalt Pub. Schs., O'Fallon, Mo., 1990—, coord. elem. sch. math., 1993—. Instr. math. Math. Learning Ctr., Portland, 1990-92; leader math. insvc. Ft. Zumwalt Pub. Schs., 1990-94. Mem. NEA, Nat. Coun. Tchrs. Math., Mo. Coun. Tchrs. Math., Math. Educators Greater St. Louis. Republican. Mem. Ch. of Christ. Avocations: water-skiing, reading, piano, children's sports. Office: Mid Rivers Elem 7479 Mexico Rd Saint Peters MO 63376

BOND, MYRON HUMPHREY, investment executive; b. Chickasha, Okla., Jan. 12, 1938; s. Reford and Jane Embick (Humphrey) B.; m. Janice Wootten, July 1, 1961; children: Richard Allen, Lori Elizabeth. BS in Petroleum Engring. summa cum laude, U. Okla., 1961, MS in Petroleum Engring., 1965. Registered profl. engr., Okla. Staff engr. Exxon Mobil, Houston, 1960—68; sr. v.p. UBS Fin. Svcs. Inc., Dallas, 1968—. Pres., chmn. Four Bees Ranch Inc., 1989—, Bond Family Inc., 1996—;dir., corp. sec. PWJC Ins. Agy. Tex. Inc., 1980—; dir. Am. Pub. Comm., Inc., 1991-92. Bd. dirs. Dallas Epilepsy Assn., 1980-82, Dallas Campfire Girls, 1980-82, Southwest NanoTechnologies Inc., 2004—. Lt. (s.g.) USN, 1961-64. Mem. Nat. Assn. Securities Dealers (pres., mem. dist. 6 com. 1994-96), Dallas C. of C., Dallas Country Club, Brook Hollow Golf Club, Phi Eta Sigma, Pi Eta Tau, Tau Beta Pi, Sigma Tau, Omicron Delta Kappa, Kappa Alpha Order. Avocations: sports, ranching. Home: 4536 Belfort Pl Dallas TX 75205-3619 Office: UBS Fin Svcs Inc 5950 Sherry Ln Ste 600 Dallas TX 75225-6551 Office Phone: 214-373-8400.

BOND, PETER DANFORD, physicist; b. Providence, Jan. 30, 1940; s. Douglas D. and Helen H. (Cannon) B.; m. Sandra E. Salim, Aug. 3, 1968; children: Jennifer, Colin; stepchildren: Anthony Shane, John Shane. BA, Harvard U., 1962; MA, Western Res. U., 1963; PhD, Case Western Res. U., 1969. Rsch. assoc. Stanford U., Palo Alto, Calif., 1969-72; from asst. physicist to acting dir. Brookhaven Nat. Lab., Upton, NY, 1972—97, acting chief info. officer, 2002—03, interim dep. dir. for sci. and tech., 2004—. Chmn. exec. com. Holifield Heavy Ion Rsch. Facility, 1981; mem. program adv. com. Super Heavy Ion Linear Accelerator, 1977-81, chmn., 1981; mem. program com. on heavy ions SUNY, Stony Brook; mem. panel to rev. maj. nuclear physics facilities Dept. Energy, 1987; mem. siting panel for Gammasphere, 1989; reviewer physics program SUNY Grad. Sch.; mem. physics divsn. adv. com. Oakridge Nat. Lab., 1992-97; mem. com. of visitors to NSF, 1994; mem. nuclear sci. adv. com. to Dept. Energy/NSF, 1994-97; mem. dean's adv. com. MIT/Lab. Nuclear Sci., 1994-99; sr. policy analyst, Office of Sci. and Tech. Policy, 1999; mem. com. of visitors Dept. Energy High Energy Physics, 2004; mem. com. Nat. Coun. on Radiation Protection, 2002-04. Contbr. numerous articles to profl. jours. FOM fellow (the Netherlands), 1983-84. Fellow AAAS (steering com. on physics 2001-03), Am. Phys. Soc. (nuclear physics div. 1977-79, program com. 1989-90, mem. selection com. Tom Bonner Prize 2000-01, chair 2001, panel on pub. affairs 2004—; chair ad hoc com. on homeland security 2002-04); mem. Sigma Xi. Avocation: athletics. Home: 7 Simpson Pl Stony Brook NY 11790-1744 Office: Brookhaven Nat Lab Directors Office Bldg 460 Upton NY 11973 E-mail: bond@bnl.gov.

BOND, RANDALL WILLIAM, music educator; b. Lawrence, Kans., Dec. 25, 1968; s. Roger William and Carolyn Christine Bond; m. Courtney Danielle Turcotte, June 5, 2004; children: Lauren Elizabeth, Lindsay Morgan, Claire Alexandra. MusB, Washburn U., 2000. Music/drama dir. Ch. of Nazarene, Lawrence, 1989—92; music tchr. Holton (Kans.) Unified Sch. Dist. 336, 2000—. Participant Nelen Hocker Theatre, Topeka, 2004—; music dir. W. Side Christian Ch., Topeka, 2003—. Mem.: NEA, Music Educators Assn., Kans. Music Educators Assn. Avocations: American muscle cars, model building. Office: Unified Sch Dist 336 901 New York Holton KS 66436

BOND, RICHARD L., food products executive; Pres., COO IBP, Inc., 1997—2001, bd. dir., 1995—2001, Tyson Foods Inc., 2001—, Co-COO, Group President, Fresh Meats and Retail, 2001—03, pres., COO, 2003—. Office: c/o Tyson Foods Inc PO Box 2020 Springdale AR 72765*

BOND, RICHARD LEE, lawyer, state senator; b. Kansas City, Kans., Sept. 18, 1935; s. Clarence Ivy and Florine (Hardison) B.; m. Sue S. Sedgwick, Aug. 23, 1958; children: Mark, Amy. BA, U. Kans., 1957, JD, 1960. City atty., Overland Park, Kans., 1960-62; adminstrv. asst. to Congressman Robert Ellsworth, Washington, 1961-66, Congressman Larry Winn, Washington, 1967-85, Congressman Jan Meyers, Washington, 1986; chmn. bd. dirs. Home State Bank, Kansas City, 1983-94; ptnr. Bennett, Lytle, Wetzler et al, Prairie Village, Kans., 1986-89; senator State of Kans., Topeka, 1985-2001, senate pres., 1997-2001. Vice chmn. Guaranty Bank and Bancshares, Kansas City, Kans., 1995-2002. Mem. Kans. Bd. Regents, 2002—. Named State Legislator of Yr. Governing Mag., 2002. Republican. Presbyterian. Avocations: gardening, tennis, hunting, fishing. Home: 9823 Nall Ave Shawnee Mission KS 66207-2915

BOND, RICHARD RANDOLPH, foundation administrator, legislator; b. Lost Creek, W.Va., Dec. 1, 1927; s. Harley Donovan and Marcella Randolph B.; m. Reva Stearns, Apr. 20, 1946; children: David, Philip, Josette, Michael. BS, Salem Coll., 1948, LHD (hon.), 1979; LHD (hon.), U. No. Colo.; MS, W.Va. U., 1949; PhD, U. Wis., 1955; postdoctoral studies, U. Mich., 1958-59. Various teaching and fellowship positions, 1949-59; dean of faculty Elmira (N.Y.) Coll., 1959-63; dean coll. of Liberal Arts U. Liberia, Monrovia, 1963-64; chief of party Cornell U. Project in Liberia, Monrovia, 1964-66; v.p. acad. affairs Ill. State U., Normal, 1966-71; pres. U. No. Colo., Greeley, 1971-81, pres. emeritus, prof. zoology, 1981-89; state rep. Colo. Gen. Assembly, Denver, 1984-90; interim pres. Front Range Community Coll., Westminster, Colo., 1991; pres. Morgan Community Coll., Ft. Morgan, Colo., 1991-96, Cmty. Found., Greeley and Weld County, 1996—2000, Bond Family Found., 1995—. Founder Nat. Student Exch., 1st No. Savs. and Loan; cons., examiner North Ctrl. Accrediting Assn., 1969-82. Author: Colorado Postsecondary Options Act., 1988; contbr. articles to profl. jours. Bd. dirs., chmn. Sunrise Community Health Ctr.; founding mem. Dream Team on Dropout Prevention; Dem. candidate for Col. 4th Congl. Dist., 1990; founder Colo. chpt. Dem. Leadership Coun., 1991—; co-chmn. Clinton Campaign, Colo., 1992; bd. dirs. Colo. chpt. Nat. Multiple Sclerosis Soc.; chmn. bd. dirs. Univ. Schs. Found., 2002—; bd. govs. Univ. Schs., 2003—; bd. of trustee Aims C.C., 2001—. With U.S. Army, 1945-47. Recipient Legislator of Yr. award DAV, 1988, Colo. Acad. Pediatrics, 1989; Mental Health award, 1990, Polit. Educator of Yr. award, Colo. Edn. Assn., 1991; fellow NSF, 1953-54, Am. Physiol. Soc., 1958, Carnegie Found., 1958-59. Mem. Am. Ornithologists Union, Am. Assn. Colls. and Univs. (bd. dirs. 1979-81), Colo. Assn. Colls. and Univs. (chmn. 1979-81), Rotary (bd. dirs. local chpt.), Sigma Xi. Independent. Mem. United Ch. Of Christ. Avocations: gardening, stamp collecting/philately, camping, genealogy. Home and Office: 5601 18th St #51 Greeley CO 80634-2925 Personal E-mail: rrbond@comcast.net.

BOND, VICTORIA ELLEN, conductor, composer; b. LA, May 6, 1945; d. Philip and Jane (Courtl) B.; m. Stephan Peskin, Jan. 27, 1974. B Mus. Arts, U. So. Calif., L.A., 1968; M Mus. Arts, Juilliard Sch. Music, 1975, D Mus. Arts, 1977; DFA (hon.), Washington and Lee U., 1992, Hollins Coll., 1995, Roanoke Coll., 1995. Condr., composer. Mem. N.Y. State Coun. Arts Music Panel, 1987-90; bd. dirs. N.Y. Women Composers. Guest condr. numerous organizations including most recently Warsaw (Poland) Symphony, York (Pa.) Symphony, Music from Penn's Woods (Pa.), 1999-00, NYC Opera Showcasing Am. Composers, 2001, Norwalk Symphony, 2002, Da Corneto Opera Co., 2003, Dallas Symphony Ray Charles Concert, 2003, Central Opera, Beijing, 2004, Ctr. for Contemporary Opera, 2004, Music Festival of the Hamptons, 2004, Chamber Opera, Chgo., 2005; music dir. New Amsterdam Symphony Orch., NYC, 1978-80, Pitts. Youth Symphony Orch., 1978-80, Empire State Youth Orch., 1982-86, Southeastern Music Ctr., 1983-84, Bel Canto Opera, 1983-86, Roanoke (Va.) Symphony Orch., 1986-95; artistic dir. Bel Canto Opera Co., 1986-88, Harrisburg Opera, 1998-03, Cutting Edge Concerts, NYC, 1999-; artistic adv., Wuhan Symphony, China, 1997-00, Opera Roanoke, 1989-95; Exxon/Arts Endowment condr., Pitts. Symphony, 1978-80, recs. include Twentieth Century Cello, Two American Contemporaries, The Frog Prince, An American Collage, Live from Shanghai, Victoria Bond: Compositions, The American Piano Concerto, Yes, 2003; commd. by Pa. Ballet, 1978, Jacob's Pillow Dance Festival, 1979, Am. Ballet Theater, 1981, Empire State Inst. Performing Arts, 1983-84, Stage One, Louisville, 1986, Ga. State U., 1986, L'Ensemble, 1990, Renaissance City Winds, 1990, Audubon String Quartet, 1990, Women's Philharm., San Francisco, 1993, Va. Explore Park and The Shanghai Symphony, 1994, D Day Found., 1994, Linda Plaut, 1994, Pianofest, 2005, Duo Gelland, 2005, Ethel, 2005, Billings (Mont.) Symphony, Elgin (Ill.) Symphony, Elements String Quartet, Indpls. Chamber Orch., Composers' Conf., Jade String Trio, others; commissions include Pianofest Duo Gelland Ethel, 2005 Bd. dirs. Am. Music Ctr. Recipient Victor Herbert award 1977, Perry F. Kendig award, 1988, ASCAP Composition award 1973—; Nat. Inst. for Music Theater grantee in opera conducting N.Y.C. Opera, 1985, Martha Baird Rockefeller grantee, 1978-79, Meet-The-Composer grantee in Composition, 1973—; Juilliard scholar, 1972-77; Juilliard fellow, 1975-77, Aspen Music Festival fellow, 1973-76; named Exxon/Arts Endowment Conductor, 1978-80, Woman of Yr. in Va., 1990, 91; featured on NBC Today show, 1990, profiled in C.S. Monitor, 1987, Wall Street Jour., 1987, others. Mem. ASCAP (awards 1975—), Am. Symphony Orch. League, Am. Fedn. Musicians, Condrs. Guild (bd. dirs. 1994—98), Internat. Alliance Women in Music, N.Y. Women Composers, Mu Phi Epsilon. Avocations: horseback riding, sailing, hiking. Personal E-mail: victoria@victoriabond.com. Business E-Mail: victoria@victoriabond.com. *I believe that our life's work is in sharing our talents and gifts with others. Our own happiness and fulfillment are in direct proportion with the amount we give of ourselves.*

BOND, WILLIAM HENRY, librarian; b. York, Pa., Aug. 14, 1915; s. Walter Loucks and Ethel (Bossert) B.; m. Helen Elizabeth Lynch, Dec. 6, 1943 (dec. Jan. 1999); children: Nancy Barbara, Sally Lynch. AB, Haverford Coll., 1937; MA, Harvard, 1938, PhD, 1941. Research fellow Folger Shakespeare Library, 1941-42; asst. to librarian Houghton Library, Harvard, Cambridge, Mass., 1946-48, curator manuscripts, 1948-64, librarian, 1965-82; lectr. bibliography Harvard, 1964-67, prof., 1967-86, librarian, prof. emeritus, 1986—. Asst. keeper manuscripts Brit. Mus., 1952-53; Sandars reader in bibliography Cambridge (Eng.) U., 1981-82. Author: Thomas Hollis of Lincoln's Inn, a Whig and His Books, 1990; editor: (Christopher Smart) Jubilate Agno, 1954, Supplement to Census of Medieval and Renaissance Manuscripts in the United States, 1962, The Houghton Library, 1942-67, 1967, Records of a Bibliographer, 1967, 18th Century Studies in Honor of Donald F. Hyde, 1970, (with Hugh Amory) The Printed Catalogues of the Harvard College Library 1723-1790, 1996. Trustee Emerson Meml. Assn., 1964-89; hon. trustee Concord (Mass.) Free Pub. Library, 1990—; trustee Historic Deerfield (Mass.) Inc., 1965-91, hon. trustee, 1991—, v.p., 1985-88. Served to lt. USNR, 1943-46. Fulbright fellow, 1952-53, Guggenheim fellow, 1982-83 Mem. Bibliog. Soc. Am. (pres. 1974-75), Bibliog. Soc. London (hon. sec. for Am. 1964-93), Grolier Club, Am. Antiquarian Soc. (councillor 1970-91, hon. councillor 1991—), Mass. Hist. Soc., Colonial Soc. Mass. (pres. 1981-93, hon. mem. 1994—), The Johnsonians, Phi Beta Kappa. Home: 109 The Valley Rd Concord MA 01742-4900

BONDAREFF, JOAN M., lawyer, retired government agency administrator; b. Utica, N.Y., Jan. 7, 1944; 1 child. Student, Cornell U., 1961-64; BA in Polit. Sci. cum laude, George Washington U., 1965; JD magna cum laude, Am. U., 1975. Bar: Md. 1975, D.C. 1978, U.S. Supreme Ct. 1979. Clk. Md. Ct. Spl. Appeals, 1975; atty. advisor for legis. and regulation Office Gen. Counsel, Dept. Commerce, Washington, 1975-76, atty. on detail to Dept. Justice, 1976-77; staff atty. NOAA, Washington, 1977-80, sr. counsel to nat. earth satellite svc., 1980-82, asst. gen. counsel for adminstrn., 1981-82, asst. gen. counsel for ocean svcs., 1982-87; sr. counsel Coast Guard and Mcht. Marine group U.S. Ho. of Reps. Mcht. Marine and Fisheries Com., Washington, 1987-94; chief counsel and acting dep. maritime adminstr. Maritime Adminstn., Dept. Transp., Washington, 1994—99; counsel maritime/marine dept. Dyer Ellis & Joseph, Washington, 2001—02; counsel maritime/marine transp. group Blame Rome LLP, Washington, 2003. Legal counsel Nat. Safe Boating Coun. Contbr. articles to law jours., including Territorial Sea Jour., Coastal Mgmt. Jour., Internat. Ship Registry Rev. Former chmn. Women's Aquatic Network. Mem. ABA (marine resources com. 1989—). Avocations: hiking, running, music, travel. Office: Blank Rome LLP 600 New Hampshire Ave NW Washington DC 20037

BONDAREFF, WILLIAM, psychiatrist, educator; b. Washington, Apr. 29, 1930; s. Leon and Gertrude Bondareff; children by previous marriage: Hyla, Sarah; m. Rita Haber Kassoy, Jan. 2, 1988. BS in Zoology, George Washington U., 1951, MS in Zoology, 1952; PhD in Anatomy, U. Chgo., 1954; MD, Georgetown U., 1962. Diplomate Am. Bd. Psychiatry and Neurology with added qualifications in geriatric psychiatry. Rsch. assoc., instr. anatomy U. Chgo., 1955; rotating intern USPHS Hosp., Balt., 1962-63; resident in psychiatry Northwestern Meml. Hosp. Inst. Psychiatry, Chgo., 1978-80; asst. prof. anatomy Northwestern U., Evanston, Ill., 1963-65, assoc. prof., 1965-69, prof., 1969-78, chmn. dept. anatomy, 1970-78; prof. psychiatry and gerontology U. So. Calif., L.A., 1981—; mem. staff U. So. Calif. Univ. Hosp., L.A., 1991—; mem. attending staff L.A. County/U. So. Calif. Med. Ctr., L.A., 1981—; mem. Hosp. Good Samaritan, L.A., 1981-96; mem. staff Norris Cancer Hosp., 1987—; mem. attending staff Cedars-Sinai Med. Ctr., 2001—. Physician/cons. VA Hosp., Downey, Ill., 1969-80, Jewish Home for Aged, Reseda, Calif., 1981-90; vis. staff mem. medicine Passavant Pavilion Northwestern Meml. Hosp., 1972-80; dir. div. geriat. psychiatry U. So. Calif., 1981—; dir. U. So. Calif.-St. Barnabas Alzheimer Disease Ctr., 1985-2001; acting dir. dept. Gerontology Research Inst. Andrus Gerontology Ctr.-U. So. Calif., 1982; staff psychiatrist Los Angeles County Hosp., 1981—; past holder various com. offices Northwestern U. Editor Mechanisms of Aging and Devel., 1970—; assoc. editor Am. Jour. Anatomy, 1970-76; mem. editl. bd. Alzheimer Disease and Associated Disorders-An Internat. Jour., 1985-95, Neurbiology of Aging, 1980-94, The Jour. of Gerontology, 1981-84, Internat. Rev. Jour. of Psychiatry, 1988—, Jour. Alzheimer's Disease, 1997-2001; contbr. articles to profl. jours. Mem. sci. adv. bd. Alzheimer's Disease & Related disorders Assn. L.A., bd.dirs., 1989—; mem. rsch. rev. com. treatment, devel. and assessment Nat. Inst. Mental Health, 1987-92. Served with USPHS, 1955-63. USPHS fellow, 1955, U. Cambridge Clare Hall vis. fellow, 1980, Hughes Hall vis. fellow, 1988; scholar Allergy Found., 1960, U. Chgo., 1953; recipient Career Devel. award Nat. Inst. Neurol. Disease and Blindness, 1966-69, Sesquicentennial award Hobart and William Smith Colls., 1972, Sandoz prize Internat. Assn. Gerontology, 1983, Alzheimer Disease and Related Disorders Assn. award, 1984; Fulbright Lectr., U. Goteborg, Sweden, 1967-68. Fellow AAAS (councilor 1970-74), Am. Psychiat. Assn. (geriatrics task force 1981), Gerontol. Soc.; mem. Am. Assn. Anatomists (chmn. local com. ann. meeting 1969), Electron Microscope Soc. Am., Am. Soc. Cell Biology, Am. Acad. Neurology (chmn. neuroanatomical scis. sect. 1971-77), Soc. Neurosci., Assn. Anatomy Chmn. (councilor 1975-77), Am. Assn. Geriat. Psychiatry (program com. 1984-89, bd. dirs. 1985-89), So. Calif. Psychiat. Soc., Internat. Psychogeriat. Assn., Cajal Club, Cosmos Club, Sigma Xi. Office: U So Calif Sch Medicine MOL 203 1237 N Mission Rd Los Angeles CA 90033-1018 Office Phone: 323-224-5056. E-mail: bondaref@usc.edu.

BONDAROOK, NINA, public relations consultant; b. N.Y.C., Sept. 19, 1955; d. Peter and Lydia Bondarook; m. Earl S. Belofsky, Apr. 14, 1989. BA in Journalism, Ariz. State U., 1977; MS in Applied Comm., U. Denver, 1990. Founder Premium PR, Millbrae, Calif., 2002. Mem. Pub. Rels. Soc. Am., Soc. Profl. Journalists. Office: 595 Market St Fl 26 San Francisco CA 94105-2802 E-mail: nina@premiumpr.com.

BONDERMAN, DAVID, investment company executive, lawyer; BA, Univ. Wash., Seattle, 1963; JD magna cum laude, Harvard Univ., 1966. Asst. prof. Tulane Univ. Sch. Law, New Orleans, 1967—68; spec. asst. to Atty. Gen. Civil Rights div., U.S. Dept. Justice, Washington, 1968—69; fellow in fgn. & comparative law Harvard Univ., 1969—70; ptnr. Arnold & Porter, Washington, 1971—83; COO Keystone Inc. (Robert M. Bass Group), Fort Worth, Tex., 1983—92; founder, principal & gen. ptnr. Tex. Pacific Group, Ft. Worth, 1993—. Mem. gov. council Wilderness Soc.; trustee Grand Canyon Trust; dir. Am. Himalayan Found.; dir. & past chmn. Univ. Wash. Found. Sheldon Fellow. Mem.: Phi Beta Kappa. Office: Tex Pacific Group 301 Commerce St Ste 3300 Fort Worth TX 76102-3128*

BONDI, BERT ROGER, accountant, financial planner; b. Portland, Oreg., Oct. 2, 1945; s. Gene L. and Elizabeth (Poynter) B.; children: Nicholas Stone, Christopher Poynter. BBA, U. Notre Dame, 1967. CPA, Colo., Calif., Wyo. Sr. tax acct. Price Waterhouse, L.A., 1970-73; ptnr. Valentine Adducci & Bondi, Denver, 1973-76; sr. ptnr. Bondi & Co., Englewood, Colo., 1976—. 50 for Colo.-1998 dir. Citizens Bank; adv. bd., dir. Guaranty Bank and Trust Co. Bd. govs. Met. State Coll. Found.; bd. dirs. Am. Cancer Soc. Denver, Colo. Youth Symphony Orch., So. Metro Denver C. of C.; mem. adv. bd. Jr. League of Denver. Mem. C. of C., Cmty. Assns. Inst., Govt. Fin. Officers Assn., Colo. Soc. Assn. Execs. (edn. com.), Home Builders Assn., Am. Inst. CPAs., Rotary (Denver), Notre Dame Club, Metropolitan Club (Denver), Castle Pines Country Club. Roman Catholic. Office: Bondi & Co 44 Inverness Dr E Englewood CO 80112-5410 E-mail: bbondi@bondico.com.

BONDI, HARRY GENE, lawyer; b. Sheridan, Wyo., Apr. 3, 1948; s. Gene and Elizabeth (Poynter) B; 1 child, Bert Gene. BS in Fin., Fairfield U., 1970; JD, U. Wyo., 1974; postgrad., Georgetown U. Law Ctr., 1977. Bar: Wyo. 1974, U.S. Dist. Ct. D.C. 1976, U.S. Tax Ct. 1976, U.S. Ct. Claims 1975, U.S. Supreme Ct. 1980, D.C. 1975, Colo. 1988, U.S. Dist. Ct. Wyo. 1977, U.S. Ct. Appeals (10th cir.) 1980. Trial atty. U.S. Renegotiation Bd., Washington, D.C., 1974-77; pub. defender Wyo. State Pub. Defender Office, Casper, 1978-79; pvt. practice Harry G. Bondi, P.C., Casper, 1977—. Author: Wyoming Labor and Employment Law, 1992, Workers Compensation in Wyoming, 1993, Wrongful Discharge Claims Under Wyoming Law, 1994, 95. Chmn. City of Casper Housing and Cmty. Devel. Commn., 1977-81; past pres. Natrona County Meals of Wheels, Inc., 1988-90, Meals on Wheels Found., 1991-94; bd. dirs. Casper Jr. Baseball League, 1994-95. Mem. Wyo. Bar Assn., Natrona County Bar Assn., Am. Trial Lawyers Assn., Wyo. Trial Lawyers Assn., Wyo. Criminal Defense Lawyers Assn., Colo. Bar Assn., D.C. Bar Assn., Federal Bar Assn., Criminal Justice Adminstrn. Panel Dist. Wyo. Avocations: hiking, biking, travel.

BONDI, JOSEPH CHARLES, JR., education educator, consultant; b. Tampa, Fla., Aug. 15, 1936; s. Joseph C. and Virginia B.; m. Patsy L. Hammer, Aug. 6, 1960; children: Pamela, Beth, Bradley. BS, U. Fla., 1958, M.Ed., 1964; Ed.D., U. Fla, 1968. Tchr., adminstr. Hillsborough County (Fla.) Pub. Schs., 1958-65; instr. U. South Fla., Tampa, 1965-66, asst. prof., 1966-68, assoc. prof., 1968-74, prof. edn., 1974—2003; ptnr. Wiles, Bondi & Assocs. Edn. cons. in field, South Africa, Hong Kong, China, Taiwan, Can., Am. Internat. Schs. Author 28 textbooks including Developing Middle Schools, 1972, Curriculum Development, 1979, 7th edit., 2005, Practical Politics for School Administrators, 1981, The Essential Middle School, 1981, 1993, 2000, 2005, Supervision: A Guide to Practice, 6th edit., 2004, The New American Middle School, 2001. Councilman City of Temple Terrace, Fla., 1970—74, mayor, 1974—78. With USNR, 1958—63. Mem.: Fla. ASCD (pres.). Republican. Lutheran. E-mail: josephbondi@aol.com.

BONDINELL, STEPHANIE, counselor, academic administrator; b. Passaic, N.J., Nov. 22, 1948; d. Peter Jr. and Gloria Lucille (Burden) Honcharuk; m. Paul Swanstrom Bondinell, July 31, 1971; 1 child, Paul Emil. BA, William Paterson U., 1970; MEd, Stetson U., 1983. Cert. elem. educator Fla., guidance counselor grades K-12 Fla. Tchr. Bloomingdale (N.J.) Bd. Edn., 1971-80; edn. dir. Fla. United Meth. Children's Home, Enterprise, 1982-89; guidance counselor Volusia County Sch. Bd., Deltona, Fla., 1988—. Coord. sch. improvement svcs., Deltona Lakes, 1996—98, Deltona Lakes, 2002—05. Sec. adv. com. Deltona Jr. HS, 1996—98, sec. PTA, 1982; vice-chmn. adv. com. Deltona Mid. Sch., 1988, chmn., 1991—92, 1991—92; mem. adv. com. Deltona HS, 1995—96; secondary sch. task force Volusia County Sch. Bd., 1986—; team leader Volusia County Sch. Accreditation Quality Assurance Team, 2003—05; mem. exec. com. Volusia County Reps.; mem. Rep. Presdl. Task Force; mem. state adv. bd. Fla. Future Educators Am., 1990—92, 2003—05. Named Deltona Lakes Tchr. of Yr., Volusia County Sch., 1991, 1996, Volusia County Schs. Dist. Sch. Accreditation Steering Com. Team Leaders, 2003—04; recipient Outstanding Ednl. Partnership award, S.W. Volusia C. of C., 1998, Sunshine State Medallion award, Fla. Pub. Rels. Assn., 1998, award, Volusia/Flagler Alcohol and Drug Abuse Prevention Coun., 1998—2005, Fla. Lottery Creative Tchg. award, 2002; Acad. scholar, Becton, Dickinson & Co., 1966, N.J. State scholar, 1966—70. Mem.: AAUW, ASCD, Internat. Platform Assn., Volusia Tchrs. Orgn., N.J. Edn. Assn., Fla. Assn. Counseling and Devel., Disvn. Learning Disabilities, Coun. Exceptional Children, Stetson U. Alumni Assn., Deltona Civic Assn., 4 Townes Federated Rep. Women's Club (sec., v.p.), Deltona Rep. Club (v.p. 1991—93). Avocations: painting, creative writing, dance. Home: 1810 W Cooper Dr Deltona FL 32725-3623 Office: Volusia County Sch Bd 2022 Adelia Blvd Deltona FL 32725-3976 E-mail: sbondine@mail.volusia.k12.fl.us.

BONDOC, ROMMEL, lawyer; b. June 23, 1938; s. Nicholas Rommel and Gladys Sue (Buckner) Bondoc; m. Ariel Guiberson, Aug. 20, 1960 (div. 1963); m. Alberta Linnea Young, Dec. 13, 1967; children: Daphne, Patience, Margaret, Nicholas. AB, Stanford U., 1959, JD, 1963. Bar: Calif. 1964, U.S. Ct. Appeals (9th cir.) 1965, U.S. Supreme Ct. 1969. Assoc. Melvin Belli, San Francisco, 1964—66, Vincent Hallinan, San Francisco, 1966—69; sole practice San Francisco, 1969—. Mem.: Calif. Attys. for Criminal Justice (bd. dir. 1975—80), No. Calif. Criminal Trial Lawyers Assn. (bd. dir. 1972—, pres. 1978—79), San Francisco Bar Assn. (judiciary com. 1982—85). Democrat. Methodist. Home: 509 Canyon Rd Novato CA 94947-4330 Office: 819 Eddy St San Francisco CA 94109-7701 Office Phone: 415-771-6174.

BONDS, BARRY LAMAR, professional baseball player; b. Riverside, Calif., July 24, 1964; s. Bobby and Pat Bonds; m. Liz Watson; 3 children. Student, Ariz. State U. With Pitts. Pirates, 1985—92, San Francisco Giants, 1993—. Formed Bonds Family Foundation. Named Nat. League Most Valuable Player, Baseball Writer's Assn. Am., 1990, 1992—93, 2001—04, Maj. League Player of Yr., Sporting News, 1990, 2001, Nat. League Player of Yr., 1990, 1991, Player of the Decade (1990's), Male Athlete of Yr., AP, 2001; named to All-Am. team, Sporting News Coll., 1985, All-Star team, 1990, 1992—98, 2000—04; recipient Gold Glove award, 1990—94, 1996—98, Silver Slugger award, 1990—97, 2000—04, Espy Award, Best Baseball Player, 1994, 2002, 2004, Espy Award, Best Male Athlete, 1994. Achievements include holds record for most home runs in a single season (73), 2001; became third player in MLB to hit 700 career home runs on Sept. 17, 2004; became MLB all-time leader in walks with 2,191 on July 4, 2004; currently #3 all-time on home run list; Member of highly athletic family: father Bobby Bonds, former MLB player; Aunt, Rosie Bonds was a member of 1964 Olympic Track Team; Godson of Willie Mays; led Nat. League in Batting Avg. (.363), 2004; oldest player to win Nat. League MVP Award (40 years old), 2004; holds MLB record with 7 league MVP awards. Office: San Francisco Giants Candlestick Point 24 Willie Mays Plz San Francisco CA 94107-2199

BONDS, JOHN WILFRED, JR., lawyer; b. Jackson, Tenn., May 6, 1943; s. John Wilfred Sr. and Louise (Robinson) B.; m. Mary Anne Hatchett, July 18, 1969; children: Kathleen Lucile, Mary Julia. BS, U.S. Air Force Acad., 1965; JD, Vanderbilt U., 1973. Bar: Ga. 1973. Commd. 2nd lt. USAF, 1965, advanced through grades to capt., 1965-70, resigned, 1970; assoc. Sutherland, Asbill & Brennan, Atlanta, 1973-79, ptnr., 1979—. Editor in chief Vanderbilt Law Rev., 1973. Mem. ABA, Ga. Bar Assn., Atlanta Bar Assn., Lawyers Club Atlanta, Order of Coif. Presbyterian. Office: Sutherland Asbill & Brennan 999 Peachtree St NE Atlanta GA 30309-3996 Office Phone: 404-853-8017. Business E-Mail: john.bonds@sablaw.com.

BONDS, PHILIPPE DALE, music educator; b. Florence, Ala., May 29, 1960; s. Jack Dale and Georgia Lou Bonds. BS, U. N. Ala., 1982, MA, 1987. Cert. class A tchg. Ala. State Bd. of Edn. Band dir. Maury County Sch., Columbia, Tenn., 1982—83, Colbert County Sch., Tuscumbia, Ala., 1983—90, Lawrence County Sch., Molton, Ala., 1990—92, Morgan County Sch., Decatur, Ala., 1992—95; band dir., adj. prof. U. W. Ala., Livingston, Ala., 1995—97; band dir., asst. prof. N. Ga. Coll. and State U., Dahlonega, Ga., 1997—98; band dir. Demopolis (Ala.) City Sch., 1998—. Cons. Marengo County Bd. Edn., Linden, Ala., 2001—04; tech. coord. Demopolis City Sch., Demopolis, Ala., 2002—. Contbr. articles various profl. jours. Mem.: NEA, Ala. Bandmasters Assn., Phi Kappa Lambda, Phi Mu Alpha Sinfonia. Republican. Presbyn. Home: 211 Commisioner Ave Demopolis AL 36732 Office: Demopolis City Schs 707 Hwy 40W Demopolis AL 36732 Office Phone: 334-285-4242. Office Fax: 334-289-2670. E-mail: philbond@bellsouth.net.

BONDURANT, DAVID WILLIAM, marketing professional; b. Kirksville, Mo., June 8, 1948; s. William George and Leila Ruth (Mulford) B.; m. Judy Helen Rindahl, Mar. 17, 1973; children: Matthew David, Erik William. BSEE, U. Mo., Rolla, 1971; BS in Physics, Northeast Mo. State Coll., 1971; MBA, U. Phoenix, 2004. Registered profl. engr., Minn. Assoc. design engr. Control Data Corp., Arden Hills, Minn., 1971-72; sr. design engr. Sperry-Univac, Eagan, Minn., 1972-75; project engr. Robertshaw Controls Co., Richmond, Va., 1975-76; prin. design engr. Sperry-Univac, Eagan, 1976-80; mgr., systems applications Honywell Solid State, Electronics Div., Plymouth, Minn., 1980-84, com. bus. devel. mgr. Colorado Springs, Colo., 1984-88; dir. new bus. devel. Ramtron Corp., Colorado Springs, 1988-95; v.p. mktg. Enhanced Memory Sys., Colorado Springs, 1995—2002; pres. Vertical Memory, 2002—. Ind. cons. Technomics Cons., Chgo., 1987. Contbr. articles to profl. jours. Mem. IEEE (pres., v.p., sec. 1977-79), Twin Cities Computer Soc., Country Club of Colo., Tau Beta Pi, Eta Kappa Nu, Phi Kappa Phi. Republican. Lutheran. Avocations: tennis, amateur radio, skiing, photography. Home and Office: 4025 Becket Dr Colorado Springs CO 80906-7681 Office Phone: 719-661-7889. Personal E-mail: dbondurant@mac.com.

BONDURANT, EMMET JOPLING, II, lawyer; b. Athens, Ga., Mar. 16, 1937; s. John Parnell and Mary Claire (Brannon) B.; m. Jane E. Fahey, Aug. 12, 1990; children by previous marriage: Emmet Jopling III, Katherine Elizabeth, Melissa Eileen, Christopher Scott, Miles Stephen. AB cum laude, U. Ga., 1958, LL.B. magna cum laude, 1960; LL.M., Harvard U., 1962. Bar: Ga. 1959. Law clk. to Judge Clement Haynsworth, Jr. U.S. Ct. Appeals, 4th Circuit, 1960-61; assoc. Kilpatrick, Cody, Rogers, McClatchey & Regenstein, Atlanta, 1962-68, ptnr., 1968-77; ptnr. firm Bondurant, Mixson & Elmore and predecessor, Atlanta, 1977—. Vis. lectr. in antitrust law U. Ga., spring 1971; pres. Atlanta Legal Aid Soc., 1972-73; vice chmn. Ga. Gov.'s Commn. on Criminal Justice Standards and Goals, 1974 Contbr. articles on antitrust and reapportionment, right to counsel, bankruptcy, and local govt. issues to profl. jours.; co-editor: Antitrust Law Developments, 1974. Mem. Joint Atlanta-Fulton County Citizens Adv. Com. on Consolidation, 1969; chmn. Atlanta Charter Commn., 1971-72; co-chmn. Com. for Sensible Rapid Transit, Atlanta, 1971-72; trustee Am. Inns of Ct. Found., 2002-; chmn. Common Cause of Ga., 2002-04; chmn. Ga. Pub. Defender Standards Coun., 2003-; chmn. bd. Ga. Appellate Resource Ctr., 2001-. Named 1 of 5 Outstanding Young Men, Atlanta Jaycees, 1970; recipient Ga. Trial Lawyer of Yr., Am. Bd. Trial Advocates (Ga. chpt.), Good Govt. award, LWV Atlanta-Fulton County, 1980, Dufree award, Calif. Western Sch. Law, 1984, Elbert P. Tuttle Jurisprudence award, 2001, Harold G. Clarke award, Ga. Indigent Def. Coun., 2001. Fellow Am. Bar Found.; mem. ABA (exec. com. Atlanta lawyers com. for civil rights), Ga. Bar Assn., Atlanta Bar Assn. (exec. com. 1975-81, Leadership award 1992), State Bar Ga. (chmn. sect. antitrust law 1972-73, chmn. jud. sys. comm. 1991—), Am. Law Inst., Am. Coll. Trial Lawyers, Am. Acad. Appellate Lawyers, Am. Judicature Soc., Ga. Law Sch. Alumni Assn. (pres. 1996-97), Lawyers Club Atlanta (sec. 1971-72), Phi Beta Kappa, Phi Delta Phi, Phi Kappa Phi, Kappa Alpha. Methodist. Home: 2930 Habersham Rd NW Atlanta GA 30305-2846 Office: Bondurant Mixson & Elmore Ste 3900 1201 W Peachtree St NW Atlanta GA 30309-3417 Office Phone: 678-891-4100, 404-881-4100. Business E-Mail: bondurant@bmelaw.com.

BONDURANT, GLENDA J., nursing educator, dean; b. Lumberton, N.C., June 26, 1962; d. Ronald H. and Jean P. Jones; m. Thomas N. Bondurant, Feb. 19, 1951. BSN, U. N.C., 1984; MSN, ECU, 1997. RN N.C. Staff nurse Moses Cone Hosp., Greensboro, 1983—86, Nash Gen. Hosp., Rocky Mount, NC, 1986—92; mem. nursing faculty Edgecombe C.C., Tarboro, NC, 1992—2002; assoc. dean allied health scis. Wilson (N.C.) Tech. C.C., 2002—. Named Bus. and Young Profl. Woman of Yr., 1992. Mem.: NCAON, N.C. Nurses Assn. (pres. 1991—92, Nurse of Yr. 1992), Sigma Theta Tau. Home: 519 Forest Acres Dr Tarboro NC 27886 Office: Wilson Tech C C 902 Herring Ave Wilson NC 27893

BONDURANT, NANCY RUTH, musician, music educator; b. Boise, Idaho, May 8, 1961; d. James Allison and Ruth Margaret Bondurant. MusB, Temple U., 1982, MusM, 1984; D in Musical Arts, U. Wash., 1997. Prin. 2nd bassoon Winston-Salem (N.C.) Symphony, 1978—79; faculty, vis. artist Pinehurst (N.C.) C.C., NC, 1986—88; vis. faculty Brevard (N.C.) Coll., 1988—89; adj. faculty Davidson (N.C.) Coll., 1991—94; lectr. U. N.C., Charlotte, 1993—94; adj. faculty Gene Nastri Cmty. Sch. Arts, Mukilteo, Wash., 1998—2001; faculty Music Ctr. of the N.W., Seattle, 1996—. Artistic dir., founding mem. Topaza, a Magical Musical Ensemble, Charlotte, 1989—95; founder, dir. Woodwind Camp, Shoreline, Wash., 1999—; solo recitalist European Internat. Festival, Geneva, 1990. Musician: (recording) Unrolling a Chinese Scroll, 2000; composer: At The Beach, 1991, Two Movements, 2003. Named winner, Rocky Ridge Concerto Competition, 1980, 1982, Magic Valley Symphony Concerto Composition, 1984, U. Wash. Concerto Competition, 1995; recipient Jack Straw Artists Assistance, Jack Straw Found., 2000; Emerging Artist grantee, Arts and Sci. Coun., 1991. Mem.: Seattle Flute Soc., Am. Fedn. Musicians, Internat. Double Reed Soc. Achievements include participating scholar in the establishment of the National Basque Music Archives. Home: 9823 238th St SW Edmonds WA 98020

BONDURANT, STUART, physician, educational association administrator; b. Winston-Salem, NC, Sept. 9, 1929; s. Stuart Osborne Bondurant; m. Susan Haughton Ehringhaus, May 5, 1991; children from previous marriage: Stuart, Margaret Lynn, Nancy Vance. BS, Duke U., 1952, MD, 1953; DSc (hon.), Ind. U., 1980. Intern Duke Hosp., Durham, NC, 1953—54, resident in internal medicine, 1954—55; resident Peter Bent Brigham Hosp., Boston, 1958—59; from asst. prof. medicine to prof. Ind. U. Sch. Medicine, Indpls., 1959—67; assoc. dir. Ind. U. Cardiovasc. Rsch. Ctr., 1961—67; chief med. br. artificial heart-myocardial infarction program NIH, Bethesda, Md., 1966—67; prof. medicine, chmn. dept., physician in chief Albany Med. Ctr. Hosp., NY, 1967—74; pres., dean Albany Med. Coll., 1974—79; prof. medicine U. NC, Chapel Hill, 1979—2004, dean Sch. Medicine, 1979—94, interim dean, 1996—97; dir. Ctr. for Urban Epidemiology Studies N.Y. Acad. Medicine, N.Y.C., 1994—96; interim exec. v.p., exec. dean Georgetown U. Med. Ctr., 2004—. Contbr. articles to med. jours. Named Citizen Laureate, Univ. Found., Albany, 1979; recipient Disting. Alumnus award, Duke U. Sch. Medicine, 1974, Merit award, Am. Heart Assn., 1975, Thomas Jefferson award, U. N.C.-Chapel Hill, 1998. Fellow: ACP (regent, pres. 1980), Royal Coll. Physicians London, Royal Coll. Physicians Edinburgh; mem.: Am. Clin. and Climatol. Assn. (pres. 1996), Assn. Am. Med. Colls. (exec. com. 1977, chmn. coun. deans 1979—82, chmn. 1993—94), Inst. of Medicine (interim pres. 1992, David Rall award 2000), Assn. Am. Physicians (pres. 1985—86), Am. Soc. Clin. Investigation (v.p. 1974). Home: 1212 Village Crossing Dr Chapel Hill NC 27517 Office: U NC Sch Medicine CB # 7000 Office of Dean Chapel Hill NC 27599-7000 Business E-Mail: sbondurant@med.unc.edu.

BONDY, JOSEPH AARON, lawyer; b. N.Y.C., Jan. 18, 1968; s. Frederick and Joan Marie Bondy; m. Meeka Jun, Sept. 6, 1997. BA in Psychology, Columbia U., 1991; JD, Bklyn. Law Sch., 1994. Bar: N.Y. 1995, U.S. Dist. Ct. (ea. and so. dist.) N.Y. 1995, U.S. Ct. Appeals (1st and 2d cirs.) 1996, U.S. Ct. Appeals (11th cir.) 1998, U.S. Ct. Appeals (4th cir.) 1999. Assoc. Law Offices of Richard Canton and Richard Jasper, N.Y.C., 1994-96; pvt. practice N.Y.C., 1996—. Mem. nat. legal com. Nat. Orgn. for Reform Marijuana Laws, Washington, 1996—; faculty mem., Nat. Criminal Def. Coll., Macon, Ga., 1998-2001; Intensive Trial Advocacy Program, Cardoza Law Sch., 1999-. Mem. Nat. Assn. Criminal Def. Lawyers (life), N.Y. State Assn. Criminal Def. Lawyers (bd. dirs., 1997-, chmn., pub. relations com., 2001), Nat. Eagle Scout Assn. Jewish. Avocations: long-distance running, camping, fishing, skiing. Office: 401 Greenwich St 5th Fl New York NY 10013 E-mail: joseph@bondylaw.com.

BONDY, PHILIP KRAMER, retired internist; b. N.Y.C., Dec. 15, 1917; s. Eugene Lyons and Irene (Kramer) B.; m. Sarah B. Ernst, Mar. 18, 1949; children: Jonathan L., Jessica, Steven M. AB, Columbia U., 1938; MD, Harvard U., 1942; MA (hon.), Yale U., 1961. Intern Peter Bent Brigham Hosp., Boston, 1942-43; mem. staff Grady Meml. Hosp., Atlanta, 1943, 46-48, chief resident in medicine, 1947-48; mem. faculty Emory U., 1947-48, 49-52, asst. prof. medicine, 1951-52; Alexander Browne Coxe fellow physiol. chemistry Yale U., New Haven, 1948-49, mem. faculty, 1948-49, 52-74, 77-88, prof. medicine, 1961, 77-88, prof. emeritus, 1988—, C.N.H. Long prof. medicine, 1965-74, chmn. dept. internal medicine, 1965-72, assoc. dean for vets. affairs, 1983-89, chmn. com. outpatient svcs., 1960-62; chmn. med. divsn. Royal Marsden Hosp., 1972-77; Cancer Rsch. Campaign prof. Inst. Cancer Rsch., London; cons. Ludwig Inst. Cancer Rsch., Zurich, Switzerland, 1972-77; assoc. chief of staff for rsch. West Haven VA Med. Ctr., 1977-83, chief of staff, 1983-89. Mem. med. vis. com. Brookhaven Nat. Labs., 1969-73, chmn., 1973; mem. program project com. NIH-Nat. Inst. Arthritis and Metabolic Disease, 1964-68, chmn., 1966-68; mem. exptl. biol. sect. breast cancer task force NIH-Nat. Cancer Inst., 1973-76; mem. adv. coun. NIDDK, 1990-94; mem. planning com. Med. Rsch. Svc. VA, 1985-88, chmn., 1986-88; mem. N.E. region planning com. VA. Editor-in-chief Jour. Clin. Investigation, 1957-62, Yale Jour. Biology and Medicine, 1978-92; editor: Diseases of Metabolism, 6th, 7th, 8th edits, Yearbook of Endocrinology and Metabolism, 1963-64; editorial bd. Conn. Medicine, 1959-61, Yearbook of Medicine, 1954-84, Medicine, 1963-85, Merck Manual, 1969-00, Clinics in Endocrinology and Metabolism, 1973-84, Cancer Topics, 1975-79. Sec. libr. bd. City of Woodbridge, Conn., 1960-67; sec. bd. dirs. Southbury Tng. Sch. Found.; sec., bd. trustees Southbury Tng. Sch.; mem. Coun. on Mental Retardation, Conn., 1997-03; cellist Hamden Symphony Orch., 1994—, prin. cellist, 1996-2004. Capt. M.C., AUS, 1943-46. Recipient Edward Sutliffe Brainard prize Columbia U., 1938, Sigma Xi prize Emory U., 1949, Rsch. Career award NIH, 1962, 66. Fellow AAAS (chmn. sect. N on med. sci. 1979), Royal Coll. Physicians, Royal Soc. Medicine (v.p. sect. oncology 1975-77); mem. ACP (master), Endocrine Soc. (councillor 1964-67, mem. publs. com. 1965-72, chmn. 1968-72), Assn. Am. Physicians, Assn. Physicians Gt. Britain and Ireland, Am. Soc. Clin. Investigation, Am. Fedn. Clin. Rsch., Nat. Assn. VA Chiefs of Staff (mem. exec. com. 1986-88), Soc. Exptl. Biology and Medicine, Interurban Clin. Club, Inst. Cancer Rsch. (London, hon.). Home: 88 Notch Hill Rd Apt 265 North Branford CT 06471

BONE, HENRY GRADY, III, physician, clinical researcher; b. Seattle, Apr. 4, 1947; s. Henry Grady Jr. and Mary Isabel (Sheehan) B. AB in Biology, Princeton U., 1968; MD with honors, U. Washington, 1972. Diplomate Am. Bd. Internal Medicine, Am. Bd. Endocrinology and Metabolism. Intern Parkland Meml. Hosp., Dallas, 1972-73; resident U. Tex., Southwestern Med. Sch. & Affiliated Hosps., Dallas, 1973-74; clin. rsch. fellow U. Tex., Southwestern Med. Schs. & Affiliated Hosps., Dallas, 1974-76; postdoctoral fellow, clin. instr. U. Calif., San Diego, 1977-78, asst. prof. medicine, 1978-84, NIH clin. investigator La Jolla, 1978-80; rsch. assoc. VA Med., Ctr., La Jolla, 1980-83; dir. clin. rsch. Ciba-Geigy Pharms., Summit, N.J., 1984-87; sr. staff physician Henry Ford Hosp., Detroit, 1987—. Lectr. grand rounds various med. ctrs., 1977—; cons. pharm. industry, 1988—, FDA, 1991—. Contbr. med. articles to profl. jours.; reviewer med. articles for profl. jours. Med. adv. panel Paget's Disease Found., 1988—, dir., sec.-treas., 1990—. Merit scholar Princeton U., 1964-68. Fellow ACP; mem. AMA, AAAS, Am.

Fedn. for Clin. Rsch., Am. Soc. for Bone & Mineral Rsch. (Dr. Boy Frame Meml. award 1989), The Endocrine Soc., Founders Soc. Detroit Inst. Art, Crawford-Armstrong Handicapped Assn., Seattle Tennis Club, Princeton Club N.Y., Detroit Yacht Club, Alpha Omega Alpha. Republican. Office: Henry Ford Hosp 2799 W Grand Blvd Detroit MI 48202-2689

BONE, ROBERT WILLIAM, newswriter; b. Gary, Ind., Sept. 15, 1932; s. Robert Ordway and Georgia Juanita (Clapp) B.; m. Sara Ann Cameron, Aug. 14, 1965; children: Christina Ann, David Robert. BS in Journalism, Bowling Green State U., 1954. Editor, tng. literature The Armor Sch., Ft. Knox, Ky., 1954-56; reporter, photographer Middletown (N.Y.) Daily Record, 1956-59, San Juan (Puerto Rico) Star, 1959-60; news editor Popular Photography Mag., N.Y.C., 1960-62; editor-in-chief Brazilian Bus. Mag., Rio de Janeiro, 1962-63; picture editor Time-Life Books, N.Y.C., 1963-68; sr. writer Fielding's Travel Guide to Europe, Mallorca, Spain, 1968-71; staff writer Honolulu Advertiser, 1971-84; free-lancer Honolulu, 1984—. Stringer Time-Life News Svc., 1981-86. Author: Maverick Guide to Hawaii, 1977, Maverick Guide to Australia, 1979, Maverick Guide to New Zealand, 1981, Fielding's Alaska and the Yukon, 1989; travel editor Honolulu mag., 1985-88, R.S.V.P. mag., 1988-89. 1st lt., U.S. Army, 1954-56. Named to Journalism Hall Fame Bowling Green State U., 1990. Mem. Soc. Am. Travel Writers, Am. Soc. Media Photographers. Democrat. Home and Office: 1053 Lunaai St Kailua HI 96734-4633 Office Phone: 808-261-1094. E-mail: travelwriter@robertbone.com.

BONEAU, C. ALAN, psychology professor, researcher; b. Cin., Feb. 2, 1926; s. Charles A. and Virginia Louise (Kircher) B.; m. Ann Mallin, Sept. 2, 1955; children: Denise Lynn, Jonathan Alan, Paul Charles. BA in Psychology with high honors, U. Cin., 1950, MA in Psychology, 1951; PhD in Exptl. Psychology, Duke U., 1957. Supr. employment testing aircraft gas turbine divsn. Gen. Electric Co., 1952-53; grad. asst., rsch. asst., univ. fellow Duke U., Durham, N.C., 1953-57, USPHS rsch. fellow, 1957-58, from asst. prof. to assoc. prof., 1958-66, asst. to dean, 1962-64; ednl. affairs officer Am. Psychol. Assn., 1966-71, dir. programs and planning, 1971-76, exec. officer, 1974-75; sr. assoc. Devel. Assocs., Inc., Arlington, Va., 1977-78; program mgr. Essex Corp., Alexandria, Va., 1978-80; prof. psychology George Mason U., Fairfax, Va., 1980-98, chair psychology dept., 1980-82, emeritus prof., 1998—; rsch. prof. Krasnow Inst. for Advanced Studies, 1998—. Faculty senate Duke U., 1962-64; rsch. psychologist Army Rsch. Inst., 1980-89. Contbr. articles to profl. jours. Treas. Sci. Manpower Commn., 1976. With USN, 1944-46. USPHS Spl. fellow Stanford U., 1965-66, citation classic recognition Current Contents, 1986. Fellow AAAS, APA (cons. editor Jour. Applied Psychology 1981-86, exec. com. editor newsletter 1981, rep. to Coun. Social Sci. Assns. 1975-76, liaison to Nat. Adv. Mental Health Coun.), Soc. for Gen. Psychology (pres. 1987), Am. Psychol. Soc., Washington Acad. Sci.; mem. Psychonomic Soc., Soc. for Computers in Psychology, Soc. for Studying Unity Issues in Psychology (pres. 1987-88), Phi Beta Kappa, Sigma Xi. Office: Dept of Psychology George Mason U Fairfax VA 22030 E-mail: aboneau@gmu.edu.

BONEPARTH, PETER, retail executive; B, U. S.C., Chapel Hill; JD, U. Va. Atty. Shea and Gould; sr. mng. dir., head investment banking Mabon Securities, 1990—94, Rodman & Renshaw, 1994—97; COO Norton McNaughton, Inc., 1997—99, pres., 1997—2001, CEO, 1999—2001; CEO, pres. Jones Apparel Group, Inc., 2002—. Office: Jones Apparel Group Corp Offices 250 Rittenhouse Cir Bristol PA 19007 Office Phone: 215-785-4000.

BONESIO, WOODROW MICHAEL, lawyer; b. Hereford, Tex., Dec. 27, 1943; s. Harold Andre and Elizabeth (Ireland) B.; m. Michaele Ann Dougherty; children: Elizabeth Eaton, Jo Kristin, William Michael. BA, Austin Coll., 1966; JD, U. Houston, 1971. Bar: Tex. 1971, U.S. Dist. Ct. (we., no., so., and ea. dists.) Tex. 1973, U.S. Ct. Appeals (5th cir.) 1973, U.S. Ct. Appeals (11th cir.) 1981, U.S. Supreme Ct. 2004. Law clk. to U.S. dist. Judge Western Dist. Tex., San Antonio, 1971-73; ptnr. Akin, Gump, Strauss, Hauer & Feld, Dallas, 1973-92, Kuntz & Bonesio LLP, Dallas, 1992—2002, Shackelford, Melton & McKinley LLP, Dallas, 2003—. Spkr. profl. confs. Bd. dirs. Grace Presbytery Devel. Bd., 1986—89; ruling elder First Presbyn. Ch., Dallas, 1999—2001, bd. dirs., 2004—. Fellow: Dallas Bar Found., Tex. Bar Found.; mem.: ABA, Tex. Mediator Credentialing Assn. (credentialed advance mediator), Nat. Assn. Rec. Artists, U. Houston Law Alumni Assn. (chpt. pres. 1982), Austin Coll. Alumni Assn. (Disting. Alumni award 2001), Common Cause Tex. (bd. dirs. 1999—), Dallas Assn. Def. Counsel, Tex. Bar Coll., Dallas Bar Assn., Am. Judicature Soc., Assn. Atty. Mediators, Am. Arbitration Assn., Fed. Bar Assn., Vocal Majority Chorus (bd. dirs. 1990—, pres. 2002—03), Lake Highlands Exch. Club, Soc. for Preservation and Encouragement Barber Shop Quartet Singing in Am. (internat. chorus champions 1975, 1979, 1982, 1985, 1988, 1991, 1994, 1997, 2000, 2003), Order of Barons, Phi Alpha Delta. Office: Shackelford, Melton & McKinley LLP 10100 N Central Expressway Ste 600 Dallas TX 75231 Office Phone: 214-242-7135. Business E-Mail: mbonesio@shacklaw.net.

BONESTEEL, MICHAEL JOHN, lawyer; b. LA, Dec. 22, 1939; s. Henry Theodore Samuel Becker and Kathleen Mansfield (Nolan) B.; children: Damon Becker, Kirsten Kathleen; m. Susan Elizabeth Schaaf, June 1, 1980. AB in History, Stanford U., 1961; JD, U. So. Calif., 1966. Bar: Calif. 1967, U.S. Dist. Ct. (ctrl. and so. dists.) Calif. 1967, U.S. Ct. Appeals (9th cir.) 1967, U.S. Dist. Ct. (no. dist.) Calif. 1969, U.S. Dist. Ct. (ea. dist.) Calif. 1983, U.S. Supreme Ct. 1989. Assoc. Haight, Brown & Bonesteel, and predecessors, L.A., 1967—71, ptnr., 1972—. Fellow Internat. Acad. Trial Lawyers, Am. Coll. Trial Lawyers; mem. ABA, State Bar Calif., Los Angeles County Bar Assn., Def. Rsch. Inst., Assn. So. Calif. Def. Counsel, Am. Soc. Most Venerable Order of Hospitaller St. John of Jerusalem, Hospitaller Order St. Lazarus of Jerusalem, Grand Priory of Am., Bel Air Bay Club, L.A. Country Club. Office: Ste 800 6080 Center Drive Los Angeles CA 90045-1574 Address: PO Box 45068 Los Angeles CA 90045-0068 Office Phone: 310-215-7100. Business E-Mail: mbonesteel@hbblaw.com.

BONET, FRANK JOSEPH, retired lawyer; b. N.Y.C., Apr. 6, 1937; s. Frank and Alexandra (Roots) B.; m. Mary Ellen Mathews, July 14, 1962; children—Catherine Ann, Frank Joseph, Elizabeth Mary, Jean Marie. BA magna cum laude, St. John's U., 1958, LL.B. (assoc. editor law rev.), 1961. Bar: Tex. 1961. With Horn & Hardart Co., N.Y.C., 1961-72, corp. sec., head corp. legal dept., 1969-72; real estate atty. J.C. Penney Co., Inc., 1972-77, sr. S.W. regional real estate atty. Dallas, 1977-89, mng. atty. real estate dept., 1989-91, also asst. corp. sec.; mng. atty. JCP Realty, Inc., Dallas, 1992-94; chief real estate counsel J.C. Penney Co., Inc., Dallas, 1994-98; now ret. Lectr. Internat. Coun. Shopping Ctrs. Contbr. articles profl. jours. Mem. N.Y. State Bar, State Bar Tex. Home: 1909 Deerfield Dr Plano TX 75023-5110 E-mail: framare@aol.com.

BONFANTE, LARISSA, classics educator; b. Naples, Italy; arrived in U.S., 1939, naturalized, 1951; d. Giuliano and Vittoria (Dompé) B.; m. Peter B. Warren, Sept. 1950 (div. 1962); children: Sebastian Raditsa, Alexandra Benfante-Warren; m. Leo Ferrero Raditsa, May 2, 1973 (dec. 2001). Student, Radcliffe Coll., 1950, U. Rome, 1951; BA, Barnard Coll., 1954; MA, U. Cin., 1957; PhD, Columbia U., 1966. Mem. faculty NYU, 1963—, prof., 1978—, chmn. dept. classics, 1978—84, 1987—90. Cons. in field; vis. mem. Inst. for Advanced Study, 1980. Author: Etruscan Dress, 1975, paperback, 2003, Out of Etruria, 1981, Reading the Past, Etruscan, 1990; author: (with Giuliano Bonfante) The Etruscan Language (transl. into Italian 1985, into Romanian 1996), 1983, 2d edit., 2002; author: Etruscan Life and Afterlife, 1986, translated to Romanian, 1996, Corpus Speculorum Etruscorum, N.Y. The Metropolitan Museum of Art, 1997; editor (with Francesco Roncalli): Antichità dall'Umbria a New York, 1991; editor: (with Judith Sebesta) The World of Roman Dress, 1994; translator: Chronology of the Ancient World (E.J. Bickerman), 1967; translator: (with Alexandra Bonf Warren) The Plays of Hrotswitha of Gandersheim, 1979; editor (with Vassos Karageorghis): Italy and Cyprus in Antiquity: 1500-450 BC, 2000; contbr. articles to profl. jours. Mem. Archaeol. Inst. Am. (gov. bd. 1982-88), Inst. di Studi Etruschi (fgn., pres. US sect.), German Archaeol. Inst. (corres. mem.). Home: 50 Morningside Dr New York NY 10025-1739 Office: NYU Classics Dept 25 Waverly Pl New York NY 10003-6701 Office Phone: 212-998-8594. Business E-Mail: lb11@nyu.edu.

BONFIELD, ANDREW R.J., pharmaceutical executive; b. London, 1962; Grad., U. Natal (Durban). Integration team SmithKline Beecham, 1989—91, dir., v.p. corp. accounts, 1991—97, dep. fin. dir., 1997—99, CFO, 1999—2000; fin. dir. BG Group, 2000—02; CFO, sr. v.p. Bristol-Meyers Squibb Co., N.Y.C., 2002—; non-exec. dir. The BOC Group, 2003—. Office: Bristol-Meyers Squibb Co 345 Park Ave New York NY 10154-0037

BONFIELD, ARTHUR EARL, lawyer, educator; b. NYC, May 12, 1936; s. Louis and Rose (Lesser) B.; m. Doris (Harfenist), June 10, 1958 (dec. 1995); 1 child, Lauren; m. Eva Tsalikian, Apr. 8, 2000. BA, Bklyn. Coll., 1956; JD, Yale U., 1960, LLM, 1961, post grad. (sr. fellow), 1961-62; DHL (hon.), Cornell Coll., 1999. Bar: Conn. 1961, Iowa 1966. Asst. prof. U. Iowa Law Sch., 1962-65, assoc. prof., 1965-66, prof., 1966-69, Law Sch. Found. disting. prof., 1969-72, John Murray disting. prof., 1972—2003, Alan D. Vestal disting. chair, 2003—, assoc. dean for rsch., 1985—. Summer vis. prof. law U. Mich., 1970, U. Tenn, 1972, U. N.C., 1974, Hofstra U., 1977, Lewis and Clark U., 1984; gen. counsel spl. joint com. state adminstrv. procedure act Iowa Gen. Assembly, 1974-75; spl. counsel adminstrv. procedure exec. br. State of Iowa, 1975; chmn. com. constl. law Nat. Conf. Bar Examiners Multi-State Bar Exam, 1977-2003; reporter 1981 Model State Adminstrv. Procedure Act, Nat. Conf. Commrs. Uniform State Laws, 1979-81; cons. Ark. State Constl. Conv., 1980; chmn. Iowa Governor's Com. State Pub. Records Law, 1983; Iowa commr. Nat. Conf. Commrs. on Uniform State Laws, 1984-2000; chmn. Iowa Gov.'s Task Force on Uniform Adminstrv. Rules, 1985-92; chmn. Iowa Gov.'s Task Force Team on Regulatory Process, Rule Making, and Rules Rev., 1999-2000. Prin. draftsman Iowa Civil Rights Act, 1965; Iowa Fair Housing Act, 1967; Iowa Adminstrv. Procedure Act, 1974,; Iowa Open Meetings Act, 1978; Iowa Civil Rights Act, 1978; Amendments to Iowa Pub. Records Law, 1984; Amendments to Iowa Adminstrv. Procedure Act, 1998; author: State Adminstrv. Rule Making, 1986; State and Federal Adminstrv. Law, 1989; contbr. numerous articles to law jours. Recipient Outstanding Svc. to Civil Liberties Award, Iowa Civil Liberties Union, 1974; Hancher Finkbine Outstanding Faculty Mem. Award, U. Iowa, 1980; Faculty Excellence Award, Iowa Bd. Regents, 1995; Outstanding Law Sch. Tchg. Award, U. Iowa, 1996; Frederick Klocksiem fellow Aspen Inst. Humanistic Studies, summer 1978. Mem. ABA (chmn. divsn. state adminstrv. law 1976-80, coun. 1980-84, chmn. sect. 1987-88, sect. adminstrv. law and regulatory practice); Am. Law Inst. (life mem.); Iowa State Bar Assn. (chmn. com. adminstrv. law 1971-85, coun. sect. adminstr. law 1990-93, 94-97, 98-99, 2000-03, 05-, reporter and mem., task force on state adminstrv. law reform 1994-96; Pres. Award Outstanding Svc. to Bar and Public 1996); Am. Coun. Learned Soc. (del. from Assn. Am. Law Sch. 1984-94). Home: 206 Mahaska Dr Iowa City IA 52246-1606 Office: U Iowa Sch Law Iowa City IA 52242 Business E-Mail: arthur-bonfield@uiowa.edu.

BONFIGLIO, THOMAS ALBERT, pathologist, educator; b. Rochester, N.Y., Oct. 17, 1942; s. Charles P. and Minnie C. (Argentiere) B.; m. Mary Barat Rice, July 2, 1966; children: Susan Marie, Amy Elizabeth, Megan Lynn. BS magna cum laude, St. John Fisher Coll., 1964; MD, U. Rochester, 1969. Diplomate Am. Bd. Pathology; cert. Nat. Bd. Med. Examiners, Internat. Bd. Cytopathology, N.Y.S. lab. dir.; lic. Ohio, N.Y. Intern in pathology U. Hosps. Cleve., 1969-70, resident in pathology, 1969-71; tchg. fellow pathology Case Western Res. U., 1969-71; chief resident in pathology Strong Meml. Hosp., Rochester, N.Y., 1971-72; instr., pathology fellow U. Rochester Med. Ctr., 1971-72, asst. prof. pathology, 1972-76, assoc. dir. cytopathology lab., assoc. dir. sch. cytotech., 1973-76, acting dir. surg. pathology, divsn., dir. cytopathology lab., 1975-76; asst. prof. pathology Case Western Reserve U., 1976-77; asst. pathologist, chief divsns. cytopathology and surg. pathology Mt. Sinai Hosp., Cleve., 1976-77; assoc. prof. pathology U. Rochester Med. Ctr., 1977-84, prof. pathology, 1984-89, prof., acting chmn. dept. pathology and lab. medicine, 1989-90, prof., chair dept. pathology and lab. medicine, 1990-97, clin. prof. pathology, 1997—2003, prof. pathology, dir. cytopathology, 2003—. Chmn. Internat. Bd. Cytopathology, 1998—; cons. pathology Rochester Gen. Hosp., 1978-97, Genesee Hosp., 1979-97; attending pathologist, dir. surg./pathology unit, 1984-85, Strong Meml. Hosp., attending pathologist, dir. anatomic pathology divsn., 1985-97, pathologist in chief, 1989-97; sr. attending pathologist, head pathology divsn. Genesee Hosp., 1997-99; dir. pathology divsn. ViaHealth, 1999-2003; sr. attending pathologist Strong Meml. Hosp., 2003—; mem. Cytotechnologist Exam. Com., 1980-83, Biol. Stain Commn., 1981-91, cytopathology exam com. Am. Bd. Pathology, 1984-89, spl. ad hoc com. cytopathology N.Y. State Dept. Health, 1988, others; v.p. Intersoc. Pathology Coun., 1988, pres., 1989; bd. dirs. Univs. Assoc. Rsch. and Edn. in Pathology; presenter papers, abstracts; participant, invited spkr., dir., panelist numerous workshops, meetings, seminars, confs., teleconfs. in field; vis. prof., guest lectr. Med. Coll. Ohio, Toledo, 1980, Dartmouth-Hitchcock Med. Ctr., Hanover, N.H., 1982, William Beaumont Army Med. Ctr., El Paso, 1984, Med. U. N.J., Newark, 1984, New Eng. Deaconess Hosp., Boston, 1985, Henry Ford Hosp., Detroit, 1989, Loyola U. Sch. Medicine, Chgo., 1990, St. Francis Hosp., Hartford, Conn., 1991, Marshall U. Sch. Medicine, Huntington, W.Va., 1991, U. Iowa Sch. Medicine, Iowa City, 1991, U. Mass. Sch. Medicine, 1994. Author: Cytopathologic Interpretation of Transthoracic Fine-Needle Biopsies, 1983, (with others) Histologic Typing of Female Genital Tract, 1994; editor: Gynecologic Cytopathology, 1997, Fine Needle Aspiration of Subcutaneous Organs and Masses, 1996; mem. editl. bd. Human Pathology, 1982-92, Am. Jour. Clin. Pathology, 1985—, Lab. Medicine, 1984-90; mem. N.Am. rev. bd., editl. adv. bd. ACTA Cytologica; contbr. articles to profl. jours.; author video Cytopathology of Fine Needle Biopsies of the Abdomen, 1985. Fellow Am. Soc. Clin. Pathologists (v.p. 1990-91, pres.-elect 1991-92, pres. 1992-93, clin. pathologists commn. on continuing edn., bd. dirs. 1985-94, chmn. nominating com. 1988, 92, rsch. and devel. com. 1985-89, chmn. quality assurance steering com. 1987-92, dep. commr. commn. on continuing edn. 1984-90, chmn. coun. cytopathology 1983-84, coun. on cytopathology 1979-84, Disting. Svc. award 1988, Ward Burdick award 2002), Coll. Am. Pathologists, Internat. Acad. Cytology (sci. program com. 1988-89, terminology com. 1992); mem. AMA, Am. Soc. Cytology (Cert. of Merit for outstanding svcs. 1987, Papanicolaou award 1991, v.p. 1984-85, pres.-elect 1985-86, pres. 1986-87, chmn. sci. program com. 1982-84, exec. com. 1980-88, numerous others), Arthur Purdy Stout Soc. Surg. Pathologists, Assn. Dirs. Anat. and Surg. Pathology (coun. 1989-95), Assn. Pathology chmn., Internat. Soc. Gynecol. Pathologists, Monroe County Med. Soc., N.Y. State Soc. Pathologists, Rochester Area Assn. Pathologists (v.p. 1978-79, pres. 1979-80), U.S. and Can. Acad. Pathology, Papanicoleau Soc. Cytology (Educator of Yr. award 2003), Alpha Omega Alpha. Roman Catholic. Avocations: fishing, boating. Home: 3666 Nibawauka Bch Canandaigua NY 14424-9725 Office: 601 ELmwood Ave Box 626 Rochester NY 14642 E-mail: tabonf@aol.com, tom_bonfiglio@urmc.rochester.edu.

BONFILS, DARCY REYNE, television producer; b. Washington, Sept. 20, 1957; d. James Robert and Marjorie (Stemm) Bonfils. BA, Middlebury Coll., 1979; MA, U. Colo., 1983. Exec. asst. Internat. Student Movement of UN, Geneva, 1980; anchor, reporter KYCU-TV, Cheyenne, Wyo, 1984-86; asst. news dir. WUFT-TV, Gainesville, Fla., 1986-87; prodr. WPEC-TV, West Palm Beach, Fla., 1987-89, WFSB-TV, Hartford, Conn., 1989-91, WBBM-TV, Chgo., 1991-92, WCBS-TV, N.Y.C., 1992-95; sr. prodr. Court TV's: Inside Am.'s Cts., N.Y.C., 1995-97; prodr. WABC-TV, N.Y.C., 1997—. Co-author: The Elvis Presley Family and Friends Cookbook, 1999; prodr.: (documentaries) Elvis: Precious Memories, 2000, (news feature) Grounding of the Golden Venture, 1993 (Emmy nomination, 1993), (news spls.) Hurricane: Eyewitness to a Storm, 2000 (Writers Guild Am. award, 2001, Emmy nomination, 2001). Mem.: NATAS, Am. Women in Radio and TV, Writers Guild Am. E-mail: darcylbon@aol.com.

BONGARD, JOSH CLIFFORD, computer scientist, researcher; b. Toronto, Canada, Apr. 17, 1974; arrived in U.S., 2003; s. Ralph and Carol Bongard. PhD, U. Zurich, 2003; Degree in Computer Sci. with honors, McMaster U., Hamilton, Ont., Can. Postdoctoral rschr. Cornell U., Ithaca, NY, 2003—. Author: How the Body Shapes the Way We Think. Office: Sibley Sch Mech and Aerospace Engring Grumman Hall 191 Cornell Univ Ithaca NY 14853 Personal E-mail: josh.bongard@cornell.edu.

BONGIORNO, JAMES WILLIAM, electronics company executive; b. Westfield, N.Y., Apr. 2, 1943; s. Samuel Salvatore and Marjorie Ruth (Hardenburg) B. Student public schs. Profl. musician, 1961—65; engr. Hadley Labs., Pomona, Calif., 1965—66, Marantz Co., Woodside, NY, 1966—67; chief engr. Rectilinear Rsch. Corp., Bklyn., 1967—68; profl. musician, writer Popular Electronics, also Audio mag., 1968—71; dir. engring. Dynaco Inc., Phila., 1972, S.A.E. Inc., Los Angeles, 1973—74; founder, pres. Gt. Am. Sound Co. Inc., Chatsworth, Calif., 1974—77; founder, 1977; pres. Sumo Electric Co. Ltd., West Hollywood, Calif., 1977—82; ind. electronic cons. Lompoc, Calif., 1982—88; founder, pres. Spread Spectrum Techs., Inc., Lompoc, Calif., 1988—. Ind. electronic cons. Patentee class A audio amplifier, FM IF-detector. Recipient State of Art Design award, Stereo Sound mag., Tokyo, 1976, 1980, 2003, High End Audio Best of CES Show award, 2003. Mem. Audio Engring. Soc., Am. Fedn. Musicians. Republican. Home and Office: 716 N G St Apt 2 Lompoc CA 93436-4530 Office Phone: 805-740-9902. Personal E-mail: sstinc@earthlink.net. *Aside from the fact that my lifetime goal has always been to design the world's finest amplifier, I also wanted it to be affordable by as many people as possible. I am happy that I have achieved this goal as there are a lot more poor people than rich people.*

BONGIORNO, JOSEPH JOHN, JR., electrical engineering educator; b. Bklyn., Aug. 3, 1936; s. Joseph John and Mildred Rose (LoPinto) B.; m. Carol Marie Olsen, Nov. 22, 1958; children: James Michael, Peter Joseph, Richard Edward, Cathryn Mary BEE, Poly. Inst. Bklyn., 1956, MEE, 1958, DEE, 1960. Asst. prof. Poly. Inst. N.Y., Bklyn., 1960-64, assoc. prof., 1964-74, prof., 1974-96, prof. emeritus, 1996—. Cons. Unisys (formerly Sperry Systems Mgmt.), Gt. Neck, N.Y., 1963-93. Contbr. articles to profl. jours. Mem. St. Aidan's Parish Sch. Bd., Williston Park, N.Y., 1967-70, 73-76, pres. 1975-76. Rsch. grantee NSF, Washington, 1972, 82, 85, Army Rsch. Office, Durham, N.C., 1993. Fellow IEEE (Control Systems Soc. best paper award 1977) Roman Catholic. Home: 36 Park Ave Williston Park NY 11596-1628 Office: Poly U 105 Maxess Rd Melville NY 11747 Office Phone: 631-755-4214. Business E-Mail: jbongior@rama.poly.edu.

BONGIOVI, JOHN FRANCIS See BON JOVI, JON

BONGOLAN-WALSH, VENA PEARL, research scientist; d. Benjamin A. and Concesa A. Bongolan; m. Carl Patrick Escamilla-Walsh, Oct. 27, 1962. MS, U. Ill., 1987. Tchg. asst. Bowling Green (Ohio) State U., 1997—2000; editl. asst. Nuc., Plasma and Radiol. Engring., U. Ill., Urbana, 2001; rschr. tchg. asst. applied math. IIT, Chgo., 2001—. Contbr. articles to profl. jours. Scholar, Nat. Sci. Devel. Bd., U. Philippines, 1976—79; Fulbright-Hayes fellow, Philippine-Am. Edn. Found., 1985—87. Mem.: Soc. Indsl. and Applied Math. Roman Catholic. Achievements include research in navier-stokes equations, ocean gravity currents, stochastic navier-stokes. Avocation: swimming. Office: Applied Mathematics IIT #10 W 32nd St Chicago IL 60616

BONHAG, AMY ELIZABETH, music educator; b. Hackensack, Nj, Mar. 30, 1980; d. Wayne Thompson and Molly Morck Bonhag. BA in Music, St. Olaf Coll., 2002. Cert. K-12 vocal music tchr. Minn., 2003, Nebr., 2003. Long term substitute Edina (Minn.) Pub. Schs., 2003—03; tchr. k-6 vocal music Omaha (Nebr.) Pub. Schs., 2003—. Musician: Intergenerational Orch. Omaha, 2004—; singer: Omaha Chamber Singers, 2003—. Mem.: Omaha Edn. Assn. (corr.; assembly rep. 2004—05), Music Educators Nat. Conf. (assoc.; mem. 2000—05). D-Liberal. Protestant-Lutheran. Avocations: computers, travel, swimming, music, exercise. Office: Omaha Public Schools 3905 N 52nd St Omaha NE 68104 Office Phone: 402-457-5905.

BONHAG, THOMAS EDWARD, insurance company executive, financial planner, financial consultant; b. Bronxville, NY, Jan. 19, 1952; s. Herman Arthur and Anne Elizabeth (Sage) B.; m. Noreen Patricia Early, Apr. 24, 1976 (div. Dec. 1981); m. Cornelia Hackett Lyons, Oct. 8, 1983. BS, Fordham U., 1973; MBA, St. John's U., 1979; postgrad., Am. Coll., 1979—84. CLU; cert. fin. planner, chartered fin. cons. Field sales rep. Colgate-Palmolive Co., N.Y.C., 1973-74; employee relations officer Chase Manhattan Bank, N.Y.C., 1974-78; agt., dist. mgr. Equitable Life Assurance Soc., N.Y.C., 1979-83, v.p. northeastern region mktg. Edison, N.J., 1984-90; sr. v.p. Kornreich Life Assocs., Inc., N.Y.C., 1990-94; CEO Winged Keel Group, Inc., NYC, 1994—95; dir. advanced planning/markets Equitable Life, NYC, 1995—98; mng. dir. The deBart Group, Inc., NYC, 1999—2005; exec. dir. Nat. Madicon Group, Inc., 2005—. Fin. cons. Am. Geriatrics Soc., N.Y.C., 1983-86; bd. dirs. Fin. Assurance Fed. Credit Union, 2001-. Mem. Hoboken (N.J.) Environ. Com., 1983-90; mayoral appointee citizens' budget adv. com. Twp. of Cranford, N.J., 1991-92; mem. Cranford Bd. Edn., 1991-94, pres., 1992-94. Mem. Soc. Fin. Svc. Profls., Nat. Assn. Ins. and Fin. Advisors, Fin. Planning Assn., Estate Planning Coun. N.Y.C. Avocations: walking, bicycling, sailing. Home: 406 Monmouth Ave Spring Lake NJ 07762-1131 Office Phone: 212-878-1689. Personal E-mail: tombonhag@msn.com.

BONHAM, HAROLD FLORIAN, research geologist, consultant; b. LA, Sept. 1, 1928; s. Harold Florian and Viola Violet (Clopine) B.; m. Sally Mae Reimer, Sept. 6, 1952 (dec. July 1999); children: Cynthia Jean Kimball, Douglas Craig, Gary Stephen; m. Linda Jean Shipp, June 14, 2000. AA in Physics, U. Calif. Berkeley, 1951; BA in Geology, UCLA, 1954; MS in Geology, U. Nev., 1963. Geologist So. Pacific Co., 1955-61; mining geologist Nev. Bur. Mines and Geology, Reno, 1963-93, acting dir., state geologist, 1993-95; cons. geologist, 1996—. Cons. UN, Can., Australia, Peoples Republic of China, 1980-90; cons. in field. Contbr. articles to profl. jour. V.p. Palomino Valley Gen. Improvement Dist., Nev., 1986-88. With USN, 1946-49, PTO. Fellow Geol. Soc. Am., Soc. Econ. Geologist, Assn. Exploration Geochemists (councillor 1988-94); mem. Geol. Soc. Nev. (hon.). Republican. Avocations: reading, computers, photography, oenology. Home: 265 Mia Dr Sparks NV 89436-7912 Business E-Mail: hbonham@infosrations.com.

BONHAM, JOHN P., music educator; m. Charlynn S. Henderson, Aug. 5, 1995; 1 child, Bethany A. B Music Edn., Oral Roberts U., 1998. Strings instr. Robert Smalls Mid. Sch., Beaufort, SC, 1998—99; band dir. Whale Br. Mid. Sch., Beaufort, 1999—2001, Mauldin (SC) H.S., 2001—04, Emerald H.S., Greenwood, SC, 2004—. Assoc. music dir. Cmty. Bible Ch., Beaufort, 1999—2001. Mem.: Music Educators Nat. Conf., SC. Band Dir.'s Assn. Republican. Mem. Ch. Of God. Avocations: camping, golf, baseball, trumpet. Office Phone: 864-941-5741.

BONHAM, RUSSELL AUBREY, chemistry educator; b. San Jose, Calif., Dec. 10, 1931; s. Russell Aubrey and Margaret Florence (Wallace) B.; m. Miriam Anne Dye, Mar. 23, 1957; children: Frances, Margaret, Anne. BA, Whittier Coll., 1954; PhD, Iowa State U., 1958. Instr. Ind. U., Bloomington, 1958-60; postdoctoral fellow Naval Rsch. Lab., 1960; asst. prof. math. U. Md., 1960; asst. prof. chemistry Ind. U., Bloomington, 1960-63, assoc. prof., 1963-65, prof. chemistry, 1965-95, prof. emeritus, 1996—; rsch. prof. chemistry Ill. Inst. Tech., Chgo., Ill., 1995—. Co-author: High Energy Electron Scattering, 1974; mem. editorial bd.: The Jour. of the Brazilian Chem. Soc., 1989-2000; contbr. over 175 articles and papers to profl. jours. Recipient Fulbright fellowship U. Tokyo, 1964-65, Guggenheim fellowship, 1964-65, Humboldt prize, 1977, 81. Fellow Am. Phys. Soc., AAAS; mem. Am. Phys. Soc., Am. Crystallographic Assn., Am. Chem. Soc., Sigma Xi.

Achievements include research on electron impact cross section measurements of molecular species of interest to low pressure processing plasmas and X-Ray scattering from gases. Office: Ill Inst Tech Dept Biol Chem Phys Scis 3101 S Dearborn Chicago IL 60616

BONHAM-CARTER, HELENA, actress; b. Eng., May 26, 1966; Ed., Westminster. TV appearances include A Pattern of Roses, Miami Vice, A Hazard of Hearts, The Vision, Arms and the Man, Beatrix Potter, Dancing Queen, Fatal Deception, A Dark Adapted Eye; films include Lady Jane, A Room with a View, Maurice, Francesco, The Mask, Getting It Right, Hamlet, Where Angels Fear to Tread, Howard's End, Mary Shelley's Frankenstein, A Little Loving, Mighty Aphrodite, Margaret's Museum, 1994, Portraits Chinois, 1995, Twelfth Night, 1995, Wings of a Dove, 1996, Revengers Comedies, 1996, Keep the Aspidistra Flying, 1997, The Theory of Flight, 1997, Fight Club, 1998, Women Talking Dirty, 1999, Novacaine, 2000, Til Human Voices Wake Us, Planet of the Apes, 2001, Heart of Me, 2001, Live from Baghdad, 2002, Big Fish, 2003, Henry VIII, 2003, Corpse Bride, 2004, Wallace & Gromit, 2004, Conversations with Other Women, 2004, Charlie and the Chocolate Factory, 2004, (voice) Corpse Bride, 2005. Office: Adam Isaccs United Talent 9560 Wilshire Blvd Beverly Hills CA 90212-2427 also: Conway Van Gelder 18-21 Jermyn St London SW1Y 6HP England

BONHAM-YEAMAN, DORIA, retired law educator; b. L.A., June 10, 1932; d. Carl Herschel and Edna Mae (Jones) Bonham; widowed; children: Carl Q., Doria Valerie-Constance. BA, U. Tenn., 1953, JD, 1957, MA, 1958; EdS in Computer Edn., Barry U., 1984. Instr. bus. law Palm Beach Jr. Coll., Lake Worth, Fla., 1960-69; instr. legal environment Fla. Atlantic U., Boca Raton, 1969-73; lectr. bus. law Fla. Internat. U., North Miami, 1973-83, assoc. prof. bus. law, 1983—2001; ret., 2001. Editor: Anglo-Am. Law Conf., 1980; Developing Global Corporate Strategies, 1981; mem. editl. bd. Attys. Computer Report, 1984-85, Jour. Legal Studies Edn., 1985-97; contbr. articles to profl. jours. Bd. dirs. Palm Beach County Assn. for Deaf Children, 1960-63; mem. Fla. Commn. on Status of Women, Tallahassee, 1969-70; mem. Broward County Dem. Exec. Com., 1982-2000; pres. Dem. Women's Club Broward County, 1981; mem. Marine Coun. of Greater Miami, 1978-94, Svc. award, 1979. Recipient Faculty Devel. award Fla. Internat. U., Miami, 1980; grantee Notre Dame Law Sch., London, summer 1980. Mem. AAUW (pres. Palm Beach county chpt. 1965-66), U.S. Coun. for Internat. Bus., No. Dade C. of C., Acad. Legal Studies in Bus., Alpha Chi Omega (alumnae club pres. 1968-71), Tau Kappa Alpha. Episcopalian.

BONIFACE, BARRY, telecommunications industry executive; BBA, So. Meth. U.; MBA in Fin., Emory U. V.p. corp. fin. dept. Prin. Fin. Securities Inc. (now First Union Securities); COO, Global Bus. Acceleration Inc.; prin. Berkshire Ptnrs. Inc., Dallas; CFO Cypress Comm., 1998, exec. v.p. network, product mgmt. and tech.; v.p. corp. devel. BellSouth Corp., Atlanta, 2001—. Office: BellSouth Corp 1155 Peachtree St NE Atlanta GA 30309-3610

BONIFACHO, BRATSA, artist; b. Belgrade, Yugoslavia, 1937; arrived in Can., 1973, naturalized, 1976. Student, Sumatovachka Sch. Art, Belgrade, 1957-59; BArch, MFA, U. Belgrade, 1965; postgrad., Acad. di Belle Arti, Italy, 1966-68, Atelier Kruger, West Germany, 1966-68. Tchr. painting and drawing Sch. Fine Arts, Belgrade, 1967-68; pvt. tutor, 1979-87. One-person shows Gallery Scollard, Toronto, 1978, Contemporary Art Gallery, Vancouver, 1979, Richmond (B.C.) Art Gallery, 1982, 93, 97, Heffel Gallery Ltd., Vancouver, 1988, 90, 91, Quan-Schieder Gallery, Toronto, 1989, 90, Fran Willis Art Gallery, Victoria, B.C., Can., 1992, 93, 94, 95, 2000, Patrick Doheny Fine Art Gallery, Vancouver, 1992, 93, 94, Artropolis, 1993, Seattle Art Fair, 1993, Threshold Gallery, Vancouver, 1993, Bau-Xi Art Gallery, Vancouver and Toronto, 1995, 96, 99, 2001, 02, 03, 04, Kimzey Miller Gallery, Seattle, 1996, Mus. History and Art, Anchorage, 1997, Gallerijk Progres, Belgrade, 2000, Contemporary Art Gallery, Zrenjanin, Yugoslavia, 2001, Gallery of the Matica Srpsick, Novi Sad, Yugoslavia, 2002, Foster/White Gallery, Seattle, 2004, 05, Art Fair, Toronto, 2004, Cologne Art Fair, Germany, 2005; juried group exhbns. in B.C., 1974-93; represented in numerous pub. and pvt. collections. Grantee, B.C. Arts Coun., 1996, 1998, 2000, Can. Coun., 1996, 1998, 1999; travel grantee, 2000, 2001, 2002, B.C. travel grantee, 1999. Office: PO Box 549 Sta A Vancouver BC Canada V6C 2N3 Office Phone: 604-254-1405. E-mail: bonifacho@telus.net.

BONIFAZ, JOHN CRISTOPHER, lawyer; b. Wilmington, Del., June 22, 1966; s. Cristobal and Deirdre (Cooney) B. BA magna cum laude, Brown U., 1987; JD cum laude, Harvard U., 1992. Bar: Mass., 1993, U.S. Dist. Ct. Mass. 1995. Community liaison Exec. Office of the Mayor, Washington, 1987-88; scheduler/adminstrv. asst. Sen. Kennedy's Re-Election Campaign, Boston, 1988; law clk. DNA People's Legal Svcs., Shiprock, N.Mex., 1990, Fla. Rural Legal Svcs., Lake Worthy, Fla., 1991; staff atty. Ctr. for Responsive Politics, Washington, 1992-93; pvt. practice Boston, 1994—; exec. dir. Nat. Voting Rights Inst., Cambridge, Mass., 1994—. Co-author: The Wealth Primary: Campaign Fundraising and the Constitution, 1994. MacArthur Fellow, 1999. Mem. Nat. Lawyers Guild (bd. dirs. Mass. chpt. 1994—). Office: 27 School St STE 500 Boston MA 02108-4303

BONILLA, HENRY, congressman, broadcast executive; b. Jan. 2, 1954; m. Deborah Knapp; children: Alicia, Austin. BA in Journalism, U. Tex., 1976. Reporter KTVV, Austin, Tex., 1976-78; reporter, prodr. KENS-TV News, 1978-80; asst. Press sec. for Gov. Dick Thornburgh, Phila., 1981; news producer WABC-TV, N.Y.C., 1982-85; asst. news dir. WTAF-TV, Phila., 1985-86; TV exec. prodr. KENS-TV, San Antonio, 1986-89; mem. appropriations com. 103rd-106th Congress from 23rd Tex. dist., Washington, D.C., 1993—. Mem. appropriations; chair agr. appropriations subcom., fgn. ops. appropriations subcom., def. appropriations subcom. Bd. v.p. San Antonio Crimestoppers; mem. adv. bd. United Way Vol. Ctr.; mem. adv. coun. Univ. Tex. Women's Athletics Dept., San Antonio Mus. Assn. Mex. Splendors Media; bd. dirs. Careers Info. and Referral Svc., San Antonio Pub. Library Found. Recipient Leadership award, 1989, Corp. Community Svc. award, 1990, Outstanding young Tex. Exec. award U. Tex. Ex-Students Assn., 1993, Pres. award US Hispanic C. of C. Tex. Hispanic C of C, Eagle award Hispanic Heritage Conf., 1993, Award for Legislative Excellence Am. Diabetes Assn., 1994, Golden Bulldog award Watchdogs of the Treas., 1994, Champion of Pvt. Property Rights award League of Pvt. Proprty Owners, 1994, Golden Flame award Vocational Home Econ. Teacher Assn. Tex., 1994, Guardian Small Bus. award Nat. Fedn. Ind. Businesses, 1994, Legislator of the Year Am. Heart Assn Tex., 1994, MLA award for Disting. Pub. Svc., Med. Library Assn., 1998, Ground Water Protector award Nat. Ground Water Assn., 2004, Congl. Support for Sci. award Inst. Food Technologies, 2004 Republican. Office: US Ho of Reps 2458 Rayburn Washington DC 20515-4323*

BONIN, JOHN PAUL, economics professor; b. Lawrence, Mass., Mar. 6, 1945; s. Ralph O. and Mildred May (Kiessling) B.; m. Hélène Boivin, July 26, 1969; children— Corinne, Jennifer BA in Econs., Boston Coll., 1966; MA in Econs., U. Rochester, 1970, PhD, 1973; MA (hon.), Wesleyan U., 1984. Asst. prof. econs. Wesleyan U., Middletown, Conn., 1970-77, assoc. prof., 1977-83, prof., 1983—, Andrews prof. econs., 2000—02, Chester D. Hubbard prof. econs. and social scis., 2002—. Vis. prof. econs. U. B.C., Vancouver, 1977-78, U. Calif.-San Diego, 1974-75, Yale U., 1989, 91; vis. rsch. scholar Birkbeck Coll., London, 1979-80; summer rsch. fellow Internat. Inst. Mgmt., Berlin, 1980; vis. sr. lectr./scholar U. Wash., Seattle, 1985; vis. lectr. Yale Sch. Orgn. and Mgmt., 1989, 91, 93; William Davidson Disting. vis. prof. U. Mich. Sch. Bus., 1998, 99; faculty affiliate, rsch. fellow William Davidson Inst., U. Mich. Bus. Sch., 1996—; cons. World Bank, Inst. for East West Studies, U.S. Dept. Treasury, UN; keynote spkr. various internat. confs. Co-translator (with H. Bonin): Advanced Exercises in Microeconomics, 1983, Economics of Uncertainty & Information, 1989; (with others): Economics of Cooperation & The Labor-Managed Economy, 1985, The Economics of Uncertainty and Information, transl. of Jean-Jacques Laffont Cours de theorie microeconomique, vol. 2, 1989, Banking in Transition Economies: Developing Market Oriented Banking Sectors in Eastern Europe, 1998; editor: Jour. Comparative Econs., 1996—; contbr. articles to profl. jours. NSF postdoctoral fellow, London, 1979-80; rsch. fellow Internat. Inst. Mgmt., Berlin, 1980; rsch. grantee Nat. Coun. for Soviet and Ea. European Rsch., 1992-93. Mem. Am. Econ. Assn., Jour. Comparative Econs. (bd. editors 1983-86, 1992—), Assn. for Comparative Econ. Studies (exec. com. 1989-91, pres. 1996), Nat. Coun. for Eurasian and East European Rsch. (bd. dirs. 1998-2002). Democrat. Roman Catholic. Home: 8 Yellow Wood St Middletown CT 06457-4927 Office: Wesleyan U Dept Of Econs Middletown CT 06457 Business E-Mail: JBonin@wesleyan.edu.

BONIN, PAUL JOSEPH, real estate company executive, bank executive; b. Malden, Mass., Mar. 6, 1929; s. Honoré Auguste and Yvonne Adrienne (Vuillaumié) B.; m. Annette Kagey, Jan. 19, 1968; children: Adam Spencer, Christopher Paul, Page Alexandra. Student, Bentley Coll., 1948-50, NYU, 1950-52, New Sch. for Social Rsch., 1962. Lic. real estate broker, N.Y. Acct. Henry W.T. Mali & Co., N.Y.C., 1951-58; budget contr., asst. account exec., developer budget control system Young & Rubicam, N.Y.C., 1958-60; v.p. Wm. Alfred White, Inc., N.Y.C., 1960-65; pres. Bonin & Barringer, Inc., N.Y.C., 1964-65; v.p. Wm. B. May & Co., Previews, Inc., N.Y.C., 1965-69; dir. acquisitions Nationwide Real Estate Co., N.Y.C., 1969-74; v.p. Landauer Assocs., Inc., N.Y.C., 1974-79, Citibank, N.A., N.Y.C., 1979-82; pres. Assocs. Mgmt., Inc., Dallas, 1982-84; dir. acquisitions The Hendrix Cos., N.Y.C., 1984-85, The Ziegelman Orgn., N.Y.C., 1985-86; sr. v.p. Crossland Svs. Bank, Bklyn., 1987-89; pres. asset mgmt. group Team Cos., N.Y.C., 1989-93; asset valuation rev. team leader, portfolio mgr. FDIC, Franklin, Hartford, Mass., Ct., 1990-2000; fin. analyst, 2000—02; loss control cons. to ins. cos., 2003—. Asset mgr. Shell Pension Fund of The Hague, The Netherlands, Electricity Coun. of Eng., London, N.Y.C.; real estate cons. Pan Am World Airways, N.Y. State Dept. Housing and Cmty. Renewal. With USN, 1946-48. Mem. Mortgage Bankers Assn., Nat. Assn. Realtors (cert. property mgr.), Inst. Real Estate Mgmt. Roman Catholic. Avocations: tennis, skiing.

BONINI, JAMES, federal official; BA in Criminal Justice, Indiana U. of Pa., 1986; MPA, U. So. Calif., 1988. Administrv. asst. South Bay Mcpl. Ct. Los Angeles County, Calif., 1987—88, sr. adminstrv. asst., 1988—89, divsn. head budget and mgmt. svcs., 1989; chief dep. ct. adminstr. Ct. Common Pleas, Montgomery County, Pa., 1990—91, dist. ct. adminstr. Berks County, Pa., 1991—96; clk. of ct. U.S. Bankruptcy Ct. No. Dist. Ind., South Bend, 1996—2003, U.S. Dist. Ct. So. Dist. Ohio, Columbus, 2003—. Office: US Dist Ct Joseph P Kinneary US Courthouse Rm 260 85 Marconi Blvd Columbus OH 43215 Office Phone: 614-719-3030.

BONINI, WILLIAM EMORY, geophysics educator; b. Washington, Aug. 23, 1926; s. John Emory and Thelma (Scrivener) B.; m. Rose Rozich, Dec. 4, 1954; children: John Allen, Nancy Mara, James Prior, Jennifer Adra. BS in Engring, Princeton, 1948, MS, 1949; PhD, U. Wis., 1957. Mem. faculty Princeton, 1953-96, prof. civil and geol. engring., 1966-70, George J. Magee prof. geophysics and geol. engring., 1970-96; prof. emeritus, 1996—; chmn. water resources program Princeton, 1971-74, chmn. geol. engring. program, 1973-96; ret., 1996. Author articles in field. Pres. Yellowstone-Bighorn Research Assn., Red Lodge, Mont., 1959-60, 71-73, v.p., 1966-71, 85-87; mem. com. sci. and arts The Franklin Inst., 1999—. Served with USNR, 1945-46. Nat. Acad. Sci. exchange scientist to Yugoslavia, 1974; NSF sr. postdoctoral fellow U. Newcastle upon Tyne, Eng., 1963-64. Fellow Geol. Soc. Am. (sec.-treas. geophysics div. 1981-83, chmn. geophysics div. 1985-86); mem. Am. Assn. Petroleum Geologists, Soc. Exploration Geophysicists, Nat. Assn. Geosci. Tchrs. (councilor-at-large 1981-83, v.p. 1983-84, pres. 1984-85), Sigma Xi (v.p. Princeton chpt. 1988-89, pres. 1989-90). Achievements include research on gravity and magnetic anomalies and crustal structure, seismic crustal studies, geophys. exploration engring. and groundwater studies, environmental geology. Home: 74 Robert Rd Princeton NJ 08540-5333 Office Phone: 609-258-3598. Business E-Mail: bonini@princeton.edu.

BONINO, FERNANDA, art dealer; b. Torino, Italy, Jan. 5, 1927; arrived in U.S., 1963; d. Francesco Pogliani and Marina Collino; m. Alfredo Bonino, July 29, 1925 (dec. Jan. 1981). M in Art, U. Italy, Torino, 1942. Dir. Galeria Bonino Ltd., N.Y.C., 1963-90, dir., pres., 1981—. Mem. Art Dealers Assn. Am. Office: Galeria Bonino Ltd 48 Great Jones St New York NY 10012-1133 Office Phone: 212-598-4262.

BONIS, LASZLO JOSEPH, marketing executive, mechanical engineer, chemist; b. Budapest, Hungary, May 31, 1931; came to U.S., 1957; s. Joseph and Ilona (Hunvald) B.; m. Eva Markovich, July 31, 1955 (div. 1981); children: Andrea Christine, Peter Anthony Laszlo; m. Cheryl E. Olsen, Dec. 28, 1985. DM Ing. Mech. Engring., U. Tech. Sci., Budapest, 1953; MSc in Metallurgy, MIT, 1959, postgrad., 1959-60. Registered profl. engr., Calif., Mass.; cert. chemist Nat. Cert. Commn. Assoc. dir. material rsch. Electronics, Inc., Budapest, 1953-56; prof. U. Tech. Sci., 1953-56; rsch. asst. MIT, Cambridge, 1957-60; exec. v.p., tech. dir. Ilikon Corp., Natick, Mass., 1960-62, pres., tech. dir., 1962-74; mgmt. cons. Tech. Fin. and Mktg., Inc., Natick, Mass., 1974—; pres., chmn., tech. dir. Composite Container Corp., Medford, Mass., 1977-88; pres. T.F.M. Cons., Dover, Mass., 1988—. Editor: (4 vols.) Fundamental Phenomena in the Material Science; contbr. articles to profl. jours.; patentee in field. Bd. dirs. The Opera Co., Boston, 1962-85, pres., 1966-85; pres. Boston Arts Coun., 1974—, Boston Opera House, 1991-94. Recipient Muse award Pub. Action for the Arts, 1984, George Washington award Am. Hungarian Found., 1984, Golden Door award Internat. Inst., 1980, Golden Diploma award Tech. U. Sci., Budapest, 2003; named One of Outstanding Young Men of Greater Boston C. of C., 1966. Fellow Am. Inst. Chemists; mem. N.Y. Acad. Scis., MIT Club. Office: TFM Cons 52 Haven St Dover MA 02030-2131 E-mail: dr.bonis@tfmconsultants.com.

BONJEAN, CHARLES MICHAEL, foundation executive, sociologist, educator; b. Pekin, Ill., Sept. 7, 1936; s. Bruno and Catherine Ann (Dancey) B. BA, Drake U., 1957; MA, U. N.C., 1959, PhD in Sociology, 1963. Mem. faculty U. Tex., Austin, 1963—2003, Hogg prof. sociology, 1974—2003, chmn. dept., 1972-74; exec. assoc. Hogg Found., 1974-79; v.p., 1979-93; exec. dir. Hogg Found., 1993—2003. Sociology editor Chandler Pub. Co., 1967-73, Crowell Pub. Co., 1973-77, Dorsey Press, 1979-88, Wadsworth Pub. Co., 1988-93; mem. coun. Intern-Univ. Consortium Polit. and Social Rsch., 1972-76; mem. steering com. Coun. Social Sci. Jour. Editors, 1975-81; 2d v.p. Conf. S.W. Found., 1984-85, 1st v.p., 1985-86, pres., 1986-87; exec. com. Grantmakers Evaluation Network, 1994-98; mem. exec. com. Grantmakers in Health, 1995-98, bd. dirs., 1993-2000; chmn. rsch. com. Coun. Founds., 1991-94, bd. dirs., 1998-2003; mem. adv. com. Am. Sociol. Found., 1992-97, chmn., 1995-97. Co-author: Sociological Measurement, 1967, Sociology: A Core Text with Adapted Readings, 1990; co-editor: Blacks in the United States, 1969, Planned Social Intervention, 1969, Community Politics, 1971, Political Attitudes and Public Opinion, 1972, The Idea of Culture in the Social Sciences, 1973, Social Science in America, 1976, The Mexican Origin People in the United States, 1985, Community Care of the Chronically Mentally Ill, 1989, Mental Health Research in Texas, 1990; editor Social Sci. Quar., 1966-94; cons. editor Am. Jour. Sociology, 1974-76, The Am. Sociologist, 1990-96; contbr. to profl. jours. Bd. dirs. Lake Travis Ednl. Found., 1986-91. Recipient tchg. excellence award U. Tex. Students Assn., 1965, Alumni Disting. Svc. award Drake U., 1979, Disting. Svc. award Southwestern Social Sci. Assn., 2001; Sigma Delta Chi scholar, 1957. Mem. Am. Sociol. Assn. (chmn. cmty. sect. 1976-78, publs. com. 1978-81, chmn. 1979-81, pres. sect. on orgns. 1983-84, chmn. dist. scholarship com. 1992-84, coun. 1985-88, exec. office and budget com. 1994-97), Southwestern Sociol. Assn. (pres. 1972-73), Southwestern Social Sci. Assn. (exec. com. 1966-97, v.p. 1992-93, pres.-elect 1993-94, pres. 1994-95, Disting. Svc. award 2001), Philos. Soc. Tex. Home: 16310 Clara Van St Austin TX 78734-3928 Business E-Mail: bonjean@mail.utexas.edu.

BON JOVI, JON (JOHN FRANCIS BONGIOVI JR.), musician, actor; b. Perth Amboy, N.J., Mar. 2, 1962; s. John and Carol Bongiovi; m. Dorothea Hurley, May, 1989; children: Stephanie Rose, Jesse James Louis, Jacob, Romeo Jon. Grad. high sch., Sayreville. Singer, songwriter band Bon Jovi, 1984—. Mem. various local bands including The Rest, The Wild Ones, Johnny and the Lechers, The Raze, Atlantic City Expressway; singer (albums)(with Bon Jovi) Bon Jovi, 1984, 7800 Fahrenheit, 1985, Slippery When Wet, 1986, New Jersey, 1988, Keep the Faith, 1992, Crossroad, 1994, These Days, 1995, Destination Anywhere, 1997, Bon Jovi, 1999, Crush, 2000, Bounce, 2002, Distance, 2003, 100,000,000 Bon Jovi Fans Can't Be Wrong, 2004; (solo albums) Blaze of Glory, 1990, Destination Anywhere, 1997; songs include Runaway, Burning Your Love, Get Ready, In and Out of Love, Hardest Part Is the Night, To the Fire, Secret Dreams, Living on a Prayer, Wanted Dead or Alive, 1987, Bad Medicine, 1988, Born to Be My Baby, 1988, Let It Rock, You Give Love a Bad Name, World in the Streets, Raise Your Hands, I'd Die for You, Bed of Roses, 1993, Midnight in Chelsea 1997, Real Life, 1999, It's My Life, 2000, Thank You for Loving Me, 2001, All About Loving You, 2003; toured Europe, Japan, 1988-89; performed USSR, S.Am., Australia, New Zealand, Hong Kong, 1989; actor (films) The Return of Bruno, 1988, Moonlight and Valentino, 1995, The Leading Man, 1996, Long Time, Nothing New, 1997, Little City, 1997, Homegrown, 1997, Row Your Boat, 1998, U-571, 2000, Pay It Forward, 2000, Vampires: Los Muertos, 2002; (TV series) The Uncle Floyd Show, 1974, Unsolved Mysteries, 1988, Sex and the City, 1998, Ally McBeal, 2002. Co-recipient Award of Merit, Am. Music Awards, 2004.

BONK, RACHAEL LOUISE, music educator; arrived in US, 1972; d. David Gary and Joan Louise Bonk. MusB, Evangel U., 1994; MusM, Ind. U., 1998. Cert. Kindermusik Instr. Music isntr. Rachael Bonk's Musical Arts, Poplar Bluff, Mo., 1998—. Mem.: Kindermusik Educators Assn., Nat. Guild of Piano Tchrs., Nat. Fed. of Music Clubs. Office: Rachael Bonks Musical Arts 3950 Hwy 67 N Poplar Bluff MO 63901 Office Phone: 573-785-7464.

BONK, SHARON CATHERINE, librarian; b. North Tonawanda, N.Y., Nov. 28, 1943; d. Joseph J. and Ann (Danylow) B. BS in Edn., SUNY, Geneseo, 1965; MA in Am. Studies, MA in Libr. Sci., U. Minn., 1969. High sch. libr. Sch. Dist. 3, Huntington, N.Y., 1965-67; social scis. selector Northeastern U. Librs., Boston, 1969-81, head, periodicals dept., 1978-82; head acquisitions dept. SUNY Albany Librs., Albany, 1978-83; asst. dir. tech. svcs. SUNY Librs., Albany, 1984-88, interim dir., 1988-89, asst. dir. rsch. svcs., 1989-90; asst. direct user svcs. Albany, 1990-93; dir. Queens Coll. Librs. CUNY, 1993—. Contbr. articles to profl. jours.; author chpts. in monographs; assoc. editor Serials Rev. Trustee Sand Lake (N.Y.) Town Libr., 1987-89; mem. users coun. OCLC, 1994-2000; mem. adv. coun. N.Y.S. Regents LSCA, 1995-97, vice chair 1996-97; bd. dirs. Met. Libr. Resources Coun., 2000-2005. Recipient Fulbright Fellowship, 1989, Chancellor's Award for Excellence in Librarianship, SUNY, 1986, Lambert Scholarship, Blackwells Coll. of Libr. Wales, U.K., 1981. Mem. Assn. Coll. and Rsch. Librs. (bd. dirs. univ. librs. sect. 2001—), Assn. for Libr. Collections and Tech. Svcs./ALA (bd. dirs. 1989-92), Beta Phi Mu. Office: Rosenthal Library Queens Coll Kisseha Blvd Flushing NY 11367

BONN, ETHEL MAY, psychiatrist, educator; b. Cin., Oct. 14, 1925; d. Stanley Ervin and Ethel May (Cliffe) B. BA, U. Cin., 1947; MD, U. Chgo., 1951. Asst. chief, then chief women's neuro-psychiat. services VA Hosp., Topeka, 1956-61, chief north service, 1961-62; assoc. dir. for clin. services Ft. Logan Mental Health Ctr., Denver, 1962-67, dir., 1967-76; clin. instr. psychiatry U. Colo. Sch. Medicine, 1963-76; field rep. Joint Commn. on Accreditation of Hosps., 1976-78; assoc. clin. prof. psychiatry UCLA Sch. Medicine, 1978-81; chief of quality assurance VA Med. Ctr.-Brentwood, L.A., 1978-81; chief psychiatry service VA Med. Ctr., Albuquerque, 1981-89; assoc. prof. psychiatry U. N.Mex. Sch. Medicine, 1981-89; prof. emeritus psychiatry sch. medicine U. N.Mex., 1989—. Cons. Fitzsimons Army Hosp., Denver, 1963-67, U. Calif. Dept Biobehavioral Scis., Los Angeles, 1978-81, VA Hosps., Ft. Lyon, Colo., Sheridan, Wyo., Tuscaloosa, Ala., 1963-67. Contbr. chpts. to books, articles to profl. jours. Recipient Dirs. commendation, VA, 1962, 81, 89, Psychiat. Adminstrs. award Am. Assn. Psychiat. Adminstrs., 1976. Fellow Am. Coll. Psychiatrists (emeritus), Am. Psychiat. Assn. (life; program com. insts. for hosp. and cmty. psychiatry 1977-81), Am. Coll. Mental Health Adminstrn. (founding), Am. Coll. Utilization Rev. Physicians; mem. AMA, Am. Hosp. Assn. (chmn. psychiat. sect. 1972-74). Avocations: travel, gardening, oil and watercolor painting, collecting rocks and minerals, photography.

BONN, RONALD SHELDON, television producer, communications educator, journalist; b. N.Y.C., June 5, 1930; s. Roy S. and Rose (Trilling) B.; m. June Weinstein, Sept. 9, 1962; children: Julia, David, Daniel. BA in Journalism, Pa. State U., 1952; postgrad., Columbia U., 1962-63. Writer, prodr. CBS News, N.Y.C., 1960-63, CBS Evening News with Walter Cronkite, N.Y.C., 1963-73, co-prodr., 1973-78; creator, exec. prodr. Universe—CBS News, N.Y.C., 1979-80; prodr. NBC News, N.Y.C., 1981-83; prodr. in charge spl. segments NBC Nightly News with Tom Brokaw, N.Y.C., 1983-88; prodr. in charge The New Cold War NBC News, 1984, medicine and sci. prodr. Sunday Today N.Y.C., 1989-92, line prodr. Tel Aviv, 1991; ind. prodr. various prodns. including NBC News Dateline, ABC News 20/20, Discovery Channel, A&E, CNN, 1993—. Guest lectr. various univs., 1965—; adj. prof. journalism U. San Diego, 2000—. Co-author: How to Help Children through a Parent's Serious Illness, 1994. Docent Maritime Mus. San Diego, 2000—. Sgt. U.S. Army, 1952-54. CBS News fellow Columbia U., 1962-63; recipient 3 Emmy awards Nat. Acad. TV Arts and Scis., 1970, 74, 84, Edward R. Murrow award Overseas Press Club Am., 1985, Edward R. Murrow Brotherhood award B'nai B'rith, 1986, Nat. Headliner award Press Club Atlantic City, 1991, White House Press Photographers award, 1991, Silver Gavel award ABA, 1992, Disting. Alumnus award Pa. State U., 1989, Am. Women in Radio and TV Commendation awards, 1991, 92. Avocations: sailing, travel. Home: 11075 Viacha Dr San Diego CA 92124 Office: Dept Comm U San Diego 5998 Alcala Park San Diego CA 92110 Office Fax: 619-260-4040. E-mail: ronbonn@sbcglobal.net.

BONNARD, RAYMOND, theater director; b. Chambersburg, Pa., May 13, 1951; m. Ricki Whitacre, Jan. 22, 1977; children: Christopher David, Alexander Whitacre. BS cum laude, Indiana (Pa.) U., 1973; MFA cum laude, Ohio U., 1976. Prodn. mgr. Mo. Reparatory Theatre, Kansas City, 1978-79; assoc. prodr. Tiffany's Attic Theatre, Waldo Astoria Theatre, Kansas City, 1979-81; prodn. stage mgr. Folly Theatre, Kansas City, 1981; mng. dir. Del. Theatre Co., Wilmington, 1981-84; producing dir. Studio Area Theatre, Buffalo, 1984-95. Asst. prof. U. Mo., Kansas City, 1978-79; respondent Am. Coll. Theatre Festival. Active Buffalo Fin. Planning Commn., Leadership Buffalo. Mem. League Regional Theatres (exec. com. 1988-91), Theatre DIst. Assn. (v.p. 1993—).

BONNEFOUX, JEAN-PIERRE, artistic director, choreographer, dancer; b. Bourg-en-Bresse France, Apr. 9, 1943; s. Laurent and Marie-Therese (Noel) Bonnefoux; m. Patricia McBride, Sept. 8, 1973. Ed., Paris Opera Sch.; ArtsD(hon.), Goucher Coll., 1987. Tchr. Sch. of Am. Ballet, N.Y.C.; choreographer, 1977—80; artistic dir. N Carolina Dance Theatre, Charlotte, NC, 1996—. Ballet artist-in-residence Goucher Coll., Towson, Md., 1984—94; artistic dir. ballet dept. Ind. U., Bloomington, 1985—96. Dancer N.Y.C. Ballet, 1970—81. Decorated Officier L'Ordre du Merite France. Office: N Carolina Dance Theatre 800 N College St Charlotte NC 28206-3227

BONNELL, BRUNO, information technology executive; Degree in Econs. and Chemical Engring., U. Paris Dauphne. Co-founder, chmn., CEO, chief crative officer Infogrames Entertainment SA (IESA), 1983—; bd. dir. Atari, Inc., NYC, 1999—, chmn. bd. dir., 2000—, CEO, 2000—04, chief creative officer, 2004—, interim CEO, 2005—. Creator SELL. Shareholder Lyons' UEFA soccer team; Olympique Lyonnais. Office: Atari Inc 417 Fifth Ave New York NY 10016 Office Phone: 212-726-6500.

BONNELL, JOHN CHARLES, literature and language professor; b. Detroit, Sept. 21, 1939; s. Leroy Carlton and Kathleen Patricia Bonnell; m. Nancy Louise Crawley, Jan. 5, 1979; m. Marel Anne Utter (div.); 1 child, Jay Michael. BA, U. Detroit, 1966; MA, U. Mich., 1967. Prof. composition and lit. Macomb C.C., Warren, Mich., 1967—. Candidate Libertarian State Rep., Mich., 2002, Libertarian County Commn., Macomb County, 2004. Liberal. Avocation: lottery analysis. Home: 16650 Martin Rd Roseville MI 48066 Office: Maconb C C 14500 E 12 Mile Warren MI 48089 Office Phone: 586-445-7367.

BONNELL, VICTORIA EILEEN, sociologist, educator; b. NYC, June 15, 1942; d. Samuel S. and Frances (Nassau) B.; m. Gregory Freidin, May 4, 1971. BA, Brandeis U., 1964; MA, Harvard U., 1966, PhD, 1975. Lectr. politics U. Calif., Santa Cruz, 1972-73, 74-76, asst. prof. sociology Berkeley, 1976-82, assoc. prof., 1982-91, prof., 1991—. Chair Berkeley Ctr. for Slavic and East European Studies, U. Calif.-Berkeley, 1994-2000, dir. Inst. Slavic, East European, and Eurasian Studies, 2002-04. Author: Roots of Rebellion: Workers' Politics and Organizations in St. Petersburg and Moscow, 1900-1914, 1983; editor: The Russian Worker: Life and Labor Under the Tsarist Regime, 1983, (with Ann Cooper and Gregory Freidin) Russia at the Barricades: Eyewitness Accounts of the August 1991 Coup, 1994, Iconography of Power: Soviet Political Posters Under Lenin and Stalin, 1997, Identities in Transition: Eastern Europe and Russia After the Collapse of Communism, 1996, Beyond the Cultural Turn: New Directions in the Study of Society and Culture, 1999, (with George Breslauer) Russia in the New Century: Stability or Disorder, 2004, (with Thomas Gold) New Entrepreneurs of Europe and Asia: Russia, Eastern Europe and China, 2004; contbr. articles to profl. jours. Recipient Heldt prize in Slavic women's studies, 1991; AAUW fellow, 1979; Regents Faculty fellow, 1978, Fulbright Hays Faculty fellow, 1977, Internat. Rsch. and Exch. Bd. fellow, 1977, 88, Stanford U. Hoover Instn. nat. fellow, 1973-74, Guggenheim fellow, 1985, fellow Ctr. Advanced Study in Behavioral Scis., 1986-87, Pres.' Rsch. fellow in Humanities, 1991-92; grantee Am. Philos. Soc., 1979, Am. Coun. Learned Socs., 1976, 90-91. Mem. Am. Assn. Advancement Slavic Studies, Am. Sociol. Assn. Business E-Mail: vbonnell@berkeley.edu.

BONNELL-MIHALIS, PAMELA GAY, library director; b. Monterey, Calif., Feb. 2, 1948; d. Dewey L. and Marlyce I. (Hansen) Scoggins; m. Verneil S. Henerson, June 18, 1966 (div. 1971); 1 child, V. Samuel Henerson III; m. Chrisman E Bonnell, Mar. 2, 1974 (div. 1983); m. Hugh R. McElroy, Nov. 10, 1990 (div. 1996); m. Stephan S. Mihalis, Oct. 5, 2002. BA, Cameron U., Lawton, Okla., 1972; MLS, U. Okla., 1972—73; CPM, S.W. Tex. State U., 1998. Libr. Met. Libr. Sys., Oklahoma City, 1974—75, Office of City Mgr., Dallas, 1977—80; dir. audience devel. Dallas Symphony Orch., 1980—81; libr. Dallas Morning News, 1981—83; libr. mgr. Plano (Tex.) Pub. Libr. Sys., 1983—91; dir. libr. svcs. Waco-McLennan County Libr. System, Waco, Tex., 1992—2001; exec. dir. Elyria (Ohio) Pub. Libr., 2002—05. Author: (book) Fund Raising for Small Libraries, 1983; contbr. chapters to books, articles to profl. jours. Gala chair Easter Seal Soc., Dallas, 1988; bd. dirs. Women's Shelter, Plano, 1991; exec. bd. Am. Heart Assn., 1997—99; chmn. Lorain County Librs. Coun., 2003—04; trustee Freedom to Read Found., 1999—, liaison, 2004—; chmn. IFRT Oboler Award Com., 2004—; mem. program com. LAMA FRFDS, 2004—; mem. ops. com. Main St. Elyria, 2004—05; trustee Dallas Symphony Orch., 1981; bd. dirs. Salvation Army, 2003—; pres. Townbluff Homeowners Assn., Plano, 1984—90, Hippodrome Theatre Guild, 1996; treas. YWCA, 1995—96. Recipient Telecom. Excellence award, Ctrl. Tex. Edn., 1997. Mem.: ALA (councilor-at-large 1990—99, pres. Intellectual Freedom Round Table 1993—94, constn. and bylaws chair 1994—97, Shirley Olofson Meml. award 1974, cert. of Spl. Thanks 1986, John Phillip Immroth award 1990), Ctrl. Tex. Women's Alliance (bd. dirs. 1992—96), Tex. Libr. Assn. (chmn. Adminstrs. Roundtable 1994—95, trustee Leroy C. Merritt Trust Fund 1997—2000, chair intellectual freedom com. 2000—02, SIRS Intellectual Freedom award 1990), Tex. Mcpl. Librs. Dirs. (pres. 1994—95), Jr. League, Leadership Waco Alumni Assn., Rotary. Avocations: reading, travel. Home: 164 Arrow Ct Elyria OH 44035 Office: Elyria Pub Libr 320 Washington Ave Elyria OH 44035 Office Phone: 440-322-0119. Personal E-mail: pbonnell39@hotmail.com. Business E-Mail: pbonnell@elyria.lib.oh.us.

BONNELLY, CLAUDE, library director; b. Quebec, Can., Feb. 4, 1946; s. Emmanuel and Gabrielle (Lepine) B.; m. Lise Lebeuf, Dec. 29, 1969; children: Mathieu, Simon. PhB, U Laval, Quebec, 1966, Lic. Philosophy, 1968; MLS, U. Montreal, Que., Can., 1973. Ref. libr. Libr. U. Laval, Sainte-Foy, Que., 1968-75, head ref. dept., 1975-78, assoc. libr., 1978-88, dir., 1988—. Can. Inst. Hist. Microprodns., Ottawa, Can. Initiative on Digital Librs. Contbr. articles to profl. jours. Mem. Assn. Rsch. Librs., Can. Assn. Rsch. Librs. (dir. 1990-91), Assn. Pour L'Advancement des Scis. et des Techniquer de la Documentation, Corp. des Bibliothecaires Profls. du Que., Can. Libr. Soc., Internet Soc. Home: 929 Brown Quebec City PQ Canada G1S 2Z6 Office: U Laval Libr Pavillon Bonenfant Sainte-Foy PQ Canada G1K 7P4 Office Phone: 418-656-2131. Business E-Mail: claude.bonnelly@bibl.ulaval.ca.

BONNER, BILLY EDWARD, physics professor; b. Oak Grove, La., Dec. 12, 1939; s. James Wilbur and Julia (Deer) B. BS, La. Tech. U., 1961; MA, Rice U., 1963, PhD, 1965. Prin. scientific officer Rutherford High Energy Lab., Didcot, Berkshire, England, 1966-70; postdoctoral fellow U. Calif., Davis, 1971-72; physicist Los Alamos (N.Mex.) Nat. Lab., 1972-85; scientific assoc. CERN, Geneva, 1983-84; prof. physics Rice U., Houston, 1985—, chmn. dept. physics, 1986-91, dir. Bonner Nuclear Lab., 1987—. Editor 3 books; contbr. articles to profl. jours. Avocations: squash, fishing, cooking. Office: Rice Univ Bonner Nuclear Labs Houston TX 77005-1892 Office Phone: 713-348-4897. Business E-Mail: bonner@rice.edu.

BONNER, DARLENE E., minister, writer; b. Reed City, Mich., July 12, 1956; d. William Gilbert Washington and Margaret Louise Taylor, William P. Taylor (Stepfather) and Phyllis Marie Washington (Stepmother); m. Algin Bonner Jr., Sept. 24, 1994; children: Marcus Lamont Washington, Clinton Lee Washington, Antonio Leshawn Washington, William Lorenzo Tate. Grad., Oceanside Coll. Cosmetology, 1980; cert. cosmetolegy, Ferris State Coll., 1981. Lic. cosmetology State of Mich., 1982, cert. nurses aide State of Mich., 1996. Cert. nurses aide Hurley Home Care and Hospice, Flint, Mich., 1996—99; founder Bonnerhouse Pub. Inc., Flint, 2002—. Pres. Young Teen Prayer Warriors, Flint, Mich., 2000—02. Author (publisher): (book of poetry) Bible Rhymes and Revelations (na, na), (novel) Distractions Decoys and The Truth, (poetry series) Prayer Warriors. Ministry, tchr., vol. River Of God Tabernacle Min, Flint, 2002—03. Avocations: swimming, writing, travel. Office: Bonnerhouse Pub Inc 445 Harriet St Flint MI 48505

BONNER, FRANCIS TRUESDALE, chemist, educator, dean; b. Salt Lake City, Dec. 18, 1921; s. Walter Daniel and Grace (Gaylord) B.; m. Evelyn Hershkowitz, Jan. 17, 1946 (dec. 1990); children: Michael David, Joan Alisa (dec.), Rachel Pearl; m. M. Jane Carlberg, Dec. 31, 1994. BA, U. Utah, 1942; MS, Yale U., 1944, PhD, 1945. Chemist Manhattan Project S.A.M. Labs. Columbia U., 1944-46; chemist Clinton Labs., Oak Ridge, 1946-47; scientist Brookhaven Nat. Lab., Upton, N.Y., 1947-48, research collaborator, 1958-88; asst. prof. chemistry Bklyn. Coll., 1948-54; Carnegie vis. fellow Harvard, 1954-55; research phys. chemist Arthur D. Little, Inc., Cambridge, Mass., 1955-58; prof. dept. chemistry SUNY-Stony Brook, 1958—, founding chmn. dept., 1958-70, dean for internat. programs, 1983-86, prof. emeritus, 1992—. Cons. editor Addison-Wesley Pub. Co., Reading, Mass., 1956-77; Rockefeller Found. adviser on curriculum, instl. devel. Universidad Del Valle, Cali, Colombia, 1961-62, 64, Ford Found. adviser, 1968; Ford Found. adviser to Universidad de Antioquia, Medellin, Colombia, 1962-64; dir. N.Y. Met. Area Ctr. Chem. Edn. Materials Study for NSF 1961-62; mem. com. for chemistry Coll. Entrance Exam. Bd., 1962-63; mem. NSF-sponsored Adv. Coun. on Coll. Chemistry, 1967-70; mem. Coll. Proficiency Exam. Com. Chemistry, N.Y. State Edn. Dept., 1963-64, 66-70; NSF sr. postdoctoral fellow Svc. des Isotopes Stables, Centre d'Etudes Nucleaires de Saclay, Gif-Sur-Yvette, France, 1964-65; vis. scientist Swiss Fed. Inst. for Water Resources and Water Pollution Control, Swiss Fed. Inst. Tech., Zurich, 1973, Kings Coll. U. London, 1987; Nat. Acad. exch. visitor, Romania, 1975; mem. grants adv. panel Fund for Overseas Grants and Edn., 1968-76; bd. dirs. Rsch. Found. State U. N.Y., 1976-88; cons. L.I. Power Authority, 1998-2003. Author: (with Melba Phillips) Principles of Physical Science, 1957, 2d edit., 1971; Contbr. numerous articles profl. jours. Mem. Ind. Rev. Panel for Decommissioning of Shoreham Nuc. Power Sta., 1992-95; mem. bd. edn. Ctrl. Sch. Dist. 6, Huntington, N.Y., 1968-72. Fellow: AAAS; mem.: AAUP, Am. Chem. Soc., Sigma Xi. Home: PO Box 2063 Setauket NY 11733-0707 Office: State U NY Dept Chemistry Stony Brook NY 11794-3400

BONNER, GERALD ANTHONY, civil engineer, consultant; b. Wicklow, Ireland, Jan. 30, 1949; m. Alice Marie Coffey, July 3, 1980; children: Anne Francis, Neil Gerald, Cormac Richard, Sean Edmund. BA, U. of Dublin, 1970, B.Engring., 1971, MS, 1973, MA, M.Engring., U. of Dublin, 1980, PhD, 1985. Chartered engr., Instn. of Engrs. of Ireland, 1978, European Orgn. for Chartered Engrs., 1980, registered profl. engr. Sr. lectr. Dublin Inst. of Tech., 1980—87; chief geotech.l engr. Brown and Root Ltd., 1987—91; sr. exec. engr. Dublin Corp., Dublin, 1992—94; head of ground engring. Ministry of Def. and Aviation, Saudi Arabia, 1994—96; sr. exec. engr. Dublin Corp., Dublin, 1996—98, project mgr. for maj. city tunnel Ireland, 1999—2001; cons. for Am., European and mid. ea. projects Parsons Transp. Group, N.Y.C., 2001—. Contbr. numerous articles to profl. jours. Mem.: ASCE, Instn. of Engrs. of Ireland, FEANI, Am. Inst. of Transp. Engrs. Achievements include research in response of underground structures to static and dynamic loading using finite element numerical analyses. Office: 100 Broadway New York NY 10005 Office Phone: 00-30-4610-29825. Personal E-mail: gerald_bonner@hotmail.com.

BONNER, HERBERT DWIGHT, construction management educator; b. Lakewood, Ohio, Sept. 5, 1942; s. Herbert C. and Ruth (H.) B. Bonner; m. Marilyn Anne Seidel, Sept. 18, 1965 (dec.). BArch, Ohio State U., 1969, MArch, 1971. Registered architect, Ohio; cert. profl. constructor. Tng. engr. H.K. Ferguson Co., Cleve., 1961-62, U.S. Steel Corp., Cleve., 1962-64, Hausman Steel Corp., Grandview, Ohio, 1964-65; tng. architect Kellam & Foley Architects, Columbus, Ohio, 1965-68; rsch. assoc. bldg. rsch. lab. Ohio State U., Columbus, Ohio, 1968-71, asst. prof., 1971-74; prof. Columbus State C.C., 1974-95; owner Bonner Constrn. Svcs., Patagonia, Ariz., 1971—. Cons. Aubon Ednl. Svcs., Columbus, 1980-85; adj. faculty mem. Caiptal U., Columbus, 1986-95; exec. dir. Associated Two Yr. Sch. Constrn., Edmonds, Wash., 1989-95. Author: Building Plans and Working Drawings, 1981; editor: Scheduling Construction Projects, 1984, Construction Equipment Operators, 1992; contbr. articles to profl. jours. Trustee Am. Coun. for Constrn. Edn., Monroe, La., 1990-95. Recipient Disting. Svc. award Assn. Bus. and Profl. Women, 1982, Nat. Assn. Women in Constrn., 1984; grantee Dept. of Def., 1970-71, 1st Community Village, 1974, Owens Corning Fiberglass, 1981-82. Mem. AIA, Am. Inst. Constructors, Ohio Horeman's Coun., Tenn. Walking Horse Beaders and Exhibitors Assn., Mid-Ohio Walking Horse Assn., Hocking County Trail Blazers. Avocations: competitive horse riding and showing, endurance riding. Office: Bonner Constrn Svcs PO Box 700 Llano TX 78643 Office Phone: 325-248-0710. Business E-Mail: bonner@threeshoesranch.org.

BONNER, JACK WILBUR, III, psychiatrist, educator, administrator; b. Corpus Christi, Tex., July 30, 1940; s. Jack Wilbur and Irldene (Turner) B.; m. Myra Lynn Taylor; children: Jack Wilbur, IV, Katherine Lynn, Shelley Bliss AA, Del Mar Coll., Corpus Christi, 1960; BA with honors, U. Tex., Austin, 1961; MD, S.W. Med. Sch., U. Tex., Dallas, 1965. Diplomate Am. Bd. Psychiatry and Neurology. Intern U. Ark. Med. Center, 1965-66; resident Duke U. Med. Center, 1966-69; assoc. in psychiatry Highland Hosp. divsn. Duke U. Med. Center, Asheville, N.C., 1971, asst. prof. psychiatry, 1972-80, dir. outpatient services, 1972-75, med. dir., 1975-81; chmn. bd. dirs., CEO, med. dir. Highland Hosp., Asheville, N.C., 1981-92; med. dir. The Oaks Psychiat. Health Sys., Austin, Tex., 1992-93, exec. med. dir., 1993-94; med. dir. Behavioral Health Svcs. Greenville (S.C.) Hosp. Sys. Univ. Med. Ctr., 1994—, adminstr. Behavioral Health Svcs., 1996—2000, acad. chair, 1999—. Asst. clin. prof. Duke U. Med. Ctr., Durham, N.C., 1982-87, asst. cons. prof. psychiatry, 1987—; clin. assoc. prof. U. N.C. Sch. Medicine, Chapel Hill, 1986-92, Quillen-Dishner Coll. Medicine, Johnson City, Tenn., 1989-92, U. Tex. Health Sci. Ctr., San Antonio, 1993-94, U. S.C. Sch. Medicine, Columbia, 1995-2004, prof. clin. neuropsychiatry and behavioral sci., 2004—. Author: (with others) The Psychology of Discipline, 1983, Unmasking the Psychopath: Antisocial Personality and Related Syndromes, 1986; contbr. articles to profl. jours. Chmn. bd. dirs. The Highland Found., 1980-93; bd. dirs. Western N.C. Med. Peer Rev. Found., 1975-78; trustee La Amistad Found., Maitland, Fla., 1985-95, N.C. Symphony, 1987-92, Cooper Riis Found., Mill Spring, N.C., 2000—. Fellow APA (Disting. Life Fellow; trustee 1999-2005, chair fin. and budget com. 2002—, Warren Williams award 2002, Nancy C.A. Roeske cert. of recognition for excellence in med. student edn. 2005), So. Psychiat. Assn. (v.p. 1984-85, chmn. bd. regents 1988-89, pres. 1992-93), Am. Coll. Psychiatrists (treas. 1992-95, 2d v.p. 1999-2000, 1st v.p. 2000-01, pres. 2002-03, E.B. Bowis award 2000); mem. AMA, Nat. Assn. Psychiat. Health Sys. (trustee 1989-94, 1st v.p. 1990-91, pres.-elect 1991-92, pres. 1992-93), Am. Group Psychotherapy Assn., Nat. Acads. Practice, Buncombe County (NC) Med. Soc. (pres. 1983), NC Psychiat. Assn. (pres. 1982-83), Nat. Anorexic Aid Soc. (nat. anorexia adv. coun. 1979-86), So. Med. Assn. (sec. sect. on neurology, neurosurgery and psychiatry 1977-80, chmn.-elect 1980-81, chmn. 1981-82), Ctrl. Neuropsychiat. Hosp. Assn. (councillor 1981-85, pres. 1983-84), Group Advancement Psychiatry (treas. 1991-99, pres. 2001-03), U. Tex. Southwestern Med. Sch. Alumni Assn. (bd. dir. 1988-95, pres. 1989-91), Benjamin Rush Soc., Phi Theta Kappa Home: Four Brookside Way Greenville SC 29605-1212 Office: Greenville Hosp Sys Behavioral Health Svcs 701 Grove Rd Greenville SC 29605-5601 Office Phone: 864-455-7834. Business E-Mail: jbonner@ghs.org.

BONNER, JOHN TYLER, biology professor; b. N.Y.C., May 12, 1920; s. Paul Hyde and Lilly Marguerite (Stehli) B.; m. Ruth Anna Graham, July 11, 1942; children: Rebecca, Jonathan Graham, Jeremy Tyndall, Andrew Duncan. Grad., Phillips Exeter Acad., 1937; BSc, Harvard U., 1941, MA, 1942, PhD (Jr. fellow 1942, 46-47), 1947; DSc, Middlebury Coll., 1970; LLD, Concordia U.; DLitt, Univ. Coll. of Cape Breton, 2005. Asst. to assoc. prof. Princeton U., 1947-58, prof., 1958-90, emeritus prof., 1990—, chmn. dept. biology, 1965-77, 83-84, 87-88. Lectr. embryology Marine Biol. Lab., Woods Hole, Mass., 1951-52; spl. lectr. U. London, 1957, Bklyn. Coll., 1966; Arnold Bernhard vis. prof. Williams Coll., 1989; Raman prof. Indian Acad. Scis., 1990; trustee Biol. Abstracts, 1958-63; mem. bd. editors Princeton U. Press, 1965-68, 71, trustee, 1976-82. Author: Morphogenesis, 1952, Cells and Societies, 1955, The Evolution of Development, 1958, The Cellular Slime Molds, 1959, The Cellular Slime Molds, rev. edit., 1967, The Ideas of Biology, 1962, Size and Cycle, 1965, The Scale of Nature, 1969, On Development, 1974, The Evolution of Culture in Animals, 1980; author: (with T.A. McMahon) On Life and Size, 1983; author: The Evolution of Complexity, 1988, Researches on Cellular Slime Molds, 1991, Life Cycles, 1993, Sixty Years of Biology, 1996, First Signals, 2000, Lives of a Biologist, 2002; editor: Growth and Form, 1961, Evolution and Development, 1981; assoc. editor: Am. Scientist, 1961—69, mem. editl. bd.: Am. Naturalist, 1958—60, 1966—68, Jour. Gen. Physiology, 1962—69, Growth, 1955—89, Differentiation, 1976—90, Oxford Surveys in Evolutionary Biology, 1982—93. Pvt. to 1st lt. USAC, 1942-46; staff aero. med. lab. Wright Field, Dayton, Ohio. Sheldon traveling fellow Panama, 1941; Rockefeller traveling fellow France, 1953; Guggenheim fellow Scotland, 1958, 71-72; recipient Selman A. Waksman award for contbns. to microbiology Theobold Smith Soc.; NSF sr. postdoctoral fellow, 1963 Fellow Am. Acad. Arts and Scis., Indian Acad. Scis. (hon.); mem. NAS, Am. Soc. Naturalists, Soc. Growth and Devel., Am. Philos. Soc., Phi Beta Kappa, Sigma Xi. Business E-Mail: jtbonner@princeton.edu.

BONNER, JOSIAH ROBINS, JR., (JO BONNER), congressman; b. Selma, Ala., Nov. 19, 1959; s. Josiah Robins Bonner; m. Janée Lambert Bonner; children: Jennifer Lee, Josiah Robins III. JB, U. Ala., 1982. Chief of staff U.S. Rep. Sonny Callahan, press sec., 1984, Congl. press sec., 1985; mem. U.S. Congress from 1st Ala. dist., 2003—. Mem. pres. adv. coun. U. Mobile; mem. bd. cmty. advisors Jr. League Mobile. Named Outstanding Alumnus in Pub. Rels., U. Ala. Coll. Comm., 2000. Mem.: Mobile Area C. of C. (bd. dirs.), U. Ala. Alumni Assn. (Mobile chpt., bd. dirs.), Leadership Mobile (bd. dirs.), Rotary Club (bd. dirs.). Republican. Episcopalian. Office: 315 Cannon HOB Washington DC 20515-0101*

BONNER, ROBERT CLEVE, federal agency administrator, lawyer; b. Wichita, Kans., Jan. 29, 1942; s. Benjamin Joseph and Caroline (Kirkwood) B.; m. Kimiko Tanaka, Oct. 11, 1969; 1 child, Justine M. BA magna cum laude, Md. U., 1963; JD, Georgetown U., 1966. Bar: D.C. 1966, Calif. 1967, Ct. Appeals (4th, 5th, 9th, 10th cirs.), U.S. Supreme Ct. Law clk. to judge U.S. Dist. Ct., L.A., 1966-67; asst. U.S. atty. U.S. Atty's Office (cen. dist.) Calif., L.A., 1971-75, U.S. atty., 1984-89; judge U.S. Dist. Ct. (cen. dist.) Calif., L.A., 1989-90; ptnr. Kadison, Pfaelzer, et al, Los Angeles, 1975-84; dir. Drug Enforcement Adminstrn., Washington, 1990-93; ptnr. Gibson, Dunn & Crutcher, L.A., 1993—2001; commr. U.S. Customs Svc. & Border Protection, Washington, 2001—. Chair Calif. Commn. on Jud. Performance, 1997-99, co-chair, Calif. Lawyers for Bush-Cheney, 2000. Served to lt. comdr. JAGC, USN, 1967-70 Fellow Am. Coll. Trial Lawyers, Fed. Bar Assn. (pres. Los Angeles chpt. 1982-83); mem. L.A. C. of C. (bd. dirs. 1999-2001), Calif. Bar Assn., DC Bar Assn. Republican. Roman Catholic. Office: US Customs Svc Hdqr 1300 Pennsylvania Ave NW Washington DC 20229

BONNER, ROBERT WILLIAM, retired lawyer; b. Vancouver, B.C., Can., Sept. 10, 1920; s. Benjamin York and Emma Louise (Weir) B.; m. Barbara Newman, June 16, 1942; children: Barbara Carolyn Massie, Robert York, Elizabeth Louise McPhee. BA in Econs. and Polit. Sci, U. B.C., 1942, LLB, 1948. Bar: B.C. 1948, created Queen's counsel 1952. With firm Clark Wilson White Clark & Maguire, Vancouver, 1948-52; atty. gen. Province of B.C., 1952-68; sr. v.p. adminstrn. MacMillan Bloedel Ltd., 1968-70, exec. v.p. adminstrn., 1970-71, vice chmn., 1971-72, pres., CEO, 1972-73, chmn. bd., 1973-74, ret., 1974; chmn. B.C. Hydro & Power Authority, 1976-85; ptnr. Bonner & Fouks, 1974-84, Robertson, Ward, Suderman, Vancouver, 1985-89. Mem. B.C. Legislature, 1952-69; mem. Energy Supplies Allocation Bd., bd. dirs. Served to maj. Royal Can. Army, 1942-45; lt. col. Res. (ret.). Mem. Can. Bar Assn., Law Soc. B.C. (life bencher), Masons, Vancouver Club, Union (Vcitoria) Club, Delta Upsilon. Social Credit Party. Home: 5679 Newton Wynd Vancouver BC Canada V6T 1H6 Office: Box 18162 2225 W 41st Ave Vancouver BC Canada V6M 2A3 Fax: 604-264-6142. E-mail: rwbonner@shaw.ca.

BONNER, WALTER JOSEPH, lawyer; b. N.Y.C., Nov. 18, 1925; s. Walter John and Marie Elizabeth (Guerin) B.; m. Maureen O'Malley; 1 child, Justin R.; children from previous marriage: Kevin P., Keith M., Barbara A., Susan E. AB cum laude, Cath. U. Am., 1951; JD, Georgetown U., 1955. Bar: U.S. Supreme Ct., D.C., Va. Law clk. to judge U.S. Ct. Appeals D.C. Circuit, 1954-55; judge U.S. Dist. Ct., Washington, 1955-56; asst. U.S. dist. atty. for D.C., 1956-60; ptnr. firm Crowell & Moring, LLP, Washington. Adj. prof. Georgetown U. Law Ctr., 1957-58, 67-83. Trustee Lawrence E. Dean Meml. Scholarship Fund, Georgetown U. Med. Ctr. Served with USNR, 1943-85, capt. Res. ret. Fellow Am. Coll. Trial Lawyers; mem. ABA, Fed, Bar Assn., Bar Assn. of D.C., Va. State Bar, Va. Trial Lawyers Assn., Res. Officers Assn., Naval Res. Lawyers Assn., Naval Res. Assn., Phi Delta Phi. Clubs: Officers and Faculty (U.S. Naval Acad.). Office: Crowell & Moring 1001 Pennsylvania Ave NW Washington DC 20004-2595 E-mail: wbonner@cromor.com.

BONNEVILLE, KATHERINE ANN, human resources specialist, consultant; b. Duluth, Minn., Apr. 21, 1960; d. Charles Albert and Patricia Jean Bonneville; children: Daniel Thomas Barthell, Sarah JoAnn Barthell. BA in Psychology, Sociology, U. Minn., Duluth, 1982; MA in Indsl. Rels., U. Minn., 1986. Compensation mgr. ING Group (formerly NWNL Co. Inc.), Mpls., 1984—91; dir. compensation NW Airlines, St. Paul, 1991—99; compensation practice leader Orgnl. Concepts Internat., Mpls., 1999—. Mem.: Nat. Assn. Stock Plan Profls., WorldatWork. Avocations: reading, travel, painting. Office: Organizational Concepts International 730 2nd Avenue South Suite 730 Minneapolis MN 55402 E-mail: kbonneville@oci-hr.com.

BONNEVILLE, RICHARD BRIGGS, retired gas industry executive; b. Chgo., July 15, 1942; s. Alfred Briggs and Grace Estelle (Burke) Bonneville; m. Mary Ann E. Pittman, July 17, 1976; children: Ann M., John B. BSME, U. Notre Dame, 1964; MBA, Harvard U., 1967. Project engr. Hamilton Std. divsn. United Techs., 1964—65; asst. to pres. Strathmore Paper divsn. Hammermill Paper, Springfield, Mass., 1966; mgr. planning Union Oil Co., Schaumburg, Ill., 1967—72; asst. to exec. v.p. Santa Fe Industries, Inc., Chgo., 1972—77, mgr. planning, 1977—79, dir. planning, 1979—84; corp. sec. Santa Fe So. Pacific Corp., 1984—88; v.p. planning Santa Fe Energy Resources, Inc., Houston, 1988—95; ret., 1995. Mem.: Pi Tau Sigma, Tau Beta Pi. Home: 920 Cranberry Hill Ct Houston TX 77079-5010

BONNEY, HAL JAMES, JR., federal judge; b. Norfolk, Va., Aug. 27, 1929; s. Hal J. and Mary (Shackelford) B.; m. Marie McBee, July 4, 1963 (div. 1979); children: David James, John Wesley. BA, U. Richmond, 1951, MA, 1953; JD, Coll. William and Mary, 1969. Bar: Va. 1969. Instr. Norfolk public schs., 1951-61; supt. Douglas MacArthur Acad., 1961-67; practiced law, 1969-71; law clk. U.S. Dist. Ct., 1969; prof. U. Va., 1964-71, Coll. William and Mary, 1969-71; U.S. bankruptcy judge Norfolk, 1971—96; ret., 1996. Adj. prof. law Regent U. Law Sch., 1987—97; prodr. Hal Bonney Prodns. Author: Overturning Applecarts, 2002. Tchr. Wesleymen Bible Class Sta. WTAR-AM, 1962-98, tchr. emeritus, 1998; tchr. Good News TV Network, 1989—; treas. Wesleymen Found., Inc., Billy Graham Crusades, 1974-76; pres. adv. coun. CBN U., 1986-95; vice-chmn. Va. Meth. Bd. Edn., Inc., 1991-99; bd. visitors Duke Div. Sch., 1991—; 1st v.p., bd. dirs. Norfolk Union Mission, 1994—; mem. City of Norfolk Task Force on Pub. Housing, 1995-96; advisor Film Sch., Regent U., 1996-2000, assoc. prodr. 2000-04; mem. City of Norfolk Parks and Recreation, commr. 2003-, chmn. 2003-; vice chair rules com. Va. United Meth. conf., 1996-2004; bd. ordained ministry United Meth. Ch., Va; active World Affairs Coun. Recipient S.A.R. Good Citizenship medal, Woodmen of the World History medal, U. Richmond Gold medal, George Washington honor medal Freedoms Found., Alli award Cultural Alliance Greater Hampton Rds., 1998; Judge Hal Bonney Day named in honor by City of Norfolk, Jan. 27, 1998. Mem. Nat. Conf. Bankruptcy Judges (pres. 1983-84, chmn. editl. bd. The Am. Bankruptcy Law Jour.), Va. State Bar, Norfolk and Portsmouth Bar Assn., Nat. Film Soc., Am. Film Inst. (Premiere Circle), Brit. Film Inst., Am. Cinematheque (moving picture ball benefit com.), James Kent Inn of Ct. (hon., pres. 1994-96), Phi Alpha Theta, Pi Sigma Alpha, Phi Alpha Delta, Masons, Shriners, Elks, Kiwanis (dir.). Home: 1357 Windsor Point Rd Norfolk VA 23509-1311 Office: The Wesleymen 5442 Tidewater Dr Norfolk VA 23509 Office Phone: 757-853-4770. Personal E-mail: bonney@cox.net.

BONNEY, RICK, science educator; b. Melrose, Mass., Sept. 20, 1954; s. Richard and Joan Morton Bonney; m. Judy Burrill, June 20, 1981; children: Jessie Bonney-Burrill, Sean Bonney-Burrill. MPS, Cornell U., 1979—81. Sr. editor Cornell Lab of Ornithology, Ithaca, NY, 1981—89, dir. of edn. and citiizen sci., 1989—2004, dir., program devel. and evaluation, 2005—. Editor: (book) Cornell Handbook of Bird Biology. Bd. mem. Vitamin L Project, Ithaca, 1999—2005. Citizen Sci. Devel., NSF, 1992—2005, Visitor Ctr. Devel., Cornell Lab of Ornithology, 2001—05, Curriculum Devel., 1995—2005. Achievements include development of Cornell Lab of Orntithology citizen science program. Office: Cornell Lab of Ornithology 159 Sapsucker Woods Rd Ithaca NY 14850 Office Phone: 607-254-2442.

BONNEY, SAMUEL ROBERT, lawyer; b. Dallas, Mar. 10, 1943; s. Herbert Staats, Jr. and Anna Margaret (Hudnall) B.; m. Margaret Reynolds Palms, Nov. 3, 1984; 1 child, Anna Beth; children from previous marriage: Samuel Robert, II, Heather Noel, Sarah Emily. BA, Austin Coll., Sherman, Tex., 1965; JD, U. Tex., 1968. Bar: Tex. 1968. Ptnr. Bonney & Bonney, Dallas, 1968—. Served with AUS, 1969. Mem. Tex. Bar Assn., Dallas Bar Assn. Clubs: Dallas Country. Office: 3838 Oak Lawn Ave Ste 800 Dallas TX 75219-4509 E-mail: bblaw@swbell.net.

BONNIE, RICHARD JEFFREY, law educator, lawyer, consultant; b. Richmond, Va., Aug. 22, 1945; s. Herbert Herman and Helene Selma (Berz) B.; m. Kathleen Ford, June 15, 1967; children: Joshua Ford, Zachary Andrew, Jessica Katherine. BA, Johns Hopkins U., 1966; LLB, U. Va., 1969. Var: Va. 1969, U.S. Dist. Ct. (ea. dist.) Va. 1969; U.S. Ct. Appeals (4th cir.) 1969, U.S. Supreme Ct. 1986. Asst. prof. law U. Va., Charlottesville, 1969-70, assoc. prof., 1973-77, prof., 1977-87, John S. Battle prof., 1987—; dir. Inst. Law, Psychiatry, and Pub. Policy, 1979—, prof. psychiatry, 2001—. Vis. fellow Inst. Criminology, Cambridge U., 1977; vis. prof. Cornell Law Sch., 1993-94, Parsons visitor Sydney Law Sch., 2005; assoc. dir. nat. Commn. Marijuana and Drug Abuse, 1971-73; reporter Nat. Conf. Commrs. on Uniform State Laws, 1972-74; cons. Spl. Action Office for Drug Abuse Prevention Exec. Office of the Pres., 1973-75; spl. asst. to U.S. Atty. Gen., 1975; mem. and sec. Nat. Adv. Coun. on Drug Abuse, 1975-80; mem. Com. on Problem of Drug Dependence, Inc., 1979-84; charter fellow Coll. Problems of Drug Dependence, 1992—; cons. Am. Psychiat. Assn., Coun. Psychiatry and Law, 1979—; mem. U.S. State Dept. Del. to investigate psychiat. practices in the Soviet Union, 1989; mem. World Psychiat. Assn. rev. team to investigate Soviet psychiatry, 1991; mem. adv. bd. permanent coordination office Reforms in psychiatry in Ctrl. and Ea. Europe, former Soviet Union, 1993—; bd. dirs. Geneva Initiative on Psychiatry, 1996-2005, Global Initiative on Psychiatry, 2005—; pres. Am. Friends of Geneva Initiatives on Psychiatry, 1997—, mem. MacArthur Found. Network on Mental Health and the Law, 1988-96; bd. dirs. Va. Capital Representation Resource Ctr., 1994-97, 2002—; mem. MacArthur Found. Network on Mandated Treatment, 2000—; mem. Max Plank Network on Aging, 2005—; co-chair, bd. dirs. Physicians and Lawyers for Nat. Drug Policy, 2004—; steering com. underage drinking Nat. Inst. Alcohol Abuse and Alcoholism, 2004—; mem. nat. commn. diversion and abuse of prescription Ctr. Addiction and Substance Abuse, 2003-04. Author: The Marijuana Conviction: The History of Marijuana Prohibition in the United States, 1974, 2d edit. 1999, Legal Aspects of Drug Dependence, 1975, Psychiatrists and the Legal Process: Diagnosis and Debate, 1977, Marijuana Use and Criminal Sanctions: Essays in the Theory and Practice of Decriminalization, 1980, Criminal Law: Cases and Materials, 1982, 2d edit., 1986, The Trial of John W. Hinckley, Jr.: A Case Study in the Insanity Defense, 1986, rev. edit., 2000, Criminal Law, 1997, 2d edit., 2004, Growing Up Tobacco Free, 1994, Mental Disorder, Work Disability and the Law, 1997, Reducing the Burden of Injury, 1999, The Evolution of Mental Health Law, 2001, Elder Mistreatment, 2002, Adjudicative Competence, 2002, Reducing Underage Drinking, 2003. Chmn. Va. Human Rights Com., Dept. mental Health and Mental Retardation, 1979-85; bd. dirs. Coll. on Problem of Drug Dependence, 1996-2000; mem. Steering Com. Underage Drinking, Nat. Inst. Alcohol Abuse and Alcoholism, 2005-, Comm. Increasing Rates of Organ Donation, 2005-, Inst. Criminology fellow Cambridge U., 1977. Fellow: Va. Law Found.; mem.: NAS (nat. assoc.), ABA (criminal justice-mental health stds. project adv. bd. 1981—87, task force on mental illness and the death penalty 2003—05), Nat. Inst. on Alcohol Abuse and Alcoholism (mem. steering com. on underage drinking 2005—), Inst. Medicine (Yarmolinsky medal 2002), Am. Acad. Psychiat. Law (Amicus award 1994), World Psychiat. Assn. (rev. team to investigate Soviet psychiatry 1991), Va. Bar Assn. (chmn. com. mentally disabled 1981—90, criminal law sect. coun. 1992—96), Am. Psychiat. Assn. (Isaac Ray award 1998, Spl. Presdl. Commendation 2003), Nat. Rsch. Coun. (com. on data and rsch. for policy on illicit drugs 1998—2000, chair com. elder abuse and neglect 2001—02, com. on law and justice 2002—, chair com. underage drinking 2002—, exec. com. divsn. com. behavioral and social scis. and edn. 2003—), Inst. Medicine of NAS (bd. neurosci. and behavioral health 1992—2001, vice chair com. preventing nicotine dependence in children and youth 1993—94, chair com. on opportunities in drug abuse rsch. 1995—96, membership com. 1995—98, chair com. injury prevention control 1997—98, com. to assess sci. base for tobacco harm reduction 1999—2001, com. to assess sys. for protection of human rsch. subjects 2000—02, chair com. to propose strategy to prevent/reduce underage drinking 2002—03, chair com. on reducing tobacco use 2004—, com. on increasing rates of organ donation 2005—). Office: U Va Sch Law 580 Massie Rd Charlottesville VA 22903 Business E-Mail: rjb6f@virginia.edu.

BONNIE, SHELBY W., computer company executive; BS in Commerce with distinction, U. Va.; MBA, Harvard U. Mng. dir. Tiger Mgmt.; CFO CNET Networks, Inc., San Francisco, 1996-97; CEO CNET Networks Inc., San Francisco, 1999—; COO CNET: The Computer Network, San Francisco, 1997-99. Office: CNET Networks Inc 235 2nd St San Francisco CA 94105-3124 Office Phone: 415-344-2000. Office Fax: 415-395-9207.

BONO, MARY WHITAKER, congresswoman; b. Cleve., Oct. 24, 1961; d. Clay and Karen Whitaker; m. Sonny Bono, Feb. 1986 (dec.); children: Chesare Elan, Chianna Maria; m. Glenn Baxley, Nov. 2001. BFA in Art History, U. So. Calif., 1984. Cert. personal fitness instr. Mem. U.S. Congress from 44th Calif. dist., 1998—; mem. energy and commerce com. Bd. dirs. Palm Springs Internat. Film Festival. Active D.A.R.E. Program, Olive Crest Home Abused Children, Tiempos de Los Ninos. Named Woman of the Yr., San Gorgonio (Calif.) chpt. Girl Scouts U.S., 1993. Republican. Avocations: outdoor activities, computer technology. Office: US House of Reps 405 Cannon Ho Office Bldg Washington DC 20515-0545*

BONO, (PAUL HEWSON), singer, songwriter; b. Dublin, May 10, 1960; m. Alison Stewart, 1982; children: Jordan, Memphis Eve, Elijah, John Abraham. Singer, songwriter U2, 1978—. Mng. dir. Elevation Partners, Menlo Park, Calif., 2004—. Albums with U2 Boy, 1980, October, 1981, War, 1983, Under a Blood Red Sky, 1983, The Unforgettable Fire, 1984, Wide Awake in America, 1985, The Joshua Tree, 1987 (Grammy award best album, best performance by group), Rattle and Hum, 1988, Achtung Baby, 1991 (Grammy award best rock group vocal, 1993), Zooropa, 1993 (Grammy nomination, Best Alternative album), Pop, 1997, The Best of 1980-1990, 1998, Million Dollar Hotel, 2000, All That You Can't Leave Behind, 2000 (Grammy awards: album of the year, best pop performance, best rock performance, best rock album, 2001), The Best of 1990-2000, 2002, Hasta la Vista Babe!: Live From Mexico City, 2000, How to Dismantle an Atomic Bomb, 2004; films/videos: Under a Blood Red Sky: U2 Live at Red Rocks, 1984, Rattle and Hum, 1988; actor in films including U2: Rattle & Hum, 1988, In Darkest Hollywood: Cinema & Apartheid, 1993, Entropy, 1999; composer of film scores including They Call it an Accident, 1982, In the Name of The Father, 1993, Golden Eye, 1995; illustrator (with daughters), Peter and the Wolf, 2003. Founder, spokesman Debt, Aids, Trade in Africa (DATA), 1999—. Named to Music Hall of Fame, UK, 2004; recipient Freedom award, Nat. Civil Rights Museum, 2004, TED prize, Tech., Entertainment, Design Conf., 2004, Grammy Award for Best Rock Performance by a Duo or Group (Vertigo), 2005. Achievements include inducted into Rock and Roll Hall of Fame as mem. of U2, 2005. Office: Regine Moylett Publicity 145A Ladbroke Grove London W10 6HJ England Address: Interscope Records 2220 Colorado Ave Santa Monica CA 90404

BONOMETTI, ROBERT JOHN, technology management and strategy executive; b. N.Y.C., Sept. 29, 1953; s. Joseph Patrick and Fortunata Mary (Barba) B.; m. Virginia Anne Scyphers, Oct. 26, 1997; stepchildren: Jessica, Michael. BS summa cum laude, U.S. Mil. Acad., 1975; MS in Physics, MIT, 1981, PhD in Physics, 1985; MBA, L.I. U., 1987. Registered profl. engr., Va. Assoc. prof. physics U.S. Mil. Acad., West Point, NY, 1985-88; program mgr. Def. Advanced Rsch. Projects Agy., Arlington, Va., 1988-93; sr. policy analyst White House Sci. and Tech. Office, Washington, 1993-95; exec. dir. tech. strategy Bell Atlantic Corp., Arlington, Va., 1995-98; pres. MGB Enterprises, LLC, Winchester, Va., 1998—; byrd prof. info. sys. and computer tech. Shenandoah U., Byrd Sch. Bus., 1999—. Industry adv. bd. Ctr. for Satellite and Hybrid Comm. Networks, U. Md., 1994-2000; chmn. rev. com. commercialization of space NASA, Washington, 1996; exec. dir. info. and comm. R & D com. Nat. Sci. and Tech. Coun., Washington, 1993-95; adj. prof. various univs., 1981—; chmn. Tek-Xam content exec. com. Va. Found. for Ind. Colls., 2000-01 Contbr. articles to profl. jours. Active animal rights and environ. orgns. Lt. col. U.S. Army, 1975—95. Recipient Laurel award Aviation Week and Space Tech., 1990; Sci. and Tech. fellow Dept. Commerce, 1993-94; Hertz Found. fellow, 1981-85. Mem. IEEE (sr.), AIAA (sr., Van Allen Conf. award, 1993), Am. Phys. Soc., Am. Astron. Soc. Avocations: music, guitar, weightlifting, tennis, running. Home and Office: Majestik Global Bus Enterprises LLC 260 Golds Hill Rd Winchester VA 22603-3129 Office Phone: 540-545-7272. Personal E-mail: athenswv@aol.com. Business E-Mail: rbonomet@su.edu.

BONOMI, FERNE GATER, public relations executive; b. Council Bluffs, Iowa, July 27, 1923; d. Roy Winfield and Leona Hazel (Bays) Gater; m. Robert Foch Bonomi, Sept. 3, 1949 (div. 1974); children: Robert Duff, David Scott; m. Wayne P. Davis, Apr. 20, 1991. BA magna cum laude, U. Iowa, 1948. Editor Silver City (Iowa) Times, 1940-41; reporter, photographer, Sunday editor Cedar Rapids (Iowa) Gazette, 1943-47; dir. pub. info. Iowa Devel. Commn., Des Moines, 1950-51; pub. info. officer Gov. William S. Beardsley, Des Moines, 1951-53; v.p. Bonomi Assocs. Inc., Des Moines, 1954-72; adminstr. Mid-Iowa Drug Abuse Coun., Des Moines, 1972-74; cons. Plain Talk Pub. Co., Des Moines, 1974-75; communications dir. Iowa Assn. Sch. Bds., Des Moines, 1975-86; owner, operator Bonomi & Co., Des Moines, 1986—. Chmn. pubs. evaluation Am. C. of C. Execs., Washington, 1977-81; mem. Universal Accreditation Bd., 2003—; presenter in field. Author: Show Me A Man, 1969; editor Iowa Sch. Bd. Dialogue, 1975-86; assoc. editor Leader's Mag., 1964-72. Active Gov.'s Com. on Employment Handicapped, 1968—74; chmn. comms. Des Moines Area Religious Coun., 1980—82. Named Iowa Sch. Communicator of Yr., Iowa Sch. Pub. Rels. Assn., 1997. Fellow Pub. Rels. Soc. Am. (developer mentoring program 1994-97, chmn. 1995, pres. Iowa chpt. 1980-82, chmn. accreditation 1982-2001, writer nat. curriculum for accreditation 1998, rev. 2003, Outstanding Contbr. award 1983, commendation for meaningful rsch. Bronze Anvil competition 1997); mem. Nat. Sch. Pub. Rels. Assn. (cert., Gold medallion 1987), Phi Beta Kappa, Alpha Delta Pi (nat. editor 1959-62, Outstanding Alumna award 1977). Mem. United Ch. Christ. Avocations: canoeing, horseback riding, church choir, dance, theater. Office: Bonomi & Co 1003 Kennedy St Ames IA 50010-4247 Office Phone: 515-233-1493.

BONOSARO, CAROL ALESSANDRA, professional society administrator, retired federal agency administrator; b. New Brunswick, N.J., Feb. 16, 1940; d. Rudolph William and Elizabeth Ann (Betsko) B.; m. Donald D. Kummerfeld, Sept. 8, 1962 (div. Jan. 1970); m. Athanasios Chalkiopoulos, Nov. 21, 1976 (div. Dec. 1991); 1 child, Melissa. BA, Cornell U., 1961; postgrad., George Washington U., 1961-62. Analytical statistician Office Mgmt. and Budget, Exec. Office of Pres., Washington, 1961-66; asst. dir. fed. programs div. U.S. Commn. on Civil Rights, Washington, 1966-68, dir. Office Fed. Programs, 1968-69, dir. tech. assistance div., 1969-71, spl. asst. to staff dir., 1972, dir. women's rights program, 1972-79, asst. staff dir. for program planning and evaluation, 1979-80, asst. staff dir. congressional and public affairs, 1980-86; pres. Sr. Execs. Assn., Washington, 1986—. Mem. adv. com. Asian Am. Govt. Execs. Network, 1996—; mem. Nat. Partnership Coun., 1997-2001. Vice chmn. Nat. Com. on Asian Wives of U.S. Servicemen, 1975-85; pres. Catholics for a Free Choice, 1980-83; chmn. bd. dirs. William Jump Found., 2003—. Mem. Exec. Women in Govt., Sr. Exec. Assn. (dir. 1981-86, chmn. bd. dirs. 1983-86) Democrat. Home: 5504 Jordan Rd Bethesda MD 20816-1366 Office: Sr Execs Assn PO Box 44808 Washington DC 20026-4808 E-mail: SEAPresident@seniorexecs.org.

BONOVITZ, SHELDON M., lawyer; BS, U. Pa., 1959; JD, Harvard U., 1962. Bar: DC 1963, Pa. 1965. Ptnr. Duane Morris LLP, Phila., 1969—, chmn. tax dept., 1972-93, mem. partners bd., 1976—, vice chmn., 1994-97, chmn., 1998—. also CEO. Former atty.-advisor to Hon. Arnold Raum, US Tax Ct.; bd. dirs. Comcast Corp., eRsch. Tech., Inc.; lectr. in law U. Pa. Law Sch., 1979-86, 93, 95, Temple U. Sch. Law, 1967-78; spkr. in field. Trustee Dolfinger-McMahon Charitable Trust, Christian R. and Mary F. Lindback Found.; bd. trustees Curtis Inst. Music, Phila. Mus. Art; bd. mem. Phila. Orch.; bd. trustees Free Liberty of Phila. Found. Fellow Am. Coll. Tax Counsel; mem. ABA (chair com. on corp. tax 1987-88), Pa. Bar Assn. (tax law sect.), Phila. Bar Assn. (chair tax sect. 1987-88), Am. Law Inst. (tax adv. group). Office: Duane Morris LLP One Liberty Pl Philadelphia PA 19103-7396 Office Phone: 215-979-1972. Office Fax: 215-979-1971. Business E-Mail: smbonovitz@duanemorris.com.

BONOW, ROBERT OGDEN, medical educator; b. Camden, N.J., Mar. 11, 1947; m. Patricia Jeanne Hitchens, Sept. 12, 1982; children: Robert Hitchens, Samuel Crawford. BS in Chem. Engring. magna cum laude, Lehigh U., Bethelehem, Pa., 1969; MD, U. Pa., Phila., 1973. Diplomate Am. Bd. Internal Medicine, subspecialty bd. on cardiovascular disease. Intern in medicine Hosp. U. Pa., Phila., 1973-74, resident, 1974-76; clin. assoc. cardiology br. Nat. Heart, Lung and Blood Inst., Bethesda, Md., 1976-79, sr. investigator, attending physician cardiology br., 1979-92, chief nuclear cardiology sect., 1980-92, dep. chief, 1989-92; Goldberg prof. medicine Northwestern U. Med. Sch., Chgo., 1992—; chief divsn. cardiology Northwestern Meml. Hosp., Chgo., 1992—; attending physician dept. medicine VA Lakeside Med. Ctr., Chgo., 1993—2003, Evanston (Ill.) Hosp., 1994—. Pfizer vis. prof. cardiovasc. medicine Yale U., 1992, U. Mass., 1998; AHA/ACC Task Force on Practice Guidelines Com. on Cardiac Radlonuclide Imaging, 1993-95; chair com. on mgmt. of patents with valvular heart disease, 1996—; vis. prof. various univs., 1982-99; mem. bd. extramural adivsors NHLBI, NIH, 2000—; mem. clin. rsch. roundtable Inst. of Medicine, Nat. Acad. Sci.; working group on methods/technologies Nat. Heart Attack Alert Program, 1994—; invited presenter at sci. sessions, symposia and acad. med. ctrs. Mem. editl. bd. Am. Jour. Cardiology, 1983—, Jour. Am. Coll. Cardiology, 1983-87, 91-95, Circulation, 1986—, Cardiovascular Imaging, 1988—, Am. Jour. Cardiac Imaging, 1990-95, Internat. Jour. Cardiac Imaging, 1990-95, Jour. Heart Valve Disease, 1982-95, Jour. Nuclear Cardiology, 1993—, Jour. Nuclear Medicine, 1994-2000, Cardiologia, 1995—, Am. Heart Jour., 1998—; contbr. over 300 publs. in med. jours. and textbooks. Recipient NIH Director's award, 1986, USPHS Commendation medal, 1990, USPHS outstanding svc. medal, 1991. Fellow ACP, Am. Coll. Cardiology (exhibits com. 1986-92, 1999-2000, program com. 1991-92, chair extramural edn. com., 1998—, bd. trustees 1999—, Disting. fellow 2000), Am. Heart Assn. (chmn. sci. session program com. 1998-2000, bd. dirs. 1999—, chmn. Coun. on Clin. Cardiology, 1999-2001, pres. 2002-03, Nat. Leadership award 2003); mem. AAAS, Am. Bd. Internal Medicine (subsplty. bd. cardiovasc. disease 1996-2001), Am. Soc. Clin. Investigation, Assn. Am. Physicians, Am. Heart Assn. Met. Chgo. (bd. govs. 1992-98, rsch. coun. 1992-98, pres. 2001-02), Am. Soc. Nuclear Cardiology (bd. dirs. 1994-98, chmn. edn. com. 1994-2000, nominating com. 1994-96), Assn. Profs. Cardiology (nominating com. 1993—, councillor 1994—, sec., treas. 1996-99, v.p. 1999-2000, pres. 2000-01), Chgo. Cardiology Group (pres. 1994-96), Am. Fedn. Clin. Rsch., Assn. Am. Physicians, Assn. Univ. Cardiologists, Ctrl. Soc. Clin. Rsch., Am Heart Assn. (pres. 2002-03), Alpha Omega Alpha. Office: Northwestern U Med Sch Cardiology Divsn 201 E Huron St Ste 10-240 Chicago IL 60611-2958

BONSACK, ROSE MARY HATEM, state legislator, physician; b. Havre de Grace, Md., Oct. 24, 1933; d. Joseph Thomas and Nasma (Joseph) Hatem; m. James P. Bonsack, Aug. 24, 1957; children: Jeanette, Karen, Thomas, David, James J. BS in Chemistry cum laude, Washington Coll., 1955; MD, Med. Coll. Pa., 1960. Intern Easton (Pa.) Hosp., 1961; physician outpatient clinic Kirk Army Hosp., Aberdeen Proving Ground, Md., 1962-74, chief outpatient clinic, 1968-72, chief dept. hosp. clinics, 1972-74; contract physician Harford County Dept. Health, Md., 1975-78; utilization rev. officer Harford Meml. Hosp., Havre de Grace, 1981-82; pvt. practice Aberdeen, Md., 1981—; mem. Md. Gen. Assembly, 1991-99, chmn. house rules and exec. nominations com., 1991-94, mem. house ways and means com., 1995-99. Coord. clinics Hypertensive Coun. Md., 1977-81; reviewer quality assurance for nursing homes in Harford County, Md. Licensing Div., 1977-81; utilization rev. officer Harford Meml. Hosp., Havre de Grace, 1981-82; med. dir. Ashley Alcoholic Rehab., Havre de Grace, 1983-84; mem. Bd. Med. Examiners Md.; mem., exec. sec. Commn. on Med. Discipline, 1985-88. V.p. St. Joan of Arc Home-Sch. Assn., 1968, pres., 1969, mem., 1968-85; v.p. No. Md. Heart Assn., 1969, pres., 1970, bd. dirs., 1973; bd. dirs. Mann House, Bel Air, Md., 1973-82, Harford County Cancer Soc., 1973-86; mem. John Carroll Home-Sch. Assn., 1974—, 1st v.p., 1975, pres., 1975; bd. dirs. John Carroll H.S., 1975—, pres. bd. dirs., 1979-85; mem. Harford County Dem. Cen. Com., 1987-90; mem. chief exec.'s coun. Harford C.C., 1990; trustee Washington Coll., 1992-99, Harford C.C., 1999—. Recipient Outstanding Contbn. to Md. Traffic Safety citation State of Md., 1969, Cert. of Merit for svc. Md. Cancer Soc., 1977, Women Helping Women award Soroptomists Harford and Cecil Counties, 1983-84, V. McCrory award for significant contbn. to enhancement of eye care in Md., Md. Optometric Assn., 1995, Alumni Citation for outstanding achievement and svc. in field of pub. svc. Washington Coll., 2000; named one of Top 100 Women in Md., Daily Record, 1996; named Harford County Living Treasure, 2004. Mem. Am. Acad. Family Physicians (bd. dirs. 1997-99, alt. del. 1990-94, del. from Md. 1994-96, chmn. chpt. affairs com. 1992—, commn. on regulations 1993-96, found. bd. dirs. 1999—), Med. Chirurgical Fac. Md., Hartford County Med. Soc. (sec. 1967, pres. 1968, v.p. 1978, Outstand Cmny. Svc. citation 1979), Md. Acad. Family Physicians (v.p. 1987, pres. 1988, Lifetime Achievement award 2003).

BONSER, CHARLES FRANKLIN, public administration educator; b. Youngstown, Ohio, Feb. 15, 1933; s. William Harley and Anita (Bromley) B.; m. Nancy A. Gebhardt, July 3, 1955; children: Catherine, Jeffrey, Andrew. BA, Bowling Green State U., 1954; MBA, Ind. U., 1961, DBA, 1965. Asst. dir. bus. rsch. Ind. U., Bloomington, 1960-63; dir. Ind. State Tax Policy, 1963-65; assoc. dir. Ind. U., bur. bus. rsch. sch. bus., asst. prof. bus. adminstrn., 1965-69, assoc. prof., 1967-81, prof. bus. adminstrn. and pub. and environ. affairs., 1971-97, assoc. dean sch. bus., 1969-71, spl. asst. to pres., 1971-72, dean sch. pub. and environ. affairs, 1972-88, dir. Inst. Devel. Strategies, 1988-97, Ameritech prof. econ. devel., 1990-97, dean emeritus, 1998—. Spl. asst. to sec. HHS, 1986; bus. econs. editor Irving Cloud Pub. Co., Chgo., 1966-91. Gov.'s designee for adminstrn. Fed. Intergovtl. Pers. Act, State of Ind., 1972-82; Ind. rep. Midwest Intergovtl. Pers. Coun., 1972-82; bd. dirs. Nat. Inst. Pub. Mgmt., Washington, 1976-82; bd. dirs. NSF Internat., Ann Arbor, Mich., 1984—. With USAF, 1955-59. Recipient Sagamore of Wabash award Gov. Ind., 1965, 74, Spl. citation U.S. CSC, 1974, 78, Spl. Citation Ind. Gen. Assembly, 1988. Mem. Nat. Assn. Schs. Pub. Affairs Adminstrn. (pres. 1976-77, mem. exec. coun. 1973-78), Am. Soc. Pub. Adminstrn. (mem. exec. coun. 1975-76, 81-82), Nat. Acad. Pub. Adminstrn. (mem. bd. trustees 1989-95), Am. Pub. Works Assn., Ind. Soc. Pub. Adminstrn. (pres. 1975-76), Beta Gamma Sigma, Pi Alpha Alpha (nat. pres. 1980—). Home: 1331 Windfield Rd Bloomington IN 47401-6183 Office: Ind Univ Spea Bldg 201 Bloomington IN 47405

BONSER, QUENTIN, retired surgeon; b. Sedro Wooley, Wash., Nov. 1, 1920; s. George Wayne and Kathleen Imogene (Lynch) B.; m. Loellen Rocca, Oct. 20, 1945; children: Wayne, Gordon, Carol, Patricia Bonser Sandell. BA in Zoology, UCLA, 1943; MD, U. Calif., San Francisco, 11947. Diplomate Am. Bd. Surgery. Intern U. Calif. Hosp., San Francisco, 1947-49, resident in gen. surgery, 1949-56; pvt. practice, Placerville, Calif., from 1956; now ret. Surgeon King Faisal Splty. Hosp., Saudi Arabia, Sept.-Oct., 1984; vis. prof. surgery U. Calif., San Francisco, 1968. Vol. physician, tchr. surgery, Vietnam, 1971, 72, 73. Capt. M.C., USAF, 1950-51. Fellow ACS; mem. H.C. Naffziger Surg. Soc. (pres. 1974-75). Home: 2590 Northridge Dr Placerville CA 95667-3416 Home Fax: 530-622-5748. Personal E-mail: qbonser@sbcglobal.net.

BONSKY, JACK ALAN, lawyer; b. Canton, Ohio, Mar. 12, 1938; s. Jack H. and Pearl E. Bonsky; m. Carol Ann Portmann, Sept. 2, 1960; children: Jack Raymond, Cynthia Lynn. AB, Ohio U., 1960; JD, Ohio State U., 1964. Bar: Ohio 1964, U.S. Dist. Ct. (so. dist.) Ohio 1969. With Metcalf, Thomas & Bonsky, Marietta, Ohio, 1964-69, Addison, Fisher & Bonsky, Marietta, 1969-70; asst. counsel GenCorp., Inc. (formerly Gen. Tire & Rubber Co.), Akron, Ohio, 1970-75, assoc. gen. counsel, 1975-86, asst. sec., 1977-86, v.p., sec., 1986; v.p., sec., gen. counsel DiversiTech Gen., Inc., 1986-87; v.p., gen. counsel GenCorp Polymer Products, 1988-94; asst. gen. counsel, dir. environ. affairs GenCorp, Inc., 1994-96; pvt. practice, 1996—. Solicitor City of Marietta, 1966-67; legal advisor City of Marietta Bd. of Edn., 1966-67; police prosecutor, Belpre, Ohio, 1969-70; comml. law instr. Am. Inst. Banking, 1969; dir. Frontier Holdings, Inc., Denver, Frontier Airlines, Denver, 1985 (merged with People Express Airlines, 1985). Mem. Marietta Income Tax Bd. of Rev., 1966-67; mem. Traffic Commn., 1966-69, chmn., 1967; mem. Marietta Civil Svc. Commn., 1969; trustee Urban League, Akron, 1978-81, pres., 1980-81; trustee Akron Comty. Svc. Ctr., 1978-81, United Way of Summit County, 1982-89; mem. Bath (Ohio) Twp. Merger Commn., 1995-96; v.p. Bath Twp. Homeowners' Assn., 1999, 2005; pres. Bath Twp. Homeowners Assn., 2000-03; bd. dirs. Washington County Soc. for Crippled Children, 1964-70, S.E. Ohio unit Arthritis Found., 1967-70, chmn., 1968-70; mem. Washington County (Ohio) Health Planning Com., 1968-70; ho. of dels. Ohio Easter Seal Soc., 1968-70; mem. econ. devel. revenue com. Bath Twp., 1999-2000. Recipient Akron Comty. Svc. Ctr. and Urban League Leadership award, 1981. Mem. Ohio Bar Assn. Home and Office: 4234 Idlebrook Dr Akron OH 44333-1726

BONTE, FREDERICK JAMES, radiologist, educator, physician; b. Bethlehem, Pa., Jan. 18, 1922; s. Frederick R. and Harriett (Stoudt) B.; m. Cecile Poetzel; children: Frederick W., Stephen J., John A., Therese A., Suzanne M., Ann E. BS, Western Res. U., 1942, MD, 1945. Diplomate: Am. Bd. Radiology (trustee 1969-75), Am. Bd. Nuclear Medicine. Intern Huntington Meml. Hosp., Pasadena, Cal., 1945-46; resident Univ. Hosp., Cleve., 1948-52; practice medicine, specializing in radiology and nuclear medicine Dallas, 1956—; mem. faculty Western Res. U. Sch. Medicine, 1952-56, asst. prof., 1952-56, chief radiotherapy and nuclear medicine, 1954-56; prof. U. Tex. Southwestern Med. Sch., Dallas, 1956—, chmn. dept. radiology, 1956-73, dean, 1973-80; dir. Nuclear Medicine Research Center, 1980—, Effie and Wofford Cain disting. chair in diagnostic imaging; Dr. Jack Krohmer prof. in radiation physics. Mem. bd. Nat. Council Radiation Protection and Measurements, 1966-71; radiology tng. com. Nat. Insts. Gen. Med. Scis., USPHS, 1966-70, residency rev. com. radiology AMA, 1966-69, adv. and rev. coms. VA, 1972—; Founding trustee Am. Bd. Nuclear Medicine, 1971-73, chmn., 1977-80; internat. cons. on med. edn. Contbr. articles to profl. jours. Capt. USAAC, 1946-48. Fellow Am. Coll. Radiology, Am. Coll. Nuclear Physicians (Pres.'s award 1997); mem. AMA (del., chmn. grad. med. edn. com., Roentgen Centennial Hartman medal 1995), Soc. Nuclear Medicine (De Hevesy Nuclear Pioneer award 1995), Am. Roentgen Ray Soc. (exec. com.), Radiol. Soc. N.Am., Sigma Xi, Alpha Omega Alpha. Achievements include research on experimental nuclear medicine and radiology. Home: 11138 Wonderland Trl Dallas TX 75229-3943 Office: 5323 Harry Hines Blvd Dallas TX 75390-9061 Office Phone: 214-648-2025. Business E-Mail: frederick.bonte@utsouthwestern.edu.

BONTOYAN, WARREN ROBERTS, chemist, lab administrator; b. Balt., Aug. 2, 1932; s. Cesario Baron and Dorothy Bertha (Hunter) B.; m. Gladys Frances Daughaday, May 3, 1958; children: Warren Wendel, Suzanne Cheri. BS, U. Md., 1956. Food and drug insp. FDA, Balt., 1956-58; rsch. chemist USDA, Beltsville, Md., 1958-60; head chemist methods devel., tng., standards and quality control lab. EPA, Beltsville, 1960-78, chief chem. and biol. investigation br., 1978-89, also dir. labs., 1978-89; the md. state chemist, chief state chemistry sect. Md. Dept. Agriculture, Annapolis, 1990—. Mem. vector and biol. control expert panel WHO.; U.S. rep. to Collaborative Internat. Pesticide Adv. Coun.; mem. expert panel pesticide chemistry FAO; cons. World Bank, 1987, Chesapeake Rsch. Consortium Inc.; chmn., organizer, participant numerous scientific symposiums. Editor: EPA Manual of Chem. Analysis of Pesticides and Devices, 1975; Contbr. articles to profl. jours. Fellow Assn. Ofcl. Analytical Chemists (pres. 1983, gen. referee pesticide formulation analysis, bd. dirs. 1978-84), Am. Inst. Chemists; mem. Am. Chem. Soc., Assn. Am. Control Ofcls., Am. Oil Chemists Soc., Alpha Chi Sigma. Office: 50 Harry S Truman Pkwy Annapolis MD 21401-8960 Office Phone: 410-841-2721. Business E-Mail: bontoywr@mda.state.md.us.

BONVENTRE, VINCENT MARTIN, lawyer, educator; b. Bklyn., Nov. 11, 1948; s. Martin Victor and Raffaela (Sabella) B.; m. Catherine L. Bonventre; children: Martin Peter, Richard Joseph, Peter John. BS, Union Coll., 1970;

JD, Bklyn. Law Sch., 1976; MA in Pub. Adminstrn., U. Va., 1981, PhD, 2002. Bar: N.Y. 1977, U.S. Ct. Mil. Appeals 1977, U.S. Supreme Ct. 1980. Acting asst. prof. govt. U. Va., Charlottesville, 1982-83; law clk. to judge N.Y. State Ct. of Appeals, Albany, 1983-86; supreme ct. jud. fellow U.S. Supreme Ct., Washington, 1986-87; prin. law clk. to judge N.Y. State Ct. Appeals, 1987-90; asst. prof. law Union U. Albany Law Sch., 1990-93, assoc., 1993-96, prof., 1996—. Instr. Cochise Coll., Sierra Vista, Ariz., 1978-80, U. Va., Charlottesville, 1980-82, asst. prof. govt., 1982-83; adj. prof. law Syracuse U., vis. prof. law, 1993, vis. prof. Maxwell Sch. Pub. Affairs, fall 1994; dir. Ctr. for Jud. Process, Albany Law Sch., 2003—; legal commentator local, state and nat. media including N.Y. Times, Nat. Pub. Radio, Fox Newschannel, ABC News, Newsday, N.Y. Law Jour., Gannett, PBS, N.Y.C. Author: Streams of Tendency on the New York Court: Ideological and Jurisprudential Patterns in the Judges' Voting and Opinions, 2003; editor State Constl. Commentary, 1996—; editor-in-chief Govt., Law and Policy Jour., 1999—; contbr. articles to profl. jours. Bd. trustees, Cath. Charities Archdiocese of Albany, 1996—. Served to capt. U.S. Army Intelligence, 1970-73, JAGC 77-80. U. Va. fellow, 1981-82. Mem. ABA, N.Y. State Bar Assn. Democrat. Roman Catholic. Avocations: pop, classical and opera music, great books, art, travel. Home: 606 Astor Ct Delmar NY 12054-9627 Office: Union U Albany Law Sch 80 New Scotland Ave Albany NY 12208-3434 Office Phone: 518-472-5856. Business E-Mail: vbonv@mail.als.edu.

BONVILLE, JOSEPH, music educator; b. Albany, NY, Oct. 30, 1953; s. Joseph R and Katherine Bonville. BS in Music Edn., Coll. of St. Rose, 1980, MS in Ednl. Adminstrn., 1991; MA in Music, Goddard Coll., 1983. Music Education Administration NY State Dept. of Edn. Fine arts coord. Watervliet Sch. Dist., NY, 1985—, h.s. band dir. Mem.: NYSSMA. Conservative-R. Cath. Avocations: martial arts, reading, movies. Office: Watervliet High School 1245 Hillside Dr Watervliet NY 12189 Office Phone: 518-629-3200. Personal E-mail: mr_bonville@yahoo.com.

BONVILLIAN, WILLIAM BOONE, lawyer; b. Honolulu, Mar. 7, 1947; s. William Doughty and Florence Elizabeth (Boone) B.; m. Janis Ann Sposato, Apr. 12, 1980; children: Raphael William Boone, Marcus Doughty. AB, Columbia U., 1969; MA in Religion, Yale U., 1972; JD, Columbia U., 1974. Bar: Conn. 1975, D.C. 1976, U.S. Supreme Ct. 1983. Law clk. to Hon. Jack B. Weinstein U.S. Dist. Ct. (ea. dist.) N.Y., 1974-75; assoc. Steptoe & Johnson, Washington, 1975-77; dep. asst. sec., dir. congl. affairs, liaison officer U.S. Dept. Transp., Washington, 1977-81; ptnr. Brown, Roady, Bonvillian & Gold, Washington, 1981-85, Jenner & Block, Washington, 1985-89; chief counsel, legis. dir. to Sen. Joseph Lieberman U.S. Senate, Washington, 1989—. Bd. editors Columbia Law Rev. 1973-74; contbr. articles to law and sci. jours. Recipient 2 outstanding Performance awards U.S. Sec. Transp., Washington, 1979, 80. Mem. Conn. Bar Assn., D.C. Bar Assn. Democrat. Episcopalian. Home: 930 Hickory Run Ln Great Falls VA 22066-1903 Office: Office Sen Lieberman 706 Hart Senate Office Bldg Washington DC 20510-0001 Business E-Mail: bill_bonvillian@lieberman.senate.gov.

BONYUET, DAVID, electrical engineer; s. King Chon and York Lan Bonyuet; m. Damaris Auxiliadora Quijada, Dec. 15, 1990; children: Dairen Carolina, Dyanne Lee. BS in Elec. Engring., IUPFAN, Maracay, Venezuela, 1984—89; Ph.D in Telecommunication, U. Politectnica de Catalunya, Barcelona, Spain, 1993—2002. Design engr. Ingenieria Electrica y Electronica Chikon Hau, Caracas, Venezuela, 1988—; instrumentation and control engr. VEPICA / WOOD Group, Caracas, Venezuela, 1991—; rsch. asst. U. Politectnica de Catalunya, Barcelona, 1994—; engring. mgr. Spectra Seriea de Venezuela, Caracas, 1998—; prin. elec. scientist Delta Search Labs, Cambridge, Mass., 2001—. Scholar, Spanish Govt., 1992—97. Mem.: IEEE, Am. Soc. for Quality. Achievements include patents pending for an apparatus to secure computers from the network and the Internet; design of Hipercheque; Short Circuit Fault Dectector for High and Middle Transmission Line; first to Virtual Reality Interface for Robot Teleoperation. Home: 62 Jensen Rd Watertown MA 02472 Personal E-mail: bonyuet@ieee.org. E-mail: bonyuet@gmail.com.

BONZAGNI, VINCENT FRANCIS, lawyer, quality assurance professional; b. Boston, Dec. 10, 1952; s. Augustine Joseph and Augusta M. (Giarla) B.; m. Marie T. Rainville, Aug. 27, 1972 (div. Sept. 1982); 1 child, Gina Theresa; m. Donna J. Bachtell, May 14, 1988; stepchildren: Allison, Neil. BS in Math., Lowell (Mass.) Tech. Inst., 1974; JD, George Mason U., 1998. Bar: Va. 1998, U.S. Dist. Ct. (ea. and we. dist.) Va., U.S. Ct. Appeals (4th cir.), U.S. Supreme Ct., 2002; notary pub. Claims adminstr. Social Security Adminstrn., 1976-79, quality assurance specialist Boston, 1979-83, disability analyst Arlington, Va., 1983-88; program adminstr. Corp. for Open Systems, McLean, Va., 1988-91; sr. hearings and appeals analyst Social Security Adminstrn., Falls Church, Va., 1991—2003; pvt. practice, 1998—. Self-employed researcher and crossword puzzle cons., 1982-2003. Author: The Mensa Book of Lists, 1992, The Mensa Book of Lists II, 1997; co-author: A History of Mensa, 1990. Treas. Maplewood Village Condo. Assn., 1989-93, 1998-2001. Mem. ABA, NRA (life), Mensa (local treas. 1986-90, local pres. 1990-91, 2000-2002, nat. historian 1989-2003, nat. SIGs officer 1989-91, internat. archivist 1992—, local ombudsman 2003—), Warren County (Va.) Bar Assn., Nat. Orgn. Social Security Claimant Reps., Nat. Puzzlers League, Phi Alpha Delta. Avocations: crossword puzzles, contests, games, trivia, genealogy. Home: 147 Mountain Top Rd Front Royal VA 22630-6013 Office: Bonzagni Law Firm PC 11-A West Prospect St Front Royal VA 22630-3223 Office Phone: 540-635-9426. Business E-Mail: bonzlaw@shentel.net.

BOO, KATHERINE, newswriter; AB (summa cum laude), Columbia U., 1988. Writer, editor Wash. City Paper, 1988—92, Wash. Monthly, 1988—92; staff writer Wash. Post, 1992—; writer New Yorker. Recipient Pulitzer prize, 2000; fellow MacArthur Found. fellow, 2002. Mem.: New Am. Found. Office: Washington Post 1150 15th St NW Washington DC 20071*

BOOCHEVER, ROBERT, judge; b. N.Y.C., Oct. 2, 1917; s. Louis C and Miriam (Cohen) Boochever; m. Lois Colleen Maddox, Apr. 22, 1943 (dec.); children: Barbara K, Linda Lou, Ann Paula, Miriam Deon; m. Rose Marie Borden, Aug. 31, 2001. AB, Cornell U., 1939, JD, 1941; HD (hon.), U. Alaska, 1981. Bar: N.Y. 1944, Alaska 1947. Law clk. Nordlinger, Riegel & Cooper, 1941; asst. U.S. atty. Juneau, Alaska, 1946—47; ptnr. firm Faulkner, Banfield, Boochever & Doogan, Juneau, 1947—72; assoc. justice Alaska Supreme Ct., 1972—75, 1978—80, chief justice, 1975—78; judge U.S. Ct. Appeals (9th cir.), Pasadena, Calif., 1980; sr. judge U.S. Ct. Appeals, Pasadena, 1986—. Mem. 9th cir. rules com. U.S. Ct. Appeals, 1983—85, chmn. 9th cir. libr. com., 1995—2001; chmn. Ala. Jud. Coun., 1975—78; mem. appellate judges seminar NYU Sch. Law, 1975; mem. Conf. Chief Justices, 1975—79, vice chmn., 1978—79; mem. adv. bd. Nat. Bank of Ala., 1968—72; guest spkr. Southwestern Law Sch. Disting. Lecture Series, 1992. Contbr. articles to profl. jours. Chmn. Juneau chpt. ARC, 1949—51, Juneau Planning Commn., 1956—61; mem. Alaska Devel. Bd., 1949—52, Alaska Jud. Qualification Commn., 1972—75; mem. adv. bd. Juneau-Douglas C.C. Capt. U.S. Army, 1941—45. Named Juneau Man of Yr., Rotary, 1974, The Boochever & Bird Chair for Study and Tchg. of Freedom and Equality, U. Calif. Sch. Law, Davis, 2000; recipient Disting. Alumnus award, Cornell U., 1989. Fellow: Am. Coll. Trial Attys.; mem.: ABA, Am. Law Inst., Am. Judicature Soc. (dir. 1970—74), Juneau Bar Assn. (pres. 1971—72), Alaska Bar Assn. (pres. 1961—62), Alaskans United (chmn. 1972), Juneau C. of C. (pres. 1952, 1955), Altadena Town and County Club, Cornell Club L.A. Office: US Ct Appeals PO Box 91510 125 S Grand Ave Pasadena CA 91105-1652 Office Phone: 626-229-7200. Business E-Mail: boochever@ca9.uscourts.gov.

BOOCOCK, STEPHEN WILLIAM, lawyer; b. Wilkinsburg, Pa., Sept. 25, 1948; s. William Samuel and Zelda Elizabeth (Heginbotham) B.; m. Carol Ann Bennett, July 11, 1970; children: Eric Alan, Allison Anne, Megan Leigh. BS in Acctg., Pa. State U., 1970; JD, U. Pitts., 1973. Bar: Pa. 1974, U.S. Dist. Ct. (we. dist.) Pa. 1973. Supervising tax specialist Coopers & Lybrand (now part of PricewaterhouseCoopers), Pitts., 1973-76; tax counsel Incom Internat., Inc., Pitts., 1977-81; asst. treas., dir. tax Allegheny Ludlum Corp., Pitts., 1981—94, asst. v.p. taxes, 1994-96; asst. v.p. taxes, chief tax officer Allegheny Technologies, Inc., Pitts., 1996—2002; dir. tax controversy svcs. Deloitte Tax LLP, Chgo., 2003—. Treas. Meadow Wood Homeowner's Assn., 1990-2001. Served to capt. U.S. Army, 1970-79; with USAR. Mem.: ABA, AICPA, IRS Adminstrv. Affairs Com., Tax Execs. Inst. (treas. Pitts. chpt. 1985—86, sec. 1986—87, sr. v.p. 1987—88, pres. 1988—89, nat. inst. dir. 1989—91, v.p. region VI 1992—93, 50th ann. task force 1993—95, membership com. 1993—97, mem. IRS adminstrv. affairs com. 1993—2003, nominating com. 1994—95, tax info. sys. com. 1995—97, mem. alternative tax sys. com. 1995—97, nominating com. 1997—98, nat. inst. dir. 1999—2001, mem. nat. exec. com. 1999—2003, nat. treas. 2001—02, nat. sec. 2002—03, v.p. region VI 1992—93), Pa. Inst. CPAs, Allegheny County Bar Assn., Pa. Bar Assn. Republican. Avocation: golf. Office: Deloitte Tax LLP 111 S Wacker Dr Chicago IL 60606-4301 Home: Ste #3C 881 N La Salle Blvd Chicago IL 60610-3259 Office Phone: 312-486-9529. E-mail: swb011@sbcglobal.net.

BOODEY, CECIL WEBSTER, JR., retired political science professor; b. Yonkers, N.Y., June 10, 1931; s. Cecil Webster and Dorothy (Mitchell) B.; m. Phyllis Ann Stensland, July 9, 1955 (dec. May 15, 2004); children: William Mitchell, John Barton, Pamela D. Ellen. BA, U. N.H., 1953; postgrad., Princeton U., 1953-54; MA, NYU, 1960. Tng. program Arabian-Am. Oil Co., Dhahran, Saudi Arabia, 1954; with N.Y. Telephone Co., Westchester, 1957-62; instr. polit. sci. Fashion Inst. Tech., N.Y.C., 1964-68, from asst. prof. to prof., 1968-95; ret., 1995; adj. prof. Fashion Inst. Tech., 1996—. Chmn. dept. social sci. Fashion Inst. Tech., N.Y.C., 1971—73; vis. prof. fgn. langs. Inner Mongolia U., Huhhot, China, 1989—90, 1996—97, 2001; lectr., China, 2000—. Treas. Richards Boys Club, Yonkers, 1962-63; v.p. Manasquan-Brielle Little League, N.J., 1969; sec. Manasquan Babe Ruth League, 1972-96; Democratic municipal chmn., Manasquan, 1970-78; pres. 11th Ward Democratic Club, Yonkers, 1962; bd. dirs. Manasquan Area Human Rels. Coun., 1973-98, Brookdale C.C., Lincroft, N.J., 1979-88; pres. Squan Soccer Club, 1980. With U.S. Army, 1954-56. Fellow Ford Found., 1953-54; Penfield scholar NYU, 1960. Mem. Am. Polit. Sci. Assn., Assn. Asian Studies, Internat. Studies Assn., Asia Soc., China Inst. in Am., Am. Profs. for Peace in the Middle East (nat. vice chmn. 1989-90), Phi Beta Kappa, Phi Kappa Phi, Pi Mu Epsilon, Pi Gamma Mu. Methodist. Home: 80 Allen Ave Manasquan NJ 08736-3426 Office: Fashion Inst Tech 7th Ave At 27th St New York NY 10001 E-mail: pcboodey@bytheshore.com. *To assist young adults to develop their qualities for critical thinking and to encourage them to participate in extra-curricular activities— these are the goals of my life.*

BOOHER, ALICE ANN, lawyer; b. Indpls., Oct. 6, 1941; d. Norman Rogers and Olga (Bonke) B. BA in Polit. Sci., Butler U., 1963; LLB, Ind. U., 1966, JD, 1967. Bar: Ind. 1966, U.S. Dist. Ct. (so. dist.) Ind. 1966, U.S. Tax Ct. 1970, U.S. Ct. Customs and Patent Appeals 1969, U.S. Ct. Mil. Appeals 1969, U.S. Ct. Appeals (D.C. cir.) 1969, U.S. Supreme Ct. 1969; cert. tchr., Ind. Rsch. asst., law clk. Supreme and Appellate Cts. Ind., Indpls., 1966; legal intern, atty., staff legal advisor Dept. State, Washington, 1966-69; staff legal adviser Bd. Vets. Appeals, Washington, 1969-78, sr. atty., 1978—, counsel, 1991—. Former counselor D.C. Penal Facilities and Shelters. Author: The Nuclear Test Ban Treaty and the Third Party Non-Nuclear States, also children's books; contbr. articles to various publs., chpts. to Whiteman Digest of International Law; exhibited crafts, needlepoint in juried artisan fairs; originator U.S. postage stamps Women in Mil. Svc., 1980-97, POWs/MIAs, 1986-96. Bd. dirs. community groups including D.C. Women's Commn. for Crime Prevention, 1980-81, Friends of Nat. Vets Mus.; pres., legal adviser VA Employees Assn.; mem. sec.'s mus. task force Dept. VA. Named Ky. Col., 1988; recipient various awards, Diisting. Svc. award, Contrbn. of Merit awards. Mem. DAV (life), VFW Aux. (life), D.C. Sexual Assault Coalition (chmn. legal com.), Life Mem. Judge Advocates Assn., U.S. Supreme Ct. Hist. Soc., U.S. Naval Inst., Nat. Mus. Women in Arts, Kennedy Ctr. Stars, Sackler/Freer Galleries (patron), Women in Mil. Svcs. to Am. Found., Bus. and Profl. Women (pres. D.C. 1980-81, nat. UN fellow 1974, nat. bd. dirs. 1980-82, 87-94, Woman of Yr. award D.C. 1975, Marguerite Rawalt award D.C. 1986), USO (DVA sec), Navy League U.S.A. (life), Am. Legion Aux. (life), Women Officers Profl. Assns., Nat. Vets. Mus. Task Force, Nat. Task Force on Women of the Mil. and Women Mil. POWS (chair Esther Peterson Tribute 1995, panel, paper moderator conf. 1997, book reviewer, contbr. to Stars & Stripes, Ex POWs Bull., others), Assn. Former Intelligence Officers (assoc.), Am. News Womens Club, Cons., Saigon Tourist, Inc., Alliance Nat. Def. (editor Advocate), OSS Soc. (assoc.).

BOOK, DAVID LINCOLN, physicist, editor, consultant; b. Boston, Aug. 4, 1939; s. M. Harold and Helen S. (Solway) B.; m. Gail Stephanie Ross, Sept. 20, 1970; 1 child, Kevin Daniel. BA, Yale U., 1959; MA, Princeton U., 1961, PhD, 1964. Rsch. physicist Gen. Atomic divsn. Gen. Dynamics, San Diego, 1964-67, Lawrence Livermore (Calif.) Lab., 1967-70; rsch. scientist GM13-GM15, U.S. Naval Rsch. Lab., Washington, 1971-91; pres. Enigmatics, Inc., Washington, 1992-2000; rsch. assoc., cons. dept. astronomy U. Md., College Park, 1992-2000; prof. physics dept. Naval Postgrad. Sch., Monterey, Calif., 2000—03. Author: Problems for Puzzlebusters, 1992; editor: Finite Difference Techniques for Vectorized Fluid Dynamics Calculations, 1981; co-editor: Nonlinear Plasma Theory, 1969; assoc. editor Applied Mechanics Reviews in Am. Soc. Mech. Engrs., 1988-91; translation editor Soc. Jour. Plasma Physics, 1975-95, Soc. Jour. Exptl. Theoretical Physics, 1985—; patentee in field. Fellow Am. Phys. Soc. (life). Avocations: frisbee, chess, writing fiction. Office Phone: 831-372-5004. E-mail: dlbook@nps.navy.mil.

BOOK, EDWARD R., retired trade association administrator; b. Cleve., May 9, 1931; s. Raymond John and Grace Elizabeth Book; m. Inga M. Scheyer, Feb. 14, 1953; children: Sandra Book Liddick, Edward R. Jr., Frederick A. BS in Hotel Adminstrn, Pa. State U., 1954. Mgr. restaurant Howard D. Johnson Co., Harrisburg, 1950-54; mgr. food and beverage, asst. mgr. Hotel Harrisburger, Harrisburg, 1956-60; v.p., gen. mgr. Hotel Bethlehem, Pa., 1960-68; gen. mgr. Hospitality Motor Inn, Cleve., 1968-69, Hotel Hershey, Pa., 1969; mng. dir. Hotel Hershey and Country Club, 1970; dir. hostelry div. HERCO, Inc. (formerly Hershey Estates), 1971, v.p., 1973-74, exec. v.p., asst. to pres., 1974, chmn. bd., pres., CEO, 1974-80, chmn., CEO, 1980-87; vice chmn. bd. dirs. Hershey Trust Co., 1985-87; exec. v.p. Travel Industry Assn. Am., Washington, 1987-89, pres., 1989-94; ret., 1994. Interim pres. USA Nat. Tourism Orgn., 1996-97; mem. travel and tourism industry adv. com. U.S. Senate Commerce Com., 1989-94; mem. adv. com. travel and tourism caucus U.S. Ho. of Reps., 1989-94; charter mem. adv. bd. HRIM program U. Del., 1990-2000; mem. nat. adv. bd. Acad. Travel and Tourism, 1994-97. Chmn. adv. com. Milton S. Hershey Med. Ctr., 1977—82; campaign chmn. Tri-County United Way, 1980, pres., 1982—83; mem. Ams. for Competitive Enterprise Sys., 1977—82; mem. devel. coun. Pa. State U., 1982—89; vice-chmn. Ctrl. Pa. SCORE, chair, 2004; mem. bd. mgrs. Milton Hershey Sch., 1974—87, Milton S. Hershey Found., 1974—87, chmn., 1981—87; trustee Pa. State U., 1977—85, vice chmn. bd., 1982—85; trustee Harrisburg Area YMCA, 1978—87; mem. exec. bd. Keystone Area coun. Boy Scouts Am., 1975—87, Capital Area coun. Boy Scouts Am., 1988—89; bd. dirs. Hwy. Users Fedn., 1993—95; bd. dirs., pres. Palmer Art Mus. Friends. With U.S. Army, 1954—56. Named Pa. Travel Man of Year, 1976, Disting. Alumnus, Pa. State U., 1986; recipient order of achievement Lambda Chi Alpha, 1976; elected to Travel Industry Hall of Leaders, 1986. Mem. VFW (life mem. post 8896), Pa. Travel Industry Adv. Coun. (chmn. 1972-76), Pa. State Hotel and Restaurant Soc. (pres. 1964), Harrisburg Area C. of C. (pres. 1975-76), Am. Hotel and Motel Assn. (industry adv. coun., long range planning com., trustee ednl. inst., resort com. 1975-87), Nat. Inst. for Food Svc. Industry (trustee 1979-82), Travel Industry Assn. Am. (bd. dirs. 1976—, chmn. 1981-82), Pa. State U. Alumni Assn. (life, pres. 1977-79), Pa. Soc. (life), Am. Legion, Lambda Chi Alpha (bd. dirs. 1998-2002). Presbyterian (elder). Home: 305 Village Hts Dr Apt 221 State College PA 16801-7685

BOOK, JOHN KENNETH (KENNY BOOK), retail store owner; b. Hillsboro, Ill., June 26, 1950; s. Vern Ray Book and Pearl Iva (Foster) Book Alford Carroll; m. Betty L. Christy, Dec. 23, 1981; children: Elizabeth Marie Dunn Rose, Leslie Michelle Dunn Edge. Assoc. in Acctg., Ky. Bus. Coll., 1974. Laborer Lexington (Ky.) Army Depot, 1968-70; machine operator A.O. Smith, Mt. Sterling, Ky., 1971-72; laborer Irvin Industries, Lexington, Ky., 1973-75; owner Kenny's Signs & Bus. Svcs., Winchester, Ky., 1977-90, Book's Bookkeeping & Tax Svc., Winchester, Ky., 1990—; rsch. bd. advisors ABI, 1990—. Active Winchester Sch. Bd., 1976, 78; candidate for commr. City of Winchester, 1977, 79, 81, 83, 87, elected commr., 1989, re-elected, 1993, 96, 98, 2000, 02, candidate for mayor, 1985; city commr., KLC, DOT; bd. dirs. Blue Grass Rails to Trails. Named to Hon. Order Ky. Cols., 1973; Road scholar Ky. Dept. Transp., 2002, Road Master, 2003; Leadership Fellow Cert., Ky. League Cities, 1999, Leadership Exec. Cert., 2000, Leadership Amb. Cert., 2001, Leadership Bronze Cert., 2003, Leadership Silver Cert., 2003. Mem. Nat. Assn. Tax Profls., Ky. Sheriffs Assn. (hon.), NATP/Am. Inst. Profl. Bookkeepers. Democrat. Office: Book's Bookkeeping & Tax Svc PO Box 840 Winchester KY 40392-0840

BOOKE, KEITH D., energy executive; BS in Acctg., Tex. Christian U. With Valero Energy Corp., San Antonio, 1983—, dir. investor rels., 1992-94, v.p. investor rels., 1994-97, v.p. adminstrn., 1997—99; exec . v.p., Chief Administration Officer Valero Engery Corp, San Antonio, 1999—. Office: Valero Energy Corp 1 Valero Pl San Antonio TX 78212-3106

BOOKER, ALVIN EUGENE, publishing executive, consultant; b. Phila., Jan. 17, 1928; s. Samuel Bear and Yetta (Stein) B.; children: Ellis Carl, Susan Barbara. BA, Temple U. Social worker YMHA, 1950-51; pres. Shopper Publs., Inc., 1952—. Office: Apt 400 1250 Greenwood Ave Jenkintown PA 19046-2957

BOOKER, BETTY MAE, poet; b. Allentown, Pa., Nov. 26, 1948; d. Harold George and Bessie (Bealer-Miller) Bartholomew; m. Samuel Efford Booker III, June 27, 1970 (dec. May 1998); children: Liesel Tamarah, Dacey Justin, Jaeson Bartholomew. BA in English, Millersville (Pa.) State Coll., 1970. Contbr. poetry to jours. and lit. mags., including Plainsong, America, Christian Century, Poetry Now. Home: 27826 Island Dr Salisbury MD 21801-2350 Office Phone: 410-596-1712. E-mail: sebefford@aol.com.

BOOKER, DANIEL I., lawyer; b. Brownsville, Pa., Nov. 14, 1947; s. Harris Taylor and Elizabeth Frances (Hulings) Booker; m. Deborah O'Neil Duff, Nov. 23, 1973; children: Daniel M., Anne R. BA, U. Pitts., 1968; JD, U. Chgo., 1971. Bar: Pa. 1972, DC 1984. Assoc. Reed Smith LLP (formerly Reed Smith Shaw & McClay), Pitts., 1971-73, 77-79, ptnr., 1979—, former head, Antitrust and Trade Regulation Practice, mng. ptnr., 1991—2000, now mem. exec. com.; trial atty., antitrust divsn. US Dept. Justice, Washington, 1973-77. Chmn. Pittsburgh Regional Alliance; bd. dirs. Allegheny Conf. Cmty. Develop., Pitts. Cultural Trust, RTI Metals, Inc., Océ-USA Holding, Inc.; mem. Jud. Coun. Pa. Contbr. articles to profl. jours. Chmn. bd. Pitts. Civic Light Opera, founding chair Acad. Musical Theater. Mem.: Acad. Trial Lawyers of Allegheny County, Allegheny County Bar Assn., DC Bar Assn. (vice chair antitrust com.), Pa. Bar Assn., ABA. Democrat. Roman Catholic. Avocations: theater, golf. Office: Reed Smith LLP 435 Sixth Ave Pittsburgh PA 15219 also: Reed Smith LLP Ste 1100 East Tower 1301 K St NW Washington DC 20005 Office Phone: 412-288-3132, 202-414-9298. Office Fax: 412-288-3063, 202-414-9299. E-mail: dbooker@reedsmith.com.

BOOKER, J. GARY, physician, researcher; b. Center, Tex., Jan. 22, 1953; s. James Julian and Sadie Rae Booker; m. Ruth Anne Martin, June 8, 1985; children: Anne, Emily. BS, La. State Univ., Shreveport, La., 1979; MD, La. State Univ. Med. Sch., Shreveport, La., 1984. Cert. psychaitry and Neurology Am. Bd. Acting chief psychiatry VA Med. Ctr., Pineville, La., 1989; asst. prof. La. State Univ. Med. Ctr., Shreveport, La., 1993—97; asst. dir. LSU Med. Ctr. Psychiatry Impatient Unit, Shreveport, La., 1995—97, med. dir., 1997; dep. corner psychiatry Corner's Office, Shreveport, La., 1998—; med. dir. Promise Hosp., Shreveport, La., 1998—; pvt. practice Shreveport, La., 1997—. Bd. mem. La. Alzheimer's Assn., 1998—2003. Petty officer 1st class USN, 1972—78. Mem.: APA, AMA, La. Psychaitric Assn., So. Med. Assn., Alpha Sigma Omicron. Presbyn. Achievements include research in prin. investagator drug rsch. clin. drug trials, 1997—. Avocations: carpentry, tree farming. Office: J Gary Booker MD 827 Margaret Pl Ste 204 Shreveport LA 71101

BOOKER, LEWIS THOMAS, lawyer; b. Richmond, Va., Sept. 22, 1929; s. Russell Eubank and Leslie Quarles (Sessoms) B.; m. Nancy Electa Brogden, Sept. 29, 1956; children: Lewis Thomas Jr., Virginia Frances, Claiborne Brogden, John Quarles. BA, U. Richmond, 1950, LLD, 1977; JD, Harvard U., 1953. Bar: Va. 1953, U.S. Ct. Mil. Appeals 1954, U.S. Supreme Ct. 1958, D.C. 1980, N.Y, 1985. Assoc. Hunton & Williams, Richmond, Va., 1956-63, ptnr., 1963-95, sr. coun., 1995—; substitute Judge 13th Dist., Va., 1996—. Lectr. in law Seinan Gakuin U., Fukuoka, Japan, 1985; vis. lectr. in law St. Thomas U., Miami, Fla., 1993; maj. gen., sr. mil. aide to Gov. of Va., 1997-2001. Mem. Va. Coun. on Human Rights, 1987; commr. chmn. Richmond Redevel. and Housing Authority, 1961-70; mem., vice chmn. Richmond Sch. Bd., 1971-80; trustee U. Richmond, 1972-2002, trustee emeritus, 2002—, rector, 1973-77, 81-85, 91-94, vice rector, 1985-87, chmn. exec. commn., 1977-81; trustee Va. Inst. Sci. Rsch., 1981-94, Richmond Symphony, 1987-92, Rouse-Bottom Found., 1989—; mem. coun. Richmond Symphony, 1995—, pres., 2004—; mem. Westminster-Canterbury Found. Richmond, 1995-2001, chmn., 1998-2001; mem. Robins Found., 1996—, Richmond Symphony Orch. Found., 1999—, Christian Children's Fund, 2000—, ChildFund Internat., 2002—, Richmond Eye and Ear Hosp., 2000—, Homeward, 2001—; chmn. Richmond Eye and Ear Found., 2001—. Fellow Am. Coll. Trial Lawyers, Am. Bar Found.; mem. ABA, Va. Bar Assn., Va. Law Found. (chmn. fellows coun. 1996-2001), Richmond Bar Assn., Westwood Racquet Club. Democrat. Baptist. Office: Hunton & Williams East Tower Riverfront Pla PO Box 1535 Richmond VA 23218-1535 Office Phone: 804-788-8496. Business E-Mail: lbooker@hunton.com.

BOOKER, RODERICK TODD, music educator, consultant; b. Tarentum, Pa., June 22, 1948; s. Mable Arlene Williams; m. Loretta N Wimbush, Feb. 24, 1974; children: Vincent, Alicia. BS, Indiana U. Of Pa., 1971, MS, 1976; PhD, Pa. State U., 1990. Cert. music tchr. Pa., prin., asst. supt., supt., asst. intermed Pa. Music tchr. Hempfield Area Sch. Dist., Greensburg, Pa., 1971—73, jr. high band dir., 1973—77, dept. chmn., 1985—; band dir. Hempfield Area H.S., Greensburg, 1977—; asst. prof. U. Pitts., Greensburg, Pa., 2000—. Author: (music educator) Student's Travel With Stunning Sub Sales, 1999; musician (magazine cover): (band directing/ fundraising activity) Conducting The Masses, 2000 (feature story in SBO mag., 2000). Mem. planning commn. Hempfield Twp. Planning Commision, Greensburg, 2000—; bd. of directors Westmoreland Symphony, Greensburg, Pa., 1987—. Mem.: Pa. Music Educators Assn. (minority rep. 1999—, bd. dirs. 1985—), Pa. State Edn. Assn. (dist. music bd. 1987—, H.S. BAND WON THE STATE AWARD FOR THE BEST JAZZ ROCK GROUP IN THE STATE IN 2002 2002). Home: 64 South Lincoln Ave Greensburg PA 15601-1225 Office: Hempfield Area HS Rd#5 Box 77 Greensburg PA 15601 Personal E-mail: rbditto2@msn.com.

BOOKHARDT, FRED BARRINGER, JR., architect; b. New Orleans, May 14, 1934; s. Fred B. and Leticia (Chevez) B. BArch, Tulane U., 1959; postgrad., U. Pa., 1960-61. Designer Freret and Wolf, Architects, 1959-60, Kenneth Ripnen, Architect, 1961-63, Francis X. Gina, Architects, 1963-64, Smith, Smith, Haines, Lundberg and Waehler, N.Y.C., 1965; ptnr., v.p. William F. Pedersen & Assocs., N.Y.C. and New Haven, 1965-77; prin. Fred B. Bookhardt, Architect, N.Y.C., 1977—. Dir. 28 E. 4th St. Housing Corp.; cons. Engring. Cons. Group, Cairo, Heliopolis and Alexandria, Egypt, 1983—; dir. The Network of Bus. & Profl. Orgns. Contbg. editor Uptown mag., New Orleans; archtl. works include: Superior Cts. Bldg., New Haven, 1974, Hall Minerals and Gems of Am. Mus. Natural History, 1976, Fed. Office Bldg., New Haven, 1978, Restaurant Claire, Key West, Fla., 1978, Woodmere Kingdom of Minerals, 1980, exec. offices So. Container Corp., Hauppauge, N.Y., 1981, Mus. Shop Am. Mus. Natural History, N.Y.C., 1982, renovation of pub. spaces lower level, 1984, employees cafeteria, 1984,

Children's Reception Ctr., 1986, Sadowsky residence, Northport, N.Y., 1987, Kaufman residence, N.Y.C., 1987, Grossman residence, Montauk, N.Y., 1983, St. Barts, W.I., 1990, Zweibel residences, N.Y.C., 1983, Ft. Lauderdale, Fla., 1984, exec. offices Bon Temps Employment Agy., N.Y.C., 1984, Dieckmann residence, Manhasset, N.Y., 1985, master plan Am. Mus. Natural History, N.Y.C., 1989, space analysis The Trotting Horse Mus., Goshen, N.Y., 1989, addition and renovation, 1990, De Roy residence, N.Y.C., 1991, Zweibel residence, Boca Raton, Fla., 1993, Kelley residence, St. James, N.Y., 1983, HIV Law Project, 1994, Hinlein residence, 1995, Price/Uribe Residence, East Northport, N.Y., 1996, Branford (Conn.) H.S. with David M. Chin, 1996-97, Mancini Residence, N.Y.C., with Charles Burke, 1998, Fitz Simons Residence, 1999, Cary Grossman Residence, 1999, Bookhardt-Gaskell Residence, New Orleans, 2000. With U.S. Army, 1954-56. Recipient Lumen award Illuminating Engrs. Soc., 1977, 1st pl. award Home Mag. ceramic tile competition. Mem. AIA, N.Y. State Assn. Architects, Architects Coun. N.Y.C., N.Y. Soc. Architects, Am. Assn. Mus., N.E. Mus. Conf., Nat. Cert. Archtl. Rev. Bd. (cert.) Home and Office: 819 Marigny St New Orleans LA 70117-8525

BOOKMAN, ALAN B., lawyer; b. New Orleans, Nov. 28, 1947; BS, Tulane U., 1969, JD, 1971. Bar: La. 1971, U.S. Dist. Ct. (ea. dist.) La. 1971, Fla. 1973, U.S. Dist. Ct. (no. and mid. dist.) Fla. 1975, U.S. Ct. Appeals (5th cir.) 1975, U.S. Supreme Ct. 1977, U.S. Ct. Appeals (11th cir.) 1981. Assoc. to ptnr. Emmanuel, Sheppard & Condon, Pensacola, Fla., 1975—. Adj. prof. Pensacola Jr. Coll. Capt. JAGC U.S. Army, 1971—74. Mem. Escambia-Santa Rosa Bar Assn. (pres. 1992-93), Fla. Bar Assn. (bd. gov. 1996-2004, exec. com., 1999-2000, 2002-, pres.-elect 2004), Escambia-Santa Rosa Bar Found. (pres. 1987-88, chmn. 1988-89, jud. nomination commn. 1st jud. dist.), Rotary. Avocation: golf. Office: Emmanuel Sheppard et al PO Drawer 1271 30 S Spring St Pensacola FL 32502-5612

BOOKMAN, ANN EDITH, director; b. N.Y.C., Apr. 28, 1948; d. John Jacob and Ruth Louise (Lowe) B.; m. Eric P. Buehrens, July 5, 1981; children: Nicholas, Emily. BA with honors, Barnard U., 1970; MA, Harvard U., 1973, PhD, 1977. Asst. dir. The Bunting Inst./Radcliffe Coll., Cambridge, Mass., 1983-89; rsch. assoc. in child and family policy Lesley Coll., Cambridge, 1990-92; dir. Ctr. for Interdisciplinary and Spl. Studies Coll. of the Holy Cross, Worcester, Mass., 1992—93; policy and rsch. dir. U.S. Dept. Labor-Women's Bur., Washington, 1993-96; exec. dir. Commn. on Family and Med. Leave, Washington, 1995-96; dir. Ctr. for Interdisciplinary and Spl. Studies Coll. of the Holy Cross, 1996—2000; vis. scholar MIT Sloan Sch. Mgmt., 2000—01; exec. dir. MIT Workplace Ctr. Sloan Sch. Mgmt., 2001—. Editor: Women and the Politics of Empowerment, 1988; author Starting In Our Own Backyards: How Working Famiiltes Can Build Cmty and Survive the New Economy Rouhedge, 2004. Gubernatorial appointee Commn. on TDI and Ins., Boston, 1988-89, Gov.'s Day Care Partnership Task Force, Boston, 1991-92; presdl. appointee U.S. Dept. Labor, Washington, 1993-96. Fellow Am. Anthropol. Assn. Democrat. Jewish. Avocation: gardening.

BOOKOFF, LESLIE, lawyer; b. Balt., June 18, 1968; BS summa cum laude, U. Md., 1990; JD cum laude, U. Pa., 1993. Bar: Md. 1993, DC 1994, registered: US Patent & Trademark Office. Ptnr. Finnegan, Henderson, Farabow, Garrett & Dunner LLP, Washington, ptnr.-in-charge, Profl. Recruitment. Mem. U. Pa. Law Rev. Office: Finnegan Henderson Farabow Garrett & Dunner LLP 901 New York Ave NW Washington DC 20001-3315 Office Phone: 202-408-4000. Office Fax: 202-408-4400. Business E-Mail: les.bookoff@finnegan.com.

BOOKOUT, JOHN FRANK, JR., oil industry executive; b. Shreveport, La., Dec. 31, 1922; s. John Frank and Lena (Hagen) B.; m. Mary Carolyn Cook, Dec. 21, 1946; children: Beverly Carolyn, Mary Adair and John Frank III (twins). Student, Iowa Wesleyan Coll., 1943, Centenary Coll., 1946-47, LLD (hon.), 1987; BSc, U. Tex., 1949, MA, 1950; DSc (hon.), Tulane U., 1978. Geologist Shell Oil Co., Tulsa, 1950-59, div. exploration mgr., 1959-61, area exploration mgr. Denver, 1961-63, The Hague, Netherlands, 1963-64, mgr. exploration and prodn. econs. dept. N.Y.C., 1965, v.p. Denver exploration and prodn. area, 1966, v.p. Southeastern exploration and prodn. region New Orleans, 1967-70; pres., chief exec. officer, dir. Shell Can. Ltd., Toronto, Ont., 1970-74; exec. v.p., dir. Shell Oil Co., Houston, 1974-76, pres., chief exec. officer, dir., 1976-88; dir., mem. exec. com. Shell Petroleum Inc., 1988—; dir. Royal Dutch Petroleum Co., 1988-93. Bd. dirs. Investment Co. Am., McDermott Internat., Inc.; past chmn. adv. bd. Inst. Bioscis. and Tech.; chmn. Tex. A&M U. Active chancellor's coun., mem. devel. bd. U. Tex.; chmn. bd. dirs. Meth. Hosp., Houston; mem. regional adv. bd. Inst. Internat. Edn.; co-chmn. media com. Econ. Summit, Houston, 1990. With USAAF, 1942-46. Decorated Air medal with 3 oak leaf clusters; comdr. Order of Orange-Nassau (The Netherlands), 1988; recipient Disting. Service award Nat. Assn. Secondary Sch. Prins., John Rogers award Southwestern Legal Fedn., 1986; named Outstanding Chief Exec. Domestic Integrated Oil Co. Wall St. Transcript, 1982-84, Disting. Alumnus U. Tex., 1981; named to Offshore Energy Ctr. Industry Pioneer Hall of Fame, 2001. Mem. Am. Assn. Petroleum Geologists (Excellence in Exploration Leadership award 1990), Nat. Petroleum Coun. (former chmn.), Houston C. of C., The Conf. Bd. (bd. dirs.), Am. Petroleum Inst. (bd. dirs., past chmn. bd., mgmt. com.), 25 Yr. Club Petroleum Industry (bd. govs. SW dist.), Internat. C. of C. (U.S. Coun., trustee), Coun. on Fgn. Rels. Inc., All-Am. Wildcatters Assn., Bus. Roundtable (mem. policy com.), Am. Coun. on Edn. (bus.-higher edn. forum mem.), The 1001 World Wildlife Fund (life). Home: PO Box 2463 Houston TX 77252-2463 Office: JKJ LLC One Shell Plz 910 Louisiana Ste 5050 Houston TX 77002

BOOKS, ROBERTA PAULA, real estate finance executive; b. Boston, Apr. 4, 1943; d. Leonard and Mary (Karsh) Books; m. Jay S. Negin, May 20, 1973; children: Martha Alice Books Negin, Samuel Benjamin Books Negin. AB in Math., Bryn Mawr Coll., 1964, AM in Physics, 1969; MBA, Harvard U., 1971; postgrad., NYU, 1966. Acct. mktg. rep. IBM, N.Y.C., 1966-69; v.p. Morgan Stanley, N.Y.C., 1971-81; spl. asst. to comptroller Office of the Comptroller of the Currency, Washington, 1977-79; mng. dir. Prudential Ins. Co. Am., Newark, 1982-86; v.p., co-head real estate capital markets Salomon Bros., N.Y.C., 1986-90; v.p. Citicorp Real Estate, N.Y.C., 1991-94; mng. dir. Chem. Bank, N.Y.C., 1994-96, Landauer Assoc., 1997—99; pres. Books Realty Capital, 1999—. Author pamphlet. Bookshop chair Bryn Mawr Club NY; mem. adv. bd. fin. and admissions coms. Green Meadow Waldorf Sch., Spring Valley, NY, 2001—; mem. music sch. com. Thurnauer Sch. Music. Mem.: Comml. Mortgage Securitization Assn., Fin. Women's Assn. N.Y. Office: Books Realty Capital 6 Demarest Ct Englewood Cliffs NJ 07632-1904

BOOKSPAN, MARTIN, broadcaster, writer; b. Boston, July 30, 1926; s. Simon and Martha (Schwartz) B.; m. Janet Sylvia Sobel, Oct. 24, 1954; children: Rachel Raissa, David Israel, Deborah Joy. BS, Harvard U., 1947; MusD (hon.), Mannes Coll. of Music, 1991; LHD (hon.), Suffolk U., 1995. Music dir. Sta. WBMS, Boston, 1946-50; concert music dir. Sta. WCOP, Boston, 1950-54; exec. dir. New Eng. Opera Theater, Boston, 1952-54; media dir. Boston Symphony, 1954-56; program dir. Sta. WQXR, N.Y.C., 1956-67; dir. concerts ASCAP, N.Y.C., 1968-83; commentator N.Y. Philharm., 1975—88, Live from Lincoln Ctr., N.Y.C., 1976—; v.p. Moss Music Group, N.Y.C., 1983-88. Cons. The Rockefeller Found., N.Y.C., 1963-67, Madison Sq. Garden, 1984-86, Nat. Westminster Bank, 1987-91; panelist Nat. Endowment for the Arts, Washington, 1978—; expert classical music Prodigy on Line Computer Svc., 1990-95; Web moderator Livefromlincolncenter.org, 1997—. Author: 101 Masterpieces Music, 1968, consumer Reports Recs., 1973, (with others) Zubin, 1978, Andre Previn, 1982. Recipient Peabody award, 1948, Letter of Merit Am. Music Ctr., 1977, Medal of Honor, Nat. Arts Club, 1984, Spl. award Concert Artists Guild, 1986, Fine Arts Radio Internat. Lifetime Achievement award, 2002. Mem. AFTRA, ASCAP, Nat. Acad. Records, Screen Actors Guild, The Bohemians, The Dutch Treat. Home and Office: Apt 1414 155 W 68th St New York NY 10023-5819 E-mail: shanasima@juno.com.

BOOMER, JOHN DANA, artist, sculptor; b. Merced, Calif., Oct. 6, 1945; Work reviewed in Nat. Sculpture Rev., Artspace, 1982, Southwest Art Mag., 1983, Fine Woodworking, Masters of American Sculpture; one-man shows and group exhbns. include Foothill Art Ctr., Golden, Colo., 1980, 83, 96, Sedona (Ariz.) Art Ctr., 1996, Albuquerque Fine Art Mus., 2000; represented in permanent collections at Albuquerque Internat. Airport, Old Jail House Art Mus., Albany, Tex., Albuquerque (N.Mex.) Art Mus. Avocations: playing guitar and harmonica, movies, hiking, reading. Home: PO Box 3207 Milan NM 87021

BOOMER, KATHLEEN MCLAUGHLIN, school system administrator; b. N.Y.C., Feb. 27, 1955; d. John Patrick and Carol McLaughlin; m. Kenneth George Boomer, Sept. 11, 1976. BA, U. Calif., Berkeley, 1977; M, St. Mary's Coll., 1986; D, U. Pacific, 1993. Adminstrv. svcs. credential Calif. Commn. Tchr. Credentialing, resource specialist Calif. Commn. Tchr. Credentialing, learning handicapped credential Calif. Commn. Tchr. Credentialing, social sci. Calif. Commn. Tchr. Credentialing. Spl. edn. tchr. Brentwood Union Sch. Dist., Brentwood, Calif., 1982—88; vice prin. Stanislaus Union Sch. Dist., Modesto, Calif., 1988—89, prin., 1989—95, supt., 2000—; dir. elem. svcs. Manteca Unified Sch. Dist., Manteca, Calif., 1995—98, asst. supt. pers., 1998—2000. Adj. prof. U. Pacific, Stockton, Calif., 1995—98. Sponsor women's leadership initiative United Way -Power of the Purse, Modesto, Calif., 2002—05. Mem.: Assn. Calif. Sch. Adminstrs. (state bd. 2001—04), Rotary Internat. Avocations: travel, reading, charity work, baseball, golf. Office: Stanislaus Union Sch Dist 3601 Carver Rd Modesto CA 95356 Office Phone: 209-529-9546.

BOOMERSHINE, DONALD EUGENE, bureau executive, development official; b. Brookville, Ohio, Oct. 5, 1931; s. Harold Everett and Elsie (Rhoads) B.; m. Marilyn Sullivan, Aug. 29, 1953 (dec.); children: Jeffrey, Alan; m. Patti Watson, May 29, 1985. BS, Bowling Green (Ohio) State U., 1953; grad., Northwestern U. Bank Mktg. Grad. Sch., 1965; M in Banking, Rutgers U. Stonier Sch. Banking, 1969-72; postgrad., U. Okla. Nat. Comml. Lending Sch., 1974. With jr. exec. program Frigidaire div. Gen. Motors Corp., Dayton, 1955-57; sr. sales rep. IBM, Dayton, 1957-61; bus. devel. rep., asst. cashier Exchange Security Bank, Birmingham, 1961-65; asst. v.p. charge nat. accounts divsn. Birmingham Trust Nat. Bank, 1965-78, v.p., 1968-71, v.p., sales mgr. Circle S div., 1978-80; v.p. community devel. Met. Devel. Bd., 1980-82; pres. Better Bus. Bur. of Cen. Ala., Birmingham, 1982—. Chmn. Bus. Tomorrow Conf. Auburn U., 1975; ednl. chmn. Assoc. Industries Ala., 1975—77; pres. Better Bus. Bur., Birmingham, 1982—; mem. Atlanta-Birmingham br. Fed. Res. Bd., 1990—97, chmn., 1993, 96; mem. bus. adv. coun. Sorrell Coll. Bus., Troy State U. Pres. North Central Ala. chpt. Muscular Dystrophy Found., 1964; trustee Birmingham YWCA, 1972—75; gen. chmn. U.S. World Youth Game, 1973; charter mem. Downtown Action Com., 1966; mem. ARC, 1967—, bd. dirs., 1968—80; mem. steering com. Mobile Coll., 1987—90; mem. adv. bd. U. South Ala., 1975-78; chmn. Am. Cancer Crusade, 1976; bd. dirs. Birmingham Children's Theatre, 1974-78, Downtown YMCA, Met. YMCA, 1992-97; mem. adv. bd. Ala. State Bd. Edn., 1976—; bd. dirs., 2d v.p. Birmingham Better Bus. Bur., 1980-82; bd. govs. Ala. Assn. Ind. Colls. and Univs.; v.p. Nat. Vet's Day, 1972—; active Leadership Birmingham; mem. Blue and Gold Bd. U.S. Naval Acad., designated info. officer, 1982—2004; mem. exec. com. Birmingham Cmty. Svc. award; founding bd. dirs. Ala. Jump Start Coalition, 2002; mem. Ala. com. Employers Support of the N.G. and Res. With USMCR, 1953-84; now col. Ret. Recipient Comdt. award U.S. Naval Acad., 1994, Comdts. Dir. award, 1999, Outstanding Broadcasters Cooperation award Ala. Broadcasters Assn., 1998, Alumni Cmty. Svc. award Bowling Green State U., 2001; Res. Day proclaimed in his honor, 1983; named to Okla. Sr. Citizen Hall of Fame, 2005. Mem. Bank Mktg. Assn. (nat. dir. 1971-75, nat. v.p. devel. 1971), Ala. Indsl. Devel. Coun., So. Indsl. Coun., World Trade Assn. Ala., Diplomats of Birmingham (founder, chmn. 1973), Marine Corps Res. Officers Assn. (nat. dir. 1974-76), Operation Native Sons and Daus. (chmn. 1972), Newcomen Soc. of U.S., Birmingham C. of C. (life), Vestavia Country Club, The Club, Touchdown Club (Birmingham, founder, dir., treas), Kiwanis (officer, dir., Birmingham 1971, Hixson fellow 2003), Vestavia Country Club, The Club, Summit Club (bd. dirs. 2004), Sigma Chi. Office: Better Bus Bur PO Box 55268 Birmingham AL 35255-5268 Home: 183 Highland Park Drive Birmingham AL 35242

BOONE, ANTHONY FOREST, artist; b. Louisville, Apr. 5, 1965; s. Nelson Bernard and Shirley Dean Boone; m. Emily Howell-Boone, Aug. 10, 1991. BA, U. Louisville, 1997, BFA, 1998; postgrad., Ind. U., 1999—2000. Ky. bus. lic. Tchrs. asst. fine arts dept. Ind. U., Bloomington, 1999—2000; owner Mus. Rock Products, Louisville, 2000—. Workshop leader McCarthy Campus, Louisville, 1995; vis. artist DePaul Transitional, Louisville, 1997; art/tech. cons. Field Mus., Chgo., 2000, Louisville Zool. Gardens, 2002—03; installation art cons. Svc. Net, Jeffersonville, Ind., 2001, City of Louisville's Lewis and Clark Bicentennial Meml., 2002; tech. cons. St. Louis Zoo, 2002; designer, fabricator display Cranbrook Inst. Sci., 2003. Spkr., lectr. Bapt. Hosp. East, Louisville, 1998—2002; active Vols. of Am., Louisville, 2000—03. Recipient Excellence award, Louisville Third Century, 1995; grantee Acad. grantee, Commonwealth Ky., Louisville, 1996; scholar Acad. scholar, Ind. U., Bloomington, 1998. Mem.: Art and Sci. Collaboratoins, Cin. Contemporary Mus., Am. Zool. Assn., Am. Assn. Mus., Internat. Sculpture Ctr. Achievements include design patents decorative rock wall panels. Avocations: paleontology, archaeology, writing, collecting and restoring Native American art. Home: 187 N Bellaire Ave Louisville KY 40206 Office: Mus Rock Products Bldg D 6330 Strawberry Ln Louisville KY 40214

BOONE, BILLY WARREN, lawyer, retired judge; b. Perryton, Tex., Feb. 6, 1955; s. Kermit George and Verna Jean (Thomas) B.; m. Celia Trimble, 1990; children: Billy Warren II, Carol Ann. BA with honors, Tex. Tech U., 1977, JD cum laude, 1980. Bar: Tex. 1980, U.S. Dist. Ct. (no. dist.) Tex. 1982, U.S. Ct. Appeals (5th cir.) 1990, U.S. Supreme Ct. 1993. Assoc. David P. Hooper & Assocs., Abilene, Tex., 1980-82; prin. Billy W. Boone, Abilene, 1982—. Part-time U.S. magistrate U.S. Dist. Ct. (no. dist.) Tex., Abilene, 1987-2003; assoc. editor Tex. Tech. Law Sch., 1979-80. Fellow Tex. Bar Found.; mem. Tex. Bar Assn., Tex. Ctr. for Legal Ethics and Professionalism, Abilene Bar Assn. (former dir.), Nat. Coun. U.S. Magistrates (mem. dist. 14D grievance com. 2003—), Order of Coif. Home: 49 Cypress Point St Abilene TX 79606-5130 Office: 104 Pine St #705 PO Box 2797 Abilene TX 79604-2797 Office Phone: 325-695-7460. E-mail: mail@bboone.com.

BOONE, BRET ROBERT, professional baseball player; b. El Cajon, Calif., Apr. 6, 1969; s. Bob Boone. Ed., U. So. Calif. Infielder Seattle Mariners, 1992-93, Cin. Reds, 1994-98, Atlanta Braves, 1999-2000, San Diego Padres, 2000—, Seattle Mariners, 2001—05, Minnesota Twins, 2005—. Recipient Am. League Gold Glove Award, 1998, 2001, 2003—04. Achievements include led Am. League in RBI's (141), 2001. Office: Minnesota Twins 34 Kirby Puckett Place Minneapolis MN 55415

BOONE, CHARLES W., physician, pathologist; b. Berkeley, Calif., Dec. 21, 1925; s. Harmon Dunscomb and Florence Celia (Chandler) B.; m. Alexandra Weekes, Dec. 21, 1992. MD, U. Calif., San Francisco, 1951; PhD, U. Calif., L.A., 1964. Fellow Coll. Am. Pathologists. Intern gen. practice UCLA, 1954-56, resident pathology, 1956-60, PhD tng. Dept. Biochemistry, 1960-64; post doctoral tng. in Cell Biology Albert Einstein Coll. Medicine, Bronx, N.Y., 1964-65; chief cell biology sect. Nat. Cancer Inst., NIH, Bethesda, Md., 1965-80; chief pathology Al Hada Hosp., Taif, Saudi Arabia, 1980-84, program dir. chemoprevention branch, Divsn. of Cancer Prevention and Control, 1984-90; divsn. chemoprevention NIH, NCI, Bethesda, 1991—. Author: (book) Cancer Prevention, 1992; contbr. over 140 articles to sci. jours. Ensign USN, 1943-45. Avocations: scuba diving, tennis, history.

BOONE, DEBORAH ANN (DEBBY BOONE), singer; b. Hackensack, NJ, Sept. 22, 1956; d. Charles (Pat) Eugene and Shirley (Foley) Boone; m. Gabriel Ferrer, 1979; children: Gabriella, Dustin Boone, Tessa Rose. Student Calif. schs. Singer: with father, Pat Boone, and family group, 1970—; profl. rec. artist, 1977—, numerous appearances (TV series) TV talk and variety programs, appeared (ABC-TV Movie of the Week TV films) Sins of the Past, 1984, star children's video Hug Along Songs; author: Debby Boone--So Far, 1988, (children's book) Bedtime Hugs for Little Ones, 1988; co-author: Tomorrow is a Brand New Day, 1989; starred in nat. tour (Broadway plays) Seven Brides for Seven Brothers, 1981—82, nat. tour Sound of Music, 1987—88, actress (plays) Camelot, 2005. Named Singing Star of Yr., Am. Guild Variety Artists, 1978, Working Mother of Yr., 1982; recipient Am. Music award, song of yr., 1977, Grammy award, best new artist, 1977, Grammy award, best inspirational performance, 1980, Grammy award, best Gospel performance for Keep the Flame Burning, 1984, Nat. Assn. Theatre Owners award, best new personality, 1980, Dove award, 1980, Dove award for album Surrender, 1984, Country Music award, best new country artist, 1977. Mem.: Ch. on the Way. Address: 4334 Kester Ave Van Nuys CA 91403-4135

BOONE, DONNA CLAUSEN, physical therapist, statistician, researcher; b. Nebraska City, Nebr., Dec. 12, 1932; d. Otto Ralph and Hallie Rae Clausen; m. Robert William Boone, Apr. 3, 1965. BA in Zoology, U. Wyo., 1954; MS in Phys. Therapy, U. So. Calif., 1980, MS in Biometry, 1983. Lic. phys. therapist, Calif. Phys. therapist Ill. Hosp. Sch., Chgo., 1955—59, Calif. Hosp., L.A., 1959—63; hemophilia specialist in phys. therapy Orthop. Hosp., L.A., 1963—78, rschr., project dir. Hemophilia Ctr., 1967—78; instr. rsch. methods U. So. Calif., L.A., 1982—83, Calif. State U., Long Beach, 1982—83; biostatistician immunulogy U. So. Calif., L.A., 0983—1987, coord., statistician Nat. Clin. Trial, Silicone Study, 1987—93; phys. therapist Huntington Meml. Hosp., Pasadena, Calif., 1993—98; cons. Hemophilia Continuous Quality Improvement, Lompoc, Calif., 1998—. Internat. lectr., cons. World Fedn. Hemophilia, Montreal, Can., 1970-78; cons. biostatis. dentistry and pharmacology U. So. Calif., L.A., 1982-83, cons. orthop., U. Buffalo, 1982-83; continuous quality improvement coach Doheny Eye Inst., L.A., 1990-92, Huntington Meml. Hosp., Pasadena, Calif., 1993-97; cons. phys. therapy working group Nat. Hemophilia Found., 2000—. Editor: Comprehensive Management of Hemophilia, 1976, (internat. newsletter) World Hemophilia AIDS Ctr., 1984-93; contbr. articles to profl. jours. Co-chair United Way Campaign Orthopaedic Hosp., L.A., chair, 1975—75; mem. Lompoc Rep. Women, 1998—, legis. chair, 2000—; vol. Rep. Campaign for Ho. of Reps., Glendale, Calif., 1996; recording sec. Santa Barbara County Rep. Women, 2000—01; lay leader St. Mary's Episcopal Ch., 1998—; bd. dirs. World Hemophilia Alliance, sec., 1996—; mem. alumni com. U. Wyo., 1999—; mem. med. adv. bd. Hemophilia Found. So. Calif., L.A., 1974—78. Grantee Fed. Govt. Agys., 1967, 73; recipient Dr. Murray Thelin award Nat. Hemophilia Found., 1976, Disting. Alumna award U. Wyo., 1979, Achievement award Alpha Chi Omega, 1980, Spl. Achievement award for treatment advances 50th Anniversary of Nat. Hemophilia Found., 1998, Donna Clausen Boone ann. award Nat. Hemophilia Found. to Phys. Therapist, 1999—. Mem. Antique Automobile Club. Republican. Episcopalian. Avocations: gardening, antique autos, travel, reading, jazz music clubs.

BOONE, J. WILLIAM, lawyer; b. Newnan, Ga., Aug. 31, 1952; s. Daniel Walter Boone Jr. and Winifred Trimble (Glover) Klein; m. Anne Elizabeth Campbell, June 28, 1986. BA cum laude, Wake Forest U., 1974; JD cum laude, Mercer U., 1977. Bar: Ga. 1977, D.C. 1979, U.S. Dist. Ct. (no. dist.) Ga. 1977, U.S. Dist. Ct. (mid. dist.) Ga. 1989, U.S. Dist. Ct. D.C. 1979, U.S. Dist. Ct. Md. 1977. Atty. U.S. Dept. Justice, Washington, 1977-83, asst. U.S. atty. Atlanta, 1983-86; ptnr., bankruptcy, reorganization Alston & Bird LLP, Atlanta, 1986—. Spkr. in field. Mem. Olympic Organizing Com.; active High Mus., Atlanta, 1983—. Capt. USAR, 1974-85. Mem. ABA (former chair. Insolvency Inst. chair, Lex Mundi Internat. Insolvency practice group 2003—), D.C. Bar Assn., Atlanta Bar Assn. (bd. dirs. 2001-05, chmn. bankruptcy sect. 1999-2000), Ga. Bar Assn. (continuing legal edn. com. 1987-88), Phi Delta Phi. Presbyterian. Avocations: sports, travel, hunting. Office: Alston & Bird One Atlantic Ctr 1201 W Peachtree St Atlanta GA 30309-3424 Office Phone: 404-881-7282. E-mail: bboone@alston.com.

BOONE, JAMES VIRGIL, retired engineering executive, researcher; b. Little Rock, Sept. 1, 1933; s. Virgil Bennett and Dorothy Bliss (Dorough) B.; m. Gloria Marjorie Gieseler, June 5, 1955; children: Clifford B., Sandra J. Smyser, Steven B. BSEE, Tulane U., 1955; MSEE, Air Force Inst. Tech., Ohio, 1959. Assoc. elec. engr. Martin Co., Balt., 1955; R&D engr. USAF, 1955-62; electronics engr. Nat. Security Agy., Ft. Meade, Md., 1962-77, dep. dir. for rsch. and engring., 1978-81; spl. asst. to gen. mgr. mil. electronics divsn. TRW, Inc., San Diego, 1981-83, asst. gen. mgr., 1983-85; dir. program mgmt. and group devel. TRW Electronic Sys. Group, 1985-86, v.p., dir. program mgmt. and group devel., 1986-87, v.p., gen. mgr. def. comm. divsn., 1987-91, v.p. gen. mgr., 1991—93; v.p. requirements and group devel. Sys. Integration Group, 1993-95, v.p. tech. and engring., 1995-96; v.p., gen. mgr. TRW Sys. Svcs. Co., 1994-96. Assoc. dir. Armed Forces Comm. and Electronics Assn., 1991-94, dir., 1994-96; mem. adv. bd. Tulane U. Coll. Engring., 1991—, pres., 2000-02; adj. prof. sch. information tech. and engring. George Mason U., 1995-96; prin. rsch. scientist C3I Ctr., 1996-99, chair acquisition com. Nat. Cryptologic Mus. Found., Inc., 1997-2002; adj. prof. Joint Mil. Intelligence Coll., 2002--. Served to capt. USAF, 1955-62. Recipient Exceptional Civilian Svc. award Nat. Security Agy., 1975, Disting. Alumnus award Tulane U. Sch. Engring., 1994. Mem. IEEE (sr.), AIAA (sr.). Republican. Presbyterian (elder). Home: 4905 Oakcrest Dr Fairfax VA 22030-4548

BOONE, MICHAEL MAULDIN, lawyer; b. Henderson, Jan. 31, 1941; s. Daniel Lacey and La Nelle Ruby (Stovall) Boone; m. Marla Hays, Aug. 2, 1969; children: Michael Hays, Maryjane Mauldin. BBA, So. Meth. U., 1963, JD, 1967. Bar: Tex. 1967. Assoc. firm Richard D. Haynes, 1967-69; co-founder Haynes & Boone LLP, Dallas, 1964, ptnr., mergers & acquisitions, corp. fin., securities transactions, 1969—, mem. mgmt. com., bd. dir. Adj. prof. law So. Meth. U. Sch. Law, 1972—88. Mem. Dallas Citizens' Coun.; trustee Abilene Christian U.; chmn. exec. bd. So. Meth. Law Sch.; bd. visitors Pepperdine U. Law Sch.; pres. sch. bd. Highland Park Independent Sch. Dist. Named a "Go-To-Lawyer" in Tex. corp./bus. law, Tex. Lawyer Mag.; named one of top corp. fin./mergers & acquisitions lawyers in Dallas, D Magazine, top 10 super lawyers, Tex. Monthly, Law and Politics Mag.; recipient Recipient Disting. Alumni award, So. Meth. U. law Sch., 1990, Next Millennium Award, Freedom's Found., Valley Forge, 1999, Justinian Award for pub. svc., 2004. Mem.: State Bar Tex. (chmn. corp. banking & bus. law sect. 1983—84), Dallas Bar Assn., ABA, Dallas Country Club, City Club, Crescent Club, Phi Delta Phi, Phi Gamma Delta. Mem. Ch. of Christ (elder). Office: Haynes and Boone LLP 901 Main St Ste 3100 Dallas TX 75202-3789 Office Phone: 214-651-5552. Office Fax: 214-200-0369. Business E-Mail: michael.boone@haynesboone.com.

BOONE, MORELL DOUGLAS, information technology educator; b. Londonderry, Northern Ireland, Dec. 15, 1942; arrived in U.S., 1946; s. Paul J. and Margaret (Hill) B.; m. Carolyn June Gallagher, July 6, 1968; children—Ian Charles, Megan Elizabeth BS, Kutztown State Coll., Pa., 1964; MS, Syracuse U., 1968, PhD, 1980. Librarian Pennridge Schs., Perkasie, Pa., 1964-66; reference librarian Hobart and William Smith Colls., Geneva, N.Y., 1968-70; lectr. Syracuse U., N.Y., 1970-72; dean learning resources U. Bridgeport, Conn., 1973-80; dir. Ctr. of Ednl. Resources Eastern Mich. U., Ypsilanti, 1980—85, dean learning resources and techs., 1986—2001, prof. interdisciplinary tech., 2001—04, prof., dir. Sch. Tech. Studies, 2004—. Cons. for internat. ednl. devel. Iran, Swaziland, Yemen, others. Presenter at profl meetings;, co-author book; contbr. articles to profl. jours.; mem. editl. bd. Innovate, Libr. Hi Tech. Chmn. Community Cablecasting Commn., Ypsilanti, 1981-84, Ypsilanti Ednl. Found., 1988-94; pres. bd. dirs. Meals on Wheels, Ypsilanti, 1998—. Named to Pennridge H.S. Wall of Fame, 2001. Mem. ALA, EDUCAUSE, Soc. Coll. and Univ. Planning, Kiwanis. Democrat. Presbyterian (elder). Avocations: gardening, reading, travel. Home: 5774 Pineview Dr Ypsilanti MI 48197-8903 Office: Eastern Mich U 122 Sill Hall Ypsilanti MI 48197 Office Phone: 734-487-1161. Business E-Mail: mboone@emich.edu.

BOONE, RICHARD WINSTON, SR., lawyer; b. Washington, July 19, 1941; s. Henry Shaffer and Anne Catherine (Huehne) B.; m. Jean Knox Logan, Dec. 17, 1966; children: Elizabeth Anne, Richard Winston, Jr., Katheryn Jeanne. BA with honors, U. Ala., 1963; JD, Georgetown U., 1970. Bar: Va. 1970, D.C. 1970, Md. 1984, U.S. Ct. Appeals (D.C. cir.) 1970, U.S. Ct. Appeals (2nd cir.) 1973, U.S. Ct. Appeals (4th cir.) 1972, U.S. Supreme Ct. 1974, U.S. Ct. Claims 1975. Ptnr. Carr, Jordan, Coyne & Savits, Washington, 1977-81; shareholder, dir. Wilkes, Artis, Hedrick & Lane, P.C., Washington, 1984—95; pres. Richard W. Boone, P.C., McLean, Va., 1984—95, The Law Offices of Richard W. Boone, 1995-97, Boone & Assocs., P.C., 1998—. Capt. USAR, 1964-67. Mem. D.C. Def. Lawyers Assn., Va. Trial Lawyers Assn., Va. Assn. Def. Attys., Barristers Assn. Avocations: model railroading, photography. E-mail: rwboone@aol.com.

BOONE, STEPHEN CHRISTOPHER, retired neurosurgeon; b. Navasota, Tex., Mar. 18, 1938; s. Berrill Harrison and Joyce (Taylor) Boone; m. Elizabeth Thompson, Apr. 9, 1960 (div. June 1979); children: Stephen, Michael, Laura; m. Susan Pate, Nov. 3, 1979; children: Christopher, Emily. BS, Duke U., 1960, MD, PhD, Duke U., 1965. Diplomate Am. Bd. Neurological Surgery. Surg. intern Duke Hosp., Durham, NC, 1965, resident in neurosurgery, 1967-72; chief neurosurgeon Brooke Army Med. Ctr., 1973-75; asst. chief neurosurgery Walter Reed Army Med. Ctr., Washington, 1975-77; from assoc. prof. to prof. neurosurgery U. N.C., 1977-82; neurosurgeon Raleigh (N.C.) Neurosurgery Clinic, 1982—2002; cons. Eastern Neurosurg. & Spine Assocs., Greenville. Brig. gen. USAR, 1962—87. Republican. Episcopalian. E-mail: scboone38@earthlink.net.

BOONSHAFT, HOPE JUDITH, public relations executive; b. Phila., May 3, 1949; d. Barry and Lorelei Gail (R ienzi) B. BA, Pa. State U., 1972; postgrad. Del. Law Sch, Kellogg Inst. Mgmt. Tng. Program writer Youth Edn., N.Y.C., 1972; legal aide to judge Phila., 1975; dir. spl. projects Guiffre Med. Ctr., Phila., 1975; senatorial campaign fin. dir. Arlen Specter, Phila., 1975; presdl. campaign fin. dir. Jimmy Carter, Atlanta, 1976; fin. dir. Dem. Nat. Com., 1977—79; dir. devel. World Jewish Congress, N.Y.C., 1978, Yeshiva U., L.A., 1979; dir. comm. Nat. Easter Seal Soc., Chgo., 1979-83; CEO Boonshaft-Lewis & Savitch Pub. Rels and Govt. Affairs, L.A., 1983-93; sr. v.p. Edelman Worldwide, 1993-95; exec. v.p. external affairs Sony Pictures Entertainement, L.A., 1995—. Spl. adv. cmty. rels. The White House, 1977-80; guest lectr. U. Ill., 1982, May Co.'s Calif. Women in Bus. Bd. dirs. L.A. Arts Coun., Los Angeles County Citizens for Economy and Efficiency in Govt. Commn., Calif. Film Commn., Spkrs. Commn. Calif. Initiative. Home: 1967 Mandeville Canyon Rd Los Angeles CA 90049-2235 Office: Sony Pictures Entertainment 10202 Washington Blvd Culver City CA 90232-3119

BOOP, RICHARD LEE, sales executive; b. Lewisburg, Pa., May 6, 1951; s. Maynard Charles and Mary Catherine (Benfer) Boop; m. Susan Marie (Katherman), July 9, 1977. AA in Indsl. Mgmt., Williamsport Area CC, 1971. Gen. mgr. QCast Aluminum, New Berlin, Pa., 1983—2001, sales mgr., 2002—, Q-E Mfg., 2002—. Scout master Boy Scouts Am., Laurelton, Pa., 1973—76. Mem.: Am. Foundry Assn., Penn. Foundry Assn. Republican. Methodist. Avocations: auto racing, hunting, fishing, reading, numismatics. Home: 1970 State Rte 235 Millmont PA 17845

BOOR, MYRON VERNON, psychologist, educator; b. Wadena, Minn., Dec. 21, 1942; s. Vernon LeRoy and Rosella Katharine (Eckhoff) B. BS, U. Iowa, 1965; MA, So. Ill. U., 1967, PhD, 1970; MS, U. Pitts., 1981. Lic. psychologist, Mo. Research psychologist Milw. County Mental Health Ctr., 1970-72; asst. prof. clin. psychologist Ft. Hays State U., Hays, Kans., 1972-76, assoc. prof., 1976-79; NIMH postdoctoral fellow in psychiat. epidemiology U. Pitts., Western Psychiat. Inst. and Clinic, 1979-81; research psychologist R.I. Hosp. and Butler Hosp., Providence, 1981-84; clin. psychologist Newman Meml. County Hosp., Emporia, Kans., 1985-93, Heartland Health Sys., St. Joseph, Mo., 1994—. Clin. psychologist Ft. Hays State U., 1972-79; asst. prof. psychiatry and human behavior Brown U., Providence, 1981-84; adj. faculty Emporia State U., 1985-94. Contbr. articles to profl. jours. U.S. Pub. Health Service fellow, 1965-67, NIMH fellow 1979-81. Home: 3018 Cambridge St Saint Joseph MO 64506-1164 E-mail: mboor@ccp.com.

BOORAEM, HENDRIK, V, education educator, historian; b. N.Y.C., May 11, 1939; s. Hendrik Booraem, IV and Dorothy Allyn Carr; m. Lynn Francis Allen (div.); children: Dorothy Allen, Hendrik VI, Anna Hollingsworth. BA, U. Va., 1961; MA, Johns Hopkins U., 1974, PhD, 1977. Instr. SUNY, Purchase, 1971—76; tchr. Strom Thurmond H.S., Johnston, SC, 1979—92; assoc. prof. Bucks County C.C., Newtown, Pa., 1992—93; asst. prof. Bucks County Cmty. Coll., Newtown, 2003—. Author: The Formation of the Republican Party in New York, 1983, The Road to Respectability, 1989, The Provincial, 1994, Young Hickory, 2002. Mem.: Newtown Hist. Assn., Holland Soc. N.Y., Authors' Guild, N.J. Gay Men's Chorus. Home: PO Box 514 Newtown PA 18940 Office: Bucks County Cmty Coll Swamp Rd Newtown PA 18940 E-mail: hendrikbooraem@comcast.net.

BOORD, JAMES EDWARD, II, music educator; b. Jan. 7, 1957; s. James Edward and Doris Jean (Bonitati) Boord; m. Kathleen Ann Kirchner, Aug. 10, 2003; children: James Edward III, Kaitlyn Emily, Christina Kirchner. BS in Music Edn., Frostburg State Coll., 1981, MEd in Adminstrn. and Supervision, 1987. H.S. band dir. Garrett County Pub. Schs., Accident, Md., 1981—94, Allegheny County Pub. Schs., Md., 1994—98, coord. music, band dir. Cumberland, Md., 1996—98; supr. music Harford County Pub. Schs., Bel Air, Md., 1998—. Mem.: Md. Music Educators Assn. (mem. exec. bd. 1998—). Avocations: fishing, golf. Home: 202 Kennedy Blvd Elkton MD 21921 Office: Harford County Pub Schs 23 N Main St Bel Air MD 21014

BOORKMAN, JO ANNE, librarian; b. San Jose, Calif., July 21, 1947; d. Charles John and Ruth Ellen (Reuss) B. BA, Scripps Coll., 1969; MS, U. Ill., 1971. Bibl. search analyst biomed. library UCLA, 1971-73, reference librarian Darling biomed. library, 1973-77; head pub. svcs. health scis. library U. N.C., Chapel Hill, 1977-80, head collections devel. health scis. library, 1980-84; head pub. svcs. Carlson health scis. library U. Calif., Davis, 1985-86, acting asst. univ. librarian health scis., 1986-87, head Carlson library, 1988—. NSF fellow, 1969-70. Fellow Spl. Librs. Assn., Med. Libr. Assn. (bd. dirs. 1988-91); mem. No. Calif. and Nev. Med. Libr. Group (pres. 1988-89, award profl. excellence 1996), Mid-Atlantic chpt. Med. Libr. Assn. (pres. 1983-84), P.E.O. Office: U Calif Carlson Health Scis Libr Davis CA 95616-5291 Office Phone: 530-752-6383. Business E-Mail: jaboorkman@ucdavis.edu.

BOORMAN, HOWARD LYON, history professor; b. Chgo., Sept. 11, 1920; s. William Ryland and Verna (Lyon) B.; m. Mary Houghton, Jan. 20, 1972 (dec.); 1 child by previous marriage: Scott A. BA, U. Wis., Madison, 1941; postgrad., Yale U., 1946-47. Divisional asst., divsn. def. materials Dept. of State, Washington, 1942-43; fgn. service officer to Peking, Hong Kong, 1947-54; rsch. assoc. Sch. Internat. Affairs, Columbia U., N.Y.C., 1955-67; prof. history Vanderbilt U., Nashville, 1967-84, prof. emeritus, 1984—. Vis. scholar Univ. Ctr. of Va., 1963. Gen. editor: Biographical Dictionary of Republican China, 4 vols, 1967-71; contbr. articles to profl. jours. Lt. USNR, 1943-46. Recipient Rockefeller Public Service award, 1954-55 Mem.: Assn. Asian Studies, Am. Polit. Sci. Assn., Am. Hist. Assn., Univ. Club (Nashville). Home: 12 Redbud Dr Nashville TN 37215-2423 Office: Vanderbilt U Dept History Nashville TN 37235

BOORSTEIN, LAURENCE, economist, educator; b. Neuilly, France, Jan. 22, 1951; arrived in U.S., 1951; s. Edward and Regula (Simons) Boorstein. BA, Columbia U., 1972, MS, 1974, CE, 1978, MBA, 1988. Sys. analyst Frederic R. Harris, Inc. engrng. divsn. Planning Rsch. Corp., NYC, 1974-77, prin. sys. engr. Frederic R. Harris, Inc. divsn., 1977-79, sr. systems planner Frederic R. Harris Engrng. Divsn., 1979-83, sr. economist Frederic R. Harris, Inc. divsn., 1983-86; sr. economist Soros Assocs., NYC, 1988-94; prin. economist DMJM Harris Inc. divsn. AECOM Tech. Corp., NYC, 1994—, Farifax, Va., 1994—. Mem.: Soc. Civil Engrs. Home: 1716 Lake Shore Crest Dr Apt 3 Reston VA 20190-3244 Office: DMJM Harris 2751 Prosperity Ave Ste 200 Fairfax VA 22031-4342 Office Phone: 703-204-6385. Personal E-mail: lboorstein@att.net. Business E-Mail: larry.boorstein@dmjmharris.com.

BOOSS, CLAIRE, freelance/self-employed editor, literary agent; d. George Frederick Charles and Muriel Elsie Booss. BA, Oberlin Coll., 1953. Mem. social svc. staff Westchester Welfare Dept., Hudson Guild, Ch. World Svc., N.Y.C., 1953—62; mem. advt. staff Benton & Bowles, Bur. Advt., 1964—71; editl. asst. Clarkson Potter Pubs., 1972—75; asst. editor Crown Pubs., 1975—77, editor, 1977—85; sr. editor Random House Pubs., 1988—95; freelance editor, lit. agt., 1996—. Consulting editor Abrams Pub., N.Y.C., 1996—97. Editor: Works of Louisa May Alcott, 1983, Scandinavian Folk and Fairy Tales, 1984, A Treasury of Irish Myth, Legend and Folklore, 1986; series editor: Children's Classics. Mem. New Chelsea Dem. Club, N.Y.C., 1958—62. Mem.: Authors Guild, Gotham Discussion Group, Appalachian Mountain Club. Avocations: reading, walking, visiting museums and galleries, theater, movies.

BOOT, JOHN C.G., economics educator; b. Semarang, Java, Indonesia, June 10, 1936; came to U.S. 1965; s. Frederik Rutger and Maria (den Tex) B.; m. A.M. Hinke Tuinman, May 22, 1965; children— Maren Caroline, Mark Frederik Abe. Ph.D., Netherlands Sch. Econs., Rotterdam, 1964. Prof. econs. and stats. SUNY-Buffalo, 1965— . Author: Quadratic Programming, 1964, others. Home: 177 Beard Ave Buffalo NY 14214-1729 Office: SUNY Amherst Campus Jacobs 325E Buffalo NY 14260-4000 Office Phone: 716-645-3254. Business E-Mail: jboot@buffalo.edu.

BOOTE, ALFRED SHEPARD, marketing researcher, educator; b. NYC, May 21, 1929; s. Alfred Denton and Katharine (Kerrison) B.; m. Joan Peterson, July 9, 1960 (div. Sept. 1963); m. Heath Drury, June 1, 1973. BA, Colgate U., 1951; MBA, Columbia U., 1953, MPhil, 1974, PhD, 1975; MA, Stanford U., 1957. Research mgr. design and market research labs., Container Corp. of Am., 1961-63; assoc. dir. mktg. research Pepsi-Cola Co., 1963-65; dir. mktg. research Far East area, PepsiCo Internat., 1965-67, dir. mktg. rsch. Worldwide, 1967-70; pvt. practice NYC, 1970—75, 1990—; cons. Arthur D. Little, Inc., Cambridge, Mass., 1975-76; gen. mgr., dir. research Decision Research Corp., Lexington, Mass., 1976-78; dir. mktg. research Singer Co., Stamford, Conn., 1978-81; mng. dir., founder Psychographics Research Corp., Inc., Bedford, N.Y., 1981-86; v.p. research Smith Stanley & Co., Inc., Darien, Conn., 1983-87. Adj. assoc. prof. sociology Hunter Coll., 1983; adj. lectr. mktg. rsch. Nichols Coll., 1985; vis. prof. mktg. Clark U., 1985-89; presenter in field. Author: An Evil Trust, 2001; mem. editl. rev. bd. Jour. of Advt., 1982-87; mem. editl. bd. Psychology and Mktg., 1983-85; contbr. articles to bus. and profl. jours. Mem. Planning Commn., Woodstock, Conn., 1985-91; mem. Regional Planning Commn. N.E. Conn., 1987-91; founder, 1st chmn. Mktg. Rsch. Soc. of Hong Kong, 1967; justice peace, Woodstock, Conn., 2001—. Served to lt. (j.g.) U.S. Navy, 1953-56. Sr. rsch. fellow, Robert C. Fischer Inst., 1999—2004. Mem. Am. Sociol. Assn., Alpha Kappa Delta, Alpha Kappa Psi. Home: 73 Bull Hill Rd Woodstock CT 06281-2311 E-mail: asb103@columbia.edu.

BOOTH, ANNA BELLE, accountant; b. Homesville, Ohio, Jan. 15, 1912; d. John Wilson and M. Pearl (Toomey) B.; m. Guy DiAmbrosio, Apr. 29, 1930; 1 child, Guy Booth. BA, Taylor Coll., 1930. Office mgr. in charge of mfg. Jacobs Tailored Clothes, Inc., Phila., 1931-41; acct., corp. cashier Lehigh Coal and Navigation Co., Phila., 1941-55; acct. Bishop & Hedberg, Phila., 1955-57; acct., office mgr. The Camax Co., Phila., 1957-60; office mgr., cashier New Eng. Mutual Life Ins. Co., Phila., 1960-67; acct. Wall & Ochs, Inc., Phila., 1967-71; comptr. Bisler Packaging Div./Pet, Inc., Phila., 1971-82; ret. Mem. Am. Soc. Women Accts. (Phila. pres. 1956-58, dir. 1952-54, 62-64, 73-75), LWV (Phila.). Home: 135 S 20th St Apt 1002 Philadelphia PA 19103

BOOTH, BETTY JEAN, retired daycare administrator, poet; b. St. Louis County, Mo., Dec. 27, 1944; d. Richard Augustus and Leoma Thelma (Atchison) Woods; m. Alfred Lee Pope Jr., Aug. 20, 1962 (div. Apr. 14, 1975); children: Wayman Maurice Woods, Aundrea Denise Walker, Juanita Rosetta Pope-Miller, Victoria Lynn Pope, Daniel Jerome Pope, Alfred Lee III Pope; m. Robert Lee Booth, Mar. 3, 1984; 1 stepchild, David Lee Griffin. Cert., United Bus. Coll., North St. Louis, Mo., 1987. Baby nurse, Ladue, Mo., 1984—89; home care worker and provider Clayton, Mo., 1989; adminstrv. asst. Grateful Home Homeless Shelter, Detroit, 1992; day care asst. Time for Happy Land Care, Detroit, 1999—. Author: Traveling on the Wing's of LIfe's Inner Circle, 2005. Recipient numerous awards for poetry. Avocations: writing, gardening, taping, reading, creating. Home: 14503 Hazelridge St Detroit MI 48205-3619

BOOTH, BONNIE NELSON, human resources consultant; b. Lynn, Mass., Aug. 28, 1942; d. Vincent Carl and Merchelle Romaine (Eastman) Nelson Student, Mary Washington Coll., 1960-61, Columbia U., 1965, Carnegie-Mellon U., 1962, 78-80; EdM in Adminstrn., Planning and Social Policy, Harvard U., 1979. Exec. sec. Kenyon and Eckhardt, Inc., N.Y.C., 1964-65; exec. sec., asst. to assoc. dir. Am. Press. Inst., Columbia U., N.Y.C., 1965; prin. sec. to chief housing sect. UN Hdqrs., N.Y.C., N.Y.C., 1965-68; adminstrv. asst. sec. UN Mission, Magadiscio, Somalia, 1968, Tripoli, Libya, 1968-69; research asst. Stockholm Sch. Econs., 1970; adminstrv. sec. to dep. dir. UN Conf. Trade and Devel./GATT, Geneva, 1970; adminstrv. asst. Harvard U., 1970-74, personnel officer dept. psychology and social relations, 1974-75; adminstrv. asst. Dravo Corp., Pitts., 1975-76; assoc. dir. admissions Chatham Coll., Pitts., 1976-77, acting dir. admissions, 1977-78; mgmt. devel. trainer and adminstr. Westinghouse Credit Corp., Pitts., 1981-86, human resources adminstr., 1986-89, human resources cons., 1989-91, pension cons., 1991-95; human resources cons. in pvt. practice Pitts., 1995—. Dem. committeewoman 7th Ward, Pitts., 1980—, vice chmn., 1990-93, chmn., 1993-94; del. Shadyside Action Coalition, 1988—, sec., 1991-92, pres., 1992-96, 98—; mgmt. vol. cons. Pitts. Fund for Arts Edn.; mem. zoning adv. com. Pitts. Zoning Code Project, 1994—. Recipient Hon. diploma for outstanding performance Internat. Seminar on Rural Housing and Community Facilities, Venezuelan Govt., 1967, Outstanding Quality Circle Facilitator award Westinghouse Electric Corp., 1985 Mem. ASTD, Lions Internatl., bd. dirs., Bloomfield-Lawrenceville Lions Club, 1999—, Internat. Assn. Quality Cirs. (pres. Pitts. chpt. 1985-90), Am. Soc. Exec. Women, Rotary. Episcopalian. Avocations: literature, art, music, film, arranging silk flowers.

BOOTH, CHERIE (CHERIE BLAIR), British barrister; b. Bury, Lancshire, Sept. 23, 1954; d. Anthony and Gale (Smith) B.; m. Anthony Charles Lynton Blair, Mar. 29, 1980; children Euan, Nicholas, Kathryn, and Leo. Grad., Lincoln's Inn, 1976; law degree, London School of Economics. Bar: 1976. Tenant New Ct. Chambers, 1977-91; barrister Gray's Inn Square, London, 1991—; appt. queen's coun., 1995; asst. recorder County Ct. & Crown Ct., 1996—99, recorder, 1999—. Fellowship John Moores Univ., Liverpool; named one of most powerful women, Forbes mag., 2005. Fellow: Royal Soc. of Arts; mem.: Internat. Soc. Lawyers for Pub. Svc. Avocations: reading, working out, attending theatre. Office: 4/5 Gray's Inn Square Gray's Inn London WC1R 5AY England*

BOOTH, DONALD RICHARD, economist, educator; b. Marble, Minn., June 1, 1931; s. Floyd James and Maude (Marquart) B.; m. Louise Hitt, Aug. 22, 1953; 1 child, David. BA, Whittier Coll., 1955; MA, Claremont Coll., 1956; PhD, UCLA, 1970. Grad. dean Chapman Coll., Orange, Calif., 1973-77, acad. dean, 1977-78, exec. v.p., 1978-79, dean, sch. of bus., 1979-81, prof. econs., 1959—, v.p. fin., 1988-89; sr. economist Claremont (Calif.) Inst., 1989—95. Bd. dirs. United Am. Bank, Westminster, Calif., Consumer Credit Counseling of Orange County, Calif. Recipient Eliot Jones award, We. Econs. Assn., 1958; Danforth Teaching fellow, Danforth Found., 1962, NSF fellow, 1970. Avocations: chess, stamp collecting/philately, swimming. Office: Chapman U One University Dr Orange CA 92866-1011 Office Phone: 714-997-6804.

BOOTH, EDGAR CHARLES, lawyer; b. Gainsville, Fla., July 13, 1934; s. Clyde V. and Bertha H. Booth; m. Anne Cawthon, Sept. 6, 1958; children: Rainey, John. BBA, U. Fla., 1956, JD, 1962. Bar: Fla. 1962. Pvt. practice, Tallahassee, 1962—. Judge small claims ct. Tallahassee, 1963-64; city judge Tallahassee, 1964-70. Capt. USAF, 1957-60. Mem. Fla. Bar Assn. Democrat. Episcopalian. Avocations: sailing, tennis, hiking, camping. Home: 900 High Rd Tallahassee FL 32304-1819 Office: PO Box 840 Tallahassee FL 32302-0840 Fax: 850-224-7442.

BOOTH, EDGAR HIRSCH, lawyer; b. Bklyn., June 8, 1926; s. Benjamin H. and Lee (Benzman) B.; m. Joan E. Blumberg, Oct. 7, 1956; children—Charles, Janet. Student, U. Va., 1944, 46-47; BA, Stanford, 1949; JD, Harvard, 1953. Bar: NY 1954. Since practiced in, N.Y.C.; assoc. Booth, Lipton & Lipton, N.Y.C., 1954-65, ptnr., 1965-84, Booth, Marcus & Pierce, N.Y.C., 1984-87, Myerson & Kuhn, N.Y.C., 1988-89, Warshaw Burstein Cohen Schlesinger & Kuh, N.Y.C., 1989-2000, of counsel, 2000—02; ret. Mem. mediators panel U.S. Bankruptcy Ct. So. Dist. N.Y. Mem. Glen Rock Bd. Edn., 1971-77, pres., 1973-74; bd. dirs. S.M. Louis Fund, Inc., N.Y.C. Served with AUS, 1944-46. Mem.: Assn. Bar City N.Y., N.Y. State Bar Assn., Am. Bankruptcy Inst. Home: 25 Belmont Rd Glen Rock NJ 07452-2305 Office: 555 5th Ave New York NY 10017-2416

BOOTH, GEORGE KEEFER, corporate financial executive; b. Rockville Centre, N.Y., July 23, 1943; s. David Conover and Nan (Tracy) B.; m. Jeanne Marie Storey, May 12, 1979; 1 child, Sarah. BA, C.W. Post Coll., 1970; MBA, Fordham U., 1973. Asst. cashier Franklin Nat. Bank, NYC, 1970-74; mgr. facilities leverage leasing Gen. Electric Credit Co., Stamford, Conn., 1974-77; corp. mgr. sales fin. Harris Corp., Melbourne, Fla., 1977-83; exec. v.p. Internat. Capital Equipment Co., NYC, 1983-85; exec. v.p., CFO, bd. dirs. Phoenixcor, South Norwalk, Conn., 1985-94; founder, mng. dir. Black Rock Capital LLC, Ireland, 1994—; dir. Black Rock Capital Ltd., England. Contbr. articles to Leasing Digest, Monitor, ELA. Served with USN, 1967—69. Mem. Equipment Leasing Assn. (industry future con. 1982-84, captive com. 1981, acctg. com. 1988, mid. market com.), Internat. Assn. Diemaking and Diecutting, Eastern Assn. Equipment Lessors, Middle Market Ind. Bus. Coun., KC, Black Rock Yacht Club (Bridgeport, Conn.; past commodore), Fayerweather Yacht Club, Oronoque Country Club, The Landings. Republican. Roman Catholic. Home: 41 Grist Mill Ln Southport CT 06890 Office: Black Rock Capital LLC PO Box 416 Fairfield CT 06824 Office Phone: 203-336-9200. E-mail: gkbooth@blackrockcapital.com.

BOOTH, GORDON DEAN, JR., lawyer; b. Columbus, Ga., June 25, 1939; s. Gordon Dean and Lois Mildred (Bray) B.; m. Katherine Morris Campbell, June 17, 1961; children: Mary Katherine McCormick, Abigail Kilgore Curvino, Sarah Elizabeth, Margaret Campbell, Celecia. BA, Emory U., 1961, JD, 1964, LLM, 1973. Bar: Ga. 1964, D.C. 1977, U.S. Supreme Ct. 1973. Pvt. practice, Atlanta, 1964-96; ptnr. Schreeder, Wheeler & Flint, Atlanta, 1995—. Bd. dirs., v.p. Stallion Music Inc., Nashville, BAA USA, Inc.; trustee, sec. Inst. for Polit. Econ., Washington. Contbr. articles to profl. jours. Trustee Met. Atlanta Crime Commn., 1977-80, chmn., 1979-80; mem. assembly for arts and scis. Emory Coll., 1971-86, chmn., 1983. Mem. Internat. Bar Assn. (coun. sect. bus. law 1974-88, chmn. aero. law com. 1971-86), State Bar Ga., Capital City Club, Piedmont Driving Club, Univ. Club (N.Y.C.), Advocates Club, Sigma Chi. Home: 3226 Paces Mill Rd SE Atlanta GA 30339-3787

BOOTH, HAROLD WAVERLY, lawyer, finance company executive; b. Rochester, N.Y., Aug. 8, 1934; s. Herbert Nixon and Mildred B. (Anderson) B.; m. Flo Rae Spelts, July 4, 1957; children: Rebecca, William, Eva, Harold, Richard. BS, Cornell U., 1955; JD, Duke U., 1961. Bar: Nebr. 1961, Ill. 1967, Iowa 1974; CLU; chartered fin. counselor; cert. fin. planner. Staff atty. Bankers Life Nebr., Lincoln, 1961-67; pres. First Nat. Bank, Council Bluffs, Iowa, 1970-74; exec. v.p., treas. Blue Cross-Blue Shield Ill., Chgo., 1974-77; pres., chief exec. officer, chmn. Bankers Life Nebr., Lincoln, 1977-84; exec. v.p. Colonial Penn Group, Phila., 1985-87; chmn., chief exec. officer VGVR Cos., 1985—. Served to 1st lt. USAF, 1955-58. Fellow Life Mgmt. Inst. (pres. 1981-84); mem. Ins. Fedn. Nebr. (past pres.) Home: 1000 Stony Ln Gladwyne PA 19035-1128

BOOTH, JANE SCHUELE, real estate company officer, real estate broker; b. Cleve. d. Norman Andrew and Frances Ruth (Hankey) Schuele; m. George Warren Booth, Dec. 6, 1968. AA, Stephens Coll., 1946; student, U. Mo., 1946—47. Lic. real estate broker, Fla. Assoc. J.M. Mathes Inc., N.Y.C., 1947-48; dept. supr. Lord and Taylor, Scarsdale, N.Y., 1948-50; art coord. J. Walter Thompson, Inc., N.Y.C., 1953-58; art buyer SSC&B Inc. Advt., N.Y.C., 1959-80; pres. Jane Schuele Booth Realty, Ocala, Fla., 1982—. Mem. Fla. Thoroughbred Fillies, Ocala, 1980—; charter mem., trustee Royal Dames for Cancer Rsch., Inc., Ocala, 1986—; treas. Ladies Aux. Fla. H.C.H. Inc., Ocala, 1986-90; bd. visitors Fla. Horsemen's Children's Home, Inc., 1983-90. Mem. Ocala/Marion County Assn. Realtors, Ocala/Marion County C. of C. (agribus./equine com.), Nat. Assn. Realtors, Fla. Assn. Realtors. Home: 1771 SW 55th Street Rd Ocala FL 34474-5933 Office: PO Box 5538 Ocala FL 34478-5538 Personal E-mail: janeschuelebooth@aol.com.

BOOTH, JOHN NICHOLLS, minister, writer, photographer; b. Meadville, Pa., Aug. 7, 1912; s. Sydney Scott and Margaret (Nicholls) B.; m. Edith Kriger, Oct. 1, 1941 (dec. Sept. 22, 1982); 1 child, Barbara Anne Booth Christie. BA, McMaster U., 1934; MDiv, Meadville/Lombard Theol. Sch., 1942; LittD, New Eng. Sch. Law, 1950. Ordained to ministry Unitarian Ch., 1942. Profl. magician, 1934-40; min. Unitarian Ch., Evanston, Ill., 1942-48, 1st Ch., Belmont, Mass., 1949-57, 2d Ch. (now 1st and 2d Ch.), Boston, 1958-64, Unitarian Ch., Long Beach, Calif., 1964-71; interim pastor N.Y.C., Gainesville, (Fla.), Detroit, 1971-73. Celebrity platform lectr. and performer on conjuring and mentalism, 1942-58; ministerial adviser to liberal students MIT, 1958-63; mem. books selection com. Gen. Theol. Library, Boston, 1960-63. Author: Super Magical Miracles, 1930, Magical Mentalism, 1931, Forging Ahead in Magic, 1939, Marvels of Mystery, 1941, The Quest for Preaching Power, 1943, Fabulous Destinations, 1950, Story of the Second Church in Boston, 1959, The John Booth Classics, 1975, Booths in History, 1982, Psychic Paradoxes, 1984, Wonders of Magic, 1986, Dramatic Magic, 1988, Creative World of Conjuring, 1990, Conjurians' Discoveries, 1992, The Fine Art of Hocus Pocus, 1995, Keys to Magic's Inner World, 1999, Extending Magic Beyond Credibility, 2001; contbr. articles to mags. and newspapers; photographer full length feature travel documentary films for TV, lecture platforms made in India, Africa, S.Am., Indonesia, South Seas, Himalayas; presented first color travelogue on TV in U.S. over NBC in N.Y.C., 1949; panel mem. radio program Churchmen Weigh The News, Boston, 1951-52; spl. corr. in Asia for Chgo. Sun-Times, 1948-49; by-line writer Boston Globe, 1954-66; producer, photographer motion pictures Heart of Africa, 1954, Golden Kingdoms of the Orient, 1957, Indonesia: Pacific Shangri La, 1957, Treasures of the Amazon, Ecuador and Peru, 1960, Adventurous Britain, 1962, South Seas Saga in Tahiti, Australia and New Guinea, summer 1966, The Amazing America of Will Rogers, 1970, Spotlight on Spain, 1975. Co-founder Japan Free Religious Assn., Tokyo, 1948; co-founder Mass. Meml. Soc., 1962, dir., 1962-64; organizer Meml. Soc. Alachua County (Fla.), 1972; pres. Long Beach Mental Health Assn., 1964-66; adv. coun. Fair Housing Found. Recipient John Nevil Maskelyne prize London Magic Cir., 1987; placed on former N.Y. Town Hall Travelogue Cinematographers Wall of Fame, 1967; named Disting. Alumnae Gallery of McMaster U.; lit. fellow Acad. Magical Arts, 1977, lifetime achievement fellow, 1990, masters fellow, 2001. Mem. Unitarian-Universalist Mins. Assn. (past dir.), Am. Unitarian Assn. (past com. chmn.), Unitarian Mins. Pacific S.W. Assn. (v.p.), Clergy Counseling Svc. So. Calif., Soc. Am. Magicians (inducted into Hall of Fame 1983), Magic Castle Hollywood, Internat. Brotherhood Magicians (hon. life), L.A. Adventurers Club (pres. 1983), Evanston (Ill.) Ministerial Assn. (pres. 1947-48). Achievements include having the first regularly scheduled TV broadcasts in U.S. by clergyperson, WBKB, Chgo., mid-1940s. Home and Office: 12032 Montecito Rd Los Alamitos CA 90720-4511 *Success often greets an imaginative, innovative approach to that which has been done in a settled way too long. An ability to time change properly and accept philosophically that which does not yield is* *to live maturely with one's own struggles and hopes. Bertrand Russell guides wisely in suggesting that a person living in a spirit that aims at creating rather than possessing has a certain fundamental happiness. Such a way of life is thereby freed from the tyranny of fear, since what one values most in one's existence is not at the mercy of outside power.*

BOOTH, JOHN THOMAS, private investor; b. NYC, Oct. 21, 1929; s. John E. and Katherine (Keeler) B.; m. Anne C. Mott, Feb. 26, 1960; children: Alison Booth Cramer, Miven Booth Trageser, Roxanna Booth Cistulli. Grad. cum laude, Deerfield Acad., 1947; BA cum laude, Amherst Coll., 1951; LLB, Harvard U., 1957. Bar: NY 1957. Assoc. firm Dewey Ballantine Bushby Palmer & Wood, N.Y.C., 1957-61; mem. buying dept. Eastman Dillon, Union Securities & Co., N.Y.C., 1961—, ptnr., 1963—; exec. v.p., dir. Blyth Eastman Dillon & Co., Inc., 1972-81; chmn. bd. Eastdil Realty, Inc., 1979-81, Am. Health Capital, Inc., 1982-86, Am. Health Capital Ventures, Inc., 1986-89; chmn. Franklin Venture Capital Inc., 1990-97, Greystone Communities, Inc., 1990—2005, Coleman, Swenson, Booth, Inc., 1997—2005. Bd. dirs. Wells Hill Ptnrs. Ltd., Litchfield Bancorp; dir., mem. investment adv. bd. Eli Whitney Conn. Innovations, Inc., 1994-2004; asst. to dir. Harvard Def. Studies Program, 1956-57; counsel NY State Assembly Com. on N.Y.C., 1960, Com. on Judiciary, 1961. Trustee Seherr-Thoss Found., White Meml. Found., Gordie Found.; mem. Litchfield HS scholarship com. Lt. (j.g.) USNR, 1951-54. Mem. Delta Kappa Epsilon, Delta Sigma Rho. Clubs: Links, University (N.Y.C.); Litchfield (Conn.) Country. Republican. Episcopalian. Office: Box 25 182 Whites Wood Rd Litchfield CT 06759-0025 Office Phone: 860-567-0873.

BOOTH, MARGARET A(NN), communications company executive; b. N.Y.C., Dec. 25, 1946; d. Herbert and Alice (Traum) B.; m. Marvin E. Schechter, Jan. 22, 1984. BS, U. Wis., 1968. Editl. asst. Bantam Books, N.Y.C., 1968-70; publicity asst. Ruder & Finn Inc., N.Y.C., 1970-71, dir. radio and TV, 1971-76, v.p., 1974-76; pres. Pub. Interest Pub. Rels., N.Y.C., 1976—, M. Booth & Assocs., Inc., N.Y.C., 1983—. Author: Promoting Issues and Ideas, 1987; contbr. articles to profl. jours. Bd. govs. Eugene Lang Coll. New Sch. for Social Rsch.; bd. dirs. N.Y. Found. Recipient YWCA Salute to Women Achievers, City of N.Y., 1985. Mem. Pub. Rels. Soc. Am., Women in Comm. (Matrix award for Pub. Rels. 1987), Women Execs. in Pub. Rels.

BOOTH, MITCHELL B., lawyer; b. N.Y.C., June 26, 1927; s. Samuel and Rose (Waxman) B.; m. Barbara C. Ribman, July 13, 1952; 1 son, Brian S. AB, Clark U., 1949; JD, NYU, 1952. Bar: N.Y. 1952. Assoc. I. Moldauer, N.Y.C., 1952—54, Sol A. Rosenblatt, N.Y.C., 1954—67; pvt. practice law N.Y.C., 1967—. Minority counsel joint legis. com. unsatisfied judgments N.Y., 1958-59, joint legis. com. preservation restoration hist. sites N.Y., 1960-64; med. malpractice mediator First Jud. Dept. Supreme Ct. State N.Y., 1980-91; bd. dirs., treas. East Hampton Mews Tenants Corp., Burgos Art Galleries Ltd., Dorolyat Corp. Asst. to chmn. Dem. law com., N.Y. County, 1961-65; rep. admissions for states of N.Y., N.J. and Conn. Clark U., 1968-71. Served to lt. USNR, 1945-46, 49-83. Mem. ABA, N.Y. State Bar Assn., Assn. of Bar of City of N.Y. (com. profl. discipline 1986-89), N.Y. Commandry, Mil. Order Fgn. Wars U.S. (life, judge advocate), Univ. Club. Home: 75 E End Ave New York NY 10028-7909 Office Phone: 212-977-2525.

BOOTH, PATRICIA VOGT (TRISH BOOTH), education consultant; b. Bklyn., Jan. 10, 1947; d. Frank C. and Evelyn (Peterson) Vogt; m. Jon V.C. Booth, Aug. 26, 1967; children: Katherine, Tyler. BA, Denison U., 1968; MA, St. Mary's U. Minn., 1991. Lamaze cert. Childbirth Educator; fellow Am. Coll. Childbirth Educators. Pvt. practice, Brattleboro, Vt., 1972-74, Lamaze Childbirth Preparation Assn., Ann Arbor, Mich., 1975-79, Childbirth Edn. Assn. of Greater Mpls., 1979-82; cons. Family Tree Clinic, St. Paul, 1982-87, perinatal edn. coord., 1982-87; co-developer and presenter basic tchr. edn. workshop Seminar Svcs., 1985-87; basic tchr. edn. workshop faculty Internat. Childbirth Edn. Assn., Mpls., 1987-92; perinatal edn. cons. pvt. practice Mpls., 1988-94; edn. cons., 1994—. Mem. Internat. Childbirth Edn. Assn. Profls. Tng. Workshop faculty, 1998-2003; founding mem. and editor Preterm Birth Prevention Consortium St. Paul, 1987-90, perinatal guidelines work group Minn. Dept. Health, 1988-89, Prenatal Care Initatives Task Force Minn., 1986-88, edn. cons. Community Clinic Consortiums Mothers-to-Mothers project, 1985-90; adv. edn. cons. Pediat. Residency Program SUNY, Syracuse, 1998—. Editor: LCPA Childbirth and Parenting Handbook, 1976, Perinatal Connection Quar., 1992-94; project editor Child Abuse MD.com, 2005; author (booklet) Before You Get Pregnant, 1986, Preparation for Pregnancy, Birth, and Early Parenting, 1992, 93, (pamphlet) Relaxation, 1986, rev. edit., 1992, 98, Breathing Awareness, 1993, rev. edit., 1998, International Childbirth Education Association Educator Certification Program Study Modules and Examination, 1994, 00, Family Centered Education: The Process of Teaching Birth, 1995, Teaching Parenting Within the Childbirth Class Curriculum: a Teacher's Guide, 1999, Pampers Childbirth Edn. Program Teacher's Companion, 2001, rev. edit., 2003, Pregnancy Q&A, 2004. Com. mem. Healthy Mothers, Healthy Babies Minn. 1985-94. Mem. Lamaze Internat., Childbirth Edn. Assn., Phi Beta Kappa. Home: 7507 Northfield Ln Manlius NY 13104-2374 E-mail: TrishBooth@aol.com.

BOOTH, PENELOPE PARTRIDGE, secondary school educator, writer, principal; b. Niskayuna, NY, Dec. 7, 1943; d. Leonard Charlton and Elizabeth Jane (Russ) Partridge; m. John Robert Booth, Sept. 10, 1966 (div. 1975); children: Elizabeth Ashley, Patricia Anne. BS in Math., Mary Washington Coll., 1965; EdM, Towson State U., 1981. Comml. supr. Chesapeake & Potomac Tel. Co., Washington, 1965-66, Richmond, Va., 1967-68; math. tchr. Havelock (N.C.) H.S., 1966-67, Jack Jouett Jr. H.S., Charlottesville, Va., 1968-70, Baltimore County Pub. Schs., Towson, Md., 1974-81, supr. math., 1987-93; prin. Catonsville (Md.) Mid. Sch., 1993-96; tchr. gifted and talented resource Office Of Math., Towson, 1981-84; chmn. math. dept. Hereford Mid. Sch., Monkton, Md., 1984-87; coord. office of math. Baltimore County Pub. Schs., Md., 1996—2004, new math. cons., 2004—. Instr. Baltimore county Pub. Schs., 1976-88, Md. Acad. Scis., Balt., 1984-86, Inst. for the Gifted Talented, Towson, 1983-85; cons. Md. State Dept. Edn., Balt., 1981-2004, Sylvan Learning, 2002-03; adj. prof. Johns Hopkins U., 1996-2004, Coll. Notre Dame Md., 1997-2003, Loyola Coll. Md., 2002-04; co-owner Conversation Pieces, 1997—. Author: Essentials of Mathematics, 1988, Consumer Mathematics, 1988, Foundations of Algebra and Geometry, 1998, (booklet) First Book of Testing. Adult leader troop 336, Girl Scouts U.S.A., Towson, 1972-88; mem. Lutherville (Md.) Recreation Coun., 1979-89; cons. Md. Math. League, 1982-87; chmn., co-founder Christa McAuliffe Scholarship Found., 1986—; mem. alumni adv. coun. Towson State U.; mem. adv. bd. MAT Program Johns Hopkins U., 1992-2002. Recipient Presdl. award NSF, 1985, Disting. Alumni award Towson State U., 1989, Educator of Yr. award Md. Coun. Tchrs. of Math., 2002. Mem. ASCD, Nat. Coun. Suprs. Math. (sec.-treas. Md. coun. 2000—), Nat. Coun. Tchrs. Math., Coun. Presdl. Awardees (scholarship chmn.), Nat. Assn. Secondary Sch. Prins., Optimists, Phi Delta Kappa, Delta Kappa Gamma (v.p.). Republican. Presbyterian. Avocations: travel, needlepoint. Home: 5301 Impatiens Ct Holly Springs NC Office Phone: 410-321-7878. Business E-Mail: pbooth5301@bellsouth.net.

BOOTH, R. COREY, information technology executive; BA, Wash. U.; MBA, Stanford U. Grad. Sch. Bus. Assoc. prin. tech. office McKinsey and Co. Bus., Chgo.; CIO and dir. office info. tech. US Securities and Exchange Commn., 2004—. Office: SEC HQ 450 Fifth St NW Washington DC 20549 Office Phone: 202-942-7040.

BOOTH, RACHEL ZONELLE, nursing educator; b. Seneca, S.C., Feb. 10, 1936; m. Richard B. Booth, Feb. 13, 1957; 1 child, Kevin M. Student, Furman U., 1953-54; diploma in nursing, Greenville (S.C.) Gen. Hosp., 1956; student, U. Alaska, 1964-66; BS in Nursing, U. Md., Balt., 1968; MS in Nursing, U. Md., 1970, PhD in Adminstrn. Higher Edn., 1978; D of Nursing Sci. (hon.), Chiang Mai U., Thailand, 1999. RN. Staff nurse VA Hosp., Murfreesboro, Tenn., 1956-57, U. Colo. Med. Ctr., Denver, 1957-58; nurse psychiatry dept. Patton State Hosp., Calif., 1958-59; staff nurse USAF Dispensary, Iraklion, Greece, 1959-60; charge nurse psychiatry Santa Rose Med. Ctr., San Antonio, 1961; staff nurse Shannon S.W. Tex. Meml. Hosp., San Angelo, 1962; supervisory clin. nurse, head nurse U.S. Dept. Health, Edn., and Welfare/USPHS/Indian Health Service, Anchorage, 1962-66; staff nurse U.S. Dept. Health, Edn., and Welfare/USPHS, Balt., 1966, 68; assoc. dir. dept. nursing U. Md. Hosp., 1970-76, dir. primary care nursing svc., 1976-81; asst. prof. Sch. Nursing U. Md., 1972-76, asst. prof. Sch. Pharmacy, 1972-80, acting assoc. dean Sch. Nursing, 1979-81, assoc. prof. Sch. Nursing, 1979, assoc. prof. clin. pharmacy, 1980-83, assoc. dean for undergrad. studies Sch. Nursing, 1981-83, co-dir. nurse practitioner program Sch. Nursing, 1972-76, chairperson grad. program dept. primary care, 1974-79; dean, Sch. of Nursing and asst. v.p. for health affairs Duke U., Durham, N.C., 1984-87; dean Sch. Nursing U. Ala. at Birmingham, University Station, 1987—. Instr. Sch. Medicine U. Md., 1972-83, program dir. primary care nurse practitioner program continuing edn., 1976-82, project dir. Robert Wood Johnson Nurse Faculty Fellowship program, 1977-82; mem. joint practice com. Med. and Surg. Faculty Md., 1974-77, mem. tech. adv. com. for physician's assts. Bd. Med. Examiners Md., 1975-80; mem. adv. com. nursing program Community Coll. Balt., 1976-79; mem. Joint Commn. on Accreditation of Hosps., pres. Md. Council Dirs. of Assoc. Degree, Diploma, and Baccalaureate Programs, 1982-83; mem. adv. bd. nursing Essex Community Coll., 1983; mem. peer rev. panel advanced nurse edn. nursing div. U.S. Dept. Health and Human Services, 1987—. Editor (with others) Hospital Pharmacy, 1971-72; asst. editor Jour. Profl. Nursing, 1984-87; contbr. articles on nursing to prof. jours. Bd. dirs. Health and Welfare Coun. Ctrl. Md., Inc., 1974-78, v.p., 1975-78; mem. health adv. com. to Pres. of Pakistan, 1981—. Recipient numerous grants for nursing adminstrn., 1972—. Mem. ANA (mem. nat. rev. com. 1975-78, v.p. 1977, chair 1978), Internat. Coun. Nurses (observer conf. 1981), Nat. Acad. Practice for Nursing (vice chairperson 1984-89), Nat. Orgn. for Nurse Execs., Nat. League for Nursing, Coun. Nat. Acad. Practice, Am. Assn. Colls. in Nursing (dean's summer seminar com. 1984-85, edn. and credentialing com. 1985-86, nominating com. 1986-87, bd. dirs. 1989-96, pres.-elect 1992-94, pres. 1994-96), N.C. Orgn. Nurse Execs. (bd. dirs. 1986-87), So. Coun. Collegiate Edn. for Nursing (exec. com. 1986-91, v.p., bd. dirs. 1991-94, pres. 1997-99), Sigma Theta Tau (chairperson nominating com. 1974, mem. 1975, rec. sec. 1980-83). Avocations: genealogy, travel, swimming. Office: U Ala at Birmingham 1530 3rd Ave S Birmingham AL 35294-0002

BOOTH, SUSAN, educational association administrator, product designer, marketing professional, researcher; d. Kyung Hi Yang and John Kent Booth; m. Martin Johnson, Jan. 4, 2002; 1 child, Makani Booth Johnson. BS, Lewis and Clark Coll., Portland, Oreg., 1984; MEd, Lesley Coll., Cambridge, Mass., 1988. Cert. elem. edn. Mass., 1988. Edn. and tech. devel. specialist Coun. for Advancement and Support of Edn., Washington, 1993—98; mgr., edn. tech. programs Nat. Sch. Bds. Assn., Alexandria, Va., 1998—2000; dir. of products and svcs. devel. Nat. Assn. of Ind. Schs., Washington, 2000—. Mem.: Am. Mktg. Assn., Greater Wash. Soc. of Assn. Exec., Am. Soc. of Assn. Exec.

BOOTH, TAMI, editor; Editor health and medicine category Little Brown, 1994—97; exec. editor health and lifestyle books IDG Books, N.Y.C. and Chgo., 1997—2000; dir. new title devel. Rodale, Inc., N.Y.C., 2000, exec. editor Women's Health Books, 2000—01, editor-in-chief Women's Health Books, 2001—. Office: Rodale Press 733 3d Ave New York NY 10017

BOOTH, WILLIAM BOLAND, JR., retired military officer, meteorologist, elementary school educator; b. Belleville, Ill., Mar. 19, 1921; s. William Boland Booth Sr. and Grace Van Eizinga; m. JoAnn Wiest, July 7, 1946; children: Cynthia Ann Booth James, William Bennett. B in Mil. Sci., U. Md., 1961; M in Edn., So. Ill. U., 1974. With USAF, 1939—41, sgt., 1941—43, warrant officer (j.g.), 1943—51, weather officer, meteorologist weather bur. forecast ctr., 1948—60, chief warrant officer, 1951—66, payroll officer, ret., 1966; tchr. Jr. HS, Mascoutah, Ill., 1968—86. Songwriter: songs Open Up Your Heart and Let Me In, poet: poems An Event or Happening, Life Gets Tedious-Doesn't It?, Survival (Hon. mention, 1990), Fishing or Golf, Take your Pick, 1997, The Candle is Burnt Out, At Least at One End, 1999, Steer Your Own Course, 1998, Affairs of The Heart, 2000, Beauty All Around You, 2000, Babe Didrikson, Zaharias, Female Athlete of the year 6 times, 2002, Leslie Townes Hope, 2003. Decorated Good Conduct Medal, Cluster, Air Force Longivity with 1 Silver Cluster, Legion of Merit, Cold War Recognition, Am. Campaign Medal, Air Force Outstanding Unit award, European Mid. East Ribbon Battle Stars for Egypt-Libya and Tunisia, Air Force Commendation Medal, WWII Victory Medal; named to, Internat. Poetry Hall of Fame, 1998. Mem.: DAV, Internat. Poetry Soc., Grand Lodge Ancient Free Accepted Masons (50 Yr. Pin 1995). Independent. Protestant-Methodist. Avocations: music, dance. Home and Office: 274 Plaza Napoli Ct Henderson NV 89074-1440 Personal E-mail: gr8poems4u@earthlink.net.

BOOTHBY, WILLIAM MUNGER, retired mathematics professor; b. Detroit, Apr. 1, 1918; s. Thomas Franklin and Florence (Munger) B.; m. Ruth Robin, June 8, 1947; children— Daniel, Thomas, Mark. AB, U. Mich., 1941, MA, 1942, PhD, 1949. Mem. faculty Northwestern U., Evanston, Ill., 1948-59; fellow Am.-Swiss Found. for Sci. Exchange, Swiss Fed. Inst. Tech., Zurich, 1950-51; assoc. prof. Washington U., St. Louis, 1959-62, prof. math., 1962-88, ret., 1988—. NSF sr. postdoctoral fellow Inst. for Advanced Study, Princeton, N.J., 1961-62, U. Geneva, Switzerland, 1965-66; professeur associe U. Strasbourg, France, 1971, 77 Author: Introduction to Differentiable Manifolds and Riemannian Geometry; co-editor: Symmetric Spaces; contbr. articles to profl. jours. Served with USAAF, 1942-46. Mem. Am., London math. Socs., Math. Assn. Am., Soc. Indsl. and Applied Math., Sigma Xi. Home: 6954 Cornell Ave Saint Louis MO 63130-3128 Office: Washington U Dept Math Saint Louis MO 63130-4899

BOOTHE, LEON ESTEL, academic administrator emeritus, consultant; b. Carthage, Mo., Feb. 1, 1938; s. Harold Estel and Merle Jane (Hood) B.; m. Nancy Janes, Aug. 20, 1960 (dec. Jan. 1997); children: Cynthia, Diana and Cheri (twins); m. Karen Ball, Nov. 11, 2000. BS (Curators' scholar), U. Mo., 1960, MA, 1962; PhD in History, U. Ill., 1966; LLD, Kyung Hee U., Korea, St. Thomas Inst. Advanced Study, 1985, Hebrew Union Coll., 1994. Tchr. history Valparaiso (Ind.) H.S., 1960-61; asst. prof. history U. Miss., Oxford, 1965-68, assoc. prof., 1968-70; assoc. prof. history George Mason Coll., U. Va. (now George Mason U.), Fairfax, 1970-73, prof. history, 1973-80, assoc. dean, 1970-71, dean, 1971-72, dean coll. arts and scis., 1972-80; provost, v.p. acad. affairs Ill. State U., Normal, 1980-83; pres. No. Ky. U., Highland Heights, 1983-96, pres. emeritus, 1996—; sr. advisor Nat. Underground R.R. Freedom Ctr., 1997-2000; prof. history No. Ky. U., 1983—. Bd. dirs. Fifth Third Bank No. Ky.; chmn. Am. Assn. of State Colls. and Univs., 1993; bd. dirs. Commn. on Internat. Edn. of Am. Coun. Edn., Nat. Underground Railroad Free Ctr., exec. com., 2001; mem. bd. trustees Am. Classical Music Hall of Fame. Former mem. adv. bd. Cin. Coun. World Affairs; trustee Cin.-Kharkiv Project, hon. mem., 1995-96; bd. dirs. Met. YMCA, Cinn., 1984—, Met. Cin. chpt. ARC, former mem., McLean County Heart Assn., McLean County United Way, INROADS/Cin., Inc., NCCJ, 1983—, Cin.'s Enjoy the Arts, 1988-90, Cin. Music Festival, Cin. Nat. Classical Music Hall Fame, Cin. Ballet, 1999—, No. Ky. U. Found., Sr. Citizens No. Ky., 1996—, May Festival, 1998—; vice chmn. No. Ky. United Way, chmn., 1988; Greater Cin. YMCA; mem. steering com. Cin. Bicentennial; chmn. Multiple Sclerosis Soc. Gifts Campaign; mem. steering and exec. coms. Cin. Youth Collaborative; co-chair blue ribbon econ. devel. study No. Ky. Area Devel. Dist.; mem. Leukemia Soc.; bd. dirs. Greater Cin. Conv. and Visitors Bur., 1989—, Kids Helping Kids, 1998—, Merc. Libr., 1998—, Festival of Arts, 1998—; bd. dirs., mem. exec. com., vice-chair cmty. edn. svcs., 1989-90, Cin. chpt. ARC, Wood Hudson Cancer Rsch. Lab. Inc., 1987-92; chmn. Ky. Bicentennial Com., 1990, chmn. steering com., 1992; chmn. Leadership Ky. Class; trustee Greater Cin. United Way and Cmty. Chest, 1991; steering com. greater Cin. summit on racism, 1994; sr. advisor Nat. Underground Railroad freedom Ctr., 1997; mem. Underground R.R. Freedom Ctr. Bd., 2000—; former bd. dirs. Am. Music Scholarship Assn., Cin. Scholarship Found., Leadership Ky. Found.; lifetime advisor to pres. Nat. Coun. for Cmty. and Justice; advisor Cin. Hispanic C. of C.; bd. dirs. Sr. Svcs. of No. Ky., 1996. NEH fellow, 1967-68; scholar Diplomat Seminars Dept. State; recipient Coll. Liberal Arts and Scis. award U. Ill., 1988, Alumni Coun. Pres.'s Spl. Recognition award No. Ky. U., 1989, Alumni award U. Mo., 1989, Walter R. Dunlevey Frontiersman award, 1994, Disting. Citizens Citation award NCCJ, Disting. Pub. Svc. award No. Ky. U. Found., 1995, Character award YMCA, 1997, Kinsman award Urban Appalachian Coun., 1998, Pres. award Pub. Rels. Soc., 2000, Lighthouse Beacon Light award, 2001, Sister Benedict Bunning award, 2003. Mem. Soc. Historians for Am. Fgn. Rels., McLean County Assn. for Commerce and Industry, Am. Assn. State Colls. and Univs. (internat. programs com. 1986-94), No. Ky. C. of C. (Walter R. Dunlevey-Frontierman award 1994), Greater Cin. C. of C. (asst. sec.-treas. 1989-93), Rotary, Masons, Leon Boothe Soc. (svc. award No. Ky. 2002), Sigma Rho Sigma, Omicron Delta Kappa, Phi Alpha Theta, Phi Delta Kappa. Office Phone: 859-572-5176. Business E-Mail: boothel@nku.edu.

BOOTHROYD, GEOFFREY, industrial and manufacturing engineering educator; b. Radcliffe, Eng., Nov. 18, 1932; arrived in U.S., 1967; s. Arthur and Annie (Fletcher) Boothroyd; m. Shirley Lewis, Apr. 10, 1954; children: Janet Kaye, Lynda Jean. BS in Engring., U. London, 1956, PhD in Engring., 1962, DSc in Engring., 1974. Apprentice Mather & Platt Ltd., Manchester, 1948—56, designer, 1956—57, English Electric Co. Ltd., Leicester, England, 1957—58; lectr., reader Salford (Eng.) U., 1958—67; prof. U. Mass., Amherst, 1967—85, U. R.I., Kingston, 1985—97, prof. emeritus. Vis. prof. Ga. Inst. Tech., Atlanta, 1964—65; cons. mfg. industries U.K. and U.S., also various pubs.; co-founder Boothroyd Dewhurst, Inc. Author: Fundamentals of Metal Machining, 1965; author: (with A.H. Redford) Mechanized Assembly (Japanese edit. 1969), 1968; author: Fundamentals of Metal Machining and Machine Tools (Spanish 1978, internat. student edit. 1979), 1975; co-author: Introduction to Engineering, 1975; author (with C.R. Poli): Applied Engineering Mechanics, 1980; author: (with C.R. Poli, L.E. Murch) Automatic Assembly, 1980; author: Handbook of Feeding and Orienting Techniques for Small Parts; author: (with L. Alting) Manufacturing Engineering Processes, 1982; author: (with P. Dewhurst) Design for Assembly Handbook, Design for Robot Assembly, 1985; author: (with W.A. Knight) Metal Machining and Machine Tools, 1991; author: Assembly Automation and Product Design, 1992; author: (with P. Dewhurst and W.A. Knight) Product Design for Manufacture and Assembly, 1994. Recipient Teaching award, Western Electric, 1969, Sr. Scholar award, U. Mass., 1982, Sci. and Tech. award, R.I. Gov., 1989, Nat. medal of Technology, U.S. Dept. Commerce Technology Admin., 1991, Providence Engring. Soc., 1991, U.K. Mensforth Internat. Gold medal, IEE, 1993, Mcht. Mfg. medal, ASME/SME, 2005; grantee NSF, 1967—87, GE, 1967, 1969, 1981, 1983, AMP Inc, 1978, 1981—84, IBM, 1983—85, AT&T, 1985, Ford Motor Co., 1984, 1986. Fellow: Soc. Mfg. Engrs.; mem.: NAE. Avocation: squash, tennis, golf, painting. Office: Boothroyd Dewhurst Inc 138 Main St Ste 2 Wakefield RI 02879-3574 Office Phone: 401-783-5840. E-mail: gboothroyd@dfma.com.

BOOTHROYD, HERBERT J., insurance company executive; b. Mason City, Iowa, Dec. 23, 1928; s. Herbert L. and Clara (Schmitt) B.; m. Barbara Elizabeth Dunne, Feb. 9, 1961; children: Diane Lea, John Herbert. AB, U. Mich., 1952, AM, 1953. Enrolled actuary, 1976. With Mass. Mut. Life Ins. Co., 1953-57; with New Eng. Mut. Life Ins. Co., Boston, 1957-87, v.p., 1967-77, sr. v.p. pension ops., 1977-82, exec. v.p. group ops., 1983-87; dir. New Eng. Pension and Annuity Co., 1980-87, pres., 1981-87; pres., dir. New Eng. Gen. Life, 1983-85. Dir. New Eng. Mut. Life Ins. Co., 1984-87, New Eng. Variable Life Ins. Co., 1984-97. Contbg. author: (book) Hammett Families, 1983, Cockrill Families of No. Virginia, 2002; contbg. author: Life and Health Insurance Handbook, 1973. Bd. dirs. New Eng. chpt. Am. Diabetes Assn., 1979-84; bd. govs. Handel and Haydn Soc., 1984-94, sec., 1986-94, overseer, 1994—2003; mem. nat. campaign com. U. Mich., 1983-90; bd. dirs. Better Bus. Bur. Ea. Mass., 1980-88, vice chmn., mem. exec. com., 1985-88. With U.S. Army, 1946—47. Fellow Soc. Actuaries; mem. SAR, Am. Acad. Actuaries, Internat. Congress Actuaries, New Eng. Hist. Geneal. Soc., Ky. Hist. Soc., U. Mich. Alumni Assn. (v.p. 1st dist. 1989-91, pres. 1991-93, nat. bd. dirs. 1997-2000, chair nat. clubs coun. 1999-2000), Phi Beta Kappa, Theta Delta Chi. Home and Office: 4205 SW 96th Dr Gainesville FL 32608 E-mail: herbbooth@aol.com.

BOOTY, JOHN EVERITT, retired theology studies educator; b. Detroit, May 2, 1925; s. George Thomas and Alma (Gamauf) B.; m. Catherine Louise Smith, June 10, 1950; children: Carol Holland, Geoffrey Rollen, Peter Thomas, Catherine Jane. BA, Wayne State U., 1952; B.D., Va. Theol. Sem., 1953, DD, 1994, U. of the South, 1997; MA, Princeton U., 1957, PhD, 1960. Ordained to ministry Episcopal Ch., 1953. Curate Christ Episcopal Ch., Dearborn, Mich., 1953-55; asst. prof. ch. history Va. Theol. Sem., 1958-64, assoc. prof., 1964-67; prof. ch. history Episcopal Theol. Sch., Cambridge, Mass., 1967-82; acting dir. Inst. Theol. Rsch., 1974-76; dean Sch. Theology U. of South, Sewanee, Tenn., 1982-85, prof. Anglican studies, 1984-90, prof. emeritus, 1990—, historiographer Episc. Ch., 1988-99. Vis. prof., rsch. Yale Div. Sch., 1985-86; Disting. vis. prof. Episcopal Divinity Sch., 1990-91, prof. emeritus, 1991—; vis. prof. Anglican studies Gen. Theol. Seminary, 1992; Trotter vis. prof. Va. Theol. Sem., 1993, 98. Author: John Jewel as Apologist of the Church of England, 1963, Yearning to be Free, 1974, Three Anglican Divines on Prayer: Jewel, Andrewes, and Hooker, 1978, The Church in History, 1979, 2d edit., 2003, The Spirit of Anglicanism, 1979, The Godly Kingdom of Tudor England, 1981, The Servant Church, 1982, What Makes Us Episcopalians, 1982, Anglican Spirituality, 1982, Meditating on Four Quarters, 1983, 2d edit., 2003, Anglican Moral Choice, 1983, The Christ We Know, 1987, The Episcopal Church in Crisis, 1988, Mission and Ministry: A History of the Virginia Theological Seminary, 1996, An American Apostle: A Biography of Stephen F. Bayne, 1997, Reflections on the Theology of Richard Hooker: An Elizabethan Addresses Modern Anglicanism, 1999; editor: The Book of Common Prayer, 1559: The Elizabeth Prayer Book, 1976, John Jewel: The Apology of the Church of England, 1963, 74, 2002, John Donne: Divine Poems, Sermons, Meditations and Prayers, 1990, The Works of Richard Hooker, vol. 4, 1982; co-editor, contbr.: The Study of Anglicanism, 1988; contbr. articles to profl. jours. Chmn. Nat. Youth Commn., P.F. Ch., 1948-50; chmn. bd. St. Luke's Jour. Theology, 1987-91, Sewanee Theol. Rev., 1991-99. Recipient Am. Philos. Soc. award, 1964; Folger Shakespeare Libr. fellow, 1964, NEH fellow, 1978-79 Mem. Soc. for Promoting Christian Knowlege (vice chmn. 1984-87). Home: 612 Mt Israel Rd Center Sandwich NH 03227-3710

BOOZER, CARLOS AUSTIN, JR., professional basketball player; b. Aschaffenburg, Germany, Nov. 20, 1981; s. Carlos Boozer; m. Cindy Boozer. BA in Sociology, Duke U., 2003. Player Cleveland Cavaliers, 2002—04, Utah Jazz, 2004—. Mem. US Olympic Basketball Team, Athens, Greece, 2004, NCAA Nat. Championship Team Duke Blue Devils, 2001. Office: Utah Jazz 301 W South Temple Salt Lake City UT 84101

BOOZMAN, JOHN, congressman; b. Shreveport, La, Dec. 10, 1950; m. Cathy Marley; 3 children. Grad., U. Ark., Fayetteville; OD, So. Coll. Optometry, 1977. Pvt. practice eye clinic, 1977; mem. U.S. Congress from 3d Ark. dist., 2001—; mem. Internat. Relations com., Transp. and Infrastructure com. and Veterans' Affairs com. U.S. Ho. Reps. Served Rogers Sch. Bd.; establisher low vision program Ark. Sch. for Blind for Little Rock; vol. optometrist area clinic. Republican. Office: 1519 Longworth HOB Washington DC 20515-0403

BOPP, JAMES, JR., lawyer; b. Terre Haute, Ind., Feb. 8, 1948; s. James and Helen Marguerite (Hope) B.; m. Cheryl Hahn, Aug. 8, 1970 (div.); m. Christine Marie Stanton, July 3, 1982; children: Kathleen Grace, Lydia Grace, Marguerite Grace. BA, Ind. U., 1970; JD, U. Fla., 1973. Bar: Ind. 1973, U.S. Supreme Ct. 1977. Dep. atty. gen. State of Ind., Indpls., 1973-75; ptnr. Bopp & Fife, Indpls., 1975-79, Brames, Bopp, Abel & Oldham, Terre Haute, Ind., 1979-92, Bopp, Coleson & Bostrom, Terre Haute, 1992—. Dep. prosecutor Vigo County, Terre Haute, 1979-86; gen. counsel Nat. Right to Life Com., Washington, 1978—; pres. Nat. Legal Ctr. for Medically Dependent and Disabled, 1984—; gen. counsel James Madison Ctr. Free Speech, 1997—; instr. law Ind. U., 1977-78. Editor: Human Life and Health Care Ethics, 1985, Restoring the Right to Life: The Human Life Amendment, 1984; editor-in-chief Issues in Law and Medicine, 1985—. Mem. congl. biomed. ethics adv.

com. Pres.'s Com. on Mental Retardation, 1987—89, mem., 1984—87, Nat. Commn. for UNESCO, 2004—; chmn. White House Conf. on Families, Washington, 1980, White House Conf. on Aging, Mpls., 1981; mem. The Federalist Soc., Free Speech & Election Law Practice Group, co-chmn. election law subcom., 1996—; bd. govs. Rep. Nat. Lawyers Assn., 2002—; alt. del. Rep. Nat. Conv., 1992, 1996, del., 2000, 2004, mem. platform com., 2000, 2004; state treas., gen. counsel Ind. Rep. State Party, 2005—; chmn. Vigo County Election Bd., 1991—93; del. Rep. State Conv., Indpls., 1980, 1982, 1984, 1986, 1990, 1992, 1994, 1996, 1998, 2000, 2002, 2004; chmn. Vigo County Rep. Ctrl. Com., 1993—97; bd. dirs. Leadership Terre Haute, 1986—89, Alliance for Growth and Progress, Terre Haute, 1993—97; chmn. bd. dirs. Hospice of Wabash Valley, Terre Haute, 1982—88. Mem. Ind. State Bar Assn., Terre Haute Rotary (bd. dirs. 1984-86). Republican. Roman Catholic. Home: 1124 S Center St Terre Haute IN 47802-1116 Office: Bopp Coleson & Bostrom 1 S 6th St Terre Haute IN 47807-3510 Office Phone: 812-232-2434. Personal E-mail: jboppjr@aol.com.

BOPP, THOMAS THEODORE, academic administrator, chemistry professor; b. Glendale, Calif., Nov. 29, 1941; s. Clarence Hardecke and Mildred Lorine (Eggers) B.; m. Judith May Creamer, June 9, 1962 (div. 1972); children: William Richard, Christopher Paul; m. Georgia Ann Kinney, Apr. 22, 1973; children: Patricia Jayne, Jon Scott. BS, Calif. Inst. Tech., 1963; PhD, Harvard U., 1968. Asst. prof. chemistry U. Hawaii, Manoa, Honolulu, 1967-72, assoc. prof. chemistry, 1972-85, prof. chemistry, 1985—, asst. v.p., 1995—2001. Chair chemistry dept., U. Hawaii, Manoa, 1992-95, chair faculty senate, 1991-92. Mem. Honolulu Symphony Chorus. Avocation: choral music. Office: Univ Hawaii Dept Chemistry Honolulu HI 96822-2275

BOR, JONATHAN STEVEN, journalist; b. Washington, Sept. 22, 1953; s. Robert Myer and Judith Anne (Harkavy) B.; m. Sally Diane Mericle, June 3, 1984; 1 child, Benjamin Andrew. BA in History, Oberlin Coll., 1975; MS in Journalism, Columbia U., 1982. Editor Millbrook Round Table, N.Y., 1976-77; editor Rhinebeck Gazette-Advertiser, N.Y., 1977; reporter Poughkeepsie Jour., N.Y., 1977-81, Syracuse Post-Standard, N.Y., 1983-87; med. reporter Balt. Sun, 1988—. Recipient Disting. Writing award Am. Soc. Newspaper Editors, 1985. Mem. Nat. Assn. Sci. Writers. Jewish. Home: 6214 Woodcrest Ave Baltimore MD 21209-3935 Office: Baltimore Sun Calvert St Baltimore MD 21225-1747

BORAH, GREGORY, surgeon, educator; b. NM, Apr. 1950; MD, Harvard U., 1978. Diplomate Am. Bd.Plastic Surgery. Prof., chief of plastic surgery U. Medicine and Dentistry NJ, Robert Wood Johnson Med. Sch., New Brunswick, NJ, 1992—. Pres. Am. Soc. Maxillofacial Surgeons, 1998—99. Contbr. more than 60 articles to profl. jours. Fellow: ACS (trustee 1999—2001); mem.: Am. Soc. Plastic Surgeons. Office: UMDNJ - Robert Wood Johnson Med Sch 1 RWJ Place New Brunswick NJ 08901

BORAS, KIM, lawyer; BA, Rollins Coll., 1986; JD, Harvard U., 1989. Bar: Calif. 1989, Fla. 1990, N.Y. 2001. Jud. clk. to Hon. Peter T. Fay, Judge, U.S. Ct. Appeals (11th cir.), 1989—90; with Latham & Watkins, L.A., 1990—, ptnr., 2001—. Office: Latham and Watkins LLC 633 W Fifth St Ste 4000 Los Angeles CA 90071

BORCHARD, WILLIAM MARSHALL, lawyer; b. N.Y.C., Nov. 19, 1938; s. Bernard Philip and Helen (Marshall) B.; m. Myra Cohen, Dec. 13, 1969; children: Jillian, Thomas. BA, Princeton U., 1960; JD, Columbia U., 1964. Bar: NY 1964, U.S. Dist. Ct. (so. and ea. dists.) NY, U.S. Ct. Appeals (2d, 3d, fed. cirs.), U.S. Supreme Ct. Assoc. Kaye, Scholer, Fierman, Hays and Handler, N.Y.C., 1964-74, ptnr., 1974-83, Cowan, Liebowitz and Latman, N.Y.C., 1983—. Author: Trademarks and the Arts, 1999, A Trademark is Not a Copyright or a Patent, 2005; mem. editl. bd. Art and the Law, 1982—, The Trademark Reporter, 1983—99. Staff sgt. USAFR, 1961-67. Stone scholar Columbia Law Sch. N.Y.C., 1962. Mem. ABA (coun. 1987-90), Am. Law Inst. (adv. com. 1986-92), Internat. Trademark Assn. (legal counsel 1988-91). Democrat. Jewish. Avocations: tennis, boating, biking. Office: Cowan Liebowitz & Latman 1133 Ave of Americas New York NY 10036-6799 Office Phone: 212-575-0671. Business E-Mail: wmb@cll.com.

BORCHARDT, MARC, nurse anesthetist; b. Southampton, N.Y., Feb. 25, 1969; s. Duke and Nancy Ann Borchardt; m. Terri Lynn Freeman, July 21, 1990. BS in Nursing, U. Fla., 1993; MN, Med. Coll. Ga., 1998. Cert. CRNA 1999. Nurse anesthetist Harbin Clinic Anesthesia, Rome, Ga., 1999—2005, Redmond Anesthesiology Assocs., 2005—. Adj. clin. instr. Med. Coll. Ga., Augusta, 2002—. Mem.: Am. Assn. Nurse Anethetists. Roman Catholic. Office: Redmond Anesthesiology Assocs 501 Redmond Rd Rome GA 30165 Home: 7 W Brook Dr Rome GA 30165 Personal E-mail: mtborch721@comcast.net.

BORCHERDING, THOMAS EARL, economist; b. Cin., Feb. 18, 1939; s. Earl Schaff and Vivian Joan (Miller) B.; m. Rhoda Jean Larson, Nov. 23, 1968; children: Matthew James, Benjamin Adam. BA, U. Cin., 1961; PhD, Duke U., 1966. Asst. prof. U. Wash., Seattle, 1966-71; assoc. prof. Va. Polytech Inst., Blacksburg, 1971-73; prof. econs. Simon Fraser U., Burnaby, B.C., Can., 1973-83; prof. law and econs. U. Toronto (Ont., Can.), 1978-79; prof. econs. Claremont (Calif.) Grad. U., 1983—. Editl. bd. CATO Jour., Washington; bd. of advisors Ind. Inst., Oakland, Calif., 1990—. Author: The Egg Board: The Social Cast of Monopoly, 1981; contbr. articles to profl. jours. NDEA fellow Duke U., 1961-64, postdoctoral fellow U. Va., 1965-66, Hoover Instn., Stanford U., 1974-75, Avery fellow Claremont U. Ctr., 1988-97. Mem. Am. Econ. Assn., Western Econ. Assn. (editor 1980-97), Can. Econ. Assn., Pub. Choice Soc., Mont Pelerin Soc., Phi Beta Kappa, Omicron Delta Epsilon, Phi Delta Theta. Home: 889 Connors Ct Claremont CA 91711-6240 Office: Claremont Grad U Sch Politics & Econs Claremont CA 91711 Office Phone: 909-621-8783. Personal E-mail: thomas_borcherding@yahoo.com.

BORCHERDS, RICHARD EWEN, mathematics professor; b. Cape Town, South Africa, Nov. 29, 1959; BA, Cambridge U., England, 1981; PhD, Cambridge U., 1983. Rsch. fellow Trinity Coll., Cambridge, England, 1983-87; asst. prof. U. Calif., Berkeley, 1987-88; rsch. fellow Cambridge U., England, 1988-92, lectr., 1992-93; prof. U. Calif., Berkeley, 1993—, Cambridge U., 1996. Contbr. articles to profl. jours. including J. Alg., Adv. Math., Duke Math. J. Recipient Fields medal 1998. Fellow: Royal Soc. Office: U Calif Dept Math 970 Evans Hall # 3840 Berkeley CA 94720-3840

BORCHERS, ROBERT REECE, physicist, science administrator; b. Chgo., Apr. 4, 1936; s. Robert Harley and Rena Josephine (Reece) B.; m. Mary Bridget Hennessy, Nov. 26, 1960; children: Patrick Joseph, Anne Marie, Robert Edward BS in Physics, U. Notre Dame, 1958; MS in Physics, Math., U. Wis., 1959, PhD in Nuclear Physics, 1962. Prof. physics U. Wis., Madison, 1962—76, vice chancellor, 1976—77, U. Colo., Boulder, 1977—79; dep. assoc., dir. MFE Program Lawrence Livermore (Calif.) Nat. Lab., 1979—83, assoc. dir. computation, 1983—91, asst. to dir. for univ. rels., 1991—93; divsn. dir. advanced sci. computing NSF, Arlington, Va., 1993—2001; chief tech. officer Maui High Performance Computing Ctr., 2001—; CEO R.R. Borchers & Assocs., 2001—04; chief scientist, ptnr. CS Cubed Group, 2004—. Mem. com. NSF, Washington, 1973-93, Nat. Acad. Sci., Washington, 1983-93. Editor Computers in Physics jour., 1987-91, chmn. editorial bd., 1991-95; contbr. numerous chpts. in books, articles on physics and computing. NSF postdoctoral fellow, 1964; A.J. Schmidt Found. fellow and scholar, 1954-60; Sloan Found. fellow, 1964-68; Guggenheim Found. fellow, 1970; recipient W.H. Kiekhofer Disting. Teaching award U. Wis., Madison, 1966; Centennial of Sci. Alumnus award U. Notre Dame, 1966 Fellow Am. Phys. Soc.; mem. IEEE Computer Soc. Avocations: golf, music. Office: MHPCC 550 Lipoa Ste 100 Kihei HI 96753 Office Phone: 703-627-3749. E-mail: marquis@bborchers.com.

BORCHERT, CATHERINE GLENNAN, minister; b. L.A., Dec. 6, 1936; d. Thomas Keith and Ruth Haslup Adams Glennan; m. Frank R. Borchert Jr., Sept. 12, 1959 (dec. Sept. 1997); children: Frank R. III, Anne Matthews, Thomas Adams. BS, Swarthmore Coll., 1958; MSLS, Western Res. U., 1959; MDiv, McCormick Theol. Sem., 1991; postgrad., Case Western Res. U. Ordained to ministry, Presbyn. Ch., 1991. Serial records libr. U. Chgo. Libr., 1959-61; ref. libr., head outreach Cleveland Heights (Ohio) Pub. Libr., 1979-86; stated clk. Presbytery of Western Res. U., Cleve., 1984-94; interim pastor Lyndhurst (Ohio) Cmty. Presbyn. Ch., 1993-94; coord. adv. com. social witness policy Gen. Assembly of Presbyn. Ch., Louisville, 1994-97; adj. faculty McCormick Theol. Sem., Chgo., 1987—, interim dean doctoral programs and continuing edn., 2000-01. Mem. exec. com. Permanent Judicial Commn. Contbr. articles to profl. jours. Bd. dirs. United Protestant Campus Min., Cleve., 1999—2002, History Assocs., Cleve., 1999—; mem. steering com. Woman 2000 Case Western Res. U., 1998—2000; alumni interviewer Swarthmore (Pa.) Coll., 1965—; mem. exec. com. Chs.' Ctr. for Theology and Pub. Policy, Washington. Mem.: Mortar Bd., Phi Alpha Theta, Beta Phi Mu. Democrat. Avocations: reading, birdwatching, choir, bike riding. Home: 13415 Shaker Blvd #9C2 Cleveland OH 44120

BORCHERT, DONALD MARVIN, philosopher, educator; b. Edmonton, Alta., Can., May 23, 1934; s. Leo Ferdinand and Lillian Violet (Bucholz) B.; m. Mary Ellen Cockrell, Dec. 27, 1960; children: Carol Ellen, John Witherspoon. AB, U. Alta., Edmonton, 1955; BD, Princeton Theol. Sem., 1958, PhD, 1966; ThM, Ea. Bapt. Theol. Sem., 1959. Teaching fellow Princeton (N.J.) Theol. Sem., 1960-61; asst. prof. Juniata Coll., Huntingdon, Pa., 1966-67, Ohio U., Athens, 1967-71, assoc. prof., 1971-75, prof. philosophy, 1975—, assoc. dean Coll. Arts and Scis., 1980-86, chmn. dept. philosophy, 1987—2002. Author: Being Human in a Technological Age, 1979, Introduction to Modern Philosophy, 1981, 7th edit., 2001, Exploring Ethics, 1986, Medical Ethics, 1992, Philosophy of Sex and Love, 1997; editor in chief: Encyclopedia of Philosophy Supplement, 1996, Compendium of Philosophy and Ethics, 1999, Encyclopedia of Philosophy, 10 vols., 2005; contbr. articles to profl. jours Assoc. Danforth Found. Nat. Humanities Inst. fellow, 1976-77; NEH Implementation grantee, 1981. Mem. Ohio Philos. Assn. (v.p. 1983-85, pres. 1985-90), Ohio Humanities Council (vice chmn. 1981-83, chmn. 1983-85). Presbyterian. Home: 9 Coventry Ln Athens OH 45701-3717 Office: Ohio U Dept Philosophy Ellis Hall Athens OH 45701 Office Phone: 740-593-4588. E-mail: borchert@ohio.edu.

BORCOVER, ALFRED SEYMOUR, journalist; b. Bellaire, Ohio, May 1, 1931; s. Joseph and Kate (Florman) B.; m. Doris E. Wellner, Sept. 13, 1958 (div. 1966); m. Linda A. Gredig, Oct. 11, 1989. BSc in Journalism, Ohio State U., 1953; MSJ, Northwestern U., 1957. Writer Northwestern U., Evanston, Ill., 1957-58; reporter, copy editor Chgo. Tribune, 1959-63, asst. travel editor, 1963-73, assoc. travel editor, 1973-79, editor travel sect., 1979-81, travel editor, columnist, 1981-93; ret., 1994. Freelance travel columnist/writer, 1994—. Author: Dollarwise Guide to Chicago, 1967; contbg. editor Fodor's Chicago, 1985-88; contbr. to Around the World with the Experts, 1970, WGN Travel Show, 1986-93; travel columnist Prodigy On-line Svc., 1990-96. Served to 1st lt. USAF, 1953-55 Recipient spl. citation George Hedmon Awards, 1965, Outstanding Achievement in Travel Writing award N.Y. Travel Writers Assn., 1976, Econ. Impact Writing award Travel Industry Assn. Am., 1983, Lowell Thomas Writing award, 1986; Gold Medal Writing award Pacific Asia Travel Assn., 1987, Cen. States Consumerism Reporting award, 1987, Alumni Svc. award Northwestern U., 1991, Cen. States Best Fgn. Series award, Cen. States Henry E. Bradshaw Meml. Writing award, 1991, Ctrl. States Fgn. Series and U.S. Article awards, 1992, Earl R. Lind Consumer Edn. award Better Bus. Bur. of Chgo., 1993, Ctrl. States Commentary award, 2004, Ctrl. States Reporting award, 2005. Mem. Soc. Am. Travel Writers (pres. 1973-74), Chgo. Headline Club (pres. 1983-84), Medill Sch. Journalism Alumni Assn. (bd. dirs. 1984-89, pres. 1989-91), Northwestern U. Alumni Assn. (bd. dirs. 1986-90), Soc. Profl. Journalists. Democrat. Jewish. Avocations: tennis, music, photography. Home and Office: 1022 Michigan Ave Evanston IL 60202-1436 Personal E-mail: aborcover@aol.com.

BORDA, RICHARD JOSEPH, retired insurance company executive; b. San Francisco, Aug. 16, 1931; s. Joseph Clement and Ethel Cathleen (Donovan) B.; m. Judith Maxwell, Aug. 30, 1953; children: Michelle, Stephen Joseph. AB, Stanford U., 1953, MBA, 1957. With Wells Fargo Bank, San Francisco, 1957-70, mgr., 1963-66, asst. v.p., 1966-67, v.p., 1967-70, exec. v.p. adminstrn. San Francisco, 1973-85; asst. sec. Air Force Manpower Res. Affairs, Washington, 1970-73; vice chmn., chief fin. officer Nat. Life Ins. Co., Montpelier, Vt., 1985-90; chmn., chief exec. officer Sentinal Group Funds, Inc., 1985-90. Former pres. Air Force Aid Soc., Washington; mem. bd. visitors Monterey Inst. Internat. Studies; govs. coun. Boys and Girls Club Monterey Peninsula; dir. Cmty. Found. Monterey County. Recipient Exceptional Civilian Svc. award, 1973, 95. Mem. USMC Res. Officers Assn., Bohemian Club, Old Capital Club, Air Force Aid Soc. (disting. counselor), Phi Gamma Delta, Cypress Point Club. Republican. Episcopalian.

BORDALLO, MADELEINE MARY (MRS. RICARDO JEROME BORDALLO), congresswoman; b. Graceville, Minn., May 31, 1933; d. Christian Peter and Mary Evelyn (Roth) Zeien; m. Ricardo Jerome Bordallo, June 20, 1953; 1 daughter, Deborah Josephine. Student, St Mary's Coll., South Bend, Ind., 1952; AA, St. Katherines Coll., St. Paul, 1953; AA hon. degree for community service, U. Guam, 1968. Presented in voice recital Guam Acad. Music, Agana., 1951, 62; mem. Civic Opera Co., St. Paul, 1952-53; mem. staff KUAM Radio-TV sta., Agana, 1954-63; freelance writer local newspaper, fashion show commentator, coordinator, civic leader, 1963; nat. Dem. committeewoman for Guam, 1964—2004; 1st lady of Guam, 1974-78, 81-85; senator 16th Guam Legislature, 1981-82, 19th Guam Legislature, 1987-88, 20th Guam Legislature, 1989-90, 21st Guam Legislature, 1991-92, 22nd Guam Legislature, 1993-94; Dem. Party candidate for Gov. of Guam, 1990; lt. gov. of Guam, 1994—2002; at-large repr. U.S. Ho. of Reps. from Guam, 2003—; mem. armed svcs., resources and small bus. coms. Del. Nat. Dem. Conv., 1964, 68, 72, 76, 80, 84, 88-92, 96, 2000-04, pres. Women's Dem. Party Guam, 1967-69; rep. Presdl. Inauguration, Washington, 1965, 77, 85, 2005; del. Dem. Western States Conf., Reno, 1965, L.A., 1967, Phoenix, 1968, conf. sec., 1967-69; del. Dem. Women's Campaign Conf., Wash., 1965, Dem. Inauguration, 1992. Pres. Guam Women's Club, 1958-59; del Gen. Fedn. Women's Clubs Convs., Miami Beach, Fla., 1961, New Orleans, 1965, Boston, 1968; v.p. Fedn. Asian Women's Assn., 1964-67, pres., 1967-69, pres. 1996-98; pres. Guam Symphony Soc., 1967-73, del. convs., Manila, Philippines, 1959, Taipei, Formosa, 1960, Hong Kong, 1963, Guam, 1964, Japan, 1968, Taipei, 1973; chmn. Guam Christmas Seal Drive, 1961; bd. dirs. Guam chpt. ARC, 1963, sec., 1963-67, fund dr. chmn., 2000; pres. Marianas Assn. For Retarded Children, 1968-69, 73-74, 84—; bd. dirs. Guam Theatre Guild, Am. Cancer Soc.; mem. Guam Meml. Hosp. Vols. Assn., 1966—, v.p., 1966-67, pres., 1970-71; chmn. Hosp. Charity Ball, 1966; pres. Women for Service, 1974—, Beauty World Guam Ltd., 1981—, First Lady's Beautification Task Force of Guam, 1983-86; pres. Palace Restoration Assn., 1983—; nominee Dem. party for Gov. of Guam, 1990. Mem. Internat. Platform Assn., Guam Rehab. Assn. (assoc.), Guam Lytico and Bodig Assn. (pres. 1983-98), Spanish Club of Guam, Inetnon Famalaoan Club (pres. 1983-86), Guam Coun. of Women's Club (pres. 1993-95), Nat. Conf. Lt. Govs. (exec. com. 1998—). Democrat. Home: Watergate E 305 N 2510 Virginia Ave NW Washington DC 20037 Office Phone: 202-225-1188. E-mail: Madeleine.Bordallo@mail.house.gov.

BORDELON, ALVIN JOSEPH, JR., lawyer; b. New Orleans, Nov. 1, 1945; s. Alvin Joseph and Mildred (Quarella) B.; m. Melanie Rose Bond; children by previous marriage: Peter Jude, Emily Aprill; m. Melanie Rose Bond. BA in English, U. New Orleans, 1968; JD, Loyola U., New Orleans, 1973. Bar: La. 1973, U.S. Ct. Appeals (5th cir.) 1975, U.S. Supreme Ct. 1983. Landman Chevron Oil Co., New Orleans, 1973-74; pvt. practice New Orleans, 1974-75; ptnr. Douglas, Favre & Bordelon, New Orleans, 1975-76, Monroe & Lemann, New Orleans, 1976-81; sr. ptnr. Bordelon, Hamlin & Theriot, New Orleans, 1981—. Labor negotiator St. Tammany Parish Sch. Bd., Covington, La., 1991—, St. Bernard Parish Sch. Bd., Chalmette, La., 1986—; instr. criminal justice Loyola City Coll., 1975-76, Loyola U. Sch. Law, 1976-77. Mng. editor Loyola Law Rev., 1972-73. Chmn. Alcoholic Beverage Control Bd., New Orleans, 1983-84; mem. Mayor's Commn. on Crime, New Orleans, 1979; pres. Faubourg St. John Neighborhood Assn., New Orleans, 1977-80. With U.S. Army, 1968-70. Recipient Outstanding Civic Leadership award La. State Senate, Baton Rouge, 1982; named Short Story Competition 1st Place winner Writer's Digest, 1993. Mem. Profl. Assn. of Dive Instrs., La. Bar Assn. Republican. Roman Catholic. Avocations: poetry and short story writing, fishing, diving. Office: Bordelon Hamlin & Theriot 701 S Peters St New Orleans LA 70130-1588 E-mail: alvinbordelon@msn.com.

BORDELON, CAROLYN THEW, elementary school educator; b. Shelby, Ohio, Dec. 28, 1942; d. Burton Carl and Opal Mae (Harris) VanAsdale; m. Clifford Charles Spohn, Aug. 28, 1965 (div. Feb. 1982); m. Al Ramon Bordelon, Oct. 26, 1985. BA in History and Polit. Sci., Otterbein Coll., 1966; MA in Edn., Bowling Green State U., 1972; postgrad., Ohio State U., 1986—. Cert. tchr. grades 1-8, Ohio. Elem. tchr. Allen East Schs., Harrod, Ohio, 1966—68, Marion (Ohio) City Schs., 1968—78, chpt. I reading tchr., 1978—86, reading recovery tchr., 1986—88, Dublin (Ohio) City Schs., 1988—. Adj. instr. reading dept. grad. studies Ashland (Ohio) U., 1996. Author: The Parent Workshop, 1992, Octopus Goes to School, 1995. Vol. Am. Heart Assn., Worthington, Ohio, 1991; mem. Rep. Nat. Com., Washington, 1994-95; mem. Royal Scots Highlanders, Mansfield, Ohio, 1976—. Recipient Excellence in Edn. award Dublin City C. of C., 1991-93, 96, 97; Dublin City Schs./Ohio Dept. Edn. Tchr. Award grantee, 1993; Martha Holden Jennings Found. scholar, 1978. Mem. Archaeol. Inst. Am., Ohio Edn. Assn., Reading Recovery Coun. N.Am., Columbus Opera Assn., Columbus Mus. Art, Phi Delta Kappa, Phi Alpha Theta. Presbyterian. Avocations: bagpiping and scottish activities, archaeology, interior design, harpsichord. Home: 3958 Fairlington Dr Columbus OH 43220-4531 Office: Griffith Thomas Elem Sch 4671 Tuttle Crossing Blvd Dublin OH 43017-3575 Personal E-mail: c.bordelonread@aol.com.

BORDELON, DENA COX YARBROUGH, retired special education educator, director; b. Gorman, Tex., June 20, 1933; d. William Thomas and Imogene (Dunlap) Cox; m. James Edgar Yarbrough, June 20, 1950 (dec.); m. Cecil J. Bordelon, Sept. 24, 1999. BA, Nicholls State U., 1964, MEd, 1971, postgrad., 1978. Supr. profl. pers., prin. schs., elem. tchr. Terrebonne Parish Sch. Bd., Houma, La., 1964-79, dir. spl. edn. svcs., 1980-91; ret., 1991. Mem.: La. Ret. Tchrs. Assn. Democrat. Methodist. Avocations: reading, theater. Home: 202 White St Houma LA 70364-2934 E-mail: cbordelon@sw.rr.com.

BORDELON, KARL JOSEPH, music educator, secondary school educator; b. Ville Platte, La., Aug. 15, 1950; s. Octave Bordelon and Hazel Morein; 1 child, Joshua Kyle. BA in Music, U. S.W. La., 1984. Cert. music educator Besse Bd. Edn., La., 1995. Tchr., dir. band various schs. Evangeline Parish Schs., La., 1974—; tchr., dir. band Midland (La.) H.S. Acadia Parish Schs., 1994—2001. Musician: The Travelers, 1965—68, Jay Randall & Epics, 1969—72, Last Flight, 1972—78, Kent Dupre, 1981—83, Moss, 1983—85, Impact, 1985—87, The Heat, 1987—91, Strollers, 1991—94, DeJa Vue, 1994—2005, Waren Storm Willie Tee & Cypress, 2005—. Bugler Vietnam Veterans, Ville Platte, La., 1996—2005; min. ch. music Our Lady Queen of All Saints Cath. Ch., Ville Platte, 1990—2005; organist Sacred Heart Cath. Ch., Ville Platte, 2000—05. Recipient Svc. as Bugler cert., Vietman Vets., 1998. Mem.: Music Educator Nat. Conf., S.W. La. Band Dirs. Assn. (assoc.), La. Assn. Educators (assoc.), Nat. Educators Assn. (assoc.). Democrat. Roman Catholic. Avocations: music, carpentry, swimming, travel. Home: 506 West LaSalle Street Ville Platte LA 70586 Office: Mamou High School 1008 7th Street Mamou LA 70504 Office Fax: 337-468-2220. Personal E-mail: karl00@centurytel.net. E-mail: karl.bordelon@epsb.com.

BORDEN, DAVID, composer, educator; b. Boston, Dec. 25, 1938; s. Raymond Borden and Natalie Mallard; m. Rebecca Lee Simmons, Dec. 8, 1994; 1 child, Gabriel. MusB, Eastman Sch. of Music, Rochester, N.Y., 1961, MusM, 1963; MA, Harvard U., 1967. Scholarship/hochschule für musik Fulbright Com., West Berlin, Germany, 1965—66; composer-in-residence Ithaca City Sch. Dist., NY, 1966—68; composer/pianist for dance Cornell U., Ithaca, 1968—87, dir., digital music program, 1987—. Dir. and rec. artist Earthquack Records, Ithaca, 1972—78; rec. artist Cuneiform Records, Silver Spring, Md., 1987—, Arbiter Records, N.Y.C. Composer: (music composition) C-A-G-E Parts 1, 2 & 3 for synthesizer ensemble, (electroacoustic music in 12 parts) The Continuing Story of Counterpoint, (electroacoustic pieces and soloists) Anagram Portraits, (choral and electroacoustic) Angels, (electroacoustic variations plus soloists) Earth Journeys, (electroacoustic cantus firmus pieces) Synergy Soundscapes. Home: 227 Enfield Falls Rd Ithaca NY 14850 Office: Cornell University Dept Music Lincoln Hall Ithaca NY 14853-4101 Business E-Mail: drb4@cornell.edu.

BORDEN, DAVID M., state supreme court justice; b. Hartford, Conn., Aug. 4, 1937; BA magna cum laude, Amherst Coll., 1959; LLB cum laude, Harvard U., 1962. Bar: Conn. 1962, U.S. Dist. Ct. Conn. 1962, U.S. Ct. Appeals (2d cir.) 1965, U.S. Supreme Ct. 1969. Pvt. practice, Hartford, Conn., 1962-77; judge Conn. Ct. Common Pleas, 1977-78, Conn. Superior Ct., 1978-83, Conn. Appellate Ct., 1983—90; assoc. justice Conn. Supreme Ct., 1990—. Chief counsel joint com. on judiciary Conn. Gen. Assembly, 1975-76; lectr. Law U. Conn. Sch. Law, 1968-70, 85-92, 94-; exec. dir. Conn. Commn. to Revise Criminal Statutes, 1963-71. Co-author: (books) Connecticut Criminal Jury Instructions, Superior Court Criminal Rules, Connecticut Criminal Law. Recipient Raymond E. Baldwin Public Service award, 1997. Mem. Conn. Bar Assn., Hartford County Bar Assn., Phi Beta Kappa. Democrat. Jewish. Avocations: hiking, reading. Office: Conn Supreme Ct 231 Capitol Ave Hartford CT 06106*

BORDEN, MARK G., lawyer; b. N.Y.C., Feb. 19, 1951; s. Arthur M. and Florence (Smiley) B. BA, Yale U., 1973; JD, Harvard U., 1976. Bar: Mass. 1976. Ptnr., mem. mgmt. com., co-chmn. Corp. dept. Wilmer Cutler Pickering Hale & Dorr, Boston. Co-author: Start-up Cos. — Planning, Financing & Operating Successful Bus. Named one of Boston's top lawyers, Boston Mag., 2002. Mem.: Boston Bar Assn., ABA, Tenacre Country Day Sch. (chmn. bd. trustees), Boston Symphony Orchestra (trustee). Office: Wilmer Cutler Pickering Hale & Dorr 60 State St Boston MA 02109-1816 Office Phone: 617-526-6675. Office Fax: 617-526-5000. Business E-Mail: mark.borden@wilmerhale.com.*

BORDEN, WILLIAM VICKERS, education educator, writer; b. Indpls., Jan. 27, 1938; s. Harold Rudolph and Elizabeth Margaret (Vickers) B.; m. Nancy Lee Johnson, Dec. 17, 1960; children: Andrew James, Sara Elise, Rachel Lynne. AB, Columbia U., 1960; MA, U. Calif., Berkeley, 1962. Instr. U. N.D., Grand Forks, 1962-64, asst. prof., 1966-70, assoc. prof., 1970-78, prof., 1978—, Chester Fritz disting. prof., 1994—98, prof. emeritus, 1999—. Playwright-in-residence Listening Winds Theatre, 1992—. Author: (plays) The Last Prostitute, 1981, Jumping, 1981, I Want to be an Indian, 1982, Loon Dance, 1984, The Only Woman Awake, 1984, When the Meadowlark Sings, 1988, Anna's Stone, 1989, Meet Again, 1990, Quarks, 1990, Turtle Island Blues, 1991, Don't Dance Me Outside, 1993, The Alien Hypothesis, 1994, Gourmet Love, Dirty Laundry, 1999, Bluest Reason, 2001, Wonderful World, 2004, Falling, 2004, Mamy Worlds, 2005, (novel) Superstoe, 1968, 96, (poems) Slow Step and Dance, 1991, Eurydice's Song, 1999; librettist: (opera) Sakakawea, 1989; fiction editor N.D. Quar., 1984-2000. Chair Grand Forks Com. on Human Rights, 1967. Mem. ASCAP, Dramatists Guild, P.E.N., Authors Guild. Home and Office: 7996 S FM548 Royse City TX 75189 Office Phone: 214-828-1202. Personal E-mail: borden@ev1.net.

BORDER, WILLIAM LAWSON, artist; b. Alton, Ill., May 31, 1933; s. Lawson Elwood and Cordelia Kelley B.; m. Laura Lea Baker, June 28, 1975; children: William Wesley, Alison Anne. Student, Pratt Inst., 1953; BFA, U. Colo., 1974. Freelance illustrator, graphic designer, N.Y.C., 1955-69, Denver, 1969-74; biol. & scientific illustrator Biol. Scis. Curriculum Study, Louisville,

Colo., 1974-82; freelance natural history illustrator Nederland, Colo., 1982-98. With U.S. Army, 1953-55. Mem. Guild Natural Sci. Illustrators, NAt. Assn. Interpretation, Rocky Mountain Nature Assn., Gilpin County Artists Assn., Art Ctr. Estes Park. Avocations: horseback riding, dry fly fishing. Home: 285 Devon Pl Boulder CO 80302-8033 Office: 463 Pine Glade Rd Nederland CO 80466-9630

BORDERS, DONNA TURNER, elementary school educator; b. Griffin, Ga., Mar. 5, 1949; d. Alvin G. and Doris (Hayes) Turner; m. Michael W. Borders, Dec. 20, 1969; children: Scott, Brent. BS in Elem. Edn., Tift Coll., 1971; MEd in Elem. Edn., Ga. State U., 1973; Edn. Specialist's degree in Early Childhood, West Ga. Coll., 1985. Cert. early childhood edn. tchr., Ga. Elem. tchr. Muscogee County Sch. Dist., Columbus, Ga., 1971-74; tchr. grade 4 Fayette County Sch. System, Fayetteville, Ga., 1975—96, tchr. early intervention, 1996—. Lead tchr. Fayette County After Sch. Program, Fayetteville, 1992-97. Mem.: Ga. Reading Assn., Profl. Assn. Ga. Educators. Avocations: hiking, gardening, reading, bicycling, travel. Office: East Fayette Elem Sch 245 Booker Ave Fayetteville GA 30215-2270 Office Phone: 770-460-3565.

BORDERS, JOHN GILLESPIE, psychotherapist, retired corporate financial executive; b. St. Louis, June 12, 1946; s. William Alexis and Kate (Thompson) B.; children: Alexandra, Clara. AB in Econs., Princeton U., 1969; MSW, Washington U., 1993. Asst. treas. Chase Manhattan Bank, N.Y.C., 1972-77; group v.p. Centerre Bank, St. Louis, 1977-86; founding ptnr. Axium Inc., St. Louis, 1987-88; pres., CEO, HealthScan, Inc., St. Louis, 1988-93; psychotherapist Youth Emergency Svc., 1992-94, St. Louis Mental Health Ctr., 1994-97, The Child Ctr., St. Louis, 1997—; actor Neighborhood Playhouse, 1971—72. Mem. psychiat. diversion term Divsn. Family Svcs., State of Mo.; field instr. Washington U., St. Louis, St. Louis U., Webster U., chief vol. officers coun. Author: Conglomerate Merger: Corporate Growth Strategy, 1969, Hound with One Red Ear, 1992; contbr. articles to profl. jours. Mem. ops. com. St. Louis Tech. Ctr., 1986-87; bd. dirs. Jefferson Nat. Expansion Meml. Assn., St. Louis, Kammergild Chamber Orch., St. Louis, Altenheim Retirement Ctr., The Thompson Ctr.; mem. exec. com., bd. dirs. Princeton U. Alumni Coun.; mem. exec. com. Project for Peaceful Sch. Learning Environment; steering com., chmn. external rels. cmty. svc. initiative Veiled Prophet Orgn., non-profit orgn. pres.'s coun. Served with U.S. Spl. Forces (Airborne) Group, 1969-70. Named one of Nation's Fifty Most Eligible Bachelors, Town & Country Mag., 1968; Eleanor Roosevelt fellow, 1993. Mem. Advance Psychoanalytic Psychotherapy Assn. (oficer, treas., bd. dirs.), coun. chief vol. officers non profit organ., Adventure Club (past pres.), Lunch Club (past pres.), Hall Commn.(past chmn.), St. Louis Country Club, Princeton Club of St. Louis (exec. com., bd. dirs.), The Generation Club, Barnes Rd. Luncheon Group Home: Twelve Highgate Rd Saint Louis MO 63132 Office: The Child Ctr 7900 Natural Bridge Rd Saint Louis MO 63121 E-mail: jborders@ccstl.org.

BORDERS, WILLIAM ALEXANDER, journalist; b. St. Louis, Jan. 11, 1939; s. William Alexis and Kate (Thompson) B.; m. Barbara D. Burkham, June 17, 1967 (div. 1984); 1 son, William Borders. BA, Yale U., 1960. Staff N.Y. Times, N.Y.C., 1960—, corr. Nigeria, 1970-72, 1972-75, 1975-79, London, 1979-82, dep. fgn. editor, 1982-83, editor Week in Rev. N.Y.C., 1983-89, sr. editor, 1989-90, news editor, 1990—. Home: 227 E 57th St New York NY 10022-2828 Office: NY Times Co 229 W 43rd St New York NY 10036-3959

BORDLEY, JAMES, IV, surgeon; b. Balt., Nov. 24, 1942; s. James III and Julia (Ross) B.; m. Dianne Redmond; children: Jessica, James V. BA, Yale U., 1965; MD, Columbia U. Physicians/Surgeon, 1970. Surg. intern Bassett Hosp., Cooperstown, N.Y., 1970-71, surg. resident, 1971-75, att. surgeon, 1978—; staff surgeon Naval Regl. Med. Ctr., Newport, R.I., 1975-77; fellow biliary and pancreatic surgery U. Wash., Seattle, 1977; instr. surgery Columbia U., N.Y.C., 1978-80, asst. prof. clin. surg., 1980—. Contbr. articles to profl. jours./publs. Lt. cmdr. USN, 1975-77. Fellow Am. Coll. Surgeons; mem. Soc. Surgery of the Alimentary Tract, Soc. Am. Gastrointestinal Endoscopic Surgeons. Office: Bassett Hosp 1 Atwell Rd Cooperstown NY 13326-1301

BORDNER, MARJORIE RICH, volunteer, educator, writer; b. McDonough Conty, Ill., Dec. 1, 1914; d. HarryR. and Merle (Turner) Rich; m. Lawrence Inman Bordner, Apr. 21, 1946; children: Larry Richard, Larrilyn Louise. BEd, Western Ill. U., 1936; EdM, U. Mo., Columbia, 1940. Tchr. various elem. and secondary schs., Ill.; instr. Western Ill. U. and Spoon River Coll.; acct., receptionist Bordner Air Conditioning-Refrigeration Co.; pres. New Eng. Women Ill. Prairie Colony, 1974-76, Fulton County Hist. and Geneal. Soc., 1974-75, 80—, Spoon River Scenic Drive Assn., 1971-74; sec. found. bd., exec. com. Western Ill. U., 1972—. Apptd. by Ill. Gov. to First Western Ill. Univ. Bd. Trustees, 1996—, Western Ill. U. Centennial Com., 1999-2000; mem. Western Ill. U. Alumni Coun., 1972—, sec., 1981—; mem. librs. bd. Western Ill. U., 2003—: mem. Fulton County Planning Commn., 1971—, Canton Bicentennial Constn. Commn., 1986—, Canton Hist. Preservation and Devel. Commn., 1986—; chmn. Fulton County Bicentennial Constn. Commn., 1973-76, 86—; sec. County Resource Devel. Exec. Coun. Fulton County, 1979—. Author: A Spoon River Portrait, 1983 (Ill. State award for excellence 1983), Fulton County, Illinois Heritage, 1987, From Cornfields to Marching Feet, Camp Ellis, Ill., 1993; contb. articles to periodicals. Recipient Disting. Alumni award Western Ill. U., 1971, Achievement award, 1980, Jefferson award, 1981, Martha Washnigton award, 1986; named hon. parade marshal Canton Friendship Festival Parade, 1976, 87, Canton July 4, 2000 parade. Mem. Ill. Hist. Soc. (life), Ill. Geneal. Soc. (life), DAR (divsn. dir., regent 1971—, sec., bd. dirs. Ill. chpt. 1977), Nat. Soc. Daus. Founders Patriots (life), Nat. Soc. Daus. Am. Colonists. Personal E-mail: mbordner@winco.net.

BORDNER, PATRICIA ANNE, insurance agent, writer; b. Red Wing, Minn., Mar. 29, 1946; d. Harold Arthur and Cecilia Helen Rodman; m. Thomas Ottis Bordner, May 18, 1981. AA, U. Minn., 1966. Cert. commercial rater U.S. Fidelity and Guaranty Co. Tchr. St. Albert the Great Elem. Sch., Mpls., 1967—68; tchr. Epiphany Edn. Ctr., Coon Rapids, Minn., 1968—70; comml. rater and acctg. clk. U. S. Fidelity and Guaranty Co., Mpls., 1971—85; ind. comml. ins. rater Coon Rapids, 1985—. Author: (poems) Hands of Time, 2000; contbr. poems to poetry contests and mags. Named Internat. Profl. of Yr., Internat. Biographical Ctr., England, 2005; named to Internat. Poetry Hall of Fame, 1996; recipient Golden Poet award, 1990, 1991, 1992, Editor's Choice award, 1993—98, 21st Century award for achiev., Internat. Biographical Ctr., England. Roman Catholic. Home: 1010 94th Ave NW Coon Rapids MN 55433-5501

BORDOGNA, JOSEPH, science foundation executive, electrical engineer, educator; b. Scranton, Pa., Mar. 22, 1933; s. Raymond and Rose (Yesu) B. BSEE, U. Pa., 1955, PhD, 1964; SM, MIT, 1960. With RCA Corp., 1958-64; asst. prof. U. Pa., Phila., 1964-68, assoc. prof., 1968-72, prof., 1972—, assoc. dean engring. and applied sci., 1973-80, acting dean, 1980-81, dean, 1981-90, dir. Moore Sch. Elec. Engring., 1976-90, Alfred Fitler Moore chair, 1979—; dir. engring. Nat. Sci. Foundation, Washington, 1991-96; COO, acting deputy dir. Nat. Sci. Found., Washington, 1996-99, dep. dir., COO, 1999—. Master Stoufer Coll. House, 1972-76; cons. industry, govt., founds.; mem. Nat. Medal of Sci. com., 1989-91; chair adv. com. for engring. NSF, 1989-91. Author: (with H. Ruston) Electric Networks, 1966, (with others) The Man-Made World, 1971; chmn. editl. bd. Engring. Edn., 1987-90. With USN, 1955—58. Recipient commendation for first space capsule recovery, 1957, Lindback award for disting. teaching U. Pa., 1967, Centennial medal Phila. Coll. Textiles and Sci., 1988, Am. Indsl. Modernization Leadership award Nat. Coalition for Advanced Mfg., 1993, Chmn.'s award Am. Assn. Engring. Socs., 1994, Engr. of Yr. award NSPE Phila., 1984, George Washington medal Engrs. Club. Phila., 1997, Gold medal Soc. Mfg. Engrs., 2001, Leadership in Tech. Mgmt. award Portland Internat. Conf. on Mgmt. of Engring. and Tech., 2003, Leadership award Semiconductor Industry Assn., 2004; inducted into Engring. Educators Hall of Fame, 1993. Fellow AAAS (chair engring. sect. 1998-99), IEEE (chmn. Phila. sect. 1987-88, pres. 1998, Centennial medal 1984), Am. Soc. Engring. Edn. (George Westinghouse award 1974), Internat. Engring. Consortium; mem. Sigma Xi, Eta Kappa Nu (eminent mem. 2005), Tau Beta Pi, Phi Beta Delta. Office: Nat Sci Found Office Dir 4201 Wilson Blvd Ste 1205 Arlington VA 22230-1859 Office Phone: 703-292-8001.

BORDY, MICHAEL JEFFREY, lawyer; b. Kansas City, Mo., July 24, 1952; s. Marvin Dean and Alice Mae (Rostov) B.; m. Marjorie Enid Kanof, Dec. 27, 1973 (div. Dec. 1983); m. Melissa Anne Held, May 24, 1987; children: Shayna Robyn, Jenna Alexis, Samantha Falyn. BA, Hamilton Coll., 1974; PhD, U. Kans., 1980; JD, U. So. Calif., 1986. Bar: Calif., 1986, US Dist. Ct. (cen. dist.) Calif., 1986, (so. dist.) Calif., 1987, US Ct. Appeals (9th cir.), 1986. Tchg. asst. biology U. Kans., Lawrence, 1975-76, rsch. asst. biology, 1976-80; post-doctoral fellow Johns Hopkins U., Balt., 1980-83; tchg. asst. U. So. Calif., LA, 1984-86; assoc. Thelen, Marrin, Johnson & Bridges, LA, 1986-87, Wood, Lucksinger & Epstein, LA, 1987-89, Cooper, Epstein & Hurewitz, Beverly Hills, Calif., 1989-93; ptnr. Jacobson, Runes & Bordy, Beverly Hills, 1994-96, Jacobson, Sanders & Bordy, LLP, Beverly Hills, 1996-97, Jacobson White Diamond & Bordy, LLP, Beverly Hills, 1997—2001, White, Bordy & Levey, LLP, LA, 2002—05, Bordy and Levey, LLP, LA, 2005—. Bd. govs. Beverly Hills (Calif.) Bar Barristers, 1988-90, chair real estate law sect. 1998-2000, exec. com. 2000—; bd. govs. Cedars-Sinai Med. Ctr., LA, 1994—; bd. dirs. Sinai Temple, 1998-2003, Jewish Fedn., LA, 2004—; cabinet United Jewish Fund/Real Estate, LA, 1995—; exec. com. Moriah Soc. for U. Judaism, 2002--; planning com. Am. Cancer Soc., 1996-2000; active Guardians of the Jewish Home for the Aging, 1995—, Lawyers Against Hunger, 1995-2002, Fraternity of Friends, 1997-99. Pre-Doctoral fellow NIH, Lawrence, 1977-80; post-doctoral fellow Mellon Found., Balt., 1980-83. Mem. ABA, State Bar Calif., LA County Bar Assn., Beverly Hills Bar Assn. (gov., barrister 1988-92, chair real estate sect. 1998-00), Profl. Network Group. Democrat. Jewish. Avocations: running, triathlons, reading. Office: Bordy & Levey LLP 1880 Century Park E Ste 615 Los Angeles CA 90067-1602 Office Phone: 310-551-9700. Business E-Mail: mjbordy@wbllaw.com.

BOREEN, HENRY ISAAC, computer company executive; b. Warsaw, Mar. 7, 1927; came to U.S., 1949; s. Isaac and Grina (Goldstein) B.; m. Lois Adele Golwyn, June 22, 1958; children: Stuart Michael Boreen, Susan Tobey Hailman. BSEE, Drexel U., 1956, MSEE, 1958, DrEngring.Sci, D Engring. Sci., Drexel U., 2002. Asst. prof. Drexel U., Phila., 1958; v.p. engr. Vector Mfg. Co., Inc., Trevose, Pa., 1958-64; chmn., CEO Solid State Sci., Inc., Montgomeryville, Pa., 1964-86; chmn. US-Tech, Inc., Valley Forge, Pa., 1987—; chmn., CEO AM Comm., Inc., Quakertown, Pa., 1990-99; chmn. Integrated Circuit Systems Inc., Valley Forge, Pa., 1993-99; with Combex, Inc., Rydal, Pa., 2000—. Bd. trustees Cardiovascular Found. New Rochelle, NY, 2002—; chmn. Combex, Inc., San Jose; bd. dirs. Integrated Cir. Sys., Inc. Co-author: Aerospace Telemetry, 1961. Recipient Centennial medal Drexel Univ., 1991. Avocations: gardening, photography, car racing, hiking, bird watching. Office: Combex Inc PO Box 4070 Rydal PA 19046

BOREI, KARIN ELISABET, librarian; b. Stockholm, Mar. 7, 1939; came to U.S., 1953; d. Hans Georg and Maj Ellen (Osterlin) Borei; children: Susan Elizabeth Hodges, Erich Michael Hodges. BA, Brown U., 1961; MLS, Drexel U., 1972; postgrad., Boston U., 1982--. Asst. libr. Univ. Mus. Libr., Phila., 1966-68; Anglo-Germanic cataloger U. Pa., Phila., 1968-72, catalog editor, 1973-76; circulation libr. U. Va., Charlottesville, 1977-79; copy cataloging coord. Boston U., 1980, systems libr., 1980-83, assoc. dir. librs., 1983-87, mem. instnl. rev. bd., 1984-91; asst. univ. libr. Boston Coll., Chestnut Hill, Mass., 1987-91, assoc. univ. libr., 1991-92; cons. Boston Libr. Consortium, 1992, Mass. State Libr., 1993; libr. dir. Trinity Coll. Vt., Burlington, 1993-98; univ. libr., dir. internat. programs Millikin U., 1999—. Organizer libr. confs.; presenter at confs., 1982—. Contbr. articles to libr. jours. Mem. ALA, Assn. Coll. and Rsch. Librs. (bd. dirs. 1990-94, White House Conf. com. 1990-92, pres. New Eng. chpt. 1988-89), Libr. Adminstrn. and Mgmt. Assn. (chmn. women adminstrs. group 1984-85), New Eng. Libr. Assn. (chmn. acad. librs. sect. 1984-85), Libr. and Info. Tech. Assn., Beta Phi Mu, Pi Lambda Theta. Office: Staley Libr Millikin U 1184 W Main St Decatur IL 62522-2039 E-mail: kborei@mail.millikin.edu.

BOREI, SVEN HANS EMIL, translator; b. Stockholm, Dec. 21, 1941; s. Hans Georg and Maj Ellen (Österlin) B.; m. Gisela Wilms Möller; children: Bethany, Rolf, Emil. AA, Valley Forge Mil. Acad., 1961; BA in English, U. Pa., 1964; postgrad., Syracuse U. English and writing tchr. Meadowbrook Sch. for Boys, Phila., 1964-65; basic skills instr. adult edn. Syracuse (N.Y.) Pub. Schs., 1965-67; assoc. dir. Ednl. and Cultural Ctr. Onondaga and Oswego Counties, Syracuse, 1966-67; English instr. Maria Regina Jr. Coll., Syracuse, 1967-68; pres., founder, trustee, CEO Ctr. for Literacy, Inc., Phila., 1968-78; literacy project coord. Appalachia Ednl. Lab., Charleston, W.Va., 1980-81; founder, pres., CEO Literacy Inst., Inc., Syracuse, 1981-88; co-prop. H.E.S. Konsult AB, Transförlag, Lerum, Sweden, 1986—; English lang. coord. Språkverket AB, Göteborg, 1987-89. Mem. Nat. Adv. Coun. on Interpreting and Translating, 2001-03; cons., presenter in field. Author: Appalachian Adult Literacy Programs Survey, 2 vols., 1981, LLA Finance Handbook, 1982, A Measure of Freedom, 1995; editor: Quality Thinking, 1998; translator: Art at Astra, 1997, Jan Johansson, a Visionary Swedish Musician, 1998, Travel Guide for Westmanland, 2000, Jazz Facts, 1999-2002, Lena Mattson, a small fairy tale, 2001, Olle Kåks, Paintings 1970-2002, 2002, Style is Fraud - Carl F. Reutersward, 2003, Sofiero Royal Residence and Glorious Garden, 2005; contbr. articles to profl. jours. Supervisory tutor trainer Laubach Literacy Action, Syracuse, 1975, master tutor trainer, 1977, regional trainer cons., 1985, bd. dirs. 1972-80; co-founder, chair Tutors for Literacy in Pa., 1975-76, W.Va. Literacy Coalition, 1980-82, Tenn. Literacy Coalition, 1982-85; mem. Lerum Mcpl. Coun., 1991-98, mcpl. exec. com., 1995-98, mcpl. bldg. bd. 1999—; bd. govs. Am.-Swedish Hist. Found., 1973-80, v.p., 1975-77, treas., 1977-78. Mem. Swedish Assn. Profl. Translators (bd. dirs. 1997-2003, vice chmn. 1998-99, chmn. 1999-2003). Avocations: music, local history. Home and Office: PL 3181 Koksås S-443 38 Lerum Sweden Office Phone: +46-302-51634. E-mail: transforlag@heskonsult.com.

BOREL, JAMES CALVIN, chemical company executive; b. Clarion, Iowa, Dec. 26, 1955; s. Ralph Jule and Phyllis Ann Borel; m. Marcia Ann Henderson, Sept. 30, 1978; children: David, Bethany. BS in Agrl. Bus., Iowa State U., Ames, 1978. Product specialist Dupont Agrl. Products, Wilmington, Del., 1981-84; sales mgr. agrl. products Dupont, Stevenage, Eng., 1984-87, mgr. agrl. products Mississauga, Can., 1987-89; gen. supt. Dupont Agrl. Products, Belle, W.Va., 1989-91, mgr. human resources Wilmington, 1991-93; regional dir. Dupont Asia Pacific, Tokyo, 1993-97; bus. dir. N.Am. DuPont Agrl. Products, Wilmington, Del., 1997—, v.p., gen. mgr. crop protection, 1997-98, pres. crop protection, 1998—2004; sr. v.p., Global Human Resources Dupont, 2004—. Avocations: golf, sailing. Office: duPont Human Resources 9046 DuPont Bldg 1007 Market St Wilmington DE 19898

BORELLI, FRANCIS J(OSEPH) (FRANK BORELLI), insurance brokerage and consulting firm financial executive; b. Bklyn., Sept. 2, 1935; s. Anthony and Ida Borelli; m. Madlyn Quadrino, June 25, 1960; children: Frank, Richard. BBA, Baruch Coll. CUNY, 1956. CPA, N.Y. With Deloitte Haskins & Sells, 1956-79, ptnr., 1968-79, mng. ptnr. in charge Bergen County, N.J. office, 1976-79; sr. v.p. fin. and adminstr., dir. Airco, Inc., Montvale, N.J., 1980-84; sr. v.p., CFO, dir. Marsh & McLennan Cos., Inc., NYC, 1984—2000. Bd. dirs. Interpub. Group, Express Scripts, Genworth Fin Bd. dirs., chmn.-emeritus Nat. Multiple Sclerosis Soc., Sedgwick Claims Mgmt. Svcs., Signal Holdings Inc.; dir. emeritus pvt. sector coun.; trustee St. Thomas Aquinas Coll.; former dir. Mid Ocean Reinsurance and United Water Resources; former nat. chmn. Fin. Execs. Internat.; chmn. Nyack Hosp. Mem. Fin. Execs. Inst., AICPAs, N.Y. State Soc. CPAs, Ridgewood Country Club, Columbus Found. Club. Home: 13 Patricia Dr New City NY 10956-2008 Personal E-mail: frankcfo@optonline.net.

BOREN, BARRY MARC, lawyer; b. N.Y.C., Apr. 16, 1950; s. Arthur Jay and Corrine Jawitz; m. Caryn J. Tanis, Dec. 16, 1989; children: Brett, Margot. BA, U. Wis.-Madison, 1972; JD, John Marshall Law Sch., 1976. Bar: Ill. 1976, U.S. Dist. Ct. (no. dist.) Ill. 1976, U.S. Ct. Internat. Trade 1977, Fla. 1978, U.S. Dist. Ct. Trial Bar (so. dist.) Fla. 1978, U.S. Ct. Appeals (7th cir.) 1978, U.S. Ct. Appeals (5th cir.) 1979, U.S. Supreme Ct. 1980, U.S. Ct. Appeals (fed. cir.) 1991, U.S. Dist. Ct. (mid. dist.) Fla. 1994, U.S. Ct. Appeals (11th cir.) 1994. Spl. asst. atty. gen. State of Ill., Chgo., 1975-77; atty. Robbins, Coe, et al, Chgo., 1977-80; pres. Ventura Ltd., Miami, Fla., 1980-90; atty. Sandler, Travis, Rosenberg, Miami, Fla., 1990-91, Andrew Parish Law Office, Miami, Fla., 1991-92, pvt. practice, Miami, Fla., 1992—. Pres. Ixora Ltd., Miami, 1988-91. Mem. Am. Assn. Exporters & Importers, Fla. Bar Assn. (internat. law sect. 1992—), Fla. Customs Brokers & Forwarding Assn. Office: 9200 S Dadeland Blvd Ste 412 Miami FL 33156-2712

BOREN, CLARK HENRY, JR., general and vascular surgeon; b. Marinette, Wis., Nov. 23, 1947; s. Clark Henry and Maryon Lillian (Peterson) Boren; children: Jenna Marie, Matthew William, Nathan Clark. BMS, Northwestern U., 1971, MD with distinction, 1973. Diplomate Am. Bd. Surgery. Resident in gen. surgery U. Calif.-H.C. Moffitt Hosp., San Francisco, 1973-79; rsch. fellow in vascular surgery Ft. Miley VA Hosp., 1976-77; vascular fellow Med. Coll. Wis./Milwaukee County Med. Complex, Milw., 1979-80; mem. staff Fox Valley Surg. Assocs., Ltd., Appleton, Wis., 1980—, pres., 1997—. Chmn. bd. United Health Wis., 1995—99. Contbr. articles to profl. jours. Mem.: AMA, ACS, Am. Assn. Vascular Surgery, Wis. Surg. Soc., Midwest Vascular Soc., Peripheral Vascular Surgery Soc., Wis. State Med. Soc., Phi Kappa Psi, Phi Eta Sigma, Phi Beta Pi, Alpha Omega Alpha. Democrat. Home: 330 W River Rd Appleton WI 54915 Office: Fox Valley Surg Assocs 1818 N Meade St Appleton WI 54911-3454 Office Phone: 920-731-8131. Business E-Mail: clark.boren@thedacare.org.

BOREN, DAN, congressman; b. Shawnee, Okla., Aug. 2, 1973; s. L. David and Janna L. (Robbins) Boren. BS in Econs., Tex. Christian U.; MBA in Internat. Bus., U. Okla. Loan processor Banc First Corp.; intern U.S. Rep. Wes Watkins, field rep.; v.p. Robbins Energy Corp.; intern Ind. Petroleum Assn.; mem. Okla. Ho. of Reps., 2003—04, U.S. Ho. Reps., 109th Congress, 2d Dist. Okla., 2005—. Pres. Seminole State Coll. Ednl. Found.; chmn. Last Frontier Coun. Boy Scout Campaign; mem. Wewoka Downtown Investment Group; bd. dirs. Jasmine Moran Children's Mus., Big Bros. Big Sisters; KIPP Found. Mem.: Wewoka C. of C. (bd. dirs.), Seminole Hist. Soc. (pres.), Rotary. Democrat. Office: 216 Cannon House Office Bldg Washington DC 20515 Office Phone: 202-225-2701.*

BOREN, DAVID LYLE, academic administrator, former senator; b. Washington, Apr. 21, 1941; s. Lyle H. and Christine (McKown) B.; m. Molly Shi, Dec. 1977; children: David Daniel, Carrie Christine. BA summa cum laude, Yale, 1963; MA (Rhodes scholar), Oxford (Eng.) U., 1965; JD (Bledsoe Meml. prize as outstanding law grad.), U. Okla., 1968. Bar: Okla. 1968. Practiced law in Seminole, 1968-74; prof. polit. sci., chair divsn. social scis. Okla. Bapt. U., Shawnee, 1969-74; mem. Okla. Ho. of Reps., 1967-75; gov. Okla., 1975-79; mem. U.S. Senate from Okla., 1979-94; pres. U. Okla., Norman, 1994—. Mem. Senate Fin. Com., Senate Agrl. Com.; chmn. Senate Select Com. on Intelligence, govt. dept. Okla. Bapt. U., 1969-74. Trustee Yale U., 1988-97. Named One of 10 Outstanding Young Men in U.S., U.S. Jaycees, 1967. Mem. Assn. U.S. Rhodes Scholars, Phi Beta Kappa. Methodist. Office: U Okla 660 Parrington Oval Rm 110 Norman OK 73019-3003

BOREN, LYNDA SUE, gifted education educator; b. Leesville, La., Apr. 1, 1941; d. Leonard and Doris (Ford) Schoenberger; m. James Lewis Boren, Sept. 1, 1961; 1 child, Lynda Carolyn. BA, U. New Orleans, 1971, MA, 1973; PhD, Tulane U., 1979. Prof. Northwestern State U., Natchitoches, La., 1987-89; propr. Colony Country House, New Llano, La., 1992-94; tchr. of gifted Leesville (La.) H.S., 1992—. Vis. prof. Newcomb Coll., Tulane U., New Orleans, 1979-83, U. Erlangen-Nuremburg, Germany, 1981-82, Middlebury (Vt.) Coll., 1983-84, Ga. Inst. Tech., Atlanta, 1985-87, Srinakharinwirot U., Bangkok, 1989-90; mem. planning com. 1st Kate Chopin Internat. Conf., Natchitoches, La., 1987-89; Fulbright lectr. USIA and Bd. Fgn. Scholars, 1981-82, 89-90. Author: Eurydice Reclaimed: Language, Gender and Voice in Henry James, 1989; co-editor, author: Kate Chopin Reconsidered, 1992; contbg. author: Encyclopedia of American Poetry, 1998; contbr. numerous articles to profl. jours. Founding mem. John F. Kennedy libr. Recipient awards for watercolors; Mellon fellow Tulane U., 1977-78; NEH seminar fellow Princeton U., 1986. Mem. MLA, AAUW, DAR, AFT, Fulbright Alumni Assn. Avocations: painting, video film documentaries, photography. Home: 1492 Fords Dairy Rd Newllano LA 71461-4530 Office Phone: 337-239-3464. Personal E-mail: alborn@peoplepc.com, schoenberger@bellsouth.net.

BOREN, WILLIAM MEREDITH, manufacturing executive; b. San Antonio, Oct. 23, 1924; s. Thomas Loyd and Verda (Locke) B.; m. Molly Brasfield Sarver, Dec. 3, 1976; children: Susan, Patricia, Janet, Jenny, Burton, Cliff. Student, Tex. A&M U., 1942-43, Rice U., 1943-44; BS in Mech. Engring., Tex. U., 1949. Vice pres., gen. mgr. Rolo Mfg. Co., Houston, 1949-54; mgr. sales engring. Black, Sivalls & Bryson, Houston, Oklahoma City, 1955-64; vice chmn., dir., mem. exec. com. Big Three Industries, Inc., Houston, 1965—; chmn. Bowen Tool Co., Houston. Bd. dirs. Engring. Adv. Coun., Tex. U.; dir. Air Liquide Am. Corp.; dir. Electric Reliability Coun. Tex. Inventor Classic Bridge game; screenwriter WWII movie Pegasus Bridge. Trustee S.W. Rsch. Inst., San Antonio; bd. dirs. Coun. Econ. Edn.; mem. chancellor's coun. U. Tex. Lt. (j.g.) USN, 1943-46. Named Disting. Grad. Engring. Dept., U. Tex., 1992. Mem. Internat. Oxygen Mfrs. Assn. (chmn.), French-Am. C. of C. (bd. dirs.), Tau Beta Pi, Pi Tau Sigma. Republican. Home: 2906 Midlane St Houston TX 77027-4912

BORENSTEIN, DANIEL BERNARD, psychiatrist, educator; b. Silver City, N.Mex., Mar. 31, 1935; s. Jack and Marjorie Elizabeth (Kerr) B.; m. Bonnie Denice Ulland, June 11, 1967; 1 child, Jay Brian. BSChemE, MIT, 1957; MD, U. Colo., 1962. Diplomate Am. Bd. Psychiatry and Neurology. Intern U. Hosp. U. Ky., 1962-63; resident in psychiatry U. Colo. Med. Ctr., 1963-66; chief resident, psychiatry instr. U. Colo. Sch. Medicine, 1965-66; psychiatry instr. U. So. Calif. Sch. Medicine, 1966-67; asst. clin. prof. psychiatry UCLA Sch. Medicine, 1972-84, assoc. clin. prof., 1984-96, clin. prof., 1996—. Founder, dir. UCLA Mental Health Program for Physicians in Tng., 1980—84; clin. assoc. L.A. Psychoanalytic Soc. and Inst., 1967—71, pres. clin. assocs., 1970—71, faculty, 1973—83, sr. faculty, 1983—; pvt. practice medicine specializing in psychoanalysis and psychiatry, West L.A., 1966—; assoc. vis. psychiatrist UCLA Ctr. Health Scis., 1973—90; cons. Medicare Program, 1995—; examiner Am. Bd. Psychiatry and Neurology; reviewer various med. and psychiat. jours., 1991—. Author: Manual of Psychiatric Peer Review, 1985, Psychiatric Peer Review: Prelude and Promise, 1985; contbr. articles to profl. jours. Bd. dirs. L.A. Child Devel. Ctr., 1981—85, Found. Advancement Psychiat. Edn. and Rsch., 1991—2005, Coop. Am. Physicians/Mutual Protective Trust, 1994—. Lt. AUS, 1957—58. Fellow: Am. Coll. Psychiatrists (com. on hon. fellowship 2002—05), Am. Psychiat. Assn. (life; coun. area VI 1977—79, com. to rev. psychiat. news 1979—81, coun. area VI, dep. rep. assembly dist. brs. 1981—82, work group on competition and legis. 1981—83, nominating com. 1982—83, assembly liaison to peer rev. com. 1982—86, assembly rep. dist. brs. 1982—89, assemly liaison to fin. and mktg. com. 1986—87, assembly corr. group on subspecialization 1986—89, assembly liaison to coun. on econ. affairs 1987—89, med. student edn. com. 1987—90, bd. liaison jud. action commn. 1989—91, bd. trustees 1989—, com. managed care 1990—92, com. mem., bd. liaison to managed care com. 1992—99, bd. liaison econ. affairs coun. 1992—2000, chmn. bd. ethics appeals, sec. 1995—97, v.p. 1997—99, pres.-elect 1999—2000, pres. 2000—01, chair med. dir. contract negotiating com. 2001, cons. bus. rels. com., chair nominating com. 2001—02, past pres. 2001—, bus. rels. com. 2002—05, fin. and budget com. 2003—, Disting. fellow); mem.: AMA (ho. dels., alt. 1998—2002, del. 2003—), Internat. Psychoanalytic Assn., Am. Psychoanalytic Assn. (com. on confidentiality 1983—96, com. on govt. rels. and ins. 1983—2000), L.A. Psychoanalytic Soc. and Inst. (co-chmn. ext. divsn. 1973—74, chmn. peer rev. com.

1975—78, curriculum com. 1980—84), Calif. Psychiat. Assn. (exec. coun. 1977—79, 1981—95, chmn. jud. com. 1986—88, bd. trustees 1989—95, Spl. Recognition award 1995), Calif. Med. Assn. (ho. of dels. psychiat. splty. rep. 1979—84, com. on mental health and mental disabilities 1979—85, alt. del. ho. del. 1984—86, del. 1986—88, com. on mental health and mental disabilities 1987—88, bd. trustees, del. 1992—2001, chmn. physicians benevolence oper. com. 1996—2001, chmn. bldg. com. 1999—2001), L.A. County Med. Assn. (chmn. mental health com. Bay dist. 1980—85, com. on substance abuse 1981—86, Bay Dist. bd. dirs. 1981—, Bay Dist. v.p. 1985—86, pres.-elect 1986—87, com. on well-being 1986—89, pres. 1987—88, exec. coun. 1988—91), So. Calif. Psychiat. Soc. (chmn. peer rev. com. 1974—77, exec. coun. 1976—89, ethics com. 1977—85, pres. 1978—79, chmn. fellowship and awards com. 1979—85, chmn. Commn. on Psychiatry and the Law 1980—81, Appreciation award 1979, 1st recipient Disting. Svc. award 1984, Outstanding Achievement award 1993, Outstanding Svc. citation 1975). Office: 151 N Canyon View Dr Los Angeles CA 90049-2721 Office Phone: 310-472-7386.

BORENSTEIN, DAVID GILBERT, internist, writer; b. Bklyn. s. Murray and Mollie (Koren) B.; m. Dorothy Regina Fait, Aug. 6, 1972; children: Sylvia, Elizabeth, Rebecca. AB, Columbia U., 1969; MD, Johns Hopkins U., 1973. Diplomate Am. Bd. Internal Medicine, Am. Bd. Rheumatology. Intern in medicine Johns Hopkins Hosp., 1973-74, resident in medicine, 1974-76; fellow in rheumatology Johns Hopkins U., 1976-78; asst. prof. medicine George Washington U., Washington, 1978-83, assoc. prof. medicine, 1983-89, prof. medicine, 1989-96, prof. neurosurgery, 1991-96, clin. prof. neurosurgery, 1997-98, clin. prof. medicine, 1997—. Cons. Vaccine Injury Compensation Program, Dept. HHS, Washington, 1993-2002, Sulzer Medica, Austin, Tex., 1997-2002, Searle, Skokie, Ill., 1997-2002, Merck-Medco, Rahway, NJ, 1997-99, OSHA, Dept. Labor, 1998-99, Merck, 1999-2004, Pfizer, 2003-04, Epicept, 2004—. Author: Low Back Pain: Medical Diagnosis, 1995, Neck Pain: Medical Diagnosis, 1996, Back in Control! A Conventional and Complementary Prescription for Eliminating Back Pain, 2001, Low Back and Neck Pain: Comprehensive Diagnosis and Management, 3d edit.; contbg. author: Low Back Pain in Rheumatology, 1997; contbg. author Low Back Pain in Rheumatology, 2d edit., 2003, Inflammatory Arthridities and Psoriatic Arthritis in the Lumbar Spine 3d edit., 2004. Mem. Appellate Jud. Nominating Commn., State of Md., 1986-94; med. adv. bd. Arthritis Found. D.C., 1986-88, bd. dirs., 1999—; med. adv. bd. Lupus Found. Greater Washington, 1992-2004. Fellow: Am. Coll Rheumatology (govt. affairs com. 1998—2004, chmn. govt. affairs com. 2001—04, bd. dirs. 2005), Am. Coll. Medicine; mem.: Rheumatism Soc. D.C. (pres. 1992—93), Internat. Soc. Study Lumbar Spine (membership com. 1999, chmn. 2002), Cosmos Club. Jewish. Avocations: skiing, squash. Office: Arthritis and Rheum Assocs 2021 K St NW Washington DC 20006-1003 Office Phone: 202-293-1470. Personal E-mail: dborenstein715@aol.com.

BORENSTEIN, MARK A., lawyer; b. Bklyn., June 26, 1951; BA, SUNY, Buffalo, 1973; JD, George Washington U., 1976; LLM, Georgetown U., 1978. Bar: Va. 1976, D,C, 1977, Calif. 1978. Law clk. to Hon. Irving Hill U.S. Dist. Ct. (cen. dist.), Calif., 1976-77; mem. Tuttle & Taylor, L.A., 1978-2000, Shapiro, Borenstein & Dupont, Santa Monica, Calif., 2000—02, Overland & Borenstein, L.A., 2002—. Lectr. U. So. Calif., 1980—82, vis. prof. law, 1997, adj. prof., 1999—. Exec. editor: George Washington Law Review, 1975-76. Inst. for Pub. Interest Representation Law fellow Georgetown U. Law Ctr., 1977-78. Mem. Phi Beta Kappa, Order of the Coif. E-mail: mborenstein@overlandborenstein.com.

BORENSTEIN, MILTON CONRAD, lawyer, manufacturing executive; b. Boston, Oct. 21, 1914; s. Isadore Sidney and Eva Beatrice B.; m. Anne Shapiro, June 20, 1937; children: Roberta, Jeffrey. AB cum laude, Boston Coll., 1935; JD, Harvard U., 1938. Bar: Mass. 1938, U.S. Dist. Ct. 1939, U.S. Ct. Appeals 1944, U.S. Supreme Ct. 1944. Pvt. practice law, Boston, 1938—; officer, dir. Sweetheart Paper Products Co., Inc., Chelsea, Mass., 1944-61, pres., 1961-83, chmn. bd., 1984; with Sweetheart Plastics, Inc., Wilmington, Mass., 1958—, v.p., 1958-84, also dir.; v.p. Md. Cup Corp., Owings Mills, 1960-77, exec. v.p., treas., 1977-84, also dir.; ptnr. Concorde Assocs., Boston. Bd. dirs. Am. Assocs. Hebrew U., 1968—; trustee Combined Jewish Philanthropies, Boston, 1969—, N.E. Sinai Hosp., Stoughton, Mass., 1974—, Ben-Gurion U., 1975-85, 87—, Boston Coll., 1979-87, chmn. estate planning coun., 1981-83, mem. coun. exec. com. 1984—, assoc. trustee, 1987-96; mem. pres.'s coun. Sarah Lawrence Coll., 1970-79; bd. overseers Jewish Theol. Sem. Am., 1971—; mem. pres. Congregation Kehillath Israel, Brookline, Mass., 1977-79, hon. pres., 1979—; mem. pres's coun. Brandeis U., 1979-81, fellow, 1981—; v.p. Assoc. Synagogues of Mass., 1980-81; exec. com. New Eng. region Anti-Defamation League, 1980—; bd. dirs., nat. governing coun. Am. Jewish Congress, 1984—; assoc. chmn. scholarship com. Harvard Law Sch., 1964-66, mem. spl. gifts com., 1990, mem. Langdell com., 1991, 92, 93, 94, 95, 96, 97, 98, 99, Boston regional campaign com., 1992, chmn. class reunion gift, 1993, 98. Recipient Community Svc. award Jewish Theol. Sem. Am., 1970, Am. Jewish Congress, 1993, Bald Eagle Outstanding Alumnus award Boston Coll., 1991; named Rofeh Internat. Man of Yr., 1996. Fellow Mass. Bar Found.; mem. ABA, Mass. Bar Assn., Boston Bar Assn. (mem. bicentennial com. 1986-87), Harvard Club (Boston and N.Y.C.), Harvard Faculty Club.

BORENSTINE, ALVIN JEROME, search company executive; b. Kansas City, Mo., Dec. 14, 1933; s. Samuel and Ella C. (Berman) B.; m. Roula Alakiotou, Dec. 31, 1976; children: Mana an dSami (twins). BS in Econs., U. Kans., 1956; MBA, U. Pa., 1960. Analyst Johnson & Johnson, New Brunswick, N.J., 1961-62; systems mgr. Levitt & Sons, Levittown, N.J., 1962-66; dir. mgmt. info. svcs. Warren Bros. Co., Cambridge, Mass., 1966-71; mgr. fin. & adminstrv. systems Esmark, Inc., Chgo., 1971-72; pres. Synergistics Assocs. Ltd., Chgo., 1972—. Mem. bus. adv. coun. Program Able, Hellenic Dimensions; mem. civic com. El Valor; mem. North Shore Cultural Ctr. Sys. and Procedures Assn. Systems and Procedures Assn. rsch. fellow, 1959-60, Eddie JAcobson Found. scholar, 1958-60. Mem.: Soc. Info. Mgmt., Assn. Sys. Mgmt. (pres Boston chpt. 1969, Disting. award 1970), Assn. Exec. Search Cons., B'nai B'rith, Carlton Club (mem. exec. svc. corps.). Home: 6033 N Sheridan Rd Chicago IL 60660-3003 Office: Synergistics Assocs Ltd 400 N State St Ste 400 Chicago IL 60610-4624 Personal E-mail: ajbsynerg@aol.com.

BORER, EDWARD TURNER, investment banker; b. Phila., Pa., Nov. 30, 1938; s. Robert Chamberlin and Helen Elizabeth (Clawges) Borer; m. Amy Hamilton Ryerson, Aug. 8, 1959; children: Edward Turher, Catherine Hamilton, Elizabeth Taft. BS, U. Pa., 1960. CFA. Rep. Hopper Soliday & Co., Inc., Phila., 1960—67, v.p. rsch., 1967—73, sec., 1971—85, sr. v.p., 1973—82, exec. v.p., 1982—84, pres., 1984—88, also bd. dirs.; dir. Montech Internat., 1994—96, Manchester (NH) Gas Co., 1965—88, pres., 1970, chmn. bd. dirs., chmn. exec. com., 1970—82; chmn. bd. dirs. EnergyNorth, Inc., 1982—; pres., dir. Phila. Corp. for Investment Svcs., 1989—95, chmn., 1995—. Dir., sec. Disaster Control, Inc., 1981—83, Omni Oil & Gas Mgmt. Co., 1981—84; founder., treas. sec., dir. Creative Info. Sys., Inc., Chadds Ford, Pa., 1967—77; v.p. Sovereign Investors, 1980—86; arbitrator NY Stock Exch., 1992—, Phila. Stock Exch., 1992—; bd. dirs. Energy North Natural Gas, Inc., Energy North Propane, Inc. Mem. Nat. Kidney Found., N.Y.C., mem. fin. com., 1995—, bd. dirs. rsch. endowment, 1996—97; chmn. West Met. Area-Wide Com.; pres. Swarthmore Home and Sch. Assn., 1973; bd. dirs. Freedom Valley coun. Girl Scouts U.S.A., 1974—75, chmn. chmn. fin. com.; bd. dirs., chmn. fin. com. Planned Parenthood Southeastern Pa., 1980—85, dir., 1988—90, treas., 1986—87; bd. dirs. Nat. Kidney Found. Del. Valley, 1990—96, treas., 1990—93, chmn., 1993—95, mem. exec. com., 1990—97; trustee George W. South Meml. Ch. of the Adv., Phila., 1978—88, vestryman, 1970—73, 1974—77, 1985—88. 1st lt. Q.M.C., AUS, 1961—62. Mem.: Phila. Stock Exch. (arbitrator 1992—), NY Stock Exch., Am. Arbitration Assn. (arbitrator 1992—), NY Soc. Security Analysts (arbitrator 1992—), Fin. Analysts Phila., Nat. Assn. Securities Dealers (arbitrator 1982—, chmn. dist. 11 and bus. conduct com. 1986), Phila. Securities Assn. (bd. dirs. 1979—83, pres. 1981—82), Fin. Analysts Fedn. (treas. 1976—77), Radley Run Country Club, Union League, Delta Upsilon. Home: 1175 S Birmingham Rd West Chester PA 19382-8092 Office: One Liberty Pl Philadelphia PA 19103

BORER, JEFFREY STEPHEN, cardiologist; b. Deland, Fla., Feb. 22, 1945; s. Lee Norton and Rita Doris (Feldt) B.; m. Brondi Beth Topchik, Sept. 16, 1978; children: Justine Isolde, Jon Andrew. BA in Govt., Harvard U., 1965; MD, Cornell U., 1969. Diplomate Am. Bd. Internal Medicine, Am. Bd. Cardiovascular Disease; cert. Bd. Nuclear Cardiology. Intern, then resident in medicine Mass. Gen. Hosp., Boston, 1969—71; clin. fellow in medicine Harvard U. Sch. Medicine, Boston, 1969—71; clin. assoc. in cardiology Nat. Heart, Lung and Blood Inst., NIH, Bethesda, Md., 1971—74, chief resident physician, 1973—74, sr. investigator, cardiology br., 1975—79; sr. Fulbright-Hays scholar, Glorney-Raisbeck fellow med. scis Guy's Hosp., U. London, 1974—75; assoc. prof. medicine Cornell U. Med. Coll., N.Y.C., 1979—82, prof., 1982—, Gladys and Roland Harriman prof. cardiovascular medicine, 1983—, prof. cardiovascular med. in radiology, 1990—, prof. cardiovascular medicine in cardiothoracic surgery, 1996—; chief cardiovascular pathophysiology divsn. N.Y. Hosp./Cornell Med. Ctr., 1996—; dir. Howard Gilman Inst. for Valvular Heart Diseases Weill Med. Coll. Cornell U., 2000—. Chmn. cardiac and renal adv. com. FDA, Washington, 1981—82, 1983—87, 2001—04, cons., 1989—2000, 2004—, mem., 1977—87, 2001—04, guest mem. Circulatory Devices Adv. Com., 2003—; mem. life scis. adv. com. NASA, Washington, 1984—88, mem. aero. med. adv. com., 1993—96, life and microgravity scis. and application adv. com., 1996—2001, biological and physical rsch. adv. com., 2001—; chmn. NASA/Mir Peer Rev. adv. com., 1993—95, NASA-NIH Biomed. and Behavioral Rsch. adv. com., 1995—2003; mem. NASA Adv. Coun., 1995—99; vis. prof. Chinese Acad. Med. Scis., Beijing, 1993—; chief divsn. cardiovascular pathophysiology N.Y. Hosp.-Cornell Med. Ctr., 1996—. Author 4 books; editor-in-chief Advances in Cardiology, 2001—, Cardiology, 2005-; mem. editl. bds. 11 med. jours.; contbr. more than 350 articles on cardiovascular disease to med. jours.; patentee in field. Sr. surgeon USPHS, 1971—79; trustee N.Y.C. Historic Properties Fund, 1984—90; mem. steering com. Assocs. of the Jewish Bd. of Family and Children Svcs., 1989—91; pres. Am. Friends of Israel Nat. Heart to Heart Assn., 1991—2004; adv. com. The N.Y. Pub. Library Dance Collection, 1999—; pres., bd. trustees Glorney Found., N.Y.C., 2001—. Recipient Investigator's award prize, European Cardiol. Soc., 1978, spl. award for contbns. to cardiology, Assn. Thoracic and Cardiovascular Surgeons of India, 1985, Wiliam A. Johnston award, Internat. Soc. Heart Rsch., 1986, spl. citation contbn. to Mir program, NASA, 1997, Pub. Svc. medal, 1999, Thomas W. Smith Meml. Lecturer, 7th World Cong. on Heart Failure, 2000, Hans-Peter Krayenbeuhl Meml. award for disting. rsch. in cardiac function, Internat. Acad. Cardiology, 2002; travelling fellow, Am. Physicians Fellowship, 1981. Fellow: ACP, N.Y. Cardiol. Soc. (pres. 1990—91), Am. Coll. Chest Physicians (chmn. cardiology forum 1985—86, exec. com. clin. cardiology sect. 1991—95), Am. Heart Assn. (established investigator 1979—84, coun. clin. cardiology and circulation), Argentine Heart Assn. (hon.), Am. Soc. Clin. Investigation, Am. Coll. Cardiology (governing coun. N.Y. chpt. 1991—93, pres. N.Y. State chpt. 1997—98, gov. 1997—2000, bd. govs. 1998—2000, bd. govs. task force on cardiovasc. econs. 1999—2000, steering com., chmn.); mem.: Heart Valve Soc. Am. (pres. 2004—), Cert. Bd. Nuc. Cardiology (bd. trustees 1996—2002, chmn. com. due process and appeals 2002—04), Am. Soc. Nuc. Cardiology (fin. com. 1995—95), Soc. Cardiac Angiography and Interventions (gov. 1995—2000), Soc. Nuc. Medicine (trustee cardiovasc. coun. 1991—94), Harvard Club N.Y.C. Avocations: athletics, theater, opera, chinese and japanese calligraphy, ancient greek history. Office: NY Presbyn Hosp Weill Cornell Med Ctr 525 E 68th St New York NY 10021-4885 Office Phone: 212-746-4646. E-mail: ero2002@med.cornell.edu, canadad45@aol.com.

BORESI, ARTHUR PETER, writer, educator; b. Toluca, Ill. s. John Peter and Eva Boresi; m. Clara Jean Gordon, Dec. 28, 1946; children: Jennifer Ann Boresi Hill, Annette Boresi Pueschel, Nancy Jean Boresi Broderick. Student, Kenyon Coll., 1943—44; BSEE, U. Ill., 1948, MS in Mechanics, 1949, PhD in Mechanics, 1953. Research engr. N. Am. Aviation, 1950; materials engr. Nat. Bur. Standards, 1951; mem. faculty U. Ill., Urbana, 1953—, prof. theoretical and applied mechanics and nuclear engring., 1959-79; prof. emeritus U. Ill. at Urbana, Urbana, 1979; Disting. vis. prof. Clarkson Coll. Tech., Potsdam, N.Y., 1968-69; NAVSEA research prof. Naval Postgrad. Sch., Monterey, Calif., 1978-79; prof. civil engring. U. Wyo., Laramie, 1979-95, head, 1980-94, prof. emeritus, 1995—. Vis. prof. Naval Postgrad. Sch., Monterey, Calif., 1986—87; cons. in field. Author: Approximate Solution Methods in Engineering Mechanics, 1991, 2d edit., 2002, Elasticity in Engineering Mechanics, 4th edit., 2000, Engineering Mechanics: Statics, 2001, Engineering Mechanics: Dynamics, 2001, Advanced Mechanics of Materials, 6th edit., 2002; contbr. articles to profl. jours. With USAAF, 1943—44, with U.S. Army, 1944—46. Fellow: ASCE, ASME, Am. Acad. Mechanics (founding, treas.); mem.: Am. Soc. Engring. Edn. (Archie Higdon Disting. Educator award 1993). Office: 3310 Willett Dr Laramie WY 82072 Business E-Mail: boresi@uwyo.edu.

BORETZ, NAOMI MESSINGER, artist, educator; b. Bklyn. BA, Bklyn. Coll.; MA in Fine Arts, CUNY; MA in Art History, Rutgers U.; postgrad., Art Students League N.Y. Exhibitions include Westminster Arts Coun. Arts Ctr., London, 1971, Hudson River Mus., N.Y., 1975, Katonah Gallery, 1976, Condeso-Lawler Gallery, N.Y.C., 1987, Carnegie-Mellon Art Gallery, Pitts., 1989, The Nelson Atkins Mus. of Art, St. Louis, 1994, Westbeth Gallery, N.Y., 1996, Mishkin Gallery, Baruch Coll., 1997, Rutgers (N.J.) U. Art Gallery, 1998, Hillwood Art Mus., N.Y., 2000, Muhlenburg Coll. Art Gallery, 2002, others, Represented in permanent collections Met. Mus. Art, NYC, Solomon R. Guggenheim Mus., Whitney Mus. Am. Art, Mus. Modern Art, DeLand Art Mus., Fla., Brit. Mus., London, Nat. Mus. Am. Art, Washington, Yale U. Art Gallery, Joslyn Art Mus., Omaha, Walker Art Ctr., Mpls., Miami U. Art Mus., Oxford, Ohio, Fogg Art Mus. Harvard U., Cambridge, Mass., Glasgow (Scotland) Mus., San Jose (Calif.) Art Mus., Asheville (N.C.) Art Mus., Princeton U. Graphic Arts Collection, N.J., Mus. S.W., Midland, Tex., Swope Art Mus., Terre Haute, Ind., others; contbr. to arts publs. Artist-fellow Va. Ctr. Creative Arts, 1973, 86, Ossabaw Found., 1975, Tyrone Guthrie Arts Ctr., Ireland, 1987, Writers-Artists Guild Can., 1988; grantee N.J. State Coun. on Arts, 1985-86. Studio: Princeton NJ

BORG, JOSEPH PHILIP, lawyer; b. NYC, Nov. 20, 1952; s. Philip Joseph and Dorothy Ann (Chircop) B.; 1 child, Chelly. BS in Polit. Sci., CCNY, 1974; JD, Hofstra U., 1977. Bar: N.Y. 1978, Ala. 1978, Fla. 1979, U.S. Dist. Ct. (no. dist.) Ala., U.S. Dist. Ct. (mid. dist.) Ala., U.S. Dist. Ct. (no. dist.) Fla., U.S. Dist. Ct. (mid. dist.) Fla., U.S. Ct. Appeals (5th cir.), U.S. Ct. Appeals (11th cir.), U.S. Supreme Ct. Asst. corp. counsel Hagan Industries, Inc., Montgomery, Ala., 1977-79; corp. counsel, legal officer First Ala. Bank of Montgomery, 1979-85; pntr. Capouano, Wampold, Prestwood & Sansone, P.A., Montgomery, 1985-94; dir. Ala. Securities Commn., Montgomery, AL, 1994—. Prof. law uniform comml. code Faulkner U.; lectr. Jones Bar Review Course, Ala. Continuing Ed. Program. Bd. dirs. Consumer Credit Counseling Svc. of Ala., Inc., 1981-85, pres., 1982-84; bd. dirs. Ala. Youth Found., 1982-85, programs chmn., 1983-84. Mem. ABA, N.Y. State Bar Assn., Ala. State Bar Assn., Fla. State Bar Assn., Am. Trial Lawyers Assn., N.Y. Trial Lawyers Assn., Montgomery County Bar Assn., Montgomery County Trial Lawyers Assn., Montgomery County Young Lawyers Assn. (sec. 1984, v.p. 1985), N.Y. Acad. Sci. Office: Ala Securities Commn 770 Washington St Ste 570 Montgomery AL 36104-3801 Office Phone: 334-242-2984. Business E-Mail: joseph.borg@asc.alabama.gov.

BORG, MALCOLM AUSTIN, publishing executive; b. NYC, Jan. 28, 1938; s. Donald Gowen and Flora (Austin) B.; m. Sandra Jean Agemian, Sept. 9, 1961; children— John Austin, Jennifer Ann, Stephen Agemian. BS, Columbia U., 1965; postgrad., Harvard Bus. Sch., 1970; LHD (hon.), Ramapo (N.J.) Coll., 1985, Fairleigh Dickinson U., 2005. Editl. trainee The Record, Hackensack, NJ, 1959-60, gen. assignment reporter, 1960-62, adminstrv. asst. to pub., 1963-64, asst. pub., 1965-66, v.p., 1967-68, exec. v.p., 1968-70, pres., 1971-78, CEO, 1971—, chmn. bd., 1975—; chmn., CEO North Jersey Media Group, Inc. (including previous co. names), 1971—. Active numerous civic orgns., 1965—; bd. dirs. Wolfeboro (N.H.) Camp Sch., 1970—; mem. Palisades Interstate Park Commn., 1974-2005; chmn. Submarine Meml. Assn., Hackensack, 1974—; mem. adv. bd. Sch. Gen. Studies, Columbia U., 1981—, chmn. 1997—, mem. nat. campaign com. Fund for Columbia, 1983-87, 92-98, mem. alumni adv. bd., 1987-95. Recipient 1st William H. Spurgeon III award Bergen council Boy Scouts Am., 1972, 1st Whitney M. Young award, 1986; Torch of Liberty award Anti-Defamation League, B'nai B'rith, 1973, ann. communications and leadership award Greater N.Y. dist. 46 Toastmasters Internat., 1976, Service to Others award N.J. div. Salvation Army, 1977, ann. community leadership award NO. N.J. Interprofl. Council, 1977, Man of Yr. award Holy Name Hosp., 1977, Editor of Yr. award Nat. Press Photographers Assn., 1985, Owl award Sch. Gen. Studies, Columbia U., 1986, Citizen's award Acad. Medicine N.J., 1986; Alumni Fedn. medal Columbia U., 1991. Mem. Newspaper Assn. Am., Am. Soc. Newspaper Editors, N.J. Press. Assn., Bergen County C. of C. (bd. dirs. 1967-74), N.J. C. of C. (bd. dirs. 1977-79), Hill Sch. Alumni Assn. (pres. 1973-76, trustee 1984-89), Advt. Coun. (bd. dirs. 1978-85), Harvard Bus. Sch. Alumni Assn. (pres. 1976-78), N.J. Srs. Golf Assn., Arcola Country Club (Paramus, N.J.), Columbia Club (N.Y.C.), Englewood Field (N.J.) Club, Mid Ocean Club (Tucker's Town, Bermuda), Harvard Club (N.Y.C.), Bath and Tennis Club (Spring Lake, N.J.), Knickerbocker Country Club (Tenafly, N.J.), Manasquan River Golf Club (Brielle, N.J.), Moselem Springs Golf Club (Fleetwood, Pa.). Avocations: golf, travel. Office: North Jersey Media Group Inc 150 River St Hackensack NJ 07601-7172 Office Phone: 201-646-4300. Business E-Mail: mac@northjersey.com.

BORG, ROBERT FREDERIC, civil engineer; b. N.Y.C., Jan. 10, 1923; s. Herman Leo and Pauline (Leibman) F.; children: Christina Borg-Gordon, Lisa Borg-Broe, Eric (dec.), Kiri Borg-Henry, Neil, Dean. *Daughter Christina, MSW from NYU, is owner of a fine antique and interior decoration shop in New York City. Her husband, Sid Gordon, is purchasing manager for Allied Beverage Group. Daughter Lisa is a physician scientist at Rockefeller University, and in private practice. Her husband, Dan Broe, is partner in MetroCommute and associated with Melrose Consulting. Daughter, Kiri, is managing director and her husband, Brian Henry, is creative director for Manhattan Creative Partners. They are respectively EVP and CEO Diligent Bd. Mem. Svcs. Son, Dean, is senior vice president and project director of Kenco Communities. His wife, Lisa, is a children's summer camp advisor. Son, Neil, resides in New York City.* B in Civil Engring., NYU, 1944, JD, 1949. Bar: N.Y. 1950; lic. profl. engr., N.Y., 1950, Ohio, 1950. Co-founder, ptnr., founding chmn. Kreisler Borg Florman Gen. Construction Co. & affiliates, Scarsdale, NY, 1955—; co-founder Kensico Construction Co., Scarsdale, 1957; field engr. Turner Construction Co., Rome, N.Y., 1942; structural engr. Chance Vought Aircraft, 1944; field engr. Spencer White & Prentis, N.Y.C., 1946-48; office engr. various gen. contractors, N.Y.C., 1948-55; pres. Kensico Construction Co., Scarsdale, 1966--. Mem. bldg. rsch. adv. bd. Nat. Acad. Engring., Washington, 1963; adj. prof. NYU, 1971-79, Pratt Inst., Bklyn., 1983-86, Columbia U., N.Y.C., 1987-90; mem. US/USSR joint com. on coop. in housing and other forms construction U.S. Dept. Housing and Urban Devel., Washington, 1976-87; mem. Sino-US Trade Delegation to China, 1993. *Attended law school at night receiving a degree in three years. Formed own business at age 32; company in business since 1955. Actively engaged full time at age 82 as chairman of company. Has built 15,000 new apartments and renovated 20,000 apartments. Completed over 300 projects including hospitals, retail facilities, religious and special projects. Helped draft the present Construction Rules of American Arbitration Association. Born on Fox Street in the South Bronx. Attributes advancement in part to education in law and engineering, entrepreneurial initiative, and personal motto, "we make our own luck".* Author (contbg.): (handbook) Building Design and Construction, 1999, Construction Project Management, Temporary Structures in Construction, 1996, Technical and Business Practices; founder (bull.) Photo Bull., De Witt Clinton H.S., N.Y.C.; editor (photo): (newspaper) Clinton News, 1940; editor-in-chief (mag.) Quadrangle, NYU Coll. of Engring., 1943; one-man shows include photography shows in various locations, 1980—2005, Gallery Show in Soho, N.Y.C., 1985, Show on Cuba, Scarsdale, N.Y., 2001, Show on World Trade Ctr., 2005, Scarsdale Libr., 2004, 2005, Mexico, San Miguel de Allende Then and Now, 2005, exhibitions include website robertfborg.com. Chmn., founder Garth Woods Conservancy, Scarsdale, N.Y., 1991— co-developer, ptnr. Bethune Tower Apts., N.Y.C., 1970, Heywood Tower Apts., 1972, Univ. Riverview Apts., 1973, Cooper Gramercy Apts., 1975, Marcus Garvey Park Village, 1976, Cove Club Apts., 1992; staff mem., docent Internat. Ctr. Photography, N.Y.C., 1994—. Served with USN, 1944-46. Finalist Entrepreneur of the Yr. award, So. New Eng., 1996, 1997, 1998, Entrepreneur of the Yr. Inst.; recipient Outstanding Builder Developer award, Associated Builders and Owners Greater N.Y., 1989—90, 1991, Builder of Yr. award, 1996, Emma Lazarus award, 1997, Disting. Alumni Recognition award, DeWitt Clinton H.S., 2001. Fellow: ASCE (mem. com. on contract adminstrn. 1952, founder, 1st chmn. constrn. group met. sect. 1962, met. sect. bd. dirs. 1962—67, chmn. tech. activities met. sect. 1963, mem. com. on contract adminstrn. 1963—67, mem. exec. com. nat. constrn. divsn. 1971, chmn., exec. com. nat. constrn. divsn. 1973—74, chmn. com. on social and environ. concerns in constrn. 2001—, master builder, constrn. Inst. ASCE 2003), Am. Arbitration Assn. (mem. nat. panel arbitrators 1957—, mem. nat. constrn. industry arbitration com. 1972—2005, chmn. 1974—76, nat. bd. dirs. 1974—84); mem.: Harbor Consortium, N.Y. Acad. Scis. Office: Kreisler Borg Florman Gen Constrn Co 97 Montgomery St Scarsdale NY 10583-5104 Office Phone: 914-725-4600. Office Fax: 914-725-0346. E-mail: kbfgeneral@aol.com.

BORG, RUTH I., home nursing care provider; d. Axel Gunner and Charlotte (Benston) B. Diploma, West Suburban Sch. Nursing, 1956; tchr.'s degree, Chgo. Conservatory, 1958; BSN, Alverno Coll., 1981. Staff nurse Boath Meml. Hosp., Chgo.; head nurse psychiatry, head nurse long-term medicine VA North Chgo. Med. Ctr.; staff nurse, night supr. intermediate care VA Clement Zabiocki Med. Ctr., Milw.; pool nurse, in-home nursing care provider Milw. County Mental Health Complex; home nurse care provider Dr. Ghonsham Sooknandan, Kenosha, Wis., 1994—99. In-home nursing care provider. Contbr. articles to profl. jours. Recipient Mary D. Bradford Disting. Alumni award, 1998. Mem.: Wis. Nurses Assn. (nominations com.). Avocation: teaching and performing music.

BORGATTA, EDGAR F., sociologist, educator; b. Milan, Sept. 1, 1924; came to U.S., 1929, naturalized, 1934; s. Edgar A. and Frances (Zinelli) B.; m. Marie Lentini, Oct. 5, 1946; children: Lynn, Kim, Lee. BA, NYU, 1947, MA, 1949, PhD, 1952. Cert. psychologist, N.Y., Vt., Wis. Instr. NYU, 1949-51, lectr., prof., 1954-59; lectr., rsch. assoc. Harvard U., 1951-54; social psychologist, asst. sec. Russell Sage Found., 1954-59; prof. sociology Cornell U., Ithaca, NY, 1959-61; Brittingham rsch. prof. U. Wis., Madison, 1961-72, chmn. dept. sociology, 1962-65, chmn. divsn. social studies, 1965-68; disting. prof. sociology Queens Coll., CUNY, 1972-77, prof Grad. Ctr., 1972-82, dir. Italian Social Sci. Ctr., 1972-77; rsch. CUNY Case Ctr. for Gerontol. Studies, 1978-81, dir. data svc., 1981-82; prof. sociology U. Wash., Seattle, 1981—93, chmn. dept., 1992—93, prof. emeritus, 1994—; dir Inst. on Aging U. Wash., Seattle, 1981-86. Cons. to bus. and govt., 1953-, Russell Sage Found., 1970-72; lectr., prof., adj. prof. sociology NYU, 1954-59; cons. editor Rand McNally & Co., 1961-74; chmn. bd. F.E. Peacock Pubs., Inc.; Nat. Inst. Gen. Scis.; spl. rsch. fellow, 1972. Editor: Research on Aging, Sociol. Methodology, Sociol. Methods and Research; co-editor: Handbook of Personality Theory and Research; editor-in-chief: Encyclopedia of Sociology, 2d edit.; contbr. articles to profl. jours. Fellow Am. Psychol. Assn., Am. Psychol. Soc.; mem. Psychometric Soc., Sociol. Rsch. Assn., Am. Sociol. Assn. (v.p. 1983), Pacific Sociol. Assn. (pres. 1985), Internat. Inst. Sociology (pres. 1984-89). Office: U Wash Dept Sociology c/o 98 Union St #608 Seattle WA 98101 Office Phone: 206-622-9158. E-mail: efborgat@att.net.

BORGER, JOHN PHILIP, lawyer; b. Wilmington, Del., Apr. 19, 1951; s. Philip E. and Jane (Smyth) B.; m. Judith Marie Yates, May 24, 1974; children: Jennifer, Christopher, Nicholas. BA in Journalism with high honors, Mich.

State U., 1973; JD, Yale U., 1976. Bar: Minn. 1976, U.S. Dist. Ct. Minn. 1976, U.S. Ct. Appeals (8th cir.) 1979, U.S. Supreme Ct. 1983, N.D. 1988, U.S. Dist. Ct. N.D. 1988, Wis. 1993. Editor-in-chief Mich. State News, East Lansing, 1972-73; assoc. Faegre & Benson, LLP, Mpls., 1976-83, ptnr., 1984—. Bd. dirs. Milkweed Edits., 1995-01; adj. prof. U. Minn. Sch. Journalism and Mass Comm., 1999. Contbr. articles to profl. jours. Recipient Freedom of Info. award, Minn. Soc. Profl. Journalists, 2002, First Amendment Award, St. Cloud State U. Dept. Mass. Comms., 2001. Mem. ABA (chmn. media law and defamation torts com. torts and ins. practice sect. 1996-97), Minn. Bar Assn., State Bar Assn. N.D., Wis. Bar Assn., Hennepin County Bar Assn. Office: Faegre & Benson LLP 2200 Wells Fargo Ctr 90 S 7th St Ste 2200 Minneapolis MN 55402-3901 Office Phone: 612-766-7501. E-mail: jborger@faegre.com.

BORGES, FRANCISCO LOPES, venture capitalist; b. Santiago, Cape Verde Islands, Nov. 17, 1951; s. Manuel L. and Maria (Lopes) B. BA, Trinity Coll., 1974; JD, U. Conn., 1978. Bar: Conn. 1979, N.J. 1979. Coun. mem. City of Hartford, Conn., 1981-85, dep. mayor, 1983-85; treas. State of Conn., Hartford, 1989-93; man. dir. of pub. fin. Financial Guaranty Ins. Co., 1993-95; man. dir. FGIC govt. svcs. GE Capital Svcs., Inc., 1995; chmn., ptnr. Landmark Partners, Inc., Simsbury, Conn. Commr. Met. Dist. Commn., Hartford, 1981—; assoc. counsel Travelers Ins. Co., Hartford, 1983; bd. dir. NAACP. Trustee Millbrook (N.Y.) Sch., 1979—; corporator St. Francis Hosp., Hartford, 1981—; vice chmn. steering com. Jr. PTA Hartford, 1984—; active U. Conn. Health Ctr. Adv. Coun., Farmington, 1982—; vice chmn. Capitol Region Coun. Govts., Hartford, 1984—; dir. Hartford Ballet Co., 1985—. Mem. Conn. Bar Assn. Democrat. Office: Landmark Partners Inc 10 Mill Pond Ln Simsbury CT 06070*

BORGES, FREDRICK MARIO, lawyer; b. Covina, Calif., Nov. 3, 1960; s. Vincent and Rose Borges. BA, Calif. State U., Fullerton, 1983; JD, Western State U., 1991. Bar: Calif. 1992. Mng. ptnr. Borges, Lauridsen & Sturm, Santa Ana, Calif., 1999—2000; gen. counsel Gateway Med. Group and Pinnacle Health Resources, Anaheim, 1999—2004; ptnr. Beam, Brobeck & West, Santa Ana, 2000—; regional counsel Concentra Health Svcs., 2000—. Arbitrator, Calif., 1993—. Contbr. articles to profl. jours. Mem.: ABA, Orange County Bar Assn., Am. Health Lawyers Assn. Avocations: stained glass, golf, drums. Office: Beam Brobeck & West 600 W Santa Ana Blvd Ste 1000 Santa Ana CA 92701 Office Phone: 714-558-3944.

BORGES, WILLIAM, III, management consultant; b. Long Beach, Calif., Nov. 21, 1948; s. William Borges Jr. and Dorothy Mae (Raymond) Morris; m. Rosalind Denise Marye, Nov. 23, 1968; children: William IV, Blake Austin. BA in Geography, Calif. State U., Sonoma, 1973; MBA, U. Phoenix, 1997. Environ. planner Mendocino County Planning Dept., Ukiah, Calif., 1976; project mgr. Engring. Sci., Inc., Berkeley, Calif., 1976-79, Santa Clara County Planning Dept., San Jose, Calif., 1979-81, Internat. Tech. Corp., San Jose, 1985-88; mgr. sales ops. Adac Labs, Milpitas, Calif., 1983-85; prin. WT Environ. Cons., Phoenix, 1988-91; project mgr. Dynamac Corp., Newport Beach, Calif., 1991-93; prin. environ. scientist Midwest Rsch. Inst., Scottsdale, Ariz., 1993-96; gen. mgr. Fitness Care, Inc., Yorba Linda, Calif., 2000—02; bus. process analyst Washoe Health Sys., Reno, 2002—. Adj. faculty U. Phoenix, Reno, 2003—. Contbr. photographs to various mags. Coord. pub. rels. Stellar Acad. for Dyslexics, Fremont, Calif., 1988. With M.I., U.S. Army, 1967-70. Mem.: Mensa. Avocations: photography, travel. Personal E-mail: wborges6@earthlink.net.

BORGMAN, GEORGE ALLAN, journalist; b. St. Louis, Jan. 22, 1928; s. Herman Francis and Martha Vivien (Wecker) B.; m. Janet Claire Ferroli, Feb. 27, 1957; children: Carole Elaine (dec.), Paul Allan, Eric Bruno; 1 child by previous marriage, Andrea Vivien Hancock (dec.). Student, U. Mo., 1945-46, 48; MusB in Music History and Lit., St. Louis Inst. Music, 1952; MusM in Musicology, Ind. U., Bloomington, 1953. Musician dance bands various locations, 1945-46, 48-50; enlisted bandsman U.S. Army, 1946-48, spl. agent mil. intelligence, 1958-79, advanced through grades to chief warrant officer 3, 1971, retired, 1979; music educator various sch. systems in Colo. and Nev., 1953-57; freelance asst. cinematographer N.Y.C., 1957-58; film editor, TV cameraman Sta. KOMU-TV, Columbia, Mo., 1958; investigator Wackenhut Corp., Boston, 1980-81; personnel security specialist (civilian) U.S. Army, Alexandria, Va., 1981-85; sportswriter Suburban World (newspapers), Needham, Mass., 1988-94; freelance jazz writer, 1988—; New England corr. and jazz writer T-J Today, 1991-92; corr., photographer, contbg. editor, columnist, reviewer Mississippi Rag, 1991—; record reviewer Cadence Mag., 1994-95; reviewer IAJRC jour., 1995—2000, The Jazz Messenger, 1994-96. Contbr. articles to profl. jours. including Joslin's Jazz Jour.; author: notes on jazz CD's. Musician Met. Wind Symphony, Boston, 1981, Fairfax (Va.) City Band, 1982-83, Canton (Mass.) Mcpl. Band/Am. Legion Band, 1980-81; assoc. mem. Westwood (Mass.) Rep. Com., 1988-89. Rated #12 Favorite Jazz Critic, Jazzbeat, 1995. Mem.: Assn. for Recorded Sound Collections, Starr-Gennet Found., Jazz Journalists Assn., Internat. Assn. Jazz Record Collectors, Disabled Am. Vets., Am. Legion. Republican. Home and Office: 158 Burgess Ave Westwood MA 02090-3010 Personal E-mail: algeob@aol.com.

BORGO, DAVID GARCIA, music educator; b. Camp Springs, Md., Feb. 8, 1970; s. Peter Anthony and Suzanne Lavon Borgo; m. Sylvia K. Garcia, July 1, 2001; 1 child, Diego Alexander. MusB in Jazz Studies, Ind. U., 1990; MA in Ethnomusicology, UCLA, 1996, PhD in Ethnomusicology, 1999. Tchg. assoc., lectr. UCLA, 1994—98; lectr. Calif. State U., Fullerton, 1997—2000, Northridge, 1998—2000, U. Calif., Riverside, 1999; asst. prof. James Madison U., Harrisonburg, Va., 2000—02, U. Calif., San Diego, 2002—. Mng. editor UCLA Ethnomusicology Publs. Dept., 1996—97; presenter in field. Musician: (CD) With and Against, 2000; contbr. chapters to books, articles to profl. jours. Office: Univ Calif San Diego Music-0326 9500 Gilman Dr La Jolla CA 92092-0326

BORGS, CHRISTIAN H., mathematical physicist; b. Dusseldorf, Germany, Apr. 12, 1957; came to U.S., 1997; s. Herwarth J. and Anneliese Borgs; m. Jennifer Tour Chayes, Sept. 2, 1993; 1 child, Claudio Ahlefelder. Diploma, Ludwigs Maximilians U. Munich, 1982, PhD, 1987; habilitation, Free U. Berlin, 1992. Postdoctoral fellow ETH Zürich, Switzerland, 1986-89; asst. prof. Free U. Berlin, 1989-93, Heisenberg prof., 1993-95; prof., head of group U. Leipzig, Germany, 1995-99; prof. math. U. Wash., Seattle, 1999—; mgr. theory group Microsoft Rsch., Redmond, Wash., 1997—. Trustee Inst. Pure and Applied Math., L.A., 1999—2004. Contbr. articles to profl. jours. Recipient Karl-Scheel prize German Phys. Soc., 1993; PhD fellow Max Planck Soc., 1983-85, Heisenberg fellow Deutsche Forschungsgemeinschaft, 1993-95; undergrad. scholar Found. of the German People, 1978-82. Mem. AAAS, Am. Math. Soc., German Phys. Soc., Internat. Orgn. Math. Physics. Avocations: travel, classical music, skiing. Office: Microsoft Rsch One Microsoft Way Redmond WA 98052 Business E-Mail: borgs@microsoft.com.

BORICK, PAUL MICHAEL, microbiologist; b. Olyphant, Pa., Sept. 27, 1924; s. Stephen G. and Tekla (Bruger) B.; m. Joan Ann O'Brien, May 12, 1956; children: Sheila, Paul, James, Kenneth, Thecla, Carl. BS in Biology, Chemistry, Scranton U., 1947; MS in Bacteriology, Syracuse U., 1951, PhD in Microbiology, 1953. Commd. 2d lt. USAF, 1950, retired, 1978; head biology labs. Wallace & Tiernan, Belleville, N.J., 1953-57; scientist-in-charge Bristol-Myers Co., Hillside, N.J., 1957-62; mgr. research and devel. Ethicon div. Johnson & Johnson, Somerville, N.J., 1962-73; dir. research and devel. Parke Davis, Greenwood, S.C., 1973-78; tech. dir., cons. Pollak & Skan Inc., Morristown, N.J., 1978-79; coordinator validation Wyeth Labs., Am. Home Products, West Chester, Pa., 1980—. Resident advisor Syracuse (N.Y.) U., 1949-53; instr. LeMoyne Coll., Syracuse, 1951-52; pres., bd. dirs. Bristol-Myers Fed. Credit Union, 1958-62; mem. adv. com. U.S. PHarmacopeia, Rockville, Md., 1968-73; lectr. Columbia U., N.Y.C, 1971-73; cons. Borick Assocs., Lakeville, Pa., 1979-80; faculty Ctr. for Profl. Advancement, New Brunswick, N.J., 1982—. Editor: Chemical Sterilization, 1973; contbr. over 40 articles to profl. jours.; patentee in field. Mem. Paupackan Lake Assn., Lakeville, 1970—; mem. adv. com. EPA, Washington, 1971-72. Mem. Am. Soc. Microbiology (pres., v.p. N.J. br. 1966-68), Am. Chem. Soc., AAAS, Am. Legion, Sigma Xi. Republican. Russian Orthodox. Avocations: fishing, photography, golf, guitar. Home: PO Box 54 Lakeville PA 18438-0054 Office: Wyeth Labs 611 W Nields St West Chester PA 19382-3520

BORIE, BERNARD SIMON, JR., retired physicist, educator; b. New Orleans, June 21, 1924; s. Bernard simon and Ruth (Lastrapes) B.; m. Martine Edith Descamps, May 2, 1957 (div. May 1964); children: Kathleen, Fabienne, Marianne. BS, U. S.W. La., 1944; MS, Tulane U., 1949; PhD, MIT, 1956; Fulbright fellow, U. Paris, 1956-57. Rsch. physicist metall. divsn. Oak Ridge Nat. Lab., 1949-53, group leader x-ray diffraction Metals and Ceramics Divsn., 1957-60, head fundamental rsch. sect., 1960-69, sr. scientist, 1969-85; prof. U. Tenn., 1963—; ret. Vis. prof. Cornell U., 1971-72, U. Calif., Berkeley, 1980. Lt. USNR, 1944-45. Fellow AAAS; mem. AIME, Am. Soc. Metals, Am. Crystallographic Assn., Sci. Rsch. Soc. Am. Achievements include research in diffraction effects of thermal motion, x-ray diffraction studies of imperfect solids; order-disorder effects in solid solutions. Home: 13 Brookside Dr Oak Ridge TN 37830-7616 Personal E-mail: bborie2@comcast.net.

BORING, KEITH A, military officer; s. Robert and Nita Boring; m. Amy Boring, Feb. 14, 1987; children: Jacob, Jessica. AS in indsl. mgmt. tech., Pensacola Jr. Coll., 1993—95. Microsoft Certified Professional Microsoft, 2003, A+ Certified Tech CompTIA, 2003, Network+ Certified Tech CompTIA, 2004, Security+ Certified Tech CompTIA, 2004, Computer Peripheral Equip Operator U.S. Dept of Labor, 1994. Cryptologic technician, spl. comm. SEAL Team 6, U.S. Navy, Norfolk, Va., 1985—87; cryptologic technician, satellite comm. NSGA Edzell, U.S. Navy, Edzell, Scotland, 1987—91; cryptologic technician, comm. NSGA Homestead, U.S. Navy, Homestead, Fla., 1991—92; cryptologic technician, instr. NTTC Corry Sta., U.S. Navy, Pensacola, Fla., 1992—95; cryptologic technician, fleet comm. Comdr. Seventh Fleet, U.S. Navy, Yokosuka, Japan, 1996—99; navy enlisted recruiter NRD Nashville, U.S. Navy, 1999—2002; cryptologic technician, computer network def. NSGA Pensacola, U.S. Navy, Pensacola, 2002—05; cryptologic technician, 5vm model mgr. CID Corry Sta., U.S. Navy, Pensacola, 2005—. Master tng. specialist NTTC Corry Sta., Pensacola, 1994—. E9/master chief U.S. Navy, 1985, Pensacola, FL. Decorated Navy Commendation medal CNRC, Comdr. 7th Fleet, Navy Commendation Medal CNET, Navy Achievement medal CNRC. Mem.: CompTIA IT Profl., Internat. Brotherhood of Magicians, Nat. Eagle Scout Assn., SAR, Chief Petty Officers Assn. Avocations: classic cars, magic. Office Phone: 850-452-6657. Personal E-mail: boringkajj@hotmail.com.

BORIS, RUTHANNA, dancer, educator, choreographer, dance therapist; b. Bklyn., Mar. 17, 1918; d. Joseph Jay and Frances (Weiss) B.; m. Frank W. Hobi (dec.) Student, Profl. Children's Sch., N.Y.C. Dir. Boris-Hobi Concert Co., 1955—57. Prin. dancer Am. Ballet, N.Y.C., 1934, Ballet Caravan, N.Y.C., 1936; prima ballerina Met. Opera Co., N.Y.C., 1939-41, Ballet Russe de Monte Carlo, N.Y.C., 1942-49; prima ballerina, choreographer-in-residence Royal Winnipeg Ballet of Can., 1957-59, dir. 1957-58; choreographer Ballet Russe de Monte Carlo, 1947, N.Y.C. Ballet, 1951; prof. dance U. Wash., Seattle, 1965-83, prof. emeritus, 1983—; adj. prof. psychiatry U. Wash., 1982; pres. exec. dir. Ctr. for Dance Devel. & Research, Albany, Calif., 1986—; choreographer: Cirque de Deux, 1947, Quelques Fleurs, 1948, Cakewalk, 1951, Kaleidoscope, 1951, Will O' The Wisp, 1951, Pasticcio, 1955, Wanderling, 1957, Ragtime, 1975, Tape Suite, 1976, Four All, 1980. Mem. adv. bd. Seattle Psychoanalytic Inst., 1975-82. Mem. Am. Guild Mus. Artists (award 1964, gov. 1942-64), Am. Dance Therapy Assn. (pres. Calif. chpt. 1986-88, mem. dance therapy credentials com. 1990-92). Office: Ctr Dance Devel & Rsch Apt 1334 555 Pierce St Albany CA 94706-1009 Office Phone: 510-528-2188. *I have always believed that each one of us has some specific mission to perform. My mission, to clarify my work and my human connections, keeps me very busy, active, curious and productive.*

BORISOFF, RICHARD STUART, lawyer; b. Rochester, N.Y., May 4, 1945; s. Samuel M. and Ida. B.; m. Risa W. Polgar, Aug. 17, 1967; children: Mindy, Dara. AB, U. Pa., 1967; JD, Columbia U., 1970. Bar: N.Y. 1971, D.C. 1981, U.S. Dist. Ct. (so. dist.) N.Y. 1973, U.S. Ct. Appeals (2nd cir.) 1973. Assoc. Paul, Weiss, Rifkind, Wharton & Garrison, N.Y.C., 1970-78, ptnr., 1978—. Mem.: ABA. Office: Paul Weiss Rifkind Wharton & Garrison LLP Ste 2320 1285 Avenue Of The Americas New York NY 10019-6064 Office Phone: 212-373-3153. E-mail: rborisoff@paulweiss.com.

BORISOV, GEORGE P., music educator; b. Krasnodar, Russia, Mar. 27, 1954; arrived in U.S., 1992, naturalized, 2000; s. Peter Vasilievich and Maria Savcichna Borisov; children: Tatiana, Basil. MA in piano performance, State Inst. Music and Tchg., Rostov-on-Don, Russia, 1976; DMA piano performance, M.Ivanovich Glinka State Conservatory, Novosibirsk, Russia, 1982; PhD in Musicology, All-Russian Inst. Arts, 1992. Cert. music tchr. Dept. Edn., N.J. Piano tchr. N.A. Rimsky Korsakov State Musical Coll., Krasnodar, Russia, 1976—86; sr. lectr. State Inst. Arts, Krasnodar, 1978—92; lectr. Ocean County Coll., Toms River, NJ, 1995—97; music dir. Immaculate Conception Roman Catholic Ch., Eatontown, NJ, 1993—2000; piano tchr. Westminster Conservatory of Rider U., Princeton, NJ, 2000—02; dir. C. Musik Sch., Colts Neck, NJ, 2000—. Author: (book) Kuban Cossack Choir, 1988, Music Culture of South Russia, 1989; contbr. articles to profl.jours.; prodr.(and narrator): (TV series, featuring musical programs) Ctrl. TV USSR and Krasnodar TV, 1984—89; founder and prodr. Music-Art Festivals, NJ, NY areas, 2002—. Recipient Cert. of Excellence, Internat. Concert Alliance, 2000. Mem.: Cecilian Music Club (Laura Conover Pedagogy award 1998, 1999), Nat. Assn. Music Tchr., Am. Guild of Piano Tchr. (Nat. Piano Auditions Honor Roll 1996—2003). Home: 81 Five Points Rd Colts Neck NJ 07722

BORISY, GARY G., molecular biology educator; b. Chgo., Aug. 18, 1942; s. Philip and Mae Borisy; children: Felice, Pippa, Alexis. BS, U. Chgo., 1962, PhD, 1966. Postdoctoral fellow NSF, Cambridge, Eng., 1966-67, NATO, Cambridge, 1967-68; asst. prof. U. Wis., Madison, 1968-72, assoc. prof., 1972-75, prof., 1975-80, Perlman-Bascom prof. life scis., 1980—2000, chmn. lab. molecular biology, 1981—2000; Leslie B. Arey prof. in cell, molecular & anatomical sci. Northwestern U. Feinberg Sch. of Medicine, 2000—. Mem. numerous panels NIH and other govt. agys., ACS, HHMI; mem. Marine Biol. Lab. Editor Jour. Biol. Chemistry, 1978-80, Jour. Cell Biology, 1980-82, Internat. Rev. Cytology, 1971-91, Cell Motility and the Cytoskeleton, 1986-94, Jour. Cell Sci., 1988—; contbr. over 100 articles to profl. jours. Recipient Romnes award U. Wis., 1975-80, NIH Merit award, 1989; grantee NIH, NSF, ACS. Fellow AAAS, Am. Acad. Arts. & Scis., 2004; mem. Am. Soc. Cell Biology, Am. Soc. Biochemistry and Molecular Biology, Sigma Xi. Office: Northwestern U Feinberg Sch 303 E Chicago Ave Chicago IL 60611*

BORITT, GABOR SZAPPANOS, history educator; b. Budapest, Hungary, Jan. 26, 1940; came to U.S., 1957; naturalized, 1963; s. Paul Szappanos Boritt and Rosa Theresia Schwartz; m. Elizabeth Lincoln Norseen, 1968; children: Norse, Jake, Daniel. BA, Yankton Coll., S.D., 1962; MA, U. S.D., 1963; PhD, Boston U., 1967. Asst. prof. Boston U., 1967-68; lectr. U. Md. Far East, 1968-70; asst. prof. Mt. Wachussets Community Coll., 1972-73, U. Memphis, 1975-76, 77-81; vis. prof. U. Mich., Ann Arbor, 1973-74, Washington U., St. Louis, 1974-75; vis. fellow Harvard U., Cambridge, Mass., 1976-77, Darwin Coll., Cambridge, Inst. U.S. Studies, U. London, 1987; assoc. prof. Gettysburg Coll., Pa., 1981—, Robert C. Fluhrer prof. Civil War Studies, 1986, dir. Civil War Inst., 1983—. Dir. Linedn 175 nat. conf. Lincoln scholars, Gettysburg, 1984, Lincoln Image exhibit, 1984-85, Confederate Image exhibit, 1987-89, Gettysburg Address 125 exhibit, 1988; Fortenbaugh Lecture Series; chmn. bd. Lincoln Prize, 1990—; co-chair adv. bd. Gilder-Lehman Inst., 1994. Author: Lincoln and the Economics of the American Dream, 1978 (award of merit 1979), Of the People, By the People, For the People, 1996; co-author: The Lincoln Image, 1984, Changing the Lincoln Image, 1985; The Confederate Image, 1987; co-author, editor: The Historians' Lincoln: Pseudohistory, Psychohistory, and History, 1988, Historians' Lincoln, Rebuttals, 1988, Lincoln: The War President, The Gettysburg Lectures, 1992, Lincoln's Generals, 1994, Why the Civil War Came, 1996; editor: Why the Confederacy Lost, 1992, War Comes Again: Comparative Vistas on the Civil War and World War II, 1995, The Gettysburg Nobody Knows, 1997; contbr. articles to N.Y. Times, LA Times, Wash. Times, Christian Sci. Monitor, profl. jours. Social Sci. Rsch. Coun. fellow, 1976-77; NEH grantee, 1984; Am. Philos. Soc. grantee, 1973, 86; Newberry Libr. grantee, 1975; Lehrman Inst., 1995-96, Rockefeller Found. Bellagio, 2003; recipient Henry E. Huntington Libr. and Art Gallery Research award, 1971, award Pa. Humanities Coun., 1984, 87. Mem. Am. Hist. Assn., Orgn. Am. Historians, Authors' Guild, Phi Alpha Theta (Hammond prize 1965). Avocation: farming. Home: Farm by Ford Plank Rd Gettysburg PA 17325 Office: Gettysburg Coll Civil War Inst Gettysburg PA 17325

BORJAS, GEORGE J(ESUS), economics professor; b. Havana, Cuba, Oct. 15, 1950; came to U.S., 1962; s. Juan V. Borjas and Edita F. Diaz; m. Jane Maureen Walsh, Nov. 11, 1989; children: Sarah Jane Irene, Timothy Jorge, Rebecca Kathryn. BS, St. Peter's Coll., Jersey City, 1971; MA, M in Philosophy, PhD, Columbia U., 1975; LHD (hon.), St. Peter's Coll., 2003. Asst. prof. Queens Coll., Flushing, N.Y., 1975-77; research assoc. Nat. Bur. Econ. Research, Cambridge, Mass., 1983—; prof. econs. U. Calif., Santa Barbara, 1978-90, San Diego, 1990-95; prof. pub. policy Kennedy Sch. Govt., Harvard U., Cambridge, Mass., 1995-97, Pferzheimer prof. pub. policy, 1998—2002, Robert W. Scrivmer prof. of econ. and social policy, 2002—. Cons. Unicon Rsch. Corp., Santa Monica, Calif., 1982-94; econs. adv. panel NSF, 1988-90; mem. Gov.'s Coun. of Econ. Advisers, 1993-98 Author: Wage Policy in the Federal Bureaucracy, 1980, International Differences in the Labor Market Performance of Immigrants, 1988, Friends or Strangers: The Impact of Immigrants on the U.S. Economy, 1990, Labor Economics, 1995, Heaven's Door: Immigration Policy and the American Economy, 1999; editor: Hispanics in the United States, 1985, Immigration and the Work Force: Economic Consequences for the United States and Source Areas, 1992, Issues in the Economics of Immigration, 2000, Rev. of Econs. and Statistics, 1998—; mem. editl. bd. Quar. Jour. Econs., 1992-98, Internat. Migration Rev., 1992—, Review of Economics and Statistics, 1997-98; contbr. articles to profl. jours. Fellow Columbia U. Alumni Fund, 1973, NIMH, U. Chgo., 1977; grantee Rockefeller Found., 1983-85, Sloan Found., 1986-93, NSF, 1986—, Russell Sage Found., 1991-93, Smith Richardson Found., 2001—; vis. scholar Harvard U., 1988-89. Fellow Econometric Soc., Soc. Labor Economists; mem. NAS (panel 1984-85, 95-97, Estrada fellow in immigration studies 2000), Am. Econ. Assn., Assn. for Pub. Policy Analysis and Mgmt. (exec. coun. 2000—). Roman Catholic. Office: Kennedy Sch Govt Harvard U 79 Jfk St Cambridge MA 02138-5801 E-mail: gborjas@harvard.edu.

BORK, ROBERT HERON, law educator, retired federal judge; b. Pitts., Mar. 1, 1927; s. Harry Philip and Elizabeth (Kunkle) B.; m. Claire Davidson, June 15, 1952 (dec. 1980); children: Robert Heron, Charles E., Ellen E.; m. Mary Ellen Pohl, Oct. 30, 1982. BA, U. Chgo., 1948, JD, 1953; LLD (hon.), Creighton U., 1975, Notre Dame Law Sch., 1982; LHD, Wilkes-Barre Coll., 1976; JD (hon.), Bklyn. Law Sch., 1984; ThD, DeSales Sch. Theology, 1990; LLD honoris causa, Adelphi U., 1990. Bar: Ill. 1953, D.C. 1977. Assoc., then ptnr. Kirkland, Ellis, Hodson, Chaffetz & Masters, Chgo., 1955-62; assoc. prof. Yale Law Sch., 1962-65, prof. law, 1965-75, on leave, 1973-75; solicitor gen. U.S. Dept. Justice, Washington, 1973-77, acting atty. gen., 1973-74; Chancellor Kent prof. law Yale Law Sch., 1977-79, Alexander M. Bickel prof. pub. law, 1979-81; ptnr. Kirkland & Ellis, Washington, 1981-82; judge U.S. Ct. Appeals for D.C. Cir., 1982—88; resident scholar Am. Enterprise Inst. for Pub. Policy Rsch., Washington, 1977, adj. scholar, 1977-82, John M. Olin scholar in legal studies, 1988-99, sr. fellow, 2000—; prof. law Ave Maria Sch. Law, 2000—03. Mem., trustee Woodrow Wilson Internat. Ctr. for Scholars, 1973-78; nominated for position assoc. justice U.S. Supreme Ct., 1987, confirmation denied by U.S. Senate; Tad and Dianne Taube Disting. vis. fellow Hoover Instn., 2003. Author: The Antitrust Paradox: A Policy at War with Itself, 1978, 2d edit., 1993, The Tempting of America: The Political Seduction of the Law, 1990, Slouching Towards Gomorrah: Modern Liberalism and American Decline, 1996, Coercing Virtue: The Worldwide Rule of Judges, 2002. With USMCR, 1945-46, 50-52. Recipient Francis Boyer award Am. Enterprise Inst., 1984, Henry Salvatori prize Intercollegiate Svcs. Inst., 1998, Named one of 75 Best Lawyers in Washington, Washingtonian Survey Mag., 2002. Fellow AAAS; mem. Federalist Soc. (co-chmn., bd. trustees). E-mail: rbork@aei.org.

BORKAN, WILLIAM NOAH, electronics executive, biomedical engineer, entrepreneur, venture capitalist, real estate developer; b. Miami Beach, Fla., Apr. 29, 1956; s. Martin Solomon and Annabelle (Hoffman) Borkan; m. Vivienne Eliane; children: Martin, Kenneth. Student, Carnegie Mellon U., 1977. Tech. Dominicks' Radio & TV Co., Miami Beach, 1971-74; computer programmer Mt. Sinai Hosp., Miami Beach, 1973-74; chief studio engr. Sta. WGMA, Hollywood, Fla., 1973-74; disc jockey Sta. WBUS-FM, Miami Beach, 1974; chief rec. engr. Dukoff Recording Studios, Miami, Fla., 1974-75; rec. studio design and constrn. TSI, Hollywood, 1975-77; chief design engr. Lumonics Co., Miami, 1974; svc. mgr. 21st Century Electronics Co., Miami, 1975; lab. tech., mem. curriculum com. elec. engring. dept. Carnegie-Mellon U.; mgr. Tech. Electronics Co., Pitts., 1976; pres. Borktronics Co., Miami, 1974-84; consulting specialist in neurobiometrics St. Barnabas Hosp., NYC, 1978-83; pres., CEO NeuroMed, Inc., 1980-85, Nice Tech., Inc., 1989-96; pres. Master Angler, Inc., 1990—. Dir. Saints Venutres Ltd, 1999—; pres. Electrovest Inc., 1985—; mng. mem. Aloha Investment Group, 2003—; cons. specialist in home automation, home theater and audio. Author publs. in field. Named Entrepreneur of Yr., Fla. Inc. Mag., 1992; grantee, Carnegie Corp., Carnegie Mellon U. Mem.: AAAS, NY Acad. Scis., Audio Engring. Soc., Assn. Advancement Med. Instrumentation, Refrigeration and Air Conditioning Engrs., Am. Soc. Heating. Achievements include numerous US and foreign patents in field; patents pending in field. Home: 3142 NE 166th St Miami FL 33160-3840 Office: Electrovest 12000 Biscayne Blvd Ste 502 Miami FL 33181-2725 Personal E-mail: bbbillfish@aol.com.

BORKO, HILDA, education educator; BA in Psychology, UCLA, 1971, MA in Philosophy of Edn., 1973, PhD in Ednl. Psychology, 1978. Elem. tchg. credential Calif., specialization in mental retardation U. So. Calif. Asst. and assoc. prof. Coll. Edn., Va. Poly. Inst. and State U., 1980—85; assoc. prof. Coll. Edn., U. Md., College Park, 1985—91, Sch. Edn., U. Colo., Boulder, 1991—94; prof. Sch. Edn. U. Colo., Boulder, 1994—. Co-author (with M. Eisenhart): (book) Designing Classroom Research: Themes, Issues, and Struggles, 1993 (Outstanding article award, 1992); contbr. articles to profl. jours. and chpts. to books. Recipient grants in field. Mem.: APA, Nat. Acad. Edn., Nat. Coun. for Tchrs. of Math., Invisible Coll. for Rsch. on Tchg., Am. Assn. Colls. of Tchr. Edn., Am. Ednl. Rsch. Assn. (pres. 2003—04), Pi Gamma Mu, Phi Beta Kappa, Phi Delta Kappa. Office: U Colo Sch Edn CB249 Boulder CO 80309 Office Phone: 303-492-8399.

BORKOVEC, VERA Z., literature and language professor; b. Brno, Czechoslovakia, Aug. 13, 1926; came to U.S., 1952; d. Josef Zanda and Jarmila (Tuscher) Martinasek; m. Alexej B. Borkovec, Aug. 29, 1951. BA, Charles U., 1949; MA, Hollins Coll., 1961, The Am. U., 1966; PhD, Georgetown U., 1973. Secondary sch. tchr. English, French Montgomery County Pub. Schs., Md., 1961-64; from asst. prof. to assoc. prof. Russian studies The Am. Univ., Washington, 1966-91, prof. emerita. Recipient Artis Bohemiae Amicis medal, Czech Ministry of Culture, 2003. Mem. Czechoslovak Soc. of Arts and Scis. (v.p. 1994—). Avocations: theater, music, poetry. Home: 12013 Kemp Mill Rd Silver Spring MD 20902-1515

BORKOWSKI, FRANCIS THOMAS, music educator; b. Weirton, W.Va., Mar. 16, 1936; s. Francis Thomas and Felicia Josephine (Pawlowski) B.; m. Kay Kaiser, Aug. 22, 1959; children: Stanley, Anne-Marie, Christian. BS, Oberlin (Ohio) Coll., 1957; M.Mus., Ind. U., 1959; PhD, W.Va. U., 1967; LLD (hon.), St. Leo (Fla.) Coll., 1989. Clarinetist Indpls. Symphony Orch., 1957-59; music dir. Bishop Kenny High Sch., Jacksonville, Fla., 1959-61; dir. bands W.Va. U., 1961-67; assoc. prof. music edn. Ohio U., Athens, 1967-69, asst. dir. Sch. Music, 1969-70, assoc. dean faculties, 1970-75; prof. music, vice chancellor, dean faculty Ind. U.-Purdue U., Ft. Wayne, 1975-78; v.p. Ft.

Wayne Philharmonic Orch., 1976-78; provost U. S.C. System, 1978-83, exec. v.p., provost, 1983-88; pres. U. South Fla., Tampa, 1988-93; chancellor Appalachian State U., Boone, NC, 1993—2003, prof. music, 2003—. Bd. dirs. Fla. Nations Bank. Author articles. Mem. nat. adv. coun. John F. Kennedy Ctr., 1978-80; pres. S.C. Orch. Assn., 1982; bd. dirs. United Way of Columbia, 1981; chmn. Moffitt Cancer Ctr. Bd., United Way Bd., Tampa; mem. urban affairs com. Nat. Assn. Land Grant Colls. Recipient Amicus Poloniae award Poland mag., 1971, award for research Sigma Xi; named Polonian of Yr., 1989, Gold medal with Diamond, INTERPROM, 1997, Commdr. of the Cross of the Rep. of Poland, 2001. Mem. Am. Coun. Edn. (bd. dirs.), Am. Assn. Higher Edn., Music Educators Nat. Conf., Phi Beta Kappa, Mortar Bd., Omicron Delta Kappa, Eta Sigma Gamma, Golden Key, Phi Beta Delta. Roman Catholic. E-mail: borkowskif@appstate.edu.

BORKOWSKI, JAMES W., lawyer; b. Staten Is., N.Y., Aug. 15, 1962; s. Edmund Lawrence and Anna Loretta (Wright) B.; m. Linda M. Borkowski, Sept. 19, 1987; children: Lauren, Matthew. BA, SUNY, 1984; JD, BU, 1987. Bar: N.Y., 1988, U.S. Dist. Ct. (so. and ea. dists.) N.Y. 1989, U.S. Ct. Appeals (2d cir.) 1991, N.J. 1992, U.S. Dist. Ct. N.J. 1992, U.S. Supreme Ct. 1996. Asst. dist. atty. Nassau County Dist. Atty., Mineola, N.Y., 1987-89; assoc. litigation dept. Windels Marx Davies & Ives, N.Y.C., 1989-94; ptnr. Stephens Hogan Rossi & Borkowski, Brewster, N.Y., 1996-98; of counsel Bleakley, Platt & Schmidt, White Plains, N.Y., 1998—. Bd. dirs. Girl Scouts Am. Westchester and Putnam, Mt. Pleasant, N.Y., 1995-96; trustee, mem. vestry St. Luke's Episcopal Ch., 1996=98, trustee The Melrose Sch., Brewster, N.Y., 1998—; town justice, Town of Southeast, N.Y., 1998—. Mem.: Putnam County Magistrates Assn. (pres. 2003—). Avocations: martial arts, tennis. Office: Bleakley Platt & Schmidt 1 N Lexington Ave Ste 700 White Plains NY 10601-1700

BORLAND, KATHRYN KILBY, writer; b. Pullman, Mich., Aug. 14, 1916; d. Paul Melbourne and Vinnie (Bensinger) Kilby; m. James Barton Borland, May 16, 1942; children— James Barton, Susan Lee. BS in Journalism, Butler U., 1937. Editor North Side Topics, Indpls., 1938-42. Author: (all with Helen Ross Speicher) Southern Yankees, 1960, Allan Pinkerton, 1962, Miles and the Big Black Hat, 1963, Everybody Laughed, 1964, Eugene Field, 1964, Phillis Wheatley, 1968, Harry Houdini, 1969, Clocks from Shadow to Atom, 1969, Good-Bye to Stony Crick, 1975, The Third Tower, 1974, Stranger in the Mirror, 1974, Good-bye, Julie Scott, 1975, To Walk the Night, 1976, These Tigers' Hearts, 1978, Irena, 1979, Pseudonyms: Alice Abbott, Jane Land. Co-recipient award for most distinguished children's book pub. by Ind. author Ind. U., 1969 Mem.: P.E.O., Theta Sigma Phi, Kappa Alpha Theta. Home: 1050 S Maish Rd Frankfort IN 46041-3213

BORLAND, VIRGINIA ANN, journalist, fashion specialist, fiber company executive; b. NYC, Mar. 8, 1929; d. Charles Peter and Margaret Elise (Swane) S.; m. J. Nelson Borland, Nov. 13, 1969 (separated 1987). BA, Wells Coll., 1951. Publicist J. Walter Thompson Advt. Agy., 1952-55, Grey Advt., 1960; fashion dir. Cunningham & Walsh, N.Y.C., 1961-85, Avtex Fibers, Inc., N.Y.C., 1986—89; fashion editor Fashion Galleria mag., NY, 1989—. Cons. fashion editor Fashion Galleria mag., KTA, MMI, BASF Fibers; N.Y. corr. Textile World; contbg. editor Style mag., Canada. Vol. pediatric ward Meml. Hosp., 1953-84. Mem. Fashion Group (gov. 1975-77, found. dir. 1983-84), Inner Circle, Color Assn. U.S.A. (chmn. women's apparel color selection com.), Round Table Fashion Execs., Fashion News Workshop, N.Y. Jr. League. Republican. Episcopalian. Home: 110 E End Ave New York NY 10028-7412 E-mail: vborland@nycrr.com.

BORLAUG, NORMAN ERNEST, agricultural scientist; b. Cresco, Iowa, Mar. 25, 1914; s. Henry O. and Clara (Vaala) Borlaug; m. Margaret G. Gibson, Sept. 24, 1937; children: Norma Jean, William Gibson. BS in Forestry, U. Minn., Minneapolis, 1937, MS in Plant Pathology, 1940, PhD in Plant Pathology, 1942; ScD (honoris causa), Punjab (India) Agrl. U., 1969, Royal Norwegian Agrl. Coll., Norway, 1970, Luther Coll., 1971, Kanpur U., India, 1972, Uttar Pradesh Agrl. U., 1971, Mich. State U., 1971, U. de la Plata, Argentina, 1971, U. Ariz., 1972, U. Fla., 1973, U. Católica de Chile, Chile, 1974, U. Hohenheim, Germany, 1976, Punjab Agrl. U., Pakistan, 1978, Columbia U., 1980, Ohio State U., 1981, U. Minn., 1982, U. Notre Dame, 1987, Oregon State U., 1988, U. Tulsa, 1991, Washington State U., 1995, Andhra Pradesh Agrl. U., India, 1996, Indian Agrl. Rsch. Inst., 1996, De Montfort U., U.K., 1997, Emory U., 1999, U. Philippines, 1999; LHD, Gustavus Adolphus Coll., 1971, Iowa State U., 1992; LLD (hon.), New Mexico State U., 1973; D. of Agr. (hon.), Tufts U., 1982; D. of Agrl. Scis. (hon.), U. Agrl. Scis., Godollo, Hungary, 1980, Tokyo U. Agriculture, 1981, U. Nacional Pedro Henríquez Turena, Dominican Republic, U. Cen. del Estes, Dominican Republic, 1983; D. Honoris Causa, U. Mayor de San Simón, Bolivia, U. de Buenos Aires, 1983, U. de Cordoba, Spain, U. Politécnica de Catalunya, Barcelona, Spain, 1986, Colegio Postgraduados, Montecillo, Mexico, 1990; PhD (hon.), U. degli Studi di Bologna, Italy, 1991, Warsaw Agrl. U., Poland, 1993, Bangladesh Agrl. U., 1998, U. LaSalle-Noroeste, Mex., 1999, U. Politécnica de Madrid, Spain, 2000, U. Américas Puebla, Mex., 2000; D. Honoris Causa, U. Autónoma Nuevo León, 2001; PhD (hon.), U. Autónoma de Chapingo, 2001, Rector U. Dubuque, 1992-93; PhD (hon.), U. Studi de Bologna, Italy, 1991, Warsaw Agrl. U., Poland, 1993; ScD (hon.), Dartmouth Coll., 2005. With U.S. Forest Service, 1935—38; instr. U. Minn., 1941; microbiologist E.I. DuPont de Nemours, 1942—44; rsch. scientist in charge wheat improvement Coop. Mexican Agrl. Program, Mexican Ministry Agr. Rockefeller Found., Mexico, 1944—60, assoc. dir. assigned to Inter-Am. Food Crop Program, 1960—63; assoc. dir. CIMMYT, 1964-82; dir. wheat research and prodn. program Internat. Maize and Wheat Improvement Ctr., Mexico City, 1964—79, acting dir., 1981, cons., 1980—; disting. prof. internat. agr. dept. soil & crop scis. Texas A&M U., College Station, Tex., 1984—. Cons., collaborator nst. Nacional de Investigationes Agricolas, Mexican Ministry Agr, 1960—64; cons. FAO, North Africa and Asia, 1960; ex-officio cons. wheat research and prodn. problems to govts. in Latin Am., Africa, Asia, 1960—; mem. Citizen's Commn. on Sci. Law and Food Supply, 1973; mem. Commn. Critical Choices for Am, 1973, Council Agr. Sci. and Tech., 1973—, Presdl. Commn. on World Hunger U.S.A., 1978—79, Presdl. Coun. Advisers Sci and Tech., 1990—93; dir. Population Crisis Com., 1971—92; asesor especial Fundacion para Estudios de la Poblacion A.C., Mexico, 1971—80; mem. adv. council Renewable Natural Resources Found., 1973; A.D. White Disting. prof.-at-large Cornell U., 1983—85; Disting. prof. Internat. Agr., Dept. Soil & Crop Scis. Tex. A&M U., 1984—; adj. prof. dept. biology Emory U., Atlanta, 1991—92; advisor The Population Inst., U.S.A., 1971—78; bd. trustees Winrock Internat. U.S.A.; life fellow Rockefeller Found., 1983—; sr. cons. CIMMYT, 1979—; hon. vis. prof. U. Minn., 1980; adj. prof. dept. biology Emory U., Atlanta, 1991—92. Named Uncle of Paul Bunyan, 1969; named to Hall of Fame, Oreg. State U. Agrl., 1981, Agrl. Nat. Ctr., Bonner Springs, Kans., 1984, Scandinavian-Am., U.S.A., 1986, Nat. Wrestling, 1992; recipient Disting. Service awards, Wheat Producers Assns., and state govts. Mexican States of Guanajuato, Queretaro, Sonora, Tlaxcala and Zacatecas, 1955—60, Recognition award, Agrl. Inst. Can., 1966, Instituto Nacional de Tecnologia Agropecuaria de Marcos Juarez, Argentina, 1968, Sci. Service award, El Colegio de Ingenieros Agronomos de Mexico, 1970, Outstanding Achievement award, U. Minn., 1959, Elvin Charles Stakman award, 1961, Disting. Citizen award, Cresco Centennial Com., 1966, Nat. Disting. Service award, Am. Agrl. Editors Assn., 1967, Genetics and Plant Breeding award, Nat. Council Comml. Plant Breeders, 1968, Star of Distinction, Govt. of Pakistan, 1968, citation and street named in honor, Citizens of Sonora and Rotary Club, 1968, Internat. Agronomy award, Am. Soc. Agronomy, 1968, Distinguished Service award, Wheat Farmers of Punjab, Haryana and Himachal Pradesh, 1969, Nobel Peace prize, 1970, Diploma de Merito, El Instituto Tecnologico y de Estudios Superiores de Monterrey, Mexico, 1971, medalla y Diploma de Merito, Antonio Narro Escuela Superior de Agricultura de la U. de Coahuila, Mexico, 1971, Diploma de Merito, Escuela Superior de Agricultura Hermanos Escobar, Mexico, 1973, award for service to agr., Am. Farm Bur. Fedn., 1971, Outstanding Agrl. Achievement award, World Farm Found., 1971, Medal of Merit, Italian Wheat Scientists, 1971, outstanding Achievement award, Minn. Athletic Club, 1971, Service award for outstanding contbn. to alleviation of world hunger, 8th Latin Am. Food Prodn. Conf., 1972, Nat. award for Agrl. Excellence in Sci., Agri-Mktg. Assn., 1982, Disting. Achievement award, Council for Agrl. Scis. and Tech., 1982, inaugural lectr., medal, Dr. S.B. Hendrick's Meml. Lectureship., 1981, other honored lectureships, dedicated in his name, Norman E. Borlaug Centro de Capitación y Formación de Agrs., Santa Cruz, Bolivia, 1983, Borlaug Hall U. Minn., 1985, Borlaug Bldg. Internat. Maize and Wheat Improvement Ctr., 1986, numerous other honors and awards from govts., ednl. instns., citizens groups. Fellow: Indian Soc. Genetics and Plant Breeding; mem.: NAS, Acad. Nat. Agronomía and Veterinaria Argentina, Chinese Acad. Agrl. Sci., Royal Soc. Eng., Internat. Food Policy Research Inst. (trustee 1976—82), Am. Council on Sci. and Health (trustee 1978—), N.I. Vavilov Acad. Agrl. Scis. Lenin Order (USSR.), Adv. Coun. Renewable Natural Resources Acad. Found. (mem. adv. coun. 1973), Coun. Agrl. Sci. and Tech., Soil Sci. Soc. Am. (hon.), Sociedad de Agronomia do Rio Grande do Sul Brazil (hon.), Royal Agrl. Soc. Eng. (hon.), Royal Soc. Edinburgh (hon.), Hungarian Acad. Sci. (hon.), Indian Nat. Sci. Acad. (hon.), Am. Acad. Arts and Scis. (hon.), Hungarian Acad. Scis. (hon.), Mexican Acad. Scis. (hon.), Am. Assn. Cereal Chemists (hon.; life, Meritorious Service award 1969), Crop Sci. Soc. Am. (hon.), Population Crisis Com., Chinese Acad. Agrl. Scis. (hon. prof. 1994), Sasakawa Africa Assn. (pres. 1986), Academia Nat. de Agronomia y Veterinaria (Argentina), Royal Swedish Acad. Agr. and Forestry (fgn. 1971), India Nat. Sci. Acad., Am. Soc. Agronomy (1st Internat. Svc. award 1960, 1st hon. life), Sigma Xi, Xi Sigma Pi, Alpha Zeta. Office: Tex A&M U 2474 Tamu Dept Soil & Crop Scis College Station TX 77843-2474

BORLIK, ROBERT W., information technology executive; BA, U. Ill.; MBA, Lake Forest Sch. Mgmt. With G.D. Searle & Co., Hewitt Assocs., United Airlines, Northwest Airlines, 1991—99; sr. v.p., chief info. officer Supervalu, Inc., Eden Prairie, Minn., 1999—. Office: Supervalu Inc 11840 Valley View Rd Eden Prairie MN 55344

BORLING, JOHN LORIN, military officer; b. Chgo., Mar. 24, 1940; s. Edward Gustav and Vivian K. (Strietelmeir) Borling; m. Myrna Lee Holmstedt, June 22, 1963; children: Lauren, Megan. BS, U.S. Airforce Acad., 1963; grad., Armed Forces Staff Coll., 1975, Nat. War Coll., 1980, Harvard U., 1991. Commd. 2d lt. USAF, 1963, advanced through grades to maj. gen., 1989, prisoner of war, 1966-73, fighter pilot, comdr., 1974-80, asst. dir. ops. HQ Pentagon Washington, 1981-82, comdr. 86th Combat Support Group Ramstein, Germany, 1982-83, comdr. 86th Fighter Group, 1983-84, exec. officer to COS NATO Mons, Belgium, 1984-86, dep. plans/analysis HQ/SAC Jt. Stategic Target Planning Staff Omaha, 1986-87, comdr. HQ 57th Air Divsn. Minot, ND, 1987-88, dep. ops. HQ SAC Omaha, 1988-91; dir. operational reg(s) HQ Pentagon, 1991-92; dep. chief of staff NATO, Norway, 1992-94, chief of staff, sr. U.S. mil. officer in Scandinavia, 1994-96; pres., CEO United Way, Chgo., 1997-98; dir. The 5th Media, Chgo., 1999—. Chmn. Performance Cons. Group, 2000—; pres., CEO SOS Am., 2000—; advisor AMSAM Biotechnologies Inc.; chmn., CEO, 100 Mission LLC, 2005—; mem. Armed Forces Policy Coun., Chgo., Coun. Fgn. Rels., Chgo., Chgo. Com.; mem. adv. com. Ill. Fatherhood Initiative, Chgo.; mentor Harris Sch., U. Chgo. Founder, charter mem. Ramstein Coun. Internat. Rels., 1983; v.p., bd. dirs. Opera Omaha, 1988—91; treas., bd. dirs. White Ho. Fellow Found., 1991—; adv. bd. Stanton Chase Internat., Maritime Trust Co.; bd. govs. Chgo. Mil. Acad.; bd. dirs. Nat. Jazz Mus., 2000; vice-chmn. Chgo. Meml. Day Parade Com., 2000; dir. Stars & Stripes Relief Fund, 2001; mem. adv. com. Kellog Sch., Northwestern U. Decorated Def. Distin. Svc. medal with oak leaf cluster, Air Force Disting. Svc. medal, Silver Star, Def. Superior Svc. medal, Legion of Merit with oak leaf cluster, DFC with oak leaf cluster, Bronze Star with V device and 2 oak leaf clusters, Air medal with 5 oak leaf clusters, Purple Heart with one cluster; named to Ill. Aviation Hall of Fame, 2004; recipient George Washington medal, Freedom Found., Valley Forge, Pa., 1975, Good Scout award, Boy Scouts Am., Chgo., 1974, Eagle Am. Hero award, Benedictine U., 2001, Patriot's award, C. of C., 2001; White Ho. fellow, 1974, Harvard U., 1998. Mem.: VFW, Air Force Assn., Assn. Grads. USAF Acad., Execs. Club Chgo., Comml. Club Chgo., Daedalians. Avocations: music, sports, reading. Office: SOS America Box 1543 Rockford IL 61110-1543 Office Phone: 405-447-2577. E-mail: jlb@100usn.com, forsosamerica@yahoo.com.

BORMES, JAMES X., lawyer; b. Aberdeen, S.D., Sept. 1, 1962; s. Robert E. and Patricia A. Bormes; m. Anne C. Hussey; children: Margaret, James, Mary, Grace. BA, St. Louis U., 1984, JD, 1988. Bar: Ill. 1988, U.S. Dist. Ct. (no. dist.) Ill. 1990, U.S. Dist. Ct. (we. dist.) Tex. 1996, U.S. Dist. Ct. (so. dist.) Ill. 2000, U.S. Ct. Appeals (7th cir.) 1991. Law clk., Judge William L. Beatty U.S. Dist. Ct. (so. dist.) Ill., Chgo., 1988—89; assoc. Joyce Kubusiak, Chgo., 1989—94, O'Brien, O'Rourke & Hogan, Chgo., 1994—98; ptnr. Law Office James X. Bormes, PC, Chgo., 1998—. Tutor Mercy Home for Boys, Chgo., 2000—. Mem.: Chgo. Athletic Assn. Roman Catholic. Office: Law Office James X Bormes PC 8 S Michigan Ste 2600 Chicago IL 60603 Office Phone: 312-201-0575. Business E-Mail: bormeslaw@sbcglobal.net.

BORN, BROOKSLEY ELIZABETH, retired lawyer; b. San Francisco, Aug. 27, 1940; d. Ronald Henry and Mary Ellen (Bortner) Born; m. Alexander Elliot Bennett, Oct. 9, 1982; children: Nicholas Jacob Landau, Ariel Elizabeth Landau, Andrew E. Bennett, Laura F. Bennett, Peter J. Bennett. AB, Stanford U., 1961, JD, 1964. Bar: DC 1966. Law clk. U.S. Ct. Appeals, Washington, 1964—65; legal rschr. Harvard Law Sch., 1967—68; assoc. Arnold and Porter, Washington, 1965—67, 1968—73, ptnr., 1974—96, 1999—2002; chair U.S. Commodity Futures Trading Commn., Washington, 1996—99. Lectr. law Columbus Sch. Law, Cath. U. Am., 1972—74; adj. prof. Georgetown U. Law Ctr., Washington, 1972—73; mem. D.C. Jud. Nomination Commn., 2005—. Pres.: Stanford Law Rev., 1963—64. Chair bd. visitors Stanford Law Sch., 1987; trustee Ctr. Law and Social Policy, Washington, 1977—96; bd. dirs. Nat. Legal Aid and Defenders Assn., 1972—79, Washington Legal Clinic for Homeless, 1993—96, Lawyers Com. for Civil Rights Under Law, 1993—96, Am. Bar Found., 1989—99, Washington Lawyers Com. for Civil Rights and Urban Affairs, 1992—96; chair bd. dirs. Nat. Women's Law Ctr., 1981—96, 2003—, bd. dirs., 1997—2002, Women's Bar Found., 1997—2002. Recipient Lifetime Achievement award, Am. Law mag., 2005. Mem.: ABA (chair sect. ind. rights and responsibilities 1977—78, chair fed. judiciary com. 1980—83, chair consortium on legal svcs. and the pub. 1987—90, bd. govs. 1990—93, chair resource devel. coun. 1993—95, state del. from DC 1994—, chair coun. Fund for Justice and Edn. 1995—96, 2005, U.S. dist. ct. jud. nomination commn. 2005), Southwestern Legal Found. (trustee 1993—96), Am. Law Inst., DC Bar (sec. 1975—76, mem. bd. govs. 1976—79), Order of Coif. Office: Arnold & Porter 555 12th St NW Washington DC 20004-1206 Office Phone: 202-942-5832. Business E-Mail: brooksley_born@aporter.com.

BORN, DANA H., dean, career military officer; BS, USAF Acad., 1983; MS, Trinity Univ., 1985; MA, Univ. Melbourne, Australia, 1991; PhD in indsl. & org. psychol., Pa. State Univ., 1994. Commd. 2d lt. USAF, advanced through grades to brig. gen., 2004; job analyst, exec. officer Occupational Measurement Ctr., Randolph AFB, Tex., 1983—86; personnel measurement psychol. USAF Exch. & Liaison office, Australian Royal Air Force, Melbourne, Australia, 1986—89; asst. prof., dept. behavioral sci. USAF Acad., Colo., 1989—91; liaison officer Pa. State Univ., 1991—94; asst. dir., recruiting rsch. & analysis Office of Asst. Sec. of Def. for Force Mgmt. Policy, Washington, 1994—97; policy analyst, aide to Sec. Office of Sec. of the Air Force, Washington, 1997—98; dep. chief, personnel issues team Office of Dep. Chief of Staff for Personnel, Washington, 1998—2000; comdr. 11th Mission Support Squadron, Bolling AFB, DC, 2000—02; prof., head Dept. Behavioral Sci. & Leadership USAF Acad., Colo., 2002—04, dean of the faculty, 2004—. Decorated Def. Meritorious Svc. Medal, Meritorious Svc. Medal with 3 oak leaf clusters, Air Force Commendation medal with oak leaf cluster, Air Force Org. Excellence award, Nat. Def. Svc. medal with bronze star. Office: Dean of the Faculty U S A F Academy CO 80840

BORN, ROBERT HEYWOOD, consulting civil engineer; b. L.A., Nov. 7, 1925; s. Robert Bogle and Mignon Mary (Heywood) B.; m. Marilyn Alice Simpson, Aug. 15, 1947; 1 child, Stefanie Born. Student, Stanford U., 1943; BE, U. So. Calif., 1949, MSCE, 1956. Registered civil engr., Calif., Ariz., Nev., Utah, Tenn., Guam; registered agrl. engr., Calif. Assoc. hydraulic engr. Calif. Dept. of Water Resources, L.A., 1949-58; chief engr., county hydraulic engr. County Flood Control/Water Conservation Dist., San Luis Obispo, Calif., 1958-70; dir., exec. v.p., regional mgr. CDM, Inc., Pasadena, Calif., 1970-78; v.p., regional mgr. Born, Barrett & Assoc./Barrett Cons. Group, Newport Beach, Calif., 1978-86, Memphis, 1978-86; prin. Robert H. Born Cons. Engrs., Memphis, 1986—88, Irvine, Laguna Niguel, Calif., 1986—88, Asheville, N.C., 1997—. Chmn. World Affairs Coun., San Luis Obispo, Calif., 1965. 1st lt. U.S. Army, 1943-47. Decorated Bronze star medal, 1944. Fellow: ASCE (life Engr. of Merit 1994); mem.: Am. Pub. Works Assn. (Floodplain Mgmt. Assn. Calif., cert. outstanding pub. works achievement 1969), U.S. Com. on Large Dams, Am. Water Works Assn. (com. chmn.), Am. Acad. Environ. Engrs. (life; diplomate). Democrat. Presbyterian. Avocations: historical research, travel. Office: Robert H Born Cons Engrs 1658 Ryamar Coves South Memphis TN 38016

BORN, SAMUEL ROYDON, II, lawyer; b. Atwood, Ill., Apr. 19, 1945; s. Samuel Roydon and Mary Elizabeth (Derr) B.; m. Brenda Alice Anderson, June 18, 1988; children: Samuel R. III, Holly Jean, Julie Chamberlain Sipe. Student, Northwestern U., 1963-64, Am. U., fall 1966; BA, Simpson Coll., 1967; JD, Ind. U., 1970. Bar: Ind. 1970, U.S. Dist. Ct. (so. dist.) Ind. 1970, U.S. Ct. Appeals (7th cir.) 1975, U.S. Dist. Ct. (no. dist.) Ind. 1990, U.S. Supreme Ct. 2003. Ptnr. Ice Miller, Indpls., 1970—. Mem. safety com. Associated Gen. Contractors Ind., 1988—. Co-author: Safety and Health Guide for Indiana Business, 1999, 5th edit., 2004; mem. bd. editors: Ind. Law Jour., 1969—70; contbr. articles to profl. jours. Mem. bd. visitors Ind. U. Sch. Law, 1988-89, 95-98; chmn. ch. cmty. athletics First Bapt. Ch., Indpls., 1975-78, trustee, 1978-80. Fellow Am. Bar Found., Ind. Bar Found., Indpls. Bar Found.; mem. ABA (mem. nat. conf. bar pres. 1987-99, ho. of dels. 1988-98, labor and employment law sect., ADR sect.), Ind. State Bar Assn. (bd. govs. 1990-99, pres. 1997-98, labor law sect., ADR sect.), Indpls. Bar Assn. (bd. mgrs. 1987-95, pres. 1988), U.S. C. of C. (occupl. safety and health adminstrv. coun. 1981-86, 2000—), Ind. C. of C. (past chmn. occupl. safety health com.), Ind. Mfrs. Assn. (pers. labor rels. com. 1982-99), Highland Golf and Country Club, Crooked Stick Golf Club, Univ. Club, Indpls. Lawyers Club, Masons, Shriners, Kiwanis, Phi Eta Sigma, Sigma Alpha Epsilon Presbyterian. Avocations: downhill skiing, golf, fly fishing, public speaking. Home: 5202 Grandview Dr Indianapolis IN 46228-1938 Office: Ice Miller 1 American Sq Indianapolis IN 46282-0020 Office Phone: 317-236-2305. Business E-Mail: born@icemiller.com.

BORN, SUZANNE, lawyer; b. Waseca, Minn., Apr. 23, 1946; BA, U. Minn., 1977; JD, Hamline U., 1980. Bar: Minn. 1980, U.S. Dist. Ct. Minn. 1980, U.S. Ct. Appeals (8th cir.) 1980, U.S. Supreme Ct. 1997. Law clk. Hon. John F. Thoreen, Stillwater, Minn., 1980-83; ptnr. Stone & Zander, Mpls., 1983-85; pvt. practice Mpls., 1985—. Adminstrv. law judge Minn. State Office of Adminstrv. Hearings, Mpls., 1989-2000. Editor Hamline Law Review, 1979-80. Mem. Mpls. Commn. on Civil Rights, 1987-92, Minn. Supreme Ct. Parental Cooperation Task Force, 1998-2000; mem. deans adv. bd. Hamlin U. Sch. Law. Recipient Disting. Svc. award Minn. Justice Found., 2000; named Super Lawyer Jour. Law and Polit., 2000, 01. Mem. Minn. Women Lawyers (pres. 1985-86, Myra Bradwell award for promoting the interests of women in the legal prof. 1998), Minn. State Bar Assn. (chair family law sect. 1999-2000), Henn. County Bar Assn. (exec. com. family law sect.). Office: 333 Washington Ave N Minneapolis MN 55401-1377 E-mail: suzanneborn@mindspring.com.

BORNET, VAUGHN DAVIS, social sciences educator, historian, researcher; b. Phila., Oct. 10, 1917; s. Vaughn Taylor and Florence Davis (Scull) Bornet; m. Mary Elizabeth Winchester, Dec. 28, 1944; children: Barbara Bornet Stumph, Stephen Folwell. BA with honors, Emory U., 1939, MA, 1940; postgrad. fellow, U. Ga., 1940-41; PhD, Stanford U., 1951. Staff Mercer U., 1946; instr. history U. Miami, 1946-48; research assoc. Inst. Am. History, Stanford U., 1951-53; dir. welfare research project Commonwealth Club of Calif., 1953-56; assoc. editor Ency. Britannica, 1958; rsch. assoc. med. econs. AMA, 1958-59; staff RAND Corp., Santa Monica, Calif., 1959-63; chmn. social scis. div. So. Oreg. U., Ashland, 1963-74, prof. history and social sci., 1963-80. Vis. prof. World Campus Afloat, spring 1969. Author: Struggle for Governmental Power in Georgia, 1754-1757, 1940, Labor and Politics in 1928, 1951, California Social Welfare, 1956, Welfare in America, 1960, Labor Politics in a Democratic Republic, 1964, Speaking Up for America, 1975; (with E.E. Robinson) Herbert Hoover: President of the United States, 1975, The Presidency of Lyndon B. Johnson, 1983 (nominee Pulitzer Prize); (juvenile) It's a Dog's Life and I Like It, 1991; (memoir) An Independent Scholar In Twentieth Century America, 1995, Thinking About the Iraq Situation, 2003, Republican, Democrat or Independent...?, 2004, When the Space Race Began, 2005; co-author The Heart Future, 1961; article United States, Ency. Brit. Yearbooks, 1957, 58; contbr. The Federal Campaign of 1864 in East Florida, 1956, Ideas in Conflict, 1958, Herbert Hoover Reassessed, 1981, The Quest for Security, 1982, Essays in Economics and Business History, 1988 Pres. So. Oreg. Symphony Assn., 1973-75; mem. U.S. Com. on Civil Rights, Oreg., 1985— . Served to lt. USNR, 1941-45, ret. comdr. Recipient Disting. Svc. awards Am., Oreg. Heart Assns., 1964, Disting. Svc. award Southern Oreg. U. Alumni Assn., 1985, Freedoms Found. award 1986. Mem. Rotary, Sigma Chi. Republican. Home: 365 Ridge Rd Ashland OR 97520-2830 E-mail: bornetvd@ashlandhome.net.

BORNHEIMER, ALLEN MILLARD, lawyer; b. Brewer, Maine, June 10, 1942; s. Millard Genthner and Gertrude Evelyn (Kinney) B.; m. Deborah Russell Hill, June 17, 1967; children: Anneliese, Charles, Elizabeth. Student, Phillips Exeter Acad., 1961; AB, Harvard U., 1965, LLB, 1968. Bar: Mich. 1968, Mass. 1971. Assoc. Dickinson, Wright, McKean & Cudlip, Detroit, 1968-70, Choate, Hall & Stewart, Boston, 1970-76, ptnr., 1976-99, mng. ptnr., 1988-95; principal, gen. counsel Cargex Properties, Inc., Boston, 2000—. Bd. dirs. Cargex Properties, Inc. and affiliated cos., Portland, Maine. Town moderator, Duxbury, Mass., 1982—, chmn. fin. com., 1974-76, mem. capital budget com., 1977; bd. dirs. Jordan Hosp., Plymouth, Mass., 1974-81; trustee North Yarmouth (Maine) Acad., 1976-79. Mem. ABA, Mass. Bar Assn., Boston Bar Assn., Am. Coll. Investment Counsel, Mass. Moderators Assn., Duxbury Yacht Club (bd. dirs. 1982-84), Harvard Club (Boston), Somerset Club (Boston). Republican. Avocations: golf, piano, sailing. Home: 15 Summerhouse Lane Duxbury MA 02332-3930 Office: 20th Fl 50 Milk St Boston MA 02109-5003 Office Phone: 617-338-0181. E-mail: allen.bornheimer@cargex.com.

BORNHOLDT, LAURA ANNA, academic administrator; b. Peoria, Ill., Feb. 11, 1919; d. John and Barbara (Kohl) B. AB, Smith Coll., 1940, MA, 1942; PhD, Yale U., 1945. Asst. prof. history Smith Coll., Northampton, Mass., 1945-52; internat. relations assoc. AAUW, Washington, 1952-57; dean Sarah Lawrence Coll., Bronxville, N.Y., 1957-59; dean women, adj. prof. history U. Pa., Phila., 1959-61; dean coll., prof. history Wellesley (Mass.) Coll., 1961-64; v.p. Danforth Found., St. Louis, 1964-73; sr. program officer Lilly Endowment Inc., Indpls., 1973-76, v.p. for edn., 1976-84; dir. office univ.-sch. rels. U. Chgo., 1984-94. Nat. adv. com. on black higher edn. and black colls. and univs. Dept. Edn., 1977-82; mem. Yale U. Council, 1977-82; emerita life trustee Coll. of Wooster, Ohio, 1967-77; trustee St. Louis U., 1971-75. Recipient Yale U. Wilbur Cross medal, 1976, Smith Coll. Alumnae medal, 1987. Mem.: Phi Beta Kappa. Home: 925 Juniper Pl Bloomington IN 47408-1285

BORNHORST, KENNETH FRANK, electromagnetics and systems engineer; b. Detroit, Feb. 5, 1929; s. Leo John and Alvina Anna (Laufersweiler) B.; m. Patricia Lucille Dreyer, July 3, 1954; children: Kenneth Jr., David L., Patricia A. BEE, U. Dayton, 1951, PhD in Engring., 1985; MEE, Poly. Inst. N.Y., 1954. Project engr. monopulse radar receiver devel. Sperry Gyroscope Co., Great Neck, NY, 1951—54; project engr. autopilot, motor, timer, gyroscope devel. Globe Industries Inc., Dayton, Ohio, 1954—60; project engr. devel. of servo guided shoe machinery United Shoe Machinery Co., Xenia, Ohio, 1960; engring. sect. head mil. equipment divsn. locator and telemetry beacon and automatic direction finder devel. NCR, Dayton, 1960—74; br. chief, analyst electromagnetic threat analysis, radar, advanced weapon sys. Nat. Aero. & Space Intelligence Ctr. USAF, Wright-Patterson AFB, Ohio, 1974—94; cons., 1995—. Radar Cross section measurement of troops and vehicles for U.S. Army, 1954-56. Mem. Tau Beta Pi. Achievements include patents for flight control system, UHF bypass capacitor, pulsed carrier radio beacon, UHF radio direction finder, low loss millimeter waveguide.

BORNINO-GLUSAC, ANNA MARIA, mathematics professor; b. Naples, Italy, Apr. 2, 1946; came to U.S., 1946; d. Bruno and Anna Maria (De Simone) B.; m. Howard Keith Wolff, July 29, 1966 (div. 1971); 1 child, Francesca Yvonne Wolff Hatzakis; m. Ronald G. Glusac, Sept. 4, 1993. BA in Chemistry, Calif. State U., Dominguez Hills, 1968, MA in Edn. Adminstrv. Svcs., 1986. Cert. standard secondary tchr., Calif., preliminary adminstrv., Calif., TFAS instr.; Calif. BCLAD credential. Tchr. math. L.A. Unified Sch. Dist., 1968—, dept. chair, 1982—84, 1990—92, coord. sch. improvement, 1998—2002, coach math. dist. K Wilmington, Calif., 2002—04, coach math. dist. 8 Gardena, 2004—. Editor: Accreditation Report, 1983. Mem. United Tchrs. L.A., Nat. Coun. Tchrs. Math., Calif. Math. Coun. Democrat. Roman Catholic. Avocations: needlecrafts, travel, reading, music. Office: 1301 W 182d St Gardena CA 90248 E-mail: amb2284@ansd.k12.ca.us.

BORNMANN, ROBERT CLARE, physician, medical consultant; b. Pitts., June 29, 1931; s. John Arthur and Iona Ann (Flanegin) B.; children: Kristin L., Elizabeth A., Jennifer C., John W. AB, Harvard U., 1952; MD, U. Penna, 1956, MS in Pharmacology, 1963. Comdr. Cape Hallett Igy Station, Antarctica, 1958-59; med. officer Underwater Swimmers Sch., Key West, Fla., 1961-62, Deepseadivscol and Experimental Dvunit, Washington, 1963-68, Deep Submergence Systems Project, Navmat, Washington, 1968-70; exchange med. officer Royal Navy Inst. of Naval Med., Gosport, UK, 1970-73; staff med. officer, oceanographer U.S. Navy, Washington, 1973-81; staff dir. Defense Med. Standardization Board, Frederick, Md., 1981-85; prin. cons. Limetree Med. Cons., Reston, Va., 1985—. Cons. Lawrence Livermore (Calif.) Nat. Lab., 1987-88, NOAA, 1987-88; mem. environ. rev. com. NASA, Houston, 1983-92. Contbr. articles and edited numerous med. jours. Fellow Aerospace Med. Assn., Royal Soc. Med.; mem. Undersea and Hyperbaric Med. Soc. (recipient C.W. Shilling award, 1988), Am. Coll. Occupational Med., Am. Assn. for Advancement of Sci., Harvard Club. Office: Limetree Med Cons 11569 Woodhollow Ct Reston VA 20191-4409

BORNS, ROBERT AARON, real estate developer; b. Gary, Ind., Oct. 24, 1935; s. Irving Jonah and Sylvia (Mackoff) B.; m. Sandra Solotkin, Mar. 30, 1958; children: Stepahnie, Elizabeth, Emily. BS, Ind. U., 1957; hon. degree, U. indpls., 1987. Account exec. Reynolds & Co., Chgo., 1957-59, Francis I duPont co., Indpls., 1960; owner, operator Borns & Co., Indpls., 1960-63; chmn. Borns Mgmt. Corp., Indpls., 1963—, Correctional Mgmt. Co., L.L.C., 1996—. Bd. dirs. Artistic Media Ptnrs. L.L.C., No. Trust Bank of Calif.; past bd. dirs. Std. Mgmt. Corp., I.W.C. Resources Corp., Indpls. Water Co., ISIPALCO Enterprises, Indpls. Power and Light Co., Mid Am. Capital Resources. Mem. bd. visitors Borns Jewish Studies Program Ind. U.; past mem. adv. bd. St. Vincent's Hosp.; past trustee St. Vincent's Hosp. Found.; bd. dirs. Barbara Sinatra Children's Ctr., treas.; bd. dirs. Indpls. Mus. Art, Ind. U. Found., Va. Waring Internat. Piano Competition, McCallum Theatre of Performing Arts; past bd. dirs. Ind. Symphony Orch., Indpls. Children's Mus. Recipient Enterprise award Indpls. Bus. Jour., 1982, Peace award State of Israel, 1979. Mem. Confrerie des Chevaliers du Tastevin, Econ. Club (bd. dirs.), Thunderbird Country Club (Rancho Mirage, Calif.). Office: Borns Mgmt Corp 21 Beachway Dr Indianapolis IN 46224-8566

BORNSTEIN, ELI, artist, sculptor; b. Milw., Dec. 28, 1922; dual citizen, U.S. and Can. m. Christina Girgulis; children: Sarah, Thea. BS, U. Wis., 1945, MS, 1954; student, Art Inst. Chgo., U. Chgo., 1943, Academie Montmartre of Fernand Leger, Paris, 1951, Academie Julian, 1952; DLitt, U. Sask., Can., 1990. Tchr. drawing, painting and sculpture Milw. Art Inst., 1943-47; tchr. design U. Wis., 1949; tchr. drawing, painting, sculpture, design and graphics U. Sask., Canada, 1950-90, prof., 1963-90, prof. emeritus, 1990—, head art dept., 1963-71. Painted in France, 1951-52, Italy, 1957, Holland, 1958; exhibited widely, 1943-; retrospective exhbn. (works 1943-64), Mendel Art Gallery, Saskatoon, 1965, one man shows, Kazimir Gallery, Chgo., 1965, 67, Saskatoon Pub. Libr., 1975, Can. Cultural Ctr., Paris, 1976, Glenbow-Alta. Inst. Art, Calgary, 1976, Mendel Art Gallery, Saskatoon, 1982, York U. Gallery, Toronto, 1983, Confedn. Ctr. Art Gallery, Charlottetown, P.E.I., 1983, Owens Art Gallery, Mt. Allison U., Sackville, N.B., 1984, Fine Arts Gallery, U. Wis.-Milw., 1984, Mendel Art Gallery, Saskatoon, 1996; represented in numerous pvt. collections; executed marble sculpture now in permanent collection, Walker Art Ctr., Mpls., 1947; commns. include aluminum constrn. for Sask. Tchr. Fedn. Bldg., 1956, structurist relief in painted wood and aluminum for, Arts and Sci. Bldg., U. Sask., 1958, structurist relief in enamelled steel for, Internat. Air Terminal, Winnipeg, Man., Can., 1962, four-part constructed relief for, Wascana Pl., Wascana Ctr. Authority, Regina, Sask., 1983, and six panel structurist relief for exterior of Synchrotron-Can. Light Source Bldg., U. Sask, 2003; also structurist reliefs exhibited, Mus. Contemporary Art, Chgo., Herron Mus. Art, Indpls., Cranbrook Acad. Art Galleries, Mich., High Mus., Atlanta, Can. House, Cultural Centre Gallery, London, 1983, Can. Cultural Ctr., Paris, 1983, Brussels, 1983, Bonn, 1984, Milw. Art Mus., 1984; model of aluminium construction, 1956 and model version of structurist relief in 5 parts, 1962, now in collection, Nat. Gallery, Ottawa, Ont., model version of Wascana commn. aquired by Can. Ctr. for Arch., Montreal; others in numerous collections.; co-editor: periodical Structure, 1958; founder, editor: The Structurist, ann. publ. 1960-72, biennial, 1972—; contbr. articles, principally on Structurist art to various publ. Recipient Allied Arts medal Royal Archtl. Inst. Can., 1968; hon. mention for 3 structurist reliefs 2d Biennial Internat. Art Exhbn., Colombia, S.Am., 1970. Address: 3625 Saskatchewan Cres S Corman Park SK Canada S7T 1B7 Office: U Sask Box 378 RPO U Saskatoon SK Canada S7N 4J8 Office Phone: 306-966-4198. E-mail: eli.bornstein@usask.ca.

BORNSTEIN, GARY A., lawyer; b. Merrick, NY, Feb. 15, 1973; BA magna cum laude, Yale Univ., 1994; JD magna cum laude, Harvard Univ., 1997. Bar: NY 1998. Law clk., Hon. Amalya L. Kearse US Ct. Appeals, 2nd Cir.; summer assoc. Cravath, Swaine & Moore LLP, NYC, 1996, assoc., 1998—2005, ptnr., litig., 2005—. Notes editor Harvard Law Rev. Mem.: ABA, Phi Beta Kappa. Office: Cravath Swaine Moore LLP Worldwide Plz 825 Eighth Ave New York NY 10019-7475 Office Phone: 212-474-1084. Office Fax: 212-474-3700. Business E-Mail: gbornstein@cravath.com.

BORNSTEIN, GEORGE JAY, literary educator; b. St. Louis, Aug. 25, 1941; s. Harry and Celia (Price) B.; m. Jane Elizabeth York, June 22, 1982; children— Benjamin, Rebecca, Joshua. AB, Harvard U., 1963; PhD, Princeton U., 1966. Asst. prof. MIT, Cambridge, 1966-69, Rutgers U., 1969-70; assoc. prof. U. Mich., Ann Arbor, 1970-75, prof. English, 1975—, C.A. Patrides prof. lit., 1995—. Cons. various univ. presses, scholastic jours., funding agys., 1970—; mem. adv. bd. Yeats: An Annual, 1982—, South Atlantic Rev., 1985-88, Rev., 1991—, Text, 1993—, Paideuma, 2003—. Author: Yeats and Shelley, 1970, Transformations of Romanticism, 1976, Postromantic Consciousness of Ezra Pound, 1977, Poetic Remaking, 1988, Material Modernism: The Politics of the Page, 2001; editor: Romantic and Modern, 1977, Ezra Pound Among the Poets, 1985, W.B. Yeats: The Early Poetry, vol. 1, 1987, vol. 2, 1994, W.B. Yeats: Letters to the New Island, 1990, Representing Modernist Texts, 1991, Palimpsest: Editorial Theory in the Humanities, 1993, W.B. Yeats: Under the Moon, the Unpublished Early Poetry, 1995, Contemporary German Editorial Theory, 1995, The Iconic Page in Manuscript, Print, and Digital Culture, 1998. Cubmaster Wolverine council Boy Scouts Am., 1977-79. Recipient good teaching award Amoco Found., 1983, Warner Rice prize for rsch. in humanities, 1988, Rosenthal award for Yeats studies W.B. Yeats Soc., 2000; fellow Am. Coun. Learned Soc., 1972-73, NEH fellow, 1982-83, fellow Old Dominion Found., 1968, fellow Guggenheim Found., 1986-87. Mem. MLA (exec. com. Anglo-Irish 1976-80, exec. com. 20th Century English 1980-85, exec. com. Poetry 1987-92, exec. com. bibliography and textual studies 1993-98, exec. com. methods of rsch. 1998-2003), Soc. Textual Scholarship (program chair 1997, exec. com. 1998-), Am. Conf. on Irish Studies (book prize judge 1991), Racquet Club, Princeton Club (N.Y.C.), Phi Beta Kappa. Home: 2020 Vinewood Blvd Ann Arbor MI 48104-3614 Office: U Mich Dept English Ann Arbor MI 48109-1003 Business E-Mail: georgeb@umich.edu.

BORNSTEIN, LESTER MILTON, retired health facility administrator; b. Boston, Feb. 19, 1925; s. Harry and Celia (Adlestein) B.; m. Marilyn Goldstein, Aug. 22, 1948; children: Aura Lynne, Michael Scott, Karen Jane. BS, Boston U., 1948; M.P.H. in Hosp. Adminstrn, Yale U., 1955. Adminstrv. resident Charles S. Wilson Meml. Hosp., Johnson City, N.Y., 1953-54; asst. dir. Barnert Meml. Hosp., Paterson, N.J., 1954-57, Newark Beth Israel Hosp., 1957-68; pres. Newark Beth Israel Med. Center, Newark, 1968-96. Served with AUS, 1943-45, ETO; to maj., Korean War 1950-53. Decorated Bronze Stars. Fellow Am. Coll. Hosp. Adminstrs., N.J. Hosp. Assn. (chmn. bd. trustees 1978-79) Home: 6 Aherne Way West Orange NJ 07052-2102 Personal E-mail: lestb@aol.com.

BORNSTEIN, MORRIS, economist, educator; b. Detroit, Sept. 4, 1927; m. Reva Rice, Apr. 7, 1962; children— Susan, Jane. AB, U. Mich., 1947, A.M., 1948, PhD, 1952. Economist U.S. Govt., 1951-52, 55-58; mem. faculty U. Mich., Ann Arbor, 1958—, prof. econs., 1964—, dir. Center Russian and E. European Studies, 1966-69. Assoc. Harvard U. Russian Rsch. Ctr., 1962-63; vis. rsch. fellow Hoover Instn., Stanford, 1969-70; cons. in field, 1959—; mem. joint com. on Eastern Europe Am. Coun. Learned Socs.-Social Sci. Rsch. Coun., 1977-80. Author: Soviet National Accounts for 1955, 1961, The Soviet Economy, 1962, 4th edit., 1974, Comparative Economic Systems, 1965, 7th edit., 1994, Economia di Mercato ed Economia Pianificata, 1973, Sistemas economicos comparados, 1973, Plan and Market, 1975, Chinese transl., 1980, The Soviet Economy: Continuity and Change, 1981, East-West Relations and the Future of Eastern Europe, 1981, The Transfer of Western Technology to the USSR, 1985, French transl., 1985, contbr. articles to profl. jours.; mem. editorial bd. Jour. Comparative Econs., 1986-88, Problems of Economic Transition, 1987-97, Soviet Economy and Post Soviet Affairs, 1988-2003, Economic Policy in Transitional Economies, 1994—, Communist Economies and Econ. Transformation, 1997-98, Post-Soviet Geography and Econs., 1997-98, Post-Communist Economies, 1999—. With U.S. Army, 1953-55. Ford Found. faculty fellow, 1962-63, Sr. Fgn. Rsch. fellow French Ministry Rsch. and Tech., 1991. Mem. Am. Econ. Assn., Assn. Comparative Econ. Studies (exec. com. 1965-67, 73-75). Office: U Mich Dept Econs Ann Arbor MI 48109-1220

BORNSTEIN, PAUL, medical educator, biochemist; b. Antwerp, Belgium, July 10, 1934; came to U.S., 1947, naturalized, 1952; s. Abraham and Mina (Ginsburg) B. BA, Cornell U., 1954; MD, NYU, 1958. Intern in surgery Yale-New Haven Hosp., 1958-59, intern in medicine, 1959-60, asst. resident in medicine, 1960-62; sr. fellow Arthritis Found. Pasteur Inst., Paris, 1962-63; rsch. assoc. NIH, Bethesda, Md., 1963-65, rsch. investigator, 1965-67; asst. prof. biochemistry and medicine U. Wash., 1967-69, assoc. prof., 1969-73, prof., 1973—, attending physician, 1968—. Mem. editl. bd. Jour. Biol. Chemistry, 1972-78, 80-85, Jour. Cell Biology, 1988-91, 94-97, Matrix Biology, 1993—; assoc. editor Arteriosclerosis, 1980-90, Collagen Related Rsch., 1981-88; contbr. articles to profl. jours. Served to sr. surgeon USPHS, 1963-67. Recipient Lederle Med. Faculty award USPHS, 1968, Rsch. Career Devel. award NIH, 1969, Macy Faculty Scholar award, 1975, Merit award NIH, 1989, Solomon Berson Alumni Achievement award NYU, 2004; Guggenheim fellow, 1985. Mem.: Internat. Soc. Matrix Biology (pres. 2001—03), Am. Soc. Matrix Biology (v.p. 2001—02, pres. 2002—03), Assn. Am. Physicians, Western Soc. Clin. Rsch., Am. Soc. Biol. Chemistry, Am. Soc. Clin. Investigation. Home: 602 34th Ave E Seattle WA 98112-4306 Office: U Wash Sch Medicine Dept Biochemistry PO Box 357350 Seattle WA 98195-7350 Office Phone: 206-543-1789. Business E-Mail: bornsten@u.washington.edu.

BORNSTEIN, STEVEN M., broadcast executive; b. Fair Lawn, N.J., Apr. 20, 1952; BS, U. Wis., 1974. Mgr. program coordination ESPN, Inc., Bristol, Conn., 1980—81, dir. program planning and qcauisitions, 1981, dir. programming, 1981—83, v.p. programming, 1983—85, sr. v.p. programming and prodn., 1985—88, exec. v.p. programming and prodn., 1988—90, pres., CEO, 1990—98, also bd. dirs.; pres. ABC Sports, N.Y.C., ABC Inc., Go.com. Mem.: Cable TV Advt. Bur., European Sports Network (dir. Lafayette Beveer bd.), Nat. Acad. Cable Programming (bd. govs.). Office: ABC Corp 77 W 66th St Fl 16 New York NY 10023-6201*

BOROCHOFF, IDA SLOAN, artist; b. July 29, 1922; d. Louis and Eva (Bistrick) Sloan; m. Charles Zachary Borochoff, Jan 11, 1942 (dec. July, 1990); children: Lynn Borochoff Gould, Jean Sue Borochoff Shapiro, Toby Ann Borochoff Bernstein, Lance Mark. Student, U. Ga., 1939-40, Ga. State U., 1940, Chgo. Sch. Interior Decorating, 1966, Allegro Sch. Ballet, Chgo., Atlanta Ballet, 1948-54, Emory U., 1971-72. Investor, owner real estate, 1941—; v.p. Designs Unltd., Inc., Atlanta, 1964—; pres. Sloan Borochoff Gallery, Atlanta, 1970—; art lectr. Met. Ednl. Svc.; art tchr. Ga. Inst. Tech., 1991. Prodr. live talk health show on cable TV, Atlanta, 1983-87. One woman shows include Lovett Sch., 1972, 75, Ga. Inst. Tech., 1972, 75, Atlanta Mdse. Mart, Saginaw Art Mus., 1998-99; group shows include Gwinnett Art Mus., Duluth, Ga., 1999, Ind. U., 1999, Purdue U., Indpls., 1999; art rev. columnist Northside Neighbor Newspapers; columnist Around Ga. with Ida. Bd. dirs. Atlanta Ballet, 1950-57; bd. dirs. Atlanta Music Club, co-editor newsletter; hostess Atlanta Arts Festival; capt. Heart Fund, 1968-76, area chmn. dr.; elected to bd. dirs. Am. Cancer Rsch. Ctr. Atlanta chpt.; active various multi-media groups; artistic dir. Atlanta Playhouse Theatre, chmn., trustee; artistic dir. Little Miss Ga. Pageant, Little Mr. Dogwood Festival Pageant; judge 17th Internat. Dogwood Festival Art Show, 1989; mem. U.S. cong. adv. bd. Am. Security Coun., 1983—; archivist nat. oral history nat. Coun. Jewish Women, 1990—; Ga. dir., chairperson Levi Hosp. Art Auction, Hot Springs, Ark., 1993-94; with Archives Exhibit Atlanta Jewish Fedn., 1994; donor Borochoff Libr. of A.A. Synagogue; com. mem., patron AJCC Book Festival, 1995-96. Recipient several art awards including Caber award, 1984; named hon. alumnus Atlanta Art Inst., 1968, One of Ten Leading Ladies of Atlanta, J.C. Singles, 19876, honored by Barbara Bush, White House, Washington, 1989, 90; City grantee, 1985. Mem. Atlanta Press Club, Atlanta Writers Club (membership com.), Atlanta Artists Club, Atlanta Women's C. of C. (chmn. fine arts 1977-78), LVW, High Mus. Art, Ga. Writers Assn., Arts High Mus. (patron), Corcoran Gallery (patron), Nat. Mus. Women in Arts (charter mem.), Internat. Platform Assn., B'nai B'rith Women (pres. chpt. 1975, mem. S.E. regional bd.), Ga. Hist. Soc., AAUW, Women in the Arts, Jockey Club, Progressive Club, Capitol Hill Club (Washington). Home: 3450 Old Plantation Rd NW Atlanta GA 30327-2426 Office: 733 Glendale Rd Scottdale GA 30079-1409

BORODYANSKAYA, YULIA M., publishing executive, consultant; b. St. Petersburg, Russia, Apr. 18, 1974; d. Mikhail P. Belzer and Olga M. Borodyanskaya; m. Roman G. Gutkovich, Sept. 23, 2002. BA in English, U. N.C., 1996. Sub rights asst. Douhleday BDD Inc., N.Y.C., 1996—98; sub rights assoc. Doubleday/Random Ho., 1998—2000; acct. exec. Rightscenter.com, 2000—01; mgr. subsidiary rights Newmarket Press, 2001—03; dir. subsidiary rights Avalon Pub. Group, 2003—. Cons. in field. Mem.: Phi Beta Kappa. Avocations: reading, skiing, travel. Office: Avalon Pub Group Inc 245 W 17th St 11th Fl New York NY 10011 Business E-Mail: yuliab@avalonpub.com.

BOROFF, HENRY JACK, federal judge, educator; b. Boston, May 31, 1951; AB magna cum laude, Boston U., 1972, JD, 1975. Bar: Mass. 1975, U.S. Dist. Ct. Mass. 1976, U.S. Ct. Appeals (1st cir.) 1979, U.S. Supreme Ct. 1987. With Friedman & Atherton, Boston, 1976-81; pvt. practice Boroff & Assocs., 1981—93; bankruptcy judge for Mass., U.S. Bankruptcy Ct., Worcester and Springfield, 1993—. Adj. prof. Western New Eng. Law Sch., 1996—, Northeastern U. Law Sch., 1998—2000; lectr. in field. Mem.: Hampden County Bar Assn., Mass. Bar Assn., Boston Bar Assn. (chair bankruptcy com. 1987—90). Office: US Bankruptcy Ct Donohue Fed Bldg 595 Main St Worcester MA 01608-2093

BORONICO, JESS STEPHEN, management science educator, dean; b. Bronx, N.Y., Oct. 23, 1956; s. Stelio and Helen (Michaels) B. BS in Math., Fairleigh Dickinson U., 1978, MS in Math., 1980; PhD in Ops. Rsch., U. Pa., 1992. Cert. AACSB Accreditation 2005. Prof. mgmt. scis. Rutgers U., Camden, N.J., 1987-88, Phila. Coll. Textiles and Scis., 1988-92, Monmouth U., West Long Branch, 1993—2001, assoc. dean Sch. Bus., 1998-2000, dean Sch. Bus., 2000-01; prof. mgmt. scis., dean Cotsakis Coll. Bus., William Paterson U., Wayne, NJ, 2001—. Cons. United Postal Svc., 1990-92, Reality Techs., 1991, N.J. Hwy. Authority, 1991-92, Kennedy Western U., Calif., 1994-97; mem. adv. bd. to various jours., 1993—. Author: Computer Simulation in Operations Management, 1996; contbg. author: The Service Productivity and Quality Challenge, 1995; editor: Studies in the Strategy and Tactics of Competitive Advantage, 2000; contbr. articles to profl. jours. Fellow U. Pa. Wharton Sch., 1983-87; recipient three Anbar citations of excellence for refereed publs., 1996-98. Mem. Inst. for Ops. Rsch. and Mgmt. Scis., Decision Scis. Inst., Am. Statis. Assn., Mensa. Avocations: softball, computer simulations. Office: Cotsakos Coll of Bus William Paterson U 1600 Valley Rd Wayne NJ 07470 E-mail: jboronic@monmouth.edu.

BOROS, JEROME S., lawyer; b. N.Y.C., Apr. 28, 1926; s. Edwin N. Boros and Margaret G. Guttman; m. Elayne N. Nossiter, Nov. 23, 1969; stepchildren: Richard, Ronald, Jill LeVine. AB, Syracuse U., 1947, MA, LLB, Syracuse U., 1950; LLM, Yale U., 1951. Bar: N.Y. 1950, D.C. Bar 1966, U.S. Dist. Ct. (so. dist.) N.Y. 1950, U.S. Ct. Appeals (D.C. cir.) 1966. Atty. CAB, Washington, 1950-53, FCC, Washington, 1953-55; assoc. Fly, Shuebruk, Gaguine, Boros & Braun, N.Y.C., Washington, 1955-62, ptnr., 1962-88, Rosenman & Colin, N.Y.C., 1988—96; of counsel Robinson, Silverman, Pearce, Aaronsohn & Berman, N.Y.C., 1996—2002; chmn. telecomm. group, of counsel Bryan Cave, 2002—. Faculty sch. speech Syracuse U., 1947; adj. prof. law NYU Sch. Law, 1971-95; chmn. Workshop on Broadcasting Practising Law Inst., 1969, lectr., 1969-76; gen. counsel Internat. Radio and TV Soc., N.Y.C., 1973-93, sec., 1973-93, gov., 1973-93; dir. Yale Law Sch. Fund, 1979-85. Acting village justice Village of Sands Point, N.Y., 1988-2000, village justice 2000—; chmn. Sands Point Cable Com., 1993—. With U.S. Army, 1944-45. Mem. City Athletic Club (gov., chmn. legal legis. com. 1959-02), Harmonie Club, 2002—. Republican. Jewish. Office: Bryan Cave 1290 Ave of Americas New York NY 10104-0199 Office Phone: 212-541-1072.

BOROVICKA, MARSHA LORRAINE, music educator; b. Ls Vegas, Nev., July 21, 1951; d. Arlo Fielding and Carrie Graff Beatty; m. Robert L. Borovicka. BA, U. Nev., 1973, MEd, 1979. Music tchr. CCSD/Jo Mackey Elem. Sch., La Vegas, Nev., 1973—75; dir. choral activities CCSD/Basic H.S., Henderson, Nev., 1975—82, CCSD/Cannon Mid. Sch., Las Vegas, Nev., 1983—85, Clark County Sch. Dist./Chaparral H.S., Las Vegas, Nev., 1985—. Choral dir. LDS Ch., Las Vegas, Nev., 1971. Musician (conductor) various choral groups. Named Tchr. of the Yr., Clark County Sch. Dist./Southland Corp., 1991. Mem. Lds Ch. Avocation: golf. Office: Chaparral HS 3850 Annie Oakley Dr Las Vegas NV 89121 Office Phone: 702-799-7580 ext. 4050. Personal E-mail: mlh554@interact.ccsd.net.

BOROWIEC, ANDREW, art educator, photographer; BA in Russian, Haverford Coll., 1979; MFA in Photography, Yale U., 1982. Instr. Parsons Sch. Design, Paris, 1980-82, 83-84; tchr. photography and art Germantown Acad., Ft. Washington, Pa., 1982-83; instr. New Sch. Social Rsch., N.Y.C., 1982-84; instr. fashion photography Lab. Inst. Merchandising, N.Y.C., 1984; dir. Sch. Art U. Akron, Ohio, 1990-95, prof. art Mary Schiller Myers Sch. Art, 1995—. Guest lectr. contemporary Am. photography U. d'Aix-Marseille, France; vis. assoc. prof. art history Oberlin (Ohio) Coll., 1990. One-man shows include Club House, UN, Geneva, 1978, Galerie Un Moment En Plus, Paris, 1981, Le Poisson Banane, Arles, France, 1981, Galerie Les Arcenaulx, Marseille, France, 1982, Radnor Gallery, Bryn Mawr Coll., Pa., 1983, Perkins Gallery, U. Akron, 1984, Midtown Y Photography Gallery, N.Y.C., 1984, Dishman Gallery, Lamar U., Beaumont, Tex., 1986, Vox Gallery, Akron, 1988, Rose Gallery, St. Edwards U., Austin, Tex., 1988, Dillingham Gallery, Ithaca (N.Y.) Coll., 1988, Exit Gallery, Reno, 1988, Canton (Ohio) Art Inst., 1989, Fla. Internat. U., North Miami, Fla., 1990, Coll. Wooster (Ohio) Art Mus., 1991, Blue Sky Gallery, Portland, Oreg., 1994, Soc. Contemporary Photography, Kansas City, Mo., 1995, 99, Regis U., Denver, 1996, O.K. Harris, N.Y.C., 1997, So. Light Gallery, Amarillo, Tex., 1999, The Print Ctr., Phila., Pa., numerous others; exhibited in group shows at Images Gallery, Cin., 1991, Ea. Mich. U., Ypsilanti, 1992, Photospiva 93, Joplin, Mo., 1993, Contemporary Artists Ctr., North Adams, Mass., 1994, U. Cin., 1995, Blue Sky Gallery, Portland, 1996, Open Space Gallery, Allentown, Pa., 1997, Cleve. Mus. Art, 1998, Silver Eye Ctr. for Photography, Pitts., 2002, numerous others; represented in permanent collections Akron Art Mus., Can. Ctr. Arch., N.Y.C., Montreal, Can., Canton Art Inst., Chgo. Art Inst., Midtown Y. Photography Gallery, N.Y.C., Yale U., New Haven, Smithsonian Am. Art Mus., Cleve. Mus. Art, Libr. Congress, Ctr. for Documentary Studies, Houston Mus. Fine Arts, Hallmark Colection, others; books: Along the Ohio, 2000; staff photographer Internat. Ctr. Photography, N.Y.C., 1979-80; freelance photography The Chronicle for Higher Edn., 1987-93; commn. by Nat. Trust Historic Preservation and Soc. Photographic Edn., 1987, Canton Art Inst., 1988-89; contbr. photography to numerous publs. Recipient Excellence award Kansas City Art Inst., 1987, Hon. Mention and Purchase award Cleve. Mus. Art, 1988, Third prize N.Mex. Photographer, 1994, Purchase prize Nat. Mus. Am. Art, 1996, Fellowship award Soc. Contemporary Photography, 1998; Nat. Endowment Arts/Arts Midwest Photography fellow, 1985; Summer Rsch. fellow U. Akron, 1988, 90, 97, 2000; Individual Artist fellow Ohio Arts Coun., 1988, 98; John Simon Guggenheim Meml. Found. fellow, 1998; Faculty Rsch. grantee U. Akron, 1986; Instl. Support grantee Ohio Arts Coun., 1988; Visual Artists Forums grantee Nat. Endowment Arts, 1988; Folk Endowment grantee U. Akron Sch. Art, 1993; Folk Endowment grantee U. Akron Mary Schiller Myers Sch. Art, 1998. Address: 1062 W Market St Akron OH 44313-7128 Fax: (330) 972-5960. E-mail: borowiec@uakron.edu.

BOROWIEC, WILLIAM MATTHEW, lawyer; b. Sierra Vista, Ariz., Dec. 21, 1962; s. Matthew William and Margaret Lynn Borowiec. BA, U. Ariz., 1987; JD, Hamline U., 1989. Bar: Ariz. 1991, U.S. Dist. Ct. Ariz. 1995. Atty. Blaser & Assocs., Tucson, 1991-93, Monroe & Assocs., Tucson, 1993, Felix & Holohan, Tucson, 1993-97; mng. ptnr. Borowiec & Borowiec, PC, Sierra Vista, Ariz., 1997—. Com. mem. Forgach House Charity Tennis Tournament, Sierra Vista. Mem. ABA, Ariz. Trial Lawyers Assn. Avocations: golf, tennis, hunting, fishing. Office: Borowiec and Borowiec 4226 Avenida Cochise Suite 5 Sierra Vista AZ 85635-2828

BOROWIK, ANN, writer; b. Providence, R.I., July 4, 1928; d. Albert de Russy and Edina (Davis) Baker; m. Val Coleman (div. 1965); m. Tom Borowik; children: Karen Borowik, Charles Coleman. Author: How Many Miles to Babylon, 1963, Lions 3: Christians, 1965, The Lottery Chronicles, 1996. Home: 310 Greenwich St Apt 3J New York NY 10013-2709

BOROWITZ, ALBERT IRA, lawyer, writer; b. Chgo., June 27, 1930; s. David and Anne (Wolkenstein) B.; m. Helen Blanche Osterman, July 29, 1950; children: Peter Leonard, Joan, Andrew Seth. BA in Classics summa cum laude, Harvard U., 1951, MA in Chinese Regional Studies, 1953, JD magna cum laude, 1956. Bar: Ohio 1957. Assoc. firm Hahn, Loeser, Freedheim, Dean & Wellman, Cleve., 1956-62, ptnr., 1962-83; ptnr. firm Jones, Day, Reavis & Pogue, Cleve., 1983-90, of counsel, 1991-94; cons., 1994—99. Author: Fiction in Communist China, 1954, Innocence and Arsenic: Studies in Crime and Literature, 1977, The Woman who Murdered Black Satin: The Bermondsey Horror, 1981, A Gallery of Sinister Perspectives: Ten Crimes and a Scandal, 1982, The Jack the Ripper Walking Tour Murder, 1986, The Thurtell-Hunt Murder Case: Dark Mirror to Regency England, 1987, This Club Frowns on Murder, 1990, Jones, Day, Reavis &

Pogue: The First Century, 1993, Unhappy Endings, 2001, Blood and Ink: An International Guide to Fact-Based Crime Literature, 2002, Terrorism for Self-Glorification: The Herostratos Syndrome, 2005, (novels) The Herostratas Syndrome, 2005, Crimes Gone By: Collected Essays of Albert Borowitz, 2005; author: (with H.O. Borowitz) Pawnshop and Palaces: The Fall and Rise of the Campana Art Museum, 1991; series editor: True Crime, Kent State Univ. Press. Hon. consul of France in Cleve., 1990-95; v.p. French-Am. C. of C. of No. Ohio, 1993-99; co-founder Borowitz True Crime Collection at Kent State U. Librs. Recipient Cleve. arts prize for lit., 1981, Gold prize for true crime Foreword Mag., 2002. Mem. Am. Law Inst., Rowfant Club (Cleve.), Union Club (Cleve.), Harvard Club (N.Y.C.), Vidocq Soc. Phila. (hon.). E-mail: alborowitz@adelphia.net.

BOROWITZ, JOSEPH LEO, pharmacologist, educator; b. Columbus, Ohio, Dec. 19, 1932; s. Joseph Peter and Anna Louise (Grundei) B.; divorced, 1985; children: Jon Joseph, Peter Joseph, Lynn Anne. BS in Pharmacy, Ohio State U., 1955; MS in Pharmacology, Purdue U., 1957; PhD in Pharmacology (NIH fellow), Northwestern U., 1960. Chief biokinetics br. Sch. Aerospace Medicine, San Antonio, 1960—62; postdoctoral fellow dept. pharmacology Harvard U. Med. Sch., Boston, 1963—64; instr., then asst. prof. pharmacology Wake Forest U. Sch. Medicine, 1964—69; assoc. prof. pharmacology and toxicology Purdue U., 1969—74, prof., 1974—; sabbatical leave to Basel, Switzerland, 1984; vis. prof. sch. pharmacy U. P.R., 2001; sabbatical leave to Cambridge, England, 1976. Contbr. articles to profl. jours. Treas. Tippecanoe County (Ind.) Comprehensive Health Planning Coun., 1971-76. Capt. USAR, 1960. Recipient award for excellence in teaching Bowman Gray Sch. Medicine, 1969, Henry Heine award for excellence in teaching Purdue U. Coll. Pharmacy, 1983; named NIH postdoctoral fellow, 1962-64; grantee NSF, 1965-68, NIH, 1971-74, 86-89, 89-94, 94-98, 1999-2004, 2004—. U.S. Army Med. Rsch., 1989-96, 97-2000. Mem.: Rho Chi. Roman Catholic. Office: Purdue U Dept Med Chem and Molec Pharmacology West Lafayette IN 47907 Business E-Mail: borowitz@pharmacy.purdue.edu.

BOROWITZ, SIDNEY, retired physics professor; b. N.Y.C., June 12, 1918; s. Morris and Rose (Cohen) B.; m. Ruth Aaron Meyer, June 20, 1943; children: Michael, Elizabeth. BS, CCNY, 1937; MS, NYU, 1941, PhD, 1948. Physicist David Taylor Model Basin, 1942-43; indsl. engr. Western Electric Co., 1943-45; instr. NYU, N.Y.C., 1946-48, asst. prof., 1950-55, assoc. prof., 1955-59, prof. physics, 1959-84, prof. emeritus, 1984—, dean, 1969-71, chancellor, 1971-77; instr. Harvard U., Cambridge, Mass., 1948-50; chief exec. officer Cistron Biotech., Pine Brook, N.J., 1981-84. Chmn. bd. dirs. Aesculapius Internat. Medicine, N.Y.C., 1987-90, Inst. for Sch. of the Future, N.Y.C., 1987—; cons. NYU, 1987-97; exec. dir. N.Y. Acad. Scis., N.Y.C., 1977-81; mem. investment adv. com. Am. Inst. Physics, 1992-97. Author: Fundamentals of Quantum Mechanics, 1967, Farewell Fossil Fuels, 1998; co-author: Essentials of Physics, 1966, A Contemporary View of Elementary Physics, 1968, Farewell Fossil Fuels, 1999. Avocation: squash. Home: 70 E 10th St New York NY 10003-5102 Office: NYU Physics Dept Washington Sq N New York NY 10003 Office Phone: 212-998-7760. Business E-Mail: sb8@nyu.edu.

BOROWSKY, PHILIP, lawyer; b. Phila., Oct. 9, 1946; s. Joshua and Gertrude (Nicholson) B.; m. Judith Lee Goldwasser, Sept. 5, 1970 (div. 1996); children: Miriam Isadora, Manuel, Nora Jo; m. Victoria Culko Smith, Oct. 17, 2004. BA, UCLA, 1967; JD, U. San Francisco, 1973. Bar: Calif. Pres. and mng. ptnr. Cartwright, Slobodin, Bokelman, Borowsky, Wartnick, Moore & Harris, San Francisco, 1987-95; pres. Law Offices Philip Borowsky, Inc., San Francisco, 1996—2002; mng. ptnr. Borowsky & Hayes LLP, San Francisco, 2002—. Mem. faculty Practicing Law Inst., N.Y.C., 1983-84; mem. adj. faculty Hastings Coll. Law, San Francisco, 1982-83; arbitrator Superior Ct., San Francisco, 1982—, Am. Arbitration Assn., 1982—, Nat. Assn. Securities Dealers, 1994—2003. Co-author: Unjust Dismissal and At-Will Employment, 1985; mem. bd. editl. cons. Bad Faith Law Update, 1986—2004. With U.S. Army, 1968—70, Vietnam. Mem.: Consumer Attys. Calif. Democrat. Office: 1 Market Plz San Francisco CA 94105-1420 Office Phone: 415-896-6800. E-mail: philip.borowsky@borowsky.com.

BORRAYO, EVELINN A., psychologist, educator; b. Guatemala City, Guatemala, Apr. 21, 1971; d. Juan A. Borrayo and Elizabeth (Reyes) de Borrayo. BS, U. Ozarks, 1993; MA, U. North Tex., 1997, PhD, 1999. Psychology intern U. South Fla., Tampa, 1998—99; rsch. assoc. Fla. Policy Exch. Ctr. on Aging, U. South Fla., Tampa, 1999—; asst. prof. psychology Colo. State U., Ft. Collins, 1999—. Mem. Nat. Surg. Adjuvant Breast and Bowel Projects Cancer Control Com., 2003. Editor (with W. Timpson, S.S. Canetto and R. Yang): Teaching Diversity: Challenges and Complexities, Identities and Integrity, 2003; prodr.: (video) Where's Maria?. Recipient award, AAUW Ednl. Found., 2003. Mem.: APA. Avocations: outdoor activities, aerobics, running, bicycling. Office: Colo State U 200 W Lake St Fort Collins CO 80523 Office Phone: 970-491-7324. Business E-Mail: borrayo@lamar.colostate.edu.

BORRECA, JOHN PETER, building materials manufacturing executive; b. N.Y.C., May 1, 1953; s. John Benedict and Ellen Loretta (McElroy) B.; m. Francine Kathleen Manetz, Apr. 24, 1976; children: Jason John, Michael Christopher. Student, CUNY, 1971-73; BA, U. South Fla., 1975. CPA, N.J. Sr. acct. The Celotex Corp., Tampa, Fla., 1975-77, plant controller Texarkana, Ark., 1978-80, mgr. ops. adminstrn. Tampa, 1982-83, dir. fin. acctg., 1983-85, v.p. fin., 1985-88; controller Insul-Coustic Div., Sayreville, N.J., 1980-82; v.p., chief fin. officer, treas. Jim Walter Corp., Tampa, 1988-90; sr. v.p., treas. and chief fin. officer The Celotex Corp., Tampa, Fla., 1990-97, pres., CEO, 1997—. Fellow N.J. Soc. CPAs, Inst. Mgmt. Accts.; mem. Fin. Execs. Inst. Democrat. Roman Catholic. Avocations: golf, swimming.

BORROFF, MARIE, English language educator; b. N.Y.C., Sept. 10, 1923; d. Albert Ramon and Marie (Bergersen) B. Ph.B., U. Chgo., 1943, MA, 1946; PhD, Yale U., 1956. Teaching asst. U. Chgo., 1946-47; instr. dept. English Smith Coll., 1948-51, asst. prof., 1956-59, asso. prof., 1959; vis. asst. prof. English Yale U., 1957-58, vis. asso. prof., 1959-6O, asso. prof. English, 1960-65, prof., 1965-71, William Lampson prof., 1971-92, Sterling prof. English, 1992-94; Sterling prof. English emeritus, 1994—; Phi Beta Kappa vis. scholar, 1973-74. Fellow Ezra Stiles Coll., Yale. Author: Sir Gawain and the Green Knight: A Stylistic and Metrical Study, 1962, (with J. B. Bessinger, Jr.); recorded dialogues read in Middle English, 1965, Sir Gawain and the Green Knight: A New Verse Translation, 1967, Pearl: A New Verse Translation, 1977, Language and the Poet: Verbal Artistry in Frost, Stevens, and Moore, 1979, Sir Gawain and the Green Knight, Patience and Pearl: Verse Translations, 2000, Stars and Other Signs: Poems, 2002; essay collection: Traditions and Rewewals Chaucer, the Gawain-Poet, and Beyond, 2003; editor: Wallace Stevens, A Collection of Critical Essays, 1963; videotaped lectures: To Hear Their Voices, Chaucer, Shakespeare and Frost, Assn. of Yale Alumni Great Tchrs. Series, Chapter Headings: Remarks Made at the Annual Initiation Ceremonies of Phi Beta Kappa, Alpha Chapter of Connecticut, 1989-1994, 1996. Bd. Govs. Yale U. Press, 1988-98. Recipient James Billings Fiske poetry prize U. Chgo., 1943; Eunice Tietjens Meml. prize Poetry mag., 1945; Margaret Lee Wiley fellow AAUW, 1955-56; Guggenheim fellow, 1969-70 Fellow Am. Acad. Arts and Scis.; mem. MLA, Acad. Am. Poets, Medieval Acad. Am., Phi Beta Kappa. Home: 31 St Ronan St New Haven CT 06511-2328 Office Phone: 203-432-2233. Business E-Mail: marie.borroff@yale.edu.

BORRONI-BIRD, CHRISTOPHER E., transportation engineer; PhD in Chemistry, Cambridge U., 1991. Post-doctoral fellowship U. Tokyo; joined Chrysler Corp., 1992; tech. mgmt. Daimler-Chrysler; dir., design and vehicle tech. interface General Motors Rsch. Lab., Warren, Mich., 2000—, dir, Hy-Wire program, lead engr., dir., Sequel (hydrogen fuel cell car). Office: General Motors Rsch Lab 30500 Mound Rd Warren MI 48090*

BORROR, DOUGLAS G., construction company executive; b. Dayton, Ohio, 1955; m. Kim Borror; children: Danielle, Donald. BA in History, Ohio State U., 1977. Lic. Real Estate Broker. With Huntington Nat. Bank, Columbus, 1977-79, Borror Corp. (now Borror Realty Co. Inc.), Dublin, Ohio, 1979—; pres. Dominion Homes, Inc., Dublin, Ohio, 1987—99, CEO, 1992—; chmn. bd. Dominion Homes, inc., Dublin, Ohio, 1999—. Bd. dir. Ohio Indemnity, Baninsurance Corp., 2004—, Columbia Gas of Ohio, Inc., Huntington Nat. Bank, Capital South Redevelopment Corp., Command Alkon Corp. Edn. chair Young President's Orgn., Columbus Chpt.; adv. bd. Goodwill Industries; bd. dir. Young President's Orgn., Internat., Wellington Sch., Recreation Unlimited; bd. trustee Ohio State U., 2004—; chmn. Columbus Riverfront Commons Corp.; bd. realtors Town of Columbus. Office: Dominion Homes Inc 5501 Frantz Rd Dublin OH 43017-7502

BORSARI, GEORGE ROBERT, JR., lawyer, commentator; b. Washington, July 30, 1940; s. George Robert and Sara Totton (Dunning) B.; m. Regis Ann Herron, Oct. 23, 1964 (div. Jan. 1985); children: George Robert, III, William Grant. BS, Va. Poly. Inst., 1962; LL.B., George Washington U., 1965. Bar: D.C. 1966. Since practiced in, Washington; ptnr. Borsari & Paxson, 1969—. Pres. Local TV Systems, Inc., 1981-89, Outdoor Inst., Inc., 1978—; chmn. Core Group Inc., 1991—. Councilman Town of Glen Echo, Md., 1969-74, mayor, 1977-81, 89-91; mem. Montgomery County (Md.) Muncipality Advisory Bd., 1972-74, Montgomery County CATV Task Force, 1973-74, 80-85, Cable TV Adv. Com., 1979-85; pres. Montgomery County chpt. Md. Mcpl. League. Served to lt. col. JAG USAR. Decorated Army Meritorious Service medal with oak leaf cluster, Army Commendation medal with 2 oak leaf clusters; recipient Presdl. commendation, 1970; St. George award Roman Catholic Archdiocese Washington, 1970; Silver Beaver award Nat. Capital Area council Boy Scouts Am., 1974 Mem. ABA (chmn. cable TV com. sect. sci. and tech. 1982-86, chmn. Broadcast Com. 1986-90, chmn. Mass Media Com. 1990-92, mem. coun. sect. sci. and tech.), D.C. Bar Assn., Fed. Comms. Bar Assn., Isaac Walton League, Kenwood Golf and Country Club (bd. govs. 2004—), Phi Delta Phi. Democrat. Home: 6107 Princeton Ave Glen Echo MD 20812-1125 Office: Borsari & Paxson 4000 Albemarle St NW Ste 100 Washington DC 20016

BORSON, SOO, geriatric psychiatrist, researcher, educator; b. San Francisco, May 4, 1942; BA, Stanford U., 1965, MD, 1969. Diplomate Am. Bd. Psychiatry and Neurology. Fellow in geriatric psychiatry U. Wash., Seattle, 1979-81, mem. faculty, 1981—, assoc. prof., 1987—. Mem. task force White House Conf. on Aging, 1981, 91. Contbr. articles to profl. publs., chpts. to books. Sec. Am. Assn. Geriatric Psychiatry, 1980-82. Fellow Gerontol. Soc. Am. (pub. policy com. 1981-83); mem. ACA (Borden award 1969, Sandoz award 1979, Dorfman award), Am. Psychiat. Assn. Office: U Wash PO Box 356560 Seattle WA 98195-6560

BORST, PHILIP WEST, academic administrator; b. Fullerton, Calif., Feb. 11, 1928; s. Richard Warner and Beatrice Ione (West) B.; m. Marguerite A. Bruns, Mar. 21, 1959; children— David, Kristin, Pamela; m. Barbara Paul, Oct. 24, 1998. AA, Fullerton Coll., 1947; BA, Stanford U., 1949, MA, 1950; postgrad., U. Calif., 1950-54; PhD (Sch. fellow), Claremont Grad. Sch., 1968. Tchr. history Carlmont High Sch., Belmont, Calif., 1954-57; asst. prof. polit. sci. and history Fullerton Coll., 1957-60, asso. prof., 1960-62, prof., 1962-67, asst. to pres., 1967-70, asst. dean instrn., 1970-72, asso. dean instrn., 1972-73, v.p. instrn., 1973-77, pres., 1977-94; retired, 1994. Mem. Assn. Calif. Community Coll. Adminstrs., Phi Delta Kappa. Democrat.

BORSTING, JACK RAYMOND, business administration educator; b. Portland, Oreg., Jan. 31, 1929; s. John S. and Ruth B.; m. Peggy Anne Nygard, Mar. 22, 1953; children: Lynn Carol, Eric Jeffrey. BA, Oreg. State U., 1951; MA, U. Oreg., 1952, PhD, 1959. Instr. math. Western Wash. Coll., 1953-54; teaching fellow U. Oreg., 1956-59; mem. faculty Naval Postgrad. Sch., 1959-80, prof. ops. research, chmn. dept., 1964-73, provost, acad. dean, 1974-80; asst. sec. def. (comptroller) Washington, 1980-83; dean Sch. Bus. U. Miami, Fla., 1983-88; Robert Dockson prof. and dean bus. adminstrn. U. So. Calif., Los Angeles, 1988-94; E. Morgan Stanley prof. bus. adminstrn. and exec. dir. Ctr. for Telecomms. Mgmt./U. So. Calif. Marshall Sch. Bus., Los Angeles, 1994—2001, prof., 2002—. Vis. prof. U. Colo. summers 1967, 69, 71; vis. disting. prof. Oreg. State U., summer 1968; bd. visitors Def. Sys. Mgmt. Coll., 1985-91, chmn., 1988-91; trustee Met Life Investor, 2000—, mem. adv. bd. Naval Postgrad. Sch., 1982-86, 98—; bd. overseers Ctr. Naval Analysis, 1984-94; trustee Aerospace Corp., 1986-92, Inst. Def. Analysis, 1990-2003; bd. advisors Elec. Power Rsch. Inst., 1999—; bd. govs., lead gov. Am. Stock Exch., 2005—. Contbr. to profl. jours. Trustee Orthop. Hosp. Found., L.A., 1992—, chmn., 1996-98, chmn. bd. dirs. 1999-2002; trustee Rose Hills Found. 1996—; gov. Town Hall of Calif., 1988-94; mem. Army Sci. Bd., 2002—. Recipient Disting. Pub. Service medal Dept. Def., 1980, 82, Disting. Svc. award Oreg. State U., 1982; disting. alumni fellow U. Oreg., 2004. Fellow AAAS, Mil. Ops. Rsch. Soc. (bd. dirs. 1965-72, pres. 1970-71), Internat. Engring. Consortium, Informs; mem. Army Sci. Bd., Inst. Mgmt. Sci., Am. Statis. Soc., Ops. Rsch. Soc. Am. (mem. coun. 1969-79, sec. 1972-74, pres. 1975-76, Kimball medal 1982, Koopmans award 2000), Internat. Fedn. Ops. Rsch. Socs. (treas. 1980-88), Calif. Club, 100 Club L.A., Sigma Xi, Pi Mu Epsilon, Beta Theta Pi. Episcopalian. Office: Marshall Sch Bus DCC 217 USC Los Angeles CA 90089-0871 Office Phone: 213-740-0980.

BORST-MANNING, DIANE GAIL, management consultant; b. Rochester, N.Y., Nov. 5, 1937; d. Howard Louis and Emily Kathleen (Crew) Borst; m. Steven Manning, Sept. 11, 1979 (dec. May 1991); m. Norman Edward Berg, Apr. 4, 1992. BA cum laude, Wagner Coll., 1959; MBA, NYU, 1966. Planner NYU Med. Ctr., N.Y.C., 1962-76, assoc. dir. planning, 1976-78, dir. mgmt. svcs., 1978-80; dir. human resources Mt. Sinai Med. Ctr., N.Y.C., 1980-85, dir. planning, 1985-86; sr. v.p. The Manning Orgn., Inc., 1986—; pres. Diane Borst Manning Assocs., Inc., 1986—. Instr. dept. health care mgmt. CUNY, 1982-92; adj. faculty Orange County C.C., 1986-88, Sarah Lawrence Coll., New Sch. Social Rsch., 1986—, St. Joseph's Coll., 1992—. Author: (cassette) Managers and Secretaries--How to Achieve Teamwork, 1980; editor: Managing Non-Profit Organizations, 1979, Regret to Inform You, 1999, My Carrier War, 2001. Chair grants Port Jervis Coun. for Arts; mem. Health Sys. Agy. Bd., N.Y.C., 1976-79; trustee Helene Fuld Sch. Nursing, N.Y.C., 1989—; mem. planning com. of bd. Mercy Cmty. Hosp., Port Jervis, N.Y.; mem. adv. bd. Inst. Bus. Industry and Govt. Orange County C.C. Fulbright fellow U.S. Govt., 1959. Mem. Am. Assn. Hosp. Planners, Assn. Am. Med. Colls. Group on Instnl. Planning, Am. Compensation Assn., Bur. Nat. Affairs (pers. policy forum 1983-84), N.Y. State Health Planning Soc., N.Y. Pers. Mgmt. Assn. (bd. dirs. 1974-76), Greater N.Y. Hosp. Assn., City Club. Avocations: gardening, auto mechanics, carpentry, real estate. Office: 40 W 55th St Apt 9D New York NY 10019-5376 E-mail: dianeborst@hotmail.com.

BORTER, JOHN PETER, retired minister; b. N.Y.C., Oct. 13, 1934; s. John and Frieda Marie (Auwaerter) Borter; m. Carol Jane Braymer, June 20, 1959; children: Linnea Elizabeth, Heidi Carol, John Theodore. BA, Maryville Coll., 1956; MDiv, Pitts. Theol. Sem., 1959. Pastor Terra Alta (W.Va.) Presbyn. Ch., 1958—60, Hanoverton (Ohio) Presbyn. Ch., 1960—64, Hillcrest Presbyn. Ch., Burgettstown, Pa., 1964—69, Slippery Rock Presbyn. Ch., Ellwood City, Pa., 1969—99; interim pastor Bessemer (Pa.) Presbyn. Ch., 2000—01, pastor emeritus, 2001—; stated supply pastor Mt. Hermon Presbyn. Ch., New Castle, Pa., 2001—. Bd. dirs. Almira Found., New Castle, People-in-Need, New Castle. Bd. dirs. Ellwood City (Pa.) Sch. Dist., 1977—81. Mem.: Rotary Club of Ellwood City (pres.-sec., Paul Harris fellow 1998). Republican. Presbyterian. Avocations: reading, gardening, travel. Home: 704 Argonne Blvd Ellwood City PA 16117-1350

BORTMAN, DAVID, lawyer; b. Detroit, Sept. 17, 1938; s. Erwin Arne and Miriam Elaine (Shapiro) B. BA, U. Mich., 1962, JD, 1965. Bar: Mich. 1965, Ill. 1971. Asst. prosecutor Wayne County, Detroit, 1965-71; staff atty. Fed. Defender, Chgo., 1971-73; trial atty. SEC, Chgo., 1974-77; sole practice Chgo., 1977-79; ptnr. Bortman, Meyer & Barasa, Chgo., 1980-90; pvt. practice L.A., 1990—. Mem. Fed. Ct. Jury Instrns. Com., Chgo., 1984—85; mem. adv. bd. Air Force Office of Pub. Affairs. Chmn. telethon com. Muscular Dystrophy Assn., Chgo., 1984; pres. Met. Chgo. Air Force Comty. Coun., 1985-88; mem. World Affairs Coun. Mem. ABA, ATLA, Acad. of TV Arts and Scis., State Bar Calif., Los Angeles County Bar Assn. (mem. lawyer referral com.), Beverly Hills Bar Assn. (entertainment law steering com.), Fed. Bar Assn. (bd. dirs. Chgo. chpt. 1985-90), Rotary, U. Mich. Club of L.A., U. Mich. Club of Chgo. (bd. govs. 1987-89), Union League of Chgo. (bd. dirs. 1986-89), Variety Club Children's Charities, Jonathan Club, Thalians Charity, West L.A. C. of C. (bd. dirs.), Century City C. of C. (bd. dirs., co-chmn. Entertainment Industry Coun.). Jewish. Home: 11908 Dorothy St Apt 102 Los Angeles CA 90049-5330 Office: 433 N Camden Dr #600 Beverly Hills CA 90210 Office Phone: 310-288-1980. Personal E-mail: davesq@earthlink.net.

BORTNICK, NEWMAN M(AYER), research chemist; b. May 14, 1921; s. Louis Benjamin and Emily Rosa (Roberts) B.; m. Lillian Ulanove, Aug. 29, 1943; children: Karl, Lynn, Wendy. BA magna cum laude, U. Minn., 1941; PhD in Organic Chemistry, 1944. Rsch. chemist Rohm and Haas Co., Phila., 1944—, head high pressure lab., 1959-66, rsch. supr. plastics, 1966-73, mgr., dir. exploratory process rsch., 1973-81, mgr. plastics rsch. dept., 1982-84, corp. rsch. fellow, 1984-90, cons., 1991—. Holder more than 100 patents in organic chemistry, polymers; contbr. articles to numerous profl. jours. Mem. Planning Comm. Springfield Twp., Pa., 1956-66; mem., pres. Bd. Sch. Dirs., Springfield Twp., 1966-73; v.p. intermediate unit 23 Montgomery County Bd. Sch. Dirs., 1971-73; bd. dirs. Carson Valley Sch., Springfield Twp., 1973—, ServiceNet, Inc., 1996—. Recipient Outstanding Achievement award U. Minn., 2000. Fellow AAAS, Am. Inst. Chemists, Royal Soc. Chemistry U.K.; mem. Am. Chem. Soc. (dir.-at-large 1983-88), Phila. Sect. Am. Chem. Soc. (chmn. 1967, councilor 1968-82, 90-99, Rsch. award 1964, Svc. award 1973), Soc. Plastics Engrs., Phi Beta Kappa, Sigma Xi, Phi Lambda Upsilon. Home: 509 Oreland Mill Rd Oreland PA 19075-2238 Office: Rohm and Haas Co PO Box 219 Bristol PA 19007-0219 E-mail: rsnrnmb@rohmhaas.com, newm2@aol.com.

BORTOLOT, GARY, writer, educator; b. Norwalk, Conn., Jan. 12, 1951; s. Richard V and Victoria P Bortolot. BA, Providence Coll., Providence, RI, 1973; MA, U. Bridgeport, Bridgeport,CT, 1977. Dir. GWB Enterprises, Norwalk, Conn., 1995—; instr. Gibbs Coll., Norwalk, Conn., 2000—; actor, 1985—95. Bd. dirs. Norwalk Cmty. Health Ctr. Mem.: Affiliated Writing Programs, MLA. Home: 501 Westport Ave Apt 294 Norwalk CT 06851

BORTON, GEORGE ROBERT, retired airline captain; b. Wichita Falls, Tex., Mar. 22, 1921; s. George Neat and Travis Lee (Jones) B.; m. Anne Louise Bowling, Feb. 5, 1944 (dec.); children: Trudie T., Robert B., Bruce M. AA, Hardin Coll., Wichita Falls, 1940. Cert. airline transport pilot, FAA flight examiner. Flight sch. operator Vallejo (Calif.) Sky Harbor, 1947-48; capt. S.W. Airways, San Francisco, 1948-55; check capt. Pacific Airlines, San Francisco, 1955-68, Hughes Air West, San Francisco, 1968-71; capt. N.W. Airlines, Mpls., 1971-82, ret., 1982. Col. USAF, 1943-73, ret. Decorated Air medal. Mem.: Airline Pilots Assn., Air Force Assn., Res. Officers Assn., Model T Club-Phoenix, Model T of Am. Club, Horseless Carriage Club. Republican. Home: Pebble Creek Resort 4053 N 162nd Ave Goodyear AZ 85338

BORTON, JOHN CARTER, JR., (TERRY BORTON), theatrical producer; b. Washington, Aug. 25, 1938; s. John Carter and Mary (Newlin) B.; m. Deborah H. Borton, June 18, 1960; children: Lynn, Mark. BA, Amherst Coll., 1960; MA, U. Calif., Berkeley, 1962; EdD, Harvard U., 1970. Cert. gen. tchr., Calif. Asst. dir. vol. program Berkeley Unified Schs., 1962-63; tchr. English, co-chmn. dept. Richmond (Calif.) Union H.S., 1963-66; cons. Phila. Bd. Edn., 1966-67, acting dir. Office Affective Devel., 1970-71, dir. dual audio TV project, 1971-77; editorial dir. Xerox Edn. Publs., Middletown, Conn., 1977-80, editor in chief, 1980-86; v.p., editor in chief Field Publs. (formerly Xerox Edn. Publs.), Middletown, 1986-91, Weekly Reader Corp. (formerly Field Publs.), Middletown, 1991-92; prodr., lead performer Am. Magic Lantern Theater, 1992—. Lectr. U. Pa., Phila., 1971-76, Phila. Coll. Art, 1976-77; cons. various sch. systems, univ./colls., founds., profl. orgns., govt. agys., 1975-77. Author: Reach, Touch and Teach: Student Concerns and Process Education, 1970, Emotionales und Soziales Lernen in der Schule, 1976; also numerous articles in profl. jours., including Weekly Reader; performer 2 records and tchr.'s manuals introducing poetry to high sch. students; author 20 scripts for The Storyphone, 1976, 80 scripts for Dual Audio, Sta. WUHY-FM, 1972-73, 14 prodns. for Am. Magic Lantern Theater. Bd. dirs. Oddfellow's Theater. Mem. League Hist. Am. Theaters, N.E. Performing Arts Assn., Magic Lantern Soc., Assn. Performing Arts Presenters, Internat. Assn. Performing Arts Young People. Avocations: carpentry, sculpture, writing, gardening. Office: Am Magic Lantern Theater PO Box 44 East Haddam CT 06423-0044 Business E-Mail: tborton@magiclanternshows.com.

BORTON, JOSEPH WALDEN, lawyer; BS in Econs., U. Oreg., 1993; JD, U. Idaho Coll. of Law, 1996. Bar: Idaho State Supreme Ct., U.S. Dist. Ct., U.S. Ct. Appeals (9th cir.). Mng. ptnr. Foley, Freeman, Borton & Stern, Meridian, Idaho, 1996—. Mentor Big Bros./Big Sisters, Boise, 2000—; bd. dirs. Meridian Edn. Found., 2003—; youth advisor Meridian Youth Coun., 2004—; mem. Meridian C. of C., pres., 2002—03. Recipient Chamber Pres.'s award, Meridian C. of C., 2001, 2002, Accomplished Under 40, Idaho Bus. Rev., 2004. Avocation: triathlons.

BORTS, GEORGE HERBERT, economist, educator; b. N.Y.C., Aug. 29, 1927; s. Elias Alexander and Etta (Silberg) B.; m. Muriel Levenson, Dec. 26, 1948; children: David, Richard, Robert. AB, Columbia U., 1947; AM, U. Chgo., 1949, PhD, 1953; AM (hon.), Brown U., 1957. Prof. econs. Brown U., Providence, 1960—. Mng. editor Am. Econ. Rev., Nashville, 1968-80, World Bus. Adv., Providence, 1990-91; co-author: Economic Growth in a Free Market, 1964. Mem. Am. Econ. Assn., Phi Beta Kappa. Home: 220 Slater Ave Providence RI 02906-3440 Office: Brown U 64 Waterman St Providence RI 02912-9029

BORUM, OLIN HENRY, retired government scientist; b. Spencer, N.C., Nov. 3, 1917; s. Oscar Henry and Marjorie Mae (Leigh) B.; m. Beatruce Star Comulada, Nov. 14, 1944; children: Pamela Leigh, Robin Olin, Denis Richard. *Daughter Pamela Leigh earned a BA from the College of William & Mary. She is a freelance writer, editor, and book agent. Son Robin attended Northern Virginia Community College. He is a GRI Realtor with Long & Foster Co., a member of the Prince William County Million Dollar Sales Club, a scuba diver, and photographer, and received a Harley Davidson national technical service award. Son Denis earned a BS from VPI and an MPA from George Washington University. He is an environmental health scientist with the EPA, a Brookings Institution Legislative Fellow with Senator Reed, and earned the EPA Science Achievement Award for Health Sciences and Silver Medal for Performance.* BS, U. N.C., 1938, MA, 1947, PhD, 1949; postgrad., U. Md., 1940-41. Rsch. chemist E.I. du Pont de Nemours & Co., Phila., 1949-50; interim rsch. asst. prof. Cancer Rsch. Lab. U. Fla., 1950; instr., asst. prof. chemistry U.S. Mil. Acad., 1952-55; rsch. adminstr. U.S. Army Chem. Corps R&D Command, Washington, 1956-60, U.S. Army Material Command, Washington, 1964-76; realtor assoc. Unique Properties, Alexandria, Va., 1974-79; realtor, assoc. broker The J. Edwards Co., Inc., Alexandria, Va., 1979-82; prin. broker Olin H. Borum Realty, 1982—. Tchr. chemistry U. Va., Arlington, Va., 1966-68. Contbr. articles to profl. jours. Adult scouter Nat. Capital Area coun. Boy Scouts Am., 1964-75, unit commr., 1968-75; sec. Mt. Vernon (Va.) Civic Assn., 1965-66; mem. Com. of 33 (nat. adv. group Nat. Sojourners, Inc.), 1962-71, chmn., 1969-71, Nat. trustee Nat. Sojourners, Inc., 1971-73. Maj. AUS, 1941-46; maj. USAF, 1951-56, lt. col., 1960-64. Recipient cert. Achievement Dept. Army, 1971; Teaching fellow U. Md., 1940-41, U. N.C., 1946-49. Fellow Am. Inst. Chemists; mem. Am. Chem. Soc., Masons, Shriners, Phi Beta Kappa, Sigma Xi. Presbyterian. Home: 9002 Volunteer Dr Alexandria VA 22309-2921 Office: 9002 Volunteer Dr Alexandria VA 22309-2921

BORUM, RODNEY LEE, finance company executive; b. High Point, N.C., Sept. 30, 1929; s. Carl Macy and Etta (Sullivan) B.; m. Helen Marie Rigby, June 27, 1953; children: Richard Harlan, Sarah Elizabeth. Student, U. N.C., 1947-49; BS, U.S. Naval Acad., 1953. Design-devel. engr. GE, Syracuse, N.Y., 1956-58, Cape Kennedy, Fla., 1956-58, missile test condr., 1958-60, mgr. ground equipment engr., 1960-61, mgr. ea. test range engring., 1961-65; adminstr. Bus. and Def. Svcs. Adminstrn.-Dept. Commerce, 1966-69; pres. Printing Industries Am., Arlington, Va., 1969-85, staff cons., 1985-86, mem. exec. com., 1969-85, dir.; pres. W.H. Rigby Cons., 1985-86; exec. v.p. Amasek Inc., Cocoa, Fla., 1986-87; assoc. Fin. Svcs. Orgn., Cocoa, Fla., 1987—. Sec. Graphic Arts Show Corp.; dir. Inter-Comprint Ltd., Strangers Cay, Ltd.; mem. governing bd. Comprints Internat.; Rep. candidate 11th dist. U.S. congress, Fla., 1988-90; ops. mgr. COVIX Corp.; mgmt. cons. 1990—; exec. v.p. Pearl of Va., Inc. Mem. exec. coun. Cub Scouts Am., 1965; bd. dirs., v.p. Brevard County (Fla.) United Fund, 1964-65; bd. dirs. Brevard Beaches Concert Assn., 1965; mem. edn. coun. bd. dirs. Graphic Arts Tech. Found., Pitts., 1970-86; trustee, founder Graphic Arts Edn. and Rsch. Trust Fund, Arlington, Va., 1978-85; candidate for U.S. Ho. of Reps. from llth dist. Fla., 1988. lst lt. USAF, 1953-56. Named Boss of Yr., C. of C., 1965; recipient Bausch and Lomb Sci. award, 1947, Am. Legion award, 1952. Mem. U.S. Naval Inst., U.S. Naval Acad. Alumni Assn., Graphic Arts Coun. N.Am. (bd. dirs. 1977—), Phi Eta Sigma. Methodist.

BORUS, JONATHAN FREDERICK, psychiatrist, educator; b. Washington, May 4, 1941; s. Joseph B. and Rosalie (Bierman) B.; m. Dixie Lee Nelson, June 13, 1964; children: Joseph S., Joshua S., Daniel A. MD, U. Ill., 1965. Diplomate Am. Bd. Med. Examiners, Am. Bd. Psychiatry and Neurology, Gen. Psychiatry, Forensic Psychiatry. Rotating intern Cook County Hosp., Chgo., 1965-66; resident in psychiatry Neuropsychiat. Inst. U. Ill., Chgo., 1966-69; rsch. psychiatrist Walter Reed Army Inst. Rsch., Washington, 1969-72; cons. psychiatrist Henry Phipps Clinic Johns Hopkins Hosp., Balt., 1972; co-dir., sr. psychiatrist Freedom Trail Clinic Erich Lindemann Mental Health Ctr., Boston, 1972-76; chief psychiat. cons. North End Health Ctr., Boston, 1972-90; dir. tng. Erich Lindemann Mental Health Ctr., Boston, 1974-76; dir. social and community psychiatry Mass. Gen. Hosp., Boston, 1975-83, chmn. com. on teaching and edn., 1983-90, dir. residency and fellowship tng. in psychiatry, 1976-90; Stanely Cobb prof. psychiatry Harvard Med. Sch., Boston, 1994—; dir. psychiatry Brigham and Women's Hosp., Boston, 1990-92, psychiatrist in chief, 1992—, chmn. dept. psychiatry, 1999—; chief of psychiatry Faulkner Hosp., 2001—; Stanley Cobb prof. psychiatry Harvard Med. Sch., 2005—. Founding mem. steering com. psychiat. epidemiology Harvard U., 1979—95, mem. mental health work group, 1982—87; founding mem., sec. Nat. Psychiatry Match Rev. Bd., Washington, 1987—91; mem. appeals bd. Accreditation Coun. for Grad. Med. Edn., Chgo., 1989—99; mem. adv. com. on mental health Nat. Acad. Scis., Inst. of Medicine, Washington, 1977—79; prin. investigator NIMH, 1975—90; vis. prof. U. Man., 1978, Lettermen Med. Ctr., 1979, U. Conn., 1984, U. South Fla., 1987, USAF Med. Ctr., 1988, Calif. Pacific Med. Ctr., 1990, Tex. A&M, 1993, U. Calif., Davis, 1997, 98, 99; mem. exec. com. Harvard Consolidated dept. psychiatry, 1992—2001, chair exec. com., 2003—05, steering com. Ptnrs. Healthcare Psychiatry, 1995—. Assoc. editor Am. Jour. Psychiatry, 1982-90; editor Acad. Psychiatry, 1989-95; edn. editor Harvard Review Psychiatry, 1993—; contbr. numerous articles to profl. jours. Mem. Beacon Hill-West End Mental Health Com., Boston, 1972-76, Lt. Gov.'s Com. for Mental Health Ins., Commonwealth of Mass., 1977-78; disting. cons. Walter Reed Army Med. Ctr., Washington, 1986-89. Maj. U.S. Army, 1969-72. Named Outstanding Psychiat. Educator, Assn. for Acad. Psychiatry, 1992; recipient Vestermark award for psychiat. edn., Am. Psychiat. Assn. and NIMH, 1997, Lifetime Achievement in Mentoring award, Harvard Med. Sch., 1998, Lifetime Achievement award, Assn. for Acad. Psychiatry, 2004. Mem.: Am. Assn. Dirs. Psychiat. Residency Tng. (treas. 1979—80, sec. 1981—82), Assn. Acad. Psychiatry (pres. 1986—88), Am. Psychiat. Assn. (Disting. Life fellow). Democrat. Jewish. Office: Brigham and Women's Hosp 75 Francis St Boston MA 02115-6106 Office Phone: 617-732-8140. Business E-Mail: jborus@partners.org.

BORWEIN, DAVID, mathematics professor; b. Kaunas, Lithuania, Mar. 24, 1924; s. Joseph Jacob and Rachel (Landau) B.; m. Bessie Flax, June 30, 1946; children— Jonathan, Peter, Sarah. B.Sc. in Engring, Witwatersrand (South Africa) U., 1945, B.Sc. Hons., 1948; PhD, University Coll. London, 1950, D.Sc., 1960. Lectr. St. Andrews U., Scotland, 1950-63; vis. prof. U. Western Ont., London, Can., 1963-64, prof., 1964-89, head math. dept., 1967-89, prof. emeritus, 1989—. Contbr. articles to profl. jours. Served with South African Forces, 1945. NSERC grantee, 1966— Fellow Royal Soc. Edinburgh; mem. London Math. Soc., Am. Math. Soc., Math. Assn. Am., Canadian Math. Soc. (chmn. research com. 1970-73, v.p. 1973-75, pres. 1985-87) Home: 1032 Brough St London ON Canada N6A 3N4 Office: Dept Math U Western Ont London ON Canada N6A 5B7 E-mail: dborwein@uwo.ca.

BORWICK, SUSAN HARDEN, musicologist, educator; d. Clyde and Edythe Brown Harden; m. Douglas Bruce Borwick, Aug. 14, 1976 (div. Apr. 20, 1996); 1 child, John Harden. MusB, MusEdnB, Baylor U., Waco, TX, 1968; PhD, Univ. NC, Chapel Hill, 1972. Asst. prof. music Baylor U., Waco, Tex., 1972—77, Eastman Sch. Music, Rochester, NY, 1977—82; assoc. prof. music Wake Forest U., Winston-Salem, NC, 1982—88, prof. music, 1988—. Chair dept. music Wake Forest U., Winston-Salem, NC, 1982—94, dir. women's studies, 2000—04, assoc. faculty Divinty Sch., 2003—04; program devel. and adminstrn. coun. Nat. Women's Studies Assn., 2000—, chair contemporary curriculum transformation project, 2001—. Author: (compact disc program notes) American Romantics: Arthur Foote and Amy Cheney Beach; composer: (sacred choral work) Morning Light, Hope: An Advent Choral Introit, (solo for voice, flute, piano) Mary's, Mary's Mary's, (sacred choral work) Benediction, (incidental music) Much Ado about Nothing; contbr. articles to profl. jours. Chair bd. of deacons Knollwood Bapt. Ch., Winston-Salem, NC, 1994—95; sec. Bapt. Women in Ministry, NC, 2000—; pres., v.p., sec. NC Assn. Music Schs., 1987—94. Grantee R. J. Reynolds Rsch. Leave, Wake Forest U., 1996, 1998, 2003—04; Travel to Collections grant, Nat. Endowment for the Humanities, 1986, William C. Archie Rsch. grant, Wake Forest U., 2000—01, 2002—03, 2004. Mem.: Soc. for Am. Music, Am. Musicological Soc., Coll. Music Soc. (life), Omicron Delta Kappa, Mu Phi Epsilon. Avocations: gardening, travel. Home: 4101 Mill Creek Rd Winston Salem NC 27106-2917 Office: Dept of Music Wake Forest Univ 7345 Reynolda Station Winston Salem NC 27109-7345 Office Phone: 336-758-5953. E-mail: borwick@wfu.edu.

BORYSEWICZ, MARY LOUISE, editor; b. Chgo. d. Thomas J. and Mabel E. (Zeien) O'Farrell m. Daniel S. Borysewicz, June 11, 1955 (dec. 2005); children: Mary Adele, Stephen Francis (dec. 1997), Paul Barnabas. BA, Mundelein Coll., 1970; postgrad. in English lit., U. Ill. 1970—71; grad. exec. program, U. Chgo., 1982. Editor sci. publs. AMA, Chgo., 1971—73; exec. mng. editor Am. Jour. Ophthalmology, Chgo., 1973—95; media cons. Fox-Wahls Design, Chgo., 1999—2004; editl. svc. cons. A.T. Kearney, Chgo., 2004—. Asst. sec., treas. Ophthalmic Pub. Co., 1985—95; guest lectr. U. Chgo. Med. Sch., 1979, Harvard U. Med. Sch., 1978, Northwestern U. Med. Sch., 1979, Am. Acad. Ophthalmology, 1976, 81, Northwestern U. Joseph Medill Sch. Journalism, 2002. Editor: Opthalmology Principles and Concepts, 7th edit., 1992, 8th edit., 1996, Documenta Ophthalmologica History Issue, 1997, 98; contbg. writer Chicago Shops, 2002, 03; contbr. articles to sci. publs. Mem. Coun. Biol. Editors (bd. dirs. 1988-91, fin. com. 1985-88, teller com. 1992-95). E-mail: mbory@aol.com.

BOSCH, JOSEPH A., human resources specialist; BS, Cornell U. Employee rels. rep. to v.p. employee rels. N.E. region PepsiCo, 1982—92; with human resources dept. So. divsn. Pizza Hut, Inc., Atlanta, 1992—97, chief people officer, 1997—2004; sr. v.p. human resources Tenet Healthcare Corp., 2004—. Served with U.S. Army. Office: Tenet Healthcare Corp 13737 Noel Rd Dallas TX 75240 Office Phone: 469-893-2200. Office Fax: 469-893-8600.*

BOSCH, MICHELE C., lawyer; b. Washington, Apr. 29, 1968; BA, U. Va., 1990; JD, Coll. William & Mary, 1993. Bar: Va. 1993, DC 1997, US Patent & Trademark Office. Ptnr. Finnegan, Henderson, Farabow, Garrett & Dunner LLP, Washington, mem. mgmt. com. Mem.: Am. Chem. Soc., Fed. Cir. Bar Assn., DC Bar Assn., Va. Bar Assn., Am. Intellectual Property Assn., ABA. Fluent in French. Office: Finnegan Henderson Farabow Garrett & Dunner LLP 901 New York Ave NW Washington DC 20001-3315 Office Phone: 202-408-4000. Office Fax: 202-408-4400. Business E-Mail: michele.bosch@finnegan.com.

BOSCH, ROBERT JOHN, JR., mechanical engineer; b. Bklyn., Oct. 15, 1945; s. Robert John and Virginia Ann (Elsbach) B.; m. Joan Suzzane Dydak, Aug. 31, 1968; children: Jennifer Anne, Jessica Anne. BME, U. Dayton, 1967; MME, Stevens Inst. Tech., 1973, MSM, 1981. Profl. engr., N.J., Utah. Assoc. engr. Gen. Dynamics Corp., Groton, Conn., 1967-69; project engr. Curtiss Wright Corp., Wood Ridge, N.J., 1969-73; project mgr. Foster Wheeler Corp., Livingston, N.J.. 1973-80; mgr. bus. devel. F.W. Energy Applications, Inc., Livingston, 1980-84; pres. Planned Mgmt. Systems, Inc., Essex Fells, N.J., 1984-86; regional mgr. Siemens Corp., N.Y.C., 1986-91; comml. dir. Foster Wheeler Energy Corp., Livingston, 1991—. Contbr. to profl. publs. Bd. dirs. Children's Aid and Adoption Soc., Hackensack, N.J., 1989—; pres. Groton Jaycees, 1969. Mem. ASME, Am. Nuclear Soc. Office: Foster Wheeler Energy Corp Perryville Corp Park Clinton NJ 08809

BOSCH, SAMUEL HENRY, computer company executive; b. Waupun, Wis., Dec. 24, 1934; s. Henry Samuel and Emma (Elgersma) B.; m. Corinne Marilyn Aardema, June 21, 1958; children: Michelle, Jonathan, David, Sara. BS in Physics, San Diego State U., 1961; MS in Physics, UCLA, 1962. Sr. rsch. engr. Gen. Dynamics, San Diego, 1962-69; mgr. mktg. Digital Equipment Corp., Maynard, Mass., 1969-77; dir. mktg. Sys. Engring. Lab., Ft. Lauderdale, Fla., 1977-79; mgr. mktg. Intel, Hillsboro, Oreg., 1979-81; dir. mktg. Metheus, Hillsboro, 1981-82; pres. ATM Techs., Beaverton, Oreg., 1982-86; pres., owner Peregrin Techs., Inc., Portland, Oreg., 1986—, Peregrin Med. Rev. Inc., Portland, 1987—. Spkr. at industry confs. Contbr. articles to sci. jours. Served with U.S. Army, 1955-57. Mem. Concord Coalition, N.W. China Coun. Mem. Oreg. Hist. Soc. Republican. Mem. Christian Ref. Ch. Achievements include patent in ATM processing. Home: 20055 NW Nestucca Dr Portland OR 97229-2821 Office: Peregrin Techs Inc 14215 NW Science Park Dr Portland OR 97229 E-mail: boschs@peregrin.net.

BOSCHERT, THOMAS NEVILLE, historian, educator; b. Memphis, Nov. 5, 1929; s. Thomas Mauldin and Edith Louise Boschert; m. Eva Ann Dickins, Mar. 25, 1952; children: Ann Carter McNeal, Neville Henry, Curtis Dickins. BA, U. Miss., 1950, MA, 1985, PhD, 1995. Instr. USAF Tech. Tng. Sch., Keesler Air Force Base, Miss., 1952—55; mgr. Duncan Grain Elevator, AAL, Duncan, 1955—64. Farm owner-operator, Duncan, 1956—83; town clk., tax collector Town of Duncan, 1984—; adj. asst. prof. history Delta State U., Cleveland, 1998—2001, vis. asst. prof. history. Contbr. articles to profl. jours. Cmty. committeeman Bolivar County Agrl. and Stblzn. Com., Cleveland, 1960—68; songleader and pianist Duncan Bapt. Ch., 1971—2004; dir. Bolivar County Farm Bur., Cleveland, 1964—76; pres. Bolivar County Hist. Soc., 1976—78. 1st lt. USAF, 1950—55, maj. (ret.) USAF, 1974—89. Recipient George Wash. Honor medal award, Freedoms Found. Valley Forge, 1968. Mem.: So. Hist. Assn., Miss. Hist. Soc. (pres. 1984—84), Am. Hist. Assn. Southern Baptist. Home: 203 Magnolia Hill PO Box 215 Duncan MS 38740 Office: Delta State University West Sunflower Road Cleveland MS 38733 Personal E-mail: thomasn@gmi.net. Business E-Mail: tboschrt@deltastate.edu.

BOSCHETTI, PHILIP J., oil industry executive; b. Yonkers, N.Y., Apr. 11, 1944; s. Anthony and Santina (Taccetta) B.; m. Linda Marie Liggio, June 11, 1966; children: Keith Philip, Scott Alan. BBA in Mktg., Iona Coll., 1966. Sales mgr. Firestone Tire and Rubber Co., NJ, 1966; fin. adminstr. William S. Paley & Co., N.Y.C., 1969-91; v.p., CFO Burnett Oil Co., Inc., Ft. Worth, 1991—. Asst. sec., treas. The Greenpark Found., Inc., N.Y.C., 1978-91, William S. Paley Found., Inc., N.Y.C., 1978-91; v.p. Burnett Ranches, Inc., Ft. Worth, 1991—, Burnett Aviation Co., Inc., Ft. Worth, 1991—, Exec. Protective Systems, Ft. Worth, 1991—; v.p., CFO Burnett Ranches, Ltd., Ft. Worth, 1992—; v.p., dir. Burnett Svcs., Inc., Ft. Worth, 1992—, Burnett Security Syst., Inc., Ft. Worth, 1994—; v.p. AJJM Capital Corp., Ft. Worth, 1996—; treas., dir. K&M, Inc., Ft. Worth, 1998-2000, Cookworks of Santa Fe, Inc., 1998-2000, Cookworks, Tex., Inc., Ft. Worth, 1998-2002; pres. CW Beverages, Inc., Ft. Worth, 1999-2002, Addison Warehouse Beverages, Inc., Ft. Worth, 1999-2002; mgr. of bd. Burnett Land, LLC; v.p., treas. Westwood Baseball Assn., 1977-88. V.p., treas. Westwood Baseball Assn., 1977-88, bd. dirs., 2000-05; v.p. Westwood Babe Ruth, 1985-88; treas. Tommy League, 1984-86; dir. Westwood Recreation Youth Football, 1984-86; mem. Westwood Inds. Club, 1976-80. Decorated Bronze star, Air medal with oak leaf cluster, Vietnamese Honor medal, Vietnamese Svc. medal, Vietnamese campaign medal w/four svc. stars, Nat. Def. Svc. medal. Mem. River Crest Country Club. Office: Burnett Oil Co Inc Burnett Plz Ste 1500 801 Cherry St Unit 9 Fort Worth TX 76102-6881

BOSCHINI, VICTOR JOHN, JR., academic administrator; b. Cleve. m. Megan Boschini; children: Elizabeth, Mary Catherine, Edward Mark, Margaret. B in Sociology and Psychology, Union Coll.; M in Coll. Student Pers., Bowling Green State U.; D in Higher Edn. Adminstrn., Ind. U. Asst. to the dir. of residence life Bowling Green (Ohio) State U., 1978—79; student adviser Western Ill. U., Macomb, 1979—82; asst. dean of students DePauw U., Greencastle, Ind., 1982—84; asst. dean studies Ind. U., Bloomington, 1984—90; assoc. provost Butler U., Indpls., 1990—97; v.p., dean student affairs, edn. prof. Ill. State U., Normal, 1997—99, pres., 1999—2003; chancellor, prof. edn. Tex. Christian U., Ft. Worth, 2003—. Bd. dir. State Farm Mutual Funds Co. Bd. .dir. Fort Worth Symphony, Tex.; bd. dir. Van Cliburn Found., Fort Worth, Tex.; bd. trustee Brite Divinity Sch. Office: Tex Christian Univ Box 297080 3861 Bellaire Cir Fort Worth TX 76109

BOSCHKEN, HERMAN L., management and public policy educator; b. San Jose, Calif., June 12, 1944; s. Herman Hoeft and Helen Lutha Boschken; m. Irene Hartung Boschken, Aug. 28, 1965; children: Steven, David. BS, U. Calif., Berkeley, 1966, MBA, 1968; PhD, U. Wash., 1972. Prof. mgmt. San Diego State U., 1973—77; prof. pub. adminstrn. U. So. Calif., L.A., 1977—81; vis. prof. bus. U. Calif., Berkeley, 1981—82; prof. orgn. and mgmt. San Jose State U., Calif., 1982—. Cons. Housing Ministry Sweden, 1983, Transp. Ministry Can., 2001. Author: Strategic Design and Organizational Change, 1988, Social Class, Politics and Urban Markets, 2002 (Best Book award Acad. Mgmt., 2003). Sr. Fulbright scholar, Umea, Sweden, 1983, Disting. European Chair, N.B., Can., 2001. Mem.: Am. Soc. Pub. Adminstrn. (editor sect. jour. 1972—95), Acad. Mgmt., Am. Polit. Sci. Assn. (Herbert Kaufman award 1990). Avocations: winemaking, skiing. Office: Dept Orgn and Mgmt San Jose State U San Jose CA 95192 Office Phone: 408-924-3563. Business E-Mail: boschken_h@cob.sjsu.edu.

BOSCHMANN, ERWIN, chemistry professor; b. Chaco, Paraguay, Jan. 1, 1939; arrived in U.S., 1959; s. David and Anna Boschmann; m. Priscilla Glee Selzer, Aug. 17, 1962; children: Heidi Kristine Boschmann Amstutz, Tonya Renee, Eric Erwin. PhD, U. Colo., 1968. Asst. prof. Ind. U.-Purdue U., Indpls., 1968-74, assoc. prof., 1974-77, prof. chemistry, 1977—, assoc. dean faculties, 1988—99, assoc. v.p., 1999—2002, Ind. U., 1998—2002; interim vice chancellor acad. affairs Ind. U. E., 2003—04; CEO Plowshares, Indpls., 2004—. Cons. Ford Found., Peru, 1968—73, Asian Devel. Bank, Indonesia, 1985—87. Author: The Electronic Classroom (Fredric Lieber Award, 1985), Ten Teaching Tools, 1987, Foundations of Life, 1991. Recipient Distng. Alumnus award, Bethel Coll., 1998; Lilly Endowment Faculty Open fellow, Indpls., 1988. Mem.: Am. Chem. Soc. Mennonite. Office Phone: 317-631-7322. Business E-Mail: erv@iu.edu.

BOSCHOK, JACKIE, labor union administrator; b. Kansas City, Mo., Apr. 24, 1952; d. John and Margaret Robey; m. Alex Boschok, July 30, 1983. Student, Culver Stockton Coll., 1970—71; BS, U. Mo., 1977. Materials facilitator Boeing Comml. Airplane Group, Seattle, 1980—2001; bus. rep. Aerospace Machinists Dist. 751, Seattle, 2001—. Chair labor and trades campaign cabinet Snohomish County United Way, Everett, Wash., 1994—97; mem. Snohomish County chpt. ARC, Everett, 2000—01. Recipient Spirit of Labor award, Snohomish County United Way, 1998; fellow, U. Mo. Columbia Sch. Agr., 1977. Mem.: Snohomish County Labor Coun. (exec. bd. 2000, v.p. 2005), Wash. State Labor Coun. (women's com. 1994—2005), Coalition Labor Union Women (nat. exec. bd. 1991—2005, rec. sec. Puget Sound chpt. 1993—2005). Office: Aerospace Machinists Dist 751 8729 Airport Rd Everett WA 98204 Personal E-mail: jackieboschok@hotmail.com.

BOSCIA, JON ANDREW, insurance company executive; b. Pitts., Apr. 15, 1952; s. Louis C. and Stella (Weryha) B.; m. Donna M. Lowar, Aug. 18, 1973; children: Nicole Marie, Brandon Jon. BA, Point Park Coll., 1973; MBA, Duquesne U., 1979. Corp. planner Consolidated Nat. Gas, Pitts., 1974-79; fin. sales rep. Westinghouse, Pitts., 1979-80; asst. v.p. Mellon Bank, Pitts., 1980-83; sr. v.p. Lincoln Nat. Pension, Ft. Wayne, Ind., 1983—98; pres. Lincoln Nat. Life Insurance Co., 1999—; ceo, pres., Lincoln Nat. Corp., Phila., 1998—2001, chmn., 1998—. Contbr. articles to profl. jours. Mem. coms. Pitts. Bd. Edn., 1974-79; chmn. coms. Arlington Park, Ft. Wayne, 1983-86; mem. START program Ft. Wayne Community Schs., 1985. PPC Found. scholar, 1973. Mem. Nat. Assn. Bus. Economists, Planning Forum. Democrat. Methodist. Avocations: jogging, racquetball, playing drums, swimming, reading. Office: Lincoln Nat Corp 1500 Market St Ste 3900 Philadelphia PA 19102-2100

BOSCKETTI, CHRISTINE FRANCES, Spanish language educator; d. Carl and Sandra Bosckett, Spanish degree, U. N.H., 1999. Cert. secondary edn. N.H. Tchr. Spanish Greenland (N.H.) Cen. Sch., 1999—2000, Whittier Regional Vocat. Tech. H.S., Haverhill, Mass., 2000—01, Londonderry (N.H.) H.S., 2001—. Office Phone: 603-432-6941.

BOSCO, ANTHONY GERARD, bishop; b. New Castle, Pa., Aug. 1, 1927; s. Joseph M. and Theresa (Pezo) B. BA, St. Vincent Sem., Latrobe, Pa.; juris canonici licentiatus, Lateran U., Rome; LLD (hon.), Duquesne U., 1971; LHD (hon.), St.Vincent Coll., 1988. Ordained priest Roman Cath. Ch., 1952. Asst. chancellor Diocese of Pitts., 1955—65, vice chancellor, 1965—67, chancellor, 1967—85, aux. bishop, 1970—87; bishop Diocese of Greensburg, Pa., 1987—2002; bishop emeritus Diocese of Greenburg, Pa., 2002—. Chmn. chmn. Cath. Comms. Found., 1984—; hon. chmn., trustee Seton Hill Coll., Greensburg, 1987; ex officio mem., bd. regents St. Vincent Sem., Latrobe, Pa., 1987—. Named Pitts.'s Man of Yr. in Religion, Pitts. Jaycees, 1975; recipient Leonardo Da Vinci award for Religion, Order of Italian Sons and Daughter, 1970. Mem.: Christian Assocs. S.W. Pa., Nat. Conf. Cath. Bishops. E-mail: abosco@dioceseofgreensburg.org.*

BOSCO, MARY BETH, lawyer; b. Jersey City, Feb. 23, 1956; BA cum laude, Yale Univ., 1978; JD with honors, George Washington Univ., 1983. Bar: DC 1983, US Dist. Ct. (ea. Ark., so. Tex., Wyo. dist.), US Ct. Appeals (8th, 10th & Fed. cir.), US Supreme Ct. Ptnr., head Govt. Contracts & Fed. Marketing practices, mem. mgmt. com. Patton Boggs LLP, Washington. Contbr. articles to profl. jours.; author (contributing): Environ. Law Handbook, 1994. Mem.: ABA. Office: Patton Boggs LLP 2550 M St NW Washington DC 20037-1350 Office Phone: 202-457-6420. Office Fax: 202-457-6315. Business E-Mail: mbbosco@pattonboggs.com.

BOSCO, PHILIP MICHAEL, actor; b. Jersey City, Sept. 26, 1930; s. Philip Lupo and Margaret Raymond (Thek) B.; m. Nancy Ann Dunkle, Jan. 2, 1957; children: Diane, Philip, Christopher, Jennifer, Lisa, Celia, John. BA in drama, Catholic U. Am., 1957. Roles include Brian O'Bannion in Auntie Mame, City Ctr., N.Y.C., 1958; Angelo in Measure for Measure, Belvedere Lake Amphitheatre, N.Y.C., 1960; Heracles in The Rape of the Belt, 1960 (Tony nomination); Will Danaher in Donnybrook, 1961; Hawkshaw in The Ticket-of-Leave Man, 1961; King Henry in Henry IV Part 1, Shakespeare Festival, Stratford, Conn., 1962; Kent in King Lear; Rufio in Antony and Cleopatra; Pistol in Henry V; Aegeon in Comedy of Errors, 1963; Benedick in Much Ado About Nothing; Claudius in Hamlet, 1964; title role in Coriolanus, 1965; Lovewit in The Alchemist, 1967; appeared in Galileo, 1967, Saint Joan, 1968, Amphitryon in 3 Zones, Tiger at the Gates, 1968, Cyrano de Bergerac, 1968, Camino Real, 1970, Operation Sidewinder, 1970, The Playboy of the Western World, 1971, An Enemy of the People, 1971, Antigone, 1971, Mary Stuart, 1971, Narrow Road Into the Deep North, 1972, Twelfth Night, 1972, The Crucible, 1972, Enemies, 1972, The Plough and the Stars, 1973, The Merchant of Venice, 1973, A Streetcar Named Desire, 1973, Mrs. Warren's Profession, 1976, Man and Superman, 1978, Whose Life Is It Anyway?, 1979, A Month In The Country, 1979, Major Barbara, 1980, Inadmissible Evidence, 1981, Hedda Gabler, 1982, Ah! Wilderness, 1983, Misalliance, 1983, Come Back, Little Sheba, 1984, Eminent Domain, 1984, Hearbreak House (Tony nominated), Caine Mutiny, 1984, Be Happy For Me, Masterclass, 1986, You Never Can Tell, 1986 (Tony nominated), A Man For All Seasons, 1986,The Devil's Disciple, 1988, (Broadway) Lend Me A Tenor, 1989, (Antoinette Perry award 1989), The Miser, 1990, Breaking Legs, 1991, (Broadway) An Inspector Calls, 1994, The Heiress, 1995, Moon Over Buffalo, 1995-96 (Tony nomination), Twelfth Night, 1998 Twelve Angry Men (Tony nominated), Chitty Chitty Bang Bang, 2005; films include: Requiem For a Heavyweight, A Lovely Way To Die, The Pope of Greenwich Village, Walls of Glass, Heaven Help Us, The Money Pit, Trading Places, 1983, Children of a Lesser God, 1986, Suspect, 1987, Three Men and a Baby, 1987, The Luckiest Man in the World, 1988, Working Girl, 1988, Dream Team, 1988, Another Woman, 1988, Blue Steel, Quick Change, FX-2, 1990, True Colors, 1990, Straight Talk, 1991, The Return of Eliot Ness, 1991, Shawdows and Fog, 1992, Attica: Line of Fire, 1993, Angie, 1993, Safe Passage, 1993, Milk Money, 1994, Nobody's Fool, 1994, It Takes Two, 1995, The First Wives Club, 1995, My Best Friend's Wedding, 1997, Critical Care, 1997, Deconstructing Harry, 1997, Shaft II, 1998, The Time Machine, 1999, Kate and Leopold, 2000; TV shows include: The Prisoner of Zenda, The Nurses, O'Brien, Hawk, The NET Play of the Month, Tribeca, Grandpa and the Globetrotters, 1987, Echoes in the Darkness, Internal Affairs, 1988, Murder in Black and White, 1989, Return of Eliot Ness, 1991, Law and Order, 1993, 95-98, Cosby, 1998, Spin City, 1999, Criminal Intent, 2001, S.V.U., 2002; (TV movie) Carriers, 1997. Served with U.S. Army, 1951-54. Recipient Critic's Circle award N.Y. Drama Critics, 1960-61; recipient Clarence Derwent award, 1966-67, Tony award nominations, 1961, 84, 87, 96, OBIE award, 1987, Emmy award, 1988, Tony award, Drama Desk award, Outer Critic's Circle award all for best leading actor, 1988-89; inductee Theater Hall of Fame, 1998. Mem. Actor's Equity Assn., Screen Actor's Guild, AFTRA Roman Catholic.

BOSCO, RONALD A., literature educator; m. Bernadette Bosco; 1 child, Daryl. Disting. svc. prof. Am. lit. and religious studies SUNY, Albany, 1975—. Lectr. in field. Contbr. articles to profl. jours. Office: SUNY English Dept Humanities 334 1400 Washington Ave Albany NY 12210

BOSE, AJAY KUMAR, chemistry professor; b. Silchar, India, Feb. 12, 1925; s. Abinash C. and Amita Kumari (Chanda) B.; m. Margaret Lois Logan, Sept. 13, 1950; children: Ryan, Ranjan, Indrani, Indira, Krishna, Rajendra. BS, U. Allahabad, India, 1944, MS, 1946; ScD, MIT, 1950; M in Engring. (hon.), Stevens Inst. Tech., Hoboken, N.J., 1963. Rsch. fellow Harvard U., Cambridge, Mass., 1950-51; lectr., then asst. prof. chemistry Indian Inst. Tech., Kharagpur, 1952-56; rsch. assoc. U. Pa., Phila., 1956-57; rsch. chemist Upjohn Co., Kalamazoo, Mich., 1957-59; assoc. prof. Stevens Inst. Tech., 1959-61, prof., 1961-83, George Meade Bond prof. chemistry, 1983-96, prof., 1996—. Founder, dir. Undergrad. Projects in Tech. and Medicine, 1972—; cons. various chem. cos. Mem. editl. bd. Jour. Heterocyclic Chemistry, 1980-83; contbr. over 300 articles to profl. jours.; patentee in field. Recipient Outstanding Achievement award Nat. Fedn. Indian Am. Assns., 1990, Ranbaxy Sci. Found. Rsch. award in Pharm. Scis., 1997, Nat. Catalyst award Chem. Mfrs. Assn., 1997, Presdl. award for excellence in sci., math. and engring. mentoring, 1999; named N.J. Prof. of Yr., Coun. for Advancement and Support of Edn. and Carnegie Found. for Advancement of Tchg., 1990. Fellow AAAS, Indian Nat. Sci. Acad.; mem. Am. Chem. Soc. (councillor 1964-70, Dreyfus award 1999), Sigma Xi. Avocation: popular sci. writing. Office: Stevens Inst of Tech Dept Chemistry & Chem Biol Castle Point Hoboken NJ 07030 Office Phone: 201-216-5547. Business E-Mail: abose@stevens.edu.

BOSE, AMAR GOPAL, electronics executive, electrical engineering educator; b. Phila., Nov. 2, 1929; s. Noni Gopal and Charlotte (Mechlin) B.; children: Vanu Gopal, Maya. SB, SM, MIT, 1952, ScD, 1956. Mem. faculty MIT, Cambridge, 1956—2001, prof. elec. engring.; chmn., CEO Bose Corp., Framingham, Mass., 1964—. Chmn., chief exec. officer Bose Corp., Framingham, Mass. Author: (with Kenneth N. Stevens) Introductory Network Theory, 1965; patentee in acoustics, nonlinear systems and communications. Fulbright fellow India, 1956-57; recipient Baker Teaching award MIT, 1964, Teaching award Am. Soc. Engring. Edn., 1965; named Inventor of Yr., Intellectual Property Owners, 1987. Fellow IEEE; mem. AAAS, Nat. Acad. Engring., Sigma Xi, Tau Beta Pi, Eta Kappa Nu Office: Bose Corp The Mountain Framingham MA 01701-9168

BOSE, BIMAL KUMAR, electrical engineering educator; b. Calcutta, India, Sept. 1, 1932; came to U.S., 1971; s. Rajendra and Nirmala (Ghosh) B.; m. Arati Ghosh, June 26, 1961; children: Papia, Amit. BE, Calcutta U., 1956, PhD, 1966; MS, U. Wis., 1960. Asst. engr. Tata Hydro Power Co., Bombay, 1956-59; asst. prof. Bengal Engring. Coll., Calcutta, 1960-71; assoc. prof. Rensselaer Poly. Inst., Troy, N.Y., 1971-76; rsch. engr. GE R & D Ctr., Schenectady, N.Y., 1976-87; prof. Condra Chair of Exellence U. Tenn., Knoxville, 1987—. Disting. scientist Power Electronics Appliance Ctr., Knoxville, 1987—; cons. PCI Ozone Corp., N.J., 1971-73, GE, 1971-76, Rsch. Triangle Inst., N.C., 1991-95, Bendix Corp., Electric Power Rsch. Inst., Lutron Electronics, UN for tech. devel. in People's Republic China and India; sr. advisor to Beijing Power Electronics R&D Ctr.; lectr. in field; hon. prof. Shanghai U. Tech., 1991, China U. of Mining and Technology, 1996, Xi'an Mining Inst., 1998. Author: Power Electronics and AC Drives, 1986, Modern Power Electronics and AC Drives, 2002; editor: Adjustable Speed AC Drive Systems, 1981, Micro Computer Control of Power Electronics and Drives, 1987, Modern Power Electronics, 1992, Power Electronics and Variable Frequency Drives, 1996; patentee in field; contbr. articles to profl. jours. Recipient Mouat Gold medal Calcutta U., 1967, Publ. award GE, 1982, Silver Patent medal GE, 1983. Fellow IEEE (life, chmn. power electronics, chmn. indsl. power converter com., Trans. Rev. chmn., static power converter com., assoc. editor Trans., neural network coun., Industry Applications Soc. outstanding achievement award 1993, Region 3 outstanding engr. award, 1994, Lamme Gold medal 1996); mem. IEEE Indsl. Electronics Soc. (Eugene Mittlemann Achievement award 1994, chmn. power electronics coun., Cont. Edn. award 1997, Millennium medal 2000, Newell award 2005). Hindu. Avocations: travel, gardening. Home: 404 Dixieview Rd Knoxville TN 37922-2609 Office: Univ of Tenn Dept Elec Engring 419 Ferris Hl Knoxville TN 37996-0001 Office Phone: 865-974-8398. Business E-Mail: bbose@utk.edu, b.bose@ieee.org.

BOSE, NIRMAL KUMAR, electrical engineer, mathematics educator; b. Calcutta, West Bengal, India, Aug. 19, 1940; came to U.S., 1961; s. Dhruba Kumar and Roma (Guha) B.; m. Chandra Bose, June 8, 1969; children: Meenekshi, Enakshi. B.Tech., Indian Inst. Tech., Kharagpur, West Bengal, 1961; MS, Cornell U., 1963; PhD, Syracuse U., 1967. Asst. prof. U. Pitts., 1967-70, assoc. prof., 1970-76, prof., 1976-86; Singer prof. elec. engring. Pa. State U., University Park, 1986-91, HRB-Systems prof. elec. engring., 1992—; vis. assoc. prof. U. Calif., Berkeley, 1973-74. Cons. RCA, Meadowland, Pa., 1968-69; spl. lectr. Coll. of Steubenville, Ohio, 1968-70; vis. assoc. prof. Am. U. Beirut, 1971, U. Md., College Park, 1972; vis. fellow Princeton U., 1996; apptd. vis. prof. Israel Inst. Tech., 1996; UN expert in neural networks to instns. and ctrs., India, 1994-95; rschr. Japan Soc. for Promotion of Sci., 1998; Humboldt guest prof. Ruhr U., Bochum, Germany, 2000-03; invited sr. mem. Inst. Math. Scis., Nat. U. Singapore, 2003. Author: Applied Multidimensional Systems Theory, 1982, Digital Filters: Theory and Applications, 1985, rev. edit., 1993; co-author: Neural Network Fundammentals, 1996; editor: Multidimensional Systems: Theory and Application, 1979, Multidimensional Systems; Progress, Directions and Open Problems, 1985, 2nd edit., 2003; founding editor-in-chief Multidimensional Sys. and Signal Processing, 1990-; co-editor: Handbook of Statistics vol. on Signal Processing and Its Applications, 1993; assoc. editor Cirs., Sys., and Signal Processing Jour., IEEE Trans. of Cirs. and Sys., Jour. Franklin Inst.; adv. com. Internat. Jour. Smart Engring. Sys. Design. Recipient Invitational fellow for rsch. in Japan, Japan Soc. for Promotion of Sci., 1998, Charles H. Fetter Univ. Endowed fellow in elec. engring., 2001—, Alexander von Humboldt Sr. U.S. Scientist Rsch. award, 1999. Fellow IEEE (chmn. cirs. and systems tech. com. on edn. 1979-85, Merit award 2000); mem. AAAS, ASEE, Am. Math. Soc., N.Y. Acad. Scis., Am. Soc. Elec. Engrs. Sigma Xi. Hindu. Avocations: table-tennis, stamp collecting/philately. Home: 1312 W Park Hills Ave State College PA 16803-3250 Office: Pa State U Dept Elec Engring University Park PA 16802 Office Phone: 814-865-3912. Business E-Mail: nkb1@psu.edu. *Development and cultivation of spiritual and intellectual resources to the best of one's ability supported by parental blessings and encouragement provide the foundation on which the edifice of an individual's contributions to science and society is constructed.*

BOSE, SHIKHA, pathologist; b. Lucknow, India, Dec. 5, 1957; arrived in U.S., 1991; d. Baidyo Nath and Sujata Ghosh; m. Swaraj Bose, Feb. 26, 1982; children: Namrata, Deepika. MBBS, King George's Med. Coll., Lucknow, 1981; MD in Pathology, All India Inst. Med. Scis., New Delhi, 1986. Diplomate Am. Bd. Anatomic Pathology, Am. Bd. Cytopathology. Sr. demonstrator All India Inst. Med. Scis., New Delhi, 1986—89, rsch. officer, 1989—91; resident/fellow Lankenau Hosp., Wynnewood, Pa., 1991—93; fellow Meml. Sloan Kettering Cancer Ctr., NYC, 1993—94; resident/fellow NYU Med. Ctr., NYC, 1994—95, Columbia Presbyn. Med. Ctr., NYC, 1995—96, clin. instr., 1996—97, asst. prof. pathology, 1997—98, UCLA, 1998—2001, Cedars Sinai Med. Ctr., L.A., 2001—. Dir., cytopathology divsn. Cedars Sinai Med. Ctr., 2002—. Contbr. articles to profl. jours., including Sci., Cancer Rsch., Oncogene, Modern Pathology, others. Fellow: Coll. Am. Pathologists; mem.: Can. Acad. Pathologists, Am. Acad. Pathologists. Office: Cedars Sinai Med Ctr 8700 Beverly Blvd # 8723 Los Angeles CA 90048 E-mail: boses@cshs.org.

BOSEKER, BARBARA JEAN, education educator; b. Milw., Dec. 2, 1944; d. Edward Herbert and Alice Margaret (Maas) B.; m. Dale Leslie Sutcliffe, Aug. 8, 1975. Student, U. Nigeria, Nsukka, 1966; BS (hon.) in secondary edn., U. Wis., Milw., 1968; MA in Anthropology, U. Wis., 1971, PhD in edn., 1978. cert. intermediate and secondary English tchr. Wis. Chemistry lab. technician Allen-Bradley Corp., Milw., 1963; coordinator Neighborhood Youth Corps., Madison, 1970; program devel. specialist Tchr. Corps., Madison, 1976-77; asst. prof. edn. Occidental Coll., 1978-80, Moorhead State U., 1980-86, assoc. prof., 1986-90, prof., 1990-95, Winona State U., 1995—. Adv. bd.: Annual Editions: Teaching English as a Second Language, 1999—; cons. Inst. Latin Am. Studies U.Tex, Austin, 1980. Grant writer Fargo-Moorhead (N.D.) Indian Center, 1980; evaluator Indian edn. grant Fargo Pub. Schs., 1985-90; contbr. articles to profl. jours. Elks Nat. and State Youth scholar U. Wis.; fellow Ford Found., 1968-69, NDEA, 1970-71, 78. Mem. NEA, Minn. Edn. Assn., Nat. Women's Studies Assn., Mortar Bd., Phi Kappa Phi, Pi Lambda Theta, Kappa Delta Pi, Sigma Tau Delta, Sigma Epsilon Sigma. Democrat. Christian Scientist. Home: 1317 Ridgewood Dr Winona MN 55987-5421 Office: Winona State U Winona MN 55987 Office Phone: 507-457-5364. Business E-Mail: bboseker@winona.edu.

BOSHES, LOUIS D., neurologist, educator, psychiatrist, researcher, historian, writer; b. Chgo. s. Jacob and Ethel (London) B.; children: Arlene Phyllis Boshes Hirschfelder, Judi Myrl; m. Natalie A. Boshes. BS, Northwestern U., 1931, MD, 1936, postgrad., 1947-51; HHD (hon.), 1976. Diplomate neurology, psychiatry, and child neurology Am. Bd. Psychiatry and Neurology. Intern Michael Reese Hosp., Chgo., 1935-36, Cook County Hosp., 1936-37; fellow psychiatry Ill. Neuro-psychiat. Inst., Chgo., 1941-42, 46-47; sr. attending neurologist and psychiatrist, chief neurology clinic Michael Reese Med. Center, 1940—; sr. attending neurologist, psychiatrist emeritus Michael Reese Hosp. Med. Ctr.; prof. neurology and psychiatry Northwestern U., 1955-63; prof. neurology U. Ill. Coll. Medicine, Chgo., 1970-78, prof. emeritus, 1978—, historian and archivist in neurology; emeritus Cook County Hosp.; attending neurologist Ill. Research and Ednl. Hosps., 1963—, dir. consultation clinic for epilepsy, 1963-78; assoc. and attending neurologist, cons. neurology Cook County Hosp., 1947—; sr. cons. neurology Downey VA Hosp., 1952-60; prof. neurology Cook County Grad. Sch. Medicine, 1970—; practice medicine specializing in neurology and psychiatry, 1975—. Med. adv. com. Cook County chpt. Nat Found., 1947-55, March of Dimes, 1956—; med. adv. com. Epilepsy Assn. Am., 1964—; bd. dirs., med. adv. com. Epilepsy Found. Am., 1964—; ambassador Internat. Bur. Epilepsy, 1969—; profl. adv. com. Nat. Parkinson Found., 1960—, Nat. Myasthenia Gravis Found., 1972—; profl. adv. bd. United Cerebral Palsy; adv. bd. Cognitive Neurology and Alzheimer's Disease Ctr. Northwestern U., 2002--. Author, contbr. to books, med. jours.; assoc. editor Diseases of the Nervous System, 1962—; editor Chgo. Neurol. Soc. Bull., Behavioral Neuropsychiatry; mem. editorial bd. Excerpta Medica, Internat. Jour. Neurology and Neurosurgery. Historian, curator, archivist neurology U. Ill. Coll. Medicine at Chgo., 1990—, historian to Central Neuropsychiatric Assn, 1975—, Lt. comdr. M.C., USNR, 1941-46. Fellow ACP, Am. Acad. Neurology, Am. Psychiat. Assn. (disting. life); mem. AMA (cons. JAMA, bd. govs. 1991—), Inst. Medicine Chgo., Pan Am. Med. Assn. (pres. sect. neurology 1973—, hon. D.Hum. 1976), Ctrl. Neuropsychiat. Assn. (pres. 1973-74, historian, curator), Ill. Psychiat. Soc. (life, sec.-treas., acting pres. 1949-50), Chgo. Neurol. Soc. (pres. 1965-66, historian 1965—, curator), Michael Reese Hosp. and Med. Ctr. Alumni Assn. (pres. 1961-62), Assn. for Rsch. in Nervous and Mental Diseases, Internat. League Against Epilepsy, Am. League Against Epilepsy, Ill. League Against Epilepsy (med. adv. com.), Ill. Med. Soc. (chmn. sect. neurology and psychiatry 1961—), Chgo. Med. Soc., World Fedn. Neurology, AAAS, Am. Med. Soc. Vienna (life), Ctrl. Assn. Electroencephalographers, Sigma Xi, Phi Delta Epsilon, Alpha Omega Alpha. Home: 3150 N Lake Shore Dr Chicago IL 60657-4829 E-mail: l.boshes@uic.edu.

BOSI, MARINA, digital audio technologist, educator; b. Piacenza, Italy; came to U.S., 1988; d. Franco and Alice Bosi; m. Richard E. Goldberg, Nov. 18, 1990. Diploma in Flute, Nat. Conservatory of Music, Florence, Italy, 1978; Diploma of Honor in Flute, Accademia Chigiana, Siena, Italy, 1982; Doctorate Laurea in Physics, U. Florence, 1987. Chargée de recherche IRCAM, Paris, 1985-87; sys. cons. Tempo Reale, Florence, 1987; DSP engr. Digidesign Inc., Menlo Park, Calif., 1988-91; project engr.-tech., mktg. and standards, R&D, bus. devel. Dolby Labs. Inc., San Francisco, 1991-97; v.p. tech., standards and strategies Digital Theater Sys. Inc., LA, 1997—2001; chief tech. officer MPEGLA, LLC, Denver, 2001—. Prof. Nat. Conservatory of Music, Venice, Italy, 1979-80; prof. computer sci. Profl. Tech. Inst., Florence, 1987-88; cons. prof. Ctr. for Computer Rsch. in Music and Acoustics, Stanford (Calif.) U., 1998—. Co-author: Introduction to Digital Audio Coding and Standards, 2002; contbr. articles to profl. jours. Recipient numerous scholarships and awards. Mem. IEEE (sr.); fellow Audio Engring. Soc. (v.p. western region U.S. and Can. 1995-97, pres. 1998-99), Am. Nat. Standards Inst., Internat. Standards Orgn., Internat. Telecomm. Union, Acoustical Soc. Am. Achievements include patents in field. Office: MPEGLA LLC 250 Steele St Denver CO 80206

BOSKEY, BENNETT, lawyer; b. N.Y.C., Aug. 14, 1916; s. Meyer and Janet (Lauterstein) B.; m. Shirley Ecker, July 3, 1940 (dec. 1998). AB, Williams Coll., 1935; LL.B., Harvard U., 1939. Bar: N.Y. 1940, U.S. Supreme Ct. 1943, D.C. 1949. Spl. asst. to Atty. Gen. U.S. Dept. Justice, Washington, 1943; advisor on enemy property U.S. Dept. State, Washington, 1946-47; atty. U.S. Atomic Energy Commn., Washington, 1947-49, dep. gen. counsel, 1949-51; ptnr. firm Volpe, Boskey & Lyons (and predecessors), Washington, 1951-96. Law clk. Judge Learned Hand, 1939-40, Justice Stanley Reed, 1940-41, Chief Justice Harlan F. Stone, 1941-43; trustee Analytic Svcs. Inc., Arlington, Va., 1962-91; adv. bd. internat. legal studies program Am. U., 1987-99. Chmn. bd. trustees Primary Day Sch., Bethesda, Md., 1969— . Served with U.S. Army, 1943-46. Mem. ABA, Am. Law Inst. (treas. 1975—, mem. coun., Am. Law Inst.-ABA com. on continuing profl. edn. 1985—), Am. Soc. Internat. Law (bd. rev. and devel. 1973-88). Office: 901 New York Ave 9th Fl Washington DC 20001 Office Phone: 202-346-4500. E-mail: bennettbos@aol.com.

BOSL, GEORGE JOSEPH, physician, oncologist; b. Cleve., Oct. 19, 1948; BS in Biology, John Carroll U., 1969; MD, Creighton U., 1973. Diplomate Am. Bd. Medicine, Am. Bd. Oncology. Intern N.Y. Hosp., 1973-74, resident in medicine, 1974-75, Sloan-Kettering Cancer Ctr., 1974-77; fellow in med. oncology U. Minn. Hosp., 1977-79; oncologist Meml. Sloan Kettering Cancer Ctr., N.Y.C., 1979—, dir. oncology, hematology fellow program, 1986-94, head divsn. solid tumor oncology, 1989-97, assoc. physician-in-chief, 1994-97, chmn. dept. medicine, 1997—; prof. medicine Cornell U., N.Y.C., 1991—. Mem. AMA, Am. Assn. Cancer Rsch., Am. Soc. Clin. Oncology, Alpha Omega Alpha. Office: Meml Sloan Kettering Ctr New York NY 10021

BOSL, PHILLIP L., lawyer; b. Feb. 27, 1945; BA, U. Calif., Santa Barbara, 1968; JD, U. So. Calif., 1975. Bar: Calif. 1975. Ptnr. Gibson, Dunn & Crutcher LLP, L.A., 1983—. Mem. U. So. Calif. Law Rev., 1973-75. Officer USCG, 1969-72. Mem. ABA, Los Angeles County Bar Assn., Fed. Bar Assn., Assn. Bus. Trial Lawyers Am., Securities Industry Assn. (compliance and legal divsn.), Inst. Corp. Counsel (gov.), Nat. Assn. Securities Dealers (arbitrator), Order of Coif. Home: 6226 Napoli Ct Long Beach CA 90803-4800 Office: Gibson Dunn & Crutcher LLP 333 S Grand Ave Ste 5000 Los Angeles CA 90071-3197 Office Phone: 213-229-7543. E-mail: pbosl@gibsondunn.com.

BOSLEY, KAREN LEE, language educator, communications educator; b. Beech Grove, Ind., Sept. 23, 1942; d. Lowell Holmes and Kathryn Gertrude (Drake) Foley; m. Norman Keith Bosley, Dec. 21, 1964; children: Mark Harold, Rachael Kathryn, Keith Lowell, Sidney Clark. AB in Lang. Arts summa cum laude, U. Indpls., 1965; MA in English, Northwestern U., 1967; MA in Journalism, Ball State U., 1984; postgrad. (Newspaper Fund fellow), U. Mo., 1973; postgrad., Ohio U., 1977. Copy editor, reporter Indpls. News, 1963-65; English tchr., yearbook adviser Beech Grove (Ind.) Jr. H.S., 1965-66; English tchr. So. Regional H.S., Manahawkin, N.J., 1967-68; prof. humanities, journalism, and English Ocean County Coll., Toms River, N.J., 1971—, student newspaper adviser, 1971—, yearbook adviser, 1999—. Part-time reporter Daily Times-Observer, Toms River, 1972—77, part-time copy editor, 1993. Contbr. articles to publs. in field. Trustee Long Beach Island Hist. Assn., Friends of Island Libr., 1975-79; pres. Long Beach I PTA; chmn. Long Beach Twp. Dem. Mcpl. Com., 1971-78; Dem. committeeman Long Beach Twp. Dist. 2, 1971-78, 85—; mem. Long Beach Twp. Recreation Commn., 1972-75; bd. dirs. Ocean County Red Cross, 1972-78, Ocean County Family Planning, Inc., 1972-78, bd. dirs. Student Press Law Ctr., 1987-2002, sec., 1998-2000, mem. adv. coun., 2002—; chmn. Cub Scout pack 32, Ocean County Coun. Boy Scouts Am.; founder, bd. dirs. Long Beach I Hist. Assn., Island Dems., Inc.; mem. adminstrv. bd. First United Meth. Ch. Beach Haven Terrace (N.J.); So. Regional H.S. Band Parent Orgn., 1995-96, pres., 1996-97, corr. sec; So. Regional Jazz Band Parents Assn., charter mem., 2001—. Mem. AAUW (pres., dir. Barnegat Light Area br.), NEA, N.J. Edn. Assn., Ocean County Edn. Assn., Faculty Assn. Ocean County Coll. (v.p. 1984-85), Coll. Media Advisers, Inc. (disting. newspaper adviser for U.S. 2-yr. colls. 1978, dir., sec.), Assn. Edn. in Journalism and Mass Comms., C.C. Journalism Assn. (dir., v.p.), Soc. Profl. Journalists, Internat. Platform Assn., Sigma Delta Chi. Home: 9 E Old Whaling Ln Long Beach Township NJ 08008-2930 Office: Ocean CC PO Box 2001 College Dr Toms River NJ 08754-2001 Office Phone: 732-255-0400 x2237. E-mail: kbosley@mac.com.

BOSMA, JENNIFER, nursing association administrator; Exec. dir. Nat. Coun. State Bds. Nursing, Chgo., 1989—.

BOSMAJIAN, HAIG ARAM, speech communication educator; b. Fresno, Calif., Mar. 26, 1928; s. Aram and Aurora (Keosheyan) B.; m. Hamida Just, Feb. 27, 1957; 1 child, Harlan. BA, U. Calif., Berkeley, 1949; MA, U. of Pacific, 1951; PhD, Stanford U., 1960. Instr. U. Idaho, Moscow, 1959-61; asst. prof. U. Conn., Storrs, 1961-65; prof. speech comm. U. Wash., Seattle, 1965—. Author: Language of Oppression (Orwell award), 1983: editor: Censorship, Libraries and the Law, 1983; Justice Douglas, 1980, Freedom of Speech, 1983, First Amendment in the Classroom Series, 1987: vol. 1, The Freedom to Read, 1987, vol. II, The Freedom of Religion, 1987, vol. III, Freedom of Expression, 1988, vol. IV, Academic Freedom, 1989, vol. V, Freedom to Publish, 1989, Metaphor and Reason in Judicial Opinions, 1992, The Freedom Not to Speak, 1999. Recipient Bicentennial of the Bill of Rights award Western States Communication Assn., 1991. Office Phone: 206-543-2660.

BOSMAN, RICHARD, artist, printmaker; b. Madras, India, 1944; Student, Byam Sch Sch. Painting/Drawing, London, 1964-69, N.Y. Studio Sch., N.Y.C., 1969-71, Skowhegan Sch. Painting, Maine, 1970. Instr. N.Y. Studio Sch., 1972, Skowhegan Sch. Painting and Sculpture, 1982, Sch. Visual Arts, N.Y.C., 1982-84. Tchr. Skowhegan Sch. Painting and Sculpture, Maine, 1982, Sch. Visual Arts, NYC, 1983—85, U. Pa., Phila., 1986, Temple U., Phila., 1987, Columbia U., NYC, 1988—90, Temple U., Phila., 1991, Rhode Island Sch. Design, Providence, 1992, SUNY, Purchase, 1993, Fairfield U., 1993, Yale U., Norfolk, Conn., 1994—98, Vassar Coll., Poughkeepsie, NY, 1995—. Exhibited in one-man shows at Galerie La Maquina Espanola, Madrid, 1990, Galerie Biedermann, Munich, Germany, 1991, Brooke Alexander, 1991, 93, 94, Galleria Toselli, Milan, 1992, Fairfield (Conn.) U. Gallery, 1993, R.I. Sch. Design Print Gallery, 1993, Timmesch Gallery, Mpls., 1993, Brooke Alexander Gallery, NYC, 1994, The Century Assn., 1996, U. Conn., 2000, Vassar Coll., 2002, Elizabeth Harris Gallery, NYC, 2003, Mark Moore Gallery, Santa Monica, Calif., 2004; group shows include Am. Fedn. ARts, N.Y.C., 1989, Walker Art Ctr. from Mpls. to Balt., 1989, U. Maine Mus. Art, Orono, 1989, Galeria La Maquina Espanola, 1989, John Berggruen Gallery, San. Francisco, 1990, Champion Gallery Champion Internat. Group, Stamford, Conn., 1992, Alice Simsar Gallery, Ann Arbor Mich., 1993, Roger Smith Hotel, NYC, 1993, Am. Acad. Arts and Letters, NYC, 1994, U. Ill., 1995, Mus. Modern Art, NYC, 1996, Columbus Mus., Ga., 1996, Walker-Kornbluth Gallery, Fairlawn, NJ, 1998, Snugharbor Cultural Ctr., Staten Island, NY, 2000, Barbara Krakow Gallery, Boston, 2002, Mark Moore Gallery, Santa Monica, Calif., 2004; works included in collections at Albright-Knox Art Gallery, Buffalo, Australian Nat. Gallery, Canberra, Bklyn. Mus., Fogg Art Mus./Harvard U., Nat. Mus. Am. Art, Washington, Weatherspoon Art Gallery, Greensboro, Detroit Inst. Art, Des Moines Art Ctr., Chrysler Mus., Norfolk, Conn., Eli Broad Family Found., L.A., Balt. Mus. Art., Australian Nat. Gallery, Canberra, Australia, others; co-author: Exit the Face, 1982; illustrator: Grasping at Emptiness, 1987, The Captivity Narrative of Hannah Duston, 1987, others. Guggenheim fellow, 1994. Address: c/o Mark Moore Gallery Bergamot Station A1 2525 Michigan Ave Santa Monica CA 90404*

BOSNER, KEVIN CHARLES, manufacturing executive, controller; b. Rochester, NY, Oct. 23, 1951; s. John A. and Sabina (Lyons) B.; m. Mary Catherine Cleary, Oct. 27, 1973; children: Richard, Alanna. BA in English and Edn., Le Moyne Coll., 1973; MBA in Fin. and Acctg., Rochester Inst. Tech., 1977. Cert. mgmt. acct. Mgr. and owner Allied Indsl. Laundry, Rochester, 1973-77, Temstad, Inc., Rochester, 1977-81; with Case Hoyt Corp., Rochester, 1981-88, corp. contr., 1986-88; v.p. fin. IMPCO, Inc., Rochester, 1988—97; contr. Germanow Simon Corp., Rochester, 1998—2002; vis. instr. acctg. SUNY Jones Sch. Bus., Geneseo, 2002—. Mem. Nat. Assn. Accts. Home: 796 Blue Creek Dr Webster NY 14580-9114 Office Phone: 585-245-5364. E-mail: bosner@genesea.edu.

BOSNIAK, MURRAY ELI, educational consultant; b. Phila., Oct. 10, 1944; s. David Bosniak and Ann Feldman; m. Kanta Nancy Stine; 1 child, Joshua; m. Linda Burr; children: Michael, Peter. BA, Temple U., Phila., 1966; MAT, Ind. U., 1968; PhD, Omega U., Newport, N.H., 2003. Cert. hypnotherapist New Eng. Inst. Hypnotherapy, 2002, lic. tchr. Pa., cert. Reiki master 2002, ordained minister 1989, cert. Sechim practitioner. Tchr. Parkway Program, Phila., 1975—84, Upward Bound, 1979—88; ednl. cons., 1986—; instr. New River C.C., 1985—98; asst. dir. Life Attaring Inst., Jacksonville, NC, 1998—2002, Alpha Learning Inst., Blacksburg, Va., 2002—. Performance poet, 1979—; actor Va. Tech. Summer Musical Ent., Blacksburg, 1992—; facilitator writing workshops, 2003—04; voice-over actor, writer Floyd Environ. Action Team; presenter in field. Co-author: (screenplays) Denial, 1993; author: Relational Teaching, 1994; contbr. articles to profl. jours. Recipient Best Tchr. award, Upward Bound, 1980, 1986; fellow Summer fellow, Pa. Advancement Sch., Phila., 1976, New River C.C., 1991. Mem.: ASCE, Nat. Rsch. in Afflective Learning Factors Assn. Avocations: golf, yoga, reading, singing, film studies. Office: Alpha Learning Inst 209 N Main St Ste C Blacksburg VA 24060 Office Phone: 540-745-3335.

BOSS, AMELIA HELEN, lawyer, educator; b. Balt., Apr. 3, 1949; d. Myron Theodore and Loretta (Oakjones) B.; m. Roger S. Clark, Mar. 3, 1979; children: Melissa, Seymour, Edward, Ashley. Student, Oxford (Eng.) U., 1968; BA in Sociology, Bryn Mawr, 1970; JD, Rutgers U., 1975. Bar: N.J, Pa., U.S. Dist. Ct. (ea. dist.) N.J., U.S. Dist. Ct. (ea. dist.) Pa., U.S. Supreme Ct., U.S. Ct. Appeals (3d cir.). Law clk. Hon. Milton B. Cranford N.J. Supreme Ct., 1975-76; assoc. Pepper, Hamilton & Scheetz, Phila., 1976-78; assoc. prof. law Rutgers U. Sch. Law, Camden, N.J., 1983-87, Temple U., Phila., 1989-91; prof. law Temple U. Sch. Law, Phila., 1991—, Charles Klein prof. law, 1999—. Vis. prof. law U. Miami Sch. Law, Coral Gables, Fla., 1985—86; Leo Goodwin disting. vis. prof. law Nova U., Sch. Law, 1998; mem. coms. Nat. Conf. Commrs. on Uniform State Laws; U.S. rep. to UN Commn. on Internat. Trade Law; dir. Inst. for Internat. Law and Pub. Policy, 2001—. Author: (books) Electronic Data Interchange Agreements: A Guide and Sourcebook, 1993, ABCs of the UCC: Article 2A, ABCs of the UCC: Article 5; editor-in-chief The Data Law Report, 1993-97, The Business Lawyer, 1998-99, ABCs of the UCC; mem. permanent editl. bd. Uniform Comml. Code; contbr. articles to profl. jours. Named among top 50 women lawyers in U.S. Nat. Law Jour., 1998. Fellow Am. Bar Found.; mem. ABA (chmn. bus. law sect. 2000-01, chmn. sect. officers conf. 2001—), Internat. Bar Assn., Am. Law Inst. (coun. 2000—), Am. Bankruptcy Inst., Am. Coll. Comml. Fin. Lawyers, Nat. Assn. Women Lawyers. Home: 309 Westmont Ave Haddonfield NJ 08033-1714 Office: Temple U Sch Law 1719 N Broad St Philadelphia PA 19122-6002

BOSS, MANLEY LEON, plant physiologist; b. Atlanta, Dec. 24, 1924; s. Herman Beryl and Florence Clara Boss; m. Helen Phyllis Ellins, Nov. 20, 1956; children: Valerie Jolly(dec.) children: Brian, Daniel. BS, U. Miami, 1949; MAgr, Inter-American Inst. Agrl. Scis., Costa Rica, 1951; PhD, Iowa State Coll., 1954. Asst. then assoc. prof. dept. botany U. Miami, Coral Gables, Fla., 1954—63; prof. dept. biology Fla. Atlantic U., Boca Raton, 1963—91, chmn. biology dept., 1968—72, asst. dean Coll. Liberal Arts, 1991—93, dean Coll. Liberal Arts, 1993—94; ret., 1994. Ecol. cons., Boca Raton, Fla., 1965—94; biostatistician/consultant, 1955—94. With U.S. Army, 1943—45, ETO. Achievements include research in cellular senescence. Home: 3308 Perimeter Rd Palm City FL 34990

BOSSART, PAUL NATHANIEL, JR., geologist, geophysicist, consultant; b. Pitts., May 24, 1930; s. Paul Nathaniel and Eugenia Evelyn (Brown) B.; m. Jean Violet Troutman, Feb. 21, 1953; children: Carla B. Kochel, Paula B. DeVore, Victoria. BS in Geology, Pa. State U., 1952; postgrad., U. Pitts., 1952-54. Registerd profl. geologist, Pa. Geophys. trainee Gulf Rsch., Odessa, Tex., 1952-54; asst. supr. seismic interpretation Canadian Gulf Oil, Calgary, Alta., Can., 1954-56; sys. geophysicist Consolidated Nat. Gas, Pitts., 1956-70; sr. geologist Peoples Nat. Gas., Pitts., 1970-79; pres. Ter-Ex, Inc., Pitts., 1979-85; pres., owner P.N. Bossart & Assoc., Inc., Pitts., 1985—. Cons. in field. Contbr. articles to profl. jours. Chmn. Pine Twp. (Pa.) Authority,

1966-79. Mem. Pitts. Assn. Petroleum Geologists, Pitts. Geological Soc., Soc. Exploration Geophysicists (emeritus). Republican. Lutheran. Home: 115 Mohawk Ln Wexford PA 15090-8831 Office: PN Bossart & Assoc Inc PO Box 55 Wexford PA 15090-0055

BOSSE, MARK THOMAS, social services administrator; b. Portsmouth, NH, Sept. 27, 1962; s. Maurice Claude and Elaine Greta (Hudon) Bosse; m. Lisa Weiss (div.); children: Joshua, Bianca. AA, St. Petersburg (Fla.) Jr. Coll., 1985; BA, U. South Fla., 1988; MBA summa cum laude, Tampa Coll., 1996. Case mgr. Gulf Coast Cmty. Care, Clearwater, Fla., 1994—96; sales mgr. Spl. Data Processing Inc., Clearwater, 1996—97, Liberti Practice Mgmt., Clearwater, 1997—99; program dir. Assn. for Retarded Citizens, San Bernardino, Calif., 1999—2000; regional program mgr. Wise Sr. Svcs., Santa Monica, Calif., 2000—01; program dir. Bridges Inc., Pomona, Calif., 2001—02; exec. dir. Marian Homes Inc., Brea, Calif., 2002—. Owner, mgr. Final Touch Cleaning Svcs., Clearwater, Calif., 1993—96. Author: Sanity Quest, 2004. Vol. firefighter Americorps, Dunedin, Fla., 1998; HIV educator for lic. facilities. Recipient Disting. Svc. award, State of Fla., 1998, Leadership and Svc. award, Fla. Commn. Cmty. Svc., 1998. Avocations: travel, reading, motorcycling. Office: Marian Homes Inc 570 W Lambert Rd Ste A Brea CA 92821 Office Phone: 714-990-6127.

BOSSELMAN, FRED PAUL, law educator; b. Oak Park, Ill., June 14, 1934; s. Fred and Beulah (Chamberlain) B.; m. Kay Wilson, 1956; children: Judith, Carol, Mark. BA, U. Colo., 1956; JD, Harvard U., 1959. Bar: Ill. 1959, Fla. 1985. Assoc. firm Ross & Hardies, Chgo., 1959-67; partner Ross, Hardies, O'Keefe, Babcock & Parsons, 1967-83, Burke, Bosselman & Weaver, Chgo., 1983-91; vis. prof. law Chgo. Kent Law Sch., Ill. Inst. Tech., 1991-92, prof., 1992—2002; prof. emeritus, 2002—. Assoc. reporter Am. Law Inst., 1969-75; dir. Met. Planning Coun. Chgo., 1971-88; commr. Housing Authority Cook County, Ill., 1973-88. Author: (with David Callies) The Quiet Revolution in Land Use Control, 1971, (with David Callies and John Banta) The Taking Issue, 1973, (with Richard Babcock) Exclusionary Zoning, 1974, In the Wake of the Tourist, 1978, (with Craig Peterson and Claire McCarthy) Managing Tourism Growth, 1999, (with Jim Rossi and Jacqueline Lang Weaver) Energy, Economics and the Environment, 2000. Dir. Sonoran Inst., 1996—; gov. Santa Lucia Conservancy, 2000—. Mem. ABA (chmn. environ. law com. sect. real property, probate and trust law 1974-77), Am. Soc. Planning Ofcls. (dir. 1977-78), Am. Planning Assn. (sec. 1978-79, pres. 1982-83), Nat. Audubon Soc. (dir. 1985-87). Home: 2715 Woodbine Ave Evanston IL 60201-1565 Office: IIT-Chicago Kent Law Sch 565 W Adams St Chicago IL 60661-3613 Office Phone: 312-906-5351. Business E-Mail: fbosselm@kentlaw.edu.

BOSSEN, WENDELL JOHN, retired financial planner; b. Vienna, S.D., Nov. 11, 1933; s. Hans Simonsen and Clara Patrina (Vorseth) B.; m. Jean Davidson, Jan. 6, 1956; children: Mark, Monica. Student, S.D. Sch. Mines, 1952. CLU. Agt. Northwestern Nat. Life Ins. Co., Mpls., 1957-61, dist. mgr., staff mgr., 1961-68, br. mgr., 1968-72, div. v.p., 1972-77; exec. v.p., chief operating officer Inter-Ocean Ins. Co., Cin., 1977-84; exec. v.p. corp. mktg. Mut. Benefit Life Ins. Co., Newark, 1984-92; pres. Internat. Corp. Mktg. Group, Hartford, Conn., 1992-99, retired, 1999. Cons. Newark Performing Arts Corp., 1986. Author: Businessmens Guide to Insurance, 1981; contbr. articles to profl. jours. Chmn. ARC, Waterstown, S.D., 1962, Northeast S.D. chpt. United Way, Waterstown, 1963, Waterstown County Reps., 1963-64; mem. exec. com. S.D. Reps., Pierre, 1964; bd. dirs. Am. Luth. Ch., Cin., 1979, Apostles' House, 1989. Recipient Danforth Found. award, 1952. Mem. Nat. Assn. Life Underwriters (pres. Watertown chpt. 1960-61, v.p. state chpt. 1961-62), Chartered Life Underwriters, Life Ins. Mktg. Research Assn. (com. chmn. 1975). Clubs: Golden Valley Country (Mpls). Lodges: Elks (pres. 1962-63), Lions (pres. 1961, 73), Kiwanis. Avocations: golf, tennis, photography. Home: 111 Sugarberry Ln Hendersonville NC 28739-6933 Office: Internat Corp Mktg Group 100 Campus Dr Florham Park NJ 07932-1006 E-mail: wbossen@aol.com.

BOSSERT, JILL AUDREY, author; b. N.Y.C., Aug. 10, 1949; d. William Thomas and Audrey Anthony (Blum) B. AA, Am. U., Paris, 1971; BA magna cum laude, NYU, 1994; MFA, Columbia U., 1997. Assoc. pub. Madison Sq. Press, N.Y.C., 1985-92; editor Rotovision, Switzerland, 1991—97. Cons. Schutz & Co. Fine Art, N.Y.C. and Greenwich, Conn., 1992-2005, Winter Antiques Show, 2003— Author stories, essays. Vol. Mark Green for Mayor, N.Y.C., 1994. Named Herbert C. Jaffa Alumni, NYU, 1994; Philip Guston fellow Columbia U., 1996. Mem. AAUW, Soc. of Illustrators (citations of merit 1992-99), Alpha Sigma Lambda. Home: 10 E 23rd St New York NY 10010-4402

BOSSERT, REX THOMAS, editor-in-chief; BA, Carleton Coll., 1979; JD, Northwestern U., 1986; MA, Stanford U., 1985, PhD in English Lit., 1988. Staff writer L.A. Daily Jour., San Francisco Daily Jour., 1989—97; assoc. editor The Nat. Law Jour., N.Y.C., 1997—99; mng. editor The N.Y. Law Jour., N.Y.C., 1999—2004; editor in chief The Nat. Law Jour., N.Y.C., 2004—. John Henry Wigmore scholar, Stanford U. fellow. Office: The National Law Journal 105 Madison Ave 8th Fl New York NY 10016 Office Phone: 212-313-9083. E-mail: rbossert@amlaw.com.

BOSSES, STEVAN J., lawyer; b. Bronx, NY, July 29, 1937; s. Fred and Frieda (Picard) B.; m. Abbye Z. Bosses, May 24, 1964; children: Donna Lynne, David Keith, Gary Philip. BME, Cornell U., 1960; LLB, Columbia U., 1963. Bar: NY 1963, U.S. Dist. Ct. (so. dist.) NY 1964, U.S. Dist. Ct. (ea. dist.) NY 1964, U.S. Dist. Ct. (ea. dist.) Mich., 1987, U.s. Dist. Ct. (we. dist.) Wis., 1981, U.S. Patent Office 1964, U.S. Ct. Appeals (2d cir.) 1970, U.S. Ct. Appeals (3d cir.) 1979, U.S. Ct. Appeals (fed. cir.) 1982, U.S. Supreme Ct. 1989. Assoc. Watson Leavenworth Kelton & Taggart, NYC, 1963—71, ptnr., 1972—81, Fitzpatrick, Cella, Harper & Scinto, NYC, 1981—. Mem. ABA, ASME, NY State Bar Assn., Am. Intellectual Property Law Assn., Fed. Bar Coun. (trustee 1989-94), Fed. Cir. Bar Assn., NY Intellectual Property Law Assn. Home: 19 Springdale Rd Scarsdale NY 10583-7330 Office: 30 Rockefeller Plz New York NY 10112-0002 Office Phone: 212-218-2257. E-mail: sbosses@fchs.com.

BOSSIDY, LAWRENCE ARTHUR, pharmaceutical company executive, former industrial manufacturing executive; b. Pittsfield, Mass., Mar. 5, 1935; m. Nancy Bossidy, 1956; children: Lynn, Larry, Paul, Pam, Nancy, Mary Jane, Lucy, Michael, Kathleen. BA in Econs., Colgate U. With GE, 1957-91; COO GE Credit Corp., 1979—81; pres. GE Services & Materials Sector, 1981—84; exec. v.p. GE, 1981—84, vice chmn., 1984—91; chmn., CEO AlliedSignal Inc., Morristown, N.J., 1991-99; CEO Honeywell Internat. Inc., 1999—2000, 2001—02, chmn., 1999—2000, 2001—02; chmn. exec. com. Merck & Co. Inc., Whitehouse Station, 2005—. Mem. bd. dirs. Merck & Co. Inc., 1992—, JPMorgan Chase, 1998—, Berkshire Hills Bancorp. Co-author: Execution: the Discipline of Getting Things Done, 2002. Mem.: Bus. Roundtable, Bus. Coun., Elfun. Roman Catholic. Office: Merck & Co 1 Merck Dr Whitehouse Station NJ 08889

BOSSON, RICHARD CAMPBELL, state supreme court justice; b. Balt., Mar. 19, 1944; s. Albert D. and Elizabeth S. (Schaeffer) B.; m. Gloria Candelaria, Jan. 9, 1971; children: Christopher, Monica. BA, Wesleyan U., Middletown, Conn., 1966; JD, Georgetown U., 1969. Bar: Conn. 1969, N. Mex. 1970, U.S. Dist. Ct. N. Mex. 1970; cert. Soccer Referee. Atty Legal Aid Soc. of Albuquerque, 1970-73; staff atty. Mexican Am. Legal Def. Fund, 1974, Latin Am. Tchg. Fellow, Fletcher Sch., Bogota, Colombia, 1975; chief of civil div. Atty. Gen. Office, Santa Fe, 1976-78; sr. ptnr. Bosson & Canepa P.A., Santa Fe, 1980—94; judge N.Mex. Ct. of Appeals, 1994—2002; justice N.Mex. Supreme Ct., 2002—, chief justice, 2004—. Mem. constl. revision commn., 1994—95; soccer referee Lead H.S. Candidate Dem. nomination for Atty. Gen of N. Mex., 1978. Reginald Heber Smith fellow. Mem. N.Mex. Trial Lawyers Assn. (bd. dirs. 1980-93), Nat. Assn. Bond Lawyers, Am. Trial Lawyers Assn. Office Phone: 505-827-4892. Business E-Mail: suprcb@nmcourts.com.

BOSSUAT, JUDY WEIGERT, music educator; d. Edward Raymond and Edith Mabel Weigert; m. Christophe Raphael Louis Bossuat, Nov. 13, 1978 (div. June 27, 1994); 1 child, Joshua Edward Joseph. MusB magna cum laude, SUNY, Potsdam, 1975; M in Suzuki Method Pedagogy, Talent Edn. Inst., Matsumoto, Japan, 1978, postgrad., 1982. Eminence tchr. credential Calif. Suzuki violin tchr. Potsdam Suzuki Talent Edn., 1973—77; dir., tchr., condr., tchr. trainer Ecole de Musique Suzuki de Lyon, Lyon, France, 1978—94; lectr. music edn. U. of the Pacific, Stockton, Calif., 1994—2005; dir., tchr. Bossuat Music Sch., Stockton, 1994—2005; string tchr. Pacific Sch., Lincoln Unified Sch. Dist., Stockton, 1995—2000; lectr. music edn. master tchr. String Project Calif. State U., Sacramento, 2002—05; instr. string pedagogy, dir. Cmty. Music Inst. U. Oreg., Eugene, 2005—. Founding mem., bd. dirs. European Suzuki Assn., 1979—94, Fedn. Musical Suzuki de France, 1980—94; v.p. Assn. Ecoles Musique Rhone, Lyon, 1984—90; European violin-viola rep. Internat. Suzuki Assn., Dallas, 1992—93; condr. Ctrl. Valley Youth Symphony Jr. Strings, 2004—; presenter in field. Author: Learning to Read Music for the Violin, 1991, Exercises for Left Hand Devel., 2000, 2d edit., 2003, composer; contbr. articles to profl. jours. Recipient medal of honor for exceptional contbn. to edn., Nat. Assembly France, 1983, medals of the city, Marseille, France, 1983, Lyon, France, 1986, Duluth, Minn., 1993, 1st prize, Regional Youth Orch. Competition, France, 1993, 2d prize, 1994. Mem.: European Suzuki Assn. (hon. life), Fedn. Musical Suzuki de France (hon. life), Suzuki Assn. No. Calif., Suzuki Assn. Ams. (Suzuki method tchr. trainer), Calif. Music Educators Assn. (orch. rep. Bay sect. 2001—02), Am. String Tchrs. Assn. (Calif. state pres. 2003—05). Office: U Oreg Cmty String Inst 1225 University of Oregon Eugene OR 97403-5693 Office Phone: 541-346-5694. Business E-Mail: jwbossuki@onebox.com.

BOST, THOMAS GLEN, lawyer, educator; b. Oklahoma City, July 13, 1942; s. Burl John and Lorene Bell (Croka) B.; m. Sheila K. Pettigrew, Aug. 27, 1966; children: Amy Elizabeth, Stephen Luke, Emily Anne, Paul Alexander. BS in Acctg. summa cum laude, Abilene Christian U., 1964; JD, Vanderbilt U., 1967. Bar: Tenn. 1967, Calif. 1969. Instr. David Lipscomb Coll., Nashville, 1967; asst. prof. law Vanderbilt U., Nashville, 1967-68; ptnr. Latham & Watkins, Los Angeles, 1968-99; prof. law Pepperdine U., 2000—. Lectr. on taxation subjects. Chmn. bd. regents, law sch. bd. visitors Pepperdine U., Malibu, Calif., 1980-2000; chmn. bd. trustees Pacific Legal Found., 2000-02. Mem. ABA (chmn. standards of tax practice com., sec. taxation 1988-90), State Bar of Calif., Los Angeles County Bar Assn. (chmn. taxation sect. 1981-82), Beach Club (Santa Monica). Republican. Mem. Ch. of Christ.

BOSTETTER, MARTIN V. B., JR., bankruptcy court judge; b. Balt., Mar. 11, 1926; s. Martin V.B. Bostetter and Louella Jane (Smith) Rice; m. Joanne Rushworth, March 28, 1955; children: Martin III, David W., Jonathan A., Lisa A. BA, U. Va., 1950, LLD, 1952. Bar: Va. 1952, Md. 1953, D.C. 1962. City prosecutor City of Alexandria, Va., 1953-57; chief judge U.S. Bankruptcy Ct. for Ea. Dist. Va., Alexandria, 1985-99. Bd. dirs. Fed. Jud. Ctr., Washington, 1984-87, chmn. edn. com. for all bankruptcy judges, Washington, 1986-89; mem. Fed. State Jud. Rels. Com. of Commonwealth of Va.; chmn. Juvenile Detention Com., Alexandria, 1957-74. Recipient Distinguished Svc. awd. Jr. C.of C., Alexandria, 1959; U.S. Courthouse named Martin V.B. Bostetter U.S. Courthouse by act of Congress, Alexandria, Va., 1998. Office: 200 N Fairfax St Alexandria VA 22314

BOSTIC, ELIZABETH ANNE, chemical engineer; b. Chestertown, Md., Mar. 3, 1981; d. Michael Raymond and Mary Catherine Bostic. BS in Chem. Engring., U. Va., 2003; postgrad. in Engring. and Tech. Mgmt., George Wash. U., 2004—. Chem. engr. Comm. Electronics Rsch. Devel. and Engring. Ctr. US Army, Fort Belvoir, Va., 2003—. Mem.: Soc. of Women Engrs., Nat. Def. Industry Assn., Nat. Rep. Com., Alpha Delta Pi Sorority (v.p. 2001—02). Office: US Army CERDEC 10125 Gratiot Rd Ste 100 Fort Belvoir VA 22060-5816 Office Phone: 703-704-1027.

BOSTIC, JAMES E., JR., paper company executive; b. SC, June 24, 1947; BS in Textile Chemistry, Clemson U., 1969, PhD in Chemistry, 1972. Sr. rsch. scientist Am. Enka Co., 1972; White House fellow, spl. asst. to sec. U.S. Dept. Agr., Washington, 1972—73, dep. asst. sec. agr., 1973—77; corp. regulatory dir. Riegel Textile Corp., 1977—81, pres. Riegel ventures divsn., 1981—82, pres. convenience products divsn., 1982—85; gen. mgr. convenience products divsn. Ga.-Pacific Corp., 1985—87, dir. sales ops. consumer tissue group, 1987—89, gen. mgr. comml. products and sys. divsn., 1989—90, v.p. Butler Paper and Mail-Well, 1991—92, group v.p. comm. papers, 1992—95, sr. v.p. environ., govt. affairs and comm., 1995—2000, exec. v.p. environ., govt. affairs and comm., 2000—03, exec. v.p. environ., govt affairs and adminstrv. svcs., 2003—. Bd. dirs. Atlanta Com. for Pub. Edn., Clemson U. Found., Progress Energy Bd., Inc.; bd. dirs., vice chmn. edn. Metro Atlanta C. of C.; trustee Ga. Conservancy, Nat. Parks Conservation Assn., The Westminster Schs.; mem. Pres. Commn. on White House Fellowships; chmn. bd. Project GRAD, Atlanta. Named Outstanding Young Men Am., 1972, 1975; recipient Disting. Svc. award, Greenville (S.C.) Jaycees, 1979, Outstanding Textile Alumnus award, Clemson U., 1983, Outstanding Pub. Servant of Yr. award, S.C. Assn. Minorities for Pub. Adminstrn., 1983, Disting. Alumni award, Clemson U. Alumni Assn., 1990, Vision 300 award, Paper Industry Mgmt. Assn., 1997, Thomas Green Clemson Acad. Engrs. and Scientists award, Clemson U., 2002, G.W. Brumley Project GRAD USA Leadership award, 2005; Doctoral Fellowship for Black Students, Ford Found., 1968. Office: 133 Peachtree St NE Atlanta GA 30303 Office Phone: 404-652-5250. Personal E-mail: jebostic69@aol.com. Business E-Mail: jebostic@gapac.com.

BOSTICK, CHARLES DENT, retired lawyer; b. Gainesville, Ga., Dec. 28, 1931; s. Jared Sullivan and Charlotte Catherine (Dent) B.; m. Susan Oliver, Sept. 8, 1956; children: Susan, Alan. Student, Emory-at-Oxford U., 1948-49; BA, Mercer U., 1952, JD, 1958. Bar: Ga. 1957, Tenn. 1974, U.S. Dist. Ct. (no. dist.) Ga. 1958, U.S. Ct. Appeals (5th cir.) 1959. Pvt. practice, Gainesville, Ga., 1958-66; asst. prof. law U. Fla., Gainesville, 1966-68, assoc. prof., 1968, Vanderbilt U., Nashville, 1968-71, prof., 1971-92, assoc. dean, dir. admissions, 1975-79, acting dean, 1979-80, dean, 1980-85; ret., 1992. Vis. prof. law U. Leeds, Eng., 1985-86, prof. law emeritus, dean emeritus Sch. Law, 1992. Served to lt. USNR, 1952-55. Mem. Tenn. Bar. Assn. Episcopalian. Office: Vanderbilt U Sch Law 21st Ave S Nashville TN 37240-0001

BOSTICK, RUSSELL M., information technology executive; b. Feb. 4, 1957; BS in Chemistry and Math., Wabash Coll.; MBA in Marketing, U. Chgo. Technology positions IBM, 1979—94, CNA Insurance, 1994—97; chief technology officer Corp. Software & Technology, Norwood, Mass., 1997—99, Chase Insurance, 1999—2005; chief information officer Zurich Life US; exec. v.p., chief information officer Conseco, Inc., Carmel, Ind., 2005—. Chmn. bd. gov. IT Resources Ctr. Office: Conseco Inc 11825 N Pennsylvania St Carmel IN 46032*

BOSTIN, MARVIN JAY, hospital and health services consultant; came to U.S., 1956; s. Samuel and Rose (Mandel) B.; 1 child, Shepard Craig. BS in Pharmacy, U. Toronto, 1955; MS in Hosp. Adminstrn., Columbia U., 1958; PhD in Pub. Adminstrn., NYU, 1972. Pharmacist New Mt. Sinai Hosp., Toronto, 1953-56; asst. adminstr. L.I. Jewish Hosp., New Hyde Park, N.Y., 1958-62; assoc. dir. Mt. Sinai Med. Ctr., Miami Beach, Fla., 1962-65; exec. v.p. E.D. Rosenfeld Assocs. Inc., hosp. and health svcs. cons., White Plains, N.Y., 1965-78; pres. M. Bostin Assocs., Inc., Stamford, Conn., 1979—. Guest scholar Brookings Instn., Washington, 1965; lectr. Sch. Pub. Health and Adminstrv. Medicine, Columbia U., N.Y.C., 1965-78, Grad. Sch. Pub. Adminstrn., 1967; lectr. Grad. Sch. Architecture and Planning, Columbia U., 1975-78; cons. to Bur. of Hearings and Appeals, Social Security Adminstrn., HEW, 1967-68; cons. task force on guidelines for constrn. and equipment of hosp. and med. facilities, USPHS, DHHS, 1987; mem. implementation work group on improving health Nat. Commn. on Children, 1992; spl. cons. to Office of Equal Health Opportunity, Office of Surgeon Gen., USPHS, 1966-67. Mem. Dade County (Fla.) Welfare Planning Coun., Miami, 1962-65; bd. dirs. South Fla. Hosp. Coun., Miami, 1963-65. Fellow APHA, Royal Soc. Health (London), Am. Assn. Healthcare Cons. (chmn. monograph series com. 1970-71, exec. com. 1972-75, profl. standards com. 1974-76); mem. Am. Hosp. Assn. (life), Forum for Health Care Planning (dir. 1982-95, treas. 1988-89, sec. 1989-90), Am. Coll. Healthcare Execs., Can. Coll. Health Svc. Execs. (fgn. affiliate), Internat. Hosp. Fedn. Address: M Bostin Assoc Inc 800 Summer St Ste 315 Stamford CT 06901-1023 Office Phone: 203-961-0511. Business E-Mail: marvin@bostin.com.

BOSTON, BETTY LEE, investment company executive, financial consultant, financial planner; b. Agana, Guam, Dec. 21, 1935; d. Homer Laurence and Bessie Margarete (Leech) Litzenberg; m. Filibert Roth Boston, Aug. 12, 1956; children: William Litzenberg, Beth Boston Tedesco, Brent Litzenberg. BA, U. Mich., 1958. CFP®. Stockbroker I.M. Simon & Co., Murray, Ky., 1976—78, 1st of Mich. Corp., Murray, Ky., 1978—86; fin. cons. J.J.B. Hilliard, W.L. Lyons, Inc., Murray, Ky., 1986—; v.p. Hilliard Lyons Inc., Murray, Ky., 1998—. Instr. adult edn. investment classes Murray State U., 1977—2000; investment commentator Sta. WKMS, Murray, 1987—. Fin. columnist Murray Ledger and Times, 2000—. Chmn. Inter-Faith Coalition Congregations, Ann Arbor, 1971-73; pres. Need Line Ch. and Cmty. Ministry, Murray, 1981-83; mem. Murray regional bd. Ky. Coun. on Econ. Edn., 1987—. Recipient Woman of Yr. award, Murray Bus. and Profl. Women, 1988. Mem. AAUW (treas. Murray br. 1982-87, pres. 1991-97), Rotary (sec. Murray club 1990-95, pres. 1998-99, Paul Harris fellow). United Methodist. Home: 917 N 16th St Murray KY 42071-1523 Office: JJB Hilliard WL Lyons Inc 414 Main St Murray KY 42071-2059 Office Phone: 270-753-3366.

BOSTON, BILLIE, costume designer, costume history educator; b. Oklahoma City, Sept. 22, 1939; d. William Barrett and Margaret Emeline (Townsend) Long; m. William Clayton Boston, Jr., Jan. 20, 1962; children: Kathryn Gray, William Clayton III. BFA, U. Okla., 1961, MFA, 1962. Asst. to designer Karinski of N.Y., N.Y.C., 1966-67; prof. costume history Oklahoma City U., 1987—. Rep. Arts Coun., Oklahoma City, 1987-90, Arts Festival, Oklahoma City, 1972-80; dir. ETC Theater, Oklahoma City SW Coll., 1979-83; actress Lyric Theatre, Oklahoma City, 1979-81; designer Casa Mahara Theatre, Ft. Worth, 1998. Exhibited in group shows at Taos, N.Mex., Santa Fe; represented in permanent collections in Dallas, Taos, Santa Fe, Tulsa, N.Y.C., La Jolla; costume designer Ballet Okla., Oklahoma City, 1979-84, Agnes DeMillie's Rodeo Ballet Okla., 1982, Royal Ballet Flanders, 1983, Pitts. Ballet, 1983, BBC's Childrens Prodn., 1984, 86, Lyric Theatre, Oklahoma City, 1987-95, Red Oak Music Theatre, Lakewood, N.J., 1988, Winter Olympics, 1988, Miss Am. Pageant, 1988, for JoAnne Worley in Hello Dolly, San Francisco Opera Circus, 1991, Jupiter (Fla.) Theatre, 1991-92, Mobile (Ala.) Light Opera, 1992, The Boy Friend, Temple U., Japan, 1995, The Sound of Music, Lyric Stage, Dallas, 1995, Annie Get Your Gun, Guys and Dolls with Vic Damone, 1995, Westbury Flash Valley Forge Music Fair, Oklahoma and Sound of Music, Casa Manana, Theatre, Ft. Worth, 1997, Singing in the Rain, Lone Star Theatre, Galveston, Tex., 1997, Most Happy Fellow, Lyric Stage Dallas, 1997, To Gillian on her 37th Birthday, Watertower Theatre, Dallas, 1998, Carousel, Annie Get Your Gun, Cinderella, Casa Manana, 1998; designer Titanic, Irving, Tex., 2003, Specture Bridegroom, Irving, 2003, Opal, Lyric Stage, Irving, 2003; designer (play) Finian's Rainbow, Lyric Stage, Dallas, Tex., 2004, Ragtime, Lyric Stage, 2004. Rep. Speakers Bur. Oklahoma City for Ballet, 1979-85; judge State Hist. Speech Tournament, Oklahoma City, 1985-87; chmn. State of Okla. Conf. on Tchr./Student Relationships, Oklahoma City, 1981. Recipient Gov.'s Achievement award, 1988, Lady in the News award, 1987; Excellence in Costume Design award Kennedy Ctr. Am. Coll. Theatre Festival XXXIV, 2001; nom. Outstanding Costume Designer Southwest, Dallas Theatre League, 2003. Mem. Alpha Chi Omega (house corp. bd. 1986-90). Methodist. Avocation: watercolorist. Home: 1701 Camden Way Oklahoma City OK 73116-5121

BOSTON, BRAD, information technology executive; BS in Computer sci., U. Ill. Former exec. Am. Nat. Bank and Trust Co. Chgo., United Airlines/Covia, Visa, Am. Express; exec. v.p., product solutions Sabre Group, Dallas, 1997—99, exec. v.p. product devel. & delivery, 1999—2000; exec. v.p. ops. Corio Inc., 2000—01; sr. v.p., chief info. officer Cisco Systems, Inc., San Jose, Calif., 2001—. Bd. advisors H-P, Harvard Group; bd. dirs. NetNumber, Inc.; mem. e-bus. adv. bd. Tex. Christian U. M.J. Neeley Sch. Bus. Named one of top tech. innovators, Info. Week mag., 2004. Office: Cisco Systems Inc 170 W Tasman Dr San Jose CA 95134

BOSTON, BRENDA ROSE, elementary school educator, administrator; b. Berwick, Pa., June 30, 1950; d. Robert L. and Sarah Marjorie (Rissmiller) B. BRE, Bapt. Bible Coll., 1972, MS in Christian Sch. Edn., 1999. Elem. supr. Bible Bapt. Ch., West Chester, Pa., 1987—.

BOSTON, DAVID, professional football player; b. Humble, Tex., Aug. 19, 1978; s. Byron and Carolyn; 1 child, Alaia. BA in Sociology, Ohio State U. Wide receiver Ariz. Cardinals, 1999—2003, San Diego Chargers, 2003, Miami Dolphins, 2004—. Office: c/o Miami Dolphins 7500 SW 30th St Davie FL 33314

BOSTON, GRETHA, actress, vocalist; b. Crossett, AK; B of Music, N Tex. State U., Denton; vocal study with vocal tech. and coaches, John Wustman, Bill Riley. Carnegie Hall debut Mozart's Coronation Mass, 1991, concert performances Beethoven's Ninth Symphony (Carnegie Hall), Handel's Messiah (Madison, Wis. & Arlington, Tex.), roles (Operas) Carmen in Bizet's Carmen, The Mother in Menotti's The Consul, Ciesca in Puccini's Gianni Schicchi, Delilah in Saint-Saens's Samson et Delilah, Maddalena in Verdi's Rigoletto (N.Y. Grand Opera), Amneris in Verdi's Aida, Azucena in Verdi's Il Trovatore, Queenie in Kern & Hammerstein's Show Boat (Tony award Best Supporting Actress in a Musical, 1995), Maria & Strawberry Woman in Gershwin's Porgy and Bess, 1993, It Ain't Nothin' But The Blues, 1999 (Tony award), appeared (TV series) Law and Order, Rosie O'Donnel, David Letterman, PBS, Today Show. Recipient 3rd place D'Angelo Young Artist Internat. Competition, 1984. Address: 250 W 57th St Ste 2223 New York NY 10107-2210

BOSTON, JAMES ROBERT, JR., lawyer; b. Dallas, Jan. 17, 1958; s. James Robert Boston Sr. and Margaret Ann (Yeager) Wolf; m. Cherrie Lynn Slatton, Aug. 10, 1981; children: Janna Cherise, Jamie Nicole. AA, Tyler Jr. Coll., 1977; BA, U. Tex., 1979; JD, South Tex. Coll. of Law, 1982. Bar: Tex. 1982, U.S. Dist. Ct. (so. dist.) Tex. 1983, U.S. Ct. Appeals (5th cir.) 1983. Briefing atty. 14th Jud. Dist. Tex. State Ct. Appeals, Houston, 1982-83; assoc. Ryan & Marshall, Houston, 1983-87, Kruse and Assocs., Houston, 1987-90; ptnr. Kruse, Laser & Boston, Houston, 1990-91; owner James R. Boston & Assocs., Houston, 1991—. Author: Liability Associated with Treating Injured Children, 1987. Fellow Tex. Bar Found.; mem. Tex. Bar Assn., Houston Bar Assn., Assn. Trial Lawyers Am., Rutherford Inst., Greater Houston Soc. Health Care Risk Mgmt., Christian Legal Soc., Order of Barristers, Phi Delta Phi. Republican. Baptist. Avocations: tennis, Tae Kwon Do, swimming, water-skiing, weightlifting. Home: 138 E Placid Hill Cir The Woodlands TX 77381-3181 Office: James R Boston & Assocs 1900 West Loop S Ste 300 Houston TX 77027-3205

BOSTON, PENELOPE J., science educator, researcher; BS, MS, PhD, U. Colo. Rsch. assoc. prof., cave and karst sci. N. Mex Tech., Socorro, N.Mex.; dir., cave and karst studies program N.Mex. Inst. Mining and Technology, Socorro, N.Mex. Contbr. articles to profl. jours. Explored the Lechuguilla cave in New Mexico at 1,567 feet down the deepest limestone cave in the US; lived for two weeks with five other chambernauts in a self-contained 24 foot capsule in the Utah desert to simulate working conditions on Mars. Office: Dept Earth & Environ Sci MSEC 346 New Mexico Tech 801 Leroy Place Socorro NM 87801 Office Fax: 505-835-5657. Business E-Mail: pboston@nmt.edu.

BOSTON, WILLIAM CLAYTON, lawyer; b. Hobart, Okla., Nov. 29, 1934; s. William Clayton and Dollie Jane (Gibbs) B.; m. Billie Gail Long, Jan. 20, 1962; children: Kathryn Gray, William Clayton III. BS, Okla. State U., 1958; LLB, U. Okla., 1962; LLM, NYU, 1967. Bar: Okla. 1961. Assoc. Mosteller, Fellers, Andrews, Snider & Baggett, Oklahoma City, 1962-64; ptnr. Fellers,

Snider, Baggett, Blankenship & Boston, Oklahoma City, 1968-69, Andrews, Davis, Legg, Bixler, Milsten & Murrah, Oklahoma City, 1972-86; pvt. practice Boston & Boston PLLC, Oklahoma City, 1986—2000. Contbr. articles to profl. jours.; mem. adv. bd. The Jour. of Air Law and Commerce, 1995-2000 Past pres. and trustee Ballet Okla.; past v.p., bd. dirs. Oklahoma City Arts Coun.; past trustee Nichols Hills (Okla.) Methodist Ch.; past trustee, chmn. Okla. Found. for the Humanities; past trustee, vice-chmn., sec. Humanities in Okla., Inc., 1992-95. With U.S. Army, 1954-56. Mem. ABA (former chmn. subcom. on aircraft fin., former chmn. aircraft fin. and contract divsn. forum on air and space law), FBA, Internat. Bar Assn., Inter-Pacific Bar Assn., Okla. State Bar Assn., Oklahoma County Bar Assn. Home: 1701 Camden Way Oklahoma City OK 73116-5121

BOSTROM, ANN HELEN HAUGERUD, public policy educator; d. Albert Ralph and Helen Augusta Haugerud; m. Douglas Kaj Bostrom, June 21, 1985; 1 child, Kaj Alexander Nelson. BA in English, U. Wash., 1983; MBA, Western Wash. U., 1986; PhD in Pub. Policy Analysis, Carnegie Mellon U., Pitts., 1990. Rsch. assoc. Bur. Labor Stats., Washington, 1991—92; asst. prof. pub. policy Ga. Inst. Tech., Atlanta, 1992—98, assoc. prof. pub. policy, 1998—; dir., decision risk and mgmt. sci. program NSF, Ballston, Va., 1999—2001; assoc. dean rsch. Ivan Allen Coll., Ga. Inst. Tech., Atlanta, 2004—. Councilor Soc. for Risk Analysis, 2001—04, chair, risk comm. splty. group, 2000—01; cons. NRC, Inst. Medicine, Transp. Rsch. Bd.; cons. bd. sci. counselors US EPA. Co-author: (book) Risk Communication: A Mental Models Approach; contbr. articles to profl. jours., chapters to books. Recipient Wall St. Jour. Student Achievement award, Coll. Bus. and Econs., Western Wash. U., 1986, Chauncey Starr award, Soc. for Risk Analysis, 1997; fellow, Lois Roth Endowment Fund, 1989—90, Fulbright Program, US Dept. State, U. Stockholm, 1989—90; Patricia Roberts Harris fellow, Carnegie Mellon U., 1988—89. Achievements include research in mental models of hazardous processes and on risk communication and decision making. Avocation: violin. Office Phone: 404-894-9629.

BOSTROM, CARL OTTO, physicist, research facility administrator; b. Port Jefferson, N.Y., Aug. 18, 1932; s. Carl Oscar and Dagmar Ester (Anderson) B.; m. Sara A. Herzog, Sept. 6, 1954; children: Robin I. Bostrom Dagan, Jennifer A. Bostrom Simmons, Carl E. BS in Physics, Franklin & Marshall Coll., 1956; MS in Physics, Yale U., 1958, PhD, 1962; ScD (hon.), Franklin & Marshall Coll., 1992. Physicist space dept. Johns Hopkins U. Applied Physics Lab., Laurel, Md., 1960-68, group supr. space dept., 1968-74, chief scientist space dept., 1974-78, assoc. head space dept., 1978-79, dept. head and asst. dir. space dept., 1979, dep. dir., 1979-80, dir., 1980-92, now dir. emeritus. Mem.-at-large adv. bd. Def. Intelligence Agy., Washington, 1982-87, 92—, chmn. sci. adv. com., 1988-92; ex officio mem. Def. Sci. Bd., Washington, 1988-92; mem. Pres. Com. on Nat. Medal Sci., 1986-91; mem.-at-large Air Force Sci. Adv. Bd., 1983-87; mem. bd. visitors Naval Surface Weapons Systems Engring. Sta. and Naval Ship Systems Engring. Sta., 1982-92; mem. external adv. bd. Ga. Tech. Rsch. Inst., 1988—. Contbr. articles to profl. jours. including Jour. Geophys. Rsch., Geophys. Rsch. Letters, Sci., Space Sci. Rev., others. Mem. BCC chpt. Izaak Walton League, Poolesville, Md., 1974-79. With U.S. Army, 1950-52. Recipient Air Force medal for exceptional civilian svc./, 1987, DOD Medal for Disting. Pub. Svc., 1992, Def. Intelligency Agy. Medal for exceptional civilian svc., 1992, NASA Disting. Pub. Svc. medal, 1992. Fellow Hudson Inst.; mem. AAAS, Am. Phys. Soc., Am. Def. Preparedness Assn., Am Geophys. Union (com. on govtl. and legis. affairs 1975-79, chmn. 1975-77), Am. Soc. Naval Engrs., Internat. Assn. Geomagnetism and Aeronomy, Cosmos Club, Navy League, Phi Beta Kappa, Sigma Xi, Sigma Pi. E-mail: cbostrom@erols.com.

BOSTWICK, JOHN, III, plastic surgeon, department chairman, medical educator; b. Bostwick, Ga., Sept. 25, 1943; MD, U. Tenn., 1966. Diplomate Am. Bd. Surgery (bd. dirs. 1996—), Am. Bd. Plastic Surgery (bd. dirs. 1995—). Intern Emory U. Hosp., Atlanta, 1966-67, resident, 1970-73, resident, plastic surgery, 1973-74; staff Crawford Long Hosp., Atlanta, 1974—, Emory U. Hosp., Atlanta, 1974—; prof. surgery Emory U., Atlanta, 1982—, chmn. plastic surgery, 1992—. Fellow ACS; mem. AMA, Am. Surg. Assn., Am. Soc. Plastic and Reconstructive Surgery, Am. Assn. Plastic Surgeons, So. Surg. Assn. Office: Emory Plastic Surgery 1365 Clifton Rd NE Atlanta GA 30322-1013 Fax: 404-778-5018.

BOSTWICK, RANDELL ARMOUR, retired food service executive; b. Niles, Ohio, Oct. 24, 1922; s. Clifton A. and May (Lloyd) B.; m. Jane Elizabeth Foster, Aug. 28, 1948; children: Suzanne Elizabeth, Sherrard, Randell A. Ed., U. Mich., Westminster Coll. Asst. traffic mgr. A&P, Youngstown, Ohio, 1948-50, asst. to div. traffic mgr. Pitts., 1952-58, div. traffic mgr., 1958-60, dir. ops., 1960-69, asst. to nat. dir. ops. N.Y. hdqrs., 1969-75; pres. subs. Super Market Service Corp., Montvale, N.J., 1975-88; corp. v.p. The Gt. A & P Tea Co., 1981-88; chmn. Supermarket Service Corp., 1988-91, ret., 1992. Served to capt. Med. Service Corps U.S. Army, 1943-46, 50-52. Presbyterian. Home: 333 River St Apt 513 Hoboken NJ 07030

BOSTWICK, ROBERT OTIS, government agency administrator; b. Mobile, Ala., Apr. 9, 1946; B, U. South Ala., 1967. Supr. Texaco Oil, Mobile, 1979-83; v.p. Midtown Restaurant Corp., Mobile, 1983-85; v.p., CEO, Signs Now, Mobile, 1985-87; v.p., dir. franchising CHECKERS Drive-In Restaurants, Mobile, 1987-89; exec. asst. to mayor Mobile, 1989—. Office: Office of the Mayor Govt Plaza 205 Government St Mobile AL 36602-2613

BOSVELD, JENNIFER, poet, writer; b. Columbus, Ohio; d. Robert O. and Maryanna Miller; m. Jim Bosveld (dec.); children: David DeRhodes, Christopher Groce, Richard Welch, Richard Groce, Raoul DeRhodes. Student, Ohio State U. Author: Elastic Elephrastic: Poets on Art/Poets on Tour, Topics for Getting in Touch: A Poetry Therapy Sourcebook, many poetry chapbooks; editor: 10 anthologies. Former bd. dirs. Disaster Rsch. Ctr., Friends of the Homeless. Recipient Pioneer award, Nat. Assn. Poetry Therapy; Individual Artist fellow, Ohio Arts Coun. Home: 81 Shadymere Ln Columbus OH 43213

BOSWELL, BILL REESER, religious organization executive; b. Cumby, Tex., Nov. 5, 1934; s. Thurman Festus and Nellie Gladys (Reeser) B.; m. Martha Raye Dawson, Feb. 23, 1958; children: Heather, Robin Boswell Music. BA, Barton Coll., Wilson, N.C., 1957; MDiv, Tex. Christian U., 1962, D Ministry, 1973. Ordained to ministry Christian Ch. (Disciples of Christ), 1957. Min. 1st Christian Ch., Brady, Tex., 1962-78, sr. min. Pampa, Tex., 1978-88; regional exec. min. Christian Ch. (Disciples of Christ) in La., Pineville, 1989—. Mem. Theta Phi. Avocations: music, blacksmithing, reading. Home: 2371 Leslie Dawson Rd La Grange NC 28551-8144 Office: Christian Church In Louisiana PO Box 191057 Little Rock AR 72219-1057

BOSWELL, G(EORGE) HARVEY, federal judge; b. Medina, Tenn., July 8, 1947; m. Jenny Lynn Butler; one child. BS, U. Tenn., 1969; JD, U. Memphis, 1979. Pvt. practice, Milan, Tenn., 1980-83; atty. Kizer, Bonds, Boswell & Crocker, 1983-93; bankruptcy judge U.S. Bankruptcy Ct. (we. dist.), Tenn., 1993—. Fellow Tenn. Bar Found.; mem. Nat. Conf. Bankruptcy Judges, Am. Bankruptcy Inst., Tenn. Bar Assn. Office: US Bankruptcy Ct 111 S Highland Ave Ste 324 Jackson TN 38301-6107 Office Phone: 731-421-9370.

BOSWELL, GEORGE MARION, JR., orthopedist, health facility administrator; b. Dallas, May 12, 1920; s. George Marion and Viola (Scarbrough) B.; m. Veta M. Fuller, Oct. 30, 1958; children: Brianna Boswell Brown, Kama Boswell Koudelka, Maia Boswell. BS, Tex. Tech U., 1940; MD, U. Tex., Southwestern Dallas, 1950. Diplomate Am. Acad. Orthopaedic Surgery. Intern Parkland Hosp., Dallas, 1950-51; resident gen. surgeryand orthopedic surgery Parkland, Baylor and Scottish Rite Hosps., Dallas, 1951-55; practice medicine specializing in orthopedics Dallas, 1955—; v.p. med. affairs Baylor Health Care System, Dallas, 1982-86; dir. orthopaedic clin. studies Baylor U. Med. Ctr., 1995—. Owner Bee Aviation Inc., Dallas, 1968—, Boswell Realty Inc., Dallas, 1971—; lectr., cons. on health care delivery. Contbr. articles to profl. jours. Prof. George M. Bowell, Jr. chair in orthopaedic surgery named in his honor Baylor U. Med. Ctr. Fellow ACS; mem. AMA, Am. Acad. Orthopaedic Surgery (Key Man U.S. Congress 1980—), Am. Hosp. Assn., Tex. Hosp. Assn. (Key Man Tex. Legislature 1980—, council on hosp. staffs), Flying Physicians (pres. Tex. 1960-64). Clubs: Cresent (Dallas). Republican. Methodist. Avocations: flying, photography, fishing, saddle making. Home: 7249 Wabash Cir Dallas TX 75214-3535 Office: Baylor U Med Ctr Wadley Tower Ste 556 3600 Gaston Ave Dallas TX 75246-2096 Office Phone: 214-348-8300. Personal E-mail: gmb51@earthlink.net.

BOSWELL, JAMES DOUGLAS, medical research executive; b. Tulsa, Feb. 12, 1942; m. Pamela Scott; children: Megan, Melanie Student, U. Okla., 1960-61; BA, U. Tulsa, 1964, MA, 1966. Indsl. relations rep. Trans World Airlines, 1966-68; dir. placement Skelly Oil Co., 1968-72, mgr. employee and pub. relations, 1972-75, gen. mgr. adminstrn., 1975-77; corp. mgr. human resources Getty Oil Co., 1977-81; v.p. employee and pub. relations L.A. Times, 1981-91; CEO House Ear Inst., L.A., 1991—, trustee, 1995—. Bd. dirs. Employers Group; pres. Skelly Oil Found., Tulsa, 1974-78, Getty Oil Co. Found., 1978-79. Bd. dirs. L.A. Boys and Girls Club, v.p., 1985; bd. dirs. L.A. Theatre Ctr., 1988-90, L.A. chpt. ARC; bd. dirs. L.A. Jr. Achievement, 1982-91, vice chmn. human resources, 1986; fellow Nat. Health Found., 1992, San Marino Cmty. Ch. Found., 1992-95; mem. Econ. Round Table, 1993, sec.-treas., 1995-96. Mem. Am. Soc. Personnel Adminstrn., Am. Psychol. Assn., Newspaper Personnel Relations Assn., Am. Newspaper Assn. (labor and personnel relations com. 1982-91). Avocations: tennis, skiing, golf. Office: House Ear Inst 2100 W 3rd St 5th Fl Los Angeles CA 90057-1922 Home: 600 Orange Grove Cir Pasadena CA 91105-2830

BOSWELL, LEONARD L., congressman; b. Harrison County, Mo., Jan. 10, 1934; s. Melvin and Margaret B.; m. Dody Boswell; 3 children. BA in Bus. Adminstrn., Graceland Coll., 1969. Commd. 2d lt. U.S. Army, 1956, advanced through grades to lt. col., resigned, 1976; mem. Iowa Senate, 1984-96, pres., 1993-97; mem. U.S. Ho. of Reps. from 3d Iowa dist., 1997—; mem. transp. and infrastucture com., agr. com., select copm. on intelligence, 1999—. Grain and livestock farmer Decatur County, 1976—. Past pres., bd. dirs. local Coop. Elevator, Lamoni. Decorated DFC (2), Bronze Star (2). Mem. VFW, Am. Legion, Cattleman's Assn., Lamoni Lions Club. Democrat. Office: US Ho of Reps 1427 Longworth HOB Washington DC 20515-0001 E-mail: Rep.Boswell.ia03@Mail.house.gov.*

BOSWELL, RUPERT DEAN, JR., retired academic administrator, mathematician, educator; b. Marshall County, Miss., Aug. 11, 1929; s. Rupert Dean and Mary Exyah (Ellis) B.; m. Grace Hadaway, Apr. 11, 1952; children: James Elton, Deanna Grace. BS, Miss. State U., 1950, MS, 1951; PhD, U. Ga., 1957. Grad. asst. Miss. State U., Mississippi State, 1950-51; instr. math. Reinhardt Coll., Waleska, Ga., 1951-53; grad. asst. U. Ga., Athens, 1953-56; assoc. prof. math. Miss. State U., 1957-61, prof., 1961-62; prof. math. Monmouth (Ill.) Coll., 1962-77; v.p. acad. affairs Rocky Mountain Coll., Billings, Mont., 1977-85; provost, prof. math. Upper Iowa U., Fayette, 1985-89; prof. math. Jacksonville (Ala.) State U., 1989-94. Mem.: AAUP, Math. Assn. Am. (chmn. com. on vis. lectrs. 1967—69, chmn. Ill. sect.), Am. Math. Soc., Fayette C. of C. (sec. 1985—87), Rotary (pres. Monmouth club 1972—73). Presbyterian. Home: 554 Queen Oak St Collierville TN 38017

BOSWELL, WILLIAM PARET, lawyer; b. Washington, Oct. 24, 1946; s. Yates Paret and Mary Frances (Hyland) B.; m. Barbara Stelle Schroeder, Sept. 6, 1969; children: Susan Anne, Sarah Mary, Christina Catherine. BA cum laude, Cath. U., 1968; JD, U. Va., 1971. Bar: Va. 1971, D.C. 1972, U.S. Ct. Mil. Appeals 1972, U.S. Supreme Ct. 1975, Pa. 1978. Atty. Peoples Natural Gas Co., Pitts., 1978-82, asst. sec., gen. atty., 1982-85, sec., gen. counsel, 1985-88, v.p., gen. counsel, sec., 1989-99; gen. counsel Hope Gas, Inc., Pitts., 1998—99; dep. gen. counsel Consol. Natural Gas Co., Pitts., 1999-2000, Dominion Resources, Inc., Pitts., 2000—04; ptnr. McGuireWoods LLP, Pitts., 2000—04; prin. William P. Boswell LLC, 2004—. Exec. com. Gas Industry Stds. Bd., 1994—97, chmn., 2001, N.Am. Energy Stds. Bd., 2002—03, named founding chmn., 2003. Pres. Borough Coun., Osborne, Pa., 1984-97, mayor, 1998—; bd. dirs. Mendelssohn Choir Pitts., 1986-2001, pres. 1997-98; trustee Laughlin Found., 1995—. Capt. JAGC, USAF, 1971-78, col. USAFR, 1978-98, ret. Decorated Legion of Merit, knight Order Malta, Equestrian Order Holy Sepulchre, Order St. Gregory, Order St. Sylvester. Mem. ABA (chair gas com. 1995-2003, chair infrastructure security com. 2003—), Pa. Bar Assn., D.C. Bar Assn., Va. Bar Assn., Am. Gas Assn. (chair regulatory com. 1996-98), Pa. Gas Assn. (chmn. 1989-90), Am. Corp. Counsel Assn. (pres. Pa. chpt. 1991-92, Excellence in Corporate Practice award 1998), Am. Soc. Corp. Secs., City Club Pitts., Army and Navy Club D.C. Republican. Roman Catholic. Avocations: reading, walking. Home: 405 Hare Ln Sewickley PA 15143-2050 Office: Dominion Tower 23 Fl 625 Liberty Ave Pittsburgh PA 15222-3142

BOSWORTH, BRUCE LEIGHTON, school administrator, educator, consultant; b. Buffalo, Mar. 22, 1942; s. John Wayman and Alice Elizabeth Rodgers; children: David, Timothy, Paul, Sheri, Skyler. BA, U. Denver, 1964; MA, U. No. Colo., 1970; EdD, Walden U., 1984. Elem. tchr. Littleton (Colo.) Pub. Schs., 1964-67, 70-81; bldg. prin. East Smoky Sch. Divsn. 54, Valleyview, Alta., Can., 1967-70; pres., tchr. St. Michael's-of-the-Mountains Sch., Littleton, 1981—. Adoption cons. hard-to-place children; ednl. cons. spl. needs children Warren United Meth. Ch. Mem. ASCD, Coun. Exceptional Children, Masons, Shriners, York Rite. Home and Office: 3500 S Lowell Blvd Apt 316 Denver CO 80236-6168 Personal E-mail: misterbura@yahoo.com.

BOSWORTH, DALE N., federal agency administrator; b. Altadena, Calif. m. Carma Bosworth; 2 children. BS in Forestry, U. Idaho. Forest supr. Wasatch-Cache Nat. Forest, Intermountain Region USDA Forest Svc., Utah, 1986—90, dep. dir. forest mgmt. Washington, 1990—92, dep. regional forester Pacific S.W. Region San Francisco, 1992—94, regional forest Intermountain Region Ogden, Utah, 1994—97, regional forester No. region Missoula, Mont., 1997—2001, chief Washington, 2001—. Mem.: Soc. for Range Mgmt., Soc. Am. Foresters. Office: USDA Forest Svc 1400 Independence Ave SW Washington DC 20250-0002

BOSWORTH, DOUGLAS LEROY, manufacturing executive, educator; b. Goldfield, Iowa, Oct. 15, 1939; s. Clifford Leroy and Clara (Lonning) Bosworth; m. Patricia Lee Knock, May 28, 1961; children: Douglas, Dawn. BS in Agrl. Engring, Iowa State U., 1962; MS in Agrl. Engring, U. Ill., 1964. With Deere & Co., Moline, Ill., 1959-94, divsn. engr. disk harrows, 1971-76, mgr. mfg. engring., 1976-80, works mgr., 1980-85, mgr. mfg., 1985-89, engring. test mgr., 1989-94; pres. WorkSpan, Inc., Mahomet, Ill., 1994—2001, Ill. Tech. Ctr., Savoy, Ill., 1995-97. Mem. Engring. Accreditation Commn., 1985—90; v.p. Skills, Inc.; mem. Assoc. Employers Bd., 1989—91; adj. engring. prof. U. Ill., Champaign-Urbana, 1995—. Active Am. Cancer Soc., Rock Island Unit; bd. dirs. United Med. Ctr., 1984—95; exec. com. Quad-City United Way, 1984—89. Mem.: Am. Soc. Agrl. Engrs. (chmn. Ill.-Wis. 1973—74, nat. bd. dirs. 1974—76, 1979—82, v.p. 1979—82, pres. elect 1991—92, pres. 1992—93, Engring. Achievement Young Designer award 1973), Rotary, Gamma Sigma Delta, Alpha Epsilon, Sigma Xi. Lutheran. Home and Office: WorkSpan Inc 1111 E Briarcliff Dr Mahomet IL 61853-9558 E-mail: dlbos@mchsi.com.

BOSWORTH, JAY L., radiation oncologist; b. N.Y.C., Oct. 23, 1945; BS, Bklyn. Coll.; MD, Albert Einstein Coll. Medicine, 1970. Cert. Therapeutic Radiology 1974. Intern Metro Hosp., N.Y.C., 1970—71; resident Bronx Mcpl. Hosp. Ctr., N.Y.C., 1971—74; former chief of divsn. radiation oncology North Shore U. Hosp., Manhasset, NY, attending physician radiation oncology, St. Francis Hosp.; radiation oncologist Nassau Radiologic Group, Manhasset, 1998—. Pres. NY Cancer Soc. Fellow: Am. Coll. Radiology; mem.: Am. Soc. Breast Diseases, Am. Urological Assn., Am. Raium Soc., Am. Soc. Therapeutic Radiology and Oncology. Office: Nassau Radiologic Group 1129 No Blvd Manhasset NY 11030-3801 Office Phone: 516-365-6544.

BOSWORTH, KATE, actress; b. L.A., Jan. 2, 1983; Actor: (films) The Horse Whisperer, 1998, Remember the Titans, 2000, The Newcomers, 2000, Blue Crush, 2002, The Rules of Attraction, 2002, Wonderland, 2003, Advantage Hart, 2003, Win a Date with Tad Hamilton, 2004, Beyond the Sea, 2004; (TV series) Young Americans, 2000. Mem.: Nat. Honor Soc. Office: United Talent Agy 5th Fl 9560 Wilshire Blvd Beverly Hills CA 90212*

BOSWORTH, STEPHEN WARREN, dean, former ambassador; b. Grand Rapids, Mich., Dec. 4, 1939; s. Warren Charles and Mina (Phillips) B.; m. Christine Holmes, June 7, 1984; children— Andrew, Allison. A.B., Dartmouth Coll., 1961; LLD (hon.), Darmouth Coll., 1986. Vice consul Am. Embassy, Panama City, Panama, 1962—63, prin. officer Colon, 1963—64; Panama desk officer U.S. Dept. State, Washington, 1964—66; econ. officer Am. Embassy, Madrid, 1967—71, Paris, 1971—74; dep. asst. sec. state, 1976-79; ambassador to Tunisia, 1979-81; dep. asst. sec. Inter-Am. affairs, 1981-82; dir. policy planning staff coun. U.S. Fgn. Svc., 1983-84; ambassador Manila, Philippines, 1984-87; pres. U.S.-Japan Found., 1988-96; exec. dir. Korean Energy Devel. Orgn., 1995-97; amb. to Republic of Korea Seoul, 1997-2001; dean Fletcher Sch. Law and Diplomacy, Tufts U., Medford, Mass., 2001—. Adj. prof. Columbia U., 1990-94. Trustee Dartmouth Coll., 1992-2002, chmn. bd. trustees, 1996-99. Recipient Dept. State Disting. Honor award, 1976, 86, Arthur S. Flemming award, 1976; named Diplomat of Yr., Am. Acad. Diplomacy, 1986 Office: Fletcher Sch Law and Diplomacy Tufts Univ Medford MA 02155 E-mail: stephen.bosworth@tufts.edu.

BOSWORTH, THOMAS LAWRENCE, architect, retired educator; b. Oberlin, Ohio, June 15, 1930; s. Edward Franklin and Imogene (Rose) B.; m. Abigail Lumbard, Nov. 6, 1954 (div. Nov. 1974); children: Thomas Edward, Nathaniel David; m. Elaine R. Pedigo, Nov. 23, 1974; stepchildren: Robert Haden Pedigo, Kevin Ian Pedigo. BA, Oberlin Coll., 1952, MA, 1954; postgrad., Princeton U., 1952-53, Harvard U., 1956-57; MArch, Yale U., 1960; PhD Honoris Causa (hon.), Kobe U., Japan, 2003. Draftsman Gordon McMaster AIA, Cheshire, Conn., summer 1957-58; resident planner Tunnard & Harris Planning Cons., Newport, R.I., summer 1959; designer, field supr. Eero Saarinen & Assocs., Birmingham, Mich., 1960-61, Hamden, Conn., 1961-64; individual practice architecture Providence, 1964-68, Seattle, 1968—2004; ptnr. Bosworth Hoedemaker Architecture and Planning, Seattle, 2004—; asst. instr. architecture Yale U., 1962-65, vis. lectr., 1965-66; asst. prof. R.I. Sch. Design, 1964-66, assoc. prof., head dept., 1966-68; prof. architecture U. Wash., Seattle, 1968-98, prof. emeritus, 1998—, chmn. dept. Seattle, 1968-72, dir. multidisciplinary program Rome, 1984-86; chief architecture Peace Corps Tng. Program, Tunisia, Brown U., summers 1965-66. Vis. lectr. Kobe U., Japan, Oct., 1982, Nov., 1990, Apr., 1993, May, 1995, June, 1998; Pietro Belluschi disting. vis. prof. U. Oreg., 1996; dir. arch. in Rome program U. Wash., Rome, 1996, prof. 2000, 2003. Bd. dirs. N.W. Inst. Arch. and Urban Studies, Italy, 1983-90, pres., 1983-85; dir. Pilchuck Glass Sch., Seattle, 1977-80, trustee, 1980-91, adv. coun., 1993—; mem. Seattle Model Cities Land Use Rev. Bd., 1969-70, Tech. Com. Site Selection Wash. Multi-Purpose Stadium, 1970, Medina Planning Commn., 1972-74, steering adv. com. King County Stadium, 1972-74; chmn. King County (Wash.) Environ. Devel. Commn., 1972-74, King County Policy Devel. Commn., 1974-77; bd. dirs. Arcade Mag., 1988-2002, pres. 1988-2000; bd. mgrs. YMCA Camping Svcs., 1998-2002; adv. bd. U. Wash Rome Ctr., 1999—. With U.S. Army, 1954-56. Winchester Traveling fellow Yale U., 1960; assoc. fellow Ezra Stiles Coll. Yale U.; mid-career fellow in arch. Am. Acad. in Rome, 1980-81, vis. scholar, Spring 1988. Fellow AIA (Seattle medalist 2003); mem. Monday Club (Seattle), Bohemian Club (San Francisco), Tau Sigma Delta. Home: 2411 25th Ave E Seattle WA 98112-2610

BOT, ADRIAN ION, immunologist; b. Teregova, Romania, June 4, 1968; came to U.S., 1994; s. Vasile and Calina B.; m. Simona Rodica, Sept. 2, 1994; 1 child, Celine. MD, U. Medicine, Timisoara, Romania, 1993; PhD, Mt. Sinai Sch. Medicine, 1998. Prin. scientist, group leader autoimmunity/vaccination dept. Alliance Pharm. Corp., San Diego, 1999—. Guest scientist Scripps Rsch. Inst., La Jolla, Calif., 1998-99; cons. in field. Contbr. articles to profl. jours.; inventor in field. Rsch. fellow Alliance Pharm. Corp., 1998-99. Mem. AAAS, Am. Assn. Immunologists, Am. Soc. Microbiology, PhD Alumni Assn. CUNY. Avocations: philosophy, physics, skiing, tennis. Office: Alliance Pharm Corp 3030 Sci Park Rd San Diego CA 92121

BOTCHEVA, LUBA, psychologist, researcher; b. Sofia, Bulgaria, Jan. 2, 1957; arrived in U.S.A., 1993; d. Bogdan Botchev and Elena Botcheva; m. Yassen Zlatkov, Oct. 26, 1990 (div. Jan. 9, 2002); children: Bogdan Zlatkov, Dimiter Zlatkov. BA in Psychology, Sofia U., Bulgaria, 1978; PhD in Devel. and Ednl. Psychology, Moscow State U., Russia, 1987; MA in Counseling Psychology, Calif. Inst. Integral Studies, San Francisco, 2000. Marriage and Family Therapy Intern Bd. of Behavioral Sci.Calif., 2000. Rsch. assoc. Stanford U., Calif., 1998—99; program dir., outcomes rsch. consulting svc. The Children's Health Coun., Palo Alto, 2001—. Post doctoral fellow in Psychiatry and Behavioral Scis. Stanford U., Calif., 1997—98; cons. Achieve, Palo Alto, Calif., 1999—2000. Editor: Sapio Rsch. Series; contbr. chapters to books, articles to profl. jours. Fellow, Ctr. for Advanced Studies in the Behavioral Sciences, 1993—94; grantee, Soros Found., 1997—99, Johann Jacobs Found., 1995—98, Spencer Found., 1998—99, Lucile Packard Found. for Children's Health, 2002—04. Mem.: APA. Achievements include research in organizational consulting and learning culture assessment. Home: 3353 Alma St #137 Palo Alto CA 94306 Office: The Children's Health Coun 650 Clark Way Palo Alto CA 94304 Office Phone: 650-617-3869. Personal E-mail: lubabb@yahoo.com. E-mail: lbotcheva@chconline.org.

BOTELHO, BRUCE MANUEL, mayor, retired state attorney general; b. Juneau, Alaska, Oct. 6, 1948; s. Emmett Manuel and Harriet Iowa (Tieszen) Botelho; m. Guadalupe Alvarez Breton, Sept. 23, 1988; children: Alejandro Manuel, Adriana Regina. Student, U. Heidelberg, Federal Republic of Germany, 1970; BA, Willamette U., 1971, JD, 1976. Bar: Alaska 1976, U.S. Ct. Appeals (9th cir.) 1976, U.S. Supreme Ct. 1979. Asst. atty. gen. State of Alaska, Juneau, 1976—83, 1987—89, dep. commr., acting commr. Dept. of Revenue, 1983-86; mayor City, Borough of Juneau, 1988—91, 2003—, dep. atty. gen., 1991—94, 2003—; atty. gen. State of Alaska, 1994—2002. Chmn. Alaska Resources Corp., 1984—86; exec. com. Conf. of Western Attys. Gen., 1997—2002. Editor: Willamette Law Jour., 1975—76; contbr. articles to profl. jours. Pres. Juneau Human Rights Commn., 1978—80, Alaska Coun. Am. Youth Hostels, 1979—81, Juneau Arts and Humanities Coun., 1981—83; pres. S.E. Alaska Area Coun. Boy Scouts Am., 1991—93, 2001—, commr. S.E. Alaska Area Coun., 1993—2000; pres. Juneau World Affairs Coun., 2000—; chmn. Gov.'s Conf. on Youth and Justice, 1995—96, Gov. Task Force on Confidentiality of Childrens Procs., 1998—2002; trustee Alaska Children's Trust, 1996—2000, Alaska Permanent Fund, 2000—02; co-chmn. Alaska Justice Assessment Commn., 1997—2002; active Commn. for Justice Across the Atlantic, 1999—; chmn. Alaska Criminal Justice Coun., 2000—02; fed. commr. Alaska Rural Jursice and Law Enforcement Commn., 2004—; Assembly mem. Borough of Juneau, 1983—86; bd. dirs. Found. for Social Innovations, Alaska, 1990—93, Alaska Econ. Devel. Coun., 1985—87, Alaska Mcpl. League, 2003—; chmn. adminstrv. law sect. Alaska Bar Assn., 1981—82. Recipient Silver Beaver award, Boy Scouts Am., 2000. Mem.: Nat. Assn. Attys. Gen. (exec. com. 1998—). Democrat. Methodist. Avocation: dance. Office Phone: 907-506-5240. Business E-Mail: botelho@gci.net, mayor@ci.juneau.ak.us.

BOTEZ, DAN, physicist; b. Bucharest, Romania, May 22, 1948; s. Emil and Ecaterina (Iacob) B.; m. Lynda Diane Arnold, Sept. 25, 1976; children: Anca, Adrian. BSEE with highest honors, U. Calif., Berkeley, 1971, MSEE, 1972, PhD, 1976; PhD (hon.), U. Politechnica, Bucharest, Romania, 1995. Fellow IBM Thomas J. Watson Rsch. Ctr., Yorktown Heights, N.Y., 1976-77; tech. staff RCA David Sarnoff Rsch. Ctr., Princeton, N.J., 1977-82, rsch. leader, 1982-84; dir. device devel. Lytel Inc., Somerville, N.J., 1984-86; chief scientist TRW Electro-Optic Rsch. Ctr., Redondo Beach, Calif., 1986, lab dir., 1986-87; sr. staff scientist TRW Rsch. Ctr., Redondo Beach, Calif., 1987-93, TRW tech. fellow, 1990-93; Philip Dunham Reed prof. elec. engring. U. Wis., Madison, 1993—; founder, bd. dirs. AlfaLight Inc., Madison, 2000—.

Author: Electro-Optical Communications Dictionary, 1983, Diode-Laser Arrays, 1994; contbr. over 240 articles to profl. jours.; holder 44 U.S. patents. Named Outstanding Young Engr., IEEE Lasers and Electro-Optics Soc., San Jose, 1984, recipient Key to Future award, 1984. Fellow IEEE (chmn. tech. com. on semiconductor lasers 1989-90), Optical Soc. Am.; mem. Phi Beta Kappa. Republican. Mem. Ea. Orthodox Ch. Avocations: racquetball, travel, photography, skiing. Home: 200 N Prospect Ave Madison WI 53726-4027 Office: U Wis Dept Elec Engring 1415 Engineering Dr Madison WI 53706-1607 Office Phone: 608-265-4643. Business E-Mail: botez@engr.wisc.edu.

BOTHMER, DIETRICH FELIX VON, curator, archaeologist; b. Eisenach, Thuringia, Oct. 26, 1918; came to U.S., 1939, naturalized, 1944; s. Wilhelm Friedrich Franz Carl and Marie Julie Auguste Karoline (Freiin von und zu Egloffstein) von B.; m. Joyce de la Bégassière, May 28, 1966; children: Bernard Nicholas, Maria Elizabeth Villalba. Student, Friedrich Wilhelms U., Berlin, 1937-38, Wadham Coll., Oxford, 1938-39; diploma classical archaeology, Oxford U., 1939; PhD in Classical Archaeology, U. Calif., Berkeley, 1944; DPhil (hon.), U. Trier, 1997. Asst. curator Greek and Roman art Met. Mus. Art, 1946-51, assoc. curator, 1951-59, curator, 1959-73, chmn., 1973-90, Disting. rsch. curator, 1990—. Adj. prof. NYU, 1966— Book rev. editor: Am. Jour. Archaeology, 1950-57; assoc. editor, 1970-76; author: Amazons in Greek Art, 1957, Ancient Art from New York Private Collections, 1961, An Inquiry into the Forgery of the Etruscan Terracotta Warriors, 1961, Corpus Vasorum Antiquorum, USA fasc. 12, 1963, Greek Vase Painting: An Introduction, 1972, Corpus Vasorum Antiquorum, USA fasc. 16, 1976, Greek Art of the Aegean Islands, 1979, A Greek and Roman Treasury, 1984, The Amasis Painter and His World, 1985, Greek Vase Painting, 1987, Glories of the Past, Ancient Art from the Shelby White and Leon Levy Collection, 1990, Euphronios, Peintre á Athènes au VI siècle avant Jesus Christ, 1990. Mem. Chancellor's Ct. of Benefactors, Oxford U. With AUS, 1943-45. Decorated Bronze Star, Purple Heart; Rhodes scholar Wadham Coll., 1938-39; Internat. House fellow U. Calif., Berkeley, 1940, Alfred B. Jordan fellow, 1940-41, Univ. fellow, 1941-42; Martin Ryerson fellow U. Chgo., 1942-43; Guggenheim Meml. Found. fellow, 1966, hon. fellow Wadham Coll.; Chevalier Légion d'Honneur, 1997. Mem. Archaeol. Inst. Am. (benefactor), Soc. Promotion Hellenic Studies (hon.), Deutsches Archaeol. Inst., Vereinigung der Freunde Antiker Kunst (Basle, Switzerland), Archaeologische Gesellschaft zu Berlin, Institut de France, Académie des Inscriptions et Belles-Lettres (fgn. assoc.), Piping Rock Club. Home: 401 Centre Island Oyster Bay NY 11771-5011 Office: Met Mus Art Fifth Ave at 82nd St New York NY 10028-0198

BOTHNER-BY, AKSEL ARNOLD, chemist; b. Mpls., Apr. 29, 1921; s. Aksel Conrad and Merle Marie (von Hagen) Bothner-B.; m. Christine Treuner, Oct. 15, 1949; children: Peter Ole, Anne Sigrun. Student, U. Nanking, China, 1939; B Chemistry, U. Minn., 1943; MS, NYU, 1947; PhD, Harvard U., 1949. Scientist Brookhaven Nat. Lab., 1949-53; fellow Am. Cancer Soc., Zurich, 1952-53; instr., lectr. Harvard U., 1953-58; cons. Retina Found., 1957-58; staff fellow Mellon Inst., 1958-71, dir., 1960-61, mem. adv. com., 1962-71; prof. chemistry Carnegie-Mellon U., 1967-77, chmn. dept., 1967-70; dean Mellon Inst. Sci., 1971-75, Univ. prof., 1977—, acting head, 1987-91, Univ. prof. emeritus, 1991—. Fulbright lectr. U. Munich, Germany, 1962-63; adj. prof. U. Pitts., 1964—; vis. prof. U. Calif. at San Diego, 1976-77; trustee MPC Corp., 1972-80; Bd. dirs. Pa. Jr. Acad. Scis., 1975-86. Contbr. articles to profl. jours. With AUS, 1943-45. Recipient Disting. Achievement award, U. Minn., 1975, IR-100 award, 1978, Pitts. award, 1988, G. Laukien award, 2002, EAS award for Achievements in Magnetic Resonance, Ea. Analyltical Symposium, 2002. Mem.: Am. Soc. Biochemistry and Molecular Biology, Am. Chem. Soc. Achievements include research in theoretical organic chemistry. Home: 6317 Darlington Rd Pittsburgh PA 15217-1835 Office: Mellon Inst 4400 5th Ave Pittsburgh PA 15213-2683 Business E-Mail: ab6d@andrew.cmu.edu.

BOTHWELL, ANTHONY PEIRSON XAVIER, SR., lawyer, educator; b. Washington, Aug. 12, 1944; s. Frederick Charles Jr. and Catherine Hannon Bothwell; m. Chung Thi Nguyen, Dec. 22, 1973 (div. Nov. 1999); children: Anthony Peirson Xavier Jr., Thomas Theodore Nguyen. BS in Fgn. Svc., Georgetown U., 1966; MS, Boston U., 1968; JD, John F. Kennedy Sch. Law, 1998; LLM with highest honors, Golden Gate U., 2000. Bar: Calif. 1999, U.S. Dist. Ct. (no. dist.) Calif. 2000, U.S. Ct. Appeals D.C. 2003. Editor AP, Miami, Fla., 1970-73; comms. coord. Fla. Power and Light Co., Miami, 1973-78; cmty. rels. mgr. Wis. Power and Light Co., Madison, 1978-83; dir. pub. affairs Lawrence Livermore Nat. Lab., Livermore, Calif., 1983-85; cons. Livermore, 1985-88; tax specialist IRS, Oakland, Calif., 1988—2001; pvt. practice San Francisco, 1999—; law prof. John F. Kennedy U. Sch. Law, Walnut Creek, Calif., 2000—. Newsroom clk. The Washington Post, 1969-70; acting news dir. Radio Sta. WBRK-AM, Pittsfield, Mass., 1967; cons. Atomic Indsl. Forum, Washington, 1981-83. Contbr. studies to profl. publs.; asst. editor: Computer World, 1967-68. City campaign chmn. Jesse Jackson for Pres., Livermore, 1988; cons. policy ethics Ams. for Energy Independence, Washington, 1980-82; cons. energy ethics com. Nat. Conf. of Cath. Bishops, Washington, 1981-83; chmn. City Coun. Adv. Com. on Energy and Environment, Livermore, 1985-87; asst. to chmn. Mass. Rep. Fin. Com., 1967-68. Recipient 1st pl. award on Commemoration of 50th Anniversary of Universal Declaration of Human Rights, San Francisco chpt. UN Assn. of USA, 1999. Mem. Internat. Bar Assn., State Bar Calif., Hist. Soc. of U.S. Dist. Ct. for No. Calif., San Francisco Bay Area chpt. Nat. Lawyers Guild (exec. bd. 1995-98), So. Poverty Law Ctr. (leadership coun.), U.S. Holocaust Mus., Rotary Internat. Democrat. Avocation: stamp collecting/philately. Office: Law Offices of Anthony P X Bothwell Ste 100 PMB 314 350 Bay St San Francisco CA 94133 E-mail: attorney@apxbothwell.com.

BOTHWELL, JOHN CHARLES, retired archbishop; b. Toronto, June 29, 1926; s. William Alexander and Anne (Campbell) B.; m. Joan Cowan, Dec. 29, 1951; children— Michael, Timothy, Nancy, Douglas, Ann. BA with honors in Modern History, U. Toronto, 1948; BD, Trinity Coll., Toronto, 1950, DD (hon.), 1972, Huron Coll., U. Western Ont., Wycliffe Coll. U Toronto, 1989; hon. sr. fellow, Renison Coll., U. Waterloo, 1988. Ordained priest Anglican Ch., 1952; curate St. James Cathedral, Toronto, 1951-53, Christ Ch. Cathedral, Vancouver, B.C., 1953-56; rector St. Aidan's Ch., Oakville, Ont., 1956-60, St. James' Ch., Dundas, Ont., 1960-65; canon missioner Niagara Diocese, 1965-69; nat. exec. dir. Anglican Ch. Can., 1969-71; co-adjutor bishop Niagara, 1971-73; bishop Diocese of Niagara, 1973-92, archbishop, 1985-91; Met. of Ont., 1985-91; ret., 1991; chancellor Trinity Coll., U. Toronto, 1991—2003. Hon. sr. fellow Renison Coll., U. Waterloo, 1988. Co-author: Theological Education for the 70's, 1969; author: Taking Risks and Keeping Faith, 1985, Living Faith Day By Day, 1990, Old-Time Religion or Risky Faith?, 1992; contbr. articles to various newspapers. Active numerous nat. and ecumenical coms.; Dir., com. chmn. Hamilton (Ont.) Social Planning Council, 1965-69, 71-75, v.p., 1975-77, pres., 1977-79; v.p. United Way, 1982, 83, pres., 1984-86; bd. dirs. Hamilton Found., 1982, v.p., 1983, pres., 1985 Inducted into City of Hamilton (Ont., Can.) Gallery of Distinction, 1993. Anglican. E-mail: jjcb@sympatico.ca.

BOTIN, ANA PATRICIA, bank executive; b. Oct. 1960; BA in economics, Bryn Mawr Coll., 1981. With credit mgmt. and financial analysis dept. J.P. Morgan, Madrid, 1981, with NYC, 1983, v.p. Latin Am. div., 1985; head banking div. capital mkts. Banco Santander, 1988, bd. dirs. and exec. com., 1989—, co-general mgr., 1991, gen. mgr. Banco Santander de Negocios, 1991, CEO Banco Santander de Negocios, 1994—99, exec. v.p., 1994—99; founder Suala Technology Capital Fund, 2000; head, cons. Coverlink, 2000; chmn., Banco Espanol de Credito (Banesto) Banco Santander, 2002—. Bd. dirs. Generali, 2004—. Named one of 100 Most Powerful Women in World, Forbes mag., 2005. Office: Banesto Avenida Gran Via Hortaleza No 3 28043 Madrid Spain*

BOTKIN, DANIEL BENJAMIN, biologist, environmental scientist, writer; b. Oklahoma City, Aug. 19, 1937; s. Benjamin Albert and Gertrude (Fritz) B.; m. Ellen Chase, Dec. 22, 1962 (div. 1976); children: Nancy, Jonathan; m. Erene Victoria Youngberg, Apr. 7, 1978 (dec. Mar. 1994); m. Jane M. O'Brien (dec. Feb. 2002); m. Diana G. Perez. BA, U. Rochester, 1959; MA, U. Wis., 1962; PhD, Rutgers U., 1968. From asst. to assoc. prof. Yale U., New Haven, 1968-76; assoc. scientist Marine Biol. Lab., Woods Hole, Mass., 1976-78; prof. biology U. Calif., Santa Barbara, 1978-92, chmn. environ. studies program, 1978-85; dir. program on global change biology dept. George Mason U., Fairfax, Va., 1993-97, prof. biology, 1993-99; pres. The Ctr. for the Study of the Environment, 1992—; rsch. prof. biology U. Calif., Santa Barbara, 1999—2004, emeritus, 2004—. Vis. prof. U. Notre Dame, 2003; disting vis. prof. Mich. State U., 2004. Author: Discordant Harmonies: A New Ecology for the 21st Century, 1990, paperback edit., 1992, Forest Dynamics: An Ecological Model, 1993, Our Natural History: The Lessons of Lewis and Clark, 1995, reprinted 2004, Passage of Discovery: The American Rivers Guide to the Missouri River of Lewis and Clark, 1999, No Man's Garden: Thoreau and a New Vision for Civilization and Nature, 2001, Strange Encounters: Adventures of a Renegade Naturalist, 2003, Beyond The Stony Mountains: Nature in the American West from Lewis and Clark to Today, 2004; (software) JABOWA, 1970, Timber: model of forest growth, 1983, 87, JABOWA-II, 1992, JABOWA-3 for Windows, 1999 JABOWA-4, 2004; co-author: Forest Succession, 1981, Environmental Studies, 1982, 87, Changing the Global Environment, 1989, Environmental Science: Earth as a Living Planet, 1995, 5th edit., 2004, The Blue Planet, 1999; contbr. articles to profl. jours., popular mags. and newspapers. Trustee Santa Barbara Bot. Garden, 1987-93; bd. dirs. Environ. Literacy Coun., Washington, 2003-, bd. trustees, Am. Folklife Ctr., Libr. Congress, 2004-; comr. US State Dept. to UNESCO. Recipient Texty award for Best Text Book, Textbook and Acad. Authors Assn., 2004, Fernow prize for Internat. Forestry, 1995, First Prize, Mitchell Internat. Prize for Sustainable Devel., 1991; named to Environ. Hall of Fame, Calif. Polytechnic U., 1995; fellow Rockefeller Bellagio (Italy) Inst., 1985, East-West Ctr., Honolulu, 1985-87, Woodrow Wilson Internat. Ctr. for Scholars, Washington, 1977-78; grantee EPA, NSF, NASA, NOAA, Mellon Found., Pew Charitable Trusts, W. Alton Jones Found., World Wildlife Fund, SOHIO Alaska Corp. Fellow AAAS; Cosmos Club, Sigma Xi (lectr. 1981-83). Avocations: photography, hiking, music. Office: 245 8th Ave #270 New York NY 10011 Office Phone: 917-747-3068. E-mail: info@naturestudy.org.

BOTKIN, JAMES W., leadership and life coach; b. Long Branch, NJ, May 15, 1943; s. Harold M. and Julia (Bishop) B.; m. Karin S. Bartow, Aug. 20, 1999; m. Rosvita Botkin; children: Alexander, Christopher. BA, Harvard U., 1965, MBA, 1968, DBA, 1973; grad., The Coaches Trng. Inst., 2003. Cert. profl. co-active coach 2004. Founder, chmn. and coach InnerCALL-Internat. Corp. Coaching Alliance, 2004—; pres. InterClass, Cambridge, Mass., 1990—2001; fellow U. Tex., Austin, 1985—. Bd. dirs. Lancaster U., England; internat. advisor New Horizons for Learning, Seattle, 1986—; internat. recognized pub. spkr. Author (with M. Elmandjra and M. Malitza): No Limits to Learning: A Report to the Club of Rome, 1979; author: (with D. Dimancescu and R. Stata) Global Stakes: The Future of High Technology in America, 1982; author: The Innovators: Rediscovering America's Creative Energy, 1984; author: (with D. Dimancescu) The New Alliance: Industry-University Partnerships, 1986; author: (with J. Matthews) Winning Combinations: Entrepreneurial Partnerships Between Large and Small Companies, 1992; author: (with Stan Davis) The Monster Under the Bed: How Business is Mastering the Opportunities of Knowledge for Profit, 1994; author: Smart Business: How Knowledge Communities Can Revolutionize Your Company, 1999. Named Hon. Citizen, Salzburg, Austria, 1977; recipient Innovator award, Rausing Fund, Lund, Sweden, 1990, Alliance award, Carnegie Corp., N.Y.C., 1986. Mem.: ICF (Internat. Coaching Fedn.), Club of Rome. Avocations: hiking, fishing, travel. Office: 26 Grozier Rd Cambridge MA 02138-3315 E-mail: jbotkin@comcast.net.

BOTKIN, MONTY LANE, computer company executive; b. Lubbock, Tex., Mar. 26, 1951; s. Louis A. and Geneva O. (Marlin) B.; 1 child, Nicholas L.; m. Ayami Honda, Oct. 26, 1996. BA, Tex. Tech U., 1975. Supr. Tex. Instruments, Inc., Lubbock, 1976-77, Abilene, Tex., 1977-78; electronic ctr. mgr. Tex. Instruments Supply Co., Palo Alto, Calif., 1978-81; mfg. mgr. home computers Tex. Instruments, Inc., Lubbock, 1981-83, mfg. mgr. calculator, 1983-87, mfg. mgr. ednl. products, 1987-90, Semi-Conductor Grp. photolithography ops. mgr., 1990-91, total quality control mgr. Lubbock Mos Memory, 1991-93; dir. mfg. Brother Industries U.S.A., Bartlett, Tenn., 1993-96, also bd. dirs.; dir. ops. Taiwan Semiconductor Mfg. Co., San Jose, Calif., 1996-2000; v.p. and gen. mgr. LAM Rsch. Corp., 2000—02; oper. officer Fujikin Inc., 2002—; exec. v.p., mng. dir., bd. dirs. Fujikin Am., Santa Clara, Calif., 2002—. Bd. dir. Fujikin of Am., exec. v.p.; bd. dir. Carten Controls Inc. and European Ops., exec. v.p. Mem. Inst. Indsl. Engrs. (sr.), Am. Soc. for Quality Control (chmn. West Tex. sect.), Am. Prodn. and Inventory Control Soc. Avocations: racquetball, photography, golf.

BOTLEY, CALVIN, lawyer, judge; b. Pineville, La., Dec. 2, 1944; s. Clifford and Lee Esther (Fontenot) B.; m. Jean Carol Norman, Jan. 20, 1968; children: Nicola Lynnette, Reginald Anthony (dec.). BA, Grambling State U., 1966; JD, Tex. So. U., 1972; LLM, U. Houston Law Ctr., 1996. Bar: Tex. 1972, U.S. Dist. Ct. (so., no., we. dists.) Tex. 1973, U.S. Ct. Appeals (5th cir.) 1973, U.S. Dist. Ct. (ea. dist.) Tex. 1975, U.S. Supreme Ct. 1975, U.S. Ct. Customs and Patent Appeals 1976, U.S. Ct. Appeals (11th cir.) 1984, U.S. Ct. Internat. Trade 1984. Asst. dist. atty. Harris County (Tex.), Houston, 1972-73; asst. atty. gen. State of Tex., 1973-78, chief Houston Regional Office, 1974-78; asst. U.S. atty. So. Dist. Tex., Dept. Justice, 1978-79; magistrate judge U.S. Dist. Ct. (so. dist.) Tex., Houston, 1979—. Chmn. criminal justice adv. council Tex. So. U., 1976-77. Bd. dirs., mem. exec. com. Houston Council on Human Relations; bd. dirs. Houston Child Guidance Ctr., bd. visitors Thurgood Marshall Sch. Law, Tex. So. U.; mem. fed. conf. com. on court security, 1988-92. Served with U.S. Army, 1966-69; Vietnam. Decorated Army Commendation medal with oak leaf cluster; recipient Pres. award Nat. Assn. Blacks in Higher Edn., 1984, Alumni of Yr. award Thurgood Marshall Sch. Law, 1994, Outstanding Achievement award Grambling State U. Polit. Sci. Honor Soc., 1981, Black and Gold Leadership award Grambling State U., 1996, Disting. Svc. award U. Houston Law Ctr., 1995, award for legal excellence NAACP, 1997, Disting. Alumni award Nat. Assn. for Equal Opportunity in Higher Edn., 1999; named to Grambling State U. Hall of Fame, 1996. Mem. ABA (Judge Edward R. Finch Law Day Speech award 1999), Tex. Bar Assn., Tex. Bar Found., Houston Bar Assn., Houston Lawyers' Assn., Fed. Magistrate Judges Assn., Houston Bar Found., Fed. Bar Assn., Nat. Geog. Soc., Coll. State Bar Tex., Masons, Rotary Internat., Phi Alpha Delta (justice Greener chpt. 1971-72, Acad. Achievement award 1972, Outstanding Mem. award 1972), Sigma Rho Sigma (pres. Grambling chpt. 1963, nat. v.p. 1964-65, nat. pres. 1965-66). Baptist. Office: US District Court 7720 US Courthouse 515 Rusk St Houston TX 77002-2600

BOTROS, NAZEIH M., adult education educator, consultant; BS, Ain Shams U., Cairo, Egypt, 1966; MSc, Am. U., Cairo, 1979; PhD, U. Okla., 1985; BA, So. Ill. U., 1998. Prof. So. Ill. U., Carbondale, 1985—. Home: 186 Sunset Dr Carbondale IL 62901 Office: So Ill U Dept Of ECE Carbondale IL 62901-6603 Office Phone: 618-453-7028. Office Fax: 618-453-7972. Personal E-mail: botrosn#siu.edu. E-mail: botrosn@siu.edu.

BOTSAI, ELMER EUGENE, architect, architecture educator, retired dean; b. St. Louis, Feb. 1, 1928; s. Paul and Ita May (Cole) B.; m. Patricia L. Keegan, Aug. 28, 1955; children: Donald Rolf, Kurt Gregory.; m. Sharon K. Kaiser, Dec. 5, 1981; 1 dau., Kiana Michelle. AA, Sacramento Jr. Coll., 1950; AB, U. Calif., Berkeley, 1954; D of Architecture, U. Hawaii, 2000. Registered architect, Hawaii, Calif. Draftsman, then asst. to arch. So. Pacific Co., San Francisco, 1953-57; designer H.K. Ferguson Co., San Francisco, 1955; project arch. Anshen & Allen Arch., San Francisco, 1957-63; prin. Botsai, Overstreet & Rosenberg, Arch. and Planners, San Francisco, 1963—79, Elmer E. Botsai FAIA, Honolulu, 1979—; of counsel Groupe 70 Internat., 1998—; chmn. dept. arch. U. Hawaii, Manoa, 1976-80, dean Sch. Arch., 1980-90, prof., 1990-99, prof. emeritus, 2000—. Lectr. U. Calif., Berkeley, 1976, dir. Nat. Archtl. Accrediting Bd., 1972-73, 79; adminstrv. and tech. cons. Wood Bldg. Rsch. Ctr., U. Calif., 1985-90, mem. profl. preparation project com. at U. Mich., Ann Arbor, 1986-87; co-author water infiltration seminar series for Bldg. Owners and Mgr. Rsch. Ctr., 1986-87; chief investigator effects of Guatemalan earthquake for NSF and AIA, Washington, 1976; steering com. on structural failures Nat. Bur. Standards, 1982-84; chmn., dir. gen. svc. Adv. Com. State of Calif. Co-author: Architects and Earthquake, Rsch. Needs, 1976, ATC Seismic Standards for Nat. Bur. of Standards, 1976, Arch. and Earthquakes: A Primer, 1977, Seismic Design, 1978, Wood-Detailing for Performance, 1990, Wood as a Building Material, 2d edit., 1991; contbr. articles and reports to profl. jour.; prin. works include expansion of Nuc. Weapons Tng. Facility at Lemoore Naval Air Sta., Calif., LASH Terminal Port Facility Archtl. Phase, San Francisco, Incline Village (Nev.) Country Club, 1365 Columbus Ave. Bldg., San Francisco, modernization Stanford Ct. Hotel, San Francisco; monument area constrn. several Calif. cemeteries. With U.S. Army, 1946—48. Recipient Cert. Honor Fedn. Archtl. Coll. Mex. Republic, 1984, Disting. Alumni award U. Hawaii, 2005; named to Wisdom Hall of Fame, 1998; NSF grantee for investigative workshop project, San Diego, 1974-80. Fellow AIA (bd. dir., 1966-71, treas. No. Calif. chpt. 1968-69, pres. 1971, nat. v.p., 1975-76, nat. pres. 1978, pres. Hawaii 1985); hon. fellow Royal Can. Inst. Arch., NZ Inst. Arch. (hon.), Royal Australian Inst. Arch. (1st arch., 1st Am.), La Societe de Arquitectos Mexicano; mem. Archtl. Sec. Assn. (hon.), Soc. Wood Sci. and Tech., Internat. Conf. Bldg. Ofcl. Home: 321 Wailupe Cir Honolulu HI 96821-1524 Office: 925 Bethel St Fl 5 Honolulu HI 96813-4393

BOTSFORD, ANNE L., social worker; b. Wharton, Tex., June 4, 1943; d. Edward Potter and Grace Pearl (Pierce) Botsford; m. Donald Harris Punetz, Mar. 27, 1983; children: Henry, Edward; 1 child from previous marriage, Alisa Pierce Young. BA, Barnard, 1966; MA, Tufts U., 1971; MSW, Adelphi U., 1978; PhD, SUNY, 1997. LCSW NY. Dir. rsch., program evaluation NY State Dept. Mental Health, Melville, NY, 1995—97; dir. social work No. Dutchess Hosp., Rhinebeck, NY, 1979—87, dir. cmty relations, 1987—91; social work supr. Columbia Presbyn. Med. Ctr., N.Y.C., 1991—93; case mgmt. supr. Ulster Assoc. for Retarded Citizens, Kingston, NY, 1993—95; assoc. prof., dir. field educators Marist Coll., Poughkeepsie, NY, 1995—. Cons. Dutchess County Office for Aging, Poughkeepsie, 1995—2002; adv. bd. Vol. of Am., Alexandria, Va., 2001—. Contbr. articles various profl. jours. Liason to polit. action com. Influencing State Policy, Alexandria, Va., 1995—. Fellowship, UCLA Ctr. on Geriatric Edn., 1999, Ctr. for Policy Rsch., Maxwell Sch., 2000. Mem.: Internat. Assn. for the Scientific Study of Intellectual Disability, Coun. on Social Work Educators, Nat. Assoc. Social Work, NY State Social Work Edn. Assn. Office: Marist Coll Dyson 380 Poughkeepsie NY 12601 Office Phone: 845-575-3000 2129. Office Fax: 845-575-3465. Business E-Mail: anne.botsford@marist.edu.

BOTSFORD, DAVID L., lawyer; b. Phila., Aug. 18, 1952; s. Thomas C. and Lois A. (Yarrison) B. BA, U. Conn., 1974; JD, So. Meth. U., 1977. Bar: Tex., 1977, U.S. Supreme Ct. 1981, U.S. Ct. Appeals (5th & 9th cir.), U.S. Dist. Ct. (all dists.), Tex.; cert. Tex. Bd. Legal Specialization, criminal law. Law clerk Emmett Colvin, Dallas, 1974-77; assoc., ptnr. Emmet Colvin, Dallas, 1978-81; briefing atty. Hon. Truman Roberts Ct. Criminal Appeals Tex., 1977-78; treas. bond trader Chgo. Bd. Trade, 1981-82; assoc. Frank Maloney, Austin, Tex., 1982-88; ptnr. Alvis, Carssow, Cummins, Hoeffner & Botsford, P.C., 1988-93, Botsford & Sauer, L.L.P., 1993-96; pvt. practice Austin, 1996—. Contbr. articles to profl. jours. Tex. Criminal Def. Lawyers Ednl. Inst. fellow, 1990. Mem.: Travis Bar Assn., Tex. Criminal Def. Lawyers Assn. (assoc. dir. 1985, 1986, dir. 1987—91, asst. sec.-treas. 1991—92, sec.-treas. 1992—93, 2d v.p. 1993—94, 1st v.p. 1994—95, pres.-elect 1995—96, pres. 1996—97, Presdl. Excellence award 1989, 1990, 1993, 1994, 1995), Tex. Assn. Bd. Cert. Specialists Criminal Law (pres. 1991—92), State Bar Tex. (criminal law exam. commn. 1985—, Coll. State Bar 1991, criminal justice sect.Outstanding Criminal Def. Lawyer of Yr. 1993), Nat. Assn. Criminal Def. Lawyers, Barristers, Order of Coif. Office: 1307 W Ave Austin TX 78701-2948 Personal E-mail: dbotsford@aol.com.

BOTSFORD, JON DOUGLAS, lawyer; b. Muskegon, Mich., Aug. 1, 1954; s. Lawrence Wayne and June Arleigh (Hanson) B; m. Joan Elizabeth Nims; children: Jackson, Tess, Matthew. BA, Mich. State U., 1976; JD, UCLA, 1979. Bar: Ill. 1979, U.S. Ct. Appeals (6th cir.) 1980, U.S. Dist. Ct. (no. dist.) Ill. 1981, Calif. 1982, Mich. 1982, U.S. Dist. Ct. (we. dist.) Mich. 1982, U.S. Supreme Ct 1984, U.S. Tax Ct. 1985. Law clk. to Hon. Albert Jengel U.S. Ct. Appeals, 6th Cir., 1979-80; atty. Jenner & Block, Chgo., 1980-82, Warner, Norcross & Judd, Grand Rapids, Mich., 1982-85, Steelcase Inc., Grand Rapids, 1985—87, sr. atty., 1987—92, asst. gen. counsel, 1992—97, gen. counsel, sec., 1997—98, v.p., gen. counsel, sec., 1998—99, sr. v.p., sec., chief legal officer, 1999—. Contbr. articles to profl. jours. Planning commr. Caledonia (Mich.) Township, 1997—99. Mem. ABA, Ill. State Bar Assn., State Bar Calif., State Bar Mich., Grand Rapids Bar Assn. Democrat. Office: Steelcase Inc 901 44th St SE Grand Rapids MI 49508-7575

BOTSKO, MICHAEL WAYNE, mathematics professor; s. Michael and Amelia Batsko; m. Donna J. Botsko, Nov. 7, 1969; 1 child, Tanya Carrie Mills. BS, Duquesne U., 1965, MA, 1967; PhD, U. Pitts., 1971. Prof. math. St. Vincent Coll., Latrobe, Pa., 1968—. Chaor math. dept. St. Vincent Coll., 1972—. Contbr. articles to profl. jours. Mem.: Math. Assn. Am. (Tchg. award 2003). Republican. Methodist. Home: 114 Stoney Brook Dr Greensburg PA 15601 Office: St Vincent Coll Dept Math Latrobe PA 15650 Business E-Mail: mike.botsko@mial.stvincent.edu.

BOTSTEIN, DAVID, geneticist, educator; b. Zurich, Switzerland, Sept. 8, 1942; naturalized, 1954; AB in Biochem. Scis. cum laude, Harvard U., 1963; PhD in Human Genetics, U. Mich., 1967. Woodrow Wilson fellow, 1963; instr. dept. biology MIT, Cambridge, Mass., 1967-69, asst. prof. genetics, 1969-73, assoc. prof. genetics dept. biology, 1973-78, prof., 1978-88; v.p. sci. Genetech, Inc., 1988-90; Stanford W. Ascherman prof. Stanford U. Sch. Medicine, Palo Alto, Calif., 1997—2003; dir., Lewis-Sigler Inst. for Integrative Genomics Princeton U., 2003—. Sci. adv. bd. Collaborative Research, Inc., 1978-87. Editor in chief Nat. Acad. Scis., 1981, Inst. Medicine, 1993, Molecular Biology of Cell, 1992—; contbr. over 230 articles to profl. jours. Recipient Career Devel. award NIH, 1972-74; Eli Lilly and Co. award in microbiology and immunology, 1978, Genetics Soc. of Am. Medal, 1988, Rosenstiel award Brandeis U., 1992, Allen award Am. Soc. of Human Genetics, 1989, Inst. of Medicine, 1993, Lifetime Contbn. to Modern Genetics award Peter Gruber Found. 2003. Mem. NAS, Genetics Soc. Am. (bd. dirs. 1984), Inst. Medicine. Achievements include proposing, with three colleagues, a method for mapping genes, leading to Human Genome Project, 1980. Office: Lewis-Sigler Inst for Integrative Genomics Carl Icahn Lab Princeton Univ Princeton NJ 08544

BOTSTEIN, LEON, academic administrator, conductor, historian; b. Zurich, Switzerland, Dec. 14, 1946; s. Charles and Anne (Wyszewianski) Botstein; m. Jill Lundquist, 1970 (div.); children: Sarah, Abigail(dec.); m. Barbara Haskell, 1982. BA (Woodrow Wilson fellow, Danforth Found. fellow, Sloan Found. fellow, Rockefeller fellow), U. Chgo., 1967; MA, Harvard U., 1968, PhD, 1985. Teaching fellow Harvard U., 1968—69; lectr. history Boston U., 1969; asst. to pres. N.Y.C. Bd. Edn., 1969—70; pres. Franconia Coll., 1970—75, Bard Coll., Annandale-On-Hudson, 1975—, Simon's Rock Coll. Bard, Great Barrington, Mass., 1979—; founder, artistic dir. Bard Music Festival, 1990—; music dir. Am. Symphony Orch., N.Y.C., 1992—, Jerusalem Symphony Orch., 2003—; artistic dir. Am. Russian Young Artists Orch., 1995—. Founder, prin. condr. White Mountain Music and Art Festival, NH, 1973—75; condr. Hudson Valley Philharm. Chamber Orch., 1989—92; guest condr. London Philharmonic, 1986—99, Philharmonia Orch., 1986, Pro Arte Chamber Orch. of Boston, 1988—89; other guest conducting appearances in Korea, Japan, Czech Republic, Philippines, Austria, Brazil, Lithuania, Romania, Scotland, Germany, Switzerland, Russia; past chmn. N.Y. Coun. Humanitities, Assn. Episc. Colls., Harper's Mag. Found.; vis. prof. Hochschule fur angewandte Kunst, Vienna, 1988; vis. faculty Manhattan Sch. Music, 1986; chmn. Salzburg Seminar, 1987; mem. nat. adv. com. Yale-New Haven Tchrs. Inst. Author: (novels) Jefferson's Children: Education and the Promise of American Culture, 1997; editor: (book) The Compleat Brahms, 1999, Musical Quar., 1992—; contbr. articles to profl. publs.; conductor: albums. Recipient

Berlin Prize Fellowship; grantee Rockefeller fellow. Fellow: Am. Acad. Arts & Scis. Office: Bard Coll Office of Pres Annandale On Hudson NY 12504 Office Phone: 845-758-7423. Business E-Mail: president@bard.edu.

BOTT, HAROLD SHELDON, accountant, management consultant; b. Chgo., Dec. 12, 1933; s. Harold S. and Mary (Moseley) B.; m. Audrey Anne Connor, May 15, 1964; children: Susan, Lynda. AB, Princeton U., 1955; MBA, Harvard U., 1959; postgrad., U. Chgo., 1960-62. Adminstrv. asst. to exec v.p. Champion Paper, Hamilton, Ohio, 1959-61; mgmt. cons. Arthur Andersen & Co., Chgo., 1961-65, mgr., 1965-71, ptnr., 1971-89. Mng. dir. mgmt. info. cons., ptnr. Andersen Cons., 1988-91; ptnr. Strategic Tng. and Recruiting Svcs. Ctr.; vice-chmn. The Assn. Mgmt. Cons., 1982-84; bd. dirs. Harvard Bus. Sch. Assocs.; faculty Grad. Sch. Bus., U. Chgo., 1994-2000; of counsel Omnitech Cons., 1994-96; pres. H.S. Bott Co., 1994-2003. Officer, pres., dir. Urban Gateways, 1965—90; treas., dir. sch. bd., pres. Kenilworth Caucus, 1990; dir. The Cradle, 2000—03, Kenilworth United Fund, 1983—89; mem. pres.'s vis. com., trustee Chgo. Theol. Sem., 2002—; bd. dirs. Orch. of Ill., 1988—89, The Joseph Sears Found., 2000—04, co-pres., 2001—; commodore Kenilworth Sailing Club, 1987—88. With USN, 1955—56. Mem. AICPA, Ill. Soc. CPA's, Kenilworth Club (treas., bd. dirs. 1975-79), Kenilworth Hist. Soc. (bd. dirs. 1995—), Indian Hill Club, Chgo. Club. Republican. Congregationalist. Home: 305 Kenilworth Ave Kenilworth IL 60043-1132 Business E-Mail: pete.bott@gsb.uchicago.edu.

BOTT, JAY CORDELL, oncologist, hematologist; b. Salt Lake City, 1947; s. Leroy J. and Blanche T. Bott; m. Julie Christiansen, 1992. BA in Chemistry, U. Utah, 1971, BA in Med. Biology, 1974, MD hons. program in internal medicine, 1975. Cert. internal medicine, hematology, oncology. Intern Naval Regional Med. Ctr., San Diego, 1975—76, resident, 1976—78, fellow in oncology, hematology, 1979—80, 1981—82; fellow in oncology U. Utah Med. Ctr., Salt Lake City, 1980—81; with Utah Valley Regional Med. Ctr., Provo, 1983—, Mountain View Hosp., Payson, Utah, 1983—, Castleview Hosp., Price, Utah, 1984—, Timpanogos Regional Hosp., Orem, Utah, 1998—; founder Oxbow Ranch, Hanna, Utah. V.p. Ctrl. Utah Med. Clinic; prior prin. investigator Nat. Surg. Adjuvant Breast Bowel Project, 1995-2004; est. one of the largest found. Quarter Horse breeding programs in U.S. Mem. Nat. Rep. Com.; missionary LDS Ch., Germany, 1967—69; tchr. Sunday Sch.; with High Cou. and Bishopric, LDS Ch. Cmdr. USNR, 1973—84. Named Utah Rep. Businessman of Yr., 2000, 2001. Fellow: ACP; mem.: Am. Cancer Soc. (past. pres. Utah Vly. chpt.), Utah County Med. Assn. (past pres.), S.W. Oncology Group, Am. Soc. Hematology, Am. Soc. Clin. Oncology, Phi Kappa Phi, Phi Beta Kappa. Avocations: ranching, hunting, classical piano, outdoorsports. Office: Ctrl Utah Med Ctr 1055 N 500 W Provo UT 84604-3305 also: Oxbow Ranch PO Box 24 Hanna UT 84031-0024 Office Phone: 801-374-2367. E-mail: cbott@centralutahclinic.com.

BOTT, JOHN CRIST, artist, educator; b. Gassaway, W.Va., Sept. 12, 1936; s. Joseph Franklin and Blanche Hannah (Crist) B.; m. Glenda Morgan, May 25, 1960 (div. Aug. 1977), 1 child, Jason; m. Kathy Hicklin, Aug. 10, 1977. BS in Art, Troy State U., 1960; MFA, U. N.C., 1969. Tchr. Bratt (Fla.) Jr. H.S., 1961-62, Forest Park (Ga.) Sr. H.S., 1962-67; grad. asst. U. N.C., 1967-68; asst. prof. Greensboro (N.C.) Coll., 1969-72, U. Evansville, Ind., 1972-76, U. So. Ind., Evansville, 1976-77; from asst. to full prof. Colby-Sawyer Coll., New London, N.H., 1977—. One-man shows include Troy (Ala.) State Coll., 1960, Clark Coll.-Atlanta U., 1966, Union South Gallery, U. N.C., Chapell Hill, 1969, Alamance County Arts Ctr., Graham, N.C., 1969, Cullis Gallery, Greensboro Coll., 1970, Stone Galleries, Davidson (N.C.) Coll., 1971, Ill. State U. Evansville, 1976; group exhibits include Amerika Haus, Nurnberg, Germany, 1959, Mobile (Ala.) Art Assn., 1962, Adair Art Gallery, Atlanta, 1966, N.C. State U., Raleigh, 1968, Greensboro Pub. Libr., 1969, Garden Gallery, Raleigh, N.C., 1969, 70, Meredith Coll., Raleigh, 1970, N.C. Mus. Art, Raleigh, 1971, 72, N.C. Artists Traveling Exhbn., 1971, Old Gallery, Evansville, 1972, Evansville Mus., 1972, Krannert Gallery, Evansville, 1973, Anderson (Ind.) Fine Arts Ctr., 1974, State Ctr. Gallery, Evansville, 1975, Mugar Gallery, New London, 1978, 79, 81, 82, 83, 84, 85, Phenix Gallery, Concord, 1982, Thronja Gallery, Springfield, Mass., 1986, Dartmouth Faculty Club, Hanover, 1987, Libr. Arts Ctr., Newport, 1988, New Harmony Gallery Contemporary Art, 1988, Ctr. for the Arts, Nashua, 1990, McGowan Fine Art, Concord, 1990, Libr. Arts Ctr., Newport, 1996, Kimball-Jenkins Mansion, Concord, 1997, Millbrook Gallery, Concord, 1997-99, 2004, Gallery Mack, 1999, 2000, 01, 02, 03, Seattle, Alpers Fine Art, Andover, Mass., 2001, many others; represented in permanent collections Troy State U., Spring Mills, Inc., Lancaster, S.C., Burlington Industries, Greensboro, Witherspoon Gallery, U. N.C., Greensboro, Sheldon Swope Gallery, Terre Haute, Ind., Bank of N.H., Concord, Chrysler Mus., Norfolk, Va., S.W. Ill. Coll., others. With U.S. Army, 1956-59. Office: Colby-Sawyer Coll New London NH 03257 Home: RR 1 Box 389C Claremont NH 03743-9400

BOTT, RAOUL, mathematician, educator; b. Budapest, Hungary, Sept. 24, 1923; s. Rudolf and Margit (Kovach) Bott; m. Phyllis Aikman, Aug. 30, 1947; children: Anthony, Jocelyn, Renee, Candace. B Engring., McGill U., Montreal, 1945, M Engring., 1946, DSc (hon.), 1987; DSc, Carnegie Inst. Tech., 1949; DSc (hon.), Notre Dame U., 1979, Carnegie-Mellon U., 1989, U. Leicester, England. Fellow Inst. Advanced Studies, Princeton U., 1949—51, 1955—57; instr. math. U. Mich., Ann Arbor, 1951—52, asst. prof., 1952—55, assoc. prof., 1957—59; prof. Harvard U., Cambridge, Mass., 1959—, W. Casper Graustein prof., 1969—99, W. Casper Graustein rsch. prof., 1999—. Author: (books and papers) in various branches of math. and its relationship to physics. Recipient Nat. Sci. medal, Pres. of U.S., 1987, Wolf prize, 2000; fellow Sloan fellow, 1956—60, hon. fellow, St. Catharines Coll., 1985. Fellow: Am. Math. Soc. (Veblen prize 1964, Steele prize 1990), Am. Acad. Arts & Scis.; mem.: NAS, French Acad. Sci., London Math. Soc. (hon.). Democrat. Roman Catholic. Avocations: music, nature. Home: 1 Richdale Ave Unit 9 Cambridge MA 02140-2610 Office: Harvard U Dept Math 1 Oxford St Cambridge MA 02138-2901*

BOTT, SIMON GREGORY, chemistry educator, researcher; b. Leicester, Eng., Oct. 7, 1962; s. Ronald William and Vivienne Mary Bott; m. Angie Rene McGuffey; children: Alexandra McGuffey, Connor. BSc, U. Bristol, Eng., 1983; PhD, U. Ala., 1986. Rschr. Oxford (Eng.) U., 1987, MIT, Cambridge, Mass., 1988—89; asst. prof. U. North Tex., Denton, 1990—97; rsch. assoc. prof. U. Houston, 1997, advisor, 2002, dir. undergrad. affairs, 2003—. Cons. Rimkus Cons., Houston, 1998. Mem.: Am. Chem. Soc. (pres. local chpt. 2002—04, councillor 2005—), Sigma Xi (local pres. 1995—97). Office: U Houston Dept Chemistry Houston TX 77204 Office Phone: 713-743-2771. Business E-Mail: sbott@uh.edu.

BOTTARI, PAUL J., lawyer; b. NYC, Apr. 26, 1951; BA, U. Notre Dame, 1973; JD, Fordham U., 1976. Bar: NY 1977, US Dist. Ct. So. Dist. NY, US Dist. Ct. Ea. Dist. NY. Ptnr. Wilson, Elser, Moskowitz, Edelman & Dicker LLP, NYC. Mem.: Am. Bd. Trial Advocates, NY State Trial Lawyers Assn. Office: Wilson Elser Moskowitz Edelman & Dicker LLP 23rd Fl 150 E 42nd St New York NY 10017-5639 Office Phone: 212-490-3000 ext. 4103. Office Fax: 212-490-3038. Business E-Mail: bottarip@wemed.com.

BOTTARO, TIMOTHY SHANAHAN, lawyer; b. Buffalo, Sept. 20, 1958; s. Samuel Domenick and Luetta May Bottaro; m. Kathleen Ann Ballard, Aug. 3, 1960; children: Patrick, Anne. BA, Creighton U., 1981; JD, U. Iowa, 1983. Bar: Iowa 1983, U.S. Dist. Ct. (no. dist.) Iowa 1983, U.S. Ct. Appeals (8th cir.) 1984. Ptnr. Rawlings & Nieland, et al, Sioux City, Iowa, 1983-95, Vriezelaar, Tigges, Edgington, Rossi, Bottaro & Boden, Sioux City, Iowa, 1995—. Chair Woodbury County Jud. Magistrate Nomination Commn., Sioux City, 1992-94. Chair Woodbury County Dem. Party, Sioux City, 1994-98; lay dir., Cathedral of the Epiphany, Sioux City, 1987—; pres., bd. trustees, Sioux City Pub. Libr., 1992-98. Recipient Libr. Pearl award Sioux City Pub. Libr., 1989, Cmty. Svc. award Iowa State Bar Assn., 2000. Mem. Am. Trial Lawyers Assn., Iowa Trial Lawyers Assn. Democrat. Roman Catholic. Avocations: bicycling, politics, walking. Office: Vriezelaar Tigges et al 421 Nebraska St Sioux City IA 51101-1311

BOTTELLI, RICHARD, retired architect; b. Orange, N.J., Apr. 20, 1937; s. Romolo and Genevieve Bottelli; m. Ann Erpenbeck, June 7, 1958; children: Richard, William, Suzanne, John. B.Arch., U. Va., 1962. Lic. architect, N.Y., N.J., Pa. Designer project mgr. romolo Bottelli, Jr., Maplewood, N.J., 1963-67; prin. Becker & Becker & Assos., N.Y.C. and London, 1967-73; propr. Bottelli Assos., Architects/Planners, Florham Park, N.J., 1973-95, ret., 1995. Is. lectr. U. Cin., 1974, So. Meth. U., 1974, Leicester (Eng.) Coll. Art, 1970; mem. adv. com. Sch. Architecture, N.J. Inst. Tech., 1982-83. Chmn. mag. editorial bd. Architecture N.J., 1974-78. Works include: Gregory park Redevel., 1965, Bankers Trust Plaza Br. Bank, N.Y.C., 1973, Hackettstown Post Office, 1976, Norman Towers, 1980, New Brunswick Sr. Citizens Housing, 1982, East Orange Sr. Citizens Housing, 1983, Springfield Mcpl. Bldg., 1990. Mem. Summit (N.J.) Planning Bd., 1971-82, chmn., 1973-82, mem. Zoning Bd., 1972-82, councilman-at-large, 1985-89; mem. N.J. Citizens Com. on Permit Coordination, 1981-85. Mem. AIA, N.J. Soc. Architects (pres. 1977), N.J. Soc. Profl. Planners, Nat. Trust Historic Preservation, Summit Tennis Club, Rotary (pres. 1987-88). Home: PO Box 1284 Grantham NH 03753-1284

BOTTELLI, ROBERTA M., music educator; b. Shelton, Wash., July 29, 1974; d. Richard Hunt and Dee Lynnette Morton; m. John C Bottelli, Oct. 10, 1998. BA, U. of Puget Sound, 1992—96; MusM, Ctrl. Wash. U., 1996; MA, Ea. Wash. U., 2000—05. Mktg. and devel. dir. Spokane Chamber Music Assn., Wash., 2003—05; dir. of string studies Whitworth Coll., Spokane, Wash. Cellist Riverside String Trio, Spokane, 2002—05; sub. cellist Spokane Symphony, 1998—2005; cellist Elan Piano Trio, Spokane, 2003—05; principle cellist Lake Chelan Bach Fest Orch., Chelan, Wash.; cellist Mid Columbia Symphony, Richland, Wash., 1997—2003, Wenatchee Symphony, Wash., 1996—2000; pvt. lesson instr. Holy Names Music Ctr., Spokane, Wash., 2000—03; adjudicator Wash. Music Educator's' Assn., Spokane, Wash., 2000—05; guest soloist Mid Columbia Symphony, 2002, Lake Chelan Bach Fest, 2004. Chamber Music fellowship, Neskowin Chamber Music, 2004. Home: 1628 E 17th Ave Spokane WA 99203 Personal E-mail: robertabottelli@comcast.net.

BOTTIGLIA, WILLIAM FILBERT, humanities educator; b. Bernardsville, NJ, Nov. 23, 1912; s. Vincent Richard and Quintilia (Mastrobattista) B.; m. Mildred MacDonald, Dec. 21, 1943 (dec. Oct. 1966); children: Martha (Mrs. Milton Morris), Janet. AB, Princeton U., 1934, AM, 1935, PhD, 1948. Instr. modern langs. Princeton U., 1934-42; engaged in industry, 1942-47; gen. mgr. J & S Tool Co., East Orange, N.J., 1946-47; asst. prof. English, St. Lawrence U., 1948; prof. Romance langs. and lits., chmn. dept. Ripon Coll., 1948-56; faculty MIT, 1956—, prof. fgn. lit. and humanities, 1960-74, head dept. fgn. lit. and linguistics, 1964-73, prof. mgmt. and humanities, 1974-78, prof. emeritus and sr. lectr. mgmt. and humanities, 1978-91. Author: Voltaire's Candide: Analysis of a Classic, 2d edit., 1964, (with others) Voltaire (Twentieth Century Views), 1968, Heroic Symphony, 1997-99, 4 vols.; editor: Reports of N.E. Conf. on the Teaching of Fgn. Langs. 1957, 62, 63. Mem.: Soc. Palmes Académiques, Dante Soc. Am., Phi Beta Kappa. Home: 34 Mary Chilton Rd Needham MA 02492-1138

BOTTITTA, JOSEPH ANTHONY, lawyer; b. Mar. 9, 1949; s. Anthony S. and Elizabeth (Bellisano) B.; m. Lynda Joan Kloss, Apr. 14, 1979; children: Michelle Emma, Gregory Joseph. BSBA, Seton Hall U., 1971, JD, 1974. Bar: US Dist. Ct. NJ 1974, US Supreme Ct. 1981. Ptnr. Rusignola & Pugliese, Newark, 1974-78; pvt. practice Joseph A. Bottitta, West Orange, NJ, 1979-88; sr. ptnr. Gilbert, Gilbert, Schlossberg and Bottitta, 1988-89; pvt. practice, 1989-95; with Bottitta and Bascelli, 1995-99. Chmn. Supreme Ct. Fee Arbitration Com. Dist. V-B., 1984-85; mem. NJ Uniform Law Commn., 1987-91, NJ Commn. Professionalism in Law, 1997-2000, NJ Supreme Ct. Profl. Responsibility Rules Com., 1999-; pres. NJ Lawyers Svc., 2000—; pres., E-Law.com, 2000—. Fellow: Am. Bar Found.; mem.: ABA, Essex County Bar Assn. (sec. 1983—84, treas. 1984—85, pres.-elect 1985—86, pres. 1986—87), NJ State Bar Assn. (trustee 1988, treas. 1994—95, v.p. 1995—97, pres.-elect 1997—98, pres. 1998—99). Republican. Roman Catholic. Office: c/o NJ Lawyers Svc 2333 Route 22 W Union NJ 07083-8517 E-mail: joeb@njls.com.

BOTTJER, DAVID JOHN, earth science and biology educator; b. NYC, Oct. 3, 1951; s. John Henry and Marilyn (Winter) B.; m. Sarah Ranney Wright, July 26, 1973. BS, Haverford Coll., 1973; MA, SUNY, Binghamton, 1976; PhD, Ind. U., 1978. NRC postdoctoral rsch. assoc. US Geol. Survey, Washington, 1978-79; asst. prof. dept. geol. sci. U. So. Calif., LA, 1979-85, assoc. prof. dept. geol. sci., 1985-91, prof. dept. earth sci., 1991—, prof. dept. biol. sci., 2003—. Rsch. assoc. Los Angeles County Mus. Natural History, 1979—; vis. scientist Field Mus. Natural History, Chgo., 1986; Paleontol. Soc. Disting. lectr., 1992-93; mem. Nat. Sci. Found. panel on earth systems history, 1997-99; sr. fellow UCLA Ctr. for the Study of Evolution and Origin of Life, 2000. Editor Palaios, 1989-96; assoc. editor Cretaceous Rsch., 1988-91; mem. editl. bd. Geology, 1984-89, 95-2000, Hist. Biology, 1988-93; co-editor Columbia U. Press Critical Moments and Perspectives in Paleobiology and Earth History (book series), 1990—; editor-in-chief Palaeo-3, 2000—. Recipient Disting. Scientist award, Ctr. for Study of Evolution and Origin of Life, UCLA, 2002. Fellow AAAS, Geol. Soc. Am., Geol. Soc. London; mem. Paleontol. Soc. (pres. 2004—), Soc. Sediment Geology (pres. Pacific sect. 2001-02), Internat. Paleontology Assn. Office: U So Calif Dept Earth Scis Los Angeles CA 90089-0001 Office Phone: 213-740-6100. Business E-Mail: dbottjer@usc.edu.

BOTTOM, DALE COYLE, marketing executive, director, management consultant; b. Columbus, Ind., June 25, 1932; s. James Robert and Sarah Lou (Coyle) B.; m. Frances Audrey Wilson, June 6, 1954 (div.); children: Jane Ellen, Steven Dale, Sharon Lynn, Carol Ann; m. Elaine McAuliffe, Aug. 20, 1988. BS, Ball State U., Muncie, Ind., 1954. Admissions counselor Stephens Coll., Columbia, Mo., 1958-61; exec. asst., then staff v.p. Inst. Fin. Edn., Chgo., 1961-67, pres., 1967-92; exec. v.p., chief fin. officer U.S. League Savs. Instns., 1985-89; chmn., dir. SAF-Systems & Forms Co.; sec.-gen. Internat. Union Fin. Instns., Chgo., 1989-95; cons. Resource Strategies Internat., Hinsdale, Ill., 1995—; assoc. v.p., dir. strategic svcs. Inland Real Estate Auctions, Inc. Bd. dirs. Savs. Instn. Ins. Group, Ltd., v.p., chief fin. officer. Chmn. bd. Barrington (Ill.) United Meth. Ch., 1981. Served as officer USAF, 1955-58; comdr. USNR (ret.), 1967-78. Recipient Award of Distinction, Ball State U., 2003. Mem. Fin. Mgrs. Soc. (dir.), Savs. Instns. Mktg. Soc. Am., Navy League, Ind. Soc. Chgo., Tavern Club (v.p. 1993), Medinah Country Club, Hinsdale Golf Club. Republican. Home and Office: 606 Burr Ridge Clb Burr Ridge IL 60527-5209 Office Phone: 630-990-5356. Personal E-mail: d.bottom@comcast.net.

BOTTOMS, ROBERT GARVIN, academic administrator; b. Birmingham, Ala., June 28, 1944; s. Dalton Garvin and Mary Inez (Cruce) Bottoms; m. Gwendolynn Jean Vickers, June 14, 1968; children: David Timothy, Leslie Clair. BA, Birmingham So. U., 1966; BD, Emory U., 1969; D of Ministry, Vanderbilt U., 1972. Chaplain Birmingham (Ala.) So. Coll., 1973—74, asst. to pres., 1974—75; asst. dean, asst. prof. church and ministry Vanderbilt U., Nashville, 1975—78; v.p. for univ. rels. DePauw U., Greencastle, Ind., 1978—79, exec. v.p. external rels., 1979—83, exec. v.p., 1983—86, acting pres., 1985, pres., 1986—. Cons. Arthur Vining Davis Found., Jacksonville, Fla., 1978—79, Luth. So. Sem., Columbia, SC, 1979—80; cons. theol. edn. The Lilly Endowment, Indpls., 1979—82; cons. Fund for Theol. Edn., N.Y.C., 1981—82; chmn. audit com. Centel Cable TV Co., Oak Brook, Ill., 1987—89; Am. ctr. for internat. leadership organizer Edn. Policy Commn. U.S.-USSR Emerging Leaders Summit, Phila., 1988. Author: Lessons in Financial Development, 1982. Chmn. com. on ch. and coll. Episcopal Diocese Ind., 1979—84; bd. advisors Vanderbilt Div. Sch., 1980—93; bd. trustees Seabury-Western Theol. Sem., 2001—; bd. dirs. Joyce Found., 1994—2002, 2004—, G.M. Constrn. Inc., Indpls., 1998—2001, The Posse Found., 2001—, Women in Govt., Washington, 2001—03, Ctr. Leadership Devel., Indpls., 2003—. Recipient CASE V Chief Exec. Leadership award, 2000. Mem.: NCAA (coun. 1989—95, subcom. eligibility appeals), Ind. Colls. Ind. Found. (bd. dirs. 1987—, nominating com. 1990—97), Great Lakes Colls. Assn. (bd. dirs. 1987—, chair 1994—96), Ind. Colls. of Ind. (bd. dirs. 1987—, exec. com. 1991—), Am. Coun. Edn. (commn. on women in higher edn. 1990—91), Assn. Governing Bds. Univs. and Colls. (coun. pres. 1997—), Nat. Assn. Schs. and Colls. United Meth. Ch. (bd. dirs. 1987—91), Nat. Assn. Ind. Colls. and Univs. (task force increasing participation of minorities in ind. higher edn. 1989—95), Nat. Coun. Chs. (governing bd. 1985—91), Chgo. Club., Cosmos Club (Washington), Univ. Club of N.Y.C., Columbia Club (Indpls.). Avocation: boating. Home: 125 Wood St Greencastle IN 46135 Office: DePauw Univ Office of Pres 313 S Locust St Greencastle IN 46135-0037 Office Phone: 765-658-4800.

BOTTORFF, DENNIS C., banker; b. Clarksville, Ind., Sept. 19, 1944; s. Irvin H. and Lucille H. B.; m. Jean Brewington, Aug. 21, 1964; children: Todd, Chad. BE, Vanderbilt U., 1966; MBA, Northwestern U., Evanston, Ill., 1968. Pres. Commerce Union Bank, Nashville; also exec. v.p. Commerce Union Corp., Nashville; chmn., chief exec. officer Commerce Union Bank and Commerce Union Corp., Nashville, 1984-87; vice chmn., chief oper. officer Sovran Fin. Corp., Norfolk, Va., 1988-89, pres., chief oper. officer, 1989-90, C&S/Sovran Corp., Norfolk, Va., 1990—, C&S/Sovran Corp. (merger Citizens & So. Corp. and Sovran Fin. Corp. 1990), 1990—; chmn., CEO, dir. 1st Am. Corp., Nashville, 1991-99; chmn., dir. AmSouth Bancorp., 1999—. Bd. advisors The Jack C. Massey Grad. Sch. Bus., Belmont, Coll., Nashville; bd. dirs. Ingram Industries, Dollar Gen. Corp. Bd. dirs. Tenn. Tomorrow; v.p., Vanderbilt Bd. of Trustees, Nashville; trustee Leadership Nashville; bd. dirs. Tenn. Performing Arts Ctr., Nashville Sports Coun. Mem. Hundred Club, Belle Meade Country Club. Presbyterian. Home: 1314 Chickering Rd Nashville TN 37215-4522 Office: Am South Bancorporation 1901 6th Ave N Birmingham AL 35288

BOTTS, GREGORY, artist; b. Harrisburg, Pa., 1952; Tchr. various schools; lectr. NY U., NY Studio Sch., Brandeis U. One-man shows include Earl McGrath Gallery, L.A., 1987, Anne Plumb Gallery, NYC, 1989—94, U. Arts Rosenwald-Wolf Gallery, Phila., 1993, Ro Snell Gallery, Santa Barbara, Calif., 1993, Tony Shafrazi Gallery, NYC, 1993, CCS Gallery UCSB, Calif., 1997, others, exhibited in group shows at Robin Lockett Gallery, Chgo., 1986, Mus. Art RISD, Providence, 1988, Richard Green Gallery, L.A., 1990, NY Studio Sch. Art Gallery, NYC, 1991, Cleve. Ctr. Contemporary Art, Ohio, 1994, Deutche Bank Lobby Gallery, NY, 1994, Baruch Coll., 1995, Art Resources Transfer, NYC, 1998, Rotunda Gallery, Bklyn., 1998, others. Recipient award, Am. Acad. Arts and Letters; grantee Adolph and Esther Gottlieb grant. Address: PO Box 164 Abiquiu NM 87510 Office Phone: 505-685-4915. E-mail: botts@cybermesa.com.*

BOTTS, JACK CHESTER, journalist; b. Ludden, ND, Oct. 11, 1924; s. Dwight Chellis and Velcia Myrtle (Swafford) B.; m. Dorris Maxine Everhart, Sept. 10, 1950; children: Jeffrey, Christian, Melanie, Michael. AB, U. Nebr., 1949; MS, Northwestern U., 1950. City desk reporter Lincoln (Nebr.) Jour., 1948-49, city editor, 1951, telegraph editor, 1952-66, editl. writer, 1957-60; asst. prof. journalism U. Nebr., 1966-68, assoc. prof., 1968-73, prof., 1973-90, chmn. dept., 1972-90; manuscript editor, 2002—. Author: The Language of News, 1994, A Pocketful of Plums, 1995, Straight and Level, 1996, Play Action, 2001, Home Place 2002, Whitestone, 2003. Sgt. USAAF, 1943-45, ETO. Named Disting. Journalist of Yr., Kappa Tau Alpha, 1990. Mem. Soc. Profl. Journalists (state pres. 1973), AP Mng. Editors (com. chmn. 1978), Phi Beta Kappa. Avocations: writing novels, building furniture, raising roses. Home: 1240 N 42d St Lincoln NE 68503 Personal E-mail: jacandorbotts@aol.com.

BOTZOW, BILL, artist, state representative; b. N.Y.C., Sept. 29, 1945; m. Ruth Botzow. BA, Princeton U., 1968. Dir. after sch. tutoring program, East Harlem, NY, 1968—70; rep. Vt. State Ho. Reps., 2003—. Chmn. Vt. Arts Coun.; treas. River Network; grant's panelist NEA, Vt. Arts Coun., N.H. Coun. on Arts, Nebr. Arts Coun.; coord. Vt.'s Art in State Bldgs., 1995—2002; bd. dir. Nat. Assembly of State Arts Agys., Gov.'s Inst. of Vt., New Eng. Found. Arts. Democrat. Home: 1225 South Stream Rd Bennington VT 05201

BOU, ENRIC, language educator; b. Barcelona, Mar. 3, 1954; arrived in U.S., 1986; s. Agustt Bou and Maria Maqueda; m. Chiara Bertola; children: Sarah, Victor. Lic., U. Autonoma, Barcelona, 1977, PhD, 1981. Prof. U. Barcelona, 1981—86, Wellesley (Mass.) Coll., 1987—96, Brown U., Providence, 1996—. Author, editor. Office: Brown Univ Box 1961 Providence RI 02912

BOUBEKRI, MOHAMED, architecture educator; Diploma in arch., U. Scis. and Tech. Oran, Algeria, 1983; MArch, U. Colo., Denver, 1985; PhD in Arch., Tex. A&M U., 1990. Lic. arch., Algeria, 1983. Jr. archtl. designer Kalik Arch., Mo., 1980—82, Electronic Transcations Assn. U., 1982—83; asst. prof. Concordia U., Montreal, Canada, 1990—93, U. Ill. Sch. Arch., Champaign-Urbana, 1993—99, assoc. prof., 1999—, chair practice and tech. faculty, 2002—. Mem.: Illuminating Engring. Soc. N.Am. (mem. daylighting com. 1995—). Office: Univ Ill Champaign Sch Arch 318 TH Buell Hall MC 621 611 E Lorado Taft Dr Champaign IL 61820

BOUCHARD, CONSTANCE BRITTAIN, medieval history educator; b. Syracuse, N.Y., May 17, 1948; d. W. Lambert and Harriet Ann (Beckwith) Brittain; m. Robert A. Bouchard, June 14, 1970. AB, Middlebury Coll., 1970; AM, U. Chgo., 1973, PhD, 1976. Lectr. U. Calif.-San Diego Ext., La Jolla, 1979-81, vis. asst. prof. dept. history, 1983, U. Calif., Irvine, 1984; instr. San Diego State U., 1985; vis. asst. prof. Kenyon Coll., Gambier, Ohio, 1987-89, 90; vis. assoc. prof. Oberlin (Ohio) Coll., 1989; asst. prof., disting. prof. medieval history U. Akron, Ohio, 1990—. Author: Spirituality and Administration, 1979, Sword, Miter and Cloister, 1987, Life and Society in the West, 1988, Holy Entrepreneurs, 1991, The Cartulary of Flavigny, 1991, Strong of Body, Brave and Noble, 1998, The Cartulary of St.-Marcel-les-Chalon, 1998, Those of My Blood, 2001, Every Valley Shall Be Exalted, 2003, The Cartulary of Montier-en-Der, 2004. Recipient Berkshire prize, Berkshire Conf., 1982; fellow NEH, 1982, 1993, Am. Philos. Soc., 1988, Guggenheim Meml. Found., 1995, Inst. for Advanced Study, 2002—03. Fellow: Medieval Acad. Am. (councillor 1989—92, Van Courtlandt Elliott prize 1978); mem.: Ohio Acad. History (councillor 1993—96, publ. prize 2002), Soc. French Hist. Studies, Am. Hist. Assn. Home: 2006 Blair Blvd Wooster OH 44691-2234 Office: Dept History U Akron Akron OH 44325-1902

BOUCHARD, GILLES, computer company executive; b. 1961; BS in engring., Ecole Centrale; master's degree, U. Calif., Berkeley. Gen. mgr. Pavilion Home PC Bus, 1998—99; v.p. worldwide ops., personal computing orgn. Hewlett-Packard, 1999—2001, v.p. and gen. mgr. bus. customer ops., 2001—02, sr. v.p. imaging and printing group ops., 2002—03, exec. v.p. and CIO, 2004—. Achievements include led the devel. of the popular Vectra VL family of bus. PCs in Grenoble, France, in the early 1990s. Office: Hewlett Packard Co 3000 Hanver St Palo Alto CA 94304

BOUCHARD, JAMES PAUL, metal products executive, sales executive; b. Kansas City, Kans., May 2, 1961; s. Robert Clayton and Helen (Clancy) B.; m. Carolyn Keegan, July 19, 1986. BBA, Loyola U., Chgo., 1984. Asst. to dist. mgr. Inland Steel Co., Chgo., 1983-85; sales rep. Denver br. Westinghouse Electric, 1985-87, U.S. Steel (divsn. USX Corp.), Milw., 1987-91, Midwest area sr. rep. Oak Brook, Ill., 1987-94, resident mgr., 1994-97, strategic planning and devel. mgr. Pitts., 1997-98, mgr. mktg., 1998, nat. mgr. pipe, tube, and container group, 1999-2000; v.p. comml. U.S. Steel-Kosice, Pitts., 2000—02; COO Mars Industries, Chgo., 2002—03; CEO Esmark, Chgo., 2003—. Bd. dirs. Esmark, Oak Brook, Ill., Electric Coating Tech., East Chicago, Ind., Bouchard Group, LLC, Hinsdale, Ill., Quaker Valley Recreation Assn., Sewickley, Pa., United Steel Group. Co-inventor patented light weight concrete, 1983. Mem. Evans Scholars Found., Strategic Leadership Forum, Pitts. Mem. Loyola U. Alumni Assn., Chgo. Dist. Golf Assn., Edgewood Valley Country Club (bd. dirs.), mem. Art Inst. Chgo., Sewickley Heights Golf Club (Pa.), Edgeworth Club Serwickley (bd. dirs.), Naples Bath and Tennis Club (bd. dirs.), Olde Fla. Golf Club Republican. Roman Catholic. Avocations: golf, basketball, baseball, football. Home: 3 Beaver St Sewickley PA 15143-1217 Office Phone: 708-756-0400. Personal E-mail: jpbouchard@esmark.com.

BOUCHARD, JASON STEVEN, music director; b. Springfield, Mass., Feb. 22, 1975; s. Raymond and Lilian Bouchard; m. Jessica Lynn Belmont, July 10, 1999. BA in Music Edn., Keene State Coll., NH, 1997; MEd, Lesley U., Cambridge, Mass., 2001; postgrad. in ednl. leadership, Ctrl. Conn. State U., New Britain, 2002. Band dir. N. Attleborough Mid. Sch., Mass., 1997—99; dir. instrumental music Enfield HS, Conn., 1999—. Judge chair ea. region CMEA, Conn., 2001—03, orchestra chair ea. region, Conn., 2004—05; band chair NCCC, Conn., 2003—04. Musician S. Hadley Cmty. Band, Mass., 2002—; judge CMEA, 2003—. Recipient Horns for Kids, 2004. Avocations: skiing, camping, music, travel. Home: 28 Middle Rd 3B Enfield CT 06082 Office: Enfield HS 1264 Enfield St Enfield CT 06082 E-mail: jbouc11232@yahoo.com.

BOUCHARD, JEFFREY B., semiconductor company executive; BS in Bus. Adminstn. and Fin., San Jose State U.; MBA, Santa Clara U. Various fin. and acctg. positions several high-tech. cos., 1983—88; various sr. fin. positions Sun Microsystems, 1988—92, worldwide ops. fin. planning and analysis mgr.; sr. fin. mgmt. positions InFocus Sys., 1993—99, dir. fin., 1995—98, dir. investor rels. and treasury, 1998—99; CFO eVineyard, 1999; v.p. fin., CFO Pixelworks, Inc., Tualatin, Oreg., 1999—. Office: Pixelworks Inc Ste 300 8100 SW Nyberg Rd Tualatin OR 97062

BOUCHARD, LESTER J., recreational therapist, consultant; s. Carol Ann Fiore and Lester Joseph Bouchard. AA in Liberal Arts, AS in Bus. Mgmt. & Adminstrn., Daytona Beach C.C., 1993; BS in Psychology, Fla. State U., 1995; MS in Exercise & Sport Sci., U. Fla., 1997, PhD in Health & Human Performance, 2000. Asst. coach men's golf U. Fla., Gainesville, 1998—99; dir. sport psychology and guidance Saddlebrook Internat. Tennis, Wesley Chapel, Fla., 2000—04; pres. Achievement Solutions, Clearwater, Fla., 2004—. Grad. tchg. asst. U. of Fla., Gainesville, Fla., 1996—2000. Author: (novels) Golf Solutions: A Step-By-Step Manual for Assessing Every Aspect of Your Game, Llowering Your Scores and Beating Your Friends; contbr. articles to profl. jours. and mags., chapters to books. Mem.: Am. Cons. League (cert. profl. cons.), U.S. Golf Assn., Assn. Advancement of Applied Sport Psychology, APA. Office: Achievement Solutions 1363 Woodcrest Ave Clearwater FL 33756 Office Phone: 727-447-9149. E-mail: dr.b@bettergolfsolutions.com.

BOUCHARD, LYNNE KATHERINE, music educator; b. L.A., June 24, 1955; d. Thomas Joseph and Anne Katherine (Gurmatakis) Bouchard; m. Daniel Ernest Winans, Apr. 6, 1985 (div.); children: Collette Jeanine Winans Engle, Ashley Anne Winans; m. Timothy Ervin Junette, May 2, 1997 (div.). Lic. practical nurse, Ariz. We. Coll., 1981. LPN; lic. instr. Kindermusik Internat. LPN Dr. David Buster, Yuma, Ariz., Dr. Abraham Injean, Yuma, Yuma County Health Dept.; pvt. piano instr. Yuma, 1987—99; tchr. music Grace Brethren Christian Sch., Waldorf, Md., 1999—2001, tchr. drama, 2000—03. Pvt. piano instr. Ivory Moon Piano Studio LLC, Waldorf, 1999—. Mem.: Md. State Music Tchrs. Assn., Port Tobacco Players, Nat. Guild Piano Tchrs. Avocations: acting, interior decorating, gardening, antiques. Home: 4575 Grouse Pl Waldorf MD 20603

BOUCHARD, THOMAS JOSEPH, JR., psychology educator, researcher; b. Manchester, N.H., Oct. 3, 1937; s. Thomas and Florence (Charest) B.; m. Pauline Marina Proulx, Aug. 13, 1960; children: Elizabeth, Mark. BA, U. Calif., Berkeley, 1963, PhD, 1966. Asst. prof. U. Calif., Santa Barbara, 1966-69, U. Minn., Mpls., 1969-70, assoc. prof., 1970-73, prof., 1973—, chmn. dept. psychology, 1985-91. Dir. Minn. Ctr. Twin and Adoption Rsch., U. Minn., 1980—. Editor (assoc.): (jour.) Jour. Applied Psychology, 1977—80, Behavior Genetics, 1982—86; contbr. articles jours. over 150 articles to profl. jours. With USAF, 1955-58. Fellow AAAS, APA, Am. Psychol. Soc.; mem. Phi Beta Kappa, Sigma Xi. Home: 1860 Shoreline Dr Wayzata MN 55391-9771 Office: Univ of Minn Dept Psychology 75 E River Rd Minneapolis MN 55455-0280 E-mail: bouch001@tc.umn.edu.

BOUCHARD, WENDY ANN BORSTEL, language educator; m. Douglas K. Bouchard, Aug. 6, 1983. BA, SUNY, Geneseo, 1978; MA, Hofstra U., 1982. Cert. secondary English tchr. N.Y. English tchr. Oneida (N.Y.) Sr. H.S., 1978—80, Mineola Jr. H.S., 1980—81, Thompson Jr. H.S., Syosset, NY, 1981—83, Roslyn (N.Y.) Jr. H.S., 1983—84, Garden City (N.Y.) Mid. Sch., 1984—2000, Garden City (N.Y.) Sr. H.S., 2000—. Mem. English program com. Mid. States Accreditation. Life mem. Girls Scouts Am. Mem.: N.Y. State English Coun., L.I. Lang. Arts Coun., N.Y. State United Tchrs., Nat. Coun. Tchrs. English. Avocations: travel, reading, swimming. Office: Garden City Sr High Sch 170 Rockaway Ave Garden City NY 11530

BOUCHER, BRADLEY ALBERT, pharmacist, educator; b. Mpls., Dec. 21, 1955; s. Dwaine Edmund and Betty Jean Boucher; m. Barbara Sue Opitz, Oct. 27, 1979; children: Alexander Albert, Andrew Bradley, Adam Nicholas. BS in Pharmacy, U. of Minn., 1979, PharmD, 1983. Registered pharmacotherapy specialist Bd. of Pharm. Specialties, 1992. Fellow U. Ky., Lexington, 1983—84; prof. of pharmacy U. Tenn., Memphis, 1996—, assoc. prof. neurosurgery, 1997—. Mem. editl. bd.: Critical Care Medicine, 2000—; contbr. articles to profl. jours., chapters to books. Treas. Houston HS Football Booster Club, Germantown, Tenn., 1999—2005. Recipient Merck award, U. of Minn. Coll. of Pharmacy, 1979, Svc. award, Am. Coll. Clin. Pharmacy, 2004. Fellow: Am. Coll. Clin. Pharmacy (hon.; treas. 1992—97, pres. 2001—02), Am. Coll. Critical Care Medicine (hon.); mem.: Am. Soc. Health-Systems Pharmacists (fellow 1983—84), Soc. Critical Care Medicine, Am. Assn. Colls. of Pharmacy, Soc. Infectious Diseases Pharmacists, Nat. Acad. Practitioners (hon.), The Rho Chi Soc. (hon.), Phi Lambda Sigma Leadership Soc. (hon.). Episc. Avocations: coaching, golf. Office: Univ Tenn 26 South Dunlap Rm 210 Memphis TN 38163 Office Phone: 901-448-4924. E-mail: bboucher@utmem.edu.

BOUCHER, BRAIN, professional hockey player; b. Woonsocket, R.I., Jan. 2, 1977; m. Melissa Boucher; 1 child, Tyler. Profl. hockey player, goaltender Phila. Flyers, 1999—2002, Phoenix Coyotes, 2002—. Goaltender Team U.S.A. World Jr. Championships, 1997, 98. Charity work Children's Miracle Network. Named to, NHL All-Rookie Team, 2000. Achievements include set NLH record for most consecutive regular season shutouts (5 games). Avocation: golf. Office: c/o Phoenix Coyotes Hockey Club Alltel Ice Dean 9375 E Bell Rd Scottsdale AZ 85260

BOUCHER, FREDERICK C., congressman, lawyer; b. Abingdon, Va., Aug. 1, 1946; s. Ralph E. and Dorothy (Buck) B. BA, Roanoke Coll., 1968; JD, U. Va., 1971. Bar: Va. 1971, N.Y. 1972. Assoc. Milbank, Tweed, Hadley, McCloy, N.Y.C., 1971-73; ptnr. Boucher & Boucher, Abingdon, Va.; state senator Va. Gen. Assembly, Richmond, 1975-79, 79-82; mem. U.S. Congress from 9th Va. dist., Washington, 1983—; mem. energy and commerce com., judiciary com.; assist. whip H. of Reps., 1985—; founder, co-chmn. house internet caucus, 1996—. Recipient Disting. Service award Va. Highlands Community Coll., Abingdon, 1984, Beamer award for Contributions to Vocational Edn., 1986, Legislator of Yr. award Vietnam Vets. Am., 1993. Mem. ABA, Assn. Bar of N.Y.C., Va. Bar Assn. Democrat. Methodist. Office: US Ho of Reps 2187 Rayburn Ho Office Bldg Washington DC 20515-4609*

BOUCHER, RICHARD A., former federal agency administrator; b. Bethesda, Md., Dec. 13, 1951; s. Melville J. and Ellen (Kaufmann) B.; m. Carolyn L. Brehm, June 19, 1982; children: Madeleine Brehm, Peter Brehm. BA cum laude, Tufts U., 1973; postgrad., George Washington U., 1976-77. Vol. Peace Corps, Senegal, 1973-75; with Agy. Internat. Devel., Guinea, 1975-76; various positions Fgn. Svc., 1977-84; econ. officer U.S. Consulate Gen., Shanghai, 1984-86; sr. watch officer US Dept. State, 1986-87, dep. dir. polit. affairs office European security and polit. affairs, 1987-89, dep. spokesman, 1989—93, acting spokesman, 1992-93, U.S. amb. to Cyprus, 1993-96; U.S. sr. ofcl. Asia Pacific Econ. Cooperation Forum, 1999—2000; asst. sec. for pub. affairs US Dept. State, Washington, 2000—05.

BOUCHER, WAYNE IRVING, management consultant; b. Bay City, Mich., Dec. 12, 1934; s. Harold Oscar and Mildred Christine (Born) B.; m. Donna Lou Collins, June 12, 1961 (div. 1973); children: Michèle Annette, Robert Alain. BA in English Lang. and Lit., U. Mich., 1956, MA in English Lang. and Lit., 1960; postgrad. in philosophy, U. Mo., 1959-61. Instr. English U. Mo., Columbia, 1958-63; asst. to pres. Rand Corp., Santa Monica, Calif., 1963-69; rsch. assoc. Inst. for the Future, Middletown, Conn., 1969-71; co-founder, v.p. The Futures Group, Glastonbury, Conn., 1971-76; dept. dir., dir. rsch. Nat. Commn. on Electronic Fund Transfers, Washington, 1976-78; sr. rsch. assoc. Ctr. for Futures Rsch., U. So. Calif., Los Angeles, 1978-84; exec. v.p. Benton Internat., Torrance, Calif., 1984-93; pres. The Ark. Inst., Little Rock, 1993-94; pres., chief ops. officer Electronic Funds Transfer Assn., Herndon, Va., 1994-95; co-founder, mng. dir. Strategic Futures Internat., Harpers Ferry, W.Va., 1995—. Author: (with J.L. Morrison and W.L. Renfro) Futures Research and Strategic Planning, 1984; Spinoza in English, 1991, 2d edit., 1999, Spinoza: 18th and 19th Century Discussions, 6 vols., 1999; editor: (with J.L. Morrison and W.L. Renfro) Applying Methods and Techniques of Futures Research, 1983; author, editor: The Study of the Future, 1977; editor (with E.S. Quade) Systems Analysis and Policy Planning, 1968; mem. editorial bd. Technol. Forecasting and Social Change, 1978-82, Futures Rsch. Quar., 1984—; contbr. articles to profl. jours. Home: 87 Lakeside Dr Harpers Ferry WV 25425-4731 Office Phone: 304-728-8280. Personal E-mail: wboucher@earthlink.net.

BOUCKAERT, CARL M., manufacturing executive; Founder, CEO Beaulieu of Am. Group, 1978—. Republican. Avocation: horseback riding. Office: Beaulieu of Am LLC 1502 Coronet Dr Dalton GA 30720

BOUDART, MICHEL, chemical engineer, consultant, chemist, educator; b. Belgium, June 18, 1924; came to U.S., 1947, naturalized, 1957; s. Francois and Marguerite (Swolfs) B.; m. Marina D'Haese, Dec. 27, 1948; children: Mark, Baudouin, Iris, Philip. BS, U. Louvain, Belgium, 1944, MS, 1947; PhD, Princeton U., 1950; D honoris causa, U. Liège, U. Notre Dame, U. Nancy, U. Ghent. Research asso. James Forrestal Research Ctr., Princeton, 1950-54; mem. faculty Princeton U., 1954-61; prof. chem. engring. U. Calif., Berkeley, 1961-64, adj. prof. chem. engring., 1994—; prof. chem. engring. and chemistry Stanford U., 1964-80, Keck prof. engring., 1980-94, Keck prof. engring. emeritus, 1994—. Co-founder Catalytica, Inc.; Humble Oil Co. lectr., 1958; AIChE lectr., 1961; Sigma Xi nat. lectr., 1965; chmn. Gordon Rsch. Conf. Catalysis, 1962. Author: Kinetics of Chemical Processes, 1968, (with G. Djéga-Mariadassou) Kinetics of Heterogeneous Catalytic Reactions, 1983; editor: (with J.R. Anderson) Catalysis: Science and Technology, 11 vols., 1981-96, (with Marina Boudart and René Bryssinck) Modern Belgium, 1990; mem. adv. editl. bd. Catal. Letters, 1989—, Catalysis Rev., 1968—, Jour. Molecular Catalysis, 1995—, Cattech, 1996—. Recipient Curtis-McGraw rsch. award Am. Soc. Engring. Edn., 1962, R.H. Wilhelm award in chem. reaction engring., 1974, Chem. Pioneer award Am. Inst. Chemists, 1991; Belgium-Am. Ednl. Found. fellow, 1948, Procter fellow, 1949; Fairchild disting. scholar Calif. Tech. Inst., 1995. Fellow AAAS, Am. Acad. Arts. and Scis., Calif. Acad. Scis.; mem. NAS, NAE, Am. Chem. Soc. (Kendall award 1977, E.V. Murphee award in indsl. and engring. chemistry 1985), Catalysis Soc., Am. Inst. Chem. Engrs., Chem. Soc., Académie Royale de Belgique (fgn. assoc.), French Nat. Acad. Pharmacy (fgn.). Home: 228 Oak Grove Ave Atherton CA 94027-2218 Office: Stanford U Dept Chem Engring Stanford CA 94305 Office Fax: 650-723-9780. Business E-Mail: mboudart@stanford.edu.

BOUDIN, MICHAEL, federal judge; b. NYC, Nov. 29, 1939; s. Leonard and Jean Boudin; m. Martha Field, Sept. 18, 1984. BA, Harvard Coll., 1961, LLB, 1964. Bar: N.Y. 1964, D.C. 1967. Law clk. to Hon. Henry J. Friendly U.S. Ct. Appeals (2d cir.), 1964—65; law clk. to Justice John Harlan U.S. Supreme Ct., Washington, 1965—66; assoc. firm Covington & Burling, Washington, 1966—72, ptnr., 1972—87; dep. asst. atty. gen. anti-trust divsn. US Dept. Justice, Washington, 1987—90; judge U.S. Dist. Ct. (D.C. dist.), Washington, 1990—92, U.S. Ct. Appeals (1st cir.), Boston, 1992—, chief judge, 2001—. Vis. prof. Harvard Law Sch., 1982—83, lectr., 1983—98, U. Pa. Law Sch., 1984—85. Contbr. articles to profl. jours. Mem.: ABA, Am. Law Inst. Office: US Ct Appeals 1st Cir 1 Courthouse Way Ste 7710 Boston MA 02210-3009 Office Phone: 617-748-4431.

BOUDOULAS, HARISIOS, cardiologist, researcher, medical educator; b. Velvendo-Kozani, Greece, Nov. 3, 1935; married; 2 children. MD, U. Salonica, Greece, 1959. Resident in internal medicine Red Cross Hosp., Athens, Greece, 1960-61, U. Salonica First Med. Clinic, 1962-66, resident in internal medicine and cardiology, 1962-66, lectr., 1969-70; postgrad. fellow, instr. div. cardiology Ohio State U. Coll. Medicine, Columbus, 1970-73, asst. prof. medicine, 1975-78, assoc. prof., 1978-80, dir. cardiac non-invasive lab., 1978-80, prof. medicine div. cardiology, 1980—, prof. pharmacy, 1984—, dir. cardiovascular rsch. div., 1983-86, dir. cardiovascular teaching and rsch. lab., 1992—; prof. medicine div. cardiology Wayne State U., Detroit, 1980-82, chief clin. cardiovascular rsch., 1980-82, acting dir. div. cardiology, 1982; chief cardiovascular diagnostic and tng. center VA Med. Ctr., Allen Park, Mich., 1980-82; chief sect. cardiology Harper-Grace Hosps., Detroit, 1982. Mem. antepistelon Athens Acad., 1998—; dir. Ctr. for Clin. Rsch., pres. sci. coun. Inst. Biomed. Rsch., Acad. of Athens. Editor in chief Hellenic Jour. Cardiology; mem. editl. rev. bd. jours. cardiology; contbr. numerous articles to med. jours. Named Disting. Research Investigator, Cen. Ohio chpt. Am. Heart Assn., Columbus, 1983. Fellow ACP, Am. Coll. Angiology, Am. Coll. Clin. Pharmacology, Am. Coll. Cardiology (trustee Ohio chpt. 1993-97), Am. Heart Assn. (coun. clin. cardiology 1989-93, coun. exec. com. 1991-93, sci. com. 1991-93), European Soc. Cardiology (sci. com. 1991-93, valvular heart disease working group 1993—), Greek Heart Assn., Am. Fedn. Clin. Rsch., Laeneck Soc. (chmn. 1991-93), Hellenic Cardiol. Soc. (pres. 2002). Office: Ohio State U Div Cardiology 1655 Upham Dr Columbus OH 43210-1251

BOUDREAU, DANIEL J., law educator, retired state supreme court justice; b. Natick, Mass., 1947; m. Faith Boudreau, 1972. BA, Boston Coll., 1969; MA, Rutgers U., 1972; JD, U. Tulsa, 1976. Pvt. practice, Broken Arrow, Okla., 1976—80; trial judge Tulsa County, Okla., 1980—92; judge, then vice-chief judge Okla. Ct. Civil Appeals, 1992-99; justice Okla. Supreme Ct., Oklahoma City, 1999—, Appellate Ct. on the Judiciary, 2001—04; prof. U. Tulsa Coll. of Law, 2004—. Office: U Tulsa Coll Law 3120 E 4th Place Tulsa OK 74104 E-mail: daniel.boudreau@oscn.net.

BOUDREAU, LYNDA L., state agency administrator; m. Jim Boudreau. Rep. Minn. Ho. of Reps., 1994—2004, speaker pro tempore. Chair, health and human svc. policy com. Office: 559 State Office Bldg 100 Rev Martin Luther Ling Jr Blvd Saint Paul MN 55155 Office Phone: 651-282-2000. E-mail: lynda.boudreau@state.mn.us.

BOUDREAU, ROBERT JAMES, nuclear medicine physician, researcher; b. Lethbridge, Alta., Can., Dec. 27, 1950; came to U.S., 1983; s. George Joseph Boudreau and Eleanor Joyce (Dalzell) Hamilton; m. Francine Suzanne Archambault, Jan. 16, 1982. BSc with highest honors, U. Sask., Saskatoon, Can., 1972; PhD, U. B.C., Vancouver, Can., 1975; MD, U. Calgary (Alta.), 1978. Diplomate Am. Bd. Nuclear Medicine. Resident in diagnostic radiology and nuclear medicine McGill U., Montreal, Que., Can., 1978-82; asst. prof. U. Minn., Mpls., 1983-87, assoc. prof., 1987-93, prof., 1993-99, prof. emeritus, 2000—, dir. grad. studies dept. radiology, 1987-91, dir. nuclear medicine divsn., 1987-2000. Author book chpts.; contbr. articles to profl. jours. Recipient Gold Key award Soc. Chem. Industry, 1972, Soc. Clin. Investigation Young Investigator award, 1978; Can. Heart Found. Med. Scientist fellow, 1976-78. Fellow Royal Coll. Physicians; mem. Soc. Chiefs of Acad. Nuclear Medicine Sects. (treas. 1989-93), Soc. Nuclear Medicine (edn. and tng. com. 1983-91, trustee 1994-95, bd. govs. ctrl. chpt. 1989—, treas. 1992-94, pres. 1994-95), Radiol. Soc. N.Am. Avocations: skiing, boating, travel, computers. Office: U Minn FUMC 500 Harvard St SE Minneapolis MN 55455-0363 E-mail: robjb@highstream.net.

BOUDREAU, THOMAS M., lawyer; b. St. Louis, 1951; BA cum laude, Maryville Coll., 1973; JD magna cum laude, St. Louis U., 1979. Bar: Mo. 1979, US Dist. Ct. Ea. Dist. Mo. 1979, US Tax Ct. 1980. Ptnr. Husch & Eppenberger, St. Louis, 1986—94; v.p., gen. counsel Express Scripts Inc., Md. Heights, Mo., 1994, sr. v.p., gen. counsel, sec., 1994—. Co-author: The Law of Lender Liability, 1990; asst. editor St. Louis U. Law Jour., 1978-79. Fellow: Am. Coll. Comml. Fin. Lawyers; mem.: ABA. Office: Express Scripts Inc 13900 Riverport Dr Maryland Heights MO 63043

BOUDREAUX, JOHN, public relations executive; b. Franklin, La., July 28, 1946; s. Abel John and Dorothy (Bourgeois) B. BA, La. State U., 1969. Reporter, copy editor Morning Advocate, Baton Rouge, 1969-71; successively reporter, copy editor, asst. city editor Houston Post, 1971-76, city editor, 1976-84; pub. rels. cons., 1984-85; sr. communications specialist IBM, Dallas, 1985-87, comm. mgr. San Francisco, 1987-88, program mgr. Westchester County, N.Y., 1988-2000; mng. editor IBM.com, 2000—03; pres. EJB Comms., 2003—. Named Outstanding Journalism Grad., La. State U., 1969. Mem. Soc. Profl. Journalists, Sigma Delta Chi (bd. dirs. Houston chpt. 1975, 83).

BOUDREAUX, KENNETH JUSTIN, economist, educator; b. New Orleans, Dec. 22, 1943; s. Aldwin John and Beverly Estelle (Swanton) B.; m. Carole Jean Barnette, May 28, 1966; 1 child, Beau Justin AB, Princeton U., 1965; MBA, Tulane U., 1967; PhD, U. Wash., 1970. Asst. prof. Sch. Bus., Tulane U., New Orleans, 1970-73, assoc. prof., 1973-78, prof., 1978—, assoc. dean faculty, 1981-83. Cons. City of New Orleans Author: Basic Theory of Corporate Finance, 1977, Finance, 1990; editorial bd. Jour. Econs. and Bus., Jour. Fin. Rsch.; contbr. articles to scholarly jours. AACSB fellow, 1969-70; recipient Wissner award Tulane U., 1972, 75, Outstanding Prof., 1972, 75, Disting. Prof., 1973 Fellow Fin. Analysts Fedn.; mem. Am. Econ. Assn., Am. Fin. Assn., Western Fin. Assn., Western Econ. Assn. Clubs: Cannon (Princeton U.), Pickwick, So. Yacht Club. Office: Tulane U Sch Bus New Orleans LA 70118 Office Phone: 504-895-8741.

BOUDREAUX, PAUL, JR., lawyer; b. Lafayette, La., Apr. 18, 1953; s. Paul and Myrna (Best) B.; m. Patricia A. Aguillard, Dec. 16, 1978 (div. 1984); 1 child, Katharina Leigh; m. Kathryn Lea Robertson, May 19, 1990. BA, Nicholls State U., 1975; JD, La. State U., 1978. Bar: La. 1978, U.S. Dist. Ct. (mid. and we. dists.) La. 1978, U.S. Ct. Appeals (5th cir.) 1981, U.S. Claims Ct. 1992. Assoc. Gaharan and Wilson, Jena, La., 1978-80, ptnr., 1980-83; assoc. Stafford, Stewart & Potter, Alexandria, La., 1983-85, ptnr., 1985—. Interviewer LaSalle Indigent Defender, Jena, 1980-81. Mem. La. Bar Assn., Rapides Bar Assn., LaSalle Bar Assn. (v.p. 1981-82, pres. 1982-83), La. Assn. Def. Counsel, La. Trial Lawyers Assn., Alexandria Exch. Club. Democrat. Avocations: hunting, fishing, ATV riding, camping, water sports. Office: 3112 Jackson St Alexandria LA 71301-4746

BOUDRIA, DON, Canadian government official; b. Hull, Quebec, Can., Aug. 30, 1949; s. Roy and Jacqueline (Lavergne) B.; m. MaryAnn Morris, Aug. 28, 1971; children: Daniel, Julie. BA in History, U. Waterloo, 1999. With Fed. Govt., 1966, chief purchasing agent; mem. Legis. Assembly, Ont., 1981; M.P.P., 1981; opposition critic of govt. svcs., 1982—83; opposition critic of cmty. and social svcs., 1981-83; opposition critic of consumer and comml. rels., 1983-84; M.P. Ho. of Commons, 1984—. Critic Fed. supply and svcs.; official opposition, mem. standing com. on Agriculture, 1984; dep. chmn. Ont. Liberal Caucus, 1984; Public Works critic, 1985; critic Can. Post. and Govt. Ops., 1988; dep. oppositon whip, 1989, asst. House leader for the Official Opposition; Sworn to the Privy Coun., 1996; Min. Internat. Cooperation, Min. Responsible La Francophonie, 1996-97; dep. govt. whip, 1993-94, chief govt. whip, 1994-96; min. of state, leader govt., House of Commons, 1997—. Mem. L'Assn. Internat. des Parlementaires de Langue Française (founding pres. Ont. sect.), Cumberland Twp. Housing Corp. (founding pres.), Sarsfield Optimist Club (founding pres.). Achievements include languages spoken and written; French, English. Avocations: history, music, skiing. Office: House of Commons 215-S Ctr Block Ottawa ON Canada K1A 0A6

BOUÉ, DANIEL ROBERT, pediatric pathologist, neuropathologist, educator; b. N.Y.C., June 22, 1958; s. Robert Charles and Dorothea Anna B.; m. Julie Marie Borgerding; children: Rachel Hope, Jenna Elizabeth, AnnaMarie Monique, Sarah Jane. BA cum laude, Carleton Coll., 1980; PhD, U. Minn., 1988, MD, 1991. Diplomate in anat. and clin. pathology and pediatric pathology Am. Bd. Pathology. Intern U. Calif., San Diego, 1991—92, resident in pathology, 1992—94, chief resident-elect, 1994—95; attending physician U. Calif./San Diego Med. Ctr., 1994—95; clin. instr. U. Calif., San Diego, 1994—95; fellow pediat. pathology Columbus Childrens Hosp., 1995—96; clin. instr. Ohio State U., Columbus, 1995—97, clin. asst. prof. pathology, 1998—2003, clin. assoc. prof. pathology, 2004—; fellow pediat. neuropathology Columbus Childrens Hosp., 1996; staff pathologist, dir. Neuropathology program Childrens Hosp., Columbus, 1997—; dir. surg. and autopsy neuropathology, muscle and nerve biopsy svcs. Interim dir. perinatal pathology and autopsy svc. U. Calif., San Diego, 1994—95; rev. pathologist/investigator Biopathology Ctr., Children's Hosp. Rsch. Found.; prin. investigator multiple grants; presenter in field. Contbr. articles to profl. jours.; referee med. jour. publs. Med. Scientist scholar U. Minn., 1982-91, G.T. Evan scholar Dept. Lab. Medicine and Pathology, 1982-85, Life & Health Ins. Med. Rsch. Fund, scholar, 1985-90; recipient J.T. Livermore Hematology award Minn. Med. Found., 1988, undergrad. med. student rsch. award 1991, Dr. Vernon D.E. Smith award, 1990. Fellow Am. Coll. Pathology, Am. Soc. Clin. Pathologists (Sheard-Sanford award 1988), Coll. Am. Pathologists; mem. Soc. Pediat. Pathology, Alpha Omega Alpha. Office: Columbus Childrens Hosp Dept Lab Med 700 Childrens Dr Columbus OH 43205-2664

BOUFFORD, JO IVEY, health science association administrator; b. Durham, N.C., July 2, 1945; BA in Psychology magna cum laude, Wellesley Coll., 1965; MD with distinction, U. Mich., 1971; DSc(hon.), SUNY, Bklyn., 1992. Diplomate Nat. Bd. Med. Examiners, Am. Bd. Pediats. Resident in social pediats. medicine Montefiore Hosp. and Med. Ctr., Bronx, N.Y., 1971-74, asst. attending physician, 1975-97, co-dir. Inst. for Health Team Devel., 1975-82, dir. residency program in social medicine, 1975-82; adminstrv. dir. Valentine Lane Family Practice, Yonkers, N.Y., 1975-82; v.p. med. ops. N.Y.C. Health and Hosps. Corp., 1982-83, v.p. med. and profl. affairs, 1983-85, exec. v.p., 1985, acting pres., 1985, pres., 1985-89; internat. fellow in comparative health sys. mgmt. King's Fund Coll., London, 1989-91, dir., 1991-93; prin. dep. asst. sec. for health Dept. Health and Human Svcs., Washington, 1993-97; dean Robert F. Wagner Grad. Sch. of Pub. Svc., New York Univ., 1997—; clin. prof. peds. NYU, 1997—, prof. pub. svc. health policy and mgmt., 2003—. Acting Asst. Sec. Health, Jan.-June 1997; adj. prof. Lehman Coll. Nursing, Bronx, 1974-80; mem. Nat. Adv. Coun. for Health Professions Edn. US-DHHS, 1976-80; mem. tech. panel on the ednl. environ. Grad. Med. Edn. Nat. Adv. Coun., 1979-80; cons. on manpower programs divsn. medicine bur. Health Professions Edn. HRSA-DHHS, 1980-88; mem. N.Y. State Coun. on Grad. med. Edn., 1987-89, N.Y. State Commn. on Grad. Med. Edn., 1985-86; mem. adv. bd. residency program in gen. preventive medicine and occupl. health Mt. Sinai coll. Medicine, 1986-89; mem. Nat. Vis. Coun. for the Health Scis. Faculty Columbia U., N.Y.C., 1988-90; mem. vis. faculty The New Sch. for Social Rsch., 1989; rep. of U.S. on exec. bd. WHO, 1994-97; mem. joint coordinating com. for Radiation Health Effects Rsch., 1994-97; U.S. staff dir. Gore-Chernomyrdin Commn. Health Com., 1994-97; various consulting positions. Mem. editl. bd. Jour. Med. Edn., 1980-86; mem. editl. adv. bd. The New Physician, 1979-89; contbr. articles to profl. jours.; presenter in field. Mem. Nat. Adv. Coun. of Agy. for Healthcare Quality and Rsch., 2000—04; bd. dirs. United Hosp. Fund, 1999—; chair sub-bd. on pub. health, Open Soc. Inst., 1998—; mem. N.Y. State Coun. on Grad. Med. Edn., 1987-89. Fellow Am. Acad. Pediats.;

mem. APHA, NAS Inst. Medicine Coun. (Robert Wood Johnson health policy fellow 1979-80), Am. Med. Women's Assn., Ambulatory Pediats. Assn., Soc. for Health and Human Values, Soc. Med. Adminstrs., Med. Adminstrs. Conf. Office: NYU Robert F Wagner Grad Sch Pub Svc 295 Lafayette St 3rd Fl New York NY 10012 Office Phone: 212-998-7410. E-mail: jo.boufford@nyu.edu.

BOUGAS, JAMES ANDREW, physician, educator, surgeon; b. Bismarck, N.D., Jan. 25, 1924; s. Andrew James and Mary (Psaltiras) B.; m. Tiina Parlin, June 27, 1953; children: Karen Louise, Tiina Maria. MD, Harvard U., 1948. Diplomate Am. Bd. Surgery, Am. Bd. Thoracic Surgery. Intern Columbia U. Svc., Bellevue Hosp., N.Y.C., 1948-50, chief resident in surgery, 1952-53; resident Presbyn. Hosp., N.Y.C., 1950-52, chief resident surgery, 1953; fellow Overholt Clinic, Boston, 1953-55, assoc., 1955-65; chief thoracic surgery U. Hosp., Boston, 1965-70; assoc. prof. surgery Boston U. Sch. Medicine, 1965—. Lectr. Tufts U. Sch. Medicine, Boston, 1965-70; chmn. Gordon Rsch. Confs., 1967-68. Contbr. articles to profl. jours. Pres. Heart Assn., Boston, 1967-69; chmn. Mass. Rehab. Commn. Adv. Com.; trustee Boston Tb Assn. With U.S. Army, 1942-44. Fellow AAAS; mem. ACS, Am. Coll. Cardiology, Am. Assn. Thoracic Surgeons, Soc. Thoracic Surgeons, Am. Coll. Cardiology, Mass. Med. Soc. (legis. com., coun.), Norfolk Dist. Med. Soc. (pres. 1989-90, Tri-State regional planning com.). Achievements include development of combined cardiac catheterization; porous metal prostheses fabrication and cardio-pulmonary physiology. E-mail: jbougas@caregroup.harvard.edu.

BOUGHAN, ZANETTA LOUISE, music educator; b. Grantham, Eng., Mar. 22, 1959; arrived in U.S., 1964; d. Peter Leonard and Alyda Venita Maria (Bellord) Snowden; m. Robert William Boughan, Nov. 3, 1995. AAS, Cochise Coll., 2003—. Pvt. piano and violin instr., Sierra Vista, Ariz., 1988—. Concertmaster Cochise Coll. Orch., Sierra Vista, 1999—2001, Pima Coll. Orch., Tucson, 2001—02; first violinist Sierra Vista Sym. Orch., 2001—02. Vol. Sierra Vista Police Dept., 2002—; ct.-apptd. spl. adv. vol. State Ariz., 2002—; vol. in Police Svc., 2002—; mem. Citizens Police Acad. Assocs., 2003—; vol. Cochise County Juvenile Ct., 2003—. With USN, 1979—84. Mem.: Ariz. Music Tchrs. Assn., Nat. Music Tchrs. Assn., Cochise Music Tchrs. Assn. (chmn. fundraising com. 1997—, sec. 1998—2000, treas. 2001—03, pres. 2003—, Profl. Develop. grant 2001), Phi Theta Kappa. Home: 4924 Marconi Dr Sierra Vista AZ 85635 Personal E-mail: zboughan@earthlink.net.

BOUGHTON, JAMES MURRAY, economist; b. Chgo., Apr. 8, 1944; s. Stanley R. and Erminie (Bloyd) B.; m. Lesley Anne Simmons. BA, Duke U., 1966; MA, U. Mich., 1967; PhD, Duke U., 1969. Asst. prof. Ind. U., Bloomington, 1970-73, assoc.prof., 1973-81, prof., 1981-83; economist Orgn. Econ. Coop. and Devel., Paris, 1973-75, cons., 1976-79; economist IMF, Washington, 1981-86, advisor, 1986-92, historian, 1992-2001, 2004—; sr. assoc. mem. St. Anthony's Coll., U. Oxford, 2000-01; asst. dir. PDR, 2001—04. Author: Monetary Policy and Federal Funds Market, 1971, Silent Revolution, 2001; co-author: Principles of Monetary Economics, 1975; co-editor: Fifty Years After Bretton Woods, Future of SDR; contbr. articles to profl. jours. V.p. Ind. Civil Liberties Union, Indpls., 1978-79; chmn. bd. dirs. Bretton Woods, Germantown, Md., 1990-93. Mem.: Am. Econ. Assn., Cosmos Club. Office: Internat Monetary Fund 700 19th St NW Washington DC 20431-0001 E-mail: jboughton@imf.org.

BOUGIE, PETER JOHN, artist, educator; b. Manitowoc, Wis., Aug. 25, 1956; s. Jerome William and Joan (Carew) Bougie. Apprentice, Atelier Lack, 1987. Dir. Bougie Studio, Mpls., 1988—; editor Classical Realism Jour., Mpls., 1996—. Exhibited in shows at Vern Carver/Beard Gallery, Mpls., Leverhouse, N.Y.C., 1996, Am. Soc. Classical Realism Guild of Artists, Newington-Cropsey Found., Hastings-on-Hudson, N.Y., 2001. Grantee R.H. Ives Grammell Studio Trust, 1994—. Mem. Am. Soc. Classical Realism Artists Guild. Roman Catholic. Avocations: bicycling, running. Office: Bougie Studio 2524 Nicollet Ave Ste 201 Minneapolis MN 55404-4248 E-mail: pbougie@pressenter.com.

BOUILLIANT-LINET, FRANCIS JACQUES, global management consultant; b. Garches, France, Aug. 20, 1932; came to U.S., 1977; s. Jacques Achille and Virginia Sutton (McKee) B.-L.; m. Carolyn Jeanine Taylor, Nov. 17, 1978. Diploma in sci., Admiral Farragut Acad., 1948; postgrad., Duke U., 1949-50. Mgmt. trainee Harry Ferguson Cos., Europe, 1951-53; sales promotion mgr. Massey-Harris-Ferguson, Paris, 1957-59; gen. programs mgr. Massey Ferguson Ltd., Coventry, Eng., 1959-63, coord. office of pres. Toronto, Ont., Can., 1963-65, group product mgr., 1966-68; dir. internat. logistics Allis Chalmers Corp., Milw., 1968-71; joint mng. dir. LePiol, s.a.r.l., Cannes, France, 1971-77; chmn. bd., chief exec. officer FBL, Inc., Hurtsboro, Ala., 1977—. also bd. dirs. Exec. dir. H.J. Crawley, Ltd., Leamington, Eng., 1961-66; bd. dirs. F.J.B., Inc., Thermal, Calif. Author: (manual) The New Product Process, 1963; trademark registrant for "Rent-a-Boss." Charter founder Ronald Reagan Rep. Ctr., Washington, 1987. With French Armed Forces, 1953-54, 56-57. Mem. Capital City Club (life), Midland (Ga.) Fox Hounds. Office: FBL Inc PO Box 298 Hurtsboro AL 36860-0298

BOULANGER, ANDREA L., academic administrator, director; b. Green Bay, Wis., Mar. 1, 1975; d. James Joseph John and Margaret Ann Boulanger. BA, U. Wis., Eau Claire, Wis., 1997; MS, We. Ill. U., 2001. Career advisor U. Wis., Madison, Wis., 2001—03; dir. career svcs. Evans Sch. Pub. Affairs U. Wash., Seattle, 2003—. Adv. Habitat for Humanity, Macomb, Ill., 1999—2001. Grantee, Wis. Academic Advising Assn., 2002, U. Wis., 2003. Mem.: Nat. Assn. Colls.s and Employers (assoc.), Am. Coll. Pers. Assn. (assoc.). Avocations: photography, bicycling, travel, camping, hiking. Office: School of Public Affairs Univ of WA 109D Parrington Hall Box 353055 Seattle WA 98195 Office Phone: 206-616-1609.

BOULDING, ELISE MARIE, sociologist, educator; b. Oslo, July 6, 1920; came to U.S., 1923, naturalized, 1929; d. Joseph and Birgit (Johnsen) Biorn-Hansen; m. Kenneth Boulding, Aug. 31, 1941; children: John Russell, Mark David, Christine Ann, Philip Daniel, William Frederic. BA, Douglass Coll., 1940; MS, Iowa State Coll., 1949; PhD, U. Mich., 1969. Research asso. Survey Research Inst., U. Mich., 1957-58, Mental Health Research Inst., 1959-60; research devel. sec. Center for Research on Conflict Resolution, 1960-63; prof. sociology, project dir. Inst. Behavioral Sci., U. Colo., Boulder, 1967-78; Montgomery vis. prof. Dartmouth Coll., 1978-79, chmn. dept. sociology, 1979-85; prof. emerita, 1985; sec. gen. Internat. Peace Rsch. Assoc., 1989-91; pres. IPRA Found., 1992-96. Mem. program adv. council Human and Social Devel. Program, UN Univ., 1977-80; mem. governing council, 1980-86. Author: (with others) Handbook of International Data on Women, 1976, Bibliography on World Conflict and Peace, 1979, Social System of Planet Earth, 1980, Women and the Social Costs of Economic Development, 1981; author: The Underside of History: A View of Women Through Time, 1975, rev. edit., 1992, Women in Twentieth Century World, 1977, Children's Rights and the Wheel of Life, 1979, Building a Global Civic Culture: Education for an Interdependent World, 1988, 90, One Small Plot of Heaven, 1990, Cultures of Peace: The Hidden Side of History, 2000; (with Kenneth Boulding) The Future: Images and Processes, 1994; editor: Peace Culture and Society: Transnational Research and Dialogue with Clovis Brigagao and Kevin Clements (eds.), 1990; New Agendas for Peace Research: Conflict and Security Reexamined (ed.), 1992; Building Peace in the Middle East: Challenges for States and Civil Society, (ed.), 1993. Internat. chair Women's Internat. League for Peace and Freedom, 1967-70; mem. Exploratory Project on Conditions for Peace, 1984-90; mem. U.S. Commn. for UNESCO, 1978-84; mem. UNESCO Peace Prize jury, 1980-87; chair bd. Boulder Cmty. Parenting Ctr., 1988-92; bd. dirs. Am. Friends Svc. Com., 1990-94, Wayland MA Coun. on Aging, 1988-2000; councillor Interfaith Peace Coun., 1995—. Recipient Disting. Achievement award Douglass Coll., 1973, Ted. Lentz Peace award, 1976, Athena award, 1983, Nat. Women's Forum award, 1985, Inst. of Def., Disarmament, Peace and Democracy award, 1990, Jack Gore Meml. Peace award Denver Am. Friends Svc. Com., 1992, Global Citizen award Boston Rsch. Ctr., 1995, Peacemaker of Yr. award Rocky Mountain Peace and Justice Ctr., 1996, World Futures Studies Fedn. award, 1997, Jane Addams Peace Activist award Women's Internat. League for Peace and Freedom, 2000; named to Rutgers Hall of Disting. Alumni, 1994; Danforth fellow, 1965-67; named Peacemaker Elder, Nat. Conf. on Peacemaking and Conflict Resolution, 1999. Mem. Am. Sociol. Assn. (Jessie Bernard award 1982, Peace and War sect. award 1994), Internat. Peace Rsch. Assn. (newsletter editor 1983-87), World Future Studies Fedn., Colo. Women's Forum. Mem. Soc. Of Friends. Home: N Hill 865 Central Ave Apt I 301 Needham MA 02492-1361

BOULEY, JOSEPH RICHARD, pilot; b. Fukuoka, Japan, Jan. 7, 1955; came to U.S., 1955; s. Wilfrid Arthur and Minori Cecelia (Naraki) B.; m. Sara Elizabeth Caldwell, July 6, 1991; children: Denise Marie, Janice Elizabeth, Eleanor Catherine, Rachel Margaret, David Caldwell, Caroline Minori. BA in English, U. Nebr., 1977; MAS, Embry Riddle Aeronautical U., 1988; grad., Fed. Law Enforcement Tng. Ctr., Artesia, N.Mex., 2003. Cert. athletics ofcl. U.S.A. Track and Field, 2001. Commd. 2d lt. USAF, 1977, advanced through grades to maj., 1988, F-117A Stealth Fighter pilot, 1991; ret. lt. col. USAFR, 2000; pilot United Airlines, 1992—. Cert. athletics ofcl. USA Track and Field, 2001—. Ct. apptd. spl. advocate Office of Guardian Ad Litem, Salt Lake City, 1996-99. Decorated DFC, Air medal (4), Air Force Commendation medal (3), Air Force Achievement medal; recipient Alumni Achievement award U. Nebr., 1998; inducted into Air Force ROTC Hall of Fame, U. Nebr., 2003. Mem. VFW, Am. Legion, DFC Soc., Airline Pilots Assn., Red River Valley Fighter Pilots Assn., Aircraft Owners and Pilots Assn. Roman Catholic. Avocations: flying, golf, running, photography. Home: 952 E Springwood Dr North Salt Lake UT 84054 Office Phone: 801-309-9149. Personal E-mail: balijo@aol.com.

BOULEZ, PIERRE, composer, conductor; b. Montbrison, France, Mar. 26, 1925; s. Leon and Marcelle (Calabre) Boulez. Student, recipient 1st prize, Olivier Messiaen at Paris Conservatory. Founder Concert du Petit Marigny, 1953—54; apptd. dir. music Jean-Louis Barrault's Theater Co., 1948; tchr., lectr., condr.; musical adviser, prin. guest condr. Cleve. Symphony Orch., 1970—71; chief condr. BBC Symphony Orch., 1970—75; musical dir. N.Y. Philharm. Orch., 1971—77; dir. Inst. de Recherche et de Coord. Acoustique/Musique, 1976—91; apptd. prin. guest condr. Chgo. Symphony Orch., 1995. Vis. prof. Harvard Univ., 1962—63; prof. Coll. de France, 1976; pres. The Ensemble Intercontemporain, 1976—97. Composer: toured Europe, North and South Am.; conducting appearances include: Edinburgh Festival, Bayreuth Festival, Salzburg Festival, Lucerne Festival; composer: Sonatina for flute and piano, 1946, Three Piano Sonatas, 1946, 1950, 1957, Le Soleil des eaux for voice and orchestra, 1947, Structures, 1952, Le Marteau sans maître, 1955, Deux improvisations sur Mallarmé, 1957, Tombeau (on text of Mallarmé), 1959, Pli selon pli, 1960, Structures II, 1962, Eclat, 1964, Domaines, 1968, Eclat/Multiples, 1970, cummings ist der dichter, 1970, explosante-fixe, 1973, Rituel, 1975, Messagesquisse, 1976, Notations I-IV, 1980, Répons, 1981, Dialogue de l'ombre double, 1986, Mémoriale, 1985, Visage nuptial, 1989, Dérive I, 1985, Anthèmes pour violin solo, 1992, explosante-fixe for large ensemble and electronics, 1993, Anthèmes for Violin Solo and Electronics, 1997, sur Incises, 1998, Notations VII, 1999, Déreive 2, 2002; author: Relevés d'apprenti, 1966, Points de Repère, 1981, le pays fertile-Paule Klee, 1989, Jalon-10 ans d'enseignement au Collège de France, 1989; musical criticism and analysis including: Penser la musique aujourd'hui, 1963. Recipient Praemium Imperiale, Japan Art Assn., 1989, Grosses Verdienstkreuz RFA, 1990, Polar Music prize, Sweden, 1996.*

BOULGER, WILLIAM CHARLES, lawyer; b. Columbus, Ohio, Apr. 2, 1924; s. James Ignatius and Rebecca (Laughlin) B.; m. Ruth J. Schachtele, Dec. 29, 1954; children: Brigid Carolyn, Ruth Mary. AB, Harvard Coll., 1948; LLB, Law Sch. Cin., 1951. Bar: Ohio, 1951, U.S. Dist. Ct. (so. dist.) Ohio 1952, U.S. Supreme Ct. 1957. Ptnr. with Thomas A. Boulger, Chillicothe, Ohio, 1951-73; ptnr. Boulger and Boulger, Chillicothe, 1974— . Pres. Ross County Welfare Assn., Chillicothe, 1954-60; mem. Chillicothe, ARC, 1958-84, chmn., 1959-63, 1985—; mem. Democratic Exec. Com., Chillicothe, 1950s. Served as pfc. U.S. Army, 1943-45, ETO. Mem. Ross County Bar Assn. (pres. 1971), Ohio Bar Assn., ABA, Sunset Club, Symposiarchs Club (past pres.). Roman Catholic. Avocations: tennis, golf. Home: 31 Club Dr Chillicothe OH 45601-1129 Office: PO Box 204 Chillicothe OH 45601-0204

BOULHOSA, MICHAEL L., lawyer; b. Yonkers, NY, June 6, 1960; BA, Fordham U., 1983; JD, Pace U., 1985. Bar: NY 1986, NY Supreme Ct., US Dist. Ct. Ea. Dist. NY, US Dist. Ct. So. Dist. NY. Ptnr. Wilson, Elser, Moskowitz, Edelman & Dicker LLP, NYC. Mem.: NY County Trial Lawyers Assn., Bronx County Bar Assn., NY State Trial Lawyers Assn., NY State Bar Assn. Office: Wilson Elser Moskowitz Edelman & Dicker LLP 23 3rd Fl 150 E 42nd St New York NY 10017-5639 Office Phone: 212-490-3000 ext. 2849. Office Fax: 212-490-3038. Business E-Mail: boulhosam@wemed.com.

BOULOT, PHILIPPE, chef; Grad., Jean Drouant Hotel Sch., Paris, 1978. With The Nikko, Paris, Four Seasons Inn on the Park, London, Four Seasons Cliff Hotel, San Francisco, The Mark Hotel, N.Y.C.; exec. chef The Heathman Restaurant, Portland, 1994—. Named N.W./Hawaii Best Chef, Am. Express. Office: The Heathman Hotel 1001 SW Broadway at Salmon Portland OR 97205

BOULT, TERRANCE E., communications educator; m. Ginger Boult. MS in Applied Math., Columbia U., 1983, MS in Computer Sci., 1984, PhD in Computer Sci., 1986. Asst. prof. computer sci. Columbia U., N.Y.C., 1986—91, assoc. prof. computer sci., 1991—94; Weissman prof. and founding chmn. computer sci. and engring. dept. Lehigh U., Bethlehem, Pa., 1994—2003; El Pomar prof. comm. and computation U. Colo., Colorado Springs, 2004—; founder, CEO Securics, Inc, Colorado Springs, 2004—; founding chief tech. officer Guardian Solutions, Inc, Bradenton, Fla., 2001—04. Contbr. articles to profl. jours. Named Presdl. Young Investigator, NSF, 1990—96, New Inventor of Yr., U. Colo. Tech. Transfer Office, 2004; recipient NCR Stakeholder award for outstanding faculty in elec. engring. and computer sci., Columbia U., Coll. Engring., 1990, Favoriate Faculty award, Lehigh U. S.T.A.R. Program, 1995, Tchg. Excellence award, Lehigh U., Coll. Engring., 1996, Engring. Faculty Rsch. award, U. Colo., Colorado Springs, 2004. Mem.: IEEE (v.p. for confs. 2001). Achievements include patents for Global Models with Parametric Offsets for Object Recovery; 3D Cardiac Motion Recovery System Using Tagged MR Images; Incompressibility Constraints for Inferring 3-D Tessellation; Separable Image Warping Methods and Systems with Spatial Lookup Tables; patents pending for imaging and biometrics technologies. Avocations: poetry, table tennis, skiing, snowboarding. Office: Univ Colo Colorado Springs 1420 Austin Bluffs Pkwy Colorado Springs CO 80933 Office Phone: 719-262-3900. Office Fax: 719-262-3900.

BOULTON, BONNIE SMITH, assistant principal, special education educator; b. Galliano, La., June 27, 1960; d. Kenneth Joseph and Geraldine Ledet Smith; m. Ross E. Boulton, May 11, 2001. BA, Nicholls State U., 1982, EdM, 1985; PhD, La. State U., 2003. Spl. edn. tchr. Lafourche Parish Schs., Thibodaux, La., 1982—87, Jefferson Parish Pub. Schs., Metairie, La., 1987—90, St. Charles Parish Schs., Destrehan, La., 1990—99; grad. asst. La. State U., Baton Rouge, 1999—2000; edn. program coord. La. Dept. Edn., Baton Rouge, 2000—01; asst. prin., spl. edn. campus supr. Eanes Ind. Sch. Dist., Austin, Tex., 2002—. Bd. dirs. La. Dyslexia Assn., 1994—98. Named to, Outstanding Young Women Am., 1985. Mem.: ASCD, Coun. for Exceptional Children. Avocations: reading, travel, gardening, cooking. Home: 11007 Major Oaks Dr Baton Rouge LA 70815-5449

BOULUD, DANIEL, chef, restaurant owner; b. France, Mar. 25, 1955; Chef, Copenhagen, European Commn., Wash., DC; owner, chef Polo Lounge, NYC, Le Régence, NYC; exec. chef Le Cirque, NYC, 1986—92; owner Daniel, NYC, 1993—, Café Boulud, NYC, 1998—, DB Bistro Moderne, City Club Hotel, NYC, 2001—. Author: Cooking with Daniel Boulud, 1993; author: (with Dorie Greenspan) Daniel Boulud's Cafe Boulud Cookbook: French American Recipes for the Home Cook, 1999; author: Letters to a Young Chef, 2003; author: (with Peter Kaminsky, Martin H.M. Schreiber) Chef Daniel Boulud: Cooking in New York City, 2002; author: (with Margaret Russell) Daniel's Dish: Entertaining at Home With a Four-Star Chef, 2003. Named Chef Yr., Bon Appétit mag.; recipient Top Table award, Gourmet mag. Office: Daniel 60 E 65th St New York NY 10021

BOUMA, JOHN JACOB, lawyer; b. Ft. Dodge, Iowa, Jan. 13, 1937; s. Jacob and Gladys Glennie (Cooper) B.; m. Bonnie Jeanne Lane, Aug. 15, 1959; children: John Jeffrey, Wendy Sue, Laura Lynne, Jennifer Ann. BA, U. Iowa, 1958, JD, 1960. Bar: Iowa 1960, Wis. 1960, Ariz. 1962, U.S. Ct. Appeals (9th cir.) 1971, U.S. Ct. Appeals (D.C. cir.) 1971, U.S. Ct. Appeals (10th cir.) 1982, U.S. Tax Ct., 1983, U.S. Supreme Ct. 1975. Assoc. Foley, Sammond & Lardner, Milw., 1960, Snell & Wilmer, Phoenix, 1962-66, ptnr., 1967—, chmn., 1983—. Contbr. articles to profl. jours. Chmn. Phoenix Human Rels. Commn., 1972-75; mem. Phoenix Commn. on LEAP, 1971-72, Phoenix Cmty. Alliance, 1991—; bd. dirs. Phoenix Legal Aid Soc., 1970-76, Ariz. Econ. Coun., 1989-93, Mountain States Legal Found., 1977-95, Valley of Sun United Way, 2004—; trustee Ariz. Opera Co., 1984-2002, pres., 1989-91; trustee Phoenix Art Mus., 1994-2000, 2002-, pres., 1996-98. Capt. JAGC, U.S. Army, 1960-62. Recipient Walter E. Craig Disting. Svc. award, 1998, Cmty. Legal Svcs. Decade of Dedication award, 1998, Disting. Achievement medal Ariz. State U. Coll. Law, 1998, Dist. Alumni Award U. Iowa, 2003. Fellow Am. Coll. Trial Lawyers; mem. ABA (Ho. of Dels. 1989—, bd. govs. 1998-2001, editl. bd. 1996-98), Maricopa County Bar Assn. (pres. 1977-78), Nat. Conf. Bar Pres. (exec. coun. 1984-91, pres. 1989-90), Western States Bar Conf. (pres. 1988-89), Ariz. Bar Assn. (pres. 1983-84), Ariz. Bar Found. (pres. 1987-88), Iowa Bar Assn., Wis. Bar Assn., Phoenix Assn. Def. Counsel (pres. 1972), Attys. Liability Assurance Soc. Ltd. (bd. dirs. 1987—, chair 2002-04), Iowa Law Sch. Found. (bd. dirs. 1986-2003), Phoenix C. of C. (bd. dirs. 1988-94), Ariz. State Coll. Law Soc. (bd. dirs., pres. 1997-2000), Ariz. Suprme Ct. Spl. Com. on Lawyer Discipline and Profl. Conduct, Order of Coif, Phi Beta Kappa, Phi Eta Sigma, Omicron Delta Kappa. Avocations: fishing, hunting, skiing, travel, golf. Home: 800 E Circle Rd Phoenix AZ 85020-4144 Office: Snell & Wilmer One Arizona Ctr Phoenix AZ 85004-2202 Office Phone: 602-382-6216.

BOUMA, LYN ANN NICHOLS, music educator; b. Lincoln, Nebr., Jan. 5, 1963; d. Raymond Joseph and Margaret Ann (Gewacke) Nichols; m. Stephen George Bouma, Jan. 25, 1964; 1 child, Claire. BMus, Nebr. Wesleyan U., Lincoln, 1985; MMus, U. Nebr., Lincoln, 1991. Choral dir. West Point (Nebr.) Pub. Schs., 1985—93, Omaha Ctrl. HS, 1993—. Mem. music ad hoc com. Nebr. Dept. Edn., Lincoln, 2000. Mem. Omaha Chamber Singers. Recipient Outstanding Tchr. award, Alice Buffett Found., 1999, Outstanding Music Alumni award, Nebr. Wesleyan U., 2002. Mem.: NEA, Music Educators Nat. Conf., Am. Choral Dirs. Assn. (life; Nebr. sec. 1992—94, chair Nebr. women's chorus 2000—04, conducted featured choirs at convs., Outstanding Young Choral Dir. 1989). Democrat. Congregationalist. Avocations: exercise, contract bridge. Home: 5123 Decatur Omaha NE 68104 Office: Omaha Ctrl HS 124 N 20th St Omaha NE 68102 Office Phone: 402-557-3361. Business E-Mail: lyn.bouma@ops.org.

BOUMA, ROBERT EDWIN, lawyer; b. Ft. Dodge, Iowa, July 19, 1938; s. Jack and Gladys (Cooper) B.; m. Susan Lawson, Nov. 26, 1963; children: James, Whitley. BA, Coe Coll., 1960; JD, U. Iowa, 1962. Bar: Iowa 1962, N.Y. 1964, Ill. 1985. Asso. Cravath, Swaine & Moore, N.Y.C., 1962-70; gen. counsel Xerox Data Systems Co., Los Angeles, 1970-73; sr. group counsel Xerox Corp., Rochester, N.Y., 1973-76; asso. gen. counsel Monsanto Co., St. Louis, 1976-78; sr. v.p., gen. counsel Household Internat., Prospect Heights, Ill., 1978-84; ptnr., chmn. firm trial dept. McDermott Will & Emery LLP, Chgo., 1984—. Trustee Coe Coll., Ill. Inst. Continuing Legal Edn. Served with USN, 1962-63, v.p. bd. dir. IA Law Sch. Found. Mem. ABA (co-chmn. com. on corp. counsel lit. sect.), Chgo. Bar Assn. Clubs: Mid-Day (Chgo.); Winter (Lake Forest, Ill.), Onwentsia (Lake Forest, Ill.); Legal of Chgo. Home: 901 Church Rd Lake Forest IL 60045-1457 Office: McDermott Will & Emery LLP 227 W Monroe St Ste 3100 Chicago IL 60606-5096 Office Fax: 312-984-7700, 312-984-7718. Business E-Mail: rbouma@mwe.com.

BOUMANN, ROBERT LYLE, lawyer; b. Holdrege, Nebr., June 9, 1946; s. John G. (dec.) and Loretta M. (Eckhardt) B. BS, U. Nebr., 1968, JD, 1974. Bar: Nebr. 1974, Colo. 1987; CPA, Nebr. Sr. tax acct. Peat, Marwick, Main and Co., Denver, 1968—71; asst. gen. counsel, asst. sec. K N Energy, Inc., Lakewood, 1974—96; pvt. practice Denver, 1996—; nat. claims mgr. Aon Risk Svcs., Inc., 1998—, Colorado Sun Power, Inc., 2004—. Treas. YMCA, Hastings, 1979-80. Mem. Nebr. Soc. CPAs, Nebr. State Bar Assn., Colo. State Bar Assn., ABA, Jaycees (treas. Hastings chpt. 1977-78), Phi Eta Sigma, Beta Gamma Sigma, Pi Kappa Alpha. Republican. Roman Catholic. Avocations: racquetball, golf. Office: 14118 W 1st Ave Golden CO 80401-5353 Office Phone: 303-782-3378. E-mail: RBoumann@comcast.net.

BOUNDS, HANK M., school system administrator; b. Hattiesburg, Miss. m. Susie Bounds; children: Will, Caroline. BS, U. So. Miss., 1991, MS in Ednl. Adminstrn., 1994; PhD, U. Miss., 2000. Prin., Lumberton, Miss., Pascagoula HS; supt. Pascagoula Sch. Dist.; state supt. edn. Miss. Dept. Edn., 2005—. Mem. S.E. Regional Adv. Bd US Dept. of Edn, mem. Nat. Forum on Edn. Statistics. With Miss. Army Nat. Guard. Recipient Nat. Reading Renaissance Award, 2003. Mem.: Nat. Assn. of Secondary Sch. Prin.'s (Adminstrv. of Yr. 2001). Office: Miss Dept Edn / Ctr HS PO Box 771 359 N W St Jackson MS 39205 Office Fax: 601-359-3513.*

BOUNDS-SEEMANS, PAMELLA J., artist; b. Milton, Del., Nov. 5, 1948; d. James Wilson Bounds and Marguerite Edna (Rickards) Bounds Carey; m. Jeffrey Wayne Seemans, Mar. 20, 1984; children: Misty Autumn, Sterling Hunter, Jordan Windsor. BA, N.Mex. Highlands U., 1971, MA, 1972. Tchr. elem. art Indian River Sch. Dist., Frankford, Del., 1973-79. Lectr. U. Md., 1981, U. Del., 1986, Del. Tech. and C.C., 1988, 75th Del. Women's Day Conf. at U. Del., U. Del. Coll. Arts and Mineralogy, 1999. Exhibited in group shows including Rehoboth (Del.) Art League, 1980, 89, 90, 92, 93, Tideline Gallery, Rehoboth Beach, Del., 1980—, Greenville, Del., 1993, Wicomico Art League, 1980, Del. Tech. and C.C., Georgetown, 1981, U. Md., 1981, Bluestreak Gallery, Wilmington, Del., 1989—, Blue Streak Art Gallery, Wilmington, 1993, Jamison Gallery, Santa Fe, 1993—, Del. Art Mus., 1996, Biennal 96 and 98 Del. Art Mus., U. Del., 1999, Am. Mus. Visionary Arts, Balt., 2000, numerous others; represented in permanent collections including Wilmington (Del.) Trust Co., Del. Nat. Bank, Sussex County Courthouse, Del. Parks and Recreation Bldg., Del. State Folklore Collection, also numerous pvt. collections; poster for mayor's office Clifford Brown Jazz Festival, Wilmington, 1998; mem. cmty. adv. editl. bd. News Jour., Gannett Papers, Wilmington, 1997-98; artist Dino Doys Rennaissance Corp. Donated art work to oncology ctr. Beebe Hosp. Found., 1995, Multiple Sclerosis Found. Del., Ronald McDonald House Del.; mem. cmty. adv. bd. News Jour. editl. Staff, 1997—; mem. parental adv. bd. U. Del., 2005. Recipient award for outstanding body of work Torpedo Factory, Alexandria, Va., 1982; fellow State of Del. Divsn. of the Arts, 1995. Mem. Nat. Mus. of Women in the Arts, Del. Art Mus., Tunnel 2d place award for most outstanding work in exhibit 1990, Popular Vote award 1980, 93, 94, 95, 96, 1st place award 1993, hon.), Del. Ctr. for Contemporary Arts, Del. Ctr. for Creative Arts, Newark Arts Alliance, Del. Nature Soc., Mothers Multiple Births (v.p. 1987), Wicomo Art League (hon. mention 1981), Univ. and Whist Club (Wilmington). Avocations: criminology, fashion, study of primitive art, psychology, gourmet cooking. Home: 1203 Greenbank Rd Wilmington DE 19808-5842

BOURDON, CATHLEEN JANE, professional society administrator; b. Sparta, Wis., July 13, 1948; d. Cletus John and Josephine Marie (Bourdon) Scheurich; children: Jill Krzyminski, Jeff Krzyminski. BA in Polit. Sci., U. Wis., 1973, MLS, 1974. Tchr. Peace Corps, Arba Minch, Ethiopia, 1969-72; asst. prof., dir. Alverno Coll. Libr., Milw., 1974-83; dep. exec. dir. Assn. Coll. and Rsch. Librs., Chgo., 1983-93; exec. dir. Ref. and User Svcs. Assn. divsn. ALA Assn. Specialized and Coop. Libr. Agys., Chgo., 1993—. Mem. ALA (pres. Staff Assn. 1987-88). Avocations: reading mystery fiction, 1940s movies. Office: Assn Specialized & Coop Libr Agys 50 E Huron St Chicago IL 60611-5295 E-mail: cbourdon@ala.org.

BOURET, PIERRE GEORGE, brokerage house executive; b. Feb. 15, 1924; m. Marie Elizabeth O'Halloran; children: Gregory Pierre, Marc Patrick, Colleen Marie. AB, Stanford U., 1948, MBA, 1949. V.p. major accounts, Dictaphone Corp. Divsn. Pitney Bowes, Rye, N.Y., 1952-89; sr. v.p. Whitehall-Parker Securities, San Francisco, 1995—. 1st lt. mil. intelligence USAR, 1943—54. Mem.: Phi Beta Kappa. Home: 1035 White Gate Rd Alamo CA 94507-2831

BOURG, LOUISE JANETTE, retired secondary school educator; b. Chgo., Oct. 2, 1947; d. Harry Francis and Alice Louise (Bate) De Boer; m. Leo J. Bourg., July 31, 1971. BA, Greenville Coll., 1969; MA, Gov.'s State U., Ill., 1973; admnstrn. cert., Gov.'s State U., 1986. Cert. tchr. secondary sch., gen. adminstrn., Ill. Tchr. French and English, internal/external rev. teams Tinley Park (Ill.) HS, 1969—2002; ret., 2002. Sec. S. Interconf. Assn. Mem. NEA, ASCD, Ill. Edn. Assn., Am. Assn. Tchrs. of French., Am. Coun. Tchrs. of Fgn. Lang. Avocations: reading, physical fitness, gardening, golf, tennis. Home: 47491 Lakeview Dr Lawrence MI 49064

BOURG, PAUL, information technology executive; Student, U. Southwestern La., 1988—90, Acad. Tech. Coll., 1990, Fla. CC, 1990—91, student, 1993—99; BS in Computer Info. Tech., Almeda U., 2005. From prodn. coord. programmer analyst Barnett Bank NA, Jacksonville, Fla., 1993—97; tech. cons. Nationsbank, Charlotte, NC, 1997, Wellspring Resources, Jacksonville, 1997, Suddath Relocation Svcs., Jacksonville, 1997; sr. programmer, technical lead Sci. Applications Internat. Corp., 1997—99; sr. programmer, cons. Cornerstone Integrated Solutions, 1999; sr. programmer analyst Am. Heritage Life, 1999—2000, Fidelity Info. Svcs., 2000—04; sr. SQL server architect EverBank Fla./RobertHalf Tech., Inc., 2004—. Home: 3482 Citation Dr Green Cove Springs FL 32043 Office Phone: 904-651-3797. E-mail: bourgp_2000@yahoo.com.

BOURGAIN, JEAN, mathematician; b. Ostende, Belgium, Feb. 28, 1954; PhD in Math, Free U., Brussels, 1977; habilitation degree, Free. U., Brussels, 1979; DSc (hon.), Hebrew U, Israel, 1991, U. Marne-la-Valle, France, 1994, Free U., Brussels, 1995. Rsch. fellow Belgium NSF, 1975—81; prof. Free U., Brussels, 1981-85; J.L. Doob prof. of mathematics U. Ill., 1985—; prof. Inst. des Hautes Etudes, Paris, 1985-95; Lady Davis prof. of mathematics Hebrew U, Jerusalem, 1988; Fairchild disting. prof. Calif. Inst. Tech., 1991; prof. Inst. Advanced Study, Princeton, NJ, 1994—. Mem. ed. bd. Annals of Mathmatics, Jour. de l'Institut de Math. de Jussieu, Publs. Mathematiques de l'IHES, Duke Math Jour., Internat. Mat. Rash. Notices, Geometrical and Functional Analysis (GAFA), Jour. d'Analyse de Jerusalem, Discrete and Continuous Dynamical Systems. Contbr. over 200 articles to profl. jours. Recipient Alumni Prize, Belgium Nat. Sci. Found., 1979, Empain Prize, Belgium NSF, 1983, Salem Prize, 1983, Damry-Deleeuw-Bourlat Prize, 1985, Langevin Prize, French Acad, Sci., 1985, E. Cartan Prize, French Acad. Sci., 1990, Ostrowski Prize, Ostrowski Found., Switzerland, 1991, Fields medal Internat. Congress of Math., 1994. Mem.: Polish Acad., Academie des Scis. Office: Sch Math Inst Advanced Study Simonyi Hall 203 Einstein Dr Princeton NJ 08540 Business E-Mail: bourgain@math.ias.edu. E-mail: bourgain@ias.edu.

BOURGAIZE, ROBERT G., economist; BA, U. Wash., 1949. Bd. dirs., sr. v.p. Peoples Nat. Bank, Seattle; pres. Central Bank, N.A., Tacoma, University Place Water Co., Epsilon Econ. Inc. Mem. Nat. Assn. Bus. Economists, English-Speaking Union U.S.A. (nat. dir.), Royal Commonwealth Soc., Am. Waterworks Assn. (life), Pacific Northwest Writers Conf., Adam Smith Econ. Found., Adam Smith Soc. (founder 1976), Theta Chi. Office: 4201 B Bridgeport Way W University Place WA 98466-4304

BOURGEAU, JEF, artist; b. Detroit, May 30, 1950; s. David Charles Bourgeau and Phyllis Louise Klapperich; m. Mary Ann Ellenwood, May 12, 1973; children: Lucie, Nicolas, Gemma. Dir. Mus. Contemporary Art, Pontiac, Mich., 1997-2000, Mus. New Art, Detroit, 2000—. Mem. adv. bd. Paint Creek Art Ctr., Rochester, Mich., 1997—. Home: 327 W Second Rochester MI 48307 Office: Mus of New Art Ste 226 1249 Washington Blvd Detroit MI 48226 E-mail: nextmuseum@aol.com.

BOURGEAULT, RONALD, art appraiser; Antiques dealer, auctioneer, 1970—; owner antiques shop, Salem, Mass.; founder, prin., chief auctioneer Northeast Auctions, Portsmouth, NH, 1987—. Appraiser Antiques Roadshow, WGBH-PBS. Lectr. in field. Named one of Power Fifty Who Mattered Most, Art & Auction Mag., 2002. Mem.: NH Antiques Dealers Assn., Nat. Auctioneers Assn., Appraisers Assn. Am. Office: Northeast Auctions 93 Pleasant St Portsmouth NH 03801 Office Phone: 603-433-8400. Office Fax: 603-433-0415. Business E-Mail: neainfo@ttlc.net.*

BOURGEOIS, LOUISE, sculptor; b. Paris, 1911; came to U.S., 1938, naturalized, 1953; m. Robert Goldwater, 1938 (dec. 1973); 3 children. Student, Sorbonne U., 1932-35; baccalaureate, Ecole des Beaux Arts, 1936-38; postgrad., Ecole du Louvre, 1936-37, Acad. Grande Chaumiere; D.F.A. (hon.), Yale U., 1977, Calif. Coll. Arts and Crafts, 1988, Moore Coll. Art, Mass. Coll. Art, 1983, Md. Art Inst., 1984, The New Sch., 1987. Instr. Md. Art Inst., Balt., 1984, New Sch. Social Rsch., N.Y.C., 1987. One-woman shows include Norlyst Gallery, 1947, Peridot Gallery, 1949, 50, 53, Allan Frumkin Gallery, Chgo., 1953, White Art Mus., Cornell U., Ithaca, N.Y., 1959, Stable Gallery, 1964, Rose Fried Gallery, 1963, 112 Greene St., N.Y.C., 1974, Xavier Fourcade Gallery, N.Y.C., 1978-80, Max Hutchinson Gallery, N.Y.C., 1980, Renaissance Soc., 1981, Mus. Modern Art, N.Y.C., 1982, retrospective Contemporary Art Mus., Houston, 1983, Daniel Weinberg Gallery, L.A., 1984, Robert Miller Gallery, 1982, 84, 87-89, 91, Serpentine Gallery, London, 1985, Maeght-Lelong, Zurich, 1985, Paris, 1985, Taft Mus., Cin., 1987-89 (travelled to The Art Mus. at Fla. Internat. U., Miami, Fla., Laguna Gloria Art Mus., Austin, Tex., Gallery of Art, Washington U., St. Louis, Henry Art Gallery, Seattle, Everson Mus. Art, Syracuse, N.Y.), Mus. Overholland, Amsterdam, The Netherlands, 1988, Dia Art Found., Bridgehampton, N.Y., retrospective Frankfurter Kunstverein, Frankfurt, Fed. Republic Germany, 1989 (travelled to Städtische Galerie im Lenbachhaus, Munich, 1990, Riverside Studios, London, 1990, Musée d'Art Contemporain, Lyon, 1990, Fondacion Tapies, Barcelona, Spain, Kunstmuseum, Berne, Switzerland, Kröller-Müller Mus., Otterlo, The Netherlands), Linda Cathcart Gallery, Santa Monica, Calif., 1990, Barbara Gross Gallerie, Munich, 1990, Karsten Schubert, London, 1990, Galerie Krinzinger, Vienna, 1990, Karsten Greve Gallery, Cologne, 1990, Ginny Williams Gallery, 1990, Monika Sprüthe Galerie, Cologne, 1990, Robert Miller Gallery 1986, 1987, 1988, 1989, 1991, Galerie Lelong, Zurich, 1991; solo exhbns. include Parrish Art Mus., Southampton, N.Y., Ydessa Hendeles Found., Toronto, 1991, 92, Milwaukee Art Mus., 1992, The Fabric Workshop, Phila., Galerie Karsten Greve, Paris, Linda Cathcart Gallery, Santa Monica, Calif., Second Floor, Reykjavik, Iceland; exhibited in numerous group shows, U.S., Europe including Sculpture Ctr., 1997, Jim Kempner Fine Art, 1997, Steinbaum Krauss Gallery, 1998, Mary Boone Gallery, 1998, Am. Craft Mus., 1998; represented in permanent collections Mus. Modern Art, N.Y.C., Whitney Mus., Met. Mus. Art, Hirshorn Mus., Musée Nat. D'Art Moderne, Paris, R.I. Sch. Design, NYU, Albright-KnAustralian Nat. Gallery, Canberra, Musée d'Art Moderne, Paris, Mus. Fine Arts, Houston, Guggenheim Mus., N.Y.C., Kunstmus. Bern, stmus. Lucerne, Albertina, Vienna, Mus. Modern Art, Vienna, Walker Art Ctr., Mpls., Storm King Art Ctr., Mountainville, N.Y., New Mus. Contemporary Art, N.Y.C., DC Moore Gallery, N.Y.C., Cheim & Read Gallery, N.Y.C., Denver Art Mus., Colo.; appeared in Limited Edition Artists Books 1990—. Recipient Outstanding Achievement award Women's Caucus, 1980, Pres.'s Fellow award R.I. Sch. Design, 1984, Skowhegan medal sculpture Skowhegan (Maine) Sch. Painting, and Sculpture, Gold medal of honor Nat. Arts Club, 1987, Creative Arts Medal award Brandeis U., 1989, Grand Prix Nat. de Sculpture French Ministry of Culture, 1991, Nat. medal arts, 1999, Wolf prize, 2003; recipient Lifetime Achievement award Coll. Art Assn., 1989, Internat. Sculpture Ctr., 1991; named Officer of Arts and Letters French Ministry of Culture, 1984. Fellow Am. Acad. Arts and Scis.; mem. Am. Acad. and Inst. Arts and Letters, Sculptors Guild, Am. Abstract Artists, Coll. Art Assn. (Disting. Artist award for lifetime achievement 1989). Office: Robert Miller Gallery 524 W 26th St Ground Fl New York NY 10001-5541*

BOURGEOIS, PATRICIA MCLIN, women's health and pediatrics nurse, educator; b. Hammond, La., Mar. 12, 1941; d. Lannie McLin and Mary (Lossett) Nicolay; m. Charles Bourgeois, June 10, 1962; children: Deborah, Cynthia, Terry Kay, Lori, Betsy. BSN, McNeese State U., 1962; MSN, Northwestern State U., Natchitoches, La., 1980. Cert. clin. nurse specialist, nursing child assessment, La. Office nurse pediatrics Green Clinic, Ruston, La., 1962-63; staff nurse ob-gyn. Lincoln Gen. Hosp., Ruston, 1963-64; staff nurse nursery St. Francis Cabrini Hosp., Alexandria, La., 1966-67; prof. maternal/child nursing La. Tech. U., Ruston, 1975—, faculty senate v.p., 2005—. Part-time office nurse Green Clinic, 1975-93; part-time resident nurse Methodist Children's Home, Ruston, 1990-97. Vice chairperson La. Coalition for Maternal/Infant Health, Baton Rouge, 1989-91; pres. Ruston Civic Guild, 1990. Recipient Inst. Regulatory Excellence fellow, Nat. Coun. State Bd. Mem. ANA (del. 1991-93), La. State Nurses Assn. (sec. 1991-93, pres. 1994-95), La. State Bd. of Nursing (apptd. mem., v.p. 2004, pres. 2005). Democrat. Roman Catholic. Office: La Tech Univ PO Box B 152 Ruston LA 71272-3178

BOURGEOIS, SUZANNE HÉLÈNE, biology educator; d. Henri Joseph Bourgeois and Gabrielle Debaerdemaker; m. Melvin Cohn, Dec. 11, 1963. DSc, U. Paris, 1962—66. Prof. The Salk Inst., La Jolla, Calif., 1974—; adj. prof. U. Calif., San Diego, 1977—2000. Com. mem. Genetics Study Sect. of the NIH, Bethesda, Md., 1972—74, Microbial Chemistry Study Sect. of the NIH, Bethesda, 1974—76; corr. editor Jour. of Steroid Biochemistry, France, 1981—93; bd. mem. NIDDK bd. of Sci. Counselors, Bethesda, 1985—87, chmn., 1987—88; mem. of the adv. com. Met. Life Found., N.Y.C., 1986—89; mem. of the sci. adv. com. on biochemistry and endocrinology Am. Cancer Soc., Atlanta, 1993. Contbr. 100 articles in profl. jours. Pub. lectr., San Diego, Calif., 1997—2004. Recipient Career Devel. Award, NIH, 1970—75, Merit Award, 1992—97; grantee rsch. grant, Nat. Inst. for Gen. Med. Sciences, 1973—83, Nat. Cancer Inst., 1983—97, Am. Cancer Soc., 1992—95. Mem.: Am. Assn. for Advancement of Sciences, Women in Cancer Rsch., The Endocrine Soc., The Am. Soc. for Biochemistry and Molecular Biology, NY Acad. of Sciences. Achievements include research in Regulation of gene expression in bacteria and animal cells; patents for Methods for reducing multidrug resistance. Office: Salk Inst 10010 N Torrey Pines Rd La Jolla CA 92037 Business E-Mail: bourgeois@salk.edu.

BOURGET, EDWIN ROBERT, marine ecologist, educator; b. Senneterre, Que., Can., July 6, 1946; s. Jean-Paul and Myrtle (O'Malley) B.; m. Paule Reny, June 16, 1969; children: Frédéric, Virginie. BSc, U. Laval, Que., 1969, MSc, 1971; PhD, U. Wales, 1974. Oceonology rschr. U. Que., Rimouski, 1974-76; adj. prof. U. Laval, 1976-80, assoc. prof., 1980-84, prof., 1984—, dir. biology dept., 1997-98, vice dean rsch. faculty sci, engring., 1998-2001; vice rector rsch. U. Sherbrooke, Que., 2001—. Author/co-author 6 books or book chpts.; contbr. numerous articles to profl. jours. Recipient Michel-Jurdant prize, Can.-French Assn. Advancement Sci., 1996; grantee in field. Mem. Groupe Interuniversitaire de recherches oceanographiques du Que. (dir. 1993-96), Natural Sci. and Engring. Rsch. Coun. (adv. bds. 1987-91), Fonds pour la Formation de Chercheurs et l'Aide a la Recherche. Office: Pavillon Central Sherbrooke PQ Canada J1K 2R1 E-mail: vrr@usherbrooke.ca.

BOURGMIGNON, ELSA, architect; b. Paris, July 28, 1975; arrived in U.S., 1998; d. Andre and Odile Bourgmignon. Mphil, Queen's Univ. Belfast, Belfast, No. Ireland, 1998; MS, Univ. Pa., Phila., Pa., 2000. Assoc. project specialist Getty Conservation Inst., L.A., Calif., 2000—. Mem.: Am. Inst. for Conservation of Historic Artistic Works, Internat. Inst. for Conservation of Historic and Artistic Works, Internat. Scientific Com, for Stone of the Internat. Coun. on Monuments and Sites (assoc.). Office: Getty Conservation Inst 1200 Getty Center Dr Ste 700 Los Angeles CA 90049

BOURGUIGNON, ERIKA EICHHORN, anthropologist, educator; b. Vienna, Feb. 18, 1924; d. Leopold H. and Charlotte (Rosenbaum) Eichhorn; m. Paul H. Bourguignon, Sept. 29, 1950. BA, Queens Coll., 1945; grad. study, U. Conn., 1945; PhD, Northwestern U., 1951; DHL, CUNY, 2000. Field work Chippewa Indians, Wis., summer 1946; field work Haiti; anthropologist Northwestern U., 1947-48; instr. Ohio State U., 1949-56, asst. prof., 1956-60, assoc. prof., 1960-66, prof., 1966-90, acting chmn. dept. anthropology, 1971-72, chmn. dept., 1972-76, prof. emeritus, 1990—; dir. Cross-Cultural Study of Dissociational States, 1963-68. Bd. dirs. Human Relations Area Files, Inc., 1976-79 Author: Possession, 1976, rev. edit., 1991, Psychological Anthropology, 1979, Italian transl., 1983; editor, co-author: Religion, Altered States of Consciousness and Social Change, 1973, A World of Women, 1980; co-author: Diversity and Homogeneity in World Societies, 1973; adv. editor: Behavior Sci. Rsch., 1976-79; assoc. editor Jour. Psychoanalytic Anthropology, 1977-87; mem. editl. bd. Ethos, 1979-89, 97—2005, 2005—, Jour. Haitian Studies, 2000—, Anthropology of Consciousness, 2002—; editor: Margaret Mead: The Anthropologist in America—, Occasional Papers in Anthropology, No. 2, Ohio State U. Dept. Anthropology, 1986; (with Barbara Rigney) Exile: A Memoir of 1939 by Bronka Schneider, 1998; contbr. articles to profl. jours. Fellow Am. Anthrop. Assn.; mem. Ctrl. State Anthrop. Soc. (treas. 1953-56, exec. com. 1995-98), Ohio Acad Sci., World Psychiat. Assn. (transcultural psychiatry sect.), Am. Ethnol. Soc., Current Anthropology (assoc.), Soc. for Psychol. Anthropology (nominations com. 1981-82, bd. dirs. 1991-93, lifetime achievement award 1999), Soc. for the Anthropology of Religion, Phi Beta Kappa, Sigma Xi. Business E-Mail: bourguignon.1@osu.edu. *It is more important to enjoy doing what you do, and to be able to do what you want to do, than to be successful. Success, if it comes, is only a by-product, nothing more.*

BOURI, MICHAEL, civil servant; b. Maghnia, Algeria, May 5, 1943; s. Hamida and Zoulikha (Senhadji) B.; m. Janet Elizabeth Powell, Feb. 1, 1965 (div.); children: Leila, Hamid; m. Naima Bouri, Mar. 1, 1994. BA, U. Algiers, 1973; MA, Am. U., Washington, 1978. Diplomatic attache Min. of Fgn. Affairs, Algiers, 1967-71, adminstr. Washington, 1972-79; asst. prof. U. Algiers, 1979-81; civil servant dept. children and families econ. self sufficiency State of Fla., Fla., 1988—. Mem. Acad. of Arts and Scis., Assn. of Govt. Economists, Inst. of Polit. Sci. Democrat. Moslem. Avocations: reading, travel. Office: State of Fla Dept of Miami 7900 NW 27th Ave Miami FL 33147 Home: 4605 Lankershim Blvd Ste 208 North Hollywood CA 91602-1874

BOURIE, ELIZABETH CONLEY, gifted resource specialist; d. Charles Duncan and Lolus Porter Conley; children: James Duncan, William Porter. BA, Coll. William and Mary, 1968; MA in Tchg., Mary Baldwin Coll., 1993. Caseworker Senator Robert C. Byrd, Washington, 1968—69; legis. asst. Gen. Svc. Adminstrn., Washington, 1969—71, Senator Richard Schweiker, Washington, 1971—74, Rep. James T. Broyhill, Washington, 1974—77; legis. rep. ADA, Washington, 1977—79; tchr. preschool Presbyn. Mtg. Ho., 1981; 5th grade tchr. H.K. Cassell Elem. Sch., Waynesboro, Va., 1993—99; differentation specialist Dixon Elem. Sch., Staunton, Va., 1997—2003; gifted resource tchr. Staunton City Schs., 2001—03; tchr. gifted program Sewells Point Elem. Sch., Norfolk, Va., 2003—, Camp Allen Elem. Sch., Norfolk, 2003—. Adj. faculty mem. MAT program Mary Baldwin Coll., Staunton, 2003—. Chmn. toast Alexandria Cmty. Y, Va., 1988, mem. bd. dirs., 1985—89; mem. vestry Grace Episcopal Ch., Port Republic, Va., 1991—93. Mem.: ASCD, Va. State Reading Assn., Internat. Reading Assn., Va. Assn. for Gifted, Nat. Assn. Gifted Children, Peo, Phi Delta Kappa. Avocations: travel, swimming, gardening, art, beading. Office: Norfolk Pub Schs 800 City Hall Ave Norfolk VA 23515 Office Phone: 757-451-4170. Business E-Mail: ebourie@nps.k12.va.us.

BOURKE, THOMAS ANTHONY, librarian, writer; b. N.Y.C., Aug. 19, 1945; s. Anthony Francis and Nora Christina (Bulman) B.; m. Graciela Adelaida Rodriguez, Aug. 18, 1990; children: Isabella A., Nora R. BA, Fordham Coll., 1966; MA, Fordham U., 1967; MS, Columbia U., 1968. Clerical aide N.Y. Pub. Libr., 1963-68, rsch. libr., 1968-80, chief microforms divsn., 1980-95; spl. asst. Ctr. for Humanities, 1995-2000; libr. Gulport (Fla.) Pub. Libr., 2001—. Reviewer Baseball History, Libr. Jour., Microform Rev., RQ, Reprint Bull., Spl. Librs. Editor-in-chief Microform Rev., 1985-90, mem. editl. bd., 1991—; asst. editor Libr. Resources and Tech. Svcs., 1991-93, cons., reviewer, 1990—; contbr. articles to profl. jours.; pub. translations from Spanish lang. to profl. libr. jours. Mem. ALA, Assn. for Info. and Image Mgmt., Libr. and Info. Tech. Assn., Assn. for Libr. Collections and Tech. Svcs. (preservation microfilming com. 1987-89, exec. com. reproduction of libr. materials sect. 1988-91), Soc. for Am. Baseball Rsch. Democrat. Roman Catholic. Avocations: writing, reading, sports. Office: Gulfport Pub Libr 5501 28th Ave S Gulfport FL 33707 E-mail: tbourke2000@yahoo.com.

BOURLAND, D(ELPHUS) DAVID, JR., linguist, educator; b. Wichita Falls, Tex., June 6, 1928; s. Delphus David and Margaret (Hawley) B.; m. Elizabeth Jagush, Oct. 16, 1981; children by previous marriages: David III, Meda, Ruskin, Ileana. AB, Harvard U., 1951, MBA, 1953; lic. in English linguistics, U. Costa Rica, 1973. Ops. analyst Ops. Evaluation Group MIT, Washington, 1955-61; with various corps., 1961-65; pres. IR Assocs., Inc., San Diego, 1965-69, Semantics Rsch. Corp., Washington, 1969-71; from instr. to assoc. prof. U. Costa Rica, San Jose, 1971-80; pres. Semantics Rsch. Corp., Wichita Falls, Tex., 1994—. Trustee Inst. Gen. Semantics, 1964-89. Author: Introduccion a la Tagmemica, 1974; co-author: An Advanced Course in Squirrelly Semantics: A Coloring Book for Some Adults, 1993, Not So Great Moments in the Lives of Great Men and Women, 1994; editor Gen. Semantics Bull., 1964-70; co-editor: To Be or Not: An E-Prime Anthology, 1991, More E-Prime: To Be or Not II, 1994, E-Prime III!, 1997; contbr. numerous articles to profl. publs. Lt. USNR, 1953-65. Korzybski fellow Inst. Gen. Semantics, 1949-50. Mem. Inst. Gen. Semantics, Internat. Soc. Gen. Semantics (contbg. editor Et Cetera, bd. dirs. 1993—, v.p. devel. 1995-97, pres. 1998—, assoc. editor 2000—), Am. Legion (comdr. dept. Panama Canal 1979-81, post comdr. Costa Rica 1980-84), Sons Am. Legion (nat. adjutant 1985, 86), Forty and Eight (nat. exec. com. 1983-86), Harvard Faculty Club, Harvard Club Boston, Wichita Falls Country Club, Sons. Confederate Vets., Wichita Falls Yacht Club. Republican. Avocation: power lifting. Home: 3301 Mockingbird Ln Wichita Falls TX 76308-2017

BOURM, ROGER MICHAEL, real estate broker, investor, property manager; b. Bellingham, Wash., May 31, 1954; s. John Milton and Gloria June Bourm; children: Matina Mary June, Allyse Nicole. A in Tech., Baylor U., 1976. Registered tech. Am. Registry Radiologic Techs., 1976; assoc. broker Wash., 1997. Registered tech St Joseph Hosp., Bellingham, Wash., 1976—79; gen. sales mgr Wilson Motors, 1979—93; assoc. broker Coldwell Banker, 1995—; owner Bourm Properties, 1995—. Chair The Arthritis Found., Bellingham, 2001—05. With U.S. Army, 1974—76. Mem.: Am. Registry Radiologic Techs., Nat. Assn. Realtors (assoc.). Home: 516 16th St Bellingham WA 98225 Office: Bourm Properties 516 16th St Bellingham WA 98225 Office Phone: 877-734-3420. Home Fax: 360-671-8868. Personal E-mail: bourm@aol.com.

BOURNE, CAROL ELIZABETH MULLIGAN, biology professor, phycologist; b. Rochester, N.Y., May 4, 1948; d. William Thomas and Ruth Townsend (Stevens) Mulligan; m. Godfrey Roderick Bourne, Dec. 21, 1968. BA in Botany/Bacteriology, Ohio Wesleyan U., 1970; MS in Botany, Miami U., Oxford, Ohio, 1978; PhD in Natural Resources, U. Mich., 1992. Lab. asst. Ohio Wesleyan U., Delaware, 1968-70; biol. lab. tech. USDA-Forest Svc., Delaware, 1970-73; grad. rsch. asst. botany dept. Miami U., Oxford, 1973-75; electron microscopist coll. medicine U. Cin., 1975-76; rsch. asst. sch. pub. health U. Mich., Ann Arbor, 1978-80, rsch. assoc. coll. medicine, 1981-83, grad. rsch. asst. sch. natural resources, 1983-86, grad. teaching asst. dept. biology, 1987; postdoctoral scientist U. Fla., Ft. Lauderdale, 1990-92; adj. instr. ecology Fla. Atlantic U. Coll. Liberal Arts, Davie, 1992-93. Adj. asst. prof. dept. biology U. Mo., St. Louis, 1994—, Washington U., St. Louis, 1994—2000, Pierre Laclede Honors Coll., U. Mo., St. Louis, 1997—; bd. dirs. CEIBA Biol. Ctr., Inc. Contbr. articles to scholarly jours. Grantee NSF, 1987-89. Mem.: Soc. for Study of Evolution, Internat. Soc. for Diatom Rsch., Phycological Soc. Am., Am. Inst. Biolog. Scis. Office: U Mo at St Louis Dept Biology One University Drive Saint Louis MO 63121-4499 E-mail: BourneC@msx.umsl.edu.

BOURNE, CHARLES PERCY, information scientist, educator; b. San Francisco, Sept. 2, 1931; s. Frank Percy and Edith (Dunlap) B.; m. Elizabeth A. Scheidtmann, Aug. 15, 1953; children— Glen Wade, Holly Ann. BS in Elec. Engring., U. Calif. at Berkeley, 1957; MS in Indsl. Engring., Stanford, 1963. Sr. research engr. Stanford Research Inst., Menlo Park, Calif., 1957-66; v.p. Information Gen. Corp., Palo Alto, Calif., 1966-70; pres. Charles Bourne & Assos., Menlo Park, 1970—; prof. in residence Sch. Library and Info. Studies; dir. Inst. Library Research U. Calif.-Berkeley, 1971-77; v.p. gen. info. div. Dialog Info. Svcs., Inc., Palo Alto, 1977-92. Research in info. scis. for libraries, schs., acads., including Library of Congress, Nat. Agrl. Library, U.S. Patent Office, Nat. Acad. Sci.; Guest lectr. univs. including U. Calif. at Berkeley, 1963-66; Sarada Ranganathan lectr., Bangalore, India, 1978; cons. corr. Nat. Acad. Sci. com. on sci. and tech. information, 1968-70; mem. adv. bd. Chem. Abstracts, 1965-68, Ency. Library and Information Scis., 1967—, Documentation Abstracts, 1968-69, Ann. Rev. Information Sci. and Tech., 1966; mem. adv. bd. World Affairs Report, 1987-90; U.S. rep. to a com. of Internat. Fedn. for Documentation, 1966-76; UNESCO cons. to Indonesia and Tanzania; Nat. Acad. Scis. cons. to Ghana, 1976; mem. U.S.-Egyptian Task Force on Tech. Info. Problems, 1976, U.S. del. UNESCO Intergovtl. Conf. Sci. and Tech. Info. for Devel., 1979; mem. Network Adv. Com. Library of Congress, 1987-92; delegate -at-large White House Conf. Lib. and Info. Svcs., 1991. Author: Methods of Information Handling, 1963, Technology in Support of Library Science and Information Service, 1980; co-author: A History of Online Information Services, 2003; contbr. articles profl. jours. Served with USMCR, 1950-51. Recipient ann. award of merit Am. Documentation Inst., 1965 Mem. Am. Soc. Information Sci. and Tech. (pres. 1970, Best Info. Sci. Book award 2004), ALA (dir. information scis. and automation div. 1966-67), Nat. Info. Standards Orgn. (bd. dirs. 1987-90). Home: 1619 Santa Cruz Ave Menlo Park CA 94025-5761

BOURNE, HENRY CLARK, JR., electrical engineer, educator, retired academic administrator; b. Tarboro, NC, Dec. 31, 1921; s. Henry Clark and Marion (Alston) B.; m. Margaret Barr Thomas, Aug. 15, 1953; children: Katherine Wimberley, Henry Clark III, Thomas Franklin, Margaret Alston. S.B., MIT, 1947, S.M., 1948, Sc.D., 1952. Registered profl. engr., Calif., Tex. Asst. prof. Mass. Inst. Tech., 1952-54; asst. prof., then asso. prof. U. Calif. at, Berkeley, 1954-63; prof. elec. engring. Rice U., Houston, 1963-77, chmn. dept., 1963-74; sect. head engring. div. NSF, Washington, 1974-75, div. dir. engring., 1977-79; dep. asst. dir. Directorate Engring. and Applied Sci., 1979-81; v.p. for acad. affairs Ga. Inst. Tech., Atlanta, 1981-86, 87-88, acting pres., 1986-87, prof. elec. engring., 1988-92, prof. elec. engring. emeritus, 1992—. Cons. editor Harper & Row, N.Y.C., 1961-67; cons. elec. engring., 1952— Author tech. papers in field of magnetics. Served to 1st lt. C.E. AUS, 1943-46. Sci. Faculty fellow NSF, 1960-61; hon. research assoc. Univ. Coll. London; Eng., 1961 Fellow IEEE, AAAS; mem. Am. Phys. Soc., Am. Soc. Engring. Edn., Sigma Xi, Tau Beta Pi, Eta Kappa Nu, Phi Kappa Phi, Omicron Delta Kappa, Beta Gamma Sigma, Delta Tau Delta. Episcopalian. Home: 173 Windrush Rd Winston Salem NC 27106

BOURNE, HENRY R., medicine, cellular and molecular pharmacology educator; b. Danville, Va., Mar. 1, 1940; m.; three children. MD, Johns Hopkins U., 1965. Instr. in medicine U. Calif., San Francisco, 1971—72, asst. prof. medicine and pharmacology, 1972—75, assoc. prof. medicine and pharmacology, 1975—81, chief, div. of clinical pharmacology, 1980—83, sr. staff mem., Cardiovascular Rsch. Inst., 1980—, prof. medicine and cellular and molecular pharmacology, 1981—, prof., chair. dept. pharmacology, 1983—91, acting chair, dept. pharmacology, 1993—94. Mem. Nat. Acad. Scis., Inst. Medicine, 2004. Office: U Calif Box 0450 513 Parnassus Ave Med Sci 1212 San Francisco CA 94143-0450 E-mail: bourne@cmp.ucsf.edu.

BOURNE, JAMES E., lawyer; b. Charleston, W.Va., Jan. 13, 1940; BA, Ind. U., 1962, JD, 1965. Bar: Ind. 1965. Law clk. to Hon. William E. Steckler, U.S. Dist. Ct. (so. dist.) Ind., 1965—67; atty. Wyatt, Tarrant & Combs, LLP, New Albany, Ind. Mem. faculty Nat. Inst. for Trial Advocacy. Fellow: Am.

Coll. Trial Lawyers; mem.: ABA, Ind. State Bar Assn. (pres.-elect 2001—02, pres. 2002—03), Leadership So. Ind., Def. Trial Counsel Ind., Def. Rsch. Inst. Office: Wyatt Tarrant Combs LLP Cmty Bank Bldg 101 W Spring St New Albany IN 47150-3440

BOURNE, KATHERINE DAY, journalist, educator; b. Lynn, Mass., Sept. 11, 1938; d. Schuyler Vandervort and Elsie Marie (Mayo) Day; m. William Nettleton Bourne; children: William Alexander, Katherine Loring. BS in Edn., Keene Tchrs. Coll., 1960; MEd, Harvard U., 1984. Tchr. Wachusett Regional High Sch., Holden, Mass., 1960-61; arts editor Bay State Banner, Boston, 1966—; dir. edn. Suffolk County House of Correction, Boston, 1979-84; edn. coord. Dept. Transitional Asst., Mass., 1984—2002, ret., 2002—. Contbr. music revs. to Christian Sci. Monitor. Dir. rels. Crime-out, Boston, 1983; mem. Gov.'s Commn. on Status of Women, 1970-74; co-founder, dir. Harvard-Radcliffe Forum Theatre, Cambridge, 1964-68; bd. dirs., mem. ARC Greater Boston, 1987-95, NAACP Boston, 1978-81. NEH journalism fellow, 1978; recipient Melnea A. Cass award Greater Boston YMCA, 1984. Mem. NAACP (life). Avocations: collecting african-american literature, aerobics, photography, stamps, art relating to black history and life. Home: 52 High St Brookline MA 02445-7707 Office: Bay State Banner The Fargo Bldg 68 Fargo St Boston MA 02210-2122

BOURNE, LYLE EUGENE, JR., psychology professor; b. Boston, Apr. 12, 1932; s. Lyle E. and Blanche (White) H. BA, Brown U., 1953. Asst. prof. psychology U. Utah, 1956-61, assoc. prof., 1961-63; vis. assoc. prof. U. Calif., Berkeley, 1961—62, vis. prof., 1968—69; assoc. prof. psychology U. Colo., Boulder, 1963—65, prof., 1965—2001, prof. emeritus, 2002—, dir. Inst. Cognitive Sci., 1979—83, chmn. dept. psychology, 1983—91; clin. prof. psychiatry U. Kans. Med. Ctr., 1967—90. Vis. prof. U. Wis., 1966, U. Mont., 1967, U. Hawaii, 1969; cons. in exptl. psychology, VA, 1965-93. Author: Human Conceptual Behavior, 1966, Psychology of Thinking, 1971, Psychology: Its Principles and Meanings, rev. edits., 1976, 79 82, 85, Cognitive Processes, 1979, rev. edit., 1986, Psychology: A Concise Introduction, 1988, Psychology: Behavior in Context, 1998; acad. editor: Basic Concept Series, Learning-Cognition Series, Scott, Foresman Pub. Co., 1970-76, Charles Merill Co., 1980-84, Advanced Psychological Texts Series, Sage Publications, 1992—; editor Jour. Exptl. Psychology: Human Learning and Memory, 1975-80; cons. editor Jour. Clin. Psychology 1975-97, Jour. Exptl. Psychology: Learning, Memory and Cognition, 1984-92, Memory and Cognition, 1984-89. Recipient Rsch. Scientist award NIHM, 1969-74. Mem.: APA (coun. editors 1975—80, coun. reps. 1976—79, chmn. early awards com. 1978—79, bd. sci. affairs 1978—81, coun. reps. 1986—89, bd. sci. affairs 1989—92, pres. divsn. 3 1992, publ. and commn. bd. 1995—), Coun. Grad. Depts. Psychology (exec. bd. 1985—89), Soc. Gen. Psychology (pres. 2001), Rocky Mountain Psychol. Assn. (pres. 1987—88), Fedn. Behavioral Psychol. and Cognitive Scis. (v.p. 1994—95, pres. 1995—97), Soc. Exptl. Psychologists (chmn. 1987—88), Psychonomic Soc. (governing bd. 1976—81, chmn. 1980—81), Sigma Xi. Home: 785 Northstar Ct Boulder CO 80304-1088 Office Phone: 303-492-4210. E-mail: lbourne@psych.colorado.edu.

BOURNE, MATTHEW, performing company executive, artistic director; BA in Dance/Theatre, Laban Centre, 1985. Dir., choreographer and artistic dir. Adventures in Motion Pictures, London, 1987—2002; founder New Adventures Dance Co., 2004—. Founder mem. Lea Anderson's The Featherstonehaughs, 1988. Stage works include: Overlap Lovers, 1987; Spitfire, 1988; Buck and Wing, 1988; The Infernal Gallop, 1989; Town & Country, 1991; The Nutcracker, 1992; Deadly Serious, 1992; The Percys of Fitzrovia, 1992; Highland Fling, 1994; Swan Lake, 1996; Cinderella, 1997; TV work includes Late Flowering Lust, 1993, Drip-A Narcissistic Love Story, 1993; choreographer As You Like It, 1989, Children of Eden, 1990, A Midsummer Night's Dream, 1991—92, The Tempest, 1991, Show Boat, 1991, Peer Gynt, 1994, Watch With Mother, 1994, Oliver!, 1994, Watch Your Step, 1995, Boutique, 1995, Roald Dahl's Red Riding Hood, 1995, A Play Without Words, 2004. Recipient Bonnie Bird award, A Place Portfolio commn. and a Barclays New Stages award for choreography, Hamburg Shakespeare Award for Arts, 2003, Nat. Dance Awards, Critics' Cir., 2004. Mailing: New Adventures Sadler's Wells Theatre Rosebery Ave London EC1R 4TN England*

BOURNE, MICHELLE LYNN, physician assistant; b. Norman, Okla., July 10, 1976; d. Mike L. Trumble and Bobbie L. Ward; m. Brandon Lawson Bourne, May 4, 2002. BS in Biology with honors, East Ctrl. Univ., Ada, Okla., 1999; MS with distinction, Univ. Okla. Health Sci. Ctr., 2001. Cert. PA-C Nat. Commn. on Cert. of Physician Asst., lic. Okla. State Bd., cert. ACLS, BLS. Optician Eyemasters, Norman, 1993—94, Okla. Optical, Ada, 1994—98; orthop. med. asst. Orthop. Jack B. Howard Ctr., Ada, 1998—99; physician asst. Emergency Medicine-Okla. U. Med. Ctr., Oklahoma City, 2001—02, Family Practice Family Health South, Oklahoma City, 2002—03, Urgent Care Am Pm Clinic, Shawnee, Okla., 2003—, Integers Marshall County Family Medicine, Madill, Okla., 2004—. Mem. 7th Ann. Ronald E. McNair Rsch. Conf., Ada, 1998—99, 7th Ann. Ronald E. McNair Summer Rsch. Internship, 1998. Fellow: Fellowship of Christian Physician Asst., Okla. Acad. of Physician Asst., Am. Acad. Physician Asst.; mem.: Christian Med. and Dental Assn., Alpha Chi. Avocations: travel, movies, pets, family, church. Office: Intergers Marshall County Family Medicine Two Hospital Dr Madill OK 73446

BOURNE, PETER GEOFFREY, physician, educator, writer; b. Oxford, Eng., Aug. 6, 1939; s. Geoffrey Howard and Gwen (Jones) B.; m. Mary Elizabeth King, Nov. 9, 1974. MD, Emory U., 1962; MA in Anthropology, Stanford U., 1969. Fellow dept. psychiatry Med. Sch.; co-dir. Alcoholism Project, Emory U., 1962-63; intern King County Hosp., Seattle, 1963-64; rsch. psychiatrist Walter Reed Army Inst.; rschr. Washington, 1964-67; chief neuropsychiat. br. U.S. Army Med. Research Team, Vietnam, 1965-66; cons. S.E. Asia Health Br. (AID), Dept. State, 1966-67; resident dept. psychiatry, Stanford U. Med. Center, Palo Alto, Calif., 1967-69; dir. mental health unit Southside Comprehensive Health Center, Atlanta, 1969-71; founder, dir. Atlanta S Ctrl. Cmty. Mental Health Ctr., 1970-71; dir. Ga. Office Drug Abuse, 1971-72; spl. adviser for health affairs to Gov. Jimmy Carter of Ga., 1971-73; asst. dir. White House Spl. Action Office for Drug Abuse Prevention, 1972-74; cons. Drug Abuse Coun., Washington, 1974-76; pres. Found. for Internat. Resources, 1975-76; Mid-Atlantic coord., dep. campaign dir. Jimmy Carter Presdl. Campaign, 1975-76; spl. asst. for health issues to U.S. Pres., Washington, 1976-78; mem. U.S. del. to Exec. Coun. UNICEF, 1977; asst. sec. gen. UN, N.Y.C., 1979-81; pres. Global Water, 1981-98; exec. v.p., pub. Devel. Internat., 1986-90; mem. U.S. Pres. Commn. on White House Fellows; head U.S. del. UN Devel. Program Governing Coun., 1978; emergency rm. physician Casualty Hosp., Washington, 1966-67; emergency room physician Kaiser Permanente Hosp., Santa Clara, Calif., 1967-69; psychiat. cons. Santa Clara County Hosp., 1968-69, San Mateo County Hosp., 1969; cons. WHO, Geneva, 1972, UN Divsn. on Narcotic Drugs, 1976; asst. prof. dept. psychiatry Emory U. Med. Sch., 1969-72, asst. prof. dept. preventive medicine and cmty. health, 1969-72; lectr. dept. psychiatry Harvard U. Med. Sch., 1974; v.p. Nat. Coordinating Coun. on Drug Abuse Edn., 1971-72; prof. psychiatry, chmn. dept. St. Georges Med. Sch., Grenada, 1979-98; pres. Peter Bourne Assocs., Washington, 1985-98. Mem. of jury The Lasker Awards, 1978—79; vice chancellor St. Georges U., Grenada, 1998—2001, vice chancellor emeritus, Grenada, 2001—; chmn. Med. Edn. Coop. with Cuba, 2000—; vis. scholar Green Coll., Oxford, England, 2001—; bd. dir. Inst. Human Virology, Balt., Nat. Grad. U., Wash., Student Partnerships Worldwide, London. Author: Men, Stress and Viet Nam, 1970; editor: Psychology and Physiology of Stress, 1969, (with R. Fox) Alcoholism: Progress in Research and Treatment, 1973, Addiction, 1974, Acute Drug Abuse Emergencies, 1976, Water Resources: Social and Economic Aspects, 1983, Fidel, A Biography of Fidel Castro, 1986, Jimmy Carter: A Comprehensive Biography from Plains to the Post-Presidency, 1997; mem. editorial bd. Psychiatry, 1968—, Am. Jour. Drug Alcohol Abuse, 1973—; contbr. articles to profl. jours. and chpts. to books. Bd. dirs. Save the Children Fedn., Inst. for So. Studies; chmn. global bd. dirs. Hunger Project; chmn., bd. trustees Council on Hemispheric Affairs, 1986—; chmn. bd. dirs. Am. Assn. World Health, 1982-98, Health and Devel. Internat., 1997—, Youth Advocate Program, 1998—, Med. Edn. Collaboration with Cuba, 1998—, Inst. Caribbean and Internat. Studies, Windward Islands Rsch. and Edn. Found. Served to capt. U.S. Army, 1964-67. Decorated Bronze Star medal, Air medal, Combat Medics badge; recipient William C. Menninger award Central Neuropsychiat. Assn., 1967, Pub. Svc. award Nat. Assn. State Drug Abuse Program Coordinators, 1974, Pub. Svc. award Assn. Chinese Ams., 1978; named one of Five Outstanding Young Men, Atlanta Jaycees, 1971, one of Five Outstanding Young Men in Ga., Ga. Jaycees, 1972. Fellow Am. Psychiat. Assn. (disting. life, chmn. task force on drugs and drug abuse edn. 1969-73); mem. AAAS, Ga. Psychiat. Assn., Washington Psychiat. Soc., Royal Soc. Medicine, Med. Assn. Ga., Soc. for Internat. Health (pres. 1988-92), Am. Med. Soc. on Alcoholism, Am. Anthrop. Assn., World Fedn. for Mental Health. Democrat. Home and Office: 2119 Leroy Pl NW Washington DC 20008-1848 Office Phone: 202-462-7266. Business E-Mail: pbourne@igc.org. *I have always felt that my training as a physician was only a starting point in using my life to touch, for the better, the lives of as large a number of people as possible, whether formulating national health policy for the President of the United States, through the United Nations, through the private voluntary agencies or the academic world. I believe that ultimate gratification can only come from the sense that one has left the world a better place than when one arrived.*

BOURNE, RUSSELL, publisher, author; b. Boston, Oct. 10, 1928; s. Standish T. and Sylvia (Russell) B.; m. Miriam Anne Young, Aug. 22, 1953 (dec.); children: Sarah Perkins, Jonathan, Louise Taber, Andrew Russell; m. Dora Grabfield Flash, Oct. 31, 1992. AB magna cum laude, Williams Coll., 1950. Reporter Life mag., 1950-53, asst. to Henry R. Luce, 1953-56; assoc. editor Archtl. Forum, 1956-59; editor Am. Heritage Jr. Library, 1959-64, Time-Life Books, Great Ages of Man, 1964-69; assoc. chief Nat. Geog. Book Service, 1969-72; partner Bourne-Thompson & Assocs., Washington, 1972-77; sr. editor Smithsonian Exposition Books, Washington, 1977-80; pub. Hearst Gen. Books, N.Y.C., 1980-81; pub., editor Am. Heritage Books, N.Y.C., 1981-83; pub. cons., 1984—. Author: View From Front Street, 1989, Red King's Rebellion, 1990, Floating West, 1992, Best of the Best Sparkman and Stephens Designs, 1995, Americans on the Move, 1995, Invention in America, 1996, Rivers of America, 1998, Gods of War, Gods of Peace, 2002. Served with CIC, U.S. Army, Berlin, 1950-52. Home and Office: 2 Fairway Dr Ithaca NY 14850-2764

BOURNEUF, HENRI JOSEPH, JR., librarian; b. Beverly Farms, Mass. s. Henri and Elizabeth (McKean) B.; m. Susan Peterson, June 19; 1 child, Anne Peterson. BA, Harvard U., 1969; MLS, Simmons Coll., Boston, 1980. Ref. libr. Widener Libr., Harvard U., Cambridge, Mass., 1980—, head ref. libr., 1995—. Democrat. Home: 78 Fresh Pond Pkwy Cambridge MA 02138-1366 Office: Widener Library Harvard Univ Cambridge MA 02138 E-mail: bourneuf@fas.harvard.edu.

BOURQUE, BOYD D., secondary school educator; Secondary tchr. Hahnville High Sch.; instr. TCP/IP and phys. networking La. State U., Baton Rouge. Recipient Tchr. Excellence award Internat. Tech. Edn. Assn., 1992.

BOURQUE, MARY LYN, psychologist, statistician, consultant; b. Lowell, Mass., May 13, 1937; d. Edward Francis and Dorothy Veronica (Christie) Bourque; m. Delwin Earl Staib, Mar. 7, 1980. AB, Emmanuel Coll., Boston, 1958; MEd, Boston Coll., 1964; EdD, U. Mass., Amherst, 1979. Tchr. h.s. Diocese of Boston, 1962—72; dir. testing Povidence. Pub. Schs., RI, 1975—79; asst. prof. U. Md. Coll. Edn., 1979—82; unit dir. Coop. Edn. Svcs., Norwalk, Conn., 1982—85; exec. dir. New Eng. Evaluation Designs, 1985—89; dir. psychometrics Nat. Assess Govt. Bd., Washington, 1989—2001; exec. dir. Mid Atlantic Psychometric Svcs., Leesburg, Va., 2001—. Chmn. tech. adv. com. Am. Bd. Certification of Tchg. Excellence, Washington, 2001—; mem. adv. panel on h.s. edn. and evaluation State of Calif., Sacramento, 2000—04; mem. adv. panel on TAKS devel. State of Tex., Austin, 2000—03. Co-author: Standard Setting Concepts, Handbook of Education Policy. Choir mem. Bridgewater Congregational Ch., Conn., 1982—89, Rockville (Md.) United Ch., 1989—96; bd. dirs., pres. Bridgewater Homeowners Assn., Conn., 1982—88, Ashton Downs Homeowners Assn., Leesburg, Va., 1993—96. Mem.: Nat. Coun. Measurement Edn. (bd. dirs. 1999—2001), Am. Ednl. Rsch. Assn. Avocations: cooking, golf, music, skiing. Home: 212 Ashton Dr SW Leesburg VA 20175 Office: MidAtlantic Psychometric Svcs 212 Ashton Dr SW Leesburg VA 20175 Office Phone: 703-771-4686. Personal E-mail: m.l.bourque@att.net.

BOURQUE, RAY, retired professional hockey player; b. Montreal, Que., Can., Dec. 28, 1960; m. Chris Bourque; children: Melissa, Christopher Ray. Defenseman Boston Bruins (NHL), 1979-2000, Colo. Avalanche, 2000—01. Mem. QMJHL All-Star 1st team, 1977-78, 78-79, NHL All-Star 1st team, 1979-80, 81-82, 83-84, 84-85, 86-87, 89-90, 93-94, 2nd team, 80-81, 82-85, 85-86, 88-89; player NHL All-Star game, 1981-86, 88-94. Recipient Calder NHL Rookie of Yr. trophy, 1980, Norris Outstanding Defenseman trophy, 1987, Frank. J. Selke trophy, 1978-79, Emile (Butch) Bouchard trophy, 1978-79, James Norris Meml. trophy, 1986-87, 87-88, 89-90, 90-91, 93-94, King Clancy Meml. trophy, 1991-92; named to Sporting News All-Star 2nd team, 1980-81, 82-83, 85-86, 88-89, Sporting News All-Star 1st team, 1981-82, 83-84, 86-87, 87-88, 89-90, 93-94; inducted to Hockey Hall of Fame, 2004 Achievements include mem. Stanley Cup Champion Colorado Avalanche, 2001.*

BOURQUE, RICHARD MICHAEL, foundation administrator; b. Omaha, Mar. 9, 1967; s. Adrian Richard Bourque and Kathleen Marrie Van Ackeren; m. Kathy J. Green, June 26, 1993. BS in Agr., U. Mo., 1990. Mgr. Lute Ranch, Ogallala, Nebr., 1991—; owner, pres. Functional Agr. Resource Techs., Inc., Ogallala, 1993—; exec. dir. Lute Family Found., Inc., Ogallala, 1994—, Heartland Philanthropy; pres. Packaging and Crating Svcs., Inc., North Platte, Nebr., 1996—. Cons. Law Office of McGinley, O'Donnell, Ogallala, 1998—; engr. Ogallala Fire and Rescue; pres. Keith County Housing Devel. Inc., Ogallala, 1997-98. Pres. Tech. Renovation Com., Ogallala, 1995-96; bd. dirs. Cmty. Redevel. Authority, Ogallala, 1996-98, Nebr. Nat. Trails Mus., Keith County, 1996—, Western Nebr. Cmty. Found. Inc., Keith County, 1996—; pres. Pub. Radio Nebr. Found., 2004—. Mem. Nebr. Cattlemen's Assn., Ogallala Yacht Club. Roman Catholic. Avocations: skiing, hunting, boating, off-road trail riding, fishing. Office: Lute Family Found Inc PO Box 187 Ogallala NE 69153-0187 E-mail: lutefound@charter.net.

BOUSFIELD, KENNETH HAROLD, civil engineer; b. L.A., Nov. 14, 1946; s. William Harold and Shirley (Burgess) Bousfield; m. Gail Nuttall, Sept. 2, 1970; children: Tara Lee, Julie, Timothy Kenneth, Kelly Jean. BSCE, Brigham Young U., 1971; postgrad., U. Utah, 1976-80. Registered profl. engr., Utah. Engr. Utah Dept. of Health, Salt Lake City, 1971-72; assoc. engr. Nielsen Maxwell & Wangsgard, Salt Lake City, 1973-76; compliance mgr. Utah Dept. of Environ. Quality, Salt Lake City, 1976—. Contbr. articles to profl. jours. Fellow: EPA; mem.: Am. Water Works Assn. Republican. Mem. Lds Ch. Office: Utah Dept Environ Quality 150 N 1950 W Salt Lake City UT 84114-4830 Business E-Mail: kbousfield@utah.gov.

BOUSLOG, ROBBIN RAYE, performing arts educator, art educator; b. Fullerton, Calif., July 17, 1952; d. Roger Leslie and Wanda Lee (Culpepper) Acton; m. Richard Bouslog, Mar. 28, 1998; 1 stepchild, Summer Nicole; m. Allan Lee Morrow, June 26, 1971 (div. Dec. 17, 1997); children: Samuel Eli Morrow, Israel Allan Morrow. AA, San Jacinto (Calif.) C.C., 1985; BA in Liberal Studies, Calif. State U., San Bernardino, Calif., 1987; MA in Edn., Claremont (Calif.) Grad. Sch., 1989. Cert. Collaborative Design Inst., 2003. Musician and choir dir. Canyon Lake (Calif.) Cmty. Ch., 1982—87; worship leader and musician Elsinore Valley Friends Ch., Lake Elsinore, Calif., 1987—97; elem. tchr. Lake Elsinore Unified Sch. Dist., 1987—96; adj. prof. Edn. dept. Hope Internat. U., Fullerton, 2001; mid. sch. tchr. Lake Elsinore Unified Sch. Dist., 1996—. Presenter visual and performing arts Lake Elsinore Unified Sch. Dist., 1987—; presenter Calif. League of Mid. Schs., San Francisco, 1996—, San Diego, 1996—. Author: (projects) Weaving in the Arts, 2000, LEUSD Visual and Performing Arts Stds., 2001. Com. mem. Tuscany Hills Homeowners Assn., Lake Elsinore, 2001; dir. Canyon Lake Choraleers, Canyon Lake, 1992. Nominee Bravo award, L.A. Music Ctr. Edn., 1994, 2002; scholar Tchrs. Honor Soc., San Jacinto C.C., 1985; Apple grant, Claremont Grad. Sch., 1987. Mem.: Calif. Music Edn. Assn., Calif. Tchrs. Assn., Calif. Art Project. Republican. Achievements include direction of nationally recognized mid. sch. choirs. Avocations: acting, music, hiking, travel, reading. Home: 30 Villa Valtelena Lake Elsinore CA 92532 Office: Lake Elsinore Unified Sch Dist 545 Chaney St Lake Elsinore CA 92530 E-mail: rickandrobbin@msn.com.

BOUSSO, RAPHAEL, physicist, educator; PhD, Cambridge U., 1998. Postdoctoral fellow Stanford U., Kavli Inst. for Theoretical Physics, Santa Barbara; fellow physics dept. Harvard U., 2002—03; assist. prof. physics dept. U. Calif., Berkeley, Calif., 2003—. Fellow Radcliffe Inst., 2002—03. Author: A Covariant Entropy Conjecture, 1999, The Holographic Principle, 2002, Light Sheets and Bekenstein's Bound, 2003; co-author: Quantization of Four Form Fluxes and Dynamical Neutralization of the Cosmological Constant, 2000. Named one of Brilliant 10, Popular Sci. mag., 2002; recipient Nat. Sci. Found. award, 2004. Office: U Calif Physics Dept 366 LeConte Hall 7300 Berkeley CA 94720 Office Phone: 510-643-9195. Business E-Mail: bousso@lbl.gov.

BOUSTANY, CHARLES W., JR., congressman, surgeon; b. Lafayette, La., Feb. 21, 1956; s. Charles and Madlyn Boustany; m. Bridget Edwards, 1979; children: Erik, Ashley. BS, Univ. Southwestern La., 1978; MD, La. State Univ., New Orleans, 1982. Surgeon, pvt. practice, Lafayette, La., 1990—2004; mem. U.S. Ho. Reps., 109th Congress, 7th Dist. La., 2005—. Mem. Lafayette Parish Rep. exec. com., 1996—2001. Bd. dir. Greater Lafayette C. of C., 2001, v.p. govt. affairs, 2002; mem. tissue adv. bd. La. Organ Procurement Agy.; bd. dir. Lafayette Gen. Med. Ctr. Mem.: Lafayette Parish Med. Soc. (pres. 2000). Republican. Office: 1117 Longworth House Office Bldg Washington DC 20515-1807 Office Phone: 202-225-2031.*

BOUSUM, JULIE KAYE, art educator; b. Vinton, Iowa, July 31, 1956; d. Glenn E. and Darlene I. King; m. Curtis J. Bousum, July 14, 1980; children: Grant R., Gelene M., Brooke R. Bachelor, Iowa State U., 1978, Master, 2002. Art instr. Green Mt. HS, Green Mt., Iowa, 1978—87; English speech, drama tchrs. coach E. Marshall HS, LeGrand, Iowa, 1987—94; art instr. Marshalltown HS, Marshalltown, Iowa, 1994—. Speech coach, judge Iowa HS Speech Assn., Des Moines, 1979—2004; treas. Marshalltown Edn. Assn., Marshalltown, Iowa, 2004—05. Landlocked Dragon, 2000, Nature Inspired Vessel, 1999. Mem.: Marshalltown Edn. Ass. Avocations: painting, gardening, pottery. Office: Marshalltown HS 1602 S 2d Ave Marshalltown IA 50158 Office Phone: 641-754-1130.

BOUTELL, AMY LEE, writer; b. Eugene, Oreg., July 14, 1976; d. Lee Gilbert Boutell and Minerva Ann Nagel. BA summa cum laude, Columbia U., 1998; postgrad., U. Tex., 2003—. Publicity asst. Thames & Hudson (W.W. Norton & Co.), N.Y.C., 1998; editor Donnaud & Assocs. Lit. Agy., N.Y.C., 1999; prodr. Hearst Corp., N.Y.C., 2000—02. Author short stories, poetry. Alumna fellow, Barnard Coll., 2003, James A. Michene fellow, U. Tex., 2003. Mem.: Phi Beta Kappa. Home: 202 E 31st St Apt B Austin TX 78705-3096

BOUTIETTE, MARY ANTONIA, language educator; b. Mishawaka, Ind., May 16, 1943; d. Ralph and Antonetta Giannuzzi; m. Darwin Garth Boutiette, June 17, 1972; children: Damien, Andraea. BA, We. Mich. U., 1965; MA, U. Notre Dame, 1968. Spanish tchr. John Adams H.S., South Bend, Ind., 1965—72, Bloomington (Minn.) H.S., 1988—89; Spanish instr. North Hennepin C.C., Brooklyn Park, Minn., 1989—. Sec. Faculty Assn., South Bend. Mem. campaign coms. DFL Party, Thief River Falls, Minn., 1970—80. Named one of Young Profl. Women of Yr., Mishawaka (Ind.) Bus. Women. Mem.: Delta Kappa Gamma (pres. 1981—84). Home: 17088 Saddlewood Trail Minnetonka MN 55345 Office: North Hennepin Cmty Coll 7411 85th Ave N Brooklyn Park MN 55445 Office Phone: 763-424-0787. E-mail: mary.boutiette@nhcc.edu.

BOUTIETTE, VICKIE LYNN, elementary school educator, reading specialist; b. Valley City, N.D., Mar. 13, 1950; BS in Elem. Edn., Valley City State U., 1972; MS in Reading, Moorhead State U., 1997; postgrad., U. S.D., 1998—. 4th-5th grade tchr. Pillsbury Pub. Sch., 1973-74; 3rd grade tchr. West Fargo Pub. Schs., 1984-90, remedial reading tchr., elem. tchr., 1993-98, Reading Recovery tchr. leader, 1998—. Sunday sch. tchr., 1975—, ch. newsletter editor, 1993—; vol. U. Minn. Hosps. and Clinics, 1991-93. Recipient Nat. Educator Award Milken Family Found., 1998, Courage award N.D. Edn. Assn., 1994, Disting. Alumni award Minn. State U. Moorhead, 2002, Alumni Merit award Valley City State U., 2000; Christa McAuliffe fellowship, 2000; named N.D. Tchr. of Yr., 1998, West Fargo Tchr. of Yr. 1997-98. Mem. NEA, West Fargo Edn. Assn. (exec. bd. 1989-90, elem. chairperson 1988-89, pub. rels. chairperson 1988-90), N.D. Edn. Assn., Valley Reading Assn. (rec. sec. 1997—), N.D. Reading Assn., Phi Delta Kappa, Alpha Mu Gamma (pres. 1972). Home: 7103 64th Ave S Fargo ND 58104-5715 Office: Westside Elem Sch 945 7th Ave W West Fargo ND 58078-1429 Fax: 701-356-2119.

BOUTIN, PETER RUCKER, lawyer; b. San Francisco, Oct. 6, 1950; s. Frank J. and Charlotte (Downey) B.; m. Suzanne Jones, Aug. 31, 1974; children: Jennifer, Lisa, Kevin. AB, Stanford U., 1972; JD magna cum laude, Santa Clara U., 1975. Bar: Calif. 1975, U.S. Dist. Ct. (no., ea., so. and ctrl. dists.) Calif. 1976, U.S. Ct. Appeals (9th cir.) 1977, U.S. Supreme Ct. 1982. Assoc. Keesal, Young & Logan, Long Beach, Calif., 1975-78, ptnr., 1978-84, mng. ptnr. San Francisco office San Francisco, 1984—. Arbitrator San Francisco Superior Ct., 1989—, Nat. Assn. Securities Dealers, San Francisco, 1980—; mediator San Francisco Superior Ct., 1989—; early neutral evaluation panel U.S. Dist. Ct., 1993—. Co-author: Am. Arbitration Assn. Arbitrator Tng. Materials, 1992; bd. editors: Securities Arbitration Commentator. Mem. Bar Assn. San Francisco, Securities Industry Assn. Compliance and Legal Divsn., Stanford Buck/Cardinal Club. Office: Keesal Young & Logan 4 Embarcadero Ctr Ste 1500 San Francisco CA 94111-4122 Business E-Mail: peter.boutin@kyl.com.

BOUTIS, TOM, artist, painter, printmaker; b. N.Y.C., Aug. 25, 1922; s. Athanasios and Olga (Toskos) B.; m. Bertha Peters, Nov. 15, 1953; 1 child, Athanasios. BFA, Cooper Union U. Artist: one-person exhbns. include Drawings, Cooper Union, N.Y.C., 1953, Paintings: Zabriesky Gallery, N.Y.C., 1955, Am. Embassy, Rome, Italy, 1957, Area Gallery, N.Y.C., 1959, 60, Art Ctr. No. N.J., Tenafly, N.J., 1968; Decade on Paper, Landmark Gallery, N.Y.C., 1976, Paper on Paper, 1978, Cylinders, Columns, Circles and Color, 1979, Shadow Drawings, 1989, Monoprints, 1981, Painting, 1972, 75, 77, 81, Paintings and Monoprints, Maurice M. Pine Libr., Fairlawn, N.J., 1985, Works on Paper, Greek Embassy, 1989; 2-man exhbns. (with Alex Katz) Tanager Gallery, N.Y.C., 1958; group exhbns. include Greek Am. artists Noemata, Bklyn. Mus., 1977, Art Callender, Cooper Union Alumni Exhbn., N.Y.C., 1978, Landmark Gallery, N.Y.C., 1972, 82, Contemporary Drawings, Louise Ross Gallery, N.Y.C., 1984, Xmas Invitation, A.I.R., N.Y.C., 1985, Works on Paper, Ann Weber Gallery, Georgetown, Maine, 1987, Gallery Artists and Friends, Am. Acad. Arts & Letters, N.Y.C., 1988, 89, Shapolsky Gallery, N.Y.C., 1988, Arsenal Invitational, Arsenal Gallery, N.Y.C., 1989, Out of the 50's Snyder Fine Art, N.Y.C., 1993, Nat. Acad. Design, N.Y.C., 1992, 93, 95, 97, 99, 2001, 03, 05, Monhegan Island Artists, The Governor's Mansion, Augusta, Maine, 1996, Works on Paper, Bergen Mus., N.J., 1998, Greek Am. Artists Queens Mus., 1999, (drawing show) Nat. Acad., 2003; represented in public collections at NYU, Everson Mus., Syracuse, N.Y., Chem. Bank, N.Y.C., Prudential Bache, N.Y.C., Resource Mgmt., N.Y.C., St. Michel's Hosp., Newark, Calvin Klein Collection, N.Y.C., Calvin Klein Works on Paper, Weisbaden German, Nieully, France, N.Y. Hilton, Broad Nat. Bank of Newark and many others. Recipient scholarship to Skowhegan

(Maine) School of Painting, 1951, Fulbright to Rome, 1955-57, Mark Rothko Found. award, 1974; grantee: N.Y. Coun. on Arts, 1975 (painting), 1979 (graphics), Nat. Endowment for the Arts, 1976, Adolf and Esther Gottleib Found., 1983, The Rockefeller Found. Residency, Bellagio, Italy, 1989. Mem. NAD. Home: 162 E 82nd St New York NY 10028-1826 Office: 195 Chrystie St New York NY 10002 Office Phone: 212-529-7303. Personal E-mail: tboutis@aol.com.

BOUTROS, LINDA NELENE WILEY, medical/surgical nurse; b. New Orleans, Aug. 31, 1951; d. Robert Vernon and Marye Dell (Adcock) Wiley; m. Eddy Boutros, Dec. 23, 1972; children: Scott, Mark, Natalie. BS in Nursing, U. S.W. La., 1973. Cert. health care risk mgr. RN, relief charge, charge nurse, med./surgical flr. Bap. Hosp., Beaumont, Tex., 1973—76; RN, coord./supr. of nursing Kelsey Seybold Clinic, Missouri City, Tex., 1982-86; RN, head nurse S.W. Pediatric Ctr., Sugarland, Tex., 1986-87; RN, nursing supr. Westshore Hosp., Tampa, Fla., 1988-89; med.-surg. nurse Centurion Hosp., Carrollwood and Tampa, 1989-90, asst. head nurse med., 1990-91, relief supr., 1991, dir. surg. nursing svcs., 1992-93; nurse mgr. surg. floor, relief house supr. Univ. Cmty. Hosp. Carrollwood, Tampa, Fla., 1993-99, RN adminstrv. supr., 1999—. Mem. ANA, Fla. Nurses Assn., Fla. Soc. Health Care Risk Mgrs. Office: Univ Cmty Hosp Carrollwood 7171 N Dale Mabry Hwy Tampa FL 33614-2670 Office Phone: 813-558-8016. Personal E-mail: lwboutros@hotmail.com.

BOUTTE, VERONICA, humanities educator; b. France, Feb. 8, 1951; BA, Nat. U., Washington, 1990; MA, Am. U., 1993; PhD, U. South Africa, 1997. Attache French Embassy, Mexico, 1970—73, Luanda, Angola, 1973—75, Havana, 1975—76, New Delhi, 1976—77, New Orleans, 1979—81, Singapore, 1982—85, Washington, 1985—92; adj. prof. Strayer U., Washington, 1998—; dir. faculty devel. The Art Inst. of Washington, 0200—. Author: The Phenomenology of Companion. Avocations: yoga, ballet, Aikido. Home: 4201 Cathedral Ave NW Washington DC 20016-4901 Office: The Art Inst of Washington 1820 N Ft Myer Arlington VA 22209

BOUTWELL, ROSWELL KNIGHT, oncology educator; b. Madison, Wis., Nov. 24, 1917; s. Paul Winslow and Clara Gertrude (Brinkhoff) B.; m. Luella Mae Fairchild, Sept. 25, 1943; children— Paul F., Philip H., David K. BS in Chemistry, Beloit Coll., 1939; MS in Biochemistry, U. Wis., 1941, PhD, 1944; DSc, Beloit Coll., 1980. Instr. U. Wis., 1945-49, asst. prof., 1949-54, assoc. prof., 1954-67, prof. oncology med. ctr. Madison, 1967—. Vis. lectr. Inst. for Environ. Medicine, NYU, summer 1966; mem. cancer study group Wis. Regional Med. Program, 1967-70; mem. adv. com. on inst. research grants Am. Cancer Soc., 1967-74, chmn., 1972-74; mem. food protection com. NRC, 1971-75; mem. lung cancer segment Nat. Cancer Inst., 1971-75; mem. adv. com. on pathogenesis of cancer Am. Cancer Soc., 1960-63; mem. Nat. Cancer Adv. Bd., 1983-90; chief research Radiation Effects Research Found., Hiroshima, Japan, 1984-86; prof. emeritus, 1988—. Mem. editorial adv. bd. Cancer Research, 1959-64, assoc. editor, 1973-83; mem. editorial bd. Jpn. J. Cancer Res., 1985—; assoc. editor: Nutrition and Cancer, 1988—; mem. sci. adv. bd. Internat. Coun. for Coordinating Cancer Rsch., 1989-92, Dermigen, 1990—. Mem. Monona Grove Sch. Bd., 1952-54; bd. dirs. Madison Gen. Hosp. Found. Recipient Kenneth P. DuBois award Soc. Toxicology, 1998, medal of honor Am. Cancer Soc., 1998. Fellow AAAS, Am. Assn. Cancer Research (dir.), Am. Soc. Biol. Chemists (Clowes award). Office: U Wis Dept Oncology McArdle Lab 1400 University Ave Rm 1125 Madison WI 53706-1526 Office Phone: 608-262-5182. E-mail: rboutwell@msn.com.

BOUTWELL, WALLACE KENNETH, JR., management consultant; b. Newton, Miss., Jan. 7, 1939; s. W. Kenneth and Elizabeth (Wilson) B.; m. Jean Youngblood, Aug. 13, 1961; children: Jennifer, Jeffrey, Julie. BS, Miss. State U., 1961; MS, N.C. State U., 1963, PhD, 1965. Systems analyst Office of Sec. Def., 1965-68; assoc. prof. agrl. econs. U. Fla., 1969, dir. budgeting, 1970; dir. planning and budgeting State Univ. System Fla., 1970-73, vice chancellor, 1973-75; co-founder, pres. MGT Am., mgmt. cons., Tallahassee, 1975—2005. Co-founder, chmn. bd. Capital Health Plan (HMO), Tallahassee, 1979—; chmn. bd. Preferred Med. Mktg. Corp.; cons. to govt. and univs. Mem. Fla. Edn. Council, 1976-77, Fla. Council on Handicapped, 1983. Bd. dirs. United Way Big Bend, 1984-90, chmn. 1989; bd. dirs. Fla. Econ. Club, 1989-96; co-founder, bd. dirs. Tallahassee 21st Century Coun., 1993-95. Served to capt. U.S. Army, 1965-67. Recipient citation Fla. Bd. Regents, 1975, Leadership Tallahassee award, 2001, Ethics in Bus. award Tallahassee Rotary Club, 2003. Home: 3431 Cedar Lane Dr Tallahassee FL 32312-1207 Office: 2425 Torreya Dr Tallahassee FL 32303-4039

BOUVIER, MARSHALL ANDRE, lawyer; b. Jacksonville, Fla., Sept. 30, 1923; s. Marshall and Helen Marion B.; m. Zepha Windle, July 11, 1938; children: Michael A., Debra Bouvier Williams, Mark A., Marshall André III, Suzanne, John A. (dec.), Wendy Bouvier Clark, Jennifer Lynn. AB, Emory U., LLB, 1949. Bar: Ga. 1948, Nev. 1960. Commd. USN, 1949; naval aviator, judge advocate; ret., 1959; atty. State of Nevada, 1959-60; pvt. practice, Reno, 1960-82, 88—; dist. atty. County of Storey, Nev., 1982-88, spl. cons. to Nev. Dist. Atty., 1991-95; pres., CEO A.G.E. Corp., 1997—. Mem. Judge Advocates Assn., Am. Bd. Hypnotherapy, Ancient and Honorable Order Quiet Birdmen, Rotary, E Clampus Vitus, Phi Delta Phi, Sigma Chi.

BOUVIER, VIRGINIA MARIE, foreign language educator, researcher, writer; b. New Haven, Conn., Nov. 9, 1958; d. Edouard Simon Pierre and Jane Marguerite (Mansfield) B.; m. James Nathaniel Lyons, Oct. 7, 1989; 1 child, Maya Alexandra Bouvier-Lyons. BA in Latin Am. Studies, Wellesley Coll., 1980; MA in Spanish, U. S.C., 1984; PhD in Latin Am. Studies, U. Calif., Berkeley, 1995. Sr. assoc. Washington Office on Latin Am., 1982-89; grad. student instr. depts. history, ethnic studies, devel. studies, Native Am. studies U. Calif., Berkeley, 1992-93; editor, intern The Emma Goldman Papers, Berkeley, 1994-95; asst. prof. dept. Spanish and Portuguese U. Md., College Pk., 1995—. Cons. C.S. Fund, Freestone, Calif., 1986, Arca Found., Washington, 1986, Levi Strauss & Co., Levi Strauss Found., San Francisco, 1992-93, World Bank, Washington, 1997. Author: (book) Decline of the Dictator: Paraguay at a Crossroads, 1988, (monographs) Alliance or Compliance: Implications of the Chilean Experience, 1983, Conditions for Chile's Plebiscite on Pinochet, 1988. Mem., treas., pres. local chpt. Amnesty Internat., Wellesley, Mass., Columbia S.C. and Washington, 1978—; cons., mem. ednl. adv. bd. Culture for Peace Project, Mayor's Office, San Francisco, 1994; mem. Oxfam, 1996—; founder Ctr. for Young Children Fgn. Lang. Devel. Com., 1997. Fellow Nat. Hist. Publs. and Records Commn., 1994-95; Gen. Rsch. Bd. grantee U. Md., 1996, Dissertation grantee Cushwa Ctr., U. Notre Dame, 1994; recipient Grant-in-Aid award Recovering the U.S. Hispanic Literary Heritage Project, U. Houston, 1997. Mem. MLA, Am. Hist. Assn., Latin Am. Studies Assn., Conf. on Latin Am. History, Coordinating Coun. for Women in History, Assn. for Documentary Editing. Office: U Md 2203 Jimenez Hall College Park MD 20742-4800

BOUYOUCOS, JOHN VINTON, research and development company executive; b. Lansing, Mich., Nov. 9, 1926; s. George John and Delia (Bemis) B.; m. Stella Wright, Sept. 29, 1953; children: Anne Stephanie, Peter Johnson, Hope Nicola; m. Kristine Thuesen Hordon, May 26, 1984. Student, U. Mich., 1944; AB, Harvard U., 1949, S.M., 1951, PhD, 1953, Harvard Bus. Sch. Smaller Co. Mgmt. Program cert., 1976. Asst. dir. Harvard Acoustics Research Lab., Harvard U., 1955-59; mgr. hydroacoustics dept. Gen. Dynamics Electronics Div., Rochester, N.Y., 1959-71; pres., chief scientist Hydroacoustics Inc., Rochester, 1972—. Patentee in field. Pres., chmn. bd. Soc. Chamber Music, Rochester, 1977-96, chmn. bd. 1996-99, chmn. emeritus, 1999—; bd. dirs., vice chmn. Rochester Philharm. Orch., 1978-89, hon. bd. dirs., 1990—. Served with U.S. Navy, 1944-46. Recipient Rochester Patent Law Assn. Inventors award, 1973. Fellow IEEE, Acoustical Soc. Am. (v.p. 1970-71; disting. svc. citation 2000); mem. Soc. Exploration Geophysicists, Audio Engring. Soc., Inst. Noise Control Engrs. Clubs: Harvard Bus. Sch. Rochester (pres. 1984). Home: 11 Elmwood Hill Ln Rochester NY 14610-3445 Office: Hydroacoustics Inc PO Box 23447 Rochester NY 14692-3447 E-mail: bcos@sprintmail.com, hai@eznet.net.

BOVA, BENJAMIN WILLIAM, writer, editor; b. Phila., Nov. 8, 1932; s. Benjamin P. and Giove (Caporiccio) B.; m. Rosa Cucinotta, Nov. 28, 1953 (div. 1973); children: Michael Francis, Regina Marie; m. Barbara Ellen Berson, June 28, 1974. BS in Journalism, Temple U., 1954; MA in Communications, SUNY Albany, 1987; EdD, Calif. Coast U., 1996. Formerly newspaper reporter; mktg. mgr. Avco Everett Rsch. Lab.; formerly tchr. sci. fiction Harvard U.; formerly tchr. sci. fiction, dir. film courses Hayden Planetarium, N.Y.C.; editor Upper Darby (Pa.) News, 1954-56; tech. editor Project Vanguard, 1956-58; motion picture scriptwriter Phys. Sci. Study Com., Ednl. Svcs., Inc., Watertown, Mass., 1958-60; mgr. mktg. Avco Everett Rsch. Lab., Avco Corp., Everett, Mass., 1960-71; editor Analog Sci. Fiction-Sci. Fact mag. Conde Nast Pub. Co., N.Y.C., 1971-78; fiction editor Omni mag., N.Y.C., 1978-79, exec. editor, 1979-81, v.p., editorial dir., 1981-82. Past mem. panel Office Tech. Assessment, U.S. Congress; lectr. Nat. Geog. Soc., major govt. and corp. exec. groups, univs.; adv. bd. Post Coll.; bd. contbrs. USA Today; publ. Galaxy Online.com, 1999-2000. Author: (fiction) The Star Conquers, 1959, Star Watchman, 1964, The Weathermakers, 1967, Out of the Sun, 1968, The Dueling Machine, 1969, Escape!, 1969, Exiled From Earth, 1971; author: (with George Lucas) THX 1138, 1971; author: Flight of Exiles, 1972, As On a Darkling Plain, 1972, When the Sky Burned, 1972, Forward in Time, 1973; author: (with Gordon R. Dickson) Gremlins, Go Home!, 1974; author: End of Exile, 1975, The Starcrossed, 1975, City of Darkness, 1976, Millennium, 1976, The Multiple Man, 1976, Colony, 1978, Maxwell's Demons, 1978, Kinsman, 1979, The Exiles Trilogy, 1981, Voyagers, 1981, Test of Fire, 1982, The Winds of Altair, 1983, Escape Plus, 1984, Orion, 1984, The Astral Mirror, 1985, Privateers, 1985, Promethians, 1986, Voyagers II: The Alien Within, 1986, Battle Station, 1987, The Kinsman Saga, 1987, Vengeance of Orion, 1988, Peacekeepers, 1988, Cyberbooks, 1989, Voyagers III, Star Brothers, 1990, Orion in the Dying Time, 1990, Future Crime, 1990; author: (with Bill Pogue) The Trikon Deception, 1992; author: Mars, 1992; author: (with A.J. Austin) To Save the Sun, 1992; author: Triumph, 1993, Empire Builders, 1993, Challenges, 1993, Sam Gunn, Unlimited, 1993, Orion and The Conqueror, 1994, Death Dream, 1994; author: (with A.J. Austin) To Fear the Light, 1995; author: Orion Among the Stars, 1995, Brothers, 1996, Moonrise, 1997, Moonwar, 1998, Sam Gunn Forever, 1998, Twice Seven, 1998, Return to Mars, 1999, Venus, 2000, Jupiter, 2001, The Precipice, 2001, The Rock Rats, 2002, Saturn, 2003, Tales of the Grand Tour, 2004, The Silent War, 2004, Powersat, 2005, Mercury, 2005, (nonfiction) The Milky Way Galaxy, 1961, Giants of the Animal World, 1962, Reptiles Since the World Began, 1964, The Uses of Space, 1965, In Quest of Quasars, 1970, Planets, Life and LGM, 1970, The Fourth State of Matter, 1971 (Best Sci. Book award ALA, 1988), The Amazing Laser, 1972, The New Astronomies, 1972, Starflight and Other Improbabilities, 1973, Man Changes the Weather, 1973; author: (with Barbara Berson) Survival Guide for the Suddenly Single, 1974; author: The Weather Changes Man, 1974, Workshops in Space, 1974, Through Eyes of Wonder, 1975, Science: Who Needs It?, 1975, Notes to a Science Fiction Writer, 1975, Closeup: New Worlds, 1977, Viewpoint, 1977, The Seeds of Tomorrow, 1977, The High Road, 1981, Vision of the Future: The Art of Robert McCall, 1982, Assured Survival, 1984, Star Peace, 1986, Welcome to Moonbase!, 1987; author: (with Sheldon Glashow) Interactions, 1988; author: The Beauty of Light, 1988, First Contact, 1990, The Craft of Writing Science Fiction That Sells, 1994, Space Travel, 1997, Immortality, 1998, The Story of Light, 2001, Faint Echoes, Distant Stars, 2004. Recipient 6 Sci. Fiction Achievement awards for best profl. editor (Hugo), E.E. Smith Meml. award for imaginative fiction New Eng. Sci. Fiction Soc., 1974, Balrog award, 1983, Inkpot award, 1985, Disting. Alumnus award Temple U., 1982, Isaac Asimov Meml. award, 1996. Fellow AAAS, Brit. Interplanetary Soc.; mem. AIAA, Nat. Space Soc. (pres. 1982-88, pres. emeritus, chmn. bd. 1988-92), N.Y. Acad. Scis., Sci. Fiction Writers Am. (charter, pres. 1990-92), Planetary Soc., Nature Conservancy, Nat. Space Club, Explorers Club, Amateur Fencer's League Am.

BOVA, VINCENT ARTHUR, JR., lawyer, consultant, photographer; b. Pitts., Apr. 25, 1946; s. Vincent A. and Janie (Pope) Bova; m. Breda Murphy, Mar. 20, 1971; 1 child, Kate Murphy Bova. BA in Bus. Adminstrn., Alma (Mich.) Coll., 1968; MPA, Ohio State U., 1972; JD, Oklahoma City U., 1975. Bar: Okla. 1975, N.Mex 1976, U.S. Dist. Ct. N.Mex 1976, U.S. Tax Ct. 1976, U.S. Ct. Appeals (10th cir.) 1976, U.S. Supreme Ct. 1979. Mktg. and systems rep., computer systems divsn. RCA, 1968-70; rsch. analyst Rsch. Atlanta, 1972-73; assoc. Threet, Threet, Glass, King & Maxwell, 1976-78; ptnr. Lill & Bova, P.A., 1978-81; pvt. practice Albuquerque, 1981—. Past pres. Bare Bulls Investment, 1982, Fumilan Investment, 1983, Toastmasters; rsch. analyst urban affairs Ohio Dept. Urban Affairs, Columbus, 1971; panel mem. N.Mex Med. Rev. Commn., 1981—, N.Mex Legal/Dental/Osteopathic Podiatry Com., 1981—; v.p. Albuquerque Com. Fgn. Rels., 2001—, pres., bd. dirs.; co-owner Albuquerque Photography Gallery. Contbr. articles to profl. jours. Bd. dirs. Rio Grande Nature Ctr.; pres., v.p. spl. projects S.W. Arts and Crafts Festival, Albuquerque, 1986—89; pol. cons. Nov. Group; mem. N.Mex Estate Planning Coun., 1978—; sec.-treas., vice-chmn., pres. adv. bd. Salvation Army, 1987—; contbr. Ctr. Home Prevention Domestic Violence, 1984—85, Ronald McDonald House, 1984; past chmn. N.Mex Workers' Compensation Monthly; mem. advt. com. Supreme Ct. Panel; mem. Edn. Forum; moot ct. judge Albuquerque. With Air N.G., 1969—75. Named one of Oustanding Young Men of Am., 1975, 1976; recipient Pacesetters award, Ohio State U., 1972. Mem.: ABA, ATLA (advanced grad. Nat. Coll. Advocacy), Photog. Soc. Am. (pres. chpt.), Profl. Photography Assn., Internat. Credit Assn. (lectr.), Image Profls. S.W. (bd. dirs., print chmn. 1996—, pres., bd. dirs., Photography award 1996, Best of Show 2000, others), Sole Practitioners Assn., N.Mex Fin. Planning Assn., Albuquerque Bar Assn., Bus. Round Table, Nat. Assn. Social Security Claimants Reps. (past state chmn.), Internat. Assn. Fin. Planners, N.Mex Trial Lawyers Assn., Nat. Def. Lawyers Assn. (staff chmn. 1986), State Bar N.Mex (mem. med. legal panel, med.-dental podiatry legal panel, rep. probate, wills and trusts ann. report), N.Mex Bar Assn. (pres. small firm and solo sect.), Ct. Practice Inst. (advanced diplomate), Profl. Photographers Am. (assoc. 8 awards 1999), Toastmasters (past pres., v.p., edn. chmn., Able Toastmaster award), Ohio State U. Alumni Assn. N.Mex (pres.), Zia Scuba Club, Millionaires Tip Club, Enchanted Lens Camera Club, Albuquerque Knife and Fork (pres., v.p., sec.-treas., bd. dirs.), Inn of Ct., Sigma Tau Gamma (pres. Albuquerque com. fgn. rels.), Phi Alpha Delta. Democrat. Presbyterian. Avocations: flower gardening, photography - video and still, computers, investing, reading. Office: 5716 Osuna Rd NE Albuquerque NM 87109-2527 Office Phone: 505-881-5225.

BOVAIRD, BRENDAN PETER, lawyer; b. N.Y.C., Mar. 9, 1948; s. John Francis and Margaret Mary (Endrizzi) Bovaird; m. Carolyn Warren Boyle, Dec. 18, 1971; children: Anne Warren, Sarah Grant. BA, Fordham U., 1970; JD, U. Va., 1973. Bar: N.Y. 1974, DC 1980, Pa. 1983, U.S. Dist. Ct. (so. and ea. dists.) N.Y. 1974, U.S. Ct. Appeals (2d cir.) 1974. Atty. Dewey, Ballantine, Bushby, Palmer & Wood, N.Y.C., 1973—82; asst. gen. counsel Campbell Soup Co., Camden, NJ, 1982—89; sr. v.p., gen. counsel, sec. Orion Pictures Corp., N.Y.C., 1989—92; counsel, mem. exec. com. Wyeth-Ayerst Internat., Inc., St. Davids, Pa., 1992—95; pres. KDH, Inc., 1994—; v.p., gen. counsel UGI Corp., Valley Forge, Pa., 1995—2003, AmeriGas Propane, Inc., Valley Forge, 1995—2003; counsel Hunt & Ayres, LLP, Phila., 2004—. Bd. dirs. Phila. Shakespeare Festival, 2004—, Phila. Vol. Lawyers for the Arts, 2005—, Young Audiences of Ea. Pa., Inc., 2005—. Mem.: MPAA, The Athenaeum Phila., Motion Picture Export Assn. Am. (bd. dirs. 1990—92), Aircraft Owners and Pilots Assn., Phila. Country Club. Office: 1818 Market St Philadelphia PA 19103 Office Phone: 215-557-8500. Business E-Mail: bpbovaird@huntandayres.com.

BOVASSO, GREGORY BERNARD, psychology educator; b. N.Y.C., Dec. 3, 1960; s. Bernard and Lucy (Papazian) B. BA, Antioch Coll., 1982; PhD, CUNY, 1989. Sr. mkt. rsch. analyst Nations Bank, Dallas, 1990-91; vis. lectr. Baylor U., Waco, Tex., 1991-92; asst. prof. Del Mar Coll., Corpus Christi, Tex., 1993-97; fellow Johns Hopkins U., Balt., 1997—. Cons. Inst. for Cultural Studies, Chevy Chase, Md., 1989-90; com. mem. Nat. Inst. Drug Abuse, Bethesda, Md., 1993-94; mem. discipline task force Corpus Christi Ind. Sch. Dist., Corpus Christi, 1993, 97. Contbr. articles to profl. jours. Office: Del Mar Coll Corpus Christi TX 78404

BOVAY, HARRY ELMO, JR., retired engineering company executive; b. Big Rapids, Mich., Sept. 4, 1914; s. Harry E. and Addibelle (Bentley) B.; m. Sue Goldston, Feb. 1, 1977; children: Mark Benson, Susan Stone C.E., Cornell U., 1936. Jr. engring. aide U.S. C.E., 1936-37; jr. metal insp., project engr. Humble Oil & Refining Co., Baytown, Tex., 1937-45; cons. engr. Houston, 1946-62; pres. Bovay Engrs., Inc., Houston, 1962-73, chmn. bd., chief exec. officer, 1974-84. Owner Bovista Farms, Tenn. and Tex.; pres. Mid-South Telecommunications Co., Inc., 1987—; endowed chair Tex. A&M U. and Cornell U. Editor: Mechanical and Electrical Systems for Buildings Pres., Sam Houston Area council Boy Scouts Am., 1963-64, exec. com. South Central region, 1973-76, bd. dirs., 1975-79, v.p., 1980-81, pres., 1981-82, mem. nat. exec. bd., 1981-84, chmn. camping/outdoor com., 1983-85, chmn. nat. audit com., 1982-87, mem. nat. adv. coun., 1985-98; chmn. Houston Commn. Zoning, 1959-60; bd. dirs. Vis. Nurse Assn., Houston, 1970-75, Retina Rsch. Found., 1998—; active United Fund Houston and Harris County; mem. Houston Adv. Council Naval Affairs, 1959; mem. Tex. Water Resources Adv. Com., 1968-71; mem. adv. com. Coastal Engring. Lab., Tex. A&M U., 1969, also mem. adv. council for Pres.; mem. engring. adv. com. Miss. State U., 1974-77; mem. Alumni Council Cornell U. Coll. Engring.; bd. visitors McDonald Obs., 1985—; mem. demand subpanel Energy Research Adv. Bd., 1985-86; mem. adv. com. rsch. programs Tex. Higher Edn. Coordinating Bd., 1992-95. Recipient Silver Beaver award Boy Scouts Am., 1965, Silver Antelope, 1976, Silver Buffalo, 1986, Disting. Svc. award SAR, 1998, George Washington Svc. award Paul Carrington chpt. SAR, 1998; named Disting. Engr., Tex. Engring. Found.; Baden-Powell fellow, World Scouting Orgn.; camping area Bovay Ranch Sam Houston Area Coun. Boy Scouts Am. Fellow ASCE, ASHRAE (ASHRAE-ALCO award); mem. Nat. Soc. Profl. Engrs. (pres. 1976, Achievement award 1987), Tex. Soc. Profl. Engrs. (pres. 1967-68), Am. Inst. Cons. Engrs. (past pres Tex. chpt.), Houston Engring. and Sci. Soc. (past 2d v.p.), Am. Rd. Builders Assn. (exec. com.), Am. Concrete Inst., Am. Wood Preservers Assn., ASTM (councilor 1960-64), Forest Products Research Soc., Tex. Forest Products Mfrs. Assn., SAME (Toulmin medal), Pres.' Assn., Newcomen Soc. N.Am., Nat. Acad. Engring., Houston Livestock Show & Rodeo (life). Clubs: Houston, Kiwanis, Cosmos, Houston Country, Petroleum. Episcopalian. Office: 3355 W Alabama St Ste 1140 Houston TX 77098-1799

BOVE, ALFRED ANTHONY, medical educator; b. Phila., Apr. 28, 1938; s. Alfred Anthony and Adeline Amelia (DeRose) B.; m. Sandra Ann Seltzer, June 25, 1966; children: Jacqueline, Christopher, Andrew. BSEE, Drexel U., 1962; MD, Temple U., 1966, PhD, 1970. Diplomate Am. Bd. Internal Medicine, Am. Bd. Cardiology, Am. Bd. Undersea Hyperb Medicine. Med. intern Temple U. Hosp., Phila., 1966-67, med. resident, 1969-70, postdoctoral fellow, 1967-69, asst. prof. medicine, 1973-81, prof. medicine, 1986—2001, prof. emeritus, 2001—; postdoctoral fellow Mayo Clinic, Rochester, Minn., 1970-71, prof. medicine, 1981-86; chief of cardiology Temple U. Med. Sch., 1986—99, chief cardiology, 2005—, assoc. dean, practice plan affairs, 1999—2001. Author: Diving Medicine, 4th edit., 2004; co-author: Diving Medicine, 1990, Exercise Medicine, 1982; editor: Skin Diver mag., 1981—; editor-in-chief: cardiology website, 2002-; contbr. articles to profl. jours. Capt. USNR, 1971-73, 98, ret. Recipient Established Investigator award Am. Heart Assn., 1975, Paul Dudley White award Assn. Mil. Surgeons of the U.S., 1998, Disting. fellow award, ACC, 2002. Fellow ACP, Am. Coll. Cardiology (state gov. 1989-92); mem. Am. Physiologic Soc., IEEE, Undersea and Hyperbaric Med. Soc. (pres. 1983, bd. trustees 2002-, Craig Hoffman award 1988, Stover-Link award 1974). Roman Catholic. Avocations: scuba diving, marathon racing. Office: Temple U Med Ctr Cardiology Sect 3401 N Broad St Philadelphia PA 19140-4105 Office Phone: 215-707-3346. Business E-Mail: bovea@tuhs.temple.edu. E-mail: fred@scubamed.com.

BOVE, JOHN LOUIS, chemistry and environmental engineering educator, researcher; b. N.Y.C., Apr. 15, 1928; s. Frank and Bridget (Randazzo) B.; m. June Althea Burns, Dec. 28, 1957; children: Adele, Catherine. BA in Chemistry, Bucknell U., 1949, MSA. in Chemistry, 1954; PhD in Chemistry, Case Western Res. U., 1973. Asst. prof. chemistry Cooper Union, N.Y.C., 1958-67, prof. chemistry and environ. engring., chmn. dept. chemistry, 1970—, dir. environ. program, 1970—; v.p. Cooper Union Research Found., 1974-80. Dep. dir. bur. tech. services N.Y.C. Air Resources, 1967-70; dir. Mid-Atlantic Consortium Air Pollution, 1970-76 Contbr. chpts., articles to profl. publs. Served with M.C. U.S. Army, 1950. Recipient Schweinburg Schweinburg Found., 1964; fellow Dow Chem. Co., 1953—; grantee NSF, 1960— Republican. Home: 125 Richards Rd Ridgewood NJ 07450-1115 Office: The Cooper Union Cooper Union 51 Astor Pl New York NY 10003-7132 E-mail: bove@cooper.edu.

BOVE, PATRICE MAGEE, elementary school educator; b. Fort Madison, Iowa, Apr. 29, 1946; d. Claude and Susie T. Magee; m. Roger E. Bove, Aug. 6, 1983; 1 child, Jonna. MusB, U. Iowa, 1968; M of Music Edn., Temple U., 1976. Tchr. elem. instrumental music Birmingham (Mich.) Sch. Dist., 1968-69; tchr. elem. music T-E Sch. Dist., Berwyn, Pa., 1969—. Co-author: Philadelphia Orchestra Student Concert Books, 1994—; contbr. MENC (Strategies for Teaching Elementary Music), 1996. Educator, writer edn. adv. com. Phila. Orch., 1994—; accompanist chorus, Wayne, Pa., 1995, Suzuki Concerts, Immaculata, Pa., 1994-97. Mem. AAUW, Nat. Assn. Music Therapy, Music Tchrs. Assn., Gordon Inst. Music Learning, Suzuki, Kodaly, Orff, Pa. Music Edn. Assn. (dist. 12 co-host elem. songfest 1995), Music Educators Nat. Conf. Avocations: reading, computers, cooking. Home: 325 Holly Rd West Chester PA 19380-4614

BOVEE, EUGENE CLEVELAND, protozoologist, emeritus educator; b. Sioux City, Iowa, Apr. 1, 1915; s. Earl Eugene and Martha Nora (Johnson) B.; m. Maezene B. Wamsley, May 18, 1942 (div. 1967); m. Elizabeth A. Moss, May 9, 1968; children— Frances, Gregory, Matthew; stepchildren— Lynne, Lisa. BA, U. No. Iowa, 1939; MS, U. Iowa, 1948; PhD, UCLA, 1950. Instr. zoology Iowa U., 1940-41; biology tchr. Greene (Iowa) H.S., Iowa, 1941-42; instr. biology U. No. Iowa, 1946-48; journalist Iowa Recorder, Greene, 1945—46; instr. zoology UCLA, 1948-50, research zoologist, 1962-68; asst. prof. biology Calif. Poly. U., 1950-52; assoc. prof. zoology, dept. chmn. N.D. State U., 1952-53; asst. prof. biology U. Houston, 1953-55; assoc. prof. U. Fla., 1955-62; prof. physiology and cell biology U. Kans., Lawrence, 1968-85, prof. emeritus, 1985—. Co-owner arts and crafts bus., 1985-96; cons. Am. Type Culture Collection, 1980-82, W.C. Brown, Pub., 1978-82. Author: (books of poems) Give Back My Body, 1994, To Tartarus and Back, 1999, Sette Bellos, 2000, A Cinquain Zoo, 2000, Old Olympian Games, 2000, Pundamonium, 2001, Biblical Limericks, 2002, Sonnets for Various Reasons, 2002, Historical Limericks, 2003, The Common Gene Pool, 2003; co-author: Historical Limericks II, 2004, Selected Poems, 2004, Various Poems, 2004, Double-Dactyl Fun, 2004; co-editor, co-author: An Illustrated Guide to the Protozoa, 1985; co-author: How to Know the Protozoa, 2d edit., 1979; Microscop. Anat. Invert., Vol. 1, 1991; editor Kans. Sci. Bull., 1974-79; contbr. chpts. to books, articles to sci. jours.; contbr. to small press lit. jours. 1st lt. MIS, U.S. Army, WWII. Research grantee NIH, 1957-62, NSF, 1970-74, NIH, NSF and ONR, 1962-68, Kans. Fed. Water Resources Inst. and U. Kans., 1968-81; recipient Disting. Alumni award U. No. Iowa, 1980. Fellow Iowa Acad. Sci.; mem. Soc. Protozoologists (hon., pres. 1979-80, v.p. 1970-71, treas. 1972-78, exec. com. 1970-81), Am. Microscop Soc. (mem.-at-large exec. com. 1959-62), Western Soc. Naturalists, Kans. Acad. Sci. (life mem., pres. 1979-80, exec. com. 1975-81), Acad. Am. Poets, Poetry Soc. Am., Kans. State Poetry Soc., Kans. Authors Club (Writing Achievement award 1996), Nat. Woodcarvers Assn., United Amateur Press Assn. Am., Sigma Xi. Home: 808 Mississippi St Lawrence KS 66044-2659

BOVEN, DOUGLAS GEORGE, lawyer; b. Holland, Mich., Aug. 11, 1943; BSE, U. Mich., 1966, JD, 1969. Bar: Calif. 1970. Ptnr. Reed Smith LLP, San Francisco, 1989—. Arbitrator Fed. and Superior Ct. Panel of Arbitrators, 1980—; panelist Superior Ct. Early Settlement Program, 1987-. Mem. ABA (mem. bus. bankruptcy, Chpt. 11 and secured creditors coms.), Am. Bankruptcy Inst., Comml. Law League Am., State Bar Calif. (insolvency law and real estate sects.), Alameda County Bar Assn., Sonoma County Bar Assn., Bay Area Bankruptcy Forum, Bar Assn. San Francisco (comml. law and bankruptcy sect., mem. arbitrator fee disputes com. 1973—), Tau Beta Pi. Office: Reed Smith LLP Two Embarcadero Ctr Ste 2000 San Francisco CA 94111 Office Phone: 415-659-5652. Business E-Mail: dboven@reedsmith.com.

BOVENDER, JACK OLIVER, JR., hospital management company executive; b. Winston Salem, N.C., Aug. 16, 1945; s. Jack Oliver Sr. and Eva Louise (Westmoreland) B.; m. Barbara Ann Tuttle; 1 child, Richard Spencer. AB, Duke U., 1967, MHA, 1969. Asst. adminstr. Community Gen. Hosp., Thomasville, N.C., 1972-75; assoc. adminstr. West Fla. Regional Med. Ctr., Pensacola, 1975-77; adminstr. Largo Med. Ctr., Largo, Fla., 1977-80, West Fla. Regional Med. Ctr., Pensacola, 1980-85; div. v.p. Hosp. Corp. Am., Atlanta, 1985-87, pres., group ops. Nashville, 1987-91; sr. v.p., operations Hospital Corp. of America, Nashville, exec. v.p., 1992—94, pres., 1997—2001, COO, 1997—2001, chmn., CEO, 2002—. Mem. editorial bd. Jour. of Health Adminstrn. Edn., Washington, 1987—, Health Adminstrn. Press, Ann Arbor, Mich., 1988—. Bd. dirs. United Way, Pensacola, 1984; sr. warden and vestryman Christ Ch., Pensacola, 1982-85. Lt. USN, 1969-72. Fellow Am. Coll. Healthcare Execs.; mem. Pensacola C. of C. (bd. dirs. 1984), Leadership Nashville, Duke U. Hosp. and Health Adminstrn. Alumni Coun. (pres. 1986-87), Duke U. Gen. Alumni Bd., Rotary (Largo, Pensacola). Republican. Episcopalian. Avocations: reading, sports. Office: HCA Health SVCS Virginia 1602 Skipwith Rd Richmond VA 23229-5205 also: Columbia/HCA 1 Park Plaza Nashville TN 37203-6527

BOVENSCHEN, WAYNE ERIC, music educator; b. Detroit, June 3, 1962; s. Ruth Rose Bovenschen; m. Tricia Ann Bailey, June 2, 1990; children: Bailey Michelle, Collin Robert, Brendan Keith. MusM in Performance, Mich. State U., East Lansing, 1988. Assoc. prof. of music Okla. State U., Stillwater, 1987—. Percussion coord. Black Gold Drum and Bugle Corps, Tulsa, Okla., 1990—93. Musician: (marching percussion ensemble arranger) Sergei Prokofiev Concerto for Piano No. 3 (arrangement) (Percussive Arts Soc. Internat. Conv. Marching Percussion Competition, 2001). Mem.: Percussive Arts Soc. (okla. chpt. pres. 2004—). R-Conservative. Office: Oklahoma State University 132 Seretean Ctr Stillwater OK 74078-4077 Office Phone: 405-744-8983.

BOVICH, EDWARD HUGH, manufacturing executive; b. N.Y.C., Sept. 20, 1924; s. Edward Francis and Beatrice Catherine (Gilmartin) Bovich; m. Michele Marie Denaro, June 6, 1953; children: Mary Beatrice Hotto, Patricia Marie Caserio, Edward Philip, John Patrick. BA in Philosophy, St. Basil's Coll. and Sem., Stamford, Conn., 1949; MA in Theology summa cum laude, Sacred Heart Major Sem., Detroit, 1999. Instr. Fordham U., 1951; spl. agt. FBI, various locations, 1951—57; dist. dir. Nat. Safety Coun., Pitts., 1957—59; exec. dir. Bd. Commerce, Wyandotte, Mich., 1959—62; dir. mktg. Wyandotte Chems. Corp. (B.A.S.F.), 1962—65, gen. mgr. cement divsn., 1966—70; pres. Wyandotte Cement Inc., 1971—77, chmn., 1977—; pres. Ind. Cement Corp., Kingston, NY, 1977—79, dir., 1978—. Mem. adv. bd. Am. Mut. Ins. Co., 1973—; spl. rep. Pa. Pres.'s Com. for Traffic Safety, 1958; chmn. emeritus Oakwood Healthcare. Author: The Art of Fundraising: What Every Healthcare Trustee Needs to Know, 1994. Trustee, chmn. Nat. Found. for Philanthropy; trustee Rotary Club Dearborn, 2000—03; trustee, vice chmn. Soc. Former Spl. Agts. of FBI Found., Quantico, Va.; chmn. The Centurions, Dearborn; pres. Sacred Heart Sch. Bd., Dearborn, 1967—68, Sacred Heart Coun., 1969—70; chmn. Chem. Industry United Found., 1969—72. Midshipman U.S. Merchant Marines USNR, 1944—46. Recipient Outstanding Lay Alumnus award, Sacred Heart Major Sem., 2001. Mem.: Soc. Former FBI Agts. (past chmn. Mich. chpt.), Dearborn Country Club (life). Republican. Roman Catholic. Home: One Morley North Pl Dearborn MI 48124

BOVIN, DENIS ALAN, finance company executive; b. N.Y.C., Nov. 4, 1947; s. Henry and Ruth (Klein) B.; m. Terry Schneider, Dec. 8, 1973; children: Michelle, Andrew. BS, MIT, 1969; MBA, Harvard U., 1971. Assoc. Salomon Bros. Inc., N.Y.C., 1971-76, v.p., 1976-81, mng. dir., 1981-92; vice chmn. Bear Stearns & Co., Inc., N.Y.C., 1992—. Vice chmn. Bus. Execs. for Nat. Security, Intrepid Mus.; bd. dirs. Ctr. for Strategic and Budgetary Analysis. Mem. exec. com. MIT Corp.; mem. Coun. on Fgn. Rels., Inc.; trustee MIT. Recipient Dept. Def. medal for Disting. Pub. Svc., 1995; named Outstanding Investment Banker, Instl. Investor Mag., N.Y.C., 1985. Mem. N.Y. Soc. for Security Analysts, Investment Assn. N.J., Bus. Exec. for Nat. Security (bd. dirs.), Bear Stearns (bd. dirs.), The Bisys Group (bd. dirs.), MIT Alumni Assn. N.Y. Office: Bear Stearns & Co 383 Madison Ave New York NY 10179- E-mail: dbovin@bear.com.

BOVING, THOMAS B., hydrologist, educator; b. Munster, Germany, Jan. 4, 1964; arrived in U.S., 1999; s. Bernhard Boving and Maria; m. Kirstina Aldona Kelertas, July 21, 1990; children: Indra, Alek, Aidan. Degree in geology, Eberhard-Karls U., 1993; PhD in Hydrology and Water Resources Mgmt., U. Ariz., 1995. Environ. hydrologist II BGT, Stuttgart, Germany, 1993—99; rsch. asst. U. Ariz., Tucson, 1996—99; prof. hydrology U. R.I., Kingston, 1999—. Mem. directorial bd. CUAHSI, Washington, 2001—04. Assoc. editor: Vadose Zone Jour., 2004—; contbr. articles to profl. jours. Mem.: Am. Geol. Soc., Am. Chem. Soc. Achievements include patents for wood-filters for removing toxic compounds from water. Office: U RI Woodward Hall Rm 315 Kingston RI 02881

BOW, STEPHEN TYLER, JR., management consultant; b. Bow, Ky., Oct. 20, 1931; s. Stephen Tyler Sr. and Mary L. (King) B.; m. Kathy O'Connor, July, 1982; children: Jerry, Jon; children by previous marriage: Sandra Bow Morris, Deborah Bow Goodin, Carol, Clara. BA in Sociology, Berea (Ky.) Coll., 1953; grad. exec. program bus. adminstrn., Columbia U., 1976. CLU. With Met. Life Ins. Co., 1953-74, 76-89; agt. Lexington, Ky., 1953-55; sales mgr. Birmingham, Ala., 1955-58; field tng. cons., 1958-59; territorial field supr., 1959-60; dist. sales mgr. Frankfort, 1960-64, Lexington, 1964-66; exec. asst. field tng. N.Y.C., 1966-67; regional sales mgr. North Jersey, 1967-72; agy. v.p., officer-in-charge Can. hdqrs., 1972-74; exec. v.p., chmn., chief exec. officer Capital Holding Corp., Louisville, 1974-76; officer-in-charge Midwestern hdqrs. Met. Life Ins. Co., Dayton, 1976-83, sr. v.p., officer-in-charge Western Hdqrs., 1983-89; chmn., CEO Southeastern Group, Inc., Louisville, 1993-94; pres., CEO Anthem Life of Ind., Indpls., 1993-95; chmn., CEO Anthem Life Ins. Cos., 1995-96; exec. v.p. Assoc. Ins. Cos., Inc., Indpls., 1993-96; chmn. Acordia of San Francisco, 1993-96; pres., CEO Delta Dental Ky., Louisville, 1989-94, Blue Cross and Blue Shield Ky., Louisville, 1989-93; vice chmn. DeHayes Group, 1996—; pres. Steve Bow and Assocs., Inc., 1996—; chmn. Victory Tech., Inc., 1998—. Past chmn. Dayton Power and Light Audit Com. Past bd. dirs. San Francisco Visitors and Conv. Bur., 1985-87, Ind. Coll. of No. Calif., Bay Area Coun., Lindsey Wilson Coll.; bd. dirs. Bay Area Boy Scouts Am., Bay Area Council, U. San Francisco; mem. adv. bd. Hugh O'Brian Youth Found.; bd. dirs. Calif. Legis. Adv. Commn. on Life and Health Ins., Metro United Way, Ky. Health Care Access Found., Greater Louisville Econ. Devel. Coun., Leadership Ky., Greater Louisville Fund for the Arts; mem. corp. council San Francisco UN Assn.; mem. bd. dirs. Ky. Home Mut., Ky. Forward, Asian Bus. League, McLaren Coll. of Bus.; past mem. San Francisco Pvt. Industry Council; past chmn. United Negro Coll. Fund of San Francisco, 1985-86; mem. exec. com. bd. dirs., v.p. county ops. United Way of San Francisco Bay Area, 1985-87; vol. chmn. U.S. Savs. Bond Campaign, Bay Area, 1987; trustee Ky. Ind. Coll. Fund, Berea Coll.; bd. dirs. Boy Scouts Am., My Old Ky. Home Coun. Recipient Outstanding Sales Mgmt. award N.Y. Sales Congress, 1972, Frederick D. Patterson award United Negro Coll. Fund San Francisco, 1986, Outstanding County Ops. Vol. award United Way of Bay Area, 1987, Bus. Appreciation award Jeffersontown, Ky. C. of C., 1993, Pres.'s award, 1993, Leadership award Internat. Women's Forum, Washington, 1993; named Citizen of Yr. Wright State U. Med. Sch., Dayton, 1982. Mem. Nat. Assn. Life Underwriters, Gen. Agts. and Mgrs. Assn., Calif. Bus. Roundtable, Nat. Assn. Corp. Dirs. (founder, former pres.), Calif. C. of C. (bd. dirs.), Ky. C. of C., Ky. Home Life Exec. Com., Am. Cancer Soc. Clubs: Lincoln of Northern Calif. Republican. Methodist. Avocations: golf, painting, reading. Home: PO Box 675905 Rancho Santa Fe CA 92067 Personal E-mail: stevebow@cox.net. *We achieve goals by thinking positively and focusing on objectives, not on problems. We achieve economic success by concentrating on serving our fellow man and finding new ways to satisfy his needs. We achieve personal satisfaction by doing more than is expected of us, and exceeding even our own expectations through determination and persistency. We achieve happiness by becoming so interested and absorbed in our work that we forget selfish, petty matters. We achieve a successful life by living each day as if our entire life is to be judged by that day alone.*

BOWA, LAWRENCE ROBERT (LARRY BOWA), former professional baseball manager; b. Sacramento, Dec. 6, 1945; m. Sheena Bowa; 1 child, Tori. Student, Sacramento City Coll. Player various minor league teams, 1966-69; player with Phila. Phillies, Nat. League, 1970-81, Chgo. Cubs, Nat. League, 1982-85, N.Y. Mets, 1985; mgr. Las Vegas Stars, 1986, San Diego Padres, 1986-88, Phila. Phillies, 2002—04. Player All-Star games, 1974-76, 78, 79, World Series, 1980. Holder major league record for highest lifetime fielding percentage for shortstop; winner Gold Glove, 1972, 78.

BOWDEN, AISHA L, elementary school educator; d. Charles and Eleanor Bowden. BFA, Howard U. Elementary Music DC Pub. Schools. Music tchr. Thomson Elem. Sch., Washington, 2000—. Recipient Key Communicator award, Arts for Every Student Program, 2003; Fulbright Groups Study Abroad grant, Fulbright, 2001. Mem.: Ubiquity, Inc. (life). Christian. Avocation: travel. Office: Thomson Elementary Sch 215 G St NE Washington DC 20002 Office Phone: 202-698-4533. Office Fax: 202-698-4533.

BOWDEN, DAVID, conductor; b. Winston-Salem, NC, Nov. 22, 1953; s. Robert Marshall and Phyllis Bowden; m. Donna Sjaardema, Aug. 17, 1974; children: Kirsten Ruth, Kristi Elisabeth. MusB, Wheaton Coll.; MusM, MusD, Ind. U. Prof. music Huntington (Ind.) Coll., 1976—83; assoc. instr. music Ind. U., Bloomington, 1983—90; dir. worship and music Evang. Cmty. Ch., Bloomington, Ind., 1984—2004; music dir., condr. Columbus Ind. Philharm., 1987—, Terre Haute (Ind.) Symphony Orch., 1997—, Carmel (Ind.) Symphony Orch., 1999—. Music dir., condr. (CD recording) Dupre Complete Music for Organ and Orchestra. Pres. Bloomington (Ind.) Pops, 1990—95; dir. WFIU, local NPR Sta., Bloomington; judge, std. awards panel ASCAP, NYC, 1999—2001. Recipient award for Adventuresome Programming, ASCAP, 1989—96; fellow, Ind. U., 1984; scholar, 1977—78, 1983—85; Nat. Merit scholar, Wheaton Coll., 1972—76. Mem.: Condrs. Guild (nat. conf. spkr. 1995—, chair new music project), Am. Symphony Orch. League (nat. conf. spkr. 1992—96), Pi Kappa Lambda. Achievements include broadcasts of orchestral perfomances on NPR Perfromance Today and PRI's Pipedreams. Avocations: running, travel, reading, basketball. Office: Columbus Ind Philharm 315 Franklin St Columbus IN 47201

BOWDEN, DEREK THOMAS, orchestra director, educator; b. Salisbury, Md., Sept. 1, 1976; s. Ervin Thomas and Donna Kay Bowden; m. Robin Radford; children: Christopher Douglas, Claire Draper-Hamilton. BS, Salisbury (Md.) U., 2000; MA, U. Del., 2004. Quality control analyst Dewberry & Davis, LLC, Fairfax, Va., 2000—01; instr. U. Del., Newark, 2001—04; mng. dir., instr. Salisbury U., 2001—. Mem. NASM accreditation com. music dept. Salisbury U., 2004—05, mem. cultural affairs com., 2004—05, active Md. Summer Ctr. for the Arts, 2001—03. Mem.: Assn. Am. Geographers, Phi Mu Epsilon. Home: 5037 Holland Rd New Church VA 23415 Office: Salisbury U 1101 Camden Ave Salisbury MD 21801

BOWDEN, DOUGLAS MCHOSE, neuropsychiatric scientist, educator, research center administrator; b. Durham, N.C., Apr. 7, 1937; s. Daniel Joseph and Charlotte (McHose) B.; m. Vivian Lee Bowden, 1966; children: Dana, Julie, Carlos, Luis. BA, Harvard U., 1959; MD, Stanford U., 1965. Staff assoc. NIMH, Bethesda, Md., 1966-69; asst. prof. psychiatry U. Wash., Seattle, 1969-73, assoc. prof. dept. psychiatry & behavioral scis., 1973-79, prof. psychiatry & behavioral scis., 1979—; core staff sci. Nat. Primate Rsch. Ctr., U. Wash., 1969—; from asst. dir. to assoc. dir. Regional Primate Rsch. Ctr., U. Wash., 1977-88, dir., 1988-94. Adj. assoc. prof. pharmacology U. Wash., 1975-79, adj. prof. pharmacology, 1979-88; rsch. fellow Japan Soc. Promotion of Sci., Japan Assn. Animal Sci., Tokyo, Tsukuba, Inuyama/Kyoto, Japan, 1989. Author: Neuronames (c) Neuroanatomical Nomenclature, 1992; editor: Aging in Nonhuman Primates, 1979; translator Traumatic Aphasia, its Syndromes, Psychology and Treatment, 1970, Primate Models of Human Neurogenic Disorders, 1976; co-author: BrainInfo website, 2001-. Surgeon USPHS, 1966-69. Fellow Gerontol. Soc. Am.; mem. Am. Soc. Primatologists, Soc. Neurosci., Gerontol. Soc., Internat. Primatological Soc. Office: U Wash Natl Primate Rsch Ct Box 357330 1705 NE Pacific St Seattle WA 98195-7330 E-mail: dmbowden@u.washington.edu.

BOWDEN, HENRY LUMPKIN, JR., lawyer; b. Atlanta, Aug. 2, 1949; s. Henry Lumpkin and Ellen Marian (Fleming) B.; m. Roberta Jeanne Johnson, June 30, 1973; children: Caroline Bruton, Henry Lumpkin III. BA, U. Va., 1971; JD, Emory U., 1974. Bar: Ga. 1974. Law clk. for Hon. Griffin B. Bell U.S. Ct. Appeals (5th cir.), Atlanta, 1974-75; ptnr. King & Spalding, Atlanta, 1975-95; prin. Bowden Law Firm, P.C., Atlanta, 1995—. Trustee Atlanta Ballet, Inc., 1976-85, chmn., 1983-84; trustee Emory U., Atlanta, 1986—; trustee Hist. Oakland Found., Inc., Atlanta, 1987-95, chmn. 1992-95; trustee Westminster Schs., Atlanta, 1995-2000. Fellow Am. Coll. Trust and Estate Counsel (state chair 1991-96), Am. Bar Found.; mem. ABA, State Bar Ga. (chair fiduciary sect. 1990-91), Atlanta Bar Assn., Lawyers Club Atlanta, Piedmont Driving Club (dir. 1996-99), Capital City Club, Nine O'Clocks (pres. 1977-78), Farmington Country Club, Gridiron Secret Soc., Homosassa Fishing Club, The Ten, Phi Beta Kappa, Omicron Delta Kappa, Phi Delta Theta. Methodist. Home: 2542 Habersham Rd NW Atlanta GA 30305-3566 Office: 191 Peachtree St NE Ste 849 Atlanta GA 30303-1741 E-mail: henrybowdenjr@bowdenlaw.com.

BOWDEN, HENRY WARNER, religion educator; b. Memphis, Apr. 1, 1939; s. Warner Hill and Jeannette Evelyn (Winn) B.; m. Karin Violet Svensson, June 9, 1962 (div. Aug. 1989); children: Robin Warner, Annika Hillery; m. Michele Clare Cairns, May 1997. AB magna cum laude, Baylor U., 1961; MA, Princeton U., 1964, PhD, 1966. Instr. faculty of arts and scis. Douglass Coll., Rutgers U., 1964-67, asst. prof., 1967-71, asst. dean acad. affairs, 1969-72, assoc. prof., 1971-79, prof., 1979—. Editor religion books Greenwood Press, 1979—; cons. Funk & Wagnells Revised Ency., 1981—83; cons., author World Book Ency., 1984—94. Author: Church History in the Age of Science: Historiographic Patterns in the United States, 1876-1918, 1971, Church History in an Age of Uncertainty: Historiographical Patterns in the United States, 1906-1990, 1991, American Indians and Christian Missions: Studies in Cultural Conflict, 1981, Dictionary of American Religious Biography, 1977, 2d edit., 1993; author, consulting editor: American National Biography; editor: Religion in America, 1970, Indian Dialogues, 1980, A Century of Church History: The Legacy of Philip Schaff, 1988, Church History: A Centennial Collection of Landmark Studies, 1988; contbr. numerous articles to profl. jours.; assoc. editor Am. Nat. Bibliography, 1989-99. Bd. dirs. Historical Soc. Episcopal Ch., 1999—. Honors fellowship Harvard U. summer session, 1960; religion fellow Princeton U., 1961-62, Roothbert fellow, 1962-64, Lilly Found. fellow, 1964-65, Rutgers Rsch. Coun. fellowship, 1969-70; Rutgers Rsch. Coun. summer grantee, 1967. Mem. Am. Soc. of Ch. History (pres. 1984, exec. sec. 1993-2004), Am. Cath. Hist. Assn., Hist. Soc. of Episcopal Ch. (bd. dirs. 1999-2005). Democrat. Episcopalian. Office: Religion Dept Rutgers Univ New Brunswick NJ 08903 E-mail: bowden-06@comcast.net.

BOWDEN, HOWARD KENT, accountant; b. New Bern, NC, 1955; s. Paul Franklin and Virginia Belle Bowden; m. Laiad Jitrak; 1 child, Kirk Adam. BSS in Acctg. and Math. summa cum laude, Campbell U., 1976. CPA Va., NC. Staff acct. Arthur Andersen & Co., Greensboro, N.C., 1976-78; mgr. McGladrey & Pullen, Fayetteville, N.C., 1978-85; assoc. prin. Thompson, Greenspon & Co., P.C., Fairfax, Va., 1985-91; sr. audit mgr. U.S. Gen. Acctg. Office, Washington, 1991-94, asst. dir., 1994—. Treas. Vander Area Crime Watch, Fayetteville, 1980. Mem. AICPA, Va. Soc. CPAs (chmn. mems. in industry and govt. com. 1993-95, chmn. acctg. and auditing procedures com. 1990-92, Chpt. Pres.'s award 1989-90, Outstanding Mem. in Bus., Industry, and Govt. award 1995-96, chpt. pres. award, 1997-98), N.C. Assn. CPAs, Inst. Mgmt. Accts. (coord. tax symposium 1982, bd. dirs. 1978-84), Assn. Cert. Fraud Examiners (cert.), Assn. Govt. Accts. (cert. govt. fin. mgr.), Lions (bd. dirs. Fairfax club 1986-90, bd. dirs. Fayetteville club 1982-85), Phi Beta Lambda, Phi Kappa Phi. Presbyterian. Avocations: baseball, tennis, softball, other sports. Home: 4337 Farm House Ln Fairfax VA 22032-1613

BOWDEN, JESSE EARLE, editor, cartoonist, journalist, educator; b. Altha, Fla., Sept. 12, 1928; s. Jesse Walden and Earlene (Rackley) B.; m. Mary Louise Clark, Feb. 4, 1951; children: Steven Earle, Randall Clark. BS in Journalism and Polit. Sci, Fla. State U., 1951; DHL, U. West Fla., 1985. Reporter, columnist Panama City (Fla.) News-Herald, 1950; sports editor Pensacola (Fla.) News-Jour., 1953-57, news editor, 1957-65, editl. page editor, 1965-66, editl. cartoonist, 1965—, editor-in-chief, 1966-97, v.p., editor, 1969-97, editor emeritus, 1998—; prof. journalist U. West Fla.; charter mem., chmn. Pensacola Hist. Commn., 1967-2001; chmn. Gulf Islands Nat. Seashore Adv. Com., 1990-93; pres. U. West Fla. Found., 1977-79, Pensacola Hist. Soc., 1978-86. Pres. West Fla. Hist. Preservation, Inc., U. West Fla., 2001—. Author: Always the Rivers Flow, 1979, Fla. Classic edit., 2002, Iron Horse in the Pinelands, 1982, Pensacola: Florida's First Place City, 1989, The Write Way, 1990, When You Reach September, 1990, Fla. Classic edit., 2005, Gulf Islands: The Sands of All Time, 1994, Earle Bowden: Drawing from an Editor's Life, 1996, Look and Tremble: A Novel of West Florida, 2000, Texas Desperado in Florida: The Capture of John Wesley Hardin in Pensacola, 1877, 2002, Embrace an Autumnal Heart, 2003; editor Emerald Coast Rev., Vol. V 1993, Vol. VI, 1995, Vol. VII, 1997, Vol. IX, 1999, Vol. X, 2001. Trustee Pensacola Jr. Coll.; bd. dirs. Fla. Hist. Soc. Served to capt. USAF, 1951-53. U. West Fla. Found. fellow, 1982; recipient Disting. Citizen award Pensacola Jr. Coll., 1966, Nat. Editl. Writing award Freedoms Found. at Valley Forge, 1967, 68, 69, 70, 72, 74, awards for editls. and cartoons, 1967, 68, 69, 72, 86, George Washington Medallion Lifetime award, 2004, DeLuna award Pensacola Founders' Day, 1979, Pensacola Kiwanis Civic award, 1982, award Am. Assn. State and Local History, 1984, Founder's award Inspiring Pensacola Bus. awards, 1992, Bob Graham Hon. AIA Archtl. Awareness award Fla. Assn. Archs., 1992, Malcolm B. Johnson Fellowship award James Madison Inst., 1994, Spirit of Pensacola award, 1998; named Pensacola Profl. Bus. Leader of Yr., 1980, J. Earle Bowden Jr. Historian award named in honor Pensacola Jr. League, 1983, Preservationist of Yr., Fla. Trust Hist. Preservation, 1985, West Fla. Lit. Hall of Honor, 1989, Dorothy Dodd Lifetime Achievement award Fla. Hist. Soc., 2000; Gulf Island Nat. Seashore Hwy. named J. Earle Bowden Way, 1997, Mary Call Darby Collins award, Fla. Sec. of State, 2002, Lifetime Achievement award Pensacola Heritage Found., 2002. Mem. Am. Soc. Newspaper Editors, Nat. Conf. Editl. Writers, Fla. Soc. Newspaper Editors (pres. 1970), Rotary. Achievements include establishment of J. Earle Bowden history endowment U. West Fla. Home: 2220 Mccutchen Pl Pensacola FL 32503-3422 Office: One NewsJour Pla Pensacola FL 32501 Personal E-mail: jeb2220@aol.com.

BOWDEN, JIM, professional sports team executive; b. May 18, 1961; m. Amy Bowden; children: J.B., Tyler, Chad. BBA, Rollins Coll., 1983. Asst. dir. player devel. and scouting Pitts. Pirates, 1985-88; asst. to sr. v.p. baseball ops. N.Y. Yankees, 1989-90; adminstrv. asst. scouting and player devel. Cin. Reds, 1982-92, gen. mgr., 1992—2003; interim gen. mgr. Washington Expos, 2004—.

BOWDEN, MARK ROBERT, writer; b. St. Louis, July 17, 1951; s. Richard Houston and Rita Lois (Keane) B.; m. Gail Louise Mclaughlin, July 24, 1955; children: Aaron Keane, William B.J., Anya Rachel, Daniel Mark, Benjamin Houston. BA, Loyola Coll., 1973. Staff reporter Balt. News-Am., 1973-79; staff writer Phila. Inquirer, 1979—2003; nat. corres. The Atlantic Monthly, 2003—. Adj. prof. Loyola Coll., Balt. Author: Doctor Dealer: The Rise and Fall of an All-American Boy and His Multimillion-Dollar Cocaine Empire, 1987, Bringing The Heat: A Pro Football Team's Quest for Glory, Fame, Immortality and a Bigger Piece of the Action, 1994, Black Hawk Down: A Story of Modern War (Hal Boyle award, Overseas Press Club, 2000), 1999, Killing Pablo: The Hunt for the World's Greatest Outlaw (Cornelius Ryan award, Overseas Press Club, 2002) 2001, Roadwork: Among Tyrants, Heroes, Rogues, and Beasts, 2004 Recipient Nat. Sci. Writing award AAAS, 1980, 1st pl. feature article Nat. Assn. Sunday Newspaper Mag. Editors, 1985.*

BOWDEN, MICHAEL TODD, literature and language educator; b. St. Louis, Aug. 1, 1950; s. Charles Robert and Harriet Joan Bowden; m. Maria Eleticia Tovar, June 20, 1981; children: Tess Gabriella, Travis Joaquin. BA in philosophy, No. Ariz. U., 1972; MFA in Creative Writing, U. Ariz., Tucson, 1980. Elem. tchr. Sierra Vista Unified Dist. Schs., Ariz., 1985—. Panelist Ariz. Commn. on the Arts, Phoenix. Author poems in various jours. and anthologies. Recipient Poetry Contest Winner, Tucson Poetry Festival, 1985; fellow, Ariz. Commn. on the Arts, 1993, 1995.

BOWDEN, VIRGINIA MASSEY, librarian; b. Houston, Tex., July 22, 1939; d. Calvin Scott and Juanita Barlow Massey; m. Charles Lee Bowden, July 2, 1960; children: Sharon Scott Bowden Davis, Ellen Maureen Bowden McIntyre. BA, U. Tex., 1960, PhD, 1994; MSLS, U. Ky., 1970. Programmer Texaco Inc., Houston, 1960-64; sr. programmer AMA, Chgo., 1964-65, C.E.I.R. Inc., N.Y.C., 1965-66, Bambergers, Newark, 1967-68; systems analyst, asst. to dir. U. Tex. Health Sci. Ctr., San Antonio, 1970-78, assoc. libr. dir., 1978-85, libr. dir., 1985—2003, libr. dir. emeritus, 2004—. Author: (with others) Handbook of Medical Library Practice, 1983; contbr. articles to profl. jours. Prse. Friends Pub. Libr., San Antonio, 1989-90. Recipient numerous grants Nat. Libr. Medicine, 1982-2003, Julia Grothaus award Bexar Libr. Assn., 1983; fellow Coun. Libr. Resources, 1978-79. Fellow Med. Libr. Assn. (Louise Darling medal 1990); mem. ALA, LWV (bd. dirs. 1983-85, 2004-2005), Acad. Health Info. Profls, Assn. Acad. Health Sci. Libr. Dirs. (bd. dirs. 1995-98), Nat. Network Librs. Medicine (bd. dirs. South Ctrl. region 1995-97), Amigos Bibliographic Coun. (trustee 1986-89), Nat. Libr. Medicine (cons. 1983-88), Tex. Libr. Assn., Coun. Rsch. and Acad. Librs. (pres. 1986-87), Tex. Coun. State Univ. Librs. (pres. 1996-98), Daus. Rep. Tex., Phi Beta Kappa (pres. San Antonio Assn. 1979). Unitarian Universalist. Home: PO Box 2968 Canyon Lake TX 78133-0016

BOWDEN, WILLIAM DARSIE, retired interior designer; b. Palo Alto, Calif., Aug. 11, 1920; s. Edmund Robert and Elisabeth (Darsie) B.; m. Anne Minor Lile, July 29, 1948; children: Darsie Minor, Raleigh Anne, Elisabeth Lile. BA, Stanford U., 1942. Jr. exec. Frederick and Nelson Dept. Store, Seattle, 1946-48; v.p., co-owner William L. Davis Co., Seattle, 1948-84. Trustee Found. for Interior Design Edn. Rsch., Plestcheeff Inst. for Decorative Arts U. Wash. Served to 1st lt. AUS, 1943-46. Fellow Am. Soc. Interior Designers (pres. Wash. chpt. 1966-67, nat. v.p. 1969-71), Furniture History Soc. (London), Phi Beta Kappa, Alpha Delta Phi. Clubs: University, Wash. Athletic. Republican. Episcopalian. Home and Office: 2030 Beans Bight Rd NE Bainbridge Island WA 98110 E-mail: bowdbxx@aol.com.

BOWDEN, WILLIAM P., JR., lawyer, bank executive; b. East Orange, N.J., Feb. 29, 1944; s. W. Paul and Catherine (Porter) B.; m. Margo Redman, June 8, 1968; children: Jennifer Porter, Peter Chandler. AB, Williams Coll., 1966; JD, Columbia U., 1969. Bar: N.Y. 1970. Atty. Davis Polk & Wardwell, N.Y.C., 1969-75, 77-80; gen. counsel, sec. Alaska Interstate Co., Houston, 1976-77; assoc. gen. counsel Citicorp, N.Y.C., 1980-85; dep. gen. counsel Marine Midland Banks, Inc., N.Y.C., 1985-91; chief counsel Office of Comptr. of Currency, U.S. Dept. Treasury, Washington, 1991-94; gen. counsel CS First Boston, Inc., N.Y.C., 1994-96, Société Générale Ams., N.Y.C., 1997—2001, Willis Group Holdings Ltd., N.Y.C. and London, 2001—. Mem. ABA, Assn. of Bar of City of N.Y., Rockaway Hunting Club, Lawrence Beach Club, Univ. Club, The Anglers Club of N.Y. Office: 7 Hanover Sq New York NY 10004-2594 also: 10 Trinity Sq London EC3P 3AX England

BOWDLER, ANTHONY JOHN, internist, educator; b. London, Eng., Oct. 16, 1928; came to U.S., 1967; s. Edward Thomas and Clara (Anthony) B.; m. Eleanor Madeleine Sladen, July 30, 1955; children: Noelle Clare, Jonathan Francis. BSc, U. Coll., London, 1949, MB, BS, 1952, MD (Bilton Pollard fellow), 1962, PhD, 1967; postgrad. (Buswell Sr. fellow), U. Rochester, 1962-64. Intern Univ. Coll. Hosp., London, 1952, casualty med. officer, 1956, registrar and rsch. fellow, 1958-62; intern Dorking Hosp., Surrey, England, 1957, Hammersmith Hosp., London, 1953, Brompton Hosp., London, 1956; sr. instr. U. Rochester, N.Y., 1962-64; sr. lectr. U. Coll. Hosp. Med. Sch., London, 1964-67; assoc. prof. medicine Mich. State U. Coll. Human Medicine, East Lansing, 1967-70, prof. medicine, 1971-80, Marshall U. Sch. Medicine, Huntington, W.Va., 1980-97, prof. medicine emeritus, 1997—. Hon. cons. Univ. Coll. Hosp., 1967. Served as surgeon lt. Royal Navy, 1953-55. Fellow ACP, Royal Coll. Physicians, Royal Coll. Pathologists; mem. AMA, Am. Fedn. Clin. Rsch., Ctrl. Soc. Clin. Rsch. (emeritus), Am. Soc. Hematology (emeritus), Am. Soc. Clin. Oncology (emeritus), Brit. Med. Assn. (life). Researcher in internal medicine. Home: 4609 Sawgrass Dr E Ann Arbor MI 48108-8644 Personal E-mail: abowdler@comcast.net.

BOWE, RICHARD WELBOURN, lawyer; b. Balt., Nov. 4, 1949; s. Richard Eugene and Virginia Welbourn (Cooley) B.; m. Mary M. Vandeweghe (dec.); children: Richard Desmond Welbourn, Hollis Baldwin. AB in Politics, Princeton U., 1971; JD, Am. U., 1976. Bar: Md. 1976, D.C. 1977, U.S. Dist. Ct. D.C. 1977, U.S. Ct. Appeals (D.C. cir.) 1977. Assoc. Howrey & Simon, Washington, 1976-78, Cladouhos & Brashares, Washington, 1978-84; group counsel Md. Cup Corp., Balt., 1984-87; ptnr. Miles & Stockbridge, Washington and Balt., 1987-93; pvt. practice law Washington, 1993—. Advisor Dingman Ctr. Entrepreneurship, U. Md., College Park, 1992—; mem. small bus. devel. com. George Mason U., Fairfax, Va., 1992—. Contbr. articles to profl. jours. Active St. Albans Sch. Parent's Assn., 1992—. Mem. ABA, Md. State Bar Assn., D.C. Bar Assn. Episcopal. Avocations: sailing, golf, reading. Office: 5100 Wisconsin Ave NW Ste 401 Washington DC 20016-4119

BOWE, RIDDICK LAMONT, professional boxer; b. Bklyn., Aug. 10, 1967; s. Dorothy Bowe; children: Riddick Jr., Ridicia, Brenda. Amateur boxer, 1982—89; professional boxer, 1989—; defeated Evander Holyfield for WBA, WBC, IBF titles, 1992; defeated Evander Holyfield for WBA, IBF Titles, 1993; defeated Herbie Hide for WBO Title, 1995; defeated Jorge Luis Gonzalez to retain WBO title, 1995; defeated Evander Holyfield to retain WBO title, 1995; defeated Andrew Golota, 1996; defeated Marcus Rhode, 2004; defeated Billy Zumbrum, 2005. Named ranked Undisputed Heavyweight Champ, 1992—93; recipient Silver super heavyweight divsn., 1988 Olympics, Seoul, Korea, ranked Undisputed Heaveyweight Champ, 1995—.*

BOWE, WILLIAM J(OHN), lawyer; b. Chgo., June 23, 1942; s. William John Sr. and Mary (Gwinn) B.; m. Catherine Louise Vanselow, 1979; children: Andrew M., Patrick D. BA, Yale U., 1964; JD, U. Chgo., 1967. Bar: Ill. 1967, Tenn. 1984. Assoc. Ross, Hardies, O'Keefe, Babcock, McDougall & Parsons, Chgo., 1967-68; assoc., then ptnr. Roan & Grossman, Chgo., 1971-78; v.p., gen. counsel, sec. The Bradford Exchange Ltd., Niles, Ill., 1979-83; asst. gen. counsel, v.p., gen. counsel United Press Internat. Inc., Nashville, 1984-85; v.p. to exec. v.p., gen. counsel, sec. Ency. Britannica, Inc., Chgo., 1986—; sec. William Benton Found., Chgo., 1987-96; pres. Merriam-Webster, Inc., Springfield, Mass., 1995-96, Ency. Britannica Ednl. Corp., Chgo., 1995-99. Part-time faculty Summer Law Inst. Kenneth Wang Law Sch., Soochow U., Suzhou, China, 2005. Mem. bd. editors Intellectual Property Studies, Chinese Acad. Social Studies, Beijing, 1996-99; contbr. articles to legal jours. Mem. The Annenberg Washington Program Anti-Piracy Project, Washington, 1988—89; bd. dirs. Internat. Anticounterfeiting Coalition, Washington, 1993—96, chmn., 1994—96; gen. counsel Gov.'s Task Force on Sch. Fin., Chgo., 1975—76; trustee Hull Ho. Assn., Chgo., 1977—79; pres., bd. dirs. Clarence Darrow Cmty. Ctr., Chgo., 1975—84; mem. bd. overseers Ill. Inst. Tech.-Kent Coll. Law, 1982—86; mem. Gov.'s Task Force on Workforce Preparation, 1991—93, Gov.'s Work Group on Early Childhood Care and Edn., 1994—95, Gov.'s Edn. Summit, 2000—02. With U.S. Army, 1968—71. Mem.: ABA, Software and Info. Industry Assn. (govt. affairs coun. 1999—), Software Publs. Assn. (govt. affairs com. 1997—99), Intellectual Property Assn. Chgo., Chgo. Bar Assn., Ill. Bar Assn., Ill. State C. of C. (bd. dirs. 1989—96, mem. edn. com. 1989—99). Office: Ency Britannica Inc 310 S Michigan Ave Ste 900 Chicago IL 60604-4216 Office Phone: 312-347-7084. E-mail: wbowe@eb.com.

BOWEN, BRUCE, professional baseball player; b. June 14, 1971; BA, Calif. State Fullerton, 1993. Guard Miami Heat, Fla., 1996—97, Boston Celtics, Mass., 1997—99, Philadelphia '76ers, Pa., 1999—2000, Miami Heat, Fla., 1999—2001, San Antonio Spurs, Tex., 2001—. Named to NBA All-Defensive Team, NBA, 2001—05, NBA Championship Team, 2005. Office: San Antonio Spurs One SBC Ctr San Antonio TX 78219*

BOWEN, CHRISTOPHER EDWARD, researcher, director; b. Jamaica, N.Y., July 24, 1947; s. James Frederick Jr. and Roseanne Marie (McGrath) B.; m. Barbara Francine Heitman, Sept. 11, 1971; children: Melissa, Jason, Heather. BA in English, St. John's U., 1970; MLS, Queen's Coll., 1974; BS in Pharmacy, St. John's U., 1979. Head libr. L.I. Press, Jamaica, 1965-77; asst. head libr. N.Y. Post, N.Y.C., 1977-88; libr. dir. Star Mag., Tarrytown, NY, 1988—2000; rsch. dir. Dark Star Mining, Bridgewater, Conn., 2000—. Mem. Spl. Librs. Assn. Office: Dark Star Mining PO Box 86 Bridgewater CT 06752 E-mail: darkstarmining@charter.net.

BOWEN, CLOTILDE MARION DENT, retired military officer, psychiatrist; b. Chgo., Mar. 20, 1923; d. William Marion Dent and Clotilde (Tynes) D.; m. William N. Bowen, Dec. 29, 1945 (dec.). *Paternal grandfather, Thomas Marshall Dent, born on a Georgia plantation, graduated from Atlanta University and Howard University Law, and was employed at US Commerce Department for 50 years. His son, William Marion, graduated Dartmouth College in 1913, on a Latin and Greek scholarship. He was the first accountant for the Supreme Liberty Life Insurance Company, Chicago. Uncle Francis M. graduated Amherst, with a law degree from Howard University. Uncle Thomas M. (Jr.) graduated Howard University, and during WWI, received a battlefield promotion to Captain for bravery in 1918. Mother, Clotilde, was a fashion designer and business owner in Chicago. Raised in Columbus by Aunt Maude (Tynes) and 1st Lt. Stephen Brady Barrows, a buffalo soldier, 10th coventry.* BA, Ohio State U., 1943, MD, 1947. Intern Harlem Hosp., N.Y.C., 1947-48; resident and fellow in pulmonary diseases Triboro Hosp., Jamaica, L.I., 1948-50; resident in psychiatry VA Hosp., Albany N.Y., 1959-62; asst. resident in psychiatry Albany Med. Ctr. Hosp., 1961-62; pvt. practice N.Y.C., 1950-55; chief pulmonary disease clinic N.Y.C., 1950-55; asst. chief pulmonary disease svc. Valley Forge Army Hosp., Pa., 1955—59; chief psychiatry VA Hosp., Roseburg, Oreg., 1962-66, acting chief of staff, 1964-66; asst. chief neurology and psychiatry Tripler Gen. Hosp., Hawaii, 1966-68; psychiatr. lcons. and dir. Rev. Br. Office Civil Health and Med. Program Uniform Svcs., 1968-70; commd. capt. U.S. Army, 1955, advanced through ranks to col., 1968, neuropsychiat. cons. USA Vietnam Medcom, 1970—71, chief dept. psychiatry Fitzsimons Army Med. Ctr., 1971-74, chief dept. psychiatry Tripler Army Med. Ctr., 1974-75; assoc. clin. prof. psychiatry U. Hawaii, 1974-75; comdr. Hawley Army Clin., post surgeon U.S. Army, Ft. Benjamin, Harrison, Ind., 1977-78, chief dept. primary care and cmty. medicine, 1978-83, chief psychiat. consultation svc. Fitzsimons Army Med. Ctr., 1983-85; chief psychiatry svc. med./regional office ctr. VA, Cheyenne, Wyo., 1987-90; staff psychiatrist Denver VA Satellite Clin., Colorado Springs, Colo., 1990-96; ret., 1996. Locum Tenens practice psychiatry, 1996—; surveyor Joint Commn. on Accreditation Healthcare Orgns., 1985-92; assoc. clin. prof. psychiatary U. Colo. Med. Ctr., Denver, 1971—; spkr. Vietnam Vets. Meml. Wall, 2001. Decorated Legion of Merit, Bronze Star, Vietnam, others; recipient Colo. Disabled Am. Vets. award, 1994-95, Pres.'s 300 Commencement award Ohio State U., 1987, Profl. Achievement award Ohio State U. Alumni Assn., 1998, Cert. of Appreciation, VFW, 2000, Am. Assn. Emergency Psychiat. award, 2001. Fellow Am. Psychiat. Assn. (disting. life), Acad. Psychosomatic Med.; mem. AMA, Nat. Med. Assn., Menninger Found (charter), Ctrl. Neuropsychiat. Assn. (Peter Bassoe fellow), S.W. Assn. of Buffalo Soldiers, Inc. Home: 1020 Tari Dr Colorado Springs CO 80921-2257 *To be successful one must always aspire to a goal just beyond his or her immediate reach.*

BOWEN, DEBRA LYNN, lawyer, state legislator; b. Rockford, Ill., Oct. 27, 1955; d. Robert Calvin and Marcia Ann (Crittenden) Bowen. BA, Mich. State U., 1976; JD, U. Va., 1979. Bar: Ill. 1979, Calif. 1983. Assoc. Winston & Strawn, Chgo., 1979-82, Washington, 1985-86, Hughes Hubbard & Reed, Los Angeles, 1982-84; sole practice Los Angeles, 1984-93; mem. Calif. State Assembly, 1992—98, Calif. State Senate, 1998—. Gen. counsel, State Employee's Retirement System Ill., Springfield, 1980-82; adj. prof. Watterson Coll. Sch. Paralegal Studies, 1985. Exec. editor Va. Jour. Internat. Law, 1977-78; contbr. articles to profl. jours. Mem. mental health law com. Chgo. Council Lawyers, 1980-82. Rotary Internat. fellow Internat. Christian U., Tokyo, 1975; Wigmore scholar Northwestern U. Sch. Law, Chgo., 1976; recipient James Madison Freedom of Information award No. Calif. chpt. Soc. Profl. Journalists, 1995. Mem. Calif. Bar Assn. (exec. com. pub. law sect. 1990-94), Mortar Bd., Phi Kappa Phi. Office: Calif Senate State Capitol Sacramento CA 95814-4906 also: Dist Office 2512 Artesia Blvd Ste 200 Redondo Beach CA 90278-3210

BOWEN, DUDLEY HOLLINGSWORTH, JR., federal judge; b. Augusta, Ga., June 25, 1941; AB in Fgn. Lang., U. Ga., 1964, LLB, 1965; profesor invitado (hon.), Universidad Externada de Bogotá, 1987. Bar: Ga. 1965, U.S. Dist. Ct. (so. dist.) Ga. 1997-. Pvt. practice law, Augusta, 1968-72; bankruptcy judge U.S. Dist. Ct. (so. dist.) Ga., Augusta, 1972-75, judge, 1979-97, chief judge, 1997—2004; ptnr. firm Dye, Miller, Bowen & Tucker, Augusta, 1975-79. Bd. dirs. Southeastern Bankruptcy Law Inst., 1976-87; mem. Ct. Security Com. Jud. Conf. U.S., 1987-92. Mem. bd. visitors U. Ga. Sch. Law, 1987-90. Served to 1st lt. inf., U.S. Army, 1966-68. Decorated Commendation medal. Mem. State Bar Ga. (chmn. bankruptcy law sect. 1977), Fed. Judges Assn. (bd. dirs. 1985-90), 11th Cir. Dist. Judges Assn. (sec.-treas. 1988-89, pres. 1991-92, chief judge So. Dist. Ga., 1997-2004). Presbyterian. Office: US Dist Ct PO Box 2106 Augusta GA 30903-2106

BOWEN, GEORGE HAMILTON, JR., astrophysicist, educator; b. Tulsa, June 20, 1925; s. George H. and Dorothy (Huntington) B.; m. Marjorie Evelyn Brown, June 19, 1948; children— Paul Huntington, Margaret Irene, Carol Ann, Dorothy Elizabeth, Kevin Leigh. BS with honor, Calif. Inst. Tech., 1949, PhD, 1952. Asso. biologist Oak Ridge Nat. Lab., 1952-54; asst. prof. physics Ia. State Coll., 1954-57; asso. prof. physics Iowa State U., 1957-65, prof., 1965-92, emeritus prof. astrophysics, 1993—. Served with USNR, 1944-46. Recipient Iowa State U. Outstanding Tchr. award, 1970, Faculty citation Iowa State U. Alumni Assn., 1971 Mem. Am. Astron. Soc., Astron. Soc. Pacific, Am. Assn. Physics Tchrs. (chmn. Iowa sect. 1966-67), Internat. Astron. Union, Sigma Xi, Tau Beta Pi. Home: 1919 Burnett Ave Ames IA 50010-4970 Office: Iowa State U Dept Physics & Astronomy Ames IA 50011-3160

BOWEN, GINGER ANN, artist; b. Amarillo, Tex., Feb. 16, 1953; d. Emmitt Lewis and Rose Hales; m. James A. Bowen; 1 child, Christian. Grad. h.s., Amarillo. Dir. adminstrns. Warner Bros. Records, Nashville, 1980—84. Exhibited in group shows at Ctrl. South Art Exhibit, 1994 (Chromatic Photo-imaging Svc. award), Catherine Lorillard Wolfe Art Club, 1995, Am. Artist Profl. League, 1995 (award, 1995), 2000—01 (Honorable Mention, 1999, Frank C. Wright Meml. award, 2001), Art Maui, 1997—98 (Purchase Pledge award, 1997), San Bernadino County Mus., 1999 (Honorable Mention, 2001), exhibitions include Calif. Art Club, 2004. Recipient First Pl. Profl., Scottsdale Artist Sch Best and Brightest Competition, 2003. Mem.: Nat. Mus. Women in Arts, Am. Artist Profl. League, Oil Painters Am. (assoc.), Calif. Art Club, Catherine Lorillard Wolfe Art Club. Avocations: travel, music. E-mail: gbowen7@cox.net.

BOWEN, HARRY ERNEST, management consultant; b. Elmira, N.Y., Jan. 31, 1941; s. Ernest William and Julia Cora (Forker) B.; m. Sandra Marie Fullerton, June 15, 1962; children: Harry Ernest Jr., Vicki Lynn Bowen Briggs, Nicholas Russel. AS in Gen. Studies, Mt. Wachusetts Coll., Gardner, Mass., 1975; BSBA, Ind. Inst. Tech., 1996. Mem. maintenance officer Intelligence and Security Command U.S. Army, Arlington Hall, Va., 1961-83; ret., 1983; assoc. dir. Martin & Stern, Inc., Chantilly, Va., 1983-89; program mgr. Paragon Sys., Inc., Centreville, Va., 1989-91; program mgr., mem. mgmt. staff Telos Fed. Sys., Sierra Vista, Ariz., 1991-96; regional mgr., project mgr., mem. mgmt. staff FC Bus. Sys., Sierra Vista, 1991-97; mem. tech. staff, dep. program mgr. Telos Corp., Ashburn, Va., 1998; v.p. sys. engring. FC Bus. Sys., Fairfax, Va., v.p. sys. engring. Sierra Vista, Ariz., 2003—. Mem. Soc. Logistics Engrs. (chmn. 1991-94, Sr. Membership award 1993), Kiwanis (pres. 1996-97)_. Republican. Avocations: bowling, swimming, coaching, walking, golf. Home: 1950 Cottonwood Dr Sierra Vista AZ 85635-6318 Office: FC Bus Sys 1234 E Fry Blvd Sierra Vista AZ 85635 Office Phone: 520-459-6227. E-mail: harry.bowen@aol.com.

BOWEN, JAMES THOMAS, career officer; b. Mason City, Iowa, May 4, 1948; s. Stanley Thomas and Marilyn Louise (Ott) B.; m. Joyce Anne Kermabon, Sept. 10, 1977; 1 child, Steven James. BBA, U. Iowa, 1969; MS, U. So. Calif., Los Angeles, 1974. Cert. project mgmt. profl. Commd. 2nd lt. USAF, 1969, advance through grades to col., 1991; student pilot 3575th Pilot Tng. Wing, Vance AFB, Okla., 1969-70; co-pilot 773rd Tactical Airlift Squadron, Clark AFB, Phillipines, 1971; pilot 6594th Test Group, Hickam AFB, Hawaii, 1971-75; acquisition program mgr. Aeronautical Systems Div., Wright-Patterson AFB, Ohio, 1976-82; chief, standoff surveillance and attack systems HQ USAF, Rsch. Devel. and Acquistion, Pentagon, Va., 1984-87; chief, acquistion plans and programs br. Air Force Inspection and Safety Ctr., Norton AFB, Calif., 1988-90; dir. projects joint tactical autonomous weapons Aero. Systems Div., Wright-Patterson AFB, Ohio, 1990-91, dir. devel. and integration F-16, 1991-94; F-16 mgmt. dir. Ogden Air Logistics Ctr., Hill AFB, Utah, 1994-95; custom sys. program mgr. Hewlett Packard and Agilent Tech. Cos., Santa Rosa, Calif., 1996-2001; site mgr. Agilent Techs., Rohnert Park, Calif., 2001—02, program mgr., 2002—. Active Rep. ctrl. com. Sonoma County; treas. bd. dirs. Blood Bank of the Redwoods; v.p. Project Mgmt. Inst. Wine Country chpt. Decorated Air medal USAF, 1972. Mem. Mil. Officers Assn. Am., Air Force Assn., Def. Systems Mgmt. Coll. Alumni Assn., Am. Mgmt. Assn., Ret. Officers Assn., Project Mgmt. Inst. Methodist. Avocations: skiing, deep sea fishing, golf. Office: Agilent Techs 1400 Fountaingrove Pkwy MS 3LS W Santa Rosa CA 95403-4902 Office Phone: 707-577-5183. Personal E-mail: jbowen@pacbell.net. Business E-Mail: james_bowen@agilent.com.

BOWEN, JEAN, retired librarian, consultant; b. Albany, N.Y., Mar. 23, 1927; d. John W. and Grace Lester (Quier) B.; m. Henry F. Bloch, June 26, 1962; 1 child, Pamela A. Bloch. AB, Smith Coll., 1948, AM, 1956; MS, Columbia U., 1957. Curator Rodgers & Hammerstein Archives of Recorded Sound, N.Y.C., 1962-67; asst. chief music divsn. N.Y. Pub. Libr., N.Y.C., 1967-85, chief music divsn., 1986-96, dir. Humanities and Social Scis. Libr., 1996-2000. Cons. Rockefeller Bros. Found., N.Y.C., 1963, N.Y.C., 67, N.Y. Philharm., N.Y.C., 1984, Schubert Archives, N.Y.C., 1982; mem. faculty Rare Book Sch. Columbia U., N.Y.C., 1984, N.Y.C., 87, N.Y.C., 91; bd. dirs. Amphion Found., N.Y.C. Contbr. articles to High Fidelity, Opera News, Am. Record Guide, Saturday Rev., MLA Notes, New Grove Dictionary of Am. Music. Mem.: Rare Book Sch. (mem. faculty, Columbia U., NYC 1984, 1987, 1991), Amphion Found. (NYC).

BOWEN, JEWELL RAY, chemical engineering professor; b. Duck Hill, Miss., Jan. 9, 1934; s. Hugh and Myrtle Louise (Stevens) B.; m. Priscilla Joan Spooner, Feb. 4, 1956; children: Jewell Ray, Sandra L., Susan E. BS, MIT, 1956, MS, 1957; PhD, U. Calif., Berkeley, 1963. Asst. prof. U. Wis., Madison, 1963-67, assoc. prof., 1967—70, prof. chem. engring., 1970-81, chmn. chem engring. dept., 1971-73, 78-81, assoc. vice chancellor, 1972-76; prof. chem. engring. U. Wash., Seattle, 1981-2000, prof. emeritus, 2001—, dean coll. engring., 1981-96. Cons. in field; adviser NSF, Dept. Def.; vis. prof. Kyoto U. Internat. Innovation Ctr., 2002; bd. dirs. Inst. for Dynamics of Explosions and Reactive Sys., 1989-, pres., 1989-95, treas., 1995-. Contbr. articles to profl. jours.; editor: 7th-10th Internat. Colloquia on Dynamics of Explosions and Reactive Systems, 1979, 81, 83, 85, chmn. program com. 18th. Mem. Wash. High Tech. Coordinating Bd., 1983—87; bd. dirs. Wash. Tech. Ctr., 1983—87, interim exec. dir., 1989—91; bd. dirs. U. Wash. Retirement Assn., 2003—05, 1st v.p., 2004—05, pres., 2005—. Recipient SWE Rodney Chipp award, 1995; NATO-NSF postdoctoral fellow, 1962-63, sr. postdoctoral fellow, 1968; Deutsche Forschungsgemeinschaft prof., 1976-77. Fellow AIAA, AAAS (com. on coun. affairs 1995-97, sect. chmn. 1996-97), Am. Soc. Engring. Edn. (deans coun. 1985-92, chmn. 1989-91, bd. dirs. 1989-94, 1st v.p. 1991, pres.-elect 1992, pres. 1993); mem. AIAA, AIChE, Am. Phys. Soc., Combustion Inst., Sigma Xi, Tau Beta Pi, Beta Theta Pi. Home: 5324 NE 86th St Seattle WA 98115-3922 Office: U Wash Dept Chem Engring PO Box 351750 Seattle WA 98195-1750 Office Phone: 206-616-8128. Business E-Mail: bowen@engr.washington.edu. E-mail: bowen5324@comcast.net.

BOWEN, JOHN METCALF, pharmacologist, toxicologist, educator; b. Quincy, Mass., Mar. 23, 1933; s. Loy J. and Marjorie (Metcalf) B.; m. Jean Alma Schmidt, Dec. 26, 1956; children: Mark John, Richard Kelley. DVM, U. Ga., 1957; PhD, Cornell U., 1960. Asst., then assoc. prof. Kans. State U., Manhattan, 1960-63; assoc., then prof. U. Ga., Athens, 1963-98, assoc. dean, dir. veterinary med. expt. sta., 1976-98. Cons. vet. medicine, 1998—. Mem. Am. Vet. Med. Assn., Soc. Neurosci., Soc. for In Vitro Biology. Office: U Ga Coll Vet Medicine Athens GA 30602-7371

BOWEN, JOHN WESLEY EDWARD, IV, lawyer; b. Columbus, Ohio, July 11, 1954; s. John Wesley Edward III and Jeanne (Lehar) B. BBA, So. Meth. U., 1976; JD, Columbia U., 1979. Bar: N.Y. 1980, U.S. Ct. Claims 1982, U.S. Supreme Ct. 1983, U.S. Dist. Ct. (so. and ea. dists.) N.Y. 1985, U.S. Ct. Appeals (fed. cir.) 1986. Trial atty. antitrust div. U.S. Dept. Justice, Washington, 1979-85; of counsel Howard & Rhone, N.Y.C., 1985-87; ptnr. Bowen & Bowen, 1989—. Dir. N.Y. Bd. of Trade, 1987-89. Contbr. articles to profl. jours. Chmn. Manhattan Jr. Assn. Commerce and Industry, N.Y.C., 1985-87, pres., 1986-87; mem. housing com. N.Y.C. Cmty. Bd. #10. Named one of Outstanding Young Men in Am., U.S. Jaycees, 1981-87. Mem. Alpha Phi Alpha. Methodist. Office: 2720 Airport Dr Columbus OH 43219-2219 Fax: (614) 418-1873. E-mail: bowenlaw@earthlink.net.

BOWEN, JONATHAN L., music educator, consultant; b. Niagara Falls, NY, Dec. 17, 1947; s. Jonathan L. and Margaret C. Bowen; m. Katherine N. Bowen, June 1, 1970; children: Heather R., Melanie R. BM, SUNY, Fredonia, NY, 1970; MM, Ithaca Coll., 1973. Music educator Magaretville Schs., NY, 1971—73, Port Byron H.S., NY, 1973—79, Homer H.S., NY, 1979—88; dir. of bands C. W. Baker H.S., Baldwinsville, NY, 1988—. All state adjudicator NY State Sch. Music Assn., 1980—; adjudicator State Edn. Dept. Summer Sch. Arts, Albany, 1990—; all state selection com. NY State Sch. Music Assn., 1995—; treas. NY State Band Dirs. Assn., 1998—2002, 2nd v.p., 2002—. Mem.: Nat. Band Assn., Onondaga County Music Educators Assn., Internat. Assn. of Jazz Educators, NY State Band Dirs. Assn. (2nd v.p., treas. 1998—2005), NY State Sch. Music Assn. (adjudicator 1980—2005). Avocations: kayaking, camping, hiking, skiing, bicycling. Home: 1626 Gunbarrel Rd Baldwinsville NY 13027 Office: Charles W Baker High Sch 29 East Oneida St Baldwinsville NY 13027 Office Phone: 315-638-6037. Home Fax: 315-638-6150. Office Fax: 315-638-6150. Personal E-mail: jbowen@bville.org.

BOWEN, JUDITH REINA, fundraising executive; b. Tampa, Fla., Aug. 15, 1940; d. Salvatore and Frances (Tyler) Reina; m. Lowell Wayne Coryell, Jan. 5, 1961 (div. Sept. 1980). BEd, Fla. State U., 1969, EdM, 1972. Program dir. Univ. Union Fla. State U., Tallahassee, 1961-65, dir. orientation, 1965-76, asst. to v.p. univ. rels., 1977-79, dir. South Fla. office Ft. Lauderdale, 1979-96; v.p. for devel. Broward C.C., Ft. Lauderdale, 1996—. Co-author: The College Admissions Game - How to Pay and Win. Active Broward Edn. Found., 1996—, Coun. for Advancement and Support Edn., 1997; mem. Broward Roundtable; grad. Leadership Fla., Leadership Broward. Mem.: Assn. Governing Bds. (program planning com.), Assn. Fundraising Profls. (Broward chpt.), Broward Hist. Soc., Execs. Assn., Tower Club. Democrat. Episcopalian. Avocations: gardening, interior design. Home: 333 Sunset Dr Apt 407 Fort Lauderdale FL 33301-2647 Office: 111 E Las Olas Blvd Fort Lauderdale FL 33301-2208

BOWEN, LINDA FLORENCE, pharmaceutical executive; b. Trenton, N.J., Apr. 21, 1960; d. Joseph John and Audrey (Würfel) Kish; m. Chris Bowen, Dec. 8, 1998. BA in English, Rutgers Coll., 1982, BS in Microbiology, 1982; MS in Drug Regulatory Affairs, L.I. Univ., 1996. Cert. US Regulatory Affairs, 2001, EU Regulatory Affairs, 2003. Microbiologist Kalipharma-Purepac Pharm., Elizabeth, NJ, 1983-85; quality assurance and regulatory affairs positions to assoc. dir. GlaxoSmithKline (formerly Block Drug Co.), Jersey City, 1985—2003; assoc. dir., regulatory affairs Bayer Healthcare, 2004—. Adj. prof. grad. QA/RA program Temple U., 1998—; mem. bd. editors Fundamentals in Can. Regulatory Affairs, 2003—04. Bd. dirs. Theatre Guild of Old Bridge, 1993—. Mem.: Drug Info. Assn., Regulatory Affairs Profl. Soc., Rho Chi. Avocations: community theater, travel, deltiology, local history. E-mail: LKish@aol.com.

BOWEN, LINNELL R., director; b. Orlando, Fla., June 16, 1940; m. Paul Ivan, Jr. Bowen; children: Julia Anne, Paul Ivan III. Student, U. Md., 1962; fundraising and devel. mgmt. program, Goucher Coll., 1990; leadership tng. course, Nat. Trust for Hist. Preserve, 1991. Tchr. U.S. history Annapolis H.S., 1962—65; dir. devel./pub. rels., dir. edn., ednl. cons. Hist. Annapolis Found., 1976—94; adj. tchr. Colonial Md. Experience Anne Arundel C.C., 1989—91; adj. tchr. fundraising for hist. preservation Goucher Coll. Ctr. for Continuing Studies, 1993—95; exec. dir. Annapolis 300, A Capital Celebration, 1994—95, Md. Hall for Creative Arts, 1996—. Bd. pres. Cultural Arts Found. Anne Arundel County, 1995—96, Jr. League Annapolis Adv. Bd., 1995—96; County exec. appt. Scenic and Hist. Rds. Commn., 1986—96; pres. Scholarship for Scholars Inc., 1991—93; steering com. Millennium Legacy Trail Art Competition, City of Annapolis Whitbread Race; active Cultural Heritage Alliance Com.; founder, dir. Annapolis Arts Alliance, 2004—05; bd. dirs. Scholarship for Scholars Inc., 1991—93, Annapolis and Anne Arundel County Conf. and Visitors Bur.; adv. com. Mitchell Gallery at St. John's Coll., 1995—2005. Named one of Md.'s Top 100 Women, 1998, 2001; recipient City of Annapolis award of commendation, Annapolis 300 Celebration, 1995, Cmty. award for Annapolis 300 Celebration, Hist. Annapolis Found., 1996, Leadership Anne Arundel Cmty. Trustee award, 1996, Lifetime Achievement award, Pub. Rels. Soc. Annapolis and Anne Arundel County, 1999; fellow Paul Harris fellow, Rotary Found., 1997. Mem.: Annapolis/Anne Arundel County (chpt. trustee), Pub. Rels. Soc. Am., Annapolis and Anne Arundel County C. of C., Anne Arundel Trade Coun. Office: 801 Chase St Annapolis MD 21401 Office Phone: 410-263-5544. Personal E-mail: anna300@aol.com. Business E-Mail: lbowen@mdhallarts.org.

BOWEN, LOWELL REED, lawyer; b. Prince Frederick, Md., Jan. 29, 1931; s. Perry Gray and Melba (Hutchins) B.; m. Marilyn Sack, June 14, 1958; children: Mark Holdsworth, David Stockbridge. BA, U. Md., 1952; LLB, U. Md., Balt., 1957. Bar: Md. 1957, U.S. Dist. Ct. Md. 1958, U.S. Ct. Appeals (4th cir.) 1959, U.S. Supreme Ct. 1964. Law clk. to chief judge U.S. Dist. Ct. Md., Balt., 1957—58; assoc. Miles & Stockbridge, Balt., 1958—65, ptnr., 1966—, mng. ptnr., 1974—91, chmn., 2001—02. Lectr. U. Md. Law Sch., 1958-63, U. Balt. Law Sch., 1965-70. Mem., chmn. various coms. Md. Commn. to Revise Annotated Code Md., Annapolis, 1973—; mem. Standing Com. on Rules of Practice and Procedure, Md. Ct. Appeals, Annapolis, 1980—; trustee, chmn. Balt. Opera Co., Inc., 1977-92; mem. Md. Humanities Coun., 1992-97; trustee, pres. Lyric Found., Inc., 1997—. 1st lt. USAF, 1952-54. Mem. ABA, Md. State Bar Assn., Maryland Club. Office: Miles & Stockbridge PC One W Pennsylvania Ave Towson MD 21204 Business E-Mail: lbowen@milesstockbridge.com.

BOWEN, MARY LU, ecumenical administrator; b. Wheeling, W.Va., Feb. 14, 1930; d. Walter Philip and Helen Elizabeth (Luthy) Wagenheim; m. Robert Edward Bowen, June 13, 1953; children: Jeanne, Thomas, Robert, David. BS in Edn., Wittenberg U., 1952; MA in Social Scis., SUNY, Binghamton, 1989. Cert. tchr., Ohio, W.Va., Tex., N.Y. Various teaching positions, 1952-80; coord. ministry with the aging Coun. of Chs., Broome County, N.Y., 1979-82, adminstrv. asst., 1982-83, asst. dir., 1984-86; assoc. for ecumenical devel. N.Y. State Coun. of Chs., Albany, Syracuse, 1990-94, regional dir. southern tier Albany, 1995-96, dir. of pub. policy, 1997—98; exec. dir. N.Y. State Cmty. of Churches, 1998—. Sec. exec. cabinet N.Y. State Coun. Chs., Albany, Syracuse, 1986-91; synodical lay rep. Evang. Luth. Ch. in Am. Region VII Coun., Phila., 1987-91, churchwide leadership team Social Min. Project, Chgo., 1990-91, sec. constituting conv. Upstate N.Y. Synod, Syracuse, 1987. Author: Reclaiming Christianity's Feminist Heritage: Reflections on Patriarchal Teachings and Women's Problems, 1989, Handbook for Clergy on Child Abuse and Neglect, 1995. Active Broome County Coordinating Coun. Child Abuse and Neglect, 1986-88, 96-98, treas. 1997; mem. Luth. Statewide Advocacy Exec. Com., Albany, 1982-90, 2000—, chmn. exec. com., 1991-99; regional adv. bd. Citizen Action N.Y., Binghamton, 1994-98; co-chmn. Interreligious Health and Justice Coalition, N.Y. Ctrl. So. Tier Region, 1994-98; Evang. Luth. Ch. in Am. Coalition for Mission in Appalachia, 1996—, chair, 2000-2001. Recipient Citizen Action N.Y. Phoenix award, 1998, Upstate N.Y. Synod Lay Discipleship award, 1999; Sr. Congl. intern, 1997. Mem.: Nat. Assn. Ecumenical Staff. Democrat. Lutheran. Avocations: travel, reading. Home: 14 Overbrook Dr Apalachin NY 13732-4234 Office: NY State Coun Chs 18 Computer Dr W Ste 107 Albany NY 12205 Personal E-mail: marylubowen@aol.com, nyscoc@aol.com.

BOWEN, PATRICK HARVEY, lawyer, consultant; b. Cin., July 7, 1939; s. Albert Vernon and Elsie Matilda (Harvey) B.; m. Karen A. Hunter; 1 child, Harvey Shaw. BA, Marietta Coll., 1961; JD, Duke U., 1964; MBA, Columbia U., 1975. Bar: N.Y. 1965, Conn. 1990. Assoc. Mudge, Rose, Guthrie & Alexander, N.Y.C., 1964-66; atty. Kennecott Copper Corp., N.Y.C., 1966-71, asst. counsel, 1971-79, asst. gen. counsel, 1979-83, asst. sec., 1980-83; sr. assoc. atty. Allied Stores Corp., N.Y.C., 1983-87, v.p., gen. counsel, sec., 1987-88, v.p., 1988-89; pvt. practice Stamford, Conn., 1990—2003, Bridgeport, Conn., 2004—. Mem. ABA, Conn. Bar Assn., NY State Bar Assn., Assn. Bar City of NY, Soc. Corp. Secs. and Governance Profls. Avocation: traditional jazz musician. Office: 602 Courtland Ave Ste 104 Bridgeport CT 06605-3324 Office Phone: 203-366-6750. Personal E-mail: phbowen@aol.com.

BOWEN, PETER GEOFFREY, arbitrator, finance educator; b. Iowa City, Iowa, July 10, 1939; s. Howard Rothmann and Lois Berntine (Schilling) B.; m. Shirley Johns Carlson, Sept. 14, 1968; children: Douglas Howard, Leslie Johns. BA in Govt. and Econs., Lawrence Coll., 1960; postgrad., U. Wis., 1960-61, U. Denver, 1963-64, U. Colo., 1994; PhD, Hamilton U., 2003. Cert.: expert witness, Denver. V.p. Perry & Butler, Denver, 1972-73; exec. v.p., dir. Little & Co., Denver, 1973; pres. Builders Agy. Ltd., Denver, 1974-75; CEO, gen. ptnr. The Investment Mgmt. Group Ltd., Denver, 1975—2005. Arbitrator NASD Dispute Resolution, Inc., 1996—, Am. Arbitration Assn., 1996—, NY Stock Exch., 2004; adj. prof. bus. Colo. Mt. Coll., 1992-2000, Daniels Coll. Bus., U. Denver, 2004—; arbitrator Eagle County Colo. Atty.'s Office, 1997-2003; continuing legal edn. lectr. on real estate syndications, 1983; adj. asst. prof. Regis U., 2000-2003. Author: A Small Business Primer for Displaced Corporate Executives, 2000, Legal and Regulatory Environment of Small Business, 2003; contbr. articles to profl. publs. Vice-chmn. Greenwood Village (Colo.) Planning and Zoning Commn., 1983-85; mem. Vail Planning and Environ. Commn., 1992-96; chmn. emeritus Vail Partnership Environ. Edn. Programs, Inc., 1993-2000; elected mem. City Council Greenwood Village, 1985-86, also mayor pro tem, 1985-86; trustee Vail Mountain Sch. Found., 1987-88. Mem. Colo. Bar Assn. (legal fee arbitration com. 2002—), Denver Bar Assn. (legal fee arbitration com. 1997—), Acad. Mgmt., Lawrence U. Alumni Assn. (bd. dirs. 1966-72, 82-86). Home: 16006 Double Eagle Dr Morrison CO 80465-9617 Personal E-mail: jsbowen@pcisys.com. Business E-Mail: pbowen2@du.edu.

BOWEN, RAY MORRIS, academic administrator, engineering educator; b. Ft. Worth, Mar. 30, 1936; s. Winfred Herbert and Elizabeth (Williams) B; m. Sara Elizabeth Gibbens, July 5, 1958; children: Raymond Morris, Marguerite Elizabeth. BS in Mech. Engring., Texas A&M U., 1958, PhD in Engring., 1961; MS in Mech. Engring, Calif. Inst. Tech., 1959. Registered profl. engr., Tex., Ky. Assoc. prof. Mech. Engring. La. State U., Baton Rouge, 1965-67; prof. Mech. Engring. Rice U., Houston, 1967-83, chmn. dept., 1972-77; dir. divsn. NSF, Washington, 1982-83, from acting asst. dir., engr. to dep. asst. dir., engr., 1990-91; prof. Engring., dean U. Ky., Lexington, 1983-89; v.p. acad. affairs Okla. State U., Stillwater, Okla., 1991-93, interim pres., 1993—94; pres. Tex. A&M U., College Station, 1994—2002, pres. emeritus, 2002—. Staff Sandia Corp., Albuquerque, 1966-67, 72, cons., 1970-78; cons. U.S. Army Ballistic Rsch. Lab, Aberdeen Proving Ground, Md., 1970. Author: Introduction to Continuum Mechanics for Engineers, 1989; co-author: Introduction to Vectors and Tensors, Vols. I and II, 1976; contbg. author: Rational Thermodynamics, 1984; contbr. articles to profl. jours. Capt. USAF, 1961-64. Fellow Johns Hopkins U., 1964-65 Soc. Scholars Johns Hopkins U., Nat. Sci. Bd., 2002-, Tau Beta Pi, Phi Kappa Phi, Sigma Xi. Office: Tex A&M Univ Evans Library Annex 252C College Station TX 77843-5000 Office Phone: 979-862-2955. Business E-Mail: rbowen@tamu.edu.

BOWEN, RHYS See QUIN-HARKIN, JANET

BOWEN, RICHARD LEE, academic administrator, political scientist, educator; b. Avoca, Iowa, Aug. 31, 1933; s. Howard L. and Donna (Milburn) B.; m. Connie Smith Bowen, 1976; children: James, Robert, Elizabeth, Christopher; children by previous marriage— Catherine, David, Thomas. BA, Augustana Coll., 1957; MA, Harvard, 1959, PhD, 1967. Fgn. service officer State Dept., 1959-60; research asst. to U.S. Senator Francis Case, 1960-62; legis. asst. to U.S. Senator Karl Mundt, 1962-65; minority cons. sub-com. exec. reorgn. U.S. Senate, 1966-67; asst. to pres., assoc. prof. polit. sci. U. S.D., Vermillion, 1967-69, pres., 1969-76, Dakota State Coll., Madison, 1973-76; commr. higher edn. Bd. Regents State S.D., Pierre, 1976-80; Disting prof. polit. sci. U. S.D., 1980-85; pres. Idaho State U., Pocatello, 1985—. Served with USN, 1951-54. Recipient Outstanding Alumnus award Augustana Coll., 1970; Woodrow Wilson fellow, 1957, Congl. Staff fellow, 1965; Fulbright scholar, 1957. Office: Idaho State U Office of Pres PO Box 8310 Pocatello ID 83209-0001 Office Phone: 208-282-3440. E-mail: bowerich@isu.edu.

BOWEN, RICHARD LEE, architect; b. Canton, Ohio, Nov. 1, 1935; s. Raymond Leed and Lillian E. (White) Bowen; m. Robin Herrington (div.); children: Richard Lee, David Herrington, Laurel Ann, Sean Andrew, Scott Andrew; m. Gail Audrey; children: Tabitha Erin, Colin Leed. BA, Case Western Res. U., 1959. Registered arch., 50 states, DC, P.R., Can., Australia, Nat. Coun. Archtl. Registration Bd.s, Archtl. Registration Coun. U.K. Pvt. practice Richard L. Bowen & Assocs. Inc., Cleve., 1963—; mng. ptnr. ComDel, 1970; pvt. practice Richard L. Bowen & Assocs. Inc., Pompano Beach, 1969—2004; pres. Enerwaste, Inc., 1992—99. Apptd. mem. Ohio State Archtl. Registration Bd., 2001—, Nat. Coun. Archtl. Registration Bds., mem. internat. registration com., mem. com. for internat. reciprocity. Prin. works include Western Campus, Cuyahoga CC, Akron State Office Bldg., West Jr. HS, John Hay HS, John Marshall HS, Cleve. Ctrl. Police Hdqs., Cleve. Hopkins Internat. Airport, FAA Regional Office Bldg., classroom and libr. bldgs. Ashtabula Campus, Kent State U., Wade Park VA Hosp., Westerly Sewage Treatment Facility Cuyahoga Regional Sewer Authority, Cuyahoga CC Manpower Skills Ctr. Ohio, Ravemna Waste Water Treatment Plant, others. Mem. Leadership Cleve.; mem. exec. com. Cuyahoga County Rep. Party, Cleve., 1963—; trustee St. Luke's Hosp. Assn., 1996—2000, Cleve. Internat. Air Show; mem. adv. bd. Cleve. Inst. Art; mem. adv. bd. knights hosp. Sovereign Order St. John Jerusalem, 2004. Recipient Energy Conservation Design award, Fla. Power Winter Garden Shoppint Ctr., 1986, Merit award, Cleve. Restoration Soc., 1992, Outstanding Achievement award, Cleve. Growth Assn., 1997, Design award, Am. Registered Architects, 2003. Mem.: AIA (design award excellence 1976, award 1979, 2000, 2002, 2003), Am. Arbitration Assn., Urban Land Inst., Am. Assn. Planners, Bldg. Ofcls. Coun. Am., Constrn. Specifications Inst., Internat. Coun. Shopping Ctrs., Guild Religious Architecture, Soc. Archtl. Historians, Am. Soc. Ch. Architecture, Royal Inst. Brit. Archs., Royal Archtl. Inst. Can., Nat. Assn. Indsl. and Office Pks. (awards 1985, 1989, 1992, 1994, 1995, 2000, 2003), Archs. Soc. Ohio (honor award 1988, 2000, 2001), Hillbrook Club, Ft. Lauderdale Yacht Club, Rowfant Club, Cat Cay Club, Useppa Island Club, Chagrin Valley Country Club, The Club, Union Club, Phi Gamma Delta. Avocations: sailing, skiing, fly and deep sea fishing. Home: 14926 Hillbrook Dr Chagrin Falls OH 44022-2634 Office: 13000 Shaker Blvd Cleveland OH 44120-2063 Office Phone: 216-377-3800. Personal E-mail: r.bowen@rlba.com.

BOWEN, SHARON Y., lawyer; BA, U. Va., 1978; MBA, JD, Northwestern U., 1982. Bar: NY 1984. Ptnr., corp. dept. Latham & Watkins LLP, NYC. Mem. adv. counsel NY Women's Bar Assn. Found., Northwestern U. Law Bd. Mng. editor Northwestern Jour. Internat. Law and Bus. Bd. dirs. NY Lawyers Pub. Interest, Inc., Harlem Sch. Arts, NYC Econ. Devel. Corp., Urban-America, Inc. Named one of Am. Top Black Attys., Black Enterprise, 2003. Mem.: ABA (mem. ho. del.), NY State Bar Assn., Bar Assn. City of NY (mem. com. corp. law). Office: Latham & Watkins LLP 885 Third Ave Ste 1000 New York NY 10022-4802 Office Phone: 212-906-1332. Office Fax: 212-751-4864. Business E-Mail: sharon.bowen@lw.com.

BOWEN, STEPHEN H., academic administrator; BA in Zoology and Philosophy, DePauw U., 1971; MA in Zoology, Ind. U., 1973; PhD in Zoology, Rhodes U., Grahamstown, South Africa, 1976. Instr. Rhodes U., 1973—76; field leader Lake Valencia Ecosys. Project U. Colo., Maracay, Venezuela, 1976—78; asst. prof. biol. scis. Mich. Tech. U., 1978—83, assoc. prof. biol. scis., 1983—89, prof. biol. scis., 1989—2001, assoc. dean Coll. Scis. and Arts, 1995—97, vice provost for instrn., 1997—2000, interim provost, sr. v.p. acad. and student affairs, 2000, vice provost for instrn., dean of distance learning, 2000—01; provost, v.p. acad. affairs Bucknell U., Lewisburg, Pa., 2001—04. Head dept. biol. scis. Mich. Tech. U., 1986—95; vis. fellow Inst. Acuicultura Torre de la Sal, Ribera de Cabanes, Spain, 1988; mem. Mich. Endangered Species Fish Tech. Adv. Com., 1986—95; mem. site rev. team Nat. Sea Grant Coll. Program, 1991; mem. tech. rev. panel Gt. Lakes Protection Fund, 1990—93; mem. tech. adv. bd. Mich. Gt. Lakes Protection Fund, 1989—92; bd. tech. experts Gt. Lakes Fishery Commn., 1989—93, co-leader lamprey ecology task area, 1994—98; mem. UN/FAO Sepik River Project Adv. Group, 1991—96; cons., evaluator North Ctrl. Assn., 1999—; cons. UN, Keweenaw Bay Chippewa, Cleve. Cliffs Iron Co. Contbr. articles to profl. jours. Grantee, State of Mich., 1980—81, 1985—86, Sport Fishing Inst., 1980—81, Office of Water Resources Tech., 1982—83, NSF Internat. Divsn., 1981, 1990, Conservation, Food and Health Found., Inc., 1987—89, Mich. Rsch. Excellence Fund, 1989—93, UN Food and Agr. Orgn., 1991, Gt. Lakes Fishery Commn., 1992—93, 1993—96, Mich. Sea Grant, 1993—95, 1995—99. Mem.: AAAS, Coun. Adminstrs. Gen. and Liberal Studies, Assn. Gen. and Liberal Studies, Nat. Assn. State and Land Grant Univs., Internat. Assn. Gt. Lakes Rsch., N.Am. Benthol. Soc. (assoc. editor jour. 1985—88), Am. Inst. Fishery Rsch. Biologists, Am. Soc. Limnology and Oceanography (chair endowment com. 1996—98), Am. Fisheries Soc. (profl. cert. rev. bd. 1996—99, assoc. editor 1981—83, cert. fisheries biologist), Ecol. Soc. Am., Am. Assn. Higher Edn.

BOWEN, STEPHEN STEWART, lawyer; b. Peoria, Ill., Aug. 23, 1946; s. Gerald Raymond and Frances Arlene (Stewart) B.; m. Joan Elizabet Logan, Jun. 18, 2005; children: David, Claire. BA cum laude, Wabash Coll., 1968; JD cum laude, U. Chgo., 1972. Bar: Ill. 1972, U.S. Dist. Ct. (no. dist.) Ill. 1972, U.S. Tax Ct. 1977. Assoc. Kirkland & Ellis, Chgo., 1972-78, ptnr., 1978-84, Latham & Watkins, Chgo., 1985—. Adj. prof. DePaul U. Masters in Taxation Program, Chgo., 1976-80; lectr. Practicing Law Inst., N.Y.C., Chgo., L.A., 1978-84, N.Y.C., 1986—. Mem. vis. com. U. Chgo. Div. Sch., 1984—2005, mem. vis. com. Sch. Law, 1991-93; mem. planning com. U. Chgo. Tax Conf., 1985—, chair, 1995-98; trustee Wabash Coll., 1996—. Fellow Am. Coll. Tax Counsel; mem. ABA, Ill. State Bar Assn., Order of Coif, Met. Club (Chgo.), Econ. Club Chgo., Phi Beta Kappa. Office: Latham & Watkins Sears Tower Ste 5800 Chicago IL 60606-6306

BOWEN, THOMAS EDWIN, surgeon; b. Lackawanna, N.y., Dec. 16, 1934; m. Margaret Marie Harrington, 1959; children: Matthew, Mark, James, John, Thaddeus, Mary Cristine. BS, St. Bonaventure U., 1961; MD, Marquette U., 1965; diploma, U.S. Army War Coll., 1985. Diplomate Am. Bd. Surgery, Am. Bd. Thoracic Surgery, Nat. Bd. Med. Examiners. Commd. 2d lt. U.S. Army, 1961, advanced through grades to brig. gen., 1988; intern Tripler Army Gen. Hosp., Honolulu, 1965-66, resident in gen. surgery, 1966-70, Vietnam, 1970-71; resident in thoracic surgery Walter Reed Army Gen. Hosp., Washington, 1971-73; dep. dir. Profl. Svcs. Directorate Office of Surgeon Gen., Washington, 1985-87; comdr., surgeon 121st Evacuation Hosp., 1987-88; assoc. prof. dept. surgery Sch. Medicine Uniformed Svcs. U. of Health Scis., Bethesda, Md., 1981—; commanding gen. Fitzsimons Army Med. Ctr., Aurora, Colo., 1988-93; assoc. clin. prof. dept. surgery U. Colo. Sch. Medicine, Denver, 1989—; assoc. prof. surgery U. So. Fla. Sch. Med.; chief of staff James A. Haley VA Med. Ctr., Tampa, Fla., 1993—. Contbr. articles to profl. publs. Chmn. Combined Fed. Campaign, Denver, 1990. Decorated D.S.M., Legion of Merit with three oak leaf clusters, Bronze Star, Alfredo Lezcano Gomez medal for Svc. to Republic of Panama; recipient Raymond Franklin Metcalf award, 1971. Mem. Assn. Mil. Surgeons, Am. Coll. Surgeons, Soc. Thoracic Surgeons, Denver C. of C., Aurora C. of C., Rotary. Roman Catholic. Avocations: beekeeping, woodworking, reading, raising animals and crops. Office: James A Haley VA Med Ctr Tampa FL 33612

BOWEN, WILLIAM GORDON, foundation administrator, economist; b. Cin., Oct. 6, 1933; s. Albert A. and Bernice (Pomert) B.; m. Mary Ellen Maxwell, Aug. 25, 1956; children: David Alan, Karen Lee. BA, Denison U., 1955; PhD, Princeton (NJ) U., 1958. Mem. faculty Princeton U., 1958-88, prof. econs., 1965-88, dir. grad. studies Woodrow Wilson Sch. Pub. and Internat. Affairs, 1964-66, provost, 1967-72, pres., 1972-88, Andrew W. Mellon Found., NYC, 1988—. Bd. dirs. Merck and Co., Inc., Am. Express Co., JSTOR, ARTstor Inc.; bd. overseers Tchrs. Ins. and Annuity Assn.-Coll. Ret. Equities Fund.; chmn. bd. dirs. Ithaka Harbors, Inc.; Romanes lectr. U. Oxford, 2000; Jefferson lectr. U. Va., 2004. Author: The Wage-Price Issue: A Theoretical Analysis, 1960, Wage Behavior in the Postwar Period: An Empirical Analysis, 1960, Economic Aspects of Education: Three Essays, 1964, (with W. J. Baumol) Performing Arts: The Economic Dilemma, 1966, (with T. A. Finegan) The Economics of Labor Force Participation, 1969, Ever the Teacher, 1987, (with J. A. Sosa) Prospects for Faculty in the Arts and Sciences, 1989, (with Neil L. Rudenstine) In Pursuit of the PhD, 1992, Inside the Boardroom: Governance by Directors and Trustees, 1994, (with T. Nygren, S. Turner, E. Duffy) The Charitable Nonprofits, 1994, (with Derek Bok) The Shape of the River: Long-Term Consequences of Considering Race in College and University Admissions, 1998, (with James L. Shulman) The Game of Life: College Sports and Educational Values, 2001, (with Sarah A. Levin) Reclaiming the Game: College Sports and Educational Values, 2003, (with Martin A. Kurzweil and Eugene M. Tobin) Equity and Excellence in American Higher Education, 2005. Trustee Ctr. for Advanced Study in Behavioral Scis., 1978-84, 89-92, Denison U., 1992-2000; regent emeritus Smithsonian Instn. Recipient Joseph Henry medal Smithsonian Instn., 1996, (with Derek Bok) Grawemeyer award in edn. U. Louisville, 2001. Mem. Am. Econs. Assn., Indsl. Rels. Rsch. Assn., Coun. on Fgn. Rels., Phi Beta Kappa. Office: Andrew W Mellon Found 140 E 62nd St New York NY 10021-8124 Office Phone: 212-838-8400.

BOWEN, WILLIAM HARVEY, bank executive, lawyer; b. Altheimer, Ark., May 6, 1923; s. Robert James and Lois Ruth Bowen; m. Mary Constance Wanasek, Aug. 31, 1947; children: Cynthia Ruth Bowen Blanchard, William Scott, Mary Patricia Bowen Barker. Student, Henderson State Tchrs. Coll., 1941-42; LL.B., U. Ark., 1949; LL.M. in Taxation, NYU, 1950; postgrad., Stonier Grad. Sch. Banking, Rutgers U., 1974. Bar: Ark. 1949, U.S. Supreme Ct. 1950. Atty. adviser U.S. Tax Ct., Washington, 1950-52; spl. asst. to atty. gen. trial sect., tax div. Dept. Justice, Washington, 1952-54; ptnr. Smith, Williams, Friday & Bowen, Little Rock, Ark., 1954-71; pres., dir. Comml. Nat. Bank, Little Rock, Ark., 1971-83, pres., dir., chief exec. officer, 1975-81, chmn., 1981-83; pres., chief exec. officer 1st Comml. Bank N.A., Little Rock, Ark., 1983-90, chmn., chief exec. officer, 1984-87, First Comml. Corp., 1984-90; chief of staff Gov. Bill Clinton, 1991-92; pres., CEO Healthsource Ark. Ventures, Inc., 1993-95; dean Sch. of Law U. Ark., Little Rock, 1995-97. Mem. staff Stonier Grad. Sch. Banking U. Del., 1976-98, bd. regents, 1977-81; memem. fed. adv. coun. Fed. Res. Bank, St. Louis, 1984-86; lectr. assemblies for bank dirs., So. Meth. U. Author: (with M. Moore) Arkansas Estate Planners Handbook, 1967. Trustee Ben J. Altheimer Found., Altheimer, Ark., 1973, Philander Smith Coll., Little Rock, 1968-80, Hendrix Coll., 1986-98, Drs. Hosp., U. Ark, Little Rock; chmn. bd. visitors U. Ark., 1979-80; state chmn. com. for employer support of N.G. and Res., nat. chmn., 1994-98; chmn. bd. Ark. Sci. and Tech. Authority, 1986-91; adv. council LWV; past chmn. Radio Free Europe Fund, Pulaski County United Fund. Served with USN, 1943-46, to lt. comdr. Res., ret. Named Little Rock Man of Yr. Ark. Dem., 1963; recipient Sales and Mktg. Exec. Man of Yr. award, 1963, Citizen-Lawyer of Yr. award Ark. Bar Found., 1971, Disting. Alumni award U. Ark., 1976 Mem. ABA (adv. com. to Treasury), Ark. Bankers Assn. (pres. 1982, chnm. legis. com. 1978-79), Am. Bankers Assn. (govt. relations council 1984—), Assn. Res. City Bankers, Ark. Bar Assn., Pulaski County Bar Assn., Beta Gamma Sigma, Sigma Alpha Epsilon, Delta Theta Phi . Clubs: Little Rock, Country of Little Rock. Lodges: Masons. Methodist. Home: 2200 Beechwood St Little Rock AR 72207-2024 Office: care Regions Bank PO Box 1471 Little Rock AR 72203-1471

BOWEN, WILLIAM JACKSON, retired gas industry executive; b. Sweetwater, Tex., Mar. 31, 1922; s. Berry and Annah (Robey) Bowen; m. Annis K Hilty, June 6, 1945; children: Shelley Ann, Barbara Kay, Berry Dunbar, William Jackson. BS, U.S. Mil. Acad., 1945. Registered profl engr, Tex. Petroleum engr. Delhi Oil Corp., Dallas, 1949-57; v.p. Fla. Gas Co., Houston, 1957-60, pres. Winter Park, Fla., 1960-74; pres., CEO Transco Cos., Inc., Houston, 1974-81; chmn. Transco Cos., Inc. (name changed to Transco Energy Co.), Houston, 1976-92; CEO Transco Energy Co., Houston, 1981-87; ret., 1992; also bd. dirs. Transco Energy Co., Houston; ret., 1992. Bd. dirs. J.P. Poindexter and Co., Inc.; mem. adv. bd. Am. Indsl. Ptnrs., N.Y.C.; hon. vice chmn. World Energy Coun. Bd. dirs. YMCA, Houston; trustee emeritus bd Baylor Coll. Medicine; trustee emeritus bd. Jesse H Jones Grad. Sch. Bus., Rice U. With AUS, 1945—49. Mem.: U.S. Energy Assn. (past chmn.). Episcopalian. Office: Williams 2800 Post Oak Blvd Level 16 Houston TX 77056-6100

BOWEN-FORBES, JORGE COURTNEY, artist, poet; b. Queenstown, Guyana, May 16, 1937; came to U.S., 1966; s. Walter and Margarita V. (Forbes) Bowen. BA, Queens Coll., Eve Leary, Guyana, 1969; MFA, Chelsea (Eng.) Sch. Design, 1972. Comml. artist Guyana Litographic, Georgetown; art dir. Corbin Advt. Agy., Bridgetown, Barbados; tech. advisor Ministry of Info. and Culture, Georgetown. Nat. juror Nat. Arts Club, N.Y.C., 1985, Nat. Soc. Painters in Casein and Acrylic. Major exhbns. include Expo 67, Can., Nat. Acad. Design, N.Y., Frye Mus., El Paso (Tex.) Mus., Wichita (Kans.) Centennial, Caribbean Festival of the Arts, Newark Mus.; 10-one-man exhbns. worldwide; works in collections including Nat. and Colgrain Collections, Guyana, El Paso Mus. Art, Kindercare Internat., Leon Loards Gallery, The McCreery Cummings Fine Art Collection, Bomani Gallery, San Francisco; poetry and articles pub. various jours.; author: Best Watercolors, 1996, Creative Watercolor, 1996; published in Best in Watercolor, Best in Oil Painting, Best in Acrylic Painting, Creative Watercolor, Splash 11, Best Contemporary Watercolors, American Poetry Annual. Recipient Silver medal of honor Allied Artists of N.Y., 1978, Gold medal of honor, 1975. Mem. Nat. Watercolor Soc. (signature mem.), Nat. Soc. Painters in Casein and Acrylics, Audubon Artists, Knickerbocker Artists (Gold Medal of Honor 1977, 79), Am. Watercolor Soc. (signature mem., High Winds medal 1984, Elsie and David Wu Ject-Key Meml. award 1998).

BOWENS, GLORIA FURR, educational administrator; b. Detroit, Apr. 15, 1927; d. Leon Lewis and Iva Rose (Talbot) Furr; B.S., Tufts Coll., 1947; Ed.M., State Coll. Boston, 1968; Ed.D., Harvard U., 1975; 1 dau., Stephanie T. Sci. tchr. Boston Pub. Schs., 1961-71, asst. to the dir. orientation for integration, 1971-73, acting dir. personnel mgmt., 1981-82, instr. med. tech., 1982—; asst. supt. schs. Roosevelt (L.I., N.Y.) Sch. Dist., 1974-77; asst. dir. urban schs. collaborative Northeastern U., Boston, 1977-79, dist. IX coordinator curriculum and competency resources, 1979-81; ptnr. antique shop, Pickering Wharf, Salem, Mass., 1982—; pres. Horizons Extended Ednl. Consulting, 1992-98. Mem. Nat. Council Adminstrv. Women Edn. (exec. bd. 1970-73), Am. Assn. Sch. Adminstrs., North Shore Antiques Assn. (treas.), Phi Delta Kappa, Alpha Kappa Alpha.

BOWER, ANNE LIEBERMAN, language educator; b. N.Y.C., May 8, 1941; d. Frank J. Lieberman and Maxine (Scheuer) Donahue; m. Roger L. Bower, Dec. 1962 (div. Dec. 1987); children, Rachael, Aviva, Issac. BS in English, Columbia U., 1963; MA in English, W.Va. U., 1985, PhD in English, 1990. Exec. sec. Pitts. Psychoanalytic Inst., 1975-77; project mgr. Greene County Indsl. Devel., Waynesburg, Pa., 1977-79, Greene County Planning Ctr., Waynesburg, 1979-81; exec. dir. Wheeling (W.Va.) Creek Watershed Commn., Wheeling and Waynesburg, 1981-86; tchg. asst. English W.Va. U., Morgantown, 1983-85, 87-90; instr. in English Waynesburg Coll., 1985-87; assoc. prof. English Ohio State U., Marion, 1990—. Spkr. Ohio Humanities Coun., Columbus, 1994-96. Author: Epistolary Responses: The Letter in 20th Century American Fiction and Criticism, 1996; editor: Recipes for Reading: Community Cookbooks, Stories, Histories, 1997, The Historical Cookbook of the American Negro, reprint, 2000, Reel Food, 2004; contbr. chpts. to books. Vol. Turning Point, Marion, 1994—, Pearl St. Sch., 2000-02, Dollars and Sense Partnership, 2001-03. Rsch. grantee Ohio State U., 1991-92, Schlesinger Libr., Radcliffe Coll., 1992, Ohio State U., 1994, Ohio Humanities Coun., 1996. Mem. MLA, Midwest MLA. Office: Ohio State U - Marion 1465 Mount Vernon Ave Marion OH 43302-5628

BOWER, BARBARA JEAN, nurse, consultant; b. Akron, Ohio, Aug. 25, 1942; d. William Howard and Maxine (Goodykoontz) Sturm; m. Howard Bower, Aug. 25, 1961 (dec. 1989); children: Nancy, Janet. BA, Elmhurst Coll., 1974, postgrad., 1987; diploma, Evang. Sch. Nursing, 1970; PhD, U. Chgo., 1993. Critical care nurse, supr. nursing Loyola U. Med. Ctr.; critical care nurse Med. Staffing Svcs., Oak Park, Ill., 1978—84; pres. Heart Care Unltd., Oak Brook, Ill., 1982—. Creator ednl. programs for cardiac patients, families and staff, 1971—. Stephen min. Christ Ch. of Oak Brook, Ill.; Republican election judge, DuPage County. Mem. AAUW, ANA, Am. Assn. Critical Care Nurses, Am. Heart Assn., Elmhurst Coll. Alumni Assn., U. Chgo. Alumni Assn., Oak Brook Exec. Breakfast Club. Avocations: rose gardening, cooking, candymaking. Office: Heart Care Unltd PO Box 3275 Oak Brook IL 60522-3275

BOWER, CHRISTOPHER JAMES, investment banker; b. Sterling, Ill., Mar. 5, 1957; s. William Joseph and Elsie Sandra (Sopko) B. BS in Acctg. and Fin., U. Colo., 1978; JD, U. San Diego, 1983. CPA, Calif. Mem. profl. staff Arthur Young and Co. Internat., Denver, 1978-79; founder, mng. dir. Pacific Corp. Group Inc., L.A., La Jolla, Calif., Chgo., 1979—. Bd. dirs. Pacific Corp. Internat., L.A.; sec. Pacific Corp. Fin. Inc., La Jolla; chmn. Pacific Corp. Advisors, Inc., La Jolla, Pacific Corp. Valuation Inc., La Jolla, 1979—. Contbr. articles to profl. jours. Mem. AICPA, Calif. State Soc. CPAs. Office: Pacific Corp Group Inc 2D Fl 1200 Prospect St Fl 2 La Jolla CA 92037-3608 Home: Ste 200 1200 Prospect St La Jolla CA 92037-3608

BOWER, DAVID NORMAN, music educator, researcher; b. Rochester, NY, Dec. 2, 1965; s. Norman Arthur and Favorite Lucille Bower. BM, SUNY Fredonia, Fredonia, NY, 1985—88; MM, Westminster Choir Coll., Princeton, NJ, 1988—90; MA, NYU, New York, NY, 1991—93; PhD candidate NYU, 2002. Music dir. Second Presbyn. Ch., Rahway, NJ, 1988—90; organist

Princeton U. Chapel, Princeton, NJ, 1988—90; music min. St John's Ch., Hazlet, NJ, 1990—91; music dir. St Peter's Ch., Belleville, NJ, 1991—93, St Ann Ch., Raritan, NJ, 1993—; music educator St Ann Sch., Raritan, NJ, 1993—; writing instr. NYU, N.Y.C., 2000—03. Contbr. articles to profl. jour. Mem.: Nat. Assn. of Music Educators, Am. Guild of Organists, Coll. Music Soc., Organ Hist. Soc. Home: 194 Wayne St #4R Jersey City NJ 07302 Office: Saint Ann Church 45 Anderson St Raritan NJ 08869-1834 Office Phone: 908-725-1008 109.

BOWER, DOUGLAS WILLIAM, pastoral counselor, psychotherapist, clergyman; b. Niagara Falls, NY, Jan. 6, 1948; s. Charles Henry Bower and Phyllis June (Rank) Ayres; m. Cheryl Stewart, May 25, 1980; children: Katherine Elizabeth, Erin Colleen. AA, Manatee Jr. Coll., Bradenton, Fla., 1969; BS, Oglethorpe U., 1972; PhD, U. Ga., 1989. RN, Ga.; ordained to ministry United Meth. Ch., 1981; cert. counselor, Ga.; life cert. diplomate Am. Psychotherapy Assn. Nurse Northside Hosp., Atlanta, 1970-80; assoc. pastor 1st United Meth. Ch., Griffin, Ga., 1980-82; pastor, pastoral counselor Oconee Street United Meth. Ch., Athens, Ga., 1982-86; dir. Counseling Ministeries, Athens, 1986—. Adj. faculty Ft. Valley State U., 1999—2001. Contbr. articles to profl. jours. Active Oglethorpe County Sr. Citizens Adv. Coun., United Way of N.E. Ga., U. Ga. Nat. Alumni Assn.; commr. Oglethorpe County, Dist. 1, 2002. Mem.: Assn. Humanist and Psychologists, Am. Psychotherapy Assn., Ga. Sheriffs Assn. (hon.). Avocations: music, walking, reading. Office: PO Box 143 Bishop GA 30621-0143 *While we may not make an impact on the world, we can and do make an impact on the immediate world around and within us. Persistence in maintaining faith, even in the face of adversity, makes a powerful impact on our immediate world.*

BOWER, FAY LOUISE, academic administrator, nursing educator; b. San Francisco, Sept. 10, 1929; d. James Joseph and Emily Clare (Andrews) Saitta; children: R. David, Carol Bower Tomei, Dennis James, Thomas John. BS with honors, San Jose State Coll., 1965; MSN, U. Calif., 1966, DNSc, 1978. Cert. pub. health nurse, sch. nurse, Calif. Office nurse Dr. William Grannis, Palo Alto, Calif., 1950-55; staff nurse Stanford Hosp., 1964-72; asst. prof. San Jose (Calif.) State U., 1966-70, assoc. prof., 1970-74, prof., 1974-82, coord. grad. program in nursing, 1977-78, chairperson dept. nursing, 1978-82; dean U. San Francisco, 1982-89, v.p. acad. affairs, 1988-89, dir. univ. planning and instl. rsch., 1989-91; pres. Clarkson Coll., 1991-97; cons. in field, 1997—; chair dept. nursing Holy Names U., 2000—. Vis. prof. Harding Coll., 1977, U. Miss., 1976; lectr. U. Calif., San Francisco, 1975; nat. exec. adv. bd. Nurse Week, 1999—; spkr., cons. in field. Author: Approaches to Teaching Primary Care, 1981, The Newman Systems Model: Application to Nursing Education and Practice, 1982, Managing a Nursing Shortage: A Guide to Recruitment and Retention, 1989, Cracking the Wall: Women in Higher Education Administration, 1993, Nurses Taking the Lead..., 1999, Care and Management of Alzheimers, vols. 1-5, 2002, Developing and Managing a Career in Nursing, 2003; (with Em O. Bevis) Fundamentals of Nursing Practice: Concepts, Roles and Functions, 1978, (with Margaret Jacobson) Community Health Nursing, 1978, The Process of Planning Nursing Care, 3d edit., 1982, (with Mae Timmons) Medical Surgical Nursing, 1995, (with others) Concepts & Issues in Nursing, 3d edit., 1996, Creating Nursings' Futures: Issues, Opportunities & Challenges, 1999; contbr. articles to profl. jours. Fellow Am. Acad. Nursing; mem.APHA (Calif. chpt.), Nurses Assn., Western Gerontol. Assn., Jesuit Deans in Nursing (chair 1982-85), Rotary (Omaha), Sigma Theta Tau (internat.pres., 1993-95. Democrat. Roman Catholic. Home: 1457 Indianhead Cir Clayton CA 94517-1239 Office Phone: 510-436-1024. Personal E-mail: fbower1@sbcglobal.net. Business E-Mail: bower@hnu.edu.

BOWER, GLEN LANDIS, federal agency administrator, lawyer; b. Highland, Ill., Jan. 16, 1949; s. Ray Landis and Evelyn Ferne Bower. BA, So. Ill. U., 1971; JD (hon.), Ill. Inst. Tech., 1974. Bar: Ill. 1974, US Ct. Mil. Appeals 1975, US Ct. Appeals (7th cir.) 1976, US Dist Ct. (so. dist.) Ill. 1977, US Dist. Ct. (cen. dist.) Ill. 1992, US Supreme Ct. 1978, US Tax Ct. 1984, US Ct. Claims 1986, US Dist. Ct. (no. dist.) Ill. 1994, US Ct. Veterans Appeals 1995. Sole practice, Effingham, Ill., 1974-83; prosecutor Effingham County, Ill., 1976-79; mem. Ill. House of Reps., Springfield, 1979-83; asst. dir., gen. counsel Ill. Dept. Revenue, Springfield, Ill., 1983-90; Presdl. apptd. chmn. US R.R. Retirement Bd., Chgo., 1990-97; asst. to Ill. Sec. of State, Chgo., 1998-99; apptd. dir. revenue State of Ill., 1999—2003; sr. advisor U.S. Small Bus. Adminstrn., Washington, 2004. Mil. aide to Gov. of Ill., 1999-2003; liaison mem. Adminstrv. Conf. of US, 1991-95; mem. Nat. Adv. Com. for Juvenile Justice and Delinquency Prevention, Washington, 1976-80, US Econ. Adv. Bd. of US Dept. Commerce, Washington, 1981-85, Ill. Gen. Assembly State Adv. Com. on Cir. Ct. Fin., Springfield, 1984; mem. Revenue Bd. Appeals, Chgo., 1985-87, chmn., 1986-87; mem. Com. of 50 on Ill. Constn., 1987-88; adv. com. on electronic tax adminstrn. IRS, 2000-2003, So. Ill. U. Pub. Policy Inst., 2000. Co-editor: Handbook on State Taxation, 1991; contbr. articles to profl. jour. Alt. del. Rep. Nat. Conv., 1972, 88, 92, 2000, 04; vice chmn. Effingham County Rep. Ctrl. Com., Ill., 1976-90; bd. dir. Dana-Thomas House Found., Springfield, Ill., 1989-90, So. Ill. U. at Carbondale Found., 1993-2002, pres.'s coun.; trustee McKendree Coll., Lebanon, Ill., 1978-81; chmn. State of Ill. Organ and Tissue Donors Adv. Bd., 1993-98. Lt. col. USAFR, 1974-99, ret. Recipient The Univ. Disting. Svc. award, 1971, Recognition citation Am. Legion, 1980, Outstanding Svc. cert. to tchg. profession Ill. Edn. Assn., 1981, Disting. Svc. award Am. Vets., 1980, 82, Presdl. citation Navy League US, 1981, Constitution award Mus. of Our Nat. Heritage, 1988, Silver Good Citizenship medal Ill. Soc. SAR, 1990, Profl. Achievement award Ill. Inst. Tech., 1993, Friend of History award Ill. State Hist. Soc., 1994, Alumni Achievement award So. Ill. U., 1994, Disting. Alumnus award So. Ill. U. Coll. Liberal Arts, 2000, Outstanding Civilian Svc. Medal, Dept. Army, 2003; named Outstanding Freshman Legislator, Ill. Edn. Assn., 1980, Legislator of Yr., Ill. Assn. Rehab. Socs., 1981, 82, One of 10 Dels. to China, Am. Coun. Young Polit. Leaders, 1988. Fellow: Am. Bar Found., Ill. Bar Found. (life); mem.: ABA, US Capitol Hist. Soc. (charter), Effingham County Mental Health Assn. (pub. affairs com. 1977—78), SBA Adv. Coun., Effingham Regional Hist. Soc. (bd. dir. 1973—77), Ill. State Hist. Soc. (v.p. 1979—81, Ralph C. Francis award 1967), Am. Coun. Young Polit. Leaders (life), Nat. Assn. Tax Adminstrs. (vice chmn. attys. sect. 1985—86, chmn. 1986—88, vice chmn. attys. sect. 1988—89), Effingham County Bar Assn. (sec. 1976—77, pres. 1983—84), Ill. State Bar Assn. (labor law sect. coun. 1976—77, sec. state taxation sect. coun. 1987—88, vice-chair 1988—89, 1988—89, chair 1989—90, sect. coun. on employee benefits 1991—98, 1991—98, sect. coun. on adminstrv. law 2000, Bd. Gov.'s award 1999), Fed. Tax Adminstrs. (bd. trustees 2001—03), Sons of Am. Revolution, Smithsonian Assocs., Abraham Lincoln Assn., Res. Officers Assn. (life), The Nat. Sojourners (life), So. Ill. Univ. Alumni Assn. (life), Am. Legion (life), Effingham County Old Settlers Assn. (pres., bd. dir. 1983—86), Art Inst. of Chgo., So. Ill. U. Carbondale Found. (bd. dir. 1993—2002), Field Mus. of Natural History, Army and Navy Club Washington D.C., Kiwanis (pres. 1977—78), Phi Alpha Delta (life). Republican. Methodist. Home: PO Box 1106 Effingham IL 62401-1106

BOWER, JAMES HOWARD, neurologist; b. Pitts., Mar. 16, 1962; s. Howard George and Doris Catherine Bower; m. Susan MacGillivray, Dec. 30, 1989; children: Leigh, Luke, Michael, Sarah. BA, Duke U., 1984; MD, N.Y. U., 1988. Diplomate Am. Bd. Psychiatry and Neurology. Gen. med. officer USN, 1988-92; neurology fellow Mayo Clinic, Rochester, Minn., 1992-96; asst. prof. Mayo Sch. Medicine, Rochester, Minn., 1998—. Contbr. several articles to profl. pubs. Lt. USNR, 1988-92. Mem. AMA, Am. Acad. Neurology. Office: 200 1st St SW Rochester MN 55905-0001

BOWER, JANIE PITTMAN, mathematics professor; b. Laurel, Miss., May 29, 1955; d. Cecil J. and Ethel J. (Sumrall) Pittman; m. Theodore E. Bower, June 23, 1978. AA, Jones Jr. Coll., Ellisville, Miss., 1975; BS, William Carey Coll., 1977; MS, Wlliam Carey Coll., Hattiesburg, Miss., 1980. Nat. bd. cert. tchr. early adolescent math. Math tchr. West Jones Jr./Sr. High Sch., Soso, Miss., 1977-79, North Forrest High Sch., Hattiesburg, 1979-80, Thames Jr. High Sch., Hattiesburg, 1980-87, Rowan Jr. High Sch., Hattiesburg, 1987—2002; tchr. Freshman Acad. Hattiesburg H.S., 2003—. Mem. algebra test com. Miss. State Dept. Edn., Jackson, 1988—; mem. textbook com. Hattiesburg Pub. Schs., 1988—; adj. faculty William Carey Coll., Hattiesburg, 1999—. Hattiesburg Edn. Found. grantee, 1988-89. Mem. Nat. Coun. Tchrs. Math. (referee jour. Math. Tchg. in Mid. Sch.), Miss. Coun. Tchrs. Math., Math. Assn. Am., Miss. Profl. Educators, Alpha Delta Kappa (past pres.) Baptist. Office: Freshman Acad Hattiesburg HS 301 Hutchinson Ave Hattiesburg MS 39401 Office Phone: 601-583-2657.

BOWER, JEAN RAMSAY, lawyer, writer; b. N.Y.C., Nov. 25, 1935; d. Claude Barnett and Myrtle Marie (Scott) Ramsay; m. Ward Swift Just, Jan. 31, 1957 (div. 1966); children: Jennifer Ramsay, Julia Barnett; m. Robert Turrell Bower, June 12, 1971 (dec. June 1990). AB, Vassar Coll., 1957; JD, Georgetown U., 1970. Bar: D.C. 1970. Exec. dir. D.C. Dem. Ctrl. Com., Washington, 1969-71; pvt. practice Washington, 1971-78, 94—; dir. Counsel of Child Abuse and Neglect Office D.C. Superior Ct., 1978-94. Mem. Mayor's Com. on Child Abuse and Neglect, 1973-94, vice chmn., 1975-79; mem. Family Div. Rules Adv. Com., 1977-94; pres., bd. dirs. C.B. Ramsay Found., 1984—; cons. child welfare issues, writer. Contbr. poetry to In a Certain Place. Mem. D.C. Child Fatality Rev. Com., 1992-; bd. dirs. Friends D.C. Superior Ct., 1994—, pres. bd. dirs., 2002-05; bd. dirs. Family and Child Svcs., Washington, 1995-2003, bd. dirs., 2004-; chair Folger Poetry Bd., 2002-, Folger Shakespeare Libr., 1998- . Named Washingtonian of the Yr. Washington Mag., 1978. Mem. Women's Bar Assn. (bd. dirs. 1993-96, found. 1986-91, Woman Lawyer of Yr. 1986), D.C. Bar Assn. (election bd. 1994-96, Beatrice Rosenberg award sect. com. 1994—), Women's Bar Assn. Found. (bd. dirs. 1986-91). E-mail: JBower3714@aol.com.

BOWER, JOHN, retired fluid mechanics engineer, commissioner; b. Somerset, Mass., Sept. 16, 1920; s. Matthew H. and Alice (Winterbom) Bower; m. Marion Louise Cadorette, Aug. 2, 1948; children: John C., Jeffrey J., Douglas J. BS, Brown Univ., Providence, RI, 1938—41. Cert. WPI, Water Works Op. & Mgmt., Worcester, Mass., 1962. Sales & engr. WW Grainger, Chgo., 1949—86; commr. Somerset Indsl. Fin. Authority, 1980—. Commr. Town of Somerset, Somerset, Mass.; chmn. Bd. of Sewer and Water Commissioners, Somerset, Mass. Warrant officer USAAF, 1942—45. Recipient State Award, Mass Consulting Engr./ Mass., 1999, Nat. Award, Nat. Assoc. Cons. Engr./ Seattle, Wash., 1999. Mem.: NY Acad. of Sci., New Eng. Water Works (life mem. for 40 yrs. svc.), Am. Water Works (life mem. for 30 yrs. svc.), RI Shriners Club (Legion of Honor), Pioneer Lodge (Master 1955). Republican. Episcopalian. Avocation: ski patrol. Home: 2742 Riverside Ave Somerset MA 02726 E-mail: JBower8175@aol.com.

BOWER, JOHN ARNOLD, JR., architect, educator; b. Phila., Apr. 22, 1930; s. John Arnold and Marie Imogene (Siegle) B.; m. Joan Wolfington, Sept. 13, 1952; children: Bradley Clark, Mark Arnold, Craig Newton. Student, Pa. State Coll., 1948-49, Ohio State U., 1949-51; BArch with honors, U. Pa., 1953. Registered architect, Pa., N.Y., N.J., Del., Md., Conn., Ill., La., S.C., N.C., Minn. Draftsman John A. Bower, Sr. Architect, Phila., 1950-51; designer Phila. Planning Commn., 1953-54; sr. designer Vincent G. Kling Architects, Phila., 1954-61; ptnr. Bower and Fradley Architects, Phila., 1961-78, Bower Lewis Thrower Architects, Phila., 1978—. Prof. architecture U. Pa.; mem. design adv. panel Dept. Housing and Community Devel., Balt., 1964—. Prin. works include Vance Hall, Wharton Grad. Ctr. (gold medal AIA Phila. chpt. 1973, design citation 1968), Internat. House (gold medal AIA Phila. chpt. 1967), Milles Sculpture Group (silver medal AIA Phila. chpt. 1972), Gallery at Market E. (cert. excellence - urban design 1978), Soc. Hill Townhouses (1st honor award Pa. Soc. Architects 1966), Princton Forrestal Village (Merit award Pa. Soc. Architects 1987), Market St. E. Transp. Mall Ctr., One Reading Ctr. Office Tower, Balt. Mus. Art. (restoration, additions), 1234 Market St. Office Bldg., 1500 Walnut St. Office Bldg., Marriott Phila. Conv. Ctr. Hotel. Albert F. Schenk travelling fellow U. Pa., 1954, fellow Fontainbleau Sch. Fine Arts-Music, Paris, 1954. Fellow AIA (nat. urban planning and design com. 1974-75, nat. com. on design 1976-78); mem. NAD (assoc.), Carpenter's Co., Hexagon Honor Soc., Tau Sigma Delta. Clubs: Germantown Cricket. Office: Bower Lewis Thrower Architects 1216 Arch St Ste 9 Philadelphia PA 19107-2835*

BOWER, JOHN LAWRENCE, ornithologist, educator; s. Mason James and Dorothe Coerr Bower. PhD, Cornell U., 1998. Assoc. prof. Western Wash. U., Bellingham, 1998—. Office: Western Washington Univ 516 High St MS 9118 Bellingham WA 98225-9118 Business E-Mail: jbower@cc.wwu.edu.

BOWER, JOHN RICHARD FENN, archaeologist, educator; b. Newton, Iowa, May 5, 1935; s. John Oates and Lillian Keithen Bower; m. Andrea Garcia Montero, Feb. 1961 (div. Aug. 1965); m. Janice Sophie Johnson, Sept. 26, 1966; 1 child, Jennifer Keithen. BA, Harvard U., 1957; MA, Northwestern U., Evanston, Ill., 1968; PhD, Northwestern U., 1973. Editor Rand McNally & Co., Skokie, Ill., 1962—67; asst. prof. Lake Forest Coll., Lake Forest, Ill., 1970—73; from asst. prof. to full prof. Iowa State U., Ames, 1973—92, prof. emeritus, 1992—; part-time lectr. U. Minn., Duluth, 1992—. Rsch. fellow Brit. Inst. of History and Archaeology in East Africa, Nairobi, Kenya, 1971; dir. archaeol excavations Serengeti Park; condr. 1st trans-Atlantic archaeol. investigations with Polish collaboration. Author: In Search of the Past, 1986; co-sr. editor Prehistoric Cultures and Environments in Africa, 1988, co-sr. author A Comparative Study of Prehistoric Foragers in Europe and North America, 2002. Lt. USN, 1957—62. Recipient Wilton Park award for internat. svc., Iowa State U., 1989; fellow Fulbright fellow, 1982. Fellow: Am. Anthropol. Assn.; mem.: AAAS, Soc. for Am. Archaeology, Duluth Cmty. Sailing Assn. (bd. dirs. 2000—), No. Lakes Archaeol. Soc. (bd. dirs. 2002—), Duluth Yacht Club (vice commodore 2002—). Democrat. Unitarian Universalist. Avocations: sailing, fly fishing, music, poetry. Office: Univ of Minn-Duluth 10 University Dr Duluth MN 55812 Home: 3496 Oyster Bay Ave Davis CA 95616-5606 Personal E-mail: jrfbower@aol.com.

BOWER, JOSEPH LYON, business administration educator; b. N.Y.C., Sept. 21, 1938; s. Morris L. and Florence (Turitz) B.; m. Nancy Milender, Feb. 16, 1958; children: Jonathan, Deborah. AB, Harvard U., 1959, MBA, 1961, D Bus. Adminstrn., 1963. Asst. prof. Grad. Sch. Bus. Adminstrn. Harvard U., Boston, 1963-68, assoc. prof. Grad. Sch. Bus. Adminstrn., 1968-71, Donald K. David prof. bus. adminstrn. Grad. Sch. Bus. Adminstrn., 1972—, sr. assoc. dean for external rels. Grad. Sch. Bus. Adminstrn., 1986-89, chmn. doctoral programs, dir. of rsch. Grad. Sch. Bus. Adminstrn., 1989-95, faculty mem. John F. Kennedy Sch. Govt. Cambridge, Mass., 1969—. Bd. dirs. Anika Rsch. Inc., Woburn, Mass., Brown Shoe Inc., St. Louis, Sonesta Internat. Hotels Corp., Boston, New Am. High Income Fund, Boston, Loews Corp., N.Y.C.; trustee TH Lee, Putnam Emerging Portfolio, Boston; chair gen. mgr. program Grad. Sch. Bus. Adminstrn., 1996— Author: Managing Resource Allocation Process, 1971 (McKinsey Found. award 1971), Two Faces of Management, 1983, When Markets Quake, 1986; co-author: Public Management: Text and Cases, 1978, Business Policy: Text and Cases, 7th edit., 1991, Business Policy: Managing Strategic Processes, 8th edit., 1995, From Resource Allocation to Strategy, 2005. Life trustee New Eng. Conservatory Music, Boston, 1984-03, DeCordova and Dana Mus. and Pk., Lincoln, Mass., 1987—. Co-recipient (with C.M. Christensen) McKinsey Found. award, 1995. Mem. Am. Econ. Assn., Coun. Fgn. Rels., St. Botolph Club (Boston), Harvard Club (N.Y.C.). Avocations: tennis, boating, golf. Office: Harvard Bus Sch Sch Bus Morgan # 467 Boston MA 02163 Office Phone: 617-495-6282. Personal E-mail: jbower@hbs.edu.

BOWER, RICHARD JAMES, minister; b. Somerville, N.J., June 9, 1939; s. Oneil A. and Mildred R. (Goss) B.; m. Helen Ann Cheek, Dec. 29, 1962 (div. 1985); 1 child, Christopher Scott. Student, Sorbonne, Paris, 1959-60; BA, Wesleyan U., 1961; MDiv, Drew U., Madison, NJ, 1965; student, Oxford U., Eng., 1983; DD, Piedmont Coll., 1999. Ordained to ministry, Congl. Christian Ch., 1965. Min. Cmty. Congl. Ch., Kewaunee, Wis., 1965-67; sr. min. Congl. Ch., Bound Brook, NJ, 1967-78, Congl. Ch. of the Chimes, Sherman Oaks, Calif., 1978-95; preaching min. Congl. Ch. Messiah, L.A., 1995-96, First Congl. Ch., L.A., 2002, 2005. Mem. exec. com., dir. Nat. Assn. Congl. Christian Chs., 1973-77, chmn., 1976-77,asst. moderator, 1981-82, moderator, 1982-83, exec. search com., 1990-91, nominating com., 1991-93, chmn., 1992-93; mem. World Christian Rels. Commn., 1993-97. Appeared on TV programs; contbr. poetry and articles to periodicals. Organizer, pres. Am. Field Svc., Kewaunee, 1966-67; dir. Children's Bur., L.A., 1981-88; bd. fellows Hollywood Congl. Ctr., 1979-82; bd. dirs. Heritage Playhouse, 1986-96. Recipient Citation for Disting. Svc., Nat. Assn. Congl. Christian Chs., 1997. Mem. Cal-West Assn. (dir., moderator 1986-87) Lodges: Bound Brook Rotary (pres. 1975-76). Democrat. Home: 365 W Alameda Ave Apt 302 Burbank CA 91506-3339 E-mail: rijabo@juno.com.

BOWER, RICHARD STUART, retired economist; b. N.Y.C., Aug. 1, 1928; s. Jacob and Elsie (Vander Beugle) Bower; m. Dorothy Ann Hagberg, June 23, 1953; children: Gari Ellen, Laura Jane, Nancy Lynne. AB, Kenyon Coll., 1949; MBA, Columbia, 1955; PhD, Cornell U., 1962. Instr. econs. Kenyon Coll., 1949-50, Alfred U., 1955-57; asst. prof. econs. and bus. Vanderbilt U., 1959-62; prof. bus. econs. Dartmouth, 1962—99; ptnr. Bower Rohr and Assocs., Hanover, 1981—2001; ret. Author: Investment and Liquidity: A Case Study of Clay Construction Products, 1965; contbr. articles to profl. jours. With USNR, 1951—55. Mem.: Am. Econ. Assn., Phi Beta Kappa, Phi Kappa Phi, Beta Gamma Sigma. Democrat. Jewish. Home: South Esker Hanover NH 03755 Office: Amos Tuck Sch Hanover NH 03755 Office Phone: 603-646-3579.

BOWER, ROBERT HEWITT, surgeon, educator, researcher; b. Omaha, Aug. 20, 1949; s. John Walter and Dorothy May (Sibert) B.; m. Debra Lea Goettsche, July 4, 1980; children: Timothy Conrad, Michael Harvey, Emily Frances. BA, Grinnell Coll., 1971; MD, U. Nebr., 1975. Diplomate Nat. Bd. Med. Examiners, Am. Bd. Surgery (dir. 1995-2001, sr. examiner 2001—). Intern U. Nebr., 1975-76, resident surgery, 1976-80, chief resident, 1979-80; clin. and rsch. fellow U. Cin., 1980-81, asst. prof. surgery, 1981-85; dir. dept. parenteral and enteral nutrition U. Hosp., 1981—, assoc. prof. surgery, 1985-95, prof. surgery, 1995—, dir. surg. residency, 1986—2002, vice chmn. edn., 1995—, dir. residency edn. program gen. surgery, 2002—. Chief surg. svc. Cin. VA Med. Ctr., 1994—. Contbr. chpts. to books and articles to profl. jours. Pres., trustee, chmn. bd. trustees Vocal Arts Ensemble of Cin.; elder, trustee Knox Presbyn. Ch. Fellow ACS, Am. Surg. Assn.; mem. Ctrl. Surg. Assn., Am. Coll. Nutrition, Soc. Am. Gastrointestinal Endoscopic Surgeons, Assn. Acad. Surgery, Am. Soc. Parenteral and Enteral Nutrition, Ohio Med. Assn., Surg. Infection Soc., Acad. Medicine Cin., Soc. Univ. Surgeons, Soc. Surgery of Alimentary Tract, Cin. Surg. Soc. (pres. 2002-03), Assn. Surg. Edn., Halsted Soc. Office: U Cincinnati Dept Surgery PO Box 670558 231 Albert Sabin Way Cincinnati OH 45267-0558 Office Phone: 513-558-4206. Business E-Mail: robert.bower@uc.edu.

BOWER, ROSE JANET, psychologist, educator; b. Pitts., Mar. 13, 1919; d. Alvin Lionel and Rose Clementina (Saller) B.; m. Albert E. Bachelet, 1993. BA, Waynesburg Pa. Coll., 1941; MA, U. Chgo., 1950, PhD, 1953. Rsch. assoc. U. Chgo., 1953-54; head dept. psychology Centenary Coll. for Women, Hackettstown, N.J., 1955-58; rsch. dir. Cath. Charities, Milw., 1958-59; rsch. assoc. Bank St. Coll. Edn., N.Y.C., 1959-61; assoc. prof. psychology and edn. Jersey City (N.J.) State Coll., 1961-68, prof., 1968-83, prof. emeritus, 1986—. Vis. assoc. prof. grad. sch. edn. U. So. Calif., L.A., 1966-67, SUNY, New Paltz, 1965. Unitarian Universalist. Avocations: walking, history, writing. Home: 35 Needle Pk Circle Queensbury NY 12804-1606

BOWER, THOMAS MICHAEL, lawyer; b. NYC, Apr. 6, 1952; s. John Joseph and Marianne Judith (Milch) B.; m. Sharon Misae Nakamoto, Dec. 1, 1979. BA magna cum laude, Cornell U., 1973; JD, Columbia U., 1976. Bar: N.Y. 1977, U.S. Ct. Mil. Appeals 1979, U.S. Dist. Ct. (so. dist. and ea. dists.) N.Y. 1980. Assoc. Bower & Gardner, N.Y.C., 1980-83, ptnr., 1984-91; prin. Newman & Bower, P.C., N.Y.C., 1991-92; of counsel Bickford, Hahn & Haley, 1993-98; ptnr. Shaub Ahmuty Citrin & Spratt, LLP, N.Y.C., 1998—2004; pvt. practice Briarcliff Manor, NY, 2004—. Lt. JAGC, USNR, 1976-80. Mem. Fedn. Def. and Corp. Counsel, Def. Rsch. Inst., Alpha Delta Phi. Office: 245 Hardscrabble Rd Briarcliff Manor NY 10510-1802 Office Phone: 888-842-4922. E-mail: tombower@thomasbower.com.

BOWERFIND, EDGAR SIHLER, JR., internist, educator, retired medical association administrator; b. Cleve., May 7, 1924; s. Edgar Sihler and Edna (Strong) B.; m. Maria Washington Tucker, Apr. 28, 1956; children— Edgar Sihler III, Ellis Tucker, Jane Strong, William Minor Lile Student, Creighton U. Med. Sch., 1945-47; MD, Western Res. U., 1949. Diplomate Am. Bd. Internal Medicine. Intern Univ. Hosps. of Cleve., 1950-51, resident in medicine, 1954-56; practice medicine specializing in internal medicine Cleve., 1957-92; mem. faculty Case Western Res. U. Sch. Medicine, Cleve., 1956-92, asst. prof. medicine, 1965-92, dir. health clinics, utilization rev., 1965-92, asst. prof. emeritus, 1992—; chief med. services Horizon Ctr. Hosp., Cleve., 1981-83. Sec. Citizens Commn. on Grad. Med. Edn., 1964-66 Sub-deacon Episcopal Diocese Ohio, 1970—; trustee The Sihler Mental Health Found. Served with AUS, 1943-46, to capt. USAF, 1951-53. Decorated Bronze Star; Ogelbay fellow in medicine U. Hosps. Cleve., 1955-56 Home: Ste 915 2181 Ambleside Dr Cleveland OH 44106

BOWERING, GEORGE HARRY, writer, consultant, language educator; b. Penticton, BC, Can., Dec. 1, 1936; s. Ewart Harry and Pearl Patricia (Brinson) Bowering; m. Angela May Luoma, Dec. 14, 1962; 1 child, Thea Claire. Student, Victoria Coll., 1953—54; BA, U. B.C., 1960, MA, 1963; postgrad., U. Western Ont., 1966—67. Asst. prof. Am. lit. U. Calgary, Canada, 1963-66; writer in residence Sir George Williams U., Montreal, 1967-68, asst. prof., 1968-71; prof. Simon Fraser U., Burnaby, 1972—2001; poet laureate of Can. Author: Mirror on the Floor, 1967, Autobiology, 1972, Flycatcher and Other Stories, 1974, Concentric Circles, 1977, A Short Sad Book, 1977, Protective Footwear, 1978, Another Mouth, 1979, Burning Water, 1980, A Place to Die, 1983, Caprice, 1987, Harry's Fragments, 1990, The Rain Barrel, 1994, Shoot!, 1994, Parents From Space, 1994, Piccolo Mondo, 1998, Diamondback Dog, 1998; poetry Points on the Grid, 1964, The Man in Yellow Boots, 1965, The Silver Wire, 1966, Rocky Mountain Foot, 1968, The Gangs of Kosmos, 1969, Touch, 1971, In the Flesh, 1973, The Catch, 1976, Particular Accidents: Selected Poems, 1981, Smoking Mirror, 1984, Kerrisdale Elegies, 1984, 71 Poems for People, 1985, Delayed Mercy, 1986, Sticks & Stones, 1989, Quarters, 1991, Urban Snow, 1992, George Bowering Selected, 1993, The Moustache, 1993, Blonds On Bikes, 1997; (poetry) His Life: A Poem, 2000, Baseball, 2003, Changing on the Fly, 2004; (essays) The Mask in Place, 1982, A Way with Words, 1982, Craft Slices, 1985, Errata, 1988, Imaginary Hand, 1988, A Magpie Life, 2001, Cars, 2002, Left Hook, 2005; author: (history) Bowering's B.C., 1996, Egotists and Autocrats, 1999, Stone Country, 2003; editor Taking the Field: The Best of Baseball Fiction, 1990, 92, Likely Stories: A Postmodern Sampler, 1992, And Other Stories, 2001, (short stories) Standing On Richards, 2004. Served with RCAF, 1954-57. Mem.: Assn. Can. TV and Radio Artists. Home: 4403 W 11th Ave Vancouver BC Canada Personal E-mail: bowering@sfu.ca.

BOWERMAN, ANN LOUISE, writer, secondary school educator, genealogist; b. Branch County, Mich., June 4, 1933; d. George Allen and Mary (Thomas) Hubbard; m. Virgil Lee Bowerman, June 4, 1954 (div. 1977); children: William Lee, Sally Ann; m. Virgil Wayne Dunkel, Jr., May 23, 1987 (div. Dec. 1996). BA, We. Mich. U., 1966, MSLS, 1971, MA, 1976. Cert. tchr. K-8, Mich., libr. sci. Tchr. Bethel #6 Sch. Dist., Coldwater, Mich., 1953—55; tchr. kindergarten Union City Schs., Mich., 1963—64; children's libr. Sturgis Pub. Libr., Mich., 1971—72; libr./media specialist Coldwater H.S., 1972—91; field rep. U.S. Census Bur., 2000—02, 2003—; media specialist libr. Union City Schs., 2002—03; ret., 1991. Mem. programming com., ann. scholarships telethon com., camera staff, video editor Cable TV Channel 31, Coldwater, 1983-90. Author: The Bater Book, 1987, A Bowerman Family History, 1998, Historic Howe, Indiana Walking Tour, 1998, The William Bowerman Family of Conneaut Township, 1998; co-author: Recommendations for High School Media Centers in Michigan, 1980 (booklet); contbr. articles to profl. jours. Mem., chair governing bd. Woodlands Libr. Coop., Albion, Mich., 1973-74, 83-86; adv. coun. Calhoun and Branch Counties Regional Ednl. Media Ctr., Marshall, Mich., 1972-91; com. mem. So. Mich. Region of Coop., Albion, 1989-91; leader All Around 4-H Club, Union City, 1954-74; mem. Sullivan Lady's Aid Soc., Union City, 1955-74,

Twin Lakes Cmty. Assn., 1997—; chair winter program com. Tibbits Arts Found., Coldwater, 1980-90; mem. Coldwater Hist. Preservation Assn., 1978-86; del. Mich. Rep. State Conv., Detroit, 1986; candidate for Branch County Commr., Coldwater, 1988; mem. Mich. Assn. for Computer Users in Learning, 1975-91; mem. cultural arts com., walking tour com. Howe (Ind.) Cmty. Assn., 1996—, pres., 2003-2004. Recipient Cert. of Appreciation, Mich. Assn. for Media in Edn., 1980, 91, Golden Apple Retirement award Coldwater H.S., 1991. Mem. Soc. Genealogists (London), New Eng. Hist. Geneal. Soc., Descendants of Founders of Ancient Windsor, Ctrl. N.Y. Geneal. Soc., DAR (good citizen selection com., treas. Coldwater br. 1997-2002, registrar 2003-04), Mich. Assn. Ret. Sch. Pers., Schenectady County Hist. Soc., Old Brutus Hist. Soc., Union City Geneal. Soc., St. Joseph County Hist. Soc. (advisor to Land Office Mus. com. 1997—), Crawford County Geneal. Soc., Coldwater Edn. Assn. (sec. 1980-90); Howe Philomath Soc., Beta Phi Mu. Avocations: travel, coin collecting/numismatics, tennis. Home: 1820 W 600 N Howe IN 46746-9406 Personal E-mail: macbater@modempool.com.

BOWERS, ANDREA, artist; b. Wilmington, Ohio, 1965; BFA, Bowling Green State U., 1987; MFA, Calif. Inst. Arts, 1992. One-woman shows include Damaged Goods, Bliss, Pasadena, Calif., 1994, Spanish Box, Santa Monica, Calif., 1996, Spectacular Appearances, Santa Monica Mus. Art, Calif., 1998, Moving Equilibrium, Sara Meltzer Gallery, NY, 1999, Intimate Strangers, 2000, Box with Dance of Its Own Making, Chouakri Brahms, Berlin, 2002, From Mouth to Ear, Goldman Tevis, LA, 2002, Virtual Arena, Sara Meltzer Gallery, NY, 2002, Magical Politics, Chouakri Brahms, Berlin, 2003, Nonviolent Civil Disobedience Training, Sara Meltzer Gallery, NY, 2004, Magazin 4 Voralberger Kunstverein, Austria, 2004, Mary Goldman Gallery, LA, 2004, exhibited in group shows at Whitney Biennial Am. Art, Whitney Mus. Am. Art, 2004, 100 Artist See God, Laguna Art Mus., San Francisco, 2003—04, Rendered, Sara Meltzer Gallery, NY, 2003, C.O.L.A. 2003, Municipal Art Gallery, Barnsdale Art PK., LA, 2003, Time-Share, Sara Meltzer Gallery, NY, 2002, Everybody Now, Bertha & Karl Leubsdorf Gallery, NY, 2001, Subject Plural, Contemporary Arts Mus., Houston, 2001, Moving Pictures, Galerie Tommy Lund, Copenhagen, Denmark, 2000, Me Mine, Luckman Fine Arts Gallery, Calif., 1999, Unfinished History, Walker Art Ctr., Mpls., 1998—99, Dave's Not Here, Three Day Weekend, LA, 1994. Regional Fellowship Visual Arts Sculpture, Western States Arts Fedn./Nat. Endowment Arts, 1995—96, Fellowship Visual Arts, City LA, 2003. Mailing: c/o Sara Meltzer Gallery 516 West 20th St New York NY 10011*

BOWERS, BEGE KAYE, literature educator, communications educator, academic administrator; b. Nashville, Aug. 19, 1949; d. John and Yvonne Bowers. BA in English cum laude, Vanderbilt U., 1971; student, U. Mich., 1985; MACT, U. Tenn., 1973, PhD, 1984. Asst. loan officer Ctr. for Fin. Aid and Placement, Baylor U., Waco, Tex., 1975-76; editorial asst. Wassily Leontief, NYU, N.Y.C., 1976-78; instr. bus. English Florence-Darlington Tech. Coll., Florence, S.C., 1979-80; tchr. English and French St. John's High Sch., Darlington, S.C., 1980-82; teaching asst. dept English U. Tenn., Knoxville, 1982-84; from asst. prof. English to prof. Youngstown (Ohio) State U., 1984—92, prof., 1992—, asst. to dean Coll. Arts and Scis., 1992-93, dir. profl. writing and editing, 1996-2000, assoc. to the dean Coll. Arts and Scis., 2001—02, asst. provost acad. programs and planning, 2002—05, interim provost, 2005, v.p. acad. affairs, 2005, assoc. provost acad. programs and planning, 2005—. Part-time freelance editor MLA, N.Y.C., 1978-80; cons. Project Arete, Youngstown and Mahoning County Pub. Schs., 1984-87, Youngstown Pub. Schs., 1986, 87-88, 90-91, Macmillan Pub. Co., 1986, Trumbull (Ohio) County Schs., 1988, Akron Beacon Jour., 1994-95, Ohio Dept. Edn., 1998-2001, Ohio Bd. Regents, 2002—; chair Mahoning Area Consortium Tech. Prep. Governing Bd., 2002—. Co-editor: CEA Critic, 1998—2002, CEA Forum, 1988—2004; co-editor: (with Barbara Brothers) Reading and Writing Women's Lives: A Study of the Novel of Manners, 1991; co-editor: (with Chuck Nelson) Internships in Technical Communication, 1991; co-editor: (with Mark Allen) Annotated Chaucer Bibliography, 1986—96, 2002 (MLA award for disting. bibliography, 2004); mem. editl. bd. South Atlantic Rev., 1987—89; editor: more than 40 pamphlets, 7 children's books, and 1 videoscript. Alumni Found. Rsch. fellow U. Tenn., 1978, dissertation fellow U. Tenn., 1983, Davis editl. fellow U. Tenn., 1984; Grad. Rsch. Coun. grantee Youngstown State U. Mem.: MLA, Am. Assn. Higher Edn., Gould Soc. (pres. faculty com. 1991—93), No. Ohio Soc. for Tech. Comm., Soc. for Tech. Comm. (Jay R. Gould award for excellence in tchg. tech. comm. 1999, Disting. Chpt. Svc. award 2001, Assoc. fellow award 2002), Assn. Tchrs. Tech. Writing, New Chaucer Soc. (asst. bibliographer 1986—), Coll. English Assn. Ohio, Coun. Editors of Learned Jours., Coll. English Assn. (exec. bd., Disting. Svc. award 1996, Lifetime Achievement award 2005), Phi Beta Kappa, Phi Kappa Phi (pres. 1991—92, sec. 1994—98, exec. bd. 1998—). Office: Youngstown State U Office of the Provost Youngstown OH 44555-0001 Office Phone: 330-941-1560. E-mail: bkbowers@ysu.edu.

BOWERS, CHRISTI C., mediator, law educator, lawyer, writer; b. Hagerstown, Md., Nov. 4, 1970; BA in Psychology, BS in Bus., Shepherd Coll., 1993; JD, MS, U. Balt., 1998, MBA, 2000. Bar: Md. 2000, cert.: Md. Inst. Continuing Profl. Edn. Lawyers (mediator), Md. Inst. Continuing Profl. Edn. Lawyers (domestic, custody and visitation mediator), Md. Inst. Continuing Profl. Edn. Lawyers (domestic property, fin. issues mediator) 2000, Md. Inst. Continuing Profl. Edn. Lawyers (advanced transformative mediator) 2002, Md. Inst. Continuing Profl. Edn. Lawyers (worker's compensation mediator) 2002, Dist. Ct. of Md. (advanced mediator) 2002. Freelance mediator - custody/visitation, civil disputes, landlord/tenant/neighbors, marriage/relationships, tng. programs for businesses, Hagerstown, 2000—; tchr.,presenter co-parenting workshop for adults and children Children of Separation and Divorce (now Nat. Family Resiliency Program), Balt., 2000—; case mgr., staff mediator family divsn. Cir. Ct. for Prince George's County, Upper Marlboro, Md., 2003—. Vol. mediator civil large and small claims cases Dist. Ct. Md., Annapolis, 2000—; vol. faculty critiquer Md. Inst. Continuing Profl. Edn. Lawyers Mediation Tng., Balt., 2001—; substitute tchr. Bd. Edn. Washington County, Hagerstown, 1999—. Author: Mediation In Maryland; editor: Resolving Issues newsletter. Exec. bd.- mem. at large Md. Coun. Dispute Resolution, Balt., 2002; bd. dirs., sec. Washington County Cmty. Mediation Ctr., Hagerstown, 2002—03. Recipient cert. appreciation for vol. mediation, Dist. Ct. of Md., 2002. Mem.: ABA, Assn. Conflict Resolution, Washington County Bar Assn., Md. State Bar Assn., Sigma Iota Epsilon (hon.). Avocations: writing, singing, travel, writing- poems, songs, guidebooks, fiction, creating things. Office: Mediation Svcs in Md PO Box 642 Hagerstown MD 21740 Office Phone: 301-730-6244. Personal E-mail: christicbo@aol.com. Business E-Mail: ccbowers@co.pg.md.us.

BOWERS, CURTIS RAY, JR., chaplain; b. Lancaster, Pa., Feb. 6, 1933; s. Curtis Ray and Oleita (Geisler) B.; m. Doris Jean, June 18, 1955; children: Sharon, William, Stephen. BA, Asbury Coll., 1958; MDiv, Asbury Theol. Sem., 1960. Pastor Methodist Ch., Cynthiana, Ky., 1956-60, Ch. of the Nazarene, Cape May, N.J., 1960-61; chaplain U.S. Army, 1961-84; dir. chaplaincy ministries Ch. of the Nazarene, Kansas City, Mo., 1984-2000. Author: Forward Edge of the Battle Area: A Chaplain's Story. Col. U.S. Army, 1961-84. Decorated Silver Star; named Srs. Double Inter-Svc. Tennis Champion, 1982; named to 327th Infantry Regimental Hall of Fame, 1998; recipient Outstanding Chaplain of Yr. award, Ch. of the Nazarene, 2000. Mem. Ch. Of The Nazarene. Avocation: tennis. Home: 3523 Portland Ave Nampa ID 83686-7993 Personal E-mail: crbowers11@juno.com.

BOWERS, DEANNA PATRICIA, secondary school educator, art educator; b. Hanford, Calif., Mar. 27, 1971; d. Douglas Edward Mattos and Patricia Gertrude Mattos Gill; m. Steven James Bowers, July 20, 2004; 1 child, Vincent; 1 child, Ethan Johnson. BA in Art Edn., Calif. State U., Long Beach, Calif., 1995; cert., U. San Diego, 2004. Tchr. Woodlake (Calif.) Union H.S., 1997—, chmn. Dept. Art, 1998—. Grantee, Paramount Farms, 1998. Mem.: NEA, Nat. Art Edn. Assn., Calif. Tchrs. Assn., Calif. Art Edn. Assn., Woodlake (Calif.) H.S. Tchrs. Assn. (v.p. 2002—). Democrat. Avocations: art, crafts, photography, travel. Office: Woodlake Union High Sch 400 West Whitney Woodlake CA 93286

BOWERS, DOUGLAS ALAN, small business owner, consultant; b. Bryn Mawr, Pa., May 19, 1946; s. William Henry and Winifred Cope (Sharpless) Bowers; m. Rebecca Elaine Sather, May 22, 1999; children: Lucas Daniel, Maya Marina. Br. mgr. Hayden Elec., Fairbanks, Alaska, 1976—77; owner Cripple Creek Svc., Fairbanks, Alaska, 1977—84, Tolovana Lodge, Alaska, 1984—. Mem., adv. com. Nenana-Minto Fish & Game, Alaska, 1994—; bd. mem. Nenana City Pub. Sch., Alaska, 1995—96; mem., adv. com. Tanavana Valley State Forest, Fairbanks, Alaska, 1995—97. Engineman 2d U.S. Coast Guard, 1965—69. Avocations: guitar, photography, fishing. Office: Box 281 Nenana AK 99760

BOWERS, FRANCIS ROBERT, literature educator; b. N.Y.C., May 4, 1920; s. William Leo and Catherine (Callahan) B. BA, Cath. U. Am., 1946, PhD, 1959; MA, Fordham U., 1952. Tchr. Ascension Sch., N.Y.C., 1946-48, St. Augustine's High Sch., Bklyn., 1948-51, St. Peter's High Sch., Staten Island, 1951-53; instr. De La Salle Coll., Washington, 1953-59; assoc. prof. English and world lit. Manhattan Coll., 1959-70, 85-89, chmn. dept., 1967-70, chmn. grad. English dept., 1961-70, dean arts and scis., 1970-80, provost, 1980-85, acad. advisor to intercollegiate athletes, 1988—2004. Author: Characterization in Narrative Poetry of George Crabbe, 1959. Trustee scholarship Cath. U., 1953-58. Finn grantee, 1962; Manhattan Coll. grantee, 1966 Mem. Phi Beta Kappa. Office: Manhattan Coll Dean Arts Office Bronx NY 10471 Office Phone: 718-862-7987.

BOWERS, GLENN LEE, retired professional society administrator; b. York, Pa., May 7, 1921; s. Elmer Frederick and Naomi Mae (Shellenberger) B.; m. Betty June Lehr, Apr. 21, 1943; children— Tina, Timothy BS, Pa. State U., 1946, MS, 1948. Wildlife biologist Pa. Game Commn., various locations, 1948-57, chief div. research Harrisburg, 1957-59, dep. exec. dir., 1959-65, exec. dir., 1965-82. Chmn. bd. dirs. Worldwide Furbearer Conf., Frostburg, Md., 1976-80 Contbr. articles to profl. jours. Served to capt. USMCR, 1942-45, PTO Recipient John Pearce Meml. award N.E. sect. Wildlife Soc., 1982; Nat. Wildlife Conservationist award Nat. Wildlife Fedn., 1982 Mem. Wildlife Soc., Internat. Assn. Fish and Wildlife Agys. (exec. com. 1972-80, pres. 1978-79, gen. counsel 1983-95, Seth Gordon award 1982), N.E. Assn. Fish and Wildlife Agys. (various offices, v.p., pres. 1965-82). Lodges: Masons. Republican. Methodist. Avocations: fishing, hunting. Home: 221 Mountain Rd Dillsburg PA 17019-1514

BOWERS, KIM, lawyer, energy executive; b. Ohio; BA, Miami Univ., Ohio; MA, Baylor Univ., Waco, Tex.; JD, Univ. Tex. Law Sch., Austin. With Kelly, Hart & Hallman, Fort Worth, Tex.; corp. counsel to sr. comml. counsel Valero Energy Corp., San Antonio, 1997—2002, mng. counsel, 2002—03, v.p. legal svc., 2003—. Office: VP Legal Svcs Valero Energy Corp One Valero Way San Antonio TX 78249

BOWERS, KLAUS D(IETER), electronics executive, researcher; b. Stettin, Germany, Dec. 27, 1929; s. Franz A. and Elisabeth (Schneider) B.; m. Roswitha U. Rau, June 15, 1964; children: Pamela, Colin. BA, Oxford (Eng.) U., 1950, MA, PhD, 1953. Research lectr. in physics Christ Ch., Oxford U., 1952-56; with AT&T, 1956-90; researcher Bell Telephone Labs., Murray Hill, N.J., 1956-59, mgr. electronics devel., 1959-66, Allentown, Pa., 1966-71; mng. dir., v.p. Sandia Nat. Labs., Albuquerque, 1971-75; exec. dir. Pa. Labs. Bell Telephone Labs., Allentown, 1975-79, v.p. Murray Hill, 1979-90. Chmn. Semiconductor Rsch. Corp., 1987-88 Author: Non Frangimur: My First Six Decades, 2004; contbr. articles to profl. jours.; patentee in field. Trustee Cedar Crest Coll., 1983-87. Fellow IEEE (Frederik Philips award 1989); mem. Nat. Acad. Engring. Home: 2890 Golf Cir Emmaus PA 18049-1735

BOWERS, MICHAEL THOMAS, chemistry professor; b. Spokane, Wash., June 6, 1939; s. John W. and Fae (Scott) B.; married, Feb. 8, 1964; children: Molly, Shelia, Melissa. BS, Gonzaga U., 1962; MS, U. Ill., 1964, PhD, 1966. Asst. prof. U. Calif., Santa Barbara, 1966-73, assoc. prof., 1973-76, prof. chemistry, 1976—. Faculty rsch. lectr. faculty senate U. Calif., Santa Barbara, 1994. Editor Internat. Jour. Mass Spectrometry, 1986—; contbr. over 300 articles to profl. jours.; editor 3 books in field; assoc. editor Jour. Am. Chem. Soc. 1st lt. U.S. Army, 1966-68. Guggenheim Found. fellow, 1994. Fellow AAAS, Am. Phys. Soc.; mem. Am. Chem. Soc. (assoc. editor jour. 1989—, Nobel laureate signature award 1989, Outstanding Achievement in Mass Spectrometry award 1996), Am. Soc. Mass Spectrometry (Disting. Contbn. award 2004), Internat. Mass Spectrometry Soc. (Thomson gold medal 1997). Roman Catholic. Avocations: golf, running. Office: U Calif Dept Chemistry Santa Barbara CA 93106 Office Phone: 805-893-2893. E-mail: bowers@chem.ucsb.edu.

BOWERS, NORMA JEAN, music educator; b. Wichita, Kans., Sept. 28, 1929; d. William Edward and Helen Marie (Braniff) Bingman; m. Marvin Bowers, 1955, (dec. 1983). BMus in Edn., James Millikin U., Decatur, Ill., 1950; MMus, No. Ill. U., 1964. Music tchr. Norris City (Ill.) Community Unit Sch., 1951-54, Aurora (Ill.) Sch. Dist. 131, 1955-57, Batavia (Ill.) Pub. Schs. #101, 1958-90; ret. Batavia (Ill.) Pub. Schs., 1990. Artist watercolor paintings, portraits on commn. Choir dir. Congl. Ch., Geneva, Ill., 1971-86. Mem. Ill. Edn. Assn., Batavia Edn. Assn. (pres. 1968-69, 82-85), NEA, Acad. Am. Educators (named outstanding educator 1973-74), Delta Kappa Gamma, Sigma Alpha Iota. Avocations: biking, travel, golf, dogs.

BOWERS, PATRICIA ELEANOR FRITZ, economist; b. N.Y.C., Mar. 21, 1928; d. Eduard and Eleanor (Ring) Fritz. Student scholar, Goucher Coll., 1946-48; BA, Cornell U., 1950; MA, NYU, 1953, PhD, 1965. Statis. asst. Fed. Res. Bank N.Y., N.Y.C., 1950-53; lectr. Upsala Coll., East Orange, N.J., 1953-59; researcher Fortune mag., N.Y.C., 1959-60; teaching fellow NYU, N.Y.C., 1960-62, instr., 1962-64; mem. faculty Bklyn. Coll., CUNY, 1964-00, prof. econs., 1974-2000, chair dept. econs., 1996-99, prof. emerita, 2000—. Author: Private Choice and Public Welfare, 1974. Sec. Friends of the Johnson Mus., Cornell U., 1989-91; Cornell Fund rep. Class of 1950, Cornell U., 2004—. Mem. Am. Econ. Assn., Econometric Soc., Met. Econ. Assn. (sec. 1963-68, pres. 1974-75), Am. Statis. Assn. (univs. chmn. ann. forecasting confs. 1970-71, 71-72), Cornell Club N.Y., Kappa Alpha Theta. Home: 145 E 16th St Apt 11-L New York NY 10003-3405

BOWERS, PAUL D., transportation company executive; b. Rome, N.Y., Aug. 28, 1948; Dir. aviation Alaska Dept. Transp. and Pub. Facilities Statewide Aviation, Anchorage, 1995—. Office: Alaska Dept Transp and Pub Facilities Statewide Aviation 4111 Aviation Dr Anchorage AK 99502-1058

BOWERS, RICHARD PHILIP, manufacturing executive; b. Reading, Pa., July 27, 1931; s. Clarence Philip and Lottie Rose (Linkowski) B.; married; children: Richard P., Karen M., Lisa Ann, Julie L. Student, St. Bonaventure U., Olean, N.Y., 1949-51. Sales engr. Bowers Battery and Spark Plug Corp., Reading, Pa., 1952-57; v.p. sales Gen. Battery Cord, Reading, Pa., 1957-64; v.p. sales and mktg. East Penn Mfg. Co., Lyon Station, Pa., 1964-67, exec. v.p., 1967-95; also bd. dirs. E. Penn Mfg. Co., Lyon Station, Pa. Pres. TBS Systems of Ala., Birmingham, 1986—, Pioneer Auto Parts, Phila., 1980—, electro Battery Co., St. Louis; chmn. bd. Taylor Battery Co., Louisville, 1986—; chmn. bd. Power Battery Toronto, Can. Pres. Green Hills Lake Recreational Assn., Green Hills, Pa., 1984-87. Served with U.S. Army, 1962-64. Named Man of Yr., Automotive Merchandising, Chgo., 1984, 89. Mem. Battery Council Internat. (chmn. convention planning com. 1986-91), Ind. Battery Mfrs. Assn. (past pres., bd. dirs.). Democrat. Roman Catholic.

BOWERS, THOMAS ARNOLD, journalism educator, dean; b. Plymouth, Ind., Sept. 27, 1942; s. Merritt Edward and Beulah Irene (Burkhart) Bowers; m. Patricia Mills Shane, July 29, 1966 (div.); children: Matthew, Lisa; m. Mary Ellen McKay Woolley, Jan. 10, 2002. BA in Journalism with distinction, Ind. U., 1964, MA in Journalism, 1969, PhD in Communication Rsch., 1971. Asst. prof. Sch. Journalism U. N.C., Chapel Hill, 1971-76, assoc. prof., 1976-80, prof., 1980-93, assoc. dean, 1980—2005, interim dean, 2005—; James L. Knight prof. Sch. Journalism and Mass Comm. U. N.C., 1993—. Cons. Meredith Coll., Raleigh, N.C., 1973, Inform, Inc., Hickory, N.C., 1981—, The Coll. Bd., N.Y.C., 1989, bd. regents U. Fla., Am. Univ. Co-author: Fundamentals of Advertising Research, 1979, 4d edit., 1991; editor Journalism Educator, 1983-88; also articles, chpts. in books. Cons. LWV, Chapel Hill, 1973, also various polit. candidates; chmn. com. United Way, Chapel Hill, 1979, 88. Capt. U.S. Army, 1965-68. Recipient Silver medal award, Triangle Advt. Fedn., N.C., 1994, Sanders award Tchg. Excellence, U. N.C., 1997; grantee, Freedom Forum, 1988—95. Mem. Assn. Edn. Journalism and Mass Communication (pres. 1988-89), Am. Advt. Fedn., Am. Acad. Advt., Newspaper Assn. Am., Phi Beta Kappa, Kappa Tau Alpha. Avocation: reading. Office: U NC Sch Jour & Mass Communication Cb 3365 Chapel Hill NC 27599-3365 Home: 17 Dartford Ct Chapel Hill NC 27517-8667 Business E-Mail: tbowers@email.unc.edu.

BOWERS, WILLIAM CHARLES, lawyer; b. Washington, Sept. 15, 1946; s. Kenneth Victor and Johnlou (Sweet) B.; children by previous marriage: William Che, Lynn Ann; m. JoAnne Kennedy, July 30, 1988; 1 child, Liam Flynn. AB, Princeton U., 1968; JD with honors, Emory U., 1975. Bar: Ga. 1975, N.Y. 1988. Law clk. to Hon. Griffin Bell, U.S. Ct. Appeals for 5th Circuit, Atlanta, 1975-76; assoc. Sutherland Asbill & Brennan, Atlanta, 1976-82, ptnr., 1982-83, Trotter, Smith & Jacobs, Atlanta, 1983-85; counsel Paul, Hastings, Janofsky & Walker, Atlanta, 1985-88; ptnr. Paul, Hastings, Janifsky & Walker, N.Y.C., 1988-90; gen. counsel GPA Capital, Shannon, Ireland, 1990-93; assoc. gen. counsel GE Capital Aviation Svcs., Stamford, Conn., 1993-95; ptnr. Winthrop, Stimson, Putnam & Roberts, N.Y.C, 1995-2000, Pillsbury Winthrop LLP, 2001—05; ptnr., chmn. Asset Securitization practice Pillsbury Winthrop Shaw Pittman, NYC, 2005—. Editor (exec. articles): Emory Law Jour. Lt. USN, 1968-72. Mem.: ABA (past chmn. Corp. Tax com.). Democrat. Episcopalian. Office: Pillsbury Winthrop Shaw Pittman 1540 Broadway New York NY 10036 Office Phone: 212-858-1106. Office Fax: 212-858-1500. Business E-Mail: william.bowers@pillsburylaw.com.

BOWERSOCK, GLEN WARREN, historian, educator; b. Providence, Jan. 12, 1936; s. Donald Curtis and Josephine (Evans) Bowersock. AB, Harvard U., 1957; BA, Oxford U., Eng., 1959, MA, DPhil, 1962; D (hon.), U. Strasbourg, 1990, Ecole Pratique Hautes Etudes, Paris, 1999, U. Athens, 2005. Lectr. ancient history Oxford U., 1960-62, vis. lectr., 1966; instr. Harvard U., 1962-64, asst. prof., 1964-67, assoc. prof. classics, 1967-69, prof. Greek and Latin, 1969-80, chmn. dept. classics, 1972-77, assoc. dean faculty arts and scis., 1977-80; prof. hist. studies Inst. Advanced Study, Princeton, N.J., 1980—; hon. fellow Balliol Coll., Oxford, 2004—. Sr. fellow Dumbarton Oaks Ctr. for Byzantine Studies, Washington, 1984—93, Ctr. for Hellenic Studies, Washington, 1976—90; cons. Ednl. Svcs., Inc., 1964, NEH, 1971—; mem. sci. com. Scuola Normale Superiore di Pisa, Italy, Istituto di Studi Umanistici, Florence, Italy; chmn. sci. com. Maison de l'Orient Mediterraneen, Lyon, France; mem. Internat. Colloquium on the Classics in Edn., 1964—66; vis. prof. Australian Nat. U., 1972, Princeton U., 1986—87, Coll. France, 1997; Sather prof. U. Calif., Berkeley, 1991; Jerome lectr. U. Mich. and Am. Acad. in Rome, 1989; syndic Harvard U. Press, 1977—81; lectr. Thompson Lectures, Pomona, 1993, Wiles Lectures, Queens U., Belfast, Northern Ireland, 1993. Author: Augustus and the Greek World, 1965, Pseudo-Xenophon, Constitution of the Athenians, 1968, Greek Sophists in the Roman Empire, 1969, Julian the Apostate, 1978, Roman Arabia, 1983, Hellenism in Late Antiquity, 1990, Fiction as History from Nero to Julian, 1994, Studies on the Eastern Roman Empire, 1994, Martyrdom and Rome, 1995, Selected Papers on Late Antiquity, 2000; editor: Philostratus' Life of Apollonius, 1970, Approaches to the Second Sophistic, 1974; editor: (with J. Clive and S. Graubard) Edward Gibbon and the Decline and Fall of the Roman Empire, 1977; editor: (with C. P. Jones) L. Robert-Martyre de Pionios, 1994; editor: (with T. J. Cornell) Momigliano-Studies on Modern Scholarship, 1994; editor: (with P. Brown and O. Grabar) Late Antiquity-A Guide to the Postclassical World, 1999; mem. editl. bd.: Arabian Archaeology and Epigraphy, Ancient Civilizations from Scythia to Siberia (Russian Acad. Scis.), Berytus, Am. Jour. Philology, 1987—95, Am. Scholar, 1981—93; editor (gen.): Revealing Antiquity. Trustee Am. Schs. Oriental Rsch., 1984—90; bd. dirs. Met. Opera Guild; adv. dir. Met. Opera Assn.; mem. nat. coun. Glimmerglass Opera, 1994—2004. Recipient James H. Breasted prize, Am. Hist. Assn., 1992, Chevalier de la Légion d' honneur; Rhodes scholar, 1957—60. Fellow: Accademia Nazionale dei Lincei, Am. Numis. Soc. (coun. 1983—96), Am. Acad. Arts and Scis.; mem.: Acad. des Inscriptions et Belles-Lettres, Russian Acad. Scis. (fgn.), German Archaeol. Inst. (corr.), Soc. Promotion Roman and Hellenic Studies (hon. Am. sec. Roman Soc.), Leschetizky Assn. Am., Am. Philol. Assn., Am. Philos. Soc. (coun. 1992—98), Johnsonians, Century Club (N.Y.C.), Knickerbocker Club (N.Y.C.), Phi Beta Kappa. Office: Inst Advanced Study Sch Hist Studies Einstein Dr Princeton NJ 08540 Office Phone: 609-734-8353. Business E-Mail: gwb@ias.edu.

BOWERSOX, THOMAS H., lawyer; b. Beatrice, Nebr., May 1, 1941; s. William H. Bowersox and Fairy (Casey) Huff; m. Barbara Mathieson, Aug. 23, 1963; children: William T., Christopher T., Elizabeth A. BBA, U. Houston, 1965, JD, 1969. Bar: U.S. Dist. Ct. (so. and ea. dists.) Tex., U.S. Ct. Appeals (5th and 11th cirs.). Instr. South Tex. Jr. Coll., Houston, 1967-72; assoc. prof. Sam Houston State U., Huntsville, 1972-74; assoc. Baker & Botts, Houston, 1975-76; from assoc. gen counsel to pres. subs. co. Zapata Corp., Houston, 1976-93, exec. v.p., 1993-94; ptnr. Bowersox, Herron & Williamson, Houston, 1996-98; of counsel Hope & Causey, Conroe, Tex., 1998—. Adv. com. energy trade policy, U.S. trade rep. industry sector Dept. of Commerce, 1989-93. Bd. dirs. Offhore Energy Ctr., Houston, 1988-92, mem. adv. bd. 1992-98; mem. adv. com. Sam Houston State U. Coll. Bus., 1985-2001. Mem. Internat. Assn. Drilling Contractors (vice chmn. contracts and risk mgmt. com. 1984-85, chmn. govt. affairs com. 1986-87, v.p. Tex. gulf coast 1989, v.p. offshore 1990-91, chmn., bd. dirs., 1992), Am. Bureau of Shipping. Avocations: golf, camping, reading. Office: Hope & Causey PO Box 3188 Conroe TX 77305-3188 Office Fax: 936-441-4674. Personal E-mail: thbowersox@earthlink.net.

BOWES, FREDERICK, III, publishing executive, consultant; b. Norwalk, Conn., Dec. 20, 1941; s. Frederick Jr. and Mary Priscilla (Herron) B.; m. Margaret Anne Hathaway, Sept. 17, 1966; children: Heather Hathaway Ezzy, Catherine Herron. AB, Dartmouth Coll., 1963; MBA, Columbia U., 1965. Fin. staff Perkin-Elmer Corp., Norwalk, Conn., 1965-70; v.p. ops. and fin. South Shore Pub. Co., North Scituate, Mass., 1970-77; cons. Graphics Mgmt., Inc., Duxbury, Mass., 1977-79; pres. Info-Graphics Inc., Braintree, Mass., 1979-80; v.p. pub. New Eng. Jour. Medicine, Mass. Med. Soc., Waltham, Mass., 1981-90; pres. Macmillan New Media, Cambridge, Mass., 1990-94, Cadmus Digital Solutions, 1995-96; pres., CEO Bowes & Assocs., Inc. dba Publist.com, 1996-2000; cons. Electronic Pub. Assocs., 2000—. Dir. Ctr. for Applied Spl. Tech. CAST, Peabody, Mass., 1999—2000. Sr. warden Parish of St. John the Evangelist, Duxbury, 1981-84; trustee, treas. Soc. St. Margaret, Boston, 1984—; trustee Mass. Bible Soc., Boston, 1983-88. Mem. Soc. Scholarly Pub. (pres. 1998), Am. Assn. Pub. Episcopalian. Avocation: birdwatching.

BOWES, HENRY EDWARD, retired communications executive; b. Merchantville, N.J., Sept. 7, 1915; s. Henry Joseph and Evaline Sarah (Humphreys) Bowes; m. Lauretta Helen Schultz, July 17, 1965; children from previous marriage: Henry, Shirley. Grad., Valley Forge Mil. Acad., 1932; student, U.S. Naval Acad., 1934-35; DBA (hon.), North Cen. Coll. With Philco Corp., 1936-62, gen. mgr. home radio div., 1955-56, v.p., gen. mgr. TV div., 1956-58, v.p. mktg., 1958-61; v.p., dir. mktg. for N.Am., dir. govt. rels. ITT, 1962-64, v.p. indsl. mktg. worldwide, 1964-66, dir. sales and distbn. ITT System, 1966-67, sr. v.p., 1967; pres., CEO McCall Corp., 1967-68; exec. v.p. Bell & Howell Co., 1969, pres., chief oper. officer, 1970-73, also bd. dirs.; ret., 1973. Chmn. exec. com. Docutel Corp.; bd. dirs. Beloit Mfg. Co., No. Telecom Corp., Embrosogrph Corp., Norton Simon, Inc. Served to col.

USAAF, World War II. Decorated Legion of Merit; recipient Disting. Alumni award, Valley Forge Mil. Acad. Mem.: Valley Forge Mil. Acad. Alumni Assn., Lost Tree Club (North Palm Beach, Fla.). Republican. Episcopalian.

BOWES, JOHN, entrepreneur, former toy and outdoor products company executive; b. San Francisco; m. Frances Bowes. Founder, pres. Kransco (sold to Mattel, 1994); owner Yakima Products Inc. (sold to Watermark), Arcata, Calif., 1994—2001, Camelbak outdoor products (sold to Bear Stearns Merchant Banking), 1995—2003. Named one of Top 200 Collectors, ARTnews Mag., 2004. Avocation: Collecting modern and contemporary art.*

BOWES, RONALD T., school system administrator; b. N.Y., Dec. 22, 1945; m. Mary Jane Bowes, Aug. 14, 1976; children: Brendan, Bridget, Conor. BA, Duquesne U., 1967, MA in Theology, 1969; PhD, Carnegie Mellon U., 1982. Cert. supt. Pa. Tchr. history Pitts. (Pa.) Pub. Schs., 1974—90; asst. supt. Cath. Schs. Diocese Pitts., Pitts., 1995—. Presenter in field. Prodr.: (films) Sports Coaching Accreditation, 2002, A Parent's Guide to Sports, 2004; contbr. articles to profl. jours. Minister St. Mary of Mercy, 1999—; various positions Saint Louise de Marillac Parish; bd. dir. Rd. Ednl. Achievement Through Choice Alliance, Harrisburg, Pa., 1994—. 1st lt. U.S. Army, 1969—71. Recipient Peace on Earth award, Pitts. City Coun., 1997, Cmty. Svc. award, The Champions Assn., 2001; fellow, Carnegie Mellon U., 1975. Mem.: KC, Chief Adminstrs. Cath. Edn., Nat. Cath. Edn. Assn. (Parental Choice award 2004), Ancient Order Hibernians, Duquesne Soc., Duquesne Century Club Disting. Grads., Sierra Club (v.p. 2001—). Republican. Roman Cath. Home: 20 East Club Dr Pittsburgh PA 15236 Office: Diocese of Pittsburgh 111 Blvd of the Allies Pittsburgh PA 15222

BOWES, WILLIAM K., JR., venture capital investment company executive; BA in econ., Stanford U.; MBA, Harvard U. Sr. v.p., dir. Blyth Eastman Dillon & Co. (formerly Blyth & Co. Inc.), Calif., 1953—78; cons. Blyth Eastman Paine Webber, 1978—80; founder US Venture Ptnrs., Calif., 1981—; bd. dirs. Xoma, Calif., 1995—. Former dir. Cetus; former bd. mem. Raychem; founding shareholder, chmn., treas. Amgen, Calif., 1984. Achievements include first employee at Amgen, Calif. 1984. Office: US Venture Ptnrs 2735 Sand Hill Rd Menlo Park CA 94025 Office Phone: 650-854-9080. Office Fax: 650-854-3018.

BOWIE, APRIL DENE'T, lawyer, arbitrator; b. Bronx, N.Y., May 09; d. A. D. and S. T. Bowie; m. K. B. Mena; 1 child, A Bowie Mena. BA, NYU, 1989; JD, Nova Southea. U., 1992; postgrad., Fordham U. Law Sch., 1992. Bar: Fla. 1997, D.C. 1998, U.S. Dist. Ct. (so. dist.) Fla. 1998, U.S. Dist. Ct. (so. and ea. dists.) NY 2002, NY 2002. Intern Hon. Cornelius Blackshear U.S. Bankruptcy Ct. (so. dist.), N.Y.C., 1992; rsch. asst. Justice George Bundy Smith Ct. of Appeals of N.Y., N.Y.C., 1994—95; atty. The Brown Law Group, P.A., Miami, Fla., 1996—; mng. atty. The Bowie Law Ctr., P.A., Ft. Lauderdale, Fla., 2000—02. Adj. prof. Fla. Meml. Coll., Miami, Fla., 1998—2000; arbitrator Nat. Assn. Securities Dealers, N.Y.C., 2001—; asst. prof. Mercy Coll., White Plains, NY, 2003—. Mem.: Westchester Bar Assn. (assoc.), N.Y. State Bar Assn. (assoc.), Am. Inns of Ct. (assoc.). Avocations: dance, singing, travel, reading, sports. Office: The Bowie Law Ctr PA PO Box 265 Scarsdale NY 10583 Office Phone: 914-815-3434. E-mail: bowiemenalaw@yahoo.com.

BOWIE, DAVID (DAVID ROBERT JONES), musician, actor; b. London, Jan. 8, 1947; s. Hayward Stenton Jones and Margaret Mary Burns; m. Angela Barret 1970 (div. 1980); 1 son, Zowie; m. Iman. Rec. artist, 1968—; motion pictures include The Man Who Fell to Earth, 1976, Just a Gigolo, 1981, Wir Kinder Von Bahnhof, 1981, Cat People, 1982, The Hunger, 1983, Merry Christmas, Mr. Lawrence, 1983, (concert film) Ziggy Stardust, 1983, Into the Night, 1985, Labyrinth (also composed music), 1986, Absolute Beginners, 1986, The Last Temptation of Christ, 1988, The Linguini Incident, 1992, Twin Peaks: Fire Walk with Me, 1992, Basquiat, 1996, Il Mio West, 1998, Everybody Loves Sunshine, 1999, Mr. Rice's Secret, 2000; composer of songs for films: The Falcon and the Snowman, 1985, Pretty Woman, 1990, Trainspotting, 1996, Grosse Pointe Blank, 1997, The Ice Storm, 1997, Moulin Rouge!, 2001, Shrek 2, 2004, Shall We Dance?, 2004 and many others; albums include Early On, 1966, Space Oddity, 1969, The Man Who Sold the World, 1970, Hunky Dory, 1971, The Rise and Fall of Ziggy Stardust and the Spiders from Mars, 1972, Aladdin Sane, 1973, Pin-ups, 1973, Images: 1966-67, 1973, Diamond Dogs, 1974, David Live, 1974, Young Americans, 1975, Station to Station, 1976, Changesonebowie, 1976, Low, 1977 (orch. adaptation by Phillip Glass, "Low Symphony" 1993), Heroes, 1977, Lodger, 1978, Stage, 1978, Scary Monsters, 1980, Changestwobowie, 1981, Let's Dance, 1983, Ziggy Stardust soundtrack, 1983, Tonight, 1984, Never Let Me Down, 1987, Sound + Vision, 1989, Black Tie, White Noise, 1993, The Singles 1969-1993, 1993, Outside, 1995, The Buddha of Suburbia, 1995, Earthling, 1997, Hours, 1999, Heathen, 2002, Reality, 2003, Diamond Dogs: 30th Anniversary Edition, 2004; (with Tin Machine) Tin Machine, 1989, Tin Machine II, 1991,; appeared in (play) The Elephant Man, Booth Theatre, N.Y.C., 1980; prodr. album by Lou Reed, Between Thought and Expression: The Lou Reed Anthology, 1992, album by Queen, Classic Queen, 1992. Recipient Grammy award for best short-form video, 1984; inducted Rock and Roll Hall of Fame, 1996.

BOWIE, DAVID BERNARD, clergyman; b. Jamaica, N.Y., Mar. 30, 1954; s. Matthew Bowie and Vanzetta Lorigné (Moore) Whittaker; m. Angela Baughman, Nov. 27, 1976; children: Courtney Alyce, Brooke Marie. BA, Talladega Coll., 1974; MDiv., Interdenominational Theological Ctr., 1983; D of ministry, Pitts. Theol. Seminary, 2000. Ordained to ministry Presbyn. Ch., 1983. Asst. Braille tchr. Erasmus Hall High Sch., Bklyn., 1975-77; employment counselor Woodward High Sch., Cin., 1978-79; student asst. pastor Westhills Presbyn. Ch., Atlanta, 1980-82; asst. pastor 1st Presbyn. Ch. East Cleveland, Ohio, 1983-84, assoc. pastor, 1984-88; stated supply pastor Heights Presbyn. Ch., Cleveland Heights, 1988-90, pastor, 1990—2001; assoc. pastor Christ the King Bapt. Ch., Dacula, Ga., 2001—03; temp. supply pastor Rice Meml. Presbyn. Ch., Atlanta. Mem. nominating com. Presbytery of Western Res., Cleve., 1985-87, moderator, 1987; mem. at-large mission coun., 1984-85, ex-officio mem., 1987, mem. com. on ministry, 1988-90, leadership devel., 1991—1993; participant study excursion Synod of Covenant, Columbus, Ohio to Cuernavaca, Mex., 1986, to C.Am., 1992,1994, to Mex. border, 1998, 2000, alt. commr., 1987, 90; mem. Ch. Devel./Redevel., Cleve., 1984-85; sem. adv. del. Gen. Assembly, United Presbyn. Ch., Houston, 1981, observer, Hartford, Conn., 1982; Clergy-Counselor Career Beginnings program Shaw High Sch., 1988-90, justice ministry 1997-2001; chaplain, Cleveland Heights Police Dept., 1998-2001; anti-racism trainer, 2000- Commr. 201st Gen. Assembly, Phila., 1989, tchr. Synod Sch., 1990, 92; mem. racial ethnic recruitment adv. com. John Carroll U., 1987-90; mem. Heights Commn. On Equity and Excellence in Edn., 1990-91, Student Svcs. Adv. Bd., 1988—2001, student mentoring program, 1988-90. Mem. Heights Clergy, Heights Interfaith Coun. (v.p. 1991—1993, pres. 1994-1996), Kiwanis, Kappa Alpha Psi. Home: 341 Hickory Haven Ter Suwanee GA 30024-6413 Office: Rice Meml Presbyn Ch 1515 Brewer Blvd SW Atlanta GA 30310

BOWIE, DEBORAH ANN, elementary school educator; b. Seoul, South Korea, Mar. 1, 1976; d. Larry J and Myong S Carbon; m. Gregory S Bowie, Dec. 5, 1998; children: Daryan J, Samuel I. BA, Murray State U., Murray, Ky., 1998; MEd, Ga. Coll. and State U., Milledgeville, 2003; postgrad., Argosy U., Sarasota, Fla., 2004—. Cert. tchr. Tex., 1999. Tchr. D. McRae Elem. Sch., Ft. Worth, 1999, Walter P. Jones Elem. Sch., Macon, Ga., 1999—2001; regular/spl. edn. tchr. Lindsey Elem. Sch., Warner Robins, Ga., 2001—. Better seeking team Lindsey Elem. Sch., Warner Robins, Ga., 2004—, instrnl. chair, 2003—04, ops./pers. decision team mem., 2001—03. Mem. Christian Fellowship Ch., Warner Robins, Ga., 2000—05. Mem.: NEA, Internat. Reading Assn. Avocations: reading, swimming, travel, singing. Office Phone: 478-929-7818. E-mail: dbowie@hcbe.net.

BOWIE, E(DWARD) J(OHN) WALTER, hematologist, researcher; b. Church Stretton, Shropshire, Eng., Mar. 10, 1925; came to U.S., 1958; s. Edgar Ormond and Ann Brown (Lorrimer) B.; m. Gertrud Susi Ulrich, Dec. 22, 1948; children— Katherine Ann, Christopher John, John Walter, James Ulrich MA, Oxford (Eng.) U., 1950, BM, BCh, 1952, DM, 1981; MS, U. Minn., 1961. House physician Univ. Coll. Hosp., London, 1953; sr. house officer Bethlem Royal and Maudsley Hosps., London, 1953-54; pvt. practice medicine Treherne, Man., Can., 1954; fellow in medicine Mayo Clinic, Rochester, Minn., 1958-60, cons. in internal medicine and hematology, 1961-90, head sect. hematology research, 1971-89; prof. medicine and lab. medicine Mayo Med. Sch., Rochester, Minn., 1974-90, prof. emeritus, 1990-96, ret., 1996. Invited spkr. Gordon Confs., 1973, 76, 78, Royal Soc., London, 1980; chmn. thrombosis coun. Internat. Soc. and Fedn. Cardiology, 1991; internat. dir. Thrombosis Vascular Tng. Ctrs. Co-author 6 books; assoc. editor Jour. Lab. and Clin. Medicine, 1976-80; contbr. chpts. to books, numerous articles to profl. jours. Recipient Judson Daland travel award Mayo Found., 1963, named Disting. Investigator, 1988, Disting. Alumnus Mayo Found., 1996. Fellow ACP, AMA, Royal Coll. Pathology; mem. AAAS, Am. Heart Assn. Internat. Soc. on Thrombosis and Haemostasis (v.p. 1980-81, Disting. Career award 1991), Am. Soc. Hematology, Internat. Com. on Thrombosis and Haemostasis (chmn. 1989-90), Ctrl. Soc. for Clin. Rsch., Am. Fedn. for Clin. Rsch., World Fedn. Haemophilia. Office: Emeritus Section Mayo Clinic Rochester MN 55905

BOWIE, LEE, academic administrator, philosopher, educator; BA in Math., Yale U.; PhD, Stanford U. Joined Mount Holyoke Coll., South Hadley, Mass., 1975, prof. philosophy, founding dir. Speaking, Arguing and Writing Program, founding co-dir. Harriet L. and Paul M. Weissman Ctr. for Leadership, v.p. student affairs, dean, 2003—. Co-editor: Thirteen Questions in Ethics and Social Philosophy, 1998, Twenty Questions: An Introduction to Philosophy, 2000. Office: Mount Holyoke College Skinner Hall Rm 213A 50 College St South Hadley MA 01075

BOWIE, NORMAN ERNEST, university official, educator; b. Biddeford, Maine, June 6, 1942; s. Lawrence Walker and Helen Elizabeth (Jacobsen) B.; m. Bonnie Jean Bankert, June 11, 1966 (div. 1980); children: Brian Paul, Peter Mark; m. Maureen Burns, Sept. 19, 1987. AB, Bates Coll., 1964; PhD, U. Rochester, 1968. Mem. faculty Lycoming Coll., Williamsport, Pa., 1968-69; asst. prof. philosophy Hamilton Coll., Clinton, N.Y., 1969-74, assoc. prof., 1974-75, U. Del., Newark, 1975-80, prof., 1980-89, dir. Ctr. for Study of Values, 1977-89; Elmer L. Andersen chairperson corp. responsibility U. Minn., Mpls., 1989—, chair dept. strategic mgmt. and orgn., 1992-95; fellow in ethics and professions Harvard U., 1996-97; Dixons prof. bus. ethics and social responsibility London Bus. Sch., 1999-2000. Lynette S. Autrey vis. prof. bus. ethics Rice U., spring 1986; vis. prof. Sch. Mgmt. U. Scranton, 1986-87, Sch. Bus. Adminstrn., Georgetown U., 1988-89; exec. v.p. seminars The Aspen Inst., 1998-99. Author: Towards a New Theory of Distributive Justice, 1971, Business Ethics, 1982, (with Ronald Duska) 2d edit., 1990, Making Ethical Decisions, 1985, University Business Partnerships: An Assessment, 1994, Business Ethics: A Kantian Perspective, 1999, Management Ethics, 2005; co-author: The Individual and the Political Order, 1977, 3d edit., 1998; editor: Ethical Issues in Government, 1981, Ethical Theory in the Last Quarter of the Twentieth Century, 1983, Equal Opportunity, 1988, Guide to Business Ethics, 2001; co-editor: Ethical Theory and Business, 1979, 7th edit., 2003, Ethics, Public Policy and Criminal Justice, 1982, The Tradition of Philosophy, 1986, Ethics and Agency Theory, 1992; co-editor Bus. and Profl. Ethics Jour., 1981-88. Mem. N.Y. Coun. for Humanities, 1974-75. NDEA fellow, 1965-68 Mem. AAUP, Acad. Mgmt., Am. Philos. Assn. (nat. exec. sec. 1972-77), Am. Soc. for Value Inquiry (pres. 1980-81), Am. Soc. Polit. and Legal Philosophy, Soc. Bus. Ethics (pres. 1988), Phi Beta Kappa. Home: PO Box 508 Trappe MD 21673-0508 Office: Carlson Sch Mgmt 321 19th Ave S Minneapolis MN 55455-0438 Office Phone: 612-625-6807. Business E-Mail: nbowie@csom.umn.edu.

BOWIE, PETER WENTWORTH, judge, educator; b. Alexandria, Va., Sept. 27, 1942; s. Beverley Munford and Louise Wentworth (Boynton) B.; m. Sarah Virginia Haught, Mar. 25, 1967; children: Heather, Gavin. BA, Wake Forest Coll., 1964; JD magna cum laude, U. San Diego, 1971. Bar: Calif. 1972, D.C. 1972, U.S. Dist. Ct. D.C. 1972, U.S. Dist. Ct. Md. 1973, U.S. Dist. Ct. (so. dist.) Calif. 1974, U.S. Ct. Appeals (D.C. cir.) 1972, U.S. Ct. Appeals (9th cir.) 1974, U.S. Supreme Ct. 1980. Trial atty. honors program Dept. of Justice, Washington, 1971-74; asst. U.S. Atty. U.S. Atty.'s Office, San Diego, 1974, asst. chief civil div., 1974-82, chief asst. U.S. atty., 1982-88; lawyer rep. U.S. Ct. Appeals (9th cir.) Jud. Conf., 1977-78, 84-87; judge U.S. Bankruptcy Ct., San Diego, 1988—. Lectr. law Calif. Western Sch. Law, 1979-83; exec. com. 9th Cir. Judicial Conf., 1991-94; com. on codes of conduct Jud. Conf. of US, 1995-2003; advisor ABA Joint Commn. to Evaluate Model Code of Jud. Conduct. Bd. dirs. Presidio Little League, San Diego, 1984, coach, 1983-84; alumni adv. bd. Sch. Law U. San Diego, 1998-2002. Lt. USN, 1964-68, Vietnam. Recipient Disting. Alumni award, U. San Diego Sch. Law, 2003. Mem. State Bar Calif. (hearing referee ct. 1982-86, mem. rev. dept 1986-90), Fed. Bar Assn. (pres. San diego chpt. 1981-83), San Diego County Bar Assn. (chmn. fed. ct. com. 1978-80, 83-85), Assn. Bus. Trial Lawyers (bd. govs.), San Diego Bankruptcy Forum (bd. dirs.), Phi Delta Phi. Republican. Mem. Unitarian Ch. Office: US Bankruptcy Court 325 West F St San Diego CA 92101-6017 Office Phone: 619-557-5158.

BOWKER, LEE HARRINGTON, sociologist, educator, writer; b. Bethlehem, Pa., Dec. 19, 1940; s. Maurice H. Bowker and Blanche E. Heffner; m. Nancy Bachant, 1966 (div. 1973); 1 child, Kirsten Ruth; m. Dee C. Thomas, May 25, 1975; children: Jessica Lynn, Gwendolyn Alice. BA, Muhlenberg Coll., 1962; MA, U. Pa., 1965; PhD, Wash. State U., 1972. Instr. in Sociology Lebanon Valley Coll., Annville, Pa., 1965-66, Allbright Coll., Reading, Pa., 1966-67; assoc. prof. Whitman Coll., Walla Walla, Wash., 1967-77; prof., assoc. dean U. Wis., Milw., 1977-82; dean grad. sch. and research Ind. (Pa.) U. of Pa., 1982-85; provost, v.p. Augustana Coll., Sioux Falls, S.D., 1985-87; dean behavioral and social scis. Humboldt State U., Arcata, Calif., 1987-97, emeritus dean, prof. sociology, 1997—2006. Cons. various pubs., colls., univs. and state agys; expert witness. Author: Prison Victimization, 1980, Humanizing Institutions for the Aged, 1982, Masculinities and Violence, 1997, The Role of the Department Chair, revised edit., 1997, Ending the Violence, rev. edit., 1998; assoc. editor Pacific Sociol. Rev., 1975-78, Justice Quar., 1983-85, Criminal Justice Policy Rev., 1984-95; contbr. articles to profl. jours. Pres. Blue Mountain Action Coun., OEO, Walla Walla, 1969-71; dir. social therapy program, Wash. State penitentiary, Walla Walla, 1971-73; bd. dirs. Milw. Bur. Community Corrections, 1979-81, Sioux Falls Symphony, 1985, United Way of Humboldt County, 1988-91. Grantee NIMH 1973, 79, 81, Washington Arts Commn. 1972, Washington Office Community Devel. 1974, Fulbright Found. 1985, Nat. Retired Tchrs. Assn./Am. Assn. Retired Persons Andrus Found. 1980; Law Enforcement Assistance Adminstrn. co-grantee, 1978. Mem.: Am. Soc. Criminology, Am. Sociol. Assn., Pacific Sociol. Assn. Home: 3513 H St Eureka CA 95503-5358 Office: Humboldt State U Sociology Faculty Arcata CA 95521 Office Phone: 707-826-4446. E-mail: dtbandlhb@cox.net.

BOWLER, MARIANNE BIANCA, federal judge; b. Boston, Feb. 15, 1947; d. Richard A. and Ann C. (Daly) B. BA, Regis Coll., 1967; JD cum laude, Suffolk U., 1976, LLD (hon.), 1994; LD (hon.), Regis Coll., 2003. Bar: Mass. 1978. Rsch. asst. Harvard Med. Sch., Boston, 1967-69; med. editor Mass. Dept. of Pub. Health, Boston, 1969-76; law clk. Mass. Superior Ct., Boston, 1976-77, dep. chief law clk., 1977-78; asst. dist. atty. Middlesex Dist. Atty.'s Office, Cambridge, Mass., 1978; asst. U.S. atty. U.S. Dept. of Justice, Boston, 1978-90, exec. asst. U.S. atty., 1988-89, sr. litigation counsel, 1989-90; magistrate judge U.S. Dist. Ct. Mass., Boston, 1990—2002, chief U.S. magistrate judge, 2002—. Chmn. bd. trustees New England Bapt. Hosp., Boston, 1990-95. Trustee Suffolk U., Boston, 1994—, Discovering Justice, 2003—; bd. dirs. The Boston Found., 1995—; dir. South Cove Nursing Facilities Found., Inc., 1995—; co-pres. Boston Coll. Inn of Ct., 1998—2002; bd. dirs. Discovering Justice, 2003-; overseer U.S.S. Constn. Mus., 2005-. Mem. Jr. League Boston, Suffolk Law Sch. Alumni Assn. (pres. 1979-80), Vincent Club, Isabel O'Neil Found., Save Venice. Democrat. Roman Catholic. Avocations: faux finishing, trompe l'oeil painting. Office: 1 Courthouse Way Ste 8420 Boston MA 02210-3010 Office Phone: 617-748-9219. Business E-Mail: honorable_marianne_bowler@mad.uscourts.gov.

BOWLER, PETER M., air transportation executive; b. May 14, 1955; children: Sarah, Anne, Sam. BS, St. Francis Xavier U., 1977; MA, Queens U., 1978; MBA, Harvard U., 1983. Divsn. mgr. sales adminstrn. Am. Airlines, 1985—86, project mgr., info. sys. planning, 1986—87, mng. dir., info. sys. strategic planning, 1987—90, mng. dir., compensation and benefits, 1990, spl. assignment, adminstrn., 1990—91, spl. assignment, corp. planning, 1991, mng. dir., food and beverage svcs., 1991—93, divsn. mng. dir., passenger sales, 1993—96, mng. dir., reservations, 1996, v.p., passenger sales, 1996—98; pres. Am. Eagle Airlines, 1998—. Office: AMR Corp 4333 Amon Carter Blvd Fort Worth TX 76155

BOWLES, BARBARA LANDERS, investment company executive; b. Nashville, Sept. 17, 1947; d. Corris Raemone Landers and Rebecca (Bonham) Jennings; m. Earl Stanley Bowles, Nov. 27, 1971; 1 son, Terrence Earl. BA, Fisk U., 1968; MBA, U. Chgo., 1971. Chartered fin. analyst. From bank official to v.p. First Nat. Bank of Chgo., 1968-81; asst. v.p. Beatrice Cos., Chgo., 1981-84; v.p. investor rels. Kraft Inc., Chgo., 1984—89; pres., founder The Kenwood Group Inc., Chgo., 1989—. Bd. dirs. Black & Decker Corp., Hyde Pk. Bank. Bd. dirs. Children's Meml. Hosp., Ga. Pacific Corp, Wis. Energy, and Dollar Gen. Corp. The Chgo. Urban League; mem. Grad. Sch. Bus. U. Chgo. Scholar United Negro College Fund, 1989. Mem. NAACP (life), Assn. Investment Mgmt. and Rsch., Chgo. Fisk trustee (1998-). Mem. United Ch. of Christ. Avocations: tennis, bridge. Office Phone: 312-368-1666. E-mail: kenwoodg@aol.com.

BOWLES, CRANDALL CLOSE, textiles executive; m. Erskine Bowles. B in Econ., Wellesley Coll.; MBA, Columbia U. Fin. analyst Springs Industries, Inc., 1973—78, exec. v.p. growth and devel., 1992, exec. v.p. textile prodn., 1993, pres. bath fashions group, 1995, pres., COO, 1997—98, CEO, chmn., 1998—; exec. v.p. Springs Co., 1978—82, pres., 1982; also bd. dirs. Bd. dirs. Deere & Co. Bd. trustees African Wildlife Found.; bd. dirs. Juvenile Diabetes Rsch. Found., Charlotte Inst. for Tech. Innovation. Mem.: Palmetto Bus. Forum, Bus. Roundtable, Bus. Coun., Am. Textile Mfrs. Inst., Excellence in Edn. Coun. Office: 205 N White St Fort Mill SC 29715-1654*

BOWLES, DAVID STANLEY, engineering educator, engineering consultant; b. Romford, Essex, Eng., June 30, 1949; m. Valerie Rosina Curd; children: Penny, Simon, Amy. BSc, City U., Eng., 1972; PhD, Utah State U., 1977. Registered profl. engr., Utah; cert. profl. hydrologist. Jr. civil engr. George Wimpey & Co., Hammersmith, London, 1967-72; rsch. asst. prof. Utah State U., Logan, 1976-80, rsch. assoc. prof., 1980-81, adj. rsch. assoc. prof., 1981-83, rsch. prof., 1983-85, prof., 1985—, assoc. dir., 1986-91, dir., 1992-96, Inst. for Dam Safety Risk Mgmt., 2000—. Vis. scientist Internat. Inst. Applied Systems Analysis, Laxenburg, Austria, 1979; br. mgr., engr. Law Engring., Denver, 1981-83; prin. Risk Assessment Cons. Engrs. and Economists (RAC), 1986—; mem. Australian Com. on Large Dams. Contbr. numerous articles to profl. jours. Bd. dirs. U.S. Soc. on Dams. Fellow ASCE, Am. Water Resources Assn.; mem. Soc. Risk Analysis, Am. Geophys. Union, Am. Inst. Hydrology, Assn. State Dam Safety Ofcls. Home: 1520 Canyon Rd Providence UT 84332-9431 Office: Utah Water Rsch Lab Utah State Univ Logan UT 84322-8200 Office Phone: 435-753-6004. E-mail: bowles@cache.net.

BOWLES, ERSKINE B., former federal official; b. Greensboro, NC, Aug. 8, 1945; s. Hargrove "Skipper" Bowles; m. Crandall Bowles; 3 children. BS in Bus. Adminstrn., U. N.C., 1967; MBA, Columbia U., 1969. With Morgan Stanley & Co., N.Y.C., Bowles Hollowell Conner & Co., Charlotte, N.C., 1975-93; adminstr. Small Bus. Adminstrn., Washington, 1993-94; asst. to the Pres. & dep. chief of staff The White House, Washington, 1994—95, chief of staff, 1996—98; ptnr. Forstmann Little & Co., N.Y.C., 1999—2001; mng. dir., co-founder Carousel Capital Co., LLC, 1999—2001, sr. advisor, 2002—; chmn. Erskine Bowles & Co. LLC, 2003—; dep. spl. envoy for Tsunami Recovery UN, 2005—. Bd. dirs. Merck & Co., 1999—2001, VF Corp., 1999—2001, First Union Corp., 1999—2001, Wachovia Corp., 2001, Krispy Kreme Doughnut Corp., 2003, Cousins Properties, 2003—, Gen. Motors Corp., 2005—. Pres. Juvenile Diabetes Found.; Dem. Senate nominee, N.C., 2002, 04. Office: Erskine Bowles & Co LLC Ste 2450 c/o Carousel Capital 201 N Tryon St Charlotte NC 28202*

BOWLES, PATRICIA MARY, secondary school educator; b. Reading, Pa., Jan. 15, 1950; d. Charles Worthington Doane and Mary Augusta (Kershner) B. BS, Kutztown (Pa.) U., 1971; MEd, Temple U., 1987. Cert. elem. tchr. and elem. prin., Pa. Tchr. visually impaired Reading (Pa.) Sch. Dist., 1972-75, adminstrv. intern, 1986-87; tchr. Berks County Intermediate Unit, Reading, 1973-93; tchr. visually impaired Reading Sch. Dist., 1993—. Account exec. United Way, Berks County, 1988—; bd. dirs. Leadership Berks, Reading, 1988—, Nat. Coun. on Alcoholism, Berks County, 1988—; pres. Leadership Berks Alumni Assn., Reading, 1987, bd. dirs., 1987—. Eleanor Long Tchr. of the Yr., Pa. Div. Visually Impaired, 1984. Mem. Assn. for Edn. and Rehab. Visually Impaired, Assn. for Supervision and Curriculum Devel., Flying Dutchmen Ski Club (trip dir. Reading chpt. 1975-76), Phi Delta Kappa, Delta Kappa Gamma. Republican. Lutheran. Avocations: snow and water skiing, dance, theater. Home: 5 Eagle Ct Reading PA 19605-3215 Office: Reading High Sch 801 N 13th St Reading PA 19604-2451

BOWLES, SUSAN MARIE, clinical pharmacist; d. Joseph Anderson Bowles, John H. McCormick (Stepfather). BS in Pharmacy, U. of Wash., Seattle, 1984; postgrad. in DPharm program, U. Colo., Denver, 2001—. Clin. pharmacist oncology/transplant Baylor U. Med. Ctr., Dallas, 1994—98; staff pharmacist Multicare Med. Ctr., Tacoma, 1984—85; clin. pharmacist oncology/medicine Va. Mason Med. Ctr., Seattle, 1985—94; clin. pharmacist medicine/transplant Baylor U. Med. Ctr., Dallas, 1998—; clin. pharmacist Emory U. Med. Ctr., Atlanta, 1987—88. Mem.: Am. Soc. Health Sys. Pharmacists, USTA, Alpha Delta Pi (correspondance sec. 1979—80). Republican. Avocations: tennis, running, skiing, golf, piano. Office: Baylor U Med Ctr 3500 Gaston Ave Dallas TX 75246 Personal E-mail: susanbowles@yahoo.com.

BOWLEY, JAMES ERIC, religious studies educator, researcher; b. Lincoln, Nebr., Aug. 30, 1962; s. Eric Herald Tonkin and Dorene Norma Bowley; m. Bonnie Epp; children: Spencer, Karissa, Austin, Sophia. BA summa cum laude, Grace Coll., 1984; Cert., Jerusalem U. Coll., 1986; MPhil, PhD, Hebrew Union Coll. Jewish Inst. Religion, 1992. Adj. prof. U. Cin., 1991—92; assoc. prof. King Coll., Bristol, Tenn., 1995—2002; assoc. prof. religious studies Millsaps Coll., Jackson, 2002—. Editor Dead Sea scrolls project Bibl. Archaeology Soc., NYC, 1992—95; editor Dead Sea Scroll Found., Jerusalem, 2002—; cons. Exploreum Mus., Mobile, Ala.; pres. grad. sch. alumni Hebrew Union Coll., Cin.; adv. Jewish Culture Orgn., Jackson, Miss. Author: (textbook) Guided Tour of Israel's Sacred Library: An Introduction to Hebrew Bible; editor: (book) The Dead Sea Scroll Concordance. Dir. Mississippians Educating for Smart Justice, Jackson, Miss., 2002—05. Hearin grantee, Millsaps Coll., 2003—04. Mem.: Soc. Bibl. Lit. Office: Millsaps Coll 1701 North State St Jackson MS 39210 Office Phone: 601-974-1328. Office Fax: 601-974-1324. E-mail: bowleje@millsaps.edu.

BOWLIN, TERRY LYNN, pharmacologist, researcher; b. Columbus, Ohio, Feb. 15, 1955; s. Britton and Gwendolyn Bowlin; m. Kathleen Ann Treadway, June 17, 1978; children: Nicole, Nicholas, Katherine. BS, Ohio State U., 1978; MS, Cleve. (Ohio) State U., 1980, PhD, 1982. Dir. immunology Marion Merrell Dow, Cin., 1983—96; v.p. rsch. Brocham Pharm., Montreal, Canada, 1996—2002; CEO Microbiotix, Inc., Worcester, Mass., 2002—. Adv. pharm. Pharma Found., Washington, 1992—; adj. prof. U. Montreal, 1997—2000, Wright State U., Dayton, Ohio, 2003—. Co-author: IL-1 Antagonist Discovery, 2000; contbr. articles to profl. jours. Rep. Kings H.S., Kings Mill, Ohio,

2003—. Fellow, Am. Cancer Soc., 1980, Cleve. Clinic, 1980, NCI, 1982. Mem.: Am. Coll. Rheumatology, Am. Assn. Immunology, Am. Assn. Cancer Rsch., Ursiline Acad. Dads Club (sec. 2004—). Republican. Methodist. Avocations: running, bicycling, skiing, golf. Home: 8466 Pond Ridge Dr Maineville OH 45039 Office: Microbiotix Inc One Innovation Dr Worcester MA 01605

BOWLING, CHARLES BRYAN, legal association administrator; b. Nurnberg, Germany, Dec. 23, 1951; s. Charles Edward and Sieglinde Bowling; 1 child, Erik Bryan. BS, U. Houston, 1995, MA, 1998; PhD in bus. administn., N. Ctrl. U., 2005. Mgmt. trainer Midcap Corp., San Antonio, outside sales; tch. adv. Motion Industries, Houston; policy procedures officer Ky. Dept. of Corrections, Frankfort, Ky. Suprv. Ky. Dept of Corrections, Frankfort, Ky., tng. coord. Coord. Citizens Corps., Bell County, Ky., 2004; Col. USA Vet. Homeland Security Svcs., Johnson City, Tenn., 2004. Avocations: running, reading, music. Home: 23 Abbey Ln Middlesboro KY 40965 Office: Ky Dept of Corrections Frankfort KY 40601 Office Phone: 606-337-7065. E-mail: chabryb@charter.net.

BOWLING, DANIEL S., III, lawyer; b. Atlanta, Oct. 19, 1955; s. Daniel Seymour and Martha (Alexander) B.; m. Elizabeth Grede, July 12, 1983; children: Daniel IV, Edward Alexander, Elizabeth. BA, Millsaps Coll., Jackson, Miss., 1977; JD, Duke U., 1980. Bar: Ga. 1980, U.S. Ct. Appeals (11th cir.) 1981, (5th cir.) 1981, (6th cir.) 1981, U.S. Dist. Ct. (no. dist., so. dist., mid. dist.) Ga. 1981, U.S. Dist. Ct. (ea. dist.) Mich. Assoc. Smith, Currie & Hancock, Atlnata, 1980-85, ptnr., 1985; various positions including labor and employment counsel, group v.p., and gen. mgr. Coca-Cola Enterprises Inc., Atlanta, 1986—2001, sr. v.p. human resources, 2001—. Mem. selection com. Fla. State Bar Pro-Bono award; former pres. Atlanta Coun. Younger Lawyers; sr. lecturing fellow Duke Law Sch. Bd. trustees Millsaps Coll.; Johnston Legacy Scholarship Found. Mem. ABA, State Bar Ga., Atlanta Bar Assn., Am. Corp. Counsel Assn., Lawyers Club Atlanta, Ansley Golf. Republican. Office: Coca-Cola Enterprises-West One Coca-Cola Pla Atlanta GA 30313*

BOWLING, GARY R., art educator; b. Lamar, Mo., Mar. 1, 1948; s. Willaim Robert and Ida Gertrude Bowling; m. Linda Jean Kruckenberg, Sept. 6, 1975; children: David Kruckenberg, Melissa Kruckenberg, Aja Kruckenberg. BS, Mo. So. State U., 1970; MFA, U. Ark., 1975. Art tchr. Independence Pub. Schs., Independence, Kans., 1970—72; architectural illustrator self employed, Fayetteville, Ark., 1973—75; drawing, painting instr. U. Ark., Fayetteville, Ark., 1974—75; chmn. Westmar Coll., Dept. of Art, Lemars, Iowa, 1975—83; artist self employed, Lamar, Mo., 1983—. Named Master Artist, Huntington Mus. of Art, 1992, Resident Artist, Buena Vista U., 1997; fellowship, Yaddo Artist Colony, 1981. Office: PO Box 207 1603 Coll St Lamar MO 64759 Office Phone: 417-682-2429. E-mail: gbowling@direway.com.

BOWLING, JOHN C., academic administrator; Pres. Olivet Nazarene U., 1991—.

BOWLING, LANCE CHRISTOPHER, recording industry executive; b. San Pedro, Calif., May 17, 1948; s. Dan Parker and Sylvia Lois (Van Devander) B. BA in Polit. Sci. and History, Pepperdine U., 1966-70, MPA, 1973. Owner, founder Cambria Master Recordings, Palos Verdes, Calif., 1972—. Editor: Joseph Wagner: A Retrospective of Composer-Conductor 1900-74, 1976, Hazards Pavilion, Jour of Soc for Preservation of South Calif. Mus. Heritage, 1985—; author: Eugene Hemmer: Composer-Pianist, 1983; prodr. over 150 classical records including works by Charles W. Cadman, Madeleine Dring, Mary Carr Moore, John Crown, Ed Bland, Florence Price, Elinor Remick Warren, Miklos Rozsa, Erich W. Korngold, Max Steiner, Ernst Gold, William Grant Still, Arthur Lange, also classical music radio station documentaries, programs for Taz Libr. Congress; contbr. Opera News, 2003 Active allocation com. Region V, United Way, LA, 1978-85; bd. dirs. Elinor Remick Warren Found., Film Music Soc., Hollywood, Calif., New World Ctr. for Arts, LA, So. Calif. Music History Resource, LA Ballet. Recipient Golden Rose award Pi Iota chpt. Phi Beta, 1988. Mem. ASCAP, Nat. Acad. Recording Arts and Scis. (classical com.), Assn. Recorded Sound Collections, Music Libr. Assn., Soc. for Preservation of Film Music, Sonneck Soc., Variety Arts Club (L.A.), Mus. Arts Club (Long Beach, Calif.), Zamorano Club (L.A.). Episcopalian. Avocations: collecting early Calif. books and ephemera, restoration of 78 RPM recordings and antique automobiles. Home: 2625 Colt Rd Palos Verdes Peninsula CA 90275-6578 Office: Cambria Master Recordings 1659 W 7th St San Pedro CA 90732-3421 Office Phone: 310-831-1322. E-mail: cambriamus@aol.com.

BOWLSBY, BOB, athletic director; b. Jan. 10, 1952; m. Candice Bowlsby; children: Lisa, Matt, Rachel, Kyle. BS, Moorhead State U., 1975; MS, U. Iowa, 1978. Asst. athletic dir. No. Iowa U., athletic dir., 1984-91, U. Iowa, Iowa City, 1991—. Chair NCAA Divsn. I Mgmt. Coun., 1997-99; mem. NCAA Divsn. I Basketball com., 2000-03, chair, 2004-05. Chmn. Big Ten Championships and awards com.; chair NCAA Olympic Sports Liaison Com., NCAA/USOC liaison com., Olympics com. mem; bd. dirs. Iowa Games. Mem. Nat. Assn. Collegiate Dir. of Athletics (exec. com.). Office: U Iowa Dir Athletics 338 Carver Hawkeye Arena Iowa City IA 52242-1020 Office Phone: 319-335-9435. E-mail: robert-bowlsby@uiowa.edu.

BOWMAN, BRUCE, art educator; b. Dayton, Ohio, Nov. 23, 1938; s. Murray Edgar Bowman and Mildred May (Moler) Elleman; m. Julie Ann Gosselin, 1970 (div. 1980); 1 child, Carrie Lynn. AA, San Diego City Coll., 1962; BA, Calif. State U., L.A., 1964, MA, 1968. Tchr. art L.A. City Schs., 1966—, North Hollywood Adult Sch., Calif., 1966—68; instr. art Cypress Coll., 1976—78, West L.A. Coll., 1969—. Seminar leader, 1986—. Author: Shaped Canvas, 1976, Toothpick Sculpture and Ice Cream Stick Art, 1976, Ideas: How to Get Them, 1985, (recording) Develop Winning Willpower, 1986, Waikiki, 1988; one-man shows include Calif. State U., L.A., 1968, Pepperdine U., Malibu, 1978, exhibited in group shows at McKenzie Gallery, L.A., 1968, Trebor Gallery, 1970, Cypress Coll., 1977, Design Recycled Gallery, Fullerton, 1977, Pierce Coll., Woodland Hills, 1978, Leopold/Gold Gallery, Santa Monica, 1980. With USN, 1957—61. Avocation: karate (black belt Tang Soo Do).

BOWMAN, BRUCE ALAN, civil engineer; b. Garmisch-Partenkirchen, Bavaria, Germany, Mar. 12, 1959; s. Walter Earl and Ingeborg Marie Bowman; m. Leslie Suzanne Thompson, Sept. 19, 1981; children: Gregory, Douglas. BS Chemistry, Ind. U., 1981; MS Ops. Rsch., USAF Inst. Tech., 1988; PhD Civil Engring., Columbia U., 1995. Analyst Office of the Dep. Chief of Staff for Pers., Hdqs., US Army, Washington, 1990—92; asst. prof. US Mil. Acad., West Point, NY, 1996—99; sect. chief and divsn. chief, joint warfighting analysis divsn. (j8) Office of the Chmn. of the Joint Chiefs of Staff, Washington, 1999—2001; prin. cons. PricewaterhouseCoopers Mgmt. Consulting LLP, Fairfax, Va., 2001—01; sr. profl. staff Johns Hopkins U. Applied Physics Lab., Laurel, Md., 2001—03; sr. scientist Anser, Inc., Arlington, Va., 2003—04; sr. cons. IBM Bus. Cons. Svcs., Fairfax, 2004; dir. sys. engring. SAIC, McLean, Va., 2005—; prin. Hilltop Cons. Ptnrs., Oak Hill, Va., 2005—. Co-chmn. sys. dynamics in nat. security conf. Nat. Def. U., Washington, 2000—00; lectr. George Washington U., Washington, 2004—; mem. tech. adv. panel Mobile Pro; mem. adv. panel Vectormax. Contbr. book Pipeline Risk Management Manual, 1996. Co- and founding exec. dir. The ACE Mentor Program of the Greater Wash. DC Met. Area, Inc., 2000; mem., bd. of directors Learning & Leadership in Families, Inc., Washington, 2001; elder Presbyn. Ch. U.S.A., 1991; youth soccer coach Springfield, Va., 1989—91, Rockland County, NY, 1992—95. Lt. col. US Army, 1981—2001. Mem.: ASCE, Mil. Ops. Rsch. Soc. (chmn. weapons of mass destruction nat. symposium 2001—01). Avocation: reading, pastels, chess, soccer, jogging. Office: IBM Bus Cons Svcs 12902 Fed Sys Pk Dr Fairfax VA 22033 Business E-Mail: bruce.bowman@us.ibm.com. E-mail: drbrucebowman@cox.net, Bruce.A.Bowman@SAIC.com.

BOWMAN, C. ALVIN, academic administrator; m. Linda Bowman; children: Laura, Natalie. BA in Speech Pathology, Augustana Coll., 1975; MS Ea. Ill. U., 1976; PhD in Speech and Hearing Sci., U. Ill., 1979. Joined dept. speech pathology and audiology Ill. State U., Normal, 1978, named chair dept. speech pathology and audiology, dir. Down Syndrome Speech-Lang. Clinic, 1994, interim provost, 2002—03, interim pres., 2003—04, pres., 2004—. Office: Ill State Univ Office of the Pres Campus Box 1000 Normal IL 61790-1000

BOWMAN, C. MICHAEL, physician; married; two children. BS in Chemistry (with honors), U. Ill., 1968; PhD in Genetics, U. Wis., 1972, MD, 1975. Diplomate Am. Bd. Pediatrics, Am. Bd. Pediatric Pulmonology. Pediat. resident Vanderbilt U., 1975-78, chief resident, 1978-79; dir. comprehensive cystic fibrosis ctr. Med. U. S.C.; divsn. head Divsn. Pediat. Pulmonolgy, Allergy & Immunology; prof. pediats. Med. U. S.C., Charleston, 2000—. Fellow Am. Acad. of Pediat., mem. Am. Bd. of Pediat., Am. Thoracic Soc. Achievements include research in lung disorders in children. Office: Med U S C Ste 281 PO Box 250561 135 Rutledge Ave Charleston SC 29425 Office Phone: 843-876-1555. Office Fax: 843-876-1583. Business E-Mail: bowmanm@musc.edu.

BOWMAN, CATHERINE MCKENZIE, lawyer; b. Tampa, Fla., Nov. 10, 1962; d. Herbert Alonza and Joan Bates (Baggs) McKenzie; m. Donald Campbell Bowman, Jr., May 21, 1988; children: Hunter Hall, Sarah McKenzie. BA in Psychology and Sociology, Vanderbilt U., 1984; JD, U. Ga., 1987. Bar: Ga. 1987, U.S. Dist. Ct. (so. dist.) Ga. 1987. Assoc. Ranitz, Mahoney, Forbes & Coolidge, P.C., Savannah, Ga., 1987-91; ptnr. Forbes and Bowman, 1991—. Bd. dirs. Greenbriar Children's Ctr., 1994-98, exec. com. 1995, pres. 1996-98; mem. distbn. com. Savannah Found., 1994-2002; ball com. Telfair Arts Acad., 2002, ball com. Historic Savannah Found., 2002; chair Savannah Country Day Sch. Fair, 2004 (PYA sec. 2005), Savannah Country Day Sch. Party, 2004. Mem. Am. Employment Law Coun., Internat. Assn. Def. Counsel, Ga. Def. Lawyers Assn., Savannah Young Lawyers Assn. (pres. 1996-97), 2000 Club (membership chair 1990-91, pres. 1992), South Atlantic Found. (bd. dirs. 1992). Home: 17 Franklin Creek S Savannah GA 31411 Office: Forbes and Bowman PO Box 13929 7505 Waters Ave Ste D-14 Savannah GA 31406-3824 Office Phone: 912-352-1190. Business E-Mail: cbowman@forbesbowman.com.

BOWMAN, CONNIE JO, secondary school educator; b. Huntington, Ind., Sept. 17, 1949; d. C. Eugene and Geraldine Celeste (Blickenstaff) Howard; m. Thomas Arthur Hess, Aug. 7, 1971 (div. June 1980); 1 child, Audrea Leigh; m. John Ezra Bowman, July 24, 1982; stepchildren: Heather Jane, Howard Thomas. BS, Manchester Coll., 1971; MAT, Purdue U., 1977. Tchr. math. Wabash (Ind.) City Schs., 1971-72, Whitko Community Schs., South Whitley, Ind., 1973-78; part-time instr. Manchester Coll., North Manchester, Ind., 1979-80; tchr. DeKalb Eastern Community Schs., Butler, Ind., 1980—. Chmn. math. dept. Eastside Jr./Sr. High Sch., Butler, 1987—. Mem. NEA, Nat. Coun. Tchrs. Math., Ind. Tchrs. Assn., Ind. Coun. Tchrs. Math. Methodist. Avocations: sewing, reading, church choir. Home: 10231 Garman Rd Leo IN 46765-9217 Office: Eastside Jr/Sr High Sch 603 E Green St Butler IN 46721-1135

BOWMAN, CYNTHIA GRANT, law educator; BA with honors, Swarthmore Coll., 1966; PhD in Polit. Sci., Columbia U., 1972; JD cum laude, Northwestern U., 1982. Law clk. to Hon. Richard D. Cudahy US Ct. Appeals (7th cir.), 1982—83; assoc. Jenner & Block, Chgo., 1983—88; vis. asst. prof. Northwestern U. Sch. Law, Chgo., 1988—89, asst. prof. law, 1989—92, assoc. prof., 1992—95, prof. law, 1995—, prof. gender studies, 2000—. Co-author: Cases and Materials on Feminist Jurisprudence: Taking Women Seriously, 2001, Women and Law in Sub-saharan Africa, 2003; contbr. articles to profl. jours. Mem.: ABA, Soc. Am. Law Tchrs., Law and Society Assn. Office: Northwestern U Sch Law 357 E Chicago Ave Chicago IL 60611 Office Phone: 312-503-6607. Office Fax: 312-503-2035. E-mail: cgbowman@law.northwestern.edu.*

BOWMAN, DANIEL OLIVER, retired psychologist; b. Holly Hill, S.C., Feb. 1, 1931; s. John Daniel and Pansy (Mizzell) Bowman. BA in Music, Furman U., 1951; MEd, U. S.C., 1952; PhD, U. Ga., 1963. Lic. psychologist, S.C. Tchr., English, French Summerville (S.C.) H.S., 1952-53; chmn. English dept., sr. guidance counselor, Boys H.S., Anderson, S.C., 1955-61; instr. psychology U. Ga., Athens, 1961-63; asst. prof. psychology The Citadel, Charleston, S.C., 1963-66, assoc. prof. psychology, counselor to corps cadets, 1966-69, prof. psychology, dir. grad. studies, 1969-77, prof., head dept. psychology, 1977-91, Arland D. Williams prof. psychology, 1991-96, prof. emeritus, 1996—. Cons. Charleston County Sheriff's Dept., 1985-94, Berkeley County Sch. System, Moncks Corner, S.C., 1977-89. Chmn. Charleston County Mental Retardation Bd., 1988-90. Mem. APA, AAUP, NASP, Am. Psychol. Soc. (charter), Southea. Psychol. Assn., S.C. Psychol. Assn. (pres. 1990-91, Outstanding Contbrs. Psychology 1988), Phi Kappa Phi (pres. 1979-80), Phi Delta Kappa. Home: 6 Fort Royal Ave Charleston SC 29407-6012 E-mail: bowmano@aol.com.

BOWMAN, DONALD EUGENE, investment advisor; b. Dayton, Ohio, July 9, 1930; s. John Peter and Delia Francis (Sink) B.; m. Mary Louise, Jan. 20, 1984; children: Clark Woodford, Marylouise Chalfant. BA, U. Wis., 1952; MBA, Loyola Coll., Balt., 1982; Exec. Advanced Mgmt. degree, Harvard U., 1974; postgrad., Stanford U., 1976. Chartered investment counselor. CEO, pres. T. Rowe Price Assn., Balt., 1956-79; founder, CEO, pres. Bowman Fin. Mgmt. Co., Balt., 1978—. Bd. dirs. Roland Park Girls Sch., 1969-75, U. Wis. Found., Madison, 1978-95, U. Balt. Found., 1978—, 4-H Found., Washington, 1988—, Wis. Alumni Assn., 1995-2000; chmn., bd. dirs. Towson U. Found., Balt., 1989-95; exec. MBA bd. dirs. Loyola Coll., Balt., 1985—; trustee Balt. Opera Co., 1996-2003; chmn. bd. St. Pauls Sch. for Girls, 1992-95; mem. adv. coun. ERISA, 1972-75; bd. govs. Investment Coun. Assn. Am., Washington, 1968-78; mem. No Load Mut. Fund Bd., 1970-78; trustee Alliance for Chesapeake Bay, 2002—; hon. chmn. Md. Nat. Rep. Bus. Adv. Coun., Presdl. Bus. Adv. Coun.; Capt. USNR, 1952-90. Recipient Bus. of Yr. award, Nat. Rep. Congl. Com., 2003, Bus. Man of the Yr. award, 2003. Mem.: Navy Mutual Aid Assn. (fin. com., audit com., employee 401K plan com., bd. dirs.). Republican. Avocations: tennis, exercise, golf. Office: Bowman Fin Mgmt Co Inc 1330 Smith Ave F Baltimore MD 21209-3703 Office Phone: 410-433-1900. Personal E-mail: dobow2000@aol.com.

BOWMAN, DOROTHY LOUISE, artist; b. Hollywood, Calif., Jan. 20, 1927; d. Bruce L. and Dorothy L. (Kalkman) B; m. Howard Hugh Bradford, Dec. 30, 1949 (div. 1965); children: Brock, Cyndra, Tal Scott, Heather, Delia, Callia. Student, Chouinard Art Inst., Calif., 1945-48, Jepson Art Inst., L.A., 1948-49; BA, Webster U., 1979. One-woman show Ventana Gallery, Big Sur, 1998; serigrapher, printmaker, painter: represented in permanent collections: Immaculate Heart Coll., L.A. County Mus., Bklyn. Mus., Long Beach Mus., Crocker Art Gallery, Mus. Modern Art, Phila., Mus. Fine Arts, San Jose State Coll., De Cordova and Danna Mus., Boston Pub. Libr., Boston Mus. Fine Arts, N.Y. Pub. Libr., Rochester Meml. Gallery, U. Wis., U. Hawaii, U. Ill., U. Kans., Santa Barbara Mus., Achenbach Found. Legion of Honor, Mus. Modern Art, Monterey, Calif., Libr. Congress, Calif. State Libr. Archives, Arquivos Historicos De Arte Contemporanea Museu De Arte Moderna, San Paulo, Brazil, Ch. of Latter Day Saints History Mus., Salt Lake City, 1987, Nat. Mus. of Women in the Arts, Washington, 2000—; twice juried internat. show 27 countries, 1987; creator animation films The Mobius World, 2000, Really O'Reiley, 2002, Never Seen Fox, 2003, Cry Baby Lion!; Traveling show Smithsonian Inst., Nat. Collection of Fine Arts, 1952; movie prodr. hist. film, Big Sur, 2002. Address: Nat Mus of Women in the Arts Archives 1250 New York Ave NW Washington DC 20005-3970 Office Phone: 831-375-5170. E-mail: dorothybowman@redshift.com.

BOWMAN, FRANK LEE (SKIP BOWMAN), retired military officer; b. Chattanooga, Tenn., Dec. 19, 1944; m. Linda Anne Rich, June 10, 1966; children: Greg, Christy. BS, Duke U., 1966; MS in Nuclear Engring., Naval Arch., MIT, 1973; LHD (hon.), Duke U. Commd ensign USN, 1966, advanced through grades to admiral, 1996; naval officer at sea on USS Simon Bolivar, USS Pogy, USS Daniel Boone, 1966-77; exec. officer USS Bremerton, USS Bremerton, 1978-80; comdr. USS City of Corpus Christi USN, 1983-86, comdr. USS Holland, 1988-90, dep. dir. ops. joint staff Washington, 1991-92, dir. polit.-mil. affairs joint staff, 1992-94, dep. chief naval ops., chief naval pers., 1994-96, dir. naval nuclear propulsion, 1996—2004; pres., CEO Nuclear Energy Inst., Washington, 2005—. Decorated Disting. Svc. medal, Defense Disting. Svc. medal, Legion of Merit with 3 gold stars, Meritorious Svc. medal with 2 gold stars, Battle E Efficiency award, four times, Navy Expeditionary medal twice, Humanitarian Svc. medal twice. Office: Nuclear Energy Inst 1776 I St NW Ste 400 Washington DC 20006*

BOWMAN, FRANK O., law educator; b. 1955; BA, Colo. Coll., 1976; JD, Harvard U., 1979. Bar: Colo. 1979. Trial atty. criminal divsn. U.S. Dept. Justice, Washington, 1979—82; spl counsel Yates & Crane, P.C., Durango, Colo., 1982—83; dep. dist. atty. Denver, 1983—86; pvt. practice Colo., 1986—87; assoc. Anderson, Campbell & Laugesen, P.C., Denver, 1987—89; dep. chief so. criminal divsn. Fla., 1989—95; spl. counsel U.S. Sentencing Commn., Washington, 1995—96; assoc. prof. law Ind. U., 1999—2002, M. Dale Palmer prof. law, 2002—. Vis. prof. Washington & Lee, 1994—95, Gonzaga, 1996—99; acad. advisor criminal law com. U.S. Jud. Conf., 1998—2001. Co-author: Federal Sentencing Guidelines Handbook; contbr. articles to profl. jours.; mem. editl. bd.: Federal Sentencing Reporter, Criminal Justice Review. Office: Ind Univ Sch Law Lawrence W Inlow Hall Rm 316 530 W NY St Indianapolis IN 46202-3225 Office Phone: 317-274-2862. Office Fax: 317-278-3326. E-mail: frbowman@iupui.edu.

BOWMAN, FREDERICK OSCAR, JR., retired cardiothoracic surgeon; b. Chapel Hill, N.C., May 24, 1928; s. Frederick Oscar and Sallie (Sanders) B.; m. Helen Roberson, 1951 (div. 1956); m. Elizabeth Wallace Schwartz, Jan. 24, 1959; children: Frederick III, John Sanders, Michael Andrew, William Albert. AB, U. N.C., 1948; MD, U. Pa., 1952. Diplomate Am. Bd. Surgery, Am. Bd. Thoracic Surgery. Intern Roosevelt Hosp., N.Y.C., 1952-53, resident in gen. surgery, 1953-54, 56-59; resident in thoracic surgery Bellevue Hosp., N.Y.C., 1959-60, Presbyn. Hosp., N.Y.C., 1960-61; instr. in surgery Coll. Physicians and Surgeons, Columbia U., N.Y.C., 1961-64, asst. prof. clin. surgery, 1964-68, assoc. prof. clin. surgery, 1968-79, prof. clin. surgery, 1979-92, prof. emeritus clin. surgery, 1992—. Attending surgeon Presbyn. Hosp., N.Y.C., 1979-91, cons. emeritus, 1991—, sect. chief pediatric cardiac surgery, 1988-91. Contbr. over 100 articles to profl. jours. Mem. U. N.C. Bd. Visitors, Chapel Hill, 1991-94. Capt. U.S. Army, 1954-56. Fellow Am. Coll. Surgeons; mem. AMA, Am. Assn. Thoracic Surgery, Soc. Thoracic Surgeons, N.Y. Soc. Thoracic Surgery (pres. 1985-86), Internat. Cardiovascular Soc., Portugese Soc. Cardiology, N.Y. Soc. Cardiology, N.Y. Heart Assn., N.Y. Surg. Soc., N.Y. Acad. Scis. Home: 12723 Morehead Govs Club Chapel Hill NC 27517

BOWMAN, HAZEL LOIS, retired English language educator; b. Plant City, Fla., Feb. 18, 1917; d. Joseph Monroe and Annie (Thoman) B. AB, Fla. State Coll. for Women, 1937; MA, U. Fla., 1948; postgrad., U. Md., 1961-65. Tchr. Lakeview H.S., Winter Garden, Fla., 1939-40, Eagle Lake Sch., Fla., 1940-41; welfare visitor Fla. Welfare Bd., 1941-42; specialist U.S. Army Signal Corps, Arlington Hall, Va., 1942-43; recreation work, asst. procurement officer ARC, CBI Theater, 1943-46; lab. technician Am. Cyanamid Corp., Brewster, Fla., 1946-47; instr., asst. prof. gen. extension divsn. U. Fla., Fla. State U., 1948-51; freelance writer, editor, indexer N.Y., Fla., 1951-55; staff writer Tampa (Fla.) Morning Tribune, 1956; staff writer, telegraph editor Winter Haven (Fla.) News-Chief, 1956-57; registrar, admissions officer U. Tampa, 1957-59; coll. counselor Atlantic States, 1959-60; registrar, freshman advisor Towson State Tchrs. Coll., Balt., 1960-62; dir. student pers., guidance, admissions Harford Jr. Coll., Bel Air, Md., 1962-64; instr., asst. prof. English, journalism York Coll., Pa., 1965-69; tchr. S.W. Jr. H.S., Lakeland, Fla., 1969-70; tchr. learning disabled Vanguard Sch., Lake Wales, Fla., 1970-82; libr. asst. Polk County Hist. and Geneal. Libr., Bartow, Fla., 1986-91. Editor, Tampa Altrusan, 1958-60, Polk County Hist. Calendar, 1986-90. Mem. Polk County Hist. Commn., 1992-99. Recipient Mayhall Music medal, 1933, Excellence in Cmty. Svc. award Nat. Soc. DAR, 1994, Outstanding Achievement award Fla. State Geneal. Soc., 2002. Mem.: AAUW (hon. 50 yr. life), Polk County Hist. Assn., Imperial Polk Geneal. Soc., Nat. Geneal. Soc., Mortar Board, Chi Delta Phi, Alpha Chi Alpha. Home: 511 NE 9th Ave Mulberry FL 33860-2620

BOWMAN, JAMES EDWARD, pathologist, educator; b. Washington, Feb. 5, 1923; s. James Edward and Dorothy (Peterson) B.; m. Barbara Taylor, June 17, 1950; 1 child, Valerie June. BS, Howard U., 1943, MD, 1946. Intern Freedmen's Hosp., Washington, 1946-47; resident pathology St. Lukes Hosp., Chgo., 1947-50; chmn. dept. pathology Provident Hosp., 1950-53, Shiraz (Iran) Med. Ctr. Nemazee Hosp., 1955-61; vis. prof., chmn. dept. pathology faculty of medicine U. Shiraz, 1959-61; dir. labs. U. Chgo., 1971-80, prof. dept. pathology, medicine, com. on genetics, biol. scis., collegiate div., 1972-93, dir., 1973-93, prof. emeritus, 1993—. Cons. pathology, div. hosp. and med. facilities HEW, USPHS, 1968; mem. Health and Hosps. Governing Commn., Cook County, 1969-72; mem. exec. com. hemalytic anemia study group NHLI, NIH, Bethesda, Md., 1973-75, Sabbatical fellow Ctr. for Advanced Study in Behavioral Scis., Stanford U., 1981-82, Ethical, Legal & Social Issues, Nat. Human Genome Program NIH/DOE. Contbr. to books and articles to profl. jours. Capt. M.C., AUS, 1953-55. Spl. rsch. fellow NIH Galton Lab., Univ. Coll., London, 1961-62. Mem. Coll. Am. Pathologists, Am. Soc. Clin. Pathologists, Am. Soc. Human Genetics, Cen. Soc. Clin. Rsch., Am. Soc. Hematology, Am. Assn. Phys. Anthropologists, Acad. Clin. Lab. Physicians and Scientists. Home: 4929 S Greenwood Ave Chicago IL 60615-2815 Office: U Chgo Dept Pathology 5841 S Maryland Ave Chicago IL 60637-1463 Business E-Mail: jbowman@uchicago.edu.

BOWMAN, JAMES KINSEY, publishing executive, rare book dealer; b. Strongsville, Ohio, Nov. 1, 1933; s. Benjamin H. and Margaret A. (Kinsey) B.; m. Judith Ann Lofton, Mar. 29, 1957; children: J. Reed, Eustacia L., Todd K. BA, Denison U., Granville, Ohio, 1956. With McGraw-Hill Book Co., N.Y.C., 1956-90, gen. mgr., v.p. coll. div., 1965-68, group v.p. higher edn., 1968-73, v.p. marketing, 1973-82, sr. v.p. adminstrn., 1982-84, sr. v.p. internat., 1984-87, v.p. gen. mgr. bookstores, 1987-90; chief exec. officer Judith Bowman Books, 1990—. Bd. dirs. Catskill Fly Fishing Ctr. and Mus., 1998-2004. Mem. Am. Assn. Pubs. (pres. coll. div. 1971-72), Slagle Trout Club (Mich.), Bedford Chowder and Marching Club (pres. 1976-77), Atlantic Salmon Fedn., Theodore Gordon Flyfishers Club (N.Y.C.), Anglers Club of N.Y., Phi Gamma Delta. Democrat. Presbyterian. Home and Office: 98 Pound Ridge Rd Bedford NY 10506-1241

BOWMAN, JEAN LOUISE, lawyer, civic worker; b. Albuquerque, Apr. 3, 1938; d. David Livingstone and Charlotte Louise (Smith) McArthur; children: Carolyn Louise, Joan Emily, Amy Elizabeth, Eric Daniel. Student, U. N.Mex., 1956-57, U. Pa., 1957-58, Rocky Mountain Coll., 1972-74; BA in Polit. Sci. with high honors, U. Mont., 1982, JD, 1985. Dir. Christian edn. St. Luke's Episcopal Ch., 1979-80; law clk. to assoc. justice Mont. Supreme Ct., 1985-87; exec. v.p. St. Peter's Cmty. Hosp. Found., 1987-91; exec. dir. Harrison Hosp. Found., Bremerton, Wash., 1991-93, St. Patrick Hosp. and Health Found., 1993—2001, Missoula Symphony Bd., 1993-99; pres. Missoula Symphony Assn., 1996-98; dir. devel. Five Valleys Land Trust, 2002—05. Bd. dirs. 1st Bank West. Trustee Rocky Mountain Coll., 1972-80; bd. dirs. Billings (Mont.) Area C. of C., 1977-80; mem. City-County Air Pollution Control Bd., 1969-74, chmn., 1970-71; del. Mont. State Constnl. Conv., 1971-72, sec., 1971-72; chmn. County Local Govt. Study Commn., 1973-76; mem. long range planning com. Billings Sch. Dist., 1978-79; bd. dirs. Billings LWV, 1970-72; pres. Helena LWV, 1988, 2d v.p. Mont. LWV, 1987-91; bd. dirs. Internat. Choral Festival, 1999—, Mont. Justice Found., 1999-2003, Friends of Flagship, 2003-04. Recipient Philanthropy Svc. award, 2004; named one of Billings' most influential citizens Billings Gazette, 1977;

Bertha Morton scholar, 1982. Mem. Mont. State Bar, Missoula Rotary (pres. 1997-98). Republican. Home: 1911 E Broadway St Missoula MT 59802-4901 Personal E-mail: jmbmsla@montana.com.

BOWMAN, JOHN J., judge; b. Oak Park, Ill., Jan. 13, 1930; 5 children. BS, U. Ill., 1952; JD, John Marshall Law Sch., 1959. Pvt. practice law, 1959-72; state's atty. DuPage County, Ill., 1973—76, circuit judge, 1976-90; presiding judge 2d dist. Ill. Ct. Appeals, Oak Brook Terrace, 1998—2000; justice 2d Dist. Appellate Ct., 1990—. With U.S. Army, 1952—54, Japan. Mem.: Alpha Tau Omega.

BOWMAN, JOHN SANDERSON, lawyer; b. Montgomery, Ala., Nov. 22, 1935; s. William Chesley Jr. and Ellen (Sanderson) B.; m. Carolyn Lawley, June 7, 1958; children: John Sanderson Jr., Mildred Lawley. BS, U. Ala., Tuscaloosa, 1958, LLB, 1960. Bar: Ala. 1960. Ptnr. Balch & Bingham, Montgomery, 1960—. Pres. Landmarks Found.; bd. dirs. Com. of 100; bd. trustees 1st United Meth. Ch. Mem. ABA, Am. Land Title Assn., Ala. Bar Assn., Montgomery C. of C. (bd. dirs. 1991—), Capital City Club (chmn. bd.). Home: 2455 Cherokee Dr Montgomery AL 36111-1609 Office: Balch & Bingham 2 Dexter Ave Montgomery AL 36104-3574 E-mail: jbowman@balch.com.

BOWMAN, JON, performing arts educator; s. Joseph Raymond and Gaye Prather Bowman; m. Beth Anne Folta, Mar. 22, 2003. MusB in Edn., Auburn U., 2000, M of Music Edn., 2002. Ala. Tchg. Cert. State of Ala., 1999. Dir. of bands Beauregard H.S., Opelika, Ala., 2001—02, Tallassee H.S., Ala., 2002—. Musician: (percussionist) Musicals for Surrounding Theaters. Upward basketball coord. Heritage Bapt. Ch., Montgomery, Ala., 2004—; scouting for events McCraney, Cottle Arts Assn., Tallassee, Ala., 2001—. Recipient Phi Mu Alpha, Delta Psi Chpt. Music Educator Yr., Phi Mu Alpha Sinfonia Frat., 2004; Music Tech. grant, Blount Found., 2005. Mem.: Music Educators Nat. Conf. (life), Ala. Bandmasters Assn. (life), Jaycees (life), Phi Mu Alpha (life; dir. of alumni affairs 2002—05). Baptist. Avocations: golf, hunting, fishing. Home: 1318 Hallwood Ln Montgomery AL 36117 Office: Tallassee High Sch 502 Barnett Blvd Tallassee AL 36078 Office Phone: 334-283-3689. Office Fax: 334-283-6210. Personal E-mail: bowmanjp1@yahoo.com. E-mail: jon.bowman@tcschools.com.

BOWMAN, KATHLEEN GILL, academic administrator; BS English & Spanish, U. of Minn., 1964, MA English Edn., 1967, PhD English Edn., 1977. Rsch. assoc. Legis. Adv. Coun. on the Econ. Status of Women, St. Paul, 1976-77; asst. dir. of grad. studies, asst prof. of edn. Reed Coll., Portland, OR, 1977-79, exec. asst. to the pres., dir. of spl. programs, 1979-82; assoc. dir., program officer Fred Meyer Charitable Trust, Portland, OR, 1982-84; assoc. v.p. for rsch. U. of Oreg., Eugene, OR, 1985-89, vice-provost for internat. affairs, 1989-94; pres. Randolph-Macon Woman's Coll., Lynchburg, VA, 1994—. Fullbright Sr. Scholar award, Japan & Korea, 1993. Office: Randolph-Macon Womans Coll Office of the Pres 2500 Rivermont Ave Lynchburg VA 24503-1555

BOWMAN, LAIRD PRICE, retired foundation administrator; b. Topeka, Jan. 28, 1927; s. Herbert Douglas and Marion Martha (Price) B.; m. Betty Lou Pote, Dec. 24, 1950; children: Bruce Pote, Susan Bowman Adams. BS, U. Kans., 1950, LLB, 1952. Bar: Kans. 1952, Mo. 1956. Law clk. chief judge U.S. Dist. Ct. Kans., 1952-53; assoc. firm McAnany, Van Cleave & Phillips, Kansas City, Kans., 1953-55; mem. firm Gage Hodges, Park & Kreamer, Kansas City, Mo., 1955-64; with Gas Service Co., Kansas City, Mo., 1964-83, asst. gen. counsel, 1968-70, sec., asst. gen. counsel, 1970-83, v.p., 1978-83, dir., 1979-83; asst. to the pres. Kans. U. Endowment Assn., U. Kans., Lawrence, 1983-91, ret., 1991. With USMC, 1945-47. Mem. Kans. Bar Assn., Mo. Bar Assn., Sigma Chi, Phi Delta Phi. Congregationalist. Home: 1120 Jana Dr Lawrence KS 66049-4418

BOWMAN, LEAH, fashion designer, consultant, photographer, educator; b. Chgo., Apr. 21, 1935; d. John George and Alexandra (Colovos) Murges; m. Veron George Broe, Aug. 31, 1954; 1 child, Michelle; m. John Ronald Bowman, Feb. 28, 1959 Diploma, Sch. of Art Inst., Chgo., 1962. Designer Korach Bros. Inc., Chgo., 1962-65; costume designer Hull House South Theatre, Chgo., 1966-67, Wellington Theatre, Chgo., 1966-67; from instr. to prof. emeritus Sch. of Art Inst., Chgo., 1967—2001, prof. emeritus, 2001—. Prodr. fashion performances and style exhbns.; vis. prof., cons. SNDT Women's U., Bombay, 1980, 85, 92, Ctrl. Acad. Arts and Design, Beijing, People's Republic of China, 1987; faculty sabbatical exhbn. Sch. of Art Inst., 1986, 93. Recipient Fulbright award, Coun. for Internat. Exchange for Scholars, India, 1980, Pres. award, Art Inst. Chgo., 1991, Honoror's award, Sch. of Art Inst., Chgo., 1998, Disting. Faculty award, Sch. Art Inst. Chgo., 2005. Office: Sch of Art Inst Chgo 37 S Wabash Ave Chicago IL 60603-3002

BOWMAN, MARJORIE ANN, family practice physician, educator; b. Grove City, Pa., Aug. 18, 1953; d. Ross David and Freda Louise (Smith) Williamson; m. Robert Choplin; children: Bridget Williamson Foley, Skyler Weston Williamson Choplin. BS, Pa. State U., 1974; MD, Jefferson Med. Coll., 1976; MPA, U. So. Calif., L.A., 1983. Intern, then resident in family practice Duke U., Durham, N.C., 1976-79; med. officer USPHS, Hyattsville, Md., 1979-82; clin. instr. uniformed svcs. U. Health Scis., Bethesda, Md., 1980-83; dir. family practice residency, prof. Georgetown U. Sch. Medicine, Washington, 1983-86; chmn. dept. family practice, prof. Wake Forest U., Winston-Salem, NC, 1986—96; prof., chmn. dept. family practice U. Pa., Phila, 1996—. Author: (Book) Stress and Women Physicians, 1985, 1990, Women in Medicine: Life and Career, 2002; editor: Archives Family Medicine, 1992—2000, Jour. Women's Health, 2001—05, Jour. Am. Bd. Family Practice, 2003—; contbr. articles to profl. jours. Fellow Am. Acad. Family Physicians; mem. AMA, Soc. Tchrs. Family Medicine (bd. dirs. 1984-88, bd. dirs. Found. 1984-99, v.p. 1988-91, pres. 1991-92), Am. Pub. Health Assn. Republican. Unitarian Universalist. Office: Univ Pa 2 Gates 3400 Spruce St Philadelphia PA 19104-4283 Business E-Mail: bowmanm@uphs.upenn.edu.

BOWMAN, PASCO MIDDLETON, II, judge; b. Timberville, Va., Dec. 20, 1933; s. Pasco Middleton and Katherine (Lohr) Bowman; m. Ruth Elaine Bowman, July 12, 1958; children: Ann Katherine, Helen Middleton, Benjamin Garber. BA, Bridgewater Coll., 1955; JD, NYU, 1958; LLM. U. Va., 1986; LLD (hon.), Bridgewater Coll., 1988. Bar: N.Y. 1958, Ga. 1965, Mo. 1980. Assoc. firm Cravath, Swaine & Moore, N.Y.C., 1958—61, 1962—64; asst. prof. law U. Ga., 1964—65, assoc. prof., 1965—69, prof., 1969—70, Wake Forest U., 1970—78, dean, 1970—78; vis. prof. U. Va., 1978—79; prof., dean U. Mo., Kansas City, 1979—83; judge U.S. Ct. Appeals (8th cir.), Kansas City, Mo., 1983—98, sr. judge, 1999—, chief judge, 1998—99. Mng. editor: NYU Law Rev., 1957—58, reporter, chief draftsman: Georgia Corporation Code, 1965—68. Col. USAR, 1959—84. Scholar Root-Tilden scholar, 1955—58; Fulbright scholar, London Sch. Econs. and Polit. Sci., 1961—62. Mem.: Mo. Bar, N.Y. Bar. Office: US Ct Appeals 8th Circuit 10-50 US Courthouse 400 E 9th St Kansas City MO 64106-2607 Office Phone: 816-512-5800.

BOWMAN, RANDALL HUNTER, reference and instruction librarian; b. Sanford, N.C., Dec. 4, 1966; s. Jimmy Tiree and Kay (Laferney) B. AA summa cum laude, Louisburg Coll., 1990; BA, U. N.C., 1992; MLIS, U.N.C., Greensboro, 1997. Info. desk asst. U. N.C., Greensboro, 1996-97; libr. intern Ctr. for Creative Leadership, Greensboro, 1996; desk supr. U. N.C., Chapel Hill, 1997; ref. libr. Gardner-Webb U., Boiling Springs, NC, 1997-2000; reference and instrn. libr. Elon U., 2000—. Lit. tutor Boiling Springs (N.C.) Elem. Sch., 1998-99; pub. coord., mem. ch. coun. Ctrl. United Meth. Ch., Shelby, N.C., 1999-2000; libr. coord. 1st United Meth. Ch., Elon, 2001—. Mem. ALA, ACRL (comm. com., instrn. chmn.), N.C. Libr. Assn., Louisburg Coll. Alumni Assn. (pres. bd. dirs. 2003-04), Phi Theta Kappa. Home: 6336 Hibiscus Ct Whitsett NC 27377 Office: Belk Libr Elon U Box 2550 Elon NC 27244 E-mail: rbowman@elon.edu.

BOWMAN, RICHARD CARL, defense consultant, retired air force officer; b. Chgo., July 5, 1926; s. Carl Elias and Lucile (Rutan) B.; m. Lois Jean Hassenauer, June 10, 1950; children: Mary Bowman Millikin, Kristin Bowman Spencer, Margaret Bowman Flaherty, Victoria Bowman Smoke, Richard Carl. BS, U.S. Mil. Acad., 1949; MS, Okla. State U., 1954; MPA, Harvard U., 1958, PhD, 1964. Enlisted in U.S. Army, 1943; commd. 2d lt. USAF, 1949, advanced through grades to maj. gen., 1975; pilot, flight comdr. Korea, 1951; mem. initial staff Air Force Acad., 1955-57, assoc. prof. polit. sci., 1959-63; mem. staff Nat. Security Council, 1964-66, Nat. War Coll., 1966—67, Office Sec. Air Force, 1967-73; dep. def. adviser to Am. ambassador to NATO, 1973-75; dir. European and NATO affairs Office Sec. Def., 1975-81, ret., 1981. Contbr. to mil. jours. Decorated Def. D.S.M. (2), Air Force D.S.M., Def. Superior Service medal, Legion of Merit (2), D.F.C., Air medal (3), Commendation medal (2); Grand Service Cross with Star W. Ger.; comdr. Order of St. Olaf (Norway, with star). Mem.: Harvard U. Alumni Assn., West Point Assn. Grads., KC (assoc. state marshall, past grand knight). Roman Catholic. Home: 7824 Midday Ln Alexandria VA 22306-2724

BOWMAN, ROGER MANWARING, real estate executive; b. Duluth, Minn., Dec. 3, 1916; s. Lawrence Fredrick and Gladys (Manwaring) B.; m. Judith Claypool, Apr. 10, 1942 (dec. 1993); Ann, David, Mary Bowman Johnson, Lawrence II. Student, U. Mich., 1934—36, Wayne State U., 1937. Pres. North Star Airways, Duluth, 1946-50, North Star Engrng. Co., Duluth, 1946-50, Superior (Wis.) Aero, 1946-50, Lawrence F. Bowman Co., Duluth, 1950-70, Gen. Cleaning Corp., Duluth, 1954-92, Bowman Corp., Duluth, 1970-83, Bowman Properties, Duluth, 1983-92; chmn. Deltona Corp., Miami, Fla., 1985-89. Cons. Topeka Group, Duluth, 1985-89; bd. dirs. Parish Corp., Minn. Power, Norwest Bank; chmn. Bowman Properties, 1988-96, Gen. Cleaning Corp., 1985—; mng. gen. ptnr. 6 ltd. partnerships, 1990—. Chmn. St. Louis County Welfare, Duluth, 1964-69, chmn. Govs. Real Estate Adv. Commn., 1968-70; pres. Duluth Devel. Corp., 1960-68; trustee Ordean Found., 1968-92; bd. dirs. Duluth Bd. Realtors, 1958-62; pres. Duluth Bldg. Owners and Mgrs. Assn. Internat., 1963-65. Lt. col. USMCR, 1940-45. Recipient Silver Beaver award Boy Scouts Am., 1959, Mayor's Commendation City of Duluth, 1976. Mem. Duluth Steam Coop. (bd. dirs. 1970-86), Duluth Bldg. Owners and Mgrs. Internat., Duluth Bd. Realtors, Real Property Adminstrs., Kitchi Gammi Club (dir. 1974-78), Northland Country Club, Boca Raton Resort and Club, Delray Beach Yacht Club. Republican. Episcopalian. Avocation: cooking. Office: 575 Wells Fargo Ctr Duluth MN 55802 Office Phone: 218-726-0161. Personal E-mail: rbowman16@aol.com.

BOWMAN, WILLIAM SCOTT (SCOTTY BOWMAN), professional hockey coach; b. Montreal, Can., Sept. 18, 1933; s. John and Jane Thomson (Scott) B.; m. Suella Belle Chitty, Aug. 16, 1969; children: Alicia Jean, David Scott, Stanley Glen, Nancy Elizabeth and Robert Gordon (twins). Student, Sir George Williams Bus. Sch., 1954; LHD, Canisius Coll., 2003. Scout exec. Club de Hockey Canadien, Montreal, 1956-66, coach, 1971-79; coach, gen. mgr. St. Louis Blues Hockey Club, 1966-71; coach, gen. mgr., dir. hockey ops. Buffalo Sabres Hockey Club, 1979-86; TV analyst Hockey Night in Can., 1987-90; dir. player devel. Pitts. Penguins Hockey Club, 1990-91, interim head coach, 1991-92, head coach, 1992-93, Detroit Red Wings Hockey Club, 1993—2002, dir. player pers., 1993—2002. Mem. Hockey Hall of Fame Selection Com. Recipient Jack Adams award, 1977, 96, Victor award for NHL Coach of Yr., 1993, 96, 2002, Stanley Cup Championship, 1973, 1976-79, 1992, 1997-98, 2002, Lester Patrick award, 2001, Can. Soc. NY award, 2001; named NHL Exec. of Yr. Sporting News, 1979-80, NHL Coach of Yr. Sporting News, 1995-96, Hockey News, 1976-77, 93-97, NHL Exec. of the Yr. Hockey News, 1996-97, NHL Coach of Yr., 1967-68, Hockey News Coach of Yr., 1968, 76, 95-96, Exec. of Yr., 1997; inducted into Hockey Hall of Fame, 1991, Mich. Sports Hall of Fame, 1999, Buffalo Sports Hall of Fame, 2000, Can. Walk of Fame, 2002, Can.'s Sports Hall of Fame, 2004, Quebed Sports Hall of Fame, 2005; holder NHL career regular season records for wins (1,244) and winning percentage (.670); holder NHL career playoffs records for wins (223) and games (353); recipient Stanley Cup as head coach Montreal Canadiens, 1973, 76-79, Pitts. Penguins, 1992, Detroit Red Wings, 1997-98, 2002; only coach in NHL history to win Stanley Cup with 3 different teams. Office: Detroit Red Wings Joe Louis Arena 600 Civic Center Dr Detroit MI 48226-4419

BOWN, CHAD PHILIPS, economics professor; BA in Econs. and Internat. Rels., Bucknell U., 1994; MS in Econs., PhD in Econs., U. Wis., 1999. Asst. prof. dept. econs. and internat. bus. Brandeis U., Waltham, Mass., 1999—. Recipient John R. Crossgrove prize in Economics, Bucknell U., 1994, Michael L. Walzer award, Brandeis U., 2001; David Granick Meml. fellow, Mellon Found., U. Wis., 1997—98, Kermit H. Perlmutter fellow, Brandeis U., 2002—03, Okun-Model fellow, The Brookings Instn., 2004—05. Mem.: Phi Beta Kappa. Office: Brandeis Univ PO Box 549110 Waltham MA 02454-9110 Office Phone: 781-736-4823. Office Fax: 781-736-2269. E-mail: cbown@brandeis.edu.

BOWNE, MARTHA HOKE, editor, consultant; b. Greeley, Colo., June 9, 1931; d. George Edwin and Krin (English) Hoke; children: Gretchen, William, Kay, Judith. BA, U. Mich., 1952; postgrad., Syracuse U., 1965. Tchr. Wayne (Mich.) Pub. Schs., 1953-54, East Syracuse and Minoa Cen. Schs., Minoa, N.Y., 1965-68; store mgr. Fabric Barn, Fayetteville, N.Y., 1969-77; store owner Fabric Fair, Oneida, N.Y., 1978-80; prodr., owner Quilting by the Sound, Port Townsend, Wash., 1987—2000, Quilting by the Lake, Cazenovia, NY, 1981—. Organizer symposium Am. Quilters Soc.; founder, pres. Quilter's Quest confs., 1994—. Mem., pres. Minoa Library, 1960-75; mem. Onondaga County Library, Syracuse, 1968-71. Mem.: Am. Quilters Soc. (editor Am. Quilter mag. 1985—95). Avocations: reading, hiking, travel, bridge, Scrabble. Home: 478 Oden Bay Dr Sandpoint ID 83864-6499 E-mail: martyidaho@sandpoint.net.

BOWNE, SHIRLEE PEARSON, credit manager; b. High Shoals Twp., NC, Mar. 11, 1936; d. Lloyd E. Pearson and Parnell (James) Garland; divorced; 1 child, Gregory Charles. Grad. h.s., Gaffney, S.C. Various secretarial positions, 1955-64; sales repr., pres. Real Estate Marketers, Inc., Tallahassee, 1964-80; chief exec. officer Shirlee Bowne Mktg. & Devel. Inc., Tallahassee, 1980-91; vice chmn. Nat. Credit Union Adminstrn., Washington, 1991-97. Cons. in field. Treas. Rep. Party Fla., 1988-91. Episcopalian. Avocation: bridge.

BOWRON, EDGAR PETERS, art museum curator, administrator; b. Birmingham, Ala., May 27, 1943; s. James Edgar Bowron and Dorothe Peters Lowles; children: James Edgar II, Clara Beatrice, St. John Grenfell. BA, Colgate U., 1965; MA, Inst. Fine Arts, NYU, 1969, PHD, 1979. Edn. lectr. Met. Mus. Art, N.Y.C., 1969-70; registrar Mpls. Inst. Arts, 1970-73; curator Renaissance and Baroque art Walters Art Gallery, Balt., 1973-78; adminstrv. asst. to dir. and curator Renaissance and Baroque art Nelson Gallery-Atkins Mus., Kansas City, Mo., 1978-81; dir. N.C. Mus. Art, Raleigh, 1981-85; Elizabeth and John Moors Cabot dir., prof. fine arts Art Mus. Harvard U., Cambridge, Mass., 1985-90; sr. curator paintings Nat. Gallery of Art, Washington, 1991-96; Audrey Jones Beck curator of European art Mus. Fine Arts, Houston, 1996—. Art adv. panel IRS, 1994—. Author: Pompeo Batoni and His British Patrons, 1982; European Paintings before 1900 in the Fogg Mus., 1990; Masterworks of European Painting in Museum of Fine Arts, Houston, 2000; editor: Selected Writings of Anthony M. Clark: Studies in Eighteenth Roman Painting, 1981, The North Carolina Museum of Art: Introduction to the Collections, 1983, Anthony M. Clark, Pompeo Batoni, A Complete Catalogue of his Works with an Introductory Text, 1985, Bernard Bellotto and the Capitals of Europe, 2001; co-editor: Art in Rome in the Eighteenth Century, 2000; contbr. articles to profl. jours. Trustee Mus. Fine Arts, Boston, 1988-90; mem. art adv. panel IRS, 1994--. Mem. NEA (arts and artifacts indemnity adv. panel 2000-04), Assn. Art Mus. Dirs. (trustee 1987-90), Master Drawings Assn. (bd. dirs. 1987—) Office: Mus Fine Arts PO Box 6826 Houston TX 77265-6826

BOWSER, JUSTINE ADELE, language educator; b. Mt. Pleasant, Pa., Aug. 3, 1973; d. Lloyd E. and Shirley L. Ansell. BA in English, Shippensburg U., Pa., 1995. Cert. tchr. English Pa., 1995. Tchr. English Allegheny-Clarion Valley Sch. Dist., Foxburg, Pa., 1995—. Advisor KEY Club Internat., 1996—. Poet:. Mem.: Kiwanis. Office: Allegheny Clarion Valley Schs PO Box 345 Rt 58 Foxburg PA 16036-0345 Home: PO Box 14 Parker PA 16049

BOWSHER, CHARLES ARTHUR, retired government official, financial executive; b. Elkhart, Ind., May 30, 1931; s. Matthew A. and Ella M. (West) B.; m. Mary C. Mahoney, Dec. 14, 1963; children: Kathryn M., Stephen C. BS, U. Ill., 1953; MBA, U. Chgo., 1956; DSc in Bus. Adminstrn. (hon.), Bryant Coll., 1984; D Pub. Svc. (hon.), George Washington U., 1993; DSc (hon.), U. Ill.-Chgo., 1994; Dr. Pub. Svc. (hon.), St. Joseph's U., 1994; DSc in Pub. Svc. (hon.), Am. U., 1996. C.P.A., Ill. Ptnr. Arthur Andersen & Co., Chgo., 1956-67, Washington, 1971-81; asst. sec. of Navy for fin. mgmt. Dept. Def., Washington, 1967-71; comptroller gen. U.S., 1981-96. Bd. dirs. DeVry Inc., Washington Mutual Investors Fund, SI Internat.; bd. govs. NASD trustee Ctr. Naval Analysis, U.S. Navy Meml. Found., Concord Coalition, Com. for a Responsible Fed. Budget. Mem. vis. com. Sch. Bus., selection com. Roger W. Jones award for Exec. Leadership; mem. nat. adv. bd. Pvt. Sector Coun.; active Bus. Execs. for Nat. Security Commn. With U.S. Army, 1953-55. Recipient Enduring Lifetime Achievement award Am. Acctg. Assn., 1996, Integrity award Office of Insp. Gen., 1996; named to Acctg. Hall of Fame, 1996. Mem. AICPA, Nat. Acad. Pub. Adminstrn., Nat. Assn. Govt. Accts., Burning Tree Club (Washington), Met. Club (Washington), Beta Alpha Psi, Pi Kappa Alpha. Home: 4503 Boxwood Rd Bethesda MD 20816-1815

BOWSHER, DENNIS JAMES, internist, cardiologist, pharmacologist; b. Beech Grove, Ind., 1953; s. Donald Andrew and Jacqueline (Brock) Barker; m. Marcia Ann Peyton, July 1, 1978; children: Karla Ann, Peyton James. BS in Chemistry cum laude, Rose Hulman Inst. Tech., Terre Haute, Ind., 1975; MD with honors, Ind. U., 1979. Intern Northwestern U., Chgo., 1979-80, resident in internal medicine, 1980-82, fellow in clin. pharmacology, 1982-84; fellow in cardiology Ind. U. Sch. Medicine, Indpls., 1984-86; mem. staff Ind. U. Med. Ctr., 1987-91, North Broward Med. Ctr., 1991—, North Ridge Med. Ctr., 1991—. Chmn. Pharmacy Com., Rsch. IRB North Broward Hosp. Dist., 1991-94, 1999—. Mem. ACA, Am. Coll. Cardiology, Am. Coll. Chest Physicians. Office: 440 E Sample Rd Ste 102 Pompano Beach FL 33064-4432

BOX, ELGENE OWEN, science educator, ecologist; b. Tex. PhD, U. NC, Chapel Hill, 1978. Prof. Dept. Geography and Inst. Ecology U. Ga., Athens, 1979—; guest rsch. prof. Tokyo U., 1992—94. Pres. Internat. Assn. Vegetation Sci., 1994—. Office: U Ga Geography Dept Cedar St Athens GA 30602-2502

BOX, LAURA DIANE CHAKRAVARTY, theater educator; d. Mary Josephine Larkin and Daniel Columbus Box, Jr.; m. Banibrata Victor Chakravarty, June 15, 1995. AA in theatre, Los Angeles City Coll., 1975—78; BA in linguistics, Calif. State U., Fullerton, 1978—80; MA in drama, San Diego State U., 1991—93; PhD in theatre, U. of Hawaii at Manoa, 1993—2000. Irving D. Suss vis. guest artist Colby Coll., Waterville, Maine, asst. prof., 2002—; postdoctoral fellow Deep Springs (Calif.) Coll., 2001—02. Dramaturg Golden Thread Productions, San Francisco, 1999—2000. Dir.(and author): (plays) The Wretched; author: Strategies of Resistance in the Dramatic Texts of North African Women: A Body of Words, 2005. Mem.: Phi Beta Delta (assoc.). Office: Colby College 4523 Mayflower Hill Waterville ME 04901 Business E-Mail: lchakrav@colby.edu.

BOXER, ALAN LEE, accountant; b. Denver, Sept. 9, 1935; s. Ben B. and Minnette (Goldman) B.; m. Gayle, Dec. 21, 1958; children: Michael E., Jodi S., Richard S. BSBA in Acctg., U. Denver, 1956. CPA, Colo. Audit mgr. Touche, Ross & Co. CPAs, Denver, 1956-60, Ballin, Milstein & Feinstein CPAs, Denver, 1960-61; prin. Alan L. Boxer, CPA, Denver, 1961-69; v.p and treas. Pawley Co., Denver, 1969-78; pres. Sci-Pro Inc., Denver, 1978-82; regional mgr. A.T.V. Systems, Inc., Denver, 1982-83; prin. The Enterprise Group, Denver, 1983-86; shareholder, pres. Allerdice, Baroch, Boxer & Co., CPAs, Denver, 1986-87; prin. Alan L. Boxer, CPA, Denver, 1987-97; dir. Boxer & Assocs. CPAs PC, 1997—. Bd. dirs. Anti-Defamation League, Denver, 1986-90, BMH Congregation, Denver, 1986-90, treas. 1990-93, v.p. 1993-98. Mem. AICPA, Colo. Soc. CPAs, Bnai Brith (pres. #171, 1982, trustee 1983-89). Democrat. Jewish. E-mail: aboxercpa@aol.com.

BOXER, BARBARA, senator; b. Bklyn., Nov. 11, 1940; d. Ira and Sophie (Silvershein) Levy; m. Stewart Boxer, 1962; children: Doug, Nicole. BA in Econ., Bklyn. Coll., 1962. Stockbroker, econ. rschr. N.Y. Securities Firm, N.Y.C., 1962-65; journalist, assoc. editor Pacific Sun, 1972-74; congl. aide to rep. 5th Congl. Dist. San Francisco, 1974-76; mem. Marin County Bd. Suprs., San Rafael, Calif., 1976-82, 98th-102d Congresses from 6th Calif. dist., mem. armed services com., select com. children, youth and families; majority whip at large; co-chair Mil. Reform Caucus; chair subcom. on govt. activities and transp. of house govt. ops. com., 1990-93; senator from Calif. US Senate, 1993—, mem. banking, housing and urban affairs com., mem. budget com., mem. environ. and pub. works com., mem. fgn. rels. com. Pres. Marin County Bd. Suprs., 1980-81; mem. Bay Area Air Quality Mgmt. Bd., San Francisco, 1977-82, pres., 1979-81; bd. dirs. Golden Gate Bridge Hwy. and Transport Dist., San Francisco, 1978-82; founding mem. Marin Nat. Women's Polit. Caucus; pres. Dem. New Mems. Caucus, 1983. Recipient Open Govt. award Common Cause, 1980, Rep. of Yr. award Nat. Multiple Sclerosis Soc., 1990, Margaret Sanger award Planned Parenthood, 1990, Women of Achievement award Anti-defamation League, 1990. Democrat. Jewish. Office: US Senate 112 Hart Senate Office Bldg Washington DC 20510-0001*

BOXER, JASON T., title company executive; b. 1970; s. Leonard Boxer. BA, U. Pa.; JD, NYU. Bar: N.Y. 1995. Real estate atty. Battle Fowler LLP; mgr. real estate dept. Loews Corp., NYC, 1998, dir. real estate, 1999, v.p. real estate NYC, 2000—. Avocation: running. Office: Loews Corp 667 Madison Ave New York NY 10021*

BOXER, JEROME HARVEY, data processing executive, consultant, accountant, management consultant, vintager; b. Chgo., Nov. 27, 1930; s. Ben Avrum and Edith (Lyman) B.; m. Sandra Schaffner, June 17, 1980; children by previous marriage: Michael, Jodi. AA magna cum laude, East L.A. Coll., 1952; AB with honors, Calif. State U., L.A., 1954. CPA, Calif.; cert. computing profl. Lab. instr. Calif. State U., L.A., 1953-54; staff acct. Dolman, Freeman & Buchalter, L.A., 1955-57; sr. acct. Neiman, Sanger, Miller & Beress, L.A., 1957-63; ptnr. Glynn and Boxer, CPAs, L.A., 1964-68; v.p., sec. Glynn, Boxer & Phillips Inc., CPAs, L.A. and Glendale, Calif., 1968-90; pvt. practice cons., 1990—. Owner Oak Valley Vineyard; instr. viticulture Cuesta Coll.; pres. Echo Data Svcs. Inc., 1978-90; instr. data processing L.A. City Adult Schs.; tchr., lectr., cons. wines and wine-tasting; instr. photography. Contbr. to Wine World Mag., 1974-82. Founding pres. Congregation Ohr Tzafon, spiritual leader, 1998—2003; mem. ops. bd. Evrywoman's Village; bd. dirs. Paso Robles Libr.; bd. dirs., v.p. So. Calif. Jewish Hist. Soc.; bd. dirs. Calif. Mid-State Fair, pres., 2005; v.p. Jewish Hist. Soc. of Ctrl. Coast; co-founder Open Space Theatre; former officer Ethel Josephine Scantland Found.; past post advisor Explorer scouts Boy Scouts Am., Eagle Scout. Recipient Youth Svc. award Mid-Valley YMCA, 1972-73. Mem.: AICPA, Ctrl. Coast Vineyard Team, Paso Robles Wine Festival Steering Com., Clowns of Am., Inc., World Clown Assn., Paso Robles Vintners and Growers Assn., Cellarmasters, Wines and Steins, Ctrl. Coast Winegrowers Assn., Am. Wine Assn., Am. Jewish Hist. Soc., Data Processing Mgmt. Assn., Assn. for Systems Mgmt., Calif. Soc. CPAs, Assoc. Students Calif. State U. L.A. (life) (hon.), Profl. Musicians of Am. (life), Cuesta Coll North County Ambs., Soc. Preservation of Variety Arts, Friends of Photography, L.A. Photog. Ctr., Acad. Model Aeros., Nat. Model Railroad Assn., Maltose Falcons Home Brewing Soc., San Fernando Valley Silent Flyers, San Fernando Valley Radio Control Flyers, Acad. Magical Arts, Internat. Brotherhood of Magicians, L.A.-Bordeaux Sister City Affiliation, Western Region Clown Assn., Paso Robles Shrine Clowns, Scottish Rite Rsch. Soc., Soc. Bacchus Am., Internat. Shrine-Clown Assn., South Coast Corinthian Yacht Club (former dir., officer), German Shepherd Dog Club Am., Pacific Mariners Yacht Club, Exch. Club, Verdugo Club, German Shepherd Dog Club Los Angeles County, Braemar

Country Club, The Invisible Lodge, Kiwanis (pres. Sunset-Echo Park 1968), So. Calif. Research Lodge, Shriner, B'nai Brith, Paso Robles Masons (32 degree, master 2004), Blue Key, Alpha Phi Omega. Home and Office: 1660 Circle B Rd Paso Robles CA 93446-9595 E-mail: jhboxer@yahoo.com.

BOXER, LAURENCE ALAN, physician, research educator; b. Denver, May 17, 1940; s. Sam G. and Tillie (Belstock) B.; m. M. Grace Jordison, Aug. 23, 1969; 1 child, David. BA, U. Colo., 1961; MD, Stanford U., 1966. Intern, resident pediatrics Yale U., New Haven, 1966-68; resident pediatrics Stanford Hosp., Palo Alto, Calif., 1968-69; fellow hematology Children's Hosp., Harvard U., Boston, 1972-74; instr. pediatrics Harvard Med. Sch., Boston, 1973-75; asst. prof. to prof. Ind. U. Sch. Medicine, Indpls., 1975-82; prof., dir. pediatric hematology/oncology U. Mich., Ann Arbor, 1982—. Mem. study sect. NIH, Bethesda, Md., 1981—; cons. Amgen, Thousand Oak, Calif., 1988—; established investigator Am. Heart Assn., Dallas, 1978-83; internat. adv. bd. U. Malaysia, Sarawak. Contbr. articles to profl. jours, chpts. to books. Maj. U.S. Army, 1969-72. NIH grantee, Bethesda, 1976—. Fellow ACP, Am. Acad. Pediatrics (E. Mead Johnson rsch. award 1983); mem. Soc. Pediatric Rsch. (pres. 1986), Am. Soc. Hematology (councellor 1988-92), Am. Soc. Clin. Investigation, Am. Soc. Cell Biology, Am. Assn. Pathologists, Am. Assn. Physicians. Republican. Jewish. Avocation: swimming. Office: U Mich L2110 Women's Hosp Ann Arbor MI 48109-0238 Office Phone: 734-764-7126. Business E-Mail: laboxer@umich.edu.

BOXER, LEONARD, lawyer; b. N.Y.C., Feb. 11, 1939; s. Max Boxer and Sally (Grill) Koffler; m. Enid Feuer, Nov. 24, 1965; children: Michael, Jason, Douglas. BS, NYU, 1960, LLB, 1963. Bar: N.Y. 1963, U.S. Dist. Ct. (so. and ea. dists.) N.Y. 1985, U.S. Supreme Ct. Assoc. Eisenberg & Weiss, Bklyn., 1964-65; ptnr. Olnick, Boxer, Blumberg, Lane & Troy, N.Y.C., 1965-86, Stroock & Stroock & Lavan, N.Y.C., 1987—. Mem. adv. bd. Chgo. Title Ins. Co., N.Y.C., 1980—; mem. exec. com., gov. NY Real Estate Bd. Trustee NYU Law Sch., 1994—; mem. spl. real estate com. Guggenheim Mus., 2004—; trustee Nat. Jewish Ctr. Immunology and Respiratory Medicine, Jewish Assn. Svcs. for the Aged, Children's Hearing Inst., N.Y. Eye and Ear Infirmary, NYU, 2000—, Cancer Rsch. Inst., 2001. Mem. N.Y. State Bar Assn., Bklyn. Bar Assn., Tax Certiorari Bar Assn. (bd. dirs. 1983-97), Beta Alpha Psi. Home: 875 Park Ave New York NY 10021 Office: Stroock & Stroock & Lavan 180 Maiden Ln Fl 17 New York NY 10038-4937

BOXER, LESTER, lawyer; b. NYC, Oct. 19, 1935; s. Samuel and Anna Lena (Samovar) B.; m. Frances Barenfeld, Sept. 17, 1961; children: Kimberly Brett, Allison Joy. AA, UCLA, 1955, BS, 1957; JD, U. So. Calif., 1961. Bar: Calif. 1962; U.S. Dist. Ct. (ctrl. dist.) Calif. 1962. Assoc. Bautzer & Grant, Beverly Hills, Calif., 1961-63; pvt. practice Beverly Hills, 1963-65, 69—; ptnr. Boxer & Stoll, Beverly Hills, 1965-69. Mem. Calif. Bar Assn., L.A. County Bar Assn., Beverly Hills Bar Assn. Office: 1801 Century Park E Ste 2513 Los Angeles CA 90067-4703 Office Phone: 310-553-3344.

BOXILL, EDITH HILLMAN, music therapist, educator, writer; b. Providence, Nov. 8, 1916; d. Maurice and Lillian Hillman; m. Roger Evan Boxill, 1965; children by previous marriage: Paul R. Epstein, Emily H. Duby. Bd. cert. music therapist. Music instr., composer, performer, N.Y.C., 1954—; dir. music therapy Manhattan Devel. Ctr., N.Y.C., 1974-87, clin. supr. music therapy interns, 1975—; lectr. then asst. prof. music therapy dept. NYU, N.Y.C., 1976-79, prof., 1980—. Adj. faculty Teach for America UCLA, 1994; adj. prof. NYU, 1980—; originator World Congresses and confs. Music Therapists for Peace, Inc., 1990—99; originator Peace Sch. Curriculum Through Music Therapy, 1993, NYU, Edith Hillman Boxill Scholarship Fund; originator worldwide Candlelight Peace Vigil Oxford U., England, 2002, originator Global Candlelight Peace Vigil, 03; originator Candlelight Global Vigil for Peace, 2005, World Congress, Australia, 2005; workshop leader UCLA, 1994; presenter in field. Archives of audiocasettes of music therapy sessions at NYU; composer, arranger, prodr. album: Music Therapy for the Developmentally Handicapped, Folkway Records, 1976, issued on CD by The Smithsonian Inst./Folkways Series; editor (jour.) Music Therapy, PeaceNotes; author: The Miracle of Music Therapy, 1997; (textbook) Music Therapy for the Developmentally Disabled, 1985 (translated into Italian, Japanese, and Korean), Manual: Students Against Violence Everywhere-S.A.V.E.-Through Music Therapy, 1998; co-author: Basic Music Therapy Competencies, 1981; videotape: A Continuum of Awareness: Music Therapy with Developmentally Handicapped, 1979; co-prodr. Earth Concert 1989, NYC; prodr.: (CD) Sing Out for Peace!; contbr. articles to profl. jours. Adv. bd. Potential Unltd. Prodns.; bd. dirs. Symphony UN., dir., coord. Music Therapy for War-Traumatized Children; founder Music Therapists for Peace, Inc., 1988; prod. (cd) Music Therapists for Peace; originator Music Therapists for Peace Day Worldwide, 1990-95, presenter, Global Vigil for Peace, Oxford U. England, 2001, Australia, 2005. Recipient Music Therapy Lifetime Achievement award, 1995, Peace and Cooperation award for Citizens of the World Internat. anthem, UN, 1998, DeWitt Clinton Masonic award, 2003, Edith Hillman Boxill award Disting. Svc., NYU, 2004—, Disting. Achievement award, 2004. Mem. ASCAP, Am. Music Therapy Assn. (hon. life, bd. dirs., chmn. legis. com., editor Music Therapy Jour. 1987-88, conf. of music therapy 1989, Disting. Svc. Music Therapy award 2004, Disting. Achievement award, 2004), Nat. Assn. Music Therapy, Am. Assn. Mental Deficiency (chair creative arts therapies), Symphony of the UN (bd. dirs.), Nat. Soc. Autistic Children, Coun. Exceptional Children, Assn. Musicians Greater N.Y., Students Against Violence Everywhere Through Music Therapy (founder, bd. dirs. 1995), Drumming Cir. For Peace (originator). Home: 375 Riverside Dr Ste 11BB New York NY 10025-2180 Office Phone: 212-865-6895. Business E-Mail: ehb2@nyu.edu.

BOYAJIAN, TIMOTHY EDWARD, public health officer, educator, consultant; b. Fresno, Calif., Feb. 22, 1949; s. Ernest Adam and Marge (Medzian) B.; m. Tassanee Bootdeesri, Apr. 23, 1987. BS in Biology, U. Calif., Irvine, 1975; M of Pub. Health, UCLA, 1978. Registered environ. health specialist, Calif. Rsch. asst. UCLA, 1978-81; lectr. Chapman U., 29 Palms, Calif., 1982-84, 88-89; refugee relief vol. Cath. Relief Svcs., Surin, Thailand, 1985-86; lectr. Nat. Univ., L.A., 1989-91; environ. health specialist Riverside County Health Svcs. Agy., Palm Springs, Calif., 1991-96; sci. tchr. South Gate (Calif.) HS, 1999—2004, Desert Hot Springs HS, 2004—05. Mem. adj. faculty U. Phoenix, 1998—; cons. parasitologist S. Pacific Commn., L.A., 1979; pub. health cons. several vets. groups, L.A., 1981-84, 97—; cons. Assn. S.E. Asian Nations, Bangkok, Thailand, 1988. Veterans rights advocate, Vietnam Vet. Groups, L.A., 1981-84. With USMC, Vietnam, 1969-71. Recipient U.S. Pub. Health Traineeship, U.S. Govt., L.A., 1977-81. Mem. VFW Avocation: writing. Home: PO Box 740 Palm Springs CA 92263-0740 Office Phone: 760-641-0707. Personal E-mail: timothy300@aol.com.

BOYAN, NORMAN J., retired education educator; b. NYC, Apr. 11, 1922; s. Joseph J. and Emma M. (Pelezare) B.; m. Priscilla M. Simpson, July 10, 1943; children: Stephen J. (dec.), Craig S., Corydon J. AB, Bates Coll., Lewiston, Maine, 1943; A.M., Harvard U., 1947, Ed.D., 1951. Instr. U.S. history Dana Hall Sch., Wellesley, Mass., 1946-48; research assoc. Lab. Social Relations, Harvard U., 1950-52; asst. prin. Mineola (N.Y.) High Sch., 1952-54; prin. Wheatley Sch., East Williston, N.Y., 1954-59; assoc. prof. edn., dir. student teaching and internship U. Wis., 1959-61; assoc. prof. edn. Stanford U., 1961-67; dir. div. ednl. labs. U.S. Office Edn., 1967-68, assoc. commr. for research, 1968-69; prof. edn. Grad. Sch. Edn., U. Calif., Santa Barbara, 1969-90, prof. emeritus, 1990—, dean, 1969-80; assoc. in edn. Grad. Sch. Edn., Harvard U., 1980-81; dir. Ednl. Leadership Inst. U. Calif., 1989-91. Vis. scholar Stanford U., 1974, 86; vis. prof. U. Ark. Program in Greece, 1977, Coll. Edn., Pa. State U., 1981, Faculty Edn. U. B.C., 1983, U. Alta., 1988, UCLA, 1991; cons. in field. Co-author: Instructional Supervision Training Program, 1978; mem. editl. bd. Harvard Edn. Rev, 1948-50, Jour. Secondary Edn, 1963-68, Jour. Edn. Rsch., 1967-82, Urban Edn, 1967-90; cons. editor, contbr. 5th edit. Ency. Ednl. Rsch., 1982; editor, contbr. Handbook Rsch. on Ednl. Adminstrn., 1988; contbr. articles to profl. jours. Served with USAAF, 1943-46. Recipient Shankland award for advanced grad. study in ednl. adminstrn., 1950, Roald F. Campbell Lifetime Achievement award U. Coun. for Ednl. Adminstrn., 1998. Mem. Am. Ednl. Rsch. Assn. (v.p. div. A 1978-80), Phi Beta Kappa, Phi Delta Kappa. Home: 1031A Calle Sastre Santa Barbara CA 93105-4439 Personal E-mail: nboyan@cox.net.

BOYANTON, JANET SHAFER, lawyer; b. Dallas, Dec. 8, 1954; d. Harvey Lee and Helen Louise (Barron) Shafer; m. Robert Earl Boyanton, May 3, 1980; 1 child, Thomas Franklin. BA, Austin Coll., 1976; MBA, Amber U., 1982; JD, Tex. Wesleyan U., 1994. Bar: Tex. 1994, U.S. Dist. Ct. (no. dist.) Tex. 1994, U.S. Supreme Ct. 2000; cert. family law mediator. Free lance writer, Dallas, 1982-92; legal asst. Law Office of Eddie Vassallo, Dallas, 1992-94; pvt. practice DeSoto, Tex., 1994—. Mem. adv. bd. Tex. Advocates for Nursing Home Residents, 1995—; vol. scouting activities Boy Scouts Am., children's choir. Mem. Nat. Acad. Elder Law Attys. (bd. dirs. Tex. chpt. 2000—). Avocations: reading, travel. Office: 211 Executive Way Desoto TX 75115-2336

BOYAR, BENJAMIN, music educator; b. NY; m. Jeanne Boyar; children: Nathan, Steven. BFA, U. NY, Buffalo; MA, Buffalo State Coll. Music educator Gateway Day Sch., Treatment Program, Willamsville, NY, 1988—90, Villa Maria Inst. of Music, Cheektowaga, NY, 1989—99, Buffalo Acad. for Visual and Performing Arts, Buffalo, 1984—2000; dir. of music Hutchinson Ctrl. Tech. H.S., Buffalo, 2000—. All-state music adjudicator woodwind, jazz and maj. orgns. NY State Sch. of Music, NY, 1985—. Assoc. Kennedy Centers' Imagination Celebration, Buffalo, 1985—95; dir. Jazz at Arts, Buffalo, 1984—2000. Recipient Music Cons., Disney Tchr. Awards mus. asst., 1994, Festival Chair, NY State Sch. Music Assn., 1988. Mem.: Internat. Jazz Educators Assn., Erie County Music Educator Assn., NY State Sch. Music Educators Assn., Music Educators Nat. Assn. Avocation: magic. Home: 225 Rosedale Blvd Amherst NY 14226 Office: Hutchinson Central Technical High School 256 South Elmwood Avenue Buffalo NY 14201 Office Phone: 716-816-3888. E-mail: banjam@adelphia.net.

BOYARSKI, ADAM MICHAEL, retired physicist; b. North Bank, Alta., Can., Apr. 14, 1935; came to U.S., 1963; s. Albert and Mary (Roskiewich) B.; m. Lorretta Sramek, June 1, 1968; children: Lisa A., Mike A. BA in Sci., U. Toronto, 1958; PhD, M.I.T., 1962. Rsch. assoc. MIT, Cambridge, 1962—63; staff physicist Stanford (Calif.) Linear Accelerator Ctr., 1963—2005; ret., 2005. Cons. in field; mem. team discovering psi family of elem. particles. Author: (software) HANDYPAK, A Histogram and Display Package, 1980; contbr. articles to scientific jours. Mem. Am. Phys. Soc. Avocations: woodworking, computers. Office: SLAC 2575 Sand Hill Rd Menlo Park CA 94025-7015 Office Phone: 650-926-2703. Business E-Mail: adam@slac.stanford.edu.

BOYARSKY, ANDREW HAROLD, surgeon, educator; b. Burlington, Vt., Feb. 18, 1952; BA, Rutgers U., 1974, MD, 1980. Diplomate Am. Bd. Surgery, Am. Bd. Surg. Critical Care. Intern U. Medicine and Dentistry N.J.-Rutgers Med. Sch., Piscataway, 1980-81, resident, 1981-85; fellow in vascular surgery Maimonides Med. Ctr., Bklyn., 1985-86; mem. staff Robert Wood Johnson Hosp., New Brunswick, NJ; assoc. prof. surgery U. Medicine and Dentistry N.J.-Robert Wood Johnson, 1993—. Office: UMDNJ-RW Johnson Med Sch Dept Surgery New Brunswick NJ 08903 Office Phone: 732-235-7920.

BOYARSKY, SAUL, medical educator, urologist; b. Burlington, Vt., July 22, 1923; s. Samuel and Ethel (Kaplan) B.; m. Rose Eisman, June 17, 1945; children: Myer William, Terry Linda Boyarsky, Hannah Gail Boyarsky. BS magna cum laude, U. Vt., 1943, MD cum laude, 1946; JD, Washington U., St. Louis, 1981. Bar: Mo. 1983. Instr. in physiology NYU, N.Y.C., 1955—56; assoc. prof. urology Albert Einstein Coll., N.Y.C., 1956-63; prof. urology Duke U., Durham, N.C., 1963-70, head divsn. genito-urinary surgery, 1970-73; prof. Washington U., St. Louis, 1970-89, head divsn. urology, 1970-73; clin. prof. surgery St. Louis U., 1991—; emeritus urologist Barnes-Jewish-Christian Hosp., Washington Hosp. Med. Ctr., St. Louis. Chmn. rsch. and tng. com. NIH, Bethesda, Md., 1968; cons. on med. devices FDA, Washington, 1969—; chmn. biomed. engring. com. AUA, Balt., 1975—90; founder Urology Lawyers Coun.; chmn. steering and curriculum com., facilitator Lifelong Learning Inst., U. Coll., Washington U., St. Louis; instr. and facilitator Duke Inst. for Learning in Retirement, 1999, 2001—03, mem. curriculum com. Author: The Neurogenic Bladder, 1967; (with others) Hydrodynamics of Micturition, 1971, Urodynamics; Hydrodynamics of the Ureter and Renal Pelvis, 1971, Ureteral Dynamics, 1972, The Care of the Neurogenic Bladder Patient, 1979, Goals in Male Reproductive Research, 1981; mem. editl. bd. Jour. of Legal Medicine. Chmn. steering com. Lifelong Learning Inst., Univ. Coll. Washington U., St. Louis. Capt. U.S. Army, 1943-50. Fellow ACS, Am. Acad. Forensic Sci., Am. Coll. Legal Medicine (former bd. govs.); mem. AAAS, AMA, ABA, AAUP, Am. Urol. Assn. (former chmn. biomed. engring. com.), Am. Assn. Clin. Urologists, Am. Assn. Genitourinary Surgeons, Am Physiologic Soc., Biomed. Urol. Assn., Internat. Continence Soc., Mo. Med. Assn., Mo., Urologic Soc., Pan-Am. Med. Assn., St. Louis Met. Med. Soc., St. Louis Urol. Soc., Societe Internationale D'Urologie, Soc. Univ. Urologists, Urodynamics Soc. (founder, 1st pres.), Am. Arbitration Assn., Am. Coll. Legal Medicine, Mo. Bar Assn., Bar Assn. Met. St. Louis, Mo. Orgn. Def. Lawyers, Urology Lawyers Coun. (founder, pres.). Jewish. Home: 6412 Mimosa Dr Chapel Hill NC 27514-9059 Personal E-mail: saulboyarsky39@msn.com.

BOYARSKY, TERRY LINDA, music educator; b. Nuremburg, Germany, Aug. 17, 1949; came to the U.S., 1950; d. Saul and Rose Sophie Eisman Boyarsky; m. Robert Watson Alcorn, May 14, 1982; 1 child, Vera Clare Alcorn. BA in Psychology, Reed Coll., 1970; BA in Eurhythmics, Cleve. Inst. Music, 1977; MA in Ethnomusicology, Kent State U., 1998. Freelance pianist, 1970—. Dalcroze eurhythmics tchr. Cleve. Inst. Music, 1976-86; Dalcroze specialist Cleve. Inst. Dance, 1977-86; vis. faculty Chautauqua (N.Y.) Inst., summers 1988-92; music and movement faculty Hathaway Brown Sch., Shaker Heights, Ohio, 1990-94; artist-in-residence, teaching artist Young Audiences of Greater Cleve., 1999—; mem. summer faculty Vandercook Coll. Music, Chgo., 2001; tchg. artist ICARE, 2002—, Kennedy Ctr. Ohio State Based Collaboratives Initiative, 2004—; presenter in field; lectr. in field. Singer: Blossom Festival Chorus, 2001—05, Akron Symphony Chorus, 2001—03. Program rev. com. Young Audiences Greater Cleve., 1997—; retreat leader Rowe Conf. Ctr., 2005; mem. adv. bd., spl. rhythmic cons. Shalhevet Folk Esemble, Cleve., 1991—95. Mem.: Dalcroze Soc. Am. (chmn. nat. conf. 1996, webmaster 1996—2001, bd. mem. 1996—, chmn. nat. conf. 2000, treas. 1996—2002), Am. Orff Schulwerk Assn. (cert. levels I and II), Cleve. Bot. Gardens. Avocations: sewing, gardening, singing. Personal E-mail: tboyarsky@ameritech.net.

BOYATT, THOMAS DAVID, former ambassador; b. Cin., Mar. 4, 1933; s. Lynn Craig Haven and Florine (Cloar) B.; m. Maxine Lorraine Shearwood, Dec. 30, 1971; children: Thomas Benton, Christopher Lynn, Jessica Allyn, Alexander Shearwood, Catherine Jordan. BA, Princeton U., 1955, MA, 1956. Vice consul Dept. State, Antofagasta, Chile, 1960-62; 2d sec. Am. Embassy, Luxembourg, 1964-66, 1st sec. Nicosia, Cyprus, 1967-70; dir. Cypriot affairs Near East Bur. Dept. State, Washington, 1970-74, assigned to Sr. Seminar, 1974-75; dep. chief mission, minister counselor Am. Embassy, Santiago, Chile, 1976-78; U.S. ambassador to Upper Volta, Ouagadougou, 1978-80, Colombia, Bogota, 1980-84; v.p. market devel. Sears World Trade Inc., Washington, 1984-87; with Dept. Treasury, 1962-64; ptnr. IRC Group, 1988-96; pres. U.S. Def. Systems, 1990-96. Trustee Princeton U., 1984-89; bd. dirs. Patterson Sch./U. Ky., Inst. for Study of Diplomacy/Georgetown U.; mem. State Dept. Adv. Com. on Leadership and Mgmt., 2004. 1st lt. SAC, USAF, 1956-59. Decorated Legion d'Honneur (Upper Volta), Gran Cruz Order of San Carlos (Colombia); recipient Meritorious Honor award Dept. State, 1969, William R. Rivkin award Am. Fgn. Service, 1970, Christian A. Herter award, 1976 Mem.: Am. Fgn. Svc. Assn. (treas.), Washington Inst. Fgn. Affairs (bd. dirs.), Acad. of Diplomacy (bd. dirs.), Am. Fgn. Svc. Assn. (pres. 1971—74, award for post-retirement contbns. to fgn. affairs 1999, Lifetime Achievement award 2001).

BOYCE, AMANDA N., psychologist; b. Kansas City, Mo., Aug. 16, 1976; d. James W. and Beatrice S. Crenshaw; m. Daniel R. Boyce, Apr. 17, 2004. BS, Truman State U., Mo., 1997; grad. in Spl. Edn., U. Kans., 2001. Tcrs. Cert. Sch. Psychologist Mo. Dept. of Elem. and Secondary Edn., 2003, Kans. State Bd. of Edn., 2001. Camp counselor- bunk coord. Ramapo Anchorage Camp, Rhinebeck, NY, 1996—97; coll. tchg. asst. U. of Kans., Lawrence, 1998—2000; sch. psychologist Kans. City, Kans. Pub. Schs., Kans., 2000—02, Swartz Creek Cmty. Schs., Mich., 2002—03; adj. instr. Washtenaw CC, Ann Arbor, Mich., 2003; sch. psychologist North Kans. City Sch. Dist., Mo., 2003—; adj. instr. Avila U., Kansas City, Mo., 2004—. Presenter North Kans. City Sch. Dist., Kansas City, 2004—, tchr. support team mem., 2003—; student improvement team coord. Kans. City Kans. Pub. Schs., Kans., 2000—02. Vol. Habitat for Humanity, Kansas City, Mo., 2001; vacation bible sch. leader Gashland Meth. Ch., Kansas City, Mo., 2001—02. Mem.: APA (student mem. 1999—2000), NASP, Kans. Assn. of Sch. Psychologists (standing mem. 1999—2001), Mo. Assn. of Sch. Psychologists (standing mem. 2004—05), Grad. Assn. of Sch. Psychologists (pres. 1999—2000), Nat. Panhellenic Coun. (rush counselor coord. 1996—97), Sigma Kappa Sorority (panhellenic rep. 1996—97). Avocation: reading. Personal E-mail: aboyce0404@yahoo.com.

BOYCE, BERT ROY, university dean emeritus, library and information science educator; b. Sharon, Pa., Jan. 10, 1938; s. Bert Roy and Julia (Loyd) B.; m. Judith Irene Warren, Aug. 25, 1968; children: Maria Natasha, Gabriel Augustus. BA in History, Marietta Coll., 1959; MS in Libr. Sci., Case Western Res. U., 1968; PhD, Cast Western Res. U., 1972. Asst. dir. Redevel. Authority, Sharon, 1966-67; rsch. analyst info. systems Libr. Congress, Washington, 1968-69; asst. prof. U. Mo., Columbia, 1972-78, chair dept. info. sci., 1976-83; assoc. prof. Sch. Libr. and Info. Sci. La. State U., Baton Rouge, 1983-85, prof. Sch. Libr. and Info. Sci., 1985—, dean Sch. Libr. and Info. Sci., 1990—. Author: Operations Research for Libraries and Information Agencies, 1991, Measurement in Information Science, 1994, Text Information Retrieval Systems, 2d edit., 1999; contbr. articles to profl. jours. Lt. USN, 1960-66, Vietnam. Sr. Fulbright-Hays scholar, Brazil, 1974. Mem. ALA (Shera Rsch. award 1988), Am. Soc. for Info. Sci. (Outstanding Info. Sci. Tchg. award 1989), La. Libr. Assn., Assn. for Libr. and Info. Sci. Edn. Democrat. Office: La State U Sch Libr and Info Sci 267 Coates Hl Baton Rouge LA 70803-0001 Business E-Mail: lsboyc@lsu.edu.

BOYCE, CAROLYN, political organization administrator; State chmn. Idaho Dem. Party, 2000—. Office: Idaho Democratic Party 988 Longmont Ave Ste 110 Boise ID 83706-3696

BOYCE, CLAYTON WINFRED, strategic communications consultant, transportation industry expert; b. Batavia, N.Y., Sept. 13, 1955; s. Sheldon William Boyce and Mary Meddie Riddle; m. Myrtha Kay Coyte, Sept. 13, 1980 (div. Oct. 1998); 1 child, Charles Randolph; m. Tracy Lynn Shaw, Aug. 31, 2002. BS in Psychology, U. Md., 1986. Reporter Germantown Courier, Phila., 1978, Saratogian, Saratoga Springs, N.Y., 1979, Daily News-Record, Harrisonburg, Va., 1980; news editor Evening Capital, Annapolis, Md., 1980—87, Knight-Ridder/Tribune News Svc., Washington, 1987-95; news copy editor Detroit Free Press, 1995; exec. editor Nat. Inst. Bus. Mgmt., 1995; editor, pub. Traffic World mag., Washington, 1996—2003; strategic comm. cons. US Dept. Transp. Office Inspector Gen., 2004—. Chmn. bd. Nat. Press Bldg. Corp., Washington, 1994-95. Deacon Plymouth Haven Baptist Church, Mt. Vernon, Va., 2003—. Named Transp. Editor of Yr., Transp. Consumer Protection Coun. Inc., 2003; recipient Editl. Excellence award, Am. Soc. Bus. Publ. Editors, 1999, 2001; N.Y. State Regents scholar, 1973. Mem. Nat. Press Club (pres. 1993-94, chmn. 1991, gov. 1989-90, treas. 1994, Courage, Leadership and Svc. award 1973), Washington Press Found. (bd. dirs. 1993-94), Friends of Nat. Journalism Libr. Found. (sec., treas. 1992-94). Baptist. Avocations: golf, reading, genealogy, running. Home: 8616 Yardley Drive Alexandria VA 22308 Office: Office of Inspector Gen / JA-40 US Dept Transp 400 7th St SW Rm 9126 Washington DC 20590 Office Phone: 202-366-6874. Office Fax: 202-366-1486.

BOYCE, CORRIE MOSBY, music educator; b. Columbia, S.C., Apr. 7, 1953; d. Rufus Levi and Emma Jo Mosby; m. W. Ray Boyce, June 21, 1975; 1 child, Ray D'Mitry. BA, Columbia Coll., 1974; MEd, Cambridge Coll., 1995. Tchr. Richland Sch. Dist. 1, Columbia, 1974—; instr. Middle Sch. Sci. Enrichment Program, Benedict Coll., Columbia, 1996—. Cluster leader Keenan Cluster Sch.'s Music Program, Columbia, 1989—90; choral music curriculum com. Richland Sch. Dist. 1, Columbia, 1998; Curriculum Leadership in the Arts participant S.C. State Dept. Edn., Columbia, 2003. Rhomania co-chairperson Beta Epsilon Sigma chpt. Sigma Gamma Rho, 1991—2002. Named Outstanding Club Woman of Yr., S.C. Fedn. of Women and Youth Clubs, Inc., 1990, United Meth. Woman of Yr., I. DeQuincey Newman United Meth. Women, 1995, Living the Legacy honoree, Nat. Coun. Negro Women, Inc., 1998. Mem.: Music Educators Nat. Conf. and affiliates, NEA and affiliates (mem. S.C. del. assembly 1993—98). United Methodist. Home: 204 Torwood Dr Columbia SC 29203 Office: Richland County Sch Dist 1 1616 Richland St Columbia SC 29201 E-mail: corrie0407@aol.com.

BOYCE, DANIEL HOBBS, finance company executive; b. Flint, Mich., Oct. 19, 1953; s. James Edward and Alice Marilyn (Hobbs) B.; m. Suzanne Kay Williams; children: Kenneth C., Geoffrey A., Stephen J. BA, U. Mich., 1974, MA, 1979. CFP. Rep. Mut. Svc. Corp., Detroit, 1982-87; br. mgr. Investment Mgmt. & Rsch. Inc., Atlanta, 1987—; co-managing ptnr. Ctr. Fin. Planning Inc., Southfield, Mich., 1988—. V.p. Southworth, Boyce & McFawn Planning Corp., Troy, Mich., 1982-85; owner, fin. planner Daniel H. Boyce Fin. Adv. Svcs., Birmingham, Mich., 1985-88; mem. adj. faculty Coll. Fin. Planning, Denver, 1985-90; mem. adv. coun. cert. program in personal fin. planning Oakland U., Rochester, Mich., 1987-2002; edn. cons. Nat. Ctr. for Fin. Edn., Denver, 1985-2001. Columnist: Money Matters, 1984—86, Personal Fin., 1987—93. Bd. dirs. Great Lakes Chamber Music Festival, 1996-98, Detroit Chamber Winds and Strings, 1992-2003, chmn. bd., 1995-98; min. music Birmingham Unitarian Ch., 1976-2001, emeritus, 2002—, bd. pres., 2003-2004. Named one of Top 200 Fin. Planners in U.S., Money Mag. and Worth Mag., 1987, 1996, 1997, 1998. Mem. Internat. Assn. Fin. Planning (bd. dirs. S.E. Mich. chpt. 1984-87, 89-91), Detroit Soc. Inst. CFPs (pres. 1986-87, chmn. 1987-88), Detroit Chamber Winds (bd. dirs., chmn. 1995-98). Office: Ctr Fin Planning Inc 40 Oak Hollow St Ste 125 Southfield MI 48034

BOYCE, DAVID S., lawyer; b. Medina, NY, 1949; AB, Cornell Univ., 1971; JD with high honors, Univ. Fla., 1977; LLM in Taxation, Georgetown Univ., 1979. Bar: Calif. 1979; cert. tax specialist Calif. Bd. of Legal Specialization. Atty.-adv. Judge Howard A Dawson Jr, US Tax Ct., 1977—79; adj. prof. law Univ. San Diego, 1980—84; now adminstrv. ptnr. LA office Jones Day. Mem.: ABA, Am. Health Lawyers Assn., LA Bar Assn., Order of Coif. Office: Jones Day Ste 4600 555 W Fifth St Los Angeles CA 90013-1025 Office Phone: 213-243-2403. Office Fax: 213-243-2539. Business E-Mail: dsboyce@jonesday.com.

BOYCE, DOREEN ELIZABETH, foundation administrator, educator; b. Antofagasta, Chile, Apr. 20, 1934; d. George Edgar and Elsie Winifred Vaughan; m. Alfred Warne Boyce, Aug. 11, 1956; children: Caroline Elizabeth, John Trevor Warne. BA with hons., Oxford (Eng.) U., 1956, MA with hons., 1960; PhD, U. Pitts., 1983; DHL (hon.), Westminster Coll., 1986, Washington and Jefferson Coll., 1993, Franklin & Marshall Coll., 2005. Lectr. and tutor in econs. U. Witwatersrand, South Africa, 1960-62; provost and dean of faculty, Mary Helen Marks prof. econs. Chatham Coll., Pitts., 1963-79; prof. econs., chmn. dept. econs. and mgmt. Hood Coll., Frederick, Md., 1979-82; pres. Buhl Found., Pitts., 1982—. Dir. and vice chair DQE Duquesne Light Co., Dollar Bank, FSB, Orbeco Analytical Svcs. Inc., Coun. Ind. Colls., Carnegie Mus.; co-founder, dir. Microbac Labs. Inc.; Pa. Gov.'s Sports and Exposition Facilities Task Force, 1995; del. White House Conf. on Small Bus., 1980; mem. Gov.'s Conf. Small Bus., 1979-82, chmn. bd. dirs., emerita trustee; mem. devel. com. Somerville Coll., 2005— Trustee Franklin and Marshall Coll., 1982-2004, Frick Edn. Commn., 1980-94, Carnegie Sci.

Ctr., 1982—, Carnegie Inst., 2005-; mem. Fed.Jud. Nominating Commn., 1977-79, Pa. Gov.'s Commn. on Financing of Higher Edn., 1983-85; bd. dirs. World Affairs Coun., 1984-96; mem. appeal com. devel. com. Somerville Coll., Oxford, Eng. Recipient Medallion of Distinction, U. Pitts., 1987, Univ. Laureate, U. Pitts., 2005; named Disting. Dau. Pa., 1996, Hon. Fellow Somerville Coll., U. Oxford, Women Who Make A Difference award, Internat. Women's Forum, 1998. Mem. Am. Econs. Assn., Am. Assn. Higher Edn., Grantmakers of Western Pa. (pres. 1984), Internat. Women's Forum, Assn. Governing Bds. Univ. and Coll. (coun. bd. chairs 2002—), Duquesne Club (bd. dirs. 2000-03, chmn., 2005-) Office: Centre City Tower 650 Smithfield St Ste 2300 Pittsburgh PA 15222-3912

BOYCE, EMILY STEWART, retired library and information science educator, retired library and information scientist; b. Raleigh, N.C., Aug. 18, 1933; d. Harry and May (Fallon) B. BS, East Carolina U., 1955, MA, 1961; MS in Libr. Sci., U. N.C., 1968; postgrad., Cath. U. Am., 1977. Libr. Tileston Jr. H.S., Wilmington, NC, 1955-57; children's libr. Wilmington Pub. Libr., 1957-58; asst. libr. Joyner Libr. East Carolina U., Greenville, NC, 1959-61, libr. III, 1962-63; ednl. supr. II ednl. media divsn. N.C. State Dept. Pub. Instrn., Raleigh, 1961-62; assoc. prof. dept. libr. and info. scis. East Carolina U., 1964-76, prof., 1976-92, chmn. dept., 1982-89; retired, 1992. Cons. So. Assn. Colls. and Schs., Raleigh, 1975-92. Active Asheville YWCA, Mediation Ctr., Botanical Gardens, Literacy Coun. Buncombe County. Mem. ALA, AAUW, N.C. Libr. Assn., Assn. Libr. and Info. Sci. Educators, Spl. Librs. Assn. Democrat. Home: 30 Creekside Way Asheville NC 28804-1763 Personal E-mail: esboyce30@charter.net.

BOYCE, GREGORY H., energy executive; BS in mining engring., U. Ariz.; completed advanced mgmt. program, Grad. Sch. Bus., Harvard U. Exec. asst. to vice chmn. Standard Oil of Ohio, 1983—84; dir. Govt. & Pub. Affairs Kennecott Corp.; pres. Kennecott Minerals Co., 1993—94, pres., CEO Kennecott Energy Co., 1994—99; CEO Energy Rio Tinto PLC, 2000—03; pres., COO Peabody Energy Corp., 2003—, CEO elect (to take office Jan. 1, 2006). Mem. Coal Industry Adv. Bd. Internat. Energy Agency; past bd. mem. Ctr. Energy & Econ. Devel., Western Regional Coun., Nat. Coal Coun., Mountain States Employers Coun., Wyo. Bus. Coun. Mem.: Nat. Mining Assn. (past bd. mem.). Office: Peabody Energy Corp 701 Market St Saint Louis MO 63101-1826 Office Phone: 314-342-7574. Office Fax: 314-342-7720. E-mail: gboyce@peabodyenergy.com.

BOYCE, JOSEPH NELSON, retired journalist, consultant, educator; b. New Orleans, Apr. 18, 1937; s. John and Sadie (Nelson) B.; m. Carol Hill, Dec. 21, 1968; children: Leslie, Nelson, Joel, Beverly. Student, Roosevelt U., Chgo., 1955-65, John Marshall Law Sch., 1965-67. Mem. Chgo. Police Dept., 1961-66; reporter Chgo. Tribune, 1966-70; corr. Time mag., 1970-73, chief San Francisco bur., 1973-79, chief So. U.S. bur., 1979-85, dep. chief Eastern U.S. bur., 1985-87; sr. editor Wall St. Jour., 1987-98, ret., 1998; media rels. cons. Dow Jones/Wall St. Jour., 1998—. Rotating faculty mem., summer program for minority journalists U. Calif., Berkeley, 1986, Berkeley, 87, Berkeley, 88, Berkeley, 89; bd. dirs. Jazzmobile, Inc., N.Y.C.; guest lectr. various colls. and univs.; vis. faculty summer program for minority journalists U. Ala.; vis. faculty Poynter Inst., 1993; William Randolph Hearst vis. prof.-in-residence Howard U., 1996; mem. adv. bd. Lyndon B. Johnson Sch. of Public Affairs U. Tex., Austin, 1998—; adj. prof. Sch. Journalism Columbia U., N.Y.C., 1999, Ind. U., Indpls., 2002, 05. Chmn. Marin County Black Leadership Forum, 1974-75; mem. Marin Justice Coun., 1977-78; bd. dirs. Jazzmobile, 1991-95. With USNR. Recipient Outstanding Black Achiever award Met. YMCA, N.Y.C., 1975; co-recipient Unity In Media award Lincoln U., 1975; Time Mag.-Duke U. fellow, 1981-82. Mem. NAACP, Nat. Assn. Black Journalists, Nat. Assn. Minority Media Execs. (bd. dirs. 1991-93), Soc. Profl. Journalists (Indpls. chpt. bd. dirs., pres. 2003-04). Episcopalian. Personal E-mail: boycevibe@aol.com.

BOYCE, MARIA WYCKOFF, lawyer; b. Houston, Tex., Aug. 30, 1963; BA cum laude, Conn. Coll., 1985; JD, Northwestern Univ., 1988. Bar: Tex. 1988, US Dist. Ct. (so., ea., no., we. dist. Tex., Colo.), US Ct. Appeals 5th cir., US Supreme Ct. Ptnr. litigation dept. & mem. exec. com. Baker Botts LLP, Houston. Editor (in chief): Jour. Criminal Law & Criminology. Mem. adv. bd. Girls Inc. of Greater Houston; bd. dir., Houston chpt. Tex. Gen. Counsel Forum. Mem.: Am. Intellectual Property Law Assn., Houston Bar Assn., Fed. Bar Assn. (pres.elect). Office: Baker Botts LLP One Shell Plz 910 Louisiana St Houston TX 77002-4995 Office Phone: 713-229-1922. Office Fax: 713-229-2722. Business E-Mail: maria.boyce@bakerbotts.com.

BOYCE, MARY C., mechanical engineer, educator; BS, Va. Polytechnic Inst., 1981; MS, MIT, 1983, PhD, 1987. Asst. prof. mechanical engring. MIT, 1987—92, assoc. prof. mechanical engring., 1992—99, prof. mechanical engring., 1999—2000, disting. alumnae prof. mechanical engring., 2000—. Named MacVicar Faculty fellow, 2000—10; recipient ALCOA Found. award, 1988, 1991, Presidential Young Investigators award, NSF, 1991—96, DuPont Faculty award, 1992—95, GenCorp Signature U. award, 1998, Keenan Innovation in Teaching award, 1998. Fellow: Am. Acad. Arts & Scis.; mem.: Materials Rsch. Soc., Am. Physics Soc., Am. Acad. of Mechanics, Am. Soc. of Mechanical Engineers (Special Achievement award 1998). Office: MIT 1-304 Mechanical Engring 77 Mass Ave Cambridge MA 02139*

BOYCE, RALPH L., ambassador; b. Washington, Feb. 1, 1952; married; 2 children. BA, George Washington U., 1974; MPA, Princeton U., 1976. Staff asst. to amb. US Fgn. Svc., Tehran, Iran, 1977—79, comml. attache Tunis, Tunisia, 1979—81, fin. economist Islamabad, Pakistan, 1981—84; spl. asst. to dep. sec. US Dept. State, Washington, 1984—88, polit. counselor Bangkok, 1988—92, dep. chief of mission Singapore, 1992—93, charge d'affaires, 1993—94, dep. chief of mission Bangkok, 1994—98, dep. asst. sec. for East Asia and Pacific Affairs Washington, 1998—2001, US amb. to Indonesia Jakarta, Indonesia, 2001—04, US amb. to Thailand Bangkok, 2004—. Fluent in Persian, French, and Thai. Office: 7200 Bangkok Pl Washington DC 20521*

BOYCE, STANLEY EDMAN, secondary school educator; b. Glendale, W.Va., Nov. 11, 1947; s. Marion Stanley and Aurelia Eudoris (Wickham) B.; m. Marlene Ann Maxwell, July 5, 1968; children: Tasha Dawn, Tanya Beth. BA in Speech, David Lipscomb Coll., 1970; postgrad, Muskingum Coll., 1975-76, Bowling Green State U., 1980; MEd, Ohio U., 1987. Jailer Coshocton County Sheriff's Office, Coshocton, Ohio, 1975; tchr. English Riverview Local Sch. Dist., Warsaw, Ohio, 1976-77; tchr. Licking County Joint Vocat. Sch., Newark, Ohio, 1977-79; guidance counselor Coshocton County Joint Vocat. Sch., 1979—. Bd. dirs., past pres., Coshocton Fed. Credit Union. With USN, 1971-75. Mem. NEA, Ohio Edn. Assn., Ea. Ohio Edn. Assn., Coshocton County Joint Vocat. Sch. Edn. Assn., Masons. Republican. Mem. Ch. of Christ. Home: 602 Hill St Coshocton OH 43812-1032

BOYD, ARTHUR BERNETTE, JR., surgeon, clergyman, beverage company executive; b. Durham, NC, June 29, 1947; s. Arthur Bernette and Mammie Lee (Chalmers) B.; m. Delphine Victoria Huffman, Mar. 14, 1981; children: Arthur III, Vicki. BA, Fla. A&M Univ., 1969; postgrad., NYU, 1970; MD, Meharry Med. Coll., 1978; postgrad., U. N.C., Chapel Hill, 1998. Cert. ATLS instr., PALS. Intern in surgery Howard Univ. Hosp., Washington, 1978-80; resident and chief resident in surgery St. Luke's Hosp., Cleve., 1981-84; fellow in liver transplant U. Pitts., 1984-85; chief adminstrv. fellow trauma/surg. critical care R.A. Cowley Shock Trauma Ctr., U. Md. Med. Sys., Cali, Colombia, 1993-94, clin. instr. surgery, sr. fellow, traumatologist Baltimore County, 1994—; co-traumatologist Prince George Cmty. Hosp., Cheverly, Md., 1994-95; chief surgeon, pres. Phoenix Med. Surgical Svc., Inc., Cleve., Carribean, 1986—; clin. instr. surgery, sr. trauma fellow Shock Trauma Ctr. U. Md. Med. Ctr., Balt., 1995-96; pres., CEO Motown Beverage Co. of Ohio, Cleve., 1988—, Towne Club Internat. of Ohio, Inc., Cleve., 1988—; pres., CEO, chmn. Star Beverage Corp., Shaker Heights, Ohio, 1997; chief adminstrv. fellow in trauma/crit. care R.A. Cowley Shock Trauma Ctr./U. Md. Med. Systems, 1993-94, clin. instr., sr. trauma rsch. fellow, 1994-95; sr. trauma fellow, clin. instr. Shock Trauma Ctr./U. Md., 1995; CEO, pres. Nat. Fin. Group, Inc., Cleve., 1997—; vice chair Star Beverage Corp., 1997. Adj. prof. anatomy and physiology Cuyhoga C.C., Cleve., 1988—; cons. surgeon other hosps. and physicians, Cleve., 1988—; continuing med. educator dept. surgery Case Western Res. U. Sch. Medicine, Cleve., 1997-98; faculty med. bd. profl. preparation course U. Mo., Kansas City, 1997. Inventor: wheelchair with mechanism to raise or lower left or right buttocks of person, hemostat that carries two sutures, synthetic covering with zipper to cover bowel when abdomen unable to be closed after surgery. Vol. Cleve. Community Action Against Addiction, 1987-88; mentor Case Western U. Inner City Program, Cleve., 1988—; judge honors sci. projects Shaker Heights Middle Sch., 1998; mem. Shaker Heights Cmty. Leaders Meetings. Fellow ACS (assoc.), Internat. Coll. Surgeons; mem. AAAS, AMA, N.Y. Acad. Scis., Nat. Med. Assn. (mentor 1990—), Assn. of Black Cardiologists, Ohio State Med. Soc., Cleve. Surg. Soc., Nat. Assn. Small Bus. Owners, Internat. Assn. Small Bus. Owners, Assn. Black Cardiologists, Greater Cleve. Ministers Alliance, Masons, Omega Psi Phi, Alpha Phi Omega. Democrat. Methodist. Avocations: reading, sports, golf. Home and Office: Motown Beverage Co 3277 Lee Rd Cleveland OH 44120-3451 also: Star Beverage Corp Ste 107 20475 Farnsleigh Rd Shaker Heights OH 44122-3850 Office Phone: 216-991-4799. Personal E-mail: aboydstar@aol.com.

BOYD, BE (BELINDA) CAROLYN, theater educator; m. John Wayne Shafer. BS in Comm. and Theater, Austin Peay State U., 1982; MFA in Acting, U. Louisville, 1986. Voice/ acting instr. U. of Louisville, 1986—89; asst. prof. of theater U. of Vt., Burlington, Vt., 1989—91; assoc. prof. if theater U. N.C., Greensboro, 1991—98; assoc. prof. of theater Tex. Christian U., Ft. Worth, 1998—2002, U. of Ctrl. Fla., Orlando, 2002—. Dir., dir.: La Lorona; actor: (actor in fires in the mirror) Fires in the Mirror (Best Actress, 2000); author: (play) Dream Keeper, Mother Of Civil Rights, In Focus: A Recollection of Black Thought. Mem.: Ctrl. Fla. Performing Arts Alliance, Assn. for Theatre in Higher Edn., Voice and Speech Trainers Assn., Am. Coll. Theatre Festival, Actor's Equity Assn., Southeastern Theatre Conf. (culteral diversity com. 1998—2000), Dramatist's Guild (assoc.). Office: U Ctrl Fla PO Box 162372 Orlando FL 32816-2372

BOYD, BENJAMIN S., lawyer; b. Springfield, Mo., Nov. 1, 1961; BA, BA, Univ. Ark., 1984, JD with high honors, 1987. Bar: Ark. 1987, Va. 1988, DC 1988, Md. 1991, US Dist. Ct. (DC, ea. & we. Va., Md., Colo. dist.), US Ct. Appeals (9th, DC cir.), US Supreme Ct. Ptnr., Nat. Hiring co-chmn. DLA Piper Rudnick Gray Cary, Washington. Office: DLA Piper Rudnick Gray Cary 1200 19th St NW Washington DC 20036-2412 Office Phone: 202-861-3942. Office Fax: 202-223-2085. Business E-Mail: benjamin.boyd@dlapiper.com.

BOYD, BEVERLY, English literature educator; b. Bklyn., Mar. 27, 1925; d. James Gray and Elspeth Kathleen (Mossop) Boyd. BA, Bklyn. Coll., 1946; MA, Columbia U., 1948, PhD, 1955. Instr. English Bklyn. Coll., N.Y.C., 1947, U. Tex., Austin, 1955-57; prof. English Radford (Va.) Coll., 1957-62; from asst. prof. to prof. English U. Kans., Lawrence, 1962—. Author: The Middle English Miracles of the Virgin, 1963, Chaucer and the Liturgy, 1967, Chaucer and the Medieval Book, 1973, Chaucer According to William Caxton, 1978, Variorum Chaucer fascicle: The Prioress's Tale, 1988, (verse) Philippine's Windows, 1988; contbr. chpts. to books. Recipient Disting. Alumna award Bklyn. Coll., 1979; Guggenheim fellow, 1969; Huntington Libr. fellow, 1960, 75. Avocation: poetry. Office: U Kans Dept Of English Lawrence KS 66045-0001

BOYD, BYRON A., labor union administrator; b. Seattle; m. Susan Boyd; 2 children. Brakeman promoted to locomotive engr. Union Pacific R.R., 1971; asst. pres. U.T. Union, mem. Local 117 Vancouver, Wash., pres., 2001—. Office: 14600 Detroit Ave Cleveland OH 44107-4250

BOYD, CAROLYN PATRICIA, history professor; b. San Diego, June 1, 1944; d. Peter James and Patricia Mae (de Soucy) B.; m. Frank Dawson Bean, Jan. 4, 1975; children: Peter Justin Bean, Michael Franklin Bean. AB with great distinction and with honors in History, Stanford U., 1966; MA, U. Wash., 1969, PhD, 1974. Tchg. asst. dept. history U. Wash., 1970-71; from instr. to prof. dept. history U. Tex., Austin, 1973-95, prof., 1995-99, assoc. dean Office Grad. Studies, 1986-88, 90-92, chair dept. history, 1994-99; dir. univ. honors program, assoc. prof. dept. history U. Md., College Park, 1989-90; prof. dept. history U. Calif., Irvine, 1999—, chair dept. history, 2004—. Lectr. in field. Author: Praetorian Politics in Liberal Spain, 1979, La política pretoriana en el reinado de Alfonso XIII, 1990, Historia Patria: Politics, History and National Identity in Spain, 1875-1975, 1997, Spanish edit., 2000; mem. editl. bd. Essays, 1992-95, Ayers, 2005-; author chpts. to books; contbr. articles to profl. jours. Recipient Summer award U. Tex. Rsch. Inst., 1997; Woodrow Wilson hon. fellow, 1966, Fulbright-Hays fellow, 1966-67, NDEA Title IV fellow, 1968-72, AAUW fellow, 1972-73, ACLS fellow, 1985; ACLS Grant-in-Aid, 1977, Am. Philos. Soc. grant, 1978, URI Rsch. grant, 1985, New Del Amo Program grant, 2000-02; fellow Woodrow Wilson Internat. Ctr. for Scholars, 2002-03. Mem. Am. Hist. Assn. (James Harvey Robinson prize com. 1992-94, John Fagg prize com. 2001-03), Soc. Spanish and Portugese Hist. Studies (gen. sec. 2000-04, mem. exec. com. 1978-80, 83-85, 96-98, chair local arrangements, program chmn. conf. 1987), Coun. European Studies, Internat. Inst. in Spain, Assn. Contemporary History. Office: U Calif Irvine Dept History Irvine CA 92697-0001 E-mail: cpboyd@uci.edu.

BOYD, CLAUDE COLLINS, educational specialist, consultant; b. Kent, Tex., May 25, 1924; s. Edward Clarke and Nora (Morris) B.; m. Frances Arline Haley, Jan. 22, 1955; children: David Chand, Anese Nasim Boyd Forsyth, Mark Kevin, Kimberly Ann Boyd Surgeon. BA, Tex. A&M U., 1948; MEd, U. Tex., 1957, EdD, 1961. Cert. elem. tchr., prin., supt., Tex. Elem. sch. tchr. Culberson County Ind. Sch. Dist., Van Horn, Tex.; elem. sch. prin. The Austin (Tex.) Ind. Sch. Dist.; elem sch. bilingual tchr. Ector County Ind. Sch. Dist., Odessa, Tex.; assoc. prof. Ind. U., Bloomington; curriculum specialist USAID, Guatemala City, Guatemala; project specialist in edn. The Ford Found., N.Y.C.; assoc. prof. edn. Pa. State U., Erie; edn. specialist Devel. Assocs., Inc., Washington; internat. edn. advisor/cons. U.S. Agy. for Internat. Devel., San Salvador, edn. adminstr., curriculum advisor La Paz, Bolivia; Dominican Republic; edn. adminstr., curriculum advisor U.S. Agy. for Internat. Devel., Dominican Republic; free-lance edn. advisor, cons., worldwide svc. Odessa, Tex.; tchr. edn. specialist InterAm. Devel. Bank, Santo Domingo, Dominican Republic. Ednl. supervision specialist InterAmerican Devel. Bank, Santo Domingo, Dominican Republic; substitute tchr. K-12, Ector County ISD, Odessa, Tex. Recipient Grand Order of Edn., Pres. of Rep. of Bolivia. Mem. ASCD, Phi Delta Kappa (past pres. Mu chpt.). Home: 2426 E 21st St Odessa TX 79761-1703

BOYD, DAVID PRESTON, business educator; b. NYC, Oct. 19, 1943; s. David Preston and Mignon (Finch) B.; m. Sally Sparks, Sept. 9, 1989. BA in English Lit., Harvard U., 1965; DPhil in Behavioral Scis., Oxford U., 1973. Asst. headmaster Dedham (Mass.) Country Day Sch., 1965-69; co-owner the Old Cambridge (Mass.) Co., 1973-77; instr. coll. bus. adminstrn. Northeastern U., Boston, 1977-78, asst. prof., 1978-82, assoc. prof., 1982-87, Patrick F. and Helen C. Walsh rsch. prof., 1985-86, chmn. human resources mgmt. dept., 1986-87, prof., 1987—, acting dean, 1987, dean coll. and grad. sch. bus. adminstrn., 1987-94. Author: Elites and Their Education National Foundation for Educational Research, 1973; mem. editl. bd. Internat. Jour. Value-Based Mgmt., Cross-cultural Mgmt.; contbr. articles to profl. jours. Past trustee Pine Manor Coll.; corporator Brookline Bancorp. Recipient Excellence in Teaching award Northeastern U., 1980; Northeastern U. grantee, 1982-84, Control Data Corp., 1983, NYU, 1985. Fellow Mass. Hist. Soc.; mem. Soc. Colonial Wars, S.R., Oxford Soc., Tennis and Racquet Club, Somerset Club, Mass Hort. Soc. (former trustee), Comml. Club, Beta Gamma Sigma, Phi Kappa Phi. Home: 14 Bristol Rd Wellesley Hills MA 02481-2727 Office: Northeastern U 304 Hayden Hall Boston MA 02115-5000 Office Phone: 617-373-4727. Business E-Mail: d.boyd@neu.edu.

BOYD, DAVID WILLIAM, mathematician, educator; b. Toronto, Ont., Can., Sept. 17, 1941; s. Glenn Kelvin and Rachael Cecilia (Garvock) B.; m. Mary Margaret Shields, Sept. 26, 1964; children: Deborah, Paul, Kathryn. BS, Carleton U., 1963; MA, Toronto U., 1964, PhD, 1966. Asst. prof. U. Alta., 1966-67, Calif. Inst. Tech., 1967-70, assoc. prof., 1970-71, U. B.C., Vancouver, Can., 1971-74, prof. math., 1974—, dept. head, 1986-89. Recipient E.W.R. Steacie Prize, 1978; I.W. Killam sr. research fellow, 1976-77, 81-82, Coxeter-James prize, 1979, Jeffery-Williams prize, 2001, CRM-Fields prize, 2005. Fellow Royal Soc. Can.; mem. Am. Math. Soc., Can. Math. Soc. Office: Univ BC Dept Math Vancouver BC Canada V6T 1Z2 E-mail: boyd@math.ubc.ca.

BOYD, EARL E., JR., councilman; b. Shoals, Ind., Aug. 29, 1943; s. Earl Ernest and Mary Louise (McCauley) Boyd; m. Barbara Jean Chattin, June 22, 1963; children: Wesley, Theresa, Kevin, Rebecca, Brian. Councilman Town of Shoals, Ind., 1996—; precinct committeeman Martin County Rep. Ctrl. Com., Shoals, Ind., 1993—, county chmn., 1997—. Named Ky. Col., Gov. Ky., 2000. Mem.: Eagles (pres. 1997—98). Home: PO Box 627 8th St Shoals IN 47581 Office: Martin County Rep Ctrl Cm 206 4th Shoals IN 47581

BOYD, ARLENE (CAREY), music educator; b. Willcox, Ariz., Dec. 6, 1929; d. Earl and Maude Yongue Allison Boyd; m. Lee M. Carey, 1949 (div. 1974); children: Joan Carey Morrison, Janet Carey Fink, Brian Earl Carey. BA in Music Edn., U. Ariz., 1951, MA in Music Edn., 1958, postgrad., 1977—78, U. Wash., 1980—81. Voice faculty Pima Cmty. Coll., Tucson, 1971—77, music tchr., 1987—91; voice faculty U. Puget Sound, Tacoma, 1978—82; tchr. voice theory Santa Fe C.C., 1982—87; pvt. voice studio, 1958—. Choral dir. various organizations. Singer (soprano soloist): Tucson Symphony, U. Ariz. Symphony, So. Ariz. Symphony, Grand Rapids Mich. Symphony, Mormon Choir with LA Philharmonic, many others. Worker for civil rights and social justice causes; tchr. youth and adult literacy. Mem.: Nat. Assn. Tchrs. Singing (founding mem.), Pi Lambda Theta, Sigma Alpha Iota. Democrat. Presbyterian. Avocation: writing. Home: 2323 E Water St #33 Tucson AZ 85719-3446

BOYD, F. ALLEN, JR., congressman, farmer; b. Valdosta, Ga., June 6, 1945; m. Cissy Boyd; children: David, John, Suzanne. BA, Fla. State U., 1969. Mem. Fla. Ho. of Reps., 1989—97, U.S. Ho. of Reps. from 2d Fla. dist., 1997—; mem. appropriations com. U.S. Congress from 2d Fla. dist., mem. mil. constrn. and the agr. com., mem. rural devel. com., mem. food and drug adminstrn. Chmn. Fla. House Dem. Conservative Caucus. With U.S. Army, 1969—71. Democrat. Office: 107 Cannon Ho Office Bldg Washington DC 20515-0902*

BOYD, HARRY DALTON, lawyer, retired insurance company executive; b. Huntington Park, Calif., June 13, 1923; s. Randall and Thelma L. (Lewis) B.; m. Margaret Jeanine Gamewell, June 13, 1948; children: Leslie Boyd Cotton, Wayne, Lynn Boyd Denby, Evan, Lance. LLB, U. So. Calif., 1949, LLM, 1960; A degree in Mgmt., Ins. Inst. Am., 1972. Bar: Calif. 1950. Pvt. practice, L.A.; assoc. Harvey & Viereck, L.A., 1952-55; assoc. gen. counsel, corp. sec. Farmers Ins. Group, L.A., 1955-77; group v.p., gen. counsel Swett & Crawford Group, L.A., 1977-83; gen. counsel, dir. Harbor Ins. Co., 1983-89; Calif. counsel Continental Ins. Co., 1987-89; of counsel Fidler & Bell, Burbank, Calif., 1990-93, Richard E. Garcia, Atty. at Law, L.A., 1994-96. Bd. dirs. FIG Fed. Credit Union, 1958-61, pres., 1960-61; mem. Sherman Oaks Property Owners Assn., 1967—, pres., 1969, 72; mem. Western Ins. Info. Svc., Spkrs. Bur., 1971-77; bd. dirs. Buffalo Reins. Co., 1983-87; expert witness in ins. litigation, 1990-2000; arbitrator reins., 1990-2000. Mem. adv. coun. Chandler Elementary Sch., 1970-73, Milliken Jr. H.S., 1973-74. With USAAF, 1943-46. Mem. Calif. Ins. Guarantee Assn. (bd. govs. 1972-77), Los Angeles County Bar Assn. (chmn. exec. com. corp. law depts. sect. 1971-72), Reins. Assn. Am. (legal com. 1979-81), Nat. Assn. Ind. Insurers (chmn. surplus lines com. 1980-82), Calif. Assn. Ins. Cos. (exec. com. 1979-83), Wilshire C. of C. (bd. dirs. 1971-79, pres. 1975), Nat. Assn. Ins. Commrs. (industry adv. com. on reins. regulation 1983-90), Am. Arbitration Assn. (arbitrator). Republican. Lutheran (pres. coun. 1964-65). Home: 24023 Rockridge CT Valencia CA 91355-3318

BOYD, HAZEL, minister; b. Huntingdon, Tenn., Sept. 09; d. Marion Homer Barnett and Lennie Victolia Hawkins; married; 6 children. Student in real estate, Columbus State Coll., Ohio. Ordained clergy Anderson Ind. Ch. of God, Ohio; cert. health aide Columbus State Coll., profl. activity dir. Cosmetologist, Columbus, Ohio; area commr. Columbus City Coun.; prison minister Columbus. Pres. PTA, 1960; judge Bd. Election; Sunday Sch. tchr., Bible tchr. Recipient various awards and citations, various orgns., including NAACP. Mem.: Greater SLAC, 50 Plus Club, Linden Kiwanis. Home: 1264 E 16th Ave Columbus OH 43211

BOYD, JAMES ROBERT, energy executive; b. Nashville, July 29, 1946; s. James Clinton and Mary Avon (Motlow) B.; m. Elise White, June 27, 1970; children: Elizabeth, Mary Franklin. BSEE, U. Ky., 1969; MBA, NYU, 1972. Sales engr. Westinghouse Electric Co., N.Y.C. and St. Louis, 1970-75, mgr. generation sales St. Louis, 1975-77, cons. planning Pitts., 1977-79, mgr. div. planning, 1979-81; mgr. strategic planning Ashland (Ky.) Oil Co., 1982-84, dir. corp. planning, 1984-86, sr. v.p., group oper. officer, 1989—2002; sr. v.p. adminstrn. Ashland Exploration, Houston, 1986-87, pres., 1987-89. Chmn. bd. dirs. Arch Coal Inc., 1998—; bd. dirs. Farmers Bank. Avocations: golf, hunting, swimming. Office: 2333 Alexandria Dr Ste 134 Lexington KY 40504 Office Phone: 859-514-6013.*

BOYD, JOHN T., engineering executive; Chmn. John T. Boyd Co., Pitts. Recipient Erskine Ramsay Gold medal Soc. Mining, Metallurgy, & Exploration, 1993.

BOYD, JOHN W., JR., farmers association leader; b. NYC; Farmer, 1983—; pres., founder Nat. Black Farmers Assn., 1995—. Achievements include founded the association to fight the racism in the USDA loan programs; led class action law suit of 1000 black farmers against the USDA in 1997 that led to a historic agreement in 1999; Staged a protest in 2003 on behalf of black farmers by traveling 200-plus miles from his farm in Virginia to Washington on a wagon pulled by his two mules, Struggle and 40 Acres. Office: Nat Black Farmers Assn 68 Wind Rd Baskerville VA 23915 Office Phone: 434-848-1865.*

BOYD, JOSEPH ARTHUR, JR., lawyer; b. Hoschton, Ga., Nov. 16, 1916; s. Joseph Arthur and Esther Estelle (Puckett) B.; m. Ann Stripling, June 6, 1938; children: Joanne Louise Boyd Goldman, Betty Jean Boyd Jala, Joseph Robert, James Daniel, Jane N. Ohlin. Student, Piedmont Coll., Demorest, Ga., 1936-38, LLD, 1963; student, Mercer U., Macon, Ga., 1938-39; JD, U. Miami, Coral Gables, Fla., 1948; LLD, Western State U. Coll. Law, San Diego, 1981. Bar: Fla. 1948, U.S. Supreme Ct. 1959, D.C. 1973, N.Y. 1982. Practice law, Hialeah, 1948-68; city atty., 1951-58; mem. Dade County Commn., Miami, Fla., 1958-68, chmn., 1963; vice mayor Dade County, 1967; justice Fla. Supreme Ct., Tallahassee, 1969-87, chief justice, 1984-86; assoc. Boyd Lindsey & Sliger P.A., Tallahassee, 1987—99. Mem. Hialeah Zoning Bd., 1946-48; juror Freedoms Found., Valley Forge, Pa., 1971, 73 Bd. dirs. Bapt. Hosp., Miami, 1962-66, Miami Coun. Chs., 1960-64; emeritus trustee Piedmont Coll. Recipient Nat. Top Hat award Bus. and Profl. Women in U.S. for advancing status of employed women, 1967 Mem. ABA, Fla. Bar Assn., Hialeah-Miami Springs Bar Assn. (pres. 1955), Tallahassee Bar Assn., Hialeah-Miami Springs C. of C. (pres. 1956), Am. Legion (comdr. Fla. 1953-54), VFW, Shriners, Masons (33 deg.), Lions, Elks, Wig and Robe, Iron Arrow, Phi Alpha Delta. Democrat. Baptist (deacon).

BOYD, JOSEPH DON, diversified financial services company executive; b. Muncie, Ind., Jan. 22, 1926; s. Joseph Cornelius and Waneta May (Barrett) B.; m. Cynthia Reiley, Dec. 28, 1957; children— Jane Elizabeth, Craig A., Michael J. AB (Rector scholar), DePauw U., 1948; MA, Northwestern U., 1950, Ed.D., 1955. Ednl. asst. First Meth. Ch., Anderson, Ind., 1948-49;

residence hall counselor Northwestern U., Evanston, Ill., 1949-50, univ. examiner, instr. edn., guidance lab. asst., 1952-54, dean men, asst. prof. edn., 1955-61; exec. dir. Ill. Scholarship Commn., 1961-80; dir. instnl. relations and research Nat. Coll. Edn., Evanston, 1981-84; pres. Joseph D. Boyd & Assocs., Deerfield, Ill., 1984—. Residence hall dir., head tennis coach, asst. basketball coach Albion Coll., 1950-52 Mem. Nat. Assn. Adminstrs. State Scholarship Programs, Phi Delta Kappa, Delta Tau Delta, Phi Eta Sigma. Clubs: Rotarian. Methodist. Home: 1232 Warrington Rd Deerfield IL 60015-3145 Office: 600 Deerfield Rd Deerfield IL 60015-3229 Office Phone: 847-940-4145. Business E-Mail: jboyd@christumcdeerfield.org.

BOYD, KATHERINE ANN, psychotherapist; b. Ranson, W.Va., Sept. 7, 1973; d. James J. and Kathleen S. Sisco; m. Glen Jr. Allan Boyd, May 25, 1996. AA in Social Sci., County Coll. of Morris, 1993; BA in Psychology, Rutgers U., 1997; MA in Counseling Psychology, Coll. of Saint Elizabeth, 2000. Behavoirist, tchr. Nat. Acad. for Child Devel., Mountain Lakes, N.J., 1993-95; mental health counselor N.W. Covenant Med. Ctr., Boonton, N.J., 1997-99; clin. therapist The RedCo Group Behavioral Health Svcs., Stroudsburg, Pa., 2000-2001; clin. specialist Newton (N.J.) Meml. Hosp. Sussex House, 2001—; behavior specialist, cons., mobile therapist Youth Advocate Programs, Inc., East Stroudsburg, Pa., 2001—. Adv. bd. for patient satisfaction N.W. Covenant Med. Ctr., 1997; mentor Coll. of Saint Elizabeth, 1999-2000. Vol. Avon Breast Cancer Crusade, N.Y., 1999-2001, Salvation Army, Dover, N.J., 1997-99, The Meth. Manor, Branchville, N.J., 1996—. Mem. ACA (assoc.), Am. Psychol. Assn., N.J. Psychol. Assn. (assoc.), N.J. Counseling Assn. (assoc.), N.J. Mental Health Counselors Assn., Am. Psychol. Soc. Methodist. Avocations: skiing, travel, equestrian, music, hiking.

BOYD, KENNETH ANDREW, music educator; b. Cutchogue, N.Y., Jan. 18, 1975; s. Judith Ann Boyd; m. Jennifer Anne Bangert, June 3, 2000. MusB in Edn., U. of Ctrl. Fla., 1998. Cert. tchr. Fla., 1998. Band dir. Meml. Mid. Sch., Orlando, Fla., 1998—99, U. HS, Orlando, 1999—2002, Olympia HS, Orlando, 2002—. Mem.: Fla. Bandmasters Assn. Office: Olympia High School 4301 S Apopka Vineland Rd Orlando FL 32835 E-mail: boydk@ocps.net.

BOYD, KENNETH R., web programmer, mathematician; b. Nov. 15, 1970; s. Lonnie and Dorothy Boyd. BS in Math., Kans. State U., 1992, MS in Math., 1998. CEO Zaimoni.com, Linn Valley, Kans., 2000—. Scholar, Barry M. Goldwater Found., 1987—89. Mem.: Am. Math. Soc. E-mail: zaimoni@zaimoni.com.

BOYD, LEONA POTTER, retired social worker; b. Creekside, Pa., Aug. 31, 1907; d. Joseph M. and Belle (McHenry) Johnston; m. Edgar D. Potter, July 16, 1932 (div.); m. Harold Lee Boyd, Oct. 1972. Grad., Indiana (Pa.) State Normal Sch, 1927; student, Las Vegas (N.Mex.) Normal U., 1933; student Sch. Social Work, Carnegie Inst. Tech., 1945, U. Pitts., 1956-57. Tchr. Creekside Pub. Schs., 1927-30, Papago Indian Reservation, Sells, Ariz., 1931-33; caseworker, supr. Indiana County (Pa.) Bd. Assistance, 1934-54, exec. dir., 1954-68; ret., 1968. Bd. dirs., hon. life mem. Indiana County Tourist Promotion; former bd. dirs. Indiana County United Fund, Salvation Army, Indiana County Guidance Ctr., Armstrong-Indiana Mental Health Bd.; cons. assoc. Cmty. Rsch. Assocs., Inc.; mem. Counseling Ctr. Aux., Lake Havasu City, Ariz., 1978-80; former mem. Western Welcome Club, Lake Havasu City, Sierra Vista Hosp. Aux., Truth or Consequences, N.M. Recipient Disting. Svc. award Indiana Jaycees, 1965, Bus. and Profl. Women's Club award, 1965. Mem.: AARP, Daus. Am. Colonists. Lutheran. Home: 520 S Higley Rd Unit 126 Mesa AZ 85206-2274

BOYD, LON VERNON, lawyer, alderman; b. Kingsport, Tenn. s. Lon and Maude Elizabeth Boyd; m. Elizabeth Lee Boyd, Dec. 15, 1956. BS, East Tenn. State U., 1951; JD, U. Tenn., 1957. Bar: Tenn. 1957. Ptnr. Boyd, Lauderback & Snodgrass, Kingsport, 1965-80; pvt. practice, Kingsport, 1957-65, 80—; alderman City of Kingsport, 1997—. Judge Sullivan County, Tenn., 1966-86, county exec., 1980-86. Pres. Sullivan County Rep. Com., 1963. With USN, from 1947, 52-54; capt. USNR, until 1982. Named Young Man of Yr., Kingsport Jr. C. of C., 1963. Mem. Tenn. Bar Assn., Kingsport Bar Assn. (pres. 1998-99), VFW, Am. Legion, Kiwanis (pres. 1964). Presbyterian. Home: 3352 Ft Henry Dr Kingsport TN 37664 Office: 154 Cherokee St Kingsport TN 37660-4308

BOYD, LORRAINE ALISON, finance educator; b. St. Stephen, Canada, Sept. 15, 1948; arrived in US, 1995; d. Garnet Allison and Diana Hartley Boyd; m. Ronald Allan Eden (div.); 1 child, Jessica Lynn Eden; m. Charles Frazer Hermann, July 8, 1995. BA with honor in econ., Mount Allison U., Canada, 1970; MA in econ., McGill U., Canada, 1973; PhD with dist. in econ., Dalhousie U., Canada, 1976. Lectr. Mt. St. Vincent U., Dept. of Econ., Halifax, Canada, 1971—74, asst. prof., 1976—80; asst. prof. to assoc. Brock U., Dept. Econ., St. Catharines, 1980—88; assoc. prof. to prof. The Norman Paterson Sch. of Internat. Affairs, Carleton U., Ottawa, 1988—95; vis. prof. Kennedy Sch. Gov., Harvard U., Cambridge, Mass., 1992—93; assoc. prof. Tex. A & M U., Dept. Mgmt., Coll. Station, Tex., 1995—2002; adj. prof. Tex. A&M U., George Bush Sch. of Gov. and Pub. Svc., College Station, Tex., 1997—; prof. Tex. A&M Dept. of Mgmt., College Station, 2002—; adj. rsch. prof. Carleton U., Norman Paterson Sch. of Internat. Affairs, Ottawa, Canada, 1995—2003; vis. prof. U. Tex., Dept. Mgmt., Austin, Tex., 2004—05. Exec. tng. Canada Customs and Revenue Agency, Ottawa, Canada, 1990—; cons. Industry Canada, Ottawa, Canada, 1990—, Bur. of Labor Statistics, US Dept. of Labor, Wash., DC, 1999—; owner, tax transfer pricing cons. firm Eden Cons., Ottawa, Canada, 1988—95, Coll. Station, Tex., 1995—. Co-editor: Multinationals and Transfer Pricing, 1985; editor: Retrospectives on Public Finance, 1991; contbr. articles various profl. jours.; co-editor: Multinationals in the Global Political Economy, 1993; editor: Multinationals in North America, 1994; author: Taxing Mutnationals: Transfer Pricing and Corporate Income Taxation in North America, 1998; co-editor: Growth, Multinationals and Governance, 2005. Founder, pres. Canadian Women Economists Network, 1991; co-founder, sec. Active Learning in Internat. Affairs, 1995; founder, pres. Women in the Acad. of Internat. Bus., 2001. Recipient Gov. General's medal, Gov. Canada, 1966; Doctoral fellowship, Canada Coun., 1974, Killam Found., 1974, Rsch. grant, Social Scis. and Humanities Rsch. Coun., 1984, 1987, Faculty fellowship, Pew Found., 1991, Rsch. grant, Social Scis. and Humanities Rsch. Coun. of Canada, 1991, Canada-US Fulbright Rsch. fellowship, Found. for Edl. Exchange between Canada and The USA, 1992, various other fellowships. Mem.: Internat. Studies Assn., Acad. of Mgmt., Acad. of Internat. Bus., Am. Econ. Assn., Canadian Econ. Assn., Internat. Inst. of Pub. Fin. Office: Tex A&M U Dept Mgmt Tamu 4221 423B Webner Bldg College Station TX 77843-4221 Office Phone: 979-862-4053. E-mail: leden@tamu.edu.

BOYD, MALCOLM, minister, writer; b. Buffalo, June 8, 1923; s. Melville and Beatrice (Lowrie) B.; life ptnr. Mark Thompson. BA, U. Ariz., 1944; B.D., Ch. Div. Sch. Pacific, 1954; postgrad., Oxford (Eng.) U., 1955; S.T.M., Union Theol. Sem., N.Y.C., 1956; DD (hon.), Ch. Div. Sch. of Pacific, 1995. Ordained to ministry Episcopal Ch., 1955. V.p., gen. mgr. Pickford, Rogers & Boyd, 1949-51; rector in Indpls., 1957-59; chaplain Colo. State U., 1959-61, Wayne State U., 1961-65; nat. field rep. Episcopal Soc. Cultural and Racial Unity, 1965-68; resident fellow Calhoun Coll., Yale U., 1968-71, assoc. fellow, 1971—; writer-priest in residence St. Augustine-by-the Sea Episcopal Ch., 1982-95. Lectr. World Council Chs., Switzerland, 1955, 64; columnist Pitts. Courier, 1962-65; resident guest Mishkenot Sha'ananim, Jerusalem, 1974; chaplain AIDS Commn. Episcopal Diocese L.A., 1989—; poet-in-residence Cathedral Ctr. of St. Paul, L.A., 1996—, hon. canon, 2002. Host (TV) Sex in the Seventies, LA, 1975; author: Crisis in Communication, 1957, Christ and Celebrity Gods, 1958, Focus, 1960, rev. edit., 2001, If I Go Down to Hell, 1962, The Hunger, The Thirst, 1964, Are You Running with Me, Jesus?, 1965, rev. edit., 1990, Free to Live, Free to Die, 1967, Book of Days, 1968, As I Live and Breathe: Stages of an Autobiography, 1969, The Fantasy Worlds of Peter Stone, 1969, My Fellow Americans, 1970, Human Like Me, Jesus, 1971, The Lover, 1972, When in the Course of Human Events, 1973, The Runner, 1974, The Alleluia Affair, 1975, Christian, 1975, Am I Running with You, God?, 1977, Take Off the Masks, 1978, rev. edit. 1993, Look Back in Joy, 1981, rev. edit., 1990, Half Laughing, Half Crying, 1986, Gay Priest: An Inner Journey, 1986, Edges, Boundaries and Connections, 1992, Rich with Years, 1993, Go Gentle Into That Good Night, 1998, Running with Jesus: The Prayers of Malcolm Boyd, 2000, Simple Grace: A Mentor's Guide to Growing Older, 2001, Prayers for the Later Years, 2002; plays Boy, 1961, Study in Color, 1962, The Community, 1964, others; editor: On the Battle Lines, 1964, The Underground Church, 1968, (with Nancy L. Wilson) Amazing Grace: Stories of Gay and Lesbian Faith, 1991; (with Chester Talton) Race and Prayer: Collected Voices, Many Dreams, 2003, (with J. Jon Bruno) In Times Like Thers--How We Pray, 2005; book reviewer: LA Times, 1979-85; contbg. editor Episcopal News; columnist Modern Maturity, 1990-2000; contbr. articles to popular mags. including Newsday, Parade, The Advocate, also newspapers. Active voter registration, Miss., Ala., 1963, 64; mem. Los Angeles City/County AIDS Task Force Malcolm Boyd Collection and Archives established Boston U., 1973; recipient Integrity Internat. award, 1978, Union Am. Hebrew Congregations award, 1980, Lazarus Project award, 2002, Louie Crew award for svc. to gay and lesbian people, 2003, Giants of Justice award Clergy and Laity United for Econ. Justice, 2004, Unitas award, Union Theol. Sem., NYC., 2005. Mem. Nat. Council Chs. (film awards com. 1965), P.E.N. (pres. PEN Ctr. U.S. West 1984-87), Am. Center, Authors Guild, Integrity, Nat. Gay Task Force, Clergy and Laity Concerned (nat. bd.), NAACP, Amnesty Internat., Episc. Peace Fellowship, Fellowship of Reconciliation (nat. com.). Episcopalian. Office: PO Box 512164 Los Angeles CA 90051-0164 Office Phone: 213-482-2040. E-mail: malcolmboyd@ladiocese.org. *The years have taught me the cost of getting involved in life. It is all a risk. One is on stage in an ever-new set without a script. The floor may give way without warning, the walls abruptly cave in. One may die at the hand of an assassin acting on blind impulse. Security, for which men sell their souls, is one of the few real jests in life. Yet the cost of not getting involved in life is higher; one has merely died prematurely. When one has stripped power of its mystique, its robes and artifices, it becomes vulnerable. When you stand up to power, you stand up to one or more individuals. Look an individual, then, in the eye, laugh, if you feel like it. This may be rightly received as a much-needed expression of human solidarity.*

BOYD, PEGGY JANE, elementary school educator; b. Arab, Ala., Apr. 4, 1950; d. Harvey H. and Adelee M. Easterwood; m. John E. Boyd, Jan. 11, 1986; children: Larry Wayne Turner Jr., Amy P. Turner. Degree in mental health tech., John C. Calhoun; BS in elem. edn., Judson Coll. Tchr. Brantley Elem., Selma, Ala., Union Grove Elem., Union Grove, Ala. Bapt. Home: 268 Country Rd 1835 Union Grove AL 35175-8469 Office: Union Grove Elem Sch 3685 Union Grove Rd Union Grove AL 35175-8469 Office Phone: 256-753-2436.

BOYD, RALPH F., JR., finance company executive, former federal agency administrator; b. Schenectady, NY, Feb. 7, 1957; BA, Haverford Coll., 1979; JD, Harvard U., 1984; LLD (hon.), Suffolk U., 2001. Law clk. Hon. Joseph H. Young U.S. Dist. Ct. Md.; assoc. Ropes & Gray, Boston, 1987—91; asst. U.S. atty. major crimes unit U.S. Attys. Office, 1992—98; ptnr. Goodwin Procter LLP, 1998—2001; asst. atty. Gen. Civil Rights Divsn. U.S. Dept. Justice, Washington, 2001—03; sr. ptnr. Alston & Bird LLP, 2003—04; exec. v.p., gen. counsel Fed. Home Loan Mortgage Corp. (Freddie Mac), McLean, Va., 2004—05, exec. v.p. community rels., 2005—; chmn. Freddie Mac Found., 2005—. Mem. exec. com. Mass. Jud. Nominating Commn., 1996—2001; mem. U.S. Magistrate Judge Selection and Rev. Panel, 1998. Office: Freddie Mac 8200 Jones Branch Dr Mc Lean VA 22102-3110

BOYD, THEOPHILUS BARTHOLOMEW, III, publishing company executive; b. Nashville, May 15, 1947; s. Theophilus B. Jr. and Mable (Landrum) B.; m. Yvette Jean Duke, May 5, 1984; children: Theophilus B. IV, LaDonna Yvette, Shalae Shantel, Justin Marriel. BS, Tenn. State U., 1969; DD, Shreveport Bible Coll., 1980; LittD (hon.), Easonian Bapt. Sem., 1983. Pers. dir. R.H. Boyd Pub. Corp., Nashville, 1969-79; pres., chief exec. officer, 1979—. Chmn. Citizens Bank, Nashville, 1982—. Vice chair Meharry Med. Coll. bd. trustees, Nashville, 1989—; trustee Fla. Meml. Coll., Miami, 1984-86; bd. dirs. Nashville Symphone Assn., 1986-87, Nashville chpt. March of Dimes, 1986—; past pres. 100 Black Men of Mid. Tenn.; v.p. fin., treas. 100 Black Men Am., 1992-94; head R.H. Boyd initiative United Way. Named Hon. Citizen, City of Dallas, 1980, Man of Yr., 1990; recipient Key to the City, Denver, 1985, New Orleans, 1986, Great Seal of U.S. award; named man of the yr. 1990 March of Dimes. Mem. Nashville Area C. of C. (exec. bd.), Kappa Alpha Psi, Sigma Pi Phi, Richland Country Club. Democrat. Baptist. Avocations: boating, marathon running. Office: RH Boyd Publishing Corp 6717 Centennial Blvd Nashville TN 37209-1017

BOYD, THOMAS MARSHALL, lawyer; b. Yorktown, Va., Sept. 10, 1946; s. Laurel Barnett and Mildred Warner Wellford (Marshall) B.; m. Torri Carol Tyler, Oct. 2, 1976; children: Brooke Warner, Tyler Randolph. BA in History, Va. Military Inst., 1968; JD, U. Va., 1971. Bar: Calif. 1973, D.C. 1974. Law clk. to Hon. A. Andrew Hauk U.S. Dist. Ct. (cen. dist.) Calif., Los Angeles, 1973-74; trial atty., atty. advisor U.S. Dept. Justice, Washington, 1974-76; assoc. counsel com. on judiciary U.S. Ho. of Reps., Washington, 1976-86; dep. asst. atty. gen. Dept. Justice Office Legis. Affairs, Washington, 1986-88, asst. atty. gen., 1988-89, dir. office policy devel., 1989-91; dep. gen. counsel Kemper Corp., Washington, 1991-93, v.p. and legis. counsel, 1993-96; v.p. for legis. affairs Investment Co. Inst., Washington, 1996-98; ptnr. Ramsey, Cook, Looper & Kurlander LLP, Washington, 1998-99, Alston & Bird, LLP, Washington, 1999—. House counsel Presdl. Transition Com. on Criminal Justice, Washington, 1980-81; pub. mem. Adminstrv. Conf. U.S., 1992-95. Co-editor U.S. Atty.'s Criminal Trial Manual, 1971; contbr. articles to profl. jours. and pub. interest articles to newspapers. Served to capt. USAF, 1968-73. Recipient Nat. Media award Delta Soc., 1985, Edmund J. Randolph award, 1988. Mem. U.S. Supreme Ct. Bar Assn., Calif. Bar Assn., D.C. Bar Assn., Army-Navy Country Club, Leland (Mich.) Country Club, Golf Club of Va. Republican. Episcopalian. Avocations: golf, jogging, writing. Office: Alston & Byrd LLP 10th Fl North Bldg 601 Pennsylvania Ave Washington DC 20004-2601 Office Phone: 202-756-3372. Business E-Mail: tboyd@alston.com.

BOYD, WILLARD LEE, academic administrator, educator, lawyer, museum director; b. St. Paul, Mar. 29, 1927; s. Willard Lee and Frances L. (Collins) Boyd; m. Susan Kuehn, Aug. 28, 1954; children: Elizabeth Kuehn, Willard Lee, Thomas Henry. BS in Law, U. Minn., 1949, LLB, 1951; LLM, U. Mich., 1952, SJD, 1962. Bar: Minn. 1951, Iowa 1958. Assoc. Dorsey & Whitney, Mpls., 1952—54; from instr. to prof. law U. Iowa, Iowa City, 1954—64, assoc. dean Law Sch., 1964, v.p. acad. affairs, 1964—69, pres., 1969—81, 2002—03, pres. emeritus, 1981—; pres. The Field Mus., Chgo., 1981—96, pres. emeritus, 1996—. Chmn. Nat. Mus. Scis. Bd., 1988—96; chair bd. dirs. Harry S Truman Libr. Inst., 1997—2001; past adv. bd. Met. Opera, Ill. Humanities Coun., Ill. Arts Coun., Chgo. Cultural Affairs Bd.; bd. dir. Nat. Arts Strategies; past pres. Nat. Com. Accrediting; past mem. adv. com. Getty Ctr. Edn. in Arts; past mem. Nat. Coun. Arts, Ill. Arts Alliance; past chmn. Am. Assn. Univs. Recipient Charles Frankel prize, Nat. Endowment for Humanities, 1989. Mem.: ABA (com. social labor and indsl. legislations 1963—65, chmn. 1965—66, coun. mem. 1975—82, mem. sect. legal edn. and admission to bar chmn. 1980—81, chmn. coun. of sect. on legal edn. and admission), Am. Assn. Univs. (past chmn.), Am. Acad. Arts and Sci., Am. Law Inst., Iowa Bar Assn. Home: 620 River St Iowa City IA 52246-2433 Office: Univ Iowa Law Sch Iowa City IA 52242-1113 Office Phone: 319-335-9004. Business E-Mail: willard-boyd@uiowa.edu.

BOYD, WILLIAM S., hotel and entertainment facility executive; s. Sam A. and Mary Boyd; 3 children. JD, Univ. Nev., Las Vegas. Pvt. practice law, 1960—75; co-founder Boyd Gaming Corp., Las Vegas, 1973, now chmn., CEO. Mem.: Am. Gaming Assn. (vice chmn.). Office: Boyd Gaming Corp 2950 Industrial Rd Las Vegas NV 89109-1150 Office Phone: 702-792-7200. Office Fax: 702-792-7313.*

BOYD, WILLIAM SPROTT, lawyer; b. San Francisco, Feb. 12, 1943; s. R. Mitchell S. and Mary (Mitchell) B.; children: Mitchell Sagar, Sterling McMicking. AB, Stanford U., 1964, JD, 1971. Bar: Calif. 1972, U.S. Dist. Ct. (no. dist.) 1972, U.S. Ct. Appeals (9th cir.) 1972, U.S. Dist. Ct. (cen. dist.) Calif. 1974, U.S. Dist. Ct. (ea. dist.) Calif. 1976. Assoc. Brobeck, Phleger & Harrison, San Francisco, 1971-77, ptnr., 1977—, of counsel. Mem. Lawyers Com for Urban Affairs, San Francisco, 1979—; bd. dirs. San Francisco Legal Aid Soc., 1980-85. Lt. USNR, 1965-68, Vietnam. Mem. ABA, Calif. Bar Assn., San Francisco Bar Assn.

BOYDA, DEBORA, advertising executive; Sr. ptnr., acct. mgr. Tatham Euro RSCG, Chgo., mng. ptnr., 1997-99; v.p., acct. dir. Leo Burnett, Chgo., 1999-2000, sr. v.p., 2000—.

BOYDSTON, JAMES CHRISTOPHER, composer; b. Denver, July 21, 1947; s. James Virgal and Mary June (Wiseman) B.; m. Ann Louise Bryant, Aug. 20, 1975. BA in Philosophy, U. Tex., 1971. Lutenist and guitarist Collegium Musicum, U. Tex., Austin, 1968-70; tchr. classical guitar Extension div. The New Eng. Conservatory of Music, Boston, 1972-73. Arranger music: S. Joplins, "The Entertainer," 1976; arranger/composer/performer cassette recording: Wedding Music for Classical Guitar, 1988; composer music: International Portraits for Classical Guitar, 1999, Baroque Suites 1-4, 2003; composer/performer/CD recording: Morsels for Classical Guitar, 2005; inventor classical guitar bridge-saddle, 1990; author original poetry included in: The World of Poetry Anthology, 1991. Avocations: astronomy, reading, building clavichords, camping. Home: 4433 Driftwood Pl Boulder CO 80301-3104

BOYDSTUN, J. HERBERT, bank executive; Pres., CEO, dir. Hibernia Corp., Hibernia Nat. Bank. Office: Hibernia Corp 313 Carondelet St New Orleans LA 70130 Office Phone: 504-533-3333. Office Fax: 504-533-2466.*

BOYE, ROGER CARL, academic administrator, journalism educator; b. Lincoln, Nebr., Feb. 8, 1948; s. Arthur J. and Matilda J. (Danca) B. BA with distinction, U. Nebr., 1970; MS in Journalism with highest distinction, Northwestern U., 1971. News editor The Quill, Chgo., 1971-73; instr. Medill Sch. Journalism, Northwestern U., Evanston, Ill., 1973-76; vis. prof. journalism Niagara U., Niagara Falls, N.Y., 1976-78; gen. mgr. The Quill, 1980-84, bus. mgr., 1984-86; asst. dean, asst. prof. Medill sch. journalism Northwestern U., 1986-92, asst. dean, assoc. prof., 1992—2004, assoc. prof., 2004—05, assoc. prof. emeritus, 2005—. Judge various journalism awards and contests, 1970s—; master comm. residential coll. Northwestern U., 1989—96, 2004—. Weekly columnist Chgo. Tribune, 1974-93; contbr. Ency. Britannica Book of the Yr. and the Compton Yearbook, 1982-99; contbg. editor The Numismatist, 2001--. Recipient Maurice M. Gould award Numismatic Lit. Guild, 1981, 92. Mem. Phi Beta Kappa, Kappa Tau Alpha. Office: Northwestern Univ Medill Sch Journalism 1845 Sheridan Rd Evanston IL 60208-0815 Office Phone: 847-491-2069. Business E-Mail: r-boye@northwestern.edu.

BOYEN, MARIAN DE See HOUTZAGER, MARIANNE

BOYER, ALBERT BRUCE, optometrist, educator; b. St. George, Utah, Feb. 9, 1954; s. Albert Cleo and Venice Vay Boyer. AS, Dixie Coll., 1977; OD, So. Calif. Coll. Optometry, 1985, BS, 1995; PhD, MS, LaSalle U., 1996. Lic. optometrist Utah, Nev., Calif., Va., contact lens certification Nat. Eye Rsch. Found. Staff dr., surg. asst. Ophthalmologist Kern & Assoc., Huntington Beach, Calif., 1986—87; staff dr. Lenscrafters 2000, Bakersfield, Calif., 1987—88; pvt. practice Reno, 1988—90; staff dr. Keller & Assocs., Las Vegas, 1990—99; prof. LaSalle U., Las Vegas, 1997—2002; CEO, pres. Vision Care 20/20, Las Vegas, 1999—. Contbr. articles to profl. jours. Served with U.S. Army, 1972—83. Recipient Top Optometrist award, Am.'s Top Optometrists Guide, 2002, Nat. Leadership award, Nat. Rep. Congress, 2003. Fellow: Am. Acad. Optometry; mem.: Am. Optometric Assn. (Optometric Recognition awards 1988—), Omicron Psi, Golden Key. Republican. Mem. Lds Ch. Achievements include new objective glaucoma testing with electro-oculagram; research in electro-oculography. Avocations: mountain hiking, restoring classic cars. Office: Vision Care 20/20 1550 N Main North Logan UT 84341 Office Phone: 435-753-3906. E-mail: albertbboyer@netscape.com.

BOYER, CARL, III, not-for-profit developer, retired mayor, municipal official, secondary school educator; b. Phila., Pa., Sept. 22, 1937; s. Carl Boyer Jr. and Elizabeth Campbell Timm; m. Ada Christine Kruse, July 28, 1962. Student, U. Edinburgh, Scotland, 1956-57; BA, Trinity U., 1959; MEd in Secondary Edn., U. Cin., 1962; postgrad., Calif. State U., Northridge, 1964-72. Tchr. Edgewood High Sch., San Antonio, Tex., 1959-60; libr. U. Cin., Cincinnati, Ohio, 1960-61; tchr. Eighth Avenue Elem. Sch., Dayton, Ky., 1961-62, Amelia High Sch., Amelia, Ohio, 1962-63; instr. Kennedy San Fernando Comm. Adult Sch., San Fernando, Calif., 1964-74, Mission Coll., San Fernando, 1971; tchr. San Fernando High Sch., San Fernando, Calif., 1963-98. Faculty chmn. San Fernando High Sch., dept. chmn.; cons. Sofia (Bulgaria) City Coun., 1991, Bandung Regency, Indonesia, 2003; key spkr. World Mayors' Conf., Jaipur, India, 1998. Author, compiler 23 books on genealogy and family history; contbr. articles to profl. jours. Councilman City of Santa Clarita, Calif., 1987-98, mayor pro tem, 1989-90, 94-95, mayor, 1990-91, 95-96; mem. Nat. League Cities Internat. Mcpl. Consortium, 1992-98; mem. revenue and taxation com. League Calif. Cities, 1992-95; sec. Calif. Contract Cities Assn., 1992-93; trustee Santa Clarita C.C. Dist., 1973-81, pres., 1979-81; bd. dirs. Castaic Lake Water Agy., 1982-84, pres. Newhall-Saugus-Valencia Fedn. Homeowners Assn., 1969-70, 71-72; pres. Del Prado Condo. Assn., Inc., Newhall, Calif.; exec. v.p. Canyon County Formation Com.; chmn. Santa Clarita City Formation Com., 1987; pres. Santa Clarita Valley Internat. Program, 1991-97, 2004—; treas. Healing the Children Calif., 1994-96, pres., 1996-99, 2003—, nat. pres., 1999-2000, vol. med. mission adminstr., 2000—. Mem. New Eng. Hist. Geneal. Soc. Republican. Methodist. Avocations: travel, photography. Home: PO Box 220333 Santa Clarita CA 91322-0333

BOYER, CAROLYN MERWIN, school psychologist; b. New Haven, Conn., Oct. 4, 1936; d. Richard Treat Merwin and Elsie Mae (Donaldson) Schuyler; m. Kenneth Sutton Boyer, Aug. 19, 1961; 1 child, Kenneth Merwin. BA in Spanish, Bucknell U., 1958; MS, So. Conn. State U., 1998. Nat. cert. sch. psychologist Milford Bd. Edn. Claims approver Equitable Life Assurance, NYC, 1961—63; libr. asst. Milford Pub. Libr., Conn., 1973—74; archtl. reporter Dodge/McGraw Hill, 1974—84; sec. Milford Bd. Edn., 1984—92, sch. psychologist, 1992—2003; ret. Reporter neighborhood news Milford Citizen, 1973—76. Exhibitions include Firehouse Art Gallery, Milford, 2004—05. Mem. diaconate bd. 1st Ch. Christ, 1980—83, 1999—2002; bd. dirs. Miles Merwin Assn., Milford, 1974—75; bd. dirs., membership chair Nat. Assn. Women Constrn., 1975—78. Mem.: Nat. Assn. Sch. Psychologists, Conn. Assn. Sch. Psychologists. Republican. Avocations: gourmet cooking, tennis, reading, walking, birdwatching. Home: 11 Anderson Ave Milford CT 06460

BOYER, DANIEL CHRISTOPHER, artist, writer, photographer; b. Hancock, Mich., Nov. 2, 1971; s. Hugh Eisenhart and Gretchen Elizabeth (Glazier) Boyer. BA, Curry Coll., Milton, Mass., 1997; Diploma, Moscow State Exhbn. Hall, 2002. Mem. editl. bd. The CTYer; Ctr. for Talented Youth Alumni Mag., Balt., 1994—96; CEO Internat. Union of Mail Artists, Tilburg, Netherlands, 2002—; curator Omphele Gallery, Calument, Mich., 2003—. Artist in residence Marquette Arts and Culture Ctr., Mich., 2003. Author: The Octopus Frets: Polit. Poems, 1994, The Tailgating Spinster, 2003; illustration in All the Days After: Critical Voices in Poetry and Artwork, 2003, contbg. author Trattato di Anatomia Patafisica, 2003, Surrealist Subversions: Rants, Images and Writings by the Surrealist Movement in the United States, 2002; one-man shows include Marquette Arts and Culture Ctr., 2004, Galerie Gora, Montreal, Can., 2001, Kerredge Gallery, Hancock, Mich., 2001, Turquoise Art Gallery, 2003, World Fine Art, N.Y., 2000, SAI Gallery Alexie, 1999, The Internet Bagel Cafe, Marquette, Mich., 1999; contbr. articles to periodicals, illustrations to newspapers and periodicals; designer covers for compact discs. Named an Hon. Alumnus, Johns Hopkins U., Balt.; recipient diploma of Excellence, 7th Internat. Ann. of Miniature Art, Art Addiction Gallery, Stockholm, Sweden, 2002. Office Phone: 906-482-4823. Personal E-mail: danielcboyer@hotmail.com.

BOYER, FORD SYLVESTER, relationship consultant, minister; b. Cadet, Mo., Jan. 12, 1934; s. Wilford Robert and Mary Elizabeth (DeClue) B.; m. Juelle-Ann Rupkalvis, May 2, 1970. BA in Psychology, USAF Inst., 1957; DD, Am. Bible Inst., Kansas City, Mo., 1977; MA, John F. Kennedy U., 1994. Ordained to ministry Servants of Christ Jesus Cath. Ch., 1979; cert. alcohol specialist. Adminstr. Getz Bros., San Francisco, 1969-73; supr. word processing U.S. Leasing Corp., San Francisco, 1977-82, dir. tng. and applications-word processing, 1982-84; computer cons Petaluma, Calif., 1984-87; massage therapist, 1985-87; pvt. practice hypnotherapy Alameda, Calif., 1987—; cons. for chem. dependency, 1987—. Contbr. articles to profl. publs.; writer, pub.: (newsletter) Starfire, 1988—; participant (TV show) Right Human Relations, San Francisco. Vol. min. Pathways Hospice, Oakland, Calif. With USAF, 1953-57, Korea. Mem. Am Coun. Hypnotist Examiners, Nat. Assn. Alcohol and Drug Abuse Counselors, Calif. Assn. Alcohol and Drug Abuse Counselors, Calif. Assn. Alcohol Recovery Homes. Avocations: writing, volunteering, music, esotericism. Home and Office: 1028 Island Dr Alameda CA 94502-6932 E-mail: fo4rd@home.com.

BOYER, HERBERT WAYNE, retired biochemist; b. Pitts., July 10, 1936; m. Grace Boyer, 1959. BA, St. Vincent Coll., Latrobe, Pa., 1958, DSc (hon.) (hon.), 1981; MS, U. Pitts., 1960, PhD, 1963. Mem. faculty U. Calif., San Francisco, 1966—, prof. biochemistry, 1976—91, prof. emeritus, 1991—. Co-founder, dir. Genentech, Inc., South San Francisco, Calif. Recipient V.D. Mattai award, Roche Inst., 1977, Albert and Mary Lasker award for basic med. research, 1980, Golden Plate award, Am. Acad. Achievement, 1981, Moet Hennessy-Louis Vuitton prize, 1988, Jerome H. Lemelson-MIT prize for excellence in invention and innovation, 1996, Nat. Tech. medal, 1989, Nat. Sci. medal, NSF, 1990. Fellow: AAAS; mem.: NAS, Am. Soc. Biol. Chemists, Am. Acad. Arts and Scis. Achievements include obtaining, with Stanley N. Cohen, first patent in the field of recombinant deoxyribonucleic acid (DNA), 1980.

BOYER, JAMES LORENZEN, internist, educator; b. NYC, Aug. 28, 1936; s. Ralph R. and Alice M. B.; m. Phoebe Bennet, Feb. 23, 1963; children: Phoebe Christine, Anna Birch. AB, Haverford (Pa.) Coll., 1958; MD, Johns Hopkins U., 1962. Diplomate: Am. Bd. Internal Medicine. Med. intern N.Y. Hosp., N.Y.C., 1962-63, resident in medicine, 1963-64, Yale-New Haven Hosp., 1966; postdoctoral fellow liver study unit Yale U., 1966-68; mem. faculty U. Chgo. Pritzker Sch. Medicine, 1972-78, prof. medicine, 1976-78, dir. liver study unit, 1972-78; prof. medicine, dir. liver study unit, chief divsn. digestive diseases Yale U. Med. Sch., 1978-96; dir. Yale Liver Ctr., 1984—, Ensign prof. of medicine, 1996—. Treas., bd. dirs. Am. Liver Found., 1976-85, chair Sci. Adv. Com., 2003-04, chmn. bd. dirs., 2004—; dep. chmn. Nat. Digestive Disease Adv. Bd., 1981-84; coun. mem. NIDDK, 1985-90. Contbr. articles to profl. jours. Chmn. bd. trustees Mt. Desert Island Biol. Lab., Salsbury Cove, Maine, 1995-2003. Lt. comdr. USPHS, 1964-66. Josiah Macey faculty scholar, 1976 Mem. Am. Assn. Study Liver Disease (pres. 1980), Am. Fedn. Clin. Rsch., ACP, Am. Gastroenterol. Assn. (councillor 1983-86), Internat. Assn. Study Liver Diseases (v.p. 1982-84, pres.-elect 1986-88, pres. 1988-90), Am. Soc. Clin. Investigation, Assn. Am. Physicians, Soc. Clin. Rsch., Am. Clin. and Climatolgic Assn. Office: Yale U Sch of Medicine 333 Cedar St New Haven CT 06510-3289

BOYER, JEFFREY N., former retail executive; BS in Fin. (hons.), U. Ill., 1980. cert. CPA., 1980. Sr. fin. mgmt. Pillsbury Co.; v.p. fin., v.p. fin. planning Kraft Foods, 1989-95; v.p. bus. devel. Diageo PLC, 1995-96; v.p. fin. Sears, 1996-98, v.p., controller, 1998-99, CFO, 1999—2001; exec. v.p., CFO Kmart Corp., Ft. Wayne, Ind., 2001.

BOYER, JOHN WILLIAM, history professor, dean; b. Chgo., Oct. 17, 1946; s. William Dana and Mary Frances (Corbley) B.; m. Barbara Alice Juskevich, Aug. 24, 1968; children: Dominic, Alexandra, Victoria. BA, Loyola U., 1968; MA, U. Chgo., 1969, PhD, 1975. From asst. prof. to assoc. prof. U. Chgo., 1975-85, prof., 1985—, Martin A. Ryerson Disting. Svc. prof., 1996—, acting dean divsn. social scis., 1992-93, dean of the coll., 1992—. Author: Political Radicalism in Late Imperial Vienna, 1981, Culture and Political Crisis in Vienna, 1995, Three Views of Continuity and Change at the University of Chicago, 1999; editor: Jour. of Modern History. Capt. USAR, 1968-80. Recipient Theodor Körner prize Theodor Körner Found., 1978, John Gilmary Shea prize Am. Cath. Hist. Assn., 1982, Ludwig Jedlicka Meml. prize Kuratorium des Ludwig-Jedlicka-Gedächtnispreises, 1996, Austrian Cross Hon. Sci. and Art, First Class, 2004; Alexander von Humboldt fellow, 1980-81. Mem. Am. Hist. Assn., Austrian Acad. Scis. (corr.). Roman Catholic. Avocation: cooking. Home: 1428 E 57th St Chicago IL 60637-1838 Office: U Chgo 1126 E 59th St Chicago IL 60637-1580 also: U Chgo Press Jour Divsn 5720 S Woodlawn Ave Chicago IL 60637-1603 Office Phone: 773-702-8576. E-mail: jwboyer@uchicago.edu.

BOYER, KAYE KITTLE, association management executive; b. Peoria, Ill., July 5, 1942; d. Keith Howard and Evelyn Pearl (Benson) Kittle; m. Jon Frederick Boyer, Mar. 20, 1965; children: Tristan Boyer Binns, Kristine Monique Hitchens. Student, Merrill Palmer Inst., Detroit, 1964; BS in Home Econs., Pa. State U., University Park, 1964; MA in Sociology, Rutgers State U., New Brunswick, 1967. Cert. assn. exec.; cert. in family and consumer scis. Creative rschr. Nat. Inst. Drycleaning, Silver Spring, Md., 1963; extension home economist Md. Coop. Extension Svc., Westminster, 1964-65; coord. human resources N.J. Coop. Extension Svc., New Brunswick, 1966-67; instr. Douglass Coll., Rutgers U., New Brunswick, 1967-70; coord., instr. pilot project Urban Coalition of Met. Wilmington (Del.) Inc., 1972; asst. to chmn. 4-H Youth Devel. Dept., Cook Coll., 1973-74; feasibility study dir. Ocean County Coll., Toms River, N.J., 1975; exec. dir. N.J. Home Economics Assn., Manalapan, 1975-86; pres. Boyer Mgmt. Svcs., Manalapan, N.J., Earleville, Md., 1984—, Palm Coast, Fla., 1984—. Mgr. Costume Soc. Am., Palm Coast, Fla., 1984—; cons. Plumpton Pk. Zool. Gardens Rising Sun, 1988-89, bd. dirs., 1990-92; cons. N.J. White House Conf., Trenton, 1980, Baltimore County Med. Assn., 1995-96, Md. Acad. Family Physicians, 1994, 97, Textile Soc. Am., 1998—; adv. com. Dept. Cmty. Edn. Rutgers U., 1979-84 Editor Exchs. Newsletter; resource dir., N.J. Programs and Svcs. Related to Adolescent Pregnancy. Vol. Soroptomist Internat. of Elkton, Md., 1987-94; bd. dirs. Cmty. Libr. of Cecilton, 1986-92; player U.S. Pub. Links Amateur, 1986; trustee Cecil County Bd. Libr. Trustees, 1998-2002. Mem. AAUW (v.p. program devel. N.J. divsn. 1984-86), Am. Assn. Family and Consumer Scis. (cert., Ruth O'Brien project grantee), Am. Soc. Assn. Execs. (cert.), Fla. Soc. Assn. Execs., Profl. Conv. Mgmt. Assn. (edn. and profl. devel. com. 1996-2001, edn. and profl. devel. working com., 2002), Internat. Assn. of Facilitators, Fla. Assn. Family and Consumer Scis., Profl. Conv. Mgmt. Assn. Edn. Found. (transition team product/svc., 2001, design task force 2000, learning ctr. task force 2000-2001, trustee 2000-2003), Penn State Alumni Assn.(chmn. strategic planning Daytona-Palm Coast chpt. 2003—), Kappa Omicron Nu (v.p. fin. 1992-93, chair constn. and bylaws com. 1994-97). Democrat. Avocation: golf. Home and Office: 107 Front St Palm Coast FL 32137

BOYER, LESTER LEROY, JR., architecture educator, consultant; b. Hanover, Pa., Apr. 6, 1937; s. Lester Leroy and Ruth Florence (Kessler) B.; m. Patricia Barbara Hayes, Dec. 28, 1958; children: Douglas Lester, Blane Edward, Darla Mae. B of Archtl. Engring., Pa. State U., 1960, MS in Archtl. Engring, 1964; PhD in Architecture, U. Calif., Berkeley, 1976. Registered profl. engr., Pa. Instr. archtl. engring. Pa. State U., 1960-64; rsch. engr. Armstrong Cork Co., Lancaster, Pa., 1964-68; course dir. Nat. Soc. Profl. Engrs., 1964-74; sr. cons. acoustics and noise control Bolt Beranek and Newman Inc., Cambridge, Mass., 1968-70; faculty Okla. State U., Stillwater, 1970-84, dir. environ. control program, 1970-84, prof. architecture, 1979-84, Tex. A&M U., College Station, 1984—96, chmn. div. design tech. Coll. Arch., 1988-90, prof. emeritus, 1999—. Fulbright scholar U. N.S.W. and U. Queensland, Australia, 1982, Tech. U., Delft, The Netherlands, 1992; dir. daylighting rsch. NSF, 1985-88; vis. researcher Solar Energy Rsch. Inst., Colo., summer 1985; cons. acoustics, environ. comfort and passive energy design, 1970—; dir. earth-sheltered bldg. rsch. Control Data Corp. and U.S. Dept. Energy, 1979-81; chair energy rsch. rev. panel on fenestration Office Energy Rsch., U.S. Dept. Energy, Washington, 1988; gen. chmn. Internat. Conf. Earth Sheltered Bldgs., Sydney, Australia, 1983; tech. chmn. Internat. Conf. Earth Sheltered Bldgs., Mpls., 1986; vis. prof., chair dept. arch. Kuwait U., 1997-98; mem. design team Benham Blair & Affiliates, Oklahoma City. Author: Earth Shelter Technology, 1987; editor: Building Design for Environmental Hazards, 1973, Earth Sheltered Building Design Innovations, 1980, Earth Shelter Performance and Evaluation, 1981, Earth Shelter Protection, 1983, Design in Geotecture, 1986, Proceedings of 5th Internat. Conf. on Underground Space and Earth Sheltered Structures, Tech. Univ. Delft, The Netherlands, 1992; contbg. author Simulating Daylight with Architectural Models, 1987. Recipient 1st Pl. Design award Nat. Energy Design competition Calif. State Office Bldg., Sacramento, 1983. Mem. ASHRAE (nat. daylighting symposium organizer 1988), Am. Solar Energy Soc. (nat. coord. passive earth cooling program 1981), Am. Underground Space Assn. (bd. dirs. 1989-92), Illuminating Engring. Soc. Lutheran. Home: HC 68 Box 19 Fort Garland CO 81133-9702 E-mail: llb@fone.net.

BOYER, LISA, basketball coach; Degree, Ithaca Coll., 1979. Asst. coach Davidson Coll., 1980-82, East Carolina, 1983-84, Miami of Ohio, 1984-95, Va. Tech., 1985-86; coach Bradley Univ., 1986-96, Phila. Rage. Named Gateway Conf. Coach of Yr., 1990.

BOYER, NAOMI ROSE, education educator, director; b. Miami, Fla., Dec. 21, 1966; d. Daniel Lee and Diane Widlan Miller; m. Gary Michael Miller, Feb. 17, 1990; children: Morgan Sara, Taryn Rose. PhD, U. South Fla., Tampa, 2001. Spl. edn. tchr. Collier County Schs., Naples, Fla., 1989—90, LA Unified Sch. Dist., L.A., Calif., 1990—91, Morongo County Sch. Dist., Joshua Tree, Calif., 1991—92; dir. of distance edn. U. South Fla.-Lakeland, Lakeland, Fla., 2001—. Contbr. articles pub. to profl. jour. Mem.: Internat. Soc. for Tech. in Edn., Assn. for Ednl. Communication Technologies, Internat. Sel-Directed Learning Symposium (chair-conference planning com. 2002—05), Am. Ednl. Rsch. Assn., Phi Kappa Phi. Democrat-Npl. Jewish. Achievements include research in Devel. of model of sSocial, self-directed learning for online enviorn. Home: 225 Foggy Creek Rd Davenport FL 33837 Office: Univ South Fla- Lakeland 3433 Winter Lake Rd Lakeland FL 33837 Office Phone: 863-667-7022. Office Fax: 863-667-7098. Personal E-mail: nboyer@lklnd.usf.edu.

BOYER, PATRICIA W., publishing executive, editor; b. Weaverville, N.C., Oct. 12, 1925; d. William Malcolm and Katherine Lotspeich Waters; m. Clyde M. Boyer, June 28, 1946 (dec. Aug. 10, 1997); children: John Gregory, Abigail, Judd Meredith, Clyde Merrill. Co-owner Boyer Ranch, Calif., 1963—97; CEO Got Solar, Inc., Oreg., 2001—; CFO H2Nation Pub. Inc., Brookings, Oreg., 2003—, Nev., 2003—; editor H2Nation Mag., Nev., 2003—. Bd. dirs. H2Nation Pub., Inc., Sparks, Nev., 2003—, Got Solar, Inc., Oreg., 2000—. Author: The Last Free Chief of the Modoc Nation: An Allegory, 2001. Mem.: Women Writing the West, Nat. Mus. of the Am. Indian at the Smithsonian, Toastmasters Internat. Avocations: music, poetry, gardening, writing, history. Office: H2Nation Publishing Inc PO Box 52080 Sparks NV 89435 Office Phone: 775-356-8411. Business E-Mail: pat@h2nation.com.

BOYER, PAUL D., biochemist, educator; b. Provo, Utah, July 31, 1918; s. Dell Delos and Grace (Guymon) Boyer; m. Lyda Mae Whicker, Aug. 31, 1939. BS, Brigham Young U., 1939; MS, U. Wis., 1941, PhD in Biochemistry, 1943; PhD (hon.), U. Stockholm, 1974, U. Minn., 1996, U. Wis., 1998. Asst. rschr. biochemistry U. Wis., 1939—43; Instr., research assoc. Stanford, 1943—45; from asst. prof. to prof. biochemistry U. Minn., 1945—56; Hill research prof. U. Minn. Med. Sch., 1956—63; prof. chemistry UCLA, 1963—89, dir. Molecular Biology Inst., 1965—83, dir. biotech. program, 1985—88, 1985-89, prof. emeritus, 1989—; chmn. biochemistry study sect. USPHS, 1962—67. Mem. U.S. Nat. Com. for Biochemistry, 1965—71. Editor: Ann. Rev. of Biochemistry, 1965—71; assoc. editor:, 1972—88; editor: Biochemical and Biophysical Research Communications, 1969—79, The Enzymes, 1970—; mem. editl. bd.: Biochemistry, 1969—76, Jour. Biol. Chemistry, 1978—83, 1987—; contbr. articles to profl. jours. Co-recipient Nobel prize for chemistry, 1997; recipient McCoy award chem. rsch., 1976, Tolman award, 1984, Rose award, Am. Soc. Chemistry and Molecular Biology, 1989, UCLA medal, 1998; fellow Guggenheim Found., 1955—56. Fellow: AAAS (v.p. biol. scis. 1985—88, council); mem.: NAS, Biophys. Soc., Am. Chem. Soc. (chmn., biochem. divsn. 1959—60, enzyme chemistry award 1955), Am. Soc. Biol. Chemists (pres. 1969—70, council mem.). Home: 1033 Somera Rd Los Angeles CA 90077-2625 Office: Dept Chem-Biochem Paul Boyer Hall 639 607 Charles E Young Dr E Box 951569 Los Angeles CA 90095-0001*

BOYER, ROBERT ALLAN, finance company executive; b. Detroit, Mar. 2, 1934; s. Robert Allan and Elizabeth (Szabo) B.; children: Jennifer, Stephen, Lorna. MBA, Cornell U., 1959. Alfred P. Sloan fellow Cornell U. Grad. Sch., Ithaca, N.Y., 1958, 59; exec. asst. to pres. Merck & Co., Inc., Rahway, N.J., 1962-68; dir. fin. TWA Corp., N.Y.C., 1969-72; nat. dir. fin. Coopers & Lybrand, N.Y.C., 1972-79; exec. dir. Sullivan & Cromwell, N.Y.C., 1979—. Chmn., founder Legal Execs. Group, Law Firm Tech. Group, 1979. Mem. congl. support com.; mem. Pres.'s Club Rep. Party, 1990. Fellow Coll. Law Practice Mgmt.; mem. ABA, Assn. Legal Adminstrs. (exec. com. 1986-87), Aircraft Owners and Pilots Assn., Yorktown Bicentennial Com. (bd. dirs., sec.), Echo Lake Country Club (Westfield, N.J.), Cornell Club (N.Y.), Cornell Club (N.J.), India House (N.Y.C.), N.Y. Acad. Scis. Clubs: Echo Lake Country (Westfield, N.J.). Republican. Presbyterian. E-mail: rboyernyc@aol.com.

BOYER, TYRIE ALVIS, lawyer; b. Williston, Fla., Sept. 10, 1924; s. Alton Gordon and Mary Ethel (Strickland) B.; m. Elizabeth Everett Gale, June 9, 1945; children: Carol, Tyrie, Kennedy, Lee. BA, U. Fla., 1953, LLB, JD, 1954. Bar: Fla. Atty. Crawford, May & Boyer, Jacksonville, Fla., 1954-58, Boyer Law Offices, Jacksonville, 1958-60; judge Civil Ct. of Record, Jacksonville, 1960-63; cir. judge 4th Jud. Cir. of Fla., Jacksonville, 1963-67; atty. Dawson, Galant, Maddox, Boyer, Sulik & Nichols, Jacksonville, 1967-73; appellate judge 1st Dist. Ct. Appeal, Tallahassee, 1973-79; chief judge 1st Dist. Ct. Appeals, Tallahassee, 1975-76; atty. Boyer, Tanzler, Blackburn & Boyer, Jacksonville, 1979-84, Boyer, Tanzler & Sussman, Jacksonville, 1984—. Adj. prof. Fla. Coastal Sch. Law, Jacksonville, 1996—, U. North Fla., 1998—; chmn. Supreme Ct. Com. on Standard Conduct Governing Judges, Tallahassee, 1976—79. Contbr. articles to profl. jours. Chmn. Duval County Hosp. Authority, Jacksonville, 1970-73, Jacksonville Bldg. Fin. Authority, 1980-81; pres. Jacksonville Legal Aid Assn., 1954-61; bd. dirs. Jones Coll., Jacksonville, 1978-85; bd. advs. Fla. Coastal Sch. Law, 1996—; adj. prof. U. North Fla., 1998—. With USN, 1942—45, PTO. Mem. ABA, Am. Judicature Soc., Fla. Bar, Amer. Bar Assn., Jacksonville Bar Assn., Fla. Acad. Trial Lawyers, Am. Bd. Trial Advs., SCV (comdr.), Mil. Order Stars and Bars (comdr.), Masons, dir., Safari Club Internat., Fla. Blue Key, Order of Coif, Phi Beta Kappa, Phi Kappa Phi. Methodist. Avocation: big game hunting. Home: 3966 Cordova Ave Jacksonville FL 32207-6019 Office: Boyer Tanzler & Sussman 210 E Forsyth St Jacksonville FL 32202-3320 Office Phone: 904-358-3030.

BOYER, TYRIE WILLIAM, judge, law educator; b. Jacksonville, Fla., Aug. 2, 1948; s. Tyrie Alvis and Elizabeth Gale Boyer; m. Lori Tofflemire Nemeyer, Nov. 6, 1997; children: Kimberly Jane Elizabeth, Kelley Deborah Leigh, R. J. Nemeyer. BSBA, U. Fla., Gainesville, 1972, JD, 1976. Cert.: Fla. Bar (civil trial Lawyer) 1983, Nat. Bd. of Trial Advocacy (civil trial advocacy) 1997, bar: Fla. 1976, U.S. Supreme Ct. 1997, U.S. Dist. Ct. (mid. dist.) Fla. 1977, U.S. Ct. of Appeals (5th and 11th cirs.) 1981. Asst. pub. defender Pub. Defender, Jacksonville, 1976—77; assoc. Mathews, Osborne, Ehrlich, McNatt, Gobleman & Cobb, Jacksonville, 1977—79; judge Duval County, Jacksonville, 2001—; ptnr. Boyer, Tanzler & Boyer, Jacksonville, 1979—2000; adj. prof. Fla. Coastal Sch. of Law, Jacksonville, Fla., 1999—. Chmn. Fla. Bar Com. on Profl. Ethics, Tallahassee, 1986—88, Fla. Bar Civil Procedure Rules Com., Tallahassee, 1998—99; chmn. Law Day Jacksonville Bar Assn., 1978—79. Author: (novels) RETRIBUTION; contbr. articles to legal jours. and outdoor publs. Dist. dir., counselor Boy Scouts of Am., Jacksonville, 2002—04; mem. Jacksonville C. of C., 1998—2000; bd. dirs. Jacksonville Cmty. Coun., Inc., 1980; bd. of advisors pre-law program U. of North Fla., 2003; advisor Family Farm, Jacksonville, 2002—05; bd. dirs. Salvation Army, Orange Park, Fla., 1995—96; bd. mem. YMCA, Jacksonville, 1977—79; bd. dirs March of Dimes, Jacksonville, 1979; chmn. Sportsmen Against Hunger, Safari Club Internat., Jacksonville, 1991; pres. student body U. of Fla., Gainesville, 1973, chief justice traffic ct., 1972. Capt. USAR, 1969—82. Named one of Outstanding Young Men of Jacksonville, Jaycees, Jacksonville, Fla., 1979, Outstanding Young Men of Am., 1980; named to Hall of Fame, U. of Fla., 1972; recipient Ethics award, Safari Club Internat., 1995, Svc. award, Filipino Travelers of Fla., 2000—01, President's award, Safari Club Internat., 2002, Fla. Blue Key, U. of Fla., 1972, John Marshall Bar Assn. Cert. of Merit, 1988, Paul Harris fellowship. Fellow: Am. Bd. of Trial Advocates (pres., v.p., sec., treas. Jacksonville chpt. 1989—92), Found. of Am. Bd. of Trial Advocates; mem.: NRA, FBA, ATLA, ABA, Jacksonville Trial Lawyers Assn., Jacksonville Bar Assn., Acad. of Fla. Trial Lawyers, Fla. Bar Assn., Clay County Bar Assn., Fla. Bd. of Trial Advocates (bd. dirs. 1992), Christian Legal Soc., Safari Club Internat. (regional v.p., bd. dirs., pres. Jacksonville chpt. 1982—2005), Nat. Alumni Assn. of the U. of Fla., South Jacksonville Rotary Internat. (bd. dirs.), Jacksonville Hist. Soc. (pres. 2005), Am. Legion, Masons, Omnicron Delta Kappa, Sigma Delta Pi (chancellor 1972), Delta Theta Phi (dean 1975). Episcopalian. Avocations: outdoor recreation, bridge. Office: Duval County Courthouse Rm 324 330 E Bay St Jacksonville FL 32202 Office Phone: 904-630-2579. Office Fax: 904-630-8358. Personal E-mail: twboyer@coj.net.

BOYES, MARY CHRISTINE, language educator; b. Providence, R.I., Sept. 3, 1964; d. David William and Sandra Lee Boyes; m. Clay Gant Blancett; 1 child, Henry Blancett. BA, Coll. William and Mary, 1986; MFA, Va.Commonwealth U., 1998. Instr. English Va. Union U., Richmond, Ala., 1998—99; asst. prof. English Ramapo Coll. N.J., Mahwah, 1999—. Mng. editor The Comparatist, Va. Commonwealth U., Richmond, 1997—98; adj. instr. English Va. Commonwealth U., 1996—99. Contbr. poetry and short stories to anthologies. Mem.: So. Humanities Coun. (exec. bd. 2000—02). Home: 119 Coles St Jersey City NJ 07302 Office: Ramapo Coll NJ 505 Ramapo Valley Rd Mahwah NJ 07430 Personal E-mail: maryboyes@hotmail.com. Business E-Mail: mboyes@ramapo.edu.

BOYES, PATRICE FLINCHBAUGH, lawyer; b. York, Pa., Aug. 1, 1957; d. Glenn Dale Flinchbaugh and Patricia Ann (Frey) Shultz. BA, Dickinson Coll., 1978; MA, U. Mich., 1980; JD, U. Fla., 1991. Bar: Fla. 1991, Fed. 1994. Law clk. Rakusin & Ivey, Gainesville, Fla., 1989; summer assoc. Hopping, Boyd, Green & Sams, Tallahassee, 1990; gen. counsel GeoSolutions, Inc., Gainesville/Tallahassee, Fla., 1986—2002; pres. Boyes & Assocs., PA, Gainesville, Fla., 1991—, Wildcat Tech. Svc., Inc., 1995-99. Pres. Wildcat Tech. Svcs., Inc., Gainesville, 1995-99. Pres. Hist. Gainesville, Inc.; chair City's Hist. Preservation Adv. Bd.; vol. Kanapha Bot. Gardens; counsel Duckpond Neighborhood Assn., Inc. Recipient Keystone Press award Pa. Soc. Newspaper Editors and Pubs., 1981, City Beautification award, 1994, Hist. Preservation award, 1994, Fla. Trust for Hist. Preservation award, 1996; grad. fellow Modern Media Inst., St. Petersburg, Fla. Mem. Fed. Bar Assn., Fla. Bar Assn. (pub. interest com. for environ. and land use sect.), 8th Jud. Cir. Bar Assn., Fla. Assn. Women Lawyers, Gainesville C. of C., Pi Delta Epsilon. Avocations: golf, historical preservation, photography, gardening, reading. Office: 4719 NW 53rd Ave Ste C Gainesville FL 32606-4356 Office Phone: 352-372-2684.

BOYETT, JOAN REYNOLDS, performing company executive; b. L.A., May 2, 1936; d. Clifton Faris Reynolds and Jean Margaret (Howard) Hauck; m. Harry William Boyett, Oct. 5, 1956; children: Keven William, Suzanne Marie Boyett Liebherr. Student, Occidental Coll., 1954-55, Pasadena Playhouse, 1955-57. Mgr. youth activities L.A. Philharm. Orch., 1970-79; dir., founder edn. divsn. Performing Arts Ctr. L.A. County, 1979-2001, v.p. edn., 1988-2001. Mem. supt.'s task force on arts edn. Calif. State Dept. Edn., 1997; cons. NEA, Washington; chmn. arts edn. task force Calif. Arts Coun., Sacramento, 1993-95; arts edn. mem. Nat. Working Group, Washington, 1992-95; mem. U.S. Sec. of Edns. Com. on Am. Goes Back to Sch. Active various coms. and task forces, L.A., Sacramento. Named Woman of Yr. L.A. Times, 1976; recipient Labor's award of honor County Fedn. Labor, L.A., 1984, Susan B. Anthony award Bus. and Profl. Women, 1986, Gov.'s award Calif. Arts Coun. and Gov., 1989, R.O.S.E. Outstanding Svc. to Edn. award, U. So. Calif., 1999, Outstanding Arts Educator award Calif. Arts Coun., 2001, Music Ctr. Club 100 Spl. Tribute award, 2001, Women in Ednl. Leadership award, 2002, Ovation award for cmty. svc. Theatre League Alliance, 2002. Mem. Calif. Art Edn. Assn. (Behind the Scenes award 1985), Calif. Dance Educators Assn. (Svc. award 1985), Calif. Ednl. Theatre Assn. (Outstanding Contbn. award 1990, nominated for Nat. Medal Arts 1996, 97). Republican. Presbyterian. Avocations: reading, attending arts events, gardening, swimming. Home: PO Box 1805 Studio City CA 91614-0805 E-mail: jarboyett@earthlink.net.

BOYINA, RAMANA PRASAD VENKATA, civil engineering educator, researcher; b. Nellore, India, Aug. 28, 1958; s. Narasimha Rao and Bhagyavati Boyina; m. Subba Lakshmi Bandhuvula, Apr. 19, 1982; 1 child, Kaysuv. BTech, Jawaharlal Nehru Technol. U., Anantapur, India, 1982; MTech, Jawaharlal Nehru Technol. U., Hyderabad, India, 1987; PhD, Indian Inst. Sci., Bangalore, 1992. Lectr. Chaitanya Bharati Inst. Tech., Hyderabad, 1982-92, asst. prof. engring., 1992-98, prof. engring., 1998—. Adj. prof. engring., Rensselaer Poly. Inst., Troy, n.Y., 1998—. Contbr. articles to profl. jours. Grantee UN Devel. Program, 1995, UNESCO, 1996, 97; rsch. grantee Govt. India, 1994-97, 97-2000. Mem. AAAS, ASCE (life), Nat. Soc. Fluid Mechs. and Fluid Power India. Hindu. Avocations: swimming, travel, cooking. Home: 50 3d Ave Seymour CT 06483 Office: Rensselaer Poly Inst 5049 JEC/110 8th St Troy NY 12180 E-mail: boyinr@rpi.edu, boyinarp@hotmail.com.

BOYKAN, MARTIN, composer, music educator; b. N.Y.C., Apr. 12, 1931; m. Susan Schwalb, 1983. AB summa cum laude, Harvard U., 1951; student, U. Zurich, Switzerland, 1951—52; MusM, Yale, 1953. Asst. prof. music Brandeis U., Waltham, Mass., 1964-67, assoc. prof. music, 1967-76, prof., 1976—, Irving G. Fine prof., 1986—. Composer-in-residence Composer's Conf., Wellesley, Mass., 1987; vis. prof. composition Columbia U., 1988-89, NYU, 1993, 2000; sr. Fulbright lectr. Bar Ilan U., Israel, 1994. Composer: String Quartets, 1949, 1965, Flute Quintet, 1953, Psalm, 1958, Prelude for Organ, 1959, Chamber Concerto for 13 Instruments, 1971, String Quartet No. 2, 1973, Piano Trio, 1975, Elegy for soprano and 6 instruments, part I, 1979, Elegy for soprano and 6 instruments, part II, 1982, String Quartet No. 3, 1984, Epithalamion for baritone, violin and harp, 1985, Shalom Rav, 1985, Fantasy Sonata for Piano, 1987, Sonata for cello and piano, 1988, Symphony for orch. with baritone solo, 1989, Piano Sonata #2, 1990, Nocturne for Cello, Piano and Percussion, 1990, Eclogue for flute, violin, cello, horn and piano, 1991, Echoes of Petrarch for flute, clarinet and piano, 1992, Voyages for Soprano and Piano, 1992, Sea-Gardens for Soprano and Piano, 1993, Impromptu for Solo Violin, 1993, Three Psalms for Soprano and Piano, 1993, Pastorale for Piano, 1993, Sonata for violin and piano, 1994, Ma'ariv Settings for chorus and organ, 1995, String Quartet No. 4, 1996, 3 Shakespeare Songs for Chorus, 1996, City of Gold for solo flute, 1996, 2d Trio for violin, cello and piano, 1997, Psalm 121 for soprano and string quartet, 1997, Usurpations for piano, 1997, Sonata for Solo Violin, 1998, Flume for Clarinet and Piano, 1998, Romanza for Flute and Piano, 1999, A Packet for Susan for Mezzo-Soprano and Piano, 2000, Second Chances Song Cycle for Mezzo Sop and Piano on Texts By Mary Oliver, 2005, Motet for Mezzo-Soprano and Viol Consort, 2000, 2d version for clarinet, viola and cello, 2005, Songlines for flute, clarinet, violin and cello, 2001, Concerto for Violin and Orchestra; author: Silence and Slow Time, 2004; mem. editl. bd.: Perspectives of New Music;

contbr. articles to profl. jours. Nat. winner Jeunesses Musicales, 1967, League-ISCM, 1983; recipient Martha Baird Rockefeller award, 1974, Fromm Found. commn., 1975, award Internat. Soc. Contemporary Music, 1983, Koussevitzky commn., 1985, AAUL, 1986, 88, rec. award Am. Acad. and Nat. Inst. Arts and Letters, 1986, Walter Hinrichsen Publ. award Am. Acad. and Inst. Arts and Letters, 1988; Paine fellow, 1951, Fulbright fellow, 1953-55, Guggenheim fellow, 1984, Sr. Fulbright fellow, 1994; grantee Nat. Endowment for Arts, 1983, and numerous others. Mem. Am. Music Ctr., Phi Betta Kappa. Home: 10 Winsor Ave Watertown MA 02472-1460 Office: Music Dept Brandeis Univ Waltham MA 02454 Business E-Mail: boykan@brandeis.edu.

BOYKIN, AMY WILLIAMS, librarian; b. Newport News, Va., Aug. 1, 1968; d. Edward Hamilton Williams, Lucy King Williams; m. Mark Julian Boykin. BA in English, Christopher Newport U., 1990; MS in Libr. Studies, U. N.C., Greensboro, 1993. Asst. reference libr. Christopher Newport U. Libr., Newport News, 1995—. Contbr. book Library Web, 1997, book Teaching Information Literacy Concepts, 2001, book Christopher Newport, 2003. Mem.: ALA, Ch. and Synagogue Libr. Assn., Mid-Atlantic Regional Archives Conf., Va. Libr. Assn., Beta Phi Mu. Baptist. Avocations: reading, cooking, crocheting. Office: Christopher Newport Univ Libr 1 University Pl Newport News VA 23606 Business E-Mail: awboykin@cnu.edu.

BOYKIN, ANNE J., dean; BSN, Alverno Coll., 1966; MSN, Emory U., 1972; PhD, Vanderbilt U., 1981. Asst. prof. Marquette U., Milw., 1973-74; assoc. prof., asst. dir. Valdosta (Ga.) State Coll., 1975-80; in-svc. educator Holy Cross Hosp., Ft. Lauderdale, Fla., 1980-81; assoc. prof. Fla. Atlantic U., Boca Raton, 1984—, dean Coll. Nursing, prof., 1996—. Dir. Christine E. Lynn Ctr. for Caring. Co-author: Nursing as Caring: a Model for Transforming Practice, 1993, 2d edit., 2001; editor: Living a Caring-Based Program, 1993, Power, Politics and Public Policy: A Matter of Caring, 1995; co-editor: Caring as Healing; Renewal through Hope, 1994; contbr. chpts. to books, articles to profl. jours. Mem. Internat. Assn. for Human Caring, Fla. Nurses Assn. (Nursing Educator award 1991), Sigma Theta Tau, Phi Kappa Phi. Office: Fla Atlantic U Christine E Lynn Coll Nursing 777 Glades Rd PO Box 3091 Boca Raton FL 33431-0991 Office Phone: 561-297-3206. Business E-Mail: boykina@fau.edu.

BOYKIN, GLADYS, retired religious organization administrator; b. N.Y.C., Dec. 10, 1929; d. Jacob Allen and Annie Mae (Alston) McClendon; m. Eugene S. Callender (div. 1963); 1 child, Renee Denise; m. John R. Strachan (dec. 1982); m. Elton Boykin, 1996. Student, NYU, 1947-49. Dep. asst. Presbyn. Ch. of East Africa, Nairobi, Kenya, 1964-67; assoc. for women's program Presbyn. Ch. of U.S., N.Y.C., 1970-83; exec. dir. United Presbyn. Women, N.Y.C., 1983-97; ret., 1997. Cons. Peace Corps, Nairobi, 1964-67, Operation Crossroads Africa, Nairobi, 1964-67, Afro-Am. Ednl. Inst., Teaneck, N.J., 1977-79, various women's orgns. in Asia, Australia, Europe, Africa. V.p. Addicts Rehab. Ctr. Bd., N.Y.C., 1957—; mem. N.Y. Coalition of 100 Black Women, N.Y.C., 1972—; v.p., bd. dirs. La. Internat. Cultural Ctr.; bd. dirs. aging resource ctr. Sister Cities of Louisville. Recipient Cert. of citation borough pres. N.Y.C., 1977, Harlem Peacemaking award Harlem Peacemaking Com., 1983, Vol. award Louisville Internat. Culture Ctr., 1996. Mem. La. C. of C., River City Assn. Bus. and Profl. Women. Avocations: music, reading, travel, needlepoint, theater. Home: 800 S 4th St Apt 2202 Louisville KY 40203-2132

BOYKIN, KEITH O., former government official, writer; b. St. Louis, Aug. 28, 1965; s. William Oliver Boykin and Shirley Ann (Hayes) Parker. BA, Dartmouth Coll., 1987; JD, Harvard U., 1992. Polit. campaign worker Dukakis for Pres., Boston, 1987-88; pub. sch. tchr. Lithonia H.S., DeKalb County, Ga., 1989; mcpl. cons. City of Pine Lawn, Md., 1989; spl. asst. to pres. The White House, Washington, 1993—94. Author: One More River to Cross: Black and Gay in America, 1996, Beyond the Down Low; Sex, Lies and Denial in Black America, 2005; Co-editor: 100 Successful College Application Essays. Recipient Young Alumni award Harvard Black Law Students Assn., Cambridge, 1994. Democrat. Mailing: PO Box 1229 New York NY 10037 E-mail: kb@keithboykin.com.*

BOYKIN, RAYMOND FRANCIS, operations management educator, consultant; b. Santa Monica, Calif., Nov. 18, 1953; s. Francis Raymond and Doris Elaine (Davis) B.; m. Shelley Lynne Ladd, July 30, 1977; children: Jennifer Lynne, Whitney Michele. BA in Quantitative Method, Calif. State U., Fullerton, 1975; MS in Mgmt. Sci., San Diego State U., 1976; PhD in Mgmt. Sci., St. Louis U., 1986. Indsl. engr. Rockwell Internat., L.A., 1976-77, sr. scientist Richland, Wash., 1977-80; sr. mgmt. scientist Monsanto Co., St. Louis, 1980-86; prof. ops. mgmt. Calif. State U., Chico, 1986—. Assoc. sr. cons. PLG, Inc., Newport Beach, Calif., 1986—; mem. tech. adv. com. State of Calif., Sacramento, 1988-90. Author, editor: Risk Analysis in the Chemical Industry, 1985; contbr. over 30 articles to profl. jours. and meetings. Mem. Soc. for Risk Analysis (chartered, ann. meeting chair 1984, 89, treas. 1989-94, Outstanding Svc. award 1994), Inst. Mgmt. Sci. (Achievement award 1984). Democrat. Avocations: golf, swimming, basketball, softball. Home: 862 Westmont Dr Chico CA 95926-7761 Office: Coll of Bus Calif State U Chico CA 95929-0001

BOYKIN, RICHARD A., tax specialist; BS summa cum laude, BA summa cum laude, PhD in Economics, U. Md. Mng. ptnr. litig. support efforts KMPG LLP, NYC, mng. ptnr. global transfer pricing svc., mng. principal internat. corp. svc. Office: KGPM LLP 345 Park Ave 36th Floor New York NY 10154 Office Phone: 212-872-7699. Office Fax: 212-872-5576. E-mail: rboykin@kpmg.com.*

BOYKIN, ROBERT HEATH, retired banker; b. Carlsbad, N.Mex., Jan. 10, 1926; s. Calvin Clay and Ruby (Heath) B.; m. Camille Inkman, Nov. 26, 1948; 1 child, Robert Heath. BBA, U. Tex., 1950, LL.B., 1953; student, Park Coll., 1943-44; spl. courses, La. State U., Tex. A. and M. Coll., Am. Mgmt. Assn. Bar: Tex. bar 1952. Tabulating supr. Tex. Edn. Agy., 1948-52; with Fed. Res. Bank of Dallas, 1953-91, asst. counsel, 1959-61, asst. counsel, asst. sec. bd., 1961-65, asst. v.p., asst. sec. bd., 1965-67, asst. v.p., sec. bd., 1967-68, v.p., sec. bd., 1968-70, sr. v.p., sec. bd., 1971-75, sr. v.p., 1976, 1st v.p., 1976-80, pres., 1981-91, ret., 1991. Sec. Conf. Pres.'s of Fed. Res. Banks, 1963-64, chmn., 1980; instr. negotiable instruments Dallas chpt. Am. Inst. Banking, 1959-61 Served as lt. (j.g.) USNR, 1943-47. Mem. Tex. Bar Assn., Tex. Bankers Assn., Delta Tau Delta, Phi Alpha Delta. Methodist.

BOYKIN, WILLIAM G., federal agency administrator, career military officer; b. Wilson, N.C., Apr. 19, 1948; Commd. U.S. Army, 1971, advanced through grades to lt. gen., 2003, comdg. gen. Spl. Forces Command Ft. Bragg, NC, 1998-2000, commdg. gen. Spl. Warfare Ctr., 2000—03; dep. under sec. intelligence US Dept. Def., Washington, 2003—. Office: US Dept Def 1000 Def Pentagon Washington DC 20301

BOYKINS, MICHAEL L., lawyer; b. Jan. 17, 1965; BS, U. Wis., 1987, JD, 1990. Ptnr., co-chmn. firm racial & ethnic diversity com. McDermott Will & Emery LLP. Fellow: Am. Coll. Investment Counsel; mem.: Chgo. Com. Minorities in Large Law Firms (bd. dir.), Econ. Club Chgo., Wis. Bar Assn., Ill. Bar Assn. Office: McDermott Will & Emery LLP 227 W Monroe St Chicago IL 60606 Office Phone: 312-984-7599. Office Fax: 312-984-7700. Business E-Mail: mboykins@mwe.com.

BOYKIW, NORMA SEVERNE, retired nutritionist, educator; b. Coalmont, Ind., Feb. 3, 1918; d. Charles Edward Goble and Ressa Naomi Johnson; m. Russel Yaroslav Alexis Boykiw, 1948 (dec. Sept. 4, 1992); children: Russel Alexis II, Mark Emerson. BS, Ind. State U., 1941. Registered Med. Asst. 1950. Dietitian asst. Ind. State U., Terre Haute, Ind., 1939—40; tchr. home econ. Wawaka Sch. Sys., Wawaka, Ind., 1941—42; nutrition tchr. Crown Point Sch., Crown Point, Ind., 1942—43; mem. staff patient diabetic diets Wesley Meml. Hosp., Chgo.; writer of diet manuals Pa., 1945—48; office mgr. Russel Boykiw, MD, Clearfield, 1948—92, ret., 1992. Ombudsman Area Agy. on Aging, Clearfield, Pa., 1999—. Compilation author Genealogy for the Goble Family, 1976;, author diet manuals Hosps. Active cmty. devel. Pa. State U., Clearfield, Pa., 1959, 1966; den mother Presbyn. Ch., Clearfield, 1967. Named Woman of the Yr., Bus. and Profl. Women, 1974, Outstanding Citizen of the Yr., Clearfield Rotary Club, 1987; grantee, Ctrl. Pa. Dist. Libr. Bd., 1968—6879. Mem.: AAUW (Outstanding Woman award 1983), Nat. Soc. Daus. of Founders and Patriots of Am., Nat. Soc. DAR, Clearfield County Hist. Soc. (grant). Democrat. Avocation: yoga. Home: 364 Bailey Settlement Hwy Clearfield PA 16830-3505

BOYLAN, ANNE MARY, historian; b. Thurles, Ireland, Apr. 9, 1947; came to U.S., 1957; d. John Felix and Brigid (Lanigan) B.; m. Peter Kolchin, June 21, 1975; children: Michael, David. BA, Mundelein Coll., 1968; MA, U. Wis., 1970, PhD, 1973. Lectr. U. N.Mex., Albuquerque, 1976-77; assoc. prof. U. Del., Newark, 1986—2002, prof., 2002—. Vis. asst. prof. U. Minn., Mpls., 1973-76; vis. lectr. U. Tex.-El Paso, 1977-79, U. N.Mex., Albuquerque, 1979-85. Author: Sunday School, 1988, The Origins of Womens Activism, 2002; contbr. articles to profl. jours. Recipient cert. of merit, Am. Assn. State and Local History, 2004; fellow Nat. Endowment for the Humanities, 1979; Alice E. Smith fellow, State Hist. Soc. Wis., 1971—72, rsch. grantee, Am. Hist. Assn., 1984, Radcliffe Rsch. Scholars Program, 1985, U. Del., 1991, 2000, Hagley Mus., 2000. Office: U Delaware Dept History Munroe Hall Newark DE 19716

BOYLAN, ELIZABETH SHIPPEE, academic administrator, biologist, educator; b. Shanghai, Nov. 29, 1946; d. Nathan M. and Elizabeth (Little) Shippee; m. Robert J. Boylan, Oct. 2, 1971; children: Elizabeth B., Emily A. AB, Wellesley Coll., 1968; PhD, Cornell U., 1972. Postdoctoral fellow U. Rochester (N.Y.) Sch. Medicine, 1972-73; asst. prof. Queens Coll. CUNY, Flushing, 1973-78, assoc. prof., 1978-82, prof. biology, 1983-95, acting asst. provost, 1988-89, asst. provost, 1989-90, assoc. provost, 1990-92; acting provost Queens Coll. CUNY, Flushing, 1992-93; assoc. provost acad. programs and planning Queens Coll., Flushing, 1994-95; provost and dean of faculty Barnard Coll., N.Y.C., 1995—, prof. biology, 1995—. Chmn. Queens Coll. Acad. Senate, 1985-88; mem. grad. faculty Grad. Ctr. CUNY, N.Y.C., 1977-95; vis. investigator Sloan-Kettering Inst. Cancer Rsch., N.Y.C., 1979-80; trustee N.Y. Met. Ref. and Rsch. Libr. Agy., Manhattan, 1989-97, chmn. fin. com. 1991-97; co-chmn. bd. trustees study com. on secondary edn. CUNY, 1987-88, co-chair vice chancellor's task force on sci., engring., tech. and math., 1988-89; panelist NSF grad. fellowship program, 1992-93; cons. to Nat. Cancer Inst., N.J. Commn. on Cancer Rsch., Endocrine Soc.; mem. breast cancer task force NCI, 1980-84; mem. adv. com. Am. Cancer Soc., 1981-85; Am. Coun. Edn. fellow Pace U., 1993-94; commr. Commn. on Higher Edn., Mid. States Assn. Colls. and Schs., 1999-2004. Contbr. and reviewer articles to profl. publs.; patentee in field. Grantee Nat. Cancer Inst., 1975-83, Am. Inst. Cancer Rsch., 1987-90, Am. Fedn. Aging Rsch., 1988-89. Mem. AAAS, AAHE, Soc. Devel. Biology, Am. Assn. Cancer Rsch., N.Y. Acad. Scis., Sigma Xi. Office: Barnard Coll Office of Provost 3009 Broadway New York NY 10027-6501 Office Phone: 212-854-2708. Business E-Mail: eboylan@barnard.edu.

BOYLAN, KEVIN BERNARD, neurologist; b. Arlington, Mass., Aug. 20, 1956; s. Charles Vincent and Edith Murial (Aho) B. BA in Social Sci. cum laude, BS in Biology, U. Calif., Irvine, 1979; MD, U. Calif., San Francisco, 1983. Diplomate Nat. Bd. Med. Examiners, Am. Bd. Psychiatry and Neurology, also Sub.-Bd. Clin. Neurophysiology, Am. Bd. Electrodiagnostic Medicine. Intern Johns Hopkins Hosp., Balt., 1983-84; fellow neurology U. Calif., San Francisco, 1984-87, fellow med. genetics, 1985-87, resident, 1987-90; fellow neuromuscular diseas Johns Hopkins Hosp, 1990-91; instr. neurology Johns Hopkins U., 1991; asst. prof. Mayo Grad. Sch. Medicine, Jacksonville, Fla., 1992—; assoc. cons. Mayo Clinic, Jacksonville, Fla., 1992-94, cons., 1994—, 1994—. Dir. EMG lab. Mayo Clinic, 1994—; dir. Muscular Dystrophy Assn. Clinic N.E. Fla., 1994— Contbr. numerous articles to profl. jours. Multiple Sclerosis fellow Nat. Multiple Sclerosis Soc., 1984-87, Charles A. Dana fellow Charles A. Dana Found., 1990-91. Mem. AAAS, Am. Soc. Human Genetics, Am. Acad. Neurology, Duval County Med. Assn. Office: Mayo Clinic Dept Neur 4500 San Pablo Rd S Jacksonville FL 32224-3899

BOYLAN, MERLE NELSON, librarian, educator; b. Youngstown, Ohio, Feb. 24, 1925; s. Merle Nelson and Alma Joy (Kepple) B. BA, Youngstown U., 1950; M.L.S., Carnegie-Mellon U., 1956; postgrad., U. Ariz., 1950-51, Ind. U., 1952. Librarian Pub. Health Library U. Calif., Berkeley, 1956-58; sci. librarian U. Ariz., Tucson, 1958-59; engring. librarian Gen. Dynamics/Convair, San Diego, 1959-61, Gen. Dynamics/Astronautics, 1961-62; assoc. librarian Lawrence Radiation Lab., U. Calif., Livermore, 1962-64, library mgr., 1964-67; chief librarian NASA Ames Research Center, Moffett Field, Calif., 1968-69; asso. dir. libraries U. Mass., Amherst, 1969-70, dir. libraries, Univ. librarian, 1970-72; dir. libraries U. Tex., Austin, 1973-77, U. Wash., Seattle, 1977-89, dir. emeritus, 1989—, prof. Sch. Librarianship, 1982-89; exec. bd. Amigos Bibliographic Council, 1974-77; mem. fin. com., governance com., user's council, computer service council Wash. Library Network, 1978—. Del. Gov.'s Conf. Librs. and Info. Svcs., 1979; sec. Texas State Bd. Libr. Examiners, 1974-77; mem. bibliographic networking and resource sharing advisory group Southwestern Libr. Interstate Coop. Endeavor, 1975-77; sec., chmn. exec. bd. Pacific N.W. Bibliographic Ctr., 1977-83; mem. com. centralzed acquisitions of libr. materials for internat. studies Ctr. for Rsch. Librs.; del. OCLC Users Coun., 1981-86. Sec. bd. trustees Littlefield Fund for So. History, 1974-77, Fred Meyer Charitable Trust; mem. adv. bd. Libr. and Info. Resources for Northwest, 1984-87. Mem. ALA, Assn. Coll. and Rsch. Librs. (legis. com. 1977-81), Assn. Rsch. Librs. (bibliographic control com. 1979-83), Spl. Librs. Assn., Am. Soc. Info. Sci., Beta Phi Mu. Home: 1354 Bellefield Park Ln Bellevue WA 98004-6854 Office: Univ of Wash Librs Suzzallo Libr Seattle WA 98195-0001

BOYLE, ANN M., dental educator, dean; BA, Case Western Reserve U., 1971; DMD, Fairleigh Dickinson U., 1975, MA in Ednl. Psychology, 1984. Cert. gen. practice Hackensack Hosp., 1976; managament cert. Harvard U., 1999. Mem. faculty Coll. Dental Med. Fairleigh Dickinson U., 1976—90, chair restorative dept., 1988—90; chair restorative dept. to assoc. dean acad. affairs Sch. Dentistry Case Western Reserve U., Cleveland, 1991—94; assoc. dean Sch. Dental Med. So. Ill. U., 1995—2002, acting dean, 2002—03, dean, prof. restorative dentistry, 2003—. Extramural pvt. practice. Fellow: Pierre Fauchard Acad., Am. Coll. Dentists; mem.: ADA (mem. commn. on Dental Accreditation), Internat. Assn. Dental Rsch., Am. Assn. Dental Rsch., Am. Dental Edn. Assn., Acad. Operative Dentistry. Office: So Ill U Sch Dental Med 2800 College Ave Bldg 273/2300 Alton IL 62002

BOYLE, ANTONIA BARNES, electronic learning consultant, writer; b. Detroit, May 21, 1939; d. James Merriam and Florence (Maiullo) B.; 1 child, Caitlin Merriam. BS in Speech, Northwestern U., 1962. Staff announcer WEFM-FM, Chgo., 1975-78; pres. Boyle Communications, Chgo., 1978-85; exec. producer Nightingale-Conant Corp., Chgo., 1985-90, Cassette Prodns. Unltd., Irwindale, Calif., 1990-92; pres. Antonia Boyle & Co., 1992—; v.p. content acquisition Youachieve.com, Inc., 1997—. Bd. dirs. WNUR-FM Alumni, Northwestern U., Evanston, Ill. Author: The Optimal You, 1990, Taping Yourself Seriously, 1991; co-author (with Jay Gordon): Good Food Today, Great Kids Tomorrow, 1994; co-author: (with Scott McKain) Just Say Yes, 1994; co-author: (with William McCurry) Guerrilla Managing for the Imaging Industry, 1997; co-author: (with William McCurry and Harold Lloyd) It's Your People...Really!, 2005; co-author: (with K.D. Sullivan) The Gremlins of Grammar, 2005. Chmn., bd. dirs. Horizons for the Blind, Chgo., 1984. Mem. Am. Fedn. Radio, TV Artists, Com.100 Northwestern U., NU Club (Chgo.). Home: 3119A Lake Ave Wilmette IL 60091-1157 E-mail: aboyleco@earthlink.com, tboyle@youachieve.com.

BOYLE, BARBARA DORMAN, film company executive; b. NYC, Aug. 11, 1935; d. William and Edith (Kleiman) Dorman; m. Kevin Boyle, Nov. 26, 1960; children: David Eric, Paul Coleman. BA in English with honors, U. Calif., Berkeley, 1957; JD, UCLA, 1960. Bar: Calif. 1961, N.Y. 1964, U.S. Supreme Ct. 1964. Atty. bus. affairs dept, corp. asst. sec. Am. Internat. Pictures, L.A., 1960-65; ptnr. Cohen & Boyle, L.A., 1967-74; exec. v.p., gen. counsel, chief op. officer New World Pictures, L.A., 1974-82; sr. v.p. prodn. Orion Pictures Corp., L.A., 1982-85; exec. v.p. prodn. RKO Pictures, L.A., 1986-87; pres. Sovereign Pictures, Inc., L.A., 1988-92, Boyle and Taylor Prodns., 1993-99, Valhalla Motion Pictures, L.A., 2000—03; chair film, TV and digital media dept. UCLA, 2003—. Lectr. in field. Exec. prodr. (film) Eight Men Out, 1987, Bottle Rocket, 1995, Campus Man; prodr. (films) Mrs. Munck, 1995, Phenomenon, 1996, Instinct, 1999; exec. prodr. The Hi Line, 1998; co-prodr. Phenomenon II, 2002; contbr. chpts. to books. Bd. dirs. UCLA Law Fund Com., L.A. Women's Campaign Fund; pres. Ind. Feature Project/West; founding mem. entertainment adv. coun. sch. law UCLA, co-chmn. 1979-80, co-chair, 2002-03. Named UCLA Law Sch. Alumni of Yr, 1999, Women in Film Crystal award, 2000. Mem. Acad. Motion Picture Arts and Scis. (exec. com.), Acad. TV Arts and Scis. (exec. com.), Women in Film (pres. 1977-78), Hollywood Women's Polit. Com., Calif. Bar Assn., N.Y. State Bar Assn. Office: UCLA Sch of Theater Film & TV 203 E Melnitz Box 951622 Los Angeles CA 90095-1622 Business E-Mail: boyle@tft.ucla.edu.

BOYLE, BRUCE JAMES, publisher; b. Mpls., Aug. 31, 1931; s. Lorille James and Norma Elizabeth (Blish) B.; m. Betty Jean Tucker, May 28, 1960; children: Katherine Ann, Julia Caroline, Amy Elizabeth. B.J., U. Mo., 1958. Copywriter Sta. KFRU, Columbia, Mo., 1958; continuity dir. KOMU-TV, Columbia, 1959; advt. salesman Better Homes & Gardens mag., 1960; advt. dir. Successful Farming mag., Des Moines, 1969-73, pub., 1973-80, Meredith Pub. Svcs., 1976-80, Meredith Video Pub., 1981-92, dir. mag. devel., 1984-92. Mem. faculty Grandview Coll., 1993-95. Bd. dirs. Youth Homes Mid-Am., 1993-99. With USN, 1951-54. Mem. Nat. Agri-Mktg. Assn. (pres. 1973-74), Farm and Indsl. Equipment Inst., Farm Equipment Mfrs. Assn. (chmn. bd. govs. 1971-72), Agrl. Pubs. Assn. (bd. dirs. 1979-81), Alpha Delta Sigma. Clubs: Wakonda Country, Okoboji Yacht, Rio Verde Country Club. Home: 3000 SW 30th St Des Moines IA 50321 E-mail: bjb718@msn.com.

BOYLE, CHRISTOPHER GEORGE, language educator, counseling administrator; b. Binghamton, N.Y., July 27, 1930; s. Edward George and Mary Giblyn B.; m. Mary Ella Morris, Dec. 30, 1951; children: Catherine Flowers, Anne Butler, Russell, Elizabeth O'Brien. AB, Amherst Coll., 1952; EdM, Harvard U., 1960. Cert. secondary tchr., Ariz., cmty. coll. tchg. cert., Ariz. English tchr., coach St. Stephen's Sch., Austin, 1952-54, Worcester (Mass.) Acad., 1954-55; English tchr., dept. head, coach St. Andrew's Sch., Middletown, Del., 1955-80; Fulbright tchr. of English U.S. Dept. of State, Helsinki, Finland, 1962-63; English dept. head, dean of studies, tchr., coach, counselor St. Gregory Coll. Preparatory Sch., Tucson, Ariz., 1980-94. Instr. Freshman English U. Del., Newark, 1970-71; part-time coll. counselor, cons. Catalina Foothills H.S., Tucson, 1997-99; advanced placement English lit exam. reader, cons., Coll. Bd./Ednl. Testing Svc., Princeton, N.J., 1965-96, workshop leader for AP English tchrs., San Jose, Calif., 1989-97; reader Scholastic Assessment Test English essays, 1967-2004. Contbr. articles to profl. jours. Mem. Del. Coun. of Tchrs. of English (pres. 1969-71). Episcopalian. Avocations: scuba diving, choral music, reading. Home: 4820-L E Fort Lowell Rd Tucson AZ 85712-1262 E-mail: cboyle727@aol.com.

BOYLE, COULTER RICHARD, IV, dean, consultant; b. Portsmouth, Ohio, Apr. 7, 1970; s. Coulter Richard Boyle, III and Judy Boyle; m. Emilee Boyle, Sept. 15, 1996; children: Abigail, Anna. BA in Comm., U. Ky., 1992, postgrad.; MA in Comm., Morehead State U., 1998. Dir. distance edn. Morehead (Ky.) State U., 1996—2000; assoc. dean continuing edn. Ea. Ky. U., Richmond, 2000—. Chair Ky. Distance Learning Steering Team, Frankfort, 2004—. Mem.: U. Continuing Edn. Assn., Assn. Continuing Higher Edn. Office: Eastern Kentucky University 521 Lancaster Ave Richmond KY 40475 Office Phone: 859-622-1224. Business E-Mail: richard.boyle@eku.edu.

BOYLE, DANIEL ROBERT, musician, delivery service executive; b. Bowling Green, Ohio, Dec. 5, 1973; s. Robert Theodore Boyle and Linda Marie (Goris) Boyle; m. Leslie Kathleen Gilbert; 1 child, Frederic Joseph. B magna cum laude, Bowling Green State U., 1996; postgrad., U. Toledo, 1997—98. Choir dir. Evergreen Local Schs., Metamora, Ohio, 1996—2000; mid. sch. choral dir. Maumee City Schs., Ohio, 2000—02; sales rep. Verizon Wireless, Findlay, Ohio, 2002—03; driver FedEx Ground, Toledo, 2003—. Organist, choir dir. St. Louis Cath. Ch., Custar, Ohio, 1981—97, Grace Luth Ch., Elmore, Ohio, 1997—. Advisor 4-H, Portage, Ohio, 1991—97. Recipient Man of Yr., Sigma Alpha Iota, Bowling Green State U., 1994; scholar Pres.'s scholar, Bowling Green State U., 1991—95. Mem.: Am. Guild Organists, Evergreen HS Future Farmers Am. (hon.), Phi Eta Mu, Golden Key, Phi Mu Alpha Sinfonia (music/ritual dir. warden 1994—95). Lutheran. Avocations: bicycling, composing music. Home: 6638 N Texas St Whitehouse OH 43571 Personal E-mail: DanandLeslie@wcnet.org.

BOYLE, E. THOMAS, federal magistrate judge; b. Paterson, N.J., Apr. 30, 1939; m. Mary Lou Kelly; two children. BS in English, Holy Cross Coll., 1961; LLB, U. Va., 1964. Bar: N.Y. 1965, U.S. Ct Appeals (2d cir.) 1974, U.S. Dist. Ct. (ea. and so. dists.) N.Y. 1974. Assoc. Mendes & Mount, N.Y.C., N.Y., 1965-66; trial counsel Legal Aid Soc. Suffolk County, N.Y., 1966-72; appellate counsel Fed. Defender Svcs., N.Y.C., 1972-75; pvt. practice Smithtown, N.Y., 1975-88; county atty. Suffolk County, Hauppauge, N.Y., 1988-92; ptnr. Boyle, Shea & Nornes, Hauppauge, N.Y., 1992-95; magistrate judge for ea. dist. N.Y. U.S. Dist. Ct., Uniondale, 1995—. Mem. Circuit Conf. Planning Com., 2001—. Office: Fed Plaza Long Island Fed Courthouse 834 Central Islip NY 11722*

BOYLE, EDWARD J., lawyer; b. Bklyn., July 3, 1941; BA, St. John's U., 1964, JD, 1967. Bar: NY 1967, US Dist. Ct. So., No., & Ea. Districts NY, US Supreme Ct., US Ct. Appeals 2nd, 7th, & 11th Circuits. Law clk. NY State Ct. Appeals, 1967—69; pvt. practice atty., 1969—75, 1977—83; chief trial counsel NY regional office SEC, 1975—77; ptnr. Wilson, Elser, Moskowitz, Edelman & Dicker LLP, NYC, 1983—. Mng. editor St. John's Law Rev., 1966—67. Mem.: ABA, Assn. of the Bar of the City of NY, NY State Bar Assn. Office: Wilson Elser Moskowitz Edelman & Dicker LLP 23rd Fl 150 E 42nd St New York NY 10017-5639 Office Phone: 212-490-3000 ext. 2392. Office Fax: 212-490-3038. Business E-Mail: boylee@wemed.com.

BOYLE, ELISABETH ESTHER, music educator; b. Fayetteville, S.C., Sept. 1, 1975; d. David Fitzgerald and Nancy Kay DeBose; m. Michael Joseph Boyle, May 25, 2002. AD in religious Edn., Founds. Bible Coll., 1997; MusB in Piano Pedagogy, Bob Jones U., 2003. Intern piano tchr. Bob Jones U., Greenville, S.C., 2000—01; owner Boyle Studio of Music, Greenville, 2002—; encore piano tchr. Stone Acad., Greenville, 2003—. Recital chair Greenville Music Tchrs. Assn., 2003—. Composer: (piano composition) The Windmill, Baroque Theme in B Minor, I Wish You Near, Melody Number Five, Without a Home, Longing, Wedding Day, Irish Jig, Mai (May), La Pluie (The Rain), (piano and orch. composition) Piano Concerto in A Minor. Pres.-elect Upstate Visual Arts, Greenville, 2003, pres., 2004—. Recipient Bach award, Nat. Guild Piano Tchrs., 1992. Mem.: Music Tchrs. Nat. Assn., Nat. Guild Piano Tchrs., Bob Jones U. Alumni Assn. Republican. Protestant. Avocations: mountain biking, travel, studying French, tennis. Office: Stone Acad 115 Randall St Greenville SC 29609

BOYLE, FRANCIS ANTHONY, law educator; b. Chgo., Mar. 25, 1950; AB in Polit. Sci., U. Chgo., 1971; JD magna cum laude, Harvard U., 1976, AM, 1978, PhD, 1983. Bar: Mass. 1977. Tchg. fellow, assoc. Harvard U. and Ctr. Internat. Affairs, 1976—78; tax atty. Bingham, Dana & Gould, Boston, 1977—78; prof. law U. Ill., Champaign, 1978—. Prof. USSR Summer U. Jurists, 1989; Parhad lectr. U. Calgary, 2001. Author: World Politics and International Law, 1985 (Outstanding Acad. Book, Choice mag. 1985-86), Defending Civil Resistance Under International Law, 1987, The Future of International Law and American Foreign Policy, 1989, The Bosnian People Charge Genocide, 1996, Foundations of World Order, 1999, The Criminality of Nuclear Deterrence, 2002, Palestine, Palestinians and International Law, 2003, Destroying World Order, 2004, Biowarfare and Terrorism, 2005;

contbr. articles to profl. jours. Mem. bur. polit.-mil. affairs (scholar-diplomat program) U.S. Dept. State, 1981; bd. dirs., coordinating coun. Lawyers Com. on Nuc. Policy, 1981—; cons. Amnesty Internat., 1983—; chmn., panel of jurists IPO Brussels Tribunal on Reagan Adminstrns. Fgn. Policy, 1984; advisor Coun. for Responsible Genetics, 1985—; cons. UN Com. on Exercise of Inalienable Rights of Palestinian People, 1987—; bd. dirs. Amnesty Internat. USA, 1988-92; gen. agent Republic of Bosnia and Herzegovina Internat. Ct. Justice with E&P Powers, 1993-94; atty of record E&P Chechen Republic of Ichkeria, 2000—; Chechen amb. to Norway, 2004—. Mem. Am. Soc. Internat. Law (ad hoc guidelines com. 1978-80, Lieber group on laws of war 1979—), Phi Beta Kappa, Sigma Xi (cert. of merit and prize in biology). Office: U Ill Coll Law 504 E Pennsylvania Ave Champaign IL 61820-6909 Office Phone: 217-333-7954. Business E-Mail: fboyle@law.uiuc.edu.

BOYLE, GERTRUDE, sportswear company executive; b. Augsberg, Germany, 1924; came to U.S., 1938; d. Paul and Marie Lanfrom; m. Neil Boyle, 1948; children: Tim, Kathy, Sally. BA in Sociology, Univ. Ariz., 1947. Pres., CEO Columbia Sportswear Co., Portland, Oreg., 1970-88, CEO, 1988-94, chmn. bd., 1994—. Named one of Best Mgrs. Bus. Week Mag., 1994, Am.'s Top 50 Women Bus. Owners Working Woman mag., Woman of Yr. Oreg. chpt. Women's Forum, 1987. Office: Columbia Sportswear Co 14375 NW Science Park Dr Portland OR 97229-5418

BOYLE, JANE J., federal judge, lawyer; b. Sharon, Pa., Dec. 15, 1954; BS, U. of Tex., Austin, 1977; JD, So Meth. U., Dallas, 1981. Asst. dist. atty. Dist. Atty.'s Office, 1981-87; asst. U.S. atty. U.S. Dist. Ct. (no. dist.) Tex., 1987-90, magistrate judge U.S. Dallas, 1990—2002, U.S. atty., 2003—04; judge US Dist. Ct. (no. dist) Tex., 2004—. Office: US Courthouse 1100 Commerce St Rm 1452 Dallas TX 75242

BOYLE, JOHN FRANCIS, lawyer; b. Oak Park, Ill., Sept. 14, 1958; s. Austin Joseph and Virginia Therese (Conahan) B.; m. Mary Anna Chiaruttini, Sept. 28, 1986; children: Elizabeth, Annie, Jack, Charlie. BS in Journalism, U. Ill., 1980, JD, 1983. Bar: Ill. 1983, U.S. Dist. Ct. (no. dist.) Ill. 1983. Assoc. atty. Epton, Mullin, Segal & Druth, Ltd., Chgo., 1983-84, McKenna, Storer, Rowe, White & Farrug, Chgo., 1984-86, Tressler, Soderstrom, Maloney & Priess, Chgo., 1986-90, Wiedner & McAuliffe, Ltd., Chgo., 1990-93, ptnr., 1993-99; staff counsel Meachum, Spahr, Cozzi & Postel, Chgo., 1999—. Mem. sch. bd. Visitation Sch., 1995—, ch. lector Visitation Ch., 1990—; soccer coach Am. Youth Soccer Orgn., Elmhurst, 1993—, Team Elmhurst, 1998—. Roman Catholic. Avocations: jogging, gardening, folk music. Office: Meachum Spahr Cozzi & Postel Wiedner & McAuliffe Ltd One S Wacker Dr Ste 3400 Chicago IL 60606 Fax: 312-443-9282. E-mail: john.boyle@libertymutual.com.

BOYLE, JOSEPH HUGH, psychiatrist; b. Hannover, Germany, Mar. 21, 1965; arrived in US, 1966; s. Dennis Edward Boyle and Kathleen Ann O'Keeffe; m. Yadira Torres, May 23, 1992; children: Romina Fabiola, Anthony Hugh. MD, Ponce Sch. Medicine, PR, 1999. Lic. NC, 2003, Ga., 2004. Resident physician, intern St. Vincent's Med. Ctr., Columbia U. Coll. Physicians and Surgeons, Bridgeport, Conn., 1999—2000; resident physician Pitt. County Meml. Hosp./Brody Sch. Medicine, Greenville, 2000—03; psychiatrist/forensic fellow Duke U., Durham/Butner, 2003—04; psychiatrist Harbin Clinic, Rome, Ga., 2004—. Cons. forensic psychiatry Harbin Clinic, Rome, 2004—. Musician: (recording) The Veldt: Marigolds. Vol. case worker Interfaith Coun., Chapel Hill, 1994—95. Psychiatrist/Forensic fellow, Duke U., Durham, Butner, 2003—04. Mem.: Am. Acad. Psychiatry and the Law, Am. Psychiat. Assn., AMA. Avocations: philosophy, politics. Office Phone: 706-233-6309.

BOYLE, KAMMER, financial planner, investment advisor; b. New Orleans, June 17, 1946; d. Benjamin Franklin and Ethel Clair (Kammer) B.; m. Edward Turner Barfield, July 23, 1966 (div. 1975); children: Darren Barfield, Meloe Barfield. BS in Mgmt. magna cum laude, U. West Fla., 1976; PhD in Indsl./Organizational Psychology, U. Tenn., 1982. Lic. psychologist, Ohio, Tenn.; reg. securities rep. InterSecurities, Inc., Nat Assn. Securities Dealers. Pvt. practice mgmt. psychology, Knoxville, 1978-81; tchg. and rsch. asst. U. Tenn., Knoxville, 1977-81; mgmt. trainer U.S. State Dept., Washington, 1978; cons. PRADCO, Cleve., 1982-83; pres., cons. Mgmt. and Assessment Svcs., Inc., Cleve., 1983-90; pres. Kammer Investment Co., Cleve., 1989-96; fin. advisor O'Donnell Securities Corp., Cleve., 1997-98. Registered securities prin., investment advisor rep. and retirement specialist Wealth Charter Group of InterSecurities, Inc., 1998-. Mem. editl. rev. bd. Jour. of Managerial Issues, 1987; author and presenter ann. Conf. APA, 1980, Southeastern Psychol. Conf., 1979, ann. Conf. Soc. Indsl./Orgnl. Psychologists, 1987, ann. conf. Am. Soc. Tng. and Devel., 1988. Mem. Jr. League Am., Pensacola, Fla., 1970-75; treas. Bar Aux., Pensacola, 1971. Recipient Capital Gifts Stipend U. Tenn., 1976-80; Walter Bonham fellow, 1980-81. Mem. APA, Cleve. Psychol. Assn., Orgn. Devel. Inst., Acad. of Mgmt., Soc. Advancement Mgmt. (pres. 1974-75), Am. Soc. Tng. and Devel. (chpt. rep. career devel. 1984-86), Cleve. Psychol. Assn. (bd. dirs. 1987-88), Real Estate Investor's Assn. (Cleve., trustee/sec. 1992-94), Mensa. Office: Wealth Charter Group Ste 200 6100 Oak Tree Blvd S Independence OH 44131

BOYLE, KEVIN GERARD, historian, educator, writer; b. Detroit, Oct. 7, 1960; s. Kevin C. and Anne Boyle; m. Victoria Lynn Getis, Jan. 4, 1992; children: Abigail Grace, Hannah Claire. BA, U. Detroit, 1982; PhD, U. Mich., 1990. Asst. prof. history U. Toledo, 1990—94; asst./assoc. prof. history U. Mass., Amherst, 1994—2002; assoc. prof. history Ohio State U., Columbus, 2002—. Author: The UAW and the Heyday of American Liberalism, 1945-1968, 1995, Arc of Justice: A Saga of Race, Civil Rights, and Murder in the Jazz Age, 2004 (Nat. Book Award for Nonfiction, 2004); co-author: Muddy Boots and Ragged Aprons: Images of Working-Class Detroit, 1900-1930, 1997; editor: Organized Labor and American Politics, 1894-1994: The Labor-Liberal Alliance, 1998. Fellow, Rockefeller Found., 1990—91, Mary Ball Wash. Chair in Am. History, J. William Fulbright Found., 1997—98, Am. Coun. Learned Socs., 2001—02, NEH, 2001—02, John Simon Guggenheim Found., 2001—02. Home: 173 N Stanwood Rd Bexley OH 43209 Office: Ohio State Univ Dept History Dulles Hall Columbus OH 43210 Office Phone: 614-292-7101.

BOYLE, KEVIN RICHARD, lawyer; b. Belleville, Ill., June 24, 1972; s. Richard E. and Janet E. Boyle. BA, Vanderbilt U., 1994; JD, U. Ariz., 1997. Bar: Calif. 1997, U.S. Ct. Appeals (9th cir.) 1998, DC 1999, U.S. Dist. Ct. (ctrl. and no. dists.) Calif. 2001. Law clk. to Hon. Melvin Brunetti U.S. Ct. Appeals (9th cir.), Reno, 1997—98; assoc. Kirkland & Ellis, Washington, 1998—99; law clk. to Hon. William H. Rehnquist U.S. Supreme Ct., Washington, 1999—2000; atty. Greene, Broillet, Panish & Wheeler, Santa Monica, Calif., 2001—05; ptnr. Panish, Shea & Boyle, L.A., 2005—. Office: Panish Shea & Boyle 11111 Santa Monica Blvd Ste 700 Los Angeles CA 90025 Office Phone: 310-477-1700. E-mail: Boyle@PSandB.com.

BOYLE, LARA FLYNN, actress; b. Davenport, IA, Mar. 24, 1970; Actress: appeared in films made for TV and for movie house distbn.: Amerika, 1987, Poltergiest III, 1988, Terror on Highway 91, 1989, How I Got into College, 1989, The Preppie Murder, 1989, The Rookie, 1990, Mobsters, 1991, Wayne's World, 1992, Where the Day Takes You, 1992, The Temp., 1993, Three of Hearts, 1993, Red Rock West, 1993, Threesome, 1994, Baby's Day Out, 1994, The Road to Wellville, 1994, Three IFS and a Maybe, 1996, Dogwater, 1997, Twin Peaks, 1989, Dead Poets Society, 1989, Men in Black II, 2002; TV appearances include The Practice, 1997-; host Saturday Night Live, 2001.

BOYLE, MICHAEL J., communications company executive; MBA, Kellogg Sch. Mgmt., 1986. Exec. Bell & Howell, IBM/Rolm, Fujitsu Bus. Comms. Sys., Phoenix Wireless Group; CEO Elcotel, 1991-97, pres., CEO Sarasota, Fla., 1999-00, pres., CEO, chmn. bd. dirs., 2000—. Office: Telular Corp Ste 109 420 Thornton Rd Lithia Springs GA 30122 Office Phone: 800-229-2326, 678-945-7770. Office Fax: 678-945-7758.*

BOYLE, PETER, actor; b. Phila., Oct. 18, 1935; m. Loraine Alterman, Oct. 1977; children: Lucy, Amy. Attended, LaSalle Coll., Phila. Former Monk Christian Bros. order. Actor in Off-Broadway shows, N.Y.C., also Second City group, Chgo., and TV commls.; appeared in films including Medium Cool, 1969, Joe, 1970, Diary of a Mad Housewife, 1970, T.R. Baskin, 1972, The Candidate, 1972, Steelyard Blues, 1973, Slither, 1973, The Friends of Eddie Coyle, 1973, Kid Blue, 1973, Crazy Joe, 1974, Young Frankenstein, 1974, Taxi Driver, 1976, Swashbuckler, 1976, F.I.S.T, 1978, The Brink's Job, 1978, Hardcore, 1979, Beyond the Poseidon Adventure, 1979, In God We Trust, 1980, Where the Buffalo Roam, 1980, Hammett, 1980, Outland, 1981, Yellowbeard, 1983, Johnny Dangerously, 1984, Turk 182, 1985, Surrender, 1987, Walker, 1987, The In Crowd, 1988, Speedzone, 1989, Funny, 1989, The Dream Team, 1989, Men of Respect, 1991, Kickboxer 2, 1991, Honeymoon in Vegas, 1992, Malcolm X, 1992, The Shadow, 1994, The Killer, 1994, Exquisit Tenderness, 1994, The Santa Clause, 1994, Katie, 1995, While You Were Sleeping, 1995, Death and Compass, 1996, Final Vendetta, 1996, That Darn Cat, 1997, Milk and Money, 1997, Species II, 1998, Dr. Dolittle, 1998, Monsters Ball, 2001, The Adventures of Pluto Nash, 2002, The Santa Clause 2, 2002, Scooby-Doo 2: Monsters Unleashed, 2004; (TV movies) Tail Gunner Joe, 1977, From Here to Eternity, In the Lake of the Woods, 1996, A Deadly Vision, 1997, Master Spy: The Robert Hanssen Story, 2002; (TV series) Joe Bash, 1986, Comedy Tonight, 1970, Everybody Loves Raymond, 1996—2005 (nominee Outstanding Supporting Actor in Comedy Series Emmy award 1999-2001, nominee Funniest Supporting Male Performer in TV Series Am. Comedy award 2000); TV guest appearances include Cagney & Lacey, 1988, Flying Blind, 1992, 93, NYPD Blue, 1994, 95, Lois & Clark: The New Adventures of Superman, 1994, 95, The X Files, 1995 (Emmy award for Outstanding Guest Actor in a Drama Sereis 1996), The Single Guy, 1996, 97, Cosby, 1997, The King of Queens, 1998, others. Recipient Emmy award, 1996.*

BOYLE, REGIS LOUISE, retired journalist educator, editor; b. Washington; d. Charles Weems and Elma (Payne) B. AB, Trinity Coll., 1933; MA, Cath. U. Am., Washington, 1934, PhD, 1939; postgrad., Columbia U., 1940. Tchr. Ea. H.S., Washington, 1936-55, Woodrow Wilson H.S., Washington, 1955-65, Walt Whitman H.S., Bethesda, Md., 1965-80; assoc. prof. journalism, chair Cath. U. Am., Washington, 1947-75; prof. U. Md., Coll. Pk., 1975-89; ret., 1989. Mem. adv. bd. Student Press Law Ctr., Arlington, Va., 1978—84. Contbg. editor: Springboard to Journalism, 1973, 2d edit., 1985. Pres. Washington chpt. Nat. Christ Child Soc., 1982-85, nat. pres., 1990-92; nat. pres. Trinity Coll. Alumnae Assn., 1955-59; v.p. Cath. U. Alumni Assn., 1951-53, 69-71. Recipient Medal of Merit, Journalism Edn. Assn., 1968, Outstanding Journalism Tchr. award So. Interscholastic Press Assn., 1981, Mary Virginia Merrick award Nat. Christ Child Soc., 1993; Dow Jones Newspaper Fund fellow W.Va. U., 1966; named Md.'s Outstanding Journalism Tchr. Balt. Sunpapers, 1972, Advisor of Yr., Coll. Media Advisors, 1974, Dow Jones Nat. Journalism Tchr. of Yr., 1980. Mem. John Carroll Soc., Order Malta (Pres.'s award 1998), Kenwood Country Club, Cosmos Club. Roman Catholic. Home: 3026 Legation St NW Washington DC 20015-1240

BOYLE, RICHARD JOHN, art historian, author; b. N.Y.C., June 3, 1932; s. James and Gertrude (Eichhorn) B.; m. Patricia Murray, June 19, 1971; 1 son, Eric; stepchildren: Rick, Cheryl, Barbara. BA, Adelphi U., Garden City, N.Y., 1954; cert. fine art, Oxford (Eng.) U., 1959; postgrad., Art Students League, N.Y.C., 1962. Profl. painter, 1959-66; curator Internat. Art Found., Newport, R.I., 1962; dir. Middletown (Ohio) Fine Arts Ctr., 1963-65; curator painting and sculpture Cin. Art Mus., 1965-73; dir. Pa. Acad. Fine Arts, 1973-82; lectr. art history Phila. Coll. Art, 1984-86, acting dir. continuing edn., 1986; lectr. art history Phila. Coll. of Textiles, 1990—; assoc. prof. Temple U., Japan, 1991-92. Adviser Nexus Gallery, Artist Coop.; lectr. Tyler Sch. of Art, Temple U., 1987—; coll. art assoc., mem. bd. advisors Creative Artists Network, 1985—; mem. artistic advisors Am. Poetry Rev., 1983—. Author: American Impressionism, 1974, John Twachtman, 1979; co-author: Genius of American Painting, 1973, Willard Metcalf, 1988, Connection With A Place: The Collection of the Brandywine River Museum, 1991; art editor: Ency. Am. History, 1973. Mem. exec. com. Phila. Devel. Corp. Served with U.S. Army, 1954-56. Benjamin Franklin fellow Royal Soc. Arts, 1976 Mem. Nat. Soc. Lit. and Art.

BOYLE, TATIANA GENNADIEVNA, research scientist; b. Khabarovsk, Russia, June 15, 1969; arrived in U.S., 1995, naturalized, 2004; d. Gennadyi Petrovich Sapozhnikov and Tamara Mikhailovna Sapozhnikova; m. David Edward Boyle, Nov. 29, 1997; 1 child, Austin Michael. MS in Biology and Chemistry magna cum laude, Khabarovsk State Pedagogical U., 1991; PhD in Biology, Russian Acad. Scis., Ecology Rsch. Inst., Khabarovsk, 1995. Sr. scientist Russian Acad. Scis., Khabarovsk, 1991—99; rsch. scientist USDA Forest Svc., Sitka, Alaska, 1997—98; sr. scientist North Pacific Mountain Flora Rsch., Portland, Oreg., 1997—. Scientist Tahoe-Baikal Inst., South Lake Tahoe, Calif., 1995—97; sr. scientist Sustainable Ecosystems Inst., Portland, Oreg., 1999—; author and editor TV series Path in the Forest, 1998. Author: Distribution and Preservation of Rare Vascular Plant Species (Khabarovsk Territory, Jewish Autonomous Region), 1994, Rare Plants of Khabarovsk Ter., 1998; contbr. chapters to books. Mem.: AAAS, Am. Inst. Biol. Scis. Achievements include research in new species habitats in Siberia and Alaska; new classification for rare plants species; development of sys. of natural protected areas for rare and endangered species in Russian Far East. Avocations: skiing, photography.

BOYLE, T.C., writer, literature educator; b. Peekskill, N.Y., Dec. 2, 1948; married; 3 children. BA U. Potsdam, 1968; MFA, U. Iowa Writer's Workshop, 1974; PhD in 19th century brit. lit. U. Iowa, 1977; LHD (hon.), SUNY, 1991. Prof. of English, founder, creaitve writing program U. of Southern Calif., 1978—. Author: stories have appeared in The New Yorker, Harper's, Esquire, The Atlantic Monthly, Playboy, The Paris Review, GQ, Antaeus, Granta, (book) Descent of Man, 1979 (St. Lawrence award for fiction, best story collection of the yr., 1980), Water Music, 1982 (Prix Passion publishers prize for best novel of the yr., 1989), Budding Prospects, 1984, Greasy Lake, 1985 (Commonwealth of Calif., Silver medal for lit., 55th ann. awards, 1986), World's End, 1987 (Commonwealth Club of Calif. gold medal for lit., best novel of the yr., 57th ann. awards, 1988, PEN/Faulkner award, best novel of the yr., 1988, Editor's Choice, N.Y. Times Book Review, one of the 16 best books of the yr., 1987), If the River was Whiskey, 1989 (Editor's Choice, N.Y. Times Book Review, one of the best 13 books of the yr., 1989, PEN Ctr. West Literary prize, best short story collection of the yr., 1989), East is East, 1990, The Road to Wellville, 1993, Without A Hero, 1994, The Tortilla Curtain, 1995 (Prix Medicis Etranger, 1997), Riven Rock, 1998, T.C. Boyle Stories, 1998 (Bernard Malamud prize in short fiction from the PEN/Faulkner Found., 1999), A Friend of the Earth, 2000, After the Plague, 2001 (Souther Calif. bookseller's assn. award for best fiction title of the yr., 2002), Drop City, 2003, (other) The Inner Circle, 2004, (book) Tooth and Claw, 2005. Recipient Nat. Endowment for the Arts fellowship, 1977, 1983.

BOYLE, TERRENCE W., federal judge; b. Passaic, NJ, Dec. 22, 1945; married; 3 children. BA, Brown U., 1967; JD, Am. U., 1970. Minority counsel housing subcom., banking and currency com. US Ho. of Reps., 1970-73; legis. asst. US Senator J. Helms, 1973; judge US Dist. Ct. (ea. dist.), NC, 1984-97, chief judge, 1997—; nominee US Ct. Appeals (4th cir.), 2005. Federal judge; b. 1945. BA, Brown U., 1967; JD, Am. U., 1970. Minority counsel housing subcom., banking and currence com. US Ho. of Reps., 1970-73; legis. asst. U.S. senator J. Helms, 1973; judge U.S. Dist. Ct. Ea. Dist., N.C., 1984-97; chief judge 1997—. Office: US Dist Ct PO Box 306 Elizabeth City NC 27907-0306*

BOYLE, TIM, apparel executive; s. Gert Boyle; m. Mary Boyle; 2 children. BS in Journalism, U. Oreg., 1971. With Columbia Sportswear Co., Portland, Oreg., 1970—, pres., CEO, 1989—. Trustee Reed Coll.; mem. Young Presidents' Orgn.; bd. dirs. Pacific Crest Outward Bound Sch., Jesuit H.S. Named one of Sports Industry's 100 Most Influential Players, Sportstyle mag., 1993—96; recipient N.W. Entrepreneur of Yr. award, Inc. Mag., 1992.

BOYLE, WILLIAM CHARLES, engineering educator; b. Mpls., Apr. 9, 1936; s. Robert and Daphne Boyle; m. Nancy Lee Hahn, Apr. 11, 1959; children: Elizabeth Lynn, Michele Jenette, Jane Lynette, Robert William. CE, U. Cin., 1959, MS in Sanitary Engring., 1960; PhD in Environ. Engring., Calif. Inst. Tech., 1963. Registered profl. engr., Wis., Ohio. With Milw. Sewerage Commn., 1955-56; civil engr. O. G. Loomis & Sons, Covington, Ky., 1956-59; asst. engr. Ohio River Valley Water Sanitation Commn., summer 1959; asst. prof. dept. engring. U. Wis., Madison, 1963-66, assoc. prof., 1966-70, prof. dept. civil and environ. engring., 1970-96, chmn. dept. civil and environ. engring., 1984-86, assoc. chair, 1988-96, emeritus prof., 1996—. Vis. prof. Rogaland Distriktshogskole, Stavanger, Norway, 1975-76; vis. prin. engr. Montgomery Engrs. Inc., Pasadena, Calif., 1988-89; cons. Procter & Gamble Co., Monsanto Co., S.B. Foot Tanning Co., Wis. Canners & Freezers Assn., Wis. Concrete Pipe Assn., Oscar Mayer & Co., Bartlett-Snow, Hide Svc. Corp., W.R. Grace & Co., Lake to Lake Dairies, Milw. Tallow, Wausau Paper Co., Packerland Packing Co., Ray-O-Vac, U.S. Army CERL, Owen Ayres & Assocs., Donohue Engrs., Davy Engrs., Carl C. Crane, Green Engring., RSE divsn. Ayres & Assocs., Schreiber Corp. Inc., Sanitaire, J.M. Montgomery, Engrs., Camp, Dresser, McKee Phila. Mixing Sys., Polkowski, Boyle, & Assocs., Rust E&I Com.; peer rev. panel on environ. engring. EPA; accreditation visitor Accreditation Bd. for Engring. and Tech., 1990—. Contbr. chapters to books, articles to profl. jours. Sr. warden St. Andrews Episcopal Ch., Madison, 1972-74, treas., 1979-85. Recipient Engring. Disting. Alumnus award U. Cin., 1986, Founders award U.S.A. nat. com. Internat. Assn. Water Pollution Rsch. & Control, 1988, commendation EPA, 1989; Mills Found. scholar U. Cin., 1954-59; USPHS trainee, U. Cin., 1959-60, fellow Ford Found., Calif. Inst. Tech., 1960-61, USPHS, Calif. Inst. Tech., 1961-63 Mem. ASCE (life, Wis. chpt., advisor U. Wis. student chpt. 1968-71, chmn. student affairs com. 1970-72, chmn. profl. activities com. 1972-74, nat., control mem. tech. coun. on codes and standards-environ. standards 1999—, chmn. environ. stds. devel. coun. 1998-2001, chair oxygen transfer standards com., 1975-2002, history and heritage com., reviewer EED Jour., Rudolf Hering medal 1975, Engring. Achievement award Wis. chpt. 1986, Engr. of Yr. award Wis. sect. 1998), Water Environment Fedn. (life, rsch. com., joint task force-pretreatment of wastewater, tech. practice com.-energy in treatment plant design, chmn. program com., bd. control, 1996-98, jour. reviewer, chmn. tech. practice com. task force on aeration, Radebaugh award 1978, Eddy award com. 1992-98, Harrison Prescot Eddy Rsch. medal 1989, chmn. rsch. symposia, editl. bd. 2004—, water environ. rsch. found. rsch. coun. 2005—, Gordon Maskew Fair medal for environ. engring. edn., 1992, Arthur Sydney Bedell award 2001), Am. Water Works Assn. (life, chmn. task group on oxygen transfer), Am. Acad. Environ. Engrs. (diplomate, life, accreditation vis. for Accreditation Bd. Engring and Tech., chmn. edn. com. 1993, trustee 1994-97, pres.-elect 1998, pres. 1999-2000, rep. bd. dirs. ABET, 1994-2000, commr. Engr. Accreditation comm. 2001-, Stanley E. Kappe award 2002), Am. Foundrymen's Soc. (com. on waste disposal, Outstanding Rsch. Paper award environ. cen. div. 1989), Sigma Xi, Theta Tau, Phi Eta Sigma, Chi Epsilon, Tau Beta Pi (advisor U. Wis. student chpt. 1994-96). Episcopalian. Avocations: photography, travel. Home: 105 Carillon Dr Madison WI 53705-4614 Office: Univ Wis 2256 Engineering Hall 1415 Engineering Dr Madison WI 53706-1607 Office Phone: 608-238-4559. Business E-Mail: boyle@engr.wisc.edu.

BOYLE, WILLIAM LEO, JR., educational consultant, retired academic administrator; b. Utica, NY, July 23, 1933; s. William Leo and Gladys (Kuney) B. AB, Colgate U., 1955; postgrad. in Spl. Mgmt. Program, Cornell U. Law Sch., 1960—61; MA, Columbia U., 1964, Profl. Diploma in Ednl. Adminstrn., 1967, EdD, 1969; LLD (hon.), Hawthorne Coll., 1979; postdoctoral, Harvard U., 1979—81; LHD (hon.), Mercy Coll., 1983; LittD (hon.), Curry Coll., 1992. Participant advanced mgmt. program, recruiter, ednl. adviser Procter & Gamble Co., Cin., 1958-60; legis. aide higher edn. com. N.Y. State Senate, Albany, 1961-62; account exec., ednl. cons. Batten, Barton, Durstine & Osborn, N.Y.C., 1962-64; assoc. dir. devel., presdl. asst. Wesleyan U., Middletown, Conn., 1964-65; program cons. Coun. for Aid to Edn., N.Y.C., 1965-70, asst. v.p., 1970-72, v.p., 1972-75; pres. Keuka Coll., Keuka Pk., NY, 1975—78, Curry Coll., Milton, Mass., 1978—92, pres. emeritus, 1992—; part-time practice as ednl. cons. to pvt. colls. and univs., Utica, 1992—. Pres., trustee 1036 Pk. Avenue Corp., NYC, 1970—74; ednl. cons. Pres. Ford Com., Washington, 1976. Author: The National Corporate Educational Support Movement, 1954-1966, 1969; contbr. articles to ednl. and profl. jours. Vice chmn. nat. bus. and industry com. Colgate U., Hamilton, NY, 1974—, mem. nat. coun., 1975—, ann. fund exec. com., 1975—, Colgate '55 class agt., 1994—, mem. maj. gifts com., established Boyle Scholarship, 1985, Boyle award in polit. sci., 1997; mem. bd. devel. com. Cmty. Found., Utica, 1992—98; established Boyle Individual Fund, Cmty. Found., Utica, 1991, Boyle Parents Meml. Fund, Cmty. Found., Utica, 2002; bd. dirs. Slocum-Dickson Found., Utica, 1991—, Family Svcs. of the Mohawk Valley, Utica, 1992—, House of the Good Shepherd, Utica, 1992—, Oneida County Hist. Soc., Utica, 1994—. Lt. USAF, 1955—58. Decorated Comdr.'s citation USAF. Mem. various ednl. and profl. orgns., also Colgate Univ. Club (N.Y.C.), Columbia Univ. Club (N.Y.C.), Ft. Schuyler Club (Utica) (bd. mgrs.), Sadaquada Golf Club (Utica), Yahnundasis Golf Club (Utica), Rotary. Home: 12 Rose Pl Utica NY 13502-5614

BOYLES, FREDERICK HOLDREN, historian; b. Gainesville, Fla., Nov. 9, 1954; s. Eugene Harry and Frances Louise (Holdren) B.; m. Deborah Anne Beverly, Aug. 21, 1976; children: Cynthia Beverly, Joseph Holdren. A in Edn. and History, Abraham Baldwin Coll., 1974; BS in Edn. and History, U. Ga., 1976; M in Recreation and Parks Adminstrn., Clemson U., 1981. Dir. trail camp Goshen (Va.) Scout Camps, 1975-79; tchr. history and geography Waycross (Ga.) City Schs., 1976-78; instr. grad. students Clemson (S.C.) U., 1978-79; outdoor recreation planner Nat. Park Svc., Atlanta, 1979-81; historian Cumberland Gap Nat. Hist. Park, Middlesboro, Ky., 1981-85; supt. Moores Greek Nat. Battlefield, Currie, N.C., 1985-89, Andersonville (Ga.)-Jimmy Carter Nat. Hist. Sites, 1989—. Adj. faculty Lincoln Meml. U., Harrogate, Tenn., 1983-84, U. N.C., Wilmington, 1987. Scoutmaster troop 231 Boy Scouts Am., Americus, Ga., 1994; elder 1st Presbyn. Ch., Americus, 1991—. Comdr. USNR, 1987, comdg. officer navy cargo handling bn. 11, Jacksonville, Fla. Named Supt. of Yr., Nat. Pk. Svc., 1998; recipient Superior Achievement award, U.S. Dept. Interior, 1980, Good Citizenship award, SAR, 1989; scholar Grad. alumni scholar, Clemson U., 1979. Mem. Sumter C. of C. (bd. dirs. 1992—), Americus Rotary Club, Burgaw N.C. Rotary Club (bd. dirs. 1988, 90), Burgaw Area C. of C. (pres. 1989). Home: 200 Webber Rd Americus GA 31719-2136 Office: Nat Park Svc 496 Cemetery Rd Andersonville GA 31711-9707 E-mail: fred_boyles@nps.gov.

BOYLES, JAMES KENNETH, retired banker; b. Louisville, Jan. 27, 1916; s. Forrest Lee and Florence (Glenn) B.; m. Hilda Margaret Rose, Sept. 13, 1940; children: Margaret, James, Douglas, Kevin. Student, Columbia U., Am. Inst. Banking, Rutgers U. With Guaranty Trust Co., N.Y.C., 1933-37; loan officer Chem. Bank, N.Y.C., 1937-50; exec. v.p. The Nat. State Bank, Elizabeth, N.J., 1950-83, dir., 1965-88. Trustee emeritus Union Coll., Cranford N.J. Served to 1st lt., inf., U.S. Army, 1942-46, ETO. Decorated 2 Bronze stars, Purple Heart. Mem. Robert Morris Assocs. (pres. 1963) Republican. Episcopalian.

BOYLL, DAVID LLOYD, broadcast executive; b. Terre Haute, Ind., Aug. 17, 1940; s. Lloyd A. and Stella Elizabeth (Ellinger) B.; m. Margie R. Coker, Apr. 14, 1962; children: Elizabeth Marie, Kelli Renae. BS in Edn., Abilene Christian U., 1964. Announcer Sta. KWKC, Abilene, Tex., 1959-64; program dir. Sta. KWKC-AM-FM, Abilene, 1964-68; sta. mgr. Sta. KFMN-FM, Abilene, 1968-74, owner, operator, 1974-80, ptnr., gen. mgr., 1980-82, Sta. KEYJ-AM-FM, Abilene, 1982-92; pres., mgr. Sta. KHXS/EZ106, Abilene, 1992-96; ptnr. KMPC-AM/KWKC-AM, Abilene, 1998—. Part-owner Sta. KYYD (now KWKC-AM), Abilene, 1995—; owner KMPC-EZ 1560, 1997—; ptnr., owner KWKC-AM, KZQQ-AM, 1998—. Pres. Abilene Downtown Assn., 1980-83; pres. Chisholm Trail coun. Boy Scouts Am., 1985-87; chmn. adv. com. Taylor County Juvenile Bd.; chmn. Abilene State Sch. Vols., 1987-90, named Vol. of Yr., 1990; chmn. local emergency planning com. Taylor County. Recipient Silver Beaver award Boy Scouts

Am., 1987, Leadership and Comms. award Toastmasters Internat., 2003. Mem. Rotary (past pres., bd. dirs. Abilene club). Republican. Home: 3949 N 9th St Abilene TX 79603-5543 Office: KZQQ/KWKC-AM 402 Cypress St Ste 510 Abilene TX 79601 Office Phone: 325-673-1455. Business E-Mail: dave@kwkc.com.

BOYNE, WALTER JAMES, writer, retired museum director; b. East St. Louis, Ill., Feb. 2, 1929; s. Walter William and Emily (Campbell) B.; m. Jeanne Quigley, Dec. 26, 1952; children: Mary Louise, Katherine Elizabeth, William James, Margaret Ann. BBA, U. Calif., Berkeley, 1958; MBA, U. Pitts., 1963; PhD (hon.), Salem Coll., 1985. Commd. 2d lt. USAF, 1952, advanced through grades to col., 1971, ret., 1974; asst. curator Nat. Air and Space Mus., Washington, 1974-75, curator, 1975-78, exec. officer, 1978-80, asst. dir., 1980-82, acting dir., 1982-83, dir., 1983-86; ret., 1986. Chmn. bd. dirs. Wingspan TV Channel; aerospace expert in residence Discover Comms.; v.p. Fighter Pilot Prodns. Author: Boeing B-52, 1981, Messerschmitt Me-262, 1980, Treasures of Silver Hill, 1982, Flying, 1979, Jet Age, 1979, De Havilland DH-4, 1983, McDonnell Douglas F-4, 1983, Vertical Flight, 1983, Leading Edge, 1986, (novel) The Wild Blue, 1986, The Smithsonian Book of Flight, 1987, The Power Behind the Wheel, 1988, Trophy for Eagles, 1989, Weapons of Desert Shield, 1991, Gulf War, 1991, Eagles of War, 1991, Air Force Eagles, 1992, Classic Aircraft, 1992, Art in Flight, 1992, Silver Wings, 1993, Clash of Wings, 1994, Clash of Titans, 1995, Beyond the Wild Blue, 1997, Beyond the Horizons, 1998, Brassey Air Combat Reader, 1999, Aces in Command, 2001, Classic Aircraft, 2001, Best of Wings, 2001, Aviation 100, 2001, Encyclopedia of Air Warfare, 2002, The Two O'Clock War, 2002, Dawn Over Kitty Hawk, 2003, Chronicle of Flight, 2003, The Influence of Air Power on History, 2003, Rising Tide, 2003, Operation Iraqi Freedom, 2003, Today's Best Military Writing, 2003; prodr., writer: (video) Beyond the Wild Blue; author, host, narrator: (video) Clash of Wings, 1998, The Sculptures of John Safer, 1998. Recipient Best Fgn. Book award Aero Club de France, 1982, Robert A. Brooks award Smithsonian Instn., 1980, Best Fiction and Non-Fiction awards Aviation Space Writers, 1987, Thomas McKean Meml. Cup, 1989, Cliff Henderson Trophy 1986, Gil Robb Wilson award AIA, 1997, Presiden'ts award for lifetime achievement Nat. Aeronautics Assn., 2005; named Elder Statesman of Aviation Nat. Aviation Assn., 1998. Mem. Daedalians, Am. Aviation Hist. Soc. (nat. advisor), Author's Guild, Sons of the Desert, Cosmos Club, Flying Aces Club Home: 21028 Starflower Way Ashburn VA 20147-4700 Office Phone: 703-689-1344. Personal E-mail: wboyne@cqi.com. *There is a pleasure in work; it is doubled if appreciated by a peer.*

BOYNES, SEAN G., dental anesthesiologist, researcher; b. Wheeling, W.Va., Apr. 19, 1978; s. William and Jennie Boynes; m. Vicki Malush, Apr. 24, 2004. BS, Lipscomb U., 1999; MS, Almeda U., 2003; DMD, U. Pitts., 2003. Diplomate Nat. Dental Bd. Anesthesiology. Faculty clin. rsch. assoc. U. Pitts., 2003—04, residen tin dental anesthesiology, 2003—. Assoc. editor: The Bull.: The Dental Soc. of Western Pa., 2004—; contbr. articles to profl. jours. Fellow: Am. Dental Soc. of Anesthesiology (assoc. Rsch. Writing award 2004); mem.: ADA (corr.), Am. Inst. of Biol. Scis. (corr.), Acad. of Gen. Dentistry (corr.), Am. Acad. of Devel. Medicine and Dentistry (assoc.), Am. Soc. of Forensic Odontolgy (assoc.), Am. Soc. of Dental Anesthesiologists (assoc.), Alpha Chi (life), Delta Sigma Delta (life). Achievements include research in the efficacy and clinical anesthetic charactics of 4% articaine with and without epinephrine when administered for dental anesthesia; sedation anesthesia education in dental schools of the United States.

BOYNTON, JAMES STEPHEN, lawyer; b. Stamford, Conn., Apr. 3, 1946; s. Horace William and Lorraine Anne (Nelsen) Boynton; m. Caroline Foster Cochran, May 9, 1970 (div. Nov. 1996); children: Caroline Lorraine, James Cochran; m. Kathleen Mary Peluso, Jan. 1, 2001. BA, Williams Coll., 1968; JD, U. Pa., 1971. Bar: N.Y. 1973, U.S. Dist. Ct. (so. dist.) N.Y. 1973. Assoc. Debevoise & Plimpton, N.Y.C., 1971-80; ptnr. Tung, Drabkin & Boynton, N.Y.C., 1980-85, Salans, N.Y.C., 1985—. Trustee Norfolk (Conn.) Land Trust, 1990—, Cushing Acad., 1993—. 1st lt. U.S. Army, 1972. Mem.: Norfolk Country Club (pres. 1985—87). Congregationalist. Home: 470 W End Ave New York NY 10024 Office: Salans 620 5th Ave New York NY 10020-2402 Office Phone: 212-632-5502. Business E-Mail: jboynton@salans.com.

BOYNTON, ROBERT MERRILL, retired psychology professor; b. Evanston, Ill., Oct. 28, 1924; s. Merrill Holmes and Eleanor (Matthews) B.; m. Alice Neiley, Apr. 9, 1947 (dec. Oct. 15, 1996); children: Sherry, Michael, Neiley, Geoffrey; m. Sheleah Maloney, Oct. 17, 1998. Student, Antioch Coll., 1942-43, U. Ill., 1943-45; AB, Amherst Coll., 1948; PhD, Brown U., 1952. Asst. prof. psychology and optics U. Rochester, N.Y., 1952-57, asso. prof., 1957-61, prof., 1961-74, founder, dir. Ctr. for Visual Sci., 1963-71, chmn. dept. psychology, 1971-74; prof. psychology U. Calif., San Diego, 1974-91, assoc. dean grad. studies and research, 1987-91; ret., 1991. Guest researcher Nat. Phys. Lab., Teddington, Eng., 1960-61; vis. prof. physiology U. Calif. Med. Center, San Francisco, 1969-70 Author: Human Color Vision, 1979, 2d edit., 1996; chmn. bd. editors Vision Research, 1982-86; contbr. articles to profl. jours. Served with USNR, 1943-45. Recipient Charles F. Prentice award Am. Acad. Optometry, 1997. Fellow AAAS, Optical Soc. Am. (dir.-at-large 1966-69, Frederick Ives medal 1995), APA, Assn. for Rsch. in Vision and Ophthalmology (trustee 1984-89); mem. NAS. Home: 376 Bellaire St Del Mar CA 92014-2207 Business E-Mail: rboynton@ucsd.edu.

BOYNTON, SANDRA KEITH, illustrator, cartoonist, stationery products executive; b. Orange, NJ, Apr. 3, 1953; d. Robert Whitney and Jeanne Carolyn (Ragsdale) B.; m. James Patrick McEwan, Oct. 28, 1978; 1 dau., Caitlin Boynton McEwan. BA in English, Yale U., 1974, postgrad. Sch. Drama, 1976-77; postgrad., U. Calif.-Berkeley Drama Grad. Sch., 1974-75. Designer Recycled Paper Products, Inc., Chgo., 1974—, v.p., 1980—; illustrator greeting cards, 1975—. Illustrator/author: Hippos Go Berserk, 1977, If At First, 1979, Gopher Baroque, 1979, The Compleat Turkey, 1980, Chocolate: The Consuming Passion, 1982, Moo, Baa, La La La, 1982, The Going to Bed Book, 1982, But Not the Hippopotamus, 1982, Opposites, 1982, A is for Angry, 1983, Blue Hat, Green Hat, 1984, Doggies, 1984, Chloë and Maude, 1985, Christmastime, 1987, Oh My, Oh, My, Oh Dinosaurs, 1993, One, Two Three, 1993, Barnyard Dance, 1993, Birthday Monsters, 1993, Pajama Time, 2000, Yay, You!: Moving Out, Moving Up, Moving On, 2001 (Publishers Weekly picture book bestseller, 2005), Philadelphia Chickens, 2002, Snuggle Puppy, 2003, Fuzzy, Fuzzy, Fuzzy!, 2003, Belly Button Book, 2005, (with Jamie MacEwan) Story of Grump and Pout, 1983, The Heart of Cool, 2001; Albums: Grunt: Pigorian Chant, 1999 (Amazon.com bestseller), (with Michael Ford): Rhinoceros Tap, 1996, Philadelphia Chickens, 2002. Mem. Soc. Of Friends. Known for creating famed birthday card greeting "Hippo Birdies Two Ewes.".*

BOYSE, PETER DENT, academic administrator; b. Saginaw, Mich., Mar. 24, 1945; s. John Wesley and Ellen Elizabeth (Dent) B.; m. Barbra Ann Meehan, Sept. 2, 1972; children: Heather, Cassandra. BA, Albion Coll., 1967; MS, U. Mich., 1969, Oreg. State U., 1973, PhD, 1987. Nuclear scientist Westinghouse, Pitts., 1969-71; dir. student activities Calif. State U., Northridge, 1973-74, epic dir., 1974-76; dir. student devel. Linn-Benton Community Coll., Albany, Oreg., 1976-79, ctr. dir., 1979-82, asst. to pres., 1982-88; exec. v.p., COO Delta Coll., University Center, Mich., 1988—92, pres., 1993—. Facilitator Emerging Leaders Inst., Ann Arbor, Mich., 1990; chair Mich. C. of C. Assn., 2000-01. Contbr. articles to profl. jours. Chair Bd. League Innovation, 2003. Mem. Am. Assn. C. of C. (mem. bd. 2001-04). Avocations: reading, golf, travel. Office: Delta Coll 1961 Delta Dr University Center MI 48710-0001 Home: 1980 E Hotchkiss Rd Bay City MI 48706-9006

BOYSEN, MELICENT PEARL, finance company executive; b. Houston, Dec. 1, 1943; d. William Thomas and Mildred Pearl (Walker) Richardson; m. Stephen M. Boysen, Sept. 10, 1961 (dec. 1973); children: Marshella, Stephanie, Stephen. Student, Cen. Mo. State, 1973-75. Owner, pres. Boysen Enterprises, Kansas City, Mo., 1973-93; fin. cons., underwriter New Eng. Life Ins. Co., Kansas City, 1978-81; owner, pres. Boysen Agri-Svcs., Kansas City, 1984-94; pres. Boysen & Assocs., Inc., Kansas City, 1987—; stockholder, pres. Am. Crumb Rubber, Inc., Kansas City, 1996—; prin. Initiatives Worldwide, Inc., Kansas City, 2002—. Cons. San Luis Rey (Calif.) Tribal Water Authority, Wind River (Wyo.) Reservation, Cheyenne River (S.D.) Sioux, Iroquois Nations (N.Y.), 1983—; founding bd. dirs., pres. Am. Indian Youth Orgn., Visible Horizons, 1987—. Founding bd. dirs. Rose Brooks Ctr. Battered Women, Kansas City, 1979-87, treas., 1979-81; exec. dir. The Flame Spirit Run, 1992; citationist, 1993; mem. Pres.'s Vol. Action Awards Program; mem. Pres.'s Bus. Adv. Coun., 2001. Recipient Women of Conscience award Panel Am. Women of Greater Kansas City. Mem. DAR, Kans. C. of C. and Industry, Kansas City C. of C. Methodist. Avocations: stamp collecting/philately, sports cars. Office: Boysen & Assocs 4112 Pennsylvania Ave Ste 202 Kansas City MO 64111-3057 Office Phone: 816-960-1900. E-mail: mboysen@boysencompanies.com.

BOYSON, MICHAEL ANDREW, investment consultant; b. Bangor, Maine, Dec. 18, 1953; s. Edward William and Gloria Patricia B.; m. Nancy Lewis Grant Boyson, May 10, 1980; children: Oscar Andrew, Elise Cook. BA, Colby Coll., Waterville, Maine, 1976. Cert. investment mgmt. analyst. Vol. U.S. Peace Corps., Rabala, Sierra Leone, 1980-82; cons. UN Devel. Program, Rabala, Sierra Leone, 1982-84; v.p. E.F. Hutton & Co., Inc., Portland, Maine, 1984-88, Shearson Lebanon Bros., Portland, Maine, 1988-95; sr. v.p. Sobmon Smith Barney, Portland, Maine, 1995—. Mem. Investment Mgmt. Cons. Assn., Chgo., 1998—. Mem. Maine Coll. Savings Bd., Augusta, 1998—, United Way Found., Portland, Maine, 1996—; pres. Greely Ski Boosters, Cumberland, Maine, 1998—, Ctr. for Cultural Exchange, Portland, Maine, 1996-99. Recipient 2nd Pl. Bradbury Mountain Hill Climb, Pownal, Maine, 2000. Mem. Woodlands Club, Bay Club, Maine Track Club. Episcopalian. Avocations: running, skiing, hiking, sailing, golf. Home: 24 Colonial Dr North Yarmouth ME 04097 Office: Solomon Smith Barney 100 Middle St Portland ME 04101 E-mail: mike_boyson@hotmail.com.

BOYTE, GEORGE GRIFFIN, lawyer; b. Humboldt, Tenn., Mar. 10, 1925; s. Hubert C. and Olga (Hogan) Boyte; m. Carol Dent, June 20, 1953; children: Katherine (Dent), Bonnie Carol (Capsuto), George Griffin Jr. BA, Vanderbilt U., 1949; JD, 1952. Bar: Tenn. 1952. Mem. firm J. Frank Warmath, Humboldt, 1952—54; ptnr. Warmath & Boyte, Humboldt, 1954—; city atty. City of Humboldt, 1973—83; mem. Tenn. Gen. Assembly, 1961—62; del Tenn. Constl. Conv., 1959, 1965. Served USMCR, 1943—45. Recipient Pub. Trust award, Humboldt Courier-Chronicle, 1976; fellow Am. Bar Found., Tenn. Bar Found. Mem.: Humboldt C. of C. (pres. 1971—72), Gibson County Bar Assn. (pres. 1968—69), Tenn. Bar Assn. (pres. 1978—79, mem. ho. of dels. 1979—82), Tenn. Def. Lawyers Assn. (v.p. 1980—), Am. Law Inst., ABA (mem. council gen. practice sect. 1974—79, ho. of del. 1980—86), Golf and Country Club (pres. local club), Rotary (pres. 1968—69). Bapt. Office: Warmath and Boyte 314 N 22nd Ave Humboldt TN 38343-3010 Home: PO Box 406 Humboldt TN 38343-0406

BOYTER, SCOTT M., academic administrator; b. Cedar City, Utah, June 19, 1947; s. Neil K. and Mae (Macfarlane) Boyter; m. Sherrie L. Bowen, Aug. 2, 1974; children: Laura Michelle, Tonia Leigh, Diana Lynn. BS, Brigham Young U., 1973, MS with high distinction, 1987. Adminstrv. asst. coll. fine arts and comms. Brigham Young U., Provo, Utah, 1973-76, bus. mgr. Sch. Music, 1976-82, bus. mgr. Coll. Fine Arts and Comm., 1982-94, asst. dean, contr. Coll. Fine Arts and Comm., 1995—. Missionary Ch. Jesus Christ LDS, Ohio, 1967—69. With USAR, 1971—2004. Recipient 1st Sgt. of the Yr. award, 96th Regional Support Command, USAR, 1996. Mem.: Am. Assn. Univ. Adminstrs., Am. Philatelic Soc., Beta Gamma Sigma. Republican. Mem. Lds Ch. Avocations: stamp collecting/philately, WWII history. Home: 331 N 875 E Orem UT 84097-5075 Office: A 501 HFAC Brigham Young Univ Provo UT 84602 Business E-Mail: scott_boyter@byu.edu.

BOYTON, RICK, theater director, actor; life ptnr. Criss Henderson. BS in Theater, Northwestern U. From casting dir. to assoc. artistic dir. Chgo. Shakespeare Theatre, 1997—2001, creative prodr., 2005—; casting dir., assoc. Jane Alderman Casting; talent agent, head feature film, TV & theatre dept. Harrise Davidson & Assoc.; artistic dir. Marriott Theatre, Lincolnshire. Lectr. Northwestern U. Actor: 1776 (Jefferson Award, acting), A Flea in Her Ear (Jefferson Award, acting); dir.: Forever Plaid. Bd. mem. Nat. Alliance for Musical Theatre; co-chmn. Festival of New Musicals, NYC, 2003—. Recipient Trailblazer Award, 2004. Office: Marriott Theatre 10 Marriott Dr Lincolnshire IL 60069*

BOZALIS, JOHN RUSSELL, physician; b. St. Louis, Sept. 19, 1939; s. George Sauter and Ruth (Russell) B.; m. Sharon Louise Sabo, June 21, 1963; children: John Jr., David L., Diana. BA, U. Okla., 1961, MD, 1965; MS, U. Mich., 1971. Diplomate Am. Bd. Internal Medicine, Am. Bd. Allergy and Immunology. Intern Henry Ford Hosp., Detroit, 1965-66, resident, 1966-68, chief resident, 1968-69; fellow in allergy-immunology U. Mich., Ann Arbor, 1969-71, instr., 1969-71; clin. asst. prof. U. Tex., San Antonio, 1972-73; pvt. practice Okla. Allergy Clinic, Oklahoma City, 1973—. Clin. instr. Coll. Medicine, U. Okla., 1973, clin. asst. prof., 1977-83, clin. assoc. prof., 1983-89, clin. prof., 1989—; mem. courtesy staff Mercy Hosp., Bapt. Hosp., Deaconess Hosp., St. Anthony Hosp., Presbyn. Hosp., Children's Hosp., Okla. Tchg. Hosp., S.W. Med. Ctr. Trustee Casady Sch., 1977-85, United Way Okla. City, chmn. profl. divsn. 1983, Okla. Health Scis. Found.; bd. dirs. Infant Ctr., 1983-86, Allied Arts Okla. City, 1984-86, 92, Hosp. Hospitality House, 1983-86; vice chmn. health scis. ctr. U. Okla. Centennial Commn.; bd. trustees McGee Eye Inst., mem. search com. for chmn. dept. ophthalmology and dir., 1991, Okla. City Mus. Art., 2003—, U. Okla. Found., 2003—; active Com. of 100, 1991; bd. trustees Okla. City Pub. Schs. Found., 1989—, Okla. Orthopedic and Arthritis Found., Inc., Bone and Joint Hosp., 1993; trustee Oklahoma City Mus. Arts, 2003—, U. Okla. Found., 2003; project dir. Schs. for Healthy Lifestyles, 1997—; chmn. legis. task force for promotion of children's health State of Okla., 2002—; pres. bd. Schs. Healthy Lifestyles, 1997—. Maj. USAF, 1971-73. Recipient Regents' Alumni award U. Okla., 1992; named Physician of Yr.-Pvt. Practice, U. Okla. Coll. of Medicine Alumni Assn., 1993, recipient dean's award, 1998. Fellow ACP, Am. Coll. Chest Physicians, Am. Acad. Allergy; mem. AMA, Am. Thoracic Soc., Okla. State Med. Assn. (del. 1993—, vice spkr. ho. dels. 1997, trustee 1993—), Okla. Lung Assn., Okla. Thoracic Soc. (pres. 1979), John M. Sheldon Soc., Okla. County Med. Soc. (editor Bull. 1978-83, chmn. orientation com. 1989—, pres. 1996, bd. trustees 1996—), Osler Soc. (pres. 1984), Okla. City Acad. Medicine, Robert M. Bird Soc., U. Okla. Coll. Medicine Alumni Assn. (chmn. rsch. com., pres. 1983-85), Okla. City C. of C. (bd. dirs. 1988-90). Republican. Episcopal. Avocations: bird hunting, golf, fly fishing, travel, gardening. Office: Okla Allergy and Asthma Clinic PO Box 26827 Oklahoma City OK 73126-0827 Office Phone: 405-235-0040. Business E-Mail: jbozalis@oklahomaallergy.com.

BOZDECH, MAREK JIRI, physician, educator; b. Wildflecken, Bavaria, Federal Republic Germany, Oct. 12, 1946; s. Jiri Josef and Zofia Jadwiga (Swiatecka) B.; m. Frances Barclay Craig, Dec. 22, 1967; children: Elizabeth, Andrew, Matthew. AB, U. Mich., 1967; MD, Wayne State U., 1972. Diplomate Am. Bd. Internal Medicine, Am. Bd. Med. Oncology, Am. Bd. Hematology. Intern and resident in internal medicine U. Wis. Hosps., Madison, 1972-75, dir. clin. hematology lab., 1978-82, dir. bone marrow transplantation, 1984-85; asst. prof. medicine U. Wis., Madison, 1978-84, assoc. prof. medicine, 1984-85; clin. fellow in hematology Moffitt Hosp. U. Calif., San Francisco, 1975-76, postdoctoral fellow in hematology Cancer Research Inst., 1976-78, research assoc. Cancer Research Inst., 1977-78, assoc. prof., 1985-89; dir. adult bone marrow transplantation U. Calif. Med. Ctr., San Francisco, 1985-89; chief oncology Kaiser Permanente Med. Ctr., Santa Rosa, Calif., 1989-91; pvt. practice specializing in oncology Hematology Redwood Regional Oncology Ct., Santa Rosa, 1991—. Contbr. articles to profl. jours. Scout leader Boy Scouts Am., Novato, Calif., 1985; bd. trustees Pacific Found. Med. Care, 1995—. Recipient Nat. Research Service award NIH, 1977-78; Wayne State U. scholar, 1971. Mem. ACP, Am. Soc. Hematology, Am. Soc. Clin. Oncology, Assn. No. Calif. Oncologists (bd. dirs. 1994-97), Sonoma County Med. Assn. (bd. dirs. 1994-96). Avocations: skiing, gardening, music, films, theater. Home: 50 La Placita Ct Novato CA 94945-1244 Office: Redwood Regional Oncology 121 Sotoyome St Ste 203 Santa Rosa CA 95405-4822 Personal E-mail: mbozdech@mindspring.com, mbozdech@yahoo.com.

BOZE, BETSY VOGEL, dean, marketing professional, educator; b. Shreveport, La., Sept. 18, 1953; d. Leroy Vogel and Betty Gray (Garrett) Vogel McDonald; children: Christopher Lee Boze, Broox Garrett Vogel Boze, Lee Gray Boze. BS in Psychology, So. Meth. U., 1974; postgrad., Am. Grad. Sch. Internat. Mgmt., 1975; MBA, So. Meth. U., 1975; PhD, U. Ark., 1984. Lectr. U. Md., 1975, 78-80; asst. prof. St. Bonaventure U., Olean, N.Y., 1977-78; instr. U. Ark., Fayetteville, 1979-83; asst. prof. Centenary Coll. of La., Shreveport, 1983-89; assoc. prof., chair U. Alaska, Anchorage, 1989-94; dean, prof. mktg. U. Tex., Brownsville, 1994—; pres. Boze & Assocs., Shreveport and Anchorage, 1983-94. Dir. Women in Mgmt. Conf., Shreveport, 1983-89; continuing edn. com. Hispanic Ednl. Telecomms. Sys., San Juan, P.R., 1995—; co-dir. Tex. Transp. Inst. Ctr. for Ports and Waterways, 1994—, HERS/Mid-Am. Summer Inst., 1996; vis. faculty Portland State U. in Khaborosk, Russia, 1994. Mem. editl. bd. Jour. for Not-for-Profit Mktg., 1990—; contbr. articles to profl. jours., chpts. to textbooks. V.p. Atlantic Mktg. Assn., Orlando, Fla., 1988-90; pres. Susitna coun. Girl Scouts U.S., Anchorage, 1992-94; pres. Wish Upon a Star, Shreveport, 1988-90; mem. program com. Commonwealth North, Anchorage, 1989-94; Tex. coord. Nat. Identification program Am. Coun. on Edn. U.S. Dept. Edn. Internat. fellow U. Hawaii, 1990. Fellow Am. Assn. State Colls. & Univs., Am. Coun. Edn.; mem. AAUP, AAUW, Leadership Tex., Petroleum Club Anchorage, Delta Delta Delta (pres. alumnae chpt. 1989-92). Methodist. Avocations: reading, swimming, backgammon. Home: 1409 Avenida Santa Ana Rancho Viejo TX 78575 Office: U Tex Brownsville 80 Fort Brown St Brownsville TX 78520-4956 E-mail: betsyboze@aol.com.

BOZELL, L. BRENT, III, communications executive; b. Washington, 1955; m. Norma Bozell; 4 children. B, Univ. Dallas, Irving. Founder, chmn. bd. dirs. Media Rsch. Ctr., 1987—; founder, chmn. Parents TV Coun. Co-editor: And That's the Way It Isn't: A Reference Guide to Media Bias; contbr. articles to newspapers including The Wall St. Journal, The Washington Post, L.A. Times, Nat. Rev., others, and syndicated columnist. Founder, pres. Conservative Victory Com.,1987—; nat. fin. chmn. Buchanan for President campaign; fin. dir., pres. Nat. Conservative Polit. Action Com. Mailing: Creators Syndicate Ste 700 5777 W Century Blvd Los Angeles CA 90045*

BOZEMAN, FRANK CARMACK, lawyer; b. Greenwood, Miss., Oct. 16, 1933; s. Frank Carmack and Mamie Hyatt (Pyle) B.; m. Mary Ireland Callcott, Dec. 29, 1961; children: Frank C. III, William Pyle, Thomas Anderson. BA, U. of South, 1955; MA, U. Va., 1956; JD, Washington and Lee U., 1960. Bar: Fla. 1960, Va. 1960. Assoc. Beggs and Lane, Pensacola, Fla., 1960-65; ptnr. Harrell, Wiltshire, Bozeman, Clark & Stone, Pensacola, 1965-75, Carlton, Fields, Ward, Emmanuel, Smith & Cutler, P.A., Pensacola, 1975-93, Bozeman, Jenkins & Matthews, Pensacola, 1993—. Editor Washington and Lee Law Rev., 1960. Chmn. Eagle Scout rev. com., Boy Scouts Am., Pensacola, 1961-63; trustee U. Of South, 1990-96. Capt. USAF, 1956-57. Mem. Am. Bd. Trial Advs. (pres. Pensacola chpt. 1989-90), Fla. Def. Lawyers Assn., Fedn. Ins. and Corp. Counsel, Register of Pre-Eminent Lawyers, Def. Rsch. Inst., Phi Delta Phi (Grad. of Yr. award 1960). Republican. Episcopalian. Avocations: sailing, gardening, civil war history and research. Home: 122 W Lloyd St Pensacola FL 32501-2637 Office: Bozeman Jenkins & Matthews PO Box 13105 Pensacola FL 32591-3105 Office Phone: 850-434-6223.

BOZEMAN, LAURA BETH, military officer, educator; b. Florrisant, Mo., Feb. 21, 1970; d. Boyd Benjamin and Dorothy Louise Carmichael; m. James Michael Bozeman, Nov. 26, 1993. MA, U. of Minn., 2001—01; BA, Tex. Christian U., 1992; diploma, Adj. Gen.'s Corps Officer Basic Course, Ft. Benjamin Harrison, Ind., 1992, Adj. Gen.'s Corps Officer Advanced Course, Ft. Jackson, S.C., 1996; cert., Combined Arms Staff and Svc. Sch., Ft. Leavenworth, Kans., 1999. Co. comdr. Alpha Co., 43d Adj. Gen. Bn., Fort Leonard Wood, Mo., 1997—99; instr. Dept. of English, West Point, NY, 2001—. Dep. adj. gen. hdqs. U.S. Army Element, Allied Land Forces Cen. Europe, Heidelberg, Baden-Wuerttemburg, Germany, 1995—96, co. exec. officer hdqs. co., 1994—95; adj./brigade s1 (pers. officer) 2d Signal Brigade, Mannheim, Baden-Wuerttemburg, Germany, 1992—94. Sponsor internat. mil. exch. program participant U.S. Army Maneuver Support Ctr., Ft. Leonard Wood, 1998—99; sponsor 4th class cadets U.S. Mil. Acad., West Point, NY, 2001—03; mem. rite of Christian initiation of adults team; host family participant, eucharistic min. Most Holy Trinity Cath. Parish, West Point, 2002—03. Capt. U.S. Army, 1992—2003. Decorated Def. Meritorious Svc. Medal, Meritorious Svc. Medal,; recipient Advanced Civil Schooling fellowship, U. S. Army, 1999—2001, 4-Yr. Army ROTC scholarship, Hdqs., U. S. Army Cadet Command, 1988. Mem.: MLA, Spaatz Assn., Adj. General's Corps Regtl. Assn. (v.p. for publicity Ozarks chpt. 1997—99, Adj. General's Corps Achievement medal 1999), Longaberger Basket Collectors Club, Sigma Tau Delta (pres. Tex. Christian U. chpt. 1991—92), Alpha Lambda Delta, Phi Beta Kappa. Roman Catholic. Avocations: travel, classic films, French language and culture. Home: HHC 8th PERSCPM Unit 15316 Box 309 Apo AP 96205-5316 Office: US Mil Acad Dept English 607 Cullum Rd West Point NY 10996 Office Phone: 011-822-7914-4353. E-mail: laura.bozeman@korea.army.mil.

BOZEMAN, THEODORE D., religion educator; b. Gainesville, Fla., Jan. 27, 1942; s. Simuel Bozeman and Kathleen Ford; m. Hannelore Bozeman, July 29, 1973. BA, Eckerd Coll., 1964; BD, Union Theol. Sem., N.Y.C., 1968; ThM, Union Sem., Richmond, Va., 1970; PhD, Duke U., 1974. Prof. U. Iowa, 1974—. Author: Protestants in an Age of Science, 1977, To Live Ancient Lives, 1988, The Precisionist Strain, 2004. NEH fellow, 1982, 95; recipient James Henley Thornwell award Presbyn. Hist. Assn., 1975. Mem. Am. Soc. Ch. History, Orgn. Am. Historians, So. Hist. Assn., Am. Hist. Assn. Office: U Iowa Dept Religious Studies Iowa City IA 52242 Business E-Mail: d-bozeman@uiowa.edu.

BOZINOVSKI, STEVO, computer science educator, researcher; s. Misko and Goluba Bozinovski; m. Liljana Bulakovska Bozinovska; children: Nevena, Adrian. BEE in Computer Sci., U. Zagreb, Croatia, 1973; MSc in Electronics, U. Zagreb, 1975, PhD in Computer Sci., 1982; diploma in Robotics and FMS, State Acad. Sci., Krems, Austria, 1993. Vis. rschr. U. Mass., Amherst, 1980—81; prof. U. Cyril and Methodius, Skopje, Macedonia, 1983—2001; assoc. prof. S.C. State U., Orangeburg, 2001—. Vis. scholar Kanazawa Inst. Tech., Japan, 1984, U. Mass., Amherst, 1995—96; vis. rschr. German Info. Tech. Ctr., Sankt Augustin, 1999, 2000; conf. organizer Biocybernetics Soc., Skopje, 1978—84; session organizer on genetics, metabolics and flexible mfg. SCI Multiconf., Orlando, Fla., 2001; guest editor Jour. Automatika, Zagreb, 1985. Author: Consequence Driven Systems, 1995; book cover pages; contbr. articles to profl. jours. Recipient Award for best paper in robotics, ETAN (Electronics, Telecommunications, Automation, and Nuclear Engineering Soc.), Nis, Yugoslavia, 1985; Fulbright Found. grantee, 1980, 1995. Mem.: IEEE, N.Y. Acad. Sci., Macedonian Biocybernetics Soc. Achievements include first to control robots using EEG and EOG signals; solve delayed reinforcement learning problem using neural network; introduce a neural feeling-based self-reinforcement learning mechanism; recognize that DNA is the cell real-time database operating system; introduce robotics metaphor in molecular genetics. Avocations: Macedonian history, comic arts. Home: 241 Wannamaker St Orangeburg SC 29115 Office: South Carolina State Univ 300 College St Orangeburg SC 29117 E-mail: sbozinovski@scsu.edu.

BOZLER, KENNETH L., information technology executive; Student in Bus. Mgmt., N.Y. Inst. Tech., Westbury. We. regional ops. mgr. Bell & Howell Co., Chgo., 1981; gen. mgr. image processing divsn. TRW, Inc., Belmont, Calif., 1989—91; region v.p. Anacomp, Inc./Image Conversion Sys. (now Lason), Medford, Mass., 1991—96; pres. and COO ScanCenters of Am., Burlington, 1996—97; v.p. sales to sr. v.p. northeast region Lason Sys., Inc.,

1997—2003; pres. and CEO Bus. Imaging Group, Inc., 2003—. Named Bus. Person of Yr., Queens, N.Y., 2000, Mgr. of Yr., Lason, 2002; named one of Top Movers of N.Y. Bus., N.Y. Newsday, 2001. Address: 9118 Woodridge Run Dr Tampa FL 33647

BOZOYAN, SYLVIA, elementary school educator; b. Aleppo, Syria, Feb. 18, 1953; arrived in U.S., 1953; d. Edward Yervant and Takouhi (Knnablian) B. BA, St. Peter's Coll., 1975; MEd, William Paterson Coll., 1978. Cert. elem. tchr. NJ, nursery sch. tchr. NJ. 1st grade tchr. Thomas A. Edison Sch., Union City, N.J., 1975—. Armenian sch. tchr. Holy Cross Armenian Ch., Union City, 1972—80, Sunday sch. tchr., 1969—. Named Outstanding Tchr. Govs. Tchr. Recognition Program, N.J., 1987-88, Outstanding Young Woman of Am., Ala., 1982, 87. Mem. Armenian Gen. Benevolent Union of Am. (sec. N.Y./N.J. Met. chpt. 1985-1995, sec., dancer ANTRANIG Dance Ensemble/exec. com. 1979—), N.J. Edn. Assn., Hudson County Edn. Assn., Union City Edn. Assn., Kappa Delta Pi, Pi Lambda Theta. Home: 1812 West St Union City NJ 07087-3311

BOZOZUK, MICHAEL, civil engineer; b. Poland, Nov. 10, 1929; married Marcelle F. M. Daoust, July 20, 1957; children: Lyne, Sylvie, Camille. BSc in Civil Engring., U. Man., Winnipeg, Can., 1952, MSc in Soil Mechanics, 1954; PhD in Geotechnical, Purdue U., 1972. Rsch. officer geotechnical section, divsn. building rsch. Nat. Rsch. Coun. Can., 1953-89; pvt. practice, 1989—96; exec. dir. Engring. Inst. Can., 1994-99. Com. soil and rock instrumentation Transp. Rsch. Bd., 1972-81, com. on founds. of bridges and other structures, 1972-81; chmn. adv. com. civil tech. Algonquin Coll., Ottawa, 1972-76; adv. com. Beaufort Sea artificial island Dept. Indian and No. Affairs, Govt. Can., 1981-84; rsch. com. silo founds. Ont. Silo Assn., 1978-82; Can. Gen. Stds. Bd. Geotextiles, 1980-85; chmn. adv. com. environ./geotechniques Sir Sanford Fleming Coll., Lindsay, Ont., 1983-87; tech. com. on founds. Can. Stds. Assn., 1983-90; mem. Can. Geosci. Coun., 1985-91; S.E. China Tour Lectr., 1986; hon. prof. Chengdu U., China, 1986; sci. advisor various orgns. and univs. Recipient Hon. award Caisse Populaire St. Genevieve, Ottawa, Can. Engring. Centennial Silver Medal, 1987, Cert. Citizenship City Calgary, 1987. Fellow Engring. Inst. Can. (Can. Paper award 1960, John B. Stirling medal 1990, Svc. award, 1999, Can. Pacific Railway Engring. Medal, 2003), Can. Soc. Civil Engrs. (fellow 1997), Can. Acad. Engring. (fellow 1999), NRC Can. (assoc. com. geotech. rsch., tech. advisor 1985-89, sec. 1989-91); mem. Geocontbns. (founding v.p. 1993-95, pres. 1999-2000), Can. Found. for Geotechnique (pres. 2001-05), Assn. Profl. Engrs. Ont., Can. Geotech. Soc. (cross Can. tour lectr. 1979, pres. 1986-90, chmn. award com. 1986-90, assoc. editor Can. Geotech. Jour. 1982-86, prize for best paper 1973, svc. award 1988, R. F. Legget Medal award 1994), Ottawa Geotech. Group (sec. 1957-59, chmn. 1976-78), Internat. Soc. Soil Mechanics and Found. Engring., Can. Geotech. Fund (treas. 1985-88), Ottawa Lapsmith Club (pres. 1995). Roman Catholic. Home and Office: 691 Sandra Ave Ottawa ON Canada K1G 2Z7

BOZZELLI, RICHARD, publishing executive; b. Apr. 15, 1958; m. Shannon T. Bozzelli; m. Nelson R., Heather L., Carter M. BS in Acctg. with honors, U. Ala., Birmingham, 1980, postgrad., NYU, 1990. CPA, Ala. Audit supr. Peat Marwick & Mitchell, 1980-84; asst. treas., dir. internal audit Bruno's Inc., 1984; audit mgr., co-dir. small bus. practice Ernst & Young (Ernst & Whinney), 1984-87; v.p., dir. Alabama Bancorp, Birmingham, 1987—; v.p., CFO EBSCO Industries, Inc., Birmingham, 1987—. Bd. dirs. PsychPartners, LLC, Primary Care Physicians Clinics, Inc.; dir. steeering com. MBA program U. Ala., Birmingham. Mem. Norton bd. Birmingham So. Coll.; mem. steering com. U. Ala.-Birmingham $20mm Capital Campaign; mem. Young Bus. Leaders of Birmingham; vol. mem. Jefferson County Commn.-Operation New Birmingham; mem. pub. affairs com. Birmingham C. of C. Recipient Class of 1994 Leadership award Nat. Multiple Sclerosis Soc., Outstanding Alumni award U. Ala. Birmingham Sch. Bus., 2003. Mem. AICPAs, Ala. Soc. CPAs (taxation com., ethics com.), U. Ala. Birmingham Nat. Alumni Soc. (bd. dirs., exec. com.), Nat. Assn. Accts. (past bd. dirs. Birmingham Magic City chpt.), Nat. TRIO Alumni Soc. (Ala. chpt.), Metro Sertoma (past mem. bd. dirs.), Beta Alpha Psi (past pres.), Omicron Delta Kappa, Alpha Lambda Delta. Home: 1205 S Cove Ln Birmingham AL 35216-3867 Office: EBSCO Industries Inc 5724 Highway 280 East Birmingham AL 35242 Office Phone: 205-991-6600.

BRAASCH, JOHN WILLIAM, retired surgeon, consultant; b. Rochester, Minn., Dec. 11, 1922; s. William Frederick and Nellie (Stinchfield) B.; m. Nancy Wheeler King, Mar. 21, 1946; children: William Frederick, Elizabeth King, Nancy Kathryn, Peggy Stinchfield. BS, Yale U., 1944; MD, Harvard U., 1946; MS in Physiology, U. Ill., 1948; PhD in Surgery, U. Minn., 1955. Diplomate Am. Bd. Surgery (bd. dirs. 1979-85). Intern St. Luke's Hosp., Chgo., 1946-47; resident in gen. surgery Mayo Clinic, Rochester, Minn., 1950-55; mem. attending staff Mpls. Gen. Hosp., 1955-57, Northwestern Hosp., Mpls., 1955-57; surg. staff New England Bapt. Hosp., Boston, 1957-80, New England Deaconess Hosp., Boston, 1957-80, Lahey Clinic Found., Boston, 1957-96; sr. cons. dept. surgery Lahey Clinic, Burlington, Mass., 1983-96, ret., 1996. Asst. clin. prof. surgery Harvard Med. Sch., Boston, 1975—. Author 3 books, several book chpts.; also numerous articles. Capt. U.S. Army, 1948-50. Recipient Balfour award for rsch. Mayo Clinic Found., Rochester, 1955. Mem. Am. Surg. Assn., Soc. for Surgery Alimentary Tract (v.p. 1987-88), Internat. Soc. Surgery, So. Surg. Soc., New England. Surg. Soc. (pres. 1984-85), Boston Sur. Soc. (pres. 1982), Surgeons Travel Club. Republican. Avocations: tennis, gardening, duplicate bridge.

BRABECK, MARY MARGARET, dean, psychology professor; BA, U. Minn., 1967, Ph.D., 1980; MS, St. Cloud U., 1970. Tchr. Bryant Jr. H.S., 1968—71; instr. U. Minn., 1971—75; instr. psychology Salve Regina Coll., Newport, RI, 1976—80; asst. prof., coord. The Human Devel. Program Boston Coll., Chestnut Hill, 1980—86, assoc. prof., 1986—92; assoc. prof., divsn. dir. Lynch Sch. Edn., Boston Coll., 1988—90, prof., chair dept. counseling, devel. psychology & rsch. methods, 1990—92, assoc. dean, 1992—95, dean, 1996—2003, prof., 1996—2003; dean The Steinhardt Sch. Edn., NYU, 2003—, prof. psychology, 2003—. Vis. prof. Brown U., Ctr. Human Devel., 1995—96; chmn. bd. Am. Assn. Colleges of Teacher Edn.; mem. Am. Psychological Assn. Bd. Ednl. Affairs, 2004—06. Recipient Kuhmerker award, Assn. Moral Edn., 1996, Boston Higher Edn. Partnership Svc. award, 2002. Office: Steinhardt Sch Edn Joseph & Violet Pless Hall NYU 82 Washington Sq E New York NY 10003 E-mail: mary.brabeck@nyu.edu.

BRACCO, LORRAINE, actress; b. Bklyn., Oct. 2, 1954; m. Harvey Keitel, 1982 (div. 1993); 1 child, Stella Keitel; m. Edward James Olmos, Jan. 28, 1994 (div. 2002); 1 child, Margaux Guerard. Studied, Actors Studio; studied with Stella Adler, Ernie Martin, John Strasberg. Model in Europe. Films include The Pick-Up Artist, 1987, Someone to Watch Over Me, 1987, Sing, 1989, The Dream Team, 1989, Goodfellas, 1990 (Acad. award nominee for best supporting actress 1990, LA Film Critics Assoc. award for best sup. actress, 1990), Talent for the Game, 1991, Switch, 1991, Medicine Man, 1992, Radio Flyer, 1992, Traces of Red, 1992, (Showtime movie) Scam, 1993, Being Human, 1994, Even Cowgirls Get the Blues, 1994, The Basketball Diaries, 1995, Hackers, 1995, Les Menteurs, 1996, Ladies Room, 1999, Tangled, 2000, Your Aura is Throbbing, 2000, Riding in Cars With Boys, 2001, Tangled, 2001, Death of a Dynasty, 2003, Max and Grace, 2004; on TV in Getting Gotti, 1996, Lifeline, 1996, The Taking of Pelham One Two Three, 1998, Sex in our Century, 2001; (TV Series) The Sopranos, 1999- (SAG award for Outstanding Performance by an Ensemble in a Drama Series, 2000); off-Broadway play Goose and Tom-Tom; Broadway play The Graduate, 2002. Mem.: bd. of dir. Riverkeeper, NY Council for the Humanities. Office: First Artists Assoc 12 W 57th St #PH New York NY 10019-3900

BRACE, MARGARET DENISE, writer; b. Takoma Park, Md., Oct. 31, 1960; d. Kenneth Earl and Margaret (Moran) Lerch; m. Keith Allen Brace, Oct. 27, 1984; children: Kelin Moran, Devra Gwynn. Student, Oxford U., 1981; BA, St. Marys Coll., 1982; MA in Spl. Edn., Loyola Coll., Balt., 1986. Cert. tchr. spl. edn., Md. Clk. CIA, McLean, Va., 1978-79; tchr. St. Michaels Grammar Sch., Silver Spring, Md., 1982-83; tchr., adminstr. Chautauqua Acad., Balt., 1983-86; spl. edn. tchr. Balt. County Pub. Schs., Balt., 1986-91; pvt. practice Balt., 1991—. Instr. Sylvan Learning Ctrs., Balt., 1986. Author: (poetry) The Voice Within, 1996, Best Poems of '97, 1997, of '98, 1998. Modeling instr. Barbizon, Bethesda, Md., 1982-84; founder Independence Day Parade, Bay Country, Md., 1996—; vol. Oliver Beach Elem. Sch., Balt., 1996—, Vacation Bible Sch., Balt., 1995—. Named to Athletic Hall of Fame, St. Mary's Coll., Balt., 1991. Mem. Profl. Disc Golf Assn., Marian Garden Club (founder 1996). Roman Catholic. Avocations: gardening, basketball, tennis, disc golf, bonsai. Home and Office: 12850 Cunninghill Cove Rd Baltimore MD 21220-1177

BRACERAS, ROBERTO M., lawyer; AB, Dartmouth Coll., 1991; JD, Yale Univ., 1994. Bar: Mass. 1994. Law clerk, Hon. Nathaniel M. Gorton US Dist. Ct., Dist. of Mass.; trial atty., criminal divsn., fraud sect. US Dept. Justice; ptnr., litig. dept. Goodwin Procter LLP, Boston, mem., diversity com. Bd. dir. Discovering Justice; Goodwin Procter liaison Boston Lawyer's Group. Mem.: Mass. Judicial Nominating Commn. Office: Goodwin Procter LLP Exchange Pl 53 State St Boston MA 02109 Office Phone: 617-570-1895. Office Fax: 617-523-1231. Business E-Mail: rbraceras@goodwinprocter.com.

BRACEWELL, RONALD NEWBOLD, engineering educator; b. Sydney, Australia, July 22, 1921; s. Cecil Charles and Valerie Zilla (McGowan) Bracewell; m. Helen Mary Lester Elliott; children: Catherine Wendy, Mark Cecil. BSc in Math. and Physics, U. Sydney, 1941, B in Engring., 1943, M in Engring. with 1st class honors, 1948; PhD, Cambridge (Eng.) U., 1950. Sr. rsch. officer Radiophysics Lab., Commonwealth Sci. and Indsl. Rsch. Orgn., Sydney, 1949—54; vis. asst. prof. radio astronomy U. Calif., Berkeley, 1954—55; mem. elec. engring. faculty Stanford U., 1955—, Lewis M. Terman prof. and fellow in elec. engring., 1974—79, now Terman prof. emeritus elec. engring. Pollock Meml. lectr. U. Sydney, 1978; Tektronix Disting. Visitor, 81; Christensen fellow St. Catherine's Coll., Oxford, 1987; sr. vis. fellow Inst. Astronomy; fellow commoner Churchill Coll., Cambridge U., 1988; Bunyan lectr. Stanford U., 1996; mem. adv. panels NSF, Naval Rsch. Lab., Office Naval Rsch., NAS, Nat. Radio Astronomy Obs., Jet Propulsion Lab. Adv. Group on Radio Experiments in Space, Advanced Rsch. Projects Agy.; govt., industry cons. elec. commn. Author: The Fourier Transform and Its Applications, 1965, 2000, The Galactic Club: Intelligent Life in Outer Space, 1974, The Hartley Transform, 1986, Two-Dimensional Imaging, 1995, Fourier Analysis and Imaging, 2003, Trees of Stanford and Environs, 2005; co-author: Radio Astronomy, 1955; translator: Radio Astronomy (J.L. Steinberg and J. Lequeux); editor: Paris Symposium on Radio Astronomy, 1959; former mem. editl. bd.: Internat. Jour. Imaging Sys. and Tech., Planetary and Space Sci., Proceedings of the Astron. Soc. Pacific, Cosmic Search, Jour. Computer Assisted Tomography, mem. bd. ann. rev.: Astronomy and Astrophysics, 1961—68; contbr. articles and revs. to jours., chapters to books. Recipient Duddell Premium, Instn. Elec. Engrs., London, 1952, Inaugural Alumni award, Sydney U., 1992; Fulbright travel grantee, 1954, William Gurling Watson traveling fellow, 1978, 1986. Fellow: AAAS, IEEE (life Heinrich Hertz Gold medal 1994, Jim Wolfensohn Suguna award 1996), Am. Acad. Arts and Scis., Astron. Soc. Australia, Royal Astron. Soc.; mem.: Order of Australia (officer), Internat. Sci. Radio Union, Astron. Soc. Pacific (life), Internat. Astron. Union, Am. Astron. Soc. (past councilor), Inst. Medicine of NAS (fgn. assoc.). Achievements include patents in field. Home: 836 Santa Fe Ave Stanford CA 94305-1023 Office: Stanford Univ 367 Packard Stanford CA 94305-9515 Office Phone: 650-723-3545. Business E-Mail: bracewell@star.stanford.edu.

BRACEY, COOKIE FRANCES LEE, minister; b. Phila., Mar. 14, 1945; d. John Daniels and Evelyn (Jarvis) Bracey. B in Social Work, Temple U., 1983; MDiv, Wesley Theol. Sem., 1990. Administrv. asst. United Meth. Ch., Phila., 1963—66, parish cmty. devel., 1984—86, local pastor Catonsville, Ellicott City, Md., 1986—90; chaplain Meth. Hosp., Phila., 1990—; pastor St. Luke Snyder Ave United Meth. Ch., Phila., 1990—92, St. Matthews United Meth. Ch., Trevose, Pa., 1992—99; sr. pastor, dir. after sch. program Mt. Carmel United Meth. Ch., 1999—; chaplain Vet. Affairs Med. Ctr., Phila., 2003; vol. chaplain Battleship New Jersey, 2004, Am. Red Cross, 2004. Missionary, Brazil, 1988, Costa Rica, 1989, Dominican Republic, 1992, Zim Babwe, Africa, 1998, El Salvador, 1998; pastor St. Matthews United Meth. Ch., Trevose, Pa., 1992; Meth. mission tour, London, 1992, Israel, 1994; adj. faculty Ea. Bapt. Theol. Sem., Wynnewood, Pa., 1994—, Henry George Sch., Phila., 1996—; mem. faculty Phila. Sch. Devel. Mins., 1997, fac. mem. Sch. of Devel. Ministries, 1997; vol. reading specialist Howe Elem. Sch., Phila., Rowen Elem. Sch., Phila., 2001; supr. Pioneers Internat., Inc., Phila., 2001; chaplain VA Med. Ctr., Phila., 2003. Mem. Multi-Cultural Task Force, Phila. 1980, Victims and Crime Task Force, Phila. Ministers Law Enforcement Support Unit, Phila. Cmty. Assistance Network; del. World Meth. Conf., Rio Janero, Brazil, 1996; chaplain CAP Aux. USAF, 1996—, Phila. Prison Sys., 1996—, ARC, 2004, Battleship N.J., 2004; mem. Phila. Mayor's Commn. on Literacy, World Affairs Coun. of Phila., Spell Binders Storytellers; missionary Zimbabwe, Africa, 1998; faculty Phila. Sch. of Developing Ministries, 1997; bd. dirs. Archives and History United Meth. Ch., 1997; del. Clergywoman Convocation, Atlanta, 1997, San Diego, 2002; cert. mentor for supr. for ministry candidates; del. Billy Graham Conv., Amsterdam, 2000, World Meth. Conf., Brighton, Eng., 2001; bd. dirs. Youth Build Charter Sch. of Phila., 1999-; bd. mem. Youth Build, 2004, Met. Christian Coun. Phila., Experience Corps, 2004; participant Ministerial Exch. Program, 2004; elected chaplain Catherine McClendon Scholarship Fund. Recipient Outstanding Clergywoman award Nat. Assn. Clergywomen, 1990, Peace & Justice award Ch. Women United, 1992, Ministry award Harry Hosier United Meth. Ch., 1992, Preacher of Yr. award, 1998. Mem. AAUW, Am. Assn. Christian Counselors, Temple Univ. Soc. Adminstrn. Alumni Assn., Asian Am. Youth Assn., Nat. Fellowship Local, Black United Meth. Preachers (v.p., treas.), Black Clergy Phila. and Vicinity (corr. sec.), Phila. Police Clergy, Coalition Prison Evangelists, Good Shepherd Mediation Program, Chaplaincy Coalition of Greater Phila., Wesley Theol. Sem. Alumni Assn., Mil. Chaplains Assn. (sec. Liberty Bell chpt.), Youth Build (bd. dirs. 2004, sec.), Met. Christian Coun. of Phila. (bd. dirs. 2004), Experience Corps (bd. mem., 2004), Ministerial Exchange Program Eng. (bd. dirs. 2005), Nat. Assn. Vets. Affairs Chaplains (vet. affairs women chaplain ann. meeting Hampton, Va. 2004), Catherine McClendon Scholarship Fund (chaplain). Democrat. Avocations: music, opera, historical researcher, board games, travel. Home: 337 Christian St Apt 3 Philadelphia PA 19147-3219 Address: 5909 North Park Ave Philadelphia PA 19141 Office Phone: 215-549-3661. Personal E-mail: bracey337@aol.com.

BRACEY, EARNEST NORTON, political science educator; b. Jackson, Miss., June 8, 1953; s. Willard and Odessa Manola (Ford) B.; m. Atsuko Konuma, Apr. 2, 1995; children: Dominique, Princess, Omar. MPA, Golden Gate U., 1979; MA, Cath. U., Washington, 1983; D of Pub. Adminstrn., George Mason U., 1993; PhD in Edn., Capella U., 1999. Commd. 2d lt. U.S. Army, 1975, advanced through grades to lt. col., 1992; ret., 1995; prof. polit. sci. C.C. of So. Nev., Las Vegas, 1996—. Adj. prof. Ctrl. Tex. Coll., Camp Zama, Japan, 1993-95; Nev. faculty alliance CC So. Nev., Las Vegas, 1996—, past chair dept. polit. sci. and history Hampton U Author: Choson, 1994, Prophetic Insight, 1999, Daniel "Chappie" James, 2003, On Racism, 2003. Mem. NAACP, Am. Soc. of Mil. Comptrs., Assn. of the U.S. Army, Retired Officer Assn. Avocations: jazz trumpeter, marathon runner, writing, poetry, american historian.

BRACH, PAUL HENRY, artist; BFA, U Iowa, 1948, MFA, 1950. Tchr. U. Mo., Columbia, 1950-51, New Sch. Social Rsch., N.Y.C., 1952-55, NYU, 1954-67, 86-90, Parsons Sch. Design, 1956-67, The Cooper Union, 1960-62, 79-82, Cornell U., 1965-67; chair dept. visual arts. U. Calif., San Diego, 1967-69; dean Sch. Art Calif. Inst. Arts, Valencia, 1969-75; chair divsn. arts Fordham U., N.Y.C., 1975-79, Empire State Coll., N.Y.C., 1979—95; Milton Avery disting. prof. Bard Coll., N.Y.C., 1993; represented by Flomenhaft Gallery, N.Y.C. Vis. artist U. N.Mex., Albuquerque, 1965; guest critic U. Minn., Mpls., Sarah Lawrence Coll., Bronxville, N.Y., Montclair (N.J.) State Coll., Art Forum Mag., 1976; vis. critic N.Y. studio program Empire State Coll., 1976—; cons. Rutgers U., New Brunswick, 1977; guest critic Bard Coll., Empire State Coll., N.Y.C., 1977; contbg. critic Art Forum Mag., 1977; vis. artist Banff (Can.) Art Ctr., 1979; contbg. critic Art in Am., 1979-2002; guest lectr. Pratt Inst., N.Y.C., 1980, Tuscon Mus. Art, 1992; vis. artist Litho Workshop, Ariz. State U., Tempe, 1981, U. N.Mex., Albuquerque, 1981; guest lectr. Tuscon Mus. Art, 1992. One-man shows at Leo Castelli, N.Y.C., 1957, 59, Cordier Ekstrom Gallery, N.Y.C., 1961-63, Kornble Gallery, N.Y.C., 1971, Andre Emmerich Gallery, N.Y.C., 1974, Jean Millant Gallery, L.A., 1974, Benson Gallery, Bridgehampton, N.Y., 1975, Lerner Heller Gallery, N.Y.C., 1978, 80, Yares Gallery, L.A., 1979, Janus Gallery, L.A., 1980, Yares Gallery, Scottsdale, Ariz., 1981, Bernice Steinbaum Gallery Ltd., N.Y.C., 1983, 85, 87, 90, 91, Elaine Horwitch Galleries, Palm Springs, Calif., 1987, Benton Gallery, Southampton, N.Y., 1987, Vered Gallery, East Hampton, N.Y., 1989, Rancho Linda Vista Gallery, Oracle, Ariz., 1992, Steinbaum Krauss Gallery, N.Y.C., 1994, McAllen (Tex.) Internat. Mus., 1995, Tucson (Ariz.) Mus. Art, 1995, Guild Hall, East Hampton, 1995, Bernice Steinbaum Gallery, Miami, Fla., 2000, others; exhibited in group shows at Wake Forest U. Art Gallery, Winston-Salem, N.C., 1988, Rose Art Mus., Brandeis U., Waltham, Mass., 1988, Anderson Gallery, Va. Commonwealth U., Richmond, 1988, Temple U., Phila., 1988, Alexandra Monet Fine Arts, New Orleans, 1989, Bernice Steinbaum Gallery, N.Y., 1990, Guild Hall Mus., East Hampton Ctr. Contemporary Art, 1990, Weatherspoon Art Gallery, Greensboro, N.Y.C., 1990, Tyler Art Gallery, Oswego, N.Y., 1990, Albright-Knox Art Gallery, Buffalo, 1990, LewAllen/Butler Gallery, Sante Fe, N.Mex., 1993, Vered Gallery, East Hampton, 1993, Steinbaum Krauss Gallery, N.Y.C., 1993, Kent (Conn.) Gallery, 1994, Andre Zarre Gallery, N.Y.C., 1995, U. Iowa, Iowa City, 2002, Flomenhaft Gallery, N.Y.C, 2005; others; represented in permanent collections at Mus. Modern Art, N.Y.C., Whitney Mus. Am. Art, N.Y.C., L.A. County Mus. Art, St. Louis Art Mus., Smith Coll. Mus., Nebr. Art Mus., Albuquerque Mus. Art, Mus. Fine Art, Santa Fe, Phoenix Art Mus., NYU, U. Iowa, others; contbr. articles to profl. jours. Fellow Djerassi Found., Woodside, Calif., 1987, 90.

BRACH, RICHARD S., lawyer; b. Mexico City, 1948; AB, Princeton U., 1969; JD, Columbia U., 1972; attended, Hague Acad. Internat. Law, Netherlands. Bar: N.Y. 1973, England & Wales (registered fgn. lawyer) 1994. Ptnr. global fin. group & Latin Am. practice group Milbank, Tweed, Hadley & McCloy, N.Y.C. Mem. ABA, N.Y. State Bar Assn., Assn. Bar City N.Y. Office: Milbank Tweed Hadley & McCloy 1 Chase Manhattan Plz Fl 47 New York NY 10005-1413 Office Phone: 212-530-5350. Office Fax: 212-530-5219. Business E-Mail: rbrach@milbank.com.

BRACHFELD, JONAS, cardiologist, educator; b. Antwerp, Belgium, Dec. 1, 1924; came to U.S., 1947; naturalized 1953. s. Chaskiel and Rosa (Spira) B.; m. Rosalind Roth, Apr. 3, 1955; children: Claude A., Renée K., Eric L. BS, Calif. Inst. of Tech., 1947; MD, U. Pa., 1952. Diplomate Am. Bd. Internal Medicine, Am. Bd. Cardiovascular Disease. Chmn. dept. internal medicine Rancocas Hosp., Willingboro, N.J., 1961-94, dir. CCU, 1972-93; founder, CEO Brachfeld Med. Assocs., Willingboro, 1969-94; prof. clin. medicine U. Medicine and Dentistry N.J., Camden, 1993—. Dir. Fellows' Clinic dept. cardiology Univ. Med. Ctr., 1997—2005. Founder Brachfeld Day Care Ctr. Jewish Geriatric Home, Cherry Hill, N.J., 1972. Fellow Am. Coll. Cardiology, Am. Heart Assn., Tau Beta Pi. Jewish. Avocation: languages (Dutch, Spanish, French, German, and Hebrew). Home: 227 Nicholson Dr Moorestown NJ 08057-2909 Office: U Med Ctr 1210 Brace Rd Cherry Hill NJ 08034 Office Phone: 856-427-7254.

BRACK, O. M., JR., language educator; b. Houston, Nov. 30, 1938; s. O. M. and Olivia Mae (Rice) B.; 1 child, Matthew Rice; m. Cynthia Alison Burns, May 22, 2004. Student, U. Houston, 1956-57; BA, Baylor U., 1960, MA, 1961; PhD, U. Tex., Austin, 1965. Asst. prof. William Woods Coll., 1964-65; asst. prof. English lit. U. Iowa, Iowa City, 1965-68, assoc. prof., 1968-73, dir. center textual studies, 1967-73; prof. English lit. Ariz. State U., Tempe, 1973—. Chmn. 18th Century Short Title Catalogue Com., 1970-73; pres. Arete Publs., Ltd., 1976-81; Albert H. Smith Meml. lectr. bibliography Birmingham (Eng.) Bibliog. Soc., 1983 vis. fellow U. Oxford Wolfson Coll., 1986-87; mem. adv. bd. 18th-Century Brit. Periodical Subject Index, 1996—, Soc. for Textual Scholarship, 1998; bd. dirs. 18th-Century Short-Title Catalogue, Inc., 1999-2000. Author: Bibliography and Textual Criticism, 1969, Samuel Johnson's Early Biographers, 1971, Hoole's Death of Johnson, 1972, Henry Fielding's Pasquin, 1973, A Catalogue of the Leigh Hunt Manuscripts, 1973, The Early Biographies of Samuel Johnson, 1974, American Humor, 1977, Twilight of Dawn, 1987, Writers, Books and Trade, 1994, Samuel Johnson in New Albion, 1997, The Macaroni Person and the Concentrated Mind, 2004, A Commentary on Mr. Pope's Principles of Morality, or Essay on Man, 2004; textual editor: Works of Tobias Smollett, 1966—; gen. editor: Works of Tobias Smollett, 1973-86; editor: English Literature in Transition, 1981-82, mem. editl. com., 1982—91; editor: Studies in Eighteenth Century Culture, 1981-86; mem. editl. com.: Yale edit. Works of Samuel Johnson, 1977—; editl. cons. The Literature of England, Scott, Foresman & Co., 1977-79, Works of David Hume, Princeton U. Press, 1990-91, Oxford U. Press, 1995-97; asst. editor: Eighteenth-Century Bibliography, 1964-73, Books at Iowa, 1966-73; editor Eighteenth Century: A Current Bibliography, 1983-90; mem. editl. com.: Age of Johnson, 1985-2003, Rocky Mountain Rev. of Lang. and Lit., 1980-98, Clarissa Project, 1987-2000. Mem. Salvation Army Coun., South Mountain Corps, 1996-2002, chair, 1999-2002. Named Grad. Coll. Outstanding Mentor, 2000; recipient Grad. Coll. Disting. Rsch. award, 1981—82, Rocky Mountains MLA Huntington Libr. award, 1986, Humanities Rsch. award, 1989—90, Faculty Achievement award, Ariz. State U. Alumni Assn., 1991; fellow, Huntington Libr., 1978, Am. Coun. Learned Soc., 1979—80, Newberry Libr., 1982, Andrew W. Mellon Fund, Huntington Libr., 1994, Huntington Libr., 1996, 1997; grantee, Am. Philos. Soc., 1967, NEH, 1993—95, 1995—98; scholar Disting. scholar, Phi Kappa Phi, 1975. Mem. MLA, Am. Soc. 18th Century Studies, East-Ctrl. Soc. 18th Century Studies, South Central 18th Century Soc. (pres. 1982-83), Western Soc. for 18th Century Studies (pres. 2000-01), Brit. Soc. 18th Century Studies, Rocky Mountain MLA, Bibliog. Soc. Am., Bibliog. Soc. U. Va., Bibliog. Soc. (London), Printing Hist. Soc., Am. Printing History Assn., Assn. for Scottish Literary Studies, Samuel Johnson Soc. So. Calif. (bd. dirs. 1989—, pres. 1994-95), The Lichfield Johnson Soc., The Johnson Soc. London, The Johnson Soc. Australian, Grolier Club, The Johnsonians (pres. 2001-02). Episcopalian. Office: Ariz State U Dept English Tempe AZ 85287-0302 Business E-Mail: om.brack@asu.edu.

BRACKEEN, JOANNE M., musician, educator, composer; b. Ventura, Calif., July 26, 1938; d. Arthur Herbert and Marie Elizabeth Grogan; m. Charles Willie Brackeen (div.); children: Deryl, Susan, Marcus, Roselle. Pianist Art Blakey Jazz Messengers, 1969—72, Joe Henderson Quartet, 1972—86, Stan Getz Quartet, 1975—77; pianist, composer Freddy Hubbard and All-Stars, 1983; band leader State Dept. Tour, 1984, JoAnne Brackeen Group, 1977—; prof. Berklee Coll. Music, Boston, 1994—. Mem. Ednl. Com., Boston. Composer, musician: albums Live at Maybeck Hall, 1989 (5 Stars Downbeat, 1989), Pink Elephant Magic, 1999 (Grammy nomination, 2000), Popsicle Illusion, 2000. Named Grand Marshall, Berklee Coll. Music, 2004; recipient, Nat. Endowments Arts, 1982; grantee, 1979; Faculty fellow, Berklee Coll. Music, 2005. Mem.: Musicians Union 802, Internat. Assn. Jazz Educators, Chamber Music Am. Avocations: yoga, swimming, pilates, meditation, chi kung. Office: Berklee Coll Music 1140 Boylston Boston MA 02215

BRACKEN, CAROLYN JEAN, artist, children's book illustrator, actress; b. Santa Monica, Calif., Nov. 21, 1944; d. Edward Vincent and Constance (Nickerson) B.; m. Henry J. Franzoni, Mar. 3, 1996. BFA, Wash. U., St. Louis, 1966. Artist Norcross Greeting Cards, N.Y.C., 1967-75; ptnr., art dept. head White, Bracken, Noonan Advt. Agy., N.Y.C., 1975; freelance artist, illustrator N.Y.C., 1975—. Illustrator over 250 children's books including Noah's Ark, 1973, Animal Crackers, 1979, Here Comes the Fire Engines, 1981, Martha's House, 1982, The Care Bear and the Terrible Twos, 1983, Fast Rolling Fire Trucks, 1984, Follow the Zookeeper, 1984, Some Busy Hospital, 1985, You Can Say No, 1985, The Busy Schoolbus, 1986, Look At My Town,

1986, New Day, 1986, Jenny's New Baby Sister, 1987, Mother Goose, 1987, All Aboard, 1988, My Trike, 1989, Gingerbread House-Easy To Make, 1989, The Story of Santa Claus, 1989, Where Is Grandma Rabbit, 1989, The Haunted House, 1991, Scary Masks, 1992, Chutes and Ladders, 1994, Tales From the Cabbage Patch (4 book set), 1995, We Like To Do Things, 1995, The Ghost Who Was Afraid Of the Dark, 1996, Our House Sticker Play, 1996, Little Chick Sticker Play, 1996, Mother Goose Rhymes, 1997, 5 books for Magic School Bus (Wet All Over, Meets the Rot Squad, Makes a Rainbow, Taking Flight, Gets Eaten), 1995-2005, Clifford the Big Red Dog books, Max and Ruby's Rainy Day, Strawberry Shortcakes Friendship Party, many books in the Magic Schoolbus Reader Series, 2003—, 5 Books in the Henry and Mudge Series, 2004—, numerous others; actress various playhouses Mem. AEA, Soc. Children's Book Writers & Illustrators. Avocations: renovating, decorating, collecting films. Home and Office: 225 Dogwood Dr Dundee OR 97115 Office Phone: 212-254-4996. E-mail: brackzoni@earthlink.net.

BRACKEN, FRANK D., retail executive; From mgmt. trainee to sr. v.p. mktg. Haggar Corp., Dallas, 1963—91, dir., exec. v.p. mktg., 1991—94, pres., COO, dir., 1994—. Office: 11511 Luna RD Dallas TX 75234-6022

BRACKEN, HARRY MCFARLAND, philosophy educator; b. Yonkers, N.Y., Mar. 12, 1926; s. Harry S. and Grace M. (McFarl) B.; m. Eva Maria Laufkotter, Dec. 24, 1949 (div.); children— Christopher, Timothy; m. Elisabeth van Gelderen, June 19, 1985 BA, Trinity Coll., Hartford, Conn., 1949; MA, Johns Hopkins, 1954; PhD, U. Iowa, 1956. Instr. U. Iowa, Iowa City, 1955-57, asst. prof., 1957-61; asso. prof. U. Minn., Mpls., 1961-63; prof. Ariz. State U., Tempe, 1963-66; prof. philosophy McGill U., Montreal, Que., Can., 1966-91. Prof. U. Calif., San Diego, 1970; vis. prof. Trinity Coll., U. Dublin, Ireland, 1972-73, 79-80; vis. prof. metaphysics U. Coll., Nat. U. Ireland, Dublin, 1972-73, 79-80; adj. faculty philosophy Erasmus U., Rotterdam, 1988-95, Rijksuniversiteit Groningen, 1990-95; adj. prof. philosophy Ariz. State U., 1995—. Author: The Early Reception of Berkeley's Immaterialism: 1710-1733, 1959, 2d edit., 1965, Berkeley, 1974; Mind and Language: Essays on Descartes and Chomsky, 1984, Freedom of Speech: Words Are Not Deeds, 1994, Descartes, 2002; mem. bd. edit. cons. History Philos. Quar., 2005—. Served with USNR, 1943-46, PTO. Recipient Acad. Freedom award Ariz. Civil Liberties Union, 1965; Edn. award J. I. Segal Found. for Jewish Culture, 1972 Mem. Am. Philos. Assn., Internat. Berkeley Soc., The Hume Soc., USS Lauderdale Assn. Home: 9107 E Avenida Las Noches Apache Junction AZ 85218-4676 E-mail: hbracken@imap2.asu.edu.

BRACKEN, MATTHEW E. S., marine ecologist; b. Corvallis, Oreg., Jan. 18, 1975; s. Barry E. and Kathleen M. Bracken; m. Cascade J. B. Sorte, June 28, 2003. BS, U. Puget Sound, 1997; PhD, Oreg. State U., 2003. Post doctoral rsch. assoc. Oreg. State U., Corvallis, 2003; vis. post doctoral rschr. U. Canterbury, Christchurch, New Zealand, 2003—04; post doctoral scholar U. Calif., Davis, 2004—. Contbr. articles to profl. jours. Recipient Markham Endowment award, Hatfield Marine Sci. Ctr., 2001; fellow, NSF, 1998—2001; Nat. Sci. scholar, U.S. Dept. Edn., 1993—96, Nat. Merit scholar, U. Puget Sound, 1993—97. Mem.: Phycological Soc. Am., Western Soc. Naturalists (Best Student Paper award 2000), Ecol. Soc. Am. Liberal. Avocations: gardening, travel, photography. Office: Bodega Marine Lab PO Box 247 Bodega Bay CA 94923 Office Phone: 707-875-1961. E-mail: mebracken@ucdavis.edu.

BRACKEN, MICHAEL PATRICK, writer, editor; b. Canton, Ohio, Sept. 7, 1957; s. William Gibson and Myrta Ann Bracken; m. Sharon Kay Johnson, Nov. 9, 1996; m. Pamela Cliff, July 2, 1993 (dec. Dec. 18, 1994); m. Karin Ann Gunn, 1978 (div. 1990); children: Ryan Mikel, Ian Patrick, Courtney Arin, Nigel Quinn. Author: (novel) All White Girls, 2001; editor: (anthology) Fedora II: More Private Eyes and Tough Guys, 2003, Hardbroiled, 2003, Small Crimes, 2004, Fedora III: Even More Private Eyes and Tough Guys, 2004; author: (gift book) In the Town of Dreams Unborn and Memories Dying, 2000; contbr. anthology, literary journal; author: (short story collection) Bad Girls, 2000, Canvas Bleeding, 2002, (novel) Deadly Campaign, 1994, (short story collection) Even Roses Bleed, 1995, (novel) Psi Cops, 1995, (short story collection) Tequila Sunrise, 2000, (novel) Just in Time for Love, 1998; editor: (anthology) Fedora: Private Eyes and Tough Guys, 2001; author: (short stories) Yesterday in Blood and Bone, 2005. Recipient Citation of Merit, Advt. Club of Waco, 1998, Judges Award, 1999, Gold ADDY, 1999, Silver ADDY, 1999, 2000, Bronze ADDY, 2001. Mem.: Advt. Club of Waco (pres. 1998—99), Pvt. Eye Writers of Am. (chair, best first novel shamus award com.), The Short Mystery Fiction Soc. (v.p. 2002—04, pres. 2004—06, Derringer Award nomination 2002, Derringer Award 2004), Horror Writers Assn., Mystery Writers of Am. (v.p., sw chpt. 2002—04), Sci. Fiction and Fantasy Writers of Am., Golden Key Internat. Honour Soc., Sigma Tau Delta. Avocation: guitar.

BRACKEN, PAUL, political science professor; b. Phila., Mar. 12, 1948; s. John Joseph and Gertrude (Logue) B.; m. Nanette Elizabeth Beattie, May 25, 1974; children: Kathleen, James, Margaret. BS, Columbia U., 1971, MS, 1976; PhD, Yale U., 1982. Rsch. asst. Fels Ctr. Govt., U. Pa., Phila., 1971-72; sr. staff Ketron, Inc., Arlington, Va., 1972-74; dir. rsch. Hudson Inst., Croton-on-Hudson, N.Y., 1974-83; asst. prof. Yale U., New Haven, 1983, assoc. prof., 1984-85, prof., 1986—. Lectr. various univs. and colls.; cons. in field. Author: Command and Control of Nuclear Forces, 1983, Fire in the East, 1999; contbr. articles to profl. jours. Mem. Commn. of Conn.'s Future, 1981-85, Inst. Social and Policy Studies, Yale U. Mem. Internat. Inst. Strategic Studies, Yale Ctr. for Internat. Studies, Coun. Fgn. Rels. Avocations: skiing, golf, amateur radio. Home: 22 Green Ln Ridgefield CT 06877-3017 Office: Yale U PO Box 1A New Haven CT 06520 E-mail: bracken7@snet.net.

BRACKEN, PAUL FRANCIS, mathematics educator; arrived in U.S., 2003; s. Paul and Marie Bracken. BS, U. Toronto, 1980; MS, U. Guelph, 1982; PhD, U. Waterloo, 1995. Rsch. assoc. U. Montreal, 1998—2001; rsch. prof. Concordia U., 2001—03; asst. prof. U. Tex., Edinburg, 2003—. Contbr. articles to profl. jours. Mem.: Am. Math. Assn. (mem. editl. bd. 1997—). Avocations: travel, reading. Office: U Tex 1201 W Univ Dr Edinburg TX 78539

BRACKEN, PEG, writer; b. Filer, Idaho, Feb. 25, 1918; d. John Lewis and Ruth (McQuesten) B.; m. John Hamilton Ohman, June 15, 1991; 1 child from previous marriage, Johanna Bracken. AB, Antioch Coll., 1940. Author: The I Hate to Cook Book, 1960, The I Hate to Housekeep Book, 1962, I Try to Behave Myself, 1963, Peg Bracken's Appendix to The I Hate to Cook Book, 1966, I Didn't Come Here to Argue, 1969, But I Wouldn't Have Missed It for the World, 1973, The I Hate to Cook Almanack - A Book of Days, 1976, A Window Over the Sink, 1981, The Compleat I Hate to Cookbook, 1986, On Getting Old for the First Time, 1996.

BRACKEN, RICHARD M., corporate financial executive; b. Richmond, Va., 1977; m. Judith Bracken; 4 children. B, 1974; M, Med. Coll. Va., 1977. Various exec. positions HCA Inc., 1981—95, pres. Pacific divsn., 1995—97, pres. western group, 1997—2001, CEO, 2001, pres., cheif fin. officer Nashville, 2002—. Mem.: Fedn. Am. Hosps. (bd. dirs.), Calif. Hosp. Assn. (bd. dirs.). Office: HCA Inc 1 Park Plz Nashville TN 37203

BRACKEN, THOMAS ROBERT JAMES, real estate investment executive; b. Spokane, Wash., Jan. 1, 1950; s. James Lucas and Frances (Cadzow) B.; m. Linda Jacobson, Sept. 9, 1972; children: Karl Forest, David Erskine. BS, Yale U., 1971; MBA, Columbia U., 1972. Sr. appraiser Prudential Ins., N.Y.C., 1972-74, mgr. real estate N.Y.C. and Newark, 1974-76, assoc. gen. mgr. Seattle, 1977-78; v.p. First City Investments, Seattle, 1978-80; pres. Fenix, Inc., Seattle, 1980-86; v.p. Washington Mortgage Corp., Seattle, 1982-85, exec. v.p., 1986-88; sr. v.p. Pioneer Bank, Lynwood, Wash., 1985-86; pres.real estate financing USL Capital, San Francisco, 1988-97; sr. v.p. real estate fin. group Orix, USA, San Francisco, 1997-98; pres. Presidio Interfunding Corp., San Francisco, 1998-99; dir. L.J. Melody & Co., San Jose, Calif., 2000—03; mem. Crossbow Capital, LLC, Los Altos, Calif., 2000—; mng. dir. The Broe Cos., San Francisco, 2003—05; sr. v.p. GMAC Comml. Mortgage Co., San Francisco, San Jose, 2005—. Mem. Nat. Assn. Indsl./Office Parks (v.p. Seattle chpt. 1981-83), Yale Assn. Western Wash. (pres. 1984-86), Urban Land Inst., Mortgage Bankers Assn. Presbyterian. Avocations: running, sports. Office: GMAC Comml Mortgage Co 550 California St 12th Fl San Francisco CA 94104 Office Phone: 415-646-7712. Personal E-mail: tombracken@msn.com.

BRACKENRIDGE, N. LYNN, not-for-profit developer; b. Youngstown, Ohio, Sept. 9, 1957; d. John Bruce and Mary Ann (Rossi) Brackenridge; m. Harry Lee Carrico, July 1, 1994. BA, Lawrence U., 1978; MS, Georgetown U., 1980. Tchg. asst. Georgetown U., Washington, 1979-81, admissions officer, 1984-85, editor, writer devel., 1985-87, asst. dir. devel., 1987-89; dir. devel. Cath. Charities U.S.A., Washington, 1989-91, Johns Hopkins U. Bologna (Italy) Ctr., 1991-92; dir. devel. and pub. rels. Nat. Ctr. for State Cts., Williamsburg, Va., 1993-97; v.p. for devel. Gateway Homes Greater Richmond (Va.), Inc., 1998-99, pres., 1999—2004; exec. dir. John Marshall Found., 2004—. Vol. Richmond Ballet, 1993-95, Leukemia Soc. Am., Hampton, Va., 1996—; bd. dirs. Ctrl. Va. chpt. Nat. Alliance for Mentally Ill, 2005—. Georgetown U. fellow, 1979-81; recipient diplome d'etudes Inst. d'Etudes Francaises de Touraine, 1976. Mem.: Nat. Soc. Fund Raising Execs. (cert. fund raising exec., chair program com., pres. 1997). Democrat. Avocations: flying small aircraft, running, reading, films, languages. Home: 9303 Cragmont Dr Richmond VA 23229-7610 Office: John Marshall Found 901 E Cary St 17th Fl Richmond VA 23219 Office Phone: 804-775-0861. Business E-Mail: lynnb@johnmarshallfoundation.org.

BRACKETT, COLQUITT PRATER, JR., judge, lawyer; b. Norfolk, Va., Feb. 24, 1946; s. Colquitt Prater Sr. and Antoinette Gladys (Cacace) B.; m. Carol Ann Roberts, Dec. 29, 2000; 1 child, Susan Elizabeth Brackett Brooks. BS, U. Ga., 1966, MA, 1968, JD, 1973, LLM, 1976; travel mktg. profl. diploma, S.E. Tourism Soc. Mktg. Coll., 1999. Bar: Ga. 1973, U.S. Dist. Ct. (so. dist.) Ga. 1974, U.S. Dist. Ct. (mid. dist.) Ga. 1977, U.S. Supreme Ct. 1980, Tenn. 1987. Assoc. Surrett & CoCroft, Augusta, Ga., 1972-74; ptnr. Surrett & Brackett, Augusta, 1974-76; faculty Sch. Law, U. Ga., Athens, 1977-82; mng. ptnr. Brackett, Prince & Neufeld, Athens, 1982-90; adminstrv. law judge Ga. Dept. Med. Assistance, Athens, 1990-98. Hearing officer Ga. State Bd. Edn., 1979-91; v.p. Mus. Dolls & Gifts, Inc., Watkinsville, Ga., 1983—; pres. Bear Country Lodge and Conf. Ctr., Pigeon Forge, Tenn., 1996— Am. Toy Mus. Assoc., 2003-; chmn. bd. Adventures in Toy Land, 1999-2000; exec. dir. Soc. Preservation of Am. Childhood Effects, 2002-; curator Toy Mus., Natural Bridge, Va., 2002-; bd. dirs. Va. Hospitality and Travel Assn., 2003-. Author: Court Administration, 1972; (monograph) The Security Inventors Protection Corporation and the Operations of SIPC, 1976; (musical play) Americanization of Mary Poppins, 1995. Pres. Athens/Clarke Mental Health Assn., 1985; chmn. bd. dirs. N.E. Ga. Mental Health Assn., 1989-90; officer of Election-Commonwealth of Va., 2002—; bd. dirs. Coalition for The Blue Ridge Pkwy., 1994-2000, Oconee Cultural Arts Found., 1995-97, Blue Ridge Pkwy. Assn., 1997-2001. Fellow Paul Harris fellow, Buchanan Rotary Club. Mem.: KC (4th deg.), ABA, Sevier County Bar Assn., Ga. Trial Lawyers Assn., Ga. Assn. Adminstrv. Law Judges (bd. dir. 1990—91), Ga. State Bar Assn., Blue Ridge/ Shenandoah Travel Mktg. Group (chmn. bd. 2004—), Ea. Nat. Parks Assn., Blue Ridge Pkwy. Assn., Shenandoah Valley Travel Assn. (bd. dir. 2003—04), Internat. Platform Assn., S.E. Tourism Soc., Soc. Am. Poets, 300 Club Roanoke, Rotary Internat., Magna Carta Barons, Cotillion Club Roanoke, Rotary (pres. elect Buchanan chpt. 2004—, Paul Harris fellow), Phi Alpha Delta. Roman Catholic. Avocations: reading, music, golf, cross country skiing. Office Phone: 540-458-3772. Office Fax: 540-291-9920. Business E-Mail: smokymts@ntelos.net, curator@awesometoymuseum.com.

BRACKETT, MARC ALAN, psychologist; s. William Joseph and Diane Brackett. BA, Rutgers U., 1991; PhD, U. N.H., 2002. Assoc. rsch. scientist Yale U., New Haven, 2003—. Author: rsch. on emotional intelligence (MENSA Edn. Rsch. award for Excellence in Rsch., 2004). Grantee Excellence in Rsch., Sigma Xi, 2001, 2002. Mem.: Soc. Personality and Social Psychology (assoc.). Achievements include development of Emotional Literacy in the Middle School: A Six Step Program to Promote Social, Emotional, and Academic Learning.

BRACKETT, MARTIN LUTHER, JR., lawyer; b. Charlotte, N.C., Feb. 23, 1947; s. Martin Luther and Helen Virginia (Smith) B.; m. Lisa Nichol; children— Martin Hunter, Alexander Jones, Amelia Kathleen, Lauren Hart. B.A., Davidson Coll., 1969; J.D., U. N.C., 1972. Bar: N.C. 1972, U.S. Dist. Ct. (we. dist.) N.C. 1973, U.S. Ct. Appeals (4th cir.) 1975. Ptnr. Bailey, Brackett & Brackett, P.A., Charlotte, N.C., 1973-83, Brackett & Sitton, Charlotte, 1983-85, Robinson, Bradshaw & Hinson, P.A., 1985—. Mem. Auditorium-Coliseum-Conv. Ctr. Authority, Charlotte, 1981-87, chmn., 1985-87. Served to capt. U.S. Army, 1972-73. Recipient Van Hecke-Wettach award U. N.C., 1972. Fellow Am. Coll. Trial Lawyers; mem. N.C. Acad. Trial Lawyers (bd. govs. 1980-86, 88-95, v.p. 1984-86). Democrat. Presbyterian. Office: 1900 Independence Ctr 101 N Tryon St Charlotte NC 28246-0100 Office Phone: 704-377-8347.

BRACKETT, PRILLA SMITH, artist, educator; b. New Orleans, Nov. 8, 1942; d. Wilson Fitch and Hannah Balch (Coffin) Smith; m. George Conrad Brackett, Sept. 28, 1968; children: Ethan Samuel, Matthew Aaron. BA in Psychology and Sociology, Sarah Lawrence Coll., 1964; MA in Sociology, U. Calif., Berkeley, 1967; MFA in Painting and Drawing, U. Nebr., 1981. Grad. tchg. asst. U. Nebr., Lincoln, 1979-81; adj. prof. Simmons Coll., Boston, 1989; instr. DeCordova Mus. Sch., Lincoln, 1992-93; adj. prof. U. Mass. Harbor Campus, Boston, 1993, Salem (Mass.) State Coll., 1993; instr. landscape workshops Arts Pro Tem, Hancock, N.H., 1993-95, 97, West Yellowstone, Mont., 1993-95. Panel coord., moderator Nat. Women's Caucus for Art, San Francisco, 1989, 95, Boston, 1996; panelist Coll. Art Assn. Nat. Conf., Chgo., 1992; guest lectr. and spkr. in field. One-woman shows include Winfisky Gallery, Salem (Mass.) State Coll., 1989, Gallery 57, Cambridge, 1989, The Bunting Inst., Radcliffe Rsch. and Study Ctr., Cambridge, 1990, Soho 20 Invitational Space, N.Y.C., 1990, Wessell Libr., Tufts U., Medford, Mass., 1990, DeCordova Mus. and Sculpture Park, Lincoln, Mass., 1993, Gallery 57, Cambridge, Mass., 1994, UMF Gallery, Farmington, Maine, 1999, duPont Gallery, Washington and Lee U., Lexington, Va., 1999, Soc. for the Protection of N.H. Forests, Concord, 2000, Berman Mus. Art, Ursinus Coll., Collegeville, Pa., 2000, Watson Gallery, Wheaton Coll., Norton, Mass., 2000, Housatonic Mus. Art, Bridgeport, Conn., 2000, Cress Gallery, U. Tenn., Chattanooga, 2001, Inst. Ecosys. Studies, Millbrook, N.Y., 2001, others; two-person exhbn. Mark Gallery, Cambridge, Mass., 2003, 04, Art Complex Mus., Duxbury, Mass., 2005; group exhbns. include Portland (Maine) Mus. Art, 1998, Creiger-Dane Gallery, Boston, 1998, Fitchburg (Mass.) Art Mus., 1998, St. Lawrence U., Canton, N.Y., 1998, U. Oreg., Eugene, 1998, Virginia Lynch Gallery, Tivarton, R.I., 2000, Berkshire Art Mus., Pittsfield, Mass., 2001, Elliot Smith Contemporary Art, St. Louis, 2002, Sonia Zaks Gallery, Chgo., 2003, Arnot Art Mus., Elmira, N.Y., others. Co-pres. Boston chpt. Amigos de las Americas, Boston, 1993-95. Recipient fellowship in painting Bunting Inst., Radcliffe Rsch. and Study Ctr., Cambridge, 1989-90, The Francine Frank fellow residency Millay Colony of the Arts, Austerlitz, N.Y., 1994, residency at Ragdale Found., Lake Forest, Ill., 1997, 98, 2nd place cash award Lancaster Mus., 1997, Lois Neelie Gill award and residency Ucross Found., Clearmont, Wyo., 1998, residency Va. Ctr. for Creative Arts, Sweet Briar, Va., 2001, 03; Vision Fund grantee, Boston Found., 1998. Mem. Coll. Art Assn., Women's Caucus for Art (coord. for exhbns. nat. conf. 1986, co-chair Boston chpt. 1987-88). Avocations: vegetable and flower gardening, hiking, going to opera, theater, dance and chamber music concerts. Home: 171 Lake View Ave Cambridge MA 02138-2131 Office: 75 Richdale Ave Ste 11 Cambridge MA 02140-2608 Business E-Mail: psb@luceatlux.com.

BRACKETT, RONALD E., investment company executive, lawyer; b. Rockford, Ill., May 10, 1942; s. F. Earl Brackett and Anne (Christenberry) Townsend; m. Susan Catherine Stichnoth, May 31, 1975; 1 child, Charles William. BA, Trinity Coll., 1964; JD, U. Mich., 1967. Bar: N.Y. 1968. Assoc. Rogers & Wells, N.Y.C., 1968-74, ptnr., 1974-91, mng. ptnr., 1984-85, cons., 1992-94; founder, prin. Associated Growth Investors, L.P., Babylon, NY, 1992—. Bd. dirs. King Kullen Grocery Co., Inc., Westbury, NY. Mem.: N.Y. State Bar Assn., Phi Beta Kappa. Office: Associated Growth Investors LP 1801 House Argyle Square Babylon NY 11702-2711

BRACKMANN, DERALD E., otolaryngologist; b. Buckley, Ill., Feb. 13, 1937; s. Otto Henry Brackmann and Anna Mina Abraham; m. Charlotte Joyce Boyden, June 21, 1959; children: David, Douglas, Mark, Steven. Student, U. Ill., 1958, MD, 1962. Diplomate Am. Bd. Otolaryngology. Intern Ill. Ctrl. Hosp., Chgo., 1962—63; resident ob-gyn. Ill. Rsch. Hosp., Chgo., 1963—64; resident Otolaryngology Los Angeles County/U. So. Calif. Med. Ctr., 1966—70, chief otology, 1981—98; staff physician House Ear Clinic, L.A., 1970—85, pres., 1985—. Chief ENT svc. St. Vincent Med. Ctr., 1971—98; clin. prof. otolaryngology U. So. Calif., clin. prof. neurologic surgery; clin. instr. House Ear Inst. Editor: Otologic Surgery, Neurotology, Neurological Surgery of the Ear & Skull Base; editl. bd.: jour. Advances in Otolaryngology-Head and Neck Surgery, Laryngoscoope, Neurotology; co-author (chpt.): Electrocochleography, 1976, Hearing Disorders, 1976, Acoustic Tumors: Diagnosis and Management, 1979, Acoustic Tumors Vol. 1 Diagnosis, 1979, Otolaryngology, 1980, Controversy in Otolaryngology, 1980, Butterworth International Medical Reviews: Otology, 1982, Disorders of the Facial Nerve, 1982, Essential Otolaryngology Head & Neck Surgery, 3d edit., 1983; author: Surgery of the Skull Base, 1983, Meniere's Disease: A Comprehensive Appraisal, 1983; contbg. editor: Neurological Surgery of the Ear and Skull Base, 1982; co-author: Gerald M. English Otolaryngology, Sensory Evoked Potentials, 1984, Cochlear Implants, 1985; author: The Facial Nerve, 1986; co-author: Ear and Skull Base, 1986, Conn's Current Therapy, 1988, Otologic Medicine and Surgery, 1988, Advances in Otolaryngology-Head and Neck Surgery, 1989; author: Operative Challenges in Otolaryngology Head and Neck Surgery, 1990, Neurosurgery Update 1: Diagnosis, Operative Technique and Neuro-Otology, 1990, Operative Techniques in Otolaryngology-Head and Neck Surgery, 1991, Surgery of Cranial Base Tumors, 1993; author: Handbook of Intraoperative Monitoring, 1994; co-author: Essential Otolaryngology, 1995, Otolaryngology, 1996; author: Atlas of Head & Neck Surgry-Otolaryngology, 1996, Disorders of the Vestibular System, 1996, Head and Neck Surgery Volume 2: Ear, 1996; co-author: Acoustic Tumors Diagnosis and Management, 2d edit., 1997, Diseases of the Ear. 6th edit., 1998, Essential Otolaryngology, 1998, Head and Neck Surgery-Otolaryngology, Vol. 2, 1998, Surgery of the Skull Base, 1998, Textbook of Clinical Neurology, 1998, Cranial Base Surgery, 1999; author: The Facial Nerve, 2000; co-author: Operative Techniques in Neurosurgery, 2001, Controversies in Otolaryngology, 2001, Surgery of the Ear, 5th edit., 2002, Essential Otolaryngology, 2003; editor: Neurologic Surgery of the Ear and Skull Base, 1982; contbg. editor: Otologic Surgery, 1994, 3d edit., 2001; co-editor: Neurotology, 1994; contbr. over 200 articles to profl. jours. Capt. USAF, 1964—66. Recipient Alumni Achievement award, U. Ill., 1997, Gold medal, Prosper Meniere's Soc., 2000; fellow, House Ear Inst. and Clinic, 1970—71. Fellow: AMA, Am. Laryngol. Rhinol. Otol. Soc., Am. Acad. Olotaryngology Head and Neck Surgery (pres. 1988, com. facial nerve disorders, pres. 1987—88); mem.: ACS, Asian Conf. Neurol. Surgeons, N.Am. Skull Base Soc. (pres. 1995—96), Rsch. Study Club, LA Soc. Otolaryngology (pres. 1986—87), Otolaryngology Soc. Australia (hon.), Royal Soc. Medicine (hon.), LA County Med. Assn., Calif. Med. Assn., Am. Otol. Soc. (task force sub-certification, pres. 1995—96), Am. Neurotology Soc. (exec. coun., pres. 1984—85), Centurion Club, Alpha Omega Alpha. Republican. Achievements include research in neurotology; cochlear implant; auditory brainstem implant. Avocations: fishing, hunting. Office: House Ear Clinic 2100 W 3rd St Los Angeles CA 90057 Office Phone: 213-483-9930. Business E-Mail: dbrackmann@hei.org.

BRADA, DONALD ROBERT, psychiatrist; b. Hutchinson, Kans., Oct. 11, 1939; s. Joseph Duane and Mary Elizabeth (Whitebread) B.; m. Carolyn Starr Cromb, Aug. 19, 1961; children: Donald Robert Jr., Stephen Andrew. AB, U. Kans., 1961, MD, 1965. Diplomate Am. Bd. Psychiatry and Neurology; Lic. Kans. State Bd. Healing Arts. Resident in psychiatry U. Kans., Kansas City, Kans., 1972; pvt. practice Hutchinson, 1976-77; med. dir., exec. dir. Horizons Mental Health Ctr., Hutchinson, 1977-87; med. dir. psychiatry St. Francis Regional Med. Ctr., Wichita, Kans., 1987-96; assoc. clinical prof. dept. psychiatry and behavior med. Sch. Med. U. Kans., Wichita, 1996—. Bd. dirs. Kans. Found. Med. Care, Topeka, Wichita Preferred Providers Assn., Pschiat. Rsch. Inst., Wichita, 1989—; mem. Govs. Mental Health Svcs. Planning Coun., 1988-94. Contbr. articles to profl. jours. Elder First Presbyn. Ch., Hutchinson, 1984-86. Col. USAF, 1964-76. Fellow Am. Psychiat. Assn.; mem. Kans. Psychiat. Soc. (pres. 1988-90), Kans. Med. Soc. (treas. 1987-90, 2d v.p. 1991-92, 1st v.p. 1992-93, pres.-elect 1993-94, pres. 1994-95), Sedgwick County Psychiat. Assn. (chmn. 1990-92). Republican. Avocations: running, golf, tennis, aerobics, travel. Home: 52 Mission Rd Wichita KS 67207-1036 Office: 1010 N Kansas St Wichita KS 67214-3124

BRADBEER, CLIVE, biochemistry educator; b. Tynemouth, Northumberland, Eng., Feb. 20, 1933; came to U.S., 1962, naturalized, 1994; s. Joseph Walter and Mary (Hall) B.; m. Wilma Jean Youngert, Sept. 1, 1960; children: Suzanne Mary, Thomas Clive. BSc with first class honors, Durham U., Newcastle Upon Tyne, Eng., 1954, PhD, 1957. Jr. rsch. biochemist U. Calif., Berkeley, 1957-59, Davis, 1959; postdoctoral fellow U. Wis., Madison, 1959-60; lectr. Queen Mary Coll., London U., 1960-62; asst. prof. Sch. Medicine, U. Va., Charlottesville, 1964-69, assoc. prof., 1969-79, prof., 1979—. Vis. scientist NIH, Bethesda, Md., 1962-64, ad hoc mem. study sect., 1980-84; vis. prof. U. Otago, Dunedin, New Zealand, 1982-83, 93. Contbr. articles to profl. jours. Mem. Am. Soc. for Biochemistry and Molecular Biology. Episcopalian. Achievements include contbns. in elucidation of the molecular mechanisms involved in utilization of vitamin B12 in microbial and animal cells. E-mail: cb7f@virginia.edu.

BRADBURN, JAMES HENRY, architectural firm executive; b. 1944; m. Gayle Bradburn. BArch, Rensselaer Polytechnic Inst. Arch. Kevin Roche and John Dinkeloo, Conn.; ptnr. C.W. Fentress J.H. Bradburn and Assocs. PC, Denver, 1980—. Bd. dir. Nat. Benevolent Assn. Colo., Christian Home Tennyson Ctr. for Children & Families, Denver. Mem.: AIA, Urban Land Inst., We. Mus. Assn., New Eng. Mus. Assn., Assn. Midwest Mus., Mountains-Plains Mus. Assn., Colo.-Wyo. Assn. Mus., Am. Assn. Mus. Office: CW Fentress JH Bradburn & Assocs PC 421 Broadway Denver CO 80203

BRADBURN, NORMAN M., behavioral science educator; b. Lincoln, Ill., July 21, 1933; s. Hubert Benjamin and Mary Celeste (Marshall) B.; m. Wendy McAneny, Dec. 15, 1956; children: Isabel Stuart, Andrew Marshall, Laura Humphreys. BA, U. Chgo., 1952, Oxford U., Eng., 1955; MA, Harvard U., 1958, PhD in Social Psychology, 1960. From asst. prof. to assoc. prof. behavioral sci. U. Chgo., 1960-67, prof., 1967—, chmn. dept. behavioral sci., 1973-79, Tiffany and Margaret Blake Disting. Service prof., 1977-99, provost, 1984-89, prof. emeritus, 1999—. Sr. study dir. Nat. Opinion Rsch. Ctr., Chgo., 1961—, dir., 1967-71, 79-84, 89-92, rsch. dir., 1992-2000, sr. fellow, 2004—; asst. dir. NSF, 2000—04. Author: (with D. Caplovitz) Reports on Happiness, 1967, The Structure of Psychological Well-Being, 1970, (with S. Sudman, G. Gockel) Side by Side: A Study of Integrated Neighborhoods, 1971, (with S. Sudman) Response Effects in Surveys, 1974, Asking Questions: A Practical Guide to Questionnaire Construction, 1982, revised edit. (with Sudman and Wansinik), 2004, Polls and Surveys: Understanding What They Tell Us, 1988, (with others) Improving Questionnaire Design and Interview Method, 1979, (with S. Sudman and N. Schwarz) Thinking About Answers, 1996. Alexander von Humboldt scholar U. Cologne (Germany), 1970-71 Fellow AAAS, Am. Statis. Assn.; mem. Internat. Statis. Inst., World Assn. Pub. Opinion Rsch., Am. Assn. Pub. Opinion Rsch. (pres. 1991-92), Am. Acad. Arts and Scis. Home: 502 N Abingdon St Arlington VA 22203-2049 Business E-Mail: bradburn-norman@norc.uchicago.edu.

BRADBURY, MICHELLE SANDY, neuroradiologist, medical researcher; b. Washington, D.C., Oct. 25, 1960; d. Stanley Morton and Rosilyn Madeline Neuder; m. John Seferian Bradbury, May 10, 1997. BA, U. Pa., 1979—82; MS, U. Md., 1983—86; PhD, MIT, 1986—91; MD, George Wash. U., 1993—97. Diagnostic Radiology Am. Bd. Radiology, 2002. Rsch. asst., dept. of nuc. medicine NIH, Bethesda, Md., 1983—85; rsch. fellow, nuc. methods group Nat. Inst. Standards and Tech., Gaithersburg, Md., 1985—86; rsch. asst., dept. radiology Mass. Gen. Hosp., Boston, 1987—91; post-doctoral fellow, contrast media lab., dept. radiology U. Calif., San Francisco, 1992—93; intramural nih rsch. fellow Nat. Eye Inst., NIH, Bethesda, 1994; surg. intern Wake Forest U., Bapt. Med. Ctr, Winston-Salem, NC, 1997—98, radiology resident, 1998—2002, neuroradiology fellow, dept. radiology, 2002—03; instr., dept. radiology Meml. Sloan Kettering Cancer Ctr., N.Y.C., 2003—. Author: (book chpt.) Scope of Diagnostic Imaging in Basic Radiology, 2nd ed., The Brain and Its Coverings in Basic Radiology, 2nd ed, (pub., The Breast Jour.) Method of combined FDG-PET and radiographic imaging of primary breast cancers, (pub.) Mesenteric Venous Thrombosis: current concepts and imaging strategies, (exhbn. (rsna) and pub.) Mesenteric venous thrombosis: diagnosis and non-invasive imaging (Commendation for publ. in Radiographics, 2000). Recipient Roentgen Resident/Fellow Rsch. Award, Radiol. Soc. of N.Am., 2002, Elias G. Theros Rsch. Award, Elias G. Theros Rsch. Fund/Prof. of Chest/Cardiac Radiology, Kerry M. Link, 2002; fellow Molecular Imaging, Meml. Sloan Kettering Cancer Ctr., 2003—. Mem.: Radiol. Soc. N.Am., Internat. Soc. Magnetic Resonance in Medicine, Am. Soc. Neuroradiology, Soc. Molecular Imaging, MIT Chpt. of NY, Tau Beta Pi, Sigma Xi. Avocations: travel, museums, piano, hiking. Home: 1365 York Ave Apt 23 D New York NY 10021 Office: Memorial Sloan Kettering Cancer Ctr 1275 York Ave New York NY 10021 Office Phone: 212-639-8938. Personal E-mail: mbrad1025@aol.com. Business E-Mail: bradburm@mskcc.org.

BRADBURY, RAY DOUGLAS, writer; b. Waukegan, Ill., Aug. 22, 1920; s. Leonard Spaulding and Esther Marie (Moberg) B.; m. Marguerite Susan McClure (dec. Nov. 24, 2003), Sept. 27, 1947; children: Susan Marguerite, Ramona, Bettina, Alexandra. DLitt, Whittier Coll., 1979. First pub. short story, 1941; stories pub. pulp mags., 1941-45. Author: (short story collections) Dark Carnival, 1947, The Illustrated Man, 1951, The Golden Apples of the Sun, 1953, Fahrenheit 451, 1953 (Commonwealth Club Calif. gold medal 1954), The October Country, 1955, A Medicine for Melancholy, 1959 (pub. in Eng. as The Day It Rained Forever, 1959), The Ghoul Keepers, 1961, The Small Assassin, 1962, The Machineries of Joy, 1964, The Vintage Bradbury, 1965, The Autumn People, 1965, Tomorrow Midnight, 1966, Twice Twenty-Two, 1966, I Sing The Body Electric!, 1969, (with Robert Bloch) Bloch and Bradbury: Ten Masterpieces of Science Fiction, 1969 (pub. in Eng. as Fever Dreams and Other Fantasies, 1970), (with Bloch) Whispers From Beyond, 1972, Harrap, 1975, Long After Midnight, 1976, The Best of Bradbury, 1976, To Sing Strange Songs, 1979, The Stories of Ray Bradbury, 1980, Dinosaur Tales, 1983, A Memory of Murder, 1984, The Toynbee Convector, 1988, Kaleidoscope, 1994; (poetry) Old Ahab's Friend, and Friend to Noah, Speaks His Piece: A Celebration, 1971, When Elephants Last in the Dooryard Bloomed: Celebrations for Almost Any Day in the Year, 1973, That Son of Richard III: A Birth Announcement, 1974, Where Robot Mice and Robot Men Run Round in Robot Towns, 1977, Twin Hieroglyphs That Swim the River Dust, 1978, The Bike Repairman, 1978, The Author Considers His Resources, 1979, The Aqueduct, 1979, The Attic Where The Meadow Greens, 1979, The Last Circus, 1980, The Ghosts of Forever, 1980, The Haunted Computer and the Android Pope, 1981, The Complete Poems of Ray Bradbury, 1982, The Love Affair, 1983, Forever and the Earth, 1984, Death has Lost Its Charm for Me, 1987; (novels) The Martian Chronicles, 1950 (pub. in Eng. as The Silver Locusts, 1951), Dandelion Wine, 1957, Something Wicked This Way Comes, 1962, Death is a Lonely Business, 1985, A Graveyard for Lunatics, 1990, Green Shadows, White Whale, 1992; (juvenile novels) Switch on the Night, 1955 (Boys Club Am. Jr. Book award 1956), R is for Rocket, 1962, S is for Space, 1966, The Halloween Tree, 1972, The April Witch, 1987, The Other Foot, 1987, The Foghorn, 1987, The Veldt, 1987, Fever Dream, 1987, The Smile, 1991; (non-fiction) Teacher's Guide: Science Fiction, 1968, Zen and the Art of Writing, 1973, Mars and the Mind of Man, 1973, The Mummies of Guanajuato, 1978, Beyond 1984: Remembrance of Things Future, 1979, Los Angeles, 1984, Orange County, 1985, The Art of Playboy, 1985, Yestermorrow: Obvious Answers to Impossible Futures, 1991, Ray Bradbury On Stage: A Chrestomathy of His Plays, 1991, Journey to Far Metaphor: Further Essays on Creativity, Writing, Literature, and the Arts, 1994, The First Book of Dichotomy, The Second Book of Symbiosis, 1995; (plays) The Meadow, 1960, Way in the Middle of the Air, 1962, The Anthem Sprinters, and Other Antics, 1963, The World of Ray Bradbury, 1964, Leviathan 99, 1966, The Day It Rained Forever, 1966, The Pedestrian, 1966, Dandelion Wine, 1967, Christus Apollo, 1969, The Wonderful Ice-Cream Suit and Other Plays, 1972, Madrigals for the Space Age, 1972, Pillar of Fire and Other Plays for Today, Tomorrow, and Beyond Tomorrow, 1975, That Ghost, That Bride of Time: Excerpts from a Play-in-Progress, 1976, The Martian Chronicles, 1977 (5 L.A. Drama Critics Circle awards), Farenheit 451, 1979, A Device Out of Time, 1986, Falling Upward, 1988; prodr. one-act plays, Royal Shakespeare Festival Theatre, The Pandemonium Theatre Co., 1963; screenwriter: (films) It Came from Outer Space, 1953, The Beast from 20,000 Fathoms, 1953, Moby Dick, 1956, Icarus Montgolfier Wright, 1962 (Academy award nomination best short film 1963), An American Journey, 1964, Picasso Summer, 1972, Something Wicked This Way Comes, 1983; (TV scripts for series) Alfred Hitchcock Presents, Jane Wyman's Fireside Theatre, steve Canyon, Trouble Shooters, Twilight Zone, Alcoa Premiere, Curiosity Shop, Ray Bradbury Television Theatre; editor: Timeless Stories for Today and Tomorrow, 1952, The Circus of Dr. Lao and Other Improbable Stories, 1956, A Day in the Life of Hollywood, 1992. Mem. adv. bd. Science Fiction Mus. and Hall of Fame. Recipient O. Henry prize, 1947, 48, Benjamin Franklin award best story, 1954, Nat. Inst. Arts and Letters award, 1954, Golden Eagle award, 1957, Mrs. Ann Radcliffe award Count Dracula Soc., 1965, 71, Writers Guild award 1974, World Fantasy award for lifetime achievement, 1977, Balrog award best poet, 1979, Aviation and Space Writers award, 1979, Gandalf award, 1980, PEN Body of Work award, 1985, Presdl. Nat. Medal of Arts, 2004. Mem. Screen Writers Guild, Sci. Fantasy Writers Am., Pacific Art Found. (v.p.), Writers Guild Am. (mem. screen writers bd.) Office: Bantam Doubleday Dell 1540 Broadway New York NY 10036-4039 Mailing: c/o Avon Books 1350 Avenue Of The Americas New York NY 10019-4702

BRADBURY, WILLIAM CHAPMAN, III, (BILL BRADBURY), state official; b. Chgo., May 29, 1949; s. William L. and Lorraine (Patterson) B.; m. Betsy Harrison (Sept. 1984); children: Abby, Zoe; m. Kathleen P. Eymann, June 7, 1986. Student, Antioch Coll., 1967-69. News reporter KQED-TV Newsroom, 1969-70; dir. pub. affairs Sta. KMPX-FM, San Francisco, 1970; mem. video prodn. group Optic Nerve, San Francisco, 1970-73; project dir. Coos Country TV, Bandon, Oreg., 1973-75; reporter, anchor Sta. KVAL-TV, Eugene, Oreg., 1975-76; news dir. Sta. KCBY-TV, Coos Bay, Oreg., 1976-78; prodr., writer, editor video news feature svc. Local Color, Langlois, Oreg., 1978-79; field prodr. PM Mag., Sta. KGW-TV, Portland, Oreg., 1979-80; mem. Oreg. Ho. of Reps., Salem, 1980-84, Oreg. Senate, Salem, 1984-95, pres., 1993-95; exec. dir. Sake of the Salmon, Gladstone, Oreg., 1995-99; sec. of state State of Oreg., Salem, 1999—. Chmn. Western Legis. Conf., Coun. State Govs., 1991, mem. ocean resources com.; founder, former chmn. Pacific Fishery Legis. Task Force. Prodr. documentaries Gorda Ridge—Boom or Bust for the Oregon Coast?, The Tillamook Burn—From Ruin to Rejuvenation, Not Guilty by Reason of Insanity, Child as Witness, Local Color, Salmon on the Run, The First Perennial Poetic Hoohaw, TV Town Hall Meetings, Common Sense, also prodr. mktg. videos and commls. for polit. candidates, hosp. Democrat. Mem. Soc. Of Friends. Avocation: white water kayaking. Office: Sec of State 141 State Capitol Bldg Salem OR 97310-0722 E-mail: bill.bradbury@state.or.us.*

BRADDOCK, DAVID LAWRENCE, health science educator; b. Glendale, Calif., Mar. 10, 1945; s. Mark Perry and Christina Bain Braddock; m. Laura Stanlye Haffer, May 1, 1976; children: Gabriel, Autumn, Adam. BA, U. Tex., 1967, MA, 1970, PhD, 1973. Spl. asst. to dir. sec.'s com. on mental retardation HEW, Washington, 1972; prin. investigator Coun. for Exceptional Children, Reston, Va., 1973-77; cons. White House Conf. on the Handicapped, Washington, 1977-78; rsch. prof., program dir. Inst. Study Devel. Disabilities U. Ill., Chgo., 1979-88, prof. cmty. health scis. Sch. Pub. Health, 1985—2001, prof. human devel., founding head dept. disability and human devel., 1988—2001, assoc. dean for rsch., 1997-98; assoc. v.p. U. Colo. Sys., 2001—; exec. dir. Coleman Inst. for Cognitive Disabilities U. Colo., 2001—; Coleman-Turner chair in cognitive disability, prof. psychiatry U. Colo. Health Scis. Ctr., Coll. Medicine, 2001—. Cons. U.S. Dept. HHS, Washington, 1972—. Author: Federal Policy Toward Mental Retardation, 1987, Residential Services and Developmental Disabilities in U.S., 1992, The State of the States in Developmental Disabilities, 7 edits., Disability at the Dawn of the 21st Century, 2002; co-author: State Law and the Education of Handicapped Children, 1972; contbr. more than 200 articles to profl. jours., monographs in field. Cons. Joseph P. Kennedy Jr. Found.; active in promoting civil and human rights of people with mental retardation and other disabilities.; bd. dirs. Spl. Olympics Internat. Fellow, Nat. Inst. on Disability and Rehab. Rsch., 1988—89; grantee U.S. Dept. HHS, U.S. Dept. Edn., Nat. Inst. on Disability and Rehab. Rsch., 1974—2004; univ. scholar, U. Ill., 1998—2001. Fellow: Am. Assn. on Mental Retardation (pres. 1993—94, editor books and monographs 1997—2002, Career Rsch. award 1998), Delta Omega; mem.: AAAS, Assn. for Retarded Citizens of U.S. (sci. adv. bd. 1987—, Disting. Rsch. award in mental retardation 1987, Franklin Smith award for disting. nat. svc. 2000). Office: Coleman Inst Cognitive Disabilities U Colo SYS 586 4001 Discovery Dr Boulder CO 80309

BRADDOCK, JENE ELIZABETH, art appraiser; b. Richmond, Ind., Sept. 13, 1946; d. Robert Louis and Mary Alice Braddock. BFA, Syracuse U., 1968. Designer, colorist Old Deerfield Fabrics, N.Y.C., 1968—71, Brunschwig and Fils Inc., N.Y.C., 1972—75, N.Y.C., 1976—79; fiber artist, 1980—83; artist, 1984—. Artist coun. Frist Ctr. for Visual Arts, Nashville, 2000—; edn. coun. Fleist Ctr. for Visual Arts, Nashville, 2002—04. Exhibitions include Festival DeVille, Nashville, 2001, Internat. Disman Competition, 2003 (1st prize in paiting, 2003). Mem. grant review panel Metro Arts Nashville, 1994—98, chair, 1997—98, 1999—2000; treas., exhbns. com., coord monthly forums Visaul Arts Alliance Nashville, 1996; coord. assemblage panel Frist Ctr. for Visual Arts, 2000. Democrat. Avocations: astrology, international travel, cooking, reading, walking. Home: 5600 Higdon Rd Joelton TN 37080

BRADDOCK, JOSEPH VINCENT, physicist; b. Hoboken, N.J., Dec. 10, 1929; s. Ralph and Rose (Rago) Braddock; m. Teresa Marquez, June 24, 1961 (dec. Nov. 1961); m. Bertha Soto, Jan. 30, 1965; children: J. Anthony, Robert T. BS in Physics, St. Peter's Coll., 1951; MS in Physics, Fordham U., 1952, PhD in Physics, 1958. Asst. prof. Iona Coll., New Rochelle, N.Y., 1958-60; co-founder, exec. BDM Internat., McLean, Va., 1960-93; trustee Potomac Found., McLean, 1988—. Cons. Def. Sci. Bd., Washington, 1975—, Dept. Army Sci. Bd., Washington, 1977-83, 93—; adv. bd. Nat. Security Agy., Ft. Meade, Md., 1977-85. Trustee Inova Hosp. Found., McLean, 1996—, Aztec Found., Alexandria, Va., 1988—, Alexandria Symphony Orch., 1990—; bd. dirs. Shrine of Immaculate Conception, Washington, 1995—. Mem. IEEE, Am. Phys. Soc. Roman Catholic. Avocations: travel, architecture, history of science and technology. Home: 1101 Saint Stephens Rd Alexandria VA 22304-1728 Office: Potomac Found 8618 Westwood Center Dr Ste 110 Vienna VA 22182 Office Phone: 703-506-1790. E-mail: jvbtpf@aol.com.

BRADDOCK, RICHARD S., internet company executive; s. Robert L. and Mary Alice (Krueger) B.; m. Susan Schulte, Feb. 14, 1978; 1 child, Christina; children by previous marriage: Jennifer, Richard, Derek BA, Dartmouth Coll., 1963; MBA, Harvard Bus. Sch., 1965. Mem. mktg. staff General Foods, White Plains, N.Y., 1965-73; mem. staff Citicorp, N.Y.C., 1973-92, sector exec. in charge of worldwide consumer fin. svcs., info. bus., investor rels., corp. pub. affairs, customer affairs, corp. advt., 1985-90, also bd. dirs.; pres. Citibank/Citicorp, N.Y.C., 1990-92; chief exec. officer Medco Containment Svcs., Montvale, N.J., 1992; spl. advisor Gen. Atlantic Ptnrs. LLC, 1996-97; non-exec. chmn. True North Communications Inc., 1997; CEO Priceline.com, 1998—2002, chmn., 1998—2004. Bd. dirs. Eastman Kodak, Lotus Devel. Corp.; chief exec. officer Medical Mktg. Group, Synetics. Bd. dirs. Cancer Rsch. Inst., N.Y.C., Lincoln Ctr., N.Y.C. Partnership; mem. Coun. on Fgn Rels. Mem. N.Y. C. of C. (bd. dirs.).

BRADDOM, RANDALL LEE, physiatrist, educator; b. Monarch, Va., Oct. 29, 1942; s. Audy Lee and Ruth Janet Braddom; m. Diana Verdun, 2001; children from previous marriage: Eric C., Steven R., Karen L. BA, DePauw U., 1964; MD, Ohio State U., 1968, MS, 1971. Diplomate Am. Bd. Electrodiagnostic Medicine, Am. Bd. Phys. Medicine and Rehab. Rotating intern Mt. Carmel Hosp., Columbus, Ohio, 1968-69; resident in phys. medicine and rehab. Ohio State Univ. Hosps., Columbus, 1969-72; physiatrist, electromyographer Rancocas Valley Hosp., Willingboro, NJ, 1972-74, Phila. Naval Med. Ctr., 1972-74; asst. prof. phys. medicine and rehab. U. Cin., 1974-75, assoc. prof., dir. phys. medicine and rehab., 1975-81; med. dir. phys. med. and rehab. St. Francis-St. George Hosp., Cin., 1987-89, Providence Hosp., Cin., 1982-89; assoc. prof., dep. chmn. rehab. medicine Temple U., Phila., 1989-91; chmn. rehab. medicine Albert Einstein Hosp., Phila., 1989-91; v.p. med. affairs Moss Rehab. Hosp., Phila., 1989-91; practitioner Rehab. Assocs., Indpls., 1991-96; med. dir. Hook Rehab. Ctr., Indpls., 1991-98; prof., chmn. phys. medicine and rehab Ind. U. Sch. Medicine, Indpls., 1991-98. Dir. Wishard Health Svcs., Indpls., Ind.; physiatrist Albert Einstein Med. Ctr. N., Phila., 1973; clin. instr. rehab. medicine Thomas Jefferson Coll. Med., Phila., 1972-74; assoc. in medicine Jewish Hosp., Cin., 1974-89; cons. phys. medicine and rehab. VA Hosp., Cin., 1975-81; dir. phys. med. and rehab. U. Hosps., U. Cin., 1975-81; assoc. clin. prof. phys. med. Ohio State U., Columbus, 1984-90; clin. assoc. prof. phys. medicine and rehab. U. Cin., Coll. Medicine, 1982-89; cons. St. Francis Hosp., Indpls., 1991-97; phys. med. and rehab. svc. chief Wishard Meml. Hosp., Indpls., 1991-2000; dir. phys. medicine and rehab. svc. Richard Roudebush VA Hosp., Indpls., 1991-97; vis. prof. Dept. Phys. Medicine and Rehab. U. Ark., 1992, U. Ky. Dept Phys. Medicine and Rehab., 1992, Dept. Internal Medicine Divsn. Phys. Medicine & Rehab. La. State U. Sch. Medicine, New Orleans, La., 1994, Baylor Coll. Medicine Dept. Phys. Medicine & Rehab., 1994, N.J. Sch. Medicine and Dentistry Dept. P.M. & R.; presenter in field; lectr. in field. Author: (with others) Physical Medicine & Rehabilitation Review, 1980; editor: Sports Medicine and Rehabilitation: A Sport-Scientific Approach, 1994, Physical Medicine and rehabilitation, 1996; contbr. articles to profl. jours. Founder, med. dir. ECCO Family Health Ctr., Inc., Columbus, 1970-72; bd. dirs. Nat. Paraplegia Found., 1975-80; med. adviser Easter Seals Soc. Southwestern Ohio, 1980-82; asst. scoutmaster Troop 291, Boy Scouts Am., 1982-84; chmn. Citizens for Our Schs. Tax Levy Campaign, Forest Hills Sch. Dist., Cin., 1985; trustee Total Living Concepts, Inc., Cin., 1977-85, Disability Svcs. Group, Inc., Cin., 1985-89; bd. examiners The Henry B. Betts award, 1991-94. Lt. comdr. USNR, 1972—74. Recipient Kiwanis Club Citizenship award, Dayton, 1960, Rsch. award Am. Paralyzed Vets. Assn., 1968, Am. Therapeutic Soc., 1968, Landacre Soc. award Ohio State U., 1978, Sidney Licht Lectureship Ohio State U., 1985, Alumni Achievement award Ohio State U., 1993, Sidney Licht Lectureship U. Minn., 1993, Randy Braddom award U. Cin. Coll. Medicine, 1989, Landwerlen award, Muscular Dystrophy Found. Ind., 1994, Lifetime Achievement award, AANEM, 2004; named Man of Yr. Columbus Citizen-Jour., 1970. Mem. Am. Acad. Phys. Med. and Rehab. (med. edn. com. 1983-86, membership recruitment group 1987, career brochure devel. group 1987, joint ann. meeting planning subcom. 1987-88, chairperson continuing med. edn. subcom. 1982-86, sci. program com. 1982-86, mktg. and comm. com. 1987-89, chairperson med. edn. com. 1986-88, sec. bd. govs. 1988-90, third-mem.-at-large 1990-91, 2nd mem.-at-large 1991-92, 1st mem.-at-large 1992-93, chair awards com. 1992-93, v.p. 1994-95, fin. com. 1994-95, chair annual meeting task force 1994-95, pres. elect 1994-95, pres. 1995-96, past pres. 1996-97, Disting. Clinician award 1997), Am. Assn. Electrodiagnostic Medicine (com. on edn. 1974-76, exam. com. 1975-76, liaision to assn. of acad. physiatrists 1988, chairperson courses com. 1986-89, pres.-elect 1989-90, bd. dirs. 1989-92, pres. 1990-91, immediate past pres.-chairperson long-range planning com. 1991-92, chmn. long range planning com. 1991-92, alt. del. AMA House of Dels. 1993-95, nominating com. 1993-94, chmn. 1994-95), Am. Assn. Electrodiagnostic Medicine, Assn. Acad. Physiatrists, Ohio State Med. Alumni Assn., AMA, Am. Bd. Electrodiagnostic Medicine (bd. dirs. 1994, long-range planning com. 1994, treas. 1995-98), Cin. Soc. of Phys. Medicine and Rehab. (pres., founder 1987-88), Internat. Med. Med. Assn. (U.S. counselor 1986-95). Presbyterian. Avocations: bicycling, writing, tennis. Office: 80 Oak Hill Rd Red Bank NJ 07701 E-mail: rbraddom@earthlink.net.

BRADEMAS, JOHN, retired academic administrator, former congressman; b. Mishawaka, Ind., Mar. 2, 1927; s. Stephen J. and Beatrice Cenci (Goble) B.; m. Mary Ellen Briggs, July 9, 1977. BA magna cum laude (Vets. nat. scholar), Harvard, 1949; PhD in Social Studies(Rhodes scholar), Oxford (Eng.) U., 1954, DCL (hon.), 2003; LLD (hon.), U. Notre Dame, Middlebury Coll., Tufts U. (others); LHD, Brandeis U., CCNY (and 46 other hon. degrees). Legis. asst. US Senator Pat McNamara; adminstrv. asst. US Rep. Thomas L. Ashley, 1955; exec. asst. to presdl. nominee Stevenson, 1955-56; asst. prof. polit. sci. St. Mary's Coll., Notre Dame, Ind., 1957-58; mem. 86th-96th Congresses from 3d Ind. Dist., 1959—81; chief dep. majority whip 93d-94th Congresses, 1973—77; majority whip 95th-96th Congresses, 1977—81; mem. com. house adminstrn., com. on edn. and labor, joint com. Libr. Congress; pres. NYU, 1981-92, fundraising campaign initiator, 1984, pres. emeritus, 1992—; mem. NY State Bd. Regents, Albany, 2004—. Chmn. bd. dirs. Fed. Res. Bank NY; dir. RCA/NBC, Columbia Pictures, Loew's Corp., Scholastic, Inc., NY Stock Exch., Rockefeller Found., Oxford U. Press-U.S.A.; past mem. bd. visitors John F. Kennedy Sch. Govt.; bd. overseers Harvard U.; mem. overseers' com. to visit Grad. Sch. Edn.; past mem. Nat. Hist. Publs. Commn., Nat. Commn. on Financing Post-Secondary Edn.; mem. Nat. Commn. Student Fin. Assistance, 1981-83, chair grad. edn. subcom., Study Nat. Needs Biomed. and Behavioral Rsch. NRC, Nat. Acad. Sci. Com. Rels. between Univs. and Govt., Nat. Commn. Financing Postsecondary Edn., Nat. Hist. Publs. and Records Commn.; bd. dirs. Am. Coun. Edn., mem. Commn. Nat. Challenges to Higher Edn., 1986-87; chmn. NY State Coun. on Fiscal and Econ. Priorities; bd. dirs. Comfidex Corp., InsurBanc, Kos Pharms., NYNEX, Texaco Inc., Alexander S. Onassis Pub. Benefit Found., Ctr. Nat. Policy, DC, Soc. Preservation Greek Heritage, Queen Sofia Spanish Inst., US-Japan Found., World Conf. Religions for Peace, Am-European Cmty. Assn.; pres. King Juan Carlos I Spain Ctr., NYU Found.; adv. bd. mem. mental illness prevention ctr., NYU Med. Ctr.; vice chmn. adv. coun. Ams., UNESCO; twentieth century fund task force mem. presdl. appointments, 1996. Author: Anarcosindicalismo y revolución en España, 1930-37, 1974, Washington, D.C. to Washington Square, 1986; co-author (with Lynne P. Brown) The Politics of Education: Conflict and Consensus on Capitol Hill, 1978. Bd. dirs. Aspen Inst., Ams. for Arts., Berlitz Internat. Inc., Carnegie Internat. Endowment Nat. Commn. on Am. and the New World, Nat. Endowment for Democracy, 1993-2001, Carnegie Commn. on Sci., Tech. and Govt., chmn. com. on Congress; mem. Nat. Commn. Pub. Svc., Nat. Adv. Coun. on Pub. Svc., US adv. coun. Transparency Internat., internat. adv. coun., mem. Ctrl. Com. World Coun. Chs., fifth assembly del. United Meth. Ch, Nairobi, 1975; bd. dirs Ctr. for Nat. Policy, chmn. exec. com.; chmn. Nat. Adv. Com. of Fighting Back, chmn. Pres.'s Com. Arts and Humanities, 1994-2001, Am. Ditchley Found., gov. Ditchley Founds.; life trustee U. Notre Dame; bd. dirs. Am. Coun. for the Arts, Acad. for Ednl. Devel., Athens Coll. (Greece), Coun. to Aid Edn.; trustee Com. for Econ. Devel., nat. commn. mem. jobs and small bus., 1986; mem. Cons. Panel to Comptr. Gen. of US, Bd. of Advisors of The Carter Ctr. Emory U., Carnegie Coun. on Ethics and Internat. Affairs, Trilateral Commn., Coun. on Spain and US, Internat. Coun., Ctrl. European U., Budapest, Am. Assocs. St. Catherine Found., Pilgrims Soc. Great Britain, Pilgrims Soc. US, VSA/arts, Internat. Adv. Coun. Pharos Trust, Cyprus; founding bd. mem. Ctr. Democracy and Reconciliation in S.E. Europe, Salonika, Greece, sr. advisor; chmn. nat. adv. com., Fighting Back, Robert Wood Johnson Found., adv. coun. David Rockefeller fellowships, NYC Partnership; hon. patron Fundación Residencia de Estudiantes, Madrid, mem. accreditation com. Red Latinoamericana de Cooperación Universitaria; dir. Am. Friends Girona Mus. and Inst., Spain; nat. adv. bd. mem. instns. democracy, Annenberg Pub. Policy Ctr., U. Pa.; first congl. delegation chair, China, 1977, first Chinese-US univ. pres. seminar attendee, Beijing, 1985; co-chmn. ind. commn., Nat. Endowment Arts, 1990. With USNR, 1945—46. Decorated chevalier of Legion of Honor, France, High Knight Comdr. of Honor Order of the Phoenix, Greece, Grand Cross of Alphonse X, Min. Edn. and Culture, Spain, 1997, Commendatore Order of Merit, Pres. Italy, 2000; recipient Disting. Svc. award Inst. Internat. Edn., 1966, Disting. Svc. award NEA, 1968, Disting. Svc. award Tchrs. Coll., Columbia U., 1969; Merit award Nat. Coun. Sr. Citizens, 1972; Disting. Svc. award Coun. of State Adminstrs. of Vocat. Rehab., 1973; Disting. Svc. award Conservation Edn. Assn., 1974; Caritas Soc. award for Outstanding Contbns. in Field of Mental Retardation, 1975, Gold medal St. Barnabas, Pres. Makarios, Cyprus, 1975; Gold Key award Am. Congress Rehab. Medicine, 1976; Disting. Svc. to Arts award AAAL, 1978; one of three recipients George Peabody award for Outstanding Contbn. to Music in Am., 1980, Town Hall Friend of Arts award, NYC, 1981, Hubert H. Humphrey award Am. Polit. Sci. Assn., 1984, Ann. Gold medal, Spanish Inst., NYC, 1985, Charles Evan Hughes Gold medal, Nat. Conf. Christians and Jews, 1985, Ellis Island medal of Honor, 1986, Nat. Govs. Assn. award, 1988, Athenagoras award for Human Rights, 1990, Gold medal of Honor City of Athens, 1991, Ann. Am. Assembly Svc. to Democracy award, 1992, Dwight D. Eisenhower medal, 1992, Disting. Svc. award, Am. Coun. Arts, 1996, Lifetime Achievement award, Ind. Coun. Humanities, 1997, Lifetime Achievement award, Cyprus Fedn. Am., 1998, Benjamin Rush award, Dickinson Coll., 1999, Nat. Svc. award, Anderson Ranch Arts Ctr., Colo., 1999, Ann. Fulbright award, Metro Internat., 2000, Lifetime Achievement for Leadership in Arts award, Ams. Arts and US Conf. Mayors, 2000, Democracy Svc. award, Nat. Endowment Democracy, 2001, Albert Gallatin medal, NYU, 2001, Disting. Svc. award, Nat. Hist. Publs. Records Commn., 2002, Global Edn. Achievement award, Fairleigh Dickinson U., 2004, Ann. Cultural award, Recording Industry Am., Disting. Svc. award, Am. Assn. U. Presses, Disting. Svc. medal, Columbia U., Disting. Svc. award in Internat. Edn., Inst. Internat. Edn., James Bryant Conant Disting. Svc. Edn. award, Edn. Commn. States, Gold Key award Am. Congress Rehab. Medicine, Disting. Svc. award, Coun. State Adminstrs. Vocat. Rehab., Humanist of Yr. award, Nat. Assn. Humanities Edn.; Named One of Top Four Most Important People in Am. Higher Edn., Change Mag., 1975; Named Humanist of Year, Nat. Assn. Humanities Edn., 1978, Pres. Constantine Karamanlis, Greece, 1981, Grand Comdr. Knights of Holy Sepulchre, Patriarch Diodoros, Jerusalem, 1982, Friend of Barcelona, Mayor Pasqual Maragall, 1993, Disting. Friend Oxford U., 1998, Post Office Named in His Honor, South Bend, Ind., 2002; Hon. fellow Brasenose, Oxford U., 1972. Fellow Am. Acad. Arts and Scis. (coun. mem., mem. European acad., 1999), Nat. Acad. Edn. (corr. mem. acad. Athens, corr. mem. acad. Argentina, 1998); mem. Phi Beta Kappa (Senator, dir.). Methodist. Office: NY State Edn Dept Bd Regents Rm 110 EB Albany NY 12234 also: NYU 53 Washington Sq S Rm 304 New York NY 10012

BRADEN, BERWYN BARTOW, lawyer; b. Pana, Ill., Jan. 10, 1928; s. George Clark and Florence Lucille (Bartow) B.; m. Betty J.; children— Scott, Mark, Mathew, Sue, Ralph, Ladd, Brad Student, Carthage Coll., 1946-48, U. Wis., 1948-49, JD, 1959. Bar: Wis. 1959, U.S. Supreme Ct. 1965. Ptnr. Genoar & Braden, Lake Geneva, Wis., 1959-63; individual practice law Lake Geneva, Wis., 1963-68, 72-74; ptnr. Braden & English, Lake Geneva, Wis., 1968-72, Braden & Olson, Lake Geneva, Wis., 1974—2002, Gagliardi O'Brien Braden Olson and Capelli, Lake Geneva, 2002—. City atty. City of Lake Geneva, 1962-64; tchr. Law Sch., U. Wis., 1977 Bd. dirs. Lake Geneva YMCA. Mem. ABA, Walworth County Bar Assn. (pres. 1962-63), State Bar Wis. (chmn. conv. and entertainment com. 1979-81, chmn. adminstrn. Justice and Judiciary com., 1986-87, bench bar rels. com., 1987-90, mem. exec. com. Wis. Bicentennial Com. on Constn.), Wis. Acad. Trial Lawyers (sec. 1975, treas. 1976, dir. 1977-79) Home: 1031 W Main St Lake Geneva WI 53147-1700 Office: 716 Wisconsin St Lake Geneva WI 53147-1826 also: PO Box 940 Lake Geneva WI 53147-0940 Office Phone: 262-248-6636. Business E-Mail: BBraden@goboclaw.com.

BRADEN, BETTY JANE, legal association administrator; b. Sheboygan, Wis., Feb. 5, 1943; d. Otto Frank and Betty Donna (Beers) Huettner; children: Jennifer Tindall, Rebecca Leigh; m. Berwyn Bartow Braden, Nov. 5, 1983. BS, U. Wis., 1965. Cert. elem. tchr., Wis. Tchr. Madison (Wis.) Met. Sch. Dist., 1965-70, 71-72, sub. tchr., 1972-75; adminstrv. asst. ATS-CLE State Bar Wis., Madison, 1978, adminstrv. asst. Advanced Tng. Seminars-Continuing Legal Edn., 1979, coordinator, 1980, adminstr. coordinator, 1980-84, adminstrv. dir., 1984-87, dir. adminstrn., bar svcs., membership, 1987—; mem. rels. and pub. svcs. dir. Legal Edn., 1992—. Speaker Bar Leadership Inst. of ABA. Mem.: LWV, Nat. Assn. Bar Execs. (program chair 1995—96, sec. 1996—98, v.p. 1998—99, pres. elect 1999—2000, pres. 2000—01), Wis. Soc. of Assn. Execs., Am. Soc. of Assn. Execs., Am. Soc. for Personnel Adminstrn., Am. Mgmt. Assn., Adminstrv. Mgmt. Soc., Meeting Planners Internat. (sec. Wis. chpt. 1981—82, pres. 1982—83). Avocations: tennis, scuba diving, reading, skiing. Home: 41 Golf Pkwy Madison WI 53704-7003 Office: State Bar of Wis 5302 Eastpark Blvd Madison WI 53718-2101 Office Phone: 608-250-6104. Business E-Mail: bbraden@wisbar.org.

BRADEN, JAMES DALE, former state legislator; b. Wakefield, Kans., Aug. 2, 1934; s. James Wesley and Olive (Reed) B.; m. Naomi Carlson, July 3, 1952 (div. Jan. 1982); children: Gregory, Michael, Ladd, Amy; m. Margie Clark Tidwell, Sept. 17, 1983; stepchildren: Richard, Lon, Dale. Grad. high sch., Wakefield. CLU, The Am. Coll. Meat cutter, Wakefield, 1952-64; ins. agt., securities broker Braden Fin. Svcs., Clay Ctr., Kans., 1964—; state rep. Kans. Ho. of Reps., Topeka, 1974-91, house majority leader, 1985-87, speaker of the house, 1987-91. Past chmn. econ. devel. com. Nat. Conf. State Legislatures, legis. coordinating council, calendar and printing com.; past chmn. assessment and taxation com.; mem. Council of State Govts. intergovtl. affairs com.; past chmn. taxation task force of Midwestern Conf. of Council State Govts.; chmn. Interstate Cooperation Commn.; former mem. State Fin. Council, Kans. Inc.; past chmn. Legis. Commn. on Kans. Econ. Devel.; past mem. Kans. Pub. Agenda Commn. Active St. Paul's Episcopal Ch., Clay Ctr.; mem. Rep. Party Exec. Com. Mem. NALU, Kans. Assn Ins. and Fin. Advisors (past pres.), Million Dollar Round Table (life), Rotary, Masons, Shriners, Elks. Episcopalian. Avocations: hunting, fishing, flying, sailing. Home: PO Box 58 Clay Center KS 67432-0058 Office: Braden Fin Svcs 1101 5th St # 58 Clay Center KS 67432-2021 Office Phone: 785-632-3601. E-mail: jbraden@classicnet.net.

BRADEN, THOMAS WARDELL, news commentator; b. Greene, Iowa, Feb. 22, 1917; s. Thomas Wardell and Louise (Garl) Braden; m. Joan E. Ridley, Dec. 18, 1948 (dec.); children: David, Mary, Joan, Susan, Nancy, Elizabeth, Thomas Wardell III(dec.), Nicholas R. AB, Dartmouth Coll., 1940, AM, 1964; LittD, Franklin Coll. Ind., 1979. Newspaperman, instr. English Dartmouth, 1946, asst. to pres. and asst. prof., 1947—48; exec. sec. Mus. Modern Art, N.Y.C., 1949; dir. Am. Com. on United Europe, 1950; editor, pub. Blade Tribune, Oceanside, Calif., 1954—68; columnist Los Angeles Times Syndicate, 1968—86; commentator CNN, CBS, NBC, 1978—89. Author (with Stewart Alsop): Sub-Rosa, 1946; author: Eight is Enough, 1975. Mem. Calif. Bd. Edn., 1959—67; past pres. Trustee Calif. State Coll., 1961—64, Dartmouth, 1964—74, Carnegie Endowment, 1970—82. With King's Royal Rifle Corps Brit. Army, 1941—44, Africa and Italy, trans. to inf. AUS, 1944, served as a parachutist office of Strategic Svc.

BRADFORD, BARBARA TAYLOR, writer, journalist; b. Leeds, Eng. came to U.S., 1964; d. Winston and Freda (Walker) Taylor; m. Robert Bradford, Dec. 24, 1963. Student pvt. schs., Eng.; D of Letters (hon.), Leeds (Eng.) U., 1990, U. Bradford, West Yorkshire, Eng., 1995; D of Humane Letters (hon.), Teikyo Post U., Waterbury, Conn., 1996. Women's editor Yorkshire (Eng.) Evening Post, 1951-53, reporter, 1949-51; editor Woman's Own, 1953-54; columnist London Evening News, 1955-57; exec. editor London Am., 1959-62; editor Nat. Design Center Mag., 1965-69; syndicated columnist Newsday Spls., L.I., 1968-70; nat. syndicated columnist Chgo. Tribune-N.Y. (News Syndicate), N.Y.C., 1970-75, Los Angeles Times Syndicate, 1975-81. Author: Complete Encyclopedia of Homemaking Ideas, 1968, A Garland of Children's Verse, 1968, How to Be the Perfect Wife, 1969, Easy Steps to Successful Decorating, 1971, Decorating Ideas for Casual Living, 1977, How to Solve Your Decorating Problems, 1976, Making Space Grow, 1979, Luxury Designs for Apartment Living, 1981, (novels) A Woman of Substance, 1979, Voice of the Heart, 1983, Hold the Dream, 1985, screen adaptation, 1986, Act of Will, 1986, To Be the Best, 1988, The Women in His Life, 1990, Remember, 1991, Angel, 1993, Everything to Gain, 1994, Dangerous to Know, 1995, Love in Another Town, 1995, Her Own Rules, 1996, A Secret Affair, 1996, Power of a Woman, 1997, A Sudden Change of Heart, 1999, Where You Belong, 2000, The Triumph of Katie Byrne, 2001, Three Weeks in Paris, 2001, Emma's Secret, 2003, Unexpected Blessings, 2004. Recipient Dorothy Dawe award Am. Furniture Mart, 1970, 71, Matrix award N.Y. Women in Comms., 1985, Spl. Jury prize for body of lit. Deauville Festival of Am. Film, 1994, Just award. Mem. Coun. Authors Guild, Nat. Soc. Interior Designers (Distng. Editl. award 1969, Nat. Press award 1971), Authors Guild Am. (mem. coun. 1989—), Am. Soc. Interior Designers. Office: Bradford Enterprises 450 Park Ave New York NY 10022-2605 Personal E-mail: bradford.ent@att.net.

BRADFORD, CARL O., judge; b. Dallas, Nov. 16, 1932; s. Montie Leroy and Vivian Ila (Milan) B.; m. Claire Solange Chaloux, Jan. 15, 1955 (dec. 1972); children: Timothy, Kathleen, Elizabeth; m. Mary Ellen Sanborn, July 7, 1973; children: Bethany, Michael. Student, U. Detroit, 1956-59; JD, U. Maine, Portland, 1962. Bar: Maine 1963, U.S. Dist. Ct. Maine 1963, U.S. Ct. Appeals (1st cir.) 1963, U.S. Supreme Ct. 1978. Asst. atty. gen. State of Maine, Augusta, 1963-64, justice Superior Ct., 1981-98, active-ret. justice Superior Ct., 1998—. Ptnr. Powers & Bradford, Freeport, Maine, 1964—81; commr. Uniform State Laws, 1972—76; mem. drafting com. Uniform Exemptions Act, 1974—76. Bd. dirs. Nat. Ctr. State Cts., Williamsburg, Va., 1997—2000; trustee Nat. Jud. Coll., Reno, 2001—, sec. bd. trustees, 2004—, chair-elect, 2005. With USN, 1951—55. Fellow Am. Bar Found., Maine Bar Found.; mem. Maine Bar Assn. (bd. govs. 1970-78, pres. 1977-78), Maine Trial Lawyers Assn. (bd. govs., sec. 1970-81), ABA (ho. of dels. 1978-81, 90-95, state bar del. 1978-81, bd. govs. 1st dist. 1990-93, bd. lisiaon to Nat. Conf. Spl. Ct. Judges 1990-91, liaison to Criminal Justice Sect. 1990-93, liaison to Nat. Conf. State Trial Judges 1991-93, chair subcom. nominations and awards com. 1991-93, bd. govs. program com. 1990-91, mem. oper. com. 1991-93, project 2000 subcom. 1991-93, bd. govs. chair compensation com. 1993, bd. govs. exec. com. 1993, bd. govs. exec. dir. search com. 1990, mem. comm. on multi-disciplinary practice 1998-2000), Nat. Conf. State Trial Judges (del. 1982-97, jud. immunity com. 1984-97, chair 1991-96, conf. vice chair 1993, chair-elect 1994-95, chair 1995-96), Am. Judicature Soc. Home: 225 Sea Meadows Ln Yarmouth ME 04096-5523 Office: Superior Ct PO Box 287 Portland ME 04112-0287 Office Phone: 207-822-4174.

BRADFORD, DANA GIBSON, II, lawyer; b. Coral Gables, Fla., Sept. 29, 1948; s. Dana Gibson and Jeanette (Ellis) B.; m. Mary E. Bradford, June 20, 1970 (div. Jan. 1982); 1 child, Jeffrey Dana; m. Donna P. Bradford, Apr. 14, 1984; 1 child, Shannon Claire. BA, U. Fla., 1970; JD, Duke U., 1973. Bar: Fla. 1973, U.S. Dist. Ct. (mid. dist.) Fla. 1974, U.S. Dist. Ct. (so. and no. dists.) Fla. 1979, U.S. Ct. Appeals (5th cir.) 1974, U.S. Ct. Appeals (11th cir.) 1982, U.S. Supreme Ct. 1977. Lawyer, ptnr. Mahoney, Hadlow & Adams, Jacksonville, Fla., 1973-82, Baumer, Bradford & Walters, Jacksonville, 1982—2000, Smith, Gambrell & Russell, LLP, Jacksonville, 2000—. Mem. Fla. Bd. Bar Examiners, 1989-94, chmn. bd., 1992-93; mem. Fla. Supreme Ct. Commn. on Professionalism, 1996-98; seminar lectr. Contbr. chpt. to book, articles to profl. jours. Mem. Leadership Jacksonville, 1982; spl. counsel Jacksonville Sports Authority. Capt. U.S. Army Res., 1972-80. Mem. ABA, ATLA, Jacksonville Bar Assn. (bd. govs. young lawyers sect. 1976-78, chmn. trial sects. 1989-90), Jacksonville Assn. Def. Counsel (pres. 1978-79), Am. Bd. Trial Advocates. Republican. Methodist. Office: Smith Gambrell & Russell LLP 50 N Laura St Ste 2600 Jacksonville FL 32202-3625 E-mail: dgbradford@sgrlaw.com.

BRADFORD, DAVID S., surgeon; b. Charlotte, N.C., Oct. 15, 1936; m. Sharon Hale; children: David Mackay, Jennifer Sutherland, Tyler Speir. BA, Davidson Coll., 1958; MD, U. Pa., 1962. Diplomate: Am. Bd. Orthopaedic Surgeons. Intern in surgery Columbia-Presbyn. Med. Center, N.Y.C., 1962-63, resident in gen. surgery, 1965-66; resident in orthopaedic surgery N.Y. Orthopaedic Hosp., Columbia-Presbyn. Med. Center, N.Y.C., 1966-68, jr. Annie C. Kane fellow orthopaedic surgery, 1968-69; research trainee orthopaedics Nat. Inst. Arthritis and Metabolic Diseases, 1969-70; prof. orthopaedic surgery U. Minn. Hosps., Mpls., 1970-90, chief of spine surgery, 1984-90; dir. Twin Cities Scoliosis Spine Ctr., Mpls., 1984—90; prof., chmn. dept. orthopaedic surgery U. Calif., San Francisco, 1991—. Mem. scientific adv. bd. Orquest, Inc. Mem. bd. editors: Spine, Spine Journal, Spine Letter, AOA News, Clinical Orthopaedics and Related Rsch., Journal of Am. Academy of Orthopaedic Surgeons, Journal of Orthopaedic Rsch.; contbr. articles to profl. jours. Mem. AMA, Am. Acad. Orthopaedic Surgeons, Am. Orthopaedic Assn., Assn. Bone and Joint Surgeons (past pres.), Orthopaedic Rsch. Soc., Scoliosis Rsch. Soc. (past pres.), British Scoliosis Soc., European Spine Deformity Soc., Internat. Soc. Orthopaedic Surgery and Traumatology, N. Am. Spine Soc., Orthopaedic Rsch. & Educational Found., Scoliosis Rsch. Soc., Spine Arthroplasty Soc., Wilson Interurban Orthopaedic Soc. Office: U of Calif San Francisco Dept Orthopedic Surgery MU-320W Box 0728 San Francisco CA 94143-0728

BRADFORD, DENNIS DOYLE, real estate broker, developer; b. Tulsa, Sept. 5, 1945; s. Doyle Earl and Elta (Price) B.; m. Richie Deloris Dawson. BSBA in Econs., U. Tulsa, 1969. Sales and mktg. rep. Xerox Corp., Oklahoma City, 1969-72; comml. loan officer Mager Mortgage Co., Oklahoma City, 1973-74; pvt. practice real estate Oklahoma City, 1973—; pres., owner Bradford Oil Co., Oklahoma City, 1977-80; pres. Blazer Oil Co., Oklahoma City, 1980—; v.p. Petro So., Inc., Tampa Fla., 1983-84; ptnr. Coachman Inns, Oklahoma City, 1981-86; chmn., CEO Coachman Inc., Oklahoma City, 1985-98; dir. Coachman Inc, San Juan, PR, 1998—2002; pres., CEO Olympic Mills Corp., Guaynabo, P.R., 1995-97; pres. West Coast Ptnrs., Inc., Bradenton, Fla., 1997—. Mem. nat. adv. coun. to U.S. SBA, Washington, 1982-92, del. to White House Conf. on Small Bus., 1986, adv. bd. Nat. SBDC, Washington, 2003—. Bd. dirs. Okla. Med. Ctr. Found., 1989-94, Salvation Army of P.R., 1996-97; bd. dirs., sec. Okla. Air and Space Mus., 1989-95, v.p. 1991-92, pres. 1992-93; mem. Local Selective Svc. Bd., Oklahoma City, 1988-94, Rep. Eagles, 1979-92, Rep. Presdl. Round Table. Mem. Nat. Cowboy Hall of Fame, Okla. Heritage Assn., Okla. County Hist. Soc., Air Force Assn., Navy League, Young Pres.'s Orgn. (chmn. 1993-94, N.Am. spl. projects officer 1993-94), World Pres.'s Orgn. (Oklahoma City chpt. chmn. 2002-04), Oklahoma City C. of C., Balloon Fedn. Am., Oklahoma City Golf and Country Club, Summit Club (Tulsa), Bradenton Country Club. Republican. Methodist. Office: West Coast Ptnrs Incn 301 NW 63rd St Ste 500 Oklahoma City OK 73116-7989 Home: 4305 17th Ave West Bradenton FL 34209 E-mail: ddb@westcoastpartners.com.

BRADFORD, GAIL IDONA, minister; b. Mobile, Ala., Sept. 12, 1947; d. Estes Paul and Doris (Roe) B.; m. Benjamin C. Lann, Jr., May 28, 1971 (div. May 1986). AA, Clarke Meml. Coll., Newton, Miss., 1967; BS, Miss. Coll., 1969; MA, La. Tech U., 1973; postgrad., Western Ky. U., 1979-82, 88-92; MDiv, So. Bapt. Theol. Sem., 1996. Cert. tchr., sch. adminstr., counselor, home economist; ordained minister United Meth. Ch. Vocat. counselor Mobile Rehab., 1970-71; tchr. kindergarten Lincoln Parish Schs., Ruston, La., 1971-73; state staff coord. Head Start, U. South Ala., Mobile, 1973-74; dep. dir. Jefferson County Com. for Econ. Opportunity, Birmingham, Ala., 1975-76; instr. vocat. edn. Lawson State C.C., Birmingham, 1977; mental health technician Commonwealth of Ky., Louisville, 1978-79; exec. dir. Tchr. Corps, Western Ky. U., Bowling Green, 1979-82; tchr. spl. edn. Jefferson County Pub. Schs., Louisville, 1982-88, tchr. vocat. home econs., 1988-92; chaplain various hosps., 1994—; dir. children's ministry PRP United Meth. Ch., Louisville, 1995-97; assoc. pastor St. Mark United Meth. Ch., 1997—; chaplain resident Norton Health Care, 1999—. Cons., condr. workshops various pub. programs, Ala., Ky., 1973—; tchr. workshops Jefferson Tech. Coll., Louisville, 1989—; mem. com. practitioners Commonwealth of Ky. Workforce Cabinet, 1990-92. Bd. dirs. Ministries United South Ctrl., Louisville, 1989—; active various Rep. campaigns, La., Ky., 1971-86; mem. nat. adv. bd. Safe Places, 1991—; mem. campaign staff Rep. John Buchanan of Ala., 1975-77; dir. counselors Hugh O'Brian Youth Found., 1989-91, 97-98, state chmn., 1991-93, state bd. sec., 1993-95, dist. dir. 1994-95. Recipient Tchr. award Louisville Commmunity Found., 1986, Leadership Edn. award Bellarmine Coll., Louisville, 1987; named Ky. col. Commonwealth of Ky., 1988. Mem. Ky. Vocat. Home Econs. Tchrs. (pres. region 6, 1990-91), Ky. Home Econs. Assn. (chmn. adult, secondary and elem. edn. 1988-92), Am. Vocat. Assn., Coun. for Exceptional Children, Am. Insts. Parliamentarians, Thomas Jefferson Parliamentarians (treas. 1986), Toastmasters (area gov. dist. 11, 1986-87, Able Toastmaster award 1984), Golden Key, Kappa Delta Pi. Methodist. Avocation: youth and adult leadership training and development. Home: PO Box 106 Cecilia KY 42724-0106

BRADFORD, J. DAVID, principal; b. Boaz, Ala., June 21, 1957; s. Eddie M. and Kathelane (Plunkett) B.; m. Karen Minnette Graves, Aug. 16, 1981; 1 child, Amanda Minnette. A, Gadsden State C.C., 1977; BS, U. Ala., 1980, EdD, 1996; MS, Jacksonville State U., 1981. Cert. secondary edn., Ala. Jr. high math tchr. Etowah County Bd. Edn., Gadsden, Ala., 1980; secondary math and computer tchr., basketball coach Gadsden City Bd. Edn., 1981—95, secondary curriculum coord., 1995—98, elem. prin., 1998—2001; secondary math tchr. Blount County Bd. Edn., Oneonta, Ala., 2001—02, elem. prin., 2002—. Math. instr. Gadsden State Community Coll., 1990—. Elder E.Gadsden Ch. of Christ, 2000—03, Oneonta Ch. of Christ, 2004—. Mem. NEA, ASCD, Nat. Coun. for Tchrs. Math., Ala. Coun. for Computer Edn., Ala. Edn. Assn., Profl. Assn. for Gadsden Educators, Ala. High Sch. Athletic Assn., Ala. Basketball Coaches Assn., Kappa Delta Pi. Mem. Ch. Of Christ. Avocations: golf, football, basketball. Home: 99 Greystone Dr Oneonta AL 35121-7095 Office: Cleveland Elem Sch 115 Stadium Dr Cleveland AL 35049

BRADFORD, JAMES C., JR., brokerage house executive; b. Nashville, July 25, 1933; s. James C. and Eleanor (Avent) B.; m. Lillian Frances Robertson, Nov., 1967; children: Jay, Bryan. BA, Princeton U., 1955. Trainee Lehman Bros., N.Y.C., 1958; ptnr. J.C. Bradford & Co., Nashville, 1959-2000; sr. mng. dir. U.B.S. PaineWebber, Nashville, 2001—. Chmn. dist. com. Nat. Assn. Securities Dealers, Atlanta, 1970-73; dir. Securities Industry Assn., N.Y.C., 1972-75; gov. Am. Stock Exch., 1986-87; bd. dirs. N.Y. Stock Exch., 1987-93, Nat. Assn. Securities Dealers Regulation. Trustee Mongomery Bell Acad., Nashville, 1968—; pres. Nashville Symphony Assn., 1969-70; pres. bd. trustees Ensworth Sch., Nashville, 1988-89. 1st lt. USAF, 1955-57. Mem. Belle Meade Country Club (bd. dirs. 1987-89), Nat. Assn. of Securities (gov. Washington 1996). Republican. Episcopalian. Office: UBS PaineWebber 3102 West End Nashville TN 37203 Office Phone: 615-750-8302. Business E-Mail: jimmy.bradford@ubs.com.

BRADFORD, JAY TURNER, insurance company executive, state legislator; b. Little Rock, Apr. 30, 1940; s. Turner and Chrystal (Jacobs) B.; 1 child, Chrystal. BA, Henderson Coll., 1963. Cert. ins. counselor. Ins. agent Metropolitan Life Co., Pine Bluff, Ark., 1963-65, McLellan Ins. Co., Pine Bluff, 1968-76; pres. Pine Bluff Ins. Exchange, 1976—. Alderman City of Pine Bluff, 1981-82; mem. Ark. State Senate, 1983—; mem. chmn. Health Labor Com., 1983—; chmn. Senate Efficiency Com.; pres. pro temArk. State Senate, Pro team Ho. of Reps., 2005-. Named Small bus. Man of Yr., 1988; recipient leadership award Leadership Pine Bluff, 1987. Mem. Soc. Ins. Agts. (cert. ins. counselor), Ind. Ins. Agts. Ark. (pres. 1981—), Subiaco Alumni Assn. (pres. 1977), Pine Bluff Civitan (pres. 1967). Democrat. Episcopalian. Office: Chmn First Ark Ins PO Box 8367 Pine Bluff AR 71611-8367

BRADFORD, MARIAH, elementary school educator, consultant; b. Bay Springs, Miss., Sept. 23, 1929; d. Glasco Hunter Bender and Georgianna Holloway; m. Demond Bradford, Sr., Apr. 15, 1960 (div. Sept. 1984); children: Anita, Demond Jr., Kelvin. BS in Home Econs., Jackson Coll., 1953; MS in Edn., Ind. U., 1973; LHD (hon.), Martin U., 1994. Cert. tchr. Miss., 1953, Ind., 1962, Ariz., 1997. Tchr. Scott County Pub. Schs., Forest, Miss., 1953—57, Meridian (Miss.) Mcpl. Separate Schs., 1957, 1959—61; county ext. agent Coop. Ext. Dept., Kosciusko, Miss., 1958—59; tchr. Ind. Pub. Schs., Indpls., 1963—92; sub. tchr. Peoria and Dysart Unified Schs., Peoria, El Mirage, Ariz., 1997—. Sec., bd. dirs. Martin U., Indpls., 1989—94; mem. bd. dirs. Indpls. Edn. Assn., 1970—78; mem. desegregation task force Ind. State Tchrs. Assn., Indpls., 1975—80. Contbr. poems to literary publs. and jours. (Editors' Choice award, 1996). Commr. Planning and Zoning, Surprise, Ariz., 1997—99; big sister Big Brothers/Big Sister, Indpls. and Phoenix, 1987—. Recipient Sagamore of the Wabash, State of Ind., Gov. Evan Bayh, 1994, Golden Apple award, Indpls. Power and Light Co. and Cmty. Leaders Allied for Superior Schs., 1992, Special Human Rights award, Indpls. Edn. Assn. Human Rights Com., 1993, Human Rights award, Indpls. Edn. Assn., 1983; grantee, Indpls. Pub. Schs. Found., 1986, DePauw U. and Dept. of Health Edn. and Welfare, 1977. Mem.: NAACP (life), Assn. Negro Bus. and Profl. Women's Clubs (founder, pres. Madame Walker chpt. 1979—89, Sojourner Truth award 1982), Ch. Nurses Auxiliary (first v.p., nat. missionary Bapt. Conv. Am., Svc. award 1998), Zion Rest Dist. Ch. Nurses Auxiliary (cons.), Household of Ruth (#6851, Grand United Order of Oddfellows). Democrat. Baptist. Avocations: writing, reading, travel, sewing, volunteering. Home: 18019 N 145th Dr Surprise AZ 85374-4222 Personal E-mail: bradfordsurp@aol.com.

BRADFORD, PETER DURGIN, elementary school educator; b. Pitts., Mar. 4, 1965; s. Edward and Nancy Dorah Bradford; m. Morag Armour Bradford, Mar. 26, 2005. BA, The Coll. Webster, 1988; MAT, John Hopkins U., 1997. Program advocate/drop-out counselor Futures Program, Balt., 1990—92; tchg. intern Tesseract Balt. City Pub. Schs., Balt., 1992—93, tchr., 1993—98, testing coach, 1998—99; tchr. Learning Inc., 1999—2002, lead tchr., 2002—. Supervisor, founder Big Show Reading Project, Balt., 1993—; supervisor Learning Inc. & Harlem Park Mentor Program, Balt., 2000—, Big Show Summer Reading Camp, Balt., 2001—. Recipient Achievement award, Project Turnaround, Md. State Penitentiary, 1990, Dedicated Tchr. award, Harlem Park Elem. Sch., 1998—99, Recognition award for founding Big Show Reading Project, Channel 2 News & Balt. Sun Newspaper, 1997, 1998, 2000. Avocations: travel, golf, camping. Office: Learning Inc 1234 W 36th St Baltimore MD 21211

BRADFORD, TUTT SLOAN, retired publisher; b. Apr. 30, 1917; s. Tutt S. and Zula (Bowen) B.; m. Elizabeth Hendley, June 30, 1941 (dec.); children: Nancy, Debbie; m. Mercedes F. Bradford, Dec. 14, 2001. Student, Wofford Coll., 1934; LLD, Maryville Coll., 2005. Pub. Cleve. Daily Banner, 1948-51; asst. to pres. Gen. Newspapers, 1951; pub. Bristol (Va.) Herald Courier, 1951-55, Maryville (Tenn.) Alcoa Daily Times, 1955-85. Bd. dir. humanities, Tenn., 1971-73; mem. devel. coun. U. Tenn., 1980-83; bd. dirs. Maryville Coll., 1974-79, 81-2003, Knoxville Symphony, Knoxville Mus. of Art, Thompson Ctr. for Cancer Survival, Lakeshore Mental Hosp., Tenn. Tech. Found.; Tenn. Resource Valley, 1988-91, 92-95, East Tenn. Found.; pres. Blount Meml. Hosp. Found., Boy's Club Found., Blount Hearing and Speech Found., 1991, Blount County Libr. Found., 1999. Pres. Blount County Indsl. Devel. Bd., 1970-72. With 9th AF AUS, 1943-45, ETO. Recipient Disting. Svc. award Bristol Jr. C. of C., 1952, Maryville-Alcoa Jr. C. of C., 1958, 73, Sequoyah Literacy award Tenn. Hist. Com., 1995, Tenn. Vol. Cmty. award Gov. Don Sunquist, 2003; named to East Tenn. Hall of Fame, Jr. Achievement, 1990; named Vol. Yr., U. Tenn., 1994, Outstanding Philanthropist Nat. Soc. Fund Raising Execs., 1991. Mem. So. Newspaper Pubs. Assn. (bd. dirs. 1968-70), Tenn. Press Assn. (pres. 1974), Knox Arts Coun. (award 1988), Blount County C. of C. (pres. 1960), Kiwanis (pres. Maryville 1967, 1987). Home: 1401 Broad Run Dr Maryville TN 37803

BRADFORD, WILLIAM DALTON, pathologist, educator; b. Rochester, NY, Nov. 2, 1931; s. William Leslie and Lenora Dee (Dalton) B.; m. Anne Bevington Harden, July 8, 1961; children— Scott Harden, Lisa Graham BA, Amherst Coll., 1954; MD, Western Res. U., 1958. Diplomate Am. Bd. Pediatrics, Am. Bd. Anatomic Pathology. Intern in pathology Boston Children's Med. Ctr., 1958-59, resident in pediatrics, 1959-61; teaching fellow in pathology Harvard Med. Sch., 1963-64; asst. prof. pathology Duke U., Durham, N.C., 1966-70, assoc. prof., 1970-81, prof., 1981—, assoc. dean, 1970-71, 74-78, 84-87, asst. to chancellor for health affairs, 1987-89, dir. pediatric pathology, 1966—, dir. pathology tng. program, 1974-2001. Pres. Durham YMCA, 1978, bd. dirs., 1976-83, 90-95; faculty chmn. of athletics Duke U., 1979-85. Lt. comdr. USN, 1961-63. Recipient Golden Apple award Student Med. Assn., 1969, 93, 95, 98, Layman of Yr. award YMCA, 1974, 78, Disting. Tchr. award Duke Med. Alumni Assn., 1989; Mead Johnson fellow, 1963-64. Mem. Internat. Acad. Pathology, Am. Assn. Pathologists, Soc. Pediatric Research, Group for Rsch. in Pathology Edn., Soc. for Pediatric Pathology (pres. 1987-88), Nat. Collegiate Athletic Assn. Council, Nat. Faculty Athletics Reps. Forum (chmn. 1985), Atlantic Coast Conf. (pres. 1982-83), Duke Med. Alumni Coun. (pres. 2000-01). Office: Duke U Med Ctr PO Box 3712 Durham NC 27710-0001 Office Phone: 919-684-5112. Business E-Mail: bradf001@mc.duke.edu.

BRADFORD, WILLIAM EDWARD, oil field equipment manufacturing company executive; b. Dallas, Jan. 8, 1935; m. JoDeane Browning, Aug. 18, 1955; children: William B., A. Kathleen, Jon E. BS in Geology, Centenary Coll., 1958; grad., Tex. A&M U., 1975. Salesman Hycalog, Inc., 1958-61; v.p., gen. ptnr. Analytical Logging, Inc., 1961-70; product mgr. Oilfield Products Group Dresser Industries, Inc., Dallas, 1970-72, mgr. Mid-cont. Oilfield Products Group, 1972-73, mgr. Europe, Africa, Middle East Oilfield Products Group, 1973-76, v.p. Security Divsn., 1976-78, pres. Security Divsn., 1980-83, group pres. Oilfield Products Group, 1983-84, v.p. ops., 1984-92, sr. v.p., 1988-92; pres. CEO Dresser-Rand Co., Corning, N.Y., 1992-95; pres., COO and dir. Dresser Industries, Inc., Dallas, ., 1995-96, pres., CEO, dir., 1996-98, chmn. pres., 1998-2000; chmn. Halliburton Co. (formerly Dresser Industries, Inc.), Dallas, 2000—. Bd. dirs. Kerr-McGee Corp., Valero Energy Corp. Mem.: Petroleum Equipment Suppliers Assn., Am. Assn. Petroleum Geologists, Soc. Petroleum Engrs., Rolling Rock Club, Northwood Country Club (Dallas). Office: Two Turtle Creek Village 3838 Oak Lawn Ave Ste 224 Dallas TX 75219

BRADLE, SUE E., music educator, editor; b. Belleville, Ill., Apr. 25, 1949; d. Ralph Leo Goodman and Alice Josephine Vunetich; m. William Ramsey Bradle, Aug. 9, 1975; children: Marc Ramsey, Margot Elaine. BS with honors, U. Ill., 1972, MS, 1977. Cert. elem. educator Ill. Educator music Duneland Schs., Chesterton, Ind., 1972—74; educator music and math. pub. schs., Chgo. area, 1974—77; editor, writer The Instrumentalist Co., Evanston, Ill., 1978—81; mgr. publicity Chamber Consortium, Chgo., 1981—82; editor, writer Media Svcs., Chgo. and Ft. Worth areas, 1982—; educator music Ft. Worth Country Day Sch., 1998—2002, Lake Country Christian Sch., 2002—. Editor: Teaching Music: The Human Experience, 1985, Faces of America, 1988. Chmn. planning and zoning com. City of Willow Park, Tex., 1986—89. Named Elem. Tchr. Yr., Lake Country Christian Sch., 2003—04. Mem.: Weatherford Music Tchrs. Assn. (pres. 1992—94), Tex. Music Tchrs. Assn., Tex. Music Educators Conf. (editor 1986—2000), Music Educators Nat. Conf., Music Tchrs. Nat. Assn. Home: 213 Sam Bass Rd Weatherford TX 76087 Office Phone: 817-236-8703. E-mail: sbradle@lccs.org.

BRADLEE, BENJAMIN CROWNINSHIELD, former executive editor; b. Boston, Aug. 26, 1921; s. Frederick J. and Josephine (deGersdorff) B.; m. Jean Saltonstall, Aug. 8, 1942; 1 son, Benjamin Crowninshield; m. Antoinette Pinchot, July 6, 1956; children: Dominic, Marina; m. Sally Quinn, Oct. 20, 1978; 1 son, Josiah Quinn Crowninshield. AB, Harvard U., 1943. Reporter N.H. Sunday News, Manchester, 1946- 48, Washington Post, 1948-51; press attachè embassy Paris, France, 1951-53; European corr. Newsweek mag., Paris, 1953-57, reporter Washington bur., 1957-61, sr. editor, chief bur., 1961-65; mng. editor Washington Post, 1965-68, v.p., exec. editor, 1968-91, v.p. at large, 1991—. Author: That Special Grace, 1964, Conversations with

Kennedy, 1975, A Good Life--Newspapering and Other Adventures, 1995. Served to lt. USNR, 1942-45. Home: 3014 N St NW Washington DC 20007-3404 Office: care Washington Post 1150 15th St NW Washington DC 20071-0001

BRADLEY, AMELIA JANE, lawyer; b. Columbia, S.C., Apr. 18, 1947; d. Hugh Wilson and Amelia Jane Bradley; m. Richard Bancroft Hovey, Apr. 1, 1977. BA, U. Va., 1968; MA, George Washington U., 1971. Bar: Va. 1976, D.C. 1985. Budget and mgmt. analyst NLRB, Washington, 1968-71, 72; clk. Cohen and Vitt, PC, Alexandria, Va., 1972-76; assoc. Cohen, Vitt & Annand, PC, Alexandria, 1976-80; White House fellow USDA, Washington, 1980-81, Office U.S. Trade Rep., Exec. Office of Pres., Washington, 1981, asst. gen. counsel, 1981-82, assoc. gen. counsel, 1982-84; prin. dep. gen. counsel Office U.S. Trade Rep., Exec Office of Pres., Washington, 1989-92; asst. U.S. trade rep. for dispute resolution Office U.S. Trade Rep., Exec. Office of Pres., Washington, 1994, legal advisor to U.S. GATT del. Geneva, 1984-87; assoc. dir. for global environment White House Office on Environ. Policy, Washington, 1994-95; assoc. dir. internat. trade and devel. Coun. on Environ. Quality, Washington, 1994—95; asst. U.S. trade rep. for monitoring, enforcement Office U.S. Trade Rep., Exec. Office of Pres., Washington, 1996—2002; dep dir. Inst. Internat. Econ. Law, Georgetown U. Law Ctr., Washington, 2004—. Chief negotiator U.S. GATT Uruguay Round Dispute Settlement Negotiating Group, 1986-87, 89-93; chmn. interagy. Sect. 301 Com., Washington, 1988-92; vis. rsch. assoc. Fletcher Sch. Law and Diplomacy, Tufts U., Medford, Mass., 1987-88; vis. rschr. Harvard U. Law Sch., Cambridge, Mass., 1988; adj. prof. Georgetown U. Law Ctr., 2003—. Mem. editl. adv. bd.: Jour. Internat. Econ. Law, 2004—. Mem., chmn. Alexandria Human Rights Commn., 1975-80; pres., trustee Alexandria Law Libr., 1978-80; founding mem. Lawyer Referral Svc., Alexandria, 1978. NEH fellow, 1978. Mem. ABA, Va. State Bar (mem., chmn. com. on legal edn. and admission to bar 1977-84), D.C. Bar (chmn. internat. trade com. 1989-90). Episcopalian.

BRADLEY, ANN WALSH, state supreme court justice; b. Richland Center, Wis. married; 4 children. BA, Webster Coll., 1972; JD, U. Wis., 1976. Former high school tchr.; atty. priv. practice, 1976—85; judge Marathon County Circuit Ct., Wausau, Wis., 1985—95; justice Wis. Supreme Ct., Madison, Wis., 1995—. Former assoc. dean and faculty mem. Wis. Judicial Coll.; former chair Wis. Jud. Conference; lecturer ABA Asia Law Initiative; commr. Nat. Conference on Uniform Laws. Bd. of visitors U. Wis. Law Sch. Fellow: Am. Bar Found.; mem.: ABA, State Bar of Wis. (Bench Bar Com.), Am. Law Inst., Am. Judicature Soc. (Harley award 2004). Office: Wis Supreme Ct PO Box 1688 Madison WI 53701-1688

BRADLEY, BETSY, museum director; BA, Millsaps Coll.; MA in English, Vanderbilt U. Dep. dir. and cmty. arts dir. Miss. Arts Commn., exec. dir., 1995—2001, Miss. Mus. Art, Jackson, 2001—. Bd. mem. Nat. Assembly of State Arts Agencies; panelist Nat. Endowment for Arts; adv. panel mem. Miss. Sch. Arts. Pres. Miss. Ctr. for Nonprofits. Named one of Top 50 Bus. Women, Miss. Bus. Jour. Office: Miss Mus Art 201 E Pascagoula St Jackson MS 39201 E-mail: mmart@netdoor.com.*

BRADLEY, BILL, former senator; b. Crystal City, Mo., July 28, 1943; s. Warren W. and Susan (Crowe) B.; m. Ernestine Schlant, Jan. 14, 1974; 1 dau., Theresa Anne. BA, Princeton U., 1965; MA, Oxford (Eng.) U., 1968. Player N.Y. Knickerbockers Profl. Basketball Team, 1967-77; U.S. senator from N.J., 1979-96; mem. fin., energy coms., spl. com. on aging, 1997—98; Disting. leadership scholar, chair U. Md., College Park; Payne Disting. prof. Inst. for Internat. Studies, Stanford U., 1997-98; campaigned for Dem. Presdl. Nomination, 1999-2000; mng. dir. Allen & Co., LLC, 2000—; chief outside advisor non-profit practice McKinsey & Co., 2000—04. Essayist CBS TV Weekend Evening News, 1997-98; sr. advisor, vice chair internat. coun. J.P. Morgan and Co., Inc., 1997-99; bd. dirs. Willis Ins. Group, Seagate Tech., 2003-, Starbucks Coffee Co.; vis. prof. pub. affairs Univ. of Notre Dame, 1998; bd. trustees Princeton U., 1998-2002; mem. Coun. Fgn. Rels. Author: Life on the Run, 1976, The Fair Tax, 1984, Time Present, Time Past, 1996, Values of the Game, 1998, The Journey From Here, 2000; host (radio talk show) American Voices, 2005-. Chmn. Nat. Civic League, 1997-98. 1st lt. USAFR, 1967-78. Rhodes scholar, 1965-67; named three-time basketball All-Am.; recipient Sullivan award as the country's outstanding amateur athlete. Democrat. Achievements include being a mem. NBA championship team, 1970, 73, Gold medal team Tokyo Olympics.

BRADLEY, BOB, professional soccer coach; b. Montclair, N.J., Mar. 3, 1958; B.History, Princeton U.; M.Sports Adminstrn., Ohio U. Head coach soccer Ohio U., Athens, 1980-81; asst. coach U. Va., 1982-83; head coach Princeton U., 1984-95; asst. coach D.C. United, 1995-97; head coach Chgo. Fire, 1997—, New York MetroStars. Named Major League Soccer's 1998 All Sport Coach of the Yr., NCAA Divsn. I Men's Coach of the Yr., 1993, winningest coach MLS history. Office: MetroStars Third Fl One Hammon Plz Secaucus NJ 07094*

BRADLEY, CHARLES MACARTHUR, retired architect; b. Chgo., Sept. 26, 1918; s. Harold Smith and Helen Francis (MacArthur) B.; m. Joan Marie Daane, July 27, 1946; children: Mary Barbara, Nancy Ann, Sally Joan, William Charles (dec.). BS in Architecture, U. Ill., 1940. With Holabird & Root, architects, Chgo., 1940-41, Giffels & Vallet, architects and engrs., Detroit, 1941-44; ptnr., corp. pres. Bradley & Bradley, architects and engrs., Rockford, Ill., 1947-2001; ret., 2001. Pres. Bradley Bldg. Corp., 1962—. Prin. works include North Sheboygan (Wis.) High Sch. and addition, 1960-68, J.F. Kennedy Middle Sch., Rockford, 1968, Singer Health Clinic, Rockford, 1964, Jacobs H.S., Algonquin, Ill., 1976, Atwood plant, Rockford, 1977, Admiral Home, Chgo., 1978, Bushnell (Ill.) Jr. H.S., 1980, Bloom H.S., 1983, Evenglow Lodge, 1984, East Aurora H.S. addition, 1992, Erie H.S., 1994; author papers on life cycling old schs., roofing procedures. Active Blackhawk coun. Boy Scouts Am. Served with C.E., U.S. Army, 1945-46. Decorated Bronze Star; recipient Meritorious Svc. award Ill. Assn. Sch. Bds., 1976. Mem. AIA (pres. No. Ill. chpt. 1962, treas. Ill. coun. 1973-74), Ill. Soc. Architects (pres. 1974), Edn. Facilities Planners Inst., Ill. Assn. Sch. Bd. Officers, Rotary, Union League, Univ. Club, Midday Club (Chgo.), Shriners, Moose, Rockford Country Club, Quail Creek Country Club, Naples Sailing & Yacht Club, Lauderdale Lakes Sailing Club, Meridian Club. Republican. Congregationalist. Home and Office: 3203 Landstrom Road Rockford IL 61107-2223 Home: 4901 Gulfshore Blvd N Naples FL 34103 Office Phone: 815-877-8500. Personal E-mail: bchuckmac@aol.com.

BRADLEY, CHARLES WILLIAM, podiatrist, educator; b. Fife, Tex., July 23, 1923; s. Tom and Mary Ada (Cheatham) B.; m. Marilyn A. Brown, Apr. 3, 1948 (dec. Mar. 1973); children: Steven, Gregory, Jeffrey, Elizabeth, Gerald. Student, Tex. Tech., 1940-42; D. Podiatric Medicine, Calif. Coll. Podiatric Medicine U. San Francisco, 1949, MPA, 1987, D.Sc. (hon.). Pvt. practice podiatry, Beaumont, Tex., 1950-51, Brownwood, Tex., 1951-52, San Francisco, San Bruno, Calif., 1952—; assoc. clin. prof. Calif. Coll. Podiatric Medicine, 1992-98. Chief of staff Calif. Podiatry Hosp., San Francisco; mem. surg. staff Sequoia Hosp., Redwood City, Calif.; mem. med. staff Peninsula Hosp., Burlingame, Calif.; chief podiatry staff St. Luke's Hosp., San Francisco; chmn. bd. Podiatry Ins. Co. Am.; cons. VA; assoc. prof. podiatric medicine Calif. Coll. Podiatric Medicine. Mem. San Francisco Symphony Found.; mem. adv. com. Health Policy Agenda for the Am. People, AMA; chmn. trustees Calif. Coll. Podiatric Medicine, Calif. Podiatry Coll., Calif. Podiatry Hosp.; mem. San Mateo Grand Jury, 1989. Served with USNR, 1942-45. Mem. Am. Podiatric Med. Assn. (trustee, pres. 1983-84), Calif. Podiatry Assn. (pres. No. div. 1964-66, state bd. dirs., pres. 1975-76, Podiatrist of Yr. award 1983), Nat. Coun. Edn. (vice-chmn.), Nat. Acads. Practice (chmn. podiatric med. sect. 1991-96, sec. 1996—), Am. Legion, San Bruno C. of C. (bd. dirs. 1978-91, v.p. 1992, bd. dir. grand jury assoc. 1990), Olympic Club, Commonwealth Club Calif., Elks, Lions. Home: 2965 Trousdale Dr Burlingame CA 94010-5708 Office: 560 Jenevein Ave San Bruno CA 94066-4408 E-mail: bradlee2@aol.com.

BRADLEY, DONALD EDWARD, lawyer; b. Santa Rosa, Calif., Sept. 26, 1943; s. Edward Aloysius and Mildred Louise (Kelley) B.; m. Marianne Stark, Apr. 22, 1990; children: Evan Patrick, Matthew Jordan, Andrea Phelps. AB, Dartmouth Coll., 1965; JD, U. Calif., San Francisco, 1968; LLM, N.Y.U., 1972. Bar: Calif. 1968, U.S. Dist. Ct. (no. dist.) Calif. 1968, U.S. Ct. Appeals (9 cir.) 1968, U.S. Tax Ct. 1972, U.S. Ct. Claims 1973, U.S. Supreme Ct. 1981. Assoc. Pillsbury, Madison & Sutro, San Francisco, 1972-77, ptnr., 1978-84; mem. Wilson Sonsini Goodrich & Rosati, Palo Alto, Calif., 1984—, gen. counsel, mem. exec. mgmt. com. Mng. dir. Wilson Sonsini Goodrich & Rosati, Palo Alto, 1995—; adj. prof. Golden State U., San Francisco, 1973-82; pres., chmn. bd. dirs. Atty.'s Ins. Mut. Risk Retention Group, Honolulu, 1986—. Capt. U.S. Army, 1969-70. Recipient Charles M. Ruddick award N.Y.U., 1972, award Bureau of Nat. Affairs, Washington, 1968. Mem. ABA, Internat. Bar Assn., Santa Clara Bar Assn., San Francisco Bar Assn., Internat. Tax Club, Peninsula Tax Club. Office: Wilson Sonsini Goodrich & Rosati 650 Page Mill Rd Palo Alto CA 94304-1050 Office Phone: 650-493-9300. Office Fax: 650-493-6811. E-mail: dbradley@wsgr.com.

BRADLEY, E. MICHAEL, lawyer; b. NYC, Apr. 13, 1939; s. Otis Treat Bradley and Marian Booth (Alling) Ward; m. Judith Allen Thompson, June 29, 1962; children: Jennifer Treat, Michael Thompson, Thomas Alcott, Samuel Allen. BA, Yale U., 1961; LLB, U. Va., 1964. Bar: NY 1965. Assoc. Davis, Polk & Wardwell, NYC, 1964-72, Brown & Wood, NYC, 1972-73, ptnr., 1974-95, mem. policy com., 1981-94, mem. exec. com., 1989-94; ptnr. Jones Day, NYC, 1995—2004, Katten Muchin Rosenman LLP, N.Y.C., 2004—. Lectr. Practicing Law Inst., NYC, 1970-79; 86, Am. Law Inst.-ABA, Phila., 1977-78; arbitrator Am. Arbitration Assn., NYC, 1975—. Contbg. editor: The Use of Experts in Corporate Litigation, 1978, Securites Law Techniques, 1985. Bd. dirs. Bennett Coll. Found., NYC, 1984—, Inst. of Ams., La Jolla, Calif., 2001—; trustee Salisbury (Conn.) Sch., 1987—. Mem. ABA, NY State Bar Assn., Fed. Bar Assn., Assn. Bar City of NY, Union Club, Coral Beach Club, Quogue Field Club, Shinnecock Yacht Club, Nat. Golf Links of Am., L.I. Wyandanch Club. Republican. Presbyterian. Office: Katten Muchin Rosenman LLP 575 Madison Ave New York NY 10022 Office Phone: 212-940-8570. Business E-Mail: em.bradley@kattenlaw.com.

BRADLEY, EDWARD JAMES, state official, computer programmer and analyst; b. Syracuse, N.Y., Jan. 3, 1946; s. Robert Carroll and Hazel Irene (Malone) B.; m. Gwen Eileen Coats, Sept. 3, 1977 (div. 1984); 1 child, Edward James II. BA cum laude, SUNY, Albany, 1971, MPA, 1980; grad., Citizens Police Acad., 1992. Specialist N.Y. State Dept. Social Svcs., 1973-78; pub. adminstr. N.Y. State Dept. Transp., Albany, 1978-81; pub. mgmt. intern N.Y. State Dept. Civil Svcs., 1981-82; personnel adminstr. N.Y. State Dept. Taxation & Fin., 1982-83; computer programmer, analyst N.Y. State Dept. Transp., 1983—. Commr. City of Albany Mcpl. Civil Svc. Commn., 1992-93, chmn., 1992-93. Author: Child and Family Genealogy Reporting System. Pres. Child and Family Enterprises, Inc., Albany, 1978-84, Traditional Am. Values, Albany, 1984-2003, Books Unbound, 1991-2003, V.O.T.E.S., 1992-2003; fundraiser United Way Am./Northeastern N.Y., Inc., 1976-78, Capital Are Coun. Chs., 1978, Birthright of Albany, Inc., 1984-88; mem. Albany County Dem. Com., 1985-93; active Pro-life Dems., Inc., 1984-94, Nat. Right-to-Life Com., Inc., 1984—, N.Y. State Right-to-Life, 1984—, Human Life Internat., 1992—; mem. nat. nominating com. Outstanding Young Ams., 1997—. With USN, 1963-66. Named one of Outstanding Young Men Am., 1982. Mem. DAV, ASPA, Am. Mgmt. Assn., Am. Pub. Welfare Assn., N.Y. State Forum for Info. Resources Mgmt., Vietnam Era Vets., Am. Legion, N.Y. Assn. Transp. Engrs., Capital Dist. Geneal. Soc. (pres. 1982-84), Nat. Spkrs. Assn., Toastmasters, Elks. Roman Catholic. Home: 1941 Western Ave Apt 1403 Albany NY 12203-7014 Office: Info Svcs Bur 2nd Fl 50 Wolf Rd Albany NY 12232-0001

BRADLEY, EDWARD R., news correspondent; b. Phila., June 22, 1941; s. Ed. R. and Gladys Bradley; divorced. BA in Edn., Cheyney (Pa.) State Coll., 1964. Radio news reporter Sta. WDAS, Phila., 1963-67, Sta. WCBS, N.Y.C., 1967-71; with CBS Television News, 1971—, stringer, 1971-73, prin. corr. in Paris, 1971, Saigon, 1972-74, Washington, 1974—75, Phnom Penh, 1975, Saigon, 1975; White House corr. CBS News, 1976—78; prin. corr. CBS Reports, 1978-81, 60 Minutes, 1981—; anchorman CBS Sunday Night News, 1976-81; anchor CBS News magazine "Street Stories", 1992—93. Anchorman: various documentaries including What's Happening to Cambodia, 1978, The Boat People, 1979, The Boston Goes to China, 1979. Recipient Du Pont award, 1978, 80, 97, George Foster Peabody Broadcasting award U. Ga., 1979, 97, George Polk journalism award, 1980, Emmy award, 1979 (3), 1983 (2), 1985, 86, 92, 93, 95. Office: CBS News 60 Minutes 555 W 57th St New York NY 10019-2925*

BRADLEY, EDWARD WILLIAM, sports foundation executive; b. Milltown, NJ, Aug. 12, 1927; s. William Ernest and Hilda (Schwendeman) B.; m. Eleanor A Massing, Apr. 12, 1952; children: Scott Richard, Gail Sharon Bradley Klewsaat, Lisa June Bradley LaMarca. BE, Panzer Coll., 1950. Dir. athletics, supr. phys. edn. and health Milltown Pub. Schs., 1951—69; fowner, pres. The Exec. Health Club, East Brunswick, NJ, 1965—84; apptd. by Gov. Florio chmn., CEO N.J. Fitness and Sports Found., Milltown, 1984—; writer Middlesex County Govt., North Brunswick, NJ, 1985—; formed Bradley, Walker, Chitwood Group Alliance, 2005—. Dir. activities Playboy Club Resort Hotel at Great Gorge, 1972; founder first sch. bicycle safety edn. program curriculum State of NJ, 1996; apptd. exec. coun. Cancer Rsch. Inst, Am. Cancer Soc., 1998; served Nat. Coalition Com. prostrate Cancer, Washington, 2002-; cons. World WIOC, 2000. Cons. Pres. Kennedy, Johnson, Carter, Nixon, Ford, Reagan, Bush; master cons., adv. Pres.'s Coun. The White House, 1988; meeting with Pres. Clinton (invitation by The White House) nat. project Stay Way, 1994; nat. dir. U.S. Army and NFL, 1993; Chief of Staff Colin Powell meeting at the White House; nat. dir. No-Shows for Charity Shows, 1996; founder Bradley Walker Chitwood Group Internat. Alliance, 2005; dist. coord., cons. Nat. Assn. Disabled Athletes; supt. recreation Borough of Milltown, 1951—64, founder sch. bicycle safety edn. prog. curriculum NJ, 1996; N.J. chmn. Nat. Network on Volunteerism, 1997; regional coord. Winter Olympic Games 2002, Salt Lake City; partnership with Arnold Schwarzenegger's Inner City Games and Mayor Oscar Goodman's Needy Youth Program, Las Vegas, 2003; VIP del. Pres.' Summit, Washington, 1997; apptd. by Gov. Kean chmn. CEO Gov.'s Coun. on Phys. Fitness and Sports, 1983—; mem. Nat. Com. for George W. Bush Pres., 2000; nat. dir., founder sch. Stay Way project Gen. Jones (Pentagon); bd. dirs. Make A Wish Found., NC, 2003; state dir. for fight against abolishing phys. edn. in NJ schs.; chmn., CEO Middlesex County Coun. on Phys. Fitness and Sports divsn. Pres.' Coun. on Phys. Fitness, 1992, NJ Youth Fitness Coalition; mem. NC Prostate Cancer Coalition, 2002; chmn. NJ Olympic XXIII Torch Relay Com., 1984; asst. torch relay U.S. Olympics XXVI, NJ and Atlanta, 1996; state coord. Olympic Torch Relay, Athens, 2004; founder, chmn. Gov.'s Blue Ribbon Panel on Fitness and Sports, David A. Sonny Werblin, pres.; pres. NJ Health Am. Fitness Leaders Award Program; mem. State of NJ Blue Ribbon Com. for Baseball in NJ; dir. Phys. Fitness and Sports for U.S. Job Corps., Edison; state-county coord. Nat. Pk. Svc., NJ Trails Relay, 1996; mem. Mission Possible task NEA-AAPERD; vice chmn., mem. exec. bd. Fairview Food and Clothing Kitchen for Needy Families, 2003; bd. dirs., dir. pub. rels. Safe Haven Shelter for Men, 2005—. Recipient U.S. Outstanding Phys. Leadership award Pres.' Coun. on Phys. Fitness and Sports by Pres. Kennedy and U.S. Jaycees, The White House, 1962, U.S. Healthy Am. Fitness Leaders award Pres.' Coun., U.S. Jaycees and Allstate, 1985, Svc. in Phys. Fitness and Sports award Montclair State Coll., 1988, Phys. Edn. award for Excellence Panzer Coll., Svc. Award Ea. Dist. AAHPERD, NJ Award for People to Watch, 1984, Jerseyan of Week award Newark Star Ledger, 1988, Honor Fellow award NJ Assn. Health, Phys. Edn. and Recreation, 1964, Young Man of Yr. award Milltown Jaycees, 1962, Sports Master award by Pres. Reagan, 1987, Svc. to the Cmty., State and Nation Award, Pres. Bush, 1992, Pres. Clinton, 1997, Pub. Svc. award State NJ and Pres.' Summit, 1997, Daily Point of Light award The White House and Point of Light Found., 1999, Pres.'s Svc. award, The White House, 2000, Outstanding Alumni award Montclair State Coll., 2000, Outstanding Gov.'s award Vol. Svc., Trenton, NJ, 2000, Outstanding Gov.'s award Vol. Svc., Raleigh, NC, 2000; honored guest Pres. Nixon, 1975, Pres. Reagan, 1987, Richard Nixon Libr., 1990-, Pres. Reagan Libr., Pres. Bush-the White House, 1991, 92, State of NJ, Pres.' Hist. Summit for 55 Yrs. Pub. Svc., Pres. Clinton, The White House, 1947-2000, Govs. NJ Leadership award Gov. Whitman, 2000, Gov. Vol. award NC Gov. Hunt, 2000, Outstanding Alumni award Montclair State U., 2000, Pres.' Svc. award, Pres. Bush, 2001, Martin Luther King Jr. award for Outstanding Cmty. Svc., 2002; named Leader of NJ State of NJ, 1998; nominated Olympic Torch Relay, Athens, Greece, 2004. Mem.: Internat. Assn. Approved Basketball Ofcls., Nat. Fitness Leadership Assn., Outstanding Phys. Fitness Leadership Congress, NJ/NC Youth Fitness Coalition Pres.' Club (corr. Honored Lifetime citation 2001), Amblers Walking Club, Court Club, Am. Legion, U.S. Jaycees, VFW (NC, NJ). Avocations: bicycling, reading, sports, Volksmarch programs. Home: NC Fitness & Sports Foundation Lambeth Walk Complex Pinkerton Corner Fairview NC 28730 Office: PO Box 2510 Wachovia Bank Complex Asheville NC 28802 also: PO Box 2145 Fairview NC 28730-2145 also: Nat Office Vols PO Box 1253 Asheville NC 28802-1253 also: NC Fitness & Sports No-Shows for Charity-Shows PO Box 2510 Asheville NC 28802-2510 also: NJ Found Office PO Box 311 Whiting NJ 08759-0311 Address: No-Shows for Charity-Shows Found Office 314 De Armond Rd Kingston TN 37763 Office Phone: 828-628-9398, 732-716-1753, 828-280-6993. Office Fax: 828-628-0590. Business E-Mail: ncnjfitnessport@aol.com, acsportsline@aol.com, gail_klewsaat@colpal.com.

BRADLEY, ELIZABETH CLAY, financial planner, educator; b. Dayton, Ky., Feb. 6, 1948; d. Glenn Washington and Margaret Elizabeth Clay; m. James D. McPhail, Aug. 16, 1970 (dec. Sept. 1990); m. Julian Bradley, May 4, 1996. BS in Home Econs., U. Ky., 1970; MS in Family Econs., Kans. State U., 1977. CFP. Tchr. Bourbon County Jr. H.S., Paris, Ky., 1970—71, Manhattan (Kans.) H.S., 1974—84; investment rep. Edward Jones, Cary, NC, 1984—2001; ret., 2001; cons. Wachovia Sec., Raleigh, NC, 2002—. Author: (workbook) Motivation Plus, 1982, The Good Life, 2001. Chair Expanding the Circle-Glenaire, Cary, 2001—04; trustee Glenaire Presbyn. Home, Cary, 2002—04; mem. 5th Ave. Presbyn. Ch.; bd. dirs. Glenaire Found., Triangle Fin. Planning Assn., 2003—04. Named Young Educator, Kans. Assn. Vocat. Home Econs. Tchrs., 1984, Small Businessperson of Yr., Cary C. of C., 1988. Mem.: Cary C. of C. (named Small Bus. Person of Yr. 1988). Avocations: walking, writing, reading, quilting, designing clothes. Home: 1917 Olde Mill Forest Dr Raleigh NC 27606 Office Phone: 919-571-2830. E-mail: eclaybradley@nc.rr.com.

BRADLEY, J. F., JR., retired manufacturing company executive; b. Wagoner, Okla., July 7, 1930; s. Jacob F. and Ilsa (Ellington) B.; m. Mary Joan Oberc, June 7, 1952 (div. 1978); children: Jeffrey F. (dec.), Michael B., Michelle J.; m. Angela C. Cutrone, Aug. 14, 1981; 1 child, Adam C.C. BBA, U. Mich., 1952; MBA, U. Detroit, 1959. Fin. analyst Ford Motor Co., Detroit, 1956-60; v.p. corp. fin. TRW Inc., Cleve., 1960-72; exec. v.p. adminstrn. and fin. Scott Fetzer Co., Lakewood, Ohio, 1972-83, dir., 1971-83; pres. Scott Fetzer Fin. Svcs. Group, Westlake, Ohio, 1983-86; chmn. Kadee Metalfab Inc., Bedford, Ohio, 1986-89, K.B.B. Enterprises Inc., Cleve., 1988-93. Trustee Ohio Coll. Podiatric Medicine, chmn., 1990-94; trustee Animal Protective League, Cleve. 1st lt. AUS, 1952-56. Mem. Masons, Shriners, Jesters, Elks, Knights Templar. Home: 7050 Lassiter Dr Cleveland OH 44129-6351 E-mail: jbradley@ocpm.edu.

BRADLEY, JAMES G., metals company executive; BSCE, Carnegie Inst. Tech.; MBA, Ind. U. Various positions U.S. Steel Corp.; v.p. ops. USS/KOBE Steel Co., Lorain, Ohio; v.p. integrated mill group Internat. Mill Svc., Horsham, Pa.; exec. v.p. ops. Wheeling (W.Va.)-Pitts. Steel Corp. subs. WHX Corp., 1995—, co-CEO, 1998—; v.p. WHX Corp., N.Y.C., 1998—; chmn., CEO Wheeling Pittsburgh Steel Corporation. Office: 1134 Market St Wheeling WV 26003*

BRADLEY, JAY CAMERON, ophthalmologist; b. Milton, Fla., Mar. 17, 1978; s. Jack Alden and Karen Sue Bradley; m. Rachael Ann Hirsch, Dec. 29, 2001. BS, Tex. Tech U., 1999; MD, Tex. Tech Sch. Medicine, 2003. Resident physician Tex. Tech U., Lubbock, Tex., 2003—. Mem.: Am. Acedemy of Ophthalmology (assoc.). Achievements include research in Multiple research projects in ophthalmology related topics. Office: Texas Tech Univ 3601 4th St Lubbock TX 79430 Office Phone: 806-743-2020.

BRADLEY, JEB E., congressman; b. Rumford, Maine, Oct. 20, 1952; m. Barbara Bradley; 4 children. BA, Tufts U., 1974. Painter, contractor; owner Natural Food Store; former mem. from dist. 8 N.H. State Ho. of Reps., former mem. environ. and agr. com., former chmn. sci., tech. and energy com.; mem. 108th U.S. Congress, 1st Dist., 2003—; mem. armed servs. com., small bus. com., veterans affairs com. Mem. Wolfeboro (N.H.) Planning Bd., 1986-90, Wolfeboro Budget Com., 1989—; mem. Chap Lakes Region Conservation Trust, 1989-90; v.p. Carpenter Sch. PTO, 1989-90. Republican. Office: 1218 Longworth HOB Washington DC 20515*

BRADLEY, JENNETTE B., state official, former lieutenant governor; b. Oct. 2, 1952; m. Michael C. Taylor. BA in Psychology, Wittenberg U. Lic. registered rep. Nat. Assn. Securitites Dealers. Exec. dir. Columbus Met. Housing Authority; sr. v.p. pub. fin. banker Kemper Securities; sr. v.p., pub. funds mgr. Huntington Nat. Bank; councilwoman Columbus (Ohio) City Coun., 1991—2002, chair parks and recreation com., chair utilities and energy generation coms., chair safety com., mem. safety and judiciary com., mem. adminstrn. com., mem. recreation and parks com., mem. health, housing and human svcs. com., mem. zoning com.; lt. gov. State of OH, 2003—05, treas., 2005—; dir. OH Dept. Commerce, 2003—05. Mem. fin., adminstrn. and intergovernmental rels. steering and policy coms. Nat. League Cities. Grad. Leadership Columbus; trustee Wittenberg U.; bd. mem., former chair Joint Columbus and Franklin County Housing Adv. Bd. Recipient Woman of Achievement award, YWCA. Republican. Office: OH Dept Treasury 30 E Broad St 9th Fl Columbus OH 43215

BRADLEY, JERRY ALAN, psychologist, consultant; b. L.A., Apr. 25, 1946; s. Norman Aaron and Kate Bradley; m. Barbara Ann Adams/Rohr, June 26, 1971; 1 child, John Nathan. BA summa cum laude, San Jose State U., 1976; postgrad., Claremont Grad. Sch., 1977—79; PhD, Am. Commonwealth U., 1993. Diplomate clinical and substance abuse psychology Am. Bd. Psychol. Specialties. Program dir. Sierra Vista, Highland, Calif., 1978—85, Vista Pacifica, Riverside, 1982—85; dir. Montclair Child Care Ctr., Montclair, 1987—89, Regency Oaks, Riverside, 1987—89; cons., staff psychologist Ea. LA Regional Ctr., Alhambra, 1989—; clin., forensic psychologist Ctr. Integral Psychology, Ventura, 1996—. Psychologist, counselor Wellspring Project, Ch. Foothills, Ventura, 1996—2005. Fellow: Am. Coll. Forensic Examiners Internat., Internat. Coll. Advanced Practice Psychologists, Prescribing Psychologists Register, Internat. Coll. Prescribing Psychologists; mem.: AAAS, APA, Am. Assn. Mental Retardation, L.A. County Psychol. Assn., Ventura County Psychol. Assn., Calif. Psychol. Assn. Avocation: music. Office: Ctr Integral Psychology 1746F S Victoria Ave #344 Ventura CA 93003 Office Phone: 805-639-4093. Office Fax: 805-639-4092. E-mail: ishecal@sbcglobal.net.

BRADLEY, JIMMY, business owner, chef; BA in Comm., U. R.I. Mem. staff DiLulio Centro, Phila.; exec. chef Savoir Fare, Martha's Vineyard, Flowers, N.Y.C., 1993; founder James Bradley Co.; co-owner It's a Wrap, 1997—; owner The Red Cat, 1999—. Office: Red Cat 227 10th Ave New York NY 10011

BRADLEY, JOHN A., career military officer; b. Lebanon, Tenn. BS in Math., U. Tenn., Knoxville, 1967; postgrad., Indsl. Coll. Armed Forces, 1978, Harvard U., 1996, Syracuse U., 2000. Commd. 2d lt. USAF, 1967, advanced through grades to lt. gen., 2004; mathematician, program analyst Hdqrs. Strategic Air Command, Offutt Air Force Base, Nebr., 1967—69; pilot combat tng. Sheppard Air Force Base, Tex., 1969—70; fighter pilot 8th Spl. Ops. Squadron, Bien Hoa Air Base, Vietnam, 1970—71; instr. pilot 50th Flying Tng. Squadron, Columbus Air Force Base, Miss., 1971—73, 47th

Tactical Fighter Squadron, Barksdale Air Force Base, La., 1973—78; chief standardization and evaluation 917th Tactical Fighter Group, Barksdale Air Force Base, La., 1978—81; asst. ops. officer, ops. officer 47th Tactical Fighter Squadron, Barksdale Air Force Base, La., 1981—83; dep. commdr. ops. 917th Tactical Fighter Group, Barksdale Air Force Base, La., 1983—85; comdr. 924th Tactical Group, Bergstrom Air Force Base, Tex., 1985—88; dep. chief of staff ops. 10th Air Force, Bergstrom Air Force Base, Tex., 1988—89; comdr. 442d Fighter Wing, Richard-Gebaur Air Force Base, Mo., 1989—93; dep. to chief of Air Force Res. Hdqrs. USAF, Washington, 1993—98; comdr. 10th Air Force, Naval Sta. Joint Res. Base, Ft. Worth, 1998—2002; dep. comdr. Joint Task Force-Computer Network Ops., U.S. Space Command, Arlington, Va., 2002; asst. to the Chmn. of the Joint Chiefs of Staff, reserve matters The Pentagon, 2002—04; chief Air Force Reserve, Washington, 2004—; comdr. Air Force Reserve Command, Robins AFB, Ga., 2004—. Decorated DSM, Def. Meritorious Svc. medal, Meritorious Svc. medal with oak leaf cluster, Legion of Merit, DFC, Air medal with 3 silver oak leaf clusters, Air Force Commendation medal, Air Force Achievement medal; recipient Def. Superior Svc. medal, Joint Meritorious Unit award with oak leaf cluster, Air Force Outstanding Unit award with "V" device & silver & bronze oak leaf cluster, Air Force Orgnl. Excellence award. Office: Hq USAF/RE 1150 Air Force Pentagon Washington DC 20330-1150

BRADLEY, JOHN ANDREW, health facility administrator; b. Hammond, Ind., Aug. 3, 1930; s. Andrew C. and Florence (Wolfe) B.; m. Judith E. Salmi, June 1, 1955; children: John Michael, Kerry Kathleen, Kelly Ann. BS, Loras Coll., 1952; MHA, St. Louis U., 1955, PhD, 1962. Asst. adminstr. Incarnate Word Hosp., St. Louis, 1958-61; from assoc. adminstr. to administr. Santa Rosa Med. Ctr., San Antonio, 1961-69; from v.p. to sr. v.p. Am. Medicorp, Inc., San Antonio, 1969-78; with Am. Healthcare Mgmt., Dallas, 1978-89, pres., 1978-84, chmn., CEO, 1985-89, Chancellor Health Systems Inc., Dallas, 1989—. Capt. AUS, 1953-57. Home: 4228 Winding Way Ct Dallas TX 75287-2767 Office Phone: 972-733-3231. E-mail: jaybrad@comcast.net.

BRADLEY, LAURENCE ALAN, psychologist; b. Cleve., Sept. 13, 1949; s. Irving and Jeanne (Weil) B.; m. Gifford Weary, Dec. 28, 1974 (div. 1979); m. Elizabeth Wrenn, Oct. 3, 1981 (div. 1991). BA cum laude in Psychology (with hons.), Vanderbilt U., Nashville, 1971; PhD in Psychology, Vanderbilt U., 1975. Clin. intern Duke U. Med. Ctr., Durham, N.C., 1975-76; asst. prof. U. Tenn., Chattanooga, 1976-77, Fordham U., Bronx, 1977-80, Bowman Gray Sch. Med., Winston-Salem, NC, 1980-82, assoc. prof., 1982-89, adminstrv. head sect. med. psychology, 1981-89; assoc. prof., dir. epidemiology, edn. & health svcs. rsch. Multipurpose Arthritis & Musculoskeletal Disease Ctr U. Ala., Birmingham, 1989-92, prof., dir. epidemiology, edn. & health svcs. rsch., 1992-99; prof., dir. neuro-behavioral medicine rsch. Multidisciplinary Clin. Rsch. Ctr., Birmingham, 1999—. Adj. assoc. prof. U. N.C., Greensboro, 1983-89; vis. behavioral scientist Orebro Med. Ctr. Hosp., Sweden, 1986-92. Co-author: Health Psychology: Clinical Methods and Research, 1991; co-editor: Medical Psychology: Contributions to Behavioral Medicine, 1981, Coping with Chronic Disease: Research and Applications, 1983; assoc. editor: Clin. Psychology, Pain, 1995—2000, editl. bd.: Health Psychology, 1999—2001, Arthritis Care and Rsch., 1995—2004, Jour. Back and Musculoskeletal Rehab., 1999—. Rsch. grantee Robert Wood Johnson Found., 1983-86, Am.-Scandinavian Found., 1986, Am. Fibromyalgia Syndrome Assoc., 1996, NIH, 1989— Fellow APA, Soc. Personality Assessment; mem. Internat. Assn. Study of Pain, Am. Pain Soc., Soc. Behavioral Medicine, Am Coll. Rheumatology, Arthritis Health Professions Assoc. (Disting. scholar, 1992), Sigma Xi, Phi Beta Kappa. Democrat. Achievements include research to determine that relaxation training and psychological therapy reduces pain behavior and number of painful joints among patients with rheumatoid arthritis, and that functional brain activity abnormalities are associated with chronic pain. Home: 3831 Clairmont Ave S Birmingham AL 35222-3607 Office: U Ala Divsn Clin Immunol and Rheumatol 805 Faculty Office Tower 510 20th St S Birmingham AL 35294-0001 Office Phone: 205-934-8550. Business E-Mail: braddog@uab.edu. E-mail: painsensation@aol.com.

BRADLEY, LAWRENCE D., JR., lawyer; b. Santa Monica, Calif., Feb. 19, 1920; s. Lawrence D. Bradley and Virginia L. Edwards; m. Joan Worthington, Feb. 1, 1945; children: Gary W., Brooks, Eric Scott. BS, USCG Acad., 1942; LLB, Stanford U., 1950. Bar: Calif. 1950, U.S. Dist. Ct. (ctrl. dist.) Calif. 1950, U.S. Dist. Ct. (so. dist.) Calif. 1967. Assoc. Pillsbury, Madison & Sutro, L.A., 1950-59, ptnr., 1959—90; ret. ptnr. Pillsbury Winthrop Shaw Pittman LLP, 1990—. Lectr. admiralty and ins. law U. So. Calif., 1952-80. Pres. Stanford Law Rev., 1949-50; assoc. editor Am. Maritime Cases, 1990-2000. Mem. adv. bd. Tulane Admiralty Law Inst., 1990—. With USN, 1942-48; served to lt. comdr. Res. Mem. ABA, Calif. Bar Assn., Maritime Law Assn. U.S. (mem. exec. com. 1974-78, chmn. cruise line com. 1991-94), Inst. Navigation, Order of Coif, Calif. Club, Chancery Club, Calif. Yacht Club, San Diego Yacht Club, Propeller Club, Transpacific Yacht Club, Tutukaka South Pacific Yacht Club. Office: Pillsbury Winthrop Shaw Pittman LLP 725 S Figueroa St Ste 2800 Los Angeles CA 90017-5443 Office Phone: 213-488-7256.

BRADLEY, LYNN HECHT, school librarian; b. Anderson, Ind. d. William Joseph and Pauline Roach Hecht; children: Carter, Will, Kate. AB, Coll. William amd Mary, 1970; MLn, Emory U., 1971; postgrad., Ga. State U., 1972—76. Children's libr. Atlanta Pub. Libr., 1970; lower/preschool libr. Lovett Sch., Atlanta, 1971—81; media specialist Douglas Co. Bd. Edn., Douglasville, Ga., 1988—93, Fulton County-Camp Creek Mid. Sch., Atlanta, 1993—. Salute to Schs. grantee, 3M Found., 2001. Mem.: ALA, Ga. Libr. Media Assn., Internat. Reading Assn. Presbyterian. Avocations: reading, walking. Office: Camp Creek Mid Sch 4335 Welcome All Rd College Park GA 30349

BRADLEY, MARILYNNE GAIL, advertising executive, advertising educator; b. Rockford, Ill., Apr. 12, 1938; d. Sherwin S. and Lillian (Leopold) Gersten; m. Charles S. Bradley, 1959 (div. Feb., 1994); children: Suzanne, Scott. BFA, Washington U., 1960; MAT, Webster U., St. Louis, 1975; MFA, Syracuse U., 1981; postgrad., St. Louis Tchrs. Acad., 1990. With Essayons Studio, St. Louis, 1968-69; tchr. Webster Groves (Mo.) H.S., 1970-98; instr. Webster Univ., Webster Groves, 1973-82, 97—, supr., 2002—; instr. U. Mo., 1980—, St. Louis U., 1978-99, Washington U., St. Louis, 1984-87. Sec. Mo. Art Edn., State of Mo., 1986-87; mem. Tchrs. Acad. 1990-92. Author, illustrator: Arpens and Acres, 1976, Packets on Parade, 1980, illustrator: St. Louis Silhouettes, 1977; editor: (videos) 12 Water Color Lessons, 1987, Techniques of American Watercolor, 1990, The Santa Fe Trail Series, 1993, Over Gauguin's Shoulder, 1994, Aboriginal Art Techniques, 1994, City of Century Homes, 1995, Australian Dreamings, 1996, Aboriginal Art - Past, Present and Future, 1996, Drawing and Painting Techniques, 1997, Line, Shape, Value, 1998, Molas, Snip and Sew: The Kuna Indians, Molas: Panamanian Traditions, 1999, The Katy Trail Series, 2000, Art Along the Katy Trail, 2000, Apre's Paris, 2001, Lewis and Clark Trail, 2001, It's Somewhere in St. Louis, 2002, St. Louis World's Fair, 2004, The Mathematics of Moorish Mosaics, 2004, Sidewalks of St. Louis, 2005. Bd. govs. Webster Groves Hist. Soc., 1965-72, 94—; mem. St. Louis Philharm. Soc., 1956-72; commr. City of Webster Groves, 1995—; co-chair Hist. Preservation Com., 2002, v.p., 2002—. Named Tchr. of Yr., 1987, Best of Show, Mo. Watercolor Soc., 2000. Mem.: Mo. Watercolor Soc. (bd. mem. 2001—), St. Louis Artist Guild (sec. 1985—86, pres. 1989—92, v.p. pres.'s coun. 1995—, treas. 2004, Disting. Woman 1987), St. Louis Woman Artists, So. Watercolor Soc. (life; sec. 1978—80, v.p. 2002—04, pres. 2004—, chair 26th ann. exhibit, chair 28th ann. exhibit, Silver Brush award, Exceptional Salute to the Masters award), Monday Club (chmn. 1979—83). Avocations: music, art, travel. Home and Office: Bradley & Assocs 817 S Gore Ave Saint Louis MO 63119-4023 Office Phone: 314-968-1439. Personal E-mail: mgbrad@aol.com.

BRADLEY, MELVIN LEROY, communications company executive; b. Texarakana, Tex., Jan. 6, 1938; s. S.T. and David Ella (Garth) B.; m. Ruth Ann Terry, Mar. 3, 1958; children: Cheryl, Eric, Jacqueline, Tracy. Student, Los Angeles City Coll., 1955, Compton Coll., 1965; BS, Pepperdine U., 1973; LLD (hon.), Shaw U., 1982, Bishop Coll., 1984, Lane Coll., 1986. Real estate broker, Los Angeles, 1960-63; dep. sheriff Los Angeles County, 1963-70; asst. to Gov. Ronald Reagan, 1970-75; dir. public relations Drew Med. Sch., Los Angeles, 1975-77; asst. v.p. United Airlines, 1977-81; sr. policy advisor to Pres. U.S., White House, 1981-82, asst. to Pres. U.S., 1982-89; pres. Garth & Bradley Assocs., Washington, 1989—. Bd. dirs. Essex Bancorp, LoanCare Servicing Ctr., SMA MicroSys. Republican. Baptist. Office: 9300 Livingston Rd Ste 213 Fort Washington MD 20744 Office Phone: 301-292-2652. Personal E-mail: garthbrad@yahoo.com.

BRADLEY, MICHAEL A., electronics company executive; Grad., Amherst Coll., Harvard U. CPA. Acct. Coopers & Lybrand; various mktg. and sales positions Teradyne, Inc., Boston, 1979; controller customer svc. divsn.; product, mktg. mgr. indsl. consumer divsn.; corp. dir. total quality mgmt.; v.p., 1992; U.S. sales mgr. semiconductor test products, 1995; mem. exec. com., 1996; CFO Terradyne, Inc., Boston, 1999—2001; pres., semiconductor divsn. Teradyne Inc., Boston, 2001—03, pres., 2003—, CEO, 2004—. Office: Teradyne Inc 321 Harrison Ave Boston MA 02118*

BRADLEY, MURRAY L(EE), librarian; b. Balt., July 20, 1941; s. Howard Lee and Isabel (Biggs) B. BS in Social Sci., Loyola Coll., Balt., 1963; MSLS with honors, Cath. U. Am., 1969; MBA with honors, Bryant Coll., 1983. Reference and circulation libr. U.S. Naval Acad., Annapolis, Md., 1964-68, asst. acquisitions libr., 1968-70, sci. and tech. libr., 1970-72, acquisitions libr., 1972-77; head readers svc. divsn. U.S. Naval War Coll. Libr., Newport, R.I., 1977-91; head rsch. reports sect. Naval Rsch. Lab., 1991-96, dep. chief libr., head info. svcs. br., 1996-99; chief of info. Patrick Henry br. Fairfax County Pub. Libr., Vienna, Va., 1999—. Assoc. editor Criarl Newsletter, 1988-91. Mem. ALA, Spl. Librs. Assn. (R.I. chpt. treas. 1978-79, D.C. chpt. nominating com. 1994, co-chair mil. librs. group 1995—, awards com. 1997), Am. Soc. Info. Sci. (sec. Chesapeake Bay chpt. 1973-74, program chmn. 1974-75, chmn. 1975-76, award of merit jury 1977-78, treas. Potomac Valley chpt. 1993-94), Beta Phi Mu. Office: Patrick Henry Library Vienna VA 22180 Home: PO Box 5555 Middleburg VA 20118-5555

BRADLEY, NOLEN EUGENE, JR., retired personnel executive, educator; b. Memphis, Nov. 29, 1925; s. Nolen Eugene and Anice Pearl (Luther) B.; m. Eloise Mullins, Jan. 7, 1947; children: Sharon (Mrs. Edward W. Vanderpool), Diana (Mrs. Wiley M. Rutledge), Nolen Eugene III, David Lee. BS, Memphis State U., 1951, MA, 1952; EdD, U. Tenn., 1966. Instr. polit. sci. Memphis State U., 1951-52; tchr. English Messick High Sch., Memphis, 1952-56; asst. dean admissions Memphis State U., 1956-64; dir. State Agy. for Title I, Higher Edn. Act, 1965, Div. Continuing Edn., U. Tenn., 1966-70; dean instrn. Vol. State Community Coll., Gallatin, Tenn., 1970-78; tutor, ednl. cons., 1978-79; pers. asst. Hoeganaes Corp., Gallatin, 1979-80, pers. mgr., 1980-82; dir. pers. Music Village U.S.A., Hendersonville, Tenn., 1984—; ret., 1981. Contbr. articles to profl. jours. Deacon Bapt. ch., 1966—. With AUS, 1944-46, ETO. Mem. Am. Assn. Sch. Adminstrs., Tenn. Adult Edn. Assn., Tenn. Edn. Assn., Omicron Delta Kappa, Pi Delta Epsilon, Phi Delta Kappa, Phi Kappa Phi. Democrat. Lion. Avocations: writing, travel, movies, reading. Home: 907 Harris Dr Gallatin TN 37066-3462 E-mail: geneloise@comcast.net.

BRADLEY, PAUL N., special education educator; b. Jackson, Miss., Mar. 10, 1950; s. Nathaniel and Amy (Bennet) Bradley; m. Karen Marie Bradley, June 17, 1989; stepchildren: Jamila, Jamal; 1 child, Kimberly Denise. BS in Social Wk., Spl. Edn., Adminstr. Leadership, Ctrl. State U., Wilberforce, Ohio, 1972; MS, U. Wis., Milw., 1977, U. Wis., 1990; JD, John Marshall Law Sch., Atlanta, 1980; MBA, Cardinal Stritch U., Milw., 1998; PhD, Walden U., 2005. Cert. K-12 learning disabled tchr. Wis., lic. dir. spl. edn./pupil svcs. Wis., secondary adminstr. Wis., ins. agt. Wis. Tchr.'s aide Juneau Acad., Milw., 1973—76; tchr. Milw. Pub. Schs., 1976—79, Atlanta Pub. Schs., 1979—81; vol. tchr. trainer U.S. Peace Corps, Kingston, Jamaica, 1981—83; supr. student tchrs. Purdue U., West Lafayette, Ind., 1983—84; supr. exceptional edn. Milw. Pub. Schs., 1984—96; tchr. Holy Redeemer Acad., Milw., 1996—97, Waukegan Pub. Schs., Ill., 1997—98; social worker Lacausa, Inc., Milw., 1998—2000; tchr. spl. edn. Racine Unified Sch. Dist., Wis., 2000—. Lic. ins. agt. Farmers Ins. Group. Cons. Big Bro. Big Sister for Pub. Edn., Milw.; coord. youth group YMCA, Milw., 2001; mem. ACLU; active Campaign Tolerance - A Project of So. Poverty Law Ctr., Montgomery, Ala., 2004; bd. dirs. Gray's Child Devel. Ctr., Milw. Recipient Commedation, Wash. Pk. H.S., 2005. Mem.: Acad. of Mgmt. Jour. Mem. Assn., The PhD Project Mgmt. Doctoral Students Assn., The Gideon Assn. Home: 9600 W Debbie Ln Milwaukee WI 53224-4618 Office: 1901 12th St Racine WI 53403 Office Phone: 262-605-9880. Business E-Mail: Pbradley@Walednu.edu.

BRADLEY, PAULA E., former state legislator; b. New Haven, Oct. 11, 1924; d. Richard Travis and Harriett (Bogenhagen) Elliott; m. William L. Bradley, 1947; children: James R. Choukas-Bradley, Dwight C., Paul W. BA, Hiram Coll., 1945; postgrad., Middlebury Coll., 1946, Hartford Seminary, 1963-64. Ret. rsch. assoc. univ. devel. Yale U.; mem. N.H. Ho. of Reps., 1992—98, 2000—02. Treas. Coos County Dem. Com., 1992—, Randolph Dem. Party, 1992—2004; chair bd. adjustment Town of Randolph, 2000—01, mem. planning bd., 2003—; mem. Gorham (N.H.) Congregational Ch.; bd. dirs. Coos County Family Health Svcs., Berlin, NH, 1993—2001, 2004—, Weeks Meml. Hosp., Lancaster, NH, 1993—95, No. Forest Heritage Park, Berlin, NH, 2001—, No. Country Coun., 2003—. Mem.: AAUW (Androscoggin br. 1990—), Randolph Mountain Club (bd. dirs. 1986—91, 1992—97, treas. 1989—91, pres. 1995—96). Democrat. Avocations: walking, gardening, choral singing. Office: 194 Randolph Hill Rd Randolph NH 03593 E-mail: wlb@ncia.net.

BRADLEY, PAULETTE NANNOS, principal; d. Arthur and Constance Nannos; m. Charles Christopher Bradley; 1 child, C. Christopher. BS, Drexel U., 1974, MS, 1983; EdD, Widener U., 2003. Cert. home economist Am. Home Econs. Assn., 1992, home econs. edn. Level II Pa. Dept. Edn., 1981, early childhood edn. level III Pa. Dept. Edn., 1983, reading specialist Pa. Dept. Edn., 1983, elem. prin. Level II Pa. Dept. Edn., 1996, secondary prin. Level II Pa. Dept. Edn., 1996, supt. Pa. Dept. Edn., 2002. Tchr. Upper Darby Sch. Dist., Pa., 1974—76, William Penn Sch. Dist., Lansdowne, 1979—80, Interboro Sch. Dist., Prospect Park, Pa., 1977—79, 1980—93, asst. prin. HS, 1993—98, elem. prin., 1998—. Adj. prof. undergrad., grad. Drexel U., Phil., 1984; dist. chair, v.p. Pa. Home Econs. Assn., 1987—94; developer grant Impact: Ptnrs. Edn., Delaware County, Pa., 1989; task force workshop facilitator Pa. Dept. Edn., Harrisburg, 1991—93; dist. student assistance team coord. Interboro Sch. Dist., Prospect Park, 1998—2002. Contbr. articles to profl. jours. Spkr., Delaware County, 1982—90; mem. Norwood Home and Sch. Assn., 1997—2005; mem., v.p. Chester Pike Kiwanis, 2000—01; scholarship com. mem. St. Luke's Greek Orthodox Ch., Broomall, 2003—05. Scholar Margaret Morton Creese scholar, Drexel U., 1973; Pa. Dept. Edn. grant vocat. edn. Mem.: Pa. Home Econs. Assn. (ea. area v.p. 1990—94), Assn. Supervision and Curriculum Devel., Pa. Sch. Bds. Assn. (corr.), Nat. Assn. Elem. and Secondary Prins. (corr.), Kappa Delta Pi, Kappa Omicron Nu, Phi Mu (pres. 1973—74). R-Liberal. Greek Orthodox. Avocations: reading, gourmet cooking, needlepoint, sewing. Office: Interboro Sch Dist Norwood Sch 558 Seneca Ave Norwood PA 19074 Office Phone: 610-237-6425. Personal E-mail: bradlepn@interborosd.org.

BRADLEY, R. TODD (TODD BRADLEY), computer company executive, communications executive; b. Balt., Nov. 29, 1958; BSBA, Towson State U., Baltimore, Md. V.p. Fed. Express; v.p., mng. dir. EMEA ops. AC Nielsen; various exec. positions to pres. NCH Promotional Svcs. subsidiary Dun & Bradstreet Corp., 1993—97; pres., CEO Transport Internat. Pool subsidiary of GE Capital Services, 1997—98; sr. v.p. Europe, Middle East and Africa region Gateway Inc., San Diego, 1998—2001, sr. v.p. U.S. consumer bus., 1999—2001, exec. v.p. global ops., 1999—2001; exec. v.p., COO Solutions Group Palm Inc., 2001—02, pres., COO Solutions Group, 2002, CEO, Solutions Group, 2001—03; CEO palmOne, Inc., Milpitas, Calif., 2003—05, advisor, 2005; exec. v.p., personal systems group Hewlett-Packard Co., Palo Alto, Calif., 2005—. Office: Hewlett-Packard Co 3000 Hanover St Palo Alto CA 94304 Office Phone: 408-503-7000.*

BRADLEY, RAYMOND STUART, education educator, researcher; BSc, Southampton U., Eng., 1969; Ms, U. Colo., Boulder, Colo., 1971, PhD, 1974; DSc, Southampton U., Eng., 2005. Head, dept. geosciences U. Mass., Amherst, Mass., 1996—2003; disting. prof. U. Mass., Amherst, Mass., 2003—05. Fellow, Am. Geophys. Union, 2005, Arctic Inst. of N.Am., 1994. Achievements include research in Authored over 100 rsch. papers and wrote or edited 11 books on climate and paleoclimatology. Office Phone: 413-545-2286.

BRADLEY, RICHARD (RICHARD BLOW), writer; b. 1964; BA, Yale Coll.; MA in Am. History, Harvard Univ. Reporter-researcher New Republic Mag., Washington; staff writer, columnist Regardie's Mag., Washington, editor-in-chief, 1992—95; co-founding editor, sr. editor George Mag., NYC, 1995—97, Washington affairs editor, 1997—99, exec. editor, 1999. Exec. editor Yale's New Jour. Mag.; author (as Richard Blow): (non-fiction) American Son: A Portrait of John F. Kennedy Jr., 2002 (#1 NY Times bestseller list, 2002); author: Harvard Rules: The Struggle for the Soul of the World's Most Important University, 2005; contbr. articles to numerous publs., online websites. Mailing: c/o Author Mail HarperCollins Pub 10 E 53rd St New York NY 10022*

BRADLEY, RICHARD EDWIN, retired academic administrator; b. Omaha, Mar. 9, 1926; s. Louis J. and Betsy (Winterton) B.; m. Doris I. McGowan, June 8, 1946; children— Diane, Karen, David. Student, Creighton U., 1946-48; BSD., U. Nebr., 1950, D.D.S., 1952; MS, State U. Iowa, 1958. Instr. State U. Iowa, 1957-58; asst. prof. Creighton U., 1958-59; asst. prof., chmn. dept. periodontics U. Nebr., 1959-62, assoc. prof., 1962-65, prof., 1965-67; assoc. dean Coll. Dentistry, 1967-68, dean, 1968-80; pres., dean Baylor Coll. Dentistry, 1980-90, pres., dean emeritus, 1990—; clin. prof. Coll. Dentistry U. Nebr. Med. Coll., Lincoln, 1990—; cons. dental edn., 199-93. Mem. Commn. A, Coun. on Dental Edn., 1986-93; pres. Am. Assn. Dental Schs., 1977-78; mem. nat. adv. com. on health professions edn. Dept. Health and Human Resources, 1982-86; pres. Am. Fund for Dental Health, 1986-87; mem. bd. of vis. Temple Univ. Sch. of Dentistry, 2001—. Editor: The New Dentist, 1992-94; contbg. editor Orban's Textbook of Periodontics, 1963; contbr. Clark's Clin., 1980. Mem. bd. visitors Temple U. Sch.Dentistry, 2001--. Served with USNR, 1944-46. Fellow AAAS, Internat. Coll. Dentists; mem. ADA, Am. Acad. Peridontology Found. (bd. dirs., pres. 1994-96), Am. Coll. Dentists (regent 1992-96, v.p. 1997-98, pres. Found. 2001-02), Sigma Xi, Omicron Kappa Upsilon. Office: U Nebraska Coll Dentistry Lincoln NE 68583-0740

BRADLEY, RICHARD JAMES, former educational association executive; b. Waltham, Mass., Aug. 18, 1929; s. Bernard E. and Mary E. (Kennedy) B.; BS, Boston U., 1951, MEd, 1959; John Hay fellow Williams Coll., summer 1962; DScEd (hon.), Nasson Coll., 1970; LHD (hon.) Endicott Coll., 1994, Am. Coll. Greece, Deree Coll., 1994; m. Joan Marcia Dick, Dec. 27, 1952; children— Pamela, Michael, Douglas. Penny. Tchr. and prin., N.H., 1954-66; dir. evaluation commn. pub. schs. New Eng. Assn. Schs. and Colls., 1966-74, exec. dir., CEO Bedford, Mass., 1974-94; pres. Dick Bradley and Assocs., Inc., Cupertino, Calif., 1995—; cons. U.S. Office of Edn., U.S. Dept. State Office Overseas Schs.; chmn. Nat. Study Sch. Evaluation, 1968-78; spkr. in field. Served in USMC, 1952-54. Mem. N.H. Prins. Assn. (pres. 1964-65), Nat. Assn. Secondary Sch. Prins. (chmn. sch. and coll. rels. com.). Roman Catholic. also: 22652 Silver Oak Ln Cupertino CA 95014-5633 E-mail: rnbrad97311@aol.com.

BRADLEY, SLATER, artist; b. San Francisco, Calif., 1975; BA, UCLA, 1998. One-man shows include, Taka Ishii Gallery, Tokyo, 2005, Matrix 216: Year of the Doppelganger, U. Calif. Berkeley Art Mus. & Pacific Film Archive, 2005, Blum & Poe, LA, 2004, Stoned & Dethroned, Team Gallery, NYC, 2004, Annandale-on-Hudson, NY, Ctr. Curatorial Studies Mus., Bard Coll., NY, 2003, Armory Photography Show, 2002, Here are the Young Men, Team Gallery, 2002, Universitatsstadt Kaiserslautern, Germany, 2002, Art + Pub., Geneva Switzerland, 2002, Arndt & Ptnr., Berlin, Germany, 2002, Video Cube, FIAS, Paris, 2001, Trompe Le Monde, Galerie Yvon Lambert, 2001, Home Town Hero, Refusalon, San Francisco, 2001, Spl. Projects Series, P.S.1, NY, 2000, Charlatan, Team Gallery, NYC, 2000, Fried Liver Attack, 1999, exhibited in group shows at Whitney Biennial, Whitney Mus. Am. Art, 2004, Premieres, Mus. Modern Art, NYC, 2004, Harlem Postcards, Studio Mus. Harlem, NYC, 2004, Statemate, Mus. Contemporary Art, Chgo., 2004, Playlist, Palais de Tokyo, 2004, When Darkness Falls, Gallery 400, U. Ill., Chgo., 2003, What am I doing Here?, ESSO Gallery, NYC, 2003, Someone to Watch Over Me, Smart Project Space, Amsterdam, Netherlands, 2003, The Passing, Galeria Helga de Alvear, Madrid, 2002, burst, Team Gallery, NYC, 2002, Art & Wellbeing-Aesthetics of Recreation, Kunsthaus Meran-Merano Arte, Italy, 2001, Dear Dead Person, Momenta, Bklyn., 2001, Friction Fiction, Echo Park Projects, LA, 2000, SoCal Car Culture, Irvine Fine Arts Ctr., Calif., 1999, Text & Numbers, Remba Gallery, LA.*

BRADLEY, THOMAS A., insurance company executive; With St. Paul Cos., Inc., St. Paul, sr. v.p. fin., CFO, 2001—04, Zurich North America, 2004—. Office: Zurich No America 550 W Washington Blvd Chicago IL 60661 Office Fax: (651) 310-8294.*

BRADLEY, VANESSA LYNN, management consultant; b. Saginaw, Mich., Apr. 8, 1967; BS in Indsl. Engring., Northwestern U., 1989; MBA, U Pa., 1993. Project engr. Gen. Motors Corp., 1989—91; project cons. Ctr. for Applied Rsch., 1992—93; v.p. Bradley Automotive Group, Ann Arbor, Mich., 1996—98; prin. A.T. Kearney, Inc., Chgo., 1993—96, 1998—. Bd. trustees Sherwood Conservatory of Music, Chgo., Providence St. Mel Coll. Prep. Sch., Chgo. Mem.: NAFE, Northwestern Alumni Club of Chgo. Office: AT Kearney Inc 222 W Adams St Chicago IL 60606 Office Phone: 312-961-1219. E-mail: vanbrad67@aol.com.

BRADLEY, WALTER D., lieutenant governor, real estate broker; b. Clovis, N.Mex., Oct. 30, 1946; s. Ralph W. and M. Jo (Black) B.; m. Debbie Shelly, Sept. 17, 1977; children: Tige, Lance, Nicole, Kristin. Student, Eastern N.Mex. U., 1964—67. Supr. Tex. Instruments, Dallas, 1967—73; mgr., salesman Nat. Chemsearch, Irving, Tex., 1973—76; real estate broker Colonial Real Estate, Clovis, 1976, Realtors Assn. N.Mex., Clovis, N.Mex., 1976—; state senator Curry County, State of N.Mex., 1990—92; lt. gov. State of N.Mex., Santa Fe, 1995—2003; dir. comml. divsn. N.Mex. State Land Office, 2004; dir. bus. and govt. affairs Dairy Farmers Am., 2005—. V.p., bd. dirs. Clovis Indsl. Commn., 1983—86, pres. econ. devel., 1987; bd. dirs. United Way, Clovis, 1984—86, Curry County Blood Adv. Bd., Clovis, 1980—85; chmn. Curry County Reps., Clovis, 1984—88, Cosmos Soccer, Clovis, 1984. Named Man of Yr., Progressive Farmer Mag., 1998; recipient Leadership award, Albuquerque NAACP, 1997, Disting. Svc. award, N.Mex. Farm and Livestock Bur., 1997, Leadership Beatification award, Keep N.Mex. Beautiful, 2000, Mark Weidler Disting. Pub. Servant award, N.Mex. Petroleum Marketers Assn., 2000, Outstanding N.Mex. Small Bus. Supporter, N.Mex. Small Bus. Devel. Ctr., 1997, Outstanding Leadership award, N.Mex. Cattle Growers' Assn., 1996. Mem.: N.Mex. Jaycees, Curry County Jaycees, Clovis C. of C., Clovis Bd. Realtors (pres. 1982, 1993), Realtors Assn. N.Mex. (v.p., bd. dirs. 1982—85, v.p. 1987—88), Lions. Republican. Baptist. Home: 904 B Colonial Pkwy Clovis NM 88101 Office Phone: 505-763-4528. E-mail: wbradley@dfamilk.com.

BRADLEY, WILLIAM BRYAN, cable television regulator; b. Charleston, W.Va., Feb. 12, 1929; s. Floyd England and Florence Clara (O'Bryan) B.; m. Virginia Vanderhoof Logan, Oct. 27, 1951; children: Christopher, Thomas, Michael, John, Mary Clare (dec.), Mary Ellen, Ann. BA in Journalism cum laude, U. Notre Dame, 1950. Supr., indsl. engr. Martin Co., Denver, 1958-61, 62-65; cons. Reynolds, Ward & Carey, Denver, 1961-62; analyst Denver City

Coun., 1965-69, staff dir., 1969-82; dir. Office of Telecommunications, Denver, 1982-94; sr. assoc. Media Mgmt. Svcs., Inc., 1994-99. Co-founder, dir., vice-chmn. Greater Metro Cable Consortium, 1992; initiated joint city-industry cable TV Tech. Stds., 1987, adopted by FCC, 1992. Participant Japanese-Am. conf. on Globalization and Cable TV, Suwa, Japan, 1991. Co-founder Nat. Assn. Telecomm. Officers and Advisors, Washington, 1980, bd. dirs., 1983-88, pres., 1985-87; chmn. telecomm. subcom. Colo. Mcpl. League, Denver, 1985-86; bd. dirs. Denver Cmty. TV, 1996-98; charter mem. The Cable Ctr., 1998. Line Officer USN, 1950-53. Roman Catholic. Avocations: chess, books.

BRADLEY GARDNER, JANICE, federal agency administrator; BA, Wake Forest U.; MA, American U. Econ. officer U.S. Embassy to Japan, 1990—92; br. chief Persian Gulf Office Leadership Analysis, 1993—95; dir. ctrl. intelligence rep. to nat. sec. coun. Exec. Office of Pres., 1995—96; spl. advisor internat. affairs Office of V.P., 1996; chief East Asia group Fgn. Broadcast Info. Svc., dep. dir.; sr. intelligence liaison US Dept. Treasury, dep. asst. sec. intelligence and analysis, asst. sec. intelligence and analysis, 2005—. Office: Dept of Treasury 1500 Pennsylvania Ave NW Washington DC 20220 Office Phone: 202-622-1841. Office Fax: 202-622-1829.*

BRADNER, HUGH, retired physics professor; b. Tonopah, Nev., Nov. 5, 1915; s. Donald Byal and Agnes Claire (Mead) B.; m. Marjorie Hall, Sept. 26, 1943; 1 child, Barbara Claire. AB, Miami U., Oxford, Ohio, 1936; PhD, Calif. Inst. Tech., 1941; ScD, Miami U., Oxford, Ohio, 1961. Grad. asst. Calif. Inst. Tech., Pasadena, 1938-41; staff U.S. Naval Ordnance Lab., Washington, 1941-43, Manhattan Project, Los Alamos, N.Mex., 1943-46; rsch. staff Radiation Lab., U. Calif., Berkeley, 1946-61; rsch. physicist Inst. Geophysics, U. Calif., La Jolla, 1961—; prof. engring. physics and geophysics U. Calif., La Jolla, 1964—79, prof. emeritus, 1979—. Mem. various adv. bd.s U.S. Navy, AEC, various univs., civic orgns.; cons. in field. Contbr. over 150 articles to profl. jours. Miami Univ. medalist, 1960. Fellow Am. Phys. Soc., Calif. Acad. Sci.; mem. AIAA, Am. Geophys. Union, Phi Beta Kappa. Achievements include several inventions including "wet suit" for divers. Home: 8515 Costa Verde Blvd # 110 San Diego CA 92122 Office: IGPP U Calif San Diego 9500 Gilman Dr La Jolla CA 92093-5004 Office Phone: 858-534-1927. E-mail: hbradner@ucsd.edu.

BRADSHAW, BASCOM KYLE, surgeon, science educator; b. Arlington, Tex., Dec. 30, 1970; s. Delbert Ray and Mary Louise Bradshaw; m. Tracy Renea Ruggles, Apr. 13, 2002. BS, U. Tampa, Fla., 1997; DO, U. North Tex., 2001; MPH, U. Tex., Galveston, 2003. Combat medic U.S. Army, 1991—94; resident in aerospace medicine Naval Aerospace Med. Inst., Pensacola, Fla., 2002—. Adj. prof. aero. sci. Embry Riddle Aero. U.-Pensacola Ctr., 2002—. Capt. U.S. Army. Decorated Meritorious Svc. medal U.S. Army, Army Commendation medal, Army Achievement medal, Coast Guard Commandant's Letter of Commendation U.S. Coast Guard; recipient Zollinger Outstanding Sr. award, Sigma Phi Epsilon, 1997, Founder's award for sleep rsch., So. Sleep Soc., 2001. Mem.: Fla. Osteo. Med. Assn., Aerospace Med. Assn., Am. Acad. Sleep Medicine (assoc.), Human Factors and Ergonomics Soc. (assoc.), Alpha Chi. Avocations: jogging, flying, cat herding, sailing. Office: Residency in Aerospace Medicine NAMI (Code 33) 340 Hulse Rd Pensacola FL 32508

BRADSHAW, BEVERLY JEAN, psychotherapist, consultant, educator; b. Denver, Dec. 25, 1946; d. William Heartsel and Shirley Marie (Powell) B. BA, U. No. Colo., 1970; MA, U. Denver, 1984; postgrad., U. Colo., Regis U. Cert. Type B profl. tchr., Colo. Recreation supr. City of Englewood (Colo.), 1968-76; communications bd. chmn. U. No. Colo., Greeley, 1968-70; tchr. Englewood Schs., 1970-83, counselor, tchr., 1984-87, counselor, 1987-92; pvt. practice, Englewood, Colo., 1991-96. Adj. prof. Arapahoe C.C., 1993—. Mayor pro tem Engelwood City Coun., 1980-87, 2000-01; mem. South Suburban Parks and Recreation Found., 1984—, chmn., 2000-02. Mem. NEA, AARP. Republican. Roman Catholic. Avocations: theater, reading, writing, carving, jewelry making. Home: 5165 S Elati Dr Englewood CO 80110-6712 E-mail: bev5165@aol.com.

BRADSHAW, CONRAD ALLAN, retired lawyer; b. Campbell, Mo., Dec. 22, 1922; s. Clarence Andrew and Stella (Cashdollar) B.; m. Margaret Crassous Sanderson, Dec. 31, 1959; children: Dorothy A., Lucy E., Charlotte L. AB, U. Mich., 1943, JD, 1948. Bar: Mich. 1948. With Warner, Norcross & Judd, LLP, ret., 2005. Lt. USNR, 1943—46. Mem. ABA, State Bar Mich. (chmn. corp., fin. and bus. law sect. 1976), Grand Rapids Bar Assn. (pres. 1970) Home: 3600 Fulton St E Grand Rapids MI 49546 Office: 900 Fifth Third Ctr 111 Lyon St NW Grand Rapids MI 49503 Office Phone: 616-752-2344. Personal E-mail: cabrad1@comcast.net.

BRADSHAW, DENIS JAMES, engineer, graphic designer; b. Franklin, Va., Dec. 31, 1948; s. Lonnie August and Marion Bradshaw; children: Matthew James, Mary Suzanne, Kimberly Lynn. BS in Indsl. Engring. and Ops. Rsch., Va. Poly. Inst. and State U., 1971, M of Engring., 1973. Instr. Va. Poly. Inst. and State U., Blacksburg, 1971—72; various engr., br. head, and divsn. dir. positions Naval Aviation Depot, Norfolk, 1973—92, prodn. engring. dept. head, 1992—94; facilities, safety and environ. office head Atlantic Ordnance Command, Yorktown, 1994—97, explosives safety dept. head, 1997—2000; gen. engr. Navy Region, Mid-Atlantic, Regional Safety Office, Virginia Beach, 2000—. Founder, owner, graphic designer Accents Media, Virginia Beach, 2002—; tchg. asst. Va. Poly. Inst. and State U., 1971—73. Photographer, Fire Hydrant on Fire. Vol. Am. Cancer Soc., Am. Heart Assn., Neighborhood Watch, Va., Virginia Beach Soccer Club; mgmt. advisor Jr. Achievement, Norfolk; min. adminstrn. Christ Cmty. Ch., Chesapeake, 1999—2004; trustee, treas., Sunday sch. tchr. various churches; team mem. Jamaica Mission Trip, 1996; bd. chmn. Tidewater Emmaus, 1998—98; bd. mem. Naval Air Rework Facility NORVA Assn., Norfolk; mem. Nat. Assn. Superintendents U.S. Naval Shore Establishments, Norfolk; com. chmn. Inst. Indsl. Engineers, Virginia Beach. Recipient Cost Reduction Diamond award, Naval Aviation Depot, 1979—87, Spl. Act award Environ. Cleanup, 1986, tchg. assistantship, Va. Poly. Inst. and State U., 1971—73; scholarship, State of Va., 1968—71. Republican. Baptist. Achievements include Naval Air Systems Command Senior Executive Management Development Program Graduate (1989); Naval Air Systems Command nominee for Arthur S. Flemming Award, sponsored by downtown Jaycees of Washington, DC granted annually to 10 career federal employees or members of the Armed Forces (1988); Developed safety sofware program that was approved for Navy-wide use (2003). Avocations: christian service, graphic design, skiing, bicycling, photography. Home: 2238 Oak Street Virginia Beach VA 23451-1312

BRADSHAW, DOVE, artist; b. NYC, Sept. 24, 1949; d. David Nelson and Jean Kathryn (Cormack) B. BFA, Boston Mus. Sch. Fine Arts, 1973. Co-artistic advisor The Merce Cunningham Dance Co., N.Y.C., 1984—. Artist in residence Pier Ctr., Orkney, Scotland, Sirius Art Ctr., Cork, Ireland, Statens Vaerksteder for Kunst, Copenhagen, 2000. One-man shows include Alan Stone Gallery, N.Y.C., 1979, S. Gering Gallery, N.Y., 1988-89, 91, 93, 95, 98, Graham Gallery, N.Y., 1979, Ericson Gallery, 1982, N.Y. Wave Hill, N.Y., 1983, PSI Mus., N.Y.C., 1991, Mattress Factory Mus., Pitts., 1990, 99, Pier Ctr., Orkney, Scotland, 1995, Stalke Gallery, Copenhagen, 1995, 96, 98, 99, 2001, 03, 04, Barbara Krakow Gallery, 1997, Mus. Contemporary Art, L.A., 1998, Larry Becker Contemporary Art, Phila. 2000, 05, Stark Gallery, N.Y., 2001, mid-career exhbn. Baruch Coll., CUNY, N.Y., 2003, Diferenca Gallery, Lisbon, 2003, Volume Gallery, N.Y., 2004, many others; group shows include Am. Ctr., Paris, Science Mus., Tokyo, 1982, Mus. Modern Art, N.Y.C., 1989, Carnegie Internat., Pitts., 1991, Met. Mus. N.Y., 1992, Art Inst. Chgo., 1992, 96, Aldrich Mus., Ridgefield, Conn., 1993, 2004, Phila. Mus., 1993, 98, 2000, Swiss Inst., N.Y.C., 1995, Baumgartner Gallery, Washington, 1998, Carnegie Mus. Art, 1997, Whitney Mus. Am. Art, N.Y., 1997, Millennium Film Theatre, 1998, Mus. Contemporary Art, L.A., 1998, U. Calif., San Diego, U. Mass. Amherst, 1999, UBU Gallery, NYU, Baruch Coll., N.Y.C., Univ. Art Mus., U. Va., Charlottsville, 2000, 05, Anastasi Bradshaw Cage Mus. Contemporary Art, Roskilde, Denmark, 2000, 04, Rooseum Contemporary Art Ctr., Malmo, Sweden, Nikolaj Contemporary Art Ctr. Copenhagen, 2002, Baruch Coll., N.Y., Volckers and Freunde Gallery, Berlin, Tanya Bonakdar, NY, 2003, Stalke Gallery, Copenhagen, 2004, Anashani Bradshaw Cage Cunningham, 2005, Slefanie Hering, Berlin, 2005, others; represented in permanent collection at Met. Mus. Art, N.Y.C., Mus. Modern Art, N.Y.C., Bklyn. Mus. Art, Whitney Mus. Am. Art, Art Inst. Chgo., Phila. Mus. Art, Ark. Art Ctr., Little Rock, Fogg Art Mus., Cambridge, Mass., Harvard U., Getty Ctr., L.A., Mus. Contemporary Art, L.A., Nat. Gallery, Washington, Carnegie Mus Art, Pitts., Mattress Factory Mus., Pitts., Internat. Le Pompidou Ctr., Paris, Pier Ctr. Orkney, Scotland, Mus. Art, Bilboa, Spain, Kunst Mus., Dusseldorf, Germany, Moderna Mus., Stockholm, Russian State Mus., St. Petersburg, Oxygen, 2002, Self Interest, 1999; prodr., dir., artist: (film) Indeterminacy, 1995; prodr. Met. Mus. postcard, 1976, 92, Met. Mus. guerilla postcard, 1978, others; artist, prodr. handmade books, including Plain Air (installation with live birds 1969, 88, 91, documentation 1991), 1969-91; author: Indeterminacy, Contingency, Equivalents, Removal, Riverstone, 1991-99. Recipient Pollock-Krasner award, 1985; grantee Nat. Endowment Arts, 1975. Mem.: Solway Jones Gallery (L.A.), Volume Gallery (N.Y.). Avocations: meditation, yoga, running, reading, gardening, landscape gardening. Home and Studio: 924 W End Ave New York NY 10025-3534 Personal E-mail: dbradshaw1@nyc.rr.com.

BRADSHAW, GLENN RAYMOND, art educator; b. Peoria, Ill., Mar. 3, 1922; s. Elza Raymond and Hilda Catherine (Johnson) B.; m. Inez Ellen Payne, June 5, 1947; children: Kristen, Todd, Lisa, Adam, Scott. BS, Ill. State U., 1947; MFA, U. Ill., 1950. Critic tchr. U. Ill., Urbana, 1947-50, prof. art, 1952-86, prof. emeritus; asst. prof. art Iowa State Tchrs. Coll., Cedar Falls, 1950-52. Master classes Springmaid Watercolor Workshop, Myrtle Beach, SC, 1986—. One-man shows include Ill. State Normal U., 1947, 50, 61, Cedar Falls Art Assn., 1951, Schermerhorn Gallery, Beloit, Wis., 1956, 57, 59, Millikin U., Decatur, Ill., 1955, Flint Art Ctr., Mich., 1957, Old Orchard Bank, Skokie, Ill., 1960, Gilman Gallery, Chgo., 1963, 65, Jane Haslem Gallery, Madison, Wis., 1966, 70, St. Louis Gallery, 1967, The Canal House, Indianapolis, 1969, Wustum Mus., Racine, Wis., 1969, Ill. State Mus., Springfield, 1972, Krannert Art Mus., Champaign, Ill., 1972, Tower Park Gallery, Peoria Hghts., Ill., 1973, 76, 78, 81, 85, Fanny Garver Gallery, Madison, Wis., 1976, 81, U. Wis., 1976, MacNider Mus., Mason City, Iowa, 1976, Prairie House, Springfield, Ill., 1980, Bicentennial Mus., Paris, Ill., 1980, Neville-Sargent Gallery, Evanston, Ill, 1980, 84, 87, 89, 91, U. San Diego, 1981, House of Art, Champaign, 1982, Humewood II Gallery, Toronto, Can., 1988, Ctr. for Vis. Arts, Wausau, Wis., 1997; group shows include Royal Watercolor Soc., London, Eng., 1962, Met. Mus. Art, N.Y.C., 1996-67, Clev. Inst. of Art, 1968, U. Colo., 1970, Am. Watercolor Soc. Invitational, Australia, 1975, Mexico City, 1989, Akron Art Inst., 1976, U. Ill. Faculty Exhibitions, Taiwan, 1981, Hong Kong, 1982, Tokyo, 1983, Albuquerque Mus. Art, 1985, June Kelly Gallery, N.Y.C., 1988, Galeri Hartl and Klier, Tubingen, Germany, 1988, L.A. County Century Gallery, 1993, Tex. Women's U., Denton, 1994, Nat. Taiwan Art Edn. Inst., 1994, Springfield Mus., 1997; represented in numerous permanent collections. With U.S. Army, 1942-45. Recipient John Young Hunter award Am. Watercolor Soc., N.Y.C., 1973, Ed Whitney Prize, 1974, Arches Paper Co. prize Long Beach Mus. Art, 1974, 1st prize Nat. Watercolor Soc., 1977, Dr. David Soletsky Memorial award Nat. Soc. of Painters in Caseinand Acrylic, N.Y.C., 1978, John J. Newman Medal and prize, 1996, William A. Paten prize Nat. Acad. Design, 1987, Schweitzer prize, 1993, Whitaker prize, 1996, 2001, Lifetime Achievement award Watercolor USA Honor Soc., 2000, others. Mem. Nat. Acad., Nat. Watercolor Soc., Am. Watercolor Soc. Studio: 6403 Pine Point Dr Mc Naughton WI 54543 Office Phone: 715-277-2401.

BRADSHAW, GLORIANNE MARIE, elementary school educator; b. Forman, N.D., Dec. 31, 1945; d. Lars and Annie Holen; m. Robert E. Bradshaw, Dec. 16, 1967 (dec.); children: Heather, Elizabeth. BS, U. N.D., 1968. Cert. tchr. Nat. Bd. Edn., 2004. Tchr. elem. sch. Ctrl. Valley Pub. Schs., Buxton, ND, 1968—70, Kennedy (Minn.) Pub. Schs., 1971—74, Valley Pub. Schs., Crystal, ND, 1980—. Contbr. articles to profl. jours. Grantee, NASA, 2001. Mem.: Internat. Reading Assn., Nat. Coun. Tchrs. English, Nat. Coun. Tchrs. Math. Home: 1411 Western Ave Grafton ND 58237 Office: Valley Elem PO Box 129 Crystal ND 58272

BRADSHAW, HOWARD HOLT, management consulting company executive; b. Phila., Feb. 28, 1937; s. Howard Holt and Imojean (Campbell) B.; m. Loretta Warren Sites, Aug. 13, 1982; children by previous marriage: Elaine Allen, Howard Holt. BA, Yale U., 1958; postgrad., Duke U., 1958-60. Cert. mgmt. cons. Western Electric Co., various locations, 1960-67; personnel mgr., head behavioral scis. cons. Celanese Fibers Co., Charlotte, N.C., 1967-72; pres. Orgn. Cons., Inc., Charlotte, 1972—. Adj. prof. Babcock Grad. Sch. Mgmt., Wake Forest U., 1997—; cons. in field. Author: Personal Power, Self Esteem and Performance, 1983, The Management of Self Esteem, 1981, Leadership and the Purpose of the Firm, 1998; editl. rev. bd. Jour. Mgmt. Issues; contbr. articles to profl. jours. Regional chmn. Constl. Party of Pa., Harrisburg, 1964-66; pres. Coordinated Planning League, Inc., Charlotte, 1972-74; exec. com. Citizens for Effective Govt., Inc., Charlotte, 1987-93; mem. Mgmt. Rev. Com., Mecklenberg County, N.C., 1990—; bd. dirs. Chemi Metals, Inc., 1991-97. Recipient Cert. of Appreciation Charlotte Police Dept., 1969, Mecklenburg County Com., 1970. Mem. ASTD, Inst. Mgmt. Cons., Am. Psychol. Assn., Soc. Indsl. and Organizational Psychology, Orgnl. Devel. Network. Republican. Presbyterian. Home: 488 Lakeview Loop Mooresville NC 28115 Office: Organization Consultants Inc 1235 East Blvd # 250 Charlotte NC 28203-5870

BRADSHAW, JAMES EDWARD (JIM BRADSHAW), consultant; b. Waco, Tex., Aug. 18, 1940; s. Leo Herman Sr. and Eleanor Rose (Cogdell) B.; m. Ouida P. Massey; children: Robin Louise, Dorenda and Dorette (twins), James E. Jr., Cogdell O'Neal. BBA in Mktg. and Fin., Baylor U., 1963. Ptnr. Cogdell's Westview, Waco, 1960-64, Kennedy-David & Assocs., Waco, 1966-68; sales rep. Fed.-Mogul Corp., Detroit, 1964-66; pres. Cogdell Auto Supply Co., Inc., Ft. Worth, 1968-77; chmn. bd. dirs. Auto Supply Co., Inc., Ft. Worth, 1979-91; mayor pro tem City of Ft. Worth, 1976-79; cons. pvt. practice, Fort Worth, Tex. Mem. adv. bd. Betty Ford Ctr., Tarrant County Coun. on Alcoholism and Drug Abuse. Former bd. dirs. Big Bros./Big Sisters Tarrant County, United Way, Jr. Achievement, Tex. Mcpl. League, Austin, 1976-78; mem. adv. bd. dirs. Betty Ford Ctr.; mem. cmty. devel. steering com. Nat. League Cities, 1978-79; chmn. Tarrant County March of Dimes, Ft. Worth, 1979, Future Pres. Orgn., Kansas City, Mo., 1974; councilman City of Ft. Worth, 1975-79, mayor pro tem 1976-79, mem. zoning commn., 1974-75; Republican. candidate 12th Congl. Dist., 1980; mem. exec. com. Tarrant County Rep. Party. Named to Ten to Watch, D mag., 1977; recipient Call to Svc. award Pres. George W. Bush, 2005 Mem. Colonial Country Club, Masons. Methodist. Avocations: golf, reading, astronomy. Home: 4729 Trail Bend Cir Fort Worth TX 76109 Office: PO Box 100338 Fort Worth TX 76185-0338 Office Phone: 817-737-0087. Personal E-mail: jimbradshaw2004@charter.net.

BRADSHAW, JEAN PAUL, II, lawyer; b. May 12, 1956; married; children: Andrew, Stephanie. BJ, JD, U. Mo., 1981. Bar: Mo. 1981, U.S. Dist. Ct. (we. dist.) Mo. 1982, U.S. Dist. Ct. (so. dist.) Ill. 1988, U.S. Ct. Appeals (8th cir.) 1986, U.S. Supreme Ct. 1987. Assoc. Neale, Newman, Bradshaw & Freeman, Springfield, Mo., 1981-87, ptnr., 1987-89; U.S. atty. we. dist. Mo. U.S. Dept. Justice, Kansas City, 1989-93; of counsel Lathrop & Gage, Kansas City, 1993-99, mem., 2000—, chair dept. health law, 2000—. Named Spl. Asst. Atty. Gen. State of Mo., 1985-89; mem., chmn. elect U.S. Atty. Gen.'s adv. com., office mgmt. and budget subcom., sentencing guidelines subcom.; mem. com. infractions NCAA Divsn. II, 2005—. Chmn. Greene County Rep. cen. com., 1988-89; pres. Mo. Assn. Reps., 1986-87; bd. dirs. Greene County TARGET, 1984-89; mem. com. on resolutions, family and community issues and del. 1988 Rep. Nat. Conv.; mem. platform com. Mo. Reps., 1988; chmn. Greene County campaign McNary for Gov., 1984, co-chmn. congl. dist. Dole for Pres., 1988, regional chmn. Danforth for Senate, 1988, co-chmn. 7th congl. dist. Webster for Atty. Gen., 1988; county chmn. U. Mo.-Columbia Alumni Assn., 1985-87; bd. dirs. Springfield Profl. Baseball Assn., Inc.; past mem. Mo. Adv. Coun. for Comprehensive Psychiat. Svcs., former bd. dirs. Ozarks Coun. Boy Scouts Am.; pres. bd. trustees St. Paul's Episcopal Day Sch., 1997-2002. Named Outstanding Recent Grad. U. Mo.-Columbia Sch. Law, 1991. Mem. ABA, NCAA (divsn. II com. Infractions, 2005—), Mo. Bar Assn., Kansas City Met. Bar Assn., U. Mo.-Columbia Law Sch. Alumni Assn. (v.p. 1988-89, pres. 1990-91), Law Soc. U. Mo.-Columbia Law Sch. Office: 2345 Grand Blvd Ste 2800 Kansas City MO 64108-2612 Business E-Mail: jpbradshaw@rathropgage.com.

BRADSHAW, JERALD SHERWIN, chemistry educator, researcher; b. Cedar City, Utah, Nov. 28, 1932; s. Sherwin H. and Maree (Wood) Bradshaw; m. Barras Biddulph, July 2, 2005; children: Donna M. Webster, Melinda C. Waterman. BS, U. Utah, 1955; PhD, UCLA, 1963. Postdoctoral Calif. Inst. Tech., Pasadena, 1962—63; chemist Chevron Rsch., Richmond, Calif., 1963—66; from asst. prof. to assoc. prof. chemistry Brigham Young U., Provo, Utah, 1966—74, prof., 1974-93, asst. chmn. chemistry dept., 1980-86, Reed M. Izatt prof., 1993-2000, emeritus prof., 2000—. Vis. prof. Nat. Acad. Sci., U. Ljubljana, Yugoslavia, 1972-73, 82, U. Sheffield, England, 1978, James Cook U., Townsville, Australia, 1988. Author 2 books; contbr. more than 400 articles to profl. jours.; patentee in field. Served with USNR, 1955-59. Recipient Utah Gov.'s medal in sci. and tech., 1991. Mem. Am. Chem. Soc. (Utah award 1989, nat. award for separations sci. and tech. 1996), Internat. Soc. Heterocyclic Chemistry (bd. advisors 1980-82), Utah Acad. Sci., Sigma Xi (ann. lectr. 1988). Republican. Mem. Lds Ch. Avocations: stamp collecting/philately, church activities. Office: Brigham Young U Dept Chemistry-Biochemistry Provo UT 84602 Business E-Mail: jerald_bradshaw@byu.edu.

BRADSHAW, JOHN ROBERT COVINGTON, III, Internet company executive; b. Carthage, N.Y., Aug. 4, 1942; s. John Covington and Selma Pauline Bradshaw; children: Sean C., Heather Hodgson. BS, U. Mo., 1968, MBS, 1970. Pres., CEO UniGlobe Fin. Inc., Clearwater, 1998—, UniGlobe Leasing., UniGlobe Multimedia; pres., owner ATM Nat. Svcs., Clearwater, Fla., 1989—. Mem. Clearwater C. of C. (chmn. resource com.), Rotary, SCORE. Avocations: boating, travel, model trains. Home: 650 70th Ave #2 Saint Petersburg Beach FL 33706-2017 E-mail: jbradshaw@uniglobemultimedia.com.

BRADSHAW, LAURENCE JAMES, artist, educator; b. St. Paul, Kans., Sept. 21, 1945; s. James Laurence and Pauline Marie (Nunnink) B.; BFA, Pittsburg (Kans.) State U., 1967, MA, 1971; MFA, Ohio U., Athens, 1973. Designer, Union Oil Co., Honolulu, summer 1967; with script dept. CBS-TV, Hollywood, Calif., 1967-69; with prodn. dept. Writers Service, Hollywood, 1969; advt. mgr. J.C. Penney Co., Pittsburg, 1970-71; grad. asst. Pittsburg State U., 1970-71; teaching asst. Ohio U., 1971-73; instr. Akron (Ohio) Art Inst., summer 1973; prof. art U. Nebr., Omaha, 1973—; dir. univ. galleries, 1974-76; visual arts rep., designer Met. Arts Council, Omaha, 1976; juror various art exhbns. including Omaha Summer Arts Festival, 1996; art dir. Akron City Scholarship Program, 1973; one-man exhbns. include U. Nebr., 1974, Pitts. State U., 1974, Barton County C.C., Great Bend, Kans., 1987, Peru (Nebr.) State Coll., 1987; group exhbns. include Museo Nazionale dell' Accademia Italia, 1983, Centre Internat. D'Art Contemporian, Paris, 1985, Esta Robinson Gallery, N.Y.C., 1982, PaulVI Inst. Arts., Washington, 1988, Internat. Print Biennial, Triennial Continents, Europe, Asia, U.S., 1997—, numerous others. Mem. ednl. adv. bd. Collegiate Press, Agora Gallery, N.Y.C., Cath. Artists of 90s, ArtistAvenue Gallery, Art Max Internat. Gallery, Anderson O'Brien Gallery; nat. bd. advisors Am. Biog. Inst., 1985—, Internat. Religious Arts Program, 1987—. Recipient Spl. award Internat. Platform Assn., 1981, Sardinian Regional prize Internat. Invitational Biennial, Calgari, Italy, 1984, Honorable Mention award Internat. Evelyn Royce Gallery, Fall River Mills, Calif., 1995, First Place award Marxhausen Art Gallery, 1995, Marilyn Offutt Sullivan award excellence in tchg., 1997, 1st place Graphic, Coastal Nat. XI, 1997, Merit award Mont. Interpretations, 1997, Honor award 47th Nat. Contemporary Realism, 1997, Pauline Law Meml. award Nat. Art Club, N.Y.C., 1997; named Outstanding Young Alumnus Pitts. State U., 1982; recipient Gold medal for artistic merit Internat. Parliament, Salsamaggiore, Italy, 1983. Mem. Visual Artists & Galleries Assn. Office: U Nebr 327 Fine Arts Bldg Omaha NE 68182-0001

BRADSHAW, MURRAY CHARLES, musicologist, educator; b. Hinsdale, Ill., Sept. 25, 1930; s. Murray Andrew and Marie (Novak) Orth; m. Doris Hogg (div.); children: Jean Marie Orth, Murray Edward Orth, Thomas Andrew Orth; m. Sharon Ann Slitton, Apr. 19, 1997. MusM in Piano, Am. Conservatory Music, Chgo., 1955, MusM in Organ, 1958; PhD in Musicology, U. Chgo., 1969. Prof. UCLA, 1996—2004. Music critic Gary Post Tribune, Ind., 1962—64; chair dept. musicology UCLA, 1993—95. Author: The Origin of the Toccata, 1972, The Falsobordone, 1978, Francesco Severi, 1981, Giroiamo Diruta The Transylvanian, 1984, Giovanni Luca Conforti, 1985, Gabriele Fattorini, 1986, Emilio d' Cavalieri, 1990, Conforti, "Breve et facile", 1999; gen. editor: Musicological Studies and Documents and Miscellanea, 2000—; contbr. articles to profl. jours. Organist, choirmaster various chs., Ill., 1948—. With U.S. Army, 1954—56. Grantee, Am. Philos. Soc., 1987; Travel grantee, NEH, 1994. Mem.: Am. Guild Organists, Am. Musicol. Soc. (pres. local chpt. 1979—81), Ctr. Medieval and Renaissance Studies. Avocations: reading, walking, dance, bridge. Home: 17046 Burbank Blvd Apt 3 Encino CA 91316-1830 Office: UCLA Dept Musicology 405 Hilgard Ave Los Angeles CA 90095-9000 Personal E-mail: mbrads3486@aol.com.

BRADSHAW, OTABEL, retired primary school educator; b. Magnolia, Ark., Oct. 27, 1922; d. Grover Cleveland and Mae (Staggs) Peterson; AA, Magnolia A&M Coll., 1950; BS in Edn., So. State Coll., 1953; MS in Edn., Henderson State U., 1975; postgrad. U. Ark.; PhD, Kensington U., 1983; m. Charles Howard Bradshaw, Aug. 14, 1948; children: Susan Charla, Michael Howard. Tchr., English and drama Walkers Creek Schs., Taylor Ark., 1945-46, primary grades Locust Bayou Schs., Camden, Ark., 1946-52, 2d grade Fairview Sch., Camden, 1962-73; tchr. 1st grade Harmony Grove Sch., Camden, 1973-83, coordinator Title IX, gifted children and handicapped; tchr. East Camden Accelerated Sch., 1983-96, ret., 1996; cons. econ. edn. workshop U. Ark., Fayetteville. Life mem., sec., historian chmn. bicentennial com. PTA; active vol. fund-raising drives Am. Cancer Soc., Birth Defects Soc.; leader Missionary Soc., Camden 1st United Methodist Ch.; mem. Camden and Ouachita County Library bd., 1974-77; active Boys Club Aux. Recipient Disting. Alumni Award So. Ark. U., 1981, Valley Forge Tchr. medal and George Washington Honor medal Freedom Found., 1973; Achievement citation Kazanian Found., 1969, citation for ednl. leadership Pres. of U.S., 1976, 77; profl. achievement citation Internat. Paper Co. Found., 1981. Mem. Assn. Supervision and Curriculum Devel. (speaker San Francisco conf.), NEA, Ark. Edn. Assn. (speaker 1969), Harmony Grove Edn. Assn. (pres. 1978-79), Nat. Council for Social Studies (mem. sexism com.), Am. Assn. Adminstrs., Alpha Delta Kappa (outstanding mem.). Club: Tate Park Garden (sec.). Home: 3188 Roseman Rd Camden AR 71701-5533

BRADSHAW, RICHARD EUGENE, government relations, energy and environment consultant; b. Rocky Mount, NC, Jan. 15, 1950; s. Harvey Edmond and Grace Darling (Cowley) B.; m. Pamela Anne Lacey, June 3, 1989. BA in Polit. Sci., U. N.C., 1974; MA in Internat. Rels., East Carolina U., 1977; postgrad., U. S.C., 1977-78. Fgn. svc. officer U.S. Dept. of State, Washington, Paris, 1978-82; dir. rsch. North Am. Telecomm. Assn., Washington, 1982-83; R&D policy cons. Washington Nichibei Cons., Washington, 1983-87; asst. prof. George Mason U., Fairfax, Va., 1987-93; sr. S & T policy analyst NSF, Washington, 1988-92; v.p. North Atlantic Rsch., Inc., Washington, 1993-94; asst. to sec. IMF, Washington, 1995-96; spl. asst. to Sec. Energy U.S. Dept. Energy, Washington, 1997-2001; v.p. Columbus Newport LLC, Arlington, Va., 2001; ptnr. Dykema Gossett PLLC, Washington, 2001—04, Stirling Strategic Svcs. LLC, Washington, 2004—. Vis. fellow George Mason U., Arlington, Va., 1996-98. Policy coord. for sci. and tech. issues Bill Clinton for Pres. Campaign, 1992; campaign staff, Clinton/Gore '96; fin. com. staff, 1997 Presdl. Inaugural. Office: Stirling Strategic Svcs LLC 1120 G St NW Ste 830 Washington DC 20005 Office Phone: 202-783-0048. Business E-Mail: rbradshaws3@earthlink.net.

BRADSHAW, RICHARD JAMES, opera company director; b. Rugby, England, Apr. 26, 1944; s. Alfred James and Florence Mary B.; m. Diana Hepburne-Scott, June 30, 1977; children: Jenny Alexandra, James Edward Merton. BA with honors, U. London, 1965; LLD honoris causa (hon.), U. Toronto, 2003. Dir. Music at Higham, 1967-77, New London Ensemble, 1972-77; internat. freelance condr. symphonies & operas, 1972—; chorus dir. Glyndebourne Festival Opera, 1975-77; resident condr. San Francisco Opera, 1977-89; chief condr., head music Can Opera Co., Toronto, 1989—, artistic & music dir., 1994—, gen. dir., 1998—. Disting. vis. faculty music U. Toronto, 1999. Decorated chevalier Order Arts and Letters (France); Conducting fellow Royal Liverpool (Eng.) Philharm. Orch., 1972; assoc. fellow Massey Coll., U. Toronto, 1995—, sr. fellow 1998—; hon fellow, Royal Conservatory Music, 2002. Office: Can Opera Co 227 Front St E Toronto ON Canada M5A 1E8 Office Phone: 416-363-6671. Business E-Mail: rbradshaw@coc.ca.

BRADSHAW, RICHARD ROTHERWOOD, engineering executive; b. Phila., Sept. 12, 1916; s. Joseph Rotherwood and Rosanna (Jones) B.; m. Audrey Grace Skinn, Oct. 3, 1940 (dec. Jan. 1981); children— Linda M., Barbara A., Vicki; m. Chanin Hale, Feb. 14, 1986. BS, Calif. Inst. Tech., 1939; MS, U. So. Calif., 1950. Pres. Richard R. Bradshaw, Inc., Van Nuys, Calif., 1946—, pres. br. office Honolulu. Contbr. articles to tech. jours., Important works include, Disneyworld Hotels, Orlando, Fla., U.S. embassy, Warsaw, Poland, U.S. Exhbn. Bldg., Moscow USSR, Taraara Hotel, Tahiti, Gulf Life Bldg., Jacksonville, Fla., Los Angeles City Airport. Recipient Alfred Lindau award Am. Concrete Inst., 1968, many others for structural design. Mem. ASCE, Internat. Assn. Bridges and Structural Engring., Am. Seismol. Soc., Cons. Engrs. Assn., Internat. Assn. Thin Shells, Am. Concrete Inst., Am. Arbitration Assn. Office: Richard R Bradshaw Inc 17300 Ballinger St Northridge CA 91325-2005 Office Phone: 818-772-1810.

BRADSHAW, ROD ERIC, personnel consultant; b. Washington, May 29, 1957; s. Howard Vernon and Ona A. (Joyce) Bradshaw; m. Rebecca Lynn Bell, Mar. 20, 1974 (div. Jan. 1981); m. Pierrette A. Newman, Dec. 2, 2000. BS, U. Md., 1973; M in Human Resource Mgmt. with honors, Pepperdine U., 1981. Pers. cons. Career Devel. Corp., Atlanta, 1977-79, regional office mgr., 1979-82, prin., mgr., 1982-93; pres. Bradshaw & Assocs., 1993—. Envoy to attending countries Atlanta Olympic Games, 1996; asst. to pres. Christopher's Corner Cmty. Assn., Marietta, Ga., 1978—79, chmn. planning com., 1979; rep. Gov.'s Environ. Symposium Smithsonian Inst., 1971; fund raiser, charter mem. High Mus. Art, Atlanta, 1979—; sponsor, adv. bd. rep. Sch. Bd. Coop. Bus. Edn. Adv. Bd.; merit badge counselor Boy Scouts Am.; nominating com. bd. mem. Buckhead Bus. Assn., Young Bucks, Outstanding Ams.; dir. cmty. affairs Atlanta Games Legacy Orgn., 1998—2000; pres. bd. dirs. Jefferson Twp., 1998—; mem. Pub. Schs. Work Bd. Learning Adv. Bd.; v.p. Windsor Gate Governance. Named One of Outstanding Young Men of Am., Atlanta C. of C., 1985; recipient J.P. Rice Scholarship, 1971. Mem.: Am. Mgmt. Assn., Nat. Assn. Pers. Cons. (v.p. Windsor gate governance), Am. Legion, Internat. Platform Assn., Atlanta Ski Club, Delta Tau Delta, Omicron Delta Kappa. Republican. Avocation: Avocations: yachting, home improvement projects, sports, politics. Home: 5717 Windsor Gate Ln Fairfax VA 22030- Office: Bradshaw & Assocs 400 Galeria Pkwy Ste 1500 Atlanta GA 30339-

BRADSHAW, TERRY (TERRY PAXTON BRADSHAW), sports announcer, former professional football player; b. Shreveport, La., Sept. 2, 1948; m. Melissa Babich, 1972 (div. 1973); m. Jo Jo Starbuck, 1976 (div. 1983); m. Charlotte Hopkins, 1983 (div. 1999); children: Rachael, Erin. Ed., La. Tech. U. Quarteback Pitts. Steelers, 1970-84; sports analyst CBS Sports Inc NFL Today, 1987-94, Fox Sports, 1995—. Author, country and western singer, entertainer, appears in numerous commls., pub. speaker; author: It's Only a Game, 2001 (NY Times Best Selling Book), Keep It Simple, 2002 (NY Times Best Seller); actor: (films) Hooper, 1978, Smokey and the Bandit II, 1980, Cannonball Run, 1981, (voice) Robots, 2005, (TV Series) Home Team with Terry Bradshaw, 1997; special guest appearances include Hardcastle and McCormick, 1985, The Sinbad Show, 1994, Blossom, 1994, Married with Children, 1995, 1996, Everybody Loves Raymond, 1997, (voice) King of Hill, 2000, Malcolm in the Middle, 2002, 8 Simple Rules...for Dating My Teenage Daughter, 2002, The Simpsons, 2005, Mad TV, 2005, several talk shows and others. Named Most Valuable Player, Super Bowl XIII, 1978, Super Bowl XIV, 1979, Most Favorite TV Sportscaster TV Guide, 1999; named to Pro Bowl, 1978, 79; inducted into Pro Football Hall of Fame, 1989; recipient Emmy award for sports studio analyst, 2000, 02; named Father of Yr. L.A., 2000; recipient Star on Hollywood Walk of Fame, 2001. Achievements include being the quarterback in Super Bowl wins of 1974, 75, 78, 79. Office: care Fox Network PO Box 900 Beverly Hills CA 90213-0900 Address: 1925 N Pearson Ln Roanoke TX 76262-9018

BRADSTOCK, JOHN, advertising executive; Pres., N.Am., Pacific Am. DDB Needham Worldwide, Inc., NYC, 1994—, vice chmn., 2000. Office: DDB Needham Worldwide Inc 437 Madison Ave New York NY 10022-7001

BRADT, HALE VAN DORN, physicist, x-ray astronomer, educator; b. Colfax, Wash., Dec. 7, 1930; s. Wilber Elmore and Norma (Sparlin) B.; m. Dorothy Ann Haughey, July 19, 1958; children— Elizabeth, Dorothy Ann. AB in Music, Princeton U., 1952; PhD in Physics, MIT, 1961. Mem. dept. physics MIT, 1961—, prof., 1972-2001, prof. emeritus, 2001—; sci. investigator Small Astronomy Satellite, NASA, 1975-79; co-prin. investigator High Energy Astronomy Obs., 1977-79; prin. investigator Rossi x-ray timing explorer ASM, 1995—2001. Co-editor: X and Gamma Ray Astronomy, 1973, The Active X-ray Sky, 1998; mem. editl. bd. Astrophys. Jour. Letters, 1974-77; author: Astronomy Methods, 2004. With USNR, 1952—54. Recipient Exceptional Sci. Achievement medal NASA, 1978, Buechner Tchg. prize MIT, 1990, Outstanding Advisor award MIT, 2004. Mem. Am. Astron. Soc. (sec.-treas. high energy astrophysics divsn. 1973-75, chmn. 1981, Rossi prize HEAD divsn. 1999), Am. Phys. Soc., Internat. Astron. Union, Sigma Xi. Office: MIT 37-587 Cambridge MA 02139

BRADWAY, TERRY, professional sports team executive; Degree, Trenton (N.J.) State Coll. Asst. dir. player pers. Balt./Phila. Stars, 1983—85; scout N.Y. Giants, 1986—92; dir. coll. scouting Kans. City Chiefs, 1992—97, dir. player pers., 1997—2000, v.p. player pers., 2000—01; gen. mgr. N.Y. Jets, 2001—. Mailing: 1000 Fulton Ave Hempstead NY 11550

BRADY, ADELAIDE BURKS, public relations agency executive, giftware catalog executive; b. N.Y.C., June 27, 1926; d. Earl Victor and Audrey (Calvert) Burks; m. James Francis Brady, Jr., June 22, 1946 (div. 1953); 1 child, James Francis. BS, Boston U., 194. Exec. v.p. Media Enterprises, 1952—55; dir. group rels. Save the Children Fedn., N.Y.C., 1955-59; dir. pub. affairs divsn. Girl Scouts U.S.A., N.Y.C., 1959-69; pres. Comm. Internat., Inc., Washington, 1969-73, Burks Brady Comm., Washington, 1972—, Adelaide's Angel Shopper Catalog Inc., Wilton, Conn., 1976—. Exec. v.p. Arts in Parks Inc., Washington, 1971—. Past bd. dirs. Lenox Hill Hosp., N.Y.C., Achievement Rewards for Coll. Scientists Found.; pres. Animal Lovers Inc. Decorated comdr. Order of St. John of Jerusalem (Eng.); recipient Silver Reel award for film The Children of Now, Save the Children Fedn. Mem. NAFE, NEA, AAUW, Nat. Assn. Women Bus. Owners, Pub. Rels. Soc. Am., Am. Women in Radio and TV, Nat. Ednl. Broadcasters Assn., Am. Soc. Profl. and Exec. Women, Women Execs. in Pub. Rels., N.Y. Press Women, Nat. Fedn. Press Women (state pres.),Women's Econ. Roundtable, DAR, Capitol Hill Club (Washington), Yacht and Country Club (Fla.), MDW Officers Club (Washington). Republican. Episcopalian. also: Yacht Country Club 3664 SE Fairway E Stuart FL 34997-6116 Office: 785 Park Ave New York NY 10021-3552

BRADY, ANDREA RASSIN, marketing executive; b. Cleve., May 21, 1963; d. Julius and Frances Balat Rassin; m. Edward L. Brady, Nov. 10, 1990; 1 child, Natalie Andrea. BS in Econs., BA in Honors English, U. Pa., 1985. Asst. brand mgr. Procter and Gamble, Cin., 1985—89; account supr. Stockton.West.Burkhardt, Cin., 1989—92; pres. The Mktg. Shop Consultants, Milford, Ohio, 1993—, IdeaSmart Devel. Svc., Milford, 2000—; dir. of mktg. GoodSports for Life, Covington, Ky., 2002—03. Spkr. to various profl. orgns. and schs., Cin., 2003—. Chair comm. com. Citizens for Excellent Schs., Milford, 2003—05; mem. bus. adv. com. Milford Schs., 2003—04; pres. Cin. Shakespeare Festival, 1995—97, Inventor's Coun. of Cin., 2001. Mem.: Ctrl. Ky. Inventor's Assn., Inventor's Coun. of Cin. (pres. 2001—). Achievements include patents in field; patents pending for. Avocations: travel, writing. Office Phone: 513-831-0664. Office Fax: 513-831-6328.

BRADY, BRUCE MORGAN, lawyer; b. Oakland, Calif., Oct. 9, 1950; s. Alfred Foster and Anne Felton (Hazlewood) B.; m. Barbara Jean Gehrett, June 8, 1974; children: Morgan G., Evan L.G. BA in Anthropology, Columbia Coll., 1972; JD, Boston U., 1975. Asst. dist. atty. King's County Dist. Atty., Bklyn., 1975-81, dep. chief criminal ct., 1980-81; assoc. Gabrini & Scher, P.C., N.Y.C., 1981-84, ptnr., 1984-90; sr. ptnr. Callan, Koster, Brady, & Brennan, LLP, N.Y.C., 1990—. Legal adv., vice-chmn. Children's Aid & Family Svcs., Paramus, N.J., 1990—; pres. Ridgewood (N.J.) Lacrosse Assn., 1993-99. Mem. N.Y. State Trial Lawyers Assn., N.Y.C. Med. Def. Bar Assn. (charter mem.). Avocations: golf, snow sports, theater, personal computing. Office: Callan Koster Brady & Brennan LLP 1 Whitehall St New York NY 10004-2109 E-mail: bbrady@ckbblaw.com.

BRADY, CHRISTINE ELLEN, education coordinator; b. Manchester, NH, Feb. 23, 1943; d. George Lewis and Lucy Eleanor (Broderick) B. BA in English, Manhattanville Coll., 1964; MA in English, U. Pa., 1966; EdD in Curriculum and Instrn., No. Ariz. U., 1987. Cert. tchr., NY, Ariz., Mass.; cert. adminstr., NY, Ariz. English instr. Bryn Mawr (Pa.) Coll., 1966-67; lang. arts tchr. Tuba City (Ariz.) H.S., 1978-82; asst. dir. Reading/Learning Ctr., Flagstaff, Ariz., 1982-83; supervisory home living specialist Apache Agy. Dept. Indian Affairs, Whiteriver, Ariz., 1983-85; English and edn. lectr. Cortland (NY) State Coll., 1988-89; asst. dir. Tchr. Ctr. Broome County, Binghamton, NY, 1990-91; English instr. Broome C.C., Binghamton, 1989-91; labor svc. rep. NY State Dept. Labor, Ithaca, 1992-94; Title I lang. arts tchr. Highland Residential Ctr. NY State Office Children and Family Svcs., Highland, 1994-98, edn. coord. S.I. Residential Ctr., 1998—2003; edn. supr. Arthur Kill Correctional Facility NY State Dept. Corrections, S.I., 2003—. Adj. faculty Met. Coll. of N.Y., 2004—. Mem.: Phi Delta Kappa (exec. bd. 1998). Office: Arthur Kill Correctional Facility NY State Dept Correctional Svcs Staten Island NY 10309 Office Phone: 718-356-7333 ext. 4330. E-mail: bradyceb@aol.com.

BRADY, DARLENE ANN, artist, designer; b. Ft. Hood, Tex., Aug. 4, 1951; d. Egbert Leo, Jr. and Eleanor Rose Marie (Wollenhaupt) B.; m. Mark M. English, 1984. BFA summa cum laude, Ohio U., 1976; MLS summa cum laude, U. Pitts, 1978, MA summa cum laude, 1980; MS in Architecture summa cum laude, U. Cin., 1986; MArch Carnegie-Mellon U., 1990. Painter stained glass artist, 1976—; ptnr. Archi-Textures, Cin., 1984—; vis. asst. prof. design U. Cin., 1984-85, grad. and teaching asst. U. Pitts., 1977-80; asst. prof. architecture Ball State U., 1993—; vis. adj. 1991; fine arts bibliographer Tulane U., 1981-83; guest curator of stained glass from Mellon Collection, U. Pitts., 1979, intern Frick Library, 1978; instr. Ohio U., winter 1976, curator B.F.A. Grad. Exhibit, 1976, asst. curator fine arts slide library, 1973-77; design cons. Procter & Gamble Miami Valley Labs., 1987-88; adj. faculty Art Acad. of Cin., 2003-04, vis. prof. U. Ill. Urbana, Champaign, 1996-98, asst. prof. arch. Ball State U., 1993-95, adj. prof.Chgo. Sch. of Architecture, U. Ill, 1991. Group exhbns. include Fest for All '81, Broussard Galleries, Baton Rouge, 1981, Assocs. Exhibit, Stained Glass Assn. Am., 1980-84, Glass on Holiday, Gazebo Gallery, Gatlinburg, Tenn., 1981, Ark.-La.-Tex. Glass Invitational, La. Tech. U. Art Gallery, 1981, Nat. Exhbn., Royal Ont. Mus., Toronto (best use of antique glass award), 1985, "Vitraux des U.S.A." Micheline Loire Gallery, Chartres, France, 1985, Corning Mus. of Glass, 1987; commns. include stained glass panel Athens Humane Soc., 1976, Athens Landscape painting for McDonald's Restaurant, 1976, Transitions stained glass windows Tompson residence, Athens, 1977. La. Cypress stained glass panels entrance door Hainesworth residence, Ruston, La., 1979, stained glass triptych Marybell Holstead residence, Ruston, 1981, solar room with 7 stained glass panels wollenhaupt residence, Lima, Ohio, 1984, skylight Union Bank, Columbus, Ind., 1985, others. Author: Stained Glass Index, 1906-77, 1979; Stained Glass: A Guide to Information Sources, 1980; Le Corbusier: An Annotated Bibliography, 1985; contbg. editor Architecture Week, 2000-02. Contbr. articles to profl. jours. Grantee Graham Found., Ball State U.; recipient Scholastic Merit award AIA. Scholar Phi Kappa Phi, 1977, J.W. Morgan, 1977, Deans fall 1978, Provost, 1978. Mem. Glass Arts Soc., Stained Glass Assn. Am. (assoc., rep. 1980-81), Beta Phi Mu, Phi Kappa Phi. Home: 1665 Pullan Ave Cincinnati OH 45223-2049

BRADY, DONNA ELIZABETH, performing company executive; b. Rockville Centre, N.J., Nov. 17, 1955; d. Frank A. and Dorothy Eleanor (Munden) B. BA, Knox Coll., 1976. Stage mgr., lighting designer Dance Edn. Svcs., Inc., Northport, NY, 1973-86; coord. Am. Dance Festival Tech. Assistance Project, N.Y.C., 1981-85; exec. dir. Performing Arts Resources, Inc., N.Y.C., 1986—, also pres., bd. dirs.; fiscal/mktg. specialist Monterey Bay Aviation, 2002—05, dir. sales and mktg., 2005—. Project staff Tech. Assistance Group/TAG Found., Ltd., N.Y.C., 1980-81; treas. N.Y. Tech. Assistance Providers Network, 1995, 96, co-chair 1997; lighting designer, stage mgr. Solomons Co. Dance, 1978-81; asst. stage mgr. Pilobolus, 1978. Bd. dirs. Artists Cmty. Fed. Credit Union, 1992-2001, sec., 1993-2000; bd. dirs., treas. Acanthus Dance, 1997—. Mem. Am. Dance Guild (bd. dirs. 1980-87, treas. 1983-87). E-mail: dbradypar@aol.com.

BRADY, EDWARD THOMAS, state supreme court justice; b. Bklyn., Nov. 1, 1943; s. Thomas and Virginia (Briggs) Brady; m. Dianne Downing; children: Thomas Robert, Ryan Ashley. Grad., Officer Candidate Sch., 1966; BA in Criminal Justice, U. Nebr., 1972; MA in Criminal Justice, CUNY, 1977; JD, U. Calif., San Diego, 1978. Bar: N.C., Ga., D.C., (U.S. Supreme Ct.), (U.S. Ct. Appeals (4th cir.)), (U.S. Ct. Appeals (5th cir.)), (U.S. Ct. Appeals (D.C. cir.)), (U.S. Army Ct. Mil. Rev.), (U.S. Ct. Mil. Appeals). Enlisted pvt. US Army, 1965; ret. as col. USAR, 1995; pvt. practice in law Fayetteville, NC, 1978—; spl. agt., criminal investigator Dept. Treas., Bur. Alcohol, Tobacco and Firearms; assoc. justice NC Supreme Ct., Raleigh, 2002—. Decorated DFC, Bronze Star medal, Air Medal with Valor Device for heroism and 2d-18th oak leaf cluster, Vietnam Cross of Gallantry with Bronze Star. Office: Justice Bldg PO Box 1841 Raleigh NC 27602

BRADY, EDWARD THOMAS, JR., lawyer, writer; b. Somerville, Mass., May 11, 1940; s. Edward Thomas Brady and Marie Florence Cashman; m. Margaret Alice Linehan, Oct. 28, 1963 (div. Dec. 31, 1979); children: Sharon Lynn, Keith Andrew. BA in Bus Adminstrn., Northeastern U., 1963; JD, Suffolk U. Law Sch., 1968. Chartered Property Casualty Underwriter The Am. Inst. of Property and Liability Underwriters, Inc. PA, 1971, Chartered Life Underwriter The Am. Coll., PA, 1977. Author Self-Employed Free Lance Author, Winchester, Mass., 2001—; atty. Self-employed Sole Practioner, Somerville, Mass., 1979—2001; gen. counsel Shelby Mut. Life Ins. Co., Shelby, Ohio, 1977—79; atty., govt. affairs and law, property-casualty dept. Travelers Ins. Co., Hartford, Conn., 1972—76; trial atty. Continental Ins. Co., Boston, Mass., 1969—72; underwriter Lumber Mut. Fire Ins. Co., Boston, Mass., 1962—67. Mem. Mass. Acad. of Trial Attys, Boston, 1984—99, ATLA, Washington, 1985—95, Mass. Trial Lawyers Assn., Boston, 1970—82. Author: (book - humorous memoir) Last In My Class (Cert., 2002), (short stories) Good Grief! About Relationships. And Other Short Stories That Make You Wish They Were Shorter (Cert., 2004), (novels) Georgie! My Georgie! The First Greek-American To Win The Medal Of Honor (Summer 2005 Scheduled Publ.), (guest columnist) Winchester Star - local Newspaper - one of 85 local town newspapers owned by Community News Corporation of Massascusetts. Tchr. Ch., Winchester, Woburn and Somerville, Mass., 1965—2001; coach Little League, Avon, Conn., 1972—76. Recipient Selected to represent State of Mass. in Nat. Track Meet at Madison Sq. Garden in NYC - 60 yard dash event., Mass. Track Coaches Assn., 1957, MVP - H.S. Baseball Team, Tri-Captain H.S. Football Team, Coaches and Teammates, respectively., 1957 -1958, Outstanding Toastmaster (Pub. Speaking) award, Toastmasters Internat., Boston, MA, 1971; scholar Coll., Athletic, for Track, Football and Baseball, Coaches and U., 1958 to 1961. Mem.: Veterans of Fgn. War Posts (hon.; non-serving mem. 2003—05). Roman Catholic. Avocations: reading, writing, walking, music, traveling. Office Phone: 781-721-4694. Personal E-mail: ponythruns@aol.com.

BRADY, HELEN JENNIFER, language educator; b. Ottawa, Ont., Can., Mar. 7, 1952; came to U.S., 1984; d. Patrick Edward Hearty and Margaret Jean (Nesbitt) B. BA, U. Toronto, 1974; MA, Princeton (N.J.) U., 1977, PhD in English Lit., 1980. Asst. prof. U. Toronto, 1980-82; instr. Marianopolis Coll., Montreal, Que., Can., 1983; asst. prof. Rhodes Coll., Memphis, 1984-88, assoc. prof., 1988—, Charles R. Glover chair English studies, 1991. Editor: (with W.H. Herendeen) Ben Jonson's 1616 Folio, 1991, (with Earl Miner) Literary Transmission and Authority: Dryden and Other Writers, 1993. Vice pres. Victoria U. Alumni Assn., Toronto, 1980-81; co-pres. Victoria U. Alumni Assn./U. Toronto, 1981-82. Princeton U. fellow, 1974-75; Can. Coun. fellow, 1975-79; Lincoln G. Hutton scholar Victoria U., 1973; recipient Jolliffe Gold medal Victoria U., 1974, Clarence Day award for outstanding teaching, 1993. Mem. Modern Lang. Assn. Office: Rhodes Coll 2000 N Parkway Memphis TN 38112-1690

BRADY, JAMES JOSEPH, labor arbitrator; b. Jersey City, Mar. 2, 1936; s. James and Anna (Shine) B.; m. Sheila Hartney, July 24, 1965; children: Matthew, Michael, James. BA, U. Notre Dame, 1959, MA in Econs., 1963, PhD in Econs., 1969. Profl. baseball player Detroit Tigers, 1955-60; asst. prof. econs. Ind. U., South Bend, 1965-69; asst. prof., assoc. prof., prof. econs. Old Dominion U., Norfolk, Va., 1969-79; dean Coll. Arts and Scis. Jacksonville (Fla.) U., 1979-83, dean Coll. Bus., 1983-84, v.p. acad. affairs, 1984-88, pres.-elect, 1988-89, pres., 1989-95, prof. econs., 1995—. Spl. magistrate Fla. Pub. Employees Rels. Commn., Tallahassee, 1985—; pvt. labor cons., Jacksonville, 1978-88; mem. Fed. Mediation and Conciliation Svc. Labor Panel, 1985—; perm. arbitrator State Fla. dept. mgmt. svcs., 1999— Author: Arbitration Principles: Layoffs, 1989; co-author: Transportation Noise Pollution, 1970. With U.S. Army, 1959-61. NASA grantee, Norfolk, Va., 1970. Mem. Am. Arbitration Assn. (labor arbitrator 1965—, comml. arbitrator 1987-89), Indsl. Rels. Rsch. Assn., Soc. Profls. in Dispute Resolution, Jacksonville C. of C. (bd. dirs. 1989—). Avocations: fishing, cooking, tennis. Home: 1072 Meadow View Ln Saint Augustine FL 32092-1055 E-mail: leftybrady@sjcgcc.com.

BRADY, JAMES WINSTON, commentator, writer, editor; b. NYC, Nov. 15, 1928; s. James Thomas and Marguerite Claire (Winston) B.; m. Florence Kelly, Apr. 12, 1958; children: Fiona, Susan. BA, Manhattan Coll., 1950. Pub. Women's Wear Daily, N.Y.C., 1964-71; editor, pub. Harper's Bazaar, N.Y.C., 1971-72; editor N.Y. mag., N.Y.C., 1977; syndicated columnist N.Y. Post, N.Y.C., 1980-83; news commentator WCBS-TV, N.Y.C., 1981-87; editor-at-large Advt. Age, N.Y.C., 1977—. Author: Superchic, 1974, Paris One, 1976, Nielsen's Children, 1978, The Press Lord, 1981, Holy Wars, 1983, Designs, 1986, The Coldest War, 1990, Fashion Show, 1992, The House That Ate the Hamptons, 2000, Warning of War: A Novel of the North China Marines, 2002, The Marines of Autumn: A Novel of the Korean War, 2000, The Marine: A Novel of War from Guadalcanal to Korea, 2003, The Scariest Place in the World: A Marine Returns to North Korea, 2005; weekly columnist Parade mag., NYC, 1986— . Served to 1st lt. USMC, 1951-52. Recipient Emmy award N.Y. TV Acad., 1975 Mem.: University (N.Y.C.). Democrat. Roman Catholic. Home: PO Box 1584 East Hampton NY 11937-0704 Office: Advt Age 220 E 42nd St New York NY 10017-5806 Business E-Mail: in_step_with@parade.com.*

BRADY, JEAN STEIN, retired librarian; b. Concord, Mass., Nov. 4, 1930; d. Walfred and Mary Selina (Jussila) Stein; m. Maurice Goodrich Klein, Feb. 22, 1957 (div. 1982); 1 child, Audrey Elaine; m. Lawrence Kevin Brady, Oct. 15, 1988. BS, Simmons Coll., 1952; cert. d'Etudes, U. Grenoble, France, 1954; MA, Northwestern U., 1957. Cert. pub. libr., N.Y. Sr. libr. N.Y. Pub. Libr., 1952-53, 57-60; cataloger Columbia U., N.Y.C., 1954-55; reference asst. Northwestern U., Evanston, Ill., 1955-57; cataloger U. W.Va., Morgantown, 1960-61; book reviewer ALA, Chgo., 1961-63; sr. cataloger Cleve. Pub. Libr., 1964-70; sr. catalog libr. Yale U. Libr., New Haven, Conn., 1970-92; cataloger Columbia U., N.Y.C., 1993-95; ret., 1995. Revision asst. Bibliographical Guide to Romance Langs. and Lits., 1956-57; reviewer: Booklist and Subscription Books Bulletin, 1961-63. Mem. Simmons Coll. Club of Cape Cod. Democrat. Episcopalian. Avocations: reading, travel, walking, swimming.

BRADY, JOHN PATRICK, JR., electronics educator, consultant; b. Newark, Mar. 20, 1929; s. John Patrick and Madeleine Mary (Atno) B.; m. Mary Coop, May 1, 1954; children: Peter, John P., Madeleine, Dennis, Mary G. BSEE, MIT, 1952, MSEE, 1953. Registered profl. engr., Mass. Sect. mgr. Hewlett-Packard Co., Waltham, Mass., 1956—67; v.p. engring. John Fluke Mfg. Co., Inc., Mountlake Terrace, Wash., 1967—73, Dana Labs., Irvine, Calif., 1973—77; mgr. engring., tech. advisor to gen. mgr. Metron Corp., Upland, Calif., 1977—78; ptnr. Resource Assocs., Newport Beach, Calif., 1978—86; prof. electronics Orange Coast Coll., Costa Mesa, Calif., 1977—99, emeritus, 1999, faculty fellow, dean tech., 1983—84, chmn. electronics tech. dept., 1994—96, chmn. acad. rank com., 1988—98. Instr. computers and elec. engring. Calif. State U., Long Beach, 1982-84; dir. measurement sci. conf. MIT, L.A., 1982-83. Contbr. articles to profl. jours. Mem. evaluation team Accrediting Commn. for Cmty. and Jr. Colls., 1982-92; mem. blue ribbon adv. com. on oversees tech. transfer U.S. Dept. of Commerce, 1974-76. With USN, 1946-48. Mem. Eta Kappa Nu, Tau Beta Pi, Sigma Xi. Office: Orange Coast Coll Costa Mesa CA 92626

BRADY, JONATHAN RICHARD, band director; b. Key West, Fla., Sept. 25, 1970; s. Barbara Ann and William George Hayes; m. Cynthia Jean Pollard, June 24, 2000. B.Mus.Edn., Winthrop U., Rock Hill, S.C., 1993; MusM in Performance, Winthrop U., 1995. Band dir. Buford H.S., Lancaster, SC, 1995—99, Battery Creek H.S., Beaufort, SC, 1999—2001, Batesburg-Leesville H.S., Batesburg-Leesville, SC, 2001—. Mem.: Music Educator's Nat. Conf. (assoc.), S.C. Band Dirs. Assn. (assoc.; marching com. mem. 2004), Omicron Delta Kappa (life), Pi Kappa Lambda (life), Phi Kappa Phi (life), Pi Kappa Phi (life). Independent. Avocations: fishing, stock car racing. Home: 178 Siddington Way Lexington SC 29073 Office: Batesburg-Leesville High School 600 Summerland Ave Batesburg-Leesville SC 29006 Office Phone: 803-532-1563. Personal E-mail: jbrady2@sc.rr.com. E-mail: jbrady@lex3.k12.sc.us.

BRADY, JOSEPH VINCENT, behavioral biologist, educator; b. N.Y.C., Mar. 28, 1922; s. James J. and Mary F. (Michaelson) B.; m. Nancy Heaton; children: Barbara Ann, Michael Joseph, Kathleen Theresa, Nancy Marie, Joanne Cecelia, Jessica Lea, Margaret Mary. BS, Fordham U., 1943; PhD, U. Chgo., 1951. Dep. dir. div. neuropsychiatry Walter Reed Inst. Research, 1951-71; prof. psychology U. Md., 1955-69; prof. behavioral biology Johns Hopkins Sch. Medicine, Balt., 1967—, prof. neurosci., 1982—; dir. Behavioral Biology Rsch. Ctr. Johns Hopkins U., Balt., 1992—; pres., chmn. bd. trustees Inst. for Behavior Resources, Balt., 1988—. Cons. pres. sci. adv. com. Merck Inst. for Therapeutic Rsch., U.S. Army Med. Rsch. and Devel. Command, NASA; assoc. chmn. Nat. Commn. for Protection Human Subjects of Biomed. and Behavioral Rsch., 1974-79; chmn. sci. adv. com. New Eng. Regional Primate Rsch. Ctr., Harvard Med. Sch., Boston, com. on problems of drug dependence NRC, com. on space biology and medicine, com. on toxicology NAS; mem. adv. com. NASA/NIH; mem. space medicine com. NAS Inst. Medicine. Contbr. articles to profl. jours. Col. M.C., U.S. Army. Fellow AAAS, APA (div. pres.), Am. Coll. Neuro-psychopharmacology, Coll. Problems Drug Dependence (pres.), Acad. Behavioral Med. Rsch.; mem. Eastern Psychol. Assn. (pres.), Soc. Behavioral Medicine (pres.), Pavlovian Soc. (pres.), Behavioral Pharmacology Soc. (pres.), Am. Soc. Pharmacology and Exptl. Therapeutics, Nat. Space Biomedical Rsch. Inst., Federated Am. Socs. Exptl. Biology. Home: Unit 610 1000 Fell St Baltimore MD 21231-3554 Office: Johns Hopkins U Behavioral Biology Rsch Ctr 5510 Nathan Shock Dr Baltimore MD 21224-6823 Office Phone: 410-550-2779. Business E-Mail: jvb@jhmi.edu.

BRADY, KATHLEEN DEMING, retired psychologist, physical therapist, educator; b. Enid, Okla., Jan. 8, 1920; d. Leon J. and Lola Faye (Hendryx) Deming; m. Roland Anderson (dec.); children: Virginia, Leon; m. Frederick S. Brady (dec. Jan. 1999); 1 child, Faye Lillian Burnaman. Student, William & Mary Coll., 1937-38, Arts Student League, NYC, 1938-39; BS cum laude, NYU, 1943; student, Pennsylvania U., 1945, Wayne State U., 1957-59; MA in Exceptional Edn., U. Fla., 1964, EdD in Psychology and Exceptional Edn., 1967. Registered Occupational Therapist, Phila., 1945; Cert. Sch. Psychologist, Occupational Therapist, Guidance. Art tchr., N.Y., Ohio and Mich.; occupational therapist U.S. Army Hosp., 1944-45; dir. occupational therapy Perry Point V.A. Hosp., 1946-55; coord. exceptional edn. program Brevard County, Fla., 1960-64; dir. guidence and counseling Satellite H.S., Brevard County, Fla., 1965-68; dir. guidence Brevard County, 1968-69; dir. guidance and counseling Orange County, 1969; psychologist Learning Disability Ctr. and Gateway Sch., 1970-72; dir. Pupil Personnel Services, High Point, N.C., 1972-73; psychologist Exceptional Edn. Program, Orlando, Fla., 1973-78; dir. Bureau Indian Affairs Special Edn. Program, Washington, 1978-80; psychologist Western Navajo Agency, Tuba City, Ariz., B.I.A. Eastern Navajo, 1983. Tchr. Brevard C.C. Fla., 1964-68, U. Fla. Gainesville, Fla., 1966-68, Fla. Ctrl. U. Orlando, 1969, U. So. Fla. Tampa, Fla., 1971-72, Rollins Coll. Orlando, 1976-77. Author: (booklet on VA rsch.) Occupational Therapy, 1950, Reflections Poems and Pictures, 2001, Renaissance Journey Poetry Book. Pres. Brevard County Coun. Exceptional Children, Brevard County Guidance Assn.; vol., greeter program James A. Haley VA Hosp. Scholar United Cerebral Palsy, U. Fla.; recipient Outstanding Achievement award Veterans Adminstrn. Mem. Nat. Assn. State Dirs. Special Edn. Home: Tampa, Fla. Died June 25, 2005.

BRADY, KEVIN, congressman; b. Vermillion, S.D., Apr. 11, 1955; m. Cathy Brady. BS, Univ. S.D., 1990. Mem. Tex. House of Reps., 1990-96, U.S. Congress from 8th Tex. dist., 1997—; mem. ways and means com. Active Saints Simon and Jude Cath. Ch. Mem.: Rotary. Republican. Office: 428 Cannon Bldg Washington DC 20515-4308*

BRADY, LUTHER W., JR., radiologist, educator; b. Rocky Mount, NC, Oct. 20, 1925; s. Luther W. and Gladys B. AA, George Washington U., 1944, AB, 1946, MD, 1948, DFA (hon.), 1988, Georgetown U., 1988; DSc (hon.), Lehigh U., 1990; MD (hon.), Toyama U., Japan, 1996; D (hon.), U. Heidelberg, Germany, 1997. Diplomate Am. Bd. Radiology (treas. 1980-82, v.p. 1982-84, pres. 1984-86). Intern Jefferson Med. Coll. Hosp., Phila., 1948-50, resident in radiology, 1954-55; resident radiology Hosp. U. Pa., Phila., 1955-56; fellow Nat. Cancer Inst., 1954-57; practice medicine, specializing in radiation oncology Phila. Asst. instr. radiology Jefferson Med. Coll. Hosp., 1954-55, U. Pa., Phila., 1955, instr., 1956-57, assoc. radiology, 1957-59; asst. prof. radiology Coll. of Physicians and Surgeons, Columbia U., NYC, summer, 1959; assoc. prof. radiology Hahnemann Med. Coll. and Hosp., Phila., 1959-62, prof., 1963—97, Disting. Univ. prof., 1997--, chmn. dept. radiation oncology, 1970—97; asst. prof. radiology Harvard Med. Sch., Boston, 1962-63; mem. med. radiation adv. com. Bur. Radiation Health, HEW, 1971-74; cons. radiation therapy various hosp.; mem. US del. to Interam. Congress Radiology, 1975, Internat. Congress of Radiology, 1981; sec. gen. Internat. Congress Radiology, 1985; med. adv. radiation therapy, med. affairs com., 1984-97; dir. Pa. Blue Shield, Camp Hill; chair Pa. Cancer Control Bd., 1989-97. Author: Tumors of the Nervous System, 1975, Cancer of the Lung, Clinical Applications of the Electron Beam; editor Cancer Clin. Trials (Am. Jour. Clin. Oncology), (with C. Perez) Principles and Practice of Radiation Oncology; editorial bd. Cancer; assoc. editor: Gynecologic Oncology, Am. Jour. Roentgenology, Cancer Research; sr. editor: Internat. Jour. Radiol. Oncology; contbr. articles on radiation therapy to profl. jour. Bd. dirs. Assn. Artists Equity of Phila., Welcome House, 1974-94, Settlement Music Sch., 1973—, Phila. Art Alliance, 1977-84; mem. oriental art com., trustee Phila. Mus. Art, 1974—, chmn. friends exec. com., 1968-72, mem. print, contemporary art and Indian art coms., 1974—; trustee Fleisher Art Meml., 1997-, Founders Award, 2003; trustee Curtis Inst. Music, 1997-, The Phillips Collection, 2003. Served to lt. M.C. USN, 1950-54. Recipient Grubbe award Chgo. Radiol. Soc., 1977, Gold medal Gilbert Fletcher Soc., 1984, Albert Soiland Gold medal U. So. Calif., 1985, del Regato Gold medal, 1986, Disting. Alumni award George Washington U., 1991, Padro Pio medal, 1993. Fellow Am. Coll. Radiology (Gold medal 1983); mem. AMA (Gold medal Disting. Svc. award 1999, Am. Roentgen Ray Soc., Am. Radium Soc. (Gold medal 1981), Am. Cancer Soc., Am. Fedn. Clin. Rsch., Am. Bd. Radiology, Am. Soc. Clin. Oncology, Am. Coll. Radiation Oncology (Gold medal 1996), Am. Soc. for Therapeutic Radiology and Oncology (Gold medal 1987), Am. Assn. for Cancer Rsch., Soc. Chmn. Acad. Radiation Oncology Program, Soc. Chmn. Acad. Radiology Dept., Assn. Pendergrass Fellows, Internat. Soc. for Radiation Oncology, Internat. Skeletal Soc., Internat. Club Radiotherapists, James Ewing Soc., Radiation Rsch. Soc., Soc. Surg. Oncology, Assn. Univ. Radiologists, Radiation Rsch. Soc., Radiol. Soc. N.Am. (Gold medal 1989), Del. Med. Soc., Med. Soc. State Pa., Pa. Radiol. Soc., Phila. County Med. Soc.(Stristmater award 1999), Phila. Roentgen Ray Soc. Clubs: Merion Cricket; Racquet, Union League (Phila.), Phila., Peale. Office: 230 N Broad St Philadelphia PA 19102-1121 also: Hahnemann U Hosp Broad & Vine MS-200 Philadelphia PA 19102 Office Phone: 215-762-1998. E-mail: Lbrady@drexelmed.edu.

BRADY, M. JANE, state attorney general; b. Wilmington, Del., Jan. 11, 1951; m. Michael Neal. BA, U. Del., 1973; JD, Villanova U., 1976. Dep. atty. gen. Wilmington and Kent County, 1977—90; chief prosecutor Sussex County, 1987—90; solo law practice, 1990—94; atty. gen. State of Del., Wilmington, 1994—. Bd. dirs. Nat. Dist. Attys. Assn., Kent/Sussex Industries. Past chair Rep Attys. Gen. Assn.; bd. dirs. Nat. Org. Victim Assistance; founder KINfolk; bd. dirs. Del. Children's Trust Fund; advisory bd. Big Bros./Big Sisters Sussex County. Named Delaware's Top Fraud Fighter, AARP Delaware, 1998. Mem.: Nat. Assn. Attys. Gen. (exec. com.). Republican. Office: Office of Atty Gen Carvel State Office Bldg 820 N French St Wilmington DE 19801-3509 E-mail: jbrady@state.de.us.

BRADY, MARY ROLFES, music educator; b. St. Louis, Nov. 26, 1933; d. William Henry and Helen Dorothy (Slavick) Rolfes; m. Donald Sheridan Brady, Aug. 29, 1953; children: Joseph William, Mark David, Douglas Sheridan, John Rolfes, Todd Christopher. Student, Stanford U., 1951—54, UCLA, 1967, U. So. Calif., 1972—73; pvt. studies with, Roxanna Byers, Dorothy Desmond, and Rudolph Ganz. Pvt. piano tchr., L.A., 1955—; TV and radio performer. Pres. Jr. Philharm. Com. L.A., 1975-76; legis. coord., bd. dirs. Philharm. Affiliates, L.A., 1978-80. Life mem. Good Samaritan Hosp., St. Vincent Med. Ctr., L.A.; trustee St. Francis Med. Ctr., 1984-88; bd. dirs. Hollygrove-L.A. Orphans Home, Inc. Mem. Am. Coll. Musicians Club, Stanford Women's Club (past bd. dirs., pres. L.A. chpt. 1977—), The Muses, Springs Country Club.

BRADY, PATRICIA G., volunteer; b. Lafayette, La., Dec. 4, 1933; d. Samuel Cooper and Camille Cora (Donlon) Grunewald; m. Robert Stratton Brady, Oct. 8, 1960; children: Sheila K. Barth, Michael S., Mary F. DeVerter. Student, U. Tex., 1951—53, U. Madrid, 1954—55; BS in Fgn. Svc., Georgetown U., 1956, MA, 1961. Bibliographer Hispanic Found. Libr. Congress, Washington, 1956—58, rsch. asst. Hispanic Law divsn., 1958—61; rep. Springfield dist. Fairfax County Group Residentiall Facilities Commn., Va., 1981—90; pres. LWV (nat. capital area), Washington, 1989—91; dir. LWV U.S., Washington, 1992—96, liaison to ABA, 1997—; mem. adv. com. to ABA Commn. on 21st Century Judiciary, 2002—03; mem. ABA Am. Jury Project, 2004—, ABA Coalition for Justice Alliance, 2005—. Mem. The Constitution Project, ABA Coalition for Justice, 1999—2003. Vice chair Fairfax County Bicentennial Commn., 1987-91; Va. coord. Belfast Children's Summer Program, Gaithersburg, Md., 1986-93. Recipient Disting. Svc. award, Nat. Ctr. State Cts., 2004. Roman Catholic. Avocations: reading, needlecrafts. Office: LWV US 1730 M St NW Ste 1000 Washington DC 20036-4508

BRADY, PATRICK, language educator, writer; b. Broken Hill, New South Wales, Australia, Oct. 27, 1933; came to U.S., 1969; naturalized, 1993; s. Patrick and Frances (Minahan) B. BA with first class honors, U. Sydney, Australia, 1953-56; D., Sorbonne, 1960. Asst. in English Poitiers (France) Tchr.'s Coll., 1957-58; lectr. in English U. Lille (France), 1959-60; lectr. in French U. Melbourne (Australia), 1961-64; sr. lectr. U. Queensland, Brisbane, Australia, 1964-68, reader in French, 1968; assoc. prof. Fla. State U., Tallahassee, 1969-72; prof. French Rice U., Houston, 1972-83, Favrot prof. French, 1983-88; Shumway chair of excellence U. Tenn., Knoxville, 1988—. Vis. prof. comparative lit. Harvard U., Cambridge, Mass., 1978; Disting. Humanities lectr. S.W. Conf. Humanities Consortium, 1980-81; state rep. Australasian Univs. Lang. and Lit. Assn., 1967-68; founder New Paradigm Press, 1991, Synthesis jour., 1995. Author: L'Oeuvre d'Emile Zola, 1967, Structuralist Perspectives, 1978, Rococo Style, 1984, Chaos in the Humanities, 1995, Feminism, 1995, (novel) Guruwari, 1995, French edit., 2004, also others; contbr. over 100 articles to profl. jours. Decorated Ordre Palmes Académiques (France); travelling scholar U. Sydney, 1958-60; Mellon Found. rsch. grantee, 1982. Mem. Am. Comparative Lit. Assn., Tenn. Writers' Alliance. Office: U Tenn Dept Modern Fgn Languages & Lit Knoxville TN 37996-0001 Office Phone: 865-588-8001. Business E-Mail: pbrady@utk.edu.

BRADY, PHILLIP DONLEY, lawyer; b. Pasadena, Calif., May 20, 1951; s. Donley L. and Evelyn M. (Dorweiler) B.; m. Kathleen Ryan; children: Ryan Donley, Conor Phillip, Sean Patrick. BA cum laude, U. Notre Dame, 1973; JD cum laude, Loyola U., Los Angeles, 1976. Bar: Calif. 1976, U.S. Ct. Appeals (D.C. cir.) 1978, U.S. Supreme Ct. 1980, U.S. Ct. Mil. Appeals 1990. Assoc. atty. Spray, Gould & Bowers, L.A., 1976-78; dep. atty gen. State of Calif., L.A., 1978-79; legis. counsel U.S. Rep. Daniel E. Lungren, Washington, 1979-81; regional dir. ACTION Agy., San Francisco, 1981-82; dir., Congl. Affairs, Immigration and Naturalization Svc. Dept. of Justice, Washington, 1982-83, assoc. dep. atty. gen., 1983-84, acting asst. atty. gen., 1984-85; dep. asst. to V.P. The White House, Washington, 1985-88, dep. counsel to Pres., 1988-89; gen. counsel Dept. Transp., Washington, 1989-91; asst. to Pres. and staff sec. The White House, Washington, 1991-93; v.p, gen. counsel Am. Automobile Mfrs. Assn., Washington, 1993—99; COO ind. rels. Nat. Automobile Dealers Assn., McLean, Va., 1999—2001, pres., 2001—. Mem. Coun. of the Administrv. Conv. of the U.S., 1988-93. Mem. ABA, Calif. State Bar Assn., FBA (chair gen. counsels sect. 1989-91, nat. coun. 1989—). Home: 5916 Colfax Ave Alexandria VA 22311-1024 Office: Nat Automobile Dealers Assn 8400 Westpark Dr Mc Lean VA 22102-3522

BRADY, RICHARD ALAN, lawyer; b. Newark, Sept. 17, 1934; s. Andrew Joseph and Katherine (Bogan) B.; m. Kathleen R. Sweeney, June 12, 1965; children: Cecilia, Kathleen, Andrew, Joshua. BS, Yale U., 1956, LLB, 1959. Bar: D.C. 1960. Ptnr. Covington & Burling, Washington, 1959—. Office: Covington & Burling 1201 Pennsylvania Ave NW PO Box 7566 Washington DC 20044-7566

BRADY, ROBERT A., congressman; b. Phila., Apr. 7, 1945; m. Debra; 2 children: Robert, Kimberly. Grad. H.S., Phila. Carpenter, Phila., 1963-65; official Carpenter's Union, Phila., 1965-98; mem. U.S. Congress from 1st Pa. dist., 1998—; mem. armed svcs. com., small bus. com. Mem. Pa. Dem. State Com., Dem. Nat. Com.; instr. Organizational Dynamics course, U. Pa. Voted in as mem. 34th Ward Dem. Exec. Com., 1967; elected 34th Ward leader, 1980, chmn. Phila. Dem. Party, 1986; appointed asst. sgt.-at-arms for Phila. City Coun., 1975-83, Phila. dep. mayor for labor in the W. Wilson Goode adminstrn., cons. to the Pa. State Senate, Pa. Turnpike commr., mem. bd. dirs. Phila. City Redevel. Authority. Democrat. Office: 206 Cannon Ho Office Bldg Washington DC 20515-3801*

BRADY, RODNEY HOWARD, diversified financial services company executive, broadcast executive, director, retired academic administrator, retired federal official; b. Sandy, Utah, Jan. 31, 1933; s. Kenneth A. and Jessie (Madsen) B.; m. Carolyn Ann Hansen, Oct. 25, 1960; children: Howard Riley, Bruce Ryan, Brooks Alan. BS in Acctg. with high honors, U. Utah, MBA with high honors, 1957; DBA, Harvard U., 1966; postgrad., UCLA, 1969-70; PhD (hon.), Weber State Coll., 1986, Snow Coll., 1991, Univ. Utah, 1997. Missionary Ch. Jesus Christ of Latter-day Saints, Great Britain, 1953-55; teaching assoc. Harvard U. Bus. Sch., Cambridge, Mass., 1957-59; v.p. Mgmt. Systems Corp., Cambridge, 1962-65, Center Exec. Devel., Cambridge, 1963-64, v.p., dir. Boston, 1964-65; v.p. Tamerand Reef Corp., Christiansted, St. Croix, V.I., 1963-65; v.p., dir. Am. Inst. Execs., N.Y.C., 1963-65; v.p., mem. exec. com. aircraft div. Hughes Tool Co., Culver City, Calif., 1966-70; asst. sec. adminstrn. and mgmt. Dept. HEW, Washington, 1970-72; chmn. subcabinet exec. officers group of exec. br., 1971-72; exec. v.p., chmn. exec. com., dir. Bergen Brunswig Corp., Los Angeles, 1972-78; chmn. bd. Uni-mgrs. Internat., Los Angeles, 1974-78; pres. Weber State Coll., Ogden, Utah, 1978-85; pres., CEO Bonneville Internat. Corp., Salt Lake City, 1985-96, also dir.; pres., CEO Deseret Mgmt. Corp., Salt Lake City, 1996—. Bd. dirs. Amerisource Bergen Corp., 1st Security Bank Corp., 1985-2000, Mgmt. and Tng. Corp., Deseret Mut. Benefit Assn., chmn.; bd. dirs. Maximum Svc. Television, Inc., Intermountain Health Care Found., Nat. Assn. Broadcasters TV Bd., 1993-96; bd. advisors Mountain Bell Telephone, 1983-87; chmn. Nat. Adv. Com. on Accreditation and Instl. Eligibility, 1984-86, mem., 1983-87; chmn. Utah Gov.'s Blue Ribbon Com. on Tax Recodification, 1984-90; cons. Dept. Def., Dept. State, Dept. Commerce, HEW, NASA, Govt. of Can., Govt. of India (and indsl. firms), 1962—. Author: An Approach to Equipment Replacement Analysis, 1957, Survey of Management Planning and Control Systems, 1962, The Impact of Computers on Top Management Decision Making in the Aerospace and Defense Industry, 1966, (with others) How To Structure Incentive Contracts— A Programmed Text, 1965, My Missionary Years in Great Britain, 1976, An Exciting Start Along an Upward Path, 1978; contbr. articles to profl. jours. Mem. exec. com. nat. exec. bd. Boy Scouts Am., 1977—; chmn. nat. Cub Scout commn., 1977-81, pres. Western region, 1981-83, chmn. nat. ct. of honor, 1984-88; mem. adv. com. program for health sys. mgmt. Harvard U., 1973-78, mem. nat. adv. coun. U. Utah, 1971—, chairperson, 1974-76, nat. adv. bd. Coll. Bus., 1985—, chmn., 1989-93, mem. adv. com. Brigham Young U. Bus. Sch., 1972—; mem. dean's round table UCLA Grad. Sch. Mgmt., 1973-78; trustee Ettie Lee Homes for Boys, 1973-79; mem. gov. bd. McKay Dee Hosp., Ogden, Utah, 1979-87; bd. dirs. Utah Endowment for Humanities, 1978-80, Nat. Legal Ctr. for the Pub. Interest, 1991—, vice chmn., 1994-95, chmn., 1995-97, Utah Shakespeare Festival, 1992-2001, Ogden C. of C., 1978-83; bd. dirs. Utah Opera Co., 1997—, Utah Symphony Orch., 1985--. 1st lt. USAF, 1959-62. Recipient Silver Antelope award Boy Scouts Am., 1976; recipient Silver Beaver award Boy Scouts Am., 1979, Silver Buffalo award Boy Scouts Am., 1982, Disting. Alumni award U. Utah, 1990. Mem. Nat. Assn. TV Broadcasters (bd. dirs.), Am. Mgmt. Assn. (award 1969), L.A. C. of C. (tax structure com. 1969-70), Salt Lake Area C. of C. (bd. dirs. 1985-88), SAR (pres. Utah chpt. 1986-87), Sons of Utah Pioneers, Freedoms Found. at Valley Forge (nat. bd. dirs. 1986—), L.A. Country Club, Alta Club, Rotary, Phi Kappa Phi, Tau Kappa Alpha, Beta Gamma Sigma. Mem. LDS Ch. (past pres. L.A. stake). Office: Deseret Mgmt Corp Eagle Gate Tower 60 E South Temple Ste 575 Salt Lake City UT 84111-1016

BRADY, ROSCOE OWEN, neurogeneticist, educator; b. Phila., Oct. 11, 1923; s. Roscoe O. and Martha (Roberts) Brady; m. Bennet Carden Manning, 1972; 2 children. Student, Pa. State U., 1941-43; MD, Harvard U., 1947; postgrad., U. Pa., 1948-49. Intern Hosp. U. Pa., 1947-48; NRC fellow U. Pa., 1948-50, USPHS spl. fellow, 1950-52; sect. chief Nat. Inst. Neurol. Diseases and Blindness, NIH, 1954-67, asst. lab. chief neurochemistry Bethesda, Md., 1967-72; chief developmental and metabolic neurology br. Nat. Inst. Neurol. Disorders and Stroke, 1972—; pres., CEO Targeted Techs., Inc., Rockville, Md. Professorial lectr. George Washington U. Sch. of Medicine, 1963—73; mem. faculty Georgetown U. Sch. of Medicine, 1965—; mem. med. staff Children's Hosp., Washington, 1992—; chmn. sci. adv. bd. Therascope, A.G., Heidelberg, Germany. Author (with Donald B. Tower): Neurochemistry of Nucleotides and Animo Acids, 1960; author: Basic Neurosciences, 1975; author: (with John A. Barranger) Molecular Basis of Lysosomal Storage Disorders, 1984; author: numerous articles. Recipient award, Gairdner Found., 1973, Lasker Found., 1982, Passano Found., 1982, Warren Alpert Found. award, 1992, MyrtleWreath award, Hadassah, 1993, Exec. Excellence award, Sr. Execs. Assn., 1993. Mem.: NAS (J.S. Kolvenko medal 1991), Inst. of Medicine, Am. Soc. Human Genetics, Am. Soc. Clin. Investigation, Am. Acad. Mental Retardation, Am. Acad. Neurology (Kotzias award 1980), Am. Soc. Biol. Chemists. Achievements include first demonstration of enzyme system for fatty acid synthesis; development of biosynthesis of myelin sheath lipids, nature of metabolic defects in Gaucher's disease, Neimann-Pick disease,Fabry's diseases and Tay-Sachs disease; enzyme replacement and gene therapy for lipid storage diseases; discovery of aberrant metabolism of sphingolipids in neoplastic diseases; role of antigenic sphingolipids in neurological diseases. Home: 6026 Valerian Ln Rockville MD 20852-3410 Office: NIH 9000 Rockville Pike Bethesda MD 20892-1260 Office Phone: 301-496-3285. Business E-Mail: bradyr@ninds.nih.gov.

BRADY, SALLY RYDER, writer, literary agent; b. Boston, May 26, 1939; d. Francis Clark and Dorothy Childs Ryder; m. Upton Birnie Brady, Nov. 17, 1962; children: Sarah, Andrew, Nathaniel, Alexander. Student, Barnard Coll., 1956-57, 59-60. Freelance writer, Hartland Four Corners, Vt., 1970—; lit. agt. Brady Lit. Mgmt., Hartland Four Corners, 1988—. Educator Harvard U., Cambridge, Mass., 1978-86. Author: (novel) Instar, 1976, (non-fiction) A Yankee Christmas, Vol. I, 1992, Vol. II, 1993.

BRADY, SHEILA ANN, manufacturing executive; b. Connersville, Ind., Dec. 11, 1935; d. Francis Elmer and Mary Eleanor (Underwood) B. BS, Ball State U., 1958; postgrad., Rutgers U., 1959-60. Art tchr. various N.J. schs., 1959-68; head dept. art Wardlaw Pvt. Boys Sch., Edison, N.J., 1968-72; asst. to pres. F.E. Brady Products, Inc., Clearwater, Fla., 1972-73; pres., treas. Brady Products, Inc., Clearwater, 1973—, chmn. bd., 1976—; pres., treas. Brady Air Controls, Inc., Muncie, Ind., 1975-84, Mountain Meadow Farms, Lake Toxaway, N.C., 1993—. Co-author: Water Systems Handbook, 5th edit. Recipient Art award City of Dunnellon, N.J., 1972; named Ky. Col., 1989. Mem. Water Systems Coun., Nat. Water Well Assn., RV Women, Carefree Club (Ft. Myers, Fla.). Avocations: composing, art, raising exotic animals. Office: Brady Products Inc 2151 Logan St Clearwater FL 33765-1312

BRADY, STEPHEN R.P.K., physician; b. New London, Conn., Oct. 13, 1955; s. Richard Harris and Jeanne Margaret (Halpin) B.; m. Marsha Anne Erickson, June 18, 1978 (div. Jan. 1993); 1 child, Ericka Anuhea; m. Elizabeth Ada Rewick, Dec. 27, 1994. AB cum laude, Harvard U., 1977; MPH, U. Hawaii, 1978, postgrad., 1979; MD, U. Pa., 1982. Diplomate Am. Bd. Internal Medicine. Intern U. Hawaii, 1982-83, resident in internal medicine, 1983-85, clin. instr. Sch. Medicine, 1986-99, clin. asst. prof. Sch. Medicine, 1999—2003, assoc. prof. Sch. Medicine, 2003—, vice-chair Dept. Native Hawaiian Health, Sch. Medicine, 2003—; physician Kaiser Clinics, Honolulu, 1985-86; physician, med. dir. Kokua Kalihi Valley, Honolulu, 1986-89; physician Waianae (Hawaii) Coast Health Svc., 1989-94; asst. med. dir., physician Am. Hawaii Cruises, Honolulu, 1989-95; physician Straub Clinic and Hosp., Honolulu, 1984—. Founding chair Hawaii Consortium for Continuing Med. Edn., U. Hawaii Sch. Medicine, 1993—. Host weekly Ask the Dr. program KHON-Fox 2 News, Hawaii, 1996—, (weekly TV program) Health in Paradise 'Olelo Channel 52, 2001-03. Cubmaster Boy Scouts Am., Kailua, Hawaii, 1995-2000. Comdr. U.S. Mcht. Marine, 1989—. Recipient Po'okela awards, 1991, 93, 95, 99, Guy Milnor award for cmty. svc., 1999; Cub Scouter award Aloha coun. Boy Scouts Am., 1999, Cubmaster award, 2000; rsch. grantee Kuakini Med. Rsch. Inst., Honolulu, 1971, Pacific Health Rsch. Inst., Honolulu, 1972-78, Children's Hosp., Phila., 1979; Paul Harris fellow, 1995; named Scot of Yr., State of Hawaii, 1999, Physician of Yr., Honolulu County Med. Soc., 2002; named one of Best Doctors in Am., 2001-04. Fellow: ACP-Am. Soc. Internal Medicine; mem.: Ahahui O Na Kauka (pres.), Soc. Epidemiologic Rsch., Hawaii Med. Assn. (chair cont. med. edn. com. 1987—, councillor), Hawaii Soc. Internal Medicine, Am. Soc. Internal Medicine, APHA, ACP, AMA, Aumoana Cmty. Assn. (v.p. 1996—), Plaza Club, Soroptimist (pres. 1998—99), Rotary, Kaneohe Yacht Club, Delta Omega. Congregationalist. Avocations: singing, running, sailing, scuba diving, music. Home: 758 Kapahulu Ave PMB 309 Honolulu HI 96816-1196 Office: Dept Native Hawaiian Health 677 Ala Moana Blvd # 1016B Honolulu HI 96813 Office Phone: 808-587-8559. E-mail: kaukaoli@hotmail.com.

BRADY, THOMAS CARL, lawyer; b. Malone, N.Y., Sept. 5, 1947; s. Francis Robert and Rosamond Ethel (South) B.; m. Joan Marie Murray, Dec. 4, 1971; children: Erin Marie, Ryan Thomas, Trevor Michael. BA, Niagara U., 1969; JD, SUNY, Buffalo, 1972. Bar: N.Y. 1973, U.S. Dist. Ct. (we. dist.) N.Y. 1973, Fla. 1981. City ct. judge City of Salamanca, N.Y., 1973; atty. County of Cattaraugus, Little Valley, N.Y., 1973-76; ptnr. Eldredge, Brady, Peters & Brooks, Salamanca and Ellicottville, NY, 1976-82; sr. ptnr. Brady, Brooks & Smith, Salamanca, 1982—96, Brady, Brooks & O'Connell, L.L.P., Salamanca, 1996—2001, Brady & O'Connell, L.L.P., Salamanca, 2001—02, Brady & Swenson, Salamanca, 2002—. Trustee St. Patrick's Roman Cath. Ch., Salamanca, 1991—; mem. N.Y. State Office Parks, Recreation and Hist. Preservation Allegany Region Commn., 1998—, vice chair, 1999—; mem. 8th Dist. Atty. Grievance Com., 1994-2000. Capt. USAR, 1969-76. Mem.: ATLA, N.Y. State Trial Lawyers Assn., Cattaraugus County Bar Assn. (pres. 1984), N.Y. State Bar Assn. (mem. ho. of dels. 2003, 2005—), Fla. Bar Assn., Kiwanis (pres. Salamanca club 1983—84). Republican. Roman Catholic. Avocations: skiing, golf, swimming, boating. Home: 6894 Woodland Dr Great Valley NY 14741-9752 Office: Brady & Swenson 41 Main St Salamanca NY 14779-0227 Office Phone: 716-945-2000. Office Fax: 716-945-3566. Business E-Mail: tbrady@bradyandswenson.com.

BRADY, TIM, dean; BS in Social Sci., Troy State U.; MS in Mgmt., Abilene Christian U.; PhD in Edn., St. Louis U. Rated pilot and navigator, air transport pilot rating. Chmn. aviation dept. Cen. Mo. State; dean instnl. advancement and external programs Parks Coll. St. Louis U.; acting dean Sch. Aviation Embry-Riddle Aero. U., Daytona Beach, Fla., 1999—, assoc. dean Sch. Aviation, dean Coll. Aviation, 2000—. Pres. Coun. on Aviation Accreditation, chmn. accreditation com. Contbr. articles to profl. jours.; lead author, editor; textbook The American Aviation Experience: A History. C-130 pilot USAF, 1958—80. Decorated D.F.C. (2). Office: Embry-Riddle Aero U Coll Aviation Bldg 600 S Clyde Morris Blvd Daytona Beach FL 32114 Office Phone: 386-226-6849. Business E-Mail: bradyt@erau.edu.

BRADY, TOM (THOMAS EDWARD PATRICK BRADY JR.), professional football player; b. San Mateo, Calif., Aug. 3, 1977; s. Thomas and Galynn (Johnson) Brady. BA, U. Mich., 2000. Quarterback New Eng. Patriots, 2000—. Named Most Valuable Player, Super Bowl XXXVI, 2002, Super Bowl XXXVIII, 2004; named to Pro Bowl, 2001, 2004; recipient Espy Award for Breakthrough Athlete of the Yr., ESPN, 2002. Achievements include drafted as a catcher by the Montreal Expos (MLB), 1995; the youngest starting quarterback in NFL history to win a Super Bowl, 2002; mem. Super Bowl Champion New England Patriots, 2002, 2004, 2005. Office: New Eng Patriots 60 Washington St Foxboro MA 02035*

BRADY, UPTON BIRNIE, editor, literary agent; b. Washington, Apr. 17, 1938; s. Francis Ignatius and Sue (Birnie) B.; m. Sally Ryder, Nov. 17, 1962; children— Sarah Schenck, Andrew Upton Birnie, Nathaniel Francis Ryder, Alexander Childs. AB, Harvard Coll., 1959. Coll. field editor Random House, N.Y.C., 1961-63; editor McGraw Hill, N.Y.C., 1963-65; mng. editor Atlantic Monthly Press, Boston, 1965-72, assoc. dir., 1972-79, dir., 1979-84, exec. editor, 1984-88; free-lance editor, cons., literary agt., 1988—. Served to lt. (j.g.) USNR, 1959-61 Mem.: PEN. Roman Catholic. Home and Office: Town Farm Hill PO Box 164 Hartland Four Corners VT 05049-0164

BRADY-BORLAND, KAREN, retired reporter, columnist; b. Buffalo, Mar. 13, 1940; d. Charles A. and Mary Eileen (Larson) B.; m. Gregg Robinson Borland, Sept. 6, 1969 (div. July 1985); children: Caitlin Luise, Kristin Robinson, Leila Nell. BA in English, Daemen Coll., 1961; MS in Journalism, Columbia U., 1962. Summer reporter Buffalo News, 1961, reporter, 1965-68, columnist, 1968-81; editor Prentice-Hall, Inc., Englewood, N.J., 1962-65;

press officer for Rep. Max McCarthy U.S. Ho. Reps., Washington, 1967; gen. assignment & features reporter Buffalo News, 1981—91, higher education reporter, 1991—2002; ret., 2002. Recipient numerous awards Buffalo Newspaper Guild, 1969-79, N.Y. State award for Major Dailies Mag. Writing AP, 1982, numerous community awards, Hilbert Coll. medal, 2002.

BRAEN, BERNARD BENJAMIN, retired psychology professor; b. Boston, Oct. 11, 1928; s. Simon Peter and Ethel (Davis) B.; m. Judith Krom; children: Philip, Eric, Benson. BA, U. Maine, 1949; MA, Boston U., 1950; PhD, Syracuse U., 1955. Diplomate clin. psychology Am. Bd. Examiners Profl. Psychology, 1962-93; lic. psychologist, N.Y., 1957-93. Chief clin. psychologist Onondaga County Child Guidance Ctr., Syracuse, N.Y., 1956-60; pvt. practice clin. psychology Syracuse, 1960-64; assoc. prof. psychology SUNY Upstate Med. Ctr., Syracuse, 1964-69, prof., 1969, Syracuse U., 1969-92; ret.; dir. grad. program in clin. psychology, dir. psychology clinic Syracuse U., 1969-83. Exec. dir. Nat. Alliance Concerned with School Age Parents, Syracuse, 1971-74, dir. research and publs., 1974-76 Contbr. articles to profl. publs., 1959—; guest editor Jour. Sch. Health, 1977. Recipient Disting. Service award Nat. Alliance Concerned with Sch. Age Parents, 1976 Fellow Am. Orthopsychiat. Assn. E-mail: bbraen@comcast.net.

BRAENDEL, DOUGLAS ARTHUR, hotel executive; b. Highland Park, Mich., Dec. 9, 1939; s. Helmuth Gunther and Constance Leah (Drysdale) B.; m. Cameron Lawry, Nov. 30, 1968; children: Jennifer Braendel Miller, Eric, Heike Lawry Batluck. BSBA, Lehigh U., 1961, MBA, 1971; Grad., Army Command and Gen. Staff, Coll., Army War Coll. Commd. U.S. Army, 1966, advanced through grades to col., 1989; bn. supply officer 24th Med. Bn., Fed. Republic of Germany, 1966-68; patient adminstr., detachment comdr. 3d Mobile Army Surg. Hosp., Vietnam, 1968-69; CFO Noble Army Community Hosp., Ft. McClellan, Ala., 1972-75; asst. prof. health adminstrn. Baylor U. Grad. Sch., San Antonio, 1975-79; exec. officer 45th Med. Battalion, Hanau, Fed. Republic Germany, 1980-82; adminstr. Army Regional Med. Lab., Landstuhl, Fed. Republic Germany, 1982-84; comdr. 10th Mobile Army Surg. Hosp., Ft. Meade, Md., 1984-86; dir. programs and evaluation Army Surgeon Gen., Washington, 1986-89; spl. asst. Office Managed Care, Health Care Fin. Adminstrn., Washington, 1989-90; CFO U.S. Army Health Svcs. Command, San Antonio, 1990-93; dir. capitation financing Office Asst. Sec. Def., Falls Church, Va., 1993-96; ret. U.S. Army, 1996; health care mgmt. cons., 1996—2000; bus. mgr. White Sulphur Springs Hotel, 2000—. Adj. instr. Park Coll., San Antonio, 1976—79, Gadsdon (Ala.) State Jr. Coll., 1973—74, Allegany (Md.) Coll., 1997—98. Vol. income tax asst. IRS, Falls Church, Va., 1986-90, Bedford, Pa., 1994—; unit commr. Boy Scouts Am., Kaiserslautern, Fed. Republic Germany, 1982-84, scoutmaster, Rochester, N.Y., and Augsberg, Fed. Republic Germany, 1965-68. Col. U.S. Army, 1966—. Decorated Def. Superior Svc. medal, Legion of Merit with oak leaf cluster, others; recipient Outstanding Author award Am. Soc. Mil. Comptrollers, 1994. Fellow Am. Coll. Healthcare Execs. (Regents award for leadership in health care 1994); mem. Assn. U.S. Army, Beta Gamma Sigma. Avocations: sailing, skiing. Office: White Sulphur Springs Hotel 4499 Milligans Cove Rd Manns Choice PA 15550 Office Phone: 814-623-5583. E-mail: braendel@bedford.net.

BRAEUTIGAM, RONALD RAY, economics professor, educational association administrator; b. Tulsa, Apr. 30, 1947; s. Raymond Louis Braeutigam and Loys Ann (Johnson) Henneberger; m. Janette Gail Carlyon, July 27, 1975; children: Eric Zachary, Justin Michael, Julie Ann. BS, U. Tulsa, 1969; MSc, Stanford U., 1971, PhD, 1976. Petroleum engr. Standard Oil Ind., Tulsa, 1966—70; staff economist Office of Telecomm. Policy, Exec. Office of Pres., Washington, 1972—73; from asst. to prof. econs. Northwestern U., Evanston, Ill., 1975—, dir. bus. instns. program, 1995—2004, Harvey Kapnick prof. Bus. Instns. dept. econs., 1990—, Charles Deering McCormick prof. tchg. excellence, 1997—2000, assoc. dean, 2004—. Vis. prof. Calif. Inst. Tech., Pasadena, 1978-79. Co-author: The Regulation Game, 1978, Price Level Regulation for Diversified Public Utilities, 1989, Microeconomics: An Integrated Approach, 2002; assoc. editor Jour. Indsl. Econs., Cambridge, Mass., 1987-90; mem. editorial bd. MIT Press Series on Regulation, Cambridge, 1980-90, Jour. Econ. Lit., 1987-91, Rev. Indsl. Orgn., 1991—2004, Microeconomics, 2005. Coach Skokie (Ill.) Indians Little League, 1985-91, Evanston Youth Baseball Assn., 1991-96. Grantee, Dept. Transp., NSF, Ameritech, Sloan Found., Mellon Found., others; sr. rsch. fellow Internat. Inst. Mgmt., Berlin, 1982-83, 91. Mem. Am. Econ. Assn., Econometric Soc., Internat. Telecommunications Soc. (bd. dirs. 1990-97), European Econ. Assn., European Assn. for Rsch. in Indsl. Econs. (exec. com. 1992—, pres. 1997-99), Soc. Petroleum Engrs. Avocations: travel, music, languages. Home: 731 Monticello St Evanston IL 60201-1745 Office: Northwestern U Dept Econs Evanston IL 60208-0001

BRAFF, ZACH, actor, director, scriptwriter; b. South Orange, N.J., Apr. 6, 1975; s. Hal and Anne Braff. BA in Film, Northwestern U., Evanston, Ill. Actor: (films) Manhattan Murder Mystery, 1993, Getting to Know You, 1999, Blue Moon, 2000, The Broken Hearts Club: A Romantic Comedy, 2000, Endsville, 2000; (TV series) Scrubs, 2001—; (TV films) My Summer as a Girl, 1994, (theatre) Macbeth, 1998, Romeo & Juliet, Twelfth Night, 2002; actor, writer, dir. (films) Garden State, 2004 (Grammy Award for Best Compilation Soundtrack, 2005). Achievements include directing and writing several short films including Lionel on a Sun Day; directing commercials and public service announcements. Office: c/o Sandra Chang Industry Entertainment 9465 Wilshire Blvd Beverly Hills CA 90212

BRAFFORD, H. WAYNE, paper company executive; B in pulp and paper sci. tech., NC State U.; MBA, Tulane U. Fin., strategic planning, gen. mgr. Internat. Paper Co., Memphis, 1975, v.p., gen. mgr., converting, specialty and pulp, 1997—2003, sr. v.p., indsl. packaging, 2003—. Chmn. The Am. Forest and Paper Assn., Printing - Writing Paper Group, 2003—. Office: Internat Paper Co 6420 Poplar Ave Memphis TN 38197

BRAFFORD, WILLIAM CHARLES, lawyer; b. Pike County, Ky., Aug. 7, 1932; s. William Charles and Minnie (Tacket) B.; m. Katherine Jane Prather, Nov. 13, 1954; children— William Charles III, David A. JD, U. Ky., 1957; LLM (fellow), U. Ill., 1958. Bar: Ky. 1957, Ga. 1965, Tax Ct. U.S 1965, Ct. Claims 1965, Ohio 1966, U.S. Ct. Appeals 1966, U.S. Supreme Ct. 1970, Pa. 1973. Trial atty. NLRB, Washington and Cin., 1958-60; atty. Louisville & Nashville R.R. Co., Louisville, 1960-63, So. Bell Telephone Co., Atlanta, 1963-65; asst. gen. counsel NCR Corp., Dayton, Ohio, 1965-72; v.p., sec., gen. counsel Betz Dearborn, inc., Trevose, Pa., 1972-97, ret., 1997. Former dir. Betz Process Chems., Inc., Betz, Ltd. U.K., Betz Paper Chem. Inc., Betz Energy Chems., Inc., Betz S.A. France, B.L. Chems., Inc., Betz GmbH, Germany, Betz Entec, Inc., Betz Ges. GmbH, Austria, Betz NV Belgium, Betz Sud S.p.A., Italy, Betz Internat. Inc., Betz Europe Inc., Primex Ltd., Barbados. Served as 1st lt. C.I.C. AUS, 1954-56. Mem. Am. Soc. Corp. Secs., Nat. Assn. Corp. Dirs. Republican. Presbyterian.

BRAFMAN, BENJAMIN, lawyer; b. N.Y.C., July 21, 1948; s. Sol and Rose (Friedman) B.; m. Lynda J. Bienenfeld, June 23, 1971; children— Jennifer, David. B.A., Bklyn. Coll., 1971; J.D. with distinction, Ohio No. Coll. Law, 1974; LL.M. in Criminal Justice, N.Y.U., 1979. Bar: N.Y. 1975, U.S. Ct. Appeals (2d cir.) 1975, U.S. Supreme Ct. 1978.manuscript editor, Ohio Northern U. Law Review, 1973-74, assoc., McGuire & Lawler, N.Y.C., 1974-76; asst. dist. atty. N.Y.C., 1976-79, mem., Brafman & Ross P.C., N.Y.C., 1979—. Mem. Assn. Trial Lawyers Am., Nat. Assn.Criminal Defense Lawyers, NY Coun. of Criminal Def. Lawyers, bd. dirs., NY Criminal Bar Assn, 1990-92; Fellow, Am.Coll. of Trial Lawyers; named "Best Criminal Defense Lawyer", New York Mag., 1997. Office: Brafman & Ross PC 26th Fl 767 Third Ave New York NY 10017

BRAGA, STEPHEN LOUIS, lawyer; b. Newport, R.I., Nov. 29, 1955; s. Manuel Louis and Nancy Rose (Lincourt) B. BA cum laude, Fairfield U., 1978; JD magna cum laude, Georgetown U. Law Ctr., 1981. Bar: D.C. 1982, U.S. Supreme Ct., U.S. Ct. Appeals (D.C., 1st, 2d, 3d, 7th, 9th and D.C. cirs.), U.S. Dist. Ct. D.C., U.S. Tax Ct. Law clk. U.S. Dist. Ct. D.C., Washington, 1981-82; atty. Miller, Cassidy, Larroca & Lewin, Washington, 1982—2000; ptnr. litigation dept. & hiring ptnr. Washington office Baker Botts LLP, Washington, 2000—. Adj. prof. Georgetown U. Law Ctr., Washington, 1993—. Democrat. Roman Catholic. Avocation: sports. Office: Baker Botts LLP The Warner 1299 Pennsylvania Ave NW Washington DC 20004-2400 Office Phone: 202-639-7704. Office Fax: 202-585-1066. Business E-Mail: stephen.braga@bakerbotts.com.

BRAGDON, PAUL ERROL, academic administrator, educator; b. Portland, Maine, Apr. 19, 1927; s. Errol Freemont and Edith Lillian (Somerville) B.; m. Nancy Ellen Horton, Aug. 14, 1954; children: David Lincoln, Susan Horton, Peter Jefferson. BA magna cum laude, Amherst Coll., 1950, DHL (hon.), 1980; JD, Yale U., 1953; LLD (hon.), Whitman Coll., 1985; DLitt. (hon.), Pacific U., 1988; DHL (hon.), Reed Coll., 1989; DHL (hon.), Lewis & Clark Coll., 2005; DSc (hon.), Oreg. Health Scis. U., 2004. Bar: N.Y. 1954. With firm Dewey, Ballantine, Bushby, Palmer & Wood, N.Y.C., 1953-58, Javits, Trubin, Sillcocks, Edelman & Purcell, N.Y.C., 1961-64; counsel Tchrs. Ins. and Annuity Assn. Coll. Retirement Equities Fund, N.Y.C., 1958-61; asst. to mayor City of N.Y., 1964-65, exec. sec. to mayor, 1965, exec. asst. to pres. City Council, 1966-67; v.p. NYU, 1967-71; pres. Reed Coll., Portland, Oreg., 1971-88; pres. emeritus, 1988—; asst. for edn. to gov. State of Oreg., 1988-91; dir. Office Edn. Policy and Planning Oreg., 1990-91; pres. Med. Rsch. Found. Oreg., Portland, 1991-94, Oreg. Grad. Inst. Sci. and Tech., Portland, 1994-98; interim pres. Lewis & Clark Coll., Portland, 2003—04. Trustee Amherst Coll., 1972-78. Recipient Torch of Liberty award Anti-Defamation League of B'nai B'rith, 1985, Presdl. Leadership award Marylhurst U., 1988, award of excellence Kaul Found., 1994, Aubrey Watzek award Lewis and Clark Coll., 1999, Simon Benson award Portland State U., 1999, Libr. Leadership award Libr. Found. Multnomah County, 2001. Mem. Phi Beta Kappa, Phi Beta Kappa Assocs., Beta Theta Pi, Arlington Club, Univ. Club. Home: 7535 SE 31st Ave Portland OR 97202-8532 Business E-Mail: paul.bragdon@reed.edu.

BRAGG, ELLIS MEREDITH, JR., lawyer; b. Washington, Jan. 30, 1947; s. Ellis Meredith Sr. and Lucille (Tingstrum) B.; m. Judith Owens, Aug. 18, 1968; children: Michael Andrew, Jennifer Meredith. BA, King Coll., 1969; JD, Wake Forest U., 1973. Bar: N.C. 1973, U.S. Dist. Ct. (we. and mid. dists.) N.C. 1974, U.S. Ct. Appeals (4th cir.) 1980, U.S. Supreme Ct. 2002. Assoc. Bailey, Brackett & Brackett, P.A., Charlotte, N.C., 1973-76; ptnr. Howard & Bragg, Charlotte, 1976-77, McConnell, Howard, Johnson, Pruitt, Jenkins & Bragg, Charlotte, 1977-79; pvt. practice, Charlotte, 2002—. Dist. chmn. Mecklenburg County Dems., Charlotte, 1978; coach youth soccer program YMCA, Charlotte, 1982-83; mem. Headstart Policy Council, Charlotte, 1985. Mem. ABA, N.C. Bar Assn., N.C. Acad. Trial Lawyers. Presbyterian. Avocations: reading, jogging, gardening. Home: 6407 Honegger Dr Charlotte NC 28211-4718 Office: 500 E Morehead St Ste 210 Charlotte NC 28202-2694 Office Phone: 704-334-0888. Personal E-mail: Bragglaw@aol.com.

BRAGG, LAWRENCE D., III, lawyer; b. 1948; BA cum laude, Yale U., 1970; JD magna cum laude, Harvard U., 1974. Bar: Mass. 1974. Law clk. Judge Edward T. Gignoux, US Dist. Ct. (Maine), 1975—76; ptnr. corp. dept. Ropes & Gray, Boston, 1983—, co-head pub. fin. practice group. Chmn. bd. Youth Enrichment Services, Boston. Mem.: Nat. Assn. Bond Lawyers, Boston Bar Assn. Office: Ropes & Gray One International Pl Boston MA 02110-2624 Office Phone: 617-951-7427. Office Fax: 617-951-7050. Business E-Mail: lawrence.bragg@ropesgray.com.

BRAGG, LYNN MUNROE, trade association administrator, former federal commissioner; b. Ft. Leonard Wood, Mo., June 15, 1954; d. Irving William and Elaine Frances (Heath) Munroe; m. Raymond Frank Bragg, Jr., Aug. 12, 1989; children: Hudson, Rachael, Braxton. BA in English, Mary Washington Coll., 1976; MS in Pub. Rels., Boston U., 1978. Speech and fin. writer Potomac Electric Power Co., Washington, 1978-80; legis. dir., legis. asst. Office of U.S. Senator Malcolm Wallop, Washington, 1981-91; dir. govtl. affairs Edison Electric Inst., Washington, 1991-94; commr. U.S. Internat. Trade Commn., Washington, 1994—2002, vice chmn., 1996-98, chmn., 1998-2000; pres. Chocolate Mfrs. Assn., McLean, Va., 2003—. Republican. Episcopalian. Avocation: golf.

BRAGG, MICHAEL ELLIS, lawyer, insurance company executive; b. Holdrege, Nebr., Oct. 6, 1947; s. Lionel C and Frances E (Klinginsmith) Bragg; m. Nancy Jo Aabel, Jan. 19, 1980; children: Brian Michael, Kyle Christopher, Jeffrey Douglas. BA, U. Nebr., 1971, JD, 1975. ChFC, CPCU, CLU; bar: Alaska 1976, Nebr 1976, U.S. Supreme Ct. 2001. Assoc. White & Jones, Anchorage, 1976-77; field rep. State Farm Ins., Anchorage, 1977-79, atty. corp. law dept. Bloomington, Ill., 1979-81, sr. atty., 1981-84, asst. counsel, 1984-86, counsel, 1986-88; asst. v.p., counsel gen. claims dept. State Farm Fire and Casualty Co., Bloomington, 1988-94; v.p., counsel, gen. claims dept. State Farm Ins. Co., Bloomington, Ill., 1994-97, assoc. gen. counsel corp. law dept., 1997—. Lectr, contbr legal seminars. Contbr, ed: articles to legal and insurance jour. Pres. McLean County Crime Detection Network, 1988—95. With USNG, 1970—76. Recipient Disting. Legal Svc. Award, Corp. Legal Times, 1998, 2003, Tort, Trial and Ins. Com. award, Am. Bar Assn., 2005. Fellow: Am. Bar Found.; mem.: ABA (various offices tort, trial and ins. practice sect. 1981—2004, vice-chmn property ins law com. 1986—91, chmn. ins. coverage litigation com. 1991—92, chmn. task force on ins. staff counsel 2000—02, coun. 2000—03, standing com. on ethics and profl. responsibility 2001—04, Staff Coun. Excellence award Torts, Trials and Ins. sect. 2005), Assn. Profl. Responsibility Lawyers, Soc. Fin. Svc. Profls., Internat. Assn. Def. Counsel, Fedn. Def. and Corp. Counsel, Def. Rsch. Inst., Assn. Corp. Counsel. Republican. Avocations: golf, tennis. Office: State Farm Ins Co Assoc Gen Counsel One State Farm Plz A-3 Bloomington IL 61710 Office Phone: 309-766-7917. Business E-Mail: buck.bragg.achk@statefarm.com.

BRAGG, ROBERT HENRY, physicist, researcher; b. Jacksonville, Fla., Aug. 11, 1919; s. Robert Henry and Lilly Camille (McFarland) B.; m. Violette Mattie McDonald, June 14, 1947; children: Robert Henry, Pamela. BS, Ill. Inst. Tech., 1949, MS, 1951, PhD, 1960. Assoc. physicist rsch. lab. Portland Cement Assn., Skokie, Ill., 1951-56; sr. physicist physics div. Armour Rsch. Found. Ill. Inst. Tech., Chgo., 1956-61; sr. mem., mgr. phys. metallurgy dept. Lockheed Palo Alto Rsch. Lab., Palo Alto, Calif., 1961-69; prof. materials sci. U. Calif., Berkeley, 1969-87, chmn. dept. materials sci. and mineral engring., 1978-81, prof. emeritus, 1987—. Faculty sr. scientist Lawrence Berkeley Lab., 1969-87, emeritus 1987—; mem. materials rsch. adv. com. NSF, 1982-86; program dir. div. materials rsch. U.S. Dept. Energy, 1981-82; cons. IBM, Siemens-Allis, NASA, NIH, NSF, NRC; vis. prof. Musashi Inst. of Tech., Tokyo, 1989, Howard U., 1999; del. 2d Edward Bouchet Internat. Conf., Accra, Ghana, 1990; rschr. Mich. U., Howard U., AT&T Collaborative Access Team, 1999. Contbr. articles to profl. jours. Pres. Palo Alto NAACP, 1967-68. With U.S. Army, 1943-46. Decorated Bronze star (2); recipient Disting. award No. Calif. sect. Am. Inst. Mining and Metall. Engrs., 1970; J. William Fulbright rsch. fellow, Nigeria, 1992-93. Fellow Nat. Soc. of Black Physicists; mem. AAUP, AAAS, Am. Phys. Soc., Am. Ceramics Soc. (chmn. No. Calif. sect. 1980), AIME (chmn. No. Calif. sect. 1970), Am. Carbon Soc., No. Calif. Coun. Black Profl. Engrs., Am. Crystallographic Assn., Sigma Xi, Tau Beta Pi. Democrat. Home: 2 Admiral Dr Ste 373 Emeryville CA 94608-1502 Office: U Calif Dept Materials Sci & Engring Berkeley CA 94720-0001 Office Phone: 510-655-6283. Personal E-mail: petebragg@aol.com. Business E-Mail: rbragg@socrates.berkeley.edu.

BRAHA, THOMAS I., oil industry executive; b. Austin, Tex., Sept. 3, 1947; s. Jacob and Valentine (Capone) B.; m. Nancy Elizabeth Rowe, Mar. 31, 1973 (div.); children: Nancy Elizabeth, Jeanne Valentine, Travis Ian. BSME, U. Tex., 1969; MBA, Temple U., 1971; postgrad., NYU, 1971-73. Engr. Davis Electronics, Inc., Austin, 1967, Whirlpool Corp., Evansville, Ind., 1968; project engr. ITE Imperial Corp., Phila., 1969-71; sr. supply analyst Mobil Oil Corp., NYC, 1971-74; pres. Western Hemisphere Bulk Oil (U.S.A.), Inc., NYC, 1974-75. Chmn. bd., CEO Braha Holding Corp., Braha Oil Corp. and Subs., Braha Estates, Inc., Braha Farms, Braha Profit and Pension Trusts; adj. faculty The Wharton Sch., U. Pa., 1996-2002; chmn. Molecular Valley Initiative of Greater Phila. Region, 2003—. Active Bryn Mawr Presbyn. Ch. Mem. ASME, Am. Mgmt. Assn., Am. Petroleum Inst., Inst. Petroleum (U.K.), Nat. Petroleum Refining Assn., Phila. Country Club. Office: Braha Holding Co PO Box 390 Bryn Mawr PA 19010-0390 Personal E-mail: tombraha@aol.com.

BRAHAM, RANDOLPH LEWIS, political science professor; b. Bucharest, Romania, Dec. 20, 1922; came to U.S., 1948, naturalized, 1953; m. Elizabeth Sommer, Dec. 15, 1954; children: Steven, Robert. BA, CCNY, 1948, MS, 1949; PhD, New Sch. for Social Research, 1952. Research assoc. YIVO-Inst. for Jewish Research, N.Y.C., 1954-59; faculty CCNY, N.Y.C., 1959—, prof. polit. sci., 1971—, disting. prof., 1987—, disting. prof. emeritus, 1992—, chmn. dept. polit. sci., 1971-81. Dir. Inst. for Holocaust Studies, Grad. Ctr. CUNY, 1980—; faculty Fairleigh Dickinson U., Hofstra U., Hunter Coll., 1956-59 Author: The Politics of Genocide, 2 vols., 1981, 2d rev. edit., 1994, The Hungarian Labor Service System, 1977, Hungarian Jewish Studies, 3 vols., 1966-73, Soviet Government and Politics, 1965, Human Rights, 1979; writer, editor, contbr. to books in field. Democrat. Home: 11407 Union Tpke Flushing NY 11375-6850 Office: CUNY Graduate Ctr New York NY 10016

BRAHAM, SANDRA ELAINE, college official; b. St. Louis, Nov. 4, 1964; d. Samuel Dale Boyd and Doris Delaine (Rice) Edmond; m. Eric Leon Braham, Oct. 18, 1995; children: Jesse, Erica, Jordan. BA in Biology, U. Mo., 1987; M in Ednl. Adminstrn., U. Tex., El Paso, 2002, EdD in Ednl. Leadership and Adminstrn., 2005. Recruitment coord. Ind. Vocat. Tech. Coll., Lafayette, 1989-92; dir. Upward Bound, U. Tex., El Paso, 1992—, dir. ednl. talent search, 1998-99, asst. v.p. for outreach programs, 1999—. Cmty. rep. editl. bd. El Paso Times, 1997—98; contbr. articles pub. to profl. jour. Edn. adv. bd. Thomason Hosp., El Paso, 1997-2000; bd. dirs. Salvation Army, El Paso, 1997-2000, YWCA, 1998—, v.p. programs, 2002-05, pres.-elect 2005—; allocation panel United Way of El Paso, 1997, 99, 2001, 03; active Leadership El Paso, 1997; bd. dirs. XII Traveler's Meml. S.W., 1999—; chair United El Paso Health and Human Svcs. Coun., 1999-2000 Recipient Disting. Club Pres. award Nat. Exch. Club, 1994, 1998 Bus. Assoc. Yr. Am. Bus. Women's Assn., Sun City chpt., Reach award YWCA, 1998, Evolution award, 2002, NAACP Civil Rights award, 2002; Upward Bound grantee U.S. Dept. Edn., 1995-99, 1999-2003, 2003—, talent search grantee U.S. Dept. Edn., 1998-2003, 2003—, Gear Up grantee U.S. Dept. Edn., 1999—; Coll. Assistance Migrant Program grantee, 2002-; Proclamation Tex. Senate, 2002. Mem. Tex. Assn. Spl. Student Svcs. Programs (pres. 2001-02), S.W. Assn. Student Assistance Programs, Leadership El Paso Alumni Assn. (bd. dirs. 1997-98), Nat. Coun. Ednl. Opportunity Assns. (instnl. mem.), U. Tex.-El Paso Profl. Women's Network, Cmty. Mentoring for Adolescent Devel. Initiative (trainer 1998-2002). Avocations: acting, singing, reading. Office: U Tex El Paso 211 Graham 500 W University Ave El Paso TX 79968-8900

BRAHMA, CHANDRA SEKHAR, civil engineering educator; b. Calcutta, India, Oct. 5, 1941; came to U.S., 1963; s. Nalinia Kanta and Uma Rani (Bose) B.; m. Purnima Sinha, Feb. 18, 1972; children: Charanjit, Barunashish. B in Engring., Calcutta U., 1962; MS, Mich. State U., 1965; PhD, Ohio State U., 1969. Registered profl. engr. Calif., Utah, N.H., Tex., Wis. Asst. engr. Pub. Works Dept., Calcutta, 1962-63; rsch. asst. Mich. State U., East Lansing, 1963-65; teaching and rsch. assoc. Ohio State U., Columbus, 1965-69; project engr. Frank H. Lehr Assocs., East Orange, N.J., 1969-70; sr. soils engr. John G. Reutter Assocs., Camden, N.J., 1970-72; asst. prof. Worcester (Mass.) Poly. Inst., 1972-74; prin. soils engr. Daniel, Mann, Johnson & Mendenhall, Balt., 1974-79; sr. engr. Sverdrup Corp., St. Louis, 1979-80, cons., 1980—; prof. Calif. State U., Fresno, 1980—2002, prof. emeritus, 2002—. Cons. Expert Resources, Inc., Peoria Heights, Ill., 1981—, The Twining Labs., Inc., Fresno, 1982—, Law Offices Marderosian and Swanson, Fresno, 1985—, Law Offices Hurlbutt, Clevenger, Long and Vortmann, Visalia, Calif., 1988—, Tech. Adv. Svcs. for Attys., Blue Bell, Pa., 1992—. Author: Fundaciones y Mechanica de Suelos, 1986; contbr. articles to profl. jours. Head sci. judge Calif. Cen. Valleys Sci. and Engring. Fairs, Fresno, 1988-2002. Recipient Outstanding Prof. of Yr. award Calif. State U., 1989, Halliburton award Calif. State U., 1991, Calif. Ctrl. Valley Outstanding Profl. Engr. award Calif. Soc. Profl. Engrs., 1993, Disting. Svc. award, 1994, Claude C. Laval Jr. award Innovative Tech. and Rsch. Calif. State U., 1991, 92, Portrait of Success award KSEE 24, Fresno, Calif., 1997, Std. of Excellence award Tau Beta Pi, 1997, Outstanding Prof. award Tau Beta Pi, 1998, Outstanding Prof. award NSPE, 1998; Brahma St. named in City of Bakersfield, Calif., 1989; Fulbright scholar, 1984; Hugh B. William fellow, Assn. Drilled Shaft Contractors, 1986, others. Fellow ASCE (v.p. 1983-84, pres. 1984-85, Outstanding Engr. award 1985, Disting Svc. award, 1986, Outstanding Prof. award 1985, Edmund Friedman Profl. Recognition award 1993); mem. ASTM, Am. Soc. Engring. Edn. (AT&T Found. award 1991, Outstanding Tchg. award 1997, AT ANDT Found. award for excellence in tchg. and rsch. 1991), Rotary (chair Clovis club 1986—, chair pub. rels. 1987, chair youth svcs. 1989, bd. dirs. 1989). Democrat. Hindu. Avocations: swimming, tennis, music, reading. Home and Office: 561 Houston Ave Clovis CA 93611-7032 Office Phone: 559-323-0316. E-mail: chandrab@csufresno.edu, csbconsultant@netscape.net, chandrab.1@netzero.net.

BRAHMBHATT, HEENA, public health researcher; d. Pushkar and Kumud Brahmbhatt. BS, Albright Coll., 1993; MPH, Johns Hopkins Sch. Pub. Health, 1996, PhD, 2002. Faculty Johns Hopkins Sch. Pub. Health, Balt., 2002—. Recipient 1st prize Nat. Maternal and Child Health Conf., Nat. Maternal and Child Health Orgn., 2002, Fogarty Young Rschr. award, Johns Hopkins Sch. Pub. Health; grantee, Elizabeth Glaser Pediatric AIDS Found., CFAR rsch. grant, Johns Hopkins Sch. Pub. Health, Gustave J. Martin Innovative Rsch. Fund; scholar Hewlett scholar. Mem.: Internat. AIDS Orgn. Office: Johns Hopkins Sch Pub Health 615 N Wolfe St Baltimore MD 21205 Business E-Mail: hbrahmbh@jhsph.edu.

BRAHMS, WILLIAM BERNARD, librarian, writer; b. Camden, N.J., Oct. 1, 1966; s. William Arthur and Jane Dilks Brahms; m. Gina-Marie Lugo, Dec. 7, 1996; children: Matthew Frederick, Giovanna Elizabeth. BA with honors, Rutgers Coll., 1989; MLS, Rutgers U., 1993. Cert. profl. libr. N.J. State Dept. Edn., 1993. Libr. intern South Brunswick (N.J.) Pub. Libr., 1992—93; refrence libr. Franklin Twp. Pub. Libr., Somerset, NJ, 1993—95, sr. reference libr., 1995—99, head adult svcs. (reference), 1999—. Com. mem. N.J. Digitization Hwy., Trenton, Highlands Regional Libr. Coop. Info. Svcs. Com., Denville, NJ; twp. historian Twp. of Franklin, Somerset. Author: (book) Images of America: Franklin Township, 1997 (Mayor's Commendation, Franklin Twp., 1998), Franklin Township, Somerset County, NJ: A History, 1998 (Mayor's Commendation, Franklin Twp., 1999); editor: Cap & Skull Centennial History and Biographical Directory, 2000. Bd. mem. Friends of the Franklin Twp. Pub. Libr., Somerset, 1993—2003; mem. Meadows Found., Somerset, 1998—, Raritan-Millstone Heritage Alliance, Somerset; bd. mem. Alumni Assn. of the Epsilon Chpt. of Delta Phi (St. Elmo's Club of Rutgers U.), New Brunswick, 1994—2003, Cap and Skull Soc. Alumni Assn., New Brunswick, 1995—2003. Named Author of the Yr., Marconi Found., 1999; recipient Cap & Skull Soc., Rutgers Coll., 1988; Henry Rutgers scholar, 1989. Mem.: ALA, Phi Eta Sigma, N.J. Libr. Assn., Omicron Delta Epsilon, Phi Beta Kappa, Delta Phi. Home: 17 Crammer Ln Hillsborough NJ 08844 Office: Franklin Twp Pub Libr 485 DeMott Ln Somerset NJ 08873 Personal E-mail: gmandwb@patmedia.net. E-mail: wbrahms@franklintwp.org.

BRAIBANTI, RALPH JOHN, political scientist, educator; b. Danbury, Conn., June 29, 1920; s. Daniel Vincent and Jane Helena B.; m. Lucy Kauffman, Feb. 19, 1943; children: Claire, Ralph Lynn. BS, Western Conn. State U., 1941; LHD (hon.), 1995; A.M., Syracuse U., 1947, PhD, 1949. Asst. prof. polit. sci. Kenyon Coll., 1949-52, assoc. prof., 1952-53; adv., civil adminstr. Ryukyu Islands, 1950; adj. lectr. George Washington U., 1951; asst. dir. Am. Polit. Sci. Assn., Washington, 1950-51; cons. Govtl. Affairs Inst., 1950-51; assoc. prof. polit. sci. Duke U., Durham, N.C., 1953-58, prof., 1958-68, James B. Duke prof. polit. sci., 1968-90, James B. Duke prof. emeritus, 1990—, founding dir., program on so. Asia, 1962—82; vis. asst.

prof. Trinity Coll., 1952; adj. lectr. Am. U., 1956; vis. asst. prof. Utica Coll., 1949; founding dir. Islamic and Arabian devel. studies, 1977-89. Scholar-in-residence Rockefeller Found., Bellagio Ctr., Italy, 1967; cons. AID, 1958-59, Ford Found., 1972, UN, 1974, Govt. Saudi Arabia, 1974—, UNESCO, 1977, Islamic Secretariat, 1980, World Bank, 1987; vis. prof. U. Kuwait, 1984; advisor on adminstrv. reform Pakistan, Malaysia, South Africa, Lebanon, Morocco, Saudi Arabia, Bangladesh; cons.; bd. advisors Nat. Coun. U.S.-Arab Rels., Moroccan-Am. Found., Mid East Policy Coun.; founding pres. Am. Inst. Pakistan Studies, 1973-78, 86, 88, Am. Inst. Yemeni Studies; bd. dirs. U.S. Mid-East Performing Arts Coun., 1995—; chmn. nat. selection com. Joseph J. Malone Postdoctoral Fellowships in Arabian Affairs; King Faisal Disting. Internat. lectr. Am.-Arab Affairs Coun., 1989-91; mem. internat. adv. com. Global Forum of Spiritual and Parliamentary Leaders on Human Survival, 1996—. Author: Research on the Bureaucracy of Pakistan, 1966, The Nature and Structure of the Islamic World, 1995, revised edit., 2000, Chief Justice Cornelius of Pakistan: Analysis, Letters, Speeches, 1999; co-author, editor: Political and Administrative Development, 1969, Pakistan: The Long View, 1976, Asian Bureaucratic Systems Emergent from the British Imperial Tradition, 1966, Tradition, Values and Socio-Economic Development, 1961, Administration and Economic Development in India, 1963, Evolution of Pakistan's Administrative System: The Collected Papers of Ralph Braibanti, 1987; co-compiler, co-editor: (with Lucy Kauffman Braibanti) The Collected Poems of Charles Henry Kauffman, 2001; gen. editor 7 vol. series on comparative adminstrn., 1968-73; bd. editors Middle East Policy, Studies in Contemporary Islam, Jour. South Asian and Mid. Ea. Studies, Comparative Politics, Politikon, Asian Forum, Jour. Pakistan Studies, Internat. Jour. Islamic and Arabic Studies. Served to capt. U.S. Army, 1942-47. Recipient citation outstanding prof. Duke Student Assn., 1972, alumni award disting. undergrad. teaching, 1979; Maxwell fellow Syracuse U., 1949, Ford Found. fellow, 1955-56, Social Sci. Rsch. Coun. fellow, 1955-56; decorated commendation medal U.S. Army, 1947. Fellow Internat. Assn. Mid. Ea. Studies (mem. exec. com. 1991—); mem. Internat. Studies Assn.-South (pres.), Am. Inst. Pakistan Studies (founding pres. 1975-77, pres. 1986-90), Internat. Cultural Soc. Korea (hon.), Am. Council for Study Islamic Socs. (bd. dirs.) Home and Office: 3805 Darby Rd Durham NC 27707-5004 *The encouragement of a profound understanding of seemingly divergent cultural systems is of critical importance. This must embrace helping newly-developed political systems appreciate their own cultural values. Only the strength of such pride can withstand the dynamic interventionism which characterizes the relations of transitorily dominant superpowers and weak, newer political entities.*

BRAID, FREDERICK DONALD, lawyer; b. N.Y.C., Aug. 10, 1946; s. Donald Michael and Margaret Anna (Fluty) B.; m. Eleanor Mae Friedman, Oct. 23, 1980; children: Andrew Harris, Roy Leal, Josh Perry, David Barnett, Steven Gabriel. BS in Econs., St. John's U., Jamaica, N.Y., 1968; JD, St. John's U., Bklyn., 1971; LLM, NYU, 1979. Bar: N.Y. 1972, U.S. Dist. Ct. (so. and ea. dists.) N.Y. 1973, U.S. Ct. Appeals (2d cir.) 1973, (D.C. and 4th cirs.) 1997, U.S. Supreme Ct. 1975. Assoc. Rains & Pogrebin, Mineola and N.Y.C., N.Y., 1971-77, ptnr., 1978-99; bd. dirs. Rains & Pogrebin, P.C., Mineola and N.Y.C., N.Y.; ptnr. Holland and Knight LLP, 2000—. Mem. adv. bd. NYU Sch. Law Ctr. for Labor and Employment Law, 1997—. Mng. editor St. John's Law Rev., 1970-71; contbr. articles to profl. jours. Served to capt. USAR, 1972—80. St. Thomas More scholar, St. John's U. Sch. Law, 1968-71. Mem. ABA, N.Y. Bar Assn., Omicron Delta Epsilon, Delta Mu Delta. Home: 17 E 96th St New York NY 10128-0783 Office: Holland & Knight LLP 195 Broadway New York NY 10007-3100 Office Phone: 212-513-3393. E-mail: fbraid@hklaw.com.

BRAILER, DAVID J., health information technology executive; b. July 16, 1959; M in mgmt. sci., PhD in mgmt. sci., Wharton Sch., U. Pa.; MD, W. Va. U. Sch. Medicine, 1986. Bd. cert. internal medicine 1989. Resident Hosp. at U. Pa.; founder CareScience, Inc. (formerly Care Mgmt. Sci.), Phila., 1993, chmn., CEO, 1993—2003; sr. fellow info. tech. and quality care Health Tech. Ctr. (HealthTech), San Francisco, 2003; nat. health info. tech. coord. US Dept. Health and Human Svc. (HHS), 2004—. Recipient Charles A. Dana Scholar, U. Pa. Sch. Medicine, Robert Wood Johnson Clinical Scholar, U. Pa., Martin Eipstein award, Nat. Libr. Medicine. Achievements include first med. student to serve on bd. trustes for AMA. Office: US Dept Health and Human Svc (HHS) 200 Independence Ave Washington DC 20201 Office Phone: 202-690-7151. Business E-Mail: david.brailer@hhs.gov.

BRAILOW, NORMA LIPTON, artist; b. N.Y., Apr. 30, 1916; d. Leon Israel Lipton and Estelle (Laiken) Rich; m. Alexander A. Brailow, Apr. 26, 1941; children: Anthony George, David Gregory. BA, Keuka Coll., 1963; MA, State U., 1970. Lic. tchr. Fashion artist Berger's Dept. Store, Buffalo, 1941-44; tchr. II, Penn Yan Acad., 1967-69; sculptor, Keuka Park, N.Y., 1970—. One woman shows include Lightner Gallery, Keuka Coll., N.Y., 1978, 82, Arnot Art Mus., Elmira, N.Y., 1979, Yates County Arts Coun., Penn Yan, N.Y., 1988; exhibited in numerous group shows Keuka Coll., Penn Yan County, Geneva, N.Y. Bd. dirs. Yates County Arts Coun., Yates Performing Arts. Mem. AAUW (bd. dirs. Yates County) Home and Office: 1714 Decourcy Ln Franklin IN 46131-7237

BRAILSFORD, JUNE EVELYN, musician, educator; b. Wiergate, Tex., Apr. 11, 1939; d. Lonnie and Jessie (Coleman) Samuel; m. Marvin Delano Brailsford, Dec. 23, 1960; children: Marvin Delano, Keith, Cynthia. BA in Music, Prairie View A & M U., Tex., 1960; MA in Music, Trenton (N.J.) State Coll., 1981; postgrad., Jacksonville State U., summer 1971, Lamar U., Beaumont, Tex., summer 1963, Juilliard Sch., summer 1994. Jr. high music tchr. Lincoln Jr. High Sch., Beaumont, Tex., 1960-61; organist/choir dir. various chs., various locations, 1962-82; dir. adult edn. Morris County Human Resources, Dover, N.J., 1980-82; band and choral dir. Zweibruecken Am. High Sch., Ger., 1982-84. Vocal soloist and pianist Am. Women's Activities, Ger., 1986-87; dir. female choir U.S. Army War Coll., 1978-79, U.S. Air Force Skylarks, Sembach, Ger., 1976-77. Commr., Beaumont (Tex.) Hist. Landmark Commn., 2003; adv. bd., Conv. and Visitors Bur., Beaumont, 2003; hostess/fundraiser Quad City Symphony Guild 75th Ur., Rock Island, 1989, Links, Inc. Beautillion Scholarship, 1989, Installation Vol. Coord. Cons., Ft. Belvoir, Va., 1990-91; minister music First Bapt. Ch., Vienna, Va., 1995; bd. dirs. S.E. Tex. Cmty. Devel. Corp.; active numerous charitable orgns. Recipient Molly Pitcher award U.S. Army F.A. Officers, 1986, Outstanding Civilian Svc. award Dept. Army, 1990, Disting. Civilian Svc. award Dept. Army, 1992. Mem. NAACP (life mem.), Rock Island Arsenal Hist. Soc. (hon. mem.), The Links, Inc., Just Good Friends, Inc., Bible Study Fellowship Internat. Baptist. Avocations: bridge, bid whist, travel, reading. Home: 7445 Prestwick Cir Beaumont TX 77707

BRAIN, GEORGE BERNARD, university dean; b. Thorp, Wash., Apr. 25, 1920; s. George and Alice Pearl (Ellison) B.; m. Harriet Gardinier, Sept. 28, 1940; children— George Calvin, Marylou. BA, Central Wash. State U., Ellensburg, 1946, MA, 1949; Ed.D., Columbia Tchrs. Coll., 1957; postgrad., U. Wash., Wash. State U., Harvard U., U. Colo., Stanford U. Tchr. math. and sci. Yakima (Wash.) secondary schs., 1946-49; instr. Central Wash. State Coll., 1949-50; elementary sch. prin. Ellensburg, 1950-51; successively elementary sch. prin., asst. supt. schs., supt. schs. Bellevue, Wash., 1951-59; vis. prof. Central Wash. State Coll., 1953, Wash. State U., 1959, U. Md., 1964; supt. schs. Balt., 1959-66; dean Coll. Edn., also dir. summer schs. Wash. State U., Pullman, 1965-85; fellow Danforth Found., 1986—. Lectr. Columbia, U. Conn., Harvard U., Ga., U. Del., Johns Hopkins, Morgan U., U. Okla., Towson State U., Stanford, Wash. U.; chmn. Fulbright Group Western European Seminar Comparative Edn., 1959; chmn. ednl. policies commn. N.E.A.; ednl. cons. (Office Edn.), 1962—; cons. Ednl. Testing Service, Princeton, N.J., 1964-67; dir. Intext Pub. Inc., Scranton, Pa., Worldbook-Childcraft (Scott-Fetzer); bd. dirs. Md. Acad. Sci., 1960-65, Nat. Edn. Found., Field Enterprises Ednl. Corp., 1970—, Pacific Am. Inst., 1977— Mem. editorial adv. bd.: Scholastics Publs, 1963—, Am. Sch. and Univ, 1960-64, Education, USA, 1964-71; mem. editorial bd.: World Book, 1966—, Jour. Tchr. Edn, 1966— . Served with USNR, 1941- 42; Served with USMCR, 1942-46; maj. lt. col. Res. Recipient Disting. Svc. award Wash. State Jr. Assn. Commerce, 1956, Disting. Svc. award in edn. NCCJ, 1963, Disting. Alumnus award Cen. Wash. U., 1989; named Man of Year Met. Civic Assn. Balt., 1962; Fulbright scholar, 1959; library named in his honor, Wash. State U., 1987. Life mem. Am. Assn. Sch. Adminstrs. (exec. com. 1964-66, pres. 1965), NEA; hon. life mem. Wash. State Assn. Sch. Adminstrs. (pres. 1959), Md. Assn. Sch. Adminstrs., Nat. Congress P.T.A.; mem. Wash. Edn. Assn. (pres. dept. adminstrn. and supervision 1957), AAAS (exec. com. commn. elementary and secondary sci. 1963-66), Assn. Supervision and Curriculum Devel., Univ. Council Ednl. Adminstrn., Nat. Joint Council Econ. Edn. (exec. com. 1963—), Nat. Conf. Profs. Ednl. Adminstrn., AAUP, Internat. Platform Assn., Nat. Council for Edn. in Health Professions, Nat. Acad. Sch. Execs., Nat. Council Fgn. Study League, Exec. Hall Fame, Phi Delta Kappa, Kappa Delta Pi. Lodges: Rotary (dir. Balt. 1964-65). Presbyterian.

BRAIN, JESSE, manufacturing executive; b. N.Y.C., Nov. 12, 1921; s. David Brain and Anna Goro; m. Marie Evelyn Richter, Mar. 17, 1951 (dec. Oct. 2002); children: Stephen L., Kenneth A., Dion T., Jeffrey S., John R., Cynthia M. LLB, Blackstone Sch. Law, 1963; MS in Indsl. Mgmt., Bklyn. Poly., 1974. Engr., designer Combustion Engring., N.Y.C., 1948—51; pvt. practice mfg. engring. cons. Farmingdale, NY, 1951—53; prodn. mgr. Republic Aviation, Farmingdale, 1953—66; dep. dir. planning and control Grumman Aerospace, Bethpage, NY, 1966—71; dir. ops. Fairchild Industries, Manhattan Beach, 1971—75; gen. mgr. fabrication Skikorsky Aircraft, Stratford, Conn., 1975—99. Author: Aircraft Parts Manufacturing, 1955, Production Control Management, 1985, Historical Aircraft of WWII, 2002. Skipper Sea Scouts Am., N.Y.C., 1938—51; vol. docent Palm Springs (Calif.) Air Mus., 1996—. With USNR, 1943—46. Named Vol. of Yr., Palm Springs Air Mus., 2003. Fellow: ASME. Avocation: writing. Home: 1924 Navajo Dr Palm Springs CA 92264

BRAIN, JOSEPH DAVID, biomedical researcher, educator, ecologist, department chairman; b. Paterson, N.J., Jan. 20, 1940; married, 1961; 3 children. SM, Harvard U., 1962, SMHyg, 1963, SDHyg, 1966. Rsch. assoc. in physiology Harvard U., Boston, 1966—68, from asst. prof. to assoc. prof., 1968—78; prof. physiology Harvard Sch. Pub. Health, Cambridge, Mass., 1978—, Cecil K. and Philip Drinker prof. environ. physiology, dir. Harvard Pulmonary Specialized Ctr. Rsch., 1977—96, dir. respiratory biol. program, 1981—93, dir. physiology program, 1993—98, chair dept. environ. health, 1990—. Mem. com. Cardiovasc. and Pulmonary Study Sect. NIH, 1975-79, program project rsch. rev. com. Nat. Heart, Lung and Blood Inst., 1980-83; bd. sci. counsellors Nat. Inst. Occupl. Safety and Health, 1992-96; dir. Ctr. Environ. Health/Nat. Inst. Environ. Health Scis. Bd. trustees Taylor U., 1984—. Fellow AAAS, Am. Physiol. Soc., Am. Thoracic Soc., Reticuloendothelial Soc., Sigma Xi. Office: Harvard U Sch Pub Health 665 Huntington Ave Boston MA 02115-6021 Office Phone: 617-432-1272. E-mail: brain@hsph.harvard.edu.

BRAINARD, CECILIA MANGUERRA, writer; b. Cebu, The Philippines, Nov. 21, 1947; came to the U.S., 1969, naturalized, 1972. d. Mariano Flores and Concepcion Cuenco Manguerra; m. Lauren Robson Brainard, Oct. 1969; children: Christopher, Alexander, Andrew. BA in Comm. Arts, Maryknoll Coll., 1968; postgrad., UCLA, 1970. Freelance writer, Santa Monica, Calif., 1981—; Freelance editor, 1992—. Lectr., instr. UCLA, UCLA Ext., and other ednl. instns., 1985—; presenter and lectr. in field. Author: Woman With Horns and Other Stories, 1988, Philippine Woman in America, 1991, Song of Yvonne, 1991, retitled When the Rainbow Goddess Wept, 1994, paperback, 1999, Acapulco At Sunset and Other Stories, 1995, Magdalena, 2002; editor: Fiction by Filipinos in America, 1993, Contemporary Fiction by Filipinos in America, 1998, Journey of 100 Years, 2000, Growing Up Filipino, 2003; co-editor: Seven Stories From Seven Sisters: A Collection of Philippine Folktales, 1992, The Beginning and Other Asian Folktales, 1995; fiction co-editor West/Word Jour., 1992; mem. editl. bd. Center-PEN Mag., 1992; author of over 250 essays and 50 stories. Cecilia's Diary, 1962-1969 Recipient Spl. Recognition award L.A. Bd. Edn., 1991, Brody Arts Fund award, 1991; named Outstanding Individual, City of Cebu, 1998; fellow in fiction Calif. Arts Coun., Sacramento, 1991. Mem. Pen Am. Ctr. Roman Catholic. Avocation: collecting antiquarian philippine books. Office: PALH PO Box 5099 Santa Monica CA 90409-5099 E-mail: cbrainard@aol.com.

BRAINARD, MELISSA, accountant; b. Buffalo, Jan. 11, 1969; d. Peter Anthony and Mary Agnes (Lazarus) Arena; m. Kevin Joseph Brainard, Sept. 25, 1993; children: Jacob Leon, Zachary Martin. BS, SUNY, Buffalo, 1991. CPA, N.Y., 1993. From staff mem. to mgr. KPMG, Buffalo, 1991-97; CFO Goodwill Industries Western N.Y., 1997-98; mgr. Deloitte & Touche, Buffalo, 1999—2002; contr. Albright-Knox Art Gallery, Buffalo, 2002—. Avocations: animals, family, running marathons. Personal E-mail: mab1696@cs.com. Business E-Mail: mbrainard@albrightknox.org.

BRAINE, DAVID THOMAS, university athletic director; b. Grove City, Pa., July 7, 1943; m. Carol Bowles; children: Jennifer, Bill, Steven, Meredith. BS, U. N.C., 1965, MS, 1966. Football coach Manatee (Fla.) H.S., 1966-67; freshman and asst. coach Va. Mil. Inst., Lexington, 1967-70; asst. coach U. Richmond, 1971-73, Ga. Tech., Atlanta, 1974-75, athletic dir., 1997—; asst. coach U. Va., Charlottesville, 1976-77, asst. athletic dir., 1978-83; from asst. to assoc. athletic dir. Fresno (Calif.) State Coll., 1983-84; dir. athletics Marshall U., Huntington, W. Va., 1985-87, Va. Tech., Blacksburg, 1988-97. Inducted Mercer County (Pa.) Hall of Fame, 1993. Office: Ga Tech Ga Tech Athletic Assn 150 Bobby Dodd Way NW Atlanta GA 30313-2551

BRAINERD, CHARLES J(ON), psychologist, mathematics professor; b. Lansing, Mich., July 30, 1944; emigrated to Can., 1971; s. Charles Donald and Geraldine Elaine (Leffler) B.; m. Susan Haske, Jan. 18, 1964 (div.); 1 dau., Tereasa Gail; m. Valerie Reyna, Oct. 5, 1985; 1 son, Bertrand. BS, Mich. State U., 1966, MA, 1968, PhD, 1970. Asst. prof. psychology U. Alta., Edmonton, Can., 1971-73, assoc. prof., 1973-76, H.M. Tory prof. social sci., 1983-86; prof. U. Western Ont., London, 1976-83, U. Ariz., Tucson, 1987—2004, U. Tex., Arlington, 2004—. Vis. prof. U. Minn., Mpls., 1980-81, So. Meth. U., Dallas, 1986-87. Author: Piaget's Theory of Intelligence, 1978, Origins of the Number Concept, 1979; editor: Alternatives to Piaget, 1978, Recent Advances in Cognitive-Developmental Theory, 1983, Springer-Verlag Series in Cognitive Development, 1979—, Devel. Rev., 2000—; assoc. editor: Behavioral and Brain Scis., 1980— . Fellow Am. Psychol. Assn., Can. Psychol. Assn. (pres. devel. psychology sect. 1986-87); mem. Psychonomic Soc., Soc. for Research in Child Devel. (assoc. editor Child Devel. 1977-80). Office: Univ Texas Psychology Dept Arlington TX 76019 Office Phone: 817-272-1202. Business E-Mail: brainerd@uta.edu.

BRAINERD, RICHARD CHARLES, human resources executive, consultant, educator; b. LA, Dec. 22, 1944; s. Calvin Richard and Charlotte Louise (Roethe) B.; m. Phyllis Jean Cottingham Wentzel, July 14, 1966, (div. Dec. 1980); children: Bret, Staci; m. Mary Keith Knopp, Mar. 31, 1984; children: Andrew, Mary Angela. BS in Bus. and Econs., U. Wis., 1968; grad. leadership devel. program, Ctr. for Creative Leadership, Greensboro, N.C., 1985. Pers. analyst Wis. Bur. Personnel, Madison, 1968-74; dir. pers., asst. adminstr. for adminstrn. Wis. Dept. Justice, Madison, 1974-80; dep. commr. pers. Minn. Dept. Employee Rels., St. Paul, 1980-85; dir. pers. Ramsey County, St. Paul, 1985-97; human resources dir. Met. Coun., St. Paul, 1997—2004; dir. human resources Am. Red Cross, St. Paul, 2004—05; cons. CPS-HR, Madison, Wis., 2004—. Instr. U. Minn. Carlson Sch. Mgmt. Employer Edn. Svc., Mpls., 1985—; co-chair, mem. exec. bd. Twin Cities Area Labor-Mgmt. Coun., Mpls., 1994—; advisor Inst. for Labor Mgmt. Studies, White Bear Lake, Minn., 1997; speaker on human rels., expert witness, 1985—, Coach Mahtomedi (Minn.) Youth Baseball Assn., 1992-97; vice chair Bd. of Pub. Works, Madison, Wis., 1979-80; vice chair, mem. fin. com. City of Mahtomedi, 1994-2003, city coun., 2004—; pres. Riverside Lions, St. Paul, Minn., 1995-98; bd. dir. ARC North Ctrl. Blood Svcs., St. Paul, Minn., 2003—. Mem. Pub. Employer Labor Rels. Assn., Minn. Pub. Employer Labor Rels. Assn., Internat. Pub. Mgmt. Assn. Human Resources (pres. 1990, bd. dirs.; hon. life, Stockberger award), St. Paul Pers. Dirs. Assn. (pres., v.p., sec.-treas.). Lutheran. Avocations: skiing, hunting, swimming, reading, writing. Home: 1823 Park Ave Mahtomedi MN 55115-1932 E-mail: richardbrainerd@comcast.net.

BRAININ, STACY L., lawyer; b. Houston, Jan. 3, 1959; BA with high honors, U. Tex., 1981, JD with high honors, 1984. Bar: Tex. 1984, admitted to practice: US Dist. Ct. (No. Dist.) Tex. 1986, US Ct. Appeals (5th Cir.) 1986, US Dist. Ct. (Ea. Dist.) Tex. 1987, US Supreme Ct. 1991. Ptnr., antitrust & white collar criminal defense Haynes and Boone LLP, Dallas. Assoc. editor Tex. Law Rev., 1983—84. Mem.: Dallas Bar Assn. (Antitrust & Trade Regulation Sect.), ABA (Litig. Sect., Criminal Justice Sect. white collar crime com. healthcare fraud subcom), Phi Beta Kappa, Order of Coif. Office: Haynes and Boone LLP 901 Main St Ste 3100 Dallas TX 75202-3789 Office Phone: 214-651-5584. Office Fax: 214-200-0373. Business E-Mail: stacy.brainin@haynesboone.com.

BRAISTED, MADELINE CHARLOTTE, artist, retired financial planner, military officer; b. Jamaica, N.Y., Nov. 23, 1936; d. Melvin Vincent and Charlotte Marie (Klos) B. AAS, Nassau C.C., 1968; BA, Hofstra U., 1973, MA, 1975; grad., U.S. Command and Gen. Staff Coll., 1985. Cert. fin. planner, 1991. Reservations agt. Airline Industry, N.Y.C., 1957-64; reservations contr. Auto Lease Industry, N.Y.C., 1964-66; nuclear medicine technician Queens Gen. Hosp., Jamaica, N.Y., 1969-70; lab. mgr. CUNY, 1970-80; owner Energy Etcetera, Flushing, N.Y., 1979-85; active duty with U.S. Army Health Profl. Support Agy., Office of Surgeon Gen., Washington, 1980-92. Author, pub. Energy Etcetera catalog, 1981-85; artist On Shore painting (honorable mention 1974). Merit badge counselor Boy Scouts Am., Queens County, N.Y., 1980-83; active PTA, Jamaica, 1980-84. Served with USMC, 1954-57, from sgt. to maj. USAR, 1975-96. Decorated Legion of Merit, Army Commendation medal with one oak leaf, Army Achievement medal with one oak leaf cluster, expert field med. badge. Mem. NAFE, APHA, Am Acad. Med. Adminstrs., Fin. Planners Assn., Am. Assn. Individual Investors, Assn. Mil. Surgeons U.S., Res. Officers Assn., Ret. Officers Assn., Nat. Art League, Rockaway Artists Alliance, Queens Coun. Arts. Roman Catholic. Avocations: painting, sculpture.

BRAITERMAN, THEA GILDA, economics professor, state legislator; b. Balt., Sept. 11, 1927; d. Isaac E. and Clara (Fink) Bloom; m. Marvin Braiterman, Mar. 21, 1948; children: Kenneth, Marta, David. BS, Johns Hopkins U., 1949; MA, U. Md., 1966; PhD, Union Inst., 1977. Assoc. prof. econs. Balt. Coll. of Commerce, 1966-73; prof. econs. New England Coll., Henniker, N.H., 1973—; mem. N.H. Ho. of Reps., 1988-94. Cons. on retirement, 1988—; selectman Town of Henniker, 1997—. Author: Workbook on Economic Theory, 1966; contbr. articles to profl. jours. Sec., bd. govs. United Way of Merrimack County, Concord, N.H., 1984-90; v.p., bd. govs. Cmty. Svcs. Coun., Concord, 1980-84. Jane Addams Peace Assn. grantee, 1976-77; Gilmore grantee New Eng. Coll., 1988-90. Mem. Am. Econ. Assn., Ea. Econ. Assn. Home: PO Box 686 Henniker NH 03242-0686 Office: New England Coll Henniker NH 03242 E-mail: theabrait@conknet.com.

BRAITHWAITE, BARBARA J., retired secondary school educator; BA, Ctrl. Mich. U., 1959; MA, U. Mich., 1960. Geography tchr. Pocono Mountain Sch. Dist., Swiftwater, Pa., 1980—2001; ret., 2001. Recipient 1st Place award Am. Express geography competition for tchrs., 1990, Outstanding Secondary Level Tchr. of the Year award Pa. Coun. Social Studies, 1992, Innovative Tchg. award State Farm Ins. Co., 1995. Mem. Pa. Geog. Alliance (steering com., tchr. cons.), Pocono Regional Geog. Alliance (co-founder, chairperson), Nat. Coun. Geog. Edn., Pa. Geog. Soc. (Tchr. Recognition award 1993, U.S., Russia, Ukraine Tchr. Excellence award 1997, Pa. Tchr. of Yr. 1999). Home: 65 Stones Throw East Stroudsburg PA 18301-9694 also: Pocono Mountain Sch Dist Swiftwater PA 18370-0200 Personal E-mail: bjb65@aol.com.

BRAITHWAITE, WILFRED JOHN, physics professor; b. Ferndale, Wash., Apr. 11, 1940; s. John Alfred and Joyce Elinor (Gunderson) B.; m. Wanda Pearl Chism, June 3, 1961 (div. 1975). BS in Physics with honors, Seattle Pacific U., 1962; MS in Physics, U. Wash., 1965, PhD in Physics, 1971; postgrad., U. Tex., 1988-89. Instr. physics Princeton (N.J.) U., 1970-72; asst. prof. physics U. Tex., Austin, 1972-79, rsch. scientist faculty, 1979-81; tech. and sci. cons. Austin, 1981-89; assoc. prof. physics U. Ark., Little Rock, 1989-95, prof. physics, 1995—. Vis. staff mem. Los Alamos (N.Mex.) Nat. Lab., 1975-76, 78-79; vis. scientist Ind. U., Bloomington, 1990-96; affiliate prof. physics U. Wash., Seattle, 1991-96; sci. assoc. PPE divsn. CERN, Geneva, Switzerland, 1992—; guest scientist Brookhaven Nat. Lab., Upton, N.Y., 1992—; lectr. in field; grant referee Ark. Sci. and Tech. Authority, 1990—; cons. for GE Corp. R&D, 2002—. Numerous unedited contbns.; jour. referee Phys. Rev. C and Phys. Rev. Letters, 1970—, Found. Physics, Assoc. Ed. Ark. Acad. Sci., 2000—. U.S. Dept. Energy rsch. grantee, 1992-95, 99—, Ark. Sci. and Tech. Authority rsch. grantee, 1993-94, 96-98; numerous grants from NSF, Dept. of Energy, Robert A Welch Found. Mem. IEEE, Am. Phys. Soc., Nat. Assn. for Rsch. in Sci. Teaching, N.Y. Acad. Sci., Ark. Acad. Sci. Achievements include rsch. of time reversal invariance; high excitation neutron particle-hole states; charge-dependent matrix elements in light nuclei; method for determining rotational symmetries of nuclear states using heavy ions; multiply-excited atomic states in helium-like and lithium-like oxygen; strength of the 3-alpha process in stellar helium burning; method for identifying antimatter stars; large isospin mixing in light nuclei via scattering comparisons of positive and negative pions near the pion-nucleon resonance; measurement limits on source sizes formed in symmetric collisions of ultra-relativistic heavy nuclei; method for separating charged kaons and pions in Time Projection Chambers via in-flight decays; instrument design for high-energy nuclear physics. Home: 1 Broadmoor Dr Little Rock AR 72204-4818 Office: Univ of Ark at Little Rock Dept Physics and Astronomy 2801 S University Ave Little Rock AR 72204 E-mail: wjbraith@comcast.net.

BRAKAS, NORA JACHYM, education educator; b. Schenectady, N.Y., Aug. 9, 1952; d. Thaddeus Michael and Theresa Mary (Patnode) J.; m. Jurgis Brakas, June 15, 1996. BS in Elem. Edn., Plattsburg State U. Coll., 1974; MS in Reading, SUNY, Albany, 1977. Cert. Advanced Study in Reading, 1986, PhD in Reading, 1990. Cert. elem. sch. tchr., reading tchr. Elem. sch. and reading tchr. Lee (Mass.) Ctrl. Sch., 1976-82; reading specialist Guilderland (N.Y.) Sch. Dist., 1988-89; rsch. asst., tchg. asst. SUNY, Albany, 1985-88, instr. reading dept., 1989-90; asst. prof. tchr. edn., reading specialist Southeastern La. U., Hammond, 1990-91, Marist Coll., Poughkeepsie, N.Y., 1991—. Presenter, spkr. in field. Contbr. articles to profl. jours. Student Literacy Corp. grantee U.S. Dept. Edn., 1991, IBM/Marist Joint Study Project grantee, 1992. Mem. Internat. Reading Assn., Soc. Children's Book Writers and Illustrators. Avocations: drawing, writing children's books, collecting antique children's books. Home: PO Box 176 Rhinecliff NY 12574-0176 Office: Marist Coll 388 F Dyson Poughkeepsie NY 12601 E-mail: Nora.Brakas@Marist.edu.

BRAKE, CECIL CLIFFORD, retired diversified manufacturing executive; b. Ystrad, Mynach, Wales, Nov. 14, 1932; came to U.S., 1967; s. Leonard James and Ivy Gertrude (Berry) B.; m. Vera Morris, Aug. 14, 1954; children— Stephen John, Richard Colin, Vanessa Elaine Chartered engr.; B.Sc. in Engring., U. Wales, 1954; M.Sc., Cranfield Inst., Bedford, Eng., 1957; grad. A.M.P., Harvard U. Sch. Bus., 1985. Mgr. research and devel. Schrader Fluid Power, Wake Forest, N.C., 1968-70, engring. mgr., 1970-75; mng. dir. Schrader U.K. Fluid Power, 1975-77; v.p., gen. mgr. Schrader Internat., 1977-78; group v.p. Schrader Bellows, Fluid Power, Akron, Ohio, 1978-82; exec. v.p. Scovill, Inc., Waterbury, Conn., 1982-86; pres. Yale Security, Inc. subs. Scovill, Inc.; group exec. Eagle Industries, Inc., Chgo., 1986—; retired, 1997. Chief oper. officer Mansfield (Ohio) Plumbing Products Inc., Hart and Cooley Inc., Holland, Mich., Caron Internat., Inc., Rochelle, Ill., Caron Internat., Inc., Rochelle, Ill., Chemineer Inc., Dayton, Ohio, Pulsafeeder Inc., Rochester, N.Y., Clevaflex Inc., Cleve., Equality Specialties Inc., N.Y.C., De Vilbiss Co., Toledo, Hill Refrigeration, Trenton, N.J., Air-Maze Corp., Bedford Heights, Ohio, Burns Aerospace Corp., Winston Salem, N.C., Atlantic Industries, Inc., Nutley, N.J., Stimsonite

Products, Niles, Ill.; ptnr., owner Prince of Wales Inc.; bd. dirs. CFI Industries. Avocations: sailing, golf. Office: Eagle Industries Inc 2 N Riverside Plz Chicago IL 60606-2600 also: 17 Harborview Rd Westport CT 06880-5061 Home: 1461 Sabal Palm Dr Boca Raton FL 33432 E-mail: cecilcliffb@aol.com.

BRAKE, JOHN RONALD, agricultural economics educator; b. Stanton, Mich., Jan. 22, 1932; s. D. Hale and Marjorie Naomi (Valentine) B.; m. Betty Jane Neitzel, Sept. 21, 1952; children— Susan Rene, Catherine Joanne, Jan Michelle, Elisa Marie. BS, Mich. State U., 1955, M., 1956; PhD, NC State U., 1959. Asst. prof. Mich. State U., East Lansing, 1959-63, assoc. prof., 1963-69, prof., 1969-1980, William I. Myers prof. agrl. fin. Cornell U., 1981-1996, ret., 1996; contr. Office Tech. Assessment, Washington, 1985; spl. advisor to CEO Farm Credit Adminstrn., Washington, 1989-90. Mem. Am. Agr. Econ. Assn. (found. bd. 1989-92). Author Farm and Personal Finance, 1968. Editor Agrl. Fin. Rev., 1983— Home: 11 Stormy View Rd Ithaca NY 14850-9774

BRAKE, TIMOTHY L., lawyer; b. St. Joseph, Mo., Apr. 8, 1948; s. Douglas E. and Ruth E. (Fahling) B.; m. Julia Marie Gerkin, Sept. 3, 1977; children: Jennifer L., Douglas M. BA in English, Regis Coll., 1970; JD, U. Mo., 1973. Bar: Mo. 1973, U.S. Dist. Ct. (we. dist.) Mo. 1973. Assoc. Margolin & Kirwan, Kansas City, 1973-79, ptnr., 1979-80; sole practice Kansas City, 1980-2001; of counsel Davis, Bethune & Jones, L.L.C., 2001—. Bd. dirs. Ozanam Home for Boys, 1990—2001, Lantz Welch Charitable Found., 1991—96. Fellow U. Mo. Law Found.; mem. Def. Lawyers Assn. (dir. western sect. 1979-80), Assn. Trial Lawyers Am., Mo. Assn. Trial Attys., Mo. Bar Assn., Kansas City Met. Bar Assn., Friends Art, Friends Zoo, Kansas City Athletic Club (dir. 1986-87), Hallbrook Country Club, Homestead Country Club. Home: 3620 Wyncote Ln Shawnee Mission KS 66205-2739 Office: 1100 Main St Kansas City MO 64105-2105 E-mail: tbrake@dbjlaw.net.

BRAKEBILL, JEAN NEWTON, career officer, nurse, educator; b. Mobile, Ala., Sept. 4, 1953; d. James Harold and Eleanor (Mrotek) Newton; m. James Arden Brakebill, Dec. 15, 1985; 1 child, Justin James. BSN, West Tex. State U., 1975; MS, Corpus Christi U., 1982; MBA in Health Adminstrn., Nat. U., 1987. RN, Tex. Staff nurse Southwestern Gen. Hosp., El Paso, Tex., 1975-76; commd. ensign U.S. Navy, 1976, advanced through grades to capt., 1998, staff nurse Naval Hosp., Charleston, SC, 1976, staff nurse Okinawa, Japan, 1978, head nurse ICU Corpus Christi, Tex., 1980-83, head nurse, clin. cons., ednl. program adminstr. Naval Hosp. San Diego, 1983-89; divsn. head med. surg. ward Naval Hosp., Long Beach, Calif., 1989-90, clin. nurse specialist inpatient nursing, 1990-91, head dept. inpatient nursing, 1991-92, head dept. command edn. and tng., 1992-93; command edn. and tng. program adminstr. Naval Med. Ctr., Portsmouth, Va., 1993-95; head dept. command staff edn. and tng. Twenty-Nine Palms Naval Hosp., Marine Corps Air Ground Ctr., Calif., 1995-98; dir. nursing svcs. Twenty-Nine Palms Naval Hosp., Calif., 1998-2001; instr. first aid, CPR ARC, 1998—. Instr. trainer BLS Am. Heart Assn., various locations, 1985—2003; advanced trauma life support educator, San Diego, 1987—91; nurse ARC, 1980—, mem. bd. execs. Morongo Basin chpt., 2001—05, chair health and safety com., 2002—05. V.p. Blessed Sacrament Elem. Sch. Bd., 2001—02, pres., 2000—02, cathecist, 2003—. Mem.: Kappa Delta. Roman Catholic. Avocations: guitar, needlecrafts, reading, swimming, art. Personal E-mail: brakebill002@earthlink.net.

BRAKEL, SAMUEL JAN, public safety executive, law educator; b. Lisse, Netherlands, Nov. 10, 1943; s. Willem Brakel and Henriette Brakel-de Hoest; children: Lia, Christian. BA, Davidson Coll., 1965; JD, U. Chgo., 1968. Rsch. fellow Am. Bar Found., Chgo., 1969—88; v.p. adminstrv. legal staff Isaac Ray Ctr., Inc., Chgo., 1988—2002; CEO Isaac Ray Forensic Group, LLC, Chgo., 2002—. Lectr. No. Ill. U. Coll. Law, DeKalb, Ill., 1988—90; adj. prof. law DePaul U. Coll. Law, Chgo., 1990—. Contbr. over 50 articles to profl. jours. in field. Office: Isaac Ray Forensic Group LLC 200 S Michigan Ave Ste 710 Chicago IL 60604 Home: 4250 N Marine Dr Chicago IL 60613 Office Phone: 312-212-9500.

BRAKELEY, GEORGE ARCHIBALD, JR., fundraising consultant; b. Washington, Apr. 18, 1916; s. George Archibald and Lillian (Fay) B.; m. Roxana Byerly; children: George Archibald III, Deborah Fay, Joan Keller. BA, U. Pa., 1938. V.p., dir. John Price Jones Co., Inc. (fund-raising counsel), N.Y.C.; pres., treas. John Price Jones Co. (Can.), Ltd., 1950-52; chmn., CEO G.A. Brakeley & Co., Ltd., 1952-61, G.A. Brakeley & Co., Inc., L.A., 1956-69; chmn., chief exec. officer Brakeley, John Price Jones Inc., 1972-83; chmn. Brakeley, John Price Jones, Inc., 1983-87, sr. cons., 1987—. Author: Tested Ways to Successful Fund Raising. Trustee Ctr. for the Study of the Presidency. Capt. C.E. AUS, WWII. Mem. Mayflower Soc., Anglers Club (N.Y.C.), Montreal Racket Club (hon.), Wee Burn Golf Club (Darien, Conn.), Royal Poinciana Golf Club (Naples, Fla.). Episcopalian. Home (Summer): 185 South Ave 26 New Canaan CT 06840

BRAKEMAN, LOUIS FREEMAN, retired university official; b. Kalamazoo, Nov. 9, 1932; s. Louis Freeman and Ruth Adelaide (Parsons) B.; m. Lori Mallett, Aug. 16, 1953; children: David, Mark, Peter, Paul, Amy. BA, Kalamazoo Coll., 1954; MA, Fletcher Sch. Diplomacy, Tufts U., 1955, PhD, 1963; LHD, Denison U., 1985. Lectr. history Brown U., 1958-59; asst. prof. polit. sci. Carroll Coll., Waukesha, Wis., 1959-62; mem. faculty Denison U., Granville, Ohio, 1962-85, prof. polit. sci., 1968-85, chmn. dept., 1965-70, dean Coll., 1970-73, provost, 1973-85, acting pres., 1974-75; dir. research project faculty devel. Gt. Lakes Colls. Assn., 1985-86; provost Stetson U., DeLand, Fla., 1987-93. Vis. prof. polit. sci. Kalamazoo Coll., 1987; vis. scholar center for Study of Higher Edn. U. Mich., 1980; dir. Regional Council Center for Internat. Students, summers 1966-68; chmn. regional selection com. Danforth Found. Assocs. Program, 1971-73; mem. Common Cause, 1972—. Co-author: Research Problems in American Politics, 1969, What One Has Within, What the Context Provides, 1989; contbr. articles to profl. jours. Pres. Volusia County Arts Coun., 1994-96, West Volusia Habitat for Humanity, 1996-98; sec. DeLand Mus. Art, 2000-01. Fulbright scholar India, 1957-58; Danforth grad. fellow, 1954-57 Mem. Nature Conservancy, Phi Beta Kappa. Presbyterian (elder). Home: 10 Northlake Dr Orange City FL 32763 E-mail: Lbrakema@earthlink.net.

BRAKEMEYER, WILLIAM DOANE, retired music educator; b. Hollywood, Calif., Oct. 21, 1944; s. Moritz Doane and Marguerite Ellen Brakemeyer. BA, San Fernando Valley State Coll., Northridge, Calif., 1968; MA, Calif. State U., San Bernardino, 1979. Cert. elem. tchr. Calif., 1969, cmty. coll./adult sch. tchr. Calif., 1989, cert. edn. for gifted and talented U. of Calif. Riverside, 2005. Tchr./music tchr. Lancaster Sch. Dist., Lancaster, Calif., 1968—72; music/English/asb tchr. Fontana USD - Alder Jr. H.S., Fontana, Calif., 1972—91; English tchr. Fontana USD - AB Miller H.S., Fontana, Calif., 1991—2004. Advanced placement coord. Fontana USD - AB Miller H.S., Fontana, Calif., 1996—2000; dist. lead music tchr. Fontana Unified Sch. Dist., Fontana, Calif., 1986—90; WASC coord. Fontana AB Miller H.S., Fontana, Calif., 2000—04; commr. Calif. Dept. of Edn. - Curriculum Devel. and Supplemental Materials Commn., Sacramento, 2002—. Composer: (sacred choral compositions) Religious choral works; arranger (musical compositions). Recipient Outstanding tchr. award, 1976. Mem.: Inland Master Chorale (v.p. of programming), Calif. Assn. for the Gifted, Phi Delta Kappa, Calif. Teachers Assn. Ret. (life), NEA Ret. (life), Fostoria Glass Collectors, Inc. (pres.), Heisey Club of Calif. (pres., treas., newsletter editor 1991—2005), Heisey Collectors of Am., Phi Mu Alpha (life; pres., treas. 1964—67). Home: 2214 Drummond St Riverside CA 92506-1532 Personal E-mail: brakemeyer@msn.com.

BRAKENSIEK, JAY CLEMENCE, county official; b. Troy, Mo., Apr. 23, 1954; s. Clemence Ernst and Juanita Geraldine (Gaylord) B.; children: Gregory Jay, Matthew James. BS in Biology, Truman State U., 1977, MA in Biosci. Edn., 1981; MS in Indsl. Hygiene, U. So. Calif., 1991, hazardous waste mgmt. cert., 2003; Exec. MBA, Peter F. Drucker Grad. Sch. Mgmt. Claremont Grad. U. Cert. tchr., Calif.; registered environ. assessor; cert. safety profl. Cardiopulmonary technologist, respiratory care practitioner Huntington Meml. Hosp., Pasadena, Calif., 1983-90; safety officer L.A. County Dept. Pub. Works, Alhambra, Calif., 1990-93; risk mgr., 1993-95; mgr. Safety and Med. Metro. Water Dist. of So. Calif., 1995—2001; deputy dir. Office Environ. Health and Safety, LA Unifed Sch. Dist., 2001—. Instr. biology Citrus Coll., Glendora, Calif., 1984-87; instr. life scis. Pasadena City Coll., 1985-88; safety officer L.A. County Dept. Pub. works, Alhambra, Calif., 1990-93; risk mgr. occupational safety Indsl. Hygiene and Workers' Comp., 1993-95; pres. J.C. Brakensiek and Assocs., 1995—. Mem. sch. bd. First Luth. Ch. and Sch., 1988-91, asbestos cons., 1990—; mem. Endowment Com., 1993-95. Nat. Inst. Occupational Health and Safety fellow U. So. Calif. Inst. Safety and Systems Mgmt., 1988, 89, 90, 91; recipient L.A. County Productivity and Quality awards cert. for Devel. and Implementation of Computerized Seach Programs for Health and Safety Regulations, 1992, Mobile Med. Monitoring Program, High Hazard Operations Rev., 1993, Devisional Safety Coord. Program, 1994, Nat. Assn. Counties Achievement award, 1994, Med. Monitoring Program. Mem. Am. Indsl. Hygiene Assn. (pres.-elect So. Calif. chpt. 2000-2001, pres. 2001-2002, law com. 1998-2001), Am. Conf. Govtl. Indsl. Hygienists, Nat. Safety Coun., Am. Soc. Safety Engrs. (v.p. Long Beach chpt. 1999-2000), Am. Soc. Safety Engrs. (nat. del. Long Beach chpt. 2000-2001, chair environ. mgmt. com., environ. practice splty. 1999-2001), County Safety Officers Orgn. Calif., U. So. Calif. Inst. Safety and Systems Triumvirate, N.E. Mo. State U. Alumni Assn., U. So. Calif. Gen. Alumni Assn., Mensa. Republican. Avocations: backpacking, photography, travel, sailing, writing. E-mail: jay.brakensiek@alumni.usc.edu.

BRAKER, GREGORY S., lawyer; b. Beaver Dam, Wis., June 19, 1962; BA magna cum laude, Evangel Coll., 1984; MA with honors, U. Md., 1987; JD, Georgetown U., 1992. Bar: Md. 1992, DC 1995, admitted to practice: US Dist. Ct. (Dist. Md.), US Dist. Ct. (DC), US Dist. Ct. (Ea. Dist.) Va., US Ct. Appeals (4th Cir.). Ptnr., Corp. Def. Dept. & Environ. Dept. Venable LLP, Washington. Lectr. in field. Co-author: The Knock on the Door: Preparing for, and Responding to, a Criminal Investigation, 1999; contbr. Mem.: Environ. Law Inst., Bar Assn. DC, ABA (Natural Resources, Environment & Energy Law Sects.), Md. State Bar Assn. Avocation: coaching youth sports teams. Office: Venable LLP 575 7th St NW Washington DC 20004 Office Phone: 202-344-4807. Office Fax: 202-344-8300. Business E-Mail: gsbraker@venable.com.

BRAKKE, MYRON KENDALL, retired research chemist, educator; b. Fillmore County, Minn., Oct. 23, 1921; s. John T. and Hulda Christina (Marburger) B.; m. Betty-Jean Einbecker, Aug. 16, 1947; children: Kenneth Allen, Thomas Warren, Joan Patricia, Karen Elizabeth. BS, U. Minn., 1943, PhD, 1947; DSc (hon.), U. Nebr., 1996. Rsch. assoc. Bklyn. Bot. Garden, 1947-52; rsch assoc. U. Ill., 1952-55; rsch. chemist U.S. Dept. Agr., Lincoln, Nebr., 1955-86. Prof. plant pathology U. Nebr., Lincoln, 1955-86. Editor: Virology, 1960-66; contbr. articles to profl. jours. Fellow AAAS, Am. Phytopath. Soc. (Award of Distinction 1988); mem. Am. Chem. Soc., Nat. Acad. Scis., Sigma Xi, Phi Lambda Upsilon, Gamma Sigma Delta, Alpha Zeta. Home: 4429-103 Columbine Dr Bellingham WA 98226 E-mail: mkbrakke@mac.com.

BRAKKEN, WILLIAM, home improvement retail executive; Exec. v.p., CFO, sec. and treas. Lanoga Corp., Redmond, Wash. Office: Lanoga Corp 17946 NE 65th St Redmond WA 98052-4963 Office Fax: (426) 882-2959.

BRAKSICK, LESLIE, academic administrator; b. Ellenville, N.Y., Feb. 21, 1965; d. Herb and Connie Wilk; 1 child, Madeleine; m. Matthew Braksick, May 10, 1991; 1 child, Austin. BA in English & Psychology, St. Bonaventure U., Olean, N.Y., 1986; MA in Indsl. Psychology, Western Mich. U., 1987, PhD in Orgnl. Behavior, 1990. Internat. cons. Western Mich. U., Kalamazoo; cons. U. Mich., Ann Arbor, sr. cons.; pres., CEO, co-founder Continuous Learning Group, Pitts. Adj. instr. W.Va. U., Morgantown; sr. cons. Ctr. Entrepreneurial Studies, Morgantown. Author: Unlock Behavior, Unleash Profits, 2000; contbr. articles to profl. jours. Bd. dirs. Heart Ctr. Children's Hosp., Pitts.; v.p. missions Presbyn. Ch. Sewickley, Pa. Mem. Assn. Behavior Mgmt. (bd. dirs.), Orgn. Behavior Mgmt. Network (awards coord.). Avocations: piano, violin, bass, tennis. Home: Backbone Rd Sewickley PA 15143 Office: Continuous Learning Group 500 Cherrington Corp Ctr Coraopolis PA 15108

BRALEY, OLETA PEARL, community health nurse, writer; b. Rochester, NY, July 19, 1944; d. Horace Everet and Ruby Doris Sullivan; m. Edward Walter Plow, June 24, 1967 (div. Jan. 10, 1990); children: James Edward Plow, John Patrick Plow; m. Franklin John Braley, Mar. 17, 1990 (dec. 1992). Lic. in cosmetology, Continental Sch. Beauty, 1966; student, Sch. Visual Arts, N.Y.C., 1963. Prodn. Kodak Park, Rochester, 1964—66; hairdresser local salons Rochester, 1966—80; money room oper. AMSA, Rochester, 1986—90; home health aide Tender Loving Care, Rochester, 1990—97; home health caretaker Via Health II, Rochester, 1992—2004, Home Care Plus, 2004—. Author: (poetry book) Best of the 90's, 1996, Best Poetry and Poets, 2002; composer: (songs) Remember, 1997, Wondering, 1997, Here to Stay, A Country Letter; featured (on-air interview) with Brian Jobel, N.Y.C., 1999, author various poems in field; lyricist: Our American Vet, 2005, staff writer: Countrywine Pub., 2005—. Recipient Editor's Choice award, Internat. Soc. Poetry, 1995—98, 2002. Avocations: music, art, writing, playing piano and cello. Home: 91 B Green Leaf Meadows Rochester NY 14612-4347

BRALY, ANGELA F., lawyer, insurance company executive; b. 1961; BBA, Tex. Tech. Univ.; JD, So. Methodist Univ. Bar: Mo. 1985. Former ptnr. Lewis Rice & Fingersh LC, St. Louis; gen. counsel RightCHOICE Managed Care Inc., St. Louis, 1999—2003; pres. & CEO Blue Cross Blue Shield of Mo., St. Louis, 2003—05; exec. v.p., gen. counsel, chief pub. affairs officer WellPoint Inc., Indpls., 2005—. Named one of 25 Most Influential Women in Business, St. Louis Bus. Jour., 2000. Mem.: ABA, Am. Health Lawyers Assn., State Bar Mo., Bar Assn. Met. St. Louis, St. Louis Health Lawyers Network. Office: WellPoint Inc 120 Monument Cir Indianapolis IN 46204 Office Phone: 317-532-6000.

BRAM, LEON LEONARD, publishing company executive; b. Chgo., Sept. 20, 1931; s. Samuel and Rose Bram; m. Doris A. Hebel, Apr. 29, 1961 (div. 1972); children: Mark James, Alexander Anton; m. Joanne Frances Casino, Sept. 30, 1978 (div. 1990); 1 child, Victoria Lynn. B.Sc., DePaul U., 1967. Various positions Chgo. Pub. Library, 1949-55, F.E. Compton Co., Chgo., 1955-63; dir. editorial rsch. Standard Ednl. Corp., Chgo., 1963-69; exec. editor F.E. Compton Co., Chgo., 1969-74; v.p., editorial dir. Primedia Reference Corp., Mahwah, NJ, 1974-97, arts adminstr., 1998, non-profit mktg. mgr., 1999—. Mem. ALA.

BRAMAN, NORMAN, automotive executive, former sports team executive; b. West Chester, Pa., Aug. 22, 1932; s. Harry and Katie (Rappaport) B.; m. Irma Miller, Sept. 30, 1956; children: Debra Braman Shack, Susan Lynn. BA, Temple U., 1955. With mktg. and sales dept. Seagrams Distbrs., N.Y.C., 1955-57; founder Keystone Stores, Phila., 1957-72; pres. Braman Enterprises, Miami, Fla., 1972—; owner Phila. Eagles, 1985—94; chmn. ARCONA, Miami, 1985-87. Mem. U.S. Holocaust Meml. Council; campaign chmn. United Jewish Appeal, Miami; bd. govs. U. Miami Med. Sch.; bd. dirs. Am. Israel Pub. Affairs Com., Miami; mem. Dade County Planning and Adv. Bd.; founder, trustee Mt. Sinai Med. Ctr., Miami; bd. govs. Tel Aviv U.; trustee United Israel Appeal Named one of Top 200 Collectors, ARTnews Mag., 2004. Mem. Greater Miami C. of C. Republican. Avocation: Collecting modern and contemporary art, especially Am. Office: Braman Enterprises 2060 Biscayne Blvd Fl 2 Miami FL 33137-5024*

BRAMBLE, JAMES HENRY, mathematician, educator; b. Annapolis, Md., Dec. 1, 1930; s. Charles Clinton and Edith (Rinker) B.; m. Margaret Hospital Hays, June 25, 1977; children: Margot, Tamara, Mary, James; 1 stepchild, Myron A. Hays. AB, Brown U., 1953; MA, U. Md., 1955, PhD, 1958; D.Sc. (hon.), Chalmers U. Tech., Göteborg, Sweden, 1985. Mathematician Gen. Electric Co., Cin., 1957-59, Naval Ordnance Lab., White Oak, Md., 1959-60; asst. prof., assoc. prof., prof. U. Md., 1960-68; prof. Cornell U., Ithaca, N.Y., 1968-94, prof. emeritus, 1994; prof. Tex. A&M U., College Station, 1994-99, disting. prof., 1999—. Dir. Center Applied Math., 1974-80; cons. Brookhaven Nat. Lab., 1976-94; vis. prof. Chalmers U. Tech., Göteborg, 1970, 72, 73, 76, 86, U. Rome, 1966-67, Ecole Poly., Paris, 1978, Lausanne, Switzerland, 1979; vis. prof. U. Paris, 1981; lectr. in field. Chmn. editorial bd. Mathematics of Computation, 1975-84; contbr. articles profl. jours. Mem. Am. Math. Soc., Soc. Indsl. and Applied Math. Office: Cornell U Dept Of Math Ithaca NY 14853 also: Tex A&M U Dept Math College Station TX 77843-0001 E-mail: bramble@math.tamu.edu.

BRAMBLE, RONALD LEE, lawyer, consultant; b. Pauls Valley, Okla., Sept. 9, 1937; s. Homer Lee and Ethyle Juanita (Stephens) Bramble; m. Kathryn Louise Seiler, July 2, 1960; children: Julia Dawn, Kristin Lee. AA, San Antonio Coll., 1957; BS, Trinity U., 1959, MS, 1964; JD, St. Mary's U., 1975; DBA, Ind. No. U., 1973. Cert. lay spkr. Meth. Ch. Mgr., guyer Fed-Mart, Inc., San Antonio, 1959—61; tchr. bus. San Antonio Ind. Sch. Dist., 1961—65, edn. coord., bus. tng. specialist, 1965—67; assoc. prof., chmn. dept. mgmt. San Antonio Coll., 1967—73; prin. Ron Bramble Assocs., San Antonio, 1967—77; pres. Adminstrv. Rsch. Assocs., Inc., 1977—82; v.p. PIA, Inc., 1982—83; v.p. fin. Solar 21 Corp., 1983—84; sr. staff Ausburn, Astoria & Seale (formerly Ausburn, O'Neill & Assocs.), San Antonio, 1984—89; pvt. practice, 1990—. Cons., comptr. TEL-STAR Sys., Inc., 1993—95; v.p. MegaTronics Internat. Corp., 1995—2003; pres. Freight Mate, San Antonio, 2003—; lectr. bus., edn. and ch. groups, 1965—. Cons. editor: Prentice-Hall, Inc., 1969—71; contbr. articles to profl. jours. Mem.: ABA, Adminstrv. Mgmt. Soc. (pres. 1966—68, Merit award 1968), Comml. Law League, Christian Legal Soc., Acad. Mgmt., Nat. Assn. Bus. Economists, Internat. Assn. Cons. to Bus., Internat. Platform Assn., Sales and Mktg. Execs. San Antonio (bd. dirs. 1967—68, Disting. Salesman award 1967), Bus. Edn. Tchrs. Assn. (pres. 1964), San Antonio C. of C., World Affairs Coun. of San Antonio, Am. Soc. Trial Cons., Toastmasters, Lions, Phi Delta Phi. Republican. Home: 127 Palo Duro St San Antonio TX 78232-3026 Personal E-mail: rlbramble@aol.com.

BRAMBLETT, GEORGE, JR., lawyer; b. Dallas, May 28, 1940; BA, So. Meth. U., 1963, LLB, 1966. Bar: Tex. 1966. Ptnr., Litig. Haynes and Boone LLP, Dallas. Spkr. in field; contbr. articles to profl. jour. Named Trial Lawyer of Yr., Dallas Bar Assn., 2001. Fellow: Am. Bar Found., Tex. Bar Found., Internat. Soc. Barristers, Am. Bd. Trial Advocates, Internat. Acad. Trial Lawyers, Am. Coll. Trial Lawyers; mem.: Tex. Assn. Def. Counsel, ABA, Phi Delta Phi. Office: Haynes and Boone LLP 901 Main St Ste 3100 Dallas TX 75202-3789 Office Phone: 214-651-5574. Office Fax: 241-200-0374. Business E-Mail: george.bramblett@haynesboone.com.

BRAME, JOSEPH ROBERT, III, lawyer; b. Hopkinsville, Ky., Apr. 18, 1942; s. Joseph Robert and Atwood Ruth (Davenport) B.; m. Mary Jane Blake, June 11, 1966; children: Rob, Blake, Virginia, John, Thomas. BA with high honors, Vanderbilt U., 1964; LLB, Yale U., 1967. Bar: Va. 1968, D.C. 2001. Assoc. McGuire, Woods, Battle & Boothe, Richmond, Va., 1967-72, ptnr., 1972-97; mem. NLRB, 1997-2000; shareholder Ogletree, Deakins, Nash, Smoak & Stewart, P.C., Washington, 2000—02, McGuire Woods, LLP, 2002—. Lectr. in field. Contbr. articles to profl. jours. Mem. adv. bd. Salvation Army, Richmond, 1980-97, chmn., 1989-91; troop com. chmn. Robert E. Lee coun. Boy Scouts Am., 1980-91; chair 10th Amendment Litig. com., Gov.'s Adv. Coun. on Federalism and Self Determination, 1994-97; gen. counsel Rep. Party Va., 1993-96. Mem. Am. Bar Found., Am. Coll. Labor and Employment Lawyers, Va. State Bar, Phi Beta Kappa. Presbyterian. Office: McGuire Woods LLP Washington Sq 1050 Conneticut Ave NW Ste 1200 Washington DC 20036-5317 Office Phone: 202-857-1718. E-mail: rbrame@mcguirewoods.com.

BRAMLETTE, DAVID C., III, federal judge; b. New Orleans, Nov. 27, 1939; BA, Princeton U., 1962; JD, U. Miss., 1965. Assoc., then ptnr. Adams, Forman, Truly, Ward & Bramlette, Natchez, Miss., 1975-91; spl. cir. judge Dist. Ct. (6th dist.) Miss., 1977, 79; fed. judge Dist. Ct. (so. dist.) Miss., 1991—. Trustee Miss. Nature Conservancy, 1990—; pres. BBCHA, 1989-90; active Arcole Hunting Camp, Ducks Unlimited, Nat. Wild Turkey Fedn.; mem. adv. bd. Natchez Lit. Celebration. Office: PO Box 928 Natchez MS 39121-0928 Office Phone: 601-442-3006.

BRAMMELL, STEPHEN HARRISON, lawyer; b. Ardmore, Okla., Dec. 5, 1957; m. Allison Brammell. BBA with distinction, U. Okla., 1979; JD, Georgetown U. Law Ctr., 1982. Bar: Okla. 1982, Tenn. 1988, Nevada 2003. Assoc. Conner & Winters, Tulsa, 1982—84; corp. staff atty. Harrah Entertainment Inc., Las Vegas, 1984—87, sr. staff atty., 1987—97, v.p., assoc. gen. counsel, 1997—99, sr. v.p., gen. counsel, 1999—. Office: Harrah Entertainment Inc Legal Dept One Harrahs Ct Las Vegas NV 89119 Home: 107 S Royal Ascot Ln Las Vegas NV 89144 Office Phone: 702-407-6000. Office Fax: 702-407-6037. Business E-Mail: sbrammell@harrahs.com.

BRAMMER, J. WILLIAM, JR., judge, lawyer; b. Des Moines, Iowa, Sept. 15, 1942; s. James W. and Mary Virginia (Steck) Brammer; m. Donna Crosby, June 20, 1964; children: Jill S., James W. III. BS, U. Ariz., 1964, JD, 1967. Bar: Ariz. 1967, U.S. Dist. Ct. Ariz. 1968, U.S. Ct. Appeals (9th cir.) 1970, U.S. Supreme Ct. 1970. Law clk. to judge Ariz. Ct. Appeals, Tucson, 1967—68; asst. atty. City of Tucson, 1968; from assoc. to ptnr. DeConcini, McDonald, Brammer, Yetwin & Lacy PC, Tucson, 1968—97; judge Ariz. Ct. of Appeals, Tucson, 1997—. Mem. com. exams. Ariz. Supreme Ct., Phoenix, 1977-84, chmn. 1982-84; mem. Commn. on Jud. Conduct, 2003—, chair, 2005—; mem. bd. govs. State Bar Ariz., 1995-97. Bd. visitors U. Ariz. Coll. Law, Tucson, 1981-84, 88—. Fellow: Ariz. Bar Found.; mem.: ABA, Law Coll. Assn. U. Ariz. (pres. 1990—91), Pima County Bar Assn. (pres. 1993—94), Morris K. Udall Inn of Ct. (pres. 2001—02). Office: Ariz Ct Appeals 400 W Congress St Ste 302 Tucson AZ 85701-1353 Office Phone: 520-628-6945. E-mail: brammer@apltwo.ct.state.az.us.

BRAMMER, LAWRENCE MARTIN, psychologist, educator; b. Crookston, Minn., Aug. 20, 1922; s. Martin G. and Edna L. (Thiesen) B.; m. Marian S. Sjolin, Feb. 11, 1945; children: Karin Marie, Kristen Lenore. BS, St. Cloud State U., 1943; MA, Stanford U., 1948, PhD, 1950. Diplomate: Am. Bd. Prof. Psychology. Psychologist Stanford U. Counseling and Testing Ctr., 1948-50; assoc. dean students Sacramento State Coll., 1950-64; prof. ednl. psychology U. Wash., Seattle, 1964-88, prof. emeritus, 1988—. Author: Therapeutic Psychology, 6th edit., 1993, Helping Relationships, 8th edit., 2002, Outplacement and Inplacement Counseling, 1984, How to Cope with Life Transitions, 1991, Caring for Yourself While Caring for Others: A Caregiver's Survival and Renewal Guide, 1999. Lt. M.S.C. AUS, 1944-46. Fulbright fellow, 1961-62 Fellow APA; mem. ACA, Queen City Yacht Club, Elks. Democrat. Lutheran. Home: 8005 Sandpoint Way NE A23 Seattle WA 98115

BRAMNIK, ROBERT PAUL, lawyer; b. N.Y.C., Nov. 17, 1949; s. Abe and Ruth (Richman) B.; m. Sheryl Ann Kalus, Aug. 12, 1973; children: Michael Lawrence, Andrew Martin. BA, CCNY, 1970; JD, Bklyn. Law Sch., 1973. Bar: N.Y. 1974, Ill. 1980, U.S. Dist. Ct. (so. and ea. dists.) N.Y. 1974, U.S. Dist. Ct. (no. dist.) Ill. 1980, U.S. Dist. Ct. (ctrl. dist.) Ill. 1982, U.S. Ct. Appeals (2d cir.) 1974, U.S. Ct. Appeals (4th cir.) 1987, U.S. Ct. Appeals (3d and 7th cirs.) 1992, U.S. Ct. Fed. Claims 1994, U.S. Supreme Ct. 1977. Sr. trial atty. NYSE, Inc., N.Y.C., 1973-75; asst. gen. counsel E.F. Hutton & Co., Inc., N.Y.C., 1975-77, Nat. Securities Clearing Corp., N.Y.C., 1977-79; with Arvey, Hodes, Costello and Burman, Chgo., 1979-86, ptnr., 1982-86, Wood, Lucksinger & Epstein, Chgo., 1987-88, Altheimer & Gray, Chgo., 1988-97, Wildman, Harrold, Allen & Dixon, Chgo., 1997—2003, Duane Morris LLP, Chgo., N.Y.C., 2003—. Lectr. Securities Industry Assn. Compliance and Legal div., N.Y.C., 1980-91, 95-2001. Vice chmn. Ill. Adv. Com. on Commodity Regulation, Chgo., 1985-89, chmn., 1989-95. Fellow: Ill. Bar Found.; mem.: ABA (coms. on futures and derivatives regulation, co-chmn. subcom. on futures commn. merchants), Nat. Futures Assn. (hearing com.

2001—, arbitrator 1991—), Nat. Assn. Sec. Dealers (arbitrator 1981—), Assn. of Bar of City of N.Y. Jewish. Office: Duane Morris LLP 227 W Monroe St Ste 3400 Chicago IL 60606 Office Phone: 312-499-0121. Business E-Mail: rpbramnik@duanemorris.com.

BRAMS, MARVIN ROBERT, economist, mental health counselor, interfaith minister, educator; b. Boston, Apr. 16, 1937; s. Leo and Sarah Brams; m. Myrna Berlin, May 15, 1960; children: Adam, Aaron. BS, Northeastern U., 1959, MBA, 1962; PhD, Clark U., 1967; M in Counseling, U. Del., 1984; postgrad., Carl Rogers Inst. Psychotherapy, 1985, Inst. Rational Emotive Therapy, 1987; MS in Spiritual Therapy, New Sem., 1990. Diplomate Am. Bd. Med. Psychotherapists; ordained as interfaith min. Columbia U., 1989; cert. Nat. Bd. Cert. Counselors; lic. mental health counselor; cert. in clin. pastoral edn. Instr. econs. Northeastern U., 1965-67; economist, prof. urban affairs and pub. policy U. Del., Newark, 1967—97, clin. psychotherapist Employee Wellness Program, 1995—97; fellow in psychoanalytic psychotherapy Harvard U., 2002—03. Econ. cons. to legal profession; vis. scholar Harvard U. Divinity Sch., 1997-99; psychiatry intern Med. Ctr. Del., 1996-97; clin. psychotherapist, VA Hosp., 1999-2001. Contbr. chpts. to books and articles to jours. and newspapers. Mem. Gov.'s Com. Del. State Fins., 1969, Gov.'s Econ. Adv. Coun., 1969-72; adv. com. property tax exemption policy Cities of Newark and Wilmington, 1972-75; mem. Del. Revenue Study Comm., 1973, Citizens Task Force on Housing, 1975, Del. Tomorrow Commn., 1974-76, New Castle County Water Supply Adv. Coun., 1975-81, Del. Revenue Study Com., 1977; fed. revenue sharing adv. com. City of Newark, 1976-78; advisor Del. Dept. Natural Resources, 1979. 1st lt. ordinance AUS, 1959-60. Fellow in urban econs. and pub. policy MIT, 1970, NSF fellow Stanford U., 1971. Mem. ACA, Assn. Humanistic Psychology, Am. Mental Health Counselors Assn., Am. Men and Women of Sci., Mass. Inst. for Psychoanalysis, Northeastern Soc. for Group Psychotherapy. Home: 110 Register Dr Newark DE 19711 Personal E-mail: brams02140@yahoo.com.

BRAMS, STEVEN JOHN, political science professor; b. Concord, N.H., Nov. 28, 1940; s. Nathan and Isabelle (Tryman) B.; m. Eva Floderer, Nov. 13, 1971; children: Julie Claire, Michael Jason. BS, MIT, 1962; PhD, Northwestern U., 1966. Research assoc. Inst. Def. Analyses, Arlington, Va., 1965-67; asst. prof. polit. sci. Syracuse U., 1967-69; asst. prof. NYU, 1969-73, assoc. prof., 1973-76, prof., 1976—. Vis. prof. U. Rochester, U. Pa., U. Mich., Yale U., U. Calif.-Irvine, U. Haifa, Inst. Advanced Studies, Vienna; cons. in field Author: Game Theory and Politics, 1975, Paradoxes in Politics: An Introduction to the Nonobvious in Political Science, 1976, The Presidential Election Game, 1978, Game Theory and the Hebrew Bible, 1980, rev. edit., 2003; author: (with Peter C. Fishburn) Approval Voting, 1983; author: Superior Beings: If They Exist, How Would We Know?, 1983, Superpower Games: Applying Game Theory to Superpower Conflict, 1985, Rational Politics: Decisions, Games and Strategy, 1985; author: (with D. Marc Kilgour) Game Theory and National Security, 1988; author: Negotiation Games: Applying Game Theory of Moves, 1994; author: (with A.D. Taylor) Fair Division: From Cake-Cutting to Dispute Resolution, 1996; author: The Win-Win Solution: Guaranteeing Fair Shares to Everybody, 1999; co-author: Applied Gamed Theory, 1979, Modules in Applied Mathematics: Political and Related Models, 1983; mem. editl. bd. Pub. Choice, 1973—90; mem. editl. bd.: Pub. Choice, 2003—; mem. editl. bd. Am. Polit. Sci. Rev., 1978—82, Jour. Politics, 1968—73, 1978—82, 1991—, Math. Social Scis., 1980—, Theory and Decision, 1982—, Jour. Behavioral Decision Making, 1987—90, Jour. Theoretical Politics, 1988—, Group Decision and Negotiation, 1991—, Control and Cybernetics, 1993—, Rationality and Society, 1999—; mem. editl. bd.: Internat. Studies Quarterly, 1999—2003, Game Theory Soc., 2004—. Social Sci. Rsch. Coun. fellow, 1964-65, Guggenheim fellow, 1986-87; Russell Sage Found. vis. scholar, 1998-99, grantee NSF, 1968-71, 73-75, 80-91, Social Sci. Rsch. Coun., 1968, Ford Found., 1984-85, Sloan Found., 1986-89, U.S. Inst. Peace, 1988-89. Fellow AAAS, Pub. Choice Soc. (pres. 2004—); mem. Am. Econ. Assn., Am. Polit. Sci. Assn., Internat. Studies Assn. (Susan Strange award 2002), Policy Studies Orgn., Peace Sci. Soc. (pres. 1990-91). Democrat. Jewish. Achievements include patents in field. Home: 4 Washington Square Vlg Apt 17I New York NY 10012-1910 Office Phone: 212-998-8510.

BRAMSON, JAMES B., dentist, dental association administrator; DDS, U. Iowa Coll. Dentistry, 1979. Pvt. practice, Mass. Grantee Hillenbrand Fellowship. Mem.: Mass. Dental Soc. (exec. dir. 1997—2001), ADA (dir. Coun. on Dental Practice 1990—97, dir. Commn. on Relief Fund Activities, sec./treas. Endowment and Assistance Fund Inc. 1990—97, exec. dir. 2001—). Office: Am Dental Assn 211 E Chicago Ave Chicago IL 60611

BRAMSON, PHYLLIS HALPERIN, artist, educator; b. Madison, Wis., Feb. 20, 1941; d. Herman and Ester (Goldberg) Halperin. BFA with high honors, U. Ill., 1963; MA in Painting, U. Wis., 1964; MFA, Sch. of Art Inst. Chgo., 1974. Prof. studio arts U. Ill., Chgo. One-woman shows include Gallerie Farideh Cadot, Paris, 1980, Marilyn Butler Gallery, Scottsdale, Ariz., 1983, Hewlett Gallery Carnegie-Mellon U., Pitts., 1985, The Renaissance Soc., Chgo., 1986, Monique Knowlton Gallery, N.Y.C., 1986, Brody's Gallery, Washington, 1987, Victorian Coll. Arts, Melbourne, Australia, 1988, G.W. Einstein Gallery, N.Y.C., 1991, Dart Gallery, Chgo., 1992, Brody's Gallery, Washington, 1993, Phyllis Kind Gallery, Chgo., 1994, Printworks Gallery, Chgo., 1997, Chgo. Cultural Ctr., 1998, Ft. Wayne Mus. Ind., 2001, Ind. U., Bloomington, 2002, Carl Hammer Gallery, Chgo., 2004, Printworks, Chgo., 2004, Littlejohn Contemporary, NY, 2004, Boulder Art Mus, Bolder, Colo., 2004, Gallery of Art U. No. Iowa, 2004, COFA Claire Oliver Fine Arts NY, 2005, others; group shows include The Renwick Gallery, Washington, 1976, The New Mus., N.Y.C., 1979, 96, Musee De Toulon (France), 1983, Seattle Art Mus., 1985, Walter Bischoff Galeries, Stutgardt, Germany, 1990, Smart Mus., Chgo., 1991, Andrew Zarre Gallery, N.Y.C., 1992, Corcoran Mus. Art, Washington, 1993, U. Art Gallery, Vermillion, S.D., 1994, P.P.O.W. Art Gallery, N.Y.C., 1995; group exhbns. include Gallery A, Chgo., 1995, David Bietzel Gallery, N.Y.C., 1995, Associated Am. Artists, N.Y.C., 1996, Mus. Contemporary Art, Chgo., 1996, Southeastern Ctr. for Contemporary Painting, 1996, Carl Hammer Gallery, Chgo., 1999, 03, Brenda Taylor Gallery, N.Y.C., 1999, The New Mus. Contemporary Art, N.Y., N.Y., 2000, Block Mus. Northwestern Ill. U., Evanston, Ill., 2000, Exit Art, N.Y.C., N.Y., 2002, Emily Davis Gallery, Myers Sch. Art U. Akron, Ohio, 2002, Zolla Lieberman Gallery, Chgo., Ill., 2002, Palm Springs (Calif.) Mus., 2002, Sheppard Gallery, U. Nev., Reno, Nev., 2002, Frist Ctr. Visual Arts, Nashville, Tenn., 2003, Nat. Acad. Mus., N.Y., N.Y., 2004 Louis Comfort Tiffany grantee, 1980, Ill. Arts Coun. grantee, 1981, 88, NEA grantee, 1976, 83, 93, Johns Simon Guggenheim grantee, 1993; Sr. Fulbright scholar, Australia, 1988; recipient Rockefeller Found. grant/residency.

BRAMSON, ROBERT SHERMAN, lawyer; b. NYC, Nov. 11, 1938; s. Oscar David and Gertrude (May) B.; m. Ruth Schaffer, June 27, 1942; children: Jonathan, Jennifer, James, Julia. B.M.E., Rensselaer Poly. Inst., 1959; JD, Georgetown U., 1963; postgrad., U. Chgo. Sch. Bus., 1963-64. Bar: Ill. 1963, Pa. 1968, NY 1984. Patent examiner US Patent Office, Washington, 1959-60; patent agt. Stevens, Davis, Miller & Mosher, Washington, 1960-63; atty. Abbott Labs., North Chgo., Ill., 1963-66, Scott Paper Co., Phila., 1966-68; ptnr., head computer and tech. law group Schnader, Harrison, Segal & Lewis, Phila., 1968-89; v.p., gen. patent and tech. counsel Unisys Corp., Blue Bell, Pa., 1989-90; founder Bramson and Pressman, Conshohocken, Pa., 1991, 95—; pres., CEO InterDigital Tech. Corp., King of Prussia, Pa., 1992-95. Adj. prof. Temple U. Law Sch., Phila. Mem. ABA, Internat. Bar Assn., Am. Law Inst., Am. Patent Law Assn., Phila. Patent Law Assn., Phila. Bar Assn. Home: 112 Booth Ln Haverford PA 19041-1752 Office: Bramson & Pressman 1100 Hector St Ste 410 Conshohocken PA 19428-2378 Office Phone: 610-260-4444. Business E-Mail: rbramson@b-p.com.

BRAMWELL, HENRY, federal judge; b. Bklyn., Sept. 3, 1919; s. Henry Hall and Florence Elva (MacDonald) B.; m. Ishbel W. Brown, Jan. 29, 1966. LLB, Bklyn. Law Sch., 1948, LLD (hon.), 1979. Bar: N.Y. bar 1948. Asst. U.S. atty., Bklyn., 1953-61; asso. counsel N.Y. State Rent Commn., 1961-63; judge Civil Ct., N.Y.C., Bklyn., 1966, 69—; asst. adminstrv. judge Kings County, Bklyn., 1974—; judge U.S. Dist. Ct., Bklyn., 1975—; U.S. Sr. Dist. judge, 1987—. Mem. Community Mayors N.Y. State; trustee Bklyn. Law Sch., 1978— Active Bklyn. Old Times Found., Inc. Served with AUS, 1942-44. Profiled in Black Judges on Justice, 1994. Mem. ABA, Nat. Bar Assn. (life), N.Y. State Bar Assn., Bklyn. Bar Assn. (trustee), Fed. Judges Assn. (founding mem.). Home: 101 Clark St Brooklyn NY 11201-2746 Office: US Dist Ct 225 Cadman Plz E Brooklyn NY 11201-1818

BRANAGAN, JAMES JOSEPH, lawyer; b. Johnstown, Pa., Mar. 5, 1943; s. James Francis and Caroline Bertha (Schreier) B.; m. Barbara Jeanne Miller, June 19, 1965; children: Sean Patrick, Erin MacKay, David Michael. BA in English Lit. with honors magna cum laude (Woodrow Wilson fellow), Kenyon Coll., Gambier, Ohio, 1965; LL.B. cum laude, Columbia U., 1968. Bar: Ohio 1968. Assoc. Jones, Day, Reavis & Pogue, Cleve., 1968-72; with Leaseway Transp. Corp., Cleve., 1972-81, gen. counsel, 1975-80, sec., 1979-81, v.p. corp. affairs, 1980-81; also officer, dir. Leaseway Transp. Corp. (subsidiaries); v.p. Premier Indsl. Corp., Cleve., 1981-82; sr. counsel TRW Inc., 1982-88; pvt. practice Cleve., 1988—; treas., gen. counsel, sec. Biomec Inc., 1998—2003. Mem. ABA, Ohio Bar Assn., Cleve. Bar Assn., Phi Beta Kappa. Office Phone: 216-751-6214. Business E-Mail: bizlaw@adelphia.net.

BRANAGH, KENNETH, actor, director; b. Belfast, Northern Ireland, Dec. 10, 1960; m. Emma Thompson, Aug. 1989 (div. 1996); m. Lindsay Brunnock, May 2003. Grad., Royal Academy of Dramatic Art, 1981; LittD (hon.), Queens U., Belfast, 1990. Co-founder Renaissance Theater Co., Eng., to 1994. Actor: (films) Coming Through, 1985, A Month in the Country, 1987, High Season, 1987, Dead Again, 1991, Swing Kids, 1993, Othello, 1995, The Gingerbread Man, 1998, The Proposition, 1998, Celebrity, 1998, The Theory of Flight, 1998, The Dance of Shiva, 1998, The Periwig-Maker (voice), 1999, Wild Wild West, 1999, How to Kill Your Neighbor's Dog, 2000, The Road to El Dorado (voice), 2000, Schneider's 2nd Stage, 2001, Alien Love Triangle, 2002, Rabbit-Proof Fence, 2002, Harry Potter and the Chamber of Secrets, 2002, Five Children and It, 2004; (TV films) Too Late to Talk to Billy, 1982, Easter 2016, 1982, A Matter of Choice for Billy, 1983, To the Lighthouse, 1983, A Coming to Terms for Billy, 1984, Ghosts, 1986, The Lady's Not for Burning, 1987, Strange Interlude, 1988, Look Back in Anger, 1989, Shadow of a Gunman, 1995, Big Al Uncovered, 2000, Conspiracy, 2001, Shackleton, 2002, Warm Springs, 2005; (TV miniseries) Maybury, 1981, Boy in the Bush, 1984, Fortunes of War, 1987; (TV series) Thompson, 1988; dir. (films) Dead Again, 1991, Swan Song, 1992, (TV films) Twelfth Night, or What You Will, 1988, dir., writer (films) In the Bleak Midwinter, 1995, Listening, 2003, actor, dir., writer Henry V, 1989, Hamlet, 1996, actor, dir., prodr. Peter's Friends, 1992, actor, dir., co-prodr. Frankenstein, 1994, actor, dir., prodr., writer Much Ado About Nothing, 1993, Love's Labour's Lost, 2000. Decorated Order of Arts and Letters (France).

BRANAM, MICHAEL A., English language educator; s. James Lloyd Branam and Patricia Ann Ewing, Kiva Beth Branam (Stepmother); m. Catherine Elaine Zenor, May 17, 1997; children: Jacob David, Grace Ann, Michael Gabriel, Mary Elizabeth. BS in Edn., Ind. U., 1995; MEd, Ind. Wesleyan U., Marion, 2002. Lic. tchr. Ind. state Ind. Bd. of Edn. Tchr. English Pike H.S., Indpls., 1997—, Ind. Wesleyan U., Marion, 2002—, Crossroads Bible Coll., Indpls., 2005—; owner, cons. Lighthouse Consulting/Crystal Shores Ednl. Svcs., Greenwood, Ind., 2000—. Ednl. spkr. Lighthouse Consulting, Greenwood, 2003—, rschr., 2000—. Contbr. ednl. papers to profl. publs. Tchr. Greenwood Christian Ch., 2000—05. Mem.: NEA (assoc.), ASCD (assoc.), Homeschool Spkr. and Vendor's Assn. (assoc.), Ind. Learning Disabilities Assn. (assoc.), Nat. Coun. Tchrs. of English (assoc.), Learning Disabilities Assn. of Am. (assoc.). Achievements include research in Educational Pedagogy. Avocations: wrestling, reading, writing. Personal E-mail: mike@hisshininglight.com.

BRANAND, CLAIRE DIANE, advertising executive, writer; d. Frank X. Dostal and Clara A. Weidmann; m. David C. Branand, May 12, 1990 (dec. Sept. 29, 2001); m. Richard M. Halpert, July 3, 1969 (div. July 20, 1973); 1 child, Wendy C. Student, Chamberlayne Jr. Coll., 1962—63; BFA, Parsons Sch. Design, 1966; student, Sch. Visual Arts, 1966—67. Layout artist R.H. Macy & Co., N.Y.C., 1966—70; freelance art dir. and writer Washington, 1974—77; prin., owner Halpert & Assocs. Advt., Washington, 1978—90; owner Branand & Assoc., Washington, 1990—. Author Skye Pub., Annapolis, Md., 1996—. Author: Overboard! A Provocative History of the U.S.S. J.P. Kennedy, Jr., 2000, Here's To Your Health! Cooking With Red Wine, 2002, Nat. Assn. Post-Polio Syndrome Newsletter. Sec. bd. dirs. Nat. Assn. Post Polio Syndrome, Washington, 1991—96. Recipient Citation, Assn. for Help of Retarded Children, 1967. Mem.: U.S. Navy League (assoc.), U.S. Naval Inst. (assoc.). Avocations: painting, writing, poetry, cooking, nutrition. Office: Skye Publishing PO Box 4562 Annapolis MD 21403 Office Phone: 410-340-2680.

BRANCA, JOHN GREGORY, lawyer, consultant; b. Bronxville, N.Y., Dec. 11, 1950; s. John Ralph and Barbara (Werle) B. AB in Polit. Sci. cum laude, Occidental Coll., 1972; JD, UCLA, 1975. Bar: Calif. 1975. Assoc. Kindel & Anderson, Los Angeles, 1975-77, Hardee, Barovick, Konecky & Braun, Beverly Hills, Calif., 1977-81; ptnr. Ziffren, Brittenham, Branca & Fischer, L.A., 1981—. Cons. N.Y. State Assembly, Mt. Vernon, 1978-82, various music industry orgns., L.A., 1981—. Editor-in-Chief UCLA-Alaska Law Rev., 1974-75; contbr. articles to profl. jours. Cons., bd. trustees UCLA Law Sch. Com., UCLA Athletic Dept., Occidental Coll., Musician's Assistance Program, 1995. Recipient Bancroft-Whitney award; named Entertainment Lawyer of Yr. Am. Lawyer mag., 1981. Mem. ABA (patent trademark and copyright law sect.), Calif. Bar Assn., Beverly Hills Bar Assn. (entertainment law sect.), Phi Alpha Delta, Sigma Tau Sigma. Avocations: art, antiques, music, real estate. Office: Ziffren Brittenham Branca & Fischer 1801 Century Park W Fl 9 Los Angeles CA 90067-6406

BRANCATO, CAROLYN KAY, economist, consultant; b. St. Louis, Sept. 20, 1945; d. John and Dorothy (Sewell) B. BA, Columbia U., 1966; PhD, NYU, 1975. Securities analyst Dominick and Dominick, Inc., 1966-69; prin. mgmt. analyst N.Y.C. EPA, 1970-73; prin. economist NSF Project, 1973-74; dir. econ. rsch. N.Y. State Legis. Inst., 1975-77; head industry analysis, fin. and energy econs. sects. Congl. Rsch. Svc., U.S. Congress, 1979-87; chief economist, exec. dir. Instnl. Investor Project Columbia Ctr. Law and Econs., 1988-93; exec. dir. Instnl. Investor Project Columbia Ctr. Law and Econs., 1991-93; chief economist Weil, Gotshal & Manges, 1987-90; dir. Riverside Econ. Rsch., 1990—; staff dir. subcoun. Corp. Governance & Fin. Markets Competitiveness Policy Coun., 1992-93; rsch. dir. corp. gov. The Conf. Bd., 1993—, dir. Commn. Pub. Trust and Pvt. Enterprise, 2002—03. Author: Getting Listed on Wall Street, 1996, Institutional Investors and Corporate Governance, 1996. Trustee Coll. Environ. Sci. and Forestry, Syracuse, N.Y., 1975-82. Fellow Royal Soc. for Encouragement of Arts. Avocations: director, playwright. Office: The Conf Bd 845 3rd Ave New York NY 10022-6601

BRANCATO, LEO JOHN, manufacturing executive; b. NYC, Oct. 27, 1922; s. Leo and Josephine (Abbruscato) B. BS in Mech. Engring, Cooper Union, 1950; MS, Columbia U., 1952. Registered profl. engr., Conn. Design engr. Ermold Co., N.Y.C., 1946-51; with Heli-Coil Corp., Danbury, Conn., 1952-70, exec. v.p., 1963-70, pres., 1970; v.p., dir. Mite-Corp., merger co. including Heli-Coil Co., Danbury, 1970-74; pres. Mite-Corp., 1974-88. Incorporator Union Savs. Bank, Danbury, 1967-92. Patentee in field of fastener tech. Trustee Danbury Hosp., 1961-2005, Union Savs. Bank Found. Inc., 1998-2005; chmn. Housatonic Regional Mental Health Council, 1965-68; commr. conservation, Danbury, 1974-79; mem. bd. visitors U. Conn. Sch. Bus. Adminstrn., 1977-89. Lt. C.E., AUS, 1943-46. Fellow ASME; mem. Princeton Club (N.Y.C.), Port Washington yacht Club (N.Y.), Tau Beta Pi.

BRANCH, GLENN, educational association administrator; b. Hackensack, N.J., Jan. 22, 1969; s. Ronald Kenneth and Susan Barbara Branch; m. Sujatha Jagadeesh, June 14, 1992; 1 child, Vikram Samuel. BA, Brandeis U., Waltham, Mass., 1990; MA, UCLA, 1992. Dep. dir. Nat. Ctr. for Sci. Edn., Berkeley, Calif., 2002—. Contbr. articles to profl. jours. Recipient Carnap Essay prize, UCLA, 1997, Robert M. Yost Tchg. award, 1995. Mem.: Am. Philos. Assn., Phi Beta Kappa. Office: National Center for Science Education PO Box 9477 Berkeley CA 94709-0477 Office Phone: 510-601-7203.

BRANCH, JOHN CURTIS, biology professor, lawyer; b. Buffalo, Okla., Oct. 1, 1934; s. Ernest Samuel and Ethel Imogene (Parsons) B.; m. Jacqueline Joyce Davis, July 20, 1960; children: Kim Renee, Karla Jean, Kay Lynn. BS, Northwestern Okla. State U., 1959; MS, U. Okla., 1963, PhD, 1965; JD, Okla. City U., 1980. Bar: Okla. 1980. Asst. prof. biology dept. Okla. City U., 1964-67, assoc. prof. biology dept., 1967-75, prof. biology dept., 1975—. With U.S. Army, 1955-57. Mem. Okla. County Bar Assn., Okla. Acad. Sci., Okla. Bar Assn., Beta Beta Beta. Methodist. Avocations: reading, sports, travel. Home: 2705 Abbey Rd Oklahoma City OK 73120-2702 Office: John C Branch PC 4912 S Western Ave Oklahoma City OK 73109-3838 also: Okla City U Dept Biology 2501 N Blackwelder Ave Oklahoma City OK 73106-1402 Office Phone: 405-634-7600.

BRANCH, JOSEPH C., lawyer; BA, Marquette U., 1967, JD magna cum laude, 1971. Bar: Wis. 1971. Ptnr. Foley & Lardner LLP, Milw., mem. mgmt. com., chmn. ins. industry practice group. Editl. rev. bd. Jour. Ins. Regulation, 1985—; bd. dirs. Fedn. Regulatory Counsel. Co-author: Insurers Operating Under Assumed or Fictitious Names: When, How & ... What?!, LLC Bandwagon: Insurers Beware. Mem.: Internat. Assn. Ins. Law, Defense Research Inst., Inc., Milw. Bar Assn., ABA (tort & ins. practice sect., com. lawyers profl. liability), State Bar Wis. (chmn. ins. com. 1980—86, bd. gov., exec. com.). Office: Foley & Lardner LLP 777 E Wisconsin Ave Milwaukee WI 53202-5306 Office Phone: 414-297-5837. Business E-Mail: jbranch@foley.com.

BRANCH, MICHELLE, musician; b. Flagstaff, Ariz., July 2, 1983; d. David and Peggy Branch; m. Teddy Landau, May 23, 2004; 1 child, Owen Isabelle. With Maverick Records, Beverly Hills, Calif., 2001—. Musician: (CD) Broken Bracelet, 2000, The Spirit Room, 2001, Breathe - The Remixes, 2002, Hotel Paper, 2003, (single) Everywhere, 2001, All You Wanted, 2001, Goodbye to You, 2003, Are You Happy Now, 2003, Breathe, 2003, (with Santana) The Game of Love, 2002 (Grammy award for Best Pop Collaboration with Vocals, 03). Recipient Grammy award for Best New Artist, 2003. Office: Maverick Recording 9348 Civic Center Dr Beverly Hills CA 90210

BRANCH, THOMAS BROUGHTON, III, lawyer; b. Atlanta, June 5, 1936; s. Thomas Broughton Jr. and Alfred Iverson (Dews) B.; m. Trudi Schroetter, Dec. 27, 1963; children: Maria Barbara, Thomas B. IV. BA cum laude, Washington and Lee U., 1958, JD, 1960. Bar: Ga. 1960, U.S. Dist. Ct. (no. dist.) Ga. 1960, U.S. Ct. Appeals (5th cir.) 1960, U.S. Dist. Ct. (mid. dist.) Ga. 1980, U.S. Ct. Appeals (11th cir.) 1980, U.S. Dist. Ct. (so. dist.) N.Y. 1984, U.S. Ct. Appeals (2d cir.) 1984, U.S. Supreme Ct. 1991. Assoc. Kilpatrick & Cody, Atlanta, 1960-63; ptnr. Greene, Buckley et al, Atlanta, 1963-79, Wildman, Harrold, Allen, Dixon & Branch, Atlanta, 1979-89, Branch, Pike & Ganz, Atlanta, 1990-95, Holland & Knight, Atlanta, 1995—. Asst. prof. Woodrow Wilson Law Sch., Atlanta, 1964-68; trustee Washington and Lee U., Lexington, Va., 1979-90, trustee emeritus, 1991—; trustee, chmn. Atlanta Lawyers Found., Atlanta, 1980-81, Atlantis Aurora, Inc., 1970-74. Mem. Citizens Adv. Council on Urban Devel., Atlanta, 1977; trustee The Children's Sch., Inc., Atlanta, 1980-85; elder, clk., trustee First Presbyn. Ch., Atlanta, 1967-79, 81-85, 97—. Fellow Am. Bar Found.; mem. ABA, Ga. Bar Assn., Atlanta Bar Assn. (mem. jud. selection and tenure com. 1988—), Am. Jud. Soc., Atlanta Lawyers Club (pres. 1976-77), Bleckley Inn of Ct. (master), Ansley Golf Club (pres., bd. dirs. 1976-87). Home: 85 Montgomery Ferry Dr NE Atlanta GA 30309 Office Phone: 404-898-8106. E-mail: tbranch@hklaw.com.

BRANCH, WILLIAM BLACKWELL, playwright, producer; b. New Haven, Sept. 11, 1927; s. James Matthew and Iola (Douglas) B.; m. Marie Louise Foster, Aug. 19, 1956 (div.); 1 dau., Rochelle Ellen. BS, Northwestern U., 1949; M.F.A., Columbia U., 1958; ABC fellow, Yale U., 1965-66. Prof. Cornell U., 1985-94. Vis. scholar, lectr. numerous univs.; vis. prof. U. Md., Baltimore County, 1979-82; U. Calif. Regents lectr., spring, 1985; vis. Luce fellow Williams Coll., fall, 1983; vis. disting. prof. William Paterson Coll. N.J., Wayne, 1994-96. Actor appearing in: Anna Lucasta, 1945, Detective Story, 1951; playwright for theatre, TV and motion pictures, 1951—; assoc. in film, Columbia Sch. of Arts, 1968-69; staff writer-producer, Channel 13, Ednl. TV, N.Y.C., 1962-64; dir. The Jackie Robinson Show, NBC, 1958-60; co-author: The Jackie Robinson Column N.Y. Post and syndication, 1959-61; screenwriter Universal Studios, 1968-69, producer, NBC News, 1972-73, pres., William Branch Assos., 1973—; works include (theatre) A Medal for Willie, 1951, In Splendid Error, 1954, A Wreath for Udomo, 1960, To Follow the Phoenix, 1960, Baccalaureate, 1975; (TV) Light in the Southern Sky, 1958 (Robert E. Sherwood TV award 1958), A Letter From Booker T., 1987; TV documentary Still a Brother: Inside the Negro Middle Class, 1968 (Emmy award nominee 1969, Blue Ribbon award Am. Film Festival 1969); documentary TV series Afro American Perspectives, 1974-83; screen Together for Days, 1971; exec. producer: Black Perspective on the News, Pub. Broadcasting System, 1978-79; author: Fifty Steps Toward Freedom, 1959; author, editor: Black Thunder: An Anthology of Contemporary African American Drama, 1992 (Am. Book award 1992), Crosswinds: An Anthology of Black Dramatists in the Diaspora, 1993. Bd. dirs. Am. Soc. African Culture, 1963-70; treas. Nat. Conf. African Am. Theatre, 1987-91; bd. dirs. Nat. Citizens Com. for Broadcasting, 1969-71; mem. nat. adv. bd. Ctr. for Book, Library of Congress, 1979-83, W.E.B. DuBois Found., 1987—. Served with AUS, 1951-53. John Guggenheim fellow, 1959-60; recipient Hannah B. Del Vecchio award Columbia, 1958 Address: 53 Cortlandt Ave New Rochelle NY 10801-2032 Office Phone: 914-235-1809.

BRANCH, WILLIAM TERRELL, urologist, educator; b. Paragould, Ark., Dec. 7, 1937; s. William Owen and Mary Rose (Dempsey) B.; m. Mary Fletcher Cox, Dec. 11, 1965; children: Ashley Tucker, William T., Steven K. BS, Ark. State U., 1964, MD, 1971. Diplomate Am. Bd. Urology. Adminstrv. asst. mental retardation planning project State of Ark., Little Rock, 1964-66; intern U. South Fla. Sch. Medicine Affiliated Hosps., Tampa, 1971-72, resident in surgery, 1972-73, resident in urology, 1973-75, chief resident in urology, 1975-76, clin. prof. urology, chmn. dept. surgery, 1976—; practice medicine specializing in urology Tampa, 1976—; mem. staff, sec. urology Tampa Gen. Hosp., 1976-78, vice chief urology, 1978-80, chief urology, 1980-82; mem. staff, co-chief surgery Meml. Hosp., Tampa, 1978-80, vice chief med. staff, 1980-82, chief med. staff, 1982-84, trustee, 1983-88, bd. dirs. Mem. adv. bd. Suncoast Ednl. Telecommunications Systems, 1982; vice chmn., bd. dirs. Meml. Hosp., 1987-88; cons. in urology James A. Haley VA Hosp., Tampa, 1978—; mem. staff St. Joseph's Hosp., Tampa, 1976—, Tampa Gen. Hosp.; cons. staff Women's Hosp., Tampa; adv. bd. Glendale Fed. Savs., 1983-85, Beneficial Harbour Island Savs. Bank, 1985-87, South Trust Bank, 1988—, also bd. dirs., exec. com., chair audit com.; chief urology, bd. mem. Tampa Outpatient Surgery Facility, 2000—; chmn. vol. faculty com. Dept. Surgery U. South Fla. Coll. Medicine; vice chmn. bd. dirs. Shriners Hosp. for Children, Tampa. Author: (with others) Mental Retardation in Arkansas, 1964-66; A Demographic Study, 1966; cons. editor Jour. Fla. Med. Assn., 1978-93. Bd. dirs. Tampa Ballet, 1980, Tampa Charity Horse Show Bd. Dirs. Assn., 1985-87, Shriners Hosp. for Children, Tampa, 2000, Tampa Outpatient Surg. Facility,United Way, Tampa, 1983-90, mem. exec. com., 1984-88; mem. med. adv. bd. Nat. Kidney Found. of Fla., Inc., 1983-90; mem. Tampa Bay Super Bowl XXV Task Force, Super Bowl XXXV Task Force; mem. adv. bd. dirs. Salvation Army; founding chmn. Kettle com., vice chmn. adv. bd. dirs., chmn., 1998-2000. Recipient Disting. Alumnus award Ark. State U., 1986. Fellow ACS (credit com. region IV, Fla. chpt. 1982-98, exec. com. Fla. chpt. 1985—, sec., treas. 1987-88, pres.-elect 1989-90, pres. 1990-92, gov. 1990-96, bd. gov. chpt. activities com. 1991-96, alt. 1993, chmn. nomination com. 1995, chmn. applications com. region IV); mem. Am. Urol. Assn., Royal Soc. Medicine (affiliate), Fla. Med. Assn. (del. 1983, 88-96), Fla. Urol. Soc. (Milton Copeland award 1976, exec. com. 1978-82), Hillsborough County

Med. Assn. (exec. com. 1978-81, treas. 1981-82, sec. 1983-84), Fla. Quality Med. Assurance, Inc. (bd. dirs., treas., chmn. exec. com. 1995, chmn. bd. govs.), Southeastern Surg. Congress, Greater Tampa C. of C. (dir. 1982-86, 87-90, chmn. med. meetings task force 1983-84, Super Star award 1983), Tampa Bay Surg. Soc. (founding mem., sec., bd. dirs. 1998, pres. 1999-2001), Tampa Hist. Soc., Hillsborough County Med. Soc. (pres. polit. action com. 1986-87, 88-89), Tampa Yacht and Country Club (gov. 1984-87), Centre of Tampa Club (founding mem. 1988-93, bd. dirs., chmn. mem. com.), Univ. Club (treas. 1998-99, sec. 1999-2000, bd. dirs. 1998-99), Ye Mystic Krewe of Gasparilla (bd. dirs. 1991-2000, 1st lt. 1988-89, lord chamberlain 1994-95, chmn. exec. com. 1995-96, capt. 1996-98), King Gasparilla LXXXVI. Home: 1002 Harbour Island Blvd # 1605 Tampa FL 33602 Office: 2919 W Swann Ave Ste 303 Tampa FL 33609-4051

BRANCH, WILLIAM THOMAS, JR., medical educator; b. Montgomery, Ala., Mar. 28, 1941; s. William Thomas and Mary Seibels (Lanier) B.; m. Carolyn Jenkins, June 9, 1967; 1 child, Katherine Mary Seibels Branch. BA, Vanderbilt U., 1963; MD, Med. Coll. Ala., 1967. Resident Peter Bent Brigham Hosp., Boston, 1967-72; staff assoc. NIH, Bethesda, Md., 1969-71; assoc. prof. Med. Sch. Harvard U., Boston, 1972-95; prof. Sch. Medicine, vice chmn. dept. medicine Emory U., Atlanta, 1995—, dir. divsn. gen. medicine, 1995—. Dir. primary care residency program Brigham & Women's Hosp., Boston, 1974-95. Editor: Office Practice of Medicine, 1982, 2d edit., 1987, 4th edit., 2003; contbr. articles to profl. jours. including New Eng. Jour. Medicine, JAMA, among others. Recipient Career award for med. edn. Soc. General Internal Medicine, 1997. Master ACP (pres.-elect). Methodist. Home: 99 Inman Cir NE Atlanta GA 30309-3384 Office: Emory U Sch Medicine 1525 Clifton Rd NE Atlanta GA 30322-4200

BRANCO, MARIA CLOTILDE, secondary school educator; b. Horta, Azores, Portugal, May 18, 1954; arrived in U.S., 1969; d. Jose Pacheco and Clotilde (Da Rosa) B. M Bilingual Edn., Southeastern Mass. U., 1979; BA in English, U. Mass., 1982. Cert. elem. and secondary tchr. Mass., adv. fied work in Portuguese and Edn. Harvard & Fitzburg Coll. & Salem State. Tchr. Falmouth (Mass.) Pub. Schs., 1976—. Adv. in field. Mem.: NEA, Falmouth Edn. Assn. (Outstanding Tchr. 2000), Mass. Tchrs. Assn., Mass. Fgn. Lang. Assn., Whaling Mus., Friends of Casa Portuguses Pub. Libr., Portuguese Club, Portuguese Am. Assn. (Outstanding Educator 2001). Home: 1235 Cove Rd New Bedford MA 02744-1110 Office Phone: 508-540-2200. Business E-Mail: mbranco@falmouthk12.ma.us.

BRAND, CHARLES MACY, history professor; b. Stanford, Calif., Apr. 7, 1932; s. Carl F. and Nan (Surface) B.; m. Mary Joan Shorrock, Aug. 7, 1954; children: Catharine, Stephen. BA, Stanford U., 1953; MA, Harvard U., 1954, PhD, 1961. Asst. prof. history San Francisco State Coll., 1962-64; asst. prof. Bryn Mawr Coll., Pa., 1964-69, assoc. prof., 1969-75, prof. history, 1975-99, chmn. dept. history, 1978-81, 96-97, prof. emeritus, 1999—. Author: Byzantium Confronts the West, 1180-1204, 1968, 2d edit., 1992; editor: Icon and Minaret, 1969; translator: Deeds of John and Manuel Comnenus (by J. Kinnamos), 1976. Served with U.S. Army, 1955-57. Dumbarton Oaks Center for Byzantine Studies fellow, 1961, 1988; Fulbright research fellow, 1968; Gennadius fellow, 1968; Guggenheim fellow, 1972 Mem. U.S. Nat. Com. for Byzantine Studies (1961), Medieval Acad. Am., Am. Hist. Assn., Byzantine Studies Conf. Home: 508 Montgomery Ave Haverford PA 19041-1409

BRAND, DONALD ALBERT, medical researcher, educator; b. New Rochelle, N.Y., Dec. 3, 1945; s. Charles Salmon and Norma Ruth Brand; m. Catherine L. Learned, Apr. 10, 1993; m. Gabriella Maresca, Sept. 12, 1964 (div.); children: Jeffrey Charles Brand-Ballard, Thomas Russell. BS, Antioch Coll., Yellow Springs, Ohio, 1968; MA, U. Wis., Madison, 1970; MPhil, Yale U., New Haven, Conn., 1975, PhD, 1976. Asst. prof., pub. health Yale U., New Haven, 1976—83, rsch. scientist, 1983—87, sr. rsch. scientist, 1987—89; sr. rschr. United Healthcare Corp., Minnetonka, Minn., 1990—95; assoc. prof., medicine N.Y. Med. Coll., Valhalla, 1996—2004, prof., medicine, 2004—. Cons. Veterans Adminstrn., Washington, 1983—86; mem., extremity radiography panel FDA, U.S. Pub. Health Svc., Rockville, Md., 1984—85; mem., site visit and spl. rev. com., trauma and burn program, nat. inst. gen. med. scis. NIH, U.S. Pub. Health Svc., Bethesda, Md., 1985; dir., primary care rsch. N.Y. Med. Coll., Valhalla, 1995—; cons., com. on assessment of practice performance Am. Bd. Internal Medicine, Phila. Contbr. articles to profl. jours. Grantee, Nat. Ctr. for Health Svcs. Rsch., U.S. Pub. Health Svc., 1979—80, Nat. Fund for Med. Edn., 1979—80, The John A. Hartford Found., 1983—87, Mar. of Dimes Birth Defects Found., 1989—90, Am. Coll. Gastroenterology, 1999—2000, Health Resources and Services Adminstrn., U.S. Pub. Health Svc., 2000—. Mem.: Soc. for Med. Decision Making. Achievements include development of several diagnostic decision aids for physicians in pediatrics, internal medicine, and trauma. Avocation: photography. Office: NY Med Coll Primary Care 600 Munger Pavilion Valhalla NY 10595 Office Phone: 914-594-4972. E-mail: donald_brand@nymc.edu.

BRAND, EDWARD CABELL, retail executive; b. Salem, Va., Apr. 11, 1923; s. William F. and Ruth (Cabell) B.; m. Shirley Hurt, June 20, 1964; children: Sylvia, Miriam, Liza, Richie, John, Edward (dec.), Marshall, Caroline. Grad., Va. Mil. Inst., 1944; HHD (hon.), Roanoke Coll., 1997, Washington and Lee U., 1999, Ferrum Coll., 2005, Va. Western Coll., 2005. Dept. of State econ. analyst, intelligence office Berlin Mil. Govt., 1947-49; v.p. Ortho-Vent Shoe Co., 1949-62; pres. Brand Edmonds Assocs. Advertising, 1962-66, chmn. bd., 1962-81; founder, pres. Stuart McGuire Co., Salem, Va., 1962-85, chmn. bd., chief exec. officer, 1973-85; chmn. emeritus, cons. Stuart McGuire Co. (merged with Home Shopping (TV) Network), 1985-86; pres. Recovery Systems, Inc., Salem, Va., 1986—. Rsch. assoc., former instr. bus. adminstrn. and sales mgmt. Roanoke Coll. Chmn. Va. State Bd. Health, 1989-93; pres., founder, chmn. Cabell Brand Ctr. for Internat. Poverty and Resource Studies of Roanoke Coll; former mem. Bus. Leadership Adv. Council.; founder, pres. Total Action Against Poverty, Roanoke Valley, 1965-95; pres. Pvt. Sector Commn. Va. Community Action Agys., 1986-88; mem. Gov.'s Commn. on Fed. Funding of State Domestic Program, 1986-88; trustee Council on Religion and Internat. Affairs, Ethics Resource Ctr., Heinz Ctr. Sci., Econs. and Environ.; bd. dirs. Roanoke Coun. Cmty. Svcs., Woodlands Conf. divsn. Woodlands Ctr. for Future Research and the Houston Area Research Ctr., Global Water, Washington, Va. Health Care Found., Richmond, Va., 1993-2000, Va. Found. for the Humanities and Pub. Policy, Charlottesville, 1993-99, Blue Ridge Pub. TV, Roanoke, Va., 1993—, Action Alliance for Va. Children and Youth, Richmond, 1994-2000, Va. Conservation Network, Richmond, 1996—; bd. trustees Western Va. Land Trust, Roanoke, Va., 1995-2000; assoc. World Resources Inst., Washington, 1985. Served from pvt. to capt. AUS, 1942-46, ETO. Decorated Bronze Star. Named Businessman in U.S. who has done most to help disadvantaged people, Vista, 1980; recipient LBJ Humanitarian nat. award, 1989, Outstanding Citizen Rotary Club, 1999. Mem. NAS (coun., pres. cir.), Social Venture Network, Direct Selling Assn. (past dir., chmn. named to Hall of Fame), U.S. C. of C., Conf. Bd. (exec. coun.), World Pres. Assn. (past dir., chmn. Argentina Conf. 1988), Newcomen Soc. N.Am., Roanoke Touchdown Club (past pres.), Valley Torch Club (past pres.), Roanoke Sales Execs. (past dir.), Rotary (past. pres. Salem). Home: 701 W Main St Salem VA 24153-3513 Office: Recovery Systems Inc PO Box 429 Salem VA 24153-0429 Personal E-mail: scbrand25@adelphia.net. Business E-Mail: CBC@CBCenter.org. *In addition to trying to do the best job I could— whether in school, business, public service, or in my family— I have felt a continuing need to improve our system and society. This has led to extensive study, travels, and a variety of extra-curricular activities. Today I have great confidence in the future of the United States and the world, but see urgent need for dramatic changes in our value systems, and need for long range planning. Our Center focuses on inter-relationship between poverty and resource limitation for sustainable development.*

BRAND, ELTON, professional basketball player; Student, Duke Univ. Profl. basketball player Chicago Bulls, 1999—2001, Los Angeles Clippers, 2001—. Founder Elton Brand Foundation, 2000—. Named Nat. College Basketball Player of the Yr., AP, 1999, First Team All-American, 1999, MVP NBA Rookie Challenge, 2000; named to NBA All-Rookie First Team, 2000, NBA All-Star Game, 2002, All-NBA Second team, 2005. Office: LA Clippers Staples Center 1111 S Figueroa St Los Angeles CA 90015*

BRAND, GEORGE EDWARD, JR., retired lawyer; b. Detroit, Oct. 25, 1918; s. George Edward and Elsie Bertie (Jones) B.; m. Patricia Jean Gould, June 7, 1947; children— Martha Christine, Carol Elsie, George Edward. BA, Dartmouth Coll., 1941; postgrad., U. Minn., Harvard U., 1941; JD, U. Mich., 1948. Bar: Mich. 1948, U.S. Supreme Ct. 1958. Mem. firm George E. Brand, Detroit, 1948-63, Butzel, Long, Gust, Klein & Van Zile, P.C., Detroit, 1963—; ptnr., dir., pres. Butzel, Long, Gust, Klein & Van Zile, 1974-89; ret. Served with USNR, 1942-46. Fellow Am. Bar Found., Am. Coll. Trial Lawyers; mem. ABA, Am. Judicature Soc., Detroit Bar Assn., VFW. Clubs: N.S.S.C. Home: 1233 Kensington Ave Grosse Pointe Park MI 48230-1101 Office: 150 W Jefferson Ave Ste 900 Detroit MI 48226-4416

BRAND, JEFFREY S., dean, law educator; AB, U. Calif., Berkeley, 1966, JD, 1969. Pub. defender Contra Costa County, Calif.; adminstrv. law judge Agricultural Labor Rels. Bd.; ptnr. Farnsworth, Saperstein and Brand, Oakland; prof. law U. San Francisco Sch. Law, dean, 1999—. Chmn. USF Center for Law and Global Justice. Former editor-in-chief Federal Litigator. Office: U San Francisco Sch Law 2130 Fulton St San Francisco CA 94117 Office Phone: 415-422-6304.

BRAND, MICHAEL, museum director; b. Australia; married; 2 children. Grad. in Asian Studies, with honors, Australian Nat. U., Canberra, 1979; MA, Harvard U., 1982, PhD, 1987. Founding head Asian art Nat. Gallery of Australia, 1988—96; asst. dir., sr. curator Queensland Art Gallery, Brisbane, Australia, 1996—2000; dir. Va. Mus. Fine Arts, Richmond, 2000—05, J. Paul Getty Ctr., LA, 2005—, J. Paul Getty Villa, Malibu, Calif., 2005—. Co-author (with Glenn D. Lowry): Akbar's India: Art from the Mughal City of Victory, 1985. Office: J Paul Getty Trust 1200 Getty Ctr Dr Los Angeles CA 90049-1679*

BRAND, OSCAR, folk singer, writer, educator; b. Winnipeg, Man., Can., Feb. 7, 1920; s. Isidore and Beatrice (Shulman) B.; m. Rubyan Saber (div.); children: Jeannie, Eric, James; m. Karen Lynn Grossman, June 14, 1970; 1 child, Jordan. BA, Bklyn. Coll., 1942; Polit. Sci. Laureate, Fairfield U., 1972; PhD (hon.), U. Winnipeg, 1987. Host, performer Folksong Festival, Sta. WNYC-AM, N.Y.C., 1945—. Pres. Harlequin Prodns., Inc., Gypsy Hill Music, Inc.; trustee Newport Festival Found.; mem. faculty Hofstra U., New Sch., 1970-80; music adviser nat. bd. YWCA; mem. creative bd. Sesame Street, Pres.'s Com. on Nutrition; cons. Bill Moyers, PBS-TV, 1983; curator Songwriters Hall of Fame. Host: (TV show) World of Folkmusic, H.E.W., 1962-68, Oscar Brand's Am. Odyssey, 1970-72, Treasure Chest, The First Look, 1965-68, (radio show) Voices in the Wind, 1974-80, 13 of Segovia, First Person Am.; star: (TV series) Let's Sing Out, Can., 1962-68, Brand New Scene, Can., 1966; artistic dir. Project America, 92d St. Y, 1998-2001; music dir. (TV series) Nat. Geog. Bicentennial, 1974, Sunday, Exploring; music advisor: (TV series) Nuclear Age, 1986-87, (PBS) Liberty, 1998; writer, dir.: (TV spl. and show) Sing, America, Sing, Kennedy Ctr. Bicentennial Celebration, 1975; composer, lyricist: (broadway show) Joyful Noise, 1966, HYMAN KAPLAN, 1968, (off-broadway show) In White America, 1965, How to Steal an Election, 1969, 2003, It's a Jungle, Bridge of Hope for lit. conf., 1969, Celebrate for N.Y. Presbytery, 1970, (off broadway show) Thunder Bay, Fun and Games, Protest, 1999, Ready Aim Sing, 1999, Ballads and Ballots, 2000, Me and Woody, 2000, (songs for film) The Fox, Sybil, The Long Riders, Blue Chips, 1994; author: Singing Holidays, 1957, Bawdy Songs, 1960, Folksongs for Fun, 1961, The Ballad Mongers, 1964, Songs of '76, 1974, When I First Came to This Land, 1975, Party Songs, 1983; rec. artist 100 albums; performer (video) At Home, 1988, Campaigns for Smithsonian, 1999; editor: Words About Music, 1980-2002; prodr. "Campaigns in Cotton", N.Y. Hist. Soc., 2004. Program coord. Nat. Hadassah, 1989-98; trustee BMI Found., 1995—; music dir. Rukeyser Guide, 1996. Served as sgt. M.C. AUS, 1942-45. Recipient Radio Pioneers of Am. award, 1986, Edinburgh, Valley Forge and Film Festival awards for documentary and ednl. films, 1946, numerous other awards include Emmy, Peabody, Freedoms Found., Scholastic for radio, TV and films, 1962-86, Lifetime Achievement award World Folk Music Assn., 1996, Peabody Personal award, 1996; honoree Coalition Against Domestic Violence (adv. bd. 1993—), United Cmty. Fund, 1997; named Illustrious Alumnus Bklyn. Coll., 2001. Mem. Nat. Acad. Popular Music (bd. dirs. 1969—). Avocations: sailing, carpentry. Office: Gypsy Hill Music PO Box 1362 Manhasset NY 11030-6362 Office Phone: 516-487-5979. E-mail: oscarbrand@oscarbrand.com, oscrbrand@aol.com. *I need more time.*

BRAND, RACHEL L., federal agency administrator, lawyer; BA, U. Minn., 1995; JD, Harvard U., 1998. Law clk. to Justice Charles Fried Mass. Supreme Judicial Ct., 1998—99; law clk. to Justice Anthony Kennedy U.S. Supreme Ct.; assoc. Cooper, Carvin & Rosenthal; assoc. counsel to Pres. The White House, Washington; prin. dep. asst. atty gen. Office of Legal Policy, U.S. Dept. Justice, Washington, 2003—05, acting asst. atty. gen., 2005, asst. atty. gen., 2005—. Editor-in-chief Harvard Jour. Law and Pub. Policy. Office: Office Legal Policy Rm 4234 Main Justice Bldg 950 Pennsylvania Ave NW Washington DC 20530-0001 Office Phone: 202-514-4601.*

BRAND, STEVE AARON, lawyer; b. St. Paul, Sept. 5, 1948; s. Allen A. and Shirley Mae (Mintz) B.; m. Gail Idele Greenspoon, Oct. 9, 1977. BA, U. Minn., 1970; JD, U. Chgo., 1973. Bar: Minn. 1973, U.S. Dist. Ct. Minn. 1974, U.S. Supreme Ct. 1977. Assoc. Briggs & Morgan, St. Paul, 1973-78, ptnr., 1978-91, Robins, Kaplan, Miller & Ciresi, LLP, 1991—. Pres. Jewish Vocat. Svc., 1981—84, Sholom Found., 1996—99; bd. dirs. Friends of the St. Paul Libr., 1997—; pres. Mt. Zion Hebrew Congregation, 1985—87. Mem. ABA, Minn. Bar Assn. (chmn. probate and trust law sect. 1984-85), Hebrew Union Coll.-Jewish Inst. Religion (bd. overseers 1987—, vice-chmn. 1996—), Am. Coll. Trust and Estate Counsel (Minn. chair 1991-96, regent 1998-2004), Ramsey County Bar Found. (pres. 1995-2000), Phi Beta Kappa, B'nai Brith. Democrat. Home: 1907 Hampshire Ave Saint Paul MN 55116-2401 Office: Robins Kaplan Miller & Ciresi LLP 2800 LaSalle Plz 800 Lasalle Ave Minneapolis MN 55402-2015 Office Phone: 612-349-8731. Business E-Mail: sabrand@rkmc.com.

BRAND, VANCE DEVOE, astronaut; b. Longmont, Colo., May 9, 1931; s. Rudolph William and Donna (DeVoe) B.; m. Joan Virginia Weninger, July 25, 1953; children: Susan Nancy, Stephanie, Patrick Richard, Kevin Stephen; m. Beverly Ann Whitnel, Nov. 3, 1979; children: Erik Ryan, Dane Vance. BS in Bus., U. Colo., 1953, BS in Aero. Engring., 1960; MBA, UCLA, 1964; grad., U.S. Naval Test Pilot Sch., Patuxent River, Md., 1963; DSc (hon.), U. Colo., 2000. With Lockheed-Calif. Co., Burbank, 1960-66, flight test engr., 1961-62, traveling engr. rep., 1962-63, engring. test pilot, 1963-66; astronaut NASA Johnson Space Ctr., Houston, 1966-92, command module pilot Apollo-Soyuz mission, 1975, comdr. STS-5 Mission, 1982, comdr. STS 41-B Mission, 1984, comdr. STS-35 Mission, 1990; chief plans Nat. Aero-Space Plane Joint Program Office, Wright-Patterson AFB, Ohio, 1992-94; asst. chief flight ops. directorate DFRC NASA, Edwards, Calif., 1994-98, dep. dir. aerospace projects, 1998—2002, acting dir. aerospace projects, 2002—04, assoc. dep. dir. for programs, 2004—. With USMCR, 1953-57. Decorated 2 Disting. Svc. medals NASA, 2 Exceptional Svc. medals, 3 Space medals; inducted into Internat. Space Hall of Fame, 1996, U.S. Astronaut Hall of Fame, 1997, Internat. Aerospace Hall of Fame, 2001. Fellow AIAA, Am. Astron. Soc., Soc. Exptl. Test Pilots. Office: M/S D2332 DFRC PO Box 273 Edwards CA 93523-0273

BRANDEIS, BARRY, apparel executive; b. May 3, 1946; s. Norman and Jennie (Yousin) B.; m. Renee Riesenberg, Apr. 4, 1971; children: Adam, Marisa. BS in Psychology, Pa. State U., 1968, MBA in Mgmt., 1970; MBA in Fin., CUNY, 1974, postgrad., 1975. Account exec. Meridian Securities Co., Bala Cynwyd, Pa., 1968-70; instr. Baruch Coll. Pace U. Grad. Sch., 1971, assoc. prof., 1975—99; asst. to chmn. Wasko Gold Products Corp., N.Y.C., 1975—77, v.p. fin., 1977—80, exec. v.p., 1980—83; group exec. Holding Capital Group, 1984—85; CEO Budoff, Inc., 1985—88; v.p. Craftex Creations, Inc., 1988—90; prin. Twin Era Ltd., 1991—. Mem. U.S. Senate Bus. Adv. Bd.; alumni bd. Pa. State U., Abington; pres. Orgn. of Student Assn., 1967, Penna Assn. of Coll. Students, 1968. Mem. AAUP, Internat. Precious Metals Inst. (charter), Assn. MBA Execs., PR C. of C. in U.S. (bd. dirs.), Internat. Platform Assn., NY Acad. Scis., Parmi Nous, Omicron Delta Kappa, Psi Chi. Home: 15 Cooper Dr Great Neck NY 11023-1908 Office: Twin Era Ltd 1410 Broadway New York NY 10018-5007 E-mail: bbxny@aol.com.

BRANDEL, ROLAND ERIC, lawyer; b. Chgo., Nov. 30, 1938; s. Eric John and Louise Catherine (Covich) B.; m. Catherine Terry, July 3, 1963 (div. July 1970). BS in Econs., Ill. Inst. Tech., 1960; JD, U. Chgo., 1966; postgrad., Columbia U., 1970. Enlisted U.S. Navy, 1960, advanced through grades to lt. comdr., ret., 1970; clk. to chief justice Calif. Supreme Ct., San Francisco, 1966-67; sr. counsel, ptnr. Morrison & Foerster, 1967—. Vis. prof. law U. Calif., Berkeley, 1974-75; consumer adv. council Fed. Res. Bd., Washington, 1976-80; vis. com. U. Chgo. Law Sch., 1983-86, Golden Gate Law Sch., San Francisco, 1983—; study groups of EFT and Negotiable Instruments Sec. of State Adv. Commn., Washington, 1983-90. Co-author: Law of EFT Systems, 1988, TIL: 4 Comp. Guide plus supplement, 1981-87, Community Reinvestment Act Manual, 1978, Financial Privacy Comp. Manual, 1979. Mem. Planning Commn. City of Berkeley, 1972-74; chmn. Waterfront Adv. Bd., Berkeley, 1973. Recipient Lifetime Achievement award, Calif. Bankers Assn., 2000, Am. Coll. Consumer Fin. Svcs. Lawyers, 2004. Mem. ABA (consumer fin. svcs. com., 1978-83, council bus. law 1982-86, 2002—, chmn. ad hoc com. payment systems 1983-88), Inst. Marine Resources (adv.bd. 1983-86), Nat. Ctr. Fin. Services (chmn. legal adv. com. 1985—, mng. com. 1983—), State Bar Calif. (chair bus. law sect., 1993-94), U. Chgo. Law Sch. Alumni (pres. 1968-94). Home: 58 Roble Rd Berkeley CA 94705-2838 Office: Morrison & Foerster 425 Market San Francisco CA 94105 Office Phone: 415-268-7093. E-mail: rbrandel@mofo.com.

BRANDENBERGER, STACY MICHELLE, music educator, secondary school educator; b. Arkadelphia, Ark., Apr. 27, 1967; d. Lewis L. and Marion F. Sims; m. Silas Andrew Brandenberger, June 9, 1990; children: Ethan, Chelsea. BM, Southwestern U., Georgetown, Tex., 1990. Elem. music tchr. Alief Ind. Sch. Dist., Houston, 1990—94, Met. Pub. Schs., Nashville, 1994—95; secondary choral tchr. Georgetown Ind. Sch. Dist., Tex., 1996—98; presch. music tchr. St. John's United Meth. Ch., Georgetown, Tex., 2003—. Elem. music com. co-chair Alief Ind. Sch. Dist., Houston, 1992—93; elem. music planning com. Nashville Met. Pub. Schs., 1994—95; private piano tchr. self employed, Georgetown, Tex., 1998—, accompanist, 1998—. Accompanist Fort Bend Boys Choir, Fort Bend County, Tex., 1992—94; dir. Children's Choir First Bapt. Ch., Georgetown, Tex., 1996—, mem. adult choir, 1996—. Finalist in Best Music Schs., Nashville Music Assn., 1994—95; named Tchr. of the Yr. Tippit Middle Sch., Georgetwn Ind. Sch. Dist., 1997—98. Mem.: Tex. Music Educators Assn. (pres. 1996—98), Nat. Guild Piano Tchrs. Baptist. Avocations: reading, singing, scrapbooks. Home: 2003 E 18th St Georgetown TX 78626 E-mail: SBrandenbe@aol.com.

BRANDENBURG, DAVID SAUL, gastroenterologist, educator; b. Linz, Austria, Apr. 12, 1948; arrived in US, 1948; s. Mayer and Syda Brandenburg; m. Bette Ellen Hirschberg, Aug. 8, 1971; children: Stacey, Mark, Marci. BA, Rutgers U., 1968; MD, Georgetown U., 1972. Bd. cert. internal medicine; bd. cert. GI. Intern, resident R.I. Hosp.-Brown U. Affiliated, Providence, 1972-75; gastroenterology fellow Emory U., Atlanta, 1975-77; pvt. practice Atlanta Digestive Diseases and Internal Medicine, 1977-82, Brandenburg and Kramer M.D., P.C., Atlanta, 1983-97; clin. asst. prof. medicine Emory U. Sch. Medicine, Atlanta, 1977—; with Atlanta Gastroenterology Assocs., 1997—. Med. dir. North Atlanta Endoscopy Ctr., Atlanta, 1986-2002; sec., v.p., pres. Ga. Soc. GI Endoscopy, Atlanta, 1980-86; chmn., med. adv. com. Ga. chpt. Crohn's and Colitis Found., Atlanta, 1995-97. Bd. trustees Temple Emmanuel, Dunwoody, Ga., 1985-91, 95-96, treas., 1988-89, v.p., 1990-91 . Fellow Am. Coll. Gastroenterology (gov. 1991-95); mem. Am. Gastroenterol. Assn., Am. Soc. Gastrointestinal Endoscopy. Office: 5671 Peachtree Dunwoody Rd Ste 600 Atlanta GA 30342-2311 Office Phone: 404-257-9000.

BRANDENBURG, MARK ANDREW, emergency physician, educator; b. Tulsa, Okla., Feb. 25, 1966; BA, W.Va. U., Morgantown, 1988; MD, U. Okla., Oklahoma City, 1992. Diplomate Am. Bd. Emergency Medicine, 1998. Intern in internal medicine U. Okla., Oklahoma City, 1992—93, intern then resident in emergency medicine, 1993—97; emergency physician St. Francis Hosp., Tulsa, 1997—; clin. assoc. prof. U. Okla. Coll. Medicine. Clin. rschr. Trauma Emergency Ctr., Tulsa, 1997—; instr. Advanced Trauma Life Support, Tulsa, 1997—, Pediat. Advanced Life Support, Tulsa, 2000—; spkr. Child Safe, Tulsa, 2000—, child injury cons., 2000—. Author: CHILD SAFE: A Practical Guide for Preventing Childhood Injuries, 2000; contbr. articles. Med. advisor Safe Kids Campaign, Tulsa, 2000—03. Fellow: Am. Coll. Emergency Medicine (life), Am. Acad. Emergency Medicine (life); mem.: Assn. Advancement Automotive Medicine (assoc.). Office: St Francis Trauma Emergency Ctr 6161 South Yale Tulsa OK 74136 Office Phone: 918-742-5059. Personal E-mail: mbrand2435@aol.com.

BRANDENBURG, RONALD WILLIAM, lawyer; b. Huron, S.D., Feb. 9, 1954; s. W. J. and Ardella K. (Ochsner) B.; m. Carol Marie Allen; children: Kelsey Kristyne, Caitlin Elizabeth, Christopher Allen. BA, Augustana Coll., Sioux Falls, S.D., 1976; JD, Loyola U., New Orleans, 1980. Bar: Minn. 1980, U.S. Dist. Ct. Minn. 1981, U.S. Claims Ct. 1991, U.S. Ct. Appeals (fed. cir.) 1992. Assoc. Newby, Dodge, Korman, Lingren, Warp & Newby, Ltd., Cloquet/Moose Lake, Minn., 1980-84; ptnr. Dodge, Warp & Brandenburg, Moose Lake, 1984-87, Hughes, Thoreen, Mathews & Knapp, St. Cloud, Minn., 1987-94; assoc. Knutson, Flynn, Hetland, Deans and Olsen, PA, 1994-95; ptnr. Quinlivan, Sherwood, Spellacy & Tarvestad, PA, 1995-98, Quinlivan & Hughes, PA, 1998—, CFO, 2004—. Vice chmn. chm. dependency adv. bd. Moose Lake Regional Treatment, 1985-90. Bd. dirs. Coalition for Concerned Citizens for Moose Lake State Hosp., 1985-87; v.p. St. Cloud Area YMCA, 1989-91, pres., 1992, bd. dirs., 2002—; divsn. chmn. St. Cloud Area United Way, 1990-91, vice chmn., 1992—, bd. dirs., 1994-2000, sec., 1997-2000. Mem. 7th Jud. Dist. Bar Assn., Minn. State Bar Assn. (mem. lawyer access and referral 1987-99), Stearns/Benton Bar Assn. Lutheran. Avocations: golf, tennis, skiing, fishing.

BRANDENSTEIN, DANIEL CHARLES, astronaut, retired military officer; b. Watertown, Wis., Jan. 17, 1943; s. Walter C. and Agnes (Holzworth) B.; m. Jane A. Wade, Jan. 2, 1966; 1 dau., Adelle. BS, U. Wis., River Falls, 1965; postgrad., U.S. Naval Text Pilot Sch., Patuxent River, Md., 1971. Commd. officer U.S. Navy, 1965, advanced through grades to capt., 1984, ret., 1993, student aviator Pensacola, Fla., 1965-67, aviator Whidbey Island, Wash., 1967-71, test pilot Patuxent River, Md., 1971-74, aviator Whidbey Island, Wash., 1974-78; astronaut NASA Johnson Space Ctr., Houston, 1978-93, chief astronaut office, 1987-93; dir. program development Loral Space Info. Sys., Houston, 1993-96; exec. v.p. Kistler Aerospace Corp., Kirkland, Wash., 1996-99; v.p. Lockheed Martin Space Ops., 1999—. Decorated Legion of Honor (France), 34 medals and awards USN, 1968-93; recipient Disting. Alumnus award U. Wis., 1982, Yuri Gagarin Gold medal Fedn. Aeronautique Internationale, 1990, Laurel Award, Space/Missiles, Aviation Week & Space Tech., 1993, Haley Space Flight award Am. Inst. of Aeronautics and Astronautics, 1993; named to Astronaut Hall Fame, 2003. Mem. AIAA (Haley Space Flight award 1993), Soc. Exptl. Text Pilots (Ivan C. Kinchloe award 1992), U.S. Naval Inst., Assn. Space Explorers. Office: PO Box 58980 Houston TX 77258-8980 Office Phone: 281-853-3314. E-mail: dan.brandenstein@lmco.com.

BRANDES, JO ANNE, lawyer; BA, U. Wis., Eau Claire; JD, Willamette U. Assoc. Herz, Levin, Teper, Chernof & Sumner, SC, 1978—81; exec. v.p., CAO, gen. counsel Johnson Diversey, Inc., Sturtevant, Wis. Dir. Johnson Family Funds, Andersen Corp. Inc. Regent emeritus U. Wis., Wis., 1996—; past mem. Gov.'s Commn. on Glass Ceiling; chmn. Wis. Child Care Coun.;

past president Racine (Wis.) Area United Found.; dir. Bright Horizons Family Solutions, Johnson Family Funds. Named Working Mother of Yr., Working Mother mag., 1994. Office: Johnson Diversey Inc 8310 16th St PO Box 902 Sturtevant WI 53177-0902

BRANDES, RAYMOND STEWART, historian, educator, dean; b. San Diego, Jan. 2, 1924; s. Theodore C. and María Rosario (Peters) B.; m. Irma Dolores Montijo, Jan. 28, 1961; children: Elena María, Elisa Anne, Laura Raquel, Claudia Reneè, Ramón Antonio, Marta Denise, Paula Nicole. BA, U. Ariz., 1961, PhD, 1965. Asst. prof. history U. San Diego, 1966-67, assoc. prof., 1967-71, prof., 1971-98, univ. archivist, 1992-98, chmn. dept., 1967-73, grad. dean, 1973-91; ret., 1998. Dir. several grants related to hist. preservation and hist. site archaeology in San Diego area. Author: Diario of Miguel Costanso, 1969, Troopers West: Military and Indian Affairs on the American Frontier, 1970, Frontier Military Posts of Arizonia, 1960, San Diego: An Illustrated History, 1982; editor Brand Book 1, San Diego Corral of Westerners, 1970, Masterplanner for Old Town State Historical Park, 1973-74, Old Town San Diego, 1821-1974, 1976, History and Archaeology of New Town, San Diego, 1985, Coronado: The Enchanted Island, 1987, 3d edit., 1999, Coronado: We Remember, 1993, The Pacific Coast League San Diego Padres, 2 vols., 1936-1957, 1997. Mem. Gaslamp Quarter Project Area Com., 1977—, chmn., 1980; v.p. San Diego Sci. Found., 1978-87, Internat. Am. Heritage Found., 2000—. With U.S. Army, 1943-46, USAR, 1950-53. Recipient medal of San Diego de Alcala, U. San. Diego, 1997; NDEA grantee, 1961-64; CETA grantee, 1978, 79; named Outstanding Prof. Social Sci. U. San Diego, 1968, 69, Disting. Historian medal U. Ariz., 1989. Mem. Mex.-Am. Educators, Nat. Coun. Pub. History, Soc. Am. Baseball Rschrs., Pacific Coast League Baseball Hist. Soc., San Diego Baseball Hist. Soc. (1st pres.), Coronado Hist. Soc. & Mus. (bd. dir.). Democrat. Roman Catholic. Home: 230 W Laurel St Apt 406 San Diego CA 92101-1464 Office Phone: 619-702-7137. Business E-Mail: rb@acusd.edu. E-mail: raybrandes@sbcglobal.net.

BRANDES, SHERRY, secondary educator; b. Washington, Mo., July 4, 1953; d. Roger Brandes and Marian Wildschuetz. BS in Edn., U. Mo., 1975, MA, 1983. Cert. in English teaching, secondary edn. Tchr. jr. high sch. English, newspaper and drama Warren County R-III Schs., Warrenton, Mo., tchr. high sch. English. Mem. NEA, Mo. Edn. Assn. (state del., state com.), Nat. Coun. Tchrs. English, Mortar Board, Phi Delta Kappa, Delta Kappa Gamma, Kappa Delta Pi. Home: 3522 Cappeln Osage Rd Marthasville MO 63357-2026

BRANDES, STANLEY HOWARD, anthropology educator, writer; b. N.Y.C., Dec. 26, 1942; s. Emanuel Robert and Annette (Zalisch) B.; m. Jane Brandes; children: Nina Rachel, Naomi Clara. BA, U. Chgo., 1964; MA, U. Calif., Berkeley, 1969, PhD, 1971. Asst. prof. anthropology Mich. State U., East Lansing, 1971-75; asst. prof. anthropology U. Calif., Berkeley, 1975-78, assoc. prof., 1978-82, prof. anthropology, 1982—, chmn. dept., 1990-93, 97-99. Dir. Barcelona Study Ctr., U. Calif. and Ill., Spain, 1981-82, Mexico City Study Ctr., 1995-96, U. Calif. Author: Migration, Kinship and Community, 1975, Metaphors of Masculinity, 1989, Forth: The Age and the Symbol, 1985, Power and Persuasion, 1988, Staying Sober in Mexico City, 2002; co-editor: Symbol as Sense, 1980. NIH fellow, 1967-71; NICHD Rsch. fellow, 1975-77; fellow John Carter Brown Libr., 1994; Am. Council Learned Socs. grantee, 1977 Fellow Am. Anthrop. Assn.; mem. Am. Ethnological Soc., Soc. for Psychol. Anthropology Office: U Calif Dept Anthropology Berkeley CA 94720-0001 Office Phone: 510-642-6945. Business E-Mail: brandes@berkeley.edu.

BRANDEWIE, RICHARD ANTHONY, laser and optics consultant; b. Sidney, Ohio; s. Leo Peter and Mary Agnes (Doorley) B.; m. Arlene Therese Warner, Aug. 29, 1959; children: Leo Peter, Frances Brandewie Geoffrion. BEE, U. Detroit, 1959; MS, Carnegie Inst. Tech., Pitts., 1960, PhD, 1963. Mem. tech. staff N.Am. Aviation, Anaheim, Calif., 1963-67; supr. lasers Rockwell Autonetics, Anaheim, 1967—79; mgr. lasers Rockwell Rocketdyne, Canoga Park, Calif., 1979-80, dir. rsch., 1980-84, program mgr., 1984-92; ind. cons. Monte Nido, Calif., 1992—. Contbr. articles to profl. jours. Dir. Edenwild Property Owners Assn., L.A., 1983, sec., 1983, pres., 1984. Recipient Esso fellowship Esso Corp., Carnegie Inst. Tech., 1961-63; recipient Nat. Sci. and Tech. award Iris Active Systems Group, 1992. Mem. IEEE, Am. Phys. Soc., Carnegie Mellon U. L.A. Alumni Assn. (dir., sec. 1980, pres. 1995-96), Sigma Xi, Eta Kappa Nu, Tau Beta Pi. Achievements include recognition as a founding father of laser radar and a major early contributor to the field of adaptive optics. Home and Office: 25760 Vista Verde Dr Monte Nido CA 91302-2164 E-mail: richbrand@ieee.org.

BRANDFORD, NAPOLEON, security firm executive; b. East Chicago, Ind, Feb. 23, 1952; m. Sharon Brandford. BA in political sci., Purdue U.; MS in Public Adminstrn., USC, 1978. Unit operator Standard Oil of Indiana, Whiting, 1974-75; asst. to transp. dir. Pacific Tel., L.A., 1976-78; chief duputy to fin. Dade County, Fla., 1978-82; v.p. Shearson, Lehman Bros., San Francisco, 1982-85; exec. v.p., dir. Grigsby Brandford & Co., Inc., San Francisco, 1985—97; founding ptnr., mgr. Southwestern and Western regions Siebert Brandford Shank & Co. LLC, N.Y.C., 1997—. Mem. fin. and investment com. Nat. Collegiate Athletic Assn.; bd. mem. Western Region Boy Scouts Am., L.A. Am. Heart Assn. Named Young Tycoon, Ebony Mag., 1988. Office: Siebert Brandford Shank & Co LLC 1999 Harrison St Ste 2720 Oakland CA 94612 Office Phone: 510-645-2245. Business E-Mail: nbrandford@sbsco.com.

BRANDHORST, WESLEY THEODORE, retired library and information scientist; b. Portland, Oreg., May 9, 1933; s. Wesley Theodore and Mary Margeurite (LaRouche) B.; m. Jane Smythe, Sept. 1, 1962; children—Tristan, Thea BA, U. Calif.-Berkeley, 1955, M.L.S., 1957. Spl. intern Libr. Congress, Washington, 1957-59; libr. Documentation Inc., Washington, 1959-61; asst. dir. NASA Sci. and Tech. Info. Facility, Washington, 1962-69; dir. ERIC Processing and Reference Facility, Washington, 1970-2000; ret., 2000. Chmn. Z39 Nat. Info. Stds. Orgn., 1985-87. Contbr. articles to profl. jours. Mem. ALA, AAAS, Spl. Librs. Assn., Am. Soc. Info. Sci. Unitarian Universalist. Avocations: tennis, running, bicycling, chess, reading. Home: 3346 Yonge Ave Sarasota FL 34235 Personal E-mail: tbrandho@att.net.

BRANDL, JOHN EDWARD, public affairs educator; b. Aug. 19, 1937; m. Rochelle Jankovich; children: Christopher, Mary Katherine, Amy. BA in Econs. with honors, St. John's U., Collegeville, Minn., 1959; MA in Econs., Harvard U., 1962, PhD in Econs., 1963. Lectr. econs. Boston Coll., 1961-62; systems analyst Office of Sec. Def., Washington, 1963-65; asst. prof. econs. St. John's U., Collegeville, 1965-67; asst. prof., rsch. assoc. Inst. for Rsch. on Poverty, dir. Systematic Analysis Program U. Wis., Madison, 1967-68; dep. asst. sec. HEW, Washington, 1968-69; from assoc. prof. to prof. pub. affairs U. Minn., Mpls., 1969—, dir. sch. pub. affairs, 1969-76, dean Hubert H. Humphrey Inst. Pub. Affairs, 1997—2002; rep. State of Minn., Mpls., 1977-78, 81-86, senator, 1987-90. Exec. bd. Ctr. for Policy Rsch. in Edn., 1986-96; vis. lectr. dept. econs. U. Philippines, 1968; vis. prof. pub. adminstrn. and pub. policy U. Sydney, Australia, 1973; teaching fellow dept. econs. Warsaw Sch. Econs., 1992-95. Author: Money and Good Intentions are Not Enough, 1998; (with A. Naftalin) Twin Cities Regional Strategy, 1981; co-editor: Public Policy and Educating Handicapped Persons, 1982; mem. editl. bd. Urban Affairs Quarterly, 1971-74, Sage Profl. Papers Adminstrv. Scis., 1972-76, Jour. Policy Analysis and Mgmt., 1981—; cons. editor Improving College and University Teaching, 1979-82; contbr. articles to pprofl. jours. Bd. dirs. Tri-Cap Community Action Agy. Inc., Mpls., 1966-67; trustee Mpls. Soc. Fine Arts, 1983-86; pres. Twin Cities Citizens' League, 1993; nat. adv. coun. St. John's U., Minn., 1975-91; chmn. Twin Cities Met. Coun. Cable TV Adv. Com., 1972-73, mem. FCC Cable Adv. Coun., 1972-73, Minn. State Planning Adv. Com., 1971-73, Gov.'s Adv. Com. on Mgmt. and Personnel Devel., 1971-76, Gov.'s Coun. of Econ. Advisors, 1971-76; Mem. study group Nat. Assessment of Student Achievement., 1986, Nat. Tchrs. Coun. Edn. Testing Svc., 1986-92, Nat. Commn. Indsl. Innovation, 1984-86; bd. dirs. policy studies orgns., 1985-90; asst. majority leader Minn. Ho. of Rep., 1983-84, minority caucus steering com., 1985-86; bd. regents St. John's U., Minn, 1991-2000. Recipient Presdl. prize Am. Evaluation Assn., 1988, Disting. Svc. award Nat. Govs. Assn., 1996 Fordham Found. prize for excellence in edn., 2005. Fellow Nat. Acad. Pub. Adminstrn.; mem. NIMH (rsch. edn. adv. com. 1980-84), Assn. for Pub. Policy Analysis and Mgmt. (v.p. 1983-84, pres. 1986-87), Am. Soc. Pub. Adminstrn. (bd. dirs. Minn. chpt. 1975-76), Cath. Econ. Assn. (coun. dirs. 1968), Harvard Grad. Soc. (coun. 1988-91), Delta Epsilon Sigma.

BRANDL, MARY-KATHERINE, mathematics professor; d. John Edward and Rochelle Ann Brandl. BA, U. Calif., Santa Cruz, 1995; MS, U. Oreg., 1997, PhD, 2001. Grad. tchg. fellow U. Oreg., Eugene, 1995—2001; asst. prof. Centenary Coll. of La., Shreveport, 2001—. Mem.: Assn. for Women in Math. (corr.), Math. Assn. of Am. (corr.), Am. Math. Soc. (corr.). Liberal. Office: Centenary Coll La 2911 Centenary Blvd Shreveport LA 71134 Personal E-mail: kbrandl@centenary.edu.

BRANDLER, JONATHAN M., lawyer; b. L.A., Jan. 8, 1946; AB, U. Calif., Berkeley, 1967; JD, U. So. Calif., 1970. Bar: Calif. 1971. Ptnr. Hill, Farrer & Burrill LLP, L.A. Lectr. Inst. Bus. Law, 1981-92. Mem. State Bar Calif. (labor law sect.), L.A. County Bar Assn. (labor law sect.). Office: Hill Farrer & Burrill LLP 1 California Plaza 300 S Grand Ave Ste 37 Los Angeles CA 90071-3110 E-mail: jbrandler@hfbllp.com.

BRANDLER, MARCIELLE Y., poet, educator; b. Riverside, Calif., June 27, 1950; d. Cecil U. and Luverne M. (Lieb) Parks. M of Profl. Writing, U. So. Calif. L.A., 1994; BA, U. Utah, 1981. Cert. lectr. L.A. C.C., 1988. Coll. educator Various colleges, Los Angeles, 1988—; dir. poetry workshop, mentor Performing Tree, Los Angeles, 2002—; vis. poet Calif. Poets in Schs., Los Angeles, 1988—2000. Author (singer, composer, producer): (cd poems with sound effects and voice) The Breathing House, poems published internationally; prodr.(featured singer/poet/emcee): (various benefit performances); author: (entertainment writer) Sierra Madre Vista & Creative Line Magazine; writer: Religion of Ethics Digest, 1997; prodr.: (pub. access TV program with Adelphia TV,) Marcielle Presents. Vol. Unitarian Universalist Ch., Pasadena, Calif., 1999—2003; mem. Foothill Enrichment Ctr., Sci. of Mind. Recipient First Pl. for poem, Eden, Mt. San Antonio Coll., 1997. Mem.: Ams. United for Separation Ch. and State (bd. mem.), Am. Fedn. Tchrs. (assoc.), Foothill Enrichment Ctr. Sci. of Mind, Alameda Writers Group (assoc.), Pasadena Opera Guild (assoc.; mem.). Achievements include Produced a film for American Film Institute; Produced a variety show for LA Coalition to End Hunger; Produced a benefit performance for the Literacy Campaign; Produced event to celebrate banned books. Avocation: poetry. Office Phone: 626-791-5867. E-mail: marcielle@dslextreme.com.

BRANDMAIER, JEFF, diversified financial services company executive; MS in info. sys., Stockton State Coll.; MBA in fin., Pace U. Mgmt. IBM; sr. mgr. KPMG Nolan, Norton & Co.; chief info. officer The Money Store, 1995—2001; sr. v.p., chief info. officer H&R Block, Inc., Kans. City, Mo., 2001—. Avocation: amateur competitive equestrian. Office: H&R Block 4400 Main St Kansas City MO 64111

BRANDMEIR, CHRISTOPHER LEE, hotel and tourism management educator; b. Seattle, Mar. 6, 1950; s. Jack W. and Betty G. (Lyman) B. BA, U. San Francisco, 1972; MBA, Nat. U., 2000; student DBA program, U. Phoenix, 2001—. Dir. coll. rels. Cogswell Coll., San Francisco, 1983-86; exec. dir. San Lorenzo (Calif.) Village, 1986-88; owner Inn Sight, Seattle, 1996—; pres., co-owner HBH Mgmt., Lopez Island, Wash., 1993-96, Inn at Swifts Bay, Lopez Island, 1988-96; instr., program mgr. hotel and tourism mgmt. Highline C.C., Des Moines, 1998—. Past chmn. San Juan Islands Tourism Resource Coun.; chmn. Acad. of hospitality and tourism mgmt. adv. bd. Seattle Pub. Schs.; pres. Lopez Island Chamber, Cascadia Coun. Hotel Restaurant and Instl. Edn. Internat.; bd. dirs., past chmn. San Juan Islands Visitor Info. Svc.; bd. dirs., fundraiser Lopez Island Cmty. Ctr. Recipient Lyons Club Svc. award. Mem. Internat. Assn. Culinary Profls. Republican. Roman Catholic. Avocations: cooking, sailing, international studies, politics. Home: 3543 Hampton Way Kent WA 98032-7027 Office: Highline CC 2400 S 240th St MS 18-1 Des Moines WA 98198-2714 Office Phone: 206-878-3710 3855. E-mail: c.brandmeir@comcast.net.

BRANDON, DAVID A., food service executive; b. 1952; With Procter & Gamble Distbg. Co., 1974-79, GFV Comm., Inc., 1979-83, COO, exec. v.p., dir., 1983-86; COO, exec. v.p., pres., dir. Valassis Inserts, Inc., Livonia, Mich., 1986—99; pres., CEO Valassis Comm., Livonia, Mich., 1989—99, chmn., 1997—99; chmn., CEO Domino's Pizza, Inc., Ann Arbor, Mich., 1999—. Office: Dominos Pizza Inc 30 Frank Lloyd Wright Dr Ann Arbor MI 48105-9757 Business E-Mail: brandod@dominos.com.

BRANDON, ELVIS DENBY, JR., financial planner; b. Nov. 28, 1927; s. Elvis Denby and Hazel Ione (Davidson) Brandon; m. Helen Holt Deupree, Apr. 25, 1953; children: Elvis Denby III, Raymond Wilson. BA with honors, Rhodes Coll., Memphis, 1950; MA, Duke U., 1952. CLU; CFP, chartered fin. cons., registered prin. NASD. Chmn. Brandon Fin. Planning Inc./Brandon Investments, Inc., Memphis, 1952—. Prodr., moderator (TV) Your Future Unlimited, 1955 (Sylvania TV award). Tchr. Shady Grove Presbyn. Ch., Memphis, 1989—; mem. pres.'s coun. and heritage soc. Rhodes Coll.; coord. Great Millennium Reunion. Mem.: Fin. Planners Assn., CFP Bd. Stds. (chmn. 1989—90, 1st chmn. internat. coun. 1992), Rotary, Racquet Club Memphis, Phi Beta Kappa. Home: 505 West Racquet Club Pl Memphis TN 38117 Office: Brandon Financial Planning Inc 5101 Wheelis Rd Ste 112 Memphis TN 38117 Office Phone: 901-324-6600. Business E-Mail: edenbybrandonjr@brandonorg.com.

BRANDON, ELVIS DENBY, III, financial planner; b. Memphis, Aug. 11, 1954; s. Elvis Denby Jr. and Helen (Deupree) B.; m. Sarah Louise Buntin, Mar. 15, 1980; children: Elizabeth Holt, William Denby, Mary Buntin. BBA, So. Meth. U., 1976; MBA, Memphis State U., 1979. Cert. fin. planner; CLU; chartered fin. cons. Mgmt. candidate First Tenn. Bank, NA, Memphis, 1979-80; sr. credit analyst Banc Texas/Dallas NA, 1980-82; asst. v.p., comml. loan officer Banc Texas/Sherman NA, 1982; pres. Brandon Investments, Inc., Memphis, 1982—; v.p. Brandon Fin. Planning, Inc., Memphis, 1982—. Adj. faculty Coll. for Fin. Planning, Denver, 1984-85. Elder Idlewild Presb. Ch. Mem.: NASD (registered prin.), Fin. Planning Assn., Soc. Fin. Svc. Profls. Presbyterian. Home: 5953 Brierdale Ave Memphis TN 38120-2345 Office: Brandon Fin Planning Inc 5101 Wheelis Rd Ste 112 Memphis TN 38117 Office Phone: 901-324-6600.

BRANDON, KATHLEEN ALMA, director; b. Cincinnati, Ohio, July 11, 1946; d. Arthur Hubert Brandon and Alma Martha Vorwerck; m. James Lee Frost, Apr. 15, 1987 (dec. June 13, 2000). BS, Ohio State U., 1969; MA, Calif. State U., Northridge, 1983. Calif. State U., L.A., 1997. Tchr., spl. edn. Franklin County Program for the Mentally Retarded, Columbus, Ohio, 1969—76, Atwater Ave. Sch., L.A., Calif., 1979—95, categorical program advisor, 1996—98; asst. prin. Los Angeles Unified Sch. Dist., L.A., Calif., 1998—99; coord. spl. edn., orthop. impaired L.A. Unified Sch. Dist., 1999—. Mem.: Computer Using Educators, Assn. Supervision and Curriculum Design, Coun. for Exceptional Children, Calif. Speech Lang. Hearing Assn., Am. Speech Lang. Hearing Assn. Avocations: reading, travel, decorating. Office: Los Angeles Unified Sch Dist 333 S Beaudry 17th Fl Los Angeles CA 90017 Personal E-mail: kate.brandon@lausd.net.

BRANDON, LIANE, filmmaker, educator; Student, St. Lawrence U., U. Edinburgh, Scotland; exchange student, U. Moscow; AB, MEd, Boston U. Ski instr., Mt. Tremblant, Canada; actress Children's Theatre, Cambridge, Mass.; film project dir. English dept. Quincy pub. schs., Mass.; prof. film-TV prodn. and media studies Sch. Edn. U. Mass., Amherst, 1973—; co-founder, mem. New Day Films, 1971—, Women in Film and Video, 1981—; co-dir. UMass Ednl. TV, U. Mass., Amherst, 1994—2004; dir. Sch. Edn. Ednl. Tech. Program, U. Mass., 1998—. Film cons. Mass. Gov.'s Commn. on Status of Women, 1974; cons. Mass. Artists Found., 1975, 82, WGBH-TV, 1992-97; judge Regional Student Acad. Awards, 1991, New Eng. Regional Emmy Awards,1992; trustee Theaterworks, 1981-83; bd. dirs. Boston Film-Video Found., 1983-87, ACLU of Mass., 1988-97; mem. adv. bd. Children's Media Found. Boston, 1993-97; guest lectr. various confs. on edn. and film to colls. and art schs. in US. Exhibited film, Mus. Modern Art, Whitney Mus. Am. Art, Chgo. Art Inst., Nat. Film Theatre, London, Internat. Womens Film Festival, Paris, Mus. Fine Arts, Boston, Libr. Congress, Washington, John F. Kennedy Ctr. Performing Arts, Washington; dir., prodr. (film) Anything You Want to Be, 1971 (Blue Ribbon Am. Film Festival award), Betty Tells Her Story, 1972, Once Upon a Choice, 1980 (Silver medal Houston Internat. Film Festival), How to Prevent a Nuclear War, 1987 (Blue Ribbon award Am. Film Festival 1988); prodr. (video) Goodnight Amherst, 1995, Fine Print, 1995, Try This At Home, 1998 (Judge's Choice award Hometown Video Festival 1999), Fresh Ink, 1998, Try This At Home: Nature Series, 2000 (award of Distinction, Communicator award); still photographer: Murder at Harvard, 2002, Act Your Age, 2002, (PBS) The Most Dangerous Woman in America, 2005. Recipient Creative Artist award AAUW, 1975, Disting. Alumni award Boston U., 1985; Careth Found. grantee, 1988, Funding Exchange grantee, 1989, Mass. Found. for Humanities and Pub. Policy grantee, 1975, Film Fund grantee, 1985. Try this at Home: Nature Series (Award of Distinction, Communicator Awards), 2000 Mem. New Eng. Screen Edn. Assn. (v.p. 1972-83), Assn. Ind. Video and Filmmakers, Women in Film and Video New Eng. (founding mem. 1981-). E-mail: brandon@educ.umass.edu.

BRANDON, RAYMOND WILSON, financial planner, securities trader; b. Memphis, Mar. 11, 1959; s. Elvis Denby Jr. and Helen (Deupree) B.; m. Dana Stallings, Sept. 21, 1996. BA, Vanderbilt U., 1981; MBA, U. Tex., 1983. CFA; CLU; cert. fin. planner; chartered fin. cons. Pres., chmn. investment com. Brandon Fin. Planning, Inc., Memphis, 1983—; v.p. ops. Brandon Investments, Inc., Memphis, 1983—. V.p. Brandon Underwriting Specialists, Inc., Memphis. Sord scholar U. Tex., 1983. Mem. Fin. Planning Assn. (pres. Memphis chpt. 1988-89), Am. Soc. Fin. Svc. Profls., Memphis Inst. Cert. Fin. Planners (bd. dirs.), CFA Inst., Rotary (Paul Harris fellow, treas., bd. dirs.), Racquet Club Memphis, Phi Beta Kappa. Presbyterian. Avocations: swimming, running, travel, magic, public speaking. Office: 5101 Wheelis Rd Ste 112 Memphis TN 38117 Office Phone: 901-324-6600.

BRANDON, WALTER WILEY, JR., retired physicist, retired aerospace engineer; b. Gainesville, Ga., Dec. 1, 1929; s. Walter Wiley and Nancy (Logan) Brandon; m. Patricia Donham, May 18, 1957; children: Dean Corbly, Miles Logan, Nancy Lynn. BA, Emory U., 1952, MS, 1953. Scientist Rohm and Haas Co., Huntsville, Ala., 1953—64, 1967—71; aerospace engr. Boeing Co., Huntsville, 1964—67; analyst U.S. Army Missile Command, Huntsville, 1972—87; aerospace engr. NASA Marshall Space Flight Ctr., Huntsville, 1987—98, ret., 1998. Tech. cons. detonation U.S. Army Missile Command, Huntsville, 1988, Morton-Thiokol Corp., Huntsville, 1988. Fellow: AIAA (assoc.); mem.: Sigma Pi Sigma (Emory U. chpt. pres. 1952—53), Sigma Xi (assoc.). Methodist. Avocations: photography, model building. Home: 1902 Colice Rd SE Huntsville AL 35801-1640

BRANDON, WILLIAM PEW, JR., social sciences educator; b. Greensboro, N.C. s. William P. and Katherine Wolff Brandon; m. Pamela Sue Fawcett, Dec. 20, 1975 BA in Philosophy and Polit. Sci.with gen. honors, Johns Hopkins U., 1963; MSc in Politics, U. London, 1967; PhD in Polit. Sci., Duke U., 1975; MPH in Health Policy and Adminstrn., U. N.C., Chapel Hill, 1976. Dir. info. svcs. evaluation and planning Orange-Chatham Comprehensive Health Svcs., Chapel Hill, N.C., 1971-75; asst. prof. preventive medicine and polit. sci. U. Rochester, N.Y., 1976-82; NEH fellow Hastings Ctr., Hastings-on-Hudson, N.Y., 1982-83; from assoc. prof. to prof. polit. sci. and pub. adminstrn. Seton Hall U., South Orange, N.J., 1984-93; Metrolina Med. Found. Disting. prof. U. N.C., Charlotte, 1994—. Vis. prof. health care adminstrn. Bernard M. Baruch Coll., CUNY, 1990; dir. rsch., fin. officer Essex and Union Adv. Bd. for Health Planning Inc., South Orange, 1992-93. Contbr. numerous articles to profl. jours., including New Eng. Jour. Medicine, Polit. Theory, Jour. Health Politics Policy and Law, others. Vol. U.S. Peace Corps, Iran, 1964-66; mem. City Planning Commn., Rochester City Govt., 1979-82; mem. N.J. State Health Planning Bd., Trenton, 1992; active Leadership Charlotte XXII, 2000-01; bd. visitors Miss Hall's Sch., Pittsfield, Mass., 2000-02; vice-chair Medlink of Mecklenberg, 2004-2005. Faculty fellow in healthcare fin. Robert Wood Johnson Found.-Johns Hopkins Med. Instn., 1985-86, GlaxoSmithKline faculty fellow, Inst. Emerging Issues, NC State U., 2004-05; grantee for rsch. on Medicaid, N.C. HHS Agy. Healthcare Rsch. and Quality, 1996-2001, 2005-2007. Mem. APHA (governing coun. 1984-86), Am. Polit. Sci. Assn., Academy for Health Svcs. Rsch., Charlotte Area Peace Corps Assn. (pres. 2003, bd. dirs. 2003-2004), Phi Beta Kappa, Sigma Xi. Office: U NC Charlotte Dept Polit Sci 9201 University City Blvd Charlotte NC 28223 Fax: 704-687-3497. E-mail: wilbrand@email.uncc.edu.

BRANDON-FALCONE, JANICE ILENE, history educator; b. Dixon, Ill., Dec. 24, 1947; d. Forrest Perrie and Genevieve Catherine (Ribordy) Brandon; m. Paul Charles Falcone, Feb. 17, 1943; children: Nicole Elizabeth, Christian Paul. BA, No. Ill. U., 1971; MA, St. Louis U., 1983, PhD, 1990; D of Humane Letters, Sureka Coll., 2004. Lab. technician St. Joseph Hosp., Elgin, Ill., 1967-77; lab. supr., dir. Reynolds County Hosp., Ellington, Mo., 1978-84; asst. dir. honors program St. Louis U., 1983-84, 85-87; assoc. prof. history N.W. Mo. State U., Maryville, 1988—. Rev. cons. Houghton Mifflin, N.Y.C., 1995, Prentice Hall-Paramount Co., N.J., 1995, 96; cons. Jour. Women's History, 1996; conf. presenter. Author: A Student Guide to These United States, 1995; author, editor: American Dreams, American Realities, 1998, 3d edit., 2001; book reviewer Am. Hist. Rev., 1994; contbr. chpt. to book and articles to profl. jours. Foster parent Mo. Divsn. Family Svcs., Maryville, 1992—93, bd. dirs., 2001—02; grant writer, participant Adult Basic Edn.-Mo. Humanities Coun., Maryville, 1994, 1996. Mem. AAUW, WILPF, Am. Hist. Assn., Am. Studies Assn., Orgn. Am. Historians. Office: NW Mo State Univ 800 University Dr Maryville MO 64468-6015

BRANDOW, STEPHEN JON, priest; b. Olean, N.Y., Dec. 25, 1960; s. David Arden and Jacqueline Delores (Johns) B. BA, Northwestern State U. La., 1983, BA in Social Work, 1985; MDiv, Notre Dame Sem., 1996. Ordained to ministry, Cath. Ch., 1996. Social worker Woodview Regional Hosp., Pineville, La., 1986; med. clk. VA Med. Ctr., Alexandria, La., 1986-91; assoc. pastor St. Rita Cath. Ch., Alexandria, La., 1996-97, Immaculate Heart of Mary Cath. Ch., Tioga, La., 1997-2000. Chaplain Ctrl. La. State Hosp., Pineville, 1997—2000, Christus St. Frances Cabrini Hosp., Alexandria, 1997—, 1997—2001, VA Med. Ctr., Alexandria, 1998—; mem. com. continuing formation of clergy Diocese of Alexandria, 1996—, sec., 1996—97. Mem. Cath. Commn. on Scouting, 1997—; bd. dir. Girl Scout Coun. of Ctrl. La., 2001—02; v.p. Attakapas Coun. Boy Scouts of Am., cmty. adv. bd. Achita Valley Coun., 2003—. Recipient Whitney Young Svc. award, Boy Scouts Am., 2002, Pelican award, Cath. Com. on Scouting, Diocese of Alexandria, 2003; James E. West fellow, Boy Scouts Am., 2002. Mem.: United Assn. Christian Counselors, La. Chaplains Assn. (bd. dirs. 1999—2002). Avocation: yoga. Home: PO Box 39 Tioga LA 71477 Office: VA Med Ctr PO Box 69004 Tioga LA 71306 Fax: 318-483-5053. E-mail: sbran62261@aol.com.

BRANDOW, THEO, architect; b. Phila., Nov. 18, 1925; s. Ralph and Minnie (Weinstock) B.; m. Selma Koss, July 22, 1945; children: Jonathan, Rinna, Shanna. Student, Girard Coll., 1935—43; BArch, U. Pa., 1949. Assoc. Oskar Stonorov, Phila., 1949-52; pvt. practice architecture Phila., 1952-78; project dir. Rochlin & Baran & Assocs., West Los Angeles, Calif., 1978-81; pres. Brandow Design Assocs., 1982-87; pvt. practice architecture Ambler, Pa., 1987—. Cons. urban renewal; vis. speaker sch. system Wellspring Ecumenical Ctr., Phila., 1966—. Prin. works include houses, apt. and office buildings, churches; design architect Benjamin Franklin House; works pub. in various mags. including Life, House and Home, Am. Home; author: Closer to Saturday, 1971, Michla, A Trilogy; also articles and lectures on Israel's Day of Atonement War of 1973; group shows include Chestnut Hill Fine Arts Festival, Phila., 1995 (1st place prize 1995), New Hope Art Festival, Pa.,

1995 (award of excellence 1995), Lansdale Festival of the Arts, Pa., 1995 (most unique craft award 1995), Woodmere Art Mus., Phila., 1996, 97, 98, 2d Fl. Gallery, Mechanicsburg, Pa., 2005; juried shows include Susquehanna Art Mus., Harrisburg, Pa., 2004. V.p. Erdenheim (Pa.) PTA, 1956; mem. Whitemarsh Valley Fair Housing Coun., 1966—; pack master local coun. Boy Scouts Am.; bd. dirs. local Jewish synagogue. With USNR, 1943-46. Recipient award World Traveling Exhibit Art in Arch., 1949, Homes for Better Living, 1957, 59, state citation Am. Home mag., 1957, nat. citation, 1958, spl. award Am. Builder mag., 1959, McCall's Congress for Better Living award, 1959, awards Nat. Assn. Home Builders, 1961, Bronze Plaque of Appreciation, Temple Beth Shalom, Mechanicsburg, 2005. Mem. AIA (awards 1957, 61). Home: 2601 #1 Market St Camp Hill PA 17001

BRANDRUP, DOUGLAS WARREN, lawyer; b. Mitchel, S.D., July 11, 1940; s. Clair L. and Ruth M. (Wolverton) B.; m. Patricia R. Tuck, Dec. 20, 1986; children: Kendra, Monika, Peter. AB in Econs., Middlebury Coll., 1963; JD, Boston U., 1966. Bar: N.Y. 1969, U.S. Dist. Ct. (so. dist.) N.Y. 1970, U.S. Ct. Appeals (2d cir.) 1970. Assoc. Donovan, Leisure, Newton & Irvine, N.Y.C., 1968-72; ptnr. Griggs, Baldwin & Baldwin, N.Y.C., 1972-80, sr. ptnr., 1980—. Mem. disciplinary com. first dept. appellate divsn. Supreme Ct. State of N.Y., 2003. Mem. Govs. Security Adv. Com., State of N.J., 1975-90. Capt. U.S. Army, 1966-68. Recipient Ellis Island medal of Honor, 1999, Order of St. John, 2002. Mem. ABA, N.Y. County Bar Assn., N.Y. State Bar Assn., Met. Club (N.Y.C., pres.), Mashomack Preserve Club. Republican. Episcopalian. Office: 57 Old Post Rd No 2 Greenwich CT 06830 Office Fax: 203-629-7983.

BRANDS, JAMES EDWIN, medical products executive; b. Lebanon, Ind., July 5, 1937; s. Edwin Herman and Pearl Irene (Brown) B.; m. Gail Marian Knight, Sept. 12, 1959; children: Jeffrey, Scot, Alan, Susan. AB, Wesleyan U., Middletown, Conn., 1959; MBA, U. Chgo., 1961; JD, Kennedy-Western U., Boise, Idaho, 1992. CPA, Mo. Staff acct., mgr. Arthur Andersen, Chgo., 1961-71, ptnr. St. Louis, 1971-82; sr. v.p. Scherer-Storz, Inc., St. Louis, 1982-86, bd. dirs.; vice chmn., CFO Scherer Healthcare Inc., Atlanta, 1982-95; exec. v.p. Scherer Sci. Ltd., Atlanta, 1986-95; chmn., CEO Marquest Med. Products, Inc., Denver, 1993-95; CFO Wilson Pest Control, Inc., Atlanta, 1997-99; sr. exec. v.p. Able Telcom Holding Corp., Atlanta, 1999—2001. Bd. dirs., pres. BodyCare Inc., Atlanta; bd. dirs. Rita Med. Sys. Inc., Fremont, Calif.; pres. Brands & Co, 1981—, Throwleigh Tech. LLC, Atlanta, 2000—. Mem. AICPA, Mo. Soc. CPAs, Bellerive Country Club (St. Louis), Country Club of the South (Atlanta). Home: 4330 Bancroft Valley Alpharetta GA 30022-5175 Personal E-mail: brandsj@bellsouth.net.

BRANDSDORFER, MARK MICHAEL, lawyer, accountant; b. Vineland, N.J., Aug. 31, 1968; s. Samuel and Ethel B.; m. Rochelle Lieberman, Nov. 20, 1994. BS with honors, Yeshiva U., N.Y.C., 1990; JD, Georgetown U., 1993. Bar: N.J. 1993, D.C. 1995, Md. 1996, U.S. Dist. Ct. N.J., N.Y. 1994, U.S. Tax Ct. 1994, U.S. Dist. Ct. D.C. 1995, U.S. Ct. Appeals (D.C. cir.) 1995, U.S. Dist. Ct. Md. 1999; CPA. Jr. acct. Karpman & Co. CPAs, N.Y.C., 1988-90; summer assoc. Eisenstat, Gabage et al., Vineland, N.J., 1992; assoc. Feldesman, Tucker et al., Washington, 1994-95; ptnr. Lieberman & Brandsdorfer LLC, Gaithersburg, Md., 1996—. Bd. dirs. PelleTech Fuels, Inc., Chaffee, N.Y., Sci. & Environ. Policy Project, Arlington, Va. Mem. ABA, D.C. Bar, Md. Bar Assn. Home and Office: 12221 Mcdonald Chapel Dr North Potomac MD 20878-2252 E-mail: mark@legalplanner.com.

BRANDT, ANTHONY KROYT, composer, educator; b. New York City, Ny, June 23, 1961; s. Nat and Yanna Kroyt Brandt; m. Karol Brandt, June 23, 1991; children: Sonya Katerine Bennett-Brandt, Gabriel Alexander Bennett-Brandt, Lucian Anthony Skye Bennett-Brandt. BA, Harvard Coll., 1983; MA, Calif. Inst. Arts, Valencia, 1987; PhD, Harvard U., 1993. Assoc. prof. Rice U., Houston, Tex., 1998—. Pres., co-founder Musiqa, Houston, 2002—. Composer: (chamber opera) The Birth of Something, 2005 (commn. Da Camera of Houston, 2005), (string quartet with voice) The Dragon and the Undying, 2004 (commn. Bowdoin Internat. Festival, 2004), (string quartet) String Quartet No. 2, 2001 (commn. Koussevitzky Found., 2000), Round Top Trio, 2003 (commn. Internat. Festival-Institute at Round Top, 2003), (TV documentary score) Crucible of the Millennium, 2001 (named best in show CHRIS, 2001). Recipient Phi Beta Kappa tchg. prize, Rice U., 2001; fellow, MacDowell Colony, 1996; Innovation grantee, Computer and Info. Tech. Inst., Rice U., 2002, Access to Artistic Excellence grantee, Nat. Endowment for Arts, 2005, Norton Stevens fellow, The MacDowell Colony, 1998, Hon. fellow, Djerassi Resident Arts Colony, 2002. Mem.: ASCAP (awards 2002—05). Achievements include design of Author, liner notes, New World, Albany and Bridge Records; Author, Sound Reasoning, web-based, interactive music appreciation course for the Connexions Project (http:/www.cnx.rice.edu), in progress. Home: 5206 Cheena Dr Houston TX 77096 Office: Rice Univ 6100 Main St Houston TX 77005 Personal E-mail: abrandt@rice.edu.

BRANDT, CARL DAVID, research virologist; b. Bridgeport, Conn., Jan. 19, 1928; s. Carl August and Hildur (Wedberg) B.; m. Elsa Lund Erickson, Apr. 25, 1964; children: Karen, Erik. BS, U. Conn., 1949; MS, U. Mass., 1951; PhD, Harvard U., 1958. Rsch. instr. dept. vet. sci. U. Mass., Amherst, 1949-52, 54; rsch. virologist Charles Pfizer & Co., Inc., Ind. and Conn., 1958—62; assoc., dept. epidemiology Pub. Health Rsch. Inst., N.Y.C., 1962—66; rsch. assoc. virology rsch. Children's Nat. Med. Ctr., Washington, 1966-79, sr. rsch. assoc., 1979-86, sr. scientist, 1986-94; ret., 1994. Instr. Georgetown U. Med. Sch., Washington, 1966-69; asst. prof. pediat. George Washington U. Med. Sch., Washington, 1969-74, assoc. prof., 1974-94, emeritus prof., 1994. Contbr. over 125 articles to profl. jours. 1st lt. USAF, 1952-54. Fellow Am. Acad. Microbiology, Infectious Diseases Soc. Am., Am. Coll. Epidemiology; mem. N.Y. Color Slide Club (bd. dirs. 1965-66), Silver Spring Camera Club (pres. 1970-71), Rock Creek Amateur Radio Assn. (pres. 1985-89). Avocations: photography, amateur radio. Home: 819 E Franklin Ave Silver Spring MD 20901-4709

BRANDT, CAROLE, theater educator, department chairman; b. Lincoln, Ill., Oct. 22, 1937; d. Clifton Perry and Mary Helen (Mitchell). BS in Speech Edn., U. Ill., 1959, MA in Theatre Art, 1962; postgrad., U. Iowa, 1968-69; PhD in Directing and Dramatic Lit., So. Ill. U., 1976. Tchr. speech and drama, play dir. pub. schs., Oak Lawn, Joliet, Maywood, Ill., 1959-65, 66-68; teaching asst. in speech U. Ill., Urbana, 1961-62; teaching asst. in rhetoric, then instr. edn. play prodn. U. Iowa, Iowa City, 1968-69; asst. prof. theatre Ill. State U., Normal, 1969-74; assoc. prof. drama Ill. Wesleyan U., Bloomington, 1975-82, dir. Sch. Drama, 1977-82; artistic dir. Cen. Sta. Dinnner, Bloomington, 1982-83, Co. ONSTAGE, Bloomington, 1983-84; prof., chmn. dept. theatre U. Fla., Gainesville, 1984-88; prof., head dept. theatre arts, exec. producer, artistic dir. Pa. State U. and Pa. Centre Stage, University Park, 1988-94; dean Meadows Sch. of the Arts, So. Meth. U., Dallas, 1994—, prof. Vis. artist, prof. Idaho State U., Pocatello, 1984; critic Am. Coll. Theater Regional and State Festivals; guest critic numerous univs. and theatres; mem. Pa. Adv. Coun. for Arts in Edn., 1990-92; exec. producer, bd. dirs. Pa. Centre Stage, 1988-92; mem. nat. com. Am. Coll. Theatre Festival, Kennedy Ctr. for Performing Arts, Washington, 1978-89, 91-93, mem. nat. exec. com., 1982-89, 91-93, nat. chmn., 1985-87. Co-author: (video tape) Adjudication 1987; dir. Nat. Evening of Scenes, Kennedy Ctr. for Performing Arts, 1986, A Chorus Line, Hippodrome State Theatre, 1987. Convener Nat. Think Tank for Change, Washington, 1990; trustee Twin Cities Ballet, Bloomington, 1982; panel mem. Ill. Arts Coun., Chgo., 1978-81; mem. reading panel Nat. Endowment for Arts, 1991-92. Recipient Theatre Educator of Yr. award Fla. Assn. for Theatre Edn., 1988; AMOCO medal of excellence Am. Coll. Theatre Festival, 1981, Kennedy Ctr. medal, 1989, 91, 93, Disting. Alumni awrd Dept. Theatre/So. Ill. U., 1996, Coll. Arts and Scis./So. Ill. U., 1997, Encomienda de la Orden de Isabel La Catolica, King Juan Carlos, 2001, Creative Arts award for excellence Dallas Hist. Soc., 2002. Fellow Coll. Fellows Am. Theatre (former dean); mem. Assn. for Theatre in Higher Edn. (founding, bd. govs. 1991—, pres. 1993-95), Nat. Assn. Schs. Theatre (panelist, evaluator 1987, 89-92, bd. dirs. 1991—, treas., v.p., pres.), Soc. for Stage Dirs. & Choreographers, Nat. Theatre Conf. (life, v.p., pres.), Fla. Theatre Conf. (pres.), Ill. Theatre Assn. (pres.). Avocations: reading, listening to music, cultural events. Office: Meadows Sch Arts/So Meth U Offfice of the Dean PO Box 750356 Dallas TX 75275-0001 Office Phone: 214-768-2880. Business E-Mail: cbrandt@mail.smu.edu.

BRANDT, EDWARD NEWMAN, JR., physician, educator; b. Oklahoma City, July 3, 1933; s. Edward Newman and Myrtle (Brazil) Brandt; m. Patricia Ann Lawson, Aug. 29, 1953; children: Patrick James, Edward Newman III, Rex Carlin. BS, U. Okla., 1954, MD, 1960, PhD, 1963; MS, Okla. State U., 1955; LHD (hon.), Med. U. S.C., Rush U.; DSc (hon.), N.Y. Inst. Tech. Intern Oklahoma City VA Hosp., 1960—61; resident U. Okla. Hosps., 1961; from instr. to prof. preventive medicine and pub. health U. Okla. Med. Ctr., Oklahoma City, 1961—70, prof., chmn. dept. biostatistics Sch. Health, 1967—68, assoc. dean Sch. Medicine, assoc. dir., 1968—70; dean Grad. Sch., prof. preventive medicine and cmty. health U. Tex. Med. Br., Galveston, 1970—72, prof., 1970—84, prof. family medicine, 1973—84, acting dean, 1972—74, assoc. dean clin. affairs, 1972—73, acting dean medicine, 1973—74, dean medicine, 1974—76, exec. dean, 1976—77; vice chancellor health affairs U. Tex. Sys., Austin, 1977—81; asst. sec. health HHS, 1981—84; pres., prof. epidemiology and preventive medicine U. Md., Balt., 1985—89; prof. internal medicine, exec. dean Coll. Medicine U. Okla., Oklahoma City, 1989—92, prof. health adminstrn. Coll. Pub. Health, 1989—96, Regents prof., 1996—2004, Regents prof. emeritus, 2004—, dir. Ctr. Health Policy, 1992—2004, chair dept. health adminstrn. and policy Coll. Pub. Health, 2000—02. Mem. primate ctr. rev. com. NIH, 1975—79, chmn., 1978—79, mem. rsch. career devel. award com., 1968—72, mem. adv. com. on rsch. in women's health, 1995—97; bd. regents Nat. Libr. Medicine, 1985—89, chmn., 1987—89; mem. exec. bd. WHO, 1982—84; chmn. adv. com. on injury control CDC, 1988—93; chmn. adv. coun. on food FDA, 1992—2000. Editor, contbr. Proc. of Conf. at U. Okla. Med. Ctr., 1968, editor Continuing Education for the Family Physician, 1974—77, AIDS and Pub. Polic Jour., 1988—91. Recipient Superior Performance award, VA Hosp., Oklahoma City, 1961, Lloyd M. Southwick Meml. award for med. writing, 1974, 1975, Spl. Appreciation award, Tex. Acad. Family Physicians, 1974, Leone award for adminstrv. excellence, 1976, Outstanding Alumni Svc. award, U. Okla. Coll. Medicine, 1977, Disting. Svc. award, U. Tex. Med. Br., 1977, 19th Ann. Stoneburner lectr., Med. Coll. Va., 1966, Disting. Leadership award, HHS, 1984, Disting. Pub. Svc. award, Dept. Def., 1986, Pub. Health award, Am. Acad. Family Physicians; scholar Triennial, Phi Kappa Phi, 1998—2001. Fellow: AAAS (chair med. scis. sect. 1992—93), Am. Coll. Cardiology (hon.); mem.: AMA (chmn. sect. on med. schs. 1979—81; chmn. com. accreditation continuing med. edn. 1979—81), Inst. Medicine NAS (governing coun. 1986—92), Philos. Soc. Tex., Okla. Acad. Family Physicians, Am. Acad. Family Physicians, Okla. Med. Assn. (chmn. com. on family violence 1993—98, chmn. coun. on state legis. 1994—), Assn. Am. Med. Colls. (exec. coun. 1986—89, Spl. Recognition award 1985), Alpha Omega Alpha, Sigma Xi, Mu Epsilon, Phi Sigma Pi, Phi Kappa Phi (nat. scholar), Alpha Epsilon Delta, Phi Eta Sigma. Office: U Okla Health Scis Ctr PO Box 26901 Oklahoma City OK 73190-0901 Office Phone: 405-271-2114.

BRANDT, FREDERIC SHELDON, dermatologist; b. June 26, 1949; BA, Rutgers U., 1971; MD, Hahnemann Med. Coll., 1975. Diplomate Am. Bd. Internal Medicine, Am. Bd. Dermatology, lic. physician N.Y., 1979, Fla., 1982, Calif., 1982. Intern NYU, N.Y.C., 1975—76, resident in internal medicine, 1976—78; resident in dermatology U. Miami, Fla., 1978—81; pvt. practice dermatology Coral Gables, Fla. Clin. assoc. prof. dept. dermatology U. Miami, Fla.; clin. rsch. investigator Collagen Corp., 2003—; lectr. in field. Contbr. articles to profl. jours. Mem.: AMA, Miami Soc. for Dermatology and Cutaneous Surgery, Internat. Soc. Cosmetic Laser Surgeons, Internat. Soc. for Dermatologic Surgery, Fla. Soc. Dermatology, Fla. Med. Assn., Dermatology Found. Leaders Soc., Dade County Med. Assn., Am. Soc. Dermatologic Surgeons, Am. Acad. Dermatology, Phi Beta Kappa. Office: 4425 Ponce De Leon Blvd Ste 200 Coral Gables FL 33146 Office Phone: 305-443-6606. Office Fax: 305-443-4890.*

BRANDT, GENE STUART, fundraising consultant; b. N.Y.C., Aug. 29, 1950; s. Eugene Charles and Elsie Virginia (Williams) B.; m. Elizabeth Holland, July 20, 1991; children: Cameron Elizabeth, Christopher Holland. AB in Polit. Sci., Knox Coll., 1972. Asst. dir. admission Knox Coll., Galesburg, Ill., 1972-74, dir. alumni affairs, 1974-76; dir. univ. devel. U. Nev., Reno, 1976-79; dir. devel. Lake Forest (Ill.) Coll., 1979-81, v.p. devel., 1981-86; v.p. external affairs Mus. Sci. and Industry, Chgo., 1986-91; pres. sci. and tech. Mus. of Atlanta, 1991-97; prin., cons., pres. TerMolen Brandt & Assocs., Inc., 1997—2003; pres. TerMolen Watkins & Brandt, LLC, 2003—. Bd. dirs., vice-chmn. Pub. Broadcasting Atlanta; bd. trustees Cazenovia Coll., 2001—, McCormick Theol. Sem., 2001—; elder Ctrl. Presbyn. Ch. Named to Outstanding Young Men of Am., 1981. Mem. Am. Assn. Mus., Assn. Fundraising Profls., Coun. for Advancement and Support of Edn., Econ. Club Chgo., Oak Park Country Club, Lahinch Golf Club (Ireland). Office: TerMolen Watkins Brandt & Assocs 500 N Dearborn St Ste 500 Chicago IL 60610-4997 Office Phone: 312-222-0560.

BRANDT, HARRY, mechanical engineering educator; b. Amsterdam, The Netherlands, Nov. 14, 1925; came to U.S., 1946, naturalized, 1962; s. Friedrich H. and Henny (Rous) B.; m. Muriel Ruth Harman, Jan. 24, 1953; children: Joyce Estelle, Marilyn Audrey, Robert Alan. BS, U. Calif.-Berkeley, 1949, MS, 1950, PhD, 1954. Supervising research engr. Chevron Research Co., La Habra, Calif., 1954-64; lectr. UCLA, 1962-64; prof. mech. engring. U. Calif., Davis, 1964—, chmn. dept., 1969-74, 86-91; dir. Internat. Pipeline Techs. Inc., Beaverton, Oreg., 1985-91; chmn. bd. Clean Energy Systems, Inc., 1997—. Cons. Lawrence Livermore Nat. Lab., 1969—, State of Calif., 1970-87, State of Alaska, 1972, Los Alamos Nat. Lab., 1988-93. Mem. ASME, Am. Welding Soc., AIAA, Sigma Xi, Tau Beta Pi. Presbyterian. Home: 26934 Middle Golf Dr El Macero CA 95618-1053 Office: U Calif Dept Mech and Aero Engring One Shields Ave Davis CA 95616 Office Phone: 530-752-0588. Business E-Mail: h.brandt@ucdavis.edu.

BRANDT, HOWARD EDWARD, physicist; b. Emerado, N.D., s. Howard Edward and Mamie Luella (Franklin) B.; m. Marilyn Kay McKinstry, Mar. 25, 1972; children: Karen, Sonja. BS in Physics, MIT, 1962; MS in Physics, U. Wash., 1963, PhD in Physics, 1970. Engr., physicist Boeing Co., Seattle, 1958-64; predoctoral rsch. asst. U. Wash., Seattle, 1964-70; physics tchr. Seattle Prep. Sch., 1971-72; physicist U. Md., College Park, 1972-73, Lulejian and Assocs., Falls Church, Va., 1973-76, Sci. Applications, Inc., McLean, Va., 1976-77, Army Rsch. Lab., Adelphi, Md., 1977—. Editor various books/conf. procs. in field, including Selected Papers on Nonlinear Optics, 1991; contbr. articles to profl. jours. Sloan Found. scholar, 1958-62; recipient Siple Silver medallion U.S. Army, 1980; Fellow US Army Rsch. Lab., 2004. Mem. Am. Phys. Soc., Am. Optical Soc., Am. Math. Soc., Math. Assn. Am., Am. Assn. Physics Tchrs. Presbyterian. Avocations: mathematics, philosophy. Home: 2713 Shanandale Dr Silver Spring MD 20904-1633 Office: Army Rsch Lab 2800 Powder Mill Rd Adelphi MD 20783-1138 Office Phone: 301-394-4143. Business E-Mail: hbrandt@arl.army.mil.

BRANDT, I. MARVIN, chemist, engineer; b. Shreveport, La., Nov. 26, 1942; s. David and Esta (Epstein) B. BS in Chemistry, Centenary Coll., 1965; postgrad., U. Tex., 1968-70. With Am. Pipe and Supply, Shreveport, 1970-73; rschr. Shell Oil, Houston, 1973-75; rsch. tech. svc. trainer NL Baroid, Houston, 1975-79; rschr., tech. svc. engr. drilling, tng. coord. Arco Oil & Gas Co., worldwide, 1979-86; specialist, project mgr. Petrolite Corp., St. Louis, 1986-90; sr. engr. drilling and completion tech., tng. mgr., environ. coord., sr. drilling engr., sr. fluids engr. Marathon Oil Co., Houston, 1990—. Cons. for drilling ops. and environ. projects Dallas, S.Am., Cen. Am., Tex., Calif., Russia, N. Sea, Mid. East, Africa, Alaska, Australia, New Zealand, China, Indonesia, Mexico, Korea, Ireland, Scotland. Contbr. articles to profl. jours.; patentee in field. Active Am. Cancer Soc., Houston, Denver, St. Louis, Morris Animal Found., Denver, Am. Heart Assn., United Way. Recipient Grad. Tching. fellowship, U. Tex., Austin, 1968-70, Robert Welch Rsch. grant, U. Tex., Austin, 1969. Mem. Soc. Petroleum Engrs. (program chmn.), Internat. Assn. Drilling Contractors (drilling com.), Am. Chem. Soc., Am. Petroleum Inst. (subcoms. for drilling and environment), Am. Assn. Drilling Engrs. (co-chmn. drilling/completion com., chmn. drilling fluids com., co-chmn. waste mgmt. com., planning com. for petro-safe offshore tech. conf. com.), N.Y. Acad. Scis., Internat. Platform Assn. Avocations: tennis, running, bicycling, music, fishing. Home: PO Box 571844 Houston TX 77257-1844 Office: 5555 San Felipe St Houston TX 77056-2723 *Life is much too serious to take so seriously.*

BRANDT, IRA KIVE, pediatrician, geneticist; b. N.Y.C. s. Charles Zachary and Hilda Eleanor Brandt; m. Dorothy Godfrey; children: Elizabeth, Laura, William, Rena. AB, NYU, 1942; MD, Columbia U., 1945. Diplomate Am. Bd. Pediatrics, Am. Bd. Med. Genetics. Intern Morrisania City Hosp., N.Y.C., 1945-46; resident Lincoln Hosp., N.Y.C., 1948-50; fellow pediatrics Yale U., New Haven, 1955-57, asst. prof., 1957-61, assoc. prof., 1961-68; chmn. dept. pediatrics Children's Hosp., San Francisco, 1968-70; clin. prof. pediatrics U. Calif., San Francisco, 1970; prof. pediatrics and med. genetics Ind. U. Sch. Medicine, Indpls., 1970-89, prof. emeritus, 1989—. Served to capt. U.S. Army, 1946-47, 52 Mem. Am. Pediatric Soc., Am. Acad. Pediatrics, Soc. Pediatric Rsch., Soc. Inherited Metabolic Disorders, Am. Soc. Human Genetics, Am. Coll. Med. Genetics. Office: Ind U Sch Medicine Dept Pediatrics 702 Barnhill Dr # 0907 Indianapolis IN 46202-5128 Business E-Mail: ibrandt@iupui.edu.

BRANDT, JENNIFER ANNE, lawyer; b. Perth Amboy, N.J., July 26, 1969; d. Sanford D. and Joan M. (Klein) B. BA highest honors, Rutgers U., 1991; JD, U. Pa., 1994. Bar: Pa. 1994, N.J. 1994, D.C. 1996. Assoc. Dilworth, Pakson, Kalish & Kauffman, LLP, Phila., 1994—98; mem. Cozen O'Connor, Phila., 1998—. Editor (sr.): Jour. Internat. Bus. Law, 1994. Named one of Lawyers on the Fast Track, Am. Lawyer Media, 2004; Arthur Littleton Fellowship, U. Pa. Mem.: ABA, N.J. Bar Assn., Pa. Bar Assn., Phila. Bar Assn. (co-chair, mem. comm.). Office: Cozen O'Connor 1900 Market St Philadelphia PA 19103

BRANDT, JOHN ASHWORTH, fuel company executive; b. Chgo., Oct. 3, 1950; s. William W. and Joan V. (Ashworth) B.; m. Debbie M. Fico, June 2, 1984; children: Briana Ashley, Bryan Ashworth. Student, U. Colo., 1969-72. Mgr. co. accounts Lincoln Wood Commodities, Chgo., 1972-74; pres. Lafayette Coal Co., Burr Ridge, Ill., 1974—, Hoosier King Coal Co., 1993—, Ind. Farms, Inc., 1996—; mem. Hoyelton LLC, 2002—; pres. Black Rsch. Coal, LLC, 2005—. Pres. Chgo. Coal Shippers, 1984—; pres. Hoosier King Coal Co.; dir. Muliganeers Non-Profit Orgn. Office: Lafayette Coal Co 200 S Frontage Rd Ste 310 Hinsdale IL 60521-6953 Office Phone: 630-986-1456.

BRANDT, JOHN HENRY, physician; b. Cleve., July 30, 1940; s. Harold Paul and Dorothy Helen (Kern) B.; m. Jon Ellison, July 30, 1963 (div. 1971); children: Sylvia Ann, Laura Ann; m. Marilyn Ruth Brandt, July 25, 1980. BA, Yale U., 1962; postgrad., Cambridge (Eng.) U., 1962-64; MD, Harvard U., 1970. Asst. to dir. Harvard Ctr. for Community Health, Boston, 1968-69; clin. fellow Med. Sch. Harvard U., Boston, 1970-73, instr. in psychiatry Med. Sch., 1973-74, 74-99; resident psychiatrist McLean Hosp., Belmont, Mass., 1970-73, dir. Waverley House, 1973-74, attending psychiatrist, 1974-90, Mass. Mental Health Ctr., 1991-99; staff psychiatrist med. dept. MIT, Cambridge, 1979-99. Active Mass. Hist. Soc., New Eng. Hist. Geneal. Soc.; mem. Trinity Ch., Boston, 1988—. Mem.: Internat. Inst., N.Y. Acad. Medicine, Mass. Med. Soc., World Boston, Lincoln Land Conservation Trust, Gore Pl., Bostonian Soc., Yale Mory's Assn., Guild of St. Luke, English Speaking Union, Clare Assn., Am. Friends Cambridge U., Harvard Musical Assn. (dir. 1990—93), Russell Trust Assn., Colonial Soc., Nichols House Mus., Trustees of Reservations, Soc. for Preservation of New Eng. Antiquities, Chief Execs. Club of Boston, Cosmos Club, Yale Club of Boston (sec. 1988—90, dir. 1990—93), Harvard Faculty Club, Boston Athenaeum, Harvard Club of Boston (chmn. Ho. com. 1989—91, v.p. 1991—93), Yale Elizabethan Club, Thursday Evening Club, Phi Beta Kappa. Republican. Episcopalian. Avocation: music. Home and Office: PO Box 530 Lincoln MA 01773-0530

BRANDT, JOHN REYNOLD, editor, journalist; b. Amarillo, Tex., Aug. 25, 1959; s. Reynold Francis Jr. and Patricia Levonne (Wallace) B.; m. Svetlana Stevovich, May 28, 1989; children: Emma Evangeline Stevovich Brandt, Aidan Reynold Stevovich Brandt. BA, Case Western Reserve U., Cleve., 1981. Sales rep. Merrell Dow Pharmaceuticals, Cleve., 1982-84, Miles Pharmaceuticals, Cleve., 1984-88, Tokos Perinatal Nursing Svcs., Cleve., 1988-89; sr. assoc. M. Zunt Assocs., Cleve., 1989-90; dir. mgmt. devel. CSA Health System, Cleve., 1990-91; assoc. editor Corp. Cleve. Mag., 1991-94; from exec. editor to pub. IndustryWeek Mag., Cleve., 1994—2000; chief editl. dir. Exec. Mag., 2000—03, pres., pub., 2001—03, editor-at-large, 2003—; pres. John R. Brandt, Inc., 2000—; CEO MPI Group, Inc., 2003—. V.p. Inst. Environ. Edn., Cleve., 1990-91. Bd. dirs. Work in N.E. Ohio Coun., 1997—; judge Workforce Excellence Awards of Nat. Assn. Mfrs., 1997—, Am. Bus. Media Neal awards, 2000. Recipient numerous awards in field from Am. Bus. Press, Assn. of Area Bus. Publs., The Press Club of Cleve., March of Dimes, Am. Soc. Bus. Press Editors. Mem. Press Club of Cleve. (dir. 1994-2001, v.p. 1996-98, pres. 1998-99). Office: 2835 Sedgewick Rd Cleveland OH 44120-1837

BRANDT, KATHLEEN See WEIL-GARRIS BRANDT, KATHLEEN

BRANDT, LAWRENCE JAY, internist, gastroenterologist, educator; b. May 20, 1944; BS in Biology cum laude, CCNY, 1965; MD, SUNY, Bklyn., 1968. Diplomate Am. Bd. Internal Medicine, Am. Bd. Gastroenterology; lic. physician, N.Y. Intern Mt. Sinai Hosp., N.Y.C., 1968-69, resident, chief resident in medicine, 1969-72, fellow in gastroenterology, 1971-72; physician divsn. gastroenterology, dept. medicine Montefiore Med. Ctr., N.Y.C., 1974—, assoc. dir. divsn. gastroenterology, 1980-85; dir. div. gastroenterology Moses divsn. Montefiore Med. Ctr., North Ctrl. Bronx Hosp., 1985-99; from instr. to assoc. prof. medicine Albert Einstein Coll. Medicine, Bronx, N.Y., 1974-85, prof. medicine, 1985—, prof. surgery, 1999—; acting dir. clin. gastroenterology Montefiore Med. Ctr./Albert Einstein Coll. Medicine, 1999—2001, dir. Gastroenterology, 2001—. Contbr. numerous articles to profl. jours. Maj. U.S. Army, 1972-74. Fellow ACP, Am. Acad. Physicians and Patients; master Am. Coll. Gastroenterology; mem. Am. Gastroenterol. Assn., Am. Soc. Gastrointestinal Endoscopy, N.Y. Gastroenterol. Assn., N.Y. Soc. Gastrointestinal Endoscopy, Phi Beta Kappa. Office: Montefiore Hosp and Med Ctr 111 E 210th St Bronx NY 10467-2401 Office Phone: 718-920-4846. Business E-Mail: lbrandt@montefiore.org.

BRANDT, RICHARD PAUL, communications and entertainment company executive; b. N.Y.C., Dec. 6, 1927; s. Harry and Helen (Satenstein) Brandt; m. Helen H. Kogel, May 31, 1975; children: Claudia, David, Matthew, Thomas, Jennifer. BS with high honors, Yale U., 1948; PhD of Comm. Arts (hon.), Am. Film Inst., 2002. With Trans-Lux Theatres Corp., 1950-54, v.p., 1952-54; with Trans-Lux Corp., Norwalk, Conn., 1950—59, v.p., 1959-62, pres., 1962-80, chmn. bd., 1974—2003, CEO, 1974-92, chmn. emeritus, 2003—; dir. Am. Book-Stratford Press, Inc., 1962-87, Brandt Theatres, 1950—85, Presdl. Realty Corp., 1972—; founding gov. Ind. Film Importers & Distbrs. Am., 1959-63, bd. dirs., 1959-69; v.p., mem. exec. com. Theatre Owners Am., 1965—78; mem. bill of rights com. Council Motion Picture Orgns., 1963-65; bd. dirs. Film Soc. Lincoln Ctr., 1968-71; mem. N.Y. State Bus. Adv. Com. on Mgmt. Improvement, 1966-70. Bd. dirs. Trans-Lux Corp.; chmn. bd. Univ. Settlement Soc., 1964-66, hon. pres., bd. dirs., 1966-77; dir. Am. Theatre Wing, 1970-99, United Neighborhood Houses, 1968-73; bd. dirs., treas. Settlement House Employment Devel., 1969-72; trustee, mem. exec. com. Am. Film Inst., 1971—, vice chmn., 1980-83, chmn. bd., 1983-86, chmn. emeritus 1986—; trustee Mus. Holography, 1979-82; mem. Tony awards mgmt. com., 1986-98; founder Live Poets Soc., 1991—. Vice chmn. bd. Coll. of Santa Fe, 1987-98; trustee Maritime Ctr., Norwalk, 1991-92; treas. bd., exec. com. Coll. of Santa Fe, 1999-2004; bd. dirs. Taos Talking Pictures

Festival, 1998-2003. Named Exhibitor of Yr., ShoWest, 1984. Mem. Nat. Assn. Theatre Owners (dir. 1957-78, exec. com. 1965-78, Sherrill Corwin award 1983), Phi Beta Kappa, Sigma Xi. Office: Trans-Lux Corp 433 Paseo De Peralta Santa Fe NM 87501-1941

BRANDT, ROBERT FREDERIC, III, retired editor, journalist; b. Louisville, Sept. 17, 1946; s. Robert Frederic Jr. and Dorothea (Burton) B.; m. Annette Floyd, Aug., 1968 (div.); m. Walda Ruth DuPriest, Sept., 1980. Student, Ea. Ky. U., 1964-66; BA, U. Ky., 1968. Copy editor The Hartford (Conn.) Courant, 1968-69, The Tampa (Fla.) Tribune, 1971-72; news editor The Miami (Fla.) Herald, 1972-78; asst. mng. editor The Washington Star, 1978-81, Newsday, L.I., N.Y., 1981-87, v.p., mng. editor, 1987—2001; ret., 2001. Bd. dirs. Guide Dog Found. for Blind, Inc., Smithtown, N.Y. Mem. Talbot County Humane Soc. (bd. dirs., chmn. shelter com.). Presbyn. Office Phone: 410-829-3737. E-mail: bbrandt1@verizon.net.

BRANDT, RONALD STIRLING, retired editor, researcher; b. Neligh, Nebr., Aug. 14, 1932; s. Ferdinand B. and Ruth G. (Thornton) B.; m. Dorothy May Rice, May 13, 1951; children: Rhonda, Rebecca, Bonita. BS, U. Nebr., 1955; MA, Northwestern U., Evanston, Ill., 1960; EdD, U. Minn., 1970. Tchr. Racine (Wis.) Pub. Schs., 1957-62, prin., 1962-64; tchr., cons. No. Nigeria Tchr. Edn. Project, Maiduguri, 1965-66; program coord. Upper Midwest Regional Edn. Lab., Mpls., 1966-68; dir. staff devel. Mpls. Pub. Schs., 1968-70; assoc. supt. Lincoln (Nebr.) Pub. Schs., 1970-78; exec. editor Ednl. Leadership, Alexandria, Va., 1978-96; asst. exec. dir. ASCD, Alexandria, 1995-97; adj. faculty George Mason U., Fairfax, Va., 2003—05. Co-author: Dimensions of Thinking, 1986, Dimensions of Learning, 1992, the Language of Learning, 1997; editor: Content of the Curriculum, 1988, Assessing Student Learning, 1998, Education in a New Era, 2000; author: Powerful Learning, 1998. 1st lt. U.S. Army, 1955-57. Inductee EdPress (Ednl. Press Assn.) Hall of Fame, Apr. 1996. Office Phone: 703-765-4779. E-mail: ronbrandt@cox.net.

BRANDT, SARA JANE, elementary school educator; b. Hutchinson, Kans., Mar. 14, 1964; d. Rollin and JoNel (Diggs) Lohmeyer; m. Larry J. Brandt, June 29, 1985. BS summa cum laude, Ft. Hays State U., 1986. Cert. in early childhood edn., English as 2d lang., Calif. Kindergarten tchr. Green Acres Sch., Dumas, Tex. Mem. Assn. Tex. Profl. Educators., Phi Kappa Phi.

BRANDT, WILLIAM ARTHUR, JR., consulting executive; b. Chgo., Sept. 5, 1949; s. William Arthur and Joan Virginia (Ashworth) B.; m. Patrice Bugelas, Jan. 19, 1980; children: Katherine Ashworth, William George, Joan Patrice, John Peter. BA with honors, St. Louis U., 1971; MA, U. Chgo., 1972, postgrad., 1972-74. Asst. to pres. Pyro Mining Co., Chgo., 1972-74; commentator Sta. WBBM-AM, Chgo., 1977; with Melaniphy & Assocs., Inc., Chgo., 1975-76; pres., cons. Devel. Specialists, Inc., Chgo., 1976—. Mem. adv. bd. Sociol. Abstracts, Inc., San Diego, 1979-83. Contbr. articles to profl. jours. Trustee Fenwick H.S., 1991-2000, Comml. Law League of Am., Internat. Coun. Shopping Ctrs., Nat. Assn. Bankruptcy Trustees, Ill. Sociol. Assn., Midwest Sociol. Soc., Urban Land Inst.; mem. Fla. del. to Dem. Nat. Conv., 1996, also mem. Dem. Party Platform Com., 2000. LaVerne Noyes scholar, 1971-74. Mem. Am. Bankruptcy Inst., Am. Sociol. Assn., Amelia Island Plantation Club, Union League Club Chgo., City Club of Miami, gov. mem. Chicago Symphony, Clinton/Gore '96 Natl. Finance Bd., mnging. trustee Democratic Natl. Comm., maj. trust mem. Democratic Senatorial Campaign Comm., life mem. Zoological Soc. of the Miami Metro Zoo. Democrat. Roman Catholic. Office: 3 First Nat Plz Ste 2300 Chicago IL 60602 also: 333 S Grand Ave Ste 2010 Los Angeles CA 90071-1524 also: 26 Broadway New York NY 10004 also: 345 California St Ste 1150 San Francisco CA 94104 Office Phone: 312-263-4141.

BRANDT, WILLIAM EDWARD, surgeon, consultant; b. Fort Wayne, Ind., Oct. 29, 1925; s. Diedrich Henry and Grace Ellen (Rohrer) B.; children: Sandra Kay, Susan Marie, William Henry, Michael Edward. BS in Anatomy and Physiology, Ind. U., Indpls., 1948, MD, 1951. Diplomate Am. Bd. Surgery. Intern Milw. County Gen. Hosp., 1951—52; resident surgery Dayton VA Hosp., Ohio, 1952—56; surgeon Linville Clinic, Columbia City, Ind., 1956—59; pvt. practice Fort Wayne, 1959—95; ret., 1995. Cons. VA, Fort Wayne, 1960—, H.H.S., Fort Wayne, 1980—. With U.S. Army, 1944-46. Fellow ACP; mem. KC (trustee 1961-65). Home: 6708 Mallard Cove Pl Fort Wayne IN 46804-2887

BRANDT, WILLIAM PERRY, lawyer; b. Phoenix, July 1, 1953; s. Joseph A. and Dorothy L. (Perry) B.; m. Elizabeth Sprague, May 16, 1987; 1 child, Elizabeth Hundley. BA, Vanderbilt U., 1974, JD, 1977. Bar: Mo. 1977, U.S. Dist. Ct. (ea., we. dist. Mo., Kans.), U.S. Ct. Appeals (8th cir. 1992), U.S. Supreme Ct. 1992. Assoc. to ptnr. Stinson, Mag & Fizzell, Kansas City, Mo., 1977—97; ptnr. Berkowitz Stanton Brandt Shaw & Williams, Kansas City, Mo., 1997—2005; ptnr., comml. litig., securities enforcement & compliance practices Bryan Cave LLP, Kansas City, Mo., 2005—. Mem. merit selection commn. US Dist Ct., 1990—91. Editor (exec.): Vanderbilt Law Rev.; contbr. chapters to books, articles to profl. jours. Ward committeeman Jackson County Rep. Party, 1988-92. Named to Best of the Bar, Kansas City Bus. Jour., 2002—04; recipient Morgan Prize, Vanderbilt Univ. Law Sch., 1977. Fellow: Am. Bar Found.; mem.: ABA, Internat. Assn. Def. Counsel, Def. Rsch. Inst., legal & compliance div. Securities Industry Assn., US Supreme Ct. Hist. Soc. (no. Mo. chmn. 1997—98), Kansas City Met. Bar Assn. (chmn. securities law com. 2000), Lawyers Assn. Kansas City (pres. 1999—2000). Episcopalian. Office: Bryan Cave LLP Ste 3500 1200 Main St Kansas City MO 64105-2100 Office Phone: 816-374-3206. Office Fax: 816-374-3300. Business E-Mail: perry.brandt@bryancave.com.

BRANDWEIN, RUTH ANN, social welfare educator, social services administrator, writer; b. Bklyn., Apr. 24, 1940; d. Charles and Kate (Berkowitz) Solin; divorced; children: Lorena Lisa Epstein, Garth Whitman. BA magna cum laude, Bklyn. Coll., 1960; MSW, U. Wash., 1970; PhD, Brandeis U., 1978. Libr. trainee Bklyn. Pub. Libr., 1960—61; substitute tchr. N.Y.C. Bd. Edn., 1961—63; recreation dir. Seattle Park Dept., 1964—66; exec. dir. Ctrl. Seattle Commn. Coun., 1967—69; rsch. assoc. Harvard U./Lab. Comm. Psychiatry, Boston, 1971—72; asst. prof., chair, comm. org. Boston U. Sch. Social Work, 1973—78; dir., assoc. prof. U. Iowa Sch. Social Work, Iowa City, 1978—81; dean Sch. Social Welfare SUNY, Stony Brook, 1981—89, prof. Sch. Social Welfare, 1981—, dir. Social Justice Ctr., 2001—; commr. Suffolk County Dept. Social Svcs., Hauppauge, NY, 1989—93; holder Spafford Endowed chair U. Utah Sch. Social Work, 1994—96. Vis. prof. U. Wash. Sch. Social Work, 2000-01; co-founder Women's Rsch. Ctr. of Boston, 1971-78; co-dir. Women's Com. of 100, 1995—; cons. U.S. Senate Subcom. on Vets.' Affairs, 1971; guardian ad litem Family Ct., Middlesex County, Mass.; expert witness Grevatt vs. U. Minn., Duluth; vis. assoc. Inst. Policy Studies, 1986-87; lead reviewer Nat. Inst. Justice, 1997-98. Author: Battered Women, Children and Welfare Reform: The Ties That Bind, 1999; editor: Affilia, 2004—; founding editor, mem. corp. bd. Affilia: Jour. Women and Social Work, 1985—, mem. editl. bd., book editor, 2004—; contbr. articles to profl. jours. and chpts. to books. Mem. Nat. Adv. Coun. Violence Against Women, 1997—2000; mem. steering com. L.I. Fund for Women and Girls, 1993—2000; mem. N.Y. Gov.'s Mental Health Coun., 1990—2002, chair, 1992—95, Suffolk County Exec. Task Force on Family Violence, 1988—94; mem. alumni bd. Brandeis U. Heller Sch., 2003—; mem. adv. bd. L.I. Housing Svcs., 2004—; bd. dirs., v.p. Kehillath Shalom Synagogue, Cold Spring Harbor, NY, 1987—90, bd. dirs., v.p., chair social action com., 2001—; bd. dirs. United Way of L.I., Melville, NY, 1982—88, mem. allocations com., 2002—05; bd. dirs. Suffolk Cmty. Coun., Islandia, NY, 1981—97; bd. dirs., mem. exec. com. Am. Jewish Congress, L.I., 1989; bd. dirs. N.Y. Civil Liberties Union, 1994—98; adv. bd. L.I. Progressive Coalition, 1998—; bd. dirs. L.I. Cmty. Found., 1994—96, Hudson- Peconic Planned Parenthood, 1997—2005; mem. action fund bd. Hudson-Peconic Planned Parenthood, 2003—, Hudson-Peconic Planned Parenthood Action Fund, 2003—; bd. dirs. Health and Welfare Coun. L.I., 1996—2001, Suffolk Coalition Against Domestic Violence, 2003—. Recipient Disting. Alumnus award U. Wash. Sch. Social Work, Seattle, 1989, Congrl. award Congressman Mrazek, Suffolk County, N.Y., Hon. Supporter award Women on the Job; Vol. Svc. award, Suffolk County Human Rights Commn., 2003, Stony Brook Hillel Found. award, 2005, Jewish Reconstructionist Fedn. award, 2005. Mem.: NASW (bd. dirs. 1991—96, 2d v.p. 1994—96, pres.-elect NY state chpt. 1997—98, pres. 1998—2000, nat. com. on women's issues 2000—03, Suffolk County Social Worker of Yr. 1989, Lifetime Achievement award 2003), Huntington NY NOW (bd. dirs. 1982—91, chair 1988—91), Coun. Social Work Edn. (chair women's commn. 1980—83, bd. dirs. 1987—89, chair internat. commn. 1988—89), NY Pub. Welfare Assn. (bd. dirs. 1990—93), Phi Beta Kappa. Office: SUNY Stony Brook Sch Social Welfare Health Sci Ctr Level 2 Rm 093 Stony Brook NY 11794-0001 Office Phone: 631-444-3176.

BRANEGAN, JAMES AUGUSTUS, III, journalist; b. Phila., June 6, 1950; s. James Augustus, Jr. and Emmeline Elizabeth (McBurney) B.; m. Stefania Pittaluga, Feb. 4, 1992. BA, Cornell U., 1972; MS in Journalism, Northwestern U., 1973. Reporter Chgo. Today, 1973-74, Chgo. Tribune, 1974-81; with Time Mag., 1981—2001, chief econs. corr. Washington bur., 1986-87, Hong Kong corr., 1987-93, European econ. corr. Brussels, 1993-97, State Dept. corr. Washington, 2001, White House corr., 1997-2001; adj. prof. Georgetown U, 2002—03, Northwestern U., 2002—03; profl. staff mem US Senate Com. on Fgn. Rels., Washington, 2003—. Co-recipient Pulitzer prize for spl. local reporting, 1976 Office: c/o Senate Fgn Rels 450 Dirksen Senate Office Bldg Washington DC 20510

BRANESCU-HURT, ANA, music educator; b. Bucharest, Romania, Jan. 3, 1972; arrived in U.S., 1979; d. Paul Doru and Smaranda Ioana Branescu; m. William David Hurt, July 3, 1993; children: Maia Elizabeth Hurt, Elie Rose Hurt. BMus, Shenandoah U., 1998. Piano coach Brockwood Park Sch., Bramdean, England, 1988—90; music tchr. Concord Instn., Yellowsprings, W.Va., 1996—97; pvt. piano studio Winchester, Va., 1996—98; piano instr. Shenandoah Conservatory, Winchester, Va., 1998—; tchr. Winchester Acad., 2002—. Performer recitals Brockwood Park Sch., 1988—90, Shenandoah U., Winchester, Va., 1995, Shenandoah Arts Coun., Winchester, Va., 1996; bd. dirs., music tchr. Winchester Jr. Acad.; sec. bd. Windsor Jr. Acad. Counselor Cmty. Outreach. Grantee Marion Park Lewis Found., Shenandoah Arts Coun., 1992—96. Mem.: Music Tchrs. Nat. Assn., Nat. Fedn. Music Clubs (sr.; v.p.). Avocations: travel, hiking, working with orphans and the homeless. Home: 146 Margaret Ln Winchester VA 22603 Office: Shenandoah Conservatory Arts Acad 203 S Cameron St Winchester VA 22601

BRANFMAN, STEVEN JAY, artist, educator; b. L.A., Mar. 5, 1953; s. Irwin Maurice and Dorisse Branfman; m. Ellen Marsha Abend, Apr. 17, 1977; children: Jared Michael, Adam Paul. BA, Cortland State U., 1974; MA in Tchg., RISD, 1975. Founder/dir. Potters Shop and Sch., Needham, Mass., 1977—; head art dept. Manitou Wabing Arts Ctr., Parry Sound, Canada, 1975—77; instr. Thayer Acad., Braintree, Mass., 1978—; artist in residence Lasell Coll., Newton, Mass., 1985—88. Founding bd. mem. Nat. K-12 Exhbn. Found., Raritan, NJ, 1999—; founding bd. dirs. Potters Coun., Westerville, Ohio, 2000—01; v.p. Studio Potter Orgn., Goffstown, NH; founding bd. dirs., adv. bd. Cortland Coll. Arts and Scis. Author: Raku: A Practical Approach, 2d edit., The Potters Professional Handbook; Represented in permanent collections Fuller Art Mus., RISD Mus. Art, Weisman Art Mus., Schein-Joseph Internat. Mus. Ceramic Art, exhibitions include National Ceramics Biennial, Guilford Handcraft Center, 2003, National Ceramics Biennial/Guilford Handcraft Ctr., 2005, National Ceramics Biennial/New Hampshire Inst. Art, 2004, Lexington Arts and Crafts Soc., 2004. Bd. dirs. alumni exec. coun. RISD; v.p. Newton Youth Soccer, 1993—97. Mem.: Nat. K-12 Ceramics Exhbn. Found., Potters Coun., Nat. Coun. Edn. in Ceramic Arts, RISD Alumni Assn. (pres. Boston chpt.). Home: 43 Chinian Path Newton MA 02459 Office: The Potters Shop 31 Thorpe Rd Needham MA 02349 Personal E-mail: sbranfpots@aol.com. E-mail: pottersshop@aol.com.

BRANHAM, C. MICHAEL, lawyer; b. Columbia, S.C., Nov. 6, 1957; s. Mack C. and Jennie Louise (Jones) B.; m. Teresa Barrett; children: Anthony, Mark. BS, Auburn U., Montgomery, Ala., 1979; JD, U. S.C., 1983. CPA; bar: S.C., cert.: (tax law specialist). Acct. Wilson, Price, Barranco & Billingsley, CPAs, Montgomery, 1979-80; law clk. Atty. Gen.'s Office, State of S.C., Columbia, 1981-82; acct. Price, Waterhouse, Columbia, 1983-86; tax lawyer Young Clement Rivers, LLP, Charleston, SC, 1986—; chmn. tax, estate planning and probate group Young Clement Rivers LLP, Charleston, SC, 1999—, firm mgmt. com., 1999—, asst. mng. ptnr., 1999—2001, mng. ptnr., 2002—. Chmn. taxation law specialization adv. bd. S.C. Supreme Ct., 1995—97; pres. Charleston Tax Coun., 1993—94; active Charleston Estate Planning Coun.; dean's adv. bd. Med. U. S.C. Nursing Sch., 1994—97, chmn. planned giving adv. coun., 1993—97; S.C. case reporter ABA sect. real property, probate and trust law, 1997—2002; mem. Bishop Gadsden Estate Planning Adv. Coun., Charleston, 1998—2002. Coach Hungryneck Internat. Soccer Assn., Mt. Pleasant, SC, 1989—99, James Island/Trident United Soccer Assn., Charleston, 1999—2000; sec., bd. dirs. S.C. Youth Soccer Assn., 2000—02; mem. Frances P. Bunnelle Found., 2000—04, chmn., 2003—04; mem. bd. dirs. Trident United Way, 2004—. Mem. ABA, AICPA, S.C. Assn. CPAs, S.C. Bar Assn., Charleston Breakfast Rotary. Avocations: soccer coaching, weightlifting. Home: 225 Dovewood Ln Vance SC 29163 Office: Young Clement Rivers LLP 28 Broad St Charleston SC 29401-3070 Office Phone: 843-724-6683. Business E-Mail: mbranham@ycrlaw.com.

BRANHAM, JENNIE JONES, artist; d. Charles Alfonzo and Louise Kilgo Jones; m. Mack Carison Branham, Dec. 17, 1953; children: Kenneth Gary, Charles Michael, Keith Robert, Laurie Lynn. BA in Art and Art Mgmt., Columbia Coll., 1986. Art gallery dir. Columbia Coll., Columbia, 1986—90; supt. of fine arts S.C. State Fair, Columbia, 1997—2000. Exhibitions include (1st Pl. Profl. Divsn., 2004), Crooked Creek Art League, Trenholm Artists Guild, Hilton Head Art League, SC State Fair, Sumpter Gallery Art, Carolina Gallery, McKissick Mus, Gallery at Nonnah's. Com. mem. Endorsing Com. for Luth. Chaplains of, Washington, 1975—81; mem. Religion & Art, Salisbury, NC, 1983—89; pres. Officers Wives Assn., Air University (Maxwell AFB), Ala., 1971—72. Mem.: Crooked Creek Art League (founding pres. 1985, Mem. of the Yr. 1995). Republican. Lutheran. Avocations: travel, reading, aerobics. Home: 109 Laurent Way Irmo SC 29063 Office: Circa Art 109 Laurent Way Irmo SC 29063 Personal E-mail: jennie2839@hotmail.com.

BRANHAM, MACK CARISON, JR., religious organization administrator, educator, minister; b. Columbia, S.C., Apr. 20, 1931; s. Mack Carison and Laura Pauline (Sexton) Branham; m. Jennie Louise Jones, Dec. 17, 1953; children: Kenneth Gary, Charles Michael, Keith Robert, Laurie Lynn. BS, Clemson U., 1953; MDiv, Luth. Theol. Sem., 1958, STM, 1963; MS, George Washington U., 1968; PhD, Ariz. State U., 1974; DD (hon.), Newberry Coll., 1990; LLD (hon.), Clemson U., 1991. Ordained to ministry Luth. Ch., 1958. Commd. 2d lt. USAF, 1953, advanced through grades to col., 1959, ret., 1979; pastor Providence Nazareth Luth. Ch., Lexington, SC, 1958-59; adminstrv. asst., registrar Luth. Theol. So. Sem., 1979-81, v.p. adminstrn., 1981-82, pres., 1982-92, pres. emeritus, 1992—. Instr., counselor in field. Editor Air Force Chaplain newsletter, 1975-77. Decorated Bronze Star, Legion of Merit; named to Order of Palmetto (S.C.). Mem.: Greater Chapin C. of C. (bd. dirs. 1998—2000, pres. 2000), Rotary (dist. gov. 2004—05). Lutheran. Home: 109 Laurent Way Irmo SC 29063 E-mail: mbranham@hotmail.com.

BRANKER, ANTHONY DANIEL JOHN, music educator, researcher, composer; b. Elizabeth, N.J., Aug. 28, 1958; s. Daniel C. and Joan P. Branker; m. Lisa A. Parris, Dec. 12, 1992; 1 child, Parris Jolean. BA in Music, Princeton U., N.J., 1980; MusM in Jazz Pedagogy, U. Miami, Coral Gables, Fla., 1983. Prof. and chair dept. of music Ursinus Coll., Collegeville, Pa., 1986—96; prof. and dir. jazz studies Hunter Coll. CUNY, N.Y.C., 1996—2000; sr. lectr. and dir. jazz studies Princeton U., NJ, 1989—. Vis. prof. music Manhattan Sch. of Music, N.Y.C., 2003—05. Composer: Spirit Song and J.C.'s Passion (Commn. from The Commn. Project, 2004), One for Dawud (Internat. Assn. Jazz Edn. Composition prize, 1986), Each On Teach One (Internat. Assn. Jazz Edn. Composition prize, 1989). Recipient Disting. Tchg. award, Inst. Arts and Humanities Edn., 1992, Presdl. Scholars Tchr. Recognition award, US Dept. Edn., 1999, Lifting Up the World with a Oneness-Heart award, Sri Chinmoy, 2003, Alumni award, Assn. Black Princeton Alumni, 2004; fellow, NEH, 1989; Fulbright Scholar, Coun. Internat. Exch. of Scholars, 2005—. Mem.: Princeton Symphony Orch. (hon.; trustee 2004—). Office: Princeton Univ Dept Music Woolworth Ctr Princeton NJ 08544 Office Phone: 609-258-2219. Office Fax: 609-258-6793.

BRANN, DONALD LEWIS, JR., school superintendent; b. L.A., Nov. 1, 1945; s. Donald Lewis and Shirley June (Scott) B.; m. m. Sari Ellen Donohoe, June 17, 1967; children: Shanonn, Rebecca. AA in Bus. Adminstrn., El Camino Coll., 1966; BS, U. So. Calif., L.A., 1968, EdD in Ednl. Adminstrn., 1982; MA in Elem. Edn., Calif. State U., L.A., 1972. Cert. tchr., sch. adminstr., Calif. Tchr. El Segundo (Calif.) Unified Sch. Dist., 1970-72, reading specialist, 1972-76, program coord., 1976-79; prin. Wilsona Sch. Dist., Lancaster, Calif., 1979-81, supt., 1981-84, Old Adobe Union Sch. Dist., Petaluma, Calif., 1984-91, Mother Lode Union Sch. Dist., Placerville, Calif., 1992-93, Wiseburn Sch. Dist., Hawthorne, Calif., 1993—. Bd. dirs. Schs. Committed To Reducing Utility Bills, Sacramento, 1983—; mem. State Supts. Small Sch. Adv. Com.; coord. El Segundo Jr. Olympics, 1972; bd. dirs. Antelope Valley Fedn. Tchrs. Credit Union, Lancaster, 1983; v.p., bd. dirs. Friends of Antelope Valley Indian Mus., Lancaster, 1982. Named One of Top 100 Sch. Execs. in N.Am., Exec. Educator, 1985. Mem. Am. Assn. Sch. Adminstrs., Sonoma County Supts. Gang of 13, Assn. Calif. Sch. Adminstrs., Small Sch. Dist. Assn. (founder, pres., treas. 1983—), Alpha Kappa Psi. Home: 640 California St El Segundo CA 90245-3216 Office: Wiseburn Sch Dist 13530 Aviation Blvd Hawthorne CA 90250-6498 E-mail: dbrann@wiseburn.k12.ca.us.

BRANN, EVA TONI HELENE, philosophy educator; b. Berlin, Jan. 21, 1929; came to U.S., 1941; d. Edgar and Paula (Sklarz) B. BA, Bklyn. Coll., 1950; MA, Yale U., 1951, PhD, 1956; HHD (hon.), Whitman Coll., 1995, Middlebury Coll., 1999. Instr. archaeology Stanford (Calif.) U., 1956-57; tutor St. John's Coll., Annapolis, Md., 1957—, dean, 1990-97; mem. Inst. for Advanced Study, 1958. Mem. U.S Adv. Commn. for Internat. Edn., 1975-77; vis. prof. Whitman Coll., Walla Walla, Wash., 1978-79; honors prof. U. Del., Newark, 1984-86. Author: Protoattic Pottery from the Athenian Agora, 1962, Paradoxes of Education in a Republic, 1979, The World of the Imagination, 1991, What, Then, Is Time, 1999, The Ways of Naysaying, 2001, Homeric Moments, 2002, The Music of the Republic, 2004, Open Secrets, 2004; translator: Greek Mathematics and the Origin of Algebra, 1968; co-translator: Plato's Sophist, 1996, Plato's Phaedo, 1998. Mem. state adv. com. U.S. Commn. on Civil Rights, Md., 1988-96. Grantee, NEH, 1987; Woodrow Wilson Ctr. fellow, 1976. Mem. Phi Beta Kappa. Democrat. Jewish. Office: St John's Coll PO Box 2800 Annapolis MD 21404-2800

BRANN, RICHARD ROLAND, lawyer; b. Olney, Ill., June 9, 1943; s. Roland John and Margaret (McVay) B.; m. Penny Sue Farrington, June 5, 1965; children: Wesley R., Patrick T. BA, Miss. State U., 1965; JD, U. Tex., 1968. Bar: Tex. 1968, U.S. Dist. Ct. (so., no., ea. and we. dists.) Tex. 1970, U.S. Ct. Appeals (5th and 11th cirs.) 1973, U.S. Supreme Ct. 1973; bd. cert. in labor and employment law Tex. Bd. Legal Specialization. Assoc. Baker & Botts, Houston, 1968-76, ptnr., 1976—. Chmn. fed. judiciary rels. com. State Bar Tex., 1996-98; chmn. Houston Mgmt. Lawyers Forum, Houston, 1981. Editor: Tex. Assn. of Bus. and C. of C. Labor Law Quar. Rev., Tex. Labor Letter; chmn. bd. editors Tex. Bd. Legal Specialization, 2000-2003. With USMC, 1961-66. Fellow Coll. Labor and Employment Lawyers; mem. ABA, Tex. Bar Assn., Tex. Bar Coll., Houston Bar Assn. (chmn. labor and employment law sect. 1997-98), Def. Rsch. Inst., Am. Employment Law Coun., Houston Club, Plaza Club, Order of Coif, Phi Kappa Phi. Republican. Methodist. Avocations: fitness activities, reading. Home: 13 Stonegate Dr Houston TX 77024-2703 Office Phone: 713-229-1563. Business E-Mail: richard.brann@bakerbotts.com.

BRANNAN, CLEO ESTELLA, retired elementary education educator; b. Turon, Kans., Feb. 22, 1924; d. Jesse Logan and Nancy Elma (Cox) Zink; m. Raymond Eugene Brannan, Aug. 4, 1946 (dec.); children: Raymond Eugene Jr., Nancy Estelle, Tricia Elaine. BS, Ft. Hays State U., 1964. Cert. elem. edn. educator Kans. Elem. tchr. Pretty Prairie (Kans.) Schs., 1943—45, Meade (Kans.) Elem. Sch., 1945—48, 1958—60, 1961—87, substitute secondary sch. tchr., 1987; ret., 1987. Contbr. articles to popular mags. Trustee Meade Pub. Libr., 1961—65, 1990—96, trustee, treas., 1990—; state bd. dirs. Friends of Kans. Librs., 1990—96. Named Kans. State Libr. Friend of the Yr., 2002. Mem. AAUW (local pres. 1985-86), Kans. Ret. Tchrs. Assn. (bd. dirs. 1991-99, state pres. 1996-97), Delta Kappa Gamma. Avocations: collecting china, travel, reading, arranging flowers. Home: PO Box 13 Meade KS 67864-0013

BRANNAN, EULIE ROSS, educational consultant; b. Norwood, Ohio, Sept. 6, 1928; s. Olin Hiram and Bernice Cleo (Beall) Brannan; m. Ruby Merle Moore, Dec. 16, 1945 (dec.); children: Stephen Earl, Deborah Brannan Watkins, Rebecca Brannan Hagan, Julie Ross Brannan-Williams; m. Willie Metta Strong, Mar. 7, 1981. AA, Ala. Christian Coll., 1947, BA, Huntingdon Coll., 1949; MS, Auburn U., 1953, EdD, 1960; postgrad., Harding Grad. Sch., 1960—63, Oxford (Eng.) U., 1981; LHD, Faulkner U., 2005. HS tchr., Montgomery, Ala., 1949-51; guidance counselor Montgomery Bible HS, 1951-53; prin. Ala. Christian HS, Montgomery, 1953-55; prof. Ala. Christian Coll., Montgomery, 1953-55, asst. to pres., 1955-56, acad. dean, 1956-69, acad. v.p., 1969-73, pres., 1973-81; field dir. Nat. Edn. Program, Huntsville, Ala., 1981-82; pres. Jefferson Christian Acad., Birmingham, Ala., 1982-90; assoc. J. Robert Clark & Assocs., 1990-91; spl. counsel to pres. Faulkner U., Montgomery, 1991—2004; involvement min. Madison (Ala.) Ch. of Christ, 2004—. Chaplain Madison Police Dept., 1996—. Mem.: Phi Delta Kappa. Home: 103 Manningham Dr Madison AL 35758-7419 Office: Madison Ch of Christ 556 Hughes Rd Madison AL 35758 Office Phone: 256-772-3911. E-mail: eulieb@bellsouth.net.

BRANNEN, JEFFREY RICHARD, lawyer; b. Tampa, Fla., Aug. 27, 1945; s. Jackson Edward and Tobiah M. (Lovitz) B.; m. Mary Elizabeth Strand, Nov. 24, 1972; 1 child, Samuel Jackson. BA in English, U. N.Mex., 1967, JD, 1970. Bar: N.Mex. 1970, U.S. Dist. Ct. N.Mex. 1970, U.S. Ct. Appeals (10th cir.) 1976, U.S. Supreme Ct. 1978. Law clk. N.Mex. State Supreme Ct., Santa Fe, 1970-71; from assoc. to pres., shareholder Montgomery & Andrews, pa, Santa Fe, 1972-93; pres. Jeffrey R. Brannen, P.A., Santa Fe, 1993—; of counsel Comeau, Maldegan, Templeman & Indall (formerly known as Carpenter, Maldegan, Templeman & Indall), Santa Fe, 1995—. Faculty Nat. Inst. Trial Advocacy, Hastings Ctr. for Trial & Appellate Advocacy, 1980-93; co-chmn. Pers. Injury Inst., Hastings, 1992. Mem. ABA, Am. Bd. Trial Advocates (N.Mex. pres. 1998), Assn. Def. Trial Attys. (state chmn. 1992—), Def. Rsch. Inst. (Exceptional Performance Citation 1989), N.Mex. Def. Lawyers Assn. (pres. 1989). Democrat. Avocations: skiing, soccer, fly fishing, travel. Office: 325 Pesco de Heralta Santa Fe NM 87501 Fax: (505) 982-4611. Office Phone: 505-983-4429. Business E-Mail: jrb@brannenlaw.net.

BRANNON, GUY EMILIO, physician; b. Bossier City, La., June 19, 1968; s. Guy Winfred and Ruby Rangel Brannon; m. Shelley Marie Lawson, Apr. 20, 1996; children: Dechlin Adair children: Grayson Alarich. BS, La. State U., Shreveport, 1991; MD, La. State U., Health Sci. Ctr., Shreveport, 1995. Diplomate La. State Bd. Med. Examiners, 1996. Intern La. State U. Med. Ctr., Shreveport, 1995—96, resident, 1996—99, chief resident, 1998—99; dir. adult psychiatric unit Brentwood-A Behavioral Health Co., Shreveport, 1999—. Asst. clin. prof. psychiatry La. State U. Health Scis. Ctr., Shreveport, 1999—; adj. prof. psychology La. State U., Shreveport, 2002—; pres., CEO PharmaComm., LLC, LaPharma, LLC. Contbr. chapters to books, articles to profl. jours. Fellow: Am. Assn. Integrated Medicine; mem.: AMA, Am. Assn. Psychiat. Medicine (diplomate), Assn. Clin. Rsch. Profls., Am. Soc. Clin. Pharmacology, La. Group Psychotherapy Soc., Am. Group Psychotherapy Assn., Am. Soc. Addiction Medicine, Am. Med. Polit. Action Com., La. Psychiat. Med. Assn. (N.W. La. chpt. v.p. 2000—01, N.W. La. chpt. pres. 2002—04, Dr. John M Bick award 1995), Am. Psychiat. Assn., So. Med. Assn., Am. Psychotherapy Assn., Am. Acad. Pain Mgmt., Mental Health

Assn. Caddo - Bossier (bd. mem. 2000—05). Achievements include research in clinical drug trials. Office: Brentwood - A Behavioral Health Company 1002 Highland Ave Shreveport LA 71101 E-mail: brentwoodoffice@aol.com.

BRANNON, JEAN ESTES, education educator; b. June 22; d. Ervin Lewis and Helen (Martin) Estes; children: Michael George, Sandra-Jean. M. Fairfield U., 1972—73. Instr. U. N.C. at Greensboro, 1974—78; prof. Alamo County Coll. Dist., 1980—2004. Cons. in field. Patentee Sa-Mitch hosp. gown. Mem. AAUP, Nat. League for Nursing, Tex. Jr. Coll. Tchrs. Assn., Sigma Theta Tau. Achievements include patents for patient hospital gown; copyright for Brannon Life Contentment Scale. Avocations: dance, music, travel. Office Phone: 210-392-4200.

BRANNON, MICHAEL GEORGE, musician; b. Atlanta; s. Lyman and Jean Brannon. Student, Guitar Inst. of the S.W., 1980-81, Berklee, Boston, 1981-84. Prof., musician, tchr., composer, writer, guitarist True Diversity, San Antonio, 1990—. Performer with recording artists Herb Ellis, Jackie King, Sam Newsome, Tommy Smith, Laszlo Gardonyi. Author: Contemporary Improvisation for Guitar, 1982. Mem. NARAS. Home: 207 Eleanor Ave San Antonio TX 78209-6703

BRANNON, RONALD ROY, retired minister; b. Aberdeen, SD, Apr. 16, 1928; s. Walter Carlos and Mary Erma (Snyder) B.; m. Rosalee Vernela Carry, July 20, 1949; children: Rhonda Lee Storer, Rodney Vaughn, Randall Roy. BA, Okla. Wesleyan U., 1950; DD, Southern Wesleyan U., 1987. Ordained to ministry Wesleyan Ch., 1951. Pastor Heber Wesleyan Ch., Miltonvale, Kans., 1949-52, First Wesleyan Ch., Wichita, Kans., 1952-68; dist. supt. Kans. Dist. of the Wesleyan Ch., 1968-83; gen. sec. Internat. Ctr.-The Wesleyan Ch. Hdqtrs., Indpls., 1982-2000; ret., 2000. Co-founder, coord. police chaplaincy, Wichita. Trustee/sec. bd. dirs. Miltonvale Wesleyan Coll., 1967-72, Okla. Wesleyan U., 1968-84, So. Wesleyan U., 1984-92; mem., sec. bd. dirs. Hephzibah Children's Home, 1983-92, chair bd. dirs., 1992—; bd. dirs. Wesleyan Investment Found., 1983—2003. Mem. Nat. Assn. Evangelicals (bd. dirs. 1970-72), Christian Holiness Assn. (treas. 1984-88). Republican. Mem. Wesleyan Ch. Home: 11388 Falling Water Way Fishers IN 46038

BRANNON, WILLIAM LESTER, JR., neurologist, educator; b. Olar, S.C., Jan. 11, 1936; s. William Lester and Lena Mae (Brigman) B.; m. Darrell Meeks, June 13, 1959; children: Debra Brannon DeMarco, William Bert, Victoria Brannon-Diaz. AB, U. S.C., 1957; MD, Med. U. S.C., 1961. Commd. ensign U.S. Navy, 1960, advanced through grades to capt., 1980; chmn. dept. neurology Nat. Naval Med. Ctr., Bethesda, Md., 1969-79; assoc. prof. neurology Georgetown U. Sch. medicine, Washington, 1969-79; prof. neurology Uniformed Svc. U. Health Scis., Bethesda, 1974-79, chmn. dept. neurology, 1978-79; dir. clin. svcs. Naval Regional Med. Ctr., Charleston, S.C., 1979-80; ret. U.S. Navy, 1980; clin. prof. neurology Med. U. S.C., Charleston, 1979-80; vice chair, dir. neurology U. S.C. Sch. Medicine, Columbia, 1980—2003, clin. prof. neurology, 2003—, disting. prof. emeritus, 2002—. Neurology cons. to attending physician U.S. Capitol and White House, 1970-79, to Surgeon Gen. U.S. Navy, 1970-79. Contbr. articles to sci. and med. reports. Fellow ACP, Am. Acad. Neurology, Am. Electroencephalography Soc. Democrat. Methodist. Avocations: tennis, photography, hiking, travel. Office: U SC Sch Medicine 3555 Harden Street Ext Columbia SC 29203-6894 E-mail: wlb@gw.mp.sc.edu.

BRANNON-PEPPAS, LISA, chemical engineer, researcher; b. Houston, Sept. 19, 1962; d. James Graham and Patricia Ann (Hightower) Brannon; m. Nicholas A. Peppas, Aug. 10, 1988. BS, Rice U., 1984; MS, Purdue U., 1986, PhD, 1988. Sr. formulations chemist Eli Lilly & Co., Indpls., 1988-91; pres., founder Biogel Tech., Indpls., 1991—2002; rsch. prof. dept. biomed. engring. U. Tex., Austin, 2002—, dir. Ctr. of Biol. and Med. Engring., 2003—. Author, editor: Absorbent Polymer Technology, 1990, mem. editl. bd.: Jour. Applied Polymer Sci., 1995—2001, Jour. Controlled Release, 1997—2001, Jour. Nanoparticle Rsch., 1998—, Biomaterials, 1999—, Drug Development and Industrial Pharmacy, 2003—. Vol. Indpls. Mus. Art, 1990—98, Humane Soc. Indpls., 1990—98, Indpls. Zoo, 1994—2000; trustee Chem. Engring. Found., 1999—2000. Recipient Harold B. Lamport award Biomed. Engring. Soc., 1989; named Outstanding Young Alumna, Kinkaid Sch., 1998. Fellow Am. Inst. of Med. and Biol. Engring.; mem. AIChE (dir. 1998-2000, exec. bd. programming coun., dir. materials divsn., chmn. subcom. biomaterials divsn. 1990-93, dir.-at-large food, pharm. and bioengring. divsn. 1992-94, 2d vice chair materials divsn. 1994-95, 1st vice chmn. materials divsn. 1995-96, chmn. 1996-97, bd. dirs. 1998-2000), Am. Chem. Soc. (membership com. 1990—), Controlled Release Soc. (treas. 1995-98, internat. planning com. 1991, bd. govs. 1992-95), Jr. League Indpls. (bd. dirs. 1992-94). Avocations: fine art, dance, travel. Office: U Tex Austin CPE 3-168a Austin TX 78712 E-mail: peppas@mail.utexas.edu.

BRANSCOMB, HARVIE, JR., lawyer; b. Dallas, Mar. 24, 1922; s. Bennett Harvie and Margaret (Vaughan) B.; m. Mary Josephine Goodearle, Dec. 28, 1951; children: Mary Margaret, Bennett Hill, Richard Lee. AB, Duke U., 1943; LL.B., Yale U., 1948. Bar: Tex. 1948, D.C. 1980, CPA, Tex. Shareholder Branscomb P.C., Attys.-at-Law, Corpus Christi, Tex., 1948—. Contbr. articles to profl. jours. Trustee emeritus Southwestern Legal Found.; trustee, chmn. Una Chapman Cox Found. Served with USNR, 1943-46. Fellow Am. Coll. Tax Counsel; mem. ABA, (chmn. tax sect. 1979-80), State Bar Tex. (chmn. sect. taxation 1961-62), Am. Law Inst., Am. Inst. CPA's, Phi Beta Kappa, Phi Delta Phi. Episcopalian. Home: 4500 Ocean Dr Apt 8B Corpus Christi TX 78412-2500 Office: 802 N Carancahua St Ste 1900 Corpus Christi TX 78470-0102 Office Phone: 361-888-9261.

BRANSCOMB, LEWIS CAPERS, JR., retired librarian, educator; b. Birmingham, Ala., Aug. 5, 1911; s. Lewis Capers and Minnie Vaughn (McGehee) Branscomb; m. Marjorie Berry Stafford, Jan. 15, 1938 (dec. 1999); children: Lewis Capers III(dec.), Ralph Stafford(dec.), Carol Jean, Lawrence McGehee. Student, Birmingham-So. Coll., 1929-30; AB, Duke U., 1933; AB in Libr. Sci., U. Mich., 1939, AM in Libr. Sci., 1941; postgrad., U. Ga., 1940; PhD, U. Chgo., 1954. Clk. Young & Vann Supply Co., Birmingham, 1933-38; order libr. U. Ga., 1939-41; libr. Mercer U., 1941-42; libr., prof. libr. sci. U. S.C., 1942-44; asst. dir. pub. svc. depts., assoc. prof. libr. sci. U. Ill., 1944-48; assoc. dir. librs., prof., 1948-52; dir. librs., prof. Ohio State U., Columbus, 1952-71, prof. Thurber studies, 1971-81, prof. emeritus, 1981—. Mem. faculty compensation and benefits com. Ohio State U., 1981-90; chmn. Adv. Coun. on Libr. Svcs. and Constrn. Act, Ohio, 1967-70; cons. Punjab Agrl. U., India, 1967, Mansfield (Ohio) Pub. Libr., 1977; mem. adv. coun. Hitachi Found., 1985-88. Author: Ernest Cushing Richardson Research Librarian, Scholar, Theologian, 1993; editor: The Case for Faculty Status for Academic Librarians, 1970; contbr. articles to profl. jours. Mem. Ohio Commn. to Abolish Capital Punishment, 1960-69; bd. dirs. Ctr. for Rsch. Librs., 1953-64, mem. exec. com., 1954-56, chmn. bd. dirs., 1961-62, mem. coun., 1965-71; chmn. bd. trustees Ohio Coll. Libr. Ctr., 1968-70, vice chmn., 1970-72. Mem. AAUP (sec.-treas. U. Ill. chpt. 1947-48; sec.-treas. Ohio State U. chpt. 1948-52, pres. 1953-54; nat. council 1952-55, co-author History of the Ohio Conf. 1949-74, chmn. com. E 1979-91, mem. exec. com. 1981-91), ALA (chmn. nominating com. 1954-55), Assn. Coll. and Research Libraries (dir. 1953-55, v.p. 1957-58, pres. 1958-59), Ohio Library Assn. (chmn. coll. and univ. sect. 1952-53, chmn. library adminstrn. sect. 1969-70, chmn. local conf. com. 1970, chmn. awards and honors com. 1974-75, chmn. notable Ohio librarians com. 1978-79, award of merit 1971, Hall of Fame 1982), Franklin County Library Assn., Acad. Library Assn. Ohio, ACLU (exec. com. Central Ohio chpt. 1958-60, 64-66), Common Cause, Thurber Circle, Thurber House (bd. trustees emeritus 1985—), Friends of Ohio State U. Libraries, Ohio State U. Retirees Assn. (exec. bd. 1983-92), Beta Phi Mu (exec. council 1955-58), Sigma Alpha Epsilon. Democrat. Home: 3790 Overdale Dr Columbus OH 43220-4749

BRANSCOMB, LEWIS MCADORY, physicist, researcher; b. Asheville, N.C., Aug. 17, 1926; s. Bennett Harvie and Margaret (Vaughan) B.; m. Margaret Anne Wells, Oct. 13, 1951 (dec. Oct. 1997); children: Harvie Hammond, Katharine C. Branscomb Kelley. AB summa cum laude, Duke U., 1945, DSc (hon.); MS, Harvard U., 1947, PhD, 1949; DSc (hon.), Poly. Inst. N.Y., Clarkson Coll., Rochester U., U. Colo., Western Mich. U., Lycoming Coll., U. Ala., Pratt Inst., Rutgers U., Lehigh U., U. Notre Dame; DEng (hon.), Colo. Sch. Mines, 1999; D Pub. Politics, Carnegie Mellon U., 2000; DSc (hon.), SUNY, Binghamton; LHD (hon.), Pace U. Instr. physics Harvard U., 1950-51; lectr. physics U. Md., 1952-54; vis. staff mem. Univ. Coll., London, 1957-58; chief atomic physics sect. Nat. Bur. Standards, Washington, 1954-60, chief atomic physics div., 1960-62; chmn. Joint Inst. Lab. Astrophysics, U. Colo., 1962-65, 68-69; chief lab. astrophysics div. Nat. Bur. Standards, Boulder, Colo., 1962-69; prof. physics U. Colo., 1962-69; dir. Nat. Bur. Standards, 1969-72; chief scientist, v.p. IBM, Armonk, N.Y., 1972-86, mem. corporate mgmt. bd., 1983-86; dir. sci. and tech. policy program Kennedy Sch. Govt., Harvard U., Cambridge, Mass., 1986-96, Albert Pratt pub. service prof., 1988-94; Aetna prof. pub. policy and corp. mgmt. Harvard U., Cambridge, Mass., 1994-96, prof. emeritus, 1996—. Mem.-at-large Def. Sci. Bd., 1969-72; mem. high level policy group sci. and tech. info. Orgn. Econ. Coop. and Devel., 1968-70; mem. Pres.'s Sci. Adv. Com., 1965-68, chmn. panel space sci. and tech., 1967-68; mem. Nat. Sci. Bd., 1978-84, chmn., 1980-84; mem. Pres.'s Nat. Productivity Adv. Com., 1981-82; mem. standing com. controlled thermonuclear rsch. AEC, 1966-68; mem. adv. com. on sci. and fgn. affairs Dept. State, 1973-74; mem. U.S.-USSR Joint Commn. on Sci. and Tech., 1977-80; chmn. Com. on Scholarly Communications with the People's Republic of China, 1977-80; mem. tech. assessment adv. coun. Office of Tech. Assessment, U.S. Congress, 1990-95; chmn. Carnegie Forum Task Force on Teaching as a Profession, 1985-86; dir. Lord Corp.; mem. pres.'s bd. visitors U. Okla., 1968-70; mem. astronomy and applied physics vis. coms. Harvard U. 1969-83, bd. overseers, 1984-86; mem. physics vis. com. M.I.T., 1974-79; mem. Pres.'s Com. Nat. Medal Scis., 1970-72; bd. dir. Am. Nat. Standards Inst., 1969-72; trustee Carnegie Instn., 1973-90, mem. Carnegie Commn. on Sci., Tech. and Govt., 1988-93; trustee Poly. Inst. N.Y., 1974-78, Vanderbilt U., 1980-2003, Nat. Geog. Soc., 1984-01, Woods Hole Oceanographic Instn., 1985-92, 93-98, LASPAU, 1999—; chmn. Nat. Info. Infrastructure-2000 steering com. NRC, 1994-95; Harvie Branscomb disting. vis. prof. Vanderbilt U., 1999-2000; rsch. assoc. Scripps Instn. Oceanography U. Calif., San Diego, 2005- Author: Empowering Technology, 1993, Confessions of a Technophile, 1995, Korea at the Turning Point, 1996, Investing in Innovation, 1998, Industrializing Knowledge, 1999, Taking Technical Risks, 2001, Making America Safer, 2002; editor Rev. Modern Physics, 1968-73. Trustee Telluride Inst., 1996-97; mem. Commn. on Global Info. Infrastructure, 1995—. USPHS fellow, 1948-49; Jr. fellow Harvard Soc. Fellows, 1949-51; recipient Rockefeller Pub. Service award, 1957-58, Gold medal exceptional service Dept. Commerce, 1961, Arthur Flemming award D.C. Jr. C. of C., 1962, Samuel Wesley Stratton award Dept. Commerce, 1966, Career Service award Nat. Civil Service League, 1968, Vannevar Bush award, nat. Sci. Bd., 2001, Proctor prize Rsch. Soc. Am., 1972, Okawa prize in Info. and Telecomm., 1998, prize for Info. and Telecomms. Ohkawa Found., 1998, Centennial medal, Harvard U., 2002. Fellow Am. Phys. Soc. (chmn. divsn. electron physics 1961-68, pres. 1979), AAAS (dir. 1969-73, 99-2003), Am Acad. Arts and Scis.; mem. NAS (coun. 1972-75, 98-2001), Nat. Acad. Engring. (Arthur Bueche award), Engring. Acad. Japan (fgn. assoc.), Russian Acad. Sci., Washington Acad. Scis. (Outstanding Sci. Achievement award 1959), Nat. Acad. Pub. Adminstrn., Am. Philos. Soc., Phi Beta Kappa, Sigma Xi (pres. 1985-86). Office: Harvard U Kennedy Sch Govt 79 J F Kennedy St Cambridge MA 02138-5801 E-mail: lbranscomb@branscomb.org. *No achievement is entirely one's own nor is there satisfaction without sharing.*

BRANSDORFER, STEPHEN CHRISTIE, retired lawyer; b. Lansing, Mich., Sept. 18, 1929; s. Henry and Sadie (Kohane) B.; m. Peggy Ruth Deisig, May 24, 1952; children: Mark, David, Amy, Jill. AB with honors, Mich. State U., 1951; JD with distinction, U. Mich., 1956; LLM, Georgetown U., 1958. Bar: Mich. 1956, U.S. Supreme Ct. 1959, U.S. Dist. Ct. (we. dist.) Mich. 1959; cwert. mediator U.S. Dist. Ct. (we. dist.) Mich., 1995-2003. Trial atty. Dept. Justice, Washington, 1956—58; atty., editor Office of Public Info., Office of Atty. Gen., 1958—59; spl. asst. U.S. Atty. for D.C., 1958—59; assoc. Miller, Johnson, Snell & Cummiskey, Grand Rapids, Mich., 1959—63, ptnr., 1963—89; dep. asst. atty. gen. civil div. U.S. Dept. Justice, Washington, 1989—92; pres. Bransdorfer & Bransdorfer, P.C., Grand Rapids, 1993—2000; ptnr. Bransdorfer & Russell, LLP, Grand Rapids, 2000—03; ret. Pres. State Bar of Mich., 1974-75, commr., 1968-75, chmn. sr. lawyers sect., 1994-95; pres. Grand Rapids chpt. Am. Inns of Ct., 1995-96; trustee Am. Inns of Ct. Found., 1997-2001; chmn. Mich. Civil Svc. Commn., 1977-78, mem., 1975-78; adv. com. 6th Cir. Jud. Conf., 1984-89; co-chair Mich. polit. leadership program Mich. State U., 1992-94; mem. comml. panel Am. Arbitration Assn., 1998-2001. Asst. editor: U. Mich. Law Rev, 1956. Pres. Grand Rapids Child Guidance Clinic, 1969-71; chmn. Kent County Coms., Griffin for Senator, 1972, Lenore Romney for Senator, 1966; mem. council legal advisers Rep. Nat. Com., 1981-89; Rep. candidate for atty. gen., Mich., 1978; trustee, v.p., Mich. State Bar Found., 1985-87, chmn., fellows, 1987-89; chmn. Mich. State Bd. Canvassers, 1985-87, Commn. on Future Directions in Health Care, West Mich., 1987-89; trustee Hist. Soc. for U.S. Dist. Ct. (we. dist.) Mich., 2002—. With U.S. Army, 1951-53. Recipient Spl. award for Superior Performance Civil Divsn., U.S. Dept. Justice, 1990. Fellow Am. Bar Found.; mem. ABA, 6th Cir. Jud. Conf. (life, mem. emeritus, sr. counsel to 6th cir. ct., 1999—), Grand Rapids Bar Assn., FBA (pres. West Mich. chpt. 1984, Disting. Life Svc. award 1989), Rep. Nat. Lawyers Assn. (bd. govs. 1985-89), Mich. Rep. Party (Svc. award 1989), Grand Rapids Barasso (Donald R. Worsfold Disting. Svc. award, 2005), Grand Rapids Bar Assn. (Donald R. Worsfold Disting. Svc. award, 2005), Rotary, Cascade Hills Country Club, Phi Kappa Phi. Presbyterian. *Life is a series of challenges. Do your best and you need not worry about the results.*

BRANSFORD, HELEN M., writer, jewelry designer; b. Nashville, Mar. 28, 1948; d. John Sterling Bransford and Helen (Trenholm) Dickinson; m. Jay McInerney; children: John Barrett III, Maisie Bransford. Cons. in field. Author: Welcome to Your Facelift, 1997; contbr. to Vogue Mag. Episcopalian. Address: 413 Lynnwood Blvd Nashville TN 37205-3434

BRANSON, ALBERT HAROLD (HARRY BRANSON), judge, educator; b. Chgo., May 20, 1935; s. Fred Brooks and Marie (Vowell) B.; m. Siri-Anne Gudrun Lindberg, Nov. 2, 1963; children: Gunnar John, Gulliver Dean, Hannah Marie, Siri Elizabeth. BA, Northwestern U., 1957; JD, U. Chgo., 1963. Bar: Pa. 1965, Alaska 1972. Atty. Richard McVeigh law offices, Anchorage, 1972-73; ptnr. Jacobs, Branson & Guetschow, Anchorage, 1973-76, Branson & Guetschow, Anchorage, 1976-82; pvt. practice Law Offices of Harry Branson, Anchorage, 1982-84, 85-89; atty. Branson, Bazeley & Chisolm, Anchorage, 1984-85; U.S. magistrate judge U.S. Dist. Ct., Anchorage, 1989—2005; ret., 2005. Instr., adj. prof. U. Alaska Justice Ctr., 1980—03; U.S. magistrate, Anchorage, 1975—76; mem. 9th Cir. Magistrate Judges Exec. Bd., 2001—04. Mem. steering com. Access to Civil Justice Task Force, 1997-98. With U.S. Army, 1957-59. Mem. Alaska Bar Assn. (bd. dirs., v.p. bd. govs. 1977-80, 83-86, pres. bd. govs. 1986, Disting. Svc. award 1992, Spl. Svc. award 1988, editor-in-chief Alaska Bar Rag 1978-86), Anchorage Bar Assn. (bd. dirs., bd. govs. 1982-86), Anchorage Inn of Ct. (pres. 1995). Democrat. Avocations: book collecting, cooking, poetry.

BRANSON, BRANLEY ALLAN, biology professor; b. San Angelo, Tex., Feb. 11, 1929; s. Branley Allan and Era Elizabeth (Rogers) B.; m. Mary Louise Lewis, June 3, 1964; 1 son, Rogers McGowan. AA, Northeastern Okla. A. and M. Coll., 1954; BS, Okla. State U., 1956, MS, 1957, PhD, 1960. Asst. prof. biology Kan. State Coll., Pittsburg, 1960-64; prof. biology Eastern Ky. U., Richmond, 1964—, found. prof., 1989-90. Contbr. articles to mags. Recipient Sci. award Okla. A. and M. Coll., 1953; named Disting. Scientist of Ky., 1984 Fellow Okla. Acad. Sci., AAAS; mem. Southwestern Assn. Naturalists (bd. govs. 1965—), Am. Malacological Union, Soc. for Study Evolution, Kan. Acad. Sci., Ky. Acad. Sci. (editor transactions), Soc. Systematic Zoologists, Am. Soc. Zoologists, Am. Soc. Ichthyologists and Herpetologists, Sigma Xi, Phi Theta Kappa, Phi Kappa Phi. Achievements include research and numerous publs. on description several species unknown animals; described structural workings lateral-line system in various fishes; olfactory system, geog. distbn. fishes and mollusks. Home: 100 Walnut Hill Dr Richmond KY 40475-3620 Office: Eastern Ky U Richmond KY 40475 E-mail: scribe11@earthlink.net. *I've had a long-term love affair with the nature of things, and the fervor doesn't seem to be lessening any with the passage of time. And strongly supported by the very real love affair with my wife and son, I've simply had the best of conditions for being creative.*

BRANSON, HARLEY KENNETH, finance company executive; b. Ukiah, Calif., June 10, 1942; s. Harley Edward and Clara Lucile Branson; 1 child, Erik Jordan. BS in Acctg. and Fin., San Jose State U., 1965; JD, Santa Clara U., 1968. Bar: Calif. 1969-98. Law clk. to judge U.S. Ct. Appeals (9th cir.), San Diego, 1968-69; pvt. practice San Diego, 1969-78; div. counsel Ralston Purina Co., San Diego, 1978-83; group gen. counsel Castle & Cooke, Inc., San Diego, 1983-85; exec. v.p., gen. counsel, corp. sec. Bumble Bee Seafoods, Inc., San Diego, 1985-89; pres., CEO Flying Palms LLC, San Diego, 1995—. Bd. dirs. Wind and Weather, Inc. E-mail: kennethbranson@gmail.com.

BRANSON, TIMOTHY E., lawyer; b. 1960; BA in Polit. Sci., Econ. with honors, Univ. Wis., Madison, 1983; JD with distinction, Univ. Iowa, 1986. Bar: Minn. 1986. Assoc. Dorsey & Whitney LLP, Mpls., 1986—93, ptnr., trial group, co-chair, ERISA litig., 1994—. Adj. prof. Hamline Law Sch., 1993. Office: Dorsey & Whitney LLP Ste 1500 50 S Sixth St Minneapolis MN 55402-1498 Office Phone: 612-343-7920. Office Fax: 612-340-8856. Business E-Mail: branson.tim@dorsey.com.

BRANT, ASHLEY FLEXON, biochemist; b. Hackensack, NJ, July 6, 1977; d. Floyd David Flexon and Julie Ann Murden; m. David Michael Brant, Mar. 22, 2003. BS, Ea. Mich. U., 2000. Genomic rsch. scientist Genomic Solutions, Ann Arbor, Mich., 2000—01; sr. assoc. scientist Pfizer Global R & D, Ann Arbor, 2001—. Contbr. chpt. to book. Mem.: Am. Soc. Mass Spectrometry (corr.). Independent. Achievements include development of analytical validation of endogenous biomarker assays. Avocations: mountain biking, cooking, hiking, outdoor activities, wine tasting. Home: 3112 Hunters Way Pinckney MI 48169 Office: Pfizer Global R&D 2800 Plymouth Rd Ann Arbor MI 48105 Office Phone: 734-622-1284. Personal E-mail: afbrant@charter.net. E-mail: ashley.brant@pfizer.com.

BRANT, HENRY, composer; b. Montreal, Que., Can., Sept. 15, 1913; s. Saul and Bertha (Dreyfuss) B.; children: Piri, Joquin, Linus; m. Katu Wilkovska, 1989. Student, Juilliard Sch. Music, N.Y.C., 1930-34; DFA (hon.), Wesleyan U., 1998. Mem. faculty Juilliard Sch. Music, 1947-55; dept. music Columbia U., 1943-53; mem. faculty Bennington (Vt.) Coll., 1957-80. Composer, condr. documentary films, U.S. Govt. OWI, State Dept., Dept. Agr. 1940-47; composer, condr. various radio network program series for NBC, CBS, ABC, 1942-46; large ensemble works include Angels and Devils, 1931, Origins: Percussion Symphony, 1952, Signs and Alarms, 1953, Antiphony 1, 1953, Millenium 2, 1954, Encephalograms 2, 1954, Ceremony, 1954, Galaxy 2, 1954, December, 1954, spatial opera Grand Universal Circus, 1956, Hieroglyphics, 1957, The Children's Hour, 1958, Mythical Beasts, 1958, Atlantis, 1960, Concerto with Lights, 1961, Barricades, 1961, Headhunt, 1962, Voyage 4; Total Antiphony, in 83 Parts, 1963, Odyssey-Why Not?, 1965, Kingdom Come, 1970, Crossroads, 1971, Immortal Combat, 1972, American Requiem, 1973, Prevailing Winds, 1974, Solomon's Gardens, 1974, Homage to Ives, 1975, A Plan of the Air, 1975, Spatial Piano Concerto, 1976, Antiphonal Responses, 1977, Trinity of Spheres, 1978, Orbits: 80 Trombones, 1979, The Secret Calendar, 1980, The Glass Pyramid, 1980, Meteor Farm, 1982, Western Springs, 1984, Fire in the Amstel, 1984, Desert Forests, 1985, Northern Lights Over the Twin Cities, 1986, Ghost Nets, 1988, Rainforest, 1989, 500: Pathways to Security, 1990, Prisons of the Mind, 1990, Hidden Hemisphere, 1992, Fourscore, 1993, Homeless People, 1993, Trajectory, 1994, Plowshares and Swords, 1996, Mergers, 1998, Ice Field, 2001 (Pulitzer prize in music 2002), Crystal Antiphonies, 2000, Glossary, 2000, Prophets, 2000, others; recs: Columbia, Desto, CRI, New World, Nonesuch, Sonic Arts, AmCam, Newport Classic. Recipient Prix Italia, 1955, Alice M. Ditson award, 1962, 64, ASCAP/Nissim award 1985, Mcpl. citations: Boston, 1983, N.Y.C., 1992; Guggenheim fellow 1946, 55, Thorne fellow, 1972; grantee: Inst. Arts and Letters, 1955, Copley, 1960, Huber, 1960, Dollard 1966, N.Y. State Coun. for Arts, 1974, NEA, 1976, ASCAP/Nissim 1984, Fromm, 1992, Koussevitzky Found., 1996. Mem. Am. Acad. Arts and Letters (life) Achievements include pioneering in development of spatial-antiphonal music. Office: c/o Carl Fischer LLC 65 Bleecker St New York NY 10012 *Undoubtedly, the answer to the riddle of existence must be: perpetual discovery.**

BRANT, JAMES WILLIAM, educational consultant, mathematician, educator; b. Indpls., Ind., Mar. 3, 1941; s. Frederick Merle Brant and Ellen Adelaide Lloyd, Harold Anthony Nelson (Stepfather); m. Nancy Kay Dreher, Jan. 3, 1962; children: James Eric, Kelly Michael, Christie Diane Barnes. BS, Ind. State, Terre Haute, 1964; MA in Liberal Studies, Valparaiso U., Ind., 1972; PhD in Arts and Sci., Columbia Pacific U., San Rafael, Calif., 1992. Tchr. secondary math. Hardin County Sch. Dist., Vine Grove, Ky., 1961—65, Duneland Sch. Sys., Chesterton, Ind., 1965—93; edn. cons., k-12 math. Nev. Dept. of Edn., Carson City, 1994—. Projects dir. math. edn., standards, assessments, and profl. edn. Nev. Dept. of Edn., Carson City, 1994—2004; conf. chair western regional conf. Nat. Coun. Tchrs. of Math., Reno, 1996—98, publicity chair ann. conf., Las Vegas, 2000—02; devel. cons.: k-3 informal assessments project W.Va. Dept. Edn., Charleston, 2002—03; dir. profl. edn., leadership, outreach svcs. and edn. programs Nev. Math. Coun., Carson City, 1994—. Project designer and editor: W.Va. Informal Assessment Program for K-3 Math., 2004 (W.Va. Dept. Edn. commendation, 2003). Recipient Achievement award, Nat. Coun. of Teachers of Math., 1998, Leadership award, Nev. Math. Coun., 2002. Episcopal. Avocations: grant writing, golf. Home: 1707 Jamie Way Carson City NV 89701 Office Phone: 775-885-1437. E-mail: drjimbrant@msn.com.

BRANT, PETER M., magazine publishing executive, real estate developer; m. Stephanie Seymour, 1995; 2 children. Chmn., CEO Brant Allen Industries, Inc., Conn.; owner Brant Publications (Interview Mag, Art in Am. Mag.), NY. Co-founder Greenwich Polo Club, Conn., 1995—. Exec. prodr.: (films) Basquiat, 1996; exec. prodr.: (films) Pollock, 2000. Bd. trustees Solomon R. Guggenheim Mus., NYC. Office: Brant Allen Industries Inc 80 Field Pt Rd Greenwich CT 06830 Office Phone: 203-661-3344. Office Fax: 203-661-3349.*

BRANT, SANDRA J., magazine publisher; m. Peter M Brant. Pub., pres. Brant Publs., N.Y.C., 1985—. Publisher, Art in America, The Magazine Antiques, Interview. Office: Brant Publs 575 Broadway New York NY 10012-3230

BRANTIGAN, CHARLES OTTO, surgeon; b. Balt., Jan. 24, 1943; s. Otto Charles and Edith May (Reinhart) B.; m. Linda Anne Reynolds, 1972 (dec. 1978); m. Kathleen Sharon Aylsworth, July 16, 1983; 1 child, Charles Aylsworth. BA in Chemistry, Cornell U., 1964; MD, Johns Hopkins U., 1968. Intern U. Colo., 1968-69, resident, 1969-70, 72-73, fellow in cardiovascular surgery Denver, 1973-74; resident in thoracic surgery Denver Gen. Hosp., 1974-75; sr. resident U. Colo. Med. Ctr., 1975-76; pvt. practice Denver, 1976—. Assoc. clin. prof. surgery U. Colo., 1976—; chief of surgery Presbyn. St. Lukes Med. Ctr., Denver, 1994—2002; dir. Denver Vascular Diagnostic Ctr., 1984—; med. dir. Denver Wound Care Ctr., 1991—2001; chief thoracic surgery Denver Gen. Hosp., 1976; asst. dir. surg. tng. program St. Joseph Hosp., Denver, 1984—86; chmn. nutritional support com. Presbyn. Med. Ctr., 1983—87; vis. prof. Mostafa Kamel Hosp., Alexandria, Egypt, 2000, El Maadi Hosp., Cairo, 2000—04. Contbr. articles to profl. jours.; author 4 books. Chmn. Hosp. Dist. Urban Design Forum, Denver, 1993—; participated in creation of Lafayette St. Historic Dist., Denver, 1987. Lt. comdr. USN, 1970-72. Recipient Spl. Citizen award Planning Office City of Denver, 1995, Historic Preservation award Historic Denver, 1988, Stephen H. Hart award Colo. State Hist. Soc., 1988, People's Choice award Capitol Hill United Neighborhoods, 1997, Ann. Love award for Hist. Preservation, Hist. Denver,

2002. Mem.: ACS, AMA, Soc. Critical Care Medicine, Am. Coll. Chest Physicians, Internat. Soc. for Cardiovasc. Surgery, Western Thoracic Surgery Soc., Am. Assn. Vascular Surgery, Am. Heart Assn., Colo. Med. Soc., Rocky Mountain Traumatologic Soc., Denver Med. Soc., Denver Brass Inc. (chmn. bd. dirs.). Lutheran. Avocations: urban land use planning, architectural historical research. Home: 2105 Lafayette St Denver CO 80205-5337 Office: 2253 Downing St Denver CO 80205-5234 Office Phone: 303-830-8822. Business E-Mail: cbrantigan@drbrantigan.com.

BRANTINGHAM, ANDRYA J., special education educator; b. Libertyville, Ill., May 27, 1965; d. John David and Betsy Ann Luther; m. Eric Lawrence Brantingham, May 24, 1997; children: Kade Pierre, JD Luke. BS, Fla. State U., 1987; MA, U. No. Colo., 1994; PhD in Curriculum Instrn., U. Wyo., 2001. Tchr. Littleton Pub. Schs., Colo., 1989—94; tchr. spl. edn. North Park Schs., Walden, Colo., 1994—96; tchr. Ouray R-1, Ridgway, Colo., 2001—03; staff devel. contractor pvt. practice, Norwood, 2004—. Bd. dirs. Wright's Mesa Ctr., Norwood; mem. exec. bd. Voyager Youth Program, Ridgway, 2003—04. Coach Spl. Olympics, Ft. Collins, Colo., 1985—87. Mem.: ASCD, Colo. Assn. Sch. Bds. Avocations: horseback riding, skiing. Home: PO Box 451 Norwood CO 81423

BRANTINGHAM, BARNEY, journalist, writer; b. Chgo., Feb. 26, 1932; s. Carl Brantingham and Frances Bell; m. Angela Mendez, Oct. 30, 1957 (div.); children: Barclay Carl, Frances, Wendy, Kenneth. Grad., U. Ill., 1954. Reporter Star Newspapers, Chicago Heights, Ill., 1957-59; editor San Clemente (Calif.) Sun-Post, 1959-60; reporter Santa Barbara (Calif.) News-Press, 1960—, columnist, 1977—. Commentator Sta. KTMS, Santa Barbara, 1989-91, Sta. KIST, Santa Barbara, 1991, SAM, 1990, 92; radio sta. feature and travel commentator KQSB, 1994-97; co-host Around the World with Arthur and Barney, Sta. KTMS, 1998, KEYT-AM, 1998-2003, Around the World, Sta. KZBN, 2003—; founding dir. Opinionated Traveler internet site www.opinionatedtraveler.com. Prodr. TV program Santa Barbara Traveler; author: The Pro Football Hall of Fame, 1988, Barney's Santa Barbara, 1989, Around Santa Barbara County with Barney, 1992; co-dir. The Opinionated Traveler Internet Site. With U.S. Army, 1955-57. Mem. Internat. Food, Wine and Travel Writers Assn. (dir. 1991-95), Am. Travel Media Assn. (bd. dirs.). Avocation: travel. Office: Santa Barbara News-Press PO Box 1359 Santa Barbara CA 93102-1359 Office Phone: 805-564-5105. Personal E-mail: barney163@cox.net. E-mail: bbrantingham@newspress.com.

BRANTINGHAM, PAUL JEFFREY, criminology educator; b. Long Beach, Calif., June 29, 1943; s. Charles Ross and Lila Carolyn (Price) B.; m. Patricia Louise Matthews, Aug. 26, 1967; 1 child, Paul Jeffrey Jr. BA, Columbia U., 1965, JD, 1968; Diploma in Criminology, Cambridge U., 1970. Bar: Calif. 1969. Asst. prof. Fla. State U., Tallahassee, 1971-76, assoc. prof., 1976-77, Simon Fraser U., Burnaby, B.C., Can., 1977-85, assoc. dean faculty interdisciplinary studies, 1980-82, prof., 1985—; dir. spl. revs. Pub. Svc. Commn. Can., Ottawa, Ont., 1985-87. Editor: Juvenile Justice Philosophy, 1974, 2d edit. 1978, Environmental Criminology, 1981, 2d edit. 1991; author: Patterns in Crime. Recipient Eisenhower Watch award Columbia U., 1966; Ford Found. fellow, 1969-70, Western Soc. Criminology fellow, 1996, Sr. fellow Fraser Inst. Mem. ABA, Calif. Bar Assn., Am. Soc. Criminology (chmn. nat. program 1978), Acad. Criminal Justice Scis., Canadian Criminal Justice Assn., Soc. for Reform of Criminal Law, Western Soc. Criminology (v.p. 2000-01, pres. 2001-02). Home: 4680 Eastridge Rd North Vancouver BC Canada V7G 1K4 Office: Simon Fraser U Sch Criminol 8888 University Dr WMC 1632 Burnaby BC Canada V5A 1S6 Office Phone: 604-291-4175. Business E-Mail: branting@sfu.ca.

BRANTLEY, JEFFREY GARLAND, health science association administrator; b. Rocky Mount, NC, Nov. 4, 1949; s. Roy Garland and Irene (Cockrell) B.; m. Mary Mathews, Nov. 21, 1981. BA in History, Davidson Coll., 1971; MD, U. N.C., 1977. Diplomate Am. Bd. Psychiatry. Resident in psychiatry U. Calif., Irvine, 1981; pvt. practice psychiatry Laguna Niguel, 1981-82, Durham, NC, 1985-87; med. dir. Hospice Orange County, Laguna Niguel, Calif., 1982; clin. dir. Durham County Mental Health Ctr., NC, 1982-89; freelance cons., educator, 1990—; dir. mindfulness-based stress reduction program Duke Ctr. for Integrative Medicine, 1998—. Clin. assoc. dept. psychiatry U. Calif., Irvine, 1981-82; consulting assoc. Dept. Psychiatry Duke U., 1983—. Author: Calming Your Anxious Mind, 2003; co-editor: Five Good Minutes: 100 Morning Practices to Help You Stay Calm and Relaxed All Day Long, 2005. Mem.: N.C. Psychiat. Assn., Am. Psychiat. Assn. Democrat. Buddhist. Avocations: spectator sports, golf, jogging, music. Home and Office: 1109 Huntsman Dr Durham NC 27713-2370 Office Phone: 919-660-6745. Business E-Mail: brant006@mc.duke.edu.

BRANTLEY, WILLA JOHN, educational administrator; b. Carthage, Miss., Aug. 24, 1956; d. Rena John; m. Harlon Dwight Bell, May 15, 1974 (div. 1979); children: Chassidy Georgina, Gerrard Dwight; m. Nicky Paul Brantley, Jan. 5, 1985 (div. 1991). Student, East Cen. Jr. Coll., 1975, Wood Jr. Coll., 1975-76; BEd magna cum laude, Jackson State U., 1979; postgrad., Miss. State U., 1979-81, 83—. Cert. elem. tchr., Miss. Counselor Miss. Band Choctaw Indian, Philadelphia, Miss., 1979; elem. tchr. Standing Pine Sch., Walnut Grove, Miss., 1979-81, prin. Philadelphia, 1983-87; ednl. specialist Chocotaw Agy., Phila., 1981-83, 87—, acting agy. supr. for edn. Philadelphia, 1981-88, agt. supt. for edn. Phila., 1990—; tchr. evaluator Pa. Dept. Edn., Philadelphia, 1990—; dir. Choctaw Dept. Edn., Philadelphia, 1990—96; substitute tchr. Oxford Elem. Sch., Batesville Job Corp., Attalla County Sch. Dist., 1996—98; legis. analysis and rsch. asst. Office of Tribal Coun., 1998—2003, exec. adminstr., 2003—. Trainers of tng. Nat. Indian Sch. Bd., Philadelphia, 1987—; curriculum specialist Bur. Indian Affairs-Choctow, Philadelphia, 1987—, staff devel. coord., 1986—; chmn. bd. ESEA, 1991; bd. dirs. Southeastern Region Visions for Edn. Vol. program implementation Save the Children Fedn., Cherokee, N.C., 1981—; planning participant nat. issues forum Kettering Found., Dayton, Ohio, 1987; mem. task force com. Office of Indian Edn. Program, Washington, 1985. Recipient cert. of recognition Save the Children Fedn., 1986. Fellow Internat. Reading Assn., Miss. Staff Devel. Coun.; mem. ASCD, Minn. Edn. Computer Consortium, Choctaw Dept. Educators (bd. dirs.), Red Water Basketball Club, Red Water Community Devel. Club, Phi Theta Kappa. Democrat. Methodist.

BRANTZ, GEORGE MURRAY, retired lawyer; b. Phila., Oct. 19, 1930; s. Louis Paul and Jeannette (Vinitz) B.; m. Joan Nadler, Mar. 29, 1953; children: Nancy Brantz Ginsberg, Amy L. Brantz Bedrick. AB, Princeton U., 1952; LLB magna cum laude, Harvard U., 1957. Bar: Pa. 1957. Ptnr. Wolf, Block, Schorr and Solis-Cohen, Phila., 1966-93; ret., 1993. Pres. Council Migration Service, Phila., 1971-73; bd. dirs. Phila. Port Corp., 1982-84. With U.S. Army, 1952-54. Mem.: Am. Law Inst., Jane Austen Soc. (treas. 1993—98). E-mail: jbrantz@comcast.net.

BRANYAN, CHERYL MUNYER, museum administrator; b. Vincennes, Ind., Apr. 27, 1970; d. Edward A. and Janet E. Munyer. BA, Ea. Ill. U., 1992, MA, 1995. Asst. curator Coles County Hist. Soc., Charleston, Ill., 1994-95, Manship Ho. Mus., Jackson, Miss., 1995-96, The Hermitage, Nashville, 1996-97; mus. adminstr. Rosalie Miss. State Soc. DAR, Natchez, 1999—2003; v.p Miss. Museums Assn., 2001—02, pres., 2002—04; dir. Hist. Jefferson Coll., Washington, Mo., 2003—. Newsletter editor Historic House Museums Affinity Group, 2000-05; bd. dirs. Natchez Hist. Soc., 2000-04. Editor SERA News, 1998-2002; co-founder, contbr. jour. Historia, 1992 Mem. Nat. Assn. Jr. Aux. (pres. 2005), Phi Alpha Theta, Sigma Tau Delta Democrat. Lutheran. Avocation: visiting museums. Office: Hist Jefferson Coll PO Box 700 Washington MS 39190 E-mail: manager@rosalie.net.

BRAS, RAFAEL LUIS, engineering educator; b. San Juan, P.R., Oct. 28, 1950; s. Rafael and Amalia Antonia (Muniz) B.; m. Patricia Ann Brown, June 29, 1974; children: Rafael Edmundo, Alejandro Luis. BSCE, MIT, 1972, MSCE, 1974, ScD in Water Resources and Hydrology, 1975; Laurea honoris causa, U. Perugia, Italy, 1991. Registered profl. engr., Mass., P.R. Asst. prof. U. P.R., Mayaguez, 1975-76; from asst. prof. hydrology to assoc. prof. MIT, Cambridge, 1976-82, prof., 1982—, head water resources and environ. engring. divsn., 1983-91, dir. Ralph M. Parsons Lab., 1983-91, dir. Minority Intro. to Eng. and Sci., 1987, William E. Leonhard prof. engring., 1988-95, Bacardi and Stockholm Water Founds. prof., 1995—2004, Edward A. Abdun-Nur prof., 2004—, head dept. civil and environ. engring., 1992—2001, faculty chair, 2002—05; assoc. dir. Ctr. for Global Change Sci., 1990—. Cons. to govt. and industry; vis. assoc. prof. U. Simon Bolivar, Caracas, Venezuela, 1982-83; vis. scholar Internat. Inst. Applied Systems Analysis, Vienna, 1983; vis. prof. Iowa Inst. Hydraulic Rsch., U. Iowa, 1989-90; mem. adv. bd. engring. divsn. NSF, 1988-91; bd. atmospheric scis. and climate NRC, 1989-93; earth scis. and applications divsn. adv. subcom. NASA, 1990, sci. team TRMM mission, 1991-94, chair Earth Sys. Sci. and Applications Adv. Com., 1998-2002; sci. steering group GCIP-Global Energy and Water Cycle Experiment, 1991-95; adv. coun. for com. Nat. Insts. for Environment; mem. adv. com. civil engring. dept. Rensselaer Poly. Inst., 2000-02; mem. adv. com. Johns Hopkins U., 1998—; mem. adv. coun. Princeton U., 1999—; mem. nominating com. Stockholm Water Prize, 1996—2004; mem. adv. com. dept. civil and environ. engring. Cornell U., 2001—; bd. dirs. Fundacion Chile, 2000-02, MIT Alumni Assn., 2002; mem. exec. com. Clarke Prize, 2002-04; mem. sci. com. Inter Poly. Sch., Milan, Italy, 2003—. Author: (with I. Rodriguez-Iturbe) Random Functions and Hydrology, 1985, 94, Hydrology: An Introduction to Hydrologic Science, 1990; editor: The World at Risk: Natural Hazards and Climate Change, 1993; editor Nonlinear Processes in Geophysics, 1996-2000; contbr. articles to profl. jours.; assoc. editor Water Resources Rsch., 1980-88, Jour. Geophys. Rsch.-Atmospheres, 1996-98; mem. editl. bd. Jour. Hydrology, Internat. Jour. Environ. Tech.; mem. editl. adv. bd. SERRA, 1998—. Recipient Walter L. Huber Civil Engring. prize, 1993, Giants in Sci. award Quality Edn. for Minorities Math., Sci. and Engring. Network, 2001, Albert Baez Jr. award and Outstanding Educator award Hispanic Engr. Nat. Achievement Awards Conf., 1999, MLK-MIT Leadership award, 2000, Clarke prize, 1998, Hispanic Engr. Nat. Achievement award hall of fame, 2003, AGU Lorenz Lecture, 2003; named to Top 100 Most Influential Hispanics, Hispanic Bus., 1997; Guggenheim fellow, 1982; P.R. Econ. Devel. Adminstrn. fellow; Gilbert Winslow Career Devel. chair MIT; Horton lectr. AMS, 1997, 1999, Kisiel Disting. lectr., 2002, William Mong Disting. lectr. U. Hong Kong, 1999-2000; NASA Pub. Svc. medal, 2002. Fellow: ASCE (task com. 1996—97, Huber prize 1993), Am. Meteorol. Soc. (Robert E. Horton lectr. 1999), Am. Geophys. Union (chmn. bd. jous. editors 1984—88, chair budget and fin. 1990—94, pres. Hydrology sect. 2003—, assoc. editor, Horton award 1981, James B. Macelwane award 1982, Lorenz lectr. 2003); mem.: NASA (Pub. Svc. medal 2002), AAAS, AMS, Soc. Presdl. Fellows Lectrs., Boston Soc. Civil Engrs., Tau Beta Pi, Sigma Xi, Chi Epsilon. Roman Catholic. Office: MIT Rm 48-213 Dept Civil Environ Engring Cambridge MA 02139 Office Phone: 617-253-2117. E-mail: rlbras@mit.edu.

BRASCHE, SARAH LEE WARNER, music educator; b. Asheville, NC, Feb. 16, 1963; d. Joseph Meed Goode and H Carolyn (Pope) Warner; m. Kevin Ray Brasche, May 19, 1985; 1 child, Mary Katerine; children: Daniel, John. BA in music, Pfeiffer U., 1985; M in music, Columbia Coll., 1993. Pvt. music tchr., Raleigh, 1985—2002; ch. musician dir. and organist, 1985—2001; choral tchr. Chapin H.S., SC, 2000—. Recipient Tchr. of the Yr., Chapin H.S., 2004—05. Mem.: Am. Choral Directors Assn., SC Music Educators Assn., Nat. Assn. for Music Edn. United Meth. Avocations: reading, travel, swimming. Office: Chapin H S 300 Columbia Ave Irmo SC 29063

BRASEL, JO ANNE, pediatrician, educator; b. Salem, Ill., Feb. 15, 1934; d. Gerald Nolan and Ruby Rachel (Rich) B. BA, U. Colo., 1956, MD, 1959. Diplomate in pediatrics and pediatric endocrinology Am. Bd. Pediatrics. Pediatric intern, resident Cornell U. Med. Coll.-N.Y. Hosp., N.Y.C., 1959-62; fellow in pediatric endocrine Johns Hopkins U. Sch. Medicine, Balt., 1962-65, asst. prof. pediats., 1965-68; asst. prof., then assoc. prof. pediatrics Cornell U. Med. Coll., N.Y.C., 1969-72; assoc. prof., then prof. pediats. Columbia U. Phys. and Surg., N.Y.C., 1972-79; prof. pediats. Harbor-UCLA Med. Ctr./UCLA Sch. Medicine, 1979—, program dir. Gen. Clin. Rsch. Ctr., 1979-93, prof. medicine, 1980—; Joseph W. St. Geme, Jr. prof. pediats. UCLA Sch. Medicine, 1999—. Mem. adv. com. FDA, Rockville, Md., 1971-75; mem. nutrition study sect. NIH, Bethesda, Md., 1974-78; mem. select panel for promotion of child health HEW, Washington, 1979-80; mem. life scis. adv. screening com. Fulbright-Hays program, Washington, 1981-84; mem. digestive disease and nutrition grant rev. group NIADDK, 1985-89; mem. U.S. Govt. Task Force on Women, Minorities and the Handicapped in Sci. and Tech., 1987-89. Recipient Rsch. Career Devel. award NIH, 1973-77, Irma T. Hirschl Trust Career Sci. award, 1974-79, Sr. Fulbright Sabbatical Rsch. award, 1980. Mem. Soc. Pediatric Rsch. (sec.-treas. 1973-77, v.p. 1977-78, pres. 1978-79), Am. Fedn. Clin. Rsch., Endocrine Soc., Am. Soc. Clin. Nutrition, Am. Inst. Nutrition, Western Assn. Physicians, Lawson Wilkins Pediatric Endocrine Soc. (bd. dirs. 1972-74, v.p. 1991-92, pres. 1992-93), Western Soc. Pediatric Rsch., Phi Beta Kappa, Alpha Omega Alpha. Office: Harbor-UCLA Med Ctr Box 446 1000 W Carson St Torrance CA 90509-2910 Office Phone: 310-222-1971. Business E-Mail: brasel@labiomed.org.

BRASELL, DOUGLAS SCOTT, music educator, consultant; b. Selma, Ala., Jan. 6, 1975; s. Travis Cecil Jr. and Colleen Woods Brasell; m. Charlotte Garrett Brasell, Mar. 25, 2000; children: Connor Matthew, Alexandra Elizabeth, Carter Garrett. MusB in Edn., Troy (Ala.)State U., 1999; MS in Edn. and Music, Troy (Ala.) State U., 2001. Dir. of bands St. James Sch., Montgomery, Ala., 2000—02; asst. dir. of bands Cairo (Ga.) H.S., 2002—03; dir. of bands Prattville (Ala.) H.S., 2003—. Founder DrumMajors.com, 1999—; owner DSB Publications LLC, Deatsville, Ala., 2005—; cons. Warner Bros. publs., 2000—. Prodr.: (DVD instructional video) The Expressive Drum Major Vol. 1 (Distributed world-wide by JW Pepper, Inc., 2005); contbr. web sites. Recipient John M. Long Acad. Achievement award, Troy U. Sch. Music, 1999. Mem.: Nat. Assn. Music Edn., Internat. Assn. Jazz Educators, Ala. Music Edn. Assn., Ala. Bandmasters Assn. Republican. Baptist. Avocations: travel, vacationing, fishing. Office: Prattville HS Band 1315 Upper Kingston Rd Prattville AL 36067 Office Phone: 334-365-0332.

BRASFIELD, ANDREW MCCOLLUM, artist; b. Houston, Mar. 25, 1970; s. Robert Hamilton (Stepfather) and Susan Kirchen Betts, McCollum Eugene Brasfield. B of Comm., Norwich U., 1992. Corr. editl. dept., news The Times Argus, Barre, Vt., 1993—94; photographer Town Talk, Media, Pa., 1999—99; music corr., photographer The Daily Local News, West Chester, 2000—01. Founder, pub. Pa.'s Path, West Chester, 2001—. *Graduating from the Military College of Vermont, he was a 4 year varsity football player. As a photographer at the 3 newspapers, he had never taken a 35mm course, and was published on many front and inside cover pages.* Author (photographer, poet, essayist, lyricist,): Phly Phishing Philadelphia with Danny Montfurnumb, musician bluesman, drummer. Bd. trustee Ctrl. Vt. Cmty. Land Trust, Barre, Vt., 1993—94. Mem.: Broadcast Music Inc. (assoc.). Achievements include Copyright holder; Poetry and Photography Chapbook ('zine); SRV & Double Trouble, Kenny Wanye Shephard, Chris Whitley 'zine. Avocation: music. Office: Any Bets Inc! 416 East Miner St - Rm C West Chester PA 19382 Personal E-mail: ambrasfield@hotmail.com.

BRASFIELD, EVANS BOOKER, lawyer; b. Richmond, Va., Sept. 21, 1932; s. George Frederick and Minna (Booker) B.; children: Evans Booker, John McDonald, Elizabeth Lee; m. Anne Dobbins Heilig, June 28, 1980; stepchildren: J. Randall Heilig, Mollie H. Storey. BA, U. Va., 1954, LLB, 1959. Bar: Va. 1959. Pvt. practice, Richmond; ptnr. Hunton & Williams, Richmond, 1965-99; gen. counsel Va. Electric & Power Co., Richmond, 1976-94, Dominion Resources, 1983-91. Pres. Children's Home Soc. Va., 1972-73, bd. dirs., 1965-91; chmn. Cen. Va. Ednl. TV Corp., 1978-84, bd. dirs., 1965-2004; bd. dirs. Richmond Cmty. Action Program, 1974-76, Richmond Area Cmty. Coun., 1973-75, Big Bros. Richmond, 1970-75, Sheltering Arms Hosp., 2001—. With USNR, 1954-56. Fellow Am. Bar Found., Va. Law Found.; mem. ABA (chmn. sect. pub. utility law 1996-97), Va. Bar Assn. (exec. com. 1981-86, pres. 1985), Richmond Bar Assn., Va. State Bar, Phi Beta Kappa (pres. Richmond chpt. 1982-83). Clubs: Country of Va., Commonwealth, (Richmond). Presbyterian. Home: 2 Ampthill Rd Richmond VA 23226-2233

BRASHARES, ANN, writer; b. Chevy Chase, Md. m. Jacob Collins; children: Sam, Nathaniel, Susannah. B in philosophy, Barnard Coll. With Daniel Weiss Associates, NYC, editor-in-chief; co-pres., editor-in-chief 17th St. Productions, NYC. Author: Steve Jobs: Thinks Different, 2001, Linus Torvalds: Software Rebel, 2001, The Sisterhood of the Travelling Pants, 2001, The Second Summer of the Sisterhood, 2003, Girls in Pants: The Third Summer of the Sisterhood, 2005. Office: c/o Random House Inc 1745 Broadway New York NY 10019*

BRASHEAR, KAREN KATHLEEN, elementary school educator; b. Pendelton, Oreg., Dec. 14, 1951; d. Elvin William and Ruby Ina (Klein) Sievers; m. Kenneth George Brashear, Sept. 1, 1973; children: Melanie Lynn, Bryan Keith. Degree in applied arts and scis., Columbia Basin Coll., 1985; BA in elem. edn., Ea. Wash. U., 1990. Cert. Am. Assn. of Christian Counselors. Loan sec. Baker Boyer Nat. Bk., Walla Walla, Wash., 1975—77; sci. specialist Richland Sch. Dist., Richland, Wash., 1982—2004, ednl. asst., 1988—90, thcr., 1990—2005. Sci. specialist Richland Schs., Richland, Wash., 1992—2005. Women's min. dir. SDA Ch., Richland, Wash., 2003—05; ropes course facilitator Columbia Basin Challenge Course, Wash. Recipient SEPAC Golden Cir. award, Richland Sch. Dist., 1996—97. Mem.: Am. Assn. of Christian Counselors. Avocations: skiing, boating, knitting, reading, travel. Home: 300 Columbia Pt Dr Richland WA 99352 Office Phone: 509-371-2680. E-mail: kbrashear@gossip.com.

BRASKET, CURT JUSTIN, systems analyst; b. Tracy, Minn., Dec. 7, 1932; s. Curt John and Mary Ann (Jenniges) B.; m. Rita Ann Bronk, July 20, 1963; children: Monica, Barbara, Rebecca. Student, U. Minn., 1950-51; BA in Math, St. John's U., Collegeville, Minn., 1954. Systems analyst Unisys (Sperry, Univac), St. Paul, 1957-88. Served with AUS, 1955-57. Mem. U.S. Chess Fedn. (life master, life mem.), Internat. Chess Fedn. (master 1983—) Achievements include being U.S. Chess master, 1953—; U.S. jr. champion, 1952; 16 times Minn. champion, 4 times North Ctrl. champion. Home: 220 Spring Valley Dr Minneapolis MN 55420-5540

BRASS, ERIC PAUL, internal medicine and pharmacology educator, academic administrator; b. Bklyn., Sept. 3, 1952; s. Edward A. and Barbara (Rosen) B.; m. Kathy E. Sietsema, Sept. 3, 1994; children: Carl, Courtney, Alexander. BSChemE, Case Western Res. U., 1974, MSChemE, 1975, PhD in Pharmacology, 1979, MD, 1980. Diplomate Am. Bd. Internal Medicine. Resident in internal medicine U. Wash., Seattle, 1980-82, fellow in clin. pharmacology, 1982-83; asst. prof. medicine and pharmacology U. Colo., Denver, 1983-89; assoc. prof. medicine and pharmacology Case Western Res. U., Cleve., 1989-93; asst. dir. Calif. Clin Trials, 1993-94; prof., chair dept. medicine Harbor-UCLA Med. Ctr., 1994—2000; prof. medicine UCLA Sch. Medicine, 1994—; dir. Harbor-UCLA Ctr. Clin. Pharm., 2000—; prof. medicine David Geffen Sch. Medicine, 1994—. Contbr. articles to sci. jours. Recipient Faculty Devel. award Pharm. Mfrs. Assn. Found., 1985; NIH rsch. grantee, 1985, 88, 93. Mem. Am. Fedn. Clin. Rsch., Am. Soc. Pharmacology and Exptl. Therapeutics, Am. Soc. Clin. Pharmacology and Therapeutics (Young Investigator award 1987), Am. Soc. Clin. Investigation. Office: Harbor-UCLA Med Ctr 1124 W Carson St Torrance CA 90502-2004 Office Phone: 310-222-4050. Business E-Mail: ebrass@ucla.edu.

BRASS, LAWERENCE MITCHELL, neurologist, epidemiologist; b. Bklyn., Apr. 10, 1956; s. Melvin Jay and Joyce Myrna Brass; m. Lori Ann Haubenstock, Sept. 12, 1987; children: Zachary, Schuyler. MD, Tufts U., 1982. Lic. physician Conn. Intern Newton-Wellesley Hosp., Newton Lower Falls, Mass., 1982—83; resident in neurology Columbia-Presbyterian Med. Ctr., N.Y.C., 1983—86; chief resident in neurology Columbia U., N.Y.C., 1985—86, stroke fellow, 1986—87; asst. prof. neurology Yale U. Sch. Medicine, New Haven, 1987—95, assoc. prof. epidemiology and public health, 1995—96, prof. neurology, epidemiology and public health, 1996—; chief neurology VA Conn. Healthcare Sys., West Haven, Conn., 1995—. Dir. cerebrovascular rsch. Ctr. for Outcomes Rsch. and Evaluation, New Haven, 1998—. Contbr. articles to profl. jours. Named one of Oustanding Young Men in Am., 1996; recipient William McKinney award, Am. Soc. Neuroimaging, 1987. Fellow: Am. Stroke Assn. (exec. com.); mem.: AMA, Am. Heart Assn. (stroke coun., outcomes and quality of care coun.), Nat. Stroke Assn. (stroke prevention bd.), Am. Acad. Neurology (chair sect. on stroke and vascular neurology). Office: Yale Med Sch Dept Neurology Box 208018 15 York St New Haven CT 06520-8018

BRASSEUR, IRMA FAYE, special education educator; b. Flint, Mich., Apr. 18, 1961; d. Ermen Massie and Geardine Herbst; m. Curtis James Brasseur (div. Jan. 25, 1996); 1 child, Cali Jean. BS in Spl. Edn., Ctrl. Mich. U., Mt. Pleasant, 1984; MA in Spl. Edn., Eastern Mich. U., Ypsilanti, 1990; postgrad., U. Kans., 1998—. Cert. tchr. Mich. Tchr. Area Edn. Agy. #7, Waterloo, Iowa, 1984—86, Davison (Mich.) Cmty. Schs., 1986—98; project coord. U. Kans., Lawrence, 2000—. Student rep. Divsn. Learning Disabilities, 1999—2002, v.p., 2001—03, pres., 2003—04. Student Initiated grantee, Office Spl. Edn. Programs, 2001. Avocations: reading, bicycling, aerobics. Office: U Kans Ctr Rsch Learning 1122 W Campus Rd Lawrence KS 66045 Business E-Mail: ibrasser@ku.edu.

BRASWELL, JODY LYNN, gifted and talented educator; b. Cin., Aug. 30, 1955; d. Edward George and Willadene B. Kraemer; m. Jimmy Billings Braswell, Dec. 22, 1974; children: Cynthia, Gina. BS in Edn., West Tex. State U., 1985; MA in Edn., Sul Ross State U., 2000. Cert. elem. edn. grades 1-8, generic spl. edn. all levels, gifted/talented endorsement, reading specialist, master reading tchr. Tchr. spl. edn. Amarillo (Tex.) Ind. Sch. Dist., 1985—86; elem. tchr. Ector County Ind. Sch. Dist., Odessa, Tex., 1989—91, tchr. spl. edn., 1995—2000, curriculum specialist, 2000—01, gifted/talented program tchr., 2001—; elem. tchr. St. John's Episcopal Sch., Odessa, 1991—95. Lead mentor Ector County Ind. Sch. Dist., Odessa, 1998—, trainer, facilitator, 2000—. Vol. Home Hospice, Odessa, 1995—; pres. Permian Basin Reading Coun., Odessa, 2000—03; bd. mem. Read Odessa, 2003—. Recipient Lifetime Achievement award, PTA, Odessa, 2000. Mem.: Tex. Classroom Tchrs., Tex. Reading Assn., Internat. Reading Assn., Delta Kappa Gamma Iota (1st v.p. 2001—). Presbyterian. Avocations: reading, music, needlecrafts, gardening. Home: 1514 E 10th Odessa TX 79761

BRASWELL, LOUIS ERSKINE, lawyer; b. Selma, Ala., Mar. 11, 1937; s. Erskine McKinley and Leota (Grubb) B.; m. Anne, June 1, 1985 (dec. Feb. 20, 1996); children by previous marriage: Margaret, Anne, Helen. AB, Birmingham So. Coll., 1959; JD, Harvard U., 1962. Bar: Ala. bar 1962. Assoc. firm Hand, Arendall, Bedsole, Greaves & Johnston, Mobile, Ala., 1963-68; ptnr. Hand Arendall LLC, Mobile, 1968—. Participant Nat. Conf. on Discovery Reform, U. Tex. Law Sch., 1982; program participant 11th Cir. Jud. Conf., 1984, others Bd. dirs. Children's Dental Clinic, Mobile, 1965-75; past pres. Friends of Mobile Publ. Libr.; bd. dirs. Jr. Achievement of Mobile; past pres. YMCA Rockies Alumni Assn.; bd. dirs. Kidney Found. South Ala., 1978-85, Ecumenical Ministries, Inc., 2001-04. With U.S. Army, 1962-63. Mem. ABA, Am. Law Inst., Ala. Law Inst., Ala. Bar Assn., Ala. Def. Lawyers Assn., Athelstan Club, Rotary Internat., Point Clear Rotary Club (bd. dirs. 1997-2000, pres. 1998-99). Presbyterian. Home: 250 N Bayview St Fairhope AL 36532 Office: PO Box 123 Mobile AL 36601-0123 Office Phone: 251-694-6300.

BRASWELL, MARK K., lawyer; b. Memphis, Dec. 16, 1963; BA with high honors, U. Tenn., 1986; JD with honors, U. Tenn. Coll. Law, 1990. Bar: Pa. 1990, Tenn. 1993. Branch chief, Enforcement Divsn. SEC; assoc. Kirkpatrick & Lockhart LLP, Washington; ptnr., Securities Regulation & Enforcement Dept. Venable LLP, Washington. Author: Conservative Pragmatism versus Liberal Principles: Warren E. Burger on the Suppression of Evidence,

1956-1986, 1987. Mem.: ABA, Tenn. Bar Assn., Phi Delta Phi, Pi Sigma Alpha. Office: Venable LLP 575 7th St NW Washington DC 20004 Office Phone: 202-344-8231. Office Fax: 202-344-8300. Business E-Mail: mkbraswell@venable.com.

BRASWELL, PAULA ANN, artist; b. Decatur, Ala., May 6, 1955; d. Andrew Leon and Dorothy Faye (Fretwell) B.; m. Roger Armand Robichaud, June 22, 1990. BA, Jacksonville State U., 1978; postgrad., New Orleans Acad. Fine Arts, 1987, U. New Orleans, 1987-88; MFA, Fla. State U., 1990. Instr. art Butler Sch., Marrero, La., 1984, Fla. Keys Coll., Tavernier, 1985; grad. instr. Fla. State U., Tallahassee, 1989-90; adj. prof. Calhoun Coll., Decatur, Ala., 1990, Chattanooga State Coll., 1991, Cleveland (Tenn.) State Coll., 1991; studio artist Knoxville, Tenn., 1991-96, Toronto, Ont., Can., 1996—. One-woman shows include Contemporary Arts Ctr., New Orleans, 1992, ARC Gallery, 1997, Propeller Gallery, 2000—01, Melt Loop Gallery, Toronto, 2004, Windsor (Ont.) Gallery Art, 2002, WARC Gallery, Toronto, 2003—04, Kabat/Wrobel Gallery, 2004, Hysteria Festival of Women, 2004, LUZ Gallery, Montreal, 2005, 5th Anniversary Loop Gallery, Toronto, 2005, Luz Gallerie, 2005, exhibited in group shows at Knoxville (Tenn.) Mus. Art, 1994—95, Combined Talents Fla. Nat., 1995, Transforming Tradition, 1996, New American Talent, 1996, Fla. State U., Mus. of the Ams., Washington, 1997, Mus. of Fine Arts, 1998, FSU Mus., 1998, Propeller Gallery, Toronto, 2000—02, WARC Gallery, 2000, 2003, Sculpture Soc. Can., 2000—01, Gallery 121, Toronto, 2000, Soul Ecology Exhibit, 2000, Propeller Ctr. for the Visual Arts, 2000—02, Sculpture Soc. Gallery, 2001, 2004, John B. Aird Gallery, 2001, 2003, Ontario Arts Coun., 2004 (Exhbn. Assn. grant, 2004). Grantee, Nat. Endowment Arts, 1991, Ont. Arts Coun., 1997, 2000, 2001—02, 2003, Can. Coun., 2002. Mem. AAUW, NOW, Women's Caucus for Arts (exhibitor), Knoxville Mus. Art (exhibitor), Knoxville Arts Coun. (exhibitor), Coll. Art Assn., Contemporary Arts Ctr. (exhibitor), People for Protection of Animals, Humane Soc. U.S. Democrat. Mem. Ch. of Christ. Avocations: gardening, environmental concerns, animal care, skiing, camping. Address: 221 Winona Dr Toronto ON Canada M6C 3S4 Office Phone: 416-654-0051. Personal E-mail: paulabrasw@aol.com.

BRATCHER, AMY, oceanographer; Degree in Marine Scis., Tex. A&M U., Galveston, Texas, 1998; degree in Oceanography, Tex. A&M U., College Station, Texas, 2002. Phys. scientist Naval Oceanog. Office, Stennis Space Ctr., Miss., 1998—2000. Mem.: Am. Geophys. Union. Office: Texas A&M University Deptartment of Oceanography College Station TX 77843-3146 Office Phone: 979-845-1056. Office Fax: 979-845-6331.

BRATER, DONALD CRAIG, dean, educator; b. Oak Ridge, Tenn., 1945; m. Stephanie Brater; 1 child, Aimee. BA in chemistry, Duke U., 1967; MD in pharmacy, Duke U. Med. Sch., 1971. Intern Duke U., 1970—71; resident in medicine U. Calif., San Francisco, 1971—73, fellow in clin. pharmacology, 1973—76; mem. faculty Southwestern Med. Sch.; joined faculty Ind. U. Sch. Medicine, 1986, chmn. dept. medicine, John B. Hickam prof. medicine, prof. pharmacology and toxicology, 1990—2000, Walter J. Daly prof., dean, 2000—. Pres. U.S. Pharmacopoeia; bd. mgrs. Inproteo, Indpls.; adj. faculty mem. Purdue U. Sch. Pharmacy; active with Indpls. U. Sch. Medicine program in Kenya. Recipient Duke Med. Alumni Award, 2000, Friends of Pharmacy Award, Purdue U. Sch. Pharmacy, 2003. Mem.: Assn. Profs. Medicine, Am. Soc. Clin. Pharmacology and Therapeutics, Assn. Am. Physicians, Am. Soc. Clin. Investigation. Office: Ind U Sch Medicine 1120 W South Dr Fesler Hall Indianapolis IN 46202-5114

BRATRUD, LINDA KAY, secondary school educator; b. Salt Lake City, May 14, 1944; d. Milton Niels and Marian Lucy (Criswell) Peterson; m. Richard L. Settle, Sept. 10, 1965 (div. Sept. 1982); children: Courtney Settle Dodson, Dana R.; m. Jeffrey C. Bratrud, Aug. 27, 1990; children: Jennifer Bratrud Stauffacher, Jeff, John. 1st diploma, U. Grenoble, France, 1964; 2d diploma, U. Paris, 1965; BA, U. Wash., 1966; MBA, U. Puget Sound, 1987. Tchr. French, South H.S., Bakersfield, Calif., 1967-68, Peninsula H.S., Gig Harbor, Wash., 1984-93; instr. French, Tacoma C.C., 1970-71; owner bookstore Smith, Settle, Bingham & Wagner, Tacoma, 1980-82; client exec. asst. Frank Russell Co., Tacoma, 1981-84. Avocations: freelance writing, gardening, golf, tennis, cooking. Address: 353 Gran Via Palm Desert CA 92260-2169

BRATT, BENJAMIN, actor; b. San Francisco, Dec. 16, 1963; m. Talisa Soto, Apr. 13, 2002; 1 child. BFA, U. Calif., Santa Barbara, 1986. Actor: (film) Bright Angel, 1991, One Good Cop, 1991, Bound by Honor, 1993, Demolition Man, 1993, The River Wild, 1994, Clear and Present Danter, 1994, Follow Me Home, 1997, The Next Best Thing, 2000, The Last Producer, 2000, Red Planet, 2000, Miss Congeniality, 2000, Traffic, 2000, Peniro, 2001, After the Storm, 2001, Abandon, 2002, The Woodsman, 2004, Catwoman, 2004, Thumbsucker, 2005, The Great Raid, 2005; (TV) Police Story: Gladiator School, 1988, Nasty Boys, 1989, Chains of Gold, 1991, Shadowhunter, 1993, Texas, 1994, Woman Undone, 1996, Exiled, 1998, (tv series) Knightwatch, 1988, Nasty Boys, 1990, Law & Order, 1995-99, After the Storm, 2001; prodr.: Follow Me Home, 1997; TV guest appearances include: Homicide: Life on the Street, 1993. Winner ALMA award as best lead actor in a TV series for Law & Order, 1998, 99. Office: ICM 8942 Wilshire Blvd Beverly Hills CA 90211-1934*

BRATT, KIRSTIN RUTH, education educator; b. Saint Cloud, Minn., Feb. 24, 1968; d. Larry Wayne and Pauline Ruth Bratt; life ptnr. Rubén Meneses; children: Sha-Narah Ruth Magby, Gabriel Magby. BA, St. Olaf Coll., 1990; MA, St. Cloud State U., 1995; EdD, No. Ariz. U., 2005. Prof. of english Ariz. Western Coll., Yuma, Ariz., 1995—2005; asst. prof. of elem. edn. Penn State Altoona, Altoona, Pa., 2005—. Office: Penn State Altoona 3000 Ivyside Pk Altoona PA 16601 Personal E-mail: krbm1968@aol.com.

BRATT, NICHOLAS, investment company executive, research and development company executive; b. Gerrards Cross, Eng., June 6, 1948; came to U.S., 1976; s. Guy Maurice and Francoise Nelly (Girardet) B.; m. Kuniko Matsui, Aug. 10, 1976; 1 child, Emi Margaret Matsui. Degree in politics, philosophy, econs., Oxford U., 1970; MIA, Columbia U., 1972. Rsch. analyst Morgan Grenfell & Co. Ltd., London, 1972-75; portfolio mgr. Morgan Grenfell S.A., Geneva, 1976, Scudder, Stevens & Clark, N.Y.C., 1976—2002, mng. dir., 1984—2002, Deutsche Asset Mgmt., N.Y.C., 2002—03; portfolio mgr. Lazard Asset Mgmt. LLC, 2003—. Pres. Scudder Internat. Fund, N.Y.C., 1982, Korea Fund, N.Y.C., 1984-2003, Scudder New Asia Fund, N.Y.C., 1987-2003, Brazil Fund, N.Y.C., 1988-2003, Scudder New Europe Fund, N.Y.C., 1990, Argentina Fund, N.Y.C., 1991-98, First Iberian Fund, N.Y.C., 1991-98, Scudder Greater Europe Fund, 1994—. Mem. N.Y. Assn. for Fgn. Investment (chmn. 1978-80), Japan Soc., Korea Soc. (bd. dirs.). Avocations: mountain climbing, skiing, tennis, paddle tennis, sailing, golf. Business E-Mail: nicholas.bratt@lazard.com.

BRATTEN, MILLIE MARTINI, editor-in-chief; m. John Bratten. With merchandising dept. Mademoiselle mag., 1975; assoc. editor Bride's mag. Conde Nast Pubs., NYC, fashion coord. menswear Bride's mag., editor accessories, fashion and beauty assoc. Bride's mag., exec. editor Bride's mag., 1991—94, editor-in-chief Bride's mag., 1994—; editl. dir. Conde Nast Bridal Group, 2002—. TV appearances in Weekend Today, Good Morning Am., Good Day N.Y., Network News, Family Values, Weddings of a Lifetime; host Romance Classics A Day of Diana; interviewed in USA Today, N.Y. Times, Washington Post, Wall Street Journal, Boston Globe, Forbes, ABC Radio Network. Mem. Am. Soc. Mag. Editors (bd. dir.), Fashion Group Internat., NY Women in Comms., Inc. (program coun. NY, past bd. dirs., v.p. membership). Office: Conde Nast Pubs 4 Times Sq 6th Fl New York NY 10036*

BRATTON, CHRISTOPHER ALAN, academic administrator, videographer, art educator; b. Akron, Ohio, July 3, 1959; s. William Raymond and Barbara Jean (Yerkey) B.; m. Dalida Maria Benfield, Oct. 7, 1994; children, Isadora and Joaquin BFA, Atlanta Coll. of Art, 1982; student, Whitney Ind. Study Program, 1984-86; MFA, U. Wis., Milw., 1994. Project dir. Rise and Shine Prodns., NYC, 1988-89; guest lectr. Sch. of Visual Arts, NYC, 1990, Sch. of the Art Inst., Chicago, Ill., 1990; vis. prof. ctr. for modern culture and media Brown U., Providence, 1991-92; faculty mem. Sch. of Art Inst., Chgo., 1992—2004, chmn. dept. video, 1993-95, chmn. dept. video, com. on exhbns. and events, instn-wide tech. initiative, 1997—98, chair dept. of film, video, and new media Chicago, Ill., 2000—01, dean undergraduate studies, 2002—04; pres. San Francisco Art Inst., Calif., 2004—. Guest lectr. in video prodn. SUNY at Old Westbury, 1986, Channel Four workshop, Derry Northern Ireland, 1986, seminars N.Y.U., panelist N.Y. Marxist Sch., Video, Edn. and Culture, N.Y.C., 1989, Literacy on the Table seminar, Video and Literacy, Bronx (N.Y.) Coun. on the Arts, 1989, Columbus in Context, Union Theol. Sem., N.Y., Mediactive Conf. Low Format Video and Media Edn., 1990; curator Teaching TV, Artists' Space, N.Y., 1990, vis. artist Hallwalls, Buffalo, Ednl. Video Ctr., N.Y.C., 1991, R.I. Sch. of Design, Providence, 1992, Gallery 400, Univ. Ill., Chgo., 1994; coord. producer Teaching TV, Deep Dish TV, 1992; presenter Hunter Coll. Roundtable on Media and Culture, N.Y.C., 1992, The Ctr. for 20th Century Studies, U. Wis., Milw., 1992; grants panelist NEA Regional fellowships, Film in the Cities, Mpls., 1993; panelist Guerilla TV, Ctr. for New TV, N.Y.C., 1993. Editor, curator: (videotape) Teaching TV, 1991; dir. (videotapes), Counterterror The North of Ireland, 1990, (Best Advocacy Work, The Atlanta Film and Video Festival 1991, Silver Apple, Oakland, Calif. Nat. Ednl. Film and Video Festival, Finalist Athens (Ohio) Festival) Framing the Panthers in Black and White (Am. Film Fest Red Ribbon, New Eng. Film and Video Fest Best Social Documentary, Australian Video Festival finalist, Hallwalls Festival of New Journalism, Buffalo, Jurors' award, Peoples Choice award The Global Africa Festival, Oakland, Calif., Spl. Jurors' award Black Maria Film and Video Fetival, East Orange, N.J., others), A Small War: The United States in Puerto Rico, 1995. Recipient fellowship in sculpture NEA, 1988, Citation Nat. Ednl. Film and Video Festival for Brooklyn, 1989, Bronze Apple for Walls and Bridges, 1990, Grand prize Internat. Youth Film and Video Festival, Warsaw for Brooklyn, 1990, Artist's Residency fellowship, Wesner Ctr. for Contemporary Art, Columbus, Ohio, 1993; grantee, Checkerboard Found., 1989, N.Y. State Coun. on the Arts, 1989, 91, J. Roderick MacArthur Found., 1989, NEA, 1990. Office: San Francisco Art Inst 800 Chestnut St San Francisco CA 94113 E-mail: president@sfai.edu.*

BRATTON, JAMES HENRY, JR., lawyer; b. Pulaski, Tenn., Oct. 9, 1931; s. James Henry and Mabel (Shelley) B.; m. Alleen Sharp Davis, Oct. 15, 1960; children: Susan Shelley McGonigle, James Henry III, Margaret Alleen Schilling. BA optime merens, valedictorian, U. South, 1952; BA, Oxford (Eng.) U., 1954, MA, 1978; LL.B., Yale U., 1956. Bar: Tenn. 1956, Ga. 1957. With antitrust div. Dept. Justice, summer 1955; since practiced in Atlanta; sr. ptnr. Smith, Gambrell & Russell. Vis. lectr. U. Ga. Law Sch., 1967; adj. prof. law Emory U., 1984-2001. Editor Yale Law Jour.; contbr. articles to profl. jours. Mem. Gov.'s Citizens Adv. Council on Environ. Affairs, 1970-74, U. South Sch. Theology Visiting Com., 2004-; trustee Pembroke Coll. Found., Inc., Trust Fund for Sibley Park, Ga. chpt. Multiple Sclerosis Soc., U. of the South, 1984-87, 95-98, Peachtree Rd. United Meth. Ch., 1997-2000, chmn. bd. trustees; bd. dirs. Soccer in the Streets, Buckhead Christian Ministry, pres., 1996; pres. Peachtree Heights West Civic Assn., 1984-99; co-chmn. Sewanee Parents Council, 1987-88; v.p. Pembroke Coll. Soc. of N.Am.; mem. Williams Parents' Fund, 1984-86; mem. parents adv. coun. Hamilton Coll., 1988-91. Named Alumnus of Yr., Sewanee Club Atlanta, 1990; John R. Crawford Disting. Svc. Award, U. of South, 2003. Fellow Lawyers Found. Ga., Am. Law Inst.; mem. ABA (standing com. on aero. law 1962-84, chmn. 1977-80), State Bar Ga. (founding chmn. environ. law sect. 1970-73), Fed. Bar Assn., Atlanta Bar Assn., Lawyers Club Atlanta, Old Warhorse Lawyers Club, Am. Acad. Polit. and Social Scis., Am. Judicature Soc., Associated Alumni U. of South (v.p. admissions 1993-95, pres. 1995-97), Yale Law Alumni Assn. (exec. com. 1976-79), Pembroke Coll. Found., Inc. (treas. 2003-), Phi Beta Kappa, Phi Delta Phi, Pi Gamma Mu, Gridiron. Democrat. Methodist. Home: 63 N Muscogee Ave NW Atlanta GA 30305-3542 Office: 1230 Peachtree St NE Atlanta GA 30309-3592 Office Phone: 404-815-3510. Business E-Mail: jbratton@sgrlaw.com.

BRATTON, WILLIAM J., police chief, former police commissioner; m. Cheryl A. Fiandaca, 1986 (div.); 1 child, David; m. Rikki Jo Klieman, April 30, 1999 B, B, postgrad., Boston State Coll.; grad. Sr. Execs. and Sr. Exec. Fellows Program, Harvard U.; grad., FBI Nat. Exec. Inst., New Eng. Inst. Law Enforcement Mgmt. Command Program, Police Exec. Rsch. Forum Sr. Mgmt. Inst. for Police. Various positions to exec. supt. Boston Police Dept., 1970-83, police commr., 1992-94; chief of police Mass. Bay Transp. Authority, 1983-86; supt. Met. Police Dept., Boston, 1986-90; chief N.Y.C. Transit Police Dept., 1990-92; police commr. N.Y.C. Police Dept., 1994-96; exec. v.p. First Security Consultants, N.Y.C., 1996—98; pres., COO Carco Group Inc, St. James, NY, 1998—2001; chief of police L.A. Police Dept., 2002—. Mem. exec. session of policing Kennedy Sch. Govt. Harvard U., 1985-92 mem. policing in 21st century work group Nat. Inst. Justice, Washington. Mem. Internat. Assn. Chiefs of Police (major cities chiefs group), Police Exec. Rsch. Forum (pres. 1994—). Office: Office of the Chief of Police 150 N Los Angeles St Los Angeles CA 90012

BRATTSTROM, BAYARD HOLMES, biology professor; b. Chgo., July 3, 1929; s. Wilber LeRoy and Violet (Holmes) B.; m. Cecile D. Funk, June 15, 1952 (div. May 1975); children: Theodore Allen, David Arthur.; m. Martha Isaacs Marsh, July 8, 1982. BS, San Diego State Coll., 1951; MA, UCLA, 1953, PhD, 1959. Dir. edn. Natural History Mus., San Diego, 1949-51, asst. curator herpetology, 1949-51; assoc. zoology UCLA, 1954-56; research fellow paleoecology Calif. Inst. Tech., Pasadena, 1955; instr. biology Adelphi U., Garden City, N.Y., 1956-60; asst. prof. Calif. State U., Fullerton, 1960-61, assoc. prof., 1961-66, prof., 1966-94, prof. emeritus, 1994—. Co-owner Horned Lizard Ranch, Horned Lizard Press; rschr., author publs. in osteology, ecology, conservation, zoogeography of vertebrates, social behavior; hon. rsch. assoc. herpetology, vertebrate paleontology Los Angeles County Mus., 1961—; pres. Fullerton Youth Mus. and Natural Sci. Ctr., 1962-64, dir., 1962-66; assoc. prof. zoology UCLA, summers 1962-63; vis. prof. zoology Sydney U., Australia, 1978, U. Queensland, Brisbane, Australia, 1984; vis. rschr. James Cook U., Townsville, Australia, 1993-94; ecol. cons. to numerous govt. agys. and pvt. corps. Author: The Talon Digs Deeply Into My Heart, 1974; author: (with M.A. Brattstrom) Aussie Slang, 2000. Recipient Disting. Teaching award Calif. State U., Fullerton, 1968, Dean's award for Outstanding Teaching and Rsch., 1992; Am. Philos. Soc. grantee to Mex., 1958, to Panama, 1959; NSF grantee, 1964-66; NSF fellow Monash U., Australia, 1966-67. Fellow AAAS (mem. coun. 1965-90), Herpetological League; mem. Am. Soc. Ichthyologists and Herpetologists (bd. govs. 1962-66, v.p. western div. 1965), Orange County Zool. Soc. (mem. bd. 1962-65, pres. 1962-64), So. Calif. Acad. Sci. (dir. 1964-67), Ecol. Soc. Am., Soc. for Study Evolution, Soc. Systematic Zoology, San Diego Soc. Natural History, Soc. Vertebrate Paleontology, Am. Soc. Mammalogists, Cooper Ornithol. Soc., Am. Ornithol. Soc., Am. Soc. Zoologists, Sigma Xi. Home: Horned Lizard Ranch PO Box 166 Wikieup AZ 85360 *My life and research has been based on an insatiable curiosity about the natural world, especially as seen in the evolutionary adaptations of animals to their environment and their interactions with each other.*

BRATVOLD, JAMES, music educator; s. Norman and Lorraine Bratvold; m. Cheryll Burkhardt, Dec. 30, 1981. BS in Edn., U. ND, 1981. Cert. educators profl. Mont. Office Pub. Instrn. Music tchr. Big Timber (Mont.) Schs., 1981—. Singer Carnegie Hall Festival Chorus, NYC, 2000; choir dir. Big Timber Luth. Ch., 1982—2005; singer Rimrock Opera Co., Billings, Mont., 2001—05. Mem.: Mont. Music Educators Assn., Mont. Choral Dirs. Assn. (clinician 1992—2005). Home: PO Box 887 Big Timber MT 59011

BRAUCHLI, ROBERT CHARLES, lawyer; b. Morristown, N.J., Nov. 11, 1945; s. Edwin Brauchli and Evelyn (Burdick) Wolford; m. Jeannette Lynne Hatcher, Jan. 18, 1992; 1 child, Holly Daniela. BA, Am. U., 1967; JD, Howard U., 1970. Bar: Ariz. 1971, U.S. Dist. Ct. Ariz. 1971, U.S. Ct. Appeals (9th cir.) 1972, U.S. Supreme Ct. 1975, White Mountain Apache Tribal Ct. 1981, U.S. Ct. Claims 1981, U.S. Ct. Appeals (fed. cir.) 1983. Staff atty. Maricopa County Legal Aid Soc., Phoenix, 1970-73; dep. county atty. County of Pima, Tucson, Ariz., 1973-78; dir. consumer fraud div., asst. atty. gen. State of Ariz., Phoenix, 1978-80; assoc. Napier and Jones, P.C., Phoenix, 1980; gen. counsel White Mountain Apache Tribe, White River, Ariz., 1980-87; ptnr. Brauchli and Brauchli, P.C., Tucson, 1987—. Mem. Indian law com. State Bar Ariz., Phoenix, 1990—; lectr. Falmouth Inst. Indian Law Studies, Falls Church, Va., 1987-89. Reginald Heber Smith fellow, 1970-72. Fellow Ariz. Bar Found. Democrat. Episcopalian. Avocations: hiking, fly fishing, skiing, bicycling, theater. Office: Brauchli and Brauchli PC 6650 N Oracle Rd Ste 110 Tucson AZ 85704-5604

BRAUDE, EDWIN SIMON, retired manufacturing executive; b. Chgo. s. Simon Arthur and Marie (Selz) B.; m. Olga Bergstad, May 4, 1951 (dec. Dec. 1992); children: Mitchell, Edwin S. Jr., Bradford, Timothy, Tammy, Teena. BSc in Civil Engring., U. Colo., 1949; postgrad., Chgo. Tech., 1959; MBA, Rockford (Ill.) Coll., 1967. From pipefitter to COO Fisher Body Div. Gen. Motors, Willow Springs, Ill.; materials mgr., mgr. mfg. Ingersoll Milling Machine Co., Rockford, 1961-71; factory mgr., v.p. mfg. NATCO, Richmond, Ind., 1972-73; plant mgr. Graphic Systems div. Rockwell Internat., Chgo. and Cedar Rapids, Iowa, 1973-76; pres., CEO Barth Industries, Cleve., 1976; corp. sr. group v.p. mfg. Nesco, Inc., Cleve., 1976—83; pres., CEO, chmn. Lester Engring., Cleve., 1977; pres., CEO Elmex, Compass Electric, BSR, Hi-Ram Group, Mich., 1979; chmn., CEO Engineered Sci. Divsn. subs. NESCO, Calif., 1981; pres. Lexington Switch and Control, Flex Cable & Kirkhof, 1983, Nat. Acme, Cleve., 1984—; v.p. ops. Acme Cleve., 1987—; pres. A.A. Gage, Ferndale, Mich., 1989—; v.p. Nesco, Inc., Mayfield Heights, Ohio, 1990—. Work with cos., Magdeburg, Germany, 1992, Novosibirsk, Siberia, 94; cons. Wolverine Diecast, 1998; chmn. bd. Wiscon Co., Memphis, 2001—; mem. MAPI Mfg. Coun. Chmn. City of Roscoe (Ill.) Zoning Commn.; mem. Roscoe Planning Bd. With USCG, 1944-46, PTO; with USAF, 1950. Mem.: Univ., Cleve. Athletic. Republican. Lutheran. Avocations: racquetball, scuba diving. Personal E-mail: esbraude@hotmail.com.

BRAUDE, MICHAEL, commodities trader, researcher; b. Chgo., Mar. 6, 1936; s. Sheldon and Nan B.; m. Linda Rae Miller, Aug. 20, 1961; children—Peter, Adam BS, U. Mo., 1957; MS, Columbia U., 1958. Vice pres. Commerce Bank, Kansas City, Mo., 1960-73; vice pres. Mercantile Bank, Kansas City, Mo., 1966-73; exec. v.p. Am. Bank, Kansas City, Mo., 1973-84; pres., CEO Kansas City Bd. Trade, Mo., 1984—2001. Bd. dirs. Midwest Trust Co., Kansas City, Mo., MGP Ingredients Inc., Atchison, Kans., NPC Internat., Pittsburg, Kans. Author: Managing Your Money, 1975, also 12 childrens books Pres. Metr. Cmty. Coll. Found., Kansas City, Mo., 1982-84; mayor City of Mission Woods, Kans., 1982-84; trustee Kans. Pub. Employee Retirement Sys., 2001—, chmn. Mem. U. Mo. Alumni Assn. (bd. dirs. 1985-87). Jewish. Avocations: running, public speaking. Home: 5319 Mission Woods Ter Shawnee Mission KS 66205-2013 Personal E-mail: lmbraude@aol.com.

BRAUDE, ROBERT MICHAEL, retired medical librarian; b. L.A., Sept. 27, 1939; s. Aaron and Dorothy (Lishner) B.; m. Sharon Helene Katz, Dec. 16, 1961; children— Michael, Daniel, Julianne BA, UCLA, 1962, MLS, MA, 1964; PhD, U. Nebr., 1987. Reference librarian Biomed Library Ctr. for Health Scis., UCLA, Los Angeles, 1964-65, head Medlars search sta., 1965-68; assoc. dir. U. Colo. Med. Library, Denver, 1968-75, dir., 1975-77, U. Nebr. Med. Library, Omaha, 1978-86; asst. dean for info. resources, Frances and John Loeb librarian Weill Med. Coll./Cornell U., 1986—; ret., 2001. Adj. faculty U. Denver, 1972-78; vis. assoc. prof. Sch. Libr. Sci., Pratt Inst., 1988—; del. White House Conf. on Libraries and Info. Services, 1979; mem. biomed. library rev. com. Nat. Library Medicine, Bethesda, Md., 1980-84, mem. panel on med. informatics long range planning project, 1985-86, mem. planning panel on outreach programs, 1988-89. Author: (continuing edn. syllabus) Planning: Strategic and Tactical, 1983, also articles and book chpts.; mem. editorial adv. bd. Bibliography of Bioethics; mem. editorial bd. ann. Statis. of Med. Sch. Librs. and U.S. and Can., 19887-93; mem. editorial bd. Jour. Am. Med. Informatics Assn. Sec.-treas. Children's Chorale, Denver, 1974-75, trustee, 1975-77 Fellow N.Y. Acad. Medicine, Med. Libr. Assn. (sec., bd. dirs. 1972-75, Janet Doe lectr. 1996, chmn. numerous coms. N.Y.-N.J. chpts., Outstanding Achievement award Midcontinental chpt. 1986, Noyes award 2002), Am. Coll. Med. Informatics; mem. ALA, Acad. Health Info. Profls. (disting.), Health Scis. Libr. Dirs. (stds. and practices com. 1980-83), Assn. Western Hosps. (chmn. hosp. librs. sect. 1976-77, membership com. 1976-77), Am. Med. Informatics Assn. (mem. editl. bd.).

BRAUDY, SUSAN ORR, writer; b. Phila. d. Bernard and Blanche (Malin) Orr. BA cum laude, Bryn Mawr Coll.; postgrad., U. Pa., Yale U. Editor, writer The New Jour. Yale U., New Haven; assoc. editor Newsweek Mag., N.Y.C.; editor, writer Ms. Mag., N.Y.C.; freelance writer N.Y. Times, N.Y.C.; v.p. Warner Bros., N.Y.C., L.A., Michael Douglas Prodns., N.Y.C., L.A. Author: (memoir) Between Marriage and Divorce, 1975, (novels) Who Killed Sal Mineo, 1984, What the Movies Made Me Do, 1984, (nonfiction) This Crazy Thing Called Love, 1991, Family Circle: The Boudins and the Aristocracy of the Left, 2003; screenwriter: (films) Scorsese Co.; Am. Zeotrope; Ixtlan; Disney. Mem.: NOW, Authors' Guild, Writers Guild of Am., PEN Club Internat., Vet. Feminists Am. Home: 240 Central Park S Apt 16B New York NY 10019-1413

BRAUER, CAMILLA THOMPSON (KIMMY THOMPSON BRAUER), civic leader; b. St. Louis, Apr. 8, 1946; m. Stephen F. Brauer; children: Blackford, Rebecca, Stephen Jr. Grad., Mary Inst., Bennett Coll., Millbrook, N.Y., 1966. Dir. St. Louis Arts & Edn. Coun., 1988—; dir., exec. com. Opera Theater of St. Louis, 1986—; dir. exec. com. Sheldon Arts Found., 1991—; trustee St. Louis Art Mus., 1989-94, chmn. bd. trustees, 1991-94, commr., 1996—; trustee Webster U., 1994—; exec. com., 1995—; chair Alexis de Tocqueville Soc., 1995, 96, 2001; v.p. exec. com. United Way of St. Louis, 1996—; bd. trustees St. Louis Symphony, 1994—, exec. com., 1995—. Recipient Internat. Barker award Variety Club, 2000; named St. Louis Post Dispatch Woman of Achievement, 1996. Mem. Naat. Soc. Fund Raising Execs. (Vol. of Yr. St. Louis 1994, Vol. of Yr. U.S. 1996), Variety Club (exec. bd. dirs. 1992—, Woman of Yr. 1992, Mo. Hist. Soc. (dir. 1991—, exec. com. 1991—). Home: 9630 Ladue Rd Saint Louis MO 63124-1311 Fax: (314) 994-1441. E-mail: camillabrauer@aol.com.

BRAUER, ETHEL MAY, secondary school educator; b. Thurmont, Md., June 16, 1946; d. Paul Arthur and Dorothy Virginia (Smith) Alexander; m. Alan Lee Brauer Sr., Apr. 26, 1969; children: Juliann Brauer Frantz, Alan L. Jr., Kelly Lynn. BA in Edn., Frostburg State U., 1968; postgrad., Hood Coll., 1990-92, Mt. St. Mary's Coll., 1994—. Cert. social studies tchr. grades 5-12, Md. Tchr. Frederick (Md.) County Bd. Edn., 1968-70, 86-87; newspaper editor Catoctin Enterprise, Thurmont, 1980-83; tchr. social studies grades 6-8 St. John Regional Cath. Sch., Frederick, 1989—. Advisor St. John Regional Cath. Student Coun., Frederick, 1989—; mem. St. John Regional Cath. Sch. Bd., Frederick, 1993—94, mid. sch. team leader, 2004—; mem. Archdiocese Social Studies Curriculum Revision Com., 1994—99, Frederick County Drug-Free Schs. Com., Newspaper in Edn. County Com.; mid sch. coord. St. John Regional Cath. Sch. Bd., 2005. Mem. Am. Legion Aux., Thurmont, 1964—, Thurmont Grange # 409, 1970—; adult leader Thurmont Jr. Grange # 35, 1975—90. Named Young Couple of the Yr., Md. State Grange, Frederick, 1972, Jr. Grange Leader of the Nation, Nat. Grange, Washington, 1979, Outstanding Young Women of Am., 1981; recipient Award of Excellence Friends of Cath. Edn., 2004, Outstanding Tchr. Am. History of Yr., Md. Soc. DAR, 2005. Mem.: Nat. Cath. Edn. Assn., Pi Lambda Theta. Republican. Methodist. Avocations: singing, reading, soccer fan, star trek fan. Home: 9817 4 Points Rd Rocky Ridge MD 21778-9726 Office: St John Regional Cath Sch 114 E 2nd St Frederick MD 21701-5360 Office Phone: 301-662-6722. E-mail: ebsjres@yahoo.com.

BRAUER, KEITH E., medical products executive; b. Palatine, Ill. BS, Ind. U., 1970; MBA, U. Mich., 1973. Assoc. fin. analyst, internat. oper. Eli Lilly, 1974—76, staff fin. analyst, pharm. divsn., 1976—77, mktg. analyst, 1977—78; bus. planning coord. Eli Lilly, Med. Devices, Diagnostics Divsn.,

1978—81, admin.; contr. Elizabeth Arden, Inc., 1981—84; v.p., fin. treas. Physio-Control Corp., 1984—86; dir. corp. affairs Eli Lilly, 1986—88, exec. dir. internat. fin., 1988, exec. dir., fin. and chief acctg. officer; v.p., CFO Guidant Corp., Indpls., 1994—. Mem.: U. Mich. Bus. Sch. Corp. Adv. Bd., Comm. Hosp. Indpls., Fin. Exec. Inst., Ind. Mus. Art (bd of trustee), Beta Gamma Sigma. Mailing: PO Box 44906 Indianapolis IN 46244 Office: Guidant 111 Monument Cl 2900 Indianapolis IN 46204-5129

BRAUER, SASHA GERRITSON, church musician, music educator; b. North Hampton, Mass., July 9, 1972; d. Stephen Lawrence Gerritson and Alicen Jean McGowan; m. Todd Lawrence Brauer, Sept. 22, 2001. MusB, Northeastern Ill. U., 1994, MusM, 1996; post master's cert., DePaul U., 1999. Exec. dir., founder L'Opera Piccola, Chgo., 1995—; dept. chair, faculty Merit Sch. Music, Chgo., 1996—; asst. to Daniel Barenboim Chgo. Symphony Orch., 1999—2001; part-time faculty Harold Washington Coll., Chgo., 2000—01; artistic dir. Happiness Club for Kids, Chgo., 2000—; part-time faculty Northeastern Ill. U., Chgo., 2000—; min. music Park Ridge Cmty. Ch., Ill., 2000—. Composer: (musical theatre work) Rumpelstiltskin, 1996. Recipient Talent award for artistic achievement, MacDowell Artists Assn., Chgo., 1991, Joan Sachs/Neill Found., Chgo., 1994, Harold Berlinger/Neill Found., 1996. Mem.: The Nation, Am. Choral Dirs. Assn. Democrat. United Church Of Christ. Avocations: professional opera singer, writing, reading. Office: L Opera Piccola 5239 N LaCrosse Ave Chicago IL 60630 E-mail: sasha@loperapiccola.org.

BRAUER, STEPHEN FRANKLIN, diplomat, manufacturing company executive; b. Sept. 3, 1945; s. Arthur John, Jr. and Jane (Franklin) B.; m. Camilla Cary Thompson, June 12, 1971; children: Blackford Fitzhugh, Rebecca Randolph, Stephen Franklin, Jr. Student, Washington and Lee U., 1963-64; BA, Westminster Coll., 1967; LLD (hon.), 1997. Sales and mktg. ofcl. Hunter Engring. Co., St. Louis, 1971-78, exec. v.p., 1978-81, pres., 1981-2001; U.S. amb. to Belgium, 2001—03. Bd. dirs. Boatmen's Trust Co., St. Louis, 1986-96; ptnr. St. Louis Cardinals baseball club, 1996—; pvt. client bd. Bank of Am., 1996—. Civilian aide Sec. Army, 1991-95; trustee Mo. Bot. Garden, 1988—; trustee Washington U., St. Louis, 1991—; mem. Mo. 21st Jud. Dist. Commn., 1992-96; hon. consul Govt. Belgium, 1987-2001; mem. nat. bd. Smithsonian Instn., Washington, 1993-99. 1st lt. C.E., AUS, 1968-70. Recipient St. Louis Regional Commerce Growth Assn. Tech. award, 1993, Recognition of Outstanding Bus. Leadership award U.S. Ho. of Reps., 1993, Dean's award Washington U. Sch. Engring., 1998, Spirit of Enterprise award Mo. Rep. Party, 1999, Henry Shaw Medal, M. Bot. Gardens, 2003. Mem. St. Louis Consular Corps., St. Louis (Mo.) Civic Progress, St. Louis Country Club, Everglades Club (Palm Beach). Republican. Episcopalian. Home: 9630 Ladue Rd Saint Louis MO 63124-1311 Office: 11250 Hunter Dr Saint Louis MO 63044-2306 Personal E-mail: sfbrauer@hunter.com.

BRAUERMAN, MELANIE, writer; b. Iowa City, Iowa, Oct. 9, 1960; d. Myles Norman Braverman and June Evelyn (Rotman) Braveman. Student, U. Iowa, 1979, The Evergreen State Coll., 1980—81. Programs adminstr. Fine Arts Work Ctr., Provincetown, Mass., 1998—. Author: (novels) Easy Justice, 1996. Recipient finalist, Mass. Cultural Coun., 1996; fellow poetry fellow, 1996. Office: Fine Arts Work Ctr 24 Pearl St Provincetown MA 02657 Home and Studio: Apt 5 633 Commercial St Provincetown MA 02657-1776

BRAUGHER, ANDRE, actor; b. Chgo., July 1, 1962; m. Amy Brabson, 1991; 2 children. MA, Julliard Coll. TV series include: Kojak (ABC Saturday Mystery), 1989-90, Homicide: Life on the Street, 1993—98 (Emmy award for Outstanding Lead Actor in a Drama Series 1998), Gideon's Crossing, 2000-01, Hack, 2002-04, Thief, 2005-; TV movies include: The Court-Martial of Jackie Robinson, 1990, Murder in Mississippi, 1990, Somebody Has to Shoot the Picture, 1990, Without Warning: Terror in the Towers, 1993, Simple Justice, 1993, Class of '61, 1993, Without Warning: Terror in the Towers, 1993, The Tuskegee Airmen, 1995, Passing Glory, 1999, Love Songs, 1999, 10,000 Black Men Named George, 2002, Soldier's Girl, 2003, Salem's Lot, 2004; film appearances include: Glory, 1989, Striking Distance, 1993, Primal Fear, 1996, Get on the Bus, 1996, City of Angels, 1998, Thick as Thieves, 1998, All the Rage, 1999, A Better Way to Die, 2000, Frequency, 2000, Duets, 2000; stage appearances include: Twelfth Night, 1989, Othello, 1990, The Way of the World, 1991, Richard II, 1994, Shakespeare in the Park, Festival in New York, Henry V.*

BRAULT, GERARD JOSEPH, French language educator; b. Chicopee Falls, Mass., Nov. 7, 1929; s. Philias J. and Aline E. (Rémillard) B.; m. Jeanne Lambert Pepin, Jan. 23, 1954; children: Francis Gerard, Anne-Marie Welsh, Suzanne Eveline Dannenmueller. AB, Assumption Coll., Worcester, Mass., 1950, DLitt, 1976; AM cum laude, Laval U., 1952; PhD, U. Pa., 1958. Teaching fellow U. Pa., 1954-56, assoc. prof. Romance langs., 1961-65, vice dean Grad. Sch., 1962-65; instr. French Bowdoin Coll., Brunswick, Maine, 1957-59, asst. prof. French, 1959-61; prof. French Pa. State U., University Park, 1965-90, Disting. prof. French and medieval studies, 1990, Edwin Erle Sparks prof. French and medieval studies, 1990-97, head dept. French, 1965-70, Edwin Erle Sparks prof. emeritus French and medieval studies, 1998—. Fellow Inst. Arts and Humanistic Studies, 1976—; dir. NDEA Summer Insts., Bowdoin Coll., 1961, 62, Assumption Coll., 1964; Fulbright fellow, Strasbourg, France, 1956-57, Fulbright rsch. scholar and Guggenheim fellow, Strasbourg, 1968-69; sr. fellow in Can. studies, Quebec City, 1984, Camargo Found. fellow, Cassis, France, 1987, 94. Author: Celestine: A Critical Edition of the First French Translation (1527) of the Spanish Classic La Celestina, 1963, Cours de langue française destiné aux jeunes Franco-Américains, 1963, rev. edits., 1965, 69, Early Blazon, 1972, rev. edit., 1997, Eight Thirteenth-Century Rolls of Arms in French and Anglo-Norman Blazon, 1973 (prix Paul Adam-Even), The Song of Roland: An Analytical Edition (named outstanding book Choice 1979), 2 vols., 1978, La Chanson de Roland: Student Edition, 1984; The French-Canadian Heritage in New England, 1986, Rolls of Arms of Edward I (1272-1307) (Aspilogia III), 2 vols., 1997 (Bickersteth medal, Riquer prize); mem. editl. bd. French Forum, 1975—, Purdue U. Monographs, 1978—; contbr. articles to profl. jours. Mem. Cath. Commn. on Intellectual and Cultural Affairs, also, Comité de Vie Franco-Américaine, Société Historique Franco-Américaine. Served with CIC, U.S. Army, 1951-53. Decorated Palmes Académiques French Ministry Edn., 1965, officer, 1975; officer, Ordre National du Mérite, 1980, Ordre des Francophones d'Amérique, 1980; recipient Faculty Scholar medal Pa. State U., 1981, Class of 1933 Humanities award, Pa. State U., 1987 Fellow Soc. Antiquaries of London, Heraldry Soc. London, Medieval Acad. Am. (adv. bd. Speculum 1972-75), Académie Internationale d'Héraldique; mem. MLA, Société Rencesvals pour l'étude des épopées romanes (pres. 1985-88, pres. Am.-Canadian br. 1970-73, editorial bd. Olifant 1975—), Am. Assn. Tchrs. French, Middle Atlantic Conf. Canadian Studies (pres. 1981-83), Internat. Arthurian Soc., Harleian Soc. (council 1987-98). Office: Pa State U Burrowes Bldg Rm 325 University Park PA 16802 Office Phone: 814-865-1492. Business E-Mail: gjb2@psu.edu.

BRAULT, JAMES WILLIAM, physicist; b. New London, Wis., Feb. 10, 1932; s. Lucian Joseph and Alvina Lucy (Boville) B.; m. Margueritte Elaine Bryan, June 29, 1952 (div. May 1986); children: Stephen Michael, Lisa Lynn, Jennifer Elaine; m. Lynda Margaret Harris Faires, July 5, 1992. BS in Physics, U. Wis., 1953; student, Cornell U., 1953-55; PhD in Physics, Princeton U., 1962. Research staff member project Matterhorn Princeton U., N.J., 1955-57, instr., 1961-64; asst. physicist Kitt Peak Nat. Obs., Tucson, 1964-68, assoc. physicist, 1969-70; physicist Nat. Solar Obs., Tucson, 1971-94; rsch. assoc. U. Colo., Boulder, Colo., 1994—. Conbtr. articles to profl. jours. Recipient Alexander von Humboldt award (Rep. of Germany), 1986-87. Fellow Optical Soc. Am.; mem. Am. Phys. Soc., Am. Geophysical Union. Democrat. Address: 1006 Honeysuckle Ln Louisville CO 80027-1096

BRAUMAN, JOHN I., chemist, educator; b. Pitts., Sept. 7, 1937; s. Milton and Freda E. (Schlitt) B.; m. Sharon Lea Kruse, Aug. 22, 1964; 1 dau., Kate Andrea. BS, MIT, 1959; PhD (NSF fellow), U. Calif., Berkeley, 1963. NSF postdoctoral fellow UCLA, 1962-63; asst. prof. chemistry Stanford (Calif.) U., 1963-69, asso. prof., 1969-72, prof., 1972-80, J.G. Jackson-C.J. Wood prof. chemistry, 1980—, chmn. dept., 1979-83, 95-96, cognizant dean phys. scis., 1999—2003. Cons. in phys. organic chemistry; adv. panel chemistry divsn. NSF, 1974-78; adv. panel NASA, AEC, ERDA, Rsch. Corp., Office Chemistry and Chem. Tech., NRC; coun. Gordon Rsch. Confs., 1989-95, trustee, 1991-95. Mem. editl. adv. bd. Jour. Am. Chem. Soc., 1976-83, Jour. Organic Chemistry, 1974-78, Nouveau Jour. de Chimie, 1977-85, Chem. Revs., 1978-80, Chem. Kinetics, 1987-89, Accts. Chem. Rsch., 1995-97, 98-2001; bd. trustees Ann. Revs., 1995—, mem. editl. adv. bd.; dep. editor for phys. scis. Sci., 1985-2000, chair sr. editl. bd., 2000—. Alfred P. Sloan fellow, 1968-70, Guggenheim fellow, 1978-79; Christensen fellow Oxford U., 1983-84, Nat. Medal of Science award, 2002. Fellow AAAS (chmn. sect. 1996-97, mem.-at-large sect. 1997-99), Calif. Acad. Scis. (hon.); mem. NAS (home sec. 2003-, Award in Chem. Scis. 2001), Am. Acad. Arts and Scis., Am. Philos. Soc., Am. Chem. Soc. (award in pure chemistry 1973, Harrison Howe award, 1976, R.C. Fuson award, 1986, James Flack Norris award 1986, Arthur C. Cope scholar, 1986, Linus Pauling medal 2002, J. Willard Gibbs medal 2003, exec. com. phys. chemistry divsn., com. on sci. 1992-97), Sigma Xi, Phi Lambda Upsilon. Home: 849 Tolman Dr Palo Alto CA 94305-1025 Office: Stanford U Dept Chemistry Stanford CA 94305-5080

BRAUMILLER, ALLEN SPOONER, gas industry executive, geologist; b. Texarkana, Tex., Feb. 1, 1934; s. Jack and Jenie (Spooner) B.; m. Patsy Lois McCoy, Dec. 23, 1955; children: Allen Spoonr, Dana Ruth Braumiller Nance, Adrienne Brevard, Colin McCoy. Student, Tulane U., 1952-53; BS, U. Miss., 1955; MS, U. Ill., 1957. Sr. exploration geologist Carter Oil Co. (merged into Humble Oil & Refining Co. 1961), 1957-69; v.p., exploration geologist Helmerich & Payne, Inc., Tulsa, 1969-96, ret., 1996; pres. Braumiller & Braumiller, Inc., Tulsa, 1995—; mgr. Est Tex. Seismic Data, LLC, Tulsa, 1996—. Geol. cons. No. Ill. Natural Gas, Urbana, 1956-57. Elder area Presbyn. ch.; mem. Philbrook Mus. Art, Tulsa, Thomas Gilcrease Mus., Tulsa. Mem. Am. Assn. Petroleum Geologists, Geol. Soc. Am., Am. Assn. Profl. Landmen, Ill. Geol. Soc., Oklahoma City Geol. Soc., Tulsa Geol. Soc., Soc. Petroleum Engrs., Archaeol. Inst. Am., Internat. Assn. Energy Advs., Internat. Platform Assn., Internat. Wine and Food Soc., Tulsa C. of C., U.S. C. of C., Nat. Trust for Historic Preservation, Knife and Fork Club, Petroleum Club (bd. dirs. 1989-92). Republican. Avocations: reef diving, cycling, swimming, gardening, music. Home: 4979 E 113th St Tulsa OK 74137-7607 also: Braumiller & Braumiller Inc Philtower Bldg 427 S Boston Ave Ste 500 Tulsa OK 74103-4118 Address: 5105 E Belle Fontaine Beach Rd Ocean Springs MS 39564 Office Phone: 918-582-2300. E-mail: patbrau@cs.com.

BRAUN, BRUCE NEAL, school system administrator; b. Milw., Wis., June 20, 1955; s. James Herbert and Verna Mae Braun; m. Jayne Louise Prichs, Apr. 29, 1978; children: Dan, Brett, Cara. Degree, Concordia Tchrs. Coll., 1978, Sagnow Valley State U., 1986. Tchr. Lutheran North HS, Macomb, Mich., 1978—81, counselor, 1981—84, guidance tchr., 1984—90; asst. prin. Lutheron Westland HS, Westland, 1990—93; prin. Goandian Lutheran, Dearborn, 1993—99; asst. supt. Mich. Dist. LCMS, Ann Arbor, 1999—. Mem. comm. com. Lutheran Bd. Assn. Conf., Detroit, 1996; program co-chair MANS Conf., Detroit, 2002; mem. mktg. bd. MANS, Lansing, Mich., 2003; writing team mem. LCMS Program, 2005; spkr. in field. Chairperson We. Wayne County, Westland, 2003; vice-chair Gospel, Cleve., 2003—; ednl. chair St. Lutheran We. Ch., Wayne, Mich., 2002; chairperson Macomb County Luthern Brotherhood, Clinton Twp., Mich., 1988. Vis. scholar Detroit Lutheran Schs. grant, Thrivent, 2002—03. Mem.: Confedex, Lutheran Edn. Assn. Lutheran. Avocations: reading, fishing, gardening, athletics. Home: 2061 W Williams Cir Westland MI 48185 Office: Lutheran Ch Mich Dist 3773 Geddes Rd Ann Arbor MI 48104

BRAUN, DAVID A(DLAI), lawyer; b. N.Y.C., Apr. 23, 1931; s. Morris and Betty Braunstein; m. Merna Feldman, Dec. 18, 1955; children: Lloyd Jeffrey, Kenneth Franklin, Evan Albert. AB, Columbia U., 1952, LLB, 1954. Bar: N.Y. 1955, Calif. 1974. Assoc. Ellis, Ellis and Ellis, N.Y.C., 1954—56, Davis and Gilbert, 1956—57; ptnr. Pryor, Braun, Cashman & Sherman, 1957—73, Hardee, Barovick, Konecky & Braun, N.Y.C., 1973, L.A., 1974—81; pres., CEO Polygram Records, Inc., N.Y.C., 1980—81; counsel Wyman, Bautzer, Rothman, Kuchel & Silbert, L.A., 1982—85; ptnr. Braun, Margolis, Burrill & Besser, L.A., 1985—87; counsel Silverberg, Rosen, Leon & Behr, 1987—89, Silverberg, Katz, Thompson & Braun, 1989—91; spl. counsel Proskauer, Rose, Goetz & Mendelsohn, 1991—93; ptnr. Monasch Plotkin & Braun, 1993—94; pvt. practice, 1994—98; sr. counsel Akin, Gump, Strauss, Hauer & Feld, L.L.P., 1998—. Adj. prof. U. So. Calif. Sch. Cinema-TV; guest lectr. UCLA Ext.; adv. com. Ctr. for Law, Media and the Arts, Columbia U. Sch. Law; internat. adv. bd. Nat. Inst. Entertainment and Media Law, Southwestern U. Sch. Law. Bd. visitors Columbia Coll., 1980-86, Columbia Law Sch., 1992-94; bd. dirs. Reprise! Broadway's Best in Concert, Musician's Assistance Program, 1994-98, Tu 'Um EST Cmty. Drug Rehab. Ctr., Rock and Roll Hall of Fame, 1985-93. Mem. Assn. of City of N.Y., L.A. County Bar Assn., Beverly Hills Bar Assn., Nat. Acad. TV Arts and Scis. (pres. N.Y. chpt. 1972-73), NATAS, Am. Arbitration Assn., Hollywood Radio and TV Soc. (bd. dirs. 1983-86), Sigma Chi, Phi Alpha Delta. Jewish. Office: Akin Gump Strauss Hauer & Feld LLP 24th Fl 2029 Century Park St Los Angeles CA 90067 Home: 1035 Alston Rd Montecito CA 93108-2407 Office Phone: 805-969-6626. Business E-Mail: dbraun@dslextreme.com.

BRAUN, EUNICE HOCKSPEIER, religious order executive, author, lecturer; b. Alta Vista, Iowa; d. George Phillip and Lydia (Reinhart) Hockspeier; m. Leonard James Braun, May 29, 1937. Student, Gates Coll., 1932-34, Coe Coll., 1941-43, Northwestern U., 1944-47. Freelance writer for mags., newspapers, 1947-52; bus. mgr. Baha'i Publishing Trust, Wilmette, Ill., 1952-55, mng. dir., 1955-71; internat. news editor Baha'i News, 1952-70; tchr. Baha'i schs., Alaska, Can., Europe and U.S., 1958—. Lectr. Baha'i Faith in U.S., Central Am., Europe, Africa, Asia, 1953—; cons. Baha'i Pub. Trust, New Delhi, India, 1972; mem. aux. bd. Continental Bd. Counselors, Baha'i Faith in the Ams., 1972-86. Author: Know Your Baha'i Literature, 1959; The Dawn of World Peace, 1963; Baha'u'llah: His Call to the Nations, 1967; From Strength to Strength, Half Century of the Formative Age of the Baha'i Faith, 1978; A Crown of Beauty, 1982; The March of the Institutions, 1984; A Reader's Guide: The Development of Baha'i Literature in English, 1986; From Vision to Victory, 1993; contbr. essays to Baha'i World, Internat. Record. Mem. Nat. League Am. Pen Women, Baha'i Faith, Iota Sigma Epsilon. Home: 1025 Forestview Ln Glenview IL 60025-4433 E-mail: sprucelawn@aol.com.

BRAUN, GUSTAV MILAN, otolaryngologist, surgeon; b. Mar. 8, 1938; BA in Chemistry, Wayne State U., 1962; MS, U. Iowa, 1971; MD, U. Mich., 1965. Diplomate Am. Bd. Otolaryngology. Intern UCLA Affiliated Hosps., 1965-66; resident in surgery Wadsworth VA Hosp., L.A., 1966-67; resident in ear, nose, throat and facial plastic surgery U. Iowa Hosps., Iowa City, 1967-71; asst. prof. facial plastic surgery and otolaryngology Sch. Medicine U. Calif., San Diego, 1974-76; pvt. practice Calif., 1977-78, Harlingen, Tex., 1979-91, Houston, 1992-2000, Mineral Wells, Tex., 2001, Palo Pinto Gen. Hosp., Mineral Wells, 2001—. Clin. asst. prof. Baylor Coll. Medicine, Houston, 1992-2001. Maj. U.S. Army, 1966-73. Fellow ACS, Am. Acad. Facial Plastic and Reconstructive Surgery, Am. Acad. Otolaryngology-Head and Neck Surgery; mem. Tex. Med. Assn, Rotary Internat. (Paul Harris fellow). Office: PO Box 1527 Mineral Wells TX 76068-1527 E-mail: gmbraun@cox-internet.com.

BRAUN, JEFFREY LOUIS, lawyer; b. NYC, Oct. 2, 1946; s. Arthur and Berta (Freimark) B.; m. Beth Essig, June 6, 1982; children: Arthur Paul, Emily Claire. BA, Rutgers U., 1968; JD, Yale U., 1971. Bar: N.Y. 1974, U.S. Dist. Ct. (so. and ea. dists.) N.Y., U.S. Tax Ct., U.S. Ct. Appeals (2d cir.), U.S. Ct. Appeals (9th cir.), U.S. Supreme Ct. Law clk. to Judge Harry Pregerson U.S. Dist. Ct. (cen. dist.) Calif., L.A., 1971—72; assoc. Paul, Weiss, Rifkind, Wharton & Garrison, N.Y.C., 1972—74, Rosenman & Colin LLP, N.Y.C., 1974—80, ptnr., 1980—2002; of counsel Kramer Levin Naftalis & Frankel LLP, N.Y.C., 2002—. Mem. N.Y. State Bar Assn. (co-chair com. on real estate litigation 2005—), Assn. of the Bar of the City of N.Y. (com. on internat. human rights 1985-88, com. on mcpl. affairs 1988-91, com. on recruitment and retention of lawyers 1992-94, long-range planning com. 1994-97), Fed. Bar Coun. (com. on cts. of the second cir. 1995—). Home: 15 Park Rd Irvington NY 10533-2008 Office: Kramer Levin Naftalis & Frankel LLP 1177 Ave of Americas New York NY 10036 Office Phone: 212-715-7830. Business E-Mail: jbraun@kramerlevin.com.

BRAUN, JEROME IRWIN, lawyer; b. St. Joseph, Mo., Dec. 16, 1929; s. Martin H. and Bess (Donsker) B.; children: Aaron, Susan, Daniel; m. Dolores Ferriter, Aug. 16, 1987. AB with distinction, Stanford U., 1951, LLB, 1953. Bar: Mo. 1953, Calif. 1953, U.S. Dist. Ct. (no. dist.) Calif., U.S. Tax Ct., U.S. Ct. Mil. Appeals, U.S. Supreme Ct., U.S. Ct. Appeals (9th cir.). Assoc. Long & Levit, San Francisco, 1957-58, Law Offices of Jefferson Peyser, San Francisco, 1958-62; founding ptnr. Farella, Braun & Martel (formerly Elke, Farella & Braun), San Francisco, 1962—. Instr. San Francisco Law Sch., 1958-69; mem. U.S. Dist. Ct. Civil Justice Reform Act Adv. Com., 1991—; spkr. various state bar convs. in Calif., Ill., Nev., Mont.; requent moderator/participant continuing edn. of bar programs; past chmn. 9th Cir. Sr. Adv. Bd., past chmn. lawyer reps. to 9th Cir. Jud. Conf.; mem. appellate lawyers liaison com. Calif. Ct. Appeals 1st dist.; jud.conf. U.S. Com. Long Range Planning; founder Jon Samuel Abramson Scholarship Endowment Stanford U. Law. Revising editor: Stanford U. Law Rev.; contbr. articles to profl. jours. Mem. Jewish Community Fedn. San Francisco, The Peninsula, Marin and Sonoma Counties, pres., 1979-80; past pres. United Jewish Community Ctrs. 1st lt. JAGC, U.S. Army, 1954-57, U.S. Army Res., 1957-64. Recipient Lloyd W. Dinkelspiel Outstanding Young Leader award Jewish Welfare Fedn., 1967, Professionalism award 9th cir. Am. Inns of Ct., 1999, John Frank award, 2005. Fellow Am. Acad. Appellate Lawyers, Am. Coll. Trial Lawyers (teaching trial and appellate advocacy com.), Am. Bar Found.; mem. ABA, Calif. Bar Assn. (chmn. adminstrn. justice com. 1977), Bar Assn. San Francisco (spl. com. on lawyers malpractice and malpractice ins.), San Francisco Bar Found. (past trustee), Calif. Acad. Appellate Lawyers (past pres., mem. U.S. Dist. Ct. Civil Justice Reform Act adv. com., Calif. Ct. of Appeals 1st Dist. Appellate Lawyers liaison com., jud. conf. of the U.S., com. on long-range planning, panelist 1994), Am. Judicature Soc. (past dir.), Stanford Law Sch. Bd. of Visitors, U.S. Dist. Ct. of No. Dist. Calif. Hist. Soc. (past pres., bd. dirs.), 9th Cir. Ct. of Appeals Hist. Soc. (past. pres.), Mex.-Am. Legal Def. Fund (honoree), Order of Coif. E-mail: jbraun@fbm.com.

BRAUN, LILIAN JACKSON, writer; Author: The Cat Who Could Read Backwards, 1966, The Cat Who Ate Danish Modern, 1968, The Cat Who Turned On And Off, 1968, The Cat Who Saw Red, 1986, The Cat Who Played Brahms, 1987, The Cat Who Played Post Office, 1987, The Cat Who Knew Shakespeare, 1988, The Cat Who Sniffed Glue, 1988, The Cat Who Had Fourteen Tales, 1988, The Cat Who Went Underground, 1989, The Cat Who Talked to Ghosts, 1990, The Cat Who Lived High, 1990, The Cat Who Knew A Cardinal, 1991, The Cat Who Wasn't There, 1992, The Cat Who Moved A Mountain, 1992, The Cat Who Went Into The Closet, 1993, The Cat Who Came to Breakfast, 1994, The Cat Who Blew the Whistle, 1995, The Cat Who Smelled a Rat, 2001, The Cat Who Went Up the Creek, 2002, The Cat Who Talked Turkey, 2004, The Cat Who Went Bananas, 2005.

BRAUN, LLOYD, Internet company executive; b. Long Island; Grad., Vassar Coll.; JD, U. Calif. Hastings Sch. Law. Atty. corp. transactions Stroock & Stroock & Lavan, 1983—84; entertainment atty. Silverberg, Rosen, Leon & Behr, 1985—89; pres. Brillstein-Grey Entertainment, 1994—98; chmn. Buena Vista TV Prodns., 1998—99; co-chmn. ABC TV Entertainment Group, 1999—2002, chmn., 2002—04; head entertainment and media div. Yahoo! Inc., 2004—. Vice chmn. Lauri Strauss Leukemia Found.; bd. trustees Vassar Coll. Office: Yahoo 701 1st Ave Sunnyvale CA 94089

BRAUN, LUDWIG, retired education educator; b. Bklyn., May 14, 1926; s. Ludwig and Wetie (Schmidt) B.; m. Eva Margaret Taylor, Sept. 7, 1947; children: Barbara Ann, Edith Elizabeth, Anne Catherine, John Ludwig. BEE, Poly. Inst. Bklyn., 1950, MEE, 1955, DEE, 1959. Elec. engr. Allied Control Co., N.Y.C., 1950-51; head electronics dept. Anton Electronics Labs., Inc., Bklyn., 1951-55; from instr. elec. engring. to prof. sys. and elec. engring. Poly. Inst. Bklyn., 1955-72; prof. engring. SUNY, Stony Brook, 1972-82, dir. bioengring. program, 1976-79, dir. personal computers in edn. lab., 1979-82; prof. computer sci., dir. acad. computing lab. N.Y. Inst. Tech., Central Islip, 1982-87; rsch. prof. NYU, N.Y.C., 1987-89; ret., 1989. Sr. fellow C.W. Post Campus, L.I.U., 1998-2004; dir. Nat. Inst. Microcomputer Based Learning, 1981-87, Intercounty Tchr. Resource Ctr., 1985-87, Mecklenburger Group, 1993-96; lectr., med. scientist Downstate Med. Ctr., 1970-82; cons. ednl. tech., 1990—, Vertol divsn. Boeing Co., GE, Ford Found., NSF, Nat. Inst. Edn., IBM, NET Schs., Inc.; tech. advisor Orton Soc., Suffolk. Author: (with E. Mishkin) Adaptive Control Systems, 1961; contbg. author: Signals and Systems in Electrical Engineering, 1962, Perry's Chemical Engineering Handbook, 1961, System Engineering Handbook, 1965, Computer Techniques in Biomedicine and Medicine, 1973, Vision Test Recommendations for American Education Decision Makers, 1990, Celebrating Success, 1995. Mem. Women's Action Alliance, 1985-88; bd. dirs. Playing To Win, Inc., 1983-90, Internat. Coun. for Computers in Edn., 1987-89. With AUS, 1944-46. First recipient Paul Pair award for contbns. to edn. through tech., Nat. Ednl. Computing Assn. Pioneer award in Ednl. Tech., 1999; fellow Global Village Schs. Inst., 1996-98. Mem. IEEE (sr. 1990), Internat. Soc. for Tech. in Edn. (bd. dirs. 1989-90), Sigma Xi, Tau Beta Pi, Eta Kappa Nu. Home: 11 Parsons Dr Dix Hills NY 11746-5217 E-mail: ludbraun@optonline.net.

BRAUN, MARK EDWARD, urban studies professor; b. Milw., Apr. 12, 1963; s. Roger Joseph and Mary Loduha Braun. BA in Econs. and History, U. Wis., 1987; MA in History, U. Wis., River Falls, 1989; PhD in Urban Studies, U. Wis., Milw., 1999. Pres. Braun Enterprises, Milw., 1990—98; urban rschr. Non-profit Data Ctr., Milw., 1998—2000; prof. SUNY, Cobleskill, 2000—. Cons. Emerlad Found., Milw., 1999—2000. Author: History of Milwaukee's Social Development Commission, 1992, Social Change and the Empowerment of the Poor, 2002; Empowerment of the Poor, Neoeclectic Movement: 1971-1985, 2005; contbr. articles to profl. jours., chapters to books. Pub. educator County Hist. Soc., Milw., 1992—95, Ctrl. Pub. Libr., Milw., 1995—96, Hist. Milw. Walking Tours, 1996—99. Mem.: Urban Hist. Assn. (assoc.), Am. Sociol. Assn. (assoc.), Urban Affairs Assn. (assoc.). Independent. Roman Catholic. Avocation: outdoor silent sports. Home: PO Box 61 Cobleskill NY 12043-0061 Office: SUNY Cobleskill Ryder Hall 106 134 Schenectady Ave Ryder Hall 106 Cobleskill NY 12043 Office Phone: 518-255-5798. Business E-Mail: braunme@cobleskill.edu.

BRAUN, MARY LUCILE DEKLE (LUCY BRAUN), physical therapist, consultant, counseling administrator, educator; b. Tampa, Fla. d. Guthrie "Gus" J. and Lucile (Culpepper) Dekle; children: John Ryan, Matthew Joseph, Jeffrey William, Douglas Edwin. AB, Brenau Coll.; MA, U. Cen. Fla.; EdD, U. Fla. Cert. disability mgmt. specialist, rehab. counselor, victim advocate; lic. mental health counselor; lic. marriage and family therapist; nationally cert. counselor. Coord. Orange County Child Abuse Prevention, Orlando, Fla., 1983-88; cons. Displaced Homemaker Program, Orlando, 1989-94, DCS, Oviedo, Fla., 1990-92. Adj. prof. U. Ctrl. Fla., Orlando, Troy State U.; clin. dir. Response Sexual Abuse Treatment Program, 1993—95; mem. adv. bd. Fla. Hosp. Women's Ctr., Orlando, 1989—; bd. dirs. Parent Resource Ctr., Orlando, Children With Attention Deficit Disorders, Orlando, 1989—91; cons. program devel. for children and adolescent treatment svcs., 1997—98; dir. clin. svcs. Rehab. and Indsl. Counseling, 1997—; cons., counselor contractor VA; counselor Share the Care Program. Author: Someone Heard, 1987, Humor Us Soup, 1989, Child Abuse and Neglect: Resource Guide for Orange County Schools, 1985, 2d edit., 1987; contbg. author: Death from Child Abuse, 1986, Personality Types of Abusive Parents, 1993, Why Children Fight, 1992. Sustaining mem. Jr. League of Greater Orlando. Program recipient Cmty. Svc. award Walt Disney World, 1987. Mem. ACA, Fla. Counseling Assn., Nat. Bd. Cert. Counselors, Phi Kappa Phi, Kappa Delta Pi, Chi Sigma Iota, Alpha Delta Pi. Avocations: scuba diving, sailing, puzzles. Office Phone: 407-423-5311.

BRAUN, MICHAEL ANDREW, radiologist; b. Shorewood, Wis., Sept. 30, 1959; s. Roger John and Mary Braun; m. Theresa Maria Dimitsopoulos, Sept. 17, 1994; children: Katherine Nicole, Alexander Joseph. BS, Marquette U., 1982; MD, U. Wis., 1986. Resident in diagnostic radiology Albany (NY) Med. Ctr., 1987—91; fellow in interventional radiology Northwestern U., Chgo., 1991—92; asst. prof. radiology Northwestern Meml. Hosp., Chgo., 1992—95; pvt. practie St. Mary's Radiologists, Milw., 1995—2000, pres., CEO, 1998—2000; med. dir. radiology St. Mary's Hosp., Milw., 1998—2002; chief interervention radiology Wis. Radiology Specialists, Milw., 2000—. Author: Interventional Radiology Procedure Manual, 1997; contbr. articles to profl. publs. Fellow: Am. Coll. Chest Physicians; mem.: Milw. Roentgen Ray Soc. (sec.-treas. 2000—02, v.p. 2003—), Soc. Interventional Radiology. Avocations: Alpine skiing, bicycling. Office: Wis Radiology Specialists 1045 Glen Oaks Ln Mequon WI 53092

BRAUN, PAUL, materials scientist, educator; PhD, U of Ill., Urbana, 1998. Assoc. prof. U of Ill., Urbana, 1999—. Contbr. articles to profl. jours. Grantee numerous grants. Office: U of Illinois 1304 West Green St Urbana IL 61801 Office Phone: 217-244-7293. E-mail: pbraun@uiuc.edu.

BRAUN, RICHARD J., lab administrator; Officer, dir., fin. svcs. Am. Express Fin. Advisors, 1976—88; CDO, dir. DST Sys., Kemper Fin. Svcs., 1976—88; exec. v.p., COO, dir. Reich and Tang L.P., 1989—91; COO, dir. EBP, Inc., 1992—94; pvt. investor, mgmt. cons., 1994—96; dir., CEO Medtox Scientific, Inc., St. Paul, 1996—2000, chmn. bd., pres., 2000—. Office: Medtox Scientific Inc 402 W County Rd D Saint Paul MN 55112

BRAUN, STANLEY, orthodontist, educator; s. Max and Sarah Braun; m. Constance Ann Belle, June 25, 1955; children: Lory Susan Wasserman, Stephen Mitchell, Mark Charles. B of Mech. Engring., NYU, 1951, MME, 1952; DDS summa cum laude, Ohio State U., 1963. Lic. Bd. Dentistry Ohio, Ind., Ill., Ky. Asst. chief engr. Master Vibrator Co., Dayton, Ohio, 1956—58; assoc. prof. of orthodontics Ind. U., Indpls., 1965—69; pvt. practice in splty. orthodontics Indpls., 1965—96; clin. prof. of orthodontics U. of Louisville, 1976—95, Vanderbilt U. Med. Ctr., Nashville, 1994—2004, U. of Ill., Chgo., 1995—98, Marquette U., Milw., 1998, St. Louis U., 1999—2001. Rsch. fellow NIH, Washington, 1963—65; cons. in orthodontics to the surgeon gen. Dept. of Health, Washington, 1965—67; editl. bd. Jour., Angle Orthodontic Soc., Edina, Minn., 1995—; guest editor seminars in orthodontics. Contbr. chpt. to textbook; mem. editl. bd.: Am. Jour. Orthodontics and Dentofacial Orthopedics, Jour. Angle Orthodontic Soc., 1995—2005; contbr. articles to profl. jours. 1st lt. USAF, 1952—54. Recipient Don Shusterman Meml. award, Ohio State U., 1963, Cert. of Recognition, NYU Orthodontic Soc., 1970, Disting. award, Am. Soc. of Dentistry for Children, 1963, Cert. of Recognition, Chgo. Dental Soc., 1965, Award of Recognition, Am. Acad. of Dental Medicine, 1975, Callahan Meml. Commn. award, Ohio State U., 1963. Mem.: Tau Beta Pi, Omicron Kappa Epsilon, Pi Tau Sigma. Achievements include Member of Engineering Team that Developed Fusing System for the First U.S. Intercontinental Ballistics Missile; design of Concrete Automatic Troweling Machine. Avocations: travel, stained glass creations, painting.

BRAUN, STEPHEN BAKER, academic administrator; b. Cleve., Nov. 3, 1942; s. William B. and Louise M. (Baker) B.; m. Retta F. Kriefall, June 16, 1974; children: Elizabeth Rachel, Christopher Baker. BS, Xavier U., 1964; MBA, Fairleigh Dickinson U., 1976; postgrad., Imperial Coll., U London, 1996, Portland State U., 2001—. Regional mgr. Northwest Airlines, Inc., St. Paul, 1967-72; v.p. Inflight Motion Pictures, Inc., N.Y.C., 1972-78; v.p., gen. mgr. Columbia Pipe & Supply, Inc., Portland, Oreg., 1978-79; exec. v.p. Golby Mfg. Co., Portland, 1979-80; v.p. fin. Timberline Software, Inc., Portland, 1980-82; pres., founder Computer Systems Supplyware, Inc., Portland, 1982-87; dean Sch. Bus. Concordia U., Portland, 1987-92, exec. v.p., 1993—; COO Concordia U. Found., Portland, 1993-2000, vice chmn., dir., 1985-2000. Mem. bd. regents Concordia U., 1986-87, 92-2000; bd. dirs. Alameda Resources Co., Tigard, Oreg.; vis. scholar grad. sch. bus. Univ. Washington, 2000—; founder, chmn. CEO Roundtable, 1994—; mem. adv. bd. Oreg. Bus. mag., 2002—; nat. keynote spkr., Defense Contract Mgmt. Agy, 2004; exec. panelist McKinsey & Co.'s Quar. Publ., 2004—; cmty. leader Fed. Reserve Bank of San Franciso, 2005—. Com. chmn. United Way, Boston, 1966; bd. dirs. German Am. Found., 1990-2000. With USN, 1964-67. Mem. Oreg. Ctr. for Entrepreneurship (pres., founder, 1986), Oreg. Enterprise Forum, Am. Mktg. Assn. (panelist 1985-88), Assn. Data Processing Systems Orgn., Rotary (long-range planning com. 1985-96, judge Oreg. Enterprise Forum, Entrepreneur of Yr. award 1998, moderator, major league baseball debate, 2003). Lutheran. Office: Concordia U 2811 NE Holman St Portland OR 97211-6099 also: Imperial Coll/Mgmt Sch 53 Princes Gate Exhibition Rd London SW7 2PG England Office Phone: 503-288-9371. E-mail: sbraun@cu-portland.edu.

BRAUN, SUSAN J., foundation administrator; married; 1 child, Alex. BA in English and Sociology, George Mason U.; MA in Health Scis., U. Md.; postgrad. in Internat. Mktg., U. Muenster, Germany. Exec. Pracon Inc. and Ctr. Econ. Studies in Medicine; various positions, Oncology/Immunology Divsn. Bristol-Myers Squibb, Princeton, NJ; pres., CEO Susan G. Komen Breast Cancer Found., 1996—. Bd. mem., staff liaison Intercultural Cancer Coun. Mem. editl. bd.: Breast Jour., C.U.R.E. Mag. Active Americorps NCCC. Recipient Frances Williams Preston award for breast cancer awareness, Vanderbilt-Ingram Cancer Ctr., 2001. Mem.: Am. Soc. Clin. Oncology, World Soc. Breast Health, Am. Soc. for Breast Disease (chair pub. policy com.). Office: Susan G Komen Breast Cancer Found 5005 LBJ Freeway Ste 250 Dallas TX 75244

BRAUN, THOMAS W., academic administrator; b. Pitts. BS in Biology, U. Pitts., 1969, DMD summa cum laude, MS in Pharmacology, U. Pitts., 1973, PhD in Anatomy, 1977. Resident in oral and maxillofacial surgery Presbyn. U. Hosp., Pitts.; instr. in anatomy at Sch. Dental Medicine U. Pitts., 1975—90, assoc. prof., chmn. dept. oral and maxillofacial surgery, 1990—93, assoc. dean hosp. affairs, 1991—96, prof., 1993—, sr. assoc. dean, 1996—99, interim dean Sch. Dental Medicine, 1999—2000, dean Sch. Dental Medicine, 2000—. Contbr. articles to profl. jours. Mem.: Pa. Soc. Oral and Maxillofacial Surgeons (past pres.), Am. Assn. Oral and Maxillofacial Surgery (mem. ho. of dels.), Am. Bd. Oral and Maxillofacial Surgery (past pres.). Office: 3501 Terrace St Pittsburgh PA 15261

BRAUN, URSULA K., gerontologist, educator, researcher; arrived in US, 1995; MD, Ruprecht-Karls U. Heidelberg, Germany, 1993; MPH, U. Tex., Houston, 2003. Diplomate Am. Bd. Internal Medicine (added qualification in geriatrics), Am. Bd. Hospice and Palliative Care. Asst. prof. medicine Baylor Coll. Medicine, Houston, 2001—; staff physician, rsch. scientist Michael E. DeBakey VA Med. Ctr., Houston, 2001—. Mem.: ACP, Gerontol. Soc. Am., Am. Geriat. Soc. (chair, spl. interest group for jr. faculty rsch. career devel. 2004—05). Office: Baylor Coll Medicine 2002 Holcombe Blvd Houston TX 77030 Office Phone: 713-794-8636. Personal E-mail: ursula.braun@gmail.com.

BRAUN, ZEV, motion picture and television producer; b. Chgo. s. Julius and Charlotte (Brandau) B.; children: Benjamin, Jonathan, Jeremy; m. MayLing Cheng, Mar. 22, 1972; 1 child, Sue-Ling. Student, Roosevelt U., Chgo., Marquette U., U. Chgo. Producer: Goldstein, 1964 (U.S. rep. Cannes Film Festival, recipient Prix de la Nouvelle Critique), Wanted: Babysitter, 1974-75, The Little Girl Who Lives Down the Lane, 1976 (Best Horror Film, Acad. Sci-Fi, Fantasy and Horror Films), Freedom Road, 1978, The Fiendish Plot of Dr. Fu Manchu, 1979-80, Marlene, 1984 (Acad. award nomination, N.Y. Film Critics award Nat. Bd. Rev. award, Nat. Soc. Film Critics award), Where Are the Children, 1985, (TV mini-series) Menendez: A Killing in Beverly Hills, 1994, Edges of the Lord, 2000; exec. prodr.: Madron, 1970, Angela, 1977, Murphy's Law, 1987, Stillwatch, 1987, Murder Ordained, 1987, Tour of Duty, 1987, 88, 89, Father Clements, 1987, (TV movie) Abducted: A Father's Love, 1996, Lethal Vows, 1999, Amber Frey: Witness for the Prosecution, 2005; co-prodr.: The Pedestrian, 1973 (Acad. award nomination, Nat. Bd. Rev. award, Golden Globe award), Bagdad Cafe, 1990, Seduction in Travis County, 1991, Split Images, 1992. Bd. dirs. Little City Found., Palatine, Ill., 1962-63; v.p., dir. Gastro-Intestinal Research Found., U. Chgo., 1964-65; v.p. City of Hope, 1970—; gen. chmn. Ann. Salute to Med. Research, 1969; chmn. bd. dirs. Internat. Kidney Inst., UCLA, 1981-83; bd. dirs. Am. Found. AIDS Rsch., 1995, Albert B. Sabin Inst. at Georgetown U., 1996, Heart Touch Project. Jewish. Office: Braun 280 S Beverly Dr Ste 500 Beverly Hills CA 90212-3908 E-mail: braunent@aol.com.

BRAUNER, GARY JULES, dermatologist, cosmetic laser surgeon; b. Bridgeport, Conn., Sept. 14, 1941; s. Charles and Frances (Rabitz) B.; m. Judith Susan Schlosser, Aug. 29, 1965; children: Lisa Michelle, Wendy Ellen. BA magna cum laude, Yale Coll., 1963; MD, Harvard U., 1967. Diplomate Am. Bd. Dermatology, Am. Bd. Pathology in Dermatopathology. Intern Jewish Hosp. of St. Louis, 1967-68; resident in dermatology Mass. Gen. Hosp., Boston, 1968-70, chief resident dermatology, 1970-71; asst. to assoc. clin. prof. dermatology Albert Einstein Coll. of Medicine, Bronx, N.Y., 1971-87; assoc. clin. prof. dermatology NY Med. Coll., Valhalla, 1987-93, Mount Sinai Sch. of Medicine, NYC, 1993—. Chief dermatology Morrisania Hosp., Bronx, 1975-76, North Ctrl. Bronx Hosp., 1976-82; chief dermatology svc. Rikers Island Health Ctr., East Elmhurst, NY, 1975-79; provisional attending physician Englewood (NJ) Hosp., 1975-78, assoc. attending physician, 1978-81, attending physician, dermatology, 1975-, chief dept. dermatology, 1992-2003; attending physician Hackensack Hosp., 1982—; asst. attending Westchester County Med. Ctr., 1987-91, Met. Hosp., NYC, 1987-95; attending physician, dermatology Pascack Valley Hosp., Westwood, NJ, 1992-, Mt. Sinai Med. Ctr., provisional attending dept. dermatology 1993-95, asst. attending, 1995—97; attending Mt. Sinai Med. Ctr., 1997-; lectr. in field. Contbg. editor Hosp. Physician, 1978—, Health Practitioner and Physician's Asst., 1978—; assoc. editor Dialogues in Dermatology, 1978-92, 95—, Jour. of the Am. Acad. of Dermatology, 1988-93, Laser Medicine and Surgery News and Advances, 1988-96; editor The Schoch Letter, 2003—; contbr. numerous articles to profl. jours. Maj. U.S. Army, 1971-74. Fellow Am. Acad. Dermatology (dir. 1992-97), Am. Soc. Dermatol. Soc.; mem. Am. Soc. of Laser Medicine and Surgery, Dermatol. Soc. Greater NY (pres. 1990-91), NY State Dermatol. Soc. (dir.), NJ State Med. Soc., Soc. for Investigative Dermatology, Assn. for Mil. Dermatologists, Internat. Soc. Tropical Dermatology, Bergen County Med. Soc., NJ Dermatol. Soc., Soc. for Pediatric Dermatology, Internat. Soc. for Dermatol. Surgery (dir. 1997-99, treas. 2000-04, sec. 2004—), Internat. Soc. for Pediatric Dermatology, Med. Coun. Skin Cancer Found., NY State Med. Soc., NY County Med. Soc. Avocations: gardening, travel, photography. Office: 125 E 63rd St New York NY 10021-7310 Office Phone: 212-421-5080. E-mail: dermlaser@aol.com.

BRAUNER, RONALD ALLAN, theology studies educator; b. Phila., Aug. 5, 1939; s. Samuel Joseph Brauner and Ann Ruth (Soloner) Levin; m. Marcia Faith Silver, Sept. 9, 1962; children: Yaakov Baruch, Miriam Aliza. Cert. in tchg., Greenberg Inst., Jerusalem, 1960; BS in Edn., Temple U., 1962; PhD, Dropsie Coll., 1974. Cert. tchr., Pa. Assoc. prof. Gratz Coll., Phila., 1967—78; acad. dean Reconstructionist Rabbinical Coll., Phila., 1972—83; dir. Brandeis-Bardin Inst., L.A., 1983—85; exec. dir. Hebrew Inst. Pitts., 1985—91; pres. Found. for Jewish Studies, Inc., Pitts., 1991—. Prof. Jewish studies Siegal Coll. Jewish Studies, 1994—. Editor Jewish Civilization: Essays and Studies, 1979-85, Straightalk, 1991—; author: Being Jewish in a Gentile World: A Survival Guide, 1995, Thinking Jewish: The Art of Living in Two Civilizations, 2001. Democrat. Office: Found for Jewish Studies 1531 S Negley Ave Pittsburgh PA 15217-1419 Office Phone: 412-521-0661. Personal E-mail: rbrauner@att.net. Business E-Mail: rbrauner@siegalcollege.edu.

BRAUNGART, RICHARD GOTTFRIED, social sciences educator, political scientist; b. Balt., Apr. 21, 1935; s. Paul Peter and Jean Mary (Stanton) B.; m. Margaret Lombard Mitchell, Aug. 29, 1964; children— Julia, Katherine, Elizabeth. BA, U. Md., 1961, MA, 1963; PhD, Pa. State U., 1969. Rsch. asst. Bur. Social Sci. Rsch., Washington, 1964; instr. sociology Pa. State U., State College, 1966-69; asst. prof. sociology U. Md., College Park, 1969-72; assoc. prof. sociology Syracuse U., NY, 1972—76, prof. sociology, 1976—2002, prof. internat. rels., 1993—2002, prof. polit. sci., 1998—2002, prof. emeritus, 2003—. Rsch. dir. President's Commn. on Campus Unrest, 1970; vis. lectr. USIA, 1971; prof. assoc. East-West Ctr., Honolulu, 1978; lectr., cons. Nat. U. Mex., 1980, USSR Acad. Scis., Moscow, 1989; German Marshall Fund U.S., Berlin and Fed. Republic Germany, 1990, China Youth Coll. for Politics, Beijing Acad. Social Scis., Shanghai Ctr. Youth Rsch., Shanghai Acad. Social Scis., Ewha U., Seoul, Han Nam U., Taejon, Republic of Korea, 1991, Vista U., U. Pretoria, Potchefstroom U., U. Orange Free State, U. Port Elizabeth, Witwatersrand U., South Africa, 1992, UN, N.Y.C., 1995, 98. Author: Family Status, Socialization and Student Politics, 1979; editor: Society and Politics, 1976, Jour. Polit. and Mil. Sociology, 1983; editor: (assoc.), 1984—; editor: Life Course and Generational Politics, 1984, 1993, The Political Sociology of the State, 1990, Critical Issues in the U.S., 1997—98; editor: (series) Research in Political Sociology, 1985—89; mem. editl. bd.:, 1989—; editor (assoc.): Western Sociol. Rev., 1976—82, Sociol. Spectrum, 1980—83; editor (book rev.) Jour. Polit. and Mil. Sociology, 1977—84; mem. editl. bd.: Sociol. Symposium, 1972—77, Polit. Behavior, 1978—84, Micropolitics, 1980—84, Quar. Jour. Ideology, 1983—90, Bangladesh e-Jour. Sociology, 2004—. With U.S. Army, 1954—56, with USAR, 1956—62. Mem. Am. Sociol. Assn. (polit. sociology sect. co-founder, treas. 1982-84, sect. coun. 1985-88, collective behavior sect. coun. 1984-86), Internat. Soc. Polit. Psychology (nominating com. 1983-84, chmn. nominating com. 1989-90. governing coun. 1989-91, chmn. search com. 1990-91), Internat. Sociol. Assn. (v.p. rsch. com. 1982-90, 98-2002, pres. com. polit. sociology 1994-98), Soc. Study Social Problems (chmn. internat. conflict and coop. divsn. 1984-86, chmn. com. stds, rsch., tchg. 1996-98), Internat. Polit. Sci. Assn. (pres. com. on polit. sociology 1994-98, v.p. rsch. com. 1998-2002). Democrat. Avocations: gardening, jogging, travel. Home: 4783 Armstrong Rd Manlius NY 13104-1418 Office: Syracuse U Dept Sociology Syracuse NY 13244-1090 E-mail: rgbraung@maxwell.syr.edu, rbraung1@twcny.rr.com.

BRAUNSDORF, PAUL RAYMOND, lawyer; b. South Bend, Ind., June 18, 1943; s. Robert Louis and Marjorie Braunsdorf; m. Margaret Buckley, June 18, 1966; children: Christopher, Mark, Douglas, Amy. BA magna cum laude, U. Notre Dame, 1965; LLB, U. Va., 1968. Bar: NY 1968, US Dist Ct (western dist) NY 1969, US Dist Ct (northern dist) NY 1980, US Ct Appeals (2d cir) 1975, US Supreme Ct 1980. Assoc. Harris Beach LLP, Rochester, 1968-75; ptnr., 1976—. Instr Nat Inst Trial Advocacy, Rochester, 1988; lectr in field. Author (contbg auth): (book) Antitrust Health Care Handbook II, 1993, Antitrust Law in New York, 1995, 2d edit., 2002. Bd dirs McQuaid Parent's Club, 1984—90, pres, 1986—87; bd dirs Mercy Parent's Club, 1989—90, Brighton Baseball, 1987—90. Republican. Roman Catholic. Avocations: tennis, photography, music. Office: Harris Beach LLP 99 Garnsey Rd Pittsford NY 14534 Office Phone: 585-419-8603. Business E-Mail: pbraunsdorf@harrisbeach.com.

BRAUNSTEIN, GLENN DAVID, physician, educator; b. Greenville, Tex., Feb. 29, 1944; s. Mervin and Helen (Friedman) B.; m. Jacquelyn D. Moose, July 5, 1965; children: Scott M. Braunstein, Jeffrey T. Braunstein. BS summa cum laude, U. Calif., San Francisco, 1965, MD, 1968. Diplomate Am. Bd. Internal Medicine, subsplty. endocrinology, diabetes, metabolism. Intern, resident Peter Bent Brigham Hosp., Boston, 1968-70; clin. fellow in medicine Harvard U. Med. Sch., Boston, 1969-70; clin. assoc., reproduction rsch. br. NIH, Bethesda, Md., 1970-72; chief resident in endocrinology Harbor Gen. Hosp. UCLA, 1972-73; dir. endocrinology Cedars-Sinai Med. Ctr., LA, 1973-86, chmn. dept. medicine, 1986—; asst. prof. medicine UCLA Sch. Medicine, 1973-77, assoc. prof., 1977-81, prof., 1981—, vice chair dept. medicine, 1986—. Cons. for AMA drug evaluations, 1990—; mem. internat. adv. com. Second World Conf. on Implantation and Early Pregnancy in Human, 1994; mem. endocrinologic and metabolic drugs adv. com. FDA, 1991-95, chmn., 1994-95, spl. advisor, 1995-2001, 04-, chmn., 2001-04; bd. mem. Am. Bd. Internal Medicine Endocrinology, Diabetes, Metabolism Subsplty., 1991-99, chmn., 1995-99, bd. dirs., 1995-99; bd. dirs. Am. Bd. Emergency Medicine. Mem. editl. bd. Mt. Sinai Jour. Medicine, 1984-88, Early Pregnancy: Biology and Medicine, 1998, Am. Family Physician, 1995—, The Am. Jour. Medicine, 1996—, Clin. Endocrinology & Metabolism, 1978-80; assoc. editor Integrative Medicine: Integrating Allopathic, Alternative and Complementary Medicine, 1997-2000. Bd. dirs. Israel Cancer Rsch. Fund, 1991-94, Cedars-Sinai Med. Ctr., 1997-2003; mem. Jonsson Comprehensive Cancer Ctr., 1991—. Recipient Gold Headed Cane Soc. award U. Calif. San Francisco Med. Ctr., 1968, outstanding achievement and cmty. svc. award Anti-Defamation League, 1997, James R. Klinenberg Chair in Medicine, 2000—; Merck scholar, 1968, Mosby scholar, 1968. Fellow ACP (mem. adv. com. to gov., So. Calif. region 1989—, credentials com. So. Calif. region 1993); mem. AAAS, Cross Town Endocrine Club (chmn. 1982-83), Endocrine Soc. (publs. com. 1983-89, long range planning com. 1986-87, recent progress hormone rsch. com. 1993-98, ann. meeting steering com. 1993-98, spl. programs com. 1998—, media adv. com. 1999-2005, chmn. 2002-05), Pacific Coast Fertility Soc. (pres. 1988), Western Soc. for Clin. Rsch., Am. Fedn. for Clin. Rsch., Am. Thyroid Assn., Am. Fertility Soc., Western Assn. Physicians (pres. 1998-99), North Am. Menopause Assn., Assn. Am. Physicians, Am. Soc. Clin. Investigations (mem. nominating com. 1989), Univ. Calif. San Francisco Sch. Medicine Alumni Faculty Assn. (regional v.p. so. Calif., mem. bd. dirs. Israel Cancer Rsch. Fund 1991-94), Phi Delta Epsilon, Alpha Omega Alpha. Office: Cedars Sinai Med Ctr Dept Med Pla Level Rm 2119 8700 Beverly Blvd Los Angeles CA 90048-1865 Office Phone: 310-423-5140. Business E-Mail: braunstein@csts.org.

BRAUNSTEIN, HERBERT, pathologist, educator; b. N.Y.C., Jan. 10, 1926; s. Max and Ida (Meyerson) B.; m. Frances Toomey, Aug. 1, 1954; children: Sheila, Mary, John, Anne. BS, CCNY and CUNY, 1944; MD, Hahnemann Med. Coll., 1950. Intern Montefiore Hosp., N.Y.C., 1950-51; resident in pathology U. Mich., Ann Arbor, 1951-52, U. Cin., 1952-55, from asst. prof. to assoc. prof. pathology, 1956-64; chmn. dept. pathology Michael Reese Hosp., Chgo.; also prof. pathology Chgo. Med. Sch., 1964-65; from assoc. prof. to prof. pathology U. Ky., Lexington, 1965-70; chmn. dept. labs. San Bernardino (Calif.) County Med. Ctr., 1970-91, also dir. sch. med. tech.; clin. prof. pathology Loma Linda (Calif.) U., 1970-91, UCLA, 1980-83; prof. in residence biomed. scis. U. Calif., Riverside, 1979-83. Author book; mem. editorial bd. Modern Pathology; contbr. articles to sci. jours., chpts. to books. Served with USNR, 1944-46, PTO. Recipient numerous research grants, Career devel. award USPHS, 1958-64. Mem. AMA, Calif. Med. Assn., San Bernardino County Med. Soc., Am. Soc. Clin. Pathologists, Coll. Am. Pathologists, U.S.-Can. Acad. Pathology, Am. Assn. Pathologists, Histochem. Soc., Phi Beta Kappa, Sigma Xi, Alpha Omega Alpha. Home: 2467 White River Way Tustin CA 92782-1467

BRAUNSTEIN, TERRY MALIKIN, artist; b. Washington, Sept. 18, 1942; d. Hiram and Dorothy (Malakoff) Malikin; m. David R. Braunstein, Jan. 17, 1965; children: Samantha, Matthew. BFA, U. Mich., 1964; MFA, Md. Inst. Art, 1968. Vis. prof. Calif. State U., Long Beach, 1989; asst. prof. Corcoran Sch. Art, 1978-86; lectr. in field. One-woman shows include Franklin Furnace, N.Y.C., 1977-79, Fendrick Gallery, Washington, 1980, Washington Project for Arts, 1976-82, Marcuse Pfeifer, N.Y.C., 1987, Tartt Gallery, Washington, 1986, 88, U. Mich., Ann Arbor, 1990, Hampshire Coll., Amherst, Mass., 1990, Hampshire Coll., Amherst, Mass., 1990, Almediterranea '92, Almeria, Spain, 1990, Long Beach (Calif.) Mus. of Art, 1991, Krull Gallery, L.A., 1992, 94, 95, 97, Troyer Fiktzpatrick, Lassman Gallery, Washington, 1995, U. Salamanca (Spain), 1996, Centro Exposicione Rodalquilar, Spain, 1998, Centro Andaluz De La Fotografia, America, Spain, 2002; exhibited in group shows at Bronx Mus., 1976, Corcoran Gallery of Art, 1973, 85, Gallery Miyazaki, Osaka, Japan, 1983, Bertha Udang Gallery, N.Y.C., 1985, Calif. State U., Long Beach, Calif., 1987, Ctr. Georges Pompidou, Paris, 1985, Calif. Mus. Photography, Riverside, 1990, Long Beach Mus. Art., 1992, Sala Arcs Gallery, Barcelona, Spain, 1990, Salas de Arenal and traveliing exhibition, Seville, Madrid, Spain and Marseille, France, 1992—, Centro Esposito della Rocca Paotina, Italy, 1994, L.A. County Mus. Art, 1995, Armand Hammer Mus., 1996, Salas De Arenal, Seville, Spain, 1997, Palazzo Del Consoli, Gubbio, Italy, 1998, Long Beach Mus. of Art, Calif., 2001; commd. pub. art works include Dirty Windows, Berlin, Germany, 1996, L.A. County Met. Transp. Authority MetroRail, 1992, L.A. County Mus. Art, 1997, 1st St. Facade, Long Beach, Calif., 1999, Bluff Erosion & Enhancement project, Long Beach, 2000—, City Hall, Long Beach, 2003, Navy Meml., 2004; represented in permanent collections at Mus. Modern Art, N.Y.C., Corcoran Gallery of Art, Washington, Long Beach Mus. Art, Mus. Contemporary Art, Chgo., Bibliotheque Nationale, Paris, Libr. of Congress, Washington, Bruce Peel Spl. Collections Libr., U. Alberta, Can., Nat. Mus. Am. Art, Washington, Mills Coll. Spl. Collections Libr., Oakland, Calif., U. Art Mus., Calif. State U., Long Beach, Getty Ctr. for Arts & Humanities, Victoria and Albert Mus., others. Recipient Visual Artists fellowship Nat. Endowment for Arts, 1985, Disting. Artist award City of Long Beach, 1992, video grant Long Beach Mus. Art, 1992, Nat. Artist's Book award Nat. Mus. Women in Arts, 1994; named disting. Vis. Prof., Calif. State U., 1989; Yaddo Artists resident, 1997, 99, 03, 05. Home: 262 Belmont Ave Long Beach CA 90803-1522 Personal E-mail: terrybraun@aol.com.

BRAUNWALD, EUGENE, physician, educator; b. Aug. 15, 1929; m. Nina H. Starr (dec.); m. Elaine R. Smith, 1993; children: Karen G., Allison, Jill. AB, NYU, 1949, MD, 1952; AM (hon.), Harvard U., 1972; MD (hon.), U. Lisbon, 1984; ScD (hon.), Mt. Sinai Med. Ctr., 1991; MD (hon.), U. Rome, 1991, U. Portg, 1992, U. Vienna, 1995, U. La Plata (Argentina), 1995, U. Rio de Janeiro, 1998, Carol Davila U., 2002, U. Athens, 2003, U. Padua, 2003, Bates Coll., 2003, Comenius U., Bratislava, 2004. Diplomate Am. Bd. Internal Medicine, Am. Bd. Cardiovascular Disease. Intern, fellow Mt. Sinai Hosp., N.Y.C., 1952—54; research fellow Columbia U. Coll. Physicians and Surgeons, N.Y.C., 1954—55; clin. assoc. cardiovascular physiology lab. Nat. Heart Inst., Bethesda, Md., 1955—57; asst. resident Osler Med. Service, Johns Hopkins Hosp., Balt., 1957—58; chief cardiology sect., chief cardiology br., clin. dir. Nat. Heart and Lung Inst., Bethesda, 1958—68; prof., chmn. dept. medicine U. Calif.-San Diego, 1968—72; Hersey prof. of theory and practice of medicine Harvard U. Med. Sch., Boston, 1972—96, Herrman Blumgart prof. Medicine, 1980—89, chmn. study group, 1984—, Disting. Hersey prof., 1996—; faculty dean for acad. programs Harvard U., Boston, 1996—2003. Chmn. dept. medicine Brigham and Women's Hosp., 1972—96, Beth Israel Hosp., 1980—89; lectr. physiology George Washington U., 1959—62; from asst. clin. prof. to clin. prof. Georgetown U. Sch. Medicine, 1960—68; lectr. medicine Johns Hopkins U., 1960—68; trustee McLear Ptnrs., 1993—96; vis. prof. numerous U.S. and fgn. univs.; lectr. in field. Co-editor: Year Book of Cardiovascular and Renal Diseases, 1965—72, Year Book of Medicine, 1973—93, Harrison's Principles of Internal Medicine, 1967—; editor: Heart Disease, 1980—; mem. editl. bds.: Ciculation, Jour. Clin. Investigation, 1964—71, Jour. Cardiovascular Pharmacology, Am. Jour. Medicine, Am. Jour. Cardiology, New Eng. Jour. Medicine, numerous others. Bd. visitors Rockefeller U., 1978—82; mem. vis. com. MIT, 1979—85, Technion U., 1979. Recipient Arthur S. Fleming award, 1965, Superior Svc. award, HEW, 1967, Disting. Achievement award, Modern Medicine, 1968, Gustav Nylin award, Swedish Med. Soc., 1970, Williams award Outstanding Chmn. and Medicine, 1987, Bristol Myers Squibb Excellence in Cardiovascular Rsch. award, 1993, J. Allyn Taylor Internat. prize, Robarts Rsch. Inst., 1993, Gold medal, European Cardiac Soc., 2004. Fellow: ACP (Phillips award 1991), Am. Coll. Cardiology (v.p. 1967, trustee 1967, 1970—75, Disting. Scientist award 1987), Am. Acad. Arts and Scis.; mem.: NAS, Internat. Soc. Cardiology, Royal Soc. Medicine, Harvey Soc., Am. Heart Assn. (bd. dirs. 1966—75, v.p. 1966—70, Rsch. Achievement award 1972, Herrick award 1981), Am. Soc. Pharmacology and Exptl. Therapeutics (John Jacob Abel award 1965), Am. Physiol. Soc., New Eng. Cardiovascular Soc. (pres. 1987—88), Assn. Univ. Cardiologists, Western Soc. for Clin. Rsch. (pres. 1971—72), Am. Fedn. Clin. Rsch. (pres. 1969—70), Am. Soc. Clin. Investigation (pres. 1974—75), Western Assn. Physicians, Assn. Am. Physicians (Kober medal 1998), Assn. Profs. Medicine (pres. 1974—75), Johns Hopkins Soc. Scholars, Alpha Omega Alpha. Office: Timi Study Group 350 Longwood Ave 1st Fl Boston MA 02115 Office Phone: 617-732-8989. E-mail: ebraunwald@partners.org.

BRAUS, IRA L., music educator, researcher; b. New York, Sept. 10, 1951; s. Harold A. and Elaine Braus. MusB, Oberlin Conservatory Music, 1974; MusM, SUNY Stony Brook, 1976; PhD, Harvard U., 1988. Instr. New Eng. Conservatory, Boston, Mass., 1985—86; vis. asst. prof. Bates Coll., Lewiston, Maine, 1991—92; asst. prof. Hartt Sch., West Hartford, Conn., 1998—2004, assoc. prof., 2004—. Wulsin fellow, Tanglewood Music Ctr., 1973. Avocations: bicycling, hiking, cooking. Office: The Hartt School 200 Bloomfield Ave West Hartford CT 06117 Office Phone: 860-768-4124. E-mail: braus@hartford.edu.

BRAVANTE, GEORGE, JR., air transportation executive; Chmn. bd. dir. Express Jet. Office: ExpressJet 1600 Smith St HQSCE Houston TX 77002

BRAVERMAN, ALAN N., lawyer; b. Mass. BA, Brandeis U., 1969; JD, Duquesne U., 1975. Bar: D.C. 1976. Assoc. Wilmer, Cutler & Pickering, 1976-82, ptnr., 1983-93; exec. v.p., gen. counsel ABC, Inc., NYC, 1993-2000; deputy, gen. counsel The Walt Disney Co., Burbank, Calif., 2000—03, sr. exec. v.p. & gen. coun., 2003—. Office: ABC Inc 500 S Buena Vista St Burbank CA 91521-0922

BRAVERMAN, DAVID GEORGE, academic dean; b. Balt., Dec. 22, 1959; s. Elliot Martin and Barbara Winifred (Kynaston) B. BA, U. Mo., 1982; MA, U. Iowa, 1987, PhD, 1990. Dir. sports programming Learfield Communications, Jefferson City, Mo., 1984-85; instr. Cornell Coll., Mt. Vernon, Iowa, 1989-90, asst. dir. residence life, 1988-90; asst. dean of coll. U. Richmond, Va., 1990—. Counselor Spl. Olympics, Richmond, 1991; bd. dirs. CARE West End Jaycees. Anson fellow Nat. Inter Fraternity Conf., 1986, Steinbeck fellow Sigma Tau Gamma, 1986. Mem. Nat. Assn. Student Pers. Adminstrs., Am. Coll. Pers. Assn. (standing com. for men 1986—), So. Assn. Coll. Student Affairs, S.E. Assn. Housing Officers, Va. Assn. Stutent Pers. Adminstrs., Va. Assn. Coll./Univ. Housing Officers, Nat. Assn. Men Against Sexism, Sigma Tau Gamma (asst. exec. dir. 1982-84, Man of Yr. award 1982). Avocations: jazz, bicycling, fishing, reading, theater. Home: 9301 Golden Way Ct Apt O Richmond VA 23294-6427 Office: U Richmond Office of Dean Richmond VA 23173

BRAVERMAN, DONNA CARYN, fiber artist; b. Chgo., Apr. 4, 1947; d. Samuel and Pearl (Leen) B.; m. William Stanley Knopf, Jan. 21, 1990. Student, U. Mo., 1965-68; BFA in Interior Design, Chgo. Acad. Fine Arts, 1970. Interior designer Ascher Dental Supply-Healthco., Chgo., 1970-72, Clarence Krusinski & Assocs. Ltd., Chgo., 1972-74, Perkins & Will Architects, Chgo., 1974-77; fiber artist Fiber Co-op Fibrecations, Chgo., 1977, Scottsdale, Ariz., 1977—. Exhibited in group shows at Mus. Contemporary Crafts, N.Y.C., 1977, James Prendergast Library Art Gallery, Jamestown, N.Y., 1981, Grover M. Herman Fine Arts Ctr., Marietta, Ohio, 1982, Okla. Art Ctr., 1982, Middle Tenn. State U., Murfreesboro, 1982, Redding (Calif.) Mus., 1983, Tucson Mus. Art, 1984, 86, The Arts Ctr., Iowa City, 1985, The Wichita Nat., 1986; in traveling exhibitions Ariz. Archtl. Crafts, 1983, Clouds, Mountains, Fibers, 1983; represented in permanent collections Phillips Petroleum, Houston, Metro. Life, Tulsa, Directory Hotel, Tulsa, Keys Estate Ariz. Biltmore Estates, Phoenix, Sohio Petroleum, Dallas, Reichold Chem., White Plains, N.Y., Rolm Telecommunications, Colorado Springs, Mesirow & Co., Chgo., Exec. House Hotel, Chgo., Cambell Estate, Ariz., Dictaphone Worldhead Quarters, Stratford, Conn., Davenport Bldg., Boston; contbr. articles to profl. jours. Avocation: photography. Home and Office: 1041 E Glenrosa Ave Phoenix AZ 85014-4435

BRAVERMAN, HERBERT LESLIE, lawyer; b. Buffalo, Apr. 24, 1947; s. David and Miriam P. (Cohen) B.; m. Janet Marx, June 11, 1972; children: Becca Danielle, Benjamin Howard. BS in Econs., U. Pa., 1969; JD, Harvard U., 1972. Bar: Ohio 1972, U.S. Dist. Ct. Ohio 1972, U.S. Supreme Ct. 1975, U.S. Ct. Appeals (6th cir.) 1980, U.S. Ct. Claims 1980. Assoc. Hahn, Loeser, Freedheim, Dean & Wellman, Cleve., 1972-75; sole practice Cleve., 1975-87; ptnr. Porter, Wright, Morris & Arthur, Cleve., 1987—96, Walter & Haverfield LLP, Cleve., 1996—. Councilman Orange Village, Ohio, 1988—, pres., 1998-2001. Capt. USAR, 1970-82. Fellow Am. Coll. Trust and Estate Counsel; mem. ABA, Ohio Bar Assn., Bar Assn. Greater Cleve. (former chmn. estate planning trust and probate sect.), Suburban East Bar Assn. (pres. 1978-80), Rotary (Cleveland Heights pres. 1980), B'nai Brith (local pres. 1978-84), Wharton Club Cleve. (pres. 1991—), Am. Jewish Congress (Ohio pres. 1992—). Avocations: golf, symphony, reading. Home: 3950 Orangewood Dr Cleveland OH 44122-7406 Office: Walter & Haverfield LLP Ste 3500 1301 E 9th St Cleveland OH 44114-1821 also: 2000 Auburn Dr Ste 200 Beachwood OH 44122 Office Phone: 216-928-2903. Personal E-mail: hbraverman@walterhav.com.

BRAVERMAN, IRWIN MERTON, dermatologist, educator; b. Boston, Apr. 17, 1929; s. Morris and Molly (Singer) B.; m. Muriel S. Freedman, June 5, 1955; children: Paula, David, Michael. AB, Harvard U., 1951; MD, Yale U., 1955. Diplomate: Am. Bd. Med. Examiners, Am. Bd. Dermatology, Am. Bd. Pathology. Practice medicine specializing in dermatology New Haven; asst. prof. dermatology Yale U., New Haven, 1962-68, assoc. prof., 1968-73, prof., 1973—. Author: Skin Signs of Systemic Disease, 1970, 3d edit., 1997; contbr. articles to profl. jours. Served to capt. U.S. Army, 1956-58. Recipient Mr. and Mrs. J.N. Taub Internat. Meml. award for research in psoriasis Baylor Med. Coll., 1980 Mem. AMA, New Eng. Dermatol. Soc. (v.p. 1990-91, pres. 1991-92), Am. Dermatol. Assn., Am. Acad. Dermatology (dir. 1980-83, Sulzberger Internat. lectr. 1989, Master of Dermatology 1993, Everett C. Fox Meml. lectr. 2001), Soc. Investigative Dermatology (bd. dirs. 1982-87, pres. elect 1991-92, pres. 1992-93, David M. Carter award for mentorship 1999), Am. Fedn. Clin. Rsch., Am. Assn. Physicians. Office: Yale U Med Sch 333 Cedar St New Haven CT 06510-3289 Office Phone: 203-785-4092. E-mail: irwin.braverman@yale.edu.

BRAVERMAN, JORDAN, columnist; b. Boston, July 4, 1936; s. Morris and Molly (Singer) B. BA, Harvard Coll., 1958; MPH, Yale U., 1963; MS of Fgn. Svc., Georgetown U., 1968. Urban planner, economist City Govt. of Quincy, Mass., 1959-61; adminstr. Nat. Blue Cross Assn., Chgo., 1963-65; economist U.S. Dept. Health Edn. and Welfare, Pub. Health Svc., Washington, 1965-67; mgmt. cons. EBS Mgmt. Cons., Washington, 1967-69; asst. to the exec. dir. Am. Pharm. Assn., Washington, 1969-72; dir. pub. policy rsch. Pharm. Mfrs. Assn., Washington, 1972-74; mng. editor Topics in Health Care Financing, Rockville, Md., 1974-75; dir. legis., policy analysis divsn. Health Policy Ctr., Georgetown U., Washington, 1975-77; cons. editor, author Washington, 1978—. Appeared numerous TV and radio shows; speech writer, lectr., pub. spkr., jour./mag. book reviewer, cons. editor VA, Washington, 1986-88, FMAS, Inc., Rockville, 1990—, others; columnist The Balt. Sun, 1990, Am. Weekly News, Washington, 1988—, Capital Jester, Washington, 1993, Internat. Med. News Svc., Washington, 1982—, Consumer Health Reporter, Washington, 1983-84, World Media Reports, 2001—, others; manuscript book referee, reviewer U. Press Am., 1982—, Rowman & Littlefield Publs. Inc., 1995—. Author: Pharmaceutical Payment Plans: An Overview, 1973, Crisis in Health Care, 1978, rev. 1980 (nominated Kulp Book award 1978), The Consumer's Book of Health: How to Stretch Your Health Care Dollar, 1982, The Education of the Osteopathic Physician, 1985, Health Maintenance Organizations: New Choices for Paying and Receiving Medical Care, 1986, Nursing Home Standards: a Tragic Dilemma in American Health, 1970, State Health Insurance Plans: Is Anyone Listening?, 1977, To Hasten the Homecoming: How Americans Fought World War II Through the Media, 1996, others; contbr. (anthologies) Echoes of Yesterday, 1994, Best Poems of 1995, Best Poems of the 90s, 1996, Best Poems of 1997, Best Poems of 1998, Thoughts by Candlelight, 1998, Outstanding Poets of 1998, A Celebration of Poets: Showcase Edit., 1998, The Blush of Morning, 1999, Nature's Echoes, 2000, (poetry anthology) The Falling Rain, 2000, American at the Millennium: The Best Poems and Poets of the 20th Century, 2000, Poetry's Elite: The Best Poets of 2000, Poetry's Elite, 2001, Under a Quicksilver Moon, 2002; contbr. poetry to Poetry.com, 2000, Best Poems and Poets, 2004, Labors of Love, 2004, Tracing the Infinite, 2004, The International Who's Who in Poetry, 2005; (cassette) The Sound of Poetry, 1995-2003, Sounds of Poetry, 2005; (photog. anthologies) Cherished Moments in Time, 1997, Candid Captures, 2001, Shadows of Thought, 2001, Best Photos of 2005; photogs. exhibited in World Sci., Washington, 1997, Internat. Photo. Hall of Fame Mus., 1997-2001; photogs. included in Editor's Choice Desk Calendar, Internat. Libr. Photograpy, 1999, Internat. Libr. Photography Desk Calendar, 1999 (Editor's Choice award 1998-99), Reflections from the Past, 1998, America at the Millennium: The Best Photos of the 20th Century, 1999, The Best Photos of 2000, Hidden Treasures, 2000 (Poetry's Elite Award, 2000, Editor's Choice award, 2001), Best Photos of 2003; contbr. articles to profl. and popular jours., govt. publs. and univs. William Stoughton scholar Harvard U., 1958-59; recipient Editors Choice award N.Am. Open Poetry Contest, 1994, 97, candidate Robert F. Kennedy Journalism award 1994, John H. Dunning prize in US History, Am. Hist. Assn., 1997, Albert J. Beveridge award in Am. History Am. Hist. Assn., 1997, Short Story award, PEN/Amazon.com, 2000; nominated Pulitzer Prize in Letters, 1996. Mem. Internat. Soc. Poets (Poet of Yr. 1996, Internat. Poet of Merit, 1997, 99, 2000, elected Hall of Fame 1997, nomination Poet of Yr. 1999, 2000, Editor Choice award, 2004, nominated Poet of Yr., 2005), Internat. Soc. Photographers (nominated disting. mem., Silver Bowl award for outstanding achievement in photography, 2004), Am.-Indian Ednl. Found. (scholarship com.), Friends of Statue of Liberty and Ellis Island, Inc. (charter), Harvard Club of Washington, Yale Club of Washington, Georgetown Club of Washington. Achievements include name being nscribed on the National Wall of Tolerance in Montgomery, Alabama, 2001; poem "Taps" was accepted into the historcial records of Arlington National Cemetery, Virginia, 2004. Avocations: trumpet, old time radio collector, theater, sports. Home: 2401 H St NW Washington DC 20037-2564

BRAVERMAN, RAY HOWARD, secondary school educator; b. Bklyn., Feb. 28, 1947; s. Irving Leonard and Josephine (Segan) B.; divorced; 1 child, Christopher Marc; m. Barbara Diane Braverman, July 30, 1994. BA in History, U. Del., 1969; MA in History, Wash. Coll., 1979; postgrad., U. Del., 1979-85. Cert. tchr., Del. Chmn. history dept., history instr. Dover (Del.) H.S., 1970—. Chmn. history dept. Dover H.S. Recipient Cert. of Appreciation U. Del., 1987, Nat. Coun. History Edn., 1991. Mem. NEA, Nat. Coun. for the Social Studies, Del. Coun. for Social Studies, Nat. Coun. for History Edn., World History Assn., Del. Edn. Assn., Capital Educators Assn., Orgn. of Am. Historians, Am. Hist. Assn. Home: 33 Elizabeth Ave Dover DE 19901-5803 Office: Dover HS One Pat Lynn Dr Dover DE 19904-2853 Office Phone: 302-672-1551 2551. E-mail: rbraver@capital.k12.de.us.

BRAVERMAN, ROBERT JAY, management consultant, educator; b. NYC, Mar. 4, 1933; s. Arthur and Ruth Edith (Beck) B.; m. Alice Glantz, Dec. 24, 1954; 1 son, John Nachum; m. Claire Hurney, Dec. 31, 1964; children: Sam, Amy. AB with honors and distinction, Columbia U., 1954; postgrad., Harvard U. Sch. Law, 1956-57, Sch. Bus., 1963. With Harbridge House, Inc. (Mgmt. Cons.), Cambridge, Mass., 1957-66; with ITT, NYC, 1966-86; sr. v.p., CEO ITT Coins Inc., NYC, 1986—. Chief exec. officer Braverman Adv. Svcs., 1986—91; prof. practice of pub. policy studies Duke U.; adj. prof. NYU, 1999—2002. Served with U.S. Army, 1954-56. Mem. Phi Beta Kappa. Home and Office: 235 W 76th St New York NY 10023-8210

BRAVO, IRENE MARIA, psychologist, educator; b. Bayamo, Cuba, Jan. 24, 1949; arrived in U.S., 1966; d. Edmundo Pedro Bravo and Irene Manuela Castro; m. Robert Quintero, Feb. 14, 1968 (div. Oct. 27, 1987); children: Robert Francis Quintero, Giselle Christine Quintero, Marguerite Irene Quintero. B in Psychology, Fla. Internat. U., 1990, M in Psychology, 1994, PhD in Psychology, 1998. Lic. psychologist Fla., mental health counselor Fla., hypnotherapist. Crisis counselor Miami Mental Health Ctr., 1994; mental health therapist South Shore Hosp., Miami, 1994—96; clin. intern Miami Heart Inst. and Cedars Med. Ctr., Miami, 1996—97; clin. coord. Adult Day Treatment Ctr., Miami, 1997—98; asst. prof. Carlos Albizu U., Miami, Fla., 1999—2003; pvt. practice Miami, 1998—; assoc. prof. Carols Albizu Univ., 2003—. Adj. instr. Fla. Internat. U., Miami, 1994—2001; presenter in field. Contbr. articles to profl. jours. Mem.: APA, Florida Psychol. Assn., Soc. Child and Adolescent Psychology. Roman Catholic. Avocations: classical music, interior decorating, films. Office: Carlos Albizu U 2173 NW 99th Ave Miami FL 33172 Business E-Mail: ibravo@albizu.edu.

BRAVO, KENNETH ALLAN, lawyer; b. Cleve., July 27, 1942; BS, Rutgers U., 1964; JD cum laude, Ohio State U., 1967. Bar: Ohio 1967, D.C. 1967. Trial atty. Criminal Divsn., U.S. Dept. Justice, 1967-69, spl. atty., 1969-79; ptnr. Benesch, Friedlander, Coplan & Aronoff, Cleve., 1979-94; of counsel Ulmer & Berne LLP, Cleve., 1994-96, ptnr., 1997—. Mem. ABA, Ohio Bar Found. (life), Ohio State Bar Assn. (coun. of dels. 1992—, bd. govs. 2001—04), Fed. Bar Assn. (bd. trustees No. dist. Ohio chpt. 2002-), Cleve. Bar Assn. (chmn. fed. ct. com. 1984-85, trustee 2001-02), Cuyahoga County Bar Assn. (chmn. fed. ct. com. 1980-82, chmn. cert. grievance com. 1986-88), Nat. Assn. Criminal Def. Lawyers, Lawyer-Pilots Bar Assn., Jud. Conf. 8th Dist. Ohio (life), Jud. Conf. 6th Cir. U.S. Ct. Appeals (life), Ohio State U. Law Alumni Soc. (pres.-elect). Office: Ulmer & Berne LLP 1300 E 9th St Ste 900 Cleveland OH 44114-1583 Office Phone: 216-931-6000. E-mail: kbravo@ulmer.com.

BRAVO, LUIS FERNANDO, investment banker; s. Fernando Ismael Bravo and Ivonne Ulrica Bianchi. BA in Econs., BS in Physics-Engring., Wash. and Lee U., 1996; MBA, U. Pa., 2003. Lic. Series 7, Series 3, and Series 63 Nat. Assn. Securities Dealers. Asst. v.p. UBS Securities, Inc., NYC, 1996—98; assoc. Bear, Stearns & Co. Inc., NYC, 1998—2001; summer assoc. Goldman, Sachs & Co., NYC, 2002; assoc. Goldman Sachs, NYC, 2003—. Recipient Wharton Way award, Wharton Student Coun., 2003; Elizabeth B. Garrett scholar, Wash. and Lee U., 1995. Mem.: Wharton Alumni Club Peru (dir., founder 2003—04), Omicron Delta Epsilon, Phi Beta Kappa, Pi Kappa Phi (treas. 1995—96, Rho chpt.). Office: Goldman Sachs & Co Inc 85 Albany St New York NY 10004 Office Phone: 212-902-4886. Office Fax: 212-428-9187. Personal E-mail: fernando.bravo@gs.com.

BRAVO, PAUL, professional soccer player; b. San Jose, Calif., July 19, 1968; Student, Santa Clara U. Midfielder San Francisco Bay Blackhawks, 1991, San Francisco Greek-Ams.; U.S. Open Cup champions, 1994; midfielder Monterey Bay Jaguars, 1995, San Jose Clash, 1996; advanced to play-offs, 1996; midfielder Colo. Rapids, Denver, 1997—; advanced to play-offs, 1997, 98. Office: 1000 Chopper CIR Denver CO 80204-5805

BRAVO, ROSE MARIE, retail executive; b. N.Y.C., Jan. 13, 1951; d. Biagio and Anna (Bazzano) LaPila; m. William Selkirk Jackey, Oct. 9, 1983. BA in English, Fordham U., 1971. Exec. trainee, dept. mgr. A&S, Bklyn, 1971—74; assoc. buyer Macy's, N.Y.C., 1974—75, buyer, 1975—79, councilor, 1979—80, adminstr., 1980—84, group v.p., 1984—85, sr. v.p., 1985—88; chmn., CEO I. Magnin, San Francisco, 1988—92; pres. Saks Fifth Ave., Inc., N.Y.C., 1992—97; CEO Burberrys Ltd., London, 1997—. Bd. dirs. Tiffany & Co. Named one of most powerful women, Forbes mag., 2005.

BRAWNER, GERALD ANDRE, paralegal; b. DC, May 12, 1965; s. Gerald Andre and Alberta Katherine Brawner; m. Joanne Smith (div.); children: DeRoy Andre, Gerald Andre III. Grad. HS, DC, 1984. Paralegal Half-Way There, DC, 1995—2004, bd. mem., 1999—2004. Cons. Washington Connection, DC, 2000—04. Democrat. Achievements include invention of water backpack and gun assembly. Avocations: reading, writing, fishing, chess.

BRAWNER, LEE BASIL, retired librarian, consultant; b. Seguin, Tex., May 1, 1935; s. Lee Basil and Thelma (Davenport) B.; m. Nancy Jayne Wallis, Dec. 6, 1958; children: Betsy Lynn, Allen Lee. Student, Tex. A. and M. U., 1953-55; BA, North Tex. State U., 1957; MA, George Peabody Coll. Tchrs., 1960. Head popular libr. and circulation dept. Dallas Pub. Libr., 1958-60, head Lakewood br., 1961-62, chief br. svcs., 1964-67; dir. Waco (Tex.) Pub. Libr., 1962-64; asst. state libr. Tex. State Libr., 1967-71; dir. Met. Libr. System, Oklahoma City, 1971-99; owner Brawner Assocs., L.L.C. Trustee AMIGOS Bibliog. Coun., 1987—90; panelist libr. bldg. awards AIA-ALA, 1990—92; mem. state adv. bd. U. Okla. Sch. Librs. and Info. Studies, 1994—. Co-author: (with Donald K. Beck, Jr.) Determining Your Public Library's Future Size: A Needs Assessment and Planning Model, 1996, Disaster Response and Planning for Libraries, 1998, In Celebration of Intellectual Freedom, 1999. Trustee, v.p. Okla. Ctr. for the Book, 1987-93; trustee Okla. Humanities Com., 1977-78; mem. Leadership Oklahoma City Alumni, 1994—; chmn. Okla. Found. for Humanities; trustee Freedom to Read Found., 1982-85, pres., 1985-86; mem. Murrah Fed. Bldg. Meml. Com., 1995—. Recipient Alumni award U. North Tex., 1989, First Amendment award Okla. Soc. Profl. Journalists, 1997-98, Downtown Now Pioneer award, 1997, Hugh M. Hefner 1st Amendment award, 1998, Angie Debo Civil Libertarian of Yr. award ACLU Union of Okla. Found., 1999, Libr. Endowment Trust 1st Lee B. Brawner Lifetime Achievement award, 2003; named to 30th Anniversary Honor Roll, ALA Intellectual Freedom to Read Found., 1999. Mem.: ACLU, ALA (coun. 1978—81, intellectual freedom com. 1979—82), Okla. Libr. Assn. (chmn. libr. devel. 1982—83, pres. 1984—85, chmn. legis. com. 1990, chmn. awards com. 1992—93, Disting. Svc. award 1983, SIRS Intellectual Freedom award 1997), Pub. Libr. Assn. (effectiveness com. 1992), Libr. Adminstrn. and Mgmt. Assn. (libr. bldg. awards com. 1987—90, 1992—93, chmn. 1990, chmn. libr. bldgs. and equipment sect. 1992), Sigma Phi Epsilon. E-mail: lobconsultant@cox.net.

BRAXTON, EDWARD K., bishop; b. Chgo., June 28, 1944; s. Cullen L. and Evelyn Braxton. Studied, Quigley Preparatory Sem., Niles Coll. Sem.; MA, STL, St. Mary of the Lake Sem., Mundelein, Ill.; PhD in Religious Studies, STD in Systematic Theology, Cath. U., Louvain, Belgium, 1975; post-doctoral fellowship, U. Chgo. Div. Sch., 1975—76. Deacon St. Raymond De Penafort Parish, Mt. Prospect, Ill.; ordained priest Archdiocese of Chgo., 1970; assoc. pastor Holy Name Cathedral, Chgo., 1970—71, Sacred Heart Parish, Winnetka, Ill., 1971—73, St. Felicitas Parish, Chgo., 1975—76; William A. Coolidge Chair of Ecumenical Thought Harvard U., 1976—77; pastoral ministry St. Paul's Parish, Cambridge, Mass., 1976—77; vis. prof. U. Notre Dame, 1977—78; chancellor for theol. affairs to Bishop James A. Hickey, Cleveland, 1978—80; spl. asst. for theol. affairs to Archbishop James A. Hickey, Washington, 1980—83; scholar in residence N.Am. Coll., Rome, 1983; dir. Calvert House Cath. Student Ctr. U. Chgo., 1983—86; ofcl. theol. cons. to William H. Sadlier Inc., NYC, 1986—92; pastor St. Catherine of Siena Parish, Oak Park, Ill., 1992—95; ordained bishop, 1995; aux. bishop Archdiocese of St. Louis, 1995—2001; bishop Lake Charles, La., 2001—05, Belleville, Ill., 2005—. Contbr. numerous articles to journals including Harvard Theological Review, Theological Studies, Louvain Studies, Irish Theological Quarterly, The New Catholic Encyclopedia, Origins, Commonweal, America, The National Catholic Reporter. Mem. US Conf. Cath. Bishops. (chmn. com. on Am. Coll. Sem. at U. Louvain; mem. com. on liturgy, com. on evangelization) Roman Catholic. Office: Diocese of Belleville The Chancery 222 S Third St Belleville IL 62220 Office Phone: 618-277-8181. Fax: 618-277-0387.*

BRAXTON, FREDERICK, music educator; b. Richmond, Va., June 19, 1945; s. Frederick and Mary Louise Braxton; 1 child, Hannah Pheobe Baxton Marks. BA in Music Edn., Va. Union U., 1978. Lic. tchr. State Bd. Edn., Va., 2004. Music tchr. Rehab. Sch. Authority, Beaumont, Va., 1979—83, Richmond Pub. Schs., 1984—; caseworker Youth Devel. Ctr., Richmond, Va., 1978. Pvt. piano tchr., Richmond, 1973—92, Richmond, 2000—; mentor Carver Elem. Sch., Richmond, 2004—05. Composer: (songs) Bee Rax's Musical Collection. Minister Mt. Sinai Holy Ch., 1995—. Specialist U.S. Army, 1965—67. Recipient Loyal Svc. award, Rehabilitative Sch. Authority Commonwealth of Va., 1981. Mem.: Va. Edn. Assn., Richmond Edn. Assn., Bus. Assn. Network Coun. Avocations: redesign old lamps, genealogy. Office Phone: 804-780-6247. Personal E-mail: beerax@aol.com.

BRAXTON, JERRY W., communications executive; With CPS divsn. Arthur Andersen and Co., 1973-76; v.p., contr., treas. Contel Corp., 1976-91; CFO Nat. Data Corp., 1992-95; exec. v.p., CFO, treas. LHS Group Inc., Atlanta, 1996—. Office: LHS Group Inc 3000 Mill Creek Ave #100 Alpharetta GA 30022-1555

BRAXTON, JOHN M., education educator; BA in Psychology, Gettysburg Coll., 1967; MA in Student Personnel Adminstrn. in higher Edn., Colgate U., 1968; DEd, Pa. State U., 1980. Asst. dir. admissions Point Park Coll., Pitts., 1971—72, Juniata Coll., Huntington, Pa., 1972—74; doctoral candidate, rsch. asst., academic advisor Pa. State U. Ctr. for the Study of Higher Edn. and Divsn. Undergrad. Studies, 1974—76; assoc. dir. instl. rsch. Wittenberg U., Springfield, Ohio, 1976—78; dir. instl. rsch. Urbana Coll., Ohio, 1978—79; asst. dir. instl. studies and planning Northeastern Ill. U., Chgo., 1979—87; vis. asst. prof. higher edn. Loyola U., Chgo., 1985—86; vis. assoc. prof. edn. U. Nebr., Lincoln, 1986; asst. prof. higher edn. Syracuse U., 1987—90, assoc. prof. higher edn., 1991—92; assoc. prof. edn. Peabody Coll., Vanderbilt U., Nashville, 1992—2000, prof. edn., 2000—. Author: (with Alan Berl) Faculty Misconduct in Collegiate Teaching, 1999, (with William Luckey and Patricia A. Helland) Institutionalizing a Broader View of Scholarship Through Boyer's Four Domains, 2002, (with Amy S. Hirschy and Shederick McClendon) Toward Understanding and Reducing College Student Departure, 2004; editor: Faculty Teaching and Research: Is There Conflict?, 1996, Perspectives on Scholarly Misconduct in Collegiate Teaching, 1999, Perspectives on Scholarly Misconduct in the Sciences, 1999, Reworking the Student Departure Puzzle, 2000; gen. editor Issues in Higher Education book series, Vanderbilt U. Press, 1996-2003; cons. editor Jour. Higher Edn., 1982-, Rsch. in Higher Edn., 1983; mem. editl. bd. Jour. of Coll. Student Retention: Rsch., Theory and Practice, 1998-, The Rev. of Higher Edn., 1982-88, Jour. of Gen. Edn., 1990-97; author and co-author various book chapters, articles, book reviews in various profl. publs. Mem. nat. peer rev. panel Nat. Insts. Health Rsch. on Rsch. Integrity Grant Program, 2002—03; mem. nat. assessment adv. group Ctr. for Inquiry in Liberal Edn., Wabash Coll., 2004—; mem. tech. rev. panel Beginning Postsecondary Students Longitudinal Study, Rsch. Triangle Inst., 2004—. Mem.: Nat. Assn. Student Personnel Adminstrs., Assn. for the Study of Higher Edn. (chair Dissertation of Yr. award selection com. 1993—95, co-chair symposium paper proposals, annual meeting 1995, bd. dirs. 1998—2000, pres. 2002—03, immediate past pres. 2003—04), Am. Ednl. Rsch. Assn. (co-chair rsch. papers, annual meeting 1987, co-vice program chair, annual meeting disvsn. J 1988, chair, Disting. Rsch. award, divsn. J 1989, mem. exec. coun., divsn. J 1995—97, chair rsch. awards com., divsn. J 1997—98, chair, exemplary pub. com., divsn. J 1997—98, program chair annual meeting, divsn. J 2000), Am. Coll. Personnel Assn. Office: Peabody Coll Dept Leadership, Policy and Orgns Higher Edn Leadership and Policy Program Box 514 Vanderbilt Univ Nashville TN 37203 Business E-Mail: john.braxton@vanderbilt.edu.

BRAY, CAROLYN SCOTT, education educator; b. May 19, 1938; d. Alonzo Lee and Frankie Lucile (Wood) Scott; m. John Graham Bray Jr., Aug. 24, 1957 (div. May 1980); children: Caron Lynn, Kimberly Anne, David William. BS, Baylor U., 1960; MEd, Hardin-Simmons U., 1981; PhD, U. North Tex., 1985. Registered med. technologist. Dir. career placement Hardin-Simmons U., 1979-82, adj. prof. bus. comm., 1981-84, assoc. dean students, 1982-85; assoc. dir. career planning and placement U. North Tex., Denton, 1985-95, adj. prof. higher edn. adminstrn., mem. Mentor program; dir. Career Ctr., U. Tex. at Dallas, Richardson, 1995-2000, prof. edn., 2000—, tchr. devel. ctr. assessment officer, 2000—. Mem. Consortium State Orgn. Tex. Tchr. Edn., 1999—; mem. adv. bd. TxBESS, 2000—. Adult Bible study tchr. 1st Bapt. Ch., Richardson, Tex., 2000—. Mem.: North Ctrl. Tex. Assn. Sch. Pers. Adminstrs. and Univ. Placement Pers. (pres. 1987—88, sec. 1988—95), Nat. Assn. Colls. and Employers (co-chair nat. conf. planning com. 1996—98), Tex. Assn. for Employer Edn. and Staffing (v.p. 1986—87, pres. 1987—88), Am. Assn. for Employment in Edn. (bd. dirs. 1989—94, treas. 1994—95, nat. conf. com. 1999, conf. com. local arrangements 1999, Priscilla A. Scotlan award for disting. svc. 1999), S.W. Assn. Colls. and Employers (life; chair ann. conf. registration 1991—92, vice chair ops. 1992—93, 4-yr. coll. dir. 1998—99, pres.-elect 1999—2000, co-chmn. tech. com.), Leadership Denton (co-dir. curriculum 1988—89, chair membership selection com., steering com. 1990, 1993—94), Denton C. of C. (pub. rels. com. 1988—95), Kappa Kappa Gamma (chpt. advisor, chair adv. bd. Zeta

Sigma chpt. 1987—93). Republican. Avocations: skiing, tennis, golf, reading. Office: U Tex at Dallas PO Box 830688 GR22 Richardson TX 75083-0688 Business E-Mail: csbray@utdallas.edu.

BRAY, COREY, intercollegiate athletics administrator, research consultant; s. Don David and Pamela Lee Bray; m. Leslie Brown Bray, July 26, 2003. BS, Pacific Luth. U., Wash., 1995; MS, U. Oreg., Oreg., 1998. Cert. Sports Mgmt. Inst., 2005. Rsch. asst. NCAA, Overland Park, Kans., 1998—99, rsch. coord. Indpls., 1999—2002, asst. dir. of rsch., 2002—03, assoc. dir. of rsch., 2003—04, rsch. cons. Summerfield, NC, 2004—05; asst. athletics dir. for adminstrn. Ea. Ky. U., Richmond, 2005—. Youth edn. through sports clinic dir. NCAA Nat. Youth Sports Corp., Indpls., 2000—04; divisoin I men's basketball tournament site control staff NCAA, 2003; men's world basketball championships event ops. control ctr. shift mgr. Ind. Sports Corp., 2002; asst. track and field coach North Eugene H.S., Eugene, Oreg., 1997, asst. basketball coach, 1995—98. Author (presenter): (testimony) Hearings Before the Secretary of Education's Commission on Opportunity in Athletics. Vol. US Swim Team Olympic Trials, Indpls., 2000; head chaperone Nat. Hershey Youth Track & Field Meet, Hershey, Pa., 1995; vol. Youthlinks Ind. Charity Golf Tournament, Indpls., 2001—04, Indpls. 500 Festival 5k Race, 2001—04, Nat. Inst. for Fitness and Sport Eco-Clean, 2003—03, Spl. Olympics Buck Buchanon Sports Festival, Kansas City, Kans., 1999, Lister Elem. Sch. and McIlvaigh Mid. Sch. Vol. Mentor Program, Tacoma, 1991—94. Recipient Psi Chi, Pacific Luth. U., 1993—95, Most Inspirational award, Pacific Luth. U. Track & Field, 1995, Most Improved award, 1992, Acad. All Am., Nat. Assn. of Intercollegiate Athletics, 1995, Acad. All League, Columbia Football Assn., 1995, Athlete Scholar award, NW Conf. of Ind. Colls., 1995, Psychology Dept. Faculty Rsch. award, Pacific Luth. U., 1995, George Fisher Scholar Athlete award, 1995, President's award Recognizing Academic and Athletic Achievement, 1993—95; scholar Morand Scholarship award, Ind. Order of Oddfellows and Rebekahs, 1992, Talent Football award, Pacific Luth. U., 1991—95, Talent Track & Field award, 1991—95; Grad. Tchg. fellow, U. of Oreg., 1996—98, Presdl. scholar, Pacific Luth. U., 1991—95, Univ. scholar, 1991—95. Mem.: Nat. Assn. of Collegiate Dirs. Athletics. Office Phone: 859-622-2125. Business E-Mail: corey.bray@eku.edu.

BRAY, DALE IRVING, civil engineering educator; b. Moncton, Can., June 1, 1940; s. Ivan Simeon and Marion Estella (Irving) B.; m. Carol Velma Cox, June 27, 1964; children: Marnie, Mark. BS in Civil Engring., U. New Brunswick, Fredericton, Can., 1963, MS in Civil Engring., 1965; PhD, U. Alberta, Edmonton, Can., 1972. Asst. prof. U. New Brunswick, Fredericton, 1965-72, assoc. prof., 1972-78, prof., 1978-98, prof. emeritus, 2004. Chmn. dept. civil engring. U. New Brunswick, 1994-98, mem. groundwater studies group, 1988—. Contbr. articles to profl. jours. Mem. Can. Water Resources Assn. (Disting. Svc. award 1995), Can. Soc. Civil Engring. (Camille A. Dagenais award 1998). Baptist. Avocations: hiking, canoeing. Office: Dept Civil Engring U New Brunswick PO Box 4400 Fredericton NB Canada E3B 5A3 Business E-Mail: dalebray@nbnet.nb.ca.

BRAY, GEORGE AUGUST, internist, researcher, educator; b. Evanston, Ill., July 25, 1931; s. George A. and Mary H. B.; m. Martha, Aug. 8, 1959 (div. July 1983); children: George, Thomas, Susan, Nancy; m. Marilyn Rice, Jan. 1, 1984. BA summa cum laude, Brown U., 1953; MD magna cum laude, Harvard U., 1957. Diplomate Am. Bd. Internal Medicine; cert. Nat. Bd. Med. Examiners, Mass. Bd. Registration Medicine, Calif. Bd. Med. Examiners, La. Bd. Med. Examiners. Intern Johns Hopkins Hosp., Baltimore, Md., 1957-58; rsch. assoc. NIH, Bethesda, Md., 1958-60; resident U. Rochester, N.Y., 1960-61; rsch. assoc. Mill Hill Nat. Inst. Med. Rsch., London, 1961-62; asst. prof. medicine Tufts U., Boston, 1964-69, assoc. prof., 1969-70, UCLA, 1970-72, prof., 1972-81, U. So. Calif., Los Angeles, 1981-89, prof. medicine and physiology, 1983-89, chief of Diabetes and Nutrition Los Angeles County USC Med. Ctr., 1981-89; prof. medicine, vice chancellor Med. Ctr. La. State U., Baton Rouge, 1989-99; exec. dir. Pennington Biomed. Rsch. Ctr., Baton Rouge, 1989-99; prof., chief clin. sci., 1999—; Boyd prof. La. State U., Baton Rouge, 1999—. Vis. prof. U. Ill., 1981; cons. FDA, 1971, 95, Can. Dept. Health and Welfare, Ottawa, Ont., 1974, Nat. Inst. on Aging; mem. adv. coun. Nat. Inst. Diabetes, Digestive and Kidney Diseases, 1985-90. Author: Obese Patient, 1976; editor: Obesity in America, 1979, Obesity in Perspective, 1976, Treatment of Obesity, 1985, 89, Obesity: Basic Aspects and Clinical Applications, 1989; contbr. articles to profl. jours. Recipient Travel award Am. Thyroid Assn., 1970, Sam E. Roberts award Kans. Nutrition Soc., 1977, Wellcome Vis. Prof. award Mich. State U., 1978, U. Chgo., 1985, Alumni Day spkr. Harvard Med. Sch., Boston, 1982, Osborne and Mendel award Am. Inst. Nutrition, 1989, E.V. McCollum award Am. Soc. Clin. Nutrition, 1989, Joseph Goldberger award in Clin. Nutrition AMA, 1994, TOPS award NAASO, 1999, W. Henry Sebrell award Weight Watchers Found., 2000, Bristol-Myers Squibb/Mead Johnson Nutrition award, 2000, Stankard Lifetime Achievement award, NAASO, 2003; grantee NIH, 1965—, Weight Watchers Found., 1979-81, Kroc Found., 1980-81; fellow NSF, 1961-62, NIH, 1962-64. Master: Am. Coll. Endocrinology (pres. 1993—95, editor Endocrine Practice 1993—95), ACP, APC (chmn.-elect con. med. spltys. 1987—88, bd. regents 1987—91, chmn. 1988—91); fellow: Am. Inst. Nutrition (Osborne-Mendal award 1988), Am. Soc. Nutrition Sci., AAAS; mem.: Johns Hopkins U. Soc. Scholars, Internat. Assn. Study Obesity (pres.-elect 1990—94, pres. 1994—98, Willendorf award 1980), Assn. Am. Physicians (hon.), Am. Soc. Clin. Investigation (hon.), N.Am. Assn. Study Obesity (chmn. organizing com. 1980—82, councilor 1984—88, pres.-elect 1988—89, pres. 1989—90, editor Internat. Jour. Obesity 1974—91, Obesity Rsch. 1991—97, TOPS award 1999, Standard Lifetime Achievement award 2003), Am. Fedn. Clin. Rsch., Am. Diabetes Assn. (bd. dirs. So. Calif. 1984—88, 1988—89), Endocrine Soc., Am. Soc. Clin. Nutrition (councilor 1982—84, v.p. 1985—86, pres.-elect 1986—87, pres. 1987—88, McCollum award 1989), Am. Assn. Clin. Endocrinology (bd. dirs. 1990—96), Peripatetic Club (hon.), Alpha Omega Alpha, Sigma Xi, Phi Beta Kappa. Avocations: medical history, travel. Office: Pennington Ctr 6400 Perkins Rd Baton Rouge LA 70808-4124

BRAY, RICHARD DANIEL, literary program director, librarian; b. Albany, N.Y., June 19, 1945; s. Harry and Sylvia Jeanette (Weiss) B.; m. Suzannah Greentree, Aug. 17, 1980. AA, Pasadena City Coll., 1966; BA, San Francisco State U., 1969; MLS, San Jose State U., 1994. Pres. Guild Books, Inc., Chgo., 1979-88; instr. English Columbia Coll.; lit. panelist L.A. Dept. Cultural Affairs, 1989-90, Calif. Arts Coun., 1989-92, NEA, 1992-94. Judge, Carl Sandburg award Friends of Chgo. Pub. Library, 1985-86. Mem. lit. adv. bd. Ill. Arts Coun., 1985-87, multi-arts adv. com. Chgo. City Arts Program, 1985-87; bd. dirs. Friends of Chgo. Pub. Libr., 1985-87, Coun. Literary Mags. and Presses, 1987-92. Mem. Am. Booksellers Assn. (edn. com. 1987-89), Nat. Writers Union, Am. Writers Congress (exec. 1981-82), Am. Libr. Assn., Calif. Libr. Assn., Multicultural Review (mem. bd. advs.), Calif. Poets and Writers (mem. bd. advs.), Librs. Index to Internet. Office: Alameda County Library 2400 Stevenson Blvd Fremont CA 94538-2326

BRAY, TIM, computer company executive; b. Can., June 21, 1955; married; 1 child. BSc with honors, U. Guelph, Ont., Can., 1981. Freelance stage mgr., Guelph, Ont., Waterloo, Canada, 1976—79; software specialist Digital Equipment Corp., Toronto, Canada, 1981—83; sys. software group leader, computer support tech. leader, digital products group Microtel Pacific Rsch., Vancouver, Canada, 1983—87; mgr. New Oxford English Dictionary Project U. Waterloo, Canada, 1987—90; part-time CEO Waterloo Maple Software, 1989—90; CEO Open Text Sys., Inc., Waterloo, 1989—91, sr. v.p. tech. Waterloo, Ont., Vancouver, 1991—96; prin. Textuality Svcs., Vancouver, 1996—99; founder, CEO Antarctica Sys., Inc., Vancouver, 1999—2002, CTO, 1999—2004; tech. dir. Sun Microsystems, Inc., Santa Clara, Calif., 2004—. Part-time lectr. Simon Fraser U., Vancouver, 1984; expert in field. Contbr. articles to profl. jours. Achievements include co-creator XML (Extensible Markup Language). Office: Sun Microsystems Inc 4150 Network Cir Santa Clara CA 95054

BRAYMAN, JEANNIE SUE, language educator; b. Omaha, Mar. 20, 1949; d. Guy M. and Lela R. (Russell) Blakey; m. John M. Brayman, Nov. 28, 1969 (dec. July 1990). BA summa cum laude, U. Nebr., 1971; MA in English, Creighton U., 1973. Lifetime teaching cert., Nebr., Iowa. Tchr. Plattsmouth (Nebr.) Community Schs., 1973-76, Metro Tech. C.C., Omaha, 1976-78, Creighton Prep. Sch., Omaha, 1978—. Various offices Met. English Lang. Arts Assn., Omaha, 1977-87; speaker in field. Contbr. articles to profl. jours. Recipient grant for summer study Nebr. Writing Project, 1978, grant Nat. Endowment for Humanities, 1991; named Outstanding Young Educator, Omaha Jaycees, 1981, Nebr. Jaycees, 1982; named Tchr. of Yr., Creighton Prep. Sch., Archdiocesan Tchr. of Yr.; named to Creighton Prep. Hall of Fame. Mem. Nat. Coun. Tchrs. English, Nebr. Coun. Tchrs. English. Avocations: reading, travel. Office: Creighton Preparatory Sch 7400 Western Ave Omaha NE 68114-1878 E-mail: jbrayman@cox.net.

BRAZDA, FREDERICK WICKS, pathologist, educator; b. New Orleans, Dec. 17, 1945; s. Fred George and Helen Josephine (Wicks) B.; m. Margaret Mary Hubbell, Sept. 8, 1973; children: Geoffrey Frederick, Gretchen Marie, Gregory Paul. Student, U. Chgo., 1962-64; BS cum laude, Tulane U., 1966; MD, La. State U., 1970. Diplomate Am. Bd. Pathology. Intern, then resident in pathology La. State U. divsn. Charity Hosp., New Orleans, 1970-75; pathologist Hotel Dieu Hosp., New Orleans, 1975-92; dir. Sch. Med. Tech., New Orleans, 1976-83; assoc. med. dir. Am. Bio-sci. Labs., New Orleans, 1985-89; tech. dir. Smith Kline Beecham Clin. Labs., New Orleans, 1990-94; pathologist, tech. dir. U. Hosp. Lab., New Orleans, 1993-95, Med. Ctr. La. at New Orleans U. Campus Lab., 1995—. Cons. St. Tammany Parish Hosp., Covington, La., Riverside Hosp., Franklinton, La, 1976-84; asst. clin. prof. pathology and med. tech. La. State U. Med. Ctr. (now La. State U. Health Scis. Ctr.), New Orleans, 1976-93, prof. clin. pathology, 1994—, dep. dir. labs. health care svcs. divsn., 1998—. Fellow Nat. Acad. Clin. Biochemistry, Coll. Am. Pathologists, Am. Soc. Clin. Pathologists; mem. AMA, AAAS, Am. Chem. Soc., Am. Assn. Clin. Chemistry, So. Med. Assn., La. Med. Soc., La. Pathology Soc., Orleans Parish Med. Soc., Greater New Orleans Pathology Soc., Clin. Lab. Mgmt. Assn., La. Civil Svc. League, Friends of City Park, Friends of Zoo, Friends of Aquarium, Friends of Charity Hosp., New Orleans Mus. Art, Les Amis du Vin, Phi Beta Kappa, Alpha Omega Alpha, Phi Beta Pi. Democrat. Roman Catholic. Home: 2805 Vivian St Metairie LA 70001-4238 Office: 2025 Gravier St Ste 200 New Orleans LA 70112-2290 Office Phone: 504-903-3978. E-mail: fbrazd@lsuhsc.edu.

BRAZE, F. DAVID, research scientist; b. Fresno, Calif. BA in Linguistics magna cum laude, Calif. State U., 1992, MA in Linguistics with distinction, 1994; PhD in Linguistics, U. Conn., 2004. Scientist Haskins Labs., New Haven, 2002—. Rsch. asst. psychology, nature and acquisition of speech code and reading U.Conn., 1995—2002. Contbr. articles to profl. jours. Recipient Human Sentence Processing Conf. Travel award, CUNY, 1996; Rodman Grad. fellow, Calif. State U., Fresno, 1992—93. Mem.: Soc. Scientific Study Reading, Linguistic Soc. Am., Cognitive Neuroscience Soc., Am. Psychol. Soc. Office: Haskins Labs 300 George St New Haven CT 06511

BRAZEAL, AURELIA ERSKINE, ambassador; b. Chgo., Nov. 24, 1943; BS, Spelman Coll., 1965; M of Internat. Affairs, Columbia U., 1967; postgrad., Harvard U., 1972. With Foreign Svc., 1968; consular and econ. officer U.S. Embassy, Buenos Aires, 1969-71; econ. reports officer Econ. Bureau U.S. State Dept., 1971-72, watch and line officer Office of Secretariat, 1973-74, desk officer Uraguay, Paraguay, 1974-77; review officer Office of Secretariat U.S. Dept. Treasury, 1977-79; econ. officer Tokyo, 1979-82; officer ECON Bur. U.S. Dept. State, 1982-84; dep. dir. Econ. Office Japan, 1984-86; mem. sr. seminar, 1986-87; min. counselor econ. affairs U.S. Embassy, Tokyo, 1987-90; U.S amb. to Micronesia, 1990-93; U.S. amb. to Kenya, 1993-96; deputy asst. sec. East Asian & Pacific Affairs, 1996-98; dean sr. seminar Fgn. Svc. Inst., Arlington, Va., 1998-99, dean leadership and mgmt. sch. and sr. seminar, 1999—2002; U.S. amb. to Ethiopia, 2002—. Office: 2030 Addis Ababa Washington DC 20521-2030*

BRAZELL, KAREN WOODARD, literature educator; b. Buffalo, Apr. 25, 1938; d. Charles Cary and Josephine Mary (Bordonaro) Woodard; m. James Reid Brazell, Aug. 27, 1961 (div. 1978); children: Katherine Ann Brazell Rivera, Stephen Reid. Student, Coll. Wooster, 1956—58, Internat. Christian U., Tokyo, 1958—60; BA, U. Mich., 1961, MA, 1962; PhD, Columbia U., 1969; D Lit (hon.), U. Puget Sound, 1993. Asst. prof. Japanese lit. Princeton U., 1969—74; assoc. prof. Cornell U., Ithaca, NY, 1974—79, prof., 1979—2000, chmn. dept. Asian studies, 1977—82, dir. East Asia program, 1987—91. Vis. prof. U. Calif., Berkeley, 1984, Nat. Inst. Japanese Lit., Tokyo, 1988-89, vis. Shinchosha prof. Columbia U., 1996. Author: Confessions of Lady Nijo, 1973 (Nat. Book Award 1974), Noh as Performance, 1977, Dance in the Noh Theater, 1981; editor: 12 Plays of Noh and Kyogen Theaters, 1988; assoc. editor Jour. Japanese Studies, 1978—; contbr. articles and book revs. to profl. jours. Trustee Cornell U., 1979-83; bd. dirs. U.S.-Japan Soc. Ithaca, N.Y., Japan Soc. N.Y.C. Performing Arts Adv. Com., 1993-2005, Japan-U.S. Partnership for Performing Arts Inc., N.Y.C., 1994-98 Fulbright-Hayes fellow, 1972-73, NEH fellow, summer 1974, Cornell U. Soc. Humanities fellow, 1976-77, Japan Found. fellow, 1978, 85, Nat. Inst. Japanese Lit. rsch. fellow, Tokyo, 1988-89. Mem. Assn. Asian Studies, Assn. Tchrs. of Japanese (exec. com. 1981-83, bd. dirs. 1989-92), Phi Beta Kappa (senator at large 1976-82, trustee found. 1977-82). Office: Cornell U Dept Asian Studies Ithaca NY 14853

BRAZIER, DON ROLAND, retired railroad executive; b. Pittsburg, Kans., Mar. 30, 1921; s. Hosie O. and Lola Frances (Tow) B.; m. June Darla Harr, Nov. 8, 1941. B.C.S., Benjamin Franklin U., Washington, 1950, M.C.S., 1951. Civilian budget officer Ordnance Corps, Dept. Army, 1940-43, 46-53; OFC asst. sec. def., 1953-67; comptroller Def. Supply Agt., 1967; dep. asst. sec. Army, 1967-68; prin. dep. asst. sec. def.-comptroller, 1968-74; treas. AMTRAK, 1974-75, v.p. fin., treas., 1975-82, exec. v.p. fin. and adminstrn., 1982-86. Dir. Washington Union Terminal; pres., dir. Chgo. Union Sta. With USAAF, 1943-46; maj. AUS ret. Decorated Meritorious Service medal; recipient Def. Disting. Civilian Service award, 1971, 73, 74

BRAZIL, AINE M., engineering company executive; Student, Univ. Coll., Galway, Ireland; BS in Engring., U. Coll. Galway, Ireland, 1977; MS in Engring., Imperial Coll. Sci. and Tech., London, 1980. Structural engr. Thornton-Tomasetti Engrs., N.Y.C., 1982, sr. assoc., 1992—97, prin., 1997—. Adj. prof. dept. civil engring. and engring. materials Columbia U. Named one of Women of Achievement, Profl. Women in Constrn., 2001.

BRAZIL, HAROLD EDMUND, political science professor; b. Bearden, Ark., Aug. 24, 1920; s. Paul Brazil and Lavenia (Govenor) Pullen; children: Leslie, Christopher, Susan, Paul, Ernest, Harold, Michael. BS, Tuskegee U., 1942; MA, Ohio State U., 1957; PhD, Ohio State U., Columbus, 1961. Placement officer VA, Columbus, 1946-49; dir. civil personnel Internat. Refugee Orgn., Fed. Republic of Germany, 1949-50; personnel officer USAF, Philippines, 1955-57, dir. research and community relations, 1957-59, command historian, 1959-62; attaché Am. Embassy, Cairo and Monrovia, Liberia, 1962-66; prof., chmn. dept. polit. sci. Sienna Coll., Loudonville, N.Y., 1966-70; co-dean sch. humanities and social sci. Rensselaer Poly. Inst., Troy, N.Y., 1970-72, prof., chmn. dept. history and polit. sci., 1972-75, prof. polit. sci., 1975-90, prof. emeritus, 1990—. Instr. Indsl. Coll. of Armed Forces, Washington, 1964, Fgn. Service Inst. of Dept. of State, Washington, 1965. Author: The Taiwan Straits Crisis of 1958, 1959, The Politics of Philippine Economic Development, 1962, A World Apart: America Military Diplomacy in S.E. Asia, 1976, The Law of the Oceans: Pursuing Order in the Twenty-First Century, 1988, The Third World, Multinationals, and the Law of the Sea Treaty, in Papers in Public Law and Comparative Political Science, 1989. Served as capt. USAF, 1942-46. Mem. Am. Internat. Polit. Sci. Assn., African Studies Assn., Inter-Univ. Seminar on Armed Forces and Soc. Home: PO Box 1560 Troy NY 12181-1560 Office: Rensselaer Poly Inst Dept Sci and Tech Studies Sage Hall Troy NY 12181

BRAZINSKY, IRV(ING), chemical engineering educator; b. NYC, Oct. 27, 1936; s. Israel and Rebecca (Singer) B.; m. Rosalie Seligson, June 14, 1959; children: Howard, Michael. BSChemE, Cooper Union, 1958; MS, Lehigh U., 1960; ScD, MIT, 1967. Chemist Freeport Sulfur Co., Port Sulfur, La., 1957; rsch. engr. NASA, Cleve., 1958, 59-61, Polaroid Corp., Waltham, Mass., 1966-69; sr. rsch. engr. Celanese Corp., Summit, N.J., 1969-76; sr. R & D engr. Halcon Internat., NYC, 1976—81; process devel. mgr. Foster Wheeler Energy Corp., Livingston, N.J., 1981-85, cons., 1985-88; adj. prof. N.J. Inst. Tech., Newark, 1971-81; assoc. prof. chem. engring. Cooper Union, N.Y.C., 1985-91, prof., 1991—, chmn. dept., 1989—. Cons. Gen. Foods Inc., Philip Morris Inc., N.Y.C. Dept. of Pers., 1985-92. Pioneer, patentee processes for heat stabilizing microporous plastic film, improving melt strength of polyester and nylon melts, and rapid chilling of beverages; contbr. articles to profl. jours. Mgr., coach Matawan Little League, 1975-81; active YMCA Indian Guides Program, 1972-80; coach Aberdeen-Matawan Basketball League, 1979-85; v.p. Matawan High Sch. Parents Athletic Assn., 1986-90. Schweinburg scholar, 1954-55; Petroleum Rsch. Fund fellow, 1958-59, A.D. Little fellow, 1963-64, Proctor & Gamble fellow, 1964-66; N.Y. State Regents scholar, 1954-58, Campbell, Reilly, Schiff and O'Rourke scholar, 1955-58. Mem. AIChE, Am. Soc. Engring. Edn., Am. Chem. Soc., Soc. Plastics Engrs., Cooper Union Fedn. of Coll. Tchrs. (v.p. 1997-2003, pres. 2003—,) Cooper Union Rsch. Found. (bd. 2001—), Soc. Rheology, N.Y. Acad. Scis., Sigma Xi. Home: 6 Rustic Ln Matawan NJ 07747-2865 Office: Cooper Union 51 Astor Pl New York NY 10003-7132 Office Phone: 212-353-4373. E-mail: rosingrustic@msn.com.

BREADY, RICHARD LAWRENCE, manufacturing executive; b. Brookline, Mass., July 7, 1944; s. John Norbert and Catherine Rosalie B.; m. Loretta Lipman, July 16, 1971; 1 child, Barrett Wynn. BA in Econs, St. Anselm's Coll., Manchester, N.H., 1965; MS in Acctg, Northeastern U., Boston, 1966; DBA (hon.), Johnson and Wales Coll., 1986. CPA Mass. With Arthur Andersen & Co., C.P.A.'s, Boston, 1966-74, audit mgr., 1969-74; ind. cons., 1974-75; treas. Nortek, Inc., Cranston, RI, 1975—77, exec. v.p., COO, 1975—77, pres., 1979—90, chmn., CEO, 1990—, also bd. dirs. Bd. dirs. Synergy Methods, Inc., R.I. Hosp., Profl. Facilities, Mgmt., Inc. Mem. U. R.I. Found.; bd. dirs. Nat. Corp. Theatre Fund, Jr. Achievement, R.I. Philharm., Coalition for Cmty. Devel.; mem. nat. coun., bd. overseers, bd. visitors Northeastern U.; corp. mem., mem. fin. com., mem. audit com. Northeastern U.; bd. overseers Moses Brown Sch.; trustee Providence Performing Arts Ctr., Trinity Repertory Co., First Night Providence, NCCJ. With USAR, 1966-67. Mem. AICPA, Nat. Assn. Mfrs., Am. Mgmt. Assn., Greater Providence C. of C., R.I. Commodores. Office: Nortek Inc 50 Kennedy Plz Ste 1700 Providence RI 02903-2393 Home: 280 Irving Ave Providence RI 02906-5544

BREAKSTONE, DONALD S., lawyer; b. Chgo., Feb. 13, 1945; s. Eugene A. and Julie K. (Kanstein) B.; m. Barbara R. Raife, Aug. 24, 1968; children: Elizabeth, Michael. BA in History, U. Mich., 1966; JD, Havard U., 1969. Bar: Ill. 1973, Ohio 1969. Editor Internat. Bur. of Fiscal Documentation, Amsterdam, The Netherlands, 1971-73; assoc. Mayer, Brown & Platt, Chgo., 1973-77, ptnr., 1977-94; v.p., gen. counsel Atty.'s Liability Assurance Soc., Inc., Chgo., 1994-97, sr. v.p., gen. counsel, 1997—. Chmn. Glencoe Village Bd. of Appeals, 1987-88. Contbr. articles to profl. jours. Mem. ABA, Chgo. Council of Lawyers. Office: Attys Liability Assurance Soc Inc 311 S Wacker Dr Ste 5700 Chicago IL 60606-6629

BREAKSTONE, KAY LOUISE, public relations executive; b. Allentown, Pa., Sept. 9, 1936; d. Morris H. and Mabel (Gruber) Senderowitz; m. Jules L. Breakstone, Dec. 3, 1960; children: Enid, Jessica. BS, N.Y.U., 1967. With N.Y. Conf. Bd., 1967-69, Bache, Halsey, Stuart, N.Y.C., 1969-70; securities analyst Dean Witter, N.Y.C., 1970-71; v.p. Burson Marsteller, Inc., N.Y.C., 1971-79, sr. v.p., 1981-87, exec. v.p., 1987-92; dir. investor rels. Kennecott Corp., Stamford, Conn., 1979-81; pres., CEO Ludgate Comm., N.Y.C., 1993—. Mem. Nat. Investor Rels. Inst. (pres. 1980-81).

BREAKSTONE, MARC L., lawyer; b. NYC, Feb. 16, 1959; BA, U. Mich., 1981; JD, Northeastern U. Sch. Law, 1986. Bar: Mass. 1986, US Dist. Ct., Dist. Mass. 1987, US Ct. Appeals, First Circuit 1987. With Sugarman & Sugarman, 1986—92; principal Breakstone, White-Lief & Gluck, 1992—. Named Mass. Lawyer Yr., Mass. Lawyer Weekly, 2002. Mem.: Mass. Bar Assn., Mass. Acad. Trial Atty., ATLA. Office: Breakstone White-Lief & Gluck PC Two Ctr Plz Ste 530 Boston MA 02108 Office Phone: 617-723-7676. Business E-Mail: breakstone@bwglaw.com.

BREAKSTONE, ROBERT ALBERT, information technology executive, consumer products company executive, consultant; b. N.Y.C., Feb. 20, 1938; s. Morris and Minnie B.; m. Eileen Fogel, Nov. 5, 1966; children: Warren, Ron, David. BS in Math., CCNY, 1960, MBA in Mgmt., 1964. Sys. engring. mgr. IBM, N.Y.C., 1960-64; dir. mgmt. sys. Continental Copper & Steel Industries, Inc., N.Y.C., 1964-68; v.p., CFO Sys. Audits, Inc., N.Y.C., 1968-70; v.p., group exec. Chase Manhattan Bank, N.Y.C., 1970-74; group v.p., bd. dirs. Chesebrough-Pond's, Inc., Greenwich, Conn., 1974-85; pres., CEO Health-Tex Inc., N.Y.C., 1985-88; exec. v.p., COO GTech Corp., West Greenwich, R.I., 1988-95; pres., CEO Landmark Internat. Group, Inc., Boca Raton, Fla., 1995—. Adj. asst. prof. Pace U. and NYU, 1964-71; adj. prof. Mercy Coll. Grad. Sch. of Bus., 1997—; bd. dirs. State of Conn. Conix Program, OSF, Inc., By Design Internat. Ltd.; bd. advisors Hoffinger Industries; spkr. in field. Bd. dirs. Stamford Mus. and Nature Ctr., Bi-Cultural Sch.; pres. United Jewish Fedn. of Stamford, 1996-98. Mem. N.Am. Soc. Corp. Planning, Am. Apparel Mfrs. Assn. (dir.), Mu Gamma Tau (pres.). Mem. N.Am. Soc. Corp. Planning, Am. Apparel Mfrs. Assn., Mu Gamma Tau (pres.). Office: Landmark International Group Inc 2432 NW 62nd St Boca Raton FL 33496 also: 95 Lyn Am St Stamford CT 06903-4527 Office Phone: 203-322-3679. E-mail: rab@landmarkinternational.com.

BREATHED, BERKELEY, cartoonist; b. Encino, Calif., June 21, 1957; s. John William Breathed and Martha Jane (Martin) de Varennes; m. Jody Boyman, May 10, 1986; children: Sophie, Milo. BA, U. Tex., 1980. Syndicated cartoonist Washington Post Writer's Group, Washington, 1980-95. Cartoonist: Bloom County, 1980-89, Outland, 1989-95; author: (compilations) Loose Trails, 1983, Toons for Our Times,1984, Penguin Dreams and Stranger Things, 1985, Bloom County Babylon: Five Years of Basic Naughtiness, 1986, Billy and the Boingers Bootleg, 1987, Tales Too Ticklish To Tell, 1988, Night of the Mary Kay Commandos, 1989, Classics of Western Literature, 1990, Politically, Fashionably and Aerodynamically Incorrect, 1992, His Kisses Are Dreamy But Those Hairballs Down My Cleavage..., 1994, One Last Peek: The Final Hits, The Special Hits, The Inside Tips, 1995, (children's books) A Wish for Wings that Work (also TV spl., home video), 1991, The Last Basselope, 1992, Goodnight Opus, 1993, Red Ranger Came Calling, 1994, Edwurd Fudwupper Fibbed Big, 2000, Flawed Dogs, 2003, Opus: 25 Years of His Sunday Best, 2004. Recipient Pulitzer prize for editorial cartooning Columbia U., 1987. Avocations: travel, animal rights, motorcycling.

BREATHITT, LINDA K., federal commissioner; b. Hopkinsville, Ky. BA in Edn., U. Ky., 1975; cert. state-local govt. exec. mgmt. pro., Harvard U. Exec. dir. Washington Office, Commonwealth of Ky., 1980-92; commr. Ky. Pub. Svc. Commn., 1993-95, chmn., 1996-97; commr. FERC, 1997—. Bd. dirs. Martin Sch. Pub. Policy, U. Ky., Tata Energy Rsch. Inst. Regulatory Studies and Governance, New Delhi. Mem. Women Execs. in State Govt., U. Ky. Alumni Assn. Methodist. Avocations: photography, scuba diving, gardening. Office: Thelen Reid & Priest LLP 701 Pennsylvania Ave NW Ste 800 Washington DC 20004

BREAULT, KEVIN D., social studies educator, researcher; b. N.Y.C., May 24, 1954; s. Roland E. and Vera A. Breault; m. Joy Dworkin, June 27, 1982 (div. Sept. 1985); m. Lynn E. Egan, July 30, 1988; 1 child, Lucy. BA, Reed Coll., 1978; MA, U. Wash., 1983; PhD, U. Chgo., 1986. Asst. prof. U. Cin., 1985-87, Washington U., St. Louis, 1988-91, U. Ill., Chgo., 1991-92; assoc.

prof. Austin Peay State U., Clarksville, Tenn., 1993-97; assoc. prof. sociology Mid. Tenn. State U., Murfreesboro, 1997-98, prof., 1998—. Author: (monograph) Four Hundred Years of Social Thought, 1986, (children's book) With Wings To Fly, 2000; contbr. articles and book revs. to profl. jours., including Am. Jour. Sociology, Jour. Interpersonal Violence, jour. Quantitative Criminology, Social Forces, Brit. Jour. Sociology, Contemporary Sociology, Sociol. Focus, Am. Sociol. Rev., Jour. Marriage and Family, Sociol. Quar., Social Sci. Rsch., also chpts. to books. Grantee U. Cin., 1986, Austin Peay State U., 1994, G.H. Weems Ednl. Found., 1997, Mid. Tenn. State U., 1999; fellow Ctr. for Advanced Study in Behavioral Scis., Ogburn-Stouffer fellow U. Chgo., 1987-88. Mem. Am. Sociol. Assn., Am. Birding Assn. Avocations: birding, travel, chess, writing young adult books. Office: Middle Tenn State U Dept Sociollogy Murfreesboro TN 37132 Home: 9413 Atherton Ct Brentwood TN 37027-8700 Office Phone: 615-898-2696. E-mail: kbreault@bellsouth.net.

BREAUX, ANNETTE LALANDE, director, elementary school educator; d. Gaston Anthony Breaux Jr. and Amy (Simon) Breaux. BS, Nicholls State U., Thibodaux, La., 1984, MEd, 1993. Tchr. Lafourche Parish Sch. Bd., Thibodaux, La., 1984—93, curriculum coord., 1993—2004; new tchr. induction coord. Nicholls State U., Thibodaux, La., 2004—. Edn. cons., Houma, La., 1998—. Co-author (with Harry K. Wong): (CD series) 10 Days to Maximum Tcaching Success, 2005, New Teacher Induction, author, 101 Answers for New Teachers, 10 Days to Maximum Teaching Success, Real Challenges, Real Solutions. Named Tchr. of Yr., LaForsche Parish Schs., 1988, Educator of Yr., Thibodaux C. of C., La., 2003. Home: 303 Sunset Ave Houma LA 70360 Office: Nicholls State U PO Box 2053 Thibodaux LA 70310 Office Phone: 985-448-4340. E-mail: annette.breaux@nicholls.edu.

BREAUX, JOHN BERLINGER, lawyer, communications professor, former senator; b. Crowley, La., Mar. 1, 1944; s. Ezra H., Jr. and Katherine (Berlinger) B.; m. Lois Gail Daigle, Aug. 1, 1964; children: John B., William Lloyd, Elizabeth Andre, Julia Agnes. BA in Polit. Sci, U. Southwestern La., 1964; JD, La. State U., 1967. Bar: La. 1967. Ptnr. Brown, McKernan, Ingram & Breaux, 1967-68; legis. asst. to Congressman Edwin W. Edwards, 1968-69, dist. asst., 1969-72; mem. 92d-99th Congresses from 7th Dist. La., 1072—1987; U.S. Senator from La. Washington, 1987—2005; mem. fin. com., 1990—2005; chief dep. whip, 1993—2005; sr. counsel Patton Boggs LLP, Washington, 2005—; Disting prof. comm. Manship Sch. Mass Comm. La State U., Baton Rouge, 2005—, sr. fellow Reilly Ctr. Media & Pub. Affairs, 2005—. Chmn. Nat. Water Alliance, 1987-88, Nat. Dem. Senatorial Campaign Com., 1989-90, founder and past chair, Dem. Leadership Coun., 1991-93; co-chmn. Nat. Bipartisan Commn. on Future of Medicare, 1998-99; co-chmn. Nat. Commn. on Retirement Policy, 1997-98; mem. Senate Rules Com.; mem. bd. dirs, CSX Corp., 2005- Co-chair senate Centrist Coalition; mem. Senate New Dems. Recipient Am. Legion award; Moot Ct. finalist La. State U., 1966; Neptune award Am. Oceanic Orgn., 1980 Mem. La. Bar Assn., Crowley Jr. C. of C., La. Jr. C. of C., Pi Lambda Beta, Phi Alpha Delta, Lambda Chi Alpha. Democrat. Office: Patton Boggs LLP 2550 M St NW Washington DC 20037 also: The Manship Sch 211 Journalism Bldg La State U Baton Rouge LA 70803

BREAZEALE, MACK ALFRED, research scientist, educator; b. Leona Mines, Va., Aug. 15, 1930; s. Carl Samuel and Maude Ella (Moore) B.; m. Joanne Morton O'Dell, Oct. 4, 1952 (dec. Nov. 1989); children: Jennifer Lee, David Mark, William Carl; m. Louise Hanna Scott, Nov. 10, 1990. BA, Berea Coll., 1953; MS, U. Mo., Rolla, 1954, Degree (hon.) in Physics, 2004; PhD, Mich. State U., 1957. Asst. rsch. prof. Mich. State U., 1957-62; assoc. prof. U. Tenn., 1962-67, prof. physics and astronomy, 1967—95; cons. solid state div. Oak Ridge Nat. Lab., 1962-71, cons. health and safety research div., 1985-87; cons. Naval Rsch. Labs., 1971-75; prin. investigator contracts Office Naval Rsch., AEC, 1963—95; disting. rsch. prof. U. Miss., 1988—; prin. scientist Nat. Ctr. for Phys. Acoustics, Miss., 1988—. Guest Inst. Basic Tech. Problems, Warsaw, Poland, 1972; vis. prof. Tech. U. of Denmark, 1977; guest U. Paris, 1977; mem. program com. Internat. Symposium on Nonlinear Acoustics, 1975, 76, 78, 81, 84, 87, 90, 93, 96, 99, 2002, 05. Contbr. articles to profl. jours. Recipient U. Mo. Alumni Merit award, 1990; Fulbright rsch. fellow Tech. U., Stuttgart, Fed. Republic Germany, 1958-59; Fulbright travel grantee, 1977-78, NATO rsch. grantee, 1978-81, 92-2001, 2004—, NSF U.S.-Italy program grantee, 1982-86. Fellow IEEE (adminstrv. com. ultrasonics, ferroelectrics and frequency control soc. 1987-89, program com. 1979—, pres. lectr., 1987, co-chair Atlanta Meeting Ultrasonics Symposium 2001, named Disting. Lectr. 1987-88), Inst. Acoustics (U.K.), Acoustical Soc. Am. (assoc. editor Nonlinear Acoustics 1977-2001, Silver medal in phys. acoustics 1988); mem. AAUP, Am. Phys. Soc., Sigma Xi, Phi Kappa Phi, Sigma Pi Sigma. Office: National Center for Physical Acoustics Coliseum Dr University MS 38677 Office Phone: 662-915-7490. Business E-Mail: breazeal@olemiss.edu. *Scientific progress ultimately depends upon absolute integrity and honesty. A scientist therefore must pursue Truth in such a manner that the path between himself and his goal can never be totally obstructed by any other human being.*

BREBBIA, CARLOS ALBERTO, engineering educator, consultant; b. Rosario, Argentina, Dec. 13, 1948; came to U.S., 1969; s. Carlos Alejandro and Elda (Eiris) B.; m. Carolyn Susan Stones, Oct. 30, 1971; children: Alexander Carlos, Isabel Elena. BS in civil engring., U. Litoral, Rosario, 1968; PhD in Civil Engring., U. Southampton, Eng., 1972; PhD (hon.), U. Bucharest, 1994. Lectr. U. Southampton, 1970-75, reader, 1976-79; assoc. prof. Princeton (N.J.) U., 1975-76; prof. U. Calif., Irvine, 1979-81; dir. Wessex Inst. Tech., Southampton, 1981—; pres. Computational Mechanics Inc., Billerica, Mass., 1984—. Mem. several adv. bds. Author 13 books; editor over 200 books; editor 3 profl. jours. Recipient Ville France medal, 1978; freeman City of London. Fellow Inst. Mech. Engring. (U.K.); mem. Liverymen of Co. of Sci. Instrument Makers. Roman Catholic. Achievements include development of the main concept of the boundary element method, of innovative computational techniques, of an industrial computer aided design code based on boundary element methods; founder of Computational Mechanics Internat., LTD, Wessex Institute of Technology. Office: WIT Ashurst Lodge Ashurst Southampton SO407AA England Office Phone: 44-2380-293223. Business E-Mail: carlos@wessex.ac.uk.

BRECHEEN, LEIGH, lawyer; d. Joel Moffat and Anne (Cutler) Brecheen; m. John James Dellaverson, Feb. 14, 1992; children: Griffin Dellaverson, Hunter Dellaverson. BA, Mills Coll., 1976; JD cum laude, Ariz. State U. Coll. Law, 1978. Bar: Ariz. 1979, Calif. 1981, Fed. Dist. Ct. L.A. 1981, N.Y. 1986. Assoc. Fennemore, Craig, von Ammon, Phoenix, 1979—81, O'Melveny & Myers, L.A., 1981—86; dir. bus. affairs Paramount Pictures, L.A., 1986—87; v.p. bus. affairs Republic Pictures, L.A., 1987—88, NBC Entertainment, Burbank, Calif., 1988—90; ptnr. Bloom, Hergott & Diemer, Beverly Hills, 1990—. Mem. bd. UCLA Law Sch. Entertainment Symposium, L.A., 1994—. Bd. dirs. Will Rogers Polo Club, L.A., 1984—87, 2003—04. Named to Super Lawyers, L.A. mag., 2004, 2005; recipient Cmty. Svc. award, Westside Women's Health Ctr., 1998. Mem.: Calif. Bar Assn., L.A. County Bar Assn., ABA (chair motion picture and TV divsn. forum of entertainment and sports 2004—). Episcopalian. Avocations: tennis, polo, skiing. Office: Bloom Hergott & Diemer 150 S Rodeo Dr 3d Fl Beverly Hills CA 90212 Office Phone: 310-859-6821. Business E-Mail: lcb@bhdrl.com.

BRECHER, ARMIN GEORGE, lawyer; b. Prague, Czechoslovakia, July 7, 1942; s. Gerhard and Eleanor Brecher; m. Elizabeth Pardue Rountree, July 2, 1966; children: Lindsay Brecher Cobb, Stefan Ryan, Alden Kelsey. BA summa cum laude, Emory U., Atlanta, 1966; LLB, U. Va., 1969. Ptnr., chair exec. com. and bd. ptnrs. Powell, Goldstein, Frazer & Murphy, Atlanta, 1969—. Mem. The ESOP Assn. Presbyterian. Office: Powell Goldstein Frazer & Murphy LLP 191 Peachtree St NE Fl 16 Atlanta GA 30303-1740

BRECHER, BERND, management consultant; b. Germany, Oct. 2, 1932; arrived in U.S., 1940; s. Jacob and Betty (Lewinsohn) B.; m. Helen Edith Casel, Feb. 1, 1959; children: Jacalyn Naomi, Alison Fay, Daniel Evan. BA, Columbia U., 1954, MS in Journalism, 1955. Dir. devel., pub. rels. and alumni affairs Coll. Physicians and Surgeons, Sch. Dentistry, Columbia U., N.Y.C., 1954-57; campaign dir., supr. John Price Jones Co., Inc., N.Y.C., 1958-67; v.p. Hamilton Coll. and Kirkland Coll., Clinton, N.Y., 1967-69; exec. v.p. John Price Jones Internat., Inc., N.Y.C., 1969-71; sr. v.p. Brakeley, John Price Jones, Inc., N.Y.C., 1971-73; pres. Bernd Brecher & Assocs., Inc., N.Y.C. and Scarsdale, 1973-93, Instl. Advancement Programs Inc., N.Y.C., Tuckahoe, Becket, Mass., 1979—. Cons., strategic planner for arts, health, edn., youth, religious, cmty., environ. and other not-for-profit instns.; exec. dir. The Grad. Ctr. Found., N.Y.C., 1994—97, Lehman Coll. Found., 2000—; cons. Lilly Endowment, Indpls., 1994—. Pres. Bd. Edn., Greenburgh, N.Y., 1977-78, Woodlands Scholarship Fund, Hartsdale, N.Y., 1965-66, Soc. Columbia Grads., 1980-85; mem. exec. com. Columbia Journalism Sch. Alumni, 1981-89; trustee Berkshire Children's Mus., 1998-2000; bd. dirs. Columbia U. Club Found., 1983—, v.p. 2003—; With U.S. Army, 1957-58. Recipient alumni medal for svc. Columbia U., 1983, Pres.'s Cup, 1981, Lion Awards, 1979, 80, 94, 99, Genesis award as a founder Alzheimer's Assn., 2005. Mem. Coun. for Advancment and Support of Edn. (Quarter Century Svc. award 1981), Assn. Fundraising Profls. (v.p. N.Y. chpt. 1987-89), Am. Assn. Cmty. and Jr. Colls., Am. Hosp. Assn., Am. Assn. Mus., Princeton Univ. Club, Univ. Club of Chgo. Avocations: theater, tennis, travel, fine dining. Home: 35 Parkview Ave Bronxville NY 10708-2953 Office: Instl Advancement Programs Inc 65 Main St Tuckahoe NY 10707-2908 Office Phone: 914-779-4092. Business E-Mail: BrecherServices@aol.com.

BRECHER, IRVING, economics professor; b. Montreal, Que., Can., Feb. 1, 1923; m. Toba Brecher, May 11, 1944; children: Richard, Thomas, Ronald, Teresa. BA, McGill U., 1943; MA, Harvard U., 1947, PhD, 1951; JD, Yale U., 1953. Tchg. fellow Harvard U., Mass., 1946—48; asst. prof. econs. McGill U., Montreal, 1948-50; Asst. prof. econs., lectr. law Northwestern U., Evanston, Ill., 1953-55; assoc. prof. McGill U., 1955—62; prof., 1962-84; chmn. dept. McGill U., 1981-84, prof. emeritus, 1985—, founding dir. Centre for Developing-Area Studies, 1963-71. Joint dir. Pakistan Inst. Devel. Econs., Karachi, 1960-61; bd. govs. Internat. Devel. Research Centre, Ottawa, 1970-73; vice chmn. Econ. Council Can., Ottawa, 1972-74; advisor various Can. and internat. orgns.; mem. staff Royal Commn. on Can.'s Econ. Prospects, Ottawa, 1955-57, Can. Royal Commn. on Banking and Fin., Ottawa, 1964-66; vis. fellow Rsch. Sch. Pacific Studies Australian Nat. U., Canberra, 1972; sr. fellow East-West Ctr. U. Hawaii, 1971-72; hon. lectr. law McGill U., 1964-66. Author: Monetary and Fiscal Thought and Policy in Canada, 1919-1939, 1957, Capital Flows between Canada and The United States, 1965, Canada's Competition Policy Revisited, 1982; co-author: Canada-United States Economic Relations, 1957, Foreign Aid and Industrial Development in Pakistan, 1972; editor: Human Rights, Development and Foreign Policy: Canadian Perspectives, 1989; co-editor: Development Planning and Policy in Pakistan, 1950-70, 1973, Equity and Efficiency in Economic Development, 1992; contbr. numerous articles profl. jours., parliamentary procs., magazines and newspapers. Bd. dirs. Can. Human Rights Found., Montreal, 1988-91, Internat. Ctr. for Human Rights and Dem. Devel., Montreal, 1990-94. Recipient Queen's Silver Jubilee medal, 1978, prize for rsch. on internat. cartels Yale Law Sch., 1962; Leave fellow Can. Council, 1971-72. Mem. Am. Econ. Assn., Can. Econs. Assn., Can. Inst. Internat. Affairs (mem. founding com.), North-South Inst. Office: McGill U-Dept of Econs 855 Sherbrooke St W Montreal PQ Canada H3A 2T7 Office Phone: 514-398-2523.

BRECHER, JOHN, newspaper editor; m. Dorothy J. Gaiter, Apr. 17, 1979; 2 children. BA in Journalism, Columbia U. With The Miami Herald, Newsweek, 1980—84; city editor The Miami Herald, 1984; sr. special writer Page One Wall Street Jour., 1990, page one editor N.Y.C., 1992—2000, columnist, Tastings (with Dorothy Gaiter). Appearances Martha Stewart Living, Today. Co-author (with Dorothy Gaiter): The Wall Street Journal Guide to Wine, 1999, The Wall Street Journal Guide to Wine New and Improved, 2002, Love by the Glass: Tasting Notes From a Marriage, 2003. Office: Dow Jones & Co 200 Liberty St Fl 11 New York NY 10281-1099*

BRECHER, KENNETH, astrophysicist, educator; b. NYC, Dec. 7, 1943; s. Irving and Edythe (Grossman) B.; m. Aviva Schwartz, Aug. 18, 1965; children: Karen, Daniel. BS, MIT, 1964, PhD, 1969. Research physicist U. Calif., San Diego, 1969-72; asst. prof. physics MIT, Cambridge, 1972-77, assoc. prof., 1977-79; assoc. prof. astronomy and physics Boston U., 1979-81, prof., 1981—, dir. Sci. and Math. Edn. Ctr., 1990—. Author, editor: (with G. Setti) High Energy Astrophysics and Its Relation to Elementary Particle Physics, 1974, (with M. Feirtag) Astronomy of the Ancients, 1979; contbr. numerous articles to profl. jours. Mem. Mass. Cultural Coun., 1989-91. Guggenheim fellow, 1979—80, W.K. Kellogg fellow, 1985—88, NRC sr. rsch. assoc., 1983—84, Exploratorium Osher fellow, 2001. Fellow Am. Phys. Soc. (chmn. astrophysics div. 1990-91); mem. Am. Aston. Soc., Internat. Astron. Union, Am. Assn. Physics Tchrs., N.Y. Acad. Scis., Sigma Xi. Home: 35 Madison St Belmont MA 02478-3535 Office: Boston U Dept Astronomy 725 Commonwealth Ave Boston MA 02215-1401

BRECHER, MICHAEL, political science professor; b. Montreal, Mar. 14, 1925; s. Nathan and Gisela (Hopmeyer) B.; m. Eva Danon, Dec. 7, 1950; children: Leora, Diana, Seegla. BA, McGill U., 1946; MA, Yale U., 1948, PhD, 1953. Mem. faculty McGill U., Montreal, 1952—, prof. polit. sci., 1963—, R.B. Angus prof. polit. sci., 1993—. Founder Shastri Indo-Can. Inst., 1968, pres., 1969, 70; vis. prof. U. Chgo., 1963; vis. prof. internat. rels. Hebrew U., Jerusalem, 1970-75, U. Calif., Berkeley, 1979, Stanford U., 1980. Author: The Struggle for Kashmir, 1953, Nehru: A Political Biography, 1959, The New States of Asia, 1963, Succession in India, 1966, India and World Politics, 1968, Political Leadership in India, 1969, The Foreign Policy System of Israel, 1972, Israel: The Korean War and China, 1974, Decisions in Israel's Foreign Policy, 1975, Studies in Crisis Behavior, 1979, Decisions in Crisis, 1980, Crisis and Change in World Politics, 1986, Crises in the 20th Century: Vol. 1, Handbook of International Crises, Vol. 2, Handbook of Foreign Policy Crises, 1988, Crisis, Conflict and Instability, 1989, Crises in World Politics, 1993, A Study of Crisis, 1997, 2000, Millennial Reflections on International Studies, 2002; contbr. over 80 articles in field to profl. jours. Recipient Watumull prize, Am. Hist. Assn., 1960, Killam awards, Can. Coun., 1970—74, 1976—79, Woodrow Wilson Found. award, Am. Polit. Sci. Assn., 1973, Fieldhouse tchg. award, McGill U., 1986, Disting. Scholar award, Internat. Studies Assn., 1995, Léon-Gérin Quebec Prize for Human Scis., 2000, Disting. Rsch. award, McGill U., 2000; Nuffield fellow, 1955—56, Rockefeller fellow, 1964—65, Guggenheim fellow, 1965—66, rsch. grantee, Can. Coun. and Soc. Sci. and Humanities Rsch. Coun. of Can., 1960, 1965, 1968, 1969—70, 1975—76, 1980—87, 1990—92, 1993—96, 2002—05. Fellow Royal Soc. Can.; mem. Internat. Studies Assn. (pres. 1999-2000), Brit. Internat. Studies Assn., World Assn. Internat. Relations, Internat., Am., Can., Israeli polit. sci. assns. Home: 5 Dubnov St Jerusalem 91043 Israel Office: McGill U Dept Pol Sci 855 Sherbrooke St W Montreal PQ Canada H3A 2T7 Office Phone: 514-398-4800.

BRECHER, MITCHELL FREDRICK, lawyer; b. Washington, July 29, 1948; s. Sam W. and Roslyn P. (Block) B.; m. Sandra L. Levinson, June 10, 1973; children— Reid Scott, Todd Loren. B.A., Franklin and Marshall Coll., 1970; J.D. with honors, George Washington U., 1973. Bar: Md. 1973, D.C. 1975, U.S. Supreme Ct. 1978, U.S. Dist. Ct. D.C. 1981, U.S. Ct. Appeals (D.C. cir.) 1981. Law clk. 5th Jud. Circuit Ct., Annapolis, Md., 1973-74; atty.-advisor FCC, Washington, 1974-81; sr. atty. GTE Sprint Communications Corp., Washington, 1981-84; asst. gen. counsel, dir. regulatory affairs Lexitel Corp., Washington, 1984-85, ALC Communications Corp., from 1985; with Bishop, Cook & Reynolds, Washington, now shareholder, telecom. law and regulation, Greenberg Traurig, Washington. Mem. Md. Bar Assn., D.C. Bar Assn., Fed Communications Bar Assn. Democrat. Jewish. Office: Greenberg Traurig LLP Ste 500 800 Connecticut Ave NW Washington DC 20006-2709 Office Phone: 202-331-3152. Business E-Mail: brecherm@gtlaw.com.

BRECHKA, FRANK TILSON, retired librarian, historian; b. N.Y.C., Sept. 30, 1930; s. Frank August and Marjorie Tilson (Connell) B. AB, Columbia U., 1952, MS, 1954, AM, 1958; PhD, U. Calif., Berkeley, 1968. Libr. N.Y. Pub. Libr., N.Y.C., 1954-57, sr. libr., 1959-61; head libr. S.I. C.C., N.Y.C., 1958-59; reference libr. Wagner Coll., N.Y.C., 1961-63, U. Calif., Berkeley, 1967-71, history libr., 1971-91, retired, 1991. Instr. history and librarianship U. Calif., Berkeley, 1970-77; cons. San Francisco Towers Libr., 1996—. Author: Gerard Van Swieten and His World, 1700-1772, 1970; contbr. articles to profl. jours. Rsch. grantee Librs. Assn. Univ. Calif., Berkeley, 1982; scholar Columbia Univ. Sch. Libr. Svc., N.Y.C., 1952-53, Fulbright, Netherlands and Austria, 1965-66. Mem. Am. Hist. Assn., Inst. for Hist. Study. Avocations: collecting books and antique maps, writing letters, travel. Home: 1661 Pine St Apt 823 San Francisco CA 94109-0409

BRECHTEL, UNDA JURKA, library director; b. Riga, Latvia, Mar. 3, 1935; came to U.S., 1951; d. Aleksanders and Irene (Stesingers) Jurka; m. Philipp Jack Brechtel Jr., Sept. 3, 1960 (div. Aug. 1986); children: Philipp Jack III, Peter Kevin. BS in Psychology, St. Thomas Aquinas, 1981; MLS, L.I. U., 1982. Reference librarian Haverstraw (N.Y.) Pub. Libr., 1982-83; libr. dir. Sloatsburg (N.Y.) Pub. Libr., 1983-85, Wanaque (N.J.) Pub. Libr., 1985-88, Oakland (N.J.) Pub. Libr., 1988-2000; ret.; libr. L.I. U., Sparkill, N.Y., 2000—. Mem. N.J. Libr. Assn., N.Y. Libr. Assn. Lutheran. Avocations: ballroom dancing, travel, gardening. Home: 1-16 Lawrence Pk Piermont NY 10968 Office Phone: 845-359-7200 5411. Personal E-mail: ubrechtel@yahoo.com.

BRECKEL, ALVINA HEFELI, librarian; b. Chgo., Dec. 6, 1948; d. William Christ and Liselotte (Herrmann) Hefeli; m. Theodore A. Breckel, Feb. 10, 1973. BFA cum laude, Bradley U., 1970; MALS, Rosary Coll. (now Dominican U.), 1973. Cert. art tchr., media libr., Ill. Tchr. art Chgo. Pub. Schs., 1971—84; libr. Oakton CC, Des Plaines, Ill., 1988—. Co-chmn. Winnetka Antiques Show, 1999, chmn., 2000, dealer chmn., 2000—; mem. North Shore Bd. Gads Hill Ctr., corr. sec., 2000—04, pres., 2004—; mem. Com. Gallery 37 in Schs., 2001—; mem. visual arts com. Chgo. Cmty. Trust Gallery Northwestern U. Settlement Assn., 2001—. Author: Looking for Glass on the Internet, 1996; editor News & Notes, 1988-89. Rep. election judge New Trier Twp., Ill., 1988; com. mem. Villagers for a Safe Winnetka, 1989; mem. women's bd. Howard Area Cmty. Ctr., 1990-95; chmn. Fuller Lane Cir., Winnetka, 1991-92, 94-95; mem. Midwestern Antiques Club, 1993—; mem. women's bd. Winnetka Cmty. House, 1995—03, historian, 1997—2003, mem. steering com., 1999—. Mem. AAUW (bd. dirs. New Trier chpt. 1989-90), Sandwich (Mass.) Hist. Soc., Winnetka Hist. Soc., Art Inst. Chgo. (life), Nat. Greentown Glass Assn., Nat. Am. Glass Club (life, founding mem. James H. Rose chpt., chpt. sec. 1992-97), Greater Chgo. Glass Collectors Club (v.p. 1995-97, pres. 1998-2000, chmn. bylaws com. 2001, chmn. nominating com. 2002), Early Am. Pattern Glass Soc. (nominating com. 1998, nat. seminar spr., 1999, spkr. Mid-States conf. 2001), Chgo. Area Shaker Interest Group, Pi Lambda Theta (life, art editor chpt. Notes 1977-84), Delta Zeta (v.p. Chgo. North Shore chpt. 1987-90), Phi Delta Kappa. Avocation: collecting and researching early American decorative arts, especially glass. Home: 185 Fuller Ln Winnetka IL 60093-4212 Office: Oakton CC 7701 Lincoln Ave Skokie IL 60077-2800

BRECKENRIDGE, BRUCE M., art educator, ceramist; b. Chgo. s. Earl George and Marjorie Duncan Breckenridge; m. Suzanne Hultquist Breckenridge, Oct. 18, 1696; children: Sarah Annessa, Ethan Hayden. B of Art Edn., Wis. State Coll., 1952; MFA, Cranbrook Acad. Art, 1953. Vis. lectr. Olivet Coll., Olivet, Mich., 1954—55; faculty Calif. Coll. Arts and Crafts, Oakland, 1961—64, Bklyn. Mus. Art Sch., 1965—68; lectr. Hunter Coll., N.Y.C., 1966—67; vis. lectr. U. Calif., Berkeley, 1967, Ariz. State U., Tempe, 1968; prof. art U. Wis., Madison, 1968—. Jr. asst. dir. Milw. Art Inst., 1951—52; installation asst. Mus. Modern Art, N.Y.C., 1964—65; asst. dir. Mus. Contemporary Crafts, N.Y.C., 1965—67. Author: (mus. catalogs) New Ceramic Forms, 1966, (review of exhbns.) Craft Horizons, 1970—71. Mem.: Nat. Coun. on Edn. in the Ceramic Arts. Home: 1715 Regent St Madison WI 53726 Office: Univ Wis Dept Art 455 N Park St Madison WI 53706 Office Phone: 608-262-6546. Business E-Mail: bmbrecke@wisc.ued.

BRECKENRIDGE, KLINDT DUNCAN, architect; b. Iowa City, Apr. 24, 1957; s. Jack Duncan and Florence (Kmiecik) B.; m. Nancy Ann Dernier, Apr. 19, 1986; children: Wilson Reid, Lauren Alessandra, Carson Duncan. BArch, U. Ariz., 1981. Registered architect, Ariz., Calif., Nev.; cert. NCARB. Architect Finical & Dombrowski, Tucson, 1981-84; pvt. practice Tucson, 1984—. Assoc. faculty Pima Community Coll. Bd. dirs., pres. Mirical Sq. Mem. AIA (treas. So. Ariz. chpt. 1997-99, pres. 1999-2000, state pres. elect 2003, com. arch. edn., pres.-elect). Democrat. Episcopalian. Avocation: running. Home: 5535 N Waterfield Dr Tucson AZ 85750-6473 Office: Brackenridge Group 700 N Stone Ave Tucson AZ 85705-8306 E-mail: breckenridge@breckenridgearch.com.

BRECKINRIDGE, JAMES BERNARD, optical engineer; s. Albert Coles and Catherine Rose (Wengler) B.; m. Ann Marie Yoder, July 24, 1965; children: Douglass E., John Brian. BS in Physics, Case Inst. Tech., 1961; MS in Optical Sci., U. Ariz., 1970, PhD in Optical Sci., 1976. Rsch. asst. Lick Obs., Mt. Hamilton, Calif., 1961-64; electron tube engr. Rauland Corp., Chgo., 1967; rsch. asst. Kitt Peak Nat. Obs., Tucson, full time, 1964-66, 68, 75-76, part time, 1969-74; mem. tech. staff Jet Propulsion Lab., Calif. Inst. Tech., 1976—, part-time faculty in applied physics, 1981—, mgr. optics sect., 1981-94; program mgr. for innovative imaging tech. and sys. Def. Program Office, 1994—99; leader NASA Team to Assess Optics Tech. in Former Soviet Union, 1992-97, mgmt. and tech. cons., 1994—; program dir. advanced tech. and instrumentation, program dir. Nat. Radio Astronomy Obs., NSF, 1999—2002; chief technologist Astron. Search for Origins, NASA, 2002—. Co-investigator NASA Spacelab 3; mem. adv. com. NASA, NSF, Dept. Def.; staff mem. Hubble Space Telescope Failure Bd., 1990, tech. mgr. Hubble Space Telescope Camera Optics Repair; mgr. advanced tech. and instruments and Nat. Radio Astronomy Obs., NSF, 1999-2002. Contbr. articles to jours. in field; 5 patents in field. Scoutmaster Boy Scouts Am.; bd. trustees United Ch. of Christ; historian Breckinridge Family Assn. Fellow Optical Soc. Am. (bd. dirs.), Royal Astron. Soc., Internat. Soc. Optical Engring. (bd. govs., pres. 1994, George W. Goddard award 2003); mem. IEEE, Am. Astron. Soc., Coun. of Scientific Soc. Pres.'s (bd. dirs. 1996), Internat. Astron. Union, Internat. Congress on Optics (U.S. chair 1999-2001), Astron. Soc. of Pacific, Breckinridge Family Assn. (pres. 1999—). Achievements include research in remote optical and infrared sensing instrumentation, interferometry, spectroscopy, image intensifiers and image analysis. Office: 4800 Oak Grove Dr Pasadena CA 91109 Home: 985 E California Blvd Ste 203 Pasadena CA 91106 Office Phone: 818-354-6785.

BRECKNER, WILLIAM JOHN, JR., retired military officer; b. Alliance, Ohio, May 25, 1933; s. William John and Frances P. (Bertchey) B.; m. Cheryl V. Carmell, Aug. 30, 1963; children: William R., Kristen C. BA, SUNY, 1976; postgrad., Harvard U., 1980. Commd. 2d lt. USAF, 1955, advanced through grades to maj. gen., 1983, various pilot and command positions, 1955-72; comdr. USAF Interceptor Weapons Sch., 1973-75; vice commandant cadets USAF Acad., Colo., 1976-79; comdr. 82d Flying Tng. Wing Williams AFB, Ariz., 1979-80; dep. chief staff logistics Hdqrs. Air Tng. Commd., Tex., 1980-83; chief staff Hdqrs. USAF Europe, 1983-84; commdr. 17th Air Force, Sembach AFB, Germany, 1984-86; ret., 1986. Mem. Colorado Springs Airport Adv. Commn.; bd. dirs. Falcon Found. Prisoner of war, Vietnam, 1972-73. Decorated D.S.M., 1986, Silver Star, 1972, Legion of Merit, 1973, Bronze Star medal, 1973, Air medal, 1968, 72, Purple Heart, 1972, 73, Republic of Vietnam Cross of Gallantry with palm, 1973 Mem. Nat. War Coll. Alumni Assn., Order Daedalians (bd. dirs.), Air Force Assn., Nam Prisoners of War Inc., Red River Valley Fighter Pilots Assn., C. of C. (chmn. mil. affairs coun. 1994-95). Lutheran. Avocations: golf, skiing, tennis. Home: 17865 Fairplay Way Monument CO 80132-8581 Office: 590 Hwy 105 Ste 266 Monument CO 80132 Office Phone: 719-481-6000. E-mail: brexgroup@earthlink.net.

BRECKON, DONALD JOHN, academic administrator; b. Port Huron, Mich., June 11, 1939; s. Robert Joseph and Margaret Elizabeth (Wade) B.; m. Sandra Kay Biehn, Sept. 4, 1959; children: Lori E., LeeAnne M., Lisa C.,

Lynanne U. AA, St. Clair County C.C., 1959; BS, Central Mich. U., 1962, MA, 1963; postgrad., U. Wis., 1965-66, Western Mich. U., 1968; MPH, U. Mich., 1968; PhD, Mich. State U., 1977. Instr. hrealth edn. Central Mich. U., Mt. Pleasant, 1963-68, asst. prof., 1968-72, assoc. prof., 1972-81, prof. health edn., 1978-81, asst. dean health, phys. edn. and recreation, 1981-82, assoc. dean edn., health and human svcs., 1982-86, dean grad. studies/assoc. provost for rsch., 1986-87; pres. Park Coll., Parkville, Mo., 1987—. Author: Hospital Health Education: A Guide to Program Development, 1982, Community Health Education: Setting, Roles and Skills, 1985, 3d rev. edit., 1994, Microcomputer Applications to Health Education and Health Science, 1986, Matters of Life and Death, 1987; contbr. articles to profl. jours. Recipient Central Mich. U. Tchg. Effectiveness awrd, 1975, Disting. Svc. award Mich. Alcoholism and Addiction Assn., 1977, Disting. Alumni award St. Clair County, 1988, Centennial award Ctrl. Mich. U., 1992, Northlander of Yr. award Kans. City Northland regional C. of C.; Mich. Dept. Edn. scholar, 1971, Yale U. Drug Dependence Inst. scholar, 1973, Midwest Inst. Alcohol Studies, Mich. Dept. Pub. Health scholar, 1974; Am. Coun. on Edn. Leadership dEvel. program fellow, 1979. Mem. Mich. Pub. Health Assn. (pres. 1976-77), Am. Pub. Health Assn., Soc. Pub. Health Edn. (pres. 1978-79), Internat. Soc. Pub. Health Edn., Coalition of Mich. Health Edn. Orgns., Mich. Alcohol and Addiction Assn., Am. Alliance for Health and Phys. Edn. Home: 7320 NW Katie Cir Kansas City MO 64152-1988 Office: Park Coll Office of Pres Parkville MO 64152

BREDAR, JAMES KELLEHER, judge; b. Omaha, Feb. 6, 1957; s. William Lorenz and Helen Dorothy (Kelleher) B.; m. Stacey Lynn Sewell, July 26, 2002. BA, Harvard U., 1979; JD, Georgetown U., 1982. Bar: Colo. 1983, Md. 1995, U.S. Supreme Ct. 1993. Nat. park ranger U.S. Dept. Interior, Estes Park, Colo., 1976-80; jud. law clk. U.S. Dist. Judge R. Matsch, Denver, 1983; dep. dist. atty. State of Colo., Craig, 1984; asst. U.S. atty. U.S. Dept. Justice, Denver, 1985-89; asst. fed. pub. defender U.S. Courts, Denver, 1989-91, fed. pub. defender Balt., 1992-98; project dir. Vera Inst. Justice, London, 1991-92; U.S. magistrate judge Balt., 1998—. Vis. scholar Yale U., New Haven, 1981-82. Author/editor: Justice Informed, 1992. Office: US Magistrate Judge 8C US Courthouse 101 W Lombard St Baltimore MD 21201-2605

BREDESEN, PHILIP NORMAN, governor; b. Oceanport, N.J., Nov. 21, 1943; s. Philip Norman and Norma (Walborn) B.; m. Andrea Conte, Nov. 22, 1974; 1 child, Benjamin. AB in Physics, Harvard U., 1967. Computer programmer Itek Corp., Lexington, Mass., 1967-70; dir. systems devel. Searle Medidata, Lexington, 1970-73, div. mgr. London, 1973-75; dir. spl. project Hosp. Affiliates Internat., Nashville, 1975-78; v.p. internat. div. INA Health Care Group, Nashville, 1978-80; chmn. and chief exec. officer HealthAmerica Corp., Nashville, 1980-86; chmn., co-founder Coventry Corp., Nashville, 1986-90; chmn. Clin. Pharms., Nashville, 1986-93; mayor Met. Govt. Nashville and Davidson County, 1991-99; pres. Bredex Corp., Nashville, 2000—02; gov. State of Tenn., Nashville, 2003—. Bd. dirs. Nashville Symphony, 1985-91, Univ. Sch. Nashville, 1986-95, United Cerebral Palsy, 1988-92, United Way of Middle Tenn., 1985-90, Tenn. State U. Found., Nashville Pub. Libr. Found., 1997—; chmn., founder The Land Trust for Tenn., 1999-2001; trustee Frist Ctr. for Visual Arts, 1998-03, chair fin. com., 2000-03; founder Nashville's Table, 1989, bd. dirs., 1989-91. Democrat. Presbyterian. Avocations: skiing, reading, computers. Home: 1724 Chickering Rd Nashville TN 37215-4908 Office: State Capitol Office Governor Nashville TN 37243-0001 Office Phone: 615-741-2001. Business E-Mail: phil.bredesen@state.tn.us.

BREDFELDT, JOHN CREIGHTON, economist, financial analyst, retired military officer; b. Oct. 31, 1947; s. Willis John and Geraldine Elizabeth (Creighton) Bredfeldt; m. Janice Elizabeth Hamilton; children: Jason Caulter, Bryan Thomas. BBA, Wichita State U., 1969, MA in Econs., 1971; PhD in Pub. Adminstrn., La Salle U., 1995; grad., Air Command and Staff Coll., 1984, Nat. Defense U., 1987. Dir. Brennan Halls Wichita State U., 1969-71; commd. 2d lt. USAF, 1971, advanced through grades to lt. col., 1987, ret., 1993; budget/cost analyst Aero. Sys. Divsn., Dayton, Ohio, 1971-76; insp. Air Force IG, Andrews AFB, Md., 1976-79; chief economist Dir. Programs AF/PRP, Pentagon, Va., 1979-83; chief cost analyst divsn. USAF Europe, 1985-87, dep. dir. program control, engine program office Dayton, 1987-89; dir. program control spl. ops. forces USAF, 1989-93; project leader for econs./fin. analyst Modern Techs. Corp., Warner Robins, Ga., 1993—. Instr. econs. Wichita State U., 1969-71; bus. prof. Bowie State Coll., 1980-83; econs. instr. European divsn. U. Md., Germany, 1985-87, Sinclair C.C., Dayton, 1988-93, Macon (Ga.) State Coll., 1994—; adj. prof. Mercer U., 1996—, Wesleyan Coll., 1998—. Contbr. articles to profl. jours. Rep., Sunday sch. tchr. Ramstein Protestant Parish Coun. Germany, 1984-86; asst. scout master Ramstein Coun. Boy Scouts Am., 1984-87, den leader Weblos, 1998, Troop 550 charter rep., 1999—; v.p. St. Timothy Lutheran Ch., Dayton, 1989-91; prayer team leader Wesley United Meth. Ch., Macon, 2004, chmn. fin. com., 2005. Mem. Assn. Govt. Accts., soc. cost Estimating and Analysis, Am. Soc. Mil. Comptrollers, Nat. Eagle Scout Assn. Personal E-mail: jeb15@cox.net.

BREE, MARLIN DUANE, publisher, author; b. Norfolk, Nebr., May 16, 1933; s. George F. and Luile Bree; m. Loris Bree; 1 child, William Marlin. BA, cert. in journalism, U. Nebr., 1955. Mng. editor Davidson Pub. Co., 1958-61; editor Greater Mpls. mag., 1962-63; pub. rels. specialist Blue Shield, 1964-67; editor Sunday Mag., Star and Tribune, Mpls., 1968-72; columnist Corp. Report, Mpls., 1973-77; publs. cons., 1978-83; co-founder, ptnr., editorial dir. Marlor Press, Inc., St. Paul, 1983-91, co-owner, pub., 1992—. Chmn. Midwest Book Awards, St. Paul, 1992. Author: In the Teeth of the Northeaster: A Solo Voyage on Lake Superior, 1988, Call of the North Wind: Voyages and Adventures on Lake Superior, 1996, Wake of the Green Storm: A Survivor's Tale, 2001, Broken Seas: True Tales of Extraordinary Seafaring Adventures, 2005; co-author: Alone Against the Atlantic, 1981; illustrator: Kids' Magic Secrets, 2003. Dir. comm. Mpls. Bicentennial Celebration, 1976. With U.S. Army, 1955-57. Named Pub. of Yr., Midwest Ind. Pubs. Assn., 1994; recipient Golden Web award, 2003-04, Writing award Boating Writers Internat., 2003, Grand Prize, Boating Writers Internat., 2004, West Marine Writer's award, 2004; honored as one of Best Ind. Pubs. in U.S., Top 101 Ind. Book Pubs., 1997. Mem.: St. Paul Sail and Power Squadron (hon.). Avocation: sailing. Office: Marlor Press Inc 4304 Brigadoon Dr Saint Paul MN 55126-3100 E-mail: marlin.marlor@minn.net.

BREECE, ROBERT WILLIAM, JR., lawyer; b. Blackwell, Okla., Feb. 5, 1942; s. Robert William Breece Sr. and Helen Elaine (Maddox) Breece Robinson; m. Elaine Marie Keller, Sept. 7, 1968; children: Bryan, Justin, Lauren BSBA, Northwestern U., 1964; JD, U. Okla., 1967; LLM, Washington U., St. Louis, 1970. Bar: Oklahoma 1967, Mo. 1970. Pvt. practice, St. Louis, 1968—. Pres., chmn. bd. dirs. Crown Capital Corp., St. Louis. Mem. ABA, Internat. Bar Assn., Mo. Bar Assn., Okla. Bar Assn., Phi Alpha Delta, Beta Theta Pi, Melrose Club, Univ. Club, Forest Hills Country Club (pres. 1978). Home: 35 Crown Manor Dr Chesterfield MO 63005-6805 Office: 540 Maryville Centre Dr Ste 12 Saint Louis MO 63141-5828 Office Phone: 314-576-4822.

BREED, ALLEN FORBES, social services administrator; b. Wisconsin Rapids, Wis., Oct. 1, 1920; s. Noel Jerub and May Belle (Forbes) B.; m. Virginia Mae Plaskett, June 24, 1945; children: Marla, Eleanor, Carol. BA cum laude, U. Pacific, 1942. With Dept. Youth Authority, State of Calif., 1945-76, supt. correctional schs., 1947-65, chief div. instns., 1965-67; chmn. Youth Authority Bd., State of Calif., 1967-76; dir. Dept. Youth Authority, State of Calif., 1967-76; vis. fellow Dept. Justice, 1976-77; spl. master U.S. Dist. Ct., R.I., 1977-78; dir. Nat. Inst. Corrections, Dept. Justice, Washington, 1978-83; chmn. bd. Nat. Council Crime and Delinquency, Washington, 1983-91, 98-99; spl. master to fed. and state cts. on prison litigation issues, 1983—. Chmn. Task Force on Corrections and mem. Joint Commn. on Juvenile Justice Standards, ABA and Inst. Judicial Adminstrn.; mem. nat. adv. com. on Juvenile Justice and Delinquency Prevention; mem. U.S. del. UN Congress on Prevention of Crime and Treatment of Offenders, Caracas, Venezuela, 1980; mem. UN Congress on Prevention Crime and Treatment of Offenders, Milan, Italy, 1985; del. Internat. Conf. on Criminology, Hamburg, Federal Republic of Germany, 1988, Internat. Conf. on Future of Corrections, Ottawa, Can., 1991—; leader del. on juvenile justice to Russia, 1989—; lectr. 1st Sino-Am. Criminal Justice Inst., People's Republic China, 1986; criminal and juvenile justice del. People's Republic China, 1992; del. Internat. Conf. Corrections, Warsaw, 1993. Contbr. articles to profl. jours., newspapers, mags. Mem. justice programs adv. com. Edna McConnel Clark Found., 1983-89; chmn. Calaveras County Libr. Commn., 2000—; vice chmn. Calaveras County Juvenile Justice Commn., 2002—; mem. Calaveras Cmty. Found., 2004—. Served to maj. USMC, 1942-45. Decorated Purple Heart. Mem. Nat. Assn. State Correctional Adminstrs. (state and nat. awards), Nat. Assn. State Juvenile Delinquency Program Adminstrs. (past pres.), Interstate Compact on Probation and Parole (past pres.), Am. Correctional Assn. (v.p. 1984-86, bd. govs. 1986-91), Am. Arbitration Assn., Nat. Coun. Crime and Delinquency (chmn. emeritus bd. dirs.), Calif. Probation, Parole and Correctional Assn. Episcopalian. Home: PO Box 698 San Andreas CA 95249-0698

BREED, RIA, anthropologist; b. Feb. 5, 1944; d. Jan Mathys and Maria Arnoldina (Gommans) Trienekens; m. David Scranton Breed, Sept. 5, 1976; children: Christian, Genevieve. Med. technologist, Profl. Sch. Venlo (Netherlands), 1962; BA in Social Anthropology, U. Amsterdam, 1972; MA in Phys. Anthropology, NYU, 1977, PhD, 1984. Clin. technologist St. Lambertus Hosp., Helmond, Netherlands, 1962—65, DePaul Hosp., Norfolk, Va., 1965—66; rsch. technician U. Amsterdam, 1968—70; rsch. technician cardiovasc. rsch. NYU Med. Ctr., NYC, 1966—68, 1972—77; rsch. assoc. NYU, NYC, 1984; head biomechanics dept. Breed Corp., 1984—88; with Automotive Tech. Internat., Denville, NJ, 1989—. Home: 48 Hillcrest Rd Boonton NJ 07005-9433 Office: Automotive Tech Internat PO Box 8 Denville NJ 07834-0008

BREEDEN, DOUGLAS TOWER, financial consultant, dean; b. Leavenworth, Ind., Sept. 29, 1950; s. Russell E. and Annabelle (Tower) B.; m. Josie Chao-Chih Pian, June 4, 1972; children: Jennifer, Laurel, Mark, David. BS in mgmt. sci., MIT, 1972; postgrad., Harvard U., 1973—74; MA in econs., Stanford U., 1976, PhD in fin., 1978. Asst. prof. fin. U. Chgo., 1978—79, Stanford U., 1979—81, assoc. prof. fin., 1981—85; vis. assoc. prof. fin. Yale U., 1981—82, Sloan Sch. Mgmt., MIT, 1984-85; area coord. for fin. and econs. Fuqua Sch. Bus., Duke U., Durham, NC, 1985—86, 1987—88, assoc. prof. fin., 1985—89, co-dir. Futures and Options Rsch. Ctr., 1987-90, prof. fin. Durham, NC, 1989—91, rsch. prof. fin., 1991—99, dean, William W. Priest Prof. Fin., 2001—; vis. prof. fin. Kenan Flagler Bus. Sch., U. NC, Chapel Hill, 2000, Dalton McMichael Prof. Fin., 2000-01; co-founder Smith Breeden Assocs., Chapel Hill, NC, 1982—, chmn. bd., 1982—2005, chmn. emeritus, 2005—, pres., 1988-2000; chmn. bd. Smith Breeden Mut. Funds, 1992-2000; chmn. bd., prin. shareholder Harrington Fin. Group, 1988—2001. Chmn., owner Wyandotte Cmty. Corp., 1989—; co-owner, Old Capital Golf Course, Corydon, IN, 1998-; chmn. bd., prin. shareholder, Cmty. First Fin. Group, 1986-; cons. Chgo. Bd. Trade, 1977-82; exec. tchr. Nomura Sch. Adv. Mgmt., Tokyo, 1987, 89-92. Editor Jour. Fixed Income, 1990-2001; assoc. editor Jour. of Fin., 1988-91, Rev. of Fin. Studies, 1987-89, Jour. Fin. Quantitative Analysis, 1985-87, Jour. Fin. Econs., 1982-88, Jour. Money, Credit and Banking, 1980-83; contbr. articles to profl. jours. Bd. dirs. Chapel Hill-Carrboro City Schs., 1989-93, Chapel Hill-Carrboro Pub Sch. Found., 1987-89; chmn. Breeden Family Found., 1989—; bd. dirs. Fund for Human Possibilities, 1995—; bd. visitors Fuqua Sch. Bus., Duke U., 1995-99; mem. deans adv. coun. Sloan Sch. Mgmt., MIT, 1999—, mem. vis. com., 1999—, mem. Pres. adv. com., 2000-01; donor Smith Breden prize Jour. of Fin., 1989—. Rotary Internat. Grad. Fellow in Bus., 1972-73, Batterymarch Fin. Mgmt. Fellow, 1981-82, Dean Witter Fellow in Fin., 1981-82. Mem. Am. Fin. Assn. (bd. dirs. 1988-91), Western Fin. Assn., Applied Capital Markets Group of Nat. Bur. Econ. Rsch. Methodist. Avocations: golf, skiing, basketball. Office: Duke U Fuqua Sch Bus One Towerview Dr Box 90120 Durham NC 27708-0120

BREEDIN, BERRYMAN BRENT, journalist, consultant, historian, public relations executive; b. Beaufort, S.C., Nov. 3, 1925; s. Berryman Brent Breedin and Jane Cunningham Dixon; m. Allain Crenshaw, Sept. 1959 (div. Jan. 1978); children: David Singleton, Sarah Breedin Chase, Amelia Breedin Twarogowski. BA, Washington and Lee U., 1947. Reporter Caller-Times, Corpus Christi, Tex., 1947-48; sports editor, columnist Daily Mail, Anderson, S.C., 1949-52; publicist, editor Clemson (S.C.) U., 1952-55, 64-66; resident mgr. Hunt Internat. Oil Co., Pakistan, 1955—58, Hunt Internat. Oil Co. Australia, 1996—97; press sec. U.S. Senator Strom Thurmond, Washington, 1958-59; info. specialist DuPont Co., Wilmington, Del., 1960-63; editor Am. Coll. Pub. Rels. Assn., Washington, 1966-71, Coun. Libr. Resources, Washington, 1972-75; dir. pub. rels. Georgetown U., Washington, 1977-79, Rice U., Houston, 1981-87; pvt. practice Columbia, S.C., 1988—; historian White House Weekly, Washington, 1998—2003. Adv. Washington D.C. Libr., 1972-76, Houston Zoo, 1981-87. Founding mem. Capital Hill Montessori, Washington, 1964, Field Sch., Washington, 1972. With USN, 1944-45. Mem. Nat. Press Club, Sigma Delta Chi. Episcopalian. Avocations: family history, sports history, movie history. Home and Office: 1829 Senate St Apt 4C Columbia SC 29201-3837 E-mail: bbreedin@sc.rr.com.

BREEDING, CARL WAYNE, lawyer; b. Whitesburg, Ky., Jan. 2, 1954; s. Carl Don and Pearl Marie (Taylor) B.; m. Mary Caufield, Sept. 7, 1974; children: Laura Taylor, Emily Allyn. BA, Transylvania U., 1976; JD, U. Ky., 1979. Bar: Ky. 1979, U.S. Dist. Ct. (ea., we. dists.) Ky. 1982, U.S. Ct. Appeals (6th cir.) 1982, U.S. Supreme Ct. 1984. Atty. Ky. Natural Resources & Environ. Protection Cabinet, Frankfort, 1979-81, dep. gen. counsel, 1981-83, gen. counsel, 1983-87; ptnr. Reece, Lang & Breeding, London, Ky., 1987-93, Breeding, McIntyre & Cunningham, P.S.C., 1993-98; with Greenebaum Doll & McDonald PLLC, Lexington, Ky., 1998—. Contbr. to profl. jours. Mem. Gov.'s Ground Water Adv. Com., Frankfort, 1986-87. Mem. ABA, Ky. Bar Assn., Fayette County Bar Assn. Republican. Home: 3 Deepwood Dr Lexington KY 40505-2105 Office: Greenebaum Doll & McDonald PLLC 229 W Main St Ste 101 Frankfort KY 40601 Office Phone: 502-875-0050. Business E-Mail: cwb@gdm.com.

BREEDLOVE, NANCY JEAN FREE, secondary school educator; b. Washington Court House, Ohio, Oct. 17, 1960; d. Robert Eugene and Nancy Marilyn (Vaughn) Free; m. Brian Frank Breedlove, Mar. 27, 1986. BA in Spanish and BS in Edn., Miami U., Oxford, Ohio, 1983; MA in Spanish Lit. and Linguistics, Ohio State U., 1986. Cert. tchr., Ohio, Wis. Tchr. Spanish Lakota High Sch., West Chester, Ohio, 1983-84, Washington Court House City Schs., 1986-92, Green Bay (Wis.) Area Pub Schs., 1992-93; tchr. Winneconne (Wis.) Community Schs., 1993—. Leader, organizer Student Travel Opportunities. Mem. NEA, Fgn. Lang. Tchrs. Assn., Order of Ea. Star, Spanish Club (officer theater prodn. Oxford, Ohio chpt. 1979-83, advisor Washington Court House chpt. 1986-92, advisor Winneconne chpt. 1993—), Sigma Delta Pi. Avocations: travel, reading, sports. Home: 2431 Newport Ct Oshkosh WI 54904-7317

BREEN, DAVID HART, lawyer; b. Ottawa, Ont., Can., Mar. 27, 1960; came to U.S., Aug. 19, 1978; naturalized, 1993; s. Harold John and Margaret Rae (Hart) B.; m. Pamela Annette Mitchell, Sept. 17, 1988; 1 child, Matthew Mitchell. BA cum laude, U. S.C., Columbia, 1982, JD, 1986. Bar: S.C., U.S. Dist. Ct. S.C., U.S. Ct. Appeals (4th cir.), U.S. Bankruptcy Ct. S.C. 1987. Law clk. to Hon. Don S. Rushing Cir. Ct. (6th cir.), S.C., 1986-87; English instr. humanities U. Coastal Carolina Coll., Conway, 1987-88; criminal law instr. Horry-Georgetown Tech. Coll., Conway, 1987-88; sr. ptnr. David H. Breen, P.A., Myrtle Beach, 1988—. C.J.A. panel atty. U.S. Dist. Ct. S.C., 1991-97; mem. family ct. adv. com. 15th Jud. Ct., 1998—. Campaign asst. Joe Clark for Prime Minister, Ottawa, 1975-76. Recipient Province of Ontario Achievement Award, 1976, Nat. Dean's List Award of Merit, 1981—82, Gold Medal - Rifle Shooting, Canada Summer Games, 1977, Provincial Champion Rifle Shooting, Ontario, 1977. Mem. ABA, ATLA, S.C. Trial Lawyers Assn., S.C. Bar Assn., Horry County Bar Assn., Am. Bankruptcy Inst., Oshawa Gun Club, Phi Delta Phi. Methodist. Avocations: swimming, computers. Home: Prestwick Country Club 2187 N Berwick Dr Myrtle Beach SC 29575-5835 Office: The Founders Ctr Ste 305 2411 Oak St Myrtle Beach SC 29577 Office Phone: 843-445-9915. Business E-Mail: davidhbreen@sc.rr.com.

BREEN, EDWARD D., manufacturing executive; married; 3 children. BS in Bus. Adminstrn. and Econs., Grove City Coll. With Gen. Instrument, 1978—88, sr. v.p. sales terrestrial products worldwide sales orgn., 1988—94, exec. v.p. terrestrial sys., 1994—96, sr. v.p. sales Broadband Networks Group, 1996—97, chmn., pres., CEO, 1997—2000; exec. v.p., pres. broadband comms. sector Motorola, 2000—01, exec. v.p., pres. networks sector, 2001—02, pres., COO Schaumburg, Ill., 2002, also bd. dirs.; chmn., CEO Tyco Internat., Portsmouth, NH, 2002—. Bd. dirs. McLeod USA Inc., Tyco Internat. Ltd. Named one of Top 15 CableFAX Mag.'s 100 most influential people in cable, 1999; recipient Vanguard award, Nat. Cable TV Assn., 1998. Office: Tyco Intl 273 Corporate Dr 100 Portsmouth NH 03801-6807

BREEN, JOHN EDWARD, civil engineer, educator; b. Buffalo, May 1, 1932; s. Timothy J. and Alice C. (Keenan) B.; m. Marian T. Killian, June 20, 1953; children: Mary L., Michael T., Dennis P., Sheila A., Sean E., Kerry T., Christopher D. B.C.E., Marquette U., Milw., 1953; DSc (hon.), Marquette U., 2004; MS in Civil Engring., U. Mo., 1957; PhD, U. Tex., Austin, 1962. Registered profl. engr., Tex., Mo. Structural designer Harnischfeger Corp., Milw., 1952-53; asst. prof. U. Mo., Columbia, 1957-59; mem. faculty U. Tex., Austin, 1959—, prof. civil engring., 1969—, J.J. McKetta prof. engring., 1977-81, Carol Cockrell Curran chair engring., 1981-84, Nasser I. Al-Rashid chair civil engring., 1984—; dir. P.M. Ferguson Structural Engring. Lab., Balcones Research Center, 1967-85. Cons. in field. Contbr. articles to profl. jours. Served to lt. USNR, 1953-56. Recipient Tchg. Excellence award Gen. Dynamics Corp., 1971, Tchg. Excellence award U. Tex. Student Assn., 1963, Teaching Excellence award Std. Oil Found. Ind., 1968, Fedn. Internat. Precontrainte medal, 1990, Internat. award of merit in structural engring. Internat. Assn. Bridge and Structural Engring., 2000, Freyssinet medal Internat. Assn. for Structural Concrete, 2002, Caquot medal French Assn. Civil Engring., 2004, John A. Roebling medal, 2005. Mem.: ASCE (T.Y. Lin medal 1985, 1989, 1991, A.J. Boase Reinforced Concrete Rsch. Coun. award 1987, Croes medal 1999), Swiss Acad. Engring., Nat. Acad. Engring., Am. Concrete Inst. (hon.; bd. dirs. 1974—77, Wason medal 1972, 1983, Raymond C. Reese Rsch. medal 1972, 1979, Kelly medal 1981, Anderson medal 1987, Raymond Davis lectr. 1978, Bloem award 1989, Alfred E. Lindau award 1994, Structural Engring. award 2002), Austin Yacht Club (commodore 1977), Sigma Xi. Democrat. Roman Catholic. Home: 8603 Azalea Trl Austin TX 78759-7501 Office: Univ Tex Ferguson Lab 10100 Burnet Rd Austin TX 78758-4445 Office Phone: 512-471-4578. Business E-Mail: jbreen@mail.utexas.edu.

BREEN, KATHERINE ANNE, speech and language pathologist; b. Chgo., Oct. 31, 1948; d. Robert Stephen and Gertrude Catherine (Bader) Breen. BS, Northwstern U., 1970; MA, U. Mo., Columbia, 1971. Cert. speech pathologist. Speech/lang. pathologist Fulton (Mo.) Pub. Schs., 1971-73; co-dir. Easter Seal Speech Clinic, Jefferson City, Mo., summer 1972, 73; speech/lang. pathologist Shawnee Mission (Kans.) Pub. Schs., 1973-96; staff St. Joseph's Hosp., Kansas City, Mo., 1978-81, Midwest Rehab. Ctr., Kansas City, 1985; pvt. practice speech therapy Deborah A. King & Assocs., 2003—. Cons. East Ctrl. Mo. Mental Health Center; guest lectr. Fontbonne Coll., St. Louis. Vol., Mid Am. Rehab. Hosp. Mem. NEA, Am. Speech and Hearing Assn., Kans. Speech and Hearing Assn., Mo. State Tchrs. Assn., Kansas City Alumni Assn. of Northwestern U. (dir. alumni admissions coun., Outstanding Leadership award 1981, Svc. award 1991), Friends of Art Nelson/Atkins Art Gallery and Mus. (vol.), Nat. Trust Historic Preservation, Kansas City Hist. Found., Zeta Phi Eta. Methodist. Home: 8318 Mackey St Shawnee Mission KS 66212-2728

BREEN, MAUREEN, language educator, writer, department chairman; b. Chgo., Nov. 6, 1947; d. Edward John and Alice (Baechle) B.; m. Dermot Putnam, July 3, 1985. BA with honors, U. Ill., Chgo., 1969; MA with honors, Ea. Mich. U., 1971; cert., U. Wis., 1995, U. Chgo., 1995, 96, Brown U., 1997. Tchr. French, Fenger H.S., Chgo., 1973-76, Hitch and Onahan Elem. Schs., Chgo., 1976-79, Lincoln Park H.S., Chgo., 1979—2001, co-chmn. dept. world langs., 1999—2001. Instr. ESL, St. Augustine Coll., Chgo., 1983-85; tchr. French, Berlitz Sch. Langs., Chgo., 1983-84; adj. prof. methods tchg. fgn. langs. in secondary schs. Roosevelt U., Chgo., 1997-98; presenter in field to confs., univs., profl. assns. Creator (learning system) Funetics; author: (plays) Une Maladie Contagieuse: Une Piece de Theatre en Trois Actes Pour la Classe de Francais, 1996; co-author: (songs) Chansons Grammaticales, 1998; contbr. articles to profl. jours., including Gifted Child Today, Roeper Rev., chpt. to book.; author: French Through Funetics, The French Creative Writing Guide, Madame Breen's Total Mastery Guide to Correcting 99 Errors Anglophones Tend to Make in Writing and Speaking French. Named Chevalier dans l'Ordre des Palmes Academiques, French Ministry of Edn., 2002; recipient My Most Inspirational Tchr. award, Disting. Citizens Soc. Internat. Greater Chgo., 1995, Outstanding Educator of Yr. award, Sheffield Assn., 1999, Svcs. Culturels Consul Gen. France scholar, U. Paris-Sorbonne III, 1976, U. Savoie, Annecy, 1980, Prix du Chapitre, Am. Assn. Tchrs. of French, others, 2000; grantee NEH, 1997. Mem. Am. Assn. Tchrs. French (award No. Ill. chpt. 2000), Ill. Coun. Tchg. Fng. Langs., Fitzgerald Literary Analysis Group, Riverside Writers Club (co-founder). Avocation: cartooning. Home: 371 Bartram Rd Riverside IL 60546-1826

BREEN, NEIL THOMAS, publishing executive; b. N.Y.C., Oct. 14, 1944; s. Neil G. and Eileen M. Breen; m. Catherine M. Breen, Dec. 2, 1978. BA, Marquette U., 1966; JD, Creighton U., 1970. Bar: Nebr. 1970, U.S. Dist. Ct. Nebr. 1970. Editor-in-chief Shepard's/McGraw Hill, Colorado Springs, Colo., 1979-86, v.p. devel., 1987-89; Thomson Legal Pub., Stamford, Conn.; pres. Callaghan & Co., Deerfield, Ill., 1989-90; v.p., gen. mgr. litigation and fed. products group, 1991-92; v.p. legal divsn. McGraw Hill Ryerson, Whitby, Ont., Can., 1993-95; pres. Law Bull. Pub. Co., Chgo., 1996—. Author: Texas Law Locator, 1973, Illinois Law Locator, 1975. Mem. ABA, Assn. of trial Laywers of Am., Ill. State Bar Assn., Chgo. Bar Assn., Can. Bar Assn. Avocations: skiing, snowshoeing, hiking. Office: Law Bulletin Pub Co 415 N State St Ste 200 Chicago IL 60610-4631

BREEN, RICHARD F., JR., law librarian, lawyer, educator; b. Providence, Aug. 1, 1940; s. Richard F. and Elizabeth (Hurlin) B.; children: Stephanie, Jonathan. AB in Econs., Dartmouth Coll., 1962; LLB, U. Maine, Portland, 1967; MLS, U. Oreg., 1973. Bar: Maine, N.H. Asst. dean U. Maine Sch. Law, Portland, 1967-70; with firm Tesreau and Gardner, Lebanon, NH, 1970-72; assoc. law libr., assoc. prof. law U. Maine Sch. Law, Portland, 1974-76; law libr., assoc. prof. law Willamette U. Coll. Law, Salem, Oreg., 1976-80, law libr., prof. law, 1980—, interim adminstrv. dean., law libr., 1986-87. Legal specialist to Albania for ABA Ctrl. and East European Law Initiative, 1995. Mem. U.S. Olympic Biathlon Tng. Team, 1963. Capt. USAR, 1962-64. Mem. Am. Assn. Law Librs., Casque and Gauntlet Honor Soc. Democrat. Congregationalist. Avocations: cross country skiing, hiking. Office: Willamette U Law Libr 245 Winter St SE Salem OR 97301-3916 Office Phone: 503-370-6386. Business E-Mail: dbreen@willamette.edu.

BREEN, STEPHEN P., editorial cartoonist; b. LA, 1970; m. Cathy Breen; 2 children. Grad., U. Calif., Riverside, 1992. Editl. cartoonist Asbury Park Press, Neptune, NJ, 1994—2001, San Diego Union-Tribune, 2001—. Caricatures, Sunday Celebs page, comic strip, Grand Avenue, hundreds of newspapers and nat. mags. Copley News Svc. Recipient John Locher Meml. award, Assn. Am. Editl. Cartoonists, Charles M. Schulz award, Scripps Howard, Pulitzer prize, 1998, hon. mention, best cartoons on internat. affairs., Overseas Press Club. Office: San Diego Union-Tribune 350 Camino de la Reina92 PO Box 120191 San Diego CA 92112-0191

BREESE, STEVEN, theater director, actor, playwright; b. Marrietta, Ohio, Aug. 15, 1956; MFA/Acting, Calif. Inst. Arts, 1981. Dir. acting program Tex. Christian U., Ft. Worth, 1993—98; dir. theater CNU, Newport News, Va.,

2000—, assoc. prof. theater, 2005—. Freelance cons./dir. various regional theaters, 1993—2000; vis. prof. Semester at Sea, Pitts., 1999—2000. Author: (plays) The Trial of Hamlet, Brotherly Love, Painted Cages (Selected in Albee New Play Workshop/Valdez, 2003), Doubletake, Character Assassinations; actor, dir.: various nat. and internat. regional theaters, 1983; actor: (plays) A Chorus Line, 1987—88, The Foreigner, 1988, Crucible, 1994, Midsummer Night's Dream, 1998, Taming of the Shrew, 1998—99, Little Shop of Horrors, Billy Bishop Goes to War; dir.: Romeo & Juliet, 1998. Recipient Best and Brightest, Tex. Christian U., 1995, 1996, 1997. Mem.: AFTRA, SAG, Actors Equity Assn. Democrat-Npl. Avocations: travel, reading, stage combat, sailing. Office: Christopher Newport Univ One University Pl Newport News VA 23606 Office Phone: 757-594-8825. E-mail: sbreese@cnu.edu.

BREESKIN, MICHAEL WAYNE, lawyer; b. Washington, Dec. 25, 1947; s. Nathan and Sylvia (Raine) B.; m. Frances Cox Lively, May 29, 1982; children: Molly Louise, Laura Rose. BA cum laude, U. Pitts., 1969; JD, Georgetown U., 1975. Bar: D.C. 1975, Colo. 1983, U.S. Dist. Ct. D.C. 1977, U.S. Dist. Ct. Colo. 1983, U.S. Ct. Appeals (D.C. cir.) 1978, U.S. Ct. Appeals (10th cir.) 1984, U.S. Supreme Ct. 1995. Mng. atty. Tobin & Covey, Washington, 1977-79; assoc. Donald M. Murtha & Assocs., Washington, 1979-80; counsel NLRB Office Rep. Appeals, Washington, 1980-83; trial atty. NLRB Denver Regional Office, 1983-88; assoc. Wherry & Wherry, Denver, 1989-91; sr. atty. The Legal Ctr. for People with Disabilities and Older People (formerly The Legal Ctr. Serving Persons with Disabilities), Denver, 1991—98; gen. counsel Assn. Cmty. Living Boulder County, Inc. (formerly the Assn. for Retarded Citizens in Boulder County, Inc.), 1998—2000; counsel Fox & Robertson, PC, Denver, 2000—02, Arc of Denver, Inc., 2002—. Presenter, lectr. in field. Adv. com. Domestic Violence Initiative for Women with Disabilities, 1997—. Recipient Outstanding Work for People with Disabilities acknowledgement Very Spl. Arts Colo., 1996; named Profl. of Yr., The Arc of Adams County, 1997; recipient Adv. of the Year award Assn. Cmty. Living in Boulder County Inc., 1996, Schenkein award Arc of Denver, Inc., 1997, award Disability Ctr. Ind. Living and Colo. Cross-Disability Coalition, 1999, Colo. Cross-Disability Coalition Meml. award for Civil Rights Legal Advocacy, 2000. Mem. ABA, Colo. Bar Assn. (disability law sect.), Arapahoe County Bar Assn., Disability Rights Roundtable. Avocations: bicycling, skiing, reading. Office: Arc of Denver 1905 Sherman St Ste 300 Denver CO 80203 Office Phone: 303-831-7733. Business E-Mail: mbreeskin@arcofdenver.org.

BREEZE, PHILIP RALEY, director; b. Barksdale AFB, La., Aug. 20, 1950; s. Robert Carey Breeze and Evelyn Louise Breeze (Cox); m. Kathryn Anne Frey Breeze; children: Nicholas Laurent, Kelly Louise. BS in Journalism, U. Fla., 1975, MA in Journalism and Comm., 1982; PhD in Comm. Mgmt., U. Ky., 1996. Asst. pub. affairs officer 82d Airborne Divsn., Ft. Bragg, NC, 1979—80; writer/editor Miss. State U., Starkville, 1982—84, U. Ky., Lexington, 1984—88; assoc. dir. of univ. rels. Va. Tech., Blacksburg, 1988—96; dir. of univ. rels. Auburn U., Montgomery, Ala., 1998—2001; dir. of licensing, mktg. and univ. rels. Kutztown U., Pa., 2001—. Chmn. comm. sect. So. Assn. of Agrl. Scientists, 1993—94. Author: (divsn. newspaper) Impact (4th Estate award for excellence in mil. journalism, 1980). Vol. leadership coun. Miller-Keystone Blood Ctr., Allentown, Pa.; mem. Kutztown Area C. of C., Pa., 2001, Reading-Berks Literacy Coun., Pa., 2004. Sgt. U.S. Army, 1977—80. Decorated Army Commendation Medal. Avocations: scuba diving, flying. Office Phone: 610-683-4114.

BREEZE, WILLIAM HANCOCK, college administrator; b. Cin., Nov. 25, 1923; s. William T. and Nancy (Hancock) B.; m. JoAnne Robertson Watson, Oct. 8, 1949 (dec. Jan. 1983); 1 child, Nancy Louise Breeze; m. Barbara L. Hall, Dec. 15, 1990. Student, Berea Coll., 1943-44; AB, Centre Coll., Danville, Ky., 1945; MA, U. Ky., 1948. Various actuarial positions Ohio Nat. Life Ins. Co., Cin., 1948-56, actuary, 1956-65, asst. to pres., 1965-67, sr. v.p., 1967-72, exec. v.p., 1972-86; v.p., gen. sec. Centre Coll., Danville, Ky., 1987-88, 89-91, acting pres., 1988-89, spl. asst. to pres. for endowment, 1991—. Bd. dirs. Ohio Nat. Life Ins. Co., 1966-88. Bd. dirs. Jr. Achievement Greater Cin., 1974-84; trustee Centre Coll., 1980-86. Served to lt. (j.g.) USNR, 1943-46, PTO. Fellow: Soc. Actuaries. Republican. Presbyterian. Avocations: reading, classical music. Home: 468 W Broadway St Danville KY 40422-1420 Office: Centre Coll Danville KY 40422 Office Phone: 859-238-5207. E-mail: breeze@centre.edu.

BREGA, CHARLES FRANKLIN, lawyer; b. Callaway, Nebr., Feb. 5, 1933; s. Richard E. and Bessie (King) B.; m. Betty Jean Witherspoon, Sept. 17, 1960; children: Kerry E., Charles D., Angie G. BA, The Citadel, 1954; LLB, U. Colo., 1960. Bar: Colo. 1960. Assoc. firm Hindry & Meyer, Denver, 1960-62, partner, 1962-75, dir., 1975; dir. firm Roath & Brega, Denver, 1975-89, Brega & Winters, Denver, 1989—. Lectr. in field; guest prof. U. Colo., U. Denver, U. Nev. (numerous states and), Can. Trustee Pres.'s Leadership Class, U. Colo., 1977— . Served with USAF, 1954-57. Mem. Colo. Trial Lawyers Assn. (pres. 1972-73), Assn. Trial Lawyers Am. (gov. 1972-79), ABA, Am. Law Inst., Am. Bd. Trial Advs., Internat. Acad. Trial Lawyers, Internat. Soc. Barristers, Cherry Hills Country Club, Denver Athletic Club. Episcopalian. Home: 4501 S Vine Way Englewood CO 80110-6027 Office: Brega & Winters PC 1700 Lincoln St Ste 1300 Denver CO 80203-4522 Office Phone: 303-866-9400. Business E-Mail: cbrega@brega-winters.com.

BREGA, KERRY ELIZABETH, physician, researcher; b. Denver, Sept. 8, 1961; d. Charles Franklin and Betty Jean Brega. BA, U. Colo., 1983, MD, 1989. Diplomate Am. Bd. Spine Surgery, Am. Bd. Neurol. Surgery. Resident in neurosurgery U. Colo., Denver, 1990-95, asst. prof. neurosurgery, 1995—; dir. neurosurgery Littleton Adventist Hosp., Denver, 1998—; asst. prof. neurosurgery U. Colo., Denver, 1995—. Bd. dirs. Donor Alliance, Denver, 1994—. Mem. Am. Coll. Spine Surgery, Am. Assn. Neurol. Surgeons, Congress Neurol. Surgeons, Colo. Neurol. Soc., Alpha Omega Alpha. Office: Littleton Adventist Hosp 7720 S Broadway Ste 220 Littleton CO 80122-

BREGLIO, JOHN F., lawyer; b. N.Y.C., June 5, 1946; s. John N. and Sylvia V. (Calucci) B.; m. Nan K. Proctor, May 22, 1976; children: Eliza Mason, Nola Keene. BA, Yale U., 1968; JD, Harvard U., 1971. Bar: N.Y. 1972, U.S. Dist. Ct. (ea. and so. dists.) 1974, U.S. Ct. Appeals (2d cir.) 1975, U.S. Ct. Appeals (D.C. cir.) 1982. Ptnr. Paul, Weiss, Rifkind, Wharton & Garrison, N.Y.C., 1971—, chair, Entertainment Dept. Adj. prof. Sch. of Arts, Columbia U.; chmn., lectr. on entertainment industry N.Y. Law Jour. Seminars, N.Y.C., 1984—88, Practising Law Inst. Bd. dirs. The Acting Co., N.Y.C., 1982-92, The Golden Fund, N.Y.C., 1989—, The Alliance for the Arts, Inc., 1989—, Am. Found. for AIDS Rsch., N.Y.C., 1994—, Young Playwrights Inc., 1995—; chmn. bd. Theater Devel. Fund, N.Y.C., 1982—; mem. adv. com. Theatre Collection Coun., Mus. of City of N.Y. Mem. ABA, N.Y. State Bar Assn., Assn. of Bar of City of N.Y., Am. Arbitration Assn. (panel arbitrators), The Century Assn. (N.Y.C.), Yale Club (N.Y.C.), Phelps Assn. (New Haven). Home: 1120 5th Ave New York NY 10128-0144 also: 41 School House Rd Waccabuc NY 10597 also: 52 W Miacomet Rd Nantucket MA 02554-4369 Office: Paul Weiss Rifkind Wharton & Garrison 1285 Avenue Of The Americas New York NY 10019-6065 Office Phone: 212-373-3391. Business E-Mail: jbreglio@paulweiss.com.

BREGMAN, ARTHUR RANDOLPH, lawyer, educator; b. Phila., Dec. 9, 1946; s. Nathan and Stella (Husock) B.; m. Patrice Rosalie Gancie, May 30, 1980. BA, Columbia U., 1968; MA, Yale U., 1969; JD, Georgetown U., 1985. Bar: DC 1985, U.S. Ct. Appeals (DC cir.) 1985, U.S. Dist. Ct. DC 1985, U.S. Claims Ct. 1985. Treas. Nat. Coun. for Soviet and E. European Rsch., Washington, 1981-83; law clk. Washington Lawyers' Com. for Civil Rights, 1983-84; assoc. Klores, Feldesman and Tucker, Washington, 1985-86; dir. Soviet and E. European Svcs. APCO, Washington, 1988-91; of counsel Steptoe & Johnson, Washington, Moscow, 1991-92, ptnr. Washington and Moscow, 1992-99, Squire, Sanders & Dempsey, Washington, 1999—2003, Salans, Washington, NY, 2003—. Adj. prof. Georgetown U. Law Ctr., Washington, 1986-89; program dir. Internat. Law Inst., Washington, 1986-91; chmn. bd. adv. U.S.-Russia Bus. Law Report, 1990—. Editor: U.S.-Soviet Contract Law, 1987. Recipient Civil Procedure prize Lawyers Coop. Pub. Co., Balt., 1982. Mem. ABA (internat. bar sect.), DC Bar Assn. Home: 3059 Porter St NW Washington DC 20008-3272 Office: 1330 Connecticut Ave NW Washington DC 20036 also: 620 Fifth Ave New York NY 10020 Office Phone: 202-457-8305. E-mail: rbregman@salans.com.

BREGMAN, DAVIS, orthopedist; b. Nov. 21, 1969; BS, MIT, 1990; MD, NYU, 1994. Diplomate Am. Acad. Pain Mgmt. Intern Lenox Hill Hosp., N.Y.C., 1994-95; resident Hosp. U. Pa., Phila., 1996-97; pres. Polo Medgroup, N.Y.C., 1996-98; med. dir. Medplaza Physicians, Huntington, NY, 1998—2002, pres., 1999—2002; med. dir. Medplaza Pain Care Ctr., 2002—. Disease prevention editor Medplaza News, Dix Hills, N.Y., 1998-99; host radio show "Your Health with Dr. Bregman," 1999-2001; developer outpatient healthcare facility, 1998; cons. Ambulatory Surgery Ctr. Devel., 1996-97; pub. spkr. on pain mgmt. topics; pioneer in use of non-surgical spinal decompression therapy. Contbr. articles to profl. jours. Named outstanding intellectual of 20th century for achievement in orthops. and pain mgmt., Hon. Chmn. of the Health Care Bus., Adv. Coun. for U.S. Congressman Tom Delay, 2001, Physician of the Yr. award, Congressman Tom Reynolds; recipient Disting. leadership award for outstanding contbns. to contemporary soc., 1999, 2000, Internat. Order Merit for svcs. to orthops. and medicine, proclamation for cmty. svc., County Exec. Robert J. Gaffney, Presdl. Seal of Honor, 2001, Businessman of the Yr. award for N.Y. State, U.S. Congressman Tom Davis, 2001. Fellow Suffolk Acad. Medicine, Am. Biog. Inst., Am. Biog. Inst. Rsch. Assn. (dep. gov.); mem. Internat. Order of Ambs., Med. Soc. State of N.Y., mem. Suffolk County Med. Soc. Office: Medplaza Physician 2829 Merrick Rd 109 Bellmore NY 11710-5725 E-mail: drbregman@doctor.com.

BREGMAN, DOUGLAS M., lawyer, educator; b. Ardmore, Pa., Oct. 21, 1949; s. Nathan and Stella Bregman; m. Brenda I. Ladell, June 17, 1973; children: Benjamin, Lauren, Daniel. BA with honors, Colgate U., 1971; JD, Georgetown U., 1974. Bar: Md. 1974, D.C. 1975, U.S. Supreme Ct. 1978. Jud. law clk. to Judge J. Dudley Digges Ct. of Appeals of Md., Annapolis, 1973-75; mem. Duckett, Orem, Christie and Beckett, Hyattsville, Md., 1975-78; instr. U. Md., College Park, 1977-81; mem. Fossett & Brugger Law Firm, Seabrook, Md., 1978; ptnr. Bregman, Berbert & Schwartz, LLC, Bethesda, Md., 1979—. Adj. prof. law Georgetown U. Law Ctr., Washington, 1992—. Co-author: Successful Real Estate Negotiations, 1987, 2d edit., 1994, Maryland Landlord/Tenant Law, Practice and Procedure, 1983, 2d edit., 1994; contbr. chpts. to books. Spl. cons., White House intern Office of Consumer Affairs, 1971; mem. Govs.'s Adv. Coun. on Landlord and Tenant Affairs, 1991-95; chmn. Com. to Retain Sitting Judges, 1998. Mem. ABA, Md. State Bar Assn. (exec. com. and bd. govs. 1982-83), Bar Assn. Montgomery County (pres. 1998-99), Prince George's County Bar Assn., D.C. Bar Assn., Montgomery County Bar Found. (treas. 1993-94). Office: Bregman Berbert & Schwartz 7315 Wisconsin Ave Ste 800W Bethesda MD 20814-3244 E-mail: dbregman@bregmanlaw.com.

BREGMAN, HOWARD, lawyer; b. Hartford, Conn., 1949; BA, Hobart Coll., 1971; JD, Case Western Res. U., 1975. Bar: Ohio 1975, Pa. 1979, Fla. 1983. Mng. shareholder Miami, Boca Raton Greenberg Traurig LLP. Editor: Case Western Res. Law Rev., 1974-75. Mem. ABA, Pa. Bar Assn., Ohio State Bar Assn., The Fla. Bar, Cleve. Bar Assn., Palm Beach County Bar Assn., Order of Coif. Office: Greenberg Traurig LLP Ste 300E 777 S Flagler Dr West Palm Beach FL 33401-6102 Office Phone: 561-650-7910. Office Fax: 561-655-6222. Business E-Mail: bregmanh@gtlaw.com.

BREGMAN, JACOB ISRAEL, environmental services administrator; b. Hartford, Conn., Sept. 17, 1923; s. Aaron and Jennie (Katzoff) B.; m. Mona Madan, June 27, 1948; children: Janet, Marcia, Barbara. BS, Providence Coll., 1943; MS, Poly. Inst. Bklyn., 1948, PhD, 1951. Rsch. chemist Fels & Co., 1947—48; head phys. chem. labs. Nalco Chem. Co., Chgo., 1950—59; supr. phys. chemistry rsch. sect. Armour Rsch. Found., Chgo., 1959—63; asst. dir. chemistry rsch. Ill. Inst. Tech. Rsch. Inst., Chgo., 1963—65, dir. chem. scis., 1965—67; dep. asst. sec. U.S. Dept. Interior, 1967—69; pres. Wapora Inc., 1969—82; v.p. Dynamac Corp., 1983—84; pres. Bregman and Co., 1984—2004, CEO, 1984—2004, treas., 2004—. Chmn. N.E. Ill. Met. Area Air Pollution Control Bd., 1962—63; chmn. Ill. Air Pollution Control Bd., 1963—67; chmn. adv. bd. on saline water conversion NATO Parliamentarians Conf., 1963; chmn. Water Resources Rsch. Coun., 1964—67; profl. lectr. George Washington U., 1980—98. Author: Corrosion Inhibitors, 1963, Surface Effects in Detection, 1965, The Pollution Paradox, 1966, Handbook of Water Resources and Pollution Control, 1976, Environmental Regulations Handbook, 1991, Environmental Impact Statements, 1992, 2d edit., 1999, Environmental Compliance Handbook, 1996, 2d edit., 1999; patentee in field; contbr. 70 articles to profl. jours. Chmn. Montgomery County (Md.) Citizens Task Force on Georgetown Br. Right of Way, 1986—90; mem. Md. Dem. State Ctrl. Com., 1974—78; treas. Montgomery Dem. Ctrl. Com., 1974—76; del. Dem. Conv., 1976; mem. plan commn. Park Forest, Ill., 1956—59; trustee, 1958—62. With AUS, 1943—46, ETO, survivor sunken troop ship "Empire Javelin", 1944. Decorated two Battle Stars, AUS. Fellow: Am. Inst. Chemists; mem.: Am. Chem. Soc., Nat. Def. Ind. Assn. (life), Soc. Am. Military Engrs. (life), VFW, Am. Legion, Phi Lambda Upsilon, Sigma Xi. Office: 5272 River Rd Ste 550 Bethesda MD 20816 Home: 6575 99th Way N #22106 Saint Petersburg FL 33708-4526 Office Phone: 301-652-4818. E-mail: bregman4827@yahoo.com.

BREGMAN, MARK, information technology executive; BS in Physics, Harvard Coll.; MS in Physics, PhD in Physics, Columbia U. Sr. mgmt. positions IBM Rsch. and IBM Japan, 1984—2000; CEO Airmedia Inc., 2000—01; exec. v.p. product ops. Veritas Software Corp., Mountain View, Calif., 2002—, chief tech. officer, 2004—, acting mgr., application and svc. mgmt. group, 2004—. Bd. overseers Fermi Nat. Accelerator Lab. Mem. vis. com. Harvard U. Lib. Mem.: Am. Physical Soc., IEEE (sr.). Office: Veritas Software Corp 350 Ellis St Mountain View CA 94043 Office Phone: 800-327-2232. Office Fax: 650-527-2908.

BREGMAN, MICHAEL EVAN, urban planner; b. Miami Beach, Apr. 8, 1966; s. Harold and Doris (Brown) B. Cert. in Planning Studies, BS in Geography, Fla. State U., 1988; MA in Urban and Regional Planning, U. Fla., 1993. Intern Miami-Dade Park and Recreation, Miami, 1992; planning technician Miami-Dade Planning and Zoning, Miami, 1993-94, sr. planner, 1994—. Mem. urban design com. Downtown Miami Main St., 1998-99; mem. Urban Environment League, Miami, 1996-97. Contbr. articles to Gold Coast Planner newspaper. Mem. Downtown Miami Citizens on Patrol, 1998-99. Mem. Am. Inst. Cert. Planners (cert. planner), Am. Planning Assn. (sec. Gold Coast 1996-97). Democrat. Avocation: Tae Kwon Do. Office: Miami-Dade Dept Planning and Zoning 111 NW 1st St Ste 1220 Miami FL 33128-1923

BREGOLI-RUSSO, MAUDA RITA, language educator; b. Iesi-Ancona, Italy; came to U.S., 1965; d. Antonio Bregoli and Libe Maria Scipioni; m. Franco Gino Russo, June 27, 1964; 1 child, Antonella. Laurea, Bologna (Italy) U., 1963; PhD in Romance Langs., U. Chgo., 1978. Vis. asst. prof. Northwestern U., Chgo., 1981-83; asst. prof. U. Ill., Chgo., 1984-90, assoc. prof., 1990—. Author: Boiardo Lirico, 1979, Renaissance Italian Plays, 1984, Impresa Come Ritratto, 1990, Teatro D'Isabella D'Este, 1997. NEH grantee, 1981. Mem. MLA, Renaissance Soc. Am., Associazione Italiana per Gli Studi Di Lingua E Letteratura Italiana. Home: 100 E Walton St Apt 19de Chicago IL 60611-1448 Office: U Ill Chgo 601 S Morgan St Chicago IL 60607-7100 E-mail: mabrer@uic.edu.

BREHL, JAMES WILLIAM, lawyer; BS engring., U. Notre Dame, 1956; JD, U. Mich., 1959. Bar: Wis. 1989; Minn. and various fed. cts. Lawyer Maun & Simon, St. Paul, 1963-2000; law practice and mediation/arbitration Nuetral Svcs., 2000—. Contbr. articles to law jours. Mem. Minn. Bar Assn. (exec. com. 1996-97), Ramsey County Bar Assn. (exec. coun. 1977-80, 87-90, pres. 1993-94). Office Phone: 651-436-5679. Fax: 651-436-5679. E-mail: jdbrehl@aol.com.

BREHM, SHARON STEPHENS, psychology professor, academic administrator; b. Roanoke, Va., Apr. 18, 1945; d. John Wallis and Jane Chappel (Phenix) Stephens; m. Jack W. Brehm, Oct. 25, 1968 (div. Dec. 1979) BA, Duke U., 1967, PhD, 1973; MA, Harvard U., 1968. Clin. psychology intern U. Wash. Med. Ctr., Seattle, 1973-74; asst. prof. Va. Poly. Inst. and State U., Blacksburg, 1974-75, U. Kans., Lawrence, 1975-78, assoc. prof., 1978-83, prof. psychology, 1983-90, assoc. dean Coll. Liberal Arts and Scis., 1987-90; prof. psychology, dean Harpur Coll. of Arts and Scis. SUNY, Binghamton, 1990-96; prof. psychology and interpersonal comm., provost Ohio U., Athens, 1996—2001; chancellor Ind. U., Bloomington, 2001—, prof. dept. psychology, 2001—, adj. prof. sch. pub. and environ. affairs, 2001—. Vis. prof. U. Mannheim, 1978, Istituto di Psicologia, Rome, 1989; Fulbright sr. rsch. scholar Ecole des Hautes Etudes en Sciences Sociales, Paris, 1981-82; Soc. for Personality and Social Psychology rep. APA's Coun. of Reps., 1995-2000, finance com., 1999—; chair governing bd. Ohio Learning Network, 1998-99. Author: The Application of Social Psychology to Clinical Practice, 1976, (with others) Psychological Reactance: A Theory of Freedom and Control, 1981, Intimate Relationships, 1985, 2d edit., 1992, (with others) Social Psychology, 1990, 4th edit., 1999, also numerous articles, and chpts. Mem. APA (fin. com. 1999—). Office: Ind U 107 S Indiana Ave Bloomington IN 47405-7000

BREIDBART, RORY STEVEN, endocrinologist; b. N.Y.C., Mar. 13, 1962; s. Murray Richard and Judith Marcia Breidbart. BS in Chemistry and Biology, Emory U., 1983; MD, Tel Aviv U., 1987. Diplomate Am. Bd. Internal Medicine, Am. Bd. Endocrinology, Diabetes and Metabolism. Resident in medicine L.I. Jewish Med. Ctr., New Hyde Park, N.Y., 1987-90, fellow in gen. internal medicine and primary care, 1990-91; fellow in endocrinology Mt. Sinai Med. Ctr., N.Y.C., 1991-93; pvt. practice, Gt. Neck, N.Y., 1993—. Clin. instr. medicine N.Y. U. Sch. Medicine, N.Shore U. Hosp., St. Francis Hosp., L.I. Jewish Med. Ctr. Recipient Physician of Yr., Metro. NY Assn. of Diabetes Educators, 2004. Fellow: ACP, Am. Coll. Endocrinology; mem.: AMA, Nassau County Med. Soc., Am. Assn. Clin. Endocrinology, Am. Diabetes Assn. Office: 29 Barstow Rd Ste 305 Great Neck NY 11021-2209 Office Phone: 516-482-0345.

BREIDEGAM, DELIGHT EDGAR, JR., battery company executive; b. Fleetwood, Pa., Oct. 3, 1926; s. DeLight Daniel and Helen Mamie (Fenstermacher) B.; m. Helen Merkel, Feb. 28, 1948; children: Daniel, Sally. LLD (hon.), Kurtztown U., 1997; attended, Gettysburg Coll., 1944-45; LLD (hon.), Moravian Coll., 1995. Chmn., CEO East Penn Mfg. Co., Inc., Lyon Sta., Pa.; mem. Battery Coun. Internat. Trustee Moravian Coll.; bd. dir. Kutztown U. Served with USAF. Recipient Grow with Berks award Reading Assn. Reators, 1994, Richard J. Caron award of excellence, 1997; named Entrepreneur of Yr., Ea. Pa./Delaware Valley, 1990, Outstanding Bus. Leader Northwood U., 2004; named to Jr. Achievement Hall of Fame, 1994, Moravian Coll. Hall of Fame. Mem. Reading-Berks C. of C. (Bus. Person of Yr. 1984), Moselem Springs Golf Club, Bonita Bay Country Club, Longleff Golf and Country Club, Saucon Valley Country Club, Huguenot Lodge, Shriners, Mason, lifetime mem. BCI Lutheran. Office: East Penn Mfg Co Inc Deka Rd Lyon Station PA 19536 Home: 214 Deysher Rd Fleetwood PA 19522

BREIER, ALAN, pharmaceutical executive; b. Toledo, May 22, 1953; m. Diane Rooney, May 30, 1981; children: Michael, Matthew. MD, U. Cin., 1980. Diplomate Am. Bd. Psychiatry and Neurology. Chief outpatient dept. Md. Psychiat. Ctr., Balt., 1987-93; chief pathophysiology and treatment unit NIH, Bethesda, Md., 1993-95, chief sect. clin. studies, 1995-97; chief med. officer, v.p. med. Eli Lilly and Co., Indpls., 1998—. Adj. prof. psychiatry U. Md., Balt., 1994—; prof. medicine Ind. U., Indpls., 1997—. Mem. editl. bd. Schizophrenia Rsch., 1994—, Biol. Psychiatry, 1999—. Recipient Lustman Rsch. award, Yale U. Sch. Medicine, 1982—84, Young Investigator award, Schizophrenia Rsch., 1987, A. E. Bennett award, Soc. Biol. Psychiatry, 1988, Joel Elkes Internat. award, ACNP, 1997. Office: Eli Lilly and Co Lilly Corp Ctr Indianapolis IN 46285 E-mail: breier_alan@lilly.com.

BREIGER, RONALD LOUIS, social sciences educator; b. NYC, Mar. 19, 1948; s. Lazarus H. and Lillian E. (Berman) Breiger; m. Linda Ruth Waugh, May 20, 1984; 1 child, David Luis Waugh-Breiger. AB, Brandeis U., 1966—70; PhD, Harvard U., 1970—75. Asst. prof. of sociology Harvard U., 1975—79, assoc. prof. of sociology, 1979—81; prof. of sociology Cornell U., Ithaca, 1981—95, dept. chmn., 1988—93, Goldwin Smith prof. sociology, 1995—2000; prof. of sociology U. of Ariz., 2000—. Vis. prof. U. of Lille-1, France, 2002. Editor: (jour.) Social Networks, 1998—; author: (collected works) Explorations in Structural Sociology (Harvard Studies in Sociology series); chair (symposium) Nat. Acad. Scis. workshop on Dynamic Network Models and Analysis. Fellow Ctr. for Advanced Study in the Behavioral Scis., 1985—86. Mem.: Nat. Sci. Found. (mem. sociology panel 1988—90), Sociol. Rsch. Assn., Internat. Network for Social Network Analysis (exec. bd. mem. 2003, mem. exec. bd. 2003—, Simmel award 2005), Am. Sociol. Assn. (exec. com., sect. on math. sociology 2000—02). Office: U Ariz Dept of Sociology Tucson AZ 85721-0027

BREIMAYER, JOSEPH FREDERICK, patent lawyer; b. Belding, Mich., May 4, 1942; s. Ronald and Crystal Helen (Reeves) B.; m. Margaret Anne Murphy, Aug. 26, 1967; children: Kathleen A., Deborah L., Elizabeth L. BEE, U. Detroit, 1965; JD, George Washington U., 1969. Bar: D.C. 1970, N.Y. 1973, Minn. 1975. Cooperative engr. Honeywell Inc, Mpls., 1962-65; patent examiner U.S. Patent and Trademark Office, Washington, 1965-70; patent atty. Eastman Kodak Co., Rochester, N.Y., 1970-73; sr. patent counsel Medtronic Inc., Mpls., 1973-90; assoc. Fredrikson & Byron, Mpls., 1990-93. Pres. Good Shepherd Home and Sch. Assn., 1984; precinct chmn. Dem. Farmer Labor Party, 1980-82. Mem. Minn. Intellectual Property Law Assn. (treas. 1986). Avocations: boating, skiing, travel. Home: 4700 Circle Down Minneapolis MN 55416-1101 Office: Breimayer Law Office 1221 Nicollet Mall Ste 206 Minneapolis MN 55403-2472 Office Phone: 612-338-1279. Personal E-mail: jfbpatent@aol.com.

BREINER-SANDERS, KAREN ELIZABETH, Spanish language educator, consultant; b. N.Y.C., June 4, 1944; d. Edwin Jerome and Val S. (Dare) Breiner; m. Arthur James Sanders, July 24, 1976; 1 child, Melisa Karena. Student, Latin Am. Inst., 1961-62; BA magna cum laude, U. Conn., 1966; MA, Brown U., 1969; PhD, George Washington U., 1980. Spanish translator, typist internat. dept. Union Carbide Corp., N.Y.C., 1962-63; tchr. Spanish, coord. modern fgn. langs. Sedgwick Jr. High Sch., West Hartford, Conn., 1966-67; tchr. Spanish, Sunset Ridge Sch., Hartford, Conn., 1969; tchr. Spanish, tutor German Cushing Acad., Ashburnham, Mass., 1969-70; tchr. Spanish and French St. Paul's Sch., Concord, N.H., 1970-73; instr. Spanish Sch. Langs. and Linguistics Georgetown U., 1973-80, core faculty Sch. Fgn. Svc., 1975, asst. prof. Spanish Sch. Fgn. Svc., 1980-90, assoc. prof. Spanish Sch. Fgn. Svc., 1990—; prof. Spanish, coord. 2d yr. Spanish Middlebury (Vt.) Coll., 1991, prof. Spanish oral proficiency, 1992, 95. Resident dir. GU summer program Cath. U. Quito, Ecuador, 1974; instr. advanced Spanish, Ball State U., 1977; presenter, lectr., cons. in field. Author: La Familia de Pascual Duarte a Travès de Su Imagineria, 1990; contbr. chpts. to books, articles to profl. jours. NDEA fellow Brown U., 1969; grantee NEH, 1986, Am. Coun. Learned Socs., 1986, Father Edmund A. Walsh Fund, Sch. Fgn. Svc., Georgetown U., 1988, 92, 94, 95, Columbian Woman Scholar George Washington U., 1976-77. Mem. MLA, Am. Assn. for Tchrs. Spanish and Portugese, Am. Coun. on Tchg. Fgn. Langs., Internat. Assn. Hispanists, Soc. for Cinema Studies, Am. Film Inst., Smithsonian Assocs., Phi Beta Kappa, Phi Delta Gamma, Phi Kappa Phi, Pi Delta Phi, Sigma Delta Pi. Avocations: reading, travel, swimming. Office: Georgetown U Sch Fgn Svc Washington DC 20057-0001

BREININ, GOODWIN M., physician; b. N.Y.C., Dec. 10, 1918; s. Louis and Mary (Mirsky) B.; m. Rose-Helen Kopelman, June 22, 1947; children: Bartley James, Constance. BS, U. Fla., 1939; A.M., Emory U., 1940, MD, 1943. Diplomate Am. Bd. Ophthalmology (dir., vice chmn., cons.). Intern U.S. Marine Hosp., Stapleton, N.Y., 1944; resident ophthalmology N.Y. U.-Bellevue Med. Ctr., 1947-51, sr. Heed fellow ophthalmology, 1954, Daniel B. Kirby prof. research ophthalmology, 1957; Daniel B. Kirby prof. ophthalmology Bellevue and U. Hosps., 1959—; chmn. dept. ophthalmology N.Y. U.-Bellevue Med. Ctr., 1959—2000; dir. eye svc. Bellevue and U. Hosps., N.Y.C., 1959—2000; chmn. med. bd. N.Y. U.-Bellevue Med. Ctr., 1975-77. Mem. vision commn. NRC, 1960-65; hon. rsch. assoc. with Sir Andrew Huxley, U. Coll., London, 1966-67; chmn. vision rsch. tng. com. Nat. Insts. Neurol. Diseases and Blindness, 1963-64; chief cons. Manhattan VA Hosp.; cons. Manhattan Eye, Ear and Throat, St. Vincent's, Beth Israel hosps., Lenox Hills Hosp.; surg. gen. USPHS; chmn. Nat. Res. Rev. Com., 1976-77; vis. prof., cons. Hailie Selassie I Univ. Found., Ethiopia, 1972; lectr. Mem. various adv. coms. relating to field, mem. med. adv. bd. Nat. Coun. to Combat Blindness; pres. Council for U.S./USSR Health Exch., 1977; mem. Am. com. Internat. Agy. for Prevention of Blindness, 1980—; pres. 2d Internat. Symposium in Visual Optics, Tucson, 1982. Author: The Electrophysiology of Extraocular Muscle, 1962; editor: Advances in Diagnostic Visual Optics, 1983; mem. editorial bd. Investigative Ophthalmology, Archives of Ophthalmology; Contbr. articles to profl. jours. Mem. bd. advisors for medicine Emory U., Atlanta; mem. coun. visitors Marine Biol. Labs., Woods Hole, Mass. Recipient Knapp medal for contbn. ophthalmology A.M.A., 1957, Edward Lorenzo Holmes lectr. citation and award for contbns. to med. sci. Inst. Medicine Chgo., 1959, Gifford lectr. and award Chgo. Ophthal. Soc., 1970, Heed Ophthalmic Found. award, 1968, Emory U. medal, 1993; Wright lectr. U. Toronto, 1972; Lloyd lectr. Bklyn. Opthal. Soc., 1971; May lectr. N.Y. Acad. Medicine, 1974; guest of honor Australian Coll. Ophthalmologists, 1974, Japanese Cong. Neuro-ophthalmology, 1979; Scobee lectr., 1977. Fellow Am. Acad. Ophthalmology and Otolaryngology (v.p. 1979, Sr. Honor award 1984), ACS, N.Y. Acad. Medicine (sec. sect. ophthalmology 1962-63, chmn. sect. 1967-68); mem. AMA (sec. sect. on ophthalmology 1966-69, chmn. 1970-71), Rsch. Ophthalmology, Am. Ophthal. Soc., N.Y. Ophthal. Soc. (pres. 1980), Harvey Soc., AAAS, Am. Commn. for Optics and Visual Physiology (chmn. 1970—), Am. Orthoptic Coun., Assn. Univ. Profs. Ophthalmology, Pan. Am. Assn. Ophthalmology, Sigma Xi, Century Assn., Practitioners Club, Charaka Club (N.Y.C.), Alpha Omega Alpha. Home: 912 Fifth Ave New York NY 10021-4159 Business E-Mail: gb7@nyu.edu.

BREIPOHL, WALTER EUGENE, real estate broker; b. Ottawa, Ill., Mar. 24, 1953; s. Eugene E. and Margaret L. (Hughes) B. Student, Ill. Valley C.C., Loyola U., Chgo., 1974. Real estate broker and devel. Breipohl Co., Ottawa, 1975—. Bd. dirs. No. Ill. Devel. Corp., Union Banc Corp., Ottawa, Union Bank, Ea. Divsn., Ottawa. Bd. dirs. Greater Ottawa, Inc., 1984—, pres., 1997; bd. dirs. Main Street U.S.A. Program, Ottawa, 1991-93, Cmty. Hosp. of Ottawa Found., 1994-97; chmn. Indsl. Devel. Commn., Ottawa, 1985-88; gov. Cmty. Hosp. Ottawa, 1986-89. Mem. Illini Valley Assn. Realtors (sec.-treas. 1983-85, President's award 1985), No. Ill. Comml. Assn. Realtors, Ill. Assn. Realtors, Nat. Assn. Realtors, Ottawa Area C. of C. and Industry (chmn. bd. dirs. 1988), Ill. C. of C. (bd. dirs. 1997, polit. action com. dir. 1998, heritage corridor dir. 1993-96), Ill.-Mich. Canal Corridor Assn. (dir. 1997), Internat. Club (Chgo.), Boat Club, Union League Club (Chgo.), Elks, KC. Republican. Roman Catholic. Home and Office: PO Box 1039 Ottawa IL 61350-6039

BREISACH, ERNST A., historian, educator; b. Schwanberg, Austria, Oct. 8, 1923; came to US, 1953; s. Otto and Maria (Eder) B.; m. Herma E. Pirker, Aug. 2, 1945; children: Nora Sylvia, Eric Ernst. PhD in History, U. Vienna, Austria, 1946; D in Econs., Wirtschafts U., 1950. Prof. Realgymnasium Vienna XIV, Austria, 1946-52; assoc. prof. Olivet Coll., Mich., 1953-57; prof. Western Mich. U., Kalamazoo, 1957-96. Author: Introduction to Modern Existentialism, 1962, Caterina Sforza: A Renaissance Virago, 1967, Renaissance Europe, 1300-1517, 1973, Historiography: Ancient, Medieval, and Modern, 1983, 2d edit., 1994, American Progressive History, 1993, On the Future of History: The Postmodernist Challenge and Its Aftermath, 2003; editor: Classical Rhetoric and Medieval Historiography, 1985. Nat. Found. for Humanities fellow, 1989-90. Mem. Am. Hist. Assn. Home: 1700 Bronson Way Apt 145 Kalamazoo MI 49009-9108 Office: Western Mich U Dept History Kalamazoo MI 49008 Personal E-mail: ebreisach@sbcglobal.net.

BREIT, JEFFREY ARNOLD, lawyer; b. Norfolk, Va., Apr. 14, 1955; s. Calvin W. and Mildred J. (Jacobs) B.; m. Suzanne Reigel, Aug. 23, 1980. BA, Tulane U., 1977, JD, 1979. Bar: Va. 1979, La. 1979, D.C. 1988, N.Y. 1991, N.C. 1991, U.S. Ct. Appeals (4th, 5th adn 11th cirs.), U.S. Supreme Ct. Ptnr. Breit, Rutter & Montagna, Norfolk, 1979-87, Breit, Drescher & Breit, Norfolk, 1987—. Adj. prof. William & Mary Sch. Law, 2004—. Contbr. articles to profl. jours. Chmn. Virginia Beach. Dem. Party, 1992—, vice chmn., 1995-97; pres. Operation Smile, Norfolk, 1987-90. Fellow Internat. Acad. Trial Lawyers; mem. ABA, ATLA (bd. govs. 1988—), Va. Trial Lawyers Assn. (pres. elect 1997-98, pres. 1998-99), La. Trial Lawyers Assn., N.C. Trial Lawyers Assn., Maritime Law Assn. U.S., Va. Trial Lawyers Assn. (pres. 1998-99). Jewish. Avocations: tennis, surfing. Home: 608 Linkhorn Dr Virginia Beach VA 23451-3917 Office: Breit Drescher & Imprevento PC 1000 Dominion Tower 999 Waterside Dr Ste 1000 Norfolk VA 23510-3304 Office Phone: 757-670-3888. Business E-Mail: JBreit@bdbmail.com.

BREIT, WILLIAM, economist, educator, writer; b. New Orleans, Feb. 13, 1933; s. Murray and Sylvia (Shor) Breit. BA, U. Tex., 1955, MA, 1956; PhD, Mich. State U., 1961. Asst. prof. La. State U., Baton Rouge, 1961—63, assoc. prof., 1964—65, U. Va., 1965—70, prof., 1970—83; E.M. Stevens disting. prof. econs. emeritus Trinity U., San Antonio, 1983—89, Vernon F. Taylor disting. prof. econs., 1999—2002. Contbr. articles to profl. jours.; author (with others): The Antitrust Penalties, 1976; author: Murder at the Margin, 1978, 1993, The Academic Scribblers, 1982, 1998, The Fatal Equilibrium, 1985, 1986, The Antitrust Casebook, 1982, 1996, A Deadly Indifference, 1998, Lives of the Laureates: Eighteen Nobel Economists, 2004. Recipient Disting. Alumni award, Mich. State U., 1998, Disting. Achievement award, S.W. Social Sci. Assn., 2002. Mem.: Am. Econ. Assn., So. Econ. Assn. (v.p. 1980—81, pres. 1985—86), Mystery Writers Am., Phi Beta Kappa (book prize 1977). Home: 438 E Hildebrand Ave San Antonio TX 78212-2501 Office: Trinity Univ 1 Trinity Pl San Antonio TX 78212-7200

BREITBARTH, S. ROBERT, manufacturing executive; b. Newark, N.J., July 15, 1925; s. Jacob and Rose (Brandman) B.; m. Laurel Patricia Stroh, Oct. 30, 1949 (dec. Jan. 1998); children: Meredith Jane, Jill Gretchen. BEE, Cornell U., 1949. V.p. Gen. Cable Corp., Greenwich, Conn., 1966-77, exec. v.p., 1976-78; pres. Gen. Cable Internat., Inc., 1978-85, also bd. dirs.; v.p. GK Technologies, Inc., 1979-82. Cons. UN Centre on Transnat. Corps., 1989-90. Treas. Stony Point Assn., Westport, Conn., 1973-75, pres., 1975-76, 87-88. Served with USAAF, 1944-46. Decorated Venezuela-Orden al Merito en el Trabajo Primera Clase, govt. Venezuela. Mem. IEEE, Spain-U.S. C. of C. (bd. dirs.), Wire Assn., Cornell Soc. Engrs., Cornell Club of N.Y. Home: 2 Stony Point Rd Westport CT 06880-5921 E-mail: r.breitbarth@att.net.

BREITENBACH, MARY LOUISE MCGRAW, psychologist, chemical dependency counselor; b. Pitts., Sept. 26, 1936; d. David Evans McGraw and Louise (Schoch) Neel; m. John Edgar Breitenbach, Apr. 15, 1960 (dec. 1963); m. Joseph George Piccoli III, Aug. 15, 1987; children: Cary Plumer Frye and Douglas Plumer (twins), Kirstin Amethyst Gretchen Leticia Piccoli. Postgrad., Oreg. State Coll., 1960-61; BA, Russell Sage Coll., Troy, N.Y., 1958; MEd, Harvard U., 1983. Lic. profl. counselor, chem. dependency specialist, Wyo.; cert. addiction specialist, level III; cert. addiction counselor II, master addiction counselor. Paraprofessional psychologist St. John's Episc. Ch., Jackson, Wyo., 1963—94; pvt. practice Wilson, Wyo., 1983—. Counselor Curran/Seeley Found. Addiction Svcs., Jackson, 1989-91, Van Vleck House/Tri-County Group Home, Jackson, 1986-89, others; provider multiple employee assistance programs local and nat. cos.; adv. com. Learning Ctr., 1997—. Trustee Teton Sci. Sch., Kelly, Wyo, 1960-76; pres. bd. govs. Teton County Mus., 1989-91, Jackson; vestry mem. St. John's Ch., Jackson. Mem.: APA, LWV, Wyo. Psychol. Assn., Wyo. Assn. Counseling and Devel., Wyo. Assn. Addiction Specialists, Nat. Assn. Alcohol and Drug Addiction Counselors. Democrat. Episcopalian. Avocations: horseback riding, reading, gardening. Home and Office: 3625 N Cheney Ln Wilson WY 83014 Office Phone: 307-733-2100.

BREITENBERGER, ERNST, scientist, educator; b. Graz, Austria, June 11, 1924; came to U.S., 1958; s. Julius Johann and Anna (Wiesinger) B.; m. Janine Dufaure, 1954 (div. 1974); children: Roland, Caroline, Gisela, Erich. Dr. phil., U. Vienna, 1950; PhD, Cambridge U., 1956. Rsch. assoc. Radium Inst., Vienna, 1950-51, Cavendish Lab., Cambridge, Eng., 1951-54; mem. faculty U. Malaya, Singapore, 1954-58, U. S.C., Columbia, 1958-63; prof. physics Ohio U., Athens, 1963-94, emeritus prof., 1994—. Guest prof. U. Bonn, W. Ger., 1969-70, U. New South Wales, Sydney, 1988. Author: Probability, Convolutions and Distributions, 1990; contbr. articles to profl. jours. Mem. Am. Phys. Soc., Math Assn., History Sci. Soc., N.Y. Acad. Sci., Gauss-Gesellschaft, Rotary Internat., Sigma Xi. Personal E-mail: brtbg@helios.phy.ohiou.edu.

BREITENFELD, FREDERICK, JR., retired educational consultant, broadcast executive; b. N.Y.C., Sept. 26, 1931; s. Frederick and Dorothy (Falk) B.; m. Mary Ellen Fitzgerald, Dec. 27, 1954 (dec. 1998); children: Ann Clark, Kathleen Ellen. BS in Engring., Tufts U., 1953, MEd, 1954; MS in TV-Radio, Syracuse U., 1960, PhD, 1963; LHD (hon.), U. Md., 1976, Salisbury State Coll., 1982, Phila. Coll. Textiles and Sci., 1987, Wesley Coll., 1992. Tchr. physics and chemistry pub. H.S., North Creek, N.Y., 1958-59; program adminstr. U. Coll., Syracuse U., 1960-61; asst. dean Syracuse U., 1961-63; resident cons. in comm. U.S. Air Force, Cape Canaveral, Fla., 1963-64; rsch. project dir. Nat. Assn. Ednl. Broadcasters, Washington, 1964-65, assoc. dir. ednl. TV stas. divsn., 1965-66; exec. dir. Md. Center for Pub. Broadcasting, Owings Mills, Md., 1966-83; CEO, pres. WHYY Inc., 1983-97. Chmn. Ea. Ednl. TV Network, 1974-76; founding chmn. Am. Program Svc., 1991, vice-chmn., 1993; vice-chmn. bd. mgrs. PBS, 1973; cons., lectr. in field; adj. prof. Cath. U. Am., 1967-72, Am. U., 1972-74; vis. prof. Syracuse U., 1976, Johns Hopkins U., 1978-83; charter mem., chmn. Nat. Univ. Consortium for Telecomms. in Tchg. Trustee Thomas Jefferson U., 1988—, Valley Forge Mil. Acad. and Coll., 1992—, Bucks County C.C., 1994—; bd. dirs. Nat. Bd. Med. Examiners, 1995-99; active Lower Makefield Twp. Zoning Hearing Bd., Bucks County, Pa., 1998-99, Pennsbury Bd. Sch. Dirs., 1998-2001. Naval aviator USNR, 1954-58. Recipient Disting. Alumnus award Radio TV dept. Syracuse U., 1967; Andrew White medal Loyola Coll., Balt., 1979; Lord Baltimore medal St. Mary's Coll., 1980; Man of Yr. award Boys and Girls Club of Phila., 1987; Globe and Anchor award USMC Scholarship Found., 1991; Williamson award for excellence in cmty. svc. Williamson Free Sch., 1993. Mem.: AFTRA, Screen Actors Guild. Home: 1525 Harvest Dr Yardley PA 19067-4234 E-mail: ricbreit@aol.com. *To live is both to care and to laugh.*

BREITMAN, LEO R., banker; Pres. Bank of New Eng., until 1990, vice chmn., 1990—91; chmn., CEO Fleet Bank Mass., 1991—. Office: Fleet Boston Financial Corp 100 Federal St Boston MA 02110-2012

BREJCHA, VERNON L., artist, art educator; b. Ellsworth, Kans. s. Charles and Adeline Brejcha; children: Amber Kay, Clay Wheaton. BS, For Hays Kans. State U., 1964, MS, 1967; MFA, U. Wis., 1972. Art instr. Edgewood Coll., Madison, Wis., 1969—72; asst. prof. Tusculum, Greeneville, Tenn., 1972—76; assoc. prof. of design U. Kans., Lawrence, Kans., 1976—2002, prof. emeritus, 2003. Glass blowing instr. Haystack Mt. Sch., Deer Isle, Maine, 1985, Penland Sch. of Crafts, Penland, NC, 1989—92. Exhibitions include various profl. bldgs. Recipient Kans Govs. Artist award, Kans. Arts Coun., 1985; fellowship, NEA, 1984. Mem.: Kans. Artist Craftsman Assn. Program Chmn., Am. Crafts Coun., Glass Art Soc. Avocation: photography. Home: 1111 E 1500 Rd Lawrence KS 66046 Office Phone: 785-842-5275.

BREKHUS, MEL G., construction executive; b. ND; BS in Engring. Sci., Univ. Mont., 1972. V.p., cement prodn. Tex. Industries (TXI), Dallas, 1989, exec. v.p., COO, cement, aggregates and concrete, pres., CEO, 2004—. Bd. dir. Portland Cement Assn. (chmn. 2001-2002); past pres. Am. Portland Cement Alliance; chmn. Innovative Paving Rsch. Found. Office: TXI 1341 W Mockingbird Ln Dallas TX 75247 Office Fax: 972-647-6700.*

BREKKE, ALAN LEE, industrial engineer; b. Havre, Mont., Aug. 6, 1946; s. Knute Charles Brekke and Doris Emily Allen. Degree in indsl. and mgmt. engring., Mont. State U., 1974. Constrn. worker Brekke & sons, Harlem, Mont., 1959-70; deliverer and stockperson Merry Mkt., Harlem, 1962-64; intern Western Interstate Commn. for Higher Edn., Sydney, Mont., 1971; indsl. engr. Mont. State U., Bozeman, 1973; indsl. engr., with program planning dept. The Boeing Co., Seattle, 1974-83; constrn. mgr. Harlem H.S., 1986-87; indsl. engr. in pvt. practice Harlem, 1983—. *His work included schedules at Boeing Aerospace Company for the Airborne Warning and Control System E-3A Sentry, Program Planning, and Control Administrator on B-1B Bomber Avionics at the Boeing Military Airplane Company where he drafted program management and planning documents submitted to the Air Force and Congress. He also provided consultation to non-Boeing persons on visionary stealth airplane technology. His suggestions affected security and generated new proposals. Alan devoted five years of 24-hour medical care to his bedridden mother.* Staff writer (centennial book) Thunderstorms and Tumbleweeds, 1989; author: Kid Curry, 1989. With EMS Blaine County III Ambulance, Harlem, 2000—. Avocations: miner, ancient languages and alphabets, genealogist, ancient history, art. Home and Office: PO Box 635 Harlem MT 59526-0635 Office Phone: 406-353-2730.

BREKKE, MICHELE ANN, aerospace engineer, aeronautical engineer; b. Rochester, N.Y., Jan. 27, 1953; d. Paul William and Janet Marie Hank; m. Robert Lee Brekke (div.); children: Joey, Jeff, Jenny. BS in Aerospace Engring., U. Minn., 1975, MS in Aerospace Engring., 1977. Instr. space shuttle ops. NASA- Johnson Space Ctr., Houston, 1977—82, payloads officer mission control, 1982—85, flight dir., 1985—88, space shuttle program mgr., 1988—94, mgr. space sta. utilization, 1994—96; space shuttle flight mgr. Nasa - Jsc, Houston, 1996—2004; NASA loaned exec. Houston Tech. Ctr., 2005—. Leader Girl Scouts of Am., Friendswood, Tex., 1995—2000; commr. Friendswood Planning and Zoning Commn., 2001—03. Named one of Am.'s 100 Young Women of Promise, Good Housekeeping Mag., 1985; recipient Hung mission plaque, Mission Control Flight Dirs., 1984, cert. of commendation, NASA Space Shuttle Program, 1993, Exceptional Achievement Medal, 1994, cert. of commendation, NASA - Johnson Space Ctr., 2000; Amelia Earhart fellow, Zonta Internat., 1975—77. Mem.: AIAA. Achievements include being first female flight director and space shuttle flight manager. Office Phone: 832-476-9297. Personal E-mail: michele.a.brekke@nasa.gov.

BREKKE, STEWART ERNEST, retired chemistry and physics educator; b. Chgo., Dec. 28, 1941; s. Herbert and Rebecca Brekke. BA, U. Ill., 1965; MA, Wayne State U., 1971; MS in Edn., Purdue U., 1987. Cert. tchr. Ill. Physics and chemistry tchr. Chgo. Pub. Schs., 1975—2001; ret., 2001. Contbr. articles to profl. jours. Mem.: Am. Assn. Physics Tchrs. (emeritus mem.), Am. Geophys. Union, Am. Phys. Soc. Achievements include invention of mathematical theory of parallelism, divergence and convergence.Nuclear vibration: the determinant of nuclear barrier heights; research in quark oscillation and oscillating-electron oscillation; a 5th quantum number; nuclear barrier height as an irregular wave; oscillating nuclear cross sections and impact parameters making them variables; reduced mass calculation must include effects of nuclear vibration; electron orbits as oscillating mechanical cloud; physics and chemistry literacy must be mathematical; success in required high school mathematical physics and chemistry for all; effects of inner city violence on student performance in high school chemistry and physics; reconstruction (partial) of the prometheia; gravitational anomalies: an attribute of each heavenly body galaxy and galactic group. Avocations: chess, tennis. Home: 2900 Maple Ave Apt 17D Downers Grove IL 60515-4134 E-mail: stewabruk@aol.com.

BREKUS, CATHERINE ANNE, historian; b. Paterson, NJ, Nov. 11, 1963; d. Gordon Lewis and Trudy Brennan Brekus; m. Erik Joseph Sontheimer, Aug. 26, 1989; children: Claire Brennan Sontheimer, Rachel Ellen Sontheimer. AB, Harvard U., Cambridge, Mass., 1985; PhD, Yale U., 1993. Assoc. prof. history of christianity U. of Chgo., 1993—. Author: (book) Strangers and Pilgrims: Female Preaching in Am. 1740-1845 (Frank and Elizabeth Brewer Prize, Am. Soc. of Ch. History). Fellow Henry Luce III Faculty Fellow in Theology, Assn. of Theol. Schools, 1999—2000, Faculty Fellowship, Pew Program in Religion and Am. Histroy, 1995—96, Charlotte W. Newcombe Dissertation Fellowship, Woodrow Wilson Found., 1991—92, Frances Hiatt Fellowship, Am. Antiquarian Soc., 1991—92. Office: University of Chicago Divinity School 1025 East 58th Street Chicago IL 60043

BRELSFORD, EDMUND MUNGER, III, musician, educator; b. Miami, Fla., Apr. 11, 1931; s. Edmund Munger Brelsford and Alice Ashby; m. Veronica Gabrielle Alewyn, Nov. 22, 1960; children: Allegra Alewyn, Oliver Ashby, Wendy Carlotta, Cecelia Van Hook, Alicia Throm. BA, U. of Miami, 1954—57; MA, Middlebury Coll., 1959—60. Prof. of fgn. languages and literatures Marlboro Coll., Marlboro, Vt., 1964—. Internat. lectr., France, Italy, Brazil, China, Cuba, Egypt, Mongolia, Ecuador, et. al. Internat. artist (concert), No., Ctrl., So. Am., Europe, Asia, Middle Ea. Chmn. The Grammar Sch., Putney, Vt., 1976—80. Machinist mate USN, 1950—54, U.S.S. Black. Decorated Korean War Theater/Combat U.S. Govt.; recipient Prix Lafayette, France-Amérique, 1957; Full Academic scholarship, French Govt., 1957—60, Rsch. grant, Partners of the Americas, 1963, Marlboro Coll., 1999. Mem.: Early Music Am., The Marlboro Recorder Workshop, Ensemble Cordiforme, New Eng. Regional Assn. of Lang. Lab. Directors, U.S.Mensa, The Appalachian Mountain Club, The Brattleboro Outing Club, The Putney Ski Club. Avocations: dance, bicycling, cross-country ski racing, theater. Home: Box 146 Marlboro VT 05344 Office: Marlboro Coll PO Box A Marlboro VT 05344

BREM, HENRY, neurosurgeon, educator, researcher; b. Paterson, N.J., Aug. 14, 1952; s. Jacob and Adele (Machabanski) B.; m. Rachel Frydman, Jan. 28, 1978; children: Andrea, Alisa, Sarah. BA, NYU, 1973; student, Harvard U., 1973-74, MD, 1978. Diplomate Am. Bd. Neurosurgery. Intern in surgery Peter Bent Brigham Hosp., Boston, 1978-79; fellow in neurosurgery Johns Hopkins Hosp., Balt., 1979-80; resident in neurosurgery Neurol. Inst. N.Y. Columbia Presbyn. Med. Ctr., N.Y.C., 1980-84; neurosurgeon Johns Hopkins U. Sch. Medicine, Balt., 1984—, prof. neurosurgery, ophthalmology and oncology, 1991—, dir. Hunterian Neurosurg. Lab., 1995—, assoc. dir. dept. neurosurgery, 1995—, Harvey Cushing profl, chmn. dept. neurosurgery, 2000. Office: Johns Hopkins Hosp Meyer 7-113 600 N Wolfe St Baltimore MD 21287-0005

BREMENSTUHL, DAVID P., elementary school educator; b. Englewood, N.J., Aug. 10, 1942; s. V. Burton and Elsie M. (Dutcher) Bremenstuhl; m. Mary Ann K. Warnock, Sept. 13, 1973; children: Heather, Erin. BS in Edn., SUNY, New Paltz, 1964, postgrad., 1967—73, U. Md., 1967—73. Cert. tchr. N.Y. State Dept. Edn., advanced profl. cert. Md. Bd. Edn. Elem. tchr. Middletown (N.Y.) Pub. Schs., 1964—66, White Plains (N.Y.) Pub. Schs., 1966—70, Irvington Pub. Schs., Irvington-on-Hudson, NY, 1971—73, Montgomery County Pub. Schs., Rockville, Md., 1973—2003, Edn. Cons. Svc., 2003—. Mem. Am. Friends Svc. Com.; founding mem. Nat. Campaign for Tolerance; active Pub. Concern Found.; mem. U.S. Holocaust Meml. Mus.; mem. leadership coun. So. Poverty Law Ctr. Recipient Lifetime Achievement award, George Washington Elem. Sch. PTA, 1970, honor Wall of Tolerance Meml., Ala. Mem.: NAACP, ACLU, NEA, Assn. Psychohistory, Montgomery County Edn. Assn., Md. State Tchrs. Assn., Nation Assoc., Interfaith Alliance, Wilderness Soc., Amnesty Internat., The Nat. Assocs., Common Cause, Doctors Without Borders, Nat. Resources Def. Coun., Oxfam Am., Sierra Club. Achievements include name inscribed on Wall of Tolerance civil rights memorial in Montgomery, Alabama. Avocations: poetry, composing music, landscape gardening. Home: 9601 Brink Rd Gaithersburg MD 20882 Personal E-mail: mbremenstu@aol.com.

BREMER, CELESTE F., judge; b. San Francisco, 1953; BA, St. Ambrose Coll., 1974; JD, Univ. of Iowa Coll. of Law, 1977; EdD, Drake U., 2002. Asst. county atty. Scott County, 1977-79; asst. atty. gen. Area Prosecutors Div., Iowa, 1979; with Carlin, Liebbe, Pitton & Bremer, 1979-81, Rabin, Liebbe, Shinkle & Bremer, 1981-82; with legal dept. Deere and Co., 1982-84; corp. counsel Economy Forms Corp., 1985-89; magistrate judge U.S. Dist. Ct. (Iowa so. dist.), 8th cir., Des Moines, 1984—; ed. D. Drake U. Sch. of Edn., 2002. Instr. Drake Univ. Coll. of Law, 1985—96. Mem. ABA, Fed. Magistrate Judge Assn., Nat. Assn. Women Judges, Am. Judicature Soc., Iowa State Bar Assn. (bd. govs., 1987-90), Iowa Judges Assn., Iowa Supreme Ct. Coun. on Jud. Selection (chmn. 1986-90), Iowa Orgn Women Attys., Polk County Bar Assn., Polk County Women Attys. Office: US Courthouse Ste 435 123 E Walnut St Des Moines IA 50309-2036 Office Phone: 515-284-6200.

BREMER, HOWARD WALTER, lawyer, consultant; b. Milw., July 18, 1923; s. Walter Hugo and Lydia Martha (Schmidt) B.; m. Caryl Marie Faust, May 28, 1948; children: Katharine, William (dec.), Thomas, Timothy, Margaret. BSChemE, U. Wis., 1944, LLB, 1949. Bar: Wis. 1949, U.S. Patent and Trademark Office 1954, U.S. Supreme Ct. 1957, U.S. Ct. Appeals (fed. cir.) 1959, U.S. Dist. Ct. (so. dist.) Ohio 1960. Patent atty. Procter & Gamble Co., Cin., 1949-60; patent counsel Wis. Alumni Rsch. Found., Madison, 1960-88; cons., Madison, 1988—. Adv. com. Coun. on Govtl. Rels., Washington, 1975-93; panel mem. Office Tech. Assessment, Washington, 1981-83; mem. Adv. Commn. on Patent Law Reform, Washington, 1991-92. Mem. internat. adv. bd. Industry and Higher Edn. Jour., 1996—; contbr. articles to profl. jours. Pres. Edgewood Campus Sch. PTA, Madison, 1967-69; adv. bd. Edgewood H.S., 1971-80, chmn. adv. bd., 1973-74. With USN, 1944-46. Recipient Alumni Appreciation award, Edgewood H.S., 1990, Hon. Recognition award, U. Wis. Coll. Agrl. and Life Scis., 2000; 5 scholarships established in his name, Assn. Univ. Tech. Mgrs., 2003. Mem. ABA (chmn. com. 1993-2001), Am. Intellectual Property Law Assn. (chmn. com. 1996-99), State Bar Wis. (chmn. intellectual property sect. 1967-68, 79-80), Wis. Intellectual Property Law Assn. (pres. 1989-90), Assn. Univ. Tech. Mgrs. (trustee 1977-78, 80-82, pres. 1978-80, com. chmn. 1985-93, mem. editl. bd. jour. 1990—, Birch award 1980, scholarship established in his name 2003). Avocations: building furniture, home maintenance, model railroading, travel, reading. Home: 1106 Brookwood Rd Madison WI 53711-3116 Office Phone: 608-263-2831. Business E-Mail: hwbremer@warf.org.

BREMER, JOHN M., lawyer; b. 1947; BA, Fordham U., 1969; JD, Duke U., 1974. Bar: Wis. 1974. From atty. law dept. to sr. exec. v.p. Northwestern Mut. Life Ins., Milw., 1974—2002, COO, 2002—. Office: Northwestern Mutual Life Ins Co 720 E Wisconsin Ave Milwaukee WI 53202-4703

BREMER, PAUL, III, (LEWIS PAUL BREMER III), former diplomat; b. Hartford, Conn., Sept. 30, 1941; s. L. Paul and Nina (Struthers) B.; m. Frances Winfield, June 11, 1966; children: Paul, Leila. BA, Yale U., 1963; cert., Inst. d'etudes Politiques, U. Paris, 1964; MBA, Harvard U., 1966. With Diplomatic Svc., 1966; exec. asst. to sec. state US Dept. State, Washington, 1974-76, dep. exec. sec., 1979-81, exec. sec., spl. asst. to sec. of state, 1981—83; dep. amb., chief of mission Am. Embassy, Oslo, 1976—79; US amb. to The Netherlands US Dept. State, The Hague, 1983—86, amb.-at-large for counter-terrorism, 1986—89; mng. dir. Kissinger Assocs., 1989—2000; chmn. Nat. Commn. on Terrorism, 1999—2001; chmn. polit. risk bus. Marsh Inc., 2000—, chmn., CEO crisis consulting practice, 2001—03; presdl. appointee Homeland Security Adv. Coun., 2002—; civilian adminstr. Iraq, head transition team Coalition Provisional Authority, Baghdad, 2003—04. Bd. dirs. Air Products and Chems. Inc., Akzo Nobel NV, Netherland-Am.

Found. Recipient Superior Honor award Dept. State, 1974, Presdl. Merit Pay award, 1983, Presdl. Medal of Freedom, 2004 Mem. Internat. Inst. Strategic Studies, Coun. on Fgn. Rels. (bd. dirs.), Netherlands-Am. Found., Conner Peripherals Inc., Air Products and Chems. Inc. Republican. Roman Catholic. Avocations: skiing, jogging, history.

BREMER, RONALD ALLAN, genealogist, editor; b. Southgate, Calif., May 2, 1937; s. Carl Leonard and Lena Evelyn (Jury) B.; childen: Blindy, Ron, Trina, Rebecca, Melinda, Aaron, Serena, Lorrie, Jennie, Elizabeth, Hans, Adam, Rachel. Student, Los Angeles Trade Tech., Cerritos Coll., Am. U., Brigham Young U.; grad., Nat. Inst. Geneal. Rsch., 1961. Prof. genealogist, 1959—; research specialist Fam. Hist. Libr., Salt Lake City, 1969-72; profl. lectr. on genealogy Salt Lake City, 1973—; pres. The Rsch. Inst. Editor Genealogy Digest mag., Salt Lake City, 1983-84, Roots Digest, 1984-85; lectr. in field. Author: World's Funniest Epitaphs, 1983; Compendium of Historical Sources, 1983; (with Bill Dollarhide) America's Best Genealogy Resource Centers, 1999. Office Phone: 801-521-3008. Personal E-mail: RonBremer@juno.com. *Money and things don't matter. Position and education mean little. Genius and slow-normal have the same opportunity. Happiness is achieving your greatest potential. Go for the goose-bumps!.*

BREMER, SUZANNE W., writer, librarian; b. LaRochelle, France, June 14, 1958; arrived in U.S., 1959; d. Edward Wood and Margret Suzanne (Fleishmann) Bremer. AA, Pine Manor Jr. Coll., Chestnut Hill, Mass., 1978; BA, Boston U., 1980; MS, Simmons Coll., 1982. Libr. Warner-Eddison Assoc., Cambridge, Mass., 1978-80, Price Waterhouse, Boston, 1981-83, Broadbased Info. Svcs., Somerville, Mass., 1983—. Vis. writer Joiner Ctr. Study War and Social Consequences, 1998—; webmaster City Newton, Mass., 1998—2001. Author: (book) Long Range Planning for Libraries, 1994; co-author: Our Bodies, Ourselves for the New Century, 1998. Bd. dirs. N.H. Automation Rev. Bd., Concord, 1982—83; mem. Catherdral Ch. of St. Paul Coun., 1998—2004. Mem.: Boston (Mass.) Athenaeum. Office: Broadbased Info Svcs 33 Columbus Ave Somerville MA 02143-2018

BREMER MARTINO, JUAN JOSE, former ambassador; b. Mexico City, 1944; Law degree, Nat. Autonomous U. Mex., 1966. Pvt. sec. to Pres. Govt. of Mex., 1972—75; dep. sec. Ministry of Presidency, 1975—76; head Nat. Fine Arts Inst., 1976—82; dep. sec. cultural affairs Ministry Edn., 1982; pres. Cervantino Internat. Festival, 1983; pres. fgn. affairs com. Chamber of Deps., 1985—88; amb. to Sweden Mexican Embassy, 1982, amb. to USSR, 1988—90, amb. to Fed. Rep. Germany, 1990—98, amb. to Spain, 1998—2000, amb. to U.S. Washington, 2001—04. Co-chair Mexican delegations XXVI Mex.-U.S. Interparliamentary Commn., Colorado Springs, Colo., 1986, XVII Mex.-U.S. Interparliamentary Commn., New Orleans, 1988; participant Commn. to Study Future of Mexican-Am. Rels., 1988; lectr. in field.

BREMNER, CEDRIC G., surgeon; b. Johannesburg, Mar. 3, 1929; arrived in US, 1993; s. James Alexander and Ida Myrle (Blackbeard) Bremner; m. cynthia Heath Tibbitts; children: Ros McCrae, Nicola Heath, Bruce McNab, Heidi Louise. MB, BChir, U. Witwatersrand, Johannesburg, 1953, ChM, 1959. Prof. surgery U. Witwatersrand, Johannesburg, 1968—78; chief surgeon Hillbrin and Coronation Hosp., Johannesburg, 1979—92; surgeon, prof. U. So. Calif., LA, 1993—. Editor: Modern Approach to Benign Esophageal Disease, 1995; author: Esophageal Diseases and Testing, 2005; contbr. articles to profl. jours. Past pres. Assn. Surgeons South Africa, Surg. Rsch. Soc. South Africa. Recipient Gold medal, Assn. Surgeons South Africa, 1990. Fellow: ACS, Royal Coll. Surgeons (Scotland), Royal Coll. Surgeons (Eng.); mem.: Soc. for Surgeons of the Alimentary Tract, Am. Surg. Soc. Avocations: hiking, fishing. Office: Univ So Calif Dept Surgery 1510 San Pablo St #514 Los Angeles CA 90033

BREMNER, JAMES DOUGLAS, psychiatrist, researcher, education educator; b. Topeka, Kans., June 5, 1961; s. James Douglas and Linnea Bremner; m. Laura Viola Vaccarino, Aug. 1, 1991; children: Sabina Francesca, Dylan Vittorio. BS, U. of Puget Sound, 1979—83; MD, Duke U. Sch. of Medicine, 1983—87. Cert. Am. Bd. of Psychiatry and Neurology, 1996, Am. Bd. of Nuc. Medicine, 2001. Assoc. prof. of psychiatry and radiology Emory U. Sch. of Medicine, 2000—; dir. Emory Ctr. for Positron Emission Tomography, 2000—. Asst. and assoc. prof. of psychiatry Yale U. Sch. of Medicine, 1992—2000. Author: (book) Does Stress Damage the Brain?. Achievements include research in brain imaging and neurobiology of mood and anxiety disorders. Home: 2125 Ponce de Leon Ave NE Atlanta GA 30307 Office: Emory U 1256 Briarcliff Rd Atlanta GA 30306 E-mail: jdbremn@emory.edu.

BREMNER, JOHN MCCOLL, agronomy and biochemistry educator; b. Dumbarton, Scotland, Jan. 18, 1922; came to U.S., 1959; s. Archibald Donaldson and Sarah Kennedy (McColl) B.; m. Eleanor Mary Williams, Sept. 30, 1950; children: Stuart, Carol. BS, Glasgow U., 1944, DSc, 1987; PhD, U. London, 1948, DSc, 1959. With chemistry dept. Rothamsted Exptl. Sta., Harpenden, Eng., 1945-59; assoc. prof. Iowa State U., Ames, 1959-61, prof. agronomy and biochemistry, 1961-75, C.F. Curtiss disting. prof. agriculture, prof. agronomy, biochemistry, 1975-93; disting. prof. emeritus, 1993—. Tech. expert IAEA, Austria, 1964-65, Yugoslavia, 1964-65. Author or co-author over 300 publs. including 30 chpts in sci. monographs. Recipient Outstanding Research award First Miss. Corp., 1979, Alexander Von Humboldt medal Alexander Von Humboldt Found., Fed. Republic of Germany, 1982, Gov.'s Sci. medal State of Iowa, 1983, Harvey Wiley award U.S. Assn. Ofcl. Analytical Chemists, 1984, Spencer medal Am. Chem. Soc., 1987, Burlington No. Found. Faculty Achievement award for Research, Gamma Sigma Delta award of merit for disting. service to agriculture, Regents award for faculty excellence, 1992, Award for Advancement of Agrl. & Food Chemistry, Am. Chem. Soc.; fellow Rockefeller Found., 1957, Guggenheim Found., 1968. Fellow AAAS, Am. Acad. Microbiology, Am. Soc. Agronomy (Agronomic Rsch. award 1985, Environ. Quality Rsch. award 1990), Soil Sci. Soc. Am. (Achievement award 1967, Bouyoucos Disting. Career award 1982, Disting. Svc. award 1993), Iowa Acad. Sci. (disting.); mem. NAS, Am. Soc. Microbiology, Brit. Soc. Soil Sci., Internat. Soil Sci. Soc., Phi Kappa Phi (centennial medalist 1997), Sigma Xi, Gamma Sigma Delta. Achievements include patent for nitrification inhibitor; development and evaluation of nitrification and urease inhibitors for control of adverse transformations of fertilizer nitrogen in soils; development of methodology for research on the nitrogen cycle and environmental problems related to agriculture; research on microbial, enzymatic, and chemical processes responsible for nitrogen transformations in soils, such as nitrification, denitrification, chemodenitrification, and urease activity. Personal E-mail: bremnerjm@msn.com.

BREMOND, DUANE BENJAMIN, marketing professional; b. San Francisco, Oct. 22, 1961; s. Walter and Bertha B.; m. Harvelin Roberts, Mar. 17, 1985 (div. 1988); 1 child, Diandra. BS in Mgmt., Pepperdine U., 2001. Congrl. aide Congresswoman Maxine Waters, L.A., 1988-95; dir. cmty. rels. AIDS Project L.A., 1995-97; asst. dir. devel. Hospitaller Found., L.A., 1997-2000; dir. mktg. and devel. Ctr. Cmty. & Family Svcs., Padadena, Calif., 2000—02; prin. Bremond & Assoc., Inglewood, Calif., 2002—. Commr. L.A. HIV & Health Svc., L.A., 1995-97. Dir. logistics Nelson Mandela Tour, L.A., 1990. With U.S. Army, 1984-87. Democrat. Home: 6002 Ladera Park Ave Los Angeles CA 90056 E-mail: breme10@yahoo.com.

BREMS, DAVID PAUL, architect; b. Lehi, Utah, Aug. 10, 1950; s. D. Orlo and Gearldine (Hitchcock) B.; m. Johna Devey Brems; children: Stefan Tomas Brems, Beret Alla Brems. BS, U. Utah, 1973, MArch, 1975. Registered architect, Utah, Calif., Colo., Ariz., Wyo., N.Mex., Idaho, Mont., Tex., Wash. Draftsman Environ. Assocs., Salt Lake City, 1971-73; draftsman/architect intern Environ. Design Group, Salt Lake City, 1973-76; architect/intern Frank Fuller AIA, Salt Lake City, 1976-77; prin. Edward & Daniels, Salt Lake City, 1978-83; pres. David Brems & Assocs., Salt Lake City, 1983-86; prin. Gillies, Stransky, Brems, Smith P.C., Salt Lake City, 1986—. Adj. prof. U. Utah Grad. Sch. Architecture, 1990-93; mem. urban design com. Assist, Inc., Salt Lake City, 1982-85, Salt Lake County Planning Commn., 1991-97, chmn., 1992-96; mem. Emigration Twp. Planning Commn., 1997—, chmn. 1997-99; mem. Emigration Masterplan Adv. Com., 1997-99; invited lectr. Wyo. Soc. Archs., 1992, sch. engring. U. Utah, 1993, 95, VA, 1993, Utah Soc. Archs., 1994, Utah Power and Light, 1994, Utah Soc. Archs., 1994, others; juror U. Utah Grad. Sch. Architecture, 1975—, Utah Soc. Am. Planning Assn., 1994—, Sunstone Symposium, 1995, Contemporary Arts Group, 1995—, others; mem. adv. com. U. Utah Grad. Sch. Architecture, 2000—. Pub. Firm Profile Intermountain Architecture, 1996, Web Mag., 1997; prin. works include solar twin homes Utah Holiday (Best Solar Design award), Sun Builder, Daily Jour., Salt Lake Tribune, Brian Head Day Lodge, Easton Aluminum, Four Seasons Hotel, Gore Coll. Bus., CMF Tooele, utah Regional Corrections Facility, St. Vincents De Paul Ctr., Steiner Aquatic Ctr., U. Utah Football Support Facility, Sports Medicine West, West Jordan Cmty. Water Park, Utah N.G. Apache Helicopter Hangar & Armory, Kashmitter I Residences, St. Thomas More Cath. Ch., Spanish Fork Cmty. Water Park, Natures Herbs, ABC Office Bldg. Divsn. of Natural Resources Bldg., Kashmitter II Residence, Litton Residence, Elliott Residence, Utah Olympic Speed Skating Oval for 2002 Olympics, Vis. Ctr. Grand Staircase Escalante Nat. Monument, Bennett Fed. Bldg., and others; ALTA Club mem., Great Salt Lake Yacht Club mem., Bear Lake Yacht Club mem., mem. Leadership Utah; mem. 2002 Olympic Energy and Water subcom., 1996—; mem. State of Utah Divsn. of Facilities Mgmt. Com. on Energy Efficient Architecture. Mem. Salt Lake City Bus. Advisory. Recipient three awards Am. Concrete Inst., 1993, Chief Engrs. Honor award U.S. Army Corps Engrs., 1994; Bronze medalist Utah Summer Games, 1991, Silver medalist, 1992, Gold medalist, 1994, Design award Dept. Def., 1995, Blue Seal award, 1995, Outstanding Project award U.S. Dept. Def., 1995, Western Mountain Region Hon. Mention St. Thomas More, 1996, Solar Today award Sun award, Energy Uses News award Dept. Natural Resources, 1996, Western Mountain Region Merit award Bennet Fed. Bldg., 2003, Western Mountain Citation award, 2003, Jewish Cmty. Ctr. Holocaust Meml., 2003; named Best Pvt. Project by Intermountain Architecture, 1994, Salt Lake County Vol. of Yr. Salt Lake County Planning Commn., 1995, Best Recreation Project Intermountain Arch., 1995, award for Sahara Office Bldg., Ceramic Tiles of Italy, 2004, award Utah Masonry Coun. Mem.: AIA (chmn. Western Mountain Regiona honor awards 1983, pres. Salt Lake chpt. 1983—84, chmn. Western Mountain Region conf. 1986, pres. Utah Soc. 1987, chmn. Western Mountain Regional honor awards 1988, com. on design 1990—, juror Colo. West awards 1992, chmn. com. on environment AIA Utah 1993, chmn. Design for Life Workshop at Sundance 1993, Utah concrete masony assoc. Emigration Canyon home 2003, Honor awards 1983, Merit awards 1983, 1985, Honor awards 1988, PCI award 1988, IFRAA award 1988, Merit awards 1988, 1993, IFRAA award 1994, Merit awards 1999, Steel Inst. award 2002, Honor award 2002, Sarnafil award 2002, Merit award 2003, Honor awards 2003, Henfagy Found. awards 2003, award Utah sect. IES for St. Thomas More, Nat. Concrete Masony award of excellence 2003), Am. Solar Soc., Am. Solar Energy Soc., Utah Soc. Architects, Black Builder Mesa Water Assn. (sec.), Acorn Hills Water Assn. (trustee), Am. Planning Assn. (juror awards 1994), Illuminating Engring. Soc. (assoc.), Utah Open Lands (S.W. Utah br.), Salt Lake Olympic Com. (environ. adv. com.), Hobie Fleet 67 (commodore 1985—86). Home: 119 N Young Oak Rd Salt Lake City UT 84108-1601

BREMSER, GEORGE, JR., electronics company executive; b. Newark, May 26, 1928; s. George and Virginia (Christian) B.; m. Marie Sundman, June 21, 1952 (div. July 1979); children: Christian Fredrick II, Priscilla Suzanne, Martha Anne, Sarah Elizabeth; m. Nancy Kay Woods, Oct. 27, 1983 (div. Feb. 1989); m. Betty Glover Lohse, Oct. 8, 1997 (dec. Mar. 2001). BA, Yale U., 1949; postgrad., U. Miami, 1959; MBA, NYU, 1962. With McCann-Erickson Inc., N.Y.C., 1952-61, asst. gen. mgr. Bogota, Colombia, 1955, gen. mgr., 1955-57, account supr. N.Y.C., 1958, v.p., mgr. Miami, Fla., 1959-61; with Gen. Foods Corp., White Plains, N.Y., 1961-71; v.p., gen. mgr. internat. div. Gen. Foods Europe, White Plains, N.Y., 1967; pres. Gen. Foods Internat., White Plains, 1967-71; group v.p. Gen. Foods Corp., White Plains, 1970-71; chmn., pres., chief exec. officer Texstar Corp., Grand Prairie, Tex., 1971-81; exec. v.p. Shaklee Corp., San Francisco, 1981-82; chmn., pres., chief exec. officer Etak Inc., Menlo Park, Calif., 1983-88, 96, chmn., 1989-96, 97—; chmn., pres., CEO Etak, Inc., Menlo Park, Calif., 1996-97, chmn., 1997-2000, CEO, 2000-01; bd. dir. Tele Atlas N.A., Inc., 2000—, chief adminstrv. officer, 2001—02. Bd. dirs. PBI Industries Inc. Trustee Union Ch., Bogota, 1956-57; Dem. county committeeman, Ridgewood, N.J., 1962-63; mem. New Canaan (Conn.) Town Council, 1969-73; founder, past pres. Citizens Com. for Conservation, New Canaan; mem. coun. Save the Redwoods League, 1987—. Served to 2d lt. USMC 1950-52, capt. Res. Mem. New Canaan Country Club, Brook Club, Yale Club (N.Y.C.), Block Island Club, Casino Club (Nantucket, Mass.), Explorers Club, Phi Beta Kappa, Beta Gamma Sigma, Beta Theta Pi. Home: Apt 3317 131 Embarcadero West Oakland CA 94607-3768 also: Mansion Beach Rd Block Island RI 02807 Office: Tele Atlas NA Inc 1605 Adams Dr Menlo Park CA 94025-1448 Office Phone: 650-328-3825 x.1294. Business E-Mail: george.bremser@teleatlas.com.

BREN, DONALD L., real estate company executive; b. 1932; BA in Bus., MBA, U. Wash. Founder, pres. Bren Company (later renamed California Pacific Homes), Newport Beach, 1958—, Mission Viejo (Calif.) Co., Newport Beach, 1963—67; CEO Irvine Co., Newport Beach, 1977—, chmn. bd., 1998—. Established Donald Bren Sch. of Environmental Sci. & Mgmt., U. Calif. Chmn. Donald Bren Found.; trustee Orange County Museum of Art, Los Angeles County Museum of Art, Calif. Inst. of Tech. With USMC, 1954—57. Named one of World's Richest People by Forbes in 2001, 02, 03, 04. Office: The Irvine Co 550 Newport Center Dr Newport Beach CA 92660-7011*

BRENCHLEY, JEAN ELNORA, microbiologist, researcher, science administrator; b. Towanda, Pa., Mar. 6, 1944; d. John Edward and Elizabeth (Jefferson) B.; m. Bernard Asbell, July 21, 1990. BS, Mansfield U., 1965; MS, U. Calif., San Diego, 1967; PhD, U. Calif., Davis, 1970; hon. degree, Lycoming Coll., 1992. Rsch. assoc. biology dept. MIT, Cambridge, 1970-71; from asst. prof. to assoc. prof. microbiology Pa. State U., Univ. Pk., 1971-77, head. dept. molecular and cell biology, dir. Biotech. Inst. University Park, 1984-87, prof. microbiology, dir. Biotech. Inst., 1984-90, prof. microbiology and biotech., 1990—; assoc. prof., then prof. biology Purdue U., West Lafayette, Ind., 1977-81; research dir. Genex Corp., Gaithersburg, Md., 1981-84. Mem. Nat. Biotech. Policy Bd., 1990-93; trustee Biosis, 1983-88; vis. scholar NIH, 1991. Editor Applied and Environ. Microbiology, 1981-85; mem. editorial bd. Jour. Bacteriology, 1974-84, Butterworth Biotech. Series, 1988-92; editor Microbiol. Revs., 1992-97. Recipient Outstanding Alumni award Manfield U., 1983; Waksman award Theobald Smith Soc., 1985; named to Pa. Hall of Fame, 1988. Fellow AAAS (nominating com. 1990-92), Am. Acad. Microbiology; mem. NAS (bioprocess com.), Am. Soc. Microbiology (pres. 1986-87, ASM Found. lectr. 1975, Alice Evans award 1996), Assn. Women in Sci., Am. Soc. Biol. Chemists, Am. Chem. Soc., Found. for Microbiology (trustee 1988-95), Sigma Delta Epsilon (hon.). Office: Pa State Univ Frear Lab University Park PA 16802

BRENCIUS, JULIE MICHELLE, music educator; b. Benton Harbor, Mich., Dec. 11, 1971; d. Charles Brent and Pamela Sue Hand; m. Mel Fredric Brencius, Apr. 10, 2004. BA in music edn., Azusa Pacific U., 1993; MusM in choral conducting, Calif. State U., Fullerton, 2002. Music tchr. John Muir H.S., Pasadena, Calif., 1996—97, Buena Pk. Sch. Dist., Calif., 1997—2001; vocal music tchr. Placentia Yocha Linda Unified Sch. Dist., Placentia, Calif., 2001—. Mem.: Southern Calif. Vocal Assn., Am. Choral Directors Assn. Avocations: flute, reading, scrapbooks. Office: 645 N Angelina Dr Placentia CA 92870

BRENDAHL, MARCIA, artist, illustrator; b. Battle Creek, Mich., Mar. 2, 1953; d. Ray LaVerne and Iris Donna (Hawkins-Eckhart) Leonard; m. Mark Eric Brendahl, Mar. 7, 1985; children: Mallorae E., Maureen E. AD in Liberal Arts, Lansing (Mich.) C.C., 1985. Ceramic tchr. Leonard's Ceramics, Lansing, 1972-83; fine artist Lansing, 1983—; art designer Lansing Sch. Dist./Kendon Elem. Sch., 1999—. Children's art tchr. Lansing Art Gallery, 1998-99, Lansing Parks and Recreation, 1999. Designer murals for stage performances, 1997—; fine art portraits of children and authors, 1989—. Vol. worker, artist Mich. Rep. Party, Lansing, 1999. Mem. Nat. Women of the Arts, Lansing Art Guild. Avocations: painting, writing short stories, photography. Home: 6888 Londal Cir Lansing MI 48911-7044

BRENDEL, BETTINA, abstract artist; b. Lueneburg, Germany; d. Robert and Xenia (Bernstein) Brendel; m. Arthur Spitzer, Mar. 4, 1949 (div. July 1965); 1 child, Violet Spitzer Lucas. Abiturium, Oberlyceum, Hamburg, Germany, 1940; student, Kunstschule, Hamburg, Germany, 1941—42; cert., Staatliche Hochschule fur Bildende Kunste, Hamburg, Germany, 1945—47; postgrad., U. So. Calif., 1955—58, New Sch. for Social Rsch., N.Y., 1968—69. Instr. UCLA Extension, 1958—61; lectr. Coll. Art Assn., Chgo., 1971, Inst. Optics, Rochester, NY, 1971; instr. UCLA Extension, 1976; lectr. U. So. Calif., 1980. Conf. participant Gulbenkian Found., Paris, Lisbon, Portugal. One-woman shows include Santa Barbara (Calif.) Mus., 1966, Spectrum Gallery, N.Y., 1967, Artcore Gallery, L.A., 1984, Long Beach Mus., 1998, Galerie Wosimsky, Germany, 1999, David Lawrence Gallery, Beverly Hills, 2000, exhibitions include nat. and internat. group shows; author: book of poems, 1977; contbr. articles to publs.; exhibitions include computer art, 1982— (prize Palm Springs, Calif., 1997, 1998), Gallery Wosimsky, Giessen, Germany, 2003; contbr. articles to profl. publs.; Represented in permanent collections Armand Hammer Mus., L.A. County Mus. Art, Long Beach Mus., Mus. Konkrete Kunst, Ingolstadt, Germany, Werner Heisenberg Inst., Munich. Recipient 1st prize, La Jolla (Calif.) Art Mus., 1958—59, Long Beach Mus. Art, 1960, Purchase prize, San Francisco Mus., 1966. Mem.: UCLA Alumni Assn., Friends of the Ctr. for History of Physics, YLEM Artists Using Sci. and Tech. (contbr. newsletter), L.A. Printmaking Soc., Archives Am. Art, Mus. Contemporary Art, L.A. County Mus. Art. Democrat. Home: 1061 N Kenter Ave Los Angeles CA 90049-1313 Office Phone: 310-476-5860. Personal E-mail: bb4art@yahoo.com.

BRENDEL, JOHN S., lawyer; b. McKeesport, Pa., May 6, 1951; BA with distinction, Cornell U., 1973; JD cum laude, Harvard U., 1976. Bar: Pa. 1977. Assoc., ptnr. Buchanan Ingersoll P.C., Pitts., 1977-95; ptnr. Cohen & Grigsby P.C., 1995-97; v.p., gen. counsel Mastech Corp., Oakdale, Pa., 1997-2000; sr. v.p. iGATE Capital Corp., Pitts., 2000—. Adj. prof. immigration law U. Pitts. Sch. of Law., Duquesne U. Sch. Law. Fulbright-DAAD fellow, 1976-77. Mem. Am. Immigration Lawyers Assn. Office: 1000 Commerce DR STE 500 Pittsburgh PA 15275-1039

BRENDER, JEAN DIANE, epidemiologist, nurse; b. Bellingham, Wash., Nov. 23, 1951; d. Otto and Jennie Wilma Tolsma; m. Dennis Ray Brender, Aug. 30, 1975; 1 child, Valerie. BSN summa cum laude, Whitworth Coll., 1974; M of Nursing, U. Wash., 1979, PhD of Epidemiology, 1983. RN Tex. Staff nurse, infection control Sacred Heart Med. Ctr., Spokane, Wash., 1974-80; instr. nursing Intercollegiate Ctr. for Nursing Edn., Spokane, 1979-80, asst. prof. nursing, 1982-84; teaching asst. epidemiology U. Wash., Seattle, 1981-82; rsch. health scientist Audie L. Murphy Vets. Hosp., San Antonio, 1984-85; staff epidemiologist bur. epidemiology Tex. Dept. Health, Austin, 1986-87, acting program dir. environ. epidemiology program, 1987, dir. environ. epidemiology program, 1987-93, dir. noncommunicable disease epidemiology and toxicology, 1993-97; infectious disease epidemiologist Bur. Disease Control, 1997-99; also state environ. epidemiologist Tex. Dept. Health, Austin, 1993-97; assoc. prof. health svcs. rsch. Tex. State U., 1999—2005; assoc. prof. epidemiology Sch. Rural Pub. Health, Tex. A&M Health Sci. Ctr., Bryan, 2005—. Bd. dirs. Agriculture Resources Protection Authority; adj. instr. allied health scis. and health adminstrn. Tex. State U., 1988-90; adj. asst. prof. epidemiology U. Tex. Health Sci. Ctr.-Houston Sch. Pub. Health, 1985-93, adj. assoc. prof., 1993—. Contbr. articles to profl. jours. Recipient H.E.A.L.T.H. award, 1994; grantee in field. Mem. APHA, Soc. Epidemiologic Rsch., Coun. State and Territorial Epidemiologists, Am. Coll. Epidemiology, Tex. Pub. Health Assn. (governing coun.). Avocations: reading, computers, church activities, skiing. Home: 6902 Alder Cv Austin TX 78750-8161 Office: Tex A&M Health Sci Ctr Sch Rural Pub Health 3000 Briarcrest Dr Ste 300 Bryan TX 77802 Office Phone: 979-862-1573. E-mail: jdbrender@aol.com.

BRENDLER, CHARLES BURGESS, urologist, educator; b. Charlottesville, Va., June 20, 1944; s. Herbert and Virginia Burgess B.; m. Lucretia Cattley Rock, June 18, 1966; children: Christopher, Amy, Emily, Peter. AB, Harvard Coll., 1966; MD, U. Va., 1974. Instr. urology Johns Hopkins U., Balt., 1980-81, asst. prof. urology, 1981-85, assoc. prof. urology, 1985-93; chief urology Balt. City Hosps., 1981-84; prof., chief urology U. Chgo., 1994—. Mem. surg. exec. com. U. Chgo. Med. Ctr., 1994—, mem. surgery edn. com., 1994—. Assoc. editor: Urologic Surgery, 5th edit., 1998; co-author: Campbell's Urology, 1985, 92, 97, 02; Urologic Surgery, 1983, 91, assoc. editor, 1998, 03; co-author Operative Urology 1990, 97, 02; contbr. articles to profl. jour. Capt. USAF, 1967-71. Mem. Am. Urol. Assn. (2d prize clin. rsch. 1983, 1st prize clin. rsch. Mid-Atlantic sect. 1991, 92), Am. Assn. Genito-Urinary Surgeons, Nat. Urol. Forum, Soc. Basic Urol. Rsch., Soc. Urol. Oncology, Am. Joint Commn. on Cancer (advisor task force on urol. cancer 1997), Alpha Omega Alpha. Democrat. Unitarian Universalist. Avocations: skiing, hiking, jogging, travel. Home: 434 W Arlington Pl Chicago IL 60614 Office: U Chgo Sect Urology 5841 S Maryland Ave Mc 6038 Chicago IL 60637-1463 Office Phone: 773-702-6105. E-mail: cbrendle@surgery.bsd.uchicago.edu.

BRENDLINGER, LEROY R., academic administrator; b. Frederick, Pa., Dec. 14, 1918; s. Claude R. and Elsie May B.; m. Virginia Steltz, Dec. 28, 1941; children: Dawn, Brian, Craig. BS, West Chester State Coll., 1946; MS, U. Pa., 1949; Ed.D., Temple U., 1959. Former tchr., East Greenville, Pa.; Ordnance Officer Candidate Sch., Aberdeen, Md.; former prin. Pottsgrove (Pa.) Schs.; former asst. supt. Montgomery (Pa.) Schs.; pres. Montgomery County Community Coll., now pres. emeritus. Chmn. SCORE, chpt. 594 Tri County area. Author: The Brendlinger Family History 1660-1994, 1995. Past pres. Montgomery County (Pa.) Health and Welfare Coun.; bd. dirs. Montgomery Hosp., Lutheran Children and Family Svc.; pres. Tri-County Area local chpt. Score 594, Pottstown, Pa. With U.S. Army, 1942-46, ETO. Recipient Outstanding Alumnus award West Chester U., 1984. Mem. Am. Assn. Jr. and C.Cs. (past pres. Pa. Commn. C.Cs.). Clubs: Brookside Country (treas. bd. govs.). Office: 340 Dekalb Pike Blue Bell PA 19422-1412

BRENDTRO, LARRY KAY, psychologist; b. Sioux Falls, S.D., July 26, 1940; s. A. Kenneth and Bernice (Matz) B.; m. Janna Agena, July 14, 1973; children: Daniel Kenneth, Steven Lincoln, Nola Kristine. BA, Augustana Coll., 1961; MS, S.D. State U., 1962; PhD, U. Mich., 1965. Prin. Crippled Children's Hosp. and Sch., Sioux Falls, 1962-63; psychology intern Hawthorn Ctr., Northville, Mich., 1964-65; instr. U. Mich., 1965; asst. prof. U. Ill., Urbana, 1966-67; pres., CEO Starr Commonwealth, Albion, Mich., 1967-81; prof. Augustana Coll., Sioux Falls, S.D., 1981-99; pres. Reclaiming Youth Internat., Lennox, SD, 1997—; dean Starr Commonwealth Rsch. Inst., 2002—. Mem. U.S. Coordinating Coun. on Juvenile Justice and Delinquency Prevention, 1997—. Co-author: The Other 23 Hours, 1969, Positive Peer Culture, 1974, 1985, Re-educating Troubled Youth, 1983, Reclaiming Youth at Risk, 1990, 2002; co-editor: Reclaiming Children and Youth, 1992—, Reclaiming Our Prodigal Sons and Daughters, 2000, Troubled Children and Youth, 2004, No Disposable Kids, 2005, Kids Who Outwit Adults, 2005, The Resilence Revolution, 2005. Lutheran. Home and Office: Reclaiming Youth Internat PO Box 57 Lennox SD 57039-0057 E-mail: courage@reclaiming.com.

BRENLY, BOB, professional sports team executive, broadcaster; Grad., Ohio U., 1977. Appeared as a catcher 1 All-Star game; catcher nine major league seasons San Francisco Giants; 3d baseman catcher Bobcats; mgr. Ariz. Diamondbacks, 2000—04. TV color analyst Ariz. Diamondbacks, broadcaster, Chgo. Achievements include became first rookie manager since 1997 to lead his team to the playoffs; Mgr. World Series Champion, 2001. Office: Ariz Diamondbacks 401 E Jefferson St Phoenix AZ 85004

BRENMAN, STEPHEN MORRIS, lawyer; b. San Francisco, Mar. 25, 1945; s. Irving I. and Vivian H. (Weiss) B.; m. Laura R. Yocum, Aug. 14, 1968; children: Jeremy S., Sara N. BS, Miami U., Oxford, Ohio, 1967; JD with distinction, Valparaiso (Ind.) U., 1970. Bar: Ind. 1970, U.S. Dist. Ct. (no. and so. dist.) Ind. 1970, U.S. Ct. Appeals (7th cir.) 1970, U.S. Supreme Ct. 1973, U.S. Tax Ct. 1973, U.S. Ct. Claims 1973. Assoc. Saul I. Ruman & Assocs., Hammond, Ind., 1970-73; ptnr. Katz & Brenman, Gary and Merrillville, Ind., 1973-78, mng. ptnr. Merrillville, 1978-99; pvt. practice Merrillville, 2000—; prin. Stephen M. Brenman, P.C. Lectr. Valparaiso U. Sch. Law, 1970; chief pub. defender Gary City Ct., 1973-78, staff coord., 1973-78; dir. and officer Dunes Volkswagen, Inc., Gary, 1977-80, Len Pollak Buick, Inc., Gary, 1977-83, Merrillville Volkswagen, Porshe-Audi, Inc., Merrillville, 1980-83; lectr. alcoholic beverage laws in Ind., miscellaneous trade orgns., 1980—; temp. probate commr., pro-tem and temp. judge Superior Ct. Lake County, Civil Divsn., East Chicago, Ind., 1980—; lectr. estate planning and right to die Congregation Beth Israel, Inc., Hammond, 1989—, Jewish Fedn., Inc., Highland, Ind., 1989—; lect. Alcoholic Beverage Server Tng., 2001-. Editor, publisher Ind. Alcoholic Beverage Laws, Rules, Regulations, Policies, Procedures & Forms, 2001; note editor Valparaiso U. Law Rev., 1969-70; contbr. articles to profl. jours. Co-chmn. Ind. Alcoholic Beverage Commn. Study Com., Rules, Regulations and Forms Rev., 1990, 2000—; election judge and commr. Lake County Election Bd., Crown Point, Ind., 1973-78; dir. Munster (Ind.) Little League, 1980-84, umpire and coach, 1980-84; bd. dirs. Munster Youth Athletic Assn., 1980-84; bd. dirs. Jewish Fedn., Inc., Highland, 1980-85, Congregation Beth Israel, Inc., Hammond, 1980-85, 2000—, chmn. bldg. com., 2000—; dir. Hoosier Boys Town, Inc., Schererville, Ind., 1990-94, dir. and officer Hoosier Boys Town Found., 1990-94; mem. Munster H.S. Booster Club, 1987—; mem., dir., officer Alpha Epsilon Pi Parents Club, Inc., Bloomington, Ind., 1990-94. Recipient Disting. Svc. award Jewish Fedn., 1980, 83, 84, Red and White Club, Munster H.S. Booster Club, 1989, Mustang Club, 1989; Valparaiso U. scholar, 1968-70. Mem. ABA (sect. bus. law, adminstrv. law and regulatory practice, subsect. alcoholic beverage law, real property, probate, trust law sects.), Nat. Assn. Estate Planners and Couns., Nat. Alcoholic Beverage Control Assn., Nat. Acad. Elder Law Attys., Nat. Assn. Criminal Def. Attys., Ind. State Bar Assn. (mem. regulatory practice and alcoholic beverage subcom., govtl. law sect.), Fed. Bar Assn., Assn. Trial Lawyers Am., Ind. Trial Lawyers Assn., Lake County Bar Assn. (chmn. legal forms com.), Am. Judicature Soc. (corp. counsel inst. mem.), Phi Alpha Delta, B'nai B'rith, Miami U. Alumni Assn., Valparaiso U. Sch. Law Alumni Assn., Zeta Beta Tau Alumni Assn. Democrat. Office: 107 West 79th Ave Merrillville IN 46410-5438 E-mail: smbpclaw@aol.com.

BRENNAN, BRIAN WILLIAM, industrial physicist; b. Troy, N.Y., May 18, 1946; s. Joseph William and Riva Mae (Angle) B.; m. Mary Ann Luciano, Aug. 31, 1968; 1 child, Joseph. B.S. in Physics, Clarkson U., 1968, M.S., 1971; Ph.D., U. Vt., 1980. Field engr. Sperry Rand Corp., Great Neck, N.Y., 1968-69; instr. computer sci. U. Vt., Burlington, 1977, rsch. asst., 1974-79, rsch. assoc., 1979-84, adj. prof., 1986-87; asst. prof. physics Norwich U., Northfield, Vt., 1982-84; sr. staff engr. Simmonds Precision, Vergennes, Vt., 1984-88; mgr. adv. engring. Simmonds Precision, Norwich, N.Y., 1988-89; dir. rsch., devel. and engring. Norwich (N.Y.) Aero Products, 1989-91; pres. B.W. Brennan & Assocs., South New Berlin, N.Y., 1989—; adj. prof. SUNY, 1993-95, Hartwick Coll., 1997; computer cons. Dean Wittier, Burlington, 1980-90; mem. adv. council Vt. Women in Tech. program, 1987-88. Bd. edn. Undilla Valley CSD 2000—. Contbr. articles to profl. jours.; patentee in field. Alderman City of Burlington, 1976-78; trustee Fletcher Free Library, Burlington, 1979-80; chmn. Burlington Civic Ctr. Com., 1979-81; chmn. Dem. Party, Burlington, 1981-83; mem. Umadilla Valley Bd. Edn.; mem. bd. of assessment rev. Town of New Berlin. Mem. Chenango Lake Property Owners Assn. (pres. 1990-2000). Avocations: hunting and fishing, skiing, hiking, golf, sailing. Home: 153 N Shore Rd South New Berlin NY 13843-9538 Office: B W Brennan Assoc 153 North Shore Rd South New Berlin NY 13843 Office Phone: 607-336-2831. Business E-Mail: bbrennan@citilink.net.

BRENNAN, DANIEL EDWARD, JR., former state judge; b. Houston, Oct. 2, 1942; s. Daniel E. and Emily (Tabor) B.; m. Ruth Miriam Gonchar, Nov. 16, 1973; children: Danna Julie, Benjamin Tabor. AA, U. State N.Y., 1974, BS, 1976; JD, U. Bridgeport, 1981; IEM, Harvard U., 1974. Bar: Conn. 1981, U.S. Dist. Ct. Conn. 1981, U.S. Supreme Ct. Exec. asst. to pres. Hunter Coll., N.Y.C., 1970-77; pres. S&B Mgmt. Systems, N.Y.C., 1977-80; ptnr. Brennan, McNamara & Baldwin, P.C., Bridgeport, Conn., 1981-96; judge Superior Ct. Conn., 1999—2004. Chief legal advisor Bridgeport Police Dept., 1983—85; chief labor counsel City of Bridgeport, 1981—85. Mem.: Conn. Bar Assn. (former chair Litigation sect.), Am. Judges Assn. (bd. govs. 2001—04). Home: 8 Beekman Pl Madison CT 06443-2475 Fax: 203-268-8498. E-mail: BDJudgeCT@aol.com, Daniel.Brennan@Jud.State.CT.us.

BRENNAN, DAVID, pharmaceutical executive; BBA, Gettysburg Coll. From sales rep. (US Divsn.) to gen. mgr. Merck and Co., Inc. and Chibret Internat. (subs. of Merck and Co., Inc.), 1975—92; joined Astra Merck (joint venture between Astra AB and Merck, then Astra Merck merged in 1998 with Astra USA of Boston to create Astra Pharm.); sr. v.p., commercialization and portfolio mgmt. AstraZeneca; sr. v.p., bus. planning and develop. Astra Pharm. L.P. (merged with Astra AB and Zeneca PLC); pres., CEO AstraZeneca LP, Wilmington, Del., also bd. dir. Mem. exec. bd. Pharma. Rsch. and Manufactures Am. Chmn. bd. dirs. Am. Heart Assn. (Southeastern Pa.); bd. dir. CEO Roundtable on Cancer. Office: AstraZeneca Pharmaceuticals LP 1800 Concord Pike PO Box 15437 Wilmington DE 19850-5437 Office Phone: 302-886-3000, 800-456-3669.*

BRENNAN, DONNA LESLEY, public relations company executive; b. Washington, Mar. 13, 1945; d. Don Arthur and Louise (Tucker) B.; m. James L Bergey, Mar. 6, 1999. BA, Denison U., 1967. Tchr. Souderton Area H.S., Pa., 1967-69; mgr. media rels. Ins. Co. N.Am., Phila., 1969-72; dir. press rels. Colonial Penn Group, Phila., 1972-75, 1975-81, dir. comm., 1981-83; v.p. corp. comm. Norstar Bancorp, Albany, NY, 1983-85; v.p. comm. Meritor Fin. Group, Phila., 1986-87; prin. Donna Brennan Assocs., 1988—. Bd. dirs. W. Vincent Land Trust, Inc. Bd. dirs. A Chance to Heal, 2005—. Mem. Pub. Rels. Soc. Am. (pres. Phila. chpt. 1988), Phila. Women's Network (founder, bd. dirs.), Pathways Pa. (vice-chmn., bd. dirs.), Forum of Exec. Women (pres. 1992-93, bd. dirs. 1989-97). Office Phone: 610-469-8765. E-mail: brennanpr@comcast.net.

BRENNAN, FRANCIS PATRICK, banker; b. Somerville, Mass., Jan. 9, 1917; s. John Joseph and Bridget (Sullivan) B.; m. Mary J. Gilhooly, July 23, 1949; children: Mary Ann, Eileen, John, Thomas. AB cum laude, Boston Coll., 1939; postgrad., Bentley Coll. Accounting and Finance, 1941. Loan officer Reconstrn. Finance Corp., Boston, 1941-42, 46-53; exec. v.p. Mass. Bus. Devel. Corp., Boston, 1954-61; chmn., chief exec. officer Union Warren Savs. Bank, Boston, 1961-87; vice-chmn. Home Owners Savs. Bank (merger Union Warren Savs. Bank), Boston, 1987-90. Bd. dirs., trustee, chmn. audit com. Boston Co. Funds, Inc.; chmn., pres., treas. Laurel Mut. Funds, 1993—; bd. dirs., exec. and fin. coms., chmn. audit and salary com. Boston Mut. Life Ins. Co., chmn. Dreyfus/Laurel Mutual Funds. Former trustee vice chmn. exec. com., chmn. fin. com. Stonehill Coll.; chmn. Mass. Bus. Devel. Corp.; mem. Sidney Farber Cancer Inst., Boston; mem. Mass. Hist. Soc.; past bd. dirs. Boston Mcpl. Research Bur., Greater Boston Real Estate Bd., Boston met. chpt. ARC. 2d lt. AUS, 1942-45, ETO. Decorated Bronze Star. Mem. Savs. Banks Assn. Mass. (pres. 1972-73), Mass. Bankers Assn. (dir.-at-large), Greater Boston C. of C. (v.p., admitted to Acad. of Disting. Bostonians 1992), Algonquin Club (Boston), Clover Club (Boston), Winchester Country Club, Madison Sq. Garden Club, Knights of Malta, Knights of Holy Sepulchre. Roman Catholic. Home: 36 Central St Winchester MA 01890-2630

BRENNAN, GERALD D. (JERRY BRENNAN), biotechnology company executive; BSBA in Acctg. and Bus. Economics, Marquette U.; JD, University of Ill. CPA Ill.; bar: Ill. Tax mgr. Coopers & Lybrand; tax counsel Premark; v.p. distributor operations and admin. Tupperware N. Am.; pres. Tupperware Canada; gen. counsel Tupperware Worldwide; CFO, COO Capcom Coin-Op, Inc.; CFO, Great Lakes fine chem. div. and Monsanto Pharma Tech Great Lakes Chem. Corp., dir. new ventures; v.p. admin. and financial operations, CFO Aastrom Biosciences Inc., 2005—. Office: Aastrom Biosciences PO Box 376 Ann Arbor MI 48106*

BRENNAN, HENRY HIGGINSON, architect; b. Chgo., Nov. 25, 1932; s. Henry D. and Ann (Higginson) Brennan; m. Margaret Butler, 1960; children: Henry Higginson Jr., Kathryn Ann Brennan Smith, Martin Timothy, Jennifer M. B.Arch., U. Ill., 1958. Registered arch., 12 states. Draftsman Westchester Constrn., White Plains, NY, 1958—59; job capt. Ketchum & Sharp, N.Y.C., 1959—61, project architect, dir. prodn., 1961—73; sr. v.p., dir. N.Y. office Welton Becket, 1973—84; ptnr. Brennan Beer Gorman/Archs., 1984—. Prin. works include master plan and design of maj. office bldgs., hotels, retail and mixed-use complexes. Mem.: AIA, Apawamis Club (Rye, NY). Office: Brennan Beer Gorman Architects 515 Madison Ave New York NY 10022-5403 E-mail: hankbrennan@bellsouth.net.

BRENNAN, JAMES F., academic administrator; b. Providence, R.I., June 11, 1945; s. Martin J. and Cecile M. B.; m. Maria Candida Martins, Aug. 10, 1968; children: Tara primis, Mikala Stewart. AB, Providence Coll., 1967; MA, U. Dayton, 1969; PhD, Kent State U., 1995. From asst. prof. to assoc. prof. SUNY, Buffalo, 1972-77; from assoc. prof. to prof. U. Mass., Boston, 1977-95; dean grad. sch. Loyola U., Chgo., 1995-2000; dean coll. arts & scis. U. Louisville, 2000—. Author: History and Systems of Psychology, 1998, Readings in the History and Systmes of Psychology, 1998; contbr. articles to profl. jours. Fellow APA; mem. Am. Psychol. Soc., Assn. Rsch. Otolaryngology, AAAS, Soc. Neurosci., Ill. Assn. Grad. Schs., Assn. Grad. Schs. in Catholic Univs., Assn. Am. Med. Colls., Sigma Xi. Office: Coll Arts & Scis U Louisville Louisville KY 40292

BRENNAN, JAMES JOSEPH, lawyer, bank executive; b. Chgo., July 14, 1950; s. John Michael and Rosemary (Rickard) Brennan; m. Donna Jean Blessing, June 2, 1973; children: Michael James, Laura Jessica. BS, Purdue U., 1972; JD, Indiana U., 1975. Bar: Ind. 1975, U.S. Dist. Ct. (so. dist.) Ind. 1975, U.S. Tax Ct. 1975, U.S. Ct. Appeals (6th cir.) 1976 U. S. Ct. Appeals (4th cir.) 1977, Ill., 1978, U.S. Dist. Ct. (no. dist.) Ill. 1978, U.S. Ct. Appeals (7th cir.) 1978, U.S. Supreme Ct. 1981. Law clk. to judge U.S. Dist. Ct. (ea. dist.), Tenn., 1975-77; ptnr. Pope, Ballard, Shepard & Fowle, Ltd., Chgo., 1977-87, Hopkins & Sutter, Chgo., 1987-91; ptnr., co-chmn. fin. svcs. group Barack, Ferrazzano, Kirschbaum & Perlman, Chgo., 1991-99; exec. v.p. corp. affairs, gen. counsel BankFinancial Corp., 2000—. Chmn. legal affairs com. Ill. Bankers Assn., Chgo., 1986, chmn. bank counsel sect., 1987; lectr. programs for bankers, bank examiners, accts. and bank counsel; participant drafting of various Ill. banking laws; adj. prof. grad. sch. bank law Ill. Inst. Tech. Kent Coll. Law, 1992-2000. Articles editor Ind. Law Rev., 1974—75; editor: Ill. Bankers Assn. Law Watch, 1988—94; contbr. articles to profl. jours. 1st recipient Disting. Bank Counsel award, Ill. Bankers Assn., 1989. Mem. Riverside Golf Club (bd. dirs. 1992-2000, sec.-treas. 1995-98), Western Golf Assn. (bd. dirs. 1998—, Evans Scholars (Purdue chpt. 1968-72, pres. 1970-71). Office: 15 W 60 Frontage Rd Burr Ridge IL 60527

BRENNAN, JOHN JOSEPH, mutual fund company executive; b. Boston, July 29, 1954; s. Francis Patrick and Mary Josephine (Gilhooley) B.; m. Catharine Barbara Joyce, May 17, 1980; children: William Thomas, Kara Boggs, Conor Hewette Bruen. AB, Dartmouth U., 1976; MBA, Harvard U., 1980. Planner N.Y. Bank for Savs., 1976-78; fin. mgr. S.C. Johnson & Son, Inc., Racine, Wis., 1980-82; asst. to the chmn. The Vanguard Group, Inc., Valley Forge, Pa., 1982-85, sr. v.p., chief fin. officer, 1985-86, exec. v.p., 1986-89, pres., 1989—96, CEO, 1996—, chmn., 1998—. Bd. dirs. ICI Mut. Ins. Co. Mem. Fin. Exec. Inst., Mut. Fund Edn. Alliance (gov. 1985—, exec. v.p. 1986—). Roman Catholic. Office: Vanguard Group Investment PO Box 2600 Valley Forge PA 19482-2600

BRENNAN, JUDITH WIATER, business owner; b. Reading, Pa. d. Edward Joseph and Eleanor Helen Wiater; m. James Edward Brennan Jr., 1967; children: James III, Theresa, Maureen, Susan. Student, U. Calif., Davis, 1964-67; cert., U. Calif., Irvine, 1992; grad., Dale Carnegie Course, 1981. Dir. pub. rels. Pacific Coast Quarter Horse Racing Assn., Inc., Los Alamitos, Calif., 1974-86; CFO Brennan Screen Printing, Inc., Santa Fe Springs, Calif., 1986—. Mem. Los Angeles County Econ. Efficiency Com., L.A., 1992-94; mem. policy bd. Pvt. Industry Coun., Cerritos, Calif., 1992-94; rep. Joint Powers Ins. Authority, La Palma, Calif., 1992-94; trustee S.E. Area Animal Control, 1994-97; mem. bd. dirs. L.A. County Sanitation Dist., 1995-96. Editor: Pacific Coast Quarter Horse Racing Assn. Newsletter, 1974-86; monthly columnist Pacific Coast Jour.; contbr. feature stories to jours. and mags. Mem. City Parks and Recreation Commn., Norwalk, Calif., 1989, City Planning Commn., Norwalk, 1989—92, City Coun., Norwalk, 1992—97, mayor, 1995—96; del. Norwalk/L.A. County Sheriff, 1992—97; mem. City Planning Commn., Norwalk, 2003; chair Art In Public Places Com., 2005; bd. advisors St. Anthony H.S., 2005; eucharistic min. St. John of God Ch., 1982—90, mem. women's coun., pres., 1974—86. Named to St. Anthony H.S. Hall of Fame, Long Beach, Calif., 2001. Mem.: Santa Fe Springs C. of C. Roman Catholic. Avocations: horses, gardening, hiking, golf. Office: Brennan Screen Printing Inc 13659-G Rosecrans Ave Santa Fe Springs CA 90670-5005

BRENNAN, LAWRENCE EDWARD, retired electronics engineer; b. Oak Park, Ill., Jan. 29, 1927; s. Lawrence John and Lillian Irene (Day) B.; m. Mary Ellen Green, Aug. 9, 1947; children: Kathleen, Marianne, Teresa, James. BSEE, U. Ill, 1948; PhD in Elec. Engring., U. Ill., 1951. Mem. tech. staff Rand Corp., Santa Monica, Calif., 1957-67; chief scientist Tech. Svc. Corp., Santa Monica, 1967-80; v.p. Adaptive Sensors, Inc., Santa Monica, 1980-93; cons. pvt. practice, Orange Beach, Ala., 1993—99; ret., 1999—. Served with USN, 1944-46. Fellow: IEEE. E-mail: lbrennan@gulftel.com.

BRENNAN, MARILYN MARGARET, music educator, director; b. Bklyn., Sept. 17, 1929; d. Milton Ernest Stevens and Margaret Elizabeth Larney; m. Basil Willoughby Brennan, Sept. 30, 1955 (dec.); children: Gwynith Amanda, Ian Hugh, Dorren Patricia, Colin Liam. Studied with Willard I. Nevins, N.Y.C., N.Y., 1952. Editl. sec. Bell Newspaper, N.Y.C., 1949; dir. music, organist Tranfiguration Episc. Ch., Bklyn., 1953—64; book reviewer Syndicate, N.Y.C., 1960; dir. music, organist St. Michael's Roman Cath. Ch., NY, 1968—75, St. Mathias Roman Cath. Ch., Queens, NY, 1975—80, St. Fidelis Roman Cath. Ch., Queens, 1980—95, Notre Dame Roman Cath. Ch., New Hyde Pk., NY, 1995—. Rd. sec. Tommy Dorsey Orch., 1948. Author, editor: The Clarion, 1978. Founder Graffiti Busters, Cypress Hills, NY, 1980—87. Mem.: Am. Guild Organists (dean 1975—85), Friends Virgil Fox (pres.), Virgil Fox Soc. (founder, pres.). Republican. Roman Catholic. Avocation: clock collecting. Home: 88 Chestnut St Brooklyn NY 11208

BRENNAN, MAUREEN, lawyer; b. Morristown, N.J., Aug. 7, 1949; BA magna cum laude, Bryn Mawr Coll., 1971; JD cum laude, Boston Coll., 1977. Bar: Pa. 1977, U.S. Dist. Ct. (ea. dist.) Pa. 1978, Ohio 1989. Atty. U.S. EPA, Washington, 1977-80; asst. dist. atty. Phila. Trial and Appellate Divs., 1980-84; in-house environ. counsel TRW Inc., 1985-87; assoc. Baker & Hostetler LLP, Cleve., 1987-91, ptnr., 1991—. Adj. prof. Case Western Res. U., Cleve., 1990-92, 2000-05. Active Cleve. Tree Commn., 1991-96, co-chair, 1993-95; trustee Clean-Land Ohio, 1990-2000; rep. Canal Heritage Corridor Com., 2000—; mem. Cuyahoga County Greenspace Working Group, 1999-2002; bd. dirs. Crown Point Ecology Ctr., 2001--. Recipient Bronze Medal for Achievement, U.S. EPA, 1980. Mem. ABA (natural resources and environ. sect., standing com. environ law 1996-98), Pa. Bar Assn. (environ. law com.), Ohio State Bar Assn. (environ. law com.), Cleve. Bar Assn. (environ. law sect., chair wetlands com. 1991-92, sect. chair 1996-97, mem. steering com. adv. OEPA on Brownfield regulations 1995-97). Office: Baker & Hostetler LLP 3200 Nat City Ctr 1900 E 9th St Ste 3200 Cleveland OH 44114-3475 Office Phone: 216-861-7957. E-mail: mbrennan@bakerlaw.com.

BRENNAN, MICHAEL, real estate company executive; B in Fin., Notre Dame U. Investment specialist CB Comml.; founding investor Tri-Net Property; pres., ptnr. The Shidler Group; COO First Indsl. Realty Trust, Inc., Chgo., co-founder, pres., CEO, 1999—, also bd. dirs. Active United Way Leadership Coun., Chgo. Humanities Coun.; campaign cabinet mem. Assn. House. Named Indsl. Property Exec. of Yr., Comml. Property News, 2000; named one of Top 100 Bus. Leaders in Am., Irish Am. Mag., 2003. Mem.: Nat. Assn. Real Estate Investment Trusts, Pres. Cir. Real Estate Roundtable, Urban Land Inst. (mem. policy and planning com.), Toqueville Soc., Young Pres. Orgn. Office: First Indsl Realty Trust Inc Ste 400 311 S Wacker Dr Chicago IL 60606

BRENNAN, MICHAEL J., lawyer; b. Mountain Lakes, New Jersey, Oct. 16, 1956; AB cum laude, with distinction in Govt., Dartmouth Coll., 1978; JD cum laude, Georgetown U. Law Ctr., 1983. Bar: Md. 1983. Ptnr., Real Estate Dept. Venable LLP, Towson, Md. Lectr. in field. Assoc. editor The Tax Lawyer, 1982—83. Bd. mem. Literary Works Inc., Chesapeake Habitat for Humanity; mem. Balt. County Leadership Program, Balt. County Loan Rev. Bd. Mem.: Dartmouth Lawyers Assn., ABA, Md. State Bar Assn., Balt. County Bar Assn. Fluent in Spanish. Office: Venable LLP 210 Allegheny Ave PO Box 5517 Towson MD 21204 Office Phone: 410-494-6271. Office Fax: 410-821-0147. Business E-Mail: jmbrennan@venable.com.

BRENNAN, MURRAY FREDERICK, surgeon, oncologist; b. Auckland, New Zealand, Apr. 2, 1940; came to U.S., 1970; m. Susan Chambers, May 26, 1973; children: Sean, Ryan, Meghan, Patrick. BSc, U. New Zealand, 1961; B Medicine B Surgery, U. Otago, New Zealand, 1964, ChM, MD, U. Otago, New Zealand, 1983, DSc (hon.), 1997; MD (hon.), U. Goteborg, Sweden, 1991. Surg. intern and resident U. Otago, 1965-69; clin. rsch. fellow Harvard Med. Sch., Boston, 1970-72; sr. resident, clin., rsch. fellow Peter Bent Brigham Hosp., Boston, 1973-75; sr. investigator, vis. scientist Nat. Cancer Inst., Bethesda, Md., 1975-81; prof. surgery, attending surgeon N.Y. Hosp./Cornell Med. Ctr., N.Y.C., 1981—; vis. physician Rockefeller U., N.Y.C., 1981-93; attending surgeon Meml. Sloan-Kettering Cancer Ctr., N.Y.C., 1981—, chmn. dept. surgery, 1985—. Fellow ACS, Royal Australian Coll. Surgeons, Brazilian Coll. Surgeons (hon.), Royal Coll. Surgeons in Ireland (hon.); mem. Inst. Medicine NAS, Royal Coll. Surgeons Edinburgh (hon.), Royal Coll. Physicians and Surgeons Glasgow (hon.), Asian Surg. Soc. (hon.), Assn. Surgeons of Gt. Britain and Ireland (hon.), Royal Coll. Surgeons Eng. (hon.), Royal Australasian Coll. Surgeons (hon.), Royal Coll. Physicians and Surgeons in Can. (hon). Office: Meml Sloan-Kettering Cancer Ctr 1275 York Ave New York NY 10021-6094

BRENNAN, NORMA JEAN, professional society administrator, director; b. Helena, Mont., Apr. 16, 1939; d. Harland Sanford Herrin and Elizabeth (Wardlaw) Brumfield; m. Anthony E. Brennan, Dec. 4, 1964 (div. Mar. 1986); children: Christopher E., Kimberly A. BA, U. Pacific, 1960. Editl. asst. Am. Rocket Soc., N.Y.C., 1961-62, asst. mng. editor, 1962-65; mng. editor AIAA, N.Y.C., 1978-80, publs. divsn. dir. N.Y.C., Washington, Reston, Va., 1980—. Mem. Young Republicans, Stockton, Calif., 1958-60; vol. Mt. Sinai Hosp., N.Y.C., 1962-64. Fellow: AIAA (Space Shuttle Flag award); mem.: Washington Women's Info. Network, N.Am. Serials Interest Group, Coun. Engring. and Sci. Soc. Execs., Assn. Am. Pubs., Coun. Sci. Editors, Soc. for Scholarly Pub. (bd. dirs.). Avocations: reading, travel, gardening. Home: 11551 Links Dr Reston VA 20190-4820 Office: AIAA 1801 Alexander Bell Dr Reston VA 20191-4344 E-mail: normab@aiaa.org.

BRENNAN, PATRICK J., lawyer; b. Bronx, NY, Oct. 28, 1963; BA, Fordham U., 1984; JD, St. John's U., 1987. Bar: NY 1988, US Dist. Ct. So. Dist. NY, US Dist. Ct. Ea. Dist. NY. Asst. dist. atty., Bronx County, NY, 1987—92; ptnr. Wilson, Elser, Moskowitz, Edelman & Dicker LLP, NYC. Mem.: NY State Bar Assn., Assn. of the Bar of the City of NY. Office: Wilson Elser Moskowitz Edelman & Dicker LLP 23rd Fl 150 E 42nd St New York NY 10017-5639 Office Phone: 212-490-3000 ext. 2302. Office Fax: 212-490-3038. Business E-Mail: brennanp@wemed.com.

BRENNAN, ROBERT LAWRENCE, educational director, psychometrician; b. Hartford, Conn., May 31, 1944; BA, Salem State Coll., 1967; M of Art in Tchg., Harvard U., 1968, EdD, 1970. Rsch. assoc., lectr. Grad. Sch. Edn., Harvard U., Cambridge, Mass., 1970-71; asst. prof. edn. SUNY, Stony Brook, 1971-76; sr. rsch. psychologist Am. Coll. Testing Program, Iowa City, 1976-79, dir. measurement rsch. dept., 1979-84, asst. v.p. for measurement rsch., 1984-92, disting. rsch. scientist, 1990-94. Dir. Iowa Testing Programs, 1994-2002; adj. faculty Sch. Edn. U. Iowa, 1979-94, E.F. Lindquist prof. edn. measurement, 1994—, dir. ctr. for advanced studies in measurement and assessment, 2002—. Author: Elements of Generalizability Theory, 1983, Test Equating Methods and Practices, 1995, Generalizability Theory, 2001, Test Equating, Scaling and Linking Methods and Practices, 2004; editor: Methodology Used in Scaling the Act Assessment and P-ACT, 1989, Cognitively Diagnostic Assessment, 1995; assoc. editor Applied Psychological Measurement, 1982—, Jour. Ednl. Measurement, 1978-83, 96—; contbr. articles to profl. jours. Harvard U. prize fellow, 1967. Fellow: APA; mem.: Iowa Acad. Edn. (pres. 1996—99), Psychometric Soc., Nat. Coun. Measurement Edn. (bd. dirs. 1987—90, v.p. 1995, pres. 1997—98, Tech. Contbn. award 1997, Career Contbn. award 2000), Am. Statis. Assn., Midwestern Ednl. Rsch. Assn. (pres. 1987—88), Am. Ednl. Rsch. Assn. (v.p. 1994—96, Divsn. D award 1980, E.F. Lindquist Career Contbn. award 2004). Home: 1925 Liberty Ln Coralville IA 52241-1071 Office: Univ Iowa 210D Lindquist Ctr Iowa City IA 52242-1533 Office Phone: 313-335-5405. Business E-Mail: robert-brennan@uiowa.edu.

BRENNAN, ROBERT WALTER, association executive; s. Walter R. and Grace A. (Mason) B.; m. Mary J. Engler, June 15, 1962; children: Barbara, Susan (twins). BS, U. Wis., 1957. Tchr., coach Waukesha (Wis.) High Sch., 1959-63; track coach U. Wis., Madison, 1963-71; exec. asst. to mayor City of Madison, 1971-73; pres. Greater Madison C. of C., Madison, 1973-2004; cons. U. Wis.-Madison Chancellor's Office, Corp. Rels., 2004—. Mem. adv. council U. Wis.-Madison Sch. Edn., 1984—; mem. Madison Urban League, 1971—; bd. dirs. Cherokee Park, Inc., Wis. Nordic Sports Found., Very Spl. Arts, Wis. Named Madison's Favorite Son, 1971. Mem. Wis. Alumni Assn. (pres. 1985-86, chmn. bd. 1986-87), "W" Club (life, cert. of merit), Theta Delta Chi. Home: 5514 Comanche Way Madison WI 53704-1026 Office: Greater Madison C of C 615 E Washington Ave Madison WI 53703-2952 Office Phone: 608-263-1394. Business E-Mail: rwbrennan@bascom.wisc.edu.

BRENNAN, STACEY LYNN, music educator; b. Englewood, N.J., Aug. 9, 1975; d. John and Valerie Heinrich. MusB in Music Edn., William Paterson U., 1997; MusM in Music Edn., Rutgers U., 2000, postgrad., 2003—. Cert. supr. N.J. Tchr. Bergenfield (N.J.) Bd. Edn., 1998—. Soprano Pro Arte Chorale, Paramaus, NJ, 1997—, St. Brendan's Roman Cath. Ch., Clifton, NJ, 1998—2004. Mem.: Am. Choral Dirs. Assn., Music Educators Nat. Conf., Music Educators Bergen County (treas. 2001—, pres. elect 2004—), Pi Lambda Theta. Office: Bergenfield Bd Edn 130 S Washington Ave Bergenfield NJ 07621

BRENNAN, SUSAN MALLICK, utilities executive; BS, U.S. Air Force Acad., 1981; MBA, Nat. U., 1989. Fin. analyst and investor rels. analyst Nev. Power Co., Las Vegas, 1992—93, mgr. reogrn. project, 1993—94, mgr. performance mgmt. and analysis, 1993—95, dir. human resources, 1995—97, dir. industry restructuring and strategic planning, 1997—99; exec. dir. customer svc. and industry restructuring Sierra Pacific Resources, 1999—2001; v.p., chief info. officer Sierra Pacific Power and Nev. Power, 2001—. Active Leadership Las Vegas, 1998, Workforce 2010 Task Force; regional pres. Am. Diabetes Assn.; bd. mem. United Blood Svcs., Found. Bd. Opportunity Village. With USAF, 1981—88. Mem.: Las Vegas C. of C. Office: Sierra Pacific/Nev Power PO Box 10100 6100 Neil Rd Reno NV 89520

BRENNAN, THOMAS EMMETT, lawyer; b. Detroit, May 27, 1929; s. Joseph Terence and Jeannette Frances (Sullivan) B.; m. Pauline Mary Weinberger, Apr. 28, 1951; children: Thomas Emmett, Margaret Ann and John Seamus (twins), William Joseph, Marybeth, Ellen Mary. LL.B., U. Detroit, 1952; LL.D., Thomas M. Cooley Law Sch., 1976. Bar: Mich. 1953. Assoc. Kenny, Radom, Rockwell & Mountain, Detroit, 1952-53; ptnr. Waldron, Brennan & Maher, Detroit, 1953-61; judge Detroit Ct. Common Pleas, 1962-63, Wayne County Circuit Ct., 1963-66; justice Mich. Supreme Ct., 1967-73, chief justice, 1969-70; adj. prof. polit. sci. U. Detroit, 1970-72; founder, pres., dean emeritus Thomas M. Cooley Law Sch., Lansing, 1972—; of counsel Riley, Roumell and Connolly, Detroit, 2002—. Mem. Mich. Commn. Law Enforcement and Criminal Justice, 1969-70; bd. dirs. Motor Wheel Corp., 1987-89. Author: Judging the Law Schools, 1997, The Bench, 2000. Founder, commr. Am. Golf League, 2000; bd. dir. Cath. League for Religious & Civil Rights, 1993—. Fellow Am. Bar Found., Mich Bar Found.; mem. ABA, Ingham County Bar Assn., State Bar Mich. (bd. commrs. 1979-83), Mich. Assn. of Professions (Disting. Citizens award 1982), Assn. of Ind. Colls. and Univs. Mich. (bd. dirs., exec. com., sec. 1990, chmn. 1991), Cath. Lawyers Soc. (Thomas More award 1987), Am. Jurisprudence Soc., Inc. Soc., Irish Am. Lawyers, Cooley Legal Author's Soc. (charter), Mich. State C. of C. (bd. dirs. 1988-94), Walnut Hills Country Club (bd. dirs. 1992-95), KC, Delta Theta Phi. Roman Catholic. Home: 12953 Grand Traverse Dr Dade City FL 33525 Office: American Golf League 34408 Perfect Dr Dade City FL 33525 Office Phone: 800-245-3791. Personal E-mail: thosbrennan@aol.com.

BRENNAN, THOMAS JOHN, city and state official, consultant, educator; b. Bklyn., Mar. 23, 1923; s. Thomas Joseph and Violet Emma (Jurgens) B.; m. Margaret Karen Jensen, Sept. 18, 1948; children: Debra Gail, Mark Kevin, Laurie Kathleen. AB, Wittenberg Coll., 1949; MGA, U. Pa., 1950. Cons. Pub. Adminstrn. Svc., Chgo., 1950—56; dep. sec. for adminstrn. Dept. Welfare Commonwealth Pa., Harrisburg, 1957—59; dep. sec. for state properties Pa. Dept. Property and Supplies, 1959—64; exec. officer Del. Dept. Mental Health, Dover, 1965—67; v.p. Exec. Mgmt. Svc., Arlington, Va., 1967—76; exec. dir. Gov.'s Justice Commn. Pa. Commn. on Crime and Juvenile Delinquency, 1976—79; dir. water utility City of New Brunswick, NJ, 1983—91, chief labor negotiator, 1988—91, pers. mgr., 1988—91, exec. officer police dept., 1989—91, pub. mgmt. cons., 1991—. Adj. instr. U. Del., 1965—67; adj. assoc. prof. Rider Coll., Lawrenceville, NJ, 1983—84, Lawrenceville, 1984—85; hearing officer N.J. Dept. Civic Svc., Trenton, 1976—2002; cons. exam. constrn., 1985—2000; cons. to staff com. UN, 1982—84; cons. various municipalities and agys.; presenter papers to profl. orgns. Bd. dirs. Bucks County Opera, Pa., 1975-80, Bucks County Play House, New Hope, Pa., 1970s; elected mem. alumni coun. Wittenberg U., 1989—; mem. Merrill's Mauraders, WWII. Decorated Silver Star, Bronze Star with 2 oak leaf clusters, Combat Infantry badge; recipient various plaques; Fels scholar U. Pa., 1948. Mem. VFW, Internat. Personnel Mgmt. Assn., Am. Pub. Works Assn. (dist. rep. Eastern Pa. bldg. and grounds com.), Am. Water Works Assn., Internat. Chief of Police Assn., Nat. Conf. State Justice Planning Adminstrn. (regional chmn., exec. com.), Criminal Justice Tng. Inst. (chmn. planning com. 1978-79), Huntington Valley Hunt (Bucks County, bd. dirs. 1975-80), Am. Legion, Upper Makefield Hist. Soc. (bd. dirs.), Wharton Alumni (Phila.), U. Pa. Emeritus Soc. (steering com. 2004—), Fraternal Order of Police. Avocations: fox hunting, pleasure riding. Home: 327 Pineville Rd Newtown PA 18940-3111

BRENNAN, WILLIAM JOSEPH, manufacturing executive; b. Buffalo, Feb. 11, 1928; s. Laurence J. and Mary Julia (Scherer) B.; m. Rita Jeanne Brooks, Dec. 27, 1947; 1 dau., Susan. BA, Bryant and Stratton Coll., 1949. With Fedders Corp., 1949—, asst. controller corp., 1962-64, dir. distbn. brs., 1965-67, v.p., dir. sales, 1967-74, v.p., dir. adminstrn., 1974-77; pres. Fedders Fin. Corp., 1977-78, group v.p. diversified products, 1978-80, v.p. fin., chief fin. officer, 1980; exec. v.p., chief fin. officer, dir. Fedders Corp., Peapack, N.J., 1986-87; pres. NYCOR Inc., Peapack, 1987-88; fin. cons. Fedders Corp., NYCOR Inc., 1988—. Bd. dirs. Fedders Corp.; chmn. bd. dirs. CSM Environ.; arbitrator NYSE. Served with AUS, 1946-47. Republican. Roman Catholic. Home and Office: 224 Whispering Woods Ct Little Silver NJ 07739 Personal E-mail: bb842@aol.com.

BRENNAN-BERGMANN, BRIDGET CATHERINE, special education educator; b. San Antonio, June 10, 1955; d. Eugene Anthony and Evelyn Joyce Brennan; m. Ernest Bergmann, Jr., Dec. 29, 1997. BS, Stephen F. Austin State, Nacogdoches, Tex., 1978; MEd, North Tex. State U., Denton, 1981. Cert. tchr. for life in areas ednl. diagnostician, physically handicapped, elem. and psychology tchr. Tchr. Stoneleigh Day Sch., Denton, 1978, Hartford County, Md., 1987—90; tchr., diagnostician Lewisville I.S.D., Tex., 1978—84, diagnostician, 1985—87; tchr., counselor Am. Sch., Guadalajara, Mexico, 1984—85; tchr., spl. edn. dept. chair Randolph Field Elem. Sch., Randolph AFB, 1990—. Vol. Therapeutic Horseback Riding, San Antonio, 2003—05; leader support group Alzheimer's Assn., Schertz, Tex., 2004—. Named Tchr. of Game, San Antonio Spurs/Rampage, 2003; recipient Carol Gray award tchr. outstanding students, Future Horizons, Arlington, Tex., 2004. Mem.: Assn. Tex. Profl. Educators, Phi Delta Kappa, Alphi Chi. Avocations: doll collecting, antiques, gardening. Office: Randolph Field Elem Sch Bldg 146 Randolph Afb TX 78148 Office Fax: 210-357-2346.

BRENNAN-SPARKS, JENNIFER ANNE, writer; b. Farnborough, Hampshire, United Kingdom, Aug. 20, 1935; arrived in U.S., 1969; d. Gordon Arthur Thomas and Lucette May (Whitburn) Pritchard; m. Arthur Joseph Sparks; children: Jonathan (dec.), Adam. Diploma, Salisbury (Eng.) Coll. Art, 1956. Woman's editor, columnist The Bangkok World, 1962-64; art dir. Marklin Advt., Bangkok, 1966-69; coord. Pacific chpt. UN Assn. USA, L.A., 1972-76; mng. dir. Pritchard, Ltd., Bangkok, 1974-75; publicity dir. Pacific chpt. UN Assn. USA, L.A., 1976-81; owner, dir. instr. The Asian Experience, Playa del Rey, Calif., 1977-83. Contbg. weekly columnist L.A. Herald-Examiner, 1979-83. Author of numerous books, including Curries and Bugles; A Memoir and a Cookbook of the British Raj, 1990, La Cucina Thailandese, 1989, Encyclopedia of Chinese and Oriental Cookery, 1989, One-dish Meals of Asia, 1986, The Cuisines of Asia, 1984, Thai Cooking, 1981, The Original Thai Cookbook, 1981. Mem. AFTRA, Royal Soc. for Asian Affairs, Am. Legion. Avocations: painting, gardening, cooking, researching. Home: 4634 36th St San Diego CA 92116

BRENNECKE, ALLEN EUGENE, lawyer; b. Marshalltown, Iowa, Jan. 8, 1937; s. Arthur Lynn and Julia Alice (Allen) B; m. Billie Jean Johnstone, June 12, 1958; children: Scott, Stephen, Beth, Gregory, Kristen BBA, U. Iowa, 1959, JD, 1961. Bar: Iowa 1961. Law clk. U.S. Dist. Judge, Des Moines, 1961—62; assoc. Mote, Wilson & Welp, Marshalltown, Iowa, 1962—66; ptnr. Harrison, Brennecke, Moore, Smaha & McKibben, Marshalltown, 1966—2000; of counsel Moore, McKibben, Goodman, Lorenz & Ellefson, LLP, Marshalltown, 2000—. Contr. articles to profl. jours. Bd. dirs. Marshalltown YMCA, 1966-71; mem. bd. trustees Iowa Law Sch. Found., 1973-86, United Meth. Ch., Marshalltown, 1978-81, 87-89; fin. chmn. Rep. party 4th Congl. Dist., Iowa, 1970-73, Marshall County Rep. Party, Iowa, 1967-70. Fellow ABA (chmn. ho. of dels. 1984-86, bd. govs. 1982-86), Nat. Jud. Coll. (bd. dirs. 1982-88), Am. Coll. Trusts and Estates Counsel, Am. Coll. Tax Counsel, Am. Bar Found., Iowa Bar Assn. (pres. 1990-91, award of merit 1987); mem. Masons, Shriners, Promise Keepers. Republican. Methodist. Avocations: golf, travel, sports. Office: Moore McKibben Goodman Lorenz & Ellefson LLP 302 Masonic Temple Marshalltown IA 50158 Office Phone: 641-752-4271.

BRENNEISE, JULIE CELESTE, music educator; b. Grass Valley, Calif., Feb. 25, 1973; d. Michael Sidney and S Carol Gates; m. John Joseph Brenneise, Oct. 30, 1999; 1 child, Richard Wallace. MusEd, UOP Conservatory of Music, 2001. Music specialist Sacramento City Unified Sch. Dist., 2002—. Office: Martin Luther King K-8 480 Little River Way Sacramento CA 95831 Office Phone: 916-433-5860. Personal E-mail: jewelsgates@yahoo.com.

BRENNEMAN, AMY, actress; b. Conn., June 22, 1964; m. Brad Silberling; 1 child, Charlotte Tucker. BA, Harvard U., 1987. Mem. Cornerstone Theater Co. Appeared in films Bye, Bye Love, 1995, Heat, 1995, Casper, 1995, Fear, 1996, in TV programs Middle Ages, 1992, NYPD Blue, 1993-94 (Emmy award nomination for outstanding guest actress in a drama series 1994), Judging Amy, 1999, (TV film) Mary Cassatt: An American Impressionist, 1999, Things You Can Tell Just By Looking at Her, 2000, Off the Map, 2003; stage appearances Saint Joan of the Stockyards, 1992. Office: Creative Artists Agy 9830 Wilshire Blvd Beverly Hills CA 90212-1825 Address: Travel Entertainment 9171 Wilshire Blvd Ste 700 Beverly Hills CA 90211 also: PMK/HBH Pub Rels 8500 Wilshire Blvd Ste 700 Beverly Hills CA 90211

BRENNEMAN, DELBERT JAY, lawyer; b. Albany, Oreg., Feb. 4, 1950; s. Calvin M. and Velma Barbara (Whitaker) B.; m. Caroline Yorke Allen, May 29, 1976; children: Mark Stuart, Thomas Allen. BS magna cum laude, Oreg. State U., 1972; JD, U. Oreg., 1976. Bar: Oreg. 1976, U.S. Dist. Ct. Oreg. 1977, U.S. Ct. Appeals (9th cir.) 1977. Assoc. Schwabe, Williamson, and Wyatt, Portland, Oreg., 1976-83, ptnr., 1984-92, Hoffman, Hart & Wagner, Portland, Oreg., 1993—. Spkr. Oreg. Self-Ins., 1978, 90; seminar instr. U. Oreg. Law Sch., Eugene, 1980. Mem. ABA, Oreg. State Bar Assn., Multnomah County Bar Assn. (spkr. 1983-84), Order of Coif, Multnomah Athletic Club, Propeller Club of U.S. (bd. dirs. 1983-85), Phi Kappa Phi, Beta Gamma Sigma. Office: Hoffman Hart & Wagner 1000 SW Broadway Fl 20 Portland OR 97205-3072 Office Phone: 503-222-4499. Personal E-mail: brennemans@hotmail.com. Business E-Mail: djb@hhw.com.

BRENNEMAN, GREGORY D., food service executive; b. 1962; m. Ronda Brenneman; 3 children. BA in Acctg. and Fin., Washburn U., Topeka, Kansas; MBA with distinction, Harvard Bus. Sch. V.p. Bain and Company, Inc., 1987—93; founder, chmn. and CEO TurnWorks, Inc., 1994—; cons. Continental Airlines Inc., Houston, 1993—95, COO, pres., 1995—2001; CEO PricewaterhouseCoopers Consulting, 2002, Burger King Corp., 2004—. Bd. dirs. Home Depot, Inc., 2000—, Automatic Data Processing, Inc. Office: Burger King 5505 Blue Lagoon Dr Miami FL 33126

BRENNEMAN, HUGH WARREN, JR., judge; b. Lansing, Mich., July 4, 1945; s. Hugh Warren and Irma June Brenneman; m. Catherine Brenneman; 2 children. BA, Alma Coll., 1967; JD, U. Mich., 1970. Bar: Mich. 1970, D.C. 1975, U.S. Dist. Ct. (we. dist.) Mich. 1974, U.S. Dist. Ct. Md. 1973, U.S. Ct. Mil. Appeals 1971, U.S. Ct. Appeals (6th cir.) 1976, U.S. Ct. Appeals (D.C. cir.) 1981, U.S. Supreme Ct. 1980. Law clk. Mich. 30th Jud. Cir., Lansing, 1970-71; asst. U.S. atty. Dept. Justice, Grand Rapids, Mich., 1974-77; assoc. Bergstrom, Slykhouse & Shaw PC, Grand Rapids, 1977—80; magistrate judge US Dist. Ct. (we. dist.) Mich., Grand Rapids, 1980—. Instr. Western Mich. U., Grand Valley State U., 1989-92. Mem. exec. bd., adv. coun. Gerald R. Ford coun. Boy Scouts Am., 1984—, v.p., 1988—92; mem. Grand Rapids Hist. Commn., 1991—97, pres., 1995—97; dir. Cmty. Reconciliation Ctr., 1991; mem. Welcome Homes for the Blind. Capt. JAGC U.S. Army, 1971—74. Recipient Disting. Alumnus award Alma Coll., 1998. Fellow Mich. State Bar Found.; mem. FBA (pres. Western Mich. chpt. 1979-80, nat. del. 1980-84), U.S. Dist. Ct. Hist. Soc. (pres. 2002-04), State Bar Mich. (rep. assembly 1984-90), D.C. Bar Assn., Grand Rapids Bar Assn. (chmn. U.S. Constn. Bicentennial com., co-chmn. Law Day 1991), Fed. Magistrate Judges Assn., Am. Inns of Ct. (master of bench Grand Rapids chpt., pres.), Phi Delta Phi, Omicron Delta Kappa, Peninsular Club, Rotary (past pres., Charities Found. of Grand Rapids v.p., Paul Harris fellow), Econ. Club of Grand Rapids (past bd. dirs.). Congregationalist. Office: US Dist Ct West Mich 110 Michigan St NW Rm 580 Grand Rapids MI 49503-2313 Office Phone: 616-456-2568.

BRENNEMAN, MARY BETH, secondary educator; b. Youngstown, Ohio, Nov. 8, 1950; d. Stanley Earle and Jane M. (Samuel) Babcock; children: Jeffrey Scott, Lisa Marie. BA summa cum laude, Miami U., Oxford, Ohio, 1973; MA, U. Mich., 1975; student, Inst. d'Etudes Francaises, Tours, France. Cert. tchr., Mich.; cert. reality therapy/choice theory. Teaching fellow U. Mich., Ann Arbor, 1973-75; French and German tchr. Sturgis Public Schs., Mich., 1975—. Chaperone for student trips to Wiesloch, Germany, 1977-79, 92; coord. Sturgis-Wiesloch Student Exch. Program, 1979-89; exchange tchr. Realschule Wiesloch, 1994. Mem. Sister Cities Affiliation Bd., 1985-89; flutist Kalamazoo Concert Band and Sturgis Wind Symphony. Mem. Sturgis Edn. Assn., Mich. Edn. Assn., Nat. Edn. Assn., Alpha Lambda Delta, Phi Kappa Phi, Phi Beta Kappa. Methodist. Avocation: flutist in concert band. Home: 408 Maplecrest Ave Sturgis MI 49091-1959 Office: Sturgis Pub Schs 216 Vinewood Ave Sturgis MI 49091-2364

BRENNEMAN, RUSSELL LANGDON, retired lawyer; b. Springfield, Ill., Aug. 15, 1928; s. Russell Langdon and Anita (Seeds) B.; m. Frederica S. Shoenfield, July 14, 1951; children: Matthew, Andrew, Amy. BA, Ohio State U., 1950; LLB, Harvard U., 1953. Bar: D.C. 1954, Conn. 1956. Assoc. Greene and Cook, Torrington, Conn., 1956-60; ptnr. Copp, Brenneman, Tighe, Koletsky and Berall, Essex, Conn., 1960-76; pres. Conn. Resources Recovery Authority, Hartford, Conn., 1976-80; ptnr. Murtha, Cullina, Richter and Pinney, Hartford, 1981—94. Vice chmn. Conn. Energy Adv. Bd., Hartford, 1974—. Author: Private Approaches to the Preservation of Open Land, 1967; contbr., editor: Land Saving Action, 1984. Bd. dirs. Conservation Law Found., Boston, 1968—1985; v.p. Conn. Forest and Park Assn., Middlefield, 1985-2000; co-chair. Gov.'s Greenways Com., Hartford, 1992; pres. Conn. Resources Recovery Authority, Hartford, 1976-1983, co-chair Conn. League of Conservation Voter, 2000—. Recipient Conservation award White Meml. Found., 1987, Oak Leaf award The Nature Conservancy, 1975; named Environ. Master, U.S. EPA Region I, 1990.

BRENNEN, STEPHEN ALFRED, management consultant; b. N.Y.C., July 07; s. Theodore and Margaret (Pembroke) B.; m. Yolanda Alicia Romero, Sept. 28, 1957; children: Stephen Robert, Richard Patrick. AB cum laude, U. Americas, Mexico City, 1956; MBA, U. Chgo., 1959. Supr. Montgomery Ward, Chgo., 1956; credit mgr. Aldens, Chgo., 1956-59; gen. mgr. Purina de Guatemala, 1964-66; pres. Purina Colombiana, Bogotá, 1967-69; founding pres. Living Marine Resources, Inc., San Diego, 1969-70; mng. dir. Central and S. Am. Ralston Purina, Caracas, Venezuela, Coral Gabels, Fla., 1970-74; pres. Van Camp Seafood Co., San Diego, 1974-79; chmn. P.S.C. Corp., Buena Park, Calif., 1979-81; pres. Inter-Am. Cons. Group, San Diego, 1981-85; chmn. Beta Enterprises Inc., 1986-91. Advisor Nat. Productivity Exch.; spl. asst. C.A.O., County of San Diego, Calif., 1987-95; mng. ptnr. Interam. Cons. Group, 1983-95; ptnr. Acad. Interpreting & Translations, Internat., 1995; assoc., owner the Montgomery Group, Inc., La Jolla. Author: Successfully Yours. Past mem. adv. bd. Mexican-Am. Found. Served with USAF. Mem. U. Chgo. in San Diego (past pres.). Roman Catholic. Personal E-mail: ybrennen@aol.com.

BRENNER, BARRY MORTON, physician; b. Bklyn., Oct. 4, 1937; s. Louis and Sally (Lamm) B.; m. Jane P. Deutsch, June 12, 1960; children: Robert, Jennifer. BS, L.I. U., 1958; MD, U. Pitts., 1962; MA (hon.), Harvard U.; DSc (hon.), Long Island U.; D.M.Sc. (hon.), U. Paris, (Pierre et Marie Curie); diploma (hon.), Charles U., Prague; fellow (hon.), Royal Coll. of Physicians, London; MD (hon.), U. Complutense, Madrid. Asst. prof. medicine U. Calif.-San Francisco, 1969-72, asso. prof. medicine and physiology, 1972-75; prof. medicine and physiology U. Calif., San Francisco, 1975-76; Samuel A. Levine prof. medicine Harvard Med. Sch., Boston; with Peter Bent Brigham Hosp., Boston, 1976—; dir. renal div. Brigham and Women's Hosp., Boston, 1979-2001, dir. emeritus, 2001—. Dir. physician-scientist program, Harvard Med. Sch., 1984-90, Harvard Ctr. for Study of Kidney Diseases, 1987-2000; cons. NIH. Editor: The Kidney, 2 vols., 1976, 7th edit., 2004, Renal Pathology, 2 vols., 1989, 2d edit., 1994, Textbook of Hypertension, 2 vols., 1990, 2d edit., 1995; Acute Renal Failure, 1985, 3d edit., 1994; co-editor Contemporary Issues in Nephrology, 1978-90; founding editor Current Opinion in Nephrology and Hypertension, 1992—; contbr. numerous articles to profl. jours. Recipient Homer W. Smith award N.Y. Heart Assn., 1984, George E. Brown award Am. Heart Assn., 1983, Merit award NIH, 1984, SKF Disting. Scientist award 1985, Donald W. Seldin and David Hume awards Nat. Kidney Found., 1995, Am. Acad. Arts and Scis., Philip S. Hench Disting. Alumnus award, U. Pitt., 1995, Novartis award Coun. High Blood Pressure Rsch. Am. Heart Assn., 2005, Novartis award for Hypertension Rsch., Am. Heart Assn.; rsch. grantee NIH, 1969-2000. Fellow AAAS, Molecular Med. Soc., Am. Acad. Arts and Scis.; mem. Am. Soc. Cell Biology, Am. Physiol. Soc., Assn. Am. Physicians (councillor), Am. Soc. Clin. Investigation (councillor, v.p.), Am. Soc. Nephrology (councillor, pres., John P. Peters award), Am. Soc. Hypertension (exec. com., pres., Richard Bright award), Internat. Soc. Nephrology (councillor, Jean Hamburger award, Amgen Internat. prize), Western Assn. Physicians, Salt and Water Club, Interurban Clin. Club, Alpha Omega Alpha, Phi Sigma. Office: 75 Francis St Boston MA 02115-6110 Office Phone: 617-732-5850.

BRENNER, BERYL H., arts therapist; b. NYC, Dec. 29, 1950; d. David and Ethel Feigenbaum; m. Laurence A. Brenner, Nov. 11, 1979; 1 child, Michael. BFA, Bklyn. Coll., 1971, MA in Art Edn., 1974. Arts, crafts dir. Dept. of the Army, Ft. Hamilton Army Base, Bklyn., 1978—90; creative arts therapist Dept. of VA St. Albans Med. Ctr., NY, 1990—92; rec., creative arts therapist VA Harbor Healthcare Med. Ctr., Rec. Svcs., Bklyn., 1992—. Lectr. Times Sq. Inc., NYC, 2002, Kingsboro C.C., Bklyn., 2002—, Metro Profl. Conf.,St. Elizabeth Ann's Adult Day Healthcare, Staten Island, 2003, VA NY Harbor Healthcare Ctr., Grand Rounds, Bklyn., 2003, Metro Profl. Conf., NYC, 2003, Chabad Ho., Binghamton U., 2004, Art Glass Show, 2004, Metro Conf., N.Y.C., 2004, Met. Jewish Adult Day Health Care, Bklyn., 2005, Grand Rounds VA Harbor Healthcare, 2005. One-woman shows include Williamsburg Arts & Hist. Ctr., Bklyn., 2003, Sapphire Lounge Gallery, N.Y.C., 2004; artist sculpture (group shows) Gallery of Contemporary Art, NYC, 1976, Artist League Bklyn., Met. Mus. Art Cmty. Gallery, 1976, 1977, Artist League Bklyn., Cork Gallery, Lincoln Ctr., 1977, 1979, The Bkly. Mus. Cmty. Gallery, 1977, Williamsburg Arts & Hist. Ctr., Bklyn., 2004, (exclusive stained glasswork) Our Lady of Guadelupe, Danbury, Conn., 1985—86, artist Temple Beth Shalom, Atlanta, 1991, (fused glass works) Robert Lehrman Gallery at Urban Glass, Bklyn., 2003, (mainchance pubs. website gallery), 2003—, (fused glass piece) Ann. Wreath Exhbn. Arsenal Gallery, NYC, 2003, (newspaper showcase) Heart as Soul, mainchance publications website gallery, 2003, Catalyst Productions. Inc., Website Gallery, 2003—; prin. works include Robert Lehman Gallery, Bklyn., 2003, Binlkey Mana Gallery, N.Y.C., 2003—, Williamsburg Art and Hist. Ctr., Bklyn., 2004—, Robert Lehman Gallery, 2004—, Primtemps, Toyko, 2004—, Washington Tech. Pk., Chantilly, Va., 2004—, Friendship Heights Art Gallery, Chevy Chase, Md., 2004—, Arsenal Gallery, N.Y.C., 2004—, Monster Gallery, Bklyn., N.Y., 2005. Recipient Ofcl. Commendation, Dept. of the Army, 1981, Exceptional Performance, 1983, Cert. of Achievement, 1984, Performance award, Dept. of Veteran's Affairs, 1991, 1992, 1993, Outstanding Rating Cert., 1994, 1995, 1996, award of excellence, "The Healing Power of Art", Manhattan Arts Internat., 2003, Cert. of Achievement, Dept. VA, 2004, Spl. Contbn. award, Dept. Va., 2005. Mem.: Am. Fedn. Govt. Employees Union, Metro (conf. com. 2003), Art Glass Assn., Nat. Capital Art Glass Guild, Glass Art Soc. Jewish. Avocations: travel, film. Office: VA Harbor Healthcare Med Ctr/Rec 800 Poly Pl Brooklyn NY 11209 Personal E-mail: Beryl2b@yahoo.com.

BRENNER, BETH FUCHS, publishing executive; Grad., U. Vt., 1980. Sales promotion coordinator Chanel, Inc., 1980-83; promotion mgr. M mag., 1983-86; adv. sales rep. New York mag., 1986-91, adv. dir., 1991-93, SELF mag., 1993-94, pub., 1994-2001, v.p., pub., 2001—. Office: SELF Magazine 4 Times Sq New York NY 10036-6562

BRENNER, DAVID H., marketing executive; m. Denise Brenner; 3 children. BBA in Mktg. summa cum laude, U. Notre Dame, 1973. With dept. gen. advt. Procter & Gamble, Cinn., 1973-76; sales promotion mgr. divsn. health care Johnson & Johnson, 1976-78, brand mgr. first aid products, 1978-80; new product devel. mgr. Kellogg's, 1980-82, past new product devel mgr., past mng. dir. bus. ops., pres. U.S. subs., 1988-91; sr. v.p. new bus. ventures Amway, Ada, Mich., 1991—. Regent Edison New Products Yr.; guest lectr. Yale U., Notre Dame U., Aquinas Coll., Grand Valley State U. Bd. trustees Grand Rapids Art Mus., Cath. Soc. Svcs., Grand Rapids, Killgoar Found. Immaculate Heart Mary Sch.; chmn. ann. fund GRAM, 1995-97. Mem. Am. Mktg. Assn., Cascade Hills Country Club, Beta Gamma Sigma.

BRENNER, DOUGLAS, editor; Exec. editor Archtl. Rec., 1980—88; arts editor House & Garden, 1989—93; exec. editor Travel & Leisure, 1993—94; editor Garden Design; dep. editor Martha Stewart Living, 1999—2000, exec. editor, 2000, editor-in-chief, editor, 2002—. Contbr. articles to newspapers. Recipient award of Excellence, Garden Writers Am., 1996. Office: Martha Stewart Living Omnimedia Advt 20 W 43d St 25th Fl New York NY 10036

BRENNER, EDGAR H., legal association administrator; b. N.Y.C., Jan. 4, 1930; s. Louis and Bertha B. (Guttman) B.; m. Janet Maybin, Aug. 4, 1979; children from previous marriage— Charles S., David M., Paul R. BA, Carleton Coll., 1951; JD, Yale U., 1954. Bar: D.C. 1954, U.S. Ct. Claims 1957, U.S. Supreme Ct. 1957. Mem. 2d Hoover Commn. Legal Task Force Staff, Washington, 1954; trial atty. U.S. Dept. Justice, Washington, 1954-57; assoc. Arnold & Porter, Washington, 1957-62, ptnr., 1962-89. Co-dir. Inter Univ. Ctr. for Legal Studies, 1999—. Co-editor: Legal Aspects of Terrorism in the United States, Terrorism and the Law, U.S. Federal Legal Responses to Terrorism, The United Kingdom's Legal Responses to Terrorism; contbr. articles to profl. jours. Commr. Fairfax County Econ. Devel. Corp., Va., 1963—78; v.p., bd. dirs. Stella and Charles Guttman Found., N.Y.C.; bd. dirs. Ams. for Med. Progress, Arlington, Va. Recipient Disting. Achievement award Carleton Coll., 2001; fellow Coll. Problems of Drug Dependency. Mem.D.C. Bar Assn., Yale Club, Explorers Club (N.Y.C.). Democrat. Home: 340 Persimmon Ln Washington VA 22747-1845 Office: 4620 Lee Hwy Ste 216 Arlington VA 22207-3400 Office Phone: 703-524-0880. Personal E-mail: edgarhbrenner@email.com.

BRENNER, EGON, academic administrator, education consultant; b. Vienna, July 1, 1925; s. Aaron and Margarethe (Adler) B.; m. Rhoda Greenberg, Dec. 24, 1950; children: Dorothy, Claudia. B.E.E., CCNY, 1944; M.E.E., Poly. Inst. Bklyn., 1949, D.E.E., 1955. Mem. faculty CCNY, 1946-81, prof. elec. engring., 1966-81, dean engring., 1971-73, acting provost, 1973-74, provost, v.p. acad. affairs, 1974-76; acting vice chancellor for acad. affairs CUNY, 1976-77, dep. chancellor, 1978-81; exec. v.p. Yeshiva U., 1981-93, prof. emeritus. Vis. prof. Tex. Tech. U., summer 1965, U. Okla., 1966 Author: (with M. Javid) Analysis of Electric Circuits, 1959, 2d rev. edit., 1967, Analysis, Transmission and Filtering of Signals, 1963. Served with AUS, 1944-46. Decorated Bronze Star. Fellow IEEE, AAAS; mem. Am. Soc. Engring. Edn., Sigma Xi, Eta Kappa Nu, Tau Beta Pi. Address: 1601 Abaco Dr Coconut Creek FL 33066 E-mail: EB1925@adelphia.net.

BRENNER, FRANK, lawyer; b. N.Y.C., Oct. 26, 1927; s. Jack and Betty (Teifer) B.; children: Jay Marlow, Matthew Adam, Amy Rebecca, Diane Rachel. BA cum laude, Lehigh U., 1948; JD, Harvard U., 1951. Bar: N.Y. 1951, U.S. Supreme Ct. 1955, U.S. Tax Ct. 1975. Asst. dist. atty., N.Y. County, 1951-55; pvt. practice N.Y.C., 1955—2003; judge N.Y.C. Criminal Ct., 1983-84. Mng. dir. InterEquity Capital Corp., 1991-98; adminstrv. judge Waterfront Commn. N.Y. Harbor, 1994-98; jud. hearing officer N.Y. State Supreme Ct., 2000-03; arbitrator Nat. Assn. Securities Dealers, 2001-; spl. referee appellate divsn. Supreme Ct., 2002-03. Mem. mediation and arbitration panel JAMS/Endispute, 1993-99. With USNR, 1945-46. Recipient commendation Brit. Royal Commn. on Capital Punishment, 1950. Fellow Am. Acad. Matrimonial Lawyers; mem. ABA (litig. sect. com. on trial complex crimes 1977-2003, criminal justice sect. com. on def. function 1979-2003, RICO subcom. on white collar crime 1982-84), N.Y. State Bar Assn. (ho. dels. 1978-83, 85-90, 92-96, fellow, bar found. 1992-2003, com. on unlawful practice law 1984-89, criminal justice sect. com. on criminal discovery 1985-2002), Assn. Bar City N.Y. (spl. com. on legal aid inquiry 1971-2, com. on penology 1972-77, com. profl. discipline 1982-85, criminal cts. com. 2002-03), N.Y. County Lawyers Assn. (dir. 1977-83, pres. coun. of assn. 1992-2002, jud. com. 1991-2002, chmn. Pres. adv. com. criminal law, 1990-2003, chmn. com. criminal law 1968-70, 80-83, com. matrimonial law

1975-80, spl. com. on selection and tenure of judges 1975-77, spl. com. to review jud. discipline 1979-80), Fund for Modern Cts. (com. on ct. facilities 1985-2002), Harvard Club (N.Y.C., Sarasota). Home: 7958 Royal Birkdale Cir Bradenton FL 34202

BRENNER, HARRY J., retail executive; From regional mgr. to exec. v.p., COO Cumberland Farms, 1981—2003, pres. Canton, Mass., 2003—. Office: Cumberland Farms 777 Dedham St Canton MA 02021

BRENNER, HOWARD, chemical engineering educator; b. N.Y.C., Mar. 16, 1929; s. Max and Margaret (Wechsler) B.; children: Leslie, Joyce, Suzanne; m. Lisa Glucksman, Sept. 8, 1995. BChemE, Pratt Inst., 1950; MChemE, NYU, 1954, D in Engring. Sci., 1957. Instr. chem. engring. NYU, 1955-57, asst. prof. chem. engring., 1957-61, assoc. prof., 1961-65, prof., 1965-66, Carnegie-Mellon U., 1966-77; prof., chmn. dept. chem. engring U. Rochester, N.Y., 1977-81; W.H. Dow prof. chem. engring. MIT, Cambridge, Mass., 1981—. Sr. vis. fellow Sci. Rsch. Coun. Gt. Britain, 1974; Fairchild Disting. scholar Calif. Inst. Tech., 1975-76, Chevron vis. prof., 1988-89; Gulf vis. prof. Carnegie-Mellon U., Pitts., 1991; Lady Davis fellow, Israel, 1995-96; vis. prof. U. Calif., Berkeley, 1996. Author: (with J. Happel) Low Reynolds Number Hydrodynamics, 1965, 2d edit., 1973, Russian edit., 1976; (with D.A. Edwards and D.T. Wasan) Interfacial Transport Processes and Rheology, 1991; (with D. A. Edwards) Macrotransport Processes, 1993; contbr. articles to profl. jours.; co-editor in chief Physico-Chem. Hydrodynamics, 1988-89. Recipient Bingham Medal Soc. Rheology, 1980, Disting. Alumni award Pratt Inst., 2001, Caribbean Congress Fluid Dynamics award, 2001; Guggenheim fellow, 1988. Fellow AAAS, NAE, AIChE (Alpha Chi Sigma award 1976, Walker award 1985, Warren K. Lewis award 1999), Am. Acad. Mechanics; mem. NAS, Am. Acad. Arts and Scis., Soc. Rheology (Bingham medal 1980), Am. Phys. Soc. (Fluid Dynamics prize 2001), Am. Chem. Soc. (Kendall award 1988, 11th ann. Honor Scroll Indsl. Engring. Chemistry Divsn. 1961), Am. Soc. Engring. Edn. (Gen. Electric Sr. Rsch. award 1996). Office: MIT Dept Chem Engring Rm 66 562 77 Massachusetts Ave Cambridge MA 02139-4307 Office Fax: 617-258-8224. Business E-Mail: hbrenner@mit.edu.

BRENNER, JANET MAYBIN WALKER, lawyer; b. Arkansas City, Kans. d. D. Arthur and Maybin (Gardner) Walker; children: Margaret Maybin Potthast, Theodore Kimball Jonas, Amanda Nash Freeman; m. Edgar H. Brenner, Aug. 4, 1979. AB, U. So. Calif.; JD, George Washington U., 1978. Bar: D.C. 1978, U.S. Dist. Ct. (D.C. cir.). Sponsor Brenner Women's Leadership com.; mem. women's com. Corcoran Gallery Art, Washington, 1969—, Pres.'s Cir., Planned Parenthood D.C., 1969—, Found. for Preservation of Hist. Georgetown. Mem. D.C. Bar Assn., Sulgrave Club (Washington). Home: 3325 R St NW Washington DC 20007-2310 also: Shadow Ridge Farm Washington VA 22747

BRENNER, LAWRENCE, medical librarian, consultant; b. Lynn, Mass., Sept. 19, 1939; m. Ruth Ida Winer. BS in Edn., Northeastern U., 1962; cert. profl. libr., Boston State U./U. Mass., 1965; registered records adminstr., Northeastern U., 1976, MPA, 1981. Registered health info. adminstr. Sr. med. libr. Boston City Hosp., 1962-94; med. record cons. ind. co. Swampscott, Mass., 1994-95; med. record cons., coord. Vencor Corp., Boston, 1995—2004; ret., 2004. Contbr. articles to profl. jours. Recipient Nat. Scholastic Art award, Nat. Scholastic/Boston Globe, 1957. Mem.: ALA, Mass. Health Info. Mgmt. Assn. (contbg. writer Bookshelf and Consultants' Corner columns, Spl. award 1997), Am. Health Info. Mgmt. Assn., Masons (past master 1987, 1999—2000). Avocations: coins, stamps, china, gardening, government. Home: 44 Elwin St Swampscott MA 01907-1065

BRENNER, MARCELLA SIEGEL, retired education educator; b. Balt., Dec. 5, 1912; d. Moses and Annie (Affachiner) Siegel; m. Morris Bernstein, July 1947 (dec. 1962); m. Abner Brenner, Oct. 1964. BS, Johns Hopkins U., 1934; MA, Am. U., 1949; EdD, George Washington U., 1962; DHL (hon.), Md. Inst. Coll. Art, 2001. Tchr. Balt. Pub. Schs., 1930-43; writer, editor USPHS, Washington, 1945-52; tchr. Lone Oak Elem. Sch., Md., 1952-54, prin., 1954-64; lectr. in edn. George Washington U., 1961, assoc. prof. Sch. Edn., 1965-83, assoc. dir. MA Tchg. Program, 1966-83, ret., 1983. Mem. staff Washington Sch. Psychiatry, 1962—; cons. U. Calif. Sch. Sys. of Washington, Tchr. Edn. and Profl. Standards Commn.; founder, dir. Mus. Edn. Program George Washington U., 1974-83; dir. Ctr. for Mus. Edn. George Washington U., 1976-79. Co-author: Interview Art and Skill, 1980, The Change Agent, 2000; contbr. articles to profl. jours. Bd. dirs. Boston Mus. Fine Arts, 1985—, Balt. Mus. Art, 1985—, B'nai Brith Klutznick Nat. Jewish Mus., 1985—, Project Interchange Dept. Am. Jewish Com., 1985—, George Washington U., 1985—; bd. Palestine Endorsement Fund, Israel Endowment Funds, Inc., 1985—. Brenner award established in her honor George Washington U., 1983; recipient Yakir Bezalel award Bezalel Acad. Arts and Design and Culture, 1988, award of appreciation State of Israel Min. Edn., 1991. Fellow Am. Orthopsychiatric Assn., Israel Mus. (hon.). Avocation: reading to visually impaired. Home: 7204 Pomander Ln Chevy Chase MD 20815-3135

BRENNER, MARK LEE, academic administrator, physiologist, educator; b. Boston, June 19, 1942; s. Harry D. and Beatrice (Price) B.; m. Ruth Abramson, Aug. 30, 1964; children: Jonathan, Tamara. BS, U. Mass., 1964, MS, 1965; PhD, Mich. State U., 1970. From asst. prof. to prof. horticultural scis. U. Minn., St. Paul, 1970—98, assoc. dean Grad. Sch., 1989-94; assoc. v.p. rsch., 1992-94; v.p. rsch. and dean Grad. Sch., 1994-98; vice chancellor rsch. and grad. edn. Ind. U.-Purdue U., Indpls., 1998—; assoc. v.p. rsch. Ind. U., Bloomington, Ind., 1998—. Cons. Abbott Labs., Chgo., 1988-89, Monsanto Corp., St. Louis, 1982-86, 88; bd. dir. Coun. Govt. Rels., ETS-GRE; v.p. bd. dirs. Assn. Accreditation Human Rsch. Protection Programs, Inc.; mem. Coun. Rsch. Policy and Grad. Edn., 1999—. Contbr. articles to profl. jours. Fellow Am. Soc. Horticultural Scis. (Outstanding Grad. Educator award 1993); mem. Am. Soc. Plant Physiologists (exec. com. 1986-89), Internat. Plant Growth Substance Assn. (sec.-treas. 1988-91), Minn. Chromatography Forum (pres. 1980-81, Palmer award 1986). Home: 8070 Lynch Ln Indianapolis IN 46250-4222 Office: Office of Vice Chancellor Rsch and Grad Edn Admin Bldg 122 355 N Lansing St Rm 122 Indianapolis IN 46202-2596 Office Phone: 317-274-1020. Business E-Mail: mbrenner@iupui.edu.

BRENNER, MARSHALL LEIB, lawyer; b. N.Y.C., Aug. 8, 1933; s. Samuel and Ruth (Novak) B.; m. Gwen A. Krakower, Aug. 9, 1959; children: Scott David, Louri Ann, Robin Lynn. BA, St Lawrence U., Canton, N.Y., 1955; JD, Bklyn. Law Sch., 1959. Bar: N.Y. 1960, U.S. Dist. Ct. (no. and ea. dists.) N.Y. 1960, U.S. Ct. Claims 1964, U.S. Supreme Ct. 1964, U.S. Dist. Ct. (so. dist.) N.Y. 1969. Assoc. Spitz & Levine, Poughkeepsie, N.Y., 1960-62; sr. ptnr. Brenner, Gordon & Lane, Poughkeepsie, 1977—. Chief appeals sect. Dutchess County Pub. Defenders Office, Poughkeepsie, 1966-78; tchr. law Marks Realtors/Appraisors, Poughkeepsie and Fishkill, N.Y., 1968-72, Robert-Mark Realtors, Hopewell Junction, N.Y., 1979-92; lectr. Dutchess County Realty Bd. for Sales/Broker Lic. Applicants, 1985—. Contbr. articles to profl. jours. Pres., bd. dirs. Sloper-Willen Community Ambulance, Wappingers Falls, N.Y., 1966-79; bd. dirs. Poughkeepsie Jewish Community Ctr., 1980-82, Dutchess County Assn. for Sr. Citizens, 1988-94, counsel, 1994—, Dutchess County Youth Bd.; mem. adv. bd. Anderson Sch., Staatsburg, N.Y., 1990-95, bd. dirs., 1995-99; mem. Pvt. Industry Coun., 1995—; exec. com., 1999—; mem. Work Force Investment Bd., 1999—, exec. bd., 2000—; mem. Town of Poughkeepsie Cablevision Com., Town of Poughkeepsie Ethics in Govt. Com. Capt. U.S. Army, 1956-63. Mem. N.Y. State Bar Assn., Dutchess County Bar Assn., N.Y. State Trial Lawyers Assn. Clubs: Harding (Poughkeepsie) (pres. 1968-69, chmn. social com. 1996—); County Players (Wappingers Falls) (bd. dirs. 1963-74). Lodges: Masons, Rotary (pres. 1973-74, 78-79, Govs. Trophy 1978). Republican. Jewish. Avocations: golf, tennis, swimming, reading, chess. Home: 7 Gwen's Way Poughkeepsie NY 12601-5654 Office: 219 Church St Poughkeepsie NY 12601-4103 Fax: 914-452-6954.

BRENNER, RAYMOND ANTHONY, priest; b. Evansville, Ind., Feb. 12, 1943; s. George Frederick and Marie Catherine (Gries) B. BA, St. Meinrad (Ind.) Coll., 1965; MDiv, St. Meinrad Sch. Theology, 1969. Ordained priest Roman Cath. Ch., 1969. Deacon Nativity Ch., Indpls., 1968; assoc. pastor St. John's Ch., Loogootee, Ind., 1969-74, Sts. Peter and Paul Ch., Haubstadt, Ind., 1974-78; pastor St. Mary's Ch., Sullivan, Ind., 1978-86, St. Joan of Arc Ch., Jasonville, Ind., 1982-86, Resurrection Ch., Evansville, 1986—2002, St. Joseph Ch., Jasper, Ind., 2002—. Mem. Cath. Charities Bd., Evansville, 1972-75; v.p. Ministerial Assn., Sullivan, 1985-86; pres. Coun. of Priests, Evansville, 1989; diocesan chaplain St. Vincent de Paul Soc., Evansville, 1990-94. Mem. Wabash Valley Human Svcs., Vincennes, Ind., 1982-86, Sullivan Housing Authority, 1983-85, Fed. Emergency Mgmt. Agy., Sullivan, 1984-86, Emergency Food Bank, Sullivan, 1984-86; spiritual advisor Evansville Cath. Cursillo, 1994—; chaplain German Twp. Vol. Fire Dept., 1998-2002, Cmty. Marriage Builders, 1997—. Mem. Optimists (chaplain Evansville Westside club 1990-2002), Elks. Democrat. Address: St Joseph Cath Ch 1020 Kundek St Jasper IN 47546-1917 E-mail: rbrenner@evansville-diocese.org. *It takes so little time to offer a smile, and the rewards are beyond imagining. Somehow they know you care and that God cares too.*

BRENNER, RENA CLAUDY, communications executive; b. Camden, N.J. d. John Lawler and Louretta (Du Fresne) Morgan; m. Edgar W. Claudy (div. 1968); 1 child, Renee; m. Millard Brenner, Nov. 6, 1971 (dec. 1975); children: Sally, Malcolm, Hugh. Student, U. Pa., 1978, U. Mich., 1983. Reporter Tribune-Telegram, Salt Lake City, 1943-45, Times Chronicle, Jenkintown, Pa., 1950-55; free-lance writer Enfield, Pa., 1955-60; pub. relations dir., advt. mgr. Gen. Atronics/Magnavox, Phila., 1960-70; mgr. corp. pub. relations ITE-Imperial, Phila., 1970-73, dir. corp. comm., 1973-76, Parker-Hannifin Corp., Cleve., 1976-83, v.p. corp. comm., 1983-85; pres. Brenner Assocs., Clearwater, Fla., 1986—. CEO Fla. Sport Dance Fedn. of Am., 1999—. Recipient Creative Direction award Phila. Club Advt. Women, 1970, Clarion award Women in Communications, 1982, Gold Key award Pub. Relations News, 1984. Mem. Bus. Profl. Advt. Assn. (life), Pub. Relations Soc. Am. (life), Nat. Investors Relations Inst. Office: Brenner Assocs 1591 Old Jacksonville Rd Warminster PA 18974-1221

BRENNER, SYDNEY, molecular biologist, researcher; b. Germiston, South Africa, Jan. 13, 1927; naturalized, British citizen; s. Morris and Lena (Blacher) B.; m. May Woolf Balkind, 1952; 3 children; 1 stepchild. MSc, U. Witwatersrand, Johannesburg, South Africa, 1947, MB, BCh, 1951; DPhil, Oxford (Eng.) U., 1954; 10 hon. degrees. Mem. sci. staff Med. Rsch. Coun., Cambridge, England, 1957-92, dir. lab. molecular biology, 1979-86, dir. molecular genetics unit, 1986-91; fellow King's Coll., Cambridge U., 1959—; hon. fellow Exeter Coll., Oxford U., 1985; rsch. scientist dept. medicine U. Cambridge Sch. Clin. Medicine, 1992-96; mem. staff Scripps Rsch. Inst., La Jolla, Calif., 1992-94; pres., dir. The Molecular Scis. Inst., La Jolla & Berkeley, Calif., 1996—; disting. rsch. prof. The Salk Inst., La Jolla, Calif., 2000—. Carter-Wallace lectr. Princeton U., 1966, 77; Gifford lectr. U. Glasgow, Scotland, 1978-79; Dunham lectr. Harvard U., 1984; hon. prof. genetic medicine U. Cambridge Clin. Sch., 1989-96; lectr. in field. Contbr. articles to sci. jours. Recipient Warren Triennial prize, 1968, William Bate Hardy prize Cambridge Philos. Soc., 1969, Albert Lasker Med. Rsch. award, 1971, Royal medal Royal Soc., 1974, Charles-Leopold Mayer prize French Acad., 1975, Gairdner Found. ann. award, 1978, Krebs medal FEBS, 1980, CIBA medal Biochem. Soc., 1981, Feldberg Found. prize, 1983, Rosenstiel award Brandeis U., 1986, Prix Louis Jeantet de Medecine, Switzerland, 1987, medal Genetics Soc. Am., 1987, Harvey prize Technion-Israel Inst. Tech., 1987, Hughlings Jackson medal Royal Soc. Medicine, 1987, Waterford Bio-Med. Sci. award Rsch. Inst. Scripps Clinic, 1988, Kyoto prize Inamori Found., 1990, Gairdner Found. Internat. award, Can., 1991, King Faisal Internat. prize, 1992, Disting. Achievement award Bristol-Myers Squibb, 1992, Albert Lasker award for Spl. Achievement in Medicine, 1996, Nobel Prize in Physiology or Medicine, 2002. Fellow Royal Soc. (Croonian lectr. 1986, Royal medal 1974, Copley medal 1991), AAS, IASc (hon.) RSE (hon.), Royal Coll. Physicians (Neil Hamilton Fairley medal 1985) Royal Coll. Pathologists (hon.); mem. Max-Planck Soc., Deutsche Acad. Natural Sci. Leopoldina (Gregor Mendel medal 1970), Am. Philos. Soc. (fgn.), Real Acad. Ciencias (Spain), Am. Acad. Arts and Scis. (fgn. hon.), NAS (U.S., fgn. assoc.), Royal Soc. South Africa (fgn. assoc.), Acad. Europa, Chinese Soc. Genetics (hon.), Assn. Physicians Gt. Brit. and Ireland (hon.); associé étranger, Académie des Scis.; corr. Scientifique Emérite de l'INSERM. Office: Molecular Scis Inst 2168 Shattuck Ave Berkeley CA 94704-1307*

BRENNER, THEODORE ENGELBERT, retired trade association executive; b. NYC, Apr. 18, 1930; s. Engelbert F.J. and Julie M. (Kierschner) B.; m. Maria T. Finn, Sept. 12, 1953; children— John Finn, Elisabeth Ann, Christopher. BCE, Manhattan Coll., 1951; MS, Johns Hopkins, 1954. Registered profl. engr., Pa., N.J. Diplomate Am. Acad. Environ. Engrs. Mgr. waste treatment dept. Permutit div. Sybron Corp., Paramus, N.J., 1959-62; prin. Hydroscience, Inc., Ft. Lee, N.J., 1963; with Soap and Detergent Assn., N.Y.C., 1963-93, v.p., tech. dir., 1970, v.p., dir. govt. affairs, 1971, pres., 1972-93; ret., 1993. Exec. dir. Joint Industry Govt. Task Force Eutrophication, 1968-70; mem. Dept. Interior Water Resources Sci., Info. Center Adv. Group, 1969-70; mem. spl. adv. com. N.Y. Temp. State Commn. on Water Resources Planning, 1964-67 Contbr.: chpt. to Advances in Environmental Sciences, Vol. II, 1969; articles to profl. jours. Mem. Rumson Bd. Edn., 1968-74, 1st v.p., 1973-74; mem. Rumson-Fair Haven Regional Bd. Edn., 1974-77, v.p., 1976-77. Served to capt. USAF, 1952-59; lt. col. ret. Mem. ASCE, AIChE, Am. Soc. Assn. Execs., Union League (N.Y.C.), Seabright (N.J.) Beach Club. Home: 5 Tyson Ln Rumson NJ 07760-1912

BRENNER, THOMAS EDWARD, lawyer; b. Hanover, Pa., Apr. 30, 1955; s. Philip F. and Ruth H. (Hoke) B.; m. Mary Small, May 26, 1979; children: Matthew D., Rebecca M., John Phillip, Donald Thomas, Catherine Jane. BA, Villanova U., 1977, JD, 1980. Bar: Pa. 1980, U.S. Dist. Ct. (cen. dist.) Pa. 1980, U.S. Ct. Appeals (3d cir.) 1980, U.S. Ct. Appeals (4th cir.) 1985, U.S. Supreme Ct. 1985. Shareholder Goldberg, Katzman P.C., Harrisburg, Pa., 1980—, also bd. dirs. Bd. dirs. Dauphin County Victim Witness Bd., Harrisburg, 1984-90, Camp Hill Soccer Assn., 1988-2002, YMCA Aquatics Club, 1991-92; sec. Capitol Area Aquatics League, 1992—; swim ofcl. PIAA, 1994—, soc., 1998-2003. Mem. ABA (com. chmn. 1984, rep. young lawyers div. 1985-86), Pa. Bar Assn. (com. chmn. 1985-86), Dauphin County Bar Assn. (com. chmn. 1985-86), Dauphin County Bar Assn. (sec. 1980, chmn. young lawyers sect. 1987, bd. dirs. 2001—), Jaycees (bd. dirs. 1987-88), Camp Hill Aquatic Club (pres. 1991—, bd. dirs. 1988—), KC. Democrat. Roman Catholic. Office: Goldberg Katzman PC 320 Market St PO Box 1268 Harrisburg PA 17108-1268 Office Phone: 717-234-4161. Business E-Mail: teb@goldbergkatzman.com.

BRENT, PATRICIA LEE, health facility administrator, writer; d. Charles Robert and Marion Helen Brent; m. George Dewey Sorenson, Mar. 12, 1988. BS, Vt. Coll., 1968; MPH, Emory U., 1981; JD, Vt. Law Sch., 1997. Cert. med. technologist Am. Soc. Clin. Pathology, 1968. Dir. profl. svcs. Alice Peck Day Meml. Hosp., Lebanon, NH, 1981—87, v.p., strategic planning, 1987—94; pres. Morgan Hill Assocs., Meriden, NH, 1998—; rsch. asst. Dartmouth Med. Sch., Hanover, NH, 1968—70, rsch. assoc., 1972—79, Stanford U. Sch. Medicine, Palo Alto, Calif., 1970—72. Mem. editl. adv. bd. compliance CCH, Inc., Chgo., 2003—. Author: (book-medicare hosp. financing policy) Inside Medicare Outliers: Keys to Policy, Payment and Compliance, (book-medicare reimbursement policy) Understanding Reimbursement for Investigational Drugs and Devices, (web-based book) Critical Access Hospitals: The Application Process, 2005; content editor, cons. (web-based ednl. product) Medicare and Medicaid Now; contbr. articles to profl. jours. and newsletters. Mem. med. ethics com. Alice Peck Day Meml. Hosp., Lebanon, 1996—; chair rev. and allocations com. United Way Upper Valley, 1992—94, bd. mem., 1992—95; Am. Lung Assn., Manchester, 1984—92; pres. Human Svc. Coun. Upper Valley, 1988—92. Mem.: Healthcare Fin. Mgmt. Assn., Healthcare Compliance Assn. (region 1 planning com. 2000—05), Am. Health Lawyers' Assn. Episcopalian. Avocations: downhill skiing, birdwatching, hiking, antiques. Office: Morgan Hill Assos PO Box 176 Meriden NH 03770 Office Phone: 603-469-3536.

BRENT, ROBERT LEONARD, radiology and pediatrics educator; b. Rochester, N.Y., Oct. 6, 1927; s. Charles and Rose (Katz) B.; m. Lillian H. Hoffman, Aug. 21, 1949; children: David A., James R., Lawrence H., Deborah A. AB, U. Rochester, 1948, MD with honors, 1953, PhD, 1955, DSc (hon.), 1988. Fellow Nat. Found., Strong Meml. Hosp., 1953-54; intern pediatrics Mass. Gen. Hosp., Boston, 1954-55; chief radiation biology Walter Reed Army Inst. Rsch., 1955-57; mem. faculty Jefferson Med. Coll., 1955—, prof. radiology, 1962—, also prof. pediatrics, Louis and Bess Stein prof. pediatrics, 1985—, emeritus chmn. pediats., 1999—; apptd. Disting. prof. Thomas Jefferson U., 1989. Hon. prof. Norman Bethume U. Med. Sci., People's Republic of China, 1992, West China U. Med. Scis., Chengdu, People's Republic of China, 1992; chmn. med. adv. bd. Nat. Found.; mem. fertility and maternal health com. FDA; mem. human embryology study sect. NIH, 1970-74; bd. trustees Health and Environ. Sci. Inst., 1991-94; pres. First Internat. Congress on Birth Defects, People's Republic of China, 1994. Editor in chief Teratology, 1976-93. Pres. Teratology Soc., 1968. Served with U.S. Army, 1955-57. Recipient Richie Meml. prize U. Rochester Med. Sch., 1953, Lindback Found. award for disting. tchg., 1968, Med. Sch. award Alpha Omega Alpha, 1952, Burlington Internat. award, 1990, Landauer award Health Physics Soc., 1995, Robley D. Evans Commemorative medal Health Physics Soc., 2001; fellow Royal Soc. Medicine, 1971-72, FitzWilliam Coll., Cambridge, 1971-72; Lady Davis scholar Hadassah Med. Ctr., Jerusalem, 1983-84. Mem. AAAS, NAS Inst. Medicine, Teratology Soc. (pres. 1967-68), Internat. Life Sci. Inst., Radiation Rsch. Soc., Am. Soc. Exptl. Pathology, Soc. Pediat. Rsch., Am. Pediats. Soc., Am. Acad. Pediats. (Merit citation 2001), Soc. Exptl. Biology and Medicine, Phila. Coll. Physicians, Phila. Pediat. Soc., Am. Assn. Immunology (emeritus), Soc. Developmental Biology, Nat. Coun. Radiation Protection, Nat. Acad. Sci. (elected Inst. Medicine 1996), Japan Teratology Soc., European Teratology Soc., Ambulatory Pediat. Assn., Sigma Xi. Office Phone: 302-651-6880. E-mail: rbrent@nemours.org.

BRENTIN, JOHN OLIN, lawyer; b. Youngstown, Ohio, Mar. 21, 1953; s. John William and Mary Ann (Ohlin) B.; m. Victoria Jane Barkate, Apr. 19, 1980; children: Steven Alexander, John Gabriel, Benjamin William. BA cum laude, Ohio State U., 1974; JD, U. Houston, 1978. Bar: Tex. 1978; U.S. dist. Ct. (so. dist.) Tex., 1978; U.S. Ct. Appeals (5th cir.) 1979; bd. cert. Estate Planning and Probate Law. Assoc. Sullins and Johnston, Houston, 1978-82, ptnr., 1983-1993; principal John O. Brentin and Assocs., Houston, 1993—. Bd. dirs. Planned Giving Coun. of Houston, 1995-98. Author: Basic Drafting of Wills and Trusts in Texas, 1993. Chmn. Econ. Devel. Coun., Bellaire, Tex., 1994-96, Planning and Zoning Bd., Bellaire, Tex., 1991-94. Mem. ABA, Houston Bar Assn., Houston Estate and Fin. Forum, Tex. Acad. Probate and Trust Lawyers, Rotary Club of Houston (pres. 1998-99). Republican. Roman Catholic. Avocation: boy scouts of am. Home: Ste 560 3700 Buffalo Speedway Houston TX 77098 Office: 3700 Buffalo Speedway Ste 560 Houston TX 77098-4711 E-mail: john@brentin.com.

BRENTLINGER, PAUL SMITH, venture capital executive; b. Dayton, Ohio, Apr. 3, 1927; s. Arthur and Welthy Otello (Smith) B.; m. Marilyn E. Hunt, June 23, 1951; children: Paula, David, Sara. BA, U. Mich., 1950, MBA, 1951. With Harris Corp., Melbourne, Fla., 1951-84, v.p. corp. devel., 1969-75, v.p. fin., 1975-82, sr. v.p. fin., 1982-84; ptnr. Morgenthaler Ventures, Cleve., 1984—. Former chmn., bd. dirs. Hypres, Inc., Elmsford, NY; chmn., bd. trustees Cleve. Inst. Art, 1992—98. Mem. Union Club, Phi Beta Kappa. Home: 2755 Eaton Rd Cleveland OH 44122-1800 Office: Morgenthaler 50 Public Sq Ste 2700 Cleveland OH 44113-2236

BRENTLINGER, WILLIAM BROCK, college dean; b. Flora, Ill., Aug. 21, 1926; s. Arthur Kenneth and Frances (Maxwell) B.; m. Barbara Jean Weir, Dec. 29, 1946; children: Gregory, Gary, Rebecca Anne, Garth, Barbara Sue. Student, Washington U., 1946-47; AB, Greenville Coll., 1950; MA, Ind. State U., 1951; PhD, U. Ill., 1959. Instr. speech Greenville Coll., 1951-59, chmn. dept., 1959-62, dean of coll., 1962-69, dean coll. fine arts and comm., 1969-92; interim pres. Lamar U., Beaumont, Tex., 1992-93, asst. to pres., 1993—. Cons. higher edn. Served with USNR, 1944-46. Recipient tchr. study award Danforth Found., 1957 Mem. Internat. Council Fine Arts Deans, Speech Communication Assn. Am., Tex. Speech Assn., Tex. Assn. Coll. Tchrs., Tex. Council Arts in Edn. (pres.), Phi Kappa Phi. Clubs: Rotary (Beaumont). Baptist. Home: 6530 Salem Cir Beaumont TX 77706-5552 Office: Lamar U PO Box 10001 Beaumont TX 77710-0001 *I have always attempted to treat people as subjects, not objects, as fellow creatures of God, and thus to be worked with not worked upon.*

BRENTS, DANIEL, architectural firm executive; b. Detroit, Dec. 25, 1938; BArch, Tex. A&M U., 1962; M in Architecture and Urban Design, Washington U., St. Louis, 1969. Registered arch., Md., Tex., Fla.; cert. Nat. Coun. Archtl. Registration Bds. Designer John S. Bolles Assoc., San Francisco, 1965-68; assoc. RTKL Assocs., Inc., Balt., 1969-72; v.p. EDI Archs., Dallas, 1972-76; sr. v.p. 3D/Internat., Houston, 1976-89; v.p. Euro Disney, S.A., Paris, 1989-92; prin. Daniel R. Brents, Inc., Houston, 1992-96, Gensler, Houston, 1996—. Mem. ULI Internat. Coun. Prin. works include Minute Maid Pk., Houston, Tex. Med. Ctr., Houston, U. Houston Main Campus, Yerba Buena Ctr., San Francisco, SpringPark, Dallas, Wintergreen Resort, Nelson County, Va., South Shore Harbor, League City, Tex., Heartland Village, Ohio, Medina (Saudi Arabia) Satellite Cmty., Asian Devel. Bank, Manila, The Philippines, IBM Corp. Hdqrs. Facilities, Southeast Asia, Spl. Econ. Zone, Shen Zhen, China, Euro Disney, Paris, Sony Center, Berlin, Philippines Centennial Expo., Hilton Americas Hotel, Houston, Tex., Dubai Internat. Fin. Ctr., Dubai. Mem. energy task force Goals for Dallas, 1975; mem. task force City of Dallas Urban Design, 1976-77, Hong Kong Am. C. of C. Community Affairs Com., 1985-87. Fellow AIA; mem. Am. Planning Assn., Am. Inst. Cert. Planners, Urban Land Inst., Tex. Soc. Archs. (internat. commn. co-chair). Office: Gensler 700 Milam St Ste 400 Houston TX 77002-2815

BRESANI, FEDERICO FERNANDO, manufacturing executive; b. Lima, Peru, Apr. 27, 1945; came to U.S., 1964; s. Federico L. and Beatriz (Ferrer) B.; m. Patricia Anne Grannis, Aug. 26, 1972; children: Christina Anne, Vianna Clarissa. BS in Elect. Engring., Milw. Sch. of Engring., 1970; MBA, Fairleigh Dickinson U., 1980. Engr. Cerro Corp., Lima, Peru, 1973-76; supr. Cerro Corp./CMP, N.Y.C., 1976-77, mgr., 1978, purchasing mgr., 1979-80; product mgr. Schumag, Inc., Norwood, N.J., 1980-82, v.p., 1982; sales, mktg. mgr. EVG, Inc., N.Y.C., 1983-85; v.p. EVG, N.Y.C., 1986-92, pres., 1992—. Mem. Wire Assn. Internat., Wire Reinforcement Inst., Latin Am. Iron and Steel Inst., Am. Concrete Inst., Concrete Reinforcing Steel Inst., Rowayton Yacht Club, Omicron Delta Epsilon. Avocations: sailing, amateur radio. Office: EVG 220 E 42nd St New York NY 10017-5806 Office Phone: 212-697-0770. Business E-Mail: f.bresani@evg-usa.com.

BRESCHER, JOHN B., JR., lawyer; b. Elizabeth, N.J., July 8, 1947; BS, Lehigh U., 1969; JD, Georgetown U., 1972, LLM, 1976. Bar: N.J. 1973, D.C. 1975. Atty. McCarter & English, Newark. Adj. prof. law Seton Hall U., 1980—84. Mem.: ABA, N.J. State Bar Assn., Essex County Bar Assn. Office: McCarter & English PO Box 652 Four Gateway Ctr 100 Mulberry St Newark NJ 07102-4004 Office Phone: 973-639-2012. E-mail: jbrescher@mccarter.com.

BRESCIA, ALICIA, science educator, vice principal; b. Reading, Pa., Jan. 19, 1947; d. Joseph John and Alice B. Heine; m. Frank J. Brescia, June 29, 1985. BA in Elem. Edn. and Biology, Coll. of St. Elizabeth, Convent Sta., NJ, 1969; MA in Sci. Edn., Columbia U., NYC, 1976. Profl. Diploma in Secondary Edn. Adminstrn. Fordham U., NYC, 1994. Tchr. Assumption Sch., Morristown, NJ, 1968—72, St. Teresa Sch., Summit, NJ, 1972—77; prin. St. Vincent Martyr Sch., Madison, NJ, 1977—81; tchr. biology and sci. Gov. Livingston HS, Berkeley Heights, NJ, 1982—85; faculty sci. in elem. edn.

Coll. of St. Elizabeth, 1983—85; tchr. sci. and biology Somers (NY) HS, 1986—93; spl. GE tchr. program Ossining (NY) HS, 1993—94; vice prin. Port Chester (NY) HS, 1994—96, chair sci. dept., 1994—98; tchr. biology The Living Environment. HS mentor Anthony Foust and Great Potential mentoring program, Port Chester, 1994—; prin. summer sch. Port Chester HS, 1996—99, mem. scholarship com., 1994—, mem. sch. improvement com., 1999—, small learning cmtys. com., 2002—; freshman acad. team Edn. Alliance and Brown Univ., 2004—. Mem. vis. com. Mid. States Assn. Colls. and Schs., 1999; bd. dirs. Heritage Hills Condo 7, Somers, 1996—2002, pres. bd., 1991, sect. leaders chair, 1996—2002. Nominee Tchr. of Yr., Port Chester Tchrs. Assn., 2000; named an Outstanding Elem. Tchr. of Am., Outstanding Elem. Tchrs. Am., 1974; grantee studies in biology, chemistry and physics, CUNY, NSF, 1971, bereavement and grief related issues, Calvary Hosp., Bronx, NY, 2002. Fellow: Assn. Supervision and Curriculum Devel., Sci. Tchrs. of N.Y. State; mem.: N.J. Sci. Tchrs. Assn., Hastings Inst. of Ethics, United Fedn. Tchrs. Roman Catholic. Avocations: gardening, travel, cooking. Office: Port Chester High School 1 Tamarack Rd Port Chester NY 10573 Office Phone: 914-934-7952.

BRESCIA, FRANK JOSEPH, medical oncologist, educator; b. Yonkers, N.Y., Feb. 24, 1942; s. Alfred Louis and Marie (Colucci) B.; m. Jane Usinger; children: Andria, Frank, Michaelann, Monica, Matthew, Joying. BS, Fordham U., 1963, MA in Philosophy, 1988; MD, N.J. Coll. Medicine, Newark, 1968. Diplomate Am. Bd. Internal Medicine, Am. Bd. Med. Oncology. Intern Cornell Med. Coll. programs North Shore Univ. Hosp., 1968-70; fellow in oncology Meml. Sloan-Kettering Cancer Ctr., N.Y.C., 1972-74; pvt. practice Millburn, N.J., 1974-80; med. dir. Calvary Hosp., Bronx, N.Y., 1980-94, Cancer Ctr. of Ga., 1994-96; assoc. prof. medicine Emory U., Atlanta, 1996-98; chief oncology Grady Meml. Hosp., Atlanta, 1996-98; prof. medicine Med. U. S.C., 1998—. Fellow Kennedy Ctr. for Bioethics, Washington, 1986—; adj. prof. Georgetown U., 1991—. Contbr. articles on clin. ethics and philosophy of care to med. jours. Maj. M.C., U.S. Army, 1970-72, Vietnam. Fellow Kennedy Ctr. Bioethics; mem. Am. Soc. Clin. Oncology. Roman Catholic. Office: Med Univ SC Clin Sci Bldg 903 96 Jonathan-Lucas St Charleston SC 29425 Office Phone: 843-792-4271. Business E-Mail: bresciaf@musc.edu.

BRESEE, JAMES COLLINS, chemical engineer; b. N.Y.C., Oct. 25, 1925; s. John James and Mabel Elizabeth (Collins) Bresee; m. Mary Kathryn Duncan, July 5, 1952 (dec. Mar. 1973); children: Kathryn Ann Bresee Brooke, Stuart James; m. Susan Lynn Austermiller, Aug. 3, 1974; children: James Michael, Benjamin Carter, Nathan John, Joanna Meghan, Andrew Paul. BSChemE, U. Ill., 1945, MSChemE, 1947; ScDChemE, MIT, 1953; JD, U. Tenn., 1971. Bar: Tenn. 1972, DC 1979. Asst. prof. chem. and nuclear engrng. MIT, Cambridge, Mass., 1951-54; br. chief and asst. dir. chem. tech. div. Oak Ridge Nat. Lab., Oak Ridge, Tenn., 1954-64, dir. civil def. rsch. project, 1964-72; asst. dir. for gen. energy devel. div. applied tech. AEC, Washington, 1972-75; dir. div. geothermal energy ERDA, Washington, 1976-77; dir. N.C. Energy Inst., N.C. State Dept. Commerce, Raleigh, 1978-81; supervisory engr. and mgr. geosci. rsch. Geothermal Tech. Div., U.S. Dept. Energy, Washington, 1982-86; mem. sr. exec. svc. Office Civilian Radioactive Waste Mgmt., U.S. Dept. Energy, Washington, 1986-98, dir. repository coordination div., 1986-88; dep. assoc. dir. for program and resources mgmt. Office Civilian Radioactive Waste Mgmt. U.S. Dept. Energy, 1988-94, acting dir. Office Human Resources and Adminstrn., Office Civilian Radioactive Waste Mgmt., 1994-96, dep. dir. Office of Program Mgmt. and Adminstrn., 1996-98, Sr. Tech. Specialist, 1998—; sr. tech. specialist DOE Office Nuc. Energy, Sci. and Tech., 2000—. Adj. prof. chem. engring. N.C. State U., 1978—81. Editor-in-chief: Geothermal Sci. and Tech., 1987—99; contbr. scientific papers to profl. publs. Mem. Oak Ridge Planning Commn., 1963—67. Lt. USNR, 1944—46, CBI. Mem.: DC Bar Assn., Tenn. Bar Assn., Sigma Xi, Phi Kappa Phi, Kappa Kappa Lambda, Beta Theta Pi. Presbyterian. Avocation: music. Home: 3213 Birchtree Ln Silver Spring MD 20906-3041 Office: US Dept Energy 1000 Independence Ave SW Washington DC 20585-0001 Business E-Mail: james.bresee@nuclear.energy.gov.

BRESKY, H. HARRY, diversified manufacturing company executive; b. 1925; Pres. Seaboard Corp., 1967—, CEO, 2001—, pres. Seaboard Flour Corp., 1987—2002. Office: Seaboard Corp 9000 W 67th St Mission KS 66202*

BRESLAW, ELAINE GELLIS, history professor; b. N.Y.C., June 27, 1932; m. Jerome Breslaw, Mar. 19, 1956 (div. May 1978); children: Joseph (dec.), Karl; m. John Muldowny, May 15, 1993. BA, Hunter Coll., 1954; MA, Smith Coll., 1956; MLS, Pratt Inst., Bklyn., 1964; PhD, U. Md., 1973. Libr. asst. Bklyn. Pub. Libr., 1959-60; reference libr. Catonsville Cmty. Coll., Md., 1964-65, Morgan State U., Balt., 1965-66, prof. history, 1966-94; vis. prof. history and adjunct U. Tenn., Knoxville, 1994—2005. Faculty assoc. John Hopkins U., Balt., 1980-97; vis. prof. history, Fulbright scholar U. West Indies, Barbados, 1989-90; project evaluator Md. Humanities Coun., Balt., 1986-87; cons. Ednl. Testing Svc., Princeton, NJ, 1981—. Author: Tituba, Reluctant Witch of Salem, 1996; editor: Records of the Tuesday Club, 1988, Witches of the Atlantic World, 2000; contbr. articles to profl. jour. Mem. Am. Hist. Assn., Southeastern Am. Soc. 18th Century Studies, Md. Hist. Soc. Home: 10900 Harbour Park Knoxville TN 37934-7009 Business E-Mail: ebreslaw@utk.edu.

BRESLIN, DARA S., anesthesiologist; b. Dublin, Ireland, Dec. 26, 1968; arrived in U.S., 2001; s. Colum A. and Eileen Breslin; m. Eimer L. Collins, Mar. 18, 2000; children: Hugo, Tommy, Amy. MBBCh, U. Coll. Dublin, 1993. Resident Coll. Anesthetists, Ireland, 1994—2000; rsch. fellow Dept. Anesthesiology The Queens U., Belfast, Ireland, 2000—01; asst. prof. Duke U., Durham, NC, 2001—, attending anesthesiologist Med. Ctr., 2001—. Mem. faculty of anesthetists Royal Coll. Surgeons, Ireland. Contbr. articles to profl. jours. Mem.: Am. Soc. Regional Anesthesia and Pain Medicine. Avocations: sports, golf. Office: Dept Anesthesiology Duke Univ Med Ctr PO Box 3094 Durham NC 27710 Office Phone: 919-681-6437.

BRESLIN, JIMMY, columnist, writer; b. Jamaica, N.Y., Oct. 17, 1929; s. James Earl and Frances (Curtin) B.; m. Rosemary Dattolico, Dec. 26, 1954 (dec. June 1981); children: James and Kevin (twins), Rosemary, Patrick, Kelly, Christopher.; m. Ronnie Myers Eldridge, Sept. 12, 1982; stepchildren: Daniel, Emily, Lucy Eldridge. Student, L.I. U., 1947-50. Syndicated columnist N.Y. Herald-Tribune, Paris Tribune, N.Y. Daily News, Newsday, L.I., NY, 1984—2004. Commentator Sta. WNBC-TV; host: (TV series) Jimmy Breslin's People, 1986; author: Can't Anybody Here Play This Game?, 1963, The Gang That Couldn't Shoot Straight, 1969, World Without End, Amen, 1973, How The Good Guys Finally Won, 1975, (with others) Forty-Four Caliber, 1978, Forsaking All Others, 1982, The World According to Breslin, 1984, Table Money, 1986, He Got Hungry and Forgot His Manners, 1988, Damon Runyon, 1991, I Want to Thank My Brain for Remembering Me, 1996, I Don't Want to Go to Jail: A Good Novel, 2001, The Short Sweet Dream of Edwardo Gutierrez, 2002, The Church That Forgot Christ, 2004; drama: The Queen of the Leaky-Roof Circuit, 1988. N.Y.C. Candidate for pres. City Council, N.Y.C., 1969; del. Democratic Nat. Conv., 1972, 76. Recipient award for nat. reporting Sigma Delta Chi, 1964, Meyer Berger award for local reporting, 1964, N.Y. Reporters Assn. award reporting, 1964, Pulitzer Prize for commentary, 1986, George K. Polk award, 1986. Mem. Screen Actors Guild, AFTRA, Writers Guild Am. Office: c/o David Black Literary Agy Ste 608 156 5th Ave New York NY 10010*

BRESLIN, MICHAEL JOSEPH, III, social services administrator, educator; b. Fountain Springs, Pa., Feb. 5, 1949; s. Michael Joseph Jr. and Barbara Ellin (Mellet) B. BS in Sociology, U. Scranton, 1971; MS in Adminstrn., Shippensburg (Pa.) U., 1984. Tchr. aide Selinsgrove (Pa.) Ctr., 1968, 69, 70; caseworker Northumberland County Children and Youth Agy., Sunbury, Pa., 1971-73; juvenile probation officer Northumberland County Juvenile Ct., 1973-74, supr., 1974-75, dir., 1976-87; dir. human svcs. Northumberland County Human Svcs., 1987-91; exec. dep. sec. Dept. Pub. Welfare, Harrisburg, Pa., 1992-95; v.p. Northwestern Corp., Harrisburg, Pa., 1995-97; sr. v.p. Northwestern Human Svcs., Harrisburg, 1997—. Adminstr. Northumberland County Mental Health and Mental Retardation Program, 1984-87; mem. adj. faculty Susquehanna U., Selinsgrove, 1989-91; cons. Tng. & Mgmt. Systems, Gibsonia, Pa., 1983-85; mem. Youth Svcs. Tng. Ctr., 1986-90. Mem. adv. bd. White Deer Run Treatment Ctr., Allenwood, Pa., 1975-77; advisor Explorer Pres. Assn., Netami dist. Boy Scouts Am., 1980-81, tng. coord. Explorer program, 1982-86, scouting coord. Explorer Post 2312, 1986-91; coord. high sch. youth program St. Michael's Ch., Sunbury, 1981-91, pres. parish coun., 1989-91; vice chmn. SSS, Sunbury, 1982-89; chmn. Sunbury Govt. Study Commn., 1989-90; bd. dirs. Hemlock coun. Girls Scouts U.S.A., 1990-95; bd. dirs. Pa. Partnerships for Children, 1996-2001, treas., 2001-2005, vice chmn., 2005—; mem. parish coun. St. Patrick Cathedral, Harrisburg, 1997-2000, fin. com., 2004—; bd. dirs. Found. for Preservation of St. Lawrence Chapel, 2005—; chair citizen rev. panel United Way Capitol Region, 1998-2000, bd. dirs., 2003—; chair Early Childhood Initiative Steering com. United Way, 1999-2005; bd. dirs. United Way Capital Region, 2003—. Named Chief Probation Officer of Yr., Juvenile Ct. Judges Commn., Harrisburg, Pa., 1985; recipient Liberty Bell award Northumberland County Bar Assn., 1986, Meritorious Svc. award Pa. Foster Parents, 1988, affiliate award Pa. Assn. County Commrs., 1990, Citizen of Yr., City of Sunbury, 1992, Pres.'s award Pa. Assn. County Human Svc. Dirs., 1994, Disting. Svc. award Juvenile Detention Ctr. Adminstrs. Pa., 1994. Mem. Nat. Juvenile Ct. Svcs. Assn. (regional rep. 1989-93), Nat. Coun. Juvenile and Family Ct. Judges (awards com.), Nat. Juvenile Detention Assn., Nat. Juvenile Ct. Svcs. Assn., Mental Health and Mental Retardation Program Adminstrs. Assn., Mental Health and Mental Retardation Adminstrs. Assn. Pa. (chmn. 1989-91). Democrat. Office: Northwestern Human Svcs 1320 Linglestown Rd Harrisburg PA 17110-2822 Home: 4515 Laurelwood Dr Harrisburg PA 17110-2829 Office Phone: 717-441-9502. E-mail: mikebreslin@comcast.net, mbreslin@nhsonline.org.

BRESLOW, ESTHER MAY GREENBERG, biochemistry professor, researcher; b. N.Y.C., Dec. 23, 1931; d. Harry Daniel and Lillian (Solomon) Greenberg; m. Ronald Charles David Breslow, Sept. 4, 1955; children: Stephanie Ruth, Karen Ann. BS with distinction, Cornell U., 1953; MS in Biochemistry, NYU, 1955, PhD in Biochemistry, 1959; postgrad., Radcliffe Coll., 1954-55. Postdoctoral fellow Cornell U. Med. Coll., N.Y.C., 1959-61, rsch. assoc., 1961-64, asst. prof., 1964-72, assoc. prof., 1972-78, prof. biochemistry, 1978—, acting chmn. dept. biochemistry, 1992-95. Mem. rev. panels NIH, Bethesda, Md., 1973—77, Bethesda, 1994—97, NSF, Bethesda, 1981—84. Mem. editorial bd. Jour. Biol. Chemistry, 1982-87, Internat. Jour. Peptide and Protein Rsch., 1981-97; contbr. articles to profl. jours. Mem. Englewood (N.J.) Bd. Health, 1986-94; mem. Dem. Mcpl. Com., Englewood, 1985-91. Eli Lilly fellow, 1954-55; USPHS fellow, 1959-61; NIH grantee, 1961—. Fellow AAAS; mem. Am. Soc. for Biochemistry and Molecular Biology, Am. Chem. Soc. (sec. div. biol. chemistry 1972-76), Harvey Soc., Sigma Xi. Home: 44 W 77th St New York NY 10024 Office: Joan and Sanford I Weill Med Coll Cornell U 1300 York Ave New York NY 10021-4805 Office Phone: 212-746-6428. Business E-Mail: ebreslow@med.cornell.edu.

BRESLOW, JAN LESLIE, scientist, educator, physician; b. N.Y.C., Feb. 28, 1943; s. Frank and Pearl (Feit) B.; m. Marilyn Ganon, June 25, 1965; children: Noah, Nicholas AB, Columbia U., 1963, MA, 1964; MD, Harvard Med. Sch., 1968. Diplomate Am. Bd. Pediatrics. Intern in pediatrics, then jr. asst. resident Children's Hosp., Boston, 1968-70; staff assoc. Nat. Heart Lung and Blood Inst., Bethesda, Md., 1970-73; from instr. to assoc. prof. pediatrics Harvard Med. Sch., Boston, 1973-83; prof. Rockefeller U., NYC, 1984-86, Frederick Henry Leonhardt prof., 1986—, lab. dir., sr. investigator. Dir. Lab. of Biochem. Genetics and Metabolism, Rockefeller U., N.Y.C., 1984—; sr. physician Rockefeller U. Hosp., N.Y.C., 1984—; mem. arteriosclerosis, hypertension and lipid metabolism adv. com. Nat. Heart, Lung and Blood Inst., 1986-90. Mem. editorial bd. Jour. Lipid Rsch., 1983-85, Arteriosclerosis and Thrombosis, 1984—, Genomics, 1987—; cons. editor Jour. Clin. Investigation, 1988-92, Jour. Biol. Chemistry, 1989-91. Served as surgeon USPHS, 1970-73. Eugene Higgins fellow Columbia U., 1963-64; recipient MERIT award Nat. Heart, Lung and Blood Inst., 1986-95, Heinrich Wieland prize, 1991, Pasarow Found. award for cardiovascular rsch., 1995. Mem. AAAS, Inst. Medicine (elected), NAS (elected), Am. Acad. Pediatr. (E. Mead Johnson award 1984), Am. Heart Assn. (coun. on arteriosclerosis 1974—, credentials com. 1984-86, award coms. 1984-87, chmn. award com. 1987-89, program com. 1986-89, exec. com. 1988—, N.Y.C. affiliate rsch. coun. 1985-87, chmn. 1987-89, chmn. policy com. 1989-91, chmn. nominating com. 1992-94, bd. dirs. 1987-90, 92—, Nat. Ctr. v.p. for rsch. 1994, bd. dirs. 1994-98, pres.-elect 1995, pres. 1996, past pres. 1997, Estab. Investigator award 1981-86, Basic Rsch. prize 1994 Nat. Ctr. Rsch. Com. (vice chmn. 1989-90, chmn. 1990-92), Rsch. program and Evaluation Com. (vice chmn. 1992-94, chmn. 1994—), Am. Soc. Clin. Nutrition, Soc. Pediat. Rsch., N.Y. Acad. Scis., Am. Fedn. Clin. Rsch., Am. Soc. Clin. Investigation (v.p. 1987-88), Internat. Arteriosclerosis Soc., Am. Soc. Biol. Chemists, Assn. Am. Physicians, Inst. of Medicine. Achievements include research in lipid and lipoprotein metabolism, genetic and environ. causes of arteriosclerosis, inborn errors of metabolism. Office: Rockefeller U Hosp Lab Biochemistry Genetics & Metabolism 1230 York Ave Box 179 New York NY 10021-6399 Office Phone: 212-327-7704. Office Fax: 212-327-7165. Business E-Mail: breslow@rockefeller.edu.

BRESLOW, LESTER, preventive medicine physician, educator; b. Bismarck, N.D., Mar. 17, 1915; s. Joseph and Mayme (Danziger) Breslow; m. Devra J.R. Miller, 1967; children: Norman, Jack, Stephen. BA, U. Minn., 1935, MD, 1938, MPH, 1941, DSc (hon.), 1988. Diplomate Am. Bd. Preventive Medicine and Public Health. Intern USPHS Hosp., Stapleton, NY, 1938—40; dist. health officer Minn. Dept. Health, 1941—43; preventive medicine officer U.S. Army, 1943—45; chief bur. chronic diseases Calif. Dept. Pub. Health, Berkeley, 1946—60, chief divsn. preventive medicine, 1960—65, dir. dept., 1965—68; lectr. U. Calif. Sch. Pub. Health, Berkeley, 1950—68; prof. pub. health UCLA Sch. Pub. Health, 1968—, chmn. dept. preventive medicine and social medicine, 1969—72, dean, 1972—80, mem. divsn. cancer control, 1980—, dir. health promotion ctr., 1988—91, dean, prof. emeritus, 1980—; dir. study Pres.'s Commn. Health Needs of Nation, 1952. Cons. Office of Technology Assessment, Nat. Heart, Lung, Blood Inst., 1977, Nat. Cancer Inst., 1981—, chmn. bd. sci. counsellors divsn. cancer prevention and control, 1982—84; chmn. Nat. Com. on Vital and Health Stats., 1979—81; mem. U.S.-China Health Scis. Com., Dept. HHS, 1982; bd. dirs., chmn. Calif. Ctr. for Health Improvement, 1998—. Editor: Ann. Rev. Pub. Health, 1979—90, Encyclopedia Pub. Health, 2002; editorial cons. in field:. Active L.A. County Pub. Health Commn., 1996—, chmn., 1997—98. Capt. U.S. Army, 1943—45. Decorated Bronze Star; recipient Lasker award, Mary Lasker Found., 1960, Porter prize, 1998, Outstanding Achievement award, U. Minn., 1970, Thomas Francis, Jr. Meml. award, U. Mich. Fellow: AAAS, ACP, Am. Coll. Preventive Medicine (Disting. Svc. award 1976); mem.: APHA (past pres., Sedgwick medal 1977, Dana award, Charles A. Dana Found. 1988, Healthtrac Found. Prize 1995, 1997), NY Acad. Medicine (Stephen Smith Achievement in Public Health award 2005), Inst. Medicine NAS (council 1978—80, chmn. bd. health promotion and disease prevention 1980—82, Lienhard award 1997), Assn. Schs. Public Health (pres. 1973—74), Am. Cancer Soc. (nat. dir., Calif. dir., chmn. adv. com. on rsch. etiology), Internat. Epidemiol. Assn. (past pres.), Am. Epidemiol. Soc., Public Health Cancer Assn. (past pres.), Am. Heart Assn. (fellow epidemiology sect.). Home: 10926 Verano Rd Los Angeles CA 90077-2224 Office Phone: 310-825-1388. Business E-Mail: breslow@ph.ucla.edu.

BRESLOW, NORMAN EDWARD, biostatistics educator, researcher; b. Mpls., Feb. 21, 1941; s. Lester and Alice Jane (Philp) Breslow; m. Gayle Marguerite Bramwell, Sept. 7, 1963; children: Lauren Louise, Sara Jo. BA, Reed Coll., 1962; PhD, Stanford U., 1967; Doctorate (honoris causa), U. Bordeaux II, 2001. Trainee Stanford U., 1965—67; vis. research worker London Sch. Hygiene, 1967—68; instr. U. Wash., Seattle, 1968—69, asst. prof., 1969—72, assoc. prof., 1972—76, prof., 1976—, chmn. dept. biostats., 1983—93; statistician Internat. Agy. Research Cancer, Lyon, France, 1972—74. Mem. Hutchinson Cancer Ctr., Seattle, 1982—; statistician Nat. Wilms' Tumor Study, 1969—2003; cons. Internat. Agy. Rsch. Cancer, Lyon, 1978—79; assoc. prof. U. Geneva, 1994—. Co-author: (Scientific publ. nos. 32 and 82 on statistics in cancer rsch.) IARC, ISI (most highly cited publication in mathematical sciences for 1993-2003). Named sr. U.S. Scientist, Alexander Humboldt Found., Fed. Republic of Germany, 1982; recipient Spiegelman Gold medal, APHA, 1978, Preventive Oncology Acad. award, NIH, 1978—83, Snedecor award, Com. of Pres.'s on Statis. Socs., 1995, R.A. Fisher lectr. award, 1995; fellow sr. Internat., Fogarty Ctr., 1990; grantee rsch., NIH, 1984—. Fellow: AAAS, Royal Statis. Soc., Am. Statis. Assn. (com. on fellows 1996—2000, N. Mantel award 2002); mem.: Internat. Biometric Soc. (regional com. 1975—78, coun. 1994—2000, v.p. 2001, 2004, pres. 2002—03), Inst. Medicine-Nat. Acad. Scis., Internat. Statis. Inst. Avocations: ski mountaineering, hiking, bicycling. Office: Univ Wash Dept Biostatistics Seattle WA 98195-7232 Business E-Mail: norm@u.washington.edu.

BRESLOW, RONALD CHARLES, chemist, educator; b. Rahway, N.J., Mar. 14, 1931; s. Alexander E. and Gladys (Fellows) Breslow; m. Esther Greenberg, Sept. 7, 1955; children: Stephanie, Karen. AB summa cum laude, Harvard U., 1952, MA, 1953, PhD, 1955. NRC fellow Cambridge (Eng.) U., 1955—56; mem. faculty Columbia U., N.Y.C., 1956—, prof. chemistry, 1962—66, S.L. Mitchell prof., 1966—, univ. prof., 1992—. Cons. to industry, 1958—; mem. medicinal chemistry panel NIH, 1964—; mem. adv. panel on chemistry NSF, 1971—; mem. sci. adv. com. GM Corp., 1982—; A.R. Todd vis. prof. Cambridge U., 1982; hon. prof. U. Sci. & Tech., China; editor Benjamin, Inc., 1962—. Author: Organic Reaction Mechanisms, 1965, 2d edit., 1969; editl. bd. Organic Syntheses, 1964—, Jour. Organic Chemistry, 1969—, Jour. Bio-organic Chemistry, 1972—, Tetrahedron, 1975—, Tetrahedron Letters, 1975—, Procs. NAS, 1984—; contbr. articles to profl. jours. Trustee Rockefeller U., 1981—; bd. sci. advisers Alfred P. Sloan Found., 1978—85. Recipient Fresenius award, Phi Lambda Upsilon, 1966, Mark Van Doren award, Columbia U., 1969, Roussel prize, 1978, Great Tchr. award, Columbia U., 1981, T.W. Richards medal, 1984, A.C. Cope award, 1987, G.W. Kenner award, U. Liverpool, Eng., 1988, Paracelsus prize, Swiss Chem. Soc., 1999, Arthur Day award, 1990, Nat. medal of Sci., NSF, 1991, Paracelsus award, New Swiss Chem. Soc., Royal Soc. London, 1990, Mayor's award in Sci., N.Y.C., 2000, Centenary lectr., London Chem. Soc., 1972. Fellow: Indian Acad. Scis. (hon. fgn.), Am. Acad. Arts and Scis., Korean Chem. Soc. (hon.); mem.: NAS (chmn. chemistry divsn. 1974—77, award in chemistry 1989), European Acad. Sci., European Acad. Scis., Royal Soc. Chemistry (London, hon.), Royal Soc. London (hon.), Chem. Soc. Japan (hon.), New Swiss Chem. Soc. (Paracelsus award 1990), Am. Chem. Soc. (pres.-elect 1995—96, pres. 1996, chmn. divsn. organic chemistry 1970, Pure Chemistry award 1966, Baekeland medal 1969, Harrison Howe award 1974, Remsen award 1977, J.F. Norris award 1980, N.Y. sect. Nicholas medal 1989, Priestley medal 1999, Bioorganic Chemistry award 2002, Willard Gibbs medal 2004, Robert Welch award 2003), Am. Philos. Soc. (coun. 1987—), Phi Beta Kappa (1st marshall 1952). Home: 44 W 77th St New York NY 10024 Office: Columbia U Dept Chemistry 116th St & Broadway New York NY 10027

BRESLOW, STEPHANIE R., lawyer; b. NYC, June 20, 1960; d. Ronald and Esther Breslow. BA cum laude, Harvard U., 1981; JD, Columbia U., 1984. Bar: Ohio 1984, NY 1986. Assoc. Cleary Gottlieb Steen & Hamilton, NYC, 1985-93; ptnr., corp. dept. Schulte Roth & Zabel LLP, NYC, 1993—, hiring ptnr., recruiting com. Spkr. in field; co-author: New York Limited Liability Companies and Partnerships, NY & Del. Business Entities: Choice Formation Operation Financing and Acquisitions. Bd. trustees The Joyce Theater, NY. Harlan Fiske Stone Scholar, 1982—84. Mem.: Pvt. Investment Fund Forum (founding mem.), Wall St. Hedge Fund Forum (steering com.), Assn. Bar City NY. Office: Schulte Roth & Zabel LLP 919 Third Ave New York NY 10022-4774 Office Phone: 212-756-2542. Office Fax: 212-593-5955. Business E-Mail: stephanie.breslow@srz.com.

BRESLOW, TINA, public relations executive; b. Phila., Feb. 18, 1946; d. Harry and Doris (Stein) Horowitz; m. Alan Breslow, Aug. 28, 1965 (div. 1970); children: Peter, Jennifer, Brett. Office mgr. Temple U. Ctr. City, Phila., 1976-79; publicist Temple U. Theater, Phila., 1979-81; mgr. pub. rels. Hershey Phila. Hotel, 1981-83; dir. pub. rels. Franklin Plaza Hotel, Phila., 1983-84; account mgr. Sommers Rosen, Inc., Phila., 1984-85; prin. Tina Breslow Pub. Relations, Phila., 1985—. Pub. rels. cons. Dock St. Beer, Phila., 1986-87, Sheraton Soc. Hill Hotel, Phila., 1985-86. Chmn. pub. rels. com. Phila. Convention and Vis. Bur., 1985; pub. rels. cons. Phila. City Planning Commn., 1988, Phila. Commn. on AIDS, 1988. Recipient Super Communicator award Women in Communication, 1984, Best New Bus. Intro. award Phila. Better Bus. Bur., 1986, Community Svs. award Hotel Sales and Mktg. Assoc. Internat., 1988, Golden Bell award, 1988, Breakfast for Champions and Olymic Fundraiser The Alexander Hotels, 1988, Woman of Distinction award, 2002; named to Wall of Fame. N.E. H.S., 2002. Mem. Phila. Pub. Rels. Assn., Pub. Rels. Soc. Am. Jewish. Office: Tina Breslow Pub Rels 2042 Rittenhouse Sq Philadelphia PA 19103-5621

BRESNAHAN, JOSEPH MICHAEL, music educator; b. Fullerton, Calif., Mar. 30, 1981; s. Robert Michael and Terri Lynn Bresnahan. B.Mus.Edn., Harding U., Searcy, Ark., 2003. Mid. sch. band dir. Vilonia Pub. Schools, Vilonia, Ark., 2003—; adj. instr. of percussion Harding U., Searcy, Ark., 2004—. Mem.: Ark. Sch. Band and Orch. Assn., Nat. Assn. for Music Edn. R-Consevative. Office Phone: 501-796-3514. Personal E-mail: drummajor4u@juno.com.

BRESNAHAN, ROGER JIANG, humanities educator, researcher; b. Chicopee, Mass., July 1, 1943; BA, Boston Coll., 1967; MA, NYU, 1968; PhD, U. Mass., 1974. Asst. prof. humanities Voorhees Coll., Denmark, S.C., 1974-78, divsn. chair, 1977-78; Fulbright sr. lectr. in Am. studies U. Philippines, 1976-77; chair dept. religious studies, core faculty Asian studies Mich. State U., East Lansing, Mich., 1978—. Editor: In Time of Hesitation, 1981, Conversations with Filipino Writers, 1990, Angles of Vision, 1992. Mem. Coll. English Assn. (hon. life, assoc. exec. sec. 1979-82), Assn. for Asian Studies, Filipino Studies Group (exec. sec. 1993-95), Soc. for Study Midwestern Lit. (corr. sec./treas. 1980—). Office: Mich State U East Lansing MI 48824-1033 Office Phone: 517-353-2930.

BRESNAN, JOAN W., literature and language professor; life ptnr. Marianne Brem. Sadie Dernham Patek Prof. in Humanities Stanford U., 2000—; Erskine Fellow U. Canterbury, Christchurch, 2005. Fellow: Am. Acad. Arts & Sci., 2004; mem.: Linguistic Soc. Am. (pres. 1999). Avocations: bicycling, photography. Office: Stanford University Builing 420 Room 22 Stanford CA 94305-2150 Office Phone: 650-723-0144. Office Fax: 650-723-5666. Business E-Mail: bresnan@stanford.edu.*

BRESS, MICHAEL E., retired lawyer; b. Mpls., Aug. 23, 1933; s. Michael J. and Anna (Tema) B.; m. Grace Billings, June 3, 1966; 1 child, Anne Ruth. BA, U. Minn., 1954, LLB, 1957. Bar: N.Y. 1958, Minn. 1959. Assoc. Donovan Leisure Newton & Irvine, N.Y.C., 1957-59, Dorsey & Whitney LLP, Mpls., 1959-64; ptnr. Dorsey & Whitney LPP, Mpls., 1964-91, of counsel, 1992-97, ret., 1998. Trustee St. Vladimir's Orthodox Theol. Sem., Crestwood, N.Y. Mem. Minn. Bar Assn., Hennepin County Bar Assn., Phi Beta Kappa. Home: 2007 W Franklin Ave Minneapolis MN 55405-2422 Personal E-mail: mbress@mn.rr.com.

BRESSAN, PAUL LOUIS, lawyer; b. Rockville Centre, NY, June 15, 1947; s. Louis Charles Bressan and Nance Elizabeth Batteley. BA cum laude, Fordham Coll., 1969; JD, Columbia U., 1975. Bar: N.Y. 1976, Calif. 1987, U.S. Dist. Ct. (so., ea. and no. dists.) N.Y. 1976, U.S. Dist. Ct. (no. and ctrl. dists.) Calif. 1987, U.S. Ct. Appeals (2d cir.) 1980, U.S. Supreme Ct. 1980, U.S. Ct. Appeals (1st and 4th cirs.) 1981, U.S. Ct. Appeals (11th cir.) 1982, U.S. Ct. Appeals (9th cir.) 1987, U.S Ct. Appeals (7th cir.) 1991, U.S. Dist. Ct. (ea. dist.) Calif. 1995; U.S. Dist. Ct. (so. dist.) Calif. 1997. Assoc. Kelley, Drye & Warren, N.Y.C., 1975-84, ptnr. N.Y.C. and Los Angeles, 1984—2003; shareholder Buchalter, Nemer, Fields & Younger, LA, 2003—. Served to lt.

USNR, 1971-72. Named One of Outstanding Coll. Athletes of Am., 1969; Harlan Fiske Stone scholar Columbia Law Sch. Mem. ABA, Calif. Bar Assn., Phi Beta Kappa. Republican. Roman Catholic. Office: Buchalter Nemer Fields & Younger 601 S Figueroa St Ste 2400 Los Angeles CA 90017 Office Phone: 213-891-5220. Business E-Mail: pbressan@buchalter.com.

BRESSLER, BARRY E., lawyer; b. Phila., Apr. 7, 1947; s. Joseph and Shirley M. (Eiseman) B.; m. Risé Sharon Cohen, June 14, 1970 (dec.); children: Allison Ivy, Michelle Amy. AB, Franklin and Marshall Coll., Lancaster, Pa., 1968; JD, U. Pa., 1971. Bar: Pa. 1971, U.S. Dist. Ct. (ea. dist.) Pa. 1973, U.S. Ct. Appeals (3d cir.) 1977, U.S. Supreme Ct. 1988, U.S. Dist. Ct. (mid. dist.) Pa. 1990. Law clk. to judge Superior Ct. Pa., Phila., 1971-73; assoc. Meltzer & Schiffrin, Phila., 1973-79, ptnr., 1979-86, Fox, Rothschild, O'Brien & Frankel, Phila., 1987-88; mem., sr. lawyer real estate litigation & creditors' rights Pelino & Lentz, P.C., Phila., 1988-2000; ptnr. Schnader, Harrison, Segal & Lewis, LLP, Phila., 2000—. Adj. instr. landlord-tenant law Delaware County C.C., Media, Pa., 1985—, Montgomery County C.C., Blue Bell, Pa., 1987—. V.p. English Ceramic Study Group, Phila.; v.p., sec. Temple Sinai, Dresher, Pa., 1991-97, 2003-04; grad. Leadership, Inc., Phila. Mem. ABA (litigation sect.), Pa. Bar Assn. (corp. banking and bus. sect.), Phila. Bar Assn. (real property sect.), Bankruptcy Conf. Ea. Dist. Pa. (treas. 1995-2000), Am. Arbitration Assn., Tau Epsilon Rho. Republican. Jewish. Avocations: tennis, ceramics, bridge. Office: Schnader Harrison Segal and Lewis LLP 1600 Market St Ste 3600 Philadelphia PA 19103-7286 Office Phone: 215-751-2050. Business E-Mail: bbressler@schnader.com.

BRESSLER, BARRY LEE, physicist, systems analyst; b. Reading, Pa., Feb. 16, 1936; s. Kenneth Russell and Lillian Mary (Good) B. BS in Physics, Ursinus Coll., 1957; MS in Physics, Va. Poly. Inst. State U., 1979, PhD in Physics, 1986. Tchr., curator insect collection Reading Pub. Mus., 1954-55; data-processing technician Philco Corp., Phila., 1956, jr. engr. Spring City, Pa., 1957-58; physicist Naval Surface Warfare Ctr., Dahlgren, Va., 1958-94, group leader, 1983-89, fellow, 1983-85, sr. scientist, 1989-94; prin. scientist EG&G Tech. Svcs., Inc., Dahlgren, 1994-95, sr. prin. scientist, 1995—. Cons. Windy Knoll Enterprises, Inc., Magnolia, Tex., 1994—; adj. prof. physics Va. Poly. Inst. State U., Blacksburg, 1994—. Scholar Bryn Mawr Coll., 1957. Mem. Am. Phys. Soc., Coleopterists Soc. (jour. referee 1991-95), Sigma Pi Sigma, Sigma Xi. Achievements include mathematical modeling and simulation, and computation of trajectories, for ballistic missiles, reentry vehicles, and interceptor missiles; determination of guidance commands for flight tests of maneuvering reentry vehicles; analysis of simulated engagements between evasively maneuvering reentry vehicles and interceptor missiles; design and optimization of reentry maneuvers; threat analysis; analysis of advanced strategic and tactical weapons systems; formulation of theoretical models for the electromagnetic pulse produced by a high-altitude nuclear burst, and for various other weapons effects; research in the quantum mechanics of many-particle systems, particularly of fermion-boson systems; education of nontraditional graduate physics students. Avocations: ecology, myrmecology, cerambycid taxonomy, Shetland sheepdogs. Home: PO Box 1345 Fredericksburg VA 22402-1345 Office: EG&G Services PO Box 552 Dahlgren VA 22448-0552 Office Phone: 540-663-9300. E-mail: BLBressler@aol.com.

BRESSLER, BERNARD, lawyer; b. NYC, Jan. 2, 1928; s. Morris and Masha (Roitman) B.; m. Teresa Stern, June 25, 1950; children: Lisa, Jeanette. BA, Rutgers U., 1949; LLB magna cum laude, Harvard U., 1952. Bar: N.Y. 1953, N.J. 1977. Atty. firm Greenman, Shea, Sandomire & Zimet, N.Y.C., 1952-60; ptnr. Bressler, Amery & Ross, N.Y.C., 1960—, Florham Park, NJ, 1981—. Dir., chmn. bd. N.J. Pub. Interest Law Ctr., 1996—; bd. trustees South St. Theatre Co., Morristown, 2003—. Author: (with others) Tax Annotations Nichols Ency. Forms, 1954-59; Editor: (with B. Meislin) New York Lawyers Manual, 1954, Harvard Law Rev., vol. 65. Campaign dir. Summit (N.J.) United Jewish Appeal, 1957-60; chmn. Summit Democrat Club, 1957; trustee Summit Civic Found.; chmn. Summit Area United Negro Coll. Fund, 1979-92. With USNR, 1945-46. Mem.: Lotos (N.Y.C.), Park Ave. Club (N.J.). Home: 3 Kimberwick Ct Morristown NJ 07960-6993 Office: 17 State St New York NY 10004-1501 also: 325 Columbia Tpke Florham Park NJ 07932-1212 Office Phone: 973-514-1200.

BRESSLER, MARCUS NATHAN, engineer, consultant; b. Havana, Cuba, July 31, 1929; came to U.S., 1942; s. Isaac and Augustine (Draiman) B.; m. Sondra Kipnes, Nov. 7, 1954; children: Eric L., Lisa A., Karen J. Lee. B of Mech. Engring., Cornell U., 1952; MSME, Case Inst. Tech., 1960. Registered profl. engr., Tenn. Stress analysis engr. The Babcock & Wilcox Co., Barberton, Ohio, 1955-66; design engr. Lenape Forge, West Chester, Pa., 1966-70; mgr., product design and devel. engr. Taylor Forge, Cicero, Ill., 1970-71; supr. codes, standards and materials TVA, Knoxville, 1971-79, sr. engring. specialist, 1979-88; pres. M.N. Bressler, PE, Inc., Knoxville, 1988—. 1st lt. U.S. Army, 1952-54, capt. USAR, 1957. Fellow ASME (life fellow, mem. boiler and pressure vessel stds. com., bd. conformity assessment, bd. nuc. codes and stds., Century Medallion 1980, Bernard F. Langer Nuc. Codes and Stds. award 1992, J. Hall Taylor medal for pressure tech. codes and stds. outstanding contbns. 1996, Dedicated Svc. award 2001). Home and Office: M N Bressler PE Inc 13508 King Lake Trail Broomfield CO 80020 Personal E-mail: mbresslerpe@juno.com.

BRESSLER, RICHARD J., former entertainment company executive; married; two children. Grad. summa cum laude, Adelphi Coll., 1979. CPA. Ptnr. Ernst & Young, Inc., 1979-88; from asst. controller to exec. v.p., CFO Time Warner, Inc., N.Y.C., 1988—95, CEO, sr. v.p., 1995—98; sr. v.p., CFO Viacom Inc., N.Y.C., 2001—05. Bd. dirs. Prep for Prep, Outward Bound; mem. Chase Nat. Adv. Bd., CFO Adv. Coun.; trustee Citizen's Budget Commn. Mem. Am. Inst. CPAs, N.Y. State Soc. Cert. CPAs.

BRESSMAN, STUART, lawyer; AB with distinction, Cornell U., 1982, JD, 1985. Bar: N.Y. 1986, U.S. Dist. Ct. (so. dist.) N.Y. 1989. Ptnr. Brown Raysman Millstein Felder & Steiner LLP, N.Y.C., 1999—. Mem.: ABA, N.Y. State Bar Assn., Assn. of the Bar of the City of N.Y. Office: Brown Raysman Millstein Felder & Steiner 900 Third Ave New York NY 10022 Office Phone: 212-895-2000.

BREST, PAUL A., law educator; b. Jacksonville, Fla., Aug. 9, 1940; s. Alexander and Mia (Deutsch) B.; m. Iris Lang, June 17, 1962; children: Hilary, Jeremy. AB, Swarthmore Coll., 1962; JD, Harvard U., 1965; LLD (hon.), Northeastern U., 1980, Swarthmore Coll., 1991. Bar: N.Y. 1966. Law clk. to Hon. Bailey Aldrich U.S. Ct. Appeals (1st cir.), Boston, 1965-66; atty. NAACP Legal Def. Fund, Jackson, Miss., 1966-68; law clk. Justice John Harlan, U.S. Supreme Ct., 1968-69; prof. law Stanford U., 1969—, Kenneth and Harle Montgomery Prof. pub. interest law, Richard E. Lang prof. and dean, 1987-99; pres. William and Flora Hewlett Found., Menlo Park, Calif., 1999—. Author: Processes of Constitutional Decisionmaking, 1992. Mem. Am. Acad. Arts and Scis. Home: 814 Tolman Dr Palo Alto CA 94305-1026 Office: William and Flora Hewlett Found 2121 Sand Hill Rd Menlo Park CA 94025 Business E-Mail: pbrest@hewlett.org.

BRESTEL, MARY BETH, librarian; b. Cin., Feb. 5, 1952; d. John Wesley and Laura Alice (Knoop) Seay; m. Michael Charles Brestel, Aug. 3, 1974; 1 child, Rebecca Michelle. BS, U. Cin., 1974; MLS, U. Ky., 1984. Libr. asst. history and lit. dept. Pub. Libr. Cin. and Hamilton County, 1974-78, children's asst. Pleasant Ridge br., 1978-81, children's asst. Westwood br., 1981-84, reference libr. sci. and tech. dept., 1984-90, 1st asst. sci. and tech. dept., 1990-92, mgr. dept., 1992—. Mem. Ohio Libr. Coun., Columbus, 2001—. Mem. United Methodist Ch. Office: Pub Libr Cin and Hamilton County Sci and Tech Dept 800 Vine St Cincinnati OH 45202-2071 Office Phone: 513-369-6938. Business E-Mail: marybeth.brestel@cincinnatilibrary.org.

BRETHAUER, WILLIAM RUSSELL, JR., claim investigator; b. Pitts., Apr. 5, 1953; s. William Russell and Cecelia Helen Brethauer; m. Barbara L. Summers, Mar. 8, 1980; children: Laura Diane, Stacey Lynn. BA magna cum laude, Thiel Coll., 1975; grad., Inst. Paralegal Tng., Phila., 1976. Cert. paralegal, casualty-property claim law assoc. Claim rep. St. Paul Cos. Inc., Ft. Washington, Pa., 1977-80, claim supr. San Jose, 1980-82, St. Paul, 1982-84, spl. claim investigator Orlando, Fla., 1984—. Intern WQED-TV, Pitts., 1974; mem. Fla. adv. com. arson prevention, Maitland, 1984—. Author: (novel) Boardwalk, 1991, (book) If I Were A Horse, They'd Shoot Me, 1993, My Enemies, Small Devils, 1993, Insurance Fraud: Deceit & Ingenuity, 1992; asst. prodr.: (multi-media program) When to Say When, 1974. Libertarian. Avocations: whitewater rafting, windsurfing, rollerblading, skiing, travel. Home and Office: PO Box 621329 Oviedo FL 32762-1329

BRETHERTON, CHRISTOPHER STEPHEN, science educator; arrived in US, 1967; s. Francis Patton and Inge Bretherton; m. Alison Catherine Cullen, Oct. 29, 1994; children: Ross, Kyle. BS, Calif. Inst. Tech., 1980; PhD, MIT, 1984. From asst. to assoc. prof. U. Wash., Seattle, 1985—96, prof., 1996—. Affiliate scientist Nat. Ctr. for Atmospheric Rsch., Boulder, Colo., 2002—; lead scientist NSF/NOAA, 2003—. Editor: Jour. the Atmospheric Scis., 1995—99; contbr. articles to profl. jours. Grantee, NSF, 1988—93. Fellow: Am. Meteorol. Soc.; mem.: Am. Geophys. Union. Avocations: hiking, mountain climbing, skiing. Office: Univ Wash Dept Atmospheric Scis PO Box 351640 Seattle WA 98195-1640

BRETON, TRACY ANN, journalist; b. N.Y.C., July 16, 1951; BA in Journalism, Polit. Sci., Syracuse U., 1973. Reporter Danbury (Conn.) News-Times, summer 1972; reporter in legal affairs Providence Jour.-Bull., 1973-99, investigative reporter, 1999—. Vis. prof. dept. English and pub. policy Brown U., 1997—. Contbr. articles to N.Y. Times, New Woman mag., other profl. and popular publs. Mem. R.I. Supreme Ct. Com. on Cameras in Courtroom, Providence. Recipient Best Feature Story for large met. newspaper award UPI, 1976, Service to Women in R.I. award Gov.'s Permanent Adv. Commn. on Women, 1977, Pulitzer Prize for investigative reporting, 1994, Master Reporter award New Eng. Soc. Newspaper Editors, 1995. Mem. U.S. Tennis Assn. (R.I. bd. dirs.), Phi Kappa Phi. Avocations: tennis, gourmet cooking, theater, travel. Home: 174 Columbia Ave Cranston RI 02905-3800 Office: Providence Jour 75 Fountain St Providence RI 02902-0050 Office Phone: 401-277-7362. E-mail: tbreton@projo.com.

BRETT, ARTHUR CUSHMAN, JR., banker; b. Bronxville, N.Y., Mar. 23, 1928; s. Arthur Cushman and Mary Kathryn (Clark) B.; m. Mary Elizabeth Cunliffe, Aug. 21, 1954; children: Margaret Brett Uzarski, Catherine Brett Main, John, Patricia, Matthew BS, Fordham U., 1953; MBA, NYU, 1959. Asst. v.p. Bowery Savs. Bank, N.Y.C., 1950-68; instl. registered rep. Salomon Bros., N.Y.C., 1968-71, 73-75, Blyth Eastman Dillon, Boston, 1971-73; v.p. Mut. Am. Life Ins. Co., N.Y.C., 1975-78; v.p. investments, sec. East River Savs. Bank, N.Y.C., 1978-80; sr. v.p., treas., chief investment officer Apple Bank for Savs., N.Y.C., 1980-92. Mem. investment com. Social Sci. Rsch. Coun., 1976-86, NYU Fed. Credit Union, 1983-89. Mem.: NY Soc. Security Analysts. Roman Catholic. Home: 2514 Redding Rd Fairfield CT 06824-1745 also: 441 Ocean Ave Stratford CT 06615-7829

BRETT, EDWARD TRACY, historian, educator; b. Oceanport, NJ, Dec. 5, 1944; s. Edward Christopher and Marion Tracy Brett; m. Donna Marie Whitson, Sept. 9, 1967; children: Tracy Brett Dunlap, Erin Marie. BA, Loyola U., 1967; MA, La. State U., 1973; PhD, Rutgers U., 1979. Asst. prof. history Coll. Santa Fe, 1981—84; prof., chmn. history dept. LaRoche Coll., Pitts., 1984—. Archbishop Oscar Romero lectr., 1992; lectr. U. Notre Dame, 1992. Author: Humbert of Romans, 1984, Murdered in Central America, 1988 (Christopher award, 88), The Catholic Press in Central America, 2003. With USN, 1967—70. Inst. for Study of Am. Evangelicals rsch. grantee, Wheaton Coll./Pew Found., 1994. Democrat. Roman Catholic. Avocations: swimming, travel. Home: 220 Kinvara Dr Pittsburgh PA 15237 Office: LaRoche Coll 9000 Babcock Blvd Pittsburgh PA 15237

BRETT, HARRY P., lawyer; b. Bklyn., June 8, 1950; BA, SUNY, Stony Brook, 1971; JD, NY Law Sch., 1978. Bar: NY 1979, US Dist. Ct. So., Ea., We., & No. Districts NY 1979, US Supreme Ct. 1993, US Ct. Appeals 2nd Cir. Criminal investigator, 1974—78; joined Wilson, Elser, Moskowitz, Edelman & Dicker LLP, NYC, 1978, now ptnr., chmn. firm hiring com., co-chmn. general liability practice group. Mem.: Am. Soc. Indsl. Security, NY State Trial Lawyers Assn. Office: Wilson Elser Moskowitz Edelman & Dicker LLP 23rd Fl 150 E 42nd St New York NY 10017-5639 Office Phone: 212-490-3000 ext. 2282. Office Fax: 212-490-3038. Business E-Mail: bretth@wemed.com.

BRETT, JAN CHURCHILL, illustrator, author; b. Hingham, Mass., Dec. 1, 1949; d. George and Jean (Baxter) Brett; m. Daniel Bowler, Feb. 27, 1970 (div. Jan. 1979); 1 child, Lia Bowler; m. Joseph Hearne, Aug. 18, 1980. Student, Colby Jr. Coll., 1968-69, Boston Mus. Fine Arts Sch., 1970; DHL (hon.), Fitchburg State Coll., 1996. Mem. bd. overseers Boston Symphony Orch., 1991—99, trustee, 1999—, Thayer Acad., Braintree, Mass. Mem.: Nat. Soc. Colonial Dames Am., Chilton Club. Office: 132 Pleasant St Norwell MA 02061-2523 E-mail: janbrett@janbrett.com.

BRETT, JAY ELLIOT, lawyer; b. Somerville, N.J., June 4, 1931; s. Mac and Blanche (Kamerman) Brett; m. Marcia Barmon, July 17, 1955; children: Peter Barmon, Julie Picard, Amy Kamerman. BS, Cornell U., 1953; LLB, Harvard U., 1958. Bar: NY 1958, US Dist Ct (we dist) NY 1959, US Ct Int Trade 1965. Ptnr. Cohen Swados Wright Hanifin Bradford & Brett, Niagara Falls, NY, 1958—2001, Blair & Roach LLP, Niagara Falls, 2001—. Vice-chmn, mem exec comt Amherst Rep Comt, NY, 1970—83; del Rep Nat Conv, Kansas City, Mo., 1976. With U.S. Army, 1953—55, Korea, maj. U.S. Army, 1961—62. Mem.: Bar Asn City Niagara Falls (pres 1979), Erie County Bar Asn, NY State Bar Asn, Assn Trial Lawyers Am, Niagara Club (bd dirs). Home: 212 Woodbury Dr Amherst NY 14226-2531 Office: Blair & Roach LLP PO Box 846 256 3rd St Niagara Falls NY 14303-0846 Office Phone: 716-285-6981. E-mail: jebtalk@aol.com.

BRETT, JOHN BRENDAN, JR., corporate advertising and public relations executive; b. Mar. 28, 1944; s. John Brendan and Vera Mae (Locke) B.; m. Alyene Maybeth Wales, Apr. 30, 1966; children: Heather Allyson, Sean Timothy. Student, U. Md., 1964-65, U. So. Miss., 1965-66; BS in Advt., U. Fla., 1969. Advt. supr. Armstrong Cork Co., Lancaster, Pa., 1969-72; mgr. advt. K-D Mfg. Co., Lancaster, 1972-75; dir. mktg. comm. Brodart Inc., Williamsport, Pa., 1975-78; mktg. comm. supr. E.I. duPont de Nemours & Co., Wilmington, Del., 1978-80, group mgr. mktg. comm., carpet fibers, 1980-85, mgr. corp. advt., 1985-87, group mgr. mktg. comm. electronics, 1987-91, sr. cons., external affairs, 1991-92; mgr. mktg. commn. and pub. affairs Sontara Tech./Dupont Nonwovens, Old Hickory, Tenn., 1992-99, global brand mgr., 1999—2001; dir. alumni rels. and grant programs Aquinas Coll., Nashville, 2001—. Mem. Idea98 & Idea2001 com. INDA Nonwovens Assn., 1997-99; mem. advt. adv. coun. U. Fla., 1984-87. Mem. editl. sounding bd. Advertising Age mag., 1985-87. Vice chmn. Del. all-star football game com. Del. Found. for Retarded Children, 1982-83, chmn., 1984, trustee, 1989-92; bd. govs. Automotive Advertisers Coun., 1975; mem. vestry St. Thomas Episc. Ch., Lancaster, Pa., 1974-75, St. David's Episc. Ch., Wilmington, 1989-92, sr. warden, 1991-92; treas. N.E. Missionary Convocation, Diocese of Mid. Tenn., Diocesesan Conv. Del., 1995; chmn. bldg. com. Country Hills Homeowners Assn., 1994-2000, sec. bd. dirs., 2000-02; mem. stewardship com. St. Timothy Luth. Ch., Hendersonville, Tenn., 2003-05 Recipient Outstanding Advt. Campaign award Am. Bus. Press/Bus.-Profl. Advt. Assn., 1974. Mem. Assn. Nat. Advertisers (corp. advt. com. 1985-86), Mid-Tenn. Classic Chevy Club (v.p. 2002, treas. 2003-04), Antique Automobile Club of Am., Alpha Delta Sigma, Kappa Tau Alpha. Avocations: outdoor photography, gardening, antique autos. Home: 170 Woodlake Dr Gallatin TN 37066 Office: Aquinas Coll 4210 Harding Rd Nashville TN 37205 Office Phone: 615-297-7545. Business E-Mail: brettj@aquinas-tn.edu.

BRETT, NANCY HELÉNE, artist; BFA, Wayne State U., 1969; MFA, Cranbrook Acad. of Art, 1972. One-woman shows include Gallery Seven, Detroit, 1976, Ericson Gallery, N.Y.C., 1980, Harm Bouckaert Gallery, N.Y.C., 1982, Hillwood Art Mus., C.W.Post, Long Island U., N.Y., 1987, L'Ecole Gallery, N.Y.C., Victoria Munroe Gallery, N.Y.C., 1989, 91, 93, Victoria Munroe Fine Art, N.Y.C, 1993, Lake George Arts Project, N.Y., 1996, The Painting Ctr., N.Y.C., 1997, Cranbrook Art Mus., 1998, Hyde Collection Art Mus., Glen Falls, N.Y., 1999; group shows include Mich. Focus, Detroit Inst. of Art and Grand Rapids Mus. of Art (Catalog), 1974, Mus. of Modern Art, Touchstone Gallery, N.Y.C., 1979, Susan Caldwell, N.Y.C., 1979, Landscape Anthology, Grace Borgenicht Gallery, N.Y.C., 1988, Lines of Vision: Drawings by Contemporary Women, Blum Helman Warehouse and Hillwood Art Mus., Long Island U. Catalog, N.Y., 1989, Notions of Place: Paintings and Drawings, Victoria Munroe Gallery, N.Y.C., 1990, The Painters, 1991, Summer Salon, 1992, Celebrating Nature, Champion Internat. Corp. Collection Exhibit., Stamford, Conn., 1991, Landscape Not Landscape, Gallery Camino Real, Boca Raton, Fla. Catalog, 1994, Bklyn. Mus. Art, Gasworks Gallery, London, Cornerstone Gallery, Manchester, U., Gallery Camino Real, Boca Raton, Fla., 1994, U. Art Mus., 1994, Gallery at Hastings-on-Hudson, Mcpl. Bldg., N.Y., 1995, West Eng., Bristol, 1996, Parsons Gallery, 1996, Bklyn. Mus. Art, 1997, Hyde Collection Art Mus., Glens Falls, N.Y., 1998, Exit Art/The first World, N.Y., 1999, Wendy Cooper Gallery, Madison, Wis., 2000, Williamsburg Art and Hist. Ctr., Bklyn., 2000, Akus Gallery, Ea. Conn. State U., Willimantic, Conn., 2000, Exit Art/The First World, N.Y.C., 2002, Sperone Westwater Gallery, N.Y.C., 2002, Courthouse Gallery, Lake George, N.Y., 2002, A.I.R., N.Y.C., 2002, numerous others; represented in pub. collections: J.P. Morgan, Morgan Guaranty Trust Co., N.Y., Champion Internat., Stamford, Conn., Amerada Hess Corp., GE, Manhattan Savings Bank, Milbank, Tweed, Hadley and McCloy, N.Y.C., Herbert F. Johnson Mus. of Art, Cornell U., Prudential Ins., Best Products, IBM, Morgan Stanley, N.Y.C., Cranbrook Acad of Art Mus., Kidder Peabody, Inc., Hosp. Corp. Am., Power Inst. of Fine Arts, Sydney, Australia, IBM, GE, Princess Cruise Lines, Marsh and McClennan Cos. Inc., Libr. of Congress, Washington. Studio: 457 Broome St New York NY 10013-2681

BRETT, PETER D., writer; b. Jackson, Mich., Apr. 23, 1943; s. Benjamin Thomas Brett and Fanchon (Hillsburg) Eidelman; m. Janet G. Brett; 1 child, Rebecca Hoffman. BS in Biology, Wayne State U., 1965; postgrad., U. Mich., 1970. Writer Peter Brett Assocs., San Rafael, Calif., 1970—. Cons. Sierra Club, San Francisco, 1975; grant writer City of Richmond, 1972; cons., tech. writer Sch. of Holography, San Francisco, 1970-72; lectr. U. Calif., San Diego, 1978. Author: Crossing Paradise, 1970 (Hopwood award 1970), Ghost Rhythms, 1976, Gallery, 1978, Borrowing the Sky, 1978. Fellow U. Colo., 1969-70. Home: 149 W Visoso Highlands Dr Tucson CA 85755 Office: Peter Brett Assocs 501 B St San Rafael CA 94901 Office Phone: 415-459-2566. E-mail: peterbrett415@aol.com, bestres@aol.com.

BRETT, THOMAS RUTHERFORD, federal judge; b. Oklahoma City, Oct. 2, 1931; s. John A. and Norma (Dougherty) B.; m. Mary Jean James, Aug. 26, 1952; children: Laura Elizabeth Brett Tribble, James Ford, Susan Marie Brett Crump, Maricarolyn Swab. BBA, U. Okla., 1953, LL.B., 1957, JD, 1971. Bar: Okla. 1957. Asst. county atty., Tulsa, 1957; mem. firm Hudson, Hudson, Wheaton, Kyle & Brett, Tulsa, 1958-69, Jones, Givens, Brett, Gotcher, Doyle & Bogan, 1969-79; judge U.S. Dist. Ct. (no. dist.) Okla., Tulsa, 1979—. Bd. regents U. Okla., 1971-78; mem. adv. bd. Salvation Army; trustee Okla. Bar Found. Col. JAG, USAR, 1953-83. Named to Okla. Heritage Assn. Hall of Fame, 2000. Fellow Am. Coll. Trial Lawyers, Am. Bar Found.; mem. Okla. Bar Assn. (pres. 1970), Tulsa County Bar Assn. (pres. 1965), Am. Judicature Soc., U. Okla. Coll. Law Alumni Assn. (bd. dirs.), Order of Coif. Democrat.

BRETTELL, RICHARD ROBSON, art historian, museum consultant, educator; b. Rochester, N.Y., Jan. 17, 1949; s. Herbert Robson and Ellen (Sackett) B.; M. Zoe Caroline Bieler, June 9, 1973. BA, Yale U., 1971, MA/PhD, 1977. Acad. program dir., asst. prof. history of art U. Tex., Austin, 1976-80; Searle curator European painting Art Inst. of Chgo., 1980-88; dir. The Dallas Mus. of Art, 1988-92; founding dir. McKinney Ave. Contemporary, 1992-93; prof. visual aesthetic studies U. Tex., Dallas, 1998—; adj. sr. curator Meadows Mus. SMU, 2003—. Adj. prof. Northwestern U., Evanston, Ill., 1984-88; vis. prof. Yale U., 1994, Harvard U., 1995; prin. organizer exhbns. The Art of the Edge: European Frames, Art Inst. Chgo., 1986, The Art of Paul Gauguin, Nat. Gallery, Washington, 1988-89, Art Inst. Chgo., Grand Palais, Paris, Pissaro: Urban Series, 1992-93, Dallas Mus. of Art, Royal Acad., Camille Pissarro in the Caribbean 1850-55, St. Thomas and the Jewish us., 1997, Impression: Painting Quickly in France, 1860-1890, Nat. Gallery London, Van Gogh Mus., Clark Inst., 2000-2001; mem. organizing com. Camille Pissarro, The Hayward Gallery, London, 1980-81, Grand Palais, Mus. Fine Arts, Boston. Author: Pisarro and Pontoise, 1990, Modern Art: Capitalism and Representation, 1999, Impression: Painting Quickly in France, 1860-1890, European Drawings from the Rbt Lehmann Collection; co-author: The Art of Paul Gauguin, 1988, Painters and Peasants in the 19th Century, 1983, A Day in the Country: Impressionism and the French Landscape, 1984, Degas in the Art Inst. of Chgo., 1984, (exhbn. catalogues) Gauguin, 1988. Bd. dirs. Mus. African-Am. Life, Dallas, 1988, DARE, 1991—; mem. Dallas Com. for Internt. Cultural Affairs, 1988. Decorated Chevalier Order of Arts and Letters (France); vis. fellow J. Paul Getty Mus., spring 1985; fellow Nat. Endowment for Humanities, summer 1980, U. Rsch. Inst. U. Tex., Austin, summer 1978, The Whiting Found, 1975-76, Samuel Kress fellow, Yale U., 1974-75. Mem. Coll. Art Assn. Am. (bd. dirs. 1986-89), Midwest Art History Assn., Soc. Archtl. Historians, Am. Assn. Museums, The Getty Grant Program (publs. com. 1987-91), Elizabethan Club. Avocation: piano playing.

BRETTHAUER, ERICH WALTER, chemist, educator; b. Denver, Sept. 12, 1937; s. Walter V. and Lucy E. B.; m. Sharlene Marie Stimpson, Oct. 10, 1966; children: Terrance Magee, Anthony Magee, Heidi, Erich Walter II. BS, U. Nev., 1960, MS, 1962. Various sci. rsch. and mgmt. positions Pub. Health Svc. and EPA, 1962-68; dir. monitoring ops. div. EPA, Las Vegas, 1978-79, dir. nuclear radiation assessment div., 1979-80, detail to U.S. radiation policy coun. Washington, 1980-81, lab. dir. Office Rsch. Devel. Enivron. Monitoring Systems Lab. Las Vegas, 1985-89, asst. administr. Office Rsch. & Devel. Washington, 1990-93; rsch. prof. U. Nev., Las Vegas, 1993-95. Congl. fellow U.S. Senate Com. on Environ. and Pub. Works, 1982—; recipient Gold medal for directing and monitoring outreach program at Three Mile Island EPA, 1979. Mem. Am. Chem. Soc., Am. Water Works Assn., Sigma Xi.

BRETTSCHNEIDER, RITA ROBERTA FISCHMAN, lawyer; b. Bklyn., Nov. 12, 1931; d. Isidore M. and Augusta T. (Singer) Fischman; m. Bertram D. Brettschneider, June 25, 1950 (dec. Nov. 17, 1986); children: Jane Brettschneider, Joseph Brettschneider; m. Bertram D. Cohn, June 30, 1991 (dec. July 2002). BA, CUNY, 1953; JD, Bklyn. Law Sch., 1956; postgrad., NYU, 1968-69, Nat. Inst. Trial Advocacy, 1976. Bar: N.Y. 1961, U.S. Dist. Ct. N.Y. 1971. Pvt. practice, Huntington, NY, 1961. Instr. women and the law C.W. Post Coll., Brookville, N.Y., 1969-70; arbitrator med. malpractice arbitration com. Suffolk County (N.Y.), 1974-76; spl. assoc. prof. philosophy and law New Coll. Hofstra U., Hempstead, N.Y., 1974-76; faculty N.Y. Law Jour. Conf. Changing Concepts in Matrimonial Law, 1976; legal advisor Am. Arbitration Assn., 1977-84; arbitrator night small claims ct. Nassau County, 1978-83; of counsel Nassau County Psychol. Assn., 1987—, Suffolk County Psychol. Assn., 1990-95. Contbr. numerous articles to profl. jours. Pres., bd. dirs. For Our Children and Us, 1992—2001. Mem. Nassau-Suffolk Women's Bar Assn. (chair judiciary com. 1974-80), Nassau County Bar Assn. (demonstrating atty. mock trial contested matrimonial action 1975), Suffolk County Bar Assn. (demonstrating atty. mock trial contested matrimonial action 1976), Am. Arbitration Assn. (legal advisor 1977-84), Nassau-Suffolk Women's Bar Assn. (pres. 1980-81). Home: 2 Crosby Pl Cold Spring Harbor NY 11724-2403 Office: Brettschneider & Brettschneider 83 Prospect St Huntington NY 11743-3306 Office Phone: 631-367-3111. Personal E-mail: vember@aol.com.

BRETZ, KELLY JEAN RYDEL, actuary, consultant; b. Wadena, Minn., Oct. 30, 1962; d. Edmund Leroy and Glenyce Clara (Andrie) B.; m. Daniel Mark Bretz Rydel; children: Michael Charles Bretz Rydel, Alexa James Bretz Rydel. BA in Math., Moorhead State U., 1984. Chartered fin. analyst; profl. risk mgr. Asst. actuary Northwestern Nat. Life Ins. Co. (now ING Reliastar), Mpls., 1984-92; assoc. actuary TMG Life Ins. Co. (Clariea part of Sun Life), Fargo, ND, 1993-94, MSI Life Ins. Co., Arden Hills, Minn., 1994, MidAm. Mut. Life Ins. Co., Roseville, Minn., 1994-95; actuarial officer Fortis Fin. Group, Woodbury, Minn., 1996—2001; v.p. and sr. portfolio mgr. US Bank, Mpls., 2001—02; ind. cons. Minn., 2002—03; dir. pricing and fin. evaluation Thrivent Fina. for Lutherans, Mpls., 2003—. Grader Soc. Actuaries' Exam 220, 1992, 93. Contbr. articles to co. jours. Organizer blood drive Mpls. Blood Bank, 1992; meal deliverer Meals on Wheels, Fargo, 1993; meal server Sharing and Caring Hands, Mpls., 1992. Fellow Soc. Actuaries (mem. fin. and investment mgmt. practice edn. com. 1995-96); mem. Am. Acad. Actuaries, Twin Cities Actuarial Club, Life Ins. Mktg. and Rsch. Assn. (fin. mktg. and svcs. com. 1993). Avocations: scuba diving, outdoor and indoor physical activies. Office: 625 Fourth Ave S Minneapolis MN 55415-1665 Office Phone: 612-340-7193. E-mail: kellybretz@aol.com.

BRETZFELDER, DEBORAH MAY, retired museum staff member; b. Hazelton, Pa., Sept. 21, 1932; d. Joseph and Rose (Smulyan) Hirsh; m. Robert Bretzfelder, Dec. 24, 1955; children: Karl, Marc. Student, Syracuse U., 1950-53. Textile colorist, designer Cohn-Hall-Marx, N.Y.C., 1954-55; fashion coordinator Hecht's Dept. Store, Washington, 1956; freelance artist Washington, 1956-58; exhibits technician Smithsonian Instn., Washington, 1958-59, supr. exhibits prodn., 1959-63, exhibits specialist Nat. Mus. Am. History, 1963-75, visual info. specialist, project mgmt. officer, 1975-83, acting chief design, 1983, chief design, 1983-87, assoc. asst. dir. exhibits and pub. spaces, 1987-88; ret., 1988. Cons. various firms., orgns., mus. personnel; instr. mus. programs; freelance photographer and exhibit designer; project dir. Contbr. works to various publs.; musician: violin sect. George Washington U. Orch., 1965—2003, violin sect. Georgetown Symphony Orch., 2003—. Mem.: Fiber Arts Study Group, Nat. Mus. Women in Arts, Nat. Soc. Hist. Preservation, Am. Assn. Mus., Tau Sigma Delta. Jewish. Home: 2748 Woodley Pl NW Washington DC 20008-1517 Office Phone: 202-232-7665. Personal E-mail: drbretzfelder@hotmail.com.

BRETZIUS, DAVID CHARLES, music educator; b. Pottsville, Pa., Dec. 21, 1954; s. Charles Edward and Mardelle Helen Bretzius; m. Karen Lee Bretzius, June 24, 1978; children: Krista, Matthew. BS in Music Edn. K-12, West Chester U., 1976, M in Music Edn., 1981. Music tchr. Phoenixville (Pa.) Area Sch. Dist., 1976—; organist 1st United Meth. Ch., Phoenixville, 1980—. Pres. Phoenixville Area Edn. Assn., 1998—2000; adj. prof. West Chester U., 2005—. Composer: (church hymn) Sing 'till sundown, 1988. Mem.: Pa. State Edn. Assn., Pa. Music Educators Assn., Phi Mu Alpha. Democrat. Methodist. Avocations: reading, sketching, composing, gardening. Home: 435 Brook Dr Spring City PA 19475 Office: Barkley Elem Sch 320 2d Ave Phoenixville PA 19460 Office Phone: 484-927-5300.

BREUER, BRADFORD R., former museum director; m. Lynne Breuer. Grad., Austin Coll. Past dir. The Alamo, San Antonio. Bd. trustees Amon Carter Mus., Ft. Worth; mem. adv. bd. Ctr. for Southwestern & Mexican Studies Austin Coll.; past pres. San Antonio Mus. Assn. Office: c/o Amon Carter Mus 3501 Camp Bowie Blvd Fort Worth TX 76107-2695*

BREUER, NANCY LOIS, management consultant; b. Paterson, N.J., Oct. 20, 1947; d. Edward Jr. and Lois Mary Breuer; m. S. Scott Bartchy, Nov. 19, 1988. BA cum laude, Middlebury (Vt.) Coll., 1969; MA, Fuller Theol. Sem., Pasadena, Calif., 1983. Instr. English Monument Mt. Regional High Sch., Great Barrington, Mass., 1969-72, South Burlington (Vt.) High Sch., 1972-77; writer Regal Books, Glendale, Calif., 1977-79; asst. dir. extended edn. Fuller Theol. Sem., Pasadena, 1979-84; dir. contract edn. ARC, L.A., 1984-89, dir. HIV/AIDS edn., 1989-91; cons., writer Breuer Cons., L.A., 1991—. Course designer, facilitator trainer Hollywood Supports, 1992—. Author: A Guide to Self Care for HIV Infection, 1991, AIDS in the Workplace: Facilitator's Manual, 1993, (with others) AIDS in the Workplace, 1994; editor jour. Pacific Ctr., 1991-94; contbr. articles to profl. jours. Mem. exec. com. Am. Lung Assn., L.A., 1984-87; commr. L.A. County AIDS Commn., 1989-91; chair AIDS in the workplace com. United Way, L.A., 1988—. Recipient Med. Category award for video U.S. Indsl. Film & Video Festival, 1992, Pro award Publicity Club L.A., 1993. Mem. ASTD, Am. Mgmt. Assn., Nat. Leadership Coalition on AIDS. Avocation: running. Office: Breuer Cons 2260 N Cahuenga Blvd Apt 207 Los Angeles CA 90068-2799

BREUER, STEPHEN ERNEST, religious organization administrator; b. July 14, 1936; came to U.S., 1938, naturalized, 1945; s. John Hans Howard and Olga Marion (Haar) B.; m. Gail Fern Breitbart, Sept. 4, 1960 (div. 1986); children: Jared Noah, Rachel Elise; m. Nadine Bendit, Sept. 25, 1988. BA cum laude, UCLA, 1959; gen. secondary credential, 1960. Tchr. L.A. City Schs., 1960-62; dir. Wilshire Blvd. Temple Camps, L.A., 1962—84; instr. Hebrew Union Coll., L.A., 1965-76, 1992—, field instr., 1977-81; dir. Edgar F. Magnin Religious Sch., L.A., 1970-80; field instr. San Francisco State U., 1970-80; exec. dir. Wilshire Blvd. Temple, L.A., 1980—2004; instr. U. Judaism, 1991; field instr. Calif. State U., San Diego; prin., exec. dir. Steve Breuer Assocs.: Consulting Nonprofits, LA, 2005—; exec. dir. Progressive Assn. Reform Day Schs., 2005—. Exec. dir. Progressive Assn. of Reform Day Schs., 2005—. V.p. L.A. Youth Programs Inc., 1967-77; youth advisor L.A. County Commn. Human Rels., 1969-72, bd. dirs. Cmty. Rels. Conf. So. Calif., 1965-85; bd. dirs. Alzheimer's Disease and Related Disorders Assn., 1984-95, v.p. L.A. County chpt., 1984-86, pres., 1986-88, nat. exec. com., 1987-95, nat. devel. chair, 1992-95, Calif. state coun. pres. 1987-92, chmn. of Calif. gov.'s adv. com. on Alzheimer's disease, 1988-97; mem. goals program City of Beverly Hills, Calif., 1985-91; bd. dirs. Pacific S.W. regional Union Am. Hebrew Congregations, 1985-88, nat. bd., exec. com., 1993-97; bd. dirs. Echo Found., 1986-88, Mazon-Jewish Response to Hunger, 1993-97, 2003-, Wilshire Stakeholders exec. com., 1987-94, Internat. Rescue Com. West Coast Bd., 1999-2005; treas. Wilshire Cmty. Prayer Alliance, 1986-88; active United Way; founded Steve Breuer Consulting for Non Profits, 2005—. Recipient Svc. award L.A. County Bd. Suprs., 1982, 87, Ventura County Bd. Suprs., 1982, 87, L.A. City Coun., 2005, Weinberg Chai Lifetime Achievement award Jewish Fed. Coun. L.A., 1986, Nat. Philanthropy Day L.A. medallion, 1993, Recognition award L.A. County Redevel. Agy., 1994, award L.A. Bus. Coun., 1997, award L.A. City Coun., 2005, Sherut L'am Svc. to People award Hebrew Union Coll., 2005; Steve Breuer Conference Ctr. named in his honor at Wilshire Blvd. Temple Camps, Malibu, 1990. Mem.: ASCD, NATA, Nata Breuer Leadership Fund, Progressive Assn. Reform Day Schs. (exec. dir. 2005—), Jewish Profl. Network, So. Calif. Conf. Jewish Communal Workers, Am. Mgmt. Assn., Jewish Communal Profls. So. Calif., Profl. Assn. Temple Adminstrs. (pres. 1985—88), L.A. Assn. Jewish Edn. (bd. dirs.), Nat. Assn. Temple Educators (Kaminker curriculum award 1973), Nat. Assn. Temple Adminstrs. (nat. bd. dirs. 1987—, v.p. 1991—93, pres. 1993—97, Svc. to Judaism award 1989, Svc. to the Cmty. award 1990, Svc. award 1994, Steve Breuer Leadership Fund established 2004), So. Calif. Camping Assn. (bd. dirs. 1964—82), Assn. Reform Zionists Am. (bd. dirs. 1993—98), People for the Am. Way, Los Angeles County Mus. Contemporary Art, Maple Mental Health Ctr. of Beverly Hills, Living Desert, Wildlife Fedn., Ctr. for Environ. Edn., Wilderness Soc., UCLA Alumni Assn, World Union for Progressive Judaism, Jewish Resident Camping Assn., Amnesty Internat. Office: Wilshire Blvd Temple 3663 Wilshire Blvd Los Angeles CA 90010-2798 Office Phone: 213-388-2401. Personal E-mail: sebwbt@aol.com. Business E-Mail: seb@wbtla.org.

BREUER, WERNER ALFRED, retired plastics company executive; b. Sinn, Hessia, Germany, Jan. 30, 1930; came to U.S., 1959; s. Christian and Hedwig (Cunz) B.; m. Gertrud Ackermann, June 21, 1950 (dec. 1998); children: Patricia, Julia, Eva-Maria. LLB, La Salle Ext. U., 1970; BS in Human Rels. and Orgnl. Behavior, U. San Francisco, 1983; MS in Bus. Mgmt., U. La Verne, 1985, DPA, 1988. Lab. supr. Dayco Corp. (Am. latex divsn.), Hawthorne, Calif., 1959-65; tech. ops. mgr. Olin Corp., Stamford and New Haven, Conn., 1965-69; gen. mgr., exec. v.p. Expanded Rubber and Plastics Corp., Gardena, Calif., 1969-96; ret., 1996; gen. mgr. Schlobohm Co. Inc., Dominguez Hills, Calif., 1989-96; ret. Cons. human resources Stabond Corp., Gardena, 1988-95. Author/composer various recordings, 1970s; contbr. articles to jours. Founder Worlds Peace and Diplomacy Forum, Cambridge, England; founding mem. Nat. Campaign for Tolerance in Am. Recipient Portfolio award, USF, Calif., 1984, Lifetime Achievement award, IBC, 2001, Am. Medal of Honor award, 2002. Mem. ASTM, ASCAP, Am. Soc. for Metals, Soc. for Plastics Engrs., N.Y. Acad. Scis., Nat. Space Soc., Planetary Soc., U. La Verne Alumni Assn. Republican. Achievements include pioneering use of plastics especcially polyurethanes in defence missiles and space and communication aviation industry; defense projects from DEW Line N.A. radar to stealth bomber, B-2 project. Home: 835 Sanctuary Cir Longmont CO 80501-2355

BREUER, WILLIAM BENTLEY, author; Frequent keynote spkr.; guest numerous radio shows and TV programs; former guest lectr. salesmanship, publicity and promotion seminars. Author: An American Saga, 1982, Bloody Clash at Sadzot, 1982 (transl. into Belgian), Captain Cool, 1983, They Jumped at Midnight, 1983, Drop Zone Sicily, 1984 (transl. into Japanese and French), Hitler's Fortress Cherbourg, 1984, Agony at Anzio, 1985 (transl. into Czechoslovakian), Storming Hitler's Rhine, 1985 (transl. into Serbo-Croatian), Death of a Nazi Army, 1985, Operation Torch, 1986, Retaking the Philippines, 1987, Devil Boats, 1987 (transl. into Japanese), Operation Dragoon, 1988 (transl. into French), The Secret War with Germany, 1988, Sea Wolf, 1989, Nazi Spies in America, 1989, Geronimo!, 1990, Hoodwinking Hitler, 1993, Race to the Moon, 1993 (transl. into Burmese, Choice award ALA 1995), The Great Raid on Cabanatuan, 1994 (made into film The Great Raid 2004), J. Edgar Hoover and His G-Men, 1995, MacArthur's Undercover War, 1994 (transl. into Polish), Feuding Allies, 1995 (trans. into Polish), Shadow Warriors, 1996, War and American Women, 1997, Unexplained Mysteries of World War II, 1997 (transl. into Polish, Czech and Chinese), Vendetta: Castro and the Kennedy Brothers, 1997 (transl. into Polish), Undercover Tales of World War II, 1998, Top Secret Tales of World War II (transl. into Japanese), 1999, Secret Weapons of World War II (trnasl. into Arabic and Chinese), 2000, Daring Missions of World War II, 2001 (transl. into Polish and Chinese), Deceptions of World War II, 2002 (transl. into Polish), The Air-Raid Warden Was a Spy, 2002, The Spy Who Spent the War in Bed, 2003, Guts!, 2005. Sgt. U.S. Army, WWII. Recipient numerous awards. Hon. mem. numerous vets. assns. Home: 3815 Westview Dr NE Cleveland TN 37312-5057

BREVERMAN, HARVEY, artist; b. Pitts., Jan. 7, 1934; s. Theodore and Sarah (Haffner) B.; m. Deborah Dobkin, June 26, 1960. BFA, Carnegie Mellon U., 1956; MFA, Ohio U., 1960. Tchr. Carnegie Mellon U., summer 1959; tchr. drawing Ohio U., Athens, 1960-61, Ill. State U., Normal, summer 1969, Falmouth (Eng.) Art Sch., 1969; prof. art Univ. at Buffalo, 1961—99, SUNY disting. prof., 1999—. Resident painter State Acad. Fine Arts, Amsterdam, 1965-66, vis. painter Kalamazoo Inst. Art, summer 1972, 73, vis. artist Oxford U., 1974, 77, U. Mich., 1978, Md. Inst. Coll. Art, 1984, 92d St. Y, N.Y.C., 1989, Coll. William and Mary, 1990, Skidmore Coll., 1990, Pont Aven Sch. Art, France, 1995, Jagiellonian U., Poland, 1997; one man shows include Albright-Knox Art Gallery, Buffalo, 1967, 89, U. Oreg., U. Ill., 1970, Canton (Ohio) Art Inst., 1971, 87, Middlebury Coll., 1973, FAR Gallery, N.Y.C., 1974, 79, Gadatsy Gallery, Toronto, 1975, 76, 79, 80, 87, Kalamazoo Inst. Art, 1976, Hackley Art Mus., Muskegon, Mich., 1977, Grand Rapids (Mich.) Art Mus., 1977, Gadatsy Gallery, Toronto, 1978, 81, 84, U. Mich., 1978, Nardin Galleries, N.Y.C., 1980, U. N.H., 1981, Art Gallery of Hamilton, 1981, Hollins U., 1982, Niagara U., 1984, Miami (Ohio) U. Art Mus., 1987, Meml. Art Gallery, Rochester, N.Y., 1988, Wenniger Gallery, Boston, 1988, St. Lawrence U., 1989, Taller Galeria Ft., Cadaqués, Spain, 1990, Babcock Galleries, N.Y.C., 1990, 91, Brigham Young U., 1993, Nina Freudenheim Gallery, Buffalo, 1994, Butler Inst. Am. Art, 1997, Yeshiva U. Mus., N.Y.C., 1997, 2002, Milton Weill Gallery, N.Y.C., 1997, Gertrude Herbert Inst. Art, Augusta, Ga., 2000, Ind. U. Sch. Fine Arts Gallery, Bloomington, 2001; group shows at Corcoran Biennial, Wash., 1963, Bklyn. Mus., 1964, Assn. Am. Artists, N.Y.C., 1965, Rijksakademie, Amsterdam, 1968, Boston Mus. Fine Arts, 1968, NAD, 1968, Pa. Acad. Fine Arts Biennial, 1969, Brit. Internat. Biennialz, Bradford, Eng., 1970, 72, FAR Gallery, 1972-74, Whitechapel Gallery, London, 1973, Pushkin Mus., Moscow, 1972, 2d Norwegian Internat. Biennial, 1974, Mus. Modern Art, Oxford, 1974, Honolulu Acad. Fine Arts, 1975, 8th Internat. Art Fair, Basel, Switzerland, 1977, Auslands Institut, Dortmund, W. Ger., 1977, Arte Fiere '78, Bologna, 1978, Art Gallery Ont., Toronto, 1979, Am. Acad. and Inst. Arts and Letters, N.Y.C., 1980, 81, NYU, 1980, Jewish Mus., N.Y.C., 1982, Queens Mus., N.Y.C., 1983, Rose Art Mus., Brandeis U., 1985, Minn. Mus. Art, St. Paul, 1985, Roger Ramsay Gallery, Chgo., 1986, Va. Mus. Fine Arts, Richmond, 1986, Lever House Gallery, N.Y.C., 1986, Albright-Knox Art Gallery, 1987, Harvard U., Carpenter Ctr., 1987, Mus. Art, San Juan, P.R., 1987, Contemporary Arts Ctr., Cin., 1988, Mus. of Fine Arts, Houston, 1988, Oakland (Calif.) Mus., 1988, 8th Print Internat., Barcelona, 1988, 4th Internat. Print Biennal, Taipei Fine Arts Mus., 1989, Inst. Contemporary Art, Boston, 1990, La Jolla Mus. Contemporary Art, 1990, Grand Palais, Paris, 1990, Yurakucho Art Forum, Tokyo, 1991, Denver Art Mus., 1991, Scottsdale Ctr. for the Arts, 1991, NAD, N.Y.C., 1992, Internat. Print Triennal, Krakow, Nüremberg, 1994, 97, 2000, 03, Mus. Applied Arts. Belgrade, 1995, XIII Premio Internat. Per L' Incisione, Biella, Torino, 1997, Bermuda Nat. Gallery, 1997, 9th Internat. Print Biennale, Varna, Bulgaria, 1997, Beijing Internat. Ex-Libris Exhbn., China, 1998, Embassy of France, La Maison Française, Washington, 1998, Florean Mus., Carbunari, Romania, 1999, 2001, 02, Mus. Civico Di Grafica, Brunico, Italy, 1999, Chateau du Puget, Alzonne, France, 1999, 12th Deutsche Internat. Grafik Triennale, Frechen, Germany, 1999, De Mini Gravura, Vitoria, Brasil, 2000, Bankside Gallery, London, 2000, Quingdao Internat. Print Biennial, China, 2000, Lahti Art Mus., Finland, 2000, Temple Gallery, Rome, 2002, Inst. for Advanced Art and Culture, Aix-en-Provence, France, 2002, 4th Egyptian Internat. Triennial, Cairo and Alexandria, 2003, 1er Concours Internat. d'Exlibris, Ankara and Istanbul, Turkey, 2003, Zeichen der Gegenwart, Vienna Art Gallery, Austria, 2003, L'Espace Melanie, Riec-Sur-Belon, Brittany and Mona Bismark Found., Paris, 2003, Internat. Print and Drawing Exhbn., Silpakorn U. Art and Culture Ctr., Bangkok, 2003, Gracefield Arts Ctr., Dumfries, Scotland, 2003-04, Adam Michewicz U., Poznan, Poland, 2005, Lefkas, Greece, 2005; also traveling exhibits in U.S., Europe, Ctrl. Am., Japan, paintings forU.S.embassies, 1976; represented in permanent collections Mus. Modern Art, N.Y.C., Whitney Mus., Art Gallery of Windsor, Ontario, Can., Albright-Knox Art Gallery, Phila. Mus., Butler Inst. Art, Youngstown, Ohio, Nat. Mus. Am. Art, Washington, Libr. of Congress, Israel Mus., Jerusalem, Bradford City Art Mus., St. Catharines Dist. Arts Coun., Ont., Can., Victoria and Albert Mus., London, Cleve. Mus., Balt. Mus. Art, Nat. Portrait Gallery, Washington, Brit. Mus., London, Hunterian Art Gallery, Glasgow, Met. Mus. Art, N.Y.C., Smithsonian Inst., Washington, others. Served with AUS, 1956-58, Korea. Grantee Louis Comfort Tiffany Found., 1962, Netherlands Govt., 1965, N.Y. Coun. Arts, 1972; named fellow NEA, 1974-75, 80-81, Va. Ctr. for the Creative Arts, 1992; elected mem. Nat. Acad. Design, N.Y.C., 1992; recipient Hassam-Speicher award Am. Acad. Arts and Letters, 1990, 91, Nat. Alumni Assn. medal of merit Ohio U., 1992, Disting. Tchg. Art award Coll. Art Assn. N.Y.C., 2003. Address: 76 Smallwood Dr Snyder NY 14226-4027

BREW, WAYNE WILLIAM, geography educator; b. Wilkes-Barre, Pa., June 16, 1958; s. John and Shirley Brew; m. Lorelle Logan Brew, Oct. 22, 1983; children: Catherine, John Logan. BS in Earth Sci., Pa. State U., 1980, BS in Geography, 1981; MA in Geography, Temple U., 1991. Sr. project geologist Roy F. Weston Inc., West Chester, Pa., 1984—2000; geography instr. Montgomery County C.C., Blue Bell, Pa., 2000—04, asst. prof. geography, 2004—. Geography coord. Montgomery County C.C., Blue Bell, 2003—; presenter in field. Mem.: Pioneer Soc. Am., Assn. Am. Geographers. Avocations: running, bicycling, field trips. Office: Montgomery County CC 340 DeKalb Pike Blue Bell PA 19422

BREWER, BARBARA BAGDASARIAN, nursing administrator; b. Providence, Apr. 18, 1950; d. Bagdasar and Grace (Sarkisian) Bagdasarian; m. Timothy F. Brewer III, May 28, 1983. BSN, U. R.I., 1972; MA in Liberal Studies, Conn. Wesleyan U., 1986; MSN, Yale U., 1988; MBA, Columbia U., 1992; PhD, U. Ariz., 2002. RN, Ariz., Conn., R.I., Ind. Staff nurse Miriam Hosp., Providence, R.I., 1972; head nurse orthopeds. unit Frisbie Meml. Hosp., Rochester, N.H., 1973-76; staff nurse St. Francis Hosp. and Med. Ctr., Hartford, Conn., 1976; clin. coord. continuing care unit Middlesex Meml. Hosp., Middletown, Conn., 1976-86; dir. cardiology svcs. Lawrence and Meml. Hosp., New London, Conn., 1988-92, v.p. ambulatory svcs., 1992-95; adminstrv. leader emergency svcs. Tucson Med. Ctr., 1996-97; rsch. assoc. U. Ariz., Coll. of Nursing, 1998—2001; predoctoral fellow NIH, 1999—2002; project dir. U. Ariz., 2001—03; v.p. quality Clarian Health Ptnrs., 2003—05; dir. profl. practice John C. Lincoln Hosp., North Mountain, 2005—. Rschr. in field. Co-author: Improving Your Skills in 12-Lead ECG Interpretation, 1990. Mem.: ANA, Ind. Nurses Assn., Am. Orgn. Nurse Execs., Sigma Theta Tau (treas. Beta Mu chpt. 2001—03). Office Phone: 602-331-5882. E-mail: bbrewe@jcl.com.

BREWER, CAREY, retired academic administrator; b. Lynchburg, Va., July 8, 1927; s. James Allen and Esther Goode (Leftwich) B.; m. Betty Ann Brighton, Sept. 3, 1949; children— Mary Elizabeth, Robert Allen, Ruth Ann, Catherine Lee. BA, Lynchburg Coll., 1949; student, Am. U., 1951; M.P.A., Harvard U., 1952, PhD, 1956. Analyst with legislative reference service Library of Congress, 1949-56; sr. def. specialist mil. ops. subcom. Ho. of Reps., 1956-60; mem. staff joint com. atomic energy U.S. Congress, 1960-61; various positions Office Emergency Planning, Exec. Office of Pres., 1961-64; pres. Lynchburg Coll., 1964-83. Lectr. Am. U., 1954-56; Mem. bd. higher edn., also mem. gen. bd., ch. fin. council Christian Ch. (Disciples of Christ); mem. Pres.'s Civil Def. Adv. Council, 1970-72; Bd. dirs. Nat. Lab. for Higher Edn.; pres. Va. Found. Ind. Colls., 1978-80 Author: Civil Defense in the United States, 1951, Implications of a National Service Program, 1952, Science and Defense, 1956, also numerous articles. Served with USNR, 1945-46. Littauer fellow Harvard, 1951-53 Mem. Council Ind. Colls. Va. (pres. 1972-74), Greater Lynchburg C. of C. (past pres.) Mem. Christian Ch. Clubs: Sphex, Waterfront Golf.

BREWER, CHARLES MOULTON, lawyer; b. Washington, June 9, 1931; BS, U. Md., 1953; JD, George Washington U., 1957. Bar: Ariz. 1959. Since practiced in, Phoenix; law clk. to Chief Justice Ariz. Supreme Ct. Levi S. Udall, 1958-59; pvt. practice, 1959—; pres. Charles M. Brewer Ltd.; airline transport pilot, 1977—. Guest lectr. Stanford U. Law Sch., Ariz. State U. Law Sch.; funded endowment Ariz. State U., 1985; mem. plaintiffs steering com. Northwest Crash Case, 1987. Contbr. articles to profl. jours. Bd. visitors Ariz. State U. Law Sch. Named one of Best Lawyers in Am. Mem.: ATLA, ABA, Atty.'s Info. Exch. Group, Fed. Bar Assn., Nat. Bar Assn., Trial Lawyers for Pub. Justice, Assn. Trial Lawyers Am., Lawyers-Pilots Bar Assn., Assn. Trial Lawyers, Internat. Acad. Trial Lawyers, Am. Bd. Trial Advs., Ariz. Trial Lawyers Assn., Maricopa County Bar Assn., Ariz. Bar Assn. Mailing: 5500 N 24th st Phoenix AZ 85016 Office Phone: 602-381-8787. Business E-Mail: cmbrewer@cmbrewer.com.

BREWER, DENNIS LEE, minister, writer; b. Owsley County, Ky., Jan. 9, 1948; s. Robert Brewer and Emma Mae Bowman; m. Lucille Sebastian, Oct. 6, 1967; children: Scottie Joe, John Bowman. BS in Edn., Ea. Ky. U., 1972; ThM, SBTS, Louisville, Ky., 1976; D of Ministry, Luther Rice Sem., Jacksonville, Fla., 1978. Pastor and county missionary Beattyville 1st Bapt. Ch., Ky., 1972—90; dir. missions Red River Assn. of Baptists, Beattyville, Ky., 1978—86; sr. pastor Unity Bapt. Ch., Richmond, Ky., 1992—. Moderator Red River Assn. of Baptists, Beattyville, Ky., 1976—80; nominating com. Ky. Bapt. Conv., Louisville, 1988—91, missions com., 1993—96, executive bd.; pres. Richmond Area Ministerial Assn., Ky., 1996—98; moderator Tates Creek Assn. of Baptists, Richmond, Ky., 2003—; pres. Lee County Ministerial Assn., Beattyville, Ky. Author: (collection of short stories) Tales From Sturgeon Creek, (historical book) The Land of Lee, (historical work) Baptist Beginnings; contbr. articles to profl. jours. Pres. Highland Pk. Homeowners Assn., Richmond, Ky., 2000—01, Lee County C. of C., Ky. Named Ky. Col., Gov. Louie B. Nunn, Hon. Col., Commr., Ky. State Police, 1986. Mem.: Kiwanis (life; Ky.-Tenn. dist. chmn. Builders Club, Disting. Lt. Gov.). R-Consevative. Southern Baptist. Office: Unity Bapt Ch 1290 Barnes Mill Rd Richmond KY 40475

BREWER, JANICE KAY, state official, property and investment firm executive; b. Hollywood, Calif., Sept. 26, 1944; d. Perry Wilford and Edna Clarice (Bakken) Drinkwine; m. John Leon Brewer, Jan. 1, 1963; children: Ronald Richard, John Samuel, Michael Wilford. Med. asst. cert. Valley Coll., Burbank, Calif., 1963, practical radiol. technician cert., 1963; D in Humanities (hon.) L.A. Chiropractic Coll., 1970. Pres., Brewer Property & Investments, Glendale, Ariz., 1970—; mem. Ariz. Ho. of Reps., Phoenix, 1983-86, Ariz. Senate, 1987-96, majority whip, 1993-96; mem. Maricopa County Bd. Suprs., 1997-2002; sec. of state State of Ariz., Phoenix, 2003-. State committeeman, Rep. Party, Phoenix, 1970, 1983; legis. liaison Arrowhead Repuolia Women; treas. Nat. Assn. Lt. Gov., 2004; bd. dirs. Motion Picture & TV Commn. Active NOW. Recipient Freedom award Vets. of Ariz., 1994; named Woman of Yr., Chiropractic Assn. Ariz., 1983, Legislator of Yr., Behaviour Health Assn. Ariz., 1991, NRA, 1992. Mem. Nat. Fedn. Rep. Women, Am. Legis. Exch. Coun. Lutheran. Office: 7th Fl State Capitol 1700 W Washington Phoenix AZ 85007-2808

BREWER, JESSE WAYNE, entomologist, educator; b. Rives, Mo., Oct. 10, 1940; s. Jesse J. and H. Faye Brewer; m. Sandra J. Ewald, Jan. 2, 1990; children: Laura E. Davis, Matthew W. PhD, Purdue U., Ind., 1968. Head dept. entomology Mont. State U., Bozeman, 1984—87, Auburn U., Ala., 1987—95, prof., 1995—. Author: about 75 refereed jour. articles in sci. jours. Mem. Orgn. of Tropical Studies, Durham, NC, 1988—2000. Grantee Vis. Scientist, Nat. Acad. of Sci., 1968, 1969, 1983, 1987. Mem.: Entomol. Soc. of Am. (exec. com. 2003—). Avocations: sports cars, hiking, skiing, snow shoeing. Home: 2114 Springwood Dr Auburn AL 36830 Office: Auburn Univ Dept of Entomology Funchess Hall Rm 301 Auburn AL 36849 Personal E-mail: brewejw@auburn.edu.

BREWER, JOHN CHARLES, journalist; b. Cin., Oct. 24, 1947; s. Harry Marion and Barbara Ann (Burrier) B.; m. Adeline Laude, Dec. 22, 1973 (div. 1994); children: Andrew John, Jeffrey Joseph; m. Ann Hagen Kellett, 1997. BS, Calif. State Poly. U., Pomona, 1970. Newsman, photographer Daily Report, Ontario, Calif., 1967-69; newsman AP, L.A., 1969-74, news editor, 1974-75, asst. chief bur. Seattle, 1975-76, chief of bur., 1976-82, L.A., 1982-86, gen. exec. membership dept. N.Y.C., 1986-88; exec. editor news svc. The N.Y. Times, 1988-90, editor in chief news svc., 1990-97; pres. N.Y. Times Syndication Sales Corp., 1990-97; publisher, editor Peninsula Daily News, Port Angeles, Wash., 1998—. Bd. dirs. Port Angeles C. of C., Olympic Meml. Hosp. Found., Port Angeles Downtown Assn. Mem. Fedn. of Fly Fishers, Northwest Steelheaders-Trout Unlimited, Nat. Steelhead Trout Assn., Rotary Internat., Kiwanis. Republican. Roman Catholic. Office: Peninsula Daily News 305 W 1st St Port Angeles WA 98362-2205 Office Phone: 360-417-3500. Business E-Mail: john.brewer@peninsuladailynews.com. *I enjoy very much being a journalist and newspaper executive. Nothing can compare with it. As for finding time for everything— the news and photo reports, relations with advertisers and subscribers, my family, my personnel, problems—always the problems—I am reminded of a woman who had eleven children. She was asked how she had time to take care of all of them. She replied that when she had one child it took 100 percent of her time, and eleven could not take more. I think there's an analogy in this.*

BREWER, JOHNNY REGINALD, music educator; b. Andalusia, Ala., Nov. 10, 1972; s. Betty and Johnny Reginald Brewer; m. Frances Jeannan Castleberry, June 12, 1999; 1 child, Jonathan Grant. MusB in Edn., Troy State U., 1998, MS, 2002. Cert. tchr. Ala., 1998. Dir. of bands Andalusia Mid. Sch., Ala., 1998—2003; asst. dir. of bands Andalusia H.S., Ala., 1998—2003; music instr. Lurleen B. Wallace C.C., Andalusia, Ala., 2003—. Dir. LBW

Ensemble, Andalusia, Ala., 2003—. Designer Red Deer Royals Show Band (marching band drill design) 1812 Overture. Dir. Lads to Leaders/Leaderettes program Evergreen Ch. of Christ, Ala., 2003—04; v.p. publicity Ala. Hiking Trail Soc., Inc., Montgomery, 2003—05. Named Tchr. of Yr., Walmart, 2002; New Tchr. Assistance grant, Ala. Power Coop., 1999. Republican. Avocations: hiking, backpacking, scuba diving, convertibles, fishing. Home: 25624 Antioch Rd Andalusia AL 36421 Office: Lurleen B Wallace CC PO Box 1418 Andalusia AL 36420 Office Phone: 334-881-2238. Business E-Mail: jbrewer@lbwcc.edu.

BREWER, KAREN, librarian; b. Janesville, Wis., Apr. 29, 1943; d. Gordon A. and Charlotte (Warren) Schultz; m. Eugene N. Brewer, June 22, 1963. BA, U. Wis., 1965, MA, 1966; PhD, Case Western Res. U., 1983. Libr. Middleton Med. Libr. U. Wis., Madison, 1966-67; libr. Med. Libr. U. Tenn., Memphis, 1968-69; libr. Cleve. Health Sci. Libr. Case Western Res. U., Cleve., 1970-76; dir. libr. Coll. Medicine Northeastern Ohio U., Rootstown, 1976-88; dir. libr. Med. Ctr. NYU, 1988—. Mem. editl. bd. Ann. Stats. Acad. Health Sci. Libr., 1986—91. Fellow N.Y. Acad. Medicine; mem. Assn. Acad. Health Sci. Librs. (sec.-treas. 1986-89, pres. 1995), Med. Libr. Assn. (bd. dirs. 1991-94), Acad. Health Info. Profls. (disting. mem.), Am. Med. Informatics Assn. Office: NYU Med Ctr Libr 550 1st Ave New York NY 10016-6402

BREWER, KELLY DEANNE, pharmaceutical sales specialist, oncological nurse; b. Lynwood, Calif., Aug. 19, 1966; d. Otis Lee and Judy Cornelia Brewer. BSN, Brigham Young U., Provo, UT, 1987. RN. Staff nurse LDS Hosp., Salt Lake City, 1988; on call staff UT Valley Regional Med. Ctr., Provo, 1988, oncology nurse, 1993—2000; oncology sales specialist Alza Pharmaceuticals, Calif., 2000—01, Ortho-Biotech, 2001, Novartis Pharmaceuticals Oncology Divsn., 2002—. Adv. bd. Alza Pharmaceuticals, Calif., 2000; ATAQ rep. Amgen, Calif.; presenter at meetings. Contbr. articles nursing publ. Treas. UT Water Ski Club. Mem.: Oncology Nursing Soc. (cert. oncology nurse 1994). Avocations: water-skiing, bicycling, hiking, skiing, cooking. E-mail: kellybrewer19@yahoo.com.

BREWER, LEWIS GORDON, judge, law educator; b. New Martinsville, W.Va., Sept. 6, 1946; s. Harvey Lee and Ruth Carolyn (Zimmerman) B.; m. Kathryn Anne Yunker, May 25, 1985. BA, W.Va. U., 1968, JD, 1971; LLM, George Washington U., 1979. Bar: W.Va. 1971, Calif. 1978. Commd. 2d lt. USAF, 1968, advanced through grades to col., 1988, dep. staff judge adv. Travis AFB, Calif., 1976—78, chief civil law San Antonio Air Logistics Ctr. Kelly AFB, Tex., 1979-83, staff judge adv. MacDill AFB, Fla., 1983—86, chief Air Force Cen. Labor Law Office Randolph AFB, Tex., 1987-88, dep. staff judge adv. Air Tng. Command, 1988-89, staff judge adv. 7th Air Force Osan AFB, Korea, 1989-91, 45 Space Wing Patrick AFB Fla., 1991-93; adminstrv. law judge W.Va. Edn. and State Employee Grievance Bd., Charleston, 1993-2000, mediator, 1994—; legal counsel W.Va. Ethics Commn., Charleston, 2000, exec. dir., 2004—. Instr. bus. law No. Mich. U., Marquette, 1972, Solano Coll., Suisun City, Calif., 1978; instr. labor law Webster U., Ft. Sam Houston, 1983. Decorated Air Force Commendation medal, Meritorious Service medal, Legion of Merit. Mem. ABA, Assn. for Conflict Resolution, W.Va. Bar Assn., State Bar Calif., W.Va. U. Alumni Assn., George Washington U. Alumni Assn. Roman Catholic. Home: 528 Sheridan Cir Charleston WV 25314-1063 Office: 210 Brooks St Ste 300 Charleston WV 25301-1826 Office Phone: 304-558-0664. Business E-Mail: lbrewer@wvadmin.gov. E-mail: mede8wv@abanet.org.

BREWER, MARILYNN B., psychology professor; PhD social psychology, Northwestern U., 1968. Dir. Inst. Social Sci. Research, UCLA; prof. psychology UCLA, Ohio State U., 1993. Editor Personality & Social Psychology Rev. Jour. Recipient Kurt Lewin Award, SPSSI, 1995, Donald T. Campbell Award for Distinguished Research Social Psychology, 1992. Fellow: Am. Acad. Arts & Sci.; mem.: Soc. Psychol. Study Social Issues (pres. 1984—85), Soc. Personality & Social Psychology (pres. 1990—91), Am. Psychol. Soc. (pres. 1993—95). Office: Dept Psychology Ohio State U 1885 Neil Ave Columbus OH 43210-1222 Office Phone: 614-292-9640. E-mail: Brewer.64@osu.edu.*

BREWER, MARK COURTLAND, lawyer; b. Hammond, Ind., Apr. 1, 1955; s. Harold Russell and Carol Joan (Odell) B. BA, Harvard U., 1977; JD, Stanford U., 1981. Bar: U.S. Dist. Ct. (ea. and we. dist.) Mich. 1983, U.S. Ct. Appeals (6th cir.) 1983. Law clk. U.S. Ct. Appeals (5th cir.), Austin, 1981-82; law clk. to justice Mich. Supreme Ct., Lansing, 1982-83; assoc. Sachs, Waldman, O'Hare, P.C., Detroit, 1983-89; mem. Sachs, Waldman & O'Hare, Detroit, 1989-95. Pres. Stanford Pub. Interest Law Found. Palo Alto, Calif., 1980-81; bd. dirs. Mich. Protection and Adv. Svc., Lansing, Mich. Contbr. articles on AIDS discrimination, drug testing, and employee privacy to profl. publs. Mem. Macomb County Dem. Com., Mich., 1982—, 12th Congl. Dist. Dem. Com. Macomb County, 1983-93, 10th Congl. Dist. Dem. Com. Macomb County, 1993—2003; chmn. Mich. Dem. Party; vice chair Dem. Nat. Com. Mem. ATLA, ABA, FBA (pres. ea. dist. Mich., bd. dirs. 1999-2000), State Bar Mich. (Outstanding Young Lawyer 1988), Mich. Trial Lawyers Assn., Assn. State Dem. Chairs (pres.), Sierra Club. Democrat. Lutheran. Office: Mich Democratic Party 606 Townsend St Lansing MI 48933-2313 Office Phone: 517-371-5410.

BREWER, NATHAN RONALD, veterinarian, consultant; b. Albany, N.Y., June 28, 1904; s. William and Rose (Johnson) B.; m. Jean Lees, Apr. 1, 1936; children: Maureen Pasik, Sandra Ginsberg, Jacquelyn Fechter. BS, Mich. State U., 1930, DVM, 1937; PhD in Physiology, U. Chgo., 1936; DSc (hon.), Chgo. Coll. Osteo. Medicine, 1977. Diplomate Am. Coll. Lab. Animal Medicine. Instr. pharmacology U. Ill., Chgo., 1935-36; veterinarian Detroit Bd. Health, 1937-38; prof. physiology Middlesex Vet. Sch., Waltham, Mass., 1938-39; pvt. practice Irvington (now Fremont), Calif., 1940-45; assoc. prof. physiology, dir. lab. animal facilities U. Chgo., 1945-69; pvt. cons. Chgo., 1969—. Contbr. articles to profl. jours. Named Man of Yr., Nat. Soc. Med. Rsch., 1956; recipient Arthur Brown award Delaware Valley Coll., 1983, Disting. Vet. Alumni award Mich. State U., 1997, Centennial award Del. Valley Coll., 1997, Rowsell award The Scientists Ctr. for Animal Welfare. Mem. Am. Assn. Lab. Animal Sci. (life, dist. svc. award 2000, pres. emeritus 2003), Am. Vet. Med. Assn. (chmn. various coms., Charles River award 1992, Animal Welfare award 2001), Nat. Acad. Sci. (chmn. parasitism com. 1953-58), Ill. State Vet. Med. Assn. (life), Chgo. Vet. Med. Assn. (life), Am. Physiol. Soc., Conf. Rsch. Workers in Animal Diseases, Ill. State Acad. Sci. (chmn. animals in rsch. com. 1968), Am. Assn. Lab. Animal Sci. (editor 1950-62, pres. 1950-55. editor emeritus, chmn. arrangements com. 1950-53, 59, 62, 66, Griffin award 1960, Ann. Nathan R. Brewer award established in his name 1994—), Nat. Acad. Sci. Inst. Lab. Animal Resources, Am. Coll. Lab. Animal Medicine (pres. 1957-59), Am. Soc. Vet. Physiologists and Pharmacologists, Am. Soc. Lab. Animal Practitioners (chmn. mgmt. practice com.), Ill. Acad. Vet. Practice. Avocation: chess. Home and Office: 10800 Tara Rd Potomac MD 20854-1340

BREWER, PETER GEORGE, ocean geochemist; b. Ulverston, Eng., Dec. 30, 1940; came to U.S., 1967, naturalized, 1982; s. Frederick and Irene (Clarkson) B.; m. Hilary Williams, Mar. 29, 1966; children: Jillian Anne, Alastair Michael, Erica Christine. BSc, Liverpool (Eng.) U., 1962, PhD, 1967. From asst. scientist to sr. scientist Woods Hole Oceanog. Inst., Mass., 1967—78, sr. scientist, 1978—91; program dir. marine chemistry NSF, 1981—83; exec. dir. Monterey Bay Aquarium Rsch. Inst., Pacific Grove, Calif., 1991—96, sr. scientist, 1996—. Leader of ocean sci. expeditions; mem. Environ. Task Force, 1992-93, NAS Ocean Studies Bd., 1986-94, Com. on Climate Change and the Ocean, 1987-90; convenor NATO A.R.I. on Chem. Dynamics of Upper Ocean, Jouy en Jossas, France, 1983; mem. NAS panel on policy implications of greenhouse gas warming: mitigation, 1989-91; mem. NAS carbon dioxide adv. com., 1982-83; vis. prof. U. Wash., 1979; mem. GEOSECS sci. adv. com., 1972-78. Assoc. editor: Geophys. Rsch. Letters, 1977-79, Jour. Marine Rsch., 1974-81, Deep-Sea Rsch., 1984-87, Jour. of Oceanography, 1994—; contbr. articles to profl. jours. Chmn. Gordon Rsch. Conf. on Chem. Oceanography, 1980; vice-chmn. Joint Global Ocean Fluxes Com., SCOR, 1987-90; mem. adv. bd. Applied Physics Lab., U. Wash., 1991-96. Grantee NSF, NASA, Office Naval Rsch., Dept. Energy. Fellow AAAS, Am. Geophys. Union. Office: Monterey Bay Aquarium Rsch Inst 7700 Sandholdt Rd Moss Landing CA 95039-0628 E-mail: brpe@mbari.org.

BREWER, PHILIP WARREN, retired civil engineer; b. Hagerstown, Md., Dec. 18, 1923; s. J. Chester and Ruth (Emmert) B.; m. Elizabeth Marvel Wynn, Aug. 29, 1947; children: Dorothy Wynn, Bruce Douglas. BS, U. Md., 1945. Hydraulic engr. Water Resources Br., U.S. Geol. Survey, College Park, Md., 1945-47; designing engr. Wash. Suburban San. Commn., Hyattsville, Md., 1947-53; sanitary engr., civil engr. Bur. Yards and Docks, Dept. Navy, Washington, 1953-68; head spl. design Naval Facilities Engring. Command, 1968-73, chief civil engr., 1973-80. Bd. dirs. Madison County Wildlife Assn., Monument River Sportsmen's Assn. (Houlton, Maine). Mem. Madison County Wildlife Assn. (bd. dirs.), Monument River Sportmen's Club (Houlton, Maine). Episcopal. Home: 2600 Barracks Rd Apt 271 Charlottesville VA 22901-2193

BREWER, RICHARD B., biotechnology company executive; BS in Biology, Va. Poly. Inst. and State U.; MBA, Northwestern U. With Genentech, Inc., 1984—95; sr. v.p. U.S. sales and mktg. Genentech Europe Ltd. and Genentech Can., Inc.; exec. v.p. ops. Heartport, Inc., 1996—98, COO; pres., CEO, dir. Scios Inc., Sunnyvale, Calif., 1998—. Mem. adv. bd. Kellogg Grad. Sch. Mgmt., Ctr. for Biotech., Northwestern U., 2001—; mem. corp. roundtable Am. Heart Assn., 1993—94, chmn. pharm. roundtable, 1994—95.

BREWER, ROBERT ALLEN, physician; b. Inpls., Jan. 29, 1927; s. Robert Dewayne and Viola Mae (Grant) B.; m. Mildred Noreen Barnett, Jan. 1, 1950 (dec. May 1997); children: Robert A. Jr., Raymond, Richard, Brian, Andrew. AA, St. Petersburg Jr. Coll., Fla., 1949; AB, Ind. U., 1952; MD, Ind U., Inpls., 1955. Emergency dept. staff physician Mound Park Hosp., St. Petersburg, Fla., 1960; staff physician Pinellas Hosp., Largo, Fla., 1961-68; pvt. practice Logansport, Ind., 1969—. Mem. Cass County Republican Com., Logansport, Ind., candidate for city coun., 1995. Capt. U.S. Army, 1957-59. Mem. AMA, Am. Acad. Family Practitioners (bd. cert. diplomate), Ind. Med. Assn., Cass County Med. Assn. Republican. Avocations: stamp collecting/philately, coin collecting/numismatics. Office: PO Box 119 831 E Broadway Logansport IN 46947-3161 E-mail: drrbrewer@kconline.com.

BREWER, ROGENNA WYNNE, writer; b. Fon du Lac, Wis., Apr. 12, 1961; d. Roger Wayne Bean and Gloria Ann (Amend) Madien; m. Jeffrey Reagan Brewer, Jan. 22, 1986; children: Todd Eugene, Tyler Wayne, Troy Roger. Interior design diploma, Southern Coll., Orlando, Fla., 1984. Bookseller, reviewer, Colo., 1990—98; writer, 1998—. Author: (book) Midway Between You and Me, 2002, Sign, Seal, Deliver, 2001 (Romantic Times Top Pick, 2001), Seal It with a Kiss, 1999 (Romantic Times Top Pick, 1999, Romantic Times Reviewers Choice nominee, 2000, Booksellers Best nominee, 2000, 3d pl. Blue Boa, 2000), Aspen Gold, 2000 (1st pl. Long Contemporary, 2000), Heart of the Rockies (working title: Puss in Boots), 1997 (1st pl. Long Contemporary, 1997). With USN, 1980—85. Mem.: Colo. Romance Writers (pres. 1997), Heart of Denver Romance Writers (founding pres. 1998), Romance Writers of Am. Avocations: reading, gardening.

BREWER, ROY EDWARD, lawyer; b. Atlanta, Dec. 22, 1949; s. Roy Mullins and Martha JoAnn (Still) Brewer; m. Catherine Elizabeth Schindler, May 5, 1979; children: Garrett Edward, Alex Winston. BA in Polit. Sci., U. Fla., 1971, MA in Polit. Sci., 1973; JD, U. Pacific, 1982. Bar: Calif. 1984, U.S. Dist. Ct. (ea. dist.) Calif. 1984, U.S. Supreme Ct. 1990. Regional planner North Cen. Fla. Regional Planning Council, Gainesville, Fla., 1975-78; dir. met. affairs Sacramento Met. C. of C., 1978-79; dir. land planning Raymond Vail and Assocs., Sacramento, 1979-84; pvt. practice Sacramento, 1984-89; ptnr. Hunter McCray Richey & Brewer, Sacramento, 1989-95, Hunter, Richey, DiBenedetto & Brewer, Sacramento, 1995—2000, mng. ptnr., 1993—2000; ptnr. The Brewer Law Firm, 2000—. Bd. dirs. Am. River Natural History Assn., 1986—90, pres., 1988—89; bd. dirs. No. Calif. Rugby Football Union, 1985—88, pres., 1985—88; chmn. Sacramento Ad-hoc Charter Comm., 1988—90; bd. dirs. Healthcare, 1987—90, chmn., 1988—89; bd. dirs. Sacramento Met. C. of C., 1985—91, pres., 1990; trustee ARC, 1989—90; chmn. Local Govt. Reorgn. Com., 1988; chair Leadership Sacramento, 2000, co-chair, 2001—03; fellow Am. Leadership Forum, Mt. Valley Chpt., 2005—; bd. dirs. Sacramento Symphony Assn., 1987—95, Am. Lung Assn., 1988—92, Sacramento Downtown Partnership, 1997—99. Named among Best and Brightest, Sacramento Mag., 1985; recipient Sacramento Regional Pride award for cmty. devel., 1991, Exceptional Performers award, Air Force Assn., 1991, Sacramentan of the Yr. award, 1991. Mem.: Am. Inst. Cert. Planners. Avocations: rugby, karate, scuba diving, snowboarding. Office: The Brewer Law Firm 980 Ninth St Ste 2050 Sacramento CA 95814 Office Phone: 916-325-5588.

BREWER, SCOTT, law educator; b. NYC; BA in Philosophy and Religious Studies, SUNY, Stony Brook, 1979; MA in Philosophy, Yale U., 1980, JD, 1988; PhD in Philosophy, Harvard U., 1997. Law clk. to Judge Harry T. Edwards US Ct. Appeals DC Cir., 1989—90; law clk. to Justice Thurgood Marshall US Supreme Ct., 1990—91; lectr. law Harvard Law Sch., Cambridge, Mass., 1988, asst. prof., 1991—98, prof., 1998—. Office: Harvard Law Sch 1563 Massachusetts Ave Cambridge MA 02138 Office Phone: 617-495-3147. Office Fax: 617-496-4866. Business E-Mail: sbrewer@law.harvard.edu.

BREWER, STEVEN GREGORY, human services administrator; b. Carlisle, Pa., Dec. 11, 1974; s. Steven Ray and Debra Ann Brewer; m. Michelle Suzanne McIntyre-Brewer; children: Aslan Steven McIntyre-Brewer, Cavan Gray McIntyre-Brewer. AA in Liberal Arts, St. Leo Coll., 1995; BA in Psychology, Shippensburg U., 2000, MS in Psychology, 2002. Program advisor III Cumberland-Perry Assn. Retarded Citizens, Carlisle, Pa., 1999—2002; grad. asst. Office Social Equity, Shippensburg U., 2000—02; human svcs. program specialist Dept. Pub. Welfare, Harrisburg, 2002—. Rschr. Pa. Legis., Harrisburg, 2004—; security for dignitaries UN, Republic of Korea, 1996—97; grad. faculty adv. com. Shippensburg U., 2001—02. Author of poems. Advocate Assn. Retarded Citizens, Carlisle, 1999—2002; civic rights advocate Shippensburg Office Social Equity, 2000—02; vol. for blind Star Libr. Program, Newville, 2003; vol. CARES homeless shelter, United Way, 2005; disaster relief vol. ARC, 2005. Sgt. U.S. Army, 1993—99. Mem.: Psi Chi. Achievements include invention of satellite tracking system. Avocations: writing, reading, bicycling. Home: 23 Oak Lane Dr Carlisle PA 17013 Office: Dept Pub Welfare Bur Long-Term Care 1401 N 7th St Harrisburg PA 17102 Office Phone: 717-772-2528. E-mail: stbrewer@state.pa.us.

BREWER, THOMAS BOWMAN, retired university president; b. Ft. Worth, July 22, 1932; s. Earl Johnson and Maurine (Bowman) B.; m. Betty Jean Walling, Aug. 4, 1951; children: Diane, Thomas Bowman Jr. BA, U. Tex., 1954, MA, 1957; PhD, U. Pa., 1962. Instr. St. Stephens Episcopal Sch., Austin, Tex., 1955-56, S.W. Tex. State Coll., San Marcos, 1956-57; from instr. to asso. prof. North Tex. State U., Denton, 1959-66; asst. prof. U. Ky., 1966-67; asso. prof. Iowa State U., 1967-68; prof. history, chmn. dept. U. Toledo, 1968-71; dean Tex. Christian U., Ft. Worth, 1971-72, vice chancellor, dean univ., 1972-78; chancellor East Carolina U., Greenville, N.C., 1978-82; v.p. acad. affairs Ga. State U., Atlanta, 1982-88; pres. Met. State Coll. of Denver, 1988-93; interim provost U. Alaska, Anchorage, 1995-97. Editor: Views of American Economic Growth, 2 vols, 1966, The Robber Barons, 1969; gen. editor: Railroads of America Series. Home: 104 Javelin Dr Austin TX 78734-5016 E-mail: TBBSR@alumni.utexas.net.

BREWER, TIMOTHY FRANCIS, III, retired cardiologist; b. Hartford, Conn., Oct. 30, 1931; s. Timothy F. Brewer Jr. and Catherine Marie (Sullivan) Brewer; m. Norma Rae Flicker, June 14, 1954 (div. Jan. 1980); children: Raymond, Donna, Timothy, Kevin, William; m. Barbara Grace Bagdasarian, May 28, 1983. BA, Yale Coll., 1953; MD, N.Y. Med. Coll., 1957. Diplomate Bd. Internal Medicine Cardiovasc. Diseases. Intern St. Francis Hosp., Hartford, 1957-58; resident in internal medicine VA Ctr., L.A., 1958-60; spl. fellow in cardiovascular diseases Cleve. (Ohio) Clinic, 1960-62; pvt. practice St. Francis Hosp., Hartford, 1962-64; assoc. dir. clin. rsch. Pfizer Inc., Groton, Conn., 1964-71; dir. Clin. Pharmacology Miles Lab., West Haven, Conn., 1971-74; pvt. practice Middlesex Hosp., Middletown, Conn., 1974-96, ret., 1996. Pres. med. staff Middlesex Hosp., Middlesex, Conn., 1981—83, chief cardiology sect., 1988—95. Fellow: ACP, Coun. on Clin. Cardiology, Am. Coll. Chest Physicians (emeritus), Am. Coll. Cardiology (emeritus); mem.: AMA (pres. South Ctrl. Conn. chpt. 1982, bd. dirs. 1980), Am. Heart Assn. (Conn. affiliate). Avocation: golf. E-mail: tfb3@earthlink.net.

BREWER, WANDA EASTWOOD, retired literature educator; b. Dec. 8, 1926; BFA, U. Denver, 1950; MA, U. No. Colo., 1961, EdD, 1968. Tchr. English Greeley Ctrl. H.S., Colo., 1961—62; prof. English U. No. Colo., 1962—91; docent Denver Art Mus., 1992—.

BREWINGTON, ARTHUR WILLIAM, retired English language educator; b. Bklyn., Nov. 10, 1906; s. Oscar and Julia (Wenisch) B.; m. Thelma Sherman, Aug. 18, 1955. AB, Asbury Coll., 1928; MA, Cornell U., 1931; PhD, Vanderbilt U., 1941. Head English dept. Tenn. Wesleyan Coll., Athens, 1929-31; instr. English Pa. State U., State College, 1932-33; prof. English and speech Memphis State U., 1940-43; inspector quality control Glenn Martin Co., Balt., 1943-45; head speech dept. Towson State U., Balt., 1945-71. Dir. drama and theater Towson State U., 1946-69. Contbr. rsch. to profl. publs. Fund-raiser, bd. dirs. Am. Heart Assn., Green Valley, 1995-96. Fulbright grantee U.S. State Dept., 1955-56, Danforth grantee, 1963. Mem. Fulbright Assn. (pres. U. Ariz. chpt. 2001-02), Kiwanis (com. chmn. 1971-95), Masons (chaplain lodge 171 1972-75), Cornell Club, Green Valley Shrine Club (pres. 1974). Democrat. Episcopalian. Avocations: theater, movies, tv, opera, symphony. Home: 69 W Cedro Dr Green Valley AZ 85614-4203 E-mail: art1110@cs.com.

BREWINGTON, JAMES, telecommunications industry executive; b. Idaho; Bachelor's Degree, Coll. Idaho; MBA, U. Seattle; Master's Degree, Stanford U. Joined AT&T, 1968; regional v.p. At&T Network Sys., 1988—90, pres. wireless bus. unit, 1990—95; pres. product realization Lucent Techs. (formerly AT&T Network Sys.), Murray Hill, NJ, 1995—96, pres. wireless network group, 1997—2001, pres. mobility solutions group, 2001—04, pres. developing markets group, 2004—. Bd. dirs. U.S.-Saudi Arabian Bus. Coun., INROADS/North Jersey, Inc.; mem. U.S./Egyptian Pres. Coun. Mem.: Cellular Telecom. Industry Assn. Wireless Found., Cellular Telecom. Industry Assn. Office: Lucent Techs 600 Mountain Ave Murray Hill NJ 07974

BREWSTER, BILL K., former congressman; b. Ardmore, Okla., Nov. 8, 1941; m. Mary Sue Nelson, 1963; children: Balynda Karel, Betsy Kecia (dec.), Bradley Kent (dec.) BS in pharmacy, Southwestern Okla. State U., 1964. Cattleman and farm co-owner; owner, pharmacist, operator Colleyville Drug. Inc. Colleyville, Okla., 1964-77; cattleman Brewster Angus Farms, 1968—; state rep. Okla., 1982-89; mem. 102nd-104th Congresses from 3rd Okla. dist., Washington, 1991-96; pres. R. Duffy Wall and Assoc., Washington, 1996—. Mem. South/West Energy Coun., 1982-90; del. Nat. Conf. of State Legislatures, 1983-90. With USAR, 1968-71. Named Disting. alumnus, Southwestern Okla. State U. Office: Capitol Hill Group 488 South Capitol St SW Ste 608 Washington DC 20003

BREWSTER, CARROLL WORCESTER, former academic administrator; b. NYC, Mar. 26, 1936; s. Carroll Harwood and Blandina (Worcester) B.; m. Ursula Mary Orange, Mar. 9, 1968 (dec. Apr. 1996); children— Abraham Carroll, Ursula Constant, Blandina Worcester. BA, Yale, 1957, LL.B., 1961; L.H.D. (hon.), Hollins Coll., 1981, Hobart and William Smith Coll., 1991; postgrad., Kings Coll., Cambridge U., 1957-58. Bar: Conn. 1962. Law clk. to chief judge U.S. Dist. Ct., Conn., 1961-62; legal asst. to Hon. Mohamed Ahmed Abu Rannat, Chief Justice of the Sudan, Khartoum, 1962-64; assoc. Tyler, Cooper, Grant, Bowerman & Keefe, New Haven, 1965-69, also U.S. commr., 1966-69; lectr. Yale Law Sch., 1967-69; coll. dean Dartmouth Coll., 1969-75; pres. Hollins Coll., Va., 1975-81, Hobart and William Smith Colls., N.Y., 1982-91; exec. dir. Hole in the Wall Gang Fund, New Haven, 1991-98. Trustee Phillips Exeter Acad., 1970-80, Anatolia Coll, 1990—, U. New Haven, 1995-2005; chmn., bd. dirs. Presiding Bishop's Fund for Wold Relief, 1986-91, The Episcopal Ch. Found., 1985-93. Editor: Sudan Law Jour. and Reports, 1961-65. Senior Fulbright scholar, U. Khartoum, Sudan, 1981-82. Home: 126 Lounsbury Rd Ridgefield CT 06877-4730

BREWSTER, CHARLES EDWARD, writer, engineer; b. Pulaski County, Ky., Jan. 24, 1941; s. Theodore and Essie Pearl Brewster; m. Norma Ruth Brewster, Nov. 5, 1962; children: Nancy Louise, Carolyn Sue, David Charles, Evelyn Ruth. A in Engring. Sci. with honors, Sinclair C.C., 1990; B with honors, Christian Bible Coll., 1990, M with honors, 1995, PhD in Theology with honors, 1996; BS in Engring., Calif. Coast U., 2000. Machine tool builder Nat. Cash Register Co., Dayton, Ohio, 1957—67; machinist Litton Industries, Woodland Hills, Calif., 1967—68, Ocean Tech., Burbank, Calif., 1968—69; tool engr., jr. engr. Inland Divsn. Gen. Motors, Dayton, 1969—73, prodn. engr., 1974—79; plant layout engr. Inland-Delco-Delphi Corp., Dayton, 1979—2000; adminstrv. manf. engr. Delphi Corp., Vandalia, Ohio, 2000—. Owner Scriptural Founds., Miamisburg, Ohio, 1996—. Author: Sophia's Unfaithful Lovers, 1996, Secrets of the Ages: Revealed, 2001, What Did God Say?, 2001. Spkr. Evangelical Edn. Ministries, Rockford, Ill., 1999—2000; New Testament Greek classes various local chs., Dayton, Ohio, 2002. Mem.: Ark Found. Dayton, Concerned Women Am. Avocations: guitar, languages, dobro, banjo. Office: Scripural Found Pub PO Box 1103 Miamisburg OH 45343

BREWSTER, ELIZABETH WINIFRED, literature educator, educator, poet, writer; b. Chipman, N.B., Can., Aug. 26, 1922; d. Frederick John and Ethel May (Day) Brewster BA, U. N.B., 1946; MA, Radcliffe U., 1947; BLS, U. Toronto, 1953; PhD, Ind. U., 1962; DLitt, U. N.B., 1982. Cataloger Carleton U., Ottawa, Ont., 1953-57; cataloger Ind. U. Library, Bloomington, 1957-58, N.B. Legis. Library, 1965-68, U. Alta. Library, Edmonton, Can., 1968-70; mem. English dept. Victoria U., B.C., 1960-61; reference libr. Mt. Allison U. Libr., Sackville, N.B., 1961-65; vis. asst. prof. English U. Alta., 1970-71; mem. faculty U. Sask., Saskatoon, Can., 1972—, asst. prof. English, 1972-75, assoc. prof., 1975-80, prof., 1980-90, prof. emeritus, 1990—. Author: East Coast, 1951, Lillooet, 1954, Roads, 1957, Passage of Summer, 1969, Sunrise North, 1972, In Search of Eros, 1974, Sometimes I Think of Moving, 1977, The Way Home, 1982, The Sisters, 1974, It's Easy to Fall on the Ice, 1977, Digging In, 1982, Junction, 1982, A House Full of Women, 1983, Selected Poems 1944-84, 2 vols., 1985, Visitations, 1987, Entertaining Angels, 1988, Spring Again, 1990, The Invention of Truth, 1991, Wheel of Change, 1993, Away from Home, 1995, Footnotes to the Book of Job, 1995, Garden of Sculpture, 1998, Burning Bush, 2000, Jacob's Dream, 2002, Collected Poems, Vol. 1, 2003, Vol. 2, 2004. Recipient E.J. Pratt award for poetry U. Toronto, 1953, Pres. medal for poetry U. Western Ont., 1980, Lit. award Can. Broadcasting Corp., 1991, Lifetime award for excellence in the arts Sask. Arts Bd., 1995, Short List award Gov. Gen., 1996, Sask. Book award for poetry, 2003. Mem. League Can. Poets (life), Writers' Union Can., Assn. Can. Univ. Tchrs. English, Order of Can.

BREWSTER, JAMES HENRY, retired chemistry professor; b. Ft. Collins, Colo., Aug. 21, 1922; s. Oswald Cammann and Elizabeth (Booraem) B.; m. Christine Barbara Germain, Jan. 23, 1954; children— Christine Carolyn, Mary Elizabeth, Barbara Anne. AB, Cornell U., 1942; PhD, U. Ill., 1948. Chemist Atlantic Refining Co., Phila., 1942-43; postdoctoral fellow U. Chgo., 1948-49; instr. Purdue U., 1949-50, asst. prof., 1950-55, assoc. prof., 1955-60, prof., 1960-91, prof. emeritus, 1991—. With Am. Field Service, 1943-45. Fellow AAAS; mem. Am. Chem. Soc., Chem. Soc. (London), Royal Soc. Chemistry, Phi Beta Kappa, Sigma Xi, Phi Lambda Upsilon. Achievements include research in bond molecular orbitals, relation optical rotation and constitution, and origins of life. Home: 334 Hollowood Dr West Lafayette IN 47906-2146 Office: Purdue U Dept Chemistry Lafayette IN 47907 E-mail: jbrewst2@Purdue.edu.

BREWSTER, KENNETH MATTHEW, marketing professional, consultant; s. Cheria Elizabeth Phelps and Kenneth Brewster. BA, U. Ky., 1993. Sales mgr. Blue Green Inc., Gatlinburg, Tenn., 1995—97; cmty. mktg. dir. Fairfield Communities, Sevierville, Tenn., 1997—99; owner Fortress One, Pigeon Forge, Tenn., 1999—2001; dir. mktg. Interval Resorts 1 LLC, Napa, Calif., 2001—. Mktg. cons. Cendant, Anaheim, Calif., 2002—03. Author: (training manual) The Road Less Traveled. Achievements include patents pending for wine Tank Locks. Avocations: music composition, international travel, scubba diving. Home: 3297 Mac Beth St Napa CA 94558 Office: RiverPointe Napa Valley 500 Lincoln Ave Napa CA 94558 Office Phone: 707-252-4200. Home Fax: 707-252-4222; Office Fax: 707-252-4222. Personal E-mail: brewnote@yahoo.com. Business E-Mail: mattb@riverpointenapa.com.

BREWSTER, MARGARET EMELIA, artist; b. Kaukauna, Wis., July 18, 1932; d. Eathen Edward and Emelia Josepha (Jennick) B. Attended, U. Wis., Fox Valley, 1951-53. Photographer, graphic artist Appleton Papers, Inc., Combined Locks, Wis., 1954-90. Exhbns. include Appleton Gallery Arts, 1965-94, Bank of Kaukauna, 1974-2003, Frances Hardy Gallery, Ephraim, Wis., 1984, 86, 93, 95, Neville Pub. Mus. Brown County, Green Bay, 1986-87, 90, 92-95, Minn. State Capital, St. Paul, 1987, Brown County Libr., Green Bay, 1988, Ctr. Visual Arts, Wausau, Wis., 1991, Milw. Art Mus., 1991-92, Outagamie County Hist. Mus., 1991-95, Bank One Lobby Gallery, Neenah, Wis., 1993-94, 96, Wis. Arts Bd. Gallery, 1994, U. Wis., Platteville, 1996, William F. Boniface Arts Ctr., Escanaba, Mich., 1996, Anderson Art Ctr., Kenosha, Wis., 1997, Atrium Gallery, Indpls., 1997, Mason St. Gallery, Green Bay, Wis., 1997-98, Colorado Springs Art Ctr., 1998, U. Wis., Marinette, 2000, Chgo. Windy City Artists, 2000, U. Wis., Oshkosh, 2001, White Bear Art Ctr., Minn., 2002, Portalwisconsin.org, 2002, Lambeau Field Atrium, 2004 Bd. dirs. Friends of the 1000 Islands Environ. Ctr., Kaukauna, 1986—, chair art fair, 1986-2005, sec., 1988-93. Mem. Kaukauna Creative Artists Group (sec. 1991-2003, chair exhibit and publicity 1991—), Nat. Mus. Women in Arts, Bay Area Watercolor Guild. Avocations: photographer, needle arts, gardening, walking, nordic skiing. Studio: 400 W Division St Kaukauna WI 54130-1120

BREWSTER, OLIVE NESBITT, retired librarian; b. San Antonio, July 19, 1924; d. Charles Henry and Olive Agatha (Nesbitt) Brewster. BA, Our Lady of Lake Coll., 1945, BS in LS, 1946. Asst. librarian aeromed. library U.S. Air Force Sch. Aviation Medicine, Randolph AFB, Tex., 1946-60; chief cataloger aeromed. library Sch. Aerospace Medicine, Brooks AFB, Tex., 1960-83, chief tech. processing, 1983-88; ret., 1988. Mem.: ALA, Mensa. Anglican. Home: 1906 Schley Ave San Antonio TX 78210-4332

BREWSTER, ROBERT CHARLES, diplomat, consultant; b. Beatrice, Nebr., May 31, 1921; s. Charles Lee and Lillian Asenath (French) B.; m. Mary Virginia Blackman, Feb. 22, 1951. Student, Grinnell Coll., 1939-41; AB, U. Wash., 1943; postgrad., U. Mex., 1946, George Washington U., 1947, Columbia U., 1946-48. Fgn. affairs analyst State Dept., Washington, 1948-49, fgn. service officer, 1949-81; 3d sec. Am. Embassy, Managua, Nicaragua, 1949-51, 2d sec., 1951-52; vice consul Am. consulate gen. Stuttgart, Germany, 1952-55; policy briefing officer ICA, staff asst. to under sec. of state for econ. affairs, 1958, spl. asst. to under sec. of state, 1959-60; assigned Nat. War Coll., 1960-61; fgn. service insp., 1961-63; counselor Am. Embassy, Asuncion, Paraguay, 1964-66; dep. exec. dir. Bur. of European Affairs, 1966-67, exec. dir., 1967-69; dep. exec. sec. Dept. State, 1969-71, dir. personnel, 1971-73; amb. Ecuador, 1973-76; coord. for Law of Sea Dept. State, 1976, dep. asst. sec. for oceans and internat. environmental and sci. affairs, 1977-78, insp. gen., 1979-81, cons., 1981-89. Mem. D.C. Commn. on Aging, 1984-85; bd. dirs. Nat. Defense Univ. Found., 1984-87; mem. Com. on Research for Security of Future U.S. Embassy Bldgs. Nat. Acad. Scis., 1985-86. With USNR, 1943-46. Mem. Nat. War Coll. Alumni Assn. (pres. 1981-83), Foggy Bottom Assn. (v.p. 1984-85, pres. 1985-87), Diplomatic and Consular Officers Ret. Clubs: Cosmos (Washington). Home: 3050 Military Rd NW 410 Washington DC 20015 E-mail: rbrewster2@earthlink.com.

BREWSTER, ROBERT GENE, concert singer, educator; b. Pinson, Ala., July 7, 1936; s. Hubert and Chrisella (Ayers) B.; m. Premala Edwards (div.); 1 child, Ravindra Robert. MusB in Piano Performance with honors, Wheaton Coll., 1958; MusM in Voice with distinction, Ind. U., 1961; PhD in Vocal Performances Practices and Musicology, Washington U., St. Louis, 1967; Konzertreife Diploma, Staatliche Hochschule fuer Musik und Darstellender Kunst, Stuttgart, Fed. Republic Germany, 1970; diploma in Lieder and Opera, Mozarteum, Salzburg, Austria, 1969. Tchr. music and French Westfield (Ala.) High Sch., 1959-60; chmn. dept. music Miles Coll., Birmingham, Ala., 1960-62; chmn. area fine arts Jackson (Miss.) Coll., 1962-63; asst. tchr. voice Washington Univ., 1963-66; touring tenor throughout Europe, 1966-73; chmn. dept. music Dillard Univ., New Orleans, 1974; chmn. dept. voice Univ. Miami, Coral Gables, Fla., 1974-82; past pres. Breff Agy., Inc., N.Y.C.; pres. European Fashion Imports, N.Y.C., 1984-88, Fashion Suite, Inc., 1988—. Guest lectr. Stanford U. in Germany, Beutelsbach, 1968-70; dozent fur gesang Berliner Kirchenmusikschule, 1970-72; founder, artistic dir. The Robert Brewster Chorale, 2004— Concert tours throughout, Europe, Asia and, The Ams.; rec. artist (album) I See the Stars, 1960; founder, artistic dir. Robert Brewster Chorale, Inc., A not-for-profit group of 30 male professional singers whose montra is healing through singing, and inspiring hope to men who have been afflicted with the HIV-AIDS virus. Seely Mudd fellow, 1964-66; Fulbright fellow, 1966-68; Deutsche Akademische Austausch Dienst award, 1968-70 Mem.: AAUP, Coll. Music Soc., Am. Musicol. Soc., Nat. Assn. Schs. Music, Fla. Vocal Tchrs. Assn., Nat. Assn. Tchrs. Singing, One Hundred Black Men, Inc., Nat. Arts Club, Phi Mu Alpha. Democrat. Episcopalian. Home and Office: 475 W 57th St Apt 18A New York NY 10019-1778 E-mail: robertgbrewster@mindspring.com.

BREWSTER, RUDI MILTON, judge; b. Sioux Falls, S.D., May 18, 1932; s. Charles Edwin and Wilhemina Therese (Rud) B.; m. Gloria Jane Nanson, June 27, 1954; children: Scot Alan, Lauri Diane (Alan Lee), Julie Lynn Yahnke. AB in Pub. Affairs, Princeton U., 1954; JD, Stanford U., 1960. Bar: Calif. 1960. From assoc. to ptnr. Gray, Cary, Ames & Frye, San Diego, 1960-84; judge U.S. Dist. Ct. (so. dist.) Calif., San Diego, 1984—98, sr. judge, 1998—. Capt. USNR, 1954-82 Ret. Fellow Am. Coll. Trial Lawyers; mem. Am. Bd. Trial Advs., Internat. Assn. Ins. Counsel, Am. Inns of Ct. Republican. Lutheran. Avocations: skiing, hunting, gardening. Office: US Dist Ct Ste 4165 940 Front St San Diego CA 92101-8902 Office Phone: 619-557-6190. Business E-Mail: Rudi_Brewster@casd.uscourts.gov.

BREWSTER, WILLIAM HOWARD, lawyer; b. Takoma Park, Md., Nov. 10, 1962; s. William and Maridell (Baker) B.; m. Karen McCue, Aug. 16, 1986; children: Kristina Baker, William Howard, Katherine Marie. BA, MA, Emory U., 1984; JD, U. Va., 1987. Bar: Ga. 1987, U.S. Dist. Ct. (no. dist.) Ga. 1988, U.S. Dist. Ct. (mid. dist.) Ga. 1992, U.S. Ct. Appeals (11th cir.) 1989, U.S. Ct. Appeals (4th cir.) 1992, (9th cir.), 2004, U.S. Supreme Ct. 1992. Assoc. Kilpatrick & Cody, Atlanta, 1987-94, ptnr., 1994—, Kilpatrick Stockton, LLP, Atlanta. Barrister Lumpkin Am. Inns of Ct., Atlanta, 1989—; adj. prof. Emory U. Sch. Law, U. Va. Sch. Law. Bd. dirs., vice chair Special Olympics, Ga.; bd. dirs. Metro Atlanta C. of C., Ga. C. of C., Ctrl. Atlanta Progress, Inc. Mem.: U. Va. Sch. Law (bd. advisors), State Bar Ga. (antitrust, intellectual property and sports & entertainment secs.), Nat. Collegiate Licensing Assn. (NCLA), Am. Intellectual Property Law Assn. (AIPLA) (trademake litig. com.), Assn. Collegiate Licensing Adminstrs. (mem. legal adv. com.), Internat. Trademark Assn. (publs. com. 1989—93), Commerce Club, Lawyers Club Atlanta. Office: Kilpatrick Stockton LLP 1100 Peachtree St NE Ste 2800 Atlanta GA 30309-4530 E-mail: BBrewster@KilpatrickStockton.com.

BREWSTER HUDSON, TATE MASON, retired language educator; b. Laurel, Miss., May 16, 1933; d. Walter Southgate and Charlotte William (Biggs) Brewster; m. Samuel Madison Hudson, Oct. 18, 1952; children: Walter Brewster, Samuel Madison III, Laura Stoddard Hudson Warren, William Mason. AA, Greenbrier Coll., 1952; BA, Coll. Wooster, 1966, MA in Teaching English, 1972; PhD, U. Akron, 1983. Cert. permanent English and reading tchr., Ohio. Tchr. English Edgewood Jr. H.S., Wooster, Ohio, 1966—80, tchr. reading, 1981—83; tchr. English Wooster H.S., 1983—96, ret., 1996. Co-instr. workshops U. Akron, Ohio, 1986-89; assessor of applicants Nat. Cert. of Early Adolescent Lang. Arts Tchrs., 1995. Clk. of session 1st Presbyn. Ch., Wooster, Ohio, 1991-1996; elder Old Stone Presbyn., Lewisburg, W.Va., 1997-2000, 2001-2003; treas. Greenbrier County Rep. Club, 2000-2005. Mem. AAUW (pres. Wooster 1973, 1998-1999, Lewisburg, 1998-2002, W.Va. state historian 1999-2003), Nat. Coun. Tchrs. English (assoc. chmn. jr. high-mid. sch. assembly 1983, chmn. 1984, editor jr. high-mid. sch. sect. English Jour. 1987), Savannah Garden Club (pres. 1999-2000), Mayflower Soc. W.Va., Nat. Soc. Colonial Dames Am. (chair patriotic svc., pres. 2001-2003, registrar 2003—, nat. roll of honor 2004), Am. Frontier Culture Mus. (bd. dirs. 1999-2002), Greenbrier Hist. Soc. (v.p. hist. affairs 1999-2004), Phi Delta Kappa. Republican. Avocations: travel, swimming, reading, bridge, gardening. Home: PO Box 847 Lewisburg WV 24901-0847 E-mail: tatehudson@verizon.net.

BREWSTER-WALKER, SANDRA JOANN, public relations executive, publishing executive, consultant, meeting planner; d. Willis Hodges and F. Wilda (Scurlock) Brewster; m. Stuart M. Walker (div. 1984); children: Jeffrey, Carlton, Cassandra. Cert., Island Drafting Sch., 1965; BA, Dowling Coll., 1972; MA, SUNY, New Paltz, 1978. Acting asst. dir. Urban Ctr., Vassar Coll., Poughkeepsie, N.Y., 1972-74; tchr. Middletown Jr. H.S., N.Y., 1974-78; elec. mfg. engr. Perkin-Elmer Corp., Norwalk, Conn., 1978-84; pub., editor Ram's Horn Pub. Co., Stamford, Conn., 1983-84; software mgr. Pergamon Press, Inc., Elmsford, N.Y., 1985-86; sr. v.p. pub. rels. Lockhart & Pettus, Inc., 1990-92; pres. Brewster Group, Inc., Stamford, 1986-92; dep. dir. Office of Comm. (apptd. by Pres. Clinton) USDA, Washington, 1993-95; pres., CEO L & P Internat., Inc., Washington, 1995—. Pub., editor Conneticut Update, 1984; editor: Augustus M. Hodges Project, 1978-86, Fairfield County Black Biograph. Index Project, 1980—; contbr. to Westchester Women mag., 1985. Mem. Town of Walkill Bicentennial Com., 1976, Bicentennial Com., Middletown Pub. Schs., 1976; mem. Circleville Pub. Sch. PTA, 1975-77, v.p., 1977-78; instr. genealogy Greater Orange YMCA, Middletown, N.Y., 1975, 77, mem. planning bd., 1976; vice chmn. to corp. campaign advisor United Negro Coll. Fund, Lower Fairfield, Conn., 1980-81; mem. John Anderson for Pres. Com., 1980; exec. dir. Conn. Legis. Black Caucus, Hartford, 1981-82; aide to State Senator J.C. Daniels, 1981-82; founder, bd. dir. Bridgeport Black History Project, 1982-83; adv. com. Conn. Democrats, 1984; inaugural com. Mayor Serrani, Stamford, 1984-85; coord. Lower Fairfield County Mondale/Ferraro Campaign, 1984; state coord. Conn. Com. to Elect Jesse Jackson Pres., 1984; Stamford coord., 1988—; mem. Conn. chpt. Coalition of 100 Black Women, 1980-81, Nat. Project Vote, 1984, adv. com. black women's exhibit L.I. and Bklyn. Hist. Soc.; vol. Alberta Jagoes for Mayor campaign, Milford, Conn., 1982, Christine M. Niedermeier for Congress Com., 1984; mem. steering com. Margaret Morton for Congress, 1987; candidate state rep. 145th dist., 1988; advance team and convention operation Clinton for President '92, Clinton/Gore '92. Named Woman of Month, Conn. Women's Mag., 1983, Working Woman of Month, Essence mag., 1983. Mem. NAFE, NOW, Coalition of 100 Black Women (Lower Fairfield chpt. 1986, 89-90), Nat. Abortion Rights Actions League, Rainbow Coalition, Nat Advance Team Clinton/Gore; YJCW-NAACP (silver life mem., 2001). Avocations: golf, tennis, painting. Office: L&P Internat Inc 611 Pennsylvania Ave SE #401 Washington DC 20003

BREWTON, WES, retired chef, retired real estate manager; b. St. Louis, Mo., Sept. 1, 1932; s. Alton Beverly Brewton and Arlene Bessie Gina Wesley; m. Dorothy Mae Lottie-Brewton (div.); children: Wesley Hopkins Jr., Wesley Andre Harris. AA in Drafting, Trade Tech., L.A., 1961; AA in Architecture, East Los Angeles, 1963. Sr. aircraft engine mechanic Republic Aviation, Long Island, NY, 1954; sr. jet engine mechanic Curtiss Wright, NJ, 1955—56, machinist, 1956—57; electromech. draftsman Douglas Aircraft, L.A., 1962—63, McDonnell Douglas, Huntington Beach, Calif., 1963—65; co-owner, archtl. draftsman Vanguard Builders, Compton, Calif., 1965—67; sr. electromech. draftsman Electronic Memories, El Segundo, Calif., 1967—68; drafting rm. supr., mgr. Microdata Corp., Huntington Beach, 1968, design svcs. mgr., 1968—70, Calif. Data, Huntington Beach, 1970—76, Data 100, Warwick, RI, 1976; founder, chef original Ho. of BBQ, Providence, 1976—83, Wes' Rib Ho., Olneyville, RI, 1983—86, Wes Brewton's Original BBQ, Providence, 1989—90; cook Virginia Mason Hosp., Seattle, 1990—91; chef, kitchen mgr. East Side Mental Health, Redmond, Wash., 1991—2000; apt. ho. mgr. Capitol Hill Housing Improvement Program, Seattle, 2004. Author: Into the Wind, 1995, Wilma, 1996. Civil rights plaintiff Brewton Versus Bd. Edn., St. Louis, 1949—50; blockwatch capt. Neighborhood Watch, Seattle, 2001. Served with USAF, 1950—54. Democrat. Baptist. Avocations: aircraft models, cooking, calligraphy, fishing. Home: 955 W 5th Ave Apt F4 Kennewick WA 99336

BREY, ERIC TRENT, hospitality and tourism educator; b. Loyal, Wis., Aug. 5, 1977; s. Duane Alfred and Paula JoAnn Brey. Postgrad., Purdue U., 2003—. Instr., rschr. Purdue U., West Lafayette, Ind. Cpl. Wis. Army N.G., 1997—2003. Decorated Army Res. Component Achievement medal, Army Achievement medal; recipient Tourism Career Iniative award; scholar, Travel Industry Assn., Meeting Profls. Internat., Purdue U.; grad. studies fellow, Okla. State U. Mem.: Am. Resort Devel. Assn., Internat. Coun. on Hospitality, Restaurant, Instl. Edn. (assoc.), Internat. Assn. Travel and Tourism Educators (assoc.). Home: 403 N Gwinn St Loyal WI 54446 Office: Purdue U 700 W State St Stone Hall B7 West Lafayette IN 47907 Personal E-mail: ebrey@purdue.edu.

BREYER, STEPHEN GERALD, United States Supreme Court Justice; b. San Francisco, Aug. 15, 1938; s. Irving G. and Anne R. Breyer; m. Joanna Hare, Sept. 4, 1967; children: Chloe, Nell, Michael. AB, Stanford U., 1959; BA (Marshall scholar), Oxford U., 1961; LLB, Harvard U., 1964; LLD (hon.), U. Rochester, 1983. Bar: Calif. 1966, D.C. 1966, Mass. 1971. Law clk. to Hon. Arthur J. Goldberg U.S. Supreme Ct., Washington, 1964—65; spl. asst. to asst. atty. gen. (antitrust) Donald Turner U.S. Dept. Justice, Washington, 1965—67; asst. prof. law Harvard U., 1967—70, prof., 1970—81, lectr., 1981—94, prof. John F. Kennedy Sch. Govt., 1978—81; asst. spl. prosecutor Watergate Spl. Prosecution Force, 1973; spl. counsel U.S. Senate Judiciary Com., 1974—75, chief counsel, 1979—81; judge U.S. Ct. Appeals (1st cir.), Boston, 1980—90, chief judge, 1990—94; Oliver Wendell Holmes lectr. Harvard Law Sch., 1992; assoc. justice U.S. Supreme Ct., Washington, 1994—. Mem. U.S. Sentencing Commn., 1985—89, Jud. Conf. of U.S., 1990—94; mem. bd. dirs. Dia Art Found, 1985—86; vis. lectr. Coll. Law, Sydney, Australia, 1975, Salzburg (Austria) Seminar, 1978, 93; vis. prof. U. Rome, 1993; Jud. Conf. rep. to Adminstrv. Conf. U.S., 1981—94. Author (with Paul MacAvoy): The Federal Power Commission and the Regulation of Energy, 1974; author: (with Richard Stewart) Administrative Law and Regulatory Policy, 1979, Administrative Law and Regulatory Policy, 3rd edit., 1992; author: Regulation and its Reform, 1982, Breaking the Vicious Circle, 1993; contbr. articles to profl. jours. Trustee U. Mass., 1974—81; bd. overseers Dana Farber Cancer Inst., Boston, 1977—94. US Army, 1957. Recipient Annual award for Scholarship in Adminstrv. Law, ABA, 1987. Mem.: ABA, Coun. Fgn. Rels., Am. Acad. Arts and Scis., Am. Law Inst., Am. Bar Found. Office: US Supreme Ct One First St St NE Washington DC 20543-0001*

BREYTSPRAAK, JOHN, JR., management consultant; b. Chgo., May 24, 1929; s. John and Grace Willets (Merrick) B.; m. Charlotte Helfand, Dec. 27, 1958. BA in Econs., Lake Forest (Ill.) Coll., 1950. Mgr. mktg. communications fibers div. Am. Cyanamid, N.Y.C., 1964-67; merchandising mgr. Vectra Fiber, Standard Oil Co. N.J., N.Y.C., 1967-69; account supr. Doyle Dane Bernbach, N.Y.C., 1969-73; mgr. mktg. svcs. Formica Corp., Am. Cyanamid, Cin., 1973-76; pres. Sanitas Wallcoverings, Am. Cyanamid, Wayne, N.J., 1976-80; gen. mgr. Chem. Light, Am. Cyanamid, Wayne, 1980-81; pres. Simmons Wallcoverings, Gulf & Western, N.Y.C., 1981-84; cons. New Bern, N.C., 1984-96; pres. Composers Music Co., New Bern, 1987-97; cons. Lacey, Wash., 1996—, South Sound Sr. Svcs., 2000—. Composer 12 musical works, 1985-89; contbr. hist. articles to Jour. of New Bern Hist. Soc., 1988-89. Pres., Craven Concerts Inc., Craven County, N.C., 1987-89; instr. U.S. Power Squadron, Craven County, 1985-87; mem. New Bern Hist. Soc., 1986-89. Avocation: landscape design. Home and Office: 1414 Sleater Kinney Rd SE Lacey WA 98503-2537

BREZ, DANTE (MOS DEF), musician, actor; b. Bklyn., Dec. 11, 1973; Host Def Poetry Jam. Actor: (films, numerous major motion pictures); musician: (albums) Black Star, 1998, Black on Both Sides, 1999, New Danger, 2004, You Know the Flex, 2004; actor: (Broadway plays) Top Dog/Underdog; (Broadway plays, Brown Sugar). Nominee Image Award, NAACP.*

BREZNAU, ANNE M., academic administrator; b. Traverse City, Mich., May 24, 1945; d. Albert J Kelsch and Lucille M Kolarik; children: John Breznar, Nathan Breznar. BA, U. Detroit, 1967, MA, 1970; DA, U. Mich., 1994. Editor Merrill-Palmer Inst., Detroit, 1967-69, pub. rels. officer, 1971-74; instr. Detroit Coll. Bus., Dearborn, Mich., 1970-71; adj. instr. Nazareth Coll., Kalamazoo, 1974-79, mem. faculty, 1980-91; divsn. chmn. Kellogg C.C., Battle Creek, Mich., 1991-99; dean acad. affairs Elizabethtown (Ky.) C.C., 1999—2001. Bd dirs Ky's Second Harvest, 2000—; Bd. dirs. Ky.'s Second Harvest, 2000—01. Mem.: Literacy Coun SS Mich (pres 1998—99), MLA, Asn Depts English (mem nat exec bd 1996—99, chmn ad hoc comt on faculty governance 1998—2000). Avocations: card playing, swimming, gardening, singing. Home: 2607 Heritage Way Wilton NY 12831-2541 E-mail: anne.breznar@esc.edu.

BRIA, SUSAN S., retired English educator, writer; b. Waterbury, Conn., Oct. 18, 1940; d. Emil P. and Susie (Spezzano) Bria. BA English, U. of Conn., Storrs, 1960—63, MA in Secondary Edn., 1965—69, Sixth yr. cert., 1986—89. English tchr. Naugatuck HS, Conn., 1963—98, dept. chair-English, 1985—96; freelance writer/ed., 1998—. Vol. spkr. Nat. Family Caregivers Assn., Md., 2002—. Author: (book) From the Heart of a Caregiver: A Spiritual Journey, 2001, (audiobook) Grandma Is Going To Live With Grandpa, 2003. Mem.: NEA, Nat. Italian Am. Found., Nat. Family Caregivers Assn. Avocations: travel, swimming, ballroom dancing, gardening, reading. Home: 127 Reservoir Road Southbury CT 06488

BRIAN, BRAD D., lawyer; b. Merced, Calif., Apr. 19, 1952; BA, U. Calif., Berkeley, 1974; JD magna cum laude, Harvard U., 1977. Bar: Calif. 1977, U.S. Ct. Appeals (3d cir.) 1978, U.S. Dist. Ct. (ctrl. dist.) Calif. 1978, U.S. Ct. Appeals (9th cir.) 1980. Law clk. to Hon. John J. Gibbons U.S. Ct. Appeals (3d cir.), 1977-78; asst. U.S. atty. Office U.S. Atty. (ctrl. dist.) Calif., 1978-81; hearing examiner L.A. City Police Commn., 1982; atty., ptnr. Munger, Tolles & Olson, L.A., 1981—. Lectr. in law U. So. Calif. Law Ctr., 1983; instr. Nat. Inst. Trial Advocacy, 1986; guest instr. Harvard Law Sch. Trial Advocacy Program, 1983; past pres. & mem. bd. dir. Legal Aid Found. Los Angeles; mem. bd. dir. Western Justice Ctr; mem. Indigent Def. Panel & chmn. Pro Se panel, U.S. Dist Ct. Los Angeles. Co-editor, Internal Corporate Investigations, 2d ed. 2002; bd. editors Harvard Law Rev., 1975-77, mng. editor and treas., 1976-77. Mem. bd. dir. Los Angeles County Music Ctr.; vice chmn. bd. dir. Joffrey Ballet, 1990—91. Named one of Top 50 Trial Lawyers in Los Angeles, Los Angeles Bus. Jour., 1999, 100 Most Influential Lawyers in Calif., Los Angeles Daily Jour., 1998—2002. Fellow, Am. Coll. Trial Lawyers; mem. ABA (chmn. pre-trial practice and discovery, litigation sect. 1987-89, liaison with fed. jud. confs. 1989-91, chair task force on civil justice reform act of 1990), Fed. Bar Assn. (past pres. L.A. chptr.), State Bar Calif., L.A. County Bar Assn. (mem. fed. practice standards com. 1980-82). Achievements include mem. U.S. All-Star baseball team, World Amateur Games, 1972; 1st Team All-Pac 8, baseball, 1974; 2d Team Academic All-American, 1974. Office: Munger Tolles & Olson LLP 355 S Grand Ave Fl 35 Los Angeles CA 90071-1560 Office Phone: 213-683-9280. Business E-Mail: brianbd@mto.com.*

BRIAND, MICHAEL, chef; Mem. staff various pastry shops, Brittany, Paris and Bern, Switzerland; chef Froggy's French Cafe, Highwood, Ill.; exec. chef Little Dix Resort, Virgin Gorda; pastry chef Ambria, Chgo., 1994—, Mon Ami Gabi. Office: Ambria 2300 N Lincoln Park W Chicago IL 60614

BRIAND-RYAN, DONNA MARIE, artistic designer; b. Inglewood, Calif., Aug. 16, 1957; d. Roland Joseph and Mary Ann (Plunkett) Levesque; m. Kenneth Leo Briand Sr., Mar. 3, 1975 (div. Feb. 1982), children: Kenneth Leo Briand Jr., Keith Allen Briand; m. Gordon Clinton Ryan, Sept. 9, 1999; 1 stepchild, Shawn Marie Ryan. A in Engring. and Fine Arts, Bristol Community Coll., Fall River, Mass., 1986; student in fashion design, Newbury Coll., 1987. Cert. artistic designer. Theatre designer Bristol Cmty. Coll. Repertory Theatre, Fall River, Mass., 1983-87; graphic freelancer Bristol Cmty. Coll. Art Ctr., Fall River, Mass., 1983-88; stage designer Bristol Cmty. Coll. Theater, Fall River, Mass., 1985—88; designer, illustrator Design-A-Line, Swansea, Mass., 1988; freelance artist Inglis, Fla., 1988—; fashion designer pvt. practice, Inglis, Fla., 1991—; printing tchr. Zula's Pl., Yankeetown, Fla., 1990—. Mem. art student adv. com. Bristol C.C. Art Ctr., Fall River, 1984-86; art tchr. Salvation Army, Fall River, 1984, Sheriff Youth Camp, Levy County, Fla., 1989. Author numerous poems. Art tchr. Salvation Army, Fall River, 1984, Sheriff's Youth Camp, Levy County, Fla., 1990. Recipient awards for individual paintings. Avocation: creations.

BRIANT, CLYDE LEONARD, metallurgist, educator; b. Texarkana, Ark., May 31, 1948; s. Clyde Leonard and Bonnie Barbara (Green) B.; m. Jacqueline Louise Duffy, July 16, 1977; children— Paul, Judith, Bonnie. BA, Hendrix Coll., Conway, Ark., 1971; BS, Columbia U., 1971, MS, 1973, Eng. Sc.D., 1974. Postdoctoral fellow U. Pa., Phila., 1974-76; staff metallurgist Gen. Electric Co., Schenectady, NY, 1976—94; prof. engring. Brown U., Providence, 1994—, Otis Randall prof., 2000—, dean engring., 2003—. Vis. scientist Rsch. Inst. for Tech. Physics, Hungarian Acad. Scis., Budapest, 1991. Editor: Embrittlement of Engineering Alloys, 1983; contbr. articles to profl. jours. Recipient Alfred Noble prize, 1980; named one of 100 Most Outstanding Young Scientists in U.S.A., Sci. Digest, 1984; overseas fellow Churchill Coll., Cambridge, Eng., 1987-88. Fellow Am. Soc. Metals; mem. AIME (Robert Lansing Hardy gold medal Metall. Soc. 1977, Rossiter W. Raymond 1979). Democrat. Home: 9 Wedgewood Ln Barrington RI 02806-3218 Office: Brown Univ Divsn of Engring Box D Providence RI 02912 Business E-Mail: Clyde_Briant@brown.edu.

BRICE, ROGER THOMAS, lawyer; b. Chgo., May 7, 1948; s. William H. and Mary Loretta (Ryan) B.; m. Carol Coleman, Aug. 15, 1970; children: Caitlin, Coleman, Emily. AB, DePaul U., 1970; JD, U. Chgo., 1973. Bar: Ill. 1973, Iowa 1973, U.S. Ct. Appeals (10th, 4th, 6th and 7th cirs.) 1975, U.S. Dist. Ct. (no. and ctrl. dists.) Ill. 1977, 1995, U.S. Trial Bar (no. dist.) 1982, U.S. Supreme Ct. 1978. Staff atty. Office of Gen. Counsel NLRB, Washington, 1974-76; assoc. Kirkland & Ellis, Chgo., 1976-79, Reuben & Proctor, Chgo., 1979-80, ptnr., 1980-86, Isham, Lincoln & Beale, Chgo., 1986-88, Sonnenschein, Nath & Rosenthal LLP, Chgo., 1988—. Legal counsel, bd. dirs. Boys and Girls Clubs Chgo., 1991—. Fellow Coll. Labor and Employment Lawyers. Roman Catholic. Home: 3727 N Harding Ave Chicago IL 60618-4026 Office: Sonnenschein Nath & Rosenthal LLP 233 S Wacker Dr Ste 8000 Chicago IL 60606-6491 Office Phone: 312-876-3112. E-mail: rbrice@sonnenschein.com.

BRICEL, MARK LEON, marketing executive; b. Ljubljana, Slovenia, Apr. 11, 1929; s. Ivan John and Ivanka (Kregar) Bricel; m. Liselotte Ringer, Mar. 10, 1951; children: Gary, Tania. Student, Air Force Acad, Mostar, Bosnia and Herzegovina, 1948, Nautical Acad., Rijeka, Croatia, 1949. Lic. pvt pilot. Exec. v.p. Toni Sailer Ski Co., Montreal, Que., Can., 1960-64; supr. G.M.

Plastic Corp., Granby, Quebec, Can., 1964-66; gen. sales mgr. G.M. Plastic Corp./GMP Sports Ltd., Granby, 1966-70, G.M.P. Sports, Inc., Westport, Conn., 1967-70; exec. v.p. House of Colonial Furniture Ltd., Montreal, 1970-75; gen. sales agt. Arcese Bros. Furniture Ltd., Missisauga, Ont., Can., 1976-96; pres. M.L. Bricel Agys. Ltd., Missisauga, 1984—, M.L Bricel Mktg. and Sales, Inc., Naples, Fla., 1991—, Progressive Mktg., Ltd., Hamilton, Bermuda, 1992—, M.L. Bricel Mktg., & Sales, Ltd., Missisauga, Ont., Can., 1999—. Dir mkt and sales Arcese Bros Furnitures Ltd, Missisauga, 1991—96, VR Furniture INc, Brampton, ON, Canada, 1997—. Lt Yugoslav Air Force, 1946—48. Recipient Silver Medal Award, FIS, 1947. Mem.: Can Owners and Pilots Asn, Blue Springs Golf Club, Royal Can Flying Clubs Asn (Blue Seal 1984). Roman Catholic. Avocations: photography, flying, golf. Office: Unit 2 2170 Dunwin Dr Mississauga ON L5L 5M8 Canada L5L 5M8 also: ML Bricel Mktg & Sales Inc 603 Serendipity Dr Naples FL 34108-2829

BRICE-O'HARA, SALLY, career military officer; b. Annapolis, Md. m. Bob Brice-O'Hara; 2 children. BA in Sociology, Goucher Coll., 1974; grad., Officer Candidate Sch., 1975; MA on Public Admin., John F. Kennedy Sch. of Govt., Harvard U.; MS in Nat. Security Strategy, Nat. War Coll.; D.Litt. (hon.), Goucher Coll., 2002. Former asst. dir. of admissions Coast Guard Academy. Former dir. personnel mgmt., fifth coast guard dist. US Coast Guard, former commanding officer of training ctr. in Cape May, former comdr. Station Cape May & Group Baltimore, former dep. comdr. of activities at Baltimore, comdr. fifth coast guard dist., 2003—05, dir., reserve and training, 2005—, mem., reserve forces policy bd., 2005—. Decorated Legions of Merit, Meritorious Service Medal, Coast Guard Commendation Medals, Coast Guard Achievement Medal. Office: US Coast Guard 2100 2nd St SW Washington DC 20593

BRICHFORD, MAYNARD JAY, archivist; b. Madison, Ohio, Aug. 6, 1926; s. Merton Jay and Evelyn Louise (Graves) B.; m. Jane Adair Hamilton, Sept. 15, 1951; children— Charles Hamilton, Ann Adair Brichford Martin, Matthew Jay, Sarah Lourena. BA, Hiram Coll., 1950; MS, U. Wis., 1951. Asst. archivist State Hist. Soc. Wis., 1952-56; methods and procedures analyst Ill. State Archives, 1956-59; records and space mgmt. supr. Dept. Adminstrn. State of Wis., Madison, 1959-63; archivist U. Ill., Urbana, 1963-95, asso. prof., 1963-70, prof., 1970—. Contbr. articles in field. Mem. gen. commn. on archives and history United Meth. Ch., 1988-96; bd. chmn. U. Ill. YMCA, 1987-89. With U.S. Navy, 1944-46. Council on Library Resources grantee, 1966-69, 70-71; Nat. Endowment for the Humanities grantee, 1976-79; Fulbright grantee, 1985; Am. Phil. Soc. grantee, 1992. Fellow Soc. Am. Archivists (pres. 1979-80); mem. Ill. Archives Adv. Bd. (chmn. 1979-84) Republican. Methodist. Home: 409 Eliot Dr Urbana IL 61801-6725 Office: 106A Arch Rsch Ctr 1707 S Orchard St Urbana IL 61801-3607

BRICK, H. BEN, librarian; b. Omaha, Nebr., June 20, 1970; s. Harold Benjamin and Judy May Brick; m. Reema Joy Isely, May 14, 1999; children: Maelin Ceili, Joyella Catherine. BS in Bible and Humanities, Grace Coll. of Bible, Omaha, 1994; BA in History, U. Nebr., 1999. Cert. pub. libr. Nebr. Libr. Commn. Libr. specialist Omaha Pub. Libr., 1996—2001, libr. I, 2001—. Chair issues and actions com. Omaha Pub. Libr., 2001. Outreach coord. Westside Ch., Omaha, 1999—2004, Sunday sch. tchr., 2000—01. Scholar, Nebr. Libr. Commn., 2003. Mem.: ALA, Nebr. Libr. Assn., Pub. Libr. Assn., History Channel Club. Baptist. Avocation: stamp collecting/philately. Office: Omaha Pub Libr 215 S 15 St Omaha NE 68102 Office Phone: 402-444-4997.

BRICKELL, CHARLES HENNESSEY, JR., marine engineer, retired military officer; b. Memphis, Apr. 13, 1935; s. Charles Hennessey and Mary Ellen (Viau) B.; m. Barbara Virginia Davis, Jan. 4, 1958; children: David Brian, Patricia Ellen, Susan Elizabeth, Timothy Paul, Joel Howard. BS in Marine Engrng., U.S. Merchant Marine Acad., 1957; MA in Bus. Mgmt., Cen. Mich. U., 1980. Enlisted USN, 1953, commd. ensign, 1957, advanced through grades to rear adm., 1984; dir. research and devel. Undersea and Strategic Warfare, and Nuclear Energy, 1984-87; dir. USN Strategic Def. Initiative Program, 1984-88; dep. dir. Navy Rsch. Devel., Test and Evaluation, 1987-88; ret. USN, 1988; gen. mgr. advanced technologies Stone & Webster Engrng. Corp., Boston, 1988-91; dir. Ops. ea. region N.Am. Energy Svcs., Issaquah, Wash., 1991-93; dir. fluids and structural mechanics Applied Rsch. Lab. Pa. State U., State Coll., 1993—. Mem. bd. advisors Applied Rsch. Lab Pa. State U., 1988-93; cons. NAS. Decorated Def. Superior Service Medal, Legion of Merit with three Gold Stars, Meritorious Service Medal with two Gold Stars. Mem. Sigma Iota Epsilon. Roman Catholic. Avocations: baseball, basketball sports officiating.

BRICKER, HARVEY MILLER, anthropology educator; b. Johnstown, Pa., June 29, 1940; s. George Harry and Florence Helen (Miller) B.; m. Victoria Evelyne Reifler, Dec. 27, 1964. BA, Hamilton Coll., 1962; MA, Harvard U., 1963, PhD, 1973. Successively instr., asst. prof., assoc. prof. to prof. anthropology Tulane U., New Orleans, 1969—. Co-author: The Analysis of Certain Major Classes of Upper Palaeolithic Tools, 1969, Excavation of the Abri Pataud: The Perigordian VI Assemblage, 1984; co-editor: Hunting and Animal Exploitation in the Later Palaeolithic and Mesolithic of Eurasia, 1993; editor: La Paléolithique Supérieur de l'abri Pataud (Dordogne), 1995; contbr. articles on French prehistory and Maya archaeoastronomy to profl. jours. Decorated Order Palmes Académiques (France). Fellow AAAS; mem. Soc. Am. Archaeology, Soc. French Prehistory. Office: Tulane U Dept Anthropology 1021 Audubon St New Orleans LA 70118-5238 E-mail: hbricker@tulane.edu.

BRICKER, JOHN TIMOTHY, pediatric cardiologist; b. East Liverpool, Ohio, Dec. 20, 1952; s. John Franklin and Rebecca Jane (Skidmore) B.; m. Janet Lynn Pearch, Aug. 25, 1973; children: Valarie, John, Susan. BA, Malone Coll., 1974; MD, Ohio State U., 1976; MBA, U. Chgo., 2002. Intrn, resident, fellow Baylor Coll. Medicine, Houston, 1976-83; asst. prof. pediatrics Baylor Coll. Medicine, Tex. Children's Hosp., Houston, 1983-88, assoc. prof. pediatrics, 1988; chief cardiology Tex. Children's Hosp., Houston, 1992—2003; chief pediatric cardiology Tex. Heart Inst., Houston, 1992—2003, vice chair pediatrics, 2003—05; chair pediats. U. Ky. Dept. Pediats., Lexington, 2005—. Editor: Current Practice of Pediatric Cardiology, 1988, The Science and Practice of Pediatric Cardiology, 1992, Cardiac Toxicity after Treatment for Childhood Cancer, 1993. Fellow Am. Acad. Pediatrics, Am. Coll. Cardiology, Am. Coll. Chest Physicians. Mem. Soc. Of Friends. Office: Univ Ky Dept Pediats 740 South Limestone J-406 Lexington KY 40536 Office Phone: 832-826-5600.

BRICKER, NEAL S., physician, educator; b. Denver, Apr. 18, 1927; s. Eli D. and Rose (Quiat) B.; m. Miriam Thalenberg, June 24, 1951 (dec. 1974); children: Dusty, Cary, Susan, Daniel Baker; m. Ruth T. Baker, Dec. 28, 1980. BA, U. Colo., 1946, MD, 1949. Diplomate Am. Bd. Internal Medicine (bd. govs. 1972-79, chmn. nephrology test com. 1973-76). Intern, resident Bellevue Hosp., N.Y.C., 1949-52; sr. asst. resident Peter Bent Brigham Hosp., Boston, 1954-55, asso. dir. cardio-renal lab., 1955-56; instr. Harvard, 1955-56; fellow Howard Hughes Med. Inst., 1955-56; from asst. prof. to prof. Washington U., 1956-72, dir. renal div., 1956-72; Mem. sci. adv. bd. Nat. Kidney Found., 1962-69, chmn. research and fellowship grants com., 1964-65, mem. exec. com., 1968-71; prof. medicine, chmn. dept. Albert Einstein Coll. Medicine, 1972-76; prof. medicine U. Miami, Fla., 1976-78, vice chmn. dept., 1976-78; Disting. prof. medicine UCLA, 1978-86; disting. prof. medicine, dir. sci. and tech. planning Loma Linda (Calif.) U., 1986-92; exec. v.p. Naturon Pharm., Riverside, Calif., 1992; clin. prof. medicine UCR/UCLA Program in Biomed. Scis., UCR, 1996—. Cons. NIH, 1964-68, chmn. gen. medicine study sect., 1966-68, chmn. renal disease and urology tng. grants com., 1969-71; vis. investigator Inst. Biol. Chemistry, Copenhagen, 1960-61; investigator Mt. Desert Island Biol. Labs.; advisor on behalf Inst. Medicine to Sen. Lowell Weicker. Assoc. editor: Jour. Lab. and Clin. Medicine, 1961-67, Kidney Internat, 1972; editorial com.: Jour. Clin. Investigation, 1964-68, Physiol. Revs, 1970-76, Am. Heart Assn. Publs. Com., 1974-79, Calcified Tissue Internat., 1978-86, Proc. Soc. Exptl. Biology and Medicine, 1978-86; editor: Supplements, Circulation and Circulation Research, 1974-79; contbr. articles to profl. jours., chpts. to books. Served with USNR, 1944-45; Served with U.S. Army, 1952-54. Recipient Gold-Headed Cane award U. Colo., 1949, Silver and Gold Alumni award, 1975; USPHS Research Career award, 1964-72; Skylab Achievement award NASA, 1974; Pub. Service award, 1975; George Norlin Silver medal award U. Colo. 1982, citation Kidney Found. So. Calif., 1984; honoree 50th Ann. Wash. U. Med. Sch. Renal Divsn., 2004. Fellow A.C.P.; mem. Am. Fedn. for Clin. Research, Central Soc. Clin. Research (council 1970-73), Assn. Am. Physicians, Am. Soc. for Clin. Investigation (pres. 1972-73, chmn. com. nat. med. policy 1973-77, Disting. Service award 1969), Internat. Soc. Nephrology (exec. com. 1966-81, v.p. 1966-69, treas. 1969-81, history honoree, video legacy honoree 2004), Internat. Congress Nephrology (pres. 1981-84), Am. Soc. Nephrology (1st pres., John Peters medal 1991), Am. Physiol. Soc., Soc. for Exptl. Biology and Medicine, Western Soc. Clin. Research, So. Soc. Clin. Investigation, Nat. Acad. Scis. (com. on space biology and medicine, ad hoc panel on renal and metabolic effects space flight 1971-72, mem. drug efficacy com. 1966-68, com. space biology, chmn. medicine in space sci. bd. 1972-81, com. chmn. 1978-81, chmn. com. renal and metabloic effects space flight 1972-74, chmn. study com. on life scis. 1976-81, mem. space sci. bd. 1977-81), Internat. Soc. nephrology, (hon.), Inst. Medicine of NAS, Internat. Soc. Nephrology, Sigma Xi, Alpha Omega Alpha. Home: 4240 Piedmont Mesa Claremont CA 91711-2332 Office: UCR/UCLA Riverside CA 92521-0121

BRICKER, RUTH, national foundation administrator, real estate developer; b. Oak Park, Ill., Mar. 23, 1930; m. Neal S. Bricker; children: Daniel Baker, Cary, Dusty, Suzanne. Student, UCLA, 1945; postgrad. in Art, U. So. Calif.; BA in Urban Planning, Antioch U., MA in Urban Planning, 1978. Cert. mediator. Staff Artforum Mag., L.A., 1966—69; we. dir. Experiments in Art and Tech., L.A., 1969—75; owner Empire Real Estate and Devel., L.A., 1975—76; mng. gen. ptnr. Orchard Pk. Devel., Loma Linda, Calif., 1988—; prodr., "Headline", "The Doc. are in" Inland Empire, Cable Sys., Calif., 2000—. Designer Trade-Off; developed programs in art and tech. for Calif. State Coll.-Long Beach, U. So. Calif., UCLA; designer laser light wall Calif. Inst. Tech.; lectr. and cons. in field. Author: Getting Rich in Real Estate Partnerships, 1983; editor, contbg. author: Experiments in Art and Technology/L.A. Jour., 1974-79; prodr. (monthly TV program) Headline; publr. Warner Books. Mem. Mayor's Housing Task Force, L.A.; Internat. Inst. Kidney Diseases; founding mem. exec. com. Sav. and Preserving Archtl. and Cultural Environment; bd. mem. Am. Found. for Pompidou Mus., Paris, Getty Mus., Archival Sec. Achievements include development of art and technology programs for the first moon landing in 1969. E-mail: ruthbricker@comcast.net.

BRICKER, VICTORIA REIFLER, anthropologist, educator; b. Hong Kong, June 15, 1940; came to U.S., 1947, naturalized, 1953; d. Erwin and Henrietta (Brown) Reifler; m. Harvey Miller Bricker, Dec. 27, 1964. AB, Stanford U., 1962; A.M., Harvard U., 1963, PhD, 1968. Vis. lectr. anthropology Tulane U., 1969-70, asst. prof., 1970-73, assoc. prof., 1973-78, prof., 1978—, chmn. dept. anthropology, 1988—91, 2003—05. Author: Ritual Humor in Highland Chiapas, 1973, The Indian Christ, The Indian King: The Historical Substrate of Maya Myth and Ritual, 1981 (Howard Francis Cline meml. prize Conf. Latin Am. History), A Grammar of Mayan Hieroglyphs, 1986, (with Gabrielle Vail) Papers on the Madrid Codex, 1997, (with Eleuterio Po'ot Yah and Ofelia Dzul de Po'ot) A Dictionary of the Maya Language as Spoken in Hocaba, Yucatan, 1998, (with Helga-Maria Miram) An Encounter of Two Worlds: The Book of Chilam Balam of Kaua, 2002; book rev. editor: Am. Anthropologist, 1971-73; editor: Am. Ethnologist, 1973-76; gen. editor: Supplement to Handbook of Middle American Indians, 1977—. Guggenheim fellow, 1982; Wenner-Gren Found. Anthropol. Rsch. grantee, 1971; Social Sci. Rsch. Coun. grantee, 1972; NEH grantee, 1990. Fellow Am. Anthrop. Assn. (exec. bd. 1980-83); mem. NAS, Am. Philos. Soc., Am. Soc. Ethnohistory (exec. bd. 1977-79), Linguistic Soc. Am., Seminario de Cultura Maya, Societe des Americanistes. Office: Tulane U Dept Anthropology New Orleans LA 70118

BRICKEY, KATHLEEN FITZGERALD, law educator; b. Austin, Tex., Sept. 16, 1944; d. Robert Bernard and Ina Marie (Daw) Fitzgerald; m. James Nelson Brickey, Aug. 22, 1969. BA, U. Ky., 1965, JD, 1968. Criminal law specialist/cons. Ky. Crime Commn., Frankfort, Cin., 1968-71; exec. dir. Ky. Judicial Conf. and Coun., Frankfort, 1971-72; adj. prof. law U. Ky., Lexington, 1972; asst. to assoc. prof. law U. Louisville, 1972-76; assoc. prof. to prof. law Washington U., St. Louis, 1976-89, George Alexander Madill prof. law, 1989-93, James Carr prof. of criminal jurisprudence, 1993—, Israel Treiman faculty fellow, 2001—02. Cons. U.S. Sentencing Commn., 1988, 91; witness U.S. Senate Com. on Judiciary, Washington, 1986. Author: Kentucky Criminal Law, 1974, Corporate Criminal Liability, 1984, 2d edit., 1992-94, Corporate and White Collar Crime, 1990, 3d edit., 2002; contbr. articles to profl. jours. Mem. Am. Law Inst., Soc. for Reform of Criminal Law, Assn. Am. Law Schs. (sect. on criminal justice chair 1989, exec. com. 1985-91, 94-95). Office: Washington U Sch Law Campus 1120 Saint Louis MO 63130 E-mail: brickey@wulaw.wustl.edu.

BRICKLEY, RICHARD AGAR, retired surgeon; b. Bluffton, Ind., Aug. 15, 1925; s. Harry Dwight and Ina (Agar) B.; m. Suzanne Slusser, Nov. 28, 1964; children: Dinah B. Olson, Sarah Jane, Richard Agar II, Laura Brickley Wakeley, Andrew John. Student, Ind. U., 1943-44; BS, B.M., Northwestern U. Med. Sch., 1947, MD, 1948. Diplomate: Am. Bd. Surgery. Intern Cook County Hosp., Chgo., 1947-49, surg. resident, 1955-56; gen. practice Bluffton, 1949-50; surg. preceptorship with Drs. Gatch and Owen, Indpls., 1950-51, 54; pvt. practice medicine, specializing in surgery Indpls., 1957-86; chmn. gen. surgery div. Meth. Hosp., Indpls., 1962-66, Winona Meml. Hosp., Indpls., 1971-73, chief of med. staff, 1974-75, bd. dirs., 1977-84. Served with M.C. USAF, 1951-53. Fellow ACS; mem. AMA, Ind. Med. Assn., Aerospace Med. Assn., Marion County Med. Soc. (chmn. bd. dirs. 1976-77), Seven-Up Club (Hillman, Mich.) (owner), Beta Theta Pi, Nu Sigma Nu. Home: 4530 Crooked Creek Ridge Dr Indianapolis IN 46228-2859 Personal E-mail: rbrickley211@comcast.net.

BRICKLIN, MARK HARRIS, magazine editor, publisher; b. Phila., Apr. 13, 1939; s. Arthur Benjamin and Rose (Gaurd) Bricklin; m. Alice Goddard Terry, Apr. 26, 1963 (div.); children: Deirdre, Brendon. BA, Temple U., 1960; postgrad., Boston U., 1961, Temple U., 1962. Teaching fellow English Boston U., 1960—61; city editor Phila. Tribune, 1962—71; freelance writer, photographer, 1962—71; with Rodale Press, Emmaus, Pa., 1971—, v.p., 1975—; exec. editor Prevention mag., 1974—97; founding editor, editorial dir. Spring mag., 1982—84; edit. dir. Men's Health mag., Emmaus, 1980—, Heart & Soul mag., Emmaus, 1994—; editor-in-chief Pets: Part of the Family, 1997—, founding editor, 1998. Journalism preceptor Pkwy. Exptl. Program Phila. Sch. Dist.; cons. book pub. Author: The Practical Encyclopedia of Natural Healing, 1976, Lose Weight Naturally, 1979, Natural Healing Cookbook, 1981, Rodale's Encyclopedia of Natural Home Remedies, 1982; co-author: Positive Living and Health, 1990, Secrets of Executive Success, 1991. Founder Prevention Walking Club, 1986. Home: 5218 W Hopewell Rd Center Valley PA 18034-9607 Office: Prevention 33 E Minor St Emmaus PA 18098-0001 E-mail: mark.bricklin@rodale.com.

BRICKMAN, JULIE R., psychologist, writer; d. Leo and Molly (Rogers) Brickman; m. Bob Magnuson Hoyk, May 31, 2002. MFA in Writing, Vt. Coll., 1998; PhD, U. Man., Winnipeg, Can., 1978. Registered psychologist Ont. Fiction faculty Spalding U., Louisville, 2001—. Freelance book reviewer San Diego Union-Tribune; writer in residence Yukon Arts Coun., 1999. Author: (novels) What Birds Can Only Whisper, 1997. Recipient Outstanding Accomplishment award, Women Helping Women, 2000; Explorations Writing grantee, Can. Coun., 1990—92. Home: 1455 Morningside Dr Laguna Beach CA 92651

BRICKMAN, KENNETH ALAN, state agency administrator; b. Hannibal, Mo., Sept. 10, 1940; s. Roy Frederick and Nita Wilma (Swearingen) B.; m. Mildred Darlene Myers, Aug. 10, 1963; children: Heather Katherine, Erik Alan. BS in Bus. and Econs., Culver-Stockton Coll., Canton, Mo., 1963; JD, U. Mo., 1970. Bar: Ill. 1970, Mo. 1970, US Supreme Ct. 1975. Ptnr. firm Scholz, Staff & Brickman, Quincy, Ill., 1970-78; pres. real estate brokerage Landmark of Quincy, Inc./Better Homes & Gardens, 1978-79; counsel, chief counsel Ill. Dept. Commerce and Cmty. Affairs, Springfield, 1980—85; gen. counsel, dep. dir. Ill. State Lottery, Springfield, 1986-91; sec.-treas., exec. v.p. La. Lottery Corp., Baton Rouge, 1991-95; exec. v.p. Iowa Lottery, Des Moines, 1995—. Served as capt. USAF, 1963-67. Mem. Culver Stockton Coll. Alumni Assn. (pres. 1979). Office: Iowa Lottery 2015 Grand Ave Des Moines IA 50312-4999

BRICKS, MAURY, financial analyst; BBA, BA, U. Tex., Austin, 1997; JD, U. Mich., 2000; MSc in Acctg. and Fin., London Sch. Econs., 2003. Bar Admission: Tex., Calif. Assoc., fin. transactions Haynes and Boone, LLP; assoc., mergers & acquisitions Cooley Godward, LLP; fin. specialist Shell Oil Co., Houston, 2003—. Recipient Emmerr E. Eagan Award, U. of Mich. Law Sch. Mem.: Order of the Coif.

BRICKSON, RICHARD ALAN, lawyer; b. Madison, Wis., Feb. 10, 1948; s. William Louis and Nancy May (Gay) B.; m. Marilyn Joan Serenco, June 20, 1971; children: Jennifer Lynne, Katherine Anne, Evan Leigh. BA, Wabash Coll., 1970; JD, Georgetown U., 1973. Bar: Mo. 1973. Staff atty. The May Dept. Stores Co., St. Louis, 1973-77, assoc. gen. counsel, 1977-79, asst. gen. counsel, 1979-81, counsel, 1981-82, counsel, sec., 1982-88, sr. counsel, sec., 1988—. Office: May Dept Stores Co 611 Olive St Saint Louis MO 63101-1721

BRIDE, JOHN W., communications executive, entrepreneur; b. Boston, Sept. 12, 1937; s. William T. and Elsie Francis (Duffy) B.; m. Marjorie McHenry, May 13, 1966 (div. 1984); children: John Hambleton, Christopher McHenry; m. Mary Eileen Kiniry, Feb. 15, 1985; 1 stepchild, Edward. BA in Econs., Norwich U., 1960; JD, U. Maine, 1964; OPM, Harvard U., 1980. Staff atty. FCC, Washington, 1964-66; account exec. Sta. KDKA-TV, Pitts., 1966-70; pres. Bride Broadcasting, Inc., Pitts., 1970-86, Chandler Broadcasting, Inc., Portland, Maine, 1970-86, Greater Portland Radio, Inc., Portland, Maine, 1972-86, B-T Satellite, Portland, Maine, 1980-96, Triangle Properties, Portland, Maine, 1980-85, Bride Communications, Inc., Portland, Maine, 1980-96, Portland Broadcast, Inc., Portland, Maine, 1987-96. Trustee John W. Duffy Trusts, Boston, 1978—2003; mem. com. fgn. rels., Portland, 1976—96; mem. adv. com. Back Cove Improvement Project, Portland, 1984—86; mem. adv. bd. Lifeline U. So. Maine, Portland, 1983—95; chair comm. adv. bd. Norwich U., 1988—98, bd. fellows, 2000—03, bd. trustees, 2003—; pres. Bride Family Found., Portland, 1980—; instr. Jr. Achievement, Portland, 1980—96, bd. dirs., 1993; treas. bd. dirs. ABC Talkradio Affiliates, N.Y.C., 1983—88; mng. ptnr. Airwave Investments, LLC, 1997—. Mem. bd. visitors U. Maine Sch. Law, 1991—. Served with U.S. Army, 1960-61. Mem.: Maine Bar Assn., Pitts. Golf Club, Harvard Bus. Club (v.p. 1984—92). Unitarian Universalist. Avocation: triathlons. Home: 83 West St Portland ME 04102-3415 Office: Airwave Investments LLC PO Box 526 Westbrook ME 04098 Personal E-mail: johnwbride@aol.com.

BRIDEGAM, WILLIS EDWARD, JR., retired librarian; b. Pottstown, Pa., Oct. 15, 1935; s. Willis Edward and M. Emma (Eberhart) B.; m. Nathalie J. Bridegam; 1 child, Martha Ann. BMus, Eastman Sch. Music, 1957; MS, Syracuse U., N.Y., 1963; MA (hon.), Amherst Coll., 1985. Med. librarian U. Rochester (N.Y.) Sch. Medicine, 1966-69, asso. dir. univ. libraries, 1969-72; dir. libraries State U. N.Y., Binghamton, 1972-75; librarian Amherst (Mass.) Coll., 1975—2004. Mem. founding com. Oberlin Group. Author: A Collaborative Approach to Collection Storage: The Five College Library Depository, 2001. Served with AUS, 1957. Mem. ALA, Assn. Coll. and Rsch. Libraries. Clubs: Grolier (N.Y.C.). Home: 53 Memorial Dr Amherst MA 01002-2533

BRIDENSTINE, LOUIS HENRY, JR., lawyer; b. Detroit, Nov. 13, 1940; s. Louis and Mary Ellen (O'Keefe) B.; m. Lucia Elizabeth Pucci, June 18, 1966; 1 child, Lucia McMullin. BS, John Carroll U., 1962; MA, U. Detroit, 1966, JD, 1965. Bar: Mich. 1966, U.S. Dist. Ct. (ea. dist.) Mich. 1966. Trial atty., atty.-advisor FTC, Washington, 1966-72; sr. legal counsel, v.p. dir. comms. Motor Vehicle Mfrs. Assn. U.S., Inc., Detroit, 1972-81; sr. v.p., gen. counsel, sec. Campbell-Ewald Co., Warren, Mich., 1981—. Exec. dir. Motorists Info., Inc., Detroit, 1977; legal affairs com. Am. Assn. Advt. Agys., N.Y.C., 1990—, chair, 2000—. Youth allocations panelist United Way Cmty Svcs., Detroit, 1991-98, chair, 1993-98, fund distbn. panelist, 1994-98, admissions compliance com. panelist, 2001-02; trustee, bd. dirs. Catholic Youth Orgn., Detroit, 1981-97, 99-2000, chair bd. dirs., 1990-92. Fellow Mich. State Bar Found. (life); mem. Mich. Bar Assn., Am. Corp. Counsel Assn., Alpha Sigma Nu, Blue Key, Detroit Athletic Club. Avocations: travel, reading. Office: Campbell Ewald Co 30400 Van Dyke Ave Warren MI 48093-2368 E-mail: lbridens@campbell-ewald.com.

BRIDESTOWE, Lord See MOORE, THOMAS

BRIDGE, BOBBE JEAN, state supreme court justice; b. 1944; m. Jonathan J. Bridge; children: Rebecca, Don. BA magna cum laude, U. Wash; MA, PhD in Polit. Sci., U. Mich.; JD, U. Wash., 1976. Superior Ct. judge King County, Wash., 1990-1999; chief judge King County Juvenile Ct., Wash., 1994-97, asst. presiding judge, 1997-98, presiding judge, 1998-99; justice Wash. State Supreme Ct., 1999—. Chmn. Judicial Info. Sys. Comm, Legislative Comm.; co-chmn. Unified Family Ct. Bench-Bar Task Force. Bd. dirs. YWCA, Becca Task Force, State Commr. on Children in Foster Care, Seattle Children's Home, Catalyst for Kids Youth Care, Tech. Adv. Com. Female Juvenile Offenders, Adv. Com. Adolescent Life Skills Program, Street Youth Law Program, Northwest Mediation Svc., Woodland Pk. Zoological Soc., Wash. Coun. Crime and Delinquency, Women's Funding Alliance, Alki Found., Privacy Fund, Seattle Arts Commn., U. Wash. Arts and Sci. Devel., Greater Seattle C. of C., Metrocenter YMCA, Juvenile Ct. Conf. Com.; mem. King County Task Force on Children and Families, Wash. State's Dept. Social and Health Svcs. Children., Youth, Family Svcs. Adv. Com., Child Protection Roundtable, Govs. Juvenile Justice Adv. Com.; chmn. State Task Force on Juvenile Issues, Coun. Youth Crisis Work Group, Families-at-Risk sub-com., Bd. Dirs. Ctr. Career Alternatives, Candidate Evaluation Com. Seattle-King Mcpl. League, Law and justice Com. League Women Voters; co-chmn. Govs. Coun. on Families, Youth, and Justice; pres. Seattle Women's Commn., Seattle Chpt. Am. Jewish Com.,bd. dirs., asst. sec.-treas. Jewish Fedn. Greater Seattle, chmn., vice chmn. Cmty. Rels. Coun. Named Judge of Yr. Wash. Women Lawyers, 1996; recipient Hannah G. Solomon award Nat. Coun. Jewish Women, 1996, Cmty. Catalyst award Mother's Against Violence in Am., 1997, Women Making a Difference award Youthcare, 1998, Annual Family Advocate award, 2002; honored "woman helping women" Soroptimist Internat. of Kent, 1999. Mem. Nat. Kidney Found., Ctr. Women and Democracy, Phi Beta Kappa. Office: Wash Supreme Ct PO Box 40929 Olympia WA 98504-0929

BRIDGE, HERBERT MARVIN, retail executive; b. Seattle, Mar. 14, 1925; s. Ben and Sally (Silverman) B.; m. Shirley Selesnick, Jan. 25, 1948; children: Jonathan J., Daniel E. BA in Polit. Sci., U. Wash., 1947. Pres. Ben Bridge Jeweler Inc., Seattle, 1955-76, chmn., 1977—. Past pres. Downtown Seattle Assn., 1980-81, Am. Jewish Com.; bd. dirs. Naval Acad. Found., Naval Undersea Mus., Alliance for Edn.; chair Puget Sound USO; chmn. sr. adv. bd. Goodwill Games of 1990; co-chair King County chpt. United Way, 2000-01. Rear adm. USNR, 1942-85. Decorated Legion of Merit with Gold Star in lieu of 2d award; recipient Israel Bonds Masada award, 1974, Am. Jewish Com. Human Rels. award, 1978, Navy League scroll hon., 1980, 96, Alumni Legend award U. Wash., 1987, Vol. of Yr. award Jewish Fedn., 1991, Humanitarian award Privacy Fund, 1991, Heritage award Mus. History and Industry, 1993, A.K. Guy Cmty. Svc. award YMCA, 1995, Cmty. Svc. award Sea 1st, 1998, Citizen of Yr. award Seattle-King County, 2001, Achievement medal Fred Hutchinson Cancer Ctr., 2003, Lifetime Achievement award Jewelry Info. Ctr., 2005; named to Nat. Jewelers Hall of Fame, 1998, Puget Sound Bus. Hall of Fame, 1999. Mem.: Greater Seattle C. of C. (past pres.), Pacific N.W. Jewelers (past pres.), Am. Gem. Soc. (head trustee 1993—2000, cert., Triple Zero award 2001, Shipley award 2003), Rotary, City Club (founder), Wash. Athletic Club (past pres.), Naval Res. Assn. (past pres.), Shriners. Democrat. Office: PO Box 1908 Seattle WA 98111-1908 Office Phone: 206-239-6868. Personal E-mail: hmbridge1@aol.com.

BRIDGE, JONATHAN JOSEPH, lawyer, retail executive; b. Seattle, Mar. 19, 1950; s. Herbert Marvin and Shirley Geraldine (Selesnick) B.; m. Bobbe Jean Chaback, May 20, 1978; children: Donald, Rebecca. BA with honors, U. Wash., 1972, JD, 1976. Bar: Wash. 1976, U.S. Dist. Ct. (we. dist.) Wash. 1976, U.S. Ct. Mil. Appeals 1977, U.S. Ct. Appeals (9th cir.) 1979, U.S. Supreme Ct. 1980. Legal service officer USN, Oak Harbor, Wash., 1976-79, staff judge adv. Bremerton, Wash., 1979-81; exec. v.p. Ben Bridge Jeweler, Inc., Seattle, 1981-90, gen. counsel, co-chief exec. officer, 1990—. Bd. dirs. Ben Bridge Corp., Seattle, Jewelers Am., N.Y.C., Jewelers Vigilance Com., N.Y., Jewelers Mut. Ins., Neenah, Wis., Assn. Wash. Bus., KUOW Pub. Radio, Seattle. Bd. dirs. King County Mental Health Bd., Seattle, 1984, Wash. Retail Assn., 1985-94, Evergreen Children's Assn., 1998—, Seattle Police Found., 2001-04; vice chmn. Seattle Urban League, 1986-88, chmn., 1988-89; pres. Am. Jewish Com., Seattle, 1986-88; counsel Pacific Northwest Jewelers Assn., 1988-2000, treas., 1990, pres., 1995-97; bd. dirs. Seattle Alliance Edn., 1990—; mem. bd. Ctr. for Career Alternatives, 1981—; precinct committeeman, 1990-96; bd. dirs. U. Wash. Law Sch. Found., 1994—, pres., 2003—. Served to lt. comdr. USN, 1972-81, Vietnam, with Res., 1981—, comdr., 1988-93, capt., 2003. Mem. ABA, Wash. State Bar Assn., Seattle/King County Bar Assn., Judge Advocates Assn., Greater Seattle C. of C., U. Wash. Alumni Assn. (bd. dirs. 1986-93), U. Wash. Law Sch. Alumni Assn. (pres. 1989-91), Wash. Athletic Club, Columbia Tower Club, City Club. Democrat. Jewish. Office: Ben Bridge Jeweler Inc PO Box 1908 Seattle WA 98111-1908 E-mail: jbridge@benbridge.com.

BRIDGE, THOMAS PETER, psychiatrist, researcher; b. Nashville, June 2, 1945; s. Thomas Gale and Hilma Elizabeth (Hartzler) B.; m. Mary L. Matthews, Dec. 15, 1969 (div. Sept. 1974); m. Beth J. Soldo, Sept. 20, 1975. BA, Duke U., 1967; MD, Med. Coll. Va., 1971. Diplomate Am. Bd. Psychiatry and Neurology. Rsch. fellow Duke U., Durham, N.C., 1972-74; clin. staff fellow NIMH, Bethesda, Md., 1977-79, chief unit on geriatrics Washington, 1980-83; sci. advisor Alcohol, Drug, and Mental Health Adminstrn., Rockville, Md., 1983-86, AIDS coord., 1986-90; chief clin. trials br. Nat. Inst. on Drug Abuse, Rockville, 1990—2000; dir. benefit risk mgmt. Johnson & Johnson, 2001—; with Huffman La Roche, 2004—. Editor: AIDS Neuropsychiatry, 1989; contbr. more than 75 articles to profl. jours. Named J.D. Lane Outstanding Investigator, USPHS, 1984; recipient New Investigator award Am. Geriatrics Soc., 1985, Sec.'s Disting. Svc. award Dept. Health & Human Svcs., 2000. Fellow Coll. Internat. Neuropsychopharmacology; mem. AAAS, Am. Coll. Neuropsychopharmacology. Achievements include patents for novel pharmacologic treatments for cognitive enhancement, chronic fatigue, and psoriasis. Home: 210 W Rittenhouse Sq Philadelphia PA 19103 Office: 340 Kingsland St Nutley NJ 07110 Business E-Mail: peter.bridge@roche.com.

BRIDGELAND, JAMES RALPH, JR., lawyer; b. Cleve., Feb. 16, 1929; s. James Ralph and Alice Laura (Huth) B.; m. Margaret Louise Bates, March 24, 1950; children: Deborah, Cynthia, Rebekah, Alicia, John. BA magna cum laude, U. Akron, 1951; MA, Harvard U., 1955, JD, 1957. Bar: Ohio 1957. Mem. internat. staff Goodyear Tire & Rubber Co., Akron, Ohio, 1953-56; ptnr. Taft, Stettinius & Hollister, Cin., 1957—; dir., mem. exec. com. Firstar Corp. and Star Bank Cin.; dir. SHV N.Am., Inc., The David J. Joseph Co., Robert A. Cline Co., Art Stamping, Inc., Seinau-Fisher Studios, Inc.; instr., lectr. in lit. U. Cin. Pres., trustee Cin. Symphony Orch.; sec., trustee Louise Taft Semple Found.; trustee Cin. Opera Co., Hillside Trust, Jobs for Cin. Grads., Cin. Inst. Fine Arts; past bd. dirs. Legal Aid Soc.; mayor, mem. coun. City of Indian Hill, Ohio, 1985-91; pres. Indian Hill Sch. Bd., 1971-77. 1st lt. USAF, 1951-53, Korea. Mem. ABA, Ohio Bar Assn., Cin. Bar Assn., Am. Arbitration Assn., Harvard Law Sch. Assn. (past pres. Cin. chpt.), Harvard Alumni Assn. (nat. v.p. 1978-85). Harvard Club (pres. 1983-84), Queen City Club, Commonwealth Club (treas. 1984-86), Queen City Optimist Club, Recess Club, Assn. Literary Scholars and Critics, Cin. Optimist Club, Cin. Literary Club. Republican. Episcopalian. Home: 8175 Brill Rd Cincinnati OH 45243-3937

BRIDGER, BALDWIN, JR., electrical engineer; b. Savannah, Ga., Sept. 18, 1928; s. Baldwin and Helen Bush (Stubbs) B.; m. Wilma Grace Martz, Mar. 21, 1953; children: Ruth Carson, John Wesley, Mary Gere. BS in Engring., Emory U., 1948; postgrad., U. Iowa, 1966-68. Registered profl. engr., Tex., Pa. Test engr. GE, Lynn, Mass., Trenton, N.J., Ft. Wayne, Ind., Schenectady, N.Y., 1948-50, design engr. Phila., 1953-65, engring. mgr. Burlington, Iowa, 1965-68, Phila., 1968-71, product planner, 1972-73; chief engr. Powell Elec. Mfg. Co., Houston, 1973-83, mgr. engring., 1983-85, mgr. application and new products engring., 1985-90, tech. dir., 1990-96; pres. Bridger Engring. Co., 1996—. Contbr. articles to tech. jours. With USN, 1951-52. Fellow IEEE (dept. chmn. 1987-88, soc. treas. 1989-90, soc. sec. 1991, soc. v.p. 1992, pres. 1993, editor, tech. jour. 1997—); mem. Phi Beta Kappa. Republican. Methodist.

BRIDGERS, WILLIAM FRANK, retired physician; b. Asheville, NC, July 26, 1932; s. John Dixon and Ruth (Norberg) B.; m. Judith Ann Ware, Nov. 27, 1974; 1 child, Jana; children from previous marriage: Jeffrey, David, Daniel. BA, U. of the South, 1954; MD, Washington U., St. Louis, 1959, fellow in preventive medicine, 1963-65. Intern Barnes Hosp., Washington U., St. Louis, 1959—60, resident, 1962—63; assoc. prof. medicine U. Miami, Fla., 1968; prof., dir. neurosci. program U. Ala., Birmingham, 1970—72, spl. asst. v.p. health affairs, 1976, chmn., prof. dept. pub. health, 1976—93, former dean, 1981—89, prof., 1981—93, univ. scholar emeritus, 1993—2003, dean emeritus, 2000—03; head Eutaw Health Policy Group, 1993—2001; ret., 2003. Staff mem. NAS, Washington, 1974; mem. governing bd. Nat. Coun. Internat. Health, Washington, 1979-87; dir. Lister Hill Ctr. for Health Policy, 1987-90; mem. com. on vital and health stats. HHS, USPHS, 1990-94. Co-editor (monthly feature) Policy Watch Am. Jour. Medicine and Am. Jour. Surgery, 1990-97; contbr. articles to profl. jours. Mem. APHA, Assn. Schs. Pub. Health (pres., mem. exec. com.), Am. Men and Women of Sci., Am. Inst. Nutrition, Am. Soc. Biol. Chemistry, Phi Beta Kappa. Democrat. Home: 2221 English Village Ln Birmingham AL 35223-1730

BRIDGES, ALAN LYNN, physicist, researcher, application developer, computer scientist; BS in Physics, Ga. Inst. Tech., 1972, MS in Physics, 1974, postgrad., 1975—78, postgrad., 1994—95. Cert. C-130J R&M HUD, BIU, MC, FMECA. Asst. research scientist Ga. Tech. Research Inst., Atlanta, 1975-78; asst. product mgr. Humphrey Instruments Inc., San Leandro, Calif., 1978; pres., cons. ETC West Ltd., 1979—; with Lockheed Aero Systems Co., 1983-88; sr. prin. engr. new bus. devel. Lockheed Electronics Co., Atlanta, 1988-90; sr. engr., program mgr. Flat Panel & Graphics Display Systems SCI Tech., Inc., Hunstville, Ala., 1990-92; software engr. specialist life cycle software support and C130JRM & S sys. engring. Lockheed Martin Aeronautical Systems Co., Marietta, Ga., 1992-2001, sr. S.W. software specialist, 1998—; reliability, supportability and safety staff engr., lead engr. vision display server Barcoview LLC, 2001—03; staff reliability/safety engr. L-3 Communication Display Sys., Alpharetta, Ga., 2003—. Mem. Lockheed Software Process Std. ISO 9000/SEI CMM software and sys. engring. CMM process action team, ACM stds. com. tech. adv. group ISO 9241. Contbg. editor Computer Tech. Rev., PC Graphics & Video Mag.; bi-monthly columnist Hardcopy, 1983-93; contbr. articles to profl. jours Mem. IEEE (sr., dir. Atlanta sect., 1987-88, sec. 1988-89, treas. 1989-90, chmn. student activities com. 1985-87, sec.-treas. computer soc. chpt. 1985-86, chmn. computer soc. chpt. 1986-89, vice-chmn. 1987-88, gen. chmn. Atlanta software tech. conf. 1987, mem P1226 ABBET com., mem. P1498/12207 stds. com., SW stds. com.), Assn. for Computing Machinery, Optical Soc. Am., Soc. Photo-Optical Instrumentation Engrs., Nat. Security Indsl. Assn. (mem. integrated diagnostic working group, co-chair integrated avionics task group), Soc. for Tech. Communications, Computer Press Assn., Soc. for Info. Display, Nat. Telesystems Conf., Control and Displays Session Orgn., Am. Nat. Standards Inst./Internat. Standards Orgn., Sigma Pi Sigma. Home: 8523 Colony Club Dr Alpharetta GA 30022-5407 Office: L-3 Comm Display Sys 1355 Bluegrass Lakes Pkwy Alpharetta GA 30004-8458 Office Phone: 770-752-5135. Personal E-mail: alan.bridges@1-3com.com.

BRIDGES, ANDREW PHILLIP, lawyer; b. Atlanta, Sept. 11, 1954; s. Glenn Jackson and Margaret Eugenia (Raymond) B.; m. J. Rebecca Lyman, July 27, 1985; children: Catherine S. Bridges-Lyman, Thomas A. Bridges-Lyman. AB, Stanford U., 1976; postgrad., Am. Sch. Classical Studies, Athens, Greece, 1977-78; JD, Harvard U., 1983; MA, Oxford (Eng.) U., 1985. Bar: Ga. 1984, Calif. 1986, U.S. Supreme Ct. 1987. Law clk. to hon. Marvin H. Shoob U.S. Dist. Ct., Atlanta, 1983-85; assoc. Farella, Braun & Martel, San Francisco, 1985-91; ptnr., head of trademarks and advt. practices group Wilson, Sonsini, Goodrich & Rosati, Palo Alto, Calif., 1991—2004; ptnr. Winston & Strawn LLP, San Francisco, 2004—. Co-chair fed. cts. com. Bar Assn. San Francisco, 1988-90; dir. Hellenic Law Soc. No. Calif., San Francisco, 1990-94; lectr. Practising Law Inst., San Francisco, 1990-97; mem. editl. bd. Intellectual Property Strategist, N.Y.C., 1994—2002; judge diocesan ct. Episcopal Diocese of Calif., San Francisco, 1995—99; arbitrator World Intellectual Property Orgn., Geneva, 1999—; early neutral evaluator U.S. Dist. Ct., San Francisco, Calif., 2002—; lectr. Fed. Judicial Ctr., Berkeley, Calif., 2002—. Contbr. articles to profl. jours. Sr. warden St. Mark's Episcopal Ch., Berkeley, Calif., 1990-92; dir. Ronald McDonald House Stanford, Palo Alto, Calif., 2002—; dir., Theatreworks, Palo Alto. Grad. fellow Rotary Found., Athens, 1977-78. Mem. Computer Law Assn., Copyright Soc. U.S.A., Internat. Trademark Assn., Phi Beta Kappa. Democrat. Avocations: mediterranean history and archaeology, classical philosophy and languages, skiing, tennis. Office: Winston & Strawn LLP 101 California St San Francisco CA 94111 Office Phone: 415-591-1482.

BRIDGES, B. RIED, lawyer; b. Kansas City, Mo., Oct. 20, 1927; s. Brady R. and Mary H. (Nieuwenhuis) B.; 1 son, Ried George. BA, U. So. Calif., 1951, LLB, 1954. Bar: Calif. 1954. Ptnr. Bonne, Bridges, Mueller & O'Keefe, L.A. and Las Vegas, 1958—. Fellow Am. Coll. Trial Lawyers, Internat. Acad. Trial Lawyers; mem. Calif. Bar Assn., Am. Bd. Trial Advs. (diplomate), Pacific Corinthian Yacht Club, Balboa of Mazatlan (Sinaloa, Mex.). Republican. Avocation: sportfishing. Home: 1001 Kensington Ct Carson City NV 89703-5431 Office: Bonne Bridges Mueller O'Keefe & Nichols 3441 S Eastern Ave Ste 402 Las Vegas NV 89109-3314 Office Phone: 775-841-0118. Personal E-mail: brb2551@aol.com.

BRIDGES, BEAU (LLOYD VERNET BRIDGES III), actor; b. Hollywood, Dec. 9, 1941; s. Lloyd Vernet and Dorothy (Simpson) B.; m. Julie Landifield 1964 (div. 1984); 2 children; m. Wendy Treece Bridges; 3 children. Attended, U. Calif. at Los Angeles. Film appearances include The Incident, For Love of Ivy, 1968, Gaily, Gaily, 1969, The Landlord, 1970, Adam's Woman, The Christian Licorice Store, 1971, Hammersmith is Out, 1972, Child's Play, 1972, Your Three Minutes Are Up, 1973, Lovin' Molly, The Other Side of the Mountain, 1975, Swashbuckler, 1976, Two-Minute Warning, 1976, Dragon Fly, 1976, Greased Lightning, 1977, Norma Rae, 1979, The Fifth Musketeer, 1979, The Runner Stumbles, 1979, Honky Tonk Freeway, 1980, Night Crossing, 1982, Love Child, 1982, Heart Like a Wheel, 1983, The Hotel New Hampshire, 1984, Iron Triangle, 1987, The Fabulous Baker Boys, 1989, (also dir.) Seven Hours to Judgment, 1988, The Wizard, 1989, Daddy's Dying...Who's Got the Will?, 1990, Married to It, 1993, Sidekicks, 1993, Nightjohn, 1996, Losing Chase, 1996, Jerry Maguire, 1996, Rocket Man, 1997, Meeting Daddy, 1998, White River Kid, 1999, Sordid Lives, 2000, Meeting Daddy, 2000, Boys Klub, 2001, Debating Robert Lee, 2004, The Ballad of Jack and Rose, 2005, Smile, 2005; TV appearances include The Man Without a Country, 1973, The Stranger Who Looks like Me, 1974, The Whirlwind, 1974, Medical Story, The President's Mistress, 1978, The Four Feathers, 1978, The Child Stealer, 1979, United States, 1980, The Kid from Nowhere, 1982, Dangerous Company, 1982, Witness for the Prosecution, 1982, The Red-Light Sting, 1984, A Fighting Choice, Outrage, 1989, Wildflower, 1991; TV film Wildflower, 1991, Million Dollar Babies, 1994, Kissenger and Nixon, 1995, Hidden In America, 1996, The Second Civil War, 1997, Inherit the Wind, 1999, The White River Kid, 1999, Common Ground, 2000, Songs in Ordinary Time, 2000, The Christmas Secret, 2000, The Agency, 2001, We Were the Mulvaneys, 2002, Sightings: Heartland Ghost, 2002, Out of the Ashes, 2003 Evil Knievel, 2004; TV mini-series Space, 1985, Without Warning: The James Brady Story, HBO, 1992 (Emmy award leading actor, 1992), The Positively True Adventures of the Alleged Texas Cheerleader-Murdering Mom, HBO, 1993 (Emmy award, Outstanding Supporting Actor in a Miniseries or Special, 1993, Golden Globe Award, Best actor in a mini-series or movie made for television, 1994), P.T. Barnum, 1999, Voyage of the Unicorn, 2001, 10.5, 2004; T.V.(also Prod.), The Denders: payback, 1997; The Defenders: Choice of Evils, 1998; T.V. Series, Maximum Bob, 1998, The Agency, 2002-03, Stargate SG-1, 2005-. Office: Creative Artists care Steve Tellez 9830 Wilshire Blvd Beverly Hills CA 90212-1825*

BRIDGES, CYNTHIA LYNN, music educator; b. Port Lavaca, Tex., Aug. 10, 1965; d. James Carlton Moses and Cheryle Lynn Hubenak; m. John Robin Bridges, Nov. 30, 1996. MusB, SW Tex. State U., San Marcos, 1987; MA, U. Hawaii, Honolulu, 1999; PhD, U. Hawaii at Manoa, Honolulu, 2005. Dir. bands Marion Ind. Sch. Dist., Tex., 1992—96; grad. asst. U. Hawaii at Manoa, Honolulu, 1997—2002; dir. bands Christian Acad., Honolulu, 2002—03; asst. prof. music Malone Coll., Canton, Ohio, 2004—. V.p. The Friends of the Royal Hawaiian Band, Honolulu, 1999—2004. Nyborg Fellowship, U. Hawaii at Manoa Music Dept., 2002. Mem.: Nat. Band Assn. Conservative. Protestant. Avocations: travel, outdoor activities, golf. Home: 5671 Birmingham Rd NE Canton OH 44721 Office: Malone Coll 515 25th St NW Canton OH 44709 Office Phone: 330-471-8219. Business E-Mail: cbridges@malone.edu.

BRIDGES, DAVID MANNING, lawyer; b. Berkeley, Calif., May 22, 1936; s. Robert Lysle and Alice Marion (Rodenberger) B.; m. Carmen Galante de Bridges, Aug. 16, 1973; children: David, Stuart. AB, U. Calif., Berkeley, 1957, JD, 1962. Assoc. Thelen, Marrin, Johnson & Bridges, San Francisco, 1962-70, ptnr., 1970-94, mng. ptnr. Houston, 1981-91. Served as lt. (j.g.) USN, 1957—59. Mem. ABA, State Bar of Tex., Tex. Bar Assn., Houston Bar Assn., Internat. Bar Assn., Houston Club, Coronado Club, Pacific-Union Club. Office: 700 Louisiana St Ste 4600 Houston TX 77002-2732 Office Phone: 713-655-0022. Personal E-mail: dbridhou@aol.com.

BRIDGES, FRANK GEORGE, physics educator; b. Saskatoon, Sask., Can., Jan. 17, 1940; came to U.S., 1964; s. Frank George and Jeanne Louise (Beveridge) B.; m. Loreen Carole Webster, June 27, 1964; children: Brent, Bradd. BSc, U. B.C., 1962, MSc, 1964; PhD, U. Calif., San Diego, 1968. Asst. rsch. physicist, lectr. U. Calif., San Diego, 1968—70, asst. prof. physics Santa Cruz, 1970—75, assoc. prof. physics, 1975—81, prof., chmn. physics dept., 1982—84, prof. physics, 1981—. Mem. many univ. coms. Contbr. numerous articles to profl. publs. Recipient numerous grants including NASA and NSF; fellowship Alexander von Humboldt Found., 1976, 1979. Fellow: Am. Phys. Soc. (presenter papers). Achievements include research in studies of the local structure about atoms in insulating and superconducting materials, using microwaves and x-ray spectroscopy; mass transfer during ice particle collisions in planetary rings; collisional properties of ice spheres at low velocities, structure of Saturn's rings. Office: U Calif Physics Dept 1156 High St Santa Cruz CA 95064-1077

BRIDGES, GEORGE S., academic administrator, sociology educator; m. Kari Tupper; children: Anna, James, Lauren, Seth. BA cum laude, U. Wash., 1972; MA in Criminology, U. Pa., 1973, PhD in Sociology, 1979. Social scientist Office of Policy and Planning Office of Atty. Gen., US Dept. Justice, 1976, asst. adminstr. Fed. Justice Rsch. Program, 1977—81; adj. prof. Inst. Criminal Justice and Criminology, U. Md., 1980—81; asst. prof. Dept. Sociology and Legal Studies Program Case Western Reserve U., 1981—82; asst. prof. Dept. Sociology U. Wash., Seattle, 1982—88, assoc. prof., 1989—97, prof., 1998—2005, acting dir. Soc. and Justice Program, 1988—89, 1992, dir., 1996—98, assoc. dean, assoc. vice provost Office of Undergraduate Edn., 1998—2001, acting dean, 2001—02, vice provost, 2001—05, dean, 2002—05; pres., prof. Whitman Coll., Walla Walla, Wash., 2005—. Dep. editor Criminology, 1984—87; author: Inequality, Crime, and Social Control, 1994; co-author: Crime and Society: Criminal Justice, 1996, Crime and Society: Crime, 1996, Crime and Society: Juvenile Delinquency, 1996, Teaching and Learning in Large Classes, 2000; contbr. articles to profl. jours. Recipient J. Francis Finnegan Meml. Prize in Criminology, U. Pa., 1974, Award for Outstanding Achievement by Scholar, Wash. Coun. on Crime and Delinquency, 1995. Mem.: Soc. Study of Social Problems, Law and Soc. Assn., Am. Soc. Criminology, Am. Sociological Assn., Am. Assn. Higher Edn., Alpha Kappa Delta, Phi Eta Sigma. Avocations: hiking, skiing. Office: Whitman Coll Memorial Bldg 303,304 345 Boyer Ave Walla Walla WA 99362 Office Phone: 509-527-5132. E-mail: bridges@whitman.edu.*

BRIDGES, JOHN FRANCIS PATRICK, healthcare educator, researcher; b. Orange, NSW, Australia, Dec. 20, 1973; arrived in U.S., 1999; s. Terrence Allen and Margaret Myree Bridges; m. Coatney Charlene Rene, Dec. 27, 2003. B Econs. with honors, Australian Nat. U., Canberra, 1996; M Econs. with honors, U. Sydney, Australia, 1997; PhD, CUNY, 2002. Rsch. asst. Nat. Bur. Econ. Rsch., NYC, 1999—2002, rsch. economist, 2004—; asst. prof. Case Western Res. U., Cleve., 2002—04; leader jr. group internat. health econ. and outcome rsch., dept. tropical hygeniene and pub. health U. Heidelberg, Germany, 2004—. Robert E. Gilleece fellow CUNY, 1999—2002. Lector, eucharistic min. St. Ann's Cath. Ch., Cleveland Heights, Ohio, 2001. Mem.: Australian Health Econs. Soc. (v.p. 1998—99, editor 2000—01). Roman Catholic. Office: INF 324 Heidelberg 69120 Germany Office Phone: 49-0-6221-564886. E-mail: healtheconomics@hotmail.com.

BRIDGES, JOHN ROBIN, retired music educator; b. Clifton F. and Glenis Bryant Bridges; m. Cynthia Lynn Moses, Nov. 30, 1996. BS in Edn., Tenn. Tech U., 1960; M in Music Edn., U. N.Tex., 1970. Permanent tchg. cert. Band dir. Tyner Jr. and Sr. H.S., Chattanooga, 1960—63; asst. band dir. Edgewood H.S., San Antonio, 1963—64; band dir. Southside H.S., San Antonio, 1964—65, Randolph AFB H.S., San Antonio, 1965—79, Douglas MacArthur H.S., San Antonio, 1979—81; band dir. and supr. Alamo Heights Ind. Sch. Dist., San Antonio, 1981—95; band and orch. dir. Trinity U., San Antonio, 1995—96; dir. bands Punahou Sch., Honolulu, 1996—2004. Music dir. San Antonio Mcpl. Band, 1985—95. Editor: Tex. Music Educator, 1978—79. Named to Tex. Bandmasters Hall Fame, 2005, Legion of Hon., John Philip Sousa Found., 2005. Mem.: Oahu Band Dirs. Assn. (pres.), Nat. Band Assn. (v.p. 1984—86, Citation 1982, Mentor award 2004), Tex. Music Educators Assn. (life; pres. 1978—79, Plaque 1979). Avocations: computer science, golf. Personal E-mail: jrbridges@neo.rr.com.

BRIDGES, JUDY CANTRELL, gifted and talented education educator; b. Dallas, Feb. 17, 1947; d. William and Jewel Alexandria (Autrey) C.; m. Gary L. Bridges, Aug. 17, 1969; children: John Drewry, Judith Alexandria. BA, Tex. Tech. U., 1969; gifted/talented endorsement, Sul Ross State U., Alpine, Tex., 1992, MEd, 1993; cert. in mid-mgmt., Sul Ross State U., 1994. Lic. secondary edn. math. and English. Tchr. New Deal (Tex.) Ind. Sch. Dist., 1969—70, Indpls. Pub. Schs., 1970, USDESEA, Zweibruecken, Germany, 1971—73, Lubbock (Tex.) Ind. Sch. Dist., 1973—76, Ector County Ind. Sch. Dist., Odessa, Tex., 1976-85, 87-90, tchr. gifted spl. edn., 1990—92, gifted/talented coord., 1992—97, dir. advanced acad. svcs., 1977—2001; ednl. cons., self employed Odessa, 2001—02; prin., dir. enchanced academic programs Midland Ind. Sch. Dist., 2002—. Acct. Walter Smith CPA, Odessa, 1977—82; real estate appraiser Appraisal Assocs., Odessa, 1985—87; vis. lectr. Sul Ross State U., Alpine, 1994, Alpine, 1997—98, Alpine, 2001; mem. gifted/talented adv. com. Region 18 Edn. Svc. Ctr., Midland, Tex., 1993—. Author: (poem) Paradigm Shifts in the West Texas Sand, 1991. Advisor, officer Jr. League of Odessa, Inc., 1980—, treas./treas. elect, 1986—88; treas. Campaign to Elect County Judge, Odessa, 1991; mem. bd. Permian H.S. Football Booster Club, 1993; dir. region I Tex. Acad. Decathlon, 1999, 2000; bd. dirs. ECISD Edn. Found., 2002—03, Odessa Symphony Guild, Odessa, Tex., 1996—98; mem. State Bd. for Educator Cert. Math. Stds. Com., 2000; chairperson math. Gifted/Talented Performance Stds. Com. Tex., 2000; dir. Tex. Assn. Gifted and Talented, 1999—2001, sec., treas., 2002, pres. elect, 2003, pres., 2004. Recipient Dept. of Def. Commendation, U.S. Dependent Edn. System, Zweibruecken, 1973, Cert. of Appreciation-Stop of Felony Odessa Police Dept., 1992. Mem. ASCD, NEA, Tex. State Tchrs. Assn. (treas. Ector County unit 1991-92), Tex. Assn. Gifted and Talented, Am. Creativity Assn., Nat. Coun. Tchrs. Math, Ptnrs. for Excellence (bd. dirs., 2002—), West Tex. Reading Coun. Baptist. Avocations: skiing, flora design, reading, travel. Home: 4243 Lynbrook Ave Odessa TX 79762-7146 Office: 1300 E Wall St Midland TX 79701 E-mail: jcbridges@sbcglobal.net.

BRIDGES, LEONARD HAL, retired history educator, writer; b. Luling, Tex., Nov. 10, 1918; s. Leonard Harold and Lyda Lois (King) B.; m. Alice Miskjian, Aug. 21, 1949; children: Lois Alice, Stephanie Ann. BJ, U. Tex., 1940; MA, Columbia U., 1947, PhD, 1950. Instr. history U. Ark., Fayetteville, 1950-53; asst. prof. U. Colo., Boulder, 1953-55, assoc. prof., 1955-60, prof., 1960-64, U. Calif., Riverside, 1964-79, prof. emeritus, 1979—. Author: Iron Millionaire: Life of Charlemagne Tower, 1952, Lee's Maverick General: Daniel Harvey Hill, 1961, reprinted, 1991, American Mysticism: From William James to Zen, 1970. Maj. U.S. Army, 1940-45, MTO. Sr. faculty fellow U. Calif., 1965; rsch. grantee Am. Philos. Soc., U. Colo., U. Calif. Avocations: writing, walking, reading.

BRIDGES, ROBERT LYSLE, retired lawyer; b. Altus, Ark., May 12, 1909; s. Joseph Manning and Jeffa Alice (Morrison) B.; m. Alice Marian Rodenberger, June 10, 1930; children: David Manning, James Robert, Linda Lee. AB, U. Calif., 1930, JD, 1933. Bar: Calif. 1933, U.S. Supreme Ct 1938. Pvt. practice, San Francisco, 1933-92; assoc. firm Thelen Marrin Johnson & Bridges, 1933-39, ptnr., 1938-92. Trustee, former chmn. U. Calif. Berkeley Found.; trustee, hon. dir. John Muir Found., 1992—. Mem. ABA, Calif. Bar Assn., San Francisco Bar Assn., Commonwealth Club of Calif., Pacific Union Club, Claremont Country Club (Oakland). Republican. Home: 3972 Happy Valley Rd Lafayette CA 94549-2426 Office: 101 Second St Ste 1800 San Francisco CA 94105-3601

BRIDGES, ROBERT RUSSELL, III, obstetrician, gynecologist; b. Chattanooga, July 27, 1954; s. Robert Russell Bridges, Jr and Jeri Foster; life ptnr. Dudley Cannada. BS, U. Ala., Huntsville, 1976, MS, 1978; MD, U. Ala., 1982. Diplomate Am. Bd. Med. Examiners, 1998. Intern, resident George Washington U. Hosp., Washington, 1982—86; pvt. practice physician Washington, 1986—. Treas. Friends of Rose Park, Washington, 1998—2005. Fellow: Am. Coll. Ob-gyn. Home: 2453 P St NW Washington DC 20007 Office: 2440 M St Nw Washington DC 20037 Office Phone: 202-333-2727.

BRIDGES, ROGER DEAN, historian; b. Marshalltown, Iowa, Feb. 10, 1937; s. Floyd F. and Beatrice Andrea (Pipher) B.; m. Karen Maureen Buckley, June 4, 1960; children: Patrick Sean, Kristin Joy, Jennifer Lynn. BA, Iowa State Tchrs. Coll., 1959; MA, State Coll. of Iowa, 1962; PhD, U. Ill., 1970; LHD, Lincoln (Ill.) Coll., 1987, Tiffin U., 1994. Tchr., libr. Keokuk (Iowa) Pub. Schs., 1959—62; instr. in history Bradley U., Peoria, Ill., 1967; asst. prof. history U. S.D., Vermillion, 1968—69; asst. editor Papers of Ulysses Grant, Carbondale, Ill., 1969—70; dir. rsch. Ill. State Hist. Libr., Springfield, 1970—76, head libr., 1976—85; dir. Ill. State Hist. Libr./Ill. Hist. Preservation Agy., Springfield, 1985—87; dir., editor Lincoln legal papers project, asst. state historian Ill. Hist. Preservation Agy, Springfield, 1987—88; exec. dir. Rutherford B. Hayes Presdl. Ctr., Fremont, Ohio, 1988—2003, exec. dir. emeritus, 2004—. Part-time instr. Ill. State U., Normal, Ill., 1974-84; adj. prof. Sangamon State U., Springfield, 1985-88, Bowling Green (Ohio) State U., 1989-2003. Author, editor: Illinois: It's History and Legacy, 1984; asst. editor: Papers of Ulysses S. Grant, vol. 4, 1972. Bd. dirs. Springfield Urban League, 1976-82, Gt. Am. People Show, New Salem, Ill., 1978-85; bd. dirs., sec., v.p. Birchard Pub. Libr. Sandusky County, Fremont, 1988-2003, 1996-99; bd. dirs., pres. Conv. and Visitors Bur. Sandusky County, Fremont, 1988-99. Nat. Hist. Publs. Commn. fellow, 1969-70;

recipient Disting. Svc. awrd Springfield Urban League, 1977. Mem. Am. Hist. Assn., So. Hist. Assn., Abraham Lincoln Assn. bd. dirs. 1985-, pres. 2004-), Orgn. Am. Historians, Soc. for Historians of Gilded Age and Progressive Era (sec., treas. 1989-2003, mem. coun. 2004-), Ill. State Hist. Soc. (bd. dirs. 2003—, Disting. Svc. award 1988), Ohio Acad. History (exec. coun. 1996-98), bd. trustees Ohioana Library Assn., 1998-2003, C. of C. of Sandusky County (bd. dirs. 1999-2002), David Davis Mansion Found. (bd. dirs. 2003-), Rotary Internat. Democrat. Baptist. Home: 2804 Mockingbird Ln Bloomington IL 61704 Office Phone: 309-664-5476. E-mail: rdbridges@verizon.net.

BRIDGES, ROY DUBARD, JR., federal agency administrator; b. Atlanta; m. Benita Louise Allbaugh; children: 2. BS in Engring. Sci., USAF Acad., 1965; MS in Astronautics, Purdue U., 1966. Commd. 2d lt. USAF, advanced through grades to maj. gen., comdr. 6510th Test Wing Edwards AFB, Calif., 1986-89, comdr. Ea. Space and Missile Ctr. Patrick AFB, Fla., 1989-90, comdr. Air Force Flight Test Ctr. Edwards AFB, 1991-93, dir. requirements Air Force Materiel Command Wright-Patterson AFB, Ohio, 1993-96, ret., 1996; dir. John F. Kennedy Space Ctr. NASA, 1997—2003; dir. Langley Rsch. Ctr., NASA, 2003—. Achievements include being a NASA astronaut, piloted Space Shuttle Challenger July and August, 1985. Office: Mail Code 106 NASA Langley Rsch Ctr Hampton VA 23681 Office Phone: 757-864-4111.

BRIDGES, WILLIAM BRUCE, electrical engineer, researcher, engineering educator; b. Inglewood, Calif., Nov. 29, 1934; s. Newman K. and Doris L. (Brown) Bridges; m. Carol Ann French, Aug. 24, 1957 (div. 1986); children: Ann Marjorie, Bruce Kendall, Michael Alan; m. Linda Josephine McManus, Nov. 15, 1986. BEE, U. Calif., Berkeley, 1956, MEE (GE Rice fellow), 1957, PhD in Elec. Engring. (NSF fellow), 1962. Assoc. elec. engring. U. Calif., Berkeley, 1957-59, grad. rsch. engr., 1959-61; mem. tech. staff Hughes Rsch. Labs. divsn. Hughes Aircraft Co., Malibu, Calif., 1960-77, sr. scientist, 1968-77, mgr. laser dept., 1969-70; prof. elec. engring. and applied physics Calif. Inst. Tech., Pasadena, 1977—2002, Carl F Braun prof. engring., 1983—2002, Carl F Braun prof. engring. emeritus, 2002—, exec. officer elec. engring., 1978-81. Lectr. U. So. Calif., L.A., 1962—64; Sherman Fairchild Disting. scholar Calif. Inst. Tech., 1974—75; bd. dirs. Phasebridge Corp., Access Laser Corp. Author (with C. K. Birdsall): (book) Electron Dynamics of Diode Regions, 1966; contbr. articles to profl. jours.; assoc. editor: IEEE Jour. Quantum Electronics, 1977—82, Jour. Optical Soc. Am., 1978—83. Mem. sci. adv. bd. USAF, 1985—89. Named Disting. Engring. Alumnus, U. Calif., Berkeley, 1995, Hon. Alumnus, Calif. Inst. Tech., 2003; recipient L. A. Hyland Patent award, 1969, Lifetime Achievement award for excellence in tchg., Assoc. Students of Calif. Inst. Tech., 2003. Fellow: IEEE (Quantum Electronics award 1988), Laser Inst. Am. (Arthur L. Schawlow award 1986), Optical Soc. Am. (objectives and policies com. 1981—86, 1989—91, bd. dirs. 1982—84, v.p. 1986, pres.-elect 1987, pres. 1988, past pres. 1989); mem.: Am. Acad. Arts and Scis., Am. Acad. Arts and Sci., Am. Radio Relay League, Nat. Acad. Scis., Nat. Acad. Engring., Phi Beta Kappa, Eta Kappa Nu (One of Outstanding Young Elec. Engrs. 1966), Tau Beta Pi, Sigma Xi. Achievements include invention of noble gas ion laser; patents in field. Office: Calif Inst Tech Moore Bldg 136-93 Pasadena CA 91125-0001 Business E-Mail: w6fa@caltech.edu.

BRIDGES-KEMP, LESLIE LAVERNE, administrative assistant; AA, Miami-Dade CC, 1981. Med. asst., sec. Dr. James W. Bridges MD, Miami, 1981—2002; adminstrv. asst. Econ. Opportunity Family Health, Miami, 2002—. Typist State Poet of Calif., Antioch, 1974—2003. Author: Anno Domini Cherokee, 2002. Catechumen Roman Cath. Ch., Miami, 2003. Scholar, Clark Coll., 1964—65. Mem.: PA Notary Publics. Roman Catholic. Avocations: computers, reading. Office Phone: 305-637-6400 15100. Personal E-mail: bobdylan6@hotmail.com. Business E-Mail: lbkemp@hcnetwork.org.

BRIDGEWATER, ALBERT LOUIS, retired science foundation administrator; b. Houston, Nov. 22, 1941; s. Albert Louis and Rita (Narcisse) B.; children: Ramesi, Akin BA in Physics, U. Calif.-Berkeley, 1963; PhD in Physics, Columbia U., 1972. Postdoctoral fellow Lawrence Berkeley Lab., Berkeley, Calif., 1970-73; staff asst. physics NSF, Washington, 1973-76, spl. exec. asst., 1976-81, dep. asst. dir., 1981-86, sr. staff assoc., 1986-88, sr. sci. assoc., 1988-2001, acting asst. dir., 1983-85. Adj. asst. prof. Howard U., Washington, 1975-76 Mem. Am. Geophys. Union, Am. Physical Soc. Avocations: reading, outdoor sports.

BRIDGEWATER, BERNARD ADOLPHUS, JR., retired retail executive; b. Tulsa, Mar. 13, 1934; s. Bernard Adolphus and Mary Alethea (Burton) B.; m. Barbara Paton, July 2, 1960; children: Barrie, Elizabeth, Bonnie. AB, Westminster Coll., Fulton, Mo., 1955; LLB, U. Okla., 1958; MBA, Harvard, 1964. Bar: Okla. 1958, U.S. Supreme Ct. 1958, U.S. Ct. of Claims 1958. Asst. county atty., Tulsa, 1962; assoc. McKinsey & Co., mgmt. cons. Chgo., 1964-68, prin., 1968-72, dir., 1972-73, 75; assoc. dir. nat. security and internat. affairs Office Mgmt. and Budget, Exec. Office Pres., Washington, 1973-74; exec. v.p. Baxter Travenol Labs., Inc., Chgo. and Deerfield, Ill., 1975-79, dir., 1975-85; pres. Brown Group, Inc., Clayton, Mo., 1979-87, 90-99, CEO, 1982-99, chmn., 1985-99, also dir.; now ret.; cons. TIAA-CREF, N.Y.C. Bd. dirs. Mitretek Sys., Inc., McLean, Va., ThoughtWorks Inc., Chgo.; adv. dir. Schroder Venture Ptnrs. LLC, N.Y.C.; cons. in field. Author: (with others) Better Management of Business Giving, 1965. Trustee Rush-Presbyn. St. Luke's Med. Ctr., 1974-84, Washington U., St. Louis, 1983-94, 95-2003, 04—, Barnes Hosp., St. Louis, 1987-90; bd. visitors Harvard U. Bus. Sch., 1987-93. Served to lt. USNR, 1958-62. Recipient Rayonier Found. award Harvard U., 1963; George F. Baker scholar, 1964 Mem. Beta Theta Pi, Omicron Delta Kappa, Phi Alpha Delta. St. Louis Country Club, Log Cabin Club, Indian Hill Country Club Office: 7701 Forsyth Blvd Ste 1000 Saint Louis MO 63105-1841

BRIDGEWATER, HERBERT JEREMIAH, JR., radio personality; b. Atlanta, July 3, 1942; s. Herbert Bridgewater and Mary Sallie (Clark) Bridgewater-Hughes. BA, Clark Coll., Atlanta, 1968; postgrad., Atlanta U.; L.H.D., Faith Coll., 1978; LL.D., Heed U., 1978. Tchr. bus. edn. and English Atlanta Pub. Sch. System, 1964-67; relocation and family svcs. cons. Atlanta Housing Authority, 1967-70; columnist, writer Atlanta Daily World, 1968—, Lovely Atlanta; consumer protection specialist FTC, Atlanta, 1970-83; pres. Bridgewater's Personnel Service, 1971—; assoc. prof. bus. edn. and mass communication Clark Coll., instr., 1983-86, Atlanta Jr. Coll., 1986—, The Univ. System of Ga., 1986—; with reservations sales Delta Airline Inc., Atlanta, 1984—. Host radio program Enlightenment (WGKA-AM), 1975-79; host pub. affairs program Confrontation WZGC FM and WIGO AM, 1975-79, WYZE AM, 1979—; TV talk show host Bridging the Gap Mem. Epilepsy Found. Am., Nat. Urban League, Big Bros. Council of Atlanta, Met. Boys Clubs of Atlanta, YMCA, NAACP; active So. Christian Leadership Conf., Ga. and nationwide civil rights movements; bd. dirs. Atlanta Dance Theater, Ralph C. Robinson Atlanta Boys Club, Proposition Theater Co., Am. Cancer Soc., Just-Us Theatre Task Force. Recipient Pres.'s award Clark Coll. United Negro Coll. Fund, 1960, 61, Best Citizens award Delta Sigma Theta, 1962, Humanitarian award Future Soc. Orgn., 1975, award Atlanta Dance Theatre, 1978-79, also; Met. Atlanta Boys Club; FTC Superior service medal, 1978; Bronner Bros. Nat. Beauticians Conv. Excellence in Communication award, 1978; named One of Most Outstanding Young Men in Am., Nat. Jr. C. of C., 1969, One of Most Eligible Bachelors in Am., 1970, One of 1,000 Successful Black Americans, 1973; both Ebony Mag.; One of 10 Outstanding Young People of Atlanta, 1977-78; One of 20 Most Progressive Young People in Atlanta, 1977; Herbert Bridgewater Day proclaimed in his honor Atlanta. Mem. Atlanta Jr. C. of C., Young Men on the Go, Clark Coll. Alumni Assn., Clark Coll. Assn., Heritage Valley Community Civic Orgn., Hungry Club Forum, Internat. Assn. for African Heritage and Black Identity (founding) Baptist (founder, chmn. bd. jr. deacons). Home: 2963 Duke Of Windsor East Point GA 30344-5606 Fax: 404 209-7287. E-mail: HerbertBridgewater@yahoo.com. *Any success which I may have achieved is attributed to my deeply rooted religious rearing which impels me to put God first in all my undertaking. Applying myself to the task with diligence, being prayerful in all my endeavors, and having a mother who is not only my backbone, but who has also stood steadfastly by my side, are the essential factors which I deem vital in my life's achievement.*

BRIDGFORTH, ROBERT MOORE, JR., aerospace engineer; b. Lexington, Miss., Oct. 21, 1918; s. Robert Moore and Theresa (Holder) Bridgforth; m. Florence Jarnberg, Nov. 7, 1943; children: Robert Moore, Alice Theresa. At, Miss. State Coll., 1935—37; BS, Iowa State Coll., 1940; MS, MIT, 1948; post grad., Harvard U., 1949. Asst. engr. Standard Oil Co., Ohio, 1940; teaching fellow M.I.T., 1940—41, instr. chemistry, 1941—43, rsch. asst., 1943—44, mem. staff divsn. indsl. cooperation, 1944—47; assoc. prof. physics and chemistry Emory and Henry Coll., 1949—51; rsch. engr. Boeing Airplane Co., Seattle, 1951—54, rsch. specialist, 1954—55, sr. group engr., 1955—58; chief propulsion sys. sect. Sys. Mgmt. Office, 1958—59, chief propulsion rsch. unit, 1959—60; founder and chmn. bd. Rocket Rsch. Corp., 1960—69, Explosives Corp. Am., 1966—69. Fellow: AIAA (assoc.), Brit. Interplanetary Soc.; mem.: AAAS, Combustion Inst., N.Y. Acad. Scis., Soc. for Leukocyte Biology, Tissue Culture Assn., Am. Assn. Physics Tchrs., Am. Inst. Physics, Am. Ordnance Assn., Am. Rocket Soc. (pres. Pacific N.W. chpt. 1955), Am. Chem. Soc., Am. Astronautical Soc. (dir.), Am. Inst. Chemists, Sigma Xi. Achievements include patents for rocket tri-propellants and explosives. Home: 4325 87th Ave SE Mercer Island WA 98040-4127 Office Phone: 206-232-4065.

BRIDGMAN, G(EORGE) ROSS, lawyer; b. New Haven, Dec. 27, 1947; s. George Ross Bridgman and Betty Jean (Soderquist) Burrows; m. Patricia Hess; children: Taylor Wilson, Katharine June, Elizabeth Honey. BA cum laude, Yale U., 1970; JD, Northwestern U., 1973. Bar: Ohio 1973, U.S. Dist. Ct. (so. dist.) Ohio 1974, U.S. Dist. Ct. (no. dist.) Ohio 1976, U.S. Ct. Appeals (6th cir.) 1984, U.S. Supreme Ct. 1990. Assoc. Vorys, Sater, Seymour & Paese, Columbus, Ohio, 1973-80, ptnr., 1980—. Mem. editorial bd. Northwestern U. Law Rev., Chgo., 1972-73. Trustee Columbus Jr. Theatre of the Arts, 1976-80, pres., 1978-80; trustee, v.p. London (Ohio) Pub. Libr., 1979-84; bd. dirs. Ctrl. Ohio Regional Coun. on Alcoholism, Columbus, 1987-89; trustee Kidscope, Columbus, 1988-89, Recovery Alliance, Columbus, 1989-97, Ohio Parents for Drug-Free Youth, 1991-99; mem. exec. bd. Simon Kenton coun. Boy Scouts Am., 1996—; mem. Columbus Symphony Chorus, 1999—. Fellow: Coll. Labor and Employment Lawyers; mem.: ABA, Nat. Assn. Coll. and Univ. Attys., Ohio Bar Assn., Columbus Bar Assn., Columbus Country Club, Capital Club. Republican. Episcopalian. Office: Vorys Sater Seymour & Pease PO Box 1008 52 E Gay St Columbus OH 43215-3161 E-mail: grbridgman@vssp.com.

BRIDGMAN, PETER ALWYN, beverage company executive; b. Brighton, Sussex, Eng., May 6, 1952; came to U.S., 1981; s. Kenneth Alwyn and Winifred Oilve (Hopper) B. BS in Econs., Bristol U., Eng., 1973. Chartered acct.; CPA, Conn. Staff acct. Peat, Marwick, Mitchell, London, 1973-77, sr. acct. Washington, 1977-79, mgr. Paris, 1979, Algiers, Algeria, 1979-81, sr. mgr. Stamford, Conn., 1981-85; with PepsiCo Internat., 1985—90; CFO PepsiCo, Central Europe, 1990—92; sr. v.p., and controller PepsiCo, North America, 1992—99, Pepsi Bottling Group, 1999—2000, PepsiCo, Inc., 2000—. Fellow Inst. Chartered Accts. in Eng.; mem. Am. Inst. CPA's, U.S. Assn. Chartered Accts. (treas. 1985-87). Avocations: tennis, squash, racquetball, theater. Office: PepsiCo Inc 700 Anderson Hill Rd Purchase NY 10577

BRIDGMAN, THOMAS FRANCIS, retired lawyer; b. Chgo., Dec. 30, 1933; s. Thomas Joseph and Angeline (Gorman) B.; m. Patricia A. McCormick, May 16, 1959; children: Thomas, Kathleen Ann, Ann Marie, Jane T., Molly. BS cum laude, John Carroll U., 1955; JD cum laude, Loyola U., Chgo., 1958. Bar: Ill. 1958, U.S. Dist. Ct. 1959. Assoc. McCarthy & Levin, Chgo., 1958, Baker & McKenzie, Chgo., 1958—96, ptnr., 1962—96. Trustee John Carroll U., 1982-88. Fellow Am. Coll. Trial Lawyers, Am. Bd. Trial Advs. (adv.), Internat. Acad. Trial Lawyers (past pres.), Union League Club, Beverly Country Club (Chgo., pres. 1983). Democrat. Roman Catholic. Home: 9400 S Pleasant Ave Chicago IL 60620-5646 Office: Baker & McKenzie 1 Prudential Plaza 130 E Randolph St Ste 3700 Chicago IL 60601-6342

BRIDSTON, PAUL JOSEPH, strategic management consultant; b. Grand Forks, ND, May 28, 1928; s. Joseph and Anna (Pederson) B.; m. Peggy C. Cullen, Aug. 26, 1955; children: Peter, Rebecca, Sarah BA magna cum laude, Yale U., 1950; MBA, Stanford U., 1952. Sec.-treas. First Fed. Savs. & Loan Assn., Grand Forks, N.D., 1955-61, pres., 1962-81, chmn. bd., 1961-82; pres. J.B. Bridston Ins. Co., 1963-80; cons. Bridston Co., 1990—. Chief Housing Guaranties Program Latin Am., AID, Washington, 1964-65; cons. U.S. Dept. State, 1968-70; asst. insp. gen. fgn. assistance, 1970; mem. N.D. Ho. Reps., 1972-74; chmn. Pioneer Mortgage Co., 1980-84; vis. prof. mgmt. U. Okla., 1988-92 Pres. Grand Forks YMCA, 1959-60, GrandForks United Fund, 1961-62; bd. dirs. Tyrone Guthrie Theatre, Mpls., 1963-69, Boys Club Am., 1963-69; chmn. Martin County Atlantic-Pacific Housing, Inc., Fla., 1984-86. With USNR, 1952-55. Mem. Nat. Savs. and Loan League (bd. dirs. 1981), U.S. Savs. League (chmn. internat. devel. com. 1968-69), Yale U. Alumni Assn., Stanford Alumni Assn., Augusta Nat. Club. Lutheran. Home: 6843 Tall Pines Rd NE Bemidji MN 56601-7095 Office Phone: 218-751-1072. Personal E-mail: pbridstn@paulbunyan.net.

BRIDWELL, BARRY DEAN, music educator, director, musician; b. Woodruff, S.C., Nov. 8, 1956; s. Gene Howard and Carolyn Edge Bridwell; m. Karen Denise Burnett, May 24, 1981; children: Keiko Savannah, Zane Micaiah, Kalika Melody. MusB, U. S.C., 1975—79, MusM, 1980—83; D of Musical Arts, U. North Tex., 1984—93. Instrumental Music Edn. S.C. State Dept. Edn., 1988. Percussion instr. Lander U., Greenwood, SC, 1982—83, U. S.C., Columbia, 1983—84; asst. dir. bands Spartanburg Sch. Dist. Five, Duncan, 1986—89; percussion instr. James F. Byrnes H.S., Duncan, 1990—92; dir. of bands Spartanburg Sch. Dist. One, Landrum, 1992—. Musician S.C. Philharm. Orch., Columbia, 1976—84, Columbia Lyric Opera, 1977—84, Columbia City Ballet, 1982—84, Columbia Town Theater, 1983—84, Greenville Symphony Orch., 1992—, Greater Spartanburg Philharm., United States, 1993—. Composer: (marching percussion) Evolution; contbr. mag. articles in Percussive Notes, The Instrumentalist; composer: (percussion ensemble) Crispy Critters, Music for Lovers of Wood. Recipient Pi Kappa Lamba, U. S.C., 1979; Nat. Merit scholarship, Celanese Corp., 1975—79. Mem.: S.C. Band Directors Assn., Music Educators Nat. Conf., Percussive Arts Soc. (pres. 1980—82, 1993—96). Mem. Christian Ch. Avocations: music, reading, movies, genealogy. Office: Landrum H S 102 Redland Rd Landrum SC 29356 Office Phone: 864-457-2834.

BRIEANT, CHARLES LA MONTE, federal judge; b. Ossining, N.Y., Mar. 13, 1923; s. Charles La Monte and Marjorie (Hall) B.; m. Virginia Elizabeth Warfield, Sept. 10, 1948. BA, Columbia U., 1947, LL.B., 1949. Bar: N.Y. 1949. Mem. firm Bleakley, Platt, Schmidt & Fritz, White Plains, 1949-71; water commr. Village of Ossining, 1948-51; town justice, 1952-58; town supr., 1960-63; village atty. Briarcliff Manor, N.Y.; also spl. asst. dist. atty. Westchester County, 1958-59; asst. counsel N.Y. State Joint Legis. Com. Fire Ins., 1968; judge U.S. Dist. Ct. (so. dist.) N.Y., N.Y.C., 1971-86, U.S. Dist. Ct. So. Dist. N.Y., White Plains, 1993—; chief judge U.S. Dist. Ct. (so. dist.) N.Y., N.Y.C., 1986-93. Adj. prof. Bklyn. Law Sch.; mem. Jud. Conf. U.S., 1989-95, mem. exec. com., 1991-95. Mem. Westchester County Republican Com., 1957-71; mem. Westchester County Legislature from 2d Dist., 1970-71. Served with AUS, World War II. Mem. ABA, N.Y. State Bar Assn., Westchester County Bar Assn., Ossining Bar Assn. Episcopalian (vestryman). Club: SAR. Office: US Dist Ct US Courthouse 300 Quarropas St White Plains NY 10601-4140

BRIEDIS, ROBERT A., lawyer; b. Ridgewood, N.J., Jan. 6, 1961; s. Ojars A. and Mirdza Briedis. BS, NYU, 1983; JD, George Washington U., 1990. Bar: N.J. 1990, N.Y. 1991, D.C. 1992, U.S. Dist. Ct. N.J. 1990. Atty. Brown Raysman & Millstein, N.Y.C., 1990-93, McCarter & English, Newark, 1993-95, Fischbein Badillo Wagner Harding, N.Y.C., 1996-98, Sidley Austin Brown & Wood LLP, N.Y.C., 1998—. Mem. Bergen County Rep. Orgn., 1998—; elected Rep. County Com., 1998, re-elected, 2000. Mem. Bar Assn. City N.Y., Beta Gamma Sigma. Office: Sidley Austin Brown & Wood LLP 875 Third Ave New York NY 10022 Fax: 212-906-2021. E-mail: rbriedis@sidley.com.

BRIEGER, GERT HENRY, medical educator; b. Hamburg, Germany, Jan. 5, 1932; arrived in U.S., 1938, naturalized, 1943; s. Carl Helmuth and Ylse (Fuchs) Brieger; m. Katharine Crenshaw, July 2, 1955; children: Heidi E., William N., Benjamin C. AB, U. Calif., Berkeley, 1953; MD, UCLA, 1957; MPH, Harvard U., 1962; PhD, Johns Hopkins U., 1968. Intern UCLA Med. Ctr., 1957—58; asst. prof. history of medicine Johns Hopkins U. Sch. Medicine, Balt., 1966—70; assoc. prof. cmty. health scis., assoc. prof. history Duke U., Durham, NC, 1970—75; prof. history of health scis., chmn. dept. U. Calif., San Francisco, 1975—84; William H. Welch prof., dir. Inst. History of Medicine Johns Hopkins U., Balt., 1984—2001, chair dept. hist. sci. med. and tech., 1993—2001, disting. svc. prof., 2002—. Author (with A.M. Harvey, S.L. Abrams and V.A. McKusick): A Model of Its Kind, A Centennial History of Johns Hopkins Medicine, 1989; editor: Medical America in the Nineteenth Century, 1972, Theory and Practice in American Medicine, 1976; co-editor Bull. of the History of Medicine, 1990—2004. Served to capt. U.S. Army, 1958—61. Mem.: Inst. Medicine, Am. Assn. History of Medicine (pres. 1980—82). Home: 10 E Lee St Baltimore MD 21202-6003 Office: Johns Hopkins U Welch Med Library Rm 320 1900 E Monument St Baltimore MD 21205-2167 E-mail: gbrieger@jhmi.edu.

BRIER, BONNIE SUSAN, lawyer; b. Oct. 19, 1950; d. Jerome W. and Barbara (Srenco) B.; m. Bruce A. Rosenfield, Aug. 15, 1976; children: Rebecca, Elizabeth, Benjamin. AB in Econs. magna cum laude, Cornell U., 1972; JD, Stanford U., 1976. Bar: Pa. 1976, U.S. Dist. Ct. (ea. dist.) Pa., U.S. Tax Ct., U.S. Ct. Appeals (3d cir.), U.S. Supreme Ct. Law clk. to chief judge U.S. Dist. Ct. Pa. (ea. dist.), Phila., 1976-77, asst. U.S. atty. criminal prosecutor, 1977-79; from assoc. to ptnr. Ballard, Spahr, Andrews & Ingersoll, Phila., 1979-90; gen. counsel Children's Hosp. of Phila., Phila., 1990—. Legal counsel Womens Way, 1979—1999; lectr. U. Pa. Law Sch., 1988-95; lectr., speaker various orgns. and seminars. Editor Stanford Law Rev., 1974-76; contbr. articles to profl. jours. Bd. dirs. U.S. Com. for UNICEF, 1994—2000, vice chmn., 1998-2000. Recipient Woman of Achievement award, March of Dimes, 2003, Leadership award, Women's Way, 2004. Fellow Am. Coll. Tax Counsel, Am. Law Inst., Am. Health Lawyers Assn. (bd. dirs. 1991-96); mem. ABA (exempt orgn. com. on tax sect., chair 1991-93, mem. health law sect., bd. dirs. 1998-, chair 2003-), Pa. Bar Assn. (tax sect., health law sect., mem. com. charitable orgn., children's rights), Phila. Bar Assn. (tax sect., health law com.). Home: 132 Fairview Rd Narberth PA 19072-1331 Office: Children's Hosp of Pa 34th St and Civic Ctr Blvd Philadelphia PA 19104

BRIERLEY, CORALE L., geological and biomining engineer; b. Mont. m. Jim Brierley. Student, Mont. State U.; BS in Biology, MS in Chemistry, N.Mex. Inst. Mining & Tech.; PhD in Environ. Scis., U. Tex., Dallas, 1981. With N.Mex. Bur. Mines; founder Advanced Mineral Techs., 1983-87; chief environ. process devel. Newmont Mining Co., 1989-91; founder, prin. Brierley Cons. LLC, Highlands Ranch, Colo., 1991—. Office: Brierley Consultancy LLC PO Box 260012 Highlands Ranch CO 80163-0012 E-mail: clbrierley@msn.com.

BRIERLEY, JAMES ALAN, biohydrometallurgy consultant; b. Denver, Dec. 22, 1938; s. Everette and Carrie (Berg) B.; m. Corale Louise Beer, Dec. 21, 1965 BS in Bacteriology, Colo. State U., 1961; MS in Microbiology, Mont. State U., 1963, PhD, 1966. Research scientist Martin Marietta Corp., Denver, 1968-69; asst. prof. biology N.Mex. Inst. Mining and Tech., Socorro, 1966-68, from asst. prof. to prof. biology, chmn. dept. biology, 1969-83; research dir. Advanced Mineral Techs., Golden, Colo., 1983-88; chief microbiologist Newmont Metall. Svcs., Englewood, Colo., 1988-2000; chief rsch. scientist biohydrometallurgy Newmont Mining Corp., 2000-01; cons. Brierley Consultancy, LLC, Highlands Ranch, Colo., 2001—. Vis. fellow U. Warwick, Coventry, Eng., 1976, vis. prof. Catholic U., Santiago, Chile, 1983; adj. prof. dept. metallurgy U. Utah, 1994-96; cons. Mountain State Mineral Enterprises, Tucson, 1980, Sandia Nat. Lab., Albuquerque, 1976, Bechtel Civil and Minerals, Scottsdale, Ariz., 1984, Newmont Gold Co., 1988, Newmont Mining Corp., 2001-04, Smith-Pachter Attys. at Law, 2002-03. Contbr. numerous articles to profl. jours.; patentee in field. Served to staff sgt. Air N.G., 1956-61. Recipient Wadsorth Extractive Metall. award, Soc. Mining, Metall. & Exploration, 2000, Honor Alumnus award, Colo. State U., 2001; grantee 32 rsch. grants. Fellow: AAAS; mem.: Nat. Acad. Engring., Mining and Metall. Soc. Am. Avocations: travel, model railroading, gardening. Home: 2074 East Terrace Dr Highlands Ranch CO 80126-2692 Office: Brierley Consultancy PO Box 260012 Highlands Ranch CO 80163-0012 E-mail: j.brierley@worldnet.att.net.

BRIERRE, MAUD, French and Spanish educator; b. Haiti; BSN, Universidad de Antioquia, Medellin, Colombia; PhD, U. Calif., Irvine. Prof. French and Spanish Saddleback Coll., Mission Viejo, Calif., 1982—. Author: (book of poetry) Signpost for Your Road, 1997, Un Bout de Chemin, 2003; contbr. articles to profl. jours. Recipient Excellence in Poetry award, Internat. Soc. Poets, 2001, Saddleback Valley award, 1986, Woman of Achievement award, Dawn Mag., 1985. Office: Saddleback College 28000 Marguerite Pkwy Mission Viejo CA 92692-3635

BRIERTON, CHERYL LYNN, lawyer; b. Hartford, Conn., Nov. 11, 1947; d. Charles Greenwood and Elizabeth (Grechko) Wootton; m. David Martin Black, Oct. 12, 1968 (div. 1978); m. John Thomas Brierton, Sept. 6, 1982 (div. 1988); 1 child, John Greenwood. BA, Wellesley Coll., 1969; JD, U. San Diego, 1982. Bar: Calif. 1983. Tchr., libr. Anglican High Sch., Grenada, West Indies, 1972-74; dep. dir. Transalpino Student Travel, Paris, 1975-76; asst. dir. adminstn. Project OZ, YMCA, San Diego, 1976-78; asst. coord. policy and advocacy Community Congress San Diego, 1978-81; field dir. Calif. Child, Youth and Family Coalition, San Diego, 1981-83; asst. exec. dir. Community Congress San Diego, 1984-85; exec. dir. Calif. Child, Youth and Family Coalition, Sacramento, 1985-86; gen. atty. Def. Logistics Agy., Def. Depot Tracy, Calif., 1986-88; atty.-advisor Dept. of the Navy, Mare Island Naval Shipyard, Vallejo, 1988-89; staff atty. San Diego Superior Ct., 1989—. Mem. faculty Nat. Juvenile Judges Conf. Dispositional Alternatives Serious Offenders, 1982, 6th and 7th Nat. Confs. Juvenile Justice, 1979-80; cons. San Diego Youth Involvement Project, 1983-84, San Diego Youth and Community Svcs., 1983-84, South Bay Community Svcs., Chula Vista, 1983. Mem. Juvenile Justice Commn., Golden Hill Neighborhood Justice Cen. Planning Bd.; mem. com. jud. process Regional Criminal Justice Planning Bd. Scholar U. San Diego 1979. Mem. MENSA. Avocations: yachting, travel. Home: 1329 Bancroft St San Diego CA 92102-2429

BRIESCH, RICHARD ALLEN, marketing educator; s. Forrest Richard and Kathryn Marie Briesch; m. Samia Sorour, Jan. 12, 2001; children: Adam Abadir, Daniel, Jasmine Abadir, Richard Charles. BS, Carnegie Mellon U., 1981; MBA, Rice U., 1991; PhD, Northwestern U., 1995. Product engr. commn. products divsn. IBM, Raleigh, 1981—84; product devel. mgr. Micom Sys., Simi Valley, Calif., 1984—88; prin. engr. Spectrum Digital, Herndon, Va., 1988—89; mgmt. cons. Briesch's Cons., 1989—99, 2000—; v.p. Pointserve, Inc., Austin, 1999—2000; cons., adv. bd. Agular Sys. Inc., Chgo., 2000—; asst. prof. Cox Sch. Bus. So. Meth. U., Dallas, 2002—. Adj. prof. Northwestern U., 1994—95; asst. prof. NYU, 1995—97; fellow Ctr. for Customer Insight U. Tex., Austin, 1997—99, asst. prof., 1997—2000, sr. lectr., 2001—02; mem. adv. bd. On-Hand Solutions, Austin, 2000—01; asst. prof. Southern Meth. U., 2002—. Contbr. articles to profl. jours. Office: So Meth U PO Box 750333 Dallas TX 75275-0333

BRIESE, MICHAEL W., writer, deacon, inventor; b. Washington, D.C., Nov. 15, 1956; s. Marion L. and Frances G. Briese. BA, U. Scranton, 1980. Cert. housing counselor via Md. Ctr. for Cmty. Devel., 2000. Ind. living specialist, Silver Spring, Md., 2000—05. Author: 101 Poems to Live By,

1998, St. Paul-Disciple, Teacher, Servant of Christ, 1998, CHARISMATA, 2002, A Prayer of the Heart, 2005. Vol. Shepherd's Table, Silver Spring, 1997—; mem. Archdiocese of Washington, 1999—. Mem.: K.C. Democrat. Roman Catholic. Achievements include patents in field of entomology. Avocations: reading, writing, walking. Home: PO Box 8242 Silver Spring MD 20907-8242

BRIFFAULT, RICHARD, law educator; BA, Columbia U., 1974; JD, Harvard U., 1977. Law clk. to Judge Shirley M. Hufstedler US Ct. Appeals, Ninth Cir., 1977—78; assoc. Paul, Weiss, Rifkind, Wharton & Garrison, 1978—80; asst. counsel to Gov. State of NY, 1980—82; faculty mem. Columbia Law Sch., NYC, 1983—, vice dean, Joseph P. Chamberlain prof. legis. Mem. Mayor Koch's Early Childhood Edn. Commn., 1985—86; counsel Gov. Cuomo's Adv. Commn. on Liability Insurance, 1986; cons. NYC Charter Revision Commn., 1987—89; mem. NYC Real Property Tax Reform Commn., 1993; cons. NY State Commn. on Constl. Revision, 1993—94; vis. scholar Taubman Ctr. for State and Local Govt., John F. Kennedy Sch. Govt., Harvard U., 1996—97. Contbr. articles to law jours. Mem.: Assn. Bar of City of NY (exec. dir. Spl. Commn. on Campaign Fin. Reform 1998—2000). Office: Columbia Law Sch Jerome Greene Hall, Rm 726 435 W 116th St New York NY 10027 Office Phone: 212-854-2638. Office Fax: 212-854-7946. E-mail: rb34@columbia.edu.

BRIGDEN, JOHN, lawyer; b. 1964; BS in elec. engring. with honors, Purdue U.; JD with honors, Georgetown U. Lic.: Va., Wash., DC, US Paten and Trademark Office. Dir. intellectual property Silicon Graphics, Inc., 1997—2000; v.p. bus. devel., gen. counsel Shutterfly, Inc., 2000—01; v.p., gen. counsel, sec. VERITAS Software Corp., Mountain View, Calif., 2001—03, sr. v.p., gen. counsel, sec., 2003—. Mem.: Calif. Bar Assn. Office: VERITAS Software Corp 222 Casbian Dr Sunnyvale CA 94089

BRIGGS, ALAN LEONARD, lawyer; b. Dayton, Ohio, Oct. 1, 1942; s. Donald M. and Helen (Barker) B.; m. Linda Ann Dobie, Sept. 10, 1966 (div. 1991); children: Jason, Aimee, Anna; m. Christine M. McCormick, 1991; 1 child, Caitlin. AB, Miami U., Oxford, Ohio, 1964; JD, Ohio State U., 1967; LLM in Patent/Intellectual Property Law, George Washington U., 1998. Bar: Ohio 1967, Calif. 1970, Fla. 1989, D.C. 1995, Va. 1995, Md. 1995. Ptnr. Murphey, Young & Smith, Columbus, Ohio, 1970-88, Squire, Sanders & Dempsey, Columbus, 1988-91, Miami, Fla., 1991-94, Washington, 1994—. Trustee Legal Aid Soc. Fellow Am. Coll. Trial Lawyers; mem. ABA, Ohio State Bar Assn. (coun. of dels. 1980-86, chmn. screening com. coun. dels. 1983-84, sect. litigation bd. govs. 1986-90), Columbus Bar Assn. (pres. 1985, chmn. litigation practice inst. 1987-90), Am. Arbitration Assn. Office: Squire Sanders & Dempsey 1201 Pennsylvania Ave NW Washington DC 20004-2491

BRIGGS, DICK DOWLING, JR., physician, educator; b. Electric Mills, Miss., Jan. 28, 1934; s. Dick Dowling and Anita (Carnathan) B.; m. Susan Hunt Davis, June 20, 1959; children: Adrienne Davis, Dick Dowling, III, Daniel Roth. BS, U. of South, 1956; MD, Washington U., 1960. Resident, fellow, chief resident U. Ala. Hosp., Birmingham, 1960-62, 64-68; prof. medicine U. Ala., Birmingham, 1964-95, emeritus eminent scholar chair, prof., dir. divsn. pulmonary critical care, 1971-92, vice chmn. dept. medicine, 1981-95, eminent scholar chair in pulmonary diseases, 1989-95; pres., CEO, med. dir. U. Ala. Health Svc. Found., P.C., Birmingham, 1988-92; corp. med. dir. Complete Health, 1985—88, Triton Health Sys., Birmingham, 1995-97; chief med. officer Best Drs. Worldwide Health Svcs., Boston, 1997—2005. Cons. VA Med. Ctr., Birmingham, 1966-2003; trustee AmSouth Funds, Birmingham, 1992—. Assoc. editor (CDROM) UpToDate, 1994—; sr. editl. bd. Archives Internal Medicine, 1985-97; contbr. articles to profl. publs. Bd. dir. Am. Bd. Emergency Medicine, 1994—2002. Recipient Pulmonary Acad. award NIH, 1972-77, Breath of Life award Cystic Fibrosis Found., 1994; named to Ala. Tennis Hall Fame, 2003. Master: ACP (Laureate award 1995), Am. Coll. Chest Physicians (pres. 1984—85, 1984—85, master fellow 2002); fellow: Am. Coll. Chest Physicians; mem.: Am. Bd. Pulmonary Disease, So. Med. Assn. (chmn. sect. medicine 1973—74), Am. Thoracic Soc. (pres. Ala. chpt. 1978—79), Assn. Pulmonary and Critical Care Medicine Program Dirs. (founding mem. 1984, pres. 1986—87), Newcomen Soc., US Tennis Assn. (pres. Ala. Tennis Assn. 1968—70, Ala. Tennis Hall of Fame 2003), Rotary Club. Episcopalian. Avocations: tennis, music, travel, wine. Home: 2925 Southwood Rd Birmingham AL 35223-1232 Office: Univ Ala Birmingham Sch Medicine 1808 7th Ave S Birmingham AL 35294-0012 Office Phone: 205-934-6015. Business E-Mail: ddbjr@uab.edu.

BRIGGS, EDWARD SAMUEL, naval officer; b. St. Paul, Oct. 4, 1926; s. Charles William and Lois Ione (Johnson) B.; m. Nanette Parks, June 7, 1949; 1 child, Jeffrey Charles. BS, U.S. Naval Acad., 1949. Commd. ensign U.S. Navy, 1949; advanced through officer ranks to vice admiral; naval aviator U.S. Navy, 1951—61, surface warfare officer, 1961—84; commanding officer USS Turner Joy, USS Jouett; asst. chief of staff plans, chief of staff U.S. 7th Fleet, 1972-73; fleet ops. officer, asst. chief staff ops. U.S. Pacific Fleet, Makalapa, Hawaii, 1973-75; comdr. Crusier-Destroyer Group 3, San Diego, 1975-77, Navy Recruiting Command, Arlington, Va., 1977-79, Naval Logistics Command, U.S. Pacific Fleet, Naval Base, Pearl Harbor, Hawaii, 1979-80; dep. comdr.-in-chief U.S. Pacific Fleet, Pearl Harbor, 1980-82; comdr. Naval Surface Force U.S. Atlantic Fleet, 1982-84; ret., 1984. Decorated Bronze Star with combat device and one star, Air medals (2), Navy Commendation medal with combat device and two stars, Legion of Merit with combat device and four stars, D.S.M.; Vietnamese Navy Gallantry medal. Mem. Surface Navy Assn., U.S. Naval Acad. Alumni Assn., Naval Inst., Navy League, San Diego Mil. Adv. Coun. Home: 3648 Lago Sereno Escondido CA 92029-7902 *Dedication to our nation and devotion to its ideals are the responsibilities of citizenship.*

BRIGGS, ETHEL DELORIA, federal agency administrator; BA, N.C. Ctrl. U., 1971; M in Counseling, U. N.C., 1972. Dir. adult svcs. Nat. Coun. on Disability, Washington, 1985—, dep. dir., acting exec. dir., exec. dir. Named One of Top 100 African-Am. Bus. and Profl. Women, Dollars and Sense Mag., 1989. Office: Nat Coun on Disability 1331 F St NW Ste 1050 Washington DC 20004-1138 Business E-Mail: ebriggs@ncd.gov.

BRIGGS, FRANKLIN HENRY, retired naval officer; b. Council Bluffs, Iowa, Mar. 7, 1933; s. Edwin Charles Briggs and Anna Maud Brandt; m. Chizuko Imaoka, Aug. 28, 1960. Student, U. Colo., 1951; BA, U. Nebr., 1955. Commd. ensign USN, 1955, advanced through grades to capt., 1976; deck and gunnery USS Essex (CVA-9), San Diego, 1955—58; asst. plans officer Comdr. Naval Forces, Yokosuka, Japan, 1958—61; ops. officer USS Paul Revere (APA-248), San Diego, 1961—63; CIC instr. Anti-Air Warfare Def. Ctr., Dams Neck, Va., 1963—66; ship employment officer Amphibious Force, Pacific, Subic Bay, Philippines, 1966—68; comdg. officer Naval Res. Ctr., Scotia, NY, 1968—70; exec. officer USS Anchorage, San Diego, 1970—72; manpower dir. Comdr. 6th Naval Dist., San Diego, 1970—72; dep. comdr. Naval Res. Readiness Command, Washington, 1974—78; Comdr. Cleve. Readiness Command, 1978—79. Decorated Vietnam Campaign medal with 10 stars, Navy Commendation medal with Combat V, Gold star, Cross of Gallantry, Expeditionary medal, Quemay-Matsu. Mem. Ikenobo Internat., Dicken's Fellowship. Conservative. Avocations: reading, history, travel, opera. Home: 890 Buen Tiempo Dr Chula Vista CA 91910-6555

BRIGGS, HENRY PAYSON, JR., headmaster; b. Boston, Apr. 14, 1932; s. Henry Payson Sr. and Eleanor Temple (Smith) B.; m. Charlin Shoenberger Devanney, Nov. 28, 1987; children from previous marriage: Payson Stewart, Heather Kavanagh. BA, Harvard U., 1954, MAT, 1959. Dir. admissions and fin. aid Harvard Coll., Cambridge, Mass., 1956-66; headmaster Western Res. Acad., Hudson, Ohio, 1966-76, Seven Hills Sch., Cin., 1976—95; interim head St. James' Episcopal Sch., L.A., 1995—96; dir. major gifts Cin. Opera, 1996-99; interim head The Potomac Sch., McLean, Va., 1999-2000, The Norfolk (Va.) Acad., 2000-01, The Ft. Worth CDS, 2001—02, St. Timothy's Sch., Balt., 2002—03, Episcopal H.S., Baton Rouge, 2004—05. Bd. dirs. Queen City Found.; former vestryman, warden Christ Episcopal Ch. Cathedral, Cin. 1st lt. U.S. Army, 1954-56. Mem. Headmasters Assn. (officer), Country Day Sch. Headmasters Assn.(former v.p.), Literary Club, Univ. Club, Tennis Club Cin. (former pres.). Avocations: education, sports, outdoors, politics. Home: 7937 Bar Harbor Dr Cincinnati OH 45255-4430 E-mail: cpbriggs@fuse.net.

BRIGGS, JACK A., realtor, real estate appraiser; b. Greenwich, Conn., Aug. 11, 1933; s. John A. Briggs and Ida H. Kay; children: William, Debbie, Jackie, Joan, Kim Christopher. Cert. in real estate and appraisal, Ft. Laurerdale U., 1972. Realtor, appraiser, Fla., 1972—. Guest instr. U. Fla., Gainesville, 1998—2002. Author: Common Sense Parenting, 1994. Vol. Advent Christian Vill, Dowling Park, Fla., 2001—; pres. Fla. chpt. Boys Town Nebr., 1986—; group leader Post-Polio Support Group, Fla., 2001—. Recipient All Am. Hero award, Baywatch Red Cross, L.A., 1994. Avocations: travel, swimming, football, chess, cards. Home: PO Box 4095 Dowling Park FL 32064 Fax: 386-658-3332.

BRIGGS, JAMES HENRY, II, engineering administrator; b. San Francisco, Dec. 25, 1953; s. Major James Henry(USMC, retired.) and Barbara (Cordes) S.; m. Niwana Alice Page, Sept. 1, 1979 (dec. Jan. 2003); children: Melanie Shannon, James Henry III. AA in Bus. Adminstrn., Albany (Ga.) Jr. Coll., 1976; BS in Computer Sci., U. N.C., Wilmington, 1979; BSEE, So. Tech., Marietta, Ga., 1985. Lic. 1st class radio telephone; registered profl. engr. Chief engr. WECT-TV, Wilmington, 1978-82; maintenance supr. Cable News Network, Atlanta, 1982-85; mgr. engring. ops. KCOP-TV, LA, 1985-87; sr. product support engr. Abekas Video Systems, Redwood City, Calif., 1987-92; dir. engring. D.T.S., Union City, Calif., 1992—97; chief engr. Sta. CSUH-TV Calif. State U., Hayward, 1997—99. Design engr. Stage Front Presentation Sys., Savannah, Ga., 1999—, CEO Charis Constrn. Co., Savannah, 2001-. Editor: Video Prodn. in the 90's. Mem. Soc. Motion Picture and TV Engr., Soc. Broadcast Engr., Greenpeace, Toastmasters Club, Lions, Golf Ptnrs. Am., Nat. Assn. Broadcastes. Avocations: model trains, music, camping, sailing, travel, bicycling, golf, tennis, gardening. Office Phone: 912-898-0681.

BRIGGS, JOHN C. C., non-profit company executive; b. Rochester, N.Y., Oct. 28, 1947; s. John Wilbur and Rosemary Risley (Carpenter) B. BA, Springfield Coll., 1970; postgrad., Colgate U., 1970-73. Exec. dir. Nat. Self-Help, Washington, 1976-81; pres., chief operating officer Activation Tng. and Devel., Washington, 1976-84, chmn., chief exec. officer Rochester, 1984—; asst. dir. Regional Council on Aging, Inc., Rochester, 1984—. Mem. steering com. U. Rochester Ctr. on Aging, 1985—, Congl. Ministry Elderly, Rochester, 1984—. Author: Coalition Building, 1978, (workbook) Power and Success, 1986, (workbook) Envisioning, 1986; contbr. articles to profl. jours. Mem. governing council Nat. Mcpl. League, N.Y.C., 1980-83; bd. dirs. Delphi Drug Abuse Ctr., Rochester, 1986, Nat. Assn. Neighborhoods, Washington, 1976-80, Community Architects, Rochester, 1973-76. Recipient Distinguished Service award United Way, Rochester, 1984. Mem.: Manhattan (Rochester)(pres. 1984-85). Democrat. Episcopalian. Avocations: organic gardening, photography, woodwork, sailing. Home: 630 Allens Creek Rd Rochester NY 14618-3408 Office: # 2 909 Burr St Jackson MI 49201-1703

BRIGGS, JOHN CHANNING, literature and language professor; b. Chgo., Feb. 5, 1948; s. Channing Matthew and Virginia Dale Briggs; m. Andrea Harrison Quest, Dec. 20, 1975; children: Emily, Christopher, Katherine. BA, Harvard U.; MA, PhD, U. Chgo. Mem. faculty U. Calif., Riverside, 1980—. Dir. inland area writing project U. Calif., 1992—, dir. entry level writing program, 1980—; mem. adv. com. Coll. Bd., NYC, 2002—04. Author: Francis Bacon and Rhetoric of Nature, 1989, Lincoln's Speeches Reconsidered, 2005. Mem.: Assn. Literary Scholars and Critics (chair curriculum com. 1992—2001), Riverside Breakfast Forum (chair 2004). Episcopalian. Office: U Calif Dept English Riverside CA 92521

BRIGGS, JOHN HAROLD, SR., music educator; b. Wilmington, Del., July 13, 1946; s. Joseph Aloysius Briggs, Jr. and Eva Lee Briggs; m. Ellen Mary Briggs, Feb. 18, 1955. BS in Music Edn., West Chester (Pa.) U., 1968; MusM in Choral Conducting, U. of Colo., 1992. Cert. tchr. State of Md., DOE, 1971. Choral music tchr. Newark (Del.) Sch. Dist., 1968—71; choral and instrumental music tchr. Wilmington (Del.) Sch. Dist., 1971—78; choral music tchr. Newcastle County Sch. Dist., Wilmington, 1978—81, Colonial Sch. Dist., New Castle, Del., 1981—2003; choral arts tchr. Prince George's County Pub. Sch., Upper Marlboro, Md., 2003—. Adult choir dir. Christ United Meth. Ch., Wilmington, 1971—89; asst. to the choral dir. U. of Del.'s Choral Union Chorus, Newark, 1991—2001; founder/conductor The Jack Briggs Singers; established Delaware All-State Jr. Chorus, New Castle County Jr. HS Choral Festival, Delaware Mid Schs. Choral Festival for Pub., Parochial, Pvt. and Religious Schs. Composer: (songs) Choral compositions included in a professional concert, 1991, singer many professional choral concerts; contbr. articles to profl. jours. Mem.: NEA, Prince George's County Edn. Assn., Md. Music Educators Assn., Md. ACDA, Am. Choral Dirs. Assn., Del. Music Educators Assn., Music Educators Nat. Conf., Colonial Edn. Assn., Del. State Educators Assn. Republican. United Methodist. Avocations: composing, travel, sports. Home: 522 Garner Ave Waldorf MD 20602 Office: Gwynn Pk Mid Sch 8000 Dyson Rd Brandywine MD 20613 E-mail: choirmaestroJack@netscape.net.

BRIGGS, M. COURTNEY, lawyer; b. Phila., Mar. 28, 1960; BA, Wesleyan U., 1982; JD with distinction, U. Okla., 1991. Asst. lit. agt. Curtis Brown Ltd., N.Y.C., 1983-86; fgn. rights assoc. Random House Inc., N.Y.C., 1986-89; assoc. Pringle & Pringle, Oklahoma City, 1991-92; sole practice Oklahoma City, 1993-94; ptnr. Derick & Briggs, Oklahoma City, 1994—. Mem. ABA, Soc. Children's Book Writers, Okla. Bar Assn. (dir. Young Lawyers divsn. 1995-98, chmn. 1997, vice-chair women in law com. 1998-99, mem. AIDS legal resources project panel 1995-99, chairperson disaster legal svcs. com. 1999). Office: Derrick & Briggs LLP Bank One Ctr 20th FL 100 N Broadway Ave Oklahoma City OK 73102-8606

BRIGGS, MICHAEL JOHN, lawyer; b. Sept. 1, 1934; BA, London U., 1957; MS in LS, U. N.C., 1965; JD, U. Wis., 1975. Alderman City of Madison, Wis., 1977-83; adminstr. law judge State of Wis., Madison, 1979-95; atty. Briggs Law Office, Madison, 1996—. Office Phone: 608-835-0914. E-mail: brigglaw@earthlink.net.

BRIGGS, NIWANA PAGE, editor, writer; b. Savannah, Ga., Oct. 6, 1957; d. William Gaines and Carolyn (King) Alexander; m. James Henry Briggs II, Sept. 1, 1979; children: Melanie Shannon(dec.), James Henry III. AA magna cum laude, Clayton State U., 1979; BA magna cum laude, U. N.C., 1982. Freelance editor The Snapdragon Group Harper Collins, San Francisco, 1989-94; legal sec. Wilson Sonsini Goodrich & Rosati, Palo Alto, Calif., 1987-89; editor, tech. writer Abekas Video Systems, Redwood City, Calif., 1989-92; proprietor Willee Gee's Used & Collectible Books, Fremont, Calif., 1992-94; exec. aide to polit. liaison World Savs. and Loan Assn., Oakland, Calif., 1992-94; exec. asst. to pres. Am. Immigation Lawyers Assn., Atlanta, 1995-96; freelance editor Atlanta, 1994-97; editor The Savannah (Ga.) Bus. Jour., 1997-99; freelance editor, writer Savannah, 1999—2001; mng. editor Enquirer Columbus Ledger, 2005—. Editl. contbns. to twelve novels, contbr. numerous articles to profl. jours. and mags. Mem. staff press office U.S. Olympic Com., Atlanta, 1996; lit. tutor, computer instr. to teenage unwed mothers Rayoc Learning Ctr., 1998; fundraiser Emergency Children's Shelter, Palo Alto, Calif., 1988-99, Savannah Onstage, 2000; mem. United Meth. Women, 1999—; mem. Republican Nat. Com., 1978—; vol. Adult Edn. Ctr., Georgetown, Ga. Mem. Telfair Acad. Arts and Scis., Am. Humane Soc. Avocations: reading, travel, antiques, baseball, opera. Home and Office: 247 Plantation Blvd Georgetown GA 39854-0602 Office Phone: 509-741-0174. Personal E-mail: niwanabriggs@aol.com.

BRIGGS, PHILIP, insurance company executive; b. Paris, Feb. 28, 1928; s. Robert E. and Madeleine (Boell) B. (parents Am. citizens); m. Jean M. Sloan, July 9, 1949; children: Karen, Heather, Peter. AB, Middlebury Coll., 1948. With Met. Life Ins. Co., N.Y.C., 1948-93, v.p., gen. mgr., 1971-73, sr. v.p., 1973-77, exec. v.p., 1977-86, vice chmn. bd. dirs., CFO N.Y.C., 1986-93; chmn. Wellchoice, Inc. (formerly Empire Blue Cross and Blue Shield), N.Y.C., 1993—2004. Fellow: Am. Acad. Actuaries, Soc. Actuaries.

BRIGGS, PHILIP JAMES, political science professor, writer; b. NYC, July 28, 1938; m. Candace Rae Kohn, Jan. 30, 1971; children: Nicola Fulham, Adam Kohn. BS, SUNY, Oswego, 1960; MA, Maxwell Sch. Citizenship and Pub. Affairs, Syracuse U., 1962, PhD, 1969. Asst. prof. social sci. SUNY Coll. Tech., Delhi, 1963-65; part-time admissions counselor Syracuse (N.Y.) U., 1967; assoc. prof. polit. sci. East Stroudsburg (Pa.) U., 1968-72, prof. polit. sci., 1972-99, dept. grad. coord.and chmn., 1977-95, faculty Fulbright adviser, 1981-82, disting. prof., faculty emeriti, 2000—. Foxhowe lectr., 1980; Commonwealth spkr. Pa. Humanities Coun., 1984—86, 1996—99; invited del. Sci. Rsch. Coun., Acad. Sci. USSR, 1979; invited participant seminar Georgetown U., 1983; invited scholar Presdl. Conf. Com., Hofstra U., 1984, 85, 87; panel co-chmn. Internat. Polit. Sci. World Congress, Paris, 1985, panel chmn., Berlin, 94; panel chmn. annual meetings Pa. Polit. Sci. Assn., 1993—99; manuscript referee Armed Forces and Soc., Chgo., 1979, Chgo., 93; cons. McGraw-Hill Book Co., N.Y.C., 1981; spkr. in field. Author: Making American Foreign Policy, President-Congress Relations from the Second World War to Vietnam, 1991, 1992, Making American Foreign Policy, President-Congress Relations from the Second World War to the Post-Cold War Era, 1994, 1995, 1997; contbg. author: series The Congress of the United States, 1789-1989; editor: Politics in America, Readings and Documents, 1972; contbr. articles and revs. to profl. publs.; (TV appearances on) C-Span, 1987, Blue Ridge Cable and Pennarama, 1991, Action News 24, Erie, Pa., 1999. Exec. dir. Rsch. Com. on Armed Forces and Soc. Internat. Polit. Sci. Assn., 1990-99; panel chmn. rsch. com. Fundacion Jose Ortega y Gasset, Madrid, 1990; panel participant Ctr. for Study of Presidency, 1995-96. With USCG, 1962, USCGR, 1962-70. Mem.: Pi Sigma Alpha.

BRIGGS, STEVE CLEMENT, lawyer; b. Vernon, Tex., Jan. 26, 1947; s. Galen Pierce and Virginia Irene (Sebert) B. BA, U. Mich., 1970; postgrad., U. Calif., Berkeley, 1970; JD, U. Colo., 1975. Bar: Colo. 1975, U.S. Dist. Ct. Colo. 1975, U.S. Ct. Appeals (10th cir.) 1976, U.S. Ct. Claims 1984. Law clk. to chief judge U.S. Dist. Ct. Colo., Denver, 1975-76; asst. atty. gen. anti-trust sect. State of Colo., Denver, 1976-78; ptnr. Hutchinson, Black, Hill & Cook, Boulder, Colo., 1978—92; judge Colo. Ct. Appeals, 1992—2000; mediator, arbitrator Jud. Arbiter Group, Inc., 2000—. Chair dean's club U. Colo. Law Sch., Boulder, 1985; bd. dirs. Vol. and Info. Ctr., Boulder, 1979-80, United Way, Boulder, 1980, Boulder Philharm., 1990—; v.p. bd. dirs. Counseling Ctr., Boulder, 1983-86. Recipient Outstanding Vol. Legal Svcs. award Eco-Cycle, 1984, Disting. Alumni award U. Colo Sch. Law, 2003. Mem. Colo. Bar Assn. (bd. govs. 1988—, exec. coun. 1990—, pres. 2004), Boulder County Bar Assn. (pres. 1986-87). Avocations: golf, travel, movies, reading. Office: Judicial Arbiter Group 1601 Blake St #400 Denver CO 80202

BRIGGS, SUSAN MILLER, surgeon; b. 1943; MD, Loyola U., 1974; MPH in Internat. Health, Harvard U., 1998. Assoc. dir. trauma svc. Matt. Gen. Hosp., attending gen. and vascular surgeon; asst. prof. surgery Harvard Med. Sch.; dir. Internat. Med. Surg. Response Team, Metro-Boston Disaster Med. Assistance Team; developer, dir. Harvard Med. Internat. Trauma and Disaster Inst., 2001—. Trauma cons. U.S. State Dept., Croatia and Bosnia, 1997. Co-editor: Advanced Disaster Medical Response: A Manual for Providers, 2003. Achievements include helping to direct on-the-scene trauma care at World Trade Ctr. disaster, Sept. 11, 2001; instrumental in relief efforts during 1999 earthquakes in Turkey. Office: Mass Gen Hosp 8 Hawthorne Pl Ste 114 Boston MA 02114

BRIGGS, VERNON MASON, JR., economics professor; b. Washington, June 29, 1937; s. Vernon Mason and Anne Maria (Cox) B.; m. Martijna Antonia Aarts, Dec. 29, 1971; children: Vernon Mason III, Kees Kanen. BS, U. Md., 1959; MA, Mich. State U., 1960, PhD, 1965. Asst. instr. econs. Mich. State U., 1960-64; asst. prof. U. Tex., Austin, 1964-68, asso. prof., 1968-74, prof. econs., 1974-78; prof. indsl. and labor relations Cornell U., Ithaca, N.Y., 1978—. Rsch. dir. Com. on Adminstrn. Tng. Programs, HEW, 1967-68; mem. Nat. Coun. Employment Policy, 1977-87, chmn., 1985-87; bd. dirs. Corp. Pub. and Pvt. Ventures, 1978-83, Ctr. for Immigration Studies, 1987—. Author: (with Ray Marshall) The Negro and Apprenticeship, 1967, The Chicanos and Rural Poverty, 1973, (with Walter Fogel and Fred Schmidt) The Chicano Worker, 1977, (with John Adams, Brian Rungeling and Lewis Smith) Employment, Income and Welfare in the Rural South, 1977, (with Ray Marshall and Allan King) Labor Economics: Wages Employment and Trade Unionism, 1980, rev., 1984, (with Felician Foltman) Apprenticeship Research: Emerging Findings and Future Trends, 1981, Immigration Policy and the American Labor Force, 1984, (with Marta Tienda) Immigration Issues and Policies, 1985, The Internationalization of the U.S. Economy, 1986, (with Leon Bouvier) The Population and Labor Force Future of New York, 1988, (with Ray Marshall) Labor Economics: Theory, Institutions and Public Policy, 1989, Mass Immigration and the National Interest, 1992, 3d edit., 2003, Immigration Policy: A Tool of Labor Economics?, 1993, (with Stephen Moore) Still an Open Door? U.S. Immigration Policy and the American Economy, 1994, Immigration and American Unionism, 2001. Recipient Jean Holloway Tchg. Excellence award, 1974 Mem. Assn. for Evolutionary Econs. (pres. 1995), Phi Sigma Kappa, Delta Sigma Pi, Omicron Delta Kappa, Omicron Delta Epsilon. Home: 332 Winthrop Dr Ithaca NY 14850-1751 Office Phone: 607-255-4375. Business E-Mail: vmb2@cornell.edu.

BRIGGS, WARD WRIGHT, classics educator; b. Riverside, Calif., Nov. 26, 1945; s. Ward Wright and Madge Elizabeth (Ravenscroft) B. BA, Washington & Lee U., 1967; MA, U. N.C., 1969, PhD, 1974. Instr. classics U. S.C., Columbia, 1973-74, asst. prof., 1974-80, assoc. prof., 1980-86, prof. classics, 1986—, Carolina disting. prof. classics, 1996—, Louise Fry Scudder prof. humanities, 1996—, interim assoc. provost, 1996-97. Vis. prof. U. Va., Charlottesville, 1988, U. Colo., 1988; fellow Inst. for Advanced Study, Princeton, 1999-2000. Author: Narrative and Simile from the Georgics in the Aeneid, 1980; editor: Letters of B.L. Gildersleeve, 1987; editor: Biographical Dictionary of North American Classicists, 1994, Soldier and Scholar, 1998; co-editor: Classical Scholarship, 1990; editor Vergilius, Jour. of Vergilian Soc. Am., 1986-95. Mem. Am. Philol. Assn., Classical Assn. Middle West and South (pres. 1988-89), Cambridge Philol. Soc., Phi Beta Kappa. Episcopalian. Home: 1904 Pendleton St Columbia SC 29201-3906 Office: Dept French and Classics U SC Columbia SC 29208-0001 Office Phone: 803-777-2765. Personal E-mail: wbriggs7@bellsouth.net. Business E-Mail: wardbriggs@sc.edu.

BRIGGS, WILLIAM BENAJAH, retired aerospace engineer; b. Okmulgee, Okla., Dec. 13, 1922; s. Eugene Stephen and Mary Betty (Gentry) B.; m. Lorraine Hood, June 6, 1944; children— Eugene Stephen II, Cynthia Anne, Julia Louise, Spencer Gentry BA in Physics, Phillips U., 1943, DSc (hon.), 1977; MSME, Ga. Inst. Tech., 1947. Aero. scientist NACA, Cleve., 1948-52; propulsion engr. regulus II, scout l.v., dynasoar, Washington rep. Chance Vought Aircraft/LTV, Dallas, 1952-64; mgr. advanced planning Marsviking, Jupiter probe McDonnell Douglas Co., St. Louis, 1964-80, dir. program devel. fusion energy, 1980-87. Mem. planetary quarantine adv. panel NASA Contbr. articles on aero. engring. and energy to profl. jours.; patentee in field Chmn. Disciples Coun. Greater St. Louis, 1969-73; chmn. bd. Christian Bd. Publs., St. Louis, 1974-91; bd. dirs. Joint Cmty. Ministries, 1987-92, Emergency Childrens Home, 1994-2000; chmn. arrangements gen. assembly/synod Disciples of Christ/United Ch. of Christ, 1993; trustee Phillips U., Enid, Okla., 1996— . With USN, 1943-46, Atlantic and West Pacific. Recipient Svc. award, Emergency Childrens Home, 2003. Assoc. fellow AIAA (dir. region 5 1974-77, v.p. mem. svcs. 1978-79); mem. VFW, Am. Nuclear Soc., Navy League. Mem. Disciples of Christ Ch. Home: 13676

Armstead Dr Saint Louis MO 63131-1513 *Facing a problem, size up the situation, determine what needs to be done, then take action. Steadfastly working your plan does produce results; just give serendipity a chance to happen.*

BRIGGS, WINSLOW RUSSELL, plant biologist, educator; b. St. Paul, Apr. 29, 1928; s. John DeQuedville and Marjorie (Winslow) B.; m. Ann Morrill, June 30, 1955; children: Caroline, Lucia, Marion. BA, Harvard U., 1951, MA, 1952, PhD, D, U. Freiburg, Germany, 2002. Instr. biol. scis. Stanford (Calif.) U., 1955-57, asst. prof., 1957-62, assoc. prof., 1962-66, prof., 1966-67; prof. biology Harvard U., 1967-73, Stanford U., 1973—; dir. dept. plant biology Carnegie Instn. of Washington, Stanford, 1973-93. Author: (with others) Life on Earth, 1973; mem. editl. bd. Ann. Rev. Plant Physiology, 1961-72; contbr. articles on plant growth and devel. and photobiology to profl. jours. Vol. Calif. State Pk. sys. Recipient Alexander von Humboldt U.S. Sr. Scientist award, 1984-85, Sterling Hendricks award USDA Agrl. Rsch. Svc., 1995, DeWitt award for partnership Calif. State Pks., 2000, Finsen medal Assn. Internat. Photobiology, 2000; John Simon Guggenheim fellow, 1973-74, Deutsche Akademie der Naturforscher Leopoldina, 1986. Fellow AAAS; mem. NAS, Am. Soc. Plant Physiologists (pres. 1975-76, Stephen Hales award 1994), Calif. Bot. Soc. (pres. 1976-77), Am. Acad. Arts and Scis., Am. Inst. Biol. Scis. (pres. 1980-81), Am. Soc. Photobiology, Bot. Soc. Am., Nature Conservancy, Sigma Xi. Avocation: Chinese cooking. Home: 480 Hale St Palo Alto CA 94301-2207 Office: Carnegie Inst Washington Dept Plant Biology 260 Panama St Palo Alto CA 94305-4101 *With gifted students, remarkable things are possible.*

BRIGHAM, BEN M., oil industry executive; Pres., CEO, chmn. Brigham Exploration Corp., Austin, 1990—. Office: Brigham Exploration Corp 6300 Bridge Point Pkwy Bldg 2 Austin TX 78730-5073

BRIGHAM, GERALD ALLEN, research physicist, consultant; b. Burlington, Vt., June 9, 1928; s. Francis Wilbur and Thelma Mary (Peria) B.; m. Sondra Claire Kay Brigham, Dec. 21, 1960; children: Stacia, Thaisa, David Allen. BS in Applied Math, U. R.I., 1954; MS in Physics, 1957; postgrad., U. Conn., 1958-62. Mathematician Aberdeen (Md.) Proving Grounds, 1954-55; instr. U. R.I., Kingston, 1955—57; rsch. physicist Electric Boat Divsn., Groton, Conn., 1957-60; cons. in acoustics Wakefield Rsch. Assn., New London, Conn., 1960-62; rsch. physicist Naval (Underwater) Ordinance Sta., Newport, RI, 1962—66; chief scientist Autonetics Divsn./Rockwell, Anaheim, Calif., 1966—71; rsch. physicist Naval Underseas Sys. Ctr., New London, 1971-73; cons., CEO, Gerald A. Brigham & Assocs. Inc., Anaheim, Calif., 1973-79; rsch. physicist Sanders Assocs., Nashua, N.H., 1979-80; cons., CEO Aquasonics, Inc., Anaheim, Calif., 1980-88; prin. engr. SubSig Divsn./Raytheon, Portsmouth, R.I., 1988-94. Instr. elec. engring. Calif. State U., Long Beach, 1968-71; cons. in applied scis., noise control, acoustics, sonar, and ocean surveillance, 1960-62, 69-71, 73-79, 80-88, 1994--. Contbr. articles to profl. jours. Sgt. USAF, 1946-49. Recipient outstanding achievement award Naval Underseas Sys. Ctr., 1973, Sanders Assn., 1981, author's award Raytheon, 1992, 93. Mem. Acoustical Soc. Am., Sigma Pi Sigma. Home and Office: 2543 E Ames Ave Anaheim CA 92806-4702

BRIGHAM, HENRY DAY, JR., retired lawyer; b. Pittsfield, Mass., Dec. 12, 1926; s. Henry Day and Gladys M. (Allen) B.; m. Catherine T. Van't Hul, Dec. 16, 1961; children: Henry Day, Johan Van't Hul, Alexander Frederick. BA, Yale U., 1947, JD, 1950. Bar: N.Y. 1951, Mass. 1966. Assoc. Milbank, Tweed, Hope & Hadley, N.Y.C., 1951-52, 54-56, Simpson Thacher & Bartlett, N.Y.C., 1956-66; v.p., gen. counsel, dir. Eaton & Howard, Inc., Boston, 1966-73, pres., 1973-79; v.p., chmn. exec. com. Eaton & Howard, Vance Sanders, Inc., Boston, 1979-81, Eaton Vance Corp., Boston, 1981—96; ret., 1996. Former trustee Eaton Vance Cash Mgmt. Fund, Boston; former v.p., trustee Eaton Vance Tax Free Reserves, Boston; former sec., clk., dir. Investors Bank & Trust Co., Boston; v.p., sec., trustee Wright Managed Income Trust, Boston, Wright Managed Equity Trust, Boston. Pres. Trustees of Donations of Episc. Diocese Mass., 1984-89; sr. warden Ch. of the Redeemer, Chestnut Hill, 1975-79; sec., bd. dirs. Chestnut Hill Assn. (Mass.), 1969—. Lt. USNR, 1952-54. Mem.: Soc. of the Cin., Assn. Yale Alumni (bd. govs.), Investment Counsel Assn. Am. (bd. govs.), Somerset Club, Longwood Cricket Club, Downtown Club, The Country Club, Tennis & Racquet Club, Harvard Club, Tarratine Club, Soc. Colonial Wars, Phi Delta Phi, Phi Beta Kappa. Episcopalian.

BRIGHI, ROBERT J., principal; Prin. Arthur W. Erskine Elem. Sch., Cedar Rapids, Iowa. Recipient Elem. Sch. Recognition award U.S. Dept. Edn., 1989-90. Office: Arthur W Erskine Elem Sch 600 36th St SE Cedar Rapids IA 52403-4314

BRIGHT, CRAIG BARTLEY, lawyer; b. Mineola, N.Y., May 23, 1931; s. Herbert Lester and Gertrude Lillian (Smith) Bright; m. Judith Alice Pollard, July 31, 1955 (dec. Aug. 1956); m. Ann Sharpe, July 18, 1959. BA summa cum laude, Colgate U., 1952; JD magna cum laude, Harvard U., 1955. Bar: N.Y. 1956, U.S. Dist. Ct. (so. and ea. dists.) N.Y. 1961, U.S. Dist. Ct. Conn. 1961, U.S. Ct. Appeals (2d cir.) 1961. Staff judge adv. Judge Adv. Gen.'s Group, 1955—57; assoc. Patterson, Belknap, Webb & Tyler, N.Y.C., 1957—64, ptnr., 1965—92. Co-author: The Law and the Lore of Endowment Funds, 1969, The Developing Law of Endowment Funds, 1974; contbr. articles to law jours. Capt. USAF, 1955—57. Mem.: ABA, Assn. of Bar of City of N.Y., N.Y. State Bar Assn. (chmn. com. on profl. ethics 1981—84), Hermitage Club Goochland, Va. Republican. Presbyterian. Home and Office: 21 Hunting Ridge Rd Manakin Sabot VA 23103-2614 Personal E-mail: cbbasb@comcast.net.

BRIGHT, DAVID FORBES, academic administrator, classicist, educator; b. Winnipeg, Man., Can., Apr. 13, 1942; s. John Hamilton and Pauline Murray (Forbes) B.; m. Marlene Joanne Mayercik, Feb. 20, 1965; children: Jennifer, Sarah. BA (hons.), U. Man., 1962; AM, U. Cin., 1963, PhD, 1967. Asst. prof. classics Williams Coll., Williamstown, Mass., 1967—70; from asst. to assoc. prof. classics U. Ill., Urbana-Champaign, 1970—85, prof. classics and comparative lit., 1985—89, chmn. dept. classics, 1977-81, 85-88, dir. comparative lit. dept., 1986—88, acting dean Coll. Liberal Arts and Scis., 1988—89; dean Coll. Liberal Arts and Scis. Iowa State U., Ames, 1989—91; dean, v.p. for arts and scis. Emory U., Atlanta, 1991—97, prof. classics and comparative lit., 1991—, chmn. dept. classics, 1999—2005, dir. comparative lit., 1999—2001. Author: Haec mihi fingebam. Tibullus in his World, 1978, Elaborate Disarray: The Nature of Statius' Silvae, 1980, Miniature Epic in Vandal Africa, 1987, The Academic Deanship, 2001; editor: Classical Texts and Their Traditions, 1984. Bd. dirs. Atlanta Ballet Co., Savoyards Light Opera, Atlanta Baroque Orch., Coun. Colls. Arts and Scis., pres. 1996-97. Woodrow Wilson Found. fellow, 1962, U. Cin. travel fellow Am. Acad. in Rome, 1965-66, Am. Council Learned Socs. fellow, 1981-82; Rsch. scholar Delmas Found., 1987. Mem. Am. Philol. Assn., Classical Assn. Middle West and South (exec. com. 1985-89, pres. 1989), Vergilian Soc. (trustee 1983-86), Soc. of Fellows Am. Acad. Rome. Episcopalian. Home: 2646 Rangewood Dr NE Atlanta GA 30345-1516 Office: Emory U Dept Classics 221F Candler Libr Atlanta GA 30322-0001 Office Phone: 404-727-4404. Business E-Mail: david.bright@emory.edu.

BRIGHT, FRANK VERNON, chemistry professor; b. La Mesa, Calif., May 10, 1960; s. Joseph Vernon and Anna Marie Bright; m. Bonnie Lee Estes, Aug. 20, 1999. BS, U. Redlands, Calif., 1982; PhD, Okla. State U., 1985; postdoctoral, Ind. U., 1985—87. Asst. prof. UB, SUNY, Buffalo, 1987—91, assoc. prof., 1991—95, prof., 1995—, ub disting. prof. of chemistry, 2002—; A. Conger Goodyear chair of chemistry UB SUNY, 2003—. Editor: (book) Supercritical Fluid Technology: Theoretical and Applied Approaches in Analytical Chemistry. Recipient Non Tenured Faculty award, 3M Inc., 1988—91, Buck Whitney medal, Ea. NY Am. Chem. Soc., 1999, Chancellor's Excellence in Tchg. award, SUNY, 2000, NY Sect. of the Soc. for Applied Spectroscopy Gold medal, Soc. for Applied Spectroscopy, 2003, Akron medal, Akron Sect. of the Am. Chem. Soc., 2003; Rsch. grant, NSF, ONR, DOE, NIH, 1987—. Mem.: Soc. for Applied Spectroscopy, Am. Chem. Soc. Achievements include patents in field. Avocations: hunting, hiking, fishing, snow shoeing, sailing. Office: Dept of Chem UB SUNY Nat Sci Complex Buffalo NY 14260-3000 Office Phone: 716-645-6800 2162.

BRIGHT, KEVIN S., producer; b. 1955; With Bright-Kauffman-Crane Prodns., Burbank, Calif. Creator, exec. prodr. Dream On, 1990-96 (Cable Ace award), Friends, 1994-2004 (Emmy nominee 1995, 96), Veronica's Closet, 1997-2000, Jesse, 1998-2000; exec. prodr. Ron Reagan Show, 1990; prodr. The Adventures of Brisco County, Jr., 1993-94; writer, prodr. Joey, 2004—. Office: Bright Kauffman Crane Prodns 4000 Warner Blvd Bldg 160 Burbank CA 91522-0001

BRIGHT, MARGARET, sociologist; b. Bentonville, Ark., Nov. 19, 1918; d. William Ray and Edna May (Woolwine) B.; m. Herman Binder, 1983. AB, U. Calif., Berkeley, 1941; MA, U. Mo., 1944; PhD, U. Wis., 1950. Lectr. rural sociology U. Mo., 1944-47; asst. project dir. U. P.R., 1950-51; acting assoc. prof. Cornell U., 1951-52; social affairs officer population br. UN, N.Y.C., 1952-54; research assoc. Bur. Applied Social Research Columbia U., N.Y.C., 1954-57; sociologist-demographer UN Tech. Assistance, Bombay, India, 1957-59; asst. prof. chronic diseases Johns Hopkins U., Balt., 1959-63, assoc. prof., 1963-68; dir. research Center for Urban Affairs, 1968-72, assoc. prof. behavioral scis., 1968-70, prof., 1970-83, prof. emerita, 1983—. Mem. U.S. Mission Coop. Health and Sanitation to, Brazil, 1960. Author: Cooperativas de Consumo de Puerto Rico: Análisis Socio-Económicó, 1957; co-author: Graduates of American Schools of Public Health, 1976; contbr. articles to profl. jours. Mem. Balt. Mayor's Task Force on Polit. Redistricting, 1971; mem. Rockefeller Commn. on Population and the Am. Future, 1970-72. Mem. Am. Pub. Health Assn. Democrat. Home: 3900 N Charles St Apt 1314 Baltimore MD 21218-1738 Office: 624 N Broadway Baltimore MD 21205-1900

BRIGHT, MYRON H., federal judge; b. Eveleth, Minn., Mar. 5, 1919; s. Morris and Lena A. Bright; m. Frances Louise Reisler, Dec. 26, 1947; children: Dinah Ann, Joshua Robert. AA, Eveleth Junior Coll, 1939; BSL, U. Minn., 1941, JD, 1947. Bar: N.D. 1947, Minn. 1947. Assoc. Wattam, Vogel, Vogel & Bright, Fargo, ND, 1947—49, ptnr., 1949—68; judge 8th U.S. Cir. Ct. Appeals, Fargo, 1968—85, sr. judge, 1985—; disting. prof. law St. Louis U., 1985—88, emeritus prof. of law, 1989—95. Lectr. Thomas Jefferson Sch. of Law, 2003—. Capt. USAF, 1942—46. Recipient Francis Rawle award, ALI-ABA, 1996, Lifetime Achievement award, U. N.D. Law Sch., 1998, Herbert Harley award, AJS, 2000. Mem.: ABA, Fed. Judges Assn., Cass County Bar Assn., Bar Assn. Met. St. Louis, U.S. Jud. Conf. (com. on adminstrn. of probation sys. 1977—83, adv. com. on appellate rules 1987—90, com. on internat. jud. rels. 1996—2003), N.D. Bar Assn. Office: US Ct Appeals 8th Cir 655 1st Ave N Ste 340 Fargo ND 58102-4952 also: Thomas F Eagleton US Courthouse 111 S 10th St Rm 26 325 Saint Louis MO 63102*

BRIGHT, REBECCA WALLER, music educator; b. Staunton, Va., July 1, 1930; d. Charles Josiah Waller, Ruth (Lewis) Waller; m. Harry Orlo Bright Jr., July 9, 1955; children: David Michael, Miriam Kay. BS, Ithaca Coll., 1952; MA in Music, Columbia U. Tchrs. Coll., 1954, EdM, 1981. Cert. cert. tchr. pub. sch. music Va., Pa., N.Y. Tchr. music Nottoway Pub. Schs., Nottoway, Va., 1952—52, Philadelphia Bd. Edn., Philadelphia, Pa., 1954—57, Long Beach Bd. Edn., Long Beach, NY, 1957—59, White Plains Bd. Edn., White Plains, NY, 1963—92; tchr. music (part-time) Mamaroneck Pub. Schs., Mamaroneck, NY, 1992—97. Solo performer throughout Europe and U.S., 1975—; choral dir. Woman's Club of White Plains, 1994—. Cons. childrens music workshops Westchester Symphony Orch., Tarrytown, NY, 1998—; chair bd. dirs. Early Learning Ctr. of White Plains; chair music com. Chatterton Hill Ch., White Plains, 1992—. Recipient Svc. award, Westchester County Sch. Music Assn., 1992, Ch. Women United, 1998, NAACP, 1993—2001. Mem.: Nat. Assn. Negro Musicians (v.p. Thomas Music Study Club 1997—), Westchester County Sch. Music Assn. (Svc. award 1992), Phi Delta Kappa, Delta Sigma Theta, Sigma Alpha Iota. Home: 220 Saxon Wood Rd White Plains NY 10605

BRIGHT, WILLARD MEAD, retired manufacturing executive, retired director; b. N.Y.C., Mar. 26, 1914; s. William Van Horn and Bernice Hartwell (Reynolds) B.; m. Martha Norris Land, May 15, 1944 (dec.); 1 child, Willard Mead; m. Virginia L. Jones, Mar. 14, 1981 (div. Aug. 1996). BS, U. Toledo, 1936, MS, 1937; postgrad., U. Pitts., 1937-38; A.M., Harvard U., 1941, PhD, 1942. Research chemist Kendall Co., Boston, Chgo., 1942-52; asst. lab. dir. Kendall Co. (Bauer & Black div.), 1944-48; lab. dir. (Theodore Clark Lab. div.), Cambridge, Mass., 1948-52; asst. research dir. Lever Bros. Co., 1952-54, research dir., 1954-60, v.p. research and devel., 1960-64; chmn. bd. W. H. Norris Lumber Co., Houston, 1957-64; treas. Border Lumber Co., Weslaco, Tex., 1957-64; v.p. R.J. Reynolds Tobacco Co., 1964-68; sr. v.p., pres. profl. products group Warner-Lambert Pharm. Co., 1968-70; pres., chief exec. officer Kendall Co., Boston, 1970-73; pres. Curtiss-Wright Corp., 1973-74, Boehringer Mannheim Corp., 1974-81; chmn. Zoll Med. Corp, 1982-96; ret., 1996. Bd. dirs. Zoll Med. Corp.; mem. adv. com. on patents U.S. Dept. Commerce, 1966-69; mem. bd. visitors dept. chemistry Boston U. Recipient Gold T award U. Toledo, 1960 Mem. N.A.M. (chmn. sci. tech. com. dir. 1970-73), Am. Chem. Soc., N.Y. Acad. Scis., Assn. Rsch. Dirs., Indsl. Rsch. Inst. (dir. 1963-69, pres. 1967-68), Dirs. Indsl. Rsch., Sigma Xi, Phi Kappa Phi, Harvard Club (Boston), Comml. Club (Boston), The Country Club (Brookline, Mass.), Bent Pine Golf Club (Vero Beach, Fla.). Home: 105 Prestwick Cir Vero Beach FL 32967-7514

BRIGHTFELT, ROBERT, diagnostic company executive; BS with distinction, MS with distinction, U. Nebr.; MBA, U. Ga. Various positions in healthcare and diagnostics DuPont Diagnostics, Dade Behring, Deerfield, Ill., group pres. for Chemistry products divsn., pres. Global Products. E-mail: brightrw@dadebehring.com.

BRIGHTMAN, SARAH, singer, actress; b. Berkhampstead, England, Aug. 14, 1960; d. Grenville and Paula (Hall) Brightman; m. Andrew Lloyd Webber (div. 1990). Student, Elmhurst Ballet Sch., Arts Edn. Sch., London. Stage appearances include (musicals) I and Albert, 1973, Cats (original cast), 1981, Nightingale, 1982, Song and Dance, 1984, Phantom of the Opera, 1986 (Drama Desk award), Aspects of Love, 1990, (requiem) Andrew Lloyd Webber's Requiem, 1985 (Grammy nomination), (operettas) Pirates of Penzance, 1983, Merry Widow, 1985; dancer, singer (dance group) Hot Gossip, 1978 (#1 record 1978); albums include: Dive, 1993, Timeless, 1997, Time To Say Goodbye, 1997, As I Came of Age, 1998, Fly, 1998, Surrender, 1998, Sings the Music of Andrew Lloyd Webber, 1998, Trees They Grow So High, 1998, Eden, 1998, La Luna, 2000, Harem, 2003. Avocations: singing, driving, swimming, writing.

BRIGHTON, GERALD DAVID, retired finance educator; b. Weldon, Ill., May 14, 1920; s. William Henry and Geneva (Ennis) B.; m. Lois Helen Robbins, June 7, 1949; children: Anne, William, Joan, John, Jeffrey. BS, U. Ill., 1941, MS, 1947, PhD, 1953. C.P.A., Ill. Instr. accountancy U. Ill., Urbana, 1947-53, prof., 1954-83, Ernst & Whinney Disting. prof., 1983-88, prof. emeritus, 1988—, dir. undergrad. acctg. program, 1978-86; staff acct. Touche, Niven, Bailey & Smart, Chgo., 1953-54. Cons. G.D. Brighton, C.P.A., Urbana, 1954—; vis. prof. U. Tex.-Austin, 1973; program specialist Dept. HUD, Washington, 1979; vice chmn. U. Ill. Athletic Assn., Urbana, 1982-86 Contbr. articles to profl. jours. Alderman City of Urbana, 1967-69; officer, bd. dirs. U. Ill. YMCA, Champaign, 1959-81, 89-95, trustee, 2002—; bd. dirs. Wesley Found., U. Ill., 1986—; treas. John Gwinn for Congress, Urbana, 1982-83, Green Meadows coun. Girl Scouts U.S., 1981-83. Served to maj. U.S. Army, 1941-46. AACSB Faculty fellow, 1978-79; recipient Bronze Tablet for high honors U. Ill., 1941 Mem. AICPA (hon.), Ill. Soc. CPAs (disting.), Am. Acctg. Assn., Assn. Govt. Accts., Govtl. Fin. Officers Assn., Nat. Tax Assn., Tax Inst. Am. Democrat. Methodist. Home: 501 Evergreen Ct Urbana IL 61801-5928 Office: U Ill 1206 S 6th St Champaign IL 61820-6978 E-mail: gbrighto@uiuc.edu. *Happiness comes very indirectly. "Seek and ye shall find." That is at best a half truth. If we rely on direct rewards for our happiness we are in trouble. At best, the string of treats will be irregular. The key is to widen one's circle. Try to rejoice in the good fortunes of your colleagues. Sometimes, jealousy gets in the way. What is the greatest satisfaction I have had from teaching? It is the occasional glimpses that I see that former students are doing well.*

BRIGHTON, JOHN A., mechanical engineer, academic administrator; b. Gosport, Ind. BS in mech. engring., Purdue U., 1959, MS in mech. engring., 1960, PhD in mech. engring., 1963. Design draftsman Schwitzer Corp., Indpls., 1952—55; instr. mech. engring. Purdue U., 1960—62; tech. staff Aerospace Corp., El Segundo, Calif., 1962; asst. prof. mech. engring. Carnegie-Mellon U., 1963—65; asst. prof. mech. engring Pa. State U., 1965—67, assoc. prof. mech. engring., 1967—77; chmn. dept. mech. engring Mich. State U., 1977-82; dir. Sch. Mech. Engring. Ga. Inst. Tech., 1982-88; dean Coll. Engring. Pa. State U., 1988-91, exec. v.p., provost, 1991—99, U. Prof., chair Tchg. and Learning Consortium, 1999—2002; provost Nat.-Louis U., Chgo., 2002—03; asst. dir. for engring. NSF, 2003—. Named Disting. Engring. Alumni, Purdue U., 2004; recipient Rodney D. Chipp Meml. Award, Soc. Women Engineers, 1992. Fellow: Am. Soc. Engring. Edn., ASME. Office: NSF 4201 Wilson Blvd Arlington VA 22230 Office Phone: 703-292-8300. E-mail: jbrighto@nsf.gov.

BRIGHTON, LOUIS ANDREW, religious studies educator; b. Saskatoon, Sask., Can., Oct. 30, 1927; s. Louis Frederick Brighton and Helen Ester Frinke; m. Mary Belle Williams; children: Stephan Louis, Anne Louise, Christine Marie, Mary Helen, Mark Andrew. BA, Concordia Coll., 1950; MDiv, Concordia Sem., 1952, STM, 1964; PhD, St. Louis U., 1991; grad., N.Y. Inst. Photography, 1965. Clergyman Holy Trinity Luth. Ch., London, 1952—58, Our Redeemer Luth. Ch., Decatur, Ill., 1958—68, St. John Luth. Ch., Lexington, Ky., 1968—74; prof. NT and bibl. langs. Concordia Sem., St. Louis, 1974—. Author: Commentary on Revelation, 1999; contbr. articles to profl. jours. Luth. chaplain London Prisons, 1957; juvenile chaplain Decatur Jail, 1958—68. Staff sgt. U.S. Army, 1946—48, Korea. Named Ky. col., Gov. Louie B. Nunn, 1970. Avocation: photography. Home: 2541 Belmont Dr High Ridge MO 63049 Office: Concordia Seminary 801 DeMun Ave Saint Louis MO 63105 Office Phone: 314-505-7127.

BRIGHTON, RUTH LOUISE, lay worker, educator; b. Harrisburg, Pa., Apr. 18, 1931; d. Paul Gerhard and Ruth Genevieve (Lee) Krentz; m. Carl T. Brighton, July 27, 1954; children: David, Susan, Andrew, Joel. BA, Valparaiso U., 1953; MS in Math., U. Wis., 1955. Cert. tchr. Tchr. Sunday sch., adult Bible class Christ Meml. Luth. Ch., Malvern, Penn., 1969—; coord. adult edn., Ea. dist. Luth. Ch.-Mo. Synod, Buffalo, 1986-89, bd. dirs., 1988-90. Bd. dirs. Concordia Pub. House, St. Louis, 1989—2001. Teaching fellow in math. U. Wis., 1953. Home: 14 Flintshire Rd Malvern PA 19355-1108

BRILES, JUDITH, writer, consultant; b. Pasadena, Calif., Feb. 20, 1946; d. James and Mary Tuthill; children: Shelley, Sheryl, Frank (dec.), William (dec.). MBA, Pepperdine U., 1980; PhD, Nova U., 1990. Brokers asst. Bateman, Eichler, Hill, Richards, Torrance, Calif., 1969-72; account exec. E. F. Hutton, Palo Alto, Calif., 1972-78; pres. Judith Briles & Co., Palo Alto, 1978-85, Briles & Assocs., Palo Alto, 1980-86; ptnr. The Briles Group, Inc., 1987—. Instr. Menlo Coll., 1986-87, Skyline Coll., 1981-86, U. Calif.-Berkeley Sch. Continuing Edn., U. Calif.-Santa Cruz Sch. Continuing Edn., U. Hawaii; mem. adv. coun. Miss Am. Pageant, 1989-95, No-nonsense Panty Hose, 1989-92, Colo. Women's News, 1993-97. Author: The Woman's Guide to Financial Savvy, 1981, Money Phases, 1984, Woman to Woman: From Sabotage to Support, 1987, Dollars and Sense of Divorce, 1988, Faith and Savvy Too!, 1988, When God Says No, 1990, The Confidence Factor, 1990 (Bus. Book of Yr, 2003), Money Guide, 1991, The Workplace Factor, 1990, Money Guide, 1991, The Workplace: Questions Women Ask, 1992, Financial Savvy for Women, 1992, The Briles Report on Women in Healthcare, 1994, Money Sense, 1995, Gender Traps, 1996, Raising Money Wise Kids, 1996, When God Says No, 1997, The Dollars and Sense of Divorce, 1998, Woman to Woman 2000, 1999 (chgo. Tribune Bus. Book of Yr.), 10 Smart Money Moves for Women, 1999(Book of Yr., 2002), Smart Money Moves for Kids, 2000 (Best How to Parenting, 2001), The Confidence Factor—Cosmic Goose Lay Golden Eggs, 2001, Stop Stabbing Yourself in the Back, 2001, Zapping Conflict in the Healthcare Workplace, 2003, Money Smarts, 2005; columnist Colo. Woman News, Denver Bus. Jour., MsMoney.com. Pres., v.p., sec., bd. dirs. foothill-DeAnza Coll. Found., Los Altos Hills, Calif., 1979-90; bd. dirs. Col. Nurses Task Force, Col. League Nursing, 1994-95; mem. adv. bd. Flint Ctr., Cupertino, Calif. Mem. NAFE (adv. bd. bus. woman'e mag. 1981-86), Peninsula Profl. Women's Network, Nat. Speaker's Assn. (bd. dirs.), WISH List (bd. dirs. 1998—), Colo. Ind. Pubs. Assn. (bd. dirs. 2002-2006); Gilda's Club (Denver bd. dirs. 2001-, pres., v.p.). Independent. Office Phone: 303-627-9179. Personal E-mail: DrJBriles@aol.com. Business E-Mail: judith@briles.com.

BRILEY, MICHAEL M., lawyer; b. N.Y.C., Feb. 4, 1945; s. John Marshall and Dorothy (DeWolf) Briley; m. Sandra Briley; children: Michael Jr., Karen. AB, Miami U., Oxford, Ohio, 1966; JD, Ohio State U., 1969. Bar: U.S. Supreme Ct., U.S. Ct. Appeals (6th cir.), U.S. Ct. Appeals (2d cir.), U.S. Ct. Appeals (D.C. cir.). Ptnr. Fuller & Henry, Toledo, 1969—84, Shumaker, Loop & Kendrick, Toledo, 1984—. Gen. counsel, corp. sec. Wacker Chem. Corp., Adrian, Mich., 1997—; examiner Ohio Bd. Bar Examinators, Columbus, 1996—. Mem.: Rockwell Springs Trout Club, Stone Oak Country Club. Independent. Avocations: golf, classical guitar. Home: 24737 W River Rd Perrysburg OH 43551 Office: Shumaker Loop Kendrick 1000 Jackson St Toledo OH 43624 Office Phone: 419-321-1325. Office Fax: 419-241-6894. Business E-Mail: mbriley@slk-law.com.

BRILL, AARON BERTRAND, nuclear medicine educator; b. N.Y.C., Dec. 19, 1928; s. Louis And Cecile (Sroge) B.; m. Joan Booth Morrison, Sept. 1, 1950; children: Paul, David, Laurie. AB, Grinnell Coll., 1949; MD, U. Utah, 1956; PhD in Biophysics, U. Calif., Berkeley, 1961. Statistician Contra Costa County Health Dept., Martinez, Calif., 1949—50; res. asst. U. Calif., Donner Lab, 1950—52; biophysicist U. Utah Pediatrics Dept., Salt Lake City, 1952-56; intern Salt Lake City Gen. Hosp., 1956-57; USPHS officer Div. of Radiol. Health, Rockville, Md., 1957-64; asst. prof. radiology dept. radiology scis. Johns Hopkins Hosp. and Sch. of Hygiene, 1961-64; assoc. prof. radiol. Vanderbilt U. Sch. Medicine, Nashville, 1964-72; assoc. prof. medicine, biomed. engring. and physics, 1964-79; prof. radiology Vanderbilt U. Sch. Medicine, Nashville, 1972-79, SUNY, Stony Brook, 1979-87; sr. scientist, nuc. medicine coord. Brookhaven (N.Y.) Nat. Lab., 1979-87; prof. nuclear medicine U. Mass. Sch. Medicine, Worcester, 1987—97. Rsch. affiliate MIT, Cambridge, 1993—; affil. prof. Worcester Polytechnic Inst., Worcester, 1995-97; rsch. prof. radiol. sci. Vanderbilt U. Sch. Medicine, Nashville, 1997—, rsch. prof. physics, adj. prof. biomed. engring., 1998—. Editor: Low Level Radiation Fact Book, 1st edit. 1982, 2d edit., 1985; editor: IEEE Trans Med. Imaging, 1986-92. Med. dir. USPHS, 1957-64, U. Calif. at Berkeley fellow, 1959-61. Fellow Inst. for elec. and electronic engring., Am. Coll. Nuclear Physicians, Am. Inst. Med. and Biol. Engring.; mem. NAS (com. on atomic casualties 1964-70, com. on biol. effects of ionizing radiation 1978-80; nat. coun. on radiation protection and measurement 1972-82, 92-97). Avocations: tennis, sailing, skiing. Office: Vanderbilt U Med Sch Dept Radiol Sci Mcn S1314 Nashville TN 37232-2675 Business E-Mail: aaron.brill@vanderbilt.edu.

BRILL, ALAN RICHARD, entrepreneur; b. Evansville, Ind., July 5, 1942; s. Gregory and Bernice Lucille (Froman) B.; children: Jennifer Leigh, Katherine Anne, Alison Elizabeth. AB, DePauw U., 1964; MBA, Harvard U., 1968. Mgmt. cons. Peace Corps, Ecuador, 1964-66; sr. acct., cons. Arthur Young & Co., N.Y.C., 1968-71; v.p. ops. Charter Med. Mgmt. Co., Inc., 1972-73; v.p. controller Hosp. Investors, Atlanta, 1972-73; v.p., treas., dir. Worrell Newspapers, Inc., Worrell Broadcasting, Inc., Charlottesville, Va., 1973-79; pres. Brill Assocs., Evansville, Ind., 1979—, Brill Media Co., Inc.,

Evansville, Ind., 1980—. Bd. visitors U. So. Ind. Sch. Bus. Mem. AICPA, N.Y. State Soc. CPAs, Evansville C. of C. (bd. dirs.), Jobs for S.W. Ind. (bd. dirs.), Beacon Group, Farmington Country Club (Charlottesville), Safari Internat. Club. Republican. Methodist. Home: PO Box 3517 Evansville IN 47734-3517 Office: Brill Media Co Inc PO Box 3353 Evansville IN 47732-3353 Business E-Mail: abo@brillmedia.com.

BRILL, DAVID R., radiologist; b. Chattanooga, Tenn., Dec. 13, 1941; s. Kenneth Grey and Prisculla (Ritchie) Brill; m. Marilyn Facka, June 17, 1972 (div. Apr. 25, 2003); m. Elizabeth Allen, Aug. 23, 2003. BA, Wesleyan U., 1963; MD, U. Mo., 1967. Diplomate Am. Bd. Radiology, Am. Bd. Nuc. Medicine. Intern Marion County Gen. Hosp., Indpls., 1967—68; resident Vanderbilt U., Nashville, 1968—71; instr. U. Tex. S.W. Med. Ctr., Dallas, 1971—72; chief nuc. medicine Geisinger Med. Ctr., Danville, Pa., 1972—2000; radiologist Chambersburg Imaging Assoc., Pa., 1998—. Advisor in nuc. medicine Pa. Blue Shield, Camp Hill, 1989—. Contbr. articles to profl. jours., chpts. to books, exhibits. Clk. of session Grove Presbyn. Ch., Danville, 1988—93. Fellow: Am. Coll. Nuc. Medicine, Am. Coll. Nuc. Physicians (pres. 1996), Am. Coll. Radiology (chmn. com. on nuc. medicine stds. 1993—98); mem.: Pa. Radiol. Soc. (pres. 1997—98), Soc. Nuc. Medicine (ho. dels. 2000—). Presbyterian. Avocations: birdwatching, jogging, adult Christian education. Office: Chambersburg Imaging Assocs 25 Penncraft Ave Chambersburg PA 17201

BRILL, DONALD MAXIM, researcher, educator; b. Elk Mound, Wis., Sept. 8, 1922; s. John James and Grace Darling (Mayo) B.; m. Meredith Joy Wright, June 25, 1955; children: John Richard, Rebecca Jean, Linda Marie, Susan Elizabeth. BS, Stout State U., 1947; MA, U. Minn., 1949; PhD, U. Wis., 1973. Tchr. Mpls. Pub. Schs., 1949-50, Eau Claire (Wis.) Pub. Schs., 1950, Chippewa Valley Tech. Coll., 1951-58; supr. Wis. Tech. Colls., Madison, 1958-65; coord. Great Cities Program for Sch. Improvement Rsch. Coun., Chgo., 1965-67; supr. rsch. Wis. Tech. Colls., Madison, 1967-70, asst. state dir., 1970-83. Adj. prof. U. Wis., Stout, 1983-86. Mem. state com. for employer support of Guard and Res., 1983-86; mem. Eau Claire Area Sch. Bd., 1989-92; founding bd. dirs. Fourth Dimension, Inc., WHEM-FM, 1994-98; primary candidate 3d Congl. Dist., Wis., 1994, mem. State Com. for Employee Support of Guarding Reserves. With U.S. Army, 1942-45, ETO. Mem. DAV (life), VFW (life), SAR (chpt. pres.), Am. Vocat. Assn. (life), The Mayflower Soc. (life). Republican. Baptist. Avocations: writing, genealogy, poetry, travel. Home: W 2745 Mitchell Rd Eau Claire WI 54701-8603 Personal E-mail: dmb316@charter.net.

BRILL, JANA ALENA, French language educator; b. Brno, Czechoslovakia, June 26, 1944; came to US, 1947; d. Vladimir Jan and Eva Marie (Tryb) Fleischer; m. Russell Martin Brill, July 19, 1969 (div. 1982); 1 child, Alexa Eva; m. Henry Michael Pinkerton, July 30, 1988; 1 child, Kate Ellen Pinkerton-Brill. BA, U. Colo., 1966, MA, 1968; PhD, U. Calif., Santa Barbara, 1983. Cert. secondary/jr. coll. French tchr., Calif.; secondary tchr., Ky. Tchr. French and German Alameda Sr. H.S., Lakewood, Colo., 1969—74; tchg. asst. U. Colo., Boulder, 1967—68; tchg. asst. and assoc. U. Calif., Santa Barbara, 1977—84; asst. prof. French U. Louisville, 1984—91; assoc. prof. French Georgetown Coll., Ky., 1991—, promotion to full prof., 1998. Cons. French in Action teaching video, 1987; dept. chair Modern and Classical Lang. and Cultures Georgetown Coll., 2003— Author: Oral Traditions: When Did the French Stop Speaking Latin?, 2005; contbr. articles to profl. jours. Mem. participatory mgmt. com. Waggener High Sch., Louisville, 1990-91; mem. adult edn. com. St. Mathew's Episc. Ch., Louisville, 1989-91. Dean's rsch. grantee U. Louisville, 1990. Mem., Am. Assn. Tchr. French, Ky. World Lang. Assn., Ky. Philol. Assn., Ky. Philol. Rev. (editl. bd. 1993), Pi Delta Phi (chpt. moderator at Georgetown Coll.) Avocations: folk music and dance, gardening.

BRILL, JANET BOND, nutritionist, educator; b. N.Y.C., Sept. 15, 1957; d. Alma Halbert and Rudolph Richard Bond; m. Samuel Brill, June 10, 1984; children: Rachel Alana, Mia Alexandra, Jason Louis. MS in Edn., U. Miami, Fla., 1986; MS in Dietetics, Nutrition, Fla. Internat. U., 1992; PhD in Exercise Phisiology, U. Miami, Fla., 2000. Cert. Exercise Test Technologist Am. Coll. Sports Medicine, 1986, registered Dietitian Am. Dietetic Assn., 1994, cert. personal trainer Nat. Strength and Conditioning Assn., 2003. Nutritionist, pvt. practice, Coral Springs, Fla., 1992—; adj. prof. U. Miami, Coral Gables, Fla., 2000—. Freelance nutrition cons., 1994—. Contbr. articles to profl. jours. Mem.: Weight Mgmt. Practice Group (founding mem.), Sports and Cardiovasc. Nutritionists Practice Group, N.Am. Assn. for the Study of Obesity, Am. Dietetic Assn., Am. Coll. Sports Medicine, Alpha Epsilon Delta Honor Soc., Golden Key Honor Soc., Phi Kappa Phi Honor Soc. Avocations: marathon running, weight training, pesco-vegetarianism. Office: 4630 N University Dr # 436 Coral Springs FL 33067 Office Phone: 954-227-0777. Personal E-mail: DrJanetBrill@aol.com.

BRILL, KENNETH C., former ambassador; b. Ft. Hood, Tex., Oct. 13, 1947; m. Mary Lee Brill; 2 children. BS, Ohio U., 1969; MS, U. Calif., Berkeley, 1973. With U.S. Fgn. svc., 1975—, posted Accra, 1976-78, staff asst. African Bur., 1978-79, desk officer, 1979-81, spl. asst. to Under Sec. for Polit. Affairs, 1981-82, dep. dir., then dir. Office of Egyptian Affairs, 1982-84, counselor for polit. affairs Amman, 1984-86, consul gen. Calcutta, 1986-89, exec. asst. to Under Sec. for Polit. Affairs, 1989-91, dep. chief of mission, charge d'Affaires New Delhi, 1991-94, spl. asst. to sec. and exec. sec. of dept., 1994, U.S. amb. to Republic of Cyprus Nicosia, 1996—99; U.S. rep. to the IAEA U.S. Dept. State, Vienna, 2001—04, U.S. rep. to the UN, 2001—04; internat. affairs advisor to the Commandant of the Industrial College of the Armed Forces. With U.S. Army, 1970-72. Recipient Disting., Superior and Meritorious Honor award U.S. Dept. State. Office: Ft Lesley J McNair Washington DC 20319-5066

BRILL, LAWRENCE JOEL, lawyer; b. Washington, Sept. 11, 1945; s. Robert Melvin and Elaine (Friedman) B.; m. Rita Joan Kopit, June 14, 1969; children: Matthew Jason. BS in Bus., Syracuse U., 1968; JD, U. Balt., 1974. Bar: Md. 1975, D.C. 1976. Legis. officer U.S. Dept. Commerce, Washington, 1972-78, spl. asst. to dep. asst. sec. textiles and apparel, 1978-79, internat. trade specialist textiles and apparel, 1979—, dir. market expansion divsn., 2000—. Atty. Pres.' Task Force on Regulatory Reform, Occupational Safety and Health, 1976. Counsel Harpers Choice Village Assn., Columbia, 1976-79, Kings Contrivance Village Assn., Columbia, 1981-83. Served with USAR, 1969-75. U.S. Dpet. Commerce Sci. and Tech. fellow, 1979-80. Mem. Md. Bar Assn. Home and Office: 9630 W Window Way Columbia MD 21046-2035 Office Phone: 301-498-6045. E-mail: lawrence_brill@ita.doc.gov, brillaw@aol.com.

BRILL, LESLEY, literature and film studies educator; b. Chgo., Sept. 3, 1943; s. Walter Henry and Fay (Trolander) B.; m. Megan Parry, Jan. 18, 1970; children: Benjamin, Calista. BA, U. Chgo., 1965; MA, SUNY, Binghamton, 1967; PhD, Rutgers U., 1971. Asst. prof. English U. Colo., Boulder, 1970-80, assoc. prof., 1981-89, chmn. dept. English, 1981-85, grad. dir., 1985-87; prof. and chmn. dept. English Wayne State U., Detroit, 1989-94. Vis. lectr. U. Kent, Canterbury, Eng., 1978-79; vis. prof. U. Paul Valery, Montpellier, France, 1984, U. de Nantes, France, 1995. Author: The Hitchcock Romance: Love and Irony in Hitchcock's Films, 1988, John Huston's Filmmaking, 1997; contbr. articles on lit. and film to profl. jours. Rockefeller Found. fellow, 1977-78. Mem. Soc. Cinema Studies. Office: Wayne State U Dept English Detroit MI 48202 E-mail: aa4525@wayne.edu.

BRILL, MARLENE TARG, writer; b. Chgo., Sept. 27, 1945; d. Irving and Genevieve (Worshill) Targ; m. Richard Benjamin Brill, Feb. 4, 1973; 1 child, Alison. BS Spl. Edn., U. Ill., 1967; MS Early Childhood Edn., Roosevelt U., 1973. Tchr. spl. edn. Dept. Mental Health, Chgo., 1967-70, Chgo. Bd. Edn., 1970-73, Wayne County Intermediate Sch., Detroit, 1973-75; curriculum specialist Cook County Office of Pub. Instrn., Chgo., 1975-78; media coord. South Metropolitan Assn., South Holland, Ill., 1979-80; writer, author MTB Comms., Wilmette, Ill., 1980—. Author: Hide-and-Seek Safety, 1985, John Adams, 1986, I Can Be a Lawyer, 1987, James Buchanan, 1988, Rainy Days and Rainbows, 1989, Why Do We Have To?, 1991, Keys to Parenting a Child with Down Syndrome, 1993, Guatemala, 1993, Allen Jay & The Underground Railroad, 1993, Trail of Tears: A Journey from Home, 1994, Keys to Parenting a Child with Autism, 1994, 2001, Guyana, 1994, Extraordinary Young People, 1996, Building the Capital City, 1996, Illinois, 1996, 2d edit., 2005, Honduras, 1996, Journey for Peace: The Story of Rigoberta Menchu, 1996, Let Women Vote, 1996, Women for Peace, 1997, Indiana, 1997, Tooth Tales from Around the World, 1998, Michigan, 1998, Diary of a Drummer Boy, 1998, The AMA Essential Guide to Asthma, 1998, Sport Success: Winning Women in Ice Hockey, 1999, Sport Success: Winning Women in Soccer, 1999, Sport Success: Winning Women in Baseball/Softball, 2000, Sport Success: Winning Women in Basketball, 2000, Margaret Knight: Girl Inventor, 2001, 25 Most Frequently Asked Questions About Discipline, 2001, Tourette Syndrome, 2001, Raising Smart Kids for Dummies, 2003, Bronco Charlie and the Pony Express, 2003, Garbage Trucks, 2004, Minnesota, 2004, Doctors, 2004, Nurses, 2005, Veteran's Day, 2005, Alzheimer's Disease, 2005, Lung Cancer, 2005, Concrete Mixers, Barack Obama, 2005. Mem. Soc. Midland Authors, Soc. Children's Book Writers and Illustrators, Author's Guild. Avocations: reading, music, drawing, crafts, walking. Office: MTB Comm 314 Lawndale St Wilmette IL 60091-3215 E-mail: mtbrill@att.net.

BRILL, RALPH DAVID, architect, real estate developer, venture capitalist; b. Nov. 24, 1944; came to U.S., 1949; naturalized, 1955; s. Walter and Irmgard (Levy) B.; children: Micah Levy, Loren Koff, Wade Sydney. Student, U. Ill., 1962-66; student urban design, Kunstskolen, Copenhagen, 1967. Registered architect; lic. real estate broker, N.Y. V.p., founder Node 4 Assocs., Inc., Bklyn., 1968-70; dir. devel. Townland Mktg. and Devel. Corp., Cherry Hill., N.J., 1970-72; pres. Ralph Brill Assocs., Garrison, N.Y., 1973—. Ptnr. Brill, Kwakami, Wilbourne, Architects, Cold Spring, N.Y.C, Telluride, Colo., 1973—93; pres. Finsky Group, Inc., 1974—88, Deer Hollow Ptnrs., 1984—, Manhattan Strategic Venture Fund, 1988—, Cara Ventures, 1988—93, White Column Farms, Pawlet, Vt., 1988—, Woodbury Tech. Ventures, 1992—, Southment Devel. Group, Inc., Montrose, Colo., 1993—; founder Manitou Realty, Cold Spring, 1976—, Swallow Comty, Cold Spring, NY, 1982—; archtl. critic Columbia U., 1969; adj. asst. prof. urban sys Fairleigh Dickinson U., 1974—76; chmn. Duchess Ptnrs., Inc., N.Y.C., 1989; bd. dirs. Brill Gmbh, Herzbrock; co-chmn. Prism Appliance Sys., Inc., 1992—96, Ster-L-Tech., Inc., 1996—2001, Studio 244, 1999—, running lights.com, 1999—. Author: The Hudson River Catalogue, 1978. Bd. dirs. Garrison Art Ctr., 1976-83, Spectra Arts, 1983-88, Chapel of Our Lady Restoration, 1977. Grantee N.Y. State Hist. Preservation, 1977, Pure Water Technologies, Inc., 1988—; recipient First Honors award Mid-Hudson AIA, 1988, 89. Mem. Soc. Indsl. Archeology, Ctr. for Hudson River Valley. Jewish. Home: PO Box 200 Garrison NY 10524-0200 Office: 77 Main St Cold Spring NY 10516-0248 also: PO Box 3559 Montrose CO 81402-3559

BRILL, YVONNE CLAEYS, engineer, consultant; b. St. Norbert, Manitoba, Can., Dec. 30, 1924; d. August and Julienne (Carette) Claeys; m. William Franklin Brill, Dec. 15, 1951; children: Naomi, Matthew, Joseph. BS, U. Manitoba, Canada, 1945; MS, U. So. Calif., 1951. Mathematician Douglas Aircraft, Santa Monica, Calif., 1945-46; research analyst Rand Corp., Santa Monica, 1946-49; group leader Marquardt Corp., Van Nuys, Calif., 1949-52; staff engr. UTC Research, East Hartford, Conn., 1952-55; project engr. Wright Aeronautical, Wood Ridge, N.J., 1955-58; mgr. propulsion systems RCA AstroElectronics, Princeton, N.J., 1966-81; staff engr., 1983-86; mgr. solid rocket motor NASA Hdqrs., Washington, 1981-83; with space engring segment Internat. Maritime Satellite Orgn., London, 1986-91; cons. Brill Assocs., Skillman, N.J., 1991—. Mem. USAF Sci. Adv. Bd., Washington, 1982-83, Nat. Acad. Engring.; Com. on Internat. Orgns. and Programs, 1992-96; apptd. mem. aerospace safety adv. panel NASA, 1994-2001. Contbr. articles to sci. jours.; patentee in field. Recipient Engr. of Yr. award, Ctrl. Jersy Engring. Couns., 1979, Diamond Superwoman award, Harpers Bazaar/DeBeers Corp., 1980, Disting. Pub. Svc. medal, NASA, 2001, Judith A. Resnik award, IEEE, 2002. Fellow AIAA (Marvin C. Demlar award 1983, WYLD award in rocket propulsion 2002), Soc. Women Engrs. (dir. student affairs 1979-80, 83-84, treas. 1980-81, Engring. Achievement award 1986, Resnik Challenger medal 1993); mem. Nat. Acad. Engring., Internat. Astronautical Acad. (academician, edn. com. 1983-85), Sigma Xi, Tau Beta Pi. Home and Office: 914 Route 518 Skillman NJ 08558-2616

BRILLIANT, ASHLEIGH ELLWOOD, cartoonist, writer; b. London, Dec. 9, 1933; came to the U.S., 1956, naturalized, 1969; s. Victor and Amelia (Adler) B.; m. Dorothy Low Tucker, June 28, 1968. BA with honors, Univ. Coll., London, 1955; MA in Edn., Claremont Grad. Sch., 1957; PhD in Am. History, U. Calif., Berkeley, 1964. Tchr. English Hollywood H.S., L.A., 1956-57; tchg. asst., reader in history U. Calif., Berkeley, 1960-63; asst. prof. history Ctrl. Oreg. Coll., Bend, 1964-65, Floating Campus divsn. Chapman Coll., Orange, Calif., 1965-67; entertainer in coffeehouses, outdoor spkr. San Francisco, 1967-68; syndicated cartoonist, dir. Brilliant Enterprises, pub. and licensing, San Francisco, Santa Barbara, Calif., 1967—. Creator Pot-Shots postcards, T-shirts, cocktail napkins, tote-bags, other items; mem. faculty Sonoma State U., Santa Barbara City Coll.; vis. scholar Ctrl. Oregon Cmty. Coll., 2002. Author: I May Not Be Totally Perfect, But Parts of Me Are Excellent, And Other Brilliant Thoughts, 1979, I Have Abandoned My Search for Truth and Am Now Looking for a Good Fantasy, 1980, Appreciate Me Now and Avoid the Rush, 1981, I Feel Much Better Now That I've Given Up Hope, 1984, All I Want Is A Warm Bed and A Kind Word, and Unlimited Power, 1985, I Try to Take One Day At A Time, But Sometimes Several Days Attack Me At Once, 1987, The Great Car Craze: How Southern California Collided With The Automobile in the 1920's, 1989, We've Been Through So Much Together and Most of It Was Your Fault, 1990, Be A Good Neighbor and Leave Me Alone, 1992, I Want to Reach Your Mind...Where is it Currently Located, 1994, I'm Just Moving Clouds Today-Tomorrow I'll Try Mountains, 1999; illustrator: The Illuminated Life, 1995, Adult Development and Aging, 1995, Give Yourself the Unfair Advantage!, 1995, Designing Effective Organizations, 1995, The Baby Boomers' Guide to Living Forever, 2000, Multiple Streams of Internet Income, 2001, Breaking Free From Boomerang Love, 2004; founder, leader Ban Leafblowers and Save Our Town, 1996. Recipient Raymond B. Bragg award, 1987, Disting. Alumnus of Yr. award Claremont Grad. U., 2000; Claremont Grad. Sch. scholar, 1956; Haynes fellow, 1962, Panama-Pacific fellow, 1963. Mem. Newspaper Comics Coun., No. Calif. Cartoonists Assn., Mensa. Home and Office: 117 W Valerio St Santa Barbara CA 93101-2927 Office Phone: 805-682-0531. E-mail: ashleigh@west.net.

BRILLIANT, ELEANOR LURIA, social work educator; b. Bklyn., Nov. 25, 1930; d. Joseph and Leah (Cohen) Luria; m. Richard Brilliant, June 24, 1951; children: Stephanie, Livia, Franca, Myron. BA, Smith Coll., 1952; MS, Bryn Mawr Coll., 1969; DSW, Columbia U., 1974. Asst. in prodn. course Harvard Bus. Sch., Cambridge, Mass., 1952—54; instr. Bryn Mawr Coll., 1969—71; adminstr., dir. Lower East Side Family Union, N.Y.C., 1974—75; dir. planning/evaluation United Way of Westchester, White Plains, NY, 1975—78, assoc. exec. dir., 1978—80; asst. prof. Columbia U., N.Y.C., 1980—84, assoc. prof., 1984—85; assoc. prof. social work Rutgers U., New Brunswick, NJ, 1986—95, prof., 1995—, mem. women's studies faculty, 1992—; dir. BSW program Rutgers U. Livingston Coll., New Brunswick, 1987—89; chair, adminstr. policy and planning area MSW program Rutgers U. Sch. Social Work, New Brunswick, 1992—97. Cons. United Way of Westchester, White Plains, 1980, Family Info. and Referral Svc. Teams, Inc., White Plains, 1980-83, 87, James Bell Assoc., 1994-96. Author: The Urban Development Corporation: Private Interests and Public Authority, 1975, The United Way: Dilemmas of Organized Charity, 1990, Private Charity and Public Inquiry: A History of the Filer and Peterson Commissions, 2000; mem. editl. bd.: Nonprofit and Voluntary Sectors Quar., 2004—. Editl. bd. Nonprofit and Vol. Sector Quarterly, 2004—; Rsch. com. Women's Philanthropy Inst., 2004—. U.S. Fulbright grantee, 1972-73, NIMH grantee 1968-69; fellow Douglass Coll., Rutgers U., 1992—. Mem. NASW (rep. to del. assembly 1987, 90, nat. treas. 1989-91), Assn. for Rsch. on Non-Profit Orgns. and Vol. Action (v.p. adminstrn./sec. 1997-99, bd. mem.-at-large 1999-01, editl. bd. Quar. 2005—), Internat. Soc. for Third-Sector Rsch., Assn. for Cmty. Orgn. and Social Adminstrn. Avocations: travel, reading, swimming. Home: 10 Wayside Ln Scarsdale NY 10583-2908 Office: Rutgers U Sch Social Work 536 George St New Brunswick NJ 08901-1167 Personal E-mail: elbrillian@aol.com.

BRILLIANT, RICHARD, art historian, educator; b. Boston, Nov. 20, 1929; s. Frank and Pauline (Apt) B.; m. Eleanor Luria, June 24, 1951; children: Stephanie, Livia, Franca, Myron. BA magna cum laude, Yale U., 1951, MA, 1957, PhD, 1960; LLB, Harvard U., 1954. Bar: Mass. 1954. From asst. prof. to prof., chmn. dept. art history U. Pa., Phila., 1962-70; prof. art history and archaeology Columbia U., N.Y.C., 1970—, Anna S. Garbedian prof. in the Humanities, 1990—; vis. Mellon prof. fine arts U. Pitts., 1971; vis. prof. Princeton U., 1986. Vis. prof. Scuola Normale Superiore, Pisa, Italy, 1974, 80, 88; chmn. governing bd. Soc. Fellows Columbia U., 1981-84; cons. Sta. WNET-TV, N.Y., 1984-89, N.Y. Hist. Soc., 2004-05; dir. Italian Acad. for Advanced Studies in Am., Columbia U., 1996-00. Author: Gesture and Rank in Roman Art, 1966, Arch of Septimius Severus in the Roman Forum, 1967, The Arts of the Ancient Greeks, 1973, Roman Art, 1974, Pompeii: A.D. 79, 1979, Visual Narratives, 1984, Portraiture, 1991, Commentaries on Roman Art, 1994, Facing the New World, 1997, My Laocoon, 2000, Un Americano a Roma, 2000; co-author: (film) The Fayum Portraits, 1988, editor Art Bull., 1990-94; co-curator exhbn. Ctr. for African Art, N.Y.C., 1990; guest curator, exhibitor Jewish Mus., N.Y.C., 1997; guest curator (exhbn.) Mpls. Inst. Arts, 2003-04. Fulbright grantee Rome, Italy, 1957-59; fellow Am. Acad. in Rome, 1960-62; Guggenheim fellow, 1967-68; NEH sr. fellow, 1972-73. Mem.: Am. Acad. Arts and Scis., N.Y. Acad. Sci., Conn. Acad. Arts and Scis., Am. Sch. Classical Studies (mng. com. 1974—2001), Coll. Art Assn. (Disting. Scholar award 2005), Mass. Bar Assn., German Archaeol. Inst. (corr.), Phi Beta Kappa. Democrat. Avocations: reading, travel, wine. Home: 10 Wayside Ln Scarsdale NY 10583-2908 Office: Columbia U Dept Art History New York NY 10027

BRILLSTEIN, BERNIE J., producer, talent manager; b. N.Y.C., Apr. 26, 1932; s. Moe and Tillie Brillstein; m. Deborah Ellen Koskoff, 1975; children: Leigh, David Koskoff, Nick Koskoff, Michael, Kate. BS in Advt., NYU. Mailroom/talent rep. William Morris Agy., N.Y.C., 1955-64; talent rep. Mgmt. III, N.Y.C., 1964-69; packager, owner, producer The Brillstein Co., L.A., 1969—; CEO Lorimar Film Entertainment, L.A., 1996—; co-chair Brillstein-Grey Entertainment, Beverly Hills, Calif., 1991-96. Exec. producer (TV) Alf, 1986, The Boys, 1989, Politically Incorrect, 1997-98, 2000-01, It's The Garry Shandling Show, The Days and Nights of Molly Dodd, The Naked Truth, 1995, Mr. Show, 1995, The Steve Harvey Show, 1996, The Dana Carvey Show, 1996, Just Shoot Me, 1997, The Martin Short Show, 1999, Primetime Glick, 2001, The Wayne Brady Show, 2001; exec. producer (films) Dangerous Liaisons, Up the Academy, 1980, Blues Brothers, 1980, Neighbors, 1981, Continental Divide, 1981, Doctor Detroit, 1983, Ghostbusters I 1984, Summer Rental, 1985, Spies Like Us, 1985, Dragnet, 1987, Ghostbusters II, 1989, Larry Sanders Show, Celluloid Closet, 1995, Cat and Mouse, Happy Gilmore, 1996, The Cable Guy, 1996, Bulletproof, 1996, What Planet Are You From? 2000, Run Ronnie Run, 2002, exec.cons. The Real Ghostbusters, 1986. Served with U.S. Army, 1953-55. Recipient Peabody awards, Emmy nominations, Cable Ace award; honoree L.A. Free Clinic, 1987. Mem. N.Y. Friars Club, Beverly Hills C. of C. (bd. dirs.), Acad. Motion Picture Arts and Scis., TV Acad. Office: Brillstein-Grey Entertainment 9150 Wilshire Blvd Ste 350 Beverly Hills CA 90212-3453

BRILMAYER, R. LEA, lawyer, educator; b. 1950; BA, U. Calif.-Berkeley, 1970, JD, 1976; LLM, Columbia U., 1978. Bar: Tex. 1978. Assoc. in law Columbia U, 1976—78; asst. prof. law U. Tex., 1978—79, U. Chgo., Chgo., 1979—81, prof., 1991; vis. prof. Yale U., New Haven, 1981—82, Nathan Baker prof., 1986—91, Howard M. Holtzmann prof. Internat. Law, 1998—; Benjamin F. Butler prof. NYU, NYC, 1991—97. Author: Justifying International Acts, 1989, American Hegemony: Political Morality in a One Superpower World, 1994, Conflict of Laws: Foundation and Future Directions, 1995. Office: Yale U Dept Law PO Box 208215 New Haven CT 06520 E-mail: lea.brilmayer@yale.edu.

BRIM, ORVILLE GILBERT, JR., former foundation administrator, writer; b. Elmira, N.Y., Apr. 7, 1923; s. Orville G(ilbert) and Helen (Whittier) B.; m. Kathleen J. Vigneron, May 30, 1944; children: John G., Scott W., Margaret L., Sarah M. BA, Yale U., 1947, MA, 1949, PhD in Sociology, 1951. Instr. sociology U. Wis., 1952-53, asst. prof., 1953-55; sociologist Russell Sage Found., N.Y.C., 1955-64, asst. sec., 1959-64, pres., 1964-72, trustee, 1964-72, cons., 1972-74; pres. Found. for Child Devel., 1974-85; mem. core study group MacArthur Found. Rsch. Program Successful Aging, 1985-89; dir. MacArthur Found. Rsch. Network on Successful Mid Life Devel., 1989—2002; pres. Life Trends, Inc., 1991—2002; vis. scholar Russell Sage Found., 1985-86; interim pres. Social Sci. Rsch. Coun., 1998-99. Vice chmn. Am. Inst. for Rsch., 1971-88, chmn. 1988-91; chmn. bd. dirs. Automation Engring. Lab., 1959-67; dir. Consumer Behavior, Inc., 1957-61; chmn. environ. panel U.S. Office Edn., 1962-64; mem. drug rsch. bd. NAS., 1964-66, adv. com. on child devel., 1971-76; mem. mental health tng. com. NIMH, 1959-62; chmn. commn. social scis. NSF, 1968-69; nat. adv. food and drug coun. HEW, 1967-69; chmn. com. on work and personality in mid. years Social Sci. Rsch. Coun., 1972-79; trustee Found. for Child Devel., 1972-85, Ctr. for Creative Leadership, 1972-78, Mental Health Law Project, 1973-77, William T. Grant Found., 1975-84, Greenwich Hosp., 1972-77 Author: Sociology and the Field of Education, 1958, Education for Child Rearing, 1959, Personality and Decision Processes, 1962, Intelligence: Perspectives 1965, 1966, Socialization after Childhood: Two Essays, 1966, American Beliefs and Attitudes Toward Intelligence, 1969, The Dying Patient, 1970, Learning to Be Parents, 1980, Ambition: How We Manage Success and Failure Throughout Our Lives, 1992; editor: Lifespan Development and Behavior, Vol. 2-6, 1979-83, Constancy and Change in Human Development, 1980, How Healthy Are We? A Nat. Study of Well-Being at Midlife, 2004; cons. editor Child Devel., 1958-61, Sociology of Edn., 1963-69, Sociometry, 1959-62; mem. publ. com. The Public Interest, 1967-75. Served as 1st lt. USAAF, 1943-46. Recipient Wilbur Lucius Cross medal Yale Grad. Sch. Assn., 1975; Kurt Lewin Meml. award Soc. Psychol. Study Social Issues, 1979 Fellow APA, AAAS, Am. Sociol. Assn., Am. Acad. Arts and Scis., Am. Orthopsychiat. Assn. (pres. 1974-75), Ea. Sociol. Soc. (pres. 1971-72); mem. Inst. Medicine of NAS, Soc. Rsch. Child Devel. (Disting. Sci. Contbns. award, 1985).

BRIMBLE, ALAN, financial planner; b. Langwith, Eng., June 5, 1930; arrived in U.S., 1967; s. Arthur George and May (Emery) B. BA with honors, St. Edmund Hall, Oxford (Eng.) U., 1952, MA, 1956. Asst. sec. Crompton Parkinson Ltd., London, 1960—62; music and arts programmes mgr. BBC-TV, 1962-67; sec., controller St. Louis Art Mus., 1969-79; dir. adminstrn. Conv. and Visitors Bur. Greater Kansas City, Mo., 1979-87; fin. cons., plan adminstr., 1987-2000. Mem. citizens com. Met. St. Louis Zoo-Mus. Dist., 1970-71; bd. dirs. Internat. Inst., St. Louis, 1970-73, Kansas City Arts Coun., 1980-84; v.p., CFO Meridian Residential Assn., 1995-99; pres. Meridian Master Assn., 1997-99. With RAF, 1948-49. Fellow, Chartered Inst. Secs. Home: 1 Boothill Cir Rancho Mirage CA 92270

BRIMELOW, PETER, journalist; b. Warrington, Eng., Oct. 13, 1947; s. Frank Sanderson and Bessie (Knox) B.; m. Margaret Alice Laws, 1980 (dec. 2004); children: Alexander James Frank, Hannah Claire Catherine. BA in history and econs. with honors, U. Sussex, Eng., 1970; MBA, Stanford U., 1972. Security analyst Richardson Securities of Can., Winnipeg, Man., 1972-73; asst. editor Fin. Post, Toronto, Ont., Can., 1973-76, columnist, contbg. editor, 1978-80, 88-90; bus. editor Maclean's mag., Toronto, 1976-78; guest writer editorial page Wall St. Jour., N.Y.C., summer 1978; econ. counsel to U.S. Senator Orrin G. Hatch of Utah, Washington, 1979-81; columnist Toronto Sun Syndicate, 1980-82; assoc. editor Barron's, N.Y.C., 1981-83, contbg. editor, 1984-86; assoc. editor Fortune, N.Y.C., 1983-84; sr. editor Forbes, N.Y.C., 1986—2001, Nat. Rev. Mag., 1993-98. Contbg. editor . Chief Exec. mag, N.Y.C., NY, 1984—86; contbg. editor. Influence mag.,

Toronto, 1984—86; columnist The Times, London, 1986—90; editor vdare-.com, 1999—; pres. Ctr. Am. Unity, 1999—; columnist CBS Marketwatch, 2002—. Author: The Wall Street Gurus: How You Can Profit from the Investment Newsletters, 1986, The Patriot Game: Canada and the Canadian Question Revisited, 1987, Alien Nation: Common Sense About America's Immigration Disaster, 1995, The Worm in the Apple: How the Teacher Unions are Destroying American Education, 2003; contbr. articles to profl. jours. Recipient Fulbright award, 1970, Nat. Bus. Writing award Royal Bank Can./Toronto Press Club, 1976, Nat. Bus. Writing citation, 1977, Gerald Loeb award, 1990; Stanford U. scholarship, 1970. Episcopalian. Office: Ctr for Am Unity PO Box 910 Warrenton VA 20188 Personal E-mail: peter@peterbrimelow.com. Business E-Mail: peter@vdare.com.

BRIMHALL, DENNIS C., hospital executive; b. Provo, Utah, Sept. 8, 1948; s. Delbert and Elinor (Brockbank) B.; m. Linda Christensen. BS in Zoology, Brigham Young U., 1972; MBA, Northwestern U., 1974. Evening adminstr. Evanston (Ill.) Hosp., 1973-74; asst. adminstr. U. Utah Hosp., Salt Lake City, 1974-79, assoc. adminstr., 1979-83; assoc. dir. Med. Ctr., U. Calif., San Francisco, 1983-88; assoc. vice chancellor Fitzsimons, Univ. of Colo. Health Sci. Center; pres., CEO U. Colo. Hosp., Univ. Colo. Health Svc. Center, Denver, 1988—. Cons. in field; bd. dirs. exec. com. Univ. Health System Consortium (UCH); bd. dirs. Accreditation Coun. of Graduate Med. Edu. (ACGME), Colo. Access; mem. adminstrn. bd. Coun. of Teaching Hosp. (COTH); mem. Joint Commn. on Accreditation of Healthcare Orgn. (JCAHO) adv. Coun. on Performance Measurement; mem., exec. adv. bd., master's program in health adminstrn. Univ. Colo. at Denver. Contbr. to several health care related articles and book chapters. Bd. dirs. Univ. Hosp. Consortium, Chgo., 1988—, Colo. Children's Campaign, Denver (past pres.), Colo. Hosp. Assn., 1990—, Nat. Conf. Christians and Jews, 1993—, Samaritan Inst., Mile High United Way, Boy Scouts of Am. (Denver coun.); active Spl. Commn. on AIDS, 1987—. Mem. Am. Coll. Hosp. Adminstrn., Colo. Hosp. Assn. (past chmn. of bd. trustees), Assn. Practitioner in Inf. Control Rsch. Found. (pres. 1993—), Denver Rotary Club. Mem. Lds Ch. Home: 5339 S Kenton Ct Englewood CO 80111-3829 Office: Univ Hosp 4200 E 9th Ave # A020 Denver CO 80220-3706

BRIMIJOIN, KAY ROTHGEB, education educator; b. Washington, June 13, 1945; d. Wade Lee and Marjorie Katherine (Miller) Rothgeb; m. Mark Pierce Brimijoin, June 23, 1967; children: William Armstrong II, Katharine Perry. BA, Conn. Coll., 1963-67; MEd, Lynchburg Coll., 1989; PhD, U. Va., 2002. Elem. tchr. Amherst Acad., Va., 1976-80, Amherst County Pub. Sch., 1982-88, coord. enrichment programs, 1988—2000. Adj. faculty U. Va., 1998—; asst. prof. Sweet Briar Coll., 2000—; mem. profl. devel. faculty ASCD. Contbr. articles to profl. jours. Grantee Va. Dept. Edn., 2000, 02, 03, 04; Commn. Arts, 1994-96, U.S. Dept. Edn., 1989. Mem. ASCD, Assn. Tchr. Educators, Internat. Reading Assn., Nat. Assn. Gifted Children (Nat. Curriculum award 1999, Doctoral Student Award 2002), Va. Assn. for Gifted (bd. dirs. 1989-98, sec. 1993-96, pres.-elect 1996-98, pres. 1998-99). Avocations: piano, cooking, hiking, reading, travel.

BRIMIJOIN, WILLIAM STEPHEN, pharmacologist, educator, neuroscientist, researcher; b. Passaic, NJ, July 1, 1942; s. William Owen and Georgiana (Macklin) Brimijoin; m. Margaret Murray Ross, June 22, 1964 (div. Nov. 2002); children: Megan Rebekkah Brimijoin-Vaules, William Owen, Alexander Ross. AB in Psychology, Harvard Coll., 1964; PhD in Pharmacology, Harvard U., 1969. Asst. prof Mayo Med. Sch., Rochester, Minn., 1972-76, assoc. prof., 1976-80, prof. pharmacology, 1980—, Winston and Iris Clement prof., 1989—; chair dept. molecular pharmacology Mayo Clinic, Rochester, Minn., 1993—2003. Cons. Mayo Clinic Rochester Minn., 1971-72, voting staff 1972—; vis. scientist Karolinska Inst. Stockholm, Sweden, 1978-79, U. Würzburg, Germany, 1987-88, Chinese Acad. Scis. Shanghai br., 1999-2004; assoc. dir., dean Mayo Grad. Sch., Rochester, 1983-87; mem. behavioral and neurosci. study sect. NIH, 1989-93, sci. adv. panel U.S. EPA, 1993-2005, sci. adv. bd. internat. conf. on cholinesterase; mem. Gulf War Grants Rev. Bd. Dept. Def., 1997-99. Mem. editl. bd. Muscle and Nerve Jour., 1980-88, Diabetes Jour., 1985-93; author: Over the River and Through the Woods, 2004; contbr. to numerous profl. jours.; patentee in field. With USPHS, 1969-71. Recipient Career Devel. award NIH, 1975, Javits Neuroscience Investigator award NINDS, 1987, Sr. Disting. U.S. Scientist award Humboldt Found., 1987-88, Mayo Disting. Investigator award Mayo Clinic, 1993. Mem. Soc. Neuroscience (social issues com. 1987), Internat. Soc. Neurochemistry, Am. Soc. Neurochemistry (program com. 1993-94), Am. Soc. Pharmacology and Exptl. Therapeutics. Avocations: languages, creative writing. Office: Mayo Clinic Dept of Pharmacology 200 1st St SW Rochester MN 55905-0002 Business E-Mail: brimijoi@mayo.edu.

BRIMMER, ANDREW FELTON, economist, consultant; b. Newellton, La., Sept. 13, 1926; s. Andrew and Vellar (Davis) B.; m. Doris Millicent Scott, July 18, 1953; 1 dau., Esther Diane. BA, U. Wash., 1950, MA, 1951; postgrad. (Fulbright fellow), U. Bombay, India, 1951—52; PhD, Harvard U., 1957; LLD, Nebr. Wesleyan U., 1968, Marquette U., 1968, L.I. U., 1969, Oberlin Coll., 1969, Tufts U., 1970, Colgate U., 1970, Atlanta U., 1970, Middlebury Coll., 1971, U. Notre Dame, 1971, Bishop Coll., 1971, Upsala Coll., 1972, U. Md., 1976, U. Mich., 1979, U. So. Calif., 1980, Washington U., 1982, Ind. U., 1991, New Sch. U., 1999, Harvard U., 1999; D.Soc.Sc., Boston Coll., 1971, Temple U., 1974; D.C.L., U. Miami, 1971, U. of the South, 1984; D.H.L., DePaul U., 1975. Economist Fed. Res. Bank, NYC, 1955—58; asst. prof. Mich. State U., 1958—61, Wharton Sch. Finance and Commerce, U. Pa., 1961—66; dep. asst. sec. Dept. Commerce, Washington, 1963—65, asst. sec. for econ. affairs, 1965—66; mem. Fed. Res. Bd., 1966—74; Thomas Henry Carroll Ford Found. vis. prof. Grad. Sch. Bus. Adminstrn. Harvard U., 1974—76; pres. Brimmer & Co., Inc., Washington, 1976—; Wilmer D. Barrett prof. econs. U. Mass.-Amherst. Bd. govs., vice chmn. Commodity Exchange, Inc.; bd. dirs. Bank of Am., Am. Security Bank, MNC Fin., Inc., Du Pont Co., Gannett Co., Inc., BellSouth Corp., Conn. Mut., Navistar Internat. Corp., Blackstone Investment Income Trust, Carr-Am. Realty, Black Rock Investment Income Fund; mem. Fed. Res. Central Banking Mission to Sudan, 1957; cons. SEC, 1962-63; chmn. Washington DC Fin. Control Bd., 1995-98; mem. Trilateral Commn.; trustee Coll. Retirement Equities Fund. Author: Survey of Mutual Funds Investors, 1963, Life Insurance Companies in Capital Market, 1962, Economic Development: International and African Perspectives, 1976, The World Banking System: Outlook in a Context of Crisis, 1985, International Banking and Domestic Economic Policies, 1986; Contbr. articles to profl. jours. Chmn. bd. trustees Tuskegee U., Com. for Econ. Devel.; bd. dirs. Interracial Council for Bus. Opportunity; mem. internat. panel UN Mgmt. and Decision Making Project, 1986-88; panel on fgn. trade stats. NAS. With AUS, 1945-46. Named Govt. Man of Year Nat. Bus. League, 1963; recipient Arthur S. Flemming award, 1966, Russworm award, 1966, Capital Press Club award, 1966, Golden Plate award Am. Acad. Achievement, 1967, Alumnus Summa Laude Dignatus U. Wash. Alumni Assn., 1972, Nat. Honoree Beta Gamma Sigma, 1971, Horatio Alger award, 1974, Equal Opportunity award Nat. Urban League, 1974, One Hundred Black Men and N.Y. Urban Coalition award, 1975, Disting. Svc. award Interracial Coun. Bus. Opportunity, 1986, Pub. Svc. award North Adams State Coll., 1987, George Washington U., 1998, Shenandoah U., 2004. Fellow Am. Acad. Arts and Scis., Nat. Assn. Bus. Economists, Ea. Econ. Assn. (v.p. 1989, pres.-elect 1990-91, pres. 1991-92), N.Am. Econ. and Fin. Assn. (v.p. 1995, pres.-elect 1996, pres. 1997, vice chair exec. com. 2004—); mem. Am. Econ. Assn. (Richard T. Ely lectr. 1982, v.p. 1989), Am. Fin. Assn., Assn. for Study Afro-Am. Life and History (pres. 1970-73, 89—), Coun. Fgn. Rels., Nat. Economists Club, Am. Statis. Assn., Soc. Govt. Economists (Disting. lectr. on econs. in govt. 1988), Omicron Delta Epsilon. Office: Brimmer & Co Inc 4400 Macarthur Blvd NW Washington DC 20007-2521 Office Phone: 202-342-6255. E-mail: afbrimmer@aol.com.

BRIMMER, CLARENCE ADDISON, federal judge; b. Rawlins, Wyo., July 11, 1922; s. Clarence Addison and Geraldine (Zingsheim) B.; m. Emily O. Docken, Aug. 2, 1953; children: Geraldine Ann, Philip Andrew, Andrew Howard, Elizabeth Ann. BA, U. Mich., 1944, JD, 1947. Bar: Wyo. 1948. Pvt. practice law, Rawlins, 1948-71; mcpl. judge, 1948-54; U.S. commr., magistrate, 1963-71; atty. gen. Wyo. Cheyenne, 1971-74; U.S. atty., 1975; chief judge U.S. Dist. Ct. Wyo., Cheyenne, 1975-92, dist. judge, 1975—. Mem. panel multi-dist. litigation, 1992-2000; mem. Jud. Conf. U.S., 1994-97, exec., 1995-97. Sec. Rawlins Bd. Pub. Utilities, 1954-66; Rep. gubernatorial candidate, 1974; trustee Rocky Mountain Mineral Law Found., 1963-75. With USAAF, 1945-46. Mem. ABA, Wyo. Bar Assn., Laramie County Bar Assn., Carbon County Bar Assn., Am. Judicature Soc., Masons, Shriners, Rotary. Episcopalian. Office: US Dist Ct 2120 Capitol Ave Rm 2603 Cheyenne WY 82001

BRIMMER, RICHARD GREEN, music educator; b. Oregon, Ohio, Sept. 14, 1960; s. George Aldrich and Margaret Ann Brimmer; m. Cecilia Marie Phillips, Aug. 21, 1981; children: Samantha, Richard II, Vincent. B of Music, Bowling Green State U., 1982, MusM, 1995. Tchr. music Cardinal Stritch High Sch., Oregon, Ohio, 1985—89, Lake Local Schs., Millbury, 1989—. Mem. BCS Music Boosters, 2002—, mem. exec. bd., 2003—. Recipient Govs. Ednl. Leadership award, State of Ohio, 2004. Mem.: Nat. Band Assn., Ohio Music Educators Assn., Nat. Assn. Music Educators. Avocations: theater, gardening. Office: Lake Local Schs 28100 Lemoyne Rd Millbury OH 43447 E-mail: lak_aca_ab@nwoca.org.

BRIN, DAVID, writer, astronomer; b. Glendale, Calif., Oct. 6, 1950; s. Herbert Henry and Selma (Stone) B; m. Cheryl Ann Brigham; 3 children. BS in Astronomy, Calif. Inst. Tech., 1973; MS in Elec. Engring., U. Calif.-San Diego, 1977, PhD in Space Sci., 1981. Electronics engr. Hughes Aircraft Co., Carlsbad, Calif., 1973-77; profl. novelist Bantam Books, N.Y.C., 1980—; postdoctoral fellow Calif. State Inst., LaJolla, Calif., 1982—85. Instr. physics, astronomy, writing San Diego State U., San Diego CC, 1982—85. Author: (novels) Sundiver, 1980, Startide Rising (Nebula award 1983, Hugo award 1983, Locus award), 1983, The Practice Effect (Balrog award), 1984, (with Gregory Benford) Heart of the Comet, 1986, Earth, 1990 (nominee Hugo award, 1994); (novellas and novelettes) The Tides of Kithrup, 1981, The Loom of Thessaly, 1981, The Postman (runner-up Hugo award 1983), 1982, Cyclops (nominee Hugo award 1985), 1984, Glory Season, 1993, Brightness Reef, 1996 (nominee Hugo award), Infinity's Shore, 1996, The Transparent Society, 1998 (Obeler Freedom of Speech award), (series) Startride Rising (Nebula award) 1983, Sundiver, 1985, The Uplift War, 1987 (Hugo and LOCUS awards for best novel, nominee Nebula award), Heaven's Reach, 1998, Foundation's Triumph, 1999, Forgiveness, 2001, Kiln People, 2002, Contacting Aliens: The Illustrated Guide to David Brins Uplift Universe, 2002; (collections) The River of Time, 1986, Otherness, 1994, Tomorrow Happens, 2003, (stories for anthologies) War of the Worlds: Global Dispatches, 1996; contbr. short stories, sci. fact articles, and sci. papers to profl. publs. Nominated for John W. Campbell award for best new author of 1982 Mem. Am. Assn. Aeronautics and Astronautics, Sci. Fiction Writers Am. (sec. 1982-84) Avocations: backpacking, music, eclecticism. Office: care Phantasia Press 5536 Crispin Way Rd West Bloomfield MI 48323-3405

BRIN, FOSTER BLAKE, psychiatrist; b. Springfield, Mass., May 23, 1948; s. Henry Brin and Gertrude Gail Scholl; m. Deborah Lynn Wood, Mar. 29, 2003; 1 stepchild, Sean Kendrick McCann; m. Martha Lynne Ehlers (dec.); 1 child, Andrew Victor. BS, U. Fla., Gainesville, 1970; MD, U. Miami, 1978. Psychiatry intern Tripler Army Med. Ctr., Honolulu, 1979—80, psychiatry resident, 1980—83; staff psychiatrist Wynn Army Comty. Hosp., Ft. Stewart, Ga., 1983—85, Cen. State Hosp., Milledgeville, Ga., 1990—2003, River Edge Behavioral Health Ctr., Macon, Ga., 2003—. Assoc. prof. dept. psychiatry Mercer U. Sch. Medicine. Physician local troop Boy Scouts Am., Warner Robins, Ga., 1995—. Capt. U.S. Army, 1979—85. Mem.: AMA, Am. Psychiat. Assn. Methodist. Avocations: stamp collecting/philately, music, album collecting. Office: River Edge Behavioral Health Ctr 175 Emery Hwy Macon GA 31217-3692 Personal E-mail: fsbrin@cox.net.

BRIN, ROYAL HENRY, JR., lawyer; b. Dallas, Oct. 9, 1919; BA, JD, U. Tex., 1941. Bar: Tex. 1941. Postgrad. fellow Harvard U., 1941—42; atty. OPA, Washington, 1942; assoc. firm Strasburger & Price, Dallas, 1946-56, ptnr., 1956—. Editor-in-chief Tex. Law Rev., 1940-41; contbr. articles to profl. jours. Fellow Am. Bar Found. (life); mem. ABA, Am. Acad. Appellate Lawyers, State Bar Tex., Tex. Assn. Def. Counsel (pres. 1981-82), Dallas Bar Assn., Dallas Assn. Def. Counsel, Def. Rsch. Inst., Internat. Brotherhood Magicians (pres. 1969-70), The Chancellors (grand chancellor), Order of Coif, Phi Beta Kappa, Phi Eta Sigma. Home: 6506 Lupton Dr Dallas TX 75225-2323 Office: 4300 Bank of Am Plz 901 Main St Dallas TX 75202-3714 Office Phone: 214-651-4604. E-mail: royal.brin@strasburger.com.

BRIN, SERGEY, information technology executive; b. Moscow, Aug. 21, 1973; BS in Math. and Computer Sci. with honors, U. Md., College Park, 1993; MS, Stanford U., 1995; MBA, Instituto de Empresa. Co-founder, pres. tech., asst. sec. Google, Inc., Mountain View, Calif., 1998—; also bd. dirs. Spkr. World Econ. Forum, Technol., Entertainment and Design Conf.; spkr. in the field. Author: (Articles) Extracting Patterns and Relations from the World Wide Web; Scalable Techniques for Mining Casual Structures; Beyond Market Baskets: Generalizing Association Rules to Correlations; co-author (with Larry Page): Dynamic Data Mining: A New Architecture for Data with High Dimensionality; guest appearence on Charlie Rose Show, CNBC, CNNfn. Named one of World's 100 Most Influential People, Time Mag., 2005; fellow NSF. Office: Google Inc 1600 Amphitheatre Pkwy Mountain View CA 94043 Office Fax: 650-618-1499.

BRINBERG, HERBERT RAPHAEL, publishing executive; b. N.Y.C., Jan. 27, 1926; s. Henry and Anna (Stambler) B.; m. Blanche Leiman, July 15, 1945; children: Amy Lynn, Todd Michael. AB, Cornell U., 1947; MS, Columbia U., 1948; PhD, NYU, 1955; DSc (hon.), Syracuse U., 1989. Research economist Conf. Bd., 1948-50; cons. economist Boni Watkins, 1951-54; asst. dir. research Licensed Beverage Industries, 1954-55; mgr. econ. research and planning Canco div. Am. Can Co., 1956-61, dir. comml. research, 1961-66, v.p. planning, 1966-71, v.p. info. tech., 1971-78; pres., chief exec. officer Aspen Systems, Rockville, Md., 1978-85, Panel Pubs., Inc., Greenvale, NY, 1982-85; mng. dir. Wolters Kluwer U.S. Corp., N.Y.C., 1978-85, pres., chief exec. officer, dir., 1986-89; pres., CEO Parnassus Assocs. Internat., Inc., 1990—; chmn. Assoc. Info. Mgrs., 1988-90. Bd. dirs. The Associated Blind; adj. prof. Baruch Coll., 1988—, chmn. bus. adv. coun. Bernard L. Schwartz Comm. Inst., 1998—; chmn. bd. visitors Sch. Info. Studies, Syracuse U., 1996—. Mem. coun. Cornell U., 1998-2003. With USAAF, 1944-45. Mem. Info. Industry Assn. (past chmn., vice chmn. 1994-98), Software and Info. Industry Assn.(bd. dirs. 1999-2001), Cornell Club N.Y.C. Office Phone: 212-348-3179. Business E-Mail: hrbrinberg@parnassusassociates.com.

BRINCKERHOFF, RICHARD CHARLES, retired manufacturing company executive; b. Middletown, NY, Apr. 4, 1931; s. Gilbert and Audrey B.; m. Barbara Wainwright Freir, Nov. 13, 1954; children: Mark Harrison, Scott Eric. AAS in Aircraft Ops., SUNY, Farmingdale, 1950; BS in Aeronautical Engring., Ind. Inst. Tech., 1956; M in Automotive Engring., Chrysler Inst., Detroit, 1958. Installation mgr. Chrysler Missile Div., Taronto, Italy, 1958-60, dir. ops. Izmir, Turkey, 1961-62; chief Bendix test conductor Kennedy Space Ctr., Fla., 1963-68; export mgr. Bendix Internat., N.Y.C., 1969-73; dir. internat. licensing Bendix Corp., Southfield, Mich., 1974-75; dir. licensing Facet Enterprises Inc., Tulsa, 1976-77, group dir. engring., 1978-79, v.p. filter group, 1980-84, exec. v.p. ops., 1985-88. Photographer: A Mobile Family's Corporate Odyssey, 1975. With USAF, 1950-54. Mem. Exptl. Aircraft Assn., Nat. Cathedral Assn., Holland Soc. NY, Nat. Silver-Haired Legislature. Republican. Episcopalian. Avocations: gardening, history, tennis, travel.

BRIND, DAVID HUTCHISON, lawyer, judge; b. Albany, Feb. 4, 1930; s. Charles Albert and Laura Stuart (Hutchison) B.; m. Shirley Jean Hodgins, Mar. 6, 1954; children: Susan Brind Morrow, Charles. AB, Union Coll., 1951; LLB, Albany Law Sch., 1954, JD, 1968; LHD, N.Y. Inst. Tech., 1971. Bar: N.Y. 1954, U.S. Supreme Ct. 1970. Atty. law divsn. N.Y. State Dept. Edn., Albany, 1954—55; ptnr. Chacchia & Brind, Geneva, NY, 1957—64; sole practice Geneva, 1964—95; presiding judge Geneva City Ct., 1974—96; ret., 1995; apptd. jud. hearing officer N.Y. State Supreme Ct., 1995—. Hearing officer N.Y. State and Local Ret. Sys., 1997—; counsel real estate N.Y. State Dormitory Auth., 1970-86; gen. counsel Geneva Gen. Hosp., 1966-85; local counsel Conrail; spl. counsel N.Y. Tchrs. Retirement Sys., 1959-72. Bd. dirs. Geneva United Way, 1965-89; campaign chmn. United Way Greater Rochester (N.Y.), 1966-69, pres., 1969-71; trustee Geneva Gen. Hosp., 1962-73; pres., 1969-71; trustee Geneva Hist. Soc., 1963-90, pres., 1968-70; chmn. Geneva Hist. Commn., 1969-89; mem. exec. bd. Finger Lakes coun. Boy Scouts Am., 1965—; bd. dirs. 7 Lakes Coun. Girl Scouts U.S.A., 1966-73; bd. dirs. Geneva Gen. Hosp. Nursing Home, pres., 1969-71; v.p. Geneva Bd. Edn., 1962-67; mem. pres.'s coun. Eisenhower Coll., 1972-79, Hobart & William Smith Colls., 1967—. Recipient Geneva Cmty. Chest/Red Cross Svc. citation, 1969, named Man of Yr., Geneva C. of C., 1971. Mem. Am. Assn. Homes for Aging, N.Y. State Sch. Bds. Assn. (law revisions com. and constnl. conv. com. 1964-68), Monroe County Jud. Com., 1976-80, Ontario County Bar Assn., N.Y. State Bar Assn. (jud. coun.), Fedn. N.Y. State Judges (pres. 1989-91), N.Y. State Assn. Jud. Hearing Officers (treas. 1995—), St. Andrews Soc. Albany, Rotary (pres. 1967-68), Finger Lakes Forum (pres. 1991—). Republican. Presbyterian. Home: 43 Delancey Dr Geneva NY 14456-2809 Office: 37 Seneca St Geneva NY 14456-0409 Office Phone: 315-789-9191. Personal E-mail: judge@novocon.net, judgedavidh@aol.com.

BRIND'AMOUR, ROD JEAN, professional hockey player; b. Ottawa, Ont., Can., Aug. 9, 1970; m. Kellie Brind'Amour; 2 children. Grad., Mich. State U. With St. Louis Blues, 1988—91; left wing/center Phila. Flyers, 1991—99, Carolina Hurricanes, 1999—, now capt., 2005—. Mem. CCHA All-Rookie Team, 1988—89; player NHL All-Star Game. Recipient CCHA Rookie of Yr. award, 1988—89. Office: Carolina Hurricanes 1400 Edwards Mill Rd Raleigh NC 27607-3624*

BRINDEL, JUNE RACHUY, writer; b. Little Rock, Iowa, June 5, 1919; d. Otto L. and Etta Mina (Balster) Rachuy; m. Bernard Brindel, Aug. 26, 1939; children: Sylvia Mina, Paul, Jill. BA, U. Chgo., 1945, MA, 1958. Prof. English Wright Coll., Chgo., 1958-81. Tchr. drama Nat. Music Camp, Interlochen, Mich., 1957—67. Author: Luap, 1971, Ariadne, 1980 (nominee Pultizer prize), Phaedra, 1985, Nobody is Ever Missing, 1984; editor: Bernard Brindel, Who Wore at His Heart the Fire's Center, 1999; contbr. short stories and poems to jours. Recipient C. S. Lewis prize, Ind. U., 1973, Lit. award, Ill. Arts Coun., Chgo., 1985; fellow, 1984, 1985. Mem.: The Writers, Soc. Midland Authors, Phi Beta Kappa. Home: 2740 Lincoln Ln Wilmette IL 60091-2234

BRINDLE, DAVID LOWELL, minister; b. Richmond, Ind., Sept. 16, 1948; s. Richard Lowell and Barbara Ann (Myers) B.; m. Linda Jean Pickard, Aug. 15, 1976; 1 child, Ruth Marie. BA, St. Meinrad (Ind.) Coll., 1972; MDiv, Earlham Sch. Religion, 1980; postgrad., United Theol. Sem., Dayton, Ohio. Ordained to ministry United Meth. Ch., 1991, Religious Soc. Friends, 2000. Pastor Fountain City (Ind.) Friends Meeting, 1981-84; grad. asst. U. Dayton, 1984-85; dir. religious edn. St. Christopher Cath. Ch., Vandalia, Ohio, 1985-86, St. Joan of Arc Cath. Ch., Hershey, Pa., 1989-90; dir. admissions Earlham Coll. Sch. Religion, Richmond, 1986-88; interim pastor Wilmington (Ohio) Friends Meeting, 1988-89; jud. assessor Tribunal, Diocese of Harrisburg, Pa., 1990-91; pastor St. Paul United Meth. Ch., Harrisburg, 1991-92, Shermans Dale United Meth. Charge, 1992-96, Mt. Olivet United Meth. Ch., Mechanicsburg, Pa., 1996-98, Wilmington (Ohio) Friends Meeting, 1998—2002, Goldsboro (NC) Friends Meeting, 2003—; assoc. sec. Friends World Com. for Consultation, London, 2002—03. Mem. Edn. Commn., Ind. Yearly Meetings of Friends, Muncie, 1981-84; chmn. Yokefellow Inst., Richmond, 1986-89; clk. Associated Com. Friends on Indian Affairs. Contbr. to religious publs. Mem. Yokefellow Internat., Oblates of St. Benedict. Democrat. Office: 700 Guilford St Goldsboro NC 27530 Home: 526 W Hooks River Rd Goldsboro NC 27530-1236 Office Phone: 919-735-5256. E-mail: davidlbrindle@aol.com. *Many of our creeds and personal beliefs begin as descriptions of our experience. We must guard against our tendency to turn descriptions into prescriptions which seek to regulate the experiences of others.*

BRINDLE, LEWIS CARVER, social services administrator, not-for-profit fundraiser; b. DuBois, Pa. s. Louis Young Brindle and Etta Lorraine Carver. BS in Edn. magna cum laude, Indiana U. Pa., 1975; MusM, Boston U., 1978. Owner Brindle Fine Catering, Boston, 1980-87; exec. asst. to pres./sec. bd. Union Theol. Sem., N.Y.C., 1988-91, major prospects officer, 1991-92; asst. dir. found. and corp. rels. NYU, 1992-95, assoc. dir. devel., 1996-2001; dir. devel. Parrish Art Mus., Southampton, N.Y., 1995-96; dir. Alberto Vilar Global Fellows Prog. in Performing Arts NYU, 2001—04; founding dir. Lewis Carver Brindle Arts Cons., N.Y.C., 2004—. Adj. faculty NYU, 2005—. Freelance opera singer, 1978-87. Episcopalian. Avocations: cooking, swimming, gardening, singing.

BRINE, KEVIN R., investment company executive; m. Madeline Brine. MBA, Stern, 1981. Ptnr. Sanford C. Bernstein & Co.; dir. Delphi Fin. Group Inc.; mng. dir. Brine Mgmt. Inc. Trustee Whitney Mus. Am. Art, bd. dir., Joan & Sanford I. Weill Med. Coll. Cornell U.; trustee NYU. Office: Brine Mgmt Inc 2001 Market St Ste 1500 Philadelphia PA 19103 Mailing: c/o Whitney Mus Am Art 945 Madison Ave New York NY 10021*

BRINEGAR, CLAUDE STOUT, retired oil industry executive; b. Rockport, Calif., Dec. 16, 1926; s. Claude Leroy Stout and Lyle (Rawles) B.; m. Elva Jackson, 1950 (div.); children: Claudia, Meredith, Thomas; m. Mary Katharine Potter, 1983 (dec. 1993); m. Karen Bartholomew, 1995. BA, Stanford U., 1950, MS, 1951, PhD, 1954; LLD (hon.), Elmira Coll., 1997. V.p. econs. and planning Union Oil (now Unocal), L.A., 1965, pres. Pure Oil divsn. Palatine, Ill., 1965-69, sr. v.p., pres. refining and mktg. L.A., 1969-73; U.S. Sec. of Transp. Washington, 1973-75; sr. v.p. adminstr. Unocal Corp., L.A., 1975-85, mem. exec. com., 1968-73, 75-92, exec. v.p., CFO, 1985-91, also bd. dirs., 1968-73, 75-95, vice chmn. bd., 1990-95. Founding dir. Conrail, Inc., 1974-75, 90-98; vis. scholar Stanford U., 1992-97. Author: monograph on econs. and price behavior, 1970; contbr. articles to profl. jours. Chmn. Calif. Citizens Compensation Commn., 1990-2002; mem. regional selection panel White House Fellows Program, 1976-83, chmn., 1983. Mem. Am. Petroleum Inst. (bd. dirs. 1976-85, 88-91, hon. life dir. 1992), Georgetown Club, Boothbay Harbor Yacht Club, Southport Yacht Club, Phi Beta Kappa, Sigma Xi. Avocation: collecting first editions of Mark Twain. Home and Office: PO Box 20246 Stanford CA 94309-0246

BRINEY, ALLAN KING, retired radiologist; b. Wilkinsburg, Pa., Nov. 17, 1921; s. Alonzo Tripp and Helen Marie (Hardman) B.; m. Gayle Diane Briney, July 4, 1986; children: Ronald A., Nancy E., Barbara A., Douglas C. BS summa cum laude, U. Pitts., 1943, MD, 1945. Diplomate Am. Bd. Radiology; lic. real estate salesperson Ariz. Intern Pitts. Hosp., 1945-46; fellow in radiology Hosp. U. Pa., Phila., 1948-51; radiologist Topeka Med. Ctr., 1951-53, Murphy Meml. Hosp., Whittier, Calif., 1953-62, Whittier Radiology Med. Group, 1953-94, Memrad Med. Group, Whittier, 1995-97; chief of staff Presbyn. Intercommunity Hosp., Whittier, 1979, radiologist, 1959-97; ret., 1997. Capt. USAF, 1946-48. Fellow Am. Coll. Radiology. Libertarian. Deist. Avocations: skiing, biking, hiking, swimming, sailing. Home: 220 Cayuse Trl Sedona AZ 86336-9797 Personal E-mail: allanking@earthlink.net.

BRING, MURRAY H., retired lawyer; b. Denver, Jan. 19, 1935; s. Alfred Alexander and Ida (Molinsky) B.; m. Constance Brooks Evert, Dec. 30, 1963 (div. June 1989); children: Beth, Catherine, Peter; m. Kathleen Delaney, May 19, 1990. BA, U. So. Calif., 1956; LLB, NYU, 1959. Bar: N.Y. 1960, D.C. 1963, U.S. Supreme Ct. 1966. Law clk. to Chief Justice Earl Warren U.S. Supreme Ct., Washington, 1959-61; spl. asst. to asst. atty. gen. civil div. Dept. Justice, Washington, 1961-62; spl. asst to dep. undersec. state Dept. State, Washington, 1962-63; dir. policy planning anti-trust divsn., 1963-65; ptnr. Arnold & Porter, Washington, 1965-87; sr. v.p., gen. counsel Philip Morris

Cos., Inc., N.Y.C., 1988-94, exec. v.p. external affairs and gen. counsel, 1994-97, vice chmn., gen. counsel, 1997-2000; ret., 2000. Editor-in-chief N.Y. Law Rev., 1958-59. Bd. dirs. Guild Hall East Hampton, NYU Law Sch. Found. Mem. ABA, Order of Coif, Phi Beta Kappa, Phi Kappa Phi. Avocations: fishing, photography, art. Office: Altria Group Inc 120 Park Ave New York NY 10017-5592

BRINGARDNER, JOHN MICHAEL, lawyer, clergyman; b. Columbus, Ohio, Nov. 7, 1957; s. John Krepps and Elizabeth (Evans) B.; m. Emily Presley, June 19, 1982; children: John Taylor, Michael Steven, Malee Elizabeth. BA, U. Central Fla., Orlando, 1979; postgrad., Mercer U., 1979; JD, Fla. State U., 1981. Bar: Fla. 1982, Calif. 1994, U.S. Dist. Ct. (mid. dist.) Fla., U.S. Dist. Ct. (no. dist.) Fla., U.S. Ct. Appeals (11th cir.). Assoc. McFarlain, Bobo, Sternstein, Wiley & Cassidy, Tallahassee, Fla., 1982-87, Finley, Kumble Wagner, Tallahassee, 1987; minister Boston Ch. of Christ, 1987-90; evangelist Bankok Christian Ch., 1990-92, Metro Manila Christian Ch., 1992-93; gen. counsel Internat. Chs. of Christ, L.A., 1993—. Bd. dirs. Eye Care Corp., Orlando, Fla., Quality Coffee Corp., Tallahassee. Mem. ABA, Fla. Bar Assn. Avocations: football, baseball, triathlons, hiking, music. Office: La International Church of Christ 3731 Wilshire Blvd Ste 810 Los Angeles CA 90010-2850

BRINGHURST, ROBERT, poet; b. L.A., Oct. 16, 1946; s. George Heber and Marion Jeanette (Large) B.; 1 child, Piper Laramie. Student, MIT, 1963—64, student, 1970—71, U. Utah, 1964—65; BA in Comparative Lit., Ind. U., 1973; MFA, U. B.C., Vancouver, Can., 1975. Vis. lectr. dept. creative writing U. B.C., Vancouver, 1975-77, lectr. dept. English, 1979-80; adj. lectr. Simon Fraser U., Burnaby, Canada, 1983-84; writer-in-residence U. Winnipeg, Canada, 1986; Can./Scotland exch. fellow U. Edinburgh, Scotland, 1989-90; Ashley Fellow Trent U., Peterborough, Canada, 1994; writer in residence U. Western Ont., 1998-99; adj. prof. Simon Fraser U., 2000—03. Conjunct prof. Trent U., 1998—; Ralph Gustafson chair in poetry Malaspina Coll., 2003. Author: Shipwright's Log, 1972, Cadastre, 1973, Stonecutter's Horses, 1974, Deuteronomy, 1974, Eight Objects, 1975, Bergschrund, 1975, Jacob Singing, 1977, Tzuhalem's Mountain, 1982, Beauty of the Weapons: Selected Poems 1972-82, 1982, Ocean/Paper/Stone, 1984, Tending the Fire, 1985, Shovels, Shoes and the Slow Rotation of Letters, 1986, Blue Roofs of Japan, 1986, Pieces of Map, Pieces of Music, 1987, Conversations with a Toad, 1987, The Black Canoe: Bill Reid and the Spirit of Haida Gwaii, 1991, 1992, The Elements of Typographic Style, 1992, The Calling: Selected Poems 1970-95, 1995, Elements, 1995, A Story as Sharp as a Knife: The Classical Haida Mythtellers and Their World, 1999, The Book of Silences, 2001, Ursa Major, 2003, The Elements of Typographic Style, 2004, Prosodies of Meaning: Literary Form in Native North America, 2004, The Solid Form of Language: An Essay on Writing and Meaning, 2004, New World Suite No. 3, 2005, The Old in Their Knowing, 2005; editor (translator): Nine Visits to the Mythworld, 2000, Being in Being: Collected Works of Skaay of the Qquuna Qiighawaay, 2001, The Fragments of Parmenides, 2003; editor: (with others) Visions: Contemporary Art in Can., 1983, Part of the Land, Part of the Water: A History of the Yukon Indians, 1987; co-author: The Raven Steals the Light, 1984, 1996, A Short History of the Printed Word, 1999, Carving the Elements: A Companion to the Fragments of Parmenides, 2004, author numerous poems, stage prodns., works for multiple voices. Guggenheim fellow in poetry, 1988, Philips fellow Am. Philos. Soc., 2000; recipient Edward Sapir prize, 2004 Mem.: Am. Philos. Soc. (Philips Fund Rsch. fellow 2000, Edward Sapir prize 2004, Lt. Gov.'s award for lit. 2005). Home: Box 51 Heriot Bay BC Canada V0P 1H0

BRINGMAN, JOSEPH EDWARD, lawyer; b. Elmhurst, N.Y., Jan. 31, 1958; s. Joseph Herman and Eileen Marie (Sheehy) B.; m. Laurie Lynn Cunningham, July 11, 1992; children: Joseph Edward Jr., Elizabeth Grace. BA, Yale U., 1980; JD, Stanford U., 1983. Bar: N.Y. 1984, Wash. 1985, U.S. Dist. Ct. (we. dist.) Wash. 1986, U.S. Ct. Appeals (9th cir.) 1986, U.S. Ct. Appeals (fed. cir.) 1988, U.S. Dist. Ct. (ea. dist.) Wash. 2000. Acting asst. prof. U. Wash. Law Sch., Seattle, 1983-85; assoc. Perkins Coie, Seattle, 1985-91, of counsel, 1992—. Dir. Perkins Coie Cmty. Fellowship, Seattle, 1990-96, chair assoc. tng. com., 1997-2000. Editor: Stanford Jour. Internat. Law, 1980-83; author Fed. Trial Practice chpt. Washington Lawyers' Practice Manual, 2002-03. Mem. Yale Alumni Schs. Com., 1980—. Nat. Merit scholar, 1976; recipient Pro Bono Publico award Trumbull Coll. (Yale U.), 1980. Mem. ABA, Wash. State Bar Assn., King County Bar Assn. (jud. screening com. 1993-96, chair fair campaign practices com. 1997-99, judiciary and cts. com. 1999-2003, sec. 2003-2004, trustee 2003-, membership com. 2003-, CLE com. 2003-2004, chair audit com. 2005). Democrat. Roman Catholic. Office: Perkins Coie LLP 1201 3rd Ave Fl 48 Seattle WA 98101-3099 Office Phone: 206-359-8501. Business E-Mail: jbringman@perkinscoie.com.

BRINK, DAVID RYRIE, lawyer; b. Mpls., July 28, 1919; s. Raymond Woodard and Carol Sybil (Ryrie) B.; m. Irma Lorentz Brink; children: Anne Carol, Mary Claire, David Owen, Sarah Jane. BA with honors, U. Minn., 1940, BSL with honors, 1941, JD with honors, 1947; LLD, Capital U., 1981, Suffolk U., 1981, Mitchell Coll. Law, 1982. Bar: Minn. 1947, U.S. Dist. Ct. Minn. 1947, U.S. Tax Ct. 1967, U.S. Supreme Ct. 1980, U.S. Ct. Appeals (D.C. Cir.) 1982. Assoc. firm Dorsey & Whitney, Mpls., 1947-53, ptnr., 1953-89, head Washington office, 1982-84, ret. ptnr. Trustee Lawyers Com. Civil Rights Under Law, 1978—; bd. dirs. Nat. Legal Aid and Defender Assn., 1978-80; U.S. panelist for Dispute Resolution under Free Trade Agreement with Can.; bd. visitors U. Minn. Law Sch., 1978-81; chmn. trust and estates dept. Dorsey & Whitney, 1956-82 Bd. editors: U. Minn. Law Rev, 1941-42; contbr. numerous articles to law jours. Bd. govs. Am. Coll. Trust and Estate Counsel Found., 1987-95. Served to lt. comdr. USNR, 1943-46. Recipient Outstanding Achievement award U. Minn., 1982 Fellow Coll. Law Practice Mgmt. (hon.), Am. Coll. Trust and Estate Counsel (regent, exec. com.); mem. ABA (gov. 1974-77, 80-83, pres. 1981-82), Ctrl. and Ea. European Legal Initiative, Com. on Law and Nat. Security, Com. on Substance Abuse, Adv. Com. to Commn. on Lawyers Assisstance Programs,Com. on Specialization, Fund for Pub. Edn. of ABA (pres. 1981-82), Am. Bar Found. (state chmn. 1977-80, gov. 1980-83), Am. Bar Retirement Assn. (pres. 1976-77), Am. Judicature Soc. (bd. dirs. 1988—), Nat. Conf. Bar Pres., Inst. Jud. Adminstrn., Am. Arbitration Assn. (trustee 1981—), Can.-U.S. Law Inst. (adv. bd. 1987—), Minn. Bar Assn. (pres. 1978-79), Internat. Mgmt. and Devel. Inst., Hennepin County Bar Assn. (pres. 1967-68), Nat. Inst. Citizen Edn. in Law (nat. adv. bd. 1982-85, chmn. 1983-84), N.W. Athletic Club, Sr. Tennis Players Club, Inc. Office: Dorsey & Whitney # 50 S 6th St Minneapolis MN 55402

BRINK, FRANK, JR., biophysicist, former educator; b. Easton, Pa., Nov. 4, 1910; s. Frank and Lydia (Wilhelm) B.; m. Marjory Gaylord, May 1, 1939; children— Patricia Brink Mayer, David Warner BS, Pa. State Coll., 1934; MS, Calif. Inst. Tech., 1935; PhD, U. Pa., 1939; D.Sc. (hon.), Rockefeller U., 1983. Instr. physiology Cornell U. Med. Coll., N.Y.C., 1940-41; instr. biophysics Johnson Research Found., U. Pa., Phila., 1941-49; assoc. prof. biophysics Johns Hopkins U., Balt., 1949-53; prof. biophysics Rockefeller U., N.Y.C., 1953-81, dean grad. studies, 1958-72, Detlev W. Bronk prof., 1974-81, prof. emeritus, 1981—. Cons. to sec. of war Dept. Army, Washington, 1941-44; mem. com. for biology and medicine NSF, Washington, 1953-59; chmn. Pres.'s Com. for Nat. Med. Sci., Washington, 1963-64 Editor Biophysics Jour., 1960-64; mem. editorial bd. various jours., 1955-71; contbr. articles on phys. chemistry of nerve cells to profl. jours. Johnson scholar U. Pa., 1935-38; Lalor Found. fellow U. Pa., 1939-40 Fellow AAAS (life); mem. AAAS, NAS, Biophys. Soc. (charter), Soc. Gen. Physiologists, Am. Acad. Arts and Scis. Avocations: reading, cycling, travel. Home: Pine Run Community Apt E-1 Ferry and Iron Hills Rds Doylestown PA 18901

BRINK, MARION FRANCIS, trade association administrator; b. Golden Eagle, Ill., Nov. 20, 1932; s. Anton Frank and Agnes Gertrude B. BS, U. Ill., 1955, MS, 1958; PhD, U. Mo., 1961. Rsch. biologist U.S. Naval Radiol. Def. Lab., San Francisco, 1961-62; assoc. dir. div. nutrition rsch. Nat. Dairy Council, Chgo., 1962-65, dir. div. nutrition rsch., 1965-70, pres., 1970-85; exec. v.p. ops. United Dairy Industry Assn., Rosemont, 1985-88, chief exec. officer, 1988-91. Vice chmn. human nutrition adv. com. USDA, 1980-81. Contbr. articles to profl. jours. Recipient citation of merit U. Mo. Alumni Assn. Mem. Am. Soc. for Nutritional Scis., Am. Soc. Clin. Nutrition, Am. Dietetic Assn., Dairy Shrine Club, Soc. for Nutrition Edn., Chgo. Nutrition Assn., Alpha Tau Alpha, Gamma Sigma Delta. Home: 444 Highcrest Dr Wilmette IL 60091-2358

BRINKEMA, LEONIE MILHOMME, federal judge; b. N.J., June 26, 1944; d. Alexander Juste and Modeste Leonie Milhomme; m. John Robert Brinkema, Dec. 22, 1966; children: Robert Aaron, Eugenie Alexandra. BA with honors, Douglass Coll., 1966; MLS, Rutgers U., 1970; JD with honors, Cornell U., 1976. Bar: D.C. 1976, Va. 1978. Trial atty. U.S. Dept. Justice, Washington, 1976-77, 1983-84; asst. U.S. atty. U.S. Atty's Office Ea. Va., Alexandria, 1977-83; prin. Leonie M. Brinkema Atty., Alexandria, 1984-85; U.S. magistrate judge U.S. Dist. Ct. (ea. dist.) Va., Alexandria, 1985-93, U.S. dist. judge, 1993—. Legal lectr. Va. State Bar Professionalism Faculty, 1990-92, No. Va. Criminal Justice Acad., 1984-85; guest lectr. Alexandria Bar Assn., Alexandria Women Attys. Assn., Va. Women Attys. Assn., U.S. Dept. Justice Advocacy Inst., Va. Law Found. Active Fairfax Choral Soc., Alban Chorale. Woodrow Wilson grad. fellow, 1966, Danforth Found. grad. fellow, 1966. Mem. ABA, Va. State Bar, D.C. Bar, Nat. Assn. Women Judges, Va. Women Attys. Assn., George Mason Inn of Ct. (master), Phi Beta Kappa. Avocation: singing. Office: US Dist Ct 401 Courthouse Sq Alexandria VA 22314-5704

BRINKER, CHARLES JEFFREY, chemistry and chemical engineering educator; b. Easton, Pa., Nov. 28, 1950; BS in Ceramic Sci. with honors, Rutgers U., 1972, MS in Ceramic Sci., 1975, PhD in Ceramic Sci., 1978. Mem. tech. staff inorganic materials chemistry Sandia Nat. Labs., Albuquerque, 1979—; disting. mem. technical staff to sr. scientist Sandia Nat. Labs, Albuquerque, 1991—; prof. chemistry and chem. engring. U. N.Mex., Albuquerque, Disting. Nat. Lab. Prof. Chemistry and Chem. Engring., 1991—, co-dir. ctr. micro-engineered materials. Co-editor: Better Ceramics Through Chemistry, 1984, 6th edit., 1994; assoc. editor Jour. Am. Ceramic Soc.; mem. editl. bd. Chemistry of Materials, Jour. Sol-Gel Sci. and Tech., Jour. Porous Materials, Current Opinion in Solid State and Materials Sci.; author: Sol-Gel Science, 1990; contbr. articles to profl. jours. Recipient Basic Energy Scis. award Dept. Energy, 1986, 92, 94, 95, Zachariasen award, 1988 Jour. Non-Crystalline Solids, 1985-87, Ralph K. Iler award in chemistry of colloidal materials Am. Chem. Soc., 1996, NOVA award Lockheed Martin, 1996, R&D 100 award, 1996, E.O. Lawrence award, 2002. Fellow Am. Ceramic Soc.; mem. Materials Rsch. Soc. (founder, co-organizer), Keramos, Nat. Academy Engring. Office: Advanced Materials Lab 1001 University Blvd SE Albuquerque NM 87106-4325

BRINKER, NANCY GOODMAN, social service administrator; b. Peoria, Ill. m. Norman Brinker; 1 child, Eric. B, U. Ill., 1968; PhD (hon.), Southern Meth. U. Founder Susan G. Komen Breast Cancer Found., 1982, Race for the Cure fitness/walk fundraising event, 1998—; founder, chair, CEO In Your Corner, Inc., 1994—98; US Amb. to Hungary US Dept. State, 2001—03. Spkr. in field; advocate for women's health issues in Congress; collaborating ptnr., Nat. Dialogue on Cancer. Author: The Race is Run One Step at a Time; co-author: 1000 Questions About Women's Health. Bd. dirs. Physicians Reliance Network, Harvard Sch. Pub. Health, NYU Med. Sch. Found., Nat. Surg. Adjuvant Breast Project, Susan Komen Breast Cancer Found., Palm Beach Fellowship of Christians and Jews, Manpower, Inc., 2004-, US Oncology, Inc., Netmarket, Inc., Meditrust Corp.; mem. Nat. Cancer Adv. Bd.; bd. govs. Nat. Jewish Coalition. Recipient Jefferson award for Hero award Coping Mag., 1996, Pub. Svc. award Oncology Nursing Soc., 1996, Greatest Pub. Svc. by a Pvt. Citizen, Am. Inst. Pub. Svc., 1997, Lifetime Achievement award Nat. Breast Cancer Awareness Month, 1997, Albert Einstein's Sarnoff Vol. award, Humanitarian of Yr. award Mt. Sinai, James Ewing Layman's award Soc. Surg. Oncology, Humanitarian of Yr. award Rep. Women's Leadership Forum, Tex. Gov. award, outstanding nat. svc., Salomon Smith Barney Extraordingary Achievement award, Champion of Prevention award, Nat. Found. for Ctrs. for Disease Control, Cino de Duca award, internat. achievements in support of breast cancer rsch.; named one of 100 Most Important Women of 20th Century, Ladies Home Jour.; named to Cancer Rsch. and Treatment Fund, Inc. Cancer Survivors Hall of Fame. Mailing: National Dialogue 2250 South Paker Rd Ste 500 Aurora CO 80014-1678*

BRINKER, NORMAN E., restaurant company executive; BS, San Diego State U. Chmn., CEO Steak & Ale Restaurants, 1966-72; restaurant group pres. Pillsbury; chmn., CEO Burger King S&A Restaurant Group, Chili's Inc., Dallas, 1983-91; chmn. Brinker Internat. Inc., Dallas, 1991—. Office: Brinker Internat Inc 6820 LBJ Fwy Dallas TX 75240

BRINKER, THOMAS MICHAEL, finance company executive; b. Phila., Sept. 8, 1933; s. William Joseph and Elizabeth C. (Feeley) B.; m. Doris Marie Carlin, Oct. 11, 1958; children: Thomas Michael, James E., Joseph F., Diane M. Student, St. Joseph's U., U. Pa.; MS in Fin. Svcs., Am. Coll., 1980; DBA, Heed U., 1990; BA in Orgnl. Mgmt., Ea. Coll., 1991. Registered investment advisor; CLU, ChFC, CFP, AEP. With Ice Capades, 1951-52, 56; with Casa Carioca, Garmisch, Fed. Rep. Germany, 1954-56; profl. ice skating tchr. and mfrs. rep. Ridley Park, Pa., 1956-60; agt., div. mgr. Prudential Ins. Co., Phila., 1960-65; gen. agt. Mut. Trust Life Ins. Co., 1965-70; pres., founder Fringe Benefits Inc., Havertown, Pa., 1970—, Fin. Foresight Ltd., Havertown, Pa., 1983—. Adj. prof. Pa. State U., 1984—, St. Joseph's U., 1985—. Host: (radio) Financial Forum, Sta. WWDB-FM, 1982-90, Sta. WCZN-AM, 1990-91, daily report on fin. foresight Sta. WFLN-FM, 1992-, WCZN-AM, 1994-, children's fin. reports on Dr. Tom on Money Matters, WPWA-AM, 1994-, WWCN, Estero, Fla., 1997, others; co-host: (radio) Fin. Foresight, Sta. WFIL-AM, Phila., 1998-2000, WWDB-AM Phila., 2001-, WPEN-AM Phila., 2003-; author: HI, I'm Tom Brinker, You're on WWDB, 1987; columnist: Financially Yours, 1983-, Dollars and $ense, 1999-; ghostwriter: Nat. Assn. Life Underwriter's Fin. Fitness campaign, 1985; columnist Dollars and $ense, 1999-; contbr., author, condr. of seminars on fin. planning; contbr. articles to profl. jours. Pres., Delaware County Estate Planning Coun., 1979-80, Pipeline Inc., Springfield, Pa., 1970-71; dir. nat. coun. Invest-in-Am., 1986; bd. dirs. Pacific Advisors Fund, Inc., 1992—, Cypress Benefit Svcs., Inc., 1997—. Recipient Nat. Quality award Nat. Assn. Life Underwriters, 1966-2002, Nat. Sales Achievement award, 1970-2000, TransAmerica Fin. Advisors award, 2003. Mem. CLU, Delaware County Life Underwriters (pres. 1975-76, 82-83), Am. Coll. Life Underwriters, Nat. Assn. Life Underwriters, Internat. Platform Assn., Nat. Assn. Ins. and Fin. Advisors (inducted into Hall of Fame, 2003), Internat. Assn. Fin. Planners (v.p. Delaware Valley chpt. 1986-88, pres. 1989-, chmn. 1990-), Million Dollar Round Table (mem. Ct. of the Table 1986-, Top of the Table 1991, 93-95, Twenty-Five Million Dollar Internat. forum 1992-93), Lake Naomi Club (v.p., mem. bd. govs. 1982, pres. 1986), KC, Manor Club, Tom Brinker's Op. Christmas Baskets (pres.), Kingsport Club, Inc. (bd. dirs., treas. 1997-). Roman Catholic. Home: 115 Locust Ave Springfield PA 19064-1619 Office: 1 N Ormond Ave Havertown PA 19083-5010 E-mail: jbrinker@brinkerorg.com.

BRINKER-GABLER, GISELA, literature educator; PhD, U. Cologne, Germany, 1973. Vis. asst. prof. U.Fla., Gainesville, 1974-75; lectr. U. Essen, Germany, 1976-80, U. Cologne, 1980-88; vis. assoc. prof. SUNY, Binghamton, 1989-93, prof., 1993—, co-dir. lit. and theory criticism, 2003—. Office: SUNY Binghamton Dept Comparative Lit PO Box 6000 Binghamton NY 13902-6000 E-mail: gisela@brinker-gabler.com, gbrinker@bin-ghamton.edu.

BRINKLEY, ALAN DAVID, provost, historian; b. Washington, June 2, 1949; s. David and Ann (Fischer) B.; m. Evangeline Morphos, June 3, 1989; 1 child, Diane Elizabeth. AB, Princeton U., 1971; PhD, Harvard U., 1979. Asst. prof. history MIT, Cambridge, 1978—82; Dunwalke assoc. prof. history Harvard U., Cambridge, 1982—88; prof. history grad. sch. CUNY, 1988—91; prof. history Columbia U., N.Y.C., 1991—98, Allan Nevins prof. history, 1998—, provost, 2003—; Harmsworth prof. Am. history Oxford (Eng.) U., 1998—99. Author: Voices of Protest: Huey Long, Father Coughlin, and the Great Depression, 1982 (Nat. Book award 1983), The Unfinished Nation: A Concise History of the American People, 1993, The End of Reform: New Deal Liberalism in Recession and War, 1995, Liberalism and its Discontents, 1998. Trustee Century Found., NYC, 1996—, chmn. bd. trustees, 1999—; trustee The Dalton Sch., NYC, 1999-05, Nat. Humanities Ctr., 2004—. Guggenheim Found. fellow, 1984-85, Woodrow Wilson Ctr. Internat. Scholars fellow, 1985, Nat. Humanities Ctr. fellow, 1988-89; Media Studies Ctr. fellow, 1993-94; Russell Sage Found., 1996-97. Fellow Am. Acad. Arts and Scis.; mem. Century Assn. Home: 435 Riverside Dr # 52 New York NY 10025 Office: Columbia U 205 Low Libr New York NY 10027 Business E-Mail: ab65@columbia.edu.

BRINKLEY, AMY WOODS, bank executive; b. Franklin, Va., Jan. 19, 1956; d. Samuel Baker and Iris (Lankford) Woods; m. Robert Gentry Brinkley, Jan. 2, 1988; 2 children. BA, U. NC, 1978. Credit analyst NCNB, Charlotte, NC, 1978-79, internat. banking officer, 1979-80, comml. banking officer Greensboro, NC, 1981-84, credit policy officer, 1985-87; sr. consumer credit policy exec. NationsBank (formerly NCNB), Greensboro, 1988—93; exec. v.p. NationsBank, 1990—99, mktg. group exec., 1993—99; pres. consumer prods. Bank Am. (formerly NationsBank), 1999—2001; chmn., risk policy Bank Am., 2001—02, deputy head, risk mgmt., 2001—02, chief risk officer, 2002—. Bd. dirs. Carolinas HealthCare Sys., Pvt. Export Funding Co. Bd. trustees Princeton Theol. Seminary; bd. advisors Partners in Out-of-Sch. Time, NC Dance Theatre, former chmn., bd. trustees; mem. U. NC bd. visitors. Mem. Women's Profl. Forum, Risk Mgmt. Roundtable, RMA Consumer Credit Execs., Phi Beta Kappa. Office: Bank Am 100 N Tryon St 18th Fl Charlotte NC 28255

BRINKLEY, CHAD ALLEN, psychologist; b. Tuscola, Ill., Nov. 4, 1971; s. Gary Ned and Laura Beth Brinkley. BS in Psychology, BS in Bus. Adminstrn., U. Ill., Urbana, 1994; PhD in Clin. Psychology, U. Wis., Madison, 2002. Staff psychologist Fed. Bur. Prisons, Houston, 2002—. Hostage negotiation team mental health expert Fed. Bur. Prisons, Houston, 2002—. Contbr. scientific papers to profl. jours. Vol. Mendota Mental Health Inst., Mendota, Wis., 1998—2001; co-chair instl. charity fund dr. Combined Fed. Campaign, Houston, 2003, mem. bd. advisors, 2004—04. Mem.: Soc. Scientific Study Psychopathy. Avocations: improvisational theater, historical recreations. Office: Federal Detention Ctr PO Box 526245 Houston TX 77052 Office Phone: 713-221-5400 5002. E-mail: cbrinkley@bop.gov.

BRINKLEY, CHARLES ALEXANDER, geologist; b. Moody, Tex., Oct. 3, 1929; s. Jess Daniel and Vera Allene (Anderson) B.; m. Jeraldine Athalene Skeeter, June 18, 1952 (dec. 1992); m. Patricia Ann McCluney, Jan. 13, 1996. Student, Temple Jr. Coll., 1947—48; BS in Geology, Midwestern State U., 1957; MS in Geology, Pa. State U., 1960. Registered profl. geologist, Ark., Fla. Checker, stock mgr. A & P Tea Co., Temple and Waco, Tex., 1947—50; office asst. John M. Mouser, ind. oil operator, Wichita Falls, Tex., 1957; grad. asst. Pa. State U., 1957—59; geologist Texaco, Inc., New Orleans and Jackson, Miss., 1959—70, dist. geologist, 1970—72, dist. stratigrapher, 1972—75; regional geologist Gen. Crude Oil Co., Houston, 1975—77, mgr. exploration West Gulf dist., 1977—79; mgr. exploration West Gulf Mobil-GC Corp., 1979; mgr. exploration, chief geologist Maralo, Inc., Houston, 1979—85; ind. petroleum geologist Houston, Kingwood, Tex., 1985; petroleum geologist, co-owner High Star Oil and Gas Exploration Co., Houston, Kingwood, Humble, Tex., 1986—. With USN, 1950-54. Fellow AAAS; mem. Am. Assn. Petroleum Geologists (cert., v.p. divsn. profl. affairs 1980-82), Soc. Econ. Paleontologists and Mineralogists (nat. gulf coast sect. and permain basin sect.), Am. Inst. Profl. Geologists (cert., sec.-treas. Tex. sect. 1985-87), Soc. Ind. Profl. Earth Scientists (cert., treas. Houston chpt. 1990), New Orleans Geol. Soc., Houston Geol. Soc., Miss. Geol. Soc., West Tex. Geol. Soc., Internat. Airline Passengers Assn., Midland Petroleum Club. Baptist. Home and Office: High Star Oil & Gas Exploration 8007 Hurst Forest Ln Humble TX 77346-1704 Fax: 281-852-8919. Office Phone: 281-852-8919. E-mail: cabrinkley@hotmail.com.

BRINKLEY, DOUGLAS, historian, writer, educator; BA, Ohio State U., 1982; MA, Georgetown U., 1983, PhD in military and diplomatic hist., 1989; PhD (hon.), Trinity Coll., Hartford, Conn. U., NOVA Southeastern U. Prof. US Navel Acad., Princeton U., Hofstra U.; Stephen E. Ambrose Prof. Hist. U. New Orleans; dir. The Eisenhower Ctr. Am. Studies; prof. history Tulane U., New Orleans, 2005—. Author: The Majic Bus: An American Odyssey, 1993, Rosa Parks, 2000, The New York Times Living History: World War II: The Axis Assault, 1939-1942, 2003, Voices of Valor: D-Day, June 6, 1944, 2004, Tour of Duty: John Kerry and the Vietnam War, 2004; co-author: Jean Monnet: The Path to European Unity, 1991, The Atlantic Charter, 1994, Witness to America, 1999, War Letters: Extraordinary Correspondence from Wars, 2001, The Mississippi and the Making of a Nation, 2002, Theodore Roosevelt, the U.S. Navy, and the Spanish-American War, 2003, Windblown World: The Journals of Jack Kerouac 1947-1954, 2004, The World War II Memorial: A Grateful Nation Remembers, 2004. Office: Tulane U Theodore Roosevelt Ctr Am Civilization Alcee Fortier, Ste 202 New Orleans LA 70118 Office Phone: 504-314-7960. E-mail: dbrinkl@tulane.edu.*

BRINKLEY, JACK THOMAS, lawyer, retired congressman; b. Faceville, Ga., Dec. 22, 1930; s. Lonnie Elester and Pauline (Spearman) B.; m. Alma Lois Kite, May 29, 1955; children: Jack Thomas Jr., Fred Alen II. Student, Young Harris Coll., 1947-49, Okla. A. and M. Coll., 1952; LL.B. cum laude, U. Ga., 1959. Bar: Ga. 1958, D.C. 1973. Sch. tchr., Ga., 1949-51; assoc. firm Young, Hollis & Moseley, Columbus, Ga., 1959-61; ptnr. firm Coffin & Brinkley, Columbus, 1961-66; mem. Ga. Ho. Reps., 1965-66; sr. ptnr. Brinkley and Brinkley, 1983-95, of counsel, 1996-2000, of counsel emeritus, 2001—; mem. 90th-97th Congresses from 3d Ga. dist.; chmn. mil. facilities and installations subcom. 97th Congress. Mem. Ga. Ho. Reps., 1965-66. Trustee Young Harris Coll. Mem. Ga. Bar Assn., Columbus Bar Assn., Young Lawyers Club of Columbus (pres. 1963-64), Blue Key, Muscogee Civitan Club (pres., 2005), Masons. Democrat. Baptist. Office: Corporate Ctr Ste 901 Columbus GA 31902 Office Phone: 706-576-5322. E-mail: jtbrink@bellsouth.net.

BRINKLEY-DUARTE, CAROL LOHMILLER, art educator; b. Phoenix, June 24, 1950; d. Benedikt and Frances Marie Lohmiller; m. Michael Carroll Brinkley (div.); 1 child, Kristen Brinkley; m. Nelson Edward Duarte, Feb. 26, 1989; 1 child, Daniel Duarte. BA in Edn. with distinction, Ariz. State U., 1972, MA in Art and Art Edn., 1973. Cert. elem. and secondary tchr. with art endorsement. Art educator Scottsdale (Ariz.) Pub. Schs., 1972—73; tchr. art 2d and 5th grade Madison Sch. Dist. #38, Phoenix, 1974—2004, educator, 2004—. Hist. site vol. Rosson House, Phoenix, 1987—88; vol. Malta Ctr., Phoenix, 1996—97, Franciscan Renewal Ctr., Scottsdale. Named Outstanding Tchr., Madison Governing Bd., 1985—88; recipient You Make the Difference award, 2002; grantee, Ariz. Commn. for Arts, 2000. Mem.: Madison Dist. Classroom Tchrs. Assn., Ariz. Art Edn. Assn., Nat. Art Edn. Assn. (nat. presenter 2005). Roman Catholic. Avocations: antiques, gardening, photography, cooking, reading. Home: 729 E Hayward Ave Phoenix AZ 85020 Office: Madison Sch Dist #38 5601 N 16th St Phoenix AZ 85016 Office Phone: 602-664-7900. E-mail: clbd2@aol.com.

BRINKMAN, DALE THOMAS, lawyer; b. Columbus, Ohio, Dec. 10, 1952; s. Harry H. and Jean May (Sandel) B.; m. Martha Louise Johnson, Aug. 3, 1974; children: Marin Veronica, Lauren Elizabeth, Kelsey Renee. BA, U. Notre Dame, 1974; JD, Ohio State U., 1977. Bar: Ohio 1977, U.S. Dist. Ct. (so. dist.) Ohio 1979. Assoc. Schwartz, Shapiro, Kelm & Warren, Columbus, 1977-82; asst. tax counsel Am. Elect. Power, Columbus, 1982; gen. counsel Worthington Industries, Inc., Columbus, 1982-99, v.p. adminstrn., gen. counsel, sec., 1999—, corp. sec., 2000—. Author: Ohio State U. Law Jour.,1975-76, editor, 1976-77. Trustee, officer Friends of Dahlberg Ctr., Columbus, 1980-86; dir., officer Assn. for Developmentally Disabled, Columbus, 1986-94. Mem. ABA, Ohio Bar Assn., Columbus Bar Assn.

Republican. Roman Catholic. Office: Worthington Industries Inc 1205 Dearborn Dr Columbus OH 43085-4769 E-mail: dtbrinkm@worthingtonindustries.com.

BRINKMAN, JOHN ANTHONY, historian, educator; b. Chgo., July 4, 1934; s. Adam John and Alice (Davies) B.; m. Monique E. Geschier, Mar. 24, 1970; 1 son, Charles E. AB, Loyola U., Chgo., 1956, MA, 1958; PhD, U. Chgo., 1962. Rsch. assoc. Oriental Inst., U. Chgo., 1963, dir. inst., 1972-81, asst. prof. Assyriology and ancient history, 1964-66, assoc. prof., 1966—70, prof., 1970—84, Charles H. Swift disting. svc. prof., 1984—2001, chmn. dept., 1969—72, Charles H. Swift disting. svc. prof. emeritus, 2001—. Ann. prof. Am. Schs. Oriental Rsch., Baghdad, 1968-69; chmn. Baghdad Schs. Com., 1970-85, chmn. exec. com., 1973-75, trustee, 1975-90; chmn. vis. com. dept. Near Ea. langs. and civilizations Harvard U., 1995-2001. Author: Political History of Post-Kassite Babylonia, 1968, Materials and Studies for Kassite History, Vol. I, 1976; Prelude to Empire, 1984; editorial bd. Chgo. Assyrian Dictionary, 1977—, State Archives Assyria, 1985—; editor in charge Babylonian sect. Royal Inscriptions of Mesopotamia, 1979-91; contbr. numerous articles to profl. jours. Fellow Am. Research Inst., in Turkey, 1971; sr. fellow Nat. Endowment Humanities, 1973-74; Guggenheim fellow, 1984-85, Emeritus fellow, Mellon Found., 2005—. Fellow Am. Acad. Arts and Scis.; mem. Am. Oriental Soc. (pres. Middle West chpt. 1971-72), Am. Schs. of Oriental Rsch., Brit. Sch. Archaeology in Iraq, Deutsche Orient Gesellschaft, Brit. Inst. Archaeology at Ankara. Roman Catholic. Home: 1321 E 56th St Apt 4 Chicago IL 60637-1762 Office: U Chgo 1155 E 58th St Chicago IL 60637-1569 Office Phone: 773-702-9545.

BRINKMAN, MICHAEL OWEN, health care consultant, educator; b. Chgo., May 15, 1936; s. Adam John and Alice Corrine (Davies) B.; m. Mary Judith Zeitz, Jan. 18, 1958; children: Stephen, Daniel, Julie, Amy, Carl, Mary Alice. BEE magna cum laude, Marquette U., 1958. Instr. Marquette U., Milw., 1957-59; engr. Wis. Electric Power, Milw., 1958-59, A.C. Electronics, Oak Creek, Wis., 1959-62; svc. engr. Nuclear-Chgo. Corp., Des Plaines, Ill., 1962-63, dir. of svc., 1963-66, plant mgr., 1966-67; gen. mgr. Electrovac, Melrose Park, Ill., 1968; mktg. analyst A.C. Electronics, Oak Creek, Wis., 1969-70; pres. On-Call Nat., Barrington, Ill., 1970-72, Hosp. Maintenance Cons., Columbus, Wis., 1972—. Co-author: (books) Clinical Engineering, 1975, Managing Your Medical Equipment, 1978, 82; contbr. numerous articles to profl. jours. Dep. committeeman Schaumburg Twp. Rep., Hoffman Estates, Ill., 1964-67; supt. Country Christian Schs., Nashotah, Wis., 1978-90, bd. dirs., 1990-95; bd. dirs. Victory Christian H.S., Neosho, Wis., 1991-2003, vol. tchr., 1991—; mem. Oconomowoc Bible Fellowship, elder, 1996—. Mem. Med. Equipment Repair Assocs. (exec. dir. 1973—), Eta Kappa Nu, Pi Mu Epsilon, Tau Beta Pi, Alpha Sigma Nu. Avocations: bible teaching, golf, stamp collecting/philately, antique glassware. Home: 443 W Prairie St Columbus WI 53925-1349 Office: Hosp Maintenance Cons Inc PO Box 309 Columbus WI 53925-0309 Office Phone: 920-623-4481. Business E-Mail: mob@gdinet.com.

BRINKMAN, PAUL DEL(BERT), retired foundation administrator, journalist, educator; b. Olpe, Kans., Feb. 10, 1937; s. Paul Theodore and Delphine Barbara (Brown) Brinkman; m. Evelyn Marie Lange, Aug. 5, 1961 (dec. June 1988); m. Carolyn L. Backer, July 27, 1990; children: Scott Michael, Susan Lynn Moeser stepchildren: Debra, Cynthia, Jeffrey. BS, Emporia State Coll., 1958; MA in Journalism (Newspaper Fund fellow), Ind. U., 1963, PhD in Mass Comm. (Scripps-Howard fellow), 1971. Editor, reporter Emporia (Kans.) Gazette, 1954-59; instr. journalism Leavenworth (Kans.) High Sch., 1959-62; lectr. Ind. U., Bloomington, 1962-65, 68-70; asst. prof. Kans. State U., Manhattan, 1965-68; prof., dean Sch. Journalism U. Kans., Lawrence, 1970-86, vice chancellor for acad. affairs, 1986-93; dir. journalism programs John S. and James L. Knight Found., Miami, 1993-2001; dean U. Colo. Sch. Journalism and Mass Comm., Boulder, 2001—02, mem. adv. bd., 2002. Balt. Sun disting. lectr. Coll. Journalism, U. Md., 1993. Bd. dirs. William Allen White Found., 1974; chmn. Big Eight Athletic Conf., 1980-81, 87-88; faculty rep. Nat. Collegiate Athletic Assn., 1978-93; mem. press fellowship adv. com. Knight Internat.; adv. bd. Journalism Sch. U. Colo.; coun. on accreditation of law schs. ABA, 1998-2004; bd. govs. Kinsey Inst., 2002—. Named Trayes Prof. of Yr. Mass Comm. Soc. divsn. Assn. Edn. Journalism, 1990; recipient Disting. Alumni award Emporia State Coll., 1978, Disting. Svc. award Ind. U., 1986. Mem. Am. Assn. Schs. and Depts. Journalism (pres. 1977-78), Inland Daily Press Assn. (chmn. edn. com. 1980-83), Assn. Edn. Journalism (chmn. publs. com. 1974-75, pres. 1980-81), Soc. Profl. Journalists, Lawrence C. of C. (v.p. 1987-88), Rotary (pres. Lawrence chpt. 1987-88), Bloomington Press Club (bd. dirs. 2002-), Indiana U. Sch. Journalism Alumni (bd. dirs. 2003-), Ernie Pyle Soc., Sigma Delta Chi, Kappa Tau Alpha. Home: 3112 Coppertree Drive Bloomington IN 47401 Personal E-mail: del.brinkman@insightbb.com.

BRINKMAN, WILLIAM FRANK, physicist, research and development company executive; b. Washington, Mo., July 20, 1938; s. William F. and Mildred A. (Bocklege) Brinkman; m. Sybille Zeldin, Sept. 17, 2002; children: David, Curtis. BS, U. Mo., 1960, PhD, 1965. Postdoctoral fellow Oxford U., 1966; mem. staff Bell Labs., Murray Hill, N.J., 1966-72, dept. head, 1972-74, dir., 1974-84; v.p. rsch. Sandia Nat. Lab., Albuquerque, 1984-87; v.p. phys. scis. rsch. Lucent Techs./Bell Labs., Murray Hill, N.J., 1987-2000, v.p. rsch., 2000—01; sr. rsch. physicist Princeton (N.J.) U., 2002—. Contbr. articles to profl. jours. on theoretical physics. Fellow AAAS, Am. Phys. Soc. (pres. 2002, George E. Pake prize 1994); mem. Am. Acad. Arts and Scis., Nat. Acad. Sci. (chmn. 8-vol. report Physics Through the 1990s), Am. Philos. Soc. Home: 20 Constitution Hill W Princeton NJ 08540 Office: Princeton Univ Dept Physics 328 Jadwin Hill Princeton NJ 08540

BRINKMEIER, ALAN JAMES, lawyer; b. Lena, Ill., Nov. 11, 1954; s. Paul W. and Blondell S. Brinkmeier; m. Gail K. Kasperski, Nov. 22, 1975; children: Alexandra Catherine, Perri Elizabeth. BA with high honors, Elmhurst Coll., 1976; JD, DePaul U., 1984. Bar: Ill. 1984, U.S. Dist. Ct. (no. dist.) Ill. 1984, U.S. Ct. Appeals (7th cir.) 1989, U.S. Supreme Ct. 1989, U.S. Dist. Ct. (cen. dist.) Ill. 1992. Paralegal Pretzel, Stouffer, Nolan & Rooney, Chgo., 1980-83; assoc. Pretzel & Stouffer, Chartered, Chgo., 1984-88, officer, 1989-92; ptnr. Merlo, Kanofsky & Brinkmeier, Ltd., Chgo., 1992—2004, Merlo, Kanofsky, Brinkmeier & Gregg Ltd, 2004—. Author book chpt.; contbr. articles to profl. publs. Leader fund drive Boy Scouts Am., 1987; v.p. funds Elmhurst (Ill.) Coll. Cabinet, 1984-93, pres. 1993-95, bd. trustees, 1996—; commr. Elmhurst Planning Zoning, 1997— Mem. ABA, Ill. State Bar Assn., Chgo. Bar Assn., DuPage County Bar Assn., Appellate Lawyers Assn., Phi Kappa Phi, Omicron Delta Kappa, Phi Alpha Delta. Office: Merlo Kanofsky Brinkmeier & Gregg Ltd 208 S La Salle St Chicago IL 60604-1000

BRINKMEYER, EUGENE, retired music educator; b. Niles, Calif., May 22, 1931; s. Elmer and Elizabeth Brinkmeyer; m. Rose Mary Brinkmeyer, Dec. 1, 1932; children: Catherine Eickhoff, Jay, Michael. BA, MusB, BTh, Yankton (S.D.) Coll., 1955; M in Sacred Music, Union Theol. Sch. Sacred Music, 1957. Min. music United Ch. of Christ, Sioux Falls, SD, 1957—60, Presbyn. Ch., Bound Brook, NJ, 1960—65; assoc. prof. music Yankton (S.D.) Coll., 1965—75, Mt. Marty Coll., Yankton, SD, 1976—2004; interim organist United Ch. Christ, Vermillion, SD, 2004—. Chmn. faculty senate Mt. Marty Coll., 1992—95, chmn. Divsn. Arts and Humanities, 1995—2001, interim academic dean, 2001—02; min. music United Ch. Christ, 1965—2000. Author: (songs) The Road to Emmaus. Adminstr. endowment Ch. Music Commns. Mem.: Yankton (S.D.) Concert Assn. (bd. dirs. 2004—05), Yankton (S.D.) Area Arts Assn. (chmn. bd. 1988—2004), Am. Guild Organists (past dean 1987—91), Mt. Marty Coll. Gregorian Club (chmn. 2002—04). Democrat. Congl. Avocations: travel, model trains, art, exercise. Home: 205 E 26 Street Yankton SD 57078 Office: Mount Marty College 1105 West 8 Yankton SD 57078 Personal E-mail: eugeneb665@aol.com. E-mail: www.mtmc.edu.

BRINKMEYER, SCOTT S., lawyer; b. Chgo., Sept. 27, 1949; BA, DePauw U., 1971; JD, St. Louis U., 1975. Bar: Mich. 1975, cert.: Am. Arbitration Assn. Nat. Panel (civil neutral arbitrator) 2004, US Dist. Ct., Western Dist. Mich. (mediator) 2005. Atty. Mika, Meyers, Beckett & Jones, PLC, Grand Rapids, Mich. Jud. law clk. Mo. Ct. appeals, 1974. Assoc. editor St. Louis U. Law Jour., 1974. Pres. Grand Rapids Rotary Dist. 290, 1997—98. Fellow: Mich. State Bar Found., Am. Bar Found.; mem.: ABA (Ho. Del. 2003—04), Grand Rapids Bar Assn., Def. Rsch. Inst., Mich. Def. Trial Counsel, State Bar Mich. (rep. assembly 1992—2004, bd. commrs. 1995—2004, exec. com. 1996—98, chair 2003—04, pres. 2003—04, sects. on environ. law, litigation, negligence law, dispute resolution, exec. com. 1999—2004). Office: Mika Meyers Beckett and Jones 900 Monroe Ave NW Grand Rapids MI 49503-1423

BRINSFIELD, JOHN WESLEY, military officer, educator; b. Atlanta, Feb. 23, 1944; s. John Wesley Brinsfield and Marietta Strout Branson; m. Patricia Tallon Brinsfield, July 6, 2002; m. Patsy Knighton, Dec. 31, 1974 (div. Apr. 2, 1986); children: Casey Marie, Cindee Marietta. BA, Vanderbilt U., 1966; MDiv, Yale U., 1969; PhD, Emory U., 1973; DMin, Drew Theol. Sem., 1983. Ordained to ministry North Ga. Conf. of the United Meth. Ch., 1969. Squadron chaplain Third Armored Cav. Rgt., Ft. Bliss, Tex., 1974—75; adj. asst. prof. history U. Tex., El Paso, 1974—75; Protestant chaplain Turkish-U.S. Logistics Detachment, Sinop, Turkey, 1975—76; instr. in world history U. of Md.-Europe, Sinop, 1975—76; instr. in ethics and world religions US Army Aviation Sch., Fort Rucker, Ala., 1976—80; asst. prof., history dept. US Mil. Acad., West Point, 1980—84; Protestant pastor Mark Twain Chapel, Heidelberg, Germany, 1985—87; chief, unit and individual tng. US Army Chaplain Sch., Ft. Monmouth, NJ, 1987—90; third army pers. chaplain US Army Ctrl. Command, Riyadh, Saudi Arabia, 1990—91; chief of pers. divsn., forces command chaplain staff US Army Forces Command, Ft. McPherson, Ga., 1991—93; historian/author Office of the Chief of Chaplains, The Pentagon, 1993—95; dir. of ethical program devel. US Army War Coll., Carlisle, Pa., 1995—99; dep. command chaplain US Army Forces Command, Fort McPherson, 1999—2002; sr. historian US Army Chaplain Sch., Fort Jackson, SC, 2002—. Adj. prof. Erskine Theol. Sem., Due West, SD, 2004—; dir. mil. family program for 320 mil. families US Army War Coll., 1995—99. Co-author: (history book) Faith in the Fight: Civil War Chaplains; author: Encouraging Faith, Serving Soldiers: A History of the US Army Chaplain Corps, 1975-1995, Religion and Politics in Colonial South Carolina, (essay on human and spiritual needs) The Future of the Army Profession; contbg. author: article on religion in the military Oxford Companion to Am. Mil. History; contbr. twenty articles on ethics and history to jours., newspapers, and magazines. Bd. dirs. Participation Ministries, Campbellsville, Ky., 1999—2003. Grad. fellow, Yale Div. Sch., 3 yr. doctoral fellow, Emory U., Woodrow Wilson fellow, Oxford U. Mem.: Yale Alumni Assn., New Eng. Hist. and Geneal. Soc., Soc. Mayflower Descs. Methodist. Avocations: tennis, genealogy, antiques, travel, scuba diving. Home: 1783 Brewer Blvd SW Atlanta GA 30310 Office: US Army Chaplain School (Historian) 10100 Lee Rd Fort Jackson SC 29207 Business E-Mail: brinsfieldj@usachcs.army.mil.

BRINSMADE, AKBAR FAIRCHILD, chemical engineering consultant; b. Puebla, Mex., May 31, 1917; s. Robert Bruce and Helen Steenbock Brinsmade; m. Juanita Phillips, June 16, 1944; children: Anne Hudson Brinsmade, Robert Bruce P., Charlotte Lynn Brinsmade. BS in Chemistry, U. Wis., 1939; MS in Chem. Engrng. Practice, MIT, 1942; postgrad., Poly. Inst. Bklyn., 1945-46, NYU, 1947-49, Tulane U., 1967-73. Registered profl. engr., N.C., La. Gen. mgr. Cia. Minera SnFrancisco y Anex., San Luis Potosi, Mex., 1939-40; sr. rsch. engr. Shell Oil Co. Inc., Houston and N.Y.C., 1942-48; project mgr. Internat. Indsl. Cons., N.Y.C. and Caracas, Venezuela, 1949-50; mng. dir. Promoters Nacional de Indsl., Caracas, 1952-57; R&D engr. Hercules Power Co., Rocket Center, W.Va., 1959-64; rsch. engrng. specialist Chrysler Space Divsn., New Orleans, 1966-69; chem. engrng. cons. to maj. U.S. and fgn. corps., 1969—. Author: (book) Travel to the Stars, 1996, (book chpts.) Solid Rocket Technology, 1967; patentee in field. Chmn. Citizens for Goldwater, Allegany County, Md., 1964. Fellow Am. Inst. Chemists; mem. NSPE (profl. engr. mem.), AIChE, Am. Chem. Soc., La. Engrng. Soc. (profl. engr. mem.), Phi Eta Sigma, Phi Lambda Upsilon, Sigma Alpha Epsilon. Republican. Lutheran. Avocations: books, history, languages, travel, tennis. Home: 486 Channel Mark Dr Biloxi MS 39531 Office Phone: 228-385-5329.

BRINSMADE, LYON LOUIS, retired lawyer; b. Mexico City, Feb. 24, 1924; s. Robert Bruce and Helen (Steenbock) B. (Am. citizens); m. Susannah Tucker, June 9, 1956 (div. 1978); children: Christine Fairchild, Louisa Calvert; m. Carolyn Hartman Lister, Sept. 22, 1979 (dec. 2003). Student, U. Wis., 1940-43; BS, Mich. Technol. U., 1944; JD, Harvard U., 1950. Bar: Tex. 1951. Assoc. Butler, Binion, Rice, Cook & Knapp, Houston, 1950-58, ptnr. in charge internat. dept., 1958-83, Porter & Clements, Houston, 1983-91; sr. counsel Porter & Hedges (formerly Porter & Clements), Houston, 1991-99. Bd. dirs. Houston br. English-Speaking Union of U.S., 1972-75. Served with AUS, 1946-47. Mem. ABA (chmn. com. internat. investment and devel. of sect. internat. law and practice 1970-76, council 1972-76, 81-82, vice chmn. 1976-79, chmn.-elect 1979-80, chmn. 1980-81, co-founder and co-chmn. com. Mex. 1982-85), Internat. Bar Assn., Inter-Am. Bar Assn. (co-chmn. sect. oil and gas laws, com. natural resources 1973-76, council 1984-87), Houston Bar Assn., State Bar Tex. (chmn. internat. law com. 1970-74, mem. council sect. internat. law 1975-78), Am. Soc. Internat. Law (exec. council 1984-86), Houston World Trade Assn. (sec., dir. 1967-70), Houston World Trade Assn. (chmn. legis. com. 1967-72), Houston C. of C. (chmn. legis. subcom. internat. bus. com. 1970-72), SAR, Allegro of Houston, Harvard Club (Houston), Sigma Alpha Epsilon. Episcopalian. Home: PO Box 1149 Wimberley TX 78676-1149 Office Phone: 512-847-2576.

BRINSON, GAY CRESWELL, JR., retired lawyer; b. Kingsville, Tex., June 13, 1925; s. Gay Creswell and Lelia (Wendelkin) B.; m. Bette Lee Butter, June 17, 1979; children from former marriage: Thomas Wade, Mary Kaye. Student, U. Ill., Chgo., 1947-48; BS, U. Houston, 1953, JD, 1957. Bar: Tex. 1957, U.S. Dist. Ct. (so. dist.) Tex. 1959, U.S. ct. Appeals (5th cir.) 1962 U.S. Dist. Ct. (ea. dist.) Tex. 1965, U.S. Supreme Ct. 1974; U.S. Dist. Ct. (no. dist.) Tex. 1990; diplomate Am. Bd. Trial Advocates, Am. Bd. Profl. Liability Attys. Spl. agt. FBI, Washington and Salt Lake City, 1957-59; trial atty. Liberty Mut. Ins. Co., Houston, 1959-62; assoc. Horace Brown, Houston, 1962-64, Vinson & Elkins, Houston, 1964-67, ptnr., 1967-91; of counsel McFall, Sherwood & Sheehy, Houston, 1992-2000. Lectr. U. Houston Coll. Law, 1964-65; mem. staff Tex. Coll. Trial Advocacy, Houston, 1978-86; prosecutor Harris County Grievance Com.-State Bar Tex., Houston, 1965-70 Served with AUS, 1943—46, ETO. Fellow Tex. Bar Found. (life); mem. Tex. Acad. Family Law Specialists (cert.), Tex. Assn. Def. Counsel, Tex. Bd. Legal Specialization (cert.), Fedn. Ins. Counsel, Nat. Bd. Trial Advocacy (cert.), Houston Ctr. Club, Phi Delta Phi. Home: 3740 Del Monte Dr Houston TX 77019-3018 Personal E-mail: gbrinson@houston.rr.com.

BRINSTER, RALPH LAWRENCE, biologist, educator; BS, Rutgers U., 1953; VMD, U. Pa., 1960, PhD in Physiology, 1964; D honoris causa, U. Basque Country, Spain, 1994; DSc (hon.), Rutgers U., 2000. Tchg.fellow U. Pa., Phila., 1961-64, instr. Sch. Medicine, 1964-65, asst. prof., then assoc. prof. Sch. Vet. Medicine, 1965-70, prof. physiology Sch. Vet. Medicine, 1970—, Rich King Mellon prof. reproductive physiology, 1975—. Lectr. Harvey Soc., 1984, Juan March Found., Madrid, 1992. Recipient Charles-Leopold Mayer prize, French Acad. Scis., 1994, March of Dimes prize, Devel. Biology, 1996, Bower award and prize, Sci., 1997, Disting. Svc. award, USDA, 1989, John Scott award, City Trusts Phila., 1997, Ernst W. Bertner award, 2001, Wolf prize in medicine, 2003. Fellow: Am. Acad. Arts and Scis.; mem.: AVMA, NAS, Inst. Medicine. Office: Univ Pa Sch Vet Medicine Philadelphia PA 19104

BRINZO, JOHN S., mining executive; b. 1942; married. BS, Kent State U., 1964; MBA, Case Western Res. U., 1968. Sr. v.p. Cleve.-Cliffs, Inc., Cleve., until 1989, exec. v.p., 1989—. Office: Cleve-Cliffs Inc 1100 Superior Ave Cleveland OH 44114-2589

BRIONES, DAVID, judge; b. El Paso, Tex., Feb. 26, 1943; m. Delia Garcia; 4 children. BA, U. Tex., El Paso, 1969; JD, U. Tex., Austin, 1971. Ptnr. Moreno & Briones, 1971-91; judge El Paso County Ct. No. 1, El Paso, 1991-94; dist. judge U.S. Dist. Ct. (we. dist.) Tex., El Paso, 1994—. Mem. Jud. Conf. Com. Adminstrn. Magistrate Judges Sys., 2003—. With U.S. Army, 1964—66. Fellow: Tex. Bar Found.; mem.: Mex.-Am. Bar Assn., El Paso Bar Assn., State Bar Tex. Office: US Courthouse Courtroom 1 511 E San Antonio Ave El Paso TX 79901-2401 Office Phone: 915-534-6744. Business E-Mail: David_Briones@txwd.uscourts.gov.

BRIONES, TERESITA LANDICHO, medical researcher, educator; d. Milagros Landicho and Carlos Briones. PhD, U. Mich., 1997. RN Mich., 1989. Clin. nurse specialist U. of Mich., Ann Arbor, Mich., 1989—95, rsch. asst., 1994—97; postdoctoral fellow Beckman Inst., Urbana, Ill., 1997—2000; assoc. prof. U. of Ill., Chgo., 2000—. Rsch. cons. Harbor -UCLA Med. Ctr., LA, 1988—89; edn. cons. Santa Monica Hosp., Santa Monica, Calif., 1985—86. Grantee Rsch., NIH, 2000 to present. Mem.: NY Acad. of Sci., Nat. Neurotrauma Soc., Am. Physiol. Soc., Soc. for Neuroscience. Achievements include research in Midwest Nursing Research Society New Investigator Award. Office: Univ Illinois 845 S Damen Ave M/C 802 Rm 750 Chicago IL 60612 Office Phone: 312-355-3142. Office Fax: 312-996-4979. E-mail: tbriones@uic.edu.

BRISBANE, ARTHUR SEWARD, newspaper publisher; b. N.Y.C., Sept. 30, 1950; s. Seward Scatcherd and Doris Mae (Fauser) B.; m. Jo Ellen Hull, Oct. 16, 1982; children: Allison Faith, Madeline Mariah, Laura Calista. AB, Harvard Coll., 1973. Child care worker McLean Hosp., Belmont, Mass., 1973-74; freelance musician, 1974-76; reporter Glen Cove (N.Y.) Guardian, 1976-77, Kansas City (Mo.) Star & Times, 1977-79, columnist, 1979-84; reporter Washington Post, 1984-87, asst. city editor, 1987-89; columnist Kansas City Star, 1990-92, editor, v.p., 1992-97, pub., pres., 1997—. Author: Arthur Brisbane's Kansas City, 1982. Avocations: tennis, reading. Office: The Kansas City Star 1729 Grand Blvd Kansas City MO 64108-1458

BRISBINE, JOANN, mental health counselor, child and adolescent mental health specialist; b. Baxter County, Ark., Aug. 22, 1947; d. Talmadge Arthur Jones and Audie Mahalia Cooper-Jones; m. Timothy Julian Runyan, Mar. 29, 1991; children: Sally Ann, Joseph Barry. MS in Applied Behavioral sci., Bastry/Leadership Inst. of Seattle, 2000—02; BA in human services, Western Wash. U., 1997—99; AA, Wenatchee Valley Coll., 1995—97. Cert. Child and Adolescent Mental Health Counselor U. of Wash., 2001, lic. mental health counselor. Vocat. counselor Work Opportunities, Lynnwood, Wash., 1991—93, Wash. Vocat. Services, Mountlake Terrace, 1993—98; tchg. asst. Everett C.C., Wash., 1997—99; child/family therapist Compass Health, Camano Island, Wash., 1999—; mental health therapist Brisbine Counseling Services, Stanwood, Wash., 2002—. Recipient Woman of the Yr., Stanwood/Camano C. of C., 2002, Cmty. Partner-Friend of WICA, Wash. Assn. of Local Women, Children and Infants Agencies, 2002, Appreciation award, Wash. Vocat. Services, 1997. Mem.: Wash. Mental Health Counselors Assn. (assoc.), Am. Mental Health Counselors Assn. (assoc.). Office: Brisbine Counseling Svcs 9631 269th St NW Stanwood WA 98292 Office Phone: 360-629-5813. Personal E-mail: timjo@whidbey.net.

BRISCOE, ANNE M., retired science educator; b. N.Y.C., Dec. 1, 1918; m. William A. Briscoe, Aug. 20, 1955 (dec. Dec. 1985); m. Theodore H. Heinly Sr., Jan. 21, 1989 (dec. Dec. 2002). MA, Vassar Coll., 1945; PhD, Yale U., 1949. From rsch. assoc. to asst. prof. Cornell U. Med. Coll., N.Y.C., 1950-56; faculty Columbia U. Coll. Physicians and Surgeons, N.Y.C., 1956—, prof. emeritus, 1987. Spl. lectr., 1987-89; lectr. Harlem Hosp. Center Sch. Nursing, 1968-77; adj. asst. prof. Hunter Coll., 1951-64, 73-75; mem. N.Y.C. Commn. on Status of Women, 1979-93, vice chair, 1982-93; non-govtl. orgn. del. to UN; adv. coun. Inst. Nuc. Power Ops., 1979-84. Contbr. articles to profl. jours. Sterling Jr. fellow, USPHS fellow, Yale U., 1949; recipient Yale medal, 1986, Susan B. Anthony award, 1989, Wilbur Cross medal Yale Grad. Sch. Sesquicentennial Convocation, 1997, Yale Fund Chmns. award, 2000. Fellow: AAAS (mem. coun. 1982—85, chmn.'s award Yale Alumni Fund 2001), Assn. Women in Sci. (editor newsletter 1971—74, nat. pres. 1974—76), N.Y. Acad. Sci. (chair women in sci. com. 1978—92, bd. govs. 1981), Am. Inst. Chemists (sec. N.Y. chpt. 1981—83); mem.: ACS, Assn. Women in Sci. Ednl. Found. (pres. 1978—82), Fedn. Orgns. for Profl. Women (treas. 1978—80), Harvey Soc., Am. Fedn. Clin. Rsch., Am. Soc. Clin. Nutrition, Yale Grad. Sch. Alumni Assn. (pres. 1981—86), Assn. Yale Alumni (assembly rep. 1978—, bd. govs. 1982—85). Home: 2116 Sea Cres Ruskin FL 33570-6128 E-mail: drannieb@aol.com.

BRISCOE, DAVID LLOYD, academic sociologist, educator; b. Mars Hill, N.C., Oct. 14, 1950; s. David and Marjorie (Ray) B.; m. Pamlir Roshell Smith. BA, U. Ark., 1980, MA, 1985; PhD, So. Ill. U., 1993. Cert. family life educator. Lectr. So. Ill. U., Carbondale, 1990-92; asst. prof. U. Ark., Little Rock, 1992-98, assoc. prof., 1998—. Mem. adv. bd. Ark. Consumer Bd., Little Rock, 1999—. Co-author: Plain Talk, 1997. Mem. exec. bd. Quapaw Coun. Boy Scouts Am., Little Rock, 1995—; mem. Martin Luther King Commn., Little Rock, 2000. Recipient Faculty Excellence award in pub. svc., Outstanding African Am. Faculty award, 2000, Legion of Honor award, 1998, Outstanding Profl. award, 2001, Eagle Scout Boy Scouts Am., 1968, Silver Beaver, 1981, Silver Antelope, 1996. Fellow Soc. Values in Higher Edn., Southwest Soc. on Aging; mem. Assn. Gerontology in Higher Edn. (exec. com. 2001). Democrat. Baptist. Avocations: camping, canoeing, martial arts, basketball. Home: 2909 W 6th Little Rock AR 72205 Office: U Ark 2801 S University Ave Little Rock AR 72204 E-mail: dlbriscoe@ualr.edu.

BRISCOE, JACK CLAYTON, lawyer; b. July 23, 1920; s. Park Harry and Elsie Gertrude (Woodward) B.; m. Dorothy Lillian Shaw, Sept. 3, 1949; children: Jacqueline Kamp, Jeffrey S., Ryd Joan. BS in Econs., U. Pa., 1943; LLB, Harvard U., 1948. Bar: Pa. 1950. Assoc. Robert C. Duffy, Phila., 1966—85; ptnr. Briscoe, Haggerty & Howard, Phila., 1966—85, Briscoe & Howard, Phila., 1986—90, Jack C. Briscoe & Assocs., Phila., 1990—. Instr. U. Pa., 1950—56; bd. dirs. Renewal Counseling, Inc., Prime Inc.; chmn. bd. dirs. Master's Plan Fin. Svcs., Inc., Zoe Consulting Inc., Cmty. Capital Adivsors Inc. Dir. Pa. Bible Soc.; elder United Presbyn. Ch. Manoa; active Fellowship Christian Athletes; mem. Rep. Presdl. Task Force; mem. bd. dirs. Faith Theol. Sem., Pa. Bible Soc.; People for People, Inc.; bd. dirs. Prime, Inc., Urban Youth Racing Sch., Inc. With USAF, 1943—46. Recipient Branch Ricky Assocs. award, Cert. Achievement award, Compulsory Arbitration Divsn. Phila. County Ct. Fellow: Harry S. Truman Libr. Inst.; mem.: Chapel of Four Chaplains (legion hon. mem.), World Affairs Coun., Missions Unltd. Inc. (bd. dirs.), Gideons Internat., Friendly Sons of St. Patrick, Pa. Soc. Harvard Law Sch. Assn., Nat. Fedn. Ind. Bus., Phila. Bar Assn., Pa. Bar Assn., ABA, Union League Club, Lawyers Club, Harvard Club. Office: Land Title Bldg Ste 2226 100 South Broad St Philadelphia PA 19110 Office Phone: 215-564-6025. Office Fax: 215-557-7651.

BRISCOE, JOHN, lawyer; b. Stockton, Calif., July 1, 1948; s. John Lloyd and Doris (Olsen) B.; m. Carol E. Sayers; children: John Paul, Katherine. JD, U. San Francisco, 1972. Bar: Calif. 1972, U.S. Dist. Ct. (no., ea. and ctrl. dists.) Calif. 1972, U.S. Supreme Ct. 1978, U.S. Ct. Appeals (9th cir.) 1981. Dep. atty. gen. State of Calif., San Francisco, 1972-80; ptnr. Washburn and Kemp, San Francisco, 1980-88, Washburn, Briscoe & McCarthy, San Francisco, 1988—2001, Stoel Rives LLP, San Francisco, 2001—, Briscoe Ivester and Bazel LLP, San Francisco, 2005—. Author: Surveying the Courtroom, 1984, rev. edit., 1999, Falsework, 1997, Tadich Grill, 2002; editor: Reports of Special Masters, 1991; contbr. articles to profl. and lit. jours. Mem.: ABA, Am. Soc. Internat. Law, San Francisco Bar Asn. Roman Catholic. Office: Stoel Rives LLP 111 Sutter St #700 San Francisco CA 94104 Office Phone: 415-617-8903. Business E-Mail: jbriscoe@stoel.com.

BRISCOE, JOHN W., lawyer; BA, Westminster Coll., 1963; JD, U. Mo., 1966. Bar: Mo. Ptnr. Briscoe, Rodenbaugh & Brannon, Hannibal, Mo.; prosecuting atty. Ralls County, Mo. Pres. Mo. Bar, bd. govs., 1990—. Pres. bd. dirs. Barkley Cemetery Assn.; active Boy Scout Am. Troop 106 Com.; bd. dirs. Hannibal C. of C.; active Truman State U. Parents Coun., 1995—97;

apptd. bd. govs. Truman State U., 1997—; active Trinity Episcopal Ch. Mem.: Hannibal Elks Club, New London Lions Club. Office: Briscoe Rodenbaugh & Brannon PO Box 446 423 S Main St New London MO 63459

BRISCOE, MARY BECK, federal judge; b. Council Grove, Kans., Apr. 4, 1947; m. Charles Arthur Briscoe. BA, U. Kans., 1969, JD, 1973; LLM, U. Va., 1990. Rsch. asst. Harold L. Haun, Esq., 1973; atty.-examiner fin. divsn. ICC, 1973—74; asst. U.S. atty. for Wichita and Topeka, Kans. Dept. Justice, 1974—84; judge Kans. Ct. Appeals, 1984—95, chief judge, 1990—95; judge U.S. Ct. Appeals (10th cir.), Topeka, 1995—. Named to Women's Hall of Fame, Univ. Kans., 2001; recipient Univ. Kans. Law Soc. Disting. Alumnus award, 2000. Fellow: Kans. Bar Found., Am. Bar Found.; mem.: ABA, Women Attys. Assn. Topeka, Kans. Bar Assn. (Outstanding Svc. award 1992), Topeka Bar Assn., Nat. Assn. Women Judges, Am. Judicature Soc., U. Kans. Law Soc., Kans. Hist. Soc., Washburn Law Sch. Assn. (hon.). Office: US Ct Appeals 10th Cir 645 Massachusetts Ste 400 Lawrence KS 66044-2235 also: US Ct Appeals 10th Cir Byron White US Courthouse 1823 Stout St Denver CO 80257*

BRISENO, KATHLEEN, education educator; d. Dominick Joseph and Rose Clare Tomaino; m. Jack Richard Briseno, Oct. 21, 1995; children: Matthew, Megan Knops. AA, Wright Coll., Chgo., 1972; BE, Northeastern Ill. Univ., Chgo., 1974; MEd, Northern Ill. Univ., Dekalb, Ill., 1979; EdD, Northen Ill. Univ., Dekalb, Ill., 2001. Cert. tchng. special and elem. edn. Ill. Spl. edn. tchr. Union Ridge Sch. Dist., Harwood Heights, Ill., 1974—79, Roselle (Ill.) Sch. Dist., 1979—80; asst. dir. spl. edn. intern Wheaton (Ill.) Sch. Dist., 1980—81; lectr. Elgin C.C., Ill., 1981; adj. faculty Nat. Coll. of Edn., Evanston, Ill., 1983, Northeastern Ill. Univ., Chgo., 1983—84; supr. student tchrs. Univ. Iowa, Iowa, 1989, Lewis Univ., Romeoville, Ill., 1989; field svc. coord., supr. student tchrs. Loyola Univ. of Chgo., Chgo., 1981—91; faculty North Ctrl. Coll., Naperville, Ill., 1990—93; supr. student tchrs., instr. No. Ill. Univ., Dekalb, Ill., 1991—92, grad. asst., 1992—93; sub. tchr. Woodridge (Ill.) Sch. Dist., 1992—94; resident supr. of student tchr. Western Ill. Univ., Macomb, Ill., 1993—94; program coord. Dekalb County Special Edn. Assn., Dekalb, Ill., 1994—97; part-time faculty Coll. of Dupage, Glen Ellyn, Ill., 1987—; asst. prof. U. Mo., 1996; ctrl. sch. spl. edn. adminstr. Naperville Sch. Dist #203, Naperville, Ill., 1997—. Reviewer and editor Merrill/Macmillan Publ. Co., Columbus, Ohio, 1990—. Author: Fall, 1993, Mandates as Reform: Who's Kidding Whom?, 2001. Legis. designee for cmty. and residential svcs. authority Ill. House of Reps. Mem.: ASCD, Coun. of Exceptional Children, Assn. of Tchr. Educators, Ill. Whole Language, No. Ill. Reading Coun., Internat. Reading Assn., Field Experience Supr. Network, Ill. Alliance of Adminstr. of Spl. Edn., Ronald Mcdonald House, Ray Graham Assn. for People with Disabilities, March of Dimes Birth Defects Found., Little Friends, YMCA, Little City Found., Boys and Girls Clubs of Chgo. Avocations: music, travel, reading. Home: 1821 Princeton Cir Naperville IL 60565 Office: Naperville Cmty Unit Sch Dist #203 203 Hillside Naperville IL 60540 Business E-Mail: kbriseno@ncusd203.org.

BRISKIN, EFREM, music educator; b. Gomel, Belarus, May 13, 1948; arrived in U.S., 1979; s. Semyon Briskin and Tsilia (Lipkina) Briskina; m. Natalya Sloina-Briskin, Aug. 4, 1973; 1 child, Michael. MusB, Leningrad State Conservatory (now St. Petersburg State Conservatory), Russia, 1969, MusM, 1971, DMA, 1973. Mem. piano faculty Petrozavodsk (Russia) Br. of Leningrad State Conservatory, 1972—79, Prep. Ctr. for Performing Arts at Bklyn. Coll., 1980—83, Lucy Moses Sch. for Music and Dance, N.Y.C., 1980—; artistic dir. Summit Music Festival, Tarrytown, NY, 1990—; mem. piano faculty Music Conservatory of Westchester, White Plains, NY, 1991—; dir. Internat. Acad. Music, St. Petersburg, Russia, 2000—. Dir. Dobbs Ferry (N.Y.) Piano Studio, 1996—; mem. Emelin Trio, N.Y.C., 1982—. Concert pianist: nat. and internat. performances, 1972—. Office: Dobbs Ferry Piano Studio 145 Palisade St Dobbs Ferry NY 10522 Office Phone: 914-328-3479. Personal E-mail: musicacad@aol.com.

BRISKIN, MADELEINE, oceanographer, paleontologist; b. Paris, Sept. 4, 1932; came to U.S., 1951, naturalized, 1956; d. Michel and Mina B. BS, CCNY, 1965; MS, U. Conn., 1967; PhD, Brown U., 1973. Prof. geology Geology-Physics Bldg., U. Cin., 1980—. Recipient award Rsch. Support, 1971-72, Support award NSF, 1978. Mem. AAAS, Am. Geophys. Union, Am. Quaternary Assn., Climap, Cin. Engrs. and Scientists Soc., Planetary Soc., Soc. Sci. Exploration, Woods Hole Oceanographic Instn., Lamont-Doherty Geol. Obs., N.Y. Acad. Scis., Sigma Xi. Achievements include discovery of 430,000 plus years astronomical cycle in deep-sea sediments; development of pulsating earth model. Office: U Cin Dept Geology Cincinnati OH 45221-0001

BRISKMAN, LOUIS JACOB, lawyer; b. Jan. 13, 1949; m. Maureen Frances O'Shaughnessy (dec. Mar. 18, 2001). BA, U. Pitts., 1970; JD, Georgetown U., 1973. Bar: Pa. 1973. Joined Westinghouse Electric Corp., 1975, chief counsel, 1978-81; v.p., sec., gen. counsel Group W Cable, Inc. (subsid. Westinghouse), 1981-83; v.p., sec., chief legal officer Group W Broadcasting Co., 1983-86; assoc. gen. counsel energy and advanced tech. & broadcasting divsn. Westinghouse Electric Corp., 1986-87, dep. gen. counsel, 1987-92, sr. v.p., gen. counsel, 1993-98; exec. v.p., gen. counsel CBS Corp., NYC, 1998-2000, gen. counsel, 2005—; exec. v.p., gen. counsel CBS TV, NYC, 2000—04; sr. v.p., gen. counsel Aetna Inc., Hartford, Conn., 2004—05. Bd. regents Georgetown U. Office: Aetna Inc 151 Farmington Ave Hartford CT 06156

BRISKMAN, ROBERT DAVID, engineering executive; b. N.Y.C., Oct. 15, 1932; s. Nathan S. and Rose L. (Fishman) B.; m. Lenora Heffner, Mar. 30, 1957; children: Laura G., Sharon L., Robert D. Jr., Douglas E. BSE, Princeton U., 1954; MS, U. Md., 1961. Registered profl. engr., D.C. Devel. engr. IBM, Poughkeepsie, N.Y., 1954-55; analyst Army Security Agy., Washington, 1956-58; chief of program support tracking and data acquisition NASA, Washington, 1959-63; asst. v.p. domestic systems Communication Satellite Corp., Washington, 1964-72; asst. v.p. space and info. systems Comsat Gen. Corp., Washington, 1973-76; dir. pre-operational program Satellite Bus. Systems, McLean, Va., 1977-79; v.p. systems implementation Comsat Gen. Corp., Washington, 1980-85; sr. v.p. engring. and ops. Geostar Corp., Washington, 1986—90; co-founder, exec. v.p. engring. Sirius Satellite Radio Inc., N.Y.C., 1991—2001, tech. exec., 2001—. Contbr. articles on satellite systems and applications, 1956—; telecommunications editor: McGraw-Hill Ency. Sci. and Tech., 1985—; patentee in field. Capt. U.S. Army, 1955-57. Recipient Founders award Electronics and Aerospace Systems Conf., 1980; named to Soc. Satellite Profls. Internat. Hall of Fame, 2001, Space Found. Technology Hall of Fame, 2002. Fellow AIAA, IEEE (v.p. tech. activities, sec.-treas., 1976-78, Centennial medal, 1984), Washington Acad. Sci., Washington Soc. Engrs. (pres. 1988-89); mem. Old Crows, Internat. Acad. Astronautics, Armed Forces Comm. and Electronics Assn., Internat. Astron. Fedn. (mem. space comms. com. 1989—, chmn. 2004—), Cosmos, Union League Clubs. Republican. Office: Sirius Satellite Radio Inc 1221 Ave of the Americas New York NY 10020 Office Phone: 212-584-5210.

BRISMAN, JENNIFER, event planning executive; BA in Exercise & Sport Sci., George Wash. U. Event planner GANZI Prodns., Prodn. Group Internat., NYC; sr. conf. prodr. Internat. Comm. Mgmt., summit dir. fin., banking & ins. divsn.; founder, pres. jennifer brisman weddings newyork inc., NYC. Mem.: NY Women in Comm. Office: Jennifer Brisman Weddings NY Inc 128 E 62d St No 1 New York NY 10021 Office Phone: 212-588-0007. E-mail: info@theweddingplanner.com.

BRISMAN, LESLIE, English literature educator; b. Bklyn., May 22, 1944; s. Benjamin and Madelein (Taruskin) B.; m. Susan Hawk, Mar. 11, 1973; children: Aviad, Shira. AB, Columbia U., 1965; PhD, Cornell U., 1969. From asst. to assoc. prof. Yale U., New Haven, 1969-79, prof., 1979—. Author: Romantic Origins, 1968, Milton's Poetry of Choice, 1973, The Voice of Jacob, 1990. Home: 5 Woodside Ter New Haven CT 06515-2020

BRISSETTE, MARTHA BLEVINS, lawyer; b. Salisbury, Md., Apr. 30, 1959; d. Reuben Wesley and Miriam Rebecca (Walters) Blevins; m. Henry Joseph Brissette III, May 24, 1980; children: Madeline Rose, William Roy. BA, U. Richmond, 1981, JD, 1983. Bar: Va. 1983, U.S. Supreme Ct. 1987. Law clk. Supreme Ct. Va., Richmond, 1983-84; atty. Dept. Justice, Washington, 1984-88; staff atty. Office of the Exec. Sec., Supreme Ct. Va., Richmond, 1988; asst. atty. gen. Office of the Atty. Gen. of Va., Richmond, 1989-92; atty., v.p. counsel Lawyers Title Ins. Corp., Richmond, 1992-97; asst. counsel State Farm Ins. Cos., 1997-99; asst. atty. gen. Office of Atty. Gen. of Va., Richmond, 1999—2001; pvt. practice Richmond, Va., 2002—05. Assoc. Ukrops Supermarkets, Inc., 2004—. Roman Catholic. Avocation: cake decorating. Home: 8307 Forge Rd Richmond VA 23228-3127

BRISTER, BILL H., lawyer, former bankruptcy judge; b. Sieper, La., Mar. 5, 1930; s. Clayton Houston and Era (Price) B.; m. Carolyn Lee McDowell, June 11, 1955; children— Jeff, Julie. B.S. in Chemistry, Northwestern State U. Natchitoches, La., 1948; J.D., U. Tex., 1958. Bar: Tex. 1957, U.S. Dist. Ct. (no. dist.) Tex. 1959, U.S. Ct. Appeals (5th cir.) 1971, U.S. Supreme Ct. 1971. Pvt. practice, Lubbock, Tex., 1958-79; bankruptcy judge U.S. Dist. Ct. (no. dist.) Tex., 1979-85; of counsel Winstead, Sechrest & Minick and predecessor firm, 1986—. Served to col. USMCR, 1951-52. E-mail: billbrist@aol.com. E-mail: billbrist@aol.com.

BRISTER, SCOTT ANDREW, state supreme court justice; b. Waco, Tex., Jan. 8, 1955; s. Miller Robbins and Annette Josephine (Scott) B.; m. Julia Upton Brister, 4 children. BA summa cum laude, Duke U., 1977; JD cum laude, Harvard U., 1980. Bar: Tex. 1980, U.S. Dist. Ct. (so. dist.) Tex. 1981, U.S. Ct. Appeals 1981 (5th cir.), U.S. Supreme Ct. 1986. Briefing atty. to presiding justice Tex. Supreme Ct., Austin, 1980-81; atty. Andrews & Kurth, Houston, 1981-89; judge 234th Dist. Ct., Harris County, Houston, 1989—98; civil administrative judge Harris County Dist. Ct., 1998—99; justice First Dist. Ct. of Appeals, Houston, 2000—01; chief justice 14th Dist. Ct. of Appeals, 2001—03; interim justice Tex. Supreme Ct., 2000, 2001, justice, 2003—. Former mem. Jud. Panel on Multidistrict Litigation, Supreme Ct. Advisory Com., Supreme Ct. Jury Task Force. Co-author Texas Pretrial Practice; author law review articles in Baylor Law Review, St. Mary's Law Jour. Mem. Phi Beta Kappa; fellow Houston Bar Found., Tex. Bar Found. Office: Tex Supreme Ct 201 W 14th St PO Box 12248 Austin TX 78711

BRISTOL, CAROLYN, retired librarian; b. Jackson, Mich., Sept. 6, 1940; d. Max Delatour and Mary Elisabeth (Grigsby) Strawn; m. William P. Bristol, June, 1962 (div. Aug. 1974); children: Shelley, Steven, Andrew. BA, U. Mich., 1962; MA, We. Mich. U., 1975, MS in Librarianship, 1980. Cert. tchr. K-12 libr. endorsement, Mich. Tchr. English Ypsilanti (Mich.) Jr. High, 1962-63; elem. libr. Kalamazoo (Mich.) Pub. Schs., 1976—80, 1983—97, 2000—01; bookseller Athena Book Shop, Kalamazoo, 1980-83; libr. Kalamazoo Ctrl. High Sch., 1997—2000; ret., 2002. Bd. dirs. Kalamazoo Folklife Orgn., 1999; elder, deacon First Presbyn. Ch., Kalamazoo, 1975-85. Mem. NEA, Mich. Assn. Media in Edn., Kalamazoo Edn. Assn., Mich. Edn. Assn., PEO Sisterhood, Beta Phi Mu. Avocations: growing flowers, reading and discussing books, folk and acoustic music.

BRISTOL, DOUGLAS, lawyer; b. Chgo., Dec. 24, 1943; s. Charles John and Josephine Eva B.; m. Maureen (dec.); 1 child, Katherine. BS, U. Wis., 1966; JD, U. Ill., 1969. Pvt. practice, Chgo. Lectr. in field; adj. prof. Kent Coll. Law. Mem. Am. Immigration Lawyers Assn. (Chgo. chpt. sec. 1987-88, treas. 1988-89, v.p. 1989-90, 1st v.p. 1990-91, pres. 1991-92, co-chmn. liaison to dir. of no. svc. ctr. 1993-94, 96-99, nat. task force 1995, founder, program dir. 1st seminar 1994-95, bd. govs. 1999-2002). Office: 321 S Plymouth Ct Ste 1525 Chicago IL 60604-3958

BRISTOL, NORMAN, lawyer, arbitrator, retired food products executive; b. Bronx, N.Y., June 14, 1924; s. Lawrence and Bell (Allchin) B.; m. Doreen Kingan, Mar. 28, 1952; children: Charles L., Norman, Alexander (dec.), Barnaby. Grad., Phillips Exeter Acad., 1941; AB, Yale, 1944; LLB, Columbia Law Sch., 1949. Bar: N.Y. bar 1950, Mich. bar 1954. Atty. Root, Ballantine, Harlan, Bushby & Palmer, N.Y.C., 1949-53; with Kellogg Co., Battle Creek, Mich., 1954-78, asst. gen. counsel, 1958-64, sec., 1960-78, gen. counsel, 1964-78, sr. v.p., 1968-75, dir., 1972-78, exec. v.p., 1975-78; atty. Howard & Howard, Kalamazoo, 1979-93. Mem. Gull Lake Comty. Schs. Bd. Edn., 1963-70, pres., 1965-67; trustee Kalamazoo Symphony Soc., Inc., 1983-94, pres., 1990-91; bd. dirs. Southwest Mich. Land Conservancy, Inc., 1996-2001. Lt. (j.g.) USNR, 1943-46. Mem. State Bar Mich., Kalamazoo Bar Assn., Am. Soc. Corp. Secs., SCORE (counsellor). Home and Office: 2962 Sylvan Dr Hickory Corners MI 49060-9319

BRISTOW, CLINTON, JR., academic administrator; b. Montgomery, Ala., Mar. 15, 1949; s. T.C. and Betty Bristow; 1 child, Maya. JD, Northwestern U., 1974, PhD, 1977; postgrad., U. Minn., 1983; MBA, Governor's State U., 1984. V.p. adminstrn. Olive-Harvey Coll., Chgo., 1980-81; dean Coll. Bus. Chgo. State U., 1985-93; pres. Chgo. Bd. Edn., 1990-92, Alcorn State U., Lorman, Miss., 1995—. Cons. in field. Contbr. articles to profl. publs. Chmn. Miss. Rhodes Scholarship Com., 1996; bd. dirs. Miss. Agr./Forestry Mus., Jackson, Chgo., Congl. Award Bd., HBCU Capital Fin. Bd.; mem. exec. com. 1890 Coun. Pres. Fellow Northwestern U. Ctr. for Urban Affairs, 1973-74; recipient Role Model award Top Ladies of Distinction, Inc., 1987, Greater Roseland Area Planning, 1990. Mem. Am. Assn. State Colls. and Univs. (state rep.), So. Assn. Colls. and Schs. (exec. com.), Nat. Collegiate Athletic Assn. (bd. of dir.), So. Edn. Found., Miss. Instns. of Higher Learning (coun. of pres.), Southwestern Athletic Conf. (past pres.). Baptist. Avocations: reading, golf, jogging. Home: 1000 Asu Dr # 719 Alcorn State MS 39096-7510 Office: Alcorn State U 1000 DR # 359 Alcorn State MS 39096 Office Phone: 601-877-6111. Business E-Mail: cbristow@alcorn.edu.

BRISTOW, ROBERT O'NEIL, writer, educator; b. St. Louis, Nov. 17, 1926; s. Jesse Reuben and Helen Marjorie (Utley) B.; children by previous marriage— Cynthia Lynn, Margery Jan Wu, Gregory Scott, Kelly Robert; m. Gail Hamiter Rosen, Aug. 25, 2003. BA in Journalism, U. Okla., 1951, MA in Journalism, 1965. Asst. advt. mgr. Altus (Okla.) Times Democrat, 1951-53; free-lance writer Altus, 1951-60; prof. English Winthrop Coll., Rock Hill, S.C., 1960-87, prof. emeritus, 1987—. Author: Time for Glory, 1968, Night Season, 1970, A Faraway Drummer, 1973, Laughter in Darkness, 1974. Served with USNR, 1944-45. Recipient award for lit. excellence U. Okla., 1969, award for novel Friends of Am. Writers, 1974 Mem. Alpha Tau Omega. Home: 613 1/2 Charlotte Ave Rock Hill SC 29730-3648 Personal E-mail: rbristow@cetlink.net.

BRISTOW, WALTER JAMES, JR., retired judge; b. Columbia, S.C., Oct. 14, 1924; s. Walter James and Caroline Belser (Melton) B.; m. Katherine Stewart Mullins, Sept. 12, 1952; children: Walter James III, Katherine Mullins (dec.). Student, Va. Mil. Inst., 1941-43; AB, U. N.C., 1947; LLB cum laude, U. S.C., 1949; LLM, Harvard U., 1950. Mem. Marchant, Bristow & Bates, 1953-76, S.C. Ho. of Reps., 1956-58, S.C. Senate, 1958-76; resident judge 5th Cir. Ct. S.C., 1976-88; ret., 1988. Nat. pres. Conf. Ins. Legislators, 1974—75. Trustee Elvira Wright Fund for Crippled Children, 1963-76; mem. bd. visitors ex officio The Citadel, Charleston, S.C., 1967-76. Served with AUS, 1943-45; ETO, brig. gen. S.C. Army N.G. Decorated Meritorious Svc. medal; recipient Order of Palmetto, 1999, Order of Cypress, 1999. Mem. ABA, Wig and Robe, S.C. Law Inst., S.C. Coun. on Holocaust, Capital City Club, Cotillion Club, Forest Lake Club, Palmetto Club, Columbia Ball Club, Sertoma, Alpha Tau Omega. Democrat. Office: PO Box 1147 Columbia SC 29202-1147

BRISTOW, WILLIAM HARVEY, JR., psychiatrist; b. Harrisburg, Pa. s. William H and Rosa Leah (St Clair) Bristow; m. Lillian H Heise; children: Jill Virginia, Lisa Ann, William H III. AB, Harvard U., 1949; MD, NYU, 1953. Diplomate Am Bd Psychiat and Neurology. Intern 4th Med. divsn. Bellevue Hosp., N.Y.C., 1953—54, resident 4th Med. divsn., 1954—55; resident dept. psychiatry N.Y. VA Hosp., N.Y.C., 1957—60; VA fellow Bellevue Psychiat. Hosp., N.Y.C., 1959—60; pvt. practice Ridgewood, NJ, 1960—. Chmn. dept. psychiat. Bergen Pines County Hosp., Paramus, NJ, 1961; former chmn. dept. psychiat. St. Joseph's Hosp., Wayne, NJ, former pres. med. bd.; former pres. med. bd., clin. dir. Ramapo Ridge Psychiat. Hosp., 1985—98, attending psychiatrist; staff psychiatrist Bergen Regional Med. Ctr., 1998—; mem. emeritus staff Valley Hosp. Fellow: Am. Psychiat. Assn. (life); mem.: AMA, Med. Soc. N.J., NYU-Bellevue Psychiat. Soc., Assn. Convulsive Therapy, N.J. Psychiat. Assn., Bergen County Med. Soc. Congregationalist. Office Phone: 201-967-4000 ext. 5712.

BRITCHER, E. DREW, lawyer; b. Ridgewood, N.J., Apr. 27, 1959; s. Warren Edwin and Dorothy Mae (Lighthiser) B.; m. Elaine M. Westerfield, Sept. 28, 1985; children: Sean Andrew and Caitlin Anne. BA, Rutgers Coll., 1981; JD, N.Y. Law Sch., 1984. Bar: N.J. 1984, U.S. Dist. Ct. N.J. 1984, N.Y. 1985, U.S. Ct. Fed. Claims 1990; cert. civil trial atty. 1994. Ptnr. Britcher, Leone & Roth LLC, Glen Rock, NJ, 2000—. Lectr. in field. Dem. committeeman State of N.J., 1993-97. Mem. ATLA (bd. govs. N.J. 1994—, pres.-elect), N.J. Bar Assn., Am. Coll. Legal Medicine, Phi Delta Phi. Democrat. Presbyterian. Avocations: golf, soccer. Office: Britcher Leone & Roth LLC 175 Rock Rd Glen Rock NJ 07452 Office Phone: 201-444-1644. E-mail: drew@medmalnj.com.

BRITCHER, MICHAEL, music educator; s. Lester and Martha Britcher; m. Michele Hassell, July 17, 1993. BS in Instrumental Music Edn., West Chester (Pa.) U., 1993; MS in Music, So. Oreg. U., 2003. Drill instr. Upper Darby (Pa.) H.S., 1990, Milton Hershey H.S., Hershey, Pa., 1990—91, Pennsville (N.J.) Sr. H.S., 1991; music tchr. James McHenry Elem. Sch., Lanham, Md., 1994, Magnolia Elem. Sch., Seabrook, Md., 1994; band and chorus dir. Thomas Johnson Mid. Sch., Lanham, 1994—95; music tchr. Springfield Elem. Sch., Rileyville, Va., 1995—98, Luray (Va.) H.S., 1995—98, Phoenixville (Pa.) Area H.S., 1998—; music instr. Downingtown (Pa.) Sr. H.S., 1992. Asst. dir. Chester County Concert Band, West Chester, 2000—03; dir. Page Valley Concert Band, Luray, 1996—98; drill designer and music arranger Phoenixville Area H.S., 1989—93. Nominee Am. Tchr. award, Disney, 2003; named Tchr. of Yr., Page Country Pub. Schs., 1997, Dir. of Yr., Cavalcade of Bands Assn., 2003—04; recipient Ray A. Kroc Tchr. Achievement award, McDonald's, 1998, citation of commendation, Pa. Ho. of Reps., 2000, 2001, 2003, 2004. Mem.: Music Educators Nat. Conf., Nat. Educators Assn., Pa. Music Educators Assn. (Dist. 12 v.p. 2003—05), Pa. State Educators Assn., Phoenixville Area Educators Assn., Kappa Kappa Psi (life; pres. and v.p. 1990—92). Avocations: reading, golf, tennis, Aikido, music. Home: 201 Parkview Blvd Spring City PA 19475

BRITO, DAGOBERT LLANOS, economics professor; b. Mex., Apr. 6, 1941; came to U.S., 1945, naturalized, 1958; s. John L. and Guadalupe G. (Llanos) B.; m. Patricia Ann Kendrick, June 29, 1968. BA, Rice U., 1967, MA, PhD, Rice U., 1970. Asst. prof. econs. U. Wis., Madison, 1970-72; asso. prof. econs. and polit. sci. Ohio State U., Columbus, 1972-75, prof., 1976-79; dir. Murphy Inst. Polit. Economy; chmn., prof. econs. Tulane U., New Orleans, 1979-84; Peterkin prof. polit. econs. Rice U., Houston, 1984—. Cons. Dept. State, Dept. Def. Author: A Dynamic Model of the Armaments Race, 1972, Strategic Nuclear Weapons and the Allocation of International Rights, 1977, Conflicts and Outbreak of War, 1985, Stock Externalities, Pigovian Taxation and Dynamic Stability, 1987, Richardsonian Arms Race Models, 1989, On the Limits of Economic Control, 1990, Externalities and Compulsory Vaccinations, 1991, The Economic and Political Incentives to Acquire Nuclear Weapons, 1993; (with M.D. Intriligator) The Economics of Disarmament, Arms Races and Arms Control, 1993, Minimizing the Risks for Accidental Nuclear War: An Agenda for Action, 1993; (with P.R. Hartley) Consumer Rationality and Credit Cards, 1995, Proliferation and the Probability of War: A Cardinality Theorem, 1996, Pricing Natural Gas in Mexico, 2002; editor: Strategies for Managing Nuclear Proliferation, 1983; assoc. editor Jour. Optimization Theory and Applications. Served with U.S. Army, 1963-66. NSF grantee, 1972, 74, 77, 78, 81; Mershon Center grantee, 1973, 78; Rice scholar Baker Inst. Mem. Econometric Soc., Public Choice Soc., Houston Philo. Soc. Office: Rice U PO Box 1892 Houston TX 77251-1892 Office Phone: 713-348-5792. Business E-Mail: brito@rice.edu.

BRITT, CAROL ANN, education educator; b. Houston, Tex., Apr. 8, 1948; d. Willard Ingram and Thelma Victoria Dowling; m. John Baker Britt, Aug. 31, 1968; children: James Austin, Nathan Andrew, John Marshall. BA, SW Tex. State U., 1969—70; MA, St. Mary's U., 1970—72. Tchr. Natalia H.S., Tex., 1971—75; adj. prof. St. Mary's U., San Antonio, 1982; adj. faculty U. of Tex. at San Antonio, 1983—92, Trinity U., San Antonio, 1986; prof. San Antonio Coll., 1992—. Evaluated PTA writing contest PTA, San Antonio, 1996—2003; treas. Daughters of the King Province VII, San Antonio, 2004—; pres., prayer chmn. Daughters of the King, St. Thomas Episcopal Ch., San Antonio, 2003—05. Recipient Outstanding Non-Tenure Track Faculty, U. of Tex. at San Antonio, 1992. Mem.: Conf. on Coll. Tchg. of English, Conf. on Coll. Composition and Commn. Episcopalian. Avocations: sewing, reading, knitting, crocheting. Home: 13907 Rocky Pine Woods San Antonio TX 78249-1830 Office: San Antonio College 1300 San Pedro San Antonio TX 78212 Office Phone: 210-733-2511. Business E-Mail: cbritt@mail.accd.edu.

BRITT, DAVID VAN BUREN, retired educational communications executive; b. Needham, Mass., July 30, 1937; s. Paul and Ellen Britt; m. Marjorie Joan Hoag, Feb. 15, 1958 (div. 1984); children: Pamela, Barbara B. Schaefer, Paul David; m. Sue Cushman, July 22, 1989. AB, Wesleyan U., 1959; MPA, Harvard U., 1967. Ops. mgmt. staff No. Trust Co., Chgo., 1959-62; legis. chief U.S. AID, Washington, 1962-68; chief programs and plans U.S. EEOC, Washington, 1968-69; dep. dir. policy planning U.S. Overseas Pvt. Investment Corp., Washington, 1969-70; ind. cons. Washington, 1970-71; from v.p. to COO Sesame Workshop, N.Y.C., 1971-90, CEO, trustee, 1990-99. Mem. Coun. on Fgn. Rels.; mem. adv. bd. Initiative on Social Enterprise, Harvard Bus. Sch., Hauser Ctr. for Non-Profit Orgns., Kennedy Sch. Govt., Harvard U.; chair bd. dirs. Kids Voting U.S.A., 2002—; trustee New World Found., N.Y.C., 1978—86, Wesleyan U., Middletown, Conn., 1989—92; bd. trustees Edn. Trust, 2005—. Recipient Disting. Alumnus award Wesleyan U., 1994. Episcopalian. Home: 1252 Harrison Point Trail Amelia Island FL 32034 Personal E-mail: dvbbritt@bellsouth.net.

BRITT, EARL THOMAS, lawyer; b. Phila., July 14, 1940; s. Earl Francis and Marie Rita (Lawless) B.; m. Maureen Wong, Dec. 26, 1964; children: Denise, Karen, Eileen, Mary, Kevin, Stephen. AB, St. Joseph's U., Phila., 1961; JD, U. Pa., 1964. Bar: Pa. 1964, U.S. Dist. Ct. (ea. dist.) Pa. 1964, U.S. Ct. Appeals (3rd cir.) 1964, U.S. Dist. Ct. Appeals (D.C. cir.) 1981, U.S. Supreme Ct. 1982. Atty. Pa. Mfrs. Assn. Ins. Co., Phila., 1964-67; assoc. Swartz Campbell & Detweiler, Phila., 1967-68; assoc., then ptnr. Duane Morris & Heckscher, Phila., 1968-92; founder, ptnr., chmn. Britt Hankins & Moughan, Phila., 1992—; judge pro tem Ct. Common Pleas, Phila., 1991—. Lectr. Comey Inst. Indsl. Rels. St. Joseph's U., 1961-92; adj. faculty Temple U. Sch. Law-Acad. Advocacy, 1994—. Mem. adv. bd. Norwood-Fontbonne Acad., 1997-2002. Mem. ABA, Pa. Bar Assn., Phila. Bar Assn. (trustee campaign for qualified judges 1989, hon. trustee 1990-91), Phila. Assn. Def. Counsel (bd. dirs. 1983-89, 93-94, pres. 1988-89), Pa. Def. Inst. (lectr. Trial Acad. 1990—), Internat. Assn. Def. Counsel, Def. Rsch. Inst., Lawyer's Club Phila. (bd. dirs. 1988-90). Republican. Roman Catholic. Home: 106 Sparango Ln Plymouth Meeting PA 19462-1115 Office: Britt Hankins & Moughan 11 E Airy St Norristown PA 19401 Office Phone: 610-277-9633. Business E-Mail: ebritt@britthankins.com.

BRITT, GLENN ALAN, media company executive; b. Hackensack, N.J., Mar. 6, 1949; s. Walter E. Britt and Helen Crupi; m. Barbara Jane Little, Oct. 25, 1975. AB, Dartmouth Coll., 1971, MBA, 1972. Contr.'s asst. Time, Inc., N.Y.C., 1972-74, fin. dir. Iran project, Time-Life Books Alexandria, Va., 1976-78, dir. video group new bus. devel. N.Y.C., 1980-81, sr. v.p. fin. video group, 1984, v.p., treas., 1986-88, v.p., CFO, 1988-90; sr. v.p., treas. Time Warner Inc., N.Y.C., 1990; exec. v.p. Time Warner Cable Group, Stamford, Conn., 1990-92; pres. Time Warner Cable Ventures, Stamford, Conn.,

1992-99, Time Warner Cable, Stamford, 1999—2001, chmn., CEO, 2001—; v.p., treas. Manhattan Cable TV, N.Y.C., 1974-76; v.p. network and studio ops. HBO Inc., N.Y.C., 1978-80, sr. v.p., CFO, 1984-86; sr. v.p. fin. Am. TV and Comm. Corp., Stamford, Conn., 1981-84. Mem. Fin. Exec. Inst., Woodway Country Club, Eastward Ho, Cape Cod National Golf Club and Country Club, Univ. Club. Avocations: skiing, gardening, golf. Office: Time Warner Cable Group 290 Harbor Dr Stamford CT 06902-7475

BRITT, GREG NELSON, music educator; b. Scottsville, Ky., Mar. 25, 1965; s. Glen Nelson and Jehree Spencer Britt. MA in Edn., Western Ky. U., 1993. Elem. music tchr. Warren County Pub. Schs., Bowling Green, Ky., 1992—99; elem. music specialist Plano Ind. Sch. Dist., Plano, Tex., 1999—. Dir. Plano Children's Chorale, Plano, 2000—. Singer Turtle Creek Chorale, Dallas, 1999—2005. Methodist. Home: 5018 N Hall St Dallas TX 75235 Office: Weatherford Elem Sch 2941 Mollimar Dr Plano TX 75075 Office Phone: 469-752-3673. Office Fax: 469-752-3601. Personal E-mail: brittg@sbcglobal.net. E-mail: gbritt@pisd.edu.

BRITT, JOHN ROY, banker; b. L. A., Oct. 9, 1937; s. Roy Arthur and Virginia Alice (Vaughn) B.; children: Jeffrey John, Belinda Lynn, Gregory Scott. BA, Claremont McKenna Coll., 1959; grad., Pacific Coast Banking Sch., U. Wash., 1973, Managerial Policy Inst., U. So. Calif., 1978. Diplomate Am. Bd. Forensic Examiners. With Security Pacific Nat. Bank, 1959-83, asst. v.p. Los Angeles, 1972-74, sr. v.p., 1974-83, adminstr. Mid City-Eastern div., 1978-83; instr. Essentials of Banking Sch., U. Notre Dame, 1979; sr. v.p. Coast Savs. and Loan, Los Angeles, 1983-85; exec. v.p., chief operating officer Pacific Inland Bank, Anaheim, Calif., 1985-86, pres., chief exec. officer, 1986-89; pres. JRB Assocs., 1990—; pres., chief exec. officer United Citizens Nat. Bank, L.A., 1992. Mem. pres.'s adv. coun. Claremont McKenna Coll., 1993; past chmn. bd. dirs., mem. exec. com. Commuter Transp. Svcs., Inc., L.A. Capt. USAR, 1959-67. Mem.: Risk Mgmt. Assn., Am. Coll. Forensic Examiners (bd. cert.). Republican. Methodist.

BRITT, MAISHA DORRAH, protective services official; b. SC; d. Charles Joseph Britt and Versena (Kennedy) Dorrah; m. W. Benjamin Williams, Dec. 14, 1963 (div. June 1976); children: Terri Rochelle, Trina Michelle. AS, BS, Phila Coll. Textiles and Sci.; MA, Antioch U., Phila., 1986; postgrad., Del. State U., 1999; PhD in Bibl. Counseling, Friends Internat. Christian U., Merced, Calif., 2002. Cert. in electronic surveillance. Police officer Phila. Police Dept., 1976-79; sgt., county detective Phila. Dist. Atty's Office, 1979-90; family devel. specialist Norristown Family Ctr., 1994—; orgn. devel. cons., cert. Christian counselor, 2002—. Founder, dir. Creative Awareness Workshop. Poet: (contbr. anthologies) Famous Poems of the Twentieth Century, 1996, Nat. Libr. of Poetry, 1998 (Editor's award). Sec. bd. Horizon House, Phila., 1988—; vol. Women Against Abuse, Phila., 1983—, mem. women's ministry Calvary Bapt. Ch., Dover; trustee Ctr. for Literacy, 1990—, vice chmn.; vol. security team program supr. Atlanta Centennial Olympic Games, 1996; tng. facilatator Ch. Women United-Womens LINC, 1999—; chair Dover Human Rels. Commn., 2002-. Inducted into Murrell Dobbins H.S. Hall of Fame, 1988; named Woman of Yr., Fedn. Bus. and Profl. Women's Clubs Inc., 1991. Mem. AAUW (pres. Dover br. 2002—), Nat. Christian Counselors Assn., County and State Detectives Assn. Pa. (exec. bd. 1990—, Leadership award 1989), Fraternal Order of Police, Internat. Police Assn., Internat. Assn. Women Police (Officer of Yr. 1989), Nat. Women's Hall of Fame, Bus. and Profl. Women's Club, Dover Century Club. Republican. Avocations: music, creative writing, creative dance, walking, photography. Address: PO Box 1381 Dover DE 19903-1381 Office Phone: 302-736-3221. E-mail: mabritt20@comcast.net.

BRITT, MARGARET MARY, finance educator; b. Balt., Jan. 21, 1951; d. Joseph John and Lottie Elizabeth (Zielinski) Britt. BA in Elem. Edn., U. Mass., 1972; BSBA, Boston U., 1979, M in Human Resource Edn., 1990; DBA in Human Resource Mgmt., Nova Southeastern U., 2002. Cert. tchr. elem. edn., music Mass., Va., N.C., vocat. tech. educator in bus. mktg. Mass. Internal auditor Digital Equip. Corp., Maynard, Mass., 1979-82, sr. fin. analyst FDP, 1982-83, sr. fin. analyst sales Stow, Mass., 1983-85, cons. trainer Maynard, 1985-87, fin. cons., trainer, 1987-90, mgr. corp. fin. edn., 1990-94; automated office instr. Mass. Job Tng., Worcester, 1995-97; sci. tchr. Holden Christian Acad., Eastern Nazarene Coll., Worcester, 1997—, instr. dept. bus. Quincy, Mass., 1998-2000, assoc. prof. dept. bus., 2000—02, asst. prof. bus. adminstrn., 2002—; assoc. prof. dept. bus. Mt. Vernon (Ohio) Nazarene U., 2003—. Part-time instr. fin. continuing edn. dept. Syracuse U., 1990—91; adj. prof. bus. Eastern Nazarene Coll., Quincy, Mass., 1994—; bd. dirs. Am. Biog. Inst.; spkr. in field. Sec. Parsons Hill Homeowners Assn., Worcester, 1985—90; presenter time mgmt. workshop MIT-Soc. Women Engrs. and Alumnae, Cambridge, 1988, 1989. Named Outstanding Young Women of Am., 1984. Mem.: AAUW, NAFE, ASTD, Nat. Mus. Women in the Arts, Inst. Internal Auditors. Avocations: walking, reading, singing, cooking. Office: Eastern Nazarene Coll 23 E Elm Ave Quincy MA 02170-2905 Home: 21 Dogwood Ter Mount Vernon OH 43050-1413 Office Phone: 740-392-6868. Business E-Mail: mbritt@mvnu.edu.

BRITT, REBECCA FAE, communications executive; b. Kirksville, Mo., Aug. 23, 1956; d. Aubrey Clarence and Marian LaVeta (Wyatt) Britt; children: Rachel Nicole, Joel Steven. BS in Bus. Mgmt. summa cum laude, Kennesaw State U., 1992. Asst. BellSouth Mobility Inc., Atlanta, 1985-87; mgr. real estate Bell South Mobility, Inc., Atlanta, 1987-91, sr. mgr. real estate and constrn., 1991-94, dir. engring. implementation, 1995—97; dir. real estate and devel. BellSouth Cellular Inc., Atlanta, 1997—98; v.p., gen. mgr. Ga. region Crown Castle Internat., Alpharetta, 1999—2001; pres., founder Britco Mgmt. Svcs., Inc., Woodstock, Ga., 2002—. Mem. Nat. Assn. Corp. Real Estate Execs., Phi Kappa Phi. Republican. Avocations: reading, poetry.

BRITT, RONALD LEROY, retired manufacturing company executive; b. Abilene, Kans., Mar. 1, 1935; s. Elvin E. and Lona H. Britt; m. Judith Ann, June 29, 1957; children: Brett G., Mark D., Melissa A. BSM.E., Wichita State U., 1963. From product engr. to product planner Hotpoint divsn. G.E. Co., Chgo., 1963-68; product planner Norge Co., Chgo., 1968; product mgr., asst. dir. engirng. Leigh Products Inc., Coopersville, Mich., 1968-74; mgr. rsch. and devel. Miami Carey divsn. Jim. Walter Corp., Monroe, Ohio, 1974-84; sr. v.p. mfg. and engring. Belvedere USA Corp., Belvidere, Ill., 1984-2001, ret., 2001. Industry rep. for electric fans Underwriters Labs. Active Boy Scouts Am., 1970-73, PTA, 1973-78; exec. adviser Jr. Achievement, 1984-85, Boone County chmn., 1968-88; bd. dirs. YMCA, Belvidere, 1990-96, vice-chmn., chmn. fin. com., 1991, v.p., 1992; trustee Dickinson County Hist. Soc., 2003—, v.p., bd. dirs. 2004Ø, pres. geneology group, 2004—; dir. on adv. bd. St. Joseph Hosp., 1990-95, 97-99, chmn. long range planning com., 1991; bd. dirs. Boone County Dist. # 100 Edn. Found., 1991-95, Abilene Kans. Airport, 2003—, Abilene City Econ. Devel. Coun., 2003—; bd. dirs. Abilene City Heritage Commn., 2003—, chair, 2005—. Served with U.S. Army, 1958-60 Recipient Inventor's award Gen. Electric Co., 1967. Mem. ASME, Home Ventilation Inst. (engring. com. 1975-84), Belvidere C. of C. (bd. dirs. 1986-89), Air Capital Corvette Club, Air Capital Carnival Glass Club, Rotary (v.p. 1999-2000, sgt.-at-arms 2001-2004, v.p. 2003-04, pres.-elect 2004-05, pres. 2005—, bd. dirs.). Republican. Methodist. Home: 619 NW 3d Abilene KS 67410

BRITTAIN, JAMES EDWARD, science and technology educator, researcher; b. Mills River, N.C., May 20, 1931; s. Randall Francis and Velma Hassie (Gillespie) B.; m. Louise Mary Lambert, March 29, 1969 (dec. Mar. 27, 1972); m. Jo Ann Layne, Apr. 14, 1973. BS, Clemson U., 1957; MS, U. Tenn., 1959; MA, Case Western Res. U., 1969, PhD, 1970. Jr. rsch. engr. U. Tenn., Knoxville, 1958-59; asst. prof. elec. engring. Clemson (S.C.) U., 1959-66; asst. prof. history of sci. and tech. Ga. Inst. Tech., Atlanta, 1969-71, assoc. prof., 1972-91, prof., 1992-94; prof. emeritus, 1994—. Author: Engineering the New South, 1985, Alexanderson: Pioneer in American Electrical Engineering, 1992, Scanning The Past: A History of Electrical Engineering and Its Pioneers, 1999, Gun Fights, Dam Sites and Water Rights, 2001; editor: Turning Points in American Electrical History, 1977. With USAF, 1950-54. Smithsonian Instn. rsch. fellow, 1972-73; recipient rsch. contract Nat. Park Svc., 1974-75; grantee NSF, 1979. Fellow IEEE (chmn. history com. 1978-79, 88-89, assoc. editor proceedings 1990-, Centennial medal 1984), Royal Soc. Arts, Radio Club Am. (Batcher Meml. prize 1989); mem. Soc. History of Tech. (mem. exec. coun. 1978-80, 89-91, Usher prize 1971). Baptist. Avocations: trout fishing, hiking, photography of historical industrial sites. Home: 189 Mountain Valley Dr Hendersonville NC 28739-9723

BRITTEN, ROY JOHN, biophysicist; b. Washington, Oct. 1, 1919; s. Rollo Herbert and Marion Hale B.; m. Jacqueline Reid, 1986 (dec. Sept. 2001); children: Gregory, Kenneth. BS, U. Va., 1941; PhD, Princeton U., 1951. Staff mem. dept. terrestrial magnetism Carnegie Instn., Washington, 1951-89; sr. research assoc. Calif. Inst. Tech., Corona del Mar, 1973-81, disting. Carnegie sr. rsch. assoc. biology, 1981-99, emeritus, 1999—. Adj. prof. U. Calif., Irvine, 1991—; discoverer repeated DNA sequences in genomes of higher organisms. Inventor in field. Named Disting. Carnegie Sr. Research Assoc. in Biology, 1981-99. Fellow Am. Acad. Arts and Scis., AAAS; mem. Nat. Acad. Scis. Office: Calif Inst Tech Kerchkhoff Marine Lab 101 Dahlia Ave Corona Del Mar CA 92625-2814 Business E-Mail: rbritten@caltech.edu.

BRITTENHAM, SKIP, lawyer; b. Port Huron, Mich. BS, USAF Acad., 1963; JD, UCLA, 1970. Bar: Calif. 1971. Sr. ptnr. Ziffren, Brittenham, Branca & Fischer, L.A., 1978—. Office: Ziffren Brittenham Branca Fischer 1801 Century Park W Los Angeles CA 90067-6406

BRITTIN, MARIE E., retired communications, psychology, speech-language and hearing science educator; b. Wichita, Kans. d. F. E. and A. M. Brittin. BS, Northwestern U.; MA, U. Iowa; PhD, Northwestern U. Lic. speech pathologist Ohio, Wash. Instr. U. Wis., Madison, 1950-53; coord. comm. disorders Tacoma Pub. Schs., 1956-64; dir. speech-language and hearing Coll. Edn. Ohio State U., Columbus, 1964-73, assoc. prof. speech-language and hearing sci., 1973-89; ret. Cons. Kent (Wash.) Pub. Schs., 1991; chair Chauncey D. Leake award for excellence in pharmacology, 1978-90; elected mem. compensation and benefits com. Ohio State U., 1985-89; adj. faculty comm. U. Wash., 1994—; adj. prof. U. Puget Sound, U. Wash., Tacoma; cons., spkr., presenter in field Editor: Ohio Jour. Speech and Hearing, 1984-85; author Family Medicine Management, 2005; contbr. articles to profl. jours. Pres., com. chair Zonta Internat., Tacoma, Columbus. Fellow Am. Speech-Lang.-Hearing Assn. (legis. coun. 1989, 90, 91, site visitor 1982-84, Ace award 1986); mem. APA, Internat. Assn. Logopedics and Phoniatrics, AAAS, Nat. Aphasia Assn., PEO, Christian Med. and Dental Assn., Ohio State U. Faculty Women's Club (pres. 1966-67), Pi Lambda Theta (pub. adv. bd. 1983-85), Delta Kappa Gamma (pres. Alpha Tau chpt. 1964, 2002-04), P.E.O. (chaplain 2002-03). Avocations: gardening, photography, biographies. Home: PO Box 1201 Puyallup WA 98371

BRITTIN, RUTH VIRGINIA, music educator, department chairman; d. Anthony N. and Helen Brittin; m. Brian F. Kendrick, Dec. 22, 1990; 1 child, Carolyn Brittin Kendrick. PhD, Fla. State U., Tallahassee, FL, 1989. Chmn. Dept. Music Edn. Syracuse (N.Y.) U., 1989—97, U. of Pacific, Stockton, Calif., 1997—. Contbr. articles to profl. jours. Mem.: Calif. Music Educators Assn. (named Outstanding U. Music Educator 2003). Office: University of the Pacific 3601 Pacific Avenue Stockton CA 95211 Business E-Mail: rbrittin@pacific.edu.

BRITTON, CLAROLD LAWRENCE, lawyer, consultant; b. Soldier, Iowa, Nov. 1, 1932; s. Arnold Olaf and Florence Ruth (Gardner) B.; m. Joyce Helene Hamlett, Feb. 1, 1958; children: Laura, Eric, Val, Martha. BS in Engring., U. Mich., Ann Arbor, 1958, JD, 1961, postgrad. Bar: Ill. 1961, U.S. Dist. Ct. (no. dist.) Ill. 1962, U.S. Ct. Appeals (7th cir.) 1963, U.S. Supreme Ct. 1970, Mich. 1989. Assoc. Jenner & Block, Chgo., 1961-70, ptnr., 1970-88; pres. Britton Info. Systems, Inc., 1991—. Lectr. DePaul U., 1988. Author: Computerized Trial Notebook, 1991, Trial By Notebook, 2002; asst. editor Mich. Law Rev., 1960. Comdr. USNR, 1952-57. Fellow Am. Coll. Trial Lawyers; mem. ABA (litigation sect., antitrust com., past regional chmn. discovery com. 1961), Ill. State Bar Assn. (chmn. Allerton House Conf. 1984, 86, 88, chmn. rule 23 com. 1985-87, chmn. civil practice and procedure coun. 1987-88, antitrust com.), Chgo. Bar Assn. (past chmn. fed. civil procedure com., mem. judiciary and computer law coms., civil practice com.), 7th Cir. Bar Assn., Def. Rsch. Inst. (com. on aerospace 1984), Mich. Bar Assn., Ill. Assn. Trial Lawyers, Order of Coif, Law Club (Chgo.), Racine Yacht Club (Wis.), Macatawa Yacht Club (Mich.), Masons, Alpha Phi Mu, Tau Beta Pi. Republican. Lutheran. Office: 411 E Washington St Ann Arbor MI 48104-2015 Office Phone: 734-747-6449. Personal E-mail: cbritton@brittonis.com. Business E-Mail: Britton@ic.net.

BRITTON, DANIEL ROBERT, art educator, artist; b. Colorado Springs, Colo., Apr. 1, 1949; s. Robert George and Virginia Lee Britton; m. Judith Marion Pechstein; 1 child, Blake Christopher. BFA, U. Colo., 1974, MFA, 1976. Instr. Ariz. State U., Tempe, 1976—78, asst. prof. art, 1979—83, assoc. prof. art, 1983—93, prof. art, 1993—. Represented in permanent collections Biblioteque Nat., Paris, Corooran Mus., Washington, Utah Mus. Fine Arts, Salt Lake City, S.M.O.C.A., Scottsdale, Ariz., Portland Art Mus., Oreg., Haggin Art Mus., Stockton, Calif., Huntsville Me. Art, Ala. With U.S. Army, 1969—71, Vietnam. Home: Chandler AZ 85226 Office: Ariz State Univ Sch Art Tempe AZ 85287

BRITTON, EDWARD CHARLES, lawyer; b. Ft. Collins, Colo., May 18, 1955; s. Charles Cooper and Maxine (Harp) B.; m. Katherine Lela Quainton, Aug. 23, 1986; children: Peter Edward Quainton Britton, Gillian Amanda Oates Britton, Matthew Joseph McDonald Britton. AB, Princeton U., 1977; BA, Oxford U., 1981; JD, Harvard U., 1983. Bar: D.C. 1987. Clk. to chief judge U.S. Ct. Appeals for 4th Cir., Balt., 1983-84; assoc. Ropes & Gray, Boston, 1984-86, Covington & Burling, Washington, 1986-92, ptnr., 1992—. Mem. D.C.Bar. Home: 5000 Glenbrook Rd NW Washington DC 20016-3225 Office: Covington & Burling 1201 Pennsylvania Ave NW Washington DC 20004-2401

BRITTON, ERNEST OTTO, landmark director; b. Cin., Aug. 21, 1959; s. Ernest Wadlington and Vernieda Iva Britton; 1 child, Kai. BA, Ea. Mich. U., 1984, MA, 1990, The Ohio State U., 1997. Program officer Ea. Mich. U., Ypsilanti, Mich., 1987—90; exec. dir. Arts Consortium Cin., 1990—93; exec. asst. to pres. No. Ky. U., Highland Heights, Ky., 1993—98; dir. external affairs Nat. Underground RR, Cin., 1998—. Campaign mgr. State Rep. 30th Dist., Cin., 1996; bd. dirs. Cin. (Ohio) Edging Pig Marathon, 2001—. Recipient Spirit of City award, Cin. (Ohio) Conv. Visitors Bur., 2005, Honorable Mention award, Priveel, 2005. Mem.: Alpha Phi Alpha. Home: 2606 Madison Rd Cincinnati OH 45208 Office: National Underground Railroad Freedom Ctr 50 E Freedom Way Cincinnati OH 45202

BRITTON, M(ELVIN) C(REED), JR., rheumatologist; b. San Francisco, Apr. 11, 1935; s. Melvin Creed and Mathilda Carolyn (Epeneter) B.; m. Mary Elizabeth Phillips, Nov. 2, 1957; children: Elizabeth Carolynne, Lisa Marie. AB, Dartmouth Coll., 1957, MS, 1958; MD, Harvard U., 1960. Diplomate Am. Bd. Internal Medicine, Am. Bd. Rheumatology, Am. Bd. Quality Assurance. Resident Dartmouth Coll. Sch. Medicine, Hanover, N.H., 1964-67; fellow Harvard U. Sch. Medicine, Boston, 1967-69; ptnr. Palo Alto (Calif.) Med. Clinic, 1969—, chmn. dept. medicine, 1990-97. Pres. med. staff Stanford (Calif.) U. Med. Ctr., 1985-87, mem. med. staff bd., 1969-87; bd. dirs. Hosp. Conf. No. Calif., 1988-92, Inst. for Med. Quality, 1998—, treas., 1999-2003, chmn. bd., 2003—; mem. Relative Value Update Commn., 1996— Contbr. articles to med. jours. Pres. Found. for Med. care Santa Clara county, Campbell, 1983-89; mem. Bay Area Lupus Found., 1978—, chmn., 1987-88, 94-95; v.p. Calif. Founds. for Med. Care, 1996, pres., CEO, 1999-2001. Fellow ACP, Am. Coll. Rheumatology (bd. dirs. 1986-89, Paulding Phelps medal 1994, mastership 2000, Disting. Svc. award 2004), Calif. Acad. Medicine (exec. com. 1996-2000, pres. 2001-03); mem. AMA (alt. del. 1988-2003, del. 2003——, chair governing coun., splty. and svcs. soc. 2004—), Calif. Med. Assn., Santa Clara County Med. Soc. (pres. 1980-81, Bd. Svc. award 1988), Arthritis Found. No. Calif. (chmn. bd. dirs. 1984-87, Disting Svc. award 1985), Vintners Club (San Francisco, v.p. 1975-78), Commonwealth Club (San Francisco). Republican. Episcopalian. Avocations: skiing, travel, enology. Office: Palo Alto Med Clinic 795 El Camino Real Palo Alto CA 94301-2726 Office Phone: 650-853-6056. Personal E-mail: rheumdc@aol.com.

BRITTON, REBECCA JOHNSON, lawyer; b. Poughkeepsie, N.Y., Aug. 12, 1963; d. Gustaf Aaron and Muriel Flewelling Johnson; m. John Harold Britton, Aug. 13, 1988; children: Sarah Catherine, Robert Aaron. BA, U. Maine, 1989; JD, Campbell U., 1992. Bar: N.C. 1992, U.S. Dist. Ct. (ea. dist.) N.C. 1992, U.S. Dist. Ct. (mid. dist.) 1995, U.S. Ct. Appeals (4th cir.) 1995, U.S. Supreme Ct. 1998. Paralegal Meiselman, Farber, Poughkeepsie, N.Y., 1982-84; office mgr. Steinberg & Kolb, Poughkeepsie, N.Y., 1984-85; clk. Beaver, Holt, Richardson, Fayetteville, N.C., 1990, assoc., 1992-97, ptnr., 1998—. Adj. prof. Campbell U. Sch. Law, Buies Creek, N.C., 1997—. Coach, atty. advisor Westover High Sch. Trial Team, Fayetteville, 1995—. Democrat. Episcopalian. Avocations: vocalist, gardening. Office: Beaver Holt Richardson 230 Green St Fayetteville NC 28301-5026 E-mail: rjb@bhr-law.com.

BRITTON, THOMAS WARREN, JR., retired management consultant; b. Pawhuska, Okla., June 16, 1944; s. Thomas Warren and Helen Viola (Haynes) Britton; m. Jerlyn Kay Davis, 1964 (div. 1970); 1 child, Natalie Dawn; m. Deborah Ann Mansour, Oct. 20, 1973; 1 child, Kimberly Ann. BSME, Okla. State U., 1966, MS in Indsl. Engring. and Mgmt., 1968. Cons. Arthur Young & Co., LA, 1968—72, mgr., 1972—76, prin., 1976—79, ptnr., 1979—88, office dir. mgmt. svcs. dept. Orange County, Calif., 1979—88; ptnr. Price Waterhouse, LA, 1988—95, ptnr.-in-charge West Coast Nat. Aerospace and Def. Industry practice, 1988—95, west coast mfg. and logistics practice, 1988—95; ptnr., chmn. US MCS Tech. Industry Practice Pricewaterhouse-Coopers, LA, 1995—2000, chmn. Global MCS Tech. Industry Practice, 1995—2000, COO MCS west bus. unit, chmn. global MCS tech. industry practice, 2000—02; ret., 2002. Lectr. in field. Mem. creative growth bd. City of San Dimas, Calif., 1976—77, chmn. Planning Commn., 1977—83; trustee World Affairs Coun. Orange County, 1980; v.p. ann. fund, pres., chmn. long range planning, bd. pres. South Coast Repertory Theater, 1982—92; trustee Providence Speech and Hearing Ctr., 1985—90, Spl. Olympics So. Calif., 1995—97; mem. devel. com. U. Calif.-Irvine Med. Sch.; chmn. Costa Mesa Arts Coun., 1984. Capt. USAR, 1971—86. Mem. LA Inst. CPAs, Mgmt. Adv. Svcs. Com., Am. Prodn. and Inventory Control Soc., Am. Inst. Indsl. Engrs., Greater Irvine Indsl. League, Okla. State U. Alumni Assn., Jonathan Club, Ridgeline Country Club, Santa Ana Country Club, Kappa Sigma. Home: 9881 Orchard Ln Villa Park CA 92861-3105 Personal E-mail: tom_britton@msn.com.

BRITZ, JOHN DOMINIC, II, political scientist, consultant; b. Pueblo, Colo., Oct. 5, 1961; s. John Dominic and Frances Ann (Krasouec) B.; m. Betsy Anne Britz, June 24; children: Samantha, Mallory. BA, U. Denver, 1985. Polit. cons. Monaghan & Assocs., Denver, 1987-89; dep. campaign mgr. Citizens for Denver's Future, 1989-90; exec. dir. House Dem. Majority Fund, Denver, 1990-91; campaign mgr. Welchert for Auditor, Denver, 1991; v.p. Welchert & Britz, Inc., Denver, 1991—. Lectr. in field. Contbr. numerous articles to profl. jours.; author tng. manuals. Mem. Denver Met. Wastewater Bd., 1998—; mem. Denver Cmty. Leadership Forum, 1993. Recipient Friend of Pub. Edn. award Phi Delta Kappa, 1999. Mem. Am. Assn. Polit. Cons. Democrat. Roman Catholic. Avocations: skiing, weightlifting, watercolor painting, drawing, fishing. Office: Welchert & Britz Inc 1701 Wynkoop St Ste 215 Denver CO 80202 Office Phone: 303-615-9725. E-mail: john@welchertandbritz.com.

BRITZ, ROBERT G., stock exchange executive; BS in Fin., Manhattan Coll.; cert. advanced mgmt., Harvard Sch. Bus. Joined NY Stock Exch., 1972, held various mgmt. positions, including mng. dir. corp. bus. devel., v.p. new listings and client svc., 1972—95, group exec. v.p., 1995—2002, pres., co-COO, exec. vice chmn., 2002—, mem. office chmn., co-chair mgmt. com. Bd. dirs. The Stanley Works; mem. office chmn. NY Stock Exch., co-chair mgmt. com.; chmn. Securities Industry Automation Corp., Sector, Inc.

BRITZ LOTTI, DIANE EDWARD, investment company executive; b. York, Pa, June 15, 1952; d. Everett Frank and Billie Jacqueline (Sherrill) Britz; m. Marcello Lotti, Sept. 9, 1978 (dec. Apr. 1990); children: Ariane Elizabeth Lotti, Samantha Alexis Lotti. BA, Duke U., 1974; MBA, Columbia U., 1982. Asst. mgr. Columbia Artists, N.Y.C., 1974-76; gen. mgr. Ea. Music Festival, Greensboro, NC, 1977-78; v.p. Britz Cobin, N.Y.C., 1979-82; pres. Pan Oceanic Mgmt., Inc., 1983-90, Pan Oceanic Advisors, Ltd., 1988-94; chair Pan Oceanic Mgmt. Ltd., 1994-2001; mng. dir. Am. Capital Ptnr., Ltd., 1996—, Erafo Ltd., 2000—; chmn. Trinity Investors Fund Inc.; founding ptnr. Circle Fin. Group LLC, 2003—, vice chmn., 2003—. Bd dirs Trinity Investors Fund Inc, Cir. Fin. LLC. Bd. advisors Turtle Bay Music Sch.; pres. Marcello Lotti Found.; mem. Nat. Com. Am. Fgn. Policy; bd. dirs. exec. com. Am. Acad. in Rome; chair Trinity bd. visitors Duke U. Mem.: Explorers Club (friend), Doubles Club, Columbia Bus Sch Club NY. Mem. Soc. Of Friends. Office: Circle Financial 17th Fl 650 Madison Ave New York NY 10022

BRIZEL, MICHAEL ALAN, lawyer; b. Monticello, N.Y., Jan. 6, 1957; s. Irving and Ruth (Marcus) B.; m. Judith Schwartz, Nov. 1, 1992. BS in Indsl. and Labor Relations, Cornell U., 1977, JD, 1980. Bar: N.Y. 1981, U.S. Dist. Ct. (ea. and so. dists.) N.Y., U.S. Ct. Appeals (6th cir.). Assoc. Burns, Summit, Rovins & Feldesman, N.Y.C., 1980-83; labor atty. Gen. Foods Corp., White Plains, NY, 1983-84, sr. labor atty., 1984-86, labor counsel, 1986-87, counsel external devel., 1987-89; sr. atty. Reader's Digest Assn., Inc., Pleasantville, NY, 1989-90, assoc. gen. counsel, 1990-96, v.p. U.S. legal affairs, assoc. gen. counsel, 1996—98, v.p., gen. counsel, 1998—2002, sr. v.p., gen. counsel, 2002—. Arbitrator small claims ct. City of White Plains, 1985-87; vis. bd. mem. Pace Law Sch., 2002-. Bd. dirs., pres. 510 E 86th St. Owners, Inc., 1985-86. Mem. ABA, N.Y. State Bar Assn. Home: 1215 Fifth Ave Apt 166 New York NY 10029 Office: Readers Digest Assn Readers Digest Rd Pleasantville NY 10570 Office Phone: 914-244-5069. Business E-Mail: michael.brizel@rd.com.

BRIZZOLARA, CHARLES ANTHONY, lawyer, director; b. Chgo., Nov. 20, 1929; s. Ralph D. and Florence H. (Hurley) B.; m. Audree Doyle, Aug. 24, 1968. BA, Lake Forest (Ill.) Coll., 1951; JD, Ill. Inst. Tech., 1957. Bar: Ill. 1959. Practiced law, Chgo., 1959-67; with Walter E. Heller & Co., also Walter E. Heller Internat. Corp. (later Amerifin Corp.), Chgo., 1967-85; v.p., sec., gen. counsel Walter E. Heller & Co., also Walter E. Heller Internat. Corp., 1974-85, sr. v.p., 1980-85; v.p. Chgo. Bears Football Club, Inc., 1975-88; mem. firm Chadwell & Kayser Ltd., 1985-90; ptnr. Michael Best & Friedrich, LLC, Chgo., 1990—2002; of counsel Berger, Newmark and Fenchel P.C., Chgo., 2003—04, Kane, Carbonara & Mendoza, Chgo., 2004—. Bd. dirs. Abacus Real Estate Fin. Co., Walter E. Heller & Co. S.E., Heller Factoring (Hong Kong) Ltd., Factoring Serfin, S.A., Chandler Leasing Corp., 1975-80; lectr. seminars Am. Mgmt. Assn. Editor: Chgo.-Kent Law Rev, 1956. Bd. dirs. Cath. Charities Archdiocese of Chgo., 1978-99, sec., 1991-94; bd. dirs. Ill. Inst. Tech. Chgo. Kent Alumni Assn., 1980-89. Served with AUS, 1952-54. Mem. Internat. Bar Assn., Ill. Bar Assn. Roman Catholic. Home: Apt 20G 253 E Delaware Pl Chicago IL 60611-1758 Office: 1 N Franklin St Chicago IL 60601 Office Phone: 312-726-2322.

BRO, RUTH HILL, lawyer; b. Brookings, SD, July 9, 1962; BA, Northwestern U., 1984; JD, U. Chgo., 1994. Atty. McBride Baker & Coles (now Holland & Knight), 1994—99, Baker & McKenzie, Chgo., 1999—2001, ptnr., 2001—. Editor: The E-Bus. Legal Arsenal: Practitioner Agreements and Checklists, 2004; co-author: Online Law, 1996, 6th edit., 2000; mem. editl. bd.: mag. The SciTech Lawyer, ABA, 2004—; contbr. articles to profl. jours. Mem.: ABA (co-chmn. e-privacy law com., mem. coun., sci. and tech. law section, info. security com.), Ill. Bar Assn., Chgo. (Ill.) Bar Assn. (computer law com.). Office: Baker & McKenzie One Prudential Plz 130 East Randolph Dr Chicago IL 60601 Office Phone: 312-861-7985. Business E-Mail: bro@bakernet.com.

BRO, WILLIAM PRICE, communications executive; b. Evanston, Ill., Apr. 7, 1946; s. Kenneth Arthur and Patricia (Welch) B.; m. Johanna Ellen Hintze, Apr. 9, 1986; children: Ellen Price, John Kenneth. BS in Bus. Mgmt. with honors, U. Phoenix, 1998. Licensed 1st class radiotelephone, FCC. Meteorologist WISN-TV, Milw., 1968-69; ops. mgr. WXCL Radio, Peoria, Ill., 1969-80; pres. Broadcast Assoc., Inc., Springfield, Ill., 1980-82, PSR Corp., Peoria, 1982-94; news anchor WHOI-TV, Peoria, 1984; pres. High Point Group, Inc., Peoria, 1994—. Advisor minority-owned radio, Peoria, 1993-96. Co-author (radio play) Peoria's War of the Worlds, 1972; author (text) How to Become an Announcer, 1973. Mem. Rep. Nat. Com., 1995-96; treas. pack 4 Cub Scouts Am., Peoria, 1996; mem. bd. Peoria Civic Opera, 1983-84; chmn. Nat. Kidney Cancer Assn., 1998—; exec. com. Ill. Valley Power Squadron, 1998—. Recipient Past Pres.'s award Peoria Heights C. of C., 1991. Mem. Peoria Radio Orgn. (founding mem.), Exptl. Aircraft Assn., Aircraft Owners and Pilots Assn., Cherokee Pilots' Assn., Rotary Club Peoria-North (sec. 1991-92), Willow Knolls Country Club (bd. dirs. 1998), Phi Theta Kappa. Republican. Unitarian Universalist. Avocations: flying, camping, boating. Home: 1013 Randolph St Winnetka IL 60093-1439

BROAD, ELI, finance company executive; b. N.Y.C., June 6, 1933; s. Leon and Rebecca (Jacobson) B.; m. Edythe Lois Lawson, Dec. 19, 1954; children: Jeffrey Alan, Gary Stephen. BA in Acctg. cum laude, Mich. State U., 1954. CPA, Mich. 1956. Cert. public acct., 1954-56; asst. prof. Detroit Inst. Tech., 1956; co-founder, chmn., pres., CEO SunAmerica Inc. (formerly Kaufman & Broad, Inc.), L.A., 1957-2001; chmn. SunAmerica Inc. (formerly Kaufman & Broad, Inc., now AIG Retirement Svcs. Inc.)), 2001—, Nat. Anchor Nat. Life Ins. Co., First SunAmerica Life Ins. Co., CalAmerica Life Ins. Co., Kaufman and Broad Home Corp., L.A., 1989-93, chmn. exec. com., 1993-95; founder, chmn. Kaufman and Broad Home Corp. (now KB Home), L.A., 1993—. Chmn. Stanford Ranch Co.; mem. exec. com. adv. bd. Fed. Nat. Mortgage Assn., 1972-73; active Calif. Bus. Roundtable, 1986-2000; co-owner Sacramento Kings and Arco Arena, 1992-99; trustee Com. for Econ. Devel., 1993-95; mem. real estate adv. bd. Citibank, N.Y.C., 1976-81; bd. dirs. Am. Internat. Group, Inc., L.A. Bus. Advisors, Sacramento Kings and ARCO Arena; co-owner Sacramento Kings & Arco Arena, 1992-99. Mem. bd. dirs. L.A. World Affairs Coun., 1988—, chmn., 1994-97, DARE Am., 1989-95, hon. mem. bd. dirs. 1995—; founding trustee Windward Sch., Santa Monica, Calif., 1972-77; bd. trustees Pitzer Coll., Claremont, Calif., 1970-82, chmn. bd. trustees, 1973-79, life trustee, 1982—, Haifa U., Israel, 1972-80, Calif. State U., 1978-82, vice chmn. bd. trustees, 1979-80, trustee emeritus, 1982—, Mus. Contemporary Art, L.A., 1980-93, founding chmn., 1980, Archives Am. Art, Smithsonian Instn., Washington, 1985-98, Am. Fedn. Arts, 1988-91, Leland Stanford Mansion Found., 1992—, Calif. Inst. Tech., 1993—, Armand Hammer Mus. Art and Cultural Ctr. UCLA, 1994-99; pres. Calif. Non-Partisan Vote Registration Found., 1971-72; chancellor's assoc. UCLA, 1971—, mem. vis. com. Grad. Sch. Mgmt., 1972-90, trustee UCLA Found., 1986-96, exec. com. bd. visitors Sch. of the Arts & Architecture, 1997—; assoc. chmn. United Crusade, L.A., 1973-76; chmn. Mayor's Housing Policy Com., L.A., 1974-75; del., spkr. Fed. Econ. Summit Conf., 1974, State Econ. Summit Conf., 1974; mem. contemporary coun. L.A. County Mus. Art, 1973-79, bd. trustees acquisitions com., 1978-81, trustee, 1995—; bd. fellows, mem. exec. com. The Claremont (Calif.) Colls., 1974-79; nat. trustee Balt. Mus. Art, 1985-91; mem. adv. bd. Boy Scouts Am., 1982-85, L.A. Bus. Jour., 1986-88; mem. adv. coun. Town Hall of Calif., 1985-87; trustee Dem. Nat. Com. Victory Fund, 1988, 92, 96; mem. painting and sculpture com. Whitney Mus., N.Y.C., 1987-89; chmn. adv. bd. ART/LA, 1989; bd. overseers The Music Ctr. of L.A. County, 1991-92, mem. bd. govs., 1996-98; mem. contemporary art com. Harvard U. Art Mus., Cambridge, Mass., 1992—; mem. internat. dirs. coun. Guggenheim Mus., N.Y.C., 1993-98; trustee Mus. Modern Art, N.Y.C.; active Nat. Indsl. Pollution Control Coun., 1970-73, Maeght Found., St. Paul de Vence, France, 1975-80, Mayor's Spl. Adv. Com. on Fiscal Adminstrn., L.A., 1993-94; bd. dirs. UCLA/Armand Hammer Mus. Art And Cultural Ctr., 1994-1999. Recipient Man of Yr. award City of Hope, 1965, Golden Plate award Am. Acad. Achievement, 1971, Housing Man of Yr. award Nat. Housing Coun., 1979, Humanitarian award NCCJ, 1977, Am. Heritage award Anti Defamation League, 1984, Pub. Affairs award Coro Found., 1987, Honors award visual arts L.A. Arts Coun., 1989; Eli Broad Coll. Bus. and Eli Broad Grad. Sch. Bus. named in his honor Mich. State U., 1991; Edythe and Eli Broad Art Ctr. named in his honor at UCLA; knighted Chevalier in Nat. Order Legion of Honor, France, 1994; recipient lifetime achievement award L.A. C. of C., 1999, visionary award Harvard Bus. Sch. Assn. So. Calif., 1999, Julius award U. So. Calif. Sch. Policy, Planning and Devel., 2001, Chmn.'s award Asia Soc. So. Calif., 2000, Visionary award KCET, 1999, Teach for Am. Ednl. Leadership award, 2001, Exemplary Leadership in Mgmt. award, UCLA, The Anderson Sch., 2002, The Alexis de Tocqueville award, United Way, 2002; Fellow Am. Acad. Arts and Scis., 2001, named one of Top 200 Collectors, ARTnews Mag., 2004. Fellow AAAS; mem. Beta Alpha Psi, Regency Club, Hillcrest Country Club (L.A.), California Club. Avocation: Collecting contemporary art. Office: Broad Foundation Ste 1200 10900 Wilshire Blvd Los Angeles CA 90024 Office Fax: 310-954-5051.*

BROAD, MARGARET CORBETT (MOLLY BROAD), academic administrator; b. Wilkes-Barre, Pa., Feb. 22, 1941; d. Stanley A. and Margaret (Kelly) Corbett; m. Robert William Broad, Aug. 25, 1962; children: Robert W. Jr., Matthew David. BA in Econs., Syracuse U., 1962, postgrad., 1971; MA in Econs., Ohio State U., 1965. Rsch. assoc. to comptr., v.p. finance Ohio State U., Columbus, 1963—65; budget and planning officer Syracuse U., NY, 1971—76; dep. dir. State Commn. Future of Postsecondary Edn. in N.Y., Albany, 1976—77; v.p. govt. and corp. rels. Syracuse U., 1977—85; exec. dir., chief exec. officer Ariz. Bd. Regents, Phoenix, 1985—92; sr. vice chancellor adminstrn. and fin. Calif. State U., 1992—93, exec. vice chancellor, COO, 1993—97; chair bd., CEO Calif. State U. Inst., 1994—97; pres. U. N.C., Chapel Hill, 1997—. Mem.: Beta Gamma Sigma, Phi Beta Kappa. Roman Catholic. Avocations: tennis, bicycling, gardening. Home: 400 E Franklin St Chapel Hill NC 27514-3707 Office: U NC Gen Adminstrn Bldg 910 Raleigh Rd Chapel Hill NC 27514-3916

BROAD, MATTHEW, lawyer; m. Cathy Broad; children: Ben, Sarah. BA bus. econ., U. Calif. Santa Barbara, 1981; JD, Hastings College of Law, 1984. Counsel-leg. dept. Boise Cascade Corp., Boise, Ill., 1984—89, assoc. gen. counsel, 1989—2004; corp. sec. OfficeMax Inc. (formerly Boise Cascade Corp.), 1989—, exec. v.p., gen. counsel, 2004—. Office: OfficeMax Inc 150 E Pierce Rd Itasca IL 60143

BROAD, MOLLY CORBETT, academic administrator; m. Robert Broad; children: Robert Jr., Matthew. BA in Econs., Syracuse U., NY, 1962, postgrad.; MA in Econs., Ohio State U., 1965; LittD (hon.), U. So. Queensland, Australia, 2000; LLD (hon.), U. Notre Dame, 2003. Budget analyst, rsch. assoc. Office of Comptr., v.p. fin. Ohio State U., Columbus, 1963—65; mgr. Office Budget and Planning, dir. Instl. Rsch. Syracuse U., 1971—76, v.p. govt. and corp. rels., 1977—85; dep. dir. NY State Commn. Future Postsecondary Edn., Albany, NY, 1976—77; exec. dir., CEO Ariz. Bd. Regents, Tuscon, 1985—92; sr. vice chancellor adminstrn. and fin. Calif. State U., Long Beach, 1992—93; pres. U. NC, Chapel Hill. Mem. bd. trustees Nat. Humanities Ctr., Research Triangle Park; hon. mem. Chapel Hill Preservation Soc., 1997; mem. bd. advisors NC Blumenthal Performing Arts Ctr.; 2000 campaign chairperson Rsch. Triangle United Way, Morrisville, NC. Named Disting. Alumna, Syracuse U.; recipient Woman of Achievement award, Syracuse, 1979, 1990 Leadership Am. award, Leadership Am., 1990, Ann. award, Leadership Calif., 1996, Arents award, Syracuse U., 1999, Tar Heel of Yr. award, U. (Chapel Hill) NC, 2001, Woman of Achievement award, Gen. Fedn. Women's Clubs (Raleigh) NC, Inc., 2003, Alexander Meiklejohn award, AAUP, 2003; fellow, Ohio State U., Syracuse U.; GM scholar. Mem.: Nat. Assn. Sys. Heads (exec. com.), Nat. Assn. State Univs. and Land-Grant Colls. (chairs info. tech, coun. of pres., bd. dirs., mem. various commns., couns., and adv. bds.), Nat. Assn. Coll. and U. Bus. Officers (adv. coun.), Microelectronics Ctr. NC (bd. dirs.), Mellon Found. (adv. bd. tech.), James B. Hunt, Jr. Inst. Ednl. Leadership and Policy (bd. dirs.), Coun. on Competitiveness (exec. com. US-Ireland bus. coalition), UNC Ctr. Pub. TV (bd. of trustees), UNC Health Care Sys. (exec. com., compensation com., bd. dirs.), U. Corp. Advanced Internet Devel. (chair emeritus, bd. dirs.), TransAtlantic Commn. Ethnicity, Race, Immigration, and Citizenship, State Higher Edn. Exec. Officers, Bus. Higher Edn. Forum (exec. com.), Rsch. Triangle Inst. (bd. govs.), Rsch. Triangle Found. (bd. dirs.), Partnership Pub. Svc. (adv. bd. govs.), Parson's Corp. (bd. dirs.), NC Inst. Medicine, NC Econ. Devel., NC Bd. Sci. and Tech., NC Biotech. Ctr. (bd. dirs.), NC Arboretum (bd. dirs.), Nat. Survey Student Engagement (exec. com.), Assn. Governing Bds. (coun. pres.), Order of Grail Valkyries, Phi Beta Kappa, Phi Kappa Phi, Golden Key, Omnicron Chi Epsilon, Beta Gamma Sigma, Eta Pi Epsilon. Home: 400 East Franklin St Chapel Hill NC 27514 Office: U NC PO Box 2688 Chapel Hill NC 27515-2688 Office Phone: 919-962-1000. Business E-Mail: mbroad@northcarolina.edu.

BROAD, WILLIAM J., science writer; b. Milw. married; 3 children. BA, Webster Coll., 1973; M in History of sci., Univ. Wis. High sch. sci. teacher, Milwaukee; writer Science mag.; with NY Times, 1983—. Author: (books) Betrayers of the Truth: Fraud and Deceit in the Halls of Science, 1983, Claiming the Heavens, 1988, Teller's War: The Top-Secret Story Behind the Star Wars Deception, 1992, Star Warriors: A Penetrating Look into the Lives of the Young Scientists Behind Our Space Age Weaponry, 1993, The Universe Below, 1993, Alien Lair, 2002; co-author: Germs: Biological Weapons and America's Secret War, 2001. Co-recipient two Pulitzer Prizes; recipient Disting. Svc. award, Univ. Wis.-Madison, 1995. Office: Science Writer New York Times 229 W 43rd St New York NY 10036

BROADBEAR, JILLIAN HELEN, medical researcher; b. Melbourne, Victoria, Australia, Dec. 24, 1966; d. William Bevis Broadbear and Patricia Helen Jose; m. John Matthew Cookson, Mar. 13, 1992; children: Kathryn Anita Cookson, Sophia Rose Cookson, James Christopher Cookson. BSc, Monash U., Clayton, Victoria, 1987; MSc, U. Mich., 1995, PhD, 1999. Rsch. asst. Austin Hosp., Melbourne U., Heidelberg, 1988—91, U. Mich., Ann Arbor, 1991—93, post-doctoral fellow, 1999—2001; sr. rsch. officer Monash U., Clayton, 2002—04, lectr., 2005—. Recipient Young Investigator Award, Internat. Soc. PsychoNeuroEndocrinology, 1998, Early Career Investigator Award, Coll. on Problems of Drug Dependence, 2001. Mem.: Endocrine Soc. Australia, Internat. Study Group Investigating Drugs As Reinforcers, Soc. for Neuroscience. Achievements include first to report endocrine changes in non-human primates in response to drug self-administration; demonstrated that cocaine-maintained behaviour is not affected when increases in stress hormone levels are blocked in non-human primates. Avocations: history, bushwalking, swimming, reading. Office: Monash Univ Wellington Rd Victoria Clayton 3800 Australia Office Phone: 011-61-3-9905-3903. Office Fax: 011-61-3-9905-3948. Personal E-mail: jillian.broadbear@med.monash.edu.au.

BROADBENT, AMALIA SAYO CASTILLO, graphic arts designer; b. Manila, May 28, 1956; came to U.S., 1980, naturalized, 1985; d. Conrado Camilo and Eugenia de Guzman (Sayo) Castillo; m. Barrie Noel Broadbent, Mar. 14, 1981 (div. Apr. 1999); children: Charles Noel Castillo, Chandra Noel Castillo. BFA, U. Santo Tomas, 1978; postgrad., Acad. Art Coll., San Francisco, Alliance Francaise, Manila, Karilagan Finishing Sch., Manila Computer Ctr.; BA, Maryknoll Coll., 1972. Designer market rsch. Unicorp Export Inc., Makati, Manila, 1975-77; asst. advt. mgr. Dale Trading Corp., Makati, 1977-78; artist, designer, pub. rels. Resort Hotels Corp., Makati, 1978-81; prodn. artist CYB/Young & Rubicam, San Francisco, 1981-82; freelance art dir Ogilvy & Mather Direct, San Francisco, 1986; artist, designer, owner A.C. Broadbent Graphics, San Francisco, 1982—. Faculty graphic design and advt. depts. Acad. Art Coll., San Francisco. Works include: Daing na Isda, 1975, (Christmas coloring) Pepsi-Cola, 1964 (Distinctive Merit cert.), (children's books) UNESCO, 1973 (cert.). Pres. Pax Romana, Coll. of Architecture and Fine Arts, U. Santo Tomas, 1976-78, chmn. cultural sect., 1975; v.p. Atelier Cultural Soc., U. Santo Tomas, 1975-76; mem. Makati Dance Troupe, 1973-74; vol. spl. events San Francisco Mus. of Modern Art. Recipient Merit cert. Inst. Religion, 1977. Mem. Alliance Francaise de San Francisco. Roman Catholic. Office: 4380A Eagle Peak Rd Concord CA 94521-3427 Personal E-mail: amybroadbent@comcast.net.

BROADBENT, ARTHUR, III, music educator; b. Hot Springs, Ark., July 29, 1958; s. Arthur Broadbent, Jr. and Blanche Broadbent. MusB Edn., Ouachita Bapt. U., 1976—80, MusM Edn., 1980—82. Lic. postgraduate profl. lic. State Bd. Edn., Commonwealth Va., 2002. Soloist/asst. dir. chancel choir First Presbyn. Ch., Norfolk, Va.; choral dir. J. A. Fair Jr./Sr. H.S., Little Rock, 1982—83, Norview Mid. Sch., Norfolk, 1984—98, Lake Taylor H.S., Norfolk, 1999—. Co-chair, all-city mid. sch. chorus Norfolk Pub. Schools, 1986—91; chair, dist. auditions VA-ACDA, Dist. II, Norfolk, 1996; chmn., dist. ii Va. Music Educators Assn., 1997—2000; chair, all-state auditions VA-ACDA Dist. II, 1997—2001; publicity/pub. rels. chair, Va. music camp 2003 Va. Music Educators Assn., 2002—. Singer: (professional core & soloist) Virginia Symphony Chorus, (opera chorus) Virginia Opera Chorus, (singer & soloist) The Virginia Chorale. Artistic com./singer rep. The Va. Chorale, Norfolk, 1996—99; artistic/edn. com. Va. Childrens Chorus, Norfolk, 1998—2000; chorus rep. Va. Opera Chorus, Norfolk, 1992—94. Mem.: Am. Fedn. Tchrs., Chorus Am., Va. Choral Directors Assn., Am. Choral Directors Assn., Music Educators Nat. Conf., Pi Kappa Lambda, Nat. Music Honor Soc., Phi Mu Alpha, Sinfonia. Home: 159 W Seaview Ave Norfolk VA 23503 Office: Norview Middle Sch 6325 Sewells Point Rd Norfolk VA 23513 Personal E-mail: baritone4u@cox.net.

BROADBENT, J. STREETT, engineering executive; b. Balt., Nov. 15, 1942; s. Walter Scott and Mabel Naomi (House) B.; m. Barbara Bea Petschke, Aug. 14, 1965; children: Kenneth Streett, Sandra Lynn. AB in Physics, Western Md. Coll., Westminster, 1964; postgrad., Johns Hopkins U., 1969-75. Applied research engr. Black & Decker, Towson, Md., 1964-67, instrumentation engr., 1967-68, test supr., test mgr., 1969-76, resident engring. mgr. Hampstead, Md., 1976-79, engring. mgr., 1979-84; real estate sales rep. Broadbent Realty, Reisterstown, Md., 1972-76; engring. mgr. Black & Decker, Towson, Md., 1985-94, sr. tech. mgr., 1994-96, sr. support sys. mgr., 1996-97; dir. Engring. Tech., 1997—2003; pres./owner Easy Streett Enterprises, LLC, Reisterstown, Md., 2003—; ptnr. Advancing Partnerships Consortium, Reisterstown, Md., 2003—04; sales rep. Bankers Life & Casualty, 2004. Treas. Greenbrier Improvement Assn., 1967—89, pres., 1969—70; fund raising com. Western Md. Coll., 1968—72; sec. Reiserstown Jaycees, 1976; com. Reiserstown Revitalization, 1976—77; treas. Md. Jr. Miss Scholarship Program, 1979—83, state chmn., 1983—92, chmn. bd., 1992—; advancement chmn. Boy Scouts Am., Reiserstown, 1985—87; adv. bd. Essex C.C., 1988—89; steering com., sub-chair logistics Partnering 2K Conf., Morgan State U., 1999—2000, IMIE external adv. com., 2002—03; adv. com. Md. Boat Act, 2005—; bd. dirs. Advancing Minorities Interest in Engring., 2003. Mem. NSPE, Instrumentation Soc. Am. (sr.), Am. Soc. for Metals, Computer and Automated Sys. Assn., Soc. Exptl. Mechanics, Soc. Plastic Engrs., U.S. Power Squadrons (Dunalk instr. 1990—), Bull/Bear Investment Club (treas. 1985-91). Avocations: boating, skiing, hunting, skeet and trap shooting, tennis. Home: PO Box 508 Reisterstown MD 21136-1324 Office: Easy Streett Enterprises LLC PO Box 508 Reisterstown MD 21136 Office Phone: 410-598-0833. Business E-Mail: streett@easystreett.com.

BROADDUS, ANDREA LYNN, environmental and transportation policy advocate; b. Washington, D.C., Dec. 27, 1971; d. Ashton Gustave and Carolyn Edith (nee Viens) Broaddus. BS in Geology and Geophysics, U. N.C., 1996; postgrad., Harvard U., 2004—. Organizer trainee Green Corps, Madison, Wis., 1996—97; campaign coord. Wisconsin's Environ. Decade, Madison, 1997—98; state coord. New Transp. Alliance, Madison, 1997—99; Milw. mgr. Bicycle Fedn. Wis., Milw., 1999—2001; cons., Grassroots organizer Citizens for a better Environment, Milw., 1999—2000; self employed Environ. Law and Policy Ctr. of the Midwest, Chgo., 1999—2000. Bd. dirs. Am. Walks, Portland, Oreg., 2003—, Walk D.C., 2003—04. Author: (report) Troubled Waters, 1997, The State of the Nation's Rail, 2004. Mem. Adv. Neighborhood Commn., 2002—04; mem. steering com. Program Dane, Madison, 1996—97; bd. dirs. Pro-Rail, Madison, 1999—2000; pres. bd. dirs. Madison Hostel, 1999—2001. Sci. Opportunity Fellfellowo, U. N.C., 1995—96, Student Rsch. grantee, Am. Pub. Power Assn., Washington, 1995—96. Avocations: bicycling, running, swimming, yoga, chess. Business E-Mail: andrea_broaddus@ksg06.harvard.edu.

BROADDUS, JOHN ALFRED, JR., retired bank executive, economist; b. Richmond, Va., July 8, 1939; s. John Alfred Broaddus Sr. and Norma (Coleman) Broaddus; m. Margaret C. Lemley, Apr. 16, 1966; children: John Alfred III, Christopher McRae. BA, Washington & Lee U., 1961; diplome, U. Strasbourg, France, 1962; MA, Ind. U., 1970, PhD, 1972; LLD (hon.), Washington and Lee U., 1993, Hampden-Sydney Coll., 2004. Intelligence rsch. specialist Def. Intelligence Agy., Washington, 1964-66; economist Fed. Res. Bank Richmond, 1970-72, asst. v.p., 1972-75, v.p., 1975-85, sr. v.p., dir. rsch., 1985-92, pres., 1993—2004. Bd. dirs. Albemale Corp., Markel Corp., Owens & Minor, Inc., T. Rowe Price Group, Inc., Faison Enterprises, Inc. Author: A Primer on the Fed, 1988; contbr. articles to publs. Pres. Richmond Meml. Hosp. Found., 1980—85; trustee Richmond Meml. Found., 1998—; mem. Gov.'s Adv. Coun. on Revenue Estimates, Va., 1993—; chmn. bd. trustees United Way of Greater Richmond, 1990; chmn. bd. govs. St. Christopher's Sch., 1992—96; trustee Va. Coun. Econ. Edn., 1994—, Va. Hist. Soc., 2001—, World Affairs Coun. Greater Richmond, 1996—; exec. com. Richmond Renaissance, 1998—; bd. dirs. Va. Commonwealth U. 1st lt. U.S. Army, 1962—64. Named Fulbright scholar, 1961. Mem.: Nat. Assn. Bus. Economists, Am. Econ. Assn., Phi Beta Kappa, Omicron Delta Kappa. Avocation: running.

BROADFOOT, ALBERT LYLE, physicist; b. Milestone, Sask., Can., Jan. 8, 1930; came to U.S., 1963; s. Morris Alexander and Lydia Georgina (Jacklin) B.; m. Katherine Eileen Deacon, Sept. 26, 1964; children: Alexander Lyle, Marilyn Louise. BE in Engring., Physics, U. Sask., Saskatoon, 1956, M.Sc. in Physics, 1960, PhD in Physics, 1963. Engr. Def. Rsch. Bd., Ottawa, Ont., Can., 1956-58; jr. physicist space div. Kitt Peak Nat. Obs., Tucson, 1963-64, asst. physicist, 1964-68, assoc. physicist, 1968-70, physicist, 1971-79; rsch. scientist, assoc. physicist Earth and Space Scis. Inst., U. So. Calif., 1979-82; sr. rsch. scientist Lunar and Planetary Lab., U Ariz., Tucson, 1982—. Home: 5231 E 17th St Tucson AZ 85711-4429 Office: U Ariz Lunar and Planetary Lab 162 Sonett Space Scis Bldg Tucson AZ 85721-0001 E-mail: alb@vega.lpl.arizona.edu.

BROADHURST, JEROME ANTHONY, lawyer; b. Cleve., Feb. 4, 1945; s. William and Estelle M. (Bozak) B.; m. Annette Lou Wilt, Sept. 3, 1966; children: Stephanie Ann, Jerome A., Elizabeth Marie. BS in Bus., U. Akron, 1967, JD, 1971. Bar: Ohio 1973, Tenn. 1987. Acctg. supr., fin. analyst B.F. Goodrich Co., Akron, Ohio, 1971-73, corp. counsel, 1973-76; counsel, asst. sec. The Weatherhead Co., Cleve., 1976-77; asst. counsel Gen. Tire and Rubber Co., Akron, 1977-80; sr. corp. atty. Holiday Inns, Inc. (subs. Holiday Corp.), Memphis, 1980-81, sec., sr. corp. atty., 1981-84; sec., assoc. gen. counsel Holiday Corp., Memphis, 1984-87, v.p., sec., assoc. gen. counsel, 1987-88; v.p., gen. counsel, sec. Perkins Family Restaurants, L.P., Memphis, 1989-91; pvt. practice law, 1991—; ptnr. Armstrong Allen, PLLC, 2000—. Mediator Tenn. Mediation/Arbitration Svc., 1994-95; adj. prof. MBA program Christian Brothers U. Sch. Bus., Memphis, 1997-99. Bd. dirs. Memphis Urban League, 1987-94; trustee Memphis Urban League Endowment Fund, 1987—. Mem. ABA (bus. law sect. com. bus. and corp. litigation 2001—, intellectual property law sect. com. on unfair comp.-trade identity 1996—, corp. gov. 2004—, small bus. 2004-, fed. regulation securities 2004-), Tenn. Bar Assn., Ohio Bar Assn., Memphis Bar Assn., Am. Soc. Corp. Secs. (corp. practices com. 1981-97, 99-2001, 2004—, pub. co. affairs com. 2003-04). Republican. Roman Catholic. Avocations: photography, jogging, racquetball. Office: Brinkley Plaza Ste 700 80 Monroe Ave Memphis TN 38103-2467 Office Phone: 901-523-8211. E-mail: jbroadhurst@armstrongallen.com.

BROADHURST, JUDITH BUCK, art gallery owner; d. Oscar Darrell and Bertha Hale Buck; m. Charles Cecil McKinney, Sept. 20, 1958 (div. Sept. 1985); children: Emry Lynne, Robin Ashley, Marc Jason; m. Jack Johnson Broadhurst, Nov. 26, 1988. RN, Rex Hosp. Sch. of Nursing, Raleigh, NC, 1958. Sales person Arras Gallery, N.Y.C., 1986—88; owner Broadhurst Gallery, Fine Art Gallery, Pinehurst, NC, 1990—. Bd. of dirs. Mus. of History, United Way, YWCA, Raleigh Fine Arts, Mus. of Art Volunteers Bd. Avocation: sculpting. Home and Office: Broadhurst Gallery 2212 Midland Rd Pinehurst NC 28374 Office Phone: 910-295-4817. E-mail: judy@broadhurstgallery.com.

BROADNAX, WALTER D., public information officer, educator; b. Starcity, Ark., Oct. 21, 1944; s. Walter and Mary Lee (Cotton) B.; m. Angel LaVerne Wheelock; 1 child, Andrea Alyce. BA, Washburn U., 1967; MPA, Kans. U., 1969; PhD, Syracuse U., 1975; Hon. Degrees, Washburn U., Topeka; Hon. Degree, Ctrl. State U. Ohio. Dir. Svc. Children, Youth and Adults, Kans., 1979-80; prin. dep. asst. sec. HHS, 1980-81; lectr. pub. mgmt. and pub. policy John F. Kennedy sch. govt. Harvard U., 1981-87, dir. innovations state and local govt., 1985-87; pres. NY State Civil Svc. Commn., 1987-90; commr. NY State Dept. Civil Svc., 1987-90; pres. Ctr. Govtl. Rsch., Inc., Rochester, NY, 1990-93; dep. sec. HHS, Washington, 1993-96; prof. school of pub affairs Univ of Md, Coll. Pk., Md., 1996-99; dean Coll. Pub. Affairs Am. U., 1999—2002; pres. Clark Atlanta U., 2002—. Bd. dirs. Keycorp, Medecision, Inc., CNA Corp. Contbr. articles to profl. jours. Trustee Syracuse U., The Coun. for Excellence in Govt. Recipient Maxwell Sch. of Citizenship and Pub. Affairs Spirit of Pub. Svc. award. Whiting scholar Washburn U. Fellow Nat. Acad. Pub. Adminstrn.; pres. ASPA (Outstanding Pub. Svc. award Nat. Capital Area chpt.), Nat. Acad. Pub. Adminstrn. (Nat. Pub. Svc. award) Avocations: reading, jogging, music. Home: 691 Beckwith St SW Atlanta GA 30314- Office: Clark Atlanta U Office of Pres Atlanta GA Office Phone: 404-880-6646. Office Fax: 404-880-8500. E-mail: wbroadnax@cau.edu.

BROADRICK-ALLEN, SANDRA CAROL, retired city manager, civic worker, consultant; b. St. Louis, May 5, 1940; d. Charles Albert Jr. and Verna Catherine (Yount) Allen; m. King Woodard Broadrick, July 4, 1975. BS, Lindenwood Coll., 1962; MA, U. Denver, 1965; PhD, U. Ill., 1975. Cert. tchr. Ill., Mo. Tchr. home econs. Princeville (Ill.) H.S., 1962-65, guidance counselor, 1965-68; dean faculty, dean students Garland Jr. Coll., Boston, 1971—75, pres., 1975-76; adminstr. Office Arms Control, Disarmament and Internat. Security, Urbana, Ill., 1981-82; campaign mgr. for state rep. from 103d legis. dist. Ill. Ho. of Reps., 1982-84; city mgr. Village of Savoy, Ill., 1985-91; adminstrv.-exec. cons., Champaign, Ill., 1992—. Editor: County Banners of the Illinois Association for Home and Community Education, 2000; mem. editl. rev. bd. Nat. Assn. for Women Deans, Adminstrs. and Counselors Jour., 1972-74. Pres. Princeville High Sch. PTA, 1966—68; moderator Princeville Cmty. Coun., 1966—68; bd. dirs. U. YWCA, Champaign, 1983—89; mem. home econs. coun. Champaign County Coop. Ext. Svc., 1985—87, treas. unit coun., 1991—92; vice chmn., pres. Ext. Edn. Found., 1992—99; mem. president's coun. U. Ill., 1998—, Busey Bank, 1998—2005; pres. Ill. Assn. Home and Cmty. Edn., 1997—2000; mem. precinct com. Champaign County Dem. Com, 1982—85; sr. high sch. youth fellowship advisor Princeville Presbyn. Ch., 1965—68. Recipient Leadership award Univ. YWCA, 1985, Outstanding Vol. award United Way Champaign County, 1986, cert. of recognition, Ill. Ho. of Reps., 1991; citizens lay advisor scholar Ritenour Sch. Dist., 1958-62, honors scholar Lindenwood Coll., 1958-62; grantee U.S. Office Edn., 1968-70. Mem. Assoc. Country Women of World (vice chmn. UN com. 1998-2001, chmn. 2001-2004, bd. dirs. 2001-2004), Scroll Soc., Rotary (charter pres. Savoy 1989-91, gov. dist. 6490 2001-02, coord. task force and adminstrv. coord. 2000-2001, dir. youth programs 2002-2003, chair R.I. Centennial Com. 2003-2005, dist. trainer 2005-2006, Paul Harris fellow 1993, multiple Spirit of Paul Harris awards, others), Phi Delta Kappa, Kappa Omicron Phi. Avocations: international travel, archaeology of lost civilizations, earthwatch and global volunteer, gardening. Personal E-mail: sandyba@net66.com.

BROADWATER, DOUGLAS DWIGHT, lawyer; b. Preston, Minn., May 31, 1944; s. George and Marion Elaine (Gleason) B.; m. Beatrice (Kinney), July 8, 1978; children: Ian Dwight, George Francis, Mark Fowler. BA, Harvard U., 1966; JD, Columbia U., 1969. Bar: NY., 1969. Staff atty. employment project Ctr. Social Welfare Policy and Law, N.Y.C., 1969—71; assoc. Cravath, Swaine & Moore LLP, N.Y.C., 1971—78, ptnr., litig., 1978—. With Vis. Nurse Svc., NY, 1991—, chmn., 1998—. Office: Cravath Swaine & Moore LLP Worldwide Plz 825 8th Ave 41st Fl New York NY 10019-7475 Office Phone: 212-474-1553. Office Fax: 212-474-3700. Business E-Mail: dbroadwater@cravath.com.

BROADWATER, JAMES E., publisher; b. Tacoma, Nov. 5, 1945; s. Robert L. and June J. B.; m. Diane K. Plummer, Apr. 22, 1967; children: James Tegan, Kelly Diane, Robert Charles, Krista Dawn. BS in Journalism, U. Fla., 1967. Acct. mgr. Young & Rubicam, Inc., Detroit, Kansas City, N.Y.C. and Houston, 1968-73; assoc. pub. Tex. Monthly Mag., Austin, 1973-78; pres., pub. Saturday Rev. Mag., N.Y.C., 1978-80; regional pub. dir. Baker Publs., Houston, 1980-85; pres. HBC, Inc., Houston, 1985-87; assoc. pub. Tex. Sportsworld Mag., 1985-86; pub. Washington Journalism Rev., 1987-92; pres. The Broadwater Co., Houston, 1993—. Mem. Mag. Pub. Assn., Nat. Press Club, Am. Mgmt. Assn., Direct Mail Mktg. Assn., Lambda Chi Alpha. Baptist. Personal E-mail: jbroadwater@sbcglobal.net. *All things are possible through Christ. Success requires that one deal in results and not succumb to the desire to rationalize excuses.*

BROADWATER, JOHN DAVID, program director, archaeologist; b. Middlesboro, Ky., Dec. 21, 1943; s. William Clinton and Dorothy Holmes (Goodloe) Broadwater; m. Sharon Gayle Thompson, Aug. 22, 1966; children: Jennifer Noelle Miller, April Renee Clark. BSEE, U. Ky., 1966; MA in Am. Studies, Coll. William and Mary, 1989; PhD, U. St. Andrews, Scotland, 2000. Cert. diving instr. P.A. Diving Instrs., 1972, marine survey archaeologist Soc. Profl. Archaeologists, 1978, pilot ultralight aircraft Va., 1988, trimix diver Internat. Assn. Nitrox and Tech. Divers, 1995, pilot DeepWorker 2000 submersible NOAA, 1999. Devel. engr. Bell Labs. Western Electric Co., Whippany, NJ, 1967—69, devel. engr. Def. Activities Divsn. Kwajalein, 1969—72; v.p. Marine Archaeol. Rsch. Svcs., Southport, NC, 1972—78; sr. underwater archaeologist Va. Dept. Hist. Resources, Yorktown, 1978—90; sanctuary mgr. Nat. Marine Sanctuary Program NOAA, Newport News, Va., 1992—, program mgr. Maritime Heritage Program, Nat. Marine Sanctuary Program, 2004—. Adj. lectr. Maritime Studies Program, East Carolina U., Greenville, NC, 1982—. Author: (book) Kwajalein, Lagoon of Found Ships, The Yorktown Shipwreck Project, (maritime archaeology series) Managing an Ironclad, In the Shadow of Wooden Walls: Naval Transports During the American War of Independence; editor: conf. proceedings; contbr. chapters to books, articles to profl. jours. Recipient Bronze medal, Nat. Oceanic and Atmospheric Adminstrn., 2000, 2003, award excellence in marine sanctuary mgmt., 2001; Caird Supplemental Fellowship grant, Nat. Maritime Mus., Scotland, 1992. Fellow: The Explorers Club; mem.: Inst. Nautical Archaeology, Adv. Coun. Underwater Archaeology (vice-chair 1985—88), Soc. Hist. Archaeology. Office: NOAA's Maritime Heritage Program Nat Marine Sanctuary Program 100 Museum Dr Newport News VA 23606 Office Fax: 757-591-7353. Business E-Mail: john.broadwater@noaa.gov.

BROADWATER, ROBERT PAUL, publishing executive, writer; b. Meyersdale, Pa., June 3, 1958; s. Paul W. and Carolyn Broadwater; 1 child, Kelly Coleen. L.A.S., Penn State U., Altoona, 1976—78. Gen. mgr. York Steak House, Altoona, 1980—90, Pizza Hut, Balt., 1990—91, The Bull Pen, Tyrone, Pa., 1991—94, Denny's Restaurant, Altoona, 1994—97; mgr. Chi Chi's Mex. Restaurant, State Coll., Pa., 1997—2004. Pub. Dixie Dreams Press, Bellwood, Pa., 2002—. Author: (book) The Bronze and the Granite, 1983, Campfires and Campaigns, 1987, Leaders in Liberty, 1991, Daughters of the Cause, 1996, Desperate Deliverance, 1998, Of Men and Muskets, 1998, From Beyond the Battlefields, 2003, Liberty Belles, 2004, Battle of Despair, 2004. Recipient History Meets the Arts, Gettysburg Tourism Agy., 2004. Mem.: Sons of Confederate Veterans (chaplain 1987—88), Descendants of Civil War Veterans (pres. 1995—96). Republican. United Ch. Of Christ. Achievements include writing a montly column on Civil War collectibles for Military Trader; author of over 80 mag. articles for, among others: Civil War Times Illustrated; America's Civil War; Military History Illustrated. Home and Office: Dixie Dreams Press 333 South 2nd Street Bellwood PA 16617 Office Phone: 814-742-8307. E-mail: DixieDreamPress@aol.com.

BROADWAY, KENNETH L., music educator, musician; m. Sherri Broadway, June 26, 2004. BM, MM, DMA, U. Ga., Athens. Instr. Augusta State U., Augusta, Ga., 1991—94; asst. prof. U. SD, Vermillion, 1994—97; assoc. prof. U. Fla., Gainesville, 1997—. Performing artist Yamaha Corp., 1995—; tympanist Gainesville Chamber Orch., 1998—; ednl. endorser ProMark Mallets, 2003—. Musician Grace United Meth. Ch., Gainesville, Fla., 2003—05. Recipient Coll. of Fine Arts Tchr. of Yr. award, 1999. Mem.: CMS, FMEA, Percussive Arts Soc. (pres., fla. chpt. 2005—). Office Phone: 352-392-0223. E-mail: kbroadway@arts.ufl.edu.

BROADWAY, NANCY RUTH, landscape design and construction company executive, consultant, model and actress; b. Memphis, Dec. 20, 1946; d. Charlie Sidney and Patsy Ruth (Meadows) Adkins. BS in Biology and Sociology cum laude, Memphis State U., 1969; postgrad., Tulane U., 1969—70; MS in Horticulture, U. Calif.-Davis, 1976. Lic. landscape contractor, Calif. Claims adjuster Mass. Mut. Ins., San Francisco, 1972—73; coord. cmty. garden City of Davis, Calif., 1976; supr. seed propagation Bordier's Wholesale Nursery, Santa Ana, Calif., 1976—78; owner, founder Calif. Landscape Co., 1978—88, Design & Mgmt. Cons., 1988—; pres. N.R. Broadway, Inc., 1998—. Actress: Visions of Murder, 1993, Eyes of Terror, 1994. NDEA fellow Tulane U., 1969-70. Fellow Am. Hort. Soc.; mem. Nat. Assn. Gen. Contractors, Calif. Native Plant Soc., Stockton C. of C. Democrat. Home and Office: 2801 Jackson St #301 San Francisco CA 94115-2156 Personal E-mail: nrbway@aol.com.

BROADWIN, JOSEPH LOUIS, lawyer; b. Nice, France, July 12, 1930; s. Samuel and Lillian Ruth (Messing) B.; m. Maria Antonia Eligio de la Puente, June 1, 1949 (div. 1974); children— David Anthony, Charles Anthony; m. Susan Elizabeth Podufaly, Oct. 24, 1980; children: Elizabeth Antonia, Samuel Edward. AB, Columbia U., 1949; LL.B., Yale U., 1952. Bar: N.Y. Assoc. Chadbourne Parke Whiteside Wolff & Brophy, N.Y.C., 1954-59, Proskauer Rose Goetz & Mendelsohn, N.Y.C., 1959-67, ptnr., 1967-70, Willkie Farr & Gallagher, N.Y.C., 1970-92; counsel Winick & Rich, P.C., N.Y.C., 1993—. Regent L.I. Coll. Hosp., Bklyn., 1971—, vice chmn. 1985—, chmn. 1991—; bd. dirs. Cobble Hill Nursing Home, Bklyn., 1979—; exec. com. W. Bklyn. Ind. Democrats, 1957-84. Served with U.S. Army, 1952-54. Mem. Assn. Bar City N.Y. Clubs: Yale (N.Y.C.). Home: 143 Henry St Brooklyn NY 11201-2501 Office: Winick & Rich PC 919 3rd Ave New York NY 10022-3902

BROBECK, JOHN RAYMOND, physiology educator; b. Steamboat Springs, Colo., Apr. 12, 1914; s. James Alexander and Ella (Johnson) B.; m. Dorothy Winifred Kellogg, Aug. 24, 1940; children: Stephen James, Priscilla Kimball, Elizabeth Martha, John Thomas. BS, Wheaton Coll., 1936, LL.D., 1960; MS, Northwestern U., 1937, PhD, 1939; MD, Yale U., 1943. Instr. physiology Yale, 1943-45, asst. prof., 1945-48, asso. prof. physiology, 1948-52; prof. physiology, chmn. dept. U. Pa., Phila., 1952-70, Herbert C. Rorer prof. med. scis., 1970-82, prof. emeritus, 1982—. Editor: Yale Jour. Biology and Medicine, 1949-52; chmn. editorial bd.: Physiol. Revs, 1963-72. Fellow Am. Acad. Arts and Scis.; mem. Am. Physiol. Soc. (pres. 1971-72), Am. Inst. Nutrition, Nat. Acad. Scis., Am. Soc. Clin. Investigation, Halsted Soc., Phila. Coll. Physicians, Sigma Xi, Alpha Omega Alpha. Home: 1343 W Baltimore Pike # C118 Media PA 19063-5519

BROBECK, STEPHEN JAMES, consumer advocate; b. New Haven, Sept. 15, 1944; s. John Raymond and Dorothy Winifred (Kellogg) B.; m. Susan Cheney Williams, May 9, 1971. BA, Wheaton Coll., 1966; PhD, U. Pa., 1972. Asst. prof. Case Western Res. U., 1970-79; exec. dir. Consumer Fedn. Am., Washington, 1980—. Vis. assoc. prof. Cornell U., 1989; adj. assoc. prof. U. Md., 1990-92. Author: The Product Safety Book, 1983, The Bank Book, 1986, The Modern Consumer Movement, 1990, Encyclopedia of the Consumer Movement, 1997; contbr. articles to profl. jours. Bd. dirs. Citizens for Tax Justice, 1980—, Coalition Against Ins. Fraud, 1993—, Alliance to Save Energy, 1994—, Jump Start Coalition, 2002—, Ctr. Study Svcs., 1998—. Mem. Am. Council Consumer Interests. Home: 4700 Connecticut Ave NW Washington DC 20008-5629 Office: Consumer Fed Am 1424 16th St NW Ste 604 Washington DC 20036-2239 Office Phone: 202-387-6121. Business E-Mail: sbrobeck@consumerfed.org.

BROCA, LAURENT ANTOINE, aerospace scientist; b. Nov. 30, 1928; arrived in U.S., 1957, naturalized, 1963; s. Paul L. and Paule Jeanne (Ferrand) Broca; m. Leticia Garica Guerra, Dec. 18, 1972; 1 child, Marie-There Yvonne. BS in Math., U. Bordeaux, 1949; lic. es Scis. in Math. and Physics, U. Toulouse, 1957; grad., Inst. Technique Profl. France, 1980; PhD of Elec. Engring., Calif. We. U., 1979; postgrad., Boston U., 1958, MIT, 1961, Harvard U., 1961. Tchg. fellow physics dept. Boston U., 1957—58; spl. instr. dept. physics N.J. Inst. Tech., Newark, 1959—60; sr. staff engr. advanced rsch. group ITT, Nutley, NJ, 1959—60; examiner math. and phys. scis. U. Paris and Caen Exam Ctr., N.Y.C., 1959—69; sr. engr. surface radar divsn. Raytheon Co., Waltham, Mass., 1960—62, Hughes Aircraft Co., Culver City, Calif., 1962—64; asst. prof. math. Calif. State U., Northridge, 1963—64; prin. engr. astrionics lab. NASA, Huntsville, Ala., 1964—65; fellow engr. Def. and Space Ctr. Westinghouse Electric Corp., Balt., 1965—69; cons. and sci. adv. electronics, phys. scis. and math. indsl. firms and broadcasting stas., 1969—80; head engring. dept. Videocraft Mfg. Co., Laredo, Tex., 1974—75; asst. prof. math. Laredo State U., 1975; engring. specialist dept. sys. performance analysis ITT Fed. Electric Corp., Vandenberg AFB, Calif., 1980—82; engring. mgr. Ford Aerospace and Comm. Corp., Nellis AFB, Nev., 1982—84, Arcata Assocs., Inc., North Las Vegas, Nev., 1984—85; sr. sci. specialist engring. and devel. EG&G-JT3, Las Vegas, 1985—. With French Army, 1951—52. Recipient Published Paper award, Hughes Aircraft Co., 1966; Fulbright scholar, 1957. Mem.: IEEE, Am. Def. Preparedness Assn., Am. Nuc. Soc. (vice chmn. Nev. sect. 1982—83, chmn. 1983—84), Air Force Assn., Armed Forces Comm. and Electronics Assn. Home: 5040 Lancaster Dr Las Vegas NV 89120-1445 Office: EG&G Spl Projects Inc PO Box 93747 Las Vegas NV 89193-3747

BROCCHINI, RONALD GENE, architect; b. Oakland, Calif., Nov. 6, 1929; s. Gino Mario and Yoli Louise (Lucchesi) B.; m. Myra Mossman, Feb. 3, 1957; 1 child, Christopher Ronald BA in Architecture with honors, U. Calif., Berkeley, 1953, MA in Architecture with honors, 1957. Registered architect, Calif., Nev. Architect, designer SMP, Inc., San Francisco, 1948-53, designer, assoc., 1956-60; assoc. architect Campbell & Wong, San Francisco, 1961-63; prin. architect Ronald G. Brocchini, Berkeley, Calif., 1964-67, Worley K Wong & Ronald G Brocchini Assocs., San Francisco, 1968-87, Brocchini Architects, Berkeley, 1987—. Lectr. Calif. Coll. Arts and Crafts, Oakland, 1981-83; commr. Calif. Bd. Archtl. Examiners, 1961-89; mem. exam. com. Nat. Coun. Archtl. Registration Bds., 1983-85. Author: Long Range Master Plan for Bodega Marine Biology, U. Calif., 1982; prin. works include San Simeon Visitor Ctr., Hearst Castle, Calif., Mare Island Med.-Dental Facillity, IBM Ednl. and Data Processing Hdqrs., San Jose, Calif., Simpson Fine Arts Gallery, Calif. Coll. Arts, Ceramics and Metal Crafts, Emery Bay Pub. Market Complex, Analytical Measurement Facility, U. Calif., Berkeley, Bodega Marine Biology Campus, U. Calif., Berkeley, Fromm & Sichell (Christian Bros.) Hdqrs., The Nature Co., Corp. Offices, Berkeley, Merrill Coll., Athletic Facilities, U. Calif., Santa Cruz, Coll. III Housing, U. Calif., San Diego, Ctr. Pacific Rim Studies, U. San Francisco, married student housing Escondido II, III, IV, Stanford (Calif.) U. With U.S. Army, 1953-55. Recipient Bear of Yr. award U. Calif., Berkeley, 1987, Alumni Citation, 1988; recipient 18 Design Honor awards for architecture, Design award State of Calif. Dept. Rehab., 1995. Fellow AIA (bd. dirs. Calif. coun., pres. San Francisco chpt. 1982); mem. Bear Backers Club (bd. dirs. U. Calif.-Berkeley athletic coun.), Berkeley Breakfast Club (bd. govs.), Order of the Golden Bear, Chi Alpha Kappa. Republican. Roman Catholic. Avocations: auto restoration, photography, sports, art. Office: Brocchini Architects Inc 2748 Adeline St Berkeley CA 94703-2251 E-mail: arcbro@pacbell.net.

BROCHIN, ROBERT M., lawyer; b. May 14, 1955; m. Cristina E. Brochin. BA, U. Fla., 1977; JD, U. Fla. Law Sch., 1980. Bar: Fla. 1981. Dep. gen. counsel Fla. Gov. Office, 1991—92, Fla. Chief Inspector Gen., 1992—93; ptnr., litig. practice group Morgan, Lewis & Bockius LLP, 1993—, chmn. recruiting com-Miami Office. Mem.: Fla. Partnership Am. (chmn.), Dade County Bar Assn., Fla. Bar Assn., Fla. Constn. Revision Commn. (1997-1998). Office: Morgan Lewis & Bockius LLP 5300 Wachovia Ctr 200 S Biscayne Blvd Miami FL 33131-2339 Office Phone: 305-415-3456. Office Fax: 305-415-3001. Business E-Mail: rbrochin@morganlewis.com.

BROCHU, CHRISTOPHER ANDREW, geologist, educator; b. Springfield, Mass., Aug. 12, 1967; s. Robert Mayo and Wynne Alyn Brochu; m. Cynthia Doreen Toll, Aug. 14, 2004. BS in Geology, U. Iowa, 1989; MS in Geol. Scis., U. Tex., 1992, PhD in Geol. Scis., 1997. Postdoctoral rsch. asst. Field Mus., Chgo., 1998—2000; asst. prof. U. Iowa, Iowa City, 2001—. Recipient Rower prize, Soc. Vertebrate Paleontology, 1996.

BROCHU, GABRIELA AVILES, biologist, researcher; b. Cordoba, Argentina, July 1, 1961; arrived in U.S., 2001; d. Alcides Ruben Aviles and Norma Olga; m. Michael Lee Brochu, Mar. 15, 2003. Degree in Biology, Nat. U. Cordoba, 1984, cert. tchr., 1986, PhD in Biol. Scis., 1991. Chief Arbovirus Lab. Nat. Inst. of Human Viral Diseases, Pergamino, Argentina, 1995—2001; rsch. asst. prof. U. of Nev., Reno, 2001—. Head aedes aegypti surveillance Ministry of Health, Cordoba, 1994—95. Contbr. chapters to books, articles to profl. jours. Recipient award, Nat. Acad. Medicine, 2000; fellow, NRC, Argentina, 1986—93. Achievements include first to first confirmed dengue cases in Argentina. Established the Arbovirus lab at INEVH, National Reference Center for dengue diagnosis and PAHO/WHO Collaborative Center. Office: Univ Nevada Nevada Genomics Ctr MS425 Reno NV 89557 Personal E-mail: gabrielaaviles@hotmail.com. E-mail: aviles@unr.nevada.edu.

BROCK, CAROLYN PRATT, chemist, educator; b. Chgo., July 25, 1946; d. Charles Stebbings and Grace (Goodman) Pratt; m. Louis Milton Brock, July 22, 1972. BA, Wellesley (Mass.) Coll., 1968; PhD, Northwestern U., 1972. Asst. prof. chemistry U. Ky., Lexington, 1972-78, assoc. prof. chemistry, 1978-87, prof., 1987—. Vis. scientist organic chemistry lab. Swiss Fed. Inst. Tech., Zurich, 1980—81, Zurich, 1988—89; bd. govs. Cambridge Crystallographic Data Centre, 2001—, vice chmn., 2003—05, chmn., 2005—. Co-editor: Acta Crystallographica, 1993; editor: Sect. B of Acta Crystallographica, 2002—; contbr. articles to profl. jours. Mem. Am. Chem. Soc., Am. Crystallographic Assn., U.S. Nat. Com. for Crystallography (sec.-treas. 1989-91), Phi Beta Kappa, Sigma Xi. Home: 133 Sycamore Rd Lexington KY 40502-1841 Office: U Ky Dept Chemistry Lexington KY 40506-0055 Office Phone: 859-257-1959. Business E-Mail: cpbrock@uky.edu.

BROCK, CHARLES LAWRENCE, lawyer, diversified financial services company executive, investment banker; b. Ottumwa, Iowa, Mar. 7, 1943; s. Charles Harlan and Betty Arlene (Ream) B.; m. Mary Jane Hipp, June 17, 1978; children: William Walker, Susanna Lawrence. BA with highest distinction, Northwestern U., 1964; JD, Harvard U., 1967; postgrad. (Rotary Found. fellow), U. Delhi (India) and India Law Inst., 1967-68; grad., Advanced Mgmt. Program, Harvard Bus. Sch., 1979. Bar: N.Y. 1968. Asso. firm Sullivan & Cromwell, N.Y.C., 1969-74; v.p., corp. sec., gen. counsel Scholastic Mags., Inc. (now Scholastic, Inc.), N.Y.C., 1974-80; interim CFO and COO Scholastic Mags., Inc., 1975-76, pub. internat. div., 1976-80; pres. Scholastic Tab Publs. Ltd., Can., 1976-80, Ashton-Scholastic Pty. Ltd., Australia, 1976-80, Ashton-Scholastic Ltd., New Zealand, 1976-80; chmn. Scholastic Publs. Ltd., U.K., 1976-80; sr. v.p., mgmt. dir. Compton Communications, 1980-82; mgr. subsidiaries Compton Advertising, 1980-82; counsel Drinker, Biddle & Reath, N.Y.C., Phila., Washington, 1982-84; ptnr. Carter, Ledyard & Milburn, 1984-95, Brock Ptnrs. and predecessor firms, 1995—; chmn., CEO Brock Capital Group LLC, 2002—. Bd. dirs., chmn. audit coms. B&H Bulk Carriers Ltd., B&H Ocean Carriers Ltd., B&H Maritime Carriers Ltd., Excel Maritime Carriers, 2002-; mem. Harvard Coll. Bd. Overseers Com. on Univ. Resources, 1992—, chmn. Harvard Bd. Overseers Nominating Com. 1996—, coun. Harvard Law Sch. Assn., 1983-85, sec., 1988-90, treas., 1990—92, exec. com., 1986—, chmn. membership com., 1987—, internat. sect., 1991—, 1st v.p., 1994-96, pres. 1996-98; bd. advisors Coll. Arts and Scis., Northwestern U., 1989—, Campaign for Gt. Tchrs. Com., 1989-90, John Evans Club, Northwestern U. 1989—; guild hall trustee Acad. of the Arts, 1990—, mem. exec. com., chmn. nominating com., 1986-90, chmn. bd., 1990-92; trustee, treas. Family Dynamics, 1981-88. Mem. editl. adv. bd. Minority Law Jour. Reunion gift chmn. Harvard Law Sch. Fund, 1967-68, vice chmn., 1975-77; trustee Harvard Law Sch. Assn. N.Y.C., 1982-85, chmn. placement com., 1983-86, v.p., 1985-96, originator, chmn. summer reception, 1982-; chmn. Harvard Community Ptnrs., 1984-86; co-chmn. ann. giving St. Barnard's Sch., 1989-95; mem. adv. bd. Minority Atty. Reporter; deacon Brick Presbyn. Ch., N.Y.C., 1973-76, regent Cathedral St. John The Divine, 1997-. Recipient Mentor award for pioneering efforts creating opportunities for minorities and women. Mem. ABA, N.Y. State Bar Assn., N.Y. County Lawyers Assn., Assn. Bar City of N.Y., Harvard Alumni Assn. (bd. dirs. 1989—, sec. 1998-2001, 1st v.p. 2001-02, 2002-2003, chmn. grad. schs. com. 1992-95), Assn. Am. Pubs., Century Assn., Harvard Bus. Club of N.Y. (v.p. 1984-86), Union Club, N.Y. Yacht Club, Down Town Assn., The Pilgrims, Piping Rock (Locust Valley, N.Y.), Maidstone Club (East Hampton, N.Y.), Ogeechee Golf Club, Phi Beta Kappa, Kappa Sigma. Home: 765 Park Ave New York NY 10021-4254 Office: 295 Madison Ave Fl 44-46 New York NY 10017 Office Phone: 212-209-3000. Business E-Mail: cbrock@brockcapital.com.

BROCK, DAVID ALLEN, retired state supreme court chief justice; b. Stoneham, Mass., July 6, 1936; s. Herbert and Margaret B.; m. Sandra Ford, 1960; 6 children. AB, Dartmouth Coll., 1958; LLB, U. Mich., 1963; postgrad., Nat. Jud. Coll., 1977. Bar: N.H. 1963. Assoc. Devine, Millimet, McDonough, Stahl & Branch, Manchester, N.H., 1963-69; U.S. atty. State of N.H., 1969-72; ptnr. Perkins, Douglas & Brock, Concord, N.H., 1972-74, Perkins & Brock, 1974-76; spl. counsel to gov. and exec. coun. N.H., 1974-76; legal counsel to gov. N.H., 1976; assoc. justice N.H. Superior Ct., 1976-78, N.H. Supreme Ct., 1978-86, chief justice, 1986—2004. Chmn. State of N.H. Legal Svcs. Adv. Commn., 1977-79; chmn. dist. ct. reform subcom. Gov.'s Commn. for Ct. System Improvement, 1974-75; chmn. N.H. Commn. Ct. Accreditation, 1986—; mem. Select Commn. on Unified Ct. System, 1980-84, chmn. N.H. Supreme Ct. Com. on Jud. Conduct, 1981-89, rules adv. com., 1985-97; mem. State N.H. Jud. Coun., 1979-87; nat. adv. bd. Leadership Inst. for Jud. Edn., 1989-96, Nat. Jud. Coll. long range planning com., 1990-91; mem. Jud. Edn. and Tech. Assistance Consortium, 1989-97; chmn. Interbranch Coun. on Substance Abuse and the Criminal Justice System, 1991-95; vice-chmn. State Justice Inst., 1994-95, co-chmn., 1995-98; v.p. Conf. Chief Justices, 1996-97, pres-elect 1997-98, pres., 1998-99; chmn.-elect Nat. Ctr. for State Cts., 1997-98, chmn., 1998-99; mem. Nat. Criminal Justice Info. Svcs. Adv. Policy Bd., 1999-2002. Bd. dirs. Manchester Cmty. Guidance Ctr., 1966-72, pres., 1969-72, policy bd., 1999-2002; chmn. Manchester Rep. Com., 1967-69; vice chmn. N.H. Rep. State Com., 1968-69; Rep. candidate U.S. Senate, 1972; del. N.H. Constl. Conv., 1974: mem. Gov.'s Commn. for Handicapped, 1978-79. Fellow ABA (edn. com. of appellate judges conf. 1981-97, appellate advocacy com. 1982-84, faculty appellate judges' seminar program 1984-89, del. ho. of dels. 1994-96), N.H. Bar Assn. (chmn. constl. revision com. 1976-77), N.H. Bar Found. (hon.).

BROCK, DEE SALA, television executive, educator, writer, consultant; b. Covington, Okla., June 7, 1930; d. Lester Edward and Vera Mae (Bowers) Sala; m. Robert Wesley Brock, June 8, 1952 (div. 1979); children: Baron Sala, Bishop Chapman, Bevin Bowers. BA, U. North Tex., 1950, MA, 1956, PhD, 1985. Tchr. high sch. Dallas Ind. Sch. Dist., 1952-66; dir. Dallas Cowboy Cheerleaders, 1960-75; mem. faculty, adminstr. Dallas County Community Coll. Dist., 1966-74, telecourse writer, producer, adminstr., 1974-75, dir. mktg. info., 1975-80; dir., v.p. PBS, Washington, 1980-89, sr. v.p. edn. Alexandria, Va., 1989-90; pres. Dee Brock & Assocs., Plano, Tex., 1991-98; pub. FAQs Press, 1999—. Bd. dirs. Pub. Svc. Satellite Consortium, U.S. Basics; adv. bd. Learning Link, 1987-90, Telcon Industry, 1990-91; chair exec. coun. U. of the World, 1989-91; adv. coun. Triangle Coalition, 1989-91; spkr. in field. Author: Writing for a Reason: Study Guide, 1974; author: (with Jeriel Howard) Writing for a Reason, 1978; author: (with Laura Derr) The World of F. Scott Fitzgerald, 1980; author: (with Deborah Burkett and Carole Wilson) Troup Goes to War: World War II, A Collection of Memories, 1999; author: (with Linda Resnik) Food FAQs: Substitutions, Yields & Equivalents, 2000; author: (with JoAnna Lewis) 100 Great Fundraising Ideas Celebrating 100 Years of Texas Library, 2002; mem. editl. bd.: Am. Jour. Distance Edn., 1987—90; prodr.: (internat. teleconf.) Out of the Red, 1991; prodr., writer: TV series and workbook Communicating in English in the Healthcare Workplace, 1994; contbr. articles to profl. jours. Trustee Coun. for Adult and Experiential Learning, 1989—99; chair spl. task force Mcpl. Libr. Friends of Libr., 1996, pres., 1997—; lay rep. N.E. Tex. Libr. Sys., 1996—, chair planning to plan com., 1997—98, adv. coun., 1998—, vice chair, 1998—2000, chair, 2000—04; chmn. Strategic Planning Com., 1999; fundraising co-chair Komen Tyler Race for the Cure, 1999; active PTA, Dallas; pres. Littera, 2002—04; v.p. cmty. rels. LWV-Tyler, 2002—03, pres., 2003—, Friends of the Troup Libr., 1998—; chair Libr. Friends, Trustees and Advs., 2001—03; bd. dirs. Tyler Civic Theatre Ctr., Coalition for the Advancement of Citizenship, 1988—90. Reynolds Econ. fellow U. N.C., 1966; Literacy award N. Tex. Reading Coun., 1980, Nat. Person of Yr. award Nat. Coun. on Community and Continuing Edn., 1985, Award for Excellence in TV Programming NEA, 1986; recipient Outstanding Career Achievement award ITC Am. Assn. Community and Jr. Colls., 1990. Mem. NEH (nat. bd. cons. 1980-85), LWV (bd. dirs., v.p. cmty. rels. Tyler chpt. 2002-03, pres. 2003—), U.S. Distance Learning Assn. (bd. dirs. 1989-91, adv. bd. 1989), So. Assn. Colls. and Schs. (project 1990 task force 1984-86), Nat. Assn. Ednl. Broadcasters (steering com. 1979-81), Assn. Ednl. Comms. Tech., Nat. Coun. Tchrs. English (pres. S.W. regional coun. 1972-74), Tex. Libr. Assn. (legis. com. 1999—, chair roundtable 2001-2003, chair pub. rels. com. 2005—). Methodist. Achievements include being co-patentee video indexing system; design of and management of PBS Adult Learning Service and PBS Adult Learning Satellite Service. Home and Office: 3529 Woods Blvd Tyler TX 75707

BROCK, DOROTHY DIXON, psychologist, psychology professor; b. St. Louis, Nov. 16, 1954; d. Arthur Roy and Dorothy Arnett Dixon. BS, Oral Roberts U., 1978; MEd, Ga. State U., 1980, PhD, 1991. Lic. psychologist Ga.; cert. tchr. Okla. Tchr. Clinton Jr. HS, Tulsa, Okla., 1978—79; co-founder Landmark Counseling Ctr., Norcross, Ga., 1981—83; contract therapist Rapha, Dunwoody, Ga., 1994—96; pvt. practice psychologist Norcross, Ga., 1995—97, 2001—04, 2005—; adj. instr. Toccoa Falls (Ga.) Coll., 1995—96, instr., 2001—02, asst. prof., 2002—, coll. counselor, 2003—04; clin. coord. New Life Clinics, Smyrna, Ga., 1997—2000. Seminar spkr., radio and TV appearances on mental health issues, 1998—. Mem.: APA, Am. Assn. Christian Counselors. Office: Toccoa Falls Coll Toccoa Falls GA 30598 Office Phone: 770-843-9077.

BROCK, HELEN RACHEL MCCOY, retired mental health and community health nurse; b. Cromwell, Okla., Dec. 10, 1924; d. Samuel Robert Lee and Ire Etta (Pounds) McCoy; m. Clois Lee Brock, Sept. 29, 1963; children: Dwayne, Joyce, Peggy, Ricki, Stacey. AS, Southwestern Union Coll., Keene, Tex., 1968; BS in Nursing, Union Coll., Lincoln, Nebr., 1970; postgrad., Vernon Regional Jr. Coll., Tex., 1972—76; MPH, Loma Linda (Calif.) U., 1983. Cert. ARC nurse. Dir. nursing Chillicothe (Tex.) Clinic-Hosp., 1970-77,

Pike County Hosp., Waverly, Ohio, 1977-79, Marion County Hosp., Jefferson, Tex., 1979-81; nurse III, nursing unit supr, patient health educator Vernon State Hosp., Maximum Security for Criminally Insane, 1981-96; retired, 1996; nurse, admissions and assessments Texhoma Community Health Svcs., 1987-94. Mem.: ANA, Tex. Nurses Assn. Home: PO Box 238 Chillicothe TX 79225-0238

BROCK, HORACE RHEA, finance educator; b. Leggett, Tex., Aug. 26, 1927; s. Hobby B. and Winona (Epperson) B.; m. Frances Euline Williams, May 24, 1955; children: Alan Howard, Mary Ann, Charles. BS, Sam Houston State U., 1946, BBA, MA, Sam Houston State U., 1951; PhD, U. Tex., 1954. Prof. U. Ark., 1954-55; disting. prof. North Tex. State U., Denton, 1965-93, chmn. dept. accounting, 1966-74, dean Coll. Bus. Adminstrn., 1983-85; dir. Chief Execs. Round Table U. North Tex., Denton, 1993—99. Adviser AID, Istanbul, Turkey, 1967-69; cons. taxation and financial reporting. Author: Introduction to Taxation, 1972, 17th edit., 1988, Cost Accounting, 1970, 7th edit., 2003, College Accounting, 1974, 11th edit., 2005, Intermediate and Advanced Accounting, 1966, Accounting for Oil and Gas Producers, 1960, Accounting for Oil and Gas Producing Companies, 1982, 5th edit., 2000 Served with USAF, 1946-49. Mem. Am. Inst. CPA's, Tex. Soc. CPA's, Beta Gamma Sigma. Home: 1900 Westridge St Denton TX 76205-6925 Office: U North Tex 302 Marquis Hall Denton TX 76203 E-mail: brocks@verizon.net, brock@unt.edu.

BROCK, JAMES RUSH, chemical engineering professor; b. Mission, Tex., Dec. 31, 1930; s. Jerome Dalton and Elizabeth (Beeler) B.; m. Mary Lou Waghorn, July 4, 1964; children: Ianthe, Alison. BA, Rice U., 1952, BS, 1953; MS, U. Wis., 1954, PhD, 1960. Registered profl. engr., Tex. Rsch. engr. Humble Oil & Refining Co., Houston, 1954-55; asst. prof. chem. engring. dept. U. Tex., Austin, 1959-62; postdoctoral fellow at Svc. de Chimie Physique II Université Libre de Belgique, Brussels, 1962-63; asst. prof. chem. engring. dept. U. Tex., Austin, 1963-65, assoc. prof., 1965-69, prof., 1969-73, 73-80, K.A. Kobe prof., 1980—2001, K.A. Kobe prof. emeritus, 2000—; vis. prof. U. Paris VI Faculty Scis., Paris, 1973, Tokyo Inst. Tech., 1988. Mem. rsch. grants adv. com. EPA, Washington, 1970—; v.p. ONG Producing Inc., Austin, 1986-2000; cons. to govt. agys. Co-author: The Dynamics of Aerocolloidal Systems, 1970; co-editor Internat. Revs. in Aerosol Physics and Chemistry, 1971-73; assoc. editor Jour. Environ. Sci. and Health, 1978—, Jour. Aerosol Sci., 1986-88; mem. editorial bd. Jour. Colloid Sci., 1965-66, Aerosol Sci. and Tech., 1984-88; contbr. more than 150 articles to profl. jours.; holder 20 patents in field. Recipient Disting. Svc. award U.S. Army Rsch. Devel. Engring. Ctr., 1987; grantee NSF. Mem. Am. Chem. Soc., Am. Assn. Aerosol Rsch. (Sinclair award 1992), Gesellschaft fur Aerosol Forschung, Tau Beta Pi, Alpha Chi Omega, Phi Lambda Upsilon. Home: 1801 Lavaca St #6E Austin TX 78701-1304

BROCK, KARENA DIANE, dancer, educator; b. L.A., Sept. 21, 1942; d. Orville DeLoss and Sallie Alice (Anderson) B.; m. Ted Kivitt, Apr. 16, 1965 (div. 1978); m. John Robert Carlyle, June 28, 1985; 1 child, Timothy John. Grad. H.S., Kansas City, Mo. Tchr. master classes Radford (Va.) Coll., U. Louisville, U. Tampa; staff tchr. Bklyn. Coll.; mem. faculty SUNY-Purchase; artistic dir., choreographer, tchr. and founder Hilton Head Dance Theater and Sch., Hilton Head Island, SC, 1985—. Guest tchr. S.C. Dance Inst., Columbia, 1993-94, Walnut Hill Sch., Boston, Savannah Ballet, Cleve. Ballet; tchr. master classes Florence, S.C., Columbia; guest choreographer Towson (Md.) U., 2000, Carolina Ballet Theatre, Greeville, S.C., 1998. Dancer, David Lichine Concert Group, L.A., 1960-61, Netherlands Nat. Ballet Co., Amsterdam, 1961-62, mem. corps, Am. Ballet Theatre, N.Y.C., 1963-68, soloist, 1968-73, prin. ballerina, 1973-79, artistic dir., prima ballerina, choreographer, Savannah (Ga.) Ballet Co., 1979-85; co-artistic dir. and choreographer Ballet South, Savannah, 1992-96; guest artist, Miami (Fla.) Civic Ballet, Macon (Ga.) Civic Ballet, Tampa (Fla.) Civic Ballet, U. Ill. Ballet Co., Champaign, San Jose (Calif.) Civic Ballet, Ballet de San Juan, P.R., Gala Ballet, Amarillo (Tex.) Civic Ballet, Maywood Ballet Co., Phila., U. Wis., Milw. Civic Ballet, Stars of Am. Ballet, various TV shows, White House, 1966, 69. Mem. adv. bd. S.C. Arts Commn., Columbia, 1988—; hon. mem. bd. dirs. Columbia City Ballet. Mem.: AFTRA, AGVA, Am. Guild Mus. Artists. Office: Hilton Head Dance Theater and Sch 24 Palmetto Business Park Rd Hilton Head Island SC 29928-3234 Office Phone: 843-785-5477. Personal E-mail: balletkbc@yahoo.com.

BROCK, KATHY, newscaster; married; 2 children. Degree in Journalism, Wash. State U. Anchor and reporter KWSU-TV, Pullman, Wash., KEPR-TV, Pasco, KCBI-YV, Boise, Idaho; weekend anchor and reporter KUTV-TV, Salt Lake City, 1984, anchor noon and 6pm news, 1985—90; co-anchor News This Morning and reporter WLS-TV, Chgo., 1990—93, co-anchor 6pm news, 1993—, co-anchor 10pm news, 2003—. TV Journalist (documentaries) Mali, West Africa, 1989 (Edward R. Murrow award, 1989, IRIS award, 1989). Office: WLS-TV 190 N State St Chicago IL 60601

BROCK, LOUIS MILTON, JR., engineering educator, researcher; b. Davenport, Iowa, Apr. 16, 1943; s. Louis Milton and Mary Elizabeth (Creech) B.; m. Carolyn Starbuck Pratt, July 22, 1972. BS, Northwestern U, 1966, MS, 1967, PhD, 1972. With Black and Veatch, Kansas City, Mo., 1962, Gen Dynamics/Convair, San Diego, 1963-64, Sargeant-Welch Co., Skokie, Ill., 1964, Am. Can Co., Barrington, Ill., 1965; prof. mech. engring. U. Ky., Lexington, 1971—. Contbr. articles to profl. jours. NSF grantee; USN/Am. Soc. Engring. Edn. fellow, 1983, 85, 87, 90; recipient rsch. award Rsch. Found. U. Ky., 1977, rsch. prof. award, 1986. Fellow ASME; mem. ASCE (corr. award 1989), Sigma Xi, Chi Epsilon. Avocations: hiking, classical music, riding, history. Home: 133 Sycamore Rd Lexington KY 40502-1841 Office: U Ky Dept Mech Engring Lexington KY 40506-0503 Office Phone: 859-257-6336 80656.

BROCK, MACON F., SR., retail company executive; Pres., COO K&K Toys; pres., CEO Dollar Tree Stores Inc., Chesapeake, Va., 1991—. Office: Dollar Tree Stores Inc 500 Volvo Pkwy Chesapeake VA 23320

BROCK, MACON F., JR., retail executive; Chmn. Dollar Tree Stores. Office: Dollar Tree Stores 500 Volvo Pkwy Chesapeake VA 23320*

BROCK, RALPH HANEY, lawyer; b. Amarillo, Tex., Aug. 6, 1948; s. Charles and Waurika (Haney) B.; m. Carolyn Frances Moore, Nov. 14, 1981. BA, Tex. Tech U., 1971, JD, 1975. Bar: Tex. 1975, U.S. Dist. Ct. (no. dist.) Tex. 1976, U.S. Ct. Appeals (5th cir.), 1978, U.S. Supreme Ct. 1979. Briefing atty. 7th Ct. Civil Appeals Tex., 1975—76; assoc. Brown & Harding, Lubbock, Tex., 1976—79; legal counsel 7th Ct. Appeals Tex., 1981—82; faculty Tex. Tech U. Sch. Law, Lubbock, 1996—97; pvt. practice Lubbock, 1979—81, 1982—. Contbr. articles to profl. jours. Mem. Tex. Bar Found. (sustaining life fellow, Dan Rugeley Price Meml. award 1999), State Bar Tex. (sect. rep. to bd. dirs. 2000-02, bd. dirs. 2002-05, chair jour. com. 1994-95, chair appellate practice advocacy sect. 1987-88, chair 1999-2000, chair women and the law sect., sec. computer sect. 1998-2000, opportunities for minorities in the profession com. 1998-2001, women in the profession com. 1998-2001, Ma'at Justice award, 1997, Pres. award 2002), ABA, ACLU, Lubbock County Bar Assn. (Pro Bono Atty. of Yr. award 1986), Lubbock County Women Lawyers Assn., Lubbock Criminal Def. Lawyers Assn., Amateur Radio Relay League, South Plains Eagle Scout Assn., Lubbock Amateur Radio Club, Phi Alpha Theta, Pi Sigma Alpha Democrat. Unitarian Universalist. Avocations: amateur radio, collecting soda pop bottles. Office: PO Box 959 Lubbock TX 79408-0959 Business E-Mail: brock@sbot.org.

BROCK, ROSLYN MCCALLISTER, association executive; BS magna cum laude, Va. Union U., 1987; M in Health Svcs. Adminstrn., George Washington U., 1989; MBA, Northwestern U., 1999. Dir. sys. fund devel. Sisters of Bon Secours Health Sys. Inc.; vice chair nat. bd. dirs. NAACP, Balt., 2001—. Vol. elem. sch. instr. Jr. Achievement; host local cable access program Cmty. Voices. Named a Future Leader, Ebony mag., 1989; named Outstanding Alumna, Va. Union U., hon. chairperson, Nat. Black Family Summit, Young Leaders fellow, Nat. Com. on U.S.-China Rels., 2003; named one of 100 Young Women of Promise, Good Housekeeping, 1987; recipient Martin Luther King, jr. medal for human rights, George Washington U. Mem.: APHA, Nat. Assn. Health Svc. Execs., The Links, Inc., Nat. Black MBA Assn., Alpha Kappa Alpha Sorority, INc. Office: NAACP 4805 Mt Hope Dr Baltimore MD 21215

BROCK, STEPHEN L., language educator, consultant; s. Daniel Gordon Brock and Alicia Marie Derks; m. Mary Lee Bortnem, Oct. 14, 1989; children: Claudia Wentworth, Etienne Leigh. BA, St. Louis U., 1986; M in English Edn., U. of Minn., 1991; MS, Creighton U., Nebr., 2001. Tchr. Omaha South HS, 1992—99; supr. internat. langs. Omaha Pub. Schs., 1999—2004. Bd. dirs., past pres. Nebr. Internat. Langs. Assn., Lincoln, Nebr., 1998—; past pres., bd. mem. Nebr. Assn. of Tchrs. of German, Omaha, 1998—2002; dir. Ctrl. States Conf. for the Tchg. of Fgn. Langs., Mpls., 2003—; presenter in field. Co-author: (instructional guide) National German Week Packet; cons. (German textbook) Deutsch Aktuell 1 & 2, presenter (conf.) Using Nonlinguistic Approaches to Improve Student Learning (Best of Nebr. award, 2001), Higher Level Thinking: Activities that Reach the Top (Best of Nebr. award, 1999). Pres. South Omaha Neighborhood Assns., 2002—04, Hanscom Pk. Neighborhood Assn., Omaha, 2000—04; pac-chair of children's action fund Omaha Edn. Assn., 1997—99; parish pastoral coun. pres. St. John's Parish Coun., Omaha, 1998—2000; dir. Police Adv. Coun., Omaha, 2002—; bd. dirs. Neighborhood Ctr. for Greater Omaha. Recipient Ten Outstanding Young Omahan's, Jaycees, 1997, STAR award, Nebr. Dept. of Edn., 1998—2003, Nebr. Outstanding Fgn. Lang. Tchr., Nebr. Fgn. Lang. Assn., 1999; fellow Fulbright Meml. Fund Tchr. Program, Japan-U.S. Ednl. Commn., 2000—01; scholar Kaufman Scholarship, U. of Minn., 1990. Mem.: South Omaha Optimists (assoc.). Roman Catholic. Avocations: wagnerian opera, haute cuisine, reading. Office: Omaha Publ Schs 3215 Cuming St Omaha NE 68131 Business E-Mail: steve.brock@loubrock.net.

BROCK, THOMAS DALE, microbiology educator; b. Cleve., Sept. 10, 1926; s. Thomas Carter and Helen Sophia (Ringwald) B.; m. Mary Louise Louden, Sept. 13, 1952 (div. Feb. 1971); m. Katherine Serat Middleton, Feb. 20, 1971; children: Emily Katherine, Brian Thomas. BS, Ohio State U., 1949, MS, 1950, PhD, 1952. Research microbiologist Upjohn Co., Kalamazoo, 1952-57; asst. prof. Western Res. U., Cleve., 1957-59, Ind. U., Bloomington, 1960-61, assoc. prof., 1962-64, prof., 1964-71; E.B. Fred prof. natural scis. U. Wis., Madison, 1971-90, prof. emeritus, 1990—, chmn. dept. bacteriology, 1979-82; pres. Sci. Tech. Pubs., Madison, 1990-94, Savanna Oak Found., 2000—. Found. for Microbiology lectr., 1971-72, 78-79 Author: Milestones in Microbiology, 1961, Principles of Microbial Ecology, 1966, Thermophilic Microorganisms, 1978, Biology of Microorganism, 7th edit., 1994, Basic Microbiology with Applications, 3d edit., 1986, A Eutrophic Lake, 1985, Thermophiles: General, Molecular and Applied Microbiology, 1986, Robert Koch: A Life in Medicine and Bacteriology, 1988, The Emergence of Bacterial Genetics, 1990, Shorewood Hills: An Illustrated History, 1999. Recipient Rsch. Career Devel. award NIH, 1962-68, Waksman award Soc. Indsl. Microbiology, 2003. Fellow AAAS; mem. Am. Soc. for Microbiology (hon. mem., chmn. gen. div. 1970-71, Fisher award 1984, Carski award 1988) Home and Office: 1227 Dartmouth Rd Madison WI 53705-2213

BROCK, WILLIAM ALLEN, III, economist, educator; b. Phila., Oct. 23, 1941; s. William and Margaret Brock; m. Joan Brock, Aug. 31, 1962; 1 child, Caroline. AB in Math. with honors, U. Mo., 1965; PhD, U. Calif., Berkeley, 1969. Asst. prof. econs. U. Rochester, NY, 1969-71; assoc. prof. U. Chgo., 1972-75, prof., 1975-81; from assoc. prof. to full prof. Cornell U., 1974-77; Romnes prof. econs. U. Wis., Madison, 1981—, F.P. Ramsey prof. econs., 1984—, W.F. Vilas rsch. prof., 1990—. Vis. assoc. prof. U. Rochester, 1973; cons. U.S. Dept. Justice, SBA, EPA, FTC. Assoc. editor: Jour. Econ. Theory, Internat. Econ. Rev., 1972—99; contbr. articles to profl. jours.; co-author (with A. Malliaris): (book) Differential Equations, Stability and Chaos in Dynamic Economics, 1989; co-author: (with D. Hsieh, B. LeBaron) Nonlinear Dynamics, Chaos and Instability: Statistical Theory and Economic Evidence, 1991. Recipient Roger F. Murray 3d Pl. prize, Inst. Quantitative Rsch. Fin., 1989; NSF grantee, 1970—2003, Sherman Fairchild Disting. scholar, Calif. Inst. Tech., 1978, Guggenheim fellow, 1987—88. Fellow: Am. Econs. Assn. (distng.), Econometric Soc.; mem.: AAAS, NAS. Office: U Wis Dept Econs 1180 Observatory Dr Madison WI 53706-1320

BROCKELSBY, JEFFREY LIND, investment executive; b. Rapid City, SD, Oct. 20, 1954; s. Earl John Brockelsby and Maude (Wagner) B. BS in Radio/TV summa cum laude, Bradley U., 1976; MS in Mass Comm., S.D. State U., 1983; Cert. in Biblical Studies, Columbia Biblical Sem., 1996. Reporter KEVN/TV, Rapid City, SD, 1976-77; press aide/campaign press sec. Se. George McGovern, Washington, 1979-81; press sec. Rep. Byron Dorgan, Washington, 1981; program dir. S.D. Democratic Party, Pierre, 1983-85; correspondent Huron Daily Plainsman, Pierre, 1985-86; congl. field rep. Rep. Tim Johnson, Rapid City, 1986-87; investment executive Brockelsby Family Trusts, Columbia, S.C., 1993—; corp. treas. Black Hills Reptile Gardens, Inc., Rapid City, 1991—. Bd. dirs. Black Hills Reptile Gardens, Inc., 1993—; polling dir. O'Connor for Gov., Sioux Falls, S.D., 1982. Author: The Brockelsbys of Crawford County Iowa-A Family History, 1991. State campaign treas. Gary Hart for Pres., 1984; field operative Paul Simon for Pres., Rapid City, 1988; cons. several polit. campaigns. Mem.: Depression and Bipolar Support Alliance. Democrat. Avocations: music, running, genealogy. Home: 164 Heritage Village Ln Columbia SC 29212-3512 Office: Brockelsby Fam Trusts 164 Heritage Village Ln Columbia SC 29212-3512

BROCKENBROUGH, EDWIN CHAMBERLAYNE, surgeon; b. Balt., July 24, 1930; s. Edwin Chamberlayne Sr. and Martha Davis (Coale) B.; m. Jean McClure, May 4, 1968; children: John, Martha, Andrew, Ann, Susan. BA, Coll. William & Mary, 1952; MD, Johns Hopkins U., 1956. Intern Johns Hopkins Hosp., Balt., 1956-57, resident, 1957-59; sr. asst. surgeon Nat. Heart Inst., Bethesda, Md., 1959-61; chief resident surgery U. Wash., Seattle, 1961-64, faculty mem. dept. surgery, 1964-75; pvt. practice Seattle, 1975-98. Clin. prof. surgery U. Wash., 1984—; pres. King County Med. Soc., Seattle, 1992; trustee Health Resources N.W., Seattle; med. dir. Pacific Vasc. Inst., 1996—. Contbr. chpt. to book and articles to profl. jours. Sr. asst. surgeon USPHS, 1959-61. Fellow ACS (pres. Wash. State chpt. 1985), Seattle Surg. Soc. (sec. 1972); mem. North Pacific Surg. Assn. (pres. 1995-96), Pacific Coast Surg. Assn., Am. Rhododendron Soc. (pres. 1977-79, Silver medal 1985). Republican. Episcopalian. Avocations: gardening, hybridizing rhododendrons, photography, culinary arts, fishing. Home and Office: 3630 Hunts Point Rd Bellevue WA 98004-1114 E-mail: nedbro@hotmail.com.

BROCKENBROUGH, HENRY WATKINS, lawyer; b. Richmond, Va., Aug. 28, 1923; s. Benjamin Willard and Kathleen Reading (Watkins) B.; m. Mary Lane Williams, Oct. 30, 1948; children: Henry Watkins, Rebecca Lane, John Reading, Willson Williams. BA cum laude, Hampden-Sydney Coll., 1944; LLB, U. Va., 1948; grad. degree, Rutgers U., 1957. Bar: Va. 1949. With Crestar Bank, Richmond, 1948-88, v.p., trust officer, 1963-67, sr. v.p., trust officer, 1967-88, spl.counsel and trust cons. to Crestar Bank, 1988-91; ptnr.unsel Taylor, Hazen, Kauffman & Pinchbeck, Richmond, 1991—2003; of counsel Pinchbeck, P.C., Richmond2003. Chmn. trust com. Va. Bankers Assn., 1970-71. Past pres. Estate Planning Coun., Richmond; chmn. bd. dirs. Tuckahoe YMCA, 1975. Lt. (j.g.) USNR, 1943-46. Mem. Va. State Bar, Va. Bar Assn., The Cohoke Club (West Point, Va., past pres.), Lambda Chi Alpha, Delta Theta Phi. Presbyterian. Home: 802 Horsepen Rd Richmond VA 23229-6725 Office: 6932 Forest HIll Ave Richmond VA 23225 Office Phone: 804-320-2439.

BROCKERT, JOSEPH PAUL, government executive, writer, editor, designer; b. Tipp City, Ohio, Sept. 17, 1954; s. Paul Edwin and Mary (Aten) B.; m. Deborah Sue Schaefer, Apr. 10, 1976; children: Jonathan Andre, Jason Anthony. BS in Journalism with honors, Ohio U., 1975. Sr. editor Linn's Stamp News, Sidney, Ohio, 1976—84; sr. stamp program specialist U.S. Postal Svc., Washington, 1984—87, program mgr. stamp design, 1987—93, coord. Citizen's Stamp Adv. Com., 1985, art dir. U.S. stamps and stationary, 1986—, designer, 1988—, mgr. Stamps OnLine website, 1999, head speechwriter, 2001, sr. writer, editor, 2002, curator spl. collections, 2003—. Guest curator Smithsonian Nat. Postal Mus., 2005—; agy. rep. Commn. Bicentennial of U.S. Constn., 1986-91. Author: Basic Knowledge for the Stamp Collector, 1978, 4th rev. edit., 1983 (Silver medal Am. Philatelic Soc. 1979, Internat. Bronze medal 1986), (with Elaine Durnin Boughner) Stamp Collecting Made Easy, 1984, 3d rev. edit., 1986; editor: The Postal Service Guide to U.S. Stamps, 20th-22d edits., 1993-95, Stamps etc., 1993—, USA Philatelic, 1996-98; composer Mass of the Good Shepherd, 2000, Good Shepherd Celebrates!, 2001; contbr. articles to profl. and hobby jours. Chmn. publicity Gunston (Va.) Elem. PTA, 1985, pres., 1986-87; budget chmn. Fairfax County (Va.) Coun. PTA, 1988-92, sec., 1992; pres. Newington Forest (Va.) Elem. PTA, 1989-91; coach Lorton Little League, 1987-88. Mem.: Am. Philatelic Soc. Roman Catholic. Avocations: music, collecting stamps, photography, composing, bowling. Home and Office: 34652 Crew Rd Pomeroy OH 45769-8907 E-mail: joseph.p.brockert@usps.gov.

BROCKETT, FRANCESCA L., retail executive; BA, Harvard U., 1982; MBA, Stanford (Calif.) U., 1986. Cons. Booz-Allen and Hamilton, Atlanta, 1982—85, McKinsey and Co., Houston, 1986—92; with PepsiCo, New Eng., 1994—95, Irvine, Calif., 1995—97, Tricon Global Restaurants, Louisville, 1997—98; from sr. v.p. strategic planning and bus. devel. to exec. v.p. Toys "R" Us, Inc., Wayne, NJ, 1998—2000, exec. v.p. strategic planning and bus. devel., 2000—. Office: Toys R Us Inc 1 Geoffrey Way Wayne NJ 07470-2030 Business E-Mail: brocketf@toysrus.com.

BROCKETT, OSCAR GROSS, theater educator; b. Hartsville, Tenn., Mar. 18, 1923; s. Oscar Hill and Minnie Dee (Gross) B.; m. Lenyth Spenker, Sept. 4, 1951; 1 dau., Francesca Lane. BA, Peabody Coll., 1947; MA, Stanford U., 1949, PhD, 1953. Instr. English U. Ky., 1949-50; asst. instr. drama Stanford U., 1950-52; asst. prof. drama Stetson U., DeLand, Fla., 1952-56; from asst. to assoc. prof. U. Iowa, 1956-63; from prof. to distinguished prof. Ind. U., 1963-78; Ashbel Smith prof. drama U. Tex., Austin, 1978-80; dean U. Tex. Coll. Fine Arts, 1978-80; DeMille prof. drama U. So. Calif., L.A., 1980-81; Waggener prof. fine arts U. Tex., Austin, 1981-87, Virginia L. Murchison Regents prof., 1987-88, holder Z.T. Scott Family Chair in drama, 1988-99, Univ. Disting. Tchg. prof., 1996—. Author 10 books; contbr. articles to profl. jours. With USNR, 1943-46. Recipient Fulbright award, 1963-64, Medallion of Honor Theta Alpha Phi, 1977, Am. Coll. Theatre Festival Gold Medallion, 1978, Career Achievement award Assn. for Theatre in Higher Edn., 1991, Spl. Citation award U.S. Inst. TheatreTech., 2001; Guggenheim fellow, 1970-71. Mem. Am. Theatre Assn. (past pres., Merit award 1979), Coll. Am. Theatre Fellows (dean. 2002-04), Am. Soc. Theatre Rsch., Internat. Fedn. Theatre Rsch., Nat. Theatre Conf., Nat. Comm. Assn., Shakespeare Assn. Am., Lit. Mgrs. and Dramaturgs of the Americas. Democrat. Episcopalian. Home: 901 W 9th St #903 Austin TX 78703 Office: U Tex Theater and Dance Dept Austin TX 78712 Office Phone: 512-232-5310. E-mail: obrockett@mail.utexas.edu.

BROCKHAUS, JOYCE PATRICA DEES, counselor, marriage and family therapist, consultant; b. Tampa, Fla., May 21, 1946; d. John Paul and Lorraine Elizabeth Dees; m. Robert Herold Brockhaus, June 13, 1970; children: Cheryl Lynn Vartanian, Robert Herold Jr. BSN, Washington U., St. Louis, 1967; MSN, U. Mo., 1971; Doctorate, St. Louis U., 1976. Mem. med. sch. faculty Washington U., St. Louis, 1983—87; dir. clin. child psychiat. nursing St. Louis Children's Hosp., 1983—87; dir. CORO, St. Louis, 1989—90; pres. Brockhaus Group, St. Louis, 1990—; mem. clin. med. faculty St. Louis U., 1990—2002, asst. prof. nursing; dir. masters program in psych. nursing U. Mo., Columbia. Pres. Family Firm Inst., Boston, 2001—02; bd. dirs. African Inst. for Family Bus., Cape Town, South Africa; family bus. cons., 1992—. Author: Nursing; contbr. articles to profl. jours. Bd. dirs. Lindbergh Sch. Dist., St. Louis, 1991—96; chairperson Cub Scout Pack 25, St. Louis, 1985—88. Named Mo. Nurse of Yr., 1985; recipient Internat. award, Family Firm Inst., 2005. Fellow: U.S. Assn. for Small Bus. and Entrepreneurship (hon.; sr. v.p. 1995—2000), Family Firm Inst. (hon.; pres. 2001—02, Barbara Hollander award 2002); mem.: Nat. Assn. Women Bus. Owners (v.p. 1990—95). Home: 10000 Hilltop Dr Saint Louis MO 63128 Office: Brockhaus Group 10000 Hilltop Dr Saint Louis MO 63128 Office Phone: 314-843-5713. Office Fax: 314-843-5113. E-mail: jpyce@brockhausgroup.net.

BROCKHAUS, ROBERT HEROLD, SR., business educator, consultant; b. St. Louis, Apr. 18, 1940; s. Herold August and Leona M. (Stutzke) B.; m. Joyce Patricia Dees, June 13, 1970; children: Cheryl Lynn, Robert Herold. BS in Mech. Engring., U. Mo.-Rolla, 1962; MSIA, Purdue U., 1966; PhD, Washington U., St. Louis, 1976. Mgr. Ralston-Purina, St. Louis, 1962-69; pres. Progressive Mgmt. Enterprises, Ltd., St. Louis, 1969—; asst. prof. mgmt. sci. St. Louis Univ., 1972-78, assoc. prof., 1978-84, prof., 1994—2004; chair in entrpreneurship Coleman Found., 1991—2004; dir. Small Bus. Inst., St. Louis Univ., 1976-86, Inst. Entrepreneurial Studies, St. Louis Univ., 1987-90; treas. CORO Found., 1987-92; exec. dir. Jefferson Smurfit Ctr. for Entrepreneurial Studies, 1990—2004; 1st v.p. Mo. Inventors Assn., 1988-94; state adminstr. Mo. Small Bus. Devel. Ctr., St. Louis, 1982-86; state dir. Mo. Small Bus. Devel. Ctrs., St. Louis, 1987-89. Schoen prof. entrepreneurship Baylor U., 1981; McAninch prof. entrepreneurship Kans. State U., 1985—87; vis. scholar So. Cross U., Australia, 1995; del. White House Conf. on Small Bus., 1986, 95; alderman City of Sunset Hills, 1998—; nat. rsch. adv. SBA, 2003; bd. dirs. U. Croatia, 2004—. Co-author: Encyclopedia of Entrepreneur, 1982: Building a Better You, 1982; Nursing Concepts for Health Promotion, 1979, Art and Science of Entrepreneurship, 1985, Entrepreneurship in the 1990's, 1991, The State of the Art of Entrepreneurialship, 1992; editor Journal of Consulting, 1988-90; co-editor: Frontiers of Entrepreneurship Research, 1990, Advances in Entrepreneurship, Firm Emergence and Growth, 1993, 95, Entrepreneurship Education, 2001; editor Family Bus. Rev., 1993-97; also contbr. articles to profl. jours. Bd. dirs. City Venture, St. Louis, 1982—86; chair Troop 25 Boy Scouts Am., 1990—93, vice chair Gravois Trl. Coun., 2000—; chair, pres. Ea. Mo. Small Bus. Week, 2002; nat. entrepreneurship rsch. advocate Small Bus. Adminstrn., 2003; bd. dirs. African Family Bus. Assn., 2004—, House Corp.; v.p. United Ch. of Christ, 1991—92, pres., 1992—93. Named extraordinary prof., Potchefstroom U., South Africa, 2000—03, Lindbergh Leader, 2001; recipient Outstanding Svc. award, Boy Scouts Am., 1994, Disting. Svc. award Gravois Trl. Coun., 2002, award of excellence, NASDAQ, 2002, Citizen of the Yr., Crestwood-Sunset Hills, 2004; Fulbright fellow, U. Waikato, New Zealand, 1985. Fellow Internat. Coun. for Small Bus. (life, sr. v.p. 1981-83, internat. pres. 1983-84, bd. dirs. 1983, v.p. 1986, exec. dir. 1987—, 2003-), Nat. Small Bus. Inst. Dirs. Assn. (nat. v.p. 1980-82, 96-97, nat. pres. 1982-83, Disting. Mentor award 2000, 2005), U.S. Assn. for Small Bus. Entrepreneurship (nat. entrepreneurship adv. 2005)); mem. Assn. Collegiate Entrepreneurs (internat. bd. dirs., exec. com. 1991-93, recipient outstanding entrepreneurship educator awd., 1992), Acad. Mgmt. (nat. prog. chmn. 1977-78, exec. com. 1993-95), Inventor's Assn. St. Louis (bd. dirs. 1989-94, 1st v.p. 1991), Family Firm Inst. (internat. conf. chair, 1995), Fenton Jaycees (treas.), Exec. Club (St. Louis, moderator 1973-86), Sunset Hills C. of C. (Citizen of Yr. 2004), Pi Kappa Alpha (dist. pres. 1969-74, faculty adv. 1990-2004, recipient disting. svc. award 1972, bd. dirs., treas., endowment found. nat. coun. for youth and religion, 1994—). Avocations: swimming, sailing, camping. Home: 10000 Hilltop Dr Saint Louis MO 63128-1512 Office Phone: 314-843-5713. E-mail: brockhau@slu.edu.

BROCKHOFT, KRISTINE LYNN, family and consumer sciences educator; d. Duane D. and June E. Nelson; m. Mike D. Brockhoft, Sept. 9, 1978; children: Nichole L., Thomas M., Christopher M., Jonathan M. BS, SD State U., 1978. Tchg. cert. SD. Family and consumer scis. tchr. Winner (SD) Sch. Dist., 1996—. Nat. exec. coun. advisor to v.p. pub. rels. Family, Career and Cmty. Leaders Am., Reston, Va., 2001—02, nat. star event lead cons., 2002—, nat. exec. coun. advisor to nat. pres., 2004—; mem. state exec. coun. advisor SD Family, Career and Cmty. Leaders Am., Brookings, 1997—, mem. bd. dirs., 2003—04, star event lead cons., 1998—; h.s. bldg. rep. Winner Edn. Assn., 1997—; mem. adv. coun. Lunchtime Solutions, Winner, 2002—. Student coun. advisor Winner H.S. Student Coun., 2002—05. Named Master

Tchr. (1 of 6 in nation), Family Economics and Fin. Edn., 2005—, Outstanding Advisor, SD Family, Career and Cmty. Leaders Am., 2002; recipient Master Advisor award, Family, Career and Cmty. Leaders Am., 1999—2000, Mentor Advisor award, 2000—01; grantee, SD Dept. Edn., 2000, 2002. Mem.: Am. Assn. Family and Consumer Scis. (assoc.; state v.p. 2003—04, cert. 1985, Top Ten Tchr. of Yr. 2003—04). Conservative. Office: Winner Sch Dist 325 S Monroe St Winner SD 57580

BROCKMAN, LESLIE RICHARD, social worker; b. St. Paul, Aug. 10, 1940; s. Leslie Blair Brockman and Mary Emma (Miller) Hemenway; m. Rosemarie Lemus, Aug. 18, 1962; 1 child, Christopher Scott. BA, Loyola U. of L.A., 1963; MS, Troy (Ala.) State U., 1977; MS in Social Work, U. Tex., Arlington, 1984. Lic. profl. counselor; lic. chem. dependency counselor, marriage and family therapist; lic. clin. practitioner ACSW; diplomate clin. social work; cert. criminal justice specialist. Exec. dir. Family Assessment Consultation Therapy Svc., Ft. Worth, 1984—; commd. 2d lt. USAF, 1963, advanced through grades to maj., retired, 1983. Fellow NASW (diplomate); mem. ACA, Am. Assn. Marriage and Family Therapists, Am. Mental Health Counselors Assn., Am. Assn. Behavioral Therapists. Home: 6400 Trail Lake Dr Fort Worth TX 76133-4810 Office: FACTS Inc 5801 Curzon Ave Ste 2B Fort Worth TX 76107-5896 Office Phone: 817-377-0808. Personal E-mail: facts@sbcglobal.net.

BROCKMANN, STEPHEN MATTHEW, education educator; b. N.Y.C., N.Y., Sept. 4, 1960; s. Karen and Henry Caruthers Brockmann. AB, Columbia U., 1978—82; MA, PhD, U. of Wis., 1983—89. Vis. asst. prof. Columbia U., 1989—90, Mich. State U., 1991—92, Brown U., 1992—93; assoc. prof. German, Carnegie Mellon U., Pitts., 1993—. Mng. editor Brecht Yearbook, Pitts., 2002—. Fellow, Alexander von Humboldt Found., 1999, 2002, 2003, 2004, German Academic Exch. Svc., 1996. Mem.: Internat. Brecht Soc., Am. Assn. of Teachers of German, MLA, German Studies Assn. Avocations: travel, hiking. Office: Carnegie Mellon University BH 160 5000 Forbes Ave Pittsburgh PA 15213

BROCKMANN, WILLIAM FRANK, retired health facility administrator; b. South Bend, Ind., Nov. 14, 1942; s. Ervin William and Elizabeth Marie (Cassidy) B.; m. Ellen Meier, June 10, 1967; children: William Edward, Rebecca Jayne. BS in Mgmt., Ind. U., 1966; MHA, St. Louis U., 1968. Administrv. asst. St. Anthony Hosp., Okla. City, 1968; asst. hosp. adminstr. Caylor-Nickel Med. Ctr., Bluffton, Ind., 1972-77, hosp. adminstr., 1977-86, pres., 1986-89, CEO, 1989—2000, mem. exec. com., 1985—2000; pres. River Ter. Estates Retirement Cmty., Bluffton, Ind., 2000—; CEO Bluffton Regional Med. Ctr., 2000—02; ret., 2002. Bd. dirs. Old First Nat. Bank. Gen. campaign mgr. Wells County United Way, 1973; past pres. Bluffton United Meth. Ch., Wells County Found.; pres., bd. dirs. Wells County Coun. on Aging; spkr. in field. Capt. M.S.C. U.S. Army, 1969—71, vietnam vet. Life fellow Am. Coll. Healthcare Execs. (Regents award, 2001); mem. Ind. Hosp. Assn. (chmn. bd. 1990-91, Disting. Svc. award, 2001), Am. Hosp. Assn. (ho. dels. 1991-93), Ind. Chi Phi Alumni Assn. (pres., 2002-). Republican. Methodist. Achievements include leading a successful merger of Wells Cmty. Hosp. and Caylor-Nickel Med. Ctr. into Bluffton Regional Med. Ctr. in 2000. Avocations: scuba diving, pool, reading, golf. Home: 1127 Ridgewood Ln Bluffton IN 46714-3827 Personal E-mail: billbrockmann@mchsi.com.

BROCKMEYER, MICHAEL F., lawyer; BA with high distinction, Univ. Ariz., 1974; JD, Univ. Md., 1977. Bar: Md. 1977. Asst. atty. gen., Md., 1978—84; chief, antitrust div. State of Md., 1984—90; ptnr., chmn. Antitrust practice group DLA Piper Rudnick Gray Cary, Balt. Adj. prof. Univ. Md. Sch. Law, 1999—; faculty mem. ALI-ABA, 1987—. Contbr. articles to profl. jours. Sch. bd. mem. Archbishop Curley High Sch. Mem.: ABA, Md. Bar Assn. Office: DLA Piper Rudnick Gray Cary 6225 Smith Ave Baltimore MD 21209-3600 Office Phone: 410-580-4115. Office Fax: 410-580-3115. Business E-Mail: michael.brockmeyer@dlapiper.com.

BROCKOVICH-ELLIS, ERIN, legal researcher; b. Lawrence, Kansas, June 1960; m. Shawn Brown, 1982 (div. 1987); 2 children; m. Steven Brockovich, 1989 (div. 1990); 1 child; m. Eric Ellis, 1999. Management trainee K-Mart, Calif.; electrical engineer trainee Fluor Engineers and Constructors; sec. E.F. Hutton, Reno; former file clerk Masry & Vititoe, Westlake Village, Calif., dir. rsch. Actor: (films) Erin Brockovich, 2000; (TV series) Challenge America, 2001, Final Justice, 2003. Named Ms. Pacific Coast, 1981; recipient Scales of Justice Award, Court TV, Special Citizen Award, The Children's Health Environmental Coalition, Mothers & Shakers Award, Redbook Magazine, Lifesaver Award, Lymphoma Research Foundation of Am. Achievements include spearheaded largest toxic tort injury settlement in U.S. history, 1996; subject of hit movie "Erin Brockovich", 2000. Office: c/o Masry & Vititoe 5707 Corsa Ave 2nd Fl Westlake Village CA 91362

BROCKWAY, DAVID HUNT, lawyer; b. Paterson, N.J., Dec. 18, 1943; s. George Pond and Lucille (Hunt) B.; m. Marilyn Bofshever, July 29, 1979. AB, Cornell U., 1968; JD, Harvard U., 1971. Bar: NY 1972, Washington 1990. Assoc. firm Donovan Leisure Newton & Irvine, N.Y.C., 1971-76; legis. atty. Joint Com. on Taxation, U.S. Congress, Washington, 1976, internat. tax counsel, 1978, deputy chief of staff, 1981, chief of staff, 1983-87; ptnr. Dewey Ballantine, Washington, N.Y.C., 1987-99, co-chmn. tax dept., 1997-99; principal-in-charge Washington Nat. Tax KPMG LLP, 1999—, bd. dir., 2003—. Mem. Am. Law Inst. Project on Sub-chpt. C., 1988—; mem. adv. bd. European Am. Tax Inst., 1989—; cons. Am. Law Inst. Project on Tax Treaties, 1989—; bd. dirs. Nat. Fgn. Trade Coun., 1993—; GE (Bermuda) Ltd., 1993-99. With U.S. Army, 1963-66. Recipient Outstanding Achievement award NYU Tax. Soc., 1998—. Mem. N.Y. State Bar Assn. (exec. com. tax sect. 1988-89, 94-99). Home: 2829 Woodland Dr NW Washington DC 20008-2743 Office: KPMG LLP 2001 M St NW Washington DC 20036-3310 Office Phone: 202-533-3036, 202-533-8542. E-mail: dbrockway@kpmg.com.

BROD, MORTON SHELVIN, oral surgeon; b. Bklyn., Apr. 19, 1926; s. Joseph and Celina (Fromberg) B.; m. Anne Turville Bigelow, June 3, 1955; children: Brian Seth, Timothy Andrew, Abbe Rena. Student, U.S. Mil. Acad., 1947-48; BA, Adelphi Coll., 1951; DDS, Columbia U., 1955. Diplomate Am. Bd. Oral Surgery, Am. Bd. Forensic Dentistry. Intern oral surgery Columbia Presbyn. Med. Ctr., N.Y.C., 1955-56; resident oral surgery Bronx VA Hosp., N.Y.C., 1956-58; pvt. practice oral surgery Norwalk, Conn., 1958-98. Attending oral surgeon chief dental service Norwalk Hosp.; attending oral surgeon Bellevue Hosp; attending surgeon Seaview Hosp., St. Barnabas Hosp., N.Y. VA Hosp.; cons. Manhattan State Hosp., Bronx State Hosp., Psychiat. Inst. N.Y., N.Y. VA Hosp.; instr. dentistry div. clin. oral physiology Columbia Sch. Dental and Oral Surgery, N.Y.C., 1957-69, asst. prof. denistry, 1969-72, assoc. prof., 1972-84, rsch. assoc. dept. stomatology, 1968-84; mem. dental mission to Govt. Anguilla, West Indies, 1969, 70, 71; assoc. prof. dentistry NYU; dir. clin. rev.-oral surgery Physicians Health Svcs.; lectr., Eng., Russia, China, Japan; assoc. prof. oral and maxio-facial surgery NYU Coll. Dentistry, 1993. Contbr. articles to profl. jours., textbooks. Sec. Westport Flood and Erosion Control Bd.; capt. CAP Flying Sharks Search and Rescu Squadron, Conn., 1968—; exec. com. Boy Scouts Am., Westport; mem. Westport Rep. Town Meeting, chmn. pub. works com.; trustee Westport-Weston br. Am. Cancer Soc.; bd. dirs. Norwalk Bd. Dental Health Clinic; dir. Westport Transit Dist., Precision Closure Corp., Auto-Grip Corp.; v.p., treas. Riverview E. Assocs. Real Estate, Inc.; mem. Southwestern Regional Planning Agy., Fairfield County adv. bd. Bridgeport Hydraulic Co. With USAF, 1943-47. Fellow Am. Coll. Oral Surgeons, Am. Soc. Oral Surgeons, Internat. Soc. Oral Surgeons, N.Y. Acad. Dentistry, Am. Coll. Forensic Examiners; mem. ADA, New Eng. Soc. Oral Surgeons, Conn. Soc. Oral Surgeons, Am. Soc. Dentistry for Children (pres. Fairfield County sect. 1962-63), Am. Acad. History Dentistry, Fedn. Dentaire Internat., N.Y. Acad. Scis., N.Y. State Dental Soc., Norwalk Dental Soc. (exec. com. 1966-67, pres. 1967-68), Christian Dental Soc., Flying Dentists Assn., Airplane Owners and Pilots Assn., Pilots Internat. Assn., Fairways Homeowners Assn. (mem. fin. and audit com.). Home and Office: 110 Gardner Dr Longmont CO 80501

BROD, ROY DAVID, ophthalmologist, educator; b. Phila., Oct. 8, 1957; s. Kenneth Lester and Carlene Marcy (Chalick) B.; m. Janice Hope Prossack, May 7, 1983; children: Jamie, Rebecca. BS in Biochemistry magna cum laude, Tulane U., 1979; MD with honors, Temple U., 1983. Diplomate Am. Bd. Ophthalmology. Intern Presbyn. U. Pa. Med. Ctr., Phila., 1983-84; resident in ophtholmology La. State U. Eye Ctr., New Orleans, 1984-87; fellow in vitreoretinal Bascom Palmer Eye Inst., Miami, Fla., 1987-88; assoc. vitreoretinal surgeon Geisinger Med. Ctr., Danville, Pa., 1988-91; pvt. practice Lancaster, Pa., 1991—. Asst. prof. Thomas Jefferson U. Sch. Medicine, Phila., 1991-92; clin. asst. prof. Pa. State U. Sch. Medicine-Hershey Med. Ctr., 1992-95, clin. assoc. prof., 1995—; presenter in field. Contbr. articles to med. jours., chpts. to books. Recipient Outstanding Tchr. award Geisinger Med. Ctr., 1990, 91; Tulane scholar, 1976, E.J. and Sarah Evans scholar, 1979, scholar Measy Found., 1982; named among Best Doctors in Am., 2000. Fellow Am. Acad. Ophthlmology (Honor award 1998); mem. AMA, Assn. for Rsch. in Vision and Ophthalmology, Vitreous Soc. (exec. com.), Retina Soc., Rsch. To Prevent Blindness, Soc. for Contemplation Fascinating Fluorescein Angiograms, Atlantic Coast Vitreoretinal Study Group, Atlantic Coast Fluorescein Angiography Club, Pa. Med. Soc., Pa. Acad. Ophthalmology, Phi Beta Kappa, Alpha Omega Alpha, Phi Eta Sigma, Alpha Epsilon Delta, Omicron Delta Kappa. Avocations: sailing, tennis, bicycling. Office: PO Box 3200 Ste 310 2108 Medical Offices Lancaster PA 17604-3200 Office Phone: 717-399-8790. E-mail: RYJN@aol.com.

BROD, STANFORD, graphic designer, educator; b. Cin., Sept. 29, 1932; s. Morris and Rebecca (Mitman) B.; m. McCrystle Wood; children: Deborah, Daniel, Michael. BS in Design, U. Cin., 1955. Graphic designer Rhoades Studio, Cin., 1955-62; tchr. exptl. typography Art Acad. Cin., 1960-75; graphic designer Lipson, Alport & Glass Assocs., Inc. and predecessor firm Lipson Jacob, Assocs. Inc., Cin., 1962-94, Wood/Brod Design, Cin., 1994—; prof. graphic design U. Cin., 1962—. Tchr. illustration and packaging Art Acad. Cin., 1991-92, 94, 96-98, 2001-05, tchr. corp. identity, 1992-97, 2002-04, tchr. advt. design, corp. design, 1994-97, tchr. visual comms., 1997-98, exhbn. design, 1999, 2002. Exhibited in group shows at Mus. Modern Art, N.Y.C., 1966, Urban Walls, Cin., 1972, City Banners, Sao Paulo, Brazil, 1975, ITC Ctr., N.Y.C., 1981, Tel Aviv Mus., 1982, Internat. Art Exhbn., Dusseldorf, Germany, 1982, Calligraphia U.S.A./USSR, 1990-96, UN, 1994; one-man shows include Skirball Mus. Hebrew Union Coll., Cin., 1989. Recipient Communications Arts awards, 1959, 64, 66, 70, 73, 76, Creativity on Paper awards, 1960-67, Internat. Typographic awards, 1965, 70, N.Y. Type Dirs. Club award, 1968, Typographic Composition Assn. awards, 1970-76. Office: 3662 Grandin Rd Cincinnati OH 45226-1117 *The more I design and paint the more I am sensitive to the movement of my pen, computer and brush, and am able to transmit the image of the subject in my head by way of my arm into my hand, and so to my work. I have become aware that pressure demands counter-pressure, and the difference between order and chaos. This points out the importance of the smallest detail, and that order is the basis of all creative work.*

BRODA-HYDORN, SUSAN, entomologist; b. Newton, N.J., Sept. 2, 1947; d. William E. and Margaret G. Hydorn. BS in Entomology with honors, U. Mass., 1969; MS in Entomology with honors, U. Fla., 1971; PhD in Entomology, U. Calif., 1977. Tchg. asst. dept. entomology U. Calif., 1973, rsch. asst. biol. control, 1974—76; rsch. assoc. dept. entomology U. Maine, 1977—79; adj. prof. dept. entomology U. Fla., 1979; instr. entomology, preventive medicine divsn. U.S. Army Acad. Health Sci., San Antonio, 1979—82; nematologist, quarantine officer, plant protection and quarantine Animal Plant Health Inspection Svc., USDA, West Hampton Beach, NY, 1984—87, identifier, entomology, 1987—95, nat. thysanoptera specialist, 1995—. Mem.: Entomol. Soc. D.C., Fla. Entomol. Soc. (hist. com. 1993—95), Entomology Soc. Am. (student awards com. 1993—96, internat. affairs com. 1997—2000). Avocations: music, organ. Home: 8319 Snowden Oaks Pl Laurel MD 20708 Office: USDA APHIS PPQ 2200 Broening Hwy Ste 140 Baltimore MD 21224 Office Phone: 240-568-9429. Office Fax: 240-568-0433. Business E-Mail: susan.broda@aphisusda.gov.

BRODBECK, WILLIAM JAN, marketing professional; b. Platteville, Wis., Feb. 14, 1944; s. Richard W. and Helen (Stoneman) B.; m. Janet Piwonka, Feb. 4, 1967; children: Allison S., Courtney K., Stephanie L. BA, Hillsdale (Mich.) Coll., 1966; PhD (hon.), Hillsdale Coll., 2004. Asst. to v.p. Hillsdale Coll., 1966-68; mgr. advt. Brodbeck Enterprises, Inc., Platteville, 1968-72, v.p., 1972-79, pres., CEO, 1980-96; pres. Relationship Mktg., Sanibel, Fla., 1996—. Gov. Uniform Product Code Coun., Dayton, Ohio, 1977-86; chmn. First Nat. Bank, Platteville, 1986-92; bd. dirs. Pegasus Ins. Svcs., Irvine, Calif Contbr. articles to profl. jours. Chmn. Third Congl. Dist. Reagan Campaign, 1976; pres. Platteville Area Indsl. Devel., 1976-79; bd. dirs. Thursday's Child, Madison, Wis., 1983-96, Wis. Shakespeare Festival, Platteville, 1986-96, CROW (Care and Rehab. of Wildlife), 1999-2002; trustee Hillsdale Coll., 1991—, chmn. presdl. search com., 1999-2000, vice chmn., 2000-03, chmn., 2003—; bd. dirs. Neenah Springs, Inc., Oxford, Wis., 1997—, Noodles and Co., Boulder, Colo., 1998—; mem. bd. govs. The Sanctuary, 1999-2004, v.p., 2001-03, pres., 2003—04; mem. nat. adv. coun. The Heritage Found., Washington, 2003-. Mem. Nat. Grocers Assn. (bd. dirs. 1977-85), Food Mktg. Inst. (bd. dirs. 1982-96, mem. efficient consumer response exec. com. 1993-96), U. Wis. Platteville Found. (pres. 1980-81), Platteville C. of C. (pres. 1972-73), Omicron Delta Kappa (chpt. v.p. 1966). Office: Relationship Mktg 2964 Wulfert Rd Sanibel FL 33957-2213 Office Phone: 239-395-8711. Personal E-mail: wjbrod@aol.com.

BRODEN, THOMAS FRANCIS, III, French language educator; b. South Bend, Ind., Nov. 19, 1951; s. Thomas F. and Joanne Marjorie (Green) B.; m. Marcia C. Stephenson, Oct. 14, 1989. AB, U. Notre Dame, Ind., 1973; AM, Ind. U., 1976, PhD, 1986; postgrad., Coll. France, Paris, 1979-80. Asst. d'anglais Lycee Henri IV and Inst. Nat. Telecomm., Paris, 1979-80, Lycee St.-Louis and Inst. Nat. Agronomique, Paris, 1981-82; lectr. French U. Notre Dame, Ind., 1984-87; vis. asst. prof. Tulane U., New Orleans, 1987-88; asst. prof. French U. Nebr., Lincoln, 1988-91, Purdue U., West Lafayette, Ind., 1991-97, assoc. prof. French, 1997—, chmn. French sect., 1999—2001. Editor Newsletter for Paris-Greimassian Semiotics, 1990-92, 97, La Mode en 1830, 2000. Notre Dame scholar, 1969-73; Rotary fellow, 1973-74, French Govt. fellow, 1981-82, PRF summer rsch. fellow; NEH grantee, 1990, Maude Hammond Fling Faculty Summer fellow, 1991. Mem. MLA, Am. Assn. Tchrs. French, Semiotic Soc. Am. (exec. bd. 1992-94), Simone de Beauvoir Soc., Toronto Semiotic Cir., Can. Semiotic Assn., Assn. Internat. de Semiotique Visuelle. Avocations: jogging, biking, gardening. Office: Purdue U Fgn Langs Stanley Coulter Hall West Lafayette IN 47907 Office Phone: 765-494-3828. Business E-Mail: broden@purdue.edu.

BRODER, DAVID SALZER, reporter, writer; b. Chgo. Heights, Sept. 11, 1929; s. Albert I. and Nina M. (Salzer) B.; m. Ann Creighton Collar, June 8, 1951; children: George, Joshua, Matthew, Michael. BA, U. Chgo., 1947, MA, 1951; LittD (hon.), Denison U., 1975, Gov.'s State U., 1994; LLD (hon.), Wabash Coll., 1977, Kenyon Coll., 1980, Cleve. State U., 1981, Wittenberg Coll., 1982, Yale U., 1984, Ind. U., 1985, Kalamazoo Coll., 1988, Rider Coll., 1989, Dartmouth Coll., 1990, Colby Coll., 1990, Lawrence U., 1991, Bates Coll., 1992, Stetson U., 1993, U. Mich., 1994, Coll. of William & Mary, 1995, Am. U., 1997, North Central Coll., 2002; D in Polit. Sci. (hon.), DePauw U., 2003; D (hon.), Ctrl. Mich. U., 2003; LHD, Clark U., 2005. Reporter Pantagraph, Bloomington, Ill., 1953-55, Congressional Quar., Washington, 1955-60, Washington Star, 1960-65, Washington bur., NY Times, 1965-66, Washington Post, 1966-75, named assoc. editor, 1975, now nat. polit. correspondent; syndicated columnist The Washington Post Writers Group. Prof. Philip Merrill Coll. Journalism, U. Md., 2001—; regular appearances on Meet the Press & Washington Week in Rev., NBC. Author: The Party's Over: The Failure of Politics in America, 1972, Changing of the Guard: Power and Leadership in America, 1980, Behind the Front Page: A Candid Look at How the News is Made, 1987, Democracy Derailed: Initiative Campaigns and the Power of Money, 2000; co-author (with Stephen Hess) The Republican Establishment: The Present and Future of the GOP, 1967, (with Bob Woodward) The Man Who Would be President: Dan Quayle, 1992, (with Haynes Johnson) The System: The American Way of Politics at the Breaking Point, 1996; contbr. numerous articles on pub. affairs to magazines and books. Former mem. U. Chgo. Alumni cabinet. Served with AUS, 1951-53. Named one of 25 most influential Washington journalists, Nat. Jour., 1997; recipient Pulitzer Prize for Disting. Commentary, 1973, White Burkett Miller Presdl. Award, 1989, 4th Estate Award, Nat. Press Found., 1990, Disting. Contributions to Journalism Award, 1993, Elijah Parrish Lovejoy Award, Colby Coll., 1990, Award for Disting. Achievement in Journalism, William Allen White Found., 1997, Lifetime Achievement Award, Nat. Soc. Newspaper Columnists, 1997, Alumni medal, U. Chgo., 2005; fellow Inst. Politics, JKF Sch. Govt., Harvard U., 1969—70, Inst. Policy Sciences and Pub. Affairs, Duke U.; Poynter Fellow, Yale U. & Ind. U., 1973. Fellow Am. Acad. Arts and Scis., Sigma Delta Chi; mem. Am. Polit. Sci. Assn. (adv. bd. Congrl. Fellows Program 1964—, Carey McWilliams Award 1983), Am. Soc. Pub. Adminstrn., Nat. Press Club, Gridiron Club. Home: 4024 27th St N Arlington VA 22207-5207 Office: Washington Post 1150 15th St NW Washington DC 20071-0002 E-mail: broderd@washingtonpost.com.

BRODER, DOUGLAS FISHER, lawyer; b. Cleve., Sept. 30, 1948; s. Harry M. and Peggy (Fisher) B.; m. Rebecca Northey, Jan. 24, 1976; 1 child, Julia N. BA, Vassar Coll., 1970; JD cum laude, Boston U., 1977. Bar: N.Y. 1978, U.S. Dist. Ct. (so. and ea. dists.) N.Y. 1978, U.S. Ct. Appeals (2d cir.) 1983, U.S. Ct. Appeals (6th cir.) 1986, U.S. Ct. Appeals (4th cir.) 1987, U.S. Dist. Ct. (ea. dist.) Mich. 1987, U.S. Supreme Ct. 1993, U.S. Ct. Appeals (9th cir.) 1997. Assoc. Lord, Day & Lord, N.Y.C., 1977-86; ptnr. Coudert Bros. LLP, N.Y.C., 1986—2002, Nixon Peabody LLP, N.Y.C., 2002—05, Kirkpatrick & Lockhart Nicholson Graham LLP, N.Y.C., 2005—. Spkr. and lectr. on continuing legal edn. Author: Antitrust Law Desk Book, 2001, A Guide to US Antitrust Law, 2005; lead editor: International Joint Ventures Professional Information Publishing Ltd., 1996; mem. editl. bd. European Competition Law Rev.; contbr. articles to profl. publs. Mem. ABA, Assn. of Bar of City of N.Y. Home: 300 Central Park W New York NY 10024-1513 Office: Kirkpatrick & Lockhart Nicholson Graham LLP 599 Lexington Ave New York NY 10022 Office Phone: 212-536-4808. Business E-Mail: dbroder@klng.com.

BRODERICK, ANTHONY JAMES, air transportation executive; b. N.Y.C., Feb. 23, 1943; s. Anthony James and Geraldine (Cummings) B.; m. Sylvia Fantasia, May 30, 1967; children: Sean, Pia. BS in Physics, St. Bonaventure U., 1964. Project mgr. pvt. industry, various locations, 1964-71; physicist U.S. Dept. Transp., Cambridge, Mass., 1971-76; staff chief environment and energy FAA, Washington, 1976-79, tech. advisor aviation standards dept., 1979-82, dep. assoc. adminstr. aviation standards dept., 1982-85, assoc. adminstr. aviation standards dept., 1985-88, assoc. adminstr. regulation and cert., 1988-96; ind. aviation safety cons., 1996—. Author numerous sci. and tech. articles; patentee in field. Recipient Arthur S. Fleming award Jaycees, 1979, Presdl. Meritorious Exec. Rank award, 1982, Sr. Exec. Svc. awards U.S. Govt., 1983-87, 89-90, 92-95, Presdl. Disting. Exec. Rank award, 1991, Aviation Week Laurel award, 1992, 2000, Flight Internat. Aerospace Personality of Yr. award, 1995, Disting. Career Svc. award Aviation Week/Flight Safety Found., 1996, RTCA achievement award, 1999, ATW Joseph S. Murphy Industry Svc. award, 2000. Fellow: Royal Aero. Soc. Roman Catholic. Home: 4711 Dumfries Rd PO Box 119 Catlett VA 20119-0119 Office Phone: 202-331-2234. E-mail: tonyb@compuserve.com.

BRODERICK, B. MICHAEL, JR., state legislator, banker; Banker, Canton, S.D.; mem. S.D. Ho. of Reps., Pierre, S.D. Mem. agr., nat. resources and transp. coms. S.D. Ho. of Reps.

BRODERICK, DANIEL P., lawyer; b. Chgo., Sept. 4, 1942; s. Joseph F. and Marcella (Jordan) B.; m. Ann Marie Beattie, July 9, 1966; children— Sean M., Brian D. B.S. in Bus. Adminstrn., U. San Diego, 1965; J.D., Georgetown U., 1972. Bar: Calif. 1973, U.S. Dist. Ct. (cen. dist.) Calif. 1974, U.S. Tax Ct. 1979. Economist, Bur. Internat. Commerce, U.S. Dept. Commerce, Washington, 1968-73; law clk. U.S. Dist. Ct. (cen. dist.) Calif., Los Angeles, 1973-74; assoc. Howser, Gertner & Brown, Newport Beach, Calif., 1974-79, ptnr., 1979— . Mem. Orange Coast Coll. Endowment Fund, Costa Mesa, Calif., 1983-84; mem. endowment fund United Way Orange County, 1983-84. Mem. Calif. State Bar. Home: 9960 Aster Cir Fountain Valley CA 92708-2309

BRODERICK, DENNIS JOHN, lawyer, retail executive; b. Pitts., Dec. 7, 1948; m. Marian Kinney. BA, U. Notre Dame, 1970; JD, Georgetown U., 1976. Bar: Ohio 1976. Assoc. Hahn, Loeser, Freidheim, Dean & Wellman, Cleve., 1976-81; staff atty. Firestone Tire & Rubber Co., Akron, Ohio, 1982—84, sr. atty., 1984—85, asst. gen. counsel, 1985—87; v.p., dep. gen. counsel for regions Federated Dept. Stores, Inc. (formerly Allied Stores Corp.), Cin., 1987-88, v.p., gen. counsel, 1988-90, sr. v.p., gen. counsel, 1990—, sec., 1993—. Served USN, 1970—73. Mem.: Black Lawyers' Assn. of Cin., Cin. Bar Assn., Am. Corp. Counsel Assn. (dir NE Ohio Chpt. 1986). Avocations: motorcycling, motorboating, horseback riding, golf. Office: Federated Dept Stores Inc 7 W 7th St Cincinnati OH 45202-2424

BRODERICK, JAMES ALLEN, painter, art educator, etcher; b. Chgo., July 25, 1939; s. James Broderick and Catherine (Cahill); m. Alice Moehelenhof, Aug. 24, 1963 (div. June 1977); children: Brian, Mark; m. Cindy Gambell, Dec. 21, 1978; children: Victoria, Catherine, Maureen. BA, St. Ambrose Coll., Davenport, Iowa, 1962; MA, U. Iowa, 1966. Asst. prof. N.W. Mo. U., Maryville, 1966-76, dir. art gallery, 1967-76, chmn. art dept., 1970-76; prof. art Tex. Tech U., Lubbock, 1976-83, chair art dept., 1976-83; prof. art U. Tex., San Antonio, 1983—, dir. visual arts divsn., 1983—2002, chmn. dept. art & art history, prof. emeritus, 2003—. One-man shows include, Iowa, Colo., Tex., Mo., Peru. Mem.: Nat. Coun. Art Adminstrs. (bd. dir. 1994—), Nat. Assn. Schs. Art & Design (accreditation reviewer 1977, v.p. 1996—99, pres. 1999—2002). Democrat. Office: U Tex San Antonio 6900 N Loop 1604 W San Antonio TX 78249-1130 Office Phone: 210-458-4352. E-mail: jbroderick@utsa.edu.

BRODERICK, JOHN CARUTHERS, retired librarian, educator; b. Memphis, Tenn., Sept. 6, 1926; s. John Patrick and Myrtle Vaughn (Newson) B.; m. Kathryn Price Lynch, Sept. 10, 1949; children: Kathryn Price, John Caruthers, Jr. AB, Rhodes Coll., Memphis, 1948; MA, U. N.C., 1949, PhD, 1953. Instr. English U. Tex., Austin, 1952-57; asst. prof. Wake Forest (N.C.) U., 1957-58, assoc. prof., 1958-63, prof., 1963-65; with Library of Congress, Washington, 1964-88, specialist, 1964-65, asst. chief, 1965-74, chief, manuscript div., 1975-79, asst. librarian for research services, 1979-88. Adj. prof. English George Washington U., 1964-84; vis. prof. U. Va., 1959, U. N.C., 1968, Cath. U. Am., 1990-91. Author: Past Imperfect, Present Tense, 2000; compiler: Whitman The Poet, 1961; editor: The Journal of Henry David Thoreau, 1981-90; contbr. to profl. jours. Adv. com. U.S. Senate Hist. Office, 1974-78; mem. Nat. Hist. Publs. and Records Commn., 1978-82, Christopher Columbus Quincentennial Jubilee Commn., 1986-88. Served with U.S. Army, 1945-46. Fellow, Coun. on Library Resources, 1971; grantee, Danforth Found., 1960, Am. Coun. Learned Socs., 1962—63. Mem. Acad. Am. Poets, Am. Antiquarian Soc., Cosmos Club, Lit. Soc. Washington, Sigma Alpha Epsilon, Omicron Delta Kappa. Home: 8005 Inspection House Rd Potomac MD 20854-3426

BRODERICK, JOHN T., JR., state supreme court chief justice; BA magna cum laude, Coll. Holy Cross, 1969; JD, U. Va., 1972. Atty. Devine, Millimet, Stahl & Branch, Manchester, NH, 1972-89; shareholder Broderick & Dean (formerly Merrill & Broderick), Manchester, 1989-95; assoc. justice NH Supreme Ct., Concord, 1995—2003, chief justice, 2004—. Mem. ct. accreditation com. NH Supreme Ct., chmn., 2004—; mem. Legal Svcs. Corp., 1993—2003. Fellow Am. Coll. Trial Lawyers, Am. Bar Found., N.H. Bar Found. (bd. dirs. 1985-91); mem. ABA (standing com. on jud. independence 2004-), Mass. Bar Assn., N.H. Bar Assn. (bd. govs. 1985-91, pres. 1990-91), N.H. Trial Lawyers Assn. (bd. govs. 1977-82, pres. 1982-83). Office: NH Supreme Ct One Noble Dr Concord NH 03301

BRODERICK, MATTHEW, actor; b. N.Y.C., Mar. 21, 1962; s. James and Patricia (Biow) B.; m. Sarah Jessica Parker, May 1997, 1 child: James Wilke Broderick. Student high sch., N.Y.C. Actor: (stage prodns.) Valentine's Day, 1980, Torch Song Trilogy, 1982 (Villager award 1982, Outer Critics Circle award 1982), Brighton Beach Memoirs, 1983 (Los Angeles Critics award 1983, Drama League award 1983, Theatre World award 1983, Antoinette Perry award 1983), Biloxi Blues, 1985, The Widow Claire, 1986-87, How to Succeed in Business Without Really Trying, 1995 (Tony award Lead Actor in a Musical, Outer Critics Cir. award, Drama Desk award), The Producers, 2001-02, 2003; (films) Max Dugan Returns, 1983, WarGames, 1983, Ladyhawke, 1985, 1918, 1985, Ferris Bueller's Day Off, 1986, On Valentine's Day, 1986, Project X, 1987, Courtship, 1987, Biloxi Blues, 1988, Torch Song Trilogy, 1988, Glory, 1989, Family Business, 1989, The Freshman, 1990, Out on a Limb, 1992, The Night We Never Met, 1993, The Lion King (voice), 1994, The Road to Wellville, 1994, Mrs. Parker and the Vicious Circle, 1994, Arabian Night (voice), 1995, The Cable Guy, 1996, Addicted to Love, 1997, Godzilla, 1998, Walking to the Waterline, 1998, Election, 1999, Inspector Gadget, 1999, You Can Count on Me, 2000, Good Boy! (voice), 2003, Marie and Bruce, 2004, The Stepford Wives, 2004, The Last Shot, 2004; (TV movies) Master Harold.and the Boys, 1985, A Life in the Theater, 1993 (Emmy nomination for best supporting actor miniseries or spl., 1994), The Music man, 2003; prodr., dir., actor: (film) Infinity, 1996. Mem. Actors' Equity Assn., SAG. Address: care CAA 9830 Wilshire Blvd Beverly Hills CA 90212-1804

BRODERICK, PATRICK A., lawyer; BA, Harvard U.; JD, Yale U. Counsel McKesson Corp., 1993—99; gen. counsel COR Therapeutics, Inc., 1999—2002; v.p., gen. counsel, sec. DaVita Inc., El Segundo, Calif., 2003—. Office: DaVita Inc 601 Hawaii St El Segundo CA 90245 Office Phone: 310-536-2400.

BRODERSON, THELMA SYLVIA, retired marketing professional; b. St. Louis, Feb. 6, 1932; d. Harry and Lillian (Fishman) B. BA, U. Denver, 1953; postgrad., Washington U., St. Louis, 2001—. Marketer Marsh & McLennan, Inc., St. Louis, 1966—85; account exec. Daniel & Henry Co., St. Louis, 1985—87; marketer G. Steven DeMaster, Inc. at Crane Agy., St. Louis, 1987—99. Prodr. Harry Fender Program Sta. KMOX-CBS, St. Louis, 1968-74; columnist The Oil Can, 1972-75. Tchr. religious sch. United Hebrew Temple, St. Louis, 1956-63. Donor Harry Fender Memorabilia to St. Louis Pub. Libr. Media Archives and Rare Books Collection, 1997. Mem.: Phi Beta Kappa. Avocations: theater, arts.

BRODEUR, CATHERINE RECKART, artist; b. L.A., May 6, 1927; d. John Charles Reckart and Catherine Hyland Burns; m. Raymond Roy Brodeur, Apr. 17, 1948; children: George, Anne, Arthur, Martha, Frances. Student, Art Student's League, N.Y.C., 1975; studied with, Daniel Greene, N.Y.C., John Howard Sanden, Jack Callahan, John Phelps, Rockport and Springfield, Mass. Art instr. Holyoke (Mass.) Home Info. Ctr., 1979, 80, 81, Wistariahurst Mus., Holyoke, 1988, 89, 90; lectr. W. Springfield (Mass.) C. of C., 1981, Holyoke Hosp., 1993; ofcl. artist USCG, 1981-91. Exhibited in group shows at Nat. Arts Club, N.Y.C., Federal Hall, N.Y.C., World's Fair, New Orleans, City Hall, Boston, New Eng. Air Mus., Windsor Locks, Conn., Berkshire Mus., Pittsfield, Mass., Governor's Island, N.Y., The Prestige Gallery, Toronto, Can., 1992, Wistariahurst Mus., Holyoke, 1992, Mus. Fine Arts, Springfield, Mass.; annual exhibits Vt. Inst. Natural Sci., Woodstock, Nature Ctr., Westport, Conn.; represented in numerous pub. and pvt. collections including Permanent Naval Art Collection, Washington, First Nat. Bank, Boston, Dominican Monastery, West Springfield; contbr. popular mags. Recipient Merit award Springfield (Mass.) Art League Nat., 1986. Mem. Pastel Soc. Am., Copley Soc. Boston, Acad. Artist's Assn. (v.p., Wilkins award 1990), Hudson Valley Arts Assn. (Margaret Fernald Dole award 1982), North Shore Art Assn. Roman Catholic. Avocation: antique collecting (oriental porcelain and pottery).

BRODEUR, MARTIN, professional hockey player; b. Montreal, Que., Can., May 6, 1972; Selected 1st round NHL entry draft N.J. Devils, 1994, goalie, 1991—. Mem. NHL All-Rookie Team, 1993—94; player NHL All-Star Game, 1996—2004; mem. Team Can., Olympic Games, Nagano, 1998, Salt Lake City, 2002, Team Can., World Cup of Hockey, 1996, 2004. Recipient Calder Meml. Trophy, 1993—94, Vezina Trophy, 2003, 2004, William M. Jennings Trophy, 1997—98, 2003, 2004. Achievements include 1st goaltender in history to record 9 consecutive 30 win seasons; set NHL record with 7 playoff shutouts, 2003; mem. Gold medal Can. Hockey team, Salt Lake City Olympic Games, 2002; mem. Stanley Cup Champion, New Jersey Devils, 1995, 2000, 2003; mem. World Cup Champion Team Can., 2004. Office: c/o New Jersey Devils 50 Rt 120 N PO Box 504 East Rutherford NJ 07073-0504

BRODEUR, RUSSELL P., design engineer; b. New Brunswick, N.J., Sept. 4, 1962; s. John H. Brodeur and Sarah Epelstein, Celine M. Brodeur (Stepmother); children: Zachary P., Jaden R. BS, Alfred U., 1984; PhD, Pa. State U., 1991. Engr. AMP Inc., Harrisburg, Pa., 1984—87; rsch. assoc. Pa. State U., University Park, 1991—94; mem. group tech. staff Tex. Instruments Inc., Attleboro, Mass., 1994—. Mem.: Am. Ceramic Soc. Avocations: water sports, skiing, travel. Home: 18 Colonial Way Rehoboth MA 02769 Office: Texas Instruments Inc 34 Forest St MS 01-42 Attleboro MA 02703 E-mail: rbrodeur@ti.com.

BRODHEAD, DAVID CRAWMER, lawyer; b. Madison, Wis., Sept. 16, 1934; s. Richard Jacob and Irma (Crawmer) B.; m. Nancie Christensen, Aug. 17, 1963; children: Compton, Peter, Christoffer. BS, U. Wis., 1956, LLB, 1959. Bar: N.Y. 1960, Wis. 1959, D.C. 1979. Assoc. firm Paul, Weiss, Rifkind, Wharton & Garrison, N.Y.C., 1959-68, ptnr., 1969—. Bd. dirs. Centennial Industries, Inc., NYC. Editor-in-chief: Wis. Law Rev. 1958-59. Trustee Collegiate Sch., N.Y.C., 1978-85; vestryman Christ and St. Stephen's Episcopal Ch., 1972-82. Mem. N.Y. State Bar, Assn. of Bar of City of N.Y., Wis. Bar. Assn., D.C. Bar Assn., ABA, Westside C. of C. of City of N.Y. (dir. 1970-83), Order of Coif, Delta Theta Phi Clubs: Washington (Conn.); Holland Soc. of N.Y. Office Phone: 212-373-3000. *Take life one day at a time. Yesterday is gone forever and tomorrow is not here. That leaves only today to deal with.*

BRODHEAD, JAMES E(ASTON), actor, writer; b. St. Louis, Jan. 30, 1932; s. James Easton II and Martha Pusey (Mithoefer) B.; m. Sue Hawes, June 21, 1963; children: William James Pusey, Daniel Alexander Hawes. BA in Speech, U. Mich., 1954. Announcer/news editor Sta. WNOP, Newport, Ky., 1954-55; actor stage and TV N.Y.C., 1955-62; copywriter/reporter Time Mag., N.Y.C. and Calif., 1963-69; pub. rels. account exec. Laurie & Assocs. and Mahoney & Assocs., L.A., 1971-74; actor Querencia Prodns., L.A. and Santa Barbara, 1974—. Bd. dirs. Western Adv. Bd., Actor's Equity, L.A., 1978-83, ANTA West, L.A., 1978-80, Western Coun. Actor's Fund Am., 1993-95, Santa Barbara Symphony, 1998-2005. Author: Inside Laugh-In, 1969; appeared in 17 films including Leadbelly, First Monday in October, Frances, Mame, Piranha, 3 Disney comedies; TV films include War & Remembrance, Helter Skelter, Gideon's Trumpet; TV series include The Judge, General Hospital, Here's Lucy, Kraft TV Theatre; more than 100 stage prodns. including Inherit the Wind, First Monday in October. Mem. Ensemble Theatre Co., Pacific Pioneer Broadcasters, Actors' Fund (life), Edwin Forrest Soc. (founding) Am. Atheists, Freedom from Religion Found., Santa Barbara Club, Sakonnet Point Club. Democrat. Avocations: reading, cooking, travel, languages. Home and Office: Querencia Prodns 506 Yankee Farm Rd Santa Barbara CA 93109-1060 Home (Summer): 6 Taylors Ln N Little Compton RI 02837-1144

BRODHEAD, RICHARD H., academic administrator; m. Cynthia Degnan Brodhead; 1 child. BA in English summa cum laude, Yale Univ., 1968, MA in English, 1970, PhD. in English, 1972. Asst. English Prof. Yale Univ., 1972—85, prof. English, 1985—90, Bird White Housum Prof. English, 1990—95, chair, English dept., 1989—93; dean Yale College, 1993—2004; A. Bartlett Giamatti prof. English Yale Univ., 1995—2004; pres. Duke Univ., 2004—. Visiting prof. Ecole Normale Superieure, Paris, 1989, Paris, 91; chair. external review committee English dept., Duke Univ., 1991; faculty mem. Yale-New Haven Teachers' Institute. Bd. mem. J. William Fulbright Foreign Scholarship Board, 2002. Recipient Bicentennial Medal, Middlebury College, 1998. Fellow: Am. Acad. Arts & Scis., 2004. Office: Duke U Office of the President 207 Allen Bldg Box 90001 Durham NC 27708*

BRODHEAD, WILLIAM MCNULTY, lawyer, retired congressman; b. Cleve., Sept. 12, 1941; s. William McNulty and Agnes Marie (Franz) B.; m. Kathleen Garlock, Jan. 16, 1965; children: Michael, Paul. AB, Wayne State U., 1965; JD, U. Mich., 1967. Bar: Mich. 1968, D.C. 1983. Tchr., Detroit, 1964-65; atty. City of Detroit, 1969-70; mem. Mich. Ho. Reps., 1971-74, 94th-97th Congresses from 17th Dist., mem. com. on ways and means, 1977-82, mem. budget com., 1979-80; chmn. Democratic Study Group, 1981-82; ptnr. firm Plunkett & Cooney P.C., Detroit, 1982—. Trustee The Skillman Found., Mich.'s Children; chair Focus: Hope-Covenant House of Mich.; dir. Citizens Rsch. Coun. of Mich. Home: 5096 Mirror Lake Ct West Bloomfield MI 48323-1534 Office: Law Offices of William Brodhead 31700 Middlebelt Rd Ste 150 Farmington Hills MI 48334 Office Phone: 248-539-7720. E-mail: wbrodhead@wbrodhead.com.

BRODIE, HARLOW KEITH HAMMOND, psychiatrist, educator, former university president; b. Stamford, Conn., Aug. 24, 1939; s. Lawrence Sheldon and Elizabeth White (Hammond) B.; m. Brenda Ann Barrowclough, Jan. 26, 1967; children: Melissa Verduin, Cameron Keith, Tyler Hammond, Bryson Barrowclough. AB, Princeton U., 1961; MD, Columbia U., 1965; LLD hon., U. Richmond, 1987; LHD (hon.), High Point U., 1992. Diplomate Am. Bd. Psychiatry and Neurology. Intern Ochsner Found. Hosp., New Orleans, 1965-66; resident in psychiatry Columbia-Presbyn. Med. Center, N.Y.C., 1966-68; clin. assoc. intramural research program NIMH, 1968-70; asst. prof. psychiatry, dir. gen. clin. research center Stanford U. Med. Sch., 1970-74; prof. psychiatry, chmn. dept. Duke U. Med. Sch., 1974-82, James B. Duke prof. psychiatry and behavioral scis., 1981—, prof. dept. psychology, prof. law, 1980—; psychiatrist-in-chief Duke U. Med. Center, 1974-82; chancellor Duke U., 1982-85, pres., 1985-93, pres. emeritus, 1993—. Mem. Pres. Biomed. Rsch. Panel, 1975; mem. Carnegie Coun. on Adolescent Devel., 1986-97; trustee Com. for Econ. Devel., 1986-93, mem. subcom. on edn. and child devel., 1990; trustee Nat. Humanities Ctr., 1988-93; mem. nat. rev. and adv. panel for improving campus race rels. Ford Found., 1990-94; mem. subcom. on Edn. on Child Devel. Com., 1990, Inst. Medicine Mental Health and Behavioral Medicine, 1981-83, chmn., 1981-82; chmn. Com. on Substance Abuse and Mental Health Issues in AIDS Rsch., 1992-95; mem. Com. on Leadership Devel., Am. Coun. on Edn., 1990-93. Co-author: The Importance of Mental Health Services to General Health Care, 1979, Modern Clinical Psychiatry, 1982; co-editor: American Handbook of Psychiatry, vols. 6, 7 and 8, 1975, 81, 86, Controversy in Psychiatry, 1978, Psychiatry at the Crossroads, 1980, Critical Problems in Psychiatry, 1982, Signs and Symptoms in Psychiatry, 1983, Consultation-Liaison Psychiatry and Behavioral Medicine, 1986, AIDS and Behavior: An Integrated Approach, 1994, Keeping an Open Door: Passages in a University Presidency, 1996, The Research University Presidency in the Late Twentieth Century, 2005; assoc. editor Am. Jour. Psychiatry, 1973-81. Recipient A.E. Bennet Rsch. award Soc. Biol. Psychiatry, 1970, Disting. Med. Alumni award Columbia U., 1985, Disting. Alumnus award Ochsner Found. Hosp., 1984, Strecker award Inst. of Pa. Hosp., 1980, N.C. award for sci., 1990, William C. Menninger Meml. award ACP, 1994. Fellow: Royal Soc. Medicine; mem.: NAS, Inst. Medicine, Internat. Soc. Sport Psychiatry, Royal Coll. Psychiatrists, Am. Psychiat. Assn. (sec. 1977—81, pres. 1982—83). Home: 63 Beverly Dr Durham NC 27707-2223 Office: Devonwood Co 3211 Shannon Rd Ste 603 Durham NC 27707

BRODIE, HOWARD, artist; b. Oakland, Calif., Nov. 28, 1915; s. Edward and Anna (Zeller) B. Student, Art Inst. San Francisco, Art Student's League, N.Y.C., U. Ghana, Accra; LHD (hon.), Acad. Art Coll., San Francisco, 1984. Mem. staff Life mag., Yank: the Army Weekly, Collier's, AP, CBS News, 1969-89; freelance artist, journalist, 1990—. Author: (book) Howard Brodie War Drawings, 1963, Drawing Fire, A Combat Artist At War, 1996; art journalist: (major wars) World War II, Korea, French Indo-China, Vietnam, (trials) Jack Ruby, Ray, Sirhan, My Lai, Charles Manson, Chicago Seven, Watergate, John Hinckley, Klaus Barbie in France, (famous people) John Wayne, Pres. Kennedy, James Jones; art at White House, 1946, 48; work represented in permanent collections Calif. Palace of Legion of Honor, San Francisco, Soc. Illustrators, N.Y., Libr. Congress, Washington, Air Force Acad., Colo.; prints, books: U.S. Army Infantry Mus., Ft. Benning, Ga., U.S. Army Mus., Presidio, Monterery, Oreg. Nat. Mil. Mus., The Hoover Instn. on War, Revolution and Peace, Anne S.K. Brown Mil. Collection Brown U. Libr., The Mus. of Books, Lenin Libr., Moscow, Gorky Sci. Libr., Moscow, Admiral Nimitz State Hist. Park, Tex., Henry E. Huntington Libr. (award), San Marina, New Britain Mus. Am. Art, Conn., West Point Libr., N.Y., Brown U. Libr., R.I.; commd. to draw The Contemporary Soldier in Action, Assn. U.S. Army, 1999; guest on Merv Griffin Show, Charles Kuralt Sunday Morning program, Ted Koppel program, Night Line; featured Andy Rooney CBS Sunday Morning program, Nostagia Network, Dennis Wholey Am. Program; featured 1 out of 7 artists (PBS Documentary) They Drew Fire, 2000, (incompanion TV book) They Drew Fire, Combat Artists of World War II, 2000. Sgt., U.S. Army. Decorated Bronze Star; recipient honor medals Freedom Found., 1957, 58, 60, 61. Office: PO Box 221940 Carmel CA 93922-1940

BRODIE, JEFFRY, band director; b. Wash., Jan. 9, 1960; s. William and Eleanor Brodie; m. Shelly Williams. BS cum laude, Towson U., Md., 1981; MA, U. Md., Coll. Pk., 1989. Substitute Dunloggin Mid. Sch., 1982; band dir., strings dir. Elkridge Elem. Sch., 1982—85; band dir. Waterloo Mid. Sch., Ellicott City, Md., 1985—87; band dir. Harpers Choice Mid. Sch., 1985—87; band dir. Ellicott Mills Mid. Sch., 1987—92, Burleigh Manor Mid. Sch., Ellicott City, 1992—. Pvt. trumpet instr., 1976—; freelance trumpet performer, 1976—; band adjudicator, clinician, 1983—; conductor Howard County All County Band, Ellicott City, Md., 2001—05, Carroll, Frederick & Charles County All County Band, 2001—05, Md. All State Band, Balt., 2005; spkr., presenter in field; presenter, advisor Oak Hill Mid. Level Inst., Ga., 2000. Performer: (trumpet) Rosebud Cafe Ragtime Ensemble, 1976—77, Prince Georges Brass Ensemble, 1976—77, Towson State U., 1977—82, Jenny Wiley State Pk., 1981, Gettysberg Symphony Orch., 1981—87. Avocations: fly fishing, hunting, travel. Personal E-mail: jbsws@comcast.net. Business E-Mail: jbrodie@hcpss.org.

BRODIE, LAWRENCE J., music educator; b. N.Y.C., Mar. 11, 1963; s. Frank and Leonora K. Brodie; m. Lynn C. Grumann, June 23, 1990; children: Mookai, Xena. MusB in Edn., Crane Sch. Music, 1985; MusM in Saxophone Performance, Ariz. State U., 1987. Cert. tchr. Ariz. Band dir. Peoria (Ariz.) Unified Sch. Dist., 1987—. Musician (saxophone): N.Am. Saxophone Alliance Region Eight Conv., 1984, 41st Ann. Coleman Chamber Music Competition, 1987 (Sauderson award, 1987), 16th Ann. Carmel Chamber Music Competition, 1987 (Florence Allan award, 1987), Laguna Beach Chamber Music Soc. Young Artist Series, 1988, Australian Tour, 1989, N.Am. Saxophone Alliance Region Two Conv., 1990; dir.: Peoria Unified Sch. Dist. Honor Band Condr., 1990, Ariz. Elem. Sch. All-State Band Guest Condr./Clinician, 1999, Deer Valley Honor Band Guest Condr./Clinician, 2002. Mem.: Basketball Ofcls. Ariz. (co-founder 2001), Nat. Fedn. State HS Assns., Nat. Assn. Sports Ofcls., Ariz. Music Educators Assn., Music Educators Nat. Conf. Avocation: NCAA basketball official. Home: 1012 W Lazy K Rd New River AZ 85087 Office: Desert Harbor Elem Sch 15585 N 91st Ave Peoria AZ 85382 Personal E-mail: l_brodie@msn.com. E-mail: lbrodie@peoriaud.k12.az.us.

BRODIE, M. J. (JAY BRODIE), architect, city planner, government executive; b. Balt., Sept. 25, 1936; s. Meyer and Sarah (Rachliss) B.; m. Georgene Ann Gonzales, May 30, 1958; children: Kimberly Brodie-Hopkins, Ellen Maria Jarrett. B.Arch., U. Va., 1958; M.Arch, Rice U., 1960. Registered architect, Md. Arch, prin. city planner, chief planner Balt. Urban Renewal and Housing Agy., Md., 1967-69; dep. commr. Dept. Housing and Comm. Devel., Balt., 1969-77, commr., 1977-84; exec. dir. Pa. Ave. Devel. Corp., Washington, 1984-93; sr. v.p. RTKL Assoc., Inc., Washington, 1993-95; pres. Balt. Devel. Corp., Md., 1996—. Mem. Urban Land Inst., 1980—; mem. Gov.'s Task Force on Housing, Annapolis, Md., 1981-83; real estate adv.; spkr. in field. Past trustee Balt. City Life Mus's.; past mem. Presidio Coun., San Francisco; past chair adv. bd. U. Va. Sch. Arch. Fellow AIA (bd. dir. Balt. chpt. 1977-78, Thomas Jefferson award 1994): mem. Am. Inst. Cert. Planners, Citizens Planning and Housing Assn. (bd. dir. 1976-77), Am. Planning Assn., Lambda Alpha, Nat. Trust for Historic Preservation. Unitarian Universalist. Avocations: ice dancing, writing, music. Home: 609 Craycombe Ave Baltimore MD 21211-2239 Office: Balt Devel Corp 36 S Charles St Fl 16 Baltimore MD 21201-3020 Office Phone: 410-837-9305. Business E-Mail: jbrodie@baltimoredevelopment.com.

BRODIE, SIMON, genetic cloning company executive; CEO Geneticas Life Science (divisions include: Allerca, Foreverpet, Genequus, The Ark, Geneticate, and Genotronica), Calif.; pres. Allerca, Los Angeles, Calif. Allerca is working to produce the world's first hypoallergenic cats; produced genetically-engineered pet fish, GloFish, which is a zebra fish implanted with a flourescent sea anemone gene. Office: Allerca 11400 W Olympic Blvd Ste 200 Los Angeles CA 90064 Office Phone: 310-312-9522. Office Fax: 310-861-5606. E-mail: info@allerca.com.

BRODIE-BALDWIN, HELEN SYLVIA, retired college and human services administrator; d. Adolphus T. and Myrtilla Brodie; m. Wilmer Baldwin, Sept. 6, 1966; 1 child, Trevor Adolphus Avery Baldwin. BA, Hunter Coll., 1956; MA, Columbia U., 1963. Asst. prof. Queensborough C.C., Bayside, NY, 1965—82, dir. counseling-student pers.; asst. prof. CUNY, 1965—82; exec. dir. Minisink Town Ho. and Camp, N.Y.C., 1979—91; asst. to the pres. York Coll. CUNY, Jamaica, NY, 1993—94; exec. dir. The Harlem Cmty. Inc., N.Y.C., 1995—97; pres., ceo Catalyst Consulting Group Internat., N.Y.C., 1999—. Cons. Nat. Conf. of Black Mayors, Atlanta, 2001—; bd. dirs. Louis Aug. Jonas Found., Rhinebeck, NY; cons. Murphy Fine Arts Ctr. Morgan State U., Balt., 2002—; adv. coun. N.Y. Women's Found., N.Y.C., 1988—94. Prodr.: (films) Lucky Devil, 2002; editor (founder): UPTOWN: The Voice of Ctrl. Harlem, 1979—84; prodr.: (plays) Show of Shows. Bd. dirs. Cmty. Bd. 10, N.Y.C., 1989—97; chmn. NYCMS Cadet Corps, Bronx, NY, 1970—79; com. chmn. N.Y.C. Mission Soc., The Cathedral Sch. of St. John the Divine, N.Y.C., YWCA-West Side, N.Y.C., 1970—74; nat. v.p. Am. Camping Assoc., 1988—90, 1992—99. Grantee, Hart Found., 1970, Am. Forum For African Studies, 1970; scholar, NYC Mission Soc., 1952—56. Mem.: Nat. Assn. Fgn. Student Advisors (com. chmn. 1970—77), Nat. Assn. Female Execs., Internat. Women's Club, Delta Sigma Theta (life; v.p.rho chpt. 1954—56). Democrat. Avocations: writing, travel. Home and Office: Catalyst Consulting Group International POBox 250786 Columbia Univ Station New York NY 10025-1509 E-mail: hsbbest@msn.com.

BRODINE, CHARLES EDWARD, physician; b. Sioux City, Iowa, May 10, 1925; s. Ivar and Dorothy B.; m. Lois Bliss, June 26, 1949; children: Stephanie Kay, Jennifer Leah, Charles Edward. BS, Iowa State U., Ames, 1948, research fellow malaria project, 1948-49; MD, Washington U., St. Louis, 1953. Intern St. Louis County Hosp., 1953-54, resident in internal medicine, 1954-55, U.S. Naval Hosp., Oakland, Calif., 1957-59; fellow in hematology, clin. instr. medicine U. Cin. and Cin. Gen. Hosp., 1955-57; head hematology svc. U.S. Naval Hosp., Oakland, 1959-61, Bethesda, Md., 1961-62, cons. in hematology, 1962-73; head divsn. rsch. hematology Naval Med. Rsch. Inst., Bethesda, 1962-66, chmn. dept. clin. investigation, 1966-70, exec. officer, 1970-73; program mgr. Navy frozen blood and trauma rsch. program research div. Bur. Medicine and Surgery U.S. Dept. Navy, Washington, 1962-71, dir. rsch. divsn., 1973-74; spl. asst. med. rsch. and devel. to Surgeon Gen. U.S. Navy, 1974-77; comdg. officer Naval Med. Rsch. and Devel. Command, Nat. Naval Med. Center, Bethesda, 1974-77; asst. med. dir. environ. health and preventive medicine Office Med. Svcs. Dept. State, Washington, 1977-90; mem. Agt. Orange Working Group, 1982-90; exec. com. Nat. Council Internat. Health, 1982-90. Bd. dirs. Gorgas Meml. Inst. Tropical and Preventive Medicine, 1973-89; mem. Bur. Medicine and Surgery Policy Council, 1974-77; med. adviser ARC, 1975-79; adv. com. Nat. Sickle Cell Disease, NIH, 1974-77; mem. com. on biomed. rsch. U.S.-Egypt Joint Working Group, 1975-77; mem. White House Working Group on Internat. Health, 1977; clin. asso. prof. dept. medicine Georgetown U., Washington, 1971—; Dept. State mem. Nat. Council for Internat. Health, 1978-89. Contbr. articles to profl. jours. Exec. com. Gorgas Meml. Inst., 1978-88. Decorated Legion of Merit for blood rsch. project, 1968; recipient Meritorious Service medal for work at Naval Med. Rsch. Inst. U.S. Dept. Navy, 1973; Robert Dexter Conrad award for outstanding sci. achievement Sec. of Navy, 1977 Mem. AMA, Assn. Mil. Surgeons (sustaining membership award 1967), Acad. Medicine of Washington (bd. dirs. 1992—), Soc. for Cryobiology (editorial bd. 1964-66), Soc. Fed. Med. Agys., Western Soc. Clin. Investigation, Soc. Med. Cons. Armed Forces. Home: 9213 Friars Rd Bethesda MD 20817-2313

BRODKEY, ROBERT STANLEY, chemical engineering educator; b. LA, Sept. 14, 1928; s. Harold R. and Clara (Goldman) B.; m. Martha Mahr, Dec. 22, 1958 (div. Nov. 1971); 1 son, Philip Arthur; m. Carolyn Patch, Dec. 6, 1975. AA in Chemistry, San Francisco City Coll., 1948; BS with highest honors, MS in Chem. Engring, U. Calif.-Berkeley, 1950; PhD in Chem. Engring. (Gulf Oil fellow), U. Wis., 1952. Rsch. chem. engr. Esso Rsch. & Engring. Co., Linden, N.J., 1952-56, Esso Std. Oil Co., Bayway, N.J., 1956-57; asst. prof. chem. engring. Ohio State U., Columbus, 1957-60, assoc. prof., 1960-64, prof., 1964-92, prof. emeritus, 1992—. Cons. on turbulent motion, mixing kinetics, rheology, 2-phase flow, fluid dynamics, image processing and analysis; expository lectr. GAMM Conf., 1975; vis. prof. Japan Soc. Promotion Sci., 1978; Clyde chair engring. U. Utah, fall 1994. Author: Transport Phemomena, A Unified Approach, 1988, reprint edit., 2004, The Phenomena of Fluid Motions, 1967, reprint edit., 1995, 2004; editor: Turbulence in Mixing Operations, 1975; contbr. articles to profl. jours.; patentee in field. Recipient Outstanding Paper of Yr. award Can. Jour. Chem. Engring., 1970; NATO sr. fellow in sci. Max Planck Institut für Strömungsforschung, Göttingen, Fed. Republic Germany, 1972; Alexander Von Humboldt Found. sr. U.S. scientist award, 1975, 83; sr. rsch. award Coll. Engring. Ohio State U., 1983, 86; Disting. Sr. Rsch. award Am. Soc. Engring. Edn., 1985; Chem. Engr. lectureship award Am. Soc. Engring. Edn., 1986; North Am. Mixing Forum award, 1994. Fellow AAAS, AIChE, Am. Phys. Soc., Am. Inst. Chemists, Am. Acad. Mechanics; mem. Am. Chem. Soc., Soc. Engring. Sci., Soc. Rheology, Sigma Xi, Phi Lambda Upsilon, Alpha Gamma Sigma, Phi Beta Delta. Office: Ohio St Univ 140 W 19th Ave Columbus OH 43210-1110 Office Phone: 614-292-2609. Business E-Mail: brodkey.1@osu.edu.

BRODKIN, ADELE RUTH MEYER, psychologist; b. NYC, July 8, 1934; d. Abraham J. and Helen (Honig) Meyer; m. Roger Harrison Brodkin, Jan. 26, 1957; children: Elizabeth Anne Brodkin Brauer, Edward Stuart. BA, Sarah Lawrence Coll., 1956; MA, Columbia U., 1959; PhD, Rutgers U., 1977. Lic. psychologist N.J. Sch. psychologist pub. schs., 1961—73; assoc. dir. Infant Child Devel. Ctr. St. Barnabas Med. Ctr., Livingston, N.J., 1977-79; clin. asst. prof. dept. psychiatry U. Medicine and Dentistry N.J., Newark, 1979-90, clin. assoc. prof., 1990-2001. Vis. scholar Hasting Ctr. for Life Scis., NY, 1979; sr. child devel. cons.; cons. Scholastic, Inc., 1988—. Author: Fresh Approaches to Working with Problematic Behavior, 2001, The Lonely Only Dog, 1998, Between Teacher and Parent, Supporting Young Children As They Grow, 1994; author: (with A.T. Jersild and E.A. Lazar) The Meaning of Psychotherapy in the Teacher's Life and Work, 1962; contbr. articles to profl. jours. Fellow, NIMH, 1962; Adelaide M. Ayer fellow, Columbia U., 1962—63, Louis Bevier fellow, Rutgers U., 1976—77. Fellow: Am. Orthopsychiat. Assn.; mem.: APA, Am. Sociol. Assn., N.J. Psychol. Assn. Home and Office: 2 Trevino Ct Florham Park NJ 07932-2724

BRODKIN, ROGER HARRISON, dermatologist, educator; b. Newark, July 31, 1932. A.B. Lafayette Coll., Easton, Pa., 1954; M.D., Jefferson Med. Coll., 1958; M.M.S. in Dermatology, NYU, 1967. Diplomate Am. Bd. Dermatology. Intern, Lenox Hill Hosp., N.Y.C., 1958-59; resident in dermatology NYU and Bellevue Hosp., N.Y.C., 1959-62; teaching asst. NYU, 1962-64, instr. dermatology, 1964-66; clin. asst. prof. U. N.J. Med. and Dental Sch., Newark, 1966-69, clin. assoc prof., 1969-79, clin. prof., 1979—; pres. Ctr. Dermatology, West Orange, N.J. Fellow ACP, Am. Acad. Dermatology, Royal Soc. Medicine, Sigma Psi. Office: Ctr Dermatology 101 Old Short Hills Rd West Orange NJ 07052-1000

BRODL, RAYMOND FRANK, lawyer, consultant, lumber company executive; b. Cicero, Ill., June 1, 1924; s. Edward C. and Lillian (Cerny) B.; m. Ethel Jean Johnson, Aug. 15, 1953; children: Mark Raymond, Pamela Jean, Susan Marie. Student, Norwich U., Northfield, Vt., 1943, Ill. Coll., 1946-48; JD, Loyola U., Chgo., 1951. Bar: Ill. 1951. Atty. law office Joseph A. Ricker, Chgo., 1951-58, Brunswick Corp., Chgo., 1958-62; sec., gen. atty. Edward Hines Lumber Co., Chgo., 1962-84, atty., cons., 1985—, sr. counselor, 2001. Democratic candidate for local jud. office, 1953, 57. Served with AUS, 1943-46. Mem. Ill. Bar Assn. Home and Office: 366 Lance Dr Des Plaines IL 60016-2628

BRODLEY, JOSEPH F., lawyer, consultant, dean; b. Washington, Sept. 22, 1926; s. Joseph and Barbara (Gross) B.; m. Angeli B. Brodley, June 4, 1960; children: Barbara Joanna, Carla Elizabeth. BA, UCLA, 1949; LLB, Yale U., 1952; LLM, Harvard U., 1953. Bar: Calif. 1953, NY 1956. Assoc. Dewey, Ballantine, N.Y.C., 1956-61; assoc. ptnr. Richards, Watson & Hemmerling, L.A., 1961-68; prof. law Ind. U., Bloomington, 1968-79; prof. law and econ., Kenison disting. scholar of law, prof. econs. Boston U., 1986—, interim dean Law Sch., 1989-90. Cons. Ford Motor Co., Dearborn, Mich., 1984, UN Devel. Project People's Republic of China, Beijing, 1992—; vis. prof. U. So. Calif., 1973, U. Mich., Ann Arbor, 1982; vis. fellow Wolfson Coll., U. Oxford, Eng., 1985; pub. testifier Ho. Subcom. Monopolies, 1977, Senate Jud. Com., Washington, 1986, 87, 90, FTC Hearings Global Competition, 1995, FTC/DOJ Hearings Antitrust and Intellectual Property, 2002; life fellow Clare Hall, U. Cambridge, Eng., 1993—; vis. scholar FTC, 2001. Contbr. articles to profl. scholarly jours. 1st lt. JAG USAF, 1953—56, Korea. Mem. Harvard Club (Boston), Yale Club, Phi Beta Kappa. Office: Boston U Sch of Law 765 Commonwealth Ave Boston MA 02215-1401 Business E-Mail: brodley@bu.edu.

BRODSKY, ALLEN, radiological and health physicist, consultant; b. Balt., Nov. 5, 1928; s. Nathan Michael and Gertrude Devera (Silberman) B.; m. Paula Fishman, June 17, 1951 (div. 1983); children: Richard, Karen, Jay; m. Phyllis Levin, Mar. 16, 1984. BS in Engring., Johns Hopkins U., 1949, MA in Physics, 1960; ScD in Biostatistics, U. Pitts., 1966. Diplomate Am. Bd. Health Physics, Am. Bd. Indsl. Hygiene, Am. Bd. Radiology. Radiol. physics fellow Oak Ridge (Tenn.) Nat. Lab., 1950; head health physics unit U.S. Naval Rsch. Lab., Washington, 1950-52; physicist region 2 FCDA, Olney, Md., 1956-57; health physicist AEC, Washington, 1957-61; rsch. assoc. Grad. Sch. Pub. Health U. Pitts., 1961-71, assoc. prof., 1966-71; radiation physicist Mercy Hosp., Pitts., 1971-75; sr. health physicist U.S. Nuclear Regulatory Commn., Washington, 1975-86; sr. scientist Sci. Applications Internat. Corp., McLean, Va., 1997—. Cons. CD, NAS, Washington, 1975; adj. prof. sch. pharmacy Duquesne U., Pitts., 1971-75; radiation sci. fellowship bd. Oak Ridge Associated Univs., 1967-70; pvt. cons., adj. prof. radiation sci. Georgetown U., Washington, 1986-. Author (and editor-in-chief): Radiation Measurement and Protection vol. I, 1979, vol. II, 1982, vol. III, 1982, vol. IV, 1986; author: Review of Radiation Risks and Uranium Toxicity, 1996; editor: Public Protection from Nuclear, Chemical and Biological Terrorism, 2004; contbr. to regulatory guides, chapters to books, articles to profl. jours. Pres. Western Pa. Profs. for Peace in Mid. East, Pitts., 1970-71; witness on radiation effects U.S. Ho. of Reps., Washington, 1978, witness on radiation studies U.S. Senate, Washington, 1978-81, expert witness U.S. Dept. Justice, Washington, 1983-84. Lt. C.E., U.S. Army, 1952-54. Named W.H. Langham lectr., U. Ky., 1979, Failla Meml. lectr., Radiol. and Med. Physics Soc., Health Physics Soc. N.Y., N.Y.C., 1987; recipient Leadership and Sci. Contbns. cert. Conf. on Bioassay, Environ., and Analytical Radiochemistry, 1986; Disting. Grad. award, U. Pitts. Graduate Sch. of Public Health, 2004. Mem. Am. Nuclear Soc. (radiation sci. and tech. award 1993), Am. Assn. Physicists in Medicine, Am. Indsl. Hygiene Assn., Am. Statis. Assn., Health Physics Soc. (chmn. standards com. 1959-61, 67-70, bd. dirs. 1967-70, pres. Western Pa. chpt. 1967-68, life mem., Disting. Svc. award 1966, pres. Balt.-Washington chpt. 1982-83, sec.-treas. govt. sect. 1988-92, Founder's award 1986, Fellow award 1992, interviewed on video for history file 2000, Robley D. Evans medal 2001). Avocations: tennis, piano, composing songs, singing, political campaigns. Home: 121 Windjammer Rd Berlin MD 21811-1902 Office Phone: 703-676-8034.

BRODSKY, BEVERLY ANNE, writer, consultant, editor; b. Phila., June 23, 1950; d. Lewis and Florence Elaine Singer; m. Bruce Brodsky, Aug. 17, 1980; 1 child, Lauren Fay. BA in Psychology cum laude, with gen. and departmental honors, Vassar Coll., 1977. Ordained to ministry L.A. Cmty. Ch. Religious Sci., 2003. Inventory, systems, & computer analyst ASO/NAVICP, Phila., 1978—98; bus. analyst NATEC, San Diego, 1998—2002; freelance book editor & writer El Cajon, 2003—; founder and propr. All One Light, 2004—; co-founder Wisdom, Wealth, Wellness, Vista, 2004—. Pres., v.p. Del. Valley Near-Death Studies, Ardmore, Pa., 1992—98. Vol. and spokesperson San Diego Hospice and Palliative Care, San Diego, 2003—05; cmty. group leader, conf. planner Inst. Noetic Scis., Petaluma, 2003—05. Scholar, Vassar Coll., 1975—76. Mem.: Internat. Assn. Near-Death Studies (leader, media cons. and spokesperson 1992—2005), Seattle Internat. Assn. Near-Death Studies (newsletter editor 2002—, bd. dirs. 2002—), Internat. Found. Survival Rsch. (donor 2004—, bd. dirs. 2004—), Phi Beta Kappa (assoc.; sec. 2001—01). Achievements include near-death experience was highlighted in Dr. Kenneth Ring's 1998 book Lessons from the Light as the concluding account; first person ever interviewed on the subject of near-death experiences on Israeli Public Radio in June 2003; near-death experience and insights were featured in McCall's magazine in 1993 and the BBC documentary, The Human Body: An Intimate Universe, in 1998. Personal E-mail: bevbrodsky@aol.com.

BRODSKY, DAVID MICHAEL, lawyer; b. Providence, Oct. 16, 1943; s. Irving and Naomi (Richman) B.; m. Stacey J. Moritz; children: Peter, Isabel, Nell. AB cum laude, Brown U., 1964; LLB, Harvard U., 1967. Bar: N.Y. 1968, U.S. Dist. Ct. (so. dist.) N.Y. 1969, U.S. Ct. Appeals (2d cir.) 1974, U.S. Dist. Ct. (ea. dist.) N.Y. 1977, U.S. Supreme Ct. 1977, U.S. Ct. Appeals (D.C. cir.) 1981, U.S. Ct. Appeals (3d cir.) 1984, U.S. Tax Ct. 1984, U.S. Dist. Ct. (no. dist.) Tex. 1986. Law clk. to U.S. Dist. judge U.S. Dist. Ct. (so. dist.) N.Y., 1967-69; asst. U.S. atty. So. Dist. N.Y., 1969-73; assoc. Guggenheimer & Untermyer, N.Y.C., 1973-75, ptnr., 1976-80; ptnr., chmn. litig. dept. Schulte Roth & Zabel, N.Y.C., 1980-99; mng. dir., gen. counsel-Ams., Credit Suisse First Boston, 1999—2002; ptnr., co-chair securities and profl. liability litigation group Latham & Watkins LLP, 2002—. Lectr. in field. Co-author: Federal Securities Litigation: A Deskbook for the Practitioner, 1997. Chmn. N.Y. Lawyers for Pub. Interest, Inc., 1991-94; bd. dirs. Equal Justice Works, N.Y. Lawyers for the Pub. Interest. Recipient Pathways to Justice award; named one of Leading Litigators in U.S., Chambers, USA. Fellow Am. Coll. Trial Lawyers (mem. access to justice com.); mem. ABA, Assn. of Bar of City of N.Y., Am. Law Inst., N.Y. County Lawyers Assn., Fed. Bar Coun., Harvard Club, Univ. Club, Scarsdale Golf Club. Jewish. Office: Latham & Watkins LLP 885 Third Ave New York NY 10022 Office Phone: 212-906-1628. Business E-Mail: david.brodsky@lw.com.

BRODSKY, DONALD W., lawyer; b. NYC, Mar. 5, 1948; BA, Duke U., 1970; JD, U. Tex., 1973. Bar: Tex. 1973, US Ct. Appeals 5th Cir., US Dist. Ct. So. Dist. Tex. Law clk. to Hon. Adrian A. Spears US Dist. Ct. We. Dist. Tex., 1973-74; shareholder Jenkens & Gilchrist, P.C., Houston, firm leader corp. & securities/energy/health practice groups. Mem. ABA, Am. Soc. Hosp. Attys., Fed. Bar Assn., State Bar Tex., Houston Bar Assn. Office: Jenkens & Gilchrist PC 5 Houston Ctr 1401 McKinney Ste 2600 Houston TX 77010 Office Phone: 713-951-3341. Office Fax: 713-951-3314. Business E-Mail: dbrodsky@jenkens.com.

BRODSKY, JOEL ALAN, lawyer; b. Chgo., July 24, 1957; s. Erwin Isadore and Sandra (Stabiner) B.; m. Darlen Rose Kil, Apr. 11, 1981 (div. 1997); children: Sarah Brina, Ilana Rachel; m. Elizabeth Younanzadeh, Mar. 28, 1998. BA, Drake U., 1979; JD, DePaul U., 1982. Bar: Ill. 1982, U.S. Dist. Ct. (no. dist.) Ill. 1983, U.S. Ct. Appeals (7th cir.) 1985, U.S. Supreme Ct. 1986. Assoc. Stone, Hughes & Theil, Chgo., 1983-89; ptnr. Brodsky & Hoxha, Chgo., 1989-96. Office: Ste 205 117 N Jefferson St Chicago IL 60661-2323 E-mail: joelbrod@aol.com.

BRODSKY, MARC HERBERT, physicist, research and publishing executive; b. Phila., Aug. 9, 1938; m. Vivian Harriet Simon, Nov. 24, 1966; children: Alexander, Emily. BA in Physics, U. Pa., 1960, MA in Physics, 1961, PhD in Physics, 1965. Rsch. staff mem. IBM T.J. Watson Rsch. Ctr., Yorktown Heights, NY, 1968-80, mgr. semicondr. physics and devices, 1980-87, program dir. Advanced Gallium Arsenide Tech. Lab., 1987-89, dir. tech. planning, 1989-91; mgr. consumer electronics, 1992-93; IEEE Tech. Adminstrn., Fellow U.S. Dept. Commerce, 1991-92; exec. dir., CEO Am. Inst. Physics, College Park, Md., 1993—. Mem. adv. coms. U. Pa. Engring. Schs., 1985—, U.S. Dept. Energy, 1986-89; mem. liaison com. to Internat. Union of Pure and Applied Physics, 1994—; mem. exec. coun. Am. Assn. Pubs. Profl. and Scholarly Pub. Divsn., 1998—. Editor: Amorphous Semiconductors, 1979, 2d edit., 1985; co-editor: Tetrahedrally Bonded Amorphous Semiconductors, 1974; contbr. numerous articles to profl. jours. Patentee in field. Trustee Mt. Kisco (N.Y.) Pub. Libr., 1986-91. Capt. U.S. Army, 1966-68. Fellow IEEE (mem. competitiveness com. 1993-94), Am. Phys. Soc. (exec. com. condensed matter div. 1981-84, edn. com. 1985-88, undergrad. prize com. 1987-88, advisor to coun. 1994—); mem. AAAS (physics nomination com. 1989-91). Avocations: photography, stamp collecting/philately, biking. Office: Am Inst Physics One Physics Ellipse College Park MD 20740-3843

BRODSKY, ROBERT FOX, aerospace engineer, educator, author; b. Phila., May 16, 1925; s. Samuel H. and Sylvia (Fox) B.; m. Patricia Wess, Jan. 24, 1959; children: Bette W., Robert D., David V., Jeffrey M. BME, Cornell U., 1947; MAero. Engring., NYU, 1948, DSc in Engring, 1950; MS in Math., U. N.Mex., 1957. Registered profl. engr., Calif., Iowa. Instr. NYU, 1948-50; supr. theoretical aerodynamics Sandia Corp., Albuquerque, 1950-56; chief aerodynamics Convair/Pomona, 1956-59; with Aerojet-Gen. Corp., 1959-71; chief engr. Space-Gen., El Monte, Calif., 1963-67; corp. mgr. european ops. Aerojet-Gen., Paris, 1969-70; mgr. systems test Aerojet ElectroSystems Co., 1970-71; prof., head dept. aerospace engring. Iowa State U., Ames, 1971-80; on faculty improvement leave with space and communications group Hughes Aircraft Co., 1978-79; sr. systems engr. TRW Space and Tech. Group, Redondo Beach, Calif., 1980-83, dir. technol. planning, 1982-86, program mgr., 1986-88; chief engr. Microcosm, Inc., Torrance, Calif., 1988-98. Adj. prof. aerospace engring. U. So. Calif., 1982-96, Nat. Technol. U., 1994-96; vis. prof. The Technion, Haifa, Israel, 1989-90, 94; lectrs. on remote sensing from space, Turin, Italy, 1988, Paris, London, Munich, 1991, Washington, 1992-94, 96, Albuquerque, 1995, L.A. & Cocoa Beach, 1996-98, 2000, Israel, 1999; cons. in field. Author: Mouldy Figge Tales, 2003, A Pilgrim Muddles Through, 2005, Songs My Mother Never Taught Me, 2005, On The Cutting Edge, 2005; assoc. editor: Handbook of Astronautics, 1991—; author chpt. on space payloads: Space Mission Analysis and Design, 1991, 2d edit., 1992; contbr. articles to profl. jours. Served with USN, 1944-46. Recipient Ednl. Achievement award AIAA/Am. Soc. Engring. Edn. Aerospace Div., 1978; NSF/NATO sr. fellow in sci., 1973 Fellow AIAA (deceleration tech. com. 1963-65, ednl. activities com. 1972-97, spacecraft sys. tech. com. 1978-82, space transp. tech. com. 1985-88, editl. adv. bd. A&A 1977-81, chmn. L.A. sect. 1986-87, Sustained Svc. award 2000), Inst. Advancement Engring; mem. NSPE, Internat. Coun. Sys. Engring., Am. Astronautical Soc., Am. Soc. Engring. Edn. (Centennial Citation 1993), Am. Soc. Aerospace Edn. (v.p. 1979-80, Educator of Yr. 1979), Rotary, Sigma Xi. Achievements include inventor space lifeboat (Time mag., Feb. 1, 1963). Home: 110 The Village Unit 410 Redondo Beach CA 90277-2546 Office Phone: 310-937-1811. Personal E-mail: rfoxbro@aol.com.

BRODSKY, SAMUEL, lawyer; b. Kansas City, Mo., June 12, 1912; s. Abraham and Anne (Brodsky) B.; m. Margery J. Bach, Oct. 17, 1944; children: Joan E., Alice E. BA, U. Tulsa, 1933; LL.B., Harvard U., 1936. Bar: N.Y. 1937. Since practiced in, N.Y.C.; law clk. to Fed. Circuit Ct. Judge Julian W. Mack, 1936-37; asst. U.S. atty. So. Dist. N.Y., 1937-43, 46, charge civil div., 1942-43, 46; partner firm Aranow, Brodsky, Bohlinger, Einhorn & Alter, 1947-79, Botein, Hays & Sklar, 1979-89; counsel Robinson, Brog, Leinwand, Greene, Genovese & Gluck, N.Y.C., 1989-97. Lectr. taxation NYU Law Sch., 1953, 56-64, Inst. on Fed. Taxation, NYU, Practicing Law Inst. Contbr. articles to profl. jours. Served to lt. USNR, 1943-46. Mem. ABA, N.Y. State Bar Assn. (past chmn. tax sect.), Harvard Law Sch. Assn. N.Y. Jewish (past pres., trustee synagogue). Home: 55 Grasslands Rd Apt B224 Valhalla NY 10595 Office: care Robinson Brog Leinwand Greene Genovese & Gluck 1345 Avenue Of The Americas New York NY 10105-0302 Office Phone: 212-586-4050.

BRODSKY, SERGEY, research scientist; b. Vladikavkaz, Russia, Apr. 15, 1967; s. Vitaly and Anna Brodsky; m. Inna Slutsky, July 9, 1993; children: Polina, Leon. MD (hon.), North Ossetian State Med. Acad., Vladikavkaz, Russia, 1992, PhD, 1995. Lic. Med. Dr. Russia, 1992. Asst. prof. No. Ossetia State Med. Acad., Vladikavkaz, Russia, 1995—96; rsch. scientist Technion - Israel Inst. of Tech., Haifa, Israel, 1997—99, SUNY at Stony Brook, NY, 1999—2002; instr. N.Y. Med. Coll., Valhalla, NY, 2002—04; asst. prof. N.Y. Med. Coll., Valhalla, NY, 2004—. Grantee Rsch. grant, Israel ministry of absorption, 1997-1999, Nat. Inst. of Health, 2004-current. Mem.: Am. Heart Assn. (Rsch. Grant 2001—03). Achievements include research in 45 Pub. In Peer-Review Jour., 2 Completed And 1 Current Rsch. Grant. Office: N Y Med Coll 95 Grassland Rd BSB R-C21 Valhalla NY 10595 Office Phone: 914-594-4731. Home Fax: 914-594-4732; Office Fax: 914-594-4732. Business E-Mail: sergey_brodsky@nymc.edu.

BRODSKY, WILLIAM J., investment company executive; b. N.Y.C., 1944; Student, Syracuse U., 1965, JD, 1968. Bar: N.Y. 1969, Ill. 1985. Atty. Model, Roland & Co., 1968-74; with Am. Stock Exch., 1974-82, exec. v.p. ops., 1979-82; exec. v.p., COO Chgo. Merc. Exch., 1982-85, pres., CEO, 1985-97; chmn., CEO Chgo. Bd. Options Exch., 1997—. Mem. internat. adv. com. Fed. Res. Bank N.Y.; mem. adv. coun. J.L. Kellogg Grad. Sch. Mgmt.; bd. dirs. Peoples Energy Corp. Bd. trustees Northwestern Meml. Healthcare, chair investment com.; trustee Syracuse U. Recipient inclusion, Jr. Achievement Chgo. Bus. Hall of Fame, 2001, Lifetime Achievement award, Anti-Defamation League, 2003. Mem. N.Y. State Bar Assn., Swiss Futures and Options Assn. (bd. dirs.), Econ. Club Chgo., Comml. Club Chgo. Achievements include: selection for inclusion into Derivatives Hall of Fame, 2000, Jr. Achievement Chgo. Bus. Hall of Fame, 2001. Office: Chgo Bd Options Exch LaSalle at Van Buren Chicago IL 60605-7413 Office Phone: 312-786-5600.

BRODWIN, MARTIN GEORGE, counselor, educator; b. N.Y.C., June 1, 1944; s. Allen Leonard and Dorothy Elaine Brodwin; m. Sandra Kaye Willadsen, Nov. 9, 1980; 1 child, Erin Rebecca. AB, UCLA, 1966; MS, Calif. State U., L.A., 1969; PhD, Mich. State U., 1973. Cert. rehab. counselor. Coord. rsch. Rancho Los Amigos Hosp., Downey, Calif., 1973—74; dir. Clin. Rehab. Svcs., L.A., 1974—79; counselor, co-owner Image Devel., L.A., 1979—88; prof., coord. rehab. counseling program Calif. State U., L.A., 1988—. Vocat. expert Office of Hearings and Appeals, Social Security Adminstrn., Pasadena, Calif., 1980—; presenter in field. Author: (book) Workshops for the Handicapped: An Annotated Bibliography, Medical Aspects of Disability: A Casebook; editor: Medical, Psychosocial, and Vocational Aspects of Disability (2nd ed.), Medical, Psychosocial, and Vocational Aspects of Disability; contbr. chapters to books, articles to profl. jours. Named Outstanding Prof. of the Yr., Calif. State U., L.A., 1996—97, Rehab. Educator of the Yr., Nat. Assn. Rehab. Profls. in the Pvt. Sector, 1996, Disting. Alumnus of the Yr. for charter coll. edn., Calif. State U. L.A. Alumni Assn., 1997; recipient Second Ann. Cinco de Mayo Career Expn. Recognition, Calif. State Dept. of Rehab., 2000, Recognition Award for Exemplary Efforts Toward Creating Employment Opportunities for Persons with Spl. Needs, Calif. State Dept. of Rehab., Employment Resources, 2000, Wang Family Excellence award for exemplary dedication, contbns. and acad. achievement, Calif. State U., 2004, Dist. Faculty Alumnus award, Calif. State U., Los Angeles Alumni Assn., 2004. Mem.: Calif. Rehab. Counseling Assn. (pres. 1997—99), Nat. Rehab. Counseling Assn., Nat. Rehab. Assn. (bd. mem. so. Calif. chpt. 1996—98), Internat. Assn. Rehab. Profls., Calif. Assn. Rehab. Profls. (treas., v.p., pres. 1975—78), Coun. on Rehab. Edn. (vice-chair 1991—95), Calif. Assn. for Counseling and Devel. (exec. coun. 1996—), Phi Kappa Phi. Office: California State Univ 5151 State University Dr Los Angeles CA 90032 Office Phone: 323-343-4440.

BRODY, AARON LEO, food and packaging consultant; b. Boston, Aug. 23, 1930; s. Nathan and Lillian (Gorman) Brody; m. Carolyn Goldstein, Apr. 11, 1953; children: Stephen, Glen, Robyn. BS, MIT, 1951, PhD, 1957; MBA, Northeastern U., 1970. Head food rsch. labs. Whirlpool Co., St. Joseph, Mich., 1957-61; packaging and product devel. mgr. Mars, Inc., Hackettstown, N.J., 1961-66; packaging coord. Arthur D. Little, Inc., Cambridge, Mass., 1967-73; new ventures mgr. Mead Packaging, Atlanta, 1973-81; mgr. mktg. devel. Container Corp. Am., Oaks, Pa., 1981-85; v.p. strategic studies Schotland Bus. Rsch. Inc., Princeton, N.J., 1985-91; mng. dir. Rubbright/Brody, Inc., Duluth, Ga., 1991-2001; pres., CEO, Packaging/Brody, Inc., 2001—. Course dir. Mich. State U., East Lansing, 1959—61; instr. Emory U., 1979; adj. assoc. prof. dept. food sci. U. Del., Newark, 1983—86; vis. prof. St. Joseph's U., Phila., 1990; adj. prof. Spring Garden Coll., Phila., 1990, U. Ga., 1995—; sr. instr. Keller Grad Sch. Mgmt., 1996—. Mem. Nat. Def. Exec. Res., 1978—88; mem. food svc. adv. com. USN, 1958—62; mem. optimal program edn., sec. DeKalb County, Ga., 1975; active Kerry for Congress campaign, 1972, Levitas for Congress campaign, 1974; mem. pres.'s coun. Spring Garden Coll., Phila., 1984—89. With U.S. Army, 1952—54. Named Packaging Man of the Yr., Nat. Inst. Packaging, Handling and Logistics Engrs.; named to Packaging Hall of Fame, 1995; recipient Willis H. Carrier award, ASHRAE, 1960, Braverman Meml. award, Israel Inst. Tech., 1976, Outstanding Alumnus award, Northeastern U., 1982; William Underwood fellow, 1955—56. Fellow: AAAS, Inst. Food Technologists (Indsl. Achievement award 1964, Riester-Davis Food Packaging Achievement award 1988, Inds. Scientist award 1994, Nicholas Appert award 2000), Packaging Inst. (v.p. 1973—79); mem.: Product Devel. and Mgmt. Assn., N.Y. Acad. Scis., Inst. Packaging Profls. (hon. Mem. of the Yr. 1994—95, cert.), Planning Execs. Inst., League Internat. Food Edn., Soc. Packaging Profls., Toastmasters, MIT Club (pres. 1977—79, mem. exec. com., v.p. ednl. coun.), Sigma Xi. Achievements include patents in field. Home: 4981 Trevino Cir Duluth GA 30096-6072 Office: PO Box 956187 Duluth GA 30095 Office Phone: 770-613-0991. Personal E-mail: aaronbrody@aol.com.

BRODY, ADRIEN, actor; b. NYC, Apr. 14, 1973; s. Elliot Brody and Sylvia Plachy. Student, Am. Acad. of Dramatic Arts, NYC, HS for the Performing Arts. Actor: (plays, off-Broadway) Family Pride in the '50s, 1986; (TV series) Annie McGuire, 1988; (TV films) Home at Last, 1988, Jailbreakers, 1994; (films) New York Stories, 1989, The Boy Who Cried Bitch, 1991, King of the Hill, 1993, Angels in the Outfield, 1994, Solo, 1996, Bullet, 1996, The Last Time I Committed Suicide, 1997, Nothing to Lose/Ten Benny, 1998, Six Ways to Sunday, 1997, The Undertaker's Wedding, 1997, Restaurant, 1998, The Thin Red Line, 1998, Oxygen, 1999, Summer of Sam, 1999, Liberty Heights, 1999, Bread and Roses, 2000, Harrison's Flowers, 2000, Love the Hard Way, 2001, The Affair of the Necklace, 2001, Dummy, 2002, The Pianist, 2002 (Acad. Award for best actor, 2003), The Singing Detective, 2003, The Village, 2004, The Jacket, 2005, King Kong, 2005.

BRODY, ALAN JEFFREY, investment company executive; b. Newark, Apr. 19, 1952; s. Robert and Marcia (Ostroff) B.; m. Miriam Kahan, May 22, 1977 BA, Northwestern U., 1974; JD, Rutgers U., 1977. Bar: N.Y. 1978, N.J. 1978. Assoc. Baer Marks & Upham, N.Y.C., 1977-80; v.p. counsel Commodity Exch. Inc., N.Y.C., 1980-81, pres., chief exec. officer, 1981-89, chmn., 1987-88; v.p. Commodities Exch. Ctr. Inc., N.Y.C., 1981-84, alternate dir., 1984-89; sr. v.p. futures div. Lehman Bros., N.Y.C., 1990-96; mng. dir. Lehman Bros. Futures Asset Mgmt. Corp., N.Y.C., 1991-96; sr. v.p. internat. divsn. Prudential Securities, Inc., N.Y.C., 1997-2000; regional dir. Europe/Middle East/Asia Pacific Prudential-Bache Internat. Ltd., London, 2001—04. Mem. commodity policy adv. com. to U.S. trade rep.; past mem. coun. Found. Internat. Futures and Commodities Inst., Geneva. Mem. ABA, N.J. Bar Assn., Assn. of Bar of City of N.Y. (commodities regulation com.), New York County Lawyers Assn., Nat. Futures Assn. (bd. dirs., exec. com. 1986-89), Futures Industry Assn. (past mem. exec. com. law and compliance div.), Am. Copper Council (past bd. dirs.), Copper Club (past bd. dirs.), Swiss Commodities & Futures Assn. (bd. dirs.) Home: 1365 York Ave Apt 33D New York NY 10021-4039

BRODY, BARUCH ALTER, medical educator, academic center administrator; b. Bklyn., Apr. 21, 1943; s. Lester and Gussie (Glass) B.; m. Dena Grosser, Aug. 15, 1965; children: Todd, Jeremy, Myles. BA, Bklyn. Coll., 1962; PhD, Princeton U., 1967. Asst. prof. MIT, Cambridge, 1967-75; assoc. prof. Rice U., Houston, 1975-77, prof., 1977—, Baylor Coll. Medicine, Houston, 1982—, dir. ctr. ethics, 1982—. Cons. NASA, 1990-91, 94—. Author: Abortion and the Sanctity of Human Life, 1975, Identity and Essence, 1981, Life and Death Decision Making, 1988, Ethical Issues in Drug Testing Approval and Pricing, 1994, The Ethics of Biomedical Research, 1998. Chmn. bd. dirs. Hebrew Acad., Houston, 1976-98; pres. Soc. Health and Human Values, 1995-96. Recipient Disting. Alumnus award Bklyn. Coll., 1991. Mem.: Inst. Medicine. Jewish. Office: Baylor Coll Medicine Ctr Med Ethics & Health Pol Houston TX 77030 also: Rice U PO Box 1892 6100 South Main Houston TX 77251

BRODY, BERNARD B., internist, educator; b. N.Y.C., June 24, 1922; s. Abraham and Sarah (Berman) B.; m. Ruth M. Miller, Jan. 15, 1954; children: Sarah, Rachel. BS, U. Wis., 1943; MD, U. Rochester, 1951. Diplomate Am. Bd. Internal Medicine, Nat. Bd. Med. Examiners. Rsch. chemist U. Chgo. and Monsanto, Dayton, Ohio, 1943-47; resident U. Rochester, N.Y., 1951-53, clin. prof. pathology and medicine, 1981-90, prof. emeritus, 1990—; resident Genesee Hosp., Rochester, 1955-56, dir. clin. labs., 1967-81, sr. v.p. med. affairs, 1975-87; pvt. practice internal medicine Rochester, 1956-67. Cons. Eastman Kodak Co., 1971-92, Robert Wood Johnson Found., 1975-80, EDMAC Assocs., Inc., 1976-83; trustee Freedom Forum, 1980-98; mem. adv. bd. Freedom Forum Media Studies Ctr., N.Y.C., 1985-98, adv. trustee Freedom Forum, 1998—. Bd. dirs. Rochester Mus. and Sci. Ctr., 1994-2003, hon. bd. dirs., 2003—; bd. dirs. Genesee Valley Med. Care, Rochester, 1962-68, Crestwood Children's Ctr., 1985-97, hon. bd., 1998—; chmn. med. adv. bd. St. Ann's Home, 1964-67; corp. mem. United Way, Rochester, 1980-87; mem. Citizens Com. Human Rels., 1980-85; v.p., mem. exec. bd. Otetiana coun. Boy Scouts Am., 1981-91; bd. dirs. Via Health Rochester Gen. Hosp., 2001-05; chmn. stewardship cabinet Lifespan, 2003—. 1st lt. U.S. Army, 1953-55. Mem. AMA, ACP, Am. Soc. Internal Medicine, Acad. Clin. Lab. Physicians and Scientists, Am. Assn. Clin. Chemistry, Sigma Xi, Alpha Omega Alpha Home and Office: 12 Huntington Brk Rochester NY 14625-1811 Office Phone: 585-381-6786. E-mail: Bbrody@rochester.rr.com. *Stay open-minded and flexible in thinking. It helps to recognize and take advantage of opportunities for adjuncts to or career enhancements or changes. It also makes for an interesting and exciting journey through life.*

BRODY, EUGENE BLOOR, psychiatrist, educator; b. Columbia, Mo., June 17, 1921; s. Samuel and Sophie B.; m. Marian Holen, Sept. 23, 1944; children: Julie Anne, James Clarke, John Holen. AB, MA, U. Mo., 1941, DSc (hon.), 1991; MD, Harvard, 1944; grad., N.Y. Psychoanalytic Inst., 1957. Resident Yale Med. Sch., 1944-46, 48-49, from instr. to assoc. prof., 1949-57;

prof. psychiatry U. Md. Sch. Medicine, Balt., 1957-76; chmn. dept., also dir. Inst. Psychiatry and Human Behavior, 1959-76, prof. psychiatry and human behavior, 1976-87, prof. emeritus, 1987—; sr. assoc. sch. of hygiene and pub. health Johns Hopkins U., 1986—. Vis. prof. U. Brazil, 1965-68, U. W.I., Kingston, Jamaica, 1972-75, U. Otago, New Zealand, 1981, James Cook U., No. Queensland, Australia, 1992; vis. prof. psychiatry Harvard Med. Sch., 1997-99; fellow Center for Advanced Studies in Behavioral Scis., Stanford, 1975-76, Inst. for Advanced Studies, Tel Aviv U., 1986; mem. adv. bd. Inst. Social Psychiatry, U. San Marcos, Peru, 1968-70; mem. nat. profl. adv. bd. psychiatry, psychology and neurology service VA, 1963-67; cons. WHO (Pan Am. Health Orgn. and Geneva, Switzerland), 1965-95; program dir. Interam. Mental Health Studies Program, 1967-69; mem. exec. bd. World Fedn. Mental Health, 1969-83, adminstrv. mem., 1972-74, mem.-at-large, 1979-81, pres., 1981-83, sec. gen., 1983-99, sr. cons., 1999—; mem. epidemiol. studies rev. com. NIMH, 1975-79, cons. clin. infant devel. program, 1979-81, hosp. rev. com., 1979-86, AIDS grant rev. com. 1987-92; mem. internat. adv. bd. Peruvian Nat. Inst. Mental Health, 1984-94, mem. editl. bd. jours., 1985-94; mem. adv. coun. Hogg Found., 1986-89; mem. sci. com. Internat. Social Sci. Coun., 1989, exec. com. 1989-91, 92-95; cons. UNESCO, 1986-93; sr. advisor Harvard Program Refugee Trauma, 1989-2004; cons. Balt. VA Med. Ctr., 1990—2004. Author: The Lost Ones, Social Forces and Mental Illness in Rio de Janeiro, 1973, Sex, Contraception and Motherhood in Jamaica, 1981, Psychoanalytic Knowledge, 1990, Biomedical Technology and Human Rights, 1993, The Search for Mental Health: A History and Memoir of WFMH, 1948-1997, 1998; editor: (with F.C. Redlich) Psychotherapy with Schizophrenics, 1952, (with R. Monroe and G. Klee) Psychiatric Epidemiology and Mental Health Planning, 1967, Minority Group Adolescents in the United States, 1968, Behavior in New Environments, 1970; cons. editor Jour. Nervous and Mental Disease, 1959-67, editor in chief, 1967—; adv. editor: Tice Med. Ency., 1967-80, Harper & Row Med. Ency., 1980-86; mem. editorial bd. Psychiatry Digest, 1967-71, Mental Hygiene, 1968-70, Social Psychiatry, 1970-81, Internat. Jour. Psychosomatic Obstetrics and Gynecology, 1984-92, Population and Environment, 1987-92; contbr. numerous articles to profl. jours. Chmn. adv. bd. Balt. chpt. Internat. Students Council, ARC, 1964-67; bd. dirs. Md. Partners of Alliance for Progress, 1965-66, Nat. Assn. Mental Health, 1964-66, mem. profl. adv. bd., 1967-71; mem. adv. bd. Inst. for Victims of Trauma, 1988-97. Served to capt. M.C. AUS, 1946-48. Fellow Am. Psychiat. Assn. (life; chmn. com. transcultural psychiatry 1966-68, rep. interam. council 1965-71, trustee 1968-71, chmn. task force family planning 1973-75, Human Rights award 1999), Am. Coll. Psychiatrists (charter), Am. Coll. Psychoanalysts (charter); mem. Assn. Behavioral Sci. and Med. Edn. (pres. 1981), Am. Psychoanalytic Assn. (life), Internat. psychoanalytic assns., Internat. Coll. Pediatrics (senate 1978-86), Internat. Assn. Psychosomatic Ob-Gyn (exec. bd. 1977-86), Peruvian Psychiat. Assn. (hon.), Peruvian Assn. Psychiatry, Neurology and Neurosurgery (hon.), Cosmos Club (Washington), West River Sailing Assn., 14 W. Hamilton St. Club (Balt.). Home: 70 Olmsted Green Ct Baltimore MD 21210-1508 Office: Jour Nervous/Mental Disease care Sheppard & Enoch-Pratt Hosp PO Box 6815 Baltimore MD 21285-6815 Personal E-mail: ebbrody@aol.com.

BRODY, EUGENE DAVID, investment company executive; b. Bklyn., Feb. 6, 1931; s. Leon K. and Ruth (Parkoff) B.; m. Jacqueline Galloway, Apr. 5, 1959; children: Jessica, Leslie. BS, U. Pa., 1952; MBA, NYU, 1963. Gen. ptnr. A.W. Jones Assocs., N.Y.C., 1965-70; v.p., bd. dirs. Downe Communications, N.Y.C., 1970-74; chief exec. officer Founders Mut. Depositor Corp., Denver, 1970-74; pres. Beekman Capital, Inc., N.Y.C., 1974—78; sr. v.p., ptnr. Oppenheimer & Co. Inc., N.Y.C., 1978—86; mng. dir. Oppenheimer Capital, 1986-96; pres. Picanet, Inc., N.Y.C., 1997—. Pub. Print Collectors Newsletter, 1971—96; trustee Manhattan Inst. for Policy Rsch., N.Y.C. Author: Odds-On Investing, 1978. Lt. USNR, 1952-55. Mem. N.Y. Futures and Options Soc. (founding dir., pres. 1978-79), University Club N.Y.C., Stamford Yacht Club, East Hampton Tennis Club. Home and Office: 2765 Deerfield Rd Sag Harbor NY 11963 E-mail: genebrody@optonline.net.

BRODY, HAROLD, neuroanatomist, educator, gerontologist; b. Cleve., May 15, 1923; s. Julius and Esther (Barowitz) Brody; m. Anne Pertz, Mar. 24, 1951; children: David Andrew, Evan Barrett. Student, LI U., 1941-43; BS, Western Res. U., 1947; PhD, U. Minn., 1953; MD, U. Buffalo, 1961. Instr. anatomy U. Minn., Mpls., 1949-50; asst. prof. U. ND, Grand Forks, 1950-54, U. Buffalo, 1954-59; assoc. prof. SUNY (merger with U. Buffalo 1961), 1959-63, prof., 1963-95; asst. dean SUNY, 1968-69; assoc. dean SUNY (merger with U. Buffalo 1961), 1969-70, Buswell rsch. fellow, 1970—, chmn. dept. anat. scis., 1971-92, disting. tchg. prof., 1995—. Vis. prof. neurophthalmology St. Mary's Hosp., Rochester, NY, 1965—75; mem. sci. bd. Buffalo Otol. Found., Buffalo, 1968—73; mem. biology coun. Canisius Coll., 1969; mem. com. rsch., demonstration White House Conf. on Aging, Washington, 1971; mem. nat. adv. coun. Nat. Inst. on Aging, NIH, 1975—79; acting dir. Ctr. Study Aging, SUNY, Buffalo, 1977—80; vis. prof. neurophthalmology U. Copenhagen, Copenhagen, 1987; disting. lectr. Anthes Wilson Abernathy, U. Toronto, Ont., Canada, 1987; vis. prof. neurophthalmology U. Copenhagen, Copenhagen, 1990—93; organizer, curator Mus. Neuroanatomy, 1994—; vis. prof. neurophthalmology U. Copenhagen, Copenhagen, 1995. Abstractor (sci. referee) Science, 1956—, Journal Gerontology, 1957—73, Journal Morphology, 1958—, (gerontology, geriat.) Excerpta Medica Section Gerontology and Geriatrics, 1959—; editor (assoc.): (sci. referee) Journal Gerontology, 1973—75; editor: (in chief), 1975—80; mem. editl. bd. (sci. edn.) Gerontology and Geriatrics Education, 1980—; editor: (jour.) Neurobiology of Aging, 1981—; rschr. (experimentation) Experimental Gerontology, 1984—. With MC AUS, 1943—46; pres. Friends Health Scis. Med. Libr., SUNY, Buffalo, 1999; trustee Erie County Meals on Wheels Legal Svcs. for Elderly. Co-recipient Lyn Millane Cmty. Svc. award, Amherst Sr. Citizens' Found., NY, 1998—99; recipient travel award, NSF, 1957, Robert W. Kleemeier Rsch. award in gerontology, Gerontol. Soc. Am., 1978; scholar Fulbright sr. rsch. scholar, Copenhagen, 1963. Mem.: AAAS, Buffalo Neuropsychiat. Soc. (pres. 1967—68), Gerontol. Soc. Am. (mem. exec. com. 1961—63, 1968—71, pres. 1974—75), Am. Aging Assn. (trustee 1970—77), Am. Geriat. Soc., Am. Assn Anatomy Chmn., Am. Assn. Anatomists, Roswell Park Med. Club (pres. 1978—79), Alpha Omega Alpha. Achievements include research on the effects of aging on human central nervous system. Home: 50 Stahl Rd Apt 301 Getzville NY 14068-1554 Office: SUNY Buffalo Main St Campus Dept Pathology and Anat Scis Rm 204 Sherman Hall Buffalo NY 14214 Office Phone: 716-829-2019. Business E-Mail: hbrody@acsubuffalo.edu.

BRODY, JACQUELINE, editor; b. Utica, N.Y., Jan. 23, 1932; d. Jack and Mary (Childress) Galloway; m. Eugene D. Brody, Apr. 5, 1959; children: Jessica, Leslie. AB, Vassar Coll., 1953; postgrad., London Sch. Econs., 1953-56. Assoc. editor Crowell Collier Macmillan, N.Y.C., 1963-67; writer Coun. Fgn. Rels., N.Y.C., 1968-69; mng. editor Print Collector's Newsletter, N.Y.C., 1971-72, editor, 1972-96, art writer, 1996—; dir., v.p. Picanet, Inc., N.Y.C., 1996—. Office: 2765 Deerfield Rd Sag Harbor NY 11963

BRODY, JANE ELLEN, journalist, researcher; b. Bklyn., May 19, 1941; d. Sidney and Lillian (Kellner) B.; m. Richard Engquist, Oct. 2, 1966; children: Lee Erik and Lorin Michael Engquist (twins). BS, N.Y. State Coll. Agr., Cornell U., 1962; MS in Journalism, U. Wis., 1963; HHD (hon.), Princeton U., 1987; LHD (hon.), Hamline U., 1993, SUNY Hlth. Sci. Ctr., 1999; LHD U. Minn. (hon.), 2000. Reporter Mpls. Tribune, 1963-65; sci. writer, personal health columnist N.Y. Times, N.Y.C., 1965—; mem. adv. council N.Y. State Coll. Agr., Cornell U., 1971-77. Author: (with Richard Engquist) Secrets of Good Health, 1970; (with Arthur Holleb) You Can Fight Cancer and Win, 1977, Jane Brody's Nutrition Book, 1981, Jane Brody's The New York Times Guide to Personal Health, 1982, Jane Brody's Good Food Book, 1985, Jane Brody's Good Food Gourmet, 1990; (with Richard Flaste) Jane Brody's Good Seafood Book, 1994, Jane Brody's Cold and Flu Fighter, 1995, Jane Brody's Allergy Fighter, 1997, The New York Times Book of Health, 1997, The New York Times Book of Women's Health, 2000, The New York Times Guide to Alternative Health, 2001. Recipient numerous writing awards including Howard Blakeslee award Am. Heart Assn., 1971, Sci. Writers' award ADA, 1978, J.C. Penney-U. Mo. Journalism award, 1978, Lifeline award Am. Health Found., 1978 Jewish. Office: NY Times 229 W 43d St New York NY 10036-3913

BRODY, KENNETH DAVID, investment banker; b. Phila., June 30, 1943; s. Herbert Brody and Esther (Forman) Brody Shimberg; m. Judy E. Donahue, Feb. 5, 1964 (div. Feb. 1974); m. Helen M. Tandler, Apr. 6, 1974 (div. Oct. 1978); m. Carolyn J. Schwenker, June 26, 1987. BSE.E. with high honors, U. Md., 1964; MBA with high distinction, Harvard U., 1971. Foreman and staff asst. Chesapeake & Potomac Telephone Co., Washington, 1964-66; with Goldman, Sachs & Co., N.Y.C., 1971-91, ptnr., 1978-91; chmn., pres. Export-Import Bank of U.S., Washington, 1993-96; founding ptnr. Winslow Ptnrs., Washington, 1996—; co-founder Taconic Capital Advisors, 1999—. Bd. dirs. Fed. Realty Investment Trust, Quest Diagnostics, Inc.; chmn. U. Md. Found., 2004—. Bd. dirs. Alvin Ailey Am. Dance Theater, N.Y.C., 1981-93, ARC, 1994-2000, St. John's Coll., 1996-97; chmn. Presdl. Commn. U.S.-Pacific Trade and Investment Policy, 1996-97; mem. investment com. George Washington U.; chair U. Md. Com. Coun. on Foreign Relations. Capt. U.S. Army, 1966-69. Baker scholar, 1970; Loeb Rhoades fellow, 1971 Mem. Coun. Fgn. Rels., Tau Beta Pi, Eta Kappa Nu, Omicron Delta Kappa, Alpha Tau Omega. Clubs: Harvard (bd. mgrs. N.Y.C.). Democrat. Unitarian Universalist. Address: 2991 Woodland Dr NW Washington DC 20008-3542 Office: Taconic Capital Advisors 450 Park Ave New York NY 10022

BRODY, LAWRENCE, lawyer, educator; b. St. Louis, Aug. 12, 1942; s. Max and Jeannette (Cohen) B.; m. Janice Dobinsky, Dec. 25, 1967; 1 child, Michael Allen. BS in Econs., U. Pa., 1964; JD, Washington U., St. Louis, 1967; LLM in Tax, NYU, 1968. Bar: Mo. Assoc. atty. Husch, Eppenberger, Donohue, Elson & Cornfeld, St. Louis, 1968-74, ptnr., 1974-86, Bryan Cave, LLP, St. Louis, 1986—, group leader Pvt. Client. Adj. prof. Washington U. Sch. Law, 1968—. Author: Missouri Estate Planning, 1988; author, editor Life Insurance Counsellor Series, 1990, 91. Fellow Am. Coll. of Trust and Estate Counsel, Am. Coll. Tax Counsel; mem. Adv. Bd. of Tax Mgmt. Office: Bryan Cave LLP One Metropolitan Square 211 N Broadway Ste 3600 Saint Louis MO 63102-2733 Office Phone: 314-259-2652. E-mail: lbrody@bryancave.com.

BRODY, MARTIN, hotel executive; b. Newark, Aug. 8, 1921; s. Leo and Renee (Kransdorf) B.; m. Florence Gropper, Nov. 22, 1946; children: Marc, Renee. BA, Mich. State U., 1943. Pres. Indsl. Feeding Co., Newark, 1951-61; pres., dir. A.M. Capital Corp., N.Y.C., 1961-71. Chmn. bd., dir. Waldorf System Inc., Boston, 1963-66, Restaurant Assocs., Inc., N.Y.C., 1964-66; chmn. bd., CEO Restaurant Assocs. Industries Inc., 1966-99; chmn. bd. St. Barnabas Corp.; dir. Jaclyn Inc., several Smith Barney mut. funds, Washington Nat. Life Ins. Co. of N.Y.; bd. dirs. Regional Planning Assn. Trustee St. Barnabas Med. Ctr.; bd. dirs. N.J. Transit Corp. Served to capt. AUS, 1943-45. Mem. Orange Lawn Tennis, Greenbrook Country (North Caldwell, N.J.), Boca Raton Hotel and Resort Club. Home: 1 Pine Valley Rd Livingston NJ 07039-8210

BRODY, MICHAEL LOUIS, lawyer; b. Chgo., July 29, 1952; s. Stanton W. and Judith Anne Brody; m. Anne Webber Epstein; children: Clare Webber, Grace Webber. BA, Wesleyan U., 1974; MA in Philosophy, U. Chgo., 1976, JD, 1979. Bar: Ill. 1979, U.S. Dist. Ct. (no. dist.) Ill. 1979, U.S. Ct. Appeals (7th cir.) 1983, U.S. Ct. Appeals (10th cir.) 1990, U.S. Ct. Appeals (6th cir.) 1990, U.S. Supreme Ct. 1992, U.S. Dist. Ct. (ctrl. dist.) Ill. 1992, U.S. Dist. Ct. Ariz. 1994, U.S. Tax Ct. 1994, U.S. Ct. of Appeals (fed. cir.) 1995, U.S. Dist. Ct. (ea. dist.) Wis. 1996, U.S. Dist. Ct. (ea. dist.) Mich. 2002. Law clk. to hon. Bernard M. Decker U.S. Dist. Ct. (no. dist.) Ill., Chgo., 1979—81; from assoc. to ptnr. Schiff Hardin & Waite, Chgo., 1981—99; ptnr. Winston & Strawn, Chgo., 1999—. Mem. adv. bd. Children and Family Rsch. Ctr., U. Ill., Champaign-Urbana, 1998—; chair juvenile law com. Chgo. Coun. Lawyers, 1997—98; co-chair policy and planning com. Adivsory Bd. to the Children's Rights Project of the Legal Assistance Found. Chgo., 1997—98; bd. mem. Roger Baldwin Found. of the ACLU, Chgo., 2002—. Mem.: ABA, Am. Intellectual Property Lawyers Assn. Office: Winston & Strawn 35 West Wacker Dr Chicago IL 60601 Office Phone: 312-558-6385. Office Fax: 312-558-5700. Business E-Mail: mbrody@winston.com.

BRODY, PETER MARTIN, lawyer; b. Bethlehem, Pa., Aug. 24, 1958; s. Arthur I. and Janice A. (Rossin) B.; m. Jenny A. Sternbach, Dec. 7, 1986; children: Sarah R., Anna E., Daniel E. AB magna cum laude, Princeton U., 1980; JD cum laude, Harvard U., 1984. Bar: Pa. 1985, D.C. 1986, Md. 1992, U.S. Dist. Ct. D.C., U.S. Ct. Appeals (D.C. cir.) 1986, U.S. Ct. Appeals (4th cir.) 1992, U.S. Supreme Ct. 1992. Law clk. to Hon. Carl McGowan U.S. Ct. Appeals, D.C. Cir., Washington, 1984-85; assoc. Rogovin, Huge & Lenzner, Washington, 1984-89, Ropes & Gray, Washington, 1989-93, ptnr. litigation dept., 1993—, co-head intellectual property practice group. Chmn. legal adv. com. Nat. Capital Multiple Sclerosis Soc., Washington, 1990—; mem. adv. com. on Criminal Justice Act procedures U.S. Ct. Appeals, Washington, 1994—. Contbr. articles to profl. jours. Mem. ABA (chmn. patent, trademark and copyright com., sect. adminstrv. law and regulatory practice 1992—), Internat. Trademark Assn. (publ. com.), D.C. Bar Assn., Internat. Wine Lawyers Assn. Avocations: swimming, bicycling, golf. Office: Ropes & Gray One Metro Ctr Suite 900 700 12th St NW Washington DC 20005-3948 Office Phone: 202-508-4612. Office Fax: 202-508-4650. Business E-Mail: peter.brody@ropesgray.com.

BRODY, RICHARD ALAN, political science educator, researcher; b. N.Y.C., Mar. 2, 1930; s. Lee and Felice Auslander; m. Marjorie Jean Brody, Aug. 23, 1964; children: Gordon Christopher, David Eric, Aaron Jed. BA, San Francisco State U., 1956, MA, 1959; PhD, Northwestern U., 1963. Asst. prof. Stanford (Calif.) U., 1962-66, assoc. prof., 1966-70, prof., 1970-95, chmn. dept., 1972-73, 74-77, prof. emeritus, 1995—. Fulbright prof. U. Leiden, The Netherlands, 1970-71; bd. overseers Am. Nat. Election Study, 1980-87. Author: Simulation Internat., 1963, Assessing the President, 1991; co-author: Reasoning and Choice, 1991 (Woodrow Wilson prize 1992); co-editor: Political Persuasion and Attitude, 1996; editor Polit. Behavior jour., 1990-97. Fellow, Ctr. Advanced Study in Behavioral Sci., 1967-68, Am. Acad. Arts and Scis., 1992; Parthemos fellow U. Ga., 1998. Mem. Am. Polit. Sci. Assn. (coun. 1977-79), Western Polit. Sci. Assn. (pres. 1987-88), Midwest Polit. Sci. Assn. Democrat. Avocations: wines, food, travel, birding. Home: 1636 Edgewood Dr Palo Alto CA 94303-2820 Office: Stanford Univ Dept Polit Sci Stanford CA 94305-6044 E-mail: Brody@Stanford.edu.

BRODY, RICHARD ERIC, lawyer; b. N.Y.C., Sept. 9, 1947; s. Harold I. and Lillian C. (Albert) B.; m. V. Jane Cohen, May 25, 1974; children: Lauren, Erica. BA, Washington and Jefferson Coll., 1969; JD, Boston U., 1975. Bar: Mass. 1975, U.S. Dist. Ct. Mass. 1975, U.S. Ct. Appeals (1st cir.) 1975, U.S. Supreme Ct. 1987. Law clk. Mass. Superior Ct., Boston, 1975-76, chief law clk., 1976-77; assoc. Sisson, Lee & Bloomenthal, Boston, 1977-78; asst. dist. atty. Atty.'s Office Middlesex County Dist., Cambridge, Mass., 1978-82; assoc. Morrison, Mahoney & Miller, Boston, 1982-85, ptnr., 1985-95, Brody, Hardoon, Perkins & Kesten, Boston, 1995—. Lectr. Nat. Inst. Trial Advocacy, trial practice series Harvard U., Mass. Continuing Legal Edn., Def. Rsch. Inst.; evaluator Middlesex Multi-Door Courthouse, Cambridge, 1989—; mediator Arbitration Forums, Inc., Tarrytown, N.Y., 1989—, cons. Liability Cons., Inc., Sudbury, 1988—; mem. nat. adv. bd. Govtl. Liability Ins., Richmond, 1985—. Trustee Mass. Civil Liability Ins., Boston, 1983-89. Named a Mass. Super Lawyer, 2004. Mem. Mass. Bar Assn. (civil litigation sect. coun.), Mass. Assn. Trial Lawyers, Boston Bar Assn., Def. Rsch. Inst., City Solicitors and Town Counsel Assn. Office: Brody Hardoon Perkins & Kesten 1 Exeter Plz Fl 12 Boston MA 02116-2848 Office Phone: 617-880-7100. Business E-Mail: rbrody@bhpklaw.com.

BRODY, ROBERT, dermatologist; b. Cleve., June 15, 1948; s. Melvin and Nancy Elizabeth Brody; m. Mary Ann Conn, July 23, 1988; children: Ian Hamilton Conn, Hartley Messing Conn, Matthew Grant Hutchinson. AB with distinction, Stanford U., 1970; MD, U. Mich., 1974. Intern in internal medicine, Cleve. Clinic, 1974-75, resident in dermatology, 1975-78; practice medicine specializing in dermatology, Cleve., 1978—; staff physician Kaiser-Permanente Med. Center, 1978-82, mem. profl. edn. com., 1978-82, chmn., 1980-82, also sec. exec. com., 1980; pvt. practice, 1982—; asst. clin. prof. Case Western Res. U. Med. Sch., 1978-80, 83—, clin. instr., 1980-83, dermatology dept. rep. to gen. faculty, 1980-82; asst. physician Univ. Hosps. Cleve., 1979—; chief dermatology divsn. St. Luke's Hosp., Cleve., 1999—. Sec., Cleve. Play House Men's Com., 1979-82; mem. ann. fund com. Stanford U., 1978—, regional co-chmn., 1981-82. Diplomate Am. Bd. Dermatology. Mem. Am. Acad. Dermatology, Cleve. Acad. Medicine. Contbr. articles to med. jours. Club: Cleve. Skating, Rowfant. Home: 2870 Glengary Rd Cleveland OH 44120-1731 Office: 3461 Warrensville Ctr Rd Cleveland OH 44122-5227

BRODY, SPENCER JOHN, pediatrician; b. Laconia, NH, Mar. 14, 1936; s. Nathan and Rose Alice (Kurinsky) B.; m. Carol; children: David, Lynn, Jeffrey, Joshua. BS summa cum laude, Tufts U., 1958; MD, Yale U., 1962; MPH, U. NH, 2004. Diplomate Am. Bd. Pediatrics, Nat. Bd. Med. Examiners. Internship and residency in pediatrics Grace-New Haven Community Hosp., 1962-65; capt., chief pediatrics 328th USAF Hosp., Richards-Gebaur AFB, Grandview, Mo., 1965-67; pediatrician Laconia, N.H., 1967-77; ptnr. Lakes Region Pediatrics, Laconia, N.H., 1977-2000; adminstr. Care and Comfort Nursing, 2000—. Active staff Lakes Region Gen. Hosp., Laconia, 1967-2000, hon. staff, 2000—, sec. staff, 1972-74, v.p. staff, 1987, pres. staff, 1975, 88-90, chief of staff, 1976, chief of pediatrics, 1977-78, 89-90. Mem. Belknap County Med. Soc. (sec. 1970-71, v.p. 1972, pres. 1973), N.H. Med. Soc. (mem. coun. on health svcs. 1984-99, chmn. 1985-93), Am. Acad. Pediatrics (N.H. chpt. alternate chpt. chmn. 1979, chpt. pres. 1983-89, exec. com. 1989-97, newsletter editor 1989-96), State of N.H. Dept. Health and Human Svcs. (mem. maternal and child health physician adv. com. 1983-96, AIDS med. adv. com. 1986-89, infant death rev. com. 1988-91). Jewish. Home: 7 Skyview Cir Meredith NH 03253 Office: Care and Comfort Nursing 61 Beacon St W Laconia NH 03246 Office Phone: 603-528-5020. E-mail: sjbrody@metrocast.net.

BRODY, THEODORE MEYER, pharmacologist, educator; b. Newark, May 10, 1920; s. Samuel and Lena (Hammer) B.; m. Ethel Vivian Drelich, Sept. 7, 1947; children— Steven Lewis, Debra Jane, Laura Kate, Elizabeth. BS, Rutgers U., 1943; MS, U. Ill., 1949, PhD, 1952. Instr., prof. dept. pharm. U. Mich. Med. Sch., Ann Arbor, 1952-66; prof. pharmacology Coll. Medicine, Mich. State U., East Lansing, 1966-90, prof. emeritus, 1990—, founding chmn. dept., 1966-86. Cons. NIH, 1969-73, NIDA, 1975-79, Internat. Soc. Heart Rsch., 1973—2002; mem. sci. adv. com. Pharm. Mfrs. Assn. Found., 1973—2002; U.S. rep. Internat. Union Pharmacology, 1973-76; mem. bd. Fedn. Am. Socs. for Exptl. Biology, 1973-76; mem. Com. Sci. Soc. Presidents. Mem. editl. bd. Jour. Pharmacology and Exptl. Therapeutics, 1965-80, specific field editor, 1981-92; mem. editl. bd. Rsch. Comm. in Chem. Pathology and Pharmacology, Molecular Pharmacology, 1972-90; editor: Human Pharmacology Molecular to Clinical, 1991, 94, 97, Ed Brody's Human Pharmacology, 4th edit., 2005; cons. Random House Dictionary of English Lang., 1964—; contbr. 300 articles to profl. jours. Served with AUS, 1943-46. Recipient Disting. Faculty award, Mich. State U., 1984; Disting. scholar, NSF-U. Hawaii, 1974. Mem. Am. Soc. Pharmacology and Exptl. Therapeutics (John Jacob Abel award 1955, mem. council 1969-72, sec.-treas. 1970, pres. elect 1973, pres. 1974, past pres. 1975, Torald Sollmann award in pharmacology 1995), Internat. Soc. Biochem. Pharmacology, Am. Coll. Clin. Pharmacology, Assn. Med. Sch. Pharmacologists (sec. 1984-86), Soc. Toxicology, Soc. Neurosci., Japanese Pharmacology Soc., AAUP, Sigma Xi, Rho Chi, Phi Kappa Phi. Home: 842 Longfellow Dr East Lansing MI 48823-2444 Office: Mich State U Dept Pharmacology East Lansing MI 48824 Business E-Mail: brodyt@msu.edu.

BRODY, WILLIAM RALPH, academic administrator, radiologist, educator; b. Stockton, Calif., Jan. 4, 1944; m. Wendy Brody; 2 children. BSEE, MIT, 1965, MSEE, 1966; MD, Stanford U., 1970, PhD in Elec. Engring., 1975. With Nat. Heart, Lung, and Blood Inst., USPHS, Balt., 1973—75; intern, then resident and fellow dept. cardiovasc. surgery Sch. Medicine Stanford U., Calif., 1970—73, tng. med. fellow cardiovasc. surgery, resident diag. radiol., 1975—77, from assoc. prof. to prof. dept. radiology, dir. rsch. labs., 1977—86; prof. Stanford U., 1982—84; founder, pres., CEO Resonex, Inc., 1984—87, chmn. bd. dirs., 1987—89; radiologist-in-chief Johns Hopkins Hosp., Balt., 1987—94; prof. radiology, provost U. Minn. Acad. Health Ctr., 1994—96, spl. asst. to pres., 1996; mem. staff depts. elec., computer engring., biomed. engring. Sch. Medicine Johns Hopkins U., 1987—94, Martin Donner prof., dir. dept. radiology, 1987—94; pres. Johns Hopkins U., 1996—. Bd, dir. Medtronic Inc.; bd. dir. Mercantile Bankshares; mem. President's Foreign Intelligence adv. bd. Contbr. articles to profl. jours. Fellow coun. cardiovasc. radiology Am. Heart Assn.; mem. internat. adv. bd. Inst. Sys. Sci., NAt. U. Singapore, 1994—97; mem. internat. acad. adv. panel, 1997; mem. sci. adv. com. Whitaker Found., 1992—97, governing com., 1997—; bd. dirs. Greater Balt. Com., 1997; trustee Goldseker Found., 1996, Balt. Mus. Art, 1997. Recipient Established Investigator award, Am. Heart Assn., 1980—84. Fellow: NAS (Inst. Medicine), IEEE, Am. Acad. Arts & Scis., Am. Inst. Med. and Biomed. Engring. (founding), Am. Coll. Cardiology, Am. Coll. Radiology; mem.: Internat. Soc. of Magnetic Resonance in Medicine. Achievements include patents in field. Office: Johns Hopkins Univ 242 Garland Hall 3400 N Charles St Baltimore MD 21218-2680*

BRODY-LEDERMAN, STEPHANIE, artist; b. NYC; d. Maxwell and Ann (Rockett) Brody. Student, U. Mich.; BS in Design, Finch Coll., 1961; MA in Painting, LI U., 1975. One-person exhbns. include James Yu Gallery, 1976, Nassau County Mus. Fine Arts, Roslyn, NY, 1978, Franklin Furnace, NYC, 1979, 55 Mercer Gallery, NYC, 1979, Kathryn Markel Fine Arts, NYC, 1979, 81, 83, Bengt Torvall, Anderson Gallery, 1980, Stockholm, 1982, Katzen/Brown Gallery, NYC, 1988, 89, Real Art Ways, Hartford, Conn., 1984, San Francisco Internat. Airport, 1986, Rastovski Gallery, NYC, 1987, Hal Katzen Gallery, NYC, 1988-89, 1991, Alfred U., 1990, Hillwood Art Mus., Brookville, NY, 1992, Casements Mus., Ormond Beach, Fla., 1994, Broward Cmty. Coll., Ft. Lauderdale, Fla., 1994, Hebrew Home for the Aged, NYC, 1994-95, Galerie Caroline Corre, Paris, 1995, La. State U., Shreveport, 1995, Marc Miller Gallery, East Hampton, NY, 1996, Pierogi 2000, Bklyn., 1996, Arlene Bujese Gallery, Easthampton, NY, 1997, 2001-03, 123 Watts Gallery, NYC, 1998, Edison CC, 2001, Ft. Myers, Fla., 2001, Hudson Opera House, Hudson, NY, 2001, Cleary, Gottlieb, Steen & Hamilton Artists Program, NYC, 2003, OK Harris Gallery, NYC, 2004, Guild Hall Mus., East Hampton, N.Y., 2004; exhibited in numerous group shows including Cont Art Mus., 1976, Mus. Modern Art, NYC, 1978, Phila. Coll. Art, 1979, Alex Rosenberg Gallery, NYC, 1980, Newark Mus., 1983, Holly Solomon Gallery, NYC, 1984, The Clocktower, NYC, 1986, Met. Mus. Art, NYC, 1986, Henry Street Settlement, NYC, 1987, Blum Helman Gallery, NYC, 1989, Queens Mus., 1989, Basel Art Fair, 1989, Midtown Payson Gallery, NYC, 1990, Caroline Corre, Paris, 1991, RI Mus. Art, 1991, Hillwood Art Mus., Brookville, NY, Am. Acad. Arts & Letters, NYC, 1992, Guild Hall Mus., East Hampton, NY, 1993, 2004, Ind. U, Terre Haute, 1993, Jewish Mus., NYC, 1994, Nat. Mus. Women in Arts, Washington, 1994, 2003, Ronald Feldman Gallery, NYC, 1995, Alternative Mus., NYC, 1995, Eugenia Cucalon Gallery, NYC, 1995, Rotunda Gallery, Bklyn., 1995, Espace Eiffel-Branly, Paris, 1996, Fotouhi Cramer Gallery, NYC, 1996, 123 Watts Gallery, NYC, 1996, San Francisco State U., 1997, Bklyn. Mus., 1997, Weatherspoon Gallery, U. NC, 1997, Gasworks Gallery, London, 1997, Parrish Art Mus., Southampton, NY, 1998, Neuburger Mus., Purchase, NY, 1998, Librairie Nicaise, Paris, 1998, Arlene Bujese Gallery, East Hampton, 1998, 2000, Generous Miracles Gallery, NYC, 1999, Montclair, NJ, Art Mus., 1999, Mpls. Coll. Art, 1999, Musee Bourdelle, Paris, 1999—, U. of the Arts, Phila., 1999, Limn Gallery, San Francisco, Bklyn. Mus., NYC, 2000, Nassau Cmty. Coll., Garden City, N.Y., 2000, Hungarian Consulate, NYC, 2001, Coll. Art and Design, Bristol, Eng., 2001, Woodstock (NY) Guild, 2002, Metaphor Gallery, Bklyn., 2002, Topkapi Mus, Istanbul, 2002, Snug Harbor Culture Ct., Staten Island, NY, 2002, 450 Art Gallery, NYC, 2002, Gracie Mansions/Javits Galleria, NYC,

2003, Chelsea Art Mus., NY, 2003, Berliner Kunstproject, Berlin, 2003, OK Harris Gallery, NYC, 2003, Nat. Mus. Woman in the Arts, Washington, 2003, Biblioteque Forney, Paris, 2004, Pratt Inst., Skylight Gallery, Bklyn., 2005; represented in permanent collections including Newark Mus., Mus. Modern Art, Prudential Ins., Bertelsmann Music Group, Guild Hall Mus., East Hampton, LI, Cooper Hewitt Mus., NYC, Grafikhuset Futura, Stockholm, Sweden, Atlanta Coll. Art, Art Gallery of Peale, Brampton, Ont., Yale U. Libr. Art and Arch., New Haven, Conn., The Jewish Mus., NYC, Carnegie Mellon Libr., Pitts., Archive Concrete & Visual Poetry, Miami Bch., Chase Manhattan Bank, NY Health and Hosp. Corp., Newark Mus., NJ, Victoria & Albert Mus., London, Doubleday Books, Saks 5th Ave. Corp., Vero Beach Ctr. for the Arts, Vero Beach, Fla., Bklyn. Mus., Montclair Art Mus., NJ, Librairie Arcade, Osaka, Japan, ArmsteaCentre Du Livre D'Artiste, Verderonne, France, Hancock Info. Group, Orlando, Fla., 2002, others; represented in public collections including the Edward Albee Found., Montauk, NY, Am. Womans Econ. Devel. Corp., NYC, Amherst Coll, Mass., Archive Concrete & Visual Poetry, Miami Beach, Fla., Art Gallery Peale, Brampton, Ontario, Can., ASCAP, NYC, Atlanta. Coll. Art., Barnes Hosp., St. Louis, Bass Mus. Art Mus. Shop, Miami Beach, Bertelsmann Music Group, NYC, Bklyn. Mus. Art, Bklyn. Union Gas, Carnegie Mellon Lib., Pitts., Ctr. for Arts, Vera Beach, Fla., Ctr. du Livre d'Artiste, Verderenne, France, Chase Manhattan Bank, Cooper Hewitt Mus., NYC, Cumberland Health Facility, Bklyn., Doubleday Books, Garden City, NY, Erasmus Haus, Basel, Switzerland, Harvard Bus. Sch., Boston, Grafikhuset Futura, Stockholm, Sweden, Guild Hall Mus., Hebrew Home for Aged, Riverdale, NY, Ins. N.Am., NYC, Libraire Arcade, Osaka, Japan, The Jewish Mus., NYC, Med. Coll. Va., Richmond, Montclair Art Mus., NJ, Mus. Fine Art, RI Sch. Design, Providence, Mus. Contemporary Art, LA, Mus. Modern Art, NYC, Nat. Mus. Women in Arts, DC, Nelson-Atkins Mus., Kansas City, Mo., Newark Mus., NY Pub. Lib., NY Health & Hosps. Corp., Prudential Ins. Co., Newark, Saks 5th Ave. Corp. Collection, Troy, Mich., SUNY-Cortland, Sydney U., Australia, Tates Mus., London, Tesseract Early Sci. Instruments, NY, Paris, Victoria & Albert Mus., London, Wadsworth Athenium Lib., Hartford, Conn., WPA Bookstore, DC, Yale U. Lib. Arts & Architecture, New Haven, Conn.; commd. series of work on paper Cmty. Rsch. Initiative on AIDS, 1999; cover painting Paris Rev. Mag., 2001; contbg. artist "Fresh" project, 2003; artist portfolio Gastronomica Mag., 2003. Recipient Hassam and Speicher purchase award Am. Acad. and Inst. Arts and Letters, 1988, Purchase award Arts in Hosps., Richmond, Va., 1994; grantee Creative Artists Pub. Svc., 1977, Ariana Found. for Arts, 1985, Artists Space, 1987, E.D. Found., 1991, Lancaster Group., US A. Comm. award, 1991, spl. opportunity stipend NY State Coun. Arts, 1992, 94, Heuss House project Lower Manhattan Cultural Coun., 1992. Studio: 822 Madison Ave Fl 4 New York NY 10021 Office Phone: 718-938-1185. Personal E-mail: sbrody1@aol.com.

BRODZINSKI, JAMES DONALD, information systems educator; b. Cleve., Dec. 7, 1950; s. Alfons Edward and Thereasa (Malafa) B.; m. Karen Ann Goyer, Sept. 30, 1972; children: Elizabeth Ann, Sarah Linda. BFA, Ohio U., 1973, MA, 1978, PhD, 1983. Vis. instr. Ohio U. Coll. Bus., Athens, 1979-80; dir. exec. tng. Hecht's, Washington, 1980-81; cons. J.D. Brodzinski, Gaithersburg, Md., 1981-83, Kennesaw, 1986—; asst. prof. bus. adminstrn. Mary Washington Coll., Fredericksburg, Va., 1982-86; assoc. prof. mgmt. Kennesaw State Coll., Marietta, Ga., 1986-90; assoc. prof., chmn. info. and decision scis. Salisbury (Md.) State U., 1990—. Cons. Arthur Andersen, Chgo., 1979-80. Contbr. articles to profl. jours. Mem. Acad. Mgmt., Am. Soc. Pers. Adminstrn., Midwest Soc. Human Resources Indsl. Rels. (bd. dirs. 1985-88, proceedings editor 1990—, program chair 1991—), So. Mmgt. Assn., Rappahannock Area Pers. Assn. (program chmn. 1985), Internat. Info. Mgmt. Assn. (founding mem., bd. dirs. 1990—, program chair 1991). Democrat. Roman Catholic. Avocations: photography, bldg.

BROECKER, WALLACE S., geophysics educator; b. Chicago, IL, Nov. 29, 1931; Attended Wheaton Coll., Wheaton, IL; AB, Columbia, N.Y.C., 1953, PhD, 1958. Asst. prof. Columbia U., N.Y.C., 1959—61, Assoc. prof., 1961—64, prof., 1964—, Newberry prof. of earth and environ. scis., 1977—. Author 6 books; contbr. articles to scholarly jours. Recipient Vetlesen prize, Columbia U., 1987, Goldschmidt award, 1986, Priestley award, Dickinson Coll., 1990, Nat. medal of Sci., 1996, Blue Planet prize, Asahi Glass Found., Tokyo, 1996. Fellow: Geol. Soc. Am. (Arthur L. Day medal 1984, Don J. Easterbrook Disting. Scientist award 2000), Geol. Soc. London (Wollaston medal 1990), Am. Geophys. Union, European Geophys. Union (Urey medal 1979, Roger Revelle medal 1995); mem.: NAS (Agassiz medal 1986), Geochem. Soc. (V.M. Goldschmidt award 1986), Am. Acad. Arts and Scis. Office: Columbia U Lamont-Doherty Earth Obs PO Box 1000 61 Rt 9W Palisades NY 10964-8000*

BROEG, BOB (ROBERT WILLIAM BROEG), writer; b. St. Louis, Mar. 18, 1918; s. Robert Michael and Alice (Wiley) B.; m. Dorothy Carr, June 19, 1943 (dec.); m. Lynette A. Emmenegger, July 23, 1977. BJ, U. Mo., 1941. With A.P., Columbia, Mo., 1939-40, Jefferson City, Mo., 1941, Boston, 1941-42; reporter St. Louis Star-Times, 1942; staff sports dept. St. Louis Post-Dispatch, 1945-85, sports editor, 1958-85, asst. to pub., 1977-85. Author: Don't Bring That Up, 1946, Stan Musial: The Man's Own Story, 1964, Super Stars of Baseball, 1971, Ol' Missou, a Story of Missouri Football, 1974, We Saw Stars, 1976, The Man Stan...Musial, Now and Then, 1977, Football Greats, 1977, The Pilot Light and the Gas House Gang, 1980, Bob Broeg's Redbirds, 1981, My Baseball Scrapbook, 1983, Front Page, 1984, Baseball From a Different Angle, 1988, Baseball's Barnum, 1989, Ol' Mizzou, A Century of Tiger Football, 1990, Bob Broeg's Redbirds, A Century of Cardinals Baseball, 1992, Super Stars of Baseball No. 2, 1993, Autobiography, Bob Broeg, Memories of Hall of Fame Sportswriter, 1995; co-author: That's a Winner, Jack Buck Autobiography, 1997, St. Louis Cardinals' Encyclopedia, 1998, The 100 Greatest Moments in St. Louis Sports, 2000; contbr. articles to profl. publs. Bd. dirs. Vets. com. Baseball Hall of Fame, 1972-2000, bd. dirs. 1975-2000; bd. dirs. Honors Ct., Nat. Football Found., 1975. Served with USMCR, 1942-45. Recipient Nat. Sportscasters, Sportswriters awards Mo., 1962-65, 67; Journalism medal U. Mo., 1971; Faculty-Alumni award U. Mo., 1969, Hall of Fame Writing award, 1980; elected to Mo. Sports Hall of Fame, 1978, Nat. Sportscasters/Sportswriters Hall of Fame, 1997, Nat. Baseball Congress Hall of Fame, 1998, Mo. Sports Legend, 2000. Mem. Baseball Writers Assn. Am. (pres. 1958), Kappa Tau Alpha, Sigma Delta Chi, Sigma Phi Epsilon, Omicron Delta Kappa. Home: 60 Frontenac Estates Dr Saint Louis MO 63131-2602 Office: Pulitzer Pub Co 900 N Tucker Blvd Saint Louis MO 63101-1069 *As a newspaperman, I seek as an epitaph only: "He was fair." Hopefully "fair" as in "just," not as in "mediocre".*

BROEK, HOWARD WINDOLPH, real estate executive; b. N.Y.C., Oct. 1, 1934; s. Howard Yates Broek and Mildred Louise Windolph; m. Berthalene Ann Arber, Mar. 30, 1963; children: Christopher John, Jennifer Louise Schnell, Gillian Sarah Gentile, Catherine Elizabeth Stemple, Alexandra Ann Jantje. B Engring., Yale U., 1956, MS, 1958, PhD, 1961. Staff physicist Argonne (Ill.) Nat. Lab., 1960-63; mem. tech. staff Bell Telphone Labs., Whippany, N.J., 1963-75, Naperville, Ill., 1975-89; sr. engr. Motorola, Arlington Heights, Ill., 1990-95; pres. Windolph Realty Co., St. Charles, Ill., 1995—. Author: Broek & Jonker Families, 1993, The Third Millenium, 2000, President's Shrink Escapes Gitmo, 2004; contbr. articles to profl. jours. Deacon Reformed Ch. in Am. NSF fellow Yale U., 1958-59. Mem. Am. Philatelic Soc., Am. Revenue Assn., Assn. for the Advancement of Dutch Am. Studies, N.Y. Geneal. and Biographical Soc., Joliet Bicycle Club, Life Extension Found. Mem. Reformed Ch. in Am. Avocations: bicycling, match and medicine stamps, skiing, hiking, oceanography. E-mail: cbroek@cox.net.

BROEKER, JOHN MILTON, lawyer; b. Berwyn, Ill., May 27, 1940; s. Milton Monroe and Marjorie Grace (Wilson) B.; m. Linda J. Broeker, Dec. 9, 1983; children: Sara Elizabeth, Ross Goddard; stepchildren: Terrance Mercil Jr., Johnny Mercil, Veronica Mercil. BA, Grinnell Coll., 1962; JD cum laude, U. Minn., 1965. Bar: Minn. 1965, Wis. 1982, U.S. Ct. Appeals (8th cir.) 1966, U.S. Dist. Ct. Minn. 1967,. U.S. Tax Ct. 1969, U.S. Ct. Appeals (5th cir.) 1971, U.S. Dist. Ct. (we. dist.) Wis. 1982, U.S. Supreme Ct. 1984. Law clk. to presiding judge U.S. Ct. Appeals (8th cir.), 1965-66; ptnr. Gray, Plant, Mooty, Mooty & Bennett, Mpls., 1966-71, Broeker, Geer, Fletcher & LaFond and predecessor firms, Mpls., 1971-91; v.p., gen. counsel NordicTrack, Inc., Mpls., 1991-94; founder Broeker Enterprises, 1992—; pres. Legal Mgmt. Strategies, Inc., Mpls., 1994—; of counsel Popham, Haik, Schnobrich & Kaufman, Ltd., Mpls., 1995-96, Halleland, Lewis, Nilan, Sipkins & Johnson, Mpls., 1996-97; pvt. practice, 1997—. Instr. U Minn. Law Sch., 1967-72; lectr. convs. and seminars, 1969—; lectr. U. Minn. Ctr. for Long Term Care Edn., 1972-77, Gt. Lakes Health Congress, 1972, Sister Kenney Inst., 1972. Contbr. articles to legal jours. Bd. dirs. Minn. Environ. Scis. Found., Inc., 1971-73; bd. dirs. Project Environ. Found., 1977-83, chmn., 1980-82; mem. alumni bd. Grinnell Coll., 1968-71; chmn. MInnetonka Environ. Quality and Natural Resources Commn., 1971-72; trustee The Writers Project, Inc., 1999-2001. Recipient Outstanding Alumni award Grinnell Coll., 1973. Mem. ABA (forum com. on health law 1978-91), Minn. Bar Assn. (chmn. environ. law com. 1970-72), State Bar Wis., Hennepin County Bar Assn. (chmn. environ. law com. 1976-77, legis. com. 1972-76, health law com. 1977-79), Am. Soc. Hosp. Attys., Minn. Soc. Hosp. Attys., Am. Health Care Assn. (legal coordinating com. 1970-75, labor com. 1973-74), Nat. Health Lawyers Assn., Minn. Thoroughbred Assn. (bd. dirs. 1991-92), Minn. Quarterhorse Racing Assn. (bd. dirs. 1994—2003, pres. 1997-99), Sierra Club (nat. dir. 1974-76, chmn. chpt. 1971-72, regional v.p. 1973-74). Home: 11402 Burr Ridge Ln Eden Prairie MN 55347-4717 Office: 8120 Penn Ave S Ste 151Q Bloomington MN 55431-1326 Office Phone: 952-886-0435. Business E-Mail: jbroeker@msn.com.

BROENING, WALTER STEPHENS, JR., journalist, history educator; b. Balt., Aug. 15, 1935; s. Walter Stephens and Evelyne (Powers) B.; m. Christine Zucker, Feb. 3, 1962; children: Alexander (dec.), John, Benjamin, Thomas. BA in Polit. Sci., Johns Hopkins U., 1959. Reporter AP, Balt., 1963-65, corr. Paris, 1965-70, Moscow, 1970-74, Lisbon, Portugal, 1974-76; asst. city editor Balt. Sun, 1976-77, op-ed page editor, 1977-85, diplomatic corr., 1985-90; news editor Internat. Herald-Tribune, Paris, 1990-96; vis. scholar in history Johns Hopkins U., Balt., 1996—. With U.S. Army, 1954-56. Mem. Johns Hopkins Club. Home: 5701 Greenleaf Rd Baltimore MD 21210-1319 Office: Johns Hopkins U Dept History 3400 N Charles St Baltimore MD 21218-2608 Personal E-mail: wsb1@verizon.net.

BROERS, LORD ALEC NIGEL, engineering educator; b. Calcutta, India, Sept. 17, 1938; s. Alec William and Constance Amy (Cox) B.; m. Mary Therese Phelan, Dec. 27, 1965; children: Mark, Christopher. BSc, Melbourne U., 1958, 59; BA in Mech. Scis., Cambridge U., 1962, PhD in Elec. Engring., 1965, ScD, 1990; DEng (hon.), Glasgow U., 1996; DSc (hon.), Warwick U., 1997; DSc (hon.), U. Mist, 2002; D. in Tech. (hon.), Greenwich U., 2000; LLD (hon.), Melbourne U., 2000; D in Univ. (hon.), Anglia Poly. U., 2000; Fellow (hon.), U. Wales, 2002; D Eng. (hon.), Peking U., 2002; LLD, U. Cambridge, 2004. Mem. rsch. staff IBM Thomas J. Watson Rsch. Ctr., Yorktown Heights, N.Y., 1965-81, mgr. electron beam tech., 1967-72, mgr. photo and electron optics, 1972-81; mgr. advanced tech. IBM East Fishkill Devel. Lab., Hopewell Junction, N.Y., 1981-84; mem. corp. tech. com. IBM Hdqrs., Armonk, N.Y., 1984; prof. elec. engring., head elec. div. dept. engring. Cambridge U., 1984-92, head dept. engring., 1992-96, vice chancellor, 1996—2003; mem. rsch. staff IBM Thomas J. Watson Rsch. Ctr., Yorktown Heights, N.Y., 1965-81. Fellow Trinity Coll., Cambridge, 1985-90; master Churchill Coll., Cambridge, 1990-96; mem. Royal Acad. Engring. Coun., 1994-96, Engring. and Phys. Scis. Coun. U.K., 1992-00; non-exec. dir. gen. bd. Lucas Industries, 1995-96; non-exec. dir. Vodafone Group, L.J. Mears LLC; chmn. Plastic Logic Ltd., Ho. Lords Sci. and Tech. Select Com., 2004-; sr. advisor Warburg Pincus; mem. Coun. Sci. and Tech. Contbr. numerous articles to profl. jours., chpts. to books; patentee in field. Recipient Am. Inst. of Physics prize for indsl. applications of physics, 1982, Cledo Brunetti award IEEE, 1985; hon. fellow Gonville and Caius Coll., Trinity Coll., Cardiff U., Imperial Coll., St. Edmund's Coll. Fellow Instn. Elec. Engrs. (hon.), Instn. Mech. Engrs. (hon.), Inst. of Physics, Royal Acad. Engring. (coun. 1992-96, 00-, v.p. 2000-01, pres. 2001—, Prince Philip medal 2000), Royal Soc.; mem. U.S. Nat. Acad. Engring. (fgn. assoc.), Australian Acad. Technol. Scis. and Engrs. (hon.), Am. Philos. Soc. (fgn. mem.). Avocations: music, small-boat sailing, skiing, tennis. Home: Saint George Wharf Apt 429 London SW8 2LZ England also: 32 Mount Hope Ave Jamestown RI 02835-1466 Office: Royal Acad Engring 29 Great Peter St Westminster SW1P 3LW England Office Phone: +44207 222 2688. E-mail: president@raeng.co.uk.

BROFFITT, JAMES DRAKE, statistician, educator; b. Indpls., Apr. 8, 1941; s. Wilgus Stanley and Virginia Elizabeth (Drake) B.; m. Barbara Helen Alford, Dec. 20, 1975; children: Daniel James, Virginia Lea. BA in Math., DePauw U., 1963; MS in Stats., Colo. State U., 1965, PhD in Stats., 1969. Statis. analyst Computer Technology, Inc., Dallas, 1969-70; asst. prof. stats. and actuarial sci. U. Iowa, Iowa City, 1970-75, assoc. prof., 1975-85, 86-88, prof., 1988—, chmn. stats. and actuarial sci., 1993—. Vis. prof. U. Western Ont., Can., 1985-86; cons. Soc. Actuaries Part 2 Actuarial Exam., Am. Coll. Testing, 1984-85, Iowa Med. Svcs., 1988. Conducted presentations in field at various univs. and confs. in the U.S. and Can.; contbr. numerous articles to profl. jours. Mem. Am. Statis. Assn., Inst. Mathematical Stats., Internat. Actuarial Assn., Soc. of Actuaries (assoc.; acad. cons. to com. which constructs compound interest exam. 1993-95), Sigma Xi, Phi Kappa Phi. Baptist. Home: 3029 E Court St Iowa City IA 52245-4907 Office Phone: 319-335-0820. Business E-Mail: james-broffitt@uiowa.edu.

BROG, DAVID, former air force officer, consultant; b. Manchester, Conn., Aug. 11, 1933; s. Israel and Pesha (Blonstein) B.; m. Verda Anna Raney, Nov. 9, 1959; children: Kai Ling, Tov Binyamin. BA, U. Pitts., 1955; MS, U. So. Calif., 1967. Commd. 2d lt. USAF, 1956, advanced through grades to col., 1978, dir. readiness and electronic combat, Hdqrs., from 1981, dep. chief staff ops. for command control and communications countermeasures, until 1982, ret., 1982; pres. IRD, Inc. (internat. R & D), domestic and internat. cons. on def. issues, Silver Spring, Md., 1982—. Contbr. articles to profl. jours. Decorated D.F.C., Legion of Merit, Air medal with 12 oak leaf clusters; named Disting. Grad. USAF Air War Coll. Mem. Red River Valley Fighter Pilots Assn. (pres.), Assn. Old Crows, Air Force Assn. Jewish. Home: 9200 Three Oaks Dr Silver Spring MD 20901-3362 Office: PO Box 877 Silver Spring MD 20918-0877 Office Phone: 301-588-3283. E-mail: davebrog@erols.com.

BROGAN, FRANCIS B., JR., lawyer; b. Ridgewood, NJ, July 16, 1949; BSBA, Georgetown Univ., 1971, JD, 1974, LLM in Tax., 1977. CPA; bar: DC 1975, US Tax Ct. 1975, bar: Fla. 1976, NJ 1977, US Supreme Ct. 1978. Co-mng. shareholder, co-chair tax group Greenberg Traurig LLP, Ft. Lauderdale, Fla. Campaign chair United Way of Broward County, 2003; past pres., bd. mem. Henderson Mental Health Ctr. Inc. Recipient John Carroll alumni svc. award, Georgetown Univ., 1991, Leader of Yr. award, Leadership Broward Found., 1998. Mem.: Am. Coll. Trust and Estate Planning Counsel. Office: Greenberg Traurig Ste 2000 401 E Las Olas Bvd Fort Lauderdale FL 33301 Office Phone: 954-765-0500. Office Fax: 954-765-1477. Business E-Mail: broganf@gtlaw.com.

BROGAN, FRANK T., academic administrator, former lieutenant governor; m. Courtney Strickland; 1 child, Colby John. BA magna cum laude, U. Cin.; M in Ednl. Leadership, Fla. Atlantic U. Supt. schs. Martin County Sch. Dist., Fla., 1988-94; commr. edn. Fla. Dept. Edn., Tallahassee, 1994-99; lt. gov. State of Fla., Tallahassee, 1999—2003; pres. Florida Atlantic U., 2003—. Former tchr., dean of students, asst. prin., prin. Martin County Sch. Dist.; chair task force Fla. Classrooms First; mem. development team Tech Prep program. Named Supt. of yr., Fla. Legislature, 1992. Republican. Office: Florida Atlantic Univ / Off of Pres Adminstrn Bldg, Rm # 339 777 Glades Rd Boca Raton FL 33431-0991 Office Phone: 561-297-3450. Office Fax: 651-297-2777.*

BROGAN, LISA S., lawyer; b. Chgo., Apr. 23, 1963; BA, Northwestern U., 1984, JD, 1987. Bar: Ill. 1987, U.S. Dist. Ct. (no. dist.) Ill. 1988, U.S. Ct. Appeals (fed. cir.) 1989, U.S. Ct. Appeals (7th cir.) 1994. Atty. Baker & McKenzie, Chgo., 1987—. Mem.: ABA, Ill. State Bar Assn., Chgo. (Ill.) Bar Assn. Office: Baker & McKenzie One Prudential Plz 130 East Randolph Dr Chicago IL 60601

BROGAN, MICHAEL DALE, gastroenterologist, educator; b. Columbus, Ohio, Aug. 2, 1951; s. Virgil Dale Brogan and Joan Elizabeth Pesola; m. Martha Ann Brogan, Apr. 15, 1981 (div. Oct. 1994); children: Katherine, Ryan; m. Karen Deering Brogan, Aug. 1, 1998. BA cum laude, Ohio State U., 1973, MD, 1978. Bd. cert. internal medicine, gastroenterology, Md. Intern in internal medicine Mt. Sinai Hosp., N.Y.C., 1978-79, resident in internal medicine, 1979-81; emergency rm. physician Holzer Med. Ctr., Gallipolis, Ohio, 1981-82; fellow in gastroenterology UCLA Med. Ctr., 1982-85, asst. prof., 1985-86; practicing physician Columbus Med. Gastroenterology, 1986—; clin. asst. prof. Ohio State U., Columbus, 1986—. Head endoscopy unit Mt. Carmel Hosp., Columbus, 1992-96; sect. head divsn. gastroenterology Riverside Hosp., Columbus, 1992-94. Contbr. numerous articles and abstracts to profl. jours. Mem. AMA, Am. Gastroenterol. Assn., Columbus Med. Assn., Alpha Omega Alpha. Avocations: personal fitness, computers, cinema. Home: 3682 Stunsail Ln Columbus OH 43221-4815 Office: Columbus Med Gastroenterology 1211 Dublin Rd 2nd Fl Columbus OH 43215-1091 Office Phone: 614-486-5207. E-mail: mbrogan@columbus.rr.com.

BROGAN, STEPHEN J. (STEVE), lawyer; b. NYC, 1952; AB, Boston Coll., 1974; JD, Univ. Notre Dame, 1977. Bar: DC 1977. Dep. asst. atty. gen. US Dept. of Justice, Washington, 1981—83; ptnr.-in-charge Jones Day, Washington, 1989—2002, mng. ptnr., 2003—, and chair adv. com. and partnership com. Chair, adv. com. Jones Day, chair, partnership com. Exec. editor Law Rev., Univ. Notre Dame, 1977. Office: Jones Day 51 Louisiana Ave NW Washington DC 20001-2113

BROGDEN, STEPHEN RICHARD, library director; b. Des Moines, Sept. 26, 1948; s. Paul M. and Marjorie (Kueck) B.; m. Melinda L. Raine, Jan. 1, 1983; 1 child, Nathan. BA, U. Iowa, 1970, MA, 1972. Caretaker Eya Fechin Branham Ranch, Taos, N.Mex., 1970-72; dir. Harwood Found. U. N.Mex., Taos, 1972-75; vis. lectr. U. Ariz., Tucson, 1975-76; rd. mgr. Bill and Bonnie Hearne, Austin, Tex., 1976-79; head fine arts Pub. Libr. Des Moines, 1980-90; dep. dir. Thousand Oaks (Calif.) Libr., 1990-99, dir., 1999—. Chair Met. Coop. Libr. Sys., 2001; bd. mem. Pacific Pioneer Broadcasters, 2005—. Author book revs., Annals of Iowa, 1980; columnist Taos News, 1973. V.p. Hospice of the Conejo, 2004—05; bd. dirs. Thousand Oaks Libr. Found., 1999—; bd. mem. Pacific Pioneer Broadcasters, 2005—. Mem. ALA, Calif. Libr. Assn., Films for Iowa Librs. (pres. 1983-86), Metro Des Moines Libr. Assn. (pres. 1980). Office: Thousand Oaks Libr 1401 E Janss Rd Thousand Oaks CA 91362-2199 Office Phone: 805-449-2660. Business E-Mail: sbrogden@mx.tol.lib.ca.us.

BROGDEN-STIRBL, SHONA MARIE, writer, researcher; b. Tuscaloosa, Ala., Sept. 3, 1948; d. Edward Henry Jr. and Esther Ruth (Coleman) Brogden; m. Robert Clark Stirbl, Mar. 30, 1990. BA, U. South Ala., Mobile, 1972; MA in English (Poetics), NYU, 1982, postgrad. Adult protective social worker Mobile County Dept. Pensions and Security, 1972-74; child protection social worker Cumberland County Child Protective Svcs., Fayetteville, NC, 1975-76; cmty. placement specialist S.I. Devel. Ctr., 1976-78, Manhattan Borough Devel. Svc., NYC, 1978-80; adminstr. Coun. on Internat. Ednl. Exch., NYC, 1981, Office of Univ. Devel., Advt. and Pub. Affairs, NYU, NYC, 1982-85; dir. advt. Office of Advt. and Pub. Affairs, NYU, NYC, 1986; cons. Meml. Sloan-Kettering, NDRI, NYU, NYC, 1986-97. Cabaret promoter. Voice recorder Book on Tape, Jewish Braille Inst., NYC, 1996; adminstrv. support Gay Men's Health Crisis, NYC, 1986; vol. Serendipity Sch. for Emotionally Disturbed Children, Sacramento, 1975; Strasberg Theatre Inst., 1977-78; founding mem. Tell It Like It Was, 1999, Ft. Bragg Semi-Reperatory Theatre Co., 1975-76, Dixie Darlings, 1966-67. Scholar NYU, 1978-82, U. So. Miss., 1966-68. Mem.: Caltech Women's Club. Christian. Achievements include patent photographic films with multiple ASA and associated camera. Avocations: poetry, art, acting, baroque violin, writing, options trading. Home and Office: 465 S Madison #109 Pasadena CA 91101 E-mail: s.brogden.1@alumni.nyu.edu.

BROGDON, BYRON GILLIAM, radiologist, educator; b. Fort Smith, Ark., Jan. 22, 1929; s. Paul Preston and Lela Florence (Gilliam) B.; m. Barbara Walkow Schreiber, June 23, 1978; 1 child, David Pope; stepchildren: William and Diane Schreiber. BS, BS in Medicine, U. Ark., 1951, MD, 1952. Intern Univ. Hosp., Little Rock, 1952-53, resident, 1953-55; resident in radiology N.C. Bapt. Hosp., Winston-Salem, 1955-56; asst. prof. radiology U. Fla., 1960-63; assoc. prof. radiology and radiol. scis., radiologist-in-charge diagnostic radiology div. Johns Hopkins U. and Hosp., 1963-67; prof., chmn. dept. radiology U. N.Mex., 1967-77; from prof. chmn. radiology to prof. emeritus U. South Ala., Mobile, 1978—96, prof. emeritus, 1996—. Sabbatical leave Univ. Coll., Galway, Ireland, 1988; cons. in forensic radiology Office Med. Exam. State Ala., 1989—; coord. internat. diagnostic course in Davos, 1984-96; mem. bd. trustees Forensic Sci. Found., 2001—, vice-chair, 2003-04. Author: Opinions, Comments and Reflections on Radiology, 1983, Forensic Radiology, 1998, a Radiologic Atlas of Abuse and Torture, Terrorism, and Inflicted Trauma (winner Highly Commended Med. Book Competition award 2003); contbr. articles to med. jours. Maj. USAF, 1953—60. Finalist Ann. Telly awards, 2004; recipient Disting. Alumnus award U. Ark., 1978, Ark. Travelers Commn. award Gov. of Ark., 1985, Disting. Achievement award Wake Forest U. Med. Alumni Assn., 1990, medal from city of Brescia, Italy, 1991, Joint Resolution of Commendation for outstanding profl. achievement Ala. Legis., 1994, Medal of Honor Leopold-Franzens U., Innsbruck, Austria, 1997, Republic of Austria Cross of Honor for Sci. and Arts 1st class, 2002, Highly Commended award, Brit. Med. Assn., 2003. Fellow Am. Coll. Radiology (pres. 1978-79, gold medal 1987), Am. Acad. Forensic Scis. (John B. Hunt award 1995, Disting. Fellow award 2001); mem. AMA (ho. of dels. 1988-95, Physician-Spkr. award 1979), Am. Roentgen Ray Soc. (life, exec. coun. 1974-75, 77-80, 84-90, 2d v.p. 1979-80, gold medal 1996), So. Radiol. Conf. (life hon., pres. 1967-68, sec. 1984-96, Eskridge lectr. 1994), Radiol. Soc. N.Am., Am. Assn. Acad. Chief Residents in Radiology (faculty advisor 1979-2002, nat. sponsor 1983-93, Malcolm Jones orator 1996), Soc. Pediat. Radiology, Assn. Univ. Radiologists (pres. 1973-74, gold medal 1985), Soc. Chmn. Acad. Radiol. Depts. (sec.-treas. 1969-70), Swiss Soc. Med. Radiology (hon., Schinz medal 1992), Internat. Skeletal Soc. (medal 2001), Country Club Mobile, Sigma Xi, Alpha Omega Alpha, Sigma Chi (Significant Sig 1999). Office: U South Ala Med Ctr Dept Radiology 2451 Fillingim St Mobile AL 36617-2238 Home: 149 Batre Ln Mobile AL 36608 Office Phone: 251-471-7868. Business E-Mail: gbrogdon@usouthal.edu. *For the physician-scientist-educator, the mere transference of knowledge or the acquisition of new data is not enough. He must participate fully in the affairs of the larger community and has a duty to help others to think about, or form an opinion on, issues they otherwise might not have considered.*

BROGI, ALESSANDRO, history professor; b. Florence, Italy, Oct. 17, 1963; arrived in U.S., 1990; s. Alberto Brogi and Manola Morandi; m. Elayne Irena Hency, May 2004; 1 child, Samuel Alexander. PhD, U. Studi Firenze, 1993, Ohio U., 1998. Full time lectr. internat. security studies Yale U., New Haven, 1999—2002; asst. prof. US diplomatic history U. Ark., Fayetteville, 2002—. Vis. lectr. U. Studi Urbino, Italy, 2001; chief cons. New Haven Festival Arts and Ideas, 2001—02; vis. prof. aul H. Nitze Sch. Advanced Internat. Studies Johns Hopkins U. Bologna Ctr., 2004—05. Author: (book) L'Italia e l'egemonia Americana nel Mediterraneo, 1996 (Finalist Premio Acqui Storia, 1997), A Question of Self-Esteem: The United States and the Cold War Choices in France and Italy 1944-1958, 2002; contbr. articles to profl. jours. Mem.: Am. Hist. Assn., Soc. Historians Am. Fgn. Rels. Avocations: swimming, tango. Office: U Ark History Dept Old Main 416 Fayetteville AR 72701 Office Phone: 479-575-5886. Office Fax: 479-575-2775. Personal E-mail: abrogi@uark.edu.

BROGLIATTI, BARBARA SPENCER, retired television and motion picture executive; b. LA, Jan. 8, 1946; d. Robert and Lottie Spencer; m. Raymond Haley Brogliatti, Sept. 19, 1970. BA in Social Scis. and English, UCLA, 1968. Asst. press. info. dept. CBS TV, L.A., 1968-69, sr. publicist, 1969-74; dir. publicity Tandem Prodns. and T.A.T. Comm. (Embassy Comm.), L.A., 1974-77, corp. v.p., 1977-82; sr. v.p. worldwide publicity, promotion and advt. Embassy Comm., L.A., 1982-85; sr. v.p. worldwide corp. comm. Lorimar Telepictures Corp., Culver City, Calif., 1985-89; pres., chmn. Brogliatti Co., Burbank, Calif., 1989-90; sr. v.p. worldwide TV publicity, promotion and advt. Lorimar TV, 1991-92; sr. v.p. worldwide TV publicity, promotion and pub. rels. Warner Bros., Burbank, 1992-97; sr. v.p. corp. comm. Warner Bros., Inc., 1997-2000; sr. v.p., chief corp. comm. officer Warner Bros. Entertainment Inc., 2000—04; exec. v.p., chief corp. comm. officer Warner Bros., 2004—05. Adv. com. acad. advancement program UCLA; bd. govs. UCLA Found., 2003—. Mem. bd. govs. TV Acad., L.A., 1984-86, UCLA Found., 2003—; bd. dirs. Nat. Acad. Cable Programming, 1992-94; mem. Hollywood Women's Polit. Com., 1992-93; mem. steering com. L.A. Free Clinic, 1997-98; mem. adv. bd. The Rape Found., 2004—. Recipient Gold medal Broadcast Promotion and Mktg. Execs., 1984. Mem. Am. Diabetes Assn. (bd. dirs. L.A. chpt. 1992-93), Am. Cinema Found. (bd. dirs. 1994-98), Dirs. Guild Am., Publicists Guild, Acad. TV Arts and Scis. (vice chmn. awards com.); adv. com. UCLA Acad. Advancement Prog.

BROGLIO, STEVEN PHILIP, physical education educator, director; b. Charleston, W.Va., Jan. 18, 1975; s. Dennis N. and Joyce R. Broglio; m. Jane Elizabeth Jester, June 5, 2004. MS, U. Pitts., 2002; diploma with highest distinction, U. N.C., Chapel Hill, 2000. Cert. athletic trainer Nat. Athletic Trainers' Assn., 2000. Clin. coord. athletic tng. U. Ga., Athens, 2002—. Named Student Rsch. awards Competition winner, NATA Found., 2003. Mem.: Nat. Athletic Trainers' Assn. Achievements include research in kinesiology of soccer heading drill; soccer headgear. Office: U Ga Dept Kinesiology 300 River Rd Athens GA 30602

BROHAWN, VIRGINIA BRIDGEMAN, music educator; b. Lockport, NY, Feb. 8, 1943; d. Ross George Bridgeman and Helene Elizabeth Mac Donald; m. Philip Brohawn, Jr., June 13, 1964; children: Jennifer, Bridget. B in music edn., West Va. Wesleyan Coll., 1964. Cert. APC tchr. Md. Music tchr. Cambridge (Md.) HS, 1964—67; choir dir. St. Paul's United Meth., Cambridge, 1968—81; music specialist St. Claire Elem., Cambridge, 1970—72; music tchr. S. S. Peter and Paul Cath., Easton, Md., 1977—81; pvt. tchr. French horn Cambridge, 1980—87; dir. choral music Cambridge-South Dorchester HS, Cambridge, 1983—2005. Found., dir. Chorus of Dorchester, Cambridge, 1975—; adj. Md. All State MMEA, 1983—2005; music adv. coun. Chesapeake Coll., Wye Mills, Md., 1986—91: Recipient Md. State Eastern Region Choral award, Md. Music Educators Assn., 1997. Mem.: NEA, Md. State Tchrs. Assn., Ea. Shore Choral Dirs. Assn., Dorchester Educators, Dorchester Arts Ctr., Dorchester Garden Club, Cambridge Yacht Club, Alpha Xi Delta. Republican. Episcopal. Achievements include Govs. Salute To Excellence for the Md. You Are Beautiful Chorus Dir. 8 citations 1993-2001. Avocations: gardening, reading, cooking, genealogy. Home: 207 Oak St Cambridge MD 21613 Office: Cambridge-South Dorchester HS 2475 Cambridge Bypass Cambridge MD 21613 E-mail: brohawnv@dcpsmd.org.

BROHN, WILLIAM DAVID, conductor, orchestrator, arranger; b. Flint, Mich. BA in Music, Mich. State U., 1955; MMus, New Eng. Conservatory Music. Played with local ensembles and performed on double bass Boston Pops Orch.; played string bass and piano with numerous musical orgns. including classical, theatrical and jazz groups; condr. nat. tours Robert Joffrey Ballet, Royal Ballet; commd. to adapt and arrange program piece for ann. Christmas concert Cleve. Orch., 1961; recreated sound track for 1938 Russian classic film Alexander Nevsky, 1987; vis. lectr. Oxford U., England. Recipient Tony award for orchestrations for Ragtime, N.Y. Drama Desk award for Miss Saigon, N.Y. Drama Desk award for The Secret Garden. Office: c/o Gershwin Theatre 222 W 51st St New York NY 10019*

BROIDE, MACE IRWIN, public information officer; b. Burlington, Vt., May 21, 1924; s. Abraham A. and Ida (Rosenberg) B.; m. Gloria Leah Goldsholl, Dec. 24, 1943; children: Cheryl Ruth Broide Light, Beverly Elaine Broide Frye, Sandra Pat Broide Banas. AB (Ernie Pyle scholar 1946), Ind. U., 1947. Polit. editor Evansville (Ind.) Press, 1947-58; senatorial adminstrv. asst., 1959-68; co-owner DeHart and Broide, Inc.; public affairs cons. Washington, 1968-78; exec. dir. com. on budget U.S. Ho. of Reps., 1978-86; pub. affairs cons., 1986-99; ret., 1999. Adj. prof. George Washington U., 1986, 87; lectr. in field. Co-author: Inside the New Frontier, 1963; contbr. articles to newspapers, mags. Sec. Nat. Dem. Senatorial Campaign Com., 1961-62; past bd. dirs. Jewish Community Coun. Evansville; past bd. govs. Nat. Dem. Club. With AUS, 1943-46. Decorated Silver Star, Bronze Star. Mem. Assn. Adminstrv. Assts. U.S. Senate (past pres.), B'nai B'rith (past pres.). Home: 4450 S Park Ave Apt 1111 Chevy Chase MD 20815-3641 Personal E-mail: mbroide@aol.com. Business E-mail: glomace25@msn.com.

BROIDO, ARNOLD PEACE, music publishing company executive; b. NYC, Apr. 8, 1920; s. Samuel S. and Ruth (Lewis) B.; m. Lucille Janet Tarshes, Mar. 5, 1944; children: Jeffrey, Laurence, Thomas. BS magna cum laude, Ithaca Coll., 1941, DMus (hon.), 1990; MA, Columbia U., 1954. Tchr. instrumental music East Jr. H.S., Binghamton, NY, 1941—42; editor, prodn. mgr. Boosey & Hawkes Inc. (music pub.), 1945—55; v.p., gen. mgr. Century Music & Mercury Music Corp., 1955—57; edn. dir. Edward B. Marks Music Corp., 1957—62; dir. publs. and sales Frank Music Corp., 1962—69; v.p. Boston Music Co., 1968—69; pres. Theodore Presser Co., 1969—95, chmn., 1995—; also dir.; chmn. Elkan-Vogel Inc., 1970—. Pres. Music Industry Coun., 1966-68, v.p., 1969-70; dir., sec. Harry Fox Agy., 1989-2000, sec.-treas., 2000—. Co-author: Music Dictionary, 1956, Invitation to the Piano, 1959; assoc. editor: Univ. Soc. Ency. of Piano Music; contbr. articles to profl. jours. Mem. Nassau County (NY) Dem. Com., 1952-63; bd. dirs. NY Citizens Com. for Pub. Schs., 1963-68, Am. Music Ctr., 1968-72, 78-83, 85-91, Am. Music Conf., 1979-80, Nat. Music Coun., 1979-85, 93—, Music Educators Nat. Conf., 1966-68; trustee ASCAP Found., 1976—, treas., 1990—; trustee Union Free Sch. Dist. 21 Bd. Edn., Rockville Centre, NY, 1963-69, sec., dist. clk., 1966-67, v.p., dist. clk., 1967-69. With USCGR, 1942-45. Recipient Disting. Alumnus award Ithaca Coll., 2001; Lowell Mason fellow MENC, 2003. Mem. ASCAP (bd. dirs. 1972—, bd. rev. 1980-82, asst. treas. 1989-90, treas. 1990—), Music Pubs. Assn. U.S. (pres. 1972-74, 80-82, bd. dirs. 1980-82, 83-92, 96-2005), Nat. Music Pubs. Assn. (bd. dirs. 1980—, sec. 1989—, treas. 2000—), Internat. Pubs. Assn. (v.p. sect. music 1972-73), Internat. Confederation Music Pubs. (v.p. 1978-88, bd. dirs. 1992—, pres. 1993-94, 96—, chmn. 1994-96, pres. 1996-98, chmn. 1998—, v.p. 2003), Internat. Fedn. Serious Music Pubs. (v.p. 1978-93, 2003-, pres. 1993-2003), Music Industry Mfrs. Assn. (dir. 1980-82), Charles Ives Soc. (bd. dirs. 1985-2003), Phi Mu Alpha Sinfonia. Office: 588 N Gulph Rd King Of Prussia PA 19406 Home: 3300 Darby Rd Apt C101 Haverford PA 19041-1094 Office Phone: 610-592-1222. Personal E-mail: abroido@presser.com.

BROILES, DAVID, lawyer; b. Ft. Worth, Feb. 23, 1938; s. Rowland and Hazel Broiles; m. Linda Broiles, Sept. 19, 1959 (div. Feb. 1, 1988); children: Jim, Lisa, Kathy; m. Patty Broiles, Nov. 10, 2000. BA, So. Meth. U., 1959, MA, 1960; PhD, Ohio State U., 1963; LLB cum laude, Yale U., 1968; LLM with distinction, Georgetown U., 1994; MLA, Tex. Christian U., 1997. Bar: Conn. 1968, Tex. 1972, U.S. Supreme Ct. 1972, U.S. Ct. Appeals (5th cir.), U.S. Ct. Appeals (D.C. cir.), U.S. Ct. Claims. Assoc. Jacobs Jacobs Grudberg & Clifford, New Haven, 1967—71; ptnr. Hooper Kerry Chappell & Broiles, Ft. Worth, 1971—78, Brown Herman Scott Dean & Miles, Ft. Worth, 1978—91, Kirkley Schmidt & Cotten, Ft. Worth, 1992—99; pvt. practice Ft. Worth, 1999—. Author: Moral Philosophy of David Hume, 1965; contbr. articles to profl. jours. Fellow: Am. Coll. Trial Lawyers; mem.: ACLU (bd. dirs. Tex. chpt.). Democrat. Avocation: travel. Home: 2400 Indian Cove Fort Worth TX 76108 Office: 100 N Forrest Park Blvd Ste 220 Fort Worth TX 76102 Office Phone: 817-335-3311.

BROITMAN, SELWYN ARTHUR, microbiologist, educator; b. Boston, Aug. 30, 1931; s. Julius Z. and Sara (Sallus) B.; m. Barbara Merle Shwartz, June 13, 1953; children: Caryn Beth, Jeffrey Z. BS, U. Mass., 1952, MS, 1953; PhD, Mich. State U., 1956. Dir. Biotech. Assocs., 1959—62; rsch. instr. dept. pathology Boston U. Sch. Medicine, 1963—64, asst. prof. dept. microbiology, 1965—69, assoc. prof. dept. microbiology, 1969—75, prof., 1975—, prof. pathology and lab. medicine, 1983—, asst. dean med. sch. admissions, 1983—; assoc. prof. nutritional scis. Henry Goldman Sch. Grad. Dentistry Boston U., 1974—. Assoc. medicine dept. medicine Harvard Med. Sch., 1969-74; spl. sci. staff pathology Boston Med. Ctr., 2000-; rsch. assoc. Mallory Inst. Pathology, Boston City Hosp., Gastro Intestinal Rsch. Lab., 1956-71; assoc. in medicine Thorndike Meml. Lab., 1969-74; chair, co-chair of various admission programs Boston U. Sch. Medicine; adv.-at-large Acad. of Advisors, 2003 Contbr. articles to profl. jours. Founding mem. Digestive Disease Found. Served with USAR 373d Gen. Hosp., 1952-66. Recipient Outstanding Teaching award Boston U. Sch. Medicine 1st Yr. Class, 1976 Fellow Am. Coll. Gastroenterology; mem. AAAS, NAS (com. diet, nutrition and cancer 1980-83), Am. Soc. Investigative Pathology, Am. Soc. Nutritional Scis., Am. Assn. Cancer Rsch., Am. Fedn. Med. Rsch., Am. Soc. Microbiology, Soc. Applied Bacteriology (Eng.), Soc. Exptl. Biology and Medicine, Nutrition Today Soc. (founding), Am. Gastroent. Assn., Boston Gastroent. Soc., N.Y. Acad. Scis., Boston Bug Club (pres. 1976), Sigma Xi. Achievements include development of post grad program, MA in med. scis., leading to MD or DMD degree 1986. Office: Boston U Sch Medicine Divsn Grad Med Scis L 317 715 Albany St Boston MA 02118 Office Phone: 617-638-5342. Personal E-mail: sabroitma@hotmail.com. *When problems cannot be resolved by the minds of this generation, the solutions must be sought in the minds of the next. The challenge is to find these young people, encourage them, and wherever possible, remove all obstacles to their learning.*

BROKAW, CLIFFORD VAIL, III, investment banker; b. N.Y.C., Sept. 17, 1928; s. Clifford Vail and Audrey (Stransom Joel) B.; m. Elizabeth Stokes Rogers, June 29, 1960; children: Clifford Vail IV, George Rogers BA, Yale U., 1950; JD, U. Va., 1956. Bar: NY 1957, U.S. Dist. Ct. 1959, U.S. Supreme Ct. 2002. Assoc. White & Case, N.Y.C., 1956-59; assoc. Blyth & Co., Inc., N.Y.C., 1959-61; assoc., then gen. ptnr. W.E. Hutton & Co., N.Y.C., 1961-67; gen. ptnr., sr. v.p. Eastman Dillon Union Securities & Co. and successor firm Blyth, Eastman, Dillon & Co., Inc., N.Y.C., 1967-77; chmn., CEO Invail Capital, Inc., N.Y.C., 1977-95; CEO IRT Corp., San Diego, 1977-95, chmn. bd., 1986-94. Bd. dirs., chmn. fin. com. Brazos River Gas Co., Mineral Wells, Tex., 1962-91; chmn. bd. Cayman Resources Corp., Tulsa, 1977-88, bd. dirs., 1992-95. Bd. advisors Marine Mil. Acad., Harlingen, Tex., 1985-91; mem. alumni assn. coun. U. Va. Sch. Law, 1976-79; founder Brokaw chair corp. law U. Va. Sch. Law, 1985, mem. dean's coun., 1990—, bus. adv. coun., 1995—; mem. indsl. adv. com. Sch. Engring and Applied Sch. U. Va., 1987-94; vestryman French Ch. du St. Espirit, 1986-88, treas., 1988-92, warden, 1989-93. Lt. col. USMCR, 1950-73. Decorated Purple Heart Mem. ABA, Suffolk County Bar assn., Pilgrims U.S., Mil. Order Carabao, Mil. Order World Wars, Mil. Order Fgn. Wars U.S., Mil. Order of Purple Heart, Nat. Inst. Social Scis. (bd. dirs. 1991-94, pres. 1992-94), Nat. Gavel Soc., Ends of Earth, Huguenot Soc. Am. (coun. 1974-80, v.p. 1986-89, pres. 1989-92), Am. Soc. Order of St. John (comdr.), U. Va. Lawn Soc., Burning Tree Club, The Meadow Club, Bathing Corp. of Southampton, Union Club (N.Y.C.), Masons, Shriners, Yale Club (N.Y.C.), Delta Theta Phi. Republican. Episcopalian. Avocations: tennis, golf. Office: PO Box 5002 Southampton NY 11969-5002

BROKAW, DOUGLAS EDWIN, music educator; b. Steubenville, Ohio, Nov. 17, 1956; s. George Marion and Barbara Ann Brokaw; m. Valeri Kay Conley, June 21, 1986; children: Jonathan Michael, Emily Rachel, Elisabeth Anne. MusB in Edn., Ohio State U., 1979; MusM, Bowling Green State U., Ohio, 1985. Cert. tchr. K-12 music Ohio Dept. Edn., 2003. Mid. sch. band dir. Wash. Ct. Ho. City Schs., Ohio, 1979—83; grad. tchg. asst. band Bowling Green State U., 1983—85; head band dir. Findlay City Schools, Ohio, 1985—89; band dir. The Am. Sch., Tegucigalpa, Honduras, 1989—91, Hopewell-Loudon Local Sch., Bascom, Ohio, 1991—95, Dalat Sch., Tanjung Bunga, Malaysia, 1995—2000, Grove City Christian Sch., Grove City, Ohio, 2000—03, Dalat Internat. Sch., Tanjung Bunga, Malaysia, 2003—. Worship musician, 1977—2004. Missionary assoc., Malaysian children's sch. tchr. Christian & Missionary Alliance, Colorado Springs, 1995—2000; ch. elder; Sunday sch. tchr. Named Outstanding Young Educator, Findlay Jaycees, 1987, Outstanding Young Am., Outstanding Young Ams., 1986. Achievements include middle School jazz band selected to perform at Ohio Music Educators' Association convention; bands consistently received Superior ratings at competition. Avocations: music, bicycling, tennis, skiing. Office: Dalat Internat Sch Tanjung Bunga Rd Penang Tanjung Bunga 11200 Malaysia

BROKAW, NORMAN ROBERT, talent agency executive; b. N.Y.C., Apr. 21, 1927; s. Isadore David and Marie (Hyde) B.; children: David M., Sanford Jay, Joel S., Barbara M., Wendy E., Lauren Quincy. Student pvt. schs., Los Angeles. With William Morris Agy., Inc., Beverly Hills, Calif., 1943—, sr. agt. and co. exec., 1951-74, v.p. world-wide ops., 1974-80, exec. v.p., dir., 1980—, co-chmn. bd., 1986-91, pres., CEO, 1989-91, chmn. bd., CEO, 1991-97, chmn. bd. worldide, 1997—. Pres. Betty Ford Cancer Ctr., Cedars-Sinai Med. Ctr., L.A., 1978—; bd. dirs. Cedars-Sinai Med. Ctr.; industry chmn. United Jewish Welfare Fund, 1975. With U.S. Army, World War II. Mem. Acad. Motion Picture Arts and Scis., Hillcrest Country Club (L.A.). Clients include former Pres. and Mrs. Gerald R. Ford, Bill Cosby, Gen. Alexander Haig Jr., Gen. Claudia Kennedy, Tony Randall, Donald Regan, Senator John Edwards, Senator James Jeffords, Attorney David Boies, C. Everett Koop, Kim Novak, Priscilla Presley, Andy Griffith, Juliette Lewis, Marcia Clark, Christopher Darden; former clients included Marilyn Monroe. Office: William Morris Agy 1 William Morris Pl Beverly Hills CA 90212-2775 also: William Morris Agy Inc 1325 Avenue Of The Americas New York NY 10019-6026

BROKAW, TOM (THOMAS JOHN BROKAW), former network news anchor; b. Webster, S.D., Feb. 6, 1940; s. Anthony Orville and Eugenia (Conley) B.; m. Meredith Lynn Auld, Aug. 17, 1962; children— Jennifer Jean, Andrea Brooks, Sarah Auld. BA in Polit. Sci, U. S.D., 1962, hon. degree, Washington U., St. Louis, Syracuse U., Hofstra U., Boston Coll., Emerson Coll., Simpson Coll., Duke U., 1991, Notre Dame U., 1993; DHL (hon.), Dartmouth Coll., 2005. Morning news editor Sta. KMTV, Omaha, 1962-65; news editor, anchorman Sta. WSB-TV, Atlanta, 1965-66; reporter, corr., anchorman Sta. KNBC-TV, Los Angeles, 1966-73; White House corr. NBC, Washington, 1973-76; anchorman Sat. Night News, N.Y.C., 1973-76; host Today show, N.Y.C., 1976-82; anchorman, editor NBC Nightly News, 1982—2004. Corr. NBC coverage US Presdl. elections, 1976, 80, anchor, 84, 88, 92, 96, 2000, 04; corr. Exposé, 1991; anchor The Brokaw Report, 1992—93; co-anchor Now with Tom Brokaw and Katie Couric, 1993—94. Corr. numerous NBC News specials, including To Be A Teacher, 1987, Wall Street: Money Greed and Power, 1987, A Conversation with Mikhail S. Gorbachev (Alfred I. DuPont award), 1987, Home Street Home, 1988, To Be An American (George Foster Peabody award), Tom Brokaw Reports: Why Can't We Live Together, 1997 (Alfred I. duPont - Columbia U. award); Author: The Greatest Generation, 1998, The Greatest Generation Speaks, 1999, An Album of Memories, 2001, A Long Way From Home, Growing Up in the American Heartland in the Forties and Fifties, 2003. Trustee Norton Simon Mus. Art, Pasadena, Calif., U. S.D. Found.; adviser Asia Soc. Named to TV Hall of Fame, 1997; recipient Peabody award, 7 Emmy awards, Nat. Headliner award, Nat. Conf. Christians and Jews, 1990, Fred Friendly First Amendment award, 1998, "Tex" McCrary Excellence in Journalism award, Congl. Medal of Honor Soc., 1999. Mem.: AFTRA (dir. 1968—72), Reporters Com. for Freedom of Press (mem. adv. com.), Sigma Delta Chi.

BROKKE, CATHERINE JULIET, mission executive; b. Mpls., Dec. 25, 1926; d. Emil John and Alma (Brye) Eliason; m. Harold Joseph Brokke, Sept. 9, 1949; 1 child, Daniel. Diploma in nursing, Luth. Deaconess Hosp., Mpls., 1947; student, Concordia Coll., Moorhead, Minn., 1948-49, Bethany Coll. Missions, Mpls., 1949-51. RN, Minn. Sch. and occupational nurse Bethany Fellowship, Mpls., 1951-75; missions sec. Bethany Fellowship Missions, Mpls., 1963-86, dir., 1986-96; retired, 1996. Instr. Bethany Coll. Missions, 1950-88. Mng. editor Message of Cross, 1990-97; composer hymns. Organist Bethany Missionary Ch., Bloomington, Minn., 1956-89; trustee STEM Ministries, 1995-2000, bd. dirs. Mem. Evang. Fellowship of Mission Agys. (trustee 1987-93), Evang. Missions Info. Svc. (bd. dirs. 1994-96). Avocations: piano, organ. Office: Bethany Fellowship Missions 6820 Auto Club Rd Ste D Bloomington MN 55438-2849 Personal E-mail: cathybrokke@att.net. Business E-Mail: cathy.brokke@bethfel.org.

BROLIN, JAMES (JAMES BRUNDERLIN), actor; b. Los Angeles, July 18, 1940; m. Jane Cameron Agee, 1967 (div. 1985); children: Josh, Jess; m. Jan Smithers (div. 1995); 1 child, Molly; m. Barbra Streisand, 1998. Student, UCLA. Regular in TV series The Monroes, 1964-65, Marcus Welby M.D, 1969-76, Hotel, 1983-88, Extreme, 1995—, (also exec. prodr.) Pensacola: Wings of Gold, 1997, Beyond Belief: Fact of Fiction, 1998, The West Wing, 1999; host Body Human 2000: Love, Sex and the Miracle of Birth, 1999; TV movie appearances include Marcus Welby M.D, 1969, Short Walk to Daylight, 1972, Class of '63, 1973, Trapped, 1973, Steel Cowboys, 1978, The Ambush Murders, 1982, Mae West, 1982, White Water Rebels, 1983, Cowboy, 1983, Beverly Hills Cowgirl Blues, 1985, Hold the Dream, 1986, Intimate Encounters, 1986, Deep Dark Secrets, 1987, Finish Line, 1989, Voice of the Heart, 1990, Nightmare on the 13th Floor, 1990, And the Sea Will Tell, 1991, Visions of Murder, 1993, Gunsmoke: The Last Ride, 1993, Parallel Lives, 1994, Hijacked: Flight 285, 1996, Marriage of Convenience, 1998; film appearances include Take Her, She's Mine, 1963, Goodbye, Charlie, 1964, Von Ryan's Express, 1965, Morituri, 1965, Our Man Flint, 1966, The Boston Strangler, 1968, Skyjacked, 1972, Westworld, 1973, Gable and Lombard, 1976, The Car, 1977, Capricorn I, 1978, Night of the Juggler, 1978, Amityville Horror, 1978, The Gringos, 1980, Pee Wee's Big Adventure, 1985, Indecent Behavior II, The Expert, 1994, Tracks of a Killer, 1995, Terminal Virus, 1995, Last Chance, 1995, Blood Money, 1996, (also dir.) My Brother's Way, 1997, Haunted Sea, 1997, Goodbye America, 1997, Beyond Belief: Fact or Fiction, 1998, A Marriage of Convenience, 1999, To Love, Honor and Betray, 1999, Traffic, 2000, The Master of Disguise, 2002, Catch Me If You Can, 2002, A Guy Thing, 2003, Cursed, 2004. Named Most Promising Actor of 1970 Fame mag., Photoplay mag.; recipient Emmy award. Avocations: licensed pilot, horse breeding, designed and built several homes, a restaurant and a bookstore. Office: Met Talent Agy care Chris Barrett 4526 Wilshire Blvd Los Angeles CA 90010-3801

BROLIN, ROBERT EDWARD, physician, surgeon; b. Holland, Mich., Apr. 12, 1948; s. Edward Magnusson Brolin and Louise A. Mann; children: Lucinda, Brian. BA, DePauw U., Greencastle, Ind., 1970; MD, U. Mich., Ann Arbor, 1974. Diplomate Am. Bd. Surgery. Asst. prof. surgery U. Medicine & Dentistry N.J.-Robert Wood Johnson Med. Sch., New Brunswick, 1980-84, assoc. prof. surgery, 1984-89, prof. surgery, 1989-2000, U. Pitts. Med. Sch., 2001—. Mem. Am. Coll. Surgeons, Am. Soc. Bariatric Surgery (pres. 2000-01), Am. Soc. Clin. Nutrition, N.Am. Assn. Study of Obesity, Soc. Univ. Surgeons, Soc. Surgery of Alimentary Tract. Avocations: jogging, stamp collecting/philately, duplicate bridge. Office: NJ Bariatrics Ste 1 4250 US Rte 1 Monmouth Junction NJ 08852 Office Phone: 732-274-3434. Business E-Mail: rbrolin@njbariatricspc.com.

BROM, LIBOR, journalist, educator; b. Ostrava, Czechoslovakia, Dec. 17, 1923; came to US, 1958, naturalized, 1964; s. Ladislav and Bozena (Bromova) B.; m. Gloria S. Mena, Aug. 31, 1961; 1 son, Rafael Brom. Ing., Czech Inst. Tech., 1948; JUC, Charles U. Prague, 1951; MA, San Francisco State Coll., U. Colo., 1962, PhD, 1970. V.p. Brom, Inc., Ostrava, 1942-48; economist Slovak Magnesite Works, Prague, Czechoslovakia, 1948-49; economist, chief planner Vodostavba, Navika, Prague, 1951-56; tchr. Jefferson County Schs., Colo., 1958-67; prof., dir. Russian area studies program U. Denver, 1967-91, prof. emeritus, 1992—; journalist, mem. editl. staff Denni Hlasatel-Daily Herald, Chgo., 1978-96; editl. staff Jour. of Interdisciplinary Studies, 1988—. Pres. Colo. Nationalities Coun., 1970-72; comptroller Exec. Bd. Nat. Heritage Groups Coun., 1970-72; mem. adv. bd. Nat. Security Coun., 1980-85; acad. bank participant Heritage Found. Author: Ivan Bunin's Proteges, Leonid Zurov, 1973, Alexander Zinoviev's Concept of the Soviet Man, 1991; co-author: Has the Third World War Already Started, 1983, Christianity and Russian Culture in Soviet Society, 1990, The Search for Self-Definition in Russian Literature, 1991; translator: Problems of Geography, 1955; author: (in Czech) In the Windstorm of Anger, 1976, Time and Duty, 1981, Teacher of Nations and Our Times, 1982, The Way of Light, 1982, On the Attack, 1983, Between the Currents, 1985, Homeland After 50 Years Nazi & Communist Occupation, 1992. V.p. Colo. Citizenship Day, 1968-69; pres. Comenius World Coun., 1976-85, World Representation of Czechoslovak Exiles, 1976-84; pres. Czech World Union, 1985-94; gen. sec. Czechoslovak Rep. Movement, 1980-91. Recipient Americanism medal DAR, 1969, Disting. Svc. award Am. by Choice, 1968, Kynewisbov Pioneer award Denver U., 1989; named Tchr. with Superlative Performance MLA, 1961, Outstanding Faculty mem. Omicron Delta Kappa, 1972, The Order of M.R. Stefanik Provisional Czechoslovak Govt. in Exile, Order of Judr. Karel Kramar, Nat. Dem. Party, Czech Republic. Mem. Am. Assn. Tchrs. Slavic and Ea. European Langs. (v.p. 1973-75), Rocky Mountain Assn. Slavic Studies (sec./treas. 1975-78, v.p. 1978-81, pres. 1982-83), Czechoslovak Christian Dem. Movement in Exile (ctrl. com. 1970-79), Dobro Slovo (hon.), Slava (hon.), Nat. Rep. Nationalities Coun. (co-chmn. human rights com. 1979-81), Phi Beta Kappa (hon.). Republican. Roman Catholic. Home: 434 A Woodview Rd Barrington IL 60010-1770 Office: Univ Denver Denver CO 80208-0001 Personal E-mail: lliborbrom@aol.com.

BROM, ROBERT H., bishop; b. Arcadia, Wis., Sept. 18, 1938; Student, St. Mary's Coll., Winona, Minn., Gregorian U., Rome. Ordained priest Roman Cath. Ch., 1963, consecrated bishop Roman Cath. Ch., 1983. Bishop of Duluth, Minn., 1983—89; coadjutor bishop Diocese of San Diego, 1989—90, bishop, 1990—. Office: Diocese of San Diego Pastoral Ctr PO Box 85728 San Diego CA 92186-5728*

BROMAN, PER FREDRIK, education educator; b. Norrkoping, Sweden, July 26, 1962; s. Allan Fredrik and Marianne Elsa Gunvor Broman; m. Nora Anne Engebretsen, Apr. 22, 1968. M in Music Edn., Ingesund Coll. of Music, Sweden, 1987; Post-Grad. Diploma, Royal Coll. of Music, Stockholm, 1992; MA, McGill U., Can., 1995; PhD, Gothenburg U., 1999. Asst. prof. Lulea U. of Tech., Pitea, Sweden, 1992—97, Butler U., Indpls., 1999. Author: (scholarly articles) Jour. of the Swedish Musicological Soc., Grove Dictionary of Music and Musicians, (scholarly book) Back to the Future: Towards and Aesthetic Theory of Bengt Hambraeus; editor: (book) Crosscurrents and Counterpoints. Sgt. Marines, 1982—83, Sweden. Grantee, Sweden Am. Found., 1990, 1991, 1994. Mem.: Swedish Musicological Soc., Coll. Music Soc., Can. U. Music Soc., Soc. for Music Theory (bd. mem., midwest chpt. 2002—), Am. Musicological Soc. Office: Butler U 4600 Sunset Ave Indianapolis IN 46208 Personal E-mail: pbroman@butler.edu.

BROMBERG, ALAN ROBERT, law educator, lawyer; b. Dallas, Nov. 24, 1928; s. Alfred L. and Juanita (Kramer) B.; m. Anne Ruggles, July 26, 1959. AB, Harvard U., 1949; JD, Yale U., 1952. Bar: Tex. 1952. Assoc. firm Carrington, Gowan, Johnson, Bromberg and Leeds, Dallas, 1952-56; atty. and cons., 1956-76; of counsel firm Jenkens & Gilchrist, P.C., 1976—; asst. prof. law So. Meth. U., 1956-58, assoc. prof., 1958-62, prof., 1962-83, Univ. Disting. prof., 1983—, mem. presdl. search group, 1971-72. Faculty adviser Southwestern Law Jour., 1958-65; sr. fellow Yale U. Law Faculty, 1966-67; vis. prof. Stanford U., 1972-73; mem. adv. bd. U. Calif. Securities Regulation Inst., 1973-78, 79-87; counsel Internat. Data Systems, Inc., 1961-65, sec., dir., 1963-65; mem. Tex. Legis. Council Bus. and Commerce Code Adv. Com., 1966-67. Author: Supplementary Materials on Texas Corporations, 3d edit, 1971, Partnership Primer-Problems and Planning, 1961, Materials on Corporate Securities and Finance— A Growing Company's Search for Funds, 2d edit, 1965, Securities Fraud and Commodities Fraud, Vols. 1-7, 1967-93, 2nd edit., 2000-05, Crane and Bromberg on Partnership, 1968, Bromberg and Ribstein on Partnership, Vols. 1, 1994-2005, Bromberg and Ribstein on Limited Liability Partnerships and the Revised Uniform Partnership Act,

1997-2005; mem. ednl. publs. adv. bd., Matthew Bender & Co., 1977-95, chmn., 1981-94; contbr. articles and revs. to law and bar jours.; adv. editor: Rev. Securities and Commodities Regulation, 1969—, Securities Regulation Law Jour, 1973—, Jour. Corp. Law, 1976—, Derivatives: Tax, Regulation, Finance, 1995-97, SMU Law Rev., 1978--. Sec., bd. dirs. Community Arts Fund, 1963-73; gen. atty. Dallas Mus. Contemporary Arts, 1956-63; bd. dirs. Dallas Theater Center, 1955-73, sec., 1957-66, fin. com., 1957-65, mem. exec. com., 1957-70, 79-85, life, 1973—, v.p., trustee endowment fund, 1974-85; trustee Found. for the Arts, 1996—. Served as cpl. U.S. Army, 1952-54. Mem. ABA (coms. commodities, partnerships, fed. regulation securities), Dallas Bar Assn. (chmn. com. uniform partnership act 1959-61, libr. com. 1981-83), Tex. Bar Assn. (chmn. sect. corp. banking and bus. law 1967-68, vice chmn. 1965-67, com. corps. 1957—, mem. com. securities 1965—, chmn. 1965-69, mem. com. partnerships 1957—, chmn. 1979-81), Am. Law Inst. (life), Southwestern Legal Found. (co-chmn. securities com. 1982-85), Tex. Bus. Law Found. (bd. dirs. 1988—, co-chmn. legis. com. 1994—). Office: So Meth U Dedman Sch Law Dallas TX 75275-0116 also: 1445 Ross Ave Ste 3200 Dallas TX 75202-2785

BROMBERG, MYRON JAMES, lawyer; b. Paterson, N.J., Nov. 5, 1934; s. Abraham and Elsie (Baker) B.; m. Lisa Murtha, Nov. 28, 1987; children—Kenneth Karl, Eric Edward, Bruce Abraham. BA, Yale U., 1956; LLB, Columbia U., 1959. Bar: N.J. bar 1960, N.Y. bar 1981. Law asst. to dist. atty., N.Y. County, 1958; law asst. U.S. atty. So. Dist. N.Y., 1958-59; asso. mem. firm Ralph Porzio, Morristown, N.J., 1960-61; ptnr. Porzio, Bromberg & Newman, Morristown, 1962-77, mng. prin., 1980-96. Atty. Morris County Bd. Elections, 1963-64; town atty., Town of Morristown, 1965-67; lectr. trial practice Rutgers Inst. CLE, 1965-94; mem. faculty Kraft-Eidson trial techniques seminar Emory U., 1997-2003. Chmn. fund and membership Morristown chpt. ARC, 1965; chmn. retail div. Community Chest Morris County, 1963; chmn. Keep Morristown Beautiful Com., 1963; mem. Morris Twp. Com., 1970-72; committeeman Morris County Democratic Com., 1962-63, 72-77; lay trustee Delbarton Sch., Morristown, 1972-75; trustee Morris Mus., 1973-79. Fellow Am. Coll. Trial Lawyers (chmn. com. on admission to fellowship 1986-91, com. on complex litigation 1992-98, com. on tchg. of trial and appellate advocacy 1998-2004), Am. Law Inst (cons. group product libility), Am. Bar Found. (life); mem. ABA, Internat. Acad. Trial Lawyers (chair N.J. 1997-99, regional chair 3d jud. cir. 1997-2000, dir. 2002—), N.J. Bar Assn. (named outstanding young lawyer 1970, chmn. joint conf. com. with N.J. Med. Soc. 1970-72), Morris County Bar Assn., Am. Judicature Soc., Trial Attys. N.J. (pres. 1976-77, Trial Bar award 1989), Internat. Soc. Barristers (N.J. State chmn., bd. govs., sec.-treas. 1996-97, v.p. 1998-00, pres. 2000-01), Found. Internat. Soc. Barristers (pres. 2002—), Internat. Assn. Def. Counsel (chair com. on toxic and hazardous substances 1994-96, dir. Def. Counsel Trial Acad. 1996), Andover Alumni Assn. N.Y.C., Columbia U. Law Sch. Assn. of N.J. (bd. dirs. 1986-95, 2001—, bd. visitors, 2005-), Phillips Acad. Alumni Coun., Yale Club (N.Y.C. and ctrl. N.J.), Chi Phi, Phi Delta Phi. Home: 9 Thompson Ct Morristown NJ 07960-6326 Office: PO Box 1997 100 Southgate Pkwy Morristown NJ 07962-1997 Office Phone: 973-538-4006. E-mail: mjbromberg@pbnlaw.com.

BROMBERG, ROBERT SHELDON, lawyer; b. Bklyn., May 3, 1935; s. Jack and Bertha (Toskey) B.; m. Barbara W. Schwartz, Apr. 1, 1978; children: Jason, David. AB, Columbia U., 1956, LLB, 1959; LLM in Taxation, NYU, 1966. Bar: N.Y. 1960, D.C. 1972, Ohio 1972, U.S. Ct. Claims 1976, U.S. Supreme Ct 1975. Practiced law, N.Y.C., 1960-66; atty. exempt orgns. br. IRS, Washington, 1966-70, Office Chief Counsel, 1970-72; partner firm Baker, Hostetler & Patterson, Cleve., 1972-79; prin. Robert S. Bromberg, L.P.A., Cleve., 1979-81, Paxton & Seasongood, Cin., 1981-85; sole practice Cin., 1985—. Lectr. tax and health law confs. Author: Tax Planning for Hospitals and Health Care Organizations, 2 vols., 1979; cons. editor: Prentice Hall Tax Exempt Organizations Service, 1973-84; nat. adv. bd. Integrated Healthcare Report; adv. bd. The Exempt Organization Tax Review; contbr. articles to profl. jours. Recipient award (5) Dept. Treasury, 1966-72, citation Am. Assn. Homes for Aged, 1973 Mem. Am. Health Lawyers Assn. (pres. 1986-87, program chmn. Ann. Tax Inst. 1975-95). Home and Office: 1144 E Rookwood Dr Cincinnati OH 45208-3334 Office Phone: 513-871-6476. E-mail: bromberg@fuse.net.

BROMBERT, VICTOR HENRI, literature educator, author; b. Germany, Nov. 11, 1923; came to U.S., 1941, naturalized, 1943; s. Jacques and Vera B.; m. Beth Anne Archer, June 18, 1950; children: Lauren Nora, Marc Alexis. BA, Yale U., 1948, MA, 1949, PhD, 1953; postgrad., U. Rome, 1950-51; HHD (hon.), U. Chgo., 1981, U. Toronto, 1997. Faculty Yale U., New Haven, 1951-75, from assoc. prof. to prof., 1958-75, Benjamin F. Barge prof. Romance lits., 1969-75, chmn. dept. Romance langs. and lit., 1964-73; Henry Putnam univ. prof. romance and comparative lit. Princeton (N.J.) U., 1975—99, dir. Christian Gauss seminars in criticism, 1984-94, chmn. Coun. Humanities, 1989-94. Summer prof. Middlebury Coll., 1951-53, Institut d'Etudes Françaises, Avignon, 1962, 64, 73, U. Colo., 1965; Christian Gauss Seminar in criticism Princeton U., 1964; vis. prof. Scuola Normale Superiore, Pisa, Italy, 1972, U. Calif., 1978, Johns Hopkins U., 1979, Columbia U., 1980, NYU, 1980, 81, U. P.R., 1983, 84, U. Bologna, Italy, 1984, Yale U., 1985; Phi Beta Kappa vis. scholar, 1986-87, 89-90; lectr. Alliance Française, humanities U. Kans., 1966; lectr. Collège de France, 1991; mem. Fulbright screening com., 1965; dir. fellowships in residence NEH, Princeton U., 1975-76, dir. summer seminar, 1979, 82, 84, 86, 88; mem. adv. com. for humanities Libr. of Congress, 1976; mem. Yale U. Coun., 1977-83; mem. ednl. adv. bd. Guggenheim Found., 1982— Author: (Literary Critiques) The Criticism of T. S. Eliot, 1949, Stendhal et la Voie Oblique, 1954, The Intellectual Hero, 1961, The Novels of Flaubert, 1966, Stendhal: Fiction and the Themes of Freedom, 1968, Flaubert par lui-même, 1971, La Prison Romantique, 1976, The Romantic Prison: The French Tradition, 1978, Victor Hugo and the Visionary Novel, 1984, The Hidden Reader, 1988, In Praise of Antiheroes, 1999, Trains of Thought: Memories of a Stateless Youth, 2002, Les Trains du Souvenir: Paris-New York-Omaha Beach-Berlin, 2005; editor: Stendhal: A Collection of Critical Essays, 1962, Balzac's La Peau de Chagrin, 1962, The Hero in Literature, 1969, Flaubert's Madame Bovary, 1969, The World of Lawrence Durrell, 1962, Ideas in the Drama, 1964, Malraux, 1964, Instants Premiers, 1973, Romanticism, 1973, Literary Criticism, 1974, Die Romanische Novelle, 1977, The Author in His Work, 1978, Essais sur Flaubert, 1979, Writers and Politics, 1983, Flaubert and Postmodernism, 1984, Writing in a Modern Temper, 1984, Literary Theory and Criticism, 1984, Hugo le Fabuleux, 1985, 19th Century Literary Criticism, 1985, Charles Baudelaire, 1987, Albert Camus, 1989, André Malraux, 1989, Gustave Flaubert, 1989, Dilemmes du Roman, 1989, Nineteenth Century French Poetry, 1990, Literature, Culture and Society in the Modern Age, 1991, Literary Generations, 1992, Dix Etudes sur Baudelaire, 1993, George Sand et son temps, 1994, Pratiques d'écriture, 1996, Stendhal et le comique, 1999, 500 Years of Theater History:, 2000, Le Metamorfosi del Ritratto, 2002, Les Modernités de Victor Hugo, 2004; contbr. articles to profl. jours. Served with M.I. AUS, 1943-45. Decorated officier Ordre des Palmes Académiques; recipient Harry Levin prize in comparative lit., 1978, Howard T. Behrman award for disting. achievement in humanities, 1979, Wilbur Lucius Cross medal for outstanding achievement, Yale Univ., 1985, Médaille Vermeil de la Ville de Paris, 1985, The Pres. award for disting. tchg., 1999; fellow Fulbright fellow, 1950—51, Guggenheim fellow, 1954—55, 1970, sr. fellow, NEH, 1973—74, Rockefeller found. resident fellow, Bellagio, Italy, 1975, 1990; grantee Am. Coun. Learned Socs., 1966. Fellow Am. Acad. Arts and Scis.; mem. MLA (editl. adv. comm. 1979-83, pres. 1989), Am. Assn. Tchrs. French, Am. Comparative Lit. Assn., Am. Philos. Soc., Soc. des Etudes Françaises, Soc. des Etudes Romantiques, Acad. Lit. Studies (pres. 1983), Soc. d'Histoire Littéraire de la France, Soc. U. per gli Studi di Lingua e Letteratura Francese, Inst. Romance Studies, Elizabethan Club (pres. 1968-70), Yale Club, Phi Beta Kappa. Home: 49 Constitution Hill W Princeton NJ 08540-6774

BROME, THOMAS REED, lawyer; b. NYC, Aug. 24, 1942; s. Robert Harrison and Mary Elizabeth (Reed) B.; m. Marie Olszewski, June 5, 1971; children: Clinton Reed, Bethan, Heather. AB, Harvard Coll., 1964; LLB, NYU, 1967. Bar: DC 1967, NY 1968. Law clk. to hon. Warren E. Burger U.S. Ct. Appeals, Washington, 1967-68; assoc. Cravath, Swaine & Moore LLP, NYC, 1968-75, ptnr., 1975—. Dir. Legal Aid Soc., NYC, 1989-98, pres., 1994-96. Mem. sch. bd., Ridgewood, NJ, 1989—92, pres., 1991—92; trustee NYU Law Ctr. Found., NY, 1992—, The Valley Hosp., Ridgewood, NJ, 2005—; pres. Ridgewood Pub. Edn. Found., NJ, 1993—96; vice chair NYU Law Ctr. Found., NY, 2001—. Mem. ABA, NY State Bar Assn., Assn. Bar of City of NY Republican. Episcopalian. Office: Cravath Swaine & Moore LLP Worldwide Plz 825 8th Ave New York NY 10019-7475 Office Phone: 212-474-1307. Office Fax: 212-474-3700. Business E-Mail: tbrome@cravath.com.

BROMLEY, BRUCE DITMAS, language educator, writer; b. N.Y.C., Sept. 23, 1956; s. Stephen Baldwin and Patricia Ann B. Student, Berklee Coll. Music, 1976-80; BA in English with honors, Columbia U., 1995; postgrad., NYU, 1995—. Poetry workship asst. dir. Phillips Brooks House Harvard U., Cambridge, Mass., 1976-80; instr. in compositional analysis Berklee Coll. Music, Boston, 1978-84; poetry reading supr. Shakespeare and Co., Paris, 1985-92; instr. English lit. Columbia U., N.Y.C., 1993-95; instr. expository writing program NYU, 1996—2003, lang. lectr. in expository writing, 2003—. Mentor in expository writing program NYU, 2000—03, lectr., 2003—. Author: (play) Sound for Three Voices, 1986, poems; composer (score and piano) Hamlet; composer, playwright in residence Oxford U. Theatre Troupe, Edinburgh Theatre Festival, Scotland, 1986-87; contbr. poems to Gargoyle Mag. Instr. Earl Hall G.E.D. program Columbia U., N.Y.C., 1995—. Recipient Master Tchr. award NYU, 2000-; Mohlberger fellow in English Lit., 2000-01. Mem. Princeton Club, Phi Beta Kappa. Home: PO Box 1573 East Hampton NY 11937-0704 Office Phone: 212-998-8860. Business E-Mail: bdb4945@nyu.edu.

BROMLEY, RICHARD, lawyer; b. Rosetown, Sask., Can., Feb. 8, 1944; s. Arthur Amos and Elsie Anna Freda (Frerichs) B.; m. Marilyn Kay Bill, Aug. 12, 1966; children: Douglas Arthur, Shannon Kimberly, Lindsay Erin. BA, U. Iowa, 1966, JD, 1968. Bar: Iowa 1968, Ill. 1969, U.S. Tax Ct., U.S. Ct. Claims, U.S. Ct. Appeals (5th, 7th, 8th and 10th cirs.), U.S. Supreme Ct. Ptnr. Foley & Lardner LLP, Chgo., chmn. ins. practice group. Lectr. Law Sch., DePaul U., Chgo., 1984-89; adj. prof. Kent. Coll. Law, Ill. Inst. Tech., Chgo., 1987-89. Editor: Iowa Law Rev., 1967-68; bd. advisors Ins. Tax Law Rev., 1989—. Bd. dirs. Chgo. Crime Commn., 1993—, Lookingglass Theatre. Mem. ABA (chmn. com. on taxation of ins. cos.), Iowa Bar Assn., Fed. Bar Assn. (ins. co. tax com.), Chgo. Bar Assn. (exec. coun. fed. tax com.), Legal Club Chgo., Cliffdwellers Club, Union League Club, Waushara Country Club (Wautoma, Wis.), Order of Coif. Lutheran. Office: Foley & Lardner LLP 321 N Clark St Ste 2800 Chicago IL 60610-4764 Office Phone: 312-832-4517. Business E-Mail: rbromley@foley.com.

BROMMER, GERALD FREDERICK, artist, writer; b. Berkeley, Calif., Jan. 8, 1927; s. Edgar C. and Helen (Wall) B.; m. Georgia Elizabeth Pratt, Dec. 19, 1948. BS in Edn., Concordia Coll., 1948; MA, U. Nebr., 1955; postgrad., UCLA, U. So. Calif., Otis Art Inst., Chouinard Art Inst.; DLitt, Concordia U., 1985. Instr. St. Paul's Sch., North Hollywood, Calif., 1948-55, Luth. High Sch., L.A., 1955-76. Assoc. Artist Workshops, Tour Agy, Springmaid Watercolor Workshops Hudson River Valley Art Workshops, Art in the Mountains Workshops, Internat. Artists Workshops. One-man shows throughout the country; group shows include Am. Watercolor Soc., Nat. Watercolor Soc., NAD, Royal Watercolor Soc., London; represented in permanent collections Claremont (Calif.) Colls., Pacific Telesis, Epcot Ctr., Orlando, Hilton Hotels, Inc., Reno, Anaheim, Las Vegas, San Francisco, Intercontinental Hotel, L.A., Harvey Mudd Coll., Claremont, Laguna Beach Mus. Art, TRW, Coca Cola Co., Ky., Concordia Coll., Nebr., Ill., Mo., Utah State U., Provo; author: College Techniques, 1994, Discovering Art History, 1981, 3d edit., 1995, The Art of Collage, 1978, Drawing, 1978, Understanding Transparent Watercolor, 1993, Landscapes, 1977, Art in your World, 1977, Watercolor and Collage Workshop, 1986, Exploring painting, 1989, Exploring Drawing, 1990, Art: Your Visual Environment, 1977, Movement and Rhythm, 1975, Space, 1974, Transparent Watercolor, 1973, Relief Printmaking, 1970, Wire Sculpture, 1968, Careers in Art, 1984, 2d edit., 2001, Emotional Content, 2003, others; editor: The Design Concept Series, 10 vols., 1974-75, Insights to Art series, 1977—; various texts; 12 video art presentations for Crystal Prodns., Inc.; set of 14 design posters for schs. and 10 watercolor posters for schsl for Crystal Prodns., Ind. Recipient prizes Am. Watercolor Soc., 1965, 68, 71, Watercolor U.S.A., 1970, 73, L.A. City Art Festival, 1970, 75, Calif. State Fair, 1975. Mem. Nat. Watercolor Soc. (treas., v.p., pres., awards 1972, 74, 78, 80), West Coast Watercolor Soc., Nat. Arts Club, Rocky Mountain Nat. Watermedia Soc., Watercolor USA Honor Soc., Nat. Art Edn. Assn., Nat. Arts (N.Y.C.), Phila. Water Color club, La. Watercolor Soc., Nat. Assn. Painters in Acrylic (hon. pres.). Republican. Lutheran. Address: 11252 Valley Spring Ln Studio City CA 91602-2611 Office Phone: 818-762-5667.

BROMSEN, MAURY AUSTIN, historian, writer, rare book dealer; b. NYC, Apr. 25, 1919; s. Herman and Rose (Eisenberg) B. BSS cum laude with spl. honors, CCNY, 1939; MA, U. Calif., Berkeley, 1941, Harvard U., 1945, doctoral postgrad. in history, 1945-50; LHD (hon.), Northeastern U., 1987. Vis. lectr. Am. history Cath. U., Santiago, Chile, 1942; instr. history CCNY, 1943-44; founding editor Inter-Am. Rev. Bibliography, 1950-53; editor, sect. chief dept. cultural affairs Pan Am. Union, Washington, 1950-54; on leave, 1953-54; adv. editor, U.S. rep. Inter-Am. Rev. Bibliography, 1956—; founder, dir. Maury A. Bromsen Assocs. (rare book, manuscript and fine art dealers), Boston, 1954—; pres., treas. Maury A. Bromsen Assocs., Inc. (rare book, manuscript and fine art dealers), 1963-89; proprietor, dir. Maury A. Bromsen Co., 1990—; hon. curator Latin Americana Collections Boston Pub. Libr., 1977; hon. curator, bibliographer Latin Americana John Carter Brown Libr. Brown U., Providence, 1996—. Vis. prof. U. Chile, Santiago, 1947; exec. sec. Medina Centennial Celebration, Washington, 1952; adv. coun. univ. librs. U. Notre Dame, 1981-84, emeritus adviser, 1984—; bd. govs. Am. Jewish Hist. Soc., 1987-92; est. Maury A. Bromsen-Simón Bolívar Room John Carter Brown Libr., Providence, 1999. Author: Simón Bolívar: A Bicentennial Tribute, 1983; editor: José Toribio Medina, Humanist of the Americas: an Appraisal, 1960, Spanish transl., 1969; research and publs. in history and bibliography of Ams. Established Medina and Harrisse rare book collections, U. Fla. Library, 1958, 63. Endowed Archibald Bromsen Meml. scholarship, CCNY, 1964; endowed Bromsen lectureship in Humanistic Bibliography, Boston Pub. Library, 1970, Maury A. Bromsen Latin Am. Acquisitions Fund, 1976, Bromsen Fund, Mass. Gen. Hosp. (Health Scis. Lib.), 1983. Decorated Orden al Mérito Bernardo O'Higgins, Knight Comdr. (Chile), Orden de Francisco de Miranda, First Class (Venezuela); elected Colonial Soc. Mass., 1985; Carnegie Endowment for Internat. Peace and U.S. Govt. Exch. fellow U. Chile, 1942; Harvard Woodbury Lowery Travelling fellow, 1946-47, Social Sci. Rsch. Coun. fellow, 1946-48; recipient Brown U. President's Medal, 2003. Mem. Antiquarian Booksellers Assn. Am., Am. Hist. Assn., ALA, Bibliog. Soc. Am., Manuscript Soc. (charter), Conf. on Latin Am. History, Academia Nacional de la Historia, Buenos Aires (corr.), Latin Am. Studies Assn., Bibliog. Soc. (London), Bibliog. Soc. U. Va., Boston Athenaeum, Harvard Coll. Library Friends, Boston Pub. Library Assocs. (hon.), Boston U. Library Assocs. (life), Iowa Library Assocs. (patron), Bell (Minn.) Library Assocs., Clements (Mich.) Library Assocs., Yale Library Assocs., Am. Hist. Soc., Am. Jewish Hist. Soc., Va. Hist. Soc. (life), N.Y. Hist. Soc., Sociedad Chilena de Historia y Geografía, The Countway Libr. of Medicine (Harvard Med. Sch., Rare Books & Special Collections subcommitte, 2003-) Filson Club (life), Phi Beta Kappa. Clubs: Harvard (Boston), Boston Athenaeum (Boston). Address: 770 Boylston St Apt 23-F Boston MA 02199-7720 Office Phone: 617-266-7060. *The true bibliographer should be more than an inventory maker and describer of the physical qualities of books and other printed material. This is but a minimal qualification of the craftsman. He ought rather to know something about the ideas to which a work relates and in what manner it supplements the known history of its field. Thereby he will make a contribution to humanism, and this should be the prime motivator of the scholarly bookman worthy of the name bibliographer.*

BROMWELL, LINDA ANNE, librarian; m. William A Winter, Feb. 14, 1981. BA in Recreation Adminstrn., Calif. State U., 1974; BA in Education, Western Wash. U., 1977; MA in Nonprofit Mgmt., Regis U., 2003. Cert. tchr. Wash., 1977. Tchr. Archdiocese Seattle, Mount Vernon, Wash., 1977—81; academic instr. Cascades Job Corps Ctr., Sedro-Woolley, Wash., 1988—91; adminstr. Skagit Valley Regional Ministry, Mount Vernon, Wash., 1994—98; coord. tng. ChildCare Resource & Referral, Everett, Wash., 1999—2001; libr. JD Ross Libr., Rockport, Wash., 2002—. Author: English Grammar Basics, 2005. Chmn. Girl Scouts - Totem Coun., Mt. Vernon, W.Va., 1988—94; liturgy chair Immaculate Heart of Mary Ch., Sedro-Woolley, Wash., 1990—96. Mem.: Alpha Sigma Nu. Independent. Roman Catholic. Avocations: reading, outdoors, travel, theater. Office: JD Ross Library 500 Newhalem Street Rockport WA 98283 Office Phone: 206-386-4477. Business E-Mail: linda.bromwell@seattle.gov.

BROMWICH, MICHAEL RAY, lawyer; b. LA, Dec. 19, 1953; s. Leo and Rose (Meyer) B.; m. Felice B. Friedman, Dec. 27, 1980; children: Daniel R., Jonah E., Kira A. AB summa cum laude, Harvard Coll., 1976; MPP, JD, Harvard U., 1980. Assoc. Foley & Lardner, Washington, 1980-83; asst. U.S. atty. U.S. Attys. Office, (so. dist.) N.Y., N.Y.C., 1983-87; assoc. counsel Office of Ind. Counsel, Iran-Contra, Washington, 1987-89; spl. counsel Office Ind. Counsel, Iran-Contra, Washington, 1990, 91; ptnr. Mayer, Brown & Platt, Washington, 1989-93; insp. gen. Dept. Justice, Washington, 1994-99; ptnr. Fried, Frank, Harris, Shriver & Jacobson, Washington and N.Y.C., 1999—. Mem. Pres. Coun. on Integrity and Efficiency, 1994-99. Mem. Phi Beta Kappa. Jewish. Office: Fried Frank Harris Shriver & Jacobson 10001 Pennsylvania Ave NW Ste 800 Washington DC 20004 also: One New York Plz New York NY 10004 Office Phone: 202-639-7297. Personal E-mail: mrbromwich@hotmail.com. Business E-Mail: michael.bromwich@friedfrank.com.

BRONAUGH, EDWIN LEE, electrical engineer, consultant; b. Salina, Kans., July 22, 1932; s. Edwin and Violet Mary (Dryden) B.; m. Geraldine Kelley, Dec. 10, 1955: children: Cecilia Ann Bronaugh Snodgrass, Dana Lea Bronaugh Weinberg. BA in Physics, Math. and Language, Tex. A&M U., Commerce, 1955. Commd. USAF, 1955, advanced through grades to capt., 1961, various comm. and ops. assignments, 1955-68; major USAFR, 1968; rsch. scientist Southwest Rsch. Inst., San Antonio, 1968-70, sr. rsch. scientist, 1970-76, rsch. dir., 1976-82; dir. R & D, tech. dir. Electro-Metrics Divsn. Penril, Amsterdam, N.Y., 1982-89; prin. electromagnetic compatibility scientist Electro-Mechanics Co., Austin, Tex., 1989-92, v.p. engring., 1992-94; prin. EdB EMC Cons., Austin, 1994—2004; lead engr. comm. devices divsn. Siemens Info. and Comm. Products, LLC, Austin, 1997-2000; ret., 2005. Author: Electromagnetic Interference Test Methodology and Procedures, 1988; contbr. over 150 articles to profl. jours.; patentee in field. Decorated Bronze Star, Air Force Commendation medal. Fellow IEEE (life; Third Millennium medal 2000); mem. IEEE Stds. Assn. (life), Electromagnetic Compatibility Soc. of IEEE (stds. com. 1980—, dir. tech. svcs. 1981-87, v.p. 1988-90, pres. 1990-92; Cert. of Appreciation 1979, Cert. of Achievement 1983, Cert. of Acknowledgement 1985, Richard R. Stoddart award 1985, Stds. Medallion 1992, Lawrence G. Cumming award 1992), Am. Nat. Stds. Inst. (vice chmn. accredited stds. com. C63 on electromagnetic compatibility 1986-2002, mem. emeritus C63 2002—), Nat. Assn. Radio and Telecom. Engrs. (sr., cert.), Electromagnetic Compatibility Soc. (hon. life.). Avocations: music, model railroads, engineering history, learning additional languages. Home and Office: 10210 Prism Dr Austin TX 78726-1364 Business E-Mail: ed.bronaugh@ieee.org.

BRONDELLO, SANDY, professional basketball player; b. Australia, Aug. 20, 1968; B.Elem.Tchg., 1990. Guard Blazers, Australia, 1995-96, BTV Wuppertal, Germany, 1996-98, Detroit Shock, 1998-99, Miami Sol, 1999—. Mem. Australian Olympic team, 1988; participant World Championships, 1990, 94; guard Austrlian Nat. Team, Women's World Championship, Germany, 1998. Named Australian Intenrat. Basketball Player of the Yr., 1992, WNBL's Most Valuable Player, 1995; recipient European Cup Most Valuable Player, 1996.

BRONFIN, FRED, lawyer; b. New Orleans, Nov. 30, 1918; children: Daniel R., Kenneth A. BA, Tulane U., 1938, JD, 1941. Bar: La. 1941, U.S. Dist. Ct. (ea. dist.) La. 1941, U.S. Ct. Appeals (5th cir.) 1951, U.S. Supreme Ct. 1973. Assoc. Rittenberg & Rittenberg, New Orleans, 1946-50; ptnr. Rittenberg, Weinstein & Bronfin, New Orleans, 1950-60, Weinstein & Bronfin, New Orleans, 1960-63, Bronfin, Heller, Steinberg & Berins, Bronfin & Heller and precessor firms, New Orleans, 1963-91; of counsel Bronfin & Heller, 1991-98, Heller, Draper, Hayden, Patrick & Horn, 1998—. With USN, 1942-46. Mem. ABA, La. Bar Assn., New Orleans Bar Assn., Order of Coif, Phi Beta Kappa. Office: Heller Draper Hayden Et Al 650 Poydras St Ste 2500 New Orleans LA 70130-6175 Office Phone: 504-568-1888. E-mail: fbronfin@hellerdraper.com.

BRONFMAN, EDGAR MILES, SR., beverage company executive; b. Montreal, June 20, 1929; naturalized, U.S., 1959; s. Samuel and Saidye (Rosner) Bronfman; m. Ann Loeb, Jan. 10, 1953 (div. 1973); children: Sam, Edgar Jr., Matthew, Holly, Adam; m. Lady Caroline Townshend (annulled Nov. 21, 1974). Student, Williams Coll., 1946—49; BA, McGill U., 1951; LHD (hon.), Pace U., 1982; LLD (hon.), Williams Coll., 1986. Chmn. Metro Goldwyn Meyer, 1969; chmn. adminstrv. com. Joseph E. Seagram & Sons, Inc., 1955-57, pres., 1957-71; chmn., CEO, pres. Distillers Corp.-Seagram Ltd., Montreal, 1971-75; chmn. The Seagram Co. Ltd. and Joseph E. Seagram & Sons Inc., 1975—94; dir. Vivendi Universal, 2000—03; co-founder Scandent Group (parent company, Cambridge Integrated Svcs. Group, Inc.), Cranbury, NJ, 1994—. Bd. dirs. Am. Technion Soc. Mem. citizens com. for N.Y.C. U.S.-USSR Trade and Econ. Coun.; chmn. Samuel Bronfman Found.; pres. N.Am. Consortium for Free Mkt. Study, World Jewish Congress; mem. exec. com. Am. Jewish Congress, Am. Jewish Com.; mem. Bus. Com. for Arts United Jewish Appeals; hon. chmn. Fedn. Jewish Philanthropies; dir. Am. com. Weizmann Inst. Sci.; mem. fin. com. Nat. Urban League; mem. internat. adv. bd. Sch. Internat. and Pub. Affairs, Columbia U.; chmn. Anti-Defamation League, N.Y.C.; bd. dels. Union Am. Hebrew Congregation; bd. dirs. Am. Com. Weizmann Inst. Sci., Israel. Named Chevalier de la Légion d'Honneur, French Govt.; named one of World's Richest People, Forbes Mag., 1999—2004. Mem.: Fgn. Policy Assn., Com. for Econ. Devel., Ctr. Inter-Am. Rels., B'nai B'rith (bd. overseers), Hundred Yr. Assn. N.Y., Coun. Fgn. Rels. Jewish.

BRONKESH, ANNETTE CYLIA, public relations executive; b. Vineland, N.J., Dec. 18, 1956; d. Manasha and Miriam (Kutlan) B.; m. Steven Silver Schwartz, Aug. 18, 1985; children: Sarah, Emily, Julie. BA, NYU, 1979. Sr. editor Instnl. Investor, N.Y.C., 1979; chief editor McGraw-Hill, N.Y.C., 1980-85; dir. Am. Stock Exchange, N.Y.C., 1985-87; v.p. pub. rels. Nikko Securities, N.Y.C., 1987-90; pres. Bronkesh Assocs., Clifton, N.J., 1990—. Mem. 100 Women in Hedge Funds. Mem. Securities Industry Assn. (pub. rels. roundtable), Fin. Women's Assn. N.Y., Phi Beta Kappa. Avocation: playing piano. Office: Bronkesh Assocs 23 Virginia Ave Clifton NJ 07012-1222 also: 23 Virginia Ave Clifton NJ 07012-1222

BRONKOWSKI, MARK JOHN, textiles executive, real estate agent; b. Hackensack, N.J., Jan. 21, 1958; s. John and Anna Bronkowski; m. Patricia Claire Bronkowski, Oct. 8, 1983; children: Brittany, James. Grad. h.s., Franklin Lakes. Lic. realtor N.J. Owner Textile Tech., Barnegat, NJ, 1976—; sales mgr. Combined Ins., Voorhees, NJ, 1989—90; sales assoc. Horizon Foods, Wall Township, NJ, 1990—91; nat. sales mgr. Net-tel, Manahawkin, NJ, 1992—97; owner, sales assoc. M & P Distributors, Barnegat, 1998—; sales assoc. TCRC, Egg Harbor Twp., NJ, 1999—, Coldwell Banker, Barnegat, NJ, 2000—; nat. sales mgr. Integrity Comm. and Utilities, LLC, Limport, Pa., 2002—. Creator (boardgame) Neighbors. Republican. Roman Catholic. Avocation: sports. Home: PO Box 715 Barnegat NJ 08005 Office: Integrity Comms and Utilities LLC PO Box 715 Barnegat NJ 08005-0715 Office Phone: 609-698-1250 24. Business E-Mail: markb@neighborsthegame.com.

BRONNER, FELIX, physiologist and biophysicist educator, painter; b. Vienna, Nov. 7, 1921; arrived in U.S., 1937, naturalized, 1943; s. Maurice and Lotte (Vogler) B.; m. Leah Horowitz, Oct. 12, 1947; children: Deborah Rachel, Ethan Samuel. BS, U. Calif., Berkeley and Davis, 1941; PhD (Quaker Oats fellow 1950-52), MIT, 1952; student, Kans. State Coll., 1938; postgrad., U. Minn., 1943, U. Va., 1946; D (hon.), Ecole Pratique des Hautes Etud, Paris, 1996. Rsch. assoc. MIT, 1952-54; Helen Hay Whitney fellow, Arthritis and Rheumatism fellow Rockefeller Inst. Med. Rsch., N.Y.C., 1954-56, asst., 1956; dir. lab. mineral metabolism Hosp. for Spl. Surgery, N.Y.C., 1957-63; asst. prof. Cornell U. Med. Coll., 1961-63; assoc. prof. physiology U. Louisville Sch. Medicine, 1963-69; prof. oral biology U. Conn., 1969-86, prof. nutritional scis., 1976-89, prof. biostructure and function, 1986-89, prof. emeritus, 1989—. Vis. scientist Weizmann Inst., Israel, 1965, 76, Varon vis. prof., 1988; vis. scientist Pasteur Inst., Paris, 1977; vis. scientist U. Cape Town Med. Sch., 1984, 88, MRC disting. vis. scientist, 1991; guest scientist INSERM, Paris, 1972, Lyon, France, 1988; cons. USPHS, 1965-68, 70-71, USDA, 1978-79, 2001—; vis. prof. Tel Aviv U. Sch. Medicine, 1976. Editor: (with C. L. Comar) Mineral Metabolism: An Advanced Treatise, 1960-69; (with A. Kleinzeller) Current Topics in Membranes and Transport, 1970-90; (with J. Coburn) Disorders of Mineral Metabolism, 1981-82; (with M. Peterlik) Calcium and Phosphate Transport Across Biomembranes, 1981; Epithelial Calcium and Phosphate Transport: Molecular and Cellular Aspects, 1984; Cellular Calcium and Phosphate Transport in Health and Disease, 1988; (with W. D. Stein) Cell Shape Determinants, Regulation, and Regulatory Role, 1989; (with D. Pansu) Calcium Transport and Intracellular Calcium Homeostasis, 1990; Intracellular Calcium Regulation, 1991; (with R. V. Worrell) A Basic Science Primer in Orthopaedics, 1991; (with M. Peterlik) Extra- and Intracellular Calcium and Phosphate Regulation: From Basic Research to Clinical Medicine, 1992; Nutrition and Health-Topics and Controversies, 1996; Nutrition Policy in Public Health, 1997; (with R.V. Worrell) Orthopaedics: Principles of Basic and Clinical Science, 1999; Nutritional Aspects and Clinical Management of Chronic Disorders and Diseases, 2003, Nutritional Clinical Management of Chronic Conditions and Diseases, 2005; (with Mary C. Farach-Carson) Bone Formation, vol. I, Topics in Bone Biology, 2003, 2d vol., 2005; mem. editl. bd. Am. Jour. Clin. Nutrition, 1968-76, Am. Jour. Physiol., 1985-97, Jour. Nutrition, 1986-95, Nutritional and Clin Mgmt. of Chronic Conditions and Diseases, 2005; contbr. articles to profl. jours.; exhibited in one-man shows, numerous juried shows, reviewed in July, 2003 ARTnews. Pres. Bur. Jewish Edn., Louisville, 1968-69. Served with AUS, 1942-46. Recipient André Lichwitz prize, Nat. Inst. Health and Med. Rsch., France, 1974. Fellow AAAS, Am. Soc. Nutritional Sci.; mem. Am. Physiol. Soc., Biophys. Soc., Harvey Soc., Soc. Exptl. Biology and Medicine, Orthop. Rsch. Soc., Am. Fedn. Clin. Rsch., N.Y. Acad. Scis., Am. Soc. Clin. Nutrition, Am. Soc. Bone and Mineral Rsch., Austrian Bone Soc. (hon.). Home: 33 Ferncliff Dr West Hartford CT 06117-1013 Office: U Conn Health Ctr Farmington CT 06030-6125 Office Phone: 860-679-2136. Business E-Mail: bronner@neuron.uchc.edu. *The past century has been a bloody, one where entire peoples were murdered. But it has also been a period of great intellectual and artistic advances. I feel privileged to have survived and to have participated in the science and art of our time.*

BRONNER, MICHAEL, advertising executive, education assistance company executive; CEO, new bus. contact Bronner Slosberg Humphrey, Boston, 1980-96; founder, chmn. Digitas (formerly Bronnercom), Boston, 1996-2000, chmn. emeritus, 2000—; founder, chmn. Upromise Inc., Needham, Mass., 2001—. Bd. dir. Children's Hospital Trust, Boys & Girls Club, Boston. Recipient Torch of Liberty award, Anti-Defamation League. Office: Digitas The Prudential Tower 800 Boylston St Boston MA 02199-8001 also: Upromise Inc 117 Kendrick St Ste 200 Needham MA 02494 Office Phone: 781-707-8400. Office Fax: 781-707-8401. E-mail: mbronner@upromise.com.

BRONSON, JAMES B., music educator; s. Burton and Katherine Bronson; m. Cynthia Helms, Mar. 5, 1968; children: Holly, Jake. B of Music Edn., Mich. State U., East Lansing, 1982; MEd, U. So. Miss., Hattiesburg, 1986. Cert. continuing edn. Mich., 1987. Asst. camp dir./instr. Blue Lake Fine Arts Camp, Twin Lake, Mich., 1980—81; music tchr./band dir. Genesee H.S., Mich., 1983—; music instr. Mott C.C., Flint, Mich., 1986—90. Head dept. fine arts Genesee Sch. Dist., Mich., 1993—; ednl. mentor Genesee H.S., Mich., 1994—; profl. musician. Musician (composer/arranger): numerous compositions. Mem. PTA Davison Cmty. Schs., Mich., 2002—04. Named Tchr. of the Yr., Genesee H.S. Student Coun., 2000. Mem.: NEA (assoc.), Miss. Cmty. Edn. Assn. (assoc.), Music Educators Nat. Conf. (assoc.), Mich. Sch. Band and Orch. Assn. (assoc.), Genesee Edn. Assn. (assoc.; v.p. 1984—91), Mich. Edn. Assn. (assoc.), U. of So. Miss. Alumni Assn. (assoc.), Mich. State U. Alumni Band Assn. (assoc.). Avocations: travel, reading, music, hiking, walking.

BRONSON, JOHN ORVILLE, JR., retired librarian; b. Memphis, Apr. 6, 1937; s. John Orville and Elinor (Sutherland) B.; m. Patricia Ann Packer, June 11, 1962; 1 stepchild, Richard Wayne McCoy; children: Victoria Patricia Elizabeth, Glenn Charles. Student, N.E. Miss. Jr. Coll., 1957-59; BS, Miss. State U., 1961; MLS, U. Miss., 1965. Field sec. Miss. Libr. Commn., 1961-63, Acacia Nat. Frat., 1963-65; instr. U. Miss., 1965-66; head libr. Calhoun Jr. Coll., Decatur, Ala., 1965-67, Chesapeake Coll., Wye Mills, Md., 1967-82, telecomms. specialist, 1982-91, coord. media tech., 1991-2000. Pres. Wye Milling Co., Inc. Editor Ala. Jr. Coll. Librarian, 1966-67. Historiographer, Easton diocese Episcopal Ch., 1980-83; pres. Talbot County Dem. Club, 1984-85; v.p., sec. congl. coun. St. Marks Luth. Ch., 1999-2004; del. Del.-Md. synod ELCA, 1998-99; bd. dirs., Integrity, Cathedral of the Annunciation, Episcopal Diocese of Md., Balt., 1999-2003. Served with USAFR, 1955-63. Mem. ALA, Md. Libr. Assn., Ala. Libr. Assn., Md. Assn. Jr. Colls., Congress Acad. Librs., Old Wye Mill Soc. (treas.) Soc. for Preservation Md. Antiquities (dir.), Upper Shore Geneal. Soc. (founder), Acacia, Masons. Home: 5506 Rockleigh Dr Arbutus MD 21227

BRONSON, PETER ROBERT, lawyer; b. Erie, Pa., Jan. 20, 1948; s. Brian Samuel and Esther Frances (Brown) B.; m. Liliane E. Steiner, Aug. 22, 1971; children: Sarah, Rivka. BA, U. Ariz., 1969; JD, Harvard U., 1972. Bar: Mass. 1973, U.S. Dist. Ct. Mass. 1977, U.S. Ct. Appeals (1st cir.) 1978. Counsel and acting exec. dir. Outdoor Advt. Bd., Commonwealth of Mass., Boston, 1973-76; sr. dep. gen. counsel Dept. of Environ. Protection, Commonwealth of Mass., Boston, 1976-91; assoc. Mirick, O'Connell, DeMallie & Lougee, Worcester, Mass., 1991-93; sole practitioner Brookline, Mass., 1993-98; zonging adminstr. Inspectional Svcs. Dept. City of Newton, Mass., 1998—2003; sole practitioner Brookline, Mass., 2003—04; adminstr. law judge Social Security Adminstrn., Cleve., 2004—. Mem.: ABA, Mass. Bar Assn. Avocations: bridge, chess. Office: Social Security Adminstrn Hearing and Appeals 7th Fl 1350 Euclid Ave Cleveland OH 44115-1827 Office Phone: 216-522-4914 X6021.

BRONSON, WILLIAM CAVOLT, JR., counselor; b. Oklahoma City, Feb. 9, 1937; s. William Cavolt and Mary Jane (Looney) B. BA, Washburn U., 1961. Cert. clin. supr., Okla., internat. alcohol drug counselor, HIV/AIDS prevention counselor, Okla. Social worker Okla. Adolescent Unit, Oklahoma City, 1964-67; supr. counseling svcs. Urban League Oklahoma City, 1967-72; exec. dir. Nat. Conf. Christians and Jews, 1972-76; social worker Dept. Human Svcs., Tulsa, 1977-79; dir. drug/alcohol svcs. Archdiocese of Okla., Oklahoma City, 1980-81; coord. Okla. Assn. for Retarded Citizens, Oklahoma City, 1981-82; coord. refugee resettlement Archdiocese of Okla., Oklahoma City, 1982-83; exec. dir. Southwest Okla. Adolescent Treatment, Lone Wolf, 1983-86; social worker Okla. Child Abuse Investigation, Oklahoma City, 1986-90; counselor drug treatment The Referral Ctr., Oklahoma City, 1990-93; clin. coord. Drug Alcohol Youth Svcs., Altus, Okla., 1995—. Author: Etiology of Violence, 2001, short stories, poem. Contbr. Nat. Dem. Conv., 2000; mem. Human Rights Campaign, Washington, 2003. Grantee U.S. Dept. Health, 1984, Kerr Found. Okla, 1982. Mem.: Am. Soc. Drug Counselors, Internat. Soc. Poets. Home: 2228 NW 118th Ter Oklahoma City OK 73120

BRONSTEIN, ALVIN J., lawyer; b. Bklyn., June 8, 1928; LLD, N.Y. Law Sch., 1951, LLD (hon.), 1990. Bar: N.Y. 1952, Miss. 1967, La. 1971, U.S. Ct. Appeals (D.C., 1st, 2d, 3d, 4th, 5th, 9th, 10th and 11th cirs.), U.S. Supreme Ct. 1961. Ptnr. Bronstein & Bronstein, Bklyn., 1952-63; pvt. practice Elizabethtown, NY, 1963-64; chief staff counsel Lawyers Constl. Def. Com., Jackson, Miss., 1964-68; fellow Inst. Politics, Kennedy Sch. Govt. Harvard U., Cambridge, Mass., 1968-69, assoc. dir. Inst. Politics, Kennedy Sch. Govt., 1969-71; ptnr. Elie, Bronstein, Strickler & Dennis, New Orleans, 1971-72; exec. dir. Nat. Prison Project, Nat. Jail Project ACLU Found., Washington, 1972-96, cons. nat. legal dept., 1996—. Cons., trial counsel CORE, NAACP, NAACP Legal Def. Fund, SCLC, SNCC, Miss. Freedom Dem. Party, Black Panther Party, Nat. Inst. for Edn. in Law and Poverty, and others; guest lectr. various law schs., 1964—; cons. various state corrections depts., 1972—; adj. prof. Am. U. Law Sch., 1973; expert witness in various prison litigs., 1978—; apptd. mem. Fed. Jud. Ctr. Adv. Com. on Experimentation in the Law, 1978-81. Contbg. author: The Evolution of Criminal Justice, 1978, Prisoners' Rights Sourcebook, Vol. II, 1980, Confinement in Maximum Custody, 1980, Sage Criminal Justice Annual, Vol. 14, 1980, Readings in the Justice Model, 1980, Our Endangered Rights, 1984, Prisoners and the Courts: The American Experience, 1985; author: (with Rudovsky and Koren) The Rights of Prisoners, 1988; author, editor: Representing Prisoners, 1981; editor: Prisoners' Self-Help Litigation Manual, 1977; contbr. articles to profl. jours. MacArthur Found. fellow, 1989; named one of the 100 most influential lawyers in Am., Nat. Law Jour., 1985, 88, 91, 94; recipient Roscoe Pound award Nat. Coun. on Crime and Delinquency, 1981, Karl Menninger award Fortune Soc., 1982, Pa. Prison Soc. award, 1991. Office: Penal Reform Internat 1120 19th St NW 8th Fl Washington DC 20036 Office Phone: 202-686-6578. E-mail: alvbron@aol.com.

BRONSTEIN, LOIS HELENE, marketing professional; b. Bklyn., Sept. 2, 1950; d. Bertram Lester and Elaine (Hoch) B.; m. Howard David Glicksman, Mar. 26, 1988. BS in Math., Pa. State U., 1972; MS in Info. Sci., Drexel U., 1973; MBA, Widener U., 1982. From mem. staff to mktg. rsch. cons. DuPont, Wilmington, Del., 1973—2000; mktg. rsch. cons. DuPont Electronic Techs., Rsch. Triangle Pk., NC, 2000—. H.W. Wilson Found. fellow, Drexel U., 1972. Mem.: Am. Mktg. Assn. Avocation: painting. Office: DuPont Electronic Technologies 14 TW Alexander Dr Research Triangle Park NC 27709 Office Phone: 919-248-5080. Business E-Mail: lois.h.bronstein@usa.dupont.com.

BRONSTEIN, LYNNE, writer; b. Dec. 30, 1950; Staff writer Showtime Mag., Santa Monica, Calif., 1998—. Freelance journalist, 1972—; freelance writer Music Connection Mag., AllMusic.com, MusicID.com, others, 2001—. Author: Astray from Normalcy, 1974, Roughage, 1977, Thirsty in the Ocean, 1980, Border Crossings, 2004; contbr. articles to mags. E-mail: tanysare@earthlink.net.

BRONSTEIN, PHIL, publishing executive; m. Sharon Stone, Feb. 4, 1998 (div. 2004); 1 adopted child, Roan. Reporter Sta. KQED-TV, San Francisco; reporter, fgn. corr. San Francisco Examiner, 1980-90, mng. editor-news, 1990—91, exec. editor, 1991—2000, sr. v.p., exec. editor, 2000—03, exec. v.p., editor, 2003—. Office: San Francisco Chronicle 901 Mission St San Francisco CA 94103*

BRONSTER, MARGERY S., retired state attorney general, lawyer; b. N.Y., Dec. 12, 1957; married; 1 child. BA in Chinese Lang., Lit. and History, Brown U., 1979; JD, Columbia U., 1982. Bar: N.Y. 1983, Hawaii 1988, U.S. Dist Ct. (So. & Ea. N.Y. & Hawaii dist.), U.S. Tax Ct., U.S. Ct. Appeals (Ninth & Eleventh cir.). Assoc. Sherman & Sterling, NY, 1982—87; ptnr. Carlsmith, Ball, Wichman, Murray, Case & Ichiki, Honolulu, 1988—94; atty. gen. State of Hawaii, 1994—99; ptnr. Bronster Crabtree & Hoshibata, Honolulu, 1999—. Co-chair planning com. Citizens Conf. Jud. Selection, 1993; chair State of Hawaii Tobacco Prevention & Control Adv. Bd. Author: Litigating a Class Action Suit in Hawaii, 2001. Mem. Violence Against Women's Act; mem. nat. gov. bd. Common Cause. Recipient Fellow of the Pacific award, Hawaii Pacific Univ., 2000, Profiles in Courage award, SW Bell Conf. We. Atty. Gen., 2000, Advocate of the Year, Hawaii Cancer Soc., 1999, Kelley-Wyman award, Nat. Assn. Atty. Gen., 1999, Top Cop award, State of Hawaii Law Enforcement Coalition, 1999, Hawaii Woman Lawyer of the Year, Hawaii Women Lawyers, 1998, Tommy Holmes award, Sex Abuse Treatment Ctr., 1998; scholar Harlan Fisk Stone. Office: Bronster Crabtree Hoshibata Suite 2300 Pauahi Tower 1001 Bishop St Honolulu HI 96813 Office Phone: 808-524-5644. Business E-Mail: mbronster@bchlaw.net.

BRONZI, PHILIP A., retired social worker, educator; s. Guesippi and Gina Bronzi; 1 child, Laura. BS in Social studies, Villanova U., 1963, MA in Polit. sci., 1965. Social worker St. Michael Parish, Atlantic City, 1985—87; ret., 1999. Mem. Chelsea Neighborhood Assn.; commr. Charter Study, Atlantic City, 1976; mayor Election Bd. Recipient grad. scholarship, Villanova Coun., 1963—65. Mem.: Sons of Italy in Am., Moose, Elks, KC (recorder 1999).

BRONZINO, JOSEPH DANIEL, electrical engineer; b. Bklyn., Sept. 29, 1937; s. Joseph Rocco and Antoinette (Saporito) B.; m. Barbara Louise McGrath, Dec. 2, 1961; children: Michael J., Melissa J., Marcella J. BSEE, Worcester Poly. Inst., 1959, PhD in Elec. Engring, 1968; MSEE, U.S. Naval Postgrad. Sch., 1961. Registered profl. engr., Conn. Instr. elec. engring. U. N.H., 1964-66, asst. prof. elec. engring., 1966-67; NSF faculty fellow Worcester Found. for Exptl. Biology, Shrewsbury, Mass., 1967-68, mem. cooperating staff, 1968-94; assoc. prof. engring. Trinity Coll., 1968-75, prof., 1975—, Vernon Roosa prof. applied sci., 1977—, chmn. dept. engring., 1981-91. Adj. faculty Boston U. Med. Sch., 1987—98; dir. and chmn. biomed. engring. program Hartford (Conn.) Grad. Ctr., 1969-97; clin. assoc. dept. surgery U. Conn. Health Ctr., Farmington, 1971-77; rsch. assoc. Inst. for Living, Hartford, 1968-97; reviewer NSF; panelist NSF Rsch. Initiation Grants; dir. Biomed. Engring. Alliance for Conn., 1997—2000; pres. Biomed. Engring. Alliance and Consortium, 2000—; lectr., spkr. in field. Author: Technology for Patient Care, 1977, Computer Application in Patient Care, 1982, Biomedical Engineering Basic Concepts and Instrumentation, 1986, Medical Technology: Economic and Ethical Issues, 1990, Expert Systems: Basic Concepts, 1990, Management of Medical Technology: A Primer for Clinical Engineers, 1992, Biomedical Engineering Handbook, 1995, 3d edit., 2005, Introduction to Biomedical Engineering, 1999, 2d edit., 2005; contbr. articles to profl. publs. Mem. Simsbury (Conn.) Planning Commn., 1977-82. Served to 1st lt. Signal Corps U.S. Army, 1961-63. Recipient Goddard award for profl. achievement, Worcester Poly. Inst., 2004. Fellow: AAAS, IEEE (sr.; regional dir. group engring. in medicine and biology 1973—78, v.p. tech. activities 1982—85, pres. 1985—86, chmn. health care engring. policy com. 1986—90, vice chmn. tech. policy coun. 1990—91, chmn. tech. policy coun., Millenium award 2000), Conn. Acad. Sci. and Engring. (v.p. 2000—02, sec. 2002—04, editor-in-chief Acad. Press Biomed. Engring. Book Series), Biol. Psychiatry, Neurosci. Soc., Am. Soc. Engring. Edn. (exec. com. divsn. biomed. engring. 1973—82, vice chmn. career devel. 1974—76, vice chmn.profl. devel. 1976—77, divisional newsletter editor 1977—79, chmn.-elect divsn. 1979—80, exec. com. 1990—91, chmn. tech. policy coun. 1992—94), Am. Inst. Med. and Biol. Engrs., Rotary (pres. Simsbury club 1971—89, Hartford Club 1989—91, pres. Simsbury club 1991—93). Republican. Roman Catholic. Achievements include rsch. in signal analysis concepts and applications, basic neurophysiol. concepts involved in identifying specific neural circuits associated with specific functions of the brain. Home: 12 Brenthaven Avon CT 06001-3941 Office: Trinity Coll Dept Engring Hartford CT 06106 Office Phone: 860-547-1995. E-mail: jdbblb@comcast.net, joseph.bronzino@beaconalliance.org.

BROOK, ADRIAN GIBBS, chemistry professor; b. Toronto, May 21, 1924; s. Frank Adrian and Beatrice Maud (Wellington) B.; m. Margaret Ellen Dunn, Dec. 18, 1954; children— Michael A., Katherine M., David L. BA, U. Toronto, 1947, PhD, 1950. Lectr. chemistry U. Sask., 1950-51; research fellow Imperial Coll., London, 1951-52, Iowa State Coll., 1952-53; lectr. chemistry U. Toronto, 1953-56, asst. prof., 1956-60, assoc. prof., 1960-62, prof., 1962-87, univ. prof., 1987-89, univ. prof. emeritus, 1989—, chmn. dept. chemistry, 1969-74. Vis. prof. U. Sussex, 1974-75, Cambridge (Eng.) U., 1982, Ind. U., 1988. Contbr. articles to profl. jours. Nuffield Overseas fellow, 1951; recipient Izaak Walton Killam Meml. prize for Sci., 1994. Fellow Royal Soc. Can., Chem. Inst. Can. (CIC medal 1985); mem. Am. Chem. Soc. (Frederic Stanley Kipping award 1973) Home: Apt 202 7 Thornwood Rd Toronto ON Canada M4W 2R8 Office: U Toronto Dept Chemistry 80 St George St Toronto ON Canada M5S 3H6 Business E-Mail: abrook@chem.utoronto.ca.

BROOK, DAVID WILLIAM, psychiatrist, researcher; b. N.Y.C., Sept. 19, 1936; s. Michael Marysson and Hilda Jeanette (Ascher) B.; m. Judith Suzanne Muser, Dec. 15, 1962; children: Adam Michael, Jonathan Edward. BA, U. Rochester, 1958; MD, Yale U., 1961. Diplomate Am. Bd. Psychiatry and Neurology; cert. addiction psychiatry; cert. in addiction medicine Am. Soc. Addiction Medicine; cert. med. rev. officer; cert. group psychotherapist Nat. Registry Group Psychotherapists. Intern U. Chgo. Hosps., 1961-62; resident Mt. Sinai Hosp., 1962-65, asst. attending psychiatrist, 1973-80, assoc. attending psychiatrist, 1980-90, attending psychiatrist (cmty. medicine), 1994—; practice medicine specializing in psychiatry N.Y.C., 1965—; clin. asst. in psychiatry Hillside Hosp., 1965-67; sch. psychiatrist N.Y.C. Bur. Child Guidance, 1967-69; asst. clin. prof. psychiatry Mt. Sinai Sch. Medicine, 1977-88, assoc. clin. prof., 1988-90, adj. assoc. prof., 1990-92; assoc. prof. psychiatry N.Y. Med. Coll., Valhalla; prof. cmty. and preventive medicine Mt. Sinai Sch. Medicine, 1994—2003, adj. prof. cmty. and preventive medicine, 2004—; assoc. prof. psychiatry N.Y. Med. Coll., Valhalla, 1990-92, prof. clin. psychiatry, 1992-94; prof. psychiatry NYU Sch. Medicine, 2004—. Adj. asst. prof. psychiatry Fordham U. Sch. Social Work, 1970-73; med. dir. Washington Sq. Inst. Psychotherapy and Mental Health, 1977-82; attending psychiatrist, acting dir. dept. psychiatry Mt. Sinai Svcs., Elmhurst Hosp. Ctr., 1989-90; attending psychiatrist Westchester County Med. Ctr., 1990-94; dir. divsn. drug abuse rsch., prevention and treatment N.Y. Med. Coll., Valhalla, 1990-94, adj. prof. clin. psychiatry, 1994-2001; prin. investigator, co-prin. investigator rsch. grants Nat. Inst. Drug Abuse; bd. examiner Am. Bd. Psychiatry and Neurology; attending psychiatrist, NYU Hosps., 2004—. Co-author, co-editor 6 books including Psychology of Adolescence, 1978, Group Therapy of Substance Abuse, 2002; contbr. over 125 articles to profl. jours., chpts. to books on group psychotherapy, adolescence, alcoholism, drug abuse and behavioral medicine; mem. editl. bd. Internat. Jour. Group Psychotherapy, Social Work in Health Care, Jour. Addictive Diseases, Jour. of Groups in Addiction and Recovery. Fellow Am. Group Psychotherapy Assn. (bd. dirs. 1992-95, 98-2001), Am. Psychiat. Assn. (disting. lfie, exec. coun. N.Y. County dist. br. 1988-91, mem. Assembly 1999—), N.Y. Acad. Medicine, Am. Soc. Addiction Medicine, Am. Psychopathol. Assn.; mem., Group Psychotherapy Found. (bd. dirs. 1992-98), Am. Acad. Addiction Psychiatrists. Office: NYU School of Medicine 215 Lexington Ave New York NY 10016 Fax: 212-263-4660. Office Phone: 212-263-4661.

BROOK, ITZHAK, pediatrician, educator; b. Haifa, Israel, June 16, 1941; came to U.S., 1974; s. Bernard and Haya (Weizbitzka) B. MD, Hebrew U., Jerusalem, 1968; MSc, Tel Aviv U., 1973. Resident pediatrics Hebrew U. Sch. Medicine, Rehovat, Israel, 1969-74; fellow infectious diseases UCLA, 1974-76; attending physician U. Calif., Irvine, 1976-77; attending physician infectious diseases Children's Hosp., Washington, 1977-80; sr. scientist Armed Forces Rsch. Inst., Bethesda, Md., 1984-92, 97—, Naval Med. Rsch. Inst., Bethesda, 1980-84, 92-97. Chmn. adv. antiinfective com. FDA, Rockville, Md., 1984-89; prof. pediatrics and medicineGeorgetown U. Sch. Medicine. Author: Pediatric Anaerobic Infection, 1984-2002; contbr. articles on infectious disease to profl. jours. Comdr. USN, 1980—. Fellow Am. Soc. Infecious Diseases, Pediatric Rsch. Soc.

BROOK, ROBERT HENRY, public health service officer, internist, educator; b. N.Y.C., July 3, 1943; s. Benjamin and Elizabeth (Berg) Brook; m. Susan Jean Weiss, June 26, 1966 (div. 1980); children: Rebecca, Daniel; m. Jacqueline Barbara Kosecoff Plaut, Jan. 17, 1982; children: Rachel, Davida. BS, U. Ariz., 1964; MD, Johns Hopkins U., 1968, ScD, 1972. Diplomate Am. Bd. Internal Medicine. Intern Balt. City Hosp., 1968—69, resident in medicine, 1969—72; project officer Nat. Ctr. Health Svcs. Rsch., HEW, Washington, 1972—74; vice-chmn. medicine UCLA, 1990—92, dir. clin. scholar program, 1974—, prof. of medicine and pub. health, 1974—; dir. health program RAND Corp., Santa Monica, Calif., 1990—, v.p., 1998—. Mem. editl. bd.: Health Adminstrn. Press, 1986—92, Jour. Gen. Internal Medicine, 1987—89, Health Policy, 1986—; contbr. articles to profl. jours. Asst. surgeon USPHS, 1972—76. Named one of one of 75 pub. health heroes of Johns Hopkins, 1991; recipient Rsch. prize, Baxter Found. Health Svcs., 1988, Glazer award, Soc. Gen. Internal Medicine; fellow Lita Annenberg Biomed. fellow, Inst. Humanistic Studies, 1981. Fellow: ACP (Rosenthal award); mem.: Johns Hopkins Soc. Scholars, Assn. Am. Physicians, Assn. Health Svcs. Rsch. (bd. dirs. 1982—89, Disting. Health Svc. Rschr. award), Am. Soc. Clin. Investigation, Inst. Medicine NAS. Democrat. Jewish. Home: 1474 Bienveneda Ave Pacific Palisades CA 90272-2346 Office: Rand Corp 1700 Main St Santa Monica CA 90401-3297 Office Phone: 310-393-0411 ext. 7368. Business E-Mail: robert-brook@rand.org.

BROOKE, AVERY ROGERS, publisher, writer; b. Providence, May 28, 1923; d. Morgan Witter and Lucy Avery (Benjamin) Rogers; m. Joel Ijams Brooke, Sept. 14, 1946; children— Witter, Lucy, Sarah. B.F.A., R.I. Sch. Design, 1945, Union Theol. Sem., 1970. Founder Vineyard Books, Inc., Noroton, Conn., 1971-88; pub., v.p. Seabury Press, N.Y.C., 1980-83. Mentor Annand Program in Spiritual Growth, Yale/Berkeley Div. Sch., 1991—96. Author: Youth Talks with God, 1959, Doorway to Meditation, 1973, How To Meditate without Leaving the World, 1975, Plain Prayers for a Complicated World, 1975, 93, Roots of Spring, 1975, As Never Before, 1976, Hidden in Plain Sight, 1978, Cooking with Conscience (under pseudonym Alice Benjamin), 1975, The Vineyard Bible, 1980, Celtic Prayers, 1981, Trailing Clouds of Glory, 1985, Finding God in the World, 1989, 2d edit., 1994, Plain Prayers in a Complicated World, 1993, Healing in the Landscape of Prayer, 1996, 2d edit., 2004; contbr. articles to religious jours. Mem. The Author's Guild, Oblate Order of the Holy Cross, Spiritual Dirs. Internat. Democrat. Episcopalian. Home: 27 Pasture Ln Darien CT 06820-5618 Office Phone: 203-655-6102. Personal E-mail: AveryRBR@aol.com.

BROOKE, EDNA MAE, retired business educator; b. Las Vegas, Nev., Feb. 10, 1923; d. Alma Lyman and Leah Mae (Ketcham) Shurtliff; m. Bill T. Brooke, Dec. 22, 1949; 1 child, John C. BS in Acctg., Ariz. State U., 1965, MA in Edn., 1967, EdD, 1975. Grad. teaching asst. Ariz. State U., Tempe, 1968-69; prof. bus. Maricopa Tech. Coll., Phoenix, 1967-72, assoc. dean instl. services, 1972-74; prof. bus. and acctg. Scottsdale (Ariz.) Community Coll., 1974-93; ret., 1993. Cons. in field. Author: The Effectiveness of Three Techniques Used in Teaching First Semester Accounting Principles to Tech. Jr. College Students, 1974. Home: 1176 E Northern Hills Dr Bountiful UT 84010-1707

BROOKE, EDWARD WILLIAM, lawyer, retired senator; b. Washington, Oct. 26, 1919; s. Edward W. and Helen (Seldon) B. BS, Howard U., 1940, LL.D., 1967; LL.B. (editor Law Rev.), Boston U., 1948, LL.M., 1949, LL.D., 1968, George Washington U., 1967, Skidmore Coll., 1969, U. Mass., 1971, Amherst Coll., 1972; D.Sc., Lowell Tech. Inst., 1967; D.Sc. numerous other hon. degrees. Bar: Mass. 1948, D.C. Ct. Appeals 1979, D.C. Dist. Ct. 1982, U.S. Supreme Ct. 1962. Chmn. Boston Fin. Com., 1961-62; atty. gen. State of Mass., Boston, 1963-66; mem. U.S. Senate from Mass., 1967-79; chmn. Nat. Low-Income Housing Coalition; former ptnr. O'Connor & Hannan, Washington; formrly of counsel Csaplar & Bok, Boston. Former pub. mem. Adminstrv. Conf. U.S.; chmn. bd. dirs. Boston Bank Commerce; bd. dirs. Meditrust, Inc., Wellesley, Mass., Grumman Corp., Bethpage, N.Y. Chmn. Boston Opera Co.; former commr. Pres.'s Commns. on Housing and of Wartime Relocation and Internment of Civilians; bd. dirs. Washington Performing Arts Soc. Served as capt. inf. AUS, World War II, ETO. Decorated Combat Infantryman's Badge; recipient Disting. Svc. award Amvets, 1952, Charles Evans Hughes award NCCJ, 1967, Springarn medal, NAACP, 1967 Fellow Am. Bar Assn., Am. Acad. Arts and Scis. Office: 6437 Blantyre Rd Warrenton VA 20187-7147

BROOKE, FRANCIS JOHN, III, retired academic administrator; b. Charleston, W.Va., Mar. 4, 1929; s. Francis John Jr. and Elizabeth (Baird) B.; m. Helen Holmes Morgan, Dec. 20, 1958; children: Francis John, Haynes Morgan, David Tucker. BA, Hampden-Sydney Coll., 1949; MA, U. Chgo., 1951; PhD, U. N.C., 1954. Instr. German Roanoke Coll., Salem, Va., summers 1950-52; teaching fellow, part-time instr. U. N.C., Chapel Hill, 1951-54; mem. faculty, to assoc. prof. German U. Va., Charlottesville, 1956-65, asst. dean. Coll. Arts & Scis., 1959-62, acting chmn. dept. modern langs., 1962-63; exec. dean, prof. German Centre Coll., Danville, Ky., 1965-68; v.p. acad. affairs Va. Commonwealth U., Richmond, 1968-74, provost, acad. campus, 1973-79, spl. asst. to pres., 1979-80, prof. German, 1968-80; pres. Columbus (Ga.) Coll., 1980-87; spl. asst. to chancellor Univ. System of Ga., Atlanta, 1988; Pacific N.W. regional rep. Presbyn. Ch. Found., Seattle, 1989-99, ret., 1999. Vice chmn. So. Humanities Conf., 1965; pres. South Atlantic region Am. Assn. Tchrs. German, 1965-67; exec. com. South Atlantic chpt. MLA, 1963-66. Mem. gen. assembly com. on theol. edn. Presbyn. Ch., 1988-90. With AUS, 1954-56. Old Dominion Found. grantee, 1960; intern acad. adminstrn. Ellis L. Phillips Found., Cornell U., 1963-64. Mem. Assn. State Colls. and Univs. (com. on humanities 1984-86, com. on urban affairs 1986-87), Omicron Delta Kappa.

BROOKE, GEORGE MERCER, JR., retired historian; b. Tokyo, Oct. 21, 1914; (parents Am. citizens); s. George Mercer and Isabel Elsie (Tilton) B.; m. Frances Fleming Bailey, June 13, 1942; children: George Mercer III, Marion Bailey Brooke Philpott. BA in Liberal Arts, Va. Mil. Inst., 1936; MA in History, Washington and Lee U., 1942; PhD in History, U. N.C., 1955. Spl. agent Md. Casualty Co., Balt., 1936-41; history instr. Va. Mil. Inst., Lexington, 1942-43, from asst. prof. to prof., 1948-80, prof. emeritus, 1980—; history instr. Washington & Lee U., Lexington, 1946-47. Author: John M. Brooke, Naval Scientist, 1980, General Lee's Church, 1984, John M. Brooke's Pacific Cruise, 1986; editor: Ironclads and Big Guns of the Confederacy: The Journal and Letters of John M. Brooke, 2002; contbr. numerous articles to profl. publs. Chmn. Citizen-Soldier Meml. Va. Mil. Inst., 1983-84, Sesquicentennial celebration, 1986-89; unit pres. Am. Cancer Soc., 1980-82; pres. Stonewall Jackson area coun. Boy Scouts Am., 1964-67. 1st lt. U.S. Army, 1943-46, PTO. Fulbright rsch. scholar Keio U., 1962-63; Fulbright teaching grantee Nat. Taiwan U., 1963; recipient Silver Beaver award Boy Scouts Am., 1967, Citizen-Scouter of Yr. award, 1989. Mem. SAR, So. Hist. Assn., Assn. for Preservation Va. Antiquities (br. pres. 1975-77), Soc. of the Cin. (standing com. 1984-87), Rockbridge Hist. Soc. (pres. 1960-62, author procs. 1989), English Speaking Union (br. pres. 1980-82), Soc. Mayflower Descs. in Commonwealth of Va., Internat. House of Japan, Am. Legion, Phi Beta Kappa, Kappa Alpha. Republican. Episcopalian. Avocations: travel, reading, walking. Home: 405 Jackson Ave Lexington VA 24450-1905

BROOKE, JOHN L., history professor; b. Mass., May 19, 1953; m. Sara C. Balderston, July 31, 1979. BA in History and Anthropology, Cornell U., 1976; MA in History, U. Pa., 1977, PhD in History, 1982. Vis. asst. prof. Amherst (Mass.) Coll., 1982-83; asst. prof. to prof. Tufts U., Medford, Mass., 1983-2001; dept. chair, 1996-97; prof. Ohio State U., Columbus, 2001—. Author: The Heart of the Commonwealth: Society and Political Culture in Worcester County, Massachusetts, 1713-1861, 1989, The Refiner's Fire: The Making of Mormon Cosmology, 1644-1844, 1994; contbr. articles to scholarly jours. Recipient award Nat. Soc. Daus. Colonial Wars, 1989, E. Harold Hugo Meml. Book prize Old Sturbridge Village Rsch. Libr. Soc., 1989, Merle Curti award for intellectual history, 1991, book prize for Am. history Nat. Hist. Soc., 1991, Bancroft prize Columbia U., 1995, ann. book prize Soc. for Historians of Early Am. Republic, 1995, ann. book award New Eng. Hist. Assn., 1995; S.F. Haven fellow Am. Antiquarian Soc., 1982, faculty rsch. fellow Tufts U., 1983, 88, Charles Warren fellow Harvard U., 1986-87, jr. fellow NEH, 1986-87, sr. fellow Commonwealth Ctr., 1990-91, fellow Am. Coun. Learned Socs., 1990-91, NEH fellow 1997-98, Guggenheim fellow, 1997-98. Mem. AAUP, Am. Antiq. Soc., Am. Hist. Assn., Orgn. Am. Historians, Mass. Hist. Soc. Democrat. Office: 164 Mt Vernon Street Arlington MA 02476

BROOKE, RALPH IAN, dental educator; b. Leeds, Eng., Apr. 25, 1934; s. Michael and Jeanette (Cohen) B.; m. Lorna Ruth Shields; children: Michael Jeremy Richard, Andrew Timothy. Baccalaureus Chirurgiae Dentium, Licentiate in Dental Surgery, Leeds U., England, 1957. Licentiate Royal Coll. Physicians, 1963. Sr. lectr. Leeds U., 1970-72; prof., chmn. dept. oral medicine U. Western Ont., London, Can., 1972-82, dean dentistry faculty, 1982-97, vice provost health scis., 1987-97. Chief dentistry Univ. Hosp., London, 1973-92. Contbr. articles to profl. jours. Fellow Acad. Dentistry Internat. (hon.), Royal Coll. Dentists Can., Royal Coll. Surgeons; mem. Nat. Dental Exam Bd. (past chmn. Can. commn. on dental accreditation), Can. Faculties Dentistry (past pres.), Can. Acad. Oral Medicine (past pres.), Can. Dental Assn. (hon.). Avocations: music, bicycling. E-mail: rbrooke@uwo.ca.

BROOKE, ROBERT LAWRENCE, lawyer; b. Bronxville, N.Y., Aug. 19, 1958; s. Ralston Lewis and Beverley Byrd Bowles B.; m. Elizabeth Lynn Burris, May 26, 1984; children: Caroline Young, Elizabeth Huntley, Anne Ralston. BA, Washington and Lee U., 1981; JD, U. Va., 1984. Bar: Va. 1984, S.C. 1996, U.S. Ct. Appeals (4th cir.), U.S. Dist. Ct. (ea. and we. dists.). Assoc. litigation sect. Hunton & Williams, Richmond, 1984-88; assoc. Troutman, Sanders, Mays & Valentine, Richmond, 1988—, ptnr. tech. and intellectual property practice group, dep. chair, 2000—. Notes editor Va. Jour. Internat. Law. Bd. dirs. Robert E. Lee coun. Boy Scouts Am., 1994-95, coun. mem.-at-large, 1996-98; mem. alumni bd. dirs. St. Christopher's Sch., 1993—, chair 2000—; pres. Richmond Assembly, 1994-96, bd. dirs., 1992-96; bd. dirs. The Parliament, 1989-92; trustee Theatre Va., 1997—. Mem. ABA (Va. membership chair 1995—, vice chair bus. torts com. 1997—, chair securities fraud and regulations subcom. comml. torts com. 1996—, chair young lawyers divsn. publs. com. 1994-96, asst. editor The Affiliate 1993-94), SAR (Va. chpt.), Va. Bar Assn. (chair young lawyers divsn. 1994-95, young lawyers divsn. exec. com. 1986-95, co-chair access to justice com. 1997—), Va. State Bar, Bar Assn. of the City of Richmond (adminstrn. justice com. 1992-95, Pro Bono Publico award 1990), Va. Assn. Def. Attys., Washington and Lee U. Alumni Assn. (pres. Richmond chpt. 1991), Phi Beta Kappa, Omicron Delta Kappa, Phi Kappa Sigma (past prse.), Country Club Va., Commonwealth Club, Fishing Bay Yacht Club, Capital Club. Republican. Episcopalian. Avocations: sailing, hunting, golf. Office: Troutman Sanders Mays & Valentine Bank of Am Ctr 23rd Fl 1111 E Main St Richmond VA 23219-3531 E-mail: rob.brooke@troutmansanders.com.

BROOKE, TAL (ROBERT TALIAFERRO), writer; b. Washington, Jan. 21, 1945; s. Edgar Duffield and Frances (Lea) B. BA, U. Va., 1969; M in Theology/Philosophy, Princeton (N.J.) U., 1986. V.p. pub. rels. nat. office Telecom Inc., 1982-83; pres., chmn. Spiritual Counterfeits Project, Inc., Berkeley, 1989—; founder End Run Pub., 1999—. Guest lectr. Cambridge U., Eng., 1977, 86, 97, 99, Oxford and Cambridge U., 1979, 84. Author: Lord of the Air: The International Edition, 1976, The Other Side of Death, Lord of the Air: The International Edition, 1979, Riders of the Cosmic Circuit, 1986, Millennial Edit., 2002, Avatar of Night, 1987, When the World Will Be As One, 1989, Lord of the Air, 1990, Virtual Gods, 1997, Conspiracy to Silence the Son, 1998, One World, 2000, The Mystery of Death, 2001. Mem. Internat. Platform Assn., Authors Guild, Soc. of The Cincinnati. Office: SCP Inc PO Box 4308 Berkeley CA 94704-0308 Office Phone: 510-540-0300. Personal E-mail: tal7@comcast.com. Business E-Mail: scp@scp-inc.org.

BROOKENS, CARL, psychologist; b. Chgo., June 13, 1943; s. John William Barnes and Alice Lee Brookens; m. Donna Joyce Helem, Aug. 28, 1966; children: Dionna Cherisse, Caron Yvonne. AA, Chgo. City Coll., 1973; BA, DePaul U., 1980; MS, Spertus Coll., 1983; MA, Roosevelt U., 1999. Lic. profl. counselor Ill., cert. counselor Nat. Bd. Cert. Counselors, forensic addictions examiner Nat. Assn. Forensic Counselors. Mgr. spl. programs State of Ill., Chgo., 1975—85, adjudicator Arlington Heights, Ill., 1985—2003, spl. agt. Chgo., 2003—. Mem.: APA, Ill. Mental Health Counselors Assn. Achievements include language competency in Russian, Mandarin Chinese, French and Arabic. Avocations: Karate (black belt), travel. Home: 33 W 59th St Westmont IL 60559 Office: State of Ill 33 S State St Chicago IL 60603

BROOKER, JEFF ZEIGLER, cardiologist; b. Columbia, SC, Nov. 1, 1941; s. Jefferson Zeigler and Virginia (Ligon) B.; m. Rhoda Arrowsmith, June 12, 1966; children: Jeff III, John, Rhoda. BS, U. S.C., 1962; MD, Med. U. S.C., 1966. Cert. in interventional cardiology, clin. cardiac electrophysiology, cardiovasc. disease and internal medicine Am. Bd. Internal Medicine. Intern, resident Hosp. U. Pa., Phila., 1966-68; resident internal medicine Stanford U. Med. Ctr., Palo Alto, Calif., 1970-71, rsch. fellow cardiology, 1971-73; staff cardiologist Tex. Heart Inst., Houston, 1973-74; assoc. dir. cardiology Providence Hosp., Columbia, S.C., 1974-81; pvt. practice cardiology Columbia, 1981—. Cons. peer rev. Jour. AMA, Chgo., 1976-77; local and regional rsch. com. Am. Heart Assn., Dallas., 1977-86. Mem. editl. bd. Jour. SC Med. Assn., Columbia, 1991—; editl. reviewer: Essentials of Echocardiography, 1977. Legis. liaison S.C. Med. Assn., Columbia, 1991-92. Lt. comdr. USN, 1968-70. Recipient Best Sci. Article award Roe Found., Columbia, 1991. Fellow ACP, Am. Coll. Cardiology, Am. Heart Assn. (coun. on clin. cardiology 1975—), Soc. for Cardiac Angiography and Interventions; mem. N.Am. Soc. Pacing and Electrophysiology, Mensa, Phi Beta Kappa, Alpha Omega Alpha. Achievements include improved method for oral dipyridamole testing for ischemic heart disease; devising a percutaneous method for inserting pacing lead into the internal jugular vein yet still implant and pulse generator on the anterior chest wall. Office: 1625 Bernardin Ave Columbia SC 29204-2003 Office Phone: 803-771-0212.

BROOKER, NORTON WILLIAM, JR., lawyer; b. Wilmington, NC, Jan. 10, 1944; s. Norton William and Mary Stewart (Aycock) B.; m. JoAnne P. Pipes, Aug. 12, 1967; children: William Thomas, Stewart Jefferson. BA, U. Ala., 1966, JD, 1968. Bar: Ala. 1968, U.S. Dist. Ct. (so. dist.) Ala. 1968, U.S. Dist. Ct. (no. dist.) Ala. 1979, U.S. Dist. Ct. (mid. dist.) 1995. Mem. Lyons Pipes & Cook, P.C., Mobile, Ala., 1968—. Spkr. in field. Active S. Oil Gas Bd. Adv., Tuscaloosa, Ala., 1986—; pres., chmn. Mobile Azalea Trail, 1972-75; vice chmn. Mobile Bay Sailing Sch., 1985—; Ala. rep. Interstate Oil and Gas Compact Commn., 1998—, spl. unitization com., 1999—. Mem. ABA, Ala. Bar Assn. (chmn. continuing edn. com. oil and gas sect. 1987-90), Mobile Bar Assn. (sec. 1975), US Sailing Assn. (sr. race officer 1989—, sr. judge 1991—, bd. dirs. 2002—), Mobile Yacht Club (commodore 1985-87), US Men's Sailing Championship (chmn. 1998-2001), Gulf Yachting Assn. Inc. (Commodore 2003). Avocations: sailing, boating, hunting. Home: 313 Shenandoah Rd E Mobile AL 36608-3318 Office: Lyons Pipes & Cook PC PO Box 2727 Mobile AL 36652-2727 Business E-Mail: nwb@lpclaw.com.

BROOKER, RICHARD I., architect; b. Boston, June 9, 1927; s. Bernard and Esther (Friedman) Brooker; m. Maria Rivalta, Sept. 3, 1966; 1 child, Niccolo. BArch, Ill. Inst. Tech., 1953. Registered arch., Mass., Colo., Mo., Ill., cert. Nat. Coun. Archtl. Registration Bd. Prin., arch. Archs. Collaborative, Cambridge, Mass., 1953-95, Boston Design Assocs., Waltham, Mass., 1995—. Prin. works include Schneider Childrens Hosp., L.I. Jewish Hillside Med. Ctr., New Hyde Park, N.Y., new constrn. and replacement project Temple U. Hosp., Phila., U.S. Postal Svc. gen. mail and bulk mail and vehicle maint. facilities, Springfield, Mass., Ctrl. Mass. Mail Processing Ctr., Shrewsbury, Mass., U.S. Postal Svc. Westchester Mail Processing/Distbn. Ctr., vehicle maint. facility, Harrison, N.Y., new facilities and renovations Cabot Corp., Billerica, Mass., hdqrs. facilities, Waltham, Mass., electron microscope lab., Billerica, Al-Hasa campus King Faisal U., Saudi Arabia, U. Baghdad, U. Tunis Sch. Law, Econ./Polit. Sci., Sch. Agri., Chott Maria Sousse, Tunisia, Ctrl. Vet. Lab., Sotuba, Mali, Saudi Arabian Mil. Assitance Program, clin. labs., med. office bldg., maternity ctr. New Eng. Meml. Hosp., Stoneham, Mass., Essex County Ho. Correction, Middleton, Mass., Kuwait Postal Svcs. complex, Kuwait City, Mass. Correctional Instn., Shirley, exec. meeting, dining rms., urology oper. rms., outpatient recovery area, patient site renovations, dialysis, cardiology, cardia oper. ste., med. office conversion, fit-up, new emergency generator plant St. Vincent Hosp., Worcester, Mass., Weehawken (N.J.) Waterfront Consultancy, Roc Harbour Master Plan and Condominium Devel., North Bergen, N.J., numerous others. With U.S. Army, 1945—46. Mem.: AIA, Mass. State Assn. Archs., Boston Soc. Archs. Home: 265 The Valley Rd Concord MA 01742-4924 Office: Boston Design Assocs Inc 393 Totten Pond Rd Waltham MA 02451-2003

BROOKER, ROBERT ELTON, JR., retired manufacturing company executive; b. L.A., Apr. 12, 1937; s. Robert Elton and Sarah (Smith) B.; m. Katherine Jones, Mar. 21, 1964; children: Robert III, Carolyn, Christopher, Alison. BS, MIT, 1959; MBA, Harvard U., 1965; PhD, Brown U., 2005. With Cummings Engine Co., 1965-81, gen. mgr. Great Lakes Foundry divsn. South Bend, Ind., 1966-69, pres. fleetguard Dallas, 1970-77, v.p. Latin Am. Miami, Fla., 1977-80, v.p. components group Columbus, Ind., 1981; pres. info. svcs. group N.L. Industries, Houston, 1981-86; pres., COO Lord Corp., Erie, Pa., 1987-90, CEO, 1990-91; pres., COO Connell Ltd. Partnership, Boston, 1993-95; dir. Dura Automotive Sys., 1995-98; ret., 1998. Dir. FCI, 1991—, Innovative Components Inc., 1998—, Dura Automotive Sys., 1995—. Author: British Military Pistols, 1603-1887, 1978, Parole Sachen, 1990; contbr. articles to profl. jours. Mem. Sea Space Symposium. Capt. USMC, 1959-63.

BROOKER, THOMAS KIMBALL, oil industry executive; b. L.A., Oct. 1, 1939; s.Robert Elton and Sally Burton Harrison (Smith) B.; m. Nancy Belle Neumann, 1966 (dec. 2003); children: Thomas Kimball Jr., Isobel, Vanessa. BA in French Lit., Yale U., 1961; MBA, Harvard U., 1968; MA in Art History, U. Chgo., 1989, PhD in Art History, 1996. Assoc. in corp. fin. Morgan Stanley & Co., Inc., N.Y.C., 1968—73, v.p., 1973—75, mng. dir., 1976—88, head Chgo. office, 1978—88; pres. Barbara Oil Co., Chgo., 1989—, bd. dirs. Bd. dirs. Arthur J. Gallagher & Co., Miami Corp., Cutler Oil & Gas Corp.; bd. govs. Midwest Stock Exch., 1980-88, vice chmn., 1986-88. Contbr. articles to profl. jours. Mem. vis. com. libr. U. Chgo., mem. vis. com. visual arts dept.; mem., chmn. com. on libr. Yale U. President's Coun., 1980-84; trustee Pierpont Morgan Libr., Gov. John Carter Brown Libr., Yale U. Libr. Assn.; vice chmn. Newberry Libr.; bd. dirs. Lyric Opera Chgo. Recipient Sir Thomas More medal U. San Francisco, 1992; assoc. fellow Saybrook Coll., Yale U. Mem. Adminstrv. Coun. (v.p.), Assn. Internat. de Bibliophilie, Bibliotheca Wittockiana (sci. com.), Bandar-Log, Caxton Club, Chgo. Club, Comml. Club, Econ. Club, River Club (N.Y.C.), Knickerbocker Club (N.Y.C.), Grolier Club (N.Y.C.), The Casino, Saddle and Cycle Club, Edgartown (Mass.) Yacht Club, The Reading Room (Edgartown), Quadrangle Club, Racquet Club, Rockaway Hunt Club, Wayfarers Club. Home: 1500 N Lake Shore Dr Chicago IL 60610-6657 Office: Barbara Oil Co 21 S Clark St Ste 3990 Chicago IL 60603-2000

BROOKER, TIMOTHY DOUGLAS, social studies educator; s. Richard A. and Lorena Jane Brooker; m. Paulita Sharlene Harp, Aug. 16, 1975; children: Brandon Richard, Nathan Paul. BA in Social Studies, John Brown U., Siloam Springs, Arkansas, 1979; MA in Diplomacy, Internat. Commerce, U. Ky., 1981, M in Pub. Policy Adminstrn., 1983; EdD, U. Ark., 1998. Cert. counselor Nat. Bd. of Cert. Counselors, 1998, residential behavioral therapist Nat. Tchg. Family Assn., 1990, lic. assoc. counselor Ark. Counseling Bd., 1996. Adj. prof. govt., bus. mgmt. Ea. Ky. U., Richmond, 1983—85; co-dir., residential behavioral therapist Ashe County Youth Svcs., Copper Kettle Ho., West Jefferson, NC, 1988—2000, West Oaks Psychiat. Inst., Houston, 1990—93, Dogwood Achievement Ctr., Inc., Siloam Springs, Ark., 1994—98; asst. prof. of govt. Oral Roberts U., Tulsa, 2001—. Adj. prof. govt., econs. John Brown U., Siloam Springs, Ark., 1993—2001; syndicated radio talk show host Demaree Media Inc., Fayetteville, Ark., 1994—2000; chair higher edn. evaluation com. Murphy Commn., Little Rock, 1996—98; vis. prof. govt. Ark. Tech. U., Russellville, 2001. Columnist: newspaper Northwest Arkansas Times. Regional chair Rep. Party Ark., Little Rock, 1993—97. Baptist. Office: Oral Roberts University 7777 S Lewis Tulsa OK 74171

BROOKHART, MAURICE S., chemist; b. Cumberland, Md., Nov. 28, 1942; married, 1965; 2 children. BA, Johns Hopkins U., 1964; PhD in Organic Chemistry, U. Calif., L.A., 1968. NATO fellow U. Southampton, 1968-69; assoc. prof., 1969-76; prof. organic chemistry U. NC, Chapel Hill, 1976—. Vis. prof. Oxford U., 1982-83. Fellow Am. Acad. Arts and Scis.; mem. Am. Chem. Soc. (award in Organometallic Chemistry 1992, Arthur C. Cope Scholar award 1994). Achievements include research in mechanistic and synthetic organometallic chemistry; applications of transition metal complexes in organic synthesis and catalysis. Office: U North Carolina Dept Chemistry Chapel Hill NC 27514

BROOKINS, OSCAR TRAVIS, economics educator; b. Benton, Miss., July 31, 1942; s. Oscar DePriest and Addie (Travis) B.; m. Kathryn Juel Weibel, Oct. 31, 1936; children: Mary Laura, Julia Akinyi. AB, DePauw U., Greencastle, Ind., 1965; MA, Northeastern U., Boston, 1967; postgrad., Purdue U., 1967-68; PhD, SUNY, Buffalo, 1976. Instr. State U. Coll., Buffalo, 1969-70, asst. prof., 1970-72; lectr. U. Ghana, Legon, 1971-74, U. Dar es Salaam, Tanzania, 1976-77; asst. prof. U. Notre Dame, Ind., 1974-81, Va. State U., Petersburg, 1982-83, Northeastern U., Boston, 1983-86, assoc. prof. econs., 1986—. Sr. Fulbright lectr. Tallinn (Estonia) Tech. U., 2000; prof. banking and fin. Mediterranean U., Turkish North, Cyprus, 2002. Mem. sch. bd. South Bend Community Sch., 1980-84; mem. library bd. Pub. Library, South Bend, 1980-84; candidate for mayor, South Bend, 1983; candidate for Boston city coun., 1989. Recipient Newsmaker award South Bend Press Club, 1981. Mem. Am. Econs. Assn., Regional Sci. Assn. Mem. African Meth. Episcopal Ch. Avocations: guitar, gardening, blues harmonica. Home: 4 Hillside St Roxbury MA 02120-3348 Office: Northeastern U 360 Huntington Ave Boston MA 02115-5000 Office Phone: 617-373-2251. Business E-Mail: o.brookins@neu.edu.

BROOKMAN, ANTHONY RAYMOND, lawyer; b. Chgo., Mar. 23, 1922; s. Raymond Charles and Marie Clara (Alberg) B.; m. Marilyn Joyce Brookman, June 5, 1982; children: Meribeth Brookman Farmer, Anthony Raymond, Lindsay Logan Christensen. Student, Ripon Coll., 1940-41; BS, Northwestern U., 1947; JD, U. Calif., San Francisco, 1953. Bar: Calif. 1954. Law clk. to presiding justice Calif. Supreme Ct., 1953-54; ptnr. Nichols, Williams, Morgan, Digardi & Brookman, 1954-68; sr. ptnr. Brookman & Talbot, Inc. (formerly Brookman & Hoffman, Inc.), Walnut Creek, Calif., 1969-92, Brookman & Talbot Inc., Sacramento, 1992—. Pres. Young Reps. Calif., San Mateo County, 1953-54. 1st lt. USAF. Mem. ABA, Alameda County Bar Assn., State Bar Calif., Lawyers Club Alameda County, Alameda-Contra Costa County Trial Lawyers Assn., Assn. Trial Lawyers Am., Calif. Trial Lawyers Assn., Athenian Nile Club, Masons, Shriners. Republican. Office: 1540 River Park Dr Ste 101 Sacramento CA 95815 also: Ste B-201 675 Ygnacio Valley Rd Walnut Creek CA 94596 also: 1746 Grand Canal Blvd Ste 11 Stockton CA 95207-8111 Office Phone: 925-932-4008.

BROOKMAN, MARC D., lawyer; b. Phila., Dec. 10, 1942; BS, Temple U., 1964, JD, 1968. Bar: Pa. 1968, US Dist. Ct. Ea. Dist. Pa., US Ct. Appeals 3rd Cir. Ptnr. Duane Morris LLP, Phila., 1979—, chair firm real estate practice group & dept., mem. firm partners bd., 1991—. Past pres. dist. coun. Urban Land Inst.; pres. Del. Valley Smart Growth Alliance; exec. com. Ctrl. Phila. Devel. Corp., 1994—, treas., 1995—96, v.p., 1996—. Mem. ABA (mem. urban, state & local govt. law sect., real property, probate & trust law sect.), Pa. Bar Assn. (mem. real property, probate & trust law sect.), Phila. Bar Assn., Urban Land Inst., Cmty. Associations Inst. (founder, past. pres. Delaware Valley Chpt.) Office: Duane Morris LLP One Liberty Pl Philadelphia PA 19103-7396 Office Phone: 215-979-1300. Office Fax: 215-979-1020. Business E-Mail: brookman@duanemorris.com.

BROOKNER, ANITA, writer, educator; d. Newson and Maude B. BA, King's Coll., 1946-49; Ed., U. London; PhD, Courtauld Inst., Paris, 1949-53. Vis. lectr. U. Reading, 1959-64; Slade prof. U. Cambridge, 1967-68; lectr. Courtauld Inst. of Art, 1964. Author: Watteau, 1968, The Genius of the Future, 1971, Greuze: The Rise and Fall of an Eighteenth Century Phenomenon, 1972, Jacques-Louis David, 1980, (novels) A Start in Life, 1981, Providence, 1982, Look At Me, 1983, Hotel du Lac, 1984 (Booker McConnell prize), Family and Friends, 1985, A Misalliance, 1986, A Friend From England, 1987, Latecomers, 1988, Lewis Percy, 1989, Brief Lives, 1991, Fraud, 1992, A Family Romance, 1993, A Private View, 1995, Altered States, 1996, Visitors, 1997, The Visitors, 1998, Soundings, 1998, Falling Slowly: A Novel, 1999, The Bay of Angels: A Novel, 2002; contbr. articles to mags.

BROOKNER, JACKIE W., sculptor, educator; b. Providence, Nov. 20, 1945; BA, Wellesley Coll., 1967; MA, Harvard U., 1968, postgrad., 1969-71. Instr. sculptor Parsons Sch. Design, N.Y.C., 1977—; instr. sculptor, vis. lectr. Harvard U., 2002; instr. sculptor N.Y. Studio Sch., N.Y.C., 1986-90, dean, 1987-88. Prin. works include Grossenhain, Germany, 2001, Dreher Park, West Palm Beach, Fla., 2004; one woman shows include Oscarsson-Hood Gallery, N.Y.C., 1982-84, Wheaton Coll., Norton, Mass., 1983, Pamela Auchincloss Gallery, N.Y.C., 1991, Miro Found., Barcelona, Spain, 1997, Hunter Mus., Chattanooga, 1994-96, Columbus (Ga.) Mus., Nat. Civil Rights Mus., Memphis. E-mail: jbrookn@aol.com.

BROOKS, A. TAEKO, historian; d. Mitsuo and Haruko Oshiro; m. E. Bruce Brooks, July 23, 1964; 1 child, E. Clement. BA, U. Hawaii, 1958, MA, 1961. Rsch. assoc. Warring States Project/U. Mass., Amherst, Mass., 1993—. Co-author: The Original Analects, 1998; contbr. chapters to books, articles to profl. jours. Mem.: Soc. for the Study of Early China, Assn. for Asian Studies, Am. Hist. Assn. Office: Warring States Project/U Mass 201C Goodell Amherst MA 01003

BROOKS, AARON LAFETTE, professional football player; b. Newport News, Va., Mar. 24, 1976; BA in Anthropology, U. Va. Football player New Orleans Saints, 2000—. Avocations: basketball, reading. Office: New Orleans Saints 5800 Airline Dr Metairie LA 70003

BROOKS, ALBERT (ALBERT EINSTEIN), actor, writer, director; b. Los Angeles, July 22, 1947; s. Harry and Thelma (Leeds) Einstein. Appeared in films Taxi Driver, 1976, Private Benjamin, 1980, Twilight Zone-The Movie, 1983, Unfaithfully Yours, 1983, Terms of Endearment, 1983, Broadcast News, 1987 (Acad. award nominee Best Supporting Actor), I'll Do Anything, 1994, The Scout, 1994, Critical Care, 1997, Out of Sight, 1998, Dr. Dolittle (voice), 1998, The In-Laws, 2003, Finding Nemo (voice), 2003; dir., writer, actor films Real Life, 1979, Modern Romance, 1982, Lost in America, 1985, Defending Your Life, 1991, Mother, 1996, Out of Sight, 1998, The Muse, 1999, My First Mister, 2001; writer, actor The Scout, 1994, Critical Care, 1997; TV appearances include The Tonight Show, Merv Griffin Show, Steven Allen Show, Gold Diggers, The Simpsons (voice only) 1993; dir., writer short films Saturday Night Live, 1975-76; recs. include Comedy Minus One, A Star is Bought (Grammy nomination).

BROOKS, ANDRÉE AELION, journalist, educator; b. London, Feb. 2, 1937; d. Leon Luis and Lillian (Abrahamson) Aelion; m. Ronald J. Brooks, Aug. 16, 1959 (div. Aug. 1986); children: Allyson, James. Journalism cert., N.W. London Poly., 1958. Journalism cert. N.W. London Poly. Reporter Hampstead News, London, 1954-58; story editor Photoplay mag., N.Y.C., 1958-60; NY corr. Australian Broadcasting Co., N.Y.C., 1961-68; elected rep. Elstree, Eng., 1973-74; contbr. columnist N.Y. Times, N.Y.C., 1978-95; freelance journalist, 1978—. Adj. prof. journalism Fairfield U., Conn., 1983—87; assoc. fellow Yale U., 1989—, founder, pres. Women's Campaign Sch., 1993—96; v.p. Minuteman Media, 1995—96; coord.-dir. Out Spain hist. curriculum, 1997—2000. Author: Children of Fast Track Parents, 1989 (Best Non-Fiction Book award, 1990), The Women Who Defied Kings: The Life and Times of Dona Gracia Nasi, 2002 (Mark Twain award, 2003, finalist Nat. Jewish Book awards, 2003), Russian Dance, 2004 (1st pl. Nat. Fedn. Press Women, 2005). Exec. bd. Am. Jewish Com., 1987—91; trustee Temple Israel, Westport, Conn., 1991—97. Named one of Am. Women Achievement, Am. Jewish Com., 1989; recipient 1st pl. news writing, Conn. Press Women, 1980,

1983, 1985—86, 1987, 1994, Outstanding Achievement award, Nat. Fedn. Press Women, 1981, 1st pl. award mag. writing, 1983, 1st pl. award, Fairfield County chpt. Women Comm., 1982—83, 1986—87, 1992, 1993, 1997, 2d pl. award in mag. writing, Nat. Assn. Home Builders, 1983, Spl. Svc. award, Conn. chpt. Am. Planning Assn., 1983, Mark Twain award, Conn. Press Club, 2003, Pioneer award, Gomez House Found., 2003, honor, Am. Sephardi Fedn., 2001. Mem.: Conn. Press Women (chmn. nominating com. 1983—86), Women Comm. (contest co-chmn. 1983—84). Office Phone: 203-226-9834. Personal E-mail: andreebrooks@hotmail.com. *Keep true to what you believe and don't become cynical or full of hate - for hate only breeds more hate.*

BROOKS, AVERY, actor, educator, musician; s. Samuel Leon and Eva Crawford Brooks; m. Vicki Bowen; children: Ayana, Cabral, Asante. BA, MFA, Rutgers U., New Brunswick, NJ; PhD (hon.), Toogaloo U., Jackson, Miss., Ind. U., Bloomington, Ind., Oberlin Coll., Oberlin, Ohio, SUNY, Buffalo, NY. Asst. prof. Rutgers U., New Brunswick, NJ, 1976—81, assoc. prof., 1981—. Artistic dir. Nat. Black Arts Festival, Atlanta, 1993—96; trustee Young Audiences of NJ, Princeton, NJ, 2001—; coun. mem. Nat. Coun. for the Shakespeare Theater, Washington, 2003—. Actor: (plays) King Lear, The Oedipus Trilogy, The Song Ministry of Rev. C.A.Tindley, The Tempest, Fences, Othello, Talented Tenth, The Ernest Green Story, The Exonerated, Roots - The Christmas Story, Paul Robeson; dir.: The Last Minstrel Show; actor: numerous others; (TV series) Spenser: For Hire, A Man Called Hawk; (TV films) Solomon Northrop's Odyssey, Spenser: Judas Goat, Spencer: A Savage Place, Spencer: Ceremony, Spencer: Pale Kings and Princesses, Star Trek: Deep Space Nine, Uncle Tom's Cabin; (films) American History X, Fifteen Minutes, The Big Hit; dir.: (TV series) Star Trek: Deep Space Nine - 9 episodes; (plays) Boogie Woogie Landscapes, For Colored Girls Who Have Considered Suicide When The Rainbow Is Enough; narrator/host (documentaries) Bible Mysteries, Discovery Channel/BBC, narrator Dinosaurs, Discovery Channel, Trackdown, ABC, Nova Series: Earthquake, WGBH-Boston, others; singer: (albums) James Spaulding Plays the Legacy of Duke Ellington, (Operas) X - The Life and Times of Malcolm X, Tania, (jazz group) Henry Threadgill, Run Silent, Run Deep, Run Loud, Run High, David Murray, The Pushkin Project; singer: (with jazz saxaphonist, David Murray) Paris Festival Banlieues Bleues, 2005; singer: (with Black Rock Coalition) Tribute to Ray Charles, Symphony Space, 2005. Recipient Disting. Artist Award, Carter G. Woodson Found., Governor's Arts Award, State of Ind., NAACP Image Award, NAACP, Lifelong Commitment to Arts & Edn., Young Audiences of DC, Wright Overstreet Award, Cin. NAACP, Black Achiever's Award, Ind. Black Expo, Rutgers U. Hall of Disting. Alumni, Rutgers U. Fellow: Am. Coll. of Theater Fellows; mem.: Actors' Equity Assn., Directors Guild of Am., Am. Fedn. of TV & Radio Artists, SAG.

BROOKS, BABERT VINCENT, publisher; b. NYC, Sept. 2, 1926; s. Babert Vincent and Florence (Goodwin) B.; m. Audrey Stephenson, Dec. 6, 1952 (div.); children: Torrey, Scott, Wendy; m. Kathryn Frazer, May 23, 1987. AB magna cum laude, Dartmouth Coll., 1947, MBA with distinction, 1949. Security analyst Arnold Bernhard & Co., N.Y.C., 1952-56; cons. Booz, Allen & Hamilton, N.Y.C., 1956-58; v.p. finance Schine Enterprises, N.Y.C., 1958-61; v.p., treas. Murray Corp. Am., N.Y.C., 1961-62; pres. Brooks, Torrey & Scott, Inc., Westport, Conn., 1962—, Westport Travel Svc., Inc., 1963, chmn., 1988-92; pres. Brooks Community Newspapers, 1974-82, chmn., 1982-99; pub. Westport (Conn.) News, 1964-99, Darien (Conn.) News-Rev., 1973-99, Fairfield (Conn.) Citizen-News, 1973-99, Norwalk Citzen News, 1997-99, Greenwich (Conn.) News, 1983-96, Inside Fairfield County, Westport, 1993-99. Sec.-treas. Airspur Corp., NYC, 1969-70; trustee King Indsl. Properties, Boston, 1965-82; bd. dirs. Westfair, Inc., Westport, Warner Investing Corp., Westport; trustee Am. Inst. Econ. Rsch., Great Barrington, Mass., 1997-2004, vice-chmn., 2002, chmn. bd. dirs., 2003-2004. Bd. dirs., treas. Dartmouth in Greenwich, 1972-81; trustee Conn. Policy and Econ. Coun. Inc., 1989-99, Norwalk Hosp., 1988-93, 95-00, Norwalk Health Svcs., Inc., 1994-2004, U. Bridgeport, 1991—, Media Rsch. Ctr., Washington, 2002—. With USNR, 1945-47. Mem. Riverside Yacht Club, Phi Beta Kappa.

BROOKS, BEN A., lawyer; b. Dallas, May 31, 1949; BBA, U. Tex., 1971; JD, So. Meth. U., 1974. Bar: Tex. 1974. Ptnr., co-head Pub. Fin. Sect Vison & Elkins LLP. Mem.: Nat. Assn. Bond Lawyers. Office: Vinson & Elkins LLP Trammell Crow Ctr 2001 Ross Ave, Ste 3700 Dallas TX 75201 Office Phone: 214-220-7921. E-mail: bbrooks@velaw.com.

BROOKS, BEN NORMAN, artist, educator; b. Belleville, Ill., May 13, 1972; s. Brooks Robert and Glauber Susan; m. Julie C. Kazmierczak, July 11, 2003. BS, SIUE, 1995; MA in Tchg., Lindenwood U., 2005. Lic. tchr. Ill. Tchr. Althoff H.S., Belleville, Ill., 1996—97, O'Fallon (Ill.) H.S., O'Fallon, Ill., 2000—. Vol. sscientist Americorps, Fairview heights, Ill., 1998. Office: O'Fallon Township Highschool 600 S Smiley st O Fallon IL 62269 Office Phone: 618-632-3507-235. Personal E-mail: brooksb@oths.k12.il.us.

BROOKS, BRUCE WILLIAM, artist, educator; b. NYC, July 10, 1948; m. Susan Beth Ross, June 24, 1982; 1 child, Olana. BFA, Pratt Inst., Bklyn., 1970, MFA, 1975. Prof. and coord. visual arts La Guardia CC, CUNY, Long Island City, 1974—. Prin. works include Sculptors at Broadway and 10th St., 1996, Trees of Blood Sabatical Works, 2004—05. Pruner NYC Parks Dept. /Trees NY. Recipient PSC/CUNY Rsch. award, CUNY Rsch. Found., 1994—95, 2002. Mem.: Bklyn. Botanical Gardens, Inner City Handball Assn. Democrat. Avocations: handball, bonsai, squash.

BROOKS, CHARLES LEE, III, computational biophysicist, educator; b. Detroit, May 14, 1956; married; 2 children. BS in Chemistry and Physics, Alma (Mich.) Coll., 1978; PhD in Physical Chemistry, Purdue U., 1982. Postdoc. fellow Harvard U., Boston, 1982-85, NIH, 1983-85; from asst. prof. to prof. Carnegie Mellon U., 1985—94, prof., 1994—; prof. molecular biology Scripps Rsch. Inst., 1994—. Mem. spl. rev. panels, site visit coms., mem. reviewers reserve Cell Biology & Biophysics Divsn. A study section, NIH; reviewer, mem. cellular and molecular biophysics panel, NSF; mem. adv. bd. Nat. Biomed. Computation Resource Inst., San Diego Supercomputing Ctr., sr. fellow, 1997; presenter in field. Mem. editl. bd. Proteins, 1995—, Biochimica et Biophysica Acta, 2000—, Physical Chemistry Chemical Physics, 2000—; editor: Jour. Computational Chemistry, 2004; contbr. over 200 articles to profl. jours.; author 1 book, several book chpts. A.P. Sloan fellow, 1990-93, AAAS, 2000; grantee Swedish Rsch. Coun., 1992. Office: Scripps Rsch Inst Dept Molecular Biology TPC6 10550 N Torrey Pines Rd La Jolla CA 92037-1000 Business E-Mail: brooks@scripps.edu.

BROOKS, DANIEL TOWNLEY, lawyer; b. N.Y.C., Apr. 15, 1941; s. Robert Daniel and Mary (Lee) B.; m. Barbara Ann Badertscher, June 16, 1973; children: Daniel Townley, Jr., Andrei Matthew. BS in Engring. cum laude, Princeton U., 1963; LLB, Stanford U., 1967, MS in Engring., 1968. Bar: Calif. 1968, U.S. Dist. Ct. (no. dist.) Calif. 1968, U.S. Ct. Appeals (9th cir.) 1968, N.Y. 1970, U.S. Ct. Appeals (2d cir.) 1972, Va. 1982, D.C. 1998. Assoc. Cadwalader, Wickersham & Taft, N.Y.C., 1968-79; atty. U.S. SEC, Washington, 1979-81; with Computer Law Advisers, Springfield, Va., 1981-85; ptnr. Cadwalader, Wickersham & Taft, Washington, 1985-98, sr. counsel, 1998-2000; sr. v.p., gen. counsel Trading Edge, Inc., Washington, 2000—. Cons. and lectr. in computer law. Mem. ABA, IEEE, Calif. Bar Assn. (inactive), N.Y. State Bar Assn., Va. Bar Assn., D.C. Bar Assn., Computer Law Assn. Inc. (bd. advisors), Assn. Computing Machinery. Home: 6106 Lorcom Ct Springfield VA 22152-1320 Office: Trading Edge Inc 140 Broadway Fl 42 New York NY 10005-1114 E-mail: dbrooks@tradingedge.com.

BROOKS, DAVID B., editor, columnist; m. Jane M. Hughes, 1986; children: Joshua, Naomi. Grad., U. Chgo., 1983. Police reporter City News Bur.; with The Nat. Rev., The Washington Times; book rev. editor Wall St. Jour., 1986—90, fgn. corr. Brussels, 1990—94, op-ed editor, 1994—95; sr. editor The Weekly Std., 1995—; op-ed columnist N.Y. Times, N.Y.C., 2003—. Contbg. editor Atlantic Monthly; commentator The Newshour with Jim Lehrer; analyst All Things Considered, The Diane Rehm Show. Author: Bobos in Paradise: The New Upper Class and How They Got There, 2000, On Paradise Drive: How We Live Now (And Always Have) in the Future Tense, 2004; editor: Backward and Upward: The New Conservative Writing, 1995; contbr. articles to publs. Office: The New York Times 229 W 43rd St New York NY 10036*

BROOKS, DAVID BARRY, resource economist; b. Easton, Mass., Feb. 15, 1934; s. Abraham and Mae (Fox) B.; m. Toby Judith Haftka, Sept. 11, 1955; children: Michael Jan, Naomi Sara. S.B. in Geology, MIT, 1955; MS in Geology, Calif. Inst. Tech., 1956; PhD in Econs., U. Colo., 1963. Geologist U.S. Geol. Survey, 1956-59; research assoc. Resources for the Future, Washington, 1961-66; asst. prof. econs. Berea Coll., 1966-67; chief div. mineral econs. Bur. Mines, Dept. Interior, 1967-70; chief Mineral Econs. Research div. Can. Dept. Energy, Mines and Resources, 1970-73; dir. Office Energy Conservation, 1974-77; dir. Ottawa office Energy Probe, 1977-82; bd. dirs. Can. Friends of the Earth, pres., 1977-81, 85-88; prin. Marbek Resource Cons. Ltd., Ottawa, Ont., Canada, 1983-88; sr. advisor Internat. Devel. Rsch. Ctr., Ottawa, 1988—2002; dir. rsch. Friends of the Earth, Canada, 2002—. Cons. Can. Internat. Devel. Agy., 1983, 85, 86, 88, UN Conf. on Human Environ., 1971-72, Labrador Resources Adv. Coun., 1979, Dept. Indian and No. Affairs, Ottawa, 1979; study team on non-renewable materials, environ. studies bd. Nat. Acad. Scis., 1972-73; mem. study team on environ. Fed. Task Force and Program Rev.; energy options adv. com. Office of Ministry of Energy, Ottawa, 1986-88; cons. Highlander Rsch. and Edn. Ctr., New Market, Tenn., 1979; exec. dir. Beaufort Sea Rsch. Coalition; bd. dirs. Ont. Hydro; keynote spkr. First Israeli-Palestinian Internat. Academic Conf. on Water, Zurich, 1992, Internat. Water Demand Mgmt. Conf., Jordan, 2004. Author: Supply and Competition in Minor Metals, 1965, Peaceful Use of Nuclear Explosives: Some Economic Aspects, 1969, Minerals: an Expanding or a Dwindling Resource?, 1973, Zero Energy Growth for Canada, 1981; co-author: Life After Oil: A Renewable Energy Policy for Canada, 1983, Watershed: The Role of Fresh Water in the Israeli-Palestinian Conflict, 1994, Water: Local-Level Management, 2002; also monographs on environ. problems of mining, water and energy conservation, water and internat. devel.; also articles. Chmn. No. Va. chpt. Congress Racial Equality, 1963-65; sec. Fed. Employees for a Democratic Soc. Served with AUS, 1957. Ashley fellow Trent U., Can., 1992. Mem.: Internat. Water Acad. Home: 1-202 Flora St Ottawa ON Canada K1R 5R7 Office: Friends of the Earth Can 300-260 St Patrick St Ottawa ON Canada K1N 5K5 Office Phone: 613-241-0085 ext. 27. Business E-Mail: dbrooks@foecanada.org.

BROOKS, DEBORAH JUNE, art educator; b. Brighton, Colo., Jan. 29, 1966; d. Ivan Lloyd and Sheryl June Brooks. BFA, Met. State Coll., Denver, 1991; MA in Edn., U. Colo., 1996. Lic. tchr. Colo. Elem. art tchr. Adams 12 Five Star Schs., Thornton, Colo., 1992—. Contract artist, instr. Butterfly Pavilion, Westminster, Colo., 2002—. Designer, painter (tidepool mural) Butterfly Pavilion, 2001; illustrator: (children's book) Tarantula Tracks: Rosie's Wild Adventure, 2004; one-woman show, Better Framer Gallery, Lakewood, Colo., 2000, exhibited in group shows at Fairplay (Colo.) Art Festival, 1996, All About Art Festival, Northglenn, Colo., 1994, Adams County Fair, 1996, 1998, others. Vol., contbr. Butterfly Pavilion, Westminster, 2000—; edn. dir. Yellow Ribbon Suicide Prevention Program, Westminster, Colo., 2003—. Named sch. of distinction, Colo. Alliance for Arts in Edn., 2001; recipient Kennedy Ctr. Sch. of Excellence of the Arts, 2001, Colo. Elem. Art Educator of Yr. award, 2005, Hon. Mention, Kennedy Ctr. Schs. Excellence in Arts, 2005; Contextual Learning grantee, Colo. Sch. to Career Partnership, 2001. Mem.: Artsource Colo., Colo. Art Edn. Assn. (nominee art tchr. of yr. 2001—02), Nat. Art Edn. Assn. Avocations: art, travel, teaching, learning.

BROOKS, DEBRA L., healthcare executive, neuromuscular therapist; b. Cedar Rapids, Iowa, Dec. 10, 1950; children: Brei, Benjamin, Bryan. BA, Coe Coll., 1973; MS, Clayton Coll., 1999, PhD, 2000. Cert. neuromuscular therapy Fla., natural therapeutics specialist N.Mex. Tchr. Cedar Rapids Cmty. Sch. Dist., 1973-92; COO NeuroMuscular Therapy Ctr., Walford, Iowa, 1994—. Educator Helping Hands Seminars, Cedar Rapids, 1992—2000, Debra Brooks' Seminars, Walford, 1993—; bus and educ consult Brooks Consults, Cedar Rapids, 1990—; mem Iowa Bd Examiners, 2001—03; chair adv. bd. ABLE, 2001—02; mem., chair Nat. Alliance State Bds., 2001—02; editl. bd. Momentum Media. Contbr. articles to profl jours and newsletters. Fundraiser, performer in musicals St Luke's Hosp, Cedar Rapids, 1978—91; fundraiser, performer in Follies Cedar Rapids Symphony, 1981—99; fundraiser, performer in telethons Variety Clubs Am, Cedar Rapids, 1989—91; mem Walford Community Develop, 1994—98; editl. bd. Tng. and Conditioning Mag. Named Outstanding Mentor of the Yr, YWCA, 2001; recipient First in Nation in Educ Award, State of Iowa, 1991, Tribute to Women of Achievement Award, YWCA, 2001. Mem.: Am. Coll. Healthcare Execs., Am. Massage Therapy Assn. (state v.p., edn. dir. 1992—94, nat. trustee Found. 1994—98, nat. bd. dirs. 1994—2002), Profl. Women's Network (chmn. 2002—03). Avocations: singing, painting, pianist, power walking, philosophy. Office: NeuroMuscular Therapy Ctr PO Box 8267 Cedar Rapids IA 52408-8267 E-mail: montanadebrabrooks@yahoo.com.

BROOKS, DERRICK DEWAN, professional football player; b. Pensacola, Fla., Apr. 18, 1973; m. Carol Brooks; children: Derrick Jr., Brianna Monai, Darius. Degree, Fla. State U., 1994, M degree, 1999. Linebacker Tampa Bay Buccaneers. Co-hosts weekly minute radio call-in show. Active March of Dimes, D.A.R.E., Audley Evans Ctr.; host Brooks Bunch; founder Derrick Brooks Charities Found. Named Number One on The Sporting News Good Guys List for cmty. work, NFL Man of Yr., 2000, Defensive Player of Yr., 2002; named to NFL Pro-Bowl, 1997-2003 Mem.: Florida State University board of trustees. Achievements include mem. Super Bowl XXXVII Champion Tampa Bay Buccaneers, 2002. Office: Tampa Bay Buccaneers 1 W Buccaneer Pl Tampa FL 33607-5797

BROOKS, DOUGLAS H., food service executive; From asst. mgr. to sr. v.p. ops. Chili's Grill & Bar, 1978—92, pres., 1994—99; COO Brinker Internat., Dallas, 1998—2004, pres., 1999—2004, chmn., CEO, 2004—. Office: Brinker Internat 6820 LBJ Freeway Dallas TX 75240*

BROOKS, EDWARD HOWARD, retired academic administrator; b. Salt Lake City, Mar. 2, 1921; s. Charles Campbell and Margery (Howard) B.; m. Courtaney June Perren, May 18, 1946; children: Merrillee Brooks Runyan, Robin Anne (Mrs. R. Bruce Pollock). BA, Stanford U., 1942, MA, 1947, PhD, 1950. Mem. faculty, adminstrn. Stanford U., 1949-71; provost Claremont (Calif.) Colls., 1971-81; v.p. Claremont U. Center, 1979-81; sr. v.p. Claremont McKenna Coll., 1981-84; provost Scripps Coll., 1987-89, pres., 1989-90; ret., 1990. Trustee EDUCOM, 1978-80, Webb Sch. Calif., 1979-90, Menlo Sch. and Coll., 1985-88; bd. overseers Hoover Instn., 1972-78; bd. dirs. Student Loan Mktg. Assn., 1973-77; active Calif. Student Aid Commn., 1984-88, chmn., 1986-88. With AUS, 1942-45. Home: 2608 Walnut Ave Manhattan Beach CA 90266 *Looking back since retirement, I have concluded that the most useful and, perhaps, enduring contribution an institutional leader can make is clearly committed efforts to make the institution better and the individuals within it better; holding everyone to even higher standards.*

BROOKS, FRANKLIN RAMON, psychologist, military officer; b. Margarita, CZ, Panama, Dec. 2, 1945; s. Sherman C. and Astrea (Bertonini) B.; m. Lenalee Bunch, July 6, 1950; children: Franklin Bryson, Marcus Ramon, Jennifer Jean; m. May 29, 1970. BS, Tex. A&M U., 1967; MS in Clin. Psychology, U. North Tex., 1971, PhD in Clin. Psychology, 1975. Cert. psychologist, Tex. 2d lt. U.S. Army, 1967, advanced through grades to col.; chief psychology svc. Frankfurt (Germany) Army Regional Med. Ctr., 1984-88, Eisenhower Army Med. Ctr., Ft. Gordon, Ga., 1988-89, chief dept. psychology, 1989-93; chief psychology svc. Brooke Army Med. Ctr., Ft. Sam Houston, Tex., 1993-95, chief dept. psychology, 1995-98, chief dept. behavioral medicine, 1998—2001; chief ops. officer Brown Sch., Laurel Ridge, 2001—02; pvt. practice San Antonio, 2002—. Clin. psychology cons. US Army Health Svc. Command, Ft. Sam Houston, 1993-95, Gt. Plains Regional Command, Ft. Sam Houston, 1995-2001; clin. dir. San Antonio Chronic Pain Inst., 2003—. Fellow Am. Coll. Forensic Examiners (diplomate); mem. APA, Am. Psychol. Soc., Assn. Mil. Surgeons US, Am. Soc. Clin. Hypnosis. Roman Catholic. Avocations: movies, racquetball. Home: 2615 Oak Leigh San Antonio TX 78232 E-mail: drfrbrooks@aol.com.

BROOKS, FREDERICK PHILLIPS, JR., computer scientist, educator; b. Durham, N.C., Apr. 19, 1931; s. Frederick Phillips and Octavia Brooks; m. Nancy Lee Greenwood, June 16, 1956; children: Kenneth Phillips, Roger Greenwood, Barbara Brooks LaDine. AB in Physics, Duke U., 1953; SM, Harvard U., 1955, PhD, 1956; D Tech. Sci. (hon.), ETH-Zurich, 1991. Engr. IBM, Poughkeepsie, NY, 1956—59, Yorktown Heights, NY, 1959—60, mgr. devel. computer System/360 Poughkeepsie, 1960—64, mgr. devel. Operating System/360, 1964—65; founder computer sci. dept. U. N.C., Chapel Hill, 1964, prof., 1964—75, chmn. dept. computer sci., 1964—84, Kenan prof., 1975—. Bd. dirs. Triangle U. Computation Ctr., 1966—84, chmn., 1975—77, N.C. Ednl. Computing Svc., 1965—; active Def. Sci. Bd., 1982—86, Nat. Sci. Bd., 1987—92. Author: The Mythical Man-Month-Essays on Software Engineering, 1975, 1995; author: (with K.E. Iverson) Automatic Data Processing, 1963, Automatic Data Processing System/360 Edition, 1969; author: (with G.A. Blaauw) Computer Architecture: Concepts and Evolution, 1997; contbr. articles to profl. jours.; inventor (with D.W. Sweeney) program interruption system, alphabetical read-out device. Trustee Durham Acad., pres., 1977—80; trustee, chmn. Trinity Sch. Durham and Chapel Hill, 2003—; chmn. exec. com. Ctrl. Carolina Billy Graham Crusade, 1972—73; mem. corp. Inter-Varsity Christian Fellowship, 1968—77. Recipient McDowell award, IEEE Computer Soc., 1970, Man of Yr. award, Data Processing Mgmt. Assn., 1970, Nat. Medal Tech., 1985, Harry Goode Meml. award, Am. Fedn. Info. Proc. Socs., 1989, Bower award and prize for achievement in sci., Franklin Inst., 1995; fellow Guggenheim Found., 1975; grantee, NSF, AEC, NIH, NASA, Def. Advanced Projects Rsch. Agy. Fellow: IEEE (John von Neumann medal 1993, Eckert-Manchly award 2004), Brit. Computer Soc. (disting.), Assn. Computing Machinery (coun. mem.-at-large 1966—70, Disting. Svc. award 1987, Allen Newell award 1994, Alan M. Turing award 1999), Am. Acad. Arts and Scis.; mem.: NAE, NAS, Royal Acad. Engring. (U.K.), Royal Netherland Acad. Arts and Scis. Methodist. Home: 413 Granville Rd Chapel Hill NC 27514-2723 Office: Univ NC Dept Computer Sci Sitterson Hall CB# 3175 Chapel Hill NC 27599-3175 Office Phone: 919-962-1931. Business E-Mail: brooks@cs.unc.edu.

BROOKS, GAIL DENISE, school system administrator, consultant; b. Camden, N.J., Oct. 24, 1951; d. Russel John and Marie Alverta (Jenkins) Brooks; 1 child, Adrienne. BA, Hofstra U., 1973; MEd, U. Pa., 1983, EdD, 1997. Tchr. Camden Bd. Edn., 1973—87, asst. prin., 1987—93, dir. curriculum & assessment, 1993—98; asst. supt. Monroe (N.J.) Twp. Bd. Edn., 1998—2004; supt. Pleasantville (N.J.) Bd. Edn., 2004—. Adj. prof. Rowan U., Glassboro, NJ, 1987—93, Rutgers U., Camden, 2004—. Mem.: Pi Lambda Theta, Phi Delta Kappa. Methodist. Home: 1596 Ormond Ave Camden NJ 08103-2941

BROOKS, GARTH (TROYAL BROOKS), country music singer; b. Tulsa, Okla., Feb. 7, 1962; s. Troyal Raymond and Colleen Carroll Brooks; m. Sandy Mahl, 1986; children: Taylor Mayne Pearl, August Anna; 1 child, Allie Colleen. BS in Avtg. and Journalism, Okla. St. Univ., 1984. Recording artist (albums) Garth Brooks, No Fences (Album of Yr. Acad. Country Music, 1991), Ropin' The Wind, 1991, Beyond the Season, The Chase, 1992, In Pieces, 1993 (Grammy nomination, Best Country Male Vocal for Ain't Goin' Down (Til the Sun Comes Up), The Hits, 1994, Fresh Horses, 1995, Sevens, 1997, The Limited Series, Double Live, 1998, In the Life of Chris Gaines, 1999, Scarecrow, 2001, (songs) The Dance (Video of Yr. award Country Music Assn., 1991, Song of Yr. and Video of Yr. awards Acad. Country Music, 1991), Friends in Low Places (Single Record of Yr. Acad. Country Music, 1991, Grammy award nomination), If Tomorrow Never Comes (Am. Music award for Country Song of Yr., 1991), The Thunder Rolls, We Shall Be Free (Video of Yr., Acad. Country Music), Somewhere Other Than The Night, Learning to Live Again, (TV spls.) This is Garth Brooks, 1992, This is Garth Brooks, Too, 1994, (TV Spls.) Garth Brooks: The Hits, 1995, Garth Brooks Live in Central Park, 1997. Named Best Male Country Music Performer, 1992, 1993, Best Male Musical Performer, People's Choice Awards, 1992, 1993, 1994, Artist of Decade, Acad. Country Music Awards, 1999; named to Grand Ole Opry; recipient Entertainer of Yr. award Acad. Country Music, 1991, 1992, 1993, 1994, Male Vocalist of Yr. award, 1991, Horizon award, Entertainer of Yr. award, Country Music Assn., 1991, 1992, Grammy award for Best Male Country Vocalist, 1992, Grammy award for Best Country Collaboration with Vocals, 1998, Best Male Musical Performer, People's Choice Awards, 1995, Am. Music Awards, Favorite Country Artist & Favorite Country Album, 2000.

BROOKS, GARY, crisis management and family business consultant; BS in Biochem. Engring. and Ind. Mgmt., MIT, 1955; MSChemE and Ops. Rsch., U. Rochester, 1959. Cert. mgmt. cons., turnaround profl. With GE Co., 1955-56, Eastman Kodak Co., 1956-64; mgr. Technomic Cons. Inc., 1968-71; divsn. exec. Scott Paper Co., 1971-76; mng. prin. turnaround cons. firm New Eng., 1976-85; founder, chmn., CEO, Allomet Ptnrs., Inc., corp. restructuring, N.Y.C., 1985—. Bd. dirs. Diomed Holdings, Inc., VRSim, Inc., Selectech, Inc.; mem. investment com. Cmty. Devel. Venture Captial Alliance; cons. in field; lectr. in field. Contbr. articles to profl. jours. Mem.: Family Firm Inst., Assn. Cert. Turnaround Profls. (1st pres.), Turnaround Mgmt. Assn. (founding mem., former bd. dirs., chair certification com.). Office: Allomet Ptnrs Ltd 370 Lexington Ave Rm 2010 New York NY 10017-6503 Office Phone: 212-370-9422. Business E-Mail: gb@allomet.com.

BROOKS, GENE (LESLIE GENE BROOKS), cultural organization administrator; b. Fletcher, Okla., June 15, 1936; s. Frank and Ethel E. (Spears) Brooks; m. Nancy E. Carman, Aug. 17, 1970; 1 child, Steven Frank. B in Music Edn., Okla. Bapt. U., 1959; M in Music Edn., U. Okla., 1962, D in Music Edn., 1968; postgrad., U. Colo. Chmn. music dept. Cameron U., Lawton, Okla., 1962-69, Midwestern State U., Wichita Falls, Tex., 1969-75, U. Ark., Little Rock, 1975-77; exec. dir. Am. Choral Dir. Assn., Oklahoma City, 1977—. Sec. gen. Internat. Fedn. Choral Music, 1982—85; dir. numerous choral festivals adn convs.; guest condr., clinician, adjudicator, spkr.; mem. juries 25th Internat. Choir Competition, Varna, Bulgaria, 38th Internat. Choral Competition, Gorizia, Italy, 1999, Gorizia, 2000, Nat. Choir Competition, New Zealand, 2000, 6th Internat. Choral Competition, Riva del Garda, Italy, 2000, World Choir Olympics, 2000, 02, Linz, Austria, World Choir Olympics, Busan, Republic of Korea, others. Recipient Disting. Alumni award, Okla. Bapt. U., 1985, Disting. Alumni award in Music, 1996, Disting. Alumni award, U. Okla., 1997. Mem.: Music Tchrs. Nat. Assn. (nat. choral chmn. 1972—75, chmn. music higher edn. 1975—77), Am. Choral Dir. Assn. (life), Coll. Music Soc. (life), Music Educators Nat. Conf. (life). Southern Baptist. Avocations: travel, skiing. Home: 18816 Woody Creek Dr Edmond OK 73003-4108 Office: Am Choral Dir Assn PO Box 2720 Oklahoma City OK 73101 Office Phone: 405-232-8161. Business E-Mail: executivedir@acdaonline.org.

BROOKS, GERALDINE, writer, reporter, correspondent; b. Sydney, Australia, Sept. 14, 1955; arrived in Eng., 1989; d. Lawrie and Gloria (Van Boss) B.; m. Anthony Lander Horwitz, Dec. 15, 1984. BA with honors, U. Sydney, 1979; MS in Journalism, Columbia U., 1983. Reporter Sydney Morning Herald, 1979-82, The Nat. Times, NSW, Australia, 1985-86; Australasian corr. Asian Wall Street Jour., NSW, 1986-87; reporter Wall Street Jour., Cleve., 1983-84, Mid. East corr. Cairo and London, 1987—. Author: Nine Parts of Desire, Foreign Correspondence Year of Wonders, 2001, March, 2005; contbr. articles to mags. Recipient Montague Grover award Australian Journalists Assn., 1979; Hal Boyle award for print reporting Overseas Press Club, N.Y.C., 1990, citation, 1991; Greg Shackleton scholar Australian Fgn. Corrs. Award Com., 1982.

BROOKS, GERLDINE MCGLOTHLIN, elementary school educator; b. Luling, Tex., Feb. 9, 1932; d. Fred Augusta and Bessie (Rutherford) McGlothlin; m. Kenneth A. Brooks, Nov. 27, 1952; children: Richard E., Kenneth A. BS in Elem. Edn., S.W. Tex. State U., 1962; postgrad., Tex. A&I U. Cert. in elem. edn., Tex. Classroom tchr. New Braunfels (Tex.) Ind. Sch. Dist., 1962-65, Pearsall (Tex.) Ind. Sch. Dist., 1965-81, Gonzales (Tex.) Ind. Sch. Dist., 1981—98, Cuero Christian Acad., 1998—2000; piano tchr., 2000—. Composer (songs) Blubonnetts All Over Texas, How Amazing is His Grace, Hemmed in by the Mountains, Take That Tree, In Our Greatest Losses, You're Not Alone, His Grace is Sufficient, Reach Out To Jesus. Mem. Nat. Fedn. Music Cubs (local pres., dist. v.p. 1989-91, treas. 1990—98), Classroom Tchrs. Nat. Edn. Assn., Tex. Ret. Tchrs. Assn. (dist. pres., 2002-2004, pres. Gonzales county chpt., 2000-02, 2004—), Gonzales Art League, Delta Kappa Gamma (treas. Gamma Pi chpt. 1969-79, pres., 1979-81, pres. Iota Xi chpt. 1988-90, Local Achievement award 1988). Office: Gozales Ind Sch Dist 1615 St Louis St Gonzales TX 78629-4330

BROOKS, GLENN ELLIS, political science professor, educational association administrator; b. Kerrville, Tex., Aug. 6, 1931; s. Glenn Ellis and Ellen (Mason) B.; m. Ann Rankin, May 31, 1953 (div. Apr. 1992); children: Elizabeth Lee, Amy Mason, Celia Brooks Brown. BA magna cum laude, U. Tex., Austin, 1953, MA, 1956; PhD with distinction, Johns Hopkins U., 1960. Sales mgr. Univ. Tex. Press, Austin, 1953-55; research assoc. Com. on Govt. and Higher Edn., Balt., 1957-59; instr. to prof. polit. sci. Colo. Coll., Colorado Springs, 1960-96, prof. and dean emeritus, faculty asst. to pres., 1968-70, chmn. dept. polit. sci., 1973-76, dean of coll. and faculty, 1979-87, dir. strategic planning, 1991-93. Rockefeller vis. lectr. U. Nairobi, Kenya, 1967-68; acad. visitor London Sch. Econs., 1972; NEH faculty fellow-in-residence Princeton (N.J.) U., 1978-79; bd. dirs. Am. Conf. Acad. Deans, 1982-85; cons. Nat. U. Lesotho, 1990, Am. Coun. Edn. Miver Program, 1992—; chief of party Fenix project Autonomous U. Puebla, Mex., 1994-96. Author: When Governors Convene: The Governors' Conference and National Politics, 1961; (with Frances E. Rourke) The Managerial Revolution in Higher Education, 1966. Contbr. chpts. to books, articles, essays to profl. publs. Bd. dirs. Colo. Humanities Program, Boulder, 1975-78, Citizens Goals for Colorado Springs, 1977—; mem. Chmn.'s Nat. Adv. Com. on Humanities in Primary and Secondary Schs. NEH, 1987—. Mem. Phi Beta Kappa, Phi Eta Sigma. Democrat. Home: 526 Observatory Dr Colorado Springs CO 80904-3970 E-mail: gbrooks@coloradocollege.edu.

BROOKS, H. ALLEN, architectural educator, author, lecturer; b. New Haven, Nov. 6, 1925; s. Harold Allen and Mildred (McNeill) B. BA, Dartmouth Coll., 1950; MA, Yale U., 1955; PhD, Northwestern U., 1957; D Engring. (hon.), Dalhousie U., 1984. Asst. prof. U. Ill., 1957-58; lectr. U. Toronto, 1958-61, asst. prof., 1961-64, assoc. prof., 1964-71, prof., 1971-86; vis. prof. Dartmouth Coll., 1969; Mellon chair Vassar Coll., 1970-71; vis. prof. Archtl. Assn., London, 1977-82, 2003. Author: The Prairie School: Frank Lloyd Wright and His Midwest Contemporaries, 1972 (recipient Alice Davis Hitchcock Book award 1973), Frank Lloyd Wright and the Prairie School, 1984, Le Corbusier's Formative Years: Charles-Edouard Jeanneret at La Chaux-de-Fonds, 1997 (Assn. Am. Pubs./Scholarly Pub. Divsn. Ann. award 1997); editor: Prairie School Architecture, 1975, Writings on Wright, 1981, The Le Corbusier Archive, 32 vols, 1982-85, Le Corbusier, 1987; editl. cons. Le Corbusier Sketchbooks, 1981-82; contbr. to numerous books and jours. With U.S. Army, 1946-47. Guggenheim Found. fellow, 1973-74; Can. Coun. fellow, 1975-76; Social Scis. and Humanities Rsch. Coun. Can. fellow, 1977-79, 83-85; Victoria U. fellow; receipent Wright Spirit award, Frank Llyod Wright Bldg. Conservency, 2002. Fellow Soc. Archtl. Historians; mem. Internat. Coun. Mus., Internat. Com. Monuments and Sites, Soc. Archtl. Historians U.S. (past pres., dir.), Soc. Archtl. Historians Gt. Britain, Soc. Study Architecture Can., Frank Lloyd Wright Bldg. Conservancy. Address: 80 Lyme Rd Hanover NH 03755-1910

BROOKS, JACK BASCOM, former congressman; b. Crowley, La., Dec. 18, 1922; s. Edward Chachere and Grace Marie (Pipes) B.; m. Charlotte Collins, Dec. 15, 1960; children: Jack Edward, Katherine Inez, Kimberly Grace. AA, Lamar Jr. Coll., Beaumont, Tex., 1941; BJ, U. Tex., 1943, JD, 1949. Bar: Tex. 1949. Mem. Tex. Legislature, 1946-50, 83rd-89th Congresses from 2nd Tex. dist., 1952-67, 90th-103rd Congresses from 9th Tex. dist., Washington, 1967-95. Author, Lamar Coll. bill, 1949. Lst lt. USMCR, 1942-46; col. Res. ret. Mem. ABA, State Bar Tex., Am. Legion, VFW, Sigma Delta Chi. Home: 1029 East Dr Beaumont TX 77706-4738 Office: 3535 Calder Ave Beaumont TX 77706-5025 Office Phone: 409-832-7508.

BROOKS, JAMES ELWOOD, geologist, educator; b. Salem, Ind., May 31, 1925; s. Elwood Edwin and Helen Mary (May) B.; m. Eleanore June Nystrom, June 18, 1949 (dec.); children: Nancy, Kathryn, Carolyn. AB, DePauw U., 1948; MS, Northwestern U., 1950; PhD, U. Wash., 1954. Research assoc. Ill. Geol. Survey, 1950; geologist Gulf Oil Corp., Salt Lake City, summers 1951-53; instr. geol. scis. So. Meth. U., Dallas, 1952-55, asst. prof., 1955-59, assoc. prof., 1959-62, prof., 1962-95, chmn. dept., 1961-70, dean, assoc. provost univ., 1969-72, provost, v.p., 1972-80, interim pres., 1980-81, prof. emeritus, 1995—, provost emeritus Dallas, 1995—; pres., trustee Inst. for Study Earth and Man, Dallas, 1981-97, vice chmn., trustee, 1997—, pres. emeritus. Chmn., trustee ISEM Found., Dallas, 2000—; cons. geologist firm DeGolyer & MacNaughton, Dallas, 1954-59. Contbr. articles to profl. jours. Trustee Hockaday Sch., 1982-88, Dallas Mus. Natural History Assn., 1984—, v.p., 1986-88, pres., 1988-90, hon. life trustee, 1990—; mem. exec. bd., internat. rep. Circle Ten coun. Boy Scouts Am., 1982—, internat. com., chmn. 1984—; bd. vis. DePauw U., 1979-83, chmn., 1983; mem. Mayor's Task Force on Fair Park, 1992; chmn. Coun. Fair Park Instns., 1992-94. Fellow AAAS, Geol. Soc. Am., Tex. Acad. Sci., Explorers Club; mem. Am. Assn. Petroleum Geologists, Dallas Geol. Soc., Sigma Xi, Sigma Gamma Epsilon, Sigma Phi. Home: 7055 Arboreal Dr Dallas TX 75231-7315 Office: Inst Study Earth and Man PO Box 750274 Dallas TX 75275-0274 Office Phone: 214-768-2325. Business E-Mail: jebrooks@mail.smu.edu.

BROOKS, JAMES L., film producer, director; b. North Bergen, NJ, May 9, 1940; s. Edward M. and Dorothy Helen (Sheinheit) B.; m. Marianne Catherine Morrissey, July 7, 1964 (div.); 1 child, Amy Lorraine; m. Holly Beth Holmberg, July 23, 1978; children: Chloe, Cooper. Student, N.Y. U., 1958-60. Writer CBS News, N.Y.C., 1964-66; writer-producer documentaries Wolper Prodns., L.A., 1966-67; founder & owner Gracie Films, 1984. Guest lectr. Stanford Grad. Sch. Communications. Creator TV series Room 222, 1968-69 (Emmy award for outstanding new series 1969); co-creator, producer TV series Lou Grant (Peabody award 1978); exec. producer, co-creator TV series Mary Tyler Moore Show, 1970-77 (Emmy award for comedy writing 1971, 74-77, Outstanding Comedy Series 1975-77, Peabody award, 1977, Writers Guild Am. winner best teleplay The Last Show, nominated best teleplay in episodic comedy, 1972, 77, TV Critics Achievement in Comedy award 1977, Achievement in Series award 1977, Humanitas 1977); writer, producer TV series Paul Sand in Friends and Lovers, 1974; co-creator, co-exec. producer TV series Rhoda show, 1974-75 (Emmy awards for outstanding writing in drama 1978-80, outstanding drama 1979, 80, 2 Humanitas for 1977, 82); writer TV show The New Lorenzo Music Show, 1976; co-writer, co-producer TV film Thursday Game, from 1971; co-creator, exec. producer TV series Taxi, 1978-80 (Emmy award for best show, best writing, 1978-79, 79-80, 80-81, TV Film Critics Circle award for achievement in comedy and in a series, 1976-77, Golden Globe awards for best comedy series, 1978, 79, 80, Humanitas prize for episode entitled Blind Date, 1979); co-exec. producer, co-writer TV series Cindy, 1978 (Writers Guild nomination for outstanding script 1978); co-creator, exec. producer TV series The Associates, 1979; exec. producer, co-exec. producer, co-creator The Tracey Ullman Show, 1986-90 (Emmy awards Outstanding Variety or Comedy series 1987, 88, 90, winner Emmy awards Outstanding Writing Variety or Music Show 1988-89), The Simpsons, 1990— (winner Emmy awards Outstanding Animated Spl., Outstanding Animated Program, winner Outstanding Animated Program); writer, co-producer film Starting Over (Writers Guild nomination for Best Screen Comedy Adaption 1979); actor film Modern Romance, 1981; producer, writer, dir. film Terms of Endearment, 1983 (Gloden Globe Best Screenplay award 1983, Acad. awards for best film, best dir., best screenplay 1984, Best Dir. award Dirs. Guild Am. 1983, winner comedy based on material from another medium, 1983, Nat. Bd. Rev. Best Picture, 1983, Golden Globe award Best Picture 1983, N.Y. Film Critics Best Picture; writer, dir., producer film Broadcast News, 1987 (winner best picture, best. dir., best screenplay N.Y. Film Critics Awards, Dirs. Guild nomination for best dir., Acad. award nomination for Best Picture and Best Screenplay); exec. producer film Big, 1988 (Peoples Choice award for favorite comedy motion picture), The War of the Roses, 1989, Say Anything, 1989; exec. producer (TV series) The Critic, 1994, What About Joan, 2001; writer, co-prodr. I'll Do Anything, 1994; dir. (play) Bklyn. Laundry; prodr. films Bottle Rocket, 1996, Jerry Maguire, 1996, As Good As It Gets, 1997, Riding in Cars with Boys, 2001; writer, dir. films Spanglish, 2004. Mem. Dirs. Guild Am., Writers Guild Am., TV Acad. Arts and Scis., Screen Actors Guild, Acad. Motion Picture Arts and Scis. Office: Gracie Films/Columbia Pictures/Sony Pictures Ent Poitier Bldg 10202 Washington Blvd Culver City CA 90232-3119*

BROOKS, JANET ELAINE, special education educator; b. Greenville, SC, May 16, 1956; d. Ernest C. Rumler and Hazel M. Powell; m. Ronald Vinson Brooks, June 7, 1980; children: Christopher Daniel, Stephanie Leigh. MusB, Wesleyan Coll., 1978; MEd, U. SC, 1980, EdS, 2001, PhD, 2004. Elem. sch. tchr., Spartanburg, SC, 1980—89; kindergarten tchr., dir. Columbia, 1990—99; tchr. spl. edn. Charleston, 1999—. Mentor clin. interns Charleston Southern U., North Charleston, SC, 2000—; mem. Coun. Exceptional Children, 2001—. Named Tchr. of Yr., Sangaree Elem. Sch., 2001—02; grantee, Berkeley Found. Edn., 2002; D.R. Holton Bright Ideas grant, 2003—04. Mem.: MADD, Assn. Curriculum and Supervision. Office: Westview Primary Sch 98 Westview Blvd Goose Creek SC 29445

BROOKS, JEANNE C., elementary school educator; b. Okinawa, Mar. 15, 1954; d. William R. and Alice L. (Stensland) Dorsett; m. Lee K. Brooks Jr., May 31, 1975; children: Chadwick, Neilson, Trey. BS, Ind. State U., 1975, MS, 1978. Cert. in elem. edn. K-8, early childhood edn. Tchr. Bibb County Pub Schs., Macon, Ga., Vigo County Sch. Corp., Terre Haute, Ind.; tchr. 4th grade Lewisville Ind. Sch. Dist., Tex. Mem. Lewisville Ind. Sch. Dist. textbook adoption com., 1987-88, 90-91, social studies curriculum writing com., 1992; student coun. faculty sponsor. Mem. LEAP (adv. bd. 1989), Lewisville Reading Coun., Tex. State Tchrs. Assn. (mentor tchr. 2003—), Phi Delta Kappa. Home: 8404 Warren Pkwy #411 Frisco TX 75034-8485

BROOKS, JEFFREY MARTIN, marketing and sales executive; b. Charlotte, NC, Oct. 14, 1958; s. Jack M. and Margaret Anne (Reap) B.; m. Kim Marke Whitaker, Sept. 26, 1981; 2 children: Justin Jeffrey Whitaker, Evan Martin Whitaker. BSBA in Acctg., East Carolina U.; MS in Econs., N.C. State U. Staff acct. Ernst & Whinney, Raleigh, N.C., 1980-82; acct. rep. Data Gen. Corp., Charlotte, 1982-85; mgr. systems mktg. AT&T, Charlotte, 1985-86; pres. Fastfly Corp., 1985-89; v.p. sales and distbn. Vanguard Cellular Systems, Inc., Greensboro, N.C., 1989-94; v.p. mktg. and sales So. Comm. (subs. So. Co.), Atlanta, 1994—97; asst. v.p. corp. mktg. BellSouth, Atlanta, 1997—2001; v.p. N.Am. channel Vigilinx, 2001—03; exec. v.p. mktg. and sales W.Va. Fiber, 2003—04; CEO Ulanji, Charleston, SC, 2004—. Cons. Charlotte Hornets, GTE. Vol. Jr. Achievement, Habitat for Humanity, YMCA Youth Sports; mem. Mt. Pisgah United Meth. Ch., Alpharetta, Ga. Mem. AICPA, Aircraft Owners and Pilots Assn., Nat. Bus. Aircraft Assn., U.S.A. Soccer, Nat. Youth Coaches Assn. Home: 9595 Autry Falls Dr Alpharetta GA 30022-3206 Office: 140 N Main St Summerville SC 29483 Office Phone: 843-553-6132. Business E-Mail: jbrooks@ulanji.com.

BROOKS, JEROME BERNARD, English and Afro-American literature educator; b. Houston, Mar. 20, 1932; s. Osburn Bernard and Agnes (Harrison) B. BA, Holy Cross Sem., Chgo., 1956, MA, 1960, Notre Dame U., 1962; PhD, U. Chgo., 1972. Instr. English Holy Cross Sem., 1962-66; lectr. English CCNY, 1968-72, asst. prof., 1972-75, assoc. prof., 1985-90, prof., 1991-95, chmn. dept. English, 1985-88, acting dean U. Affairs, 1988-89, dep. to the pres., 1991-95, prof. emeritus, 1996—. Cons. NEH, Washington, 1985, U. Mo. Press, Columbia, 1986; bd. dirs. N.Y. Alliance for Pub. Schs., Transp. Rsch. Consortium, Rice H.S.; vis. prof. English, Bard. Coll., Annandale-on-Hudson, N.Y. Author: Black Women Writers 1950-80, 1984; contbr. World Authors Encyclopedia, 1986, The Paris Review, 1994; co-editor Continuities mag., 1973-76. NEH grantee, 1979; named Fulbright Sr. Lectr. at U. Madagascar, USIA, 1976-78. Mem.: Princeton Club, Univ. Club of Chgo. Democrat. Roman Catholic. Avocation: play classical piano. Office: CUNY Dept English 138th St and Convent Ave New York NY 10031 E-mail: jbrooksx@msn.com.

BROOKS, JERRY ROBERT, small business owner; b. Gainesville, Tex., Dec. 28, 1925; s. Clay Younger and Mary Irene (Simmons) Brooks. BS in Econs., U. North Tex., 1948, MS in Econs., 1950. Lic. pvt. pilot 1946. Tool designer Nat. Supply divsn. ARMCO Stl., Inc., Gainesville, 1955—82; owner, mgr. Brooks Engring. Co., Gainesville, 1982—. Contbr. articles to profl. jours. Mem. Gainesville Arts Coun., 1981—84. With USAAF, 1944—45. Recipient Internat. award merit, 1st Internat. Inventors Exhbns., 1965, 2d Internat. Inventors Exhbns., 1966, Gold Medal award, 3d Internat. Inventors Exhbns., 1967, Bronze medal, 20th Internat. Exhbn. New Inventions and Products, 1971. Mem.: AIAA, Planetary Soc., Nat. Space Soc. Achievements include nine patents in diverse fields. Avocation: musician (play trumpet). Home: 1716 Merrywood Way Gainesville TX 76240-5142 Office: Brooks Engring Co 921 N Grand Ave Gainesville TX 76240

BROOKS, JOAE GRAHAM, psychiatrist; b. Boston, June 14, 1926; d. Collins and Hannah Slade (Benton) Graham; m. Bernard Charles Brooks, Jan. 11, 1976; children by previous marriage: Anne Benton Millman, Jane Graham Selzer. Nursing degree, Mass. Gen. Hosp. Sch. Nursing, 1947; AB with distinction, U. Rochester, 1950, MD, 1954. Diplomate Am. Bd. Psychiatry and Neurology. Intern in medicine Duke Hosp., Durham, N.C., 1954-55; resident in psychiatry Mass. Mental Health Ctr., Boston, 1955-57; resident in child psychiatry Beth Israel Hosp., Boston, 1957-59, mem. staff, 1959-97; pvt. practice Brookline, Mass., 1959-97. Cons. New Eng. Home for Little Wanderers, Boston, 1959-75, Kimberly Clark Corp., 1983-97; asst. clin. prof. psychiatry Harvard U. Med. Sch., Boston, 1978-97; vol. psychiatrist Sr. Friendship Ctr. Health Clinic, Naples, Fla., 1998—; mem. Bd. Registration in Medicine of Mass., 1991-95. Author: No More Diapers! A Guide to Toilet Training, 1971, 2d edit., 1991, When Children Ask About Sex-A Guide for Parents, 1975, I'm A Big Kid Now! A Guide to Toilet Training for Children and Parents, 1989. Distinguished fellow APA (life), Acad. Child and Adolescent Psychiatry (life); mem. Mass. Psychiat. Soc., New Eng. Coun. Child Psychiatry (bd. dirs. 1979-82, pres. 1987-89). Home: 5950 Almaden Dr Naples FL 34119-4627 Office Phone: 239-263-7425.

BROOKS, JOHN EDWARD, college president; b. Boston, July 13, 1923; s. John Edward and Mildred (McCoy) B. BS in Physics, Coll. Holy Cross, 1949; postgrad. in geophysics, Pa. State U., 1949-50; MA in Philosophy, Boston Coll., 1954, MS in Geophysics, 1959; S.T.D. in Dogmatic Theology, Gregorian U., Rome, Italy, 1963; H.H.D. (hon.), St. Ambrose Coll., 1976; D.Sc. (hon.), Worcester Poly. Inst., 1980; D Humanities, Assumption Coll., 1990; HHD (hon.), St. Anselm Coll., 1993; D Humanities (hon.), U. New England, 1994, Anna Maria Coll., 1994, Coll. of the Holy Cross, 1994. Joined Soc. of Jesus, 1950; ordained priest Roman Catholic Ch., 1959; instr. math. and physics Coll. of Holy Cross, Worcester, Mass., 1954-56, instr. theology, 1963-64, asst. prof., 1964-67, assoc. prof. religious studies, 1967-93, chmn. dept. theology, 1964-69, Loyola prof. humanities, 1993—, v.p., dean coll., 1968-70, pres., trustee, 1970-94, pres. emeritus, 1994—, sec. com. ednl. policy, 1968-70, chmn., 1970-94. Participant bibl. and archeol. consortium Jewish Inst. on Religion, Hebrew Union Coll., 1968; inst. acad. deans Am. Coun. Edn., St. Louis U., 1968; trustee St. Peter's Coll., Jersey City, 1969-75, Canisius Coll., Buffalo, 1974-80, Spring Hill Coll., Mobile, Ala., 1981-94, Anna Maria Coll., Paxton, Mass., 1998—, St. Sebastian's Sch., Needham, Mass., 1998-; mem. Mass. Postsecondary Edn. Commn., Mass. 1202 Commn., 1974-77; mem. exec. com. New Eng. Colls. Fund, 1974, 78; mem. Mass. Pub./Pvt. Forum; mem. Worcester Downtown Devel. Corp., Mass. Biotech. Rsch. Inst., 1985—; bd. visitors Air U., 1978-86; bd. dirs. Worcester Mcpl. Rsch. Bur., Inc. Community trustee United Way Cen. Mass.; consortium dir. Social Svcs. Corp., Worcester; bd. dirs. Worcester Mechanics Hall Assn.; mem. commn. govtl. rels. Am. Coun. on Edn., 1989-92. With U.S. Army, 1942-46. Mem. Assn. Jesuit Colls. and Univs. (bd. dirs. 1970-94), Assn. Ind. Colls. and Univs. in Mass. (v.p. 1972-73, chmn. coms., exec. com.), New Eng. Assn. Schs. and Colls. (sec.-treas. 1985-92, pres.-elect 1993, pres. 1994), Econ. Club (pres. Worcester chpt. 1977-78, exec. com. 1978-86), Delta Epsilon Sigma, Alpha Sigma Nu. Office: Coll of Holy Cross Ciampi Hall Worcester MA 01610 Office Phone: 508-793-3656. Business E-Mail: jbrooks@holycross.edu.

BROOKS, JOHN WHITE, lawyer; b. Long Beach, Calif., Sept. 3, 1936; s. John White and Florence Belle (O'Grady) B.; m. Elizabeth Ann Bellmore, June 21, 1958; children: Stephen Sanford, John Tinley. AB, Stanford U., 1958, LLB, 1966. Assoc. Luce, Forward, Hamilton and Scripps, San Diego, 1966-71, ptnr., 1971-81, sr. ptnr., 1981—2004, sr. internat. counsel, 2004—; founding chmn. Internat. Svcs. Group, 1989—. Mem. Internat. Coun. Inst. Ams., Pacific Coun. Internat. Policy. 1996-98; panelist Ctr. for Internat. Comml. Arbitration, 1987—; bd. dirs. Union of Pan-Asian Communities, 1989-98, Ctr. for Dispute Resolution, 1986—; chmn. Pacific Rim Adv. Coun., 1984-91. Author: Passport Pal, The Pacific Rim, 1996-2000, The Heads Up Report; contbr. articles to profl. jours. Mem. Commn. of the Californias, 1977—79; chmn. San Diego Regional Yr. 2000 Working Group, 1998—2000; dir. Corp. Fin. Coun. of San Diego, 1977—82, chmn., 1980—81; bd. visitors Stanford Law Sch., 1978—80. With USN, 1958—63. Alfred P. Sloan scholar, Stanford U., 1958, Rocky Mountain Mineral Law Found. Research scholar, 1966. Mem. ABA (bus. law sect., com. on internat. commercial transactions, subcom. on Asia-Pacific law and internat. bus. structures and agreements, com. on negotiated transactions, internat. law sect., subcom. on multinat. corps., com. on internat. comml. transactions), Calif. Bar Assn. (bus. law sect. com. on corps. 1977, vice chmn. com. on internat. practice 1986-87, exec. com. internat. law sect. 1987), San Diego County Bar Assn., Internat. Bar Assn. (com. on issues and trading in securities 1980-89, com. on procedures for settling disputes 1980—, com. on bus. orgns. 1989—), Inter-Pacific Bar Assn. (com. on internat. trade), Am. Arbitration Assn. (panel of arbitrators 1975-96), State Bar Calif. Avocations: greenhouse gardening, horse competitions, helicopters, wine, food. Office: Luce Forward Hamilton & Scripps 600 W Broadway Ste 2600 San Diego CA 92101-3372 Office Phone: 619-699-2410. Business E-Mail: jwbrooks@luce.com.

BROOKS, JOLI, music educator; b. Sanford, N.C., Aug. 2, 1961; d. Edwin H. and Joyce Simpson Brooks; m. James E. Gillentine, Dec. 20, 1997. MusB, East Carolina U., 1983, M in Sch. Adminstrn., 2003. Cert. Nat. Bd. Profl. Tchg. Stds. Orch. dir. Jacksonville (N.C.) H.S., 1997—. Mem.: N.C. Am. String Tchrs. Assn., N.C. Music Educators Assn. (orch. sect. chair 2004—), Mensa. Office: Jacksonville HS 1021 Henderson Dr Jacksonville NC 28540 Office Phone: 910-346-4011 ext 3. Office Fax: 910-989-2046. E-mail: jaxorchestra@hotmail.com.

BROOKS, JUANITA ROSE, lawyer; b. Merced, Calif., May 9, 1954; BA, San Diego State U., 1974; JD, Yale U., 1977. Bar: Calif. 1977, Supreme Ct. Cailf., U.S. Supreme Ct., U.S. Ct. Appeals (9th cir.), Atty. Fed. Defenders San Diego, Inc., San Diego, 1977-80; pvt. practice, 1980-93; ptnr. McKenna & Cuneo, L.L.P., San Diego, 1993-2000; prin. Fish & Richardson, P.C., San Diego, 2000—. Adj. prof. Calif. Western Sch. Law, 1984-86, Nat. Criminal Defense Col. 1979—, Nat. Inst. Trial Advocacy, 1982—. Contbr. articles to profl. jours. Appeared numerous television programs including Good Morning Am., Today, CBS Morning News. Recipient Silver Tongue award, San Diego, 1999; Named One of the Best Lawyers in Am., San Diego Mag, 2001, 2005, One of the Top Women Litigators in Calif., San Francisco Daily Journ. & LA Daily Journ., 2002-05, One of Calif. Top 25 IP Lawyers, San Francisco Daily Journ., 2003, 2005. Mem. ABA, Calif. Bar Assn., Nat. Assn. Criminal Defense Lawyers (bd. dirs. 1993—), Am. Trial Lawyers Assn., Am. Acad. Healthcare Attys. Office: Fish & Richardson PC 12390 El Camino Real San Diego CA 92130-2081 Office Phone: 858-678-4377. Business E-Mail: brooks@fr.com.

BROOKS, KATHLEEN, journalist; b. Atlanta, Jan. 25, 1957; d. William Chesley and Sara (Brooks) Howton. BA, Stephens Coll., Columbia, Mo., 1978. Mktg. asst. The Laitram Corp., New Orleans, 1978-79; reporter Daily Home, Talladega, Ala., 1979-80, copy editor, 1980-81; asst. wire editor, reporter Gastonia (N.C.) Gazette, 1981, wire editor, 1981-84; asst. wire editor Comml. Appeal, Memphis, 1984-88, Washington editor, 1988-91, nat. editor, 1991—. Methodist. Office: The Comml Appeal 495 Union Ave Memphis TN 38103-3221 E-mail: brooks@gomemphis.com.

BROOKS, KENNETH N., forestry educator; m. Pamela Naylor; children: Marianne, Robin, Cherie, Nicole. BS in Range Sci., Utah State U., 1966; MS in Watershed Mgmt., U. Ariz., 1969, PhD in Watershed Mgmt., 1970. Hydrologist North Pacific Divsn. Corps of Engrs., Portland, Oreg., 1971-73, Tng. and Methods br. Hydrologic Engring. Ctr., Davis, Calif., 1973-75; asst. prof. dept. forest resources U. Minn., St. Paul, 1975-79, assoc. prof., 1979-85, prof., 1985—, dir. grad. studies in natural resources sci. and mgmt., 1987—; fellow Environment and Policy Inst. East-West Ctr., Honolulu, 1983—84. Cons. nat. and internat. agencies and firms including Food and Agrl. Orgn. of UN, U.S. Agy. for Internat. Devel., World Bank; condr. workshops in field; Fulbright lectr., Taiwan, 1997-98. Co-author: Guidelines for Economic Appraisal of Watershed Management Projects, 1987, Watershed Management Project Planning, Monitoring and Evaluation: A Manual for the ASEAN Region, 1989, Hydrology and the Management of Watersheds, 1991, 3d edit. 2003, Challenges in Upland Conservation: Asia and the Pacific, 1993, Dryland Forestry, 1995; contbr. articles to profl. jours. Am. Inst. Hydrology (chmn. bd. registration 1995-2003, sec. 1992), Soc. Am. Foresters (chmn. water resources working group 1991-93), Am. Water Resources Assn. (dir. West North Ctrl. dist. 1987-90), Western Snow Conf., Internat. Soc. Tropical Foresters, Xi Sigma Pi, Sigma Xi, Phi Kappa Phi. Office Phone: 612-624-2774. E-mail: kbrooks@umn.edu.

BROOKS, KIX (LEON ERIC BROOKS), musician; b. Shreveport, La., May 12, 1955; m. Barbara Brooks; children: Molly, Eric. Grad., La. Tech. Staff songwriter Tree Pub.; songwriter Highway 101, The Nitty Gritty Dirt Band; with Brooks & Dunn, 1988—; rec. artist Arista, 1991—. Prodr. clothing line "Panhandle Slim Western Wear" with Ronnie Dunn. Singer: (single) Baby, When Your Heart Breaks Down, 1983, (solo album) Kix Brooks, 1993, (albums) (with Ronnie Dunn) Brand New Man, 1991 (Acad. Country Music award Album of Yr., 1992), Hard Workin' Man, 1993 (Grammy award Best Country Vocal Performance by Duo or Group for "Hard Workin' Man", 1993), Waitin' on Sundown, 1994, Borderline, 1996 (Grammy award Best Country Vocal Performance by Duo or Group for "My Maria", 1996), Greatest Hits Collection, 1997, If You See Her, 1998, Tight Rope, 1999, Super Hits, 1999, Steers and Stripes, 2001, It Won't Be Christmas Without You, 2002, Red Dirt Road, 2003, Greatest Hits Collection: Volume II, 2004, (singles) Boot Scootin' Boogie, 1992, We'll Burn That Bridge, 1993, Rock My World (Little Country Girl), 1993, (songs) (8 Seconds (soundtrack) Ride 'Em High, Ride 'Em Low, 1994, (with Hank Thompson) Hooked on Honky Tonk, 1997, (with Reba McEntire) If You See Him, If You See Her, 1998; background vocals, chorus: albums T-r-o-u-b-l-e (Travis Tritt), 1992, appears on: albums Common Thread: The Songs of the Eagles, 1994 (Country Music Assn. Album of Yr., 1994). Named Top New Vocal Duo or Group, Acad. Country Music, 1991, Entertainer of Yr., 1995, 1996, 2001, Top Vocal Duo, 1991—97, 2000—03, 2005, Vocal Duo of Yr., Country Music Assn., 1992—99, 2001—03, Vocal Group of Yr., 2004, Entertainer of Yr., 1996, Favorite Band, Duo or Group-Country Music, Am. Music Awards, 2004. Office: Brooks and Dunn PO Box 120669 Nashville TN 37212-0669

BROOKS, LILLIAN DRILLING ASHTON (LILLIAN HAZEL CHURCH), adult education educator; b. Grand Rapids, Mich., May 27, 1921; d. Walter Brian and Lillian Church; m. Frederick Morris Drilling, 1942 (div. Apr. 1972); children: Frederick Walter, Stephen Charles, Lawrence Alan, Lynn Anne; m. Richard Moreton Ashton, Aug. 25, 1973 (dec. 1990); m. Ralph J. Brooks, May 21, 1994. Student, Grand Rapids Jr. Coll., 1939-41, Wayne State U., 1941-42, Grand Rapids Art Inst., 1945-49, UCLA, 1964-69, Loyola Marymount Coll., Westchester, Calif., 1970-73; life tchg. credential, U. So. Calif., Long Beach, 1973. Life teaching credential, Calif. Decorator John Widdicomb Furniture Co., 1945-49; tchr. art Inglewood Sch. Dist., Calif., 1965-73; tchr. adult edn. art Downey Unified Sch. Dist., 1973-95; tchr. art Assn. Retarded Citizens and Mentally Disadvantaged Students Downey Cmty. Health Ctr., 2003—04. Art tchr. institutionalized adults ages 18 to 60, 2000-2004; lectr. Downey Art League, 1990-92, Whittier (Calif.) Art Assn., 1991, h.s. and mid. sch. lectr., 1994-95; judge Children's Art Exhibit, Downey, 1992; participant Getty Found., San Francisco, 1993, Getty Found., Cranbrook, 1994, Getty Conf. on Aesthetics, 1995, Cin. U., 1992, El Segundo, 1994; mem. state accreditation com. Inglewood and Downey United Sch. Dists., 1966-70, 75-80, 85—; owner A & B Furniture Svc. Ctr., 1995—. One-woman shows include El Segundo Mcpl. Libr., 1965, Pico Rivera Art Gallery, 1978, Downey Art Mus., 1999; exhibited in group shows at Fairlane Show, Dearborn, Mich., 1959, Jane Lessing Art Gallery, 1966, Westchester Mcpl. Libr., 1971, Inglewood City Hall, 1973, Aegina Sch., Greece, 1973, Downey Mus. Art, 1992, 99-2000; represented in permanent collection U. Mich., Calif. Senate Bldg. Pres. bd. dirs. Downey Art Mus., 1996-2002, dir. Mus., 1998, vol. dir., 1999, bd. dirs. 1998-2000; art commr. City of Dearborn, Mich., 1954-59; former pres. Dearborn Art Inst., Pacific Art Guild; pres. Downey Art League, 1991-94, v.p., 1999-2000; pres. Exhbn. Ch., 1995, v.p. 1996-98; vol. dir. Art Mus., 1998-99; lectr. on art as a career local Downey high and mid. schs.; juried children's art shows; vol. tchr. basic art; judge art shows. Recipient Certs. of Appreciation for contbn. of leadership Coord. Coun. Downey, Downey Governing Bd., Downey Bd. Edn., 1997, 2002, Cmty. Svc. award for Outstanding Svc. Downey Rotary, 1994, Cert. of Recognition Calif. State Assembly, 1999, Downey Coord. Coun., 1998-99, award 2002; named Tchr. of Yr., Masons, Downey, 1986; painting chosen to represent dist. in state capital, 1999-2001. Mem. Calif. Coun. on Art Edn. (parliamentarian Downey 1990-92, Calco Excellence in Tchg. award 1991, various certs.). Avocations: reading, hiking, international travel, photography, painting. Home: 9318 Fostoria St Downey CA 90241-4020

BROOKS, LINTON FORRESTALL, federal agency administrator; b. Boston, Aug. 15, 1938; m. Barbara Julius; children: Julie, Kathryn. BS in Physics, Duke U., 1959; MA in Govt. and Politics, U. Md., 1972; disting. grad., USN War Coll., 1979. Commd. USN, advanced through grades to capt.; dir. arms control NSC, 1984—89; dep. head del., amb.; head U.S. del. on nuc. and space talks, chief strategic arms reductions negotiator State Dept.; asst. dir. strategic and nuc. affairs U.S. Arms Control and Disarmament Agy.; v.p., asst. to Pres. for policy analysis Ctr. Naval Analyses, Alexandria, Va., 1993—2001; dep. adminstr. def. nuc. nonproliferation Dept. Energy, Washington, 2001—02; acting under sec. of energy for nuclear security US Dept. of Energy, 2002—03, under sec. of energy for nuclear security, 2003—; acting adminstr. Nat. Nuclear Security Adminstrn., Washington, 2002—03, adminstr., 2003—. Cons. strategic arms reductions Clinton Adminstrn. Contbr. articles to profl. jours. Mem.: Phi Beta Kappa. Office: US Dept Energy Forrestal Bldg 1000 Independence Ave SW Rm 7A-199 Washington DC 20585

BROOKS, MARTIN, electronic media company executive; b. N.Y.C., Aug. 26, 1950; s. Kenneth and Ruth (Schubert) Brooks; m. Stacey Savage, May 30, 1973 (div. 1980); 1 child, Kerin. BFA, NYU, 1973. Sr. prodn. engr. Cinema Sound, N.Y.C., 1971—78; chief rec. engr. G&T Harris, N.Y.C., 1978; mgr. rec. ops. CBS Pub., N.Y.C., 1978—81, mgr. audio visual devel., 1981—83, mgr. software devel., 1983—84, dir. software devel., 1984—86; exec. editor, electronic publ. R.R. Bowker/Reed Reference Pub., N.Y.C., 1986—90, v.p. New Providence, NJ, 1991—95; sr. v.p. electronic pub. Reed Reference Pub., New Providence, 1995—96; id. cons. N.Y. Intermedia Authority, 1996—98; dir. front end devel. and ops. Bol.Com Bertelsman, N.Y.C., 1998—2002; id. cons. N.Y. Intermedia Authority, 2002—. Engr., prodr. radio program Crawdaddy Rock Rev., 1978; owner, developer JimmyVivino.com, Jerry Vivino.com websites; ind. cons. films, theater evaluation svc. Dolby Distbr. Svcs. divsn. Dolby Labs. Editor (and designer): (cd-rom) Books in Print Plus, 1986, Books in Print with Book Reviews Plus, 1987, Variety's Video Directory Plus, 1986, Enviro Energyline Abstracts Plus, 1991, Library Reference Plus, 1992, Children's Reference Plus, 1992, Global Books in Print Plus, 1994, Libros en Venta, 1995, ABMS Medical Specialists Plus, 1995, Advertiser and Agency Ped Books Plus, 1995, Corporate Affiliations Plus, 1995, Martindale-Hubbel Law Directory, 1995; prodr.(and designer): (software) Class II, 1984, Adventures in Science Series, 1985; contbr. 77-WABC radio spl., 2002. Mem.: Optical Pub. Assn. (bd. dirs.), Soc. Motion Picture and TV Engrs., Audio Engrng. Soc. Home: 11220 72nd Dr Forest Hills NY 11375-5661 Office Phone: 917-887-6450. E-mail: mbrooks@newyorkkintermedia.com.

BROOKS, MATTHEW WAYNE, agrichemical regulatory chemist, consultant; b. Springfield, Mass., Oct. 13, 1961; s. Donald Wayne and Helen Brooks; m. Laura McKenna Kehoe, June 18, 1988; children: Sierra, Wyatt. BS, U. Mass., 1983, MS, 1986, PhD, 1992. Chief chemist Mass. State Pesticide Analysis Lab., Amherst, 1986-88; sr. rsch. chemist FMC Co., Princeton, N.J., 1993-98; sr. chemistry cons. JSC, Inc., Arlington, Va., 1998—2001; dir. Ag-Chem. Consulting, LLC, 2002—. Author: (book chpt.) Encyclopedia of Agrichemicals, 2001; contbr. articles to profl. jours. Pres. Mercer County Literacy Vols., Princeton, 1995-98; treas. Montgomery Wood Homeowners Assn., Princeton, 1995-98; driver Meals on Wheels, Fairfax, Va., 2000-2001; grant reviewer United Way, Trenton, N.J., 1997-98. Mem. Am. Chem. Soc. Democrat. Office: Ag-Chem Cons LLC 12208 Quinque Ln Clifton VA 20124 E-mail: mwbrooks01@yahoo.com.

BROOKS, MEL, film producer, actor, film director, scriptwriter; b. June 28, 1926; Author: sketch Of Fathers and Sons in New Faces of 1952, 1957, sketch Shinbone Alley; co-author: sketch All American, 1962; writer (TV series) Your Show of Shows, also Caesar's Hour, The Sid Caesar, Imogene Coca, Carl Reiner, Howard Morris Special, 1967 (Emmy award for outstanding writing achievement in a comedy-variety), co-creator Get Smart, recordings include 2000 Years, 2000 and One Years, 2000 and Thirteen Years, 2000 Year Old Man in the Year 2000, 1997 (Grammy award for Best Spoken Word Album Comedy, 1998), writer, dir. (motion pictures) Producers, 1968 (Acad. award for Best Original Screenplay), writer, dir., star The Twelve Chairs, 1970, co-writer, dir., star Blazing Saddles, 1974, Silent Movie, 1976, co-writer, dir. Young Frankenstein, 1974, co-writer, dir., prodr., star Robin Hood: Men In Tights, 1993, Dracula: Dead and Loving It, 1995, prodr., dir., co-writer and star High Anxiety, 1977, Spaceballs, 1987, Life Stinks, 1991, writer, dir., prodr., star History of the World-Part I, 1981, writer, narrator The Critic, 1964 (Acad. award for best animated short subject); actor: (films) (voice) Robots, 2005; actor, prodr. To Be or Not To Be, 1983; prodr.: 84 Charing Cross Road, 1987; prodr.: The Elephant Man, 1980, Frances, 1982, My Favorite Year, 1982, Fly I, 1986, Fly II, 1989; guest actor (TV series) Mad About You (Emmy award for outstanding guest actor in a comedy series, 1997, 1998, 1999), co-writer, composer, prodr. (Broadway musical) The Producers, 2001 (3 Tony awards). Office: c/o The Culver Studios 9336 Washington Blvd Culver City CA 90232-2628

BROOKS, MICHAEL, music archivist; Book trade editor, advt. exec., 1960; worked on jazz reissues CBS Records, 1971; with SNUM, 1976; reissue prodr. spl. products divsn. Columbia, 1977; chief prodr. mail-order record divsn. Time-Life, 1981; prodr., archivist CBS Records and Sony Music, 1987—. Prodr.: (albums) The Lester Young Story, Vol. 3 (Grammy award Best Hist. Repackage Album, 1978), (with Jerry Korn) Billie Holiday-Giants of Jazz (Grammy award Best Hist. Reissue, 1979), (with George Spitzer) Hoagy Carmichael-From Stardust To Ole Buttermil Sky (Grammy award Best Hist. Album, 1981); album notes writer: albums A Bing Crosby Collection, Vols. I & II (Grammy award Best album notes, 1978), master engr. with others: albums Louis Armstrong-The Complete Hot Five & Hot Seven Recordings (Grammy award Best Hist. Album, 2000), compilation prodr.: albums Lady Day - The Complete Billie Holiday On Columbia 1933-1944 (Grammy award Best Hist. Album, 2001). Named Grammy award for liner notes on Count Basie reissue Super Chief, 1972. Office: Sony Music Entertainment 550 Madison Ave New York NY 10022-3211

BROOKS, MICHAEL PAUL, retired urban planning educator; b. Topeka, June 13, 1937; s. Paul Edward and Gladys Leora (Nansen) B.; m. Shirley Birdeen Rhoad, June 8, 1958 (div. Aug. 1983); children: David, Timothy, Susan.; m. Ann DeWitt Watts, Feb. 18, 1984. BA magna cum laude, Colgate U., 1959; M in City Planning, Harvard U., 1961; PhD, U. N.C., 1970. Dir. rsch. The N.C. Fund, Durham, 1963-66, dir. planning and program devel., 1966-67; lectr. dept. city and regional planning U. N.C., Chapel Hill, 1967-70, assoc. prof., 1970-71; prof. dept. urban and regional planning U. Ill., Urbana, 1971-78, head dept., 1971-78; dir. Bur. Urban and Regional Planning Rsch., 1971-77; dean Coll. Design, Iowa State U., Ames, 1978-84, Sch. Architecture and Environ. Design, SUNY, Buffalo, 1984-87, Sch. Community and Pub. Affairs, Va. Commonwealth U., Richmond, 1987-91, spl. asst. to provost for strategic planning, 1991—93, prof. dept. urban studies and planning, 1993—2003, ret., 2003. Cons. in field. Commr. Research Triangle Regional Planning Commn., Chapel Hill, N.C., 1969-71 Mem. Am. Planning Assn. (pres. 1979-80), Am. Inst. Cert. Planners, Assn. Collegiate Schs. Planning (pres. 1976-77) Democrat. E-mail: mkbrks@comcast.net.

BROOKS, PETER (PRESTON), literature educator, department chairman, writer; b. NYC, Apr. 19, 1938; s. Ernest and Mary Caroline (Schoyer) B.; m. Margaret Elisabeth Waters, July 18, 1959 (div. 1995); 3 children; m. Rosa Ehrenreich, May 15, 2001. BA, Harvard U., 1959, PhD, 1965; postgrad., U. Coll. London, 1959-60, U. Paris, 1962-63; MA (hon.), Yale U., 1975; Doctor (hon.), Ecole Normale Supérieure, 1997; MA (hon.), U. Oxford, 2001. Instr. French Yale U., 1965-67, asst. prof., 1967-72, assoc. prof., 1972-75, prof. French and comparative lit., 1975—, Chester D. Tripp prof. humanities, 1980-2001, dir. The Lit. Major, 1974-79, dir. Whitney Humanities Ctr., 1980-91, 96-01, chmn. dept. French, 1983-88, chmn. dept. comparative lit., 1991-97, Sterling prof. comparative lit. and French New Haven, 2001—04; univ. prof. English and law U. Va., Charlottesville, Va., 2004—. Eastman vis. prof. U. Oxford, 2001—02. Author: The Novel of Worldliness, 1969, The Child's Part, 1972, The Melodramatic Imagination, 1976, Reading for the Plot, 1984, Body Work, 1993, Psychoanalysis and Storytelling, 1994, World Elsewhere, 1999, Troubling Confessions, 2000, Realist Vision, 2005; co-editor: Law's Stories, 1996, Whose Freud?, 2000; contbg. editor Partisan Rev., 1972-88; mem. editl. bd. Yale French Studies, 1966—; chmn. Yale Jour. Criticism, 1987—. Acad. advisor Marlboro Co., 1975—; regional chmn. Mellon Fellowships in Humanities, 1982-84; trustee Hopkins Sch., New Haven, 1983-88; mem. adv. coun. West European program The Wilson Ctr.; mem. adv. bd. Stanford Humanities Ctr., 1996-2001; mem. humanities adv. coun. N.Y. Pub. Libr. Decorated Officier des Palmes Académiques, 1986; Marshall fellow, 1959, Morse fellow, 1967, Guggenheim fellow, 1973, Am. Coun. Learned Socs. fellow, 1980, NEH fellow, 1988. Fellow Am. Acad. Arts and Scis.; mem. MLA (exec. coun. 1993-97), Am. Phil. Soc., Yale Club, Elizabethan Club (New Haven), Century Assn. Democrat. Office: Univ Va Dept English PO Box 40012 Charlottesville VA 22904-4121 Office Phone: 434-924-8877.

BROOKS, PHILIP COOLIDGE, JR., archivist, curator, historian; b. Dec. 1, 1940; s. Philip Coolidge and Dorothy Hamilton (Holland) Brooks; m. Susan Mary Fox, Dec. 21, 1965; 1 child, Anthony Franklin Coolidge. BA, U. Kans., 1962, MA, 1966; Exchange fellow, U. Reading, Eng., 1962—63, postgrad., 1964—65, Stanford U. Law Sch., 1963—64. Mus. specialist polit. history Smithsonian Instn., Washington, 1967—71; asst. to exec. dir. Nat. Archives, Washington, 1971—74, asst. to asst. archivist, pub. programs, 1974—83, also curator archives reception room, acting dir. edn. div., 1979—83, sr. archives specialist, records centers, 1983—96, devel. officer, 1986—87; ret., 1996. Historian archivist Pres. Inaugural Com., 1968, 89, 93. Contbr. articles on history to profl. jours. Mem. Gadsby's Tavern Acquisitions Commn., Alexandria, Va., 1974—78, Historic Records Adv. Com., Alexandria, 1975—77; vice chmn. Historic Alexandria Resources Com., 1983—97, chmn., 1995—97; mem. Alexandria Libr. Co., 1989—; vice chmn. Alexandria Assn., 1976—78; chmn. Alexandria Ad Hoc Lyceum Com., 1981—82, The Lyceum Co., 1983—87, vice chmn., 1987—91; mem., vice chmn. Alexandria Bicentennial Commn., 1972—83; chmn. Alexandria Mus. Task Force, 1979—80, Alexandria 250th Anniversary Com., 1997—2000; dir. RROC Found., 1984—92; pres. Rolls-Royce Found., 2000—03; mem. adv. Coun. Internat. Nontheatrical Events, 1989—97. Recipient Commendable Service award, Nat. Archives, 1976, Archivist's Achievement awards, 1985, 1996, Appreciation cert., City Alexandria, 1976, 1981, 1984, Va. Senate Joint Resolution of Commendation, 2000, Rolls-Royce Found. Commendation, 2003. Mem.: Nat. Trust Historic Preservation, Am. Assn. State and Local History, Am. Assn. Museums, Rolls Royce Owners Club (dir. 1978—84, editor The Flying Lady 1986—89, v.p. regions 1992—94), Bentley Drivers Club (rep. 1968—), Lambda Chi Alpha. Home: 3908 Col Ellis Ave Alexandria VA 22304-1704

BROOKS, PHILIP RUSSELL, chemistry educator, researcher; b. Chgo., Dec. 31, 1938; s. John Russell and Louise Jane B.; children: Scott, Robin, Christopher, Steven. BS, Calif. Inst. Tech., 1960; PhD, U. Calif., Berkeley, 1964. Rsch. assoc. physics dept. U. Chgo., 1964; from asst. to assoc. prof. chemistry Rice U., Houston, 1964-75, prof., 1975—. Editor: State-to-State Chemistry, 1977. Vol. Boy Scouts Am., Houston, 1970—. Recipient Humboldt prize Alexander von Humboldt Found., 1985; predoctoral fellow NSF, 1960-63, postdoctoral fellow, 1963-64, Alfred P. Sloan fellow, 1970-74, John Simon Guggenheim fellow, 1974-75, Vis. Erskine fellow U. Canterbury, 1991, JSPS fellow Japan Soc. Promotion Sci., 1992. Fellow Am. Phys. Soc.; mem. Am. Chem. Soc. Achievements include research on chemical reaction dynamics. Home: 1026 Glourie Cir Houston TX 77055-7504 Office: Rice U Chemistry Dept MS60 6100 Main St Houston TX 77005-1892 E-mail: brooks@python.rice.edu.

BROOKS, PHILLIP, advertising executive; b. 1955; With Affiliate of Excellence Co., Mpls., 1976—, now pres.; with Excellence Co., Mpls., pres., CEO. Office: The Excellence Co 600 Lakeview Point Dr Saint Paul MN 55112-3494

BROOKS, RICHARD C., electrical engineer, federal official; b. Phila., Aug. 31, 1945; BEE with honors, U. Va., Charlottesville, 1967; MSE, Johns Hopkins U., 1970; PhD, U. Mo., Columbia, 1973; MBA, Va. Poly. Inst., 1978. Registered profl. engr., Va., 1972. Chief, integrated systems lab. Nat. Weather Svc./NOAA, Silver Spring, Md., 1989—96; dep. dir., systems acquisition office Nat. Oceanic & Atmospheric Adminstrn. (NOAA), Silver Spring, 1996—2002; dir., satellite & ground systems program NESDIS/Nat. Oceanic & Atmospheric Adminstrn. (NOAA), Suitland, Md., 2002—. Troop com. Boy Scouts Am., Arlington, Va., 1984—2003. Lt U.S. Pub. Health Svc., 1968—70, Baltimore, Maryland, Lcdr U.S. Pub. Health Svc. Reserve, 1970—99. Mem.: IEEE (sr.). Achievements include research in image processing and pattern recognition. Avocation: skiing. Office: NOAA Dept Commerce 4401 Silver Hill Rd FB4 Rm 3301 Suitland MD 20746 Office Phone: 301-457-5277. Business E-Mail: richard.brooks@noaa.gov.

BROOKS, RICHARD DICKINSON, lawyer; b. Daytona Beach, Fla., Sept. 17, 1944; m. Betty Jane Huba, Aug. 28, 1971; children: Hillary Ann, Richard Jason. BA, Marietta (Ohio) Coll., 1967; JD, Case Western Res. U., 1972. Bar: Ohio 1972, U.S. Dist. Ct. (so. dist.) Ohio 1975, U.S. Ct. Appeals (6th cir.) 1993. Atty. Bridgewater Robe Brooks & Keifer, Athens, Ohio, 1972-87, Arter & Hadden, Columbus, Ohio, 1987—2003, Bailey Cavalieri LLC, Columbus, 2003—. Coach Upper Arlington Cub Scout Baseball, Columbus, 1989-90; pres. A.T.C.O. Inc. Sheltered Workshop, Athens, 1986; bd. dirs. Athens C. of C., 1984-87. Sgt. U.S. Army, 1968-70, Vietnam. Fellow Am. Bar Found., Ohio Bar Found. (pres. 1988); mem. ABA, Ohio Bar Assn. (exec. com. 1979-83), Columbus Bar Assn. (environ. law com.), Athens County Bar Assn. (pres. 1978-79), Ohio CLE Inst. (bd. dirs. 1989-90), Ohio State Legal Svcs. Assn. (bd. dirs. 1982—). Avocations: basketball, tennis, fishing, furniture restoration. Office: Bailey Cavalieri LLC 10 W Broad St Ste 2100 Columbus OH 43215-3422 Office Phone: 614-229-3285. E-mail: richard.brooks@baileycavalieri.com.

BROOKS, RICHARD J.G., music educator, composer; b. Syracuse, N.J. s. Donald D. and Ethel Mae Brooks. BS in Music Edn., SUNY, Potsdam, 1966; MS in Composition, Binghamtom U., 1971; PhD in Composition, NYU, 1981. Prof., chair music dept. Nassau C.C., Garden City, NY, 1975—2004. Co-author: Layer Dictation, 1979; composer: over 70 original works. Composer fellow, Nat. Endowment for the Arts, Washington, 1983. Mem.: Soc. Composers, Inc. (chair exec. com. 1977—82, exec. com. 1978—), Am. Composers Alliance (pres. 1993—2002).

BROOKS, RODNEY ALLEN, information technology executive, educator; b. Australia; BSc in Pure Math., Flinders U., South Australia, 1974, MSc in Pure Math., 1977; PhD in Computer Science, Stanford U., 1981. Founder Lucid, 1984, Artificial Creatures (now a subsidiary of iRobot), 1991—; rsch. scientist Carnegie Mellon U., 1983, Artificial Intelligence Lab, MIT, 1983; co-founder ISRobotics (now iRobot Corp.), Burlington, Mass., 1990—; prin. arch., chief tech. officer iRobot Corp., Burlington, Mass.; joined computer sci. faculty MIT, 1984, Fujisu prof. computer sci. and engrng., elec. engrng. and computer sci. dept.; dir. MIT Computer Sci. and Artificial Intelligence Lab. (MIT CSAIL). Cray lectr. U. Minn.; Mellon lectr. Dartmouth Coll.; Hyland lectr. Hughes; Forsythe lectr. Stanford U.; vis. lectr. Cornell U., Free U. of Brussels, NEC Rsch. Lab., Princeton, NJ, Electro Tech. Lab., Tsukuba, Japan; bd. dir. Intelligent Inspection Corp. Frequently profiled and quoted in articles and news stories for Good Morning America, Scientific American, Discover, Learning Channel shows, and Nightline for expertise in Artificial Intelligence; contbr. articles in profl. jours.; co-founding editor International Journal of Computer Vision, mem. editl. bds. for Adaptive Behavior, Artificial Life, Applied Artificial Intelligence, Autonomous Robots and New Generation Computing, appeared in "Fast, Cheap and Out of Control", 1996; co-editor (with Pattie Maes): Artificial Life IV: Proceedings of the Fourth International Workshop on the Synthesis and Simulation of Living Systems, 1994; co-editor: (with Luc Steels) The Artificial Life Route to Artificial Intelligence: Building Embodied Situated Agents, 1995; author: Model-Based Computer Vision, 1984, Programming in Common LISP, 1985, Cambrian Intelligence: The Early History of the New AI, 1999, Flesh and Machines: How Robots Will Change Us, 2002. Recipient Computers and Thought award, Internat. Joint Conf. on Artificial Intelligence. Fellow: AAAS; mem.: Am. Assn. for Artificial Intelligence (founding fellow), Nat. Acad. Engrng. Office: MIT CSAIL The State Ctr 32 Vasser St 32-G430 Cambridge MA 02139 also: iRobot Corp 63 South Ave Burlington MA 01803 Office Phone: 617-253-5223, 781-345-0200. Office Fax: 617-253-0039, 781-345-0201. Business E-Mail: brooks@csail.mit.edu.*

BROOKS, ROGER G., lawyer; b. Poughkeepsie, NY, Dec. 25, 1961; AB, Princeton Univ., 1984; MA, JD, Univ. Va., 1987; MDiv, Regent Coll., Vancouver, BC, 1995. Bar: NY 1989. Law clk., Hon. John D. Butzner, Jr. US Ct. Appeals, 4th Cir.; assoc. Cravath, Swaine & Moore LLP, NYC, 1988—92, 1995—99, ptnr., litig., 1999—. Articles editor Va. Law Rev. Mem.: Assn. Bar of City of NY. Office: Cravath Swaine & Moore LLP Worldwide Plz 825 Eighth Ave New York NY 10019-7475 Office Phone: 212-474-1072. Office Fax: 212-474-3700. Business E-Mail: rgbrooks@cravath.com.

BROOKS, ROGER KAY, insurance company executive; b. Clarion, Iowa, Apr. 30, 1937; s. Edgar Sherman and Hazel (Whipple) B.; m. Marcia Rae Ramsay, Nov. 19, 1955 (div. Sept. 1989); children: Michael, Jeffrey, David; m. Saulene Richer, Mar. 17, 1990. BA in Math., magna cum laude, U. Iowa, 1959. Actuarial asst. Central Life Assurance Co., Des Moines, 1959—64, asst. sec., 1964-68, v.p., 1968-70, exec. v.p., 1970-72, pres., COO, 1972—94; CEO AmerUs (merger of Central Life and American Mutual), 1994—. Mem. Des Moines Devel. Com. Named to Iowa Bus. Hall of Fame, Iowa Ins. Hall of Fame; recipient Alexis de Toqueville Soc. award, United Way, Ctrl. Iowa, 2004. Fellow Soc. Actuaries; mem. Greater Des Moines C. of C. (past chmn.), Actuaries Club of Des Moines (past pres.), Phi Beta Kappa. Presbyterian (elder). Club: Des Moines (past pres.). Office: AmerUs Group PO Box 1555 Des Moines IA 50306-1555 Office Phone: 515-362-3660. Business E-Mail: roger.brooks@amerus.com.*

BROOKS, ROGER LEON, retired academic administrator; b. El Dorado, Ark., Apr. 14, 1927; s. Roger Spurgeon and Lumae (Jackson) B.; m. Martha Edwina Withers, Aug. 25, 1950; children:Leslie, Roger, Geoffrey, Stephen, Douglas. BA, Baylor U., 1949; MA, U. Ill., 1950; PhD, U. Colo., 1959. Instr. English U. Colo., 1955-57, 58-60; prof. Tex. Tech U., Lubbock, 1960-64, assoc. dean Grad. Sch., 1964-67; dean Coll. Arts and Scis., East Tex. State U., Commerce, 1967-72; pres. Howard Payne U., Brownwood, Tex., 1972-79; v.p. adminstrv. affairs Houston Bapt. U., 1979-87; dir. Armstrong Browning Libr., Baylor U., 1987-96. Cons. Victorian Studies, 1967, Choice, 1970, Can. Coun., 1971. Editor: Studies in Browning and His Circle, 1987-96, Robert Browning and Victorian Culture, 1992, Elizabeth Barrett Browning and Victorian Culture, 1994; contbr. articles to profl. jours. Pres. bd. advs. Baylor U., 2000-02, libr. fellow, 2002—. With USNR, 1945-51; lt. col. USMC, 1972-87, ret. Rsch. grantee U. Colo. at Oxford and Brit. Mus., 1957-58, Tex. Tech. U. at Bibliotheque Nationale, Paris, 1964, Am. Philos Soc. at N.Y. Public Libr., 1963, Brit. Mus., 1980, the Suratt-Lewis Libr. award, 1997. Mem. London Browning Soc., Grolier Club (N.Y.C.), Westlake Club (Houston). Office: Baylor U Armstrong Browning Lib Waco TX 76798

BROOKS, SCOTT J., rehabilitation services professional, writer; b. Sheboygan, Wis., 1955; BS in Psychology and Philosophy, U. Wis., Oshkosh, Wis., 1979; MA in Cmty. Human Svcs., U. Wis., Green Bay, Wis., 1983; MA in Ednl. Policy Studies, U. Wis., Madison, Wis., 1985. Lic. profl. counselor Wis. Academic adv. U. Wis., Madison, 1986—91; coord. academic advising We. Wyo. C.C., Rock Springs, Wyo., 1991—92; counselor Divsn. Vocat. Rehab., Oshkosh, Wis., 1994—. Author: The Taste of Pitch, 2005. Avocations: writing, painting. Home: 2912 Heise Rd Omro WI 54963-9495 Office: Divsn Vocational Rehabilitation 315 Alg Oshkosh WI 54963

BROOKS, SHELLY ANN, minister, osteopath; b. Ft. Worth, May 24, 1962; d. Donald Lee and Florine Estelle B. BS, Tex. Wesleyan U., 1984; DO, U. North Tex., 1988; MDiv, So. Meth. U., 1994. Diplomate Tex. Bd. Med. Examiners; ordained elder Meth Ch. Family practice intern Family Practice Ctr., Waco, Tex., 1988-89; family practice physician MediCenter, 1989-92; assoc. pastor Ctrl. United Meth. Ch., 1992-94; pastor 1st United Meth. Ch., Ranger, 1994—97, Alvarado, 1997—. Bd. dirs. Ctrl. Tex. Sr. Adult Ministries, Waco, 1994. Recipient McFadden scholarship, 1980-84, Am. Osteo. Assn. scholarship, 1984-85, Nicholson scholarship, 1989-94. Mem. Ctrl. Tex. Conf. United Meth. Ch., Tex. Osteo. Med. Assn., Tex. Med. Found. Avocations: walking, bicycling, horseback riding. Office: 1st United Meth Ch PO Box 364 Alvarado TX 76009 Home: PO Box 2226 Brownwood TX 76804-2226

BROOKS, SUSAN W., prosecutor; Grad., Miami U.; JD, Ind. U., 1985. Ptnr. McClure, McClure & Kammen, 1985—97; dep. mayor City of Indpls., 1998—99; of counsel Ice Miller Law Firm, Indpls., 2000—01; U.S. atty. (so. dist.) Ind. US Dept. Justice, 2001—. Office: 10 W Market St Ste 2100 Indianapolis IN 46204 Office Phone: 317-226-6333.

BROOKS, TERRY, writer, former lawyer; b. Sterling, Ill., Jan. 8, 1944; s. Dean Oliver and Marjorie Iantha (Gleason) B.; m. Barbara Ann Groth, Apr. 23, 1972; children: Amanda Leigh, Alexander Stephen. AB, Hamilton Coll., 1966; LL.B., Washington and Lee U., 1969. Mem. firm Besse, Frye, Arnold, Brooks & Miller Sterling, 1969. Author: The Sword of Shannara, 1977, The Sword of Shannara: Panamon Creel and Keltset (rec.), 1978, The Elfstones of Shannara, 1982, The Wishsong of Shannara, 1985, Magic Kingdom for Sale/Sold, 1986, The Tangle Box: A Magic Kingdom of Landover Novel, 1994, Antrax: The Voyage of the Jerle Shannara, 2001, Morgawr: The Voyage of the Jerle Shannara, 2002, High Druid of Shannara: Jarka Ruus, 2003, High Druid of Shannara: Tanequil, 2004 (Publishers Weekly Bestseller). Mem. Am., Ill., Whiteside County bar assns., Office: 2850 SW Yancy St PO Box 229 Seattle WA 98126*

BROOKS, TIMOTHY H., broadcast executive; b. Exeter, N.H., Apr. 18, 1942; s. John W. R. and Olive P. (Bradbury) B. BA, Dartmouth Coll., 1964; MS, Syracuse U., 1969. Promotion asst. Sta. WTEN-TV, Albany, N.Y., 1966-68; sales promotion supr. Sta. WCBS-TV, N.Y.C., 1969-70; sr. rsch. analyst NBC Owned Stas. Div., N.Y.C., 1970-72; mgr. ratings rsch. NBC-TV Network, N.Y.C., 1972-76, dir. TV network rsch., 1978-82, dir. program rsch., 1982-88; asst. dir. rsch. and mktg. TV Advt. Reps., Inc., N.Y.C., 1976-77; sr. v.p., media rsch. dir. N.W. Ayer Inc., N.Y.C., 1989-90; v.p. rsch. USA Networks, N.Y.C., 1991-94, sr. v.p. rsch., 1994-99, Lifetime TV., N.Y.C., 2000—03, exec. v.p. rsch., 2003—. Adj. prof. communications L.I. Univ., Greenvale, N.Y., 1979-88. Author: The Complete Directory to Prime Time TV Stars, 1987, Lost Sounds: Blacks and the Birth of the Recording Industry, 1890-1919, 2004; co-author: The Complete Directory to Prime Time Network and Cable TV Shows, 1946-present, 1979 (Am. Book award 1980, Broadcast Preceptor award San Francisco State U. 1981), TV's Greatest Hits, 1985, TV in the '60s, 1985, The Columbia Master Book Discography, 1999 (Assoc. Recorded Sound Collections award for Excellence, 2000); also numerous articles on history of TV and recording industry. Capt. U.S. Army, 1964-66, Vietnam, USAR, 1966-74. Recipient Jack Hill award for excellence and integrity in media rsch., CableTV Advt. Bur., 1995. Mem. Assn. for Recorded Sound Collections (bd. dirs. 1979-97, pres. 1982-84, contbg. editor jour. 1986—, compiler Current Bibliography 1979—, founder ARSC awards for excellence in pub. rsch. on recs., chmn. awards com. 1989-97, Lifetime Achievement award 2004), Media Rating Coun. (exec. com., chmn. cable comm. 1993-96, chmn. 1997-99), Advt. Rsch. Found. (bd. dirs. 1995-2000, chmn. video electronic media coun. 1995—, chmn. 1998-99), Radio-TV Rsch. Coun., Cable and Telecomms. Assn. for Mktg. (chmn. rsch. com. 2003-), Cabletelevision Advt. Bur. (mem. rsch. com. 1991—), Record Rsch. Assocs., City of London Phonograph and Gramophone Soc., TV Assn. Progammers L.Am. (founding mem.). Avocations: hiking, camping. Office: Lifetime TV Worldwide Plaza 309 W 49th St New York NY 10019-7316 Business E-Mail: brooks@lifetimetv.com.

BROOKS, VALERIE CLARE, special education educator; b. Shawano, Wis., Mar. 18, 1978; d. Edwin Francis Christensen and Rhonda Jean Strehlow; m. Christopher James Brooks, July 21, 2001; 1 child, Kaitlin Audrey. BS in Edn., U. Wis., 2001. Cert. spl. edn. LD 6-12, CD 6-12 tchr. Wis., 2001, D/HH K-12 tchr. Wis., 2005. Spl. edn. tchr. Shawano-Gresham Sch. Dist., Wis., 2001—. Dept. chairperson Shawano Cmty. H.S., Wis., 2004—. Home: PO Box 698 113 E Park St Bonduel WI 54107 Office: Shawano Cmty HS 220 Cty B Shawano WI 54166 Office Phone: 715-526-2175. Personal E-mail: valchris@athenet.net.

BROOKS, VELMA, entrepreneur, small business owner; Grad., Madam C.J. Walker Beauty Coll., Dallas, 1968; student, Bethune Cookeman Coll., Daytona Beach, Fla., Prairie View A&M U., Tex.; AA, El Centro C.C., Dallas, 1970; student, Internat. Aviation Travel Acad., Arlington, Tex., Loreal Sch. of Color, Paris, 1976. Cosmetology instr., ednl. dir. Madam C.J. Walker Beauty Coll., Dallas, 1974; salon owner, mgr. Velma B's Coiffures, Dallas; operator Neighborhood Beauty Salon, Dallas; tchr., technician Mme C.J. Walker Products Mfg. Co., Chgo.; artistic ednl. dir. Simpson's Labs., Houston; mktg. and sales dir. Diamite Direct Sales Corp., Santa Barbara, Calif.; outside sales rep. Mayo Travel Svcs., Dallas, Oak Cliff Travel Agy., Dallas. Named Legends in Bus., Ban of Am., 1997, Bus. Woman Against the Odds, Smithsonian Inst., Bus. Woman of the Yr., Theta Nu Sigma; recipient 1st place Rose D'or Championship, The Golden Rose Paris Festival, Vienna, Austria, 1974, Bus. Woman of the Yr., South Dallas Bus. and Profl. Women's Club, Pylon nat. Businessman's League, Psi Lambda, Trail Blazer award, Venture Advisors, Inc./Tex. State Assn. Beauty Culturist League, Outstanding Ednl. Contbn. award, Internat. Beauty Show Group/Advanstar Prodns., award for dedicated mentor and svc., Dallas Ind. Sch. Dist., 25 Yrs. Svc. in Indsl. Career Tech., Tex. Cosmetology Assn./Nat. Cosmetology Assn., Legacy award, Urban League Greater Dallas, 2004.

BROOKS, WALTER S., dermatologist; b. Cleve., July 16, 1956; s. John R. and Christel W. (Plogsties) B.; m. Debra A. Hart, Aug. 29, 1981; children: Aaron S., David J.H., Arielle N. BA magna cum laude, U. Rochester, 1978, MD, 1982. Resident in internal medicine Rochester (N.Y.) Gen. Hosp., 1982-85; resident in dermatology U. Pitts., 1985-88; clin. instr. dermatology to clin. asst. prof. dermatology U. Rochester, 1989—; dermatologist pvt. practice, Rochester, 1988—. Trustee Rochester Acad. Medicine, 1996—99; vice-chair campaign Leadership Soc. Demratology Found., 1997; chair Upstate N.Y. Leadership Soc. Dermatology Found., 2002—; amb., dermatology del. People to People, China, 2000. Del. People to People Internat., 2003, Global Peace Initiative, 2003. Recipient Leadership award Dermatology Found. Soc., 1995. Fellow Am. Acad. Dermatology; mem. Nat. Bd. Med. Examiners, Buffalo-Rochester Dermatol. Assn. (pres. 1995-96), Rochester Dermatol. Soc. (pres. 1996-98). Conservative. Non-Denominational. Avocation: photography. Home: 22 Silver Fox Dr Fairport NY 14450-8666 Office: 730 Weiland Rd Rochester NY 14626-3919 Office Phone: 585-719-9600. Business E-Mail: wbrooks@rochester.rr.com.

BROOKS SHOEMAKER, VIRGINIA LEE, librarian; b. Oklahoma City, Sept. 16, 1944; d. Leo B. and Eloise Gilreath; m. Phil Ashley Brooks, Aug. 10, 1972 (dec. Oct. 1982); 1 child, Philip Brooks; m. Gene Darrel Shoemaker, Feb. 16, 1986; children: Rob Shoemaker, Julie Shoemaker, Donna Shoemaker, Gary Shoemaker. Student, Oklahoma City C.C., 1980; BS, U. Ctrl. Okla., 1988, M in Sch. Media, 1991, postgrad., 2000—; attended, Okla. State U. With Dept. Human Svcs., Oklahoma City, 1970-75, State Dept. Librs., Oklahoma City, 1980-87; substitute tchr. Oklahoma City Schs., 1989-91, 1995; vol. libr. Children's Libr., Children's Hosp., Oklahoma City, 1992—; libr. vol. Corpus Christi Sch. Libr., 1998—; vol. children's sect. First Bapt. Libr.; vol. Libr. for Blind. Sponsor World Vision, Seattle, 1994—; active cub scouts Boy Scouts Am.; vol. Habitat for Humanity, Vista Care Hospice; project transformation First Bapt. Good Shepherd Children's Dental Clinic; vol. Vista Care Hospice, 2002—; project transformation Wesley Meth.; active, life mem. Meth. Ch. of the Servant; women mission groups Wesley Meth., First Bapt. Ch.; vol. children's sect. First Bapt. Libr.; reading sch. libr. tutor First Bapt. Good Shepherd Children's Dental Clinic. Recipient Adopt-a-Park award, Oklahoma City Beautiful award, 1985—88, Omniplex Sci. Mus., Oklahoma City, 1986—89. Mem.: Omniplex Sci. Mus. (Adpot-a-Park award 1986—89), Internat. Reading Assn. (reading tutor city schs.), Coun. Exceptional Children, Zool. Soc., Classen Alumni Assn., U. Ctrl. Okla. Alumni Assn. Baptist. Avocations: piano, reading, creative writing, dogs and cats, making greeting cards. Personal E-mail: doggytown14@webtv.net.

BROOKS-TURNER, MYRA, music educator; b. Knoxville, Tenn., Jan. 13, 1933; d. Paul David and Lilli Ray Brooks; m. Ronald J. Turner, June 11, 1960; children: Stacy Turner Steele, Cheryl Turner Walker, Teresa Turner Basler. Student of piano, voice and composition, Juilliard Sch. Music, 1945—51; BMus in Piano, So. Meth. U., 1955, MusM in Theory and Composition, 1956, postgrad. in Piano, 1957—58. Educator Dallas Indep. Schs., Tex., 1956—60; choral music specialist Knoxville City Schs., Tenn., 1960—65; composer-in-residence Birmingham Children's Theatre, Ala., 1965—68; music instr. Mercer U. Music Prep. Sch., Atlanta, 1975—77; instr. composition Maryville Coll. Prep. Sch. of the Arts, Tenn., 1978—80; music instr. U. Tenn., Knoxville, 1990—92; owner Myra Brooks Turner Studio of Music, Knoxville, Tenn., 1992—. Freelance writer, pub. MBT Prodns., Knoxville, 1993—; French instr. Ossoli Cir., 2004—. Composer, prodr.: (musicals) Make Way for Love, 1955; Uh-Uh, 1956; Javaho Junction, 1958; composer, dir. The Green Dragon, 1965—68 (Seattle Nat. Playwriting First Place award); 450 music pieces, 1993—2004; contbr. articles to profl. jours. Music worship leader Epis. Ch. of Ascension, Knoxville, Tenn., 1992—93. Recipient Cultural Arts award, Tenn. Arts Commn., 1982. Mem.: Tenn. Fed. Music Clubs (state jr. counselor 1978—88, officer, state bd. 1978—89, Ea. Tenn. divisional v.p. 2002—, officer, state bd. 2002—, East Tenn. divsn. jr. counselor 2002—, editor State Piano Competition Book 2003, 2004—06), Nat. Fed. Music Clubs (jr. festivals bulletin advisor 1982—90), Knoxville Music Tchrs. Assn. (sec., bd. mem. 2000—01, Composer of Yr. 1978, 2001), Tenn. Music Tchrs. Assn. (state jr. counselor 2005—), Nat. Music Tchrs. Assn., Ossoli Circle, Knoxville Writer's Group, Tuesday Morning Musical Club (pres. 1990—91), U. Tenn. Faculty Women's Club, Pi Kappa Lambda Nat. Music Honorary, Mu Phi Epsilon Internat. Frat. (pres. 1973—74, pres. Atlanta Alumnae, Music Therapy award 1974), Alpha Delta Pi. Republican. Episcopalian. Avocations: study of French, study of Italian, photography, interior decorating. Business E-Mail: MyraBrooksTurner@aol.com.

BROOMAN, DAVID J., lawyer; b. Hackensack, N.J., Dec. 25, 1956; s. Bankston T. and Hildegard Brooman; m. Gardenia L. Brooman, July 26, 1958; children: David J., Richard W., Kyle M., Luke A. BA, Rutgers U., 1979; JD, Villanova U., 1982. Bar: Pa., 1982, NJ, 1983, U.S. Dist. Ct. (ea. and mid. dists.) Pa., N.J., U.S. Dist. Ct. N.J., U.S. Ct. Appeals (3d cir.). Ptnr. Cohen Shapiro Polisher Shiekman & Cohen, Phila., 1988-95; ptnr., environ. law group Drinker Biddle & Reath, Phila., 1995—, now mng. ptnr, mem. mgmt. com. Bd. dirs. Delaware Valley Child Care Coun., Phila., 1986-94; v.p., bd. dirs. Pa. Resources Coun., Media, 1990-98. Named Outstanding Child Adv., Support Ctr. Child Advs., Phila., 1995. Mem.: ABA, Phila. Bar Assn., Pa. Bar Assn. Office: Drinker Biddle & Reath One Logan Sq 18th & Cherry Sts Philadelphia PA 19103-6996 Office Phone: 215-993-2210. Office Fax: 215-993-8585. Business E-Mail: david.brooman@dbr.com.

BROOME, BURTON EDWARD, retired insurance company executive; b. NYC, July 10, 1935; s. Burton Edward and Ann Loretta (Wall) B.; m. Anne Curtis, June 21, 1974; 1 child, Chelsea Anne. BSc, Fordham U., 1963; MBA, U. Calif., Berkeley, 1964. Ins. examiner Crum & Forster, N.Y.C., 1956-60; audit mgr. Price Waterhouse, N.Y.C., 1960-74; v.p., contr. Transamerica Corp., San Francisco, 1974-99; mem. oper. com. ARC Reins. Corp., Honolulu, 1993-99; ret., 1999. Mem. profl. acctg. program U. Calif., Berkeley, 1982-99; bd. dirs. Transamerica HomeFirst Corp., San Francisco, 1994-98, River Thames Ins. Co., London, 1994-98. Chmn. adv. coun. SEC and Fin. Reporting Inst., U. So. Calif., L.A., 1982-99. With U.S. Army, 1954-55. Mem. Fin. Exec. Inst.

BROOME, CLAIRE VERONICA, epidemiologist, researcher; b. Tunbridge Wells, Kent, England, Aug. 24, 1949; came to U.S., 1951; d. Kenneth R. and Heather C. (Platt) B.; m. John F. Head, Apr. 2, 1988; children: Gabriel K., Steven G. BA, Harvard U., 1970, MD, 1975. Diplomate Am. Bd. Internal Medicine. Dep. chief spl. pathogens br. Ctrs. for Disease Control, Atlanta, 1979-80, chief meningitis, spl. pathogens br., 1981-90, assoc. dir. sci., 1991-94, acting dir., nat. ctr. injury prevention and control, 1992-93, dep. dir., 1994-99, sr. advisor to dir. for health info. sys., 1999—. Cons. vaccine devel. AID, 1988—, WHO, NIH, various univs.; mem. steering com. on encapsulated bacterial vaccines, WHO, Geneva, 1989-91, chmn., 1992-96; mem. adv. com. on vaccines FDA, Washington, 1990-94; mem. sci. adv. group experts global program on vaccines and immunizations World Health Orgn., 1996—. Contbr. numerous articles to profl. jours. Recipient M. C. Rockefeller fellowship, 1970-71, Meritorious Svc. medal USPHS, 1986, Disting. Svc. medal USPHS, 1996, 2000, John Snow award Am. Pub. Health Assn., 2000; rsch. grants NIH, FDA, Dept. of State. Fellow Infectious Diseases Soc. Am. (Bristol-Myers Squibb award 1993); mem. ACP, Inst. of Medicine, Am. Epidemiologic Soc., Am. Soc. Microbiology, Common Cause, Phi Beta Kappa, Alpha Omega Alpha. Avocation: tennis. Office: Ctrs for Disease Control # D68 Atlanta GA 30333

BROOME, DAVID A.J., instrument company executive; b. Leicester, England, Feb. 21, 1932; arrived in U.S., 1957; s. Albert Leonard and Mabel Isabel Broome; m. Caroline Margaret Mason, Oct. 27, 1956; children: Richard, Deborah, Mark, Christopher. Apprentice J.W. Walker, London, 1948—55, reed voicer, 1955—57, Austin Organs Inc., Hartford, Conn., 1957—78, v.p., tonal dir., 1978—98; ptnr. Broome & Co LLC, Windsor Locks, Conn., 1999—. Cons. and lectr. in field. Mem.: Organ Hist. Soc., Am. Guild Organists, Am. Inst. Organ Builders. Avocations: gardening, chess, hiking, bridge. Office: Broome & Co LLC 12 Copper Dr Windsor Locks CT 06096

BROOME, KATHRYN, secondary school educator; b. Natchez, Miss., Dec. 7, 1950; d. Jackson Daniel and Edna Louise (Barrett) B.; m. John Bridges, Dec. 23, 1997. BS, Miss. State Coll. for Women, 1973; M English Edn., Miss. Coll., 1995. Tchr. Columbia (Miss.) Pub. Schs., 1973-74, Larmar County Schs., Hattiesburg, Miss., 1974-77, Monroe County Schs., Hamilton, Miss., 1977-84, Jackson (Miss.) Pub. Schs., 1984—. Real estate agt. Century 21 Eddie Rosamond Realty, Jackson, 1997-98, Re/Max Properties, Jackson, 1998—; student coun. sponsor Powell Middle Sch., Jackson, Miss., 1991—, team leader 8th grade 1991-92; varsity cheerleader sponsor Hamilton H.S., 1979-80, 95. Mem. Jackson pub. schs. supts. orgn. for student coun. Jackson Pub. Schs., 1991-93; rep. Parent/Tchr. Student Assn., Jackson, 1997; supporter United Way. Grantee IBM, 1996, Jackson Pub. Schs., 1997, Entergy, 1997, Tchr. Talk, 1997, Bell South, 1997, Jr. League, 1997. Mem. Miss. Fedn. Tchrs., Jackson Fedn. Tchrs., Jackson Assn. of Realtors, Jr. Beta Club, Sigma Tau Delta. Republican. Baptist. Avocations: people, animals, swimming, painting, cooking. Office: Jackson Public Schs 662 S President St Jackson MS 39201-5601 Home: 2411 Knox St Gulfport MS 39503-3618

BROOME, MARION, dean; BSN, Med. Coll. Georgia, 1973; MN in Family Health Nursing, U. S.C., 1977; PhD in Child and Family Devel., U. Georgia, 1984; post-doctoral studies, U. Ala., 1986—88. Nursing sci. study section NIH, 1997—2001; assoc. dean, prof. rsch. U. Ala., 1999—2004; cons. Ind. U. Sch. Nursing, 2004—, dean, 2004—. Pres. Soc. Pediatric Nurses; bd. dirs. Assn. Care of Children's Health, Midwest Nursing Rsch. Soc. Office: Ind U Sch Nursing Office Ednl Svcs 1111 Middle Dr NU 117 Indianapolis IN 46202-5107

BROOME, OSCAR WHITFIELD, JR., finance educator; b. Monroe, NC, Feb. 3, 1940; s. Oscar Whitfield and Irma (Hinson) B.; m. Julia Carol Renegar, June 14, 1964; children: Christine Irma, Michael Whitfield. AB, Duke U., 1962; MS, U. Ill., 1964, PhD, 1971. Prof. acctg. U. Va., Charlottesville, 1967-91, prof. law, 1998—, Frank S. Kaulback Jr. prof. commerce, 1991—, assoc. dean, 1992-98, interim dean, 1997, dir. grad. studies, 1986-92, dir. Ernst & Young master's program, 1998—2001; exec. dir. Inst. Chartered Fin. Analysts, Charlottesville, 1978-84. Faculty fellow Price Waterhouse & Co., N.Y.C., 1964; vis. prof. U. Tex., Austin, 1975, Duke U., Durham, N.C., 1977-78, Tulane U., New Orleans, 2002; vis. rsch. scholar, Lancaster (Eng.) U., 1994; adminstr. exams. Inst. CFAs, 1973-77; bd. regents Coll. Fin. Planning, 1984-89, chmn., 1987-89; mem. CPA Exam. Rev. Bd., 1984-87, chmn., 1986-87; mem. exams. com. Nat. Assn. State Bds. Accountancy, 1995-2000, 04—; bd. dirs. Internat. Bd. Stds. and Practices for CFPs, 1989-91; mem. vis. adv. com. DePaul U. Sch. Accountancy, 1991-97; mem. Va. Bd. Accountancy, 2003—. Named Outstanding Educator Va. Soc. C.P.A.'s, 1979; recipient Outstanding Faculty award Z Soc., 1988. Mem. AICPA (bd. examiners 1977-82), Assn. for Investment Mgmt. and Rsch. (investment analysis stds. bd. 1984-86), Nat. Assn. Accts. (pres. chpt. 1974), Phi Beta Kappa, Phi Kappa Phi, Beta Gamma Sigma, Beta Alpha Psi, Omicron Delta Kappa.

BROOMFIELD, ROBERT CAMERON, federal judge; b. Detroit, June 18, 1933; s. David Campbell and Mabel Margaret (Van Deventer) B.; m. Cuma Lorena Cecil, Aug. 3, 1958; children: Robert Cameron Jr., Alyson Paige, Scott McKinley. BS, Pa. State U., 1955; LLB, U. Ariz., 1961. Bar: Ariz. 1961, U.S. Dist. Ct. Ariz. 1961. Assoc. Carson, Messinger, Elliot, Laughlin & Ragan, Phoenix, 1962-65, ptnr., 1966-71; judge Ariz. Superior Ct., Phoenix, 1971-85, presiding judge, 1974-85; judge U.S. Dist. Ct. Ariz., Phoenix, 1985—, chief judge, 1994-99; judge Fgn. Intelligence Surveillance Ct., 2002—. Faculty Nat. Jud. Coll., Reno, 1975-82. Contbr. articles to profl. jours. Adv. bd. Boy Scouts Am., Phoenix, 1968-75; tng. com. Ariz. Acad., Phoenix, 1980—; pres. Paradise Valley Sch. Bd., Phoenix, 1969-70; bd. dirs. Phoenix Together, 1982—, Crisis Nursery, Phoenix, 1976-81; chmn. 9th Cir. Task Force on Ct. Reporting, 1988—; space and facilities com. U.S. Jud. Conf., 1987-93, chmn., 1989-93, chmn. security, space and facilities com., 1993-95, budget com., 1997—, chmn. economy subcom., 2003—; founding mem. Sandra Day O'Connor Inn of Ct., 1988-94. Recipient Faculty award Nat. Jud. Coll., 1979, Disting. Jurist award Miss. State U., 1986. Mem. ABA (chmn. Nat. Conf. State Trial Judges 1983-84, pres. Nat. Conf. Met. Cts. 1978-79, chmn. bd. dirs. 1980-82, Justice Tom Clark award 1980, bd. dirs. Nat. Ctr. for State Cts. 1980-85, Disting. Svc. award 1986), Ariz. Bar Assn., Maricopa County Bar Assn. (Disting. Pub. Svc. award 1980), Ariz. Judges Assn. (pres. 1981-82), Am. Judicature Soc. (spl. citation 1985), Maricopa County Med. Soc. (Disting. Svc. medal 1979), Rotary. Office: US Dist Ct Sandra Day O'Connor Cthse 401 West Washington St #626 SPC 61 Phoenix AZ 85003-2158 Office Phone: 602-322-7540. Business E-Mail: robert_broomfield@azd.uscourts.gov.

BROOTEN, DOROTHY, nursing educator, former dean; b. Hazleton, Pa. married; two children. BSN, U. Pa., 1966, MSN, 1970, PhD in Ednl. Adminstrn., 1980. Assoc. prof. nursing Thomas Jefferson U., 1972-77; from asst. to assoc. prof. nursing U. Pa., 1977-88, prof. nursing, chair Health Care of Women & Childbearing, 1980-93, dir. Ctr. for Low Birthweight, Sch. Nursing, 1990-96, Overseers prof. perinatal nursing, 1990-96; dean, prof. Frances Payne Bolton Sch. Nursing Case Western Res. U., Cleve., 1998—2000; prof. Florida International Univ., 2001—, assoc. dir. graduate program, School of Nursing, 2003—. Cons. Sch. Medicine, U. Utrecht, The Netherlands, 1989, Ministry of Health, Malawi, Africa, 1991. Recipient Contbrn. to Nursing Sci. award ANA, 1988. Mem. Inst. Medicine-NAS, Am. Acad. Nursing (mem. gov. coun. 1988-91). Achievements include research on low birthweight prevention, postdischarge care of low birthweight infants, health care delivery. Office: Fl Internat U Rm ACII230 11200 SW 8th St Miami FL 33199

BROOTEN, KENNETH EDWARD, JR., lawyer, writer; b. Kirkland, Wash., Oct. 17, 1942; s. Kenneth Edward Sr. and Sadie Josephine (Assad) B.; m. Patricia Anne Folsom, Aug. 29, 1965 (div. Apr. 1986); children: Michelle Catherine, Justin Kenneth; m. Judy Diane Robinette, July 14, 2001. Diploma, Lewis Sch. Hotel, Restaurant and Club Mgmt., Washington, 1963; student, U. Md., 1964-66; AA with honors, Santa Fe C.C., Gainesville, Fla., 1969; BS in Journalism with highest honors, U. Fla., 1971, MA in Journalism and Communications with highest honors, 1972, JD with honors, 1975; law student, U. Idaho, 1972-73; diploma in internat. law, Polish Acad. Scis., Warsaw, 1974; postgrad. in Internat. Law, Trinity Coll.,Cambridge (Eng.) U., 1974. Bar: Fla., D.C., U.S. Dist. Ct. (no., mid. and so. dists.) Fla., U.S. Dist. Ct. D.C., U.S. Tax Ct., U.S. Ct. Appeals (5th, 9th, 11th and D.C. circs.), U.S. Supreme Ct., Trial Counsel Her Majesty's Govt. of United Kingdom in U.S. Asst. to several congressmen U.S. Ho. of Reps., Washington, 1962-67; adminstrv. asst. VA Cen. Office, Washington, 1967; adminstrv. officer VA Hosp., Gainesville, Fla., 1967-72; ptnr. Carter & Brooten, P.A., Gainesville, Fla., 1975-78, Brooten & Fleisher, Chartered, Washington and Gainesville, Fla., 1978-80; pvt. practice, Washington and Gainesville, 1980-86, Washington, 1987-88, Washington and Orlando, Fla., 1988-91, Washington and Winter Park, Fla., 1991-98; ret., 1998. Spl. counsel, acting chief counsel, dir. Chief Counsel Select Com. Assassinations U.S. Ho. of Reps., 1976-77; counsel Her Majesty's Govt. of U.K. (in U.S.). Author: Malpractice Guide to Avoidance and Treatment, 1987; episode writer TV series Simon and Simon; nat. columnist Pvt. Practice, 1988-90, Physicians Mgmt., 1991-93; commentator Med. News Network, 1993-94; contbr. more than 250 articles to profl. jours.; composer. Served with USCGR, 1960-68. Named one of Outstanding Young Men Am., U.S. Jaycees, 1977; Paul Harris fellow, 2002. Mem. Fla. Bar Assn., D.C. Bar Assn., Assn. Former Intelligence Officers, Sigma Delta Chi. Episcopalian. Avocations: writing, marksmanship, dangerous game hunting. Address: The Oxbow Ranch Bascom FL 32423-9361 Office Phone: 850-569-5881. Personal E-mail: kbrooten@aol.com.

BROPHY, DENNIS RICHARD, psychology and philosophy educator, administrator, clergyman; b. Milw., Aug. 6, 1945; s. Floyd Herbert and Phyllis Marie (Ingram) B. BA, Washington U., 1967, MA, 1968; MDiv, Pacific Sch. Religion, 1971; PhD in Indsl. & Orgnl. Psychology, Tex. A&M U., 1995. Cert. coll. tchr., Calif. Ednl. rschr. IBM Corp., White Plains, NY, 1968—71; edn. minister Cmty. Congl. Ch., Port Huron, Mich., 1971—72, Bethlehem United Ch. Christ, Ann Arbor, Mich., 1972—73, Cmty. Congl. Ch., Chula Vista, Calif., 1974; philosophy instr. Southwestern Coll., Chula Vista, 1975; assoc. prof. psychology & philosophy Northwest Coll., Powell, Wyo., 1975—96, prof., 1996—, assessment testing coord., 1999—. Chmn. social sci. divsn., 1992-95; religious edn. cons. Mont.-No. Wyo. Conf. United Ch. of Christ. Mem. APA (Daniel Berlyne award 1996), Wyo. Coun. Humanities, Soc. Indsl. Orgnl. Psychology, Soc. Tchg. of Psychology, Yellowstone Assn. United Ch. Christ, Phi Beta Kappa, Phi Kappa Phi, Sigma Xi, Omicron Delta Kappa, Theta Xi, Golden Key Nat. Honor Soc. Faculty Outstanding Svc. award, 2003. Home: 533 Avenue C Powell WY 82435-2401 Office: Northwest Coll 231 W 6th St Powell WY 82435-1898 Office Phone: 307-754-6133. E-mail: dennis.brophy@northwestcollege.edu.

BROPHY, JAMES DAVID, JR., humanities educator; b. Mt. Vernon, N.Y., Oct. 5, 1926; s. James David and Mildred (Stall) B.; m. Elizabeth Bergen, Mar. 26, 1951; children: Sheila, David, Katharine, Elizabeth, James Mark. Student, MIT, 1944-45; BA, Amherst Coll., 1949; MA, Columbia U., 1950, PhD, 1965; postgrad., U. Dijon, 1950-51. Instr. English Iona Coll., New Rochelle, N.Y., 1951-58, asst. prof., 1958-64, asso. prof., 1964-68, prof., 1968—, chmn. dept., 1968-71, 80-82, emeritus prof., 1992—. Author: Edith Sitwell, 1968, W.H. Auden, 1970; Editor: The Achievement of Galileo, 1962, Modern Irish Literature, 1972, Contemporary Irish Writing, 1983, New Irish Writing, 1988. Served with USNR, 1945-46. Fulbright fellow France, 1950-51; N.Y. State scholar in internat. studies, 1965; recipient Pro Operis medal Iona Coll., 1971, Bene Merenti award, 1981, Pro Multis Annis award, 1991; Nat. Endowment for Humanities grantee, 1973; Wilton Park asso., 1979 Mem. Milton Soc. Am., English Inst., Columbia Club N.Y. Home: 39 Oceanview Dr Southampton NY 11968-4215 E-mail: j-ebrophy@worldnet.att.net.

BROPHY, JERE EDWARD, education educator, researcher; b. Chgo., June 11, 1940; m. Arlene Sept. 21, 1963; children: Cheryl, Joseph. BS in Psychology, Loyola U., Chgo., 1962; MA in Human Devel., U. Chgo., 1965, PhD in Human Devel., 1967; Doctorate (hon.), U. Liege, 2004. Rsch. assoc., asst. prof. U. Chgo., 1967-68; from asst. to assoc. prof. U. Tex., Austin, 1968-76; staff devel. coord. S.W. Ednl. Devel. Lab., Austin, 1970-72; prof. Mich. State U., East Lansing, 1976-92, co-dir. Inst. for Rsch. on Tchg., 1981-93, univ. disting. prof., 1993—. Co-author: Teacher-Student Relationships: Causes and Consequences, 1974; editor (book series) Advances in Research on Teaching, 1989—. Fellow Ctr. for Advanced Study in the Behavioral Scis., 1994. Fellow: APA, Internat. Acad. Edn., Am. Psychol. Soc.; mem.: Nat. Soc. for the Study of Edn., Nat. Coun. for the Social Studies, Nat. Acad. Edn., Am. Ednl. Rsch. Assn. (Palmer O. Johnson award 1983, Presdl. citation 1995). Office: Mich State U 213B Erickson Hall East Lansing MI 48824-1034

BROPHY, JERE HALL, manufacturing executive; b. Schenectady, Mar. 11, 1934; s. Gerald Robert and Helen Dorothy (Hall) B.; m. Joyce Elaine Wright, Aug. 18, 1956; children: Jennifer, Carolyn, Jere. BS in Chem. Engring, BS in Metall. Engring, U. Mich., 1956, MS, 1957, PhD, 1958. Asst. prof. Mass. Inst. Tech., 1958-63; sect. supr. nickel alloys sect. Paul D. Merica Research Lab., Inco, Inc., Suffern, N.Y., 1963-67, research mgr. non-ferrous devel., 1967-72, asst. mgr., 1972-73, mgr., 1973-77; dir. research and devel. and dir. Paul D. Merica Research Lab., Inco, Inc. (Inco Research and Devel. Center), 1978-80; dir. advanced tech. initiation INCO Ltd., N.Y.C., 1980-82; v.p., dir. Materials and Mfg. Tech. Ctr. TRW Inc., Cleve., 1982-86, v.p. mfg. and materials devel. automotive sect., 1986-88; v.p. technology Brush Wellman Inc., Cleve., 1988-96; cons., 1996—. Author: (with J. Wolff) Thermodynamics of Structure; Contbr. (with J. Wolff) tech. articles to profl. jours. Fellow Am. Soc.

Metals, AAAS; mem. Am. Inst. Mining and Metall. Engrs. (dir. IMD div. 1973-76), Am. Mgmt. Assn. (research and devel. council 1975-87). Clubs: Edgewater Yacht. Episcopalian. Home and Office: 31905 Jackson Rd Chagrin Falls OH 44022-1707

BROPHY, JEREMIAH JOSEPH, retired finance company executive, retired military officer; b. N.Y.C., Mar. 19, 1930; s. John Joseph and Mary Margaret (Moran) B.; m. Jane Guthrie, June 4, 1955; children: John, Sandy, Greg, Elizabeth, Diane, Stephen. Student, Manhattan Coll., 1947-48; BS, U.S. Mil. Acad., 1953; postgrad., Army Command and Gen. Staff Coll., 1963, Army War Coll., 1969, Monmouth Coll., 1981. Commd. 2d lt. U.S. Army, 1953; advanced through grades to brig. gen., 1976; advisor 12th Vietnamese Inf. Rgt., Vietnam, 1963-64; comdr. 1st Bn., 327th Inf. 101st Airborne Divsn., Vietnam, 1969-70; comdr. U.S. garrison Aschaffenburg, Germany; comdr. 3d Brigade, 3d Inf. divsn., 1973-75; comdr. U.S. garrison Baumholder, Germany; asst. comdr. 8th Inf. div., 1976-78; dep. comdr. Combined Arms Tng. Devels. Agy., 1978-80; dep. comdr. U.S. Army Tng. Ctr. Ft. Dix, N.J., 1980-83; stockbroker Merrill, Lynch, Pierce, Fenner & Smith, Nashville; agt. Franklin Life Ins. Co.; exec. v.p. Gen. Trust Co.; divsn. mgr. Waddell & Reed Inc., Nashville, 1983-94; cert. fin. planner BMA Fin. Svcs. Inc., Nashville, 1995—2001. Decorated D.S.M., Bronze Star valor with oak leaf cluster, Purple Heart, Legion of Merit with oak leaf cluster, Vietnamese Cross of Gallantry (3 awards), Meritorious Svc. medal, Army Commendation medal with oak leaf cluster. Mem. Assn. Grad. U.S. Mil. Acad., West Point Soc. Mid. Tenn., Mil. Officers Assn. Am. (Mid Tenn. chpt. bd. dirs., pres. 1998). Roman Catholic. Home: 6071 Bethany Blvd Nashville TN 37221-4314 E-mail: planner30@aol.com.

BROPHY, JOSEPH THOMAS, computer company executive; b. N.Y.C., Oct. 25, 1933; s. Joseph R. and Mary (Mitchell) B.; m. Carole A. Johnson, June 8, 1957; children: Thomas J., David W., Patricia J., Maureen A., Kathleen M. BS cum laude, Fordham U., 1957; grad. sr. exec. program, MIT, 1987. Paramedic St. Clares Med. Ctr., N.Y.C., 1955-57; mathematician Vitro Labs., West Orange, N.J., 1957; dir. mgmt. info. systems Prudential Ins. Co., Newark, 1957-67; v.p. Huggins & Co. (cons. actuaries and mgmt. cons.), Phila., 1967-68; v.p., chief actuary Bankers Nat. Life Ins. Co., 1968-72; pres. Travelers Ins. Co., Hartford, Conn., 1972-93; chmn. Workgroup on Elect Data Interchange, Washington, 1992-95; cons. Actuarial Scis. Assocs., Somerset, N.J., 1993—; owner, dir. Solution Point, 1996—. Bd. dirs. Engineered Bus. Sys., Travtech, Inc., Travelers TPA, Inc., Ctr. Corp. Health, U.S. Behavioral Health, Travelers Health Sys., Conservco, Accent Color Scis.; cons. in field, 1967—; enrolled actuary Employee Retirement Income Security Act (ERISA). Author: A User's Guide to Project Management. Tech. editor: Actuarial Digest. Pres. St. Patrick's Pipe Band, Inc.; bd. dirs. Cath. Family Svcs., Conn. Opera, Conn. Acad. for Edn. in Math., Sci. and Tech., Hartford Grad. Ctr.; corporator St. Francis Hosp.; chmn. adv. bd. info. scis. Grad. Bus. Sch., Fordham U., Bronx, N.Y.; advisor Actuarial Studies, Hartford U., Sch. Pub. Health, Harvard U.; trustee St. Joseph Coll., Conn. With USMCR, 1949-50, AUS, 1952-54. Recipient Disting. Info. Sci. award Data Processing Mgmt. Assn., 1986. Fellow Soc. Actuaries; mem. Am. Acad. Actuaries, Acoustical Soc. Am., Hartford Actuaries Club, N.Y. Actuaries Club, Am. Arbitration Soc. (arbitrator), Greater Hartford C. of C. (bd. dirs.), Hartford Club, Internat. Brotherhood of Magicians, Telemedicine 200, Lake Sunapee Yacht Club. Home: 154 Garnet Hill Rd PO Box 701 Sunapee NH 03782-0701 Office: Actuarial Scis Assocs 270 Davidson Ave Somerset NJ 08873-4140

BROPHY, MARY O'REILLY, environmental scientist; b. N.Y.C., Aug. 3, 1948; d. Luke Edward and Regina (Mahoney) O'Reilly; children: Robert, Sara, Lena. Student, Fordham U., 1966—68; BS, U. Mich., 1970, MS, 1972, PhD, 1979. Rsch. asst. prof. Health Sci. Ctr., Syracuse, NY, 1979-84; environ. toxicologist Syracuse Rsch. Corp., 1984-86; pres. ARLS Cons., Inc., Syracuse, 1993—; sr. indsl. hygienist N.Y. State Dept. Labor, Syracuse, 1987—2000; environ. specialist N.Y. State Dept. Transp., Binghamton, 2000—. Adj. asst. prof. SUNY Sch. Pub. Health, Albany, 1990—; adj. prof. chemistry LeMoyne Coll., 1998; dir. Am. Bd. Indsl. Hygiene, Lansing, Mich., 1995—2001; mem. Z10 com. Am. Nat. Stds. Inst., 2001—; mem. adv. bd. N.Y. State Inst. for Health and the Environment, 2001—. Author: An Ergonomics Guide to VDTs, 1994, (with others) Occupational Ergonomics, 1996; contbr.: ILO's Encyclopedia of Occupational Health and Safety, 1998, Implications of Hormesis for Industrial Hygienists, 2003, Health Risk Assessment at Brownfield Redevelopment Sites, 2003, Groundwater Effects From Highway Tire Shreds, 2004, others; contbr. articles to profl. jours. Mem. Syracuse (N.Y.) Peace Coun. Mem. Am. Indsl. Hygiene Assn., Am. Assn. Govtl. Indsl. Hygienists, Human Factors & Ergonomics Soc., N.Y. State Assn. Transp. Engrs. (Broome County Brownfields com.). Avocations: Karate, fly-fishing, dance, folk harp. Home: 7705 Farley Ln Manlius NY 13104-9571 Office Phone: 607-721-8138. Personal E-mail: Mary_Brophy@sln.suny.edu. Business E-Mail: mbrophy@dot.state.ny.us.

BROPHY, THOMAS ANDREW, lawyer; b. Phila., Apr. 24, 1952; s. Joseph Aloysius and Berenice (Trainor) B.; m. Anne Corr, Oct. 4, 1975; children: Colleen, Patricia, Jessica, Mary Elizabeth, Anne. BA in English, U. Dayton, 1974; JD, Temple U., 1981. Bar: Pa. 1982, U.S. Dist. Ct. (ea. dist.) Pa. 1982, U.S. Ct. Appeals (3d cir.) 1982. Assoc. Marshall, Dennehy, Warner, Coleman & Goggin, Phila., 1982-87, ptnr., 1987—2005, pres., CEO, 2005—. Author: How to Evaluate and Settle Personal Injury Cases, 1989; contbr. articles to law rev. Athletic coach St. Monica's Track Club, Berwyn, Pa., 1990-2004. Mem.: Montgomery Bar Assn., Product Liability Coun., Am. Bd. Trial Advocates, Phila. Bar Assn. Roman Catholic. Avocations: reading, track and field. Home: 265 Keller Rd Berwyn PA 19312-1449 Office: 1845 Walnut St Philadelphia PA 19103-4708 Office Phone: 215-575-2600. E-mail: tbrophy@mdwcg.com.

BRORBY, WADE, federal judge; b. Omaha, 1934; BS, U. Wyo., 1956, JD with honor, 1958. Bar: Wyo. County and prosecuting atty. Campbell County, Wyo., 1963—70; ptnr. Morgan Brorby Price and Arp, Gillette, Wyo., 1961—88; judge U.S. Ct. Appeals (10th cir.), Cheyenne, Wyo., 1988—2001, sr. judge, 2001—. With USAF, 1958—61. Mem.: ABA, Wyo. Bar Assn. (commr. 1968—70), Def. Lawyers Wyo., Am. Judicature Soc., Campbell County Bar Assn. Office: US Ct Appeals 10th Cir O'Mahoney Fed Bldg Rm 2018 PO Box 1028 Cheyenne WY 82003-1028 also: Byron White US Courthouse 1823 Stout St Denver CO 80257*

BROSCOE, PETER A., mortgage company executive, consultant; b. NYC, Sept. 6, 1963; s. Joseph Edward and Joan Broscoe; married, Aug. 24, 1984; children: Clark, Ashley, Prescott, McKenzie, Chase. BS in Music Bus. Adminstrn., St. Joseph's Coll., Rensselaer, Ind., 1985. Cert. direct endorsed underwriter Housing Urban Devel. Pres., CEO Mortgage Express, Inc., Greenwood, Ind., 1994—; mng. mem. Trinity Title Svcs., Greenwood, 1999—; mem. Broscoe Group Properties, Greenwood, 1999—, Express Mortgage LLC, Greenwood, 2003—. Bd. dirs. Premiere Credit of N.A., Indpls. Chmn. bd. Greenwood Christian Acad., 2002—; chmn. bd. Area Youth Ministry, Indpls., 2002—. Named one of Top 40 Most Influential People Under 40 in Ind., Indpls. Bus. Jour., 2003. Mem.: Ind. Assn. Mortgage Brokers, Nat. Assn. Mortgage Brokers. Republican. Office: Mortgage Express Inc Ste A 374 Meridian Parke Ln Greenwood IN 46142 Business E-Mail: peter@mortgageexp.com.

BROSELOW, LINDA LATT, medical office technician, aviculturist; b. Harrisburg, Pa., July 9, 1940; d. Herman and Ricci (Buch) Latt; m. Robert Joel Broselow, Nov. 26, 1966; children: Andrew M., Katherine, Jordan. BS, Pa. State U., 1962; MA, Columbia U., 1965. Vol. Peace Corps, Ankara, Turkey, 1962-64; office mgr. Robert J. Broselow, M.D., Lubbock, Tex., 1984-88, med. office technician, 1990-98. Vol. South Park Hosp., Lubbock, 1986-87, Ronald McDonald House, Lubbock, 1990-92. Mem. ASPCA, MADD, Am. Diabetes Assn., Am. Assn. Ret. Persons, Audubon Soc., Arkadashlar, Assn. of Univ. Women, League of Women Voters. Avocation: reading. Home: 4609 9th St Lubbock TX 79416-4710 Office: 4609 9th St Lubbock TX 79416 Fax: 806-795-2005. Personal E-mail: mamoollbb@sbcglobal.net.

BROSHAR, ROBERT CLARE, architect; b. Waterloo, Iowa, May 20, 1931; s. Clare McDanel and Stella Mae (Scott) B.; m. Joyce Elaine Lukes, June 27, 1953; children: Scott, Michael, Matthew, Patrick, Elizabeth. B.Arch., Iowa State U., 1954. Ptnr. Henry & Broshar, 1960-62, Thorson, Brom, Broshar, Snyder (architects), Waterloo, 1963-96. Bd. dirs., pres. Blackhawk County YMCA, 1972-75; chmn. bd. dirs. Goodwill Industries, 1995-96; mem. Gov.'s Com. Employment of Handicapped, 1975-79; bd. dirs. Central Gardens North Iowa, 2003—; vice-chmn. Rivercity Soc. for Historic Preservation., 2003. 1st lt. AUS, 1954-56. Recipient Disting. Svc. award Iowa Easter Seal Soc., 1976, Leon Chatelain award Nat. Easter Seal Soc., 1983, Iowa State U. Alumni Achievement award, 1982, Arch. Excellence award Master Builders of Iowa, 2001; named Iowa State U. Parent of Yr., 1980. Fellow: AIA (Iowa pres. 1972, nat. dir. 1975—78, nat. v.p. 1979—81, 1982, nat. pres. 1983, Iowa Medal of Honor 1992), Royal Archtl. Inst. Can. (hon.); mem.: Soc. Archs. Guatemala (hon.), Soc. Archs. Mex. (hon.), Rotary (Paul Harris fellow), Phi Kappa Phi, Tau Sigma Delta, Delta Upsilon, Tau Beta Pi, Knight of St. Patrick Engring. Soc., Iowa State U. Order of Knoll. Republican. Methodist. Home: 15340 Dodge Ave Clear Lake IA 50428-8773 Personal E-mail: rojobro@netins.net.

BROSILOW, COLEMAN BERNARD, chemical engineering educator; b. Phila., Nov. 14, 1934; s. Samuel and Ethel (Stein) B.; m. Rosalie Ziegleman, Feb. 18, 1962; children— Rachelle, Benjamin. BS, Drexel U., 1957; M.Ch.E., Poly. Inst. N.Y., 1959, PhD, 1962. Systems engr. Am. Cyanamid Co., Process Analysis Group, Wayne, N.J., 1962-63; asst. prof. chem. engring. Case Western Res. U., Cleve., 1963-67, assoc. prof., 1967-73, prof. chem. engring., 1973—2001, prof. emeritus, 2001—, chmn. dept. chem. engring., 1980-84. Chmn. bd. Control Soft Corp., 1985-2001, now bd. dirs.; vis. prof. chem. engring. The Technion, Haifa, Israel, 1971-72, Ben Gurion U., Israel, 2000; cons. in field. Contbr. articles to profl. jours.; editl. bd.: Am. Inst. Chem. Engrs. Jour, 1980-85, Techniques of Model-based Control, 2002; patentee in field. Founding mem. bd. trustees Solomon Schecter Day Sch. of Cleve., 1978—, pres., 1978-84. . Fellow AIChE (computing in chem. engring. award 1989); mem. Sigma Xi, Tau Beta Pi, Phi Lambda Upsilon. Jewish. Home: 25 Shoham St Rehovot 76227 Israel Office: Ben Gurion U of the Negev Dept Chem Engring PO Box 653 Be'er Sheva 84105 Israel E-mail: cbb@po.cwru.edu, cbb@case.edu.

BROSIUS, KAREN, museum director; Attended, Butler U., Ecoles d'arts Americaines, Juilliard Sch. Music; MA summa cum laude, Hunter Coll., CUNY. Rschr. Rsch. Found. of City of NY; pub. affairs officer Pierpont Morgan Libr.; sr. philanthropic, arts, and comm. exec. Altria Group, Inc, NYC, dir. corp. affairs, dir. corp. contbns. and pub. affairs, dir. media rels.; dir. Columbia Mus. Art, SC, 2004—. Bd. dirs. Arts & Bus. Coun., ArtTable. Bd. mem. Funders Concerned About AIDS, Nat. AIDS Fund, City Harvest. Mem.: Am. Assn. Mus., Nat. Endowment Arts. Office: Columbia Mus Art PO Box 2068 Columbia SC 29202 E-mail: Kbrosius@columbiamuseum.org.*

BROSKOSKE, STEPHEN L., information technology educator; b. Nanticoke, Pa., June 28, 1963; s. Ronald and Theresa Broskoske. B of Edn., Coll. Misericordia, 1985; MS, Wilkes U., 1989; EdD, Lehigh U., 2000. Assessment and tech. devel. specialist, program specialist Luzerne County C.C., Nanticoke, Pa., 1986—98; asst. prof. Coll. Misericordia, Dallas, 2000—. Mem., past pres., adv. bd. Luzerne/Wyo. Counties Area Agy. Aging, Wilkes-Barre, Pa., 1992—; mem., faculty senate Coll. Misericordia. Sec., bd. trustees First United Meth. Ch., 2003, dir. music, organist, 1984; mem., found. bd. Luzerne/Wyo. Counties Area Agy. Aging, Wilkes-Barre, 2004. Grantee, U.S. Dept. Edn., 2001—04. Mem.: Pa. Assn. Colleges and Tchr. Educators, Pa. Assn. Ednl. Comm. and Tech. Avocations: music, bicycling, flight simulations. Office: Coll Misericordia 301 Lake St Dallas PA 18612 Office Phone: 570-674-6761.

BROSLOVSKY, LEWIS, physician; b. Lakewood, N.J., June 24, 1948; BA in Biology, Gettysburg Coll., 1970; MD, U. Bologna, Italy, 1977. Intern Brookdale Hosp. Medical Ctr., Bklyn., 1977-78, resident ob-gyn, 1978-81; attending ob-gyn Cmty. Gen. Hosp., Sullivan Co. Harris, N.Y., 1982-92; chmn. dept. ob-gyn. Horton Med. Ctr., Middletown, N.Y., 1992—. Fellow ACOG, Am. Soc. Colposcopy and Cervical Pathology; mem. Am. Assn. Gynecologic Laparoscopists. Office: 75 Crystal Run Rd Ste 200 Middletown NY 10941 also: 18 Old Monticello Rd Ferndale NY 12734-5201 also: 155 Crystal Run Rd Middletown NY 10941 also: 254 Route 17K Ste 201 Newburgh NY 12550-8300 Office Phone: 845-703-6999. E-mail: lbroslovsky@crystalrunhealthcare.com.

BROSNAHAN, JAMES (JEROME), lawyer; b. Boston, Jan. 12, 1934; s. James Jerome and Alice B. (Larkin) B.; m. Carol Simon, Nov. 8, 1958; children: Amy Rebecca, James Jerome III, Lisa Katherine. BBA, Boston Coll., 1956; LLB, Harvard U., 1959. Bar: Ariz. 1960, U.S. Ct. Appeals (9th cir.) 1961, Calif. 1963 (chmn. fed. courts commn. 1974-75), U.S. Dist. Ct. (no. dist.) Calif. 1964, U.S. Supreme Ct. 1970, U.S. Dist. Ct. (cen. dist.) Calif. 1974. Asst. U.S. atty. U.S. Dist. Ct. Ariz., Phoenix, 1961-63, U.S. Dist. Ct. (no. dist.) Calif., San Francisco, 1963-66; assoc. to ptnr. Cooper, White & Cooper, San Francisco, 1966-75; ptnr. Morrison & Foerster, San Francisco, 1975—. Spl. counsel Calif. Legislature Join Sub-Com. Crude Oil Pricing, 1973-74; chmn. Fed. Ctrs. com. State Bar Calif., 1974; chmn. del. U.S. Ct. Appeals (9th cir.) Jud. Conf., 1977-78, lawyer rep., 1977-79; mem. jud. coun. Calif. Adv. Com. on Gender Bias in the Cts., 1987-90; frequent lectr., panelist continuing legal edn. programs, various orgns., schs., and pub. interest groups. Author: Trial Handbook for California Trial Lawyers, 1974; contbr. articles to profl. jours. Treas. Mexican-Am. Legal Def. Fund, San Francisco, 1981-83, nat. bd. dirs. 1980-84; bd. dirs. ACLU, keynote speaker 1987; bd. dirs. Sierra Club Legal Def. Fund, 1974-77; bd. dirs. Legal Svcs. for Children, Inc., 1984—; civil adv. bd. Racketeer-Influenced and Corrupt Orgns., 1985—. With USAF, 1960. Named one of five best attys. in San Francisco, San Francisco Examiner, 1980, one of 7200 best attys. in Am., 1987, one of 100 Powerful lawyers Nat. Law Jour., 1988, 1998, Legend of Law, Lawyers Club, San Francisco, 2002, one of the Top Ten Lawyers in Bay Area, San Francisco Chronicle, 2005; recipient Am. Legal Def. and Edn. Legal Svcs award, 1985, MALDEF Legal Svcs. award, 1985, Polit. Parties and Dem. award, Meiklejohn award, 1986, Father Moriarty Cen. Am. Refugee Recognition award, 1987, Wm. O. Douglas award, 1988, Faculty award Nat. Inst. Trial Advocacy, Tree of Life award Jewish Nat. Fund, William J. Brennan Jr. award, U. Va., 2003, Champion of Justice award Loyola Law Sch. Marymount U., 2005. Fellow Am. Coll. Trial Lawyers (Samuel E. Gates Award, 2000), Internat. Acad. Trial Lawyers, Internat. Soc. Barristers, ABA Found.; mem. ABA (adv. com. to pres.-elect program on competency and contg. legal edn. 1979, active numerous panels, programs, convs., Pro Bono Publico award, 1987, sect. on individual rights and responsibilities), Calif. Bar Assn. (chmn. panel on cross-exam 1981), Am. Law Inst., Am. Bd. Trial Advs. (named Trial Lawyer of Yr., 2001), Nat. Inst. for Trial Advocacy (bd. trustees 1992), Bar Assn. San Francisco (past pres. 1977), Practicing Law Inst. (bd. dirs. 1975-77, chmn. com. on employment of minority 1988), Am. Judicature Soc. (bd. dirs.), Calif. Attys. for Criminal Justice (bd. dirs. 1981-83, San Francisco bail projects 1987—), Am. Bd. Criminal Lawyers, Com. on Minority Employment, Am. Lawyers Newspapers Group, Inc. (nat. bd. of contbrs. 1988—), Harvard Law Sch. Alumni Assn., U.S. Supreme Ct. Hist. Soc. Nat. Products Unit Lawyers Coop. (Am. jurists editorial adv. bd.). Clubs: Barristers (San Francisco) (pres. 1968). Office: Morrison & Foerster LLP 425 Market St San Francisco CA 94105-2482 Office Phone: 415-268-7000. E-mail: jbrosnahan@mofo.com.

BROSNAHAN, LEGER NICHOLAS, language educator; b. Kansas City, Mo., Dec. 11, 1929; s. Earl Francis and Helen Rose Mottin Brosnahan; m. Irene Teoh, Nov. 4, 1967; children: L. Nicholas Jr., Jennifer Ru-chao. AB, Georgetown U., 1951; MA, Harvard U., 1952, PhD, 1957. Instr. Northwestern U., Evanston, Ill., 1957-61; asst. prof. Hawaii U., Honolulu, 1961-63; rschr. U. Paris, 1963-64; vis. prof. U. Lyons, France, 1964-65; asst. prof. U. Md., College Park, 1965-68; from assoc. prof. to prof. Ill. State U., Normal, 1968—2002; ret. Vis. prof. Myagi-Kyoiku Dai, Sendai, Japan, 1968-69, Moscow Linguistics U., 1992-93, Changshin Coll., Masan, Korea, 1996; rschr. Usedcom, Tokyo, 1969-70. Author: Japanese and English Gesture, 1990, Chinese and English Gesture, 1991, Standard American English Behavior, 1997, Russian and English Nonverbal Communication Mosco, 1998. Sgt. U.S. Army, 1952-54.

BROSNAHAN, ROGER PAUL, lawyer; b. Kansas City, Mo., Aug. 9, 1935; s. Earl and Helen (Mottin) Brosnahan; m. Jill Farley, Aug. 2, 1956; children: Paul, Connor, Helen, Farley, Tracy, Hugh, Lee. BS, St. Louis U., 1956; LLB, Mich. U., 1959. Bar: Mo. 1959, Minn. 1959, U.S. Supreme Ct. 1971, U.S. Dist. Ct. Appeals (8th cir.) 1975, U.S. Dist. Ct. Appeals (6th cir.) 1984, U.S. Dist. Ct. Appeals (10th cir.) 1999. Ptnr. Streater, Murphy, Brosnahan & Langford, Winona, Minn., 1959-78, Kutak, Rock & Huie, Mpls., 1979-82, Robins, Kaplan, Miller & Ciresi, Mpls., 1982-93, Brosnahan, Joseph & Suggs P.A., Mpls., 1993-99; prin. Law Offices of Roger P. Brosnahan, Winona, 1999—2005. Mem.: ABA (state del. 1976—88), Nat. Conf. Bar Pres. (pres. 1980—81), Minn. Bar Assn. (pres. 1974—75), Minn. Trial Lawyers Assn. Democrat. Roman Catholic. Office: Roger P Brosnahan Inc 116 Center St Winona MN 55987 Fax: 507-457-3001. Office Phone: 507-457-3000. E-mail: rpbros@mwt.net.

BROSNAN, CAROL RAPHAEL SARAH, retired art association administrator; b. Paterson, NJ, July 19, 1931; d. Basil Roger and Mary Ellen Carroll (McDonald) B. Piano student of, Iris Brussels, 1940—53; student, George Washington U., Washington, 1956—61, U. Va., 1975, U. Oxford (Eng.), 1975; BA in History, George Washington U., 1981, MA in History, 1987. Adminstrv. clk. Dept. Army, Def., Pentagon, Office asst. chief staff intelligence, Washington, 1955-58; clk. fgn. sci. info. program NSF, Washington, 1958-60, adminstrv. clk., 1960-65, adminstrv. fellowship clk. grad. fellowship program, 1965-72; staff asst. to Jane Alexander, chmn. Nat. Endowment Arts, Washington, 1972-94; ret., 1994. Music tchr. (piano), Paterson, 1945—53; pianist at recitals U.S., Heidelberg, Germany. With WAC U.S. Army, 1953—55. Recipient Young People's Concerts award, 1945. Hon. fellow Harry S. Truman Libr. Inst. Nat. Internat. Affairs, 1975. Mem. Am. Legion, Am. Hist. Assn., Nat. Assn. Uniformed Svcs., Acad. Polit. Sci. (contbg. 1978-81), Am. Classical League, Friends Bodleian Libr. (Oxford U.), Luther Rice Soc. George Washington U. (life), Heritage Soc. (life), Phi Alpha Theta. Home: 6030 Sunset Ridge Ct Centreville VA 20121-3051 Office: Nat Endowment for Arts 1100 Pennsylvania Ave NW Washington DC 20004-2501

BROSNAN, PIERCE, actor; b. Navan, County Meath, Ireland, May 16, 1953; m. Cassandra Harris, Dec. 27, 1977 (dec. Dec. 28, 1991); m. Keely Shay Smith, Aug. 4, 2001. Stage appearances include Wait Until Dark, The Red Devil Battery Sign, Filumena, (London); film appearances include The Mirror Crack'd, The Long Good Friday, 1982, Nomads, 1986, The Fourth Protocol, 1987, The Deceivers, 1988, Mr. Johnson, 1989, The Lawnmower Man, 1991, Mrs. Doubtfire, 1993, Love Affair, 1994, Robinson Crusoe, 1995, GoldenEye, 1995, Mars Attacks!, 1996, The Mirror Has Two Faces, 1996, Dante's Peak, 1997, Tomorrow Never Dies, 1997, The Nephew, 1998, (voice) The Quest for Camelot, 1998, Grey Owl, 1999, The Thomas Crown Affair, 1999, The World is Not Enough, 1999, The Match, 1999, The Tailor of Panama, 2000, Die Another Day, 2002, Laws of Attraction, 2004, After the Sunset, 2004, others; TV appearances include Murphy's Stroke, The Manions of America, Nancy Astor, Remington Steele, Noble House, Around The World in 80 Days, 1989, Murder 101, 1991; prodr. The Nephew, 1999, The Thomas Crown Affair, 1999, The James Bond Story, 1999; TV guest appearances include The Professionals, 1977, Moonlighting, 1985, Muppets Tonight!, 1996.

BROSS, ALBERT LOUIS, JR., artist; b. Newark, June 29, 1921; s. Albert L. and Ann Rita (Sinkovits) B.; m. Barbara Ann Tries, Apr. 12, 1946; children: Albert L. III, Eric A. Student, Art Students League N.Y., N.Y.C., 1939-42, 46-49. Lectr. Talens & Son (Holland), Union, N.J., 1965-70, Langnickle Inc., N.Y.C., 1968-72. Art instr. Art Ctr. of the Oranges, East Orange, N.J., 1962-67, Cranford (N.J.) Art Assn., 1960-62, Summit (N.J.) Art Assn., 1965-72, YWCA Adult Sch., Summit, 1950-72. Staff sgt. U.S. Army, 1942-46, PTO. Recipient Lt. Melvin Brewer award Hudson Valley Art Assn., 1977, Philip Shumaker award Hudson Valley Art Assn., 1991, Oil award Interant. Miniature Art Exhbn., 1985-86, Seascape award, 1986, Landscape award, 1991. Mem. Art Students League N.Y. (life), Hudson Valley Art Assn., Miniature Art Soc. N.J., Associated Artists N.J., Chaffee Art Ctr. Republican. Avocations: cooking, target shooting, gardening. Home: PO Box 282 New Vernon NJ 07976-0282

BROSTRON, JUDITH CURRAN, lawyer; b. Chgo., Feb. 2, 1950; d. Norman William and Marianne Cecelia (Baron) Curran; m. Kenneth C. Brostron, Nov. 22, 1989. Diploma Nursing, Evanston (Ill.) Hosp., 1971; BA, Nat. Coll. Edn., Evanston, 1981; JD, Chgo.-Kent Coll. Law, 1985; LLM, St. Louis U., 1999. Bar: Mo. 1985, U.S. Dist. Ct. (ea. dist.) Mo. 1985, Ill. 1986. Staff nurse Evanston Hosp., 1971-78, St. Francis Hosp., Evanston, Ill., 1979-81; assoc. Lashly & Baer, P.C., St. Louis, 1985-91, ptnr., 1991—. Mem. ABA, Am. Soc. Law Medicine, Mo. Bar Assn., Ill. Bar Assn. Avocations: running, golf, gardening. Office: Lashly & Baer P C 714 Locust St Saint Louis MO 63101-1699

BROSZ, MARGARET HEADLEY, pediatrics nurse; b. Dover, NJ, Dec. 31, 1951; d. Charles E. and Carolyn (Cobb) H.; m. Walter J. Brosz, May 28, 1978. Student, Douglass Coll., New Brunswick, N.J., 1970-72; BS in Nursing, Cornell U., 1974; MS, Boston Coll., Chestnut Hill, Mass., 1978. Cert. trainer medication adminstrs. Nurse Vis. Nurse Assn. Boston, 1974-76; pediatric nurse practitioner Wrentham (Mass.) State Sch., Boston Children's Hosp., 1978-80; staff nurse pediatrics ICU Thomas Jefferson U. Hosp., Phila., 1980-81; employee health clinician Children's Hosp. Phila., 1981-83; nurse mgr. The Woods Svcs., Langhorne, Pa., 1983—. Vol. interpreter Pennsbury Manor, Morrisville, Pa.; former bd. dirs. Pennsbury Soc. Mem. Devel. Disabilities, 1996—2001. Mem.: Devel. Disabilities Nurses Assn.

BROTHERS, CAROLYN IRENE, elementary and secondary educator; b. L.A., Aug. 28, 1956; d. Seldon R. and Grace Rose B. BA in Psychology, U. Calif., Irvine, 1978; postgrad., U. Calif., Riverside, 1985; MA in Sch. Counseling, U. La Verne, 1988. Cert. resource specialist, dance; pupil pers. credential, learning handicapped credential, multiple subject credential. Resource specialist San Jacinto (Calif.) Unified Sch. Dist.; dance instr. Coastline Community Coll., Fountain Valley, Calif.; resource specialist Garden Grove (Calif.) Unified Sch. Dist.; assoc. prof. reading Chapman U., 2000—, dir. Reading Ctr., 2000—01. Mentor, tchr. and trainer Tchrs. for Zoophonics; instr. Nat. U.; activities dir. Chapman Univ., 2000—04, math reading supr. Contbr. articles and poetry to jours. Recipient Gold and Silver award World of Poetry; Victress Bower grantee. Mem. ASCD, Calif. Assn. Resource Specialists (chpt. pres., bd. dirs. region e, state treas. region 4), Garden Grove Edn. Assn. (recipient WHO award 1999), San Jacinto Tchrs. Assn. (treas.), Jr. League of Orange County (tng. chmn., Treas. of League award 2001). Home: 2525 Avenita Alpera Tustin CA 92782-9027

BROTHERS, JOHN ALFRED, retired oil company executive, chemicals executive; b. Huntington, W.Va., Nov. 10, 1940; s. John Luther and Genevieve (Monti) B.; m. Paula Sprague Benson, June 21, 1975. BS, Va. Poly. Inst., 1962, MS, 1965, PhD, 1966; postgrad advanced mgmt. program, Harvard U., 1981. With Internat. Nickel Co., 1962-64; with Ashland Oil, Inc., Ky., 1966—, sr. v.p., 1983-87; sr. v.p., group operating officer Ashland Oil Inc., 1987-97; with Ashland Chem. Co., Columbus, Ohio, 1974-88, pres., 1983-88; exec. v.p. Ashland, Inc., 1997-99; ret., 1999. Adj. prof. engring. Ohio State U., 1978—; pres. bus. adv. coun., 1981—. Bd. dirs. Columbus Mus. Art, Columbus Children's Hosp., Ohio Dominican Coll., 1984—. NSF fellow, 1965-66; named Outstanding Young Man U.S. C. of C., 1972 Mem. Am. Petroleum Inst., Chem. Mfrs. Assn., Columbus C. of C. (bd. dirs.), Tau Beta Pi, Phi Kappa Phi. Clubs: Scioto Country, Rolling Rock, Double Eagle Golf, Hole-in-the-Wall Golf, Mill Reef, Columbus. Republican.

BROTHERS, JOYCE DIANE, television personality, psychologist; b. N.Y.C. d. Morris K. and Estelle (Rapoport) Bauer; m. Milton Brothers, July 4, 1949; 1 child, Lisa Robin. BS, Cornell U., 1947; MA, Columbia U., 1950, PhD, 1953; LHD (hon.), Franklin Pierce Coll., Gettysburg Coll., Lehigh U., 1994, Mt. St. Mary Coll., 1998. Asst. in psychology Columbia U., N.Y.C., 1948-52; instr. psychology Hunter Coll., N.Y.C., 1948-52; ind. psychologist, writer, 1952—. Co-host: TV program Sports Showcase, 1956; appearances: TV program Dr. Joyce Brothers, 1958-63, Consult Dr. Brothers, 1960-66, Ask Dr. Brothers, 1965-75; hostess (TV syndication) Living Easy with Dr. Joyce Brothers, 1972-75; columnist TV syndication, N.Am. Newspaper Alliance, 1961-71, Bell-McClure Syndicate, 1963-71, King Features Syndicate, 1972—, Good Housekeeping mag., 1962—; appearances Sta. WNBC, 1966-70; radio program Emphasis, 1966-75, Monitor, 1967-75, Sta. WMCA, 1970-73, ABC Reports, 1966-67, NBC Radio Network Newsline, 1975—; news analyst radio program, Metro Media-TV, 1975-76, news corr., TVN, Inc., 1975-76, Sta. KABC-TV, 1977-82, Sta. WABC-TV, 1980-82, 86-88, Sta. WLS-TV, 1980-82, NIWS Syndicated News Service, 1982-84, The Dr. Joyce Brothers Program, The Disney Channel, 1985, Sta. KCBS-TV News, 1987—; contbr. CBS News, 2003—, MSNBC, 2003—; spl. feature writer Hearst papers, UPI; current affairs spl. corr. Fox TV Syndication, 1990-97; featured on A&E's Biography, 1999; author: Ten Days to a Successful Memory, 1959, Woman, 1961, The Brothers System for Liberated Love and Marriage, 1975, How to Get Whatever You Want Out of Life, 1978, What Every Woman Should Know About Men, 1982, What Every Woman Ought to Know About Love and Marriage, 1988, The Successful Woman, 1989, Widowed, 1990, Positive Plus: The Practical Plan to Liking Yourself Better, 1994. Co-chmn. sports com. Lighthouse for Blind; door-to-door chmn. Fedn. Jewish Philanthropies, N.Y.C.; mem. fund raising com. Olympic Fund; mem. People-to-People Program. Winner $64,000 Question TV Program, 1956, $64,000 Challenge, 1957; recipient Mennen Baby Found. award, 1959, Newhouse Newspaper award, 1959, Am. Acad. Achievement award, Am. Parkinson Disease Assn. award, 1971, Deadline award Sigma Delta Chi, 1971, Pres.'s Cabinet award U. Detroit, 1975, Woman of Achievement award Women's City Club Cleve., 1981, award Calif. Home Econs. Assn., 1981, award Distrubutive Edn. Clubs Am., 1981, Golden Gavel Excellence in Comm. award Toastmasters, 1982, Pub. Svc. award Ridgewood Women's Club, 1987, Women Who Make a Difference award Sen. Bill Bradley, 1990, Gt. Am. award Bards of Bohemia, 1993, Diamond award, 1994, George M. and Mary Jane Leader Healthcare Achievement award, 1995, Nat. Cmty. Svc. award McQuade Children Svcs., 1998, Presdl. citation Am. Psychol. Assn., 2002. Mem. Sigma Xi. Office: NBC Westwood One Radio Network 1700 Broadway New York NY 10019-5905

BROTHERS, LYNDA LEE, lawyer; b. Palo Alto, Calif., Nov. 21, 1945; BS in genetics, U. Calif., Berkeley, 1968; MS in biochemical genetics, U. Va., 1971; JD, Golden Gate U., 1976. Bar: Calif. 1976, Wash. 1986. Counsel com. sci. and tech. subcom. environment and atmosphere US Ho. of Reps., Washington, 1977-79; dep. asst. sec. for environment US Dept. Energy, Washington, 1979-81; asst. dir. solid, hazardous and radioactive waste and air pollution Wash. Dept. Ecology, Olympia, 1984-86; with Heller, Ehrman, White & McAuliffe, Seattle, 1986-90; ptnr. Davis, Wright & Tremaine, Seattle, 1990—2000, Sonnenschein Nath & Rosenthal LLP, San Francisco, 2000—. Mem. Bd. on Radioactive Waste Mgmt. NRC, 1989—96. Mem. editorial bd. Golden Gate U. Law Rev., 1976; contbr. articles to sci. and legal jours. Mem. N.W. Citizens' Forum on High Level Nuclear Waste at Hanford, 1986-88; pres. Washington Environ. Found., 1983-90. Office: Sonnenschein Nath & Rosenthal LLP 685 Market St, 6th Fl San Francisco CA 94105 Office Phone: 415-882-0344. Office Fax: 415-543-5472. Business E-Mail: lbrothers@sonnenschein.com.

BROTHERS, THOMAS EDWARD, surgeon; b. Sturges, Mich., Dec. 5, 1957; s. Paul Lavere and Barbara Jean (Johnson) B.; m. Lisa Kaye Von Moll, May 12, 1984; children: Brittany Leigh, Kelly Nicole. BA, Kalamazoo (Mich.) Coll., 1980; MD, U. Mich., 1983. Diplomate Am. Bd. Surgery, Am. Bd. Surg. Critical Care, Am. Bd. Gen. Vascular Surgery. Intern U. Mich., Ann Arbor, 1983-84, resident, 1984-89, fellow in vascular surgery, 1989-91; mem. staff Med. U. Hosp., Charleston, S.C.; assoc. prof. Med. U. S.C. Contbr. articles to profl. jours. Fellow ACS, Assn. VA Surgeons; mem. AHA (bd. dirs. Trident divsn. S.C. region), Coller Soc., Perpheral Vascular Surgery Soc., So. Soc. Vascular Surgery, Soc. Univ. Surgeons, Internat. Soc. Cardiovascular Surgery.

BROTHERTON, NAOMI, artist; b. Galveston, Tex., Apr. 8, 1920; d. Vernon Smart and Hunter Smith Macon; B.A., Baylor U., 1941; m. Lem Brotherton, Nov. 20, 1941; children— Betty Brotherton Crudden, Robert James. Tchr. watercolor painting various workshops, 1962—; ptnr. Artisan's Studio-Gallery, Dallas; 41 one-woman shows since 1955, including: Oak Cliff Soc. Fine Arts, Dallas, 1961, Western N.Mex. U., Silver City, 1967, Baylor U., 1967, S. Ark. Art Center, El Dorado, 1969, Irving (Tex.) Art Center, 1972, 1995, Artisans Studio-Gallery, Dallas, 1981, Carlsbad (N.Mex.) Art Mus., 1984,1997, St. Edward's U., 1985; group shows include: Panhandle Plains Hist. Mus., Canyon, Tex., 1968, Laguna Gloria Gallery of Tex. Fine Arts Assn., Austin, 1969, Barnwell Art Center, Shreveport, La., 1974, Galleria de Arte de Saltillo (Mex.), 1978, Artisans Studio-Gallery, Dallas, 1981, 82, Dallas Public Library, 1980; awards in competitive shows include: Tex. Watercolor Soc., 1954, 66, 81, Tex. Fine Arts Assn., Dallas, 1963, 65, 67, 69, 70, 73, 74, Tex. Fine Arts Assn. State-wide, Austin, 1965, 67, 70, 73, 74, Southwestern Watercolor Soc., Dallas, 1964, 66, 67, 68, 69, 71, 72, 79, 81, Artists and Craftsmen Assoc. of Dallas, 1983, 84, Coppini Acad. Fine Arts, 1982, 83; numerous others; represented in permanent collections: Baylor U., Ft. Worth Public Schs., S. Ark. Art Center, Brownsville (Tex.) Art Center, Pecos (Tex.) Art Center, Carlsbad Mus. and Art Ctr., others. Mem. Tex. Watercolor Soc. (charter), Southwestern Watercolor Soc. (pres. 1967-68), Okla. Watercolor Assn., West Tex. Watercolor Soc., Western Fedn. of Watercolor Socs., Beta Sigma Phi. Episcopalian. Co-author: Variations in Watercolor, 1981.

BROTMAN, BARBARA LOUISE, journalist, writer; b. N.Y.C., Feb. 23, 1956; d. Oscar J. and Ruth (Branchor) Brotman; m. Chuck Berman, Aug. 28, 1983; children: Robin, Nina. BA, Queens Coll., 1978. Writer, columnist Chgo. Tribune, 1978—. Recipient Ill. Newspapers Column Writing award, UPI, 1984, Peter Lisagor award, Sigma Delta Chi, 1984; John S. Knight fellow for profl. journalism, 2004. Avocation: broomball. Office: Chgo Tribune Co 435 N Michigan Ave Chicago IL 60611-4066

BROTMAN, DAVID JOEL, architectural firm executive, consultant; b. Balt., Jan. 21, 1945; BS in Architecture, U. Cin., 1968. Registered arch. Ariz., Calif., Colo., D.C., Fla., Ga., Hawaii, La., Md., N.J., N.Y., Nev., Ohio, Oreg., Tex., Utah. Arch. Locke & Jackson, Balt., 1968, The Archtl. Affiliation, Towson, Md., 1968-75; joined RTKL, Balt., 1975-79, arch. Dallas, 1979-90, v.p., 1984—2000, exec. v.p., mng. dir. LA, 1990-2000, vice chmn., 1994-2000; prin. Sunset Consultants, Malibu, Calif., 2000—. Tchr. U. Tex. Sch. Architecture, Arlington, Catonsville (Md.) C.C.; arbitrator Am. Stock Exch., N.Y. Stock Exch., Nat. Assn. Security Dealers. Prin. works include Galleria at South Bay, Redondo Beach, Calif., Eton Sq. (Design Tex. Soc. Archs., 1986), Computer Sci. Corp., Fairfax County, Va., AT&T Customer Tech. Ctr., Dallas (Honor award Dallas chpt. AIA 1988), Tysons Corner Ctr., McLean Va. (Design award Monitor Ctrs. and Stores of Excellence 1989, Design award Internat. Shopping Ctrs. 1989, Exceptional Design award Fairfax County, Va. 1990, Modernization Excellence award Bldgs., 1990, Excellence award Urban Land Inst. 1992), St. Andrews (Scotland) Old Course Hotel, Tower City Ctr., Cleve., Eastland Shopping Ctr., Melbourne, Australia, Morley City Shopping Ctr., Perth, Australia, Dong An Market, Beijing, Desert Passage at Alladin, Las Vegas, Sci. and Tech. Mus., Shanghi, 825 Market St., San Francisco, many others; contbr. articles to profl. jours. Mem.: AIA (pres. Calif. coun. 2004, Calif. regional dir.), Urban Land Inst., Nat. Coun. Archtl. Registration Bds., Internat. Coun. Shopping Ctrs. Office Phone: 310-457-6048. Personal E-mail: sunset100@verizon.net.

BROTMAN, JEFFREY H., wholesale distribution executive; b. 1942; married; 2 children. BA in polit. sci., U. Wash., JD, 1967. Ptnr. Lasher-Brotman & Sweet, 1967-74; with ENI Exploration Co., 1975-83; co-founder Costco Wholesale Corp., 1983, chmn. bd., chief exec. officer, 1983-88, chmn. bd., 1988—93, vice chmn., 1993—94, chmn., 1994—. Dir. Starbucks, 1988—99, Garden Botanika, 1989—98, Seattle-First Nat. Bank, 1990—99, The Sweet Factory, Inc., 1992—98. Trustee Seattle Art Mus., 1990—, Seattle Found., 1991—, U. Wash. Med. Ctr. Bd., 1991—, King County United Way Bd., 1996—; co-chair King County United Way Campaign Bd., 1997—, chair, 1997; regent U. Wash., 1998—2004, v.p. bd. regents, 2002—03, chair bd. regents, fin. and audit com., 2000—. Office: Costco Wholesale 999 Lake Dr Issaquah WA 98027

BROTMAN, MARTIN, gastroenterologist; b. Winnipeg, MB, Canada, June 26, 1939; MD, U. Manitoba, 1962. Diplomate Am. Bd. Internal Medicine, Gastroenterology Am. Bd. Internal Medicine. Intern Winnipeg Gen. Hosp., 1962—63; resident internal medicine Mayo Grad. Med. Sch., Rochester, Minn., 1963—65, fellow gastroenterology, 1965—67; med. adminstr. San Francisco; pvt. practice; chmn. med. dept. Calif. Pacific Med. Ctr., San Francisco, 1992—95, pres., CEO, 1995—. Clin. prof. med. U. Calif. San Francisco, 1982—. Mem.: AMA, ASGE, AASLD, Am. Soc. Internal Medicine, Am. Coll. Physicians, Am. Gastroentrol. Assn. (pres.-elect 2001—02, pres. 2002—03). Home: 2333 Buchanan P-1200 San Francisco CA 94115 Office: California Pacific Med Ctr PO Box 7999 San Francisco CA 94120 Address: Pacific Internal Med Assocs 2100 Webster St #423 San Francisco CA 94115-2380

BROTMAN, PHYLLIS BLOCK, advertising executive, public relations executive; b. Balt., Mar. 23, 1934; d. Sol. George and Delma (Herman) Block; m. Don N. Brotman, Aug. 16, 1953; children: Solomon G., Barbara Brotman Kaylor. Student, Balt. Jr. Coll., U. Va., Mary Washington Coll. Assoc. Channel 13 TV, 1953-55; free-lance pub. rels., 1960-66; coord. pub. rels. Md. Coun. Edni. TV, 1965-66; pres., CEO Image Dynamics, Inc., Balt., 1966—. Lectr., cons. Md. Gen. Assembly Legis. Info. Program, 1968-70; panelist TV and radio; bd. dirs., bd. trustees Notre Dame Coll., Md.; bd. visitors Elon Coll., N.C., Towson U., Md. Columnist Balt. Bus. Jour., 1965. State chair U.S. Olympics Com. Mid-Atlantic Region, 1989-92; chair, com. mem. Greater Balt. Com., 1985-87, econ. devel. coun., 1990-91; adv. bd. Nat. Aquarium Balt., 1988—; bd. dirs. Nat. Adv. Rev. Bd., 1988-89, Balt. Symphony Orch., 1989-2001, mktg. com. 75th ann. season, 1991; active Balt. Pub. Rels. Coun.; chair adv. bd. Children and Youth Trust Fund, 1989—; bd. dirs. Internat. Visitors Ctr., co-chair mktg. com., 1990—; founding mem. Chamber Symphony San Francisco, 1984, bd. dirs., 1984-91; pub. rels. com., pres. adv. coun. U. Md. Sys., 1988—; 20th ann. conf. com. Internat. Urban Fellows Program Johns Hopkins Inst. Policy Studies, 1989-90; cmty. resources bd. Jr. League Balt., 1982-87; bd. dirs. New Directions for Women, 1979, 87-90, Stella Maris Hospice Oper. Corp., 1985-87, Jewish Family and Childrens Soc., 1980-83, Nat. Coun. Jewish Women; mem. comm. United Way Ctrl. Md., 1981-83; mktg. and pub. rels. com. Balt. Mus. Art, 1982-84, hon. com. Joshua Johnson Coun. and Endowment Fund, 1988; active U. Md. Endowments Com., 1978-79; nat. commr. B'nai B'rith Youth Commn.; bd. electors Balt. Hebrew Congregation, pres. parents assn., religious sch. com., bd. congregation; past bd. dirs. Assoc. Placement and Guidance Bur., Levindale Home and Infirmary Ladies Aux., Sinai Hosp. Aux., Nat. Jewish Welfare Fund; chair Balt. County Econ. Devel. Commn., 1987-91; appointed commn., 1980; appointed Mayors Commn. Telecomm., 1987-90; appointed State of Md. Legis. Compensation Commn., 1979—, Mayor Balt. Bus. Delegation for Balt. Conv. Ctr., 1979; bd. trustees Loyola Coll. Balt., 1986-93, treas., 1981, 82-83; bd. adv. Towson State U., 1989—, bd. vis., mem. adv. coun. Sch. Bus. & Econs., 1983-85; Found. bd. dirs. Mary Washington Coll., 1985-87, 88-92, speaker jr. class ring ceremony, 1981; mem. exec. com. Inst. Politics and Govt. Coll. Continuing Edn. U. So. Calif.; commencement speaker U. Ky. Coll. Dentistry, 1982; chmn. panel State Dept. Edu., 2001-2002; mem. Bd. Edn. Visionary Panel, 2001—, chmn. support task force; bd. visitors Towson U.; chmn. Sch. Comms. Recipient Cert. Achievement, Young Womens Leadership Coun., Cert. Appreciation for svc. to Md. Gen. Assembly by Md. Senate, Cert. Achievement in profession Md. Ho. Dels., Legis. Info. Program Pub. Rels. Soc. Am. Md. Chpt., Cert. Appreciation pub. svc. Md. Area Residences Youth, Pub. Rels. award Great Chesapeake Balloon Race Pub. Rels. Soc. Am., Md. Chpt., Leadership award nat. svc. to profession Internat. Orgn. Women Execs., 1980, Dedicated Svc. award Jewish Family and Children, 1983, Pres. Citation pvt. sector initiatives, 1985, Guardian of Menorah Internat. award B'nai B'rith, 1986; named one of Balt. Most Powerful Women, Balt. Mag., Balt. Outstanding Women Mgts. WMAR-TV, U. Balt., 1983, Woman of Yr., Arlene Rosenbloom Wyman Guild-U. Md. Cancer Ctr., 1984, B'nai B'rith Internat., 1985, 94, Avon Products, Inc., 1990, Media Advocate of Yr. for Md. U.S. Small Bus. Adminstrn., 1985, Most Admired company Balt. Mag., 1987-89, Entrepreneur of Yr. Balt. County Econ. Devel., 1990, Save-A-Heart Humanitarian of Yr., 1991, Balt. County Woman of Yr., 2004. Mem. Am. Assn. Adv. Agencies (chair mid-Atlantic region 1981-82, gov. eastern region 1982-84, chair 1986-87, bd. dirs., gov. rels. com. 1982-87), Am. Assn. Polit. Cons. (pres. 1976-80, bd. dirs. 1974-76, 80—), Nat. Coun. Jewish Women (life, bd. dirs.), Pub. Rels. Soc. Am. (Md. chpt. nat. chair roundtable 1987-88, co-chair nat. conf. 1980, v.p. 1968, Silver Anvil award 1988, Lifetime Achievement award 1993), Am. Adv. Fedn. (co-chair pub. rels. com. 1986-88, nat. govt. rels. coun. 1982—, chair legis. com. 1981), Meeting Planners Internat. (co-chair pub. rels. 1978-80, task force election by-laws 1979), Adv. Assn. Balt. (bd. dirs. 1974-76), Md.-DC-Del. Press Assn. (co-chair assocs. sect. 1982-83), Am. Trauma Soc. (nat. bd. dirs. 1981-87, Md. bd. dirs. 1982-89), Balt. County C. of C. (co-chmn. pub. rels. 2003—, mem. legis. com., 2002—), Beta Gamma Sigma, Alpha Sigma Nu, Balt. Md. C. of C. (v.p. membership 1991—, v.p. leadership Md. bd. govs. 1992-93, v.p. ctrl. dist. 1985-91, legis. conf. chair 1990, exec. com. 1986—, bd. dirs. 1984—), Balt. County C. of C. (bd. dirs. 2004-, Woman of Yr. 2004), Ctr. Club Balt. (bd. dirs., comm. chair 1983—, pres. 2003—). Avocations: tennis, flying, wine tasting. Home: 8105 Mcdonogh Rd Baltimore MD 21208-1005 Office: Image Dynamics Inc 8105 Mcdonogh Rd Baltimore MD 21208-1005 Office Phone: 410-363-1565. Personal E-mail: pbbrotman@comcast.net.

BROTMAN, RICHARD DENNIS, counselor; b. Detroit, Nov. 2, 1952; s. Alfred David and Dorothy G. (Mansfield) B.; m. Debra Louise Hobold, Sept. 9, 1979. AA, East LA Jr. Coll., 1972; AB, U. So. Calif., 1974, MS, 1976. Lic. marriage, family and child counselor, Calif.; cert. counselor, Calif. Instructional media coord. Audiovisual divsn. Pub. Libr., City of Alhambra, Calif., 1971-78; clin. supr. Hollywood-Sunset Cmty. Clinic, L.A., 1976—; client program coord. North Los Angles County Regional Ctr. for Devel. Disabled, 1978-81; sr. counselor Eastern L.A. Regional Ctr. for Devel. Disabled, 1981-85; dir. cmty. svcs. Almansor Edn. Ctr., 1985-87; tng. and resource devel. Children's Home Soc. Calif., 1987-90; program supr. Pacific Clinics-East, 1990-94; assoc. dir. clin. svcs., dir. clin. svcs. Alma Family Svcs., 1994—2002; probable cause hearing officer Orange County (Calif.) Health-care Agy., 1986—. Corp. dir. San Gabriel Mission Players, 1973-75. Mem. Am. Assn. for Marriage and Family Therapy (approved supr.), Calif. Pers. and Guidance Assn., Calif. Rehab. Counselors Assn. (officer), San Fernando Valley Consortium of Agys. Serving Devel. Disabled Citizens (chmn. recreation subcom). L.A. Aquarium Soc. Democrat. Home: 3515 Brandon St Pasadena CA 91107-4542 Office Phone: 626-577-9728. Personal E-mail: brieftherapy@sbcglobal.net.

BROTMAN, STANLEY SEYMOUR, federal judge; b. Vineland, N.J., July 27, 1924; s. Herman Nathaniel and Fanny (Melletz) B.; m. Suzanne M. Simon, Sept. 9, 1951; children: Richard A., Alison B. BA, Yale U., 1947; LLB, Harvard U., 1950. Bar: N.J. 1950, D.C. 1951. Pvt. practice, Vineland, 1952-57; ptnr. Shapiro, Brotman, Eisenstat & Capizola, Vineland, 1957-75; judge U.S. Dist. Ct. N.J., Camden, 1975—; acting chief judge Dist. Ct. of V.I., 1989-92; judge U.S. Fgn. Intelligence Surveillance Ct., 1997—2004. Mem. N.J. Bd. Bar Examiners, 1970-74. Chmn. editl. bd. N.J. State Bar Jour, 1969-74; contbr. articles to profl. jours. Trustee Newcomb Hosp., Vineland, 1953-68. With U.S. Army, 1943-45, 51-52. Fellow Am. Bar Found., Jud. Conf. U.S. (space and facilities com. 1987-93); mem. ABA (ho. of dels. 1975-80, state del. 1982-93, mem. judicial immigration edn. project, chmn. adv. com. 1996—), Nat. Conf. Fed. Trial Judges (exec. com. 1984-87, chmn.-elect 1986-87, chmn. 1987-88, chmn. standing com. jud. selection, tenure and compensation 1988-92, chmn. steering com. of nominating com. 1992-93, standing com. Fed. Jud. Improvements 1992-2003), Am. Judicature Soc. (dir. 1995-2000), N.J. State Bar Assn. (pres. 1974-75), Cumberland County Bar Assn. (pres. 1969-70), Assn. of Fed. Bar of State of N.J., Harvard U. Law Sch. Assn. N.J. (pres. 1974-75), Fed. Judges Assn. (v.p. 1993-97), Yale U. Alumni Assn., Am. Legion, Jewish War Vets., Yale Club, B'nai B'rith, Masons, Shriners. Office: MH Cohen US Courthouse 6030 MH Cohen US Courthouse 4th and Cooper St Camden NJ 08102 Office Phone: 856-757-5062. E-mail: sbrotman@yahoo.com.

BROTMAN, STEVEN, venture capitalist; b. 1968; m. Paula M. Brotman; 3 children. BS in econ., Duke U., 1990; JD/MBA with honors, Wash. U., 1995; grad. studies, Columbia U. Law and Bus. Sch. Investment banking analyst Pauli and Co.; rsch. analyst Bear Stearns; CEO, chmn. AdOne Classified Network, 1994—98; founder, mng. dir. Silicon Alley Venture Ptnrs., 1998—. Named to Top 40 under 40 among NY businessmen, 1995, Top 25 Players Shaping Silicon Alley, Crain's, 1997, Tech 100, 2001. Avocations: golf, technology, books. Office: Silicon Alley Venture Ptnrs 152 W 57th St 20th Fl New York NY 10019 Office Phone: 212-967-6545. Office Fax: 212-898-9044. Business E-Mail: steve@savp.com.

BROTMAN, STUART NEIL, management consultant, lawyer, educator; b. Passaic, N.J., Dec. 5, 1952; s. William and Edith (Berkowitz) B.; m. Gloria Z. Greenfield, June 9, 1985; children: Daniel Greenfield, Rachel Greenfield, Gabriel Greenfield. BS, Northwestern U., 1974; MA, U. Wis., 1975; JD, U. Calif.-Berkeley, 1978. Bar: Calif. 1978. Spl. asst. to the asst. sec. of commerce for comm. and info. Nat. Telecom. and Info. Adminstrn., Washington, 1978-81; pres. Comm. Strategies Inc., Cambridge, Mass., 1981-84; pres. Stuart N. Brotman Comm., Lexington, Mass., 1984-, pres. Museum TV & Radio, 2004-05; adj. assoc. prof. Boston U. Sch. Law, 1990-1997; adj. prof. internat. law Fletcher Sch. Law and Diplomacy, Tufts U., 1990-97; lectr. Knight-Bagehot Program Grad. Sch. Journalism Columbia U., 1998—; lectr. and rsch. fellow Harvard Law Sch., 1997—; adj. fellow Ctr. for Strategic and Internat. Studies, 1999-2000; Eisenhower fellow, 2000-; mem. editl. adv. com. Fed. Comm. Law Jour., 1986-94, EuroWatch: Econs., Policy and Law in the New Europe, 1992—, Transnat. Data and Comm. Report, 1991-94; counsel Winthrop, Stimson, Putnam & Roberts, N.Y. 1993-95, Morrison & Foerster, San Francisco, 1996-97. Mem. adv. com. UCLA Comm. Law Program, 1986-92; mem. nat. adv. coun. Northwestern U. Sch. Comm., 1990—; bd. dirs. Boalt Hall Alumni Assn., U. Calif., Berkeley, 2000-03; mem. comm. arts adv. bd., U. Wis., Madison 2003—; mem. New England Steering Com., Eisenhower Fellowships, 2003—. Editor: The Telecom. Deregulation Sourcebook, 1987, Telephone Company and Cable Television Competition, 1990; author: Broadcasters Can Negotiate Anything, 1988, Communications Law and Practice, 1995; editl. adv. bd. Internat. Jour. Comm. Law and Policy, 1999—, Jour. of Biolaw and Bus., 2004—; contbg. editor Cable Comm., Kitchener, Ont., Can., 1983-95, Cable Comm. Mag.; adv. bd. Jour. Sci. and Tech. Law, 1996—; contbr. articles to profl. jours. Annenberg Washington Program sr. fellow, 1988-94, sr. fellow Edward R. Murrow Ctr. for Internat. Comm., 1994-97; bd. dirs. U.S.-Israel Sci. and Technology Found., 2001-04, chmn. 2003-04, Boalt Hall Alumni Assn.; chmn. Envivio Inc., 2000-02. Mem. ABA (chmn. internat. comm. law com. internat. law and practice sect., 1992-95, internat. legal edn., 1995-96), Fed. Comm. Bar Assn., Northwestern U. Alumni Assn. (Merit award 1996), Cosmos Club, Nat. Press Club. Democrat. Jewish. Personal E-mail: sbrotman@brotman.com.

BROTODININGRAT, SOEMADI DJOKO MOERDJONO, ambassador; b. Solo, Central Java, June 13, 1941; married; 2 children. With Dept. Fgn. Affairs of Republic of Indonesia, 1965—, staff/head of sect., Directorate of Info., 1965—71, 3d sec./2d sec. Indonesian Embassy Brussels, 1971—75, dep. dir. Directorate of Social and Cultural Rels., 1975—78, 1st sec., counsellor Indonesian Permanent Mission to UN N.Y.C., 1978—82, dep. dir. Directorate of Multilateral Econ. Coop., 1982—84, minister counselor Indonesian Permanent Mission to UN N.Y.C., 1984—88, dir. multilateral econ. coop., 1988—91, amb. extraord. and plenipotentiary, Permanent Rep. of Republic of Indonesia to UN and other internat. orgns. Geneva, 1991—95, dir. gen. for fgn. econ. rels., 1995—98, amb. extraord. and plenipotentiary Republic of Indonesia to Japan and to Fed. States of Micronesia, 1998—2002, amb. to U.S. Washington, 2002—. Office: Embassy of Indonesia 2020 Massachusetts Ave NW Washington DC 20036

BROTT, WALTER HOWARD, retired cardiac surgeon, educator, retired military officer; b. Alamosa, Colo., Sept. 5, 1933; s. Walter Hugo and Viola Helen (Roscher) B.; m. Marie Helen Kuzniewski; children: Cheryl Marie, Michelle Marie, Kevin Walter. BA, Yale U., 1955; MD, U. Kans., 1959. Diplomate Am. Bd. Surgery, Am. Bd. Thoracic Surgery. Commd. 1st. lt. U.S. Army, 1959, advanced through grades to col., 1974; intern Walter Reed Army Med. Ctr., Washington, 1959; resident in gen. surgery William Beaumont Gen. Hosp., El Paso, Tex., 1960-64; resident in thoracic surgery Fitzsimmons Army Med. Ctr., Denver, 1967-69; comdr. 3d Surg. Hosp., Vietnam, 1969, 18th Surg. Hosp., 1970; asst. chief thoracic and cardiovascular surgery Walter Reed Army Med. Ctr., 1971-76, chief cardiothoracic surgery, 1977-84; ret. U.S. Army, 1982. Chief surg. cons. Surgeon Gen. Army, Washington, 1976-77; prof. surgery and subsequent clinical prof. surgery Uniformed Svcs. U. Health Scis., 1976—; assoc. clin. prof. surgery U. Tenn., Knoxville, 1984-94, hon. clinical prof., 1994—; mem. joint rev. com. Coun. for Perfusion Edn. and Accreditation, 1981-87. Contbr. articles to profl. jours.; chmn.: NATO editorial bd. Emergency War Surgery Handbook, 1977-82. Mem. physicians' panel Heritage Found., 1991—. Decorated Legion of Merit with oak leaf cluster; decorated Bronze Star (U.S.), Cross of Gallantry (Vietnam); recipient Cert. of Achievement Surgeon Gen. U.S., 1978 Fellow ACS (grad. edn. com. 1977-78); mem. AMA (cons. panel coun. allied health edn. accreditation 1981-87), Walter Reed Assn., Soc. Thoracic Surgeons, Washington Med. Soc., Thoracic and Cardiovascular Surgeons, Thoracic Surgery Program Dirs. Assn., Am. Assn. for Thoracic Surgery, Assn. Med. Cons. to Armed Forces, Assn. Mil. Surgeons, Heritage Found. (Physicians Coun.), Internat. Platform Assn., Alpha Omega Alpha. Clubs: Yale (Washington); Marine Meml. Lutheran. *Using those opportunities to better the life of one's fellow man not only gives gratification in itself but enhances the person spiritually and occasionally materially by God's rewards.*

BROTTO, MARCO A. DE PAULA, education educator, researcher; b. Vitoria, Brazil, June 5, 1962; s. Julio Sarcinelli and Ruth de Paula Brotto; m. Leticia Souza Brotto, May 23, 1997; children: Victor P, Andre P, Gabriella P. PharmM, Fed. U. Ceara, Brazil, 1991; PhD, Trinity Coll., London, Eng., 1999. Rsch. fellow Med. Coll. of Ga., Augusta, Ga., 1994—98; instr. Case Western Res. U., Cleve., 2000—03; asst. prof. UMDNJ-Robert Wood Johnson Med. Sch., Piscataway, NJ, 2003—. Lab. dir. Case Western Res. U., Cleve., 1999—2003. Coord. Bahai Faith, Atlanta, 1994—97. Recipient Sci. Reviewer, Various Internat. Sci. Jour., 1999-present; grantee Faculty Minority Grant, Nat. Inst. of Health-NIH, 2003—; Rsch. Fellowship, Aha, NIH, 1993-1998. Mem.: Am. Physiol. Soc. Bahai Faith. Achievements include research in muscle fatigue, stress and cardiac physiology. Office: UMDNJ-Robert Wood Johnson Medical School 675 Hoes Ln Piscataway NJ 08854 Office Phone: 732-235-5068. Office Fax: 732-235-4483. Business E-Mail: brottoma@umdnj.edu.

BROTTON, JOYCE DUPRAS, English language educator; m. Charles Michael Brotton, Oct. 26, 1968; children: Charles Michael, Ann Brotton Harvey. BA, George Mason U., 1992, MA, 1993, D in Arts, 2002. Intelligence processing U.S. Dept. of Def., Washington, 1963—68; prof. English, program head No. Va. C.C., Annandale, Va., 1994—. Exec. sec. Adv. Bd., Cert. in Profl. Writing, Annandale, Va., 1999—; coord., cert. in profl. writing No. Va. C.C., Annandale, Va., 1999—, adj. faculty; conf. chair Va. English Discipline Peer Group of C.C. English Tchrs., 2002, head English Program. Prodr.(narrator): (televised video) The Theory of Editing, The Practice of Editing, Writing User Manuals; contbr. articles to profl. jours.; author: Revising Life Through Literature: From the Reformation through Post Modernism, 2004. Chair, scholarship awards Greenbriar Woman's Club, Fairfax, Va., 1995—; speaker-world lit. and profl. writing Speakers Bur., No. Va. C.C., Annandale, Va., 1998—. Mem.: Assn. Tchrs. of Tech. Writing (assoc.), Two-Year Coll. English (assoc.; presenter 1997—2001), Golden Key. Avocations: world travel, theater, reviewing books. Office: Northern Va Cmty Coll 8333 Little River Turnpike Annandale VA 22003 Business E-Mail: jbrotton@nvcc.edu.

BROTZEN, FRANZ RICHARD, materials scientist, educator; b. Berlin, July 4, 1915; arrived in U.S., 1941; s. Georg and Lena (Pacully) Brotzen; m. Frances Burke Ridgway, Jan. 31, 1950; children: Franz Ridgway, Julie Ridgway. BSMetE, Case Inst. Tech., 1950, MS, 1953, PhD, 1954. Salesman a Quimica Bayer Ltda., Rio de Janeiro, 1934-41; mfrs. rep. R.G. Le Tourneau, Inc., Longview, Tex., 1947-48; sr. rsch. assoc. Case Inst. Tech., Cleve., 1951-54; mem. faculty Rice U., Houston, 1954—, prof. materials sci., 1959—88, prof. emeritus, 1988—, dean engring., 1962-66, master Brown Coll., 1977-82. Vis. prof. Max Planck Inst., Stuttgart, Germany, 1960—61, Stuttgart, 1973—74, Fed. Poly. Inst., Zurich, Switzerland, 1966—67, U. Lausanne, Switzerland, 1981. Contbr. scientific papers to profl. jours. Chmn. Houston Contemporary Arts Assn., 1964—65. Served to 1st lt. U.S. Army, 1942—46. Recipient Sr. Scientist award, West German Govt., 1973—74; Guggenheim fellow, 1960—61. Fellow: Am. Soc. Metals (chmn. Houston chpt. 1980—81); mem.: AIME, Soc. Engring. Sci., Am. Phys. Soc., Sigma Xi, Tau Beta Pi. Home: 2701 Bellefontaine St # H Houston TX 77025 Office: Rice U Dept Materials Sci PO Box 1892 Houston TX 77251-1892 Office Phone: 713-348-3563.

BROUDE, MARK ALLEN, lawyer; b. Skokie, Ill., June 26, 1964; s. Richard F. and Paula G. Broude; m. Susan Zuckerman, Mar. 21, 1992; 1 child, Jacob. BA, Williams Coll., 1986; JD, U. Chgo., 1989. Bar: N.Y. 1990, U.S. Dist. Ct. (so. dist.) N.Y. 1992. Assoc. Shearman & Sterling, N.Y.C., 1989-92; from assoc. to ptnr. Schulte Roth & Zabel LLP, N.Y.C., 1992—. Contbr. articles to profl. jours. Mem. ABA, N.Y. State Bar Assn., Internat. Bar Assn., Assn. Bar City N.Y. Office: Schulte Roth & Zabel LLP 919 3d Ave New York NY 10022

BROUDE, RICHARD FREDERICK, lawyer, educator; b. L.A., June 6, 1936; s. Leo Martin and Frances (Goldman) B.; m. Paula Louise Galnick, June 8, 1958; children: Julie Sue, James Matthew, Mark Allen. BS, Washington U., St. Louis, 1957; JD, U. Chgo., 1961. Bar: Ill. 1961, Calif. 1971, N.Y. 1989. Prof. law U. Nebr., Lincoln, 1966-69, Georgetown U., Washington, 1969-71; ptnr. Commons & Broude, L.A., 1974-77, Irell & Manella, L.A., 1977-80, Sidley & Austin, L.A., 1980-87, White & Case, L.A., 1987-90, Mayer, Brown & Platt, N.Y.C., 1990-99. Adj. prof. law U. So. Calif., L.A., 1978-90, St. Johns U., 2000—; adv. panel World Bank Insolvency Initiative; cons. OECD Forum for Asian Insolvency Reform. Author: Reorganizations Under Chapter 11, 1986—, Cases and Materials on Land Financing, 3rd, 1985; editor: Insolvency and Finance in the Transportation Industry, 1993, Collier Internat. Bus. Guide; mem. editl. bd.: Collier on Bankruptcy, contbg. editor: Collier Bankruptcy Practice Guide. Fellow Am. Bar Found., Am. Coll. Bankruptcy; mem. ABA (com. on bus. bankruptcy), Am. Law Inst. (advisor Transnat. Insolvency Project), Internat. Bar Assn. (chair insolvency and credit rights com. 1996-2000), Bar Assn. of City of N.Y., Calif. Bar Assn., Nat. Bankruptcy Conf. (conferee, chair com. on internat. aspects, vice chair legis. com.). Office: Richard F Broude PC 400 E 84th St # 22A New York NY 10028-5611 Office Phone: 917-301-3468. E-mail: rfbroude@broudepc.com.

BROUDE, RONALD, music publisher; b. N.Y.C., Oct. 15, 1941; s. Irving and Anne Broude; m. Janyce Ingalls, Aug. 19, 1982. AB, Columbia Coll., 1962; MA, Columbia U., 1962, PhD, 1967. Pres., exec. editor Broude Bros. Ltd., N.Y.C. and Williamstown, Mass., 1973—; trustee Broude Trust for the publ. musicological editions, N.Y.C., 1981—. Mem. exec. bd. Early Music Am., 1994-98. Mem.: Soc. Textual Scholarship (mem. exec. bd. 1989—, exec. dir. 2004—).

BROUGHTON, CAROLYN MILES, multimedia executive, public relations executive; b. Cambridge, Mass., Mar. 2, 1958; d. David Alan and Martha Jean (Butler) Miles; m. George C. Broughton, May 7, 1988; 1 child, Christiana Marie. AA, Am. Coll., Paris, 1979; BA in Radio and TV Communications, George Washington U., 1982; MA in Human Resources Devel., Webster U., 1996. TV reporter Sta. WHSV-TV3, Harrisonburg, Va., 1981-82, Sta. WJKS-TV17, Jacksonville, Fla., 1982-85, Sta. WJXT-TV4, Jacksonville, 1985-89; pub. rels. coord. City of Jacksonville, 1989—. Pres. Broughton & Assocs. Disabilities Cons., Jacksonville, Fla., 1994—. Vol. P.A.C.E. Ctr. for Girls, Jacksonville, 1989—, Gateway coun. Girl Scouts USA, 1999—. Recipient Cmty. Svc. Fla. Emmy award, 1987, Golden Palm award 1997 (2), 2000, Image award (3), 1998, Image Awds. (6), 1999, Silver Quill Awd., 1998, Image award (3), 2000, Mayor's award, 2001. Mem. City County Communicators and Mktg., Fla. Govt. Communicators, Internat. TV and Video Assn., U.S. Fencing Assn. Avocations: internet, web content and design, photography, fencing, volunteerism. Office: 6999 Merrill Rd Ste 2 Jacksonville FL 32277-2690 E-mail: brough@mediaone.net.

BROUGHTON, JAMES WALTER, real estate development executive, consultant; b. Atlantic City, Dec. 16, 1946; s. Walter Lennie and Janet Caroline (Mossman) B.; m. Sharon Carter, Mar. 10, 1980; children: Jennifer Christine, Matthew James. Student, U. Colo., Colorado Springs, 1967-68, U. Md., 1968-70, U. Colo., Denver, 1972-73. Asst. regional sales dir. Del E. Webb Corp., Denver, 1972-76; dir. mktg. Interval Internat., Miami, Fla., 1981-82; exec. dir. Time Sharing Inst., Miami, 1981-82; pres. J. Broughton, Inc., Miami, 1976-83, Spectrum Mktg. Group, Denver, 1983-84, Ocean Resourts Devel. Co., Ventura, Calif., 1984-85; sr. v.p. Fairfield Cmtys., Inc., Atlanta, 1985; chmn., pres., CEO, Lexes Enterprises, Inc., Las Vegas, Nev., 1985—. Bd. dirs. Consol. Resorts, Inc., PC Cons., Inc., Sea-Shore, Inc., Internat. Cruise and Excursion Gallery; pub. Time Sharing Ency., 1981, Time Sharing Ind. Rev., 1981. Contbr. articles to profl. jours. With USAF, 1964-71. Mem. Am. Resort Devel. Assn. (bd. dirs. 1985—, exec. com. 1988—, chmn. meetings coun. 1991—, resort devel. forum 1993—, treas. 1993—, recruitment award 1983, NTC svc. award 1987, Leader of Yr. award 1991, Industry Visionary Leader of Yr. award 1993), Nat. Time Sharing Coun. (chmn. 1984-86, bd. govs. 1984-92, recruitment award 1984), Interval Internat. (adv. bd. 1982-91), Urban Land Inst. (recreational devel. coun. 1993—). Republican.

BROUGHTON, MARGARET MARTHA, mental health nurse; b. London, Ky., Feb. 1, 1926; d. Edward Broughton and Stella Alice Johnson; m. Louis Kurt Henkel, May 17, 1947 (div. Nov. 1957); children: Gretchen Maria Henkel Clark, Suzanne Henkel Guthrie, Elizabeth Henkel Stark, David Lawrence Henkel, John Arthur Henkel. RN, Christ Hosp. Sch. Nursing, Cin., 1947; BA in Religious Studies, U. Calif., Santa Barbara, 2003. Staff nurse, psychiatric nurse to asst. supt. psychiatric nurse and instr. Camarillo (Calif.) State Hosp., 1958—70; mental health nurse I and II, insvc. instr. Ventura County Mental Health, Calif., 1973—88; part-time spiritual group facilitator Hillmont Psychiatric Ctr., Ventura, Calif., 1995—. Democrat. Universalist Unitarian. Avocations: singing, reading, walking. Home: 980 Terracina Dr Santa Paula CA 93060 E-mail: phoenixrise@vcnet.com.

BROUGHTON, PHILLIP CHARLES, lawyer, director; b. Findlay, Ohio, Sept. 21, 1930; s. Harold C. and Marian (Pierson) B.; children: Margaret Crockett, Phillip Charles, Anne Duvall, Elizabeth Cox. BA, Bowling Green U., 1953; JD, U. Mich., 1957; LLM, NYU, 1962. Bar: N.Y. 1957. Practiced in, N.Y.C., 1957—; mem. firm Thacher, Proffitt and Wood, 1957-93, of counsel, 1993—. Pres., bd. dirs. Midgard Found., N.Y.C.; pres., bd. trustees Asheville (N.C.) Art Mus.; trustee United Way Asheville, N.C. Mus. Art, Achilles Meml. Fund. Mem. ABA.

BROUGHTON, ROBERT STEPHEN, engineering educator, consultant; b. Corbetton, Ont., Can., June 29, 1934; s. Arthur Stephen and Luella Margaret (Gray) B.; m. Ruth Mabel Smith, May 11, 1957; children: G. Anne, Sharon Mae, Heather Louise, Stephen Russell. BS in Agr., U. Toronto, 1956, B in Applied Sci., 1957; MCE, MIT, 1959; PhD in Drainage Engring., McGill U., Montreal, 1972; LLD (hon.), Dalhousie U., Halifax, N.S., Can., 1989. Cert. profl. engr., Ont., Que. Jr. engr. John Deere Plow Co., Welland, Ont., 1956; rsch. asst. MIT, Cambridge, 1957-59; hydraulic engr. conservation br. Ont. Govt., Toronto, 1959-61; lectr. in agrl. engring. McGill U., 1962-63, asst. prof. agrl. engring., 1963-66, assoc. prof., 1966-74, prof., 1974-98, prof. emeritus, 1998—. From v.p. to pres. Can. Soc. Agrl. Engring., 1968-75, chmn. drainage rsch. com.; speaker farmers' meetings. Author, editor book in field; contbr. over 130 articles to publs. Tchr. Sunday sch. Beaurepaire United Ch., Beaconsfield, Que., 1965-72, clk. of session, 1973-78. Recipient Internat. Achievement award Can. nat. com. Internat. Commn. Irrigation and Drainage, 1993, Genie award, 1994, Mastery for Svc. award Mc Gill U., 1995, Lifetime Achievement cert. for drainage of agrl. lands Can. Nat. Com. irrigation and Drainage, 2004; named to Internat. Drainage Hall of Fame, 1994. Fellow Can. Soc. Agrl. Engring. (Maple Leaf award 1978, James Beamish award 1989), Am. Soc. Agrl. Engrs., Ordre des Ingénieurs du Que.; mem. Assn. Profl. Engrs. Ont., Corrugated Plastic Pipe Assn. (life). Mem. United Ch. Can. Achievements include research on design and construction of subsurface drainage systems for control of waterlogging and salinity of irrigated lands, assisted with irrigation and drainage projects in India, Pakistan, Egypt, Trinidad, El Salvador, Barbados, Canada, etc. Office: McGill U Macdonald Campus 21111 Lakeshore Rd Sainte-Anne-de-Bellevue PQ Canada H9X 3V9 Business E-Mail: robert.broughton@mcgill.ca.

BROUILLETTE, DAN R., former federal agency administrator; b. Paincourtville, La. m. Adrienne Brouillette; 2 children. Grad., U. Md. Legis. dir. to Congressman Billy Tallzin, 1989—97; sr. v.p. R. Duffy Wall & Assocs., 1997—2000; asst. sec. congl. and intergovtl. affairs U.S. Dept. Energy, Washington, 2001—03; ptnr. Alpine Group Inc., 2000—01, 2003; staff dir. U.S. Ho. Energy & Commerce com., Washington, 2003—. With U.S. Army. Office: The Comm on Energy & Commerce 2125 Rayburn Ho Office Bldg Washington DC 20515

BROUN, ELIZABETH, art historian, curator; b. Kansas City, Mo., Dec. 15, 1946; d. Augustine Hughes and Roberta Catherine (Hayden) Gibson. BA, U. Kans., 1968, PhD, 1976; cert. advanced study, U. Bordeaux, France, 1967. Curator prints and drawings Spencer Mus. Art, Lawrence, Kans., 1976-83; asst. prof. U. Kans., Lawrence, 1978-83; asst. dir. chief curator Nat. Mus. Am. Art, Washington, 1983-88, acting dir., 1988-89; dir. Smithsonian Am. Art Mus. (formerly Nat. Mus. Am. Art), Washington, 1989—. Author: exhbn. catalogues Prints of Zorn, 1979, Prints and Drawings of Pat Steir, 1983, Patrick Ireland; Drawings 1965-85, 1986, Albert Pinkham Ryder, 1989; co-author: Benton's Bentons, 1980, Engravings of Marcantonio Raimondi, 1981. Woodrow Wilson fellow, 1968-69; Ford. Found. fellow, 1970-72 Mem. Phi Beta Kappa Office: MRC 970 PO Box 37012 Washington DC 20013-7012 Office Phone: 202-275-1515.

BROUNTAS, PAUL PETER, lawyer; b. Bangor, Maine, Mar. 19, 1932; s. Peter Nicholas and Penelope (Spiropoulos) B.; m. Lynn Barrett Thurston, Sept. 7, 1963; children— Paul Peter, Jennifer VanWoert, Barrett Penelope AB summa cum laude, Bowdoin Coll., 1954; BA, Oxford (Eng.) U., 1956, MA, 1960; LLB, Harvard U., 1960. Bar: Mass. 1960. Assoc. Hale and Dorr LLP, Boston, 1960-64, jr. ptnr., 1964-68, sr. ptnr., 1968—2002, sr. counsel, 2003—04, Wilmer, Cutler, Pickering, Hale & Dorr, Boston, 2004—. Guest presenter Harvard U. Bus. Sch., Cambridge, Mass., 1981-87; corp. sec. various corps.; panelist, lectr. corp., venture capital and securities law. Author: Boardroom Excellence: A Common Sense Perspective on Corporate Governance, 2003. Overseer Bowdoin Coll., Brunswick, Maine, 1974-82, pres. bd. overseers, 1979-82, trustee, 1983-96, chmn. bd. trustees, 1993-96; chmn. com. for Michael S. Dukakis Gov. of Mass., 1976-88; chmn. Dukakis for Pres. Com., 1987-88; mem. corp. Children's Hosp. Med. Ctr., Boston, 1965-87, Boston Mus. Sci., 1966-91, Mass. Gen. Hosp., Boston, 1983-94; mem. bd. overseers Newton Wellesley Hosp., 1990-96; mem. Marshall Scholar Selection Com. N.E. Region, 1973-75, 88-92; mem. Weston Planning Bd., Mass., 1967-72, chmn., 1970-72; chmn. Met. Boston Citizen's Coalition for Cleaner Air, 1969-71; bd. dirs. Mass. Ctrs. of Excellence Corp., 1985-87. Served with U.S. Army, 1956-58. Marshall scholar, 1954 Mem. ABA, Mass. Bar Assn., Boston Bar Assn., Assn. Marshall Scholars and Alumni (treas. 1965-71, bd. dirs. 1988-90). Avocations: skiing, golf. Office: Wilmer Cutler Pickering Hale and Dorr LLP 60 State St Boston MA 02109-1816 Office Phone: 617-526-6620. E-mail: paul.brountas@wilmerhale.com.

BROUS, THOMAS RICHARD, lawyer; b. Fulton, Mo., Jan. 7, 1943; s. Richard Pendleton and Augusta (Gilpin) B.; m. Patricia Catlin, Sept. 12, 1964; (dec. Sept. 1999); children: Anna Catlin Brous, Joel Pendleton Brous; m. Mary Lou McClelland Kroh, Sept. 8, 2001. BSBA, Northwestern U., 1965; JD cum laude, U. Mich., 1968. Bar: Mo. 1968, U.S. Dist. Ct. (we. dist.) Mo. 1968, U.S. Ct. Mil. Appeals 1968, U.S. Supreme Ct. 1971. Assoc. Watson & Marshall L.C., Kans. City, Mo., 1968-78, ptnr., 1978-96, mng. ptnr., 1992-94; shareholder Stinson, Mag & Fizzell, P.C., Kans. City, Mo., 1996—2002; ptnr. Stinson Morrison Hecker LLP, Kans. City, 2002—. Mem. steering com. U. Mo. Kansas City Law Sch. Employee Benefits Inst., 1990—2001, chmn. 1992-93; with Ctrl. Mtn. Tax Exempt and Govtl. Entities Coun. IRS, 1997—. Author: Chapter 26, III Missouri Business Organizations, 1998; asst. editor Mich. Law Rev., 1966-68. Mem. vestry St. Andrews Episcopal Ch., Kansas City, 1974-77, Grace & Holy Trinity Cathedral, 1994—, chancellor, 1998—; trustee Mo. Repertory Theatre, Inc., Kansas City, 1990—, pres., 1995-98; v.p., treas. Barstow Sch., Kansas City, 1982-86; dir. Met. Orgn. to Counter Sexual Abuse, Kansas City, 1992-95. Capt. U.S. Army, 1968-72. Mem. ABA, Univ. Club (pres. 1988-89), Greater Kansas City Soc. Hosp. Attys., Kansas City Met. Bar Assn., Heart of Am. Employee Benefit Conf., The Mo. Bar Assn. (vice-chair employee benefits com. 1997-2000), Mo. Soc. Hosp. Attys., Delta Upsilon, Beta Gamma Sigma. Episcopalian. Avocations: reading, hiking, gardening. Office: Stinson Morrison Hecker LLP 1201 Walnut Ste 2800 Kansas City MO 64106 Office Phone: 816-691-3368. E-mail: tbrous@stinsonmoheck.com.

BROUSSARD, MALCOLM JOSEPH, pharmacist, consultant; b. Lake Charles, La., Mar. 14, 1953; s. Roy Joseph and Liller Leeova (Tubbs) B. BS in Biology, McNeese State U., Lake Charles, 1975; BS in Pharmacy, Xavier Coll. Pharmacy, 1978. Registered pharmacist. Staff pharmacist Hotel Dieu Hosp., New Orleans, 1978-80, JoEllen Smith Meml. Hosp., New Orleans, 1980-85; asst. dir. pharmacy St. Jude Med. Ctr., Kenner, La., 1985-91; dir. pharmacy MacKinnon Ctr., Metairie, La., 1991-93; pharmacist St. Jude Med. Ctr., Kenner, La., 1994—99; exec. dir. La. Bd. Pharmacy, 1999—. Founder, pres. Parenteral Therapy Svcs., Inc., Harvey, La., 1985—90; v.p. Lapalco Pharmacy, Inc., 1987—90, South La. Med. Supply Co., Inc., 1987—90; pharmacy cons. La. State Bd. Nursing, New Orleans, 1980—93; externship preceptor Xavier Coll. Pharmacy, 1980—99, vis. instr., 1982—83, asst. prof., 1991—99. Bd. dirs. New Orleans Pharmacy Mus., 1988—99; mem., advisor La. Pharmacists Polit. Action Com., 1984—99. Mem. Am. Pharm. Assn., Am. Soc. Hosp. Pharmacists (state del. 1991-93), La. Pharmacists Assn. (pres. 1983-84, Pres.'s award 1984, Pharmacist of Yr. 1985), La. Soc. Hosp. Pharmacists (pres. 1988-89), S.E. La. Soc. Hosp. Pharmacists (pres. 1981-82, Pharmacist of Yr. 1984), Rho Chi, Phi Lambda Sigma. Republican. Roman Catholic. Avocation: skiing. Home: 2510 Gates Cir Apt 12 Baton Rouge LA 70809-1032 Office Phone: 225-925-6496. Business E-Mail: mbroussard@labp.com.

BROUSSARD, MICHAEL LLOYD, literary agent; s. Lloyd James Broussard and Glenda Carolyn Lott. BA, S.W. Tex. State U. Lit. agt. Dupree Miller & Assocs., Dallas. Agt. Art Smith (Back to Table), 2001, Crucial Conversation, 2002 (NY Times Bestseller list), Heidi Swanson Cookbook 1.0, 2004 (NY Times Bestseller list). Avocations: skiing, fishing, movies, reading, pool. Office: Dupree Miller & Assocs 100 Highland Pk Vill #350 Dallas TX 75205

BROVER-LUBOVSKY, BELLA, musicologist; d. Mirra (Kipnis) and Mark Brover; m. Nahum Lubovsky, Sept. 10, 1962; children: Iliya Lubovsky, Dana Lubovsky, Ilan Lubovsky. BA in Music Theory and Piano, Sch. Music Kishinev, 1981; MA in Musicology, Moldavian State Consevatory, 1986; PhD of Musicology, Hebrew U., 2000. Rschr. and lectr. Hebrew U., Jerusalem, 2001—03; vis. asst. prof. Sch. Music U. Ill., Urbana, 2003—. Lectr. Magid Inst. for Adult Edn., Jerusalem, 1995—2003, Rubin Acad. Music and Dance, Jerusalem. Author: (academic) Estro armonico. Organization of Tonal Space in the Music of Vivaldi and his Contemporaries. Mem. Israel U. Women Assn., Jerusalem, 2000—01. Recipient Postdoctoral Prize for Study in Italy, Vigevani Found., 2003—04; fellow Salter New Program in Musicology, Hebrew U., 2001—03; grantee Orzen Postdoctoral Rsch., Hebrew U. Jerusalem, 2003—04; Individual Rsch. fellow, Newberry Libr., 2004—05. Mem.: Israel Musicological Soc., Soc. Music Theory, Am. Soc. Eighteenth-Century Studies, Soc. Eighteenth-Century Music, Am. Musicological. Soc. Office: School of Music Univ Ill 1114 W Nevada St Urbana IL 61801 Office Phone: 972-2-5883954. Business E-Mail: msbrover@mscc.huji.ac.ie. E-mail: lubovsky@uiuc.edu.

BROVITZ, RICHARD STUART, lawyer; b. Rochester, N.Y., Aug. 20, 1951; s. Murray H. and Rifka R. (Rotenberg) B.; m. Joan F. Zarkower, Aug. 11, 1974; children— Justin, Jessica. B.S. cum laude with honors in Acctg., Sch. Mgmt., Syracuse U., 1973, M.S., 1973, J.D. cum laude, Coll. Law, 1976. Bar: N.Y. 1977, U.S. Dist. Ct. (we. dist.) N.Y. 1977, U.S. Tax Ct. 1979. Assoc. Wegman, Mayberry, Burgess & Feldstein, Rochester, 1977-79; assoc. Fix Spindelman, Turk, Himelein & Shukoff, Rochester, 1979-81, ptnr., 1982—, mng. principal, 1985—. Pi Mu Epsilon math. scholar Syracuse U. Mem. ABA, N.Y. State Bar Assn., Monroe County Bar Assn. (chmn. Rochester life underwriters com.), Justinian Hon. Law Soc., Beta Gamma Sigma, Beta Alpha Psi, Phi Kappa Phi. Office: Fix Spindelman Brovitz Turk Himelein & Shukoff Two State St Rochester NY 14614

BROWAR, LISA MURIEL, librarian; b. N.Y.C., Jan. 22, 1951; d. Elliott Andrew and Shirley (Kahn) Browar. B in English Lit., Ind. U., 1973, MLS, 1977; M in English Lit., U. Kans., 1976; postgrad., Ind. U.-Purdue. U., Indpls., 2001—. Cert. in fund raising mgmt. 2001. Asst. curator Beinecke Libr. Yale U., New Haven, 1979-81, archivist Sterling Meml. Libr., 1981-82; curator spl. collections Vassar Coll. Libr., Poughkeepsie, N.Y., 1982-87; asst. dir. rare books and manuscripts N.Y. Pub. Libr., N.Y.C., 1987-96; dir. The Lilly Libr., Ind. U., Bloomington, 1996-2001; libr. for English and Am. lit., philosophy and film studies Main Libr., Ind. U., Bloomington, 2001—02; univ. libr. New Sch. U., N.Y.C., 2002—. Editor RBM: A Jour. of Rare Books, Manuscripts, and Cultural Heritage, 1999-2003. Mem. ALA, Assn. Coll. and Rsch. Librs. (sec. rare books and manuscripts sect. 1987-89, chair, 1994-95, editor 1999—), Soc. Am. Archivists, Bibliog. Soc. Am., Grolier Club. Democrat. Avocations: opera, theater, photography. Office: Fogelman Libr 65 Fifth Ave New York NY 10011 Office Phone: 212-229-5598 ext. 3149. Business E-Mail: browarl@newschool.edu.

BROWDE, ANATOLE, electronics company executive, consultant; b. Berlin, June 10, 1925; came to U.S., 1940, naturalized, 1946; s. Alexander and Rebecca (Braude) Kutisker; m. Jacqueline Rousseau, Mar. 10, 1973; children: David, Elizabeth, Richard. BEE, Cornell U., 1948; postgrad., Northwestern U., 1948, Columbia U., 1951-52; MLA, Washington U., St. Louis, 1994, MA, 1996, PhD in History, 1999. Engr. Capehart-Farnsworth Corp., Ft. Wayne, Ind., 1948-51, Arma Corp., Bklyn., 1951-53; project engr. BOMARC, Westinghouse Electric Co., Balt., 1953-55; assoc. dir. missile dept. Avco Corp., Cin., 1955-59; with McDonnell Douglas Corp., 1959-90, v.p. engring. and mktg., 1979-81; v.p., gen. mgr. info. systems div. McDonnell Douglas Electronics Co., St. Charles, Mo., 1981-82, v.p. Microelectronics Ctr., 1982-87; v.p. ops. McDonnell Douglas Electronics Systems Co., 1987-89, dir. ops. integration, 1989-90; pres. Browde Cons. Inc., St. Louis, 1990—97. Adj. prof. Maryville U., St Louis, 1992—. Chmn. secondary schs. com. Cornell U., 1968-1976, mem. univ. council, 1971-77, 79—; trustee First Unitarian Ch., St. Louis, 1977-80, chmn., 1979-80, chmn. fin. com., 1985-1989. Mem.: Cornell (St. Louis), Cornell U. Coun. Republican. Unitarian Universalist. Achievements include development of Mercury, Gemini Spacecraft electronics, 1961-68, airborne collision avoidance system, 1968-72. Home: 12031 Carberry Pl Saint Louis MO 63131-3124

BROWDER, FELIX EARL, mathematician, educator; b. Moscow, July 31, 1927; s. Earl and Raissa (Berkmann) Browder; m. Eva Tislowitz, Oct. 5, 1949; children: Thomas, William. SB, MIT, 1946; PhD, Princeton U., 1948; MA (hon.), Yale U., 1962; D (hon.), U. Paris, 1990. C.L.E. Moore instr. math. MIT, 1948—51, vis. assoc. prof., 1961—62, vis. prof., 1977—78; instr. Boston U., 1951—53; asst. prof. Brandeis U., 1955—56; from asst. prof. to prof. Yale U., 1956—63; prof. math. U. Chgo., 1963—72, Louis Block prof. math., 1972—82, Max Mason disting. svc. prof., 1982—87, chmn. dept., 1972—77, 1980—85; v.p. rsch. Rutgers, The State U. NJ, 1986—91; univ. prof. Rutgers U., New Brunswick, 1986—. Vis. mem. Inst. Advanced Study, Princeton (N.J.) U., 1953—54, 1963—64; vis. prof. Princeton U., 1968, Inst. Pure and Applied Math., Rio de Janeiro, 1960, U. Paris, 1973, 1975, 1978, 1981, 1983, 1985; sr. rsch. fellow U. Sussex, 1970, 1976, England; Fairchild Disting. visitor Calif. Inst. Tech., Pasadena, 1975—76; spkr. Internat. Congress of Math., 1970, Sci. Bd. Santa Fe Inst., 1986—98, U.S. Nat. Med. Sci., 1999. Contbr. theorems to books, including Nonlinear Problems, 1966, Functional Analysis and Related Fields, 1970, Nonlinear Operators and Nonlinear Equations of Evolution in Banach Spaces, 1976, Nonlinear Functional Analysis and Its Applications, 1986. With U.S. Army, 1953—55. Fellow Guggenheim, 1953—54, 1966—67, Sloan Found., 1959—63, NSF sr. postdoctoral fellow, 1957—58. Fellow: AAAS (chmn. sect. A 1982—83); mem.: NAS (coun. mem. 1992—95), Math. Assn. Am., Am. Math. Soc. (editor bull. 1959—68, 1978—83, mem. coun. 1959—72, 1978—83, mng. editor 1964—68, 1980, exec. com. counl 1979—80, colloquium lectr. 1970, pres. 1999—2001), Am. Acad. Arts and Scis., Sigma Xi (pres. chpt. 1985—86). Achievements include development of linear and nonlinear partial differential equations; nonlinear functional analysis and fixed point and mapping theorems. E-mail: browder@math.rutgers.edu.

BROWDER, JOHN GLEN, former congressman, educator; b. Sumter, SC, Jan. 15, 1943; s. Archie Calvin and Ila (Frierson); m. Sara Rebecca Moore; 1 child, Jenny Rebecca. BA in History, Presbyn. Coll., 1965; MA in Polit. Sci., PhD in Polit. Sci., Emory U., 1971. Asst. in pub. relations Presbyn. Coll., Clinton, S.C., 1965; sportswriter The Atlanta Jour., 1966; investigator U.S. Civil Service Commn., Atlanta, 1966-68; prof. polit. sci. Jacksonville (Ala.) State U., 1971-87; mem. Ala. Ho. of Reps., Montgomery, 1982-86; sec. of state State of Ala., Montgomery, 1987-89; mem. 101st-104th Congresses from 3d Ala. dist., Washington, 1989-96; disting. vis. prof. nat. security affairs Naval Postgrad. Sch., Monterey, Calif., 1997—; eminent scholar in Am. democracy Jacksonville State Univ., Ala., 1999—. Contbr. articles to newspapers, profl. jours.; author: Study Guide for The Future of American Democracy, 2004. Mem. Am. Polit. Sci. Assn., So. Polit. Sci. Assn. Democrat. Methodist. Office: Naval Postgrad Sch NS/BG Nat Security Affairs Dept Monterey CA 93943 E-mail: igbrowder@nps.navy.mil.*

BROWDER, WILLIAM BAYARD, lawyer; b. Urbana, Ill., Sept. 6, 1916; s. Olin Lorraine and Nellie Sheldon (Taylor) B.; m. Mary Bain Lehmann, Sept. 6, 1942 (dec. Feb. 1984); children: David Sheldon, Wendy Elisabeth, Amy Spence (dec.); m. Betty M. Kennedy, Jan. 5, 1985 AB, U. Ill., 1938, JD, 1941; LLD, MacMurray Coll., Jacksonville, Ill., 1979, Ill. Coll., 1990. Bar: Ill. 1941. Atty. I.C.R.R., 1941-47, Union Tank Car Co., Chgo., 1948-81, sec., 1952-77, dir., 1954-81, gen. counsel, 1956-79, v.p., 1965-74, sr. v.p., 1974-81; v.p., dir. Trans Union Corp., 1969-81, gen. counsel, 1969-79, sr. v.p., 1974-79, sr. v.p. law, 1979-81; v.p., dir. Ecodyne Corp., 1972-81. Dir. Procor, Ltd., 1952-81 Mem. Citizens Com. To Study Police-Community Relations in Chgo., 1966-67; chmn. Com. To Study Financing Community Colls. in Ill., 1974-75; pres. Chgo. Crime Commn., 1965-67; mem. adv. com. U. Ill. Coll. Commerce and Bus. Adminstrn., Champaign-Urbana, 1969-73; mem. Ill. Racing Bd., 1973-74; mem. Ill. Bd. Higher Edn., 1975-91, chmn., 1979-91; pres. Wilmette United Fund, 1962; life trustee YMCA-U Ill., 1966—, chmn.,

1967-79; bd. dirs. Mid Am. chpt. ARC, 1963-65, Wilmette Pub. Libr., 1964-67, Northwestern Meml. Hosp., 1970-75; mem. U. Ill. Found., 1969—, bd. dirs., 1973-79, mem. pres.'s coun., 1974—; mem. Ill. Gov.'s Task Force on Pvt. Sector Initiatives, 1983-86, Ill. Gov.'s Commn. on Sci. and Tech., 1983-87; mem. Ill. Gaming Bd., 1993-99; bd. dirs. organized crime com. Chgo. Crime Commn.; trustee Trinity United Meth. Ch., chmn. bd. trustee, 1973-85. Mem. Am., Ill. bar assns., U. Ill. Law Alumni Assn. (pres. 1968-71), Chgo. Legal Club, Order of Coif, Union League Club (Chgo.) (dir. 1974-76), Westmoreland Country Club (Wilmette, Ill.) (sec., dir. 1979), Phi Beta Kappa, Phi Eta Sigma, Beta Theta Pi, Phi Alpha Delta. Methodist. Home: 521 E Orange Grove Ave Sierra Madre CA 91024-2616

BROWDY, JOSEPH EUGENE, lawyer; b. Bklyn., July 23, 1937; s. Philip and Fannie (Asherowitz) B.; m. Anita Sue Rubenstein, June 18, 1958; childrenF: Jennifer, Daniel. BA, Oberlin Coll., 1958; LLB, NYU, 1961. Bar: N.Y. 1962, D.C. 1982. Assoc. Paul, Weiss, Rifkind, Wharton & Garrison, N.Y.C., 1962-71, ptnr., 1972-97, of counsel, 1998—. Adj. asst. prof. real estate NYU, 1976-86; lectr. in field. With U.S. Army Res., 1961-62. Mem. Assn. of Bar of City of N.Y. (com. real property law, chmn. subcom. on leasing 1989-92), Am. Coll. Real Estate Lawyers, Order of Coif, Phi Beta Kappa. Office: Paul Weiss Rifkind Wharton & Garrison 1285 Avenue of the Americas New York NY 10019-6065 Office Phone: 212-373-3039. Business E-Mail: jbrowdy@paulweiss.com.

BROWER, CHARLES NELSON, lawyer, judge; b. Plainfield, N.J., June 5, 1935; s. Charles Hendrickson and Mary Elizabeth (Nelson) B.; children: Michael Claudio Joseph Hutchings, Carmen Désirée Ponti, Frederica Anne Amity, Jasmin Maria Plekavich, Charles Hendrickson II. BA cum laude, Harvard U., 1957, JD, 1961; cert. Parker Sch. Comp. & Internat. Law, Columbia U., 1962. Bar: N.Y. 1962, D.C. 1970, U.S. Supreme Ct. 1967, U.S. Ct. Appeals (D.C. cir., 2d, 5th, 6th, 7th, 8th, 9th, 11th and fed. cirs.), U.S. Ct. Internat. Trade, U.S. Dist. Ct. (so. and ea. dists.) N.Y., U.S. Dist. Ct. D.C. Assoc., then ptnr. White & Case LLP, N.Y.C., 1961-69; asst. legal adviser European affairs Dept. State, Washington, 1969-71, dep. legal adviser, 1971-73, acting legal adviser, 1973; ptnr. White & Case LLP, Washington, 1973-84, 88-00, spl. counsel, 2001—05; mem. 20 Essex St. Chambers, London, 2001—. Judge Iran-U.S. Claims Tribunal, The Hague, 1984—88, 2001—, substitute judge, 1983—84, 1988—2000; dep. spl. counselor to the Pres., Washington, 1987; counsel and advocate for U.S., 92, Costa Rica, 98, Internat. Ct. Justice, The Hague; mem. Register of Experts UN Compensation Commn., 1991—; mem. sec. of state adv. com. on internat. law, 1996—; mem. panels of arbitrators and conciliators Internat. Ctr. for Settlement of Investment Disputes, 1998—; judge ad hoc Inter-Am. Ct. of Human Rights, 1999—. Fulbright scholar, Rheinische Friedrich-Wilhelms-Universitaet, Bonn, and Hochschule fuer Politik, Berlin, 1957—78. Mem. ABA (chmn. sect. internat. law 1981-82, mem. ho. of dels. 1982, 84-98, bd. govs. 1985-88, mem. nominating com. 1992-94), Internat. Law Assn. (hon. v.p. Am. br.), Internat. Bar Assn., Am. Soc. Internat. Law (v.p. 1994-96, pres. 1996-98, hon. v.p. 1998—2004), Am. Law Inst., Assn. of Bar of City of N.Y., Coun. Fgn. Rels., Inst. Transnat. Arbitration (chmn. adv. bd. 1994-2000), Ctr. for Am. and Internat. Law (trustee 1996—), Met. Club, Chevy Chase Club. Episcopalian. Home and Office: Parkweg 13 2585 JH The Hague Netherlands Office: White & Case 701 Thirteenth St NW Washington DC 20005 Office Phone: 31 70 3520064. E-mail: cbrower@20essexst.com.

BROWER, DAVID JOHN, lawyer, urban planner, educator; b. Holland, Mich., Sept. 11, 1930; s. John J. and Helen (Olson) B.; m. Lou Ann Brown, Nov. 26, 1960; children: Timothy Seth, David John, II, Ann Lacey. BA, U. Mich., 1956, JD, 1960. Bar: Ill. 1960, Mich. 1961, Ind. 1961, U.S. Supreme Ct. 1971. Asst. dir. div. community planning Ind. U., Bloomington, 1960-70; rsch. prof. dept. city and regional planning U. N.C., Chapel Hill, 1970—, assoc. dir. Ctr. for Urban and Regional Studies, 1970-94; pres. Coastal Resources Collaborative, Ltd., Chapel Hill and Manteo, N.C., 1980—; counsel Robinson & Cole, Hartford, Conn., 1986—. Vis. prof., Vt. Law Sch., South Royalton, summers, 1994—. Author: (with others) Constitutional Issues of Growth Management, 1978; Growth Management, 1984, Managing Development in Small Towns, 1984, Special Area Management, 1985, Catastrophic Coastal Storms, 1989, Understanding Growth Management, 1989, Coastal Zone Management: An Evaluation, 1991, An Introduction to Coastal Zone Management, 1994, rev. edit. 2002, Natural Hazard Mitigation, 1999. Fellow Am. Inst. Cert. Planners (Coll. of Fellows); mem.Am. Planning Assn. (bd. dirs. 1982-85, chmn.-founder planning and law div.). Democrat. Episcopalian. Home: 612 Shady Lawn Rd Chapel Hill NC 27514-2009 Office: U NC CB # 3140 Chapel Hill NC 27599-0001 E-mail: brower@email.unc.edu.

BROWER, JAMES CALVIN, graphic artist, painter; b. Clarksburg, W.Va., Dec. 30, 1914; s. Leroy Cooper and Margaret Wood (Watkins) B.; m. Elsie Margaret Day, Sept. 19, 1936; children: James Lawrence, Sandra Joan, Margaret, Linda Ann, Beth. Grad. high sch., Charleston, W.Va., 1932. Pvt. practice, Huntington, W.Va., 1933-43, Toledo, 1952—; ptnr., art dir. Brower, Brownsberger and Burda, Toledo, 1944-51; dir. art and design Meeks Heit Pub. Co., 1992-99. Author, illustrator: Mood and Mode, 2003; illustrator: Education for Sexuality, 1970, Human Sexuality, 1982, Education for Sexuality and HIV/AIDS, 1993, Blowpipes, Northwest Ohio Glassmaking in the Gas Boom of the 1880s, 2002, Mood & Mode, A Selection of Transparent Watercolors, 2003; paintings featured in The Creative Artist, 1990, The Best of Watercolor 2, 1997, The Best of Watercolor Composition, 1997. Recipient Pres. award Okla. Watercolor Soc., 1987, Past Pres. award San Diego Watercolor Soc. Internat. Exhbn., 1989. Mem. Ohio Watercolor Soc. (hon.; signature mem., bd. dirs. 1986-92, publicity chmn. 1986-92, Gold medal 1984, Charles Burchfield Meml. award 1991, Exhbn. award 1992, made hon. mem. 2001), Northwestern Ohio Watercolor Soc. (pres. 1983-84, Gold medal 2003), Nat. Water Color Soc. (signature mem., Artist's Mag./Liquitex award 1990, Mem.'s Exhbn. awards 1996, 98), Ky. Watercolor Soc. (artist mem.), Ga. Watercolor Soc. (signature mem., Gold award Nat. Exhbn. 1990), Transparent Watercolor Soc. Am., Toledo Fedn. Art Soc. (pres. 1987-88), Tile Club Toledo, Toledo Artists Club (gold medal 1998). Republican. Presbyterian. Avocations: chess, bridge. Home and Office: 2222 Grecourt Dr Toledo OH 43615-2918 Office Phone: 419-536-3984.

BROWER, JANICE KATHLEEN, library and information scientist; b. Chgo., July 29, 1952; d. Gerald B. (dec. Dec. 2000) and Emily (Kavicky) B. AA, Lincoln Coll., 1973; BS, Ill. State U., 1975; postgrad., U. Okla., 1984-86. Libr. assoc. Chgo. Pub. Libr., 1975-80, 81-83; libr. technician U. Okla. Biol. Sta., Norman, 1987; libr. technician III Jim E. Hamilton Correctional Ctr. Okla. Dept. of Corrections, Hodgen, 1987—. Lutheran. Avocations: reading, walking, visiting historical sites and museums, architecture. Office: Jim E Hamilton Correctional Ctr 53468 Mineral Springs Rd Hodgen OK 74939-3064 Office Phone: 918-653-7831 372. Business E-Mail: janice.brower@doc.state.ok.us. E-mail: jkbrower@alltel.net.

BROWER, ROBERT CHARLES, rehabilitation counselor, small business owner; b. Allendale, N.J. s. William P. and Adele B.; m. Hilja Kristiansen, Dec. 21, 1963; children: Robert K., Kristine D. BA in Psychology, Rutgers U., 1963; MDiv, Luth. Theol. Sem., Phila., 1966; postgrad. in counselign, Princeton Theol. Sem., 1970-71; postgrad. in Bus. Adminstrn., N.Y. Inst. Tech., 1993—. Cert. rehab. counselor, disability mgmt. specialist, case mgr., N.Y., U.S. Dept. Labor; ordained to ministry Lutheran Ch., 1966. Pastor St. Paul Luth. Ch., E. Windsor, N.J., 1966-71; psychiatric rehab. counselor N.Y. State Office of Vocations., Cen. Islip, 1971-73; coord. Rehab. Inst., Mineola, St. James, N.Y., 1973-74; program dir. and mental health clinic adminstr. Skills Unlimited, Oakdale, N.Y., 1974-78; dist. mgr. Intracorp subs. CIGNA, Woodbury, White Plains, N.Y., 1978-83; mgr. disability mgmt. svcs. Nat. Ctr. Disability Svcs. (formerly Human Resources Ctr.), Albertson, N.Y., 1984-90; pres. Brower Rehab. Svcs., Inc., Medford, N.Y., 1990—. Adj. prof. Sch. Counseling, Rsch., Spl. Edn. and Rehab., Hofstra U., Uniondale, N.Y., 1988-2001; speaker in field. Cert. Disability Mgmt. Specialist Commn.,(bd. dirs., treas. 1993-94, vice chair 1994-95, chair 1995-96), rep. to Found. for Rehab. Cert., Edn. and Rsch., 1993-94, 99-2003, chair govt. affairs and pub. rels. com., treas. found., treas., vice chair, 1994-95, chair, 1995-96. Mem. AAUP, Internat. Assn. Rehab. Profls., Internat. Rehab. Assn. (chmn. commn. for certification of disability mgmt. specialists commn.), Nat. Rehab. Profls. in Pvt. Sector, Profl. Rehab. Assn. L.I. and N.Y.C. (Rehab. Profl. of Yr. in Ancillary Care 1994), Assn. Blauvelt Descendants (pres. 1998-2005), Delta Mu Delta Avocations: sailing, photography. Home: 37 Crooked Pine Dr Medford NY 11763-4329

BROWMAN, DAVID L(UDVIG), archaeologist; b. Dec. 9, 1941; s. Ludvig G. and Audra (Arnold) B.; m. M. Jane Fox, Apr. 24, 1965; children: Lisa, Tina, Becky. BA, U. Mont., 1963; MA, U. Wash., 1966; PhD, Harvard U., 1970. Hwy. archaeologist Wash. State Hwy. Dept., Olympia, 1964-66; field dir. Yale U., New Haven, 1968-69; tutor Harvard U., 1969-70; mem. faculty Washington U., St. Louis, 1970—, prof. archeology, 1984—, chmn., 1986—. Dir. Cons. Survey Archeology, St. Louis, 1976—, Inst. Study of Plants, Food and Man, Kirkwood, Mo. 1979-84: cons. St. Louis Dept. Parks and Recreation, 1978—. Editor/author: Advances in Andean Archaeology, 1978, Economic Organization of Prehispanic Peru, 1984, Risk Management and Arid Land Use Strategies in the Andes, 1986, New Perspectives on Americanist Archaeology, 2002; editor: Cultural Continuity in Mesoamerica, 1979, Early Native Americans, 1980. Charter mem. Confluence St. Louis, 1983; mem. Gov.'s Adv. Coun. Hist. Preservation, 1982-89, sec. 1989-91. NSF fellow, 1967, grantee, 1974-75, 85—. Fellow AAAS; mem. Soc. Profl. Archaeologists (sec.-treas. 1981-83, grievance coord. 1997-98), AAUP (chpt. pres. 1980-82), Registry Profl. Archaeologists (grievance coord. 1998-99), Mo. Assn. Profl. Archaeologists (v.p. 1981-82), Mo. Archaeology Soc. (trustee 1977—), Sigma Xi (chpt. pres. 1985-). Roman Catholic. Avocations: hiking, gardening. Office: Washington U Campus Box 1114 Saint Louis MO 63130-4899 Office Phone: 314-935-5231.

BROWN, A. HAYDEN, animal scientist, educator; s. A. Hayden and Imogene Wanda Brown; m. Helen Virginia Gann, Nov. 9, 1977; 1 child, Ashley. BSc, Tenn. Tech. U., 1968; MSc, U. Tenn., 1974, PhD, 1976. Cert. Am. Coll. Animal Genetics, registered Am. Registry Profl. Animal Scientist. Prof. U. Ark., Fayetteville, Ark., 1977—. Mem. editl. bd.: Jour. Animal Sci., 2001—03; contbr. articles to profl. jours. Named to American Cattle Breeders Hall Fame, 1982. Mem.: American Registry Profl. Animal Scientists (pres. 1999—2000), Sigma Xi. Office: University Arkansas AFLS B 106 Fayetteville AR 72701 Business E-Mail: hbrown@uark.edu.

BROWN, ABBIE HOWARD, education educator, researcher; b. Bklyn., Mar. 5, 1960; s. Ronald Wallace and Shirley Ann B. MA, Columbia U., 1988; PhD, Ind. U., 1999. Tchr. Bank Street Sch. for Children, N.Y.C., 1985-88, Ridgewood (N.J.) Pub. Sch., 1988—95; assoc. instr. Ind. U., Bloomington, 1995—99; asst. prof. edn. Wash. State U., Pullman, 1999—2002; assoc. prof. edn. Calif. State U., Fullerton, 2002—. Faculty mem. Walden U., Mpls., 1996—. Author: Multimedia Projects in the Classroom, 2002, Technology and the Diverse Learner, 2004; contbr. articles to profl. jours. Avocations: science fiction, comic books. Home: 911 W Imperial Hwy Unit D La Habra CA 90631-7009

BROWN, ADAM MICHAEL, music educator; b. Cin., Aug. 21, 1981; s. Bruce Wayne and Sara Jean Brown. MusB in Music Edn., U. of North Tex., Denton, 2003. Band dir. Mason H.S., Mason, Ohio, 2003—. Percussion arranger Fairfield H.S., Ohio, 2001—03; percussion instr. Keller H.S., Tex., 2002—03. Ch. treas. Fairfield Missionary Ch., Fairfield, Ohio, 2005. Coll. of Music Percussion scholar, U. of North Tex., 1999—2003, Bd. of Regents scholar, 1999—2003, Internat. scholar, Avedis Zildjian Cymbal Corp., 2002—03. Mem.: Internat. Assn. for Jazz Edn., NEA, Music Educators Nat. Conf., Percussive Arts Soc. Avocations: music, sports, travel. Home: 1642 Oak Valley Court Fairfield OH 45014 Office: Mason High School 6100 S Mason-Montgomery Road Mason OH 45040 Office Phone: 513-398-5025 30981. Personal E-mail: untdrum99@aol.com. E-mail: browna@mason.k12.oh.us.

BROWN, ALAN CHARLTON, retired aeronautical engineer; b. Whitley Bay, Eng., Dec. 5, 1929; came to U.S., 1956; s. Stanley and Dorothy (Charlton) B.; m. Gweneth Evelyn Bowler, July 26, 1952; children: Yvonne, Christine, Diane, Maureen. Diploma aeronautics, Hull (Eng.) Tech. Coll., 1950; MS, Cranfield (Eng.) Inst Tech., 1952, Stanford U., 1965; DSc (hon.), Cranfield (Eng.) U., 2001. Apprentice Blackburn Aircraft Ltd., Brough, Eng., 1945-50; aerodynamicist Bristol (Eng.) Aeroplane Co., 1952-56; rsch. scientist U. So. Calif., L.A., 1956-58, Wiancko Engring. Co., Pasadena, Calif., 1958-60, Lockheed Missiles & Space Co., Palo Alto, Calif., 1960-66; group leader Lockheed Aero. Sys. Co., Burbank, Calif., 1966-69, dept. mgr., 1969-78; chief engr. F-117A Lockheed Aerospace Sys. Co., Burbank, Calif., 1978-82, dir. stealth tech., 1982-89; dir. engring. Lockheed Corp., Calabasas, Calif., 1989-92. Fellow AIAA (Aircraft Design award 1990), NAE, Royal Aero. Soc. Democrat. Avocations: music, model aircraft. Home: 388 Aptos Ridge Cir Watsonville CA 95076-8518 Personal E-mail: alnbrown@cruzio.com.

BROWN, ALAN CRAWFORD, lawyer; b. Rockford, Ill., May 12, 1956; s. Gerald Crawford and Jane Ella (Herzberger) B.; m. Dawn Lestrud, Apr. 16, 1998; children: Parker Crawford, Sydney Danielle, Sarah Kate, Drew Kristen, Connor Austin. BA magna cum laude, Miami U., Oxford, Ohio, 1978; JD with honors, U. Chgo., 1981. Bar: Ill. 1981, U.S. Dist. Ct. (no. dist.) Ill. 1981, U.S. Tax Ct. 1986. Assoc. Kirkland & Ellis, Chgo., 1981-87; sr. assoc. Coffield Ungaretti Harris & Slavin, Chgo., 1987-89; ptnr. McDermott, Will & Emery, Chgo., 1989—2001, Neal, Gerber & Eisenberg, Chgo., 2001—. Deacon Northminster Presbyn. Ch., Evanston, Ill., 1989-92; apiarist Chgo. Botanic Garden, Glencoe, Ill., 1988-97; active Kenilworth (Ill.) Union Ch. Mem. Order of Coif, Phi Beta Kappa. Office: Neal Gerber & Eisenberg Ste 2200 Two North LaSalle St Chicago IL 60602-3801 E-mail: acbrownesq@aol.com, abrown@ngelaw.com.

BROWN, ALBERTA MAE, nurse; b. Columbus, Ohio, Nov. 11, 1932; d. Sylvester Clarence and Malinda (Mason) Angel; m. Norman Brown, Dec. 19, 1967 (dec. Jan. 1989); children: Charon, Charles, Stevan, Carole. Grad., Antelope Valley Coll., 1961; AA, L.A. Valley Coll., 1975; BS, Calif. State U., 1981. Nurses aid, vocat. nurse, respiratory therapist St. Bernardines Hosp., 1965-69, Good Samaritan Hosp., L.A., 1969-70, Midway Hosp., L.A., 1973-81; allergy nurse, instr. respiratory therapy VA Hosp., L.A., 1970-93; also acting dept. head; nurse, respiratory splty. unit Jerry L. Pettis Meml. Hosp., Loma Linda, Calif., 1984-93; with Wadley Regional Med. Ctr., Texarkana, Tex., 1993-94; rehab. nurse Robert H. Ballard Rehab. Hosp., San Bernardino, Calif., 1994-98; nurse Ballard Rehab Hosp., San Bernardino, 1998—. Instr. L.A. Valley Med. Technoogists Sch., Compton Coll., 1979, Summit Coll., Colton, Calif., 2004—. Patentee disposible/replaceable tubing for stethoscope. Mem. Am. Assn. Respiratory Therapy, Nat. Honor Soc., Social-Lites, Inc. of San Bernardino Club, Order Ea. Star, Eta Phi Beta. Democrat. Baptist. Office: Robert H Ballard Rehab Hosp 1760 W 6th St San Bernardino CA 92411-2466

BROWN, ALICE ELSTE, artist; b. Balt., Nov. 5, 1922; d. Albert John and Anna Emily (Rosenbauer) Elste; m. Charles Hammond Brown, Nov. 30, 1946 (dec. Sept. 1994); children: Charles Hammond Jr., Barbara Brown Lander, Laurie Ellen. RN, U. Md., 1944; BS in Nursing Edn., Johns Hopkins U., 1949; BA in Art, Coll. Notre Dame, Balt., 1978; MA in Painting and Art Edn., Towson U., 1984. RN Md. Nurse, head nurse U.S. Army Nurse Corps, U.S., Europe, 1944-46; pub. health nurse Balt. Health Dept., 1950-52; artist Balt., 1960—; artist-in-residence Pyramid-Atlantic Studios, Balt., 1987-92. Adj. instr. drawing and design Coll. Notre Dame, 1980. One-woman shows include Roland Park Libr., 1965, Greater Balt. Med. Ctr., 1964, exhibited in group shows at Md. Fedn. Art, 1970—79, Jewish Cmty. Ctr., 1970, Towson YMCA, 1960, Easton (Md.) Acad. Arts, 1977, Coll. of Notre Dame, 1980, Western Md. Coll., Westminster, 1990, Pyramid Atlantic, Washington, 1990, Rehoboth (Del.)Art League, 1996—. Home nursing tchr. ARC, Balt., 1950s; asst. leader, leader Girl Scouts Am., Balt., 1960s; vol. docent Balt. Mus. Art, 1970s. 1st lt., U.S. Army Nurse Corps, 1944-46. Recipient Pi Lambda Theta award, Johns Hopkins U., 1949, Steinbugler award in art, Coll. Notre Dame, 1978. Mem. Nat. Mus. Women in the Arts (charter mem.), Md. Art Place, Rehoboth Art League (Thomas McFarland Skelly Meml. award 1998), Johns Hopkins U. Alumni Club. Democrat. Avocations: walking, reading, archaeology, environmental concerns.

BROWN, ALTON C., television personality, chef; b. LA, July 30, 1962; m. DeAnna Brown; 1 child, Zoey. Degree in Drama, U. Ga.; degree in Culinary Arts, New England Culinary Inst. Cameraman; dir. commercials and corp. films; writer, director, host Good Eats, 1998—. Author: I'm Just Here for the Food, 2002. Avocations: bicycling, reading, cooking. Office: Be Square Prodns Inc 2721 Idlewood Dr NE Atlanta GA 30303

BROWN, AMY LEE, wealth planner, educator; b. Royal Oak, Mich., Aug. 26, 1971; d. William Bernard and Loralee Ellsworth Brown. BS in Fin. magna cum laude, U. Akron, 1998. Cert. fin. planner (CFP), chartered fin. cons. (ChFC), divorce fin. analyst (CDFA), chartered life underwriter (CLU). Various fin. positions, 1988—2001; sr. fin. planner Szarka Fin. Mgmt., North Olmsted, Ohio, 2001—03; fin. svcs. profl. Skylight Fin. Group, Cleve., 2003; asst. v.p. and sr. wealth planner Fifth Third Bank, Cleveland. Tchr. cert. fin. planner edn. courses. Office: Fifth Third Bank 600 Superior Ave E Cleveland OH 44114 Office Phone: 216-274-5122. Business E-Mail: amy.brown@53.com.

BROWN, ANDREAS LE, retail executive, art gallery owner; b. Coronado, Calif., Apr. 29, 1933; s. Harvey Clair and Helene Celeste (Kimball) B. AB, Calif. State U., San Diego, 1955; postgrad., Stanford U., 1955-57; DFA (hon.), Calif. State U., 2005. Mem. faculty Calif. State U., 1960-63; staff rsch. fellow Humanities Rsch. Ctr., U. Tex., 1963-65; appraiser rare books, 1965-67; owner, pres. Gotham Book Mart & Gallery Inc., N.Y.C., 1967—, Sorer Realty Corp., N.Y.C., 1989—. Author: A Creative Century, 1970, (with Hal Morgan) Prairie Fires and Paper Moons, 1981; contbg. editor Antaeus; mem. adv. bd. Paris Rev. Trustee Edward Gorey Charitable Trust; adv. Anthony Found., Houston; With U.S. Army, 1958-59. Recipient Disting. Alumnus award, Calif. State U., San Diego, 2003. Mem. Manuscript Soc., Antiquarian Booksellers Assn. Am., Am. Booksellers Assn., Internat. League Antiquarian Booksellers, Sigma Chi, Grolier Club (N.Y.). Achievements include specializing in modern rare books and manuscripts. Home and Office: 16 E 46th St New York NY 10017 Office Phone: 212-719-4448. Office Fax: 212-719-3481. Business E-Mail: gothambookmart@verizon.net.

BROWN, ANGELIA, poet; b. Barnesville, Ga., Jan. 5, 1968; d. Charlie Fred and Elizabeth Brown; children: Demarius, Marcus, Jalessa Freeman, David Freeman. Poet: Nature, 1992, In Memory of Those We Love and Cherish, 1993, Love That Is Meant to Be, 1994, Love, 1997, Our Love, 1997, A Friendship, 1998 (Accomplishment of Merit award, 1998), Life, 1998 (Editors Choice award, 1998), All About Angelia and the Lord, 1998, Watch Them Dogs, 2003 (Editors Choice award, 2003). Mem.: NAFE. Methodist. Avocations: gardening, art, baking, bookmaking. Home: 128 Roger Brown Dr Barnesville GA 30204

BROWN, ANN W., not-for-profit developer; m. Donald Brown, 1959; 2 children Student, Smith Coll., 1955-58; BA, George Washington U., 1959; LLD (hon.), Smith Coll., 2000. Past v.p. Consumer Fedn. Am.; chmn. bd. Pub. Voice, 1983-94; chmn. U.S. Consumer Product Safety Commn., 1994—2001, Safer Am. for Everyone, Palm Beach Gardens, Fla., 2001—. Nat. and local chmn. consumer affairs com. Ams. for Dem. Action; past chmn. adv. bd. Washington Consumer Protection Office. Named Washingtonian of Yr., Washingtonian Mag., 1989, Govt. Communicator of Yr., Nat. Assn. Govt. Communicators, 1995, Outstanding Alumna, George Washington U., 1996; recipient Champion of Safe Kids award, Nat. Safe Kids Campaign, 1994, Philip Hart Pub. Svc. award, Consumer Fedn. Am., 1999, Excellence in Pub. Svc. award, Am. Acad. Pediat., 2000, Nat. Working Parent award, Lokoff Found., 2000, Crystal Slipper award, 2002. Avocations: tennis, movies. Home and Office: SAFE Safer Am for Everyone 2734 Rhome Dr Palm Beach Gardens FL 33410 Office: SAFE Safer Am for Everyone 1776 I Street NW Ste 900 Washington DC 20006

BROWN, ANNA RIDGWAY, elementary school educator, assistant principal; b. Hartwell, Ga., July 13, 1960; m. Kevin Gregory Brown, Apr. 9, 1983; children: Ginny, Drew. BS, MEd, U. Ga., 1985; ABD, Nova Southeastern U., 2003. Cert. tchr. Nat. Bd. for Profl. Tchg. Stds., 2001. Tchr. Hart County Mid. Sch., Hartwell, Ga., 1985—2004, asst. prin., 2004—. Reach to Teach faculty Ga. Profl. Stds. Commn., Atlanta, 2003—; presenter in field. Exec. com. mem. Ga. Nat. Bd. Certification Program, Atlanta, 2001—05. Recipient Outstanding Educator award, Hart County Ret. Tchr. Assn., 2002, Hart County Ret. Tchrs. Assn., 2003; scholar Nat. Bd. Certification, Nova Southeastern U., 2004; Tchr. scholar, Horace Mann, 2003. Mem.: ASCD, Ga. Mid. Sch. Assn., Profl. Assn. Ga. Educators (sys. rep., dist. com. mem. 2003—05, pres.-elect 2005, Outstanding Mem. award 2004, grad. scholar 2003). Home: 304 Lakeshore Dr Hartwell GA 30643 Office: Hart County Middle School 176 Powell Rd Hartwell GA 30643 Office Phone: 706-856-7241. Business E-Mail: abrown@hart.k12.ga.us.

BROWN, ANNE MILLION, retired elementary school educator; b. Greeneville, Tenn., July 23, 1949; d. Herbert Blaine and Mary Ann (Williamson) Million; m. Joe L. Brown, Mar. 5, 1972; 1 child, Susan Leigh. Bachelor, East Tenn. State U., 1972, Master, 1985. Cert. elementary tchr., Tenn. 3d grade tchr. Greene County Sch. Bd., Greeneville, 1972—2003; ret., 2003. Mem. reading textbook com. Greene County Sch. Bd., 1988-89, 94-95, chairperson for 3d grade tchrs., 1988-89, reporter for 3d grade tchrs. group, 1987-88. Ch. leader Cedar Grove United Meth. Ch., Chuckey, Tenn., 1994-95; girl scout leader Washington County, Tenn., 1984-85, 85-86; leader Just-Say-No Club, Doak Sch., 1984-89; mem. Home Demonstration Club, Washington County, 1974-80; dir. Concerned Citizens of Doak, 1987-88, reporter, 1986-87. Named Tchr. of Yr., Doak Sch., 2002—03. Mem. NEA, Tenn. Edn. Assn. (rep.), Greene County Edn. Assn. (faculty rep. 1985-86, 84-85, newsletter com. 1986), Horse Creek Ruritan Club Republican. Home: 148 Bill Martin Rd Chuckey TN 37641-2048

BROWN, APRIL SCHLEA, pharmacist; b. Lansing, Mich., Nov. 4, 1966; d. William Robert and Kathleen Louise Pederson; m. Steven James Brown, Sept. 26, 1991; children: Jordan Elizabeth, Stephanie Taylor, Ciera Nicole. Student, Edison C.C., 1998; grad., Fla. Gulf Coast U., 2000; postgrad., Palm Beach Atlantic U., 2001—. Life Insurance Agent Dept. of Profl. Regulation, FL; Nuclear Technician Troxler Nuc. Electronics. Radiol. tech. coord. SW Fla. Regional Med. Ctr., Ft. Myers, 1986—87; owner Caravan Med./ Dental Supply, 1995—97, AS Brown Resource Group, 1998—2000, AS Brown Meteoritics, N.Y.C., 1999—2000; exec. prodr. New Park Pictures, 2003—. Creative cons. Young Punks Films, Tallahassee, 1994—97; editl. advisor Duchess Publications, Cape Coral, 1998—; creative cons. SMD studios, 2001—. Author: What About Hooters. America's Introduction to the Hilarious Reality of Hooters., The Publishing List; co-author: If.A book for people with way too much time on their hands. Legislative policy Fla. Pharmacy Assn., Tallahassee, 2001—02; nat. leadership inst. Wyeth-Pharmaceuticals, Washington, 2002—02. Recipient Nat. Leadership award, Nat. Assn. Chain Drug Stores; Marcus Family scholar, 2003. Mem.: Fla. Pharmacy Assn. (leadership award 2003), Union Concerned Scientists, Am. Assn. Publishers, Am. Assn. Pharm. Scientists, Am. Pharm. Assn. (chpt. pres. 2002—03), Phi Delta Chi. Avocations: piano, flute, writing, meteoritics & the cosmos (chondrites, stony-irons; unified theory, wave vs. particle), independent research (starlink cry9c gene; governmental rule/ illuminati), language/ religion (ancient hebrew, arabic, cuneiform; jewish, muslim). Personal E-mail: asbrowngroup@cs.com.

BROWN, ARNOLD, management consultant; b. Boston, Aug. 18, 1927; s. Frank and Frances Brown; children: Pamela, Cynthia, Derek. BA honors, UCLA, 1950. Asst. dir. Sales Promotion Mut. Benefit Life Ins. Co., Newark,

1957—61; v.p. Inst. Life Ins., N.Y.C., 1961—77; chmn. Weiner, Edrich, Brown, Inc., N.Y.C., 1977—. Guest lectr. Harvard Bus. Sch., Duke U., Wharton Sch. Co-author: Supermanaging, 1984, Office Biology, 1993, Insider's Guide to the Future, 1997, FutureThink, 2005; contbr. articles to profl. jours. With USN, 1944—46. Mem.: World Future Soc. (dir.). Office: 200 E 33rd St New York NY 10016-4874 Business E-Mail: weinerbrown@earthlink.net.

BROWN, ARNOLD, physical therapy consultant; b. N.Y.C., Apr. 8, 1930; s. Murray and Tessie Brown; m. Alice L. Kahn, July 31, 1955; 1 child, Alan. BS in Edn., Panzer Coll., 1951; cert. in phys. therapy, Columbia U., 1952; MA in Psychology, Ball State U., 1972. Lic. phys. therapist, Ind. Staff phys. therapist VA Hosp., East Orange, N.J., 1954-55; sr. phys. therapist Cerebral Palsy Clinic, Union City, N.J., 1955-56; chief phys. therapist Mobility, Inc., New Rochelle, N.Y., 1956-57, Inland Steel Co. Hosp., East Chicago, Ind., 1957-67, Ball Meml. Hosp., Muncie, Ind., 1967-84; dir. phys. therapy Profl. Med. Svc., Clay County, Ind., 1984-86, St. Anthony Hosp., Michigan City, Ind., 1986-93; ret., 1993; cons. physical therapy, 1993-96. Cons. Lake County Assn. Retarded Children, Gary, Ind., 1963-67; insvc. instr. Ball Meml., St. Anthony Hosp., 1967-93; instr. Michigan City High Schs., Health Care Practicum, 1987-93; adj. clin. prof. phys. therapy Andrews U., Berrien Springs, Mich., 1987-93; clin. supr. student affiliations Ball State U., 1975-83, clin. instr. Ball State U., 1981-83; clin. supr. student affiliations Ind. U., 1975-83; mem. adv. bd. Vis. Nurse Assn., Muncie, 1972-78; tchr. health care practicum Michigan City H.S.'s, 1987-93. Author: Physiological and Psychological Considerations in Management of Stroke, 1976; author/instr.: Orientation to Physical Therapy, 1979, Body Mechanics, 1987(videotapes); contbr. to profl. jours. Bd. dirs. Nat. Multiple Sclerosis Soc., 1974-77, Easter Seal Soc., Muncie, 1976-78. With U.S. Army, 1952-54. Recipient Vocat. Dirs. award A.K. Smith Career Ctr., Michigan City, 1993. Mem. Am. Phys. Therapy Assn. (mgmt. sect.). Avocations: piano, walking, exercise, reading. Home: 2 Buckingham Ct Apt 2 Michigan City IN 46360-1588

BROWN, ARNOLD LANEHART, JR., pathologist, educator, dean; b. Wooster, Ohio, Jan. 26, 1926; s. Arnold Lanehart and Wilda (Woods) B.; m. Betty Jane Simpson, Oct. 2, 1949; children— Arnold III, Anthony, Allen, Fletcher, Lisa. Student, U. Richmond, 1943—45; MD, Med. Coll. Va., 1949. Diplomate Am. Bd. Pathology. Intern Presbyn.-St. Luke's Hosp., Chgo., 1949-50, resident, 1950-51, 53-56, asst. attending pathologist, 1957-59; practice medicine specializing in pathology Rochester, Minn., 1959-78; cons. exptl. pathology, anatomy Mayo Clinic, Rochester, 1959-78, also prof., chmn. dept., 1968-78; prof. pathology U. Wis., Madison, 1978—, dean Med. Sch., 1978-91. Mem. nat. cancer adv. coun. NIH, 1971-74, HEW, 1972-74; chmn. clearing house on environ. carcinogens Nat. Cancer Inst., 1976-80, chmn. com. to study carcinogenicity of cyclamate, 1975-76; mem. Nat. Com. on Heart Disease, Cancer and Stroke, 1975-79; mem. com. on safe drinking water NRC, 1976-77; mem. award assembly Gen. Motors Cancer Rsch. Found., 1978-83, vice chmn., 1982-83; co-chmn. panel on geochemistry of fibrous materials related to health risks Nat. Acad. Scis.-NRC, 1978-80; chair working group Internat. Agy. for Rsch. on Cancer, Lyon, France, 1979, 83, 87. Contbr. articles to profl. jours. Bd. sci. counselors Nat. Inst. Environ. Health Scis., NIH Nat. Toxicology Program, 1992—. With USNR, 1943-45, 51-53. Nat. Heart Inst. postdoctoral fellow, 1956-59 Mem. Am. Soc. Exptl. Pathology, Internat. Acad. Pathology, Assn. Am. Med. Colls. (chmn. coun. deans 1984-85). Home: 211 2Nd St NW Apt 1503 Rochester MN 55901-2896 Personal E-mail: arnoldbro@msn.com.

BROWN, ARTHUR EDMON, JR., retired army officer; b. Manila, Nov. 21, 1929; s. Arthur Edmon and Grace E. M. (Montgomery) B.; m. Jerry Deane Cook, June 6, 1953; children: Marian Brown Shope, Nan Brown Irick, Arthur Edmon III. BS, U.S. Mil. Acad., 1953; M.Public and Internat. Affairs, U. Pitts., 1965. Commd. 2d lt. U.S. Army, advanced through grades to gen.; mem. faculty U.S. Army War Coll., 1970-73; comdr. 1st Brigade, 1st Infantry Div. Fort Riley, Kans., 1973-75; mem. gen. staff Dept. Army, Washington, 1975-78; asst. div. comdr. 25th Infantry Div. Hawaii, 1978-80; dep. supt. U.S. Mil. Acad., West Point, 1980-81; comdr. U.S. Army Readiness and Moblzn., Region IV, Fort Gillem, Ga., 1981-83; dir. army staff Dept. Army, Washington, 1983-87; vice chief of staff U.S. Army, 1987-89, retired. Decorated Def. D.S.M., Army D.S.M. with oak leaf cluster, Bronze Star with 3 oak leaf clusters, Silver Star, Legion of Merit with 3 oak leaf clusters. Episcopalian. Home: 35 Fairway Winds Pl Hilton Head Island SC 29928-5547 also: 3302 N St NW Washington DC 20007-2807 Personal E-mail: aebjr@adelphia.net.

BROWN, ARTHUR EDWARD, physician; b. Trenton, NJ, June 7, 1945; s. Milton Charles and Jeanne Ruth (Swern) B.; m. Jo Frances Meltzer, Nov. 24, 1985. BS, Bucknell U., 1967; MD, Jefferson Med. Coll., 1971. Intern, resident Roosevelt Hosp., NYC, 1971-72, 74-76; trainee Nat. Cancer Inst., 1976-77; fellow infectious diseases Meml. Sloan-Kettering Cancer Ctr., NYC, 1976-78; clin. asst. physician Cornell U., Weill Med. Coll., NYC, 1978-82, asst. prof. medicine and pediat., 1979-85, assoc. prof. clin. medicine and pediat., 1985—94, prof. clin. medicine and pediat., 1994—; asst. attending physician Meml. Hosp. for Cancer and Allied Diseases, NYC, 1982—89, assoc. attending physician, 1989—93, attending physician, 1993—; asst. attending pediatrician NY Presbyn. Hosp., NYC, 1979—85, assoc. attending pediatrician, 1985-94, attending pediatrician, 1994—2004. Vis. assoc. physician The Rockefeller U. Hosp., NYC, 1995—96; cons. Anti-Infective Drugs adv. com FDA, USPHS, DHHS, 1997—; med. dir. Employee Health Svc. Meml. Sloan-Kettering Cancer Ctr., NYC, 2002—, chief, 2003—. Editor: Infectious Complications of Neoplastic Diseases Controversies in Management, 1985, Infections in Oncology, 1993-2000; consulting editor Am. Jour. Medicine, 1984-86; mem. editl. bd. Antimicrobial Agts. and Chemotherapy, 1985-87, European Jour. Clin. Microbiology and Infectious Diseases, 1993-2005, Infections in Medicine, 1995—, Microbial Drug Resistance, 1996—; contbr. numerous articles to profl. jours. Trustee The Peddie Sch., Hightstown, NJ, 1999—. Surgeon, USPHS, 1972-74. Recipient 2d pl. HeSCA Print Festival, 1985, Bronze Plaque award Film Coun. Columbus, 1985, Bronze medal Internat. Film & TV Festival, NYC, 1985, Semi-Finalist Am. Jour. Nursing Media Festival, 1986. Fellow ACP (councillor NY chpt. 2000-02, 05—, NY chpt. pub. health com. 2000—, NY chpt. nominating com. 2004), Soc. Healthcare Epidemiology Am., Infectious Diseases Soc. Am. (state and regional bd. dirs. 1995-98); mem. AAAS, Am. Fedn. for Med. Rsch., NY County Soc. Internal Medicine (pres. 1994-96), NY State Soc. Internal Medicine (dir. 1995-2000), NY Soc. Infectious Diseases (sec., treas. 1993-97; v.p. 1997-98, pres.-elect 1998-99, pres. 1999-2000), Am. Soc. Microbiology, NY Acad. Scis., Am. Soc. Clin. Oncology, Internat. Immunocompromised Host Soc., NY Soc. Tropical Medicine, Multinat. Assn. of Supportive Care in Cancer. Achievements include research on AIDS, management of infectious complications of neoplastic diseases. Office: Meml Sloan-Kettering Cancer Ctr 222 E 70th St New York NY 10021 Office Phone: 212-434-5103. E-mail: brown2@mskcc.org.

BROWN, AUTRY, psychology professor, clergyman; b. Watson, Okla., May 1, 1924; s. Solon Lemley and Bessie Jane (Wilhelm) B.; m. Opal Irene Landers, Sept. 5, 1942 (dec.); children: Juanice, Rebecca, Steven, Deborah; m. Betty Parsons, Sept. 7, 2002. BA, Eastern N.M. U., 1950; M of Div., New Orleans Bapt. Theol. Sem., 1955, MRE, 1956, EdD, 1968; postgrad., Colo. State U., 1970, Southwest Mo. State U., 1985. Ordained to ministry Bapt. Ch., 1942. Pastor Bookcliff Bapt. Ch., Grand Junction, Colo., 1957-61, Carrollton Ave. Bapt. Ch., New Orleans, 1962-64, Immanuel Bapt. Ch., Ft. Collins, Colo., 1964-72; asst. prof. psychology Mo. Bapt. U., St. Louis, 1972-74, Southwest Bapt. U., Bolivar, Mo., 1974-76, prof. psychology, 1978-89, dir. counseling services, 1978-89; disting. prof. psychology, 1989—; cons. family ministry Colo. Bapt. Gen. Conv., Denver, 1976-78. Author: Church Family Life Conference Guidebook, 1973; contbr. books, profl. jour. Recipient Spl. Services award Bd. Trustees New Orleans Bapt. Theol. Sem., 1972. Mem. Am. Assn. Marriage and Family Therapy, Mo. Assn. Marriage and Family Therapy (Spl. Service award 1984, treas. state exec. bd. 1979-83), Ozark Assn. Marriage and Family Therapy (pres. 1985-86), Mo. Assn. Counseling and Devel., Fellows Menniger Found. Avocation: collecting antique barbed wire. Home: 1526 W Laverne St Bolivar MO 65613 Office: Christian Tng Inst 1526 W Laverne St Bolivar MO 65613 E-mail: autrybrown@microcare.net, sabrown@sbuniv.edu.

BROWN, B. ANDREW, lawyer; b. Charleston, W.Va., Mar. 10, 1957; BA in History, Stanford U., 1979; MPA, Harvard U., 1981; JD, MA in Philosophy, Duke U., 1986. Bar: Minn. 1989. Legis. aide Sen. Gary Hart, Washington, 1981-82; atty. Donovan, Leisure, Newton & Irvine, Washington, 1986-88, Wilkie, Farr & Gallagher, Washington, 1989, Dorsey & Whitney, Mpls., 1990—, ptnr., 1995—, and co-chmn., environ., natural resources, energy practice group. Office Phone: 612-340-5612. Office Fax: 612-340-8800. Business E-Mail: brown.andrew@dorsey.com.

BROWN, BARBARA BERISH, lawyer; b. Washington, June 26, 1946; d. Alfred Edward and Sylvia (Kaufman) B.; m. Robert F. Berish, Mar. 26, 1988; 1 child, Jared. BA, Radcliffe-Harvard, 1968; JD, Yale U., 1971. Law clk. to Hon. J. Joseph Smith US Ct. Appeals, Conn., 1971-72; staff atty. Defender Assn. Phila., 1972-74; atty. Women's Law Project, Phila., 1974-76; assoc. Litvin, Blumberg, Matuson & Young, Phila., 1976-80; ptnr. Pepper Hamilton & Scheetz, Washington, 1981—84; mng. ptnr. Paul Hastings Janofsky & Walker, Washington, 2000—. Co-author: Legal Guideto Human Resources, 1984, 3d rev. edit., 2005. Mem. ABA (com. co-chair, CEO coun. mem. labor and employment law sect.). Office: Paul Hastings Janofsky & Walker 875 15th St NW Washington DC 20005 Office Phone: 202-551-1717. Office Fax: 202-551-0117, 202-551-0117. Business E-Mail: barbarabrown@paulhastings.com.

BROWN, BARBARA FLETCHER, lawyer; b. Hartford, Conn., Oct. 20, 1937; d. Irving Abner and Frances Edith Fletcher; m. John Wilson brown, June 7, 1959; children: Alison Hilary, Meredith Leslie. Student, Wells Coll., Aurora, N.Y., 1955-57; BA with honors and distinction, St. Joseph Coll., West Hartford, Conn., 1959; JD, U. San Diego, 1976. Bar: Calif. 1977, U.S. Dist. Ct. (so. dist.) 1977, U.S. Ct. Appeals (9th cir.) 1977. Asst. U.S. atty. U.S. Atty.'s Office-So. Dist. Calif., San diego, 1977-80; assoc. Brennan LaRocque, Rancho Bernardo, Calif., 1980-81; ptnr. LaRocque Brown & Campbell, Rancho Bernardo, 1981-83; sole practitioner La Jolla, Calif., 1983-87; ptnr. Brown & Brown, San Diego, 1988—. Judge pro tem San Diego County SuperiorCt., 1986-89, 91-94. Bd. dirs. Legal Aid Soc. San diego, 1978-81. Mem. AAUW, San Diego County Bar Assn. (exec. com. 1986-89, 91-94, rec. sec. 1987-91), State Bar Calif. (mem. com. on fed. cts. 1978-81), Lawyers Club of San Diego (bd. dirs. 1978-80, pres. 1980-81, adv. bd. 1986-88), Calif. Women Lawyers (bd. dirs. and exec. com. 1980-82), San Diego Trial Lawyers Assn., La Jolla Rotary Club. Office: Brown & Brown 4370 La Jolla Village Dr San Diego CA 92122-1249

BROWN, BARBARA JEANNE, librarian; b. Charles City, Iowa, Oct. 9, 1941; d. William Howard and Marion Beatrice (Katcher) B. BS, Iowa State U., 1963; MS, Columbia U., 1964. Asst. circulation librarian Cornell U., Ithaca, N.Y., 1964-66, asst. reference librarian undergrad. library, 1966-68, assoc. reference librarian, 1968-71; head of reference and pub. services Washington and Lee U., Lexington, Va., 1971-76, univ. librarian, 1985—; asst. librarian gen. reader services Princeton (N.J.) U., 1976-80; assoc. dir. program coordination Research Libraries Group Inc., Stanford, Calif., 1980-85. Bd. dirs. S.E. Library Network, Atlanta, 1986-90, OCLC User's Coun., 1992—; vice chair, chair-elect, ACRL Coll. Librs. sect. Mem. ALA, Assn. Coll. and Research Libraries, Va. Library Assn., Reference and Adult Services Div. (bd. dirs. 1976-78). Office: Washington & Lee U U Libr Lexington VA 24450-0303

BROWN, BARBARA JUNE, hospital and nursing administrator; b. Milw., Aug. 17, 1933; d. Carl W. and Nora Anne (Damrow) Rydberg; children: Deborah, Robert, Andrea, Michael, Steven, Jeffrey. BSN, Marquette U., Milw., 1955, MSN, 1960, EdD, 1970. RN, Wis.; cert. nurse adminstr. advanced. Adminstr. patient care Family Hosp., Milw., 1973-78; assoc. clin. prof. U. Wash., Seattle, 1980-87; assoc. adminstr. nursing Virginia Mason Hosp., Seattle, 1980-87; assoc. exec. dir. King Faisal Specialist Hosp., Riyadh, Saudi Arabia, 1987-91; adj. prof. Univ. Ariz., 2001—. Project dir. NIH, Sexual Assault Treatment Ctr., Milw., 1975-78; lectr., cons., 1974—. Founder, editor-in-chief: Nursing Adminstrn. Quar., 1976—; editor-in-chief, regional v.p. Nurse Week, Mountain West, 2000—04; editor-in-chief: Modern Nurse, 2005—. Vol. ski instr. for disabled, Winter Park, Colo. Fellow: Nat. Acad. Practice, Am. Acad. Nursing (governing coun.); mem.: ANA, Grand County Pub. Health and Emergency Svcs. (chmn. health adv. com. 1994—96), Nat. League Nursing (bd. govs. 2002—05, bd. dirs.), Am. Orgn. Nurse Execs., Sigma Theta Tau. Office Phone: 520-825-5629. Personal E-mail: naqbb@aol.com.

BROWN, BENJAMIN A., investment advisor; b. N.Y.C., Feb. 13, 1943; s. Horace A. and Lillian A. (Hurwitz) B.; m. Elinore Carole Abravanel, Aug. 8, 1968; children— Adam Howard, Dina Lauren BBA in Acctg., Adelphi U., 1964; MBA in Fin. and Investments, Baruch Coll. CUNY, 1971. Registered investment advisor prin.-fin. mgmt. svcs. Acct. Samuel Greiff C.P.A., Atty., Forest Hills, N.Y., 1963-66; v.p. research dept. Walston & Co., N.Y.C., 1967-73; treas. ENSERCH Corp., Dallas, 1974-78, v.p. fin., 1978-82, v.p. fin. relations, 1982-96. V.p. Enserch Exploration, Inc., 1995-96; v.p. fin. and investor rels. EEX Corp., Houston, 1997-98; chief investment officer, mng. dir. Fin. Mgmt. Svcs., Dallas, 1999—. Mem. Am. Assn. Individual Investors, N.Y. Soc. Security Analysts, DAC Country Club, Univ. Club Houston. Avocations: walking, golf, coin collecting/numismatics, oenology. Home: 5200 Keller Springs Rd Apt 621 Dallas TX 75248-2744 Office: Candy & Schonwald Bldg 3116 Live Oak St Ste 201 Dallas TX 75204-6190 Office Phone: 214-826-6660. *I strive everyday to give more than I take and spend less than I make. My success and happiness are entirely attributable to a very loving and supportive family, including a perfect mate for more than 37 years, two children that reflect the best qualities parents could wish for, a mother and brother that are always there for me, in-laws that most can only dream about and two extraordinary grandchildren.*

BROWN, BENJAMIN ANDREW, retired journalist; b. Red House, W.Va., Apr. 30, 1933; s. Albert Miller and Mary Agnes (Donegan) B.; m. Joanne Gretchen Harder, May 22, 1956; children: Benjamin Andrew, Gretchen, Mark, Betsy Brown Larson. BS in Journalism, Fla. State U., 1955. Sportswriter Charleston (W.Va.) Daily Mail, 1955-57; with AP, 1957-93, gen. exec. N.Y.C., 1976-78, 82-93, chief bur. Los Angeles, 1978-82; assoc. Am. Newspapers Cons., Ltd., Milw., 1993-95. Bd. dirs. Last Chance Press Club, Helena, Mont., 1969; v.p. Minn. Press Club, 1975. Office: PO Box 3012 Paso Robles CA 93447-3012 Personal E-mail: babrown@charter.net.

BROWN, BENJAMIN F., IV, charitable foundation executive; b. Temple, Tex., June 24, 1930; s. Benjamin F. Brown and Mary Lestelle Hunt; m. Clara M. Lovett, June 1, 1980. BA, Baylor U., 1950; MA, U. Colo., 1953; PhD, Harvard U., 1966. Asst. prof. Calif. State U. Sonoma, 1962—66; prof. U. Kans., Lawrence, 1966—79; prof. history U. Florence, Italy, 1969—71; sr. analyst CIA, McLean, Va., 1980—94; CEO B & L Charitable Found., Phoenix, 1998—. V.p. Biltmore Greens Assn., 2004—; bd. dirs. Phoenix Symphony, 2004—. Recipient Marraro prize, Am. Hist. Assn., 1977; fellow Guggenheim Found., Rome, 1977—78; Fulbright fellow, U. Rome, 1954—55. Democrat. Episcopalian. Avocations: photography, travel, genealogy. Home: PO Box 32547 Phoenix AZ 85064 E-mail: gettone@cox.net.

BROWN, BETSY ETHERIDGE, academic administrator; b. Statesville, N.C., Aug. 2, 1950; d. Guy Wetmore and Elizabeth (Hackney) Etheridge; m. Homer L. Brown, Aug. 13, 1972 (dec. Mar. 1987); 1 child, Elizabeth Leigh (dec. July 1992); m. Lawrence C. Timbs, Jr., July 30, 1995. BS in English, Appalachian State U., 1972; MA in English, Ohio State U., 1974, PhD in English, 1978. Cert. tchr., N.C. Asst. prof. English Pa. State U., University Park, 1978-85; asst. to v.p. Queens Coll., Charlotte, N.C., 1987-89, Winthrop U., Rock Hill, S.C., 1990-92, assoc. v.p., 1992-94, dean Coll. Arts and Scis., 1994—2001; assoc. v.p. acad. affairs U. N.C., Chapel Hill, 2001—. Bd. mem. Cmty. Bd. for Women's Svcs., Rock Hill, 1994—, WNSC Cmty. Adv. Bd., 1998—, Roanoke Island Commn., 2002—. Recipient Mgmt. Devel. Program award Harvard Grad. Sch. Edn., 1992, Forum award Am. Coun. on Edn.-Nat. Idenfification Program, 1995; Fulbright grantee, Bonn, Germany, 1994. Mem. AAUW, S.C. Women in Higher Edn. Adminstrn. (bd. sec. 1994—). Office: U NC Office of Pres PO Box 2688 Chapel Hill NC 27515-2688

BROWN, BILLYE JEAN, retired nursing educator; b. Damascus, Ark., Oct. 29, 1925; d. William A. and Dora (Megee) B. BSNEd, U. Tex. Med. Br., Galveston, 1953; MSNEd, St. Louis U., 1958; EdD, Baylor U., 1975. Asst. prof. U. Tex. Med. Br. Sch. Nursing, 1958-60; assoc. prof. U. Tex. Nursing Sch., Austin, 1960-67, assoc. dean, prof., 1968-72, dean, prof., 1972-89; prof. emeritus Sch. Nursing U. Tex., 1989—; mem. Nat. Adv. Council Nurse Tng., 1982-87. Nat. League for Nursing fellow, 1957-58; recipient Alumni Merit award St. Louis U., 1981; Am. Acad. Nursing fellow, 1984. Mem. ANA, Am. Assn. Colls. Nursing (pres. 1982-84, Sister Bernadette Armiger award 1990), Tex. League Nursing, Tex. Nurses Assn. (Nurse of Yr. 1980), Sigma Theta Tau (pres. 1989-91, Internat. Mary T. Wright Founders award 1999), Phi Kappa Phi (life).

BROWN, BLANCHE Y., secondary school educator, genealogist, researcher; b. Saint Mary's, W.Va., Feb. 2, 1918; d. Lewis Frederick and Edna Clara (Walker) Yost; m. Vincent Robert Brown, June 1, 1946; children: Susan Elizabeth, Roberta Ann Brown Pugh. BA, Marietta Coll., 1939; postgrad., Columbia U., 1946, 47. Cert. secondary tchr. in sci. and English. Pers. supr. Packard Electric divsn. Gen. Motors Corp., Warren, Ohio, 1940-44; tchr. bus. edn. New Matamoras (Ohio) H.S., 1945-49; fin. sec. St. Paul's United Meth. Ch., Houston, 1949-50; pers. dept. Olin Chem. Corp., Pasadena, Tex., 1951-53; tchr. biology Pasadena H.S., 1958-78. Co-editor: Grandview Township's First Trustees Journal--1803-1843, 1991; editor Matamoras Area Hist. Soc. Newsletter, 1987-99. Recipient First Families of Ohio award Ohio Geneal. Soc., 1989, Award of Achievement Ohio Hist. Soc. for Matamoras Area Hist. Soc. Newsletter, 1992. Mem. Tex. Ret. Tchrs. Assn. (life), Nat. Soc. DAR (Marietta, Ohio chpt. schs. chmn. 1988-94, corr. sec. 1995-99, nat. Photography award 1989), Matamoras Area Hist. Soc. (genealogy and local history coord. for Sesquicentennial Celebration 1846-1996, Bicentennial Celebration 1797-1997), VFW Aux. (life), AAUW. Republican. Methodist. Avocations: photography, artwork with shells, writing. Home: 733 Main St New Matamoras OH 45767-6013

BROWN, BOB (ROBERT JOSEPH BROWN), former state official; b. Missoula, Mont., Dec. 11, 1947; s. Clifford Andrew and Jeanne M (Knox) Brown; m. Susan Kay Stoeckig, Sept. 20, 1975; children: Robin Sue, Kelly Charlynn. BS in History, Mont. State U, 1970, BS in Polit. Sci., 1974; MEd, U. Mont., 1988. Cert. secondary tchr. State rep. Mont. Ho. Reps., Helena, 1971—74; senator 2d dist. Mont. State Sen., Helena, 1974—96; tchr. history Whitefish H.S., 1990—91; Tchr. govt., history Big Fork (Mont.) High Sch., 1979—86; tchr. history, econs. Flathead High Sch., Kalispell, Mont., 1986—89; instr. Flathead Valley C.C., 1990, 1994, dir. U. Mont. Ext., 1991—98; dir. govt. & pub. relations Columbia Falls Aluminum Co., 1998—2000; sec. state State of Mont., 2001—04. With USN, 1972—73. Mem.: Mont. Edn. Assn. (Golden Gavel award 1979), Packyderm, Rotary, Am. Legion, Kiwanis, Moose, Phi Delta Kappa. Republican. Avocation: fishing.

BROWN, BOBBY (ROBERT BARESFORD BROWN), vocalist, actor; b. Boston, Feb. 5, 1969; s. Herbert and Carole Brown; m. Whitney Houston, July 18, 1992; children: Bobbi Kristina, 3 children from previous relationships. Singer with New Edition, 1983—86, 1996—97. Singer (solo albums) Dance...Ya Know It, 1989, King of Stage, 1987, Don't Be Cruel, 1988, Bobby, 1992, Forever, 1997, Remixes in the Key of B, 1993, Greatest Hits, 2000, (albums with New Edition) New Edition, 1994, All for Love, 1985, Christmas All Over the World, 1985, Home Again, 1996, (singles) Candy Girl, 1983, On Our Own (theme from Ghostbusters II), 1989, (with Ja Rule) Thug Luvin, 2002; actor (films) Ghostbusters II, 1989, Knights, 1993, Panther, 1995, Nemesis II, 1995, Nemesis III-Pray Harder, 1995, A Thin Line Between Love and Hate, 1996, Go for Broke, 2001, Two Can Play that Game, 2001; actor (reality TV series) Being Bobby Brown, 2005. Recipient Grammy award for Best R&B Vocal Performance, Am. Music award, Soul Train Music award, People's Choice award, 1989. Address: Madd Mobb c/o Nippy Inc 2160 N Central Rd Fort Lee NJ 07024

BROWN, BOYD ALEX, physicist, researcher; b. Columbus, Ohio, Sept. 25, 1948; s. Frank L. and E. Catherine (Chenoweth) B.; m. Mary J. Hohenstein, July 21, 1984; children: Elizabeth Lorraine, Mark Alexander. BA in Physics, Ohio State U., 1970; MS in Physics, SUNY, Stony Brook, 1971, PhD in Physics, 1974. Research fellow Japan Soc. for the Promotion of Sci., Tokyo, 1974-75; research assoc. Mich. State U., East Lansing, 1975-78; research officer Oxford U., Eng., 1978-82; assoc. prof. physics Mich. State U., East Lansing, 1982-90, prof. physics, 1990—. Contbr. more than 400 articles to physics jours. Recipient Humboldt sr. rsch. fellow, 1991—, Dist. Faculty award, 2004 Fellow Am. Phys. Soc.; mem. The Am. Phys. Soc., Sigma Pi Sigma. Avocations: music, books. Office: Mich State U Cyclotron Lab East Lansing MI 48824

BROWN, BRITT, retired publishing company executive; b. Long Beach, Calif., Apr. 23, 1927; s. Harry Britton and Victoria (Eaton) B.; m. Anne Louise McCarthy, June 19, 1948; children— Cathy Lynn, Cynthia Ann, Britt Murdock, Bruce McCarthy. Student, U. So. Calif., 1944-46; BA, U. Kans., 1947. Classified advt. salesman Wichita (Kans.) Eagle (now Wichita Eagle & Beacon Pub. Co.), 1947-50, classified mgr., 1952-55, advt. dir., 1956-62, v.p., sec., 1963-71, pub., pres., 1971-73, chmn., 1973-79. Served with USMCR, 1944-46, 50-51. Mem. Sigma Delta Chi, Kappa Alpha.

BROWN, BRUCE ANDREW, lawyer; b. Cleve., Oct. 16, 1959; s. Andrew and Ruby Louise (Bishop) B. BA, Brown U., 1981; JD, Columbia U., 1984. Bar: N.Y. 1985, Ohio 1990. Assoc. Proskaver Rose Goetz and Mendelsohn, N.Y.C., 1983-86, Finley, Kumble Wagner Heine Vnderberg Manley Myerson & Casey, N.Y.C., 1986-87; pvt. practice B. Andrew Brown & Assocs., Cleve., 1987—. Mem. NAACP, Urban League (bd. dirs. 1988—), Omega Psi Phi. Democrat. Moslem. Avocation: golf. Office: B Andrew Brown & Assocs 1300 Bank One Ctr 600 Superior Ave E Cleveland OH 44114-2611

BROWN, BRUCE BADEN, accountant; b. Seattle, Dec. 1, 1933; s. Charles Elric and Mabel Enid (Coleman) Brown; m. Lois Jean Bellemans-Brown, 1963 (div. 1979); 3 children; m. Teresita Grimarez Brown, 1981 (div. 1985); 1 child; m. Lois Jean Bellemans-Brown, 1991. BBA, U. Wash., 1960. Cert. enrolled agt. U.S. Treasury. Various to v.p. Weather Master of Wash., Lynnwood, 1975—77; sr. planning and programs analyst Saudi Aramco, Dhahran, Saudi Arabia, 1977—93; owner Lighthouse Tax Svc., Mukilteo, Wash., 1995—. Tax and bus. cons. Lighthouse Tax Svc., 1997—; property developer Puget Sound Hills No. 2, 1977—79. Author: Desert Duel, 1999. Officer Mukilteo Hist. Soc., 1995—2004; dir. Mukilted Lighthouse Festival Assn., 2004—05; coun. mem. City of Mukilteo, Wash., 1999—2003. Cpl. U.S. Army, 1951—54, Germany. Named Mukilteo Citizen of Yr., 2002; recipient Appointed Commr., Mukilteo Civil Svc., 2004. Home: 312 Cornelia Ave Mukilteo WA 98275 Office: Lighthouse Tax Svc 312 Cornelia Ave Mukilteo WA 98275 Office Phone: 425-348-6448. E-mail: Bruceb33@aol.com.

BROWN, BRUCE MAITLAND, philanthropy consultant; b. Bryn Mawr, Pa., Sept. 2, 1947; s. Charles Stuart and Margaret (Houston) B.; m. Elaine Eldredge, Sept. 3, 1983; 1 child, Carter Houston Brown. BA, Lawrence U., 1969; MA, U. Ky., 1973. Program analyst FDA, Rockville, Md., 1973-75, exec. secretariat, 1975-78, spl. asst., 1978-82, dep. dir., press ofc., 1982-86; v.p. communications Council for Responsible Nutrition, Washington, 1986-87; v.p. for charitable trusts CoreStates Trust and Investment Group, 1987-93; cons. Inst. for Nonprofit Excellence, Radnor, Pa., 1993-95. Meteorologist Sta.

WCAU-Radio, Phila., 1965; news dir., sports broadcaster Sta. WLFM-Radio, Appleton, Wis., 1965-69; aide U.S. Senator Hugh Scott, Washington, 1969; pub. rels. contr. Fellowship of Reconciliation, Nyack, N.Y., 1982; writer speeches FDA commrs., 1979-82; cons. Sewell C. Biggs Mus. Am. Art, 1994; bd. advisors Wayne Art Ctr., 1994—, chmn., 2002—; cons. Transworld Commerce Alliance, 1994-96; bd. dirs. PhilaPride, Inc., 1993-97; adv. bd. Endow-a-Home, Resources for Human Devel., 1993-98; exec. bd. Am. Edn. Media Ctr., 1995—, v.p., 1998—; lectr. Assn. Fundraising Profls. and Villanova U. Office Continuing Edn., LaSalle U. Nonprofit Ctr., Greater Phila. Cultural Alliance, 1993—, sec.-treas., 1998-2005. Trustee Lawrence U., 1994—97; bd. dirs. sec.-treas. Hoxie Harrison Smith Found., 1994—; rev. panelist cmty. devel. fund United Way Southeastern Pa., 1995—97; co-pres., bd. dirs. Brooke Valley Conservancy Assn., 1988—95; officer Paint Br. Farms Civic Assn., Colesville, Md., 1978—83; founder, trustee HBE Found., 1988—; mem. non-profit MBA adv. coun., lectr. MBA in Nonprofit Mgmt. bd. visitors Ea. Univ., 1990—; mem. adv. bd. Ctr. for Urban Resources, 1992—2000, Presbyn. Children's Village, mem. adv. com., 1994—2003, bd. dirs., 2003—; trustee Bryn Mawr Rehab. Found., 1997—98; mem. beneficiary adv. bd. Trusts and Estates Group, 1998—; mem. adv. coun. Esperanza Health Ctr., 1998; mem. devel. com. Camphill Village, Kimberton Hills, 1998—2003; mem. devel. adv. com. Fellowship of Reconciliation, 1996—; mem. Phila. bd. World Vision's Love for Children, 1996—97; treas. 1702 Found., 2003—; bd. trustees Resources Com. of Episc. Acad., Merion, Pa., 1995—98; sec. bd., mem. audit com., mem. ch. found. bd. Episcopal Diocese Pa., 1998—2003; bd. dirs. Resources for Better Families, 1994—97, Bermuda Artworks Found. Bd., 1992—96, Chester Rural Cemetery Assn. Bd., 1998; treas. bd. dirs. Kearsley, 1996—2000; mem. adv. bd. Del. County Hist. Soc., 1999—. With U.S. Army, 1969—71. Mem.: Del. Valley Grantmakers (founding bd. dirs., v.p. 1989—91), The Assemblies, Bay Head Yacht Club, Merion Cricket Club, Skytop Club. Orthodox Anglican. Avocations: reading, gardening, meteorology, soccer, swimming.

BROWN, BRYAN D., career military officer; b. Oct. 20, 1948; BA, Cameron U.; MS in Bus., Webster U. Commd. U.S. Army, advanced through grades to gen., 2003; dir. requirements and strategic assessments U.S. Spl. Ops. Command (USSOCOM), MacDill AFB, Fla., 1996-98, dep. comdr., 2002—03, comdr., 2003—; commdg. gen. Joint Spl. Ops. Command, Ft. Bragg, NC, 1998—2000; comdg. gen. U.S. Army Spl. Ops. Command, Ft. Bragg, NC, 2000—02. Decorated Disting. Svc. Medal, Legion of Merit, Disting Flying Cross, Bronze Star Medal, Air Medal with "V" Device, Joint Svc. Commendation Medal, Armed Forces Expeditionary Medal. Office: US Spec Ops Command MacDill AFB Tampa FL 33621*

BROWN, C. HAROLD, lawyer; b. Mendenhall, Miss., July 28, 1931; children: Tracey Gwen, Terry Lynne, Allison Anne, Harold Allen. BA, Vanderbilt U., 1957; LLB, U. Tex., 1960. Bar: Tex. 1960. Sr. ptnr. Brown Pruitt Peterson & Wambsganss, P.C., Ft. Worth, 1960—. Pres. A.J. and Jessie Duncan Found.; past chmn. Ft. Worth Civil Svc. Commn.; past chmn. bd. dirs., past pres. Tarrant County Conv. Ctr., 1980; active Com. for Greater Tarrant County; past bd. dirs. Ft. Worth Camp Fire Girls, Nat. Com. for Adoption, Gladney Ctr. Hall of Fame, Adopt a Spl. Kid/Tex., Tex. Assn. Licensed Children's Svcs.; mgr. campaign R.M. Stovall for Mayor of Ft. Worth, 1969, 71, 73, Richard T. Andersen for Tarrant County Commr., 1972, 76, 80, 84, Senator Al Gore for Pres., Tarrant County, Tex., 1988; past deacon U. Christian Ch., Ft. Worth. Sgt. U.S. Army, 1953-55. Recipient cert. Carnegie Hero Fund Commn., 1972; named Outstanding Young Texan, 1976; named to Gladney Ctr. Hall of Fame. Fellow Tex. Bar Found. (life), Southwestern Legal Found., Tarrant County Bar Found. (life), Ft. Worth-Tarrant County Bar Assn. (charter, life, bd. dirs. family law sect. 1978-80); mem. ABA, Tex. Bar Assn., Tarrant County Probate Bar, Ft. Worth Jr. Bar Assn. (pres. 1963), Am. Acad. Adoption Attys., Am. Acad. Hosp. Attys., Nat. Health Lawyers Assn., Pro Bono Coll. of State Bar of Tex., Badge and Shield, Vanderbilt U. Alumni Assn. (pres. 1966-67), Am. Brittany Club (Hall of Fame), Ridotto Club (pres. 1974), Petroleum Club, River Crest Country Club, Steeplechase Club, Nat. Commodore Club (adm.), Rotary, Masons, Shriners, Jesters, Alpha Tau Omega, Phi Delta Phi. Office: Brown Pruitt Peterson & Wambsganss PC 201 Main St Ste 801 Fort Worth TX 76102-3817 Office Phone: 817-338-4888. E-mail: brownpruittlaw@ad.com.

BROWN, C TIMOTHY, insurance company executive; Regional mgr., west ctrl. region Aetna Inc., gen. mgr., Ohio, Ky., W. Va., market v.p., western Pa., regional counsel, ctrl. and northeast regions; various positions Am. Gen. Ins. Co., Dallas; sr. v.p., mid. market accounts and health care delivery Aetna Inc, 2001—. Office: Aetna Inc 151 Farmington Ave Hartford CT 06156

BROWN, CAMERON, insurance company consultant; b. Chgo., Sept. 29, 1914; s. George Frederic and Irene (Larmon) B.; m. Dorothea Fruechtenicht, May 10, 1947 (div. Feb. 1965); children: Reid L., Deborah Sue; m. Jean McGrew, Dec. 22, 1965; 1 dau., Sophia Lyn. AB, U. Ill., 1937; grad., Indsl. Coll. Armed Forces, 1941. Vice pres. R. B. Jones & Sons, Inc., 1938-41; dir. Geo. F. Brown & Sons, Inc., Chgo., 1947-79, v.p., 1947-50, exec. v.p., 1950-53, pres., 1953-64, chmn., chief exec. officer, 1964-76; dir. Interstate Nat. Corp., 1968-79, pres., 1968-74, chmn., 1970-76; dir. Nat. Student Mktg. Corp., 1970-79, pres., 1970-72, chmn., 1970-75; dir. Interstate Fire & Casualty Co., 1952-79, exec. v.p., 1953-56, pres., 1956-74, chmn., 1970-76; dir. Chgo. Ins. Co., 1957-79, pres., 1957-74, chmn., 1970-76; dir. Interstate Reins. Corp., 1957-79; pres. Cameron Brown Ltd., 1976—. Underwriting mem. Lloyd's of London, 1971-95; sec., dir. Ill. Ins. Info. Svc., 1967-76. Contbg. author: Property and Liability Handbook, 1965. Pres. Chgo. area Planned Parenthood Assn., 1969-72; bd. dirs. Planned Parenthood Fedn. Am., 1976-79; active John Evans Club, Northwestern U., U. Ill., Pres.'s Club, U. Ill. Found., U. Chgo. Pres.'s Club. Lt. col. Gen. Staff Corps AUS, 1941-45. Decorated Bronze Star with oak leaf cluster. Mem. Lloyd's Broker Assn. (chmn. 1959-60), Nat. Assn. Ind. Insurers (bd. govs. 1961-77). Ill. St. Andrews Soc., Surplus Line Brokers Assn. (chmn. 1954), Confrerie des Chevaliers du Tastevin (officer-comdr. Chgo. and L.A.), Commanderie de Bordeaux (Maitre emeritus at Chgo., Santa Barbara, bd. govs. 1973—), Conseiller de Bordeaux, Chgo. Club, Exec. Club (dir. 1969-73, 1st v.p. 1970-71), Econ. Club, Mid-Am. Club, Casino Club Chgo., Army-Navy Country Club, Old Elm Club, Shoreacres Club, Onwentsia Club, Pine Valley Golf Club, Birnam Wood Golf Club, The Valley Club, Hon. Co. Edinburgh Golfers, Royal and Ancient Golf Club St. Andrews, Psi Upsilon. Home: 1400 N Green Bay Rd Lake Forest IL 60045-1110 also: 2004 Sandy Pl Santa Barbara CA 93108-2226

BROWN, CARLTON E., college president; m. T. LaVerne Ricks-Brown; children: Kwame, Jamila. BA in English, U. Mass., 1971, EdD in Multicultural Edn., 1979. Faculty Sch. of Edn. Old Dominion U., Va., 1979-87; various to Dean Sch. Edn. Hampton U., 1987-90, dean Sch. Liberal Arts and Edn., 1990-96, v.p. for planning, dean Grad. Coll., 1996-97; pres. Savannah (Ga.) State U., 1997—. Mem. bd. Hampton City Sch. Bd., 1992-97, vice-chair 1995-97; bd. dirs. Savannah Econ. Devel. Coun., 1998—, Nat. Assn. for Equal Opportunity, 1999—; vice chair Savecon Devel. Authority, 2002—. Mem. Savannah C. of C. (bd. dirs. 1999—), Savannah Econ. Devel. Authority (chmh. 2004), Youth Futures Assn. (vice chmn. 2004). Office: Savannah State Univ PO Box 20449 Savannah GA 31404-9707 E-mail: brownce@savstate.edu.

BROWN, CAROL, make-up artist; b. Stockholm, Nov. 26, 1949; d. Julius C. and Violet (Moten) B. Student, Mt. St. Mary's Coll., 1968-72, European Exch. Program, 1972-74, L.A. Valley Coll., 1974-76. Cert. make-up artistry tchr., Calif. Makeup-artist Spelling Entertainment, Paramount, Disney, NBC, others, L.A., 1977—; CEO Natural to Knockout.com., L.A., 1996—; founder, CEO Carol Brown Natural Empowerment Found., L.A., 2000—. Aesthetic cons. C.B. Enterprises, 1990—; instr. Fred Segal Beauty, 1990—; spkr. in field; mem. adv. bd. Denise Roberts Found.; mem. speakerservices.com. Author: Natural to Knockout Makeup Application Beauty Guide, 2001. Vol. L.A. Mission, 1989—, Jenesee Ctr., L.a., 1996—, Sickle Cell Disease Assn. Am., L.A., 1996—. Recipient Outstanding Tech. Achievement award L.A. Black Media Coalition, 1989. Mem.: NATAS (mem. Emmy awards com. 1985—90, mem. show com. 1985—90, mem. exec. peer group com. 1985—93, 3 Emmy awards, 7 Emmy award nominations), NAACP, Assn. Image Cons. Internat., Colour Soc. Australia, Internat. Alliance Stage and Theatrical Emmployees, Aesthetics Internat. Assn. Office: Carol Brown Natural Empowerment Found PO Box 79083 Los Angeles CA 90079

BROWN, CAROL A., librarian; b. Cleve., July 11, 1950; d. Stanley and Bernice (Prorok) Przybyla; m. Richard Brown, May 25, 1979. BS, Kent State U., 1972; MLS, Case Western Res. U., 1973. Mgr. libr. svcs. Consol. Natural Gas, Cleve., 1973—2000; cons. The Info. Edge, 2000—. Bd. dirs. Cleve. Area Met. Libr. System, 1991—. Mem. Am. Gas. Assn. (chmn. libr. svcs. com. 1981-82, vice chmn. libr. svcs. com. 1991-92), Cleve. Area Met. Libr. System (pres. bd. 1985-86), Am. Soc. Info. Scis., Spl. Librs. Assn. Office: 14220 Indian Creek Dr Cleveland OH 44130-6858 Office Phone: 440-234-8101. E-mail: myinfolady@yahoo.com.

BROWN, CAROL ROSE, artist; BFA, Cornell U. Solo shows include The Witkin Gallery, N.Y.C., Charles Lucien Gallery, N.Y.C., Rettig Y Martinez, Santa Fe, The Little Gallery, Ithaca, N.Y., Korn Gallery, Drew U., Madison, N.J.; exhibited in group shows at Etherton-Stern Gallery, Tucson, Missoula (Mont.) Mus. Fine Arts, Parrish Mus., Southampton, N.Y., Provincetown (Mass.) Art Assn. and Mus., Whitney Mus. at Stamford (Conn.), The Torrey (Utah) Gallery; represented in collections U.S. Embassy, Athens, Greece, Rabat, Morrocco, Ashgabat, Turkmenistan. Individual fellow Nat. Endowment for the Arts, 1994. Personal E-mail: carolrosebrown@aol.com.

BROWN, CAROLYN RICE, dancer, choreographer, writer, filmmaker; b. Fitchburg, Mass., Sept. 26, 1927; d. James Parker and Marion Burbank (Stevens) Rice; m. Earle Brown, June 28, 1950 (div.). BA cum laude, Wheaton Col., 1950; student, Marion Rice Studio of Dance, Fitchburg, Mass., 1931-46, Julliard, N.Y.C., 1952-53, Metropolitan Opera Ballet Sch., 1953-65, Merce Cunningham Studio, 1952-72; Doctor Fine Arts (honorary), Wheaton Col., 1974. Principal dancer Merce Cunningham Dance Co., N.Y.C., 1953-73; freelance choreographer and tchr. various cities and countries, 1973-90; self-employed filmmaker, 1975-78; choreographer Centre Choreographique, Anger, France, 1976; dean of dance Sch. of Arts, SUNY, Purchase, 1980-82; guest artist Die Palucca Schule, Dresden, East Germany, 1985, Bartholin Internat. Ballet, Copenhagen, 1987; sr. fellow Dept. Theatre Arts U. Minn., Mpls., 1988-89, 90; regents lectr. Dept. Dramatic Art U. Calif., Berkeley; artistic cons. Merce Cunningham Dance Co., 1998—. Choreographer numerous works, 1967-90; contbr. articles to profl. jours.; dir., prodr. (film) Dune Dance, 1978. Recipient Dance Magazine award, 1969, 100th Anniversary Disting. Svc. award Wheaton Coll., 1970, Choreography awards Nat. Endowment for the Arts, 1973, 75, 76, choreography fellowship John Simon Guggenheim Found., 1983. Mem. Merce Cunningham Dance Found., Phi Beta Kappa; bd. mem. Found. for the Contemporary Performance Arts, 1967-2001. Office: Cunningham Dance Found 463 West St New York NY 10014-2010

BROWN, CARROLL, retired diplomat, association executive, consultant; b. Selma, Ala., Oct. 5, 1928; s. Jack Crisman and Bessie (Bedsole) B.; m. Elvira DiMiceli, Apr. 2, 1953; children: David, Suzanne. AB, Columbia U., 1951, MA, 1953; postgrad., Johns Hopkins U., 1964-65. Joined Fgn. Service, 1957; posts include Yugoslavia, Poland, Washington, Austria; dep. dir. for Eastern European affairs Dept. State, Washington, 1974-76; dep. chief mission Am. embassy, Warsaw, 1976-79; consul gen. Düsseldorf, Fed. Republic Germany, 1979-81, Munich, Fed. Republic Germany, 1981-84; dir. Office Can. Affairs Dept. State, Washington, 1984-86, acting dep. asst. sec., 1986; mem. U.S. delegations to 41st and 42nd UN Gen. Assemblies, N.Y.C., 1986; pres., bd. dirs. Am. Council on Germany, 1988-99; owner ind. cons. firm, 1999—2002. Adv. bd. World Policy Inst. With USN, 1953-57. Decorated comdr.'s cross Order of Merit (Germany); recipient Meritorious Honor award and Superior Honor award U.S. Dept. State. Mem. Fgn. Svc. Assn., Diplomatic and Consular Officers, Ret., Coun. Fgn. Rels., Univ. Club. Home: 114 E 71st St # 3E New York NY 10021 E-mail: cbrown123@earthlink.net.

BROWN, CECELIA MARY, library and information scientist, educator; b. Sarnia, Ontario, Can., Sept. 29, 1958; d. William and Mary Josephine Brown; m. Lee Richard Krumholz, June 14, 1987; children: Aleze Sarah Brown Krumholz, Talya Blythe Brown Krumholz. PhD, U. Ill., 1988. Assoc. prof. U. Okla., Norman, Okla., 1996—. Mem.: ALA, Okla. Libr. Assn., Spl. Libr. Association, Am. Soc. Info. Sci. and Tech. (Best Paper award 2004), Beta Phi Mu. Office: University of Oklahoma 401 W Brooks Norman OK 73019 Office Phone: 405-325-3921. Office Fax: 405-325-7648. E-mail: cbrown@ou.edu.

BROWN, CECILY, artist; b. London, 1970; Attended, NY Studio Sch., 1992; BA in Fine Arts, First Class Honors, Slade Sch. Art, London, 1993; B-TEC Diploma in Art & Design, Epsom Sch. Art, Surrey, England, 1987; attended Drawing & Printmaking classes, Morley Coll., London, 1987—89. Exhibitions include Fete Worse Than Death, Laurent Delaye, London, 1994, Eagle Gallery, London, 1995, Taking Stock, NY, 1996, Deitch Projects, NY, 1997, Janice Guy Gallery, NY, 1997, Vertical Painting, P.S. 1 Contemporary Art Ctr., NY, 1999, Pleasure Dome, Jessica Fredericks Gallery, NY, 1999, Facts & Fictions, Galleria in Arco Turin, Italy, 1999, At Century's End: John P. Morrissey Collection 90's Art, Mus. Contemporary Art, Fla., 1999, Deitch Projects, NY, 2000, The Skin Game, Gagosian Gallery, Beverly Hills, Calif., 2000, Serenade, Victoria Miro Gallery, London, 2000, Gagosian Gallery, NY, 2000, Emotional Rescue: Contemporary Art Project Collection, Ctr. Contemporary Art, Seattle, 2000, Days of Heaven, Contemporary Fine Arts, Berlin, 2001, Directions, Hirshhorn Mus. & Sculpture Garden, Washington, DC, 2002, Off, Murray Guy, NY, 2003, Whitney Biennial Am. Art, Whitney Mus. Am. Art, 2004. Mailing: c/o Gagosian Gallery 555 West 24th St New York NY 10011*

BROWN, CHARLES DICKSON, not-for-profit fundraiser, consultant; b. Jacksonville, Fla., Jan. 23, 1953; s. Charles Dickson Brown and Margaret Alma Baines; m. Robin Gail Mamlet, Dec. 22, 1997; 1 child, Padgett Tift. BA, Princeton U., 1975. Assoc. dir. animal giving Princeton U., NJ, 1979—88; dir. devel. Pennington Sch., NJ, 1988—91, Lawrenville Sch., NJ, 1991—97; v.p., ptnr. A.T. Kearney Exec. Search, NY, 1997—98; dir. external affairs Solomon R. Guggenheim Mus., NY, 1998—99; exec. dir. devel. Johns Hopkins U., Balt., 1999—2000; dir. med. devel. Stanford U., Palo Alto, Calif., 2000—. Contbr. chapters to books. Trustee Trust Hidden Villa, Los Altos Hills, Calif., 2002—, Sequoia Fund, Visalia, Calif., 2003; advisor Raise the Frequency, San Francisco, 2003. Mem.: The Brook, Nassau Club. Independent. Episcopalian/Buddhist. Avocations: running, reading, cello, piano, fundraising. Home: 730 Josina Ave Palo Alto CA 94306 Office: Stanford Med Alum Assoc 2700 Sand Hill Rd Menlo Park CA 94025-7020 E-mail: cdbrown@stanford.edu.

BROWN, CHARLES DODGSON, lawyer; b. N.Y.C., Dec. 31, 1928; s. James Dodgson and Leonora Rose (Nichols) B.; m. Martha Lockhart Spindler, Apr. 5, 1963; children: Gregory Spindler, William Howard. BA, NYU, 1949, JD, 1952. Bar: N.Y. 1952, U.S. Dist. Ct. (so. and ea. dists.) N.Y. 1955, U.S. Supreme Ct. 1958, U.S. Ct. Appeals (2d cir.) 1968. Counsel, former ptnr. Thacher Proffitt & Wood, N.Y.C., 1954—. Co-author: Equipment Leasing, 1995—. Chmn. zoning bd. Asharoken, N.Y., 1965, alt. chmn. environ. bd., 1967, trustee, 1967, village justice, 1980—; chmn. Boy Scout Am., Northport, N.Y., 1989—; elder 1st Presbyn. Ch., Northport; mem. admiralty law inst. faculty Tulane U. Sch. Law, 1999. With U.S. Army, 1952-54. Mem. ABA, N.Y. Bar Assn., Maritime Law Assn. U.S. (proctor in Admiralty 1956, former chair to marine fin. com. 1996-2000), N.Y. State Magistrate Assn., Suffolk County Magistrate Assn., Northport Tennis Club. Republican. Avocations: scuba diving, wind surfing, tennis. Office Phone: 212-912-7655. Personal E-mail: cbrown2@optonline.net. Business E-Mail: cbrown@tpw.com.

BROWN, CHARLES E., retail executive; Degree in Mgmt. Sci., Duke U. CPA. Various positions KPMG; v.p., controller Pizza Hut (subs. PepsiCo), 1989—94; v.p., CFO Aramark Corp., 1994—95; sr. v.p., CFO Denny's, Inc., 1996—98; from sr. v.p. fin., controller to exec. v.p., CFO Office Depot, Inc., Delray Beach, Fla., 1998—2001, exec. v.p., 2001—, CFO, 2001—. Office: Office Depot Inc 2200 Old Germantown Rd Delray Beach FL 33445

BROWN, CHARLES EARL, lawyer; b. Columbus, Ohio, June 6, 1919; s. Anderson and Ruth (Keeran) B.; m. Mary Elizabeth Hiett, May 23, 1959; children: Douglas Charles, Rebecca Ruth. AB, Ohio Wesleyan U., 1941; JD, U. Mich., 1949. Bar: Ohio 1949. Pvt. practice, Toledo; assoc. Zachman, Boxell, Bebout & Torbet, 1950-53; ptnr. Brown, Baker, Schlageter & Craig (and predecessors), 1953-90, of counsel, 1990-95, Shindler, Neff, Holmes & Schlageter, 1996—. Chmn. steering and exec. coms. Auto Trim Wholesalers div. Automotive Service Industry Assn., 1960-68 Lucas County Rep. Exec. Com., 1968-92; trustee, sec. Joseph J. and Marie P. Schedel Found., 1963-93, pres., 1993—. Capt. AUS, 1941-46; col. Res. ret. Decorated Bronze Star; recipient John J. Pershing award U.S. Army Command and Gen. Staff Coll., 1963 Fellow Am. Bar Found. (state chmn. 1978-84), Ohio State Bar Found. (trustee 1987-92), Am. Coll. Trust and Estate Counsel; mem. ABA, Ohio Bar Assn. (bd. govs. real property sect. 1953-76, coun. of dels. 1973-84, exec. com. 1984-87), Toledo Bar Assn. (past mem. exec. com.), Sixth Cir. Jud. Conf. (life), Toledo Area C. of C. (past trustee, com. chmn.), Res. Officers Assn., Assn. U.S. Army, Phi Beta Kappa. Congregationalist (past chmn. trustees). Lodge: Masons (32 deg.). Home: 3758 Brookside Rd Toledo OH 43606-2614 Office: 1200 Edison Plaza 300 Madison Ave Toledo OH 43604-1561

BROWN, CHARLES EUGENE, retired electronics company executive; b. Huntingburg, Ind., Oct. 31, 1921; s. Lemuel C. and Bertha (McCormack) B.; m. Elizabeth Sherman McAllister, Aug. 16, 1952; children— Deborah, Judith, Robert, Sarah BS, Ind. U., 1948, MBA, 1950. Corp. staff Glidden Co., Cleve., 1949-59; dir. indsl. relations Cleve. Pneumatic Tool Co., 1959-62, Honeywell, Inc., Mpls., 1962—68; dir. employee relations Honneywell, 1968—73; v.p. employee relations Honeywell, Inc., Mpls., 1973—80, v.p. exec. human resources, 1980-85, sr. staff v.p., 1985-86. Bd. dirs. Family and Children's Services, Mpls., Honeywell Retiree Vol. Program. Served with U.S. Army, 1942-45, ETO Decorated Purple Heart Mem.: Minneapolis, Interlachen Country. Home: 5601 Dewey Hill Rd Unit 219 Edina MN 55439

BROWN, CHARLES FREEMAN, II, lawyer; b. Boston, Mar. 7, 1914; s. Arthur Harrison and Nellie Abigail (Kenney) B.; m. Caroline Gotzian Tighe, Nov. 12, 1949 (dec. Jan. 1951); m. Pamela Judith Wedd, Nov. 29, 1952; children— Penelope Susan, Nicholas Wedd. AB, Harvard U., 1936, LL.B., 1941. Bar: Mass. 1941. Assoc. atty. Sherburne, Powers & Needham, Boston, 1941-43; asst. gen. counsel, gen. counsel OSRD, Washington, 1943-47; counsel rsch. and devel. bd. and mil. liaison com. Sec. Def., Def. Dept., rep. govt. patents bd., counsel Def. Prodn. Bd., dep. asst. sec. gen. for prodn. and logistics NATO detailed from Washington, London, Paris, 1947-53; asst. to pres. Hydrofoil Corp., Annapolis, Md., 1953-54; asso. gen. counsel CIA, Washington, 1954-60; v.p., treas. Sci. Engring. Inst., Waltham, Mass., 1960-66; dep. gen. counsel NSF, Washington, 1966-73, gen. counsel, 1973-76, chmn. interim compliance panel, 1970-71. Cons., 1976— Trustee Belmont (Mass.) Day Sch., 1963-66; bd. dirs. Hillcrest Children's Ctr., Washington, 1978-87, pres., 1980-83; pres. Cleveland Park Book Club, 1980-83, 91-94; bd. dirs. Cleveland Park Hist. Soc. Recipient Disting. Service award NSF. Mem. Fed. Bar Assn., Cosmos Club. Home and Office: 3050 Military Rd NW Washington DC 20015

BROWN, CHERYL, music educator; b. Santa Cruz, Calif., Feb. 13, 1958; d. Robert Sterling Brown and Billie Cornett; 1 child, Connor Wilton. BA in Music Performance, Am. Cons. Music, 1984; MA in Music Edn., Northeastern Ill. U., 1992. Sch. music tchr. Chgo. Pub. Schs., 1991—95, Addison (Ill.) Sch. Dist., 1995—; writer, pub. gen. music curriculum Lisle, Ill., 1994—. Jazz pianist, luxury hotels, country clubs, Chgo., 1981—. Author: (sch. music texts) Activities for the General Music Class, 1994, Holiday Activities for the General Music Class, 1995, Spell the Riddle Book, 1998. Mem.: NEA, Ill. Educators Assn. Democrat. Avocation: outdoor activities. Home: 2768-C Wayfaring Ln Lisle IL 60532

BROWN, CHRISTOPHER JERMAINE, education educator; b. Hattiesburg, Miss. m. Kim Stewart; 1 child, Carrington. Ed S Specialist in Edn. Adminstrn., U. So. Miss., Hattiesburg. Adminstr. Hattiesburg Pub. Schs., Hattiesburg, Miss., 2001.

BROWN, CHRISTOPHER PATRICK, health care administrator, educator; b. Phoenix, June 7, 1951; s. Charles Francis and R. Patricia (Quinn) B.; m. Tracey Ann Wallenberg, May 23, 1987; 1 child, Ryan Matthew. AA in Biol. Scis., Shasta Coll., Redding, Calif., 1976; AS in Liberal Arts, SUNY, Albany, 1977; grad. Primary Care Assoc. Program, Stanford U., 1978; BA in Community Svcs. Adminstrn., Calif. State U., Chico, 1982; M. in Health Svcs., U. Calif., Davis, 1984. Gen. mgr. Pacific Ambulance Svc., El Cajon, Calif., 1974; primary care assoc. Family Practice, Oregon-Calif., 1978-82; cons. Calif. Health Profls., Chico, 1982-84; bus. ops. mgr. Nature's Arts, Inc., Seattle, 1985-86; instr. North Seattle C.C., 1984-89, program dir., 1986-89; asst. dir. Pacific Med. Clinic North, Seattle, 1990-92; dir. Pacific Med. Clinic Renton (Wash.), Pacific Med. Ctr., 1992-95; dir. ops./physician svcs. St. Luke's Regional Med. Ctr., Boise, Idaho, 1995-97, adminstr. ambulatory care, 1997-98; adminstr. St. Luke's Meridian (Idaho) Med. Ctr., 1997-98; COO, sr. v.p. Medford (Oreg.) Clinic, 1998-2000; pres./cons. Integra Healthcare Solutions, 2000—. Mem. Butte County Adult Day Care Health Coun., Chico, 1982-84; bd. dirs., pres. Innovative Health Care Svcs., Chico, 1982-84; bd. dirs. Highline W. Seattle Mental Health Ctr., 1985-90, v.p. 1988-90; tech. adv. com. North Seattle C.C., 1992-93; bd. dirs. ARC, 1997-98; commr. planning commn. City of Central Point, Oreg., 2004-05. Mem. Internat. Platform Assn., Soc. Ambulatory Care Profls., Med. Group Mgmt. Assn., Multispecialty Group Exec. Soc., Accreditation Assn. for Ambulatory Health Care (accreditation surveyor 1996-97). Avocations: gardening, woodworking, church activities. Home: 345 Orth Dr Central Point OR 97502 E-mail: cbrown3394@aol.com.

BROWN, CLIFFORD BRYANT, financial consultant; b. Trenton, N.J., Dec. 7, 1970; s. Clifford and Dorothy Mae Brown; 1 child, Bryanna D. AA, So. Calif. Internat. Coll., 1995. Fin. cons. Ind. Capital Mgmt., Huntington Beach, Calif., 1994-95; fin. advisor Prudential, N.Y.C., 1996-98, Manhattan Planning Group, N.Y.C., 1998—. Vol., Hale Ho., N.Y.C. Sgt., USMC, 1989-95; mem. USMCR. Fellow Nat. Assn. Life Underwriters; mem. Harlem C. of C. Baptist. Avocations: travel, golf, basketball. Office: Innovative Retirement Solutions 60 E 42nd St 49th Fl New York NY 10165-0006

BROWN, CLIFTON, agricultural products supplier, director; b. 1946; Farmer, Trenton, N.C., 1967—; pres. Jones County Cotton Gin, Inc., Trenton, N.C. Office: Jones County Cotton Gin Inc 888 Nobles Ln Trenton NC 28585-7540

BROWN, COLLEEN, broadcast executive; BA bus admin and pol sci, U Dubuque, Iowa; MBA, U Colo. Gen. mgr. Sta. KPNX-TV, Phoenix, till 1998; v.p. broadcast Lee Enterprises, 1998-99, pres. Davenport, Iowa, 1999—2000; sr v.p. bus dev Belo Corp, Dallas, 2000—. Mem. March of Dimes. Mem. Young Press Assn. Office: AH Belo Corp 400 S Record St PO Box 655237 Dallas TX 75265-5237

BROWN, CONNELL JEAN, animal scientist, educator, retired animal scientist; b. Everton, Ark., Mar. 6, 1924; s. Clarence Jackson and Winnie Dee (Trammell) B.; m. Erma Dexter (Taylor), May 19, 1946; children— Craig Jay, Mark Allen BSA., U. Ark., 1948; MS, Okla. State U., 1950, PhD, 1956. Asst. prof. dept. animal sci. U. Ark., Fayetteville, 1950-57, assoc. prof., 1957-62, livestock sect. leader, 1978-81, prof., 1962-86, Univ. prof., 1986-90, prof. emeritus, 1990—; lectr. Internat. Stockmans Short course, 1980. Contbr.

articles to profl. jours. Served with USAAF, 1943-46; PTO. Recipient Rsch. award Performance Registry Internat., 1977, U. Ark. Coll. Agr. Rsch. award, 1981, Disting. Svc. award Ark. Cattlemans Assn., 1985; named to Am. Polled Hereford Assn. Hall of Merit, 1986, Ark. Agrl. Hall of Fame, 1994. Fellow AAAS, Am. Soc. Animal Sci. (pres. so. sect. 1975, leadership award so. sect. 1975); mem. Am. Genetics Assn., N.Y. Acad. Scis., So. Assn. Agrl. Scientists (bd. dirs.), Am. Registry Profl. Animal Scientists (pres. Ark. chpt. 1989), Kiwanis (dist. pres. 1984-85, lt. gov. 1992-93), Sigma Xi (pres. 1986-87), Gamma Sigma Delta (pres. 1967-68). Home: 188 Cydnee St Fayetteville AR 72703-3710 E-mail: cjb36@cox-internet.com.

BROWN, CORRINE, congresswoman; b. Jacksonville, Fla., Nov. 11, 1946; 1 child, Shantrel. BS, Fla. A&M U., 1969, MS, 1971; EdS, U. Fla., 1974. Prof. Fla. Community Coll., 1977—82, guidance counselor, 1982—92; mem. Fla. Ho. of Reps, 1982—92; del. Nat. Dem. Conv., 1988; mem. U.S. Congress from 3rd Fla. dist., 1993—; mem. transp. and infrastructure com., vet. affairs com. Mem. Sigma Gamma Rho. Democrat. Baptist. Home: 314 Palmetto St Jacksonville FL 32202-2619 Office: US Ho of Reps 2444 Rayburn Ho Office Bldg Washington DC 20515-0903

BROWN, COURTNEY ALLISON, composer, writer, singer; b. Sept. 9, 1975; d. Charles and Yolanda Faye Brown; 1 adopted child, Benjamin Joseph. BS in Psychology, Tulane U., 1997; student, So. Christian U. Residential counselor Meth. Home for Children, New Orleans, 1997—98, case mgr., 1998—2000; mental health specialist Hope Haven Residential Treatment Ctr., Marrero, La., 2000; case mgr., supr. Quality Ind. Svc. Coords. La., Kenner, 2000—. Composer: (songs) Thank You Lord for Just Being There, 1995, By His Stripes, 1995, Lord You're Holy, 1999, United Saints Gospel Music, 2001, (albums) Anointed Voices Strictly For Praise & Worship, 1999, All Things, 2004; author: Letters From A Concerned Friend, 2004; editor: Hullabaloo Viewpoint, 1994—95; editl. writer: Women of Excellence mag., 2002—03. Democrat. Baptist. Home: 2430 Dubreuil St New Orleans LA 70117 Office: 5060 Rochester Blvd Marrero LA 70072

BROWN, DALE, JR., obstetrician, educator, health facility administrator; b. Balt., Oct. 14, 1937; s. Dale and Louise (McCormick) B.; m. Eleanor Bartlett Moore, 1965; children: Stephen, Chris (dec.). BS, U. N.Mex., 1959, post-grad., 1960; MD, U. Tex., Galveston, 1964. Diplomate Am. Bd. Ob-Gyn (examiner 1991—). Intern Charity Hosp., New Orleans, 1964-65, resident, 1965-68; pvt. practice Amarillo, Tex., 1970-71, Houston, 1971-76, 1977—; mem. staff The Meth. Hosp.; assoc. chief ob-gyn, chief obstetrics St. Luke's Episcopal Hosp., 1984—, head residents, 1992—, chief staff, 1995-97. Clin. instr. Tulane Med. Sch., 1967-68; from instr. to assoc. clin. prof. Baylor Coll. Medicine, 1972-91, clin. prof., 1991—; cons. neonatal mortality com. Tex. Children's Hosp., 1986—. Contbr. articles to profl. jours. Mem. bd. deacons First Prebyn. Ch., 1976-86, chmn. diaconate bd., 1985-86, mem. bd. elders, 1987—; Active Audubon Soc., 1978—, Wilderness Soc., 1981—. Mem. AMA (Recognition award 1982-95, 85-88, 88-91, 91-94, 94-97), ACOG (Recogintion award 1982-85, 85-88, 88-91, 91-94), ACS, Internat. Coll. Surgeons, Internat. Soc. Advancement Humanistic Studies Gynecology, Internat. Soc. Study of Vulvovaginal Disease (asst. sec., treas. 1979-87, sec. gen. 1987-93, pres. elect 1993-95, pres. 1995-97),Am. Fertility Soc., Inst. Study of Vulvar Disease (bd. dirs., treas. 1988—), Ctrl. Assn. Obstreticians and Gynecologists (chmn. local arrangements com. 1976, mem. selection and presentation of papers com. 1980), So. Med. Assn., Tex. Med. Assn., Tex. Obstet. and Gynecol. Soc., Houston Obstet. and Gynecol. Soc., Houston Surgical Soc., Harris County Med. Assn., Seward Wills Obstet. and Gynecol. Soc., Conrad Collins and Pernol Ob-Gyn Soc., Tex. Flyfishing Club, Doctor's Club, Houston City Club, River Oaks Country Club, Mu Delta. Office: 6624 Fannin St Ste 2180 Houston TX 77030-2341

BROWN, DALE PATRICK, retired advertising executive; b. Richmond, Va., Aug. 11, 1947; d. Thomas Windom and Helen (Curtis) Patrick. BA in Journalism, U. Richmond, 1968, MA in English, 1978. Reporter city news sect. Richmond Times-Dispatch, 1968-71; free-lance writer, 1971-73; v.p., supr. pub. rels. account The Martin Agy., Richmond, 1973-77, account supr. advt., v.p., 1977-79, v.p., supr. advt. account, then group v.p. and sr. v.p., 1983-89; mgr. communications svcs. Mobil Chem. Co., Richmond, 1979-81; mgr. communications Whittaker Gen. Med., Richmond, 1981-83; exec. v.p. The Stenrich Group, Richmond, 1989-90; pres., chief exec. officer Sive/Young & Rubicam, Cin., 1990-98. Trustee U. Richmond, 1992-2004, hon. trustee, 2004—, mem. exec. com., 1999-2001, vice chair acad. program com., 2002-04; mem. devel. bd. Good Samaritan Hosp., 1992-95, Leadership Cin.; bd. dirs. Met. Growth Alliance, 1997-99, Downtown Cin. Inc., 1995-98, Midwest Strategic Trust, 1993-97, Ohio Nat. Life Ins. (exec. com.), bd. dirs. Frisch's Inc., 1998—, Mercantile Libr., 2000—, Cin. C. of C., 1995-98; chair Acad. Career Women of Achievement, 1996-2001; bd. govs. Cin. chpt. Am. Assn. Advt. Agys., 1990-98. Recipient 2 AAF Silver medals, 1988, 96, Richmond Advt. Person of Yr. award Advt. Club Richmond, 1988, Woman of Achievement award Cin. YWCA, 1993, Human Rels. award Am. Jewish Com., Cin. chpt., 1996, various others including Addy, Effie, Clio awards N.Y. Art Dirs. Club. Mem. Pub. Rels. Soc. Am., Advt. Club Cin., Queen City Club (bd. dirs.), Comml. Club of Cin. Avocations: reading, travel, arts. Home: 1231 Martin Dr Cincinnati OH 45202-1737

BROWN, DALE SUSAN, retired federal agency administrator, academic administrator, consultant, writer; b. NYC, May 27, 1954; d. Bertram S. and Beatrice Joy (Gilman) Brown. BA, Antioch Coll., 1976. Rsch. asst. Am. Occupational Therapy Assn., Rockville, Md., 1976-79; writer Pres.' Com. on Employment of People with Disabilities, Washington, 1979-82, program mgr. handicapped concerns com., 1982—85, program mgr. labor com., 1985, 96-98, program mgr. work environment and tech. com., 1988-94, program mgr. com. on libr. and info. svcs., 1984-86, youth devel com., 1986-88, new products devel. team, 1987-90, agy. rep., 1991-93, with interagy. tech. assistance coordinating team, 1992-94; program mgr. Job Accomodation Network, 1997-99; mgr. Nat. Conf. of Youth with Disabilities, 2000; policy advisor Office Disability Employment Policy Dept. Labor, 2001—05, mem. youth team, 2002—05, ret., 2005—. Cons. in field, gen. assembly speaker nat. conv. Gen. Fedn. Women's Clubs, 1981, mem. Rehab Svcs. Adminstrn. Task Force on Learning Disabilities, 1981-83. Author: Pathways to Employment for People with Learning Disabilities, 1991, Working Effectively with People Who Have Learning Disabilities and Attention Deficit Hyperactivity Disorder, 1995, I Know I Can Climb the Mountain, 1995, Learning Disabilities and Employment, 1997, Learning A Living Guide to Planning Your Career and Finding A Job for People with Learning Disabilities, Attention Deficit Disorder and Dyslexia, 2000, Job-Hunting Tips for the So-Called Handicapped, 2001, Steps to Independence for People with Learning Disabilities, 2005, (films) They Could Have Saved Their Homes, 1982; dir.: (videotape) Part of the Team People with Disabilities in the Workforce, 1990; co-editor: Learning Disabilities Quar. Americans with Disabilities Act and Learning Disabilities, 1992; mem. editl. bd. Perceptions, 1981—83, Learning Disabilities Focus, 1988—90, In the Mainstream, 1994—98; guest editor: Learning Disabilities Rsch. and Practice, 1990—96; guest editor Learning Disability and Career Development, 2002; guest editor: Career Planning and Adult Devel. Jour., 2002. Gy. rep. interagy. com. Handicapped Employees, 1998—99; bd. dirs. Closer Look Nat. Info. Ctr., Washington, 1980—83; bd. dir. Am. Coalition for Citizens with Disabilities, 1985—86; mem. Congl. Task Force Rights and Empowerment of Ams. with Disabilities, 1988—90; profl. adv. bd. Nat. Attention Deficit Disorder Assn., 1996—99; bd. dir. Coun. on Quality and Leadership, 2000—; adv. bd. Internat. Ctr. for Disability Resources on the Internet, 2003—; chair conf. on Info. Tech. for User With Disabilities, 1989; spl. asst. for people with disabilities Federally Employed Women, 1991—92; blue ribbon panel Nat. Telecomm. Access for People with Disabilities, 1989—94; pres. Assn. Learning Disabled Adults, Washington, 1979—80; del. Nat. Writer's Union, 1999; rep. com. on fed. govt. as model employer, com. on youth with disabilities Presdl. Task Force on Employment of Adults with Disabilities, 1999—2002; judge, Ten Outstanding Young Ams. U.S. Jr. C. of C. Jaycees, 2003. Named one of Ten Outstanding Young Ams., U.S. Jr. C. of C. Jaycees, 1994; recipient, Margaret Byrd Rawson award, 1989, Personal Achievement award Women's Program USDOL, 1989, Individual Achievement award, Nat. Coun. on Communication Disorders, 1991, Spl. Achievement award, Pres.'s Com. on Employment of People with Disabilities, 1991, Gold Screen award, Nat. Assn. Gov. Communicators, 1991, Arthur S. Fleming award, 1992, Voices Campaign award, 2004, Honor award, Dept. of Labor, 2004; grantee, Found. for Children with Learning Disabilities, 1982. Mem.: Inter Agency. Com. on Handicapped Employees (rep. 1989—91), Learning Disabilities Assn. Am. (bd. dirs. 1986—91), Nat. Assn. Govt. Communicators (Blue Pencil award 1986), Nat. Network of Learning Disabled Adults (founder, pres. 1980—81), ALA. Democrat.

BROWN, DALE WEAVER, clergyman, theology studies educator; b. Wichita, Kansas, Jan. 12, 1926; s. Harlow J. and Cora Elisa (Weaver) Brown; m. Lois D. Kauffman, Aug. 17, 1947; children: Deanna Gae, Dennis Dale, Kevin Ken. BA, McPherson Coll., 1946; BD, Bethany Theol. Sem., 1949; post grad., Drake U., 1954-56, Northwestern U. and Garrett Bibl. Inst., IL., 1956-58; PhD, Northwestern U., IL., 1962. Ordained to ministry Ch. of Brethren, 1946; pastor Stover Meml. Ch. of Brethren, Des Moines, 1949-56; dir. religious life, asst. prof. philosophy and religion McPherson Coll., 1958-62; assoc. prof. Christian theology Bethany Theol. Sem., Oak Brook, Ill., 1962-70; prof. Christian theology Bethany Theol. Sem., 1970-94. Del. standing com. Ch. of Brethren, 1954; moderator Middle Iowa Dist., 1952-53, mem. dist. and regional bds., gen. bd., 1960-62, moderator-elect. ann. conf., 1970-71, moderator, 1971-72. Author: In Christ Jesus: The Significance of Jesus as the Christ, 1965, Four Words for World, 1968, So Send I You, 1969, Brethren and Pacifism, 1970, The Christian Revolutionary, 1971, Flamed by the Spirit, 1978, Understanding Pietism, 1978, rev. edit., 1996, Berea College: Spiritual and Intellectual Roots, 1982, What About the Russians, 1984, Biblical Pacifism, 1986, Bibical Pacifism, new edit., 2003, Another Way of Believing--A Brethren Theology, 2005. Mem. Am. Acad. Religion, Internat. Bonhoeffer Soc., Fellowship of Reconciliation, Am. Theol. Soc. Home: 1101 E College Ave Elizabethtown PA 17022-2236 Office Phone: 717-361-9020. Personal E-mail: dwb1926b@aol.com. E-mail: dbrown1101@comcast.net.

BROWN, DALLAS COVERDALE, JR., retired military officer, historian, educator; b. New Orleans, Aug. 21, 1932; s. Dallas Coverdale and Rita Sydney (Taylor) B.; m. Joyce Regina Bush, July 26, 1955, (div. Aug. 1985); children: Dallas Coverdale, III, Leonard, Jan, Karen, Barbara; m. Elizabeth Taylor Vance, Sept. 3, 1985 BA in History and Polit. Sci. (Disting. Mil. Grad. 1954), W.Va. State Coll., 1954; MA in Govt., Ind. U., 1967, postgrad. in Def. Lang. Inst., 1966; grad., Command and Gen. Staff Coll., 1968, USA Russian Inst., 1970; disting. grad., Naval War Coll., 1974. Commd. 2d lt. U.S. Army, 1954, advanced through grades to brig. gen., 1978; service in Korea, W. Ger., Vietnam; dep. chief staff intelligence U.S. Army Forces Command, 1978-79; dep. vice dir. fgn. intelligence Def. Intelligence Agy., 1979-80; dep. comdr. U.S. Army War Coll., Carlisle Barracks, Pa., 1980-84; ret., 1984; assoc. prof. history W.Va. State Coll., Institute, 1984-96. Mem. bd. advisors W.Va. State Coll., 1990-91; mem. W.Va. Gov.'s Higher Edn. Advocacy Team, 1992-93, Savannah (ga.) Coun. on World Affairs Inc., 2000-; fgn. affairs coun. Hilton Head, 1999—; bd. dirs. WPBY-TV (PBS), 1995-96. Constituent U.S. Army War Coll. Found.; mem. Mil. Adv. Coun., Ctr. for Def. Info. Decorated Def. Superior Service medal, Meritorious Service medal (2), Joint Service Commendation medal, Army Commendation medal, Meritorious Unit Commendation, Master Parachutist badge, Aircraft Crewman badge; named Alumnus of Yr. W.Va. State Coll., 1978; named to W.Va. State Coll. ROTC Hall of Fame, 1980 Mem. Assn. U.S. Army, Ret. Officers Assn., Nat. Eagle Scout Assn., Sun City Vets. Assn. (comdr. 1999-2000, trustee 2000—), W.Va. State Coll. Alumni Assn., Alpha Phi Alpha, Alpha Lambda Boule, Sigma Pi Phi, Pi Alpha Theta, Pi Sigma Alpha, Rocks Club. Unitarian Universalist. Achievements include first African American general officer in field of military intelligence. Home: Sun City Hilton Head 17 Devant Dr E Bluffton SC 29909-4537 Personal E-mail: dallas17@hargray.com.

BROWN, DAN, writer; b. NH, June 22, 1964; m. Blythe Brown. Grad., Phillips Exeter Acad., Amherst Coll., 1986. Former English teacher Phillips Exeter Academy. Author: Matter, 1996, Digital Fortress, 1999 (Publishers Weekly Bestseller paperback list, 2005), Angels and Demons, 2000 (Publishers Weekly Bestseller paperback), Deception Point, 2001 (Publishers Weekly Bestseller paperback, 2005), The Da Vinci Code, 2003 (#1 NY Times Bestseller, #1 Publishers Weekly Bestseller). Named one of Time Mag. 100 Most Influential People, 2005. Office: c/o Random House Publicity 1745 Broadway New York NY 10019*

BROWN, DANIEL, curator, executive secretary; b. Cin., Nov. 4, 1946; s. Sidney H. and Genevieve Florence (Elbaum) B. AB cum laude, Middlebury Coll., 1968; AM, U. Mich., 1970; postgrad., Princeton U., 1971-72. Dir. cultural events U. Cin., 1972, spl. asst. to pres., 1973; v.p., corp. sec. Brockton Shoe Trimming Co., Cin., 1974—, sec. treas., 1997—; curator Maple Knoll Villag Retirement Cmty., KZF Gallery, 2003—. Curator KZF Gallery, Cin., 1987—94, 2004—, Design Studio, 1998—99, Katz and Dawgs Gallery, 1989—90, Antiques Design Ctr., 1998—, U. Clubs Ann. Art Exhibit, Antique & Design Studios, 1999—, Christ Hosp., 1999—, Regional Women Mid-Career Artists, 2000, 537 Gallery, 2000—, Maple Knoll Retirement Cmty., 2000, Univ. Club, 2005—; instr. Art Acad. Cin., 1980, 1988—; prin. Daniel Brown, Inc., Cin. and Columbus, 1999—; panel leader Midwest Coll. Art Assn. Conv., 1995; curator, art adv. St. Joseph Orphanage, 2002—; art critic Cin. Mag., 1980—83, Cin. Herald, 1992—94, Cin. Art Acad. Newsletter, Provincetown Arts, 1988—90, USA Arts; editor, co-pub., co-owner The Blue Book of Cin., 1998—; commentator Sta. WKRC-TV, Cin.; art and music critic Sta. WCP-TV, Cin., 1986—88; arts editor, essayist Cin. City Beat, 1994—95; guest curator New Art from Academe: An Overview The Cen. Exch., Kansas City, Mo., 1988, Lyrical Abstractions, 1989, Design of the Future, 1989, Contemporary Landscape Kancabco Co., Cin., 1988, No. Ky. U., 1989, The Arts Consortium, 1991—94, Cuba Now Carnegie Arts Ctr., 1996; guest co-curator Tangeman Fine Arts Gallery, U. Cin., 1987, guest curator, 88; permanent curator KZF Art Gallery, Cin., 1987—95; guest co-curator Artist at Mid-Career: A Dialogue Between Columbus and Cin., 1989—90; curator Liberties Restaurant, Cin., 1990—93, Fifth Third Bank, Cin., 1991—92, African-Am. Mus., 1992—93, African Am. Artists, 1994; guest spkr. Arts Consortium, 1994; guest critic dept. painting and drawing U. Cin., 1993—, lectr. lit. Inst. for Learning in Retirement, 2004—; corr. editor Dialogue Mag., 1986—90, art reviewer, 1983—; lead editorialist The Arts Consortium Newsletter, 1992; monthly editorialist Antenna Newspaper, 1995—; lectr., curator art exhbns. The Christ HOsp. and the Maple Knoll Retirement Cmty., 1999—; Chinese painting tchr. Art Acad., 2004; cons. in field; exec. editor The Blue Chip Rev., 2004—. Author: David Bumbeck: The Romantic Classicist, 1989, Tom Bacher: High Tech American Impressionist, 1989, The Universe Watching: The Art of Nancy Fletcher Cassell, 1990, John Stewart: A Retrospective, 1991, Bukang Kim: Journey to the East, 1992, Hustlers, 1992-93, The Evolution of Form, Bukang Kim: A Retrospective, 1995, Robert Knipschid: Four Decades of Painting, 2002; columnist Art Acad. News, 1990-94, Cin. Post, 1991, Downtowner, 1991-95, Everybody's News, 1994; editor-in-chief Antenna Arts Mag., 1996-98, The Bluechipreview.com, 2004—. Mem. exhbns com. Contemporary Arts Ctr.; sec., bd. dirs. Mercantile Libr., 1985-91, treas., 1986, chmn. programs com., 1987—, Young Wing; trustee Contempory Arts Ctr., 1984-87, co-chmn. artists adv. bd., 1987, Vocal Arts Ensemble, 1984, Enjoy the Arts, 1985-88, v.p., 1986; mem. bd. advisors Cin. Artists Group Effort, 1986-88; guest curator Carnegie Arts Ctr., Covington, Ky., 1986—; juror art competitions, Cin. and Columbus, Ohio, 1986-87, Mansfield, Ohio, Kansas City, Mo.; mem. citizens' adv. com. Art Acad. of Cin., 1989—, trustee, 1991—; trustee Art Acad. Cin. Coop. Gallery, 1990; co-chmn. fine art com. The Arts Consortium, cin., 1990—, curator, 1991—; sole juror Art Acad. Alumni Juried Exhbn., 1992; trustee UMOJA Artists' Group, 1994; curator KZF Gallery, 2004—. Recipient The Critic's Purse award Dialogue mag., 1985. Mem. Internat. Soc. Art Critics (N.Y. and Paris chpts.), Univ. Club (art com. 1990-91, guest curator 1992), Visiting Nurses Assn. of Cin. (bd., 2004—). Home: 3493 Brookline Ave #3 Cincinnati OH 45220 Office Phone: 513-751-3134.

BROWN, DANIEL EDWARD, social sciences educator; b. Newark, Aug. 10, 1950; s. Jack and Dorothy Brown; m. Annie Yu, May 30, 1981; children: Aaron Keith Ho-Mun, Elena Kathleen Lok-Mun. BA, Brown U., 1972; MA, Cornell U., 1972, PhD, 1978. Prof. U. Hawaii, Hilo, 1977—, chair, social scis. divsn., 1999—2003. Coord. rsch. and grad. studies U. Hawaii, 2004—. Author: Fundamentals of Human Ecology; contbr. articles numerous scientific journals. Rsch. And Tng. Support grant, NIH, 1981-2004, Rsch. Support grant, Am. Heart Assn., 1993-1995; 1997-1999, Nat. Ctr. for Minority Health and Health Disparities, 2004—. Mem.: Soc. for the Study of Human Biology, AAAS, Am. Assn. of Phys. Anthropologists, Human Biology Assn. (past pres. 2001—05). Avocation: hiking. Office: U Hawaii 200 W Kawili St Hilo HI 96720-4091 Office Phone: 808-974-7468.

BROWN, DANIEL STEWART, JR., communications educator, university official; b. Abington, Pa., June 9, 1959; s. Daniel Stewart and Lucille Mae (Freeman) B.; m. Susan Kay Shrum, Dec. 31, 1988. BA, Bob Jones U., 1982; MA, Miami U., Oxford, Ohio, 1983; PhD, La. State U. and A&M Coll., 1987. Instr. speech Pensacola (Fla.) Christian Coll., 1983-84; asst. prof. comm. Miami U., 1987-88; dir. devel. Maranatha Christian Schs., Columbus, Ohio, 1988-90; asst. prof. comm. arts Bryan Coll., Dayton, Tenn., 1990-94, assoc. prof., 1994-97, chmn. divsn. humanities, 1993-97, dir. honors program, 1995-97; assoc. prof. comm., dir. Ind. Wesleyan U., Indpls., 1997—. Contbr. articles and book revs. to profl. publs.; dir. Destiny in Dayton, 1991, 92. Mem. planning com. Tenn. Strawberry Festival, Dayton, 1993; mem. devel. dist. planning com. Tenn. Humanities Coun., 1996; vol., bd. dirs. Women's Care Ctr., 1995—, chmn., 1996-97. Recipient Apex award Comm. Concepts, 1991. Mem. Nat. Comm. Assn., Religious Comm. Assn., Kiwanis (v.p. Dayton, Tenn. 1994-95, pres. 1995-96, bd. dirs. Noblesville-Sunrisers 1999—), Phi Delta Kappa. Republican. Presbyterian. Avocations: landscaping, cooking. Office: Ind Wesleyan U 3777 Priority Way South Dr Indianapolis IN 46240-1491 E-mail: dbrown@indwes.edu.

BROWN, DARMAE JUDD, librarian; b. Sept. 14, 1952; d. William Robert and Dorothy Judd (Curtis) B. BA, W. Va. Wesleyan Coll., 1974; MA, U. Denver, 1975, M of Computer Info. Systems, 1992. Searching assoc. Bibliog. Ctr. for Rsch., Denver, 1975-76; libr. N.E. Colo. Regional Libr., Wray, 1976-81; head tech. svcs. Ector County Libr., Odessa, Tex., 1981-84, Waterloo (Iowa) Pub. Libr., 1984-89; sys. coord. Aurora (Colo.) Pub. Libr., 1989—2002; head tech. svcs. Saline County Libr., Benton, Ark., 2003—. Vestry mem. St. Stephen's Episcopal Ch., 2001-02. Mem.: ALA, Sigma Alpha Iota, Beta Phi Mu. Personal E-mail: darmae@bemail.com.

BROWN, DARRELL JAMES, publishing executive; b. Abilene, Tex., Feb. 13, 1959; s. Don J. and Alma K. Brown; m. Patricia Lee Stevens, Apr. 2, 1983; children: Tova Lee, Devon Justice. BS in Psychology, U. Mo., 1981. Dir. retail dept. The May Cos., St. Louis, 1981; vice chmn., editor LEADERS Mag., N.Y.C., 1981—; v.p. Dormann Pub., Inc., N.Y.C., 1984—; v.p., sec. SIPA News Svc., N.Y.C., 1984—, Internat. Bd. Indsl. Advisors, N.Y.C., 1984—; pres. Global Change Inc., 1996—. Lectr., career guidance counselor in youth field. Founding exec. bd. mem., sec., treas. Acacia Frat., U. Mo., Columbia. Mem. The Young People's Leadership Found. (pres.), Scottish Rite Mason (33rd degree), Order of De Molay (Legion of Honor). Avocations: tennis, skiing. Office: Leaders Mag 59 E 54th St New York NY 10022-4211

BROWN, DAVID, motion picture producer, writer; b. N.Y.C., July 28, 1916; s. Edward Fisher and Lillian (Baren) B.; m. Liberty LeGacy, Apr. 15, 1940 (div. 1951); 1 son, Bruce LeGacy; m. Wayne Clark, May 25, 1951 (div. 1957); m. Helen Gurley, Sept. 25, 1959. AB, Stanford U., 1936; MS, Columbia U., 1937. Apprentice San Francisco News and Wall St. Jour., 1936; night editor, asst. drama critic Fairchild Publs., 1937-39; editorial dir. Milk Research Council, 1939-40; assoc. editor Street & Smith Publs., 1940-43; assoc. editor, exec. editor, editor-in-chief Liberty mag., 1943-49; editorial dir. Nat. Edn. Campaign, A.M.A., 1949; assoc. editor, mng. editor Cosmopolitan mag., 1949-52; mng. editor, story editor, head scenario dept. 20th Century-Fox Film Corp. Studios, Beverly Hills, Calif., 1952-56, mem. studio exec. com., 1956-60, producer, 1960-62; v.p., dir. story operation 20th Century Fox Film Corp., Beverly Hills, Calif., 1964-69, exec. v.p. creative operations, 1969-70, dir., 1968-70; exec. v.p. creative operations, dir. Warner Bros., 1971-72; ptnr. Zanuck/Brown Co., N.Y.C., 1972-87; owner Manhattan Project Ltd., 1987—; pres. Island World, 1990-92; exec. story editor, head scenario dept., editorial v.p. New Am. Library World Lit., Inc., 1963-64. Final judge for best short story pub. in mags. Benjamin Franklin Mag. ann. awards, 1955-58. Author: Brown's Guide ot Growing Gray, 1987, Let Me Entertain You, 1990, The Rest of Your Life is the Best of Your Life, 1991; contbr. Am. mag., Collier's, Harper's, Sat. Evening Post, Reader's Digest, Journalists in Action, 1963, others; editor: I Can Tell It Now, 1964, How I Got That Story, 1967; prodr.: (films) The Sting, 1973, The Sugarland Express, 1974, The Eiger Sanction, 1975, Jaws, 1977, MacArthur, 1977, Jaws II, 1978, The Island, 1980, Neighbors, 1981, The Verdict, 1982, Target, 1985, Cocoon, 1985; exec. prodr.: Driving Miss Daisy, HBO Women and Men, 1 and 2, 1990, 1991, The Player, 1992, A Few Good Men, 1992, Watch It, 1993, The Cemetery Club, 1993, Canadian Bacon, 1994, Kiss The Girls, 1997, The Saint, 1997, Deep Impact, 1998, Angela's Ashes, 1999, Chocolat, 2000, Along Came a Spider, 2001; prodr.: (plays) A Few Good Men, TRU, The Cemetery Club, The Shawl, Mr. Goldwyn, Sweet Smell of Success, Vanilla, Dirty Rotten Scoundrels. Trustee com. on film Mus. Modern Art, N.Y.C. Served as 1st lt., M.I. AUS, World War II. Mem. Acad. Motion Picture Arts and Scis. (recipient Irving G. Thalberg Meml. award 1991), Producers Guild Am. (David O. Selznick Lifetime Achievement award 1993), Nat. Press Club (Washington), Coffee Ho. Club (N.Y.C.), Bd. of Visitors Columbia U. Grad Sch. of Journalism, Players Club (N.Y.C.), Dutch Treat (N.Y.C.), Century Assn. (N.Y.C.), N.Y. Friars Club. Office: Manhattan Project Ltd 1775 Broadway Ste 410 New York NY 10019-1903 E-mail: dbrown1775@aol.com. *Success, after all, is no more and no less than doing well what one wants to do most-regardless of where such an endeavor places one in the hierarchy of society.*

BROWN, DAVID G., academic administrator; AB in Econs. with honors, Denison U., 1958; PhD, MA in Econs., Princeton U., 1961. From asst. to assoc. prof. econs. U. N.C., Chapel Hill, 1961-66; Am. Coun. on Edn. fellow U. Minn., 1966-67; provost, v.p. for acad. affairs Drake U., 1967-70; provost, exec. v.p. for acad. affairs Miami U., 1970-82; pres. Transylvania U., 1982-83; spl. cons. Assn. Governing Bds., 1983-84; chancellor U. N.C., Asheville, 1984-90; provost Wake Forest U., Winston-Salem, NC, 1990—98, v.p., dean Internat. Ctr. for Computer Enhanced Learning, 1998—2003, provost emeritus, 2004—; interim pres. Ga. Coll. and State U., 2003; coord., Inter-Instl. Collaborative Atlantic Coast Conf., 2002—. Chair Asheville's Econ. Devel. Summit, 1986, Nat. Small Pub. Ivys Conf., 1988, coord. Interinstl. Academic Collaborative, Atlantic Coast Conf. Univs., 2001-; leader numerous workshops. Author: The Market for College Teachers, 1965, The Mobile Professors, 1967, Leadership Vitality, 1979, Leadership Roles of Chief Academic Officers, 1984, (monograph) Economic Development: 1987 and Beyond, 1986, Electronically Enhanced Education, 1999, Always in Touch, 1999, Interactive Learning, 2000, Teaching with Technology, 2000, Ubiquitous Computing, 2003, Developing Faculty to Use Technology, 2003; contbr. articles and papers to profl. bulls. and jours., also book chpts. Recipient Big A award Asheville Area C. of C., 1990; named one of 100 Young Leaders of the Acad., Change Mag., 1978; rsch. grantee Carnegie, 1979, U.S. Dept. Edn., 1965, NSF, 1965. Mem. Nat. Assn. State Univs. and Land Grant Colls. (chair coun. on acad. affairs 1975-76), Nat. Coun. Chief Acad. Officers (chair ACE 1978-80), Nat. Am. Assn. for Higher Edn. (chair 1981-82), Nat. Higher Edn. Colloquium (chair 1984-86), Phi Beta Kappa, Omicron Delta Kappa. Office: Wake Forest Univ 439 Vanderbilt Rd Asheville NC 28803 Office Phone: 828-274-0828. E-mail: brown@wfu.edu.

BROWN, DAVID NELSON, lawyer; b. Harrodsburg, Ky, May 29, 1940; s. Irmel Nelson and Pauline (Harmon) Brown; m. Lois Aileen Everett, June 20, 1964; 1 child, Ian Richard. AB, Cornell U., 1963; JD, U. Chgo., 1966. Bar: DC 1967. Assoc. Covington & Burling, Washington, 1966—74, ptnr.,

1974—, mgmt. com., 1989—93. Comment editor: U. Chgo. Law Rev. Mem.: ABA, Cosmos Club, Order of Coif. Episcopalian. Office: Covington & Burling 1201 Pennsylvania Ave NW Washington DC 20004-2401 Office Phone: 202-662-5238.

BROWN, DAVID RANDOLPH, electrical engineer; b. L.A., Oct. 31, 1923; s. Gilbert and Blanche Mabel (Phillips) B.; m. Sally England, Dec. 17, 1944; children: Philip, Ellen, Polly, Ann. BSEE, U. Wash., 1944; SMEE, MIT, 1947. Group leader MIT Lincoln Lab., Lexington, Mass., 1951-58; assoc. tech. dir. MITRE Corp., Bedford, Mass., 1958-63; lab. dir. SRI Internat., Menlo Park, Calif., 1963-85, staff scientist, 1985-93. Fellow IEEE. Avocation: genealogy. Home: 1470 Sand Hill Rd Apt 309 Palo Alto CA 94304-2031 Personal E-mail: drbrown@alum.mit.edu.

BROWN, DAVID RICHARD, school system administrator, minister; b. Manhattan, Kans., Oct. 22, 1929; s. Marion Arthur and Dorothy (Bailey) B.; m. Jeanette Christine Phoenix, July 28, 1962; children: David M., Mark, Thomas. BA, U. So. Calif., 1951; MDiv, U. Chgo., 1955; postgrad., U. So. Calif., 1956, 57. Ordained minister, Presbyn. Ch. Assoc. pastor Federated Community Ch., Flagstaff, Ariz., 1957-59; minister of edn. Lakeside Presbyn. Ch., San Francisco, 1959-62; pastor of edn. 1st Presbyn. Ch., Medford, Oreg., 1962-69, pastor Newark, Calif., 1969-75; founder, pastor Community Presbyn. Ch., Union City, Calif., 1975-89; founder, supt. Christian Heritage Acad., Fremont, Calif., 1984—2000; organizing pastor New Life Presbyn. Ch., Fremont, 1989—99; asst. prof. Chabot Coll., Hayward, Calif., 1975-80; pastor New Life Presbyn. Ch., Castro Valley, Calif., 1999—. Moderator Presbytery of No. Ariz., 1959, Presbytery of No. Calif., 2001—02; religion editor The Valley Citizen, Danville, Calif., 2000—. Dir.: various Shakespearian theatrical prodns., 1982—84 (Thesbian award, 1984). Pres. Boys Christian League, L.A., 1953-54, Coconino Assn. for Mental Health, Flagstaff, 1958-59; chaplain Mozumdar YMCA Camp, Crestline, Calif., 1952-56; chmn. Tri-City Citizens Action Com., 1986-90. Recipient plaque, KC, 1989. Mem. Rotary (chpt. pres. 1988-89, Paul Harris fellow 1989). Avocations: skiing, stamps, choir, drama. E-mail: revdavidbrown@sbcglobal.net.

BROWN, DAVID RONALD, lawyer; b. Turtle Creek, Pa., Jan. 25, 1939; s. James R. and Mary A. (Barnes) Brown; m. Debra W. Brown; children: Michelle, Adrienne, Aaron, Eden, Jeremy. Student, Brown U., 1956-57; BS, U. Pitts., 1960; JD, Duquesne U., 1967. Bar: Penn. 1968, U.S. Dist. Ct. (we. dist.) Penn. 1967, U.S. Ct. Appeals (3d cir.) 1972, U.S. Tax Ct. 1986. Rschr. phys. chemistry Mellon Inst., Pitts., 1960-66; real estate lawyer Redevel. Authority of Allegheny County, Pitts., 1966-69; ptnr. Litman, Litman, Harris & Brown, Pitts., 1969-2000, Sherrard, German & Kelly, Pitts., 2000—. Lectr. Robert Morris Coll., 1978-84. Councilman Borough of Turtle Creek, Penn., 1963-67. Mem. ABA (real property and probate sect., bus. law sect.), Pa. Bar Assn., Allegheny County Bar Assn. (com. legal svcs. 1973-74, real property sect., probate and trust law sect.). Home: 1 Trimont Ln Apt 660 D Pittsburgh PA 15211-1157 Office: Sherrard German & Kelly 28th Fl 2 PNC Plaza Pittsburgh PA 15222 Office Phone: 412-355-0200. Business E-Mail: dbrown@sgkpc.com.

BROWN, DAVID RUPERT, engineering executive; b. Chgo., Sept. 11, 1934; s. Hugh Stewart and Sara (Daniels) B.; m. Mary Heaton Nicolaus, Sept. 6, 1958; children: David R. Jr., Robert N., Sara D. BSME, Purdue U., 1956; MBA, U. Akron, 1968. V.p. engrng. Diamond Power Specialty Co., Lancaster, Ohio, 1974-77, v.p. ops., 1977-80, pres., 1980-82; sr. v.p., group exec. Babcock & Wilcox, Lancaster, 1982-85, Barberton, Ohio, 1985-87, v.p., gen. mgr., 1987; with Worldwide Procurement Inc., Akron, Ohio, 1987-90; v.p. mktg. Stock Equipment Co., Chagrin Falls, Ohio, 1990-95. With U.S. Army, 1957-58. Mem. ASME, Pi Tau Sigma, Tau Beta Pi. Home: 1717 Brookwood Dr Akron OH 44313-5072 E-mail: DBrown2020@aol.com.

BROWN, DAVID T., manufacturing executive; m. Nancy Brown; 2 children. B in Econs., Purdue U., 1970. Salesman Procter & Gamble, Shearson Hammill, Eli Lilly; with Owens Corning, 1978—, v.p. roofing and asphalt divsn., pres. roofing and asphalt divsn., 1994—96, pres. bldg. materials sales and distrbn., 1996—97, v.p. then pres. insulating sys. bus., 1997—2001, COO, 2001—02, CEO, pres., 2002—. Office: 1 Owens Corning Pkwy Toledo OH 43659

BROWN, DAVID WARFIELD, management educator, lawyer, academic administrator; b. Evanston, Ill., Aug. 16, 1937; s. Lloyd Warfield and Nancy (Coleman) B.; m. Alice Bean, Feb. 29, 1964; children: Peter Bean, Sarah Alice. BA, Princeton U., 1959; JD, Harvard U., 1963. Bar: N.Y. 1966. Assoc. Patterson, Belknap & Webb, N.Y.C., 1966-69; chief-of-staff Congressman Edward I. Koch, Washington and N.Y.C., 1969-74; v.p. Rand Inst., N.Y.C., 1974-75; chmn. N.Y. State Commn. Investigation, N.Y.C., 1975-78; dep. mayor City of N.Y.C., 1978-79; commr. Met. Transp. Authority, N.Y.C., 1979-85; ptnr. Hawkins, Delafield & Wood, N.Y.C., 1980; pres. Blackburn Coll., Carlinville, Ill., 1989-91; prof. profl. practice (mgmt.) Milano Grad. Sch. Mgmt. and Urban Policy, New Sch. U., N.Y.C., 1996—2004; cons. Kettering Found. Lectr., adj. prof. pub. mgmt. Sch. Mgmt., Yale U., New Haven, 1979-89. Author: When Strangers Cooperate: Using Social Conventions to Govern Ourselves, 1995, Organization Smarts, 2002; co-editor: Higher Edn. Exch.; contbr. articles to profl. jours. Capt. USAR, 1963-65. English Speaking Union scholar, London, 1959-60. Mem. Assn. of Bar of City of N.Y., Kettering Found. (assoc., vis. scholar 1991-92). Home and Office: PO Box 1266 Taos NM 87571-9998

BROWN, DAVID WILLIAM, economist, educator, consultant; b. Meriden, Conn., Nov. 10, 1931; s. William Horace and Elsie Miriam (Lovett) B.; m. Jean Margaret Young, Dec. 27, 1956; children: Cheryl Maurine, Kevin William. BS with distinction and honors, U. Conn., 1953; MS, Cornell U., 1954; PhD, Iowa State U., 1956. Asst., assoc. prof. U. Tenn., Knoxville, 1956-58, internat. prof., 1968-82; vis. prof. U. Malaya, Singapore, 1958-60; extension economist, asst. to dean Texas A&M U., College Station, 1961-63; team leader, tech. adv. Iowa Iowa-USAID program, Puno and Lima, Peru, 1963-66; vis. prof. Iowa State U., Ames, 1967-68; chief situation, outlook svc. UN Food and Agriculture Orgn., Rome, 1982-87; sr. economist food crops project, Acad. Ednl. Devel. USAID, Jakarta, Indonesia, 1988-90; social scis. specialist, adj. prof. U. Ill.-USAID project, Peshawar, Pakistan, 1990-94. Adj. prof. econs., tech. and humanities Salve Regina U., 1999-01; vol. career counselor Peace Corps, 1967-82; vol. economist R.I. Ctr. for Comml. Agr., 1995-2003, R.I. Conservation Dists., 1995—, R.I. Dept. Transp. Watch, 1995—, mem. exec. bd. 2002—; mem. Naval Installation Restoration Adv. Bd., Newport, 1996—; counselor Interactivity Found., 1996—. Mem., programmer, spkr. Coun. Internat. Visitors, Newport, R.I., 1994—; mem. Planning Bd., City of Newport, 1996-2000; mem. Aquidneck Island Planning Commn., 1996-2000; mem. R.I. Tree Coun., 1996—; mem. Newport Tree Commn., 2002—, chmn., 2003—; mem. EPA/TAG Aquidneck Island Citizen's Adv. Bd., 1996-2003, Aquidneck Island Affordable Housing Planning Group, 2003—; founding mem. R.I. People's Energy Coun., 2002—. Mem. Am. Econ. Assn., Union of Concerned Scientists. Avocations: socio-economic history, folk music, urban forestry. Home: 421 Bellevue Ave Apt 4C Newport RI 02840-6944 Personal E-mail: djbrown2@prodigy.net.

BROWN, DEAN NAOMI, state official, geologist; b. Fairbanks, Alaska, Mar. 9, 1944; d. James Heuston and Betty (Jefford) Alexander; m. Jim McCaslin Brown, Sept. 1, 1963 (div. 1987); children: Robin Wendy, Shelly Reneé. BS in Geology, U. Wis., 1967. Lectr. geology U. Ind., Kokomo, 1971-72; geologist, landman Amax Coal Co., Indpls., 1974; asst. and field constrn. engr. Trans-Alaska pipeline Fluor Alaska, Inc., 1975-76; environ. geologist Civil Engr./AK, Wasilla, 1977; various positions to acting dir. agr. Alaska Dept. Natural Resources, 1978-87; office mgr. Northwind Aviation, Anchorage, 1987-88; geologist Placer Dome U.S., Inc., Nome, Alaska, 1988; journeyman carpenter Ensearch Corp., Bradley Lake, Alaska, 1989; from no. regional mgr. div. land and water mgmt. to Dep. State Forester Alaska Dept. Natural Resources, Anchorage, 1990—2003, acting dir. agr., 2003—04, dep. state forester, 2004—. Adj. prof. natural resource econs. Alaska Pacific U., 1991, 93; vice-chair Alaskan-Chinese Timber Commn., 1993, Gov.'s Mktg. Alaska Forest Products Coun.; del. Coun. Western State Foresters, 1994-95, Nat. Assn. State Foresters, 1994; co-chair Dept. Nat. Resources Computer Group, 1996—; des. Statewide Emergency Response Commission, 1997—; mem. AK Wildland Fire Coord. Group, 1996—, chair, 1999—, Gov.'s Transition Team-Valley, 2002. Vol. Iditarod Trail Com. Recipient cert. of appreciation City of Valdez, Alaska, 1976, Anchorage Sch. Dist., 1983, 4-H Leaders, Palmer, Alaska, 1987, cert. of achievement Susitna coun. Girl Scouts U.S.A., 1982, Outstanding Achievement award Alaska Dept. Natural Resources, 1986. Mem. Aircraft Owners and Pilots Assn., Alaska Airman's Assn., Pacific Rim Arabian Horse Assn. (charter mem. 1997—), Alaska Horse Breeders Assn. (bd. dirs. 1984-90), Ninety-Nines. Avocations: flying, horse breeding and showing, painting, photography, gold mining. Home: PO Box 870366 Wasilla AK 99687-0366 Office: Alaska Dept Natural Resources 550 W 7th, Ste 1450 Anchorage AK 99501-5925 Office Phone: 907-269-8476. E-mail: dean_brown@dnr.state.ak.us.

BROWN, DEBORAH ELEANOR, minister; b. Carmel, Calif., Jan. 20, 1940; d. Charles Edward and Lois Eleanor French; m. Ronald Earl Brown; children: Cynthia Liegh Brown Cockrill, Gregory Scott. B, Occidental Coll., L.A., Calif., 1961; MDiv, Episc. Theol. Seminaty of Southeast, Austin, Tex., 1989. Ordained priest Episc. Ch., 1990. Primary elem. tchr. Long Beach Unified Sch. Dist., Long Beach, Calif., 1961—62; tchr. Pueblo Unified Sch. Dist., Pueblo, Colo., 1965—66, New Ulm Sch. Dist., New Ulm, Minn., 1970—77; assoc. rector St. Christopher's Epsicopal Ch., Roseville, Minn., 1992—96, interim rector, 1996—98; asst. interim rector St. John's the Evangelist Episcopal Ch., Mpls., 1998—99; interim rector St. Luke's Episcopal Ch., Mpls., 2000—01; pre-interim rector St. Clementis Episcopal Ch., St. Paul, 2001—; supply priest Episcopal Diocese of Minn., 2001—. Chaplian Eagan Police Dept., Eagan, Minn., 1995—, coord. chaplain program, 1999—; co-coord. vol. Gen. Con. of Episc. Ch., Mpls., 2003; co-coord. deacon/laity Episcopal Diocese of Minn., Mpls., 2002—. Rep. Eagan Police Dept. Eagan Health Cmty. Inst., Eagan, Minn., 2001—03, Eagan Pk. and Recreation Master Plan, Eagan, Minn., 2005—. Recipient Award of Merit, Eagan Police Dept., 2000. Democrat. Episc. Avocations: reading, knitting, art.

BROWN, DEL M. MAUHRINE, lawyer, educator; b. Ft. Meade, Md., May 26, 1965; BA, U. Md., 1987, JD, 1991. Bar: Va. 1993, U.S. Dist. Ct. (ea. dist.) Va. 1994, U.S. Ct. Appeals (4th cir.) 1994. Tchg. asst. Sch. Law U. Md., Balt., 1990, instr., 1991, assoc. dir. devel., mem. faculty College Park, 1991-92; Asper fellow, law clk. Md. Ct. Spl. Appeals, Balt., 1991; pvt. practice Virginia Beach, Va., 1993—; asst. prof., dir. recruitment Norfolk (Va.) State U., 1993-98; assoc. Poindexter and Brown, 1995-98; asst. pub. defender Office Pub. Defender Portsmouth, Va., 1998—2000. Vis. prof. U. Minn., Mpls., 1994. Editor: report N.J. Gov.'s Commn., 1991. Bd. dirs. Md. Women's Polit. Caucus, College Park, 1989—91; candidate Va. Ho. Dels., 1995, 1997. Mem.: ABA (mem. planning bd. young lawyers divsn. 1993—94), Va. Bar Assn. (6th cir. rep. young lawyers divsn.), Va. Trial Lawyers Assn., Hopewell Bar Assn., Golden Key, Delta Sigma Theta, Omicron Delta Kappa. Avocations: tennis, rollerblading. Office: 700 Gittings St Ste 100 Suffolk VA 23434 Office Phone: 757-925-2489 127. Personal E-mail: dmmbesaia@yahoo.com.

BROWN, DENISE, poet; b. Chgo., Oct. 7, 1963; d. Earl L. and Dorothy Grier; married; 3 children. Author: (poetry) A Treasury of Great Poems, 1998, poems. Recipient Editor's Choice award, 1999, Cert. of Recognition, 2001, The Diamond Homer award, 1998.

BROWN, DENISE SCOTT, architect, urban planner; b. Nkana, Zambia, Oct. 3, 1931; arrived in U.S., 1958, naturalized, 1971; d. Simon and Phyllis (Hepker) Lakofski; m. Robert Scott Brown, July 21, 1955 (dec. 1959); m. Robert Charles Venturi, July 23, 1967; 1 child, James C. Student, U. Witwatersrand, South Africa, 1948—51; diploma, Archtl. Assn., London, 1955; M of City Planning, U. Pa., 1960, MArch, 1965; DFA (hon.), Oberlin Coll., 1977, Phila. Coll. Art, 1985, Parsons Sch. Design, 1985; LHD (hon.), N.J. Inst. Tech., 1984, Phila. Coll. Textiles and Sci., 1992; DEng (hon.), Tech. U. N.S., 1991; HHD (hon.), Pratt Inst., 1992; DFA (hon.), U. Pa., 1994; LittD (hon.), U. Nev., 1998; D. Arch. (hon.), U. Miami, 1997; DFA (hon.), Lehigh U., 2002. Registered architect, U.K. Asst. prof. U. Pa., Phila., 1960—65; assoc. prof., head urban design program UCLA, 1965—68; with Venturi, Rauch and Scott Brown, Phila., 1967—, ptnr., 1969—89; prin. Venturi, Scott Brown and Assocs. Inc., Phila., 1989—. Vis. prof. arch. U. Calif., Berkeley, 1965, Yale U., 1967—70; asst. prof. U. Pa., 1960—65, vis. prof. Sch. Fine Arts, 1982, 83; Eliot Noyes design critic in arch. Harvard U., Cambridge, Mass., 1989—90; mem. visitors com. MIT, 1973—83; mem. adv. com. dept. arch. Temple U., 1980—2001; cons. to dean search com. Sch. Arch. Washington U., St. Louis, 1992; mem. adv. bd. dept. arch. Carnegie Mellon U., 1992—; mem. jury Prince of Wales Prize in Urban Design Grad. Sch. Design Harvard U., Cambridge, 1993; mem. bd. overseers U. Librs. U. Pa., 1995—2004. Author: Urban Concepts, 1990; co-author: Learning from Las Vegas, 1972, (rev. edit.), 1977, A View from the Campidoglio: Selected Essays, 1953-84, 1985, Architecture as Signs and Systems for a Mannerist Time, 2004; contbr. numerous articles to profl. jours.; prin. works include campus plans U. Mich., Dartmouth Coll., Tsinghua U., Beijing, city plans Miami Beach, Memphis, plans for U. Pa. Perelman Quadrangle, Nat. Gallery, London, Hotel du Dept. de la Haute Garonne, Toulouse, France, others. Policy panelist design arts program NEA, 1981—83; mem. bd. adv. Architects, Designers and Planners for Social Responsibility, 1982—; mem. capitol preservation com. Commonwealth of Pa., Harrisburg, 1983—87; trustee Chestnut Hill Acad., Phila., 1985—89; hon. vice patron The Royal Soc. for the Encouragement of Arts, Manufacture and Commerce in the U.S., 2004; mem. curriculum com. Phila. Jewish Children's Folkshul, 1980—86; bd. dirs. Ctrl. Phila. Devel. Corp., 1985—, Urban Affairs Partnership, Phila., 1987—91. Decorated commendatore Order of Merit Italy, chevalier de l'Ordre des Arts et des Lettres France; co-recipient The Phila. award, 1993, Luminary award, 2005; named to Germantown Hall of Fame, Germantown Hist. Soc., Pa., 2002; recipient Chgo. Architecture award, 1987, U.S. Presdl. award, Nat. Medal of Arts, 1992, Hall of Fame award, Interior Design mag., 1992, The Benjamin Franklin medal, Royal Soc. for Encouragement of Arts., Mfg. and Commerce, 1993, Topaz medal, Am. Coll. Schs. of Architecture/AIA, 1996, Giants of Design award, House Beautiful Mag., 2000, Joseph Pennell medal, Phila. Sketch Club, 2000, Vincent J. Scully Prize, Nat. Bldg. Mus., 2002, Edith Wharton Women of Achievement award for Urban Planning, 2002, Soc. for Environ. Graphic Design Fellow award, 2003, Visionary Woman award, Moore Coll. Art and Design, 2003, The Franklin Founder Bowl, The Franklin Celebration, 2005, Harvard Radcliffe Inst. medal, 2005. Mem.: Germantown Historical Soc. of Phila., Germantown Jewish Centre (Germantown Hall of Fame 2002, Soc. for Environ. Graphic Design Fellow award 2003), Royal Soc. Encouragement of Arts, Mfg. and Commerce (hon. vice patron 2004), Soc. Archtl. Historians (bd. dirs. 1981—84), Soc. Coll. and Univ. Planning, Archtl. Assn. London, Am. Planning Assn., Archs. Designers and Planners for Social Responsibility, Am. Acad. Arts and Scis., Royal Inst. Brit. Archs., Athenaeum of Phila., Carpenters Co. of City and County of Phila., Internat. Women's Forum. Democrat. Jewish. Office: Venturi Scott Brown & Assocs Inc 4236 Main St Philadelphia PA 19127-1696

BROWN, DENNY L., utilities executive; Various mgmt. positions Stagg Systems, IBM; v.p., chief information officer info. svcs. Pinnacle West Capital Corp., Ariz. Pub. Svc. Comp., Phoenix, 2001—. Office: Pinnacle West Capital Corp Arizona Pub Svc Comp 400 N Fifth St Phoenix AZ 85072-3999 Office Phone: 602-250-1000.*

BROWN, DEVIN, professional basketball player; b. Dec. 30, 1978; BA, Texas-San Antonio, 1998—2002. Guard San Antonio Spurs, Tex., 2002—05. Named to Rocky Mountain Revue All-Tournament Team, 2004, First Team, Reebok Pro Summer Team, 2003, NBA Championship Team, NBA, 2005. Office: San Antonio Spurs One SBC Ctr San Antonio TX 78219*

BROWN, DONALD ARTHUR, lawyer; b. Washington, Feb. 1, 1929; s. Louis S. and Rose (Kliban) B.; m. Ann Winkelman, July 13, 1959; children: Cathy, Laura. BA in Econs., George Washington U., 1949, LL.B. (Case Club oral argument competition winner), 1952, LL.M., 1958. Bar: D.C. 1952. Sr. partner Brown, Gildenhorn & Jacobs (and predecessor), Washington, 1955—. Mem. faculty Practising Law Inst.; faculty Harvard U. Sch. Bus., Cambridge, Mass., 1984-93, Yale U. Sch. Mgmt., New Haven, 1986, George Washington U. Sch. Bus., Washington, 1994—; guest lectr. Am. U., Nat. Assn. Real Estate Counselors, Nat. Assn. Real Estate Investors; pres., sec. JBG Constrn., Inc.; partner JBG Assocs.; v.p., treas. JBG Properties, Inc.; trustee, gen. counsel Nat. Bank Rosslyn, Arlington, Va.; mem. minority enterprises com. SBA; finance com. Housing Devel. Corp.; mem. Model Cities Com. D.C.; apptd. by Pres. of U.S. commr. Internat. Cultural and Trade Ctr., 1988. Co-author: Understanding Real Estate Investments, 1967; contbr. articles to profl. jours. Exec. bd. Forest Hills Citizens Assn.; bd. dirs. D.C. Jr. C. of C.; mem. Friends Kennedy Center, Friends Corcoran Gallery, Big Bros. Orgn. D.C.; bd. dirs. Washington Area Tennis Patrons Found., 1964—, pres., 1973-75, Fed. city council; trustee Woodley House, psychiat. half-way house, Washington, 1973—, pres. bd. dirs., 1975—; trustee U. D.C., Sidwell Friends Sch., The Phillips Collection, 1984—; mem. art adv. council Washington Conv. Ctr. com. D.C. Conv. Ctr. Served as officer USNR, 1952-55. Named Washingtonian of Yr., Washingtonian mag., 1989. Mem. ABA, Fed. Bar Assn., D.C. Bar Assn., Washington Bd. Realtors (chmn. lawyer-realtor liaison com. 1972, chmn. investment property com. 1970), Economics Club of Washington, Burning Tree Club. Jewish (bd. mgrs. congregation 1962, treas. 1965). Club: Georgetown (Washington). Home: 2734 Rhone Dr Palm Beach Gardens FL 33410-1280 Office: Brown Gildenhorn & Jacobs 5301 Wise Ave NW Washington DC 20015

BROWN, DONALD DAVID, biology professor; b. Cin., Dec. 30, 1931; s. Albert Louis and Louise (Rauh) B.; m. Linda Jane Weil, July 2, 1957; children: Deborah Lin, Christopher Charles, Sharon Elizabeth. MS, MD, U. Chgo., 1956, D.Sc. (hon.), 1976, U. Md., 1983; DSc (hon.), U. Cin., 1992. Staff mem. dept. embryology Carnegie Instn. of Washington, Balt., 1963—, dir., 1976-94; prof. dept. biology Johns Hopkins U., 1968—. Pres. Life Scis. Research Found. Served with USPHS, 1957-59. Recipient U.S. Steel Found. award for molecular biology, 1973, V.D. Mattia award Roche Inst., 1975, Boris Pregel award for biology N.Y. Acad. Scis., 1976, Ross G. Harrison award Internat. Soc. Developmental Biology, 1981, Bertner Found. award, 1982, Rosenstiel award for biomed. sci., 1985, Louisa Gross Horwitz award, 1985, Feodor Lynen award U. Miami Winter Symposium, 1987. Fellow Am. Acad. Arts and Scis., AAAS; mem. Nat. Acad. Scis. (mem. coun. 1994-97), Soc. Devel. Biology (pres. 1975), Am. Soc. Biol. Chemists, Am. Soc. Cell Biology (pres. 1992, E.B. Wilson award 1996), Am. Philos. Soc. Home: 5721 Oakshire Rd Baltimore MD 21209-4217 Office: Carnegie Instn Washington 3250 San Martin Dr Baltimore MD 21218 E-mail: brown@ciwemb.edu.

BROWN, DONALD DOUGLAS, transportation executive, consultant, retired military officer; b. Montreal, Que., Can., Aug. 1, 1931; came to U.S., 1938; s. Donald Bannerman and Hilda Taylor (Noel) B.; m. Joan Teresa McAndrews, Aug. 7, 1954; children— Cathy J. Brown Peinhardt, James D., Nancy J. Brown May. BA, Columbia U., 1954; MBA, Syracuse U., 1965. Commd. officer U.S. Air Force, 1955, advanced through grades to maj. gen., 1979, ret., 1987, wing chief aircrew standardization Phan Rang Air Base, Vietnam, 1968-69, chief Weapon System Support div. in Directorate of Supply, then dir. logistics plans Scott AFB, Ill., 1973-75, asst. dep. chief of staff for logistics, 1975-76, from vice comdr. to comdr. McChord AFB, Wash., 1976-77, asst. dep. chief of staff for ops. Mil. Airlift Command Scott AFB, Ill., 1979-80, dep. chief of staff for plans, 1980-83, dep. chief of staff for ops. Mil. Airlift Command, 1983-84, comdr. 22d Air Force, Mil. Airlift Command Travis AFB, Calif., 1984-87, ret., 1987; chmn. bd. Evergreen Air Ctr. Inc. Cons. in aviation/logistics mgmt. Decorated Disting. Service medal with oak leaf cluster, Legion of Merit with oak leaf cluster, D.F.C. with oak leaf cluster, Bronze Star, Air medal with 4 oak leaf clusters, Republic of Vietnam Cross of Gallantry with palm Mem. Air Force Assn., Nat. Def. Transp. Assn. (appted. to bus. practices com.), Beta Gamma Sigma. Office Phone: 253-588-2149.

BROWN, DONALD JAMES, JR., lawyer; b. Chgo., Apr. 21, 1948; s. Donald James Sr. and Marian Constance (Scimeca) B.; m. Donna Bowen, Jan. 15, 1972; children: Megan, Maura. AB, John Carroll U., 1970; JD, Loyola U., Chgo., 1973. Bar: Ill. 1973, U.S. Dist. Ct. (no. dist.) Ill. 1973, U.S. Tax Ct. 1982. Asst. to state's atty. Cook County, Ill., 1973-75; assoc. Baker & McKenzie, Chgo., 1975-82, ptnr., 1982-95, Donohue, Brown, Mathewson & Smyth, Chgo., 1995—. Office: Donohue Brown et al 140 S Dearborn St Chicago IL 60603-5202

BROWN, DONALD ROBERT, psychology professor; b. Albany, NY, Mar. 5, 1925; s. J. Edward and Natile (Rosenberg) B.; m. June Gole, Aug. 14, 1945; children: Peter Douglas, Thomas Matthew, Jacob Noah. AB, Harvard U., 1948; MA, PhD, U. Calif.-Berkeley, 1951. Mem. faculty Bryn Mawr Coll., 1951-64, prof. psychology, 1963—. Sr. research cons. Mellon Found., Vassar Coll., 1953-63; part-time vis. prof. Swarthmore Coll., U. Pa., also U. Calif.-Berkeley, 1953-61; fellow Center Advanced Study Behavioral Scis., 1960-61; prof. psychology, sr. research scientist, dir. Center Research Learning and Teaching, U. Mich., 1964—; cons. Peace Corps, 1965-71; hon. research fellow Univ. Coll., London, 1970-71; Fulbright sr. research fellow Max Planck Inst., Berlin, 1982; Netherlands Basic Sci. fellow, Leyden, 1983 Author: articles, chpts. in books; editor: Changing Role and Status of Soviet Women, 1967, Frontiers of Motivational Psychology, 1986; co-editor: Frontiers of Mathematical Psychology, 1990. Served with AUS, 1943-46, ETO. Fellow Am. Psychol. Assn., Chinese Acad. Sci.; mem. Soc. Psychol. Study of Social Issues, AAAS, AAUP, Sigma Xi, Psi Chi. Home: 2511 Hawthorne Rd Ann Arbor MI 48104-4031 Business E-Mail: donrobro@umich.edu.

BROWN, DONALD WESLEY, lawyer; b. Cleve., Jan. 2, 1953; s. Lloyd Elton Brown and Nancy Jeanne Hudson. AB summa cum laude, Ohio U., 1975; JD, Yale U., 1978. Bar: Calif. 1978, U.S. Dist. Ct. (no. dist.) Calif. 1978, U.S. Dist. Ct. (cen. dist.) Calif. 1990. Assoc. Brobeck, Phleger & Harrison, San Francisco, 1978-85, ptnr., 1985—2003, Covington & Burling, San Francisco, 2003—. Democrat. Home: 2419 Vallejo St San Francisco CA 94123-4638 Office: Covington & Burling One Front St San Francisco CA 94111 Office Phone: 415-591-7063. Business E-Mail: dwbrown@cov.com.

BROWN, DOROTHY M., academic administrator; Prof. history Georgetown U., Washington, 1966—98, interim provost, 1998—99, provost, 1999—. Former chair history dept. Georgetown U. Office: Georgetown U Office of the Provost Box 571014/ ICC 650 Washington DC 20057-1014

BROWN, DUDLEY EARL, JR., psychiatrist, educator, health science association administrator, federal agency administrator, retired military officer; b. Berryville, Va., Apr. 10, 1928; s. Dudley Earl and Rosa Lee (Costello) B.; m. Lelia Adrienne Motley, June 22, 1953; children: Lelia Brown Farr, David, Kevin. BA, Washington and Lee U., 1949; MD, Med. Coll. Va., 1953. Diplomate Am. Bd. Psychiatry and Neurology. Commd. lt. (j.g.) M.C. USN, 1953, advanced through grades to rear adm., 1974; intern Naval Hosp., Portsmouth, Va., 1953-54, resident in neuropsychiatry Bethesda, Md., 1957-60; svc. in Vietnam; commdg. officer Nat. Naval Med. Ctr., Bethesda, 1975-76, Naval Regional Med. Ctr., San Diego, 1976-78; fleet surgeon U.S. Pacific Fleet and staff surgeon, comdr.-in-chief U.S. Forces, Pacific, Pearl Harbor, Hawaii, 1978-80; ret., 1980; dep. asst. chief med. dir. for profl. svcs. VA Ctrl. Office, Washington, 1980-82; assoc. dep. chief med. dir. VA, Washington, 1982-87; asst. prof. clin. psychiatry U. Pa. Med. Sch., 1967-70; prof. clin. psychiatry Uniformed Svcs. U. Health Scis., Bethesda, 1981—, Med. Coll. Va., Va. Commonwealth U., Richmond, 1987—2004; dir. health policy studies, dir. Washington office Abt Assocs. Inc., 1987-93, v.p., 1992—, mng. v.p., 1993—2001. Sci. adv. bd. Ctr. Prisoner of War Studies, 1998-04. Contbr. to med. jours. Decorated Legion of Merit; recipient Meritorious Svc. medal, Navy Commendation medal, VA Disting. Svc. medal, Disting. Alumnus Med. Coll. Va., 1993. Fellow ACP, Am. Psychiat. Assn., Am. Coll.

Psychiatrists; mem. Washington Psychiat. Soc., Nat. Health Coun. (bd. dirs. 1989-94), Assn. Mil. Surgeons U.S., Soc. Med. Cons. to Armed Forces (v.p. 1988-89, pres. 1989-90), Phi Gamma Delta, Alpha Epsilon Delta. Presbyterian. Home: 2415 Black Cap Ln Reston VA 20191-3027 Office: Abt Assocs Inc 4800 Montgomery Ln Ste 600 Bethesda MD 20814-3460 Office Phone: 703-264-1953. Personal E-mail: dearlbown@aol.com.

BROWN, EARL KENT, historian, minister; b. Kent, Ohio, July 26, 1925; s. Earl Royal and Bernice Blanche (Howard) B. BA, Columbia U., 1948; S.T.B., Boston U., 1953, PhD (Howard fellow 1953-54, United Methodist Ch. Dempster fellow 1954-55), 1956. Ordained to ministry United Meth. Ch., 1957. Asst. prof. history Baldwin Wallace Coll., 1956-63, asso. prof., 1963; assoc. prof. church history Boston U., 1963-70, prof., 1970-86, prof. emeritus, 1986—. Vis. prof. Case Western Res. U., 1961, Union Theol. Sem., Manila, 1970, United Theol. Coll., Bangalore, India, 1978, U. Manchester, Eng., 1979. Author: Women of Mr. Wesley's Methodism, 1983; Contbr. articles to acad. jours., religious periodicals. Fulbright fellow, 1962 Mem. Phi Beta Kappa. Home: Merrill Gardens #354 2261 Tuolumne Street Vallejo CA 94589 Office Phone: 707-643-6474.

BROWN, EDDIE C., investment company executive; married; 2 children. BSEE, Howard U., 1961; MSEE, NYU, 1968; MBA, Ind. U., 1970. Chartered fin. analyst; chartered investment counselor, Md. Engr. Titan missile project Martin Marietta Co., 1961; design engr. systems devel. div. (spl. cirs.) IBM Corp., 1963-68; mgr. investment systems, asst. to pres. Irwin Mgmt. Co., 1970-73; v.p., portfolio mgr. T. Rowe Price Assocs., 1973-83; v.p., mem. investment adv. com. T. Rowe Price Tax-Free Income Fund, 1973-83; pres. Brown Capital Mgmt. Inc., Balt., 1983—. Panelist Wall Street Week with Louis Rukeyser; bd. mem. Mercantile Bankshares Corp., Municipal Mortgage Equity. Bd. dirs. Community Found. of Greater Balt. Area; mem. Greater Balt. Com.'s Pub. Policy Coun., Ind. U. Sch. of Bus. Dean's Adv. Coun., Pres.'s Round Table. 1st lt. Signal Corps U.S. Army, 1961-63. Consortium for Grad. Study in Mgmt. fellow; IBM study program resident. Mem. Md. Acad. Scis., C. of C. of U.S. (small bus. coun.), Inst. Chartered Fin. Analysts (chartered), Fin. Analysts Fedn., Balt. Soc. Security Analysts, Beta Gamma Sigma, Sigma Iota Epsilon. Office: Brown Capital Management 1201 North Calvert St Baltimore MD 21202

BROWN, EDGAR HENRY, JR., mathematician, educator; b. Chgo., Dec. 27, 1926; s. Edgar Henry and Viola (Offen) B.; m. Gail Hamilton, June 13, 1954; children: Jessica, Nicholas. BS, U. Wis., 1949; MS, Wash. State U., 1951; PhD, MIT, 1954. Instr. Washington U., St. Louis, 1954-55, U. Chgo., 1955-57; Office Naval Res. fellow Brown U., 1957-58; from mem. faculty to prof. Brandeis U., Waltham, Mass., 1958—63, prof. math., 1963—, chmn. Dept. Math., 1960—62, 1978—80. Instr. math. Inst. Advanced Study, 1962—63, Math. Inst., Oxford, England, 1965—66, vis. prof., 1994; instr. math. U. Coll., London, 1973—74; vis. prof. Princeton U., 1971; vis. prof. New Coll. Oxford and Kings Coll. Cambridge (England) U., 1982—83; sr. rsch. fellow Jesus Coll., Oxford, 1986—87; vis. prof. Yale U., 1993. Served with USNR, 1944-46. Fellow, NSF, 1962—63, Guggenheim Found., 1965—66, Brit. SRC Rsch. Coun., 1973—74, 1982—83. Mem. Am. Math. Soc., Am. Acad. Arts and Sci. Home: 32 Fisher Ave Newton MA 02461-1117 Office: Brandeis U MS 050 Waltham MA 02454 Business E-Mail: brown@brandeis.edu.

BROWN, EDWARD J, III, bank executive; B in indsl. mgmt., Ga. Inst. Tech.; M in fin., Harvard U., 1972. Credit analyst and various positions NationsBank, 1972—79, sr. v.p., dir. So. dept., 1979—80, sr. v.p. specialized industries divsn., 1980—82, Tampa Bay area exec., 1982—84, Tampa Bay region exec., 1984—85, mid. market group exec., 1985—88, pres. corp. banking, 1988, pres. global fin., 1997; pre. global capital raising and global capital markets Bank Am. Corp. (formerly NationsBank), 1998—2000; pres. global corp. and investment banking Bank Am. Corp., 2000—. Bd. dirs. Inst. Internat. Fin., Carolinas Health Care Sys., PGA TOUR Golf Course Properties. Commr. San Francisco Asian Art Mus. Office: Bank Am Corp 100 N Tryon St Charlotte NC 28255

BROWN, EDWARD JAMES, SR., utilities executive; b. Ft. Wayne, Ind., Sept. 30, 1937; s. William Theodore and Jane Elizabeth (Dix) Brown; m. Margaret Bessey, June 17, 1989; children: Edward James Jr., Elena Emily. BA, Yale U., 1959; MA, Fordham U., 1962. CFA. Fin. writer E.F. Hutton & Co., N.Y.C., 1970-71; economist N.Y. Power Authority, N.Y.C., 1971-74, prin. economist, 1974-80, mgr., customer svcs., 1980-83, mgr. spl. projects, 1983-86, dir. strategic planning, 1986-93, dir. new bus., 1993-94. Mem. mgmt. com. Iroquois Gas Transmission Sys., 1989—94. Pres. Park Ave. Meth. Trust, N.Y.C., 1981—; dir. Friends of Shakers, Inc., Sabathday Lake, Maine, 1980—, pres., 1982—84, treas., 1995—; trustee United Soc. Shakers, Sabathday Lake, 1982—84, 1995—, John St. Meth. Episcopal Trust Soc., N.Y.C., 1982—; bd. dirs. Meth. Ch. Home for Aged, Riverdale, NY, 1995—2001, 2003—, mem. investment com., 1983—, co-chmn., 1994—2003, treas., 1996—2001, pres., 2003—, Meth. Ch. Home Fund, 1996—99; bd. dirs., treas. John Wesley Towers, 1999—; bd. dirs. Yorkville Emergency Alliance, N.Y.C., 1982—88; mem. internat. adv. coun. Mus. Am. Folk Art, N.Y.C., 1988—2001; dir., chmn. investment com. United Meth. City Soc., N.Y.C., 1999—, chartered fin. analyst. Mem.: Assn. Investment Mgmt. and Rsch., N.Y. Soc. Security Analysts. Home: 500 E 85th St New York NY 10028-7407

BROWN, EDWIN WILSON, JR., preventive medicine physician, educator; b. Youngstown, Ohio, Mar. 6, 1926; s. Edwin Wilson and Doris (McClellan) B.; m. Patricia Ann Currier, Aug. 9, 1952; children: Edwin Wilson, John Currier, Wende Patricia. Student, Carnegie Inst. Tech., 1943, Amherst Coll., 1943—44, Houghton Coll., 1946—47; MD, Harvard U., 1953, MPH (Nat. Found. fellow), 1957. Rsch. fellow U. Buffalo, 1953-54; intern E.J. Meyer Meml. Hosp., Buffalo, 1954-55; resident pub. health Va. Dept. Health, 1955-56; tchr. medicine specializing in preventive medicine Boston, 1958-61, Hyderabad, India, 1961-63; assoc. med. dir. People-to-People Health Found., Washington, 1965-66; assoc. prof. medicine Ind. U.-Purdue U., Indpls., 1966-85, dir. divsn. internat. affairs, 1966-74, assoc. dean student svcs., dir. internat. svcs., 1979-85; pres. Internat. Med. Assistance, Inc., Indpls., 1986—. Med. dir. Ind. Dept. Correction, 1974-76; sr. med. edn. advisor King Faisal U., Dammam, Saudi Arabia, 1977-78; field dir. Harvard Epidemiol. Project, Egedesminde, Greenland, 1956-57; asst. prof. preventive medicine Sch. Medicine Tufts U., 1958-61; dep. chief staff Boston Dispensary, 1961; vis. prof. preventive medicine Osmania Med. Coll., Hyderabad, India, 1961-63; asst. dir. divsn. internat. med. edn., dir. AAMC-AID project internat. med. edn. Assn. Am. Med. Colls., Evanston, 1963-65; exec. sec. Study Group on Childhood Accidents, Boston, 1959-61; rsch. assoc. Sch. Pub. Health, Harvard U., 1959-60; dir. Curtis Pub. Co., Inc.; cons. Boston City Health Dept., 1959-60, WHO, 1973-74; chmn. bd. dirs. Med. Assistance Programs, Inc. Contbr. articles to profl. jours. Bd. dirs. Paul Carlson Found., Campus Teams, Iran Found., CARE/MEDICO, Internat. Students Inc. Served with AUS, 1944-46, ETO. Recipient Pub. Svc. award Vets. Day Coun. Indpls., 1996, Patriarch of Antioch's award Knight Comdr. of Order of St. Mark, 1998. Fellow Am. Pub. Health Assn.; mem. Assn. Tchrs. Preventive Medicine, Indian Assn. Advancement Med. Edn., Mass. Med. Soc., Internat. Policy Forum (bd. govs.), Nat. Policy Coun., Rotary Internat., Sigma Xi. Home and Office: 8153 Oakland Rd Indianapolis IN 46240-2747 Office Phone: 317-257-7454. Personal E-mail: Ed@TheBrowns.com, imaindy@aol.com.

BROWN, ELIZABETH ELEANOR, retired librarian; b. Charlotte, Mich., Aug. 29, 1921; d. Delbert Francis and Katherine Eleanor (Griffith) Brown. AB, Albion Coll., 1943; MLS, Pratt Inst., 1953. Info. specialist Enjay Co., N.Y.C., 1943-50; reports indexer Bakelite Co., Bound Brook, N.J., 1950-52; reference libr. IBM, Poughkeepsie, NY, 1953-69, Yorktown Heights, N.Y., 1953-69, info. retrieval specialist, libr. White Plains, N.Y., 1969-82, ret., 1982. Vol. Nat. Archives Rocky Mountain Region, 1986—; mem. del. spl. librs. to Russia and Czech Republic Citizen Amb. program People to People Internat., 1995. Mem.: DAR, ALA, Spl. Librs. Assn. (sec.-treas. engring. divsn. 1968—70, chmn. tech. sci. group N.Y.C. chpt 1970—71, archivist 1970—72, founding mem. and past pres. Hudson Valley chpt.), Am. Chem. Soc., Remsen-Steuben Hist. Soc., Eaton County Geneal. Soc., Kalamazoo Valley Geneal. Soc., Wales, Ireland, Scotland and Eng. Family Hist. Soc., Internat. Soc. Brit. Genealogy and Family History, Gen. Soc. Mayflower Descs., Pilgrim John Howland Soc., New Eng. Hist. Geneal. Soc., Colo. Geneal. Soc., Colo. Mayflower Soc., Gwynedd Family History Soc., Columbine Geneal. and Hist. Soc., Welsh-Am. Geneal. Soc., Colo. Welsh Soc., Grand Traverse Area Geneal. Soc., Rowe Hist. Soc., Mortar Bd., Alpha Lambda Delta, Phi Beta Kappa, Delta Zeta. E-mail: browneeb21@aol.com.

BROWN, ELIZABETH SCHMECK, fashion historian; b. Ancon, Panama, Sept. 7, 1918; d. Henry Penuel and Pansy Blossom (Logan) Schmeck; m. Walter Daniel Brown, July 29, 1944; children: David Henry, Walter Daniel Jr., Edward Logan, Kenneth Maclin. Student, U. Tex., 1935—37; BS, Cornell U., 1940, MS, 1945; student, Art Students League N.Y. Cert. family and consumer scis. AAFCS. Instr. textiles and clothing, curator costume collection Coll. Home Econs. Cornell U., Ithaca, NY, 1941—45; assoc. home economist McCall Pattern Co., N.Y.C., 1963—65; assoc. Uno Pattern Co., N.J. and Pa., 1972—74; lectr. on hist. dress, 1972—; appraiser of hist. dress, 1978—. Contbr. articles to profl. publs.; curated exhbns., NJ Divsn. on Women, Trenton, Kemmerer Mus., Bethelehem, Pa., Antiques at the Armory, Phila., Rutgers Inst. for Rsch. on Women, New Brunswick, N.J., N.J. Hist. Commn. Mem. Montgomery Twp. Bd. Edn., Skillman, NJ, 1969—81, various offices, including pres., 1975—77; legis. chmn., pres. Somerset County Sch. Bds. Assn., Somerville, NJ, 1977—80; testified to State Legis. and Bd. Edn. for mandate of Family Life Edn.; active N.J. Network Family Life, 1983—2002; mem. adv. coun. Family, Career, and Cmty. Leadership Am., 2001—; bd. dirs. Costume and Textile Group N.J., 2001—; bd. dir. (former treas.) Wesley Found., 1984—, Princeton U.; mem. PTA, Pitts.; pres. Whittier Sch., Park Ridge, Ill.; founding com. River-Ridge Council, Broomall, Pa. Fellow: Costume Soc. Am. (treas. 1980—86, bd. dirs. several terms 1982—, Bd. of Dir., several terms 1982—2004, corr. sec. 1986—92, pres. region II 1993—97, v.p. internal rels. 1998—2003, parliamentarian, bd. dirs.); mem.: AAUW (pres. Princeton br. 1973—75), N.J. Assn. Family and Consumer Scis. (state pres.'s unit nom. com., divsn. chair, apparel and textiles, archives and history), Am. Assn. Family and Consumer Scis. (nat. leader 1992), Van Harlingen Hist. Soc. (former trustee), Hist. Soc. Princeton (collections com.), Internat. Textile and Apparel Assn., N.J. Assn. Mus., PTA Pitts. (various offices), Internat. Sewing Machine Collectors Soc., Am. Assn. State and Local History, Cornell Alumni Assn., Princeton YWCA (vol. Friday Club 1968—2000), Y Canoe Club, Cornell Woman's Club (Pitts.) (pres., chair sec. sch. com.), Friday (com. mem. 2000—), Cornell Woman's Club (Chgo.), Cornell Woman's Club (Phila.), Phi Kappa Phi, Kappa Omicron Nu, Alpha Lambda Delta. Achievements include testified to State legislature and Bd. of Edn. for mandate of Family Life Edn; in process in 3-5 yrs. of giving my costume collection to the collection at the Coll. of Human Ecology there. Avocations: costume collection of over 2000 items, collecting antique paper patters, collecting antique sewing machines and other sewing items. Home and Office: 45 Whippoorwill Way Belle Mead NJ 08502 E-mail: ebrown@nerc.com.

BROWN, EPHRAIM TAYLOR, JR., lawyer; b. Birmingham, Ala., Aug. 31, 1920; s. Ephraim Taylor and Lida (Otts) B.; m. Clara DeBardeleben Ebaugh, Oct. 21, 1949; children: Ephraim Taylor III, Clara DeBardeleben, Lida Otts. AB, Princeton U., 1941; LLB, Cornell U., 1943. Bar: Ala. 1943. Pvt. practice, Birmingham; assoc. Cabaniss, Johnston, Gardner, Dumas & O'Neal, 1943-52, ptnr., 1952-91; of counsel, 1992—. Chmn. spl. com. Revision Probate Laws Ala., 1967; chmn. bd. bar examiners Ala. State Bar, 1967-79. Bd. dirs. Childrens Fresh Air Farm; trustee, elder, deacon local Presbyn. ch. Fellow Am. Coll. Trust and Estate Counsel; mem. ABA, Ala. Bar Assn. (pres.), Birmingham Bar Assn., Ala. Law Inst. (mem. counsel), Birmingham Country Club, Sigma Alpha Epsilon. Home: 12 Cross Creek Park Birmingham AL 35213-2302 Office: PO Box 830612 2001 Park Pl Ste 700 Birmingham AL 35203-4804

BROWN, ERIC JOEL, biomedical researcher; b. Ann Arbor, Mich., Sept. 27, 1950; s. Bernard and Shirley (Mark) B.; m. Marion Glynn Peters, Apr. 2, 1983; 1 child, Abigail. AB, Harvard Coll., 1971; MD, Harvard Med. Sch., 1975. Intern, then resident Beth Israel Hosp., Boston, 1975-77; clin. assoc. LCI/NIAID/NIH, Bethesda, Md., 1977-79, expert, 1979-81, sr. investigator, 1981-85; assoc. prof. Washington U., St. Louis, 1985-90, co-dir. divsn. infectious diseases, 1989-99, prof., 1990-99; prof. medicine and immunology U. Calif., San Francisco, 1999—. With USPHS, 1981-85. Fellow Infectious Diseases Soc.; mem. Soc. for Clin. Investigation, Am. Assn. Physicians. Office: U Calif San Francisco PO Box 2140 San Francisco CA 94143-2140 E-mail: ebrown@medicine.ucsf.edu.

BROWN, ERNEST L., education educator; b. Pensacola, Fla., June 24, 1932; s. Annie B. (Brown) Pate. BS, Fla. A&M U., 1954, MEd, 1966; postgrad., U. Okla., 1970; PhD, Fla. State U., 1975. Cert. tchr. math. and sci., cert. vis. tchr., cert. in ednl. leadership, Fla. Tchr. math. and sci. Escambia County (Fla.) Sch. Bd., Pensacola, 1957-68, vis. tchr., 1968-70; prin. N.B. Cook Elem. Sch., Pensacola, 1970-74; grad. asst. Fla. State U., Tallahassee, 1973-74, interim prin. Developmental Rsch. Sch., 1974-75, prin., 1975-86; dir. Developmental Rsch. Sch. Fla. A&M U., Tallahassee, 1986-89, dir. student tchg., 1989-91, assoc. prof. of ednl. leadership, 1991—. Mem. adminstrv. coun., mem. adv. bd. Developmental Rsch. Sch. Fla. State U., 1974-86; mem. task force on lab. schs. Fla. State Dept. Edn., Tallahassee, 1980; mem. state adv. com. Fla. Statewide Com. on Program Assessment, Tallahassee, 1979-80; mem. rev. com. Fla. Ednl. Leadership Exam program U. South Fla., Tampa, 1993. Contbr. articles to edn. publs. NSF fellow Bklyn. Coll., 1959, Kellogg Found. fellow, 1965-66. Mem. Phi Delta Kappa, Kappa Alpha Psi (life, alumni), Sigma Pi Phi. Democrat. Baptist. Avocations: golf, sports, music, reading. Home and Office: 3049 Knotty Pine Dr Pensacola FL 32505-1853 Personal E-mail: ebro505@cox.net.

BROWN, FLORA BRYANT, history professor; b. Columbia, N.C., Feb. 24, 1954; d. Chatmon and Sadie Leary Bryant; 1 child, Sterling Miles. BA, St. Augustine's Coll., 1976; MA, U. N.C., 1978; PhD, U. S.C., 1990. Instr. history St. Augustine's Coll., Raleigh, NC, 1979—85; prof. history Elizabeth City State U., 1990—. Vis. instr. N.C. Ctrl. U., Durham, 1978—79. Sec. Links, Inc., Elizabeth City, 1998—2002; mem. Elizabeth City Sch. Found., 1997—2002; bd. dirs. Sommerset Hist. Site, Criswell, 1990—92. Named Vol. of Yr., H.L. Trigg Cmty. Sch.; Fulbright-Hayes scholar, India, 1982. Fellow: N.C. Assn. Historians, Am. Hist. Assn. Methodist. Avocations: reading, sewing, swimming, skiing. Office: Elizabeth City State U 1704 Weeksville Rd Elizabeth City NC 27909 Office Phone: 252-335-3367.

BROWN, FRANCES LOUISE (GRANDMA FRAN), artist, art gallery director; b. Indpls., Oct. 19, 1925; d. Harley and Lenore (Spencer) Netherland; m. C.G. Clarkson, July 24, 1943 (div. Aug. 1967); children: James E. Clarkson, John B. Clarkson, Deborah L. Cromis. Thomas L. Currey, June 9, 1972 (dec. May 1978); m. George L. Brown, Jr., Mar. 3, 1982; 1 stepchild, Nancy Snow. BS in Edn., Miami U., 1968; MA in Edn., Ball State U., 1970. Tchr. elem. sch. Liberty Elem. Sch., Ind., 1968—71; tchr. Ball State U., Muncie, Ind., 1971—72; instr. Colby C.C., Kans., 1972—75; gallery owner, primitive artist Grandma Fran Art Gallery (formerly Currey Studio Gallery), Berryville, Ark., 1975—. Author: Now Hear This, 1974; works exhibited at Nat. Mus. Am. Art, Washington, Wichita (Kans.) Art Assn. Gallery, Ark. Coll., Batesville, South Ark. Art Ctr., El Dorado, Harding Coll., Searcy, Ark., U. Ark., Fayetteville, Eureka Springs (Ark.) Hist. Mus., Western State Coll. Colo., Gunnison, MacMurray Coll., Jacksonville, Ill., Colby (Kans.) Coll., Claremore (Okla.) Coll., Warren Hall Coutts III, Meml. Art Gallery, Inc., El Dorado, Kans., Masur Mus. Art, Monroe, La., Nebr. State Hist. Soc. Mus., Lincoln, Ind. State Mus., Indpls., Ozark Folk Ctr., Mountain View, Ark., Ft. Smith (Ark.) Art Ctr., Ctr. for So. Folklore, Memphis, Rogers (Ark.) Hist. Mus., Albrecht Art Mus., St. Joseph, Mo., Shiloh Mus., Springdale, Ark., Intenrat. Ctr. Contemporary Art, Paris, John Judkyn Meml. Mus., Eng., Mykonos (Greece) Folklore Mus., Musees Royaux des Beaux-Arts de Belgique, Brussels, Setagaya Art Mus., Tokyo, Fukuoka (Japan) Art Mus.; represented in permanent collections Smithsonian Instn., Washington, Mus. Am. Folk Art, N.Y.C., Nebr. State Hist. Soc. Mus., Lincoln, Ind. State Mus., Indpls., Ozark Mountain Folk Ctr., Mountain View, Ctr. for So. Folklore, Memphis, Setagaya Art Mus., others; paintings recognized in various books, newspapers and articles. Avocations: pilot, sewing, reading, fishing, cooking. Home and Office: Grandma Fran Art Gallery 3331 Highway 62 W Berryville AR 72616-8948 Office Phone: 870-423-2073.

BROWN, FRANK, social sciences educator; b. Gallian, Ala., May 1, 1935; s. Tom and Ora L. (Lomax) B.; m. Joan Drake, July 6, 1963; children: Frank G., Monica J. BS, Ala. State U., 1957; MS, Oreg. State U., 1962; MA, U. Calif., Berkeley, 1969, PhD, 1970; grad. studies, Tenn. State U., U. Puget Sounds, San Francisco State U., Calif. State U., East Bay, SUNY, Buffalo. Chem., physics tchr. Oakland Pub. Schs. (Calif.), 1962-68; assoc. dir. N.Y. State Commn. on Higher Edn., N.Y.C., 1970-72; dir. Urban Inst., prof. CCNY, 1971-72; prof., coll. master SUNY, Buffalo, 1972-77; dean U. N.C., Chapel Hill, 1983-90, Cary C. Boshamer prof. edn., dir. ednl. rsch. and policy project studies for rsch. in social sci., 1990—. Vis. scholar U. Calif., Berkeley; dir. sponsored rsch. Ford Found., N.Y.C., SUNY, Nat. Inst. Edn., Spencer Found., Buffalo, NSF, Washington, Rockefeller Found., US Dept. Edn., IBM Corp., Burroughs Corp.; speaker, presenter in field. Author: (with others) Fleischmann Commn. Report, Vols. I & II, 1973, Vol. III, 1974, Minority Enrollment in U.S. Institutions of Higher Education, Readings on the State of Education in Urban America, 1991, Challenges of Urban Education and Efficacy of School Reform, 2003; contbr. articles to Ednl. Forum, Ednl. Researcher, Jour. Negro Edn., Jour. Black Studies, Am. Sch. Bd. Jour., numerous others; book series editor: Educational Excellence, Equity; editor: Emergent Leadership; book review editor: Education and Urban Society; editorial bds. Afro-Am. History in NY State, Brigham Young U. Edn. & Law Jour., Jour. Black Students, Jour. Negro Edn., Jour. Ednl. Policy, Edn. and Urban Soc., Jour. Equity and Leadership, NABSE Jour., NOLPE Law, others. Bd. dirs. Buffalo Urban League, Langston Hughes Black Culture Ctr., Buffalo; trustee White Rock Bapt. Ch., Durham, N.C.; founder, first chair Black Faculty/Staff caucus CUNY, SUNY, U. N.C., Chapel Hill. With U.S. Army. Grad. fellow Tenn. State U., San Francisco State U., Washington U., Oreg. State U., U. Calif.-Berkeley, fellow Rockefeller Found., 1979. Mem. NAACP, Am. Assn. Colls. for Tchr. Edn. (bd. dirs.), Am. Edn. Fin. Assn., Am. Ednl. Rsch. Assn. (sec. div. A, v.p., com. on minority affairs), Assn. Sch. Bus. Ofcls. Internat., Edn. Law Assn., Assn. Social and Behavioral Scientists, Nat. Alliance Black Sch. Ednl. Fin. Assn. of Sch. Bus. Assn., Educators, Nat. Assn. Multicultural Edn., Nat. Orgn. Legal Problems of Edn. (editorial bd. 1979-80, bd. dirs. 1990—), Politics of Edn. Assn., Phi Delta Kappa, Alpha Phi Alpha (chpt. pres.). Democrat. Baptist. Office: U NC 121B Peabody Hall CB 3500 Chapel Hill NC 27599-3500 Office Phone: 919-962-2522. Office Fax: 919-966-1533. Business E-Mail: fbrown@email.unc.edu.

BROWN, FRANK BEVERLY, IV, lawyer; b. Bryan, Tex., June 1, 1945; s. Frank B. III and Kathleen (Mangum) B.; m. Janice Parks, July 19, 1980; children: Frank Parks, Caroline Paige. BBA, U. Tex., 1967, JD, 1975. Bar: Tex. 1976; CPA, Tex. Assoc. Daugherty, Kuperman, Golden & Morehead, Austin, Tex., 1976-80, ptnr., 1980-84, Armburst & Brown, Austin, 1984-90, Strasburger & Price, Austin, 1990-97, Armbrust & Brown, Austin, 1997—. Capt. USAF, 1967-73. Mem. Tex. Bar Assn. (tax sect., bus. law sect.), Travis County Bar Assn. (corp. and real estate sects.). Presbyterian. Avocations: racquetball, skiing, flying. Office: Armbrust & Brown 100 Congress Ave Ste 1300 Austin TX 78701-2744 Office Phone: 512-435-2302. Business E-Mail: fbrown@abaustin.com.

BROWN, FREDERIC JOSEPH, army officer; b. Fort Sill, Okla., July 18, 1934; s. Frederic Joseph and Kathryn (Richardson) B.; m. Harriette Anne Upham, July 7, 1956; children: Kathryn, Harriette, Judith. BS, U.S. Mil. Acad., 1956; MA, Grad. Inst. Internat. Studies, U. Geneva, 1963, PhD, 1967. Commd. officer U.S. Army, advanced through grades to lt. gen.; comdr. 1st squadron 4th cav., 1969-70; mem. staff NSC, 1972-73; comdr. 1st Tiger brigade 2d Armored Divsn., Ft. Hood, Tex., 1975-76; comdr. U.S. Army Tng. Ctr. Armor, Ft. Knox, Ky., 1977-78; asst. divsn. comdr. 8th Inf. Div. Baumholder, Germany, 1978-81; dep. chief of staff tng. U.S. Army Tng. and Doctrine Command, Ft. Monroe, Va., 1981-82; commdg. gen., chief armor U.S. Army Armor Ctr., Ft. Knox, Ky., 1983-86; comdr. 4th U.S. Army, Ft. Sheridan, Ill., 1986-89. Asst. prof. dept. polit. scis. US Mil. Acad., West Point, NY; mem. adj. rsch. staff Inst. Def. Analyses; cons. in tng. tech. and devel.; advisor, cons. advanced individual, team learning and knowledge mgmt. Dept. Def. Tng. fgn. armies, 1995—; advisor Dept. Army design advanced learning future Army, 1997—; army mentor knowledge mgmt. Battle Command Knowledge Sys., 2003-. Author: Chemical Warfare--A Study in Restraints, 1968 The United States Army in Transition II: Landpower in the Information Age, 1993; co-author: The United States Army in Transition, 1973; author numerous papers on info. age tng. for Inst. for Def. Analyses, 1989-05; co-prodr. TV series on U.S. Army post-Vietnam All We Could Be, 1995-02; developer advanced tng. policies and programs for U.S. Army Force XXI, 1996-98; designer Army R & D of advanced learning and leader devel., 2000. Decorated D.S.M. with oak leaf cluster, Silver Star, Legion of Merit; Olmsted scholar, 1961-63 Mem. Coun. Fgn. Rels., Internat. Inst. Strategic Studies. Home: 6317 Stoneham Ln Mc Lean VA 22101-2346 Office: Inst Def Analyses Joint Advanced Warfighting Program 1801 N Beauregard St Alexandria VA 22311-1701 *The essence of satisfaction is service to others. In my case, the opportunity to defend the values and wealth of our great nation.*

BROWN, FREDERICK CALVIN, retired physics professor; b. Seattle, July 6, 1924; s. Fred Charles and Rose (Mueller) B.; m. Joan Schauble, Aug. 9, 1952 (dec. Mar. 2003); children: Susan, Gail, Derek. BS, Harvard U., 1945, MS, 1947, PhD, 1950. Physicist Systems Research Lab., Harvard (NDRC), 1945-46; staff physicist Naval Research Lab., Washington, 1950; physicist Applied Physics Lab., U. Wash., 1950-51; asst. prof. Reed Coll., Portland, Oreg., 1951-55, U. Ill., Urbana, 1955-58, assoc. prof., 1958-61, prof., 1961-87, prof. emeritus, 1987—; assoc. Center for Advanced Study, 1969-70; prin. scientist, area mgr. Xerox Palo Alto (Calif.) Rsch. Ctr., 1973-74; prof. physics U. Wash., Seattle, 1987-99, prof. emeritus, 1999—; ret., 2000. Vis. mem. St. Johns Coll., Oxford, Eng., 1964-65; cons. prof., applied physics dept. Stanford U., 1973-74 Author: The Physics of Solids-Ionic Crystals, Lattice Vibrations and Imperfections, 1967; Contbr. articles profl. jours. Recipient Alexander von Humboldt sr. scientist award U. Kiel, 1978; NSF sr. postdoctoral fellow Clarendon Lab., Oxford, 1964-65 Fellow Am. Phys. Soc. Achievements include being innovator in use of synchrotron radiation for spectroscopy; first observation of polaron mobility and mass in ionic crystals, luminescence and lifetime of point defects such as F-centers, charge density waves in layered crystals, and early photoemission experiments on high temperature superconductors. Home: 5915 25th Ave W Everett WA 98203-1468

BROWN, FREDERICK GRAMM, psychology professor; b. Madison, Wis., Apr. 6, 1932; s. Fred E. and Meda I. (Gramm) B.; m. Barbara A. Thaller, June 23, 1956; children: Jeffrey S., Kirk F., Daniel H. BA, U. Wis., 1954, MA, 1955; PhD, U. Minn., 1958. Asst. prof. U. Mo., Columbia, 1958-61; asst. prof. psychology Iowa State U., Ames, 1961-64, assoc. prof. psychology, 1964-68, prof. psychology, 1968—97, Univ. prof., 1993—97, Univ. prof. emeritus, 1997—; vis. scholar Ednl. Testing Service, 1985-86. Author: Measurement and Evaluation, 1971, Guidelines for Test Use, 1980, Measuring Classroom Achievement, 1981, Principles of Educational and Psychological Testing, 3d edit., 1983 Fellow Ctr. for Advanced Study in Behavioral Scis., 1967-68, U.S. Office Edn., 1967-68 Fellow APA, Am. Psychol. Soc.; mem. Am. Ednl. Rsch. Assn., Nat. Coun. Measurement in Edn., Phi Beta Kappa. Home: 2616 Kellogg Ave Ames IA 50010-4725

BROWN, FREDERICK LEE, b. Clarksburg, W.Va., Oct. 22, 1940; s. Claude Raymond and Anne Elizabeth (Kiddy) B.; m. Shirley Fiille Brown; children: Gregory Lee, Michael Owen-Price, Kyle Stephen, Kathryn Alexis. BA in Psychology, Northwestern U., 1962; MBA in Health Care Adminstrn., George Washington U., 1966; LHD (hon.), U. Mo., 1995. Vocat. counselor Cook County Dept. Pub. Aid, Chgo., 1962-64; from adminstrv. resident to v.p.

ops. Meth. Hosp. Ind., Inc., Indpls., 1965—72, v.p. ops., 1972-74; exec. v.p., COO Meml. Hosp. DuPage County, Elmhurst, Ill., 1974-82, Meml. Health Svcs., Elmhurst, 1980-82; pres., CEO CH Health Techs., Inc., St. Louis, 1983-93, Christian Health Svcs., St. Louis, 1986-93, CH Allied Svcs., Inc., St. Louis, 1988-93, BJC Health Sys., St. Louis, 1993—98, vice-chmn., 1999—2000; pres., CEO Christian Hosp. NE-NW, 1982—88, No. Ariz. Healthcare, Flagstaff, 2003—04. Adj. instr. Washington U. Sch. Medicine, St. Louis, 1982—2001; mem. chancellor's coun. U. Mo., 1990—94; mem. exec. com. HealthLink, Inc., 1986—92; pres., CEO Village North, Inc., 1986—93; chmn. shareholder comm. com. Am. Healthcare Systems, Inc., 1985—86, vice chmn., 1992; bd. dirs. Commerce Bank St. Louis, Am. Excess Inc. Ltd.; mem. corp. assembly Blue Cross Blue Shield Mo., 1991—95; vis. scholar, exec. in residence The George Washington U., 2001—02. Contbr. articles to profl. jours. Co-chmn. hosp. divsn. United Way Greater St. Louis, 1983, chmn., 1984, chmn. health svcs. divsn., 1985—86, vice chmn. region, 1988, bd. dirs., 1986—2001, exec. com., 1991—, chmn. audit com., 1992—2001; active Kammergild Chamber Orch., 1984—88, v.p., 1985—88, bd. dirs., 1987—91; active Mo. Heart Inst., 1988—92, Alton Meml. Hosp., 1987—91, bd. dirs., 1987—91; mem. exec. bd. St. Louis Area coun. Boy Scouts Am., 1989—2000, activities coun. chmn., 1993—95; chmn. Friends of Scouting Campaign, 1991—92; mem. medicaid budget task force Mo. Dept. Social Svcs., 1990; mem. emergency rm. svcs. task force St. Louis Regional Med. Ctr., 1985; mem. corp. assembly Blue Cross Blue Shield of Mo., 1991; bd. dirs. Sold on St. Louis, 1991—93, St. Louis Reg. Commerce & Growth Assn., 1993—98; bd. trustees Webster Hills Math. Ch., 1990—92, communion steward, 1987. Fellow Am. Coll. Healthcare Execs. (chmn. credentials com. 1978, chmn. task force governance and constituencies 1986-88; mem. Gold Medal award com. 1985, com. on ethics 1989-91, chmn. awards and testimonials com., 1992-93, bd. regents 1991-93, gov. dist. V, 1993-98); mem. Am. Acad. Med. Adminstrs. (life, state dir. 1988—, Health Care Exec. of Yr. 1990, Statesman in Healthcare, 1992), Hosp. Pres.'s Assn., Advt. Club Greater St. Louis, Am. Hosp. Assn. (coun. on mgmt. 1987, alt. del. for healthcare systems 1988-90, del. to ho. of dels. for health care systems 1991, fin. com. chair 1995, chair-elect 1998, chmn. 1999), APHA, George Washington U. Alumni Assn. for Health Svcs. Adminstrn. (preceptor 1975-93, Alumnus of Yr. award 1981, Frederick Gibbs award, 1993), Hosp. Assn. Met. St. Louis (bd. dirs. 1984-94, chmn. bd. 1988-89, sec. 1985-86, treas. 1987, chmn. coun. on pub. affairs and comm. 1985, vice chmn. 1987, various coms.), Greater St. Louis Health Care Alliance (co-chair 1992-96), Mo. Hosp. Assn. (mem. coun. on rsch. and policy devel. 1983-88, chmn. coun. on multi-instnl. hosps. 1986-88, mem. dist. coun. pres.'s 1986-89, bd. dirs. 1988-92, chmn. bd. trustees 1990), Ctrl. Ea. Profl. Rev. Orgn. (bd. dirs. 1982-85, various coms.), St. Louis Met. Med. Soc. (lay advisor 1990-92), Healthcare Execs. Study Soc., Internat. Health Policy and Mgmt. Inst. (bd. dirs. 1988—), Am. Protestant Health Assn. (bd. dirs. 1988-93, chmn. 1992-93), Pinnacle Peak Country Club, Forest Highlands Country Club. Republican. Home: 8409 E La Junta Rd Scottsdale AZ 85255-2859 also: 724 Forest Highlands Flagstaff AZ 86001 Office Phone: 928-607-3069. Personal E-mail: fredlbrown@cox.net.

BROWN, GARY CHRISTIAN, ophthalmologist, director; b. Mineola, NY, May 14, 1949; m. Melissa M. Brown; children: Heather, Heidi, Kathryn. BS, Colgate U., 1971; MD, SUNY Upstate Med. Ctr., Syracuse, 1975. Intern Grady Hosp./Emory U., Atlanta, 1975-76; resident Wills Eye Hosp., Phila., 1976-79, fellow, 1979-81, dir., 2003—; physician Retinovitreous Assocs., Wyndmoor, Pa., 1981—, practice, Bethlehem, Pa., Huntington Valley, Cherry Hill, NJ. Pres., chmn. bd. dirs. Pa. Physician Health Plan, Inc., Harrisburg, 1994-96; prof. Jefferson Med. Coll.; spkr. in field; co-dir. Center for Value Based Medicine Author and co-author medical texts, 3 novels, over 350 sci. papers in field; editor: Current Science in Ophthalmology, 1992-96. Mem. AMA, Am. Acad. Ophthalmology (sr. honor award 1994), Pa. Med. Soc., Pa. Acad. Ophthalmology (pres.), Wills Eye Ex-Resident Soc. (pres. 1996), Wills Eye Hosp. Soc., Ophthalmologic Club of Phila. (pres. 1985), Phi Beta Kappa, Alpha Omega Alpha. Office: Retinovitreous Assocs 910 E Willow Grove Ave Wyndmoor PA 19038-7910 also: Wills Eye Hosp 840 Walnut St Philadelphia PA 19107 Office Phone: 215-233-4300.

BROWN, GARY SANDY, electrical engineering educator; b. Jackson, Miss., Apr. 13, 1940; s. John Leo and Welma (Kelley) B.; m. Mary Kathleen Connaughton, Mar. 16, 1970; children: Joshua John, Nathan Matthew. BSEE, U. Ill., 1963, MS, 1964, PhDEE, 1967. Grad. rsch. asst. Antenna Lab. U. Ill., Urbana, 1963-67; mem. tech. staff TRW Systems Group, Redondo Beach, Calif., 1969-70; sr. engr. Rsch. Triangle Inst., Durham, N.C., 1970-73; sr. scientist Applied Sci. Assocs., Apex, N.C., 1973-85; prof. elect. engring. Va. Poly. Inst. and State U., Blacksburg, 1985—, apptd. Bradley disting. prof. electromagnetics, 2002. With Wallops Flight Facility, NASA, Wallops Island, Va., 1974; cons. Naval Rsch. Lab., Washington, 1988-91, Decision Scis. Applications, Arlington, Va., 1988-91, DTI Inc., Torrance, Calif., 1987-91, Applied Physics Lab., Laurel, Md., 1987-88, Waste Policy Inst., Blacksburg, Va., 1991—, Motorola Corp., Chandler, Ariz., 1991-93; mem. NATO AGARD Electromagnetic Propogation Panel, 1993—; dir. Electromagnetic Interactions Lab. Contbr. chpts. to books, articles to profl. jours. Capt. U.S. Army, 1967-69. Recipient Best Paper awards R.W.P. King, 1978, Schelkunoff, 1999, Bradley Disting. Prof. Electromagnetics, 2002. Fellow IEEE (Third Millenium award 2000); mem. Antennas and Propagation Soc. of IEEE (pres. 1988), Am. Geophys. Union (editor's citation Radio Sci., Am. sects. 1986), Internat. Union of Radio Sci. (mem.-at-large 1987, sec. U.S. nat. com. 1997-99, chair U.S. nat. com. 2000-2002), NATO AGARD Sensors and Propagation Panel. Avocations: backpacking, jogging. Office: Va Poly Inst & State U Bradley Dept Elec & Computer Engr Blacksburg VA 24061

BROWN, GEORGE E., judge, educator; b. Hammond, Ind., July 27, 1947; s. George E. and Violet M. (Matlon) B.; m. Patricia A. Schneider, June 6, 1970; children: Janet M., Elizabeth A. BS, Ball State U., 1969; JD, DePaul U., 1974; grad., Ind. Jud. Coll., 1996, grad., 2002. Bar: Ind. 1974, Ill. 1974, U.S. Dist. Ct. (no. dist.) Ind. 1979, U.S. Supreme Ct. 1977, U.S. Tax Ct. 1977. Pvt. practice, LaGrange & Lake Counties, Ind., 1974-84; judge LaGrange County Ct., 1984-87, LaGrange Superior Ct., 1988—. Part-time chief dep. prosecutor LaGrange County, 1975—77; adj. faculty Tri-State U., Angola, Ind., 1991—2004. Vol. Jr. Achievement, 1997—. Mem.: ABA, Nat. Conf. State Trial Judges (criminal justice com.), Ind. Judges Assn. (com. protective orders), LaGrange County Bar Assn. (pres. 1978), Ind. State Bar Assn. (ho. of dels., com. on improvements in the jud. sys., written publs. com.), Rotary (past dir., v.p. 1999—2000, pres. 2000—01, bd. dirs. 2002—). Office: Lagrange Superior Ct Courthouse Lagrange IN 46761 Office Phone: 260-499-6363.

BROWN, GEORGE EDWARD, JR., visual arts educator, soccer coach; b. Ft. Worth, Tex. s. George Edward and Lenita M. Brown; m. Misty M. Brown, May 25, 1991; children: Macey, Brittney. BA, Tex. Wesleyan U., Ft. Worth, 1988—91. Visual arts educator Richland Mid. Sch., Ft. Worth, 1993—99, Birdville H.S., Ft. Worth, 1999—. Fine arts dept. chair Birdville H.S., Ft. Worth, 2003—; mem. art educators adv. bd. Tex. Wesleyan U., Ft. Worth, 2003—. Mem.: Assn. Tex. Profl. Educators, Tex. Assn. Soccer Coaches, Nat. Art Edn. Assn. Republican. Baptist. Avocations: running, fishing, hunting. Office: Birdville HS 9100 Mid-Cities Blvd Fort Worth TX 76180 Home: 5332 Texas Dr Fort Worth TX 76180

BROWN, GEORGE LESLIE, legal association administrator, consultant, retired manufacturing executive, retired lieutenant governor; b. Lawrence, Kans., July 1, 1926; s. George L. and Harriett Alberta (Watson) B.; m. Modeen; children: Gail Brown Chandler, Laura Nicole, Kim Doreen, Cynthia Renee; stepchildren: Ronnie, Carol, Angela, Sharolyn, Nyra. BJ, U. Kans., 1950; postgrad., U. Colo., 1950-51; A.M.P., Harvard Bus. Sch., 1980. Mem. writing staff Denver Post, 1950-65; asst. exec. dir. Denver Housing Authority, 1965-69; exec. dir. Met. Denver Urban Coalition, 1969-75; lt. gov. Colo. Denver, 1974-79; v.p. Grumman Corp., N.Y., 1979-90; assoc. Whitten & Diamond (formerly Lipsen, Whitten & Diamond), Washington, 1990-94; dir. Prudential Securities, 1994-97; of counsel Moser and Moser Law Firm, 1994—; v.p. L. Robert Kimball, Archtl. Engrs.; sr. v.p. Greenwich Ptnrs. Bd. dirs. Davis and Elkins Coll., Washington Trade Ctr., Joint Ctr. for Polit. Studies, Boys Choir of Harlem, Coll. Aeros., Air Force Meml. Found. Mem. Colo. Ho. of Reps., 1955, Colo. Senate, 1956-74. Served with USAAF, 1944-46. Recipient Adam Clayton Powell award for polit. achievement, 1975, Opportunities Industrialization Center Nat. Govt. award, 1975; George Brown Urban Journalism scholarship established at U. Kans. William Allen White Sch. Journalism, 1976 Mem. Kappa Alpha Psi. Office: Greenwich Partners 1090 Vermont Ave NW Ste 800 Washington DC 20005-4961

BROWN, SIR GEORGE NOEL, judge; b. Gales Point Village, Belize, June 13, 1942; s. Noel Todd and Elma Priscilla (O'Brien) B.; m. Eleanor Marie Williams, June 5, 1962 (div. May 1972); children: Georgia Yvette Marie, Aubrey Noel David, Marsha Elizabeth, Roxanne Patricia; m. Magdalene Elizabeth Bucknor, Aug. 24, 1974. Cert. in pub. adminstrn., Carlton U., Ottawa, Ont., Can., 1970; LLB with 2d class honors, U. W.I., Barbados, 1976; cert. in legal edn., Norman Manley Law Sch., Kingston, Jamaica, 1978; cert. in legis. drafting, Commonwealth Secretariat Law Sch., Nairobi, Kenya, 1979. Customs examiner Belize Customs and Excise Dept., Belize City, 1960-67; clk. of cts. Belize Magistrates Cts., Belize City, 1967-69; adminstrv. asst. Belize Ministry Trade and Industry, Belize City, 1970-72; lay magistrate, various cities, Belize, 1972-73; crown counsel Atty. Gen.'s Ministry, Belmopan, Belize, 1978-81, solicitor gen., 1981-84; puisne judge Belize Supreme Ct., Belize City, 1984-90, chief justice, 1990-98; law revsion commr. Law Revision Office, Belize City, 1998-99; legal cons., 2000—. Dep. gov. gen. Gov. Gen's. Office, Belize, 1986—95; mem. Belize Adv. Coun., 1986—88, sr. mem., 1988—2002; mem. prison parole bd., 1998—2000; chmn. bd. dir. Tubal Trade and Vocat. Inst., 2003—; chmn. Nat. Rehab. Com., 2003—, mem., 2004—. Mgr., coach primary and secondary sch. soccer teams, Belize City, 1986-99, 1st divsn. and semi-pro soccer club, Belmopan and Belize City, 1981-2000; sec., chmn. Belize Harbour Regatta Com., Belize City, 1958-85. Decorated Knight Order of Brit. Empire, 1991. Mem. Belize Bar Assn. (sec. 1979-81). Seventh Day Adventist. Avocations: yachting, soccer, drama, cricket. Home: 6203 Cor Park Ave Seashore Dr PO Box 236 Belize City Belize Office: Welch House 76 Dean St PO Box 1117 Belize City Belize Office Phone: 501-227-7063.

BROWN, GEORGE STEPHEN, physics professor; b. Santa Monica, Calif., June 28, 1945; s. Paul Gordon and Frances Ruth (Moore) B.; m. Nohema Fernandez, Aug. 8, 1981 (div. 1992); 1 child, Sonya; m. Julie Claire Dryden, Mar. 22, 1997. BS, Calif. Inst. Tech., 1967; MS, Cornell U., 1968, PhD, 1973. Mem. tech. staff Bell Labs., Murray Hill, N.J., 1973-77; sr. research assoc. Stanford (Calif.) U., 1977-82, rsch. prof. applied physics, 1982-91; prof. physics U. Calif., Santa Cruz, 1991—, chair dept. physics, 1996-2000, vice provost, 2000—. Assoc. dir. Stanford Synchrotron Radiation Lab., Stanford, 1980-91. Mem. editorial bd. Rev. Sci. Instruments, 1983-86; contbr. articles to profl. jours. Fellow Am. Phys. Soc. Avocation: music performance. Home: 115 Quarry Ct Santa Cruz CA 95060-2056 Office: U Calif Dept Physics Santa Cruz CA 95064

BROWN, GERALD CURTIS, retired military officer, engineering executive; b. Worcester, Mass., Aug. 10, 1942; s. Victor Curtis and Ethel (Dean) B.; m. Alelaide M. Forshey, June 28, 1964 (div.); children: Deborah Ann, Suzanne Marie; m. Jean Jennings, Aug. 1, 1998. BS, U.S. Mil. Acad., West Point, N.Y., 1964; MS, U. Ill., 1970. Registered profl. engr., Tex., Md., D.C., Fla., Ill. Commd. 2d. lt. U.S. Army, 1964, advanced through grades to brig. gen., 1988; capt. 18th Engr. Brigade, Vietnam, 1966-67; maj. 1st Air Cavalry Div., Vietnam, 1970-71; assoc. prof. history U.S. Mil. Acad., West Point, 1974-77; bn. comdr. 82d Combat Engr. Bn., Bamberg, Fed. Republic Germany, 1978-80; dist. engr. Balt. Dist., Corps Engrs., 1982-84; staff engr. U.S. Army Tng. and Doctrine Command, Ft. Monroe, Va., 1984-86; mil. exec. Office Undersec. Army, Washington, 1986-88; fellow Harvard U., Cambridge, 1988-89; comdg. gen. U.S. Army Corps Engrs., North Atlantic Div., N.Y.C., 1989-92; dir. Environ. programs Dept. of Army, The Pentagon, Washington, 1992-94; ret. U.S. Army, 1994; v.p. Sverdrup Civil, Inc., Falls Church, Va., 1994-95; v.p., mgr. Ea. Ops. Sverdrup Environ., Inc., Balt., 1995-98; v.p. Sverdrup Civil, Inc., Falls Church, 1998-99; program mgr. Parsons Brinckerhoff, London, 2000—01; assoc. dir. for ops. Fermi Nat. Accelerator Lab., Batavia, Ill., 2001—. Natl. Defense Exec. Reserve; Fed. Emerg. Mgmt. Agency, chmn. bd. of vis., fed. Emerg. Mgmt. Inst., Md., 1998-2000; founder, pres. Army Corps Engrs. Meml. Corp. Contbr. articles to mil. jours. Fellow Soc. Am. Mil. Engrs. (v.p. 1989-92, bd. dirs. 1993-96, founder, chmn. Acad. Fellows 1995-96); mem. ASCE, Army and Navy Club (Washington), Union League Club (Chgo.). Avocations: golf, opera, reading. Office: Fermi Natl Accelerator Lab PO Box 500 MS 200 Batavia IL 60510-0500 Office Phone: 630-840-8529. Business E-Mail: gcbrown@fnal.gov.

BROWN, GERALD EDWARD, physicist, researcher; b. Brookings, S.D., July 22, 1926; BA, U. Wis., 1946; MS, Yale U., 1948, PhD, 1950; DSc, U. Birmingham, 1957; DSc (hon.), U. Helsinki, 1982, U. Birmingham, 1990, U. Copenhagen, 1998, Ohio State U., 2005. Prof. physics U. Birmingham, 1959-60, Nordic Inst. Theoretic Atomic Physics, 1960-85, Princeton U., 1964-68, SUNY, Stony Brook, 1968-74, leading prof., 1974-88, dist. prof. physics, 1988—. Lectr. math physics, 1955-58; reader U. Birmingham, 1958-59; dir. nuclear astrophysics Inst. Theoretical Physics NSF, U. Calif., 1960. Recipient Boris Pregel award N.Y. Acad. Sci., 1976, Tom W. Bonner prize Nuclear Physics, 1982, Sr. Dist. Sci. award Alexander von Humboldt Found., 1987, John Price Wetherill medal Franklin Inst., Phila., 1992, Max-Planck medaille German Phys. Soc., 1997, Hans A. Bethe prize nuclear physics and astrophysics Am. Physics Soc., 2001, Wilbur Lucius Cross medal Yale Grad. Sch. Arts and Scis., 2003. Office: SUNY Inst Theoretical Physics Stony Brook NY 11794-0001

BROWN, GERALD EUGENE, minister; b. Garden City, Kans., July 16, 1949; s. Alva E. and Louise I. (Newcomb) B.; m. Susan L. McConnell, Nov. 14, 1970; children: Patricia, Mark Thomas, Robert. BA cum laude, S.W. Mo. State U., 1972; M Div. cum laude, Midwestern Bapt. Theol. Sem., 1975; D of Ministry, Nazarene Theol. Sem., 2000. Ordained to ministry Christian Ch., 1974. Pastor Ludlow (Mo.) Bapt. Ch., 1973-75; dir. Christian ministries Tabernacle Bapt. Ch., Kansas City, Mo., 1975-79; minister Longview Chapel Christian Ch., Lee's Summit, Mo., 1980-87, Antioch Community Ch., Kansas City, Mo., 1987—. Bd. dirs. Clay-Platte Emergency Relief Assn., pres., 1989-91; asst. chaplain Lee's Summit Community Hosp., 1986-87; chaplain intern VA Med. Ctr., Kansas City, 1990-91; organizing dir. The Shepherd's Ctr. of Lee's Summit, 1985-87; mem. instnl. rev. bd. NKC Hosp., 1996--. Sec. Flood Relief Task Force, Kansas City, 1977-78; exec. dir. Emergency Assistance Coalition, Inc., Kansas City, 1980-84; mem. Mayor's Task Force on Energy, Kansas City, 1983-84; mem. ch. rels. commn. Internat. Coun. Cmty. Chs., 1988-91, moderator, 1990-91, mem. ecumenical rels. commn., 1993--; spiritual care coord. Kansas City chpt. Red Cross Disaster Svcs., 1998-2002. Mem. Internat. Coun. Community Chs. (ch. rels. commn. 1988—, moderator 1990—), Northland Ministerial Alliance (v.p., pres.-elect 1988, pres. 1989-90). Democrat. Home: 613 NE 44th St Kansas City MO 64116-1809 Office: Antioch Community Ch 4805 NE Antioch Rd Kansas City MO 64119-3499 E-mail: accgerald@highstream.net. *God has given us the means to peace in our world; it falls to us to make those means effective in our world.*

BROWN, GERALDINE, nurse, freelance writer; b. Clemson, S.C. d. Isaac and Gladys (Patterson) B. AS in Nursing, U. D.C., 1973; real estate cert., Long and Foster Inst., 1984; cert. in TV broadcasting, Columbia Sch., 1987; BSN, Bowie State U., 1989, MA in Comm., 1991, MSN, 1997; PhD, Howard U., 1994. RN, D.C., FCC Third Class License. Supr. staff nurse Walter Reed Hosp., Washington, 1970—76; supr. clin. nurse Dept. Human Svcs., Washington, 1976—78, cmty. health nurse, 1978—84; nursing instr. Phillips Bus. Sch., Alexandria, Va., 1984—85; pvt. nurse Washington, 1973—; faculty Howard U. Coll. Nursing, 1994—. Dir. pub. affairs Bible Way Chs. Worldwide, Inc., Washington, 1978-91; soc. columnist As It Happens, Charlotte (N.C.) Post, 1964-66; soc. editor Washington Cafe Soc. mag, 1971; contbr. feature stories Capital Spotlight newspaper, 1978—; mem. faculty Coll. Nursing, Howard U., 1994—. Asst. organizer DC Mayor's United Nations Day, 1980; vol. Met. Boys and Girls Clubs, Washington, 1980—; vol. Nursing Instr., The Washington Saturday Coll., 1982-84; Co. ARC, 1973—, Big Sisters of the Washington Met. Area, 1988—. Recipient certs. of excellence Govt. of D.C., 1978-84; cert. of appreciation Mayor of D.C., 1980, Meritorious Pub. Svc. award, 1980; svc. trophy Washington Saturday Coll., 1984. Mem. ANA, NAACP, Nat. Coun. Negro Women, Smithsonian Inst. (assoc.), Nat. Black Nurses Assn., Washington Urban League, Chi Eta Phi, Sigma Theta Tau. Democrat. Avocations: stamp collecting/philately, travel, poetry. Office Phone: 202-244-0313. Business E-Mail: G.Brown2@worldnet.att.net.

BROWN, GERALDINE REED, lawyer, management consultant; b. LA, Feb. 18, 1947; d. William Penn and Alberta Vernice (Coleman) Reed; m. Ronald Wellington Brown, Aug. 20, 1972; children: Kimberly Diana, Michael David. BA summa cum laude, Fisk U., 1968; JD, Harvard U., 1971, MBA, 1973. Bar: N.Y. 1974, U.S. Dist. Ct. (so. and ea. dists.) N.Y. 1974, U.S. Ct. Appeals (2d cir.) 1974, U.S. Supreme Ct. 1977, N.J. 1992, U.S. Dist. Ct. N.J. 1992, Pa. 1993. Assoc. White & Case, N.Y.C., 1973-78; atty. J.C. Penney Co., Inc., N.Y.C., 1978-88; pres. The Reed-Brown Cons. Group., Montclair, N.J., 1989—; counsel Spooner & Burnett, N.Y.C., 1993-98. Asst. prof. bus. law Montclair State Coll., 1990-92; adj. prof. bus. law Kean Coll. NJ, 1989-94; adj. prof. Law Sch. Seton Hall, 1995; dir., sec., gen. counsel Renaissance Jr. Golf, Inc., Newark; instr. Hudson County C.C., Bergen C.C., Entrepreneurial Tng. Inst.; mem. com. on women and the cts., com. on fee arbitration NJ Supreme Ct. Bd. dirs. Coun. Concerned Black Execs., N.Y.C., 1977-88, Studio Mus. in Harlem, N.Y.C., 1980-81; mem. Montclair (N.J.) Devel. Bd., 1985-88, ad hoc com. on Montclair Econ. Devel. Corp., 1985-88; sec., bd. trustee Montclair YWCA, 1989-97, United Hosps. Med. Ctr., vice chmn., 1991-93, trustee, 1989-97, exec. com., chair bylaws com., chair strategic planning com., pers. com.; former sec. bd. trustees, chair human resources com. Ramapo Coll., 1993-04, trustee, 1993-04; chair bylaws com., N.J. United Minority Bus. Brain Trust; trustee Essex County Ct. Apptd. Spl. Advocates, 1989-93, Jr. League of Montclair, Newark Mental Health Resources Ctr., Montclair, N.J., 1991-96; trustee, sec. Montclair Early Childhood Corp., 1997-98; trustee, sec. St. Marks United Meth. Ch., Pineridge Corp., United Meth. Homes; mem. bd. dirs. Equal Opportunity Fund NJ Commn. Higher Edn. Fellow NY State Bar Found.; mem. ABA (several coms. sect. corp., banking and bus. law, sect. internat. law and practice), NJ Bar Assn. (mem. bus. orgns. com.), Essex County Bar Assn., NY State Bar Assn. (mem. Ho. of Dels. 2005-, exec. com. CLE, legis. liason 1981-90, vice chmn. 1988-90, exec. com. of corp. counsel sect., chmn. com. on SEC, fin. corp. law and governance, chair com. atty. professionalism 1994-97, mem. task force on profession, com. rev. of cts. and professions), Assn. of Bar of City of NY (corp. law com. 1978-81), NY County Lawyers Assn. (corp. law com.), Exec. Women of NJ, Harvard Bus. Sch. Club, Harvard Law Sch. Assn. (trustee, v.p. NJ chpt.), Coalition 100 Black Women, Harvard Bus. Sch. Black Alumni Assn., Harvard Law Sch. Black Alumni Assn., Harvard Club (NYC), Phi Beta Kappa, Delta Sigma Theta (past chair social action com. Montclair alumnae chpt., past chair rules com., parlimentarian) Home and Office: The Reed-Brown Cons Group 180 Union St Montclair NJ 07042-2125 Office Phone: 973-509-8243. Personal E-mail: rbcg1@aol.com.

BROWN, GILES TYLER, history professor, lecturer; b. Marshall, Mich., Apr. 21, 1916; s. A. Watson and Ettroile (Kent) B.; m. Crysta Beth Cosner, Nov. 21, 1951 (dec. July 1992). AB, San Diego State Coll., 1937; MA, U. Calif., Berkeley, 1941; PhD, Claremont Grad. Sch., 1948. Tchr., counselor, Binet intelligence tester San Diego City Schs., 1937—46; chmn. social sci. divsn. Orange Coast Coll., Newport Beach, Calif., 1948—60; prof. history, chmn. social sci. divsn. Calif. State U., Fullerton, 1961—66, also chmn. history dept., dean grad. studies, 1967—83, assoc. v.p. acad. programs, 1979—83. Lectr. in field; cons. gerontology; participant Wilton Park Conf., Eng., 1976; mem. instl. rsch. bd. So. Calif. Coll. Optometry, 1980-97; past chmn. Hist. Landmarks Com. Orange County; mem. nat. task force Assessment Quality Masters' Degree, Coun. Grad. Schs., 1981-83. Author: Ships That Sail No More, 1966; Contbr. to: Help in Troubled Times, 1962; contbr. articles to profl. jours. Trustee, past pres., past chmn. bd. World Affairs Coun. Orange County; past pres. U. Calif.-Irvine Friends Libr.; nat. bd. dirs., past nat. pres. Travelers Century Club; emeritus bd. dirs. Pacific Symphony Orch. Named Citizen of Yr., Orange Coast Coll., 1993; recipient hon. medal, DAR, 1977, Nat. Soc. Daus. Colonial Wars, 1984, Golden Orange award, World Affair Coun. of Orange County, 2002. Mem. AAAS, SAR, Am. Hist. Assn. (Pacific History award 1950), We. Assn. Grad. Schs. (exec. com. 1981-83), Phi Beta Kappa, Phi Delta Kappa, Phi Alpha Theta, Phi Beta Delta (hon. internat. scholar), Kappa Delta Pi, Explorers, Masons. Baptist. Home: 413 Catalina Dr Newport Beach CA 92663-4105

BROWN, GLENDA ANN WALTERS, ballet director; b. Buna, Tex., July 22, 1937; d. Jesse Olaf and Kathryn Jeanette (Rogers) Walters; m. David Dann Brown, Dec. 13, 1958 (div. 1995); children: Kathryn, Jean, Vanessa Lea. Grad. h.s., Beaumont, Tex. Mem. Melody Maids, Beaumont, 1950-60; asst. tchr. Widman Sch., Beaumont, 1952-55; owner, tchr. Walters Sch. of Dance, Jasper, Tex., 1955-59; assoc. tchr. Emmamae Horn Sch., 1964-81, artistic dir., 1981—; assoc. dir. Allegro Ballet Houston, 1974-81, artistic dir., 1981—; owner, dir. Allegro Acad. Dance, Houston, 1981—. Dir. Regional Dance Am., Nat. Craft Choreography Conf., 1987—2001; mem. adv. bd. Dance Tchr. Mag., 1998—2003; founder, dir. Glenda Brown Choreography Project, 2002—. Dance panel Cultural Arts Coun., Houston, 1979, Tex. Commn. on the Arts, 1988-90; sec. Riedel Estates Civic Club, Houston, 1975-78; Rep. poll worker, Houston, 1970-81; bd. dirs. Austrian Alps Performing Arts Festival, 1996-98; coord. First Nat. Regional Dance Am. Festival, 1997, bd. dirs. Tanzsommer/Austria, 1998—. Mem. Dance Masters Am. (exam. chair chpt. 3 1980-86), Regional Dance Am. S.W. (exec. v.p. 1981-2001), Dance Am., Nat. Assn. Regional Ballet (bd. dirs. 1985-88), Regional Dance Am. (nat. bd. dirs., v.p. 1988-95, pres. 1995-2001, dir. emeritus 2002—). Methodist. Avocations: camping, singing, golf, travel. Office: Allegro Ballet and Dance Acad 1570 S Dairy Ashford St Ste 200 Houston TX 77077-3870 Office Phone: 281-496-4670. E-mail: glendabrown@ev1.net.

BROWN, GORDON EARL, surgeon, consultant; b. Highland Park, Mich., Mar. 4, 1931; s. Cecil E. and Margaret Glenn (Thurston) B.; m. Christina Cordell Knauss, Feb. 1, 1990. AB, Kenyon Coll., 1953; MD, Columbia U., 1957; MPA, Pa. State U., 1995. Intern U. Va. Hosp., 1957-58; resident gen. surgery Cedars Sinai Hosp., L.A., 1963-66, L.A. County Harbor Gen. Hosp., 1966-68; surg. registrar Selly Oak Hosp., Birmingham, England, 1968-69; pvt. practice gen. surgery Bishop, Calif., 1971-82; gen. surgeon Whitaker Corp., 1982-84, Locum Tenens, 1984-86, Lancaster (Pa.) Cardiothoracic Surgeons, 1986-88; cons. Blue Shield of Pa., Camp Hill, 1988—. Med. advisor QA and I Cmty. Gen. Hosp., Reading, Pa., 1995-97. Capt. USAF, 1959-62. Home and Office: 4651 Harborview Dr Erie PA 16508-3043 Office Phone: 814-860-8454.

BROWN, GREGORY K., lawyer; b. Warren, Ohio, Dec. 9, 1951; s. George K. and Dorothy H. (Gaynor) B.; m. Joy M. Feinberg, Apr. 10, 1976. BS in Bus. & Econs., U. Ky., 1973; JD, U. Ill., 1976. Bar: Ill. 1976. Assoc. atty. McDermott, Will & Emery, Chgo., 1976-80, Mayer, Brown & Platt, Chgo., 1980-84; ptnr. Keck, Mahin & Cate, Chgo., 1984-93, Oppenheimer Wolff & Donnelly, Chgo., 1994-97, Seyfarth, Shaw, Fairweather & Geraldson, Chgo., 1997-2000, Gardner, Carton & Douglas, Chgo., 2000—. Contbg. author: The Handbook of Employee Ownership Plans, 1989, Employee Stock Ownership Plans, 1989 Active Chgo. Coun. Fgn. Rels. Named One of the Top Benefits Lawyers Nat. Law Jour., 1998. Mem.: ABA (chair employee stock ownership plan com., tax law sect. Nat. Ctr. Employee Ownership, Employee Stock Ownership Plan Assn. chair legis. and regulatory adv. c 1997—99), Chgo. Bar Assn. (chmn. employee benefits com. 1988—89). Avocations: basketball, bicycling, golf, opera, theater. Office: Gardner Carton & Douglas 191 N Wacker Dr Chicago IL 60606-1698 E-mail: gkbrown@gcd.com.

BROWN, GREGORY MICHAEL, psychiatrist, educator, researcher; b. Toronto, Mar. 27, 1934; s. Norbert Joseph and Nellie Shaw (Diack) B.; m. Audrey Christina Shute, June 18, 1960; children: Jacqueline Anne Embleton, David Michael, Mary Catherine Brown Lutsch, Paul Douglas, Barbara Suzanne French, Joyce Christina, Patricia Elizabeth, Anne Marie; m. Elizabeth Mary East, July 14, 2000. BA, U. Toronto, 1955, MD, 1959, diploma in Psychiatry, 1964; PhD, U. Rochester, 1971. Intern St. Michael's Hosp., 1959-60; resident in medicine Shaughnessy Hosp., Vancouver, 1960-61; resident in psychiatry various hosps., Ont., 1961-64; ward physician Toronto Psychiat. Hosp., 1964-66; courtesy staff Peel Meml. Hosp., Brampton, Ont., 1964-66; fellow in clin. investigation dept. psychiatry U. Toronto, 1964-66, clin. tchr. in psychiatry, 1968-69, asst. prof. to assoc. prof., 1969-75, prof., 1975-77, prof. dept psychiatry, prof. dept. physiology, 1989-99, prof. Inst. Med. Sci., 1991-99, prof. emeritus, 1999—; prof. depts. neuroscis. and psychiatry McMaster U., 1977-87, staff psychiatrist Med. Ctr. Hamilton, Ont., 1977—, chmn. dept. neuroscis., 1977-87, prof. dept. neuroscis., 1987-88, prof. dept. biomed. scis., 1988-89, prof. emeritus, 1989—; external examiner dept physiology U. Hong Kong, 1990-92; instr. medicine and psychiatry U. Rochester Sch. Medicine, N.Y., 1966-69; staff psychiatrist Clarke Inst. Psychiatry, Toronto, 1968-77, 90—, dir. rsch., 1990—, v.p. rsch., 1995-96, head neuroendocrinology rsch. sect., 1996-99; clin. scientist Ctr. Addiction and Mental Health, Toronto, 1999—. Pres., CEO CIDtech Rsch. Inc., Cambridge, Ont., Canada, 1984—, chmn., 2004—. Co-author: Frontiers in Neurology and Neuroscience Research, 1974, Clinical Neuroendocrinology, 1977, Neuroendocrinology and Psychiatric Disorder, 1984, The Pineal Gland: Endocrine Aspects, Advances in the Biosciences, 1985, Clinical Neuroendocrinology, 1988; assoc. editor Can. Jour. Physiology and Pharmacology, 1973-78; mem. editorial bd. Psychoneuroendocrinology, 1978-89, Jour. Pineal Rsch., 1981-89, Psychiatry Rsch., 1979—, Jour. Psychiatry and Neuroscience, 1990—; mem. exec. editorial bd. Progress in Neuro-Psychopharmacology and Biological Psychiatry, 1989—; mem. editorial bd. Biological Signals, 1991—; contbr. to books; contbr. articles to profl. jours. Named Rsch. assoc. Ont. Mental Health Found., 1968—, Traveling fellow Ont. Mental Health Found., 1966-68; recipient numerous rsch. awards, McNeil Lab. award, 1975, John Dewan award Ont. Mental Health Found., 1980, Heinz Lehmann award Can. Coll. Neuropsychopharmacology, 1983. Fellow APA, Royal Coll. Physicians, Royal Soc. Can.; mem. Can. Psychiat. Assn., Ont. Psychiat. Assn., Am. Psychosomatic Soc. (councillor 1978-82), Can. Med. Assn., Ont. Med. Assn., Soc. Psychoneuroendocrinology (councillor 1981-87), Endocrine Soc., Can. Coll. Neuropsychopharmacology (chmn. publ. com. 1986-89), Can. Soc. Endocrinology and Metabolism (councillor 1981-83), Can. Soc. Clin. Investigation. Roman Catholic. Avocations: photography, music, theater. Home: 100 Bronte Rd Unit 422 Oakville ON Canada L6L 6L5 Office: CIDtech Rsch Inc 1200 Franklin Blvd Cambridge ON Canada N1R 6T5 Office Phone: 519-621-3334 x202.

BROWN, GREGORY NEIL, academic administrator, forester, educator; b. Detroit, Feb. 10, 1938; s. Robert Octavus and Dorothy Etta May (Kingsbury) B.; m. Patricia Lee Talbott, Dec. 16, 1961 (div. 1974); children: Kathryn Duket, Julie Ann, Deborah Louise; m. Janeth Christine Hartman, May 24, 1974 (dec. 1997); children: Kimberly Suzanne, Kevin Scott; m. Laura Jean Dale, June 27, 1998. BS, Iowa State U., 1959; MF, Yale U., 1960; DF, Duke U., 1963. Plant physiologist Oak Ridge Nat. Lab., 1963—66; asst. prof. forestry to prof. U. Mo.-Columbia, 1966—77, dir. grad. studies Sch. Forestry, 1969—74; prof. Iowa State U., Ames, 1977—78; dept. head, prof. U. Minn.-St. Paul, 1978—83; dean, prof. U. Maine-Orono, 1983—86, acting v.p. acad. affairs, 1986-87, 91-92, v.p. rsch. and pub. svc., 1987—92; dean, prof. Coll. Natural Resources, Va. Poly. Inst. and State U., Blacksburg, 1992—2004, interim dean Coll. Agrl. and Life Scis., 2003; ret., 2004. Assoc. dir. Maine Agrl. Exptl. Sta., Orono, 1983-86, acting pres., 1992; assoc. dir. Va. Agrl. Exptl. Sta., Blacksburg, 1992-2004, interim provost, 1995; chair, bd. dirs. Powell River Project, 1996-2004; mem. sci. adv. bd. Nat. Ctr. Housing and the Environment, 2002—. Author-editor: Seedling Physiology and Reforestation Success, 1984; editor: International Directory of Woody Plant Physiologists, 1974-84, Jour. Forest Sci., 1979-82; editl. bd.: Renewable resources Jour., 2002—. Contbr. articles to profl. jours. Scoutmaster Boy Scouts Am., 1965-66; mem. Forestry Rsch. Adv. Coun., U.S. Sec. Agr., 2000-2002. Mem. Soc. Am. Foresters (chmn. physiology working group 1983-84), Nat. Assn. Profl. Forestry Schs. and Colls. (north Ctrl. rsch. chmn. 1981-82, nat. sec. treas. 1984-85, nat. pres. elect 1986-87, 94-95, pres. 1996-97), Internat. Union Forest Orgns. (chmn. working parties 1970-86), Nat. Assn. State Univs. and Land-Grant Colls. (chair bd. on natural resources 1997, chair U.S. geol. survey partnership com. 1997-2000), Soc. for Preservation and Encouragement of Barbershop Quartet Singing in Am. (pres. 1973-74), Sigma Xi, Xi Sigma Pi, Gamma Sigma Delta (jr. faculty award 1971). Lutheran. Home: 1227 Old Fort Rd Fairview NC 28730 Personal E-mail: browngn@charter.net.

BROWN, GREGORY Q., electronics executive; BA in Econs., Rutgers U. Pres. Ameritech New Media Inc., 1994—96, Ameritech Custom Bus. Svcs.; joined Micromuse, 1999, chmn., CEO; exec. v.p., pres., CEO comml., govt. and indsl. solutions sector Motorola, Inc., 2003—. Bd. dirs. R.R. Donnelley & Sons Co., Micromuse, Inc. Mem. bd. overseers Rutgers U. Office: Motorola Inc 1303 E Algonquin Rd Schaumburg IL 60196*

BROWN, GWENDOLYN WILLIAMS, music educator; b. Danville, Ky., Aug. 3, 1945; d. Edward Pendleton Williams, Sr. and Mattie (Pride) Williams; m. Albert Sylvester Brown, Jr., Feb. 14, 1976; 1 child, Lydia Ruth; m. John Davidson Reynolds, Aug. 4, 1964 (div. Aug. 1, 1968). BA, CSULA, Los Angeles, Calif., 1964—67, tchg. credential, 1994. Banker Wells Fargo Bank, Pasadena, Calif., 1968—75, Oakland, Calif., 1968—75, Berkeley, Calif., 1968—75; sales clk., music dept. Marshall Fields, Skokie, Ill., 1976—78; clerical substitute Arcadia Unified Sch. Dist., Arcadia, Calif., 1987—89; bible class, tchr. First A.M.E. Ch., Pasadena, Calif., 1989—92; substitute tchr. Pasadena Unified, Pasadena, Calif., 1989—93, Arcadia Unified, Arcadia, Calif., 1989—93; children's choir dir. First A.M.E. Ch., Pasadena, Calif., 1990—94; choral music tchr. Monrovia Unified Sch. Dist., Calif., 1993—. Soloist, opera workshop Merritt Coll., Oakland, Calif., 1971—75; Western Opera Co. chorus San Francisco Opera, San Francisco, 1981; Phil Reeder Oakland Choraleers Oakland Choraleers, Oakland, Calif., 1986. Mem. First A.M.E. Ch., Pasadena, Calif., 1984—, First A.M.E. Heritage Com., Pasadena, Calif., 2000—. Recipient Outstanding Student Tchr., Calif. State Univ./Los Angeles, Calif., 1993—94, African Am. Artist award, First A.M.E. Ch., Pasadena Youth Usher Bd./ Calif., 2000. Mem.: Am. Choral Dir. Assn. (mem. 1994—), Music Educators Nat. Conf. (mem. 1994—), Kappa Delta Pi (mem. 1995—, v.p. 1996—98). Democrat. African Methodist Episcopalian. Avocations: reading, photography, sewing, knitting, crocheting. Home: 44 W La Sierra Drive Arcadia CA 91007-4019 Office: 325 E Huntington Drive Monrovia CA 91016

BROWN, HANK, academic administrator, former senator, foundation administrator; b. Denver, Feb. 12, 1940; s. Harry W. and Anna M. (Hanks) B.; m. Nana Morrison, Aug. 27, 1967; children: Harry, Christy, Lori. BS, U. Colo., 1961, JD, 1969; LLM, M in Tax Law, George Washington U., 1986. Bar: Colo. 1969; CPA, 1988. Asst. pres. Monfort of Colo., Inc., Greeley, 1969—70, corp. counsel, 1970—71; v.p. Monfort Food Distbg., 1971—72, v.p. corp. devel., 1973—75, v.p. internat. ops., 1975—78, v.p. lamb div., 1978—80; mem. Colo. State Senate, 1972—76, asst. majority leader, 1974—76; mem. 97th-101st Congresses from Colo. 4th dist., 1981—90; U.S senator from Colo. Washington, 1991—96; pres. U. No. Colo., Greeley, 1998—2002, Daniels Fund, 2002—, Univ. Colo. statewide sys., Denver, 2005—. Chmn. Fgn. Rel. subcom. Near Ea. and South Asian affairs, Judicorp subcom. on constl. law. With USN, 1962—66. Decorated Air medal, Vietnam Svc. medal, Nat. Defense medal, Naval Unit citation. Republican. Congregationalist. Office: The Daniels Fund 101 Monroe St Denver CO 80206 Office Phone: 970-941-4444.*

BROWN, HAROLD, federal agency administrator, director; b. N.Y.C., Sept. 19, 1927; s. A.H. and Gertrude (Cohen) B.; m. Colene Dunning McDowell, Oct. 29, 1953; children: Deborah Ruth (Mrs. Eric Ploumis), Ellen Dunning (Mrs. Ray Merewether). AB, Columbia U., 1945, A.M., 1946, PhD in Physics (Lydig fellow 1948-49), 1949; 11 hon. degrees. Research scientist Columbia U., 1945-50, lectr. physics, 1947-48, Stevens Inst. Tech., 1949-50; divsn. leader E.O. Lawrence Radiation Lab. U. Calif., Berkeley, 1950-60, staff mem., group leader E.O. Lawrence Radiation Lab., 1952-60; dir. Lawrence Livermore (Calif.) Lab., 1960-61; dir. def. rsch. and engring. Dept. Def., Washington, 1961-65; sec. Dept. Air Force, Washington, 1965-69; pres. Calif. Inst. Tech., Pasadena, 1969-77; sec. US Dept. Def., Washington, 1977-81; disting. vis. prof. Sch. Advanced Internat. Studies Johns Hopkins U., Md., 1981-84, chmn. Fgn. Policy Inst., 1984-92, counselor Ctr. Strategic & Internat. Studies, 1992—; ptnr. Warburg, Pincus & Co., N.Y.C., 1990—. Bd. dirs. Cummins Engine Co., Mattel, Inc., Evergreen Holdings, Inc.; mem. Polaris Steering Com., 1956-58; mem. Pres.'s Sci. Adv. Com., 1960-61; sr. sci. advisor Conf. Discontinuance Nuclear Tests, 1958-59; U.S. del. SALT, Helsinki, Vienna and Geneva, 1969-77; chmn. Tech. Assessment Adv. Coun. to U.S. Congress, 1974-77; chmn. Commn. on Roles and Capabilities of U.S. Intelligence Comty., 1995-96; mem. exec. com. Trilateral Commn., 1973-76, trustee, 1992—; trustee Rand Corp., 1983-92, 93—; mem., ind. panel investigating abuses at Abu Ghraib prison, 2004. Author: Thinking About National Security: Defense and Foreign Policy in a Dangerous World, 1983. Trustee Beckman Found., 1982-95, chmn., 1993-95; trustee Rockefeller Found., 1983-93. Decorated Medal of Freedom; named One of 10 Outstanding Young Men U.S. Jaycees, 1961; recipient Medal of Excellence Columbia U., 1963; Joseph C. Wilson award in internat. affairs, 1976, Enrico Fermi award U.S. Dept. Energy, 1992. Mem. NAE, NAS, Am. Phys. Soc., Am. Acad. Arts and Scis., Bohemian Club, River Club, Met. Club, Phi Beta Kappa. Office: Ctr for Strategic & Intl Studies 1800 K St NW Ste 400 Washington DC 20006-2202

BROWN, HAROLD EUGENE, retired magistrate; b. Damascus, Ark., Jan. 6, 1935; s. Amos Eugene and Hazel Gladys (Thomas) B.; m. Carolyn Marie Sanders, Aug. 26, 1972; children: James Daryl, Deena Leigh, Cynthia Marie. Student, U. Md. Overseas Divsn., Verdun, France, 1962-64, Germanna C.C., 1978-84. Enlisted U.S. Army, 1954, advanced through grades to sgt. maj., 1977; White House liaison Chief of Staff Army, Washington, 1969—73; dep. dir. Def. Coop. Agy., New Delhi, 1973—77; post sgt. maj., co. comdr Fort A.P. Hill, Bowling Green, Va., 1977—81; magistrate 15th dist. Supreme Ct. Va., Fredericksburg, 1982—2002, apptd. chief magistrate, 1987—2000, apptd. magistrate VI, 2000—02; ret., 2002. Marriage commr. Commonwealth Va., 1984. Bd. dirs., former dir. Rappahannock Coun. Domestic Violence; bd. dirs. Rappahannock United Way. Decorated Cross of Gallantry (Republic of Vietnam). Mem. Am. Judges Assn., Va. Magistrates Assn., Va. Cmty. Criminal Justice Assn., Ret. Sgts. Maj. Assn. Avocations: golf, photography, computer programming. Home: 21 Rosewood Dr Fredericksburg VA 22408-1521 Office Phone: 540-840-5170. Personal E-mail: hebrown5@aol.com.

BROWN, HARRY JOE, real estate developer; s. Harry Joe Brown and Sally (Eilers); m. Karen Somerville (div.); 1 child, Morgan; m. Katherine Nelson (div.); 1 child, Esme. Studied at, Yale U., Oxford U. Head, develop. 20th Century Fox; pres. Brown Co., NYC. Writer: movie Duffy; prodr.: (plays) Zoo Story, Krapp's Last Tape; co-author (with Richard Meier and Alastair Gordon): (book) American Dream: The Houses at Sagaponac: Modern Living in the Hamptons, 2003. Recipient won final, Paradise Island Pro-Am Backgammon Competition. Achievements include initiating the residential development of "The Houses at Sagaponac" in Southhampton, Long Island, NY. Office: Brown Co Inc 461 Park Ave S New York NY 10016 Office Phone: 212-683-4400.

BROWN, HELEN GURLEY, editor-in-chief; b. Green Forest, Ark., Feb. 18, 1922; d. Ira M. and Cleo (Sisco) Gurley; m. David Brown, Sept. 25, 1959. Student, Tex. State Coll. for Women, 1940—41, Woodbury Coll., 1942; LLD, Woodbury U., 1987; DLitt, L.I. U., 1993. Exec. sec. Music Corp. Am., 1942—45; exec. sec. William Morris Agy., 1945—47; copywriter Foote, Cone & Belding (advt. agy.), Los Angeles, 1948—58; advt. writer, account exec. Kenyon & Eckhardt (advt. agy.), Hollywood, Calif., 1958—62; editor-in-chief Cosmopolitan mag., 1965—97, Cosmopolitan Internat. Edits, 1997—. Author 8 books. Named 1 of 25 most influential women in U.S., World Almanac, 1976—81; recipient Francis Holmes Achievement award for outstanding work in advt., 1956—59, Disting. Achievement award, U. So. Calif. Sch. Journalism, 1971, Spl. award for editl. leadership Am. Newspaper, Woman's Club, Washington, 1972, Disting. Achievement award in journalism, Stanford U., 1977, Matrix award in mag. category, N.Y. Women in Comm., 1985, Henry Johnson Fisher award, Mag. Pubs. of Am., 1995, Helen Gurley Brown Rshc. Professorship established name, Northwestern U. Medill Sch. Journalism, 1986, inducted into Pubs.' Hall of Fame, 1988. Mem.: AFTRA, Am. Soc. Mag. Editors (Hall of Fame award 1996), Authors League Am., Eta Upsilon Gamma. Office: Cosmopolitan The Hearst Corp 224 W 57th St New York NY 10019 Office Phone: 212-649-3555.

BROWN, HENRY E., JR., congressman; b. Bishopville, SC, Dec. 20, 1935; m. Billye Beaver; 3 children. D. Bus. Admin. (hon.), The Citadel, 1998. Ret. v.p. Piggly Wiggly Carolina Co.; mem. SC House Reps., 1985-2000, US Congress from 1st SC Dist., 2001—. Mem. Congressional com. Transportation and Infrastructure, Budget, Veterans' Affairs; apptd. to Ways and Means com., 1989, chmn., 1995; chmn. Joint Tax Study Com.; mem. Budget and Control bd., Legislative Audit Coun., Joint Bond Review com.; served on Hanahan City Coun., 4 yrs., Hanahan Planning Com., 4 yrs. Mem. Cooper River Bapt. Ch. Served SC N.G., 9 yrs. Named Legislator Yr., SC Assn. Sch. Librs., 1998-99, Natl. Rep. Legislators Assn, 1999, SC Vocat. Dirs. Assn., 1999, Ind. Colls. of SC, 1995, SC Coll. Legislators, 1995, Outstanding Legislator, SC Sch. Bd. Assn., 1997. SC Legislator Yr., SC Assn. Realtors, 1997; named Servant Yr., SC Chamber, 1995, SC Taxpayers Watchdog, SC Treas. Office; awarded Order of Palmetto, State of SC, 2000; recipient Dir. award, SC Dept. Revenue, Guardian of Small Bus. award, SC Chap. NFIB, 1996. Past dir. Crime Stoppers, Berkeley Chamber of Commerce; Hammerton Lodge #332 A.F.M., North Charleston Rotary Club. Republican. Office: US Congress from 1st SC Dist 1124 Longworth Ho Office Bldg Washington DC 20515*

BROWN, HERBERT GRAHAM, entrepreneur; b. Opelousas, La., Nov. 22, 1923; s. T.G. and Mamie (Walker) B.; m. Diane Fontenot, Oct. 18, 1953; children: Deborah, Graham, Jared, Greg, Donna. Student, U. So. La., 1944, Eckerd Coll., St. Petersburg, Fla., 1985. Owner, prin. appliance and furniture stores, La. and Fla., 1939-89, rice and cattle farm, La., 1948-89, Browns Thrift City, La., 1961-70; owner, developer shopping ctrs. and apartments, various locations, 1955-89; chmn. bd. Checker Drive-in Restaurants, 1989—95; pres. Am. Bank, La., 1954-63; sr. v.p. Jack Eckerd Corp., Fla., 1970-72; owner, ptnr., developer K-Marts, Mobile Home Parks, shopping ctrs., Fla. and La., 1970-89. Dist. gov., R.I., 1968-69; vice chmn. ARC, United Way; pres. Fla. & La. vol. Boy Scouts Am.; trustee, vice chmn. Morton F. Plant Hosp., Clearwater, Fla.; world chmn. R.I. Health Hunger & Humanity Com., 1981-86; U.S. chmn. Polio Plus Campaign Com., 1986-88; chmn. bd. dirs. Checkers, 1989-95. Cpl. U.S. Army, 1943-45. Recipient Silver Medallion Brotherhood award NCCJ, Silver Beaver award Boy Scouts Am., Boy Scout Distinguished Citizen award, State of La., 2001, Humanitarian of Yr. award Fla. Mar. of Dimes, Goodwill Industries, Watson Clinic, Medulla Al Merito Rotario, Columbia, Meritorious Svc. award Rotary Internat., Svc. to Mankind award Sertoma; elected to Tampa Bay BUs. Hall of Fame; named Entrepreneur of Yr., State of Fla., named Mr. Clearwater, 2000-2001, Clearwater Chamber of Commerce. Mem. Heartbeat Internat. (bd. dirs.), La. C. of C. (bd. dirs., pres.), Rotary Internat. (bd. dirs. 1978-80, trustee Rotary Found., pres.-elect 1994-95, pres. 1995-96, chmn. Rotary Found. 2000-01, Disting. Svc. award 1986-87). Republican. Roman Catholic. E-mail: hgb@herbertgbrown.com.

BROWN, HERBERT RUSSELL, lawyer, writer; b. Columbus, Ohio, Sept. 27, 1931; s. Thomas Newton and Irene (Hankinson) B.; m. Beverly Ann Jenkins, Dec. 2, 1967; children: David Herbert, Andrew Jenkins. BA, Denison U., 1953; JD, U. Mich., 1956. Assoc. Vorys, Sater, Seymour and Pease, Columbus, Ohio, 1956, 60-64, ptnr., 1965-82; treas. Sunday Creek Coal Co., Columbus, 1970-86; assoc. justice Ohio Supreme Ct., Columbus, 1987-93. Mem. Ohio Ethics Commn., 2002-04, Ohio Public Defender Commn., 2004-; examiner Ohio Bar, 1967-72, Multi-State Bar, 1971-76, Dist. Ct. Bar, 1968-71; commr. Fed. Lands, Columbus, 1967-68, Lake Lands, Columbus, 1981; bd. dirs. Thurber House, 1992-94, Sunday Creek Coal Co.; adj. prof. Ohio State U. Coll. Law, 1997-2000; panelist Am. Arbitration Assn., 1993—. Author: (novels) Presumption of Guilt, 1991, Shadows of Doubt, 1994, (plays) You're My Boy, 1999, Peace with Honor, 2000, Mano A Mano, 2000, Power of God, 2002; mem. editl. bd. U. Mich. Law Rev., 1955-56. Trustee Columbus Bar Found., 1993—2003, pres., 2001—02; candidate Ohio State Legis.; deacon, mem. governing bd. 1st Cmty. Ch., 1966—80; bd. dirs. Ctrl. Cmty. House Columbus, 1967—75. Capt. JAGC U.S. Army, 1956—57. Recipient Disting. Alumni citation, Denison U., 2003. Fellow Am. Coll. Trial Lawyers; mem. Ohio Bar Assn., Columbus Bar Assn., Colo. Bar Found. (trustee 1993-2003, pres. 2001-02). Democrat. Office: 5 E Long St Columbus OH 43215

BROWN, HERSHEL M., retired newspaper publisher; b. Phila., Jan. 7, 1923; s. Paul and Sarah (Magil) B.; m. Lorraine Rose Blofson, Apr. 21, 1944; children: Susan R., Stephen J.(deceased), Adam L. Student, U. Pa., Phila., 1940-42; BS in Bus., Northwestern U., Evanston, Ill., 1944; MS in Journalism, Northwestern U., 1947. Reporter, editorial writer, music critic Globe Times, Bethlehem, Pa., 1947-48; rewrite, asst. to Sunday editor, music critic Post Gazette, Pitts., 1949-50; advt. copywriter, account exec., plans bd. chmn., v.p./exec. supr. Al Paul Lefton Co. Inc., Phila., Chgo., L.A., 1950-68; pub. Register News, Bordentown, N.J., 1968-96; pres. Lorraine Pub. Inc., Bordentown, N.J., 1968-96. V.p., trustee Jenkintown (Pa.) Music Sch.; pub. rels. dir. Co-Opera Co. Phila., 1950-57; bd. mem. Farnsworth Ave. Revitalization Project, Bordentown, N.J., 1984-90; mem. artists selection com. Cmty. Concerts Bordentown, Inc., 1982-96. Lt. USNR, 1944-46. Recipient 1st pl. awards Pa. Newspaper Pubs., 1948, N.J. Press Assn., 1971, 78. Mem.: Am. Newspaper Guild, Merchandising Execs. Club Chgo., Sigma Delta Chi. Jewish. Avocations: piano, cello, concerts, theater, record collecting, swimming.

BROWN, HILTON, artist, educator, writer; b. Momence, Ill., Sept. 22, 1938; s. Oswald E. and Maud M. (Shronts) B. Student, Goodman Theater/Art Inst. Chgo, 1956-58, U. Chgo., 1959-60, U. Ill., Chgo., 1961-62; cert. in fine arts, 1962; Diploma in Fine Arts, BFA in Painting, Sch. of Art Inst. Chgo., 1962, MFA in Painting, 1963. Instr. drawing/painting Sch. Art Inst. Chgo., 1962-65; asst. prof. fine art Sch. Fine Arts Washington U., St. Louis, 1965-68; asst. prof. fine arts Goucher Coll., Towson, Md., 1968-70, assoc. prof. fine arts, 1970-75, prof. and chair dept. visual arts, 1975-78; vis. assoc. prof. art history U. Del., 1974-78, prof. art conservation Newark, 1978-84, Mayer prof. artists techniques, 1984-88, prof. art, art history and art conservation, 1988-92, Harriet T. Baily prof. art, art conservation, art history and mus. studies, 1992—. Cons., lectr. Nat. Tchr. Inst./Nat. Gallery of Art, Washington, 1990—2000. Author: (exhbn. catalog) The Art and Archives of Ralph Mayer, 1984; co-author (exhbn. catalog) Milk and Eggs: The American Revival of Tempera Painting, 1930-1950, 2002; co-curator (exhbn.) Brandywine River Mus., Akron Art Mus., Spencer Mus., U. Kans., 2002; one person show Susan Isaacs Gallery, Wilmington, Del., 1990; 135 invitational and juried shows, 1961-2004; work in mus. collections Balt. Mus. of Art. Sec. bd. dirs. Gay and Lesbian Alliance of Del., Wilmington, 1991-93; co-chair Lesbian, Gay, Bisexual Caucus of Commn. to Promote Racial and Cultural Diversity, U. Del., 1992-99, chair faculty senate com. on diversity and affirmative action, 1993-95, 97-98. Democrat. Anglo-Catholic. Avocations: reading, gardening. Office: Univ of Delaware Mus Studies 207 Mechanical Hall Newark DE 19716 Office Phone: 302-831-8237. Business E-Mail: hilton@udel.edu.

BROWN, HOLMES, public relations executive; b. Prescott, Kans., Oct. 2, 1914; s. Frank Emerson and May Holmes Brown; m. Mary Ellen Lynch, Oct. 17, 1938; children: Holmes Cheney, Hamilton Frank, James Emerson. BS, Iowa State U., 1936; postgrad., GE Inst., 1936-39. Mgmt. technician GE, various locations, 1936-43; with pub. rels. Am. Locomotive, N.Y.C., 1945-50; pub. affairs exec. Colonial Williamsburg (Va.) Found., 1950; pub. rels. exec. Ford Motor Co., Dearborn, Mich., 1952-60; asst. to Sgt. Shriver War on Poverty, Washington, 1964-66; v.p. Am. Airlines, N.Y.C., 1966-68; pub. affairs officer Continental Group, N.Y.C., 1968-75; v.p. Continental Group Found., N.Y.C., 1975-79; pres., chmn. The Inst. for Applied Econs., N.Y.C., Va., 1979—. Prodr. nat. nutrition program GE Co., 1941-43; pres., chmn. N.Y. Bd. of Trade, 1979-85. Editor: How to Get the Most Our of the Food You Buy, 1942; prodr. Headstart Ednl. Guide Books, 1965; author: Can You Trust Network Evening News; author (newspaper article) Nixon's Enemy List, 1973. Pres. Fund for New Priorities, N.Y., 1977, bd. dirs., 1976-99. Recipient Outstanding Alumni award Iowa State U., 1957, Leadership award Fund for New Priorities, 1978, Silver Anvil award Am. Pub. Rels. Soc., 1959. Mem. Admirals Club (life), Nat. Press Club, Boars Head Sports Club, The Goodwin Soc. Colonial Williamsburg, The Nat. Hist. Soc., Va. Hist. Soc. Democrat. Episcopalian. Avocations: farming, tennis, sculpting, track, history. Home: High Mowing Farms 1894 Stillhouse Creek Rd Afton VA 22920-2043 Office: Inst for Applied Econs 1 Ednam Vlg Charlottesville VA 22903-4636 Office Phone: 434-971-8333. E-mail: holmesmb@iqworks.net.

BROWN, IFIGENIA THEODORE, lawyer; b. Syracuse, N.Y., Mar. 14, 1930; d. Gus and Christine Theodore; m. Paul Frederick Brown, Sept. 16, 1956; 1 child, Paul Darrow. BA, Syracuse U., 1951, LLB, JD, 1954. Bar: N.Y. 1956. Acting police justice Village of Ballston Spa, NY, 1960—62; sr. ptnr. Brown & Brown, Ballston Spa, 1958—95; ptnr. Brown Brown & Peterson Esqs, Ballston Spa, 1995—2000; of counsel Brown, Peterson, Craig and Thomas, Ballston Spa, 2000—. Chmn. N.Y. State Bd. Real Property Svcs., Albany, 1996—. Mem. Charlton Sch. Bd., 1989-93, Ballston Spa Libr. Bd., 1991-94; founder, pres. Saratoga County Women's Rep. Club; vice-chmn. Saratoga County Rep. Com., 1958-72. Mem. N.Y. State Bar Assn., Saratoga County Bar Assn. (treas. 1983-84, pres. 1984-85), Zonta (pres. Saratoga County 1962, 90), Order Ea. Star. Republican. Greek Orthodox. Avocations: church choir, piano. Home: 42 Hyde Blvd Ballston Spa NY 12020-1608 Office: Brown Peterson Craig and Thomas One E High St Ballston Spa NY 12020 Office Phone: 518-885-9292.

BROWN, J. MARTIN, oncologist, educator; b. Doncaster, Eng., Oct. 15, 1941; married; 2 children. BSc, U. Birmingham, 1963; MSc, U. London, 1965; DPhil in Radiation Biology, Oxford U., 1968. NIH fellow radiation biology Stanford U. Med. Ctr., Calif., 1968-70, rsch. assoc., 1970-71, from asst. prof. to assoc. prof., 1971-84, prof., dir. divsn. radiation biology, 1984—, dir. Cancer Biology Rsch. Lab., 1985—. Sr. fellow Am. Cancer Soc. Dernham, 1971-74; mem. adv. com. biol. effects of ionizing radiations NAS, 1971—. Recipient Bruce F. Cain Meml. award, Am. Assn. Cancer Rsch., 1999. Mem. AAAS, Am. Assn. Cancer Rsch., Am. Soc. Therapeutical Radiology & Oncology, Brit. Inst. Radiology, Brit. Assn. Cancer Rsch., Radiation Rsch. Soc. (9th Rsch. award 1980). Achievements include research in mammalian cellular radiobiology, tumor radiobiology, experimental chemotherapy, bioreductive cytotoxic agents, radiation carcinogenesis. Office: Stanford U Med Sch Cancer Biology Rsch Lab Dept of Radiation & Oncology GK103 Stanford CA 94305-5468

BROWN, J'AMY MARONEY, journalist, media consultant, investor; b. Oct. 30, 1945; d. Roland Francis and Jeanne (Wilbur) Maroney; m. James Raphael Brown, Jr., Nov. 5, 1967 (dec. July 1982); children: James Roland Francis, Jeanne Raphael. Student, U. So. Calif., 1963-67. Reporter L.A. Herald Examiner, 1966-67, Lewisville Leader, Dallas, 1980-81; editor First Person Mag., Dallas., 1981-82; journalism dir. Pacific Palisades Sch., L.A., 1983-84; freelance writer, media cons., 1984-88; media dir., chief media strategist Tellem Inc., 1990-92, comm. cons., issues mgr., 1992—. Press liaison U.S. papal visit, L.A., 1987; pres., CEO and owner PRformance Group Comm., 1995—; auction chmn. Assn. Pub. Broadcasting, Houston, 1974, 75; vice chmn. Dallas Arts Coun., 1976-80; vice chmn. Met. March of Dimes, Dallas, 1980-82; del. Dallas Coun. PTAs, 1976-80; bd. dir., pres. continuing edn. adv. bd. Santa Barbara City Coll.; pres. Montecito Assn., bd. dir., Women's Econ. Ventures, Santa Barbara Visual Arts Alliance; mem. core-coun. Santa Barbara Coun. on Self-Esteem; coord. specialist World Cup Soccer Organizing Com.; dir. J.M. Brown Charitable Found. Columnist: Santa Barbara News Press, 2004—05, Montecito Jour., 2004—05. Recipient UPI Editors award for investigative reporting, 1981. Mem. NAFE, Pub. Rels. Soc. Am. (accredited), Women Meeting Women, Women in Comm., Am. Bus. Women's Assn., Goleta Valley Art Assn., Santa Barbara C. of C. (media com.). Republican. Roman Catholic. Home: 1143 High Rd Santa Barbara CA 93108-2430 Office Phone: 805-969-5515.

BROWN, JACK A., state representative, rancher, real estate broker; b. St. Johns, Ariz., May 2, 1929; m. Beverly Van Camp Agr. and econs. degree, Brigham Young U., 1953. Mem. Ariz. Ho. Reps., 1963-74, 87-96, Dem. leader, 1969-72, asst. minority leader, 1989-92; mem. Ariz. Ho. Reps. 5th dist., 2004—; minority leader Ariz. Senate, 1997—2004. Former chair State Water Quality Control Coun. Mem. Apache City Bd. Realtors, Cattle Growers, Farm Bur., Ariz. Acad., State Chamber, Kiwanis. Democrat. also: PO Box 220 Saint Johns AZ 85936-0220 Office: Ariz Ho Reps 1700 W Washington St Ste H Phoenix AZ 85007-2844 Fax: 602-542-3429. Office Phone: 602-926-4129. Office Fax: 602-417-3010. Business E-Mail: jbrown@azleg.state.az.us.

BROWN, JACK D(ELBERT), chemist, researcher; b. Boise, Idaho, June 21, 1954; s. Robert and Shirley Fay (Piper) Brown; m. Leslie Anne Terry, June 21, 1981; children: Lauren Anne, Justin Andrew. Student, Boise State U., 1973-76; BS, Utah State U., 1983, PhD, 1987. Postdoctoral rschr. Colo. State U., Ft. Collins, 1986-88; sr. rsch. chemist Syntex Chems. Inc., Boulder, Colo., 1988-90, prin. rsch. chemist, Tech. Ctr., 1990—99, disting. scientist, 1999—2002, Tech. Ctr. Roche Colo. Corp., Boulder, 1998—; mgr. devel. Boehringer Ingelheim Chem., Inc., 2002—. Co-author: (book) Metabolism of Food Disaccarides, 1983; contbr. articles to profl. jours. Explorer scout advisor Boy Scouts Am., Boulder, 1991. Mem.: AAAS, N.Y. Acad. Scis., Am. Chem. Soc., Sigma Xi. Achievements include co-inventor. Home: 5731 FireLight Ter Moseley VA 23120 Office: Boehringer Ingelheim Chem 2820 N Normandy Dr Petersburg VA 23805 Office Phone: 804-698-7202. Business E-Mail: jbrown@bichemical.com. E-mail: jackandleslie@comcast.net.

BROWN, JACK H., supermarket company executive; b. L.A., June 14, 1939; Student, San Jose State U, UCLA. V.p. Sages Complete Marktes, San Bernardino, Calif., 1960-67, Marsh Supermarkets, Yorktown, Ind., 1971-77; pres. Pantry Supemarkets, Pasadena, Calif., 1977-79; pres. mid-west divsn. Cullum Cos., Dallas, 1979-81; pres., CEO Stater Bros. Markets, Colton, Calif., 1981—; also chmn. bd. dirs. Trustee U. Redlands, Calif.; bd. dirs. Goodwill Industries of inland Empire, San Bernardino; bd. councillors Calif. State U., San Bernardion. With USNR, 1956-62. Recipient Horatio Alger award Disting. Ams., 1992, Bus. Exec. of Yr. award U. so. Calif., 1993; Calif. State U., San Berardino Sch. Bus. named in his honor, 1992. Mem. Western Assn. Food Chains (v.p., bd. dirs., pres. 1987-88), Calif. Retailers Assn. (bd. dirs.), Food Mktg. Inst. (vice chmn.), So. Calif. Grocers Assn., Food Employers Coun. (bd. govs.), Life Savs. and Loan Assn. (dir.), Elks. Republican. Presbyterian. Office: Stater Bros Markets 21700 Barton Rd Colton CA 92324*

BROWN, JACK SIDNEY, music educator, musician; b. Washington, Mar. 20, 1963; s. Francis Oakley and Alma Faye (Thrower) Brown; 1 child, Kevin Sidney. BA in Music Edn., Miss. Coll., Clinton, 1986; MA in Musicology, Calif. State U., Long Beach, 1997. Tchr. Dallas Ind. Sch. Dist., 1987—89, Long Beach Unified Sch. Dist., Calif., 1990—96, Emmett Sch. Dist., Idaho, 1996—2000, Meridian Sch. Dist., 2000—. Composer and performer: recordings Live From Left Of Center, Headin' West; performer: New Arrivals; dir.: (recordings) By His Grace. Precinct chair Idaho Dem. Party, Meridian, 2002—; choir dir. First Congl. United Ch. of Christ, Boise, 1996—. Mem.: NEA (govt. rels. com. 2004—), Music Educators Nat. Conf., Am. Choral Directors Assn. (state r&s chair - jazz choir 2002—). Congregationalist. Avocations: bicycling, music, hiking, reading, gardening. Home: 1687 E Cougar Creek Meridian ID 83642 Office: Meridian High School 1900 W Pine Ave Meridian ID 83642 Office Phone: 208-888-4905 3146. Office Fax: 208-888-5273. Personal E-mail: pignbear@aol.com. E-mail: brownjs@meridianschools.org.

BROWN, JAMES, singer, broadcasting executive; b. Pulaski, Tenn., June 17, 1928; Former pres. J.B. Broadcasting, Ltd., James Brown Network. Chmn. James Brown Enterprises, James Brown Prodns. Leader musical group, Famous Flames, from 1956; now solo performer, rec. artist with cos.including King, Smash Records, Polydor; recs. include At the Apollo, Pure Dynamite, Original Disco Man, Please, Please, Raw Soul, Sex Machine, I Got You (I Feel Good), Get on the Good Foot, The Popcorn, There It Is, I Got the Feelin', Soul on Top, Hot on the One, Poppa's Got a Brand New Bag, Gravity, The Big Payback, Living in America; more than 75 albums including: Live At The Apollo, 1962, Hot Pants, 1971, Best Of, 1975, Body Heat, 1977, Special, 1981, Soul Syndrome, 1980, Bring It On, 1983, Gravity, 1986, I'm Real, 1988, Love Overdue, 1991, Love Power Peace: Live at the Olympia, Paris 1971, 1992, Papa's Got a Brand New Bag, 1992, A Payback, 1992, Universal James, 1992, The Greatest Hits of the Fourth Decade, 1992, Try Me, 1996, Hooked on Brown, 1996; U.S. tours include performances at Apollo, NYC, Howard U., Washington; author (autobiography) I Feel Good: A Memoir of a Life of Soul, 2005. Recipient 44 Gold Record awards; Grammy award, 1965, 1986; inducted into Rock and Roll Hall of Fame, 1986. Address: care Bros Mgmt Assocs 141 Dunbar Ave Fords NJ 08863-1551*

BROWN, JAMES BENTON, lawyer; b. Pitts., Jan. 18, 1945; s. Sidney J. and Marian R. (Bailiss) B.; m. Susan M. Brenner, Aug. 6, 1967; children: Jessica Lynn, Joshua David. BA, U. Louisville, 1967; JD, Duquesne U., 1971. Bar: Pa. 1971, U.S. Dist. Ct. (we. dist.) Pa. 1971, U.S. Ct. Appeals (3d cir.) 1974, U.S. Supreme Ct. 1982. Dir., ptnr. Cohen & Grigsby, P.C., chair labor and employment grup. Lectr. Pa. Bar Inst.; mediator Justus ADR; arbitrator Am. Arbitration Assn. Commr. Port of Pitts. Commn.; bd. dirs. Jewish Assn. Aging. Mem. ABA, Fed. Bar Assn., Pa. Bar Assn. (past vice chmn. labor and employment law sect.), Allegheny County Bar Assn., Internat. Assn. Def. Counsel. Democrat. Home: 100 Denniston St # 1 Pittsburgh PA 15206 Office: 15th fl 11 Stanwix St Ste 15 Pittsburgh PA 15222-1312 Office Phone: 412-297-4900. Business E-Mail: jbrown@cohenlaw.com.

BROWN, JAMES CHANDLER, retired academic administrator; b. Garden City, N.Y., Aug. 5, 1947; s. Harry Chandler and Lillian Marie (Cutter) B. BA, Susquehanna U., Selinsgrove, Pa., 1970; License es Lettres, Geneva U., 1978; postgrad., Stanford U., 1984. Rsch. asst. Geneva U., 1972—79; asst. Galerie Jan Krugier, Geneva, 1978—81; coord. pubs. So. Oreg. State Coll., Ashland, 1982-84; dir. pubs. So. Oreg. U., 1984—2001, emeritus faculty, 2003—; resident dir. Oreg. Ctr., Oreg. Univ. Sys., Lyon, France, 2001—03. Cons. in field. Author: How to Sharpen Your Publications (brochure, Case award) 1985, College Viewbook (booklet), 1985. Sec. bd. dirs. Schneider Mus. Art, Ashland, 1985-94, Alliance Francaise of Portland, 2005—. Canton of Geneva grantee, 1974-79; awardee, Coun. for Advancement and Support of Edn., 1987-88, 95, 98, 2000, 01. Mem. Coun. for Advancement and Support of Edn., Omicron Delta Kappa Leadership Soc., Coun. of Mgrs. Methodist. Avocations: reading, hiking, cross country skiing, photography. Home: 121 NW Howard Ln Dallas OR 97338

BROWN, JAMES JOSEPH, manufacturing executive; b. N.Y.C., Apr. 4, 1928; s. Peter J. and Mary (O'Neil) B.; m. Mary E. McKeon, Dec. 30, 1961; children: Patricia, James, Carolyn, Denise, Erin. BS, Fordham U., 1952. C.P.A., N.Y. Acct. Touche, Ross, Bailey & Smart (C.P.A.s), N.Y.C., 1952-54; sr. acct. Price Waterhouse & Co. (C.P.A.s), Caracas, Venezuela and N.Y.C., 1954-63; mgr. internal audit Litton Industries, 1963-65; sr. v.p., chief fin. officer dir. Kidde, Inc., 1965-82; chmn. bd. Am. Desk Mfg. Co., 1982-97. Served with AUS, 1946-48. Named Alumni Man of Year, Fordham U. Coll. Bus. Adminstrn., 1971 Mem. AICPA, N.Y. State Soc. CPAs, Econ. Club N.Y. Clubs: Treasurers of N.Y, Ridgewood Country, N.Y. Athletic. Office: 441 Weymouth Dr Wyckoff NJ 07481-1216 E-mail: jbrown9778@aol.com.

BROWN, JAMES KNIGHT, lawyer; b. Rainelle, W.Va., Sept. 25, 1929; s. Hugh Allen and Florence Catherine (Knight) B.; m. Sarah Elizabeth Droste, June 21, 1952; children: Carolyn, Patricia, Julia. BS, W.Va. U., 1951, LLB, 1956. Bar: W.Va. 1956, U.S. Ct. Appeals (4th and 6th cir.), U.S. Supreme Ct. Assoc. Jackson & Kelly, Charleston, W.Va., 1956-62, ptnr., 1962-98; mem. Jackson & Kelly PLLC, Charleston, 1999—2001, of counsel, 2001—. Former W.Va. adv. bd. dirs. BB&T Corp. 1st lt. USAF, 1951-53. Fellow Am. Bar Found., W.Va. Bar Found.; mem. ABA, W.Va. State Bar (pres. 1975-76), Order of Coif, Phi Beta Kappa. Democrat. Presbyterian. Avocations: woodworking, golf. Office: Jackson & Kelly PLLC 1600 Laidley Tower Charleston WV 25301-2189

BROWN, JAMES MILTON, law educator; b. Streator, Ill., July 16, 1921; BA, U. Ill., 1943; JD, U. Fla., 1963. Bar: Fla. 63, DC 68. Pres., gen. mgr. J.C. Ames Lumber Co., Streator, 1947—61, Brown-Vissering Constrn. Co., Streator, 1956—61; Sterling fellow Yale Law Sch., 1964—65; assoc. prof. law U. Miss., 1964—65; prof. law George Washington U., Washington, 1965—92, prof. emeritus, 1992—, dir. land use mgmt. and control program Nat. Law Ctr., 1965—92, sr. staff scientist Program of Policy Studies, 1965—82. Commr. Md. Nat. Capital Park and Planning Commn., 1991—2002; mem. various panels NAS; cons. in field. Contbr. articles to legal jours. Mem.: ABA, Fla. Bar Assn., DC Bar Assn., Order of Coif, Lambda Alpha, Phi Delta Phi. Home: 10035 Weeks Dr Brooksville FL 34601 Office: James Martin Brown 211 South Main St Brooksville FL 34601 Personal E-mail: profjmb@bellsouth.net.

BROWN, JAMES NELSON, JR., retired accountant; b. Bronx, Apr. 17, 1929; s. James Nelson and Agnes Mary (Cummins) B.; m. Lila Barbara Watt, Dec. 12, 1950; children: Constance Ellen Brown Buttacavole, Nelson Arthur, Richard John. BSBA, Drake U., 1956. CPA; cert. internal auditor, fraud examiner. Sr. acct. Arthur Andersen & Co., N.Y.C., 1956-61; asst. v.p., dir. internal auditing Salomon Inc., N.Y.C., 1961-86, asst. v.p., dir. projects mgmt. dept., 1986-91, asst. v.p. environ. litigation dept., 1991-93, v.p., mgr. environ. litig. dept., 1994-97; cons. environ. litig. dept Citigroup, Inc., N.Y.C., 1998—2002. Com. chmn. Cub Scouts, 1973-75; troop com. chmn. Boy Scouts Am., Carteret, N.J., 1976-77, 88-90, com. mem., 1978-87. Sgt. AUS, 1947-52. Mem. AICPA, VFW, Am. Mgmt. Assn., N.J. Soc. CPAs, Nat. Assn. Cert. Fraud Examiners, Inst. Internal Auditors, Am. Legion, Elks. Republican. Roman Catholic. Personal E-mail: Jnbrownjr@aol.com.

BROWN, JAMES ROBERT, retired air force officer; b. Bozeman, Mont., June 17, 1930; s. Marley Robert and Ann Louise (Pace) B.; m. Sandra Shores, Dec. 19, 1964; children: James V., Brian R. BS, Mont. State U., 1953; grad., Squadron Officer Sch., 1962, Air Command and Staff Coll., 1964, Indsl. Coll. of Armed Forces, 1974. Commd. 2d lt. U.S. Air Force, 1953, advanced through grades to lt. gen., 1984, undergrad. pilot tng. program Williams AFB, Ariz., 1954-54, bomb comdr., intelligence officer 20th Fighter-Bomber Wing Royal Air Force Station Wethersfield, England, 1955—58, fighter gunnery, instr. pilot, acad. instr. Nellis AFB, Nev., 1958—60, fighter weapons sch., rsch. and devel. project officer, instr. pilot, 1960—62, flight evaluator Tactical Air Command Langley AFB, Va., 1962-63, flight comdr., instr. pilot Davis-Monthan AFB, Ariz., 1964-66, tour duty Vietnam, 1966—67, dir. tng. analysis and devel. Davis-Monthan AFB, Ariz., 1967-71, staff action officer tactics br. chief, acting chief tactical div. for Directorate of Plans and ops. Washington, 1971-75, dir. ops. 388th Tactical Fighter Wing Korat Royal Thai AFB, Thailand, 1975-76, vice comdr. 3d Tactical Fighter Wing Clark Air Base, Philippines, 1976, comdr. 3d Tactical Fighter Wing, 1976-78, comdr. 313th Air div. and 18th Tactical Fighter Wing Kadena Air Base, Japan, 1978-81, dep. chief of staff for ops. Ramstein Air Base, Ger., 1981, asst. chief staff ops. Supreme Hdqrs. Allied Powers, Europe Mons, Belgium, 1981-84, comdr. Allied Air Forces So. Europe, dep. comdr. in chief U.S. Air Forces in Europe Naples, Italy, 1984-86; vice comdr. Langley AFB Tactical Air Command, Va., 1986-88; ret., 1988; dir. aviation programs East Inc., Chantilly, Va., 1991-94, 97—. Decorated D.D.S.M., D.S.S.M., Legion of Merit with oak leaf cluster, Bronze Star medal, Air Medal with four oak leaf clusters, Air Force Commendation medal with oak leaf cluster, Def. Superior Service medal Avocations: golf, bike riding, walking, horseback riding. Home: 1591 Stowe Rd Reston VA 20194-1602 Office Phone: 703-263-0477. E-mail: tfabyanic@eastinc.us.

BROWN, JAMES RUSSELL, III, librarian; b. Charlottesville, Va., May 23, 1947; s. James Russell Jr. and Helen Irene (Elliott) B.; m. Ingrid Veltman (div.); 1 child, Ethan; m. Gail Bonnie Beskin, June 19, 1983. AB in Biology summa cum laude, Boston U., 1968; PhD in Sociology, Boston Coll., 1987; MS in LS, Long Island U., 1992. Cert. pub. libr., N.Y. Lab. technologist R.I.S.T. Labs., East Northport, N.Y., 1977-80, Dianetics Lab., Syosset, N.Y., 1980-87, St. Luke's Hosp., N.Y.C., 1987-90; libr. Glen Cove (N.Y.) Pub. Libr., 1990-95, Shelter Rock Pub. Libr., Albertson, N.Y., 1995—. Local 1199 shop steward St. Lukes Hosp., 1988-90; Teamsters Local 810 shop steward Glen Cove Pub. Libr., 1993-95. Mem. state com. NY State Green Party, 2002—. Tufts U. Latin Am. teaching fellow, Guatemala and Mex., 1972-74. Mem. ALA, N.Y. Libr. Assn., Nassau County Libr. Assn., South Shore Audubon Soc. (bd. dirs. 2005—), Beta Phi Mu (bd. dirs. 1994-98, archivist 1995-99). Avocations: hiking, backpacking. Home: 422 E Market St Long Beach NY 11561-2318 Office: Shelter Rock Pub Libr 165 Searingtown Rd Albertson NY 11507-1521 E-mail: jrb398@yahoo.com.

BROWN, JAMES SHELLY, lawyer; b. Trenton, NJ, May 5, 1945; s. Alexander Aloysius and Madlyn (Shelly) B.; m. Margaret Lee Martin, June 6, 1987; children: Elizabeth Paige, Kristen Blaire. BA, Hoftsra u., 1968; JD, Fordham U., 1972. Bar: NY 1973. Asst. dist. atty. County of NY, NYC, 1972-78; atty. Bower & Gardner, Esqs., 1978—94; ptnr. Wilson, Eiser, Moskowitz, Edelman and Dicker, NYC, 1994—. Hearing officer NYC Off Track Betting Corp., 1978—84. Fellow Am. Coll. Trial Lawyers; mem. NY State Bar Assn., Assn. of Bar of City of NY, Fed. Bar Coun. Avocation: tennis. Home: 31 Old Parish Rd Darien CT 06820-4319 Office: Wilson, Elser, Moskowitz, Edelman & Dicker LLP 23rd Fl 150 E 42nd St New York NY 10017-5639 Office Phone: 212-490-3000 2303. Office Fax: 212-490-3038. E-mail: brownj@wemed.com.

BROWN, JAMES THOMPSON, JR., computer information scientist, logistics specialist; b. Orange, N.J., Jan. 3, 1935; s. James Thompson and Marjorie (Hale) B.; m. Alice Beasley, Oct. 3, 1959; children— Kathryn, James. B.M.E., Cornell U., 1957; M.S., Stanford U., 1964. Applied sci. rep. IBM Corp., Schenectady, N.Y., 1957-59, corp. staff mem., White Plains, N.Y., 1960-68; cons. Case & Co., Stamford, Conn., 1969-74, dir., 1975-83, pres., 1983-84; pres. Tom Browne & Co., Wilton, Conn., 1985—; developer optimum buying and inventory mgmt. sys. and svc. pricing techniques; designer warehouse and distbn. sys. Life mem. Rep. Inner Circle. Mem. Internat. Assn. Chain Stores (adviser, speaker 1971—), Nat. Grocers Assn. (adviser 1983—), Am. Inst. Indsl. Engrs. (sr. mem.), Inst. Ops. Rsch. and Mgmt. Scis., Landmark Club, Cornell Club (N.Y.), Capitol Hill Club. Republican. Home: 135 Middlebrook Farm Rd Wilton CT 06897-2019 Office: Tom Brown & Co PO Box 431 Wilton CT 06897-0431 *One of my guiding principles is not to try to solve a problem until I understand it. Understanding often means getting your hands dirty. And when I do understand, take the time to carefully think out the solution.*

BROWN, JAMES W., gastroenterologist; b. Detroit, May 20, 1938; BS, U. Nebr., 1960; MD, Northwestern U., Chgo., 1964. Diplomate Am. Bd. Internal Medicine, Am. Bd. Internal Medicine in Gastroenterology. Gastroenterologist Wenatchee (Wash.) Valley Clinic, 1970—; chief gastroenterology U.S. Naval Hosp., San Diego. Vice-chmn., bd. dirs. Wenatchee Valley Clinic, 1992-95, chmn., CEO, 1996-2001; bd. dirs. NCW Cmty. Bank, Wenatchee. Contbr. articles to profl. jours. Chmn. bd. dirs. Mustard Seed Neighbor Ctr., Wenatchee, 1990-92, bd. dirs. 1989-95, 2004-. Lt. comdr. USN, 1968-70. Fellow Am. Coll. Gastroenterology; mem. Alpha Omega Alpha. Methodist. Avocations: cooking, hiking, reading, physical fitness, travel, golf.

BROWN, JAMES WARD, mathematician, educator, author; b. Phila., Jan. 15, 1934; s. George Harold and Julia Elizabeth (Ward) B.; m. Jacqueline Read, Sept. 3, 1957; children: Scott Cameron, Gordon Elliot, AB, Harvard U., 1955; AM, U. Mich., 1958, PhD (Inst. Sci and Tech. predoctoral fellow), 1964. Asst. prof. math. U. Mich., Dearborn, 1964-66, assoc. prof., 1968-71, prof., 1971—, acting chmn. dept., 1974, 85. Asst. prof. Oberlin Coll., 1966-68; editorial cons. Math. Rev., 1970-85; dir. NSF Grant, 1969 Author: (with R.V. Churchill) Complex Variables and Applications, 7th edit., 2004, Internat. Student edit., 1996, Japanese edit., 2004, Spanish edit., 2004, Chinese edit., 2005, Korean edit., 1992, Greek edit., 1993, Fourier Series and Boundary Value Problems, 6th edit., 2001, internat. student edit., 1993, Japanese edit., 1980; contbr. articles to U.S. and fgn. sci. jours. Recipient Disting. Faculty award U. Mich.-Dearborn, 1976, Disting. Faculty award Mich. Assn. Governing Bds. Colls. and Univs., 1983 Mem. Am. Math. Soc., Research Club of U. Mich., Sigma Xi. Home: 1710 Morton Ave Ann Arbor MI 48104-4522 Office: 4901 Evergreen Rd Dearborn MI 48128-1491

BROWN, JAN HOWARD, lawyer; b. Bklyn., Nov. 13, 1948; s. Monroe and Ruth B.; m. Deborah Lugo, Sept. 28, 1981 (dec. Feb. 26, 1992); children: Richard, Andrew; m. Elizabeth Jo Spaeth, Mar. 3, 1996. BA, Antioch Coll., 1973; JD, Western New Eng. Coll., 1976. Bar: N.Y. 1978, U.S. Dist. Ct. (so. dist. and ea. dist.) N.Y. 1978. Internat. lectr. U.S. immigration. Contbg. author: Visa Processing Guide, 1998—. Mem. Am. Immigration Lawyers Assn., N.Y. State Bar Assn. (chmn. immigration law com.). Office: Jan H Brown PC 225 W 57th St Ste 400 New York NY 10019 Office Phone: 212-397-2800. E-mail: jhb@janhbrown.com.

BROWN, JANICE ROGERS, federal judge, former state supreme court justice; b. Greenville, Ala., May 11, 1949; m. Allan Brown (dec.); 1 child, Nathan; m. Dewey Parker. BA, Calif. St. U., Sacramento, 1974; JD, UCLA, 1977; LLM, U. Va., 2004. Dep. legis. counsel Calif. Legis. Counsel Bur., 1977—79; dep. atty. gen. Calif. Dept. Justice, 1979—87; deputy sec., gen. counsel Calif. Business, Transportation & Housing Agy., 1987—90; sr. assoc. Nielsen, Merksamer, Parrinello, Mueller & Naylor, Sacramento, 1990—91; legal affairs sec. to Gov. Pete Wilson State of Calif., Sacramento, 1991—94; assoc. justice Calif. Ct. Appeals (3rd dist.), Sacramento, 1994—96, Calif. Supreme Ct., San Francisco, 1996—2005; judge US Ct. Appeals (DC cir.), 2005—. Adj. prof. law U. Pacific, 1998—99. Achievements include being the first African-American woman to serve on the Calif. Supreme Court. Office: US Ct Appeals 333 Constitution Ave NW Washington DC 20001

BROWN, JANINE, lawyer; b. Wheeling, W.Va., Oct. 5, 1961; BA with distinction, Univ. Mich., 1982; JD high honors, Duke Univ., 1986. Bar: Ga. 1986. Ptnr., chair, tech. group Alston & Bird LLP, Atlanta. Named a Ga. Super Lawyer, 2004; named one of the Top 50 Female Super Lawyers., 2004. Office: Alston & Bird LLP One Atlantic Ctr 1201 W Peachtree St NW Atlanta GA 30309-3424 Office Phone: 404-881-7834. Office Fax: 404-881-7777. Business E-Mail: jbrown@alston.com.

BROWN, JARED, theater director, educator, writer; BFA, Ithaca Coll., 1960; MA Theatre, San Francisco State Coll., 1962; PhD Theatre, U. Minn., 1967. Instr. creative writing St. Paul Pub. Sch. System, 1962-63; teaching asst. U. Minn., 1963-64, instr. Communication Dept., 1964-65; from asst. prof. to prof. dept. theatre Western Ill. U., 1965-89, acad. dir. Semester in London, 1979-80; dir. Sch. Theatre Arts, Prof. Theatre Arts Ill. Wesleyan U., 1989—2002; adj. prof. Ill. State U., 2003—. Aided devel. (policies, curriculum), Theatre Dept. Western Ill. U., 1971; panel discussant Western Ill. U., 1973, 1974; chmn. panel Ill. Theatre Assn. Convention, 1976; panel discussant Assn. Theatre in Higher Edn. Convention, 1987; disting. faculty lectr. Western Ill. U., 1986, dir. grad. program dept. theatre, 1975-89, chmn. directing, theatre history and playwriting programs, dept. theatre, 1972-89; mem. panel judges to award NEH Summer Stipends, Ill., 1990; mem. panel to award NEH Fellowship Grants, 2004; judge Am. Coll. Theatre Festival, 1973-74, 89-90; mem. various theatre coms. Ill. Wesleyan U.; mem. various coms. Univ., Coll. Fine Arts, Dept. Theatre Western Ill. U.; spkr., presenter in field. Author: The Fabulous Lunts, A Biography of Alfred Lunt and Lynn Fontanne, 1986, (Barnard Hewitt award 1987), Zero Mostel: A Biography, 1989, The Theatre in America During the Revolution, 1995, Alan J. Pakula: His Films and His Life, 2005, also 11 plays; dir. 100 plays including The Merchant of Venice, Hedda Gabler, Henry IV, La Ronde, Death of a Salesman, Cat on a Hot Tin Roof, A Streetcar Named Desire, Who's Afraid of Virginia Woolf, You Can't Take It With You, Brighton Beach Memoirs, Inherit the Wind, Peter Pan, Bye Bye Birdie, Guys and Dolls, Kiss Me Kate, 110 In The Shade, Annie, Funny Girl, Broadway Bound, Tartuffe, Antigone, She Loves Me, Noises Off, Sight Unseen, Bedroom Farce, Once in a Lifetime; appeared in My Fair Lady, Western Ill. U., 1978, On The Twentieth Century, 1986, Russian Dressing, 2005, various radio and TV programs; contbr. chpts. to texts, 20 scholarly articles to profl. jours. Recipient stipend NEH, 1988, DuPont award for tchg. excellence, 1997; named Best Dir., The Pantagraph, 1991, 92, 94, 96; grantee Ill. Arts Coun., 1980, 81, 87, Western Ill. U., 1983-85, 86-87, 89, Cultural Arts Devel. Fund, 1980-89, Ill. Wesleyan U., 1990, Artistic/Scholarly Devel. grantee, 1999, 2002. Mem. Nat. Collegiate Players, Phi Kappa Phi, Theta Alpha Phi. Home: 18 Chatsford Ct Bloomington IL 61704-6220 Office: Sch Theatre Arts Ill Wesleyan U Bloomington IL 61702 Office Phone: 309-664-0708. E-mail: jbrown@iwu.edu.

BROWN, JASON MARTIN, music educator; b. Dover-Foxcroft, Maine, Nov. 16, 1975; s. Joel Eric and Paula Bea Brown. MusB in Music Edn., U. Maine, 2000. Cert. educator Maine, 2003. Band dir. M.s.a.d. #45, Washburn, Maine, 2000—01; chorus dir., music tchr. M.s.a.d. #64, East Corinth, 2001—02, M.s.a.d. #4, Guilford, 2002—04; band dir. Foxcroft Acad., Dover-Foxcroft, 2004—. Organist United Ch. Christ, Monson, Maine, 2002—. Mem.: MENC. Conservative. Methodist. Avocations: reading, sports, travel. Home: 89 Pleasant St Dover Foxcroft ME 04426 Office: Foxcroft Acad 975 W Main St Dover Foxcroft ME 04426 Office Phone: 207-564-8351. Personal E-mail: brownjaso@yahoo.com. E-mail: jason.brown@foxcroftacademy.org.

BROWN, JASON WALTER, neurologist, educator, researcher; b. N.Y.C., Apr. 14, 1938; s. Samuel Robert and Sylvia (Brown) B.; children: Jonathan Schilder, Jovana Millay; m. Carine Hoeusler; 1 child, Ilya. BA, U. Calif.-Berkeley, 1959; MD, U.S.C., 1963. Intern St. Elizabeth's Hosp., Washington, 1963-64; resident in neurology UCLA, 1964-67; practice medicine specializing in neurology N.Y.C., 1970—; instr. Boston U. Med. Sch., 1969-70; asst. clin. prof. Columbia-Presbyn. Hosp., N.Y.C., 1970-75; vis. asst. prof. neurology Albert Einstein Coll. Medicine, N.Y.C., 1972-75; vis. assoc. prof Rockefeller U., N.Y.C., 1978-79; clin. assoc. prof. neurology NYU, 1975-79, clin. prof., 1979—; pres. Inst. Research in Behavioral Neurosci. Vis. scholar N.Y. Psychoanalytic Inst., 1993—. Author: Aphasia, Apraxia and Agnosia, 1972, Mind, Brain and Consciousness, 1977, Life of the Mind, 1988; editor: Jargonaphasia, 1982; English Translation of Aphasie by Arnold Pick (Aphasia), 1973, Neuropsychology of Visual Perception, 1989, Classics in Neuropsychology: Apraxia and Agnosia, Self and Process, 1991, Time, Will and Mental Process, 1996, Mind and Nature, 2000, The Self-Embodying Mind, 2002; contbr. numerous articles on neurology to med. jours.; mem. editl. bd. Jour. Nervous and Mental Disease, Aphasiology, Advances in Neurolinguistics. Grantee NIH; fellow Alexander von Humboldt Found., 1979—, World Rehab. Fund, 1982, Founds. Fund for Research in Psychiatry, 1974-75. Jewish. Home and Office: 66 E 79th St New York NY 10021-0244 E-mail: drjbrown@hotmail.com.

BROWN, JAY MARSHALL, retired secondary school educator; b. Bklyn., July 26, 1933; s. Sidney and Bertha (Swirsky) Brown; m. Merle Thelma Kaminsky, Nov. 4, 1956; children: Sidney Matthew, Ellen Beth Factor. BS in Journalism, NYU, 1955, MA in Am. Civilization, 1960; postgrad., Yeshiva U., 1958-60, U. Conn., West Hartford, 1968-70; 6th yr. profl. diploma, So. Conn. State Coll., 1977. Pub. rels. dir, asst. credit mgr. Colonial Sand & Stone Co., N.Y.C., 1955-60; employment counselor N.Y.C. Dept. Welfare, 1960-63; attendance tchr. Bd. Edn., N.Y.C., 1963-65; youth dir. Jewish Community Ctr., Rochester, N.Y., 1965-67; exec. dir. Conn. Valley Regional B'nai B'rith

Youth, New Haven, 1967-70; resource tchr. Sheridan Mid. Sch., Bd. Edn., New Haven, 1970-72; learning ctr. tchr. Bd. Edn., New Haven, 1972-74; social studies tchr. Troup Mid. Sch., Bd. Edn., New Haven, 1974-80; history tchr. Hillhouse HS, Bd. Edn., New Haven, 1980-93; ret., 1993. Tchr. U.S. history New Eng. Acad. Jewish Studies, New Haven, 1984—85; specialist audio-visual and media Quinnipiac Coll., Hamden, Conn., 1982. Contbr. articles to profl. jours. Chmn. clear sch. mission com., effective sch. steering com. Hillhouse HS, New Haven, 1984, sch. planning and mgmt. team, 1988—91, coord. teenagers adv. program, 1989—91, faculty senate, 1991—93; acting pres. Alliance Mentally Ill, 1993—94, pres., 1995—; mem. Commn. on Disabilities Town of Hamden, 2001—04, chair Commn. on Disabilities, 2002—03; corr. sec. Jewish Hist. Soc., New Haven, 1980—81; v.p. Regency Hills Condo Assn., 1994—95; active Mental Health Month Com., 1995—99; family resource ctr. com. Consultation Ctr., 1994—98; coord. Mental Health Network Spkrs. Bur., 1996—98; facilitator Journey of Hope Ednl. Program, 2002—04; vice chmn. Regional Mental Health Bd., Catchment Area 7, 1997—2004, chmn., 2004—; rev. and evaluation team State Regional Mental Health Bd. Dist. 2, 1996—2000, vice chmn., 1997—2000, chmn., 2004—; bd. govs. Inst. Learning and Retirement, 1998—2000; coord. New Haven County's Mental Illness Awareness Week, 1998—2003, People Helping People Program, 1998—2003; mem. Hamden Commn. Disability Rights and Obligation, 2001—04; chmn. Hamden Commn. Disability Rights, 2002—03; active Hamden Dem. Town Com., 1974—76; pres. Brotherhood Mishkan Israel, 1976—78, 1983—89, 2001—02, sec., 1997—98, treas., 1998—2001, 2004—; asst. treas. Congregation Mishkan Israel, 1983—84, chmn. budget com., 1987—88, chmn. house and property com., 1979—84, trustee, 1978—84, 1986—92, 1994—2003, libr., archivist, 1981—84, pers. com., 1996—2002, abatement com., 1997—98, ops. com., 1999—2002. Recipient Man of Yr. award of Merit, Congregation Mishkan Israel's Brotherhood, 1978, People Helping People award, Sears and NAMI, 2001. Mem.: New Haven County Ret. Tchrs. Assn. (v.p. 1994—95, sec. 1997—2003), Phi Delta Kappa. Democrat. Jewish. Avocations: stamp collecting/philately, polit. items, sports items, cmty. svc. Home: 25 Wright Ln Hamden CT 06517-2126 Personal E-mail: jay_m_brown@sbcglobal.net, cac7@sbcglobal.net.

BROWN, J.E., lawyer, consultant; b. Dec. 10, 1940; BS, Tex. A&I U., 1963; JD, U. Tex., 1967. Mem. Tex. Senate, 1980—2002; chmn. natural resources com., sunset adv. com., natural resources interim com., water resources devel. com., Gulf States Marine Fisheries Commn., Tex. Water Found. Mem. Criminal Justice Com., So. Legis. Conf. Energy Commn., Am. legis. Exch. Coun. Telecom. Commn., Nat. Conf. State Legis. Comm. and Info. Policy, Legis. and Congl. Redistricting Com., Fin. Com., Nominations Com., Vets. Affairs and Mil. Installations Com., alt. Environ. com., Legal Com. Interstate Oil and Gas Compact Commn.; past chmn. Energy Coun.; adj. prof. U. Tex. Sch. Law. Office Phone: 512-457-0600. Business E-Mail: busterbrown@austin.rr.com.

BROWN, JEAN WILLIAMS, former state supreme court justice; b. Birmingham, Ala. m. E. Terry Brown; 2 children. Grad. with honors, Samford U., 1974; JD, U. Ala., 1977. Bar: Ala. 1977, U.S. Ct. Appeals (11th cir.), U.S. Supreme Ct. Law clerk Tucker, Gray & Thigpen; asst. atty. gen. criminal appeals divsn., chief extradition officer Ala. Atty. Gen.'s Office; judge Ala. Ct. Criminal Appeals, 1997-99; justice Supreme Ct. Ala., 1999—2005. Mem.: Bench and Bar Legal Honor Soc. Office: Ala Supreme Ct 300 Dexter Ave Montgomery AL 36104-3741 Office Phone: 334-221-6488.

BROWN, JEANETTE GRASSELLI, retired director; b. Cleve., Aug. 4, 1928; d. Nicholas W. and Veronica (Varga) Gecsy; m. Glenn R. Brown, Aug. 1, 1987. BS summa cum laude, Ohio U., 1950, DSc (hon.), 1978; MS, Western Res. U., 1958, DSc (hon.), 1995, Clarkson U., 1986; D Engring. (hon.), Mich. Tech. U., 1989; DSc (hon.), Wilson Coll., 1994, Notre Dame Coll., 1995, Kenyon Coll., 1995, Mt. Union Coll., 1996, Cleveland State U., 2000, Kent State U., 2000, Ursuline Coll., 2001; DSc, Youngstown State U., 2003; DSc (hon.), U. Pecs, Hungary, 2002. Project leader, assoc. Infrared Spectroscopist, Cleve., 1950-78; mgr. analytical sci. lab. Standard Oil (name changed to BP Am., Inc. 1985), Cleve., 1978-83, dir. technol. support dept., 1983-85, dir. corp. rsch. and analytical scis., 1985-88; disting. vis. prof., dir. rsch. enhancement Ohio U., Athens, 1989-95; ret., 1995. Bd. dirs. AGA Gas, Inc., USX Corp., McDonald Investments, BDM Internat., BF Goodrich Co., Nicolet Instrument Corp.; mem. bd. on chem. sci. and tech. NRC, 1986-91; chmn. U.S. Nat. Com. to Internat. Union of Pure and Applied Chemistry, 1992-94; mem. joint high level adv. panel U.S.-Japan Sci. and Tech., 1994-2001, Ohio Bd. Regents, 1995—, chmn., 2000-2002; vis. com. Nat. Inst. Stds. and Tech., 1988-91. Author, editor 8 books; editor: Vibrational Spectroscopy; contbr. numerous articles on molecular spectroscopy to profl. jours.; patentee naphthalene extraction process. Bd. dirs. N.E. Ohio Sci. and Engring. Fair, Cleve., Martha Holden Jennings Found., Cleve. Clinic Found., Sci. Svc. Inc.; chair bd. dirs. Cleve. Scholarship Programs, Inc., 1994-2000; trustee Holden Arboretum, Cleve., 1988—, Edison Biotech Ctr., Cleve., 1988-95, Cleve. Playhouse, 1990-96, Garden Ctr. Greater Cleve., 1990-93, Mus. Arts Assn., 1991—, Gt. Lakes Sci. Ctr., 1991—, Rainbow Babies and Children's Hosp., 1992-95, Nat. Inventors' Hall of Fame, 1993—, Ohio U., 1985-94, chmn. 1991-92; chair steering com. Mellen Ctr. Cleve. Clinic, 1996—; chair bd. dirs. ideastream, PBS, NPR. Recipient Disting. Svc. award Cleve. Tech. Soc. Coun., 1985; named Woman of Yr. YWCA, 1980; named to Ohio Women's Hall of Fame State of Ohio, 1989, Ohio Sci. & Tech. Hall of Fame, 1991, Humanitarian award Nat. Conf. Cmty. Justice, 2000, Medal of Honor, Ellis Island, 2002. Mem. Am. Chem. Soc. (chair analytical divsn. 1990-91, Garvan medal 1986, Analytical Chem. award 1993, Encouraging Women into Careers in Sci. award 1999), Soc. for Applied Spectroscopy (pres. 1970, Disting. Svc. award 1983), Coblentz Soc. (bd. govs. 1968-71, William Wright award 1980), Royal Soc. Chemistry (Theophilus Redwood lectr. 1994), Phi Beta Kappa, Iota Sigma Pi (pres. fluorine chpt. 1957-60, nat. hon. mem. 1987). Republican. Roman Catholic. Avocations: swimming, dance, music. Home: 150 Greentree Rd Chagrin Falls OH 44022-2424

BROWN, JEANETTE L., environmental protection administrator; BBA, Morgan State U., 1980; postgrad., Am. U., Washington. Intern Navy Regional Contracting Ctr., Washington, 1978; with Navy Automatic Data Processing Selection Office, Joint Cruise Missile Project/NAV AIR; dep. dir. Office of Small and Disadvantaged Bus. Utilization, EPA, Washington, dep. dir. Office of Acquisition Mgmt., dir. Office of Acquisition Mgmt.; dir. small and disadvantaged bus. EPA, Washington.

BROWN, JEANNETTE ELIZABETH, retired science educator; d. Ada May Fox - Brown and Frederick Brown. BA, Hunter Coll., 1952—56; MSc, U. of Minn., 1956—58. Jr. chemist CIBA Pharm. Co., Summit, NJ, 1958—69; rsch. chemist Merck & Co. Inc., Rahway, NJ, 1969—95; vis. prof. of chemisty NJ. Inst. of Tech., Newark, 1993—95; N.J. Statewide Systemic Initiative coord. N.J. Inst. of Tech., Newark, 1995—98; N.J. statewide systemic initiative regional dir. NJ. Inst. of Tech., Newark, 1998—2002; ednl. cons. Self Employed, Hillsborough, NJ, 2002—. Chmn. Project SEED Com. Am. Chem. Soc., Washington, 1986—88; mem. of com. on equal opportunities in sci. NSF, Washington, 1991—98; mem. Black U. liason com. Merck & Co. Inc., Rahway, NJ, 1978—85. Mem. Cmty. Devel. Corp., Irvington, NJ, 2001—03; coun. mem. NJ. Assn. United Ch. of Christ, Montclair, NJ, 1998—2003; mem. Homesharing Bd., Bridgewater, NJ, 1998—2002. Recipient Women Chemist Com. Regional Award for Diversity, Am. Chem. Soc., 2002, Hunter Coll. Hall of Fame, Hunter Coll. Alumni Assn., 1991, Women in Sci. Videotape, Sch. of Dentistry U. of Mich., 1981; Tchg. Assistantship, U. of Minn., 1956—58, Dreyfus Chemistry Program, Camille and Henry Dreyfus Found., 2000—03. Mem.: AAAS, Am. Chem. Soc. (councilor North Jersey sect. 1982—), NY Acad. of Sci., Assn. for Women in Sci., Nat. Orgn. for Profl. Advancement of Black Chemists and Chem. Engineers, Iota Sigma Pl (life). Protestant United Ch. Of Christ. Achievements include patents for synthesis of 12-Oxo-Trans (E) 10-Dodecanoic acid useful as a plant bioregulant; dipetidase inhibitors; use of pyrollidino ethano as a coccidiostat. Avocations: travel, gardening, exercise, swimming.

BROWN, JEFF, pharmaceutical executive; s. Joseph W. and Helen A. Brown; m. Kristen Brown, July 2, 2004. B Microbiology, U. NH, 1994; MBA, Babson Coll., 1997. Mgr. global sterilization and microbiology systems Haemonetics, Corp., Braintree, Mass., 1995—2000; mgr. worldwide sterilization and microbiology Johnson & Johnson, Norwood, Mass., 2003—. Prin. Sterility Svc. Cons., Mass., 1998—2003. Co. campaign coord. United Way, Norwood, Mass., 2003—04. Vis. scholar Sci. Award scholar, County of Plymouth Mass., 1990; Pell Grant, 1990. Mem.: Assn. Advancement Med. Instrumentation (assoc.), Am. Soc. Microbiology (assoc.), Toastmasters (corr.; sgt. at arms 1999—2000). Achievements include development of first templated sterilization documents in medical device industry. Office: Johnson & Johnson 325 Paramount Dr Raynham MA 02767 E-mail: eop8@yahoo.com.

BROWN, JEFFREY MONET, lawyer; b. Columbus, Ohio, July 4, 1953; s. Charles Ernest Brown and Barbara (Metzler) Dible; m. Rita Zoia, May 9, 1981; 1 child, Jessica Marie. BA, Wittenberg U., 1975; JD, Ohio State U., 1979. Bar: Ohio 1979; U.S. Dist. Ct. (so. dist.) Ohio 1979. Legal intern Columbus Dept. Law, 1978-79; ptnr. Crabbe, Brown, Jones, Potts & Schmidt, Columbus, 1979—, mng. ptnr., 1991—. Mem. devel. commn. City of Columbus, 1990-91; commr. Ohio Supreme Cts. Bd. Commrs. on Grievances and Discipline, 1993-96. Bd. dirs. Rosemont Ctr. for Troubled Youth, Columbus. Mem. ABA, Am. Law Firm Assn., Computer Law Assn., Ohio State Bar Assn., Columbus Bar Assn., U.S. Trademark Assn., Columbus Apt. Assn., Ohio Apt. Assn., Ohio Assn. Civil Trial Attys., Columbus Claims Assn. Avocations: golf, fishing, motorcycling. Office: Crabbe Brown Jones Potts & Schmidt 500 S Front St Ste 1200 Columbus OH 43215-7631 E-mail: JBrown@CBJPS.com.

BROWN, JEREMY EARLE, advertising executive; b. Richmond, Va., Nov. 25, 1946; s. Earle Palmer and Barbara Brown; m. Sally McHugh, Feb. 2; children: Jeremy, Amy, Sarah, Tucker. BA in Drama and Fine Arts, Washington and Lee U., 1969; MBA, Harvard U., 1973. Account exec. Leo Burnett Cos., Chgo., 1973-74; former pres. Earle Palmer Brown, Bethesda, Md.; now chmn., CEO The Earle Palmer Brown Cos., Bethesda, 1974—. Mem. Washington Bd. Trade. Mem. Am. Assn. of Advt. Agys. (bd. dirs.), Young Pres.'s Orgn. (exec. com.), Am. Mgmt. Assn., Phi Gamma Delta. Clubs: Georgetown, The Advertising of Met. Washington (past pres., Silver Medal) (Washington); Columbia Country (Chevy Chase). Address: North Pier 401 E Illinois St # 500 Chicago IL 60611-4363

BROWN, JERRY (EDMUND GERALD BROWN JR.), mayor, former governor; b. San Francisco, Apr. 7, 1938; s. Edmund Gerald and Bernice (Layne) B.; m. Anne B. Gust, June 18, 2005 BA in Latin/Greek, U. Calif., Berkeley, 1961; JD, Yale U., 1964. Bar: Calif. 1965. Research atty. Calif. Supreme Ct., 1964-65; atty. Tuttle & Taylor, Los Angeles, 1966-69; sec. state State Calif., Sacramento, Calif., 1970-74, gov., 1975-83; chmn. Calif. Dem. Party, 1989-90; Dem. candidate for Pres. of United States, 1992; mayor Oakland, Calif., 1999—. Practiced law, LA. Author: (book) Dialogues, 1988. Trustee Los Angeles Community Colls., 1969. Democrat. Office: 1 Frank Ogawa Plz 1 City Hall Plz 3rd Fl Oakland CA 94612 Office Phone: 510-238-3141. Office Fax: 510-238-4731. Business E-Mail: officeofthemayor@oaklandnet.com.*

BROWN, JERRY A., federal bankruptcy judge; b. Detroit, Jan. 31, 1932; m. Florence Freedman; three children. BA, Murray State Univ., 1954; LLB, Tulane U., 1959. Bar: La. 1959, Ky. 1959, U.S. Ct. Appeals (5th cir.) 1960, U.S. Ct. Appeals (11th cir.) 1981, U.S. Dist. Ct. (ea. dist.) La. 1960, U.S. Dist. Ct. (we. dist.) La. 1961, U.S. Dist. Ct. (mid. dist. La.) 1973, U.S. Dist. Ct. (we. dist.) Ky. 1981. Law clk. to Hon. John Minor Wisdom U.S. Ct. Appeals (5th cir.), 1959-60; assoc. Monroe & Lemann, New Orleans, 1960-63, ptnr., 1963-90; spl. counsel Bronfin & Heller, New Orleans, 1991-92; bankruptcy judge U.S. Bankruptcy (ea. dist.) La., New Orleans, 1992—. With U.S. Army, 1954-56. Office: US Bankruptcy Ea Dist 500 Poydras St Rm B-741A New Orleans LA 70130-3319 Office Phone: 504-589-7886.

BROWN, JERRY MILFORD, health products executive; b. Anderson, S.C., Apr. 30, 1938; s. James Milford and Jane Elizabeth (McCord) B.; m. Alice Alberta Thompson, July 30, 1960; children: John Milford, Allen Thompson, James Milford II. BS, Furman U., 1960; MA in Biology, Wake Forest U., 1963, Temple U., 1967; PhD in Physiology, Dental Sch., U. Md., 1972. Commd. lt. U.S. Army, 1960, advanced through grades to lt. col., 1980; rsch. instr. Hahanemann Med. Coll., Phila., 1967-68; sect. leader, exptl. medicine divsn. Biomed. Lab., Edgewood Arsenal, Md., 1967-68; instr. anatomy Med. Sch., U. Md., Balt., 1970-77; sect. leader exptl. medicine divsn. U.S. Army Rsch. Inst. Environ. Medicine, Natick, Mass., 1973-76; dep. dir. U.S. Army Med. Intelligence and Info. Agy., Ft. Detrick, Md., 1976-80; dir. internat. health affairs Dept. Def., Washington, 1980-84; chief plans ops. security 2d Gen. Hosp., Germany, 1984-87; med. coord. Fed. Emer. Mgmt. Agy., Washington, 1987-90; nat. disaster med. system staff, bd. govs. Nat. Coun. Internat. Health, 1980-90; cons. and spl. asst. to the pres. Bio Tech. Gen. Corp., Iselin, N.J., 1991-99; pres., chief oper. officer NeuroSurg. Internat., 1995—; v.p., chief oper. officer M/D Frontiers, Springfield, Va., 1990—; pres. Automated Med. Products, Inc., Springfield, Va., 1990—; pres. CEO Automated Med. Products Corp., 1997—; mgr. Precision Med. Manufacturing L.L.C., Wheeling, Ill., 2002—. V.p. Automated Systems, 1991—; assoc. dir. rsch. nat. study ctr. trauma and emer. medicine U. Md.; U.S. mem. Internat. Com. Mil. Medicine and Pharmacy, 1981-87, U.S. mil. mem. Joint Civil/Mil. Med. Working Group U.S., NATO, 1981—; mem. program planning com. Internat. Assembly Emer. Med. Svcs., Balt., 1984; congress lobbyist; cons. in field. Contbr. articles to med. jours.; pub. books in field of philately. Commr. Explorer Scouts, Natick, Mass., 1975-76; trustee Cardinal Spellman Philatlic Mus., Weston, Mass., 1980-97. Decorated Meritorious Svc. medal with oak leaf clusters, Legion of Merit; recipient gold medal, Res. Officers Assn., 1960. Mem. Electron Microscopy Soc. Am., Am. Stamp Dealers Assn., Ctrl. Atlantic Stamp Dealers Assn. (pres. 1977-81), Rsch. and Engring. Soc. Am., Balt. Philatelic Soc., Sigma Alpha Epsilon, Sigma Xi. Republican. Baptist. Office Phone: 732-602-7717. Personal E-mail: btgc@mindspring.com. E-mail: jbrown@automatedmedproducts.com.

BROWN, JESSICA, music educator; b. Urbana, N.Y., Mar. 2, 1979; d. Laurence Arthur and Hope Cook; m. Joseph Lee Brown, June 2, 2001. MusB in Edn., Taylor U., 2000; MusM in Performance, Ball State U., 2002. Cert. music tchr. N.Y. State Bd. of Edn., 2002, Ind. Bd. of Edn., 2000. Music tchr. Big Flats Elem. Sch., Big Flats, NY, 2002—; pvt. piano tchr. Savona, NY, 1999—. Ch. musician Victory Highway Ch., Painted Post, NY, 2002—. Missionary World Gospel Mission, Horseheads, NY, 2002—03. Mem.: Music Teachers Nat. Assn. (treas. 2001—02), Music Educators Nat. Conf., Phi Delta Kappa. Avocations: backpacking, gardening, cooking, quilting, animals. Home: 57 W Lamoka Ave Horseheads NY 14879 Office: Big Flats Elementary Sch 543 Maple St Big Flats NY 14814 Personal E-mail: jessicabrown21@juno.com.

BROWN, JIM (JAMES NATHANIEL BROWN), community activist, actor, retired professional football player; b. St. Simon's Island, Ga., Feb. 17, 1936; s. Swinton and Theresa B.; m. Sue Jones, 1958 (div. 1972); children: Kim and Kevin (twins), Jim; m. Monique Gunthrop, 1997. BA, Syracuse U., 1957. Fullback Cleve. Browns Profl. Football Team, 1957-65; founder Negro Industrial Economic Union (now Black Economic Union), 1965—, Vital Issues, 1986—, Amer-I-can, 1989—; spl. con. Cleve. Browns, 1993—. Mem. Commn. on the Status of African Am. Males, 1994. Actor: (films) Rio Conchos, 1964, The Dirty Dozen, 1967, The Mercenaries, 1968, Ice Station Zebra, 1969, The Split, 1968, Riot, 1969, 100 Rifles, 1969, ...tick...tick...tick..., 1970, The Grasshopper, 1970, El Condor, 1970, Kenner, 1971, Superbug, 1971, Slaughter, 1972, Black Gunn, 1972, Slaughter's Big Rip-off, 1973, I Escaped from Devil's Island, 1973, The Slams, 1973, Three the Hard Way, 1974, Take a Hard Ride, 1975, Adios Amigo, 1976, Gus, 1976, I Will, I Will ... For Now, 1976, Kid Vengeance, 1977, Fingers, 1977, The Wild One, 1977, One Down, Two to Go, 1982, The Running Man, 1987, I'm Gonna Git You Sucka, 1988, L.A. Heat, 1989, Crack House, 1989, Killing American Style, 1990, Twisted Justice, 1990, The Divine Enforcer, 1991, Original Gangstas, 1996, Mars Attacks!, 1996, He Got Game, 1998, Small Soldiers (voice), 1998, Any Given Sunday, 1999, On the Edge, 2002, She Hate Me, 2004, Animal, 2005; (TV movies) Lady Blue, 1985, Hammer, Slammer & Slade, 1990, Sucker Free City, 2004; (TV appearances) I Spy, 1967, Police Story, 1977, CHiPs, 1979, 1983, T.J. Hooker, 1983, 1984, Knight Rider, 1984, The A-Team, 1986, Highway to Heaven, 1988, Good Sports, 1991, Between Brothers, 1998, Arli$$, 2000, Soul Food, 2004; actor, prodr. Pacific Inferno, 1979; exec. prodr. Richard Pryor Here and Now, 1983; author: Off My Chest, 1964, Out of Bounds, 1989. Founder Black Economic Union. Recipient numerous Nat. Football League awards including Rookie of the Year, 1958, Player of Year, 1959, 64, Jim Thorpe Trophy, 1959, Back of the Decade, 1960; Hickock Belt as Profl. Athlete of Yr., 1964; named to Pro Bowl 1958-65; recipient Bert Bell Memorial Award, 1964; named to Pro Football Hall of Fame, 1971, Coll. Football Hall of Fame, 1995; named Player of the Century, Sports Illustrated, 1999.*

BROWN, JOBETH GOODE, food products executive, lawyer; b. Oakdale, La., Sept. 15, 1950; d. Samuel C. Goode and Elizabeth E. (Twiner) Baker; m. H. William Brown, Aug. 4, 1973; 1 child, Kevin William. BA, Newcomb Coll. Tulane U., 1972; JD, Wash. U., 1979. Assoc. Coburn, Croft & Putzell, St. Louis, 1979-80; staff atty. Anheuser-Busch Cos. Inc., St. Louis, 1980-81, exec. asst. to v.p. sec., 1982-83, asst. sec., 1983-89, sec., v.p., 1989—. Trustee Anheuser-Busch Found., St. Louis, 1989—, Girls, Inc. of St. Louis; bd. dirs. Met. Assn. Philanthropy. Mem. ABA, Mo. Women's Forum, Mo. Bar Assn., Bar Assn. Met. St. Louis, Am. Soc. Corp. Secs. (pres. 1992), Algonquin Golf Club, Order of Coif. Republican. Presbyterian. Office: Anheuser-Busch Cos Inc 1 Busch Pl 202-6 Saint Louis MO 63118-1852

BROWN, JOE BLACKBURN, judge; b. Louisville, Dec. 9, 1940; s. Knox and Miriam (Blackburn) B.; m. Marilyn McGowen, Aug. 10, 1963; children: Jennifer Knox, Michael McGowen. BA cum laude, Vanderbilt U., 1962, JD, 1965. Bar: Ky. 1965, Tenn. 1972, U.S. Supreme Ct. 1979. Asst. U.S. atty. Dept. Justice, Nashville, 1971-73, 1st asst. U.S. atty., 1974-81, U.S. atty., 1981-91, spl. asst. U.S. trustee, 1991-98; U.S. magistrate judge, U.S. Dist. Ct. (mid. dist.) Tenn., Nashville, 1998—. Lectr. law Atty. Gen.'s Advocacy Inst., 1982—; vice chmn. Atty. Gen.'s Adv. Com., 1986-87, chmn. subcom. on sentencing guidelines, mem. subcom. on budget and office mgmt., 1982-91; instr. math. and bus. law Augusta (Ga.) Coll., 1966-69; instr. law Nashville Sch. Law, 1999—. Contbr. articles to legal jours. Bd. dirs. Mid-Cumberland Drug Abuse Coun., Nashville, 1977-86; asst. scoutmastr Boy Scouts Am.; vestryman St. David's Episcopal Ch., sr. warden, 1982, 90; ch. atty. Episcopal Diocese of Tenn., 1995-98; lt. col. CAP, 1996—. Maj. U.S. Army, 1965-71; col. JAGC, USAR ret. Decorated Legion of Merit, Meritorious Svc. medal with 3 oak leaf clusters; recipient Disting. Svc. award Atty. Gen.'s Adv. Com., 1988. Fellow Tenn. Bar Assn., Nashville Bar Found.; mem. FBA (treas. 1978), Nashville Bar Assn. (bd. dirs. 1995-97, exec. com. 1996-97, v.p. 1997, bd. dirs. 2004—), Radio Amateur Transmitting Soc. (pres. 1997-98), Nat. Assn. Flight Instrs., Profl. Assn. Div Instrs., Ky. Bar Assn., NRA (life, Disting. Riflemen award), Harry Phillip Inn of Ct. (master of bench and bar 1994—), Order of Coif, Phi Beta Kappa. Republican. Home: 3427 Woodmont Blvd Nashville TN 37215-1421 Office: US Courthouse Rm 797 801 Broadway Nashville TN 37203-3816 Business E-Mail: joe_b_brown@tnmd.uscourts.gov.

BROWN, JOHN B., III, former federal agency administrator; married; 2 children. BA, SUNY, Brockport, 1968. Spl. agt. Bur. Narcotics and Dangerous Drugs, 1972—84, DEA, Mexico, 1984—88, group supr. Miami, Fla., group supr. Caribbean enforcemend group, inspector and gen. inspector, deciding ofcl. for disciplinary matters, 1995—97; dor. El Paso Intelligence Ctr., Tex., 1997—2002; deputy adminstr. DEA, U.S. Dept. Justice, Alexandria, Va., 2002—03, acting adminstr., 2003.

BROWN, JOHN HOWARD, economics educator; b. Warren, Ohio, Feb. 4, 1952; s. Howard Graham and Mary Elizabeth (Longfellow) B.; m. Joan Ellen Broome, Dec. 14, 1978; 1 child, Paul Joseph. BA, Buchtel Coll. Arts & Scis., 1978, MA, 1982; PhD in Econs., Mich. State U., 1989. Vis. instr. U. Akron, Ohio, 1983-84, Albion (Mich.) Coll., 1987-88; vis. lectr. Mich. State U., East Lansing, 1988-89; asst. prof. econs. U. Nev., Las Vegas, 1989-94, Ga. So. U., Statesboro, 1994—. Mem. 3d World Cliometric Congress, Munich, 1997; sec. gen. transp. and pub. utilities group AEA, 2001—. Mem. editl. bd.: Rev. Indsl. Orgn., 2004—; contbr. articles to profl. jours. Bus. and econs. fellow U. Pitts., Czech Republic, 1993. Mem. Am. Econ. Assn., Indsl. Orgn. Soc., Am. Law and Econs. Assn. (presenter ann. meetings 1999), Cliometric Soc. Avocation: golf. Office: Ga So Univ Sch Econ Devel PO Box 8152 Statesboro GA 30460 Office Phone: 912-681-0896. Business E-Mail: jbrown@georgiasouthern.edu.

BROWN, JOHN LAWRENCE, JR., eletrical engineering educator; b. Ellenville, N.Y., Mar. 6, 1925; s. John Lawrence and Grace Evelyn Brown; m. Marjorie Anne Schnelle, June 15, 1957 (div. Mar. 1969). BS, Ohio U., 1948; PhD, Brown U., 1953. Asst. prof. Pa. State U., State College, 1951-53, assoc. prof., 1953-60, prof. engring. rsch., 1960-69, prof. elec. engring., 1969-88, prof. emeritus, 1988—. Stocker vis. prof. Ohio U., Athens, Ohio, 1988-90. Author numerous papers in profl. jours. With U.S. Army, 1943-46, Prince vis. fellow Ariz. State U., Phoenix, 1982-83, Gen. Lew Allen Rsch. Chair Air Force Inst. Tech., Dayton, Ohio, 1984-85. Fellow IEEE (life); mem. Math. Assn. Am., Acoustical Soc. Am. Avocations: tennis, book collecting. Home: 1431 Curtin St State College PA 16803-3020 Office Phone: 814-865-2212. Business E-Mail: jlb6@psu.edu.

BROWN, JOHN LOTT, former university president, retired educator; b. Phila., Dec. 3, 1924; s. John Lott and Carolyn Emma (Francis) B.; m. Catharine Hertfelder, June 11, 1948; children: Patricia Carolyn, Judith Elliott, Anderson Graham, Barbara Smith. BSEE, Worcester (Mass.) Poly. Inst., 1945, DSc (hon.), 1984; MA, Temple U., 1949; PhD, Columbia U., 1952. Personnel tng. and personnel mgr. Olney foundry Link-Belt Co., Phila., 1948-50; tech. dir. air force contract, dept. psychology Columbia U., 1952-54; head psychology div., aviation med. lab. Naval Air Devel. Ctr., Johnsville, Pa., 1954-59; dir. grad. tng. program physiology, 1962-65; asst., then asso. prof. physiology U. Pa. Med. Sch., 1955-65; prof. physiology and psychology Kans. State U., 1965-69; dean Grad. Sch., 1965-66, v.p. acad. affairs, 1966-69; prof. optics and psychology, dir. center visual sci. U. Rochester, N.Y., 1969-78; pres. U. South Fla., Tampa, 1978-88, prof. psychology, physiology and opthalmology, 1978-92, prof. indsl. engring., 1988-92, interim dir. Ctr. for Microelectronic Rsch., 1993-94, pres. emeritus, 1988—; interim pres. Worcester Poly. Inst., 1994-95. Chmn. com. vision NRC-Nat. Acad. Scis., 1965-70; chmn. vision rsch. program com. Nat. Eye Inst., 1975-78; trustee Worcester Poly. Inst., 1970-83, mem. alumni coun., 1975-76; trustee Illuminating Engring. Rsch. Inst., 1974-79; mem. U.S. nat. com. Internat. Commn. Optics, 1977. Author chpts. in books, also monographs, articles, 1953—; cons. editor: Perception and Psychophysics, 1972-90; editorial adv. bd.: Vision Research, 1971-77. Bd. dirs. Pub. Broadcasting Svc., 1980-83, Mid-Am. Inst. Profl. Devel., 1980-82, Fla. Gulf Symphony, 1979-81, Tampa Gen. Hosp. Found., 1980-81, Smith-Kettlewell Eye Rsch. Inst., 1991-97; mem. Fla. Council 100, 1978-88; mem. corp. bd. Tampa Performing Arts Hall, 1980-88; chmn. Tampa Bay Area R&D Authority, 1979-86, Tampa Bay Area Fgn. Affairs Com., 1979-92; chmn. bd. dirs. H. Lee Moffitt Cancer Ctr. and Rsch. Inst., 1984-88, Exec. Svc. Corp. of Tampa Bay, 1989-97, pres., 1994. With USNR, 1943-46, comdr., 1947-69. Recipient Research Career Devel. award NIH, 1961-62, Robert Goddard award Worcester Poly. Inst., 1969; sr. research fellow USPHS, 1959-61; grantee NIH; grantee NSF; grantee Office Naval Research; grantee Nat. Eye Inst.; grantee NIMH; grantee NASA. Fellow Optical Soc. Am. (exec. coun. Rochester chpt. 1975-76, assoc. editor jour. 1972-77), Am. Psychol. Assn., AAAS; mem. Assn. Rsch. Vision and Ophthalmology (pres. 1978), Soc. Neurosci., Psychonomic Soc., Fla. Assn. Colls. and Univs. (pres. 1988-89), Sigma Xi, Tau Beta Pi, Psi Chi, Phi Eta Sigma, Phi Kappa Phi, Omicron Delta Kappa, Phi Gamma Delta. Mem. Soc. Of Friends. Home: 105 Kendal Dr Oberlin OH 44074-1905 Personal E-mail: jlottb@aol.com.

BROWN, JOHN PATRICK, publishing executive, financial consultant; b. N.Y.C., Oct. 14, 1925; s. Patrick and Emma A (McCarrick) B.; m. Caroline T. Hopkins, Oct. 17, 1959 (dec. Nov. 2002); children: John Patrick, Anne B. Loftus. BBA, St. John's U., Jamaica, N.Y., 1949; MBA, N.Y.U., 1960. C.P.A., N.Y. Accountant Arthur Young & Co., C.P.A.s, N.Y.C., 1950-58; asst. treas. Paramount Pictures Corp., 1962-65; controller, treas. Washington Star, 1966-76; v.p. fin., treas. Bergen Evening Record Corp., N.J., 1976-82; dir. fin. and adminstrn. Washington Times, 1982-88. Adj. prof. acctg. Am. U., U. Va., Va. Tech. Served with AUS, 1944-46. Mem. AICPA, Fin. Execs. Inst., Internat. Newspaper Fin. Execs. Clubs: Metropolitan (Washington). Roman Catholic. Home and Office: 4230 Embassy Park Dr NW Washington DC 20016-3619

BROWN, JOHN WILFORD, health products executive; b. Paris, Tenn., Sept. 15, 1934; s. Albert T. and Treva (Moody) B.; m. Rosemary Kopel, June 7, 1957; children: Sarah Beth, Janine. BSChemE, Auburn U., 1957. Process engr. Ormet Corp., Hannibal, Ohio, 1958-62; sr. engr. Thiokol Chem. Corp., Marshall, Tex., 1962-65; with Squibb Corp., Princeton, NJ, 1965-72, asst. to pres., 1970-72; pres. Edward Weck & Co. divsn. Squibb Corp., NYC, 1972-77; chmn. bd. dirs. Stryker Corp., Kalamazoo, 1979—, pres., CEO, 1979—2003. Mem. Am. Chem. Soc., Health Industries Mfg. Assn. (bd. dirs.). Democrat. Mem. Ch. of Christ. Office: Stryker Corp 2725 Fairfield Ave Kalamazoo MI 49048-2605

BROWN, JOHN Y., III, former state official; BA in History magna cum laude, Bellarmine Coll., Louisville, Ky., 1988; JD with distinction, U. Ky. Coll. Law, Lexington, 1992. Summer assoc. Stoll, Keenon & Park Law Firm, Lexington, Ky., 1990, Brown, Todd & Heyburn Law Firm, Louisville, 1991; dir. franchising Roasters Franchise Corp., Fort Lauderdale, Fla., 1992-94; sec. of state Commonwealth of Ky., Frankfort, 1996—2003. Grad. asst. Dale Carnegie Tng., 1987-92. Mem. ABA, Ky. Bar Assn. Democrat.

BROWN, JONATHAN, art historian, art educator; b. Springfield, Mass., July 15, 1939; s. Leonard Melvin and Jeanette (Levy) B.; m. Sandra Backer, July 22, 1966; children: Claire, Michael, Daniel. AB, Dartmouth Coll., 1960; M.F.A., Princeton U., 1963, PhD, 1964; MA (hon.), Oxford U., 1981. Mem. faculty Princeton, 1965-73, asso. prof. art and archaeology, 1971-73; asso. prof. art NYU, 1973-75, prof., 1976-84, Carroll and Milton Petrie prof., 1984—; dir. Inst. Fine Arts, 1973-78; Slade prof. fine arts Oxford (Eng.) U., 1981-82. Vis. mem. Inst. Advanced Study, Princeton, N.J., 1978-79; adv. com. dept. European paintings Met. Mus. Art, 1974-79; adv. bd. Master Drawings jour.; bd. dirs. Fundacion Duques de Soria, 1990—; curator Am. Philos. Soc., 1992-98, Velazquez in New York Museums, 1999, Los siglos de oro en los virreinatos de America, 1550-1700, 1999, Velazquez, Rubens, Van Dyck: Pintores Cortesanos del Siglo XVII, 1999, El Greco: Themes and Variations, 2001, (with Sir John Elliott) La almoneda del siglo, 2002, Princeton U. Art Mus., The Frick Collection; Andrew W. Mellon lectr. in fine arts Nat. Gallery of Art, 1994; mem. adv. com. Mus. del Prado. Author: Prints and Drawings by Jusepe de Ribera, 1973, Zurbaran, 1973, Murillo and His Drawings, 1976, Images and Ideas in Seventeenth Century Spanish Painting, 1978, A Palace for a King: The Buen Retiro and the Court of Philip IV, 1980; (with J.H. Elliott) also articles on Spanish art, (with others) El Greco of Toledo, 1982, Velazquez, Painter and Courtier, 1986, (with R.G. Mann) Spanish Paintings of the Fifteenth through Nineteenth Centuries, National Gallery of Art, 1990, The Golden Age of Painting in Spain, 1991, Kings and Connoisseurs: Collecting Art in 17th Century Europe, 1995, (with C. Garrido) Velázquez. The Technique of Genius, 1998, Painting in Spain, 1500-1700, 1998; editor: Picasso and the Spanish Tradition, 1996, Franklin and Condorcet: Two Portraits from the American Philosophical Society, 1997, Velázquez, Rubens y Van Dyck, 1999; co-editor: Sources and Documents in the History of Art: Italy and Spain 1600-1750, 1970, Los siglos de oro en los virreinatos de América, The Sale of the Century, 2002. Recipient Medalla de Oro de Bellas Artes, Gov. of Spain, 1986; Fulbright fellow, 1964-65; Am. Council Learned Socs. fellow, 1968-69; Nat. Endowment Humanities fellow, 1978-79; Guggenheim fellow, 1980-81; Order of Isabel la Catolica, 1986, Gran Cruz de Alfonso X el Sabio, 1996, Premio Elio Antonio Nebrija U. de Salamanca, 1997. Mem. AAAS, Coll. Art Assn. Am. (Arthur Kingsley Porter prize 1971), Hispanic Soc. Am. (corr.), Am. Philos. Soc., Real Academia de Bellas Artes (Madrid, corr., Valencia, corr.). Home: 71 Battle Rd Princeton NJ 08540-4945 Office: 1 E 78th St New York NY 10021-0119

BROWN, JOSEPH W., JR., (JAY BROWN), insurance company executive; Grad. in Probability and Stats., Northern Ill. U., 1974. Pres., CEO Fireman's Fund Ins. Co., 1975-92; chmn., pres., CEO Talegen Holdings, Inc., 1992-98; chmn., CEO MBIA Inc., 1998—2004, dir., 1986—, chmn., 2004—. Bd. dir. Safeco Corp., Oxford Health Plan. Fellow: Property Casualty Acturial Soc.; mem.: Soc. of Chartered Property and Casualty Underwriters, Am. Acad. of Actuaries. Office: MBIA Ins Inc 113 King St Ste 1 Armonk NY 10504-1610*

BROWN, JOSEPH WENTLING, lawyer; b. Norfolk, Va., July 31, 1941; s. Edwin Wallace and Nancy Jack (Wentling) B.; m. Pamela Jones, Aug. 18, 1966; children: Tyree, Palmer, Jeffrey, Hunter. BA, U. Va., 1965; LLB, Washington and Lee U., 1968. Bar: Nev. 1969, D.C. 1976, U.S. Dist. Ct. Nev. 1969. Pres. Jones Vargas Law Firm, Las Vegas, 1997—. Commr. Nev. Dept. of Wildlife, 1979-85, Nev. Athletic Commn., 2003-; mem. U.S. Fgn. Claims Settlement Commn., 1981-87; bd. dirs. State Justice Inst., 1988-89; mem. Bd. of Litigation, Mountain States Legal Found., 1978-82. Editor: Washington and Lee Lawyer, 1967-68. Bd. dirs. Nev. Devel. Authority, Las Vegas C. of C., Nev. Cath. Cmty. Svcs., Wells Fargo Bank, Nev.; dep. counsel Rep. Nat. Conv., 1984; mem. Rep. Nat. Com., 2002—. Served with USMCR, 1963-69. Mem. ABA, ATLA, Nev. Bar Assn., Clark County Bar Assn., Spanish Trail Country Club, Rotary. Republican. Roman Catholic. Home: 8 Tapadero Ln Las Vegas NV 89135 Office: Jones Vargas 3773 Howard Hughes Pkwy Suite 300 S Las Vegas NV 89109 Office Phone: 702-862-3300. Business E-Mail: jnb@jonesvargas.com.

BROWN, JOSEPH WILLIAM, retired lawyer; b. Evanston, Wyo., Sept. 19, 1919; s. James Jr. and Mary (Duncombe) Brown. BS, U. Wyo., 1943, JD, 1947. Bar: (Patent) 1947. Patent agt. Shell Devel., Calif., 1946-54, mgr. polymer divsn., 1954-72, mgr. patents Houston, 1972-80, ret., 1980. Capt. U.S. Army, 1944—46. Home: 698 E 2320 N Provo UT 84604-1749

BROWN, JOY ALICE, social services administrator; b. Redmesa, Colo., Mar. 19, 1917; d. Ezra E. and Alice M. (Pinkerton) Walker; m. Clayton Henry Brown, Apr. 9, 1941; children: Kimleigh Clayton, Loraleigh Joy. BA, Highlands U., 1958; MA, U. No. Colo., 1967, EdD, 1970. Tchr. La Plata County, Colo., 1936-41; prin. Bayfield (Colo.) pub. schs., 1942-46; tchr. Aztec (N.Mex.) pub. schs., 1946-63; spl. edn. coordinator primary schs. Palmer, Alaska, 1963-67; lab. sch. supr. U. No. Colo., 1967-70; assoc. prof. edn. N.Mex. State U., 1970-75; dir. Open Door Center, Las Cruces, N.Mex., 1975—. Cons. Tex. Edn. Service Center, Roswell (N.Mex.) schs.; sec. Dona Ana Human Services Consortium, 1977. Contbr. articles on edn. to profl. jours. Recipient Community Service award Las Cruces Eastside Center, 1972; Outstanding Contribution award N.Mex. Council of Exceptional Children, 1977. Mem. NEA, Council for Exceptional Children, Nat. Assn. Retarded Citizens, Phi Delta Kappa. Home: 34081 Country Rd M Mancos CO 81328

BROWN, JOYCE F., academic administrator; b. N.Y.C., July 7, 1946; d. Robert E. and Joyce Cappie Brown; m. H. Carl McCall, Aug. 13, 1983. BA, Marymount Coll., 1968; MA, NYU, 1971, PhD, 1980. From vice chancellor to prof. emeritus CUNY, 1983—98, prof. emeritus, 1998—. Dep. mayor pub. and cmty. affairs, N.Y.C., 1990; pres. Fashion Inst. Tech. SUNY, 1998—; bd. dirs. Polo Ralph Lauren. Dir. N.Y.C. Outward Bound Ctrl. Pk. Conservancy, women's com., Paxar Corp.; trustee Marymount Coll.; dir. Boys Harbor Inc., 1987—. Office: Fashion Inst Tech Seventh Ave at 27th St New York NY 10001-5992

BROWN, JUDITH, academic administrator; BA, U. Calif., Berkeley, 1968, MA, 1971; PhD in History, Johns Hopkins U., 1977. Asst. prof. history U. Md., Balt. County, 1977—82, Stanford U., Palo Alto, Calif., 1982—92, prof., 1991—95; Allyn and Gladys Cline prof. history, dean Sch. Humanities Rice U., Houston, 1995—2001; v.p. acad. affairs, provost Wesleyan U., Middletown, Conn., 2001—. Author: In the Shadow of Florence: Provincial Society in Renaissance Pescia, 1982, Immodest Acts: The Life of a Lesbian Nun in Renaissance Italy, 1986. Office: Wesleyan U 3d Fl North Coll 237 High St Middletown CT 06459

BROWN, JUDITH OLANS, lawyer, educator; b. Boston, May 29, 1941; d. Sidney and Evelyn R. (Lefkovitz) Olans; m. James K. Brown, Oct. 5, 1969. AB magna cum laude with distinction, Mt. Holyoke Coll., 1962; LL.B. cum laude, Boston Coll., 1965. Bar: Mass. 1965. Law clk. Supreme Jud. Ct., 1965-66; assoc. Foley, Hoag and Eliot, Boston, 1966-69; chief counsel Mass. Dept. Community Affairs, Boston, 1969-70; atty. adv. Office of Regional Counsel, HUD, Boston, 1970, asst. regional counsel, 1971, assoc. regional counsel, 1971-72; instr. Boston U. Law Sch., 1971, Northeastern U. Sch. Law, Boston, 1972, assoc. prof., 1972-75, prof., 1975-98, prof. emerita, 1998—. Vis. prof. Law Sch., Boston Coll., 1992. Contbr. articles to legal jours.; article and book rev. editor: Boston Coll. Indsl. and Comml. Law Rev., 1964-65. Mem. steering com. Lawyers Com. for Civil Rights under Law (emeritus); trustee Kimball Union Acad.1993-2003. Loeb fellow, 1972—73. Mem.: Order of Coif, Phi Beta Kappa. Home: PO Box 82 Plainfield NH 03781-0082 E-mail: jbrown@fcgnetworks.net.

BROWN, JULIE KATHARINE, social historian, photographic historian; d. Robert F. and Margaret (Hahn) McGraw; m. John Paul Brown, 1968; children: Margaret Ellen, Paul Francis. BA, Boston Coll., 1962; MA, U. Rochester, 1966; PhD, U. Queensland, Brisbane, Australia, 1985. Cert. tchr. NY. Post doctoral fellow dept art and art history U. Rochester, NY, 1989—90; resident scholar/visitor program/sr. rsch. fellow Smithsonian Instn., Washington, 1991—; fellow NEH, 1994—95; rsch. fellow Mo. Hist. Soc., St Louis, 2002; fellow Smithsonian Instn. Ctr. for Edn. and Mus. Studies, Washington, 2002—. Author: Making Culture Visible: The Public Display of Photography at Fairs, Expositions and Exhibitions in the United States, 1847-1900. Amsterdam: Gordon & Breach, 2001, Contesting Images: Photography and the World's Columbian Exposition, 1984, J. K. Brown and Margaret Maynard. Fine Art Exhibitions in Brisbane 1884-1916, 1980, Recovering Representations: Health Exhibits and Sites of Health at Internat. Expositions in the US, 1876-1904. Pisano scholar, NIH Mus., Bethesda, Md., 2002, Huntington Libr. fellow, San Marino, Calif., 2005. Personal E-mail: jkbrown@aol.com.

BROWN, JUNE EVELYN, librarian, documentalist; b. Ipswich, Suffolk, Eng., June 29, 1925; came to U.S., 1946; d. Frederick George and Evelyn Claudia (Barker) Laws; m. Ronald Martin Brown, Apr. 14, 1945 (dec. Aug. 1980); children: Erica Karen, Diane Rosemary. Nat. diploma design, Leicester (Eng.) Coll. Arts and Tech., 1944; BA, Alfred U., 1969; MLS, SUNY, Geneseo, 1970. Libr. asst. Herrick Libr. Alfred (N.Y.) U., 1960-69, acquisitions libr., 1969-77, univ. libr., 1977-87; Peace Corps vol., documentalist Ministry Econ. Devel., Tourism and Energy, St. John's, Antigua and Barbuda, 1987-89. Libr. trustee, So. Tier Libr. System, N.Y., 1989-96. Contbr. articles on libr. acquisitions, binding procedures and children's lit. to profl. jours. U.S. Dept. Edn. fellow, 1969. Mem. ALA, Nat. Libr. Assn., Libr. Assn. Antigua and Barbuda, N.Y. Libr. Assn., Antigua Artists Soc. (sec. 1987-89). Republican. Episcopalian. Avocations: painting, gardening, travel. Home: 30 Sayles St Alfred NY 14802-1324

BROWN, JUNE GIBBS, retired government official; b. Cleve., Oct. 5, 1933; d. Thomas D. and Lorna M. Gibbs; children: Ellen Rosenthal, Linda Windsor, Victor Janezic, Carol Janezic. BBA summa cum laude, Cleve. State U., 1971, MBA, 1972; postgrad., Cleve. Marshall Law Sch., 1973-74; JD, U. Denver, 1978; postgrad. Advanced Mgmt. Program, Harvard U., 1983. Cert. govt. fin. mgr., 1995; CPA, Ohio. Real estate broker, officer mgr. N.E. Realty, Cleve., 1963-68; staff acct. Frank T. Cicirelli, C.P.A., Cleve., 1970-71; asst. to comptr. S.M. Hexter Co., Cleve., 1971; grad. tchg. fellow Cleve. State U., 1971-72; dir. internal audit Navy Fin. Ctr., Cleve., 1972-75; dir. fin. sys. design Bur. of Land Mgmt., Denver, 1975-76; project mgr. Bur. of Reclamation, 1976-79; insp. gen. Dept. Interior, Washington, 1979-81, NASA, Washington, 1981-85; v.p. fin. and adminstrn. Sys. Devel. Corp., a Burroughs Co., 1985-86; assoc. adminstr. for mgmt. NASA, 1986-87; insp. gen. U.S. Dept. Def., Arlington, Va., 1987-90; dep. insp. gen. USN-CINCPACFLT, 1990; insp. gen. USN Pacific Fleet, Pearl Harbor, Hawaii, 1991-93, HHS, Washington, 1993-2001; inspector gen. HHS, SSA, Washington, 1995-96; ret., 2001. Bd. dirs. Fed. Law Enforcement Tng. Ctr., 1984-85, Interagy. Auditor Tng. program Dept. Agr. Grad. Sch., 1983-85; chmn. interagy. com. on Info. Resource Mgmt., 1984-85; mem. bd. advisors Nat. Contract Mgmt. Assn., 1987-89, NSF, 2002-; mem. Pres.'s Coun. on Integrity and Efficiency, 1993-2001, vice chair, 1994-97, 1998-2001, rep. Nat. Intergovtl. Audit Forum, 1994-98; bd. dirs. Insps. Gen. Auditor Tng. Inst. Mem. bd. advisors Howard U. Sch. Bus., 1987-89. Recipient award Am. Soc. Women Accts., 1969, 70, 71, Raulston award Cleve. State U., 1971, Pres.'s award Cleve. State U., 1971, Outstanding Achievement award U.S. Navy, 1973, Career Svc. award Chgo. region Fed. Exec. Bd., 1974, Outstanding Contbn. to Fin. Mgmt. award Denver region Fed. Exec. Bd., 1977, Donald L. Scantlebury award Joint Fin. Mgmt. Improvement Program, 1980, Outstanding Svc. award Nat. Assn. Minority CPA Firms, 1980, NASA Exceptional Svc. medal, 1985, Outstanding Achievement in Aerospace award, 1987, Woman of Yr. award, YWCA 1988, Bur. Land Mgmt., Dept. Interior, 1975, Disting. Pub. Svc. award Dept. Def., 1989, Meritorious Civilian Svc. award U.S. Navy, 1993, Nat. Capital Area chpt./Govt. Exec. Mag. award for leadership, 1994, George Washington U. Pi Alpha Alpha Pub. Svc. award, 1996; named Disting. Alumni Cleve. State U., 1990, named Outstanding Fellow of Coun. for Ethical Org. for Creating the Standards for Healthcare Compliance, 2001 Fellow Nat. Acad. Pub. Adminstrn. (standing panel exec. orgn. and mgmt., pub. svc. panel); mem. AICPA (mem. govt. auditing stds. 1996-99), Assn. Govt. Accts. (nat. pres. 1985-86, nat. exec. com. 1977-87, vice chmn. nat. ethics com. 1978-80, 90, chmn. fin. mgmt. standards bd. 1981-82, service award 1973, 76, 93, outstanding achievement award 1979, Robert W. King Meml. award 1988, dir. Hawaii chpt. 1991-93, Nat. Pres.'s award 1999, Disting. Fed. Leadership award 1998), Hawaii Soc. CPAs (bd. dirs. 1991-93), Am. Accts. Assn., Nat. Contract Mgmt. Assn. (bd. advisors 1988-90), NASA Alumni Assn., Women in Aerospace, ASPA (at-large mem. nat. coun. 1994-98, Profl. Responsibility Exemplary Practice award 1990, pres.-nat. capital area chpt. 1989), Exec. Women in Govt., Beta Alpha Psi. Personal E-mail: igjgb@yahoo.com.

BROWN, KAREN KENNEDY, judge; b. Houston, May 23, 1947; BA, U. Pa., 1970; JD, U. Houston, 1973. Bar: Tex. 1973, U.S. Ct. Appeals (5th cir.) 1974, U.S. Dist. Ct. (so. dist.) Tex. 1975, U.S. Supreme Ct. 1980, U.S. Ct. Appeals (11th cir.) 1981. Law clk. to Hon. John Brown, Houston, 1973-75; law clk. to Hon. Woodrow Seals, 1975-76; asst. fed. pub. defender So. Dist. Tex., Houston, 1976—82; pvt. practice Houston, 1982—83; magistrate judge U.S. Dist. Ct. (so. dist.) Tex., 1984-90, bankruptcy judge Houston, 1990—. Episcopalian. Office: US District Court PO Box 61252 Rm 4202 515 Rusk Ave Houston TX 77208

BROWN, KAREN RIMA, orchestra manager, Spanish language educator; b. N.Y.C., Apr. 26, 1943; d. Alexander and Leona (Rosenfeld) Jaffe; m. Russell Vernon Brown, Aug. 13, 1966; children: Stephanie Leona and Gregory Russell. BA, Colby Coll., 1965; MA, U. Wis., 1968. Tchg. asst. U. Wis., Madison, 1965—66, instr. Spanish Janesville, 1966—68, Baraboo, 1968—70, Eau Claire, 1970—71, Ohio U., Zanesville, 1978—98, assoc. prof., 1998—; mgr. Southeastern Ohio Symphony, New Concord, 1977—99. Lectr. Spanish Muskingum Coll., New Concord, 1984, 97-99; mem., music panelist Ohio Arts Coun., Columbus, 1979-83, 90-93; pres. S.E. Ohio Regional Arts Coun., Zanesville, 1978-80; mem. Univ. Internat. Coun. Ohio U., Athens, 2003-. Bd. dirs. Muskingum County Visitors and Conv. Bur., Zanesville, 1987-90, bd. sec., 1989-90; bd. dirs. Assn. of Two Toledos, 1984-87, Ohio Citizens Com. for Arts, Canton, 1979-84; mgr. emeritus Southestern Ohio Symphony Orch., 1999—. Mem. Am. Assn. Tchrs. Spanish and Portuguese, Ohio Valley Fgn. Lang. Alliance, Bus. and Profl. Women, Phi Beta Kappa, Phi Sigma Iota, Sigma Delta Pi (hon.). Democrat. Avocations: travel, consultant to arts organizations, mentor for gifted high school students. Office: Ohio Univ-Zanesville 1425 Newark Rd Zanesville OH 43701-2695

BROWN, KATHE, recreational therapist, counselor; d. Stanley Joseph Kazmierczyk and Anna Baran; m. Robert Arthur Brown, Nov. 9, 1969; children: David Asher, Ariel Claire. BSc, Penn State U., University Park, 1966. Owner Integrated Touch Therapy, Princeton, NJ, 1998—. Vol. Princeton Hospice, 2000—. Avocations: tennis, travel. Home: 12 Rosewood Ct Princeton Junction NJ 08550 Personal E-mail: tchspirit@aol.com.

BROWN, KATHERINE YVONNE BAINES, occupational therapist, educator; b. Chgo., Nov. 8, 1974; d. Keith Rouse and Roberta B. (Baines) Wheeler; m. Irving Brown, II, Jan. 18, 2000; children: Sydney Yvonne Kailee, Irving DeVaughn; 1 child, Anthony DeVaughn Rodgers. BS, Chgo. State U., 1996; MEd, Purdue U., 1999; EdD, Nat. Louis U., 2005. Lic. occupl. therapist Ill., cert. Ind., Tenn., develop. therapist Ill.; lic. tchr. & sch. counselor K-12 Ind., cert. Tenn., physical agent Tenn., fund development Ctr. Non-profit Mgmt., early intervention specialist Ill., thermal physical agent modalities Tenn. Occupl. therapist level I Therapeutic Work Ctr., Chgo., 1996; occupl. therapist level II Provider's Therapeutic Svcs., Chgo., 1996, St. Joseph Hosp. & Medical Ctr., Joliet, Ill., 1996; occupl. therapist Jackson Park Hosp. & Medical Ctr., Chgo., 1997; activity therapy supr. Advocate Christ Hosp. & Medical Ctr., Oak Lawn, Ill., 1997—98; ind. contractor mental health, 1998—2001; counselor Alexian Brothers Behavioral Health Ctr., Hoffman Estates, Ill., 1998—2001; graduate asst. Purdue U., Hammond, Ind., 1998—2000, tchg. asst.-supr., 1999, practicum supr., 1999; home health occupl. therapist St. Catherine Hosp., East Chgo., 2000—01; mental health counselor The Children's Connection Therapeutic Sch., Chgo., 2000—01; occupational therapist Baptist Ch., Nashville, 2001—05; occupl. therapist Baptist Hosp., 2001—05, temp. occupl. therapist, 2002. Adj. prof. Nashville State CC, 2002—; acad. coord. clinical & FW edn., asst. prof. Belmont U., Nashville, 2002—04, mktg. info. group mem., 2002—04, search com. mem. Coll. health Scis. for assoc. dean & chair, 2002—05, advisor honor society, 2002—05, curriculum com. mem., 2002—05, recruitment rep., 2002—05, judge debate competition, 2002, mktg. task force, 2002—04, social events task force, 2002, adj. prof., 03, faculty senate rep., 2003—04, mktg. com. Coll. Health Scis., 2002—04, search com. mem. Coll. Health Scis. for asst./assoc. prof., 2003—05, Dr. Martin Luther King Jr. com. mem., 2003—05, Dr. Martin Luther King Jr. sub-com. chair, 2003—05, asst. prof. Coll. Health Scis., Sch. Occupl. Therapy, 2004—, accreditation review com. mem., 2004—05, graduation com. mem., 2005; alumni career specialist Purdue U., 2004—05. Contbr. articles to profl. jours. Advocate Luth. Gen. Hosp. Good Times Classic, 1996, Food/Clothes Drive & Toys for Tots Program, 1997, Christ Hosp. & Medical Ctr. Psychiatry & Substance Abuse Performance Improvement Com., 1997—98, Christ Hosp. & Medical Ctr. Annual Assoc. Picnic Com., 1997—98, Chase Corp. Challenge, Health Care Team, 1998; vol. Aids Walk, Chgo., 1998; advocate Good Samaritan Hosp. Autumn Classic, 1998; delta com. 18th Ave Enrichment Ctr., 2003—04; governance facilitator Nat.-Louis U., 2004—05; co-chair 18th Ave Enrichment Ctr., 2004—05; mem. W.A. Bass Mid. Sch. Adopt a Family Program, 2004. Nominee Galloway Empowerment award, Nat. Coalition 100 Black Women, Inc., 2005; recipient Advisor Appreciation award, Delta Sigma Theta Sorority, Inc., 2004, Excellence for Exemplary Tchg. Higher Edn. award, Tenn. Occupl. Therapy Assn., 2003. Mem.: Kellogg Elec. Rsch. Acad. (3d v.p. 1999—2000, 1st v.p. 2000—01, pres. 2001), Tenn. Occupl. Therapy Assn. (exec. bd. mem. 2002—04, treas. 2002—04), R.H. Boyd African Am. Leadership Soc. (steering com. 2005), Kellogg Sch. PTA (fin. com. mem. 1997—2001), Lakeview PTO (1st pres. 2002—03), Lakeview YMCA, Psi Configuration Psychology Club (pres. 1999). Avocations: reading, flute. Home: 3044 Summercrest Trail Antioch TN 37013

BROWN, KATHLEEN, bank executive, lawyer; d. Edmund G. and Bernice Brown; m. George Rice (div. 1979); children: Hilary, Alexandra, Zebediah; m. Van Gordon Sauter, 1980; 2 stepsons. BA in History, Stanford U., 1969; JD, Fordham U. Sch. Law, 1985. Mem. L.A. Bd. Edn., 1975-80; with O'Melveny & Myers, N.Y.C., then L.A.; commr. L.A. Bd. Pub. Works, 1987-89; elected Treas. of Calif., 1990-94; exec. v.p. Bank of Am., L.A., 1994-99, pres. Pvt. Bank West, 1999—. Co-chmn. Capital Budget Commn., Washington, 1997—. Mem. Pacific Coun. on Internat. Policy, Stanford Inst. for Internat. Studies; dir. Children's Hosp. L.A., San Francisco Ballet. Democrat.

BROWN, KATHRYN ANN, music educator; b. Tigerton, Wis., Feb. 3, 1972; d. Clarence Herbert and Janice Marie Natzke; m. Bryan Lee Brown; children: Riley Michael, Alexandra Kathryn. BA, U. Wis. Green Bay, 1995; M in Music Edn., U. Wis., 2001. Music educator intern Luxemburg-Casco Sch. Dist., Wis., 1995—96; music educator long-term substitute W. DePere Sch. Dist., Wis., 1996; music educator, choral dir. Gillett Sch. Dist., Wis., 1996—2005. Summer music camp instr. U. Wis., Green Bay, 1997—2002, summer music clinic instr., Madison, 1999; cons. Creative Memories Ind., 2003—; pvt. voice and piano instr., 1993—. Dir.: Singing in Wisconsin, 2001, 2004; actor: Steel Magnolias, 1999, 1940s Radio Hour, 1999, Coping, 2000. Mem.: Wis. Choral Dirs. Assn. (summer music camp instr. 1996, membership chmn. 1999—2004), Wis. Music Educators Assn., Wis. Sch. Music Assn. (State Honor Treble Choir Sectional Coach 2000, 2001), Am. Choral Dirs. Assn., Main Str. Revue Cmty. Theater (bd. dirs. 2000—01). Avocations: scrapbooks, singing. Personal E-mail: bkrabrown@bayland.net.

BROWN, KAY (MARY KATHRYN BROWN), retired state official, consultant, political organization worker; b. Ft. Worth, Dec. 19, 1950; d. H. C., Jr. and Dorothy Ruth (Ware) Brown; m. William P. Dougherty, Dec. 15, 1978 (div. 1984); m. Mark A. Foster, Aug. 24, 1991; 1 adopted child, Kathryn Yucui. BA, Baylor U., 1973. Reporter UPI, Atlanta, 1973-76; reporter, feature writer Anchorage Daily Times, 1976-77; reporter, co-owner Alaska Adv., Anchorage, 1977; aide, rschr. Alaska State Legislature, Juneau, 1979-80; dep. dir. divsn. of oil and gas (formerly divsn. minerals and energy mgmt.) Alaska Dept. Natural Resources, Anchorage, 1980-82, dir., 1982-86; elected Alaska Ho. of Reps., 1986-96; exec. dir. Alaska Conservation Alliance and Voters, 1997-2000; ret.; Alaska comms. dir. Dem. Nat. Com., 2005—. Del. White Ho. Conf. Libr. and Info. Svcs., 1991. Co-author: (book) Geographic Information Systems: A Guide to the Technology, 1991; talk radio host, 1996—2000. E-mail: kaybrown@alaska.net.

BROWN, KEITH, musician, educator; b. Colorado Springs, Colo., Oct. 21, 1933; s. Kenneth Vernon and Audrey Lucille (Nelson) B.; m. Leslee Joanne Scullin, June 13, 1954 (div. Jan. 1991); children: Robert Vernon, Lise Joanne, Kristin Patricia; m. Joann Alexander, May 14, 1994. B.Mus., U. So. Calif., 1957; M.Mus., Manhattan Sch. Music, 1964. Trombonist Indpls. Symphony Orch., 1957-58; mem. faculty, solo trombonist Aspen Festival, 1957-69; trombonist N.Y. Brass Quintet, 1958-59; prin. trombonist Casals Festival, San Juan, P.R., 1958-80; assoc. prin. trombonist Phila. Orch., 1959-62; prin. trombonist Met. Opera Orch., 1962-65; performed with Chamber Music Soc. of Lincoln Ctr., 1969-88; participant Marlboro Festival, 1970-73; dir. instrumental activities, prof. music, condr. univ. orch. Temple U., Phila., 1965-71; prof. emeritus, condr. Ind. U., Bloomington, 1971-97; condr., music dir. Bloomington Symphony Orch., 1975-80; chmn. brass dept., condr. Music Acad. of West, 1978-82, 85-87; co-founder Ensemble Mediation, 1998—. Artistic dir., condr. Camerata Orch., Bloomington, 1989-96; artistic/mus. dir. InterAm. Youth Orch. of the Festival Casals, San Juan, P.R., 1989-91. Regular guest condr. Orquesta Sinfonica Venezuela, coach, adv., guest condr, Orquesta Nacional Juvenil and Orquesta Sinfonica Simon Bolivar, Caracas, 1979—; coach, adviser Joven Orquesta Nacional de Espana, 1984-94; bd. advisers N.Y. Cornet and Sacbut Ensemble, 1984—; tchr. master classes, lectr., recitalist (1st western trombonist), conservatories in, Beijing and Shanghai, China, 1982, Beijing, 1988; guest condr. Sapporo (Japan) Symphony Orch., 1990, Orquesta del Principado de Asturias, Spain, 1991; author 10 vols.

orchestral studies for trombone and tuba, numerous edits. of solos, brass ensembles, study materials, 1960—. Served with U.S. Army, 1953-56. Recipient spl. award Asociacion Musical, Caracas, Venezuela, 1979, Alumni award U. So. Calif. Sch. Music, 1957; Nat. Arts assoc. Sigma Alpha Iota, 1995. Mem. Internat. Trombone Assn., Phi Mu Alpha Sinfonia, Pi Kappa Lambda, Kappa Kappa Psi (hon.) Clubs: Rotary. Methodist. Avocations: tennis, sailing. Home: 2925 Olcott Blvd Bloomington IN 47401-2403 Business E-Mail: brownk@indiana.edu.

BROWN, KEITH LAPHAM, retired ambassador; b. Sterling, Ill., June 18, 1925; s. Lloyd Heman and Marguerite (Briggs) B.; m. Carol Louise Liebmann, Oct. 1, 1949; children: Susan, Briggs (dec.), Linda, Benjamin. Student, U. Ill., 1943-44, Northwestern U., 1946-47; LLB, U. Tex., 1949. Bar: Tex., Okla., Colo. Assoc. Lang, Byrd, Cross & Ladon, San Antonio, 1949-55; v.p., gen. counsel Caulkins Oil Co., Oklahoma City, 1955-70, Denver, 1955-70; founder, developer Vail Assocs., Colo., 1962; pres. Brown Investment Corp., Denver, 1970-87; developer Colo. State Bank Bldg., Denver, 1971; amb. to Lesotho Dept. State, 1982-84, amb. to Denmark Copenhagen, 1988-92; ret., 1992; chmn. Brown Investment Corp., Denver, 1993—. Mem. adv. bd. Ctr. for Strategic and Internat. Studies. Chmn. Rep. Nat. Fin. Com., 1985-88; hon. trustee, past pres. bd. Colo. Acad.; mem. Am. Acad. Diplomacy. Ensign USN, 1943-46. Mem. Coun. Am. Ambs. (pres.), San Antonio Country Club, Bohemian Club. Republican. Presbyterian. also: 11 Auburn Pl San Antonio TX 78209-4739 Office: 1490 Colo State Bank Bldg 1600 Broadway Denver CO 80202-4927 Office Phone: 303-830-7379.

BROWN, KENNETH LLOYD, lawyer; b. N.Y.C., Sept. 28, 1927; s. Edythe Schneider; m. Freya Dorothy Finkelstein, July 10, 1954; children: Ivy Hope Brown Hill, Patrice Shari Brown. BS, NYU, 1951; LLB, St. John's U., Bklyn., 1954. Bar: NY 1955. Pvt. practice, Forest Hills, N.Y., 1955-61; asst. corp. counsel City of N.Y., 1962-78; ptnr. Rivkin, Radler & Kremer and predecessor firms, Uniondale, N.Y., 1977-98; pvt. practice Jamaica, N.Y., 1998—. Dem. dist. leader Queens County Dem. Orgn., Forest Hills, until 1982; mem. Forest Hills Jewish Ctr. With U.S. Army, 1945-47. Mem. Queens County Bar Assn. (various coms.), Am. Legion, Jewish War Vet. Post, Continental Regular Dem. Club (founder), Robert F. Kennedy, Jr. Dem. Club, B'nai B'rith, Masons, Knights of Pythias. Avocation: politics. Home: PO Box 457 Flushing NY 11375-0457 Office: 15049 Hillside Ave Jamaica NY 11432-3319 Office Phone: 718-297-7711.

BROWN, KENNETH MACKINNON, lawyer; b. Honolulu, Oct. 28, 1946; s. Kenneth Stirling and Chandler (Darden) B.; m. Janet Gail Davis, Feb. 3, 1968; children: Jennifer Darden, Matthew Chapin MacKinnon. BA, U. N.H., 1968; JD, Washington U., 1973. Bar: N.H. 1973, U.S. Dist. Ct. N.H. 1973, U.S. Ct. Appeals (1st cir.) 1974. Assoc. Winer, Lynch & Pillsbury, Nashua, N.H., 1973-76; ptnr. Kahn & Brown, Nashua, 1976-95, Sullivan & Gregg, P.A., Nashua, 1995—. Pres. bd. dirs. N.H. Legal Assistance, Concord, 1978-80; chmn. bd. Rivier Coll. Paralegal Adv. Bd., Nashua, 1984—; bd. dirs. N.H. Assn. for Mental Health, Concord, 1978-81, N.H. Soc. Protection of Forests, Concord, 1983-88. Mem. N.H. Bar Assn. (mem. Interest on Lawyers' Trust Accounts com. 1984-99, chmn. 1998-99), Assn. Trial Lawyers Am., N.H. Trial Lawyers Assn. Clubs: Nashua Country (N.H.). Avocations: golf, family. Home: 29 Baxter Rd Hollis NH 03049-5943 E-mail: brownk@sgpa-law.com.

BROWN, KENT NEWVILLE, ambassador; b. Oakland, Calif., May 7, 1944; s. Victor B. and Mary E. (Shaver) B.; m. Norma Giorno, Dec. 29, 1995; children from previous marriage: Steven D., Karen E. BA, U. Calif., Davis, 1964, MA, 1966. 3rd sec. U.S. Embassy, Panama, 1967-69, 2nd sec. Prague, Czechoslovakia, 1970-73; watch officer to exec. secretariat U.S. Dept. of State, Washington, 1973-74; fellow Hoover Instn., Stanford, Calif., 1974-75; officer Soviet desk U.S. Dept. of State, Washington, 1976-80; 1st sec. U.S. Embassy, Moscow, 1980-83; sr. advisor U.S. Arms Control Del., Vienna, Austria, 1984-88; office dir. Strategic Nuc. Policy U.S. Dept. of State, Washington, 1989-90; polit. advisor Supreme Allied Comdr. Europe, Belgium, 1990-92; amb. U.S. Embassy, Tbilisi, Georgia, 1992-95; dir. pers. U.S. Dept. of State, Washington, 1995-96; v.p. govt. rels. Ea. Europe J.T. Internat., Geneva, 1996—. Bd. dirs. NATO workshop, Menlo Park, Calif. Bd. dirs. U.S.-Russia Bus. Coun. Mem. Internat. Inst. for Strategic Studies. Office: 12 Ch de Rieu Geneva 17 Switzerland

BROWN, LAMAR BEVAN, lawyer; b. Tooele, Utah, Apr. 26, 1951; s. John B. and Reva M. B.; children: Sean La Mar, Kyle Ross, Ian Lawrence. BA, Utah State U., 1974; JD, We. State U., 1980. Bar: Calif. 1980, U.S. Dist. Ct. (so. dist.) Calif. 1980, U.S. Ct. Appeals (9th cir.) 1986, U.S. Dist. Ct. (no. and ctrl. dist.) 1992. Assoc. Law Offices George Andrews, San Diego, 1980-82, Higgs, Fletcher & Mack, San Diego, 1982-90, Law Offices Craig McClellan, San Diego, 1990-95; mem. McClellan & Brown, San Diego, 1995—. Mem. Consumer Attys. Calif., Consumer Attys. San Diego, Western Trial Lawyers Assn., San Diego County Bar Assn. Democrat. Office: McClellan & Brown 1144 State St San Diego CA 92101-3529 E-mail: lamarbrown@aol.com.

BROWN, LARRY DOUGLASS, research consultant; b. Greenville, Miss., July 10, 1955; s. Bobby Jene and Jo Ann B.; m. Rebecca Askew, Aug. 7, 1985; children: January Adkins, Benjamin, Nicholas, Caroline. PhD, DeMontfort U., 1998; advanced diploma, Oxford U., 2003. Cons. PRI Bus. and Polit. Cons., London, 1996-2000; rsch. cons. art and hist. rsch. PRI, Little Rock, Ark., also London, 1996—. White collar crime investigator Ark. State Police, 1980-96. Author: Crossfire: Witness in the Clinton Investigation, 1999. Ark. dir. criminal justice issues George Bush presdl. campaign, 1988, Little Rock, 1988; mem. drug and alcohol abuse coun. mem. Gov. Bill Clinton, 1984 Scholastic achievement award U.S. Dept. Justice, 1978; recipient Cert. of Recognition Gov. Bill Clinton, 1984. Fellow Acad. of Polit. Sci., Nat. Troopers Coalition (vice-chmn. 1988-90, Spl. Svc. award 1990), Ark. State Police Assn. (pres. 1986-90), Am. Polit. Sci. Assn. Baptist. Home: 5217 Country Club Blvd Little Rock AR 72207 Office: 6301 C Street 5 Little Rock AR 72205 Office Phone: 501-563-2469. Personal E-mail: prillc@earthlink.net.

BROWN, L(ARRY) EDDIE, tax specialist, real estate agent, accountant, financial planner; b. Aug. 31, 1941; s. Earl and Lois Ovoca (Norrod) B.; m. Lillian Virginia Edwards, Feb. 9, 1965; children: Clifford Bruce, Michael Dwayne, Jennifer Noelle. BBA, Ga. State U., 1974, MBA, 1976. Cert. tax profl.; accredited tax advisor; accredited bus. acct.; enrolled agt. Mgmt. trainee Citizens Bank, Cookeville, Tenn., 1963-65; office mgr. Redisco, Tampa, Fla., 1965-67; methods analyst Delta Air Lines, Atlanta, 1967-83; owner Brown Enterprises, College Park, Ga., 1971—95, Fayetteville, Ga., 1995—. Pres. So. Heritage Properties, Inc., 1984—; instr. Ga. State U., 1976-80. Bd. dirs. Ga. Spl. Olympics, Atlanta, 1983-90; Ga. del. White House Conf. on Small Bus., 1995, Congl. Small Bus. Summit, 1998, 2000. With USAF, 1959-63. Mem. Nat. Soc. Tax Profls. (Ga. state com. 1994-99), Nat. Assn. Tax Practitioners (Ga. bd. dirs. 1994-98), Nat. Soc. Pub. Accts., Ga. Assn. Pub. Accts. (bd. govs. 1994-2001, 1st v.p. 1996-97, pres. 1997-99, chpt. pres. 1993-95), Fin. Planners Assn., Nat. Assn. Securities Dealers, Ga. Assn. Realtors, Civitan Club (pres. Airport-Southside, Atlanta 1982-83, treas. Airport Area, Atlanta 1979-81, Civilian of Yr. chpt. 1982, bd. dirs. Ga. dist. north 1984-86, trustee Ga. dist. North Found. 1985-88), Masons. Mem. Lds Ch. Office: Brown Enterprises 392 Glynn St N Fayetteville GA 30214-1191 Office Phone: 770-719-4440. E-mail: taxpco@brownenterprises.com.

BROWN, LAUREN EVANS, zoologist, researcher, educator; b. Waukesha, Wis., Sept. 4, 1939; s. Winston Dever and Julianne Evelyn Brown; m. Jill Rae Hollingshead, Feb. 21, 1968; children: Lara Nell, Kara Anne Nash, Evan Saxon. BS in Biology, Carroll Coll., 1961; MS in Zoology, So. Ill. U., Carbondale, 1963; PhD in Zoology, U. Tex., Austin, 1967; postgrad., U. Melbourne, Australia, 1968. Lab asst., zoology Carroll Coll., Waukesha, Wis., 1957—61; rsch. asst. biochem. Dairyland Food Lab., Waukesha, 1960; tchg. asst. genetics Mark Twain Inst., St. Louis, 1961; tchg. and rsch. asst. So. Ill. U., Carbondale, 1961—63, rsch. asst. Pine Hills Field Sta. Pine Hills Swamp, Ill., 1963; tchg. and rsch. asst. U. Tex., Austin, 1963—67; asst. prof. to assoc. prof. Ill. State U., Normal, 1967—77, prof., 1977—2002, prof. emeritus, 2002—, curator amphibians and reptiles, 1990—, maj. prof. for numerous MS and PhD students, chair sect. ecology, evolution, ethology and systematic biology, 1978—79, interdisciplinary studies, 1996—, adj. prof., 2002—. Endangered species and environ. cons., 1966—; chair undergrad. and grad. curriculum coms. Ill. State U., 1974—83, mem. athletic coun., 1992—95, rsch. grant evaluation com., 1977—81, curriculum infusion program mem., 1995—2002, mem. univ. libr. com., 1997—2002, chair libr. com., 1998—2002, mem. exec. com., u. libr., 1999—2002, mem. focus group to evaluate univ. pres., 2001, mem. focus group for underrepresented groups, u. office for diversity and affirmative action, 2001—02, mem. adv. coun. family campaign, 2002—04, hon. libr., 2002—; mem. Houston Toad Recovery Team US Fish and Wildlife Svc., 1978—84, 1998—; affiliate profl. scientist Ill. Natural History Survey, Champaign, Ill., 1997—; presenter in field. Co-author: Recovery Plan for the Houston Toad, 1984; editor: Herpetologica, 1978—81, Alytes, 2000—; mem. editl. bd.: Ill. Natural History Survey, 1999—; contbr. numerous articles to profl. jours., chapters to books. Grantee in field, 1962—. Mem.: Mo. Herpetological Assn., Chgo. Herpetological Soc., Md. Herpetological Soc., Internat. Soc. for the History and Bibliography of Herpetology, N.Am. Native Fishes Assn., Ill. Ornithol. Soc., Coleopterists Soc., Coun. Biology Editors, Internat. Soc. Study and Conservation Amphibians (mem. editl. bd. 2000—, mem. bd. councillors 2003—), Am. Soc. Ichthyologists and Herpetologists, Declining Amphibian Populations Task Force, Soc. Study Amphibians and Reptiles (conservation com.), Herpetologists' League (bd. trustees 1979—80), Am. Rabbit Breeders Assn. (chair libr. com. 2001—02). Achievements include rediscovery of the near extinct Houston Toad in Lost Pines. Avocations: hiking, breeding and rearing animals, genealogy, swimming. Home: 15958 E 2550 North Rd Hudson IL 61748-9391 Office: Ill State Univ Dept Biological Sci Campus Box 4120 Normal IL 61790-4120 Office Phone: 309-438-5990.

BROWN, LAURENCE DAVID, retired bishop; b. Fargo, ND, Feb. 16, 1926; s. John Nicolai and Ada Amelia (Johnson) B.; m. Virginia Ann Allen, Sept. 6, 1950; children: Patricia Ann, Julia Louise, Claudia Ruth. BS, U. Minn., 1946; BA, Concordia Coll., 1948; M of Theology, Luther Theol. Sem., 1951. Ordained to ministry Evang. Luth. Ch., 1951. Pastor Our Savior's Luth. Ch., New Ulm, Minn., 1951-55; nat. assoc. youth dir. Evang. Luth. Ch., Mpls., 1955-60; nat. youth dir. Am. Luth. Ch., Mpls., 1960-68; instn. dir. Tchr. Tng., U. Minn., Mpls., 1968-69; exec. dir. Freedom from Hunger Found., Washington, 1969-73; sr. pastor St. Paul Luth. Ch., Waverly, Iowa, 1973-79; bishop Iowa Dist. Am. Luth. Ch., Des Moines, 1979-89, N.E. Iowa Synod, Evang. Luth. Ch. in Am., Waverly, 1989-92; prof. religion Wartburg Coll., Waverly, Iowa, 1992-93; interim sr. pastor Ctrl. Luth. Ch., Mpls., 1994-95, Calvary Luth. Ch., Mpls., 1996-97; ret. Bd. regents Luther Coll., Decorah, Iowa, 1989-92, Wartburg Coll., 1988-92, Wartburg Theol. Sem., Dubuque, Iowa, 1988-91, Self-Help, Inc., 1989-94. Author: Take Care: A Guide for Responsible Living, 1983; contbr. articles to profl. jours. Lt. USN, 1943-46. Lutheran. Avocation: reading. Home: 7500 York Ave S #916 Edina MN 55435

BROWN, LAURIE MARK, physicist, researcher; b. Bklyn., Apr. 10, 1923; s. William and Elvira (Fleischman) B.; m. Judith Kobrin, Dec. 27, 1942 (dec. May 1963); children: Joanna Lisa, Julie Elena; m. Brigitte Dziumbla-Winzeler, June 6, 1969; children: Judith, Jean. AB, Cornell U., 1943, PhD, 1951. Mem. faculty physics Northwestern U., Evanston, Ill., 1950—, prof., 1961-93, prof. emeritus, 1993—. Mem. Inst. for Advanced Study (NSF fellow), Princeton, 1952-53; cons. Argonne Nat. Lab., 1960-70; vis. prof., Vienna, 1966, Rome, 1967, São Paulo, 1972-73 Editor and author profl. books; contbr. articles to profl. jours. Fulbright research scholar Italy, 1958-60 Fellow Am. Phys. Soc. (chmn. div. history of physics 1983-84, 2001-2002). Home: 724 Noyes St Evanston IL 60201-2847

BROWN, LAVEDA PAGE, consultant; b. Madisonville, Tex., Jan. 9, 1956; d. William Sr. and Frankie Bell Hardy; m. Gregory Arnold Page (dec. 1979); children: Gregory D., Bettina D. Student, El Centro Jr. Coll., 1975-77, Abilene Christian U., 1990, Cisco Jr. Coll., 1991-92. Cert. bus. devel. specialist. Owner, mgr. Master' Touch, Dallas, 1988-91; procurement specialist Abilene (Tex.) Christian U. Caruth Small Bus. Devel. Ctr., 1992-94; bus. cons., procurement specialist McLennan C.C., Small Bus. Devel. Ctr., Waco, Tex., 1994—. With Affiliated Computer Svcs., Dallas, 1989-90; advisor Sign of the Times, Waco. Mem. Tex. Econ. Devel. Coun., Austin, 1999-00 Recipient Distinction award Tex. Assn. Minority Bus. Enterprise, 1995, Adv. Yr. Fort Worth Small Bus. Admstrn., 1998. Mem. Am. Bus. Women Assn. (v.p. mktg. 1999-00, top recruiter dist. II award 2000), Nat. Purchasing Assn., Nat. Contract Mgmt. Assn., Svc. Corps Retired Execs. (procurement specialist), Tex. Assn. Procurement Ctrs. (legis. com. 1994-96), Gtr. Waco C. of C. (com. mem. 1999-00). Republican. Mem. Lds Ch. Avocations: reading, ceramic, cross stitching, gardening. Office: McLennan Cmty Coll Small Bus Devel Ctr 401 Franklin Ave Waco TX 76701-2127 E-mail: ljbrown@mclennan.edu.

BROWN, LAWRENCE CHARLES, lawyer; b. Johnson City, N.Y., Apr. 5, 1951; s. Charles Hugh and Cora Rose (O'Connor) B.; m. Constance Angela Grimes, July 28, 1973; children: Jason P., Christina M. BS, Cornell U., 1973; MA, SUNY, Albany, 1974; JD, Syracuse U., 1977. Bar: N.Y. 1978, U.S. Dist. Ct. (we. dist.) N.Y. 1978, U.S. Dist. Ct. (so. dist.) N.Y. 1986, U.S. Tax Ct. 1987, U.S. Court Appeals (2nd Circuit) 1998, U.S. Supreme Court 1998. Assoc. Phillips, Lytle, Hitchcock, Blaine & Huber, Buffalo, N.Y., 1977-78, Hodgson, Russ, Andrews, Woods & Goodyear, Buffalo, 1978-82; ptnr. Lipsitz, Green, Fahringer, Roll, Salisbury & Cambria, Buffalo, 1982-94, Kavinoky & Cook, LLP, 1994-96; prin. Law Offices of Lawrence C. Brown, Buffalo, 1996—. Bd. dirs. Fund for Pub. Edn./Comml. Law Found., treas., 2002-04, sec., 2004—; advisor high sch. moot ct. teams for state bar program; presenter in field. Rsch. editor Syracuse U. Law Rev., 1976-77; mem. editl. bd. Comml. Law Jour., 1998-2002, Comml. Law Bull., 1998-2004, bd. editors DePaul Bus. and Comml. Law Jour., 2002-; contbr. articles to profl. jours. Mem. ABA, N.Y. State Bar Assn., Erie County Bar Assn., Comml. Law League Am. (nat. vice chmn. practice and procedure com. 1989-91, nat. vice chmn. uniform laws com. 1990—, nat. chmn. uniform laws com. 1992-95, advisor 1995-2002), Pi Kappa Alpha. Methodist. Avocation: public speaking. Office: 385 Cleveland Dr Buffalo NY 14215 Office Phone: 716-831-1994. E-mail: lcbrown36000@cs.com, brownl724@aol.com.

BROWN, LAWRENCE HAAS, retired banker; b. Evanston, Ill., July 29, 1934; s. Robert C. and Alice (Haas) B.; m. Ann Ferguson, June 23, 1956; children— Michael, Kenneth, Russell Student, Cornell U., Ithaca, N.Y., 1952-54; BBA, U. Mich., 1956. Sr. v.p. No. Trust Co., Chgo., 1958-89, ret., 1989. Chmn. Pub. Securities Assn., N.Y.C., 1980; vice chmn. Mcpl. Securities Rulemaking Bd., Washington, 1982; bd. dirs. Nuveen Funds. Pres. Highwood (Ill.) Pub. Libr., 1993—97; bd. dirs. United Way of Highland Park/Highwood. Lt. USN, 1956—58. Mem.: Exmoor Country (Highland Park, Ill.) (pres. 1984-85); Municipal Bond (pres. 1977). Republican. Presbyterian. Avocations: tennis, curling, golf. Home: 201 Michigan Ave Highwood IL 60040-1808 Personal E-mail: ablbcurler@aol.com.

BROWN, LAWRENCE HARVEY (LARRY BROWN), professional basketball coach; b. Brooklyn, NY, Sept. 14, 1940; Student, U. North Carolina, Chapel Hill, NC, 1959-63. Amateur basketball player Akron Goodyears, Akron, OH, 1963-65; asst. coach U. North Carolina, Chapel Hill, NC, 1965-67; player New Orleans (ABA), New Orleans, 1967-68, Oakland (ABA), Oakland, CA, 1968-69, Washington (ABA), 1969-70, Virgina Squires (ABA) - Denver Nuggets (ABA), 1970-71, Denver Nuggets (ABA), Denver, 1971-73; head coach Carolina Cougars (ABA), 1972-74, Denver Nuggets (ABA), 1974-76, Denver Nuggets (NBA), Denver, 1976-79, UCLA, Los Angeles, CA, 1979-81, New Jersey Nets (NBA), Newark, 1981-83, U. Kansas, Lawrence, KS, 1983-88, San Antonio Spurs (NBA), San Antonio, 1988-92, Los Angeles Clippers (NBA), Los Angeles, CA, 1992-93, Indiana Pacers (NBA), Indpls., 1993-97, Phila. 76ers (NBA), 1997—2003, Detroit Pistons (NBA), 2003—05, New York Knicks (NBA), 2005—. Mem. Am. Basketball Assn. All-Star Team, 1968—70, U.S. Olympic Team, 1964, Am. Basketball Assn. Championship Team, 1969; asst. coach U.S. Olympic Team, 2000, head coach, 04. Named Most Valuable Player, ABA All-Star Game, 1968, ABA Coach of Yr., 1973, 1975, 1976, IBM Coach of Yr., NBA, 2001; recipient Espy Award for Best Coach/Manager, ESPN, 2004. Achievements include coached NBA Championship Team, 2004; only coach in history to win NCAA and NBA Titles. Office: c/o New York Knicks 2 Penn Plaza New York NY 10001*

BROWN, LEE KELVIN, pulmonary, critical care and sleep medicine physician, physician, researcher; b. Bklyn., Apr. 25, 1950; s. Bernard and Rosalind Schneider Brown; m. Carol Jean Yormack, Aug. 27, 1972; children: Matthew Ian, Douglas Elliot. BEE, MIT, 1972; MD, Mt. Sinai Sch. Medicine, NY, 1976. Diplomate internal medicine Am. Bd. Internal Medicine, 1979, pulmonary disease Am. Bd. Internal Medicine, 1982, critical care medicine Am. Bd. Internal Medicine, 1987, sleep medicine Am. Bd. Sleep Medicine., 1993. Resident medicine Mt. Sinai Hosp., NYC, 1976—79; fellow pulmonary disease Mt. Sinai Med. Ctr., Miami, Fla., 1979—81; assoc. prof. medicine Mt. Sinai Sch. Medicine, NYC, 1981—93; assoc. program dir. St. Joseph's Hosp. Med. Ctr., Phoenix, 1993—97; prof. clin. medicine U. Ariz., Tucson, 1994—97; chair divsn. sleep medicine Lovelace Health Sys., Albuquerque, 1997—2003; exec. dir. Program Sleep Medicine Health Sci. Ctr. U. N.Mex., Albuquerque, 2003—, assoc. chief, outpatient svcs. Divsn. Pulmonary, Critical Care Medicine Sch. Medicine, 2003—, prof. medicine, pediat. Sch. Medicine, 2003—, vice chair Dept. Internal Medicine Sch. Medicine, 2004—. Mem., comm. tech. com. Am. Acad. Sleep Medicine, Westchester, Ill., 1995—96; liaison, State Health Care Am. Coll. Chest Physicians, 1996—97; mem., continuing med. edn. com. Am. Acad. Sleep Medicine, Westchester, Ill., 1997—99, chair, mem. com., 1997—2001; clin. practice com. Am. Thoracic Soc., 1999—2000; del., N.Mex. Med. Soc. Greater Albuquerque Med. Assn., 2000—03; comm. com. Am. Thoracic Soc., NYC, 2000—03; editl. bd., chest The Cardiopulmonary Critical Care Jour., Park Ridge, Ill., 2001—03; assoc. editor, AASM Bull. Am. Acad. Sleep Medicine, 2002—03; mem. physician recruitment, retention com. Greater Albuquerque Med. Assn., 2002—03; chair, publ. com. Am. Acad. Sleep Medicine, Westchester, 2002—03; vice chair, sleep network Am. Coll. Chest Physicians, 2002—03; bd. dirs. Am. Thoracic Soc., NYC, 2002—, chair, coun. chpt. rep., 2003—, mem., clin. problems assembly planning com., 2003—. Author: (3 peer reviewed sci. papers) American Journal of Medicine, 1980—91, 10 review articles, various, (peer reviewed sci. paper) Journal of Applied Physiology, 1983, (13 peer reviewed scientific papers) Chest, The Cardiopulmonary and Critical Care Journal, 1985—2003, 18 chapters in textbooks, various, (peer reviewed sci. paper) Respiration Physiology, 1990, Lung, 1995, (4 peer reviewed sci. papers) American Journal of Respiratory and Critical Care Medicine, 1995—2003, (5 editls.) Chest, The Cardiopulmonary and Critical Care Journal, 1997—2003, (2 peer reviewed sci. papers) Archives of Internal Medicine, 1997—98, (peer reviewed sci. paper) Neurology, 1998, American Journal of Kidney Disease, 1999, Sleep Medicine, 2000, Sleep, 2000, Clinical Genetics, 2003. Asst. scoutmaster Boy Scout Troop 40, 1994—97; physician vol. Phoenix Open Golf Tournament, 1995—96; v.p. Rosalee Ranch Homeowners Assoc., Scottsdale, Ariz., 1996—97. Recipient Scholarships, Engring. Scholarship, Grumman Aerospace Inc., 1968—72, Tau Beta Pi Engring. Honor Soc., Tau Beta Pi, 1972, Eta Kappa Nu Elec. Engring. Honor Soc., Eta Kappa Nu, 1972; fellow Pulmonary WinterCourse fellow, Fla. Lung Assoc., 1980—81. Fellow: ACP, Am. Coll. Chest Physicians (chmn. sleep network 2004—, Alfred Soffer Award for Editorial Excellence 2003), NY Acad. Medicine, Am. Acad. Sleep Medicine, Am. Coll. Critical Care Medicine. Achievements include research in respiration and neurological disease; pulmonary physiology; sleep disorders. Avocations: hiking, amateur radio, computer science. Office: Univ NMex Bldg #2 1101 Medical Arts AveNE Albuquerque NM 87120 E-mail: lkbrown@alum.mit.edu, lkbrown@salud.unm.edu.

BROWN, LEE PATRICK, retired mayor, federal official, protective services official, educator; b. Wewoka, Okla., Oct. 4, 1937; s. Andrew and Zelma (Edwards) B.; m. Yvonne Carolyn Streets, July 14, 1958 (dec.); children: Patrick, Torri, Robyn, Jenna; m. Frances M. Young, Dec. 29, 1996. BA, Fresno State U., 1960; MA, San Jose State U., 1964; MS, U. Calif., 1968; PhD in Criminology, U. Calif., Berkeley, 1970; D of Pub. Affairs (hon.), Fla. Internat. U., 1982; LLD (hon.), John Jay Coll., 1985; HHD (hon.), Portland State U., 1990; LHD (hon.), Fresno State U., 1994; LLD (hon.), SUNY Brockport, 1995; doctorate (hon.), Howard U., Wiley Coll.; Doctorate (hon.), Paul Quinn Coll., 2002. Officer San Jose (Calif.) Police Dept., 1960-68; prof. Portland (Oreg.) State U., 1968-72; assoc. dir. Urban Affairs Inst. Howard Inst., Washington, 1972-75; sheriff Sheriff's Dept., Mulnomah County, Oreg., 1975-76; dir. Dept. Justice Services, Mulnomah County, 1976-78; commr. Dept. Pub. Safety, Atlanta, 1978-82; chief of police Houston Police Dept., 1982-90; police commr. N.Y.C., 1990-92; prof. Tex. So. Univ., 1992-93; dir. Nat. Drug Control Policy, Washington, 1993-96; mem. Pres. Cabinet, 1993-96; prof. Rice Univ., Houston, 1996-98; mayor City of Houston, 1998—2004; vis. scholar Rice U., 2004—05; chmn., CEO Brown Group Internat. Adj. prof. U. Houston, U. Tex. Health Sci. Ctr., Houston, Tex. So. U., Houston; vis. prof. Dalian Sch. Tech., China; hon. prof. Beijing Normal Sch., Tongji U.; guest prof. Tianjin U., China; cons. U.S. Dept. Justice, Washington, Police Found., Washington, various state and local govts., Houston; chmn. Nat. Minority Adv. Council on Criminal Justice; mem. Nat. Adv. Commn. on Criminal Justice Standards and Goals, Washington, Nat. Commn. on Higher Edn. for Police, Washington, Commn. on Accreditation for Law Enforcement Agencies, Washington, Presdl. Task Force, 1993—. Co-author: Attitudes of Black Police Officers, 1976, Police and Society, 1981; editor: Neighborhood Team Policing, 1976, Violent Crime, 1981; author of numerous articles and book chpts. Bd. dirs. Boy Scouts Am., United Way, Urban League, Blue Bonnet Bowl, "Just Say No", Peoples Workshop for Visual and Performing Arts, Houston, 1987—, Nat. Black Child Devel. Inst., Washington, 1987—, Nat. Alliance Against Violence, N.Y., 1986—, Sheltering Arms, Houston, 1985—; task forcemem. Nat. Ctr. for Missing and Exploited Children, Washington, 1986—; adv. bd. Nat. Inst. Against Prejudice and Violence, Balt., 1987—; mem. Police Activities League, Houston, 1987—; mem. adv. policy bd. Nat. Incident Based Reporting System, 1988—; mem. adv. com. Fannie Mae, Washington, 1999; bd. dirs. Police Found., 2000; mem. U.S. Conf. of Mayors, Mayors and CEOs. Recipient Peace and Justice award Martin Luther King Jr., 1981, Nat. Law Enforcement award Nat. Black Police Assn., 1982, Disting. Alumnus award Fresno State U., 1983, Police Leadership award, Police Exec. Research Forum, 1987, Liberty Bell award Houston Young Lawyers Assn., 1987, August Vollmer award Am. Soc. Criminology, 1988, Cartier Pasha award Cartier Internat., 1992, Exemplary Leader award Am. Leadership Forum, 1994, Mikey Leland Lifetime Achievement award Mickey Leland Ctr. for World Hunger; named to Gallup Hall of Fame by Gallup, Inc., 1993; named Mgr. of Yr., Nat. Mgmt. Assn., Practitioner of Yr., Nat. Assn. of Blacks Criminal Justice, 1984, Communicator of Yr. Washington News Service, 1986, Father of Yr. Nat. Father's Day com., 1991, Politician of Yr. Libr. Jour., Technologist of Yr., Pub. Tech., Inc., 2002, Alumnus of Yr., U. Calif., Berkeley, 2005; named one of 100 Most Influential Black Ams., Ebony Mag., 2003; rsch. fellow Harvard U., 1988; Berkeley fellow, 2002. Mem. Internat. Assn. Chiefs of Police (past pres.), Nat. Orgn. of Black Law Enforcement Execs. (v.p. 1985, Robert Lamb Jr. Humanitarian award 1987), Police Exec. Research Forum, Internat. Narcotic Enforcement Officers Assn., Nat. Forum for Black Pub. Adminstrs., N.Y. Police Chiefs Assn., Tex. Police Assn., Tex. Criminal Justice Task Force, Nat. Police Athletic League, Mich. State U. (adv. council nat. neighborhood foot patrol ctr.), Nat. Research Council (com. on research on law enforcement and the adminstrn. of justice, com. on status of Black Ams.), Harvard U. (com. exec. session on community policing), Nat. Council on Crime and Delinquency (bd. dirs.), Nat. Acad. Pub. Adminstrn. (Nat. Pub. Svc. award 1988), Am. Soc. Pub. Adminstrn. (Nat. Pub. Svc. award 1988), Am. Leadership Forum, Forum Club of Houston (bd. dirs. 1987—), Calif. Alumni Club of Tex., Houston Bus. and Profl. Men's Club, Alpha Phi Alpha (Award of Merit 2000), Sigma Pi Phi. Democrat. Avocations: travel, reading, writing. Office Fax: 832-366-1584. Personal E-mail: leepbrown1@aol.com.

BROWN, LEON CARL, historian, educator; b. Mayfield, Ky., Apr. 22, 1928; s. Leon Carl and Gwendolyn (Travis) B.; m. Anne Winchester Stokes, Aug. 29, 1953; children: Elizabeth Boone, Joseph Winchester, Jefferson Travis. BA, Vanderbilt U., 1950; postgrad., U. Va., 1950-51, London Sch. Econs., 1951-52; PhD, Harvard, 1962. Fgn. Svc. officer., Beirut, 1954-55, Khartoum, Sudan, 1956-58; asst. prof. Mid. Ea. studies Harvard U., Cambridge, Mass., 1962-66; assoc. prof. Nr. Ea. history and civilization Princeton (N.J.) U., 1966-70, Garrett prof. fgn. affairs, 1970-93, Garrett prof. emeritus, 1993—, chmn. dept. Nr. Ea. studies, 1969-73, dir. program Nr. Ea. studies, 1969-73, 80-93. Author: (with C.A. Micaud and C.H. Moore) Tunisia: The Politics of Modernization, 1964, The Tunisia of Ahmad Bey, 1974, International Politics and the Middle East, 1984, Religion and State: The Muslim Approach to Politics, 2000; editor: State and Society in Independent North Africa, 1966, From Madina to Metropolis: Heritage and Change in the Near Eastern City, 1973, (with Norman Itzkowitz) Psychological Dimensions of Near Eastern Studies, 1977, Centerstage: American Diplomacy Since World War II, 1990, (with Cyril E. Black) Modernization in the Middle East, 1992, Imperial Legacy: The Ottoman Impact On The Balkans & The Middle East, (with Matthew Gordon) Franco-Arab Encounters, 1996, Diplomacy in the Middle East, 2001; translator with commentary: The Surest Path; The Political Treatise of a 19th Century Muslim Statesman, 1967. Served with USAAF, 1945-46. Mem. Middle East Studies Assn. (pres. 1975-76) Home and Office: 191 Hartley Ave Princeton NJ 08540-5613 Personal E-mail: lcbrown@princeton.edu.

BROWN, LEONARD ASHLEIGH (SMOKEY), JR., lawyer; b. Newberry, S.C., July 24, 1969; s. Leonard Ashleigh and Sarah Gibson B.; m. Amy Durr, May 16, 1992; 1 child, Courtney. BA in History, Presbyn. Coll., 1991; JD, U. S.C. Sch. Law, 1997. Bar: S.C. Assoc. Welch Law Firm, Greenwood, SC, 1997—2001; owner, ptnr. Law Office of Smokey Brown, SC, 2001—; mcpl. judge Town of Chapin, SC, 2001—. Prosecutor City of Greenwood, 1998-2001, Lander U., Greenwood, 1999-2001; radio broadcaster Lander U. baseball, 1999-2000. Pres. Broken Ridge Homeowner's Assn., Greenwood, 1998-2000. Mem. ATLA, S.C. Assn. Criminal Def. Lawyers, S.C. Trial Lawyers Assn., Supreme Ct. Hist. Soc., Lake Murray-Irmo Rotary Club, Greater Irmo C. of C. Methodist. Avocations: baseball, historical traveling, hunting, reading, scuba diving. Office: Law Office Smokey Brown PC 7434 Forest Ct Irmo SC 29063-1545 also: 216 Rolling Creek Cir Irmo SC 29063-8383

BROWN, LES (LESTER LOUIS), journalist; b. Indiana Harbor, Ind., Dec. 20, 1928; s. Irving H. and Helen (Feigenbaum) B.; m. Jean Rosalie Slaymaker, June 12, 1959; children: Jessica, Joshua, Rebecca. BA in English, Roosevelt U., Chgo., 1950. Entertainment industry reporter, reviewer theatrical events Chgo. bur. Variety, 1953-55; asso. editor Downbeat mag., 1955; co-founder, operator folk music cabaret The Gate of Horn, Chgo., 1956; Chgo. bur. mgr. Variety, 1957-65; editor radio-TV dept. N.Y.C., 1965-73; asst. mng. editor, 1973; radio-TV corr. N.Y. Times, 1973-80; editor in chief Channels mag., 1980-87; sr. v.p. editorial devel. C.C. Pub., N.Y.C., 1987-91; pub. TV Bus. Internat. mag., 1988-91, editor in chief, 1990-91; columnist, 1992—; pub. World Guide, 1990. Cons. Revson Found., 1978, Ctr. for Comm., NYC, 1991-2003, World Alliance TV for Children, 1993-2001, Golden Rose Montreux TV Festival, 1994-2001, Monte Carlo TV Festival, 1994-2001; lectr. creative writing and entertainment industries Columbia Coll., Chgo., 1959-62, scholar-in-residence, 1985; lectr. comm. Hunter Coll., NYC, 1973-75, New Sch., NYC, 1977-83, Columbia U., 1994-96; lectr. Fordham U., 1995-2002, dir. TV Pantheon Oral History Project, 1996; Poynter fellow in modern journalism Yale U., 1977, lectr., 1978-80; assoc. fellow Morse Coll., 1978-86; Presdl. fellow Aspen Inst., 1978; bd. dirs. Dore Schary Awards, World TV and Radio Coun. UNESCO; sr. fellow Freedom Forum Media Studies Ctr. Columbia U., 1992-93. Author: lyrics Abilene, 1963, Television: The Business Behind The Box, 1971, Electric Media, 1973, New York Times Encyclopedia of Television, 1977, Keeping Your Eye on Television, 1979; Les Brown's Encyclopedia of Television, 1982, Fast Forward: The New Television and American Society, 1983, Les Brown's Encyclopedia of Television, 1992; also articles. Mem. Film-TV adv. bd. N.Y. State Coun. on Arts, 1975; pres. Media Commentary Coun. Inc. With AUS, 1951-53. Recipient Silver Cir. award N.Y. Chpt. Nat. Acad. TV Arts and Scis., 1996. E-mail: tvmaven@cloud9.net.

BROWN, LESTER B., social worker, educator; b. Whitmire, S.C., Jan. 11, 1943; s. William Barney and Minnie Eugenia (Vaughn) Brown. AB in Psychology, U. Chgo., 1969, AM in Social Work, 1971, PhD in Social Treatment, 1980. Sr. child care counselor, therapist Nicholas J. Pritzker Ctr. and Hosp., Chgo., 1964-68, 69; social worker I Ill. Dept. Children and Family Svcs., Chgo., 1967-70, social worker II, 1971; group homes social worker Jewish Children's Bur., Chgo., 1971-73; social worker, field instr. Jackson Park Hosp., Chgo., 1973, clin. dir., 1973-74, cons., 1975-77, SUNY, Albany, 1981, asst. prof. social work, chmn. undergrad. social welfare, 1981-86; prof. social worker Wayne State U., 1986-89; assoc. prof. social work Calif. State U., Long Beach, 1989-95, prof. social work and Am. Indian studies, 1995—. Lectr. U. Wis., Milw., 1977—78, instr., 1978—80; lectr. U. Chgo., 1977—78; guest lectr. Boston Coll., 1981; cons., presenter in field. Author: (book) Two Spirit People: American Indian Lesbian Women and Gay Men, 1997, Aging Gay Men, 1997, Brief Treatment and a New Look at the Task Central Approach, 2003; contbr. articles to profl. jours., chapters to books; mem. editl. bd. Health Care Mgmt. Rev., 1981—84. Bd. dirs. Capital Dist. Travelers Aid Soc., 1983—86; condr. workshops ethnic sensitive work Pittsfield Sch. Dist., Mass., 1984; participant workshops mental health and child welfare; mem. com. Urban League. Grantee, SUNY, 1981, U.S. HHS, 1981, Sch. Social Welfare, 1982. Mem.: NASW, Coun. Social Work Edn., Acad. Cert. Social Workers. Democrat. Avocation: baking/cooking. Home: 810 Orizaba Ave Long Beach CA 90804-4926 Office: Calif State U Long Beach Social Work 1250 N Bellflower Blvd Long Beach CA 90840-0006 Office Phone: 562-985-4984. Personal E-mail: lbbrown@netscape.com. Business E-Mail: lbrown2@csulb.edu.

BROWN, LESTER RUSSELL, research and development company executive; b. Bridgeton, NJ, Mar. 28, 1934; s. Calvin C. and Delia (Smith) B.; m. Shirley Ann Woolington, June 12, 1960 (div.); children: Brian, Brenda. BS in Agrl. Sci., Rutgers U., 1955; MA in Agrl. Econs., U. Md., 1959; MPA, Harvard U., 1962; LHD (hon.), Dickinson Coll.; LLD (hon.), U. Md.; LHD (hon.), Franklin Coll.; LLD (hon.), Williams Coll., Rutgers U.; LHD (hon.), Glassboro State Coll., Tufts U.; LLD (hon.), Coll. of Wooster; LHD (hon.), Clark U., Ripon Coll., Otterbein Coll.; DSc (hon.), U. Pisa, McGill U.; LLD (hon.), U. Notre Dame; D of Pub. Svc. (hon.), Northland Coll.; LHD (hon.), St. Lawrence U.; DSc (hon.), Claremont Coll.; D of Social Sci. (hon.), Villanova U.; DSc (hon.), Westminster Coll., Utah, Westminster Coll., Pa., U. Conn., Ohio State U. With Dept. of Agr., 1958—69, adminstr. internat. agr. devel. service, 1966-69; adv. to sec. U.S. Dept. Agr., Washington, 1965—69; sr. fellow Overseas Devel. Council, 1969-74; pres., founder Worldwatch Inst., Washington, 1974-2000, Earth Policy Inst., Washington, 2001—. Faculty Salzburg Seminar in Am. Studies, 1971, 1974; guest scholar Aspen Inst., summers 1972-74; sr. adv. Japanese Ministry Agr., Forestry, & Fishery; vice chmn. Adv. Com. of the U.S. China Assoc. Environ. Edn.; hon. prof. U. Shanghai, China, 2003; hon. prof. U. Shanghai, 2003, Chinese Acad. Scis., 2005. Author: Man, Land and Food, 1963, Increasing World Food Output, 1965, Seeds of Change, 1970, World Without Borders, 1972, In the Human Interest, 1974, (with Gail Finsterbusch) Man and his Environment: Food, 1974, (with Erik Eckholm) By Bread Alone, 1974 (Christopher award), The Twenty-Ninth Day, 1978 (Ecologia Firenze award), (with Colin Norman and Christopher Flavin) Running on Empty, 1979, Building a Sustainable Society, 1981, State of the World, 1984-2001, (with others) Vital Signs, 1992-2001, (with Hal Kane) Full House, 1994, Who Will Feed China?, 1995, Tough Choices: Facing the Challenge of Global Food Scarcity, 1996; editor: (with Ed Ayres) World Watch Reader, 1998, (with Flavin and Sandra Postel) Saving the Planet, 1991, (with Gardner and Halweil) Beyond Malthus, 1999, Eco-Economy: Building an Economy for the Earth, 2001 (Peka award 2004), (with Larsen and Fischlowitz-Roberts) The Earth Policy Reader, 2002, Plan B: Rescuing a Planet Under Stress and a Civilization in Trouble, 2003, Worldwatch Issue Alert, 2000-01, Eco-Economy Updates, 2001-, Outgrowing the Earth: The Food Security Challenge in an Age of Falling Water Tables and Rising Temperatures, 2005, others; (permanent exhibit) The Works of Lester R. Brown, Cook Coll., Rutgers U., 2005; contbr. articles to profl jours. Mem. adv. com. Inst. Internat. Econs.,UN Found., Eco-Policy Ctr./Rutgers U.; mem. bd. advisors Internat. Fund for China's Environment; bd. dirs. Inst. for Sustainable Devel., Poland; treas. and bd. mem. Farview Found.; mem. adv. coun. Internat. Fund for Agrl. Rsch.; advisor Clean Up the World Project, Australia, Internat. Coun. Earth Day 2000; mem. adv. bd. Ctr. for a New Am. Dream; mem. nat. adv. bd. Population Connection (formerly Zero Population Growth); mem. adv. com. Internews; mem. adv. bd. Green House Network; bd. patrons Internat. Network Green Planners; mem. steering com. Ecol. Cities Project, U. Mass.; dir. Japan for Sustainability; mem. adv. coun. Ecology channel. Recipient Superior Svc. award Dept. Agr., 1965, Arthur S. Flemming award, 1965, A.H. Boerma award UN Food and Agrl. Orgn., 1981, UNEP Environ. Leadership medal, 1982, Lorax award Global Tomorrow Coalition, 1985, award World Wildlife Fund for Nature Internat., 1989, UN Environment prize, 1987, A Bizzozero award U. Parma, 1991, Humanist of Yr. award, 1991, Pro Mundo Habitabili award King Carl XVI Gustaf, Sweden, 1991, Delphi Internat. Cooperation award, 1991, Cervia Ambiente prize, Italy, 1992, Robert Rodale Lectr. award, 1992, Environmentalist of Yr. award Japan Jaycees, 1992, Cert. Spl. Recognition Assn. Am. Geographers, 1993, Blue Planet prize Asahi Glass Found., 1994, J. Sterling Morton Arbor Day award, 1995, Pub. Svc. award Fedn. Am. Scientists, 1995, Disting. Achievement award Heylar House Alumni Assn. Rutgers U., 1995, Rachel Carson Environ. Achievement award Nat. Nutritional Foods Assn., 2000, Bruno H. Schubert Found. environment award, 2001, Natural Bus. Leadership award, 2002, Excellence Adv. award Internat. Fund for China's Environment, 2002, Italian Presdl. medal, 2003, Georg and Greta Borgström prize Royal Swedish Acad. Agriculture & Forestry, 2005, Claire Matzger Lilienthal Disting. Lectr. award Calif. Acad. Scis., 2005; selected as 100 Who Made A Difference The Earth Times, 1995, 100 Champions of Conservation, Audubon Soc., 1998; named one of People of the Century The Daily Jour., NJ, 2000, One of 500 Most Influential People in US in Fgn. Policy World Affairs Coun. Am., 2003, One of 30 Global Visionaries Planet Mag., 2005; named to Bridgeton HS Disting. Alumni Hall of Fame, 2005. Fellow World Bus. Acad.; mem. Coun. Fgn. Rels., World Future Soc., Cosmos Club, Sierra Club (adv. coun. for excellence in environ. engring.). Office: Earth Policy Inst Ste 403 1350 Connecticut Ave NW Washington DC 20036-1995 Office Phone: 202-496-9290. Business E-Mail: epi@earth-policy.org.

BROWN, LILLIAN HILL, retired academic administrator; b. Newport News, Va., Nov. 24, 1932; d. Charlie Wyatt and Caroline Melinda (Rowlett) Hill; m. Louis Franklin Brown, June 30, 1956; children: Avery L., Colin H. BS, Va. State Univ., 1955; MS, U. Bridgeport, 1967, profl. 6th yr. degree, 1983; post grad., So. Conn. State Univ., 1985. Chmn. guidance and pers. svcs. Wilby H.S., Waterbury, Conn., team mem. student assistance team, coord. natural helpers program, proctor SAT coll. bds. prog. Mem. pres.'s adv. bd. Teikyo Post U.; admission advisor com. Naugatuck Valley Comty.-Tech. Coll.; adv. bd. to bd. govs. for higher edn. in Waterbury; adv. panel Racial Imbalance Regulations of Pub. Schs. in Conn.; regional adv. bd. dirs. Bank Boston. Bd. trustees St. Margaret's-McTernan Sch.; bd. dirs., chmn. nominating com. Waterbury Symphony Orch.; trustee, chair nominating com. The Antiquarian and Landmark Soc.; bd. dirs. Children's Comty. Sch.; chmn. bd. dirs. Waterbury chpt. ARC; bd. trustees, chmn. scholarship com. The Waterbury Found.; bd. mgrs., mem. The Waterbury Club; mem. devel. com. Waterbury Hosp. Health Network, Inc.-Waterbury Hosp.; mem. oral history project African Ams. in Waterbury; co-chair Leavenworth Soc./United Way; vestry bd., chalice bearer St. John's Episcopal Ch.; life mem. NAACP; mem. Waterbury chorale; co-founder In Search of Excellence A Scholarship Fund for African Am. Students; incorporator Child Guidance Clinic; co-chair United Way-Leavenworth Soc.; adv. regional bd. Bank Boston. Recipient Plaque for Outstanding Leadership in Cmty., Tribute to Conn. Women, Plaque for Outstanding Leadership in Cmty., Alpha Kappa Alpha, Achievement award Nat. Assn. Negro Bus. and Profl. Woman's Clubs, Inc., Cmty. Svc. award Waterbury Jaycees, 1991, St. John's Order of the Eagle, 1995, Humanitarian Svc. award Anderson's Boys Club, 1999, Cmty. Svc. Vol. of Yr. United Way CNV, 2001. Mem. NEA (life), Conn. Edn. Assn., Waterbury Tchr. Assn., Pupil Pers. and Guidance Assn., The Sch. Counselor (Conn. chpt.), Phi Delta Kappa (Plaque for Dedicated Svc. to U. of Conn. chpt. 1993), Delta Sigma Theta (charter mem. New Haven alumnae chpt., Waterbury alumnae chpt. v.p. 2001)., Waterbury Chorale (v.p.), The Links, Inc. (charter mem. Waterbury chpt.). Avocations: domestic and foreign travel, collecting lladro porcelain, chorale singing, collecting porcelain dolls of color. Home: 59 Timber Ln Waterbury CT 06705-3608

BROWN, LISA ROCHELL, academic administrator; b. Akron, Ohio, Feb. 14, 1962; d. James Allen and Elaine (Foster) B.; 1 child, Bridjette Nicole. BS in Biology, U. Akron, 1986, MPA, 1991. Coord. peer counseling program U. Akron, 1986-90, rsch. assoc., 1991-92; coord. minority admissions and retention programs Miami U., Oxford, Ohio, 1990-91; dir. intercultural rels. Edinboro U. of Pa., 1992-99; assoc. dir. playground safety and injury prevention Columbus (Ohio) Children's Hosp., 1999—. Ind. cons. Lorain (Ohio) County C.C., 1992—; faculty advisor Alliance for Racial Identity and Cultural Acceptance, Intercultural Diplomats. Bd. dirs. Booker T. Washington Ctr., Hamilton, 1990-91, Walking in Black History, JFK Cmty. Ctr., Erie, Pa., 1998; chair scholarship com. Arlington Christian Acad., Akron, 1991-93; chair Met. Erie Intervention Program, 1994—. Recipient Dr. MLK Jr. Day of Svc. award Corp. for Nat. Svc., 1998; grantee Erie Ins. Group Inc., 1996-98, Erie Cmty. Found., 1997, Pa. State Sys. Higher Edn., 1997. Mem. Alpha Kappa Alpha. Mem. Ch. of God. Avocations: aerobics, singing, exercise, reading, basketball. Office: Columbus Childrens Hosp Columbus OH 43205

BROWN, LORENE B(YRON), retired library educator; b. Plant City, Fla., Nov. 9, 1933; d. Benjamin and Sallie (Barton) Byron; m. Paul L. Brown, Aug. 1, 1974. BS, Fort Valley State Coll., 1955; MSL.S., Atlanta U., 1956; PhD, U. Wis., 1974. Cataloguer N.C. Central U., Durham, 1956-58, Gibbs Jr. Coll., St. Petersburg, Fla., 1958-60, Fort Valley State Coll., Ga., 1960-65, Norfolk State U., Va., 1965-70; assoc. prof., dean Atlanta U., 1970-89, prof., 1989—2003; dir. Info. Retrieval Workshops, Atlanta, 1976-78; evaluator Coop. Coll. Library Ctr., Atlanta, 1979-82; cons. United Bd. Coll. Devel., Atlanta, 1976-79. Mem. southeastern/Atlantic regional adv. coun. Nat. Network Librs. Medicine, 2001—03. Author: Subject Access for African American Material, 1995. Mem. Friends of Library, Atlanta, 1982. Recipient Rachel Schenk award Library Sch. U. Wis., Madison, 1971; So. Fellowship Found. fellow Atlanta, 1972-74 Mem. ALA, Am. Soc. for Info. Sci., Assn. Library and Info. Sci. Edn., Ga. Library Assn., Met Atlanta Library Assn., Beta Phi Mu. Democrat. Baptist. Home: 855 Flamingo Dr SW Atlanta GA 30311-2402

BROWN, LOWELL SEVERT, physicist, researcher; b. Visalia, Calif., Feb. 15, 1934; s. Volney Clifford and Anna Marie Evelyn (Jacobson) B.; m. Shirley Isabel Mitchell, June 23, 1956; 1 son, Stephen Clifford. AB, U. Calif., Berkeley, 1956; PhD (NSF predoctoral fellow 1956-61), Harvard U., 1961; postgrad., U. Rome, 1961-62, Imperial Coll., London, 1962-63. From rsch. assoc. to assoc. prof. physics Yale U., 1963-68; mem. faculty U. Wash., Seattle, 1968—, prof. physics, 1970-2001, prof. emeritus, 2001—; mem. staff Los Alamos (N.Mex.) Sci. Lab., 2001—. Vis. prof. Imperial Coll., London, 1971-72, Columbia U., N.Y.C., 1990; vis. scientist Brookhaven Nat. Lab., summer, 1965-68, Lawrence Berkeley Lab., summer 1966, Stanford Accelerator Ctr., summer, 1967, CERN, Geneva, summer, 1979, Inst. for Theoretical Physics, U. Calif., Santa Barbara, winter 1999; mem. Inst. Advanced Study, Princeton, N.J., 1979-80; cons. Los Alamos Nat. Lab., spring 1999, vis. scientist, 1991; vis. physicist Deutches Elektronen-Synchrontron, Hamburg, 1986 Author: Quantum Field Theory, 1992; mem. editl. bd. Phys. Rev., 1978-81; editor Phys. Rev. D, 1987-95; contbr. articles to profl. publs. Trustee Seattle Youth Symphony Orch., 1986—95. Postdoctoral fellow NSF, 1961-63; sr. post-doctoral fellow, 1971-72; Guggenheim fellow, 1979-80 Mem. Ferrari Club of Am. (dir. Northwest region 1999-2003). Home: 621 Halona Santa Fe NM 87505 Office: X-7 MS F699 PO Box 1668 Los Alamos NM 87545 Personal E-mail: lowellb@ferrariclub.com.

BROWN, LYN, newscaster; married; 2 children. With Sta. WSOC-Radio, Charlotte, NC, 1976—80; anchor, corr. Sta. WTNH-TV, New Haven, 1980—84, CNN, N.Y.C., 1984—88, CBS News, 1988—90; co-anchor Sta. WNYW-TV, N.Y.C., 1990—. Recipient Emmy, 1992. Office: WNYW 205 E 67th St New York NY 10021

BROWN, LYNETTE RALYA, journalist, publicist; b. Beloit, Wis., Dec. 15, 1926; d. Lynn Louis and Ethel Clara (Meeker) Ralya; m. Donald Adair Brown, Jr., Dec. 20, 1947; children: Donald Adair III, Alison Laura, Julia Carol. BA in Journalism, Mich. State U., 1948, MA in Journalism, 1985; MA in Mass Comm., Wayne State U., 1983. Actress, publicist Grand Traverse Playhouse, Traverse City, Mich., 1946 (summer), N.Y. Summer Playhouse, Mackinac Island, Mich., 1947 (summer); writer WILS Radio, Lansing, Mich., 1947-48; writer, performer WJBK Radio, TV, Detroit, 1948-49; editor Denby Ctr. News, Detroit, 1949-51; freelance writer Oakland County, Mich., 1952-78; editor Henry Ford Mus., Dearborn, Mich., 1979-81; writer, reporter Legal Advertiser Newspaper, Detroit, 1983-85; publicist Bloomfield (Mich.) and Birmingham (Mich.) Pub. Librs., 1986-89; freelance writer, publicist Lynette Brown Comm., Birmingham, Mich., 1989—. Columnist: (newspaper) At the Libraries, 1986-89; solo performer Elizabeth Cady Stanton, 1995—. Probation sponsor Dist. Ct. Mich., 1960-70; publicist Oakland County Vol. Bur., 1979-82; leader sr. high/jr. high youth group Drayton Ave. Presbyn. Ch., Oakland County, 1952-54, 62-66, Pine Hill Congl. Ch., Oakland County, 1968-71, Northbrook Presbyn. Ch., Oakland County, 1976-77; polit. campaign worker Rep. candidates and non-partisan jud. candidates, 1952—; Cub Scout leader Royal Oak Emerson Sch., Oakland County, 1961-64; Girl Scout troop leader Bloomfield Twp. Meadow Lake Sch., Oakland County, 1966-71; dir. Martha Griffiths Project, 1989-. Grantee N.Y. State's Thanks Be To Grandmother Winifred Found., 1996, Elizabeth Kummer Award AAUW Mich., 2002. Mem. AAUW (chair women's issues, pub. info. dir. 1995-2000, state projects dir. 2000—), Oakland County C. of C. (Athena award 1995), Mich. Women's Studies Assn. (bd. dirs. 1999—). Home and Office: 6120 Westmoor Rd Bloomfield Township MI 48301 Office Phone: 248-626-5414.

BROWN, MABEL (WELTON), lawyer; b. Geneseo, Ill., Dec. 7, 1916; d. Harry E. and Mabel (Welton) B. BA, Oberlin Coll., 1938; JD, U. Chgo., 1941. Bar: Ill. Ptnr. Brown and Brown, Geneseo, 1941-44; sole owner Brown & Brown, Geneseo, 1944-81; sr. ptnr. Brown and Ray, Geneseo, 1981—. Atty. Green River Spl. Drainage Dist., Henry and Bureau Counties, Ill.; chmn. Geneseo Planning Commn., 1961-68, bd. dirs. Geneseo Hist. Assn., 1987—. Mem. ABA, Ill. Bar Assn., Henry County Bar Assn. (pres. 1973-76). Republican. Methodist. Office: Brown and Ray 115 N State St Geneseo IL 61254-1345 Office Phone: 309-944-5115.

BROWN, MARGARET ANN, lawyer; b. Mobile, Ala., 1952; BA, Univ. Va., 1974, JD, 1977. Bar: La. 1977, Va. 1986. Ptnr., practice group leader, real estate fin. Troutman Sanders LLP, McLean, Va. Mem.: ABA, Fairfax Bar Assn., La. State Bar Assn. Office: Troutman Sanders LLP Ste 500 1660 Industrial Dr Mc Lean VA 22102 Office Phone: 703-734-4336. Office Fax: 703-448-6506. Business E-Mail: ann.brown@troutmansanders.com.

BROWN, MARGARET DEBEERS, lawyer; b. Washington, Sept. 24, 1943; d. John Sterling and Marianna Hurd (Hill) deBeers; m. Timothy Nils, Aug. 28, 1965; children: Emeline Susan, Eric Franklin. BA magna cum laude, Radcliffe Coll., 1965; postgrad., Harvard U., 1965-67; JD, U. Calif., Berkeley, 1968. Bar: Calif. 1969, U.S. Ct. Appeals (9th cir.) 1971, U.S. Ct. Appeals (D.C. cir.) 1986, U.S. Ct. Appeals (2d cir.) 1987, U.S. Supreme Ct. 1972. Assoc. White, Hamilton, Wyche, Shell & Pollard, Petersburg, Va., 1968-70, Heller, Ehrman, White & McAuliffe, San Francisco, 1970-73; sole practice San Francisco, 1973-77, 98—; atty. Pacific Telephone (name changed to Pacific Bell), San Francisco, 1977-83, sr. atty., 1983-85; sr. counsel Pacific Telesis Group, 1985-98, ret. Elder, deacon, sec.-treas. of deacons Calvary Presbyn. Ch., San Francisco; bd. dirs. No. Calif. Presbyn. Homes and Svcs chmn. 2003-. Mem. Calif. State Bar (mem. com. bar examiners 1994-98, chair subcom. on petitions and litigation 1996-98), San Francisco Bar Assn. (chmn. corp. law dept. sect. 1993, judiciary com. 1993-96, nominating com. 1993), Harvard Club of San Francisco (v.p. schs. 1998—2003, bd. dirs.), Radcliffe Club of San Francisco (bd. dirs.), Phi Beta Kappa. E-mail: mdbk@pge.com.

BROWN, MARGUERITE JOHNSON, music educator; b. El Paso, Tex., Mar. 31, 1940; d. Don Lee and Eloise (Watson) Johnson; m. R. Don Lumley, Dec. 1961 (div. July 1982); children: Jessica Lumley Rodela, Jeffrey Tate Lumley; m. Gilbert Bivins Brown, Oct. 27, 1989; 1 stepchild, Erich Michael. MusB in Piano Pedagogy with honors, U. Tex., 1962; M in Liberal Arts with honors, So. Meth. U., 1974. Tchr., group piano Dallas Ind. Sch. Dist., 1965-72; tchr. music theory Canal Zone Coll., Panama Canal Zone, 1977-79, musical theater accompanist, 1975-79; tchr. class piano Del Mar Coll., Corpus Christi, Tex., 1980-82; tchr., edn. dir. piano & keyboard Coast Music Co., Corpus Christi, Tex., 1982-87; tchr. class piano, theory Del Mar Coll., Corpus Christi, Tex., 1987-90, performance accompanist, 1993-94; owner, piano tchr. pvt. Studio 88, Corpus Christi, Tex., 1994—2001; resident music dir. Monastery St. Clare, Brenham, Tex., 2001—. Mem.: Nat. Guild Piano Tchrs. (adjudicator), Nat. Guild Piano Tchrs., Dallas Music Edn. Assn. (pres. piano divsn. 1969—71), Music Tchrs. Nat. Assn., Corpus Christi Music Tchrs. Assn. (pres. 1995—97), Nat. Fedn. Music Clubs. Office: Monastery Saint Clare 9288 Hwy 105 Brenham TX 77833-7269 Home: 9280 Highway 105 Brenham TX 77833-7269 E-mail: margueritejohn@cs.com.

BROWN, MARK D., medical educator; MD, Jefferson Med. Coll., 1961, PhD, 1965. Cert. Orthopaedic Surgery Am. Bd. of Orhopaedic Surgery, 1972. Prof., chmn. Miller Sch. of Medicine, U. Miami, Dept. Orthopaedics & Rehab., Miami, Fla., 1973—. Lcdr NAVY, 1961—73. Office: U Miami Sch Medicine PO Box 016960 (R-2) Miami FL 33101 Office Phone: 305-243-6725. E-mail: mbrown@med.miami.edu.

BROWN, MARK E., manufacturing executive; b. Peosta, Iowa; BA, U. Iowa. Acct. Whirlpool Corp., 1973, mgr., Columbia (SC) plant, 1988; controller N. Am. Appliance Group/Whirlpool, 1991—93, v.p., procurement, 1993—95, gen. mgr. mktg., 1995—96; controller Whirlpool Asia, Hong Kong, 1996—97; corp. v.p. controller Whirlpool Corp., 1997—99, exec. v.p., CFO, 1999—2002, sr. v.p., global strategic sourcing, 2002—. Office: Whirlpool Corp 2000 N M-63 Benton Harbor MI 49022*

BROWN, MARK MALLOCH, international organization official; married; 4 children. Grad. in History, Cambridge (Eng.) U.; M in Polit. Sci., U. Mich. Polit. corr. Economist Mag., 1977—79; with UN High Commr. for Refugees, 1979-83; founder, editor The Economist Devel. Report, 1983-86; ptnr. Sawyer-Miller Group, 1986—94; dir. external affairs World Bank, 1994—96, v.p. external affairs and v.p. UN affairs, 1996—99; admin. UN Devel. Program UN, NYC, 1999—, chief of staff to sec. gen., 2005—. Dir. field ops. for Cambodian refugees, Thailand, 1979-81; dep. chief emergency unit, Geneva, 1981; vice-chmn. bd. Refugees Internat., Washington; mem. Soros Adv. Com., Bosnia, 1993-94; chmn., UN sec-gen. task force on UN comm. reform, 1997. Contbr. articles to profl. jours. Recipient (UN High Commr. for Refugees and staff) Nobel Peace prize, 1981, named one of most influential people, TIME mag., 2005. Office: UN Devel Program External Affairs 1 United Plaza New York NY 10017 Fax: 202-522-2644.

BROWN, MARK T., philosopher, educator; b. Neosho, Mo., July 18, 1948; s. Clarence W. and Marguerite T. Brown; m. Glenda C. Wagner, July 23, 1987; 1 child, Hilary T. PhD in Philosophy, U. Kans., 1987. Prof. philosophy U. Wis. Colls., Wausau, 1987—. Contbr. articles to profl. jours. Mem.: Am. Philos. Assn. (assoc.). Achievements include research in ethical analysis of issues in reproductive medicine and the philosophical implications of psychopathology. Home: 518 South 7th Ave Wausau WI 54401 Office: Univ Wis Colleges 518 South 7th Ave Wausau WI 54401 Office Phone: 715-261-6266. Business E-Mail: mbrown@uwc.edu.

BROWN, MARY ELLEN, former state legislator, accountant; b. Hartland, Maine, July 26, 1952; d. Justin O. and Ernestine (Garnett) Humphrey; m. Gary R. Brown, June 6, 1971; children: John A., Jessica I. AA, Franklin Pierce C.C., Concord, N.H., 1978. Pvt. practice Automated Bookkeeping Svcs., Pittsfield, NH, 1976—; realtor historic properties and distinctive homes Pembroke. Author: Out of Season, 1997, Messages From Mothers to Daughters, 2001, The Impeachment Trial of the New Hampshire Surpreme Court Justuce, 2002, Promoting Your Book in New Hampshire, 2004, others; contbr. articles to newspapers, mags. State legislator, N.H., 1995-96; pres. Chichester (N.H.) PTO, 1979, Tax Payers Assn., 1996. Mem. Internat. Women's Writers Guild, Nat. Soc. Pub. Accts., N.H. Wildlife Fedn., Go N.H. (polit. group), N.H. Writers Project. Avocations: writing, fishing, gardening.

BROWN, MARY EVELYN, music educator; b. Hagerstown, Md., May 29, 1953; d. John Michael and Evelyn Jane (Yeide) Aurand; children: Sarah Kathryn, Rachel Allison. BA in music, Hood Coll., 1975; MusM in music edn., Butler U., 1980. Cert. English Tenn. State U., 1985, tchg. Md., Pa., Ind., Tenn., Mich. Vocal music tchr., choral dir. Schuylkill Valley Sch. Dist., Leesport, Pa., 1975—76; vocal music tchr. Carmel-Clay Schs., Carmel, Ind., 1976—85, Tippecanoe County Schs., Ind., 1981—85, Nashville Pub. Schs., Nashville, 1983—89; English tchr. Anglo-English Sch., Hamburg, Germany, 1989—90; vocal music tchr. Phila. Pub. Schs., Phila., 1991; vocal music tchr., choral dir. Ferndale Pub. Schs., Ferndale, Mich., 1992—. Pvt. piano, voice instr. Coord. CROP Walk, Hood Coll., 1973—74. Grantee, Met. Nashville Pub. Edn. Found., 1987, 1988, Ferndale Edn. Found., 1998—2005. Mem.: NEA, Mich. Sch. Vocal Music Assn., Am. Choral Dirs. Assn., Music Edn. Nat. Conf. Avocations: reading, writing, singing, walking.

BROWN, MARY ROSE, energy executive; B in Comm., S.W. Tex. State U. V.p. pub. rels. Atkins Agy., 1983—97, Valero Corp., San Antonio, 1997—, sr. v.p. corp. comm. Office: Valero Corp Hdqs One Valero Place San Antonio TX 78212-3186*

BROWN, MATTHEW A., state official; b. Providence; m. Marisa Brown. BA, Columbia U.; JD, Yale Law Sch. Founder and exec. dir. Democracy Compact, 2000—02; Sec. of State State of RI, 2003—. Exec. dir. City Year, Democracy Compact. Democrat. Office: 217 State House Providence RI 02903

BROWN, MATTHEW S., lawyer; b. Chgo., Jan. 29, 1955; BA magna cum laude, Conn. Coll.; JD, Georgetown U., 1978. Bar: Ill. 1978. Ptnr. Katten Muchin Zavis Rosenman, Chgo. Mem.: ABA, Chgo. Bar Assn. Office: Katten Muchin Zavis Rosenman 525 West Monroe St, Ste 1600 Chicago IL 60661 Office Phone: 312-909-5207. Office Fax: 312-577-8726. E-mail: matthew.brown@kmzr.com.

BROWN, MEREDITH M., lawyer; b. N.Y.C., Oct. 18, 1940; s. John Mason Brown and Catherine (Screven) Meredith; m. Sylvia Lawrence Barnard, July 17, 1965; 1 child, Mason Barnard. AB, Harvard U., 1961, JD, 1965. Bar: N.Y. 1965, U.S. Ct. Appeals (2d cir.) 1966, U.S. Dist. Ct. (so. dist.) N.Y. 1976. Law clk. to Hon. Leonard P. Moore U.S. Ct. Appeals (2d cir.), N.Y.C., 1965-66; assoc. Debevoise & Plimpton, N.Y.C., 1966—72, ptnr., 1973—2004, of counsel, 2004—05, co-chair corp. dept., 1993—2002, chair or co-chair mergers and acquisitions group, 1985—2004. Author: (with others) Takeovers: A Strategic Guide to Mergers & Acquisitions, 2d edit., 2004, Global Offerings, 1994, Privatisations, 1994, Mechanics of Global Equity Offerings, 1995, International Mergers and Acquisitions: An Introduction, 1999; contbr. articles to profl. publs. Mem. ABA (bus. law sect.), Assn. of Bar of City of N.Y. (chmn. profl. responsibility com. 1987-90), Internat. Bar Assn. (co-chmn. com. on issues and trading of securities, sect. on bus. law 1994-98, co-chmn. capital markets forum, sec. bus. law 1998-2002). Home: 79 Tipping Rock Rd Stonington CT 06378 E-mail: mmbrown@debevoise.com.

BROWN, MERRILL MARK, publishing executive, corporate planner; b. Phila., Aug. 2, 1952; s. Fred R. and Gertrude (Katz) B.; m. Barbara S. Kappalman, May 25, 1980; children: Jessica, Rachel. BA in Polit. Sci., Washington U., St. Louis, 1974. Reporter Media Gen. News, Winston-Salem, N.C., 1974-75, Washington corr., 1975-78; fin. writer Washington Star, 1978-79, Washington Post, 1979-82, N.Y. corr., 1982-84; dir. bus. devel. Washington Post Co., 1984-85; exec. editor Channels Mag., N.Y.C., 1985-87, editor, 1987-88, editor-in-chief, 1989—; sr. v.p. Ct. TV, 1990-94; editor in chief MSNBC.com, 1996—, now sr. v.p., editor in chief, 2000—. TV commentator with appearances on NBC, CNN, other networks. Contbr. World Book Year Book, 1982-86; free-lance writer. E-mail: Merrill.Brown@MSNBC.COM.

BROWN, MICHAEL ARTHUR, lawyer; b. San Angelo, Tex., Oct. 15, 1938; s. Edwin Michael and Sadie Beatrice (Johnson) B.; m. Carol Ann Campbell, Dec. 20, 1958 (div. Mar. 1978); children: Michael Paul, Michele Louise; m. Teresa Ann Boyd, Feb. 24, 1979; 1 child, Matthew Arthur. BBA, LLB magna cum laude, St. Mary's U., 1961; LLM, Georgetown U., 1970. Bar: Tex. 1962, U.S. Supreme Ct. 1967, D.C. 1974, U.S. Ct. Appeals (5th cir.) 1975. Commd. 2nd lt. U.S. Army, 1961, advanced through grades to maj., 1966, resigned, 1969; ret. as Col. USAR, 1991; dep. asst. gen. counsel U.S. Dept. Commerce, Washington, 1969-73; gen. counsel U.S. Consumer Product Safety Commn., Washington, 1973-76, exec. dir., 1976-79; dep. gen./enforcement counsel U.S. EPA, Washington, 1982-83; ptnr. Schmeltzer, Aptaker & Sheppard, Washington, 1979-82, 84-90, Thelen, Marrin, Johnson, Washington, 1990-91, McCutchen, Doyle, Brown & Enersen, Washington, 1991-97, Brown & Freeston, Washington, 1997—. Named one of Outstanding Young Lawyers U.S., Jr. C. of C., 1969. Mem. D.C. Bar Assn., Tex. Bar Assn. Avocation: snow and water skiing. Office: Brown and Freeston 3201 New Mexico Ave NW Washington DC 20016-2756 E-mail: mab@brown-freeston.com.

BROWN, MICHAEL DEWAYNE, former federal agency administrator, lawyer; b. Guymon, Okla., Nov. 11, 1954; s. Wayne E. and R. Eloise B.; m. Tamara Ann Oxley, July 19, 1973; children: Jared Michael, Amy Aryann. Student, Southeastern State Coll., 1973-75; BA in Pub. Adminstrn./Polit. Sci., Cen. State U., Edmond, Okla., 1978; JD, Oklahoma City U. Sch. Law, 1981. Bar: Okla. 1982, Colo. 1992, U.S. Dist. Ct. (no. and we. dists.) Okla. 1982, U.S. Ct. Appeals (10th cir.) 1982, U.S. Ct. Appeals (D.C. cir.) 1987. Assoc. Long, Ford, Lester & Brown, Enid, Okla., 1982-87; pvt. practice Enid, Okla., 1987—; gen. counsel & dep. dir. Fed. Emergency Mgmt. Agy. (FEMA), Wash., DC, 2001—02; under sec. Preparedness & Response (FEMA dir.) U.S. Dept. Homeland Security, Wash., DC, 2003—05. Adj. prof. state and local govt. law legis. Oklahoma City U.; cons. No. Okla. Devel. Assn., Enid, 1983-91; gen. counsel Alpha Oil Co., Duncan, Okla., 1985, Physicians Mgmt. Svc. Corps., 1985-90, Physicians of Okla., Inc., Physicians Med. Plan Okla., Inc., City Nat. Bank & Trust Co., 1987-88, Stanfield Printing Co., 1987—, Hammell Newspapers, Inc., 1987-90, Dillingham Ins., 1989-91, Suits Rig Corp., Suits Drilling Co., 1989-91; chmn. bd. dirs. Okla. Mcpl. Power Authority, Edmond, 1982-88, judges & stewards commr. Internat. Arabian Horse Assn., 1991—. Councilman City of Edmond, 1981; cons. Okla. Reps., Oklahoma City, 1983; bd. dirs. Okla. Christian Home, Edmond, 1985; Rep. nominee 6th Dist. U.S. Congress, 1988; co-chmn. Nat. Challengers Polit. Coalition, 1989-91; trustee, co-chair fin. com. Theodore Roosevelt Assn., 1994—. Michael D. Brown Hydroelectric Power Plant and Dam named in his honor, Kaw Reservoir, Okla., 1987. Mem. Okla. Bar Assn. (assoc. bar examiner 1984—), MD Physicians Okla., Ariz. and La., MD Physicians of Tulsa. Mem. Christian Ch. (Disciples Of Christ). Avocations: travel, photography, reading, wilderness adventures, swimming.

BROWN, MICHAEL JAY, lawyer; b. 1955; AB cum laude, Harvard Coll., 1976; JD, Boston Univ., 1979. Bar: Wash. 1979. Atty., corp. fin., securities practice group Bogle & Gates PLLC, 1997—99; ptnr., corp. dept. Dorsey & Whitney LLP, Seattle, 1999—, and co-chair, emerging companies group. Bd. adv. The Accessibility Group Inc. Mem.: Nat. Assn. Bond Lawyers, NASD Bd. of Arbitrators, Wash. State Bar Assn. (exec. com., editor, bus. law sect. 1989—96). Office: Dorsey & Whitney LLP Ste 3400 US Bank Ctr 1420 Fifth Ave Seattle WA 98101 Office Phone: 206-903-8811. Office Fax: 206-903-8820. Business E-Mail: brown.michael@dorsey.com.

BROWN, MICHAEL K., lawyer; b. Woodside, NY, Aug. 13, 1956; m. Martha Brown; 3 children. AB, Georgetown U., 1978; JD, U. San Francisco, 1982. Bar: Calif. 1982. With Crosby, Heafey, Roach & May (combined with Reed Smith LLP, 2003), LA, 1982—2002, mng. ptnr., LA office, 1991—94, mem. exec. com., 1991—2002, chair, LA Product Liability Group, 1996—2000, chair, LA Comml. Litig. Group, 2000—01, chair, Complex Litig. Practice Group, 2002; ptnr., mem. exec. com. Reed Smith LLP, LA, 2003—. Mem. Product Liability Adv. Coun., Inc. Bd. governors U. San Francisco Law Soc., 1989—91; bd. counselors U. San Francisco Sch. Law, 1991—; legal policy adv. bd. Wash. Legal Found. Mem.: Food and Drug Law Inst., Def. Rsch. Inst. (mem. drug and med. device com.), Assn. So. Calif. Def. Counsel, LA County Bar Assn., Internat. Assn. Def. Counsel (mem. legis. jud. and govtl. affairs com. 2000—, vice chair drug, device and biotech com. 2000—02, 2004—), Internat. Trademark Assn., Assn. Bus. Trial Lawyers (bd. governors LA chpt. 2000—04), ABA. Office: Reed Smith LLP 355 S Grand Ave Ste 2900 Los Angeles CA 90071-1514 Office Phone: 213-457-8018. Office Fax: 213-457-8080. Business E-Mail: mkbrown@reedsmith.com.

BROWN, MICHAEL LANCE, lawyer; b. Pearsall, Tex., Jan. 3, 1950; s. Alanson Wesley and Ruth (Gillis) B.; m. Nela Laura Thomas, May 12, 1971; 1 child, Robert Allen. BA, U. Tex., 1972, JD, 1975. Bar: Tex. 1975, La. 1981, U.S. Ct. Appeals (5th and 11th cirs.) 1981, U.S. Dist. Ct. (so. dist.) Tex. 1982, U.S. Dist. Ct. (we. dist.) Tex. 1984, U.S. Supreme Ct. 1984, U.S. Dist. Ct. (no. dist.) Tex. 1986, U.S. Dist. Ct. (ea. dist.) Tex. 1987; cert. oil, gas and mineral law Tex. Bd. Legal Specialization, 1987. Lease analyst Exxon Co. U.S.A., Houston, 1975-77; staff atty. land dept. Coastal Corp., Houston, 1977-79; law dept. Getty Oil Co., Houston, 1979-81; ptnr. Dohoney & Collier (and predecessor firm), Houston, 1981-86; pvt. practice Houston, 1986-89; ptnr. Brown & Adkins, Houston, 1989—. Mem. ABA, Houston Bar Assn., Am. Assn. Petroleum Landmen, Houston Assn. Petroleum Landmen, Downton Optimist Club, Houston Club, Phi Beta Kappa. Methodist. Home: 1508 W Clay St Houston TX 77019-4914 Office: 712 Main St Ste 2120 Houston TX 77002-3206 E-mail: attorneybrown@msn.com.

BROWN, MICHAEL RICHARD, minister; b. Columbus, Ohio, Mar. 2, 1959; s. Cornelius Paul Brown and Pearl Elizabeth (Baker) Buck; m. Christine Elaine Stanley, Aug. 23, 1980; 1 child, Stephanie Nicole. BA in Bible and Religion, Huntington Coll., 1981, M in Ministry, 1983, postgrad., 1984. Ordained to ministry Ch. of United Brethren in Christ, 1983. Min. Monroe United Brethren Ch., Ind., 1982—89, Franklin United Brethren Ch., New Albany, Ohio, 1989—. Dir. Adams County Soccer Clinic, Decatur, Ind., 1984—85; chmn. Adams County Child Protection Team, Decatur, 1985; mem. Hoosiers for Better Schs., A-Plus Program; soccer coach New Albany Mid. Sch., 1989—2003; nat. bd. mem. Looking Unto Jesus Churches, Philippines; chmn. bd. dirs. Ch. Planting Ctrl. Conf. United Brethren Ch.; bd. dirs. Camp COTUBIC, 1996—2002; v.p. Adams County Energy Assistance Inc., 1986. Named one of Outstanding Young Men of Am., 1985. Mem. New Albany Ministerial Assn. (v.p. 1994, pres. 1991, 94, conf. supt. Columbus dist. 1995-97). Republican. Avocations: soccer coach, running. Home: 6695 Albanyview Rd Westerville OH 43081-9236 Office: Franklin United Brethren Ch 7171 Central College Rd New Albany OH 43054-9303

BROWN, MICHAEL ROBERT, lawyer; b. Worcester, Mass., Apr. 5, 1938; s. Walter David and Ethel Fay (Berman) B.; m. Susan Fay Lappin, July 8, 1962; children: Laura, Pamela. BA, Bowdoin Coll., 1959; JD, Columbia U., 1962. Bar: Mass. 1963, N.Y. 1968. Staff atty. NLRB, Washington, 1963-66; assoc. Simpson, Thacher & Bartlett, N.Y.C., 1966-70; ptnr. Herrick & Smith, Boston, 1970-84, Goldstein & Manello, Boston, 1984-90, Palmer & Dodge, Boston, 1990—2002, Seyfarth Shaw, Boston, 2002—. Adj. prof. employment law Sch. Law Suffolk U., Boston, Selectman, Wellesley, Mass., 1992-95. Fellow Coll. Labor and Employment Lawyers; mem. ABA, Mass. Bar Assn., Boston Bar Assn. Office: Seyfarth Shaw Two Seaport Ln Boston MA 02210-2028 Office Phone: 617-946-4907. Business E-Mail: mrbrown@seyfarth.com.

BROWN, MICHAEL ROBERT, healthcare corporation executive; b. Joliet, Ill., Aug. 9, 1960; s. Robert Raymond and Virginia A. (Bianchi) B. AAS, Joliet Jr. Coll., 1980; BS, No. Ill. U., 1983, MBA, 1996. Acctg. supr. northern region DeKalb (Ill.) Genetics, 1982-85; fin. analyst Baxter Healthcare Corp., Deerfield, Ill., 1985, sr. fin. analyst, 1985-87, sr. consols. analyst, 1987-88, mgr. acctg. svcs., 1988-89, mgr. corp. acctg., 1989-93, dir. fin. planning McGaw Park, Ill., 1993-95, asst. contr. renal divsn., 1995-99, v.p. fin. renal divsn., 1999—2003, dir. fin., medication delivery, 2003—05, dir. corp. audit, 2005—. Vol. Jr. Achievement, United Way; bd. exec. advisors No. Ill. U. Mem. Inst. Mgmt. Accts., Chgo. Coun. Fgn. Rels., No. Ill. U. Alumni Assn., No. Ill. U. Exec. Club. Avocations: music, tennis. Personal E-mail: mrbrown9@aol.com.

BROWN, MICHAEL ROBERT, communications educator, poet; b. Phila., Apr. 20, 1940; s. Edwin W. Brown and Tybertus J. Wallick; children: John, Timothy, Kenneth, David. BA, U. Scranton, 1962; EdM, Temple U., 1966; PhD, U. Mich., 1971. Cert. secondary English Pa. Asst. prof. U. Ill., Chgo., 1976—80; prof. North Park Coll., Chgo., 1980—82; assoc. prof. English Chgo. State U., 1983—91; lectr. U. R.I., Kingston, 1991—92; prof. comm. Mount Ida Coll., Newton, Mass., 1992—. Vis. prof. Suwon (South Korea) U., 1986—87. Author poetry. Home: 3 Bay Dr Buzzards Bay MA 02532 Office: Mount Ida Coll 777 Dedham St Newton MA 02459 Office Phone: 617-928-4548. E-mail: michaelbrown@lifename.com.

BROWN, MICHAEL STUART, geneticist, educator, science administrator; b. Bklyn., Apr. 13, 1941; s. Harvey and Evelyn (Katz) Brown; m. Alice Lapin, June 21, 1964; children: Jane Elizabeth, Ellen Sarah. BA, U. Pa., 1962, MD, 1966; DSc (hon.), Rensselaer Poly. Inst., 1982, U. Chgo., 1982, U. Pa., 1986, U. Buenos Aires, 1988, U. Paris, 1988, So. Meth. U., 1993, U. Miami, 1996; DSc (hon.), Rockefeller U., 2001. Intern, then resident in medicine Mass. Gen. Hosp., Boston, 1966-68; served with USPHS, 1968-70; clin. assoc. NIH, 1968-71; asst. prof. U. Tex. Southwestern Med. Sch., Dallas, 1971-74; Paul J. Thomas chair in med. Jonsson Ctr. Molecular Genetics, 1977—; W. A. (Monty) Moncrief Disting. Chair in Cholesterol and Arteriosclerosis Rsch. Southwestern Med. Sch. of biomed. scis., 1989—. Mem. med. adv. bd. Scripps Inst.; bd. dirs. Pfizer Inc., 1996—, Regeneron, Inc., 1991—. Co-editor: The Metabolic Basis of Inherited Disease, 1983. Recipient Pfizer award, Am. Chemical Soc., 1976, Passano award, Passano Found., 1978, Lena Annenberg Hazen award, 1982, Albert Lasker Med. Rsch. award, 1985, Horwitz prize, 1985, Nobel prize in physiology or medicine, 1985, Nat. Med. Sci., U.S. Govt., 1988, Albany Med. Ctr. prize in medicine, 2003. Mem.: Royal Acad. Scis. (fgn.), Harvey Soc., Assn. Am. Physicians, Am. Soc. Clin. Investigation, Nat. Acad. Scis. (Lounsbery award 1979). Office: UT Southwestern Med Ctr Dept Molecular Genetics 5323 Harry Hines Blvd Dallas TX 75390-9046 E-mail: mike.brown@utsouthwestern.edu.*

BROWN, MIKE, professional sports team executive; b. 1935; s. Paul and Katie Brown; m. Nancy Brown; children: Katie Blackburn, Paul. BS in Business, Dartmouth Coll., 1957; JD, Harvard Law Sch. Asst. gen. mgr. Cin. Bengals; gen. mgr., 1992; pres., chmn. & owner Cin. Bengals, 1991—. Address: Cincinnati Bengals 1 Paul Brown Stadium Cincinnati OH 45202-3418*

BROWN, MORRIS, lawyer; b. Rahway, N.J., Mar. 16, 1928; s. Frank and Celia (Roth) B.; m. Sylvia Cohen, Aug. 2, 1953; children: David H., Alan S. BA, George Washington U., 1951; LLB, Harvard U., 1955. Bar: N.J. 1956, U.S. Dist. Ct. N.J. 1956. Law clk. to Judge Thomas F. Meaney U.S. Dist. Ct. for N.J., 1955-56; assoc. Wilentz, Goldman & Spitzer, Woodbridge, N.J., 1956-67, ptnr., 1967—. Mem. adv. commn. on profl. ethics N.J. Supreme Ct., 1983-95. Assoc. editor N.J. Law Jour., 1985-91. V.p. Temple Neve Shalom, Metuchen, N.J., 1971-73, bd. dirs. 1973, 75; co-chmn. United Jewish Appeal, 1971; v.p. No. Middlesex County YMHA, 1972-73; interim pres. Jewish Fedn. No. Middlesex County, 1975; trustee John F. Kennedy Med. Ctr. Edison, N.J., 1975—. with USN, 1946-48. Mem. ATLA-N.J. (pres. 1976-77), N.J. State Bar Assn., N.J. Trial Lawyers Assn., Middlesex County Bar Assn., Middlesex County Trial Lawyers Assn. (pres. 1970-72), Am. Bd. Trial Attys., Am. Coll. Trial Lawyers. Democrat. Home: 9 Fairway Ln Ocean NJ 07712-3634 Office: Wilentz Goldman & Spitzer PA PO Box 10 90 Woodbridge Ctr Woodbridge NJ 07095-1304 Office Phone: 732-855-6060. Business E-Mail: brownm@wilentz.com.

BROWN, MURRAY, economist, educator; b. Alden, NY, July 4, 1929; s. Leo and Sarah Brown; m. Barbara Ellen Kingon, June 4, 1954; 1 child, Erica Sara. PhD, The Grad. Faculty, The New Sch., 1956. Prof. SUNY, Buffalo, 1967—96; assoc. Il Centro Di Studi e Piani Economici, Rome, 1965—. Pres. AAUP, Buffalo. Author: The Theory and Measurement of Technological Change, Coalitions in Oligopolies. Pres. AAUP, Buffalo, 1989—94. Fellow, Ford Found., 1961, Guggenheim Found., 1966; Hiram J. Halle fellow, The New Sch., 1955, Fulbright fellow, 1981, Disting. Fulbright fellow, 1987. Mem.: Econometric Soc. (assoc.). Avocations: skiing, running. Home: 80 Fairlawn Dr Amherst NY 14226 Personal E-mail: mbrown@buffalo.edu.

BROWN, MYRA SUZANNE, school librarian; b. Gainesville, Fla., Jan. 6, 1949; d. Samuel Jackson and Myra Frances (Whiddon) B.; m. Roman Jonas Yoder, Jan. 5, 1973 (dec.); m. Jeremy Gallaudet Hole, May 3, 1986. Student European divsn., U. Md., West Berlin, 1967-69; BA, U. South Fla., 1971; MSLS, Fla. State U., 1972; postgrad., U. Cin., 1974. Libr. asst. Strozier Libr., Fla. State U., Tallahassee, 1973, libr. serials dept., 1973; libr. sci. and tech. dept. Pub. Libr. of Cin. and Hamilton County, 1973-74; libr. assoc. II Coll. Design, Architecture and Art Libr. U. Cin., 1975-77; assoc. univ. libr. State U. Sys. of Fla. Extension Libr., St. Petersburg, Fla., 1979-81, Edn. Libr. U. Fla. Librs., Gainesville, 1982-84, head and edn. bibliographer, 1984-90; asst. dept. chair humanities and social scis. svcs. dept. Smathers Librs. U. Fla., Gainesville, 1990—92, head and edn. bibliographer Edn. Libr., 1992—2002, asst. edn. libr., 2002—, univ. libr., 2002—. Mem. reference liaisons discussion group Rsch. Librs. Group, Inc., 1990-92; reviewer Gale Rsch. Co., Inc., 1988—Ednl. Librs., 1995—; participant rsch. panel Univ. Microfilms Internat., 1992; mem. nat. user group Libr. of Congress Cataloging Distbn. Svc., 1992-96; cons. Mus. Fine Arts Libr., St. Petersburg, Fla., 1981-82, Design, Architecture and Art Libr., U. Cin., 1975-77; participant focus group ISI, 1998, 99; participant rsch. panel Libr. Supplies, 1999; cons. New Bus. Devel. Edn. titles Gale Rsch., 1998, 99. Mem. editl. bd. Edn. Librs., 1999—; contbr. World Architecture Index: A Guide to Illustrations, 1991; contbr. chpts. to books, articles to profl. jours. Aux. mem., vol. Shands Hops. of U. Fla., Gainesville, 1993-96, nominating com., 1995-96, sustaining mem., 1997—; advocate for homeless; mem. outreach com. Holy Trinity Episcopal Ch.; advocate for animal rights; vol. Interfaith Hospitality Network, 2003—; co-chair Holiday Bazaar-Jewelry Room, 2004—; mem. exec. bd. Cedar Creek Homeowners Assn., 2004—, v.p., 2004-2005. Mem. ALA (chmn., planner, moderator preconf. and conf. program, mem. divsns. 2000—, reference svcs. in medium-sized rsch. librs. discussion group 1992—2001, presenter), Spl. Librs. Assn. (info. tech. divsn., 1979-93, edn. divsn. Fla. chpt. 1979—, discussion list mgr., developer 1994-2000, chair nominations com., 2004, presenter at ann. confs.), Am. Ednl. Rsch. Assn., Fla. Ednl. Rsch. Assn., U. Fla. Librs. Assn. (v.p. 1983-84), Phi Delta Kappa (historian 1993-94). Democrat. Episcopalian. Avocations: animal welfare concerns, advocacy for the homeless, art, fashion consulting. Office: Smathers Librs of U Fla Edn Libr 1500 Norman Hall PO Box 117016 Gainesville FL 32611-7016 Office Phone: 352-392-0707. Business E-Mail: msbrown@ufl.edu.

BROWN, NANCY ELLEN, language educator, writer; b. Inglewood, Calif., May 2, 1960; d. Robert Alexander and Elizabeth (Collins) B.; life ptnr. Susan Mary Allen. AA in Gen. Studies, Cypress (Calif.) Coll., 1985; BA in French, Calif. State U., Fullerton, 1986; MA in Multicultural Edn., Calif. State U., Dominquez Hills, 1991. Profl. clear multi-subject credential with lang. emphasis, Spanish bilingual cultural specialist credential, Calif.; nat. bd. cert. tchr. Bilingual tchr. L.A. Unified Sch. Dist., 1986—, mem. site leadership coun., 1989—, grant and proposal writer, 1990—. Pvt. cons. Best Practice Partnership, 1998—. Mem. ASCD, Calif. Assn. for Bilingual Edn., United Tchrs. L.A. (chpt. chmn. 1989—). Democrat. Home: 6714 La Marimba St Long Beach CA 90815 Office: Hawaiian Avenue Sch 540 Hawaiian Ave Wilmington CA 90744-4998 E-mail: sinetag@earthlink.net.

BROWN, NANCY FIELD, editor; b. Troy, N.Y., Feb. 20, 1951; d. Robert Grant and Barbara Katherine (Field) B. BS in Journalism, Mich. State U., East Lansing, 1974. Asst. editor Mich. Am. Legion, Lansing, 1974-76, State Bar of Mich., Lansing, 1976-78, editor, 1976—, sr. dir. pubs., 1995-98, asst. exec. dir. publs., 1998—. Mem. Nat. Assn. Bar Execs. (cons. pubs. com. Chgo. chpt. 1989—), Mich. State U. Alumni Assn., Nat. Assn. Desktop Pubs., Am. Soc. Assn. Execs. Presbyterian. Avocations: reading, writing, photography, travel. Office: State Bar of Mich 306 Townsend St Lansing MI 48933-2012

BROWN, NORA M., elementary school educator; Tchr. Dr. James H. Naylor Sch., Hartford, Conn., 1973—; area coord., sec., third v.p. Hartford Fedn. Tchrs., 1994—2000; serves on Nat. Bd. Profl. Tchg. Stds. Office: Dr James H Naylor Sch 639 Franklin Ave Hartford CT 06114-3089 Office Phone: 860-695-4620. E-mail: norabrown1@aol.com.

BROWN, NORMAN DONALD, history professor; b. Pitts., June 28, 1935; s. Donald Madden and Regina Deborah (Koehler) B.; m. Betty Jane Aldrich, Apr. 2, 1966; children: David, Tracy. BA summa cum laude, Ind. U., 1957; MA, U. N.C., 1959, PhD, 1963. Instr. history U. Tex., Austin, 1962-65, asst. prof., 1965-69, assoc. prof., 1969-83, prof., 1983-84, Barbara White Stuart Centennial prof. Tex. history, 1984—. Author: Daniel Webster and the Politics of Availability, 1969, Edward Stanly, 1974, Hood, Bonnet, and Little Brown Jug, 1984; editor: One of Cleburne's Command, 1980, Journey to Pleasant Hill, 1982. Woodrow Wilson fellow, 1957. Fellow: Tex. State Hist. Assn. (coun. 1989—93, 2d v.p. 1997—98, 1st v.p. 1998—99, pres. 1999—2000, coun. 2000—02); mem.: Civil War Preservation Trust, Civil War Round Table Assocs., Soc. Civil War Historians (adv. bd. 1986—), Soc. Historians Early Am. Republic, So. Hist. Assn., Orgn. Am. Historians, Sons of Union Vets. of the Civil War, Phi Kappa Phi, Phi Alpha Theta, Phi Beta Kappa. Democrat. United Methodist. Avocation: book and stamp collecting. Home: 2607 Barton Skyway Austin TX 78704-4602 Office: Univ Tex Dept History Austin TX 78712

BROWN, OLEN RAY, medical microbiology and toxicology educator, researcher, consultant, writer; b. Hastings, Okla., Aug. 18, 1935; s. Willis Edward and Rosa Nell (Fulton) B.; m. Pollyana June King, Aug. 30, 1958; children: Barbara Kathryn, Diana Carol, David Gregory. BS in Lab. Tech., Okla. U., 1958, MS in Bacteriology, 1960, PhD in Microbiology, 1964. Diplomate Am. Bd. Toxicology. Instr. Sch. Medicine, U. Mo., Columbia, 1964-65, asst. prof., 1965-70, assoc. prof., 1970-77, prof. dept. molecular microbiology and immunology, 1981-96, rsch. prof., 1996—2001; joint appointments, prof. depts. microbiology and biomed. scis. Coll. Vet. Medicine, U. Mo., 1977-96, prof. biomed. scis., 1987-96. Guest lectr. Ross U., St. Kitts, W.I., 1984, 88; asst. dir. Dalton Rsch. Ctr., U. Mo., 1974-78, Dalton rsch. investigator grad. sch., 1968—; grant peer reviewer for program projects SCOR and Superfund grants NIH, 1979, Nat. Inst. Environ. Health Scis., Dept. Commerce, EPA, 1986, 90-99, Am. Inst. Biol. Scis. for Dept. Def., USAMRMC, Fund for Improvement of Secondary Edn., 2002; cons. drug abuse policy office White House, 1982, Immunol. Vaccines, Inc., Columbia, 1984—, Lab. Support, Inc., Chgo., 1988-89, Ea. Rsch. Group, Lexington, Mass., 1991—, Teltech, Mpls., 1992—, Scis. Internat., Inc., Alexandria, Va.; judge top 100 products for 1996, 99, Rsch. and Devel. Mag. Author: Laboratory Manual for Veterinary Microbiology, 1973, The Art and Science of Expert Witnessing, 2002; co-author: elem. and advanced lab. manuals for med. microbiology, 2 vols., 1978, 79; contbr. Progress in Clinical Research,

Vol. 21, 1978, 79, Oxygen, 5th Internat. Hyperbaric Conf., Vols. I, II, 1974, 79, numerous articles to profl. jours.; book and film critic AAAS, Washington, 1986—; item preparer Am. Coll. Test, Med. Coll. Admissions Test, 1981—; mem. editorial staff Biomed. Letters, 1981—; responder Sci. and Math. Helpline for Mus. Sci. Discovery, Harrisburg, Pa., 1996—, reviewer profl. jours. Track and field ofcl. U. Mo. and Big Eight Conf., Columbia, 1979-86. Investigative rsch. grantee Office Naval Rsch., Dept. Def., 1968-81, NIH, 1976-88, NIEHS, 1981-94, 95—, USAID, 1983-86, Nat. Inst. Dental Health Scis., 1989-92. Fellow Am. Inst. Chemists (cert. chemistry and chem engring., profl. program bd. 1989-90, sd com. chemistry and environ. concerns); mem. Top One Percent Soc., Soc. Toxicology, Internat. Soc. Study Xenobiotics, Am. Chem. Soc., Am. Heart Assn., Internat. Soc. Exposure Analysts, Nat. Space Soc., Oxygen Soc., Columbia Track Club (sec.-treas. 1979-82). Avocations: long-distance running, painting. Office: U Mo Dalton Rsch Ctr Columbia MO 65211-0001 Office Phone: 573-449-7444. Business E-Mail: browno@missouri.edu.

BROWN, OMER FORREST, II, lawyer; b. Somerville, NJ, Mar. 4, 1947; s. George Alvin and Frances (Schnitzler) B.; m. Sandra J. Cannon, Apr. 3, 1982. AB, Rutgers U., 1969; JD, Cornell U., 1972. Bar: NJ 1972, DC 1974, U.S. Supreme Ct. 1976. Dept. atty. gen. dept. law and pub. safety State of NJ, Trenton, 1972-75; sr. trial atty. US Dept. Energy, Washington, 1979-83; ptnr. Davis Wright Tremaine, Washington, 1987-96, Harmon, Wilmot & Brown, LLP, Washington, 1997—. Bd. dirs., sec. VideoTakes, Inc., Arlington, Va., 1986—; vis. lectr. Cornell U. Law Sch., 1993-95, 2002; mem. OECD Contact Group on Nuc. Safety Assistance for Eastern Europe, 1994—; mem. G-7 Joint Task Force on Ukrainian Nuc. Legis., 1996—. Contbr. numerous articles on energy, environ. and ins. law to legal jours.; mem. scientific and editl. commn., Internat. Jour. Nuc. Law, 2004-. Capt. USAR, 1969—75. Recipient Class of 1931 award Rutgers U. Alumni Assn., 1979, Loyal Son of Rutgers award, 1980. Mem. ABA (various offices tort and ins. practice sect. 1981-96, coord. group on energy law 1995-99), Internat. Bar Assn., Fed. Bar Assn., DOE Contractor Atty. Assn., Univ. Club (Washington). Democrat. Roman Catholic. Address: PO Box 419 Saint Michaels MD 21663-0419 Office Phone: 202-842-4711. E-mail: omerb@aol.com.

BROWN, OWSLEY, II, diversified consumer products company executive; b. Louisville, Sept. 10, 1942; s. William Lee Lyons and Sara (Shallenberger) B.; m. Christina Lee, Oct. 26, 1968; children— Owsley, Brooke Lee, Augusta Wilson BA, Yale U., 1964; MBA, Stanford U., 1966. Asst. treasurer Brown-Forman Corp., 1968—70, asst. v.p., 1970—71, bd. dir., 1971—, v.p., 1971—75, treasurer, 1975—80, sr. v.p., CFO, 1980—83; pres. Brown-Forman Beverage Co., 1983—86, chmn., CEO, 1986—93; CEO Brown-Forman Corp., 1993—2005, chmn., 1995—. Pres. Actors Theatre, 1985, 89-90; bd. dirs. Greater Louisville Fund for Arts. 1st lt. U.S. Army, 1966-68. Mem. Pendennis Club, Louisville Country Club, Filson Club. Republican. Episcopalian. Office: Brown-Forman Corp 850 Dixie Hwy Louisville KY 40210-1091*

BROWN, PAMELA S., attorney general; BA in Cultural Anthropology, U. Wash., 1982, JD with honors, 1988. Tech. dir, news dir., news ed. KOMO TV, ABC, Seattle, 1981—85; Rule 9 atty., King County prosecutors and Wash. State, atty. gen., consumer protection div., 1986—87; criminial def. atty. Seattle, 1987—89; criminal prosecutor, off. of atty. gen. No. Mariana Islands, 1989—90, chief sen. legal counsel, 1990—94; ptnr. Long & Brown, attys. at law, 1994—98; pvt. practice, 1998—99; fed. ombudsman, off. of ombudsman, off. of insular affairs US Dept. of Interior, Saipan, 1999—2001; of counsel Teker Civille Torres and Tang attys. at law and MP mng. atty. for Saipan Off., Labor, Immigration and Civil Litig., Saipan, 2001—02; legal counsel to gov. No. Mariana Islands, Saipan, 2002—03, atty. gen., 2003—. Mem. Am. Bar Assn., Commonwealth Bar Assn. Office: Off of Atty Gen Hon Juan A Sablan Meml Bldg Caller Box 10007 Capitol Hill Saipan MP 96950 Office Phone: 670-664-2341. Office Fax: 670-664-2349. Personal E-mail: pbrown52@hotmail.com.

BROWN, PAMELA WEDD, artist; b. Cauderan, Gironde, France, Nov. 21, 1928; came to U.S., 1953; d. William Basil and Nora Marsh (van Nostrand) Wedd; m. Charles Freeman Brown, Nov. 29, 1952; children: Penelope Susan, Nicholas Wedd. Student, Ecole des Beaux Arts, Paris, 1947-48, Academie Julian, 1946-51. Free lance fashion illustrator, Paris, 1947-48; dir. arts and crafts YWCA, Toronto, Ont., Can., 1951; dir. Washington Womens Arts Ctr., 1987-88; dir., pres. Washington Printmakers Gallery, 1990-91; co-pres. Studio Gallery, 1992-94. Artist in residence The Art Barn, Washington, 1986. Designer book plate Nat. Mus. Women in Arts Libr., 1985; represented in permanent collections Libr. of Congress, NIH, Nat. Mus. Am. History, Nat. Mus. Women in Arts. Precinct capt. Bd. of Elections and Ethics, Washington, 1970-80. Recipient First prize drawing, Academie Julian, Paris, 1947, Purchase award, Jr. League, Newport News, Va., 1971. Mem. Studio Gallery D.C. (assoc.), Art League (Equal award 1980, 82, 85, 88, 2000, 02), Woman's Nat. Dem. Club. Avocations: music, tennis, sailing, dance. Home: 3050 Military Rd NW # 636 Washington DC 20015

BROWN, PATRICIA IRENE, retired law librarian, lawyer; b. Boston; d. Joseph Raymond and Harriet A. (Taylor) B. BA, Suffolk U., 1955, JD, 1965, MBA, 1970; MST, Gordon Conwell Theol. Sem., 1977. Bar: Mass. 1965. Libr. asst. Suffolk U., Boston, 1951-60, asst. libr., 1960-65, asst. law libr., 1965-85, assoc. law libr., 1985-92; ret., 2009; human resources counselor Winthrop (Mass.) Sr. Ctr., 1993—; counselor Winthrop Sr. Ctr. Author: A League of My Own: Memoir of a Pitcher for the All-American Girls Professional Baseball League, 2003. Dir. Referral/Resource Ctr., Union Congl. Ch., Winthrop, Mass.; vol. health benefits counselor Mass. Dept. Elder Affairs, 1994-99; counselor Winthrop Sr. Ctr., 2000— First Woman inducted into Nat. Baseball Hall of Fame, Cooperstown, N.Y., 1988, All- Am. Girls Profl. Baseball League, 1950-51. Mem. Assn. Am. Law Librs., Am. Congl. Assn. (bd. dirs.), Mass. Bar Assn. Avocations: television and movie history, walking, computers. Home: 1100 Governors Dr Apt 26 Winthrop MA 02152-3254 Personal E-mail: pbrown@suffolk.edu.

BROWN, PATRICK O., molecular biologist, educator; BA, U. Chgo., PhD, 1980, MD, 1982. Pediat. resident Children's Meml. Hosp., Chgo.; rschr. U. Calif., San Francisco; assoc. prof. biochemistry Stanford (Calif.) U. Sch. Medicine. Recipient award in molecular biology NAS, 2000. Office: Stanford Sch Medicine 300 Pasteur Dr Stanford CA 94305

BROWN, PAUL A., physician, business executive; b. Boston, Apr. 1, 1938; s. Morton G. and Helen C. (Appleton) B.; m. Cynthia R. Shrier, June 4, 1961; children: Richard, Mark. AB, Harvard U., 1960; MD, Tufts U., Boston, 1964. Intern Tufts New Eng. Med. Ctr., Boston, 1964-65; resident in pathology Columbia Presbyn. Hosp., N.Y.C., 1965-69; chmn., chief exec. officer Metpath Inc., Teterboro, N.J., 1970-83, chmn., 1983-84, Sci/Med Advances Corp., Teaneck, N.J., 1983-88, Hearx Ltd., West Palm Beach, Fla., 1986—. Chmn., chief exec. officer Permark Corp., Hacksensack, N.J., 1985-89; lectr. pathology Columbia U., 1981— Trustee Tufts U., 1978—; mem. vis. com. Boston U. Sch. of Medicine, 1987—2000, Tufts U. Sch. Medicine, 1978—82; com. vis. physicians chmn. bd. overseers, 1983—95. Home: 1744 S Ocean Blvd Palm Beach FL 33480-5105 Office: Hearx 1250 Northpoint Pkwy West Palm Beach FL 33407 Office Phone: 561-478-8770 x123. Business E-Mail: pbwon@mearx.com.

BROWN, PAUL FREMONT, aerospace engineer, educator; b. Osage, Iowa, Mar. 10, 1921; s. Charles Fremont and Florence Alma (Olson) B.; m. Alice Marie Culver, Dec. 5, 1943; children: Diane, Darrell, Judith, Jana. BA in Edn. and Natural Sci., Dickinson State Coll., 1942; MS in Cybernetic Systems, San Jose State U., 1971. Profl. quality engr., Calif., 1978; cert. reliabilty engr., Am. Soc. Quality Control, 1976. Test engr., supr. Boeing Aircraft Corp., Seattle, 1948-56; design specialist, propulsion systems Lockheed Missiles and Space Co., Sunnyvale, Calif., 1956-59, supr. system effectiveness, 1959-66, staff engr., 1966-76, mgr. product assurance Hubble Space Telescope Program, 1976-83; v.p. rsch., devel. Gen. Agriponics Inc. of Hawaii, 1971-76; owner Diversatek Engrng. and Product Assurance Cons., 1983—. Instr., lectr. San Jose State U. Author: From Here to Retirement, 1988, The Winds of Hope, 2002; contbr. articles to profl. jours. Active in United Presbyn. Ch., 1965—; scoutmaster Boy Scouts Am., 1963-65. Served to 1st lt. USAF, 1943-46. Recipient awards for tech. papers, Lockheed Missiles and Space Co., 1973-75. Mem. Am. Soc. Quality Control, AIAA, Toastmasters Club (Sunnyvale, Calif.), Calif. Writers' Club (pres. South Bay br. 1993-94). Home and Office: 19608 Braemar Dr Saratoga CA 95070-5046 E-mail: anp3943@aol.com.

BROWN, PAUL M., lawyer; b. Jan. 10, 1938; s. I. Harry and Rose L. (Kresge) B.; m. Helga J. Fischer, Aug. 4, 1962 (div. 1977); children: Stephanie J., William A.; m. Ruth Reiter, June 28, 1986. Student, Williams Coll., 1955-57; BS in Econs., U. Pa., 1959; LLB, Columbia U., 1962. Bar: N.Y. 1963, U.S. Ct. Appeals (2d cir.) 1963, U.S. Dist. Ct. (so. and ea. dists.) N.Y. 1964, U.S. Dist. Ct. Mass. 1981, U.S. Ct. Appeals (3d cir.), U.S. Ct. Appeals (1st cir.) 1982, U.S. Dist. Ct. (we. dist.) N.Y. 1983, U.S. Ct. Appeals (6th cir.) 1983, U.S. Dist. Ct. R.I. 1985, U.S. Dist. Ct. (ea. dist.) Mich. 1986. Assoc. Berman & Frost, N.Y.C., 1963-66; ptnr. Havens, Wandless, Slitt and Tighe, N.Y.C., 1966-74, Whitman and Ransom, N.Y.C., 1975-94, Parson & Brown, N.Y.C., 1994-99, Satterlee Stephens Burke & Burke, N.Y.C., 1999—. Councilman Closter, N.J., 1970-74; police commr. Closter, 1970-73; trustee No. Valley Regional H.S., Demarest, N.J., 1972. With USAR, 1962-68. Mem. Assn. of Bar of City of N.Y., N.Y. State Bar Assn., Fed. Bar Coun., Am. Arbitration Assn. (panel of arbitrators), Univ. Club, Columbia Golf & Country Club, Las Campanas (N.Mex.) Club. Democrat. Office: Satterlee Stephens Burke & Burke 230 Park Ave New York NY 10169-0079 Office Phone: 212-404-8786. E-mail: pbrown@ssbb.com.

BROWN, PAUL NEELEY, federal judge; b. Denison, Tex., Oct. 4, 1926; s. Arthur Chester and Nora Frances (Hunter) B.; m. Frances Morehead, May 8, 1955; children: Paul Gregory, David H. II. JD, U. Tex., 1950. Assoc. Keith & Brown, Sherman, Tex., 1951-53, Brown & Brown, Sherman, 1953; asst. U.S. atty. for Ea. Dist. Tex. Texarkana and Tyler, Tex., 1953-59; U.S. atty. Ea. Dist. Tex., Tyler, 1959-61; ptnr. Brown & Brown and Brown Brothers & Perkins, Sherman, 1961-65, Brown and Perkins, Sherman, 1965; sole practice, Sherman, 1965-67; ptnr. Brown & Hill, Sherman, 1967, Brown Kennedy Hill & Minshew, Sherman, 1967-71, Brown & Hill, Sherman, 1971-76, Brown Hill Ellis & Brown, Sherman, 1976-85; U.S. dist. judge U.S. Dist. Ct. (ea. dist.) Tex., Sherman, 1985—, sr. US dist. judge, 2001. Served with USN, 1944-46, 50-51. Fellow Tex. Bar Found.; mem. Rotary. Presbyterian. Office: US Dist Ct Fed Bldg 101 E Pecan St Sherman TX 75090-5989

BROWN, PAUL SHERMAN, lawyer; b. June 26, 1921; s. Paul Michael and Norma (Sherman) Brown; m. Ann Wilson, Feb. 7, 1959; 1 child, Paul S. BS in Commerce, St. Louis U., 1943, JD cum laude, 1951. Bar: Mo. 51, U.S. Dist. Ct. (ea. dist.) Mo. 51, U.S. Ct. Appeals (8th cir.) 51, U.S. Supreme Ct. 66. Shareholder Brown & James, P.C., St. Louis, 1980—. Instr. St. Louis U. Night Law Sch., 1978—; lectr. in field; mem. com. on civil pattern jury instructions Mo. Supreme Ct. Contbr. articles to profl. jours. Fellow: Internat. Soc. Barristers, Internat. Acad. Trial Lawyers, Am. Coll. Trial Lawyers; mem.: ABA (vice-chmn. com. consumer products liability 1977—78), Am. Judicature Soc., Bar Assn. Met. St. Louis (pres. 1970—71), Lawyers Assn. St. Louis, Am. Bd. Trial Advocates, Mo. Bar Assn. (bd. govs. 1963—67), Order of Woolsack, St. Louis Amateur Athletic Assn. (bd. dirs. 1974—76, pres. 1976—78), Alpha Sigma Nu. Roman Catholic. Home: 7331 Kingsbury Blvd Saint Louis MO 63130-4143 Office: Brown & James 1010 Market St Ste 18 Saint Louis MO 63101-2270

BROWN, PERRY JOE, university dean; Student, Foothill Coll., Los Altos, Calif., 1962-63; BS in Forestry, Utah State U., 1967, MS in Forest Recreation, 1968, PhD in Outdoor Recreation & Social Psych, 1971; postgrad., U. Mich., 1968, 69-70. Lectr. forest sci. Utah State U., Logan, 1968-71, asst. prof. forest sci., 1971-73; from asst. prof. recreation resources to asst. dean Colo. State U., 1973—82; assoc. dean instrn., continuing edn. and internat. programs Oreg. State U., 1988-94; dean Coll. Forestry and Conservation U. Mont., Missoula, 1994—, prof. forest resources, 1994—, dir. Mont. Forest and Conservation Expt. Sta., 1994—. Social sci. project leader Oreg. State U.-Nat. Park Svc. Coop. Park Studies Unit, 1990-93; interim dir. Oreg. Tourism Inst., Oreg. State Sys. Higher Edn., 1987-89; mem. adv. bd. Va. Poly. Inst. and State U. Coll. Forestry and Wildlife; mem. numerous panels and task forces NAS, regional planning commns., fed. and state agys. and domestic and internat. profl. orgns.; profl. cons. to numerous fed., state and internat. land mgmt. agys., univs., cos. and the Forest Ecosystem Mgmt. Assessment Team social sci. team; leader Rocky Mountain Coop. Ecosys. Studies Unit; mem. nat. adv. bd. Nat. Forest Found., 2002—. Editor Utah Tourism and Recreation Rev., 1972-73; assoc. editor Jour. Leisure Rsch., 1977-79, Jour. Leisure Scis., 1982-85; mem. editl. bd. Jour. Forest and Landscape Rsch., 1993-99; author over 110 books, articles, papers and reports including 2 books and 16 book chpts. Recipient Cert. of Appreciation, USDA Forest Svc., 1988. Fellow Acad. Leisure Scis.; mem. Soc. Am. Foresters, Human Dimensions in Wildlife Study Group, Internat. Union Forestry Rsch. Orgns. (leader forest recreation, landscape planning and nature conservation sect. 1986-96, dep. coord. divsn. 6 1996—), Nat. Assn. Profl. Forestry Schs. and Colls. (western region chair, exec. bd. 1996-97, pres.-elect 1998-00, pres. 2000-02, past pres. 2002—). Office: U Mont Coll Forestry and Conservation Missoula MT 59812-0001

BROWN, PETER C., movie theater company executive; b. 1959; Founder, chmn. Entertainment Properties Trust, 1997—2003; CFO AMC Entertainment Inc., Kansas City, Mo., co-chmn., 1998—99, chmn., CEO, pres. Mo., 1999—. Bd. dir. Nat. Assn. Theatre Owners, Nat. CineMedia, Midway Games Inc. Office: AMC Entertainment Inc 920 Main St Kansas City MO 64105 Office Phone: 816-221-4000.*

BROWN, PETER DAVID GILSON, German language educator; b. Alton, Ill., Oct. 18, 1943; s. Weir Messick and Vivian Virginia (Bauer) B.; m. Elaine Greenblatt, Sept. 10, 1966 (div. Aug. 1970); 1 child, Stephanie; m. Susan Roberta Jensen, Sept. 11, 1970 (div. Mar. 1992); 1 child, Andrew J.B. BA summa cum laude, Columbia Coll., 1964; MA, Columbia U., 1965, PhD, 1971. Instr. of German Columbia U., N.Y.C., 1967-71, Barnard Coll., N.Y.C., 1968-71; asst. prof. German SUNY, New Paltz, 1971-74, assoc. prof. German, 1974-86, prof. German, 1986—99, disting. svc. prof. German, 1999—. Dir. SUNY Acad. Summer Program, Hamburg/Stade, Fed. Republic Germany, 1974-98; mem. editorial adv. bd. Peter Lang Pub., NYC, 1986—, United U. Professions (v.p. academics, New Paltz Chpt., 2005-). Author: Oskar Panizza: His Life and Works, 1983; editor: (series of 100 vols.) Studies in Modern German Literature, 1985—, Studies in German Jewish History, 1995—, Women in German Literature, 1997—, Das Liebeskonzil: eine Himmels-Tragödie in fünf Aufzügen, 2005; contbr. articles to profl. jours. Chmn. Mid-Hudson Nuclear Opponents, New Paltz, N.Y., 1974-80; legis. coord. Safe Energy Coalition of N.Y. State, Albany, 1974-75; bd. dirs. Environ. Planning Lobby, Albany, 1976-77, Hudson River Sloop Clearwater, Poughkeepsie, N.Y., 1981-83. Recipient Advanced German Studies Prize German Consulate, 1963, Experienced Faculty Travel award NYS/UUP, 1987; Woodrow Wilson fellowship Woodrow Wilson Found., 1964; Tech. Assistance Study grant U.S. Dept. Energy, 1980, SUNY Chancellor's Award for Excellence in Teaching, 1993, Bundesverdienstkreuz, 1999, Tchr. of Yr. award, 2000. Mem. Am. Assn. of Tchrs. of German, Modern Lang. Assn. of Am. Avocations: poetry, piano playing, photography. Office: SUNY Dept Fgn Langs 414 Jacobson Faculty Tower New Paltz NY 12561-2499 Office Phone: 845-257-3492. E-mail: brownp@newpaltz.edu.

BROWN, PETER STEWART, lawyer; b. Jersey City, Jan. 8, 1951; s. George John and Marie Therese (Coyne) B.; m. Charlotte Anne Tileston, Mar. 31, 1978; children: Christopher, Olivia, Emma. BA summa cum laude, Drew U., 1974; JD, Harvard U., 1977. Bar: N.Y. 1977, U.S. Dist. Ct. N.Y. (so. dist.) 1978. Assoc. Winthrop, Stimson, Putnam & Roberts, N.Y.C., 1977-84, ptnr. London, 1985—; sr. v.p., gen. counsel Arrow Electronics, Melville, NY, 2001—. Office: Arrow Electronics 3414 B Bush St Melville NY 11747

BROWN, PHILIP ALBERT, lawyer; b. Gettysburg, Pa., June 12, 1949; s. Clyde Raynor and Jean (McCullough) B.; m. Donna Leslie Lohr, May 25, 1985; 1 child, Andrew Raynor. BA in History, George Washington U., 1971; JD, U. Mich., 1974. Bar: Ohio 1974. Assoc. Vorys, Sater, Seymour & Pease, Columbus, Ohio, 1974-81, ptnr., 1981—. Arbitrator Nat. Assn. Security Dealers: mem. Ohio civil legal needs assessment implementation com. Ohio Supreme Ct., 1991-94. Trustee Legal Aid Soc. Columbus, 1985-91, pres. 1989-90; trustee Ohio State Legal Svcs. Assn., 1994—; mem. Nat. Coun. for Arts and Scis. of George Washington U. Fellow Columbus Bar Found.; mem. Phi Beta Kappa. Avocation: fishing. Office: Vorys Sater Seymour & Pease 52 E Gay St Columbus OH 43215-3161

BROWN, PRESTON, lawyer; b. NYC, Oct. 6, 1936; s. John Mason and Catherine (Meredith) B.; m. Betsey G. Pinckney, Oct. 9, 1965 (div. Mar. 1982); children: Catherine St. George, John Preston; m. Eva N. Kasten, June 10, 2000. AB, Harvard U., 1958, LLB, 1961. Bar: N.Y. 1962, D.C. 1969, U.S. Supreme Ct. 1974. Assoc. Davis, Polk & Wardwell, N.Y.C., 1961-67; adminstrv. asst., del N.Y. State Constl. Conv., Albany, 1967; spl. asst. to under sec. HUD, Washington, 1967-69; resident counsel Curtis, Mallet-Prevost, Colt & Mosle, Washington, 1969-75, ptnr., 1975—. Contbr. articles to profl. jours. Bd. dirs. Goodwill Industries Am., Washington, 1969-75, Young Audiences of D.C., 1985-92, 93-99, 2000-2004, pres., 1989-92. Mem.: Met. Club (Washington), Knickerbocker Club (N.Y.C.). Episcopalian. Home: 2231 48th St NW Washington DC 20007-1036 Office: Curtis Mallet-Prevost Colt & Mosle 1200 New Hampshire Ave NW Ste 430 Washington DC 20036 Office Phone: 202-452-7373. E-mail: pbrown@cm-p.com, PresBrown3@msn.com.

BROWN, PRISCILLA ANN, elementary school educator; b. Augusta, Ark., July 18, 1961; d. Richard and Lucy Ann (Roberts) Brown. BSE, Ark. State U., 1985; MS in Edn., Harding U., 1990; post grad., Howard U., PhD in African Am. Lit., 2005. Tchr. Pulaski County Pub. Schs., Little Rock, 1985—87, Augusta (Ark.) Pub. Schs., 1987—90; instr. English and Edn. Harding U., Searcy, Ark., 1990—93; tchg. asst. Howard U., Washington, 1993—96; coordinating adminstr. Sheridan Sch., Washington, 1996—2000, tchr., 2000—. Author: Heartstreams: Poems from the Delta, 2003; contbr. articles to profl. publs. Democrat. Avocations: quilting, theater, walking. Home: 162 Uhland Terrace NE Washington DC 20002 Office: The Sheridan School 4400 36th St NW Washington DC 20008 E-mail: annbrown@priscillaannbrown.com.

BROWN, R. LARRY, human resources specialist, transportation executive; b. Jackson, Tenn. BA, Lane Coll.; JD, U. Memphis. Supervisory trial atty. EEOC, 1980—82; asst. U.S. atty. we. dist., Tenn., 1982—87; mng. dir. litigation FedEx Express Corp., Memphis, v.p. legal, sr. v.p., chief human resources officer, 1999—. Bd. dirs. Yes Found., Ptnrs. in Pub. Edn. Office: FedEx Express Corp 3610 Hacks Cross Rd Memphis TN 38125 Office Phone: 901-369-3600. Office Fax: 301-395-2000.*

BROWN, RALPH SAWYER, JR., retired lawyer; b. Cohasset, Mass., July 21, 1931; s. Ralph Sawyer and Rosemary (Wyman) B.; m. Elizabeth Atkinson Rash, June 12, 1953; children— Lucy Victoria Phillips, Alexander Sawyer Batson. BA, Swarthmore Coll., 1954; LLB, Harvard U., 1957. Bar: Mass. bar 1957, N.Y. State bar 1963. Assoc. Hutchins & Wheeler, Boston, 1957-62, Carter, Ledyard & Milburn, N.Y.C., 1962-68; ptnr. Janklow & Traum, N.Y.C., 1968-71; sec., asst. gen. counsel Indian Head, Inc., N.Y.C., 1971-76, v.p., treas., 1976-79; v.p., gen. counsel, sec. Esquire, Inc., N.Y.C., 1979-83, sr. v.p., gen. counsel, sec., 1983-84; assoc. counsel Paramount Communications Inc., N.Y.C., 1984-93, sr. counsel, 1993-94. Bd. mem. Concert Artists Guild, Correctional Assn. NY, NY Soc. Libr., Osborne Assn. Mem. Phi Beta Kappa. Home: 160 W 86th St Ph 4 New York NY 10024-4074 E-mail: rsbrown160@aol.com.

BROWN, RAY KENT, biochemist, physician, educator; b. Columbus, Ohio, Apr. 7, 1924; s. Ray Stemen and Grace (Nunemaker) B.; m. Gertrude Lydia Harris, Jan. 25, 1947 (dec. Feb. 1998); children— Kimberly Brown, Kitene Kading, Kevin; m. Dorothy Skinner, Mar. 19, 1998. BA, Ohio State U., 1944, MD, 1947, MS, 1948; PhD, Harvard U., 1951. Intern Boston City Hosp., 1947-48; sr. asst. surgeon USPHS, Bethesda, Md., 1951-53; asst. dir. div. labs. and research N.Y. State Dept. Health, Albany, 1953-59, assoc. dir. div., 1959-63; asst. prof. biochemistry Albany Med. Coll., 1954-56, assoc. prof., 1956-61, prof., 1961-63, Wayne State U. Sch. Medicine, 1963-96, chmn. dept. biochemistry, 1963-87, prof. emeritus, 1996—. Mem. Highland Twp. (Mich.) Planning Commn., 1968-96. Served with U.S. Army, 1943-45, with USPHS, 1951-53. Mem. Am. Soc. Biol. Chemistry (Travel award 1958, 61, 64), Am. Assn. Immunologists, Biochem. Soc. Gt. Britain, Am. Chem. Soc. Home: 3820 Middle Rd Highland MI 48357-3044

BROWN, REBECCA ANN, French educator; b. Springfield, Ohio, Dec. 13, 1952; d. Russell Raymond and Virginia Grace (Ingels) Schulte; m. Keith Daniel Brown, June 19, 1976; 1 child, Michael Joseph. BA, Ohio Dominican Univ., 1975; MA, Coll. Mt. St. Joseph, 1988. Cert. tchr. Ohio. Tchr. English Pleasant High Sch., Marion, Ohio, 1975-80, tchr. French, 1975—, advisor fgn. travel with students, 1976—; advisor Nat. Hon. Soc., 2000—. Mem. Ohio Edn. Assn., Ohio Fgn. Lang. Assn., Pleasant Assn. Tchrs. (pres. 1980-81). Avocations: travel, reading, music, art, photography. Office: Pleasant High Sch 1101 Owens Rd W Marion OH 43302-8423 E-mail: rebecca_B@treca.org.

BROWN, REGINALD JUDE, federal agency administrator; BS, U.S. Mil. Acad., 1961; MPA, Harvard U., 1965. Dir. adminstrn. Mitre Corp., McLean, Va., 1972-73; dep. adminstr. Office of Food, Cost of Living Coun., Washington, 1973-74; assoc. dir. Def. Manpower Commn., Washington, 1974-75; prin. analyst Congl. Budget Office, Washington, 1975-77; exec. dir. Pres.'s Commn. on Mil. Compensation, Washington, 1977-78; dir. Energy Div., Office of Price Monitoring, Coun.on Wage and Price Stability, Washington, 1979; exec. v.p. DECA Group Inc., Miami, Fla., 1979-81; sr. fellow Ctr. for Strategic and Internat. Studies, Washington, 1982-89; asst. adminstr. U.S. AID, Washington, 1989—93; asst. secy. army manpower reserve affairs U.S. Dept. Defense, Washington, 2001—. Co-author: The Lessons of Wage and Price Controls, 1977; contbr. articles to jours. in field. Decorated Bronze Star, Meritorious Svc. medal. Republican. Office: US Dept Defense Manpower Reserve Affairs 111 Army Pentagon Washington DC 20310-0111

BROWN, RENEE, sports association executive; b. Henderson, Nev. Grad., U. Nev., Las Vegas. Asst. coach women's basketball U. Kans., Stanford U., Calif., San Jose State U., Calif.; asst. coach USA Basketball Women's Nat. Team, Colorado Springs, Colo., 1995—96; dir. player pers. Women's Nat. Basketball Assn., N.Y.C., 1996—99, sr. dir. player pers., 1999—2000, v.p. player pers., 2000—. Office: Women's Nat Basketball Assn Olympic Tower 645 Fifth Ave New York NY 10022

BROWN, RICHARD CHRISTOPHER, retired epidemiologist; b. Gainesville, Fla., Jan. 16, 1932; s. Joseph P. and Mildred Smith Brown; m. Linda Dickinson, July 2, 1960 (div. Dec. 1984); children: Douglas R., Jennifer Brown Kirkham. AB, Western Res. U., 1953; MD, U. Fla., 1962; MPH, U. Calif., Berkeley, 1967. Diplomate Am. Bd. Preventive Medicine. Pub. health inspector Polk County Health Dept., Lakeland, Fla., 1956-57; rotating intern Va. Mason Hosp., Seattle, 1962-63; resident in preventive medicine Fla. Dept. Health, West Palm Beach, Fla., 1963-64; resident in internal medicine U.S. VA Hosp., Portland, Oreg., 1964-66; epidemiologist USPHS, Window Rock, Ariz., 1967-68; asst. prof. preventive medicine U. Okla. Med. Sch., Oklahoma City, 1967-68; staff physician Morton Plant Hosp., Clearwater, Fla., 1968-91, Bay Pines (Fla.) VA Med. Ctr., 1991—2001. Dir. Hernando County Health Dept., Brooksville, Fla., 1987-88; med. dir. Bay Pines VA Domicilary. Contbr. articles to profl. jours. Bd. dirs. ARC, Clearwater, Fla., 1970; spl. expert witness Agy. for Health Care Adminstrn., State of Fla. Bd. Medicine, Tallahassee, 1997-98. Asst. surgeon USPHS, 1962-67. Recipient Rsch. award Am. Geriatrics Soc., Lederle Lab., 1965, Physician Recognition award AMA, 1969. Fellow Am. Coll. Preventive Medicine; mem. Am. Coll. Epidemiology,

Fla. Soc. Preventive Medicine (past pres.), Delta Tau Delta. Democrat. Episcopalian. Avocation: triathlon and marathon running. Home: 1157 Granada St Clearwater FL 33755-1054

BROWN, RICHARD E., music educator; b. Kingsport, Tenn., Feb. 15, 1967; s. Donald E. and Joyce M. Brown; m. Meredith Rae Dean; children: Valerie, Julia. BS in Instrumental Music Edn., U. Tenn., Knoxville, 1989; MA in Ednl. Leadership and Policy Analysis, East Tenn. State U., 1994. Cert. instrumental music tchr. Tenn., sch. adminstr. Tenn. Band dir. Va. Jr. H.S., Bristol, 1989—90; asst. band dir. Dobyns-Bennett H.S., Kingsport, Tenn., 1990—94; band dir. John Sevier Mid. Sch., Kingsport, 1994—. Guest music condr., clinician, band contest adjudicator various sch. dists., Southeastern U.S. Ch. camping leader Holston Presbytery Camp, Banner Elk, NC, 1989—2003; com. mem. Waverly Rd. Presbyn. Ch., Kingsport. Named Kingsport Mid. Sch. Tchr. of the Yr., Kingsport City Schools, 2001; recipient Arts Leadership award, Greater Kingsport Arts Coun., 2004. Mem.: NEA, East Tenn. Sch. Band and Orch. Assn., Music Educator's Nat. Conf. Presbyterian. Achievements include design of middle school band recruiting and retention methods; middle school band concert formats; development of middle school band grading and awards systems. Avocations: historic home renovation, antique automobile restoration, canoeing, kayaking. Office: John Sevier Mid Sch 1200 Wateree St Kingsport TN 37660 Office Phone: 423-378-2450. Office Fax: 423-378-2430. Personal E-mail: richardbrown67@yahoo.com. E-mail: rbrown@k12k.com.

BROWN, RICHARD EDWIN, chemistry educator, researcher; b. Bloomington, Ill., May 28, 1939; s. Clyde Jacob and Mildred (Lape) B.; m. Bette Jo Remus; children: Katherine Marie, Laura Jo. BS, U. Ill., 1962; PhD, Ind. U., 1967. NIH postdoctoral fellow Uppsala (Sweden) U., 1967-69; postdoctoral rschr. Queen's U., Kingston, Ont., Can., 1969-71, asst. prof., 1971-73, Champlain Regional Coll., Lennoxville, Que., Can., 1973-74, State U. Campinas, Sao Paulo, Brazil, 1974-77; mgr. computing user svcs. SUNY, Buffalo, 1977-80; assoc. prof. Mich. Technol. U., Houghton, 1980-93, prof., 1993—. Mem. Am. Chem. Soc. (program dir. Great Lakes regional meeting 1989), Sigma Xi. Office: Mich Technol U Dept Chemistry Houghton MI 49931 Office Phone: 906-487-2383. Business E-Mail: rebrown@intu.edu.

BROWN, RICHARD HARRIS, former information technology executive; b. New Brunswick, N.J., June 3, 1947; s. Harris Ransford and Winifred (Clelland) Brown; m. Christine Demier, Sept. 27, 1969; children: Ryan, Allison. BS in Communications, Ohio U., 1969. Comml. rep. Ohio Bell, Columbus, 1969—71, comml. mgr., 1971—74, dist. comml. mgr. Toledo and Cleve., 1974—80, div. mgr. Cleve., 1980—81; v.p. engring. & ops. United Telephone System, Inc. subs. United Telecommunications, Inc., Westwood, Kans., 1981—82; v.p. ops. United Telephone Co. of Midwest, Overland Park, Kans., 1982—83; v.p., COO United Telephone Co. of Fla., Apopka, 1983—87; sr. v.p. human resources & adminstrn. United Telecommunications, Inc., Shawnee Mission, Kans., 1987, sr. v.p. ops., 1987—89, exec. v.p., chief info. & planning officer, 1989; vice chmn., bd. dirs. Ameritech, 1993—95, Chgo., 1993—95; pres., CEO H&R Block, Inc., Kansas City, Mo., 1995—96; CEO, bd. dirs. Cable and Wireless PLC, London, 1996—98; chmn., CEO EDS (Elec. Data Systems), Plano, Tex., 1998—2003. Bd. dirs. Vivendi Universal, Home Depot, Inc., DuPont; mem. Pres.'s adv. com. on trade and policy negotiations, Pres.'s nat. security telecom. adv. com. Trustee Ohio U. Found., Athens, 1989—, So. Meth. U.; vice chmn. Chgo. United Way Campaign, 1994. With USNG, 1969—74. Named Outstanding Alumnus, Coll. of Interpersonal Comms., Ohio U., 1988. Mem.: U.S.-Japan Bus. Coun., U.S.-France Bus. oun., Bus. Coun., The Bus. Roundtable, Execs. Club, Econ. Club, Comml. Club, Shoreacres Country Club, Chgo. Club.

BROWN, RICHARD HOLBROOK, library director, historian, researcher; b. Boston, Sept. 25, 1927; s. Joseph Richard and Sylvia (Cook) Brown. BA, Yale U., 1949, MA, 1952, PhD, 1955. Instr. history U. Mass., Amherst, 1955—59, asst. prof., 1959—62; assoc. prof. No. Ill. U., De Kalb, 1962—64; dir. Amherst Project, Amherst and Chgo., 1964—72; dir. rsch. and edn. Newberry Libr., Chgo., 1972—83, acad. v.p., 1983—94, sr. rsch. fellow, 1994—. Vis. prof. history and edn. Northwestern U., Evanston, Ill., 1971—84; cons. NEH, 1977—; bd. dirs. Chgo. Metro History Fair, 1977—, pres., 1984—91; cons. Ctr. Study So. Culture, U. Miss., 1979—; mem. Ill. Humanities Coun., 1980—86, chmn., 1982—83. Author: The Hero and the People, 1964, The Missouri Compromise: Political Statesmanship or Unwise Evasion?, 1964; gen. editor: Amherst Project Units in American History, 25 vols., 1964—75. Recipient George Washington Eggleston prize, Yale U., 1955; Andrew Mellon Postdoctoral fellow, U. Pitts., 1960—61. Mem.: Orgn. Am. Historians, Social Sci. Edn. Consortium (pres. 1975—77), Am. Antiquarian Soc. Democrat. Roman Catholic. Office: The Newberry Libr 60 W Walton St Chicago IL 60610-3380 Office Phone: 312-255-3594. Business E-Mail: brownr@newberry.org.

BROWN, RICHARD L., lawyer; b. N.Y.C., Nov. 9, 1944; s. S. Robert and Frances S. B.; children: Jesselyn Alicia, Justin Alexander, Jeremy Brandon, Matthew Tyler, Garrett William. BA, Emory U., 1966; JD, NYU, 1969. Bar: N.Y. 1969, D.C. 1973, U.S. Ct. Appeals (D.C. cir.) 1974, U.S. Ct. of Claims 1980, U.S. Supreme Ct. 1980. Atty., advisor FCC, Washington, 1969-72; assoc. firm Farrow, Cahill, Kaswell & Schildhause, Washington, 1972-75; sr. ptnr. Brown Nietert & Kaufman, Chartered, Washington, 1975—. Gen. counsel Community Antenna TV Assn., 1972-75; pres. Alaskan Cable Network, Inc., Fairbanks, 1980-85; v.p., gen. counsel Soc. for Pvt. and Comml. Earth Stas., 1980-86; chmn. bd. trustees Rock Creek Internat. Sch., Washington, 2999-2002. Author: Low Power TV Handbook, 1981, licensing manual for land mobile radio-TV, 1980; co-author: The Satellite Earth Station Zoning Book, Questions & Answers About Satellite Earth Stations, The Business of Private Cable Television, The Low-Power TV Manual; contbr. articles to profl. jours. Pres. Sudden Cardiac Arrest Survivors Network, 2000—04. Mem. ABA, Fed. Communications Bar Assn. Office: Brown Nietert & Kaufman Chartered 2000 L St NW Ste 817 Washington DC 20036

BROWN, RICHARD LEE, lawyer, director; b. Ft. Worth, Dec. 7, 1925; s. Marvin H. and Janie (McIntosh) B.; m. Elizabeth McPherson, Nov. 19, 1949; children: Beverly Elizabeth, Leigh Ann (dec.). Student, Rice U., 1942-43; LLB, U. Tex., 1949; LLM, George Washington U., 1954. Bar: Tex. 1949. Asst. dist. atty., Tarrant County, 1949- 50; spl. atty. Chief Counsel's Office, IRS, Washington, 1953-56; partner Friedman & Brown, 1956-60, Stone, Parker, Snakard & Brown, 1961-66, Law, Snakard, Brown & Gambill, 1967-81, 83-84; of counsel Bishop Payne Harvard & Kaitcer, Ft. Worth, 1984-89, 91—; judge Ct. Appeals Tex. 2d Dist., 1981-83; chief civil div. Tarrant County Dist. Atty's Office, 1989-91. Former mem. bd. commrs. Pub. Housing Authority Ft. Worth, chmn., 1976-77; Chmn. bd., chmn. competition Van Cliburn Internat. Piano Competition, 1966-69. Served with AUS, 1944-46; Served with U.S. Army, 1950-53. Decorated Bronze Star medal, Combat Infantry badge and 3 battle stars. Fellow Tex. Bar Found. (life); mem. Tex. Bar Assn., Tarrant County Bar Assn. (pres. 1977-78) Office: 1800 Bank of Am Bldg 500 W 7th St Fort Worth TX 76102-4700 Office Phone: 817-335-4911.

BROWN, RITA MAE, writer; b. Hanover, Pa., Nov. 28, 1944; d. Ralph and Julia Ellen B. AA, Broward Jr. Coll., 1965; BA, NYU, 1968; cinematography degree, Sch. Visual Arts, N.Y.C., 1968; PhD, Inst. Policy Studies, 1976; DLitt, Wilson Coll., 1992; LLD (hon.), William Woods U., Fulton, Mo., 2000; LLD (hon.), York (Pa.) Coll., 2003; LHD (hon.), Franklin Pierce Coll., 2002. Photo editor Sterling Pub., N.Y.C., 1969-70; lectr. Fed. City Coll., Washington, 1970-71; rsch. fellow Inst. Policy Studies, Washington, 1971-73; pres. Am. Artists Inc., Charlottesville, Va., 1980—. Vis. mem. faculty in feminist studies Goddard Coll., Plainfield, Vt., 1973—; mem. lit. panel NEA, 1978-81; Hemingway judge for 1st fiction PEN Internat., 1983; blue ribbon panelist Prime Time Emmy Awards, 1984, 86; tchr. Nebr. Summer Writers Conf., U. Nebr., Lincoln, 2003, 04. Author: (translator) Hrotsvitra: Six Medieval Plays, 1971, (novels) The Plain Brown Rapper, 1972, The Hand That Cradles the Rock, 1971, Songs to a Handsome Woman, 1973, Rubyfruit Jungle, 1974, In Her Day, 1976, Six of One, 1977, Southern Discomfort, 1982, Sudden Death, 1983, High Hearts, 1986, Starting from Scratch, 1987, Bingo, 1988, Wish You Were Here, 1989, Rest in Pieces, 1991, Murder at Monticello, 1993, Venus Envy, 1993, Dolley, 1994, Paydirt, 1995, Riding Shotgun, 1996, Murder, She Meowed, 1996, Loose Lips, 1998, Outfoxed, 2000, Mrs. Murphy Mysteries, 2001, Outfoxed, 2000, Alma Mater, 2001, Hotspur, 2002, Full Cry, 2003, Whisker of Evil, 2004, Cat's Eyewitness, 2005, The Hunt Ball, 2005; (poetry) The Poems of Rita Mae Brown, 1987; TV series include I Love Liberty, 1982, Long Hot Summer, 1985, My Two Loves, 1986, The Alice Marble Story, 1986, Southern Exposure, 1990, Cat on the Scent, 1999, Loose Lips, 1999, Outfoxed, 2000, Pawing Through The Past, 2000; TV films include The Girls of Summer, 1989, Selma, Lord, Selma, 1989, Passing Through, 1993, A Family Again, 1994, others; (cable TV) The Mists of Avalon, 1986, The Nat Turner Story-African American Anthology, 1993, The Wall, K-9, 1993; (films) Slumber Party Massacre, 1982, Sweet Surrender, 20th Century Fox, 1986, Table Dancing, 1987, Mary Pickford, 1998. Former exec. officer NOW; bd. dirs. Human Rights Campaign Fund, N.Y.C., 1986; co-founder Radical Lesbians; founder Redstockings Radical Feminist Group, Nat. Gay Task Force, Nat. Women's Polit. Caucus. Recipient Award for Best Variety Show on TV Writers Guild Am., 1982, Outstanding Alumni, Am. Assn. Cmty. Colls., 1999, Outstanding Alumna, Broward Cmty. Coll., 1999, Literary Lion award N.Y. Pub. Library, 1986, Emmy award nomination for The Long Hot Summer, ABC mini-series, 1985; Emmy nomination for best variety show I Love Liberty, 1982; named Charlottesville favorite author The Observer, 1990, Athlete of the Week, The Observer, 1990. Mem. PEN Internat., Oak Ridge Foxhunt Club (Master of Foxhounds). Office: care of The Wendy Weil Agy 232 Madison Ave Ste 1300 New York NY 10016-2901 E-mail: waywardwomen@aol.com.*

BROWN, ROBERT ALAN, geologist, educator; b. LA, June 11, 1934; s. Carl Clayton and Olive (Hirst) B.; m. Marcia Louise Jobe, Dec. 12, 1957; children: Vanessa, Morgan, Tristin. BS, U. Calif., Berkeley, 1957, MS, 1963; PhD, U. Wash., 1969. Fellow U. Wash., Seattle, 1969-70, Nat. Ctr. Atmospheric Sci., Boulder, Colo., 1970-71; rsch. prin. investigator U. Wash. Polar Sci. Ctr., Seattle, 1971-73; prof. atmospheric sci. U. Wash., Seattle, 1983—. Adj. prof.: Naval Postgrad. Sch., 1983, Fraunhofer Inst., Garmish, Germany, 1991, U. Concepcíon, Chile, 1996, 2003, Ecole Poly., Paris, 1997. Author: Analytic Methods in Planetary Boundary Layer Models, 1973, Fluid Mechanics of the Atmosphere, 1991, The Tree or the Panzaic Plea, 2005; co-author: The Panzaic Principle, 1971, Microwave Remote Sensing for Ocean and Marine Weather Forecast Models, Ency. of Earth System Science, Surface Waves and Fluxes: Current Theory, Polar Oceanography, 1990; editor Pacific Ocean Remote Sensing Congress book series, 1992—, Remote Sensing of the Pacific Ocean with Satellites, 1998; contbr. over 80 articles to profl. jours. 1st lt. U.S. Army, 1957-59. Recipient Disting. Sci. award, Pan Ocean Remote Sensing Confs., 2000. Fellow Am. Meteorol. Soc.; mem. Am. Geophys. Union, Am. Oceanographic Soc., Sigma Xi, Phi Kappa Psi. Democrat. Office: U Wash Dept Atmospheric Sci PO Box 351640 Seattle WA 98195-0001 Office Phone: 206-543-8438. Business E-Mail: rabrown@atmos.washington.edu.

BROWN, ROBERT ARTHUR, academic administrator, chemical engineering professor; b. San Antonio, July 22, 1951; s. Ralph and Lillian (Rilling) B.; m. Beverly Ann Lamb, June 22, 1972; children: Ryan Arthur, Keith Andrew. BS, U. Tex., 1973, MS, 1975; PhD, U. Minn., 1979. Instr. U. Minn., Mpls., 1978; from asst. prof. chem. engring. to provost MIT, Cambridge, 1979—88, provost, 1988—2005, dean Sch. of Engring., 1996-98, co-dir. supercomputer facility, 1989-94; pres. Boston (Mass.) U., 2005—. Cons. Lincoln Labs., Lexington, Mass., 1985-87, Mobil Solar Energy, Waltham, Mass., 1982-93. Contbr. over 160 articles to profl. jours. Recipient Outstanding Jr. Faculty award Amoco Oil Co., 1981, Camille and Henry Dreyfus Tchr.-Scholar award 1983; named one of Outstanding Young Texans-Execs. U. Tex., 1991. Mem. AAAS, NAE, NAS, AIChE (Allen P. Colburn award 1986, Profl. Progress award 1996), Soc. Indsl. and Applied Math., Am. Assn. Crystal Growth (Young Author award 1985), Am. Phys. Soc., Am. Acad. Arts and Scis. Office: Boston U Office of Pres One Sherborn St Boston MA 02215 Business E-Mail: rab@mit.edu, rabrown@bu.edu.*

BROWN, ROBERT CHARLES, college administrator; b. Coushatta, La., Feb. 9, 1945; s. John Theodore Brown and Bobby (Best) Campbell; m. Jill Lestage, June 8, 1968; children: Charles Hugh, Martha Ruth, John Lestage. BA, Northwestern State U., 1967; MA, La. State U., 1969, PhD, 1976. Instr. econs. Northwestern State U., Natchoches, La., 1969-71; lang. prof. Wingate Coll., N.C., 1976-80; prof. econs. McMurray Coll., Abilene, Tex., 1980-86, asst. to pres., 1982-84, v.p., 1984-86; bus. sch. dean Mo. State Coll., 1987—; pres. Ark. Tech. U., 1993—. Mem. Taylor County Red Cross Bd., Abilene, 1983-84. U.S. Dept. Labor fellow, 1975-76. Mem. Am. Econ. Assn., So. Econ. Assn., blue Key, Phi Kappa Phi. Democrat. United Methodist. Avocation: model railroads.

BROWN, ROBERT DALE, wildlife science educator, department head; b. Red Bluff, Calif., July 31, 1945; s. Charles Arthur and Carol Joyce (Dale) B.; m. Regan Mensch, June 30, 1981; children: Alex, Jason, Adam. Student, U. Calif., Davis, 1963—65; BS, Colo. State U., 1968; PhD, Pa. State U., 1975. From asst. prof. to assoc. prof. Tex. A&I U., Kingsville, 1975-81; from assoc. rsch. scientist to rsch. scientist C. Kleberg Wildlife Rsch. Inst., Kingsville, 1981-87; dept. head Miss. State U., Starkville, 1987-93, Tex. A&M U., College Station, 1993—, coord. Gulf Coast Coop. Ecosys. Studies Unit, 2002—. Dir. Inst. for Renewable Resources, College Station, 1995—. Editor: Antler Development in Cervidae, 1983, Translocation of Wild Animals, The Biology of Deer, 1991. Lt. col. USMCR, 1968—93. Mem. Am. Inst. Nutrition, Wildlife Soc. (pres.-elect), Am. Fisheries Soc., Nat. Assn. Univ. Fish and Wildlife Programs (past pres.), Soc. for Range Mgmt. Episcopalian. Avocations: scouting, hunting, fishing, scuba, sailing. Office: Tex A&M U # 2258 Dept Wildlife Fisheries Sci College Station TX 77843-2258 Office Phone: 979-845-1261. E-mail: rdbrown@tamu.edu.

BROWN, ROBERT E., transportation executive; b. Croydon, Eng., 1945; BS, Royal Mil. Coll., Kingston, Can.; postgrad., Harvard U., 1983. With Can. Armed Forces, Atomic Energy Can., Pub. Svc. Commn., Treasury Bd., Coun. Maritime Premiers, 1976-78; assoc. dep. mininster Dept. Regional Indsl. Expansion; v.p. corp. devel. Bombardier, Inc., Montreal, Canada, 1987-89, sr. v.p. corp. devel. and strategic planning, 1989-90; pres. Canadair, 1990-92, Bombardier Aerospace Group-N.Am., 1992-96, pres., COO, 1996-99; pres., CEO Bombardier, Inc., Montreal, Canada, 1999—2002; chmn. Air Can., 2003—. Bd. dirs. Nortel Networks Corp.; pres., CEO CAE, Inc., Montreal.

BROWN, ROBERT FATH, philosopher, educator; b. St. Louis, June 6, 1941; s. John Pickens and Georgia Fath Brown; m. Ann Lee Werthmuller, June 21, 1963 (div. Nov. 1996); children: Nathan, Kristy, Grace; m. Mary Ann Harkins, Oct. 31, 1997; stepchildren: Erin Bagnatori, Kyle Bagnatori. BA, DePauw U., 1963; student, Union Theol. Sem., N.Y.C., 1963—70; MA, Columbia U., 1967, PhD, 1971. From instr. to assoc. prof. philosophy U. Del., Newark, 1970—86, prof. philosophy, 1986—, dir. univ. honors program, 1989—98. Vis. lectr. philosophy Hull U., England, 1980—81. Author: The Later Philosophy of Schelling, 1977; co-translator: Hegel: Lectures on the Philosophy of Religion, 1984—87, editor and co-translator: Hegel: Lectures on the History of Philosophy, vol. III, 1990. Recipient Del Tufo award, Del. Humanities Coun., 1993. Mem.: Am. Acad. Religion, Soc. Philosophy Religion, Am. Philos. Assn. Independent. Avocation: birdwatching. Home: 4 Washington St Newark DE 19711-7105 Office: Dept Philosophy Univ Delaware Newark DE 19716

BROWN, ROBERT G., lawyer; b. Boston, Apr. 29, 1956; s. Roger Ellis and Ida Margaret (Roherty) B.; m. Margaret H. Brown Dec. 11, 1991. AA, Cape Cod C.C., 1976; BA, Northeastern U., 1979; JD, Suffolk U., 1982. Counsel Barnstable Conservation Found., Inc., 1983-1990, Hyannis (Mass.) Fire Dist., 1985-93, Cotuit (Mass.) Fire Dist., 1985-88, West Barnstable (Mass.) Fire Dist., 1987—, Old King's Hwy Region Hist. Dist. Com., 1984—, Mass. Dept. Correction, Boston, 1989-95. Dir. Barnstable Conservation Found. Inc., 1983-85. Mem. Barnstable Town Meeting, 1975-87, Barnstable Planning Com., Barnstable Charter Com., 1976-77, Barnstable Planning Bd., 1979-85. Mem. Mass. Bar Assn. (small firm mgmt. sect. coun. 1991-93), Mass. Acad. Trial Attys., Barnstable County Bar Assn., Phi Alpha Delta. Office: 86 Willow St Yarmouth Port MA 02675-1758

BROWN, ROBERT GROVER, engineering educator; b. Shenandoah, Iowa, Apr. 25, 1926; s. Grover Whitney and Irene (Frink) B. BS, Iowa State Coll., 1948, MS, 1951, PhD, 1956. Instr. Iowa State Coll., Ames, 1948-51, 53-55, asst. prof., 1955-56, assoc. prof., 1956-59, prof., 1959-76, Disting. prof., 1976-88, Disting. prof. emeritus, 1988—; research engr. N. Am. Aviation, Downey, Calif., 1951-53. Cons. various aerospace engring. firms., 1956— Author: (with R.A. Sharpe, W.L. Hughes) Lines, Waves and Antennas, 1961, (with J.W. Nilsson) Linear Systems Analysis, 1962, (with Patrick Y.C. Hwang) Introduction to Random Signals and Applied Kalman Filtering with MATLAB Exercises and Solutions, 3d edit., 1997. Fellow IEEE, Inst. Navigation (Burka award 1978, 84, Weems award 1994). Home: 2601 S Lakeview Dr Clear Lake IA 50428-2910

BROWN, ROBERT JOHN, social sciences educator, consultant; b. Stillwater, Minn., June 15, 1935; s. Lindsay and Bertha Brown; m. Janet Rae Johnson, Aug. 22, 1959 (div.); m. Jacquelyn Marie Heidtke, Apr. 24, 1992; children: Anthony, Daniel, Linda Richie, Michael, Andrew. BS, Winona (Minn.) State U., 1957; MA, U. Minn., 1958, PhD, 1964. Cert. tchr. Minn., sch. counselor Minn. Tchr.-counselor, coach Farmington (Minn.) Pub. Schs., 1958—60; guidance dir. Sch. Dist. 192, Inver Grrove Heights, Minn., 1960—63; instr. U. Minn., Mpls., 1963—64; prof. leadership and policy U. St. Thomas, Mpls., 1964—; spl. asst. to the sec. U.S. Dept. Edn., Washington, 1981—85. Scholar in residence Nat. Assn. Secondary Sch. Prins., Reston, Va., 1990—91; editl. adv. com. Rowman and Littlefield Edn. Press, Lanham, Md., 2000—05; charter sch. adv. bd. State Dept. of Edn., St. Paul, 2003—05. Author: (monograph) Reflections on the Education Activities of the Business Roundatable, 1991, The Entrepreneurial Education, 2000; editor: (book series) Innovations in Education, 2001—; creator and co-exec. prodr. (TV series) Critical Issues in Education. State senator Minn. Legislature, St. Paul, 1967—77; mem. State Bd. Edn., St. Paul; Minn. nat. committeeman Rep. Party, Washington, 1979—81; organizer, co-chmn. Nat. Educators for Reagan-Bush, Washington, 1984; state chmn. Minn. Rep. Party, St. Paul, 1973—75; bd. dirs. DeLaSalle H.S., Mpls. Fellow Tozer Found., 1957—58; grantee Nat. Conf. on Rural Edn., Control Data Corp., C.C. Cooperation in Human Svc. Delivery, Comprehensive Employment and Tng. Act; scholar Tozer Found., 1953—57. Mem.: Nat. Assn. Secondary Sch. Prins. (state bd. dirs.), Am. Edn. Rsch. Assn. Republican. Roman Catholic. Home: 405 W County Rd C Roseville MN 55113 Office: U St Thomas 1000 Lasalle Ave Minneapolis MN 55403-2009 Office Phone: 651-962-4992. Office Fax: 651-962-4169. Personal E-mail: bobjbrown@comcast.net. E-mail: rjbrown@stthomas.edu.

BROWN, ROBERT LAIDLAW, state supreme court justice; b. Houston, June 30, 1941; s. Robert Raymond and Warwick (Rust) B.; m. Charlotte Banks, June 18, 1966; 1 child, Stuart Laidlaw. BA, U. of the South, 1963; MA in English and Comparative Lit., Columbia U., 1965; JD, U. Va., 1968. Bar: Ark. 1968, U.S. Dist. Ct. (ea. and we. divs.) Ark. 1968. Assoc. Chowning, Mitchell, Hamilton & Burrow, Little Rock, 1968-71; dep. prosecuting atty. 6th Jud. Dist., Prosecuting Atty. Office, Little Rock, 1971-72; legal aide Office Gov. Dale Bumpers, Little Rock, 1972-74; legis. asst. U.S. Senator Dale Bumpers, Washington, 1975-76; adminstrv. asst. Congressman Jim Guy Tucker, Washington, 1977-78; ptnr. Harrison & Brown, P.A., Little Rock, 1978-85; pvt. practice law, 1985-90; assoc. justice Ark. Supreme Ct., Little Rock, 1991—. Contbr. articles to profl. jours. Trustee U. of the South, Sewanee, Tenn., 1983-89, bd. regents, 1989-95. Fellow ABA, Ark. Bar Found (cert. of recognition 1981); mem. Ark. Bar Assn. Episcopalian. Office Phone: 501-682-6864. Business E-Mail: Robert.Brown@arkansas.gov.

BROWN, ROBERT MUNRO, museum director; b. Riverside, N.J., Mar. 4, 1952; s. James Wendell and Janet Elizabeth (Munro) B.; m. Mary Ann Noel, June, 1973 (div. 1977); m. Claudia Leslie Haskell, Jan. 14, 1978. BA in Polit. Sci. cum laude, Ursinus Coll., 1973; MA in Social Scis., Rivier Coll., 1978; PhD in Early Am. History, U. N.H., 1983. Grad. asst. dept. history U. N.H., Durham, 1979-83, instr., 1983-84; site curator T.C. Steele State Hist. Site Ind. State Mus. System, Nashville, Ind., 1984-91; exec. dir. Hist. Mus. at Ft. Missoula, Mont., 1991—. Hist. interpreter Strawberry Banke, Portsmouth, N.H., 1980-83; instr. Rivier Coll., Nashua, N.H., 1986-91, N.H. Coll., Nashua and Salem, 1986-91; supr. pub. programs Mus. Am. Textile History, North Andover, Mass., 1985-91; sec.-treas. Western Mont. Heritage Ctr./No. Rockies Heritage Ctr., 1992-93; mem. grad. com. U. Mont., 1993; mem. steering com. Ft. Missoula, 1993; reviewer Inst. Mus. and Libr. Svcs., 1993--; reviewer Am. Assn. Mus.-Mus. Asessment Programs, 1997—; mem. Mont. Com. of the Humanities Spkrs. Bur., 1995—; lectr., presenter, chair panels in field. Contbr. articles to profl. jours. Trustee Historic Harrisville, N.H., 1989-91; bd. dirs. United Peoples Found., 1991-93, v.p., 1993; mem. planning com. Western Mont. Heritage Ctr., 1991, U. Mont. Centennial Celebration, 1992, Leadership Missoula, 1992; active open space, parks and resource planning and mgmt. project team City of Missoula, 1993; mem. blue ribbon task force Five Valleys Luth. Retirement Cmty. Planning Com., 1994, Western Mont. Vol. Ctr. Coun., 2004-05. Grantee, Mass. Coun. on Arts and Humanities, 1986, 1987, 1988, Int. Mus. Svcs., 1988, 1989, 1990, 1991, 1993, 1995, 1997, 1999, AT&T, 1988, Am. Wool Coun., 1988, BayBank, 1989, Am. Yarn Assn., 1989, North Andover Arts Lottery Coun., 1989, 1990, Mass. Cultural Coun., 1990, Greater Lawrence Cmty. Found., 1991, Mass. Arts Lottery Coun., 1991, Gallery Assn. for Greater Art, 1991, 1992, 1994, 1995, 1996, 1997, 1998, Mont. Comm. for Humanities, 1991, 1992, 1993, 1994, 1995, 1996, 1997, 1998, 1999, 2000, 2001, 2002, Sinclair Oil Co., 1991, Mont. Rail Link, 1992, 1998, 1999, 2001, 2002, 2003, U. Mont. Found., 1992, Pepsi-Cola Co., 1992, 1993, 1994, 1995, 1996, 1997, Coca-Cola Bottling Co., 1998, Cmty. Med. Ctr., 1999, St. Patrick Hosp., 1999, U.S. WEST Found., 1992, 1995, The Missoulian, 1992, 1995, Champion Internat., 1992, Mont. Cultural Trust, 1993, 1995, 1997, Missoula Rotary, 1993, Tex. Mus. Austin, 1993, Inst. Mus. Svcs., 1993, 1995, 1997, 1999, 2002, Zip Beverage Co., 1994, Bitterroot Motors, 1994, 1995, 1996, 1997, 1998, Grizzly Hackle, 1994, University Motors, 1995, 1996, Earl's Distbg., 1996, Norwest Bank, 1996, 1997, 1998, ALPS, 2001, 2002, Southgate Mall, 2002; scholar, U. N.H., 1979—83; rsch. grantee, 1982, Kellogg Found. fellow, 1987. Mem.: Greater Boston Mus. Educator's Roundtable (steering com. 1988—90), Mtn. Plains Mus. Assn. (Mont. state rep. 1995—97, ann. meeting local arrangements chair 1997, chmn. scholarship com. 1998, sec. 1998—2000, chmn. scholarship com. 1999—2004, ann. meeting program co-chair 2000, treas. 2001—04), Western Mont. Fundraisers Assn. (charter 1991, v.p. 1993—95, pres. 1995—97), Mus. Assn. Mont. (panelist 1994), Mont. Hist. Soc., Assn. Records Mgrs. and Adminstrs. (charter Big Sky chpt. 1992—94), Am. Hist. Assn., Am. Assn. State and Local History (state membership rep. 1996—98, state awards chair 2001—, program com. 2003, mem. coun. 2005—), Am. Assn. Mus. (small mus. adminstrs. com., Mountain-Plains regional rep. 2000—03), Kiwanis (Sentinel chpt.), Masons (Missoula chpt.), Phi Alpha Theta. Democrat. Avocations: canoeing, cross country skiing, snowshoeing. Home: 216 Woodworth Ave Missoula MT 59801-6050 Office: Hist Mus at Ft Missoula Ft Missoula Bldg 322 Missoula MT 59804 Business E-Mail: ftmslamuseum@montana.com.

BROWN, ROBERT WALLACE, mathematics professor, educator; b. Portland, Oreg., May 20, 1925; s. Bert and Stella (Conway) B.; m. Doris Arrilda Burroughs, Sept. 4, 1948; children: Robert Wallace, Janice Dianne. BS, Pacific U., 1950; MS, Oreg. State U., 1952, PhD, 1958. Mathematician, Nat. Bur. Standards, Corona, Calif., 1952-54; Mathematician Boeing Co., Seattle, 1958-66; vis. asso. prof. Oreg. State U., Corvallis, 1966-67; prof. math. U. Alaska, Fairbanks, 1967-82, head dept., 1967-77, 79-82; vis. prof. math. Lewis and Clark Coll., Portland, Oreg., 1982-85; ret., 1985. Contbg. author: Error in Digital Computation, 1965. With USNR, 1942—45. Mem. Math. Assn. Am., Am. Math Soc., AAAS, Sigma Xi, Pi Mu Epsilon, Sigma Pi Sigma. Home: 20755 SW Prindle Rd Tualatin OR 97062-9701

BROWN, ROBERT WAYNE, lawyer; b. Allentown, Pa., July 6, 1942; s. P.P. and Rose (Ferrara) B.; m. Rochelle Kaplan, Oct. 23, 1977; m. Shelley Sherman, Mar. 3, 1973; children: Courtney Sherman, Robin Thea, Ryan Palmer; m. Lupe Pearce, Nov. 22, 1996. AB, Franklin and Marshall Coll., 1964; JD, Cornell U., 1967. Bar: Ill. 1969, Pa. 1971. VISTA atty. Cmty. Legal Svcs., Detroit, 1967-68; asst. prof. law U. Ill., 1968-70; ct. adminstr., law clk. Lehigh County Ct. Common Pleas, 1971-72; ptnr. Gross & Brown, Allentown, 1972-76; pvt. practice law Allentown, 1976-77; sr. ptnr. Brown & Brown, Allentown, 1977-82, Brown, Brown & Solt, Allentown, 1982-85, Brown, Brown, Solt & Krouse, Allentown, 1985-89, Brown, Brown, Solt & Ferretti, Allentown, 1989—; city solicitor Allentown, 2002—. Instr. bus. law Muhlenburg Coll., 1973-76; pub. defender Lehigh County, 1973-74; adv. bd. PNC Bank. Active Rape Crisis Coun. Lehigh Valley, 1978-84, Lehigh County Pre-trial Svcs., 1975-82; bd. dirs. Hispanic Am. Orgn., 1982-90, treas., 1983-86; bd. dirs. Lehigh County Sr. Citizens, 1980-88, pres., 1984-86; bd. dirs. Lehigh County Legal Svcs., 1973-77, Boys and Girls Club Allentown, 1994-2002, pres., 1998-2000; founding trustee Robert Clemente Charter Sch., 1998—. Recipient Cmty. Svc. award Hispanic Am. Orgn., 1985, Human Rels. Commn. award, Allentown, 1986; Lindback scholar Franklin and Marshall Coll., 1963-64. Mem. ABA, Pa. Bar Assn., Lehigh County Bar Assn., Order of Coif, Rotary (bd. dirs. Allentown 1998—, pres. 2004—), Club of Allentown. Democrat. Home: 225 Parkview Ave Allentown PA 18104-5323 Office: 1425 W Hamilton St Allentown PA 18102-4224 Office Phone: 610-433-6771. E-mail: rwbrown@onemain.com.

BROWN, ROGER GORDON, lawyer; b. Sedalia, Mo., Mar. 19, 1952; s. Virgil Brown and Kathryn Virginia Brown; m. Corrine Marion White, May 26, 1979 (div. Nov. 1994). BA, U. Mo., 1974, MA, 1976; JD, Gonzaga U., 1979. Assoc. Bushman, Nett & Gallaher, Jefferson City, Mo., 1980—82; ptnr. Bushman, Nett, Gallaher & Brown, Jefferson City, 1982—87; owner, sr. atty. Roger Brown & Assocs., Jefferson City, 1987—. Pres. Mo. Assn. Trial Attys., Jefferson City, 1996—97, Cole County Bar, 1995. Democrat. Avocations: gardening, coaching baseball. Home: 4601 Tanner Bridge Rd Jefferson City MO 65101 Office: Roger Brown & Assocs 216 E McCarty Jefferson City MO 65101 E-mail: rgblaw@socket.net.

BROWN, ROGER H., academic administrator; m. Linda Mason. BS, Davidson Coll., 1978; MBA, Yale U. Pres. Berklee Coll. Music, Boston, 2004—. With CARE and UNICEF, Thailand, Cambodia; co-dir. Save the Children, Sudan, 1985—86; co-founder Bright Horizons Family Solutions, 1986, CEO, 1986—2002; co-founder Horizons Initiative, Boston, bd. mem. Stand for Children; mgmt. cons. Bain and Co. Co-author: Rice, Rivalry, and Politics. Mem. gov. bd. Nat. Assn. for Edn. of Young Children; chairperson NAEYC Commn. on Accreditation. Named Nat. Entrepreneur of Yr., Ernst and Young/USA Today, 1996, Best Entrepreneur, BusinessWeek, 1997; named one of the 25 Friends of the Family, Working Mother mag., 1997; recipient Caring Corporation Award, Child Care Action Campaign, 1999. Office: Berklee Coll Music 1140 Boylston St Boston MA 02215 Office Phone: 617-266-1400.*

BROWN, RONALD, retired stockbroker; b. Aug. 30, 1930; s. Arthur S. and Eleanor (Smith) B.; m. Patricia Joan Milner, Aug. 2, 1952; children: Mitchell Ronald, Valerie Patricia. BS, Purdue U., 1953; MBA, NYU, 1957. Security analyst E.W. Axe & Co., Tarrytown, N.Y., 1955-56, Stillman, Maynard, N.Y.C., 1956-61; instl. salesman Clark Dodge & Co., N.Y.C., 1961-67; gen. ptnr. Buttonwood Assocs., Jersey City, 1967-71; pres. Personal Investment Mgmt. Co., Mahwah, N.J., 1971-72; asst. v.p., account exec. E.F. Hutton N.Y.C., 1972-77; sr. v.p. Dean Witter Reynolds, Inc., 1979-97; ret., 1997. Contbr. articles to profl. jours. Rockland County Rep. committeeman, 1958-60. With U.S. Army, 1953-55. Mem. N.Y. Soc. Security Analysts Inst., Chartered Fin. Analysts, N.Y. Athletic Club, Assn. Investment Mgmt. and Rsch., Kappa Sigma, Scarsdale Golf Club. Home: 100 W 57th St New York NY 10019-3302 E-mail: dufferon@nyc.rr.

BROWN, RONALD C., hotel executive; LLB, Osgoode Hall Law Sch., Toronto, Can.; LLM, London Sch. Econs. Exec. v.p., CFO Can. Pacific Hotels and Resorts; exec. v.p. fin. and planning, chmn. Doubletree Hotels Corp., 1990; pres. Doubletree Corp., 1994; sr. v.p., CFO Starwood Lodging Trust, Phoenix, 1995-98; exec. v.p., CFO Starwood Hotels and Resorts Worldwide, Inc., White Plains, NY, 1998—2003, exec. v.p., strategy, 2003—. Pres. Sonoran Hotel Advisors. Office: Starwood Hotels and Resorts 1111 Westchester Ave White Plains NY 10604

BROWN, RONALD DELANO, endocrinologist; b. Grosse Pointe, Mich., Dec. 28, 1936; s. Carroll Bradley and Alice Ruth (Chapper) B.; m. Marylee Ethel Lucas, July 27, 1957; children: Linda Diane, Kent William, Mark Steven. BS with distinction, U. Mich., 1959, MD with distinction, 1963. Diplomate Am. Bd. Internal Medicine, subspecialty in endocrinology and metabolism; lic. physician Mich. Intern Detroit Gen. Hosp., 1963-64; asst. resident in medicine U. Calif. Med. Ctr., San Francisco, 1966-68; chief resident in medicine San Francisco Gen. Hosp., 1968-69; fellow in endocrinology Vanderbilt U., Nashville, 1969-71, instr. medicine, 1969-71, asst. prof. medicine, 1971-73; assoc. prof. medicine Baylor Coll. Medicine, Houston, 1973-74, Mayo Med. Sch., Rochester, Minn., 1975-80; prof. medicine Health Scis. Ctr., U. Okla., Oklahoma city, 1980-93; clin. staff St. Joseph's Mercy Hosp., Clintown Twp., Mich., 1993—. Dir. U. Okla. Hypertension Ctr., 1986-93; chief clin. hypertension Health Scis. Ctr., U. Okla., 1980-93; chief hypertension VA Hosp., Oklahoma City, 1980-86; dir. multidisciplinary hypertension rsch. tng. program (NIH), Mayo Clinic, Rochester, 1977-80; chief endocrinology Ben Taub Hosp., Houston, 1973-74, assoc. dir. clin. rsch. ctr., 1973-74; coord. Tenn. Mid-South Regional Hyper-Control Program, Vanderbilt U., 1971-73; lectr. in field. Editl. bd. Jour. Clin. Endocrinology and Metabolism, 1987-91; reviewer for Life Scis., Annals of Internal Medicine, Jour. Lab. Clin. Medicine, Am. Jour. Medicine, Endocrinology, Mayo Clinic Proceedings, Steroids; contbr. 58 articles to profl. jours. Capt. USAF, 1964-66. Fellow ACP. Am. Coll. Endocrinologists; mem. Am. Soc. Hypertension, Am. Assn. Clin. Endocrinologists, Phi Kappa Phi, Phi Lambda Upsilon, Alpha Omega Alpha. Avocation: nursery. Office: Ronald D Brown MD 7237 1st St Marine City MI 48039-2801

BROWN, RONALD MALCOLM, engineering corporation executive; b. Hot Springs, SD, Feb. 21, 1938; s. George Malcolm and Cleo Lavonne (Plumb) B.; m. Sharon Ida Brown, Nov. 14, 1964 (div. Apr. 1974); children: Michael, Troy, George, Curtis, Lisa, Brittney. AA, Southwestern Coll., 1970; BA, Chapman U., 1978. Commd. USN, 1956, advanced through grades to master chief, 1973, ret., 1978; engring. mgr. Beckman Inst., Fullerton, Calif., 1978-82; mfg. engring. br. mgr. Northrop Corp., Hawthorne, Calif., 1982-83; dir. of ops. Transco, Marina Del Rey, Calif., 1983-85; v.p. engring. and design Decor Concepts, Arcadia, Calif., 1985-87; design dir. Lockheed Aircraft Corp., Ontario, Calif., 1987-97; v.p. engring. and program mgmt. Ducommon Inc., Carson, Calif., 1997—2003; pres. Basic Cons., Inc., Brea, Calif., 2003—. Mem. Rep. Nat. Com. and Pres.'s Club. Mem. Soc. Mfg. Engrs., Inst. Indsl. Engrs., Nat. Trust for Hist. Preservation, Fleet Res. Assn., Am. Film Inst., Nat. Mgmt. Assn. Avocations: golf, running, racquetball. Office: 101 W Central Brea CA 92821 Personal E-mail: greatr@aol.com.

BROWN, ROSA ELIZABETH, social worker, writer; b. Newport News, Va., Nov. 25, 1943; d. Marcellus Lee and Corrine Harris; m. Rufus Brown, Oct. 29, 1976; 1 child, Derek Vaughn Gatling. BA, Va. State U., Petersburg, 1966. Ordained prophetess and assoc. pastor New Vision Internat. Ministry, N.J. Team leader Lee Internat./Adminstrn. for Children Svcs., N.Y.C., 1996—99; social worker III Orange County Dept. of Social Svcs., Hillsbprough, NC, 1993—94; family svc. specialist Divsn. of Youth and Family Svcs., Newark. Author: (novels) God Has Another Plan, Be Encouraged, Jehovah Shammah: The God in the Storm, Send Judah First, Selah!. Enumerator, asst. crew leader U.S. Census Bur., East Orange, NJ, 2000. Recipient 4-yr. state scholarship, State of Va., 1962—66. Democrat. Pentecostal. Avocations: reading, writing, singing, liturgical dancing. Home: 128 Hillyer St East Orange NJ 07017 Office Phone: 862-264-3613. Personal E-mail: rosa_pwg@yahoo.com.

BROWN, ROSELLEN, writer; b. 1939; BA, Barnard Coll., 1960; MA, Brandeis U., 1962. MS prof. in Am. and English lit. Tougaloo Coll., 1965—67; prof. creative writing Goddard Coll., Plainfield, Vt., 1976; vis. prof. creative writing Boston U., 1977—78; prof. creative writing U. Houston, 1982—85, 1989—96; prof. Grad. Creative Writing Program Sch. Art Inst. Chgo., 1997—. Author: The Autobiography of My Mother, 1976, Tender Mercies, 1978, Before And After, 1992, Civil Wars, 1994 (Janet Heidinger Kafka award for best novel), Half a Heart, 2000, short stories, poetry. Recipient award in Lit., Am. Acad. Arts and Letters; fellow, Radcliffe Inst., MacDowell Colony, Guggenheim Found., Ingram Merrill Found., Bunting Inst., Howard Found. Office: Sch Art Inst Chgo 4th Fl 37 S Wabash Chicago IL 60603-3103

BROWN, ROWLAND CHAUNCEY WIDRIG, library and information scientist, consultant; b. Detroit, Oct. 11, 1923; s. Rowland Chauncey and Rhea (Widrig) B.; m. Kathleen Heather Sayre, May 18, 1946; children: Stephanie Anne Kugelman, Geoffrey Rowland Sayre (dec.), Kathleen Heather. BA cum laude, Harvard U., 1947, JD, 1950; sr. in mgmt. Sloan Sch., MIT, 1969; D. Humane Letters (hon.), Ohio Dominican Coll., 1999; D. in cmty. devel., Franklin U., 2005. Bar: D.C. 1951. Counsel Econ. Sablzn. Agy., 1950-52; staff counsel SBA, 1954; counsel Machinery and Allied Products Inst., Washington, 1955-59; with Dorr Oliver, Stamford, Conn., 1959-70, pres., 1968-70; pres., chief exec. officer Buckeye Internat., Inc., Columbus, Ohio, 1970-80; chief exec. officer Online Computer Libr. Ctr., Columbus, 1980-89; with R. Brown & Assocs., Columbus. Adv. bd. tchg. and learning Ohio State U. Sr. internat. cons. Coun. for Ethics Econs. inter-profl. panel on tech. and ethics; hon. trustee Columbus Cmty. Cable Access; bd. dirs., visitor's bd. Ohio Dominican Coll.; trustee Coun. for Pub. Deliberation, Civic Life Inst. Decorated Air medal (3), Purple Heart, Korean Republic citation. Mem. Am. Soc. Info. Sci., Am. Assn. for Higher Edn., N.Y. Harvard Club, Columbus Club, Torch Club, Columbus Rotary. Home and Office: R Brown & Assoc 2711 Edington Rd Columbus OH 43221-2502 E-mail: rcwbrow@columbus.rr.com.

BROWN, ROXANNE (JERENE ROXANNE BROWN), sales executive; b. L.A., July 5, 1947; d. John Phillip and Margaret Leona (Dalryrnple) Ortiz; m. Terry Lee Wood, May 7, 1966 (div. Sept. 1969); 1 child, Tiffany Christine Wood Suraco; m. Christopher Corey Brown, July 17, 1984 (dec. Sept. 1984); children: Jason Michael and John Charles (twins); m. Richard L. Gibbs, Apr. 18, 1996 (dec. Feb. 2000). Student, Casper Coll., 1977. Info. operator Gen. Telephone, Baldwin Park, Calif., 1965-67, long distance operator Santa Maria, Calif., 1967-69; office mgr. Monroe Calculator, Las Vegas, Nev., 1972-74; mgr. Exch. Club, Salt Lake City, 1977-81, Pouches Inc., Salt Lake City, 1981-82; asst. producer KSTU TV 20, Salt Lake City, 1982-84; sec. ADVO - Sys., Inc., Orange, Calif., 1984-85, terr. sales rep., 1985-88, major account exec. Garden Grove, Calif., 1988-95; v.p. JRB & Assocs., Long Beach, Calif., 1995—. Cons. Rice - Urmana Advt., Huntington Beach, Calif., 1989-91. Bd. dirs. ACLU, Salt Lake City, 1977; precinct worker Voter Registrar, Huntington Beach, 1988, Long Beach, Calif., 1990; bd. dirs., sec. Alamitos Bay Beach Peninsula Preservation Group, 1996-98. Mem.: ACLU, SAG, Platform Speakers Assn., Alamitos Bay Garden Club (v.p., ways and means com. 1996—98). Avocations: sculpting, photography, sailing. Home: 77 Ximeno Ave Long Beach CA 90803-3056 E-mail: rocknsand@yahoo.com.

BROWN, RUTH GEISLER, engineer; b. Beaver Falls, Pa., Mar. 17, 1924; d. Carl Charles and Emily (Pletz) Geisler; m. Stuart Fife Brown, Apr. 13, 1944. Student, Johns Hopkins U., 1960—70. Svc. rep. Bell. Tel. of Pa., Pitts., 1942—43; draftsman to group engr. Martin Marietta Co., Middle River, Md., 1944—49, 1950—63; design draftsman Bendix Radio, Balt., 1949—50; engring. staff assoc. missile programs and microelectronics Johns Hopkins U./Applied Physics Lab., Laurel, Md., 1963—75, sr. engring. staff, supr. hybrid ops., 1975—79, divsn. staff, 1979—81, electronic design supr., 1981—83, engring. design supr., 1983—90; ret., 1990. Mem.: NAFE, Internat. Electronic Packaging Soc., Internat. Soc. Hybrid Microelectronics. Republican. Home: 12628 W Parkwood Dr Sun City West AZ 85375-4626

BROWN, SANDRA, writer; b. Waco, Tex., Mar. 12, 1948; m. Michael Brown; children: Ryan, Rachel. Mgr. Merle Norman Cosmetics Studios, Tyler, Tex., 1971-73; weather reporter KLTV-TV, Tyler, 1972-75, WFAA-TV, Dallas, 1976-79; model Dallas Apparel Mart, 1976-87. Author: (romance novels) Breakfast in Bead, 1983, Heaven's Price, 1983, Relentless Desire, 1983, Tempest in Eden, 1983, Temptation's Kiss, 1983, Tomorrow's Promise, 1983, In a Class by Itself, 1984, Send No Flowers, 1984, Bittersweet Rain, 1984, Sunset Embrace, 1984, Words of Silk, 1984, Riley in the Morning, 1985, Thursday's Child, 1985, Another Dawn, 1985, 22 Indigo Place, 1986, The Rana Look, 1986, Demon Rumm, 1987, Fanta C, 1987, Sunny Chandler's Return, 1987, Adam's Fall, 1988, Hawk's O'Toole's Hostage, 1988, Slow Heat in Heaven, 1988, Tidings of Great Joy, 1988, Long Time Coming, 1989, Temperatures Rising, 1989, Best Kept Secrets, 1989, A Whole New Light, 1989, Another Dawn, 1991, Breath of Scandal, 1991, Mirror Image, 1991, French Silk, 1992, The Silken Web, 1992, Honor Bound, 1992, A Secret Splendor, 1992, Shadows of Yesterday (also published as Relentless Desire), 1992, Three Complete Novels, 1992, Charade, 1994, The Witness, 1995, "TEXAS!" series: Texas! Lucky, 1990, Texas! Sage, 1991, Texas! Chase, 1991, Texas! Trilogy, 1992, (as Laura Jordan) Hidden Fires, 1982, The Silken Web, 1982, (as Rachel Ryan) Love Beyond Reason, 1981, Love's Encore, 1981, Eloquent Silence, 1982, A Treasure Worth Seeking, 1982, Prime Time, 1983, (as Erin St. Claire) Not Even for Love, 1982, A Kiss Remembered, 1983, A Secret Splendor, 1983, Seduction By Design, 1983, Led Astray, 1985, A Sweet Anger, 1985, Tiger Prince, 1985, Above and Beyond, 1986, Honor Bound, 1986, The Devil's Own, 1987, Two Alone, 1987, Thrill of Victory, 1989, Exclusive, 1996, Fat Tuesday, 1997, Unspeakable, 1998, The Alibi, 1999, Stand Off, 2000, The Switch, 2000, The Crush, 2002 (NY Times Bestseller), Hellow Darkness, 2003, White Hot, 2004 (Publishers Weekly Bestseller, 2005), Chill Factor, 2005. Recipient Am. Bus. Women's Assn's Disting. Circle of Success award, B'nai B'rith's Disting. Literary Achievement award, A. C. Greene award, Romance Writers Am. Lifetime Achievement award. Mem.: Literacy Partners, Novelists, Inc, Internat. Assn. Crime Writers, Mystery Writers Am., Author's Guild.

BROWN, SANDRA JEAN, special education educator; d. John Francis and Ruth Hilda Daley; m. John Franklin Brown, Jr., Aug. 10, 1996; children: Sean Edward Mountjoy, Erin Lynn Mountjoy, Sara Anne Davis children: Eric Robert Mountjoy. BS, Calif. State Coll., 1969; MEd, Converse Coll., 1995. Cert. Nat. Bd. Profl. Tchg. Stds., 2004. Kindergarten tchr. Butler County Sch. Dist., Zelienople, Pa., 1969—71; title one math tchr. Shiprock Consol. Sch. Dist. 22, N.Mex., 1978—80; owner, operator A&W Root Beer Restaurant, Cortez, Colo., 1980—81; case mgr. Billings Fairchild Ctr. Intermediate Care Facility, Okla., 1985—87; missionary Gen. Bd. Global Ministries United Meth. Ch., Winterhaven, Calif., 1987—90; spl. edn. tchr. San Pasqual Unified Sch. Dist., Winterhaven, Calif., 1987—90, Spartanburg County Sch. Dist. Seven, SC, 1991—2000, Spartanburg County Sch. Dist. Five, Duncan, 2000—; spl. edn. resource tchr. Shiprock Consol. Sch. Dist. 22, N.Mex. Editor, creator, operator (bi-weekly tribal newspaper) Ute Mountain Ute Indian Tribe, Towoac, Colo., 1976—78. Participant Am. Heart Assn. Ride-a-Thon, Myrtle Beach, SC, 1995—2004; vol. Habitat for Humanity, Spartanburg, 1997—2000; chairperson Reidville Rd. United Meth. Ch. Readiness Ctr., Moore, SC, 1993. Fed. Perkins grant, 2001. Methodist. Avocations: gardening, horseback riding, camping. Office: James F Byrnes HS 150 E Main St PO Box 187 Duncan SC 29334 Office Phone: 864-949-2355.

BROWN, SANDRA LEE, arts management consultant, watercolorist; b. Chgo., July 9, 1943; d. Arthur Willard and Erma Emily (Lange) Boettcher; m. Ronald Gregory Brown, June 21, 1983; 1 child, Jon Michael. BA in Art and Edn., N.E. Ill. U., 1966; postgrad., No. Ill. U. Cert. K-9 tchr., Ill. Travel agt. Weiss Travel Bur., Chgo., 1959-66; tchr. Chgo. Sch. Sys., 1966-68, Schaumburg (Ill.) Sch. Dist. 54, 1968-94, creator coord. peer mentoring program for 1st-yr. tchrs., 1992-96; cons. Yardstick Ednl. Svcs., Monroe, Wis., 1994—2003; exec. dir. Monroe Arts Ctr., 1996—2001, Monroe Area Coun. for the Arts, Madisonville, Tenn., 2002—03; arts mgmt. cons. Helping Hands, Non-Profit Consulting, Knoxville, Tenn., 2003—, Tenn. Arts Commn. Arts cons.; mem. adv. bd. Peer Coaching and Mentoring Network, Chgo. suburban region, 1992-94; peer cons. Schaumburg Sch. Dist. 54, 1988-94. Exhibited in group shows Court House Gallery, Woodstock, Ill., Millburn (Ill.) Gallery, Gallerie Stefanie, Chgo., Monroe Arts Ctr., 1997. Campaign chmn. for mayoral candidate, Grayslake, Ill., 1989; campaign chmn. for trustee Citizens for Responsible Govt., Grayslake, 1991. Mem. Lakes Region Watercolor Guild, Delta Kappa Gamma (chmn. women in arts Gamma chpt. Ill. 1992-94, Alpha Mu chpt. 1995-97), Cmty. Arts League (Athens, Tenn.). Avocations: gardening, musician for barn dances, pre-war Appalachian, blues and cajun music, research collecting 78 rpm records. Home and Office: Helping Hands Non-Profit Consulting PO Box 1456 Athens TN 37371 *Life's greatest limitations are internal. Resolve those, and external experience transforms into opportunity.*

BROWN, SARA NORDHOLM, social work educator; b. Fergus Falls, Minn., Jan. 28, 1941; d. David E. and Sara Evelyn (Nelson) Nordholm; m. Dudley J. Brown, June 15, 1963; Sara (Brown) Dunlap, Kirsten Leona, Jesse Chanda. BA in Sociolgy, St. Olaf Coll., 1963; student, U. Beirut, Lebanon, 1962; MSW, Columbia U., 1965; PhD in Family Rels. and Child Devel., Okla. State U., 1982. Lic. social worker, Okla. Med. social worker St. Lukes Hosp., N.Y.C., 1965-66; instr. Mbereshi Secondary Sch., Zambia, 1970-73, U. Benghazi, Libya, 1974-77; tchg. assoc. Okla. State U., Stillwater, 1978-80, asst. prof., 1980-81; prof. Northeastern State U., Tahlequah, Okla., 1981—2001, chmn. dept., 1983-97; ret., 2002; prof. emeritus Northeastern State U., 2002—. Adminstr. Child Welfare Tng. Grant, Tahequah, Okla., 1984-90, Child Abuse Prevention Rsch, Tahlequah, 1986-90; presenter, planner Cherokee Nation Women's Conf., Tahlequah, 1989. Contbr. articles to profl. jours. Founding mem. Child Abuse Prevention Task Force, Tahlequah, 1983; bd. dirs. Help-In-Crisis, Tahlequah, 1981-85, Habitat for Humanity, Tahlequah, 1990—,Lusaka, 2005, Zambia, 2005, Tahlequah Food Pantry, 1998—; mediator Agr. Mediation, State of Okla., 1988—. Recipient Cert. Social Planning Aging Svc. Eastern Okla. Devel. Dist., Tahlequah, 1985, Appreciation award, Cherokee Nat. Employment & Tng., Tahlequah, Okla., 1986, Outstanding Alumni award, Okla. State U. Women's Coun., Stillwater, 1987; named Cherokee Nation Early Childhood Advocate of Yr., 1999; named to Muskogee (Okla.) Hall of Fame, 1984, NSU Faculty of the Yr. for Svc. Contbns., 1995. Mem.: NASW (v.p. 2001—, bd. dirs. Okla. chpt., Lifetime Achievement award 2000), AAUW (v.p. local br. 1988—89, pres. 2003—05, host 2 delegations of Russian profls. 2003—04), Baccalaureate Social Work Program Dirs. Assn., Okla. Health and Welfare Assn. (bd. dirs. 1987—90), Okla. Lic. Social Workers, Coun. Social Work Edn., Columbia U. Sch. Social Work Alumni (bd. dirs.). Methodist. Home: PO Box 1412 Tahlequah OK 74465-1412 E-mail: browns@nsuok.edu.

BROWN, SARAH M., artist, art gallery owner; b. Longview, Tex., Jan. 30, 1935; d. Phil Uhls and Fannie Belle (Keating) B. BFA with honors in figure drawing and figure painting, U. Chgo. and Art Inst. Chgo., 1957; student, Tulane U., 1960, Odyssey Studio, Atlanta, 1978, Nat. Watercolor Seminar, 1980. Tchr. ceramics Pensacola Fla. Jr. Coll., 1958; dir. art dept. Pensacola Fla. Adult Vocat. Sch., 1958-59; owner S. Brown Studio-Gallery, New Orleans, 1959-63, Atlanta, 1963-89, Roswell, Ga., 1986-89, Sarah Brown Studio-Gallery, Atlanta, 1989—. Founder Sarah Brown Art Tours, 1973-, The Little Brown Press, 1976-; condr. seminars in field, represented by Richard James Galleries, Charleston, S.C., Southeastern Interiors, Eatonton, Ga. One-woman shows include Longview (Tex.) Art Assn., Pensacola Art Assn., Douglasville Cultural Arts Ctr., 1995, exhibited in group shows at Nat. We. Small Painting Exhbn., 1982 (Best of Show, 1st place), Palm Beach Galleries (3rd place show, 1st place We. category), NLAPW Ga. State Competition (1st place oils), Midwest Armory Art Exhibn., Chgo., Johnson Galleries, Three Arts Club, Southside Arts Festival, Delgado Mus., New Orleans, Pensacola Quadricentennial, Royal Orleans Hotel, New Orleans, Piedmont Art Festival, Berman Lipton Interiors, Atlanta Artists Group Show, Jr. C. of C., Am. Painters in Paris, Winter Park (Fla.) Outdoor Art Festival, Festival of the Masters, Lake Buena Vista, Fla., Knickerbocker Artists 31st Annual, N.Y.C., Catherine Lorillard Wolfe Art Club Exhibit, Nat. We. Small Painting Exhbn., Bosque Farms, N.Mex., Palm Beach Galleries, New Orleans, ABC Art and Frame Show, Atlanta, Wildlife Fedn., 1994, Safari Internat. Exhbn., Galleria Mall, Atlanta, 1995, Callawolde Cultural Arts Ctr., 2001, Decor Art Expo, 2003, commns. include A.H. Stephens Meml., Crawfordville, State of Ga. Dept. Natural Resources, Warm Springs Lodge, Elijah Clarke Mus., New Echota Historic Site, Hofwyl Plantation, Savannah, Ga., SouthEastern Wildlife Expo, Charleston, SC, 2005, Represented in permanent collections former Pres. Jimmy Carter, Sen. Geraldine Ferraro, Reynolds Plantation and Great Waters, Eatonton, Ga., St. Ives Country Club, featured art in mags., exhibitions include Cultural Art Ctr., Atlanta, 2001. Founder Mitzi Brown Drama Fund, Shamrock H.S., Atlanta, 1974. Mem. Nat. League Am. Pen Women, Nat. Mus. Women in the Arts (charter), Portrait Soc. Am., Inc., Atlanta High Mus., Atlanta Zool. Soc., Ga. Wildlife Fedn. Office: Sarah Brown Studio-Gallery 2947 Lookout Pl NE # 2 Atlanta GA 30305-3217 Office Phone: 404-262-7304. E-mail: sarahbrownstudio@comcast.net.

BROWN, SELMA, artist; b. Chgo., Dec. 22, 1935; d. William and Sima (Wolf) Quateman; m. Selah Brown (div. 1975). Student, U. Ill., 1952-54, Mexico City Coll., 1955, Chgo. Art Inst., 1956, San Francisco Art Inst., 1978; student in mask carving, Anon Home Sch., Bali, Indonesia, 1982; student, Zhe Jiang Art Acad., Hangzhou, China, 1987. Illustrator, designer Spencer Press, Chgo., 1956-57, Sci. Rsch. Assn., Chgo., 1957-58; book design/layout artist Scott Foresman, Chgo., 1958-59; tchr. Layton Sch. of Art, Milw., 1958-59, Alvarado Pub. Sch., San Francisco, 1974, Haight Ashbury Workshop, San Francisco, 1975; art dir. St. Elizabeth Youth Advocates, Oakland, Calif., 1993. Executed mural children's Community Sch., Van Nuys, Calif., San Francisco Art Commn., San Francisco Bd. Edn., CETA Program, others; designer stage sets for theatrical prodns. (Bay Area Critics award 1980). Bd. dirs. Precita Eye Mural Collective, San Francisco, 1985—. Avocations: tai chi, travel. Home: 96 Carl St San Francisco CA 94117-3951

BROWN, SEYMOUR R., lawyer; b. Cleve., Oct. 24, 1924; s. Leonard and Ella (Rubinstein) B.; m. Madeline Kusevich, July 8, 1956; children: Frederic M., Thomas R., Barbara L. N. Rybicki. BA, Case-Western Res. U., 1948; JD, Cleve. State U., 1953. Bar: Ohio 1953. Prin. Seymour R. Brown & Assocs., Cleve.; ptnr. Brown-McCallister Real Estate, Residential & Comml. Constrn., Melbourne, Fla., 1973-81. Spl. counsel to atty. gen. State of Ohio, 1963-70. Editor, pub.: Gt. Lakes Architecture, 1955-59. Chmn. CSC, University Heights, Ohio, 1978-82, 84-86, mem., 1976-2003; mem. exec. com. Cuyahoga County Rep. Orgn., 1966-2003; pres. Nat. Permanent Endowment Fund, Inc., 1988-92. With AUS, 1943-45. Decorated Purple Heart, Bronze Star; named to Ohio Mil. Hall of Fame, 2003. Mem. Ohio Bar Assn., Cleve. Bar Assn., Am. Arbitration Assn. (comml. arbitration panel), Zeta Beta Tau (nat. dir., nat. pres. 1978-80), Masons. Office: 1344 Continental Ave Melbourne FL 32940-6702 Office Phone: 216-721-7124. Business E-Mail: srb2@gbronline.com.

BROWN, SHARON WEBB, art educator; b. Whitesburg, Ky., Nov. 20, 1942; d. Chester and Doris Adams Webb; m. Bob Brown, May 19, 1973; children: Alyn, Ashley Susan. BA, Georgetown (Ky.) Coll., 1964. Art tchr. Jefferson County Schs., Louisville, 1964—72; art coord. Louisville City Schs., Louisville, 1972—73; tchr. fine arts, dept. chair Marshall County Schs., Benton, Ky., 1975—. Editor: Hallowed Hollows, 2001, Women in God's Word, 2001, God's Specialty, 2002; actor: (plays) Harvey, 2001, 2002, Do Not Go Gentle, 2002. Elder Presbyn. Ch., Calvert City, Ky. Mem.: Women in the Arts, Speed Mus. (bd. dirs. 1972—73), Commonwealth Yacht Club (rec. sec. 1993—2004). Republican. Avocations: travel, literature, painting. Home: POBox 641 Calvert City KY 42029 Office: Marshall County Schools 416 High School Road Benton KY 42025 Personal E-mail: sbrown@marshall.k12.ky.us.

BROWN, SHEBA ANN, elementary school educator; b. Miss., 1951; married; 1 child, Joshua. BS in Elem. Edn., U. So. Miss., 1973. Tchr. 4th grade Biloxi (Miss.) Pub. Schs., 1973-74; tchr. 3d grade Ferncrest Acad., New

Orleans, 1974-75, Cifton Ganus Pvt. Sch., New Orleans, 1975-78; tchr. 4th grade Putnam County Schs., Palatka, Fla., 1986-87; tchr. multi-age primary class Biloxi Pub. Schs., 1987—. Condr. workshops; presenter in field. Recipient Beverly Briscoe award Biloxi Schs., 1990, Enhancement award City of Biloxi, 1995, Leo Seal Tchr. Recognition award, 1999; named Miss. Tchr. of Yr., 1995, Women at the Top Coast Mag., 1996. Mem. Internat. Reading Assn., Nat. Coun. Tchrs. English, Jeff Davis PTA (treas.), Delta Kappa Gamma. Home: 135 Travia Ave Biloxi MS 39531-5328

BROWN, SHERROD, congressman, retired state official; b. Mansfield, Ohio, Nov. 9, 1952; s. Charles G. and Emily (Campbell) B.; m. Connie Schultz; children: Emily, Elizabeth. BA, Yale U., 1974; MA in Edn., Ohio State U., 1979, MA in Pub. Adminstrn., 1981. Mem. Ohio Ho. of Reps., Mansfield, 1975-82; Sec. of State State of Ohio, Columbus, 1983-91; mem. U.S. Congress from 13th Ohio dist., Washington, 1993—; mem. energy and commerce com., internat. rels. com. Instr. Ohio State U., Mansfield, 1978-79 Author: Congress from the Inside, 1999, Myths of Free Trade, 2004. Active India Caucus. Recipient Eagle Scout Am. 1966, Friend of Edn. award, 1978 Mem. Nat. Assn. Secs. State Democrat. Lutheran. Office: US Ho of Reps 2332 Rayburn Ho Office Bldg Washington DC 20515-3513*

BROWN, SHIRLEY MARGARET KERN (PEGGY BROWN), interior designer; b. Ellensburg, Wash., Mar. 30, 1948; d. Philip Brooke and Shirley (Dickson) Kern; m. Ellery Kliess Brown, Jr., Aug. 7, 1970; children: Heather Nicole Coco, Rebecca Cherise, Andrea Shirley Serene, Ellery Philip. BA in Interior Design, Wash. State U., 1973. Apprentice then interior designer L.S. Higgins & Assocs., Bellevue, Wash., 1969-72; interior designer ColorsPlus Interiors, Inc., Bellevue, Wash., 1972, Strawns Office Furniture & Interiors, Inc., Boise, 1973-75, Empire Furniture, Inc., Tulsa; owner Inside-Out Design Co., Ltd., Boise, 1973-82; interior designer Architekton, Inc., Tulsa, 1984-86, Johnson Brand Design Group, Inc., 1986-87, Ellery Brown & Assocs. Arch., 1987—, Seattle Design Ctr.-Visions & Studio Programs, Scottsdale, Ariz., 1998—, Mehagian's Fine Furniture, Scottsdale, Ariz., ASID Designers' Showhouse, 2000, Ladlows Fine Furniture, 2003—. Lectr. in field. Contbr. articles to profl. jours.; featured designer Ariz. Lifestyle mag., 2002. Pres. PTA, co-chair capital bond prin. sel. com., enrollment rev. com., 1989-95; bd. dirs. Paradise Valley Young Life; designer West Valley Child Crises Ctr., Inc.; contributing designer West Valley Child Crisis Ctr. Recipient Seattle Design Ctr. Marjorie Siegel award, 1997, Phoenix Home and Garden Mag. ASID Showhouse, 2000. Mem.: AAUW, Nat. Soc. Interior Designers, Am. Soc. Interior Designers (dir. chpt. 1976—77, presdl. citation Oreg. chpt. 1977, chmn. Boise subchpt. 1977—79, sec. 1980—81, chmn. Wash. chpt. step workshop chmn. 1993—97, NCIDQ chmn. 1993—97, Wash. state presdl. citation 1995, presdl. citation Oreg. chpt. 1995—96, Wash. state presdl. citation 1996, 1997, bd. dirs. North Ariz. chpt. 2003—, Showhouse Mehagian's Designer award Phoenix Home and Garden Mag. 2000, bd. dirs. Ariz. chpt. 2003—), Jr. League Phoenix, Wash. State U. Alumni Assn., Idaho Hist. Co., Jr. League Seattle, Zonta, Alpha Gamma Delta. Republican. Presbyterian. Office: Ladlows Fine Furniture 16000 N Scottsdale Rd Scottsdale AZ 85254 Office Phone: 480-609-5083. Personal E-mail: azbrowns@hotmail.com.

BROWN, SHIRLEY MARK, retired science administrator; b. Phila., Apr. 25, 1924; d. Paul and Bertha Evelyn (Zucker) Mark; m. Bernard Beau, Sept. 1, 1947; children: Eric Joel, Aimee Susan. BA, Temple U., Phila., 1945, MA, 1947. Rsch. chemist U. Mich., Ann Arbor, 1947-50; instr. Upsala Coll., East Orange, 1960-74; acad. planner Rutgers U., New Brunswick, N.J., 1974-80, assoc. dir. Waksman Inst., 1980-88; exec. dir. Rutgers Rsch. and Ednl. Found., New Brunswick, 1980-94; assoc. dir. Office of Corp. Liaison and Technol. Transfer Rutgers U., 1988-91, adminstr. corp. contracts, 1991-94. Ct. mediator Union County, 2003—05. Sec. Joint Civic Com. Westfield 1962-66, Com. for Human Rights Westfield 1967-70; publicity chairperson. PTA Westfield 1963-67; counselor State Health Ins. Program, Union County, 2000-05; vol. Zimmerli Art Mus., Rutgers U., 1994-2005, bd. dirs., 2003-05. Mem. LWV, Assn. Univ. Technol. Mgrs., Nat. Coun. Univ. Rsch. Adminstrs., Soc. Rsch. Adminstrs. Avocations: travel, theater, art, bridge. Home: 146 Tudor Oval Westfield NJ 07090-2245 Personal E-mail: smb146@msn.com. E-mail: smb146@msn.org.

BROWN, SHONA, information technology executive; BS in computer systems engring., Carleton U.; MA in econ. and philosophy, Oxford U.; Phd in indsl. engring. and engring. mgmt., post-doctorate in indsl. engring. and engring. mgmt., Stanford U. Prof. dept. indsl. engring. and grad. sch. bus. Stanford U.; former ptnr. Global Strategy Practice McKinsey and Co.; v.p. bus. ops. Google Inc., 2003—. Author: Competing on the Edge: Strategy as Structured Chaos. Office: Google Inc 1600 Amphitheatre Pky Mountain View CA 94043 Office Phone: 650-623-4000. Office Fax: 650-618-1499.

BROWN, STEPHANIE CECILE, librarian, writer; b. Pasadena, Calif., Mar. 23, 1961; d. Harry Francis and Anne Catherine (Murray) B.; m. Derek Lawrence Christiansen, Dec. 1, 1991; children: Nathaniel, Thomas. BA, Boston U., 1984; MFA, U. Iowa, 1986; MLS, U. Calif., Berkeley, 1987. Libr. specialist Orange County Pub. Libr., 1989—. Author: Allegory of the Supermarket, 1998; contbr. poetry to profl. publs. Recipient Jessica Maxwell Meml. Poetry prize Am. Poetry Rev., 1994; NEA fellow, 2001. Roman Catholic. Office: San Clemente Libr 242 Avenida Del Mar San Clemente CA 92672

BROWN, STEPHEN D., lawyer; b. Boston, 1949; BA, Williams Coll., 1971; JD, Villanova U., 1976. Bar: Mass. 1976, Pa. 1978. Law clk. to Hon. Daniel H. Huyett, 3d U.S. Dist. Ct. (ea. dist.) Pa., 1976-78; ptnr. Dechert LLP, Phila. Editor-in-chief Villanova U. Law Rev., 1976. Office: Dechert LLP 1717 Arch St Ste 4000 Philadelphia PA 19103-2793 Office Phone: 215-994-2240. E-mail: stephen.brown@dechert.com.

BROWN, STEPHEN F., health facility administrator; BS, U. Ala. Joined Am. Med. Internat., 1976; CIO Am. Med. Internat. (now Tenet Healthcare Corp.), 1990—95; sr. exec. v.p., CIO Tenet Healthcare Corp., Santa Barbara, Calif., 1995—99, exec. v.p., CIO, 1999—. Active The Wharton Sch., Info. Week mag., CEO mag., The Healthcare Collaboration Group, Sheldon I. Dorenfest and Assocs. Consulting; mem. adv. bd. Nat. Health Founds. Ctr. for Health Info. Tech. Contbg. author: Financial Information Systems Manual, 1992. Office: Tenet Healthcare Corp 13737 Noel Rd Ste 100 Dallas TX 75240

BROWN, STEPHEN HAYZE, JR., social worker; b. Chgo., Sept. 7, 1954; s. Stephen Hayze Brown and Barbara Elizabeth Grandpré; m. Judith Eileen McCain, Mar. 5, 1997; 1 child, Javon. BS in Biology, Chgo. State U., 1981; diploma hematology and phlebotomy, Med. Careers Inst. Rsch. asst. Chgo. State U., 1980; instr. anatomy U. Ill. Coll. Dentistry, Chgo., 1982; ind. landscaping contractor, 1982-86, 87-89; tchr. Chgo. Bd. Edn., 1986-87; case mgr. Ill. Dept. Human Svcs., Chgo., 1999—. Assemblyman 44th Ward Assembly, Chgo., 1976-77. Ill. State scholar, 1972, Nat. Merit/Achievement scholar, 1972. Mem. Nat. Space Soc., The Planetary Soc. Roman Catholic. Avocations: music, science fiction, philosophy, comparative religion, astronomy.

BROWN, STEPHEN IRA, philosophy professor; b. Bklyn., July 14, 1938; s. Milton Frank and Ruth (Mittman) B.; m. Eileen Thaler, June 12, 1960; children: Jordan David, Sharon Jean. AB, Columbia Coll., 1960; MA in Teaching (Sloan fellow 1960-61), Harvard U., 1961, Ed.D., 1967. Instr. math. and edn. Simmons Coll., Boston, 1962-65; asst. prof. edn. Harvard U., 1966-72; vis. prof. Hebrew U., Jerusalem, 1970-71; asso. prof. Syracuse (N.Y.) U., 1972-73; mem. faculty SUNY, Buffalo, 1973-98, prof. math. edn., 1979-98, prof. philosophy of edn., 1982-98, prof. emeritus, 1998—. Vis. prof. U. Ga., Athens, 1979-80; vis. scholar Harvard U., Cambridge, Mass., 1993-94; participant ethics workshops Coll. Jewish Studies, Buffalo, 1974-76. Author: Some Prime Comparisions, 1978, Student Generations, 1987, Posing Mathematically, 1996, Reconstructing School Mathematics: Problems with Problems and the Real World, 2001; co-author: The Art of Problem Posing, 1983, rev. edit., 2005; co-author: Mathematics, Pedagogy and Secondary Teacher Education, 1996; co-editor: Progresssive Education: A Movement and Its Professional Journal, 1988, Problem Posing: Reflections and Applications, 1993; editor: Creative Problem Solving, 1989; mem. rev. bd. Ednl. Theory, 1983-87; mem. editl. bd. Math. Tchr., 1977-80, For Learning of Math., 1980-97; mem. adv. bd. Humanistic Math. Network Jour., 1995-2003; contbr. articles to profl. jours. Mem. adv. council Inst. Jewish Life, 1973-75. Grantee Dewey Found., 1979-80, NSF. 1983-86, 90-97; John Dewey sr. fellow, 1986-87. Fellow Philosophy Edn. Soc.; mem. John Dewey Soc. (bd. dirs. 1976-78), Math. Assn. Am., Nat. Council Tchrs. Math., Phi Beta Kappa, Phi Delta Kappa. Home: 86 Sherbrooke Ave Williamsville NY 14221-4606 Business E-Mail: sibrown@buffalo.edu. *I attribute a large part of my success to lack of clarity and specificity with regard to goals, to ambiguity and vagueness with regard to principles, to a sense of humor which provides distance between a taken for granted reality and my personal world, and to a general disinclination to analyze what accounts for my success.*

BROWN, STEPHEN LEE, retired insurance company executive; b. Providence, July 6, 1937; AB, Middlebury Coll., 1958. CLU. With John Hancock Fin. Svcs. Inc. and John Hancock Life Ins. Co., Boston, 1958-2001, pres., chief ops. officer, vice chmn. bd., 1987-92, chmn., CEO, 1992-2000, chmn., 2000-2001. Trustee emeritus Wang Ctr. for Performing Arts; bd. dirs. Alfred P. Sloan Found., Palm Beach (Fla.) Civic Assn. 1st lt. U.S. Army, 1956—59. Fellow: Soc. Actuaries; mem.: Chartered Life Underwriter. Office: John Hancock Fin Svcs Inc John Hancock Place PO Box 111 Boston MA 02117-0111

BROWN, STEPHEN PAT, artist; b. Greeley, Colo., Aug. 26, 1950; s. Carl Adrian Brown and Mildred Louise (Van Beber) Ballard; m. Gretchen Anna Treitz, June 12, 1982; children: Rushton Jeremiah Treitz. Student, Inst. of European Studies, Vienna, Austria, 1969; postgrad., Skowhegan (Maine) Sch. of Painting, 1972; BFA, Colo. State U., 1972; MFA, Bklyn. Coll., 1978. Asst. prof. Hartford U., 1988—. Guest artist La. State U., 1979; guest artist, lectr. Cortland (N.Y.) U., 1982; bd. dirs. painting Nat. Dance Inst. Mural, N.Y.C., 1984-85; insr. Pratt Inst., N.Y.; instr. aesthetic edn. program Cooper-Union, N.Y.C., 1984; artist in residence Parsons Sch. of Design, N.Y.C., instr., 1987; artist in residence Arts Ptnrs., N.Y.C. Bd. of Edn., 1985-87; guest lectr. Pa. State U., State College, 1988—; instr. Sch. of Art Chautauqua (N.Y.) Inst., 1988; guest lectr. Grad. Art Dept. Bklyn. Coll., N.Y., 1989, Am. U., 1989. One-man shows include Bowery Gallery, N.Y.C, 1978, Alex Rosenberg Gallery, N.Y.C., 1981, 82, Cortland U., 1982, Artists Choice Mus., N.Y.C., 1983, 84, N.Y. Studio Sch., 1984, One Penn Pla., N.Y.C., 1985, Sherry French Gallery, N.Y.C., 1986, Nat. Acad. of Design, N.Y.C., 1986, Allan Stone Gallery, N.Y.C., 1987, Prince St. Gallery, Rockefeller Gallery, SUNY at Fredonia, 1988; group show Allan Stone Gallery, 1989; collections appear at Hosta Museum, New Bntain Museum of American Art, The Speed Museum, The Albany Museum, Mattatuck Museum. Bd. Govs. Painting scholar Art Students League, N.Y.C., 1973, Charles B. Shaw Painting scholar Bklyn. Coll., 1978; Yaddo fellow Saratoga Spring, N.Y., 1981, fellow Millay Colony for the Arts, 1981; recipient, Academy Award in Art, American Academy of Arts and Letters, 1994, Academy Award for Painting, American Academy of Arts and Letters; elected, National Academy of Design, 1999 Democrat. Mem. Pilgram Covenant Ch. Office: 47 Barnard Rd Granville MA 01034-9514 also: Hartford U 200 Bloomfield Ave Hartford CT 06117-1545*

BROWN, STEPHEN PHILLIP, judge; b. Birmingham, Ala., June 29, 1941; s. William P. and Milledge (Anderson) B.; m. Dorothy Louise Ogden, Aug. 6, 1967; children: Katherine, Phillip, Stephen. Student, Auburn U., 1963; LLB, Walter F. George Sch. Law, 1967. Bar: Ga. 1967, U.S. Dist. Ct. (mid. dist.) Ga. 1967, U.S. Ct. Appeals (11th cir.) Ga. 1967, U.S. Supreme Ct. 1967. Atty., regional counsel IRS, NYC, 1967-69; ptnr. Brown, Katz, Flatau & Hasty, Macon, Ga., 1969-95; judge Superior Ct. Macon Jud. Cir., 1996—. Rep. Ga. House of Reps., Atlanta, 1971-74. Democrat. Methodist. Avocations: organic gardening, woodworking. Home: 2434 Wesleyan Dr N Macon GA 31210-6043 Office: Superior Ct Bibb City 310 Bibb County Courthouse Macon GA 31201 Office Phone: 478-621-6328. E-mail: pbrown@co.bibb.ga.us, fpbrown@cox.net.

BROWN, STEPHEN S., telecommunications industry executive; B in Bus. Mktg., Tex. Tech. U.; M in Mgmt. Info. Sys., Naval Post Grad. Sch. Dir. sys. integration GE Aerospace; dir. enterprise integration and telecom. Pillsbury; CIO Imation; v.p., CIO Micron Electronics; sr. v.p., CIO Carlson Cos., Minnetonka, Minn., 2000—. With USMC. Office: Carlson Cos 701 Carlson Pkwy Minnetonka MN 55305 Office Phone: 763-212-1330.

BROWN, STEVEN HARRY, engineering executive; b. Phila., Sept. 16, 1948; ABS, Temple U., 1970, BS, 1971; MA, West Chester (Pa.) U., 1974. Diplomate Am. Acad. Health Physics (panel examiner 1988-91, appeals com. 1999-2001). Health physicist Temple U., Phila., 1969-71; tchr. phys. sci. Phila. Sch. Dist., 1971-76; mgr. radiation protection Westinghouse Electric Corp., Lakewood, Colo., 1976-80; mgr. western regional office Radiation Mgmt. Corp., Phila., 1980-82; prin. safety analysis engr. Rockwell Internat., Golden, Colo., 1982-83, program mgr. waste isolation pilot project, 1983-85; sr. project mgr. West Valley Demonstration Project Dames and Moore, West Valley, NY, 1985-87; dir. Radiol. Svcs., 1987-92; v.p. govt. svcs. Internat. Tech. Corp., Englewood, Colo., 1992—2002; v.p. DOE programs Shaw Group, Centennial, Colo., 2003—. U.S. rep. Internat. Conf. on Radiation Hazards in Mining, Beijing, 1986. Mem. Nat. Health Physics Soc. (pres. Rocky Mountain chpt. 1982-83), Am. Nuc. Soc. Office: Shaw Group 9201 E Dry Creek Rd Centennial CO 80112 Office Phone: 303-793-5200.

BROWN, SUSAN L., internet and marketing services professional; b. Mansfield, Ohio; d. Ernest B. and Lizabeth Mainzer; m. James C. Brown, Sept. 25, 1977 (div. Sept. 1998); children: Lizabeth Anne, Alex Campbell. BS, Northwestern U., 1970; postgrad., Stanford U. Dir. mktg. MicroPro, San Rafael, Calif., 1981-85; pres., cons. Brown Comms., San Mateo, Calif., 1985-97; dir. consumer internet svcs. HealthCenter.com, San Francisco, 1997—, comm. and mktg. strategy cons., 2002—03, CISCO Sys., 2003; info. tech. tng. enterprise application cons. Kaiser Permanent, 2003—. Bd. dirs. Kollage Cmty. Sch. Arts, San Francisco/San Carlos, Calif., 1998-99; spkr., panelist, mem. seminars. Prodr., dir. documentary Growing Up Violent, 1984; prodr., dir. corp. video SF3, 1990; prodr., dir. TV show Action!, 1983. PTA pres. Ctrl. Elem. Sch., Belmont, Calif., 1995-96. Mem. AAUW, LWV, Commonwealth Club, Planned Parenthood. Avocations: watercolor painting, strength training, reading, gardening.

BROWN, SUSAN LOUISE, philosopher, educator; b. Quanitico, Va., Jan. 1, 1955; d. John Bomar and Margaret G. Brown; 1 child, Codi E. AA, St. Petersburg Jr. Coll., 1995; BA, U. West Fla., 1998, MA, 2000; student, U. W. Fla., 2001—. Assoc. prof. Kaplan U., Boca Raton, Fla., 2002—; instr. philosophy U. West Fla., Pensacola, 2001—. Vol. Santa Rosa Sch. Dist., Milton, Fla., 1995—2001; chair Title I Parent Adv. Bd., Santa Rosa County, Fla., 2001—02, mem., 2003—04. Fellow, Coll. Profl. Studies, U. West Fla., 2001. Office: Univ West Florida 11000 University Parkway Pensacola FL 32514 Office Phone: 850-474-2671.

BROWN, TERRENCE CHARLES, art association executive, researcher, lecturer; b. N.Y.C., Oct. 2, 1949; s. Robert Carl and Ruth Carothers Johnson; m. Catherine Simms Citarella, Apr. 24, 1982; children: Peter Huston, Christopher Simms. BA, Vanderbilt U., Nashville, 1971. Curator Soc. Illustrators Mus. Am. Illustration, N.Y.C., 1972-83; dir. Soc. Illustrators, N.Y.C., 1983—. Instr. Sch. Visual Arts, N.Y.C., 1995—2000. Contbr.: 200 Years of American Illustration, 1976, The Illustrator in America: 1880-1980, 1984 Served to capt. USAR, 1971-79 Office: Soc of Illustrators 128 E 63rd St New York NY 10021-7303 Business E-Mail: dir@societyillustrators.org.

BROWN, THEODORE LAWRENCE, chemistry professor; b. Green Bay, Wis., Oct. 15, 1928; s. Lawrence A. and Martha E. (Kedinger) B.; m. Audrey Catherine Brockman, Jan. 6, 1951; children: Mary Margaret, Karen Anne, Jennifer Gerarda, Philip Matthew (dec.), Andrew Lawrence. BS in Chemistry, Ill. Inst. Tech., 1950; PhD, Mich. State U., 1956. Mem. faculty U. Ill., Urbana, 1956—, prof. chemistry, 1965-93, prof. chemistry emeritus, 1993—, vice chancellor for rsch., dean Grad. Coll., 1980-86, dir. Beckman Inst. for Advanced Sci. and Tech., 1987-93. Vis. scientist Internat. Meteorol. Inst., Stockholm, 1972; Boomer lectr. U. Alta., Edmonton, Can., 1975; Firth vis. prof. U. Sheffield, Eng., 1977; mem. bd. govs. Argonne Nat. Lab., 1982-88, Mercy Hosp., Urbana, 1985-89, Chem. Abstracts Svc., 1991-96, Arnold and Mabel Beckman Found., 1994—, Am. Chem. Soc. Pub., 1996-2001. Author: (with R.S. Drago) Experiments in General Chemistry, 3d edit., 1970, General Chemistry, 2d edit., 1968, Energy and the Environment, 1971, (with H.E. LeMay and B.E. Bursten) Chemistry: The Central Science, 1977, 10th edit., 2005, Making Truth: Metaphor in Science, 2003; assoc. editor Inorganic Chemistry, 1969-78; contbr. articles to profl. publs. Mem. Govt.-Univ.-Industry Roundtable Coun., 1989-94; bd. dirs. Champaign County Opportunities Industrialization Ctr., 1970-79, chmn. bd. dirs., 1975-78. With USN, 1950-53. Sloan rsch. fellow, 1962-66, NSF sr. postdoctoral fellow, 1964-65, Guggenheim fellow, 1979. Fellow AAAS, Am. Acad. Arts and Scis.; mem. Am. Chem. Soc. (award in inorganic chemistry 1972, award for disting. svc. in advancement of inorganic chemistry 1993), Philosophy of Sci. Assn., Cognitive Sci. Soc., Sigma Xi, Alpha Chi Sigma. Home: Apt 203 10751 Crooked River Rd Bonita Springs FL 34135-1727 E-mail: tlbrown1@earthlink.net.

BROWN, THERESA JOLEE, music educator, director; b. Hattiesburg, Miss., Mar. 18, 1966; d. Malcolm Douglas and Diane Dobres (Curtis) Courtney; m. Thomas Anthony Brown, June 27, 1998. BA, Clark Coll., Dubuque, Iowa, 1990. Tchr. music Farley-Bankston Cath. Sch., Farley, Iowa, 1990—92; tchr. music and choral dir. Southwestern Wis. Cmty. Schs., Hazel Green, Wis., 1992—. Mem.: Wis. Sch. Music Assn., Am. Choral Dirs. Assn. Office: Southwestern Wis Cmty Schs 1415 Fairplay Hazel Green WI 53811 Home: 302 1st Ave SE Farley IA 52046

BROWN, THOMAS ANDREW, retired aircraft/weaponry manufacturing executive; b. Iowa City, Iowa, July 24, 1932; s. Charles Valentine and Mary Clementine (Proestler) B.; m. Louise Grafton Baggott, Aug. 31, 1957; children: James, Mary, Catherine. BA, State U. Iowa, 1953; BA with honors, Oxford U., 1955; MA, Harvard U., 1958, PhD, 1962. With Rand Corp., 1962-74, assoc. head info. sci., 1966-74, dir. strategic studies Washington, 1983-85; asst. v.p. Sci. Applications, Inc., Los Angeles, 1974-77; dep. asst. sec. of def. program analysis and evaluation Dept. Def., Washington, 1977-81; ptnr. Booz, Allen & Hamilton, Bethesda, Md., 1981-83; mgr. strategic studies Northrop Corp., 1985-94. Served with USAF, 1955-57. Recipient Disting. Pub. Svc. medal Dept. Def., 1981; Rhodes scholar, 1953-55; NSF fellow, 1957-61 Home: 21912 234th Ave SE Maple Valley WA 98038-8423 Personal E-mail: LittleTom@aol.com.

BROWN, THOMAS CARTMEL, JR., lawyer; b. Marion, Va., June 20, 1945; m. Sally Guy Lynch; children: Sarah Preston, Taylor Cardwell. AB, Davidson Coll., 1967; JD, U. Va., 1970. Bar: Va 1971. Assoc. Boothe, Prichard & Dudley, Alexandria, Va., 1971-76, ptnr., 1976-86, McGuireWoods LLP and predecessors, McLean, Va., 1986—. Mem. lawyers com. Nat. Ctr. State Cts., 1993—2003, Warren E. Burger Soc.; sec., gen counsel Potomac KnowledgeWay, 1995—99; bd. dirs. No. Va. Charitable Health Care Found., 2005—. Mem. Va. Child-Day Coun., Richmond, 1987—91, No. Va. Roundtable, 1995—2001; pres. Alexandria Libr. Co., 2002—04; bd. dirs. Alexandria chpt. ARC, 1982—88; mem. exec. bd. Nat. Capital Area Coun. Boy Scouts Am., 2002—. Fellow: Va. Law Found. (bd. dirs. 1997—2005, pres. 2003), Am. Bar Found.; mem.: Va. State Bar (chmn. bus. law sect. 1987—88, chmn. health law sect. 2002—03), Va. Bar Assn. (pres. 1992), Omicron Delta Kappa. Office: McGuireWoods LLP 1750 Tysons Blvd Ste 1800 Mc Lean VA 22102-4231 Office Phone: 703-712-5393. Business E-Mail: tbrown@mcguirewoods.com.

BROWN, THOMAS HUNTINGTON, neuroscientist; b. N.Y.C., June 13, 1945; s. Thomas Huntington and Elvira R. (Crandall) B. BA in Molecular Biology, MA in Psychology, Calif. State U.-San Jose, 1972; PhD in Neurosci., Stanford U., 1977. Postdoctoral fellow Stanford U., Calif., 1977-79; asst. rsch. scientist Beckman Rsch. Inst., Duarte, Calif., 1979-82, assoc. rsch. scientist, 1982-86, rsch. scientist, 1986-88; prof. dept. psychology Yale U., New Haven, 1988—. Mem. joint appt. dept. cellular molecular physiology Yale U., 1992—, dir. Ctr. for Theoretical and Applied Neurosci., 1992-96; adviser NIH, NIMH study sects., 1982-83, 89-94, 94-98, mem. NIH-IFCN5 study sect., IFCN1 study sect., 1998—. Mem. editl. bd. Behavioral Neurosci. Jour., 1983-89, Network: Computation in Neural Systems, 1990-92, Synapse, 1990-2002, Hippocampus, 1990-93, Psychobiology, 1997-2000; contbr. articles to sci. jours., 1976—. Recipient Epilepsy Found. Am. award, 1980, McKnight Found. Scholar's award, 1981, McKnight Found. Career Devel. award 1984, Muscular Dystrophy Found. fellow, 1977, NIH fellow, 1978; grantee in field, 1980—. Mem. AAAS, Am. Psychol. Assn., Am. Psychol. Soc., Am. Physiol. Soc., N.Y. Acad. Sci., Conn. Acad. Sci. Engring., Soc. Neurosci., Internat. Neurol. Network Soc. Office: Yale U Dept Psychology PO Box 208205 New Haven CT 06520-8205 Office Phone: 203-432-7008.

BROWN, THOMAS PHILIP, III, lawyer; b. Washington, Dec. 18, 1931; s. Raymond T. and Beatrice (Cullen) B.; m. Alicia A. Sexton, July 28, 1955; children: Thomas, Mark, Alicia, Maria, Beatrice. BS, Georgetown U., 1953, LL.B., 1956. Bar: D.C., Md. Pvt. practice law, 1958—. Author monograph and articles on legal malpractice. Pres. Cath. Youth Orgn. of Washington, 1972. Served to 1st lt. USMCR, 1955-58. Mem. Bar Assn. D.C. (pres. 1986, bd. dirs. 1987), Barristers Club, Columbia Country Club. Home: 5610 Wisconsin Ave Apt 208 Chevy Chase MD 20815 Office: Unit 2 5247 Wisconsin Ave NW Washington DC 20015

BROWN, TIMOTHY ALAN, town manager; b. Valparaiso, Ind., Jan. 10, 1961; s. Charles M. and Nanette Kuehl Brown; m. Lori S. Herbst, Aug. 10, 1985; children: Bradley Alan, Suzanne Marie. BA in Urban and Regional Planning, Ball State U., Muncie, Ind., 1983; BS in Geography, Ball State U., 1983. Cartographer dept. geography Ball State U., Muncie, Ind., 1982—83; city planner and park supt. City of Angola, Angola, Ind., 1983—86; town mgr. Town of Merrillville, Merrillville, Ind., 2004—, planning and bldg. adminstr., 1986—96; town mgr. Town of Cedar Lake, Cedar Lake, Ind., 1996—2004. Mem. past pres., dist. dir. Jaycees, Merrillville, Ind., 1987—2001; pres. Cedar Lake Hist. Assn., 2004—; elder First Christian Ch. of Highland, Highland, Ind., 2000—03; bd. dirs. Christmas in Sept., South Lake County, 1998. Master: Masons; mem.: Ind. Mcpl. Mgmt. Assn. (pres. 1999), Merrillville C. of C. (pres. 2004—), Ind. Planning Assn., Leadership NW Ind. (corr.; mem. and spkr. 2000), Slovak Club. D-Conservative. Avocations: collecting glass insulators, fishing, civil war history & biographies. Office: Town of Merrillville 7820 Broadway Merrillville IN 46410 Office Phone: 219-769-5711. Office Fax: 219-756-6170. E-mail: townmgr@townofmerrillville.com.

BROWN, TINA, journalist, television personality; b. Maidenhead, Eng., Nov. 21, 1953; d. George Hambley and Bettina Iris May (Kohr) Brown; m. Harold Evans, Aug. 20, 1981; children: George Frederick, Isabel Harriet. MA, Oxford U.; D (hon.), The London Inst., 2001. Columnist Punch Mag., London, 1978; editor in chief Tatler Mag., London, 1979—83, Vanity Fair Mag., N.Y.C., 1984—92; editor New Yorker mag., N.Y.C., 1992—98; chmn., editor-in-chief Talk Media, 1998—2002; weekly columnist The Wash. Post, 2003—, Salon.com, 2003—; host, Topic A with Tina Brown CNBC, 2003—. Author: (plays) Under the Bamboo Tree, 1973 (Sunday Times Drama award), Happy Yellow, 1977, (book) Loose Talk, 1979, Life As A Party, 1983. Named Most Promising Female Journalist, Young Journalist of Yr., 1978, Comdr. Brit. Empire, Her Royal Highness Queen Elizabeth, 2000; recipient Kathrine Pakenham prize, Sunday London Times, 1973, Mag. Editor of the Yr., Age Mag., 1988, USC Disting. Achievement in Journalism award, USC Journalism Alumni Assoc., 1994. Office: Attn Betty Greif 447 E 57th St New York NY 10022

BROWN, TOD DAVID, bishop; b. San Francisco, Nov. 15, 1936; s. George Wilson and Edna Anne (Dunn) B. BA, St. John's Coll., 1958; STB, Gregorian U., Rome, 1960; MA in Theology, U. San Francisco, 1970, MAT in Edn., 1976. Dir. edn. Diocese of Monterey, Calif., 1980—82, chancellor, 1982—89, vicar gen., chancellor, 1983—89; pastor St. Francis Xavier, Seaside, Calif., 1977—82; bishop Roman Catholic Diocese of Boise, Idaho, 1989—98; appointed and installed bishop Roman Cath. Diocese of Orange, Calif., 1998. Past mem. 3rd millenium com. U.S. Conf. Cath. Bishops, past chmn. com. on ecumenical and interreligious affairs, past mem. com. on mission, pastoral practices, past chair laity com.; chmn. subcom. interreligious affairs U.S. Conf. Cath. Bishop; mem. Episcopal bd. govs. N.Am. Coll. Named Papal Chaplain Pope Paul VI, 1975. Mem.: The Sovereign Mil. Hospitaller Order of St. John of Jerusalem of Rhodes and of Malta, The Equestrian Order of the Holy Sepulchre of Jerusalem, Canon Law Soc. Am. (past mem. Bishop's com. on liturgy, econ. concerns of the Holy See, Ea. Chs.), Cath. Biblical Assn., Cath. Theol. Soc. Am. Roman Catholic. Avocations: films, travel, reading, exercise. Office: Diocese of Orange Marywood Ctr 2811 E Villa Real Dr Orange CA 92867-1932 Office Phone: 714-282-3000.

BROWN, TOM CHRISTIAN, newspaper publisher; b. Nampa, Idaho, July 24, 1947; s. Frank Thomas and Esther (Ulrich) B.; m. Carol Burroughs, May 31, 1969; children: Brian J., Maree C. BA in History with honors, Oreg. State U., 1969; MS in Journalism, Northwestern U., 1970. Reporter Corvallis (Oreg.) Gazette-Times, 1969; reporter, asst. city editor Billings (Mont.) Gazette, 1970-74; ops. mgr. Mont. Std., Butte, 1974-76; gen. mgr. Missoulian, Missoula, Mont., 1976-80, pub., 1980-86, Concord (N.H.) Monitor, 1987—2005; CEO, pres. Newspaper of New Eng., 2005—. Bd. dirs., v.p. Newspapers of New Eng., Concord; pres. Page Buying Coop, Phila., 1994—, chmn. bd., 1996-2001; bd. dirs. East Oregonian Pub. Co. Bd. dirs. United Way, Concord, 1989-96, 98—, Capital Ctr. for Arts, 1998—2004, Missoula YMCA, 1984-86; pres. Missoula Symphony, 1985, Mont. Press Assn., Helena, 1985; v.p. N.H. BBB, Concord, 1995-99; 2d v.p. Pacific N.W. Newspaper Assn., Portland, 1986; mem. Concord Task Force on Racism. Mem. Newspaper Assn. Am., New England Newspaper Assn. (com. chair 1994-2004, bd. dirs. 2004—), Merrimack C. of C. (bd. dirs. 1993-98, 99—), Missoula C. of C. (bd. dirs. 1977-84, v.p. 1983), Rotary (bd. dirs. Missoula chpt. 1976-79), Sigma Delta Chi. Avocations: running marathons, skiing, hiking, climbing, reading. Home: 15 Dwinell Dr Concord NH 03301-2542

BROWN, TOMMIE FLORENCE, social work educator; b. Rome, Ga., June 25, 1934; d. Phillip and Mary Louise (Murden) B. BA, Dillard U., 1957; MSW, Washington U., St. Louis, 1964; DSW, Columbia U., 1984. Social svc. supr. Tenn. Dept. Pub. Welfare, Chattanooga, 1964-67, dir. tng., 1967-71; asst. prof. sociology U. Tenn., Chattanooga, 1971-73, head social work dept., 1973-82, UC Found. assoc. prof. social work, 1982—; mem. Tenn. Ho. of Reps., Nashville, 1992—, mem. commerce, conservation and environ. coms., 1992-94, mem. edn. com., 1995—, sec. fin. ways and means com., 1995—. Named Nat. Social Worker of Yr., NASW, 1971. Democrat. Baptist. Home: PO Box 3258 Chattanooga TN 37404-0258 Office: Tenn Gen Assembly Legislative Plz Ste 36 Nashville TN 37243-0128

BROWN, TONI CYD, secondary school educator, elementary school educator; b. Billings, Mont., Apr. 22, 1950; d. Alec Wilbert and Ruth Isabel (Uline) Brown; children: Marykitt Higdon, Elizabeth Higdon BA in English, U. Wyo., 1972; MA in English, 1979, BA in Elem. Edn., 1988. Cert. Comml. pilot, 1995, instrument ground instr. Tchr. Billings Sch. Dist. #2, 1973-77; admissions counselor Rocky Mt. Coll., Billings, 1977-78; tchr. Gillette Campus No. Wyo. C.C., 1979-80, dir. Region III Developmentally Delayed Presch. Prog., 1980; tchr. various grades Campbell County Sch. Dist., Gillette, 1980-88, tchr. gifted resource rm., 1988-89, tchr. mid. sch. English comm., career, acad. competition, 1989-2000; cons., 2000—. Vice chair Challenger Learning Ctr. and Scis. Complex of Wyo.; cons. in field; lectr. in aerospace edn. and gifted edn. with learning disabilities Former chairman bd. dirs. High Plains Energy Tech. Ctr. Found. Named Campbell County Am. Legion Educator of the Yr., 1988, Outstanding Educator of Yr. Fed. Aviation Adminstrn., 1990, Crossfield Tchr. of Yr. finalist, 1993, Air Force Assn. Rocky Mountain Region Tchr. of Yr., 1995, Nat. Air Force Assn. McAuliffe award; Space Acad. grantee Internat. Ninety-Nines, 1987; Wyo. Christa McAuliffe fellow, 1990; recipient Civil Air Patrol Rocky Mountain Region Brewer award, 1994. Mem. Am. Quarter Hourse Assn., Internat. Arabian Horse Assn., Campbell County Reading Assn., Wyo. Reading Assn., Wyo. Sci. Tchrs. Assn. (Elem. Sci. Tchr. of Yr. 1988), Aircraft Owners and Pilots Assn., Civil Air Patrol, Exptl. Aircraft Assn., Ninety Nines, Inc., U. Wyo. Alumni Assn., Women's Sports Found., Wyo. Writers/Poets, Am. Legion Aux., Delta Kappa Gamma (mem. scholarship com.). Avocations: flying, breeding and training horses, piano, poetry. Home and Office: 2610 S Douglas Hwy Ste 180-326 Gillette WY 82718-6468 E-mail: tcb@vcn.com.

BROWN, TONY ERSIC, record company executive; b. Greensboro, N.C., Dec. 11, 1946; s. Floyd Everett and Mattie Agnes (Nance) B.; m. Janie Breeding (div. July 1975); children: Brandi, Brennan; m. Gina Lou Morrison, Apr. 19, 1979 (div. Apr. 1992). Grad. high sch., Durham, S.C. Mem. band Oak Ridge Boys, Nashville, 1972-75, Elvis Presley, Nashville, 1975-77, Emmylou Harris, Nashville, 1977-80; mgr. artists and repertoire RCA Records, Hollywood, Calif., 1978-80; dir. artists and repertoire Nashville, 1983-84; mem. band Rosanne Cash, Nashville, 1980-83; sr. v.p. artists and repertoire MCA Records, Nashville, 1984-87, exec. v.p., head of A & R, 1987—, now pres. Songwriter Silverline Music, 1972—. Active Leadership Nashville, 1987. Mem. Nat. Acad. Rec. Arts and Scis. (bd. dirs., Grammy award 1980, 83, 85, Producer of Yr. 1991), Country Music Assn., Acad. Country Music, Nashville Entertainment Assn., Gospel Music Assn. (Dove award 1972). Office: MCA Records 60 Music Sq E Nashville TN 37203-4325

BROWN, TRISH EILEEN See VERNAZZA, TRISH

BROWN, TRISHA, dancer; b. Aberdeen, Wash., Nov. 25, 1936; BA in Dance, Mills Coll., Calif.; D (hon.), Mills Coll., 1997; PhD in Fine Arts (hon.), Oberlin Coll. Founder, artistic dir. Trisha Brown Dance Co., N.Y.C., 1970—; founding mem. Judson Dance Theater; choreographer Grand Union Improvisation Group, 1970-76. Lectr. Mills. Coll., Calif., Reed Coll., Oreg., NYU, N.Y.C., Goucher Coll., Md., Carnegie Mellon U., Pa.; condr. workshops and seminars throughout world. Choreographer Untitled, 1961, Trillium, 1961, Lightfall, 1963, Untitled Duet, 1963, Part of a Tango, 1963, Target, 1964, Rulegame Five, 1964, Motor, 1965, Homemade, 1965, Inside, 1966, Skunk Cabbage, 1967, Saltgrass and Waders, 1967, Medicine Dance, 1967, Snapshots, 1968, Ballet, 1968, Falling Duet, 1968, Sky Map, 1969, Dance with Duck's Head, 1968, Yellow Belly, 1969, Leaning Duets, 1970, The Stream, 1970, Man Walking Down the Side of a Building, 1970, Accumulation 4 1/2, 1971, Walking on the Wall, 1971, Leaning Duets II, 1971, Falling Duet II, 1971, Rummage Sale and the Floor of the Forest, 1971, Planes, 1968, Roof Piece, 1971, Primary Accumulation, 1972, Accumulating Pieces, 1973, Group Accumulation, 1973, Roof and Fire Piece, 1973, Spanish Dance, 1973, Structured Pieces, 1973, Figure 8, 1974, Drift, 1974, Spiral, 1974, Pamplona Stones, 1974, Locus, 1975, Line Up, 1976, Water Motor and Splang, 1978, Glacial Decoy, 1979, Opal Loop, 1980, Son of Gone Fishin', 1981, Set and Reset, 1983 (N.Y. Dance and Performance award, 1984), Lateral Pass, 1985 (N.Y. Dance and Performance award, 1986), Carmen, 1986, Newark, 1987, Astral Convertible, 1989, For M.G.: The Movie, 1991, Astral Converted, 1991, Another Story as in Falling, 1993, If you couldn't see me, 1994, Foray Forêt, 1990, You Can See Us, 1995, M.O., 1995, Twelve Ton Rose, 1996; featured (TV series) M.O., Sta. WNET-TV, N.Y.C., Dance in America, Sta. WGBH-TV, Boston, Dancing on the Edge, Making Dances; exhibitions include Venice Biennale, Toulon Mus., exhibited in group shows at Musée de Marseille, Numerals: Math. Concepts in Contemporary Art, The Pluralist Decade, New Notes for New Dance, Art and Dance: Images From the Modern Dialogue. Mem. Nat. Coun. on Arts, 1994. Decorated chevalier Ordre des Arts et des Lettres; recipient Creative Arts award, Brandeis U., 1982, Dance Mag. award, 1987, Samuel H. Scripps Am. Dance Festival award, 1994, Prix de la Danse la Société des Auteurs et Compositeurs Dramatiques award, 1996, Nat. medal of Art, 2003; fellow, Guggenheim Found., 1975, 1984, NEA Creative Artists Svc. Program, 1977, 1981—84; grantee, NEA, N.Y. State Coun. on Arts; MacArthur fellow, 1991. Mem.: Am. Acad. Arts and Letters (Nat. medal of Art 2003). Office: Trisha Brown Co care Rebecca Davis 625 W 55th St New York NY 10019-3560*

BROWN, TROY ANDERSON, JR., retired electric power industry executive; b. Tampa, Fla., July 7, 1934; s. Troy Anderson and Valerie Aldona (Mohler) B.; m. Jean Thompson, Aug. 22, 1962; children: Troy Anderson, III, George Albert, Douglas Alan. AB, Harvard U., 1956; JD, U. N.C., 1959. Bar: Fla. bar 1959. With Raybro Electric Supplies Inc., Tampa, 1960-99, exec. v.p., 1964-74, pres., 1974-99. Bd. dirs. Bay Cities Bank. Mem. exec. com. Tampa Com. 100, 1975, U. South Fla. Found., 1974-75; chmn. bd. fellows U. Tampa, 1978; bd. dirs., vice chmn. Tampa Mus., 1977-79; bd. dirs. Tampa YMCA, 1977-79, Tampa Marine Inst., 1976-77. With USAFR, 1959. Mem.: Tampa Mchts. Assn. (bd. dirs. 1980), Pres. Round Table Tampa (pres. 1971), Exch. Club Tampa (pres. 1970), Greater Tampa C. of C. (gov. 1968—74), Nat. Assn. Elec. Distbrs. (bd. dirs. 1989—91), Harvard Club N.Y.C., Harvard Club of Fla. (pres. 1984), Tampa Yacht and Country Club (bd. dirs. 1982—83), Ye Mystic Krewe Gasparilla, Jesters, Shriners. Episcopalian. Home: 1013 S Skokie St Tampa FL 33629-5237

BROWN, TYESE ANDREA, music educator; d. Andrew Percy and Elois Smith Brown. B of Music Edn., Howard U., 1993; MA, NYU, 1999. Cert. tchr. music K-12. Telemarketer Americana Portraits, West Orange, NJ, 1992; substitute tchr. Orange Bd. Edn., Orange, NJ, 1994—95, South Orange and Maplewood (N.J.) Bd. Edn., 1994—95; music dir. Jersey Explorer Mus., East Orange, 1997—99; music tchr. K-4 Jersey City (N.J.) Bd. Edn., 1999—2000; music tchr. grades 3-5 Montclair (N.J.) Bd. Edn., 2000—02; music tchr. grades 7-8 North Plainfield (N.J.) Bd. Edn., 2002—03; music tchr. grades K-7 Roselle (NJ) Bd. Edn., 2003—. Music competition judge NAACP ACT-SO Competitions, Charlotte, N.C. and Atlanta, Ga., 1996—99; soprano vocal judge Ctrl. Jersey Music Educators Assn. Jr. Competitions, 2002, NJ Music Educators Assn., 2002; music dir. Hillside's Traveling Troupe, Montclair, 2000—02. Composer: (songs) The Winds of Yesterday, 1984 (Instrns. Experience Exposures award, 1984), The Ancient Springs, 1985. Music dir. AmeriCorps, Jersey City, 1997—99. Named Gifted Musician of Essex County, Instrns. Experience Exposure, 1984; recipient Gifted Student scholarship, Geraldine R. Dodge Found., 1984, Musician of Yr. award, Newark Comty. Sch. Arts, 1982—88. Mem.: ASCAP (songwriter/pub. mem.), Music Educators Nat. Conf., NYU Alumni Assn., Howard U. Alumni Assn., Kappa Delta Pi, Pi Lambda Theta. Avocations: drawing, reading, composing music, swimming, bowling. Office: ASCAP 1 Penn Plz New York NY 10019 also: Roselle Bd Edn 710 Locust St Roselle NJ 07203 E-mail: tyenote@aol.com.

BROWN, VALERIE ANNE, psychiatric social worker, educator; b. Elizabeth, N.J., Feb. 28, 1951; d. William John and Adelaide Elizabeth (Krasa) B. BA summa cum laude (fellow), C.W. Post Coll., 1972; MSW (Silberman scholar), Hunter Coll., 1975; PhD, Am. Internat. U., 1996. Diplomate Am. Bd. Examiners, Am. Bd. Clin. Social Work, Nat. Assn. Social Work; cert. addictions specialist; cert. master hypnotherapist; cert. psychophilogic integration therapist. Social work intern Greenwich House Counseling Ctr., N.Y.C., 1973-74, Metro Cons. Ctr., N.Y.C., 1974-75; sr. psychiat. social worker, co-adminstr. Essex County Guidance Ctr., East Orange, N.J., 1975-80; pvt. practice psychiat. social work, psychotherapy, 1979—. Sr. psychiat. social worker John E. Runnells Hosp., Berkeley Heights, N.J., 1980-86; dir. social work Northfield Manor, West Orange, N.J., 1987; clin. coord. Project Portals East Orange Gen. Hosp., 1987-88; asst. dir. ARS/Century House Riverview Med. Ctr., Red Bank, N.J., 1988-93; sr. clin. case mgmt. specialist Prudential Ins. Co., Woodbridge, N.J., 1993; clin. dir. Greenhouse-KMC, Lakewood, N.J., 1994-2000, Shoreline-KBH, Toms River, N.J., 1996-2000; tech. advisor Nat. Comm. Network, 1988—; mental health clinician III UMDNJ-UBHC, Edison, N.J., 2000—; instr. Brookdale Coll., 1991—; co-founder Women's Growth Ctr., Cedar Grove, N.J., 1979; counselor Passaic Drug Clinic, 1978-80; field instr. Fairleigh Dickinson U., Madison, N.J., 1981-86, Brookdale Coll., 1989-92; field supr. Union Coll., Cranford, N.J., 1986; instr. Sch. Social Work, NYU, N.Y.C., 1980-83, asst. prof., 1983-85; evaluator Intoxicated Driver Resource Ctr., Essex County, N.J., 1987-88. Alt. Monmouth County profl. adv. bd.; founding mem. Nat. Campaign Tolerance of So. Poverty Law Project, 2004. Named Dist. Alumnae Mother Seton Regional H.S., Clark, N.J., 1997. Mem. NASW (Whittman Lifetime Achievement nominee 1997-98), Psi Chi, Pi Gamma Mu, Sigma Tau Delta. Avocations: reading, swimming, travel. Office: 20 Ellsworth Ct Red Bank NJ 07701-5403

BROWN, VANDELLA, librarian; b. Senatobia, Miss., Apr. 23, 1952; d. Whitfield Sr. and Lue Walter (Heffner) Brown. BA, Memphis State U., 1977; MLS, U. Iowa, 1983; PhD, U. Berkley, 2004. Libr. asst. Main Libr. Memphis/Shelby County, 1977-82; rschr. U. Iowa, Iowa City, 1982-83; libr. mgr. Memphis/Shelby County Pub. Libr., 1983-93, Columbus (Ohio) Met. Pub. Libr., 1993-98; libr. dir. E. St. Louis (Ill.) Pub. Libr., 1998-2000; network dir. Ill. State Libr., 2000—. Mem. adv. coun. Ill. State Libr., 1999. Author: (book) Celebrating the Family: Steps to Planning a Family Reunion, 1991, African-American Fiction: A Slamming Genre, 1997; rschr. Roots: The Second Generation, 1977. Pres. Reunion Ho. Family Reunion, Memphis, 1989—; regional OCLC network dir. adv. exec. com., 2001—03; ex-official mem. users exec. bd. Ill. OCLC; dir. Libr. Diversity Program, 2003—. Named Outstanding Supporter, Memphis State Black Student Assn., 1983; recipient letter of Recognition, City of Memphis Mayor, 1993. Mem.: ALA (mem. Black Caucus 1987), Ill. Libr. Assn. (chair diversity and racial com.), Sangamon County Hist. Soc. Democrat. Mem. Ch. Of Christ. Avocations: miniature book collecting, reading, gardening. Office: 300 S 2nd St Springfield IL 62701-1703 Office Phone: 217-785-9075. Office Fax: 217-782-1877. Personal E-mail: vandellabrown@aol.com. Business E-Mail: vbrown@ilsos.net.

BROWN, VICKI KNASEL, newswriter; b. New Albany, Ind., Feb. 28, 1955; d. Wayne Wells Knasel and Harletta Mae Troglio; m. Calvin Don Brown, Oct. 8, 1976; children: Christopher Daniel, Kara Michelle. BA, Hardin-Simmons U., 1977. Reporter, soc. editor Snyder (Tex.) Daily News, 1983—87; missionary to Tanzania Internat. Mission Bd., SBC, Richmond, Va., 1987—94; lifestyles editor, reporter Mineral Wells (Tex.) Index, 1993—95; news and info. writer Weatherford (Tex.) Coll., 1995—97; pub. rels. dir. Palo Pinto Gen. Hosp., Mineral Wells, 1998—99; editor The Graham (Tex.) Leader, 1999—2001; news writer Word & Way, Jefferson City, Mo., 2002—. Freelance writer, 1983—; freelance spkr., 2002—. Author: (book/workbook) Youth on Mission, Vol. 3: Come, Go with Me, 1997. Recipient Anson M. Jones award, Tex. Med. Assn., 2001, Cmty. Svc. Series award, North and East Tex. Press Assn., 2001, 3rd award Best Investigative-In Depth Series, Nat. Newspaper Assn., 2001. Office: Word & Way Ste 400 3236 Emerald Ln Jefferson City MO 65109 Office Phone: 573-635-5939 x205.

BROWN, W. DOUGLAS, lawyer; b. 1946; BA, Lafayette College, 1968; JD, U. Va., 1971. Atty.-legal dept. Air Product & Chemicals Inc., Allentown, Pa., 1975—80; gen. counsel, sec. Catalytic Inc. (subsidiary of Air Products), 1980—83; v.p., sec. Stearns-Catalytic World Corp. (subsidiary of Air Products), 1983—87, Am. Ref-Fuel (jointly owned by Air Products and Browning-Ferns Industry), 1987—96, sr. v.p., sec., 1996—97; v.p., gen. counsel, sec. Air Products & Chemicals Inc., 1990—99, v.p. adminstrn. Gases and Equipment Group, 1997—99. Office: Air Products & Chemicals Inc 7201 Hamilton Blvd Allentown PA 18195-1501

BROWN, W. MILLER, faculty dean; B, Amherst Coll.; cert. of advanced study, U. Paris; PhD, Harvard U. Lectr. in French Boston U., 1960—63; tchg. fellow Harvard U., Cambridge, Mass., 1963—65; prof. philosophy Trinity Coll., Hartford, Conn., 1965—, dean of faculty. Past chmn. dept. philosophy Trinity Coll., past ombudsman; former vis. prof. U. Kent, Canterbury, England; former mem. Soc. Fellows U. Durham, England; lectr. Hartford Classical Magnet Program. Office: Trinity Coll 300 Summit St Hartford CT 06106-3100

BROWN, WADE EDWARD, retired lawyer; b. Blowing Rock, N.C., Nov. 5, 1907; s. Jefferson Davis and Etta Cornelia (Suddreth) B.; m. Gilma Baity (dec.); m. Euzelia Smart (dec.); children: Margaret Rose, Wade Edward, Sarah Baity Otey. Student, Mars Hill Coll., 1928; JD, Wake Forest U., 1931. Bar: N.C. 1930. Pvt. practice, Boone, N.C., 1931—; ret. Chmn. N.C. Bd. Paroles, Raleigh, 1967-72; cons. Atty. Gen., N.C. Dept. Justice, 1973; with student legal svcs., Appalachian State U. Author: Wade E. Brown: Recollections and Reflections, 1997. Mem. N.C. Senate, 1947-49, N.C. Ho. of Reps., 1951-53, Boone Merchants Assn.; mayor Town of Boone, 1961-67; chmn. Watauga County Hosp.; mem. gen. bd. Bapt. State Conv. N.C.; trustee Wake Forest U., now trustee emeritus; trustee Appalachian State U., Bapt. Found. N.C. Bapt. State Conv.; founder Watanga County Pub. Libr., 1996—. Office: PO Box 1776 Boone NC 28607-1776

BROWN, WALTER REDVERS JOHN, physicist; b. Toronto, Ont., Can., Aug. 22, 1925; s. Ernest Redvers and Rita Mary (Brooks) B.; m. Anita Catherine Goggio, June 5, 1948 (div. 1972); children: Paul, Susan, Patricia, Judith; m. Beth Susan Southard, Oct. 12, 1974; 1 child, Amy. BS, U. Toronto, 1947; MS, U. Rochester, 1949. Sr. physicist Eastman Kodak Co., Rochester, N.Y., 1947-55; rsch. assoc. Boston U., 1955-57; asst. to dir. rsch. Itek Corp., Lexington, Mass., 1957-62; v.p. R & D United Carr Inc., Boston, 1962-69; exec. v.p. Ealing Corp., Cambridge, Mass., 1969-71; pres. Daedalon Corp., Salem, Mass., 1971—. Patentee in field. Fellow Optical Soc. Am. (Adolph Lomb medal 1956); mem. Eastern Yacht Club, St. Botolph Club. Roman Catholic. Home: 120 Atlantic Ave Marblehead MA 01945-3049 Office: Daedalon Corp PO Box 2028 Salem MA 01970-6228 Office Phone: 978-744-5310. E-mail: DAEDALON@COVE.COM.

BROWN, WENDY ELAINE, communications consultant; b. Los Alamos, N.Mex., Apr. 28, 1956; d. Leon J. and Dorothy (Stern) B.; m. Richard Swanson; children: Tasmin Amanda Swanson, Nathaniel Richard Swanson. BA, Northwestern U., 1978. Software engr. Prime Computer Inc., Natick, Mass., 1978-80; systems programmer Dialcom, Silver Spring, Md., 1980-85; systems programmer, analyst APA, Falls Church, Va., 1985-86; mem. tech. staff Corp. for Open Systems, McLean, Va., 1986-89; cons. PSC Internat. Inc., McLean, Va., 1989-95, BAE Systems (formerly Digitalnet), Annapolis Junction, Md., 1995—. Author: OSI Dictionary of Acronyms, 1992. Democrat. Jewish. Avocations: sewing, electronic networking. Home: 9417 Russell Rd Silver Spring MD 20910-1445 Office: BAE Systems Ste 210 141 National Business Pkwy Annapolis Junction MD 20701-1003 E-mail: wbrowns@gmail.com.

BROWN, WENDY WEINSTOCK, nephrologist, educator; b. NYC, Dec. 9, 1944; d. Irving and Pearl (Levack) Weinstock; m. Barry David Brown, May 2, 1971 (div. Sept. 1995); children: Jennifer Faye, Joshua Reuben, Julie Aviva, Rachel Ann. BA, U. Mass., 1966; MD, Med. Coll. of Pa., 1970; MPH, St. Louis U., 1999. Diplomate Am. Bd. Internal Medicine. Intern U. Ill. Affiliated Hosps., Chgo., 1970-71; resident in internal medicine The Med. Coll. Wis. Affiliated Hosps., Milw., 1971-74; gen. practitioner Vogelweh (W. Germany) Health Clinics, 1975-76; fellow in nephrology Med. Coll. of Wis. Milw. County Med. Complex, Milw., 1976-78; staff physician St. Louis VA Med Ctr., 1978—2003, acting chief, hemodialysis sect., 1983-85, chief dialysis/renal sect., 1985-90, dir. clin. nephrology, 1990—2003; staff physician St. Louis U. Hosps., 1978—2003, St. Louis City Hosp., 1982-85, St Mary's Health Ctr., St. Louis, 1994—2003; chief of staff VA Tenn. Valley Healthcare Sys., Nashville, 2003—. Assoc. prof. internal medicine St. Louis U. Health Sci. Ctr., 1985—98, prof. internal medicine, 1998—2003; prof. medicine Meharry Med. Coll. Vanderbilt Univ., 2003—. Reviewer Clin. Nephrology, Nephrology, Dialysis and Transplantation, Am. Jour. Nephrology, Am. Jour. Kidney Disease, Jour Am. Geriatric Soc., Jour. Am. Soc. Nephrology, Geriatric Nephrology and Urology, Kidney Internat.; med. editor NKF Family Focus; mem. editl. bd. Clin. Nephrology, Geriatric Nephrology, Internat. Urology and Nephrology, Advances in Renal Replacement Therapy; editor-in-chief: Advances in Chronic Kidney Disease, 2004-; contbr. articles to profl. jours. Mem. adv. coun. Mo. Kidney Program, 1985-91, chmn., 1988-89; numerous positions Nat. Kidney Found., 1984—, nat. chmn., 1995-97; bd. dirs. United Way, St. Louis, 1994-2003, Nat. Kidney Found. Ea. Mo. and Metro East, Inc., 1980-94; bd. dirs. Combined Health Appeal Greater St. Louis, Inc., 1988, pres., 1989-92; bd. dirs. Combined Health Appeal Am., 1991-98, sec., 1992-96, vice chmn., 1996-98. Named Casual Corner Career Woman of Yr., 1986, Combine Health Appeal of Am. Vol. of Yr., 1991, Olympic Torch Bearer, 1996, St. Louis Health Profl. of Yr., 1997; recipient Upjohn Achievement award, Med. Coll. Wis. Affiliated Hosps., 1972, Cert. of Leadership, St. Louis YWCA, 1989, Chmn.'s award, Nat. Kidney Found. of Ea. Mo. and Metro East, 1990, award of excellence, 2002, Chmn.'s award, Nat. Kidney Found., Washington, 1990, Martin Wagner award, Nat. Kidney Found., 1999, award of excellence, Nat. Kidney Found. Ea. Mo. and Metro East, 2002. Fellow ACP, AHA; mem. Am. Soc. Nephrology, Internat. Soc. Nephrology, Coun. on Kidney in Cardiovascular Disease, Am. Heart Assn., St. Louis Soc. Am. Med. Women's Assn., St. Louis Internists (v.p. 1983-84, pres. 1984-85), Women in Nephrology (pres. 2000-02), Internat. Soc. for Peritoneal Dialysis, Am. Geriatrics Soc., Soc. for Exec. Leadership in Acad. Medicine (bd. dirs., program chair 1999—), Alpha Omega Alpha. Jewish. Home: 1728 Glen Echo Rd Nashville TN 37215-2910 Office: VA Tenn Valley Healthcare Sys 1310 24th Ave S Nashville TN 37212-2637 Office Phone: 615-327-5330. Business E-Mail: wendy.brown@med.va.gov.

BROWN, WESLEY ERNEST, federal judge; b. Hutchinson, Kans., June 22, 1907; s. Morrison H. H. and Julia (Wesley) B.; m. Mary A. Miller, Nov. 30, 1934 (dec.); children: Wesley Miller, Loy B. Wiley; m. Thadene N. Moore. Student, Kans. U., 1925-28; LLB, Kansas City Law Sch., 1933. Bar: Kans. 1933, Mo. 1933. Pvt. practice, Hutchinson, 1933-58; county atty. Reno County, Kans., 1935-39; referee in bankruptcy U.S. Dist. Ct. Kans., 1958-62, judge, 1962-79, sr. judge, 1979—. Apptd. Temporary Emergency Ct. of Appeals of U.S., 1980-93; dir. Nat. Assn. Referees in Bankruptcy, 1959-62; mem. bankruptcy divsn. Jud. Conf., 1963-70; mem. Jud. Conf., U.S., 1976-79. With USN, 1944-46. Mem. ABA, Kans. Bar Assn. (exec. council 1950-62, pres. 1964-65), Reno County Bar Assn. (pres. 1947), Wichita Bar Assn., S.W. Bar Kan., Delta Theta Phi. Office: US Dist Ct 414 US Courthouse 401 N Market St Wichita KS 67202-2089

BROWN, WILLIAM A., lawyer, mediator, arbitrator; b. Memphis, Nov. 6, 1957; s. Winn D. Sr. and Annie Ruth (Hurt) B.; m. Mary Lee Walker, Dec. 27, 1980. BBA, U. Miss., 1978, JD, 1981. Bar: Miss. 1981, U.S. Dist. Ct. (no. and so. dists.) Miss. 1981, U.S. Dist. Ct. (we. dist.) Tenn. 1987. Ptnr., pres. Walker, Brown & Brown, P.A., Hernando, Miss., 1981—. Bd. dir. The Baddour Ctr. Pres. DeSoto Literacy Coun., Hernando, 1988, Am. Cancer Soc., Hernando, 1988, DeSoto County Econ. Devel. Coun., 1995—96; mem. Leadership 2000, 1990—91; dir. Hist. DeSota Found., 2005—; chmn. Ch. Coun. Hernando United Meth. Ch., 2002—04; vice-chmn. Hernando Preservation Commn., 1997—2000, chmn., 2001—; chmn. design com. Main St. Project, 1997—2000; allocations chmn. United Way of Mid-South DeSoto County; dir. DeSoto Health and Wellness Ctr., Baddour Meml. Ctr. James O. Eastland scholar, 1978-81; Paul Harris fellow Rotary Internat., 1997. Mem. Miss. Bar Assn. (bd. dirs. young lawyers sect. 1988-89, Bd. Bar Commrs. 2002-05), DeSoto County Bar Assn. (v.p. 1988-89, pres. 1996-98), Rotary (pres. Hernando chpt. 1989-90), Boy Scouts Am., N.W. Miss. (membership chmn. 1990, activities chmn. 1991). Methodist. Avocations: gardening, design and construction projects. Home and Office: Walker Brown & Brown PA PO Box 276 Hernando MS 38632-0276

BROWN, WILLIAM DOUGLAS, chemicals executive, lawyer; b. 1946; BA, Lafayette Coll., 1968; JD, U. Va., 1971. Bar: Pa. 1972. Various Air Products and Chems., Inc., Allentown, Pa., 1975—, v.p. adminstrn. air products gases and equipment group, 1997, v.p., gen. counsel, sec., 1999—. Mem. mgmt. com. Air Products and Chems., Inc., mem. corp. exec. com. Mem. ABA. Office: Air Products and Chems Inc 7201 Hamilton Blvd Allentown PA 18195-1526

BROWN, WILLIAM ERNEST, dentist; b. Benton Harbor, Mich., Aug. 29, 1922; s. William Ernest and Gertrude (Eliot) B.; m. T.N. McDonald, Oct. 21, 1944 (dec. July 1969); children: Judith M. Brown Smith, Wendy E. Brown Kerschbaum, Terrence N.; m. E.M. Tyree, Sept. 11, 1970 (dec. Jan. 2000). DDS, U. Mich., 1945, MS, 1947. Practice pediatric dentistry, Ann Arbor, Mich., 1947-62; part-time tchr. U. Mich., 1947-62; from asst. prof. to prof. dentistry, assoc. dir. W.K. Kellogg Found. Inst. Grad. and Postgrad. Dentistry, 1962-69; dean Coll. Dentistry, U. Okla., Oklahoma City, 1969-87; acting provost Health Scis. Ctr. U. Okla., 1973-75. Author: Oral Health, Dentistry and the American Public, 1974, Dental Education in the United States, 1976. Mem. City of Ann Arbor Human Rels. Commn., 1960-66, chmn., 1965-66; chmn. bd. dirs. ARC, Oklahoma County chpt., 1991-93; pres. Cmty. Coun. Ctrl. Okla., 1998-2000; bd. dirs. United Way of Metro Oklahoma City, 1998-2000; mem. Hall of Honor com. U. Mich. Dental Sch., 2003—. Recipient Gies Editorial award, 1965, 67 Mem. ADA, Am. Assn. Dental Schs. (pres. 1984-85), Am. Acad. Pediatric Dentistry, Am. Soc. Dentistry for Children. Home: 1666 Coburn Dr Ann Arbor MI 48108-9626 E-mail: driffl22@aol.com.

BROWN, WILLIAM HILL, III, lawyer; b. Phila., Jan. 19, 1928; s. William H. Jr. and Ethel L. (Washington) B.; m. Sonya Morgan Brown, Aug. 29, 1952 (div. 1975); 1 child, Michele D.; m. D. June Hairston, July 29, 1975; 1 child, Jeanne-Marie. BS, Temple U., 1952; JD, U. Pa., 1955. Bar: Pa. 1955, D.C. 1972, U.S. Ct. Appeals (3d cir.) 1959, U.S. Ct. Appeals (4th cir.) 1978, U.S. Dist. Ct. (ea. dist.) Pa. 1957, U.S. Ct. Appeals (10th cir.) 1986, U.S. Ct. Appeals (5th cir.) 1988, U.S. Dist. Ct. D.C. 1994, U.S. Ct. Appeals (D.C. cir.) 1994, U.S. Ct. Appeals (fed. cir.) 1997, U.S. Ct. Appeals (8th cir.) 2002. Assoc. Norris, Schmidt, Phila., 1955-62; ptnr. Norris, Brown, Hall, Phila., 1962-68, Schnader, Harrison, Segal & Lewis, Phila., 1974—, mem. exec. com., 1983-87; chief of frauds Dist. Atty.'s Office, 1968, dep. dist. atty., 1968; commr. EEOC, Washington, 1968-69, chmn., 1969-73. Lectr. S.W. Legal Found., Practising Law Inst., Nat. Inst. Trial Advocacy; bd. dirs. United Parcel Svc., Inc., 1983-2003, mem. audit com., 1988-2003, chair, 1996-2003, Lawyers Com. Civil Rights Under Law; chmn. Phila. Spl. Investigation Commn. MOVE; pres. Nat. Black Child Devel., Inc., 1986-90; bd. dirs. Cmty. Legal Svcs., 1986—; mem. exec. com. Schnader, Harrison, Segal & Lewis, 1983-87; bd. dirs., mem. exec. com. Lawyers Com. Civil Rights Under law, 1977—, co-chair, 1991-93; mem. Commn. on Comml. Operation of U.S. Customs Svc., 1994-98. Contbr. articles to profl. jours. Bd. dirs. Mid. States Colls. and Secondary Schs., 1983-89, Main Line Acad., 1982—, Nat. Sr. Citizens Law Ctr., 1988-94; mem. nat. bd. govs. Am. Heart Assn., 1994-96, mem. audit com., mem. pub. affairs policy com., bd. dirs., 1986-94, mem. audit com., mem. pub. affairs policy com.; mem. adv. com. on appellate ct. rules Supreme Ct. Pa., 1989-95. With USAF, 1946-48. Recipient award of merit Fed. Bar Assn., Columbus, 1971, NAACP award, 1971, Dr. Edward S. Cooper award Am. Heart Assn., 1995, Whitney M. Young Jr. Leadership award Urban League, 1996, Whitney North Seymor award Lawyers Com. for Civil Rights Under Law, 1996, Champions for Social Justice and Equality award Black Law Students Assn. Rutgers-Camden, 1997, Fidelty award, 1998, Earl G. Harrison Pro Bono award, U. Pa. Disting. Law Alumni award, 2000, Earl G. Harrison Pro Bono award, 2001, Equal Employment Opportunity Commn. Spirit of Partnership award 2003, Lawyers' Com. for Civil Rights Under Law Lifetime Achievement award, 2004. Fellow Internat. Acad. Trial Lawyers, Am. Law Inst.; mem. ABA, Phila. Bar Assn. (Fidelity award 1990), D.C. Bar Assn., Pa. Bar Assn., Fed. Bar Assn., Nat. Bar Assn., Inter-Am. Bar Assn., World Assn. Lawyers (founding mem.), Am. Arbitration Assn. (past bd. dirs.), Barrister's Assn. Phila., Inc. (J. Austin Norris award 1987), Citizens Commn. on Civil Rights, NAACP (bd. dirs. legal def. and ednl. fund), Alpha Phi Alpha (Recognition award 1969); hon. mem., United Parcel Svc. Legal Dept., 2003. Republican. Episcopalian. Office: Schnader Harrison Segal & Lewis 1600 Market St Suite 3600 Philadelphia PA 19103-7286 Office Phone: 215-751-2434. Business E-Mail: wbrown@schnader.com.

BROWN, WILLIAM L., banker; b. Hendersonville, N.C., Feb. 1, 1922; s. William W. and Sarah (Maxwell) B.; m. Helen Presbrey, August, 1947; children: Kathryn H., Richard P., Steven J., Melissa M. Student, Mars Hill Coll., Newbury Coll.; MBA, Harvard, 1947. With First Nat. Bank Boston/Bank of Boston Corp., 1949-89, asst. v.p., 1949-59, v.p., 1959-66, sr. v.p., 1966-69, exec. v.p., 1969-71, bd. dirs., 1969-92, dir. of corp., 1970-92, pres., COO, 1971-83, chmn., CEO, 1983-87, ret., 1989. Bd. dirs. Gen. Cinema Corp., Chestnut Hill, Mass., Ionics, Inc., Watertown, Mass., N.Am. Mortgage Co., Santa Rosa, Calif.; trustee Bradley Real Estate Trust, Boston. Hon. life overseer Children's Hosp. Med. Ctr., Boston; trustee assoc. Boston Coll., Marine Biol. Lab., Woods Hole, Mass.; trustee, mem. corp. Mus. Sci.; bd. dirs. Jobs for Mass., Inc., John F. Kennedy Libr. Found., Ret. Artery Bus. Com., Ret. Friends of Post Office Sq.; mem. corp. Northeastern U. Lt. USNR, World War II. Office: Bank of Boston MS/01-28-02 100 Federal St Fl 8 Boston MA 02110-1898

BROWN, WILLIAM ROBERT, trade association administrator, consultant; b. Delaware, Ohio, Jan. 19, 1926; s. Omar Lloyd and Olive Ida (Johnson) B.; m. Dorothy Judd Curtis, Dec. 30, 1950; children— Darmae Judd, Ann Barlett Brown Nutt. BA, Ohio Wesleyan U., 1948; MA; research scholar, Ohio State U., 1949. Asst. Inst. Practical Politics, Ohio Wesleyan U., 1947-48; research dir. Mo. State C. of C., 1950-64; govtl. research dir. Del. State C. of C., 1964-65; assoc. research dir. Council of State Chambers of Commerce, Washington, 1965-78, pres., 1979-90, Commerce Service Ctr., Inc., 1986-90; cons., 1991—. Editor: State Tax Report, 1969-81, Jud. Report, 1969-81, Property Tax Report, 1979, State UC Report, 1984-90, State Chamber News, 1988-90. Trustee Nat. Found. for Unemployment Compensation and Workers Compensation; precinct chmn. Rep. Party, 1968-70; pres. Friends of the Railroad, 1980-89. Recipient BNA Tax Mgmt. award for disting. svc. in state and local tax law. Mem. Nat. Tax Assn., Estero (Fla.) C. of C. (exec. dir. 1998-2000), Bonita-Estero Rep. Club (pres. 1999-2001), Phi Beta Kappa, Pi Sigma Alpha, Kappa Delta Pi, Sigma Chi. Methodist. Home: 4160 Gunnison Ct # 821 Estero FL 33928 E-mail: aquilla@ix.netcom.com.

BROWN, WILLIAM SAMUEL, JR., communication sciences and disorders educator; b. Pottstown, Penn., Apr. 25, 1940; s. William Samuel and Elizabeth (Gallager) B.; m. Elaine Kay Whitehouse, Aug. 18, 1962; children: William Samuel III, Allen Reed. MA, SUNY, Buffalo, 1967, PhD, 1969. Speech therapist Crawford Cty. Schools, Meadville, Penn., 1962-65; rsch. asst. SUNY, Buffalo, N.Y., 1965-68; prof. U. Fla., Gainesville, Fla., 1970—. Contrib. numerous publications to scientific jours. Postdoctoral fellow U. Fla, Gainsville, 1968-70. Fellow Internat. Soc. Phonetic Sci. (coun. rep. 1980—), Am. Speech-Lang.-Hearing Assn., Acoustical Soc. Am.; mem. Am. Assn. Phonetic Sci. (exec. sec. 1980—). Republican. Presbyterian. Office: U Fla IASCP Dauer 63 Gainesville FL 32611

BROWN, WILLIAM VIRGIL, internal medicine educator; b. Royston, Ga., Sept. 25, 1938; m. Alice Brown; 2 children. BA in Physics and Chemistry, Emory U., 1960; MD, Yale U., 1964. Diplomate Am. Bd. Internal Medicine, Am. Bd. Endocrinology. Intern, asst. resident Osler Med. Svc. Johns Hopkins Hosp., Balt., 1964—66; clin. assoc. Nat. Heart and Lung Inst., Bethesda, Md., 1966—69; fellow in endocrinology and metabolism Yale-New Haven Hosp., 1969—70; asst. prof. medicine U. Calif. Dept. Medicine, San Diego, 1970—74, assoc. prof. medicine, 1974—78; dir. lipid rsch. clinic U. Calif., San Diego, 1972—78; prof. medicine Mt. Sinai Sch. Medicine, N.Y.C., 1978—87, dir. divsn. arteriosclerosis and metabolism, 1978—87; pres., CEO Medlantic Rsch. Found., Washington, 1987—91; Charles Howard Candler prof. internal medicine, dir. divsn. arteriosclerosis and lipid metabolism Emory U., Atlanta, 1991—, pres. faculty coun. and univ. senate, 1998—99; chief of medicine Atlanta VA Hosp., 1998—. Chmn. Gordon Conf. on Lipid Metabolism, 1984; metabolism study sect. NIH, 1985; pres. Am. Bd. Clin. Lipidology, 2005—. Assoc. editor: Correct Controlled Clinical Trials, 2000—. Fellow, Alexander von Humboldt. Fellow: ACP (master physician); mem.: Nat. Lipid Assn. (pres. 2002—), Am. Bd. Bioanalysis (high-complexity clin. lab. dir.), Southeastern Lipid Assn. (pres. 1997—99), Am. Soc. Exptl. Biology, Am. Soc. Clin. Investigation, Am. Fedn. Clin. Rsch., Am. Heart Assn. (mem. physiology study sect. 1978—80, mem. credentials com. arteriosclerosis coun. 1978—80, chmn. credentials com. arteriosclerosis coun. 1979—82, mem. nutrition com. 1981—86, mem. several rsch. con., chmn. nutrition com. 1982—86, bd. dirs. 1983, vice chmn. edn. and cmty. program com., nat. pres. 1991—92, gold heart award 1996, R. Bruce Logue award 2000, fellow arteriosclerosis coun., fellow epidemiology and preventive cardiology coun.; numerous others), Alpha Omega Alpha, Phi Beta Kappa. Achievements include research in study of the structure and metabolism of lipoproteins; study of the lipolytic enzymes, including their molecular and kinetic characteristics, diagnosis and treatment of the hyperlipoproteinemias; the relationship of lipoprotein metabolism to atheromatous vascular disorders. Office: Atlanta VA Hosp 1670 Clairmont Rd Decatur GA 30033-4004 Fax: 404-235-3005. Office Phone: 404-235-3001. E-mail: w.virgil.brown@med.va.gov.

BROWN, WILLIE LEWIS, JR., former mayor, former state legislator, lawyer; b. Mineola, Tex., Mar. 20, 1934; s. Willie Lewis and Minnie (Boyd) B.; children: Susan, Robin, Michael. BA, San Francisco State Coll., 1955; LL.D., Hastings Coll. Law, 1958; postgrad. fellow, Crown Coll., 1970, U. Calif.-Santa Cruz, 1970. Bar: Calif. 1959. Mem. Calif. State Assembly, Sacramento, 1964-95, speaker, 1980-95, chmn. Ways and Means Com., 1971-74; chmn. revenue and taxation com., 1976-79; Democratic Whip Calif. State Assembly, 1969-70, majority floor leader, 1979-80, chmn. legis. black caucus, 1980, chmn. govtl. efficiency and economy com., 1968-84; mayor San Francisco, 1995—2004. Mem. U. Calif. bd. regents, 1972, Dem. Nat. Com., 1989-90; co-chmn. Calif. del. to Nat. Black Polit. Conv., 1972, Calif. del. to Nat. Dem. Conv., 1980; nat. campaign chmn. Jesse Jackson for Pres., 1988. Mem. State Legis. Leaders Found. (dir.), Nat. Conf. State Legislatures, NAACP, Black Am. Polit. Assn. Calif. (co-founder, past chmn.), Calif. Bar Assn., Alpha Phi Alpha, Phi Alpha Delta Democrat. Methodist.*

BROWNA, JO MCINTYRE, nurse; d. Cornelius Daniel McIntyre and Josephine Rafferty McIntyre; children: Marc L., Patrick J. Diploma in Nursing, Albert Einstein Med. Ctr., Phila., 1972. Cert. oper. rm. nurse, Assn. of Oper. Rm. Nurses, 1992, RN 1st asst., Assn. of Oper. Rm. Nurses, 1998. Mgr., staff Virtua Health Sys., Voorhees, NJ, 1993—2003; tech. support rep. Medtronic Neurol., Phila., 2000—03. Nurse 1st asst. various hosp. affiliations, NJ, 2001—. Recipient Excellence Leadership award, Dale Carnegie, 1997. Mem.: Assn. of Oper. Rm. Nurses, Am. Assn. of Neurol. Surgeons (assoc.). Achievements include working with other RNFAs to change N.J. laws prohibiting RNFAs to work in N.J; having N.J. ins. cos. value our roles and have mandatory reimbursement from all ins. cos; support of legislature to vote for Medicare reimbursement. Home and Office: Jo Browna PC 13 Dori Court Erial NJ 08081

BROWNBACK, SAM, senator, lawyer; b. Parker, Kans., June 12, 1956; m. Mary; children: Abby, Andy, Liz, Mark, Jenna. BS in Agrl. Econs. with honors, Kan. State U.; JD, U. Kans. Farm broadcaster KKSU; ptnr. law firm, N.Y.C.; instr. law Kans. State U.; city atty. Ogden and Leonardville, Kans.; sec. agr., Washington; mem. 104th Congress from 2nd Kans. dist., Washington, 1994-96; U.S. Senator from Kans. Washington, 1996—. Mem. judiciary, com., sci. and transp., fgn. rels., govtl. affairs, joint econ. coms.; fellow U.S. Trade Rep. Carla Hills, 1990-91, mem. intergovtl. adv. com.; spkr. on trade, agr., leadership, motivation, mem. com. health, edn., labor and pensions. Co-author: 2 books; contbr. numerous articles. Pres. Kans. Prayer Breakfast; developer Family Impact Statement; vice chmn. Riley County Rep. Com. Recipient Hon. Am. Farmer degree, FFA; named Outstanding Young Person, Osaka, Japan Jaycees, Kansan of Distinction, 1988. Republican. Office: US Senate 303 Hart Senate Office Bldg Washington DC 20510-0001*

BROWN-BANKS, JENNIFER ELAINE, writer, educator; b. Chgo., June 29, 1961; d. Major Harding and Arabella Brown Neal; m. Leandrew Banks; 1 child, Jaremy Dortch. AA, Robert Morris Coll., Chgo., 1994; student, North Park U., Chgo., 1996-98; BA, Chgo. State U., 2002. Sr. analyst No. Trust Bank, Chgo., 1979-93; acctg. coord. St. Edmund's, Chgo., 1995-2000; feature writer Single Living Mag., Chgo., 1995—; office mgr. Schindler Comm., Chgo., 2000—03. Contbg. author: Chocolate for a Woman's Heart, 1998, Chocolate for a Woman's Spirit, 1999. Recipient Vision award Brainerd Cmty. Devel., Chgo., 1994. Mem. Poets United to Advance the Arts (founder, pres.). Roman Catholic. Avocations: reading, poetry, music. E-mail: jenniferwriter@yahoo.com.

BROWNE, ARTHUR, newspaper editor; BA, Boston Coll.; JD, St. John's U. Various editl. positions The Daily News, NYC, 1973—2000, editl. page editor, 2003—; founding editor Petplace.com, 2000—00; enterprise editor Bloomberg News, 2002—03. Adj. faculty Columbia U. Sch. Journalism, 2004. Co-author: I Koch. Mem.: Am. Soc. Newspaper Editors. Office: NY Daily News Inc 450 W 33rd St New York NY 10001-2603

BROWNE, DALLAS, anthropologist, educator; b. Chgo., Oct. 9, 1944; s. William Eldridge and Ann (Sherman) Browne; m. Imelda M. Siedentopf, Apr. 8, 1972; children: Eldridge, La Salle, Hubert, William. BA, Northeastern U., 1966; MA, U. Ill., 1971, PhD in Anthropology, 1983. Asst. prof. Wabash Coll., Crawfordsville, Ind., 1980—82, Colby Coll., Waterville, Maine, 1983—85, York Coll. CUNY, 1985—91; assoc. prof. anthropology So. Ill. U., Edwardsville, 1991—. Cons. evaluation Kenya Govt., 1976; with UNICEF; hon. consul, Tanzania. Author: Current Discourse on Dilemmas Facing Developing Nations, 2005. Capt. U.S. Army. Fellow, Ford Found., 1971, Inst. Study Racism, 1980, Ctr. Polit. Studies and Inst. Social Rsch., 1984. Mem.: St. Louis Consular Corps (pres.), Midwest Latin Am. Assn., Midwest African Studies Assn. (pres.-elect), World Affairs Coun., Am. Com. Fgn. Rels., Eugene Redman Writers Assn., Midwest Assn. Latin Am. Studies, New Eng. Black Studies, Assn. Black Anthropologists, Soc. Urban Anthropology, Am. Anthropol. Assn. Avocation: building models of famous inventions. Office: Dept Anthropology Box 1451 S Ill U Edwardsville Edwardsville IL 62026-0001

BROWNE, DIANA GAYLE, artist, social worker; b. San Francisco, Aug. 31, 1924; d. Clarence Luther and Elsa Henrietta (Ericson) Sidelinger; m. Alfred B. Britton Jr., Sept. 2, 1942 (div. 1960); children: Alfred B. Britton III, Kathryn H. Lumbert, Patrick Luther Britton; m. James Stuart Browne M.D., May 19, 1963; children: Bruce Petter Browne, Julia Regina Browne. Student, Stanford U., 1947; BA with great distinction with honors, San Jose State U., 1949; MSW, U. Calif., 1958; BFA, San Francisco Art Inst., 1973. LCSW Calif. Clinical social worker Dept. Mental Health, Sacramento, 1958-59; clin. social worker U. Calif. Med. Ctr., San Francisco, 1960-61, Langley Porter Neuropsych. Inst., San Francisco, 1961-65, Napa State Hosp., 1980-85; postgrad. Inst. for Clin. Social Work, Berkeley, 1981-83; freelance artist Mill Valley, Calif., 1966-80, 1985—. Mem. Acci Gallery, Berkeley, 1977-91, Alliance Women Artists, 1988-89. Recipient Merit award Calif. State Fair Fine Arts Div., 1989, Marin Arts Guild, Larkspur, Calif., 1977-79, Art award Marin County Fair, 1977-78, 89-90. Mem. AAUW, DAR, Calif. Soc. Printmakers, Calif. Watercolor Assn. (signature mem., membership chmn. 1986-88, Merit award 1987), Marin Soc. Artists, Outdoor Art Club (Mill Valley), Alpha Chi Omega (pres. Santa Clara County alumnae 1949-51, Marin County alumnae 1966-68). Avocations: computer graphics, photography, geneology. Personal E-mail: goldengate4@sbcglobal.net.

BROWNE, DONALD VICTOR, broadcast executive; b. Passaic, N.J., May 16, 1943; s. Donald James and Roseanna (Hopp) B.; m. Maria Junquera, May 9, 1981; children: Christopher Barret, Ryan Alexander. BS in Mktg., Fairleigh Dickinson U., 1971. Traffic expediter CBS News, NYC, 1967-70, prodr., 1970-71, reporter, assignment editor, 1971-75, prodr., dep. bur. chief Atlanta, 1975-79; bur. chief, Fla., L.Am. NBC News, Miami, Fla., 1979-88, bur. chief, L.Am., S.E. US, 1988-89, exec. news dir. NYC, 1989-90, exec. v.p., 1990-93; pres., gen. mgr. Sta. WTVJ-TV, NBC, Miami, 1993—2003; COO Telemundo Network, Hialeah, Fla., 2003—05, pres., CEO, 2005—. With USCG, 1967-73. Office: Telemundo Network 2290 W 8th Ave Hialeah FL 33010

BROWNE, DOUGLAS ALAN, music educator, director; b. Mineola, N.Y., Nov. 2, 1946; m. Susan Evelyn Kamp, June 29, 1968; 1 child, Joshua Douglas. MusB, Houghton (N.Y.) Coll., 1968; MA, West Tex. State U., 1974; MusD, U. Mo., 1984. Choral dir. Elba (N.Y.) Ctrl. Sch., 1968—69, Robert E. Lee H.S., Midland, Tex., 1974—79; dir. of choirs Grove City (Pa.) Coll., 1981—. Dir. music East Main Presbyn. Ch., Grove City, Pa., 1983—2000. Specialist U.S. Army, 1969—72, Vietnam. Mem.: Pa. Music Educators Assn., Music Educators Nat. Conf., Am. Choral Dir. Assn. Avocations: bicycling, skiing, racquetball, travel. Home: 25 Straffordshire Ct Grove City PA 16127 Office: Grove City College 100 Campus Dr Grove City PA 16127 Office Phone: 724-458-2088. Personal E-mail: susandoug@zoominternet.net. E-mail: dabrowne@gcc.edu.

BROWNE, FREDERICK DOUGLAS, physiologist, educator; b. Springfield, Ohio, June 3, 1929; s. Charles David and Ruth Noami Browne; m. Joyce Louise Burton, June 11, 1955; children: Fred, Sharon, Michael, Regina, Stephan, Monica. BS, U. Dayton, 1956; MS, Miami U., Ohio, 1958; postgrad., Case Western Res. U., 1963-66; EdD, Nova U., 1981. Ordained permanent deacon Maronite Cath. Ch., 1992. Rschr. artificial organs and exptl. heart surgery Cleve. Clinic, 1958-63; predoctoral fellow Coll. Medicine Case Western Res. U., Cleve., 1963-66; instr. sci. Cleve. Bd. Edn., 1966-69; asst. prof. St. John's Coll., Cleve., 1969-73; instr. Sch. Anesthesia Cleve. Clinic, 1973-74; prof. anatomy and physiology Cuyahoga C.C., Warrensville, Ohio, 1973-92; chair/CEO Rameso, Inc., Copley, Ohio, 1993—. Contbr. articles to profl. jours. Pres., Bd. Cath. Edn., Diocese of Cleve., 1972-73; chmn. Civil Svc. Commn. Warrensville Heights, Ohio, 1970-72; councilman Warrensville Heights, 1982-85; bd. dirs. Summit County Cath. Social Svc.; mem. precinct com., AMA minority affairs com., Rep. Nat. Conv., 2004. 2d lt. U.S. Army, 1952-54. NIH fellow, 1963-66. Mem. AAUP, AMA, Nat. Assn. Advancement Sci., N.Y. Acad. Scis., Ohio Coll. Biology Tchrs. Assn., Secular Franciscan, Alpha Phi Alpha. Republican. Personal E-mail: hrida02@aol.com.

BROWNE, G.M. WALTER SHAWN, journalist, publisher; b. Sydney, Australia, Jan. 10, 1949; s. Walter Francis and Hilda Louise (Leahy) B.; m. Raquel Emilse Facal, Mar. 9, 1973; 1 stepson, Marcello Garcia. Grad. high sch. Chess player, 1957—; U.S. jr. champion, 1966; Australian champion, 1968-69; U.S. Open champion, 1971-73; Nat. Open champion, 1971-73, 75, 84, 86-87, 91, 94-95, 2002; U.S. champion, 1974-78, 80-83; Pan-Am. champion, 1974; Internat. German champion, 1975; mem. U.S. Olympic Team, 1974, 78, 82, 84; Nat. and U.S. Open Blitz chess champion, 1989; Pan-Pacific Blitz chess champion, 1991. Columnist Chess Life & Rev., Berkeley, Calif., 1973—; lectr. in field; commentator at 1999 Fide World Championship, Las Vegas, Nev. Publisher: Strongest International Chess Tourneys, 1978-85. Named Internat. Master Fedn. Internat. des Eshecs, 1969, Internat. Grandmaster, 1969; winner German Open Championship, Mannheim, 1975; 1st pl. Venice, 1971; 1st pl. Rejkavik, Iceland, 1978; 1st pl. Wijk Am. Zee, Holland, 1974, 80; 1st pl. Santiago, 1981; 1st pl. Indonesia, 1982, Gjovik, 1983, Naestved, 1985, 2d-3d World Open, Phila., 1988; only 11 time winner Nat. Open, Can. Open champion, 1991, U.S. class champion, 1991, 7 time Am. Open champion; winner N.Am. Open 1991, 93, 94, 96; inducted into U.S. Hall of Fame, 2003, Sr. US Champ, Las Vegas, 2005. Mem. World Blitz Chess Assn. (pres., founder, pub., editor quar. mag. Blitz Chess 1988-2003). Address: 8 Parnassus Rd Berkeley CA 94708-2041 E-mail: wbkingchess@aol.com.

BROWNE, HARRY, writer, financial planner; b. NYC, June 17, 1933; s. Edson Bradford and Cecil Margaret (Davis) B.; m. Gloria Frances Maxwell, June 9, 1953 (div. 1964); 1 child, Autumn Lee; m. Pamela Lanier Wolfe, Nov. 2, 1985. Grad. high sch., Van Nuys, Calif. Various sales and advt. positions, L.A., 1956-67; investment advisor U.S., Can. and Switzerland, 1967—; dir. pub. policy DownsizeDC.org, currently; cons. Permanent Portfolio, currently; sr. polit. analyst Free Market News Network, currently. Cons. Permanent Portfolio Fund, Austin, Tex., 1982—. Author: How You Can Profit from the Coming Devaluation, 1970, How I Found Freedom in an Unfree World, 1973, You Can Profit From a Monetary Crisis, 1974, Harry Browne's Complete Guide to Swiss Banks, 1976, New Profits from the Monetary Crisis, 1978, Investment Rule #1, 1985, Why the Best-Laid Investment Plans Usually Go Wrong, 1987, The Economic Time Bomb, 1989, (with Terry Coxon) Inflation-Proofing Your Investments, 1981, Why Government Doesn't Work, 1995, Fail-Safe Investing, 1999, The Great Libertarian Offer, 2000, A to Z: 872 Libertarian Soundbites You Can Use Right Now, 2004. Libertarian Party cand. for U.S. Pres., 1996. With U.S. Army, 1953-56. Libertarian. Avocations: classical music, opera, reading, sports, television, good food & wine. Office: 2825 Sawyer Bend Rd Franklin TN 37069-1701*

BROWNE, JACKSON, singer, songwriter; b. Heidelberg, West Germany; s. Clyde Browne. Joined Nitty Gritty Dirt Band, 1966. Musician, songwriter: albums Jackson Browne (Saturate Before Using), 1972, For Everyman, 1973, Late for the Sky, 1974, The Pretender, 1976, Running on Empty, 1977, Hold Out, 1980, Lawyers in Love, 1983, Lives in the Balance, 1986, World in Motion, 1989, I'm Alive, 1993, Everywhere I Go, 1994, Looking East, 1996, The Naked Ride Home, 2002, co-wrote: Take it Easy (with Glen Frey for the Eagles). Recipient Founders award, ASCAP, 2004. songs "These Days" and "Shadow Dream Song", were recorded by Tom Rush, Nico, Gregg Allman and others; inducted Rock and Roll Hall of Fame, 2004.

BROWNE, JEFFREY FRANCIS, lawyer; b. Clare, South Australia, Australia, Mar. 1, 1944; came to U.S., 1975; s. Patrick Joseph and Irene Kathleen (Cormack) B.; m. Deborah Mary Christine West, Aug. 28, 1971; children: Veronique Namur Irene, Jeffrey James, Nicholas Patrick, Sophie Christina, Amy Elizabeth. LLB, Adelaide U., South Australia, 1966; LLM, Sydney U., Australia, 1968, Harvard U., 1976. Bar: South Australia 1969, Australian Capital Territory 1973, N.Y. 1978, Victoria 1982, New South Wales 1983, Western Australia 1983. Assoc. High Ct. Australia, Canberra, Australian Capital Territory, 1967-68; diplomat Dept. Fgn. Affairs, Canberra, 1969; 2d sec. Australian High Commn., London and Malaysia, 1970-71, acting high commr. Ghana, 1972; counsel nuclear tests case Internat. Ct. Justice, 1973-74; assoc. Sullivan & Cromwell, N.Y.C., 1976-81, ptnr., 1983—; gen. counsel Alcoa of Australia, Melbourne, 1981-82. Bd. dirs. Compinvest Pty. Ltd. Mem. Law Inst. Victoria, Australian Mining and Petroleum Law Assn., Law Coun. Australia (chmn. fin. and securities subcom., internat. trade and bus. law com.), Inst. Dirs. of Australia, Internat. Bar Assn. (sect. on energy and natural resources), Am. C. of C. in Australia (bd. dirs.), Am. Soc. Internat. Law, N.Y. Yacht Club, Melbourne Club. Office: Sullivan & Cromwell 125 Broad St Fl 28 New York NY 10004-2489 also: 101 Collins St Melbourne Victoria 3000 Australia E-mail: brownej@sullcrom.com.

BROWNE, JOHN CHARLES, retired physics researcher, former national research laboratory executive; b. Pottstown, Pa., July 29, 1942; s. Charles Ignatius and Mary Agnes (Titzer) B.; m. Susan Mary Mazzarella, Dec. 30, 1972 (div. Dec. 1984); children— Christopher Ryan, Adam Charles; m. Marti Moore, May 4, 1985; 1 child, Courtney Keese. BS, Drexel U., 1965; PhD, Duke U., 1969; DSc (hon.), Drexel U., 1998. Instr. Duke U., Durham, N.C., 1969-70; staff scientist Lawrence Livermore Lab., Calif., 1970-79; group leader Los Alamos Nat. Lab., 1979-81, div. leader, 1981-84, assoc. dir., 1984-93; dir. Los Alamos Neutron Sci. Ctr., Los Alamos, 1993—97; lab. dir. Los Alamos Nat. Lab., 1997—2003, sr. scientist, 2003, ret, 2003; owner JCB Sci. Cons., LLC, 2005—. Contbr. articles to profl. jours. NASA fellow, 1965-67 Fellow AAAS, Am. Phys. Soc. Avocations: skiing, tennis. Office Phone: 435-668-7265. E-mail: jcbrowne729@msn.com.

BROWNE, (EDMUND) JOHN PHILLIP, oil industry executive; b. Hamburg, Germany, Feb. 20, 1948; s. Edmund and Paula Browne. MA in Physics, Cambridge U., Eng., 1969; MS in Bus., Stanford (Calif.) U., 1980; DEng (hon.), Heriott Watt U.; DTech (hon.), Robert Gordon U.; DSc (hon.), Warwick U.; LLD (hon.), U. Dundee; DSc (hon.), U. Hull, U. Leuven; LLD (hon.), U. Notre Dame, U. Thunderbird; DSc (hon.), U. Cranfield; LLM (hon.), U. Sheffield, Colo. Sch. Mines, Mendeleyer U., Buckingham U.; DSc, Cranfield. Registered profl. engr., U.K. Petroleum engr. Brit. Petroleum Co.,

London, N.Y., Calif. and Alaska, 1969-79, regional petroleum engr., 1979-80, comml. mgr., 1981-83, group treas., 1984-86; chief exec. BP Finance Internat., 1984; mgr. forties field Brit. Petroleum Co., Aberdeen, Scotland, 1983-84; exec. v.p., CFO, CEO Standard Oil Co. of Ohio, Cleve., 1986-87; CEO Standard Oil Prodn. Co., 1987-89; chief fin. officer BP America, Inc., Cleve., 1987-89; mng. dir., chief exec. officer BP Exploration, London, 1989-95; mng. dir., bd. The Brit. Petroleum Co., PLC, 1991-98, group chief exec., 1995-98, BP Amoco (now BP p.l.c.), 1998—. Nonexec. dir. Redland PLC, 1992-96, Smithkine Beecham, 1995-99, Intel Corp., 1997—, Goldman Sachs, 1999-; mem. supervisory bd. Daimler-Chrysler AG, 1997-2001; chmn. adv. bd., judge Inst. Mgmt. Studies, Cambridge, Eng., Tsinghua Sch. Econs. and Mgmt., Beijing, China. Emeritus chmn. adv. bd. Stanford Grad. Sch. Bus., 1997; trustee Brit. Mus., 1995—; v.p. Prince of Wales Bus. Leaders Forum; hon. fellow St. John's Coll., Cambridge. Created knight, 1998, life peer, 2001; Trevelyan open scholar. Fellow Royal Acad. Engring., Inst. Mining and Metallurgy, Inst. Chem. Engrs. (hon.); mem. Athenaeum Club (London), Judge Inst. Mgmt. Studies, Cambridge (chmn.), Internat. Adv. Bd. Tsinghua Sch. Economics and Mgmt., Beijing (chmn.). Avocations: ballet, opera, photography, pre-columbian art.

BROWNE, JOSEPH PETER, retired librarian; b. June 12, 1929; s. George and Mary Bridget (Fahy) B. AB, U. Notre Dame, 1951; STL, Pontificum Athenaeum Angelicum, Rome, 1957; STD, Pontificum Athenaeum Angelicum, 1960; MLS, Cath. U. Am., 1965. Joined Congregation of Holy Cross, Roman Cath. Ch., 1947, ordained priest, 1955. Asst. pastor Holy Cross Ch., South Bend, Ind., 1955-56, libr., prof. moral theology Washington, 1959-64; mem. faculty U. Portland, Oreg., 1964-73, 75—, dir. libr., 1966-70, 76-94, dean Coll. Arts and Scis., 1970-73, assoc. prof. libr. sci., 1967-95, prof. emeritus, 1995—, regent, 1969-70, 77-81, chmn. acad. senate, 1968-70. Prof., head dept. libr. sci. Our Lady of Lake Coll., San Antonio, 1973-75; chmn. Interstate Libr. Planning Coun., 1977-79. Mem. Columbia River chpt. Huntington's Disease Soc. Am., 1975-90, pres., 1979-82; pastor St. Birgitta Ch., Portland, 1993-2005; chmn. Archdiocesan Presbyteral Coun., 1994-98, 2000-02; mem. coll. of cons. Archdiocese of Portland, 1995-2005. Recipient Culligan award U. Portland, 1979. Mem. ALA, Cath. Libr. Assn. (life, pres. 1971-73), Cath. Theol. Soc. Am., Pacific N.W. Libr. Assn. (pres. 1985-86), Oreg. Libr. Assn. (life, pres. 1967-68), Nat. Assn. Parliamentarians, Oreg. Assn. Parliamentarians (pres. 1985-87), Mensa Internat., All-Ireland Cultural Soc. Oreg. (pres. 1984-85), Ancient Order of Hibernians, KC. Democrat. Home: 5410 N Strong St Apt 3 Portland OR 97203-5731 Business E-Mail: browne@up.edu.

BROWNE, JOY, psychologist, radio personality; b. New Orleans, Oct. 24, 1950; d. Nelson and Ruth (Strauss) B.; Carter Thweatt, June 9, 1966 (div. 1979); 1 child, Patience. BA, Rice U.; PhD, Northeastern U.; postgrad., Tufts U. Registered psychologist, Mass. With rsch./optics dept. Sperry Rand, Boston, 1966-68; engr. space program Itek, Boston, 1968-70; head social svcs. dept. Boston Redevel. Authority, 1970-71; staff psychologist South Shore Counselling Assocs., Boston, 1971-82; on-the-air psychologist Sta. WITS, Boston, 1978-82, Sta. KGO, San Francisco, 1982-84; host, news Sta. KCBS, San Francisco, 1984-85; on-air psychologist Sta. WABC, N.Y.C., 1985-87, ABC Talkradio, N.Y.C., 1987-92, WOR Radio Network, N.Y.C., 1992—, Sta. WABC-TV, 1995-97, Dr. Joy Browne Show, Syndicated Eyemark Entertainment, 1999—. On-air psychologist WCBS-TV Five O'Clock News, 1999; dir. Town of Hull Adolescent Outreach Program; cons. human sexuality PBS, 1994—. Author: The Used Car Game, 1971, The Research Experience, 1976, Nobody's Perfect, 1988, Why They Don't Call When They Say They Will and Other Mixed Signals, 1989, Dating for Dummies, 1998, 9 Fantasies That Will Ruin Your Life, 1998, It's a Jungle out There Jane! Understanding the Male Animal, 1999, Getting Unstuck: 8 Simple Steps To Solving Any Problem, 2002. Named One of 25 Outstanding Broadcasters USA Today, 1995-96, 100 Most Influential Talkers, Legend La., 1996, Best Female Talk Show Host, Nartash, 1996, 97, Female Talk Show Host of Yr., Vanity Fair Hall of Fame, 1996. Mem. APA (bd. dirs. 1994-97), Phi Kappa Phi (Communicator of Yr. award 1992). Office: c/o WOR Radio 1440 Broadway Fl 23 New York NY 10018-2390

BROWNE, JUANITA MARIA, academic administrator, social sciences educator; b. Springfield, Mass., Sept. 25, 1937; d. Frederick A. and Creola Crenshaw Brown; children: Andrew Griffin III, Anne-Marea Griffin-Holt, Aimee Desiree Griffin-Munnings, E. Tsekani. BA in English, Edn. and Sociology, Am. Internat. Coll., 1966; EdM in English Edn., Temple U., Phila., 1971, PhD in History, 1973; PhD in Ministerial Edn. with distinction, Mason U., 1991; Ednl. Specialist, Point Loma Nazarene U., 1996; EdD in Ednl. Leadership, No.Ariz. U., 1997, U. San Diego, 2004; post doctoral, Harvard U., Cambridge, Mass., San Diego State U. Cert. tchg. with 18 endorsements, life credential coll. instr. Calif. Dir. Black studies Atlantic Cmty. Coll., Atlantic City, 1969—71; exec. dir. human rels. City of Atlantic City, 1970; prof. cross-cultural studies Grossmont Coll., El Cajon, Calif., 1975—2000; academic v.p. C.H. Mason U., San Diego, 1991—93; founder and pres. Imani Kuumba Coll., 1993—; adj. prof. Springfield Coll., Sch. Human Resource. Cons. Mayoral and Gov.'s Com. of Human Rels., Mass., N.J. Pub. Broadcasting; co-chair Coun. on Civil Rights Orgns. Author: African Am. Roots: A Study of Blacks in the Bible, African Am. Roots, The Black Woman: A History, "The Black Woman" ERIC Resources in Edn., I Thought I heard My People Cry...An account of a pilgrimage to Goree I., Senegal, West Africa, U.S. History, Black Perspectives, Am. Culture; contbr. articles to newspapers. Del. African Am. - Am. Summit, Johannesburg, 1997, Ghana, 1999; mem. bd. PLNU Health Promotion Ctr.; active civil rights campaigns of 1960's; mem. St. Stephen's Ch. of God in Christ, 1977—. Recipient honors, F.B.I., 1996, U.S. State's Attorney's Office, 1997, Nat. Black Bus. and Profl. Women, Nat. MaHogany mag., 2002, Nat. Black Evangelists Orgn., 2002, U.S. Navy, 2002, Edn. award, Nat. Coalition of 100 Black Women, 1994, Ebony Excellence award Edn., 1994, Outstanding Cmty. Svc., Chapel of Four Chaplains, Temple U., Outstanding Contbn., Assn. Study of Negro Life and History, Outstanding Svc, to Non-Traditional Student, Outstanding Educator, Sen. Waddie Deddah, Outstanding Achievement in Field of Edn. A.I.D. Inc., 7th Ann. Black Achievement awards, Leadership commendation, City of San Diego, 2002, Commitment to Diversity commendation, 2002. Mem.: NAACP, Gamma Beta Phi. Office: Imani Kuumba Coll andGrad Sch 7317 El Cajon Blvd La Mesa CA 91941 Office Phone: 619-461-4500. Office Fax: 619-461-3900.

BROWNE, LOVETIE W., special education educator, small business owner; b. Monrovia, Liberia, Jan. 12, 1965; arrived in U.S., 1993; d. Archibald J. Browne and Susannah B. Blackmon-Telewoda; m. Saye D. Gbalazeh, Sept. 15, 1984 (div. May 3, 2000); children: Saye M., Lovetie F. BS in Elem. Edn., Cuttington U. Coll., Suokoko, Liberia, 1988; MS in spl. edn., Coppin State Coll., Balt., 1995; cert. adv. study in edn., Coll. of Notre Dame, Balt., 2002. Cert. std. tchg. NJ, adv. profl. tchg. Md. Elem. sch. tchr. Archdiocese of Monrovia, Liberia, 1988—93; spl. edn. tchr. Balt. City Pub. Sch., 1994—. CEO My Heart's Appeal Inc., Balt., 1996—. Author: (book) A Sibling's Vow, 2001. Recipient Tchr. of Excellence award, Balt. City Coun. of PTAs Inc., 1997, Crystal award, Victor E. Ward Edn. Fund, 2002. Mem.: Nat. Edn. Assn., Coun. on Exceptional Children, Coppin State Coll. Alumni Assn. (parliamentarian 2002—). Democrat. Pentacostal. Achievements include founder, My Heart's Appeal, non-profit orgn. providing edn. and vocational assistance to mentally retarded children in West Africa. Avocations: reading, writing, humanitarian affairs, hearing people's stories, lifetime learning. Home: 1909 Greenberry Rd Baltimore MD 21209 E-mail: Blovetie@aol.com.

BROWNE, MALCOLM WILDE, journalist; b. N.Y.C., Apr. 17, 1931; s. Douglas Granzow and Dorothy Rutledge (Wilde) B.; m. Huynh thi Le Lieu, July 18, 1966. Student, Swarthmore Coll., 1948-50, N.Y.U., 1950-52. Cons. chemist, tech. writer, 1952-56; newsman, copy editor Middletown (N.Y.) Daily Record, 1958-60; with Balt. bur. A.P., 1960-61; chief Indochina corr., 1961-65; Saigon corr. ABC, 1965-66; freelance writer and corr. N.Y.C., 1966-68; corr. New York Times, Buenos Aires, 1968-71, S. Asia, 1971-73, Eastern Europe, 1973-77, sci. corr., 1977-81; sr. editor Discover mag., 1981-84; sci writer N.Y. Times, 1985-00, retired, 2000; McGraw prof. writing Princeton (N.J.) U., 1995-96. Author: The New Face of War, 1965, Muddy Boots and Red Socks, 1993. Served with AUS, 1956-58. Recipient First prize World Press Photo award The Hague, 1963, Pulitzer prize fgn. corr., 1964, Overseas Press Club award, 1964, Sigma Delta Chi award, 1964, Louis M. Lyons award, 1964, Nat. Headliners Club award, 1964; A.P. Mng. Editors award, 1964, Grady-Stack medal Am. Chem. Soc., 1992; Edward R. Murrow Meml. fellow Coun. on Fgn. Rels., 1966-67. Mem.: Sigma Xi. Address: 36 E 36th St New York NY 10016-3463

BROWNE, MICHAEL L., insurance company executive; Pres., CEO Harleysville Insurance. Office: Harleysville Group Inc 355 Maple Ave Harleysville PA 19438-2297 Office Phone: 800-523-6344.*

BROWNE, MICHAEL LEON, lawyer; b. Beaumont, Tex., Sept. 2, 1946; s. Ernest Jewell and Marjorie Jane (Heisig) B.; m. Elizabeth Oswald, Feb. 22, 1969; children: Sarah Skelton, Patrick Michael; m. Anne Farrell, Dec. 28, 2000. AB, Princeton U., 1968; JD, U. Pa., 1974. Bar: Pa. 1974. Law clk. to presiding justice U.S. Dist. Ct. (ea. dist.) Pa., 1974; assoc. Dilworth, Paxson, Kalish, Levy & Coleman, Phila., 1974-75; spl. asst. to U.S. Sec. of Transp., 1975-77, dep. under sec. transp., 1976-77; assoc. Dilworth, Paxson, Kalish, Levy & Kauffman, Phila., 1977-78, ptnr., 1979-80; ins. commr. Commonwealth of Pa., 1980-83, chmn. Gov.'s task force on health care cost containment, 1981-83; ptnr. Reed Smith LLP, Phila., Pitts., Washington, 1983—, mem. exec. com., 1987—2000, mng. ptnr. Delaware Valley Region, 1993—2000, chair internat. ins. practice group, 2001—. Bd. dirs. Harleysville Ins. Co. Del. Rep. Nat. Conv., 1984, 88, 92, 96; mem. nat. fin. com. Rep. Party; co-chmn. Pa. fin. com. for George Bush for Pres., 1987-88; trustee Temple U. Decorated Bronze Star with Combat V. Mem. ABA, Pa. Bar Assn., Phila. Bar Assn. Office: Reed Smith Shaw & McClay 2500 One Liberty Pl Philadelphia PA 19103

BROWNE, RAY, congressman, insurance agent; b. Washington, Dec. 8, 1938; s. Woodrow Lee and Mary Isabelle (Manning) B.; m. Barbara Lee Andrus, May 17, 1979; children: Ray II, Molly Lee. Student, U. Md., 1959-62. CLU; ChFC. Life ins. agt., gen. agt. Aetna Life & Casualty, Washington, Cleve., Charleston, W.Va., 1964-82; ins. broker The Browne Co., Washington, 1982—; shadow rep. from D.C. U.S. Ho. of Reps., Washington, 2001—. Vis. lectr. John Carroll U., Cleve., 1972-77; speaker in field. Contbr. polit. and bus. commentary to newspapers, articles to profl. jours. Adv. neighborhood commr. Washington Govt., 1989-90; mem. drug strategy team Washington Govt., 1989-90; vice chair Hurt Home Bd., Washington, 1987-89; candidate for City Coun., Washington, 1990; del Dem. Nat. Com., 2004; mediator Washington Superior Ct., 1985-88; mem. parish coun. Holy Trinity Cath. Ch., Washington, 2001-2004. With USN, 1956-58. Mem. Nat. Assn. Life Underwriters (dir. No. Va. 1964-66), Greater Washington Chpt. CLU (bd. dirs., sec., treas., v.p., pres. 1982-91), Million Dollar Roundtable (life, Big Brothers and Big Sisters Merit award), Mensa, U. Md. M Club, Alpha Tau Omega (Silver Circle award 1984). Democrat. Roman Catholic.

BROWNE, RAY BROADUS, popular culture educator; b. Millport, Ala., Jan. 15, 1922; s. Garfield and Annie Nola (Trull) B.; m. Olwyn Orde, Aug. 21, 1952 (dec.); children— Glenn, Kevin; m. Alice Pat Matthews, Aug. 25, 1965; 1 child, Alicia. AB, U. Ala., 1943; A.M., Columbia U., 1947; PhD, UCLA, 1956. Instr. U. Nebr., Lincoln, 1947-50; instr. U. Md., College Park, 1956-60; asst. prof., assoc. prof. Purdue U., Lafayette, Ind., 1960-67; prof. popular culture Bowling Green (Ohio) State U., 1967—, Univ. disting. prof., 1975—. Author, editor: Melville's Drive to Humanism, 1971, Popular Culture and the Expanding Consciousness, 1973, The Constitution and Popular Culture, 1975, Dominant Symbols in Popular Culture, 1990, The Many Tongues of Literacy, 1992, Continuities in Popular Culture, 1993, The Cultures of Celebrations, 1994, Preview 2001: Popular Culture Studies in the Future, 1996, Lincoln-Lore: Lincoln in Contemporary Popular Culture, 1996, Pioneers in Popular Culture Studies, 1998, The Defining Guide to United States Popular Culture, 2000, The Detective as Historian, 2000, Mission Underway: The History of the Popular Culture Association/American Culture Association and Popular Culture Movement, 2002, Popular Culture of the Civil War and Reconstruction, 2003, Murder on the Reservation: American Indian Crime Fiction, 2004, Popular Culture Studies Across the Curriculum, 2005, others; creator, editor Jour. Popular Culture, 1967-82, Jour. Am. Culture, 1977-82. Served with U.S. Army, 1942—46. Mem. Popular Culture Assn. (founder, sec., treas. 1970—), Am. Culture Assn. (sec.-treas. 1977—). Democrat. Avocation: scholarly research. Home: 210 N Grove St Bowling Green OH 43402-2335 Office: Bowling Green U Jour Popular Culture Bowling Green OH 43403-0001 Office Phone: 419-372-7861. Business E-Mail: rbrowne@bgnet.bgsu.edu.

BROWNE, RICHARD CULLEN, lawyer; b. Akron, Ohio, Nov. 21, 1938; s. Francis Cedric and Elizabeth Ann (Cullen) Browne; m. Patricia Anne Winkler, Apr. 23, 1962; children: Richard Cullen, Catherine Anne, Paulette Elizabeth, Maureen Frances, Colleen Marie. BS in Econs., Holy Cross Coll., 1960; JD, Cath. U. Am., 1963. Bar: Va. 1963, U.S. Ct. Claims 1963, U.S. Ct. Customs and Patent Appeals 1963, D.C. 1964, U.S. Ct. Mil. Appeals 1963, U.S. Ct. Appeals (D.C. cir.) 1964, U.S. Supreme Ct. 1966, U.S. Ct. Appeals (fed. cir.) 1982, U.S. Ct. Appeals (9th cir.) 1983, U.S. Ct. Appeals (6th cir.) 1991, U.S. Ct. Appeals (7th cir.) 1998. Assoc. Browne, Beveridge, DeGrandi & Kline, Washington, 1963-68, ptnr., 1968-72, Shaffert, Miller & Browne, Washington, 1972-74; sr. counsel Office of Enforcement EPA, Washington, 1974-76; asst. chief hearing counsel U.S. Nuclear Regulatory Commn., Washington, 1976-78; sole practice Washington, 1978-79; ptnr. Winston & Strawn, Washington, 1980-2001, of counsel, 2001—. Lectr. U. R.I., 1975, Washburn U., 1978, Legal Ins., CSC, 1975—78, Hofstra U., 1987—, Nat. Inst. for Trial Advocacy, 1986—. Del. Montgomery County Civic Fedn., 1970—74; chmn. Citizens Adv. Com. on Rockville Corridor, 1972—77; mem. Montgomery County Potomac River Basin Adv. Com., 1972—74; chmn. Cath. U. Am. Fund, 1996—2001. Capt. JAGC USAF, 1963—66, capt. USAFR, 1966—69. Named Disting. Mil. Grad., Holy Cross Coll., 1960; recipient In Hoc Signo award, 2004. Mem.: Centesimus Annus Pro Pontifice Found. (v.p. 2004—), Cath. U. Gen. Alumni Assn. (bd. govs. 1992—, chair Gibbons medal com. 1995—2001, exec. com. 1995—2001), Cath. U. Law Sch. Alumni Soc. (bd. dirs. 1991—98, pres. 1992—93, bd. visitors 1998—), Coll. Holy Cross General Alumni Assn. (bd. dirs. 1971—78, alumni senate 1978—97, nominations and elections com. 1995—2004, bd. dirs. 1997—, pres. 2002—03). Republican. Home: 7203 Old Stage Rd Rockville MD 20852-4438 Office: Winston & Strawn 1700 K St NW Washington DC 20006 E-mail: rbrowne@alumni.holycross.edu.

BROWNE, SPENCER IVAN, mortgage company executive, Internet company executive; b. 1949; married. BS, U. Pa., 1971; JD (cum laude), Villanova U., 1974. Spl. counsel SEC, 1974—79; ptnr. Brownstein Hyatt & Farber, Denver, 1983-84; pres., dir. MDC Holdings, Inc., 1984-96; pres., CEO, dir. Asset Investors Corp., 1988-96; pres., CEO & dir. Comml. Assets, Inc., 1994-96; with Strategic Asset Mgmt. LLC, Denver, 1996—. Bd. dirs. Annaly Mortgage Mgmt., Delta Fin. Corp., Nexus Resources Inc., Internet Commerce Group. Office: Strategic Asset Mgmt LLC 575 N Shore Dr Miami Beach FL 33141 Office Phone: 303-748-1994. Personal E-mail: sibsam@aol.com. E-mail: spencer@nexusresources.com.

BROWNE, STANHOPE STRYKER, lawyer; b. Colorado Springs, Colo., July 22, 1931; s. Samuel Stanhope Stryker and Florence Jeanette (Reynolds) B.; m. Elizabeth Whitney Sturges, Sept. 12, 1964; children: Katrina C., Whitney R. AB, Princeton U., 1953; LL.B., Harvard U., 1956. Bar: Pa. 1957. Assoc. Dechert LLP, Phila., 1956-65, ptnr., 1965-97, of counsel, 1998—, resident ptnr. Brussels, 1972—76. Lectr. internat. law. Contbr. articles to profl. jours. Chmn. Penn's Landing Corp., Phila., 1981-97, Com. to Preserve Am.'s Birthplace, 1965-72; vice chmn. World Affairs Council, 1978-90; bd. dirs. Phila. 1976 Bicentennial Corp., 1971-72, Greater Phila. Movement, 1970-71, Phila. Port Corp., 1984-90, Ecole Française Internationale de Philadelphie, 1991-99, The Ch. Found., 1998-01, French Heritage Soc., Inc., 1999-05; mem. exec. com. Cen. Phila. Devel. Corp., 1968-72, 77-99; mem. Phila. Dist. Export Council US Dept. Commerce, 1983-96; vice pres. Pa. Prison Soc., 1962-69; pres. Greater Phila. Council of Chs., 1966-67; mem. Diocesan Coun. Episcopal Diocese of Pa., 1967-71; rector's warden St. Peter's Ch., 1983-90, mem. bd. fgn. parishes Episcopal Ch., 2005-; chmn. Democrats Abroad, Belgium, 1975-76, Pa. Internat. Trade Conf., 1977-79; mem. adv. commn. Independence Nat. Hist. Park, Phila., 1969-72; hon. consul of France in Phila., 1986-96; mem. vestry Am. Cathedral in Paris, 2001-02. Recipient Pub. Service and Polit. Courage award Southeastern Pa. chpt. Ams. for Democratic Action, 1965; decorated Nat. Order of Merit, France, 1998. Mem. Phila. Bar Assn., French-Am. C. of C. (bd. dirs. Phila. chpt. 1989-2001), Phila. Com. on Fgn. Rels., Brook Club (N.Y.C.), Phila. Club (bd. dirs. 1988-92), Phi Beta Kappa Democrat. Episcopalian. Office: Dechert LLP 4000 Bell Atlantic Tower 1717 Arch St Philadelphia PA 19103-2793 also: Circa Ctr 2929 Arch St Philadelphia PA 19104 Personal E-mail: stanlibby@verizon.net.

BROWNELL, BLAINE ALLISON, educational association administrator, former academic administrator, history professor; b. Birmingham, Ala., Nov. 12, 1942; s. Blaine Jr. and Annette (Holmes) B.; m. Mardi Ann Taylor, Aug. 21, 1964; children— Blaine, Allison. BA, Washington and Lee U., 1965; MA, U. N.C., 1967, PhD, 1969. Asst. prof. Purdue U., West Lafayette, Ind., 1969-74; assoc. prof., chmn. dept. U. Ala., Birmingham, 1974-78, prof., 1980-90, dean grad. sch., 1978-84, dean social and behavioral scis., 1984-90; provost, v.p. for acad. affairs U. North Tex., Denton, 1990-98; exec. dir. Ctr. Internat. Programs and Svcs. U. Memphis, 1998-2000; pres. Ball State U., Muncie, Ind., 2000—04; CEO U21pedagogica Ltd., Charlottesville, Va., 2004—05. Sr. fellow Johns Hopkins U., Balt., 1971-72; Fulbright lectr. Hiroshima U., Japan, 1977-78; dir. U. Ala. Ctr. Internat. Programs, 1980-90. Author: The Urban Ethos..., 1975, City in Southern History, 1977, Urban America, 1979, 2d edit., 1990, The Urban Nation 1920-80, 1981; editor Jour. Urban History, 1976-90, assoc. editor, 1990-95. Mem. Birmingham City Planning Commn., 1975-77, Jefferson County Planning Commn., 1975-77, Dallas Com. Fgn. Rels., 1990-98; chmn. Birmingham Coun. on Fgn. Rels., 1988-90, Charlottesville Com. Fgn. Rels., 2004—. Mem. Am. Hist. Assn., Orgn. Am. Historians, So. Hist. Assn., Philos. Soc. Tex. Home: 4640 Mockernut Ln Earlysville VA 22936

BROWNELL, EDWIN ROWLAND, banker, civil engineer, land surveyor; b. Tampa, Fla., Sept. 19, 1924; s. Clarence DeWolf and Helen Lucy (Hill) B.; m. Helen Marie Kegel, Jan. 22, 1948 (dec. Apr. 1967); 1 child, Nancy; m. Blanche Rosina Parisi, Dec. 26, 1967; children: Elizabeth, Elaine, Evelyn. BCE, U. Fla., 1947. Registered profl. surveyor, Fla., Ark., Ga., Miss., Nev., N.D., S.D., S.C., Tenn., W.Va. Cadastral engr. City of Miami, Fla., 1948-53; pres., CEO, chmn. E.R. Brownell & Assocs., Inc., Miami, 1953-93, real estate salesman, 1975—; founding dir. Total Bank, 1983—85, Am.'s Bank, 1980—83; pres., chief exec. officer, chmn. Brickellbanc Savs. Assn., Miami, 1985-89, also bd. dirs.; pres. Tri-County Engring. Co., 1983-89, Naples (Fla.) Title and Abstract Co., 1st Title and Abstract Co. Chmn. surveying com. U. Fla., Gainesville, 1974—, mem. pres.'s coun.; mem. nat. engring. degree accreditation team Nat. Coun. Engring. Examiners, Md., 1985-95, mem. team evaluating engring. readiness U.S. Armed Forces, 1980-81; chmn. engring. adv. com. Fla. Bd. Regents, Tallahassee, 1982-85; vice-chmn. legal grievance com. Fla. Bar, 1992-94. Elected county surveyor State of Fla., Dade County, 1956-60; chmn. Zoning Bd. Adjustment, Coral Gables, Fla., 1978-87; chmn. Coral Gables Planning and Zoning Bd., 1987-95; mem. Coral Gables Code Enforcement Bd., 1995-97, City of Coral Gables Historic Preservation Com., 1997, City of Coral Gables Constrn. Regulation Bd., 1997-2005; bd. dirs. Boys Club of Miami, 1980-83, Salvation Army South Fla., dir., 1990-94 Named Man of Yr., Dade County, Fla., 1989. Master Am. Contract Bridge Assn. (nat.); fellow Am. Congress Surveying and Mapping (hon. life, pres. 1980-81, Surveying Excellence award 1977, Miami Man Yr. 1990, Presdl. award 1994), NSPE, Nat. Soc. Profl. Surveyors (pres. 1978-79), Fla. Surveying and Mapping Soc. (hon., life), Profl. Surveyors and Mappers (pres. 1981), Fla. Soc. Profl. Land Surveyors (hon. life mem., Fla. Land Surveyor of Yr. 1973, pres. 1972, pres. Dade County chpt. 1965-69, hon., life mem. Dade County chpt. 1993); mem. AIA, NSF, Profl. Surveyors of Fla. (bd. dirs., chmn. 1993-94), Am. Soc. Photogrammetry and Remote Sensing (Presdl. citation 1982, 91, Merit award 1992), Am. Soc. Photogrammetry Found. (vice chmn. 1985-91), Am. Mil. Engrs., Am. Planning Assn., Internat. Geog. Info. Found. (vice-chmn.), Miami Bd. Realtors, Fla. Engring. Soc. (bd. dirs. 1992-94), Fla. Planning and Zoning Assn. (S. Fla. chpt.), Fla. Assn. Cadastral Mappers, Bus. Inc., Sierra Club (pres. 1977), Com. of 100, Bus. Inc., Granada Golf Assn., 10th Holers Golf Assn. (treas. 1995-96, pres. 1996-97, pres. 2003-04), Coral Gables Country Club Fleet, Coral Gables 30 Yr. Club, Coral Gables Fin. Club (pres. 1998-01), U. Miami Yacht Club, Century Club Coral Gables (exec. sec., treas. 1993-96), Coral Gables Country Club (dir., pres. 1991-97, chmn., vice chmn. found. 1992-94, pres. fin. club 1998-02), Riviera Country Club 9 (fin. com.), Holly Hills Country Club (NC), Computer Club Coral Gables (bd. dirs.), U. Miami Sailing Club, Kiwanis (pres. Southwest Miami chpt. 1979-81), Elks, Duplicate Bridge Nat. Master, Lambda Alpha Internat., Kappa Alpha Republican. Roman Catholic. Avocations: golf, bridge, travel. Home: 1207 Sorolla Ave Coral Gables FL 33134-3515 E-mail: ebrow40862@aol.com.

BROWNELL, F. WILLIAM, lawyer; b. Ashland, Wis., July 18, 1952; BS, Georgetown Univ., 1974, MS, JD, Georgetown Univ., 1978. Bar: DC 1978, lic.: US Ct. Appeals, DC 1979, US Supreme Ct. 1983, US Ct. Appeals, 11th Cir. 1987, US Ct. Appeals, 2nd, 7th Cir. 1988. Ptnr., resources, regulatory, environ. law Hunton & Williams LLP, Washington. Mem.: ABA, Phi Beta Kappa. Office: Hunton & Williams 1900 K St NW Washington DC 20006-1109 Office Phone: 202-955-1555. Office Fax: 202-778-2201. Business E-Mail: bbrownell@hunton.com.

BROWNELL, GORDON LEE, physicist, researcher; b. Duncan, Okla., Apr. 8, 1922; s. Roscoe David and Mabel (Gourley) B.; m. Anna-Liisa Kairento; children: Wendy Silverman, Peter G., David L., James K., Piia Kairento, Janne Kairento. BS, Bucknell U., Lewisburg, Pa., 1944; PhD, Mass. Inst. Tech., 1950. Mem. faculty MIT, 1950—, prof., 1970-91, prof. emeritus, 1991—; dir. Physics Rsch. Lab., Mass. Gen. Hosp., Boston, 1950—. Bd. dirs. Neuroresearch Found. Served to lt. (j.g.) USNR, 1944-46. Fellow Am. Phys. Soc., Am. Nuclear Soc., Am. Coll. Radiology (hon.); mem. Am. Assn. Physicists in Medicine (Coolidge award 1987), Soc. Nuclear Medicine (Paul C. Aebersold award 1975), European Soc. Nuclear Medicine (de Hevesy medal 1979, 2003), Inst. Med. Nat. Acad. Clubs: Union Boat (Boston). Home: 45 Warren St Salem MA 01970-3132 Office: Mass Gen Hosp Physics Rsch Lab Boston MA 02114 also: MIT Cambridge MA 02139 E-mail: g.brownell@verizon.net.

BROWNELL, KELLY DAVID, psychologist, educator; b. Evansville, Ind., Oct. 31, 1951; s. Arnold Buffum and Margaret Elizabeth (Egly) Brownell; m. Mary Jo Gabriele, Aug. 20, 1977; children: Matthew Joseph, Kevin David, Kristy Elizabeth. BA, Purdue U., 1973; PhD, Rutgers U., 1977. Lic. clin. psychologist Conn. Postdoctoral fellow Brown U., Providence, 1977; from asst. prof. to assoc. prof. U. Pa., Phila., 1977—87, prof., 1987-90; prof. psychology Yale U., New Haven, 1991—, prof. epidemiology and pub. health, chair dept. psychology, 2003—, dir. Yale Ctr. Eating and Weight Disorders, 1994-2000, master of Silliman Coll. Author: (book) Handbook of Eating Disorders, 1986, Handbook of Behavioral Medicine, 1988, Eating Disorders in Athletes, 1991, Eating Disorders and Obesity, 1995, vol. 2, 2002, Behavioral Medicine and Women, 1998, Food Fight, 2004; contbr. articles to profl. jours. Recipient Cattell award, N.Y. Acad. Scis., 1978, Choice award, ALA, 1989. Fellow: APA (pres. divsn. health psychology 1989—90), Acad. Behavioral Medicine Rsch., Soc. Behavioral Medicine (pres. 1988—89); mem.: Assn. Advancement Behavior Therapy (pres. 1988—89). Office: Yale U Dept Psychology Box 208205 New Haven CT 06520-8205 Office Phone: 203-432-7790. E-mail: kelly.brownell@yale.edu.

BROWNELL, PATRICIA JANE, social worker, educator; b. Platteville, Wis., July 14, 1943; d. Richard and Thelma (Rowe) B.; m. James Gale Collins, Mar. 5, 1996. BA, U. Wis., 1967; MSW, Fordham U., 1978, PhD,

1994. Cert. social worker, N.Y. Caseworker dept. social svcs. Human Resources Adminstrn., N.Y.C., 1967-73, project coord. office spl. housing svcs., 1973-77, project mgr. office adminstrv. svcs., 1977-78, grants mgr., rsch. asst., sr. planner policy/program devel., 1978-83, exec. asst. to exec. dep. and dep. commr. home care svcs., 1983-90, dir. spl. projects office exec. dep. commr. family support, 1990-94, dep. dir. non-residential svcs. domestic violence program, 1994, adv. to exec. dep. commr. family support adminstrn., 1995—; from instr. to adj. prof. Fordham U. Grad. Sch. Social Svc., N.Y.C., 1990-94, asst. prof., 1995—. Vis. prof. behavioral sci. dept. Police Acad./N.Y.C. Police Dept., 2001—; adv. bd. Mary's House, 2000—; sec. DW Fin. Mgmt. Agy., 1995-97; cons. N.Y.C. Dept. for the Aging, 1998—; rsch. assoc. Ctr. for Hispanic Mental Health Rsch., 2000—; ad hoc coord. Fordham-St. James Field Placement and Cmty. Practice Project, 2000—; steering com. Interdisciplinary Ctr. for Family and Child Advocacy, 1997—; dir. profl. devel. Interdisciplinary Tng. for Pub. Child Welfare Workers and Supr. to Improve Child Welfare Svcs., 1997-2000; liaison Influencing State Policy, 1997— Co-author: Work with Older People: Challenges and Opportunities, 1994, Helping Battered Women: New Perspectives and Remedies, 1996, Social Work in Juvenile and Criminal Justice Settings, 2d edit., 1997, Multicultural Perspectives in Working with Families, 1997; (with E.P. Congress and I. Abelman) Battered Women and their Families: Intervention and Treatment Strategies, 1998; (with J. Berman) To Grandmother's House We Go and Stay: Perspectives on Custodial Grandparents, 2000; (with M. Moch) Social Work in the Era of Devolution: Toward a Just Practice, 2001; mem. editl. bd. (newsletter) Victimization of the Elderly and Disabled: Preventing Abuse, Mistreatment and Neglect, 1997—; contbr. articles to profl. jours. Bd. dirs. Fund for the Advancement Social Svcs., 1998—; steering com. N.Y.C. Elder Abuse Coalition, 1995—. Faculty Rsch. grantee Fordham U., 1996-97, 99—, N.Y.C. Dept. for the Aging grant, 1999—; Ravazzin scholar Ravazzin Ctr. for Social Work Rsch. in Aging, 1998—; Rational Emotive Inst. fellow, 1995; recipient Linda Mills Meml. award N.Y. State Divsn. Parole, 1993, Faculty Merit award, 1996-2000. Mem. NASW (welfare reform task force N.Y. chpt. 1994—, nominating com., del. assembly 2000—), State Soc. on Aging N.Y. (nominating com. 1999—, exec. com., co-chair social policy com. 2001—) Avocations: reading, yoga, drawing. Office: Fordham U Grad Sch Social Svc 113 W 60th St New York NY 10023 E-mail: brownell@fordham.edu.

BROWNELL, WILLIAM EDWARD, biophysics professor, researcher; b. Augusta, Ga., Oct. 17, 1942; s. Harold Cox Brownell and Loris Irene Miller; m. Nancy Jane Schulson, May 1, 1968; children: Isaac Franklin-Miller, Mia Frances Irene, Aaron Schulson. BS, U. Chgo., 1968, PhD, 1973. Instr. US peace corps Edo Coll., Benin City, Nigeria, 1965—66; asst. to assoc. prof. U. Fla., Gainesville, 1974—85; assoc. to full prof. Johns Hopkins Sch. Medicine, Baltimore, Md., 1985—94; prof., jake and nina kamin chair Baylor Coll. Medicine, Houston, 1994—. Invited prof. U. Geneva, 1982—83; INSERM rsch. prof. U. Montpellier, France, 1984; adj. prof. Rice U., Houston, 2000—. Recipient Claude Pepper award, NIH, NIDCD, 1990-1997, Kresge, Mirmelstein Sci. Merit award, 1994, Spl. Friends of People with Hearing Loss award, Self Help for Hard of Hearing, 1995, Med. and Biol. Scis. Disting. Svc. Alumni award, U. Chgo., 1997, Michael E. DeBakey Excellence in Rsch. award, 2001; Rsch. grants, NIH, NSF, 1975—, Rsch. stipend, Roche Rsch. Found., 1982-1983, Fulbright scholar, French Fulbright Program, 1984. Mem.: Am. Physiol. Soc., Biophysical Soc., Soc. for Neuroscience, Assn. Rsch. in Otolaryngology (pres. 2004—05), Sigma Xi. Achievements include discovery of outer hair cell electromotility; voltage dependent lipid lateral diffusion. Avocations: travel, motorcycling, in-line skating.

BROWNER, CAROL M., former federal agency administrator; d. Michael Browner and Isabella Harty Hugues; m. Michael Podhorzer; 1 child, Zachary. Grad., U. Fla., 1977, JD, 1979. Gen. counsel govt. ops. com. Fla. Ho. of Reps., 1980; with Citizen Action, Washington; chief legis. aide environ. issues to Sen. Lawton Chiles, 1986—88; legis. dir. to Sen. Al Gore, Jr., 1988-91; sec. Dept. Environ. Regulation, Fla., 1991-93; administr. EPA, Washington, 1993—2000; principal The Albright Group L.L.C., 2001—. Mem. adv. coun. Harvard Med. Sch., Ctr. for Health and the Global Environment. Democrat. Office: The Albright Group 901 15th St NW Ste 1000 Washington DC 20005

BROWNFIELD, WILLIAM R., ambassador; b. Fort Bragg, N.C., May 1952; m. Kristie A. Kenney. BA, Cornell U., 1974; Student, U. Tex. Sch. of Law, 1976—78; grad., Nat. War Coll., 1993. Entered fgn. svc. U.S. Dept. State, 1979, polit. adviser to comdr.-in-chief U.S. So. Command, 1989—90, counselor for humanitarian affairs Geneva, 1995—98, prin. dep. asst. sec. for internat. narcotics and law enforcement, 1998—99, dep. asst. sec. of state for Western Hemisphere Washington, 1999—2002, U.S. amb. to Chile, 2002—04. Office: Am Embassy Caracas-Venezula Apo AA 34037

BROWN-GRAYSON, RON, foundation administrator, writer; s. Elizabeth Clara Turner-Frank and Howard Joseph Frank (Stepfather), Robert Lynn and Katie Lou Brown (Stepmother). Grad., Nat. Conservatory Dramatic Arts, 1985, William Esper Studios (Sanford Meisner Acting Technique) - NYC Conservatory, 1993; MDiv, Sch. Of Universal Resonance & Creative Empowerment, N.Mex., 2002, D, Sch. Of Universal Resonance & Creative Empowerment, 2002. Exec. asst. to exec. dir. Nat. Crime Prevention Coun., Washington, 1987—91; mgr. theatre N.Y. Theatre Workshop, New York City, 1991—96; pres., co-founder Source Legacy Found., Rio Rancho, N.Mex., 2002—. Pres. bd. dirs. Source Legacy Found., Rio Rancho, 2002—; actor stage, TV, comml. and film work. Author: (book, published) The Source Legacy Workbook - Volume One, (television pilot) Milagros, (play) Straight Down Christopher Street, I Will Come Back, (book) The Source Legacy Workbook - Vol. Two, The Source Legacy Workbook - Vol. Three, (novel) The Indigo Triptych. Mem.: AFTRA, Actors' Equity Assn. Office: Source Legacy Foundation PO Box 15126 Rio Rancho NM 87174-0126 Office Phone: 505-891-7699. Personal E-mail: sourcelegacy@aol.com.

BROWNING, CHRISTOPHER R., historian, educator; b. Durham, N.C., May 22, 1944; s. Robert Willard and Eleanor (Oechsli) B.; m. Jennifer Jane Horn; children: Kathryn, Anne. BA, Oberlin Coll., 1967; MA, U. Wis., 1968, PhD, 1975. Instr. history Allegheny Coll., Meadville, Pa., 1969-71; asst. prof. history Pacific Luth. U., Tacoma, 1974-79, assoc. prof., 1979-84, prof., 1984-97, disting. univ. prof., 1997-99; Frank Porter Graham prof. history U. N.C., Chapel Hill, 1999—. J.B. and Maurice C. Shapiro sr. scholar in residence U.S. Holocaust Mus., 1996, Ina Levine scholar, 2002-03; George Macaulay Trevelyan lectr. Cambridge U., 1999; George L. Mosse lectr. U. Wis., Madison, 2002. Author: The Final Solution and the German Foreign Office, 1978, Fateful Months, 1985, Ordinary Men, 1992 (Nat. Jewish Book award 1993), The Path to Genocide, 1992, Nazi Policy, Jewish Workers, German Killers, 2000, Collected Memories: Holocaust History and Post-War Testimony, 2003, The Origins of the Final Solution, 2004 (Nat. Jewish Park award 2004). Woodrow Wilson fellow, 1967-68, Alexander von Humboldt fellow, Germany, 1980-81, Fulbright rsch. fellow, Israel, 1989, Inst. for Advanced Studies fellow, Princeton, N.J., 1995. Office: U NC Dept History Chapel Hill NC 27599-0001

BROWNING, COLLEEN, artist, educator; b. U.K. came to U.S., 1949; d. Langley and Violet (Cairnes) B.; m. Geoffrey Wagner. Cert., Spade Sch. Art, Eng. Instr. art CCNY, Prat Inst., N.Y.C., Nat. Acad. Design, N.Y.C. One-woman shows include Kennedy Galleries, N.Y.C., Wichita Art Mus., 1987, Butler Inst. Am. Art, 1991, Nev. Mus. Art, 1994, So. Alleghenies Mus. Art, 1997; featured in articles in N.Y. Times, Newsweek, Glamor mag., others; author: Working Out a Painting, 1988. Recipient Art award Butler Inst. Art, Youngstown, Ohio, Nat. Acad. Design, N.Y.C. Office: Kennedy Galleries 40 W 57th St New York NY 10019-4001

BROWNING, COLLEEN APPLEGATE, elementary school educator; b. Ribolt, Ky., Mar. 26, 1938; d. Glen Carl and Lena May (Spence) Applegate; m. John Turner Browning, Oct. 20, 1956. BA, Morehead State U., 1962; MA, Purdue U., 1966, Ednl. Specialist, 1974. Cert. in elem. edn., K-6, 7-8, reading K-12, neurologically impaired K-12, elem. adminstrn., supervision K-6, Ind.; elem. edn. 1-6, reading K-12, Fla. Elem. tchr. Tippecanoe Sch. Corp., Lafayette, Ind., 1962-72, diagnostic tchr., 1972-75; media specialist Lafayette Sch. Corp., 1975-79, learning resource tchr., 1979-90, 91-93; elem. tchr. Marion County Sch. System, Ocala, Fla., 1990-91. Fund-raiser Pub. Schs. Found., Lafayette, 1988-89. Purdue U. fellow, 1972. Mem. AAUW, NEA (adv. bd. pubs. 1976—), Tippecanoe Edn. Assn. (officer/com. 1962-75), Ind. State Tchrs. Assn. (workshop dir. 1972-75), Environ. Edn. Assn. (treas. 1970-72), Friends of the Libr., C. of C. of Lafayette, Lafayette Edn. Assn., Greater Lafayette Coun. of Internat. Reading Assn. Avocations: sewing, horseback riding, biking, reading. Home: 2215 NE 6th Pl Ocala FL 34470-9207

BROWNING, JAMES ROBERT, federal judge; b. Great Falls, Mont., Oct. 1, 1918; s. Nicholas Henry and Minnie Sally (Foley) Browning; m. Marie Rose Chapell. BA, Mont. State U., Missoula, 1938; LLB with honors, U. Mont., 1941, LLD (hon.), 1978, Santa Clara U., 1989. Bar: Mont. 1941, D.C. 1953, U.S. Supreme Ct. 1952. Spl. atty. antitrust div. Dept. Justice, 1941—43, spl. atty. gen. litigation sect. antitrust div., 1946—48, chief antitrust dept. N.W. regional office, 1948—49; asst. chief gen. litigation sect. antitrust div. Dept. Justice (N.W. regional office), 1949—51, 1st asst. civil div., 1951—52; exec. asst. to atty. gen. U.S., 1952—53; chief U.S. (Exec. Office for U.S. Attys.), 1953; pvt. practice Washington, 1953—58; lectr. N.Y.U. Sch. Law, 1953, Georgetown U. Law Center, 1957—58; clk. Supreme Ct. U.S., 1958—61; judge U.S. Ct. Appeals 9th Circuit, 1961—76, chief judge, 1976—88, judge, 1988—2000, sr. judge, 2000—. Reed justice com. on continuing edn., tng. and adminstrn. Jud. Conf. of U.S., 1967—68, com. on ct. adminstrn., 1969—71, chmn. subcom. on jud. stats., 1969—71, com. to study the illustrative rules of jud. misconduct, 1969, com. on the budget, 1971—77, adminstrn. office, subcom. on budget, 1974—76, mem., 1976—88, exec. com. of conf., 1978—87, com. to study the illustrative rules of jud. misconduct, 1985—87, com. to study U.S. jud. conf., 1986—88, com. on internat. conf. of appellate judges, 1987—90; David T. Lewis disting. judge-in-residence U. Utah, 1987; Blankenbaker lectr. U. Mont., 1987; Sibley lectr. U. Ga., 1987; lectr. Human Rights Inst., Santa Clara U. Sch. Law, Strasbourg. Editor-in-chief: Mont. Law Rev. Dir. Western Justice Found.; chmn. 9th Cir. Hist. Soc. 1st lt. U.S. Army, 1943—46. Decorated Bronze Star; named to, Order of the Grizzly, U. Mont., 1973; recipient Devitt Disting. Svc. to Justice award, 1990; scholar in residence, Santa Clara U., 1989, U. Mont., 1991. Mem.: FBA (bd. dirs. 1945—61, nat. coun. 1958—62), ABA (judge adv. com. to standing com. on Ethics and Profl. Responsibility 1973—75), Am. Soc. Legal History (adv. bd. jour.), Am. Judicature Soc. (chmn. com. on fed. judiciary 1973—74, bd. dirs. 1972—75, Herbert Harley award 1984), Inst. Jud. Adminstrn., Am. Law Inst., Mont. Bar Assn. (Jameson award 2001), D.C. Bar Assn., Nat. Lawyers Club (bd. govs. 1959—63). Office: US Ct Appeals 9th Cir PO Box 193939 San Francisco CA 94119-3939 *Notable cases include: pro bono case Bell vs. U.S., 349 U.S. 81, 1955.**

BROWNING, JANE LOUISE, social services administrator; b. Omaha, Dec. 7, 1947; d. Dale Paul and Esther Lucille (Quick) Schmidt; m. John William Browning III, July 29, 1978; children: John William IV, Paul Cornelius. Student, Northwestern U., 1966-68; BA in English Lit. cum laude, U. Tex., Dallas, 1978. Citizen advocacy coord. The Arc of Denver, 1972-74; pub. info. specialist The Arc of the U.S., Arlington, Tex., 1974-78; asst. dir. Ark. Endowment for Humanities, Little Rock, 1979-82, exec. dir., 1982-89; pres., CEO Word Work, Little Rock, 1989-90; dir. devel. The Arc of Md., Annapolis, 1991-95; exec. dir. Md. Coalition for Inclusive Edn., Balt., 1995-96; dir. divsn. membership & publs. NASW, Washington, 1997-98; exec. dir President's com. on mental retardation, Washington, 1999—2000; dep. dir. Nat. Assn. Women Judges, 2001; exec. dir. Learning Disabilities Assn., 2001—. Exec. com. Ark. Developmental Disabilities Coun., Little Rock, 1982-87; appointee, mem. Pres.'s Com. on Mental Retardation, Washington, 1994-2000; mem. nominating com. The Arc-U.S. The Arc-U.S. Congress States, 1997—. Co-author: (textbook) An Arkansas History for Young People, 1991, 3d edit., 2002. Mem. PEO, Am. Soc. Assn. Execs. Democrat. Episcopalian.

BROWNING, JAY D., energy executive; BBA in Fin., MBA, JD, Tex. Tech. U. Atty., corp./transactional divsn. Baker & Botts, LLP, Austin, Tex.; assoc., corp. and securities divsn. Akin, Gump, Strauss, Hauer & Feld, LLP, San Antonio; various legal pos. Valero Energy Corp., San Antonio, corp. sec., mng. atty. corp. law, v.p., 2002. Office: Valero Corp Hdqrs One Valero Way San Antonio TX 78249

BROWNING, PETER CRANE, packaging company executive; b. Boston, Sept. 2, 1941; s. Ralph Leslie and Nancy (Crane) Browning; m. Carole Ann Shegog, Dec. 14, 1963 (div. 1974); children: Christina, Jennifer; m. Kathryn Anne Klucharich, July 27, 1974; children: Kimberley, Peter. AB in History, Colgate U., 1963; MBA, U. Chgo., 1976. Salesman, mktg. mgr. White Cap divsn. Continental Can, Northbrook, Ill., 1964-75; mgr. mktg. Conally Venture divsn. Continental Can, 1975-79; gen. mktg. and sales mgr. Bondware divsn. Continental Can, 1979-81, v.p., gen. mgr., 1981-84; v.p. gen. mgr. White Cap. div. Continental Can, 1984-86, exec. v.p., oper. officer, 1987-89; pres. Gold Bond Bldg. Products div. Nat. Gypsum Co., Charlotte, NC, 1989-90; pres., chmn., CEO Nat. Gypsum Co., Charlotte, 1990-93; exec. v.p. Sonoco Products Co., Hartsville, SC, 1993-96, pres., COO, 1996-98, pres., CEO, 1998-2000. Chmn. bd. dirs. Nucor corp., Wachovia Corp., Lowe's Cos., Inc., Phoenix Cos., Inc., Acuity Brands, Inc., ENPRO Industries; dean McColl Grad. Sch. Bus. Queens U., Charlotte, 2002—05. Life mem. coun. Grad. Sch./U. Chgo. Mem.: DeBordieu Country Club, Quail Hollow Country Club. Republican. Episcopalian. Avocations: mountain climbing, running, reading. Home: 2038 Providence Rd Charlotte NC 28211

BROWNING, ROBERT DAVID, music educator; b. Honolulu, June 11, 1965; s. Benjamin M. and Mary Helen Browning; m. Connie Turner Browning, July 13, 1992; children: Ashley, Elizabeth. B in Music Edn., U. Cin., 1987; MusM in Conducting, James Madison U., Harrisonburg, 1993. Cert. music tchr., K-12 State of Ohio. Band dir. Sunman-Dearborn Mid. Sch., St. Leon, Ind., 1988—91, Lauderdale County Schs., Ripley, Tenn., 1993—94; tchg. asst. James Madison U., Harrisonburg, Va., 1991—93; band dir., music tchr., chair music dept. Moeller HS, Cin., 1994—. Profl. trumpeter, Cin., 1983—; pvt. trumpet instr., Cin., 1985—. Recipient Tchg. Assistantship, James Madison U., 1991—93. Mem.: Music Educators Nat. Conf. Avocations: reading, philosophy, history, literature, physical fitness. Office: Moeller HS 9001 Montgomery Rd Cincinnati OH 45242 Office Phone: 513-792-3350.

BROWNING, ROBERT LYNN, retired theology studies educator; b. Gallatin, Mo., June 19, 1924; s. Robert W. and Nelle J. (Trotter) B.; m. Jean Beatty, Dec. 27, 1947 (dec. 1977); children: Gregory, David, Peter, Lisa; m. Jackie L. Rogers, Aug. 26, 1979. BA, Mo. Valley Coll., 1945; MDiv, Union Theol. Sem., 1948; PhD, Ohio State U., 1960; postgrad., Columbia U., 1951—53, Oxford U., 1978—79, postgrad., 1984—85. Ordained to ministry Disciples of Christ Ch., 1947, transferred to United Meth. Ch., 1949. Min. edn. Old Stone Ch., Meadville, Pa., 1946—51, Cmty. Ch. at Cir., Mt. Vernon, NY, 1951—53, North Broadway United Meth. Ch., Columbus, Ohio, 1953—59; prof. Christian edn. Meth. Theol. Sch., Delaware, Ohio, 1959—72, William A. Chryst prof. Christian edn., 1972—89, prof. emeritus, 1989—. Sr. counselor Coun. for Ethics in Econs., 1989—; pres. Meth. Conf. on Christian Edn., 1967-69; exec. dir. Commn. on Role of The Professions in Soc., Fellow Acad. for Contemporary Problems, 1974-76, commn. bd., 1976—; mem. Ohio Ethics Commn., 1999—. Author: Communicating with Junior Highs, 1968, Guidelines for Youth Ministry, 1970, What on Earth Are You Doing, 1966; (audiotape with Charles Foster) Communicating the Faith with Children, 1971, Ways the Bible Comes Alive, 1975, Ways Persons Become Christian, 1976 (with Charles Foster, Everett Tilson) Looking at Leadership with the Eyes of Biblical Faith, 1978, (with Roy Reed) The Sacraments in Religious Education and Liturgy: An Ecumenical Model, 1985, Models of Confirmation and Baptismal Affirmation: Liturgical and Educational Issues and Designs, 1995, Forgiveness, Reconciliation and Moral Courage: Motives and Designs for Ministry in a Troubled World, 2004; contbg. author: An Introduction to Christian Education, 1966, Counseling and Psychotherapy: Classics on Theories and Issues, 1975, Foundations for Christian Education in an Era of Change, 1976, Preventing Adolescent Alienation: An Interprofessional Approach, 1983, Children, Parents and Change, 1984, Interprofessional Education, 1987, Congregations: Their Power to Form and Transform, 1988, Handbook for Families, 1998, Personal Narratives About the History of Methodist Christian Education in the Twentieth Century, 1999; editor: Integration: Objective Studies and Practical Theology, Proc. Assn. Profl. Edn. for Ministry, 1981, The Pastor as Religious Educator, 1989; contbr. articles on religious edn. to profl. jours. Bd. dirs. Southside Settlement, columbus, 1968-74, Tray-Lee Ctr., Columbus, 1955-59, Ohio State U. Wesleyan Found., 1960-78, vice chmn., 1976-78; bd. ministry ohio West Conf. United Meth. Ch., 1982-89. With USN, 1942-45. Recipient Paul Hinkhouse award Religious Pub. Rels. Coun. Am., 1971. Mem. Assn. for Profl. Edn. for Ministry (editor proc. 1980-82), Religious Edn. Assn., Assn. for Profs. and Rschrs. in Religious Edn. (pres. 1989), United Meth. Profs. Christian Edn. Home: 6613 Hawthorne St Worthington OH 43085-3071 Fax: 614-885-2059. E-mail: bobbrowni@cs.com.

BROWNING, ROY WILSON, III, former mortgage banking executive; b. Enid, Okla., Mar. 27, 1952; s. Roy W. Jr. and Geraldine L. (Green) B.; m. Ann Karlene Trousdale, May 31, 1974; children: Kamden, Karina, Christopher. BS in Acctg., Phillips U., 1974. CPA, Okla., Kans. Audit Arthur Andersen & Co., Oklahoma City, 1974-81; treas., CFO, Clements Energy, Inc., Oklahoma City, 1981-82; CFO, Atlas Investment Corp., Oklahoma City, 1982-85; exec. v.p. Metmor Fin., Inc. subs. Met. Life Ins. Co., Overland Park, Kans., 1985-95; exec v.p., CFO, Greenpoint Mortgage Corp, Charlotte, NC, from 1995. Trustee Phillips U., Enid, 1993—. Mem. AICPA, Kans. Soc. CPA's, Mortgage Bankers Assn. Am. (chmn. fin. mgmt. com. 1994), Hallbrook Country Club, Rotary (bd. dirs. Overland Park 1986—). Republican. Mem. Ch. of Nazarene. Avocations: golf, travel, reading. Office: GreenPoint Mortgage Corp 5032 Parkway Plaza Blvd Charlotte NC 28217-1962 Home: 19356 E Fair Pl Aurora CO 80016-3822

BROWNING, TERRI L., secondary school educator; b. Winfield, Kans., Aug. 9, 1956; d. G. Norman and Veloris Chamberlain; m. Jim L. Browning; children: Lacey M., Skye B. Callison. BA, Kans. Newman U., 1994. English tchr. Oxford (Kans.) H.S., 1994—. No. Ctrl. Assn. bldg. chair Oxford Jr.-Sr. H.S., 1996—; coord. dist. leadership team Unified Sch. Dist. 358, Oxford, 2000—. Pres., bd. dirs. Oxford Pub. Libr. Bd., 1994—2004; ministries com. First United Meth. Ch., Oxford, 2000—04. Mem.: Kans. Assn. Tchrs. of English (bd. dirs. 2004—). Democrat. Home: PO Box 383 Oxford KS 67119 Office: Oxford HS 501 N Water Oxford KS 67119 Office Phone: 620-455-2410.

BROWNING WRIGHT, DIANA M., psychologist, consultant; d. Al Browning and Margaret Couch; m. Dale Stuart Wright (div.); children: LIndsay L. Wright, Brendan Wright. BA in Social Scis., San Diego State U., 1971; MS in Counseling, Calif. State U., LA, 1982; student, Waseda U., Tokyo, 1983—86. Lic. ednl. psychologist Calif. Bd. Behavioral Examiners, cert. sch. psychologist Calif., behavior analyst Calif., advanced tng. and specialization-behavior analysis Calif. Assn. Sch. Psychologists; tchr. Calif. Mental health officer Iowa Security Med. Facility, Iowa City, 1972; tchr. All Sts. Sch., Cedar Rapids, Iowa, 1972—74, Iowa City Schs., 1975—78; classroom cons. Los Angeles County Schs., 1980—82; cons. Spl. Edn. Resource Network, 1985—86; consulting psychologist Tokyo, 1985—86; sch. psychologist El Monte (Calif.) City Sch. Dist., 1986—88, Arcadia (Calif.) Unified Sch. Dist., 1988—91; pvt. practice ednl. psychologist Calif., 1988—; trainer, behavior analyst, sch. psychologist Diagnostic Ctr. So. Calif. Calif. Dept. Edn., LA, 1991—; dir. Positive Environments Network Trainers, LA, 1999—. Adj. asst. prof. Calif. State U., LA, 1986—95, Long Beach State U., 1995—96; trainer, cons. Santa Clarita Preschool Project, 1995—96; project dir. Pasadena Unified Sch. Dist., 1996—97; project dir., cons. LA Unified Sch. Dist., 1996; faculty LRP Scpl. Edn. Nat. Conv., 2000—. Contbg. editor: Nat. Assn. Sch. Psychologists, 2000—; contbr. articles to profl. jours. Recipient cert. of Appreciation for Svc. to Individuals with Autism, Autism Soc. Am., 1993, Commitment to Welfare of Children plaque, Calif. Assn. Sch. Psychologists, 1994, cert. of Recognition for Outstanding Contbn. to Field of Spl. Edn., S.W. SELPA, 1998, Meritorious Work in Spl. Edn., Calif. State Fedn./Coun. Exceptional Children, 1999, cert. of Recognition, Calif. Assn. Resource Specialists and Spl. Edn. Tchrs., 1999—2002; Dick Dodge scholar, 1980—82, Belva Owens scholar, 1980—82, Mabel Wilson Richards scholar, 1980—82. Office: Calif Dept Edn 4339 State University Los Angeles CA 90032

BROWN LEATHERBERRY, THOMAS HENRY, performing company executive, glergyman; b. Wilmington, Del., June 24, 1930; s. Glenn Ford and Rita (Leatherberry) Brown; m. Grace L. Wilson, Mar. 1, 1950 (div. 1978), m. Wendolyn M. King, Oct. 8, 2002; children: Linda Henry, Patricia Williams, Lucinda Brown, Martha Baccus, Tommy Jr. (dec.), Jason James. Student, Carnegie Hall Sr. Drama Sch., N.Y.C., 1961; A. in Engring. Comms., N.Y. Sch. Announcing, N.Y.C., 1968; BA in Behavioral Sci. and Bibl. Edn., U. Del.; M Bibl. Theology, Ea. Bapt. U.; DD (hon.), Trinity Coll., Knoxville, Tenn., 1970. Artist, comedian Mantan Moreland, N.Y.C., 1959-62; road mgr., negotiator Langston Hughes Prodns., N.Y.C., 1963-66; dir. music Chs. of God in Christ, Bklyn., 1968-78; dir. arts Gospel Arts Coalition, Inc., Wilmington, 1978—; pastor Bible Way House of Prayer Worldwide Inc., Wilmington, 1989—; minister of music Bibleway Mid-Atlantic Diocese, Balt., 1990—. Dir. asst. Alvin Ailey Dancers, N.Y.C., 1963; disk jockey Sta. WWRL, N.Y.C., 1969, tchr. Christina Cultural Arts, Wilmington, 1983-89; music dir. World Christian Fellowship, 1989—. Dir. recs. Rite Enterprise Rec. Co., 1954; actor Prodigal Son, 1963, Black Nativity, 1964; asst. to producer (TV) MD, 1967; stage dir., program mgr. Gospel Music shows, CBS-TV, 1967; author (radio) America Calls, 1967, Israel Radio Calls, 1967; dir., engr. RCA Inst. TV, Sta. ABC-TV, 1968. Program dir. Y.M.C.A., Wilmington, 1978-81; entertainer for Gov. Dupont, State of Del., 1980; dir. gospel music coun. 6602, City of Wilmington, 1983. With U.S. Army, 1950-53. Named State Leader, African Am. Proclamation Inc., Phila., 1983; recipient Attestation Pilgrimage award, Minister of Courison, Jerusalem, 1983, award of Grand Performance, Jewish Community Rels. Com., Wilmington, 1988. Mem. BMI, Am. Guild Authors and Composers, Trinity Coll. Alumni Assn., Am. Legion (chaplain Brandywine, Del.), VFW (life), Masons (grand music dir. 1989—, past worshipful master, illustrious master, imperial dep. chaplain 1997—, past grand high priest, 33 degree, hon. past emperial potentate, 2002, royal select master thrice, Ill. master), Order Ea. Star (past worthy patron), Shriners, Elks (Appreciation award Paul Lawrence Dunbar lodge #106 1981), Heroines of Jericho (grand Joshua), Honor Guard Assn. (lt. col.), Del. Phylaxis Soc. (pres.), Epsilon Delta Psi (life). Democrat. Avocations: football, basketball, movies, playing organ and piano.

BROWNLEE, CHRISTINE, elementary school educator; b. Houston, Miss., Dec. 7, 1948; d. Thomas Larry and Glynder Brownlee. *Parents, Thomas and Glynder Brownlee, started selling fruits and vegetables on a truck in 1967. They later moved into a building in 1978, which is currently Brownlee and Son's Market. Thomas and Glynder have been married sixty years. They have received numerous awards including Small Business awards from the Urban League and NAACP. Father was nominated by a news channel to go to Washington D.C. for an award. They have sponsored a Little League baseball team for twenty years.* BS, Ball State U., 1974; M, Ind. U., 1978; attended, Aenon Bible Coll., 1996—97. Cert. tchr. Ind. Tchr. Ft. Wayne (Ind.) Sch., 1974—99; bus. mgr. New Beginnings, Indpls., 1998—2000, bd. mem., 1997—2000; substitute tchr. Pike Twp., Indpls., 2005; mem. Black Sch. Educator Internat., Cosmopolites. Tchr. Alpa Time, Ft. Wayne, 1989; homebound tutor, Ft. Wayne, 1989—93; tchr. John Dixie Learning Acad., Ft. Wayne, 1990—93. Mem. NAACP, 2003—04; bd. mem. Christ Ch. Apostolic, Inc., 2005. Mem.: Urban League, Pi Lambda Theta. Avocations: travel, shopping.

BROWNLEE, DAVID A., lawyer; BA, Yale Univ., 1962; MA, Oxford Univ., England, 1964; LLB, Yale Univ., 1968. Bar: Pa. 1969, Supreme Ct. Pa., US Dist. Ct. (no. NY & we. Pa.), US Ct. Fed. Claims, US Tax Ct., US Ct. Appeals

(2d, 3d & 6th cir.). Law clk. Justice Thomas W. Pomeroy, Jr., Pa. Supreme Ct.; ptnr. & gen. counsel Kirkpatrick & Lockhart Nicholson Graham LLP, Pitts. Mem. Pitts. Bd. Edn.; past chmn. Gov. merit selection com. for state ct. judges, Allegheny County, Pa. Rhodes scholar. Fellow: Am. Bar Found.; mem.: ABA, Am. Law Inst., Pa. Bar Assn., Allegheny County Bar Assn. (mem. profl. ethics com.). Office: Kirkpatrick & Lockhart Nicholson Graham LLP Henry W Oliver Bldg 535 Smithfield St Pittsburgh PA 15222-2312 Office Phone: 412-355-6446. Office Fax: 412-355-6501. Business E-Mail: dbrownlee@klng.com.

BROWNLEE, DELPHINE, actress, musician; b. Paris, July 19, 1930; d. John Donald and Carla (Oddone) B.; m. Dan Oluf Eriksen, Apr. 24,1954 (div. June 1958); 1 child, Lynn Michele; m. Theodore Robert Bashkow, Sept. 12, 1960. Grad., Neighborhood Playhouse, N.Y., 1949. Tchr. pvt. studio, 1977—; adj. prof. Montclair State U., 1981-84; faculty Conservatory Hackley Sch., 1985-90, Mt. Kisco Sch. Music. Several voice overs for TV and radio commercials, recitals at Carnegie Recital Hall, opera performances with Singers Theatre; original cast of Man of La Mancha, Fade-Out, Fade-In, Here's Love, Carnival, others. Mem. N.Y. Singing Tchrs. Assn., N.Y. State Music Tchrs. Assn., Nat. Coun. Jewish Women (past pres. No. Westchester sect. 1971-73), Actor's Equity Assn., Screen Actors Guild, Am. Federations TV and Radio Artists. Avocations: gardening, reading, birdwatching. Home: 92 Jay St Katonah NY 10536-3729

BROWNLEE, DONALD EUGENE, II, astronomer, educator; b. Las Vegas, Nev., Dec. 21, 1943; s. Donald Eugene and Geraldine Florence (Stephen) B.; m. Paula Szkody. BS in Elec. Engring, U. Calif., Berkeley, 1965; PhD in Astronomy, U. Wash., 1970. Research assoc. U. Wash., 1970-77, asso. prof. astronomy, 1977-89; asso. geochemistry Calif. Inst. Tech., Pasadena, 1977-82; prof. astronomy U. Wash., 1989—. Cons. NASA, 1976— Author papers in field, chpts. in books. Grantee NASA, 1975; recipient J. Lawrence Smith medal Nat. Acad. of Sciences, 1994. Mem. AAAS, Internat. Astron. Union, Am. Astron. Assn., Meteoritical Soc. (Leonard medal 1996), Com. Space Rsch. Dust, NAS (NASA PI stardust mission). Office: U Wash Dept Astronomy Seattle WA 98195-0001

BROWNLEE, JOHN L., prosecutor; BA, Washington and Lee U., 1987; MBA, Golden Gate U.; JD, Coll. William and Mary, 1994. Law clk. U.S. Dist. Ct. (we. dist.) Va., 1994—96; asst. U.S. atty. D.C., 1997—2001; assoc. Woods, Rogers and Hazelgrove, Richmond, Va., 2001; U.S. atty. we. dist. Va U.S. Dept. Justice, 2001—. Lt. U.S. Army, 1987—91, capt. JAG USAR, 1991—. Office: 180 W Main St Abingdon VA 24210

BROWNLEE, LES (R. LESTER BROWNLEE), former civilian military employee; Degree, U. Wyo.; MBA, U. Ala.; grad, U.S. Army War Coll. Commd. 2d lt. US Army, advanced through grades to col.; mem. Rep. staf Senate Armed Svcs. Com., 1987—2001; prin. profl. staff mem. for Army and M.C. Corps program Spl. Ops. Forces and Drug Interdiction Policy and Support, 1987—96; nat. security advisor to Sen. John Warner US Senate, 1993—96; staff dir. Spl. Ops. Forces and Drug Interdiction Policy and Support, 1996—2001; under sec. US Army, Washington, 2001—04, acting sec., 2003—04. Decorated Silver Star, Bronze Star, Purple Heart.

BROWNLEE, PAULA PIMLOTT, higher education consultant; b. London, Eng., June 23, 1934; came to US, 1959; d. John Richard and Alice A. (Ajamian) Pimlott; m. Thomas H. Brownlee, Feb. 10, 1961; children: Kenneth Gainsford, Elizabeth Ann, Clare Louise. BA with honors, Somerville Coll., Oxford (Eng.) U., 1957, PhD in Organic Chemistry, 1959. Postdoctoral fellow U. Rochester, N.Y., 1959-61; rsch. chemist Am. Cyanamid Co., Stamford, Conn., 1961-62; lectr. U. Bridgeport, Conn., 1968-70; asst. prof., then assoc. prof. Rutgers U., N.J., 1970-76, assoc. dean, then acting dean Douglass Coll., 1972-76; dean faculty, prof. chemistry Union Coll., Schenectady, N.Y., 1976-81; pres., prof. chemistry Hollins U., Va., 1981-90; pres. Assn. Am. Colls. and Univs., Washington, 1990-98; prin. Pres.' Group, LLC, 1997—2003; founding prin. Nat. Acad. for Acad. Leadership. Bd. dirs. Acad. Search Consultation Svc. Contbr. articles and chpts. to profl. publs. Sr. trustee U. Rochester; vice chair bd. trustees Buena Vista U. Hon. fellow Somerville Coll., Oxford, Eng., 1996—. Mem. Am. Chem. Soc., Cosmos Club, Sigma Xi. Episcopalian. Office Phone: 540-869-7066. Personal E-mail: pbrownlee@direcway.com.

BROWNLEE, ROBERT CALVIN, pediatrician, educator; b. Due West, S.C., Mar. 13, 1922; s. Robert Calvin and Eleanor Louise (Pressly) B.; m. Judith Frances Irby; children: Eleanor Koets, Susan, Katherine Chambers, Jonathan, Robert Calvin. AB, Erskine Coll., 1943; MD, Vanderbilt U., 1945. Diplomate Am. Bd. Pediat. (pres. 1975), Am. Bd. Family Practice. Intern Vanderbilt U. Hosp., Nashville, 1945-46, resident, 1948-49, U. Va., Charlottesville, 1949-50; chief resident Vanderbilt U., Nashville, 1950-51; practice medicine, specializing in pediat. Christie Pediatric Group, Greenville, S.C., 1951-70; dir. pediat. Greenville Hosp. Sys., 1970-75; assoc. exec. sec. Am. Bd. Pediat., Chapel Hill, N.C., 1976, exec. sec., 1977-87, pres., 1987-92. Clin. prof. pediat. U. Pa., 1976-78; prof. pediat. U. S.C., 1971-75; clin. prof. U. N.C., 1978-96. Contbr. articles to med. jours. With AUS, 1943-45; with M.C. USAF, 1946-48, 53. Mem. Am. Acad. Pediat., Ambulatory Pediat. Assn. Presbyterian. Home: 1045 Fearrington Post Pittsboro NC 27312

BROWNLEE, ROBERT HAMMEL, lawyer; b. Chester, Ill., Dec. 15, 1951; s. Robert Mathis and Geneva (Hammel) B.; m. Sue F., June 17, 1978. BS, So. Ill. U., Carbondale, 1973; JD, Vanderbilt U., Nashville, 1976. Bar: Mo. 1976, Ill. 1977, U.S. Dist. Ct. (ea. and we. dists.) Mo. 1976, U.S. Dist. Ct. (so. and cen. dists.) Ill. 1977, U.S. Ct. Appeals (8th cir.) 1979, Ky. 1999, U.S. Supreme Ct. 1999. Assoc. Thompson & Mitchell, St. Louis, 1976-82; ptnr. Thompson Coburn, St. Louis, 1982—. Mng. editor Vanderbilt Law Review, Nashville, 1975-76; mem. Bar Assn. of Met. St. Louis, 1976—, Ill. State Bar Assn., Springfield, Ill., 1977—, Am. Bankruptcy Inst., 1988—, Ky. Bar, 1999—. Co-author: Rights of Secured Creditors in Bankruptcy, 1987, Lender Liability in Missouri, 1988, Protection of Secured Interests in Bankruptcy, 1989, Litigation in Bankruptcy Proceedings, 1994, Interlocutory Appeal Issues Before the Bankruptcy Reform Commission, 1996; Author: Bankruptcy Impact on Commercial Leases, Advanced Missouri Real Estate Law, 1997, updated, 1999, 2001, Impact of the Bankruptcy Review Commission's Report on Creditor Issues, 1997, Vendor Protection in Maritime Bankruptcy Reorganizations, 2003, The Sarbanes-Oxley Act of 2002: Potential Impacts on Future Administration of Large Chapter II Cases, 2003. Mem. Friends of the St. Louis Zoo., 1986—, St. Louis Bot. Garden Sponsors, 1987—; builder of the community United Way of Greater St. Louis, 1988—. Fellow Am. Coll. Bankruptcy Lawyers; mem. ABA (litigation sec. 1976—, co-chair jury instrn. subcom. of bankruptcy and insolvency com. 1994-99, bus. sec. 1976—, vice-chair claims trading subcom. bus. bankruptcy com. 1998-2001, chmn. subcom. adminstrn., U.S. trustee and jurisdiction and venue 2002-), Mo. Athletic Club, Mo. Bankers Assn. (chmn. legal adv. bd. 1997-98). Avocations: fishing, american art pottery, antiques, gardening. Office: Thompson Coburn LLP 1 US Bank Plz Ste 2600 Saint Louis MO 63101-1643 Office Phone: 314-552-6017. Business E-Mail: rbrownlee@thompsoncoburn.com.

BROWNLEE, THOMAS MARSHALL, manufacturing executive; b. Omaha, Nebr., Oct. 11, 1926; s. John Templeton and Reed (Marshall) B.; children: Linda Sue, Thomas John, Curtis Marshall, Reed Ann; m. Lenora A. Hollingsworth, Mar. 31, 1994. BSBA, U. Nebr., 1950. Asst. mgr. Daytona Beach (Fla.) C. of C., 1950, Tampa (Fla.) C. of C., 1952-53; exec. mgr. Tallahassee C. of C., 1953- 58; exec. v.p. Greater Columbia (S.C.) C. of C., 1959-63, Winston-Salem (N.C.) C. of C., 1963-64, Orlando Area (Fla.) C. of C., 1964-78; chmn. Brownlee Lighting Co., Orlando, 1978—. Mem. energy policy com. Orange County (Fla.) Schs.; mem. Fla. Energy Action Com.; mem. energy com. Nat. League Cities Contbr. articles to profl. jours. Bd. dirs. Loch Haven Art Mus.; bd. dirs. Chamber Inst., U. Ga.; mem. Orlando City Council.; pres. Christian Service Ctrs. Daily Bread. Served with USNR, 1944-46; as 1st lt. AUS, 1951-52. Mem. Fla. Energy Mgmt. Assn. (pres.), Illuminating Engring. Soc. (pres. Ctrl. Fla. chpt., bd. dirs., pres. internat. soc. 1996), Am. C. of C. Execs. Assn. (hon., pres. 1966), S.C. C. of C. Execs. Assn., Fla. C. of C. Execs. Assn. (pres. 1971), Better Bus. Bur. Ctrl. Fla. (chmn.), Knights Temple, Scottish-Am. Soc. Ctrl. Fla. (bd. dirs.), Orlando Scottish Games (exec. coun.), St. Andrews Soc. Ctrl. Fla. (pres.), Coun. Scottish Clans and Assn., Scottish Coalition (chmn.), Caledonian Found., Country Club Orlando, Univ. Club, Tiger Bay Club (pres.), Clan Hamilton Soc. (Fla. commr.), Rotary, Phi Delta Theta. Episcopalian. Office: Brownlee Lighting 4600 Dardanelle Dr Orlando FL 32808-3832 Office Phone: 407-297-3677. Business E-Mail: tmbrownlee@brownlee.com.

BROWNLEE, WILSON ELLIOT, JR., history professor; b. Lacrosse, Wis., May 10, 1941; s. Wilson Elliot Sr. and Pearl (Woodings) Brownlee; m. Mary Margaret Cochran, June 25, 1966; children: Charlotte Louise, Martin Elliot. BA, Harvard U., 1963; MA, U. Wis., 1965, PhD, 1969. Asst. prof. U. Calif., Santa Barbara, 1967-74, assoc. prof., 1974-80, prof. history, 1980—2002, spl. advisor to systemwide provost, 1995, assoc. systemwide provost, 1996, prof. emeritus, 2002—. Vis. prof. Princeton U., NJ, 1980—81; chmn. dept. history U. Calif., Santa Barbara, 1984—87, acad. senate, 1983—84, Santa Barbara, 1988—90, systemwide acad. senate, 1992—93; dir. U. Calif.-Santa Barbara Ctr., Washington, 1990—91; chmn. exec. com. dels. Am. Coun. Learned Socs., N.Y.C., 1988—90, bd. dirs., Nat. Coun. on Pub. History, Boston; bicentennial lectr. U.S. Dept. Treasury, 1989; faculty rep. U. Calif. Bd. Regents, 1991—93; adj. prof. history Calif. State U., 1997—99; mem. bd. control U. Calif. Press, 1996—99; co-organizer Conf. on History of Reagan Presidency U. Calif., Santa Barbara and Vanderbilt U., 2002; adj. prof. sch. pub. policy Pepperdine U., 2004. Author: Dynamics of Ascent, 1974, 2d edit., 1979, Progressivism and Economic Growth, 1974, Federal Taxation in America: A Short History, 1996, 2d edit., 2004; co-author: Essentials of American History, 1976, 4th edit., 1986, America's History, 1987, 3rd edit., 1997; editor: Women in the American Economy 1976, Funding the American State, 1996; co-editor: The Reagan Presidency: Pragmatic Conservatism and Its Legacies, 2003; contbr. articles to profl. jours., chpts. to books. Pres. Assn. for Retarded Citizens, Santa Barbara, 1982—84, 1st v.p. Sacramento, 1983—84; pres. Santa Barbara Trust for Hist. Preservation, 1986—87, 1995—97, 2002—03; trustee Las Trampas Inc., 1994—97, Calif. State Parks Found., 2002—05; assessment appeals bd. Santa Barbara County, 2002—; chmn. schs. com. Harvard Club, Santa Barbara, 1971—80, 1985—86. Recipient Spl. Commendation, Calif. Dept. Pks. and Recreation, 1988, Oliver Johnson award for Disting. Svc., U. Calif. Acad. Senate, 1988; fellow Woodrow Wilson Ctr., Washington, 1987—88; Charles Warren fellow, Harvard U., 1978—79. Mem.: Am. Hist. Assn., Orgn. Am. Historians, Econ. History Assn., Am. Tax Policy Inst. Office: U Calif Dept History Santa Barbara CA 93106 Business E-Mail: brownlee@history.ucsb.edu.

BROWNLIE, ROBERT WILLIAM, lawyer; b. Sasebo, Japan, Mar. 5, 1962; s. Robert Philip and Sachiko (Sugita) B.; m. Perla Esteban, Jan. 7, 1989. BA in Economics, U. Calif. San Diego, 1985; JD, U. Calif. Davis, 1988. Bar: Calif. 1988, U.S. Dist. Ct. (so., ea. ctrl. & no. dist. Calif.), U.S. Ct. Appeals (5th, 9th cir.), US Ct. Fed. Claims, US Supreme Ct. Rsch. asst. U. Calif. Davis Sch. of Law, 1986-87, teaching asst., 1987-88; summer assoc. Gray, Cary, Ames & Frye, San Diego, 1987, assoc., 1988-90, Milberg, Weiss, Bershad, Specthrie & Lerach, San Diego, 1990-92, Gray, Cary, Ware & Freidenrich, San Diego, 1992-95, mem., 1995—2004; ptnr., co-chmn. Securities Litigation practice group DLA Piper Rudnick Gray Cary, San Diego, 2005—. Contbr. articles to profl. jours. Pres., v.p., bd. dirs. Asian Bus. Assn., San Diego, 1994-98; bd. dirs. San Diego Mediation Ctr., 1994-95; fin. com. mem. San Diego Automotive Mus., 1993-95. Mem. ABA (mem. class action and derivative litigation com.), Nat. Asian Pacific Am. Bar Assn. (bd. dirs. 1997-99), Calif. Bar Assn., San Diego County Bar Assn. (legis. com. mem. 1988-95), Pan Asian Lawyers Assn. of San Diego (v.p., pres., bd. dirs. 1995-99), Order of Coif, Phi Kappa Phi. Democrat. Avocations: automobile enthusiast, golf, travel, sailing, boating. Home: 1450 Woodglen Ter Bonita CA 91902-4283 Office: DLA Piper Rudnick Gray Cary Suite 1100 4365 Executive Dr San Diego CA 92121 Office Phone: 858-638-6886. Office Fax: 858-677-1401. Business E-Mail: robert.brownlie@dlapiper.com.

BROWNLOW, FRANK WALSH, literature and language professor; b. Dundonald, Northern Ireland, Sept. 2, 1934; came to U.S., 1959; s. Frank and Katherine Georgina (Darroch) B. BA, Liverpool (Eng.) U., 1956; PhD, U. Birmingham, Eng., 1963. From instr. to assoc. prof. English U. Mich., Ann Arbor, 1959-61, 63-69; lectr. U. Western Ont., London, Can., 1961-63; from assoc. prof. to prof. Mt. Holyoke Coll., South Hadley, Mass., 1969—. Vis. assoc. prof. Dartmouth Coll., Hanover, Mass., 1968-69. Author: Two Shakespearan Sequences, 1977, Shakespeare, Harsnett and the Devils of Denham, 1993, Robert Southwell, 1996; editor: John Skelton: The Book of the Laurel, 1991; contbr. articles on Shakespeare, Skelton, Byron, Herbert, Chesterton, also others, to profl. jours. Mem.: Renaissance English Text Soc., Byron Soc. Avocation: music. Office: Mt Holyoke Coll Dept English South Hadley MA 01075 Office Phone: 413-538-2126. Business E-Mail: fbrownlo@mtholyoke.edu.

BROWN MANRIQUE, GERARDO, architect, educator; b. Mex., Mar. 30, 1949; s. Gerardo and Maria Enriqueta (Manrique de) Brown. BArch, BS in Bldg. Scis., Rensselaer Polytech. Inst., 1971; MArch, Cornell U., 1974. Registered architect, Okla., Ohio; cert. NCARB. Project designer O.M. Ungers, Architects, Ithaca, N.Y., 1971-73; jr. designer James M. Sink & Assocs., Houston, 1974; asst. prof. U. Okla. Sch. Architecture, 1974-78; pvt. practice Oxford, Ohio and Norman, Okla., 1976—; asst. prof. Miami U. Dept. Architecture, Oxford, 1978-82, assoc. prof., 1982-87, prof., 1987—. Vis. scholar Miami U. European Ctr., Luxemburg, 1986, 97-98. Author: The Ticino Guide, 1989, The Guidebook of Housing Design, 1992; pub., editor Interalia Design Books; contbr. articles to profl. jours. Bd. dirs. Oxford Mile Sq. Neighborhood Assn., 1985-92; exec. sec. Historic and Archl. Preservation Commn., Oxford, 1980-82. Recipient Fulbright Lecturing award Nat. U. Buenos Aires, 1988, Grant Graham Found., 1988, 91, 96; named Willard K. Martin Disting. Vis. Critic, U. Oreg., 1991. Mem. Guild of Bookmakers. Office: Miami U Dept Architecture Oxford OH 45056 Office Phone: 513-529-7222. E-mail: brownmg@muohio.edu.

BROWN-OLMSTEAD, AMANDA, public relations executive; b. Oct. 7, 1943; Founder ABOA (formerly a divsn. Shandwick PLC), 1972; pres., CEO A Brown Olmstead Assocs., Atlanta. Mem. Atlanta Pub. Rels. Seminar Group. Mem. nat. bd. dirs. Episcopal Media Ctr.; bd. dirs. Ctrl. Atlanta Progress, Councilors for The Carter Ctr., Atlanta Bot. Garden; mem. adv. bd. Sheperd Spinal Ctr., U. Miss. Bus. Sch.; mem. adv. guild Clark U.; pres. Ga. chpt. Internat. Women's Forum; mem. exec. com. Regional Bus. Coalition. Named a Recognized Woman of Achievement, Internat. Women's Forum; named one of The Ten Outstanding Atlantans; named to Georgia Pub. Rels. Hall of Fame; recipient Gold medal, N.Y. Film and TV Festival; YWCA honoree, Salute to Women of Achievement. Fellow: Pub. Rels. Soc. Am. (mem. Counselors Acad., mem. eligibility bd., Silver Anvil award); mem.: Order of the Phoenix, Leadership Atlanta. Achievements include being featured in Mademoiselle magazine, Business Week, Savvy, Atlanta Weekly, Atlanta magazine, and Movers and Shakers in Georgia. Office: A Brown Olmstead Assocs 274 W Paces Ferry Rd NW Atlanta GA 30305-1167

BROWNRIGG, JOHN CLINTON, lawyer; b. Detroit, Aug. 7, 1948; s. John Arthur and Sheila Pauline (Taffe) B.; children: Brian M., Jennifer A., Katharine T. BA, Rockhurst Coll., 1970; JD cum laude, Creighton U., 1974. Bar: Nebr. 1974, U.S. Dist. Ct. Nebr. 1974, U.S. Tax Ct. 1977, U.S. Ct. Appeals (8th cir.) 1990. Ptnr. Eisenstatt, Higgins, Kinnamon, Okun & Brownrigg, P.C., Omaha, 1974-80, Erickson & Sederstrom, P.C., Omaha, 1980—. Lectr. law trial practice Creighton U. Sch. Law, Omaha, 1978-83; dir. Legal Aid Soc., Inc., Omaha, 1982-88, pres., 1987-88, devel. coun., 1989—; dir. Nebr. Continuing Legal Edn., Inc., 1991-93. Chmn. law sect. Archbishop's Capital Campaign, Omaha, 1991; dir. Combined Health Agys. Drive, 2001-03. Sgt. USAR, 1970-76. Fellow Nebr. State Bar Found. (dir. 1991-93); mem. Nebr. State Bar Assn. (pres. 1992-93), Nebr. Assn. Trial Attys., Omaha Bar Assn. (pres. 1990-91). Avocations: golf, bicycling, hiking. Office: Erickson & Sederstrom PC Ste 100 10330 Regency Parkway Dr Omaha NE 68114-3761

BROWNRIGG, WALTER GRANT, cartoonist, corporate financial executive, consultant; b. Boston, Oct. 26, 1940; children by previous marriage: Elizabeth Grant, Christopher Hertel; m. Judith Courtney Hamilton, Apr. 28, 1984; children: Carter Grant, Taylor Hamilton, Kelsey Anderson. AB in History cum laude, Princeton U., 1962; MBA, Columbia U., 1964. Asst. plant mgr. Berwick Weaving, Inc., Pa., 1964-72; asst. to v.p. Frank & Stessel, Inc., N.Y.C., 1972-73; sr. assoc. Drake Sheahan/Stewart Dougall, Inc., N.Y.C., 1973-76; exec. dir. Greater Hartford (Conn.) Arts Council, 1976-79; dir. Am. Council Arts, N.Y.C., 1979-83; cartoonist, creator Grantland, 1984—; pres. Grantland Enterprises, Inc., 1991. Spkr., cons. in field. Author: Effective Corporate Fundraising, Corporate Fundraising: A Practical Plan of Action. Mem. Charlottesville Rotary Club, Beta Gamma Sigma.

BROWNSON, JACQUES CALMON, architect; b. Aurora, Ill., Aug. 3, 1923; s. Clyde Arthur and Iva Kline (Felter) B.; m. Doris L. Curry, 1946; children: Joel C., Lorre J., Daniel J. BS in Architecture, Ill. Inst. Tech., 1948, MS, 1954. Instr., asst. prof. architecture Ill. Inst. Tech., 1949-59; prof. architecture, chmn. dept. U. Mich., 1966-68; chief design C.F. Murphy Assocs., Chgo., 1959—61; project arch., chief designer Chgo. Civic Ctr. Archs., 1961—68; dir. state bldg. divsn. State of Colo., Denver, 1986—88; pvt. practice Denver, 1988—. Former mng. arch. Chgo. Pub. Bldg. Commn.; past dir. planning and devel. Auraria Ctr. for Higher Edn., Denver; bd. dirs. Capital Constrn., Denver; guest lectr. architecture in U.S. and Europe. Prin. works include Chgo. Civic Ctr., Lake Denver, Colo., 1985, Chgo. Tribune/Cabrini Green Housing, 1993; author: History of Chicago Architects, 1996, Oral History of Jacuqes Calmon Brownson, 1996. Recipient award for Geneva House Archtl. Record mag., 1956; Design award for steel framed factory Progressive Architecture mag., 1957. Home and Office: 659 Josephine St Denver CO 80206-3722

BROWNSON, KENNETH C., dean; b. Hazleton, Pa., Apr. 16, 1945; s. Kenneth George and Mary Louise (Dennion) B. AAS in Nursing, Del. Tech. and C.C., 1978; BS in Profl. Arts, St. Joseph's Coll., Standish, Maine, 1984; MS in Mgmt., The Am. Coll., 1986; MS in Psychology, Calif. Coast U., 1989; EdD in Adult and Nontraditional Edn., Newport U., 1991; Cert. in Cmty. Health Edn., Calif. Coll. Health Sci., 1999. RN, Del., Pa.; cert. psychiat. and mental health nurse; cert. allied health instr. Evening supr., asst. head nurse intensive/critical care unit Riverside Hosp., Wilmington, Del., 1980-83; staff RN, nurse/counselor crisis svc. unit Crozer-Chester Med. Ctr., Chester, Pa., 1983-94; pres. Adult Edn. Resource, New Castle, Del., 1987—; dean undergrad. studies Greenwich U., Australia, 1989—2001; prof. social studies Am. Pub. U. Sys., 2001—. Mem. adv. bd. Insvc. Tng. Inst., 1991—99; v.p., bd. dirs. Brandywine Counseling, Inc., Wilmington, 2001—04. Mem. editl. bd. Health Care Mgr.; author: College at Home for Nurses and All Healthcare Professionals, 2002; contbr. articles to profl. jours. With USN, 1965-69, Vietnam. Recipient First Place, Feature Writing, Am. Med. Technologists, 2003, 2004. Home and Office: 33 W 4th St New Castle DE 19720-5092 E-mail: kbrownson@comcast.net.

BROWNSON, MARY LOUISE, counselor, educator, artist; b. Detroit, Dec. 8, 1927; d. Max Curt Poppe and Hilda Caroline Larson; m. Elwyn James Brownson, Dec. 30, 1950 (div. Sept. 1979); children: Elwyn James, Richard, Matthew, Mary. B of Design, U. Mich., Ann Arbor, 1950; MS, No. Mont. Coll., Havre, 1976. Cert. secondary sch. tchr. Mont., 1972. Instr. Wittenburg U., Springfield, Ohio, 1950—53, No. Mont. Coll., Havre, 1963—71; drug and alcohol counselor Alcohol Svcs. Ctr., Boise, Idaho, 1979—80; migrant career placement counselor Boise State U., Idaho, 1981—85; mgr. Ctr. Use, Boise Sr. Ctr., Idaho, 1985—88; employment counselor Fed. Cmty. Treatment Ctr., Boise, Idaho, 1988—90; mgr. activities Hillcrest Retirement Ctr., Boise, Idaho, 1990—94. Represented in permanent collections, Kent State U. Collection. Pres. PTA, Havre, Mont.; Dem. candidate for state legislature Havre, Mont. Mem.: AAUW (pres.), LWV (pres. 1999—2003). Democrat. Unitarian-Universalist. Avocations: gourmet cooking, swimming, reading, painting. Home: 3820 Sheringham Dr Boise ID 83704

BROWNSON, SUE MCPHERSON, music educator; b. Burlington, N.C., Apr. 7, 1958; d. William Steadman and Versa (Price) McPherson; children: Patrick Michael, Jessica Sue. BM, N.C. Sch. of the Arts, Winston-Salem, 1980; AS Sci., Coll., Burlington, N.C., 1985. Private music tchr., Winston-Salem, NC, 1980—81; actress The Lost Colony, Manteo, NC, 1981; music tchr. Happy Acres Ranch, Jacksonville, 1982—85; lab. technician Roche Labs., Burlington, NC, 1985—87; sheet music dept. head Flesher Higher Music, Aurora, Colo., 1987—93; minister of music Aurora First Presbyn. Ch., Colo., 1987—93; music tchr. Elbert County Charter Sch., Elizabeth, Colo., 1997—2002; music tchr. voice and piano Brownson Music Studio, Elizabeth, Colo., 2000—. Mem.: Douglas Elbert Music Tchrs. Assn. (chair nominations com. 2000), Am. Coll. Musicians. Republican. Presbyn. Achievements include Students in voice and piano are divsn. winners and hon. mentions in local music competitions. Avocation: gardening. Home: 35711 Darting Bird Ride Elizabeth CO 80107 Office: Brownson Music Studio 35711 Darting Bird Ride Elizabeth CO 80107

BROWNSTEIN, ALAN P., health foundation executive, consultant; b. N.Y.C., Sept. 20, 1944; s. Charles S. and Thelma S. (Blauweiss) B.; m. Patricia Marie Rosenberg, June 15, 1968; children— Joshua B., Jeremy S. BS, SUNY-Buffalo, 1967, MSW, 1969; MPH, U. Mich., 1973. Dir. health policy and legisl. research Local 1199, Drug and Hosp. Union/Nat. Union Hosp. and Nursing Home Employees, RWDSU, AFL-CIO, N.Y.C., 1970-72; dep. dir. Office Comprehensive Health Planning, Exec. Office Human Services Mass., Boston, 1973-75; dir. office grants mgmt. and devel. N.Y.C. Health and Hosps. Corp., 1975-77; asst. dir. dept. for the community Community Service Soc. N.Y., N.Y.C., 1977-80; dir. Council of Home Health Agys. and Community Health Services, Nat. League for Nursing, N.Y.C., 1980-81; exec. dir. Nat. Hemophilia Found., N.Y.C., 1981-94; pres., CEO Am. Liver Found., Cedar Grove, N.J., 1994—. Expert witness U.S. Congress, 1971-95; cons. Citizens' Com. for Children, N.Y.C., 1979-81, Blue Cross Mass., Boston, 1981, Office Maternal and Child Health, USPHS, Rockville, Md., 1983; mem. adj. faculty in health econs., hosp. and healthcare mgmt. program Sch. Bus. Adminstrn., Adelphi U., Garden City, N.Y., 1979-81, mem. profl. adv. bd., 1977-81; mem. adj. faculty in health svcs. mgmt. New Sch. for Social Rsch., N.Y.C., 1979; mem. nat. adv. com. Nat. Pediatric HIV Resource Ctr. Co-author monographs: Consumers Guide to Health Insurance, 1974; Consumers Guide to Nursing Homes, 1975. Contbr. chpts. to books, articles to profl. jours. Vice pres. Health Systems Agy. Bd. G., Queens, N.Y., 1979-81; v.p. Jamaica Estates Assn., N.Y., 1980-92, Friends of Cunningham Park, Queens, 1983-85; bd. dirs. Cmty. Health Charities, 2002—. Recipient Faculty Fund for Social Work Students award SUNY-Buffalo Sch. Social Welfare, 1969, Disting. Alumni award SUNY Buffalo, 1993; fellow NIMH, 1967-69, USPHS, 1972-73 Mem. APHA, Pub. Health Assn. N.Y.C. (bd. dirs. 1979-82), World Fedn. Hemophilia, Nat. Health Coun. (bd. dirs. 1988—), Digestive Disease Nat. Coalition (bd. dirs. 1994—), Am. Soc. of Assn. Execs., Nat. Ctr. for Non-Profit Bds., Health Care Quality Alliance (bd. dirs. 1996-2001). Office: Am Liver Found 75 Maiden Ln Ste 603 New York NY 10038

BROWNSTEIN, ANDREW RICHARD, lawyer; b. Waterbury, Conn., Oct. 22, 1953; s. Jack and Edith (Wortman) B.; m. Elise Jaffe; children: Alexander, Julia. BA, BS in Econs., U. Pa., 1975, MBA, 1976; JD, Harvard U., 1979. Bar: N.Y. 1980, U.S. Ct. Appeals (3rd cir.) 1980. Law clk. to Hon. Leonard I. Garth U.S. Ct. Appeals (3d cir.), 1979-80; assoc. Wachtell, Lipton, Rosen & Katz, N.Y.C., 1980-85, ptnr., corp. dept., 1985—, chmn. diversity com. Adj. prof. securities law Rutgers U. Sch. Law,1983; chmn. Ray Garrett Jr. Corp. & Securities Law Inst., Northwestern Univ. Sch. Law, 1998-99. Articles editor, Harvard Law Rev.; contbr. articles to profl. jours. Mem. ABA (securities regulation and bus. law divsn.), N.Y.C. Bar Assn., Phi Beta Kappa,

Beta Gamma Sigma. Office: Wachtell Lipton Rosen & Katz 51 W 52nd St Fl 29 New York NY 10019-6150 Office Phone: 212-403-1233. Office Fax: 212-403-2233. Business E-Mail: arbrownstein@wlrk.com.

BROWNSTEIN, BARBARA LAVIN, geneticist, educator, director; b. Phila., Sept. 8, 1931; d. Edward A. and Rose (Silverstein) Lavin; m. Melvin Brownstein, June 1949 (div. 1955); children: Judith Brownstein Kaufmann, Dena. Asst. editor Biol. Abstracts, Phila., 1957-58; research fellow dept. microbial genetics Karolinska Inst., Stockholm, 1962-64; assoc. Wistar Inst., Phila., 1964-68; assoc. prof. molecular biology, dept. biology Temple U., Phila., 1968-74, prof., 1974-96, prof. emeritus Seattle, 1996—, chmn. dept., 1978-81, provost, 1983-90; sr. assoc. Ctr. Ednl. Rsch. U. Wash., Seattle, 1994—. Vis. scientist dept. tumor cell biology Imperial Cancer Rsch. Fund Labs., London, 1973-74; bd. dirs. Univ. City Sci. Ctr., Greater Phila. Econ. Devel. Coun., Forum Exec. Women; program officer NSF, 1992-93; sr. assoc. Inst. Ednl. Inquiry, Seattle, 1994—. Bd. dirs. Lopez Island Sch., 2001—. Recipient Liberal Arts Alumni award for excellence in teaching Temple U., 1980; recipient Outstanding Faculty Woman award Temple U., 1980 Fellow AAAS; mem. Am. Soc. Cell Biology, N.Y. Acad. Sci., Assn. Women in Sci., NSF (program officer 1992-93). Home: PO Box 835 Lopez Island WA 98261 Office: Inst Ednl Inquiry 124 E Edgar St Seattle WA 98102 Office Phone: 360-468-4885. E-mail: bbrownst@msn.com.

BROWNSTEIN, ELIZABETH SMITH, writer; d. Frank Edward and Grace Hanrahan Smith; m. Arnold Wallace Brownstein, Oct. 12, 1967 (div. 1973). BA in Polit. sci., Wellesley Coll., 1952; MSc in Internat. Rels., London Sch. Econs. and Polit. Sci., 1967. Chief TV rschr. CBS, 1952—56, chief TV rschr. Meet the Press, 1958—60; dir. The Experiment in Internat. Living, N.Y.C., 1960—66; assoc. prodr., writer Evening Edit. with Martin Agronsky, 1971—76; exec. prodr., program devel. mgr., asst. program mgr. WETA-TV, Washington, 1976—82. Author: If This House Could Talk, 1999, Lincoln's Other White House, 2005; dir. rsch.: (TV series) Smithsonian World, 1982—87; coord. prodr.: Smithsonian Video Collection, 1989—92. Mem.: Soc. Woman Geographers (sec. nat. exec. coun. 1990—96, Washington Group rep. 1996—2002, 2004—05, v.p. 2005—), Alumni and Friends of London Sch. Econs. (exec. v.p. 1977—80, bd. dirs. 1977—, pres. 1980—82), Washington Press Club (bd. govs. 1979—83), Nat. Press Club. Democrat. Unitarian. Avocations: walking holidays, swimming, reading, films. Home: 4201 Cathedral Ave NW Washington DC 20016*

BROWN-WAITE, VIRGINIA (GINNY BROWN-WAITE), congresswoman; b. Albany, NY, Oct. 5, 1943; m. Harvey Waite; children: Jeannine Bradford, Danene Mitchell, Lorie Sue Busiere. BS, SUNY, 1976; MS, Russell Sage Coll., 1984. Legis. dir. NY State Senate, 1970—87; commr. Hernando County Bd. of Commr., 1991—93; mem. Fla. State Senate, 1992—2002, U.S. Ho. of Reps. from 5th Fla. dist., 2003—; mem. fin. svcs. com., govt. reform com., vet. affairs com. Adj. prof. Springfield Coll.; owner Mr. Donut franchise. Active W Hernando GOP, United Way; bd. dirs. Hernando County Spouse Abuse Ctr. Mem. Bus. and Profl. Women's Club, Suncoast MG Club. Republican. Roman Catholic. Office Phone: 202-225-1000.

BROWNWOOD, DAVID OWEN, lawyer; b. L.A., May 24, 1935; s. Robert Scott Osgood and Ruth Elizabeth (Bellamy) B.; m. Sigrid Carlson, Mar. 3, 1956 (div. 1972); children: Jeffrey Owen, Kirsten, Scott David, Daniel Stuart; m. Susan Sloane Jannicky, July 4, 1975; 1 child, Mary Ruth Bellamy; stepchildren: Bradbury, Stephanie Ellington. AB with distinction, Stanford U., 1956; LLB magna cum laude, Harvard U., 1964. Bar: Calif. 1965, N.Y. 1969. Law clk. Ropes & Gray, Boston, 1963; assoc. McCutchen, Doyle, Brown & Enersen, San Francisco, 1964-66; lectr. law U. Khartoum, Sudan, 1966-67, Kenya Inst. Adminstrn., Lower Kabete, 1967-68; assoc. Cravath, Swaine & Moore, N.Y.C., 1968-72, ptnr., 1973—2003, sr. counsel, 2003—, recruiting ptnr., 1978-82, mng. ptnr. for legal staff, 1983-86; ptnr. in charge London office, 1995—2001. Treas. N.Y. Law Inst., 1978-83, chmn. exec. com., 1983-88, pres., 1988-93. Mem. editorial bd. Harvard U. Law Rev., 1963-64. Nat. chair Harvard U. Law Sch. Fund, 1991—93; bd. dirs. Royal Oak Found., 2003—, treas., 2004—; pres. Benjamin Franklin House Found., 2002—; dir. Literacy Assistance Ctr., N.Y.C., 1983—94, co-chmn. bd. dirs., 1987—94; trustee Greenwich (Conn.) Country Day Sch., 1985—92, v.p., 1986—88, pres., chmn. bd. trustees, 1988—92; co-chmn. Harvard U. Law Sch. 25th Reunion Gift, 1988—89, 40th Reunion Gift, 2003—05; N.Y. regional com. campaign Harvard Law Sch., 1991—95; com. on univ. resources Harvard U., 1991—, mem. Harvard law sch. vis. com., 1995—2001; keystone regional vice chair centennial campaign Stanford U., 1986—92; exec. com. Stanford U. N.Y. Coun., 1992—95; vice chmn. Stanford U. N.Y. Major Gifts Com., 1993—95; co-chair Stanford U. Ea. Coun., 1993; bd. govs. Stanford Assocs., 1993—95, pres., chmn. bd. govs., 1994—95; bd. advisors Stanford U. Trust (U.K.), 1995—2002; mem. nat. bd. Outward Bound USA, 1993—96; trustee Greenwich Libr., 2003—; bd. dirs. Stanford U. Alumni Assn., 2004—. 1st lt. USAF, 1956—61, fighter pilot Air Def. Command, capt. USAFR, Mass. Air N.G., 1961—66. Recipient Centennial medallion Stanford U., Stanford Assocs. award. Fellow Am. Bar Found., N.Y. State Bar Found., Fgn. Policy Assn.; mem. ABA, N.Y. State Bar Assn., Assn. Bar City N.Y., The Pilgrims, Round Hill Club, Field Club, Sankaty Head Club, Siasconset Casino Assn., Harvard Club Home: 296 Old Church Rd Greenwich CT 06830 also: 61 Orange St Nantucket MA 02554 Office: Cravath Swaine & Moore 825 8th Ave Fl 46 New York NY 10019-7416 Office Phone: 212-474-1218. Business E-Mail: dbrownwood@cravath.com.

BROXMEYER, HAL EDWARD, medical educator; b. Bklyn., Nov. 27, 1944; s. David and Anna (Gurman) B.; m. C. Beth Biller, 1969; children: Eric Jay, Jeffrey Daniel. BS, Bklyn. Coll., 1966; MS, L.I. U., 1969; PhD, NYU, 1973. Postdoctoral student Queens U., Kingston, Canada, 1973-75; assoc. rschr., rsch. assoc. Meml. Sloan Kettering Cancer Ctr., NYC, 1975-78, assoc., 1978-83, assoc. mem., 1983; asst. prof. Cornell U. Grad. Sch., NYC, 1980-83; assoc. prof. Ind. U. Sch. Medicine, Indpls., 1983-86, prof. medicine, microbiology and immunology, 1986—; sci. dir. Walther Oncology Ctr., Indpls., 1988—, chmn. microbiology and immunology, 1997—, Disting. prof., 2004—. Mem. hematology II study sect. NIH, Bethesda, Md., 1981-86, 95-2000, chair, 1997-2000; adv. com. NHLBI, NIH, Bethesda, 1991-94; chmn. bd. sci. counselors Nat. Space Biomed. Rsch. Inst., 1998—, mem. coun., 1999—, MSAB; bd. dirs. Nat. Disease Rsch. Interchange; co-chmn. Sect. Hematopoiesis, Faculty of 1000 Medicine. Assoc. editor Exptl. Hematology, 1981-90, Jour. Immunology, 1987-92, Stem Cells, 1996-97, Brit. Jour. Haematology, 1998—; editor Jour. LeuKocyte Biology, 1995—; sr. editor Stem Cells and Development (previously Jour. Hematotherapy and Stem Cell Rsch.), 2000-; mem. editl. bd. Blood, 1983-87, Biotech. Therapeutics, 1988-95, Internat. Jour. Hematology, 1991—, Jour. Lab. Clin. Medicine, 1992—, Jour. Exptl. Medicine, 1992—, Annals Hematology, 1993—, Cell Transplantation, 1994—, Critical Rev. Oncology/Hematology, 1995—, Stem Cells, 1998—, Jour. Blood and Marrow Transplantations, 1998—, Cytokines, Cellular and Molecular Therapy, 1998—, Current Trends Immunology, 2004—; contbr. more than 590 articles to profl. jours. Ednl. com. Leukemia Soc. Am., Indpls., 1983—; nat. career devel. study sect. Leukemia and Lymphoma Soc., NY, 1991—95, 2000—. Recipient Founder's Day award NYU, 1973, Merit award Nat. Cancer Inst.; Leukemia Soc. Am. award, 1987-95, Spl. Fellow award, 1976-78, Scholar award, 1978-83, Gold medal City of Paris, 1993, World of Difference award Ind. Health Industry Forum, 1997, Landsteiner award Am. Assn. Blood Banks, 2002, Health Care Heroes award Indpls. Bus. Jour., 2002, Prestigious External award recognition IUPUI, 2003, Disting. Alumni award L.I. U., Bklyn. Ctr., 2005. Mem. AAAS, NY Acad. Scis., Soc. for Leukocyte Biology, Am. Assn. Cancer Rsch., Am. Assn. Immunologists, Internat. Soc. Exptl. Hematology (pres. 1990-91), Internat. Soc. Stem Cell Rsch., Am. Soc. Hematology (coun. mem. 2000-05), Am. Fedn. Clin. Rsch., Am. Soc. Blood and Marrow Transplantation. Avocation: competitive Olympic-style weightlifting. Home: 1210 Chessington Rd Indianapolis IN 46260-1630 Office: Ind U Sch Medicine 950 W Walnut St Rm 302 Indianapolis IN 46202-5181 Fax: 317-274-7592. Office Phone: 317-274-7510. E-mail: hbroxmey@iupui.edu.

BROYLES, CHRISTINE ANNE, art educator; d. H.C. and Dorothy E. Lippstreuer; m. Robert E. Broyles, Dec. 30, 1989. BFA, B in Art Edn., U. South Fla., 1981. Cert. tchr. Fla., Nat. Assn. Underwater Instrs. Intern Charlotte County Pub. Schs., Port Charlotte, Fla., 1981, sci. tchr. Lemon Bay H.S., 1981—83, art instr. grades 6-8 L. A. Ainger Mid. Sch. Rotonda West, Fla., 1984—; adult edn. tchr. (arts and GED) Charlotte County Adult and Cmty. Edn., Englewood, Fla., 1982—85; adult edn. tchr. (arts) Sarasota (Fla.) Vocat. and Tech. Sch., 1982—85, Venice (Fla.) Area Art League, 1982—86; freelancer, guest writer Suncoast Media Group, Venice, 1982—. Layout editor Charlotte County Lit. and Fine Arts Mag., Port Charlotte, 1999—2001; mem. supt.'s roundtable forum Charlotte County Pub. Schs., Port Charlotte, 1999—2001, secondary fine arts liason, 1998—, dept. head (elective subjects) L. A. Ainger Mid. Sch., Rotonda West, 2000—, EXCEL mentor tchr., Port Charlotte, 1999—, mem. code of student conduct com., 1999, mem. pupil progression plan com., 99, mem. student assistance team, 2000; trainer Beacon Learning Ctr., Panama City, Fla., 2001—; webmaster, co-creator, editor The Art Web; dir. instrnl. pers. Charlotte County Classified and Tchrs. Assn., Punta Gorda, 1995—96, v.p., 1996—98; mem. specification and validation com. Fla. Tchr. Certification Exam, 1984, 2004, tech. and lit. coun., 1999—; facilitator Profl. Learning Cmty., 2004—; presenter in field. Author: (teacher resource book) Art Across the Curriculum. Named Educator of Yr., Sunshine Rotary of Englewood, 1998, Tchr. of Yr. (local), Wal-Mart, 1998, Sam's Club, 1998; recipient Best of Show award, Arts and Humanities Coun. Port Charlotte, 1999; grantee, Fla. Arts and Humanities Coun., 1996—98, Fla. Arts and Humanities Coun., 2002—04; scholar, Am. Legion Aux., 1975—80; arts program scholar, Fla. Ctr. for Tchrs., 2000. Mem.: Fla. Art Edn. Assn., Fla. League Tchrs., Nat. Art Edn. Assn. Avocations: scuba diving, travel, arts, antiquing. Office: L A Ainger Mid Sch 245 Cougar Way Rotonda West FL 33947 Office Phone: 941-697-5800.

BROYLES, DEBORAH J., lawyer; b. Worcester, Mass., July 8, 1963; BA, Mt. Holyoke Coll., 1985; JD, Harvard U., 1993. Bar: Calif. 1993, US Ct. Appeals (9th Cir.), US Dist. Ct. (No. Dist.) Calif., US Dist. Ct. (Ea. Dist.) Calif., US Dist. (Ctrl. Dist.) Calif., US Dist. Ct. (So. Dist.) Calif. Ptnr., Diversity Com. Thelen Reid & Priest LLP, San Francisco. Mem.: Charles Houston Bar Assn., Nat. Bar Assn., Nat. Employment Law Coun., Calif. Minority Counsel Program (steering com. 2004—05), Calif. Assn. of Black Lawyers (ann. convention co-chmn. 1996, v.p.-north 1998—99, jud. appointments com. 1999—2002), Bar Assn. San Francisco, ABA. Office: Thelen Reid & Priest LLP 101 Second St Ste 1800 San Francisco CA 94105-3601 Office Phone: 415-369-7203. Office Fax: 415-371-1211. Business E-Mail: djbroyles@thelenreid.com.

BROYLES, JEFFREY LYNN, school psychologist; b. Springfield, Ohio, Sept. 18, 1957; s. Franklin Deland and Ruth Ann Broyles; m. Pamela Gaye White, June 21, 1981; children: Myranda, Meredith. BS, Wright State U., 1981, MS, 1983, MEd, 1984; PhD, Miami U., 2001. Cert. tchr., prin., counselor, sch. psychologist, supt. Tchr. MEdway Elem. Sch., New Carlisle, Ohio, 1981—84; sch. counselor Westlake Elem. Sch., 1985—86; asst. prin. Olice Br. Mid. Sch., 1997—98; dir. human resources Miami County E.S.C., Troy, 2002—03; sch. psychologist Troy City Schs., 2004—. Adj. instr. Wright State U., Dayton, 2000—, Urbana U., 2001—, Clark State C.C., Springfield, 2004—. Avocations: weightlifting, bicycling, reading.

BROYLES, STEPHEN DOUGLAS, public information officer; b. Columbus, Ohio, Sept. 7, 1947; s. Enoch Ernest and Georgina Marie (Weaver) B; m. Kay Lyn Porter, May 31, 1968; children: Paul Douglas, Leora Marie. BA, Ohio State U., 1969; MA, Webster Coll., 1978; DPA, U. Ala., 1995. Commd. 2d lt. U.S. Air Force, 1969, advanced through grades to lt. col., 1989; chief mgmt. support divsn. Def. Comms. Agy., Stuttgart, West Germany, 1983-87; dep. base comdr. USAFE, San Vito Air Base, Italy, 1987-89; chief seminar divsn. Air U., Maxwell AFB, Ala., 1989-92; ret. U.S. Air Force, 1992; asst. mgr. Pizza Hut Delivery, Montgomery, Ala., 1993-94; city adminstr. City of Muenster, Tex., 1995-2000; dean adminstrv. svcs. North Ctrl. Tex. Coll., 2000—. Mem. Am. Soc. Pub. Adminstrs., Kiwanis (pres. 1996-98). Avocations: reading, tai chi, swimming, hiking. Home: 407 W 9th St Muenster TX 76252-2241 Office: North Ctrl Tex Coll Gainesville TX 76240-4699 Office Phone: 940-668-3300. Business E-Mail: sbroyles@nctc.edu.

BROYTMAN, VLADISLAV I., hygenist; b. Moscow, Oct. 6, 1948; arrived in U.S., 1998; s. Iosif Broytman and Frida Tsvick; m. Nadezhda Broytman, Dec. 13, 1969; children: Natalya, Nick. Diploma, Med. Inst., Russia, 1973; PhD, Med. Inst., St. Petersburg, Russia, 1984; ScD, VAK, Moscow, 1994. Physician Sanitary Epidemiology Sta., Russia, 1973—85; chief Indsl. Hygiene Lab. Sci. Rsch. Indsl. Hygiene and Occupl. Diseases, Russia, 1985—90, pres. Moscow, 1990—98; v.p. Art of Life, Inc. Ambulance, Phila., 2002—. Contbr. over 135 articles to profl. jours.; author: 4 monographs. Recipient Gold medal, Russia, 1989. Mem.: Hygienist Assn., N.Y. Acad. Sci. Achievements include patents in field. Home: 2375 Woodward St Apt 307ET Philadelphia PA 19115

BROZAK, EDITH See MCMANN, EDITH

BROZOWSKI, LAURA ADRIENNE, mechanical engineer; b. Yokohama, Japan, May 12, 1960; arrived in U.S., 1961; d. John and Muriel Sydney (Jackson) Brozowski. BSME, U. Calif., 1982; MSME, Calif. State U., 1987; MBA, Pepperdine U., 1988. Registered profl. engr., Calif.; cert. profl. mgr. Inst. Cert. Profl. Mgrs. Engring. scientist United Tech. Corp. Pratt & Whitney, Canoga Park, Calif., 1982—. Author: in field. Recipient Space Achievement Mid Career award, Rotary Nat., Rotary Nat. award for Space Achievement, 2003, Stellar award, 2003. Fellow: Inst. Advancement Engring.; mem.: NSPE, ASME, Nat. Mgmt. Assn. Avocations: music, continuing education, dance.

BRU, ABELARDO E., food products executive; BS in Mech. Engring., CCNY; AMP in Fin. Adminstrn., Mex. Inst. Banking and Fin.; AMP, Kellogg's Bus. Sch. With Ford Motor Co., Avon Products; various positions Pepsico, Inc., 1976—, pres., gen. mgr. Sabritas, 1992—99, chmn., CEO, Frito-Lay N.Am., 1999—. Mem. global leadership coun. Frito-Lay Co. Office: Pepsico Inc 7701 Legacy Dr Plano TX 75024

BRUBAKER, CRAWFORD FRANCIS, JR., federal agency administrator, aerospace scientist, consultant; b. Fruitland, Idaho, Apr. 23, 1924; s. Crawford Francis and Cora Susan (Flora) B.; m. Lucile May Christensen, May 5, 1945; children: Eric Stephen, Alan Kenneth, Craig Martin, Paul David. BA, Pomona Coll., 1946; MBA, U. Pa., 1948. Office mgr. Lockheed Calif. Co., Burbank, 1948-54, sales adminstr., 1954-57, with fighter contracts divsn., field office rep., 1959-65, asst. dir. fighter sales, 1965-69, dep. mgr. bid and proposals, 1969-74, mgr. govt. sales, 1974-76; dir. internat. mktg. devel. and policy Lockheed Corp., Burbank, 1976-83; dep. asst. sec. for aerospace U.S. Dept. Commerce, Washington, 1983-87; internat. aerospace cons., 1987—. Vice chair bd. trustees So. Calif. Presbyn. Homes; vice chmn. Industry Sector Adv. Com., Washington, 1979-83; mem. Aero. Policy Rev. Com., Washington, 1983-87. Vice chmn. So. Calif. Dist. Export Coun., L.A., 1980-83, 88-91, chmn., 1992-93. Lt. (j.g.) USN, 1943-45, PTO. Mem. AIAA, Am. Def. Preparedness Assn., Sigma Alpha Epsilon. Republican. Presbyterian. Avocations: coin collecting/numismatics, golf, fishing, photography. E-mail: fordbaker@romres.org, cfbrubaker@romres.org.

BRUBAKER, JAMES EDWARD, mechanical engineer; b. Chgo., Feb. 24, 1935; s. Samuel James and Mary Louise (Alward) B.; m. Phyllis Ann Evans, Aug. 18, 1956; children: David, Richard, Lisa, Mark. BS in Gen. Engring., U. Ill., 1956. Instr. engring. U. Ill., 1956-57; mgr. mechanism and core barrel devel. advanced submarine project Bettis Atomic Power Lab., Pitts., 1959-75; cog. engr. head access area and refueling equipment Clinch River Breeder Reactor, Pitts., 1975-83; project engr. Peacekeeper (MX) Missile Project, Advanced Reactor Divsn., 1983—85; prin. engr. West Valley Nuc. Demonstration Project. Advanced Reactor Divsn., 1985-87; prin. engr. Tomahawk missile sys., naval environ. equipment, 1987-95; sr. project engr. advanced submarine reactor pumps Machinery Tech. Divsn. Westinghouse Elec. Corp., Pitts., 1996—2000. Cons. in field. Patentee in field; editor Mechanism Design Manual and Mil. Specification for Naval Reactor CRDMs. Recipient Environ. Protection commendation U.S. Navy, 1995. Mem. Pleasant Hills Athletic Assn. (pres. 1976-77), Lions Club Internat. (14-B dist. gov. 2005—), Phi Kappa Tau. Republican. Avocations: tennis, golf, reading, travel.

BRUBAKER, KAREN SUE, small business owner; b. Ashland, Ohio, Feb. 5, 1953; d. Robert Eugene and Dora Louise (Camp) Brubaker; m. Philip J. Potter, Oct. 10, 2003. BSBA, Ashland U., 1975; MBA, Bowling Green State U., 1976. Supr. tire ctr. ops. B.F. Goodrich Co., Akron, Ohio, 1976-77, supr. tire ctr. acctg., 1977-79, asst. product mgr. radial passenger tires, 1979-80, product mgr. broadline passenger tires, 1980-81, group product mgr. broadline passenger and light truck tires, 1981-83, mktg. mgr. T/A high tech radials, 1983-86; product mktg. mgr. B.F. Goodrich T/A radials The Uniroyal Goodrich Tire Co., Akron, Ohio, 1986-91; product mktg. mgr. Michelin performance tires Michelin Americas Small Tires, Akron, Ohio, 1991-95; ind. EcoQuest Internat. distbr. DBA Indoor Air Repair & Water, Fairlawn, Ohio, 1996—. Sect. chmn. indsl. divsn. United Way, Akron, 1983-86; mem. adv. coun. to trustees Coll. Bus. and Econs, Ashland U., 1990-92; vol. Hospice Vis. Nurses Svcs., 1995--; fund raiser Nat. Heart Assist and Transplant Fund/Judi Reali Transplant Fund, 1996. Recipient Alumni Disting. Service award Ashland Coll., 1986; Alpha Phi Clara Bradley Burdette scholar, 1975. Mem. Am. Mktg. Assn. (pres. Akron/Canton chpt. 1982-83, Highest Honors award 1983, nat. bd. dirs., v.p. bus. mktg. 1984-86, v.p. profl. chpts. 1987-89), Sales and Mktg. Execs. (v.p. membership, 1998-99), Akron Women's Network, Zonta Internat. (membership dir. 1987-94, 96—), Beta Gamma Sigma, Omicron Delta Epsilon. Home: 822 Village Pkwy Fairlawn OH 44333-3297 Office Phone: 330-666-9330. Personal E-mail: airwaves@bigplanet.com.

BRUBAKER, LAUREN EDGAR, minister; b. Birmingham, Ala., Oct. 8, 1914; s. Lauren Edgar and Nora (Drake) B.; m. Leonte Saye, June 6, 1944; children: Lauren Eugene, Edward Saye; m. Patricia Barnett, July 23, 1994. AB, Birmingham So. Coll., 1935; MDiv, Princeton Theol. Sem., 1938, postdoctoral, 1946-47; STM, Union Theol. Sem., N.Y., 1942, ThD, 1944. Ordained to ministry Presbyn. Ch., 1938. Asst. pastor in, Parkersburg, W.Va., 1938-41; grad. asst. Union Theol. Sem., 1941-43; chaplain U.S. Army, 1943-46; grad. instr. Princeton Theol. Sem., 1946-47; prof. philosophy and religion, chaplain Parsons Coll., Fairfield, Iowa, 1947-49. Assoc. prof. U. S.C., Columbia, 1949-58, prof., 1958-79, Disting. prof., 1979-80, Disting. prof. emeritus, 1980—, univ. chaplain, 1949-94, chmn. dept. religious studies, 1949-80; adj. prof. Luth. Theol. So. Sem.; moderator Univ. Forum on S.C. Ednl. TV, 1965-73. Contbr. articles to profl. jours. Dir. S.C. Coun. Human Rels., 1966-69; exec. committeman Columbia and Richland County Dem. party, 1950-60. Served to maj. AUS, 1943-46. Mem. AAUP (past officer), Inst. Religion (dir. 1960-63), S.C. Acad. Religion (founder 1968, pres. 1968), Am. Acad. Religion (pres. 1959), Presbyn. Edn. Assn. South, Columbia Ministers Assn. (pres. 1972), Assn. Coll. and Univ. Religious Affairs (bd. dirs. 1985-86), Columbia Forum Internat. Affairs (pres. 1971), Columbia Coun. for Internat. (bd. dirs., pres. 1986, 87), Nat. Assn. Coll. and Univ. Chaplains, Soc. Bibl. Lit. (past officer), Christian Jewish Congress S.C. (sec. 1982-90), Columbia CROP WALK (treas. 1983-98), Common Cause of S.C. (dir. 1988-2000, sec. 1989-96), Exec. Club Columbia (pres. 1960-61), Kiwanis (pres. 1986-87), Omicron Delta Kappa (faculty adviser 1968-71), Pi Gamma Mu, Phi Kappa Phi, Tau Kappa Alpha. Achievements include research on the teaching of religion in accredited colleges and universities. Home: 10450 Lottsford Rd Apt 4207 Mitchellville MD 20721-2752

BRUBAKER, LINDA, gynecologist; b. Oak Park, Ill., Oct. 30, 1955; d. George Albert and Marian Constance Tetzlaff; m. Warren Earl Brubaker, June 25, 1983; children: Aleah, Anita, Keene. BA with honors, U. Ill., Chgo., 1977; post grad., U. Chgo., 1978; MD, Rush U. Rush Med. Coll., Chgo., 1984. Cert. Am. Bd. Ob-Gyn., lic. physician and surgeon Ill. Post sophomore fellow dept. pathology Rush U. Rush Med. Coll., Chgo., 1982—83; resident ob-gyn. Rush Presbyn. St. Luke's Med. Ctr., 1984—88, chief resident ob-gyn., 1987—88, adjunctive attending and fellow urogyne, 1988—90; instr. Rush Med. Coll., 1988—90, asst. prof. urogynecology, 1990—95, asst. prof. gen. surgery, 1993—95, assoc. prof. dept. ob-gyn. conjoint dept. surgery, 1995—99, prof. dept. ob-gyn. conjoint dept. surgery, 1999—2000; consulting provisional MacNeal Hosp., Berwyn, 1991—93; provisional Vencor Hosp., Chgo. and Northlake, 1992—95; gen. Ill. Masonic Med. Ctr., Chgo., 1995—2000; asst. attending Rush Presbyn. St. Luke's Med. Ctr., 1990—98, sr. attending, 1998—2000, Loyola U. Med. Ctr., Maywood, 2000, prof. dept. ob-gyn., 2000—, prof. dept. urology, 2000—. Dir. Divsn. of Female Pelvic Medicine and Reconstructive Surgery Loyola U. Med. Ctr., Maywood, Ill., 2000—; vis. prof. Dept. Ob-Gyn. Karolinska Inst. Danderyd Hosp., Stockholm, 1999, Dartmouth-Hitchcock Med. Ctr., Lebanon, NH, 2002; presenter to profl. seminars and confs. Contbr. scientific papers, articles to profl. jours. Named Urogynecologist of Yr., Nat. Assn. Continence, 2002; recipient Faculty Tchg. award, 1992, Ortho Pharmaceutical/CREOG, 1998; grantee, NIH/NICHD, 2001—06, NIH/NIDDK, 2001—06, Eli Lilly & Co., 2002—. Fellow: ACS, ACOG (Outstanding Svc. on Edn. Commn. 1998). Avocations: sports, reading, orchids. Office: Loyola Univ Med Ctr 2160 S First Ave Maywood IL 60153

BRUBAKER, ROBERT LORING, lawyer; b. Louisville, May 22, 1947; s. Robert Lee and Betty (Brock) B.; m Jeannette Marie Montgomery, Dec. 21, 1968; children: Benjamin Brock, Anne Montgomery. BA, Earlham Coll., 1969; JD, U. Chgo., 1972. Bar: Ohio 1972, U.S. Dist. Ct. (so. dist.) Ohio 1973, U.S. Ct. Appeals (6th cir.) 1975, U.S. Supreme Ct. 1978, U.S. Ct. Appeals (D.C. cir.) 1979, U.S. Ct. Appeals (3d, 4th and 7th cirs.) 1995. Asst. atty. gen. Atty. Gen.'s Office State of Ohio, Columbus, 1972-76; assoc. Porter Wright Morris & Arthur, Columbus, 1976-78, ptnr., 1979—. Editor: Ohio Environmental Law Handbook, 1990, 2d edit., 1992, 3d edit., 1994, Deposition Strategy, Law and Forms: Environmental Law. Mem. ABA (natural resources, energy and environ. law sect., pub. utility sect., standing com. on environ. law), Ohio Bar Assn. (environ. law com.), Air and Waste Mgmt. Assn. (chmn. S.W. Ohio chpt. 1990-91, chmn. East Ctrl. sect. 1991-92), Columbus Bar Assn. (environ. law com.), Nat. Coal Coun. Home: 2661 Wexford Rd Columbus OH 43221-3217 Office: Porter Wright Morris & Arthur 41 S High St Ste 2800 Columbus OH 43215-6194 Office Phone: 614-227-2033. Business E-Mail: rbrubaker@porterwright.com.

BRUBAKER, WILLIAM ROGERS, sociology educator; b. Evanston, Ill., June 8, 1956; s. Charles William and Elizabeth (Rogers) B. BA summa cum laude, Harvard U., 1979; MA, Sussex U., Eng., 1980; PhD, Columbia U., 1990. Prof. UCLA, 1994—, assoc. prof. sociology, 1991-94. Author: The Limits of Rationality, 1984, Citizenship and Nationhood in France and Germany, 1992, Nationalism Reframed, 1996, Ethnicity Without Groups, 2004; editor: Immigration and Politics of Citizenship in Europe and North America, 1989. Jr. fellow Soc. Fellows Harvard U., 1988-91; MacArthur fellow, 1994-99; NSF Young Investigator awardee; Guggenheim fellow, 1999-2000. Office: U Calif Dept Los Angeles Dept of Sociology 264 Haines Hall Los Angeles CA 90095

BRUBAKER, WILLIAM W., JR., federal agency administrator, civil engineer; b. May 13, 1949; m. Sandra Ann Squaglia; children: Taralyn, William W. III. BS in Civil Engring., U. Va., 1972; MS in Civil Engring., Ga. Inst. Tech., 1975; MS in Bus. Adminstrn., Boston U., 1978. Registered profl. engr., Minn., Fla. Gen. engr. South Railroad, Atlanta, 1972-75; civil engr. U.S. Army Corps Engrs., 1976-92; gen. engr., mem. fed. sr. exec. svc. NASA, Washington, 1992—, dir. facilities engring., 1995—. Mem. exec. com. Constrn. Industry Inst.; adv. com. mem. civil engring. dept. U. Va. Decorated Meritorious Civilian Svc. medal U.S. Army, 1992; recipient Fed. Engr. of the Year award NSPE, 1997. Fellow ASCE; mem. Soc. Am. Mil. Engrs.

BRUBECK, DAVID WARREN, musician; b. Concord, Calif., Dec. 6, 1920; s. Howard and Elizabeth (Ivey) Brubeck; m. Iola Whitlock, Sept. 21, 1942; children: David Darius, Michael, Christopher, Catherine, Daniel, Matthew.

MusB, U. Pacific, 1942; postgrad. study with Darius Milhaud, Mills Coll., 1946-49; PhD (hon.), U. Pacific, Fairfield U., U. Bridgeport, Mills Coll., Niagara U., Kalamazoo Coll., U. Duisburg, Germany, U. Nottingham, England, Cleve. Inst. Music. Leader Dave Brubeck Octet, Trio and Quartet, 1946—, 3 month tour Europe and Middle East for U.S. Dept. State, followed by tours Australia, Japan, and USSR, recordings with Atlantic Record Co., Columbia Record Co., Decca, Horizon, Concord Jazz, Fantasy Records, Music Masters, GRP, Telarc Records, Time Out (1st jazz LP to receive Gold Record); composer: (ballets) Points on Jazz, Glances, (orchestral) Elementals, They All Sang Yankee Doodle, (flute and guitar) Tritonis, (piano) Reminiscences of the Cattle Country, Four by Four, Chromatic Fantasy Sonata, (oratorios) Beloved Son, The Light in the Wilderness, Voice of the Holy Spirit, (cantatas) Gates of Justice, Truth Is Fallen, La Fiesta de la Posada, (chorus and orchestra) Pange Lingua, Mass: To Hope, I See, Satie, Four New England Pieces, Lenten Triptych, In Praise of Mary, Joy in the Morning, (choral) Earth Is Our Mother, and over 100 jazz compositions including Blue Rondo a la Turk, In Your Own Sweet Way, The Duke. Decorated John Gense award NYC; named to Nat. Medal of the Arts, 1994, Hollywood Walk of Fame, 1994, Am. Jazz Hall of Fame, 1995; recipient NEA Jazz Master award, jazz polls conducted by Downbeat, Melody Maker, Cashbox, Billboard and Playboy mags., 1952—55, first jazz musician on cover of Time Mag., 1954, B.M.I. Jazz Pioneer award, 1985, Compostela Humanitarian award, 1986, Conn. Arts award, 1987, Am. Eagle award Nat. Music Coun., 1988, Officier de L'Ordre des Arts et Lettres, Govt. France, 1988, Ct. Bar Assn. award, 1992, Simon's Rock Disting. Achievement, 1992, Lifetime Achievement award NARAS, 1996, Lugano award, Switzerland, 1996, Cyril Magnin award, San Francisco, 1997, Spirit of the City award, NYC, 1999, James Smithson award, Smithsonian Inst., 2000, Calif. Golden State award, 2000, Bocconi Univ. medal, Milan, 2000, Honor Cross for Sci. and Art, 1st Class, Austrian Govt., 2002; Duke Ellington fellow Yale U., 1992. Mem.: Phi Mu Alpha. also: care Sutton Artists Corp 20 W Park Ave Ste 305 Long Beach NY 11561-2019 Office: Derry Music Co PO Box 150270 San Rafael CA 94915*

BRUCE, CAROL ELDER, lawyer; b. East Orange, NJ, June 7, 1949; BA, George Washington U., 1971, JD, 1974. Bar: DC 1975. Law clk. to Hon. Harold H. Greene, Chief Judge DC Superior Ct.; asst. & ind. counsel, Fraud and Major Crimes Divsn. US Dist. Atty. Office, Washington; ptnr., Corp. Def. Dept. & Comml. Litig. Dept. Venable LLP, Washington. Mem., Lawyer Counseling Panel US Dist. Ct. (Dist. DC); faculty Georgetown U., Washington. Bd. adv. George Washington U. Law Ctr., Washington. Named a Top Washington Lawyer, criminal def., Washingtonian Mag., 2004, Leading Lawyer, litig., Legal Times, 2003. Master: Edward Bennett Williams Am. Inn of Ct. (charter mem.); fellow: Am. Coll. Trial Lawyers (internat. affairs com.); mem.: DC Bar Assn. (bd. gov.). Office: Venable LLP 575 7th St NW Washington DC 20004 Office Phone: 202-344-4717. Office Fax: 202-344-8300. Business E-Mail: cebruce@venable.com.

BRUCE, CHRISTINE ANN, special education educator, gifted and talented educator; d. Raymond Earnest Bunce and Lois May Rodney; m. Jonathan Green (div.). BS, Millersville U., 1972, MEd, 1974; PhD, Pa. State U., 1999. Tchr., team leader Lampeter-Strasburg Sch. Dist., Pa., 1972—82; sch. counselor Warwick Sch. Dist., Lititz, 1982—99, dir. pupil svcs., 1991—99; dist. coord., EEL counseling, spl. edn., gifted svcs. Sch. Dist. Lancaster, 1999—. Adj prof. Pa. State U., Great Valley, 2003—, Harrisburg, 2003—; chair IU113 Student Assistance Program, Lancaster, 1991—93; mem., dist. rep. Children and Youth Liaison, 1990—93; mem. Lancaster Book Challenge. Bd. pres., vol. Big Bros./Big Sisters, Lancaster, 1985—; bd. trustees Hugh O'Brien Youth Leadership, 1989—93. Mem.: ASCD, Tchrs. of English as 2d Lang., Nat. Assn. Bilingual Edn., Am. Counselor Assn. Avocations: travel, theater, reading, gardening. Office: Lancaster Sch Dist 251 S Prince St Lancaster PA 17601

BRUCE, DAVID LIONEL, retired anesthesiologist, educator; b. Champaign, Ill., Oct. 27, 1933; s. Lionel Harry and Freda Eleanor (Tipsword) B.; m. Geraldine Zawasky, Nov. 24, 1956 (div. 1967); children: Ellen Marie, Brian David; m. Sharon Jean Wells, Jan. 18, 1985 (div. 2004). Student, U. Ill., 1951-54, MD, 1960. Diplomate Am. Bd. Anesthesiology. Intern Ill. Rsch. and Ednl. Hosp., Chgo., 1960-61; resident U. Pa., Phila., 1961-64; asst. prof. anesthesiology U. Ky. Med. Ctr., Lexington, 1964-66; from asst. prof. to prof. Northwestern U. Med. Sch., Chgo., 1966-77; prof. U. Calif., Irvine, 1977-81; prof. anesthesiology NYU Med. Sch., 1981-84; prof. U. Miss. Med. Ctr., Jackson, 1984-90, chmn. dept., 1985-90; dir. outpatient surgery Athens (Ga.) Regional Med. Cr., 1990-92; prof. anesthesiology U. South Fla., Tampa Gen. Hosp., 1992-93; med. dir. surg. svcs. Tampa Gen. Hosp., 1993; med. dir. outpatient surgery ctr. Athens (Ga.) Regional Med. Ctr., 1993-95. Cons. FDA, Rockville, Md., 1972-75, mem. adv. com., Bethesda, Md., 1973-77. Author: Klaus and Max: Their Friendship Defied Hitler, 2000; contbr. numerous articles to profl. jours. Cpl. U.S. Army, 1954-56. Recipient Rsch. Career Devel. award USPHS, 1967-72 Fellow Royal Soc. Medicine (Eng.) (travelling fellow 1975); mem. Am. Soc. Anesthesiologists. Avocations: music, writing.

BRUCE, DUNCAN ARCHIBALD, investor, writer; b. Pitts., Feb. 19, 1932; s. Archibald Duncan Bruce and Marian Colley; m. Tamara Bruce, Dec. 4, 1965; children: Jennifer, Elizabeth. BS in Econs., U. Pa., 1954. Pres. Edgewood Holdings, Inc., N.Y.C., 1989—2002, Normandie Holdings, Ltd., N.Y.C., 1996—. Author: (book) The Mark of the Scots, 1996, The Scottish 100, 2000, King Arthur Revisited, 2001, The Great Scot, 2004. Hon. chieftan Bonnie Brae Scottish Games, Millington, NJ, 1990. Recipient Ellis Island medal of honor, Nat. Ethnic Coalition Orgns., 1998, Odom Heritage award, Scottish Weekend, 2002, Nat. Tartan Day award, Scottish Coalition, 2003. Fellow: Soc. Antiquaries Scotland; mem.: Caledonian Found., Burns Soc. City of N.Y. (past trustee), Scottish Heritage USA (bd. dirs.), St. Andrew's Soc. N.Y. (historian, bd. mgrs., pres., chmn. 250th ann. com., mem. exec. com.), Am. Scottish Found. (bd. dir., treas., v.p., past hon. sponsoring com.), Mask and Wig Club, An Ceud Fear. Home: 185 E 85th St Apt 35D New York NY 10028-2150

BRUCE, ESTEL EDWARD, lawyer; b. Hutchinson, Kans., Nov. 23, 1938; s. Kenneth Dean and Josephine (Vigna) B.; m. Marnell Elaine Higley, Aug. 9, 1960; children: Anthony Dean, Caroline Bruce Macaulay. BA summa cum laude, Yale U., 1960, LLB magna cum laude, 1966. Bar: D.C. 1967, U.S. Ct. Appeals (1st, 2d, 3d, 4th, 5th, 6th, 8th, 9th, 10th, D.C. and Fed. cirs.), U.S. Supreme Ct. 1969. Law clk. for Justice Potter Stewart of U.S. Supreme Ct., 1966—67; assoc. Covington & Burling, Washington, 1967-73, ptnr., 1973—; adj. prof. constitutional law Georgetown U. Law Center, 1970-75. Mem. Appellate Judges Conf., Com. on Appellate Practice, 1993-2000; mem. faculty ABA Appellate Inst., 1992-2000. Mem. adminstrv. bd. Cornell Lab. Ornithology, 1998-2004; bd. dirs. Young Concert Artists Washington, 2003—, Washington Area Lawyers for the Arts, 1993-99, Yale Law Sch. Fund, 1992-98, Audubon Nat. Soc., 1986-92. Lt. jg. USN, 1960—63. Mem.: ABA, Edward Coke Appellate Inn of Ct. (v.p. 2000—02, pres. 2002—03), D.C. Bar Assn., Am. Acad. Appellate Lawyers, Am. Law Inst., Chevy Chase Club, Met. Club, Phi Beta Kappa, Order of Coif. Home: 2701 Foxhall Rd NW Washington DC 20007-1128 Office: Covington & Burling 1201 Pennsylvania Ave NW Washington DC 20004-2401 Office Phone: 202-662-5284. Personal E-mail: ebruce@cov.com.

BRUCE, JACKSON MARTIN, JR., lawyer; b. Milw., Apr. 10, 1931; s. Jackson Martin and Harriet (Edgell) B.; m. Lilias M. Morehouse, June 30, 1954; children: Lilias Stephanie, Andrew Edgell. AB magna cum laude, Harvard U., 1953, JD cum laude, 1957; MA with 1st class honors in Law, Cambridge U., 1955. Bar: Wis. 1957, Fla. 1973. Assoc. Quarles & Brady, Milw., 1957-64, ptnr., 1964-96; shareholder Dunwody, White & Landon, Naples, Fla., 1996—; counsel Michael Best & Friedrich, Milw., 1996—. Mem. joint editl. bd. Uniform Trusts and Estates Acts; contbr. articles to profl. jours. Bd. dirs. Living Ch. Found., Inc., 1965-98; trustee Univ. Sch. Milw., 1973-79. Fellow Am. Coll. Trust and Estate Counsel (bd. regents 1976-82, treas. 1990-91, sec. 1991-92, v.p. 1992-93, pres. 1994-95); mem. ABA (bd. govs. 1994-97, chmn. sect. real property, probate and trust law 1984-85, ho. dels. 1988-97, ethics com. 1998-2001), State Bar Wis. (chmn. bd. govs. 1979-80), Am. Bar Found., Am. Law Inst., Internat. Acad. Estate and Trust Law (mem. exec. coun. 1980-86), Nat. Conf. Bar Pres., Town Club, Milw. Club (bd. dirs. 1985-2001), The Club Pelican Bay. Home: 6101 Pelican Bay Blvd Apt 1201 Naples FL 34108-8183 also: 9008 N Bayside Dr Milwaukee WI 53217-1913 Office: Dunwody White & Landon 4001 Tamiami Trl N Ste 200 Naples FL 34103-3591 also: Michael Best & Friedrich 100 E Wisconsin Ave Ste 3300 Milwaukee WI 53202-4107 Office Phone: 239-263-5885, 414-225-4963. Business E-Mail: jbruce@dwl-law.com, jmbruce@michaelbest.com.

BRUCE, JAMES DONALD, academic administrator; b. Livingston, Tex., June 28, 1936; s. Vivian Eugene and Edna Lee (St. Clair) B.; m. Eleanor MacLaren, Nov. 25, 1959; children: David MacLaren, Heather MacLaren, Nathaniel MacLaren. BSEE, BS in Math., Lamar State Coll. Tech., Beaumont, Tex., 1958; SMEE, MIT, 1960, ScD, 1964. Mem. faculty MIT, Cambridge, 1964—, assoc. dean engring., 1971-78, dean, 1977-78, prof. elec. engring., 1973—, dir. indsl. liaison, 1979-82, dir. info. sys., 1983-86, v.p. for info. sys., chief info. officer, 1986—, program mgr. reengring adminstrv. process, 1994-98. Found. New Eng. Acad. and Rsch. Network (NEARnet), 1988—95, mem. steering com., 1988—95; bd. dirs. BBN Tech. Svcs., Inc., 1993—95; mem. network planning and policy adv. coun. Univ. Corp. for Advanced Internet Devel. (UCAID), 1998—2002, chmn. network planning and policy adv. coun., 1999—2002, mem. bd. trustees, 1999—; cons. to govt. and industry; mem. adv. com. elec. engring. Lamar U., 1993—; mem. tech. adv. com. Mass. Divsn. Capital Planning and Ops., 1993—95; mem. total quality edn. com. to sec. edn. Commonwealth of Mass., 1993—95; founder Marketplace Network, Inc., bd. dirs. Trustee Harvard Coop. Soc., 1974-84, 93-96; trustee Park St. Congrl. Ch., Boston, 1977-83, vice chmn. bd. trustees, 1979-81, chmn., 1981-83, deacon, 1985-96, elder, 1997-99, moderator-elect, 2003. Postdoctoral fellow, Ford Found., 1964—65. Sr. mem. IEEE; mem. Am. Soc. Engring. Edn., Consortium for Sci. Computing (trustee, mem. exec. com., 1984-90, vice chmn. 1986-88), Eta Kappa Nu, Tau Beta Pi. Home: 12 Woodpark Cir Lexington MA 02421-7208 Office: MIT 77 Massachusetts Ave Rm 10-219 Cambridge MA 02139-4307 E-mail: jdb@mit.edu.

BRUCE, JAMES EDMUND, retired utilities executive; b. Boise, Idaho, June 23, 1920; s. James E. and Bessie (Barcus) B.; m. Lois I. Stevens, Aug. 24, 1946; children: James E., IV, Steven, Robert, David. Student, Coll. Idaho, 1937-39; BA, Portland U., 1941; postgrad., Georgetown U., 1941-42; LLB, U. Idaho, 1949. Bar: Idaho 1948. Asst. atty. gen. State of Idaho, 1948-49; dep. pros. atty. Ada County, Idaho, 1949-51; with Idaho Power Co., Boise, 1951-87, v.p., 1968-74, pres., chief operating officer, 1974-76, pres., chief exec. officer, 1976-85, chmn., 1985-87, ret., 1987. Dir. Albertson's Inc., First Security Corp., 1981-93; chmn. Blue Cross of Idaho, 1988-90. Bd. dirs. Mountain States Legal Found., 1977-88; mem. St. Alphonsus Found., Boise State U. Found., Bishop Kelly Found., Boise Park Bd., 1958-78; chmn. Idaho State Lottery; Idaho chmn. U.S. Savs. Bonds, 1976-85; chmn. bd. trustees St. Alphonsus, 1985-2002; trustee Coll. Idaho, YMCA, Idaho Nature Conservancy; pres. Ada County Hwy. Dist. Commn. With U.S. Army, 1942-46. Mem. ABA, Boise Execs. Assn., Edison Electric Assn. (dir. 1978-85), N.W. Electric Light and Power Assn. (pres. 1982), Boise C. of C., Arid Club, Crane Creek Country Club, Rotary, Elks, K.C. Roman Catholic.

BRUCE, JOHN ALLEN, foundation executive, educator; b. Kansas City, Mo., Sept. 17, 1934; BA, Wesleyan U., Middletown, Conn., 1956; MDiv., Gen. Theol. Sem., N.Y.C., 1959; PhD, U. Minn., 1972. Ordained to ministry Episcopal Ch., 1959. Clergyman, 1959-68; prof. U. Ala., Tuscaloosa, 1972-74; exec. dir. E.C. Brown Found., Portland, Oreg., 1974-98. Cons. to philanthropies and corp. programs; clin. prof. community medicine Sch. Medicine, Oreg. Health Scis. U., Portland, 1976-01. Author, editor various scholarly publs.; exec. prodr. ednl. films on family life, health and values. Bd. dirs., officer various cmty. orgns. Served to lt. USN, 1964-67. Recipient awards from med. orgns. and related groups. Mem. Cosmos Club. Republica. Home: 4909 Mulholland Dr Lake Oswego OR 97035-4393

BRUCE, JOHN ANTHONY, artist; b. L.A., Apr. 8, 1931; s. Merle VanDyke and Katherine Mary (Butler) B.; children: Marsha Lee, Margaret Lorren, James Cole, Glenn Allen, Mark Corwin, Leslie Ann. BA in Psychology and Art, Calif. State U., L.A., 1965. Design engr. N.Am. Aviation Corp., Downey, Calif., 1952-57; comml. artist Aerojet Gen. Corp., Sacramento, 1957-59; advt. mgr. Flow Equipment Co., Santa Fe Springs, Calif., 1959-63; art dir. Barnes-Champ Advt., Santa Ana, Calif., 1963-66, Long Beach (Calif.) Ind. Press Telegram News, 1970-73. Freelance art cons. Epcot project Walt E. Disney Enterprises, Glendale, Calif., 1976-77. Permanent collections Smithsonian Inst., Washington, D.C.; one man shows Ghormley Gallery, L.A., 1966, Les Li Art Gallery, L.A., 1970, Upstairs Gallery, Long Beach, Calif., 1973, El Prado Gallery, Sedona, Ariz., 1987; group shows Newport Beach Invitational, Newport Beach, Calif., 1964, Laguna Beach Art Festival, Laguna Beach, Calif., 1962, 63, 64, 65, Butler Inst. Am. Art, Youngstown, Ohio, 1970, Allied Artists, N.Y.C., 1988; currently exhibiting with Bartfield Gallery, N.Y.C., New Masters Gallery, Carmel, Calif. With U.S. Army, 1949-52, Korea. Recipient John B. Grayback award Am. Profl. Artists League, 1988, Best of Show award Gene Autry Mus. AICA Show, 1996, San Dimas Festival of Western Art, 1996, Best of Show Chgo. Windy City Artists, 1999, numerous others. Republican. Studio: 5394 Tip Top Rd Mariposa CA 95338-9609

BRUCE, JUDITH ESTHER, retired music educator, elementary school educator; b. St. Louis, Oct. 16, 1945; d. Charles Edward and Helen Ruth (Yost) Poleos; m. Roy N. Bruce; children: Rory, Robert, Joshua. BS in Edn., Southeast Mo. State U., 1967; MA in Theatre, Lindenwood U., 1992, MFA in Theatre, 1994. Tchr. vocal music Springdale Elem. Sch., Mo., 1967—77, DeSmet Elem. Sch., Florissant, Mo., 1977—85; tchr. vocal and MIE Yamaha Walnut Grove Elem. Sch., Ferguson, Mo., 1985—2002. Talent chmn., benefit charity shows, Christian Hosp. Aux., St. Louis, 1977-2000 Recipient Hall of Fame award, St. Louis Suburban Music Educators Assn., 2002—03. Mem.: St. Louis Suburban Music Educators Assn., Music Educators Nat. Conf., St. Louis Suburban Music Edc. Assn. (Hall of Fame award 2002—03, 2002—03), Ferguson-Florissant Cmty. Tchrs. Assn., Mo. State Tchrs. Assn. (treas. Ferguson-Florissant dist. chpt. 1985—2002), Raintree Arts Coun. of Lincoln and Pike Counties, White Shrine. Home: 17534 Highway NN Bowling Green MO 63334 E-mail: bruce45@earthlink.net.

BRUCE, LADY ANNE, vocational school educator; b. Jackson, Miss., Apr. 16, 1958; d. Jerry Clay and Jeannine Jacks Stone; m. Robert Alan Bruce, June 9, 1990; children: Laurel Anne, Alan Clay. BS, Miss. State U., 1980, MEd, 1985. Nat. bd. cert. tchr. Nat. Bd. for Profl. Tchg. Stds. Miss., 2002. Mktg. and coop. edn. instr./DECA advisor Iuka H.S., Iuka, Miss., 1984—91; coop. edn. instr., DECA advisor Tishomingo County H.S., Iuka, Miss., 1991—95; mktg. instr., DECA advisor Bay H.S., Bay St. Louis, Miss., 1996—2002; lodging and hospitality instr., DECA advisor Hancock County Vocat. Ctr., Kiln, Miss., 2002. State officer advisor Miss. DECA, Jackson, 2000—02; curriculum writing team Rsch. and Curriculum Unit, Starkville, 2003—05. Asst. girl scout leader troop 340 Girl Scouts, Diamondhead, Miss., 1997—2005; legislative com. Delta Kappa Gamma, Diamondhead, Miss., 2000—02; sunday sch. tchr. St. Thomas Episcopal Ch., Diamondhead, Miss., 1997—2003; world fellowship chairperson Delta Kappa Gamma, Diamondhead, Miss., 2002—04. Recipient Dist. Mktg. Tchr. of the Yr., Miss. Assn. of Mktg. Teachers, 1987, 1988, 2001, Star Tchr., Miss. Econ. Coun., 1990, 2000, DECA Dist. Advisor of the Yr., Miss. DECA, 1999, Hancock County Tchr. of the Yr., Hancock County Sch. Dist., 2005. Mem.: Miss. DECA (hon. life mem.), Miss. Assn. of Career and Tech. Edn. (assoc.), Miss. Assn. Mktg. Educators (assoc.; pres. 1990—91), Assn. for Career and Tech. Edn. (assoc.). Episcopalian. Avocations: travel, needle work, reading. Office: Hancock County Vocat Ctr 7180 Airport Rd Kiln MS 39556 Office Phone: 228-467-3568. Office Fax: 228-466-4944. Personal E-mail: ladybruce@hotmail.com.

BRUCE, MARINO ANTON, sociologist, educator; b. South Boston, Va., Feb. 4, 1968; s. Paul and Vernell Bruce (Stepmother), Annie Bruce; m. Dorothy Janice Warren; children: Leslial Renee Franklin, Larueal Janiece Hughes children: Antonia Janielle. BA in Econs., Davidson Coll., 1989; PhD, N.C. State U., 1997. Asst. prof. sociology U. Wis., Madison, Wis., 1998—2004, NIH rsch. fellow, 2003—05; assoc. prof. family and cmty. medicine Meharry Med. Coll., Nashville, 2005—. Personal E-mail: marinobruce@yahoo.com.

BRUCE, MARY HANFORD, academic administrator, educator, writer; d. Francis Hamilton Baldy and Frances Lawson Waterfield; m. Guy Steven Bruce, Mar. 23, 1991; m. David Allan Terry, Oct. 6, 1962 (div. Jan. 8, 1980); children: David Hamilton Terry, John Hanford Terry. PhD, Ariz. State U., Tempe, 1986. Cert. tchr. Ariz., Tenn., Tex. Lectr. Memphis State U., 1968—69, Ariz. State U., Tempe, 1982—85; sr., Fulbright scholar Ecole Normale Superieure, Yaomde, Cameroon, 1988—90; dir. internat. children's reading, writing and tchg. program Monmouth Coll., Reading, England, 2001—04. Dir. Associated Programs of Midwest Program, Harare, Zimbabwe, 1995; writer-in-residence U. Dar es Salaam, Tanzania, 2004; group leader student trip, Munich, 05. Author: Holding to the Light, 1992, Dr. Sally's Voodoo Man, 2003, (short stories) Twin Bead, Echoes, Voodoo Faust, Swaying, C'est Le Parfum, They Only Laughed Later, numerous poems. Grantee, Mellon Found. Global Ptnrs., Kenya, 2000, 2002, Mellon Found. Global Ptnrs., Tanzania, 2004—; Fulbright scholar, Ecolé Normabe Superiere, Univ. Yaounde, Cameroon, Africa, 1988—90. Mem.: AAUP, Associated Writing Programs. Home: 511 E Boston Monmouth IL 61462 Office: Monmouth Coll 700 E Broadway Monmouth IL 61462 Office Phone: 309-457-2183. Business E-Mail: mary@monm.edu.

BRUCE, MELISSA DANIELLE, music educator; b. Rock Hill, SC, Jan. 20, 1981; s. Danny Ray and Deborah (Taylor) Bruce. MusB, Gardner-Webb U., 2004. Lic. tchr. NC. Secretarial asst. Gardner-Webb U., Boiling Springs, NC, 2004; music tchr., dir. Thomas Jefferson Classics Acad., Mooresboro, NC, 2004—. Vacation bible sch. tchr. First Ch. of Nazarene, Kings Mountain, NC, 1998—, Sunday sch. tchr., 1999—2003, Nazarene Youth internat. sec., 2002—. Recipient Symphonic Band award, Gardner-Webb Univ., 2003—04, First Chair Music Dept. award, 2003. Mem.: NC Music Educators' Assn. (treas. Gardner-Webb chpt. 2003—04). Avocations: composing, bicycling, tennis, softball, clarinet. Office: Thomas Jefferson Classical Acad 2527 Hwy 221-A Mooresboro NC 28114

BRUCE, PETER WAYNE, lawyer, insurance company executive; b. Rome, N.Y., July 12, 1945; s. G. Wayne and Helen A. (Hibling) B.; m. Joan M. McCabe, Sept. 20, 1969; children: Allison, Steven. BA, U. Wis., 1967; JD, U. Chgo., 1970; postgrad., Harvard Bus. Sch., 1986. Bar: Wis. 1970. Atty. Northwestern Mut. Life Ins. Co., Milw., 1970-74, asst. gen. counsel, 1974-80, gen. counsel, sec., 1980—, v.p., 1983-87, sr. v.p., gen. counsel, sec., 1987-90, sr. v.p. ins. ops., 1990-95, exec. v.p. ins. ops. & adminstrn., chief compliance officer, 1995-98, exec. v.p. accumulation products and long term care, 1998-2000, sr. exec. v.p. ins. ops. and long term care, 2000, sr. exec. v.p., 2000—. Bd. dirs. Northwestern Mut. Life Ins. Co., Milw., Northwestern Long-Term Care Ins. Co., Alverno Coll. Badger Meter Found., Growth Design Corp. Former chmn. Alverno Coll., Curative Rehab. Ctr., former mem. Shorewood Civic Improvement Found.; chair Milw. Archdiocese Resource Devel. Coun.; bd. dirs., chair Curative Found.; mem. Milw. Archdiocese Cath. Cmty. Found.; mem. Village of Shorewood (Wis.); mem. Village Shorewood Cmty. Devel. Assn., Wis. Equal Justice Fund; former mem. Planning and Devel. Commn. Mem. Wis. Bar Assn., Milw. Bar Assn., Am. Law Inst. Office: Northwestern Mut Life Ins Co 720 E Wisconsin Ave Milwaukee WI 53202-4703

BRUCE, ROBERT VANCE, historian, educator; b. Malden, Mass., Dec. 19, 1923; s. Robert Gilbert and Bernice Irene (May) B. Student, MIT, 1941-43; BS, U. N.H., 1945; MA, Boston U., 1947, PhD, 1953. Instr. U. Bridgeport, Conn., 1947-48; master Lawrence Acad., Groton, Mass., 1948-51; rsch. asst. to Benjamin P. Thomas, Washington, 1953-54; mem. faculty Boston U., 1955—, assoc. prof. history, 1960-66, prof., 1966-84, prof. emeritus, 1984—. Vis. prof. U. Wis., Madison, 1962-63. Author: Lincoln and the Tools of War, 3d edit., 1989, 1877, Year of Violence, 3d edit., 1989, Bell: Alexander Graham Bell and the Conquest of Solitude, 3d edit., 1995, Brit. edit., 1973, Japanese edit., 1991, Lincoln and the Riddle of Death, 1982, The Launching of Modern Am. Sci., 2d edit., 1988 (Pulitzer prize 1988); contbg. author: Lincoln the War President, 1992, Feeding Mars, 1993, War Comes Again, 1995, The Lincoln Enigma, 2001; contbr. articles to profl. jour. With AUS, 1943-46. Guggenheim fellow, 1957-58; Henry E. Huntington fellow, 1966; recipient Pulitzer Prize in history, 1988. Fellow AAAS, Soc. Am. Historians; mem. Orgn. Am. Historians (life mem.), AAAS, Lincoln Group of Boston (pres. 1969-74), Phi Beta Kappa. Democrat. Home: 3923 Westpark Ct NW Olympia WA 98502 E-mail: yov1877@webtv.net.

BRUCE, THOMAS ALLEN, physician, educator; b. Mountain Home, Ark., 1930; s. Rex Floyd and Dora Madeline (Fee) B.; m. Dolores Fay Montgomery; children: T.K. Montgomery, Dana Fee Thomas. BSM., MD, U. Ark., 1955, DSc (hon.), 1995. Intern Duke Hosp., 1956-57; resident medicine Bellevue Hosp., N.Y.C., 1957, Meml. Center Cancer and Allied Diseases, N.Y.C., 1958, Parkland Meml. Hosp., Dallas, 1958-59; cardiopulmonary trainee Southwestern Med. Sch. of U. Tex., 1959-60; cardiac research fellow Hammersmith Hosp. and U. London Postgrad. Med. Sch., London, 1960-61, Harvard Bus. Sch., 1974. From instr. to prof. medicine Wayne State U., 1961—68, also asst. dean Sch. Medicine; prof. medicine, head cardiovascular sect. U. Okla. Med. Ctr., 1968—74; prof. medicine, dean Coll. Medicine U. Ark. Med. Scis., 1974—85, emeritus prof., 1997—, dean pro tem Coll. Pub. Health, 2001—02, prof. health policy and mgmt., 2001—; dean pro tem U. Ark. Clinton Sch. Pub. Svc., 2003—04, assoc. dean, 2004—; med. dir. Barton Rsch. Inst., 1974—85; coord. Sino-am. Med. Exch. Program, 1979—85; rsch. support rev. com. NIH, 1983—85; program dir. W.K. Kellogg Found., 1985—97; co-chair session 312 Salzburg Seminar, Austria; mem. History of Medicine Assocs.; chair nat. adv. bd. cmty. health leadership program Robert Wood Johnson Found., 2004—; policy adv. bd. Ark. Ctr. for Health Improvement; chmn. bd. trustees Watershed Found.; adj. staff Ark. Cmty. Found.; chair bd. dirs. Heifer Project Internat., 2003. Rsch. and publs. on cardiovascular disease including left ventricular function in cardiac denervation, coronary heart disease, myocardial metabolism relating to phospholipids in graded cardiac ischmia, med. edn. with particular reference to rural health care, health promotion and disease prevention, primary health care, community-based pub. health. Master gardener, chmn. garden docents Wildwood Park Performing Arts; exec. bd. Ark. Com. on Fgn. Rels.; bd. dirs. Garvan Woodland Gardens. Recipient Ark. Gov. Meritorious Achievement award, Lugene Chilcote award, 1999, Double Helix award U. Ark. Med. Sci., 2001, Lucy Lockett Cabe award Wildwood Park for the Performing Arts, 2001, Giving Tree Soc. award, 2003, Ctrl. High Mus. Appreciation award, 2001, Ark. Ctr. for Health Improvement award, 2002, Sen. David Pryor Carelink award, 2004, Bruce Commons Dedication award U. Ark. Med. Scis. Coll. Publ Health, 2004, Martin Luther King Salute to Greatness award, 2005; Profl. of Yr., U. Ark. at Little Rock, 2003; inductee U. Ark. Med. Scis. Coll. Medicine Hall of Fame, 2004. Fellow: ACP, Am. Coll. Cardiology; mem.: AMA, APHA, Leila Arboretum Soc. (pres. 1989—92), Am. Rhododendron Soc., Ark. Caduceus Club, Alpha Omega Alpha, Sigma Xi. Home: 6 Spy Glass Ln Little Rock AR 72212-4418

BRUCE, THOMAS EDWARD, thanatologist, psychology professor; b. Vinton, Iowa, Dec. 3, 1937; s. George Robert and Lucille Etta (Aurner) B.; children: Scott Thomas and Suzanne Laura. BA, U. No. Iowa, 1961, MA, 1964; postgrad., U. Colo., 1968-71; MA, U. San Francisco, 1985. Lic. psychology educator, counselor, Calif. Tchr. various Iowa high schs., 1961-65; sociologist, counselor Office Econ. Opportunity, Denver, 1965-66; social sci. educator Arapahoe Coll., Littleton, Colo., 1966-69; lectr. U. Colo., Boulder, 1968-71; psychology educator Sacramento City Coll., Calif., 1972—. Thanatology cons. for hospices, survivor support groups, No. Calif., 1984—. Author: Grief Management: The Pain and the Promise, 1986,

Thanatology: Through the Veil, 1992; contbr. articles to profl. publs. Co-founder, bd. dirs. Bereavement Resources Network, Sacramento, 1983-87; profl. dir. Children's Respite Ctr., Sacramento, 1985-88; pres.-elect., bd. dirs. Hospice Care of Sacramento, 1979-85. With U.S. Army, 1955-58. Recipient Pres.'s award Nat. Hospice Orgn., 1985. Mem. Sacramento Mental Health Assn. (Vol. Svc. award 1985, 87), Assn. for Death Edn. and Counseling, Thanatology Found., Am. Fedn. Tchrs., Faculty Assn. Calif. C.C.'s, Pi Gamma Mu, Phi Delta Kappa. Avocations: music, visual arts, travel, reading. Office: Sacramento City Coll 3835 Freeport Blvd Sacramento CA 95822-1318 Office Phone: 916-558-2294. E-mail: brucete@yahoo.com.

BRUCE, WILLIAM A., airport executive; BS in Polit. Sci., UCLA, 1967; MPA, Calif. State U., L.A., 1971. Budget analyst, chief negotiator employee rels. City of L.A., 1969-80, various other positions, 1980-99; dir. airports adminstrn. L.A. World Airports, 1999—. Office: Los Angeles Dept Airports 1 World Way Los Angeles CA 90045-5803

BRUCH, CAROL SOPHIE, law educator; b. Rockford, Ill., June 11, 1941; d. Ernest and Margarete (Willstätter) B.; m. Jack E. Myers, 1960 (div. 1973); children: Margarete Louise Myers Feinstein, Kurt Randall Myers. AB, Shimer Coll., 1960; JD, U. Calif.-Berkeley, 1972; Dr. honoris causa, U. Basel, 2000. Bar: Calif. 1973, U.S. Supreme Ct. 1980. Law clk. to Justice William O. Douglas U.S. Supreme Ct., 1972-73; acting prof. law U. Calif., Davis, 1973—78, prof., 1978—2001, rsch. prof., prof. emeritus, 2001—05, chair doctoral program in human devel., 1996—2001, disting. prof. emeritus, 2005—. Acad. vis. law dept. U. Munich, 1978-79, 92, U. Cologne, 1990, U. Cambridge, 1990, London Sch. Econs. and Polit. Sci., 1991, Kings Coll., London, 1991; vis. prof. U. Calif., Berkeley, 1983, Columbia U., 1986, U. Basel, 1994, vis. Fulbright prof. Hebrew U., Jerusalem, 1996-97; vis. fellow Fitzwilliam Coll., Cambridge, Eng., 1990, U. Calif. Humanities Rsch. Inst., Irvine, 1999, vis. scholar Inst. for Advanced Legal Studies (Univ. London), 1991, UCLA Ctr. Study of Women, 2004-05; cons. to Ctr. for Family in Transition, 1981, Calif. Law Revision Commn., 1979-82, NOW Legal Def. and Edn. Fund, 1980-81; lectr., legis. drafting and testimony, 1976—; mem. U.S. del. 4th Inter-Am. Specialized Conf. on Pvt. Internat. Law, OAS, 1989. Contbr. articles to legal jours. Editor Calif. Law Rev., 1971; editorial Bd. Family Law Quar., 1980-87; Representing Children, 1995—, Am. Jour. of Comparative Law, 2001—; lectr. in field. Mem. adv. com. child support and child custody Calif. Commn. on Status of Women, 1981-83, child support adv. com. Calif. Jud. Coun., 1991-94, adv. com. on private internat. law U.S. Dept. State, 1989—, internat. child abduction steering com. Internat. Ctr. for Missing and Exploited Children (London), 1999-2001; host parent Am. Field Service, Davis, 1977-78. Max Rheinstein sr. rsch. fellow Alexander von Humboldt Found., Fed. Republic Germany, 1978-79, 92, Fulbright fellow, Western Europe, 1990, Fulbright Sr. Scholar, Israel, 1997, Disting. Pub. Svc. award U. Calif. Davis Acad. Senate, 1990. Mem. ABA, Calif. State Bar Assn., Am. Law Inst., Internat. Soc. Family Law (exec. coun. 1994-2000, 2002—), Order of Coif. Democrat. Jewish. Office: U Calif Sch Law 400 Mrak Hall Dr Davis CA 95616-5201

BRUCH, RUTH E., information technology executive; BA in fin., U. Iowa. Contr. Davenport Bank and Trust Co., Iowa; with ctr. bus. innovation Ernst & Young; v.p. and dir. IT planning First Bank Sys. (now US Bank), St. Paul; v.p. and mng. dir. info. sys. Continental Bank (now Bank Am.), Chgo.; prin. JGA Consulting, Barrington, Ill., 1991—93; from dir. info. tech. strategic planning to v.p. and CIO Union Carbide Corp., Danbury, Conn., 1993—99; pres. and COO Zonetrader.com, Chgo., 1999—2000; v.p. and CIO Visteon Corp., Dearborn, Mich., 2000—02; sr. v.p. and CIO Lucent Tech., Murray Hill, NJ, 2002—. Bd. dir. Mellon Fin. Corp., 2003—; tech. adv. bd. Blue Star Solutions. Home: Chgo. Office: Lucent Tech Inc 600 Mountain Ave Murray Hill NJ 07974

BRUCH, VIRGINIA IRENE SULLIVAN, librarian, writer; b. Hickman, Ky., May 26, 1921; d. Thomas Terrell and Virginia Irene (Helm) Sullivan; BS, Murray U., 1943; m. Truman Elwood Bruch, Feb. 18, 1944; dau., Susan Irene (Mrs. Richard Lyons Rose). Librarian, Union City (Tenn.) High Sch., 1943-44; librarian, cataloger FTC Army Library, Washington, 1949-55; librarian, cataloger Army Library, Washington, 1955-65, chief catalog sect., 1965-71, chief tech. svcs. br., 1971-80; rsch. curator Boyhood Home of Robert E. Lee, Alexandria, Va., 1983—. Recipient prize Fed. Poet, 1956, first place essay category creative writing contest Va. Highlands Festival, 1976; Outstanding Performance award Army Library, 1979. Mem. Spl. Libraries Assn., A.L.A., Nat. Geneal. Soc., Va. Hist. Soc., Tenn. Hist. Soc., Ky. Hist. Soc., Louisville Hist. Soc., Filson Club. Mem. Christian Ch. (librarian 1960-72). Author: Proud Wanderers: My Mother's Family, 1981; Beneath the Oaks of Ivy Hill, 1982; contbr. to Am. Poetry mag., Poet Lore, Driftwood, Christian Herald, Fed. Poet, Badge of Honor, Family Heritage.

BRUCK, ARLENE FORTE, secondary school educator; b. Kingston, N.Y., June 26, 1945; d. Machileo and Lillian (Turco) Forte; m. Laurence J. Bruck; children: Jennifer Lynn, Jason Scott. BA in Latin, Coll. Mt. St. Vincent, Riverdale, N.Y., 1967; MS in Psychology, SUNY, New Paltz, 1971. Cert. in social studies, Latin, elem. edn. Tchr. 2d grade Kingston Schs. Consol., 1967-74, tchr. Latin, psychology and sociology, 1984—. Mem. Mid-Hudson Social Studies Coun., 1992—. Placement chair Jr. League, Kingston, 1982-84; vol. Girl Scouts, Tillson, N.Y., 1981-86, Athletes Against Drugs, Kingston, 1984-87. NEH fellow, 1992; recipient Gender Equity fellowship, Mary Dodge McCarthy award for gen. excellence, 1967, Mid-Hudson Social Studies Coun. Excellence in Tchg. award, 1994, Nat. Honor Soc. Tchr. Recognition award, Wall of Tolerance honoree, Southern Poverty Law Ctr.; named Outstanding Young Woman, 1974, Internat. Biog. Ctr. Woman Yr., 1996-97; N.Y. State Regents scholar, 1963-67, AAUW scholar, 1963-67. Mem. APA, AAUW (v.p. 1970-74, sec. 1975-77, pres. program 1994, pres. 1995-96), N.Y. State Assn. Fgn. Lang. Tchrs. Roman Catholic. Avocations: reading, gourmet cooking, travel. Home: 39 Beth Dr Kingston NY 12401-6148 Office: Kingston High Sch 403 Broadway Kingston NY 12401-4617

BRUCK, BILL, finance company executive; b. Dayton, Ohio, Aug. 1, 1951; s. Emil J. and Lucy A. (Lombardi) B.; m. Jacqueline Youden, June 6, 1984 (div. Dec. 1987); m. Anita M. Brack, June 15, 1996; 1 child, Abby Elizabeth. AB, Brown U., 1973; MA, Duquesne U., 1974; PhD, U. Fla., 1977. Lic. clin. psychologist, Va. Asst. prof. psychology Seattle U., 1978-79, West Ga. Coll., Carrollton, 1979-81; prin. Leadership Resources, Inc., Fairfax, Va., 1981-83; assoc. prof. psychology Marymount U., Arlington, Va., 1983-91, dir. instnl. rsch., 1986-91, prof. psychology, 1991-99; owner/operator Bill Bruck & Assocs., Falls Church, Va., 1986—2003; prin. Caucus Systems, Inc., Arlington, Va., 1999-2001; ptnr. Q2Learning LLC, 2001—. Author: Special Edition Using WordPerfect Office, 1994, Special Edition Using PerfectOffice 3, 1995, Special Edition Using Novell GroupWise 4, 1995, Using Corel WordPerfect Suite 7, 1996, Using Corel WordPerfect Suite 8, 1997, The Essential Book for Microsoft Office 95, 1996, The Essential Book for Microsoft Office 97, 1997, The Essential Book for Microsoft Office 2000, 1999, Make Your Mouse Roar, 2001, Taming the Information Tsunami, 2002. Mem. APA. Avocations: martial arts, racquetball, gardening, folk music. Office: 2686 Hillsman St Falls Church VA 22043 Office Phone: 877-751-2200. Personal E-mail: billbruck@yahoo.com. Business E-Mail: bill@bruck.com.

BRUCK, NICHOLAS, economist, educator; b. Yugoslavia, May 25, 1932; Austrian citizen, 1955-62; came to U.S., 1957; s. Nikolaus and Anna (Biebel) B.; divorced; children: Maria, Maya, Max, Thomas. BA, Vienna Sch. Econs., 1953, MBA, 1956, PhD, 1960; MA in Econs., Duke U., 1954. Econ. analyst Western Electric Co., N.Y.C., 1957-58, 1960-62; prof. econs. St. John's U., Jamaica, N.Y., 1962-66, Am. U., Washington, 1980-82; economist U.S. Bur. Labor Stats., Washington, 1966-67; chief fin. studies Inter-Am. Devel. Bank, Washington, 1968-79; sr. indsl. devel. officer UNIDO, Vienna, 1979-80; sr. fin. economist, seminar dir. Econ. Devel. Inst., World Bank, Washington, 1982-94; pres. Internat. Devel. Enterprise Assocs., Washington, 1994—; owner, operator Mimosa Farm, Potomac, Md., 1970—99. Instr. Hofstra U., L.I. U., Manhattan Coll., 1963—66, U. Colo., Boulder, Inst. Shipboard Edn., 1980; Fulbright vis. prof. San Carlos U., Guatemala, 1967—68; adj. prof. Johns Hopkins U., Balt., 1976—78, Georgetown U., Washington, 1977—78; professorial lectr. George Washington U., Washington, 1985—2000; cons. in field. Editor: Capital Markets under Inflation, 1982, Banking and Investment Financing, in Russian, 2 vols., 1995; contbr. articles to profl. jours. Bd. dirs. Am. Coun. Voluntary Agys. for Fgn. Svc., 1963-73, German World Alliance, 2001—; chmn. World Assn. Trainers in Devel., 1992—; spl. advisor World Fedn. Devel. Banks, 1995—; sec. gen. Danube Swabian Assn. of U.S.A. and Can., 1957-58. With JAGC, U.S. Army, 1958-60 Fulbright scholar, 1953-54, grantee, 1967; Ford Found. fellow, 1965. Mem. Am. Econ. Assn., Soc. for Internat. Devel. (chmn. work group on financing devel. 1975-79, 80-81, bd. dirs. 1980-86, v.p. Washington chpt. 1981-82), Nat. Economists Club (founding, 1968-). Office: IDEA PO Box 57467 Washington DC 20037-0467 Office Phone: 310-762-0133. E-mail: ideas@attglobal.net.

BRUCK, ROBERT IAN, education educator; b. NYC, June 25, 1952; s. Sidney Wolfgang and Sylvia Bruck; m. Debra Sue Schlessel, June 17, 1973; children: Isaac Samuel, Sarah Anne, Sonia Rose. BA, SUNY College, Buffalo; PhD, Syracuse U., 1974—78. Postdoctoral fellow Cornell U., 1977—79; asst./assoc prof. NC State U.; sci. advisor to the gov. of NC, 1990—92; prof. and dir. environ. sci. NC State U., 1994—, dist. prof., 2004—. Academic adv. bd. EPA, Washington, 1995—2002. Recipient Order Of The Longleaf Pine, State Of NC, 1992, The NC award For Sci., 1997, Outstanding achievement award, NC State U., 1997, Disting. alumnus award, SUNY Buffalo, 1997, Alumni Outstanding Tchr. award, NC State U., 1998. Mem.: Am. Phytopathological Soc. Democrat-Npl. Jewish. Avocations: mountain climbing, photography. Home: 1301 Larkhall Ct Cary NC 27511 Office: North Carolina State University Box 7106- Center For Earth Observation Raleigh NC 27695 Personal E-mail: bob_bruck@ncsu.edu.

BRUCKEN, ROBERT MATTHEW, retired lawyer; b. Akron, Ohio, Sept. 15, 1934; s. Harold M. and Eunice B. (Boesel) B.; m. Lois R. Gilbert, June 30, 1960; children: Nancy, Elizabeth, Rowland, Gilbert. AB, Marietta Coll., 1956; JD, U. Mich., 1959. Bar: Ohio 1960. Assoc. Baker & Hostetler, Cleve., 1960-69, ptnr., 1970—2004; ret., 2004. Trustee Lakeside Assn., 1979-97, Marietta Coll., 1983—; sec., treas. Leader Shape, Inc., 1990—. Served with AUS, 1959-60. Mem. ABA, Ohio State Bar Assn. (chmn. probate and trust law sect. 1981-83), Cleve. Bar Assn. (chmn. probate ct. com. 1973-75), Am. Coll. Trust and Estate Counsel, Phi Beta Kappa. United Church Of Christ. Office Phone: 216-861-7552. Business E-Mail: rbrucken@bakerlaw.com.

BRUCKER, PAUL C., academic administrator, physician; Pres. emeritus Thomas Jefferson U., Phila., 1990—2004. Office: Thomas Jefferson U Rm 303 Curtis Bldg 1015 Walnut St Philadelphia PA 19107-5567 Office Phone: 215-955-3790. Business E-Mail: paul.brucker@jefferson.edu.

BRUCKERT, LUCINDA GETTY, artist; b. Niskayuna, N.Y., Oct. 28, 1952; d. George Clinton and Mary Wheeler (Walker) Getty; 1 child, Anita Genet Bruckert. Grad. h.s., 1970. Freelance artist, Clay, N.Y., 1977-89; comml. driver Cicero-North Syracuse (N.Y.) Sch. Dist., 1989—; owner Handcrafted Glass, Clay, 1995—. Designer cross-stitch. Recipient 2d Place Masters award Old Forge Art Show, 1979, 3d Place, 1970, 79. Avocations: gardening, painting. Home: PO Box 5195 Syracuse NY 13220-5195

BRUCKHEIMER, JERRY, producer; b. Detroit, Sept. 21, 1945; m. Linda Bruckheimer. Grad., U. Ariz. Former prodr., art dir. advt. agy.; co-founder Don Simpson/Jerry Bruckheimer Films, 1983. Assoc. prodr. (films) Culpepper Cattle Company, 1972, Rafferty and the Gold Dust Twins, 1975; prodr. (films) American Gigolo, 1980, Young Doctors in Love, 1982; (with George Pappas) Farewell My Lovely, 1975; (with Dick Richards) March or Die, 1977; (with William S. Gillmore) Defiance, 1980; (with Ronnie Caan) Thief, 1981, Cat People, 1982; (with Don Simpson) Flashdance, 1983, Beverly Hills Cop, 1984, Thief of Hearts, 1984, Top Gun, 1986, Beverly Hills Cop II, 1987, Days of Thunder, 1990, Bad Boys, 1995, Crimson Tide, 1995, Dangerous Minds, 1995; The Rock, 1996, Con Air, 1997, Enemy of the State, 1998, Armageddon, 1998, Gone in 60 Seconds, 2000, Coyote Ugly, 2000, Remember the Titans, 2000, Pearl Harbor, 2001, Black Hawk Down, 2001, Bad Company, 2002, Kangaroo Jack, 2003, Pirates of the Caribbean: The Curse of the Black Pearl, 2003, Bad Boys II, 2003, King Arthur, 2004, National Treasure, 2004; exec. prodr. (films): (with Don Simpson) The Ref, 1994, Soldier of Fortune, 1997, Dangerous Minds, 1995, (TV films) Max Q, 1998, Swing Vote, 1999; exec. prodr. (TV series): C.S.I., The Amazing Race (Emmy award for Outstanding Reality/Competition Program 2003, 04), 2001-, CSI: Crime Scene Investigation, 2000, CSI: Miami, 2002, Without a Trace, 2002, Profiles From the Front Line, 2003, Skin, 2003, Cold Case, 2003-, Fearless, 2004, CSI: NY, 2004-, Just Legal, 2005-. Recipient ShoWest award Prodr. of Yr., 1999, David O. Selznick Lifetime Achievement award Prodrs. Guild of Am., 2000; named one of 50 Most Powerful People in Hollywood Premiere mag., 2003-05. Office: Jerry Bruckheimer Films 1631 10th St Santa Monica CA 90404-3705*

BRUCK LIEB PORT, LILLY, retired consumer advisor, broadcaster, columnist; b. Vienna, May 13, 1918; came to U.S., 1941, naturalized, 1944; d. Max and Sophie M. Hahn; m. Sandor Bruck, Mar. 7, 1943; 1 child, Sandra Lee (Mrs. John David Evans III); m. David L. Lieb, Dec. 7, 1985; m. Charles S. Port, Nov. 22, 1998. PhD in Econs., U. Vienna; postgrad., Sorbonne, Paris, Sch. of Econs., London, Sch. of Bus., Columbia U., 1941-42, Sch. of Social Work, NYU, 1964-66. Dir. consumer edn. Dept. Consumer Affairs, City of N.Y., 1969-78; project dir. Am. Coalition of Citizens with Disabilities, 1977-78; consumer advisor, broadcaster In Touch Networks, N.Y.C., 1978-90; consumer affairs commentator Nat. Pub. Radio, 1980-82; ret. Author: Access, The Guide to a Better Life for Disabled Americans, 1978; contbr. articles to disability and rehab. to books, ency. and mag. Presid. Scarsdale Hadassah, 1960-68. Chmn. Westchester county, Bonds for Israel, 1960-68; trustee Kol AMI-JCC, White Plains, N.Y.; assoc. Jewish Mus.; sponsor Lilly Bruck Lieb Creative Writing Program, Purchase Coll., SUNY; mem. pres.'s coun. White Plains (N.Y.) Hosp. Recipient Woman of Yr. award Anti Defamation League, 1972. Democrat. Home: 25 Murray Hill Rd Scarsdale NY 10583-2829 E-mail: lblone@aol.com.

BRUCKNER, DANIEL RAYMOND, history educator; b. Waynesburg, Pa., July 30, 1947; s. Raymond Oscar and Aldene Grooms Bruckner; m. Sandra Gesko Bruckner, Aug. 3, 1973. BA, Waynesburg (Pa.) Coll., 1969; MA, W.Va. U., 1973. Social studies tchr. Thomas Stone H.S., Waldorf, Md., 1973—2001; substitute tchr. High Point H.S., Beltsville, Md., 2001—. Mem. history adv. bd. Harper Collins Pub., N.Y.C., 1988—92; mem. world history adv. bd. Prentice-Hall, Inc., N.Y.C., 1994—2000. Mem. Greenpeace, Inc., Washington, 1976—, Clean Water Action, Washington, 1984—, Children's Wish Found., Atlanta, 1992—. Sgt. U.S. Army, 1969—72, Vietnam. Recipient Outstanding award, McDonald's, Inc., 1990; bus. fellow, Washington Bd. of Trade, 1985. Mem.: Md. Humanities Coun., Md. Hist. Soc., Am. Hist. Assn. Democrat. Roman Catholic. Avocations: reading, collecting small flags, collecting classic films, genealogy. Home: 5022 Geronimo St College Park MD 20740 Office: High Point HS 3601 Powdermill Rd Beltsville MD 20705 Office Phone: 301-572-6400. E-mail: brucknerdan03@aol.com.

BRUCKNER, MARTHA, academic administrator; Bachelor's degree, Master's degree, U. Nebr., Omaha; Doctorate, U. Nebr., Lincoln. Assoc. supt. for ednl. svcs. Millard (Nebr.) Pub. Schs.; tchr. h.s., asst. prin., prin. pub. schs.; assoc. prof., chairperson ednl. adminstrn. U. Nebr., Omaha. Contbr. articles to profl. jours. Recipient award, Nebr. Coun. Sch. Adminstrs., Nebr. Schoolmasters Orgn. Mem.: ASCD (pres.-elect 2003—, bd. dirs., budget liaison, organizer student chpt. U. Nebr., Omaha). Office: Don Stroh Adminstrn Ctr 5606 S 147th St Omaha NE 68137*

BRUCKNER, WILLIAM J., lawyer; b. Atlanta, Mar. 28, 1944; s. William Paul and Ruth (Seibert) B.; m. Lucy Clark, June 27, 1970; children: Heather, Christina. BS, The Citadel, 1966; JD, U. Ga., 1969. Bar: Ga. 1970, S.C. 1982, U.S. Dist. Ct. (no. and mid. dists.) Ga., U.S. Ct. Appeals (5th cir.), U.S. Supreme Ct. Asst. solicitor Solicitor's Office County of Fulton, Atlanta, 1971-73; labor solicitor So. Bell, Atlanta, 1973-82, gen. atty. Columbia, S.C., 1982-83, Atlanta, 1983-86; ops. and litigation counsel BellSouth Enterprises, Atlanta, 1986; assoc. gen. counsel Bell South Enterprises, Atlanta, 1990—; gen. atty. human resources divsn. Bell South Corp., Atlanta, 1986-90, assoc. gen. counsel, 1993—. Mem. Atlanta Soc., 1990—; bd. dirs. Ashford-Dunwoody YMCA, Atlanta, 1986-87, Horizon Theater, Atlanta, 1990—. Capt. U.S. Army, 1970-71. Mem. Atlanta Lawyers Club, Greater Atlanta U. Ga. Club (pres. 1990, trustee Ga. Student Ednl. Fund, chmn. ACCA legal office mgmt. com.), Buckhead Club. Roman Catholic. Avocations: photography, sports. Home: 11315 Bowen Rd Roswell GA 30075-2238 Office: Bell South Corp 1155 Peachtree St NE Ste 1700 Atlanta GA 30309-7629

BRUCKSTEIN, ALEX HARRY, internist, gastroenterologist, geriatrician; b. Germany, Dec. 2, 1949; came to U.S., 1950; s. Jacob and Rose B., m. Dorothy Krausman, Mar. 23, 1973; children: Tammy, Sharon, Sarah, Michael. BS in Chemistry, CCNY, 1971; MD, Albert Einstein Coll. Medicine, 1975. Diplomate Am. Bd. Internal Medicine, Am. Bd. Gastroenterology, Am. Bd. Internal Medicine- Geriatrics. Intern in internal medicine Roosevelt Hosp., N.Y.C.; resident in internal medicine St. Luke's Hosp., N.Y.C.; resident in gastroenterology VA Hosp., N.Y.U., N.Y.C.; pvt. practice internal medicine, gastroenterology Staten Island, N.Y. Hosp. affiliations: Doctors' Hosp. Staten Island, N.Y., Staten Island U. Hosp. N., Staten Island U. Hosp. S., St. Vincent's Hosp., Staten Island; vis. clin. fellow Columbia U. Dept. Medicine, 1975-78, NYU Dept. Medicine, 1978-80; clin. asst. prof. medicine N.Y. Med. Coll., 1983-90, SUNY Health Sci. Ctr. at Bklyn., 1990—. Fellow ACP, Am. Coll. Gastroenterology; mem. AMA, Med. Soc. State N.Y., Richmond County Med. Soc., Am. Gastroent. Assn., N.Y. Soc. Gastrointestinal Endoscopy, N.Y. Acad. Gastroenterology, Am. Geriatrics Assn. Office: 2627 Hylan Blvd Staten Island NY 10306-4339 Office Phone: 718-667-3200. Personal E-mail: sevenbr@aol.com.

BRUDER, GEORGE FREDERICK, lawyer; b. Ann Arbor, Mich., June 4, 1938; s. George G. and Mary Louise (Pfisterer) Bruder; m. Jean Riley, July 10, 1965; children: Roxanne, Stephanie. AB, Dartmouth Coll., 1960; JD, U. Chgo., 1963. Bar: D.C. 1964. Counsel FPC, Washington, 1964—67; counsel Long Lines Dept. AT&T, Washington, 1967—68; assoc. Debevoise & Liberman, Washington, 1968—70, ptnr., 1971—75, Bruder, Gentile & Marcoux, Washington, 1976—97. Mem.: Fed. Energy Bar Assn. Democrat. Episcopalian. Home: 8 E Lenox St Chevy Chase MD 20815-4211 E-mail: gfbruder@erols.com.

BRUDER, HAROLD JACOB, artist, educator; b. N.Y.C., Aug. 31, 1930; s. Julius and Della (Wlodinger) B.; m. Anet Sirna, July 15, 1979; 1 child, Dellan; children from previous marriage: David, Shari. Cert., Cooper Union, 1951. Mem. faculty Kansas City Art Inst., 1963-65, Pratt Inst., 1965-66; prof. art Queens Coll., Flushing, N.Y., 1965-95, chmn. art dept., 1982-85, prof. emeritus, 1995—. Artist-in-residence, Aspen, Colo., 1967; one-man shows include, Robert Isaacson Gallery, N.Y.C., 1962, Forum Gallery, N.Y.C., 1968, 69, 72, 76, 79, Durlacher Bros., N.Y.C., 1964, 1967, William and Mary Coll., 1979, Queens Coll., N.Y.C., 1974, Queens Mus., N.Y.C., 1982, Armstrong Gallery, N.Y.C, 1984, 86, Contemporary Realist Gallery, San Francisco, 1988, Mitchell Algus Gallery, N.Y.C., 2004, Queens Coll. Art Ctr., 2005; group exhbns. include, Whitney Mus., 1970, Balt. Mus., 1970, Butler Inst., 1972, Cleve. Mus., 1974, Phila. Mus., 1976, represented in permanent collections, Hirshhorn Mus., Washington, Sheldon Meml. Gallery, Lincoln, Nebr., N.J. State Mus., Trenton; contbr. articles to profl. jours. NEA grantee, 1985 Studio: 1123 Broadway #811 New York NY 10010 Home: 500 W 56th St Apt 2506 New York NY 10019 Studio: 1123 Broadway #811 New York NY 10010 E-mail: dellan580257058@aol.com.

BRUDNER, HARVEY JEROME, physicist; b. NYC, May 29, 1931; s. Joseph and Anna (Fiddelman) B.; m. Helen Gross, Dec. 18, 1963; children: Mae Ann, Terry Joseph, Jay Scott. BS in Engring. and Physics, NYU, 1952, MS, 1954, PhD, 1959; postgrad., U. Md., 1954-56, CCNY, 1958, Columbia U., 1959-61. Electronics engr. Bendix Corp., Teterboro, N.J., 1952; physicist U.S. Naval Ordnance Lab., White Oak, Md., 1953-54; sr. physicist Emerson Rsch. Labs., Washington, 1954-57; prin. physicist Emerson Radio, Jersey City, 1957-61; rsch. assoc. NYU Inst. Math. Scis., N.Y.C., 1957-60; guest scientist Rockefeller Inst. for Med. Rsch., N.Y.C., 1960-61; sr. rsch. assoc. Am. Can Co., Princeton (N.J.) Lab., 1964-67; v.p. R & D Westinghouse Learning Corp., N.Y.C., 1967-71, pres., 1971-76; also dir.; mem. adminstrv. com. Westinghouse Electric Corp., Pitts., 1971-76; pres. Westinghouse Electric Corp. (Westinghouse Learning Group), 1971-76, H.J.B. Enterprises, N.Y.C., 1961—, Med. Devel., Inc., N.Y.C., 1962; dir. Ideal Sch. Supply Corp., Ednl. Products, Inc., Document Reading Svcs., Ltd., Linguaphone Inst. Ltd., Info. Synergy, Inc., Cambridge Learning Connection, Inc.; chmn. new devels. com. Project Aristotle; acting dir. Gottscho Info. Center, Coll. Engring., Rutgers U.; prof. math., physics, dean sci. and tech. NY Inst. Tech., 1962-64; instr. atomic physics NYU, 1953-54. Cons. Nat. Inst. Edn., Mass. Inst. Tech., Rutgers U., Worcester Poly. Inst., Poly. Inst. N.Y., Nat. Inst. Community Devel., U.S. Ho. of Reps. Com. on Sci. and Tech.; mem. adv. com. Middlesex County Coll., 1966—, Paterson State Coll., 1975; mem. exec. planning com. tng. adv. sect. Nat. Security Indsl. Assn., 1966; nat. adv. bd. Am. Coll. in Jerusalem; dir. computers in edn. study Nat. Inst. Edn., 1979; bd. dirs. World Learning and Communications, 1978— Editl. commentator Another Opinion, Sta. WCBS, N.Y.C., N.Y. Power Authority; author: Semiconductor Physics, 1954, College Technical Mathematics, 1967, Algebra and Trigonometry-A Programmed Course with Applications, 1971, On Fermat's Last Theorem, 1979, Fermat and The Missing Numbers, 1994, How the Babylonians Solved Numbered Triangle Problems 3600 Years Ago, 1998; columnist Light-On Series: Ednl. Tech. Mag., Source Data: Datamation Mag.; chmn. editl. adv. bd. Tech. Horizons in Edn. Jour.; participated Borough Highland Park March, 2005; contbr. articles to mags., jours., and newspapers. Mem. steering com. Project PROCEED, NSF, Mcpl. Alliance Com., Highland Park, 1990—; capt. long-range planning com. Highland Park Sch. Bd.; trustee Ross Hall Heights Assn., 1966; chmn., pres. Joyce Kilmer Authority, New Brunswick, NJ, 1985—, Joyce Kilmer Centennial Commn., New Brunswick, 1986; coord. WABC-TV News, N.Y.C., Joyce Kilmer Trees, 1994; coord. program Fermat and Babylonian Rectangles, Sta. WCTC, 1994; apprd. to Mcppl. Alliance Against Drugs and Alcohol, 1990—99; apptd. to Middlesex County Mcpl. Alliance Network, 1995—; coord. Project DATE (Drugs, Alcohol, Tobacco, Education), Rutgers U. N.J. Forum, 1995—, New Brunswick Cmty. Bridge Project, 2001, Vets. Day Project, 2001; pres. Highland Park Centennial Commn., 2002—; dir. cir. George Street Playhouse. New Brunswick, 2002—. Recipient cert. Americanism Vets. Alliance of Raritan Valley, 1992, award Kiwanis Internat., 1993, Raritan-Millstone Heritage Alliance, 1998, 2 Nobel Laureate awards Sta. WCTC, 2003, award Mayor Robert Wood Johnson, Highland Park, Triangles from Rectangles award The Daily Targum, 2004; named Knight, Order of the Swan, 1996, New Brunswick Historical Assn., 2003, Grand Marshall, Vets. Alliance Meml. Day Parade, May 31, 2004. Fellow IEEE (life, ednl. adminstrn. com., solar standards com., photovoltaic subcom.), mem., Am. Phys. Soc., Soc. Motion Picture and TV Engrs., Internat. Fedn. Med. Electronics, AAAS, Electronic Industries Assn. (edn. com.), Am. Ednl. Research Assn., Adult Edn. Assn. U.S.A., N.Y. Acad. Scis., Am. Mgmt. Assn. (ednl. adv. com.), Math. Assn. Am., Am. Soc. Tng. and Devel., Council Ams., Am. Judicature Soc., Am. Math. Soc., Am. Soc. Curriculum Devel., Knight, Order of the Swan, Sigma Xi, Sigma Pi Sigma, Tau Beta Pi. Clubs: Chemists (N.Y.C.); N.Y. Univ., The Midtown Exec. and Chemists' Club, N.Y.C., Toastmasters. Home: 812 Abbott St Highland Park NJ 08904-2909 Office: Joyce Kilmer Centennial Commn 17 Joyce Kilmer Ave New Brunswick NJ 08901-2507 Office Phone: 732-572-0524. Office Fax: 732-572-0524. Personal E-mail: hjbe@aol.com. *I have tried: to play a constructive part in permitting others to make a positive contribution to society; to achieve a proper mix of idealism, reason, and faith in my decision making; to apply science and technology for the betterment of humanity.*

BRUDNER, HELEN GROSS, social sciences educator; b. NYC; d. Nathan and Mae (Grichtman) Gross; children: Mae Ann, Terry Joseph, Jay Scott. BS, NYU, 1959, MA, 1960, PhD, 1973. Tchr. NYC Bd. Edn., 1959-60; instr. Pratt

Inst., Bklyn., 1959-61; asst. prof. history NY Inst. Tech., NYC, 1961-63, dir. guidance, 1962-63; assoc. prof. Fairleigh Dickinson U., Rutherford, NJ, 1963-73, prof. history, polit. sci. Teaneck, NJ, 1974—, dir. Honors Coll. Rutherford, NJ, 1972-84, chmn. dept. social sci., 1980-88, pres. univ. senate, 1975-78, asst. provost, 1983—, dean, 1984, dir. grad. programs, assoc. dir. Sch. History, Polit., Internat. Studies, 1995—, dir. lang. grad. studies, pres. acad. senate, 1996—; v.p. HJB Enterprises, Highland Park, NJ, 1970—. Vice-chmn. bd. dirs. WLC Inc., Highland Park, 1990-, Casitas De Monte Corp., Calif., treas., 2005; vice-chmn. Casitas De Monte Assoc., Palm Springs, Calif., 2000-04, treas., 2005; cons. auto ednl. systems, 1971-; participant bd. trustees F.D.U.; spkr. NJ Com. Humanities. Contbr. articles to profl. jours. constl. law, transfer tech., futurism. Active women politics project NSF, 1981; active consortium project women Am. history NEH Woodrow Wilson Found., 1980, Consortium Global Interdependence, Princeton, 1984; bd. dirs. Options Spkrs. Bur., NJ Credit Union League, NJ Credit Union Shared Network, WLC Inc.; mem. Mcpl. Alliance Highland Park, Hist. Preservation Commn., Highland Park; chmn. bd. dirs. Fairleigh Dickinson U. Fed. Credit Union, 1987—; vice chmn. NJ Adv. Com. on Women Vets., 1993-; design selection com. NJ Korean Vets. Meml. Recipient Woman Yr. award Am. Businesswomen's Assn., 1980, Meritorious Svc. award NJ Credit Union League, 1997, Cert. Spl. Congrl. Recognition, 2000, NJ Divsn. Mil. and Vet. Affairs award, 2004 Mem. Am. Judicature Soc., Am. Hist. Soc., Acad. Polit. Sci., Phi Alpha Theta, Phi Sigma Alpha. Office: Fairleigh Dickinson U Sch History, Polit Internat Studies Teaneck NJ 07666 Address: PO Box 1407 Highland Park NJ 08904

BRUDVIG, GLENN LOWELL, retired library director; b. Kenosha, Wis., Oct. 14, 1931; s. Lars L. Brudvig and Anna Elizabeth (Hillesland) B. Lovejoy; m. Myrna Winifred Michael, Oct. 1, 1953; children— Gary Wayne, Lee Anthony, James Lowell, Kristin Elizabeth BA in Edn., U. N.D., 1954, MA, 1956; MALS, U. Minn., 1962. Tchr. pub. schs. Mahnomen and Herman, Minn., 1954-55, 56-58; librarian, archivist U. N.D., Grand Forks, 1958-62, asst. librarian, 1962-63; supr. dept. libraries U. Minn., Mpls., 1964, dir. bio-med. libr., 1964-83; dir. librs. Calif. Inst. Tech., Pasadena, 1983-95, ret., 1995. Instr. library sci. U. N.D., Grand Forks, 1962-63; asst. dir. for research and devel. U. Minn., Mpls., 1968-79, instr. library sci., 1968-71, dir. Inst. Tech. Libraries, 1982-83; cons. Nat. Library of Medicine, Bethesda, Md., 1971-75. Contbr. articles to profl. jours. Served with U.S. Army, 1951-52 Nat. Library of Medicine grantee, 1967-79. Home: 15 Eagle Ridge Rd Saint Paul MN 55127-6411 E-mail: Gandmbrudvig@aol.com.

BRUELL, CAROL, science educator; b. Jersey City, Jan. 24, 1957; d. Joseph Stanley Borkowshi and Eve Biale; m. Clifford Joseph Bruell; children: Kirsten, Katie, Kelsey. BA in biology, Blackburn Coll., 1979; MA in zoology, So. Ill. U., 1984; MS in devel. psychol., U. Conn., 1986; MEd, U. Mass., 2001. Biology tchr. US Peace Corps, Ghana, 1979—80; rsch. coord. Ctr. for Human Genetics, Boston, 1986—91; outdoor edn. tchr. Horizons for Youth, Sharon, Mass., 1980—81; tchr, naturalist Mass. Audubon Soc., Barre, Mass., 1981; life sci. tchr. Chelmsford Pub. Sch., Chelmsford, Mass., 1999—2001; HS biology tchr. Chelmsford HS, Chelmsford, Mass., 2001—. Vol. Chelmsford Pub. Libr., Chelmsford, Mass., 1994—95; leader Girl Scouts USA, Chelmsford, Mass., 1997—2002. Biotechnology grant, Mass. Bio. Edn. Coun., 2003, Arts & Tech. grant, Chelmsford Arts and Tech. Fund, 2004. Mem.: Mass. Assn. of Biology Tchrs. Home: 7 Penni Ln North Chelmsford MA 01863 Office: Chelmsford HS 200 Richardson Rd North Chelmsford MA 01863 Office Phone: 978-251-5100. Business E-Mail: bruellc@chelmsford.k12.ma.us.

BRUEMMER, DAVID JONATHAN, robotics engineer; b. San Antonio, Sept. 6, 1976; s. Wayne C and Beth A. (Vanderveer) Bruemmer; m. Heather Anne Mateyak, June 6, 1998; children: Ethan John children: Lucy Elizabeth. BA in Computer Sci. and Religion with honors, Swarthmore Coll., 1998. Def. advanced rsch. program agy. cons. Strategic Analysis, Arlington, Va., 1999—2000; tech. dir. for unmanned ground vehicles Idaho Nat. Lab., Idaho Falls, 2000—. Dept. energy rep. Autonomy Levels for Unmanned Sys. Working Group, 2003—; program chair ACM/IEEE Conf. on Human Robot Interaction, Salt Lake City, 2004—; program com. Am. Nuc. Soc. Conf. on Robotics and Remote Sys. for Hazardous Environments, Salt Lake City, 2004—. Guest editor: Intelligent Sys. Mag.; contbr. articles to profl. jours. and encyclopedias. Recipient Tech. Innovation award, Am. Assn. for Artificial Intelligence, 2003, Winner Robot Rescue Competition, 2003; Class of 1934 scholar, Swarthmore Coll., 1995. Mem.: Robotics Foundry (charter mem. 2003—04), Sigma Xi (life), Phi Beta Kappa (life). Achievements include development of military man portable autonomous demining robot; common operating picture interface for future combat systems small unmanned ground vehicle; autonomous robotic indoor mapping system for remote characterization of hazardous environments; invention of robot swarm for spill finding and perimeter formation; autonomous navigation system for military unmanned ground vehicles. Avocations: cycling, soccer. Home: 608 Cedar Ridge Dr Idaho Falls ID 83404 Office: Idaho Nat Lab 2525 N Fremont Dr Idaho Falls ID 83415 Office Phone: 208-526-4078. Personal E-mail: bruedj@inel.gov.

BRUEMMER, FRED, writer, photographer; b. Riga, Latvia, June 26, 1929; emigrated to Can., 1951, naturalized, 1956; s. Arist and Dorothea (Wahl) B.; m. Maud van den Berg, Mar. 31, 1962; children: Aurel, Rene. Student Fed. Republic Germany schs.; DLitt (hon.), U. N.B., Can., 1989. Self-employed writer-photographer specializing in arctic and antarctic regions, 1961—; books include The Long Hunt, 1969, Seasons of the Eskimo, 1971, Encounters with Arctic Animals, 1972, The Arctic, 1974, The Life of the Harp Seal, 1977, Children of the North, 1979, Summer at Bear River, 1980, The Arctic of the World, 1985, Arctic Animals, 1986, Seasons of the Seal, 1988, World of the Polar Bear, 1989, (with Eric S. Grace) Seals, 1991, The Narwhal, 1993, (with Angèle Delaunois), Les Animaux du Grand Nord, 1993, (with Karen Pandell) Land of Dark, Land of Light, 1993, Arctic Memoires: Living with the Inuit, 1993, (with Angèle Delaunois) Nanook and Naoya: The Polar Bear Cubs, 1995, Kotik: The Baby Seal, 1995, (with Thomas D. Mangelsen) Polar Dance, 1996, Seals in the Wild, 1998, Glimpses of Paradise: The Marvel of Massed Animals, 2002. Decorated Order of Can.; Recipient Queen Elizabeth II Silver Jubilee medal, 1978, Canadian Anniversary Commemorative medal, 1993. Fellow Arctic Inst. N.Am., Royal Can. Acad. Art, Travel Journalists Guild, N.Am. Nature Photography Assn. (Lifetime Achievement award 2003). Address: 2 Strathearn South Montreal West Montreal PQ Canada H4X 1X4 Office Phone: 514-482-5098. E-mail: fredbruemmer@yahoo.ca.

BRUEMMER, RUSSELL JOHN, lawyer; b. Decorah, Iowa, Apr. 23, 1952; s. John William and Marion Jean (Wartinbee) B. BA, Luther Coll., 1974; JD, U. Mich., 1977. Bar: Minn. 1978, D.C. 1980, U.S. Dist. Ct. D.C. 1981, U.S. Supreme Ct. 1990, N.Y. 2001. Law clk. Judge William H. Webster, U.S. Ct. Appeals (8th cir.), 1977-78; spl. asst. to the dir. FBI, Washington, 1978-80, chief counsel congl. affairs, 1980-81; assoc. Wilmer, Cutler & Pickering, Washington, 1981-84, ptnr., 1985—87; counsel to Dir. of Ctrl. Intelligence CIA, Washington, 1987-88, gen. counsel, 1988-90; ptnr. Wilmer, Cutler & Pickering, Washington, 1990—; ptnr., chmn. Fin. Inst. dept. Wilmer Cutler Pickering Hale & Dorr, Washington, 2004—. Spkr. in field. Editor-in-chief U. Mich. Jour. Law Reform; mem. editl. bd. Electronic Banking Law and Commerce Report; contbr. articles to profl. jours. Recipient Meritorious Intelligence Officer award, 1988, Disting. Intelligence medal, 1990, CIA, Disting. Svc. award Luther Coll., 2004. Mem. ABA (banking law com. 1982—, subcom. on bank holding cos. and nonbanking activities, chmn. 1985-87, chmn. subcom. on securities activities 1994-96, 98-99, standing com. on law and nat. security 1995-98, corp. compliance com., vice-chmn. subcom. on developing codes of conduct 2003—), Am. Law Inst., Fed. Bar Assn. (mem. exec. com. banking law com.), Order of the Coif. Republican. Lutheran. Home: 4024 40th St N Arlington VA 22207-4608 Mailing: Wilmer Cutler Pickering Hale & Dorr LLP 2445 M St NW Washington DC 20037-1487 Office: Wilmer Cutler Pickering Hale & Dorr LLP 1899 Pennsylvania Ave NW Washington DC 20006 Office Phone: 202-663-6804. Office Fax: 202-663-6363. Business E-Mail: russell.bruemmer@wilmerhale.com.

BRUEN, JAMES A., lawyer; b. South Hampton, N.Y., Nov. 29, 1943; s. John Francis and Kathryn Jewell (Arthur) B.; m. Carol Lynn Heller, June 13, 1968; children: Jennifer Lynn, Garrett John. BA cum laude, Claremont Men's Coll., 1965; JD, Stanford U., 1968. Bar: Calif. 1968, U.S. Dist. Ct. (no., ea., so. and cen. dists.) Calif. 1970, U.S. Ct. Claims 1972, U.S. Tax Ct. 1972, U.S. Ct. Appeals (9th cir.) 1972, U.S. Supreme Ct. 1973, Ariz. 1993. Atty. FCC, Washington, 1968-70; asst. U.S. atty. criminal div. Office of US. Atty., San Francisco, 1970-73, asst. U.S. atty. civil div., 1973-75, chief of civil div., 1975-77; ptnr. Landels, Ripley & Diamond, San Francisco, 1977-2000, Farella Braun & Martel LLP, San Francisco, 2000—. Faculty Practising Law Inst. Def. Rsch. Inst., ABA/Am. Law Inst. Co-author: Pharmaceutical Products Liability, 1989; contbg. editor: Hazardous Waste and Toxic Torts Law and Strategy, 1987-92; contbr. numerous articles to profl. jours. Mem. ABA (vice chmn. environ. quality com. nat. resources sect. 1989-93, co-chmn. enforment litigation subcom. environ. litigation com. litigation sect. 1990-92), Am. Inn of Ct. (master-at-large), Internat. Soc. for Environ. Epidemiology. Avocations: scuba diving, travel. Office: Farella Braun & Martel Russ Bldg 30th Fl 235 Montgomery St San Francisco CA 94104 Fax: 415-954-4480. Business E-Mail: jbruen@fbm.com.

BRUEN, JOHN DERMOT, management consultant; b. Glen Cove, NY, Oct. 19, 1930; s. John D. and Kathleen M. (Halferty) B.; m. Ann Theone Lee, June 22, 1957; children: Michael J., Kathleen A., Thomas L., Lisa M. BS, U. Md., 1959; MBA, U. Pitts., 1963; grad., Naval War Coll. Command and Staff Course, 1966, Army War Coll., 1972. Enlisted in U.S. Army, 1948, commd. 2d lt., 1953, advanced through grades to lt. gen., 1983; service in Korea, Germany, Azores, Thailand and Vietnam; dir. resources and mgmt. Office Dep. Chief Staff Logistics Hqrs., DA, 1977—79; comdr. Mil. Traffic Mgmt. Command Washington, 1979-83; comdr. 21st Support Command Europe, 1983-86; ret., 1986; pres. Bruen & Assocs., Springfield, Va., 1986—; vice chmn. internat. U.S. Computer-Aided Acquisition and Life-Cycle Support Industry Steering Group, 1991—95; hon. col. U.S. Army Transp. Corps Regt., 1997—2001. Contbr. articles on leadership, mgmt. to profl. jours. Decorated Def. D.S.M., Army D.S.M., Legion of Merit with two oak leaf clusters, Bronze Star with one oak leaf cluster, Meritorious Svc. medal with one oak leaf cluster, Army Commendation medal with one oak leaf cluster; decorated grand officer Order of the Crown (Belgium); named to U.S. Inf. Officer Candidate Sch. Hall of Fame, 1979, U.S. Army Transp. Corps Hall of Fame, 2000; recipient Computer-Aided Acquisition and Life-Cycle Support Meritorious Svc. award, 1996. Mem. U.S. Army Transp. Corps Regiment Assn. (pres. 1997-2001), Nat. Def. Transp. Assn., Assn. U.S. Army, Mil. Officers Assn. Am. (bd. dirs. 1986-94). Roman Catholic. Office: 6104 Greenlawn Ct Springfield VA 22152-1314 Office Phone: 703-644-7072. Personal E-mail: jdbruen@aol.com.

BRUENE, BARBARA JANE, artist, educator; b. Waterloo, Iowa, June 22, 1936; d. Hazen M. and Mary Lisle Fallgatter; m. Roger Julius Bruene, June 10, 1956; children: Jim, Bruce. BA, U. No. Iowa, 1958; MA, Iowa State U., 1978; MFA, Drake U., Des Moines, Iowa, 1986. Gallery dir. Coll. of Design Gallery, Iowa State U., Ames, 1988—98; faculty Dept. Art and Design, Iowa State U., Ames, 1975—98, assoc. prof. emerita, 1998—. One-woman shows include Calligraphic Paintings and Artist's Books, Ball State U., Muncie, Ind., 2000, exhibitions include Alpha Mark traveling exhbn., 1999—2001, Artist's Books, Corcoran Gallery of Art, Washington, 1999, numerous other group and solo exhbns. Avocations: reading, travel. Home: 2122 Greeley St Ames IA 50014

BRUENE, WARREN BENZ, electronics engineer; b. Beaman, Iowa, Nov. 1, 1916; s. Fred Karl and Luella Lydia (Benz) B.; m. Mildred Clare Meyer, July 13, 1941; children: Julia Beth Bruene James, Jo Carol Bruene Lilley. BSEE, Iowa State U., 1938. Registered profl. engr., Tex, 1971-2004. Design engr. Collins Radio Co., Cedar Rapids, Iowa, 1939-46, project engr., 1946-54, group head, 1954-57, dept. staff, 1957-60, dept. head, 1960-61, div. staff, Richardson, Tex., 1961-73; div. staff Rockwell Internat., Richardson, 1973-84; sr. engr. Electrospace Systems, Inc., Richardson, 1984-90; pvt. practice radio engring. cons. Dallas, 1990—. Vis. com. U. Tex., Austin, 1966-72. Co-author 7 tech. books; contbr. articles to profl. jours. Inventor 22 patents. Named Engr. of Yr., Preston Trail chpt. Tex. Soc. Profl. Engrs., 1975, profl. achievement citation in engring. Iowa State U., 1993. Fellow IEEE (sect. chmn. 1958-59, region dir. 1962-63), Toastmasters (Richardson) (area gov. 1969). Republican. Methodist. Avocations: economics, amateur radio, technical writing. Home: 7805 Chattington Dr Dallas TX 75248-5307

BRUENGER, SUSAN ANN, music educator; b. Belleville, Ill., Sept. 26, 1953; d. Walter Oliver and Dolores Marie Dill; m. David Charles Bruenger, Nov. 7, 1974. BMus, So. Ill. U., Edwardsville, 1975; MMus, U. N. Tex., Denton, 1989, PhD in Music Edn., 1999. Elem. music tchr. Megner Sch., Afton, Mo., 1971—79; music dir. Laboure HS, St. Louis, 1975—76; music dept. chair Althoff HS, Belleville, Ill., 1980—86; music tchr. Little Elm (Tex.) Mid. Sch., 1986—87; choral music supr. Denison (Tex.) Ind. Sch. Dist., 1992—95; music coord. Incarnate Word Acad., St. Louis, 1997—2001; asst. prof. U. Tex., San Antonio, 2001—. Contbr. articles to profl. publs. Mem.: Tex. Music Educators Conf., Coll. Music Soc., Am. Choral Dirs. Assn., Music Educators Nat. Conf., Phi Delta Kappa, Phi Kappa Lambda, Phi Kappa Phi. Office: Univ Texas - Music Dept 6900 N Loop 1604 West San Antonio TX 78249 Office Phone: 210-458-5322. Business E-Mail: sbruenger@utsa.edu.

BRUESCHKE, ERICH EDWARD, physician, researcher, educator; b. nr. Eagle Butte, S.D., July 17, 1933; s. Erich Herman and Eva Johanna (Joens) B.; m. Frances Marie Bryan, Mar. 25, 1967; children: Erich Raymond, Jason Douglas, Tina Marie, Patricia Frances, Susan Eva. BS in Elec. Engring, S.D. Sch. Mines and Tech., 1956; postgrad., U. So. Calif., 1960-61; MD, Temple U., 1965. Diplomate Am. Bd. Family Practice, also cert. in geriatrics. Intern Germantown Dispensary and Hosp., Phila., 1965-66; mem. tech. staff Hughes Research and Devel. Labs., Culver City, Calif., 1956-61; practiced gen. medicine Fullerton, Calif., 1968-69; dir. research Ill. Inst. Tech. Research Inst., Chgo., 1970-76; research asst. prof. Temple U. Sch. Medicine, 1965-69; mem. staff Mercy Hosp. and Med. Center, Chgo., 1970-76; vis. prof. Rush Med. Coll., Chgo., 1974-76, prof., chmn. dept. family practice, 1976—95, program dir. Rush. Christ family practice residency, 1978-93, vice dean, 1992—93, acting dean, 1993-94, dean, 1994-2000, v.p. univ. affairs, 2000—02; trustee Anchor HMO, 1976-81, v.p. med. and acad. affairs, 1981—; trustee Synergon Health Systems, 1993-98; vice chmn., bd. dirs. Rush Presbyn. St. Lukes Health Assocs., disting. prof. medicine, 2002—, Rush Med. Coll. of Rush U., 2002—. Sr. attending Presbyn.-St. Luke's Hosp., Chgo., 1976—2003, vis. attending, 2003—; med. dir. Chgo. Bd. of Health West Side Hypertension Ctr., 1974—78; bd. dirs. Comprehensive Health Planning Met. Chgo., 1971—74, Fedn. of Ind. Ill. Colls. and Univs., West Suburban Higher Edn. Consortium; adv. com. Edn. to Careers, Health and Medicine/Chg. Bd. Edn. Editor-in-chief Disease-a-Month, 1998-2003; assoc. editor Primary Cardiology, 1979-85; cons. editor for family practice Hosp. Medicine, 1986-2003; med. editor World Book/Rush Presbyn. St. Lukes/Med. Ency., 1987-2003; contbr. articles to profl. jours. Served with USAF med. corps, 1966-68. Named Physician Tchr. of Yr. Ill. Acad. Family Physicians, 1988, alumni of yr. Temple U. Sch. Medicine, 1996. Fellow Am. Acad. Family Physicians, Inst. of Medicine of Chgo.; mem. IEEE (chmn. Chgo. sect. Engring. in Medicine and Biology group 1974-75), Internat. Soc. for Artificial Internal Organs, Am. Fertility Soc., Am. Occupational Med. Assn. (recipient Physician's recognition award 1969, 72, 75), Chgo. Med. Soc., Am. Heart Assn., Assn. for Advancement Med. Instrumentation, N.Y. Acad. Scis., Sigma Xi, Phi Rho Sigma, Eta Kappa Nu, Alpha Omega Alpha. Home: 319 N Lincoln St Hinsdale IL 60521-3442 *It is important to be courageous and do what you really want to do rather than what is expected or what seems to be currently popular. If life is approached with a spirit of goodwill and one is strong enough to follow one's own desires, then the contribution made and the success achieved can be a credit to humanity and also a source of endless enjoyment. The real secret of life is self-discipline; this allows the tempering of short-term needs with the necessary long-term planning to achieve a stable life and a meaningful contribution to humankind.*

BRUESEWITZ-LOPINTO, GAIL C., marketing professional; b. N.Y.C., May 17, 1956; d. Arthur George and Blanche Juliana (Dobos) Bruesewitz; m. Joseph LoPinto, Sept. 1990; children: Frank Joseph LoPinto, Joseph Arthur LoPinto. BA in Eng. Lit., SUNY, Binghamton, 1978. Mem. promotion and artist devel. staff Columbia Records/CBS Records, Inc., N.Y.C., 1979-82, dir. nat. dance music mktg., 1982-89; nat. dir. Ear Candy Records, 1990-91; prodn. coord. AIG Risk Mgmt., Inc. divsn. Am. Internat. Group, Inc., N.Y.C., 1991-96, Swiss Reins. Am. Alternative Risk Transfer Div., N.Y.C., 1996-98; meeting and event specialist corp. comm. Swiss Re New Markets, N.Y.C., 1999-2000; mktg. coord. Am. Home Assurance Co. AIG, 2004—. Rep. record divsn.Women's Orgn. coun. CBS, Inc., N.Y.C., 1980—82; mem. adv. bd. dance/music New Music Seminar, N.Y.C., 1989—; auction benefit co-chair First Presbyterian Ch., Sag Harbor, NY, 2002; mem. adv. bd. dance/music LoPinto Prodns., N.Y.C., 2000—04; meeting and event planning cons., 2000—04; co-chair catalog com. Grace Ch. Sch Scholarship Benefit Auction, 2002. Editor: (newsletter) Brueser's Boogie Backpage, 1983—90. Active Big Sisters, Binghamton (N.Y.) Social Svcs. Dept., 1975—78; bd. dirs. Camp Wilbur Herrlich, Pawling, NY, 1990, Mt. Tremper (N.Y.) Luth. Camp and Retreat Ctr., 1976—78; asst. Sunday sch. tchr. 1st Presbyn. Ch., Sag Harbor, 2000—. Named N.Y. rep., Mademoiselle mag., 1975. Democrat. Lutheran. Avocations: sailing, ballet, jazz. Office: Am Home Assurance Co 20th Fl 175 Water St New York NY 10038 Office Fax: 212-458-1300. Business E-Mail: gail.lopinto@aig.com.

BRUESKE, CHARLOTTE, poet, composer; b. Plainview Township, Minn., Jan. 1, 1934; d. Layton Floyd and Berneta Dallas (Thompson) B. AA, Pasadena City Coll., 1976; BA, Calif. State U., Fullerton, 1984; postgrad., Fuller Theol. Sem. Author: Once in a Coon's Age, 1989, The Ancestors of Gottlob August Bruss and Bertha Pauline Goede, 1989, A Search for the Records of the Orphans of Dannan, 1990; composer, lyricist numerous works, including Evergreen, 1990, Every New Day, 1991, Lift Up One Another, 1991, Where the Red Ferns Abound, 1995, To Touch This World by Love, 1996, Because of Love, 1997, Poems of the Seasons, To Every Life, 1998; co-author: (with J'hana Brueske) I Heard a Robin Sing Today, 1997, Consider the Lilies, 1997, Life Friend, 1998, Where Love Abides, 1998, The Bells in the Steeple, 1999, Anthology of Love: Morning Light, The Hug of Heaven, Break Not The Morn At Dawning, 2001, Anthology: Still I See the Dawn, Healing Hands, Sunset, 2002, Seasons of the Heart, 2003, Mosaics of Love, 2004, A Heart for God, 2005 Recipient Cert. of Merit Virginia Baldwin/Talent Assocs., 1977. Democrat. Mem. Reformed Ch. Am. Home: PO Box 134-321 Big Bear Lake CA 92315

BRUESS, CHARLES EDWARD, lawyer; b. St. Paul, Oct. 15, 1938; s. Edward Charles and Eleanor Mabel (Hammersten) B.; m. Jean Ellen Gustafson, Aug. 26, 1962; children: Steven Charles, Karen Jean. BA, U. Minn., 1959; student, Ohio U., 1959-60; JD, Ind. U., 1963. Bar: Ind. 1963, U.S. Dist. Ct. (so. dist.) Ind. 1968, U.S. Supreme Ct. 1966. Assoc. Barnes, Hickam, Pantzer & Boyd, Indpls., 1967-71; ptnr. Barnes & Thornburg (formerly Barnes, Hickam, Pantzer & Boyd), Indpls., 1972-94, of counsel, 1995-96, ret., 1996; dep. clk. U.S. Dist. Ct. (so. dist.) Ind., 1999—. Trustee Eagle-Union Community Sch. Corp., Zionsville, Ind., 1978-90; dir. Tri-County Ctr. Inc., 1991-94, Zionsville Pub. Libr., Leasing Corp., 1992—; bd. dirs. Hussey-Mayfield Meml. Pub. Libr. Found., 1999—. Fellow Ind. Bar Found.; Lawyers Club (Indpls.). Republican. Methodist.

BRUFF, HAROLD HASTINGS, law educator, former dean; b. 1944; BA in Am. History and Lit., Williams Coll.; JD magna cum laude, Harvard U. Law faculty Ariz. State U., Tempe, 1971-79; sr. atty.-advisor Office of Legal Counsel, U.S. Dept. Justice, 1979-81; cons. to chmn. Pres.'s Commn. on the Accident at Three Mile Island, 1981; law faculty U. Tex., Austin, 1983-85, John S. Redditt prof. law, 1985-92; Donald Rothschild rsch. prof. George Washington U. Law Sch., Washington, 1992-96; dean U. Colo. Sch. Law, Boulder, 1996—2003, Charles Inglis Thomson prof. law, 2003—. Contbr. articles to profl. jours. Mem. ABA, Phi Beta Kappa. Office: U Colo Boulder Sch Law 208 Fleming Law Bldg Campus Box 401 Boulder CO 80309-0001 E-mail: Harold.Bruff@colorado.edu.

BRUGAROLAS, JAMES BRUFAU, oncologist; b. New Yok, Mass., Oct. 16, 1969; MD, U. of Navarra, Spain, 1993; PhD, MIT, Cambridge, Mass., 1997. Diplomate Am. Bd. Internal Medicine with subspecialty in oncology, 2001. Staff physician Dana-Farber Cancer Inst., Boston, 2003—; instr. in medicine Harvard Med. Sch., Boston, 2003—. Recipient Young Investigator award, Dept. of Medicine, Brigham and Women's Hosp., 2004, Claudia Adams Barr award, Dana-Farber Cancer Inst., 2003—05; grantee KO8 grantee, NIH, 2005—. Mem.: Sigma Xi. Office: Dana-Farber Cancer Institute 44 Binney St Boston MA 02115-6084 Office Phone: 617-632-4742. Office Fax: 617-632-4760. E-mail: james_brugarolas@dfci.harvard.edu.

BRUGGEMAN, TERRANCE, biotechnology company executive; Postgrad., U. Chgo. CEO Network Mgmt., Syscon; COO eBilities.com; CEO Diversa Corp.; chmn. bd., pres., CEO Provasis Therapeutics, Inc., San Diego.

BRUGGEMAN, TERRANCE JOHN, corporate financial executive; b. Mandan, N.D., Oct. 20, 1946; s. George Edward and Marcella Merle (Gray) B.; m. Nancy Ellen Hohman, June 28, 1969 (div. 1997); children: Todd M., Megan P; m. Dianne Dyer, 2003. BA, U. Notre Dame, 1968; postgrad. bus. adminstrn., U. Chgo., 1968-70. Div. mgr., v.p. Continental Ill. Nat. Bank, Chgo., 1968-77; asst. treas. Gould Inc., Rolling Meadows, Ill., 1977-78, treas., 1978-80, v.p., treas., 1980-81; chmn. Gould Fin. Inc., Rolling Meadows, 1978-81; v.p. fin. and adminstrn. AM Internat., Inc., Chgo., 1981-85; mng. dir. Dean Witter Reynolds, Inc., 1985-86; sr. mng. dir. Bear, Stearns and Co., Inc., N.Y.C., 1986-89; sr. v.p., bd. mem., chief ops. officer Lear Siegler Inc., Livingston, N.J., 1989-90; sr. v.p., bd. dirs., chief fin. officer chief ops. officer Grimes Aerospace and FL Industries, Livingston, 1989-90; mng. ptnr. Three Cities Rsch., Inc., N.Y.C., 1990-93; chmn., pres. and CEO Network Mgmt. Inc., Fairfax, Va., 1993-97; chmn., CEO Piatl Holdings Inc., Mt. Laurel, N.J., 1993-99; chmn., pres., CEO Syscon Corp., Falls Church, Va., 1995-96; chmn., CEO Norcross Safety Products, Oak Brook, Ill., 1996, Red Ball Inc., Louisville, 1996, So. Cross O'Fallon Bldg. Products, St. Louis, 1996, Red Giraffe, Louisville, 1996; chmn., CEO, pres. Diversa Corp., San Diego, 1996-99; chmn., pres., CEO Provasis Theraputics, Inc., San Diego, 1999—2002; pres., dir., CEO Sure Beam Corp., San Diego, 2003—04; chmn. Somanta Inc., 2004—. Bd. dirs. Yulex Corp., Harnifschfeger Industries, Inc. SGI, Inc., Silver Eagle Transport, Inc., Stationers Distbg., Inc., Alpha Wire Inc., Miss Erika Inc., Garden Ridge Pottery Corp., Pameco Holding Inc., Curtis Industries Inc., Gulf Coast Lubrication. Bd. dirs. Lincoln Park Zool. Soc., 1972—, pres., CEO, 1984-87; bd. dirs. North Shore Youth Health Svc., 1979-80, N.Y. Zool. Soc./The Wildlife Conservation Soc., 1987-96, Biocom, 1999—, Chmn.'s Roundtable, 1999—, The Burnham Inst., 2002-, Calif. State U. San Marcos, 2003-, Amen Clinics, Inc., 2005-. Mem. Fin. Execs. Inst., Am. Assn. Zool. Parks and Aquariums, Chgo. Club, Notre Dame Club. Home: 10 Old Course Drive Newport Beach CA 92660-9025 Office Phone: 949-706-3697. Personal E-mail: tbruggeman@cox.net.

BRUGGER, DAVID JOHN, media consultant; b. Bethlehem, Pa., Feb. 5, 1943; s. Vincent Francis and Frances Stephanie (Miller) Brugger; m. Joanne Kay Strouf, Oct. 26, 1973. BA in Journalism, Duquesne U., 1965; MS in Theater, CUNY, 1968; postgrad., Drake U., 1973-74, Harvard U., 1980. Exec. prodr. Sta. KDIN-TV, Des Moines, 1968-70; prodn., ops. mgr. Iowa Pub. Broadcasting Network, Des Moines, 1970-71, network ops. mgr., 1971-73, dir. adminstrn., 1973-77; gen. mgr. Sta. WUFT-TV-FM, Gainesville, Fla., 1977-81; dir. Broadcast Svc. Corp. Pub. Broadcasting, Washington, 1981-83; v.p. Telecomm Corp. Pub. Broadcasting, Washington, 1983-87; sr. v.p. Corp. Pub. Broadcasting, Washington, 1987; pres., bd. dirs. Assn. Am.'s Pub. TV Stas., Washington, 1988-2000; pres. Global Media Consulting, Washington, 2000—. Lectr. Fundacion Agnel Ramos, Hato Rey, PR, 1990; mem. consumer adv. com. FCC, 2003—; cons. in field. Prodr.: (TV program) Interracial Dating and Marriage, 1967 (N.E.T. award, 1968); exec. prodr. (TV program) The Bicycle, 1968 (Ohio State award, 1968). Mem. coun. Salvation Army. Named to Hall of Fame, Boys and Girls Clubs Am., 1992; recipient Disting.

Svc. award, Ea. Pub. Radio Network, 1984, Disting. Grad. award, Ctrl. Cath. H.S., 1998, Lowell award, Pub. Broadcasting, 2000; Bklyn. Coll. TV Ctr. scholar, 1965. Mem.: Soc. Profl. Journalists, Greater Washington Soc. Assn. Execs., Am. Soc. Assn. Execs. (Excellence in Govt. Rels. award 1992), US-Indonesia Soc. (mem. world affairs coun.), USIA Pvt. Sector Ctr., Nat. Boys Club Alumni Assn. (award 1988), Asia Soc., Nat. Friends Pub. Broadcasting, Cosmos Club. Roman Catholic. Avocation: international cultures.

BRUHN, JOANN MARIE, radiologic technologist, writer, speaker; b. Perham, Minn., Oct. 3, 1952; d. Raymond Ellsworth and Donna Jeanne (Peterson) Bruhn; children: Mark Schermerhorn, Justin, Craig Schermerhorn-(dec.). Student, Bernice Robe Studio, Detroit Lake, Minn., 1981; cert., Meritcare Sch. Radiologic Tech., Fargo, N.D., 1987. Registered technologist Am. Registry Radiologic Technologists. Piano tchr., Vergas and Moorhead, Minn., 1978—86; music coord. Moorhead Healthcare Ctr., Moorhead, 1985—86; registered radiologic technologist Healtheast/St. John's Hosp., St. Paul, 1987—. Presenter original music. *Following the death of her youngest son, Craig, in 1995, she became inspired to share this story of grief and healing along with original music that was brought to her to assist in the healing process. It is her ministry to help others through their pain and grief with her presentations and workshops that feature this healing music. It is her vision to help bring peace and understanding to as many people as she can in the remainder of her lifetime, through her "Sundance Project."* Author: Sundance, The Story of Craig, 2002; composer: piano compositions, 1986—. Vol. pianist Leukemia and Lymphoma Soc., Wayzata, Minn., 2003; vol. spkr. Am. Cancer Soc., Minn., 2004; vol. pianist, spkr. White Bear Lake (Minn.) United Meth., 1987—; vol. pianist, organist Vergas United Meth. Ch., 1968—81. Mem.: Am. Registry Radiol. Technologists, Am. Soc. Radiologic Technologists. Avocations: songwriting, piano and vocal performance, kayaking, swimming, bicycling. Home and Office: Sundance Project 4372 Greenhaven Dr Saint Paul MN 55127 Office Phone: 651-762-1412. E-mail: joannbruhn@hotmail.com.

BRUICE, THOMAS C., chemist, educator; b. LA, 1925; BS, U. So. Calif., 1950, PhD, 1954. Postdoctoral fellowship UCLA; asst. prof. biochemistry Yale Med. Sch., 1955—58; assoc. prof. biochemistry Johns Hopkins Med. School, 1958—60; prof. chemistry Cornell U., 1960—64, U. Calif., Santa Barbara, 1964—95, rsch. prof. chemistry and biochemistry, 1995—. Contbr. articles to profl. journals. Served USN, 1943—46. Recipient Richard C. Tolman Medal of So. Calif. Sect., Am. Chem. Soc., 1979, Repligen Medal, 1987, Arthur C. Cope Scholar Award, 1987, Alfred Bader Medal, 1988, Renaud Award of Mich. State Sect., 1988, James Flack Norris Award, 1996, Career Devel. Award, NIH, 1956, Lifetime Investigator Award, 1962, MERIT Award, 1990, 1997; Guggenheim Fellow, 1979—80. Fellow AAAS, Royal Soc. Chemistry; mem. NAS (Award in Chem. Sciences, 2005), Am. Acad. Arts and Sciences. Office: U Calif Santa Barbara Dept Chemistry and Biochemistry 9510 Santa Barbara CA 93106-9510 Office Phone: 805-893-2044. Office Fax: 805-893-4120. Business E-Mail: tcbruice@chem.ucsb.edu.*

BRUININKS, ROBERT H., academic administrator, psychologist, educator; b. Mich. m. Susan Andrea Hagstrum; children: Robert, Brian, Brett. BS in Spl. Edn., Music and Social Sci., Western Mich. U., 1964; MA, Vanderbilt U., 1965, PhD in Edn., 1968. Joined as asst. prof. ednl. psychology U. Minn., 1968, Emma M. Birkmaier prof. ednl. leadership Mpls., 1991—94, dean Coll. Edn. and Human Devel., 1991—97, exec. v.p., provost, 1997—2002, pres., 2002—, prof. ednl. psychology. Dir. Devel. Disabilities Office Govs. Coun. on Developmental Disabilities, State Planning Agy., Minn., 1974—76; mem. J. William Fulbright Fgn. Scholarship Bd., 2003—. Contbr. chapters to books, articles to profl. jours. Trustee Com. for Econ. Devel. Named Minnesotan of Yr., Minn. Monthly Mag., 2004; recipient Disting. Alumni award, Mich. U. Alumni Assn., 2004; nat. leadership fellow, Kellogg Found., 1981—84. Fellow: APA, Am. Psychol. Soc., Am. Assn. on Mental Retardation (pres. 1990—91, Edn. award 1996); mem.: Nat. Assn. State Univs. and Land-Grant Colls. (bd. dirs.). Office: Univ Minn 202 Morrill Hall 100 Church St SE Minneapolis MN 55455 Office Phone: 612-626-1616. Business E-Mail: upres@umn.edu.

BRUINSMA, GOSSE, research and development company executive; Sr. med. mgmt. Forest Labs., Clin Trials Rsch., Ltd., Zambon Ltd.; gen. mgr., v.p. Chrysalis Clin. Svcs. Internat., Switzerland; v.p. devel. Crucell BV (formerly IntroGene BV); chief adminstrv. officer, treas., COO, dir. Axonyx Inc.; pres. Axonyx Europe.

BRUKARDT, GARY, health facility administrator; Undergrad., Univ. Wisc.; grad., Am. Grad. Sch. Internat. Mgmt. With St. Luke's Med. Ctr., Phoenix, Presbyterian St. Luke's Med. Ctr., Denver; found., sr. officer Partners Nat. Health Plans; with VHA; chmn., pres. Healthnet, 1991—96; exec. vice-pres. Baptist Healthcare Affiliates, Nashville, 1991—96; pres., CEO Renal Care Group, 1996—. Office: Renal Care Group Ste 600 2525 West End Ave Nashville TN 37203 Office Phone: 615-345-5500, 615-345-5505.

BRULEY, DUANE FREDERICK, academic administrator, consultant, engineer; b. Chippewa Falls, Wis., Aug. 3, 1933; s. Casper Sepharald and Hazel Ella (Kuehn) B.; m. Suzanne Bigler, June 14, 1959; children: Scott, Randall, Mark. Student, Eau Clare (Wis.) State U., 1951-53; BSChemE, U. Wis., 1956; grad., Oak Ridge (Tenn.) Sch. of Reactor Tech., 1957; M in Mech. Engring., Stanford U., 1959; PhD in Chem. Engring., U. Tenn., 1962. Registered profl. engr., S.C. Nuclear engr. Union Carbide Nuclear Co., Oak Ridge, Tenn., 1956-59; head tennis coach U. Tenn., 1961; prof. chem. engring., head tennis coach Clemson (S.C.) U., 1962-73; head chem. engring., head tennis coach Tulane U., New Orleans, 1973-77; head tennis profl. Timberlane Country Club, Gretna, La., 1973-76; v.p. acad. affairs, asst. tennis coach Rose Hulman Inst. Tech., Terre Haute, Ind., 1977-81; head biomed. engring., dir. rehab. engring. ctr. La. Tech. U., Ruston, 1981-84; dean sch. of engring., prof. engring. sci. Calif. Poly U., San Luis Obispo, 1984-91; program dir. biochem. and biomass engring. NSF, Washington, 1987-90, sect. head bioengring. and environ. systems, 1989-90; pres. Synthesizer, Inc., 1988—; dean engring. U. Md., Baltimore County, 1991-94, dir. bioengring., rsch. prof., 1994—2005, prof. emeritus, 2005—. Vis. prof. Princeton (NJ) U., 1970, U. Yamagata (Japan), U. Hokkido, 1975, U. Minn., 1997; adj. prof. dept. chem. engring. U. Louisville, 2002—; cons. Westvaco, Charleston, S.C., 1964-67, DuPont, Ponchartrain, La., 1974-79, Am. Enka Corp., 1970-71, Milliken and Co., 1978-79, Exxon, Baton Rouge, La., 1978-79, El Paso Products Co., 1980-82, Electronics Assocs., Inc., Long Branch, NJ, 1984-88, CRAY Rsch., 1986, EDS, 1995; varsity football and tennis U. Wis., Eau Claire, football adv. coun., 2003—; semi profl. football Chippewa Marines, 1952-53; co-program dir. Nat. Heat Transfer Conf., Balt., 1997, chmn. conf. coord. com., 1998; chmn. nat. heat transfer coord. com. AIChE/ASME, 1998, Nat. Heat Transfer Ann. Conf., 1999; dir. ann. Biodownstream Processing Symposium ASME/AIChE, 2003-05. Author: (chpt.) Mathematics of Microcirculation, 1980; editor: Oxygen Supply, 1973, Oxygen Transport to Tissue, 1973, 83, 88, 91, 92, 94, 98, Hyperthermia, 1988, Protein C and Related Anticoagulants, 1990; rsch. editorial bd.: Biomedical Instrumentation and Technology, 1993-97; contbr. articles to profl. jours.; co-developer BWK Technique for high speed numerical integration. Cons. ARC; narrator five part TV series on biomed. engring., 1982, TV Biomed. Engring. Sta. WEAU, Eau Clare, Wis., 1982; keynote spkr. First Cray Acd., Rsch. Louisville, 2001; recorded for Wis. Pub. TV Network Biotechnology/Bioengring.; head tennis profl. Montebello Tennis Club, 1989-90; referee Sunshine Cup Internat. Jr. Tennis Tournament, Miami, 1966-69. Recipient Ann. Rsch. award La. Tech. U., 1983, Gold medal downhill skiing Nat. Standard Race, 1987, Alumni Disting. Svc. award U. Wis., Eau Claire, 1992, Spl. Opportunity award in Bioengring. The Whitaker Found., 1994—, Disting. Alumni award Chippewa Falls (Wis.) H.S., 2004; named 2d Winningest Tennis Coach in Atlantic Coast Conf. history, 1990, one of Outstanding Educators of Am., 1972; NSF GOALIE grantee with ARC-Protein C, 2001-2004. Fellow AIChE (chmn. heat transfer energy conversion divsn., chmn. com. for Donald Q. Kern award 1997, chmn. com. for Max Jakob Meml. award 1997, Disting. spkr.), Am. Inst. Med. and Biol. Engring. (founding fellow acad. coun.),mem. ASME (exec. bd., bioprocess engring. program, chmn. bioprocess engring. subdivsn., Disting. spkr.); mem. Internat. Soc. on Oxygen Transport Tissue (co-founder 1973, pres. 1983, exec. com., founder, chmn. com. Melvin H. Knisely award 1983—, keynote spkr. 25th anniversary Milw., 1997, 26th ann. meeting, Budapest, Hungary 1998, keynote spkr. Bari, Italy 2004, editor in chief Kluwer/Plenum, Oxygen Transport to Tissue, Advances and Exptl. Medicine and Biology 1999—; named Duane F. Bruley award in his honor), NY Acad. Scis., Calif. Soc. Profl. Engrs. (hon.), Soc. Automotive Engrs. (Ralph R. Teetor Ednl. award 1986), Nat. Soc. Profl. Engrs., Am. Soc. Engring. Edn. (1st Pl. Rsch. award 1967, Biomed. Instrumentation and Tech. Outstanding Rsch. Paper award 1966, 97), La. Engring. Soc. (Charles M. Kerr Pub. Rels. award 1983), U.S. Profl. Tennis Assn. (Disting. Svc. award), U.S. Tennis Assn. (hon. life), Sigma Xi, Tau Beta Pi. Avocation: tennis (#1 mens 35 doubles and #3 mens 35 singles in SC). Home: 7345 Swan Point Way Columbia MD 21045-5010 Office Phone: 410-455-3693.

BRUMBACK, CHARLES TIEDTKE, retired newspaper executive; b. Toledo, Sept. 27, 1928; s. John Sanford and Frances Henrietta (Tiedtke) B.; m. Mary Louise Howe, July 7, 1951; children: Charles Tiedtke Jr., Anne Meyer, Wesley W., Ellen Allen. BA in Econs., Princeton U., 1950; postgrad., U. Toledo, 1953-54. CPA, Ohio, Fla. With Arthur Young & Co., CPAs, 1950-57; bus. mgr., v.p., treas., pres., CEO Sentinel Star Co. subs. Tribune Co., Orlando, Fla., 1957-81; pres., CEO Chgo. Tribune subs. Tribune Co., 1981-88, pres., COO, 1988-90, CEO, 1990-95, chmn., 1993-95. Bd. dirs. Avid Tech., Inc. Life trustee Northwestern U., Chgo. Hist. Soc.; trustee Culver Ednl. Found.; trustee Northwestern Meml. Hosp., chmn., 1987-90. 1st lt. U.S. Army, 1951-53. Decorated Bronze star. Mem. Fla. Press Assn. (treas. 1969-76, pres. 1980, bd. dirs.), Am. Newspaper Pubs. Assn. (bd. dirs., treas. 1991-92), Newspaper Assn. Am. (bd. dirs., sec., 1992-93, vice chmn. 1993-94, chmn. 1994-95), Comml. Club Chgo., Chgo. Club. Home: 1400 Harbor Dr Sarasota FL 34239 Office: Tribune Co 435 N Michigan Ave Chicago IL 60611-4066 Office Phone: 312-222-3014. Personal E-mail: charlie435@aol.com. Business E-Mail: cbrumback@tribune.com.

BRUMBACK, CLARENCE LANDEN, physician; b. Denver, Apr. 19, 1914; s. Carl Alvin and Hildur Athelia (Landen) B.; m. Lucile Leslie Gillie, June 17, 1943; children— Richard, Carl. AB, U. Kans., 1936, MD, 1943; MPH, U. Mich., 1948. Diplomate Am. Bd. Preventive Medicine. Intern U.S. Marine Hosp., San Francisco, 1943-44; dir. pub. health Laclede County, Mo., 1947, AEC, Oak Ridge, 1948-50; dir. Palm Beach County (Fla.) Health Dept., 1950-86; coord. grad. edn. Palm Beach County Health Dept., 1986-2000. Clin. prof. U. Miami; adj. prof. Fla. Atlantic U., Boca Raton, Fla.; trustee Am. Bd. Preventive Medicine, 1969-78. Mem. editl. bd. Jour. Public Health Policy, 1981-88; contbr. articles to profl. jours. Bd. dirs. Palm Beach County chpt. A.R.C., Am. Lung Assn. S.E. Fla., Heart Assn. Palm Beach County, Community Mental Health Center Palm Beach County, Palm Beach County unit Am. Cancer Soc., Palm Beach County Mental Health Assn., Palm Beach County Health Dept., 1950-86; pres. YMCA of Palm Beaches, 1970. With AUS, 1944-47. Recipient Meritorious Svc. award Fla. Public Health Assn., 1968; Merit award State of Fla., 1972; Physician of Yr. award Am. Assn. Public Health Physicians, 1975, Lifetime Achievement award, 2000. Fellow APHA (Sedgwick Meml. medal 1989, mem. exec. bd. 1964-70), Am. Coll. Preventive Medicine, Royal Soc. Health; mem. AMA (Dr. Nathan Davis award 1993), Fla. Med. Assn. (cert. of Merit award 1995), Palm Beach County Med. Soc., Rotary, Elks. Democrat. Lutheran. Home: 1242 Devonshire Way Palm Beach Gardens FL 33418-6864 Office: 826 Evernia St West Palm Beach FL 33401-5708

BRUMBACK, ROGER ALAN, neurologist, researcher; b. Washington, Feb. 15, 1948; s. Oscar Benjamin and Frances Elaine (Neufeld) B.; m. Mary Helen Skinner, Apr. 26, 1969; children: Darryl Wyatt, Audrey Christine, Owen Eliot. BS in Pre-Medicine, Pa. State U., 1967; MD, Pa. State U., Hershey, 1971. Diplomate Nat. Bd. Med. Examiners; Am. Bd. Pediatrics; in Child Neurology, Am. Bd. Psychiatry and Neurology; in Anatomic and Neuropathology, Am. Bd. Pathology; cert. clin. electroencephalography. Pediatric intern Johns Hopkins Hosp., Balt., 1971-72, pediatric asst. resident, 1972-73; fellow in pediatrics Johns Hopkins U. Sch. Medicine, Balt., 1971-73; asst. resident neurology Barnes Hosp., St. Louis, 1973-74; fellow in pediatric neurology Washington U., St. Louis Children's Hosp., 1973-75; clin. assoc. neurology and exptl. neuropathology med. neurology br. Nat. Inst. Neurol. and Communicative Disorders and Stroke, Nat. Insts. of Health, Bethesda, Md., 1975-77; clin. instr. neurology and pediatrics U. Pitts., 1977-78; asst. prof. neurology U. N.D., Fargo, 1978-79, asst. prof. pediatrics, 1978-82, assoc. prof. neurology, 1980-82; resident/fellow anatomic pathology and neuropathology svcs. Strong Meml. Hosp., U. Rochester (N.Y.), 1982-86; assoc. prof. pathology U. Okla., Oklahoma City, 1986-89, chief neuropathology sect. Health Scis. Ctr., 1987-2000, prof. pathology, 1989-2000; interim chmn., dept. pathology Okla. U., Oklahoma City, 1999-2000; prof. pathology, chmn., dept. pathology Creighton U. Med. Ctr., St. Joseph Hosp., Omaha, 2001—, prof. psychiatry, 2003—. Chief neurology svc. V.A. Med. Ctr., Fargo, 1978-82; dir. Muscular Dystrophy Assn. Clinic, Fargo, 1978-82, co-dir., Oklahoma City, 1988-91; adj. assoc. prof. pediatrics U. Okla., 1986-90, adj. assoc. prof. psychiatry and behavioral scis., 1986-91, adj. prof. pediatrics, 1990-2000, adj. prof. psychiatry and behavioral sci., 1991-2000, adj. prof. neurology 1991-2000, adj. prof. orthopaedic surgery, 1996-2000, David Ross Boyd prof. pathology, 1997-2000, adj. prof. geriatric medicine, 1998-2000; clin. care cons. dermatology br. Nat. Cancer Inst., 1987-2000; chief pathology and lab. med. svc. VHA Nebr.-Western Iowa Health Care Sys., Omaha, 2001-. Author (with W.H. Olson, G. Gascon, L.A.Christoferson): Practical Neurology for the Primary Care Physician, 1981; author: (with J.W. Gerst) The Neuromuscular Junction, 1984; author: (with R.M. Herndon) The Cerebrospinal Fluid, 1989; author: (with M.H. Brumback) The Dietary Fiber Weight Control Handbook, 1989; author: (with R.W. Leech) Hydrocephalus: Current Clinical Concepts, 1991; author: Neurology and Clinical Neuroscience, 1993; author: (with W.H. Olson, G. Gascon, V. Iyer) Handbook of Symptom-Oriented Neurology, 2nd edit., 1994; author: (with R.W. Leech) Neuropathology and Basic Neuroscience, 1995; author: (with C.E. Coffey) Textbook of Pediatric Neuropsychiatry, 1998; author: (with W.A. Weinberg, C.R. Harper) Attention, Behaviour, and Learning Problems in Children: Protocols for Diagnosis and Treatment, 2001; chief editor: Jour. Child Neurology, 1986—, mem. editl. bd.: Jour. Geriatric Psychiatry and Neurology, 1994—. With USPHS, 1975-77. Alumni fellow, Penn. State U., 2001. Mem. Am. Acad. Neurology, Am. Assn. Electrodiagnostic Medicine, Am. Assn. Neuropathologists, Am. Acad. Pediats., Am. Neurol. Assn., Child Neurology Soc., Coun. Biology Editors, Coll. Am. Pathologists, Internat. Child Neurology Assn., Soc. for Exptl. Neuropathology (sec.-treas. 1988-93, pres. 1995-97), Behavioral Neurology Soc. (councillor 1990-91, sec.-treas. 1991-93, pres. 1993-95), Alpha Omega Alpha. Republican. Lutheran. Avocation: genealogy. Office: Creighton U Med Ctr Pathology Dept 601 N 30th St Omaha NE 68131 E-mail: rogerbrumback@creighton.edu.

BRUMBAUGH, HARLEY AARON, retired music educator, conductor, composer, poet; b. Renton, Wash., Oct. 23, 1934; s. Aaron Emery and Alice Jane Brumbaugh; m. Catherine Terry Aldridge, June 14, 1958; children: Blaine Harley, Heidi Lynn Magstadt. B of Edn., Ctrl. Wash. U., 1957, M of Music Edn., 1962. Cert. tchr. Wash., 1957. Supr. music Ketchikan Sch. Dist., Ketchikan, Alaska, 1959—62; dir. instrumental music Port Angeles Sch. Dist., 1962—63; dir. choral music Renton Sch. Dist., 1963—72; prof. music Bellevue C.C., 1972—92. Trumpeter Seattle Opera Orch., 1966—67; festival condr. Tacoma All-City Honor Choir, 1982—86, All Southeastern Alaska Massed Choir, Ketchikan/Skagway, 1974—78, All-Bellevue Massed Choir, 1975, Olympic Penninsula Massed Choir, Chimacum, 1979; condr. Celebration Singers Australian Youth Music Festival, Melbourne, 1983; condr. Celebration Singers, Nandi, Fiji, 1985, U. Mex. Concert Series, Mexico City, 1981, Tahiti Typhoon Benefit Radio Broadcast, Papeete, French Polynesia, 1983; lead trumpet/vocalist Kings Of Swing jazz band White Nights Festival, St. Petersburg, Russia, 1992; v.p. Wash. Jazz Educator's Assn., Yakima, 1970—72; trumpeter Seattle Symphony, Seahawks Band, Sonic Six, Seattle World's Fair Band; trumpet player Marion Hutton, Eartha Kitt, Morey Amsterdam, Kay Starr, Frankie Laine, Vick Schoen; trumpeter Mel Torme, Nelson Riddle, Lawrence Welk, Tex Beneke, Tenn. Ernie Ford; lead trumpet in Seattle bands Jackie Souders Orch., Max Pillar, Norm Hougy, Archie Kyle, Hank Ohstus, Ted Carper, Red Shepherd, Ben Blakeman, Reg Hudman, Terry King, The Many Sounds of Nine Orch.; leader Harley's Horns-A-Plenty!; v.p. Puget Sound Choral Director's Assn., Seattle, 1973—75; co-founder Wash. Assn. of Cmty. Bands, Bellevue, 1986; v.p. East Side Musician's Assn., 1995—97; nat. chmn. for cmty. and two yr. colleges Music Educator's Nat. Conf., Chgo., 1977—78; chmn./clinician NW Music Educator's Conf., Portland, 1972—73; clinician Wash. Music Educator's Conf., Yakima, 1970; mem./singer Seattle Opera Chorus, 1964—65; guest appearances on Saturday with Saldonia, The Don Lane Show, The Daryl Somers Show, 1982—83. Composer: Drums of God, No Greater Love, Tattered Sandals, Four Riverside Reflections, Molly Malone (arrangement), 1970-1974; author: (poems) Riverside Reflections; composer (performer): (musical score for documentary video) Snoqualmie Falls Mill Town Images; dir.(producer): (television bicentennial musical) Sounds of Freedom!. Dir., founder The Valley Cmty. Players, Renton, Wash., 1965; co-founder Wash. Assn. of Cmty. Bands, Bellevue, 1986; condr. Renton City Concert Band, 1985—2003; founding mem. entertainment bd. Renton River Days Ann. Festival, 1985—2001; co-founder/prodr. Snoqualmie Valley Arts Live, 1992—96; founder Celebration Singers; founding mem. Bellevue Jazz Festival, 1974. With U.S. Army, 1957—59. Named Honored Citizen of Yr., Greater Renton C. of C., 2003; named to State of Wash. Music Educator's Hall of Fame, 1998; recipient Golden Acorn award, Renton PTA, 1964—65, Exemplary Status, Wash. C.C. Humanities Assn., 1965, Man of the Yr. Arts, Bellevue Mcpl. Arts Commn., 1985, Musical Expression award, Evergreen Safety Coun., 1987, Life Achievement award, Bellevue Lion's Club, 1992, BRAVO award, Renton Mcpl. Arts Commn., 2002. Mem.: Internat. Trumpet Guild, Poets West, Wash. State Hist. Soc., Snoqualmie Valley Hist. Soc. (life; bd. 2003). Avocations: professional musician, church choir director, history, reading, walking, seminars. Home: 524 Orchard Avenue NE North Bend WA 98045 Personal E-mail: hcbrum@earthlink.net.

BRUMBY, JAMES REMLEY, III, (KNOX BRUMBY), retired priest; b. Marietta, Ga., Apr. 24, 1921; s. James Remley and Martha Louise Brumby; m. Vesta Frances Palmer, Aug. 20, 1971; m. Ferrell Louise West, Dec. 24, 1944; children: Ferrell Lynora, Martha Suzanne; stepchildren: Dana, Christine, Liana, Erik, Jenny. At, U. Fla., 1940—42; BA, U. of the South, Sewanee, Tenn., 1948, MDiv, 1951. Priest-in-charge St. Johns Episcopal Ch., Brooksville, Fla., 1951—53, St. Margarets Episcopal Ch., Inverness, Fla., 1951—53; asst. Holy Trinity Episcopal Ch., West Palm Beach, Fla., 1953—54; vicar Holy Spirit Ch., West Palm Beach, 1953—55, rector, 1955—60, St. Mary's Ch., Daytona Beach, Fla., 1960—66; canon missioner Diocese S. Fla., Ft. Lauderdale, 1966—70; chmn. dept. of missions Diocese Fla., Ft. Lauderdale, 1966—70; founder, priest Ch. Atonement, Ft. Lauderdale, 1966—70; supply priest Diocese Fla., Tallahassee, 1970—88; priest-in-charge Ch. Ascension, Carrabelle, Fla., 1988—2003. Dept. Christian edn. Diocese S. Fla., Orlando, 1952—58, dept. promotions, 1954—56, chair dept. young people, 1954—56, dept. mission and ch. ext., 1957, chair dept. camps and conf., 1958—66, mem. exec. bd., 1960—66; mem. Youth Bd. Provence IV, 1956—59; pres. Palm Beach Ministerial Assn., 1957—58, Volusia County Ministerial Assn., Daytona Beach, 1962—63; trustee Univ. South, Sewanee, Tenn., 1963—69, chair trustees com. to make student body co-ed, 1969, acting dir. ch. rels., 1984—90; founder, chmn. bd. Louttit Manor for Elderly, Daytona Beach, 1964—66; hon. canon St. Lukes Cathedral, Orlando, 1966; dep. to Gen. Conv., 69; mem. diocesan coun. Diocese Fla., 1996—2000, canon Apalachee regional coun. ministry, mem. exec. bd., 1996—2000. Author: (book) I Am a Part of All I Have Met, 1999. Lt. col. USAAF, 1942—45 USAR, 1946—58. Democrat. Avocations: painting, sailing, flying. Home: Village of Shell Point 67 Connie Dr Crawfordville FL 32327

BRUMFIELD, JACK, communications executive; Grad., Alliane Coll. Pa. Various positions N.Y. Govs. Office, N.Y. Power Authority; with Winner/Wagner & Assocs., N.Y.C., L.A.; sr. exec. v.p. Stoorza Ziegaus & Metzer, San Diego, 1995-2000; gen. mgr. Stoorza Comm., L.A., 2000—. Mem. Ctrl. City Assn. L.A. (govt. rels. com., bd. dirs.).

BRUMFIELD, WILLIAM CRAFT, Slavic studies educator, photographer, writer; b. Charlotte, N.C., June 28, 1944; s. Lewis F. and Pauline Elizabeth (Craft) B. BA, Tulane U., 1966; PhD in Slavic langs., U. Calif., Berkeley, 1973. Vis. lectr. U. Wis., Madison, 1973-74; asst. prof. Harvard U., Cambridge, Mass., 1974-80; assoc. prof. Tulane U., New Orleans, 1984-91, prof. Slavic langs., 1992—. Resident dir. Am. Coun. Tchrs. of Russian Pushkin Inst. Program, Moscow, 1979-80; co-dir. Summer Inst. for Coll. Faculty, NEH, 1994; advisory dir. Russian Children's Welfare Soc.; lectr. on architecture, photography and lit. at museums and univs throughout U.S. and Europe. Author: Gold in Azure: One Thousand Years of Russian Architecture, 1983, The Origins of Modernism in Russian Architecture, 1991, A History of Russian Architecture, 1993, 2004 (Notable Book of Yr. NY Times Book Rev., 1993), An Archtl. Survey of St. Petersburg: 1840-1916, 1994, Lost Russia: Photographing the Ruins of Russian Architecture, 1995, Landmarks of Russian Architecture: A Photographic Survey, 1997; editor, contbr.: Reshaping Russian Architecture: Western Technology, Utopian Dreams, 1990, Christianity and the Arts in Russia, 1991, Russian Housing in the Modern Age: Design and Social History, 1993, Commerce in Russian Urban Culture: 1861-1914, 2001, Zhilishche V Rossii: vek XX, 2001, Predprinimatelstvo i gorodskaia kultura V Rossii, 2002, Vologda Album, 2005; contbr. articles to profl. jour.; photog. exhbns. include Duke U. Mus. Art, 1996, New Orleans Mus. Art, 1996, U. Mich. Mus. Art, 1997, Arkhangelsk Mus. Art, 1999, Shchusev Mus. Architecture, Moscow, 2001; represented in permanent collections at Photographic Archives, Nat. Gallery Art, Washington, Libr. Congress, New Orleans Mus. Art; elected to Russian Acad. of Architecture, 2002. Woodrow Wilson fellow, 1966, NEH fellow Nat. Humanities Ctr., 1992-93, fellow Harvard Russian Rsch. Ctr., 1980-81, John Simon Guggenheim fellow, 2000-2001; NEH Collaborative Fellowship Am. Coun. for Internat. Edn., 2001-02; sr. exch. scholar Internat. Rsch. Exchs. Bd./Am. Coun. Learned Socs. U.S.-USSR Exch., Moscow, 1983-84, rsch. scholar Kennan Inst., Washington, 1989; grantee Samuel H. Kress Found., 1996-97, grantee Nat. Coun. for Eurasian and East European Rsch., 1999-2000; elected to Russian Acad. Architecture, 2002. Mem. Am. Assn. Advancement Slavic Studies, Soc. Archtl. Historians, Inst. Modern Russian Culture (head photography sect.), Am. Coun. Tchrs. of Russian, Soc. of Historians of East European and Russian Art and Architecture, Russian Acad. Architecture, Phi Beta Kappa. Office: Tulane U Slavic Dept 305 Newcomb Hall New Orleans LA 70118 Office Phone: 504-865-5276. Business E-Mail: brumfiel@tulane.edu.

BRUMIT, JO ANN, sheet metal manufacturing executive; 4 children. With KARLEE, 1982—, CEO & chmn. Garland, Tex. Recipient Entrepreneur of Yr. for Mfg. by INC. Mag., Ernst & Young, 1991, Amb. of Yr. Award, Hogan Ctr. for Performance Excellence, 1994, 1999, Dir. of Yr., Garland Chamber of Commerce, 1997, Athena Award, 2000, Malcolm Baldridge Nat. Quality Award, 2000. Mem.: Hogan Quality Roundtable, Garland Ind. Sch. Dist. (bus. sch. ptnr.), Richland Cmty. Coll. Middle Mgmt. Prog. (adv. bd. mem.), Baylor Healthcare System Found. (bd. dirs.), Sch. to Career Bd., Tex. Work (source bd. mem.), Tex. Quality Found. (adv. bd., Tex. Quality award 1999). Office: Karlee PO Box 461207 Garland TX 75046-1207 E-mail: jabrumit@karlee.com.

BRUMIT, LAWRENCE EDWARD, III, oil field service company executive; b. Brunswick, Ga., Feb. 5, 1950; s. Lawrence Edward Jr. and Felicite (Smith) B.; m. Leila Ann Parker, Feb. 21, 1976; children: Mary Louise, Lawrence Edward IV. BS in Petroleum Engring., Mont. Tech., 1974. Field engr. Dowell, Farmington, N. Mex., 1974; service engr. Dowell Schlumberger, Warri, Nigeria, 1975, mgr., Cork, Ireland, 1976, tech. engr., Galeota, Trinidad, 1977, mgr., San Fernando, Trinidad, 1978-79, tng. ctr. mgr., Pau, France, 1980, div. mgr. S.W. Africa, Luanda, Angola, 1981-82, tech. mktg. mgr., Paris, 1983-84, v.p., region mgr., Paris, 1984-86, pres. compagnie de services, 1985—, mgr., v.p. Europe Africa, 1986-88; dir. personnel Schlumberger Ltd. Drilling and Pumping Svcs., Paris, 1988-90; v.p., gen. mgr. Dowell Schumberger North Am., Houston, 1991-95, rancher Flying "B" Ranch, 1995—; bd. dirs. Mont. Tech. Found., 1993-96. Recipient All Conf. Baseball Outstanding Coll. Athlete of Am. award Frontier Conf., 1969-71, 72, No. 1 Player and Capt. award, 1971. Mem. Soc. Petroleum Engrs. Romann Catholic. Avocations: flying; golf. Home: 4425 Sundown Rd Missoula MT 59804-7109

BRUMLEY, LARRY GENE, music educator; b. Ada, Okla., Jan. 23, 1946; s. Joe Bailey and Margie Maurine Brumley; m. Elizabeth Ann Aldrich, Dec. 30, 1967; children: Michael, Gary, Philip. B.Music Edn., Tex. Christian U., 1972; MA with distinction, Calif. State U., Fresno, 1977. Tchr. choir and band Terra Bella Elem. Sch., Calif., 1972—73; tchr. choir and orch. Porterville HS, Calif., 1973—81; percussionist Bakersfield Philharmonic, Calif., 1962—64, Riverside Symphony, Calif., 1964—66, U.S. 4th Army Band, San Antonio, 1967—69, Tulare County Symphony, Tulare, Calif., 1972—81, Marshall Symphony, Tex., 1981—; prof., dir. choirs and voice Panola Coll., Carthage, Tex., 1981. Bd. dirs. Shreveport Chamber Singers, 1986—; drummer in "light jazz" combo; asst. dir. 1st Presbyn. Ch., Ft. Worth, 1970—72; music dir. First United Meth. Ch., Porterville, Calif., 1972—81, North Highlands United Meth. Ch., Shreveport, La., 1986—98, First United Meth. Ch., Carthage, Tex., 1998—; chorus master Shreveport Opera, 1986—88; condr. Shreveport Chamber Singers, 1986—; choral adjudicator Heritage Festivals, Inc., Salt Lake City, 1986—. Ad hoc mem. curriculum revision com. Tex. Coord. Bd. of Colls. and Univs.; county chmn. Rep. Party of Panola County, 1995—2003; bd. dirs. Shreveport Summer Music Festival, 1981—, Marshall Symphony, 1984—. With U.S. Army, 1966—69. Mem.: Tex. Jr. Coll. Tchrs. Assn., Tex. Music Educators Assn., Am. Choral Dirs. Assn., Am. Fedn. Musicians, Tex. Two-Year Coll. Choral Dirs. Assn. (pres. 1982—83, regional rep. 1990—93), Lions (past bd. dirs.). Republican. Methodist. Avocations: golf, travel, reading, cuisine dining. Home: 1128 Oakwood Carthage TX 75633 Office: Panola College 1109 W Panola St Carthage TX 75633-2341 Office Phone: 903-693-2061. E-mail: lbrumley@academicplanet.com.

BRUMLEY, TOM, museum director, artist; Installation coord. New Mus. Contemporary Art, NYC, dir. ops. Office: New Mus Contemporary Art 556 W 22nd St New York NY 10011 E-mail: tbrumley@newmuseum.org.*

BRUMM, JAMES EARL, lawyer, import/export company executive; b. San Antonio, Dec. 19, 1942; s. John Edward and Marie Oletha (Gault) B.; m. Alicia Joan Pine, Aug. 17, 1968 (div. Mar. 1991); children: Christopher Kenji, Jennifer Kimiko, Laurie Kiyoko; m. Yuko Tsuchida, Apr. 17, 1991. AB, Calif. State U., Fresno, 1965; LLB, Columbia U., 1968. Bar: N.Y. 1969. Assoc. Reid & Priest, N.Y.C., 1968-72, Logan, Takashima & Nemoto, Tokyo, 1973-76; exec. v.p., gen. counsel, dir. Mitsubishi Internat. Corp., N.Y.C., 1977—; pres. Mitsubishi Internat. Corp. Found., N.Y.C., 1992—. Bd. dirs. Brunei LNG, Tembec, Inc., Mitsubishi Corp., Japan, 1995—2002. Trustee Spuyten Duyvil Nursery Sch., Bronx, NY, 1991—95; bd. dirs. Sanctuary for Families, 2000—; bd. visitors Columbia Law Sch., 1998—; mem. nat. bd. visitors Calif. State U., Fresno, 2005—; bd. dir. Jr. Achievement Internat., 1997—2000, Internat. Sch. Svcs., 1997—99, Forest Trends, 2003—, Am. Bird Conservancy, 2003—. Mem. ABA, Internat. Bar Assn., Assn. Bar City N.Y. (chmn. com. on internat. trade 1990-93, chmn. task force on internat. legal svcs. 1998-2001, rep. to Internat. Bar Assn. 2001—), Univ. Club, Nippon Club. Home: 255 W 84th St Apt 6C New York NY 10024-4327 Office: Mitsubishi Internat Corp 655 3d Ave New York NY 10017 Office Phone: 212-605-2565. Business E-Mail: james.brumm@mitsubishicorp.com.

BRUMMEL, MARK JOSEPH, religious organization administrator; b. Chgo., Oct. 28, 1933; s. Anthony William and Mary (Helmreich) B. BA, Cath. U. Am., 1956, STL, 1961, MSLS, 1964. Joined Order of Claretians, Roman Cath. Ch., 1952; ordained priest Order of Caretians, Roman Cath. Ch., 1960; librarian, tchr. St. Jude Sem., Momence, Ill., 1961-70; asso. editor U.S. Cath. mag., Chgo., 1971-72; editor U.S. Cath. Mag., 1970—2002; dir. St. Jude League, Chgo., 1970—2002. Treas. Eastern Province Claretians, 1998—, also bd. dirs.; bd. dirs. Chgo. Family Health Ctr. Editor Today mag., 1970-71; contbr. article to publ. Chmn. bd. Eighth Day Ctr. for Justice, Chgo., 1988-92; bd. dirs. Assn. of Chgo. Priests, 1994-96; mem. Ill. Cath. Conf., 1993-96. Mem. Cath. Press Assn. (St. Francis De Sales award 1996), Associated Ch. Press (v.p. 1985-87). Avocation: photography. Home: 205 W Monroe St Chicago IL 60606 Office: Claretian Missionaries 205 W Monroe St Fl 7 Chicago IL 60606-5033 Office Phone: 312-236-7782. E-mail: mark_brummel@claret.org.

BRUMMET, RICHARD LEE, accounting educator; b. Ewing, Ill., Mar. 16, 1921; s. George Otto and Iva Talitha (Smith) B.; m. Nellie Eldora Riddle, Aug. 6, 1942; children— Carmen, John. B.E., Ill. State U., 1942; MS, U. Ill., 1947; PhD, U. Mich., 1956. Prof. Cornell U., 1954-55; prof. U. Mich., 1955-69, dir. mgmt. edn., 1966-68; Willard J. Graham distinguished prof. U. N.C., 1970-86, dir. M in Acctg. degree program, 1984-86, prof. emeritus, 1986—. Cons. Ford Found., Cairo, Egypt, 1963-64; vis. prof. Netherlands Sch. Econs., 1969, U. South Africa, 1974, U. New South Wales, Australia, 1976; cons. in field. Author: Overhead Costing, 1957, Cost Accounting for Small Manufacturers, 1953; 197l, Record Keeping for Small Home Builders, 1952, The Metal Finishing Industry, 1966; Contbr. articles to profl. jours. Served to capt. AUS, 1942-46. Mem. Am. Inst. C.P.A.'s (council 1975-77), Am. Acctg. Assn. (treas. 1967-69, pres. 1974-75), Inst. Mgmt. Accts. (v.p. 1970-71, pres. 1979-80, chmn. 1980-81, Disting. Service award for Educators, 1988) Pioneer in social accounting, human resources accounting. Nat. Assn. Accts. annual Disting. Service award for Educators named in his honor. Home: 322 Cedar Berry Ln Chapel Hill NC 27517 Office Phone: 919-967-1628. Personal E-mail: lbrummet@fusionbb.net.

BRUMMUND, ELIZABETH JENNY, elementary school educator; b. Providence, R.I., Nov. 12, 1961; d. John Thurber and Janet Christina Bartlett; m. Douglas Eric Brummund, Apr. 25, 1987; children: Douglas Dale, Christina Ann. BA, U. R.I., 1983; MA in Tchg., Conn. Coll., 1991. Cert. tchr. Conn. Kindergarten, transitional 1st tchr. Chariho Regional Dist., Ashaway, RI, 1985—91; elem. tchr. No. Stonington Christian Acad., RI, 1997—2001; grade 4 tchr. Stonington Pub. Schs., RI, 2001—. Ch. sch. tchr. United Congregational Ch., Pawcatuck, Conn., 1987—. Recipient Outstanding Young Ch. Woman, Ch. Women United, 2005. Democrat. United Ch. Of Christ. Avocations: reading, book collecting, decorating. Home: 30 Mary Hall Rd Pawcatuck CT 06379 Office: Stonington Pub Schs Deans Mill Elem 35 Deans Mill Rd Stonington CT 06378

BRUN, HENRY, publishing executive; b. N.Y.C., Feb. 11, 1940; BA, Bklyn. Coll., 1958-62; MS, Pace U., 1975. Supr. N.Y.C. Sch. Sys., 1962-90; prin. John Jay H.S., Bklyn., 1990-94; COO Amsco Sch. Pubs. Inc., N.Y.C., 1994-95, pres., 1995—. Author: Women of the Ancient World, The Retreat from Imperialism, Global Studies: Civilizations of the Past and Present, The World Today, America Today, Global History: The Growth of Civilizations. Mem. Am. Archeol. Assn., Soc. Antiquaries Newcastle upon Tyne, Soc. Promotion Roman Studies. Office: Amsco Sch Pubs Inc 315 Hudson St New York NY 10013-1009

BRUNALE, VITO JOHN, aerospace engineer; b. Mt. Vernon, N.Y., July 2, 1925; s. Donato and Antoinette (Wool) B.; m. Joan Florence Montuori, Apr. 23, 1949; 1 child, Stephen. AAS, Stewart Aero. Inst., 1948; BSAE, Tri-State U., 1958; MSME, U. Bridgeport, 1966; DSc, Nev. Inst. Tech., 1973; PhD (hon.), Internat. U., Spain, 1987; DSc, Pacific Western U., 1984. Rsch. engr. Norden Labs., White Plains, N.Y., 1948-55; instr. Tri-State U., Angola, Ind., 1955-58; engring. cons. Norden Div. United Aircraft, Norwalk, Conn., 1958-67; chief engring. cons. Singer-Kearfott Corp., Pleasantville, N.Y., 1967-73; chief engr. Diagnostic/Retrieval Systems, Mt. Vernon, N.Y., 1973-76; tech. problem mgr. Fairchild Republic Co., Farmingdale, N.Y., 1977-87; sr. tech. expert Sikorsky Aircraft, 1987—. Cons. in field; engring. tutor to coll. students; v.p. Lithoway, Inc., 1969-73; lectr. in field; tech. guest speaker numerous tech. soc. meetings.; participant engring. exchange program, USSR, People's Republic China. Contbr. articles to profl. jours. including Product Engring., Aviation Week, Environ. Scis. Participant U.S.A. Citizen Amb. Program. Served with USAAF, 1943-45. Decorated Purple Heart (3), Air medals, D.F.C. Tri-State U. tcht. fellow, 1955-58; NSF grantee; recipient Aircraft Design award, 1948, Inst. Aero. Sci. Lecture award, 1948, Norden Rsch. award, 1963, Cost Reduction award, 1965, Singer Engring. award, 1970, 72, Fairchild outstanding achievement award, 1985, 86, 87, Fairchild award of excellence, 1984, Am. Biographical Inst. and Research Assn. Outstanding Performance award, 1989, Aircraft Recognition award, 1986, citation N.Y. State Assembly, 1988, Conspicuous Service Cross N.Y. State, 1988, Prisoner of War medal, 1988, others; honoree Nat. Air and Space Mus.; named to Wisdom Hall of Fame, 1998. Mem. AIAA (award 1973, Aviation award 1994, Sr. Mem. award 1994, Merit award 1998, membership award 1998, award 1998), VFW, DAV, K.C., U.S. Naval Inst., Air Force Assn., Am. Ordnance Asssn., Inst. Environ. Sci., Nat Space Inst., Newman Club, Internat. Students Assn., Internat. Platform Assn., World Inst. of Achievement. Roman Catholic. Achievements include patent (with others) for Bearing Spin Rail Test; development of method of discriminate displacement for equilibrium of structures, of the position point vibration isolation technique, of the vapress vibration system, of advanced techniques for structural and vibration analyses, of the Doppler-Inertial-Loran system, of state of the art mathematical and structural analyses techniques, of Mars Doppler Lander system, computer time studies, anti-corrosion methods; resolution of 140 technical problems on the Fairchild A-10 aircraft, of more than 30 technical problems with the Saab-Fairchild 340; solution of Grumman A-6A radar tracking problem in Vietnam; elimination of technical problems on LEM inertial guidance; rsch. in mfg. productivity, co-planer structural analyses. Home: 459 Bronxville Rd Bronxville NY 10708-1102 Office: Main St Bronxville NY 10708-1102

BRUNDA, DANIEL DONALD, retired aerospace engineer, consultant, inventor, writer; b. Lansford, Pa., Oct. 22, 1930; s. Michael Theodore and Ella (Jurba) B. BSME, Lehigh U., 1952, MSME, 1953; postgrad., Johns Hopkins U., 1955, Princeton U., 1958—65, Drexel U., 1983. Registered profl. engr., N.J.; cert. expert witness and cons. Engr. Bell Aircraft aerodynamicist Glenn L. Martin, Balt.; devel., test, evaluation and performance propulsion engr. Bell Aircraft Glenn L. Martin & Curtiss Wright, Princeton, NJ, 1953—57; aerospace engr. rsch. U.S. Naval Air Propulsion Ctr., Ewing, NJ, 1957—72, local mgr. ind. R&D, 1972—83; powerline radiation energy engring. cons. Ewing, 1978—. Dep. dir. gen. Internat. Biog. Inst. in the Americas, 2000, sci. adv. to dir. gen., 2003; founder Electromagnetic Powerline Radiation Engrs., Am. Biog. Inst., 2000. Author: Powerline Radiation, Your Genes, Hereditary Diseases, The Unified Nature of Electromagnetic Radiation Energy and Control, and the Radiation Limits of Human Beings, 2003, Design of Safe Electric Transmission and Distribution Lines, 2003; contbr. over 20 articles to profl. jours. Internat. amb. of goodwill World Peace and Diplomacy Forum, 2003. Recipient Lifetime Achievement award, IBC, 2002, World Lifetime Achievement award, Am. Biog. Inst., 2002. Fellow Bioelectromagnetic Soc. (assoc.); mem. ASME (life), AIAA, Am. Biographical Inst. Rsch. Assn. (lifetime dep. gov., named Amb. of Grand Eminence 2002, World Lifetime Achievement award 2002,DiVinci Diamond award 2004). Achievements include research, and patents on powerline radiation, which determined the molecular weight, radiation limits, inductive impedance of average adult human beings; proved that powerline radiation is a cause of cancer and many other diseases; explained mathematically Volta's electrophonic effect 1800 A.D.; discovered Brunda's Absorbance Law and the Absorbance of DNA. Home and Office: Powerline Radiation Energy Engring Cons 106 W Upper Ferry Rd Ewing NJ 08628-2724 Office Phone: 609-882-2598.

BRUNDAGE, GERTRUDE BARNES, pediatrician; b. Neptune, N.J., May 13, 1941; d. John Holt and Mary Downey (Chatham) B. BS in Chemistry, Marietta Coll., 1964; MD, Jefferson Med. Coll., 1971. Diplomate Am. Bd. Pediatrics. Chemist Lederle Labs., Pearl River, N.Y., 1964-67; intern pediatrics Harrisburg (Pa.) Polyclinic Hosp., 1971-72; resident pediatrics Wilmington (Del.) Med. Ctr., 1972-74; pediatrician St. Barnabas Med. Ctr., 1974—; chief dept. pediat. Hosp. Ctr. at Orange, 1990—98. Moderator Presbytery of Newark, 1996; active 1st Presbyn. Ch., elder, trustee, 1982—87, 1989—92, 2004—. Mem. AMA, N.J. Med. Women's Assn., Am. Med. Women's Assn., Essex County Med. Soc., Med. Soc. N.J., Alpha Gamma Delta. Republican. Presbyterian. Avocations: choral singing, needlecrafts, gardening. Home: 18 Farrington St West Caldwell NJ 07006-7716 Office: Gertrude B Brundage MD 572 Park Ave East Orange NJ 07017-1904 Office Phone: 973-678-1214. E-mail: trudyb18@comcast.net.

BRUNDAGE, JEFFREY J., human resources specialist, air transportation executive; m. Diane Brundage; 3 children. Attended, Johnson and Wales Coll. Pilot Pocono Airlines, Atlantic Coast Airlines; sr. collective bargaining coord. Airline Pilots Assn. Internat.; mng. dir. employee rels. for flight function Am. Airlines, 1999—2001, v.p. employee rels., 2001—04, sr. v.p. human resources, 2004—. Office: AMR Corp 4333 Amon Carter Blvd Fort Worth TX 76155 Office Phone: 817-963-1234. Office Fax: 817-967-9641.*

BRUNDAGE, RITA S., retired elementary school educator; b. Hamtramck, Mich., Oct. 1, 1946; d. Rustico Aguigam and Rosie Miguel Sibucao; m. Arthur Lester Brundage, Sept. 23, 1972. BA in Elem. Edn., U. South Fla., 1968. Classroom tchr. DeSoto Elem. Sch., Tampa, 1968—75, alternative edn. tchr., 1975—79, classroom tchr., 1979—86, ESEA reading tchr., 1986—92, accelerated literacy learning tchr., 1992—96; match resource tchr. Bing Elem. Sch., Tampa, 1996—98; lead tchr. B.C. Graham Elem. Sch., Tampa, 1998—2003; lead arts tchr. Muller Elem. Magnet Sch., Tampa, 2003—05. Author: (guide for tchrs.) Alternative Reading Strategies, 1980. Office: Muller Elem Magnet 13615 N 22d St Tampa FL 33613 Office Phone: 813-558-1355. E-mail: RBrundage@webtv.net.

BRUNDAGE, RUSSELL ARCHIBALD, retired data processing executive; b. N.Y.C., N.Y., Feb. 16, 1929; s. Eugene Columbus and Sophia Catherine (Gillies) B.; m. Barbara Jane Nelson, May 18, 1958; children: Russell Archibald, Nelson David, Beth Ellen, Paul Winston. BA, Washington Sq. Coll., NYU, 1957. With U.S. Fgn. Service, State Dept., 1950-55; applied sci. writer IBM Corp., N.Y.C. and White Plains, N.Y., 1957-60; with Colonial Penn Group, Phila., 1960-81, v.p., 1972-81; pres. Colonial Penn Group Data Corp., 1970-77; v.p. Nat. Assn. Plans, Inc., 1971-81; v.p. data processing SAI Group, Inc., 1982; pres. SAI Data Services Div., 1983-86; v.p. MIS Mut. Assurance Co., Phila., 1989-94; v.p. Green Tree Ins. Co., Phila., 1989-94; v.p., bd. dirs. Valley Ins. Co., Phila., 1990-92, Green Tree Ins. Co., Phila., 1992-94. V.p. Am. Loyalty Ins. Co., Gahanna, Ohio, 1989-94, also bd. dirs.; v.p., sec. Mut. Assurance Co., Green Tree Ins. Co., Am. Loyalty Ins. Co., 1991-94. Chmn. Lee Magisterial Dist. Republican Com., Fairfax County, Va., 1966; bd. dirs. S.E. Pa. chpt. Am. Heart Assn., 1993-96. Served with USAF, 1947-50. Mem. Vets. 7th Regt. N.Y., St. Andrews Soc. Phila. Republican. Presbyterian (Ret. Elder, Active Deacon). Home: 23 Wincrest Dr Phoenixville PA 19460-5735

BRUNDAGE, THOMAS CHARLES, geologist, consultant; b. Eureka, Calif., Aug. 15, 1947; s. William John and Katherine Melva Brundage; m. Diane Clair de Ford, Feb. 6, 1949; 1 child, Robin Summer Daugherty. BA, Humboldt State U., 1970. Cert. geologist Oreg. Bd. Geologist Examiners, registered Calif., Oreg. Geologist No. Geotech. Inc., Eureka, Calif., 1980—87; prin. geologist Brundage Geol. Consulting, Fortuna, Calif., 1988—96, Pacific Watershed Assocs., McKinleyville, Calif., 1997—2004; owner, mgr. Soil Lab., Arcada, Calif., 1988—; prin. geologist Consulting Geologist, Arcada, Calif., 2004—. Mgr. water sys. Fickle Hill Water Group, Arcada, Calif., 1996—; cons. Strategic Alliance Group, Eureka, Calif., 2000—. Mem. adv. bd. North Coast Regional Land Trust, Arcada, Calif., 2001—; active local polit. campaigns, 1985—; bd. dirs. Sanctuary Forest Inc., Whitethorn, Calif., 1994—. Lt. U.S. Coast Guard, 1971—74. Mem.: Assn. Engring. Geologists. Democrat. Avocations: backpacking, swimming, landscaping, building, dance.

BRUNDIGE, ROBERT WILLIAM, JR., lawyer; b. Dayton, Ohio, Feb. 4, 1944; s. Robert W. and Elizabeth (Marquardt) B.; m. Katherine D. Muller, Dec. 18, 1971; children: Elizabeth, Allyson. BA, Yale U., 1966; JD, Vanderbilt U., 1969. Bar: N.Y. 1970, U.S. Dist. Ct. (so. and ea. dists.) N.Y. 1972, U.S. Tax Ct. 1973, U.S. Ct. Appeals (2d cir.) 1975, U.S. Ct. Appeals (11th cir.) 1983, U.S. Ct. Appeals (5th cir.) 1985, U.S. Supreme Ct. 1996, N.J. 1997, U.S. Dist. Ct. N.J. 1997, U.S. Ct. Appeals (3rd cir.) 2000. Assoc. Sage, Gray, Todd & Sims, N.Y.C., 1969-75, ptnr., 1976-86, Hughes, Hubbard & Reed, LLP, N.Y.C., 1987—. Mem. Vanderbilt Law Sch. Nat. Alumni Bd., Nashville, 1993-98; del. Yale U. Assn. of Yale Alumni, 1994-98; mem. Yale Alumni Fund, 1971—; mem. Yale Club of Bergen County and Vicinity, 1977—; presenter in field. Author: (with others) The McGraw-Hill Construction Business Handbook, 2d edit., 1985; mem. adv. bd. Vanderbilt Jour. Transnational Law, 2000—; contbr. article to profl. jours. Trustee Ridgewood Pub. Edn. Found., 1990-97, pres., 1990-93; pres. dean's coun. Vanderbilt U. Law Sch., Nashville, 1996—. Recipient Disting. Svc. award Vanderbilt Law Sch., 1995. Mem. ABA (sect. litigation, chmn. subcom. on commodities 1984-86). Episcopalian. Avocations: tennis, fly fishing, gardening. Home: 251 Palmer Ct Ridgewood NJ 07450-2316 Office: Hughes Hubbard & Reed 1 Battery Park Plz Fl 17 New York NY 10004-1405

BRUNEAU, WILLIAM JOSEPH, JR., minister, career counselor; b. New Haven, Feb. 27, 1947; s. William Joseph Bruneau and Erma Luca Schipritt; m. Barbara Boynton, Mar. 28, 1970; children: Heidi Bruneau Hayes, Michael William. BA in Bibl. Studies, Breadloaf Bible Coll., Burlington, N.C., 1985; MDiv, Earlham Sch. Religion, Richmond, Ind., 1994. Ordained to ministry Elim Fellowship, 1981, The Christian and Missionary Alliance, 1987. Vice pres. World Harvest Evangelism of New Eng., Durham, Conn., 1977-80; founder, dir. The Storefront St. Ministry, Meriden, Conn., 1981—; assoc. pastor The Ch. of the Living God, Farmington, Conn., 1981-85; pastor The Community Ch. of the Cross, Richmond, Ind., 1985-91, Moreland (Ind.) Friends Meeting, 1991-95; sr. career advisor Bernard Haldane Assocs., Indpls., 1995-98; sr. pastor Penn Friends Ch., Cassopolis, Mich., 1998—; chaplain Cass County Sheriff's Dept., 1998—. Evangelist World Harvest Evangelism, Madurai, India, 1979; chmn. Christian Life and Witness, So. New Eng. Billy Graham Crusade, 1984-85; chaplain Wayne County Jail, Richmond, 1986-94; founder, dir. The "Fire Escape" radio/concert ministry, Richmond, 1987—. Columnist Sr. Life Mag., 1990-95. Bd. dirs. Richmond Jr. Players, 1987, Mental Health Assn. Wayne County, Richmond, 1990—95. William W. Wildman Found. scholar, 1991. Mem. ASTD, Richmond Ministerial Assn. (bd. dirs., pres. 1987), Wayne County C. of C. (co-chmn. promotion and advt. devel. 1987, chmn. Quality of Life Com. 1988), Cass/Vandalia C. of C. (pres., bd. dirs. minority coalition). Home: 509 E State St Cassopolis MI 49031-1132 Office: Penn Friends Ch 19107 Quaker St Cassopolis MI 49031-9492 Office Phone: 269-445-8546. Personal E-mail: gratefuldad21@hotmail.com. *The Church must not live in isolation from its surroundings. If we expect our communities to hear and respond to the message of Christ, then the church must hear and respond to the voice of its community. To be heard we must also hear.*

BRUNELL, MARK ALLEN, professional football player; b. L.A., July 17, 1970; m. Stacy Brunell; 4 children. BA in History, 1992. 2nd quarterback Green Bay Packers, 1994—95; quarterback Jacksonville Jaguars, 1995—2003, Washington Redskins, 2004—. Staged inaugural Mark Brunell Charity Golf Tournament to benefit Wolfson Children's Hosp.; spokesman Leukemia Soc. Am., 1996; active Fellowship Christian Athletes. Named Most Valuable Player Rose Bowl, 1991, NFL Offensive Player of Week, 1996, AFC Offensive Player of Week, 1996, Pro Bowl AFC, 1997, 1998, 2000, Pro Bowl MVP, 1997. Avocations: hunting, fishing, golf. Office: c/o Washington Redskins 21300 Redskins Park Dr Ashburn VA 20147

BRUNELL-JOINER, KARLEA, academic administrator, educator; b. Burlington, Vt., Dec. 21, 1970; d. Donald Raymond and Elveta Ceclia Brunelle; m. Gregory Joiner, June 20, 1998; 1 child, Jack Joiner. BA, St. Michael's Coll., Colchester, Vt., 1992; MEd, Rutgers Univ., New Brunswick, N.J., 1993; PhD, Fla. State Univ., Tallahassee, Fla., 1999. Monitor Rutgers Univ., Piscataway, NJ, 1993, career counseling asst., 1993; counselor Kilgore Jr. CC, Kilgore, Tex., 1994; acad. advisor Fla. State Univ., Tallahassee, 1994—97, peer adv. coord., 1996—98, acad. support svc. coord., 1998—99; dir. of first yr. student devel. Western New Eng. Coll., Springfield, Mass., 1999—2002; asst. dean of studies Assumption Coll., Worchester, Mass., 2002—. Adj. faculty Springfield Coll., Mass., 2000—01, Western New Eng. Coll., Springfield, Mass. Vol. adv. Cath. student union Fla. State Univ., Tallahassee, 1996; dir. Cath. student ctr. Kilgore Jr. CC, Tex., 1996. Mem.: Nat. Orientation Dir. Assn., Nat. Acad. Advt. Assn., Nat. Assn, Student Personnel Adminstr., Am. Coll. Personnel Assn. Avocations: golf, skiing, scrapbooks. Office: Assumption Coll 500 Salisbury St Worcester MA 01609

BRUNELLO-MCCAY, ROSANNE, sales executive; b. Cleve., Aug. 26, 1960; d. Carl Carmello and Vivan Lucille (Caranna) B.; m. Walter B. McCay, Feb. 26, 1994; children: Angela Breanna, Mikala Bell. Student, U. Cin., 1978—81, Cleve. State U., 1981—82. Indsl. sales engr. Alta Machine Tool, Denver, 1982; mem. sales./purchases Ford Tool & Machine, Denver, 1982-84; sales/ptnr. Mountain Rep. Enterprises, Denver, 1984-86; pres., owner Mountain Rep. Ariz., Phoenix, 1986—; pres. Mountain Rep. Oreg., Portland, 1990—, Mountain Rep. Wash., 1991—, Mountain Rep. Calif., Sunnyvale, 1997—, San Clemente, 1998—, Port Clinton, Ohio, 1999—; we. regional sales mgr. Offshore Internat., Inc., Tucson, 2002—. Sec. Computer & Automated Systems Assoc., 1987, vice chmn., 88, chmn., 89. Active mem. Rep. Party, 1985—; mem. Phoenix Art Mus., Grand Canyon Minority Coun., 1994; vol. Make-A-Wish Found. fund raiser, 1995—; founder Ariz. Sonora Corridor Network. Named Mrs. Chandler Internat., Mrs. Ariz. Internat. Orgn., 1996, Mrs. East Valley U.S., 1997; finalist Mrs. Ariz. Internat., 1996, Ms. Ariz. 2000, Ms. U.S. Continental Pageant. Mem. NAFE, Soc. Mfg. Engrs. (pres. award 1988), Computer Automated Assn. (sec. 1987, vice chmn. 1988 chmn. 1989), Manufacturers and Agents Nat. Assn. (chair-elect 2002), Nat. Hist. Soc., Italian Cultural Soc., Tempe C. of C., Vocat. Ednl. Club Am. (mem. exec. bd., pres. 1987—). Roman Catholic. Avocations: sports, aerobics, dance, skiing, golf, tennis. Office: Mountain Rep Ariz 410 S Jay St Chandler AZ 85225-6253 Office Phone: 480-899-1900. Business E-Mail: rosanne@mtnrep.com.

BRUNER, JEROME S., law educator; BA, Duke U., 1937; PhD, Harvard U., 1941. Prof. NYU, Sch. of Law, NYC, 1998—; prof. Psychology Harvard U.; watts prof. Oxford U.; Meyer vis. prof. NYU Sch. of Law, NYC, 1991. Founder Head Start. Author: The Process of Education, 1961, Acts of Meaning, 1991, Minding the Law, 2000. Recipient Internat. Balzan prize, CIBA Gold medal for Dist. Rsch., Dist. Scientific award, Am. Psychological Assn. Mem.: Pres. Sci. Adv. Com., Nat. Acad. Edn. Office: NYU Sch of Law Vanderbilt Hall 40 Washington Sq S New York NY 10012 Office Phone: 212-998-6463. Business E-Mail: jerome.bruner@nyu.edu.

BRUNER, NANCY J., publishing executive; B, N.Mex. State U.; MFA, U. So. Calif. With US West Media Group, Denver; cons. dir. bus. devel. Spring Multimedia, Kansas City; dir. new media Seattle Times, now v.p. new media. Office: Seattle Times PO Box 70 Seattle WA 98111-0070

BRUNER, PHILIP LANE, lawyer; b. Chgo., Sept. 26, 1939; s. Henry Pfeiffer and Mary Marjorie (Williamson) B.; m. Ellen Carole Germann, Mar. 21, 1964; children: Philip Richard, Stephen Reed, Carolyn Anne. AB, Princeton U., 1961; JD, U. Mich., 1964; MBA, Syracuse U., 1967. Bar: Wis. 1964, Minn. 1968. Mem. Briggs and Morgan P.A., Mpls., St. Paul, 1967-83; founding shareholder Hart and Bruner P.A., Mpls., 1983-90; ptnr. Faegre & Benson, Mpls., 1991—, head constrn. law group, 1991—2001. Adj. prof. William Mitchell Coll. Law, St. Paul, 1970-76, U. Minn. Law Sch., 2003-; lectr. law seminars, univs., bar assns. and industry; chmn. Supreme Ct. Minn. Bd. Continuing Legal Edn., 1994-98. Co-author: Bruner and O'Conner on Construction Law, 7 vols., 2002; contbr. articles to profl. jours. Mem. Bd. Edn., Mahtomedi Ind. Sch. Dist. 832, 1978-86; bd. dirs. Mahtomedi Area Ednl. Found., 1988-94, 2002—, pres., 1988-91, 2002—; bd. dirs. Minn. Ch.

Found., 1975—, pres., 1989-97; chmn. constrn. industry adv. bd. West Group, 1991—. Served to capt. USAF, 1964-67. Decorated Air Force Commendation Medal; recipient Disting. Service award St. Paul Jaycees, 1974; named One of Ten Outstanding Young Minnesotans, Minn. Jaycees, 1975. Fellow Am. Coll. Constrn. Lawyers (founding mem., bd. govs. 1999-2002, sec. 2003-2005, pres.-elect 2005-2006), Nat. Contract Mgmt. Assn., Am. Bar Found.; mem. ABA (chmn. internat. constrn. divsn. forum com. on constrn. industry 1989-91, chmn. fidelity and surety law com. 1994-95, regional chmn. pub. contract law sect. 1990-96, receipient Forum com Cornerstone award, 2005), Internat. Bar Assn., Inter-Pacific Bar Assn. (vice chmn. internat. constrn. com. 1995-97), Fed. Bar Assn., Minn. Bar Assn. (vice chmn. litigation sect. 1979-81), Wis. Bar Assn., Hennepin Bar Assn., Am. Arbitration Assn. (nat. panel arbitrators), Mpls. Club. Presbyterian. Home: 8432 80th St N Stillwater MN 55082-9331 Office: Faegre & Benson 2200 Wells Fargo Ctr 90 S 7th St Minneapolis MN 55402-3901 Office Phone: 612-766-7412. E-mail: pbruner@faegre.com, Philipbruner@hotmail.com.

BRUNER, WILLIAM EVANS, II, ophthalmologist, educator, researcher; b. Cleve., Oct. 10, 1949; s. Clark Evans and Pauline (Schrenk) B.; m. Susan Lee Fraser, June 7, 1975; children: Amanda Lee, Andrew Evans. BA, Wesleyan U., 1971; MD, Case Western Res. U., 1975. Diplomate Am. Bd. Ophthalmology. Intern in surgery Univ. Hosps., Cleve., 1975-76, resident in ophthalmology, 1976-79; fellow in cornea and anterior segment surgery Johns Hopkins Hosp., Balt., 1979-81; asst. prof. ophthalmology Case Western Res. U., Cleve., 1981-89, assoc., 1989-93, assoc. clin. prof., 1993-96, clin. prof., 1996—. Sr. editor; manual of Corneal Surgery, 1987; contbr. chpts. to med. textbooks and articles to profl. jours. Trustee Case Western Res. U, Cleve., Hawken Sch., Gates Mills, Ohio. Recipient Alfred S. Maschke award Case Western Res. U. Sch. Medicine, 1975. Fellow Am. Acad. Ophthalmology; mem. Wilmer Residents Assn., cleve. Acad. Medicine, Alpha Omega Alpha, Tavern Club, Cleve. Skating club, The Kirtland Club. Avocations: skiing, boating, sailing, golf, music. Home: 2906 Weybridge Rd Shaker Heights OH 44120-1874 Office: 1611 S Green Rd Cleveland OH 44121-4128 E-mail: bruner2020@aol.com.

BRUNETT, ALEXANDER J., archbishop; b. Detroit, Jan. 17, 1934; s. Raymond and Cecilia Gill Brunett. BA, Sacred Heart Seminary; STL in Sacred Theology, STB, Pontifical Gregorian U. ordained priest July 13, 1958. Assoc. pastor St. Rose of Lima Parish, Detroit, 1959—61, St. Alphonsus Parish, Dearborn, 1961—62; chaplain U. Mich., Ann Arbor, 1962—64, Ea. Mich. U., Ypsilanti, 1968; academic dean St. John's Provincial Seminary, Plymouth, 1969—73; dir. Div. of Ecumenical and Interreligious Affairs Archdiocese of Detroit, 1973—91; pastor St. Aidan Parish, Livonia, Shrine of Little Flower Parish, Royal Oak, 1991—94; ordained bishop Diocese of Helena, 1994; archbishop Diocese of Seattle, 1997—. Mem. Internat. Roman Cath.-World Meth. Dialogue; co-chair Anglican-Roman Cath. Internat. Commn.; chmn. Archdiocesan Theol. Commn.; vicar N.W. Wayne Vicariate, Archdiocese of Detroit; nat. chmn. Third Jewish-Christian Dialogue, Detroit. Editl. writer Mich. Cath. newspaper. Bd. trustees Cath. Near East Welfare Assn.; mem. bd. dirs. St. Patrick Seminary, Menlo Park, Calif., Mundelein Seminary, Ill. Recipient DOVE Award, Ecumenical Inst. for Jewish-Christian Studies, 1996. Mem.: Nat. Assn. of Diocesan Ecumenical Officers (pres. 1974—81), US Conf. of Cath. Bishops Com. on Ecumenical and Interreligious Affairs (chmn. 1996). Office: Archdiocese of Seattle 910 Marion St Seattle WA 98104-1274*

BRUNETT, EMERY WALTER, pharmacist, educator; b. Ovando, Mont., Dec. 3, 1927; s. Elbe James and Mary Katherine (Betzler) B.; m. Iris Eileen Stephens, Dec. 27, 1970; children: Emery Jr., Katherine, Stephenie, Barbara. BS in Pharmacy, U. Mont., 1953, MS in Pharmacy, 1956; PhD, U. Wash., 1966. Registered pharmacist, Mont., Wyo. Instr. U. Mont., Missoula, 1956-57, vis. asst. prof., 1964-65; instr. U. Wash., Seattle, 1958-59; asst. prof. Drake U., Des Moines, 1966-69; asst. prof., assoc. prof. U. Wyo., Laramie, 1969-94, assoc. prof. emeritus, 1994—. Pres. Laramie Citian Club, 1983, sec., 1985-97. Sgt. U.S. Army, 1946-48. Mem. Elks, Am. Legion, Laramie Sunrise Rotary (charter pres. 1996-97, sec. 1997-2003), U. Wyo. Retirees (pres. 1997-98, treas. 1999-2002), Rho Chi, Kappa Psi, Phi Sigma, Phi Lambda Sigma. Democrat. Lutheran. Avocation: outdoors.

BRUNETTI, MELVIN T., federal judge; b. Reno, 1933; m. Gail Dian Buchanan; children: Nancy, Bradley, Melvin Jr. Attended, U. Nev., 1951-53, 1956-57, 1960; JD, U. Calif., San Francisco, 1964. Mem. firm Vargas, Bartlett & Dixon, 1964-69, Laxalt, Bell, Allison & Lebaron, 1970-78, Allison, Brunetti, MacKenzie, Hartman, Soumbeniotis & Russell, 1978-85; judge U.S. Ct. Appeals (9th cir.), Reno, 1985-99, sr. judge, 1999—. Mem. Council of Legal Advisors, Rep. Nat. Com., 1982-85. Served with U.S. Army N.G., 1954-56. Mem. ABA, State Bar of Nev. (pres. 1984-85, bd. govs. 1975-84). Office: US Ct Appeals Ste 506 US Courthouse 400 S Virginia St Reno NV 89501-2194*

BRUNETTI, WAYNE HENRY, utilities executive; b. Cleve., Oct. 13, 1942; s. Henry Joseph and Lillian (Lupo) B.; m. Mary Kelly, Aug. 17, 1963; children: Kelly Christine, Andrew Wayne. BSBA in Acctg., U. Fla., 1964; program for mgmt. devel., Harvard U., 1974. Acct. Fla. Power and Light Co., Miami, Fla., 1964-68, systems analyst, 1968-69, project coordinator, 1969-72, mgr. property acctg., 1972-73, mgr. corp. acctg., asst. comptroller, 1973-77, asst. to v.p. pub. affairs, 1977-80, dir. energy mgmt., 1980, v.p. energy mgmt., 1980-83, v.p. divs., 1983-84, group v.p., 1984-87, exec. v.p., 1987-91; pres., CEO Mgmnt. Systems Internat., Fla., 1991-94; pres., COO Public Svc. Co. of Colo., 1994-96, CEO, 1996; chmn., pres., CEO New Century Energies, Inc., Denver, 2000; pres. Xcel Energy, 2001—03, chmn, CEO, 2001—05. Mem. Sec. Energy Nat. Petroleum Coun., 2002—03. Mem.: Minn. Bus. Partnership, Inc., Juran Ctr. for Leadership and Quality (exec. adv. bd.), Capital City Partnership (bd. dirs.). Democrat. Roman Catholic.

BRUNGRABER, ROBERT J., civil engineer, educator; b. Dec. 20, 1929; s. Louis Rudolph and Beatrice Emogene B.; m. Ruth Ann Rupp, June 13, 1951; children: Robert Lyman, Margaret Ruth. BSCE, U. Mich., 1951; MS, Cornell U., 1956; PhD, Carnegie Inst. Tech., 1963. Field engr. Porter-Urquhart-Skidmore, Owings & Merrill, cons. engrs., Casablanca, Morocco, 1951—53; instr. Cornell U., Ithaca, NY, 1953—56; rsch. engr. Alcoa Rsch. Labs., New Kensington, Pa., 1956—60; asst. prof. civil engring. Princeton U., 1962—66; assoc. prof. civil engring. Union Coll., Schenectady, NY, 1966—68; prof. civil engring. Bucknell U., Lewisburg, Pa., 1968—, presdl. prof., 1979—92, prof. emeritus, 1992—. Founder, pres. Slip-Test, Inc., 1976; structural cons. Borough Hall, Princeton, NJ, 1966; Intergovtl. Pers. Act appointee Nat. Bur. Stds., 1974—76; dir., treas., mem. nat. exec. com. Nat. Inst. Bldg. Scis., 1976—81. Contbr. articles to profl. publs. Mem.: ASTM (Charles H. Irvine award, Merit award), ASCE (chmn. com. lightweight alloys of metals structural divsn. 1969—73), Moles, Cosmos Club, Nassau Club, Phi Kappa Phi, Sigma Xi, Phi Gamma Delta, Chi Epsilon, Tau Beta Pi. Achievements include patents for in field; research in structural applications of alumninum, particularly welded applications, pile foundations, and slip resistance of footwear and/or walkway surfaces; supr. design and constrn. of Stephen J. Potter Meml. Lab., Union Coll., 1967; stuctural test facility at Bucknell U., 1985 (now named R.J. Brungraber Structural Test Facility); design of original system for reinforcing obsolete steel truss bridges; invention of NBS-Brungraber device for measuring the slip-resistance of footwear and/or walkway surfaces. Office Phone: 732-449-1789. E-mail: sliptestinc@verizon.net.

BRUNI, STEPHEN THOMAS, museum director; b. Phila., Feb. 3, 1949; s. Eugene Thomas and Frances Isabel (McMorran) B.; m. Barbara Natalie Plunket, May 13, 1949; children: Christopher Stephen, Katherine Elizabeth. BA, George Washington U., 1971. Curatorial asst. Del. Art Mus., Wilmington, 1972-74, program asst., 1974-77, adminstrv. asst., 1977-79, mgr. support svcs., 1979-82, asst. dir. adminstrn., 1982-84, dep. dir. adminstrn., 1984-85, acting dir. adminstrn., 1985-86, exec. dir., 1986—. Mem. arts selection com. Del State Arts Coun., 1985-86, State Divsn. Librs., 1984-86; mem. Gov.'s Arts Adv. Com., 1983-85; mem. adv. bd. Siena Hall and Seton Villa, Creative Artists Network; bd. dirs. Studio Group, Inc. Mem. bd. Literacy Vols. Am. (affiliate Wilmington Libr.). Mem. Am. Assn. Mus., Assn. Art Mus. Dirs., Bd. Greater Wilmington Conv. and Visitors Bur. Avocations: skiing, racquet sports, golf, bicycling. Office: Del Art Mus 2301 Kentmere Pky Wilmington DE 19806-2019*

BRUNIE, CHARLES HENRY, investment manager; b. N.Y.C., July 17, 1930; s. Charles Henry and Olivia (Swanston) B.; m. Jean Isbell Corley, June 23, 1965; stepchildren: William Corley, Jean Corley Yankus, Ellen Corley. BA, Amherst Coll., 1952; MBA, Columbia, 1956. Analyst N.Y. Life Ins. Co., N.Y.C., 1956-60, Faulkner, Dawkins & Sullivan, 1960-63, Oppenheimer & Co., N.Y.C., 1963-65, gen. ptnr., 1965-82, mem. exec. com., 1969-82; chmn. Oppenheimer Capital, 1969-96, chmn. emeritus, 1996-2000; trustee Manhattan Inst., 1978—, chmn. bd., 1980-1990, chmn. emeritus, 1990—; chmn. Brunie Assocs., N.Y.C., 2001—. Served with AUS, 1952-54. Mem. N.Y. Soc. Security Analysts, Chartered Financial Analysts, Mont Pelerin Soc., Delta Upsilon. Clubs: Knickerbocker (N.Y.C.), Doubles (N.Y.C.), Annabell's (London), Bronxville Field, Siwanoy Country (Bronxville). Home: 21 Elm Rock Rd Bronxville NY 10708-4202 Office: Brunie Assocs 600 3d Ave 17th Fl New York NY 10016

BRUNIG, ROBERT ARTHUR, lawyer; b. New Orleans, Feb. 15, 1946; s. Arthur John and Marie Louise (Engelhardt) B.; m. Donna Jean Bahn, Aug. 2, 1968 (div. Dec. 1980); children: Jennifer Lynn, Adam Robert, Scott Arthur. AA, Concordia Luth. Coll., Austin, Tex., 1965; BA with high distinction, Concordia Sr. Coll., 1967; M. in Div., Concordia Sem., St. Louis, 1971; JD magna cum laude, Washburn U., 1976. Bar: Kans. 1976, Minn. 1976, U.S. Dist. Ct. Kans. 1976, U.S. Dist. Ct. Minn. 1977, U.S. Ct. Appeals (8th cir.) 1979, U.S. Tax. Ct. 1984, U.S. Supreme Ct. 1985, D.C. 1987, U.S. Dist. Ct. D.C. 1987, U.S. Ct. Appeals (D.C. cir.) 1990, U.S. Ct. Appeals (3d cir.) 1996, Tex. 1998, U.S. Dist. Ct. (so., ea., no. and we. dists.) Tex. 1999, U.S. Ct. Appeals (5th cir.), U.S. Ct. Appeals (10th cir.) 2003. Pastor Zion Lutheran Ch., Vassar, Kans., 1971-76; law clk. to judge U.S. Dist. Ct., St. Paul, 1976-78; assoc. O'Connor & Hannan, Mpls., 1978-83, ptnr., 1983-94; shareholder Moss & Barnett, P.A., Mpls., 1994—97; with U.s. SEC, Ft. Worth, 1997—2003; sole proprietor Brunig & Assocs., Southlake, Tex., 2003—. Chmn. merit selection panel magistrates/bankruptcy judges U.S. Dist. Ct., Minn., 1984, mem. merit selection panel, magistrate, 1989; bd. dirs. Coffey County Hosp. Assn., Burlington, Kans., 1971-76; bd. advisors Hilltop Nursing Home, Lyndon, Kans., 1971-76. Bd. dirs. Coffey County Hosp. Assn., Burlington, Kans., 1971-76; bd. advisors Hilltop Nursing Home, Lyndon, Kans., 1971-76. Mem. ABA, Minn. State Bar Assn., Hennepin County Bar Assn., DC Bar Assn., Tex. Bar Assn. Lutheran. Home and Office: 918 Strafford Dr Southlake TX 76092-7110 Office Phone: 817-329-7210. E-mail: rabrunig@yahoo.com.

BRUNING, JAMES LEON, academic administrator, educator; b. Bruning, Nebr., Apr. 1, 1938; s. Leon G. and Delma Dorothy (Middendorf) Bruning; m. E. Marlene Schaff, Aug. 24, 1958; children: Michael, Stephen, Kathleen. BA, Doane Coll., 1959; MA, U. Iowa, 1961, PhD, 1962. Chmn. dept psychology Ohio U., Athens, 1972-76, acting dean arts and scis., 1976-77, assoc. dean, 1977-78, vice provost, 1978-81, provost, 1981-93, trustee prof., 1993—, v.p. regional higher edn., 1998—99, dir. Enterprise project, 2002—03. Planning cons. NCHEMS, Boulder, Colo., 1979—80; provost Shawnee (Ohio) State U., 1996. Author: (book) Computational Handbook of Statistics, 1997, Research in Psychology, 1970; contbr. articles to profl. jours. Chair task force Ohio Bd. Regents, 1994—95. Grantee, Esso, 1963—64, NIMH, 1963—66, EPDA, 1974—75, OBOR, 1989—91. Mem.: APA (vis. scientist), AAAS, Midwestern Psychol. Assn., Sigma Xi. Democrat. Lutheran. Home: 6148 Melnor Dr Athens OH 45701-3577 Office: Ohio U Psychology Dept Athens OH 45701 Business E-Mail: bruningj@ohio.edu.

BRUNING, JON CUMBERLAND, state attorney general; b. Lincoln, Nebr., Apr. 30, 1969; s. Roger Howard and Mary Genevieve (Cumberland) B.; m. Deonne Leigh Niemack, July 8, 1995, two children, Lauren Caroline, Jon Cumberland Jr. BA with high distinction, U. Nebr., 1990, JD with distinction, 1994. Bar: Nebr. 1994, U.S. Dist. Ct. Nebr. 1994, U.S. Ct. Appeals (8th cir.) 1994. Pvt. practice, Papillion, Nebr., 1993-97; mem. Nebr. Legislature from 3rd dist., Lincoln, 1997—2002; atty. gen. State of Nebr., 2003—. Mem., Gretna United Methodist Church, Nebr. State Bar Assoc., Phi Beta Kappa. Republican. Methodist. Home: 17501 Riviera Dr Omaha NE 68136-1951 Office: State Capitol 2115 State Capitol PO Box 98920 Lincoln NE 68509

BRUNK, SAMUEL FREDERICK, oncologist; b. Harrisonburg, Va., Dec. 21, 1932; s. Harry Anthony and Lena Gertrude (Burkholder) B.; m. Mary Priscilla Bauman, June 24, 1976; children: Samuel, Jill, Geoffrey, Heather, Kirsten, Peter, Christopher, Andrew, Paul, Barbara BS, Ea. Mennonite Coll., 1955; MD, U. Va., 1959; MS in Pharmacology, U. Iowa, 1967. Diplomate Am. Bd. Internal Medicine, Am. Bd. Internal Medicine in Med. Oncology. Straight med. intern U. Va., Charlottesville, 1959-60; resident in chest diseases Blue Ridge Sanatorium, Charlottesville, 1960-61; resident in internal medicine U. Iowa, Iowa City, 1962-64, fellow in clin. pharmacology (oncology), 1964-65, 66-67, asst. prof. internal medicine, 1967-72; assoc. prof. internal medicine, 1972-76; fellow in medicine (oncology) Johns Hopkins U., Balt., 1965-66; clin. assoc. prof. med. Okla. State U. Coll. Osteo; vis. physician bone marrow transplantation unit Fred Hutchinson Cancer Treatment Ctr., U. Wash., Seattle, 1975; practice medicine specializing in med. oncology Des Moines, 1976-94; attending physician Iowa Luth. Hosp., 1976-94, Iowa Meth. Med. Ctr., 1976-94, Charter Hosp., 1976-94, Mercy Hosp. Med. Ctr., 1976-94; dir. med. oncology Hahne Regional Cancer Ctr., DuBois, Pa., 1994; attending physician DuBois Regional Med. Ctr., 1994; dir. Pa. Cmty. Cancer Care, 1995; attending physician St. Mary's Regional Med. Ctr., 1994; med. oncologist cancer treatment ctrs. Am. Southwestern Regional Med. Ctr., Tulsa, Okla., 1995—2001, chief med. oncology cancer treatment ctrs. Am., 2002—; attending physician Meml. Med. Ctr., Tulsa, Okla., 1995—. Chief of staff Iowa Luth. Hosp., 1990, chmn. dept. internal medicine, 1988; cons. physician Des Moines Gen. Osteo. Hosp., 1976-94; prin. investigator Iowa Oncology Rsch. Assn. in assn. with N. Cen. Cancer Treatment Group and Ea. Coop. Oncology Group, 1978-83; prin. investigator Iowa Oncology Rsch. Assn. Cmty. Clin. Oncology Program, 1983-84; mem. cancer care com. St, Mary's, Pa., 1995. Contbr. articles to profl. jours. Bd. dirs. Iowa div. Am. Cancer Soc., 1971-89, Johnson County chpt., 1968-72. Mosby scholar, U. Va., 1959 Fellow ACP, Am. Coll. Clin. Pharmacology; mem. AMA, Okla. Medical Soc., Tulsa County Medical Soc., Am. Soc. Clin. Oncology, Raven Soc., Alpha Omega Alpha. Roman Catholic. Home: 2929 E 69th St Tulsa OK 74136-4541

BRUNK, THOMAS WALTER, art historian; b. Romeo, Mich., Nov. 25, 1949; s. Norman Brunk and Margie Velma Smith. MA in Art and Archtl. History, Norwich U., 1992; PhD in Art History, Union Inst., 1997. Clk. coord. Rouge Steel Co., Dearborn, Mich., 1971—. UAW Local 600, 1971—; founder, pres. Indian Village Hist. Collections, Inc., Detroit, 1973—92; pres. Stapleton Found. for Health Edn., Wayne State U., Detroit, 1980—95, Detroit Masonic Temple Libr. and Mus., Detroit, 2001; prof. archtl. history Coll. for Creative Studies, Detroit, 2001; adj. prof. archtl. history Merrill-Palmer Inst. Wayne State U., Detroit, 2003—. Guest curator Mich. State U., Detroit, 1976, Detroit Inst. Arts, 1976, Detroit Hist. Mus., 1978, 79, 81, 84, U. Mich. Mus. Art, Ann Arbor, 1995—96; pres. The Pewabic Soc., Inc., Detroit, 1988—89; adj. prof. archtl. history Merrill-Palmer Inst.. Wayne State U., 2003; instr. art history Coll. for Creative Studies, Detroit, 2001—. Author: Arts and Craft in Detroit 1906-1976: The Movement, The Society, The School, 1976, Pewabic Pottery: Marks and Labels, 1978, Pewabic in Architecture, 1979, Dichotomy, 1980, 1981, 1999, Bulletin of the Detroit Institute of Arts, 1981, The Acanthus Club, 1981, Leonard B. Willeke: Excellence in Architecture and Design, 1986, A Tribute to Edgar Louis Yaeger, 1988, American Craft, 1989, Selected Works By Contemporary Hispanic Artists in Michigan, 1989, The Grosse Pointe Artists Association, 1992, The Grand American Avenue 1850-1920, 1994, Tonnancour, 1994, 1997, Painting with Fire, 1995. Mem.: Mich. Archival Assn., Detroit Inst. Arts Founders Soc., Alliance Francaise Detroit, Soc. Archtl. Historians (pres. The Saarinen (Mich.) chpt. 1989—93, 1998—), The Players, Acanthus Club, Witenagemote Club, The Scarab Club (pres. 1990—92), Algonquin Club Detroit and Windsor, Prismatic Club, Masons, Scottish Rite. Avocations: historic preservation, ceramics, photography, genealogy, travel. Home: 1479 Seminole Ave Detroit MI 48214-2708 Office: Detroit Masonic Temple Libr and Mus 500 Temple Ave Detroit MI 48201-2659 Office Phone: 313-331-4930. Personal E-mail: brunk@spamcop.net.

BRUNK, WILLIAM EDWARD, astronomer; b. Cleve., Nov. 24, 1928; s. Edgar Rea and Mabel Mowbray (Pearson) B.; 1 dau., Anna Kathryn. BS, Case Inst. Tech., 1952, MS, 1954, PhD, 1963. Aero. research scientist Lewis Flight Propulsion Lab., NACA, Cleve., 1954-58; aerospace engr. Lewis Research Center, NASA, Cleve., 1958-64; staff scientist for planetary astronomy NASA Hdqrs., Washington, 1964-65, program chief planetary astronomy, 1965-77, discipline scientist planetary astronomy, 1977-82, chief planetary sci. br., 1982-85; mgr. solar system sci. Univ. Space Rsch. Assn., Washington, 1985-94; ret., 1994. Recipient Exceptional Service medal NASA, 1985. Fellow AAAS; mem. Am. Astron. Soc. (Harold Mazursky Meritorious Svc. award 1995), Internat. Astron. Union; Mem. Sigma Xi. Home: 4802 51st St W Apt 710 Bradenton FL 34210-5107 E-mail: webrunk@earthlink.net.

BRUNK-CHAVEZ, BETH LYNNE, language educator; b. Lima, Ohio, July 22, 1970; d. Raymond Lawrence and Mary Kathleen Brunk; m. Eduardo Antonio Chavez, May 12, 2001; children: Jackson Raymond, Carter Harrigan. BA in Advt., N.Mex. State U., 1992; MA in English, U. Tex., El Paso, 1995; PhD in English, U. Tex., Arlington, 1999. Tchg. asst. U. Tex., El Paso, 1993-95, Arlington, 1995-99; asst. prof. James Madison U., Harrisonburg, Va., 1999—2002, U. Tex., El Paso, 2002—. Cons. Prentice Hall Publ., N.J., 2000; textbook author McGraw Hill. Mem. MLA, Nat. Coun. Tchrs. of English, Rhetoric Soc. Am., Popular Culture Assn. Avocations: cooking, exercise activities. Home: 6600 Grand Ridge Dr El Paso TX 79912 Office Phone: 915-747-5731. E-mail: chavezb@sbcglobal.net.

BRUNKHORST, ROBERT JOHN, computer programmer, analyst; b. Waverly, Iowa, Dec. 5, 1965; s. John Blaine and Edna C. (Atkins) B.; m. Kris Nielsen, Sept. 12, 1992; 1 child, Karalynn Kristine. BS in Computer Sci., Loras Coll., 1989. Computer programmer Century Cos. Am., Waverly, 1990—, computer analyst. Press intern Sen. Charles Grassley, Washington, fall 1986. State rep. State of Iowa, 1992—; organizer Solid Waste Adv. Com., Waverly, 1990—; active Boy Scouts Am., N.E. Iowa, 1982—. Mem. Jaycees, Farm Bur. Home: 413 10th St NE Waverly IA 50677-2739

BRUNNER, GEORGE MATTHEW, management consultant, former business executive; b. Newark, Jan. 17, 1925; s. Mathias J. and Mary E. (Fuith) B.; m. Ruth E. Owens, Nov. 16, 1953. AB in Chemistry, Columbia U., 1949, MChemE, 1950. Devel. engr. J.T. Baker Chem. Co., Phillipsburg, N.J., 1950-53; plant mgr. Internat. Minerals & Chem. Corp., Niagara Falls, N.Y. and Houston, 1953-62; mfg. engring. mgr. Gen. Foods Corp., Hoboken, N.J., Houston and Lafayette, Ind., 1962-71; v.p. mfg. W.R. Grace & Co., St. Simons Islands, Ga., 1971-73; pres., chief exec. officer S.A. Schonbrunn & Co., Inc., Palisades Park, N.J., 1973-82; v.p. ops. Am. Maize Products Co., Stamford, Conn., 1982-84; mgmt. cons., 1984—. Served with AUS, 1943-45. Decorated Purple Heart. Mem. Nat. Coffee Assn. (dir.), Pres.'s Assn., Am. Chem. Soc., Am. Inst. Chem. Engrs., Electrochem. Soc., 5th Armored Div. Assn. (pres. 1980-81). Patentee in field. Home and Office: 1221 Clays Trl Oldsmar FL 34677-4866

BRUNNER, KATHLEEN MARIE, humanities educator; b. Torrance, Calif., Nov. 5, 1953; d. Earl Allen and Patricia Nellie Brunner. MA in Comparative Lit., U. Wash., Seattle, 1990—92, PhD in Comparative Lit., 1990—97, MA in Romance Langs. & Lit., 1993—94. Reader U. Wash., Seattle, 1991—94, tchg. asst., 1994—96; lectr. Alliance Francaise de Seattle, 1999—2004; instr. Highline C.C., Des Moines, Wash., 2001—02. Bd. dirs., past pres., past v.p., past sec. Alliance Francaise, 1998—2004; bd. dirs., sec. French-American C. of C. Pacific-Northwest, Seattle, 1999—; bd. dirs., v.p., admin. Nat. French Contest Alaska, B.C. and Alta. chpt. Am. Assn. Tchrs. French, Washington, 1999—; adv. bd. dept. French studies U. Wash., Seattle, 2003—. Contbr. articles to profl. jours. Recipient Vignernon d'honneur du Beaujolais, Union Interprofessionel des vins du Beaujolais, 2002; Study Grant, French Govt., 2000. Mem.: MLA, Wash. Assn. Lang. Tchng., Soc. Prof. Français and Francophone Am., Groupe D'Etudes Sartriennes. Avocations: swimming, travel, photography. Business E-Mail: brunnerk@lanepowell.com.

BRUNNER, KIM M., insurance company executive, lawyer; b. 1949; BA, Augustana Coll.; JD, Univ. Ariz. Chief counsel Ill. Ins. Dept.; atty. Nationwide Ins. Co.; with State Farm Ins. Cos., Bloomington, Ill., 1987—, assoc. gen. counsel, 1991-93, v.p.-counsel, 1993-97, sr. v.p., gen. counsel, 1997—. Co-chmn. Civil Justice Reform Group; mem. bd. overseers RAND Inst. for Civil Justice. Office: State Farm Ins Cos 1 State Farm Plz Bloomington IL 61710-0001

BRUNNER, LILLIAN SHOLTIS, nurse, writer; b. Freeland, Pa. d. Andrew J. and Anna (Tomasko) Sholtis; m. Mathias J. Brunner, Sept. 8, 1951; children: Janet Brunner Cramer, Carol Ann Brunner Burns, Douglas Mathias. RN, diploma, U. Pa., 1940, BS, 1945, LittD (hon.), 1985; MS in Nursing, Case-Western Res. U., 1947; ScD (hon.), Cedar Crest Coll., 1978. RN, Pa. Head nurse U. Pa. Hosp., Phila., 1940-42, operating room supr., 1942-44, head, fundamentals of nursing dept., 1944-46; asst. prof. surgical nursing Yale U. Sch. Nursing, New Haven, Conn., 1947-51; surgical supr. Yale-New Haven Hosp., 1947-51; Lillian Sholtis Brunner chair med.-surg. nursing U. Pa., 2001. Rsch. project dir. Sch. Nursing Bryn Mawr (Pa.) Hosp., 1973-77; co-founder History of Nursing Mus., Pa. Hosp., Phila., 1974; mem. bd. overseers Sch. Nursing U. Pa., 1982-88; bd. overseers emeritus, 1988—; chmn. nursing adv. Presbyn.-U. Pa. Med. Ctr., Phila., 1970-88, 90-93, trustee, 1976-88, 90-95, vice chmn. bd. trustees, 1985-88; mem. com. profl. advisory Vis. Nurse Assn., Lancaster, Pa., 1996-99; sec. Glen Coun., Willow Valley Manor North, 1997-2000. Author: Manual of Operating Room Technology, 1966, (with others) Lippincott Manual of Nursing Practice, 1974, 4th edit., 1986, Textbook of Medical and Surgical Nursing, 1964, 6th edit., 1988; mem. editl. bd. Jour. Nursing and Health Care, Nursing 1978-1999, Nursing Photobook Series, 1978-90. Bd. dirs. Presbyn. Found. for Phila., 1995-99. Recipient Disting. Alumnus award Frances Payne Bolton Sch. Nursing, Case Western Res. U., 1980, Alumni award for merit Soc. Alumni Assns., U. Pa., and Am. Dream Achievement award Class of '45, U. Pa., 1995, Mentor award, Millersville U. Sch. Nursing, 2004. Fellow: Am. Acad. Nursing (Living Legend award 2002); mem.: Nurses Alumni Assn. U. Pa. Hosp., Philanthropic Ednl. Orgn., Nat. League for Nursing (judge nat. writing contest 1982—84, Disting. Svc. award 1979), ANA, Acad. U. Pa., Ben Franklin Soc., Internat. Old Lacers Soc., Nat. League Am. Pen Women (sec. Phila. chpt. 1972—76, nat. sec. 1984—88), Pi Lambda Theta, Pi Gamma Mu, Sigma Theta Tau. Home and Office: Apt J-411 645 Willow Valley Sq Lancaster PA 17602-4871 Office Phone: 717-464-6247.

BRUNNGRABER, ERIC HENRY, banker; b. Madison, Wis., Feb. 12, 1957; s. Eric G. and Lois M. (Ihde) B.; m. Ann M. Roberson, May 30, 1987. BSBA in Fin., U. Mo., 1979; MBA in Fin., St. Louis U., 1982; diploma, U. Del., 1991. Asst. to chmn. Cass Bank & Trust Co., St. Louis, 1979-82, mgr. spl. projects, 1982-84, asst. v.p. comml. lending, 1986-88, v.p., treas., 1989-92, exec. v.p., 1993—; mgmt. cons. Cass Bus. Cons., St. Louis, 1984-86; v.p., sec. & CFO Cass Comml. Corp., Bridgeton, Mo. Mem. Robert Morris Assocs. Office: Cass Comml Corp 13001 Hollenberg Dr Bridgeton MO 63044

BRUNO, CATHY EILEEN, management consultant, former state official, social sciences educator; b. Binghamton, N.Y. d. Martin Frank and Beverly Carolyn (Hamlin) Piza; m. Frank L. Delaney (div.); m. Paul R. Bruno, May 5, 1990. BA, SUNY, Binghamton; MSW, Syracuse U. Psychiat. social worker Broome Devel. Ctr., Binghamton, 1973-74, 76, congl. legis. aide, 1975; asst.

dir. Bur. Program and Fiscal audits N.Y. State Office Mental Retardation and Devel. Disabilities, Albany, 1976-80; statewide coord. Intermediate Care Facilities for Developmentally Disabled, 1980; cert. coord. Western County Svc. Group, 1980-83, Upstate unit dir. Bur. Cert. Control, 1983-85; dir. ICF/DD Survey and Rev., 1985-89; area dir. Bur. Program Cert., 1989-95; dir. Bur. Transitional Svcs., 1995-97, mgmt. cons., 1997—. Adj. instr. SUNY Sch. Social Welfare, Albany, 1982-83; adj. faculty C.C. of Southern Nev., Las Vegas, 1998. Vol. U. Nev. Coop. Ext. Master Gardener program, 1997—; bd. dirs. Worldwide AIDS Movement, 2000—01. Mem. Am. Mgmt. Assn. Home and Office: 293 Canyon Spirit Dr Henderson NV 89012-3472

BRUNO, GRACE ANGELIA, accountant, retired educator; b. St. Louis, Oct. 11, 1935; d. John E. and Rose (Goodwin) B. BA, Notre Dame Coll., 1966; MEd, So. Ill. U., 1972; MAS, Johns Hopkins U., 1983; PhD, Walden U., 1985. CPA, Mo., Md., N.J. Tchr. Sch. Sisters of Notre Dame (SSND) of St. Louis, 1962-80; pres. Bruno-Potter, Inc., Avon By The Sea, N.J., 1981—. Asst. treas., instr. acctg. Coll. of Notre Dame of Md., Balt., 1978-80, treas., 1979-80; asst. prof. acctg. Georgian Ct. Coll., Lakewood, N.J., 1985-91; fin. advisor James Harry Potter gold medal award ASME, N.Y.C., 1980—. Elected to Internat. Platform Assn., 1987. Mem. AICPA, N.J. Soc. CPAs, St. Louis Bus. Educators (treas. 1972-73), Johns Hopkins Univ. Faculty Club. Democrat. Roman Catholic. Home and Office: 419 3rd Ave Avon By The Sea NJ 07717-1244 Office Phone: 732-776-7334. E-mail: gbruno4u@optonline.net.

BRUNO, HAROLD ROBINSON, JR., retired journalist, writer; b. Chgo., Oct. 25, 1928; s. Harold R. and Tallulah H. (Kandel) B.; m. Margaret E. Christian, Nov. 12, 1959; children: Harold, Daniel. BS in Journalism, U. Ill., 1950. Reporter Advt. Age, Chgo., 1950; sports editor DeKalb (Ill.) Chronicle, 1950-51; reporter City News Bur., Chgo., 1953-54, Chgo. American, 1954-60, Newsweek mag., 1960-63, bur. chief Chgo., 1963-66, news editor N.Y.C., 1966-71, chief polit. corr. Washington, 1971-78; polit. dir. ABC News, Washington, 1978-97, polit. analyst, 1997-98; ret., 1998; sr. polit. analyst Politics.com, 1999-2000. Adv. bd. Internat. Programs and Studies, pres.'s coun., U. Ill.; adv. bd. Washington Ctr. for Politics and Journalism; moderator Vice Presdl., 1992. Columnist Firehouse mag; Contbr. articles to various publs. Bd. dirs. Chevy Chase Fire Dept.; adv. bd. Presdl. Classroom for Young Ams.; mem. Port Chester (N.Y.) Vol. Fire Dept.; dir., chmn. Fallen Firefighters Found., Nat. Fire Acad. With U.S. Army, 1951-53. Recipient Lowell Thomas award Internat. Platform Assn., 1984, Pres. award Internat. Assn. Fire Chiefs, 1999; Fulbright scholar, 1956-57; named Fire Svc. Person of Yr. Cong. Fire Svc. Inst., 1995. Mem. Nat. Fire Protection Assn., Nat. Vol. Fire Coun., AFTRA, Chgo. Newspaper Reporters Assn., Friendship Fire Assn., U. Ill. Alumni Assn. (bd. dirs., Illini achievement award 1984), Bethesda-Chevy Chase Rescue Squad Alumni, Soc. Profl. Journalists, Chgo. Press Vets. Assn. (Press Vet. of Yr. award 1999), Internat. Assn. Fire Fighters (hon.), Tau Delta Phi. Jewish. Home: 3414 Cummings Ln Chevy Chase MD 20815-3238

BRUNO, JOSEPH L., state legislator; BS, Skidmore Coll. Mem. N.Y. State Senate, Albany, 1976—, chmn. senate elections com., 1989-93, chmn. senate ins. com., 1985-89, vice chmn. legis. commn. on solid waste mgmt., 1985-89, chmn. senate com. on consumer protection, 1979-84, pres., 1995—. State senate majority leader, 1995—; asst. majority leader for conf. ops., 1989-95; chmn. senate commerce, econ. devel. and small bus. com., 1993-95; chmn. legis. com. on pub.-pvt. cooperation, 1989-95 Mem., chmn. Rensselaer County Rep. Com., 1974-77; past pres. N.Y. State Assn. Young Reps.; mem. Italian Cmty. Ctr., Troy, N.Y., Troy Boy's Club, Troy Music Hall Assn. Mem. N.Y. State Sheriffs Assn. (hon.), St. Mary's Acad. Alumni Assn. (past pres), N.Y. State Jaycees (past v.p.), Soc. ofthe Friends of St. Patrick (bd. dirs.), VFW (Brunswick Post 831), Elks. Office: NY State Senate State Capitol 909 Legislative Office Bldg Albany NY 12247

BRUNO, LOUIS VINCENT, principal; b. Allegheny County, Pa., Feb. 10, 1959; s. Thomas E. and Anna Marie (Lavra) B. BS in Elem. Edn., U. Pitts., 1981, MEd in Mentally/Physically Handicapped, 1982, cert. secondary prins., 1990; EdD, Sch. Leadership, U. Pitts., 2004. Cert. tchr. expectations and student achievement/gender/ethnic expectations and student achievement coord., learning potential assessment device instr., instrumental enrichment trainer. Tchr. Steel Valley Sch. Dist., Munhall, Pa., 1981-82; adult living program instr. United Cerebral Palsy Assn., Pitts., 1982; from learning disabilities tchr. to asst. prin. Wilkinsburg (Pa.) Sch. Dist., 1982—98, asst. prin. Wilkinsburg (Pa.) Mid. Sch., 1998—; prin. 8th Linton Mid. Sch., Pitts., 1999—. Mem. adv. bd. TV and Video Tchrs. Assn. of Western Pa. Home: 301 Mcgregor Dr Verona PA 15147-3433 Office Phone: 412-795-3000 157. Personal E-mail: loubruno@aol.com. Business E-Mail: lbruno@phsd.k12.pa.us.

BRUNO, PHILIPPE M., lawyer; b. 1955; JD in Civil Law, Univ. Grenoble Law Sch., 1977, LLM in European Integration, 1978, PhD in European and Internat. Law cum laude, 1989; LLM in Internat. and Comparative Law, Georgetown Univ., 1984. Bar: France 1980, Va. 1987, DC 1998. Assoc., litig. Criffo & Olivier, Grenoble, France, 1980—82; European cons. Busby, Rehm and Leonard PC, 1982—84, assoc., 1984—88, Dorsey & Whitney LLP, Washington, 1988—94, ptnr., internat. dept., 1995—2004; ptnr., global trade practice group Greenberg Traurig LLP, Washington, 2005—. Lectr., European and civil law Univ. Grenoble, France, 1980—82. Office: Greenberg Traurig LLP Ste 500 800 Connecticut Ave NW Washington DC 20006 Office Phone: 202-331-3193. Office Fax: 212-331-3101.

BRUNO, SUSAN ELIZABETH, secondary school educator; b. Freeport, N.Y., June 19, 1946; d. Nicholas Stephen and May Elizabeth (McCarthy) B. BS in Edn., Fordham U., 1968; MA, Hofstra U., 1972. Cert. tchr., N.Y. Tchr. Massapequa (N.Y.) Sch. Dist. 23, 1968—. Office: Massapequa Sch Dist 23 4925 Merrick Rd Massapequa NY 11758-6201 Office Phone: 516-797-6110.

BRUNS, DAVID EUGENE, medical educator, researcher; b. St. Louis, Dec. 12, 1941; s. Eugene H. and Ellen E. (Johnson) B.; m. M. Elizabeth Hirst; children: Elizabeth, David. BSChemE, Washington U., 1963, AB, 1965; MD, St. Louis U., 1973. Diplomate Nat. Bd. Med. Examiners; lic. Va. State Bd. Medicine. Instr. pathology Sch. Medicine Washington U., St. Louis, 1973-77, vis. prof. pathology, 1985-86; asst. prof. U. Va., Charlottesville, 1977-81, assoc. prof. dept. pathology, 1981-90, prof. pathology Sch. Medicine, 1990—, assoc. dir. clin. chem. and toxicology, 1977—2003, assoc. dir. molecular diagnostics, 1986—, dir. clin. chemistry, 2003—. Lectr. in field. Author, editor, with Lo and Wittwer: Molecular Testing in Laboratory Medicine, 2002; editor: Clin. Chemistry, 1990—; co-editor: Yearbook of Pathology and Laboratory Medicine, 1995—97; contbr. articles to profl. jours.; author, editor (with Burtis and Ashwood): Tietz Textbook of Clinical Chemistry and Molecular Diagnostics, 4th edit., 2005. Bd. dirs. Little League Baseball, Charlottesville. Recipient St. Louis-San Francisco Railroad Scholarship, Washington U., 1959—63; Rsch. Grant award, NIH, Am. Cancer Soc., Am. Dairy Coun. Mem.: Am. Assn. Clin. Chemistry (Outstanding Contbns. to Rsch. award 1987, Outstanding Contbns. to Clin. Chemistry award 1998, Norman Kubasik award 2001, Presdl. Citation 2001, Bernard Gerulat award 2001, Miriam Reiner award 2003, Speaker Award 2003, Presdl. Citation 2005), Acad. Clin. Lab. Physicians and Scientists (mem. exec. coun. 1990—93, pres. 2003—04), Assn. Clin. Scientists (pres. 1985—86, Sunderman award 1987). Achievements include patents for immunochemical assays for human amylase isoenzymes and related monoclonal antibodies, 1993; identification of toxicity of polyethylene glycol. Avocations: travel, reading, theater. Business E-Mail: dbruns@virginia.edu.

BRUNS, NICOLAUS, JR., retired agricultural products supplier, lawyer, educator; b. NYC, Sept. 27, 1926; s. Nicolaus and Emily Marie (Hawkins) B.; m. Joan-Carol Littleton, Aug. 29, 1959; children: Nicolaus III, Gregory. BS, U. Miami, Fla., 1947; JD, Georgetown U., 1949, LL.M., 1952. Bar: D.C. 1950, Ill. 1965, U.S. Supreme Ct. 1965, N.Y. 1980. Spl. asst. U.S. Navy Dept., Washington, 1950-57; sr. trial atty. U.S. Dept. Justice, Washington, 1957-65; sr. atty. Internat. Minerals and Chem. Corp., Skokie, Ill., 1965-70, asst. gen. counsel, 1970-74, gen. counsel ops., 1974-79, v.p., sec., assoc. gen. counsel Northbrook, Ill., 1979-87; sr. v.p., sec., gen. counsel IMC Fertilizer Group Inc., Northbrook, Ill., 1987-90; antitrust policy coun. U.S. C. of C., Washington, 1981-90. Adj. prof. Loyola U., Chgo., 1980-81, Lake Forest Grad. Sch. Mgmt., Ill., 1981—2003; cert. arbitrator Am. Arbitration Assn., Nat. Assn. Securities Dealers, 1990—. Adminstrv. asst. to v.p. Boy Scouts Am., N.E. Ill. area, 1967, 80; pres. Fund for Perceptually Handicapped, Skokie, Ill., 1976, Concerned Help in Learning Devel., Highland Park, Ill., 1974-75. With U.S. Army, 1945-46. Mem. ABA (antitrust and securities com.), Chgo. Bar Assn., Fed. Bar Assn., Am. Soc. Corp. Secs. (bd. dirs. 1985-87, pres. Midwest region 1984), K.C. (past grand knight Washington coun.), Mich. Shore Club (Wilmette, Ill.), Harbour Ridge Club (Stuart, Fla.). Republican. Roman Catholic. Home: 2500 Indigo Ln Apt 348 Glenview IL 60026 also: 2532 NW Seagrass Dr Palm City FL 34990-4884

BRUNS, WILLIAM JOHN, JR., business administration educator; b. Pasadena, Calif., July 13, 1935; s. William John and Carol Jane (Stalder) B.; m. Barbara Jean Dodge, Apr. 12, 1957 (div. 1980); children: Robert William, John Richard, David James, Michael Alan.; m. Sharon Merle McKinnon, July 16, 1982; 1 child, Anastasia Catherine. BA, U. Redlands, Calif., 1957; MBA, Harvard U., 1959; PhD, U. Calif. at Berkeley, 1963; DBA (hon.), U. Redlands, Calif., 1976. Asst. prof. econs., then asst. prof. econs. and indsl. adminstrn. Yale U., 1962-66; asso. prof., then prof. accounting U. Wash., 1966-72; prof. bus. adminstrn. Harvard U., 1972-93, Henry R. Byers prof. bus. adminstrn., 1993—2001, emeritus, 2001—; vis. prof. bus. adminstrn. Northeastern U., 2001—. Cons. to industry. Author: Accounting for Decisions: A Business Game, 1966, Accounting and Its Behavioral Implications, 1969, Introduction to Accounting: Economic Measurement for Decisions, 1971, A Primer on Replacement Cost Accounting, 1976, Cases in Management Accounting, 1981, 85, Accounting and Management: Field Study Perspectives, 1987, Performance Measurement, Evaluation, and Incentives, 1992, The Information Mosaic, 1992, Accounting for Managers: Text and Cases, 1994, 3d edit., 2005; book rev. editor: Accounting Rev, 1967-69; mem. editorial bd., 1969-72, 76-78; advisory editor: Addison-Wesley Pub. Co; mem. editorial bd.: Accounting, Orgns., and Soc, 1975-79, Jour. of Managerial Issues, 1993—. Mem. Quinnipiac council Boy Scouts Am., 1964-66; Chief Seattle council, 1966-72, Algonquin council, 1972-81. Danforth grad. fellow, 1957-62; Danforth assoc., 1967-89. Mem. Am. Acctg. Assn., Inst. Mgmt. Accts. Home: 46 Garden Rd Wellesley MA 02481-3015 Office: Harvard Bus Sch Soldiers Fld Boston MA 02163-1317 E-mail: wbruns@hbs.edu.

BRUNSDALE, MITZI LOUISA, (MALLARIAN), English language educator, book critic; b. Fargo, N.D., May 16, 1939; d. Gregory Starn and Phyllis (Grobe) Mallarian; m. John Edward Brunsdale, Dec. 2, 1961; children: Margaret Louisa, Jean Ellen and Maureen Lois, twins. BS (hon.), N.D. State U., 1959, MS, 1961; PhD, U. N.D., 1976; post grad., Ind. U., 1976. Grad. asst. Ind. U., 1959-60; instr. English and French Mayville State Coll., ND, 1961; instr. English Mayville State Coll., ND, 1975-76; asst. prof. Mayville State Coll., ND, 1976-78, assoc. prof., 1978-83; prof. Mayville State U., ND, 1983—, chmn. divsn. liberal arts, 1998—2003. Book critic, Houston Post, 1971-85; book reviewer, Chgo. Tribune, 1987—, The Armchair Detective, 1995-98, Publishers Weekly, 1996—, The Strand Mag., 1998—; state sec., treas. N.D. Am. Coun. on Edn. Nat. Identification Program Bd. Author: Sigrid Undset: Chronicler of Norway, 1988, Dorothy L. Sayers: Solving the Mystery of Wickedness, 1991, James Joyce: The Short Fiction, 1993, James Herriot, 1996, Student Companion to George Orwell, 2000. Contbr. articles to profl. jour. and reference ency. Sec. twentieth Dist. N.D. Rep. Com., 1963-70; chmn. N.D. Humanities Coun., 1980, 81-82; grant rev. panelist NEH; corr. sec. N.D. Fedn. Rep. Women, 1990-92. Mem., MLA, D.H. Lawrence Soc., Am. James Joyce Soc., Phi Kappa Phi, Sigma Alpha Iota, Kappa Alpha Theta. Home: RR 1 Box 9 Mayville ND 58257-9706 Office: Mayville State Coll Dept English Mayville ND 58257 Office Phone: 701-788-4782.

BRUNSEN, WILLIAM HENRY, finance educator, consultant, researcher; b. Friend, Nebr., Aug. 18, 1940; s. William H. and Lorene Lavern (Schrock) B.; m. Judith Elaine Williamson, Feb. 22, 1964; children: William Eric, Lori Elaine. BS in Econs., Eastern N.Mex. U., 1968; MA in Econs., U. Nebr., 1972, PhD in Fin., 1976. Cert. mgmt. acct. Legis. asst. Nebr. Legislature, Lincoln, 1971-80; fin. officer Peterson Constrn., Lincoln, 1980-83; asst. prof. fin. Western Carolina U., Cullowhee, NC, 1983-85, No. Ariz. U., Flagstaff, 1985-87; prof. fin. Ea. N.Mex. U., Portales, 1987—. Co-author: Commercial Banking, 1985; contbr. articles to profl. jours. With USAF, 1961-65. Fulbright scholar, West Berlin, Fed. Republic Germany, 1968-69. Mem. Fin. Mgmt. Assn., S.W. Fin. Assn., Nat. Assn. Accts., Inst. Cert. Mgmt. Accts. Avocation: reading. Home: PO Box 2024 Portales NM 88130-2024 Office: Eastern NMex U PO Box 2024 Portales NM 88130-2024

BRUNSVOLD, BRIAN GARRETT, lawyer, educator; b. Mason City, Iowa, Apr. 10, 1938; s. P.O. and Arlene J. (Garrett) B.; m. Mary Sue Willey, Nov. 28, 1963; 1 child, Laura Ann. BSChemE, Iowa State U., 1960; JD, George Washington U., 1967. Bar: Va. 1967, D.C. 1967. Law clk. U.S. Ct. Claims, Washington, 1966-67; atty. firm Finnegan, Henderson, Farabow, Garrett & Dunner, Washington, 1967—. Professorial lectr. in law George Washington U., Washington, 1975-96. Co-author: Drafting Patent License Agreements, 1984, 91, 98, 2004. 1st lt. C.E., U.S. Army, 1961-63, Korea. Mem. Licensing Execs. Soc. (trustee 1987-89, counsel 2000-03, Cert. of Merit 1988). Avocations: tennis, hunting, fishing. Office: Finnegan Henderson Farabow Garrett & Dunner 901 New York Ave NW Washington DC 20001 Office Phone: 202-408-4000. Business E-Mail: brunsvob@finnegan.com.

BRUNSVOLD, MARY HELEN SUSAN (CHICA BRUNSVOLD), artist; b. Ypsilanti, Mich., Mar. 6, 1940; d. Norman Leroy and Mary Helen (Norburn) Willey; m. Brian Garrett, Nov. 28, 1963; 1 child, Laura Ann Hynes. BS in Design, U. Mich., 1961, MA in Art, 1962. Cert. secondary tchr., Mich. Gen. illustrator Ctrl. Intelligence Agy., Langley, Va., 1962-67, Indsl. Coll. of Armed Forces, Washington, 1967-68; tchr. art Fairfax (Va.) County Adult Svc. and Recreation, 1969-71, Barcroft Recreation, Falls Church, 1974-82. Art tchr. studio, Falls Church, Va., 1976-80; panelist, workshop leader Ohio Watercolor Soc., Cuyahoga Falls, 1997, 99, 2002; art in the embassies program mem. US State Dept One-woman shows include Art League, Torpedo Factory Art Ctr, 1996, Atrium Gallery Children's Nat. Med. Ctr., Washington, 1997, Artists' Mus., Strathmore Hall Arts Ctr., Bethesda, Md., 1997, Burroughs/Chapin Art Mus., Myrtle Beach, S.C, 1997, Ellen Noel Art Mus., Odessa, Tex., 1998, Touchstone Gallery, Washington, 1998, Forseyth Gallery Tex. A&M U., 1999, San Angelo Art Mus., Tex., 2000, Northwood Univ., Cedar Hill, Tex., 2000, The Art Sta., Stone. Mt., Ga., 2001, Paine Arts Ctr. and Gardens, Oshkosh, Wis., 2001, Atrium Gallery of Fairfax INOVA Hosp., Fairfax, Va., 2002, Longwood U., Farmville, Va., 2003, Goodyear Cottage, Jekyll Island, Ga., 2003, This Century Gallery, Williamsburg, Va., 2003, Black Rock Ctr. of Art, Germantown, Md., 2005, Visual Arts Ctr. N.W. Fla., 2005, Broadway Gallery, Fairfax. Pres. Lake Barcroft Swim Team, Falls Church, 1965-69; membership chmn. Barcroft Recreation Ctr., Falls Church, 1975-88; pres. Lake Barcroft Woman's Club, Falls Church, 1975-76; tchr. Sunday sch. Faith Luth. Ch., Arlington, Va., 1976-80; active art in the embassies program US State Dept Recipient Arts in Miss. award, Miss. Watercolor Soc., 1995, Harrison Cady award, Am. Watercolor Soc., 1999. Mem. Nat. Mus. Women in Arts (charter), Nat. Watercolor Soc. (signature), N.W. Watercolor Soc. (signature), Va. Watercolor Soc. (signature), Potomac Valley Watercolorists (charter, pres. 1993-95), Art League Lutheran. Avocations: singing, photography, tennis. Home: 3510 Wentworth Dr Falls Church VA 22044-1309 Personal E-mail: artbychica@juno.com.

BRUNT, DEWEY HILLERY, III, civil engineer, educator; b. Jennings, La., Oct. 31, 1947; s. Dewey Hillery and Margaret Ruth Brunt; m. Gloria Ann Robinson, June 26, 1976; children: Jonathan, Christopher. BSCE, U. Houston, 1975, MSCE, 1979. Lic. profl. engr., Tex., 1980. Study mgr. US Army Corps Engrs., Galveston, Tex., 1975—82, engring. mgr., project mgr., 1982—95, chief, engring. mgmt. br., 1995—95, chief, constrn. & profl. services br., 1998—2001, chief, project engring. sect., 2001—. Adj. prof. math. Coll. of the Mainland, Texas City, Tex., 1981—. Pres. League City Intermediate Sch. Band Boosters Assn., Tex., 1975—76; pres., treas. Clear Creek H.S. Band Boosters Assn., League City, Tex., 1996—2000; dir., chmn. bd. Galveston Govt. Employees Credit Union, 1997. Petty officer 2d class USN, 1971—72. Decorated Vietnam Svc. medal USN, Vietnam Campaign medal Republic of South Vietnam; recipient Commander's award, Corps of Engineers, 1992, 1994, Martin Luther King, Jr. award, Galveston Dist. BEP, 2002. Mem.: Tex. C.C. Teachers Assn., Western Dredging Assn. Office: US Army Corps Engrs 2000 Fort Point Rd Galveston TX 77550 Office Phone: 409-766-3170.

BRUNT, HARRY HERMAN, JR., psychiatrist; b. Phila., Jan. 22, 1921; s. Harry Herman and Ann (Zurbrugg) B.; m. Zoe M. Bower, July 2, 1944; children: Marianne Brunt Tallman, Margaret B. Griffin, Jane. BS with honors, Va. Poly. Inst., 1942; MD, U. Pa., 1945. Diplomate: Am. Bd. Psychiatry and Neurology. Intern, Lankenau Hosp., 1946; resident psychiatry Trenton (N.J.) State Hosp., VA Hosp., Coatesville, 1948-52; practice medicine specializing in psychiatry Trenton, 1952, Princeton, N.J., 1952-54, Hammonton, N.J., 1954-69, Long Branch, N.J., 1969-74; acting asst. clin. dir. Trenton State Hosp., 1952; asst. supt. N.J. Neuropsychiat. Inst. Princeton, 1952-54; med. dir. Ancora State Hosp., 1954-69; dir. dept. psychiatry Monmouth Med. Center and Pollak Clinic, Long Branch, 1969-74, Jersey Shore Med. Ctr., 1980; pvt. practice, 1974—. Assoc. prof. psychiatry Jefferson Med. Coll., 1952-66; instr. psychiatry U. Pa., 1953-65; adj. asso. prof. psychiatry Temple Med. Sch., 1968-70; prof. psychiatry Hahneman Med. Coll., 1970-74; clin. prof. psychiatry Robert Wood Johnson Med. Sch., New Brunswick, N.J., 1971-96. Cons. bur. family services Dept. Health, Edn. and Welfare Dept., 1960-68. Served to capt. M.C. AUS, 1946-48. Fellow ACP, AAAS, Am. Psychiat. Assn. (dist. life, chmn. future planning com. assembly dist. brs., mem. policy com. area III 1968, recorder 1969, speaker 1971-72, trustee 1972-73, 74-75), Am. Geriatric Soc., Am. Coll. Psychiatrists (founding); mem. AMA, Monmouth County Med. Soc. (exec. com.), N.J. Neuropsychiat. Assn. (past pres.), Med. Soc. N.J. (chmn. coun. mental health), Beach Haven Yacht Club (commodore 1992-93), Alpha Kappa Kappa, Phi Kappa Phi. *I have obtained a great deal of satisfaction from helping others throughout my life but little of this would have been possible without my family's backing and sacrifice. The family is still what makes life worth living.*

BRUNT, MANLY YATES, JR., psychiatrist; b. Winston-Salem, N.C., Nov. 7, 1926; s. Manly Yates and Jessie Corina (Evans) B.; M.D., Wake Forest U., 1948; m. Jacklyn Beatrice Bray, Dec. 2, 1961; children— Diane Strachan, William Bray, Douglas Evans, Kenneth Sherman. Intern, Grad. Hosp. U. Pa., 1949-50; exec. med. officer Inst. of Pa. Hosp., Phila., 1952-62, mem. sr. attending staff, 1968—, prin. investigator Behavior Research Lab., 1957-61; mem. faculty U. Pa., 1953-68; dir. emeritus dept. psychiatry Bryn Mawr (Pa.) Hosp., past pres. staff and chmn. exec. com. Pres. Community Nursing Bur. Met. Phila., 1961-64; bd. dirs. Main Line Health Care Group, Inc. Served with M.C., AUS, 1950-52. Diplomate Am. Bd. Psychiatry and Neurology. Mem. AMA, Am. Psychiat. Assn., Am. Psychoanalytic Assn., Phila. Coll. Physicians and Surgeons, Wake Forest U. Med. Alumni Assn. (pres. 1985), Alpha Omega Alpha. Republican. Presbyterian. Clubs: Merion Cricket, Phila. Skating and Humane Soc., Little Egg Harbor Yacht. Mailing: 1084 E Lancaster Ave Bryn Mawr PA 19010

BRUNTON, DANIEL WILLIAM, mechanical engineer; b. Ft. Wayne, Ind., Sept. 25, 1956; s. Paul Edward and Margaret Alice (Rice) B.; m. Carol Marie Pryor, Feb. 19, 1994; children: Edward Daniel, Ann Marie. BS, UCLA, 1978, MS in Engring., 1980, M of Engring., 1986. Mem. tech. staff Hughes Missiles Group, Canoga Park, Calif., 1978-89, dept. mgr., 1989-93; mech. engr. dept. mgr. Litton Itek, Lexington, Mass., 1993-94; sr. engr. Raytheon Missile Sys., Tucson, 1994-97, engring. fellow, 1997—. Mem. Soc. Photonic Instrumentation Engrs., Tau Beta Pi. Achievements include 3 patents on optical design, optical material testing, and mechanisms. Office: Raytheon Missile Sys PO Box 11337 Tucson AZ 85734-1337

BRUS, LOUIS EUGENE, physical chemist; b. Cleve., Aug. 10, 1943; s. Victor John and Mary Alicia (Megede) B.; m. Marilyn Drennan, Apr. 10, 1970; children: Michael, Christina, Elizabeth. BS in Chem. Physics, Rice U., Houston, 1965; PhD in Chem. Physics, Columbia U., 1969. Disting. mem. tech. staff AT&T Bell Labs., Murray Hill, NJ, 1973—96; assoc. dir., Thomas A. Edison prof. Columbia U., 1996—. Chmn. bd. trustees Gordon Rsch. Conferences, 2001. Mem. editorial bd. Jour. Phys. Chemistry, Chem. Phys. Letters; contbr. articles to profl. jours. Lt. Naval Rsch. Lab. USN, 1969—73. Hutchinson lectureship, Rochester U., 1991, Welsh lectureship, 1988; Kistiakowsky lectureship, Harvard U., 1993, Irving Langmuir prize, Am. Physical Soc., 2001, Chemicals Materials prize, Am. Chemical Soc. & Dupont, 2005. Fellow Am. Phys. Soc. (Irving Langmuir Prize in Chem. physics 2001); mem. NAS, Am. Chem. Soc. (Chemistry of Materials Prize 2005). Achievements include research in quantum effects in semiconductor crystallites, resonance raman investigations of transient chemical species, carbon nanotubes and organic electronics, local electromagnetic field enhancement, transition metal oxide nanocrystals and electric force microscopy. Office: Columbia Radiation Lab 1001 Schapiro Ctr Columbia Univ 530 W 120th St Mail Code 8903 New York NY 10027 also: Columbia U Dept Chemistry Havermeyer Hall MC 3125 3000 Broadway New York NY 10027 Business E-Mail: brus@chem.columbia.edu.

BRUSCA, RICHARD CHARLES, biologist, researcher, educator, science administrator; b. L.A., Jan. 25, 1945; s. Finny John and Ellenora C. (McDonald) B.; m. Caren Irene Spencer, 1964 (div. 1971); children: Alec Matthew, Carlene Anne; m. Anna Mary Mackey, 1980 (div. 1987); m. Wendy Moore, 1998. BS, Calif. Poly. State U., 1967; MS, Calif. State U., L.A., 1969; PhD, U. Ariz., 1975. Curator, rschr. Aquatic Insects Lab., Calif. State U., L.A., 1969—70; resident dir. U. Ariz. and U. Sonora (Mex.) Coop. Marine Lab., 1970—71; prof. biology U. So. Calif., L.A., 1975—86; head Invertebrate Zoology sect. Los Angeles County Mus. Natural Hist., 1984—87; Joshua L. Baily curator, chmn. dept. invertebrate zoology San Diego Natural History Mus., 1987—93; prof., dir. grad. program in marine biology U. Charleston, SC, 1993—98, assoc. dir. Grice Marine Lab., 1993—98; rsch. prof. dept. ecology and evolutionary biology and Ctr. for Insect Sci., U. Ariz., 1998—; exec. dir. Ariz.-Sonora Desert Mus., Tucson, 2001—. Dir. acad. programs Catalina Marine Sci. Ctr., U. So. Calif., 1978—82; field rschr. No., Ctrl. and So. Ams., Polynesia, Australia, New Zealand, Antarctica, Saharan and Sub-Saharan Africa, Europe; bd. dirs. Orgn. for Tropical Studies, Slocum-Lunz Found., Intercultural Ctr. for the Study of Deserts and Oceans, Sonoran Sea Aquarium, Tucson; mem. panels NAS/NSF; chairperson adv. com. Smithsonian Instn.; adv. com. Systematics Agenda 2000; chairperson adv. com., inland waters crustacea specialist Internat. Union for Conservation of Nature Species Survival Commn.; mem. adv. bd. All Species Found., 2001; mem. adv. bd. Sch. Renewable Natural Resources U. Ariz., 2003—. Author: Common Intertidal Invertebrates of the Gulf of California, 1980; co-author: A Naturalist's Seashore Guide, 1978, Invertebrates, 1990, 2d edit., 2003, Isopod Systematics and Evolution, 2001, Seashore Guide to Northern Gulf of California, 2004, Distributional Checklist of the Microfauna of the Gulf of California, 2005; contbr. over 150 articles to sci. jours. Recipient U.S. Antarctic Svc. medal, 1965, numerous rsch. awards; granteee NSF, Nat. Geog. Soc., Charles Lindberg Found, David & Lucile Packard Found., NOAA, Nat. Park Svc., Dept. Def., Am. Philos. Assn., others. Fellow: AAAS, Linnean Soc. London; mem.: Soc. for Systematic Biology, Assn. Sea of Cortez Rschrs. (hon.; life), Crustacean Soc. (pres.), U. Edinburgh Biogeography Study Group, Willi Hennig Soc., S.Am. Explorers Club, Sigma Xi. Avocations: photography, Mexican and Mesoamerican indigenous art and culture, Latin American politics. Office: Ariz-Sonora Desert Mus 2021 N Kinney Rd Tucson AZ 85743 Office Phone: 520-883-3007. Business E-Mail: rbrusca@desertmuseum.org.

BRUSCA, ROBERT ANDREW, economist; b. Detroit, Mar. 14, 1950; s. Andrew Adam and Doris Rita (Lozon) B.; m. Kathleen Hays. BA, U. Mich., 1973; MA, Mich. State U., 1976, PhD, 1977. Chief economist Fed. Res. Bank of N.Y., N.Y.C., 1977-82; economist, fedwatcher Irving Trust Co., N.Y.C.,

1982-85; chief economist, exec. v.p. The Nikko Securities Co Internat., Inc., N.Y.C., 1986-99; cons. N.Y.C.; chief economist Ecobest Cons., N.Y.C. Adj. prof. Columbia U., 1978—; appeared frequently on TV, radio as fin. specialist, 1983—. Author (column) Money Current, Fin. World mag., 1987-88, Econ. Currents, 1988—; columnist for CNBC.com.; contbr. articles in field. Mem. Money Marketeers NYU (bd. dirs. 1966—, pres.). Avocations: golf, basketball, reading, travel. Home: 357 West End Ave Apt One New York NY 10024-6815 Office Phone: 212-875-8637.

BRUSCH, JOHN LYNCH, physician, educator, hospital administrator; b. Boston, Nov. 3, 1943; s. Charles and Margaret Agnes (Lynch) Brusch; m. Patricia Gahan, May 12, 1973; children: Amy Claire, Meaghan, Patrick. BS, Tufts U., 1965, MD, 1969. Diplomate Am. Bd. Internal Medicine, Am. Bd. Infectious Disease, Am. Bd. Geriatrics. Intern New Eng. Med. Ctr., Boston, 1969-70, resident in medicine, 1970-71, resident in infectious disease, 1971-74; asst. chief medicine Brighton Pub. Health Svc. Hosp., Boston, 1974-76; pvt. practice physician Cambridge, Mass., 1976—; chief medicine Youville Hosp., Cambridge, 1991—, dir. cmty. medicine, 1995—; clin. assoc. medicine Mass. Gen. Hosp., Boston, 1996—; med. dir. transitional care unit, chief medicine Somerville Hosp., 1999—, med. dir., 2001—. Assoc. chief medicine Cambridge Health Alliance, 1999—, dir. hosp. bd., 2003—; asst. prof. medicine Harvard Med. Sch., 2001—; bd. dirs. North Cambridge Coop Bank. Co-author: (book) Infective Endocardits; assoc. editor: Infectious Disease Practice, 1984—, mng. editor: Emedicine, 2001—; contbr. articles to profl. jours. With USPHS, 1974—76. Fellow: ACP; mem.: Equestrian Order of Holy Sepulchre, Am. Soc. Microbiology, Longwood Cricket Club. Home: 52 Radcliffe Rd Belmont MA 02478-3340 Office: Cambridge Hosp 1493 Cambridge St Cambridge MA 02139-1099 Office Phone: 617-661-1800. Personal E-mail: jbruschmd@aol.com.

BRUSH, GEORGE W., college president; b. Boonton, N.J., Sept. 4, 1921; s. George W. and Adele (Tillotson) B.; m. Dorothy E. Mackallor, Sept. 24, 1942; children: Elithe, Lawrence, Kathleen, Sharon, George III, Charles, Nancy, Elizabeth. BS, Fairleigh-Dickinson U., 1960; MA, NYU, 1964, EdD, 1969. Cert. airframe and powerplant tech. FAA. Dir. tng. Teterboro (N.J.) Sch., 1947-50; dir. admissions Coll. Aeros. (formerly Acad. Aero.), Flushing, N.Y., 1950-66, exec. dean, 1966-80, v.p., 1980-83, pres., 1984-90, pres. emeritus, 1990, trustee, 1990-94. Cons. cmty. colls., N.Y. and N.J., 1965—, N.Y. State Bd. Regents, 1971-85; visitor Middle States Assn. Colls. and Schs., 1975—; faculty cons. Excelsior Coll., Albany, N.Y.; chair bd. trustees Plaza Coll., N.Y.C. Chmn. Maywood Planning Bd., N.J.; arbitrator Better Bus. Bur., Bergen County, N.J., 1976—; trustee, edn. chair N.J. Aviation Hall of Fame and Mus. Staff sgt. U.S. Army, 1944-46. Recipient disting. alumni award Coll. Aeros., adminstrs. award FAA, 1990, Disting. Svcs. award U. of State of N.Y.; named vol. of yr. Bergen County, 1992; elected to N.J. Aviation Hall of Fame, 2002. Mem. AIAA, FAA (Frank Taylor award 1995), Aviation Writers Assn., Am. Legion, Wings (bd. govs. 1986-89, chmn. edn. com.), K of C, HOAI (pres. Estero chpt.). Home and Office: 21030 Butchers Holler Estero FL 33928-2201

BRUSH, JOHN EDWIN, education educator; b. Jefferson, Pa., Aug. 2, 1919; s. Edwin Charles and Irene Humphrey Brush; m. Miriam Watson Kelly, Aug. 21, 1942; children: Jonathan, Kamala, Steven, Timothy. B, U. Chgo., 1942, M; PhD, U. Wisc. Instr. St. Louis U., Mo., 1949—51; prof. Rutgers U., New Brunswick, NJ, 1951—86, emeritus prof., 1986—2005. Author: (book) Population of New Jersey, 1956. Fellowship, J. S. Guggenheim Meml., 1957—58, fellowship and travel, Am. Inst. Indian Studies, 1965—66. Mem.: Assn. for Asian Studies, Assn. Am. Geographers. Home: 214 Meadford Leas Medford NJ 08055

BRUSH, STEPHEN GEORGE, historian, educator; b. Bangor, Maine; s. Edward Newcomb and Lillian Maynard (Hatfield) B.; m. Phyllis Egbert; children: Denise, Nicholas. AB in Physics, Harvard U., 1955; DPhil in Physics, Oxford (Eng.) U., 1958. Postdoctoral fellow Imperial Coll., London, 1958-59; physicist Lawrence Radiation Lab., Livermore, Calif., 1959-65; rsch. assoc. Harvard Project Physics, Cambridge, Mass., 1965-68; lectr. Harvard U., Cambridge, Mass., 1966-68; assoc. prof. U. Md., College Park, 1968-71, prof., 1971—, Disting. univ. prof. History of Sci., 1995—. Author: The Kind of Motion We Call Heat, 1976, Statistical Physics and the Atomic Theory of Matter, 1983, History of Modern Science, 1988, History of Modern Planetary Physics, 1996; co-author: Physics, The Human Adventure: From Copernicus to Einstein and Beyond, 2001; co-author: Introduction to Concepts and Theories in Physical Science, 1973, 2d rev. edit.; author, editor: Kinetic Theory, 1965, vol. II, 1966, Vol. III, 1972, The Kinetic Theory of Gases: An Anthology of Classic Papers with Historical Commentary, 2003; editor: Resources for the History of Physics, 1972; co-editor: History in the Teaching of Physics, 1972, Maxwell on Saturn's Rings, 1983, Maxwell on Molecules and Gases, 1986, Maxwell on Heat and Statistical Mechanics, 1995. Recipient History of Geology award Geol. Soc. Am., 2004; Rhodes scholar, Oxford U., 1955-58; NSF grantee, 1965—; Guggenheim fellow, 1999-2000. Fellow AAAS, Am. Phys. Soc. (councillor 1987-90); mem. History of Sci. Soc. (pres. 1990-91, Pfizer award 1977, Hazen Edn. prize 2001). Achievements include theoretical research calculation showing that a system of charged particles (plasma) will condense from gas to solid under conditions of high pressure and low temperature. Office: U Md Dept History Inst Phys Sci and Tech College Park MD 20742-0001 Office Phone: 301-405-4846. Business E-Mail: brush@ipst.umd.edu.

BRUSHABER, GEORGE KARL, academic administrator, minister; b. Milw., Dec. 15, 1938; s. Ralph E. and Marie C. (Meister) B.; m. N. Darleen Dugar, Jan. 27, 1962; children: Deanna Lyn Dalberg, Donald Paul. BA, Wheaton Coll., 1959, MA, 1962; MDiv, Gordon-Conwell Theol. Sem., 1963; PhD, Boston U., 1967. Ordained to ministry Bapt. Gen. Conf., 1966. Prof. philosophy, chair dept. Gordon Coll., Wenham, Mass., 1963-72; dir. admissions and registration Gordon-Conwell Theol. Sem., 1970-72; v.p., acad. dean Westmont Coll., Santa Barbara, Calif., 1972-75; v.p., dean of coll. Bethel Coll., St. Paul, 1975-82; pres. Bethel U., St. Paul and San Diego, 1982—. Staley Found. lectr. Anderson U., Sioux Falls Coll.; sec. for higher edn. Bapt. Gen. Conf., Arlington Heights, Ill., 1982—; cons., evaluator Minn. Humanities Commn., St. Paul. Editor Gordon Rev., 1965-70; pub., founding editor Christian Scholar's Rev., 1970-79; exec. editor Christianity Today, 1985-90, chmn. sr. editors, 1990-2000; contbr. articles to religious jours. Bd. dirs. Youth Leadership, Mpls., 1982—, Fairview Elders' Enterprises Found., 1989—, Scripture Press Ministries Found., 1994—; adv. bd. Mpls./St. Paul Salvation Army, 1992--; chair bd. Scripture Press Ministries, 1994—; adv. coun. Evang. Environ. Network, 1994—; mem. Commn. on Minorities in Higher Edn. Am. Coun. Edn., 1995-99. Mem. Nat. Assn. Evangs. (trustee 1982—), Assn. Pres. Ind. Colls. and Univs., Minn. Pvt. Coll. Coun. (bd. dirs. 1982—), Minn. Consortium Theol. Sems. (bd. dirs. 1982—), Cook Comm. Internat. (bd. dirs. 1998—), Coun. Ind. Colls. (bd. dirs. 1984-89), Am. Philos. Assn., Evang. Theol. Soc., Am. Assn. Higher Edn., Swedish Coun. Am. (bd. dirs. 2000—), Am. Assn. of Pres. of Indenp. Coll. and Univ., Soc. Christian Philosophers, Christian Environ. Assn., Christian Coll. Consortium (bd. dirs.), Fellowship Evang. Sem. Pres., Minn. Club, North Oaks Country Club. Home and Office: Bethel Univ 3900 Bethel Dr Saint Paul MN 55112-6902

BRUSHWOOD, MACK LEWIS, labor union administrator; b. Columbia, Mo., Oct. 17, 1918; s. Malcolm Lewis and Alberta Lillian Brushwood; m. Edith June Gibbs, Dec. 21, 1943; 1 child, David Mack. Degree in Practical Bus. in Adminstrn., Am. Tech., 1938. Asst. mgr. J.J. Newberry, Columbia, Mo., 1937—41, Jefferson City, 1939, Alma, Mich., 1939—41; claims supr. Dept. Labor Divsn. Employment Security, Columbia, Mo., 1946—85, supr., 1977. Supr. Mo. Dept. labor, Columbia, Mo., Jefferson City, Mo. With USAF, 1941—45. Mem.: AARP (chpt. pres. 1984—86, dist. dir. 1986—91, dist. dir., local pres.), Assn. Ret. State Employees (pres.), Nat. Coun. Silver Haired Legislature (life), Voiture 292 40/8 (life), Am. Legion (life; point comdr., 8th dist. adjutant). Protestant. Home: 2512 Fleetwood Dr Columbia MO 65202

BRUSIC, KEN, editor; m. Pam Brusic; 1 child, Mike. BA in English, U. Denver; MA, U. Colo., 1972. With Boulder Daily Camera; journalism fellow U. Mich.; city editor Wichita Eagle and Wichita Beacon, 1978—79; assoc. prof. U. Mont., Missoula; spl. projects editor The Patriot Ledger, Quincy, Mass.; mng. editor The Sun of San Bernardino, Balt. News Am.; projects editor Orange County Register, Santa Ana, Calif., 1989—90, asst. mng. editor, 1990—92, mng. editor, 1992—97, exec. editor, 1997—2002, editor, 2002—; sr. v.p. Freedom Comm., Inc. Head of content Freedom Orange County Info., 2002. Avocations: motorcycling, reading, running. Office: Orange County Register PO Box 11626 625 N Grand Ave Santa Ana CA 92711

BRUSKEWITZ, FABIAN W., bishop; b. Milw., Sept. 6, 1935; STD, Gregorian Univ., Rome, 1969. Ordained priest Roman Catholic Ch. 1960. Bishop Diocese of Lincoln, Nebr., 1992—. Office: Chancery Office PO Box 80328 Lincoln NE 68501-0328*

BRUST, DAVID, physicist; b. Chgo., Aug. 24, 1935; s. Clifford and Ruth (Klapman) B. BS, Calif. Inst. Tech., 1957; MS, U. Chgo., 1958, PhD, 1964. Rsch. assoc. Purdue U., Lafayette, Ind., 1963—64, Northwestern U., Evanston, Ill., 1964—65, asst. prof. physics, 1965—68; theoretical rsch. physicist U. Calif. Lawrence Radiation Lab., Livermore, 1968—73. Cons. Bell Telephone Lab., Murray Hill, N.J., 1966. Campaign coord. No. Calif. Scientists and Engrs. for McGovern, 1972. NSF travel grantee, 1964; NSF rsch. grantee, 1966-68. Mem. Am. Phys. Soc., Am. Assn. Coll. Profs., Internat. Solar Energy Soc., Astron. Soc. of Pacific, Nature Conservancy, Calif. Acad. Sci., Commonwealth Club. of Calif., World Affairs Coun. No. Calif., Commonwealth Club Anza Borrego Desert, Natural History Assn., Planetary Soc., Sierra Club, Sigma Xi. Office: PO Box 13130 Oakland CA 94661-0130

BRUST, JOHN CALVIN MORRISON, neurology educator; b. Syracuse, NY, Aug. 20, 1936; s. John C.M. and Constance (Cook) B.; m. Mary Duncan, Oct. 23, 1965; children: Mary Duncan, Frederick Eliot Noyes, James Charles Morrison. AB, Harvard U., 1958; MD, Columbia U., 1962. Diplomate Am. Bd. Psychiatry and Neurology. Intern Presbytn. Hosp., N.Y.C., 1962-63, resident in neurology, 1966-69, attending in neurology, 1969—, Harlem Hosp. Ctr., N.Y.C., 1969-75, dir. dept. neurology, 1975—; prof. clin. neurology Columbia U., N.Y.C., 1975—. Author: Neurological Aspects of Substance Abuse, 1993, 2d edit., 2004, The Practice of Neural Science, 1999; contbr. over 200 articles to profl. jours. Lt. USNR, 1962-65. Fellow Am. Acad. Neurology; mem. Am. Neurol. Assn., Am. Clin. and Climatological Assn., Century Assn., N.Y. Practitioners Soc., Alpha Omega Alpha. Office: Harlem Hosp Ctr Dept Neurology 506 Lenox Ave Dept New York NY 10037-1802 Office Phone: 212-939-4244. Business E-Mail: jcb2@columbia.edu.

BRUSTAD, ORIN DANIEL, lawyer; b. Chgo., Nov. 11, 1941; s. Marvin D. and Sylvia Evelyn (Peterson) B.; m. Ilona M. Fox, July 16, 1966; children: Caroline E., Katherine L., Mark D. BA in History, Yale U., 1963, MA, 1964; JD, Harvard U., 1968. Bar: Mich. 1968, U.S. Dist. Ct. (so. dist.) Mich. 1968. Assoc. Miller, Canfield, Paddock and Stone, Detroit, 1968-74, sr. ptnr., 1975—, chmn. employee benefits practice group, 1989-96, dep. chmn. tax dept., 1989-93. Bd. dirs. Electrocon Internat., Inc., Ann Arbor, Mich. Mem. editl. adv. bd. Benefits Law Jour.; contbr. articles to profl. jours. Fellow Am. Coun. Employee Benefits Counsel (charter); mem. ABA, Mich. Bar Assn., Detroit Bar Assn., Mich. Employee Benefits Conf. Avocations: sailing, skiing, reading, piano. Home: 1422 Macgregor Ln Ann Arbor MI 48105-2836 Office: Miller Canfield Paddock & Stone 150 W Jefferson Ave Fl 25th Detroit MI 48226-4432 E-mail: odbrusta@aol.com, brustad@millercanfield.com.

BRUSTEIN, LAWRENCE, finance company executive; b. Liberty, N.Y., Oct. 11, 1936; s. Leo and Rae (Smoller) B.; m. Ellen Gloria Sheppard, June 20, 1965; children: Jacqueline, Michael. BS, U. Buffalo, 1958. CPA, N.Y. With Irving Handel & Co., CPAs, N.Y.C., 1959-62, Robert Simons & Co., CPAs, N.Y.C., 1962-64, E&L Distbrs., Inc., 1964-66, Barney's, N.Y.C., 1966-68; controller Holly Stores div. K-Mart, North Bergen, N.J., 1968-70; v.p., treas. Marcade, Jersey City, 1970-86; exec. v.p. Modells, N.Y.C., 1987—. Editl. adv. bd. Retail Tech mag. Exec. v.p. Reform Temple of East Brunswick, 1977— . Mem. AICPA, N.Y. State Soc. CPAs, Internat. Mass Retail Assn. (chmn. fin.). Home: 15 Rolling Meadows Blvd S Ocean NJ 07712 Office: Modells 498 7th Ave Fl 20 New York NY 10018-6704 Office Phone: 212-822-1011. Personal E-mail: brustein@aol.com.

BRUSTEIN, ROBERT SANFORD, literature and language professor, theater director, writer; b. N.Y.C., Apr. 21, 1927; s. Max and Blanche (Haft) B.; m. Norma Ofstrock, Mar. 25, 1962 (dec.); children: Daniel Anton; m. Doreen Beinart, Dec. 20, 1996; stepchildren: Jean Beinart, Peter Beinart. BA, Amherst Coll., 1948, LittD; postgrad., Yale Drama Sch., 1948-49, U. Nottingham, Eng., 1953-55; MA, Columbia U., 1950, PhD, 1957; LittD, Lawrence U.; LLD, Beloit Coll., 1975; ArtsD, Bard Coll., 1981; LHD, Emory U., 1983; Arts D, Marlboro Coll., 1995, Middlebury Coll., 1996, Hebrew Coll., 1997. Instr. English Cornell U., 1955-56; instr. drama Vassar Coll., 1956-57; faculty Columbia, 1957-66, prof. English and comparative lit., 1965-66; prof. English Yale U., New Haven; dean Yale U. (Sch. Drama); founder, artistic dir. Yale Repertory Theatre, 1966-79; dir. Loeb Drama Centre; also founder, artistic dir. Am. Repertory Theatre Co.; prof. English Harvard U., 1979—. Drama critic New Republic, 1959-67, 78—, contbg. editor, 1959-79; guest theatre critic London Observer, 1972-73; contbr. to N.Y. Times, 1972—; directed and adapted plays including: Ghosts, 1982, Six Characters in Search of an Author, 1984, The Changeling, 1985, Tonight We Improvise, 1986, Right You Are, 1987, The Father, 1990, When We Dead Awaken, 1992, The Seagull, 1994, The Cherry Orchard, 1995, The Wild Duck, 1996, The Master Builder, 1999, Enrico IV, 2001, Lysistrata, 2002; panel mem. Nat. Endowment for Arts, 1969-72, 81-84; created, adapted Shlemiel the First, 1994. Author: The Theatre of Revolt: Studies in the Modern Drama, 1964, Seasons of Discontent: Dramatic Opinions 1959-1965, 1965, The Third Theatre, 1969, Revolution as Theatre: Notes on the New Radical Style, 1971, The Culture Watch, 1975, Critical Moments, 1980, Making Scenes, 1981, Who Needs Theatre, 1987, Reimagining American Theatre, 1991, Dumbocracy in America, 1994, Cultural Calisthenics, 1998, The Siege of the Arts, 2001, Letters to a Young Actor, 2005, (plays) Demons, 1995, Nobody Dies on Friday, 1996, Poker Face, 1999, The Face Lift, 1999, Chekhov on Ice, 2000, Three Farces and A Funeral, 2000, Divestiture, 2001, Spring Forward, Fall Back, 2004, Letters to a Young Actor, 2005; editor: The Plays and Prose of Strindberg, 1964; contbr. articles to profl. jours. Trustee Sarah Lawrence Coll., 1973-77. Served with U.S. Mcht. Marine, 1945-47. Recipient George Jean Nathan award dramatic criticism, 1962, 87, George Polk Meml. award outstanding criticism, 1965, Eliot Norton award, 1984, award in criticism Jersey City Jour., 1967, award Outstanding Achievement in Am. Theater, New Eng. Theater Coun., 1985, Tiffany award for excellence in theatre Internat. Soc. Performing Arts Adminstrs., 1987, Thomas De Gaetan award UITT, 1991, Disting. Svc. to Arts award Am. Acad. Arts and Letters, 1995, ATHE award for lifetime achievement in the theatre, 2000, named to Theater Hall of Fame, 2002; Fulbright fellow, 1953-55; Guggenheim fellow, 1961-62; Ford Found. fellow, 1964-65, Nat. Arts Journalism Program sr. fellow Columbia U., 2003. Mem. Am. Acad. Arts and Scis., Am. Acad. Arts and Letters. Office: Harvard U Loeb Drama Center Cambridge MA 02138 Office Phone: 617-429-1021. E-mail: brustein@fas.harvard.edu.

BRUSTEIN, WILLIAM IRVING, sociology educator; b. Fairfield, Conn., July 13, 1947; s. Louis I. and Flora Eva Brustein; m. Yvonne Christine Ramey, Feb. 14, 1981; children: Arielle Lauren, Maximilian Samuel. BA, U. Conn., 1969; MA, John Hopkins U., 1971; PhD, U. Wash., 1981. Asst. prof., then assoc. prof. sociology U. Utah, Salt Lake City, 1981—88; assoc. prof. sociology U. Minn., Mpls., 1989—94, prof., Morse alumni disting. tchg. prof. sociology, 1994—2000, adj. prof. polit. sci., 1994—2000, dir. Ctr. for European studies, 1992—95, chair dept. sociology, 1995—98, disting. McKnight univ. prof., 2000—01; prof. sociology, history and polit. sci. U. Pitts., 2001—, UCIS prof. internat. studies, 2001—, dir. Univ. Ctr. Internat. Studies, 2001—. Panelist sociology program NSF, Washington, 1998-2000; vis. scholar London Sch. Econs. and Polit. Sci., 1999. Author: The Social Origins of Political Regionalism: France, 1849 to 1981, 1988, The Logic of Evil: The Social Origins of the Nazi Party, 1925-1933, 1996 (James S. Coleman Disting. Contbn. to Rational-Choice scholarship 1997), Roots of Hate: Anti-Semitism in Europe before the Holocaust, 2003; editor: Nazism as a Social Phenomenon, 1998; cons. editor Am. Jour. Sociology, 1998-2000. Bd. dirs. Jewish Family Svc., St. Paul, 1991-95, Hillel, Mpls., 1998-2000; exec. bd. Student Project for Amity Among Nations, Mpls., 1998-2000. Grantee NSF, Washington, 1999. Mem. Am. Sociol. Assn. (coun. mem. polit. sociology and comparative hist. sociology 1987-90, 88-91, chair rational choice sect. 2004-05, chair PhD granting depts. 1996-98), Am. Polit. Sci. Assn., Assn. Internat. Edn. Adminstrs. (exec. com. 2003—), Nat. Assn. State Univs. Land-Grant Colls. (task force internat. edn. 2003—, chair acad. affairs com., exec. com. 2005—), Phi Beta Kappa, Assn. for Studies in Internat. Edn. (bd. dirs., 2004—). Democrat. Avocations: coaching boys soccer, reading, international travel, skiing. Home: 5 Old Timber Trail Pittsburgh PA 15238 Office: Office of Dir U Pitts Univ Ctr Internat Studies 4G40 Wesley W Posvar Hall Pittsburgh PA 15260 Fax: 412-624-4672. Office Phone: 412-648-7374. Business E-Mail: brustein@ucis.pitt.edu.

BRUTCHIN, PATRICIA M., artist, art educator; b. Eldorado, Kans., May 8, 1955; d. Bill and Virginia Roads Brutchin; m. David L. Strebel, Oct. 21, 1991. BFA, Wichita State U., 1985; MFA U. Cin., 1987. Substitute fine arts instr. Wilmington City Schs., Ohio, 1991—93, Norwood City Schs., Cin., 1991—93; adj. instr. Wilberforce U., Ohio, 1993—94; asst. prof. Clark State Cmty. Coll., Springfield, Ohio, 1994—99; instr. sculpture Springfield Mus. Art, 1999, U. Wis., Stevens Pt., 1999; instr. Ill. Inst. Art, Schaumburg, Ill., 1999—; represented by Moonstone Gallery, Lake Geneva, Wis., Firehouse Fine Arts Gallery, Crystal Lake, Ill. Pvt. instr. Brutchin Studios, Wilmington, Ohio, 1993—94. One-woman shows include, Carnegie Arts Ctr., Covington, Ky., 1989, Books and More Fine Arts Gallery, Wilmington, 1997, Springfield Mus. of Art, 2000, Ind. U., Southbend, 2001, exhibited in group shows, Cin. Art Club, 1992, Ohio State Fair, 1995, Pump House Art Gallery, Chillicothe, Ohio, 1997, Art House, Oak Park, Ill., 2001, represented in pub. and pvt. collections. Recipient 1st place award, Springfield Art Mus., 1996, 2d place award, 1997; grantee Individual Artist grantee, City of Cin., 1992—93; scholar Clayton Staples scholar, Wichita State U., 1984—85, Jr. and Ivey Jay Honors scholar, 1995, Wolfstein scholar, U. Cin., 1996. Home and Studio: 10 Baldwin Ct Lake In The Hills IL 60102

BRUTON, JOHN MACAULAY, trade association executive, consultant; b. Mexico City, Nov. 13, 1937; s. Edmund Macaulay and Byrd (Grant) B.; m. Frances McMillan Marks, Nov. 25, 1960; children: Alexander, Macaulay, Brinley. BA, Duke U., 1959. Pres., gen. mgr. Grant Advt. de Panama, Panama City, 1970-72, Mexico City, 1972; comm. dir. Am. C. of C. of Mex., Mexico City, 1972-74, gen. mgr., 1974-77, exec. v.p., CEO, 1977—2002, councillor, 2002—; sr. mng. dir. Manatt Jones Global Stratagies, Mexico City, 2003—. V.p. exec. mgmt. Assn. Am. C. of C. in Latin Am., L.A., Washington, 1985-88, v.p. membership svc., 1988—. Bd. dirs. Am. Benevolent Soc., Mex., 1964-68, Am. Soc. Mex., 1975-78, 80-84; adv. bd. Jr. League Mexico City, 1978—; bd. trustees Fomento Educacional A.C., 1988—, treas., 1993—. Mem. Univ. Mex. (bd. dirs. 1979-83, pres. 1981-82). Episcopalian. Home: Ameyalcalli Ocotepec 80 10200 Mexico City Mexico Office: Edificio Omega Campos Eliseo 5 345-5 Mexico City Mexico E-mail: jbruton@manattjones.com.

BRUTON, REBECCA ANN, mayor, commissioner; b. Arkansas City, Kans., Dec. 12, 1949; d. Robert Thomas and Gloria JoAnn (Jackson) Bush; m. Ronald Dean Bruton, Sept. 23, 1973. BS, Southwestern Coll., Winfield, Kans., 1975; grad. Inst. Mcpl. Leadership, Wichita State U., 2001. Elem. tchr. USD #471, Dexter, Kans., 1977—88; owner, sec. Bruton's Towing and Salvage, Arkansas City, 1988—; mayor, city commr. City of Arkansas City, 1999—2003; founder A Piece of the Garden Ministries, 1989—. Bd. trustees S. Ctrl. Kans. Regional Med. Ctr., Arkansas City, 2000—03; bd. dirs. Strother Field Commn., Arkansas City, 2000—03. Preacher Medicalodge East, Arkansas City, 1992—2001. Named Vol. of Yr., Medicalodge East, 1999—2000. Mem.: Kans. Sunshine Coalition Open Govt. (charter mem.), Kans. Taxpayers Assn. Avocations: Bible study, reading. Office: Bruton's Towing and Salvage 1800 South Fourth Arkansas City KS 67005 E-mail: actycomm@ArkCity.org.

BRUTTOMESSO, KATHLEEN ANN, dean, nursing educator, researcher; b. Torrington, Conn., Apr. 28, 1935; d. Thomas F. and Margaret (Gleeson) McMahon; div.; children: Raymond I. Jr., Cheryl A., Robert I., Charles A., Douglas A. BS, St. Joseph Coll., West Hartford, Conn., 1956; MS, Boston Coll., 1959; DNSc, Boston U., 1987. RN, Conn., Mass., Ill., N.J. Staff nurse, head nurse, supr. Mass. Gen. Hosp., Boston, 1956-59; supr. Charlotte Hungerford Hosp., Torrington, 1963-64; instr. Seton Hall U., South Orange, N.J., 1975-77; assoc. prof. U. Conn., Storrs, 1977—, interim dean. Researcher in field. Contbr. articles to profl. jours. Boston U. scholar, 1980-81. Mem. ANA, Conn. Nurses Assn., Conn. Nurses Found. (charter mem.), Ea. Nursing Rsch. Soc., Sigma Theta Tau (Mu chpt. Gamma Nu chpt., charter mem.).

BRUUN, PER MOLLER, civil engineer, consultant; b. Skagen, Denmark, Feb. 28, 1917; arrived in U.S., 1952; s. Niels Bruun and Marie Moller; m. Elizabeth Bruun, Sept. 29, 1943; children: Brita, Niels. MSCE, Tech. U. Denmark, 1941, DSc, 1954; D (hon.), U. Santander, 1978, U. Iceland, 1996. Coastal engr. Ministry of Pub. Works, Denmark, 1941—49, Ministry Edn., Denmark, 1949—54; chmn. coastal engrs. U. Fla., Gainesville, 1954—67; chmn. port engrs. Tech. U. Norway, Trondheim, 1967—78; cons. Hilton Head, SC, 1978—. Author: Coast Stability, 1954, Port Engineering, 1973, 4th edit., 1990, Design and Construction of Mounds for Breakwaters and Coastal Protection, 1985, Tidal Inlets and Littoral Drift, 1960, 3d edit., 1978; contbr. articles to profl. jours. Artilleryman Danish Armed Forces, 1941—42, artilleryman Danish Armed Forces, 1945—46. Named Knight of Icelandic Falcon, 1994; recipient Coastal award, Internat. Orgn. Coastal Dynamics, 2001, Internat. Coastal Conf. award, ASCE, 2002, Medal of Honor, Fla. Shore and Beach Preservation Assn., 1992. Fellow: ASCE (life); mem.: Norwegian Acad. Tech. Scis., Danish Acad. Tech. Scis., Danish Assn. Hydraulic Rsch. (hon.), Fla. Shore Protection Assn. (hon.). Avocation: writing. Home: 34 Baynard Cove Hilton Head Island SC 29928

BRUVOLD, KATHLEEN PARKER, retired lawyer; BS in Math., U. Denver, 1965; MS in Math., Purdue U., 1967; JD, U. Cin., 1978. Bar: Ohio 1978, U.S. Dist. Ct. (so. dist.) Ohio 1978, U.S. Dist. Ct. (ea. dist.) Ky. 1979. Mathematician bur. rsch. and engring. U.S. Post Office, 1967; instr. math. Purdue U., West Lafayette, Ind., 1967-68, asst. to dir., tng. coord., programmer Adminstrv. Data Processing Ctr., 1968-71; instr. math. Ind. U., Kokomo, 1969-70; pvt. practice Cin., 1978-80; asst. dir. Legal Adv. Svcs. U. Cin., 1980-89, assoc. gen. counsel, 1989—2002; asst. atty. gen. State of Ohio, 1983—2002; ret., 2002. Chair Ohio pub. records com. Inter-univ. Coun. Legal Advisors, 1980-84; presenter various confs. and symposiums. Active com. group svcs. allocation United Way and Community Chest; v.p. Clifton Recreation Ctr. Adv. Coun., 1983-84; vice chair Cin. Bilingual Acad. PTA, 1989-90. U. Denver scholar, Jewel Tea Co. scholar; Nat. Merit finalist. Mem. ABA, Nat. Assn. Coll. and Univ. Attys. (bd. dirs., co-chair taxation sect., com. ann. meeting arrangements, program com., publs. com., bd. ops. com., JCUL editl. bd. nominations com., honors and award com., intellectual property sect., com. continuing legal edn. 1992-2002), Ohio Bar Assn., Cin. Bar Assn. (com. taxation, program chmn. 1985-86, sec. 1986-87, com. computer law). Home: 536 Evanswood Pl Cincinnati OH 45220-1527

BRUYA, JOHN ROBERT, art educator; b. Oakland, Calif., Aug. 17, 1941; s. William Clement and Margurite Alene (Giesa) B.; m. Marilyn Catherine Rosera; children: Sara Allison, Kristen Catherine. BA in Edn., Eastern Wash. U., 1963; MFA, U. Wash., 1970. Tchr. art Wendler Jr. High Sch., Anchorage, 1964-67; instr. U. Wash., Seattle, 1970-71; prof. art Slippery Rock (Pa.) U., 1971—. Mem. craft adv. com. Pa. Coun. Arts; sabbatical rschr., France, 1999-2000. Recipient Top Ten Sr. Yr. Eastern Wash. U., Cheney, 1963; named

Artist of Yr. Butler County (Pa.)/Music & Arts Festival, 1985. Mem. Am. Craft Coun., Soc. N.Am. Goldsmiths, Pa. Art Edn. Assn. (Outstanding Pa. Higher Edn. Art Educator 1994), Associated Artists Pitts. (bd. dirs. 1972-75), Pitts. Craftsmen's Guild (bd. dirs. 1971-75). Democrat. Roman Catholic. Avocations: gourmet cooking, raising bonsai. Home: 326 State St Grove City PA 16127-1629 Office: Slippery Rock U Art Dept Slippery Rock PA 16057 E-mail: robert.bruya@sru.edu.

BRUYANT, PHILIPPE PIERRE, medical researcher; arrived in U.S., 2001; BS in Cell Biology, U. Lyon, France, 1988, BS in Physiology, 1989, MS in Neuroscis., 1991, PhD, 1997. Rsch. assoc. U. Lyon, 1998—2001; postdoctoral fellow U. Mass., Worcester, 2001—02, rsch. instr., 2002—. Reviewer Jour. Nuc. Medicine. Mem.: IEEE Nuc. and Plasma Scis., Soc. Nuc. Medicine. Achievements include research in methods to improve medical images quality: noise reduction, motion compensation. Office: U Mass Dept Nuc Medicine 55 Lake Ave North Worcester MA 01655 Office Phone: 508-856-4313. E-mail: philippe.bruyant@umassmed.edu.

BRUZELIUS, NILS JOHAN AXEL, journalist; b. Stockholm, Feb. 27, 1947; came to U.S., 1958; s. Axel Sture and Constance (Brickett) B.; m. Lynne A. Weil, Aug. 10, 2002. BA in History, Amherst Coll., 1968. Reporter, bur. chief Middlesex News, Framingham, Mass., 1968-70; reporter, state house corr. AP, Boston, 1970-73; med./mental health writer Boston Globe, 1973-79, investigative reporter, 1979-81, asst. met. editor, 1981-86, health and sci. editor, 1986-99, fgn. editor, 1999—2001; sr. editor sci. desk Nat. Pub. Radio, Washington, 2002—; dep. nat. editor sci. Washington Post, 2002—. Mem. Boston Globe investigative team receiving Disting. Investigative Reporting award Investigative Reporters and Editors Assn., 1979, Disting. Journalism citation Scripps-Howard Found., 1979, Pulitzer prize for spl. local reporting, 1980; Knight Sci. Journalism fellow MIT, 1992-93. Mem.: Investigative Reporters and Editors, Nat. Assn. Sci. Writers, Ocean Cruising Club. Home: 133 D Street SE Washington DC 20003 Office Phone: 202-334-7204. Business E-Mail: njbruzelius68@alumni.amherst.edu.

BRYAN, A(LONZO) J(AY), retired service club official; b. Washington, N.J., Sept. 17, 1917; s. Alonzo J. and Anna Belle (Babcock) B.; m. Elizabeth Elfreida Koehler, June 25, 1941 (div. 1961); children: Donna Elizabeth, Alonzo Jay, Nadine; m. Janet Dorothy Onstad, Mar. 15, 1962 (div. 1977); children: Brenda Joyce, Marlowe Francis, Marilyn Janet. Student. Retail florist, Washington, NJ, 1941-64; with WalMart Corp., 1989—2005. Fund drive chmn. ARC, 1952; bd. dirs. Washington YMCA, 1945-55, N.J. Taxpayers Assn., 1947-52; mem. Washington Bd. Edn., 1948-55. Mem. Washington Grange, Sons and Daus. of Liberty, Soc. Am. Florists, Nat. Fedn. Ind. Businessmen, Florists Telegraph Delivery Assn., C. of C., Masons, Tall Cedars of Lebanon Club, Jr. Order United Am. Mechanics, Kiwanis (pres. Washington N.J. 1952, lt. gov. internat. 1953-54, gov. N.J. dist. 1955, sec. 1957-64, sec. S.E. area Chgo. 1965-74, editor The Jersey Kiwanian 1958-64, internat. staff 1964-85, sec.-treas. Rocky Mountain dist. 1989, pres. South Denver 1990-91, editor Rocky Mountain Kiwanian 1990-96), Breakfast Club (Chgo., pres. 1981-82). Methodist. Home: 8115 S Poplar Way B 203 Centennial CO 80112-3174

BRYAN, ARTHUR LEE, music educator; b. Berkeley County, SC, Feb. 6, 1951; s. Robert Marion and Alnetha McKelvey Bryan; children: Shay'La Yvonne Bryan-Harris, Arthur Lee Bryan,II, Jonathan Lamont. BA in Music Edn., Tex. Coll., 1975. Texas Teacher Certificate (Provisional - All - Level - Music) Tex. Edn. Agy., 1975. Instr. music Tex. Coll., Tyler, Tex., 1978—81, dir. choir, 1978—81, admissions counselor, 1978—81; staff sgt. U.S. Army, Fort Hood, Tex., 1981—2001; bandsmen, trumpet player 2nd Infantry Divsn. Band, Eighth Army Band, Camp Casey, 1982—2001; bandsmen, trumpet player 1st Cavalry Divsn. Band, Fort Hood, Tex., 1982—2001; bandsmen, trumpet player Eighth Army Band, Seoul, 1982—2001; dir. bands Fairway Middle Sch., Killeen, Tex., 2001—; ret. U.S. Army, 2001. Mem. Ancient Egyptian Arabic Order Nobles Mystic Shrine, Killeen, Tex., 1985—2002. Decorated Meritorious Svc. Medal Dept. of the Army, NATO Metal NATO; recipient Coined For Excellence, Commdg. Gen. for UNC; CFC; US Forces Korea, 1998, Commdg. Gen. For III CORPS and Ft. Hood, 1997, Command Sgt. Maj. of the Army, 1996, Coined for Excellence, Commanding Gen. for III CORPS and Fort Hood, 1998, 1999. Mem.: VFW, NEA (assoc.), Tex. Bandmasters Assn. (assoc.), Music Educators Nat. Conf. (assoc.), World Kido Fedn., Korea Kido Assn., N.G. Assn. Tex. (life), 1st Cavalry Divsn. Assn. (life), US Taekwondo Union, Masons, Alpha Kappa Mu, Phi Mu Alpha Sinfonia (assoc.), Omega Psi Phi (life; past basileus 1986—2002, past chaplain, keeper of records and seal). Democrat. Episcopalian. Home: 2404 Edgefield Street Killeen TX 76549 Office: Fairway Middle School 701 Whitlow Avenue Killeen TX 76541 Personal E-mail: arthurbryan@earthlink.net. E-mail: arthurbryan@hotmail.com.

BRYAN, BARBARA DAY, retired librarian; b. Livermore Falls, Maine, May 20, 1927; d. Lorey Clifford and Olga Elvira (Bergquist) Day; m. Robert S. Bryan, June 24, 1950. BA in Psychology, U. Maine, 1948; MS in Library Sci., So. Conn. State U., 1964. Catalog dept. asst. Yale U. Library, New Haven, 1948-49; departmental library cataloger Harvard U., Cambridge, Mass., 1949-51; descriptive cataloger Yale U. Library, New Haven, 1951-52; cataloger Fairfield (Conn.) Pub. Library, 1952-54, reference librarian, 1954-57, asst. librarian, order librarian, 1957-65; asst. dir. libraries Fairfield U., 1965-74, university librarian, 1974-96, u. libr. emerita, 1996—. Mem. Conn. State Libr. Bd., Hartford, 1978—92, chair, 1987—92; bd. dirs. Bibliomation, Inc., Stratford, Conn., 1987—91. Pres. Friends Nyselius Libr., Fairfield U., 1998-2000, mem. exec. bd., 2001—; commr. Fairfield Hist. Dist. Commn., 2003—. Named Conn. Libr. Assn. Libr. of Yr., 1988; recipient Disting. Alumnus award, So. Conn. State U. Sch. of Libr. Sci., 1979. Mem. ALA (life, Conn. chpt. councilor 1977-80), Assn. Coll. and Rsch. Librs. (constn. and by-laws com. 1986-90, mem. coll. libr. sect. stds. com. 1991-95), New Eng. Libr. Assn. (mem. com. 1981-85, coun. mem. 1975-77), Conn. Libr Assn. (legis. com. 1996—), Fairfield Hist. Soc. (libr. vol.), Conn. Audubon Soc., Oak Lawn Cemetery Assn. (bd. dirs. 1994—), Assn. Conn. Libr. Bds. (bd. dirs., chair legis. com. 1996—), Inst. Ret. Profl. (adv. bd. 1998-2001, 05-), Fairfield U. Retirees Assn. (pres. 2003-04), Phi Beta Kappa, Phi Kappa Phi. Democrat. Avocations: reading, walking. Home: 999 Merwins Ln Fairfield CT 06824-1919

BRYAN, BARRY RICHARD, lawyer; b. Orange, N.J., Sept. 5, 1930; s. Lloyd Thomas and Amy Rufe (Swank) B.; m. Margaret Susannah Elliot, July 24, 1953; children— Elliot Christopher, Peter George (dec.), Susannah Margaret, Sallie Catharine. BA, Yale U., 1952, JD cum laude, 1955; diploma in comparative legal studies, Cambridge U., Eng., 1956. Bar: N.Y. 1959. Legal advisor to gen. counsel Sec. of U.S. Air Force, Washington, 1956-58; assoc. Debevoise & Plimpton, N.Y.C., 1958-62, ptnr., 1963-93, presiding ptnr., 1993-98, of counsel, 1999—2002. Served to 1st lt. USAF, 1956-58. Fulbright scholar Trinity Coll., Cambridge U., 1956. Mem. ABA, Assn. of Bar of City of N.Y., Union Internationale des Avocats, Country Club of New Canaan, Fishers Island Club, Order of Coif, Phi Beta Kappa. Episcopalian. Home: PO Box 197 Isabella Beach Rd Fishers Island NY 06390 Office: Debevoise & Plimpton 919 3rd Ave Fl 43 New York NY 10022 Office Phone: 212-909-6508.

BRYAN, COLGAN HOBSON, aerospace engineering educator; b. Trenton, SC, Oct. 7, 1909; s. John William and Mary (Hobson) B.; m. Sara Lucille Turbeville, June 18, 1938 (dec. Nov. 17, 1975); 1 son, Colgan Hobson; m. Carol Lindsay Smelley, July 14, 1979 (dec. Sept. 20, 1993). BS in Elec. Engring, U. S.C., 1932; M.Ed., Duke U., 1940; MS in Aero. Engring, Ga. Inst. Tech., 1948. Registered profl. engr., Ala. Faculty U. Ala., 1942—, prof. aerospace engring., 1948—, chmn. dept., 1952—; research scientist NASA, 1962; on leave with U. Tenn. Space Inst., 1968-69. Cons. to industry, 1941-. Mem. Ala. Aero. Commn., 1944-48. Recipient Charles Henry Ratcliff award for excellence in teaching, 1976, Outstanding Faculty award Delta Tau Delta, 1976, George H. Denny Outstanding Faculty award Sigma Chi, 1976, Disting. Engring. fellow, 2002; established Colgan H. Bryan Aerospace Engring. Scholarship, 1991. Fellow AIAA (assoc.; Disting. Svc. award 1980, Disting. fellow 2002, award for excellence in tchg. 2003); mem. NSPE, ASME, AAUP, NEA, Am. Soc. Engring. Edn., Am. Ordnance Assn., Ala. Soc. Profl. Engrs. (Engr. of Yr. award Tuscaloosa chpt. 1990), Ala. Edn. Assn., Acacia (life), Kiwanis (pres. Tuscaloosa 1966, Service award 1966, Disting. Service award 1977), Pi Tau Chi (faculty adviser). Episcopalian. Achievements include research projects in theoretical and applied aerodynamics, energy (solar and wind). Home: 2825 Bimini Pl Tuscaloosa AL 35406 Office: U Ala PO Box 861461 Tuscaloosa AL 35486-0013 Office Phone: 205-348-7307.

BRYAN, GREYSON, lawyer; b. LA, 1949; BA with Distinction and Honors, Stanford U., 1971; JD cum laude, Harvard U., 1976. Bar: Calif. 1976, NY 1978, DC 1985, Japan (Gaikokuho-Jimu-Bengoshi, withdrew in 1990) 1987. Dir. tng. Harvard Law Sch. Internat. Tax Program, 1979—81, rsch. assoc., 1981—82; adj. prof. law, regulation internat. bus. UCLA Sch. Law, 1994—97; adj. prof. internat. bus. law UCLA Anderson Grad. Sch. Mgmt., 1995—98; established, partner-in-charge O'Melveny & Myers LLP, Tokyo, 1987—90, co-chair global practice group, 1990—94, ptnr. litig. Los Angeles, Calif., coordinates internat. practice, head litig. dept. internat. practice group. Cons., Office of Tax Analysis US Dept. Treasury; mem. litig. dept. of yr. American Lawyer; founding mem. Pacific Coun. on Internat. Policy. Articles editor Harvard Internat. Law Jour.; contbr. articles to profl. jours. Assoc. and acting dir. Volunteers in Asia, Inc., 1971—73; mem. bd. student advisors Harvard U.; chmn. Asia Soc. So. Calif. Ctr., 1992—2001; bd. visitors Stanford U. Inst. Internat. Studies, 1995—2004. Sheldon Traveling Fellow, 1976—77, sr. fellow, UCLA Sch. Pub. Policy and Social Rsch., 1998—99. Mem.: Am. Law Inst. (mem. tax advisory group, fed. income tax project 1982—84), DC Bar. Office: O'Melveny & Myers LLP 1999 Avenue of the Stars 7th Fl Los Angeles CA 90067-6035 Office Phone: 310-246-8444. Office Fax: 310-246-6779. Business E-Mail: gbryan@omm.com.

BRYAN, HENRY C(LARK), JR., retired lawyer; b. St. Louis, Dec. 8, 1930; s. Henry Clark and Faith (Young) B.; m. Sarah Ann McCarthy, July 28, 1956; children— Mark Pendleton, Thomas Clark, Sarah Christy Nussbaum. AB, Washington U., St. Louis, 1952, LL.B., 1956. Bar: Mo. 1956. Law clk. to fed. judge, 1956; assoc. McDonald & Wright, St. Louis, 1956-60; ptnr. McDonald, Bernard, Wright & Timm, St. Louis, 1961-64, McDonald, Wright & Bryan, St. Louis, 1964-81, Wright, Bryan & Walsh, St. Louis, 1981-84; pvt. practice law, 1984-96; ret., 1996. V.p., dir. Harbor Point Boat & Dock Co., St. Charles, Mo., 1966-80, Merrell Ins. Agy., 1966-80. Served to 1st lt. AUS, 1952-54 Mem. ABA, Mo. Bar Assn., St. Louis Bar Assn. (past chmn. probate and trust sect., marriage and div. law com.), Kappa Sigma, Phi Delta Phi Lodges: Elks. Republican. Episcopalian. Home: 41 Ladue Ter Saint Louis MO 63124-2047

BRYAN, HENRY COLLIER, clergyman, retired secondary school educator; b. Atlanta, Apr. 10, 1941; s. Thomas Harper and Rubye (Collier) B. Student, Temple U., 1959-63, 64, 70; BEd, Cheyney U., 1962; postgrad., Va. Union U., 1965-66; MDiv, Ea. Bapt. Theol. Sem., 1968; postgrad., Howard Law Sch., 1962-63, U. Alaska, Juneau, 1990. Cert. math. tchr., Phila.; ordained to ministry Am. Bapt. Ch., 1968. Tchr. math. Masterman Demonstration Sch., Phila., 1968-71, Phila. High Sch. for Girls, 1971-97; ret., 1997. Chaplain Alpha Phi Alpha Fraternity, Phila, 1968—. Assoc. min. Zion Bapt. Ch., 1967-68; asst. min. Wynnefield United Presbyn. Ch., 1969-72; Charter mem. North br. Y's Men Assn., Phila., 1972—; bd. dirs. Cherry Hill (N.J.) Civic Assn., 1992—. Recipient Outstanding Young Men Am. award Wynnefield Presbyn. Ch., Phila., 1971. Mem.: ASCD, NAACP (life), NSTA (life), Pa. Coun. Tchrs. Math., Pa. Coun. Suprs. Math., Nat. Coun. Suprs. Math., Math. Assn. Am., Phila. Fedn. Tchrs. (bldg. rep. Girls' H.S. 1996—97), Phila. Health Computer Users Group (life), Am. Baptist Mins. Coun. (life), Nat. Coun. Tchrs. Math. (life), Assn. Tchrs. Math. Phila. (life), Alpha Phi Alpha (life), Phi Delta Kappa (life). Avocations: computers, electronics, sports, chess, world travel. Home: 17 W Brook Dr Cherry Hill NJ 08003-1109

BRYAN, J(AMES) P(ERRY), JR., energy executive; b. Houston, Jan. 17, 1940; s. James Perry Bryan Sr. and Gretchen (Smith) Josey; m. Mary Jon Lewis, Jan. 24, 1964; children: Alicia and John Bracken. BA, U. Tex., 1962, LLB, 1965; BFT, Am. Inst. Foreign Trade, 1966. V.p. Morgan Guaranty Trust Co., N.Y.C., 1966-69; v.p. dir. investment banking Dominick & Dominick, N.Y.C, Houston, 1969-74; pres., CEO The MortgageBanque, Inc., Houston, 1974-78; v.p., regional dir. corp. fin. dept. E.F. Hutton & Co., Inc., Houston, 1978-81; chmn., CEO Torch Energy Advisors, Inc., Houston, 1981—; Neuvo Energy Energy Assets Internat. Corp., Houston, 1987—95; chmn. & CEO Bellwether Exploration Co., Houston. Bd. dirs. Torch Energy Advisors, Inc., Bellwether Exploration Co., Neuvo Energy Co., Park Nat. Bank, Torchmark Corp., Republic Waste Inds. Founder, editor Internat. Law Jour.; contbr. reviews and articles on Tex. history to mags. and jours. Chmn. endowment fund, other offices Tex. State Hist. Assn.; chmn. fund raising com., past. chmn., pres. Tex. Hist. Found.; chmn. devel., adv. bd. Inst. Texan Cultures; trustee Nita Stewart Haley Meml. Libr.; past trustee, chmn. nominating com. Harris County Heritage Soc; mem. adv. bd. Bazoria County Hist. Mus.; founding chmn., past bd. dirs. South Main Ctr. Assn.; founder, bd. dirs. Collector's Inst.; bd. dirs. The Book Club of Tex.; chmn., dir. fund raising River Oaks Bapt. Sch., others. Mem. ABA, Tex. Bar Assn., Houston Bar Assn., Univ. Tex. Ex-Students Assn. (life), Philos. Soc. Tex., Houston Country Club, Tex. Breakfast Club (treas. Houston), Tejas Club, Argyle Club, Nat. golf Links Am., Phi Delta, Delta Phi Epsilon. Office: Torch Energy Advisors Inc 1221 Lamar St Ste 1175 Houston TX 77010-3039

BRYAN, JOHN HENRY, food and consumer products company executive; b. West Point, Miss., 1936; BA in Econs. and Bus. Adminstrn., Rhodes Coll., Memphis, 1958. Joined Bryan Foods, 1960; with Sara Lee Corp. (formerly known as Consol. Food Corp.), Chgo., 1960—; from exec. v.p. to pres. Sara Lee Corp. (formerly known as Consol Food Corp.), Chgo., 1974, CEO, 1975—2000, chmn. bd., 1976—2000, also bd. dirs.; consultant Sara Lee Corp., Chgo., 2001—. Bd. dirs. GM Corp., BP Amoco Corp., Bank One, Goldman Sachs Group, Inc. Chmn. bus. adv. coun. Chgo. Urban League; bd. govs. Nat. Women's Econ. Alliance, Chgo.; trustee, vice chmn., exec. com. U. Chgo., Rush-Presbyn.-St. Luke's Med. Ctr.; trustee Com. Econ. Devel.; trustee, treas. Art Inst., Chgo.; chmn. Catalyst, Chgo. com. Chgo. Coun. on Fgn. Rels.; mem. trustee's coun. Nat. Gallery Art, Washington; mem. Pres.'s com. on the arts and humanities; bd. dirs. Bus. Com. for Arts. Decorated Legion of Honor France, Order of Orange Nassau The Netherlands, Order of Lincoln medallion; named Man of Yr., Harvard Bus. Sch. Club Chgo., Exec. Yr., Crain's Chgo. Bus., 1992; named to Jr. Achievement Chgo. Bus. Hall of Fame, 1992, Miss. Hall of Fame, 1992; recipient Nat. Humanitarian award, NCCJ, William H. Albers award, Food Mktg. Inst. Mem.: Bus. Roundtable, Bus. Coun., Grocery Mfrs. Assn. (sr.; past chmn. bd.). Office: Sara Lee Corp 3 1st Nat Plz 70 W Madison St Ste 4500 Chicago IL 60602-4260

BRYAN, JOHN RODNEY, management consultant; b. Berkeley, Calif., Dec. 29, 1953; s. Robert Richard and Eloise (Anderson) Putz; m. Karen Nelson, Jan. 20, 1990. BA in Chemistry, U. Calif., San Diego, 1975; MBA, Rutgers U., 1985. Agt. Prudential, San Diego, 1975-79; sales mgr. Herman Schlorman Showrooms, L.A., 1980-83; pvt. practice mgmt. cons. Basking Ridge, N.J., 1983-85; mgmt. cons. The Brooks Group, Hollywood, Fla., 1985-89; pvt. practice San Diego, 1988—. With Western Productivity Group, 1990-95; pres. eProcesses Consulting, Inc., 1999—, with Kaufman Global, 2005—. Elder La Jolla Presbyn. Ch., 1991—; chmn. bd. Allicance for African Assistance, 2004—. Mem. Inst. Indsl. Engring., Rutgers Club So. Calif., Beta Gamma Sigma. Avocations: singing, golf. Address: 6265 Hurd Ct San Diego CA 92122-2917 E-mail: jbryan@eprocessesinc.com.

BRYAN, JOHN STEWART, III, newspaper publisher; b. Richmond, Va., May 4, 1938; s. David Tennant and Mary Davidson Bryan; m. Alice Pyle Zimmer, 1963 (div. 1985); children: Elizabeth Talbott, Anna Saulsbury; m. Lisa-Margaret Stevenson, 1993. BA, U. Va., 1960; LHD (hon.), Hampden-Sydney Coll., 1997, Emory and Henry Coll., 1999, Coll. of William and Mary, 2001, Randolph Macon Coll., 2004. Former advt. salesman Burlington (Vt.) Free Press; former reporter The Tampa (Fla.) Times; pub. The Tampa Tribune and Times, 1976—77, Richmond Times-Dispatch, Richmond News Leader, 1978—. Bd. dirs. Media Gen., Inc., Richmond, vice-chmn., exec. v.p., 1985—, chmn., pres., CEO, 1990—2005, chmn., 2005—; bd. dirs. Mut. Ins. Co., Bermuda. Past pres. or chmn. Tampa Bay Art Ctr., Tampa Citizens Safety Coun., Tampa United Way, Gulf Coast Symphony, Jr. Achievement Richmond, Goodwill Industries Richmond, United Way Greater Richmond; trustee Va. Found. Ind. Coll., chmn., 1993—95; trustee Va. Performing Arts Found., Thomas Jefferson Found., George C. Marshall Found., World Affairs Coun. Richmond, Va. Hist. Soc.; former dir., trustee Episc. H.S., U. Tampa, St. Catharine's Sch., Hoover Instn. at Stanford, Tampa Bay Buccaneers, Tampa Rowdies, Richmond C. of C., Maymont Found., Valentine Mus. With USMC, 1960—62. Mem.: S.R., SAR, Va. Bus. Coun., World Bus. Coun., Soc. Profl. Journalists, Newspaper Assn. Am. (dir. 1990—93, 1997—), Newspaper Advt. Bur. (chmn. 1991—92), Va. Press Assn. (bd. dirs. 1980—86), So. Newspapers Pub. Assn. (found. chmn. 1978—79, pres. 1981—82), Fla. Press Assn. (life; pres. 1971—72, Disting. Svc. award 1975), Fla. Soc. Newspapers Editors (life), Soc. Colonial Wars, Soc. Cin., Fla. Coun. of 100, Farmington Country Club, Tampa Yacht and Country Club, Commonwealth Club, Country Club Va., Bohemian Club. Home: 4608 Sulgrave Rd Richmond VA 23221-3119 Office: Media Gen Inc PO Box 85333C Richmond VA 23293-5333

BRYAN, KAREN SMITH, lawyer; BA in Psychology, Bryn Mawr Coll., 1972; MA, UCLA, 1973; JD, U. So. Calif., 1979. Bar: Calif. 1979. With Latham & Watkins LLP, L.A., 1979—, ptnr., 1987—. Mem. planning com. U. So. Calif. Tax Inst. Named So. Calif. Super Lawyer, 2003—05; named one of Am.'s Leading Bus. Lawyers, Chambers & Ptnrs., 2003, 2004, 2005. Mem.: ABA (corp. tax com. and ind. income tax com.). Office: Latham & Watkins LLP 633 W Fifth St Ste 4000 Los Angeles CA 90071 Office Phone: 213-485-1234. Business E-Mail: karen.bryan@lw.com.

BRYAN, KIRK, JR., meteorologist, oceanographer, researcher; b. Albuquerque, July 21, 1929; married, 1956; 2 children. BS, Yale U., 1951; PhD in Meteorology, MIT, 1957. Rsch. assoc. meteorologist Woods Hole Oceanography Inst., 1958-61; rsch. meteorologist Gen. Circulation Rsch. Lab. U.S. Weather Bureau, 1961-68; oceanographer Geophys. Fluid Dynamics Lab., NOAA and Princeton (N.J.) U., 1968-94; vis. lectr. Princeton U., 1968-94, rsch. scientist, 1994-96, sr. rsch. scholar, 1996—. Mem. panel climatic variation global atmosphere rsch. program NAS, 1972-74; chmn. working group numerical models Sci. Com. Ocean Rsch., 1975-77. Fellow Am. Meteorol. Soc., Am. Geophys. Soc., Am. Geophys. Union (pres. oceanography sect., Maurice Ewing award 1993); mem. Russian Acad. Sci. (fgn.). Achievements include research in dynamic meteorology, physical oceanography, and general circulation of the atmosphere and oceans. Home: 700 Hollinshead Spring Rd Apt C205 Skillman NJ 08558-2037 Office: Princeton Univ Program Atmos and Ocean Sci Sayre Hall Princeton NJ 08544-1003 Office Phone: 609-258-3688. Business E-Mail: kbryan@splash.princeton.edu.

BRYAN, LAWRENCE DOW, college president; b. Barberton, Ohio, Jan. 30, 1945; s. W. Richard and Celia A. (Evans) B.; m. Marjorie Napier, June 15, 1968; children: Mark Evans, Alexa Marie. BA, Muskingum Coll., 1967; MDiv., Garrett Theol. Sem., 1970; PhD, Northwestern U., 1973. Tchg. asst. Nat. Coll. Edn., Evanston, Ill., 1969-71; biog. rsch. fellow Garrett Theol. Sem., Evanston, 1972-73; asst. prof. religious studies, chaplain McKendree Coll., Lebanon, Ill., 1973-77, asst. v.p. acad. affairs, 1977-78, dean, 1978-79, assoc. prof., 1978-79; prof. philosophy and religion, v.p., dean Franklin (Ind.) Coll., 1979-90; pres. Kalamazoo Coll., 1990-96, MacMurray Coll., Jacksonville, Ill., 1997—. Trustee Parkstone Group of Funds, 1994-98. Mem. Forum for Kalamazoo County, 1990-94, Kalamazoo Symphony Orch. Bd., 1990-96; pres. Heyl Found., Kalamazoo, 1990-96; bd. dirs. Bronson Hosp., 1991-96; trustee Interlochen Ctr. for Arts, 1994-97; pres. Jacksonville Main St. Bd. Dirs. Mem. Internat. Bonhoeffer Soc., Fed. Ind. Ill. Colls. and Univs., Rotary, Phi Sigma Tau, Delta Sigma Rho-Tau Kappa Alpha, Alpha Psi Omega, Theta Alpha Phi. Methodist. Business E-Mail: president@mac.edu.

BRYAN, RICHARD H., lawyer, educator, former senator; b. Washington, July 16, 1937; m. Bonnie Fairchild; 3 children. BA, U. Nev., 1959; LLB, U. Calif., San Francisco, 1963. Bar: Nev. 1963, DC 2002. Dep. dist. atty., Clark County, Nev., 1964—66; pub. defender, 1966—68; counsel Clark County Juvenile Ct., 1968—69; mem. Nev. Assembly, 1969—73, Nev. Senate, 1973—79; atty. gen. State Nev., 1979—83, gov., 1983—89; senator from Nev. U.S. Senate, 1989—2001; ptnr., mem. exec. com. Lionel, Sawyer & Collins, 2001—. Former mem. U.S. Senate coms. on commerce, sci. and transp., Dem. Policy Com., Fin. Com., Banking, Housing and Urban Affairs Com., Senate Nominating Steering and Coord. Com., Select Com. on Intelligence; adj. prof. polit. sci. U. Nev., Las Vegas, 2001—. Former pres. Clark County Legal Aid Soc.; bd. dirs. Las Vegas C. of C.; bd. trustees Nev. Devel. Authority, 2001—. 2d lt. U.S. Army, 1959—60. Recipient Disting. Svc. award, Vegas Valley Jaycees. Mem.: ABA, Coun. of State Govts. (past pres.), Am. Judicature Soc., Clark County Bar Assn., Elks, Masons, Lions, Phi Alpha Theta, Phi Alpha Delta. Democrat. Office: Lionel Sawyer & Collins 1700 Bank Am Plaza 300 S 4th St Las Vegas NV 89101*

BRYAN, ROBERT ARMISTEAD, university administrator, educator; b. Lebanon, Pa., Apr. 26, 1926; s. Morris Armistead and Katherine (Maulfair) B.; m. Kathryn Elizabeth Williams, Feb. 3, 1953; children: Lyla, Matthew. BA, U. Miami, 1950; MA, U. Ky., 1951, PhD, 1956. Teaching asst. U. Ky. at Lexington, 1950-54, instr., 1956-57; lectr. extension div. U. Calif., Tokyo, Japan, 1955-56; dean advanced studies, dir. sponsored rsch. Fla. Atlantic U., 1969-70; mem. faculty, adminstrn. U. Fla., Gainsville, 1957-90, prof. English, 1968-90, dean faculties, 1970-71, assoc. v.p. acad. affairs, 1971-75, v.p. acad. affairs, 1975-85, provost, 1985-89, interim pres., 1989-90, ret., 1990; interim pres. U. Cen. Fla., 1991-92, U. South Fla., 1993-94. Reader Coll. Bd. Exams., Ednl. Testing Svc., 1958-61; cons. So. Assn. Schs. and Colls., 1965-73, also chmn. visitation com., 1966-67; cons. HEW, Nat. Assn. of State Univs. and Land Grant Colls., 1990-91; cons. Fla. Bd. Regents, 1994-95; trustee Bethune-Cookman Coll., 1994-2001; mem. Fla. Postsecondary Edn. Planning Commn., 1996-2000. Bibliographer: Twentieth Century Literature, 1958-61. Served with U.S. Mcht. Marine, 1944-47, with AUS, 1954-56. Decorated Royal Order North Star (Sweden) Mem. MLA, Southeastern Renaissance Conf., S. Atlantic Mod. Lang. Assn., Sigma Chi. Episcopalian. Home: 5000 SW 25th Blvd Apt 4122 Gainesville FL 32608 E-mail: rbryan@gator.net.

BRYAN, ROBERT J., federal judge; b. Bremerton, Wash., Oct. 29, 1934; s. James W. and Vena Gladys (Jensen) B.; m. Cathy Ann Welander, June 14, 1958; children: Robert James, Ted Lorin, Ronald Terence. BA, U. Wash., 1956, JD, 1958. Bar: Wash. 1959, U.S. Dist. Ct. (we. dist.) Wash. 1959, U.S. Tax Ct. 1965, U.S. Ct. Appeals (9th cir.) 1985. Assoc., then ptnr. Bryan & Bryan, Bremerton, 1959-67; judge Superior Ct., Port Orchard, Wash., 1967-84; ptnr. Riddell, Williams, Bullitt & Walkinshaw, Seattle, 1984-86; judge U.S. Dist. Ct. (we. dist.) Wash., Tacoma, 1986—. Mem. State Jail Comm., Olympia, Wash., 1974-76, Criminal Justice Tng. Com., Olympia, 1978-81, State Bd. on Continuing Legal Edn., Seattle, 1984-86; mem., sec. Jud. Qualifications Comm., Olympia, 1982-83; chair Wash. Fed.-State Jud. Coun., 1997-98; mem. 9th Cir. Jud. Coun., 2001-03. Author: (with others) Washington Pattern Jury Instructions (civil and criminal vols. and supplements), 1970-85, Manual of Model Criminal Jury Instructions for the Ninth Circuit, 1992, Manual of Model Civil Jury Instruction for the Ninth Circuit, 1993. Chmn. 9th Ct. Jury Com., 1991-92; bd. dirs. Fed. Jud. Ctr., 2000-04. Served to maj. USAR. Mem.: 9th Cir. Dist. Judges Assn. (sec.-treas. 1997—99, v.p. 1999—2001, pres. 2001—03). Office: US Dist Ct 1717 Pacific Ave Rm 4427 Tacoma WA 98402-3234

BRYAN, SCOTT, business owner, chef; Intern under Bob Kinkaid, The Harvest, Boston; chef 21 Fed., Nantucket, Gotham Bar & Grill, N.Y.C., Square 1, San Francisco; staff meat sta. Restaurant Bouley, N.Y.C.; sous chef Le Bernardin; mem. staff Lespinasse; exec. chef Soleil, N.Y.C.; chef Alison on Dominick St., N.Y.C.; co-owner, chef Siena (formerly Luma), N.Y.C.; co-owner Indigo, N.Y.C., 1996; co-owner, exec. chef Veritas, N.Y.C., 1999—. Named one of the country's Best New Chefs, Food & Wine mag., 1996. Office: Veritas 43 E 20th St New York NY 10003

BRYAN, SHARON ANN, lawyer; b. Kansas City, Mo., Dec. 18; d. George William and Dorothy Joan (Henn) Goll; children: Lisa Ann, Holly Renee. BJ, U. Mo., 1963; diploma, Stanford Radio and TV Inst., 1961; postgrad., NYU Sch. Arts and Sci., 1963-64; cert. personal fin. planning profl., UCLA, 1986; JD, U. So. Calif., 1989. Cert. specialist in family law. Proofreader, copy editor Cadwalader, Wickersham and Taft, N.Y.C., 1963-64; manuscript editor, writer nonsci. sects. N.Y. State Jour. Medicine, Med. Soc. State N.Y., N.Y.C., also mng. editor Staffoscope, 1965-66; manuscript editor Transactions, editor Perceiver Am. Acad. Ophthalmology and Otolaryngology, Rochester, Minn., 1969-72, hist. writer, 1972-82; atty. Burkley, Moore, Greenberg & Lyman, Torrance, Calif., 1989-91; with Christopher M. Moore & Assocs., 1991-99, Moore, Bryan & Schroff, 1999—. Writer publicity articles Ft. Lee (Va.) Cmty. Theatre; mediator Dept. 2 Superior Ct. of Calif., Ctrl. Dist. and Dept SWJ, S.W. Dist. Author: Pioneering Specialists: History of the American Academy of Ophthalmology and Otolaryngology, 1982. Vol. honor roll soc. Meml. Sloan-Kettering Cancer Ctr.; active N.Y. Hosp. Women's League, 1965-67; docent L.A. County Mus. Natural History, 1982-86; vol. Harriet Buhai Ctr., 1990-97; pres. Malaga Cove Homeowners Assn., 1999-2000. Mem.: NOW, ATLA, ABA, Assn. Cert. Family Law Specialists (bd. dirs. 2003—, editor newsletter 2004, 2005), South Bay Women Lawyers Assn. (rec. sec. 1994—95, pres. 1996—97), Los Angeles County Bar Assn. (exec. com. L.A. delegation 1996—98, family law sect. exec. com. 2001—04, L.A. del. to State Bar Calif. 2004), Women's Lawyers Assn. L.A (bd. govs. 1991—97, chmn. family law sect. 1993—97), N.Y. Acad. Scis., Am. Med. Writers Assn. (editor conv. bull. 1966), Kappa Alpha Theta (chmn. membership com. N.Y. chpt. 1966), Kappa Tau Alpha. Home: 533 Via Del Monte Palos Verdes Estates CA 90274-1205 Office: 21515 Hawthorne Blvd Ste 490 Torrance CA 90503 Office Phone: 310-540-8855. Business E-Mail: sharon@mbslawcorp.com.

BRYAN, THOMAS LYNN, lawyer, educator; b. Wichita, Kans., June 10, 1935; s. Herbert Thomas and Ruth Marjorie (Williams) B.; m. Virginia Alice Cooper, June 13, 1981; children from previous marriage: Victoria Lynne Hague, Douglas Edward BA, U. Kans., 1957; LLB, Columbia U., 1960. Bar: N.Y. Assoc. Willkie Farr & Gallagher, N.Y.C., 1960-66, ptnr., 1967-92; adj. prof. Stetson U. Coll. Law, 1993-97. Co-author: Business Acquisitions, 1971, 2d edit. 1981 Mem. Longboat Key Club, Phi Beta Kappa Republican. Avocations: sports, golf, theater. Mailing: 77 Lakewood Ave Ho Ho Kus NJ 07423-1507 Address: 3448 Mistletoe Ln Longboat Key FL 34228-4146

BRYANS, HENRY S., lawyer; b. Bryn Mawr, Pa., 1946; BA, Yale Univ., 1968; JD, Univ. Pa., 1971. Bar: Pa. 1972, Del. 2004. Law clerk, Hon. Henry J. Friendly, chief judge US Ct. Appeals (2d cir.); joined Drinker Biddle & Reath LLP, Phila., 1972, ptnr., bus., fin. dept., firm gen. counsel. Lectr. in field. Mem.: Am. Law Inst. Office: Drinker Biddle & Reath LLP One Logan Sq 18th & Cherry Sts Philadelphia PA 19103-6996 Office Phone: 215-988-2823. Office Fax: 215-988-2757. Business E-Mail: henry.bryans@dbr.com.

BRYANS, RICHARD W., lawyer; b. Demver, May 29, 1931; s. William A. and Ruth W. (Waldron) B.; m. Carol Jean, Feb. 17, 1955; children: Richard W., Bridget Ann. BS, Denver U., 1954, JD, 1955. Bar: Colo., U.S. Supreme Ct. 1971. Sole practice, Boulder, Colo., 1958-63; ptnr. Kelly, Stansfield & O'Donnell, Denver, 1963-92, Bryans & Bryans, Denver, 1993—. Served to lt. (j.g.) USNR, 1955-58. Office: 1177 Grant St # 308 Denver CO 80203-2362

BRYANT, ANNA LAYNE, supervisor; b. Sanford, NC; d. Zoilie Aubrey and Judith Thomas Ray; m. Derek Lloyd Bryant, July 29, 2000; 1 child, Eleanor Layne. BA, Appalachian State U., 1998; MBA, Mid. Tenn. State U., 2003. Network operator NC Rsch. and Edn. Network, Research Triangle Park, 1998—2000; coord. videoconferencing and telecourses Mid. Tenn. State U., Murfreesboro, 2000—. Vol. Nashville Area Habitat for Humanity, 2001—, Nashville Area Room in the Inn, 2001—. Mem.: Beta Gamma Sigma. Democrat. Presbyterian. Office: Mid Tenn State U 1301 E Main St Murfreesboro TN 37132

BRYANT, ANNE LINCOLN, educational association executive; b. Jamaica Plain, Mass., Nov. 26, 1949; d. John Winslow and Anne (Phillips) B.; m. Peter Harned Ross, June 15, 1986; stepchildren: Charlotte Ross, George Ross. BA in English, Secondary Edn., Simmons Coll., 1971; EdD in Higher Edn., U. Mass., 1978. Intern U. Mass., Amherst, 1972; asst. to dean Springfield Tech. C.C., 1972-74; dir. Nat. Assn. Bank Women Ednl. Found., Chgo., 1974-86; v.p. P.M. Haeger, Chgo., 1978-86; exec. dir. AAUW, Washington, 1986-96, also exec. dir. Ednl. Found., Legal Advocacy Fund; exec. dir. Nat. Sch. Bds. Assn., Washington, 1996—. Contbr. articles to profl. jours. Mem. exec. com. Simmons Coll., Boston, 1971—; adv. commr. Edn. Commn. States, 1986—; mem. bd. govs. UNA of U.S.A., 1991—97, Ind. Sector, 1988-94, Hosp. Corp. Am., 1993-94. Recipient William H. Cosby Jr. award U. Mass., 1983; named Woman of Yr. for Edn., YWCA, 1976. Fellow Am. Soc. Assn. Execs. (bd. dirs. 1985-88, Key award 1992); mem. Am. Assn. for Higher Edn. (bd. dirs. 1980-87). Episcopalian. Avocations: tennis, skiing, reading, walking. Office: NSBA 1680 Duke St Alexandria VA 22314 E-mail: alb3@nsba.org.

BRYANT, ARTHUR H., lawyer; b. Harrisburg, Pa., Aug. 11, 1954; s. Albert Irwin and Marjorie (Weinrib) B.; m. Nancy Kaye Johnson, Aug. 17, 1991; 1 stepchild, Vinnie Johnson; 1 child, Wallace Johnson Bryant. AB with hons., Swarthmore Coll., 1976; JD, Harvard U., 1979; D (hon.), Ripon Coll., 1998. Bar: Pa. 1981, U.S. Dist. Ct. (ea. dist.) Pa. 1981, U.S. Ct. Appeals (3d cir.) Pa. 1981, U.S. Ct. Appeals (11th cir.) Ga. 1985, U.S. Ct. Appeals (6th cir.) Ohio 1986, U.S. Ct. appeals (D.C. cir.) 1986, U.S. Ct. Appeals (9th cir.) Calif. 1987, U.S. Ct. Appeals (7th cir.) Ill. 1988, U.S. Ct. Appeals (5th cir.) Tex. 1988, D.C., 1989, U.S. Supreme Ct. 1989, U.S. Ct. Appeals (1st cir.) 1996. Intern Rosenman, Colin & Freund, N.Y.C., 1978, N.Y. Civil Liberties Union, N.Y.C., 1978, Cambridge & Somerville Legal Svcs., Cambridge, Pa., 1979; law clk. U.S. Dist. Ct. (so. dist.), Tex., 1979-80; atty. Kohn, Savett, Marion & Graf., Phila., 1980-84; staff atty. Trial Lawyers for Pub. Justice, Washington, 1984-87, exec. cir., 1987—. Recipient George Moscone Meml. award Consumer Atty. Assn. L.A., 2003; named one of 20 young lawyers making a difference in the world ABA Barrister mag., 1991, one of 50 most influential people in coll. sports Coll. Sports Mag., 1994, one of 45 lawyers whose vision and commitment are changing lives The Am. Lawyer, 1997, one of 100 most influential lawyers in Am. Nat. Law Jour., 2000; recipient Wasserstein Pub. Interest law fellowship, 1996; Honored by Oreg. Trial Lawyers Asn., renamed pub. svc. award to Arthur H. Bryant Pub. Justice Award, 2003. Mem. ABA (Pursuit of Justice award 2003), ATLA. Achievements include honored by Oregon Trial Lawyers Association renaming its public service award The Arthur H. Bryant Public Justice Award 2003. Office: Trial Lawyers Pub Justice 555 Twelfth St Ste 1620 Oakland CA 94607 Office Phone: 510-622-8150.

BRYANT, BARBARA EVERITT, academic administrator, researcher, retired marketing professional, retired federal agency administrator; b. Ann Arbor, Mich., Apr. 5, 1926; d. William Littell and Dorothy (Wallace) Everitt; m. John H. Bryant, Aug. 14, 1948; children: Linda Bryant Valentine, Randal E., Lois. AB, Cornell U., 1947; MA, Mich. State U., 1967, PhD, 1970; HonD, U. Ill., 1993. Editor art Chem. Engring. mag. McGraw-Hill Pub. Co., N.Y.C., 1947-48; editl. rsch. asst. U. Ill., Urbana, 1948-49, free-lance editor, writer, 1950-61; with continuing edn. adminstrn. dept. Oakland Univ., Rochester, Mich., 1961-66; grad. rsch. asst. Mich. State U., East Lansing, 1966-70; sr. analyst to v.p. Market Opinion Rsch., Detroit, 1970-77, sr. v.p., 1977-89; dir. Bur. of the Census, U.S. Dept. Commerce, 1989-93; rsch. scientist Sch. Bus. Adminstrn., U. Mich., 1993—. Author: High School Students Look at Their World, 1970, American Women Today & Tomorrow, 1977, Moving Power and Money: The Politics of Census Taking, 1995; contbr. articles to profl. jours. Mem. U.S. Census Adv. Com., Washington, 1980—86, Mich. Job Devel. Authority, Lansing, 1980—85; state editor LWV of Mich., 1959—61; bd. dirs. Roper Ctr. for Pub. Opinion Rsch., 1993—2004; mem. nat. adv. com. Inst. for Social Rsch., U. Mich., 1993—. Fellow: Am. Statis. Assn.; mem.: Am. Assn. Pub. Opinion Rsch., Am. Mktg. Assn. (pres. Detroit 1976—77, midwestern v.p. 1978—80, v.p. mktg. rsch. 1982—84, found. trustee 1993—2001), Rotary, Cosmos Club. Republican. Presbyterian. Avocation: swimming. Home: 1505 Sheridan Dr Ann Arbor MI 48104-4051 Office: U Mich Sch Bus Ann Arbor MI 48109-1234 Office Phone: 734-763-9062. Business E-Mail: bryantb@umich.edu.

BRYANT, BERTHA ESTELLE, retired medical/surgical nurse; b. Va., Jan. 11, 1927; d. E.F. and Julia B. (Dowling) Bryant, Diploma, Sibley Meml. Hosp., Washington, 1947; BS, Am. U., 1948; MA, Tchrs. Coll., Columbia U., 1962. Staff nurse, head nurse NIH, Bethesda, Md., 1954-59; asst. dir. nursing USPHS Alaska Native Hosp., Mt. Edgecumbe, 1959-61; instr. Sch. Nursing, U. Mich., 1962-64; chief div. clin. nursing Bur. Nursing, D.C. Dept. Public Health, Washington, 1964-65; commd. Nurse Corps, USPHS, 1965, nurse dir., capt., 1974—. Nurse cons., hosp. facilities services br., div. hosps. and med. facilities Bur. Health Services, HEW, Silver Spring; nurse cons., social analysis br., div. health services research and analysis Nat. Center Health Services Research, Health Resources Adminstrn., HEW, Rockville, Md.; nurse cons. div. extramural research Nat. Center Health Services Research, Office Asst. Sec. Health, HHS, Hyattsville, Md., 1977-81 Contbr. articles to profl. jours. Mem. AAUW, Assn. Mil. Surgeons U.S., Commd. Officers Assn. USPHS

BRYANT, CLIFTON DOW, sociologist, educator; b. Jackson, Miss., Dec. 25, 1932; s. Clifton Edward and Helen (Dow) B.; m. Nancy Ann Arrington, Sept. 13, 1953; m. Patty Maurine Watts, Feb. 1, 1957; children: Melinda Dow, Deborah Carol, Karen Diane, Clifton Dow II. Student, U. Miss., 1950-53, BA, 1956, MA, 1957; postgrad., U. N.C., Chapel Hill, 1957-58, La. State U., 1958-60, PhD, 1964. Vis. instr. dept. sociology and anthropology Pa. State U., summer, 1958; instr., rsch. assoc. dept. sociology and anthropology U. Ga., 1960-63; asst. prof., assoc. prof., chmn. dept. sociology and anthropology Millsaps Coll., Jackson, Miss., 1963-67; summer research participant, tng. and tech. project Oak Ridge Asso. Univs., summer 1967; prof., head dept. sociology and anthropology Western Ky. U., Bowling Green, Ky., 1967-72; prof. sociology Va. Poly. Inst. and State U., Blacksburg, 1972—; head dept. Va Poly. Inst. and State U., Blacksburg, 1972-82. Vis. prof. Xavier U., Philippines, 1984-85; vis. prof., vis. rsch. scholar Miss. Alcohol Safety Edn. Program, Miss. State U., (summer), 1985; vis. Fulbright prof. dept. grad. inst. sociology Nat. Taiwan U., Taipei, Republic of China, 1987-88; vis. scientist U.S. Army summer faculty rsch. and engring. program, 1993; participant Fulbright-Hays Seminar Abroad program, Hungary, 1993, China, 1998. Author: Khaki-Collar Crime: Deviant Behavior in Military Context, 1979, Sexual Deviancy and Social Proscription, 1982; editor and contbr.: Deviant Behavior: Occupational and Organizational Bases, 1974, The Social Dimensions of Work, 1972, Sexual Deviancy in Social Context, 1977, Deviant Behavior: Readings in the Sociology of Norm Violations, 1990; editor-in-chief: The Encyclopedia of Criminology and deviant Behavior, 4 vols., 2001, Death and Dying: A Reference Handbook, 2 vols., 2003; co-editor, contbr.: Deviancy and the Family, 1973, The Rural Work Force: Nonagricultural Occupations in America, 1985; compiler: Handbook of Audio-Visual Resources to Accompany Social Problems Today, 1971; editor: Social Problems Today: Dilemmas and Dissensus, 1971; co-editor: Introductory Sociology: Selected Readings for the College Scene, 1970; editor in chief Deviant Behavior: An Interdisciplinary Jour., 1978-91; editor So. Sociologist, 1970-74; mem. editorial bd. Criminology: An Interdisciplinary Jour, 1978-91; chmn. editorial policy bd., founding editor-in-Chief Deviant Behavior: An Interdisciplinary Journal, 1992—; chmn. editorial bd. Sociol. Symposium, 1968-80; assoc. editor Sociol. Forum, 1979-80, Sociol. Spectrum, 1981-85; mem. bd. adv. editors Sociol. Inquiry, 1981-85, assoc. editor, 1997—; bd. editors Society and Animals, 1997—; assoc. editor spl. issue Marriage and Family Relations, fall 1982, Sociological Inquiry, 1997—; contbr. chpts. to books, articles, book reviews to profl. publs. Served to 1st lt., M.P. U.S. Army, 1953-55. Recipient E. Gordon Ericksen Outstanding Grad. Faculty award sociology dept. Va. Poly. Inst. and State U., 1992, 93, spl. award for continuing contbn. to undergrad. tchg. enterprise, 1992, Undergraduate Tchg. Excellence award, 1995-96, 2001. Mem. Am. Sociol. Assn., Am. Soc. Criminology, So. Sociol. Soc. (pres. 1978-79, Disting. Book award 2001), Mid-South Sociol. Assn. (pres. 1981-82, Disting. Career award 1991), Rural Sociol. Soc., Soc. Anthropology of Work, Internat. Sociol. Assn., Inter-Univ. Seminar on Armed Forces and Society, So. Assn. Agr. Scientists, Omicron Delta Kappa, Phi Kappa Phi, Alpha Phi Omega, Alpha Kappa Delta, Pi Kappa Alpha, Phi Beta Delta. Presbyterian. Home: 1724 E Ridge Dr Blacksburg VA 24060-8568 Office: Va Poly Inst State U Dept Sociology Blacksburg VA 24061 E-mail: cbryant@vt.edu.

BRYANT, DANIEL JAMES, food and beverage company executive, former federal agency administrator; b. 1965; married; 2 children. BA, Am. U., JD, 1992; MA, Oxford (Eng.) U. Law clk., spl. asst. U.S. Dept. Justice, 1987—92; speech writer former Atty. Gen. William Barr; policy dir. First Freedom Coalition, 1994—95; majority counsel Crime Subcom., 1995—99; majority chief counsel House Judicary Com. Crime Subcom., 1999—2001; asst. atty. gen. legis. affairs U.S. Dept. Justice, Washington, 2001—03, counselor, sr. adv. to atty gen. legal and policy matters, 2003, asst. atty. gen. Office Legal Policy, 2003—05; v.p. pub. policy & fed. govt. affairs Pepsi Co., Inc., Purchase, NY, 2005—. Mem. gov. affairs com. permanent subcom. investigations U.S. Senate. Office: PepsiCo Inc 700 Anderson Hill Rd Purchase NY 10577

BRYANT, DAVID J., lawyer; b. Fostoria, Ohio, Dec. 17, 1961; BS, U. Ill., 1984; JD, Northwestern U., 1987. Bar: Ill. 1987. Ptnr. comml. real estate law Katten Muchin Zavis Rosenman, Chgo. Mem.: ABA, Pension Real Estate Assn., Nat. Assn. Real Estate Investment Trusts, Chgo. Bar Assn. Office: Katten Muchin Zavis Rosenman 525 W Monroe St, Ste 1600 Chicago IL 60661 Office Phone: 312-902-5380. Office Fax: 312-577-8665. E-mail: david.bryant@kmzr.com.

BRYANT, DEBRA DEON, mathematics educator; d. Herman Glen and Reba Williams (Stepmother); m. Bruce Bryant, Sept. 10, 1994; children: Heather, Dustin, Rachel Dilldine. EdD, U. of Tenn., 1992—98. Assoc. prof. Tenn. Tech U., 1990—. Dir. Cumberland Plateau Regional Sci. & Engring. Fair, Cookeville, Tenn., 2003—. Office: Tenn Tech Univ 55 Univ Dr FH 407 Box 5171 Cookeville TN 38505 Office Phone: 931-372-3668. Home Fax: 931-372-6275; Office Fax: 931-372-6275.

BRYANT, DONALD L., JR., insurance and benefits company executive; b. Mt. Vernon, Ill., June 30, 1942; s. Donald Loyd and Eileen (Gallaway) B.; m. Barbara Frances Murphy, July 9, 1981; children: Derek Lawrence, Christina Murphy, Justin Donald. BA, Denison U., Granville, Ohio, 1964; JD, Washington U., St. Louis, 1967. CLU, Chartered fin. cons. Chmn., chief exec. officer Donald L. Bryant Assocs., St. Louis, 1968-75, Bryant Group, Inc., St. Louis, 1975—. Owner family vineyard, Napa Valley, Calif. Pres. Herbert Hoover Boys Club, St. Louis, 1987—; active Arts and Edn. Coun. Greater St. Louis, 1983—, Dance St. Louis, 1988—, Opera Theatre St. Louis, 1985—, Boy Scouts Am., 1972—, St. Louis Art Mus., 1990; bd. trustees Mus. Modern Art. Named Outstanding Alumni, Sch. of Law Washington U., 1990; named one of Top 200 Collectors, ARTnews Mag., 2004. Mem. Million Dollar Round Table (life), The Internat. Forum, Assn. Advanced Life Underwriters, St. Louis Assn. Life Underwriters, Estate Planning Coun. St. Louis, Mo. Bar Assn., ABA, Bellerive Country Club (St. Louis) (golf champ 1976), Vintage Club (Indian Wells, Calif.), Winged Foot (Mamaroneck, N.Y.), Castle Pines (Castlerock, Calif.), Meadowood (Napa Valley, Calif.), Sunningdale Golf. Republican. Presbyterian. Avocations: wine, golf, collecting abstract expressionism, especially de Kooning, contemporary art. Office: Bryant Group Inc 701 Market St Ste 1200 Saint Louis MO 63101-1884 Office Fax: 314-231-4859.

BRYANT, DONALD LOYD, insurance company executive; b. Orchard, Iowa, Jan. 30, 1919; s. Lester E. and Bessie (Farless) B.; m. Eileen Galloway, May 11, 1941; children: Donald Loyd, Hedy E. Bryant Garlock, Brenda K., Becky Bryant Hubert. B.Ed., So. Ill. U., 1940. With War Manpower Commn., Mt. Vernon, Ill., 1940; agt., dist. mgr. Equitable Life Assurance Soc. U.S., Elgin and Carbondale, Ill., 1946-54, agy. mgr. St. Louis, 1954-69, v.p., chief agy. staff ops. N.Y.C., 1969-71, v.p. corp. relations, 1971-72, sr. v.p. corp. relations, 1972-74, exec. v.p., spl. asst. to pres., 1974-78, exec. v.p., 1978-81. Bus exec.-in-residence Tex. Christian U., Ft. Worth, 1980—; cons. Nat. Exec. Services Corp.; bus. exec.-in-residence So. Ill. U. Served to lt. USN, 1942-46. Recipient Alumni Achievement award So. Ill. U., 1964, 88. Mem.: Quail Ridge Golf and Tennis (Boynton Beach, Fla.). Presbyterian. Home and Office: 1489 Partridge Pl N Boynton Beach FL 33436-5409 *On each job, behave as though you will be on that job for the remainder of your working life. In this way you avoid mistakes because you'd have to live with those mistakes. You are careful to pick good associates because you will have to live with them forever. You give security to your subordinates, command their loyalty, because they sense you'll be there forever. Ironically you'll then do such a superior job that you'll be promoted over and over while behaving as though you'll be on your job forever.*

BRYANT, FRED BOYD, psychology educator; b. Princeton, N.J., Nov. 26, 1952; s. George Macon and Merrilee (Miles) B.; m. Linda Sue Perloff, July 12, 1980; children: Hilary Jacyln, Erica Lindsay. BA, Duke U., 1974; MA, Northwestern U., Evanston, 1977, PhD, 1980. Postdoctoral fellow Inst. for Social Rsch., U. Mich., Ann Arbor, 1979-82; asst. prof. Loyola U., Chgo., 1982-85, assoc. prof., 1985-90, prof., 1990—. Rsch. cons. in field, 1982—; legal cons., N.Y., Ill., 1985—. Editor: Methodological Issues in Applied Social Psychology, 1992; contbr. numerous articles to profl. jours. Mem. APA, Am. Evaluation Rsch. Assn., Midwestern Psychol. Assn. Office: Loyola U Dept Psychology 6525 N Sheridan Rd Chicago IL 60626-5344 Office Phone: 312-508-3033. E-mail: fbryant@luc.edu.

BRYANT, G(ARY) DAVID, lawyer; b. Norman, Okla., Apr. 23, 1949; s. Harry Edgar and Nola Eulene (Lair) B.; m. Sandra; children: Kimberly Dae, Charity Suzanne. BA in Philosophy and English, U. Okla., 1973; JD, Oklahoma City U., 1975. Bar: Okla. 1975, U.S. Dist. Cts. (no., we. and ea. dists.) Okla. 1975, U.S. Ct. Appeals (7th and 10th cirs.) 1981, U.S. Supreme Ct. Pvt. practice, Oklahoma City, 1975-78; assoc. Linn & Helms, Oklahoma City, 1978-83; ptnr. Kline, Kline, Elliott & Bryant, Oklahoma City, 1983—. Trustee Chpt. 7 U.S. Bankruptcy Panel, 2001—. Mem. ABA (litigation and antitrust sects.), Okla. Bar Assn. (litigation sect.), Assn. Trial Lawyers Am. (civil litigation sect.), Okla. Trial Lawyers Assn. (civil litigation sect.). Democrat. Office: Kline Kline Elliott & Bryant 720 NE 63rd St Oklahoma City OK 73105-6405 Office Phone: 405-848-4448. E-mail: dbryant@klinefirm.org.

BRYANT, GEORGE BERNARD, music educator, musician; b. Nyack, NY, June 17, 1939; s. Geroge Bernard Bryant Sr. and Margaret Beirne. MS, Juilliard Sch. of Music, 1962. Pvt. music tchr., Nyack, 1962—; music dir. St. Ann's Roman Cath. Ch., Nyack, 1966—; organist Temple Beth Torah, Upper Nyack, NY, 1978—. Adjudicator, judge Nat. Guild Piano Tchrs., 1995—. Recipient Exec. Arts award, County of Rockland, NY, 1989; George Bryant Organ scholarship named in his honor, 1997—. Mem.: Nat. Pastoral Musicians, NY State Music Tchrs. Assn. (v.p. 1986—), Rockland County Music Tchrs. (bd. dirs. 1962—). Home: 133 1st Ave Nyack NY 10960

BRYANT, GREGORY ALEXANDER, bishop; b. Atlanta, Ga., Dec. 9, 1953; s. Silas Johnson and Mildred Bryant; m. Yvonne De Bryant, Oct. 26, 1996 (div.); children: Antwoine, Gregory Jr., Titus, Sheranda, Shawana, Tiffany. BA in religious arts, Jacksonville Theological Seminary, 2001, MA in religious studies; PhD in religious studies, Christ is the Answer U., 1995. Founder, pastor The Fountain of Praise, Atlanta, 1976—; founder, pres., CEO The More Than Conquerors Fellowship, Inc., Atlanta, 1985—; founder, pastor The Trumpet In Zion, Douglasville, Ga., 1985—, Shield of Faith Ministries, Carrollton, Ga., 2004—; founder, bishop Fountain of Life Ministries, McDonough, Ga., 2004—; founder Healing Streams Ministries, Newnan, Ga., 2005. Counselor Am. Assn. of Christian Counselors; founder New Directions with a Positive Change, Atlanta, 2004—, Camp Praise for Inner City Children, Atlanta. Author: Stongholds, 2003, My Warfare is Not With You, 2003, Let Your Haters Be Your Motivators, 2003. Serving and counseling Hosea Williams Feed the Hungry, Atlanta, 1994—. Recipient various proclamations and congratulatory letters of acknowledgement, 1983—2004. Mem.: SCLC, NAACP, Urban League, Rainbow Push. Achievements include 1st African Am. preacher on regualr TV, Atlanta Ga., 1980. Avocations: football, fishing, travel, reading, boating. Office: The More Than Conquerors Fellowship Internat Inc 770 N Elizabeth Pl Atlanta GA 30318 Office Phone: 404-794-9514. E-mail: fountainofpraisemtc2004@yahoo.com.

BRYANT, HUBERT HALE, lawyer; b. Tulsa, Jan. 4, 1931; s. Roscoe Conkling and Curlie Beatrice (Marshall) B.; m. Elnora Geraldine Roberson, Oct. 25, 1952; children: Cheryl Denise, Tara Kay. BA, Fisk U., 1952; LLB, Howard U., 1956. Bar: Okla. 1956, U.S. Dist. Ct. (no. dist.) Okla 1956, U.S. Ct. Appeals (10th cir.) 1967, U.S. Supreme Ct. 1980. Individual practice law, Tulsa, 1956—67, 1981—84, 1986—. Asst. city prosecutor, City of Tulsa, 1961-63, chief city prosecutor, 1963-67, asst. U.S. atty., No. Dist. Okla., 1967-77, U.S. atty., 1977-81; mcpl. ct. judge City of Tulsa, 1984-86. Trustee 1st Bapt. Ch., Tulsa, 1970-75, 96-2002; bd. dirs. Tulsa Urban League, 1962-64. Recipient Outstanding Alumni award Howard U. Sch. Law, 1981, 30 Yr. Outstanding African Am. Lawyer award Met. Tulsa Urban League, 1997. Mem. NAACP, Nat. Bar Assn. (Named to Hall of Fame), Okla. Bar Assn., Tulsa County Bar Assn., Okla. Trial Lawyers Assn., Nat. Set, Masons (named Mason of Yr. local chpt. 1963, Outstanding Citizen award 1978), Sigma Pi Phi, Alpha Theta Boule, Alpha Phi Alpha. Democrat. Home: 1818 N Boston St Tulsa OK 74106 Office: 2623 N Peoria Ave Tulsa OK 74106-2512 Office Phone: 918-428-6665.

BRYANT, JACQUELINE SHIM, lawyer; b. Cross Roads, St. Andrews, Jamaica; BS, Northwestern U., 1985; JD, UCLA, 1989. Bar: Ill. 1990, U.S. Dist. Ct. (no. dist.) Ill. 1990. Assoc. Levin & Funkhouser, Chgo., 1989-91; sole practitioner Chgo., 1991-95; atty. Aronberg Goldgehn Davis & Garmisa, Chgo., 1995-99, D'Ancona & Pflaum LLC, Chgo., 1999-2001. Contbr. chpt. to book. Trustee Northwestern U., 1993-97. Mem. ABA, Asian-Am. Bar Assn., Women's Ednl. Aid Assn. (bd. dirs. 1991—), Northwestern Alumni Assn. (bd. dirs. 1993—), John Evans Club (bd. dirs. 1993—), Jr. League of Chgo., Coun. of 100. Office: D'Ancona & Pflaum LLC 111 E Wacker Dr Ste 2800 Chicago IL 60601-4209 E-mail: jackiebryant@nualumni.com.

BRYANT, J(AMES) BRUCE, lawyer; b. Dettlebach, Fed. Republic Germany, Jan. 23, 1961; came to U.S., 1964; s. John Thomas and Doris Jean (Hazenbuahler) B.; 1 child, James Bruce II. BA, Northwestern State U., Natchitoches, La., 1984; MJ, La. State, 1986; JD, Miss. Coll., 1989. Bar: Miss., Tex. 1995, U.S. Dist. Ct. (no. and so. dists.) Miss., U.S. Ct. Appeals (5th cir.) La. 1991, U.S. Dist. Ct. (we. dist.) La. 1994; cert. supervisory techniques, La. State Univ., 2003. With residential life La. State U., Baton Rouge, 1985-86; law libr. worker Miss. Coll. Sch. Law, Jackson, 1986-87; clk. Brunini Law Firm, Jackson, 1987-88; ptnr. Cook & Bryant, Bay St. Louis, Miss., 1989-90; assoc. Cook, Yancey, King & Galloway, Shreveport, La., 1990-93; prof. bus. law La. State U., 1991-92, prof. paralegal sci., 1994-96; staff atty. State of La. Office of Support Enforcement, Shreveport, 1993-95; atty. Storm Operating Co. Inc. of La., 1994-98; sr. regional atty. State of La. Dept. Health and Hosps., Shreveport-Bossier City, La., 1995—; prof. comms. law, pub. rels and advt. Northwestern State U., 1996—; spl. asst. dist. atty. 1st Jud. Dist., Caddo Parish, La., 1998—. Bd. dirs. Extra Mile; cons. Wyman Fed. Credit Union, Geismar, La., 1989-90, Comml. Nat. Bank, Shreveport, 1990-93; owner, pres. Showbizzz Entertainment Agys., Shreveport, 1992—; v.p. Godfather Prodns., Inc., Shreveport-Bossier City, La., 1994—; owner La. Ctr. for Law and Justice, 1995—; spl. asst. dist. atty. Caddo Parish, 1998—; owner, pres. Dreamworks Internat., 1999—. Editor, author (with others): Art & Bylaws for Moot Court, 1989; contbr. to The Silence Within, 2000. Del. Republican Dist. IV, 1994—; bd. dirs. Shreveport Little Theatre, 1995-2000, Extra Mile, 1996—; vol. N.W. La. Coalition for Mentally Ill, 1995—, pres., 2002-05; vol. Shreveport/Bossier Svc. Connection, 2001—; liaison officer Gov.'s Health Consortia; mem. L.A. Pro Bono Project, Tex. Bar Assn. Pro Bono Project (Outstanding Svc. Award 2002); liason Govs. Health Consortia, 2004—; rewrite subcom. La. Legislation MR/DD, 2004-05, mem. legis. subcom. on involuntary commitment. Recipient Outstanding Svc. award, Tex. State Bar Pro Bono Project, 2002. Mem. ABA, La. Bar Assn. (mem. health law sect.), Miss. Pro Bono Project, Miss. Bar Assn., Assn. Trial Lawyers Am., La. Trial Lawyers Assn., Hancock County Bar Assn. (social chmn.), Shreveport Bar Assn. (comml. litigation sect., editor newsletter), TKE Alumni Assn. (pres.), Univ. Club (mem. com. 1994—). Roman Catholic. Avocations: martial arts, weightlifting, skiing, shooting. Home: PO Box 444 Shreveport LA 71162-0444 Office: La Ctr for Law and Justice 711 Texas Advocates Bldg Shreveport LA 71120

BRYANT, JERRY DOYLE, lawyer; b. Whitley City, Ky., Mar. 12, 1947; s. Fred and Myrtle Roberta (Vanover) B.; B.S., Cumberland Coll., 1969; J.D., Ind. U., 1973; m. Melanie Griffin, Sept. 30, 1995; children, Laura, Jennifer, Jeremy, Connor. Mgr., Sears Roebuck & Co., Cin., 1969-70; indsl. relations rep. Westinghouse Co., Bloomington, Ind., 1970-72; admitted to Ohio bar, 1974, Fla. bar, 1984, Ky. bar 1985; individual practice law, Wilmington, Ohio, from 1974; vis. asst. prof. Wilmington Coll., 1975-79; spl. coun. Ohio Atty Gen., 1975-90; judge Wilmington Mcpl. Ct., 1985. Chmn. Clinton County Bd. Elections, 1976-80; mem. exec. com. Dem. party, Wilmington, 1975-97. Mem. Am. Bar Assn., Am. Trial Lawyers Assn., Ohio Bar Assn., Ky. Bar Assn., Fla. Bar Assn., Clinton County Bar Assn. (pres.), Wilmington C. of C. Democrat. Methodist. Lodges: Eagles, Rotary, Masons, Shriners. Home: 14 Morningline Ln Wilmington OH 45177-9220 Office: 21 N South St Wilmington OH 45177-2211

BRYANT, JOHN, utilities executive; Economist Unilever; corp. planner Brit. Oxygen Co.; mgr. worldwide ops. ind. oil svc. and mfg. co.; with Brit. Sugar Corp, 1989; mgr. ind. power bus. Midlands Electricity plc, 1991; v.p. Cinergy Corp., Cin., 1998—; pres. Cinergy Global Resources, Cin., 1998—. Office: Cinergy Corp 139 E 4th St Cincinnati OH 45202

BRYANT, JOHN A., food products executive; b. Brisbane, Queensland, Australia, Nov. 6, 1965; m. Alison Bryant; 5 children. B Commerce, Australian Nat. U.; MBA, U. Pa. Various leadership positions Deloitte & Touche, Marakon and A.T. Kearney; with Kellogg Australia and Kellogg Europe Kellogg Co., 1998—, v.p. Kellogg N.Am. strategy devel./bus. understanding, v.p. fin. planning cereal, 1998, v.p. trade mktg., mem. sales leadership team Kellogg USA, 2000, sr. v.p., CFO Kellogg USA, 2000—02, sr. v.p., 2002, exec. v.p., CFO, 2002—, responsible for natural and frozen foods divsn. Kellogg USA, 2003—; pres. Kellogg Internat., 2004—. Recipient Palmer Grad. scholarship, Wharton Sch., U. Pa. Mem.: Securities Inst. Australia (assoc.), Inst. Chartered Accts. Australia (assoc.). Office: Kellogg PO Box 3599 1 Kellogg Sq Battle Creek MI 49016-3599

BRYANT, JOHN BRADBURY, economics professor, consultant; b. July 7, 1947; s. Royal Calvin and Martha Preble (Jones) B.; m. Evelyn Sandra Seltzer, June 24, 1973; 1 child, Aryn Royale. BA, Oberlin Coll., 1969; MS, Carnegie-Mellon U., 1973, PhD, 1975. Economist, bd. govs. FRS, Washington, 1974-77; sr. economist Fed. Res. Bank, Mpls., 1977-81; assoc. prof. U. Fla., Gainesville, 1980-81; cons. Fed. Res. Bank, Dallas, 1983-86, 91-92; Fox assoc. prof. Rice U., Houston, 1981-84, Fox prof. econs., 1984—, prof. mgmt., 1987—. Vis. scholar Hoover Inst., Stanford U., 1988-89; vis. fellow Center, Tilburg U., Netherlands, 1998-99. Contbr. articles to profl. jours., books. Office: Rice U Dept Econs MS22 6100 Main St Houston TX 77005-1892 Business E-Mail: jbb@rice.edu.

BRYANT, JOHN HOWARD, writer; b. Indpls., Ind., Aug. 24, 1938; s. Howard Gustav Bryant, Ruth Irene (Dunkin) Bryant; m. Kathe Bryant, Apr. 8, 1961; 1 child, Jeffrey Conan. BA in Philosophy cum laude, Marian Coll., Indpls., 1991; A in Logotherapy, V.E. Frankl Inst. Logotherapy, 1999; postgrad., Earlham Sch. Religion, Richmond, Ind. Instr. philosophy Ind. State U., 2002—03, lectr. philosophy, Ind. Sch. Medicine, Internat. Soc. for Value Inquiry, 2003, World Congress Phil., Istanbul, Turkey, 2003. Writer, lectr., advisor to PhD candidates and post-doctoral rschrs., China, 2004; presenter in field. Author: International Magazine of Electronics Technology, 1977, Proceedings of National Conference on Ethics in America, 1994—95, Korean Journal of Thinking and Problem Solving, 1997—2000, 2003, 2004, Sophia: A Journal for Philosophy Theology and Cross-Cultural Philosophy of Religion and Ethics, 2002—03, Australian Friend, 2002, Ariadne's Web, 2003, 2004, Bulletin of the Russian Philosophical Society, 2003, Quaker Life, 2003, World Philosophy, 2004, A Guided Conversation on Global Ethics, Axiology and Ethics; contbr. chapters to books, articles to jour. Recipient Outstanding Leadership award, Plainfield Kiwanis, Inc., 1976; grantee, Ind. State U. Found., Terre Haute, 2003, Fudan U., Shanghai, China, 2004. Mem.: Inst. Noetic Sci., Gandhi-King Soc., Concerned Philosophers for Peace, Nat. Coun. Excellence in Critical Thinking, Viktor Frankl Inst. Logotherapy. Mem. Soc. Of Friends. Home: 1323 Almond Ct Plainfield IN 46168

BRYANT, JOSEPHINE HARRIET, library director; b. Oshawa, Ont., Can., Dec. 3, 1947; d. Donald Joseph and Margaret Mary (Quilty) B.; children: David Joseph, Michael Andrew. BA, U. Toronto, Ont., 1969, BLS, 1970, MLS, 1974; diploma in Pub. Adminstrn., U. Western Ont., London, 1988. Libr. Ont. Hydro, Toronto, 1970-74; libr. supr. Brampton Pub. Libr. and Art Gallery, 1974-77, br. head, 1977-79; regional dir. Fairview North York Pub. Libr., 1983-85, mgr. century libr., 1986, dep. dir., 1986-88, CEO, 1988-98; city libr. Toronto Pub. Libr., 1998—. Co-chair faculty info. sci. fundraising com., dean's adv. com. U. Toronto. Mem. ALA, Can. Libr. Assn., Ont. Libr. Assn., Inst. Pub. Adminstrn., Urban Libr. Coun., Public Libraries Internat. Network. Avocation: golf. Office: Toronto Pub Libr 789 Yonge St Toronto ON Canada M4W 2G8 Office Phone: 416-393-7032. Business E-Mail: jbryant@torontopubliclibrary.ca.

BRYANT, KAREN WORSTELL, financial advisor, investment company executive; b. Cadillac, Mich., Sept. 7, 1942; d. Harley Orville and Rose Edith (Bell) Worstell; children: Lynda Jean Bashoor, Tracey Jo Taylor, Cynthia Jill Warren, Troy Thomas; m. Robert Melvin Bryant, Nov. 29, 1968. Student, Cen. Mich. U., 1963-67, Mich. State U., 1966, Johns Hopkins U., 1982-83, Loyola U., 1983. Sales rep. Xerox Corp., Southfield, Mich., 1972-74; cons. and employment contracts IBM World Trade Asia, The Policy Study Grp., Johnson & Johnson Internat., Tokyo, Japan, 1974-79; area sales mgr. Universal Plastics, McLean, Va., 1979-81; exec. product mgr. The Western Union Telegraph Co., Upper Saddle River, N.J., 1981-86; dir. mktg. and sales support The Nat. Guardian Corp., Greenwich, Conn., 1986-88; v.p., fin. cons. Salomon Smith Barney, Paramus, N.J., 1988-97; sr. v.p., fin. advisor Morgan Stanley, Pearl River, NY, 1997—. Guest lectr. for orgns.; guest on TV documentaries. Mem.: Nature Conservancy, World Wildlife Fedn., NY State Horse Coun. Avocations: horseback riding, power boating, decorating, horticulture. Home: 6 Christmas Hill Airmont NY 10952 Office: Morgan Stanley Box 1726 One Blue Hill Plz 1st Fl Pearl River NY 10965-2535 Office Phone: 845-731-2535. E-mail: karen.bryant@morganstanley.com.

BRYANT, KEITH LYNN, JR., history professor; b. Oklahoma City, Nov. 6, 1937; s. Keith Lynn and Elsie L. (Furman) B.; m. Margaret A. Burum, Aug. 14, 1962; children: Jennifer Lynne, Craig Warne. BS, U. Okla., 1959, MEd, 1961; PhD, U. Mo., 1965. From asst. prof. to prof., assoc. dean U. Wis., Milw., 1965-76; prof. Coll. Liberal Arts Tex. A&M U., College Station, 1976-88, head dept. history Coll. Liberal Arts, 1976-80, dean, 1980-84; prof. history U. Akron, Ohio, 1988-2000, head dept., 1988-95, prof. emeritus, 2000—. Cons. So. Ry., NEH. Author: Alfalfa Bill Murray, 1968, Arthur E. Stilwell, Promoter with a Hunch, 1971, History of the Atchison, Topeka and Santa Fe Railway, 1974, William Merritt Chase: A Genteel Bohemian, 1991, Culture in the American Southwest, 2001; co-author: A History of American Business, 1983; bd. editors Western Hist. Quar., 1984-87, Southwestern Hist. Quar., 1980-87; editor Railroads in the Age of Regulation, 1900-1980, 1988. Various offices local Rep. Party, Okla., Tex.; chmn. Bush for Pres., Brazos County, 1979-80. Served to 1st lt. U.S. Army, 1959-60. Recipient William H. Kiekhofer award U. Wis., 1968, George W. and Constance M. Hilton book award Ry. and Locomotive Hist. Soc., 1990, David P. Morgan Article award Ry. and Locomotive Hist. Soc., 1998; grantee Am. Philos. Soc., 1968, NEH, 1984. Mem. So. Hist. Assn. (chmn. Frank Owsley book award com. 1988), Western History Assn., Tex. Hist. Assn., Lexington Group, S.W. Conf. Humanities Consortium (pres. 1982-83). Presbyterian. Home: PO Box 5366 Bryan TX 77805-5366

BRYANT, KERI LYNN, German language educator; b. Stockton, Calif., June 14, 1964; d. Larry Jean and Jessie Anne (Leimbach) B. BA, Kenyon Coll., 1987; MA, Columbia U., 1987, U. Pa., 1991, PhD, 1994. German instr. High Mowing Sch., Wilton, N.H., 1987-89; lectr. U. Pa., Phila., 1994-95; asst. prof. German Murray (Ky.) State U., 1995—. Co-author: Alles Klar?, 1996. Mem. MLA, AAUW (v.p. 1996—), Am. Assn. of Tchrs. of German. Avocations: travel, crafts, music. Home: 1217 Maple St Hays KS 67601-3414 Office: Murray State Univ Dept Fgn Lang PO Box 9 Murray KY 42071-0009

BRYANT, KOBE, professional basketball player; b. Phila., Aug. 23, 1978; s. Joe "Jellybean" and Pam Bryant; m. Vanessa Laine, Apr. 18, 2001; 1 child, Natalia. Player L.A. Lakers, 1996—. Mem. NBA Championship team, 2000, 01, 02. Named National High School Player of the Year (Lower Merion H.S.), 1996, All-NBA defensive, 1999—2000, MVP, NBA All-star game, 2002; named to NBA All-star game, 1998, All-NBA 3d team, 1999, All-NBA 2d team, 2000, 2002, All-NBA 1st team, 2003, NBA All-star game, 2000—04. Achievements include went straight to NBA right out of high school; being the youngest player ever (19 yrs. of age) in NBA All-star game, 1998. Office: LA Lakers 555 N Nash St El Segundo CA 90245-2818

BRYANT, L. GERALD, management consultant; b. Norman, Okla., July 27, 1942; s. Lewis Cullen and Ludie A. (Skacel) B.; m. Linda Sue Farris, June 12, 1964; children: David Graham, Heather Leigh. BBA, U. Okla., 1964; MHA, Washington U., St. Louis, 1968. Acct. Pan-Am. Petroleum Corp., Tulsa, 1964-66; adminstrv. asst. Baylor U. Med. Ctr., Dallas, 1968-70, adminstr. C.P.C.H., 1970-72, assoc. dir., 1972-75, assoc. dir. planning and budget, 1975-80, sr. v.p., 1980-81, Baylor Health Care System, Dallas, 1981-84, COO, exec. v.p., 1984-92, exec. v.p. strategy devel., 1992—2000; pres. Bryant Consulting Group, 2000—. Bd. dirs. Regional Health Planning Agy., Irving, Tex., 1979—83; adj. faculty Wahington U. Sch. Med., St. Louis, 1983—2000, U. Ala., Birmingham, 1992—2000, Trinity U., San Antonio, 1996—2000; active Blue Ribbin Task Force on Health Care Reform, Tex. Hosp. Assn., 1992—93; devel. bd. dirs. Allied Bank, Dallas. Contbr. chpts. to books. Bd. dirs. Arthritis Found. Dallas, 1980-84; bd. dirs. Preservation Dallas, 1995—; deacon Wilshire Bapt. Ch., Dallas, 1976—; bd. dirs. Dallas Sci. Pl., 1995—. Fellow Am. Coll. Health Care Execs.; mem. Am. Hosp. Assn. (coun. regents 1994—, ho. of dels. 1996—, region 7 policy bd. 1994—), Tex. Hosp. Assn. (coun. on health planning 1981-84, coun. on pre-paid health plans 1984—), Am. Soc. Hosp. Planning, Am. Mgmt. Assn. Lodges: Rotary. Republican. Baptist. Avocations: antique furniture collecting, travel, gardening. Home and Office: 8722 Rocky Cove Cir Dallas TX 75243-7530

BRYANT, LAWRENCE M., history educator; b. Atlanta; s. George McBride Bryant and Mary Germaine Garner; m. Marcia Langley, Aug. 31, 1968; 1 child, Justin. BA, Emory U., 1965; MA, U. Iowa, 1968, PhD, 1978. Instr., assoc. prof. Spring Hill Coll., Mobile, Ala., 1975-85; prof. history Calif. State U., Chico, 1987—. Vis. prof. Stanford (Calif.) U., 1985-87. Author: King and City in Renaissance France, 1986. Founder Friends of History, Chico, 1997. Andrew Mellon fellow, Harvard U., Cambridge, Mass., 1984-85, NEH fellow, 1993-94; Alumni fellow awardee U. Iowa, 2002. Mem. Am. Hist. Assn., French Hist. Studies (pres. 1999-93), Renaissance Soc. Am., Soc. Ct. Studies (bd. dirs. 1998—, exec. coun. 1992-95), 16th Century Soc. Democrat. Avocation: swimming. Office: Chico State U History Dept Chico CA 95929-0735 E-mail: lbryant@csuchico.edu.

BRYANT, LELAND MARSHAL, business and nonprofit executive; b. Gainesville, Ga., Apr. 28, 1950; s. William Marcus and Pierre Lou (Milner) B.; children: Shauna, Natalie, Marcus, Jacob. Student, Vanderbilt U., 1968-70; BBA with hons., U. Tex., 1972; MBA, U. Pa., 1978. CPA, Tex. Acct. Arthur Andersen and Co., Dallas, 1978-81; exec. v.p. Walter Bennet Comms., Dallas, 1981-89; pres. Grand Canyon Railway, Flagstaff, Ariz., 1989-97; v.p., CFO, Grand Canyon (Ariz.) Assn., 1997—. Pres. Fray Marcos Hotel, Flagstaff, 1995-97. Bd. dirs. Grand Canyon Nat. Park Found., 1995—; nat. adv. bd. No. Ariz. U., Flagstaff, 1994-97. Mem. AICPA, Grand Canyon Assn. (bd. dirs. 1995-97), Nat. Parks Conservation Assn. (nat. adv. coun. 1995-98). Republican. Office: Grand Canyon Assn PO Box 399 Grand Canyon AZ 86023-0399

BRYANT, LINDA ANN, art educator, artist, poet; b. Globe, Ariz., Apr. 15, 1935; d. Arnold Lester Brantley and Evelyn Maud Cole; m. Richard Hudson Bryant, Jan. 4, 1960 (div. Aug. 1969); 1 child, Lisa Shannon. BFA in Painting, Ariz. State U., 1969; MA in Art Therapy, Prescott (Ariz.) Coll., 1995. Cert. tchr. K-12, secondary tchr. 7-12. Art tchr. Phoenix Country Day Sch., Paradise Valley, 1971—. Coord. 7th grade Phoenix Country Day Schs., Paradise Valley, founder mid. sch. literary mag.; selection com. mem. Ariz. Arts and Humanities, Phoenix. One women shows include The Downtown Gallery, 1996, Gallery Three, 1989, 90, 91, Alwun House, 1984, Scottsdale Ctr. for the Arts, 1981; represented in permenant collections. Recipient Rex L. Allison chair for excellence in tchg. Phoenix Country Day Sch., 1995, Excellence award for lit. mag. Nat. Coun. English Tchrs., 1998. Mem. NEA. Avocations: photography, wilderness trips, canoeing. Office: Phoenix Country Day Sch 3901 E Stanford Dr Paradise Valley AZ 85253-7500

BRYANT, MARCHELLE DIONNE, performing arts educator; b. Detroit, June 20, 1974; d. Mary Lee and Willie Thomas Bryant. Bachelors, Marygrove Coll., 1998. Tchr. Acad. of Detroit Schs./Cherry Hill Sch. of Performing Arts, Inkster, 1998—2001, St. Cecilia, Detroit, 2001—. Tutor summer camp St. Cecilia Sch./Bryant-Hogan Summer Camp, Detroit, 2002—03. Mem. choir Peace Bapt. Ch., Detroit, 2001—04. Mem.: Sigma Tau Delta (life). Democrat. Baptist. Office: St Cecilia Sch 6327 Burlingame Detroit MI 48208 Personal E-mail: sugaplum0072003@yahoo.com.

BRYANT, MYNORA J., not-for-profit fundraiser; Grand basileus Sigma Gamma Rho. Office: Ste 200 1000 Southhill Dr Cary NC 27513 Office Phone: 919-678-9721.*

BRYANT, PAUL T., electronics engineer; b. Washington; s. Herbert Arnold and Lucy Mae Bryant; m. Sharon Lynn Wilson; children: Matthew Paul, Andrew Paul. BS in Elec. Engring., U. Md., 1964; Program Mgmt. Cert., Def. Sys. Mgmt. Coll., 1981. Engr. Value Engring., Alexandria, Va., 1964-66; electronic design engr. White Electromagnetics Inc., Rockville, Md., 1966-68; sys. engring. dept. head Litton Industries, College Park, Md., 1968-76; electronic warfare program mgr. Naval Electronic Sys. Command, Washington, 1976-84; advanced concepts sect. head Naval Rsch. Lab., Washington, 1984-91; engring. sect. head NASA, Greenbelt, Md., 1991-97, engring. br. head, 1997—. Patentee in field. Chmn. Bowie Postal Customer Adv. Coun., Md., 1994-98; bd. mem. Takoma Park Cmty. Svc. Ctr., Md., 1994-98. Recipient letter of appreciation U.S. Postal Svc., 1994, Joint Spl. Ops. Com., 1988. Office: NASA-Goddard Space Flight Ctr Code 565 Greenbelt MD 20771-0001 Home: 11628 Leda Ln New Port Richey FL 34654-6238

BRYANT, RICHARD MILES, retired clinical psychologist; b. Princeton, Ill., June 6, 1932; s. Miles William and Amanda (Kaar) B.; m. Patricia Ruth Patton, Aug. 20, 1955; children: Richard Miles, Jr., William Patton, Melissa Ruth. BA, Washington U., St. Louis, 1954; student, U. Iowa, 1954-55; PhD, U. Tex., 1958. Diplomate Am. Bd. Profl. Psychology. Chief clin. psychology sect. Mental Hygiene Consultation Svc., Ft. Leonard Wood, Mo., 1958-60; supr. psychol. svcs. Juvenile Residential Treatment Program State Hosp., Fulton, Mo., 1960-63; part-time asst. prof. psychology Lincoln U., Jefferson City, Mo., 1960-63; spl. lectr. William Woods Coll., Fulton, Mo., 1960-63; sr. clin. psychologist Children's Med. Ctr., Tulsa, 1963-64, dir. psychol. svcs., 1964-75; pvt. practice clin. psychology Tulsa, 1975-90; ret., 1990. Past chmn. Okla. Bd. Examiners Psychologists. Mem. Am. Psychol. Assn., Okla. Psychol. Assn. (sec.-treas. 1969-71, pres. 1972-73), Am. Soc. Clin. Hypnosis, Tulsa Psychol. Assn. (past pres.), Sigma Xi, Kappa Alpha. Home: 5353 S Joplin Ave Tulsa OK 74135-7560

BRYANT, RUTH ALYNE, banker; b. Memphis, Jan. 12, 1924; d. James Walter and Leola (Edgar) B. Student, Rhodes Coll. (formerly Southwestern Coll.), Memphis, 1941-43; LHD (hon.), U. Mo., St. Louis, 1990. Clk. Fed. Res. Bank of St. Louis (Memphis Br.), 1943-47, exec. sec., 1947-68, asst. cashier, 1968-69, asst. v.p., 1969-73, v.p., 1973-90. Trustee chancellor's coun. U. Mo., St. Louis, 1979—, chmn., 1985-88; pres. Premiere Performances, 1990-96, vice chmn., 1996-98, bd. dirs., 1998; mem. adv. bd. Salvation Army, St. Louis, 1983-91, DePaul Health Ctr., St. Louis, 1984-87; adv. coun. Hope Ctr., St. Louis, 1987, chmn., 1990-91; chmn. adv. coun. Riverway Sch., 1989-95; bd. dirs. Assocs. of St. Louis U. Librs., 1977—, pres., 1983-85; bd. dirs. The Vanderschmidt's Sch., 1980-86, Internat. Edn. Consortium, 1988-92; bd. dirs. St. Louis Merc. Libr., 1989—, sec., 1990-92, v.p., 1992-94, pres., 1994-2000; trustee Mo. Coun. on Econ. Edn., 1989-93; bd. dirs. Dance St. Louis, 1992—2003, v.p., 1993-94, English Lang. Sch., 1993-97; mem. devel. bd. U. Mo. Press, 2002—; bd. dirs. Ctr. French Colonial Studies, 1994-, pres. 2003-. Fellow: Winston Churchill Meml.; mem.: Bank Mktg. Assn. (dir. Mo.-Ill. chpt. 1976—79), English Speaking Union (bd. dirs. 1989—, 1989—, v.p. 1992—96, nat. bd. dirs. 1995—96, pres. 1997—, nat. bd. dirs. 1998—2004), Nat. Assn. Bank Women (editor Woman Banker 1959—62, v.p. so. region 1967—68, pres. 1970—71, trustee ednl. found. 1974—75), Mo. Bankers Assn. (mktg. and pub. rels. com. 1974—76), Am. Inst. Banking (nat. women's com. 1962—63, pres. Memphis chpt. 1968—69), Alliance Francaise of St. Louis (exec. v.p. 2001—03, pres. 2003—), Nat. Soc. Arts and Letters, Rhodes Coll. Internat. Alumni Assn. (exec. bd. 1999—2000), Univ. Club (St. Louis), The Venerable Order of St. John in Jerusalem (comdr.). Home: 625 S Skinker Blvd Apt 202 Saint Louis MO 63105-2301

BRYANT, THOMAS LEE, magazine editor; b. Daytona Beach, Fla., June 15, 1943; s. Stanley Elson and G. Bernice (Burgess) B.; m. Patricia Jean Bryant, June 30, 1979. BA in Polit. Sci., U. Calif., Santa Barbara, 1965, MA in Polit. Sci., 1966. Fgn. svc. officer U.S. Dept. State, Washington, Buenos Aires, 1967-69; radio broadcaster KDB Sta., Santa Barbara, Calif., 1969-72; magazine editor, now editor-in-chief Road & Track, Newport Beach, Calif., 1972—. Mem. Internat. Motor Press Assn., Motor Press Guild, Sports Car Club of Am. Avocations: golf, trap and skeet shooting. Office: c/o Hachette Filipacchi Mags Inc 1499 Monrovia Ave Newport Beach CA 92663-2752

BRYANT, TIMOTHY CLARK, investment brokerage executive; b. Akron, Ohio, Apr. 11, 1943; s. Alan Willard and Clara Sherman (Clark) B.; m. Mary Esther Snell, Jan. 17, 1981. AB, Dartmouth Coll., 1967; MBA, U. Chgo., 1971; MS in Taxation, DePaul U., 1975. CPA, Ill. Dir. fin. and adminstrn. Fibre Box Assn., Chgo., 1975-77, Akers Packaging Co., Middletown, Ohio, 1977-78; dir., sec., treas. CompuShop, Inc., Dallas, 1978-80, dir., 1980-85; v.p. fin., dir. Rubicon Corp., Richardson, Tex., 1980-82, Automated Mgmt. Inc., Dallas, 1982-83, Avian Corp., Clearwater, Fla., 1983-85, pres., bd. dirs., 1985-87; v.p. investments A.G. Edwards and Sons, 1990—. Chmn. bd. dirs. Adventures Away, Inc., Chgo., 1983-87; pres., treas., bd. dirs. Talk2 Corp., Clearwater, 1987-90; cons. Nevada Brake Corp., 1985-91, So. Conf. Bur., Inc., 1987-90, Innovative Products Group, Inc., 1987-90. With U.S. Army, 1965-66, Korea. Mem. AICPA, Chgo. Yacht Club, Vinoy Club. Home: 307 Brightwaters Blvd NE Saint Petersburg FL 33704-3709 Office: A G Edwards & Sons 700 Central Ave Saint Petersburg FL 33701 Office Phone: 727-550-2222.

BRYANT, WARREN F., retail executive; Sr. v.p. supermarket divsn. Dillon Co. Inc., pres., CEO, 1995—99; sr. v.p. Kroger Co., 1999—2002; CEO, pres. Long Drug Stores Corp., 2002—, acting COO, 2003—. Office: 141 N Civic Dr Walnut Creek CA 94596*

BRYANT-SALA, KAREN, music educator; d. William D. Bryant and Rosemary Oshel; m. John C. Sala (div.); 1 child, John Douglas Sala. B in Music Edn., Murray State U., 1967; MusM, North Tex. State U., 1968. Music tchr. Gibson City (Ill.) Unit Schs., 1969; prof. music John A. Logan Coll., Carterville, Ill., 1970—. Mem.: NEA, Am. Assn. for Women in C.C. (pres. 2002—03), Am. Choral Dirs. Assn., Music Educators Nat. Conf., Ill. Music Edn. Assn., Sigma Alpha Iota. Baptist. Office: John A Logan Coll 700 College Rd Carterville IL 62918

BRYAR, PAUL, ophthalmologist, educator; BA, Georgetown U., Washington, D.C., 1989; MD, U. Ill., Chgo., 1994. Diplomate Am. Bd. Ophthalmology. Asst. prof. ophthalmology and pathology Northwestern U. Feinberg Sch. of Medicine, Chgo., 1999—; physician and surgeon Northwestern U. Med. Sch., Dept. Ophthal., Chgo., 1999—. Internship Internal Med. Northwestern U. Med. Sch., Chgo., 1994—95, Res. Ophthal., 1995—98; Fell. Ophthal. Pathol. U. Wisc., Madison, 1998—99; physician Nr. North Health Svc. Corp., Chgo., 1999—2003. Named Ophthalmogy Tchr. of the Yr., Chgo. Curriculum in Ophthalmology, 2002; Rsch. grantee, Ill. Soc. for the Prevention of Blindess, 2003. Fellow: Am. Acad. of Ophthalmology; mem.: Assn. for Rsch. in Vision and Ophthalmology, Alpha Sigma Nu, Alpha Omega Alpha. Achievements include Investigating role of Nerve Growth Factor in ocular surgical healing. Avocations: running, travel. Office Phone: 312-695-8150.

BRYCE, ROBERT W., lawyer; b. Defiance, Ohio, Jan. 10, 1954; s. F. William and Jeanette A. Bryce; m. Francelia A. Yagelski, Aug. 16, 1975; children: Bobbi Ann, Christa Jean, Teresa Marie. BS, Mich. State U., 1976; JD, U. Toledo, 1980. Bar: Ohio 1981, U.S. Dist. Ct. (no. dist., we. divsn.) Ohio 1983, U.S. Ct. Appeals (6th cir.) 1993, cert.: Nat. Bd. Trial Advocacy (bd. cert. civil trial adv.). Jr. high sci. tchr. Toledo Pub. Schs., 1976—80; biology tchr. Montpelier (Ohio) H.S., 1980—81; asst. county prosecutor Defiance County, 1981—83; civil trial atty. Frank W. Cubbon, Jr. & Assocs., Toledo, 1983—88, Huffman, Gallagher, Schlageter & Breier, Oregon, Ohio, 1988—92, Schlageter, Breier & Bryce, Oregon, 1992—2003, Schlageter & Bryce Co., L.P.A., Oregon, 2003—; examiner Nat. Bd. Trial Advocacy, Civil Ethics, 2003, Nat. Bd. Trial Advocacy, Med. Negligence, 2004; lectr. Nat. Bus. Inst., 2003. Trustee Anthony Wayne Sch. Edn. Found., Whitehouse, Ohio, 1997—2000. Named Ohio Super Lawyer, Cin. Mag., 2003. Mem.: Toledo Bar Assn. (mem. fee grievance com. 1986—88, mem. common pleas ct. com. 1988—90, mem. grievance com. 1998—2000), Ohio State Bar Assn., Ohio Acad. Trial Lawyers (trustee 1996—98), Am. Acad. Trial Lawyers, Sons Am. Legion (adj. 2003—), Mich. State Alumni Assn., Fraternal Order Eagles, Sigma Chi. Avocations: skiing, golf, entomology, landscaping. Home: PO Box 2666 11015 Stiles Rd Whitehouse OH 43571 Office: Schlageter & Bryce Co LPA 715 S Coy Rd Oregon OH 43616 Office Phone: 419-691-2435.

BRYCE, WILLIAM DELF, lawyer; b. Georgetown, Tex., Aug. 7, 1932; s. D.A. Bryce and Frances Maxine (Wilson) Bryce Bakke; m. Sarah Alice Riley, Dec. 20, 1954; children: Douglas Delf, David Dickson. BA, U. Tex., 1955; LLB, Yale U., 1960. Bar: Tex. 1960. Briefing atty. Tex. Supreme Ct., Austin, 1960-61; sole practice, 1961—. Lectr. U. Tex., 1965—66. Editor, Tex. Supreme Ct. Jour. Served to 1st lt. USAF, 1955—57. Fellow Tex. Bar Found. (sustaining; life); mem. ABA, State Bar Tex., Travis County Bar Assn., Williamson County Bar Assn., Rotary Internat. (dist. 5870 gov. 1999-2000). Home: 308 E University Ave Georgetown TX 78626-6813 Office: 511 S Main St Georgetown TX 78626-5609

BRYCHTOVA, JAROSLAVA, sculptor; b. Semily, Czechoslovakia, 1924; m. Stanislav Libensky (dec. Feb. 2002). Student, Acad. Applied Arts, Prague, Czechoslovakia, 1945—51, Acad. Fine Arts, Prague, 1947—50. Designer Zeleznobrodské sklo, Zelezny Brod, Czech Republic, 1950—84. Guest lectr. Pilchuck Summer Sch., Stanwood, Wash., Ctr. Creative Studies, Detroit, others; presenter in field. also: Heller Gallery 420 W 14th St New York NY 10014-1064 Office Phone: 212-414-4014.

BRYDGES, THOMAS EUGENE, lawyer; b. Niagara Falls, N.Y., June 1, 1942; s. Earl W. and Eleanor M. (Mahoney) B.; m. Melissa May, May 26, 1990; children: Andrew MacLeod, Elizabeth Hendricks. BA in History, Syracuse U., 1971, JD, 1973. Bar: N.Y. 1974, U.S. Dist. (we. dist.) N.Y. 1974, U.S. Ct. Appeals (2d cir.) 1978. Assoc. Jaeckle, Fleischmann & Mugel, Buffalo, 1973-78, ptnr., 1979—. Bd. dirs., sec. Theodore Roosevelt Inagural site, 1999—. Author: (with others) Employment Discrimination Law, 1980—. Trustee Daemen Coll., Amherst, N.Y., 1988—; bd. dirs., v.p. Art Park & Co., Lewiston, N.Y., 1976—. Capt. U.S. Army, 1962-68, Vietnam. Decorated Bronze Star, Air medal, Army Commendation (2). Mem. ABA (labor sect.), Erie County Bar Assn. (bd. dirs. 2002--), N.Y. Bar Assn. (labor law com.). Office: Jaeckle Fleischmann & Mugel 12 Fountain Plaza Buffalo NY 14202 Office Phone: 716-843-3812. E-mail: tbrydges@jaeckle.com.

BRYFONSKI, DEDRIA ANNE, publishing company executive; b. Utica, NY, Aug. 21, 1947; d. Lewis Francis and Catherine Marie (Stevens) B.; m. Alexander Burgess Cruden, May 24, 1975 BA, Nazareth Coll., Rochester, N.Y., 1969; MA, Fordham U., 1970. Editorial asst. Dial Press, N.Y.C., 1970-71; editor Walker & Co., N.Y.C., 1971-73; from editor to v.p., assoc. editl. dir. Gale Rsch. Co., Detroit, 1974—84, from sr. v.p., editl. dir. to pres., CEO, 1984—98; pres. Gale Pub. Gale Group, Farmington Hills, Mich., 1999—2002; exec. v.p. Thomson Gale, Farmington Hills, 2003—. Author: The New England Beach Book, 1974; editor: Contemporary Literary Criticism, Vols. 7-14, 1977-80, Twentieth Century Literary Criticism, vols. 1-2, 1977-78, Contemporary Issues Criticism, vol. 1, 1982, Contemporary Authors Autobiography Series, vol. 1, 1984 Bd. dirs. Friends of Detroit Pub. Libr., 1980-89, pres., 1984-86; bd. dirs. Friends of Librs. U.S.A., 1995—. Mem. ALA, Assn. Am. Pubs. (chmn. libraries com. 1983-85, exec. council gen. pub. div. 1985-87, co-chmn. joint com. resources and tech. services div. 1983-85). Home: 546 Lincoln Rd Grosse Pointe MI 48230-1218 Office: Thomson Gale 27500 Drake Rd Farmington MI 48331-3535

BRYK, ANTHONY S., education educator; BS Summa Cum Laude, in chem., Boston Coll., 1970; EdD, Harvard Grad. Sch Edn., 1977. Instr. to asst. to assoc. prof. Harvard Grad. Sch. Edn., 1973—85; vis. assoc. prof. U. Chgo., Edn. and Sociology Dept., 1984—85; assoc. prof. to prof. U. Chgo, Dept. Edn. and Coll., 1985—2000; Marshall Field IV prof. U. Chgo., Dept Sociology, 1997—; fellow Stanford U., Ctr. for Advanced Studies in Behavioral Sci., 2002—. Founding dir. Consortium on Chgo. Sch. Rsch.; prin. investigator Ctr. for Rsch. Edn of Students at Risk, Johns-Hopkins U., Howard U. Recipient Sch. Reform Achievement award, Chgo. Assn. Local Sch. Coun., 1998, Philomethia Club Boston Coll. award, 1970, The Palmer A. Johnson award, Am. Ednl. Rsch. Assn., 1991, Willard Waller award, Am. Sociol. Assn., 1991—93. Mem.: Nat. Acad. Edn., Am. Statis. Assn., Am. Ednl. Rsch. Assn., Am. Sociol. Assn., Sigma Xi, Alpha Sima Nu. Office: Harvard U 1313 E 60th St 23A Chicago IL 60637

BRYNER, ALEXANDER O., state supreme court chief justice; b. Tientsin, China, 1943; m. Carol Crump; 2 children. BA, Stanford U., 1966, JD, 1969. Law clk. to Chief Justice George Boney Alaska Supreme Ct., 1969-71; legal editor Bancroft Whitney Co., San Francisco, 1971; with Pub. Defender Agy., Anchorage, 1972-74; ptnr. Bookman, Bryner & Shortell, 1974; Alaska dist. ct. judge Anchorage, 1975-77; U.S. atty. Alaska, 1977-80; chief judge Alaska Ct. Appeals, 1980-97; state supreme ct. justice Alaska Supreme Ct., Anchorage, 1997—2003, state supreme ct. chief justice, 2003—. Office: Alaska Supreme Ct 303 K St Anchorage AK 99501-2013

BRYNN, EDWARD PAUL, former ambassador; b. Pitts., Aug. 1, 1942; s. Walter Bruggeman and Mary Margaret (Callahan) B.; m. Jane Cooke, Apr. 1, 1967; children: Sarah, Edward, Kiernan, Anne-Elizabeth, Justin-Oliver. BS in Fgn. Svc., Georgetown U., 1964; MA in History, Stanford U., 1965, Phd in History, 1968; MLitt, Trinity Coll., Dublin, Ireland, 1968, PhD in Politics, 1977. Prof. history USAF Acad., Colorado Springs, Colo., 1968-72, 76-78; polit. officer Am. Embassy, Colombo, Sri Lanka, 1973-75, Bamako, Mali, 1978-80; staff mem. Senate Select Com. on Intelligence, Washington, 1981-82; dep. chief of mission Am. Embassy, Nouakchott, Mauritania, 1982-85, charge d'affaires Moroni, Comoros, 1985-87, dep. chief of mission Yaounde, Cameroon, 1987-89, amb. Ouagadougou, Burkina Faso, 1990-93; prin. dep. asst. sec. Bur. of African Affairs, 1993-95; amb. Am. Embassy, Accra, Ghana, 1995—98; internat. affairs advisor Nat. War Coll., Washington, 1998-99; assoc. provost internat. programs U. N.C., Charlotte, 1999—. Chmn. Charlotte World Affairs Coun., 2002—. Author: Crown and Castle, 1979, Church of Ireland, 1980. Lt. col. USAFR, 1990. Mem. Am. Fgn. Svc. Assn. Home: 3306 Lakewood Edge Dr Charlotte NC 28269 Office Phone: 704-687-2414. E-mail: ebrynn@email.uncc.edu.

BRYSON, GARY SPATH, cable television and telephone company executive; b. Longview, Wash., Nov. 8, 1943; s. Roy Griffin and Marguerite Elizabeth (Spath) B.; m. Bobbi Bryson; children: Kelly Suzanne, Lisa Christine. AB, Dartmouth Coll., 1966; MBA, Tuck Sch., 1967. With Bell & Howell Co., Chgo., 1967-79, pres. consumer and audio-visual group, 1977-79; chmn. bd., CEO Bell & Howell Mamiya Co., Chgo., 1979-81; exec. v.p. Am. TV & Communications Corp., subs. Time, Inc., Englewood, Colo., 1981-88; v.p. diversified group US West, Englewood, 1988-89, pres. cable communications div., 1989-92; pres., CEO TeleWest Internat., 1992-93; pres. SkyConnect, Boulder, 1994-96. Comm. cons., 1996—. Mem. Phi Beta Kappa, Sigma Alpha Epsilon. Republican. Lutheran. Home: PO Box 2097 Edwards CO 81632 E-mail: gsbryson@earthlink.net.

BRYSON, JOHN E., utilities executive; b. N.Y.C., July 24, 1943; m. Louise Henry BA with distinction, Stanford U., 1965; student, Freie U. Berlin, Federal Republic Germany, 1965-66; JD, Yale U., 1969. Bar: Calif., Oreg., D.C. Asst. in instrn. Law Sch., Yale U., New Haven, 1968-69; law clk. U.S. Dist. Ct., San Francisco, 1969-70; co-founder, atty. Natural Resources Def. Council, 1970-74; vice chmn. Oreg. Energy Facility Siting Council, 1975-76; assoc. Davies, Biggs, Strayer, Stoel & Boley, Portland, Oreg., 1975-76; chmn. Calif. State Water Resources Control Bd., 1976-79; vis. faculty Stanford U. Law Sch., Calif., 1977-79; pres. Calif. Pub. Utilities Commn., 1979-82; ptnr. Morrison & Foerster, San Francisco, 1983-84; sr. v.p. law and fin. So. Calif. Edison Co., Rosemead, 1984; exec. v.p., chief fin. officer Edison Internat. and So. Calif. Edison Co., 1985-90, chmn. of bd., CEO Rosemead, 1990-99; chmn., pres., CEO Edison Internat., 2000—. Lectr. on pub. utility, energy, communications law.; former mem. exec. com. Nat. Assn. Regulatory Utility Commrs., Calif. Water Rights Law Rev. Commn., Calif. Pollution Control Financing Authority; former mem. adv. bd. Solar Energy Research Inst., Electric Power Research Inst., Stanford Law Sch.; bd. dirs. Pacific Am. Income Shares Inc., The Boeing Co., Walt Disney Co. Mem. bd. editors, assoc. editor: Yale U. Law Jour. Past bd. dirs. World Resources Inst., Washington, Calif. Environ. Trust, Claremont U. Ctr., Grad. Sch., Stanford U. Alumni Assn.; bd. dirs. The Keck Found.; former trustee Stanford U., 1991. Woodrow Wilson fellow Mem. Calif. Bar Assn., Oreg. Bar Assn., D.C. Bar Assn., Nat. Assn. Regulatory Utility Commrs. (exec. com. 1980-82), Stanford U. Alumni Assn. (bd. dirs. 1983-86), Phi Beta Kappa. Office: Edison Internat 2244 Walnut Grove Ave Rosemead CA 91770-3714*

BRYSON, LOUISE HENRY, broadcast executive; m. John E. Bryson. Grad., Pomona Coll., 1993. Former sr. v.p., FX Networks; exec. v.p., distbn. & bus. devel. Lifetime Television. Past dir. & chmn. KCET TV, LA; past dir. So. Calif. Public Radio; dir. Investment Co. of Am. Vice chmn. J. Paul Getty Trust; mem. bd. councilors Annenberg Sch. for Comm., Univ. So. Calif. Office: Lifetime Television 309 W 49th St New York NY 10019*

BRYSON, NANCY S., lawyer; b. 1951; BA in History, Boston U.; JD, Georgetown U. Bar: DC. Staff atty., asst. counsel for appellate litig. US Dept. of Labor, Occupl. Safety and Health Divsn. Solicitor's Office, 1975—79; trial atty., asst. chief land and natural resources divsn. environ. def. sect. US Dept. of Justice, 1979—84; ptnr., natural resources and environment group Crowell & Moring LLP, Washington, 1998—2002, co-chair, biotechnologies practice; gen. counsel USDA, Washington, 2002—05. Vol. mediator US Dist. Ct., DC; lectr. in the field of environ. law. Contbr. articles in environ. law.

BRYSON, WILLIAM CURTIS, federal judge; b. Houston, Aug. 19, 1945; m. Julia Penny Clark; 2 children. AB magna cum laude, Harvard Coll., 1969; JD, U. of Tex. Sch. of Law, 1973. Law clk. to Justice Henry Friendly U.S. Ct. of Appeals, 2d Cir., 1973—74; law clk. to Justice Thurgood Marshall U.S. Supreme Ct., 1974—75; atty. Miller, Cassidy, Larroca & Lewin, 1975—78; asst. to the Solicitor Gen. U.S. Dept. of Justice, 1978—79; chief Appellate Sect., Criminal Divsn., 1979—82; spl. counsel Organized Crime & Racketeering Sect., Criminal Divsn., 1982—86; dep. solicitor gen., 1986—94; dep. assoc. atty. & acting assoc. atty. gen., 1994; cir. judge Fed. Cir., Washington, 1994—. Office: US Ct of Appeals for the Fed Cir 717 Madison Pl NW Washington DC 20439*

BRYSON, WILLIAM HAMILTON, law educator; b. Richmond, Va., July 29, 1941; s. William Alexander and Lillian Sutton (Wilkinson) B. BA, Hampden_Sydney Coll., 1963; LLB, Harvard U., 1967; LLM, U. Va., 1968; PhD, Cambridge (Eng.) U., 1972. Bar: Va. 1967. Asst. prof. U. Richmond Sch. Law, 1973-76, assoc. prof., 1976-80, prof., 1980—; Blackstone prof. law U. Richmond Sch. Law, 2001. Adv. com. on rules of ct. Jud. Council Va. Author: Equity Side of the Exchequer, 1975, Legal Education in Virginia 1779-1979: A Biographical Approach, 1982, Virginia Civil Procedure, 1997, Virginia Circuit Court Opinions, 1985—, Virginia Law Books, 2000, Samuel Dodd's Reports, 2000, Cases Concerning Equity, 2001; mem. editl. bd., asst. editor Am. Jour. Legal History, 1999—. William Senior scholar, 1970-72; Max Planck Inst. fellow, Frankfurt, Germany, 1972-73; Fulbright grant, 1963, Am. Coun. Learned Socs. grant, 1980; recipient Yorke prize Cambridge U., 1973 Fellow Royal Hist. Soc.; mem. Selden Soc. (Va. corr.), Va. Hist. Soc., Va. Bar Assn., Am. Soc. Legal History (bd. dirs. 1981-84), John Marshall Inn of Ct. (exec. com.), Phi Beta Kappa. Episcopalian. Office: U Richmond Sch Law Richmond VA 23173

BRZEZINSKI, ZBIGNIEW, political science educator, writer, former national security advisor; b. Warsaw, Mar. 28, 1928; came to U.S., 1953, naturalized, 1958; s. Tadeusz and Leonia (Roman) B.; m. Emilie Anna Benes, June 11, 1955; children: Ian, Mark, Mika. BA with 1st class honors in Econs. and Polit. Sci., McGill U., 1949, MA in Polit. Sci., 1950; PhD, Harvard U., 1953. Inst. govt. and research fellow Russian Research Center, Harvard U., 1953-56; asst. prof. govt., research assoc. Russian Research Center and Center Internat. Affairs, Harvard U., 1956-60; assoc. prof. public law and govt. Columbia U., 1960-62, prof., 1981-89. Dir. Rsch. Inst. Internat. Change, 1962-77; mem. faculty Russian Inst., 1960-77; dir. Trilateral Commn., 1973-76; asst. to pres.for nat security affairs, Nat. Security Coun. 1977-81; ofcl. Nat. Security Coun., 1977-81; counselor Ctr. Strategic and Internat. Studies, 1981—; prof. Nitze Sch. Advanced Internat. Studies, Johns Hopkins U., 1989—; mem. policy planning coun. U.S. Dept. State, 1966-68, Pres.'s Fgn. Intelligence Adv. Bd., 1987-91; mem. Joint Com. Contemporary China, Social Sci. Rsch. Coun., 1961-62; guest lectr. numerous pvt. and govt. instns. 1953—, participant internat. confs., 1955—. Author: The Permanent Purge-Politics in Soviet Totalitarianism, 1956, The Soviet Bloc— Unity and Conflict, 1960, Ideology and Power in Soviet Politics, 1962, Alternative to Partition, 1965, Between Two Ages, 1970, The Fragile Blossom, 1971, Power and Principle, 1983, Game Plan, 1986, The Grand Failure: The Birth and Death of Communism in the Twentieth Century, 1989, Out of Control, 1993, The Grand Chessboard, 1997, The Choice: Global Domination or Global Leadership, 2004; co-author: Totalitarian Dictatorship and Autocracy, 1957, Political Power: USA/USSR, 1964 (German edit. 1966), also numerous articles.; editor, co-author, contbr.: Political Controls in the Soviet Army, 1954; Editor, co-author, contbr.: Africa and the Communist World, 1963, Dilemmas Of Change In Soviet Politics, 1969, Dilemmi Internationazionali In Un-epoca. Teconetronica, 1969; columnist: Newsweek, 1970-72; co-editor: Russia and the Commonwealth of Independent States: Documents, Data and Analysis, 1997. Mem. hon. steering com. Young Citizens for Johnson, 1964. Recipient Presdl. Medal of Freedom, 1981, U Thant award, 1995, Order of White Eagle, Poland, 1995. Fellow AAAS; mem. Coun. Fgn. Relations. Clubs: Metropolitan (Washington). Office: Ctr Strategic & Internat Studies 1800 K St NW Washington DC 20006-2202

BRZOWSKI, BRIAN KEITH, plastic surgeon; BS in Biochemistry, U. Ga., 1984; MD, Med. Coll. Ga., 1988. Diplomate Am. Bd. Surgery, Am. Bd. Plastic Surgery. Commd. USAF, 1984, advanced through grades to major; resident gen. surgery Wilford Hall USAF Med. Ctr., San Antonio, 1988—93; ret. USAF, 1997; fellow plastic surgeon Mayo Clinic, Rochester, Minn., 1997—99; pvt. practice Ogden, Utah, 1999—. Mem.: AMA, Am. Soc. Plastic Surgery, Am. Coll. Surgeons, Utah Med. Assn. (mem. taskforce for office-based surgery 2001). Office: Brzowski Plastic Surgery 1525 E 600 S Ste C Ogden UT 84405

BRZOZOWSKI, RICHARD JOSEPH, retired artist; b. New Britain, Conn., Sept. 9, 1932; s. Joseph Peter and Genevieve (Sutula) B.; m. Dorothy Caruso, Jan. 19, 1956; children: Richard, David. Student, Paier Sch. of Art. Staff artist Miller, Johnson Co., Meridan, Conn., 1959-80, creative dir., 1980-90; ret. Mem. Am. Watercolor Soc. (corr. sec./2nd v.p. 1989—, bd. dirs. 1988-89), Copley Soc. of Boston, Allied Artist N.Y., Conn. Watercolor Soc. (bd. dirs. 1967-69), Nat. Soc. for Painters in Casein and Acrylics (bd. dirs.). Democrat. Roman Catholic. Avocation: fine art. Home: 13 Fox Rd Plainville CT 06062-1808

BRZUSTOWICZ, JOHN CINQ-MARS, lawyer; b. Rochester, N.Y., Feb. 1, 1957; s. Richard J. and Alice (Cinq-Mars) B.; m. Diane Day, Aug. 22, 1981; children: Richard Reed, Megan Day, Emily Day-Hanson. BA, Coll. Wooster, 1979; JD, Case Western Res. U., 1985; cert., Cornell Inst. Labor Rels., 1982. Bar: Pa. 1985, U.S. Dist. Ct. (we. dist.) Pa. 1985, U.S. Ct. Appeals (3d cir.) 1986, U.S. Supreme Ct. 1990. Asst. to dir. Inst. Am. Music U. Rochester, Rochester, 1979-82; assoc. Peacock, Keller, Yohe, Day & Ecker, Washington, Pa., 1985-88, Sable, Makoroff & Libenson, Pitts., 1988-90; pvt. practice Brzustowicz Law Offices, McMurray, Washington, Pa., 1990-94; shareholder Day, Brzustowicz & Malkin, P.C., McMurray, Pa., 1995—. Chmn. bd. dirs. Inst. for Am. Music of Eastman Sch. Music, 1997-2000; chmn. law libr. Washington County (Pa.) Bar, 1992; mem. com. Jud. Inquiry Bd., Pa., 1991-94. Co-author: Pennsylvania School Law, 1992, Pennsylvania Administrative Law, 1987; editor: So You Want to Be A Lawyer, 1990; advisor on PBC documentary: Life of Howard Hanson, An American Masterpiece, 1987. Pres. Newman Club, Coll. Wooster, 1976-79; v.p. Young Reps., Wooster, Ohio, 1977-79; co-founder, officer Wooster Polo and Hunt Club, 1976-79; bd. dirs. Hanson Inst. Am. Music of Eastman Sch. Music, 1996, Washington County Fund, 1998-2000, Pyramid Gallery, Rochester, N.Y., 1997—; mem. fin. com. JFK Sch., 1998—2005. Recipient Merit award Inst. Am. Music, 1981, Outstanding Scholar award Rotary, Albert H. Robbins award for Meritorious Svc. in Advancement of Am. Art, 2000. Mem.: KC, ATLA, ABA, Pa. Young Lawyers for Washington County (state rep. 1988), Washington County Bar Assn. (legis. com. 2001—), Allegheny County Bar Assn., Pa. Bar Assn. (del. 1992), Wash. C. of C., Peters Twp. C. of C. Roman Catholic. Avocations: reading, woodworking, biology. Home: 56 Mckennan Ave Washington PA 15301-3531 Office: 3821 Washington Rd Mc Murray PA 15317-2964 Office Phone: 724-942-3789. Personal E-mail: dexterdawg@aol.com, dandblaw@adelphia.net.

BRZUSTOWICZ, STANISLAW HENRY, dental educator; b. Bklyn., Apr. 30, 1919; s. John Stanislaw and Victoria (Szutarski) B.; m. Wanda Frances Seglow, July 3, 1949; children: Robert, Thomas, Michael, Linda. BS, St. John's U., 1940; DDS, Columbia U., 1943. Pvt. practice, Bklyn., 1947-74, New Hyde Park, NY, 1963-93; prof. clin. dentistry Columbia U. Sch. Dental and Oral Surgery, N.Y.C., 1946-87, prof. emeritus clin. dentistry (operative), 1987—; course dir. preclin. operative dentistry, attending dentist Presbyn. Hosp., N.Y.C., 1974—89; spl. lectr. in dentistry, 1990—. Bd. dirs., v.p. Prospect Pattern & Machine Works, Inc., Bklyn., 1962-72; bd dirs., sec. to bd. Atlas Savs. & Loan Assn., Bklyn., 1962-94. Contg. author Differential Diagnosis of Mouth Diseases, 1943 Served to capt. U.S. Army, 1943-46 Mem. ADA, N.Y. State Dental Soc., 2d Dist. Dental Soc., Nat. Med. and Dental Soc., Cath. Dentist Guild (joint program dental care for indigent children with Cath. Guardian Soc. 1949-54), Roger Bacon Sci. Soc., Kosciuszko Found., Holy Name Soc., Omicron Kappa Upsilon. Republican. Roman Catholic. Home: 58 Executive Dr New Hyde Park NY 11040-1014 Office: Columbia U Sch Dental and Oral Surgery 630 W 168th St New York NY 10032-3795

BU, RULEI, artist, educator; b. Shanghai, July 23, 1970; arrived in U.S., 1998; s. Xinnong Bu and Grace Gao. BFA, Shanghai U., 1993. Tchr. Shanghai U., 1993—98; artist Rockville, Md., 1998—2000; pres. A A Studio, Inc., Germantown, Md., 2001—. One-man shows include Rockville City Hall, 1999, Gaithersburg (Md.) City Hall Gallery, 2000, Strathmore Hall Arts Ctr., Md., 2000, NIH, 2000, Dumbarton Concerts Gallery, Washington, 2000, Rockville (Md.) Arts Pl., 2000, Glenview Mansion Art Gallery, Md., 2001, Kensington Art Gallery, 2002, Framer's Choice Gallery, 2001, 2002, 2003, 2004, Weinberg Ctr. Arts, 2002, Gaithersburg Arts Barn, 2003, Alvear Studio, Wash., DC, 2004. Recipient Clemente Family award, The Art League, Alexandria, Va., 2000, Marshall award, 2002, JoAnn Rose award, League of Reston (Va.) Artists, 2001, 1st pl. award, The Delaplaine Visual Arts Edn. Ctr., Frederick, Md., 2001. Mem.: Montgomery County Art Assn. (1st pl. 1999, 2001, 2004), Rockville Art League (1st pl. 1999, 2000, 2002, 2003), Gaithersburg Fine Arts Assn. (1st pl. 1999, 2000, 2001, Sharon Sage award 2003, 1st pl. 2004). Office: A A Studio Inc 13915 Schaeffer Rd Boyds MD 20841 Office Phone: 301-916-5991. E-mail: ruleibu@hotmail.com.

BUATTA, MARIO, interior designer; b. N.Y.C., Oct. 20, 1935; s. Felix and Olive B.; student Wagner Coll., 1953-54, Cooper Union, 1958-59, Parsons Sch. Design, Europe, 1961; Ph.D. (hon.), Wagner Coll. Asst. decorator B. Altman & Co., N.Y.C., 1959-61, Elisabeth Draper Inc., N.Y.C., 1961, Keith Irvine and Co., N.Y.C., 1962; pvt. practice interior decorating, N.Y.C., 1963—, works include: Protocol Offices of 1964 World's Fair, exec. offices Met. Opera House at Lincoln Center, N.Y.C.; dean of design Chgo. Merchandise Mart Design Community. Bd. dirs. East Side House Settlement, N.Y.C.; past bd. dirs. Kips Bay Boys Club, N.Y.C., Fashion Inst. Tech., N.Y.C.; work in process includes: redecoration of Blair House, the White House Guest House. Bd. dirs. Royal Oak, Nat. Trust Gt. Britain, The Hist. House Trust, N.Y.C.; chmn. Winter Antiques Show, East Side House Settlement benefit; hon. chmn. Cooper Hewitt Mus., Decorative Arts Soc. Mem. Am. Soc. Interior Designers. Designs included in numerous publs. Inducted into Interior Design Hall of Fame; Giant of Design award Ho. Beautiful Mag., 2002, Pratt Legend award Pratt Inst., 2003. Office: 120 E 80th St New York NY 10021-0306

BUBE, RICHARD HOWARD, retired materials scientist, educator; b. Providence, Aug. 10, 1927; s. Edward Neser and Ella Elvira (Baltteim) B.; m. Betty Jane Meeker, Oct. 9, 1948 (dec. Apr. 2, 1997); children: Mark Timothy, Kenneth Paul, Sharon Elizabeth, Meryl Lee; m. Mary Anne Harman, Sept. 9, 2000. Sc.B., Brown U., 1946; MA, Princeton U., 1948, PhD, 1950. Mem. sr. research staff RCA Labs., Princeton, N.J., 1948-62; prof. materials sci. and elec. engring. Stanford U., 1962-92, prof. emeritus, 1992—, chmn. dept., 1975-86, assoc. chmn. dept., 1990-91. Cons. to industry and govt. Author: A Textbook of Christian Doctrine, 1955, Photoconductivity of Solids, 1960, The Encounter between Christianity and Science, 1968, The Human Quest: A New Look at Science and Christian Faith, 1971, Electronic Properties of Crystalline Solids, 1974, Electrons in Solids, 1981, 3d edit., 1992, Fundamentals of Solar Cells, 1983, Science and the Whole Person, 1985, Photoelectronic Properties of Semiconductors, 1992, Putting It All Together: Seven Patterns for Relating Science and Christian Faith, 1995, One Whole Life: Personal Memoirs of Richard H. Bube, 1995, Photoinduced Defects in Semiconductors, 1996, Photovoltaic Materials, 1998; also articles; editor Jour. Am. Sci. Affiliation, 1969-83; mem. editl. bd. Solid State Electronics, 1975-94, Christians in Sci.; assoc. editor Ann. Rev. Materials Sci., 1969-83. Fellow Am. Phys. Soc., AAAS, Am. Sci. Affiliation; mem. Am. Soc. Engring. Edn. (life), Internat. Solar Energy Soc., Sigma Xi. Evangelical. Home: 753 Mayfield Ave Stanford CA 94305-1043 *I find no contradiction or conflict between science and Christian faith, but rather a marvelous compatibility that touches all aspects of life.*

BUBENCIK, JOHN WILLIAM, II, civil engineer, consultant; b. Little-Falls, NY, Apr. 24, 1958; s. William John and Dorothy Bubencik; life ptnr. Regina Marie Zamblauskas; 1 child, Stephanie Lynn Santoro. AS, Herkimer County CC, NY, 1979; BS, State U. at Albany, 1981. Engineering Level IV, Nat. Inst. Cert. in Engring. Tech., 2001, NETTCP-Concrete Technician, North East Tech., 2002, NETTCP-Hot Mix Asphalt Paving Inspector, North East Tech., 2001, NETTCP-Siols and Aggregate Inspector, North East Tech., 2001, cert. Nuclear Density Gauge, Field Safety Corp., 2000, Concrete, Am. Concrete Inst., 2001, Federal Railroad Adminstrn., Fed. RR Adminstrn., 1998, Railroad Crossing, Tex. A&M U., 1992. Laborer, driver I.L. Richer Co., Richfield Springs, NY, 1976—79; apprentice, elec., mech., archtl. Shadow Brook Farms, Schuyler Lake, NY, 1976—83; spl. projects coord. NY Susquehanna and We. RR, NY, NJ, Pa., 1982—87; ctrl. divsn. engr. Guilford Transp., NH, Maine, Mass., Conn., 1998—99; constrn. engr. Daniel, Mann, Johnson, Mendenhall and Harris, Milford, Conn., 1999—. Consulting engr. II Arch. Engrs. Conglomerate, Milford, Conn., 1999—. Fellow: St. Labre Indian Sch. (hon.), Disabled Am. Vets. (assoc.); mem.: Paralyzed Vets. Am. (hon.), Law Enforcement Officers Legal Defence Fund (assoc.), Help Hospitalized Vets. (assoc.), Nat. Police & Trooper Assn. (assoc.), Law Enforcement Alliance of Am. (assoc.), Am. Fedn. of Police & Concerned Citizens (assoc.), Concerns of Police Survivors (assoc.). Avocation: travel. Home: East Lake Rd PO Box 6 Schuyler Lake NY 13457 Office: DMJM and Harris Harborwalk 22 Broad Stt 2nd Floor Milford CT 06460 Office Phone: 203-410-0697. Home Fax: 203-874-2868; Office Fax: 203-874-2868. Personal E-mail: exavierII@37.com. E-mail: john.bubencik@dmjmarris.com.

BUBENIK, JAN, cancer researcher, biology professor; b. Brno, Czech Republic, Apr. 23, 1940; s. Jan and Terezie (Klimentová) B. MD, Charles U., Prague, Czechoslovakia, 1962; PhD, Acad. Scis., Prague, 1965, DSc, 1973. Sr. investigator Acad. Scis., Prague, 1965-72, chief dept., 1972—; dep. dir. Inst. Molecular Genetics, Prague, 1990—; assoc. prof. Charles U., 1992-95, Komenius U., Bratislava, Slovakia, 1993—. Vis. scientist Stockholm U., 1969-70, Cancer Ctr., Houston, 1992-93; vis. prof. Fibiger Inst., Copenhagen, 1985, 92; prof. cellular and molecular biology Charles U., 1995—. Contbr. over 230 articles to profl. jours.; mem. editl. bd. Internat. Jour. Oncology, Neoplasma, Gene Therapy, Jour. Cancer Rsch. and Clin. Oncology, Microbiologica, Jour. Exptl. and Clin. Cancer Rsch., others. Recipient State prize in medicine Czechoslovakia, 1985, Yamagiwa-Yoshida award Internat. Union Against Cancer, 1991, E. Nuti prize for cancer rsch. Assn. Promozione Study Immunology of Tumor, Rome, 1992. Mem. European Cytokine Soc., Internat. Endotoxin Soc. (charter mem.), NY Acad. Scis., European Assn. for Cancer Rsch. (exec. com.). Roman Catholic. Avocations: sport fishing, scuba diving. Office: Czech Acad Sci Flemingovo nám 2 166 37 Prague 6 Czech Republic Office Phone: 4202-20183234. Business E-Mail: bubenik@img.cas.cz.

BUBLÉ, MICHAEL, singer; b. 1975; Signed to 143 Records (Reprise), 2001. Singer: (albums) Michael Bublé, 2003 (double platinum, #1 in Canada), Down With Love Soundtrack, 2003, Let It Snow, 2003, Spider-Man 2 Original Motion Picture Soundtrack, 2004, It's Time, 2005, (CD/DVD) Come Fly With Me, 2004. Office: Reprise Records Warner Brothers Records Inc 3300 Warner Blvd Burbank CA 91505*

BUBLITZ, DEBORAH KEIRSTEAD, pediatrician; b. Boston, Feb. 28, 1933; d. George and Dorothy (Kingsbury) Keirstead; m. Clark Bublitz, June 1, 1958; children: Nancy B. Dyer, Susan B. Schooleman, Philip K. Bublitz, Caroline D. Bublitz, Elizabeth E. Bublitz. BS, Bates Coll., 1955; MD, Johns Hopkins U., 1959. Resident St. Louis Children's Hosp., 1959-60, U. Colo. Health Sci. Ctr. and Dept. Health and Hosps., Denver, 1968-74; pvt. practice Littleton, Colo., 1974—; asst. clin. prof. pediatrics U. Colo. Health Sci. Ctr. and Children's Hosp., 1975-87, assoc. clin. prof. pediatrics, 1987—. Creditials com. Swedish/Porter Hosp., Englewood, Colo., 1985-87, chief dept. pediatrics, 1985-87; med. assoc., advisor LaLeche League, 1975—. Author: (with others) Clinical Pediatric Otolaryngology, 1986. Fellow Am. Acad. Pediatrics; mem. AMA, Colo. Med. Soc. (women's governing coun. 1990-96, asst. chair women's governing coun. 1993-94, chair, 1994-95), Arapahoe Med. Soc., Am. Women's Med. Assn. Episcopalian. Avocations: painting, gardening, bird watching, grandchildren. Home: 5621 Blue Sage Dr Littleton CO 80123-2713 Office: Littleton Pediatric Med Ctr 206 W County Line Rd Ste 110 Highlands Ranch CO 80129-2319 E-mail: littletonpeds@uswest.net.

BUBRICK, MELVIN PHILLIP, surgeon; b. Chgo., June 2, 1944; m. Barbara Lynn Jacobs, Jan. 26, 1969; children: Jerome Bradley, Ellen Jeanne, Dena Beth. BA with honors, U. Ill., 1964, MD, 1968. Diplomate Am. Bd. Surgery, Am. Bd. Colon and Rectal Surgery; lic. Minn. Intern in surgery Univ. Hosps., Madison, Wis., 1968-69; resident in gen. surgery Hennepin County Gen. Hosp., Mpls., 1969-74; postdoctoral fellow colon and rectal surgery U. Minn. Health Scis. Ctr., Mpls., 1974-75; clin. instr. div. colon and rectal surgery U. Minn., Mpls., 1975-77, clin. asst. prof., 1977-78, clin. asst. prof. dept. surgery, 1978-80, asst. prof., 1980-87, assoc. prof., 1987—; chief surgery, program dir. surg. residency Hennepin County Med. Ctr., 1988-94; pres., CEO Hennepin Facility Assocs., 1995—2000, chmn. bd. dirs., 1991—2001. V.p. Mpls. Med. Rsch. Found., 1991-2000; chmn. bd. dirs. Hennepin Faculty Assocs., 1991—2000, CEO, 1991-2001. Author: (with others) Conn's Therapy, 1985, The Pancreas. Principles of Medical and Surgical Practice, 1985, Applied Therapeutics: The clinical use of drugs, 4th rev. edit., 1988; contbr. over 90 articles to Minn. Med. jour., Am. Surg. jour., Diseases of Colon and Rectum, Surgery, others. Bd. dirs. Mpls. Med. Rsch. Found., Inc., 1981-89. Mem. AMA, ACS, Am. Assn. Surgery of Trauma, Am. Soc. Colon and Rectal Surgeons (co-chair Self Assessment Exam. Com. 1984-85), Am. Soc. Microbiology, Assn. Program Dirs. of Surgery, Cen. Surg. Assn., Collegium Internat. Chirurgiae Digestivae, Soc. Surgery of Alimentary Tract, Minn. Assn. Pub. Teaching Hosps., Minn. Surg. Soc., Minn. Med. Assn., Mpls. Surg. Soc., Hennepin County Med. Soc. (mem. and chair various coms. 1975—, Hennepin faculty assoc. 1983—). Achievements include rsch. in assessment of bursting strength and healing of intestinal anastomoses, predictive value of surface oximetry in assessing healing in irradiated bowel, use of antibiotic microspheres for infected vascular grafts and peritonitis, clinical and anatomic assessment of first rib-clavicular decompression on subclavian catheters and pacemaker leads, influence of nutritional deficits in intestinal anastomotic strength, iron chelation with a Deferoxamine (DFO) conjugate in hemorrhagic shock.

BUC, NANCY LILLIAN, lawyer; b. Orange, NJ, July 27, 1944; d. George L. and Ethel Buc. AB, Brown U., 1965, LLD (hon.), 1994; LLB, U. Va., 1969. Bar: Va. 1969, N.Y. 1977, D.C. 1978. Atty. Fed. Trade Commn., Washington, 1969-72; assoc. Weil, Gotshal & Manges, N.Y., 1972-77, ptnr., 1977-78, Washington, 1978-80, 81-94, Buc & Beardsley, Washington, 1994—; chief counsel FDA, Rockville, Md., 1980-81. Mem. recombinant DNA adv. com. NIH, 1990-94, reduced risk tobacco products core com. Life Scis. Rsch. Office, 2005-; consensus panelist NIH Consensus Devel. Conf. on Effective Med. Treatment of Heroin Addiction, 1997; adj. prof. law Georgetown U. Law Ctr., 2000-02 Mem. editl. bd. Food Drug and Cosmetic Law Jour., 1981-87, 94-97, Jour. of Products Liability, 1981-92, Health Span: The Jour. of Health, Bus. & Law, 1984-95. Mem. adv. com. on new devels. in biotech. 1986-89, mem. adv. com. on govt. policies and pharm. R & D, 1989-93, Office of Tech. Assessment, Washington, mem. com. to study drug abuse medications devel. and rsch., 1993-95; mem. com. on contraceptive R&D, Inst. Medicine, Washington, 1994-96; trustee Brown U., 1973-78, 1998-2004, fellow, 1980-92. Recipient Disting. Svc. award Fed. Trade Commn., Washington, 1972, Award of Merit FDA, Rockville, 1981, Sec.'s Spl. citation HHS, Washington, 1981, Ind. award Associated. Alumni of Brown U., 1991. Mem. ABA (mem. spl. com. to study FTC 1988-89), Nat. Partnership for Women and Families (bd. dirs.). Office: Buc & Beardsley 919 18th St NW Ste 600 Washington DC 20006-5507 Office Phone: 202-736-3610. Business E-Mail: nlb@bucbeardsley.com.

BUCCI, THOMAS VINCENT, music educator, pianist, composer; b. Providence, Sept. 7, 1926; s. Vincent Anthony and Anna Bucci; m. Catherine Elizabeth Conway; children: Thomas, Anne Cignoli, Vincent, Kathleen Ball, David. Bachelor's degree, New England Conservatory of Music, 1951, Master's degree, 1961. Cert. tchr. Maine. Instrumental music supr. Portland Maine Sch. Dept., 1952—81; mem. piano faculty U. So. Maine, Gorham, 1971—. Organist St. Joseph's, Portland, 1965—. Composer: (work for viola and piano) Concertante, 1976, (chorus and piano composition) Three Sketches, 1978, (work for chorus and orch.) Four Longfellow Pieces, 1996, (orch. piece) Italian Folk Fantasy, 1987, (trumpet trio) Trio for Trumpets, 1979, (work for chorus and orch.) MASS, 1978. Accompanist Maine All-State Chorus; music adjudicator Music Educators Assns., 1965—90; mus. dir. Portland Lyric Theater, 1952—65; guest condr. Portland Youth Orch., 1965—75; piano soloist Portland Symphony, 1965—80. Staff Sgt. U.S. Army. Recipient commn. for chorus and organ piece, 1st Congl. Ch. on Meeting House Hill, 1978, commn. for brass quintet, R.I. Philharm. Orch., woodwind quintet premier, Kennedy Ctr. Mem.: Nat. Educators Assn., Maine Music Educators, Music Educators Nat. Conf., Italian Heritage Club. Home: 140 Abby Ln Portland ME 04103 Personal E-mail: tbucci@maine.edu.

BUCHAN, ALAN BRADLEY, rail transportation executive, consultant; b. N.Y.C., Mar. 1, 1936; s. Harold Bradley and Grace Viola (Lahrs) B.; m. Janet Lucille Riemersma, Feb. 20, 1960; children: Robert Michael, Richard Steven, Kathleen Ann. BCE, Norwich U., 1957; MLA, cert. in Hist. Preservation, U. Pa., 1992. Track supr. The Pa. R.R., various locations, 1964-66, indsl. engr. Phila., 1966-68; tng. supr. Penn Cen. Transp. Co., Phila., 1968-69; dir. tng. and safety Franklin Mint, Inc., Franklin Center, Pa., 1969-71; dir. mgmt. devel. N.Y.C. Transit Authority, Bklyn., 1971-72; sr. cons. Cole, Warren and Long, Phila., 1972-74, Transp. and Distbn. Assocs., Media, Pa., 1974-77, v.p., 1977-86, pres., 1986-89, TSD, Inc., Phila., 1986-89; v.p. transp. Day & Zimmermann, Inc., Phila., 1986-89; prin. Alan Buchan & Assocs., Mount Laurel, N.J., 1989—. Vis. lectr. U. Pa., 1993; open space program adminstr. County Burlington, N.J., 1992-98. V.p., trustee Whitesbog Preservation Trust, 1993-97; chmn. adv. bd. N.J. Historic Sites Coun., 1998-2005, bd. dirs., chair bldg. and grounds com. YMCA Camp Ockanickon; bd. dirs. Pa. R.R. Tech. and Hist. Soc., pres., 2003. Mem. Chi Epsilon. Republican. Episcopalian. Avocation: model making. Home: 785 Cornwallis Dr Mount Laurel NJ 08054-3209 E-mail: abbuchan1@comcast.net.

BUCHAN, DOUGLAS CHARLES, gas industry executive, government agency administrator; b. Bklyn., Aug. 4, 1936; s. Charles J. and Amelia P. (Petraca) B.; 1 son, Paul Douglas. Student, U. Fla., 1954—56. Pres. Buchan Gas Co., St.Petersburg, Fla., 1955-86, Buchan Oil Co., St.Petersburg, 1966-89, Grill Parts Distbrs., 1982-86, Site Mgmt., 1983—; dep. asst. sec. energy U.S. Dept. Energy, Washington, 1989—. Mem. U.S. Senate Bus. Adv. Com., 1984—, Petr Equipment Inst., Common Ground Alliance, Pinellas County Gas Bd., Pinellas County Plumbing and Mech. Bd., So. Bldg. Code Congress. Pres. Pinellas County Rep. Ivory Club; chmn. Pinellas campaign Reagan-Bush, Fla. campaign George Bus for Pres. 1st lt. U.S. Army, 1958-65. Mem. Internat. Code Coun. Energy Tng. Network, Nat. Oil Jobbers Coun., Nat. Liquified Petroleum Gas Assn., Nat. Assn. Fire Investigators, Nat. Fire Protection Assn., Fla. Petroleum Marketers Assn. (v.p.), Oil Fuel Inst. Fla (pres., chmn. bd.), St. Petersburg Yacht. Episcopalian. Home: 1067 42nd Ave NE Saint Petersburg FL 33703-5235 Office: US Dept Energy 1000 Independence Ave SW Washington DC 20585-0001 E-mail: buchandoug@msn.com.

BUCHAN, JONATHAN EDWARD, JR., lawyer; b. Mullins, S.C., Sept. 1, 1950; s. Jonathan Edward and Margaret Alice (Liles) B.; m. Suzette Rogers Phillips, Nov. 22, 1986; 1 stepchild, Geoffrey Eliot Eloge; 1 child, Caroline Phillips. AB magna cum laude, Princeton U., 1972; JD, Duke U., 1978. Bar: N.C. 1978. Co-founder, sr. editor, Osceola News Weekly, Columbia, SC, 1973—74; govt. reporter Charlotte Observer, Columbia, SC, 1974—75; govt. editor Charlotte (NC) Observer, 1983—84; ptnr. Helms Mulliss & Wicker and predecessor firms, Charlotte, 1984—. Mem. adj. faculty dept. mass media law Wake Forest Law Sch., 1992-2002; bd. dirs. Legal Svcs. for So. Piedmont, Inc., 1993-98. Co-author: 50-State Survey of Libel Law, N.C. Sect., 1981—; contbg. author: North Carolina Media Law Handbook, 2001. Pres., bd. dirs. Hospice at Charlotte, Inc., 1982-88; adv. bd. Trust for Pub. Land, Carolinas. 2001—. Mem.: Mecklenburg County Bar Assn. (pres. 2004—05). Avocations: fly fishing, tennis, reading. Home: 2342 Thetford Ct Charlotte NC 28211-3268 Office: Helms Mulliss & Wicker PO Box 31247 201 N Tryon St Ste 3000 Charlotte NC 28202-1157 Office Phone: 704-343-2063. Personal E-mail: Buchan247@aol.com. Business E-Mail: jon.buchan@hmw.com.

BUCHANAN, BRUCE, II, political science professor; b. Shelby, Mont., July 28, 1945; s. Neil and Dorothy Jean (Gallup) B.; m. Susan Safford Bright, June 10, 1964 (div. June 1976); m. Stephanie Ann Sokolewicz, Jan. 3, 1981; children: Kathryn Elaine, Douglas Neil, Jacqueline May. BA, Stanford U., 1967; MA, Yale U., 1969; MPhil, 1970, PhD, 1972. Prof. U. Ga., Athens, 1973-74, U. Tex., Austin, 1974—. Author: The Presidential Experience, 1978, The Citizens Presidency, 1987,Electing A President, 1991, Renewing Presidential Politics, 1996, Presidential Campaign Quality, 2004, The Policy Partnership, 2004. Exec. dir. Markle Commn. on Media and Electorate, 1988-90; rsch. dir. Markle Found. Presdl. Election Study, 1992, dir. Markle Presdl. Watch, 1996. Mem. Am. Polit. Sci. Assn. (award for best paper on presidency 1997), Presidency Rsch. Group. Avocations: cello, sports, gardening. Home: 1304 Wilshire Blvd Austin TX 78722-1127 Office: U Tex Dept Govt Austin TX 78712-1087 Office Phone: 512-232-7212. Business E-Mail: bruceb@mail.la.utexas.edu.

BUCHANAN, BRUCE G., computer scientist, educator; b. St. Louis, July 7, 1940; AB, Ohio Wesleyan U., 1961; MA, Mich. State U., PhD in Philosophy, 1966. Rsch. assoc. computer sci. Stanford U., Palo Alto, Calif., 1966-71, rsch. computer scientist, 1972-76, adj. prof. computer sci., 1976—; univ. prof. computer sci., prof. philosophy, intelligent systems and medicine U. Pitts. Mem.: AAAI, AAAS, Am. Assn. Artificial Intelligence (pres. 2000—01), NAS Inst. Medicine. Office: U Pitts Dept Computer Sci 205 Mineral Industries Bldg Pittsburgh PA 15260-3803

BUCHANAN, DAVID ROBERTS, medical educator; s. John and Roberta Buchanan; m. Lacinda Rene Hummel, June 28, 1997. MD, U. Chgo., 1996. Cert. Am. Bd. Internal Medicine. Dir. med. student programs John Stroger Hosp. Cook County, Chgo., 2002—04; head sect. social medicine John Stroger Hosp. Cook County, Rush U., Chgo., 2003—. Advocacy fellow, Open Soc. Inst., 2002—04.

BUCHANAN, EDNA, writer, retired journalist; b. Paterson, NJ; Journalist Miami Beach (Fla.) Daily Sun, 1965-70; became journalist The Miami (Fla.) Herald, 1970. Author: Carr: Five Years of Rape and Murder, 1979, The Corpse Had a Familiar Face: Covering America's Hottest Beat, 1987, Nobody Lives Forever, 1990, Never Let Them See You Cry: More From Miami, America's Hottest Beat, 1992, Contents Under Pressure, 1992, Miami, It's Murder, 1994, Suitable for Framing, 1995, Act of Betrayal, 1996, Margin of Error, 1997, Pulse, 1998, Garden of Evil, 1999, You Only Die Twice, 2001, Cold Case Squad, 2004, Shadows, 2005; contbr. articles to popular mags. Recipient Green Eye Shade award Soc. Profl. Journalists, 1982, Pulitzer prize for gen. reporting, 1986, George Polk Career award, 2001. Mem. United Ch. of Christ. Office: care Don Congdon Assocs 156 5th Ave Ste 625 New York NY 10010-7002

BUCHANAN, EDWARD A., education educator; b. Newark, Aug. 28, 1937; s. Osborne B. and Edna Dorothy (Weber) B.; m. Gladys J. Buchanan, Aug. 28, 1965; children Roger, Becky. AB, Rutgers U., 1959; MRE, N.Y. Theol. Sem., 1962; PhD, So. Bapt. Theol. Sem., 1970. Tchr. Ctrl. Sch., Middlesex, NJ; assoc. prof. psychology and edn. Grand Rapids Bapt. Coll., Mich.; dean acad. affairs, prof. Lancaster Bible Coll., Pa.; prof. edn., dir. continuing edn. Bethel Theol. Sem., St. Paul; sr. prof. edn. Southeastern Bapt. Theol. Sem., Wake Forest, NC, assoc. dean ministry studies. Author (handbook) The Bible, 2004, Christian Heritage, 2004; contbr. articles to profl. jours. Mem. APA, ASCD, Am. Ednl. Rsch. Assn., Nat. Soc. Study of Edn. Home: 1113 Silent Brook Rd Wake Forest NC 27587-7145 Office: Southeastern Bapt Theol Seminary 122 N Wingate Wake Forest NC 27587 E-mail: gedbuc@earthlink.net, ebuchanan@sebts.edu.

BUCHANAN, J. VINCENT MARINO, lawyer; b. Ft. Knox, Ky., Feb. 15, 1951; s. Robert Samuel and Jeanice (Moran) Buchanan; m. Gilda Lee; children: Thomas Marino, Maria Antonia, Kendra Marina. Student, U.S. Mil. Acad., 1969—71; BA, Bowling Breen State U., 1972; JD, U. Toledo, 1975. Lic. annuity life and health ins. agt.; bar: Ohio 1976, U.S. Dist. Ct. (no. dist.) Ohio 1977, U.S. Ct. Appeals (6th cir.), U.S. Tax Ct. Mng. atty., ptnr. Buchanan & Assocs., Risingsun, Ohio, 1976—; gen. ptnr. Real Estate Diversified, G.P. Sec., bd. dirs. Ohio Hispanic Inst., Bowling Green, Ohio, 1983—86; bd. dirs. Advs. Basic Legal Equality, Toledo, 1981—88. Mem.: ABA (exec. com. family law divsn.), N.W. Ohio Rivers Coun., Lions, Elks, Am. Legion. Roman Catholic. Home: 21148 Dunbridge Rd Dunbridge OH 43414 Office: Buchanan & Assocs 8500 Us Highway 23 Risingsun OH 43457-9632

BUCHANAN, JAMES MCGILL, economist, educator; b. Murfreesboro, Tenn., Oct. 2, 1919; s. James McGill and Lila (Scott) Buchanan; m. Anne Bakke, Oct. 5, 1945. BS, Middle Tenn. State Coll., 1940; MA, U. Tenn., 1941; PhD, U. Chgo., 1948; D honoris causa (hon.), U. Giessen, 1982, U. Zurich, 1984, George Mason U., U. Valencia, New U. Lisbon, 1987, Ball State U., 1988, City U., London, 1988, Lycoming Coll., 1992, Free U., Rome, 1993, U. Bucharest, 1994, Acad. Econ. Studies, Romania, 1994, U. Catania, 1994, U. Porto, 1995, U. Valladolid (Spain), 1996, Fuanceso Marroquin U., Guatemala, 2001. Assoc. prof. U. Tenn., 1948—50, prof. econs., 1950—51; prof. Fla. State U., 1951—56, U. Va., 1956—62, Paul G. McIntyre prof. econs., 1962—68, chmn. dept., 1956—62; prof. UCLA, 1968—69; Univ. Disting. prof. Va. Poly. Inst., 1969—83, prof. emeritus, 2000—; Univ. Disting. prof. George Mason U., 1983—99, prof. emeritus, 1999—; adv. dir. Ctr. for Pub. Choice, 1969—; assoc. prof. Francesco Marroquin U., Guatemala, 2001. Fulbright rsch. scholar, Italy, 1955—56; Ford Faculty rsch. fellow, 1959—60; Fulbright vis. prof. Cambridge U., 1961—62. Author (with C.L. Allen and M.R. Colberg): Prices, Income and Public Policy, 1954; author: Public Principles of Public Debt, 1958, The Public Finances, 1960, Fiscal Theory and Political Economy, 1960; author: (with G. Tullock) The Calculus of Consent, 1962; author: Public Finance in Democratic Process, 1966, The Demand and Supply of Public Goods, 1968, Cost and Choice, 1969; author: (with N. Devletoglou) Academia in Anarchy, 1970; editor (with R. Tollison): Theory of Public Choice, 1972; editor: (with G.F. Thirlby) LSE Essays on Cost, 1973; author: The Limits of Liberty, 1975; author: (with R. Wagner) Democracy in Deficit, 1977; author: Freedom in Constitutional Contract, 1978, What Should Economists Do?, 1979; author: (with G. Brennan) The Power to Tax, 1980, The Reason of Rules, 1985; author: Liberty Market and State, 1985, Economics: Between Predictive Science and Moral Philosophy, 1987, Explorations in Constitutional Economics, 1989, Economics and Ethics of Constitutional Order, 1991; editor: Better than Plowing, 1992, Ethics and Economic Progress, 1994; editor: (with Yong Yoon) Return to Increasing Returns, 1994; author: Post-Socialist Political Economy, 1997; author: (with R. Congleton) Politics By Principle, Not Interest, 1998; author: Collected Works of James Buchanan, Vols. I-XIII, 2000, Collected Works of James Buchanan, Vols. XIV-XIX, 2001, Collected Works of James Buchanan, Vol. XX, 2002. Lt. USNR, 1941—46. Decorated Bronze Star; recipient Seidman award, 1984, Nobel Prize in Econs., 1986. Fellow: Am. Acad. Arts and Scis.; mem.: Mt. Pelerin Soc. (pres. 1984—86), Western Econ. Assn. (pres. 1983), So. Econ. Assn. (pres. 1963), Am. Econ. Assn. (exec. com. 1966—69, v.p. 1971, dist. fellow 1983—). Achievements include development of the contractual and constitutional bases for the theory of economic and political desision-making. Home: PO Box G Blacksburg VA 24063-1021 Office: George Mason U Buchanan House Mail Stop 1 E6 Fairfax VA 22030-4443

BUCHANAN, JOHN DONALD, retired physicist, retired radiobiologist; b. Mesa, Ariz., Oct. 1, 1927; s. John Freeborn and Marguerite (Brimhall) B.; m. Donna Marie Smith, Aug. 27, 1955; children— Margaret MacNeil, John Michael, Andrew Tierney, David Brimhall. BS in Chemistry, U. Ariz., 1949. Diplomate Am. Bd. Health Physics. Sr. chemist Tracerlab, Inc., Richmond, Calif., 1950-59; staff assoc. Gen. Atomic divsn. Gen. Dynamics Corp., San Diego, 1959-62; mgr. nuc. applications and measurements Teledyne-Isotopes Inc., Palo Alto, Calif., 1962-71; mgr. applied rsch. Internat. Nutronics Inc., Palo Alto, 1971-73; supr. radiol. monitoring programs NUS Corp., Rockville, Md., 1973-75; sr. health physicist, radiochemist U.S. Nuc. Regulatory Commn., Washington, 1975-94. Author papers on radiation protection, radioanalytical chemistry, radioactivity measurements, radioisotope applications. Served with USNR, 1945-46. Fellow AAAS, Am. Inst. Chemists, Health Physics Soc.; mem. Am. Nuc. Soc., Am. Chem. Soc., Am. Acad. Health Physics, Phi Lambda Upsilon, Phi Delta Theta. Home: 7508 Dew Wood Dr Rockville MD 20855-1007

BUCHANAN, JOHN E., JR., museum director; b. Nashville, July 24, 1953; BA in English Lit. with honors, U. of the South, 1975; MA in Art History, Vanderbilt U., 1979. Exec. dir. Lakeview Mus. of Arts and Scis., Peoria, Ill., 1982-86; dir. The Dixon Gallery and Gardens, Memphis, 1986; exec. dir. Portland Art Mus., Portland, Oreg. Contbr. articles to profl. jours. Former bd. dirs. Peoria City Beautiful, Peoria Mayor's Commn. on the Arts and Humanities, Ill. Valley Pub. Telecomms. Corp., Arts, Culture and Entertainment Com., Chgo. World's Fair, 1992, Number Art mag., Memphis Visitor and Conv. Bur.; mem. art competition com. Nat. Civil Rights Mus., Memphis; adv. bd. Moss Lecture Series, Rhodes Coll., Children's Mus. of Memphis, Pub. TV and Radio, WKNO; bd. dirs. Internat. Festival; chmn. 1994 Annual Meeting, Southeastern Mus. Conf. Recipient Thomas W. Briggs Cmty. Svc. award 1990. Mem. Assn. of Art Mus. Dirs., Am. Assn. of Mus. (state rep.), Southeastern Mus. Conf., Am. Ceramics Circle, The Dixon Gallery and Gardens (life), Midwest Mus. Conf. (former program com. mem.). Office: Portland Art Museum 1219 SW Park Ave Portland OR 97205-2486*

BUCHANAN, JOHN LYNN, retired broadcast executive; b. Garland, Tex., Aug. 19, 1920; s. William Irl and Kathryn Raney Buchanan; m. Stella West, Oct. 31, 1947; children: John Lynn II, Elizabeth Ann Ashurst. Grad., Ryan Sch. Aeronautics, San Diego, 1941; student in engring., North Tex. State U.; student, U. Minn., NYU. Autopilot, radio-compass test engr. C5 Bombsight Sperry Gyroscope Co., N.Y.C.; B-29 aircraft field engr. Honeywell, 1943—46; assigned Pacific Air Svc. Command, Manila; B-29 tr. command 2d A.F. Hdqrs., Colorado Springs; instr. 313th, 314th, 315th, 73d, 58th & 509th wings in high level precision bombing technique using Honeywell autopilot and Norden bombsights B-29 XX A.F. Hdqrs., Guam, Tinian; indsl. sales engr. Honeywell, N.Y.C. and Phila., 1947—50; sta. mgr. KTLN, Denver, 1950—55; founder, owner Sta. KWBY, Colorado Springs, 1954; founder Sta. KSSS, Colo. Springs, 1955, Sta. KDAB, Denver, 1959, Sta. KKSN, Dallas-Ft. Worth, 1960; pres. Ameco Cable-TV, Inc., Phoenix, 1959—65; v.p. acquisitions Am. Cable TV (subs. Ameco, Inc.); founder Diversified Media Brokers, Dallas, 1966; ret., 1985. Contbr. poems to anthologies including Anthologies Internat. Libr. Poetry, Famous Poets (Bards of Burbank) and Noble Ho. London. Founding mem. U.S. Air Mus., Duxford, England, Smithsonian Udvar-Hazy Air & Space Ctr. Wall of Honor; docent Pima Air and Space Mus., Tucson; mem. Rep. Nat. Com., presdl. task force, 2004. Instr. pilots, bombardiers, flight engrs. USAF, 1941—46. Mem.: Ariz. Air and Space Assn., USAF Assn., Nat. Cable TV Assn., Nat. Assn. Broadcasters, Sigma Chi (life).

BUCHANAN, JOHN MACHLIN, biochemistry professor; b. Winamac, Ind., Sept. 29, 1917; s. Harry James and Eunice Blanche (Miller) B.; m. Elsa Nilsby, Dec. 11, 1948; children: Claire Louise, Stephen James, Lisa Renee, Peter Nilsson. AB, De Pauw U., 1938, D.Sc., 1975; MS, U. Mich., 1939, D.Sc., 1961; PhD, Harvard, 1943. Instr. dept. physiol. chemistry Sch. Medicine U. Pa., 1943-46, asst. prof., 1946-49, assoc. prof., 1949-50, prof., 1950-53; NRC fellow Med. Nobel Inst., Stockholm, 1946-48; prof., head div. biochemistry dept. biology Mass. Inst. Tech., 1953-67, Wilson prof. biochemistry, 1967-88, Wilson prof. emeritus, 1988—. Lectr. Harvey Soc., 1958 Mem. editorial bd.: Jour. Biol. Chemistry, 1961-67, Jour. Am. Chemistry Soc, 1961-72, Physiol. Revs, 1957-60, 65-71. Civilian with Nat. Def. Research Com., 1943; mem. subcom. blood and related substances NRC, 1951-55, mem. med. fellowship bd., 1954—; mem. sci. adv. bd. Boston Biomed. Rsch. Inst., 1975-93, Papanicoulaou Cancer Research Inst., 1975-81. Fellow Guggenheim Meml. Found., 1964-65; leave of absence to Salk Inst. Biol. Studies LaJolla, Calif. Mem. Am. Soc. Biol. Chemists (sec. 1969-72), Am. Chem. Soc. (Eli Lilly award in biol. chemistry 1951), Internat. Union Biochemists (mem. nat. com.), Nat. Acad. Scis., Am. Acad. Arts and Scis., Sigma Xi. Home: 56 Meriam St Lexington MA 02420-3622 Personal E-mail: enb@mymailstation.com.

BUCHANAN, JOHN MACLENNAN, Canadian provincial official; b. Sydney, N.S., Can., Apr. 22, 1931; s. Murdoch William and Flora Isabel (Campbell) B.; m. Mavis Forsyth, Sept. 1, 1954; children: Murdoch, Travis, Nichola, Natalie, Natasha. BSc, Mt. Allison U., cert. engring., 1954; LLB, Dalhousie U., Halifax, N.S., 1958; DEng (hon.), N.S. Tech. Coll., 1979; LLD (hon.), St. Mary's U., 1982; DCL, Mt. Allison U., 1981; LLD (hon.), St. Francis Xavier U., 1986; D Polit. Sci. (hon.), U. de St. Anne, 1989. Bar: Called to bar, created queen's counsel 1972. Pvt. practice, Halifax, 1958-71; mem. N.S. Legislative Assembly, Halifax, from 1967; min. public works, then fisheries; premier of N.S., 1978-90. Created Queen's Counsel, 1972; leader Progressive Conservative Party in N.S., from 1971; elected mem. legis. assembly for Halifax-Atlantic provinces gen. election, 1967, 70, 74, 78, 81, 84, 88, apptd. Privy Coun., 1972; apptd. to Senate of Can., 1990, bd. dirs. Legal Aid for N.S. Barristers Assn. Active Boy Scouts Am., pres. exec. oun., chmn. policy bd., 1978-90. Mem. Can. Bar Assn., N.S. Barristers Assn., Can.-U.S. Parliamentary Assn. (bd. dirs.), Royal Can. Legion, Buchanan Soc. of Glasgow, Scotland (bd. dirs.), Halifax Club, City Club, Lions, Masons, Shriners, Odd Fellows. Progressive Conservative. Mem. Progressive Ch. Can. Office: The Senate Ottawa ON K1A OA4 Canada

BUCHANAN, J(OHN) ROBERT, physician, educator; b. Newark, Mar. 8, 1928; s. John Hamilton and Elsie (Castles) Buchanan; m. Susan Townsend Carver, Oct. 27, 1962; children: Ross, Allyn. AB cum laude, Amherst Coll., 1950; MD, Cornell U., 1954; postgrad., Inst. Arthritis and Metabolic Diseases, USPHS, 1956—57, postgrad., 1960—61. Diplomate Am. Bd. Internal Medicine, Nat. Bd. Med. Examiners. Intern N.Y. Hosp., N.Y.C., 1954—55, resident physician, 1955—58, physician to outpatients, 1960—62, from asst. to assoc. attending physician, 1962—71, attending physician, 1971—76, assoc. dir. welfare med. care project, 1961—64; capt. U.S. Army Med. Corps, 1958—60; vis. asst. physician Rockefeller Inst. Hosp., N.Y.C., 1960—61; assoc. vis. physician Bellevue Hosp., N.Y.C., 1965—68; fellow Cornell U., 1956—57, instr. medicine, 1961—63, asst. prof. medicine, 1963—67, asst. dir. comprehensive care and teaching program, 1961—64, asst. to chmn. dept. medicine, 1964—65; assoc. dean Cornell U. (Med. Coll.), 1965—69, dean, 1969—76, clin. assoc. prof. medicine, 1967—69, assoc. prof., 1969—71, prof., 1971—76; pres. Michael Reese Hosp. and Med. Center, Chgo., 1977—82; prof. medicine Pritzker Sch. Medicine, U. Chgo., 1977—82, assoc. dean, 1978—82; gen. dir. Mass. Gen. Hosp., Boston, 1982—94, gen. dir. emeritus, 1994—; prof. medicine Harvard Med. Sch., Boston, 1982—. Mem. com. on sci. policy Sloan-Kettering Inst., 1969—76, State of Ill. Med. Determination Bd., 1980—82; adminstrv. bd. Coun. Tchg. Hosps., 1984—89; mem. composite com. U.S. Med. Licensing Exam sponsored by Nat. Bd. Med. Examiners, Fedn. of State Bd. Med. Examiners, and Ednl. Coun. Fgn. Med. Grads.; sr. program cons. prepaid managed health care program Robert Wood Johnson Found., 1982—85; bd. dirs. Charles River Labs., i-STAT, chmn., 1999—2003; trustee Ednl. Commn. Fgn. Med. Grads., 1989—96, vice chmn., 1992—93, chmn., 1994—96; bd. dirs. MetCare. Chmn. nat. adv. coun. Children's TV Workshop, 1974—75; trustee Cornell U., 1970—76, China Med. Bd. of N.Y., Inc., 1970—99, vice-chmn., chmn., 1989—99; bd. mgrs. Meml. Hosp., 1969—76; mem. adv. com. Edwin L. Crosby and W.K. Kellogg Found. Fellowships, 1979—80; trustee Ctr. for

Effective Philanthropy, 1981—85, Aga Khan U., Karachi, Pakistan, 1985—; mem. coordinating com. Boston Bus. Roundtable, 1994; bd. dirs. Pub. Health Rsch. Inst. of N.Y.C., 1969—76, Winnifred Masterson Burke Relief Found., 1972—80, 1982—88; trustee Goodspeed Musicals, 2002—. Fellow: APHA, ACP; mem.: Vol. Hosps. Am. (bd. dirs. 1990), Pvt. Industry Coun. Boston, Mass. Hosp. Assn. (chmn.-elect 1989—90, chmn. 1990—91), N.Y. Acad. Medicine, Ill. Hosp. Assn. (chmn. 1979—80), Inst. Medicine NAS, Assn. Med. Schs. N.Y. N.J. (trustee 1970—76, pres. 1972—76), Assn. Am. Med. Colls. (coun. deans 1969—77, chair elect 1975—76, mem. assembly 1976—77, exec. coun. 1985—89, coun. tchg. hosps. 1988—94, chmn. 1988—90, 1991—92, liaison cmty. med. edn. 1982—88, chmn. 1983—91), N.Y. Acad.Medicine, N.Y. County Med. Soc., N.J. State Med. Soc., Harvey Soc. Home: PO Box 669 5 Chestnut Hill Rd Killingworth CT 06419 Personal E-mail: jrobertbuchanan@aol.com.

BUCHANAN, LOUISE, political organization worker, consultant; d. James Ellis and May (Hall) Buchanan. BA, Blue Mountain Coll., 1958; MA, Carver Sch. Missions and Social Work, 1960. Exec. dir. Bapt. Good Will Ctr., Charleston, SC, 1960—65; comty. organizer Inner City Meth. Coun., Louisville, 1965—66; neighborhood coord. Comty. Action Commn., Louisville, 1966—71; supr. comty. resources Ky. Dept. Child Welfare, Louisville and Frankfort, Ky., 1971—74; exec. asst. to Rep. Jack Kemp U.S. Ho. Reps., Washington, 1974—76, exec. asst. to Rep. Joe Early, 1976—93; cons. child advocacy Washington, 1993—; mem. adv. bd. Efforts from Ex-Convicts, Washington, 1978—96; exec. bd. pres. Life Pieces to Masterpieces, Washington, 1997—; mem. adv. bd. Congl. Chorus, Washington, 1989—. Organizer Capitol Hill Staffers for Hungry and Homeless, Washington, 1976—93; trainer benefit walks For Love of Children, Washington, 1988; active Arlingtonians for Better County, 1997; mem. Common Cause, 1989—; coord. Capitol Hill Women's Polit. Caucus, Washington, 1976—83; mem., v.p. Park Spring Bd. Park Spring Condo Assn., 1999—. Recipient Keys to City of Worcester, Mass., Worcester City Coun., 1986, 1988, outstanding Svc. award, Efforts from Ex-Convicts, 1992, Leadership award, Life Pieces to Masterpieces, 2002. Democrat. Presbyterian. Avocations: music, writing, travel, tennis, being a loyal friend. Home: # 201 5075 7th Rd S Arlington VA 22204 Office: Consulting for Creative Change # 201 5075 7th Rd S Arlington VA 22204 Office Phone: 703-820-7293. Personal E-mail: lbuch44@msn.com.

BUCHANAN, LOVELL, entertainer; b. Ephrata, Pa., Mar. 22, 1949; s. Virginia (Eidemiller) Windham; m. Marie Veronica Sheetz. BS cum laude, Millersville (Pa.) U., 1977. Cert. tchr. Pa. Machinist Alcoa Corp., Lancaster, Pa., 1973-74; tchr. Manheim Twp. Sch. Dist., Lancaster, 1978-81, Downingtown (Pa.) Sch. Dist., 1982-83; tech. trainer Hamilton Tech. Co., Lancaster, 1984-88; pres. FunFoolery Prodns. Creator Dimmer the Million Dollar Robot, Prof. Funfoolery character, Chuckles the Clown (permanent collection Clown Hall of Fame, Delevan, Wis.), Whistling Willie, Chef Percy Produce, Juan D. Waiter, Monsieur Von Juggle; It's Magic, 1978, Optical Illusions, 1998 (permanent collection Ripley's Believe It or Not Mus., Atlantic City, N.J.); author: The Fun Foolery Book of Magic, 2002. With USN, 1968—72, Vietnam. Decorated Gallantry Cross. Mem.: World Clown Assn., Internat. Jugglers Assn., Soc. Am. Magicians, Internat. Brotherhood Magicians, Humane League (Appreciation award 1985), Epsilon Pi Tau. Republican. Home: 2726 Chapel Rd Lancaster PA 17603-5917

BUCHANAN, MARY BETH, prosecutor; BA, Calif. U. Pa., 1984; JD, U. Pittsburgh Sch. Law, 1987. Assoc. Strassburger, McKenne, Gutnick and Potter, Pittsburgh, 1987—88; asst. U.S. atty. civil divsn. (We. dist.) Pa. US Dept. Justice, 1988—92, asst. U.S. atty. criminal divsn. (We. dist.) Pa., 1992—2001, U.S. atty., 2001—, dir. exec. office U.S. Attorneys Washington, 2004. Mem. adv. com. U.S. Sentencing Commn., 2002—03; chair adv. com. U.S. Attys., 2003—04. Recipient Athena award, Pitts. C. of C., 2004, Susan B. Anthony award, Women's Bar Assn., 2002. Office: US Attorney 633 US Post Office & Courthouse Pittsburgh PA 15219

BUCHANAN, PATRICK JOSEPH, journalist, political commentator; b. Washington, Nov. 2, 1938; s. William Baldwin and Catherine E. (Crum) B.; m. Shelley Ann Scarney, May 8, 1971. AB in English cum laude, Georgetown U., 1961; MS in Journalism, Columbia U., 1962. Editorial writer St. Louis Globe-Dem., 1962-64, asst. editorial editor, 1964—65; exec. asst. to Richard M. Nixon, 1966-69; spl. asst. to Pres. Nixon, 1969-73; cons. to Presidents Nixon and Ford, 1973-74; commentator NBC Radio Network, 1978-82; columnist TV Guide, 1975—77; syndicated columnist NY Times Spl. Features, 1975-78, Chgo. Tribune-NY News Syndicate, 1978-85; White House Comm. Dir. Pres. Ronald Reagan, Washington, 1985-87; syndicated columnist Tribune Media Svcs., 1987-91, 93-95, Creators Syndicate, 1997—99, 2001—. Co-host Buchanan-Braden Show, Sta. WRC, 1978-83, columnist; co-host Crossfire (TV show) Cable News Network, 1982-85, 87-91, 93-95, 97-99; panelist The McLaughlin Group, NBC/PBS, 1982-85, 88-92, 97-99, 2001—, After Hours WTOP-TV, 1979-1982; moderator Capital Gang (TV Show) Cable News Network, 1988-91; co-host Buchanan and Press, MSNBC, 2002-2003; editor-in-chief newsletter PJB-From the Right, 1990-91; co-founder, editor The Am. Conservative, 2002—; candidate for Rep. Nomination for Pres., 1992, 96, Reform Party candidate for Pres., 2000; founder, chmn. The Am. Cause, 1993-95, 97-99, 2001—, Pat Buchanan & Co., Mut. Broadcasting System, 1993-95; polit. analyst MSNBC, 2003-. Author: The New Majority, 1973, Conservative Votes, Liberal Victories, 1975, Right from the Beginning, 1988, America Asleep, 1991, The Great Betrayal, 1998, A Republic, Not an Empire, 1999, Death of the West, 2002, Where the Right Went Wrong, 2004. Mem. Pres.'s Commn. White House Fellowships, 1969-73; v.p. Am. Coun. of Young Polit. Leaders, 1974-75, 76-79. Named Knight of Malta, 1987. Independent. Roman Catholic.

BUCHANAN, PHILLIP HOGE, lawyer, foundation administrator, educator; b. Pearisburg, Va., Dec. 17, 1960; s. Wiley Blake Jr. and Mary Ella (Hedrick) B.; m. Katharine Berkeley Bernard, Aug. 23, 1997. BS in Mgmt., Va. Tech., 1983; JD, Washington and Lee U., 1988. Bar: Va. 1988, U.S. Dist. Ct. (ea. dist.) Va. 1988, U.S. Ct. Appeals (4th cir.) 1988, U.S. Supreme Ct. 1992. Territory mgr., dir. health products info., dist. mgr. Mid-Atlantic div. Ralston-Purina Co., Charlotte, N.C., 1983-85; atty. Willcox & Savage, P.C., Norfolk, Va., 1988-92; officer, in-house counsel FCFT, Inc., Bluefield, W.Va., 1992; dir. will and trust programs, dir. planned giving, sr. dir. devel. Va Tech., Blacksburg, 1992—2001; pvt. practice Blacksburg and Charlottesville, Va., 1992—; sr. philanthropic advisor, atty. Duke U., Durham, NC, 2002—, dir. Office Gift Planning, 2002—. Judge Va. Acad. Decathlon, U. Va., 1999, 2000. Mem. fin. com. United Way of the Va., Montgomery County Christmas Store; bd. dirs., mem. fin. com. Va. United Methodist Found.; mem. devel. com. N.C. Meth. Children's Homes; mem. Durham Estate Planning Coun., Nat. Com. on Planned Giving, N.C. Planned Giving Coun, Duk U. Estate Planning Coun.; AF parent chair Durham Montessori Sch.; fin com. N.C. Meth. Children's Home. Recipient Am. Electric Power Co. Scholarship. Mem. ABA (mem. forum on constrn. industry, environ. sect., sports and entertainment law, young lawyers sect., litigation sect.), Fed. Bar Assn. (mem. transp. law sect.), Va. Bar Assn., Va. State Bar (young lawyers sec. 1988, vice-chair for S.E. regional trial competition), Norfolk-Portsmouth Bar Assn. (young lawyers sect., pub. rels. com.), Masons, Scottish Right, Shriners, Ducks Unltd. Methodist. Avocations: fishing, skiing, scuba diving, Karate, golf. Office: Duke Univ PO Box 90606 2127 Campus Dr Durham NC 27708 Office Phone: 919-681-0467.

BUCHANAN, RHONDA LEE DAHL, Hispanic literature educator; b. Alexandria, Va., Oct. 23, 1954; d. Ronald Lee and Dorothy Mae (Smith) Dahl; m. Robert Martin Buchanan, June 7, 1975. BA, Western Md. Coll., 1976; MA, U. Colo., 1978, PhD, 1982. Vis. asst. prof. Ind. U., New Albany, 1983-84, U. Louisville, 1984-85, asst. prof., 1985-89, assoc. prof., 1989—. Author: A Jungian Interpretation of El otoño del patriarca, 1982; contbr. articles to profl. jours. Mem. MLA, Assn. Colombianists, Ballet Español (bd. dirs., chmn. grants com. 1987-91). Office: U Louisville Dept Classical Modern Ln Louisville KY 40292-0001

BUCHANAN, RICHARD KENT, electronics company executive; b. Schenectady, Sept. 10, 1951; s. Richard Linton and Jeanette (Dunn) B.; m. Diane Carolyn Laffler, Oct. 14, 1984; 1 child, Lindsay Sarah. BSEE, USAF Acad., 1973; MBA, Harvard U., 1980. Commd. 2d lt. USAF, 1973, advanced through grades to capt., 1976; resigned, 1978; mgmt. cons. Bain and Co., Boston, 1979-82; corp. dir. strategy Gen. Instrument Corp., N.Y.C., 1982-84; mgr. strategic planning GE Med. Systems Group, Milw., 1984-86, mgr. mktg. magnetic resonance, 1986-87, product gen. mgr. magnetic resonance bus. unit, 1987-89; dir. strategic mktg. Motorola Communications Sector, Schaumburg, Ill., 1989-91; dir. internat. networks svcs. Motorola Land Mobile Sector, Schaumburg, Ill., 1991-94; v.p., gen. mgr. Am. Parts Divsn., Motorola, Schaumburg, Ill., 1994-97, Radio Products Group, N.Am. Divsn., Motorola, Rolling Meadows, Ill., 1997-2000; v.p., gen. mgr. Global eBusiness, Motorola, Deer Park, Ill., 2000—05; v.p. corp. tech. and devel, chief growth officer Harris Corp., Melbourne, Fla., 2005—. Contbr. numerous articles on time div. multiple access comm. systems to profl. jours. Scholar, NSF, 1968. Mem. IEEE, N.Y. Acad. Scis. Republican. Avocations: skiing, travel, art, swimming. Home: 1076 Aberdeen Rd Palatine IL 60067-4313 Office: Harris Corp 1245 NASA Blvd Melbourne FL 32919 Personal E-mail: rkentb333@aol.com.

BUCHANAN, RICHARD N., dean, dental educator; m. Patricia Buchanan; children: Jennifer, Brian. Grad., U. Tex., Austin; DMD, U. Pa. Sch. Dental Medicine, 1969. Dental officer US Mil. Acad.; pvt. dental practice; instr. Georgetown U. Sch. Dentistry, 1972—73; mem. faculty U. Tex. Health Sci. Ctr., San Antonio, 1973—89, chair dept. gen. practice, assoc. dean academic affairs, interim dean, spl. cons. strategic planing Grad. Sch. Biomedical Sciences; exec. assoc. dean NJ Dental Sch., U. Medicine & Dentistry NJ, Newark, 1989—91, acting dean, 1990—91, dean, 1991—96, Baylor Coll. Dentistry, Tex. A&M Sys. Health Sci. Ctr., Dallas, 1996—2000, dir. advanced clin. edn., 2001—02; sr. fellow Ctr. for Ednl. Policy & Rsch. Am. Dental Edn. Assn., Washington, DC, 2000—01; dean SUNY Buffalo Sch. Dental Medicine, 2002—, prof. restorative dentistry, 2002—. Reviewer Jour. Dental Edn. Fellow: Internat. Coll. Dentists, Am. Coll. Dentists; mem.: Am. Dental Edn. Assn., ADA, S.W. Acad. Restorative Dentistry, Omicron Kappa Upsilon. Office: SUNY Sch Dental Medicine 3435 Main St 325 Squire Hall Buffalo NY 14214

BUCHANAN, ROBERT MCLEOD, lawyer; b. N.Y.C., Oct. 4, 1932; s. Albert William and Elizabeth (McLeod) B.; m. Jane Vidaud Britton, July 6, 1957; children: Robert M. Jr., Jamy B. Buchanan Madeja, Stephen S., Genevra V. Buchanan Casais. BA, Dartmouth Coll., 1954; JD, Harvard U., 1959. Bar: N.Y. 1960, Mass. 1969, U.S. Supreme Ct. 1973. Assoc. Debevoise & Plimpton, N.Y.C., 1959-68; ptnr. Sullivan & Worcester LLP, Boston, 1968-2000, of counsel, 2000—. Contbr. articles on antitrust law to profl. jours. Moderator Town of Weston, Mass., 1980—, mem., chmn. fin. com., 1975-80; chmn. weston Hist. Dist. Study Com., 1973. With U.S. Army, 1954-56. Mem. Mass. Bar Assn. (ethics com. 1986—), Boston Bar Assn. (chmn. antitrust com. 1980-86), Harvard Faculty Club. Unitarian Universalist. Avocations: reading, guitar playing, kayaking. Office: Sullivan & Worcester LLP 1 Post Office Sq Ste 2100 Boston MA 02109-2129 Office Phone: 617-338-2861. Business E-Mail: rbuchanan@sandw.com.

BUCHANAN, ROBIN BYINGTON, school system administrator; b. Columbus, Ohio, Jan. 20, 1953; d. Eugene Clare (Stepfather) and Patricia Clark Battels, Robert Clifford and Betty Byington (Stepmother); m. Brooks Wayne Buchanan, June 28, 1980; children: Nathan Brooks, Daniel Clark. AA, Wingate Coll., 1972; BA, Meredith Coll., Raleigh, N.C., 1974; Masters, Appalachian State U., Boone, N.C., 1978; Ednl. Specialist, postgrad. in Edn., Western Carolina U., Cullowhee, N.C., 2003—. Cert. early childhood edn. tchr. N.C. Dept. of Pub. Instrn., 1974, prin. N.C. Dept. of Pub. Instrn., 1981, supt. N.C. Dept. of Pub. Instrn., 2003. Tchr. Montgomery County Schs., Troy, NC, 1974—75, Mitchell County Schs., Bakersville, NC, 1975—86, asst. prin., 1986—96, prin., 1997—2000, asst. supt., 2000—04, assoc. supt., 2004—. Ext. adv. coun. Mitchell County Agrl. Ext., Bakersville, NC, 2000—; bd. dirs. Mitchell County 4-H, Bakersville, NC, Mitchell County Communities in Schs., Spruce Pine, NC. Mem. Mitchell County Juvenile Crime Prevention Coun., Bakersville, NC, 1990; vol. leader Mitchell County 4-H, Spruce Pine, NC, 1994—2005; sanctuary choir mem. First Bapt. Ch., Spruce Pine, NC, 1988, children's Bible drill dir., 1993—2001, Sunday sch. dept. dir., 1994, Sunday sch. dir., 1996—2000, youth Bible drill dir., 2002, deacon, 2005—. Mem.: ASCD, N.C. Prins. and Asst. Prins. Assn., N.C. ASCD, N.C. Assn. of Sch. Administrs., Delta Kappa Gamma, Phi Kappa Phi, Pi Lambda Theta. Avocations: reading, walking. Office: Mitchell County Schs 72 Ledger School Rd Bakersville NC 28705

BUCHANAN, SIDNEY A., sculptor; b. Superior, Wis., Sept. 12, 1932; s. Sidney Allison and Dorothy Buchanan; m. Midori Marouka Buchanan, Apr. 16, 1971 (div.); 1 child, Patrick. BA, U. Minn., 1962; MA, N.Mex. Highlands, 1963. Prof. U. Nebr., Omaha, 1965—95. Lectr. Joslyn Art Mus., Omaha, Am. Inst. Architects; artist-in-residence Opera Omaha; mem. artist rev. panel Artists-in-Sch. Cmty., 1978. One-man shows include Sheldon Meml. Art Gallery, Lincoln, Nebr., 1971, Sioux City Art Ctr., 1976, exhibited in group shows at Neuberger Mus. Art, Purchase, NY, 2000, prin. works include sculpture, Omaha, 1975. With U.S. Army, 1956—58. Avocations: classical music, poetry, travel. Home: 1202 S 62d St Omaha NE 68106

BUCHANAN, TERRY LYNN, elementary school educator; b. Florence, Ala., Sept. 25, 1954; d. Orlan Kenneth and Mary Elizabeth Irons; m. Terry Lynn Buchanan, Mar. 12, 1976; children: Trent, Ty, Tucker. BS in Edn., U. N.Ala., 1975, M in Edn., 1979, cert. in edn. specialist, 1989. Tchr. Lauderdale County Bd. Edn., Florence, 1976—. Named 4-H Leader of Yr., Auburn Ext., Ala., 1983. Mem.: NEA, Ala. Edn. Assn., Lauderdale County Edn. Assn. (treas. 1994—99). Home: 197 Blaze Dr Florence AL 35632 Office: Brooks Elem Sch PO Box 9 Killen AL 35645

BUCHANAN, THERESA CARROLL, judge; b. Alexandria, Va., Aug. 27, 1957; BS, U. Va., 1979; JD, Coll. of William and Mary, 1982. Pvt. practice law, 1983-91; asst. U.S. atty. U.S. Dist. Ct. (ea. dist.) Va., Alexandria, 1991-96, magistrate judge, 1996—. Mem. Fed. Bar Assn., Va. State Bar Assn., Alexandria Bar Assn.

BUCHANAN, WALTER WOOLWINE, electrical engineer, educator, academic administrator; b. Lebanon, Ind., Oct. 6, 1941; s. Eugene Neptune and Amy Malvina (Woolwine) B.; m. Carol Ann Saunders, Dec. 28, 1968 (div. 1978); children: William Saunders, John Douglas; m. Charlotte Jane Drake, 1985. BA, Ind. U., 1963, JD, 1973, PhD, 1993; BS in Engring., Purdue U., 1982, MS in Elec. Engring., 1984. Bar: Ind.; registered profl. engr., Ind., Fla., Tenn., Oreg., Mass. Aerospace engr. Martin Co., Denver, 1963-64, Boeing Co., New Orleans, 1964-65; audit coord. Ind. Tax Bd., Indpls., 1970-73; atty. VA, Indpls., 1973-79; electronics engr. Naval Avionics, Indpls., 1979-86; asst. prof. Ind. U.-Purdue U., Indpls., 1986-93, U. Ctrl. Fla., Orlando, 1993-95; assoc. prof., chair Mid. Tenn. State U., Murfreesboro, 1995-96; prof., dean Oreg. Inst. Tech., Klamath Falls, 1996-99; prof., dir. Northeastern U., Boston, 1999—2005; prof. and J.R. Thompson chair Tex. A&M U., College Station, 2005—. Evaluator Accreditation Bd. for Engring. and Tech., Balt., mem. tech. accreditation commn., 1998—2003, mem. exec. com., 2004—; grants reviewer NSF, Washington; cons. in field. Mem. editl. bd. Jour. Engring. Tech.; mem. editl. bd.: Nat. Engring. Tech. Ednl. Clearinghouse, Internat. Jour. of Modern Engring.; contbr. over 100 articles to profl. publs. Faculty coun. Ind. U.-Purdue U., Indpls., 1989-92, exec. com., 1991-92; fundraiser Ind. U. Found., Indpls.; tech. com. Ind. Bus. Modernization Corp., Indpls., 1990-93; vestry St. Paul's Ch., Klamath Falls, Oreg., 1998-99; vestry King's Chapel, Boston, Mass., 2004-05. Lt. comdr. USN, 1965-69, Vietnam. Recipient Glenn W. Irwin award, Peter Marbaugh award Ind. U.-Purdue U. Indpls., 1988; Wright scholar Ind. U., 1961; Rsch. grantee Ctr. on Philanthropy, 1992, Fla. Engring. and Indsl. Experimentation Sta., 1993, NSF, 2004. Fellow: Am. Soc. for Engring. Edn. (exec. bd. ednl. rsch. and methods divsn. 1986—92, exec. com. engring. tech. divsn. 1994—, bd. dirs. 2003—05, internat. engring. tech. Listserv adminstr., past chair, Centennial award 1993, Frederick J. Berger award 2000, James H. McGraw award 2003, rsch. grantee); mem.: NSPE (educator, exec. bd., past sec., Profl. Engr. in Edn. award 1993, 1997), IEEE (sr.; com. tech. accreditation activities, past chair, press electronics tech. editl. bd.), Mass. Soc. Profl. Engrs. (pres. 2005), Engring. Tech. Coun. (exec. com. 2002—, chair elect 2004—), Indpls. Sci. and Engring. Found. (bd. dirs. 1988—92), Profl. Engrs. in Oreg. (pres. elect 1999, past chair engring. edn.), Soc. Mfg. Engrs. (sr.), Tenn. Soc. Profl. Engrs. (past chair engring. edn.), Fla. Engring. Soc. (past chair engring. edn.), Ind. Soc. Profl. Engrs. (past chair engring. edn.), Engring Tech. Leadership Inst. (exec. coun.), Ancient and Honorable Arty. Co. Mass., Univ. Faculty Club (bd. dirs. 1988—93), Scientech Club (bd. dirs. 1990—92), Order of Engr., Engring. and Sci. Hall of Fame, Phi Beta Delta, Delta Phi Alpha, Tau Alpha Pi (past pres.). Republican. Episcopalian. Achievements include systems test evaluation on the Apollo booster rocket. Home: 2240 Rockingham Loop College Station TX 77845-4854 Office: Tex A&M Univ Dept Engring Tech and Indsl Distbrn 3367 TAMU College Station TX 77843-3367 Business E-Mail: buchanan@entc.tamu.edu.

BUCHANAN, WILLIAM H., JR., retired lawyer, venture capitalist; b. Summit, N.J., July 2, 1937; s. William Hobart and Margaret R. B.; m. Eleanor A. Lincoln, June 18, 1966; children: Diana A., Jessica R. AB, Princeton U., 1959; LL.B., Harvard U., 1963. Bar: N.Y. 1964. Assoc. firm Shearman & Sterling, N.Y.C., 1963-70; v.p., sec., gen. counsel Reuben H. Donnelley Corp., N.Y.C., 1970-91, sr. v.p., chief legal counsel, 1991-97; asst. sec., assoc. gen. counsel Dun & Bradstreet Corp., N.Y.C., 1976-79, v.p., sec., assoc. gen. counsel, 1979-91, v.p. law, 1991-96, v.p. law, sec., 1996-97; pres. Spencer Trask Spin-Off Group LLC, 1998—2001; exec. v.p. Spencer Trask Intellectual Capital Co. LLC, 1999—2001; ret., 2001. Served with USMCR, 1959-60. Mem. Am. Soc. Corp. Secs. (pres. N.Y. regional group 1979-80, nat. treas. 1979-83, bd. dirs. 1983-86). Clubs: Princeton (N.Y.C.); New Canaan Field, Port Royal Club, Naples, Fl., Grey Oaks County Club, Naples, Fl. Republican. Presbyterian.

BUCHBERG, AKIVA, product designer, consultant; b. Tel Aviv, Jan. 3, 1953; s. Mordechai Marcus and Rachel (Resnick) Buchberg; m. Dominique Batsheva Dolo, Sept. 15, 1977; 1 child, Thomas M. Pres. Akido Ltd., Tel Aviv, 1977—86; pres. & COO Abaco S.A., Paris, 1986—91; chmn. & CEO Wrapco Internat. N.V., Curacao, Netherlands Antilles, 1992—2000; pres. & CEO B.I.H. Inc., Miami, Fla., 1993—2003. Active cons. M.G.A. Tech. Group, France, International Paper, United States, Israeli Aircraft Industries, Israel, Burger King Corp., United States, RayKay Inc., Japan, Cartier, Paris, Kabbalah Center Internat., many others, 1986—2003. Achievements include more than 250 U.S. and international patents; inventor products, new technologies for high speed machines. Home and Office: 1717 Ferrari Dr Beverly Hills CA 90210

BUCHBINDER, ELLEN MAUD, allergist; b. N.Y.C., 1950; MD, Tulane U., 1978. Diplomate Am. Bd. Allergy and Immunology. Intern New England Deaconess Hosp., Boston, 1978-79, resident Bsoton, 1979-81; with Mt. Sinai Hosp., N.Y.C. Asst. clin. prof. Mt. Sinai Sch. Medicine. Allergy & Immunology fellow Mass. Gen. Hosp., Boston, 1981-83. Fellow ACP, Am. Acad. Allergy and Immunology, Am. Coll. Allergy and Immunology; mem. AMA. Office: 111 E 88th St Ph B New York NY 10128-1173

BUCHELE, WESLEY FISHER, retired agricultural engineering educator; b. Cedar Vale, Kans., Mar. 18, 1920; s. Charles John and Bessie (Fisher) B.; m. Mary Jagger, June 12, 1945 (dec. 2000); children: Rod, Marybeth, Sheron, Steven. BS, Kans. State U., 1943; MS, U. Ark., 1951; PhD, Iowa State U., 1954. Registered profl. engr., Iowa, Calif. Jr. engr. John Deere Tractor Works, Waterloo, Iowa, 1946-48; asst. prof. U. Ark., Fayetteville, 1948-51; agrl. engr. USDA, Ames, Iowa, 1954-56; assoc. prof. Mich. State U., East Lansing, 1956-63; prof. Iowa State U., Ames, 1963-89, prof. emeritus, 1989—; ret., 1989. Vis. prof. U. Ghana, Legon, 1968-69, Beijing Agrl. Engring. U., 1983-84; vis. scientist Commonwealth Sci. and Indsl. Rsch. Orgn., Australia, Internat. Inst., Tropical Agr., Ibadan, Nigeria, 1979-80, Internat. Rice Rsch. Inst., Manila, 1991-92; cons. engr. Detroit Arsenal, Ordnance Corps, Waterways Exptl. Sta., Corps of Engrs., U.S. Steel Corp., GM, Detroit, 1974-76; bd. dirs. Farm Safety 4 Just Kids, Earlham, Iowa, Self-Help, Inc., Waverly, Iowa, JAC Tractor Co. Author 18 books; inventor 23 patents. Mem. Ames Energy Com., 1974-75; advisor Living History Farm, Urbandale, Iowa, 1965—, bd. govs., 1984—. Maj. U.S. Army, 1943-46, PTO; maj. Ordnance Corps, USAR, 1946-69, ret. Named Eminent Engr., Iowa Engring. Soc., 1989; recipient Outstanding Engring. award, U. Ark., 2005, Disting. Alumni 7th Coll. Engring., 2005. Fellow Am. Soc. Agrl. Engrs. (bd. dirs. 1978-80, McCormick-Case award 1988, Henry A. Wallace award for significant contbn. to agr. 2003, Outstanding Engring. Alumni award 2005), Nat. Inst. Agrl. Engrs.; mem. AAAS, Soc. Automotive Engrs., Am. Soc. Agronomy (mem. com. 1961-65), Steel Ring, Internat. Assn. Mechanization of Field Experiments (v.p. 1964-93), Internat. Platform Assn., Osborne Club, Toastmasters. Avocations: photography, travel, golf, inventing, writing. Home and Office: 239 Parkridge Cir Ames IA 50014-3645 Office Phone: 515-292-2933. Personal E-mail: wbuchele@msn.com.

BUCHEN, DAVID A., lawyer; b. 1964; BA in Philosophy, U. Calif., 1985; JD with honors, George Washington U., 1989. Bar: 1989. Atty. Fulbright & Jaworski LLP; corp. counsel Bausch & Lomb Surgical (formerly Chiron Vision Corp.), 1995—98; corp. counsel, sr. corp. counsel Watson Pharmaceuticals, Inc., Corona, Calif., 1998—2000, asst. sec., 1999—2002, v.p., sr. corp. counsel, 2000, v.p., assoc. gen. counsel, asst. sec., 2000—02, sr. v.p., gen. counsel, sec., 2002—. Office: Watson Pharmaceuticals Inc 311 Bonnie Cir Corona CA 92880

BUCHENROTH, STEPHEN RICHARD, lawyer; b. Bellefontaine, Ohio, Feb. 8, 1948; s. Richard G. and Patricia (Muller) B.; m. Vicki Anderson, June 6, 1974; children: Matthew Brian, Sarah Elizabeth. BA, Wittenburg U., Springfield, Ohio, 1970; JD, U. Chgo., 1974. Bar: Ohio 1974, U.S. Dist. Ct. (so. and no. dists.) Ohio 1974, U.S. Ct. Appeals (6th cir.) 1974. Ptnr. Vorys, Sater, Seymour & Pease, Columbus, Ohio, 1974—. Author: Ohio Mortgage Foreclosures, 1986, Ohio Franchising Law, 1990, also chpts. in books. Trustee, v.p. Godman Guild Assn., Columbus, 1977-83; trustee, sec. Neighborhood Homes, Inc., Columbus, 1977-85; mem. bd. rev. Worthington Pers., 1981—; pres. Worthington Alliance for Quality Edn., 1989-91; bd. advisors paralegal program Capitol U. Law Sch., 1991-2004; pres. chmn. bd. trustees Worthington Edn. Found., 1997-98; mem. Ohio Supreme Ct. Commn. on CLE, 1994-2000, chmn., 1999; bd. advisors C.H.A.D.D. of Ctrl. Ohio, 1993-97; trustee Wittenberg U., 2000—, vice chmn 2005—. Recipient Cmty. Svc. award, Legal Assts. Ctrl. Ohio, 1987. Mem.: ABA (forum com. franchising), Am. Coll. Real Estate Lawyers, Columbus Bar Assn. (pres. 1992—93, bd. govs., Bar Svc. medal 2000), Ohio State Bar Assn. (chmn. 2003—05, coun. dels., chmn. legal assts. com., bd.govs. real property sect., real property specialty bd. 2003—). Republican. Lutheran. Home: 2342 Collins Dr Columbus OH 43085-2810 Office: Vorys Sater Seymour & Pease 52 E Gay St PO Box 1008 Columbus OH 43215-3161 Office Phone: 614-464-6366. Business E-Mail: SRBuchenroth@vssp.com.

BUCHER, STEVEN JOHN, lawyer; b. Sioux Falls, S.D., July 17, 1955; s. Clifford and Eva M. (Scott) B.; m. Donna L. Hallberg; children: Bert S., Ellen L. BS in Social Sci. and Secondary Edn., Black Hills State Coll., Spearfish, S.D., 1978; JD, U. S.D., 1981. Bar: S.D. 1981. Ptnr. Miller & Bucher Law Offices, Plankinton, S.D., 1982-90; sole practice Plankinton, 1991—. Bd. dirs. Plankinton Devel. Co. Mem. State Bar S.D., Tri County Bar Assn. Democrat. Methodist/Roman Catholic. Office: Bucher Law Office 109 N Main St Plankinton SD 57368-2013

BUCHHOLZ, DEBBY, lawyer; Bachelor's, U Calif San Diego; JD, Harvard Law Sch. Gen. counsel John F. Kennedy Ctr. Performing Arts, Washington; gen mgr La Jolla Playhouse, La Jolla, Calif., 2003—. Office: La Jolla Playhouse 2910 La Jolla Village Dr PO Box 12039 La Jolla CA 92039

BUCHHOLZ, LEE WILLIAM (LEROY WILLIAM BUCHHOLZ), retired music educator; b. Nemaha County, Nebr., Feb. 3, 1937; s. Otto and Anna Buchholz; m. Lois Bremmer Buchholz, June 5, 1960; children: Renee, Erik, Heidi, Brad. BMusEd, Wartburg Coll., Waverly, Iowa, 1959; MusEdM, U. No. Iowa, Cedar Falls, 1971. Tchr. Orange Twp. (later consolidated with Waterloo Public Sch.), Waterloo, Iowa, 1959—68, Columbus Cmty. Schs., Columbus Junction, Iowa, 1968—98; adult literacy coord. Kirkwood C.C., Washington, Iowa, 1998—. Adj. faculty Drake U., Des Moines, 1983—2000, Iowa Wesleyan U., Mt. Pleasant, Iowa, 1984—2000. Mem.: NEA, Am. Choral Dirs. Assn., Iowa State Edn. Assn., Washington Area Habitat for Humanity (bd. mem. 2000—, pres.), Optimists (bd. mem. (Washington Iowa chpt.) 1998). Republican. Lutheran. Avocations: singing, theater, gardening. Home: 905 S 10th Ave Washington IA 52353-1305 Office: Kirkwood Washington Ctr 111 Westview Dr Washington IA 52353 Office Phone: 319-653-4655. E-mail: lbuchholz@lisco.com.

BUCHHOLZ, RONALD LEWIS, architect; b. Milw., Jan. 14, 1951; s. Raymond LeRoy and Della (Krause) B.; m. Mary Lou Stockhausen, May 20, 1972; children; Lauren Robert, Geoffrey Alan. BS in Architecture, U. Wis., Milw., 1973, cert. pub. mgr., 1995. Registered architect, Wis. Archtl. appraiser Am. Appraisal Co., Milw., 1973; plan examiner, bur. bldgs., structures Wis. Dept. Industry, Labor & Human Rels., Madison, 1973-76, staff architect, 1976, architect, adminstrv. code cons., bur. code devel., 1976-80, dep. dir., 1980-83, asst. dir., 1983-87, asst. office divsn. codes & applications, 1987-89, dep. divsn. adminstr. divsn. safety & bldgs., 1989-96, Wis. Dept. Commerce, Madison, 1996—. Instr. U. Wis., Madison Ext., also. state cert. courses for bldg. and dwelling insps.; mem. Wis. Bldg Code Adv. Rev. Bd., 1976-89, Fire Prevention Coun., 1978-89, adv. com. Alternative Energy Tax Credits, 1978, 80, Dept. Devel. Permit Ctr., 1984-89; mem. Interagy. Com. on Spills of Hazardous Materials, 1981-82, Flood Hazard Interagy. Coord. Coun., 1985-90; mem. adv. com. Wis. Elec. Supply, 1984-86; state rep. U.S. EPA Study Group for Underground Storage Tank Regulations, 1987-90. Author tech. reports. Vol. leader Boy Scouts Am.; coach Madison Area Youth Soccer Assn., 1984-87; basketball coach Madison Parochal Sch. League, 1984-95; mem. U. Wis. Cert. Pub. Mgr. Program Policy Bd., sec. 1999-2001, chair, 2002-. With U.S. Army N.G., 1970-76. Mem. Resdl. Facilities Coun. (exec. sec. 1976-78), Wis. Soc. Cert. Pub. Mgrs. (pres. 2000-01, bd. dirs. 1998—), Internat. Code Coun., Am. Acad. Cert. Pub. Mgrs. (pres. 2004), Nat. Eagle Scout Assn., KC. Roman Catholic. Home: 2587 Monument Ct Fitchburg WI 53711-5470 Office: 4th Fl 201 W Washington Ave Madison WI 53703-2760 Fax: 608-266-9946. Office Phone: 608-266-1817. E-mail: rbuchholz@commerce.state.wi.us.

BUCHHOLZ, TODD, journalist, social sciences educator, consultant; Degree econ., JD, Cambridge, Harvard. Pres. G7 Group, Inc.; assoc. dir. econ. policy The White House, Washington, 1989—92; mng. dir. Tiger Mgmt., N.Y.C.; econ. commentator (TV), contbg. editor Worth mag. Worth Capital Pub., L.P., N.Y.C.; tchr. econs. Harvard; journalist Wall Street Jour., Forbes, Reader's Digest. Advisor Soros Fund, Goldman Sachs, Tiger Mgmt., Pres.; lectr. in field; spkr. IBM, U.S. C. of C. Author: From Here to Economy, 1996, New Ideas From Dead Economists, 1999, Market Shock, 9 Economic and Social Upheavals that Will Shake the Financial Future, 1999; author Global Markets column Worth mag.; commentator PBS Nightly Bus. Report, ABC News, CNN; appeared on CNN, CNBC, CBS, PBS's Newshour, Firing Line with William F. Buckley, Jr.; contbg. editor: Worth mag. Named one of 21 Top Speakers of the 21st Century, Successful Meetings mag.; recipient Allyn Young Teaching prize, Harvard U.

BUCHHOLZ, WILLIAM JAMES, communications executive, educator; b. Ladysmith, Wis., July 17, 1945; s. James Fossegard and Hazel Winnefred (Crandell) B.; m. Dorothy Ann Kostka, June 17, 1967; children: Christopher, Jeffrey. BA, U. Wis., Eau Claire, 1967; MA, Ohio U., 1968; PhD, U. Ill., 1976. Grad. asst. U. Ill., Urbana, 1972-76; asst. prof. English, bus. communication, info. design Bentley Coll., Waltham, Mass., 1976-83, assoc. prof., 1983-91, prof., 1991—, dir. undergrad./grad. bus. communication programs, 1988-95, co-chmn. dept. English, 1993; chmn. dept. English, 1995-2000; cons. in corp. comm. and internet Waltham, Mass., 1978—; chmn. dept. info. design and corp. comm., 2001—. Mgr. pubs. Scholastech Inc., Cambridge, Mass., 1983-9; cons. in field. Author: Writing in Business and Manufacturing, 1998, Truth and Taste: Revisiting High Ethical Standards, 1994, Ontology, 2005; editor, author: Communication Training and Consulting in Business, Industry and Government, 1983; co-editor, contbr.: The Challenge of Change, Managing Communications and Building Corporate Image in the 1990s, 1989, Global Communications: Applying Resources Strategically, 1990; co-editor: New Corporate Relationships, 1991; contbr. articles to profl. jours., chpts. to books With USN, 1968-72. Grantee FIPSE, 1986, 87; fellow NDEA-IV, 1967-68, inst. fellow Bentley Coll., 1991-92. Mem.: Boston IA, Phi Sigma Epsilon. Roman Catholic. Avocations: personal computing, swimming, cross country skiing, reading, travel. Home: 44 Raffaele Dr Waltham MA 02452-0313 Office: Bentley Coll Grad Ctr 175 Forest St Waltham MA 02452-4713 Office Phone: 781-891-2216. E-mail: wbuchholz@bentley.edu.

BUCHI, MARK KEITH, lawyer; b. Salt Lake City; m. Denise Kimball, June 4, 1973; 7 children. BS, MBA, U. Utah, 1974, JD, 1978. Bar: Utah 1978. Divsn. chief tax and bus. Utah Atty. Gen. Office, Salt Lake City, 1980-83, asst. atty. gen., 1978-83; chmn. Utah Tax Commn., Salt Lake City, 1983-86; atty. Holme Roberts & Owen, Salt Lake City, 1986-88, ptnr., 1988-89, mng. ptnr., 1989-95, chmn. firmwide exec. com., 2000—01. Mem. tax recodification commn. Utah State Tax Commn., Salt Lake City, 1984-91; mem. Utah Govs. Tax Rev. Commn., Salt Lake City, 1991—; mem. exec. com. Multistate Tax Commn., Boulder, Colo., 1985-86. Mem. tax platform com. Utah Rep. Party, 1986. Mem. ABA, Utah Taxpayers Assn. (chmn. 1992, bd. dirs. 1990—). Mem. Lds Ch. Avocations: golf, water skiiing, fishing, gardening, carpentry. Office: Holme Roberts & Owen LLP 299 S Main St #1800 Salt Lake City UT 84111-2219 E-mail: buchim@hro.com.

BUCHIN, JEAN, psychologist, educator; b. NYC, Aug. 15; d. Mac and Celia Jacobs; children: Peter J., John D. BA, CUNY, 1941; MA, Columbia U., 1948; PhD, NYU, 1965. Tchr. NYC Pub. Schs., 1946—61; counselor, asst. prof. CUNY, 1962—84; mgmt. tng. cons. Met Life Ins. Co., N.Y.C., 1980—86; cons. assessment programs N.Y.C. Divsn. Pers., Sci. and Tech. Adv. Bd., N.Y.C., 1982—90. Mem. Nat. Bd. Cert. Counselors, Nat. Bd. Cert. Career Counselors; asst. prof. coord. Which Way With Women program Baruch Coll.; vis. asst. prof. NYU; cons. NYC Tchrs. Consortium; mem. Spkrs. Bur., Child Abuse Ctr.; cons. N.J. Human Resources Divsn.; career cons. AARP; lectr., leader workshops 53d St. Y., NYU, Queens Coll., A.W.E.D., leader workshops Marymount Coll.; mediator ABA; cons. Child Abuse Ctr. Author: Singular Parent, Noah's Ark Minus One. Washington Sq. Coll. fellow. Mem. AAUP, ACA, APA (pres. Tri State chpt. divsn. 35), Ea. Psychol. Assn., Met. NY Assn. for Applied Psychology, Bus. and Profl. Women, Career Devel. Specialists Network.

BUCHIN, STANLEY IRA, management consultant, finance educator; b. NYC, Sept. 7, 1931; s. K. and Bertha (Handman) B.; m. Jacqueline Thurber Chase, Sept. 14, 1957; children: Linda C., David L., Gordon T. SB, MIT, 1952; MBA, Harvard U., 1956, DBA, 1962. Asst. to treas. Bay State Abrasives, 1956-58; rsch. asst. Harvard Bus. Sch., 1958-59, rsch. assoc., 1959-60, instr., 1960-61, lectr., 1961-62, asst. prof., 1962-66, assoc. prof., 1966-69; pres. Applied Decision Sys., Wellesley, Mass., 1969-78; v.p. Temple, Barker & Sloane, Inc., Lexington, Mass., 1975-80, sr. v.p., 1980-90; prin. Arthur D. Little, 1991-99. Pres. Boston-Bermuda Cruising Ltd., 1992-97, Gen. Ship Cruising Corp., 1994-97; vis. lectr. Templeton Coll. Oxford (Eng.), 1991-93; prof. Arthur D. Little Sch. Mgmt., 1992—; assoc. prof. Boston U., 1997—; chmn. acad. policy com. Met. Coll., long-range planning com. Mass. Sch. Profl. Psychology. Author: E-Book about Business Strategy, 2000, E-Book about Marketing, 2001. Trustee, chmn. long range planning com. Mass. Sch. Profl. Psychology. With Chem. Corps, U.S. Army, 1952-54; bd. dirs., Barbin-Harper LLC, 2003—; bd. advisors Earthwatch. IBM fellow, 1962-63; George F. Baker scholar, 1956. Mem. Am. Mktg. Assn., Inst. Mgmt. Sci., Fin. Mgmt. Assn., Harvard Club Boston, Tau Beta Pi. Republican. Congregationalist. Home: Union Wharf # 304 Boston MA 02109-1206 Office: 808 Commonwealth Ave Boston MA 02215-1206 Office Phone: 617-353-0932. Business E-Mail: sbuchin@bu.edu.

BUCHMAN, KENNETH WILLIAM, lawyer; b. Plant City, Fla., Nov. 20, 1956; s. Paul Sidney and Beryle (Solomon) B.; m. MarDee H. Buchman, May 9, 1985; 1 child, Katherine Elizabeth. AA, U. Fla., 1976, BBA, 1978, JD, 1981. Bar: Fla. 1981; U.S. Dist. Ct. (Mid. dist.) Fla. 1981; U.S. Ct. Appeals (11th cir.) 1986; U.S. Supreme Ct. 1988; bd. cert. city, county, local govt. law., 1996. Ptnr. Buchman and Buchman, Plant City, 1981-85, Buchman and Buchman, PA, Plant City, 1985-91; pvt. practice Plant City, 1991-2000; asst. city atty. City of Plant City, 1982-91, city atty., 1991—. City atty. San Antonio, Fla., 1995-2000; mem. exec. coun. city, county and local govt. law sect. Fla. Bar., 1997—2005, chair, 2003-04; cle com. Fla. Bar Assn., 2004—. Mem.: Plant City Bar Assn., Fla. Mcpl. Attys. Assn. (steering com. 1999—2002, exec. bd. 2002—04, treas. 2004—), Kiwanis Club of Plant City (pres. 1986—87), Masons. Jewish. Office: 302 W Reynolds St Plant City FL 33566-3314

BUCHMAN, M. ABRAHAM, lawyer; b. Bklyn., Oct. 25, 1916; s. Judah Louis and Augusta Buchman; m. Ann P. Buchman, July 25, 1950; 1 child, Amy. BA cum laude, NYU, 1935; LLB cum laude, St. Lawrence U., 1938, JSD summa cum laude, 1939. Bar: N.Y. 1939, U.S. Dist. Ct. (so. dist.) N.Y. 1946, U.S. Ct. Appeals 1949, Supreme Ct. U.S. 1964. Plant mgr., contr. Atlas Import & Export Co., 1931-39; ptnr. Buchman & O'Brien, N.Y.C., Washington, 1940—, San Francisco; owner Buchman Law Offices, Edison, NJ. Cons. to sec. USAF, 1946-52; cons. to State Dept. at various meetings Coun. of Europe on prep. of conv. for wines and spirits; cons. Am. Wine Assn., 1993—, Vermouth Inst., Inc., 1943-64, Internat. Vermouth Inst., 1964—, Fedn. Italiana Industriali, Produttori ed Esportatori di Vini, Acquavit, Liquori, Sciroppi, Aceti ed Affini, 1962—; Am. Beverage Alcohol Assn., 1963—. Maj. USAF, 1942-46. Fellowship in adminstrv. law named in his honor Columbia U. Law Sch., 1985—. Mem. ABA, FBA (pres. Empire State chpt. 1995-97), Assn. ICC Practitioners, Fed. Bar Coun., Internat. Bar Assn., Phi Beta Kappa. Home: 5301 Woodlands Blvd Tamarac FL 33319-3025 Office: Buchman & O'Brien LLP 10 E 40th St Rm 708 New York NY 10016-0200 also: 1331 Pennsylvania Ave NW Washington DC 20004-1710 also: 505 Sansome St San Francisco CA 94111-3106

BUCHMAN, MARK EDWARD, bank executive; b. Caldwell, N.J., June 19, 1937; s. Samuel Joseph and Dorothy Eunice (Friedland) B.; m. Mary Angela Dolan, June 6, 1964 (div. 1991); children: Jennifer Ann, Romy Ellen; m. Arletta Martin, Mar. 18, 2002. BS, U. Pa., 1959; AMP, Harvard U., 1977. Sr. v.p., dep. gen. mgr. Mfrs. Hanover Trust Co., N.Y.C., 1962-82; exec. v.p. Union Bank, Los Angeles, 1982-88; pres. Govt. Nat. Mortgage Assn., Washington, 1988-89; prin. Buchman & Assocs., 1989-90; pres., CEO Bank of L.A., 1990-92, Liberty Bank, Honolulu, 1993-94. Mem. pres.'s council U. Pa., 1984—; Pacific Asia Mus., Pasadena, Calif., 1983-85. Served to lt. (j.g.) USN, 1959-62. Mem. Coun. on Fgn. Rels., Japan-Am. Soc. So. Calif. (pres.), Calif. Bankers Assn. (pres. 1986-87), Assn. Res. City Bankers, Calif. Club, Vintage Club, Bel-Air Country Club. Republican. Avocations: tennis, skiing, golf, bridge. Home: 225 Delfern Dr Los Angeles CA 90077-3544 Office Phone: 310-472-4677. Personal E-mail: shibuihito@aol.com.

BUCHMAN, SETH BARRY, lawyer, publishing executive, columnist; b. N.Y.C., Jan. 4, 1955; s. Lewis Charles and Mari Lynn (Wahrman) B.; m. Blaise Hughes Miller, June 14, 1980. BA in English, Hobart Coll., 1977; JD, Bklyn. Law Sch., 1981. Bar: N.Y. 1982. Pvt. practice, N.Y., 1982—; pub. Stare Decisis, N.Y., 1982—. Mem. ABA (award 1981), Assn. Trial Lawyers Am. (essay award 1981). Avocations: painting, sculpting, gardening, songwriting.

BUCHMANN, ALAN PAUL, lawyer; b. Yonkers, NY, Sept. 5, 1934; s. Paul John and Jessie Gow (Perkins) B.; m. Lizabeth Ann Moody, Sept. 5, 1959. BA summa cum laude, Yale U., 1956; postgrad, U. Munich, 1956-57; LLB, Yale U., 1960. Bar: Ohio 1960, U.S. Dist. Ct. (no. dist.) Ohio 1963, U.S. Ct. Appeals (6th cir.) 1968, U.S. Supreme Ct. 1977, Fla. 1996. Assoc. Squire, Sanders & Dempsey, Cleve., 1960-70, ptnr., 1970-96; pvt. practice St. Petersburg, Fla. Contbr. articles to profl. jours. State chmn. Ohio Young reps., 1970-71, nat. committeeman, 1971-74; exec. com. Cuyahoga County Reps., 1969-95, fin. com., 1987-94; mem. Selective svc. Bd., 1967-75; trustee Cleve. Internat. Program, 1979-82, 94-95; pres. English Speaking Union, 1981-83. Recipient Robert A. Taft award Young Reps., 1969, Outstanding State Chmn. award, 1971, James A. Rhodes award, 1974; Fulbright fellow U. Munich, 1956-57. Mem. ABA (chmn. pub. utility law sect. 1989-90, sect. del. 1996—, coord. com. on legal edn. 1991-97, nominating com. 2003—, mem. credentials com. 2004—), Fla. Bar Assn., Ohio State Bar Assn., St. Petersburg Bar Assn., Hillsborough County Bar Assn. Office Phone: 727-363-3026. E-mail: bbuchmann1@aol.com.

BUCHMANN, MOLLY O'BANION, choreographer, educator; b. Baton Rouge, Nov. 22, 1949; d. James Dennis and Annie Laurie (Joffrion) O'Banion; m. Fred J. Buchmann, Aug. 23, 1969; children: F. Jason (dec.), Dennis Andrew. BS in Secondary Edn., La. State U., 1971, MS in Dance, 1973. Artistic dir. Baton Rouge Ballet Theatre, 1976—; choreographer Baton Rouge Little Theatre, 1983—; tchr. dance Baton Rouge Magnet H.S., 1979-85; owner, mgr. The Dancers' Workshop, Baton Rouge, 1973—; dir. dance Scotlandville Magnet H.S., 1986-98; dance dir., profl.-in-residence dept. theatre La. State U., Baton Rouge, 1999—. Vis. artist Arts and Humanities Council of Greater Baton Rouge, 1976; choreographer Aubin Lane Dinner Theatre, Baton Rouge, 1980-82; mem. cultural caucus steering com. La. State Div. of Arts, cons., 1986. Editor La. Dance News, 1976-77. Choreographer numerous ballets. State of La. Div. Arts Choreographic grantee, 1982; Baton Rouge Alumni Fedn. scholar, 1967; recipient Mayor-Pres.'s award for excellence in the arts. Mem. Southwest Regional Ballet Assn. (bd. dirs., sec. 1984-88, parliamentarian 1993). Democrat. Roman Catholic. Office: Baton Rouge Ballet Theatre PO Box 82288 Baton Rouge LA 70884-2288 Business E-Mail: mbuchm1@lsu.edu.

BUCHSBAUM, KAREN FUSON, public relations executive, consultant; b. New Bern, N.C., Dec. 26, 1953; d. Robert Henderson and Amelia Carmen Fuson; m. Frederick Joel Buchsbaum, Nov. 23, 1979; 1 child, Ashley. BS in Comms., U. Tenn., Knoxville, 1975. Asst. dir., pub. info. dir. Greater Tampa (Fla.) Bicentennial Coun., 1975-76; dir. pub. rels. St. Francis Hosp., Miami Beach, Fla., 1977-79; dir. advt., comms. and pub. rels. Cedars Med. Ctr., Miami, Fla., 1979-84; prin., co-owner Comms. Strategies, Inc., Coral Gables, Fla., 1984—2002; comm. cons., 2002—. Bd. visitors U. Tenn. Coll. Comms., Knoxville, 1987—; mem. pub. rels. adv. coun. U. Miami, Coral Gables, 1997-2002. Advisor Crime Watch Am., 1994-95; pres. Epilepsy Found. South Fla., Miami, 2000-2002; pres. Carver Elem. Sch. PTA, Coral Gables, 1992-93; participant Leadership Miami, 1984; pub. rels. chair spl. events Gulliver Schs. Parents Assn., 2001-03; pub. rels. chair charity golf tournament Kidney Found. South Fla., 2002. Recipient award Nat. Health Info. Coun., 1999,2000, Pub. Rels. award, 1988-94, 98—, Fla. Hosp. Assn., 1978, 80, 81, 82, 83, 84, 86, 88, 89, 91, 92, 93, 96, 97, 98, 99, 2000, touchstone award Am. Soc. Hosp. Mktg. and Pub. Rels., 1986, Health and Medicine award for direct mktg. videos Telly Awards, 2000, Cardiovascular Comms. award Am. Heart Assn., 1998, 99, Healthcare Mktg. Report awards 1988, 89, 90, 91, 92, 93, 94, 98, 99, 2000, 2001. Fellow Pub. Rels. Soc. Am. (accredited, chmn. Sunshine dist. 1989, pres. Miami chpt. 1983, MacEachern award 1986), South Fla. Hosp. Pub. Rels. and Mktg. Assn. (pres. 1979), Fla. Soc. for Healthcare Pub. Rels. and Mktg. (bd. dirs. 1979-84). Avocations: travel, reading, antiques, golf, dance. Home: 13627 Deering Bay Dr # 804 Coral Gables FL 33158

BUCHSBAUM, NORMAN ROBERT, lawyer; b. Mt. Vernon, N.Y., Sept. 25, 1941; s. Abraham and Sophie (Forrest) B.; m. Roxanne Layton, Jan. 1, 1967; children— Jeffrey, Emily. A.B., Dartmouth Coll., 1963; LL.B., Yale U., 1966; cert. Uppsala (Sweden) U., 1967. Bar: Ga. 1966, Md. 1968, U.S. Dist. Ct. (no. dist.) Ga. 1966, U.S. Dist. Ct. Md. 1968, U.S. Ct. Appeals (4th cir.) 1968, U.S. Ct. Appeals (3d cir.) 1981, U.S. Ct. Appeals (5th cir.) 1966, U.S. Ct. Appeals (8th cir.) 1976, U.S. Ct. Appeals (7th cir.) 1982, U.S. Ct. Appeals (D.C. cir.) 1986, U.S. Supreme Ct. 1974. Mem. Shawe & Rosenthal, Balt., 1968-75; ptnr. Weinberg & Green, Balt., 1975-80, Jackson, Lewis Schnitzler & Krupman, Balt., 1981-84; instr. Indsl. Relations Labor Studies Ctr., U. Balt.; served with Am. embassy, Stockholm, 1967. Mem. ABA, Ga. Bar Assn., Md. Bar Assn. Republican. Jewish. Clubs: Dartmouth of Md., Merchants, Center, Yale of Maryland. Contbg. editor The Developing Labor Law, Mercer Law Rev. Office: 400 E Pratt St Suite 600 Baltimore MD 21202

BUCHSBAUM, PETER A., judge; b. Bklyn., Dec. 27, 1945; s. Arnold and Rose (Chanes) B.; m. Elaine Frey, Dec. 24, 1967; children: Matthew, Andrew, Aaron. AB, Cornell U., 1967; JD, Harvard U., 1970. Law sec. to Chief Justice Hon. Joseph Weintraub, Trenton, 1970-71; lawyer N.J. State Tax Policy Commn., Trenton, 1971-72; staff counsel ACLU, Newark, 1972-74; asst. dep. pub. adv. N.J. Dept. Pub. Adv., Trenton, 1974-79; lawyer Warren, Goldberg, & Berman, Princeton, N.J., 1979-84; ptnr. Sterns Herbert and Weinroth and Hannoch Weisman, Princeton, 1984-91, Greenbaum, Rowe, Smith, Ravin & Davis, Woodbridge, NJ, 1991—2004; judge Superior Court of N.J., 2004—. Spl. counsel N.J. State League Mcpl., Trenton, 1988—94; counsel Boroughs of High Bridge and Flemington, NJ, 1986—2004; commr. N.J. Law Rev. Commn., Newark, 1994—2004; adj. faculty Rutgers-Camden (N.J.) Law Sch.; former cons. APA Growing Smart Project. Columnist: N.J. Reporter Mag., Princeton, 1982—2000, State and Local Law News ABA, 1996—2004; co-editor: State and Regional Comprehensive Planning, 1993; reporter: Land Use Law and Zoning Digest Mag.; contbr. articles to profl. jours. Bd. dirs. Hunterdon County United Way, 1999-2004, Hunterdon County Housing Corp., Flemington, N.J., 1992-2004; mem. twp. com. West Amwell Twp., N.J., 2001-04; ptnr. N.J. State Dem. Com., 1997-2004 Mem. ABA (coun. sect. on state and local govt. law), Am. Coll. Real Estate Lawyers, N.J. State Bar Assn. (chmn. land use law sect. 1986-87, sect. trustee 1983-96, Media award, 1987). Jewish. Avocations: gardening, writing. Home: 126 Bowne Station Rd Stockton NJ 08559-1907 Office: Superior Ct of NJ Hunterdon County Justice Ctr 65 Park Ave Flemington NJ Business E-Mail: pbuchsbaum@aol.com.

BUCHTA, RICHARD MICHAEL, pediatrician; b. Binghamton, N.Y., Feb. 8, 1941; s. Martin Joseph and Pauline (Perchinsky) Buchta; m. Diane Zirilli; children: Richard Jr., Daniel, Kymberley Rusch. BS, Le Moyne Coll., Syracuse, N.Y., 1963; MD cum-laude, Stritch-Loyola, Chgo., 1967. Lic. G16721, Calif., cert. Am. Bd. of Pediat., 1973, Am. Bd. of Pediat., sub-bd. Adolescent medicine, 2001, pediat. adv. life support 1996. Internship U.S. Naval Hosp., San Diego, 1967—68, pediat. residency, 1968—70; fellowship Children's Hosp. of L.A., 1973—74; asst. chief to pediat. U.S. Naval Hosp., Camp Pendleton, Calif., 1970—73; clin. instr. pediat. Univ. Calif., San Diego, 1972—74; pvt. practice LaJolla, Calif., 1974—83; attending physician Univ. Calif., San Diego, 1978—81, 1996—99; head divsn. Pediat. Scripps Clin., 1985—. Dir. med. edn. pediat. U.S. Naval Hosp., Camp Pendleton, Calif., 1970—73, dir. adolescent clin., 1970—73; asst. clin. prof. pediat. Univ. Calif., San Diego, 1975—79; supr. pediat. svc. Hillcrest Receiving Home, San Diego, 1975—83; clin. prof. Univ. Calif., San Diego, 1985—; physician U.S. Triathlon Team, 1985—87; cons. in field; lectr. in field. Contbr. articles publ. to profl. jour., chapters to books, scientific papers. Mem. Nat. Dem. Com., Washington, 1993—, Amnesty Internat. USA, 1987—; med. adv. bd. Medwell Group, 2002—; mem. Carter Ctr., Atlanta, 1995—; mem. Scripps Office for the Protection Rsch. Subjects Com. Scripps Clin. Academic Affairs, 1999—; scientific adv. bd. Physicians Nutraceutical Lab., Calif., 2000—. Ensign USN, 1966, lt. USN, 1967—71, lt. comdr. USN, 1971—77, hon. discharge USN, 1973, with USNR, 1973—87, comdr. USNR, 1977—83, capt. USN, 1983—87, ret. USNR, 1987. Mem.: N. Am. Soc. for Pediat Gyn., Physicians for Social Responsibility, Soc. for Adolescent Medicine, Am. Acad. of Pediat., Jesuit Cmty. Office: Scripps Clin Dept Pediat and Adolescent Medicine 3811 Valley Ctr Dr San Diego CA 92130 Home: 13403 Caminito Carmel Del Mar CA 92014 Office Phone: 858-764-3040.

BUCHWALD, AMY ANNAMARIA, pharmacologist, researcher; d. Gyula and Anamaria Formanek; m. Peter Sandor Buchwald, May 16, 1986; children: Zoltan, Zsuzsa. PhD, U. Fla. Gainesville, 2001; BS, Babes-Bolyai U., 1986. Tchr. Scoala Generala Capusu-Mare, Capus, Romania, 1996—89; redactor Radio-Tv Cluj, 1991—93; scientist Kos Pharm., Inc., Miami-Lakes, Fla., 2001—02, sr. scientist Weston, Fla., 2002—. Contbr. articles to profl. jours. (Hon. Mention, 1998). Mem.: Am. Assn. Pharm. Scientists. Office: Kos Pharmaceuticals Inc 2200 North Commerce Pkwy ste 300 Weston FL 33326-3258

BUCHWALD, ART, columnist, writer; b. Mt. Vernon, NY, Oct. 20, 1925; s. Joseph and Helen (Kleinberger) B.; m. Ann McGarry, Oct. 11, 1952; 3 children. Student, U. So. Calif., 1945-48. Former correspondent Variety mag., Paris; former columnist European edit., NY Herald Tribune; now syndicated columnist Tribune Media Services. Author: Paris After Dark, 1950, Art Buchwald's Paris, 1954, The Brave Coward, 1957, A Gift From the Boys, 1959, More Caviar, 1958, Un Cadeau Pour Le Patron (Prix de la Bonne Humeur 1958), Don't Forget to Write, 1960, Art Buchwald's Secret List to Paris, 1963, How Much Is That in Dollars?, 1961, Is It Safe to Drink the Water?, 1962, I Chose Capitol Punishment, 1963, And Then I Told the President, 1965, Son of the Great Society, 1966, Have I Ever Lied to You, 1968, The Establishment Is Alive and Well in Washington, 1969, Counting Sheep, 1970, Getting High in Government Circles, 1971, I Never Danced at the White House, 1973, The Bollo Caper, 1974, I Am Not a Crook, 1974, Irving's Delight, 1975, Washington is Leaking, 1976, Down the Seine and Up the Potomac, 1977, The Buchwald Stops Here, 1978, Laid Back in Washington, 1981, While Reagan Slept, 1983, You CAN Fool All of the People All the Time, 1985, I Think I Don't Remember, 1987, Whose Rose Garden Is It Anyway?, 1989, Lighten Up, George, 1991, Leaving Home: A Memoir, 1993, I'll Always Have Paris, 1996, Stella in Heaven: Almost a Novel, 2000, We'll Laugh Again, 2002. Served as sgt. USMCR, 1942-45. Recipient Pulitzer Prize for Outstanding Commentary, 1982 Mem. Am. Acad. Arts and Scis., Am. Acad. Humor Columnists.*

BUCHWALD, HENRY, surgeon, educator, researcher; b. Vienna, June 21, 1932; arrived in U.S., 1939, naturalized; s. Andor and Renee (Franzos) B.; m. Emilie D. Bix, June 6, 1954; children: Jane Nicole, Amy Elizabeth, Claire Gretchen, Dana Alexandra. BA summa cum laude, Columbia U., 1954, MD, 1957; MS in Biochemistry, PhD in Surgery, U. Minn., 1967. Diplomate Am. Bd. Surgery. Intern Columbia/Presbyn. Med. Ctr., N.Y.C., 1957-58; resident fellow in surgery U. Minn., Mpls., 1960-67; asst. prof. surgery U. Minn. Med. Sch., Mpls., 1967-70, assoc. prof., 1970-77, prof. surgery, prof. biomed. engring., 1977—, dir. grad. surg. tng., resident tng. program, in-tng. exam., chmn. credentials com.; chair Gwen and Sarah Davision Wangensteen Chair in Express Surgery, 2001—. Pres. Minn. Inventors Hall of Fame, 1989-92, chmn. bd. dirs. 1992-94; vis. prof., lectr. McLaren Gen. Hosp., Flint., Mich., 1979, Buffalo Surg. Soc., Mpls., 1980, G.P. Wratten Surg. Symposium, Washington, 1980, Frontiers of Medicine Series, Chgo., 1980, Minn. Endocrine Club, Mpls., 1980, Symposium on Surgery, Tokyo, 1980, Northwestern Med. Assn., Sun Valley, Idaho, 1981, Mayo Clinic, Rochester, Minn., 1981, BSG/Glaxo Internat. Tchg. Day, Norwich, Eng., 1982, Mass. Gen. Hosp., Boston, 1983, SUNY, Stony Brook, 1984, D.C. Gen. Hosp., Washington, 1984, L.A. Surg. Soc., 1987, Sch. Dentistry, Dept. Continuing Edn., U. Minn., 1988, others; Alfred Strauss vis. lectr., Chgo., 1989; dir. postgrad. course Bariatric Surgery Primer, ACS; spkr., cons. in field.; presenter numerous confs. and symposia. Author: (with others) Hepatic, Biliary and Pancreatic Surgery, 1980, Lipoproteins and Coronary Atherosclerosis, 1982, Atherosclerosis: Clinical Evaluation and Therapy, 1982, Nutrition and Heart Disease, 1982, Advances in Vascular Surgery, 1983, Advances in Surgery, 1984, others; contbr. Gibbon's Surgery of the Chest, 4th edit., 1983, Hardy's Textbook of Surgery, 1983, Implantable Pumps: ASAIO Primers in Artificial Organs, 1987; contbr. over 300 articles to profl. jours., trans.; mem. editorial bd. Chirurgia Generale, Jour. Clin. Surgery, Infu-Systems Internat., Diabetes, Nutrition and Metabolism, Obesity Surgery Jour. Am. Soc. Artificial Int. Orgn., Jour. Bacteriol. Surgery, Online Jour. Current Clin. Trials, also guest editor other jours. Capt. SAC, USAF, 1958-60. Recipient Inventor of Yr. award Minn. Inventors Hall of Fame, 1988, 90, Clin. Scholar award U. Minn., 1991, Diehl award U. Minn.; recipient numerous rsch. grants univs., Nat. Heart and Lung Inst., Nat. Cancer Inst., Nat. Inst. Arthritis, Metabolism and Digestive Diseases, NIH, med. founds., pharm. cos., corps., 1956—. Fellow ACS (gov. 1999—, Samuel D. Gross award 1969), Am. Surg. Assn., Soc. Univ. Surgeons, Ctrl. Surg. Assn. (program com. 1982-85, chmn. 1984-85, treas. 1992-94, pres. 1997-98), Assn. Acad. Surgery (Disting. Svc. award 1976), Epidemiology Coun. and Cardiovasc. Coun. Am. Heart Assn. (established investigator), Am. Coll. Cardiology, Soc. Surgery Alimentary Tract, Soc. Clin. Trials (program com. 1984-85); mem. AAAS, Minn. Surg. Assn. (First Clin. Rsch. award 1965), Mpls. Surg. Assn., Minn. Heart Assn., Am. Assn. History Medicine, Am. Soc. Artificial Internal Organs (program com. 1984-87, sect. editor Trans.), Internat. Study Group Diabetes Treatment with Implantable Insulin Delivery Devices (sec.-gen. 1984-88, chmn. 1989-94), St. Paul Surg. Soc. (hon.), Am. Coll. Nutrition (mem. editorial bd.), Am. Soc. Bariatric Soc. (pres. 1998-99), Internat. Soc. Obesity Surgery (pres. 2003-04), Paleopathology Club, Alpha Omega Alpha. Avocations: running, riding, tennis, reading, chess. Office: 420 Delaware St SE Minneapolis MN 55455 Office Phone: 612-625-8413. Business E-Mail: buchw001@umn.edu.

BUCHWALD, JED ZACHARY, environmental health researcher, science history educator; b. N.Y.C., June 25, 1949; BA, Princeton U., 1971; MA, Harvard, 1973, PhD, 1974. Instr., dir. Inst. History Philosophy Sci. and Tech. U. Toronto, 1974—92; prof., dir. Dibner Inst. for History of Sci. and Tech. MIT, 1992—2001; Doris & Henry Dreyfuss prof. of history Calif. Inst. Tech., Pasadena, 2001—. Author: (book) The Creation of Scientific Effects, 1994; co-editor: Isaac Newton's Natural Philosophy, 2000, Histories of the Electron, 2001; contbr. articles to profl. jours. Named MacArthur fellow, John D. and Katherine T. MacArthur Found., 1995; recipient award for excellence in environ. health rsch., Lovelace Inst., Albuquerque, 1995. Office: Calif Inst tech Div Humanities & Soc Sci MC 101-40 Pasadena CA 91125*

BUCHWALD, NAOMI REICE, federal judge; b. Kingston, N.Y., Feb. 14, 1944; BA cum laude, Brandeis U., 1965; LLB cum laude, Columbia U., 1968. Bar: N.Y. 1968, U.S. Ct. Appeals (2d cir.) 1969, U.S. Dist. Ct. (so. and ea. dists.) N.Y. 1970, U.S. Supreme Ct. 1978. Litigation assoc. Marshall, Bratter, Greene, Allison & Tucker, N.Y.C., 1968-73; asst. U.S. atty. So. Dist. N.Y., N.Y.C., 1973-80, dep. chief civil divsn., 1976-79, chief civil divsn., 1979-80; U.S. magistrate judge U.S. Dist. Ct. (so. dist.) N.Y., N.Y.C., 1980-99, chief magistrate judge, 1994-96, U.S. dist. judge, 1999—. Editor Columbia Jour. Law and Social Problems, 1967-68. Recipient spl. citation FDA Commrs., 1978, Robert B. Fiske Jr. Assn. William B. Tendy award, Outstanding Pub. Svc. award Seymour Assn., Columbia Law Sch. Class of 1968 Excellence in Pub. Svc. award, 1998. Mem. Fed. Bar Coun. (trustee 1976-82, 97-2000, v.p. 1982-84), N.Y. State Bar Assn., Assn. of the Bar of the City of N.Y. (trademarks and unfair competition com. 1988-89, mem. long range planning com. 1993-95, litigation com. 1994-96, ad hoc com. on jud. conduct 1996-99; prof., jud. ethics com. 2002-2004), Phi Beta Kappa, Omicron Delta Epsilon. Office: US Ct House Foley Square New York NY 10007-1316

BUCHWALD, NATHANIEL AVROM, neurologist, physiologist; b. N.Y.C., July 19, 1925; s. Solomon Sanders and Nellie (Miller) B.; m. Caroline L. Wakefield, Apr. 8, 1989; children: Amanda, Scott, Raina. BS in Chemistsry, U. Miami, Fla., 1946; PhD in Neurosci., U. Minn., 1953. Instr. Sch. of Medicine Tulane U., New Orleans, 1953-57; from asst. prof. to prof. Sch. of Medicine UCLA, 1957—, dir. mental retardation rsch. ctr. Neuropsychiat. Inst., 1971—. Cons. in field; mem. sci. bd., chair Huntington Disease Found., 1977-83. Contbr. over 150 articles to profl. jours. Grantee USPHS, 1955—. Mem. Am. Physiol. Soc., Nat. Mental Retardation Ctrs. Dirs. Orgn., Soc. for Neurosci., Internat. Brain Rsch. Orgn. Office: UCLA Sch Medicine 1608 Abbotsbury St Thousand Oaks CA 91361 Personal E-mail: cbuchwald@mindspring.com.

BUCHWALD, PETER SANDOR, science association director; b. Kolozsvar, Transylvania, Romania, Feb. 27, 1963; arrived in U.S., 1992; s. Péter Szilard and Margit (Török) Buchwald; m. Amy Formanek, May 16, 1986; children: Zoltan, Zsuzsa. BS, U. Babes-Bolyai, Kolozsvar, Romania, 1986; PhD, U. Fla., 1997. Tchr. Petru Maior Lyceum, Gherla, Romania, 1986—90, Brassai Samuel Lyceum, Cluj, Romania, 1990; computerized info. mgr. RMDSz, Cluj, 1990—92; rsch. assoc. U. Fla., Gainesville, 1992—97, post doctoral rsch. assoc., 1998—2000; sr. rsch. scientist IVAX Rsch., Inc., Miami, 2000—03, assoc. dir. drug discovery, 2003—. Contbr. over 60 articles to profl. jours., chapters to books; author: (software program) LinBiExp, QLOGP, Soft Drug Design, 1999. Mem.: AAAS, Am. Assn. Pharm. Sci., Am. Chem. Soc., Phi Kappa Phi. Achievements include development of simple molecular size-based model for organic liquids and water. Office: IVAX Rsch Inc 4400 Biscayne Blvd Miami FL 33137

BUCHY, JIM, food products executive; b. Greenville, Ohio, Sept. 24, 1940; s. George Jacob and Amba (Armbruster) B.; m. Sharon Lynn Steinvall, 1965; children: Kathryn, John. BS, Wittenberg U., 1962. Pres. Charles G. Buchy Packing Co., Greenville, 1977—; mem. Ohio Ho. of Reps., Columbus, 1983—2000. Mem. Greenville Bd. Edn., 1980-82; dist. del. Rep. Nat. Conf.; mem. Darke County (Ohio) Rep. Exec. Com.; chmn. Darke Econ. Found., 1977-82; bd. dirs. Greenville Indsl. Park; past pres. Darke County Rep. Men's Club. Mem. Darke County C. of C., Rotary, Phi Mu Delta. Home: North Broadway PO Box 899 Greenville OH 45331-0899

BUCK, BERNESTINE BRADFORD, retired school counselor; b. Altheimer, Ark., July 25, 1924; d. Henry Walker and Dora Lois Bradford; BA, Stowe Tchrs. Coll., 1950; MEd, U. Mo., 1973; m. Joseph Wellington Buck, Oct. 1, 1950; children: Stanley W., Linda Carol, Debra Lois. Tchr. pub. schs., St. Louis, 1950-73, sch. counselor, 1973-87. Committeewoman, St. Louis 20th Ward, 1988-89; mem. U. Mo. scholarship com., 1974-84, Antioch Bapt. Ch. scholarship com., 1980-86, Coro Reinvest Program, 1988. Mem. Am., Mo. personnel and guidance assns., St. Louis Guidance Assn. (pres. 1979-80), Mo. Guidance Assn. (exec. council 1980-81, v.p. elem. sect.), Alpha Kappa Alpha. Baptist.

BUCK, D. RUTH, legal research and writing educator; b. 1952; BA, U. Va., 1974; MEd, U Va., 1976; JD, U. Va., 1985. Bar: Ga. 1986, Va. 1986. Assoc. Neely & Player, Atlanta, 1985—86; asst. dir. com. continuing legal edn. Va. Law Found., 1986—88; instr. legal writing U. Va. Sch. Law, 1988—90, asst. prof., 1990—94, assoc. prof., 1994—2000, prof., 2000—, co-dir. legal rsch. & writing program, 1988—. Office: U Va Sch Law 580 Massie Rd Charlottesville VA 22903-1789 Office Phone: 434-924-1042. E-mail: drb7c@virginia.edu.

BUCK, EARL WAYNE, private investigator, motel owner; b. La Porte City, Iowa, Jan. 15, 1939; s. Edwin Earl and Uleta Pearl (Purdy) B.; m. Maxine E. Parker, Oct. 19, 1969; children: Brian, Douglas, Stuart, Teresa. LLB, La Salle U., 1969. Asst. mgr. Chgo. br. Atwell, Vogel & Sterling, Scarsdale, N.Y., 1965-70; pvt. detective, Sioux City, Iowa, 1968-74; mgr. Milw. br. Atwell, Vogel & Sterling, Scarsdale, N.Y., 1970; sr. auditor Comml. Union Ins. Co., Chgo., 1970-74; police chief McHenry Shores (Ill.) Police Dept., 1973-79; self-employed ins. investigator McHenry, Ill., 1980-88, Rapid City, S.D., 1988—; owner Corral Motel, Rapid City, 1988—. Liquor liability investigator for various ins. cos., 1980-88; farm owner, 1986-96; owner High Plaines Detective Agy., 1990-. Chmn. McHenry Shores (Ill.) Zoning Commn., 1972, Police Support Subcom., C. of C. Pub. Safety Com.; key contact Help Abolish Legal Tyranny; active Rapid City Police Res., 1989-90, North Rapid Civic Assn., 1991—, pres., chmn. bd., 1993-94; active Pennington County Air Quality Bd., 1990-93, chmn., 1992-93. With U.S. Army, 1957-61. Recipient Police Meritorius Service award Vill. of McHenry Shores, 1979. Mem. Midwest Ins. Auditors Assn., McHenry County Police Chief's Assn., Rapid City Police Officers Assn., Rapid City Area Hospitality Assn. (bd. dirs.), Rapid City Area C. of C. (safety com. 1989-91), Am. Legion, Fed. Weed and Seed Program Rapid City (steering com.), NRA, Moose, Black Hills Sr. Games. Republican. Lutheran. Avocations: flying, amateur archaeology, photography, fishing, hunting. Office Phone: 605-342-7511. E-mail: buckwayne9@wmconnect.com.

BUCK, GURDON HALL, lawyer, urban planner, mediator; b. Hartford, Conn., Apr. 10, 1936; s. Richard Saltonstall and Aloha Frances (Hall) B.; children: Keith Saltonstall, Frances Josephine, Daniel Winthrop; m. Martha Finder, 1996. BA in English, Lehigh U., 1958; JD, U. Pa., 1965. Bar: Conn. 1965, U.S. Dist. Ct. 1966, U.S. Ct. Appeals (2d cir.) 1966. Assoc. Shipman & Goodwin, Hartford, 1965-67; v.p., counsel R. F. Broderick & Assocs., Hartford, 1968-69; ptnr. Pelgrift, Byrne, Buck & Connolly, Hartford and Farmington, Conn., 1969—78, Byrne, Buck & Steiner and predecessor Byrne & Buck, Farmington, 1975-78; ptnr. counsel real estate and land use sects., chmn. common interest group Robinson & Cole, Farmington and Hartford, 1979—2002, sr. counsel, 2003—. Author: Condominium Development, Forms with Commentary, 1990, 2d edit., 1992; prin. co-author: The Connecticut Condominium Manual, 1972, Real Estate Brokers Community Associations Handbook, rev. edit., 1982, Connecticut Common Interest Ownership Manual, 1984, 2d edit., 2005, The Alaska Common Interest Ownership Manual, 1985, Attorney's and Lenders Guide to Common Interest Communities, 1989, 2nd edit., 1999; contbr. articles on zoning, condominiums, planned unit devels. to profl. jours.; columnist various newspapers. Lt. USCGR, 1958-62. Recipient Disting. Svc. award Glastonbury (Conn.) Jaycees, 1968. Mem. ABA (common interest com. law com., real property and probate, joint editl. bd. real property laws, adv. Uniform Planned Cmty. Act, Model Real Estate Coop. Act, Uniform Common Interest Ownership Act), Am. Law Inst. (advisor, Restatement on Property 3d Servitudes), Am. Coll. Real Estate Lawyers (bd. dirs. 1986-92, common ownership com.), Anglo-Am. Real Property Inst. (bd. govs. 1994-96), Cmty. Assns. Inst. (nat. trustee 1982-88, pres. Conn. chpt. 1980-83, sec. 1986-89, bd. dirs. 1992-98, pres. rsch. found. 1980-83, Century Club, Byron Hanke Disting. Svc. award, Acad. of Authors), Am. Planning Assn., Am. Inst. Cert. Planners, Internat. Bar Assn. (panelist common ownership consumer protection 1987), Conn. Bar Assn. (chmn. com. opinions, chmn. real estate sect., chair Pub. Svc. Recog. Com., Ethics com., pro bono com., ed. Conn. Bar Jour.), Statewide Legal Svcs. (bd. dirs., pres. 1998-), Hartford County Bar Assn., Conn. Assn. Homebuilders Orgn. (developer's coun.). Office: 280 Trumbull St Hartford CT 06103-3507 Office Phone: 860-275-8222. Personal E-mail: gbuck@rc.com. *The common interest community is the mutual sharing of resources and lives through the land. It is as old as civilization itself and as modern as the latest marketing techniques.*

BUCK, HENRY WILLIAM, JR., obstetrician, gynecologist; b. Kansas City, June 4, 1934; s. Henry William Sr. and Nina Irene (Krebs) B.; m. Barbara Laviece Mallory, Sept. 6, 1963; children: Mallory Renee, Andrew William. BA, U. Kans., 1956, MD, 1960. Cert. Am. Bd. Ob.-Gyn. Gynecologist emeritus Student Health Svc. U. Kans., Lawrence, head gynecology dept. Student Health Svc., 1987—; pvt. practice Lawrence, 1967—87. Pres. bd. dirs. Douglas County Citizens' Com. on Alcoholism, Lawrence, 1983—; chmn. task force HPV disease Am. Coll. Health Assn. Capt. USAF, 1965—67. Fellow ACS, Am. Coll. Ob-Gyns.; mem. AMA, Kans. Med. Soc., Kans. Ob-Gyn. Soc. (pres. 1980-81), Kappa Sigma, Omicron Delta Kappa. Republican. Lutheran. Avocations: photography, music, writing, travel. Home and Office: 306 Homestead Dr Lawrence KS 66049-2000 Office Phone: 785-843-5610.

BUCK, JAMES MAHLON, JR., venture capitalist; b. Bryn Mawr, Pa., Apr. 27, 1925; s. J. Mahlon and Grace Irene (Knapp) B.; m. Elia Garrett Durr, Sept. 15, 1953; children: Caroline Buck Rogers, James M. III. AB in Econs., Princeton U., 1946. Ops. mgr. Smith, Kline and French, Inc., Phila., 1948-56, v.p. ops., 1956-65; chmn., chief exec. officer The Drug House, Inc., Phila., 1965-77; chmn. Alco Health Services Group, Valley Forge, Pa., 1977-83; pres., CEO TDH Capital Ptnrs., Radnor, Pa., 1977—. Mem. adv. bd. Phila. Phillies, 1981—. With U.S. Army, 1943-45, ETO. Mem.: Merion Golf (Ardmore, Pa.); Merion Cricket (Haverford, Pa.). Republican. Presbyterian. Avocations: tennis, golf, music, spectator sports. Home: 121 Rose Ln Haverford PA 19041-1724 Office: TDH Capital Corp PO Box 8234/Radnor Ct 259 N Radnor Chester Rd Ste 210 Radnor PA 19087-5259 also: Phila Phillies PO Box 7575 Philadelphia PA 19101-7575

BUCK, JOE (JOSEPH FRANCIS BUCK), sportscaster; b. St. Petersburg, Fla., Apr. 25, 1969; s. Joseph Buck; m. Ann Buck; 2 children. BA in English, Ind. U., 1991. Announcer St. Louis Cardinals, 1991—; lead play-by-play announcer MLB on Fox, 1996—; play-by-play announcer NFL on Fox, 1994—97, lead play-by-play announcer, 2002—. Recipient Emmy award for Outstanding Sports Personality for play-by-play, 1999—2003. Achievements include became the youngest play-by-play announcer to call a World Series, 1996; has announced World Series, 1996, 98, 2000, 01, 02, 03, MLB All-Star Game, 1997, 99, 2001, 02, 03, 04, Mark McGwire's record breaking 62nd home run, 1998; son of Jack Buck, Hall of Fame broadcaster, and former voice of the St. Louis Cardinals. Office: c/o William Morris Agy 1325 Avenue of the Americas New York NY 10019

BUCK, JOHN E., printmaker; b. Ames, Iowa, Feb. 14, 1946; m. Deborah Butterfield; 2 children. BFA, Kans. City Art Inst., 1968; MFA, U. Calif., Davis, 1972. Instr. in sculpture Mont. State U., Bozeman, 1976-90. Sculptor and print maker: solo exhibitions include: Kans. City (Mo.) Art Inst., John Buck, 1988, Fine Arts Mus. San Francisco, John Buck: Woodblock Prints, 1993— (travels), Palm Springs Desert Mus., 1994, John Buck: Sculpture, 1994, The Contemporary Mus., Honolulu, John Buck: A Survey Exhibition, 1995, Lewis and Clark Coll., Portland, Oreg., 1999, Madison Art Ctr., 1999, Holter Mus. of Art, Helena, Mont., 2000, Mus. of Northwest Art, La conner, Wash., 2000, Sangre De Cristo Arts Ctr., Pueblo, Colo., 2003, Boulder Mus. Contemporary Art, Boulder, 2005, Jackson Hole Ctr. for Arts, Wyo., 2005; group exhibits Seattle Art Mus., Seattle, Calif. Permanent Collection, 1992, Newport Harbor Art Mus., Newport Beach, Calif., Beyond the Bay, 1993, Laguna Gloria Art Mus., Austin, Human Nature, Human Form, 1993, The Oakland (Calif.) Mus., Here and Now, 1994; commissions include: Ahmanson Commercial Devel., Chgo., 1991, Prin. Fin. Group, Des Moines, Iowa, 1989, Swedish Hosp., Seattle, 1999, Meridian Plz., Sacramento, 2001; represented by Zolla/Lieberman Gallery, Chgo., Greg Kucera Gallery, Seattle, DC Moore Gallery, N.Y.C., Imago Galleries, Palm Desert, Calif. Recipient Individual Artist's award NEA, 1980, awards in the visual arts, Nat. Artists Award, 1984. Office Fax: 406-585-9757.

BUCK, LAWRENCE PAUL, former history professor, academic administrator; b. Pittsburg, Kans., Oct. 6, 1944; m. Judy L.; children: David L., Laura T. BA, Wichita State U., 1966; MA, Ohio State U., 1967, PhD in History, 1971. Asst. prof. Widener U., Chester, Pa., 1971-77, assoc. prof. history, 1977-85, prof. history, 1985—, dean Coll. Arts and Scis., 1981-84, acad. v.p., provost, 1984—2004, acting pres., 1994, 2001—02. Author: Die Haltung der Nurnberger Bauernschaft im Bauernkrieg, 1970, Opposition to Tithes in the Peasants' Revolt, 1973, Civil Insurrection in a Reformation City, 1976, Demands for Reform by Urban Dissidents During the German Peasants' Revolt, 1977, The Reformation, Purgatory, and Perpetual Rents in the Revolt of 1525 at Frankfurt am Main, 1985; translator: Monemvasia: The Town and Its History, 1981; co-editor: The Social History of the Reformation; contbr. articles to profl. jours., book chpts. Rsch. grantee Am. Philos. Soc., 1973, NEH, 1974. Mem. Am. Soc. Reformation Rsch., 16th Century Study Conf. Office: Widener U Humanities Divsn One University Pl Chester PA 19013 Business E-Mail: lawrence.p.buck@widener.edu.

BUCK, LESLIE ELIZABETH, mathematics educator, poet; b. Amherst, Mass., June 15, 1962; d. Lucien Alan and Beverly Elizabeth Buck; 1 child, Elise L. BA in Math., Dowling Coll., 1984—87; MS in Math., Adelphi U., 1989—92; MS in Environ. Engring., Poly. U., 1992—2000. Fundamentals engring., NY State Edn. Dept., Profl. Licensing divsn., 1999. Wildlife rehabilitator Volunteer's for Wildlife, Huntington, NY, 1991—; prof. math. Suffolk County C.C., Riverhead, NY, 1992—; tchg. asst./phd candidate Poly. U., Bklyn., 1995—2000; grad. rsch. intern Air Force Office Sci. Rsch., Tyndall Air Force Base, Panama City, Fla., 1996; engring. aide Suffolk County Dept. Pub. Works, Yaphank, NY, 1996—97; environ. engr. Fanning, Phillips, & Molnar, Ronkonkoma, NY, 1997—99. Jour. reviewer Am. Math. Assn. of Two Yr. Colleges (AMATYC), Tex., 1999—. Author: (rsch. presentation) 4th Ann. N.E. Regional Student Environ. Conf.; author: (rsch asst.) (rsch.) Modeling of Organohalide Reactions in Aqueous B12/Ti(III) Systems, Environ. Sci. and Toxicology (SETAC), Jour. of Environ. Sci. Health; author: (conf. presentation) New York State Math. Assn. of Two Yr. Colleges (NYSMATIC). Wildlife rehabilitator ind., East Moriches, NY, 1991; vol. Nature Conservancy, Shelter Island, NY, 1999—2000; swimmer Swim for Life, Province Town, RI, 2000—01; organizer/swimmer Swim for Wildlife, Huntington, NY, 2001—02; educator/vol. Not In Our Name, N.Y.C., 2002. Recipient, Nat. Dean's List, 1986—87; fellow, Adelphi U., 1989—92, Poly. U., 1995—99; grantee Math. and Nursing, NSF, 2000, The Art of Math., 2001; scholar, Women's nat. Farm and Garden Assn., 1996. Mem.: ACLU, Math. Assn. Am., Am. Math. Assn. Two Yr. Colleges, Water Environment Fedn., Nat. Groundwater Assn., NY State Math. Assn. Two Yr. Colleges, Nat. Arbor Day Soc., Bioneers, Wilderness Soc., Nat. Parks and Recreational, Nature Conservancy, Oxfam Am., Green Peace, Coun. of Indian Nations, Earth Save, Tau Beta Pi, Pi Mu Epsilon. Green Party. Avocations: swimming, woods watching, organic gardening, poetry, yoga. Office: Suffolk County C C 121 Speonk-Riverhead Rd Riverhead NY 11901-3499 Business E-Mail: buckl@sunysuffolk.edu.

BUCK, LINDA B., physician, medical educator; b. Seattle, Jan. 29, 1947; BS in Psychology, U. Wash., Seattle, 1975; BS in Microbiology, U. Wash., 1975; PhD, U. Texas Southwestern Med. Ctr., Dallas, 1980. Postdoctoral fellow Columbia U., 1980—84; assoc. Howard Hughes Medical Inst., 1984—91, asst. investigator, 1994—97, assoc. investigator, 1997—2000; asst. prof. neurobiology Harvard U., Boston, 1991—96, assoc. prof. neurobiology, 1996—2001, prof. neurobiology, 2001—02; mem., dir. Buck Lab Fred Hutchinson Cancer Rsch. Ctr., Seattle, 2002—; affiliate prof. physiology & biophysics U. Wash. Sch. of Medicine, Seattle. Contbr. articles to profl. jours. Recipient McKnight Scholar award, McKnight Endowment Fund for Neuroscience, 1992, Takasago award for Rsch. in Olfaction, Takasago Corp., 1992, Lewis S. Rosenstiel award for Disting. Work in Basic Med. Rsch., 1997, Louis Vuitton-Moet Hennessy Sci. for Art prize, R. H. Wright award in Olfactory Rsch, 1996, Unilever Sci. award, 1996, The Lewis S. Rosentiel award for Disting. Work in Basic Med. Rsch., 1997, Kenji Nakanishi award for Rsch. in Olfaction, Gairdner award, Toronto, 2003, Perl/U. NC Neuroscience Prize, 2003; co-recipient of Nobel Prize in Medicine, 2004. Fellow: Am. Assn. for the Advancement of Sci., 2002; mem.: NAS, 2003. Achievements include discovery of (with Richard Axel) the odorant receptors and the organization of the olfactory system. Office: Basic Scis Divsn Fred Hutchinson Cancer Rsch Ctr A3-020 1100 Fairview Ave N PO Box 19024 Seattle WA 98109-1024 Office Phone: 206-667-6316. Office Fax: 206-667-1031. E-mail: lbuck@fhcrc.org.

BUCK, MICHAEL, statistician, medical researcher; s. Buck. BS in Computer Sci., Brigham Young U., 2003. Database arch. Hewlett-Packard, Boise, Idaho, 2001—03; rschr. med. informatics Intermountain Health Care, Salt Lake City, 2003—. Grantee, Nat. Libr. Medicine, 2003—. Mem.: IEEE, Healthcare Info. and Mgmt. Sys. Soc., Am. Med. Informatics Assn. Mem. Lds Ch. Achievements include research in identifying adverse drug event risks in the geriatric population. Personal E-mail: mike.buck@utah.edu.

BUCK, RICHARD CRAIG, family practice physician; b. Frankfort, Ind., Sept. 14, 1941; s. Morris Edward and Josephine (Fickle) B.; m. Patricia Joan Reser, Dec. 22, 1962; children: Gregory Edward, Paige D'Lee. BS, Ind. U., 1963; MD, Ind. U., Indpls., 1966. Diplomate Am. Bd. Family Practice. Intern Meml. Hosp., South Bend, Ind., 1966-67, family practice resident, 1969-71; pvt. practice in family medicine South Bend, 1971—. Chief family practice Meml. Hosp., South Bend, 1979-80, 1985; active staff Meml.Hosp. South Bend, Ind., St. Joseph Med. Ctr., South Bend, Ind. Lt. U.S. Navy, 1967-69. Mem. AMA, Am. Acad. Family Practice, Ind. State Med. Assn. Avocations: camping, canoeing, skiing. Home: 16825 Hampton Dr Granger IN 46530-6907 Office: 51916 US 31 N South Bend IN 46637

BUCK, THOMAS RANDOLPH, retired lawyer, retired diversified financial services company executive; b. Washington, Feb. 5, 1930; s. James Charles Francis and Mary Elizabeth (Marshall) B.; m. Alice Armistead James, June 20, 1953; children: Kathryn James, Thomas Randolph, Douglas Marshall, David Andrew; m. Sunny Clark, Sept. 15, 1971; 1 child, Carey Virginia; m. Yvonne Brackett, Nov. 27, 1981. BA summa cum laude, Am. U., 1951; JD, U. Va., 1954. Bar: Va. 1954, Ky. 1964, Fla. 1974. Asst. gen. atty. Seaboard Air Line R.R. Co., 1958-63; sec., gen. counsel Am. Comml. Lines. Inc., Houston, 1963-68; asst. gen. counsel Tex. Gas Transmission Corp., 1968-72; sec., gen. counsel Leadership Housing Inc., 1972-77; pres. law firm Buck and Golden, P.A., 1975-92; exec. v.p., gen. counsel Buck Fin. Svcs., Inc., Ft. Lauderdale, Fla., 1992-99; ret., 1999. Chmn. Hanover Bank Fla.; adj. prof. bus. law Broward C.C., Fla. Bd. dirs. Sheridan House for Youth; trustee Fla. Bapt. Found. Served to capt. USMCR, 1954-58. Mem. Assn. ICC Practitioners (nat. v.p., mem. exec. com.), Maritime Law Assn. U.S., Am. Judicature Soc., Omicron Delta Kappa, Alpha Sigma Phi, Delta Theta Phi. Clubs: Kiwanian, Propeller of U.S. Home: 2222 Woodbine Dr Tallahassee FL 32309 Personal E-mail: trbuck2yb@earthlink.net.

BUCKAWAY, WILLIAM ALLEN, JR., lawyer; b. Bowling Green, Ky., Dec. 3, 1934; s. William Allen and Kathryn Anne (Scoggin) B.; m. Bette Joan Cross, July 27, 1963; 1 child, William Allen III. AB, Centre Coll. of Ky., 1956; JD, U. Louisville, 1961. Bar: Ky. 1961, U.S. Dist Ct. (we. dist.) Ky. 1961, U.S. Dist. Ct. (ea. dist.) Ky. 1986, U.S. Ct. Appeals 2004, U.S. Supreme Ct. 1975. Assoc. Tilford, Dobbins, Caye & Alexander, Louisville, 1961-78; ptnr. Tilford, Dobbins, Alexander, Buckaway & Black LLP, Louisville, 1978—; gen. counsel, corp. sec. Clean Coal Power Resources Inc., 2003—. Atty. Masonic Homes of Ky., Louisville, 1985—; gen. counsel Kosair Charities. Elder 2d Presbyn. Ch., Louisville, 1975; emeritus mem. bd. govs. Lexington (Ky.) unit Shriners Hosp. for Crippled Children, 1986, sec., 1989-94; mem. children's oper. bd. Kosair Children's Hosp., 1986-99; mem. bd. govs. Norton Health Care, Louisville, 1999—. With USNR, 1956-58. Named Disting. Alumnus, U. Louisville Sch. Law, 1986, Centre Coll., 1986. Mem. SAR (pres. Ky. soc. 1999-2000, pres. Louisville-Thruston chpt. 2002-03), Nat. Eagle Scout Assn., Soc. of the Cin. in State of Va., Sons Confederate Vets. (adj. John Hunt Morgan Camp 1993-96), Masons (33 deg., past master Crescent Hill lodge 1967, chmn. jurisprudence and law com. imperial coun. Shrine of N.Am. 1989-91), Kosair Shrine Temple (potentate 1986), Rotary, Soc. Colonial Wars (Ky. coun.), Soc. War of 1812 (pres. Ky. soc. 1998-2000, judge adv. gen., gen. soc. 2003—), Sigma Chi, Phi Alpha Delta. Home: 1761 Sulgrave Rd Louisville KY 40205-1643 Office Phone: 502-584-1000. Personal E-mail: bbuckaway@aol.com. Business E-Mail: wbuckaway@tilfordlaw.com.

BUCKELEW, LARRY C., lab administrator; b. 1953; Grad., U. Calif., Berkeley, 1975. Exec. positions Am. Hosp. Supply, Baxter, Sunrise Med., TFX Med.; pres. Gambro Healthcare U.S., Lakewood, Colo., 2000, pres., CEO, 2000—. Chmn. Renal Leadership Coun.; founding mem., bd. dirs. Kidney Care Ptnrs.; mem., exec. com. Gambro AB.

BUCKELEW, RICHARD ALLAN, historian, educator; b. San Antonio, May 17, 1961; s. Richard Estell and Virginia Anne Buckelew; m. Kelly Ann McCrary, Feb. 26, 1983; children: Ryan Allan, David Michael, Bradley Keith, Brooks Andrew. BA in History, U. Ark., Monticello, 1993; PhD in History, U. Ark., 1999. Cert. EMT-paramedic U. Tex. Health Sci. Ctr. Tchg. asst., instr. U. Ark., Fayetteville, 1995—99; asst. prof., dept. chair Bethune-Cookman Coll., Daytona Beach, Fla., 1999—. Recipient C. Vann Woodward award for Best Non-Fiction, U. Ark. Press, 1995; Mary Hudgins Rsch. grantee, U. Ark., 1996, 1997, Fulbright Coll. Travel grantee, 1996, 1997, Summer Rsch. grantee, Bethune-Cookman Coll., Rsch. Found., 2003. Mem.: Port Orange Hist. Trust (assoc.), Halifax Hist. Soc. (assoc.), Fla. Hist. Soc. (assoc.), Am.

Hist. Assn. (assoc.), Assn. for Study African Am. Life and History (assoc.), Ark. Hist. Assn. (assoc.), So. Hist. Assn. (assoc.), Phi Alpha Theta (life; v.p. 1998—99). Democrat. Baptist. Avocations: travel, reading, sports, computers. Home: 5807 Wales Ave Port Orange FL 32127 Office: Bethune Cookman Coll 640 Mary McLeod Bethune Blvd Daytona Beach FL 32114-3099 Office Phone: 386-481-2445. Office Fax: 386-481-2442. Personal E-mail: drbuckelew@cfl.rr.com. E-mail: buckeler@cookman.edu.

BUCKELS, MARVIN WAYNE, savings and loan association executive; b. Sterling, Colo., Feb. 11, 1929; s. Harvey and Myrl (Tarr) B.; m. Doris Torrance, Aug. 1, 1959; children: Lisa K., Devon Carol. BA, U. Denver, 1951; MS, U. Wis., 1952. With Beatrice Foods, Denver, 1952-55; loan counselor Midland Fed. Savs. and Loan Assn., Denver, 1955-56, treas., 1956-62, exec. v.p., 1962-85, Western Capital Investment Corp., Denver, 1985-91. Vice-chmn. Colo. Bd. Vocat. Edn., 1967; pres. Adult Edn. Coun. Met. Denver, 1970; bd. dirs. Auraria Higher Edn. Ctr., 1975-79, vice chmn. bd., 1977-78; bd. dirs. Auraria Found., 1992—, treas., 1997—; bd. dirs. Rocky Mountain Hosp., 1979, pres., 1980; chmn. Colo. Postsecondary Edn. Facilities Authority, 1981-2005; bd. dirs. Denver Civic Ventures, Inc., 1986, chmn., 1987-90; legis. policy com. Colo. Assn. Commerce and Industry, 1986-89; treas. Colo. Pub. Affairs Coun., 1987-89; bd. dirs. Colo. Symphony Orch., 1990-2000, treas., 1990-96; chmn. The Downtown Denver Partnership, 1991-92. With U.S. Army, 1946-48. Mem. U.S. Savs. and Loan League, Colo. Savs. and Loan League (legis com.), Am. Savs. and Loan Inst. (past pres. Denver chpt.), Contrs. Soc. (past pres. Denver chpt., nat. bd. govs.), Sys. and Procedures Assn. (past pres. Denver chpt.), Adminstrv. Mgmt. Soc. (past pres. Denver chpt.), Denver Metro C. of C. (past chmn. spl. task force studying sch. bond issue, mem. pub. affairs coun. 1991-93, loaned exec. Nat. Alliance Businessmen's program), Phi Beta Kappa. Democrat.

BUCKENMAIER, CHESTER, III, military officer, anesthesiologist; Chief, regional anesthesia section Walter Reed Army Med. Ctr., Washington. Dir. Army Regional Anesthesia Fellowship. Lt. Col. U.S. Army. Nominee Rave award in Medicine, WIRED, 2005. Office: Walter Reed Army Med Ctr Regional Anesthesia Section Anesthesia & Operative Svc 6900 Georgia Ave NW Washington DC 20307 Office Phone: 202-782-0039. Business E-Mail: chester.buckenmaier@na.amedd.army.mil.*

BUCKHOLZ, ROBERT E., JR., lawyer; b. New Haven, 1955; AB, Dartmouth Coll., 1976; JD, Columbia U., 1979. Bar: NY 1980. Assoc. Sullivan & Cromwell, NYC, 1980—87, ptnr., 1987—, now mng. ptnr., corp. and fin. practice area. Mem.: ABA. Office: Sullivan & Cromwell 125 Broad St Fl 28 New York NY 10004-2489 Office Phone: 212-558-4000. Business E-Mail: buckholzr@sullcrom.com.

BUCKI, CARL LEO, judge; b. Buffalo, July 11, 1953; s. John Ferdinand and Adeline (Graczyk) B.; m. Deborah Colleen Bruch, July 22, 1978; 1 child, Craig R. BA magna cum laude, Cornell U., 1974, JD cum laude, 1976. Bar: NY 1977, US Dist. Ct. (we. dist.) NY 1978. Confidential clk. NY Ct. Appeals, Buffalo, 1976-77; assoc. Moot & Sprague, Buffalo, 1977-83, ptnr., 1983-90, Cohen, Swados, Wright, Hanifin, Bradford & Brett, 1990-93; judge US Bankruptcy Ct. we. dist. NY, 1993—. Editor: The American Constitution From a Polish Ethnic Perspective, 1990; contbr. articles to profl. jours. Pres. Polish Cmty. Ctr., Buffalo, 1978—80, St. Gregory the Great Sch. Bd., Amherst, NY, 1991—96, chair, 1992—95; v.p. Parents Anonymous of Buffalo, 1981; bd. mgrs. Buffalo and Erie Hist. Soc., 1993—, vice-chair, 1995—96, chair, 1996—2001; nat. bd. dirs. Polish Union Am., Buffalo, 1982—86, nat. atty., 1986—93; bd. dirs. Polish Arts Club, 1997—99. Named citizen of yr. Ampol Eagle Newspaper, Buffalo, 1977, 98. Mem. ABA (exec. com. young lawyers divsn. 1987-89), NY State Bar Assn. (mem. exec. com. young lawyers sect. 1984-91, chmn. 1988-89, mem. Ho. Dels. 1989-91, nominations com. 1990-94), Erie County Bar Assn. (chmn. comml. bankruptcy law com. 1987-90), Nat. Conf. Bankruptcy Judges (cir. rep. bd. govs. 2001-04), Profl. Businessmen's Assn. (pres. 1981), Chopin Singing Soc. Home: 225 Halston Pky East Amherst NY 14051-1856 Office: U S Bankruptcy Ct 300 Pearl St Buffalo NY 14202-2510 Personal E-mail: carlbucki@aol.com.

BUCKINGHAM, AMYAND DAVID, chemistry professor; b. Sydney, NSW, Australia, Jan. 28, 1930; s. Reginald Joslin and Florence Grace (Elliot) B.; m. Jillian Bowles, July 24, 1965; children: Lucy Elliot, Mark Vincent, Alice Susan. BSc with honors, Sydney U., 1951, MSc, 1953; PhD, Cambridge U., Eng., 1956, ScD, 1985. Cert. chemist; cert. physicist. Lectr., tutor Christ Ch., Oxford, Eng., 1955-65; lectr. Oxford U., 1958-65; prof. theoretical chemistry Bristol (Eng.) U., 1965-69; prof. chemistry Cambridge (Eng.) U., 1969-97, prof. emeritus, 1997—; fellow Pembroke Coll., Cambridge, 1970-97, emeritus fellow, 1997—. Author: Laws and Applications of Thermodynamics, 1964; editor: Organic Liquids, 1978, Principles of Molecular Recognition, 1993; editor Molecular Physics, 1968-72, Internat. Revs. in Phys. Chemistry, 1981-89, Chem. Physics Letters, 1978-99. Trustee Henry Fund, 1976—. Decorated comdr. Brit. Empire. Fellow Royal Soc. (coun. 2000-01, Hughes medal 1996), Royal Soc. Chemistry (Faraday medal, 1998), Inst. of Physics (Harrie Massey medal, 1995), Optical Soc. Am. (Townes Award 2001), Am. Phys. Soc., Royal Australian Chem. Inst. (Rennie medal 1958); mem. AAAS (hon.), NAS (fgn. assoc.), Am. Chem. Soc., Internat. Acad. Quantum Molecular Sci., Internat. Union Pure and Applied Chemistry (com. phys. chemistry and biophys. chemistry divsn., v.p. 2001-03), Royal Swedish Acad. Scis. (fgn.). Avocations: cricket, travel. Office: Univ Chem Lab Lensfield Rd Cambridge CB2 1EW England E-mail: adb1000@cam.ac.uk.

BUCKINGHAM, BARBARA RAE, social studies educator; b. Union City, Ind., Jan. 27, 1932; d. Ray E. and Edith A. (Wagner) B. BA cum laude, Hanover Coll., 1954; MA, Ind. Univ., 1956. Tchr. City Sch. Dist., Marion, Ohio, 1956-64, social studies educator Rochester, NY, 1966—. Editor: Revonah, 1954; art work Aldelphean, 1959. Vol. Peace Corps, Ethiopia, 1964-66, Mary Cariola Children's Ctr., Christian Heritage Homes, Hope Hall, Congresswomen Louise Slaughter Campaign, 1996-97, 96-98; mem. governing bd. Rochester Returned Peace Corps Vols., 1968-76; com. mem. Councilwoman Letvin, Gates, N.Y., 1980; steering com. Pub. Affairs Forum, Hanover, 1952, DAR. Mem. AAUW (pres. 1958-59), DAR, Rochester Tchrs. Assn., Nat. Peace Corps Assn., Friends of Ethiopia, Rochester Tchr. Assn. (election com.), Pi Gamma Mu (Outstanding Grad. award 1954), Gamma Sigma Pi, Alpha Phi Gamma. Democrat. Presbyterian. Avocations: travel, art work. Home: 64 Lyellwood Pkwy Rochester NY 14606-4532

BUCKINGHAM, BETTY JO, library media consultant; b. Aug. 6, 1927; d. Irvin Amos and E(lsie) Dean (Webb) B. BA, Iowa State Tchrs. Coll., 1948; MS in Libr. Sci., U. Ill., Urbana, 1953; PhD, U. Minn., 1978. Tchr. English Earlham (Iowa) Cmty. Sch., 1948-50; tchr., libr. Harlan (Iowa) Cmty. Sch., 1950-54; libr. Ft. Madison (Iowa) Cmty. H.S., 1954-60, Kurtz Jr. H.S., Des Moines, 1960-64; cons. Iowa Dept. Edn., Des Moines, 1964—94. Lectr. U. Minn.-Mpls., 1970. Author, editor: Growth Notes for School Media Specialists, New Iowa Standards for Library Media Programs, 1989, Selection of Instructional Materials, A Model Policy and Rules, 1980, 1994; author: Weeding the Library Media Center Collections, 1984, Weeding the Library Media Center Collections, 1994, Planning the School Library Media Center Budget, 1984, Planning the School LIbrary Media Center Budget, 1994; editor: Iowa and some Iowans, 1995, Women at the Well, 1987, Plan for Progress in the Library Media Center, P-K12, 1991; joint compiler in field:; contbr. articles to profl. jours.; author: History of Local Church, 1994, Church District, 2002, Lenten and Advent Dramas, 1996—. Mem. steering com. women's caucus Ch. of the Brethren, 1977-80, editor Cistern periodical, 1980-87, Femailings periodical, 1994-97, bd. dirs. No. Plains dist., 1984-91, 2002-, conf. moderator, 1990-91, conf. sec. 2002—. Mem. ALA, NEA, Am. Assn. Sch. Librs. (past sec., pres., councillor 1984-85), Iowa Ednl. Media Assn. (cons. 1973-83), Iowa Libr. Assn., Intellectual Freedom Found., Women's Fellowship Prairie City (past pres.), Beta Phi Mu, Kappa Delta Pi. Democrat. Avocations: reading, classical music, writing. Home: 10048 Highway F70 W Prairie City IA 50228-8471

BUCKINGHAM, DAVID COWAN, judge; b. Murray, Ky., Oct. 29, 1951; s. Robert Ray and Betty Sue (Hutson) B.; m. Dianne Lee Armstrong, July 10, 1982; 1 child, Tyler Daniel. BA, Murray State U., 1974; JD, U. Louisville, 1977. Bar: Ky. 1977. Asst. county atty. Calloway County, Murray, 1978-81; sole practice Murray, 1978-81; dist. judge 42nd Judicial Dist., Murray, 1982-86; circuit judge 42nd Judicial Cir., Murray, 1987-96; judge Ct. of Appeals, 1997—. Mem. Ky. Bar Assn., Calloway County Bar Assn. Democrat. Mem. Ch. of Christ. Avocations: golf, baseball card collecting. Office: 312 S 8th St Murray KY 42071-2428 Office Phone: 270-753-4324.

BUCKINGHAM, DEIDRE LYN, writer, musician; b. Endicott, N.Y., Apr. 18, 1973; d. Richard Paul and Doris May (Mlynar) Moore; m. Jeff K. Buckingham, June 9, 1995. AA in Office Tech., Cedarville (Ohio) Coll., 1993, BA in Profl. Writing, 1995. Tech. writer Ont. Sys. Corp., Muncie, Ind., 1995-97. Author: Snapdragon's Dance, 2004. Caption editor Deaf Video Comm. Am., Lisle, Ill., 1997-99. Recipient Pres.'s award for lit. excellence Iliad Press, 1997, Editor's Choice award Internat. Libr. Poetry, 2003; Mari Heyduck scholar Women in Comm., 1994. Avocations: writing poetry and essays, recording original music.

BUCKINGHAM, EDWIN JOHN, III, lawyer; b. Grand Forks, N.D., Sept. 15, 1947; s. Edwin John Jr. and Kathryn Ruth (Aird) B.; m. Cheryl Ann Pantalone, 1971; 1 child, Emma Nicole. AB, Yale U., 1969, JD, 1972. Bar: N.Y. 1973, Tex. 1978. Assoc. Shea Gould Climenko & Kramer, N.Y.C., 1972-74; assoc. gen. counsel Celanese Corp., N.Y.C., 1974-77; mgr. legal affairs Solvay Polymers, Inc., Houston, 1977-79, dir. legal affairs, 1979-81, gen. counsel, v.p., 1981—, Solvay Am., Inc., Houston, 1984—. Sec. Wessex Civic Assn., Houston, 1986-88. Named Chevalier de l'Ordre de Leopold, Belgium. Mem. ABA, Am. Corp. Counsel Assn., Tex. Bar Assn., Tex.-Mex. Bar Assn. Avocations: fencing, birding. Office: Solvay Am 3333 Richmond Ave Houston TX 77098-3007 Office Phone: 713-525-6080.

BUCKINGHAM, ELIZABETH C., lawyer; b. 1964; AB magna cum laude, Smith Coll., 1985; JD, Harvard Univ., 1988. Bar: DC 1988, Minn. 1994. Ptnr., co-head, trademark and litig. group Dorsey & Whitney LLP, Mpls. Articles editor Harvard Jour. on Legis., 1987—88, lectr., writer in field. Mem.: Minn. Intellectual Property Lawyers Assn., Internat. Trademark Assn., Midwest Intellectual Property Inst., WomenVenture (bd. dir. 2000—), Phi Beta Kappa. Office: Dorsey & Whitney LLP Ste 1500 50 S Sixth St Minneapolis MN 55402-1498 Office Phone: 612-343-2178. Office Fax: 612-340-8856. Business E-Mail: buckingham.elizabeth@dorsey.com.

BUCKINGHAM, LORIE, automotive executive; BA in Math. and Chemistry, SUNY, Potsdam. Dir. enterprise IT solutions Union Carbide Corp., Danbury, Conn., 1993—99; former chief info. officer Zonetrader.com, Chgo.; dir. global software solutions Visteon Corp., Dearborn, Mich., 2000—02, v.p., chief info. officer, 2002—. Office: Visteon Corp 1700 Rotunda Dr Dearborn MI 48120

BUCKINGHAM, SHELLEY MARIE, music educator; b. Canton, Ohio, Jan. 3, 1976; d. Kenneth Albert and Ruth Marie Carver; m. David Wesley Buckingham, June 26, 1999. Bachelors Degree, Bowling Green State U., 1998. Band tchr. grades 5-12 Greeneview Local Schs., Jamestown, Ohio, 1998—99; band tchr. grades 6-12 Fremont (Ind.) Local Schs., 1999—2000, Elkhart (Ind.) Cmty. Schs., 2000—. Mem.: NEA, Ind. State Tchrs. Assn., Music Educators Nat. Conf., Ind. Bandmasters Assn., Ind. State Sch. Members Assn. Office: West Side Middle School 101 S Nappanee Elkhart IN 46514 Office Phone: 574-295-4815. Personal E-mail: s_buckingham@hotmail.com.

BUCKINGHAM, VIRGINIA, editor; m. David Lowy; 1 child, Jack. B in Comms., Boston Coll., 1987. Dep. press sec., asst. press sec. to Gov. Weld and Lt. Gov.; press. sec. to Gov. Weld and Lt. Gov. Cellucci, 1994-95; campaign mgr. Gov. Weld's bid for U.S. Senate; chief of staff to Gov. Cellucci and Lt. Gov. Swift, 1997-2000; exec. dir., CEO Mass. Port Authority (Massport), East Boston, 2000—01; dep. editl. page editor Boston (Mass.) Herald, 2003—.

BUCKLAND, ARTHUR RENWICK, research and development company executive; b. Bellefonte, Pa., June 1, 1948; s. John Alexander Channing and Miriam Helen (Renwick) Buckland; m. Eunice Sue Kan Chen; 1 child, Marc C.C. BSEE, Syracuse U., 1970; MBA, Harvard Bus. Sch., Boston, 1976. Pres. Emartex Schlumberger, Paris, 1982—90, Lax Electronics, London, New York, 1990—91; CEO Four P. Systems, San Diego, 1991—92, CP Clare, Boston, 1992—2001, Engim, Boston, 2001—03, ABS, Boston, 2003—04, Doo Mgmt, Boston, 2004—. Bd. dirs. Several private cos., 1975—. Corporator Emerson Hosp., Concord, Mass., 1999—; leader Boy Scouts Am., Concord, Mass., 1996—; coach U.S. LaCrosse, Concord, Mass., 2000—. Named Entrepreneur of the Yr. NASDAQ, E&Y, others, 1996, Eagle Scout, Boy Scouts Am., N.J., 1962. Mem.: IEEE, Nat. Assn. Corp. Dirs. (pres. 1999—), Nashawatac Golf Club, Eta Kappa Nu, Tau Beta Pi. Achievements include speaks 5 langs.; IPO's on NASDAQ of L.S.E; completed 35 MIA Transactions worth over 7 billion; raised $150 million in private and public capital while starting nine companies. Avocations: cuisine, fine arts, sports, travel. Office: Doo Mgmt 263 Elm St Concord MA 01742 Office Phone: 978-287-0188. Office Fax: 978-287-0388. E-mail: art@buckland.com.

BUCKLAND, BARRY CHRISTOPHER, chemical engineer; b. London, Jan. 6, 1948; BSc, Manchester (Eng.) U., 1970; MSc, U. Coll. London, 1971, PhD in Biochem. Engring., 1974. Biochem. engr. Abbott Lab., Chgo., 1974-77; sr. engr. Lederle Lab., Pearl River, N.Y., 1977-80; dir. Fermentation Pilot Plant, Merck & Co. Inc., Rahway, N.J., 1980-86, biochem. process R&D, 1986-90, sr. dir., 1990-93, exec. dir., 1993-96; v.p. Bio Process R&D, Merck & Co. Inc., 1996—. Vis. prof. Univ. Coll., London, 1989—, Rutgers U., 1990—. Fellow Am. Inst. Med. & Biol. Engring., Internat. Inst. Biotechnology (lectr. 1995); mem. AICE (dir. Food, Pharm. & Bioentring. Divsn. 1993-95), Am. Chem. Soc. (lectr. 1994), Nat. Acad. Engring. Office: PO Box 4 West Point PA 19486-0900 E-mail: barry_buckland@merck.com.

BUCKLAND, JON (JONNY), musician; b. London, Nov. 11, 1977; Student, U. Coll. London. Lead guitarist Coldplay, 1998—. Musician: (albums) Parachutes, 2000 (Grammy award: Best Alternative Music Album, 2001), A Rush of Blood to the Head, 2002 (Grammy awards: Best Alternative Music Album, 2002, Best Rock Performance By A Duo Or Group With Vocal for song "In My Place", 2002, Record Of The Yr. for song "Clocks", 2003), Live 2003, 2003. Office: Capital Records 1750 North Vine St 10th Floor Hollywood CA 90028

BUCKLAND, KAREN WISSER, music educator; b. Allentown, Pa., Apr. 9, 1959; d. Donald Wesley and Ethel Cecelia Wisser; m. James Patrick Buckland, June 6, 1998. MusB, Mansfield U., 1981; MusM, U. S.C., 1984, D in Musical Arts, 1997. Freelance musician/tchr., Columbia, SC, 1981; organist, pianist Spring Valley Presbyn. Ch., Columbia, 1986—2001, Charleston So. U., Summerville, SC, 1997—2000; asst. prof. music Presbyn. Coll., Clinton, SC, 2002; organist, pianist First Presbyn. Ch., Clinton, 2001—. Dir., founder Musical Achievement Day, Clinton, 2000—; artistic dir. piano clinic Presbyn. Coll., Clinton, SC, 2002—, dir. keyboard studies, artistic dir., 2002—; founder, artistic dir. concert series First Presbyn. Ch., Clinton, 2002—; guest lectr. S.C. Music Educators Conf., Charleston, 2004; adjudicator and lectr. in field. Musician, co-founder: Ludlamshöhle Ensemble, 2003—. Belk fellow, Presbyn. Coll., 2004—. Mem.: S.C. Music Educators Assn., Music Educators Nat. Conf., Music Tchrs. Nat. Assn., S.C. Music Tchrs. Assn. (dir. H.S. state auditions 2002—04, v.p. state conf. 2005—), Sigma Alpha iota, Pi Kappa Lambda. Republican. Avocations: cooking, pistol shotting, reading, genealogy. Office: Presbyn Coll Music Dept 503 S Broad St Clinton SC 29325

BUCKLAND, MICHAEL KEEBLE, librarian, educator; b. Wantage, Eng., Nov. 23, 1941; came to U.S., 1972; s. Walter Basil and Norah Elaine (Rudd) B.; m. Waltraud Leeb, July 11, 1964; children: Anne Margaret, Anthony Francis. BA, Oxford U., 1963; postgrad. diploma in librarianship, Sheffield U., 1965, PhD, 1972. Grad. trainee Bodleian Library, Oxford, Eng., 1963-64; asst. librarian U. Lancaster (Eng.) Library, 1965-72; asst. dir. for tech. svcs. Purdue U. Libraries, West Lafayette, Ind., 1972-75; assoc. prof. Sch. of Info. Mgmt. and Sys. U. Calif., Berkeley, 1976-79, dean, 1976-84, prof., 1979—2003, prof. emeritus, 2004—, asst. v.p. library plans and policies, 1983-87; v.p. Ind. Coop. Library Svcs. Auth., 1974-75. Co-dir. Electronic Cultural Atlas Initiative, 2000—; vis. scholar Western Mich. U., 1979; vis. prof. U. Klagenfurt, Austria, 1980, U. New South Wales, Australia, 1988. Author: Book Availability and the Library User, 1975, (with others) The Use of Gaming in Education for Library Management, 1976, Reader in Operations Research for Libraries, 1976, Library Services in Theory and Context, 1983, 2d edit., 1988, Information and Information Systems, 1991, Redesigning Library Services, 1992; editor: Historical Studies in Information Science, 1998, Robert Gitler and the Japan Library School, 1999. Fulbright Rsch. scholar U. Tech., Graz, Austria, 1989. Mem. ALA, Am. Soc. Info. Sci. (pres. 1998), Assn. Libr. and Info. Sci. Edn., Calif. Libr. Assn. Office: U Calif Sch Info Mgmt And Sys Berkeley CA 94720-0001

BUCKLER, MARILYN LEBOW, school psychologist, educational consultant; b. N.Y.C., Mar. 18, 1933; d. Herman and Gertrude (Abolitz) Lebow; m. Sheldon A. Buckler, June 1, 1952 (div. 1978); children: Julie, Eve, Sarah Buckler Welcome. BS cum laude, NYU, 1954; MEd in Counseling, Northeastern U., 1970. Cert. ednl. psychologist, Mass.; sch. guidance counselor, Mass., sch. psychologist, Mass. Kindergarten tchr. Washington Pub. Schs., 1955-56, Stamford (Conn.) Pub. Schs., 1956-58; guidance counselor Framingham (Mass.) Pub. Schs., 1969-70; sch. psychologist, guidance counselor Carlisle (Mass.) Pub. Schs., 1970-95; parent program cons. Reach out to Schs. program Wellesley Coll.-Stone Ctr., 1993—. Tchr. parenting course Middlesex C.C., Bedford, Mass., 1990—, cons. LEAP program, 1992-93; workshop leader, creator parenting courses, various pvt. schs. and orgns., Mass., 1990—; spl. project cons., workshop specialist "Families First" Wheelock Coll., 1995—. Mem. ACA, Mass. Sch. Counselor Assn., Mass. Sch. Psychologists Assn., Pi Lambda Theta. Avocations: films, cooking, travel, reading.

BUCKLER, SHELDON A., technology company executive; b. NYC, May 18, 1931; s. Morris H. and Mollie M. (Smith) B.; m. Dorothea J. Chandler, June 30, 1978; children: Julie, Eve, Sarah. BA, NYU, 1951; PhD, Columbia U., 1954. Rsch. assoc. U. Md., 1954-56; rsch. group leader Am. Cyanamid Co., Stamford, Conn., 1956-62; mgr. organic unit AMF, Springdale, Conn., 1962-64; with Polaroid Corp., Cambridge, Mass., 1964-94, vice-chmn. bd., 1990-94; chmn. bd. Commonwealth Energy Sys., Cambridge, 1995-99. Chmn. bd. Lord Corp., 2000—; bd. dirs. Parlex Corp. Contbr. articles to profl. jours.; patentee in field. Trustee Va. Union U., 1973-75; chmn. bd. Mass. Eye and Ear Infirmary, 1996-02. With U.S. Army, 1954-56. Recipient Maurice Holland award Indsl. Rsch. Inst., 1998. Mem. Am. Chem. Soc., Phi Beta Kappa. Office: Lord Corp 111 Lord Dr Cary NC 27511-7923 Office Phone: 800-524-2885 ext. 6228. Personal E-mail: sheldonbuckler@comcast.net.

BUCKLES, BRADLEY A., trade association administrator; BA, U. Wyo., 1971; JD, Washburn U., 1974. Bar: Kans. 1974. Chief counsel U.S. Bur. Alcohol, Tobacco, Firearms and Explosives, 1974—95, dep. dir., 1996—99, dir., 1999—2003; exec. v.p. Anti-Piracy Unit Rec. Industry Assn. Am., Washington, 2003—. Office: RIAA Ste 300 1330 Connecticut Ave NW Washington DC 20036 Business E-Mail: bbuckles@riaa.com.

BUCKLES, JUDITH ANN, dental educator, program administrator; b. Francisville, Ind., Feb. 15, 1940; d. Lawrence Melvin and Mary Rosella Johnston; m. Edward Donald Buckles, Jan. 27, 1962; children: Dawn Marie, Erica Danielle, Erin Nichole. Cert. dental nurse, Elkhart (Ind.) U. Medicine and Dentistry, 1959; AAS, Purdue U., 1986, BS with honors, 1991. Cert. dental asst. Dental asst. Francis A Jones, DDS, Lafayette, Ind., 1959-69, Raymond Price, DDS, Lafayette, 1969-73; program supr., sr. instr. Ivy Tech. State Coll., Lafayette, 1973—. Religious instr. St. Ann Ch. and Shrine, Lafayette, 1980-95; asst. with fund raising St. Ann Rosary Soc., Lafayette, 1979—, St. Ann Social Club, Lafayette, 1994—, St. Ann Parish Coun., 2000-. Fellow Am. Dental Assts. Assn., Nat. Assn. Dental Assts., Ind. Dental Assocs. Assn., Lafayette Dental Assts. Assn., German-Am. Club, Phi Kappa Phi. Avocations: collecting antique depression glass ware, collecting cookbooks, collecting boyd bears and angels, collecting porcelain dolls, collecting german dishes. Office: Ivy Tech State Coll 3101 S Creasy Ln Lafayette IN 47905-6299

BUCKLES, MICHAEL KIM, music educator, musician; s. Billy Paul and Kwang Ja Buckles; m. Boriana Kojouharova, June 12, 2003. BA, Tulane U., 1993; MusM, Cleve. Inst. of Music, 1995; D of Mus. Arts, La. State U., 2003. Registered Suzuki instr. Suzuki Assn. of the Ams. Sect. violinist La. Philharm., New Orleans, 1995—98; instr. of violin and viola Xavier U., New Orleans, 1996—98; Suzuki instr. prep. dept. U. of New Orleans, 1996—2002; instr. of violin and viola Dillard U., New Orleans, 2000—02; asst. prof. of upper strings and music edn. McNeese State U., Lake Charles, 2002—; concertmaster Lake Charles (La.) Symphony, 2002—. Musician: Three Songs from Shindler's List, Symphonie Concertante by Haydn. Dir. Lake Charles Area Youth Orch., 2002—. Recipient Mayor's award, Lake Charles Area Youth Orch., 2004. Mem.: La. Music Educators Assn. (orch. divsn. chair 2004—), La. Music Tchrs. Assn. (string chmn. 2003—04, string chair 2003—), Suzuki Assn. of the Ams., Music Tchrs. Nat. Assn. Office: McNeese State Univ Box 92175 Lake Charles LA 70609 Office Phone: 337-475-5034. Office Fax: 337-475-5063. Business E-Mail: mbuckles@mcneese.edu.

BUCKLES, ROBERT HOWARD, retired investment company executive; b. Champaign, Ill., June 30, 1932; s. Renick Hull and Ethel Maxine Buckles; m. Linda Carol Porter, Dec. 27, 1958; children: Meredith Ann, Christopher John. BA, Stanford U., 1953; MBA, Harvard U., 1957. Security analyst Lehman Corp., N.Y.C., 1957-65, v.p., 1965-69, exec. v.p., 1969-73, pres., 1973-84, also bd. dirs.; pres. Gas Properties, Inc., 1973-84; exec. v.p., dir. Lehman Mgmt. Co., 1973-84; pres., chief investment officer Rothschild Asset Mgmt. Inc., 1984-87; mng. dir. Rothschild, Inc., 1984-87; chief investment officer, sr. mng. dir. Furman Selz Capital Mgmt., 1987-97. Dir. One William St. Fund.; bd. dirs. Assn. Publicly Traded Investment Funds. Contbr. articles to profl. publs. With security agy. AUS, 1954-56. Mem. N.Y. Soc. Securities Analysts. Home: 425 E 58th St Apt 35C New York NY 10022-2300

BUCKLES, STEPHEN GARY, economist, educator; b. Kansas City, Mo., June 11, 1943; s. Orland and Leighfern (Emry) B.; m. Mary Parker Harmon, Nov. 28, 1970. AB, Grinnell Coll., 1965; PhD, Vanderbilt U., 1976. Economist Joint Coun. Econ. Edn., N.Y.C., 1970-74; prof. U. Mo., Columbia, 1976-88; pres. Nat Coun. Econ. Edn., N.Y.C., 1989-94; prof. econs., sr. lectr. Vanderbilt U., Nashville, 1994—. Vis. prof. Vanderbilt U., 1983; tchr. NYU, 1972-74; past chair individual investors adv. com. N.Y. Stock Exch.; mem. mgmt. team, standing com. 2006 Econs. Nat. Assessment. Recipient tchg. awards U. Mo., 1986-87, John Schramm Leadership award Nat. Assn. Econ. Educators, 1989, Student's Choice award Vanderbilt, 1996, William Forbes award for Pub. Awareness, 1998, Marvin Bower award in econ. edn., 2002. Office: Vanderbilt U Dept Econs Nashville TN 37235 Office Phone: 615-322-0199. E-mail: stephen.buckles@vanderbilt.edu.

BUCKLEW, NEIL S., former academic administrator, educator; b. Morgantown, W.Va., Oct. 23, 1940; s. Douglas Earl and Lanah L. (Martin) B.; children— Elizabeth, Jennifer, Jeffrey. AB, U. Mo.; MS, U. N.C.; PhD (grad. fellow), U. Wis. Dir. personnel Duke U., 1964-66; dir. employee relations U. Wis., 1966-70; prof., v.p. Central Mich. U., Mt. Pleasant, 1970-76; prof., provost Ohio U., Athens, 1976-80; pres. U. Mont., Missoula, 1981-86, W.Va. U., 1986-95, prof. Morgantown, 1995—. Vis. rsch. fellow Pa. State U.;

arbitrator in field. Author: Public Sector Collective Bargaining, Planning in Higher Education. Mem. Nat. Assn. State Univs. and Land Grant Colls. Office: West Va U PO Box 6025 Morgantown WV 26506-6025 Business E-Mail: nbucklew@wvu.edu.

BUCKLEY, CLAUDE LANGFORD, artist; b. Madrid, May 15, 1959; came to U.S., 1972; s. Fergus Reid and Elizabeth Hanna (Howell) B.; divorced; children: Ian Howell, Aidan Michael. BFA, U. of the South, 1980. Aartist, 1980—. Works include portrait of H.R.M. Juan Carlos de Borbon, King of Spain. Mem Springdale Hall. Roman Catholic. Avocations: photography, outdoor activities. Home: PO Box 1421 Camden SC 29020-1421

BUCKLEY, DONALD GRAY, librarian; b. Springfield, Mass., June 21, 1952; s. Donald Gray and Josephine Baggarley Buckley. AB, Colby Coll., Waterville, Maine, 1975; MA, Simmons Coll., Boston, 2003. Bookmobile libr. Westfield (Mass.) Athenaeum, 1976—87, br. libr., 1987—90, circulation mgr., 1990—97, sys. libr., 1997—2000, asst. dir., 2000—03; pub. svc. mgr. Cerritos Libr., Calif., 2003—05, support svcs. mgr., 2005—. Mem. circulation task force CWMARS Libr. Group, Paxton, Mass., 1996—2001, mem. vendor options com., 2000—02; Legislative Libr. Day trip organizer Mass. Libr. Assn., 2003. Pres. Western Mass. Colby Club, 1987—94; assoc. class agent class of 1975 Colby Coll., 1998—. Mem.: Am. Libr. Assn., Pub. Libr. Assn., Calif. Libr. Assn., Beta Phi Mu. Avocations: tennis, running, cross country skiing, languages. Home: 231 7th St #B Seal Beach CA 90740 Office: Cerritos Libr 18025 Bloomfield Ave Cerritos CA 90703

BUCKLEY, FRANCIS H., economist, law educator, lawyer; b. Saskatoon, Sask., Canada, Aug. 4, 1948; s. F.J. and H.B. Buckley; m. Esther Goldberg; 1 child, Sarah. BA, McGill U., Montreal, Canada, 1969, LLB, 1974; LLM, Harvard U., 1975. Bar: Ont. 1982. Asst. prof. McGill Univ., 1977—82, assoc. prof., 1984—89; assoc. Osler Hoskin & Harcourt, Toronto, 1982—84; prof. George Mason Univ., Arlington, Va., 1989—; dir. Law & Econ. Ctr., George Mason Univ. Vis. Olin fellow Univ. Chgo. Law Sch., 1988—89; vis. prof. Sorbonne, Paris, 1999—2001. Author: The Morality of Laughter, 2003; editor: The Fall and Rise of Freedom of Contract, 1999; contbr. articles to prof. jour. Office: George Mason Law and Econs Ctr 3301 N Fairfax Dr Arlington VA 22201

BUCKLEY, FREDERICK JEAN, lawyer; b. Wilmington, Ohio, Nov. 5, 1923; s. William Millard and Martha (Bright) B.; m. Josephine K. Buckley, Dec. 4, 1945; children: Daniel J., Fredrica Buckley Elder, Matthew J. Student, Wilmington Coll., 1941-42, Ohio State U., 1942-43; AB, U. Mich., 1948, LLB, 1949; LLD (hon.), Wilmington Coll., 2004. Bar: Ohio 1950, U.S. Dist. Ct. (so. dist.) Ohio 1952, U.S. Supreme Ct. 1978, U.S. Ct. Appeals (6th cir.) 1981, Fla. 1982, U.S. Dist. Ct. (mid. dist.) Fla. 1991; cert. cir. ct. mediator, Fla.; cert. arbitrator Fla. state and fed. cts. Assoc. G.L. Schilling, Sr., Wilmington, 1951-52; ptnr. Schilling & Buckley, Wilmington, 1953-56; sole practice Wilmington, 1956-62; sr. ptnr. Buckley, Miller & Wright, Wilmington, 1962—2002. Chmn. The Wilmington Savs. Bank, 1971—2003; solicitor City of Wilmington, 1954-63. Contbr. articles in field. With AUS, 1943-46, ETO. Joint program Mich. Inst. Pub. Adminstrn. fellow, 1948. Fellow Am. Coll. Trial Lawyers; mem. ABA, Am. Arbitration Assn. (comml. panel), Ohio State Bar Assn., Clinton County Bar Assn., Fla. Bar, Fla. Acad. Profl. Mediators, Collier County Bar Assn., Ohio State Bar Found. Republican. Methodist. Office Phone: 239-434-8475.

BUCKLEY, GEORGE W., sporting goods executive; PhD in Engring., U. Southhampton (Eng.). Various mgmt. positions Brit. Railways Bd., GEC Turbine Generators Ltd., Detroit Edison Co.; past pres. elec. motors divsn. Emerson Elec. Co.; pres. Mercury Marine unit Brunswick Corp., Fond du Lac, Wis., 1997-2000, chmn. & CEO Lake Forest, Ill., 2000—. Bd. dirs. Tyco Internat. Ltd, 2002—. Office: Brunswick Corp 1 N Field Ct Lake Forest IL 60045-4811

BUCKLEY, JACQUELYN ANASTAISA, educational psychologist, researcher; b. Elk Grove Village, Ill., Feb. 21, 1972; d. John and Betty Buckley; m. David Edward Ludwa, Dec. 27, 1997. BA, St. Mary's Coll., Notre Dame, Ind., 1994; PhD, U. Wis., 2002. Asst. rsch. prof., rsch. fellow U. Nebr., 2002—04; NIH rsch. fellow Johns Hopkins U., Balt., 2004—. Contbr. articles to profl. jours., posters to profl. confs. Vol., tchr. Teach for Am., Pharr, Tex., 1994—97; vol. Teach for Am. Alumni Orgns., Madison, Lincoln, and Balt., 1997—2005, Habitat for Humanity, Madison, 1997—2001. Recipient rsch. fellowship, NIH, 2004—06, Grad. Student Rsch. award, U. of Wis. Dean's Club, 2000. Mem.: APA (Cert. of Merit, Psychologist in Pub. Svc. award 2001), Soc. for Prevention Rsch., Nat. Assn. Sch. Psychologists (cert. in sch. psychology), Psi Chi. Avocation: running. Home: # 404 7111 Woodmont Ave Bethesda MD 20814 Office: Johns Hopkins U 624 N Broadway Baltimore MD 21205 Office Phone: 410-955-0412. Personal E-mail: jbuckley97@hotmail.com.

BUCKLEY, JAMES W., librarian; b. LA, Aug. 16, 1933; s. George W. and Alta L. (Hale) B.; m. Margaret Ann Wall, Aug. 7, 1965; children: Kathleen Ann, James William, John Whitney. AA, Los Angeles Harbor Coll., 1953; BA, Calif. State U., Long Beach, 1960; MLS, U. So. Calif., 1961, M in Pub. Adminstrn., 1974. Cert. tchr., Calif. Libr. West Gardena br. Los Angeles County Pub. Libr., 1961-62, librarian Carson br., 1962-63; libr. Montebello (Calif.) Regional Libr., 1963-68; regional librarian Orange County (Calif.) Pub. Libr., 1968, dir. pub. services, 1969-74; county librarian San Mateo County (Calif.) Libr., 1974-77, Marin County (Calif.) Libr., 1978; city librarian Torrance (Calif.) Pub. Libr., 1979—. Exec. dir. Calif. Nat. Libr. Week, 1970; tchr. pub. svc. Coll. San Mateo, 1975; chmn. Met. Coop. Libr. Sys., 1989-90, Calif. Libr. Assn. Assembly, 1993-95. Served with U.S. Army, 1955-57. Mem. ALA, Am. Soc. Pub. Adminstrn., Calif. Libr. Assn., Rotary. Office: Torrance Pub Libr 3301 Torrance Blvd Torrance CA 90503-5014 E-mail: jbuckley@tornet.com.

BUCKLEY, JEREMIAH STEPHEN, lawyer; b. San Francisco, Oct. 12, 1944; s. Jeremiah Stephen and Flora (Saur) Buckley; m. Deborah Stanley, Nov. 5, 1983. AB, Fairfield U., 1966; JD, U. Va., 1969. Bar: Conn. 1969, D.C. 1972, U.S. Supreme Ct 1980. VISTA vol. Wayne County Legal Svcs., Detroit, 1969-70; asst. counsel govt. ops. com. U.S. Ho. of Reps., Washington, 1971-73; minority counsel housing subcom. U.S. Senate, Washington, 1973-77, minority staff dir. banking com., 1977-79; ptnr. Leighton, Lemov, Jacobs & Buckley, Washington, 1979-84, Thacher Proffitt & Wood, Washington, 1984-93, Goodwin Procter LLP, Washington, 1994—2003, Buckley Kolar LLP, Washington, 2003—. Co-author: The Law of Electronic Signatures and Records, 2004. Mem.: ABA, Fed. Bar Assn., Electronic Fin. Svcs. Coun., Exchequer Club, Millwood Golf Club, Kenwood Golf Club. Office: 1250 24th St NW Washington DC 20037 Office Phone: 202-349-8000. Business E-Mail: jbuckley@buckleykolar.com.

BUCKLEY, JOHN JOSEPH, JR., healthcare executive; b. Evanston, Ill., Oct. 5, 1944; s. John Joseph and Mary Ruth (Smith) B.; m. Sarah Amelia Puceloski, May 16, 1970; children: Ruth Mary, Patricia Kimberly, John Joseph III AB, Kenyon Coll., 1966; MBA, George Washington U., 1969. Asst. adminstr. Maricopa County Gen. Hosp., Phoenix, 1969-71, St. Joseph's Hosp. and Med. Ctr., Phoenix, 1971-74, assoc. adminstr., 1974-76, v.p., 1976-79, pres., 1984-88, St. Anthony's Hosp., Amarillo, Tex., 1979-84, St. Anthony's Devel. Corp., Amarillo, 1982-84; chief operating officer Harrington Cancer Ctr., Amarillo, 1982-84; sr. v.p. Mercy Health System, Cin., 1988-91; pres. So. Ill. Healthcare Enterprises, Carbondale, Ill., 1992—2001, Jack Buckley & Assocs., College Station, Tex., 2001—; interim pres., CEO St. Mary's Hosp. of East St. Louis, Ill., 2002; interim COO, St. Joseph Campus of Via Christi Med. Ctr., Wichita, Kans., 2003; interim CEO St. Joseph Regional Health Ctr., Bryan, Tex., 2003—04, CEO, 2004—, pres., 2005—. Pres. So. Ill. Hosp. Svcs., Health Svcs. of So. Ill., Regional Health Plan, 1992-2001. Active Amarillo Alliance of Cmty. Svc. Execs., Amarillo Area Acad. Health Ctr. Corp., Amarillo Area Hosp. Home Care, Amarillo Found. Health and Sci., Panhandle chpt. Tex. Soc. to Prevent Blindness, Amarillo Jr. League, Children's Oncology Svcs. of Tex. Panhandle; Amarillo diocesan coord. health affairs; mem. adminstrv. com. Amarillo; pres. Mercy Svcs. Corp., 1984-88; bd. dirs. Greater Phoenix Affordable Health Care Found., 1984-88; trustee Kenyon Coll., Gambier, Ohio, 1991-95, mem. alumni coun., 1998-2003, pres., 2001-02; mem. SI Edge, 1995-2003. Fellow: Am. Coll. Health-care Execs. (regent Ariz. 1984—88, regent So. Ill. 1998—2002); mem.: Ariz. Hosp. Assn., Ariz. Kidney Found., Cath. Health Assn. U.S., Ill. Hosp. Assn. (trustee 1995—2001, chmn. 2000), Tex. Hosp. Assn. (trustee 1983—84), Alumni Assn. of George Washington U. Health Svcs. Mgmt. and Policy (pres. 1995—97), Delta Phi (pres. alumni assn. 1988—2000). Republican. Roman Catholic. Office: St Joseph Regional Health Ctr 2801 Franciscan Dr Bryan TX 77802-2544 Office Phone: 979-776-2446. Business E-Mail: jbuckley@st-joseph.org. E-mail: jackbuckleyjr@earthlink.net.

BUCKLEY, JOSEPH PAUL, III, computer technician; b. Chgo., July 6, 1949; s. Joseph Paul and Helen (Lavelle) B.; m. Patricia Nemeth, June 17, 1972; children: Megan, Michael, Patrick, Thomas. BA, Loyola U., Chgo., 1971; MS in Detection of Deception, Reid Coll. Detection of Deception, Chgo., 1973. Lic., Ill. Detection of deception examiner John E. Reid & Assocs., Inc., Chgo., 1971—, chief polygraph examiner, 1978-80, dir. Chgo. office, 1980-82, pres. corp. Chgo., Milw., 1982—. Chmn. Ill. Detection of Deception Examiner Com., 1978-82; mem. adv. com. Office of Tech. Assessment, 1983 Co-author: Criminal Interrogation and Confessions, 1st edit., 1962, 4th edit., 2001, The Investigator Anthology, 1999, Essentials of the Reid Technique, 2004; contbr. articles to profl. jours. Mem. Am. Polygraph Assn. (v.p. 1979-80, chmn. pub. rels. com. 1979-80, 84-95, awards), Ill. Polygraph Soc. (v.p. 1981, pres. 1982-83), Am. Acad. Forensic Scis., Am. Mgmt. Assn., Am. Soc. Indsl. Security (investigations com. 1983-89), Spl. Agts. Assn., Internat. Pers. Mgmt. Assn., Internat. Assn. Chiefs Policy, Chgo. Crime Commn. Office: 250 S Wacker Dr Ste 1200 Chicago IL 60606-5841 Office Phone: 312-876-1600. E-mail: jbuckley@reid.com.

BUCKLEY, MICHAEL FRANCIS, lawyer; b. Saranac Lake, N.Y., Nov. 1, 1943; s. Francis Edward and Marjorie (Mooney) B.; m. Mary Thornton, June 26, 1965; children: Sean, Kathleen. BA, Dartmouth Coll., 1965; JD, Cornell U., 1968. Bar: N.Y. 1969, Fla. 1982, U.S. Dist. Ct. (we. dist.) N.Y. 1970. Assoc. Harter, Secrest & Emery, Rochester, N.Y., 1968-75, ptnr., 1976—. Contbg. author: Estate Planning and Probate in New York, 1985; co-editor: Administration of New York Estates, 1990. Bd. dirs. Highland Hosp. Found., Rochester, 1981-95, pres., 1984-87; bd. dirs. Highland Hosp., 1987—, pres., 1992-94; bd. dirs. Highland Health Sys., Inc., 1995-97, Strong Ptnrs. Health System, Inc., 1997—, YMCA of Greater Rochester, 1997—2005, Highland Cmty. Devel. Corp., 1998-2002, Highland Living Ctr., Inc., 1998-2002, Rochester Area Cmty. Found., 1999—, James P. Wilmot Found., Inc., 2000—, U. Rochester Med. Ctr., 2000—, James P. Wilmot Cancer Ctrs., 2005-. Fellow Am. Coll. Trusts and Estates Counsel; mem. N.Y. State Bar Assn. (exec. com. trusts and estates law sect. 1988-92), Monroe County Bar Assn. (chmn. trusts and estates sect. 1984-85, banking liaison com. 1985-86), Fla. Bar Assn., Estate Planing Coun. Rochester, Internat. Assn. Fin. Planners. Roman Catholic. Avocations: basketball, platform tennis. Home: 571 Thomas Ave Rochester NY 14617-1432 Office: Harter Secrest & Emery 1600 Bausch & Lomb Pl Rochester NY 14604-2711 Office Phone: 585-231-1173. Business E-Mail: mbuckley@hselaw.com.

BUCKLEY, REBECCA HATCHER, allergist, immunologist, pediatrician, educator; b. Hamlet, NC, Apr. 1, 1933; d. Martin Armstead and Nora (Langston) Hatcher; m. Charles Edward Buckley, III, July 9, 1955; children: Charles Edward IV, Elizabeth Ann, Rebecca Kathryn, Sarah Margaret. BA, Duke U., 1954; MD, U. NC, 1958. Intern Duke U. Med. Ctr., Durham, NC, 1958-59, resident, 1959-61, pediat. allergist and immunologist, 1961—. Dir., chair exam. com. Am. Bd. Allergy and Immunology, Phila., 1971—73, co-chair bd. dirs., 1982—84; chair Diagnostic Lab. Immunology, 1984—88; mem. staff Duke U. Med. Ctr., asst. prof. pediat. and immunology, 1968—72, assoc. prof. pediat., 1972—79, prof. pediat., 1976—79, prof. immunology, J. Buren Sidbury prof. pediat., 1979—. Contbr. articles to profl. jours. Fellow: AAAS (chair med. scis. sect. 2001—03); mem.: NAS, Inst. Medicine of NAS, Am. Pediatric Soc. (coun. mem. 1991—, pres. 1999—2000, chmn. immune deficiency found. med. adv. com. 2003—), Southeastern Allergy Assn. (pres. 1978—79), Am. Acad. Pediat. (Bret Ratner award 1992), Soc. Pediatric Rsch., Am. Assn. Immunologists, Am. Acad. Allergy and Immunology (exec. com. 1975—82, pres. 1979—80, hon. fellow award 1999). Republican. Episcopalian. Home: 3621 Westover Rd Durham NC 27707-5032 Office: Duke U Med Ctr PO Box 2898 Durham NC 27710 Office Phone: 919-684-2922. Business E-Mail: buckl003@mc.duke.edu.

BUCKLEY, RICHARD BENNETT, asset management company executive; b. Providence, Nov. 7, 1942; s. Alfred and Helen (Searles) B.; m. Karen Owen, May, 1982; 1 child, Owen Searles. BA, Denison U., 1965; JD, Syracuse U., 1968; Exec. MBA, U. New Haven, 1982. Bar: U.S. Supreme Ct. 2001. Successively asst. dean, dir. placement, dean admissions, lectr. ins. law, assoc. dean, dir. placement, dir. admissions, asst. prof. law Syracuse (N.Y.) U., 1968-74, assoc. prof., 1974-77; pres. Schiavone Tire & Rubber Reclamation Corp., New Haven, 1978-80, Schiavone Sports, New Haven, 1978-80; v.p. Cowen Asset Mgmt., N.Y.C., 1980-87, spl. ltd. ptnr., 1986-92, sr. v.p., 1987—, exec. v.p., 1990—; dir., 1992-98; also bd. dirs.; dir. S.G. Cowen, N.Y.C., 1999-00; sr. v.p. Prudential Securities Inc., New Haven, 2000—04; of counsel Law Offices of Joshua Brown, 2004—. Chmn. bd. dirs. Founders Bank, New Haven, 1984-95; mentor Sch. Orgn. and Mgmt. Yale U., New Haven, 1987-89; bd. dirs. Saab Fin. Auto Receivables Corp., Saab Fin. Auto Receivables Corp. II, Saab Fin. Auto Receivables Corp. III, Saab Fin. Svcs. Corp., adv. New Oxford Dictionary of Am. English, cons. Heartland Energy Inc., 2004 Author: Handbook on Profl. Ethics and Responsibility, 1973; mng. editor Ins. Counsel Jour., 1971-87; spl. subject advisor New Oxford Dictionary of American English; contbr. legal articles to profl. jours. Trustee First Congl. Ch., Guilford, Conn., 1996, chmn. 2003, Hamden Hall Country Day Sch. Assoc. fellow, Berkeley Coll. Yale U., 2002—. Mem. ABA, Order of Coif, Quinnipiack Club (pres. 1992-93), Rotary (pres. 1987-88, Spl. Pers. award 1982-83, Rotarian of Yr. 1985-86). Avocations: sailing, skiing, tennis, fly fishing. Home: 34 Grove Hill Rd Guilford CT 06437-3126 Office: Mercantile Manor 35 Elm St New Haven CT 06511 Office Phone: 203-562-0000.

BUCKLEY, ROBERT JOHN, academic research administrator; b. N.Y.C., Jan. 12, 1949; s. John Patrick and Mary Elizabeth (Carroll) B.; m. Lillian Perez, Apr. 28, 1973. BA, Fordham U., 1970; MBA, NYU, 1976. Asst. dir. devel. Hunter Coll. CUNY, 1970-72, asst. to dean programs in edn., 1972-77, dir. office research adminstrn., 1977—. Chair coun. grants officers CUNY, 1984-86, 88—. Mem. Nat. Coun. Univ. Rsch. Adminstrs., Soc. Rsch. Adminstrs., Assn. Univ. Tech. Mgrs. Office: CUNY Hunter Coll 695 Park Ave New York NY 10021-5024

BUCKLEY, ROBERT JOHN, music educator; b. Aurora, Ill., Sept. 3, 1974; s. Robert F. and Louanne Linda Buckley. BS in Music Edn., U. Ill., 1998, M of Music Edn., 2002. Dir. band Rotolo Mid. Sch., Batavia, Ill., 1998—. Asst. for student tchr. Rotolo Mid. Sch., 2005. Percussionist Holy Cross Contemporary Choir, Batavia, 2001—. Mem.: NEA, Music Educators Nat. Conf., Nat. Band Assn.

BUCKLEY, ROBERT MATTHEW, electrical engineer; b. Bklyn., Nov. 14, 1947; s. Matthew Louis and Catherine Sienna Buckley; m. Linda Susan Montagne, May 16, 1971; children: Christopher, Kevin, Michael. BSc, N.Y. Inst. Tech., 1972; MAS, Embry Riddle U., 2004; postgrad., Nova Southeastern U. Engring. asst. N.Y. Telephone, Bklyn., 1972-74; project engr. PRD, Syosset, N.Y., 1974-77; engr. Citibank, Melville, N.Y., 1977-81; engring. specialist ILS Divsn. Grumman Aerospace, Bethpage, N.Y., 1981-84; engring. mgr. AIL, Deer Park, N.Y., 1984-85; v.p. engring. TTI, Ronkonkama, N.Y., 1985-90; v.p. ATTI, Hauppague, N.Y., 1990—. Contbr. articles to profl. jours. Leader Boy Scouts Am., Medford, N.Y., 1985; pres. NYPMAC, Medford, 1987-89. With USMCR, 1969-71. Mem. IEEE. Roman Catholic. Achievements include patent for video display and analyzer, new phase noise measurement technique, new use for phase noise measurement, and patent for generating programmable spectrally pure doppler signals. Office: ATTI 110 Ricefield Ln Hauppauge NY 11788-2008 Office Phone: 631-231-8777. E-mail: rbuckley@nova.edu.

BUCKLEY, SAMUEL OLLIPHANT, III, lawyer; m. Jennifer Nell Willis; children: William Paul, Samuel Olliphant, Matthew, Mary Beth. BS in Chemistry, La. State U., 1969; JD, Loyola U., New Orleans, 1977. Bar: La. 1977, U.S. Dist. Ct. (ea. dist.) La. 1977, U.S. Dist. Ct. (mid. dist.) La. 1978, U.S. Ct. Appeals (5th crct.) 1979, U.S. Ct. Appeals (11th crct.) 1981, U.S. Dist. Ct. (we. dist.) La. 1987, Colo. 1993. Dir. environ. Witco Chem. Corp., Gretna, La., 1970-77; assoc. Jones, Walker, Waechter, Poitevent, Carrere & Denegre, New Orleans, 1977-82, ptnr., 1982-92, of counsel, 1992-97, Cater & Willis, New Orleans, 1997—. Assoc. prof. environ. law Loyola U. Law Sch., 1984-87. Lead article editor Loyola U. Law Rev., 1976-77. Mem. Friends of Audubon Zoo, New Orleans; vestry mem. Christ Ch. Cathedral, 1997—2003. Mem. ABA (vice chmn. urban law com. 1980-81, solid and hazardous waste com. 1981-85, biotech. com. 1991-92), La. Bar Assn. (vice chmn. environ. law sect. 1980-82, chmn. 1982-86), Am. Chem. Soc., Loyola U. Law Alumni Assn. (bd. dirs. 1979-80), Nat. Audubon Soc. Democrat. Episcopalian. Avocations: skiing, golf. Home: 319 Fairway Dr New Orleans LA 70124-1020 Office: Cater & Willis 3723 Canal St New Orleans LA 70119-6140 E-mail: sbuckley@bellsouth.net.

BUCKLEY, SUSAN, lawyer; b. Rockville Center, N.Y., Dec. 24, 1951; BA, Mt. Holyoke Coll., 1973; JD, Fordham U., 1977. Bar: N.Y. 1978, D.C. 1980. Ptnr. Cahill Gordon & Reindel LLP, N.Y.C., 1985—. Mem. ABA, N.Y. State Bar Assn. (com. on media law 1992-95), Bar Assn. N.Y.C. (com. comm. law 1986-89). Office: Cahill Gordon & Reindel LLP 80 Pine St Fl 17 New York NY 10005-1790 Office Phone: 212-701-3000.

BUCKLEY, THOMAS HUGH, historian, educator; b. Elkhart, Ind., Sept. 11, 1932; s. Bernard Leroy and Martha B. (Swoveland) B.; m. Julie Griffith; children: Christopher, Kathryn, Elizabeth, Thomas, Barbara. Student, Northwestern U., 1950-53; AB, Ind. U., 1955, MA, 1956, PhD (grad. fellow), 1961. From instr. to prof. U. S.D., 1960-69; vis. prof. Ind. U., 1969-71; prof., chmn. dept. U. Tulsa, 1971-81, chmn. humanistic studies, 1975-81, Jay Walker research chair Am. History, 1981—, assoc. dean Grad. Sch., 1995-2000; cons. on overseas edn. to Nat. Edn. Corp. Author: The United States and the Washington Conference, 1921-1922, 1970 (award as best first book by an historian 1971); co-author: American Foreign and National Security Policies, 1914-1945, 1987; editor: Research and Roster Guide of Soc. Historians of Am. Fgn. Relations, 1980-86; contbr. chpts. in books. Postdoctoral fellow Stanford U., 1968, U. Wis., 1983, Brown U., 1986, U. Tex., 1991; Fulbright fellow, U. Western Australia, 1986. Mem. Orgn. Am. Historians, Soc. Historians of Am. Fgn. Relations, Tulsa Com. Fgn. Relations, Phi Alpha Theta, Lambda Chi Alpha. Republican. Methodist. Home: 1301 Terrace Dr Tulsa OK 74104-4409 Office: Univ Tulsa Dept History Tulsa OK 74104 Office Phone: 918-631-2824. E-mail: thomas-buckley@utulsa.edu. *Success comes in the race of life not always to the swiftest but to those who keep on running.*

BUCKLEY, VINCENT H., lawyer; BA, Rice U., 1947; LLB, U. Tex., 1950. Various legal and mgmt. positions Dow Chemical, asst. gen. counsel, gen. counsel Pacific region, pres., gen. mgr. oil and gas divsn.; with Lock, Liddell, and Sapp, 1990—2002; exec. v.p., gen. counsel, bd. dirs. Adams Resources & Energy, Inc., Houston, 2002—. Office: Adams Resources & Energy Inc 4400 Post Oak Pky Ste 2700 Houston TX 77027 Office Phone: 713-881-3600. Office Fax: 713-881-3491.

BUCKLEY, VIRGINIA LAURA, editor; b. N.Y.C., May 11, 1929; d. Alfred and Josephine Marie (Manetti) Iacuzzi; m. David Patrick Buckley, July 30, 1960; children: Laura Joyce, Brian Thomas. BA, Wellesley Coll., 1950; MA, Columbia U., 1952. Tchr. English Bennett Coll., Millbrook, N.Y., 1954-56, Berkeley Inst., Bklyn., 1956-58; copy editor World Pub. Co., N.Y.C., 1959-69; children's book editor Thomas Y. Crowell, N.Y.C., 1971-80; editl. dir. Lodestar Books, N.Y.C., 1980-97; contbg. editor Clarion Books, N.Y.C., 1997—. Author: State Birds, 1986; contbr. articles to profl. jours. Mem. ALA Home: 33 Brook Ter Leonia NJ 07605-1504 Office: Clarion Books 215 Park Ave S New York NY 10003-1603 E-mail: vbuckley@worldnet.att.net.

BUCKLEY, WENDELL DEAN, music educator; b. Hayfield, Pa., Nov. 23, 1921; s. Jay Keith and Rose Miller Buckley; m. Joan Naglestad Buckley, June 7, 1957; children: David W., Julie A. BA, MusB, Oberlin Coll., 1950, MusM, 1951; PhD, U. Iowa, 1965. From instr. to prof. music Concordia Coll., Moorhead, Minn., 1954—92, prof. music emeritus, 1992—. With USAF, 1942—46. Mem.: Rotary, Pi Kappa Lambda. Office: Concordia Coll Music Dept 901 8th St S Moorhead MN 56562-0001

BUCKLEY, WILLIAM ELMHIRST, publishing consultant; b. Rahway, N.J., Oct. 6, 1913; s. John A. and Margaret Elsie (Elmhirst) B.; m. Virginia Smith, Aug. 2, 1941; children: Carolyn E., William Elmhirst Jr. Student, U. Pa., 1932-34. Jr. exec. Quinn & Boden Co., Inc. (book mfrs.), Rahway, N.J., 1935-42, Doubleday & Co., N.Y.C., 1945-49; with Henry Holt & Co., N.Y.C., 1949-58, v.p., dir., 1951-58; v.p. sales World Pub. Co., Cleve., 1958-60; v.p. book div. McCall Corp., N.Y.C., 1960-62; v.p. Curtis Pub. Co., N.Y.C., 1962-68, dir. book div., 1962-68; asst. to pres. Cowles Communications, Inc., 1968-72; chmn. Cowles Book Co., 1968-72; chmn., pres. Cambridge Book Co. (subsidiaries Cowles Communications Inc.), 1968-72; publishing cons., 1972—. Served to lt. comdr. USNR, 1942-45. Mem. Phi Delta Theta. Clubs: Dutch Treat (N.Y.C.); Soc. Four Arts (Palm Beach, Fla.), The Beach Club (Fla.).

BUCKLEY, WILLIAM FRANK, JR., magazine editor, writer; b. NYC, Nov. 24, 1925; s. William Frank and Aloise (Steiner) B.; m. Patricia Taylor, July 6, 1950; 1 child, Christopher Taylor. Student, U. Mexico, 1943; BA, Yale U., 1950; LHD (hon.), Seton Hall U., 1966, Niagara U., 1967, Mt. St. Mary's Coll., 1969, U. SC, 1985, Converse Coll., 1988, U. South Fla., 1992, Adelphi U., 1995, Yale U., 2000; LLD (hon.), St. Peter's Coll., 1969, Syracuse U., 1969, Ursinus Coll., 1969, Lehigh U., 1970, Lafayette Coll., 1972, St. Anselm's Coll., 1973, St. Bonaventure U., 1974, U. Notre Dame, 1978, NY Law Sch., 1981, Colby Coll., 1985; DScO (hon.), Curry Coll., 1970; LittD (hon.), St. Vincent Coll., 1971, Fairleigh Dickinson U., 1973, Alfred U., 1974, Coll. William and Mary, 1981, William Jewell Coll., 1982, Albertus Magnus Coll., 1987, Coll. St. Thomas, 1987, Bowling Green State U., 1987, Coe Coll., 1989, St. John's U., Minn., 1989, Grove City Coll., 1991. Instr. Spanish lang. Yale U., New Haven, 1947-51; assoc. editor Am. Mercury, NYC, 1952; founder, pres., editor-in-chief Nat. Rev., NYC, 1955-90, editor-at-large, 1991—2004; syndicated columnist, 1962—; host weekly TV show Firing Line, 1966-99; Froman disting. prof. Russell Sage Coll., 1973. Lectr. New Sch. Social Rsch., 1967-68; vis. lectr. Yale U., 1996-97. Author: God and Man at Yale, 1951, (with L. Brent Bozell) McCarthy and His Enemies, 1954, Up from Liberalism, 1959, Rumbles Left and Right, 1963, The Unmaking of a Mayor, 1966, The Jeweler's Eye, 1968, The Governor Listeth, 1970, Cruising Speed, 1971, Inveighing We Will Go, 1972, Four Reforms, 1973, United Nations Journal, 1974, Execution Eve, 1975, Saving the Queen, 1976, Airborne, 1976, Stained Glass, 1978 (Am. Book Award for Best Mystery, 1980), A Hymnal, 1978, Who's On First, 1980, Marco Polo, If You Can, 1982, Atlantic High, 1982, Overdrive, 1983, The Story of Henri Tod, 1984, The Temptation of Wilfred Malachey, 1985, See You Later Alligator, 1985, Right Reason, 1985, High Jinx, 1986, Racing Through Paradise, 1987, Mongoose, R.I.P., 1988, On the Firing Line, 1989, Gratitude, 1990, Tucker's Last Stand, 1991, WindFall, 1992, In Search of Anti-Semitism, 1992, Happy Days Were Here Again, 1993, A Very Private Plot, 1994, The Blackford Oakes Reader, 1995, Brothers No More, 1995, Buckley: The Right Word, 1996, Nearer, My God, 1997, The Lexicon, 1998, The Redhunter, 1998, Let Us Talk of Many Things, 2000, Spytime, 2000, Elvis in the Morning, 2001, Nuremberg, 2002, Getting It Right, 2003, The Fall of the Berlin Wall, 2004, Miles Gone By: A Literary Autobiography, 2004, Last Call for Blackford Oakes, 2005; editor:

The Committee and Its Critics, 1962, Odyssey of a Friend: Whittaker Chambers' Letters to William F. Buckley, Jr., 1954-1961, 1970, American Conservative Thought in the Twentieth Century, 1970, (with Charles Kesler) Keeping the Tablets, 1988; contbr. to Racing at Sea, 1959, The Intellectuals, 1960, What is Conservatism?, 1964, Dialogues in Americanism, 1964, Violence in the Streets, 1968, The Beatles Book, 1968, Spectrum of Catholic Attitudes, 1969, Great Ideas Today Annual, 1970, Essays on Hayek, 1976; also periodicals. Conservative Party candidate for mayor, NYC., 1965; mem. USIA Adv. Commn., 1969-72; pub. mem. US del. to 28th Gen. Assembly UN, 1973. Served to 2d lt., inf. AUS, 1944-46. Recipient Best Columnist of Yr. award, 1967, Disting. Achievement award in journalism U. So. Calif., 1968, Emmy award for outstanding program achievement NATAS, 1969, Cleveland Amory award for best interviewer/interviewee TV Guide, 1974, Bellarime medal, 1977, Americanism award Young Rep. Nat. Fedn., 1979, Carmel award Am. Friends of Haifa U., 1980, Creative Leadership award NYU, 1981, Lincoln Lit. award Union League, 1985, Shelby Cullom Davis award, 1986, Lowell Thomas Travel Journalism award, 1989, Julius award for outstanding pub. svc. U. So. Calif. Sch. Pub. Adminstrn., 1990, Gold medal award Nat. Inst. Social Scis., 1992, Presdl. Medal of Freedom, 1991, Adam Smith award Hillsdale Coll., 1996, Clare Boothe Luce award Heritage Found., 1999, Henfy Salvatori award Claremont Inst., 2000, Phillips Found. Lifetime Achievement award, 2002, Alexander Hamilton award Manhattan Inst., 2004. Fellow Soc. Profl. Journalists, Sigma Delta Chi; mem. Mont Pelerin Soc., New York Yacht Club, Phila. Soc. Republican. Roman Catholic. Office: Nat Rev 215 Lexington Ave New York NY 10016-6023*

BUCKLIN, DONALD THOMAS, lawyer; b. Providence, July 11, 1938; s. Elmer F. and Anne (Scott) B.; m. Kathryn L. Alfera, Nov. 30, 1963; children: Donald R., Heather Anne. BS in Acctg., Providence Coll., 1960; JD cum laude, Am. U., 1967. Bar: Va. 1968, D.C. 1968. Supervisory acct. GAO, 1960-67; law clk. to judge U.S. Dist. Ct. D.C., 1967-68; asst. U.S. atty. for D.C. Dept. Justice, Washington, 1968-71; ptnr. Rowley & Scott, Washington, 1971-74, Truitt, Fabrikant, Bucklin & Lenzner, Washington, 1974-76, Wald, Harkrader & Ross, Washington, 1977-85, Squire, Sanders & Dempsy, 1986—. Contbg. author: Antitrust Counseling and Litigation Techniques, 1984. Served to 1st lt. USAR, 1960-68. Fellow Am. Coll. Trial Lawyers; mem. ABA (criminal law sect. white collar crimes and offenders 1976-77, litigation sect. com. on liaison with state and local bar assns.), D.C. Bar Assn. (treas. Criminal Practice Inst. 1972-73, exec. coun. young lawyers sect. 1973-75, Young Lawyer of Yr.), D.C. Bar (litigation sect. steering com., treas. 1985, bd. govs. 1986-89, bd. dirs., exec. com. 1989—, pres. 1995-96). Office: Squire Sanders & Dempsey 1201 Pennsylvania Ave NW PO Box 407 Washington DC 20044-0407

BUCKLIN, LOUIS PIERRE, business educator, consultant; b. N.Y.C., Sept. 20, 1928; s. Louis Lapham and Elja (Barricklow) B.; m. Weylene Edwards, June 11, 1956; children: Randolph E., Rhonda W. Student, Dartmouth Coll., 1950; MBA, Harvard U., 1954; PhD, Northwestern U., 1960; PhD with honors (hon.), Stockholm Sch. Econs., 2001. Asst. prof. bus. U. Colo., Boulder, 1954-56; instr. in bus. Northwestern U., Evanston, 1958-59, assoc. dean Grad. Sch. Bus. Adminstrn., 1981-83; prof. bus. adminstrn. U. Calif., Berkeley, 1960-93, prof. emeritus, 1993—. Mem. ASUC Aux. Enterprise Bd., 1999—, chmn., 2000-2001; vis. prof. Stockholm Sch. Econs., 1983, INSEAD, Fontainebleau, France, 1984, Erasmus U., Rotterdam, Netherlands, 1993-94, Cath. U. Leuven, Belgium, 1994; prin. Bucklin Assocs., Lafayette, Calif., 1975—; adv. bd. Gemini Cons., San Francisco, 1987-94. Author: (books) A Theory of Distribution Channel Structure, 1966, Competition Evolution in the Distrubutive Trades, 1972, Productivity in Marketing, 1979; editor: Vertical Marketing Systems, 1971, (books) Channels and Channel Institutions, 1986, (journal) Jour. of Retailing, 1996—2001. Mem. City of Lafayette Planning Commn., 1990-93. Capt. USMC, 1951-53, Korea. Recipient Alpha Kappa Psi Found. award for best paper in Jour. Mktg., 1993, Lifetime Recognition for scholarly contbns. to retailing Soc. for Mktg. Advances, 2001. Mem. Inst. for Ops. Rsch. Mgmt. Scis., Am. Mktg. Assn. (Paul D. Converse award 1986). Democrat. Avocations: travel, microcomputers, photography. Office: U Calif Haas Sch Bus Berkeley CA 94720-0001 E-mail: pbucklin@haas.berkeley.edu.

BUCKLO, ELAINE EDWARDS, United States district court judge; b. Boston, Oct. 1, 1944; married. AB, St. Louis U., 1966; JD, Northwestern U., 1972. Bar: Calif. 1973, U.S. Dist. Ct. (no. dist.) Calif. 1973, Ill. 1974, U.S. Dist. ct. (no. dist.) Ill. 1974, U.S. Ct. Appeals (7th cir.) 1983. Law clk. U.S. Ct. Appeals (7th cir.), Chgo.; pvt. practice, 1973-85; U.S. magistrate judge U.S. Dist. Ct. (no. dist.) Ill., Chgo., 1985-94, judge, 1994—. Spkr. in field. Contbr. articles to profl. jours. Mem. jud. conf. com. on adminstrn. Magistrate Judge Sys., 1998-2004; mem. vis. com. No. Ill. U. Sch. Law, 1994—; mem. Northwestern U. Law Bd., 1996-99. Mem. ABA (standing com. law and literacy 1995-98), FBA (v.p. 1990-92, pres. Chgo. chpt. 1992-93), Women's Bar Assn. Ill. (bd. dirs. 1994-96), Chgo. Coun. Lawyers (pres. 1977-78). Office: US Dist Ct No Dist Everett McKinley Dirksen Bldg 219 S Dearborn St Ste 1446 Chicago IL 60604-1794

BUCKMAN, JAMES EDWARD, lawyer; b. N.Y.C., Oct. 2, 1944; s. John Burr and Mary Dolores (Ullery) B.; m. Nancy Lee McLaughlin, Aug. 23, 1969; children: Elizabeth Ahern, Anne Tracy, Julia Walsh. AB, Fordham U., 1966; JD, Yale U., 1969. Bar: N.Y. 1969, Ga. 1974, U.S. Dist. Ct. (no. dist.) Ga. 1974. Assoc. Dewey, Ballantine, Bushby, Palmer & Wood, N.Y.C., 1969-72; asst. gen. counsel Gable Industries, Inc., Atlanta, 1972-74; assoc. then ptnr. Troutman, Sanders, Lockerman & Ashmore, Atlanta, 1974-85, ptnr., 1990-92; exec. v.p., gen. counsel Days Inns of Am., Inc., Atlanta, 1985-89, HFS Inc., Parsippany, N.J., 1992-96; now vice chmn., gen. counsel Cendant Corp, Parsippany, 1996—. 1st lt. USAFR, 1969-75. Mem. ABA, Atlanta Bar Assn., State Bar Ga. Roman Catholic. Avocation: running. Office: Cendant Corp 9 W 57th St 37th Fl New York NY 10019

BUCKMAN, THOMAS RICHARD, foundation executive, educator; b. Reno, May 3, 1923; s. Thomas Eli and Georgia Christina (Damm) B.; m. Gunhild Margareta Malmkjell, May 1, 1948; children: Anne Christina, Carol Erica. BA, U. Pacific, 1947; MA, U. Minn., 1951, B.L.S. (H.W. Wilson scholar), 1953. Clk., Permit Office for Germany, Allied High Commn., Stockholm, 1949-50; sr. clk. U. Minn. Libr., 1952-53; asst. reference libr. Oreg. State U. Libr., 1953-54; King Gustav V fellow in Sweden, Am. Scandinavia Found., 1954-55; asst. libr. Modesto (Calif.) Jr. Coll. Libr., 1955-56; head acquisitions dept. U. Kans. Libr., 1956-60, assoc. dir., 1960-61, dir. libraries, 1961-68, lectr. in Scandinavian, 1958-61; prof. bibliography, univ. libr. Northwestern U., Evanston, Ill., 1968-71; pres. Found. Ctr., N.Y.C., 1971-91, sr. advisor, 1991-93; pres., chmn. Engring. Info. Found., 1995—. Past chairperson bd. dirs. Telecom. Coop. Network, E.S.T.C., N.A., Engring. Info., Inc. Editor, translator: Modern Theatre: Seven Plays and an Essay (by Pär Lagerkvist), 1966; editor: Bibliography and Natural History, 1966, University and Research Libraries in Japan and the United States, 1972; contbr. articles to profl. jours. With USNR, 1943-46. Guggenheim fellow, 1964-65, Scandinavian studies fellow U. Minn., 1952, H.W. Wilson scholar, 1953. Mem. ALA (chmn. internat. rels. adv. com. for liaison with Japanese librs. 1967-71, dir. internat. rels. office 1966-67), Soc. for Advancement of Scandinavian Study (sec.-treas. 1959-69), Am. Scandinavian Found. (bd. dirs. 1978-82). Home: 30 Lincoln Plz Apt 30S New York NY 10023-7126 Office: Engring Info Found 180 W 80th St Ste 207 New York NY 10024-6301

BUCKMAN, WILLIAM H., lawyer; b. 1953; married. BS, Stockton State Coll.; JD, Rutgers U. Bar: NJ 1978, cert.: NJ Supreme Ct. (Criminal Def. Atty.) 1989. With pub. defender's office, Gloucester County, NJ; pub. defender Rutland, Vt., 1995—97; prin. William H. Buckman Law Firm, Moorestown, NJ. Mem. Nat. Orgn. Reform Marijuana Laws. Contbr. articles to profl. jours. Named to Ten Leaders of Criminal Def. Law of So. NJ, 2004—. Mem.: NACDL, NY Assn. Criminal Def. Lawyers, Pa. Assn. Criminal Def. Lawyers, Burlington County Bar Assn., Assn. Criminal Def. Lawyers NJ. Office: William H Buckman Law Firm 714 E Main St Ste 1B Moorestown NJ 08057 Office Phone: 856-608-9797. Office Fax: 856-608-6244. E-mail: wbuckman@whbuckman.com.

BUCKMASTER, JIM, online community bulletin board company executive; b. in BioChemistry summa cum laude, Va. Tech; studied medicine and classics, U. Mich. Lead web developer Inter-University Consortium for Polit. and Soc. Rsch., U. Mich.; dir. web develop. dotcom Creditland, Quantum Corp.; CTO, lead programmer Craigslist, San Francisco, pres., CEO, 2000—. Bd. transportation, San Francisco. Built the world's first multi-terabyte database-driven public website at the University Michigan; Craigslist is a network of local community bulletion boards, where millions of people research subjects such as: jobs, housing, goods & services, events, friendships, and advice. Office: Craigslist 1319 9th Ave San Francisco CA 94122-2308 Office Phone: 415-566-6394. Office Fax: 415-504-6394. Business E-Mail: jim@craigslist.org.

BUCKMASTER, MATTHEW TOBE, music educator, musician, small business owner; b. Naples, Fla., July 25, 1978; s. Harvey Elba and Barbara Munson Buckmaster; m. Ana Parris, Aug. 13, 2000. MusM, U. South Fla., 2001, PhD, 2005; MusB, Fla. So. Coll., 2000. Cert. tchr. Fla., 2002. Musician Walt Disney World, Lake Buena Vista, Fla., 1998—; tchg. asst. U. South Fla., Tampa, 2000—01; musician Busch Gardens, Tampa, 2000—02; adj. prof. Southeastern Coll., Lakeland, 2001—; band dir. Kathleen H.S., 2002—03; co-owner B and B Pub., 2004—; asst. dir. athletic bands U. South Fla., 2005—. Treas. Ctrl. Fla. Trombone Soc., 2004—. Composer: (musical arrangement) Londonderry Air, The Rite of Spring. Va. Bridges Doctoral fellow, U. South Fla., 2003-2005. Mem.: Fla. Bandmaster's Assn., Coll. Music Soc., Music Educator's Nat. Conf., Internat. Trombone Assn., Phi Kappa Lambda, Phi Mu Alpha Sinfonia (chpt. pres. 1998—99, Sinfonia Found. scholar 1999). Independent. Avocations: travel, basketball. Home: 7537 Jessamine Dr Lakeland FL 33810 Office Phone: 813-974-7144. Personal E-mail: mattbuckmaster@hotmail.com.

BUCK-MOORE, JOANNE ROSE, nursing administrator, educator; b. Cambridge, Mass., Jan. 3, 1939; d. Joseph J. and Louise L. (Buck) Verrochio; m. C. Edwin Buck (dec.); m. Donald P. Moore (dec.); children: Marie-Louise, Victoria, Katrina, Edwin. ASN, Middlesex C.C., Bedford, Mass., 1977; BSN magna cum laude, Worcester (Mass.) State Coll., 1980; MSN, U. R.I., 1983. RN, Mass. Dir. nursing Ctr. for Rehab. at Columbus, East Boston, Mass., Mt. Pleasant Hosp., Lynn, Mass.; nurse mgr. and program dir. Commonwealth of Mass. Dept. of Mental Health, Boston. Course instr. Palm Beach C.C., Fla. Atlantic U.; lectr. at schs., clubs, seminars, confs.; legal cons. and expert witness. Author: Management by Objective: A Handbook for Nurses. Mem. ANA (cert. mental health nurse), Sigma Theta Tau. Home: 18 Faulkner Hill Rd Acton MA 01720-4211

BUCKMORE, ALVAH CLARENCE, JR., computer scientist, ballistician; b. Lewiston, Maine, Sept. 11, 1944; s. Alvah Clarence and Mary (Begin) Buckmore; m. Lolita F. Laurina. Student, Holyoke C.C., Nat. Radio Inst., Famous Writers Sch., U. Mass. Cert. firearms instr.; lic. amateur radio operator. CEO, chief scientist Buckmore Enterprises, Westfield, Mass., 1974—; developer math./engring. software database for microcomputer Calculated Solutions (formerly SC Applied Tech. Inc.), Columbia, S.C. Mgmt. cons. firearms industry; instr. Mass. Mil. NCO Acad., 1976; mem. Mass. State Rifle and Pistol Team, 1976. Contbr. Collier's Ency., articles to profl. jours. Mem. Mass. Rep. Party, Rep. Presdl. Task Force, Mass. Rep. Senate Com., at-large del., 1992—; comm. officer, dir. RACES for Mass. Emergency Mgmt. Agy., Area III, 1996-98. Recipient Internat. Recognition award, 1979; NSF fellow, 1978—. Mem. AAAS, Computer Soc. of IEEE, NRA (life), DAV (life), Am. Def. Preparedness Assn., Nat. Assn. Federally Lic. Firearms Dealers (mem. sr. coalition), Assn. for Computer Tng. and Support, Math. Assn. Am., Am. Radio Relay League, Soc. Amateur Radio Astronomers, Amateur Radio Satellite Corp., Vietnam Vets. Am. (mem. vets. coun. Liberty chpt. 219 1988), Am. Fedn. Police, Am. Legion, N.Y. Acad. Scis., Mount Tom Amateur Repeater Assn. Achievements include development of amateur radio satellite communications, of parallel processing techniques, algorithms, and code for ballistic applications; over 38 major discoveries made in ballistics, including the discovery of 3 new sciences: time physics, the study of the physical properties of time; force-fields, the study of the absorption, displacement, projection, or reflection of kinetic energy; and ballistic signatures, the study of the physical characteristics of a bullet in terminal flight. Address: 18 Tannery Rd Westfield MA 01085-4822 Personal E-mail: k1tma@hotmail.com. *Since the age of 15 years it has been my consistent objective in life to develop a genuine ability to think, talk and use information properly and, over these years—which include the experience of my serving as an illegal POW with only partial official recognition—I have wavered very little, if at all.*

BUCKNALL, MALCOLM RODERICK, artist; b. Twickenham, Middlesex, U.K., Feb. 1, 1935; arrived in U.S., 1958; s. Eric Herbert and Mary McCauley Bucknall; m. Carolyn Foreman, Dec. 14, 1931; children: Christopher, Timothy, Andrew. Student, U. Viswa-Bharati, Bengal, India, 1954—55; diploma in design, Chelsea Art Sch., London, 1958; BFA with honors, U. Tex., 1961; MFA, U. Wash., 1963. Artist Greenwich Village Art Ctr., N.Y.C., 1961—63, Bryant Gallery, New Orleans, 1968—69, Graham Gallery, Houston, 1984—92, Martin Rathburn Gallery, San Antonio, 1992—98, D. Berman Gallery, Austin, Tex., 2000—. Posters, music artwork, painting, drawing. Pvt. U.S. Army, 1955—57. Recipient Bronze medal, Inst. Am. Art, 1972, Best Artwork on Music Release award, Nat. Poll A.P. Mag., 1994; fellow, NEA, 1985—86; Visual Artists fellow, Nat. Mus. Am. Art, Washington, 1996. Avocations: Scrabble, walking, cooking. Home: 4205 Shoal Creek Austin TX 78756

BUCKNALL, WILLIAM L., JR., human resources professional; BS, U. New Haven, 1965; MS in Mgmt., MIT. Various positions including corp. dir. salaried employee relations United Technologies Corp., Hartford, Conn., 1966-92, v.p. human resources and orgn., 1991—92; sr. v.p. human resources and orgn., 1992—. Mem. dean's adv. coun. MIT Sloan Sch. Mgmt.; mem. adv. bd. Ctr. Advanced Human Resource Studies Cornell U.; bd. dirs. Labor Policy Assn. Mem. nat. corp. com. United Negro Coll. Fund. Mem.: Nat. Acad. Human Resources. Office: United Technologies Corp United Technologies Bldg 1 Financial Plz Hartford CT 06101 Office Phone: 860-728-7000.*

BUCKNER, ELMER LA MAR, insurance executive; b. Provo, Utah, Apr. 27, 1922; s. Elmer R. and Altis LaVern (Maxfield) B.; m. Melba Hale, Oct. 3, 1945; children: Lynda, Brent, Terry, Kathy, David. BS, Brigham Young U., 1946; HHD (hon.), Weber State U., 1994. CLU. Ptnr. Buckner-Radmall Ins. Counselors, Ogden, Utah, 1947-62, co. inc. pres., 1962-85. Mem. Utah Ho. of Reps., 1965-67, Utah Senate, 1967-75, asst. majority leader, 1971-75. Bd. govs. ARC, 1956-62, mem. exec. com., 1961-62; mem. gen. bd. Young Men's Mut. Improvement Assn., LDS Ch., 1957-58, young men's gen. bd., 1980, regional rep., 1981-87; bishop Ogden 55th Ward, 1958-63, pres. Ogden LDS Temple, 1987-90; 2d counselor Weber Heights Stake presidency, 1963-68; pres. Weber State Coll. Stake, 1968-73, Sacramento mission, 1975-78; former dir. Citizens Com. for Hoover Report; mem. Com. on Religion in Am. Life Inc.; former mem. adv. com. FOA; v.p. Lake Bonneville coun. Boy Scouts Am., 1968-69, pres., 1970, program chmn. Western region, 1973-75; mem. alumni bd. Brigham Young U., 1959-63, pres., 1961-62; v.p. Ogden Area United Fund, 1962, pres. No. Utah, 1963; chmn. Utah Cancer Crusade, 1970; v.p. Utah Cancer Soc., 1971, Utah div. Am. Cancer Soc.; del. Rep. Nat. Conv., Chgo., 1960, chmn. Weber County Reps., 1960-64; elector Utah State Reps., 1964; mem. Utah Bd. Regents Higher Edn., 1981-85; bd. dirs. western region bd. Boy Scouts Am., 1986-2002, pres. area II coun., 1985-87. 1st lt. USAAF, World War II; 23 missions. Recipient Silver Beaver award Boy Scouts Am., 1967, Silver Antelope award, 1983; Disting. Alumni award Weber State Coll., 1983, Alexis de Tocqueville award United Way Am., 1987, Alumni Disting. Svc. award Brigham Young U., 1991; named Utah Ins. Agt. of Yr., 1973. Mem. U.S. C. of C. (bd. dirs. 1955-56), U.S. Jaycees (pres. 1954-55), Utah Jaycees (pres. 1952-53), Ogden C. of C. (bd. dirs. 1980, pres. 1982, Utah Hall of Fame award 1989), Ogden Jaycees (pres. 1950), Jr. Chamber Internat. (treas. 1956), Weber Coll. Alumni Assn. (pres. 1958-59), Kiwanis (pres. Ogden club 1967), Sigma Gamma Chi (internat. pres. 1967-69). Home: 1550 Country Hills Dr Ogden UT 84403-2512 E-mail: elbuckner@comcast.net.

BUCKNER, JOHN KNOWLES, investor; b. Springfield, Mo., Sept. 8, 1936; s. Ernest Godfrey and Mary Helen (Knowles) B.; m. Lorraine Catherine Anderson, Sept. 22, 1962; children: John Knowles, Allison. BA, Williams Coll., 1958; MS, Mass. Inst. Tech., 1960; PhD, nuclear engring., Stanford U., 1965; grad., Advanced Mgmt. Program, Harvard, 1974. Mgr. analysis dept. EG&G Inc., Bedford, Mass., 1966-70; dir. electronic data processing, controller, v.p. financial ops. Eastern Gas & Fuel Assos., Boston, 1970-77; exec. v.p., chief operating officer, dir. Waters Assos., Inc., Milford, Mass., 1977-80; v.p., chief fin. officer Prime Computer, Inc., Natick, Mass., 1980-83; sr. v.p., chief fin. officer EG & G, Inc., Wellesley, Mass., 1983-86; vice chmn., chief fin. officer Control Data Corp., Mpls., 1986-89; chmn. Pensco Pension Svcs. Inc., San Francisco, 1989-98, Bohdan Automation, Inc., Mundelein, Ill., 1994-98. Contbr. articles on engring., data analysis and systems to profl. jours. AEC spl. fellow nuclear sci. and engring., 1959, 62-65 Mem.: Assn. Univs. for Rsch. in Astronomy (bd.d ir. 2003—), Sigma Xi, Phi Beta Kappa, Chi Psi. Office: Pensco Pension Svcs Inc 450 Sansome St 14th Fl San Francisco CA 94111-3306 *My present success, such as it is, has resulted from a willingness and ability to work hard, motivate others, and apply my own training and ideas to the particular task at hand, irrespective of the nature of the field of endeavor. My approach has always been to attain a level of technical and managerial competence necessary to bring about change. Generally, my goal is to make a contribution in as many areas of human conduct as my diligence and native ability will allow.*

BUCKNER, JOYCE, psychologist, educator; b. Benton, Ark., Sept. 25, 1937; d. Waymond Floyd Pannell and Willie Evelyn (Wright) Whitley; m. John W. Buckner, Aug. 29, 1958 (div. 1970); children: Cheryl, John, Chris; m. Sanford Reitman, Aug. 13, 1994. BA, Ouachita Bapt. Coll., 1959; MS in Edn., Henderson State U., 1964; PhD, North Tex. State U., 1970. Lic. psychologist, Tex., marriage and family therapist; cert. Nat. Registry Health Svc. Providers in Psychology; master trainer in imago relationship therapy. Assoc. prof. U. Tex., Arlington, 1970-80, chmn. dept. edn., 1976-78; pvt. practice Arlington, 1974—. Dir., chief profl. officer Southwest Inst. Relationship Devel.; appeard on tv shows including Oprah; spkr. in field. Author: Making Real Love Happen: The New Era of Intimacy. Mem. APA, Nat. Assn. for Imago Relationship Therapy (pres.), Nat. Speakers Assn., Am. Assn. Marital and Family Therapy. Avocations: dance, travel, art. Home: 4118 Bishop Creek Court Arlington TX 76016 Office Phone: 817-478-5257. E-mail: joybuckner@aol.com.

BUCKNER, MELISSA SPIRT, lawyer; b. Orange, N.J., Jan. 10, 1969; d. Nathan and Nena Lela (Mih) Spirt; m. David Marc Buckner, Apr. 5, 1997. BA in English and Polit. Sci., Rutgers Coll., 1991, JD, 1994. Bar: Fla. 1994, N.J. 1994, D.C. 1997. Legal intern to Hon. Nicholas H. Politan U.S. Dist. Ct. N.J., Newark, fall 1993; assoc. Stoldt & Horan, Hackensack, N.J., 1994-95; staff atty. King & Spalding, Atlanta, 1995-96; atty. U.S. Dept. HHS Office of Gen. Counsel, Washington, 1997-98; program dir. Human Svcs. Coalition, Miami, 1999—2002; regional dir. Lawyers for Children Am., 2002—. Mem. com. on pub. interest law, chmn. moot ct. bd. Rutgers Law Sch., Newark, 1993-94; Regional dir., Lawyers for Children America, Inc., 2002-. Pres. Rutgers Coll. Governing Assn., New Brunswick, N.J., 1990-91, mem. univ. senate, 1989-91; mem. Nat. Coun. Jewish Women, v.p. pub. affairs, v.p. comty. affairs, 2000—; mem. Jr. League of Miami, 1997—; mem. Miami Fellows Initiative, 2001-2003. Mem. Fla. Bar Assn. (supreme rules com.), Juvenile Rules Com., Order of Barristers. Office: Lawyers for Children Am 200 S Biscayne Blvd Ste 4000 Miami FL 33131 Office Phone: 305-577-4771. E-mail: melissa.buckner@steelhector.com.

BUCKNER, NATHAN ANDREW, music educator, musician; b. Eugene, Oreg., July 29, 1964; s. Paul Eugene and Kay Lamoreux Buckner. MusB, Juilliard Sch., 1987; MusM, Ind. U., 1989; D in Musical Arts, U. Md., 1996. Assoc. prof. piano U. Nebr., Kearney, 1997—. Pianist Sandhill Trio, Kearney, 1998—; founding mem. Delmarva Piano Festival, Rehoboth Beach, Del., 1992—. Editor: Philip Antony Corri: Complete Piano Music, 1997. Mem.: Music Tchrs. Nat. Assn., Phi Kappa Phi. Home: 409 W 32d St Kearney NE 68845 Office: U Nebr at Kearney Kearney NE 68849 Business E-Mail: bucknern@unk.edu.

BUCKNER, PHILIP FRANKLIN, newspaper publisher; b. Worcester, Mass., Aug. 25, 1930; s. Orello Simmons and Emily Virginia (Siler) B.; m. Ann Haswell Smith, Dec. 21, 1956 (div. Nov. 1993); children: John C., Frederick S., Catherine A.; m. Mary Emily Aird, Dec. 15, 1995 (div. Sept. 1997). AB, Harvard U., 1952; MA, Columbia U., 1954. With Bay State Abrasive Products Co., 1954-59; Reporter Lowell (Mass.) Sun, 1959-60; pub. East Providence (R.I.) Post, 1960-62; asst. to treas. Scripps League Newspapers, Seattle, 1964-66, divsn. mgr., 1966-71; pres. Buckner News Alliance, Seattle, 1971—. Pub. daily newspaper group including Carlsbad (N.Mex.) Current-Argus, 1971-90, Pecos (Tex.) Enterprise, 1971—, Fontana (Calif.) Herald-News, 1971-89, Banning and Beaumont (Calif.) Gazette, 1971-74, Lewistown (Pa.) Sentinel, 1971-93, Tiffin (Ohio) Advertiser-Tribune, 1973-93, York (Pa.) Daily Record, 1978-2004, Winsted (Conn.) Citizen, 1978, Excelsior Springs (Mo.) Standard, 1978, Oroville (Calif.) Mercury-Register, 1983-89, Corona (Calif.) Independent, 1984-89, Minot (N.D.) News, 1989-93, York (Pa.) Dispatch, 2004—. Avocation: mountain climbing. Office: Buckner News Alliance 2101 4th Ave Ste 1870 Seattle WA 98121-2345

BUCKNER, ROBERT EARLE, music educator, consultant; b. Norfolk, Va., May 8, 1945; s. Leo Lafayette Buckner, Jr. and Lois Liner Buckner; m. Donna Lyn Dupree, May 30, 1981; children: Michael Aaron, Ginger Lee Zsambeky, Andrew Christian, Kristin Erin Moore, Lyn Dupree Metzger. BS in Music Edn., We. Carolina U., 1967. Dir. bands Sylva-Webster (N.C.) H.S., 1966—79; prin., owner United Music Enterprises, Waynesville, NC, 1979—; dir. bands East Tenn. State U., Johnson City, Tenn., 1987—91; dir. athletic bands We. Carolina U., Cullowhee, NC. Cons. Disney Corp., Orlando, Fla., 1981—86; bd advisors Bands Am., Indpls., 1981—86; cons. Pygraphics, Inc, Argyle, Tex., 1981—; show designer Carolina Crown Drum and Bugle Corps, Charlotte, NC, 1993, U.S. Marine Drum and Bugle Corps, Washington, 1982—99; guest condr. N.C. All-State Band. Recipient Lowell Mason Music Edn. award, Music Educators Nat. Conf., 2005. Mem.: Music Educators Nat. Conf., N.C. Music Eduators Conf., N.C. Bandmaster Assn., Coll. Band Dirs. Nat. Assn., Phi Kappa Phi. Democrat. Episcopalian. Avocations: golf, skiing, reading. Office Phone: 828-227-2259.

BUCKNER, SALLY BEAVER, language educator, writer; b. Statesville, N.C., Nov. 3, 1931; d. Henry George and Foda Leigh (Stack) Beaver; m. Robert Lynn Buckner, Aug. 21, 1954; children: George Robert, Sally Lynn, Theodore Warren. AB in English, U.N.C., Greensboro, 1953; MA in English, N.C. State U., 1970; PhD in Curriculum and Instrn., U. N.C., Chapel Hill, 1980. Tchr. Arlington Jr. H.S., Gastonia, N.C., 1953-54, Protestant Sch., Goldsboro, N.C., 1962-65; journalist Raleigh Times, N.C., 1966-68; tchg. asst. N.C. State U., Raleigh, 1968-70; prof. English Peace Coll., Raleigh, 1970-98. Mem. scholar's adv. bd. MotheRead; chair N.C. Writers' Conf., 1988-89. Author: (poetry collection) Strawberry Harvest, 1986; editor: (anthology) Our Words, Our Ways, 1991, 95, Word and Witness: 100 Years of North Carolina Poetry, 1999. Mem. Legis. Study Commn. for Emotionally Disturbed Children, N.C., 1970-71, Women's Good Will Com., Goldsboro, N.C., 1963-65; co-chair arts edn. panel Dept. Cultural Resources, Raleigh, 1977-81; bd. dirs. N.C. Autism Soc., 1969-73, N.C. Lit. and Hist. Soc., 1981-86. Recipient Ragan-Rubin award N.C. English Tchr.'s Assn., 1993, Sam Ragan award, St. Andrew's Coll, Laurinburg, N.C., 1993, R. Hunt Parker award N.C. Lit. and Hist. Soc., 1999; named Alumnae Disting. Prof., Peace Coll., 1991. Mem. N.C. Poetry Soc. (poet laureate festival chair 1988-89), N.C. Lit. Hall of Fame (chair selection com.). Democrat. Baptist. Avocations: music, gardening, reading. Office Phone: 919-782-3636. E-mail: quenell@mindspring.com.

BUCKSBAUM, JOHN, real estate development company executive; BS in Econs., U. Denver. Pres. Gen. Growth Calif.; CEO Gen. Growth Properties, Inc., 1999—, also bd. dirs. Mem. exec. com. Wharton Sch. Adv. Bd., Urban Land Inst., bd. govs.; bd. dirs. World TEAM Sports, U.S. Ski Team Found.

Mem. Internat. Coun. Shopping Ctr. (bd. dirs. Ednl. Found.), Nat. Assn. Real Estate Investment Trusts, Nat. Realty Coun. (exec. com.), U. Calif. Real Estate Ctr. Office: Gen Growth Properties inc 110 N Wacker Dr Chicago IL 60606-1511*

BUCKSBAUM, MATTHEW, real estate investment trust company executive; b. Marshalltown, Iowa, Feb. 20, 1926; s. Louis and Ida (Gerwin) B.; m. Carolyn Swartz, Aug. 3, 1952; children: Ann B. Friedman, John. BA in Econ., U. Iowa, 1949. Owner, operator Regional Supermarket Chain, Marshalltown, 1949-54; owner, developer Pvt. Real Estate, Iowa, 1954-64; chmn. Gen. Growth Properties, Chgo., 1964—. Trustee, past chmn. Aspen (Colo.) Music Festival and Sch.; bd. dirs. Chgo. Symphony Orch., Lyric Opera Chgo. Sgt. USAF, 1944-46, PTO. Mem. Internat. Coun. Shopping Ctrs. (past chmn.), Urban Land Inst., Nat. Assn. Real Estate Investment Trusts. Jewish. Office: General Growth Properties Inc 110 N Wacker Dr Chicago IL 60606-1511 Office Phone: 312-960-5123. Office Fax: 312-960-5463.

BUCKSBAUM, MELVA, foundation administrator; m. Martin Bucksbaum (dec.); 1 child, Mary; m. Raymond J. Learsy. Mgr. Martin Bucksbaum Family Found., 1995—; dir. Robert I. Goldman Found., 1996—; bd. mem. Am. Friends of Israel Mus., NY, The Jewish Mus., NY, Hirshhorn Mus. & Sculpture Garden, Washington, Save Venice, New York & Venice; visiting com. Grad. Sch. Design, Harvard U. Named one of top 200 collectors (with Raymond Learsy), ARTnews Mag., 2004; recipient Gertrude Vanderbilt Whitney Award for outstanding arts patronage & philanthropy, 2004. Mem.: Whitney Mus. Am. Art (trustee 1996—, vice chmn. 2004—), Tate Gallery (Internat. Com.). Avocation: collector of contemporary art. Mailing: 646 Willoughby Way Aspen CO 81611 also: c/o Whitney Mus Am Art 945 Madison Ave New York NY 10021*

BUCKSPAN, RANDY JAY, plastic surgeon; b. Nurnberg, Fed. Republic Germany (parents Am. citizens), Oct. 9, 1954; s. Harold and Betty Jane (Marker) B.; m. Amy Denise Boynton, May 2, 1981; children: Elizabeth Anne, Caitlin Elaine, Andrew David. BS in Chemistry, U. Tex., Austin, 1976; MD, U. Tex., Galveston, 1980. Diplomate Am. Bd. Plastic Surgery. Resident in gen. surgery Vanderbilt U. Hosp., Nashville, 1980-85; fellow in plastic surgery U. Ky., Lexington, 1985-87. Contbr. articles to med. jours. Mem. AMA, ACS, Am. Soc. Plastic and Reconstructive Surgeons, Southeastern Soc. Plastic and Reconstructive Surgeons, Tampa Bay Soc. Plastic Surgeons Avocations: tennis, golf, fishing. Home: 219 Miramar Blvd NE Saint Petersburg FL 33704-3823 Office: 1607 Dr Martin Luther King Jr St N Ste B Saint Petersburg FL 33704 Office Phone: 727-822-6531. Business E-Mail: drbuckspan@tampabayplasticsurgery.net.

BUCKSTEIN, CARYL SUE, writer; b. Denver, Aug. 10, 1954; d. Henry Martin and Hedvig (Neulander) B. BS in Journalism, U. Colo., 1976. Editor Rifle (Colo.) Telegram, 1976; corr. So. Colo. Pueblo (Colo.) Star-Jour. and Chieftain, 1977-84; corr. The Denver Post, 1985; staff editor Nat. Over-the-Counter Stock Jour., Denver, 1985-89; writer Rocky Mountain News, Denver, 1990-92; editor Urban Spectrum, Denver, 1993; contbg. writer Boulder (Colo.) County Bus. Report, 1992—. Bd. mem. Holiday Project, Denver, 1996; mem. exec. bd. Denver Newspaper Guild, 1998. Recipient 1st Place Gen. Assignment Bus. Articles, Colo. Press Women, Denver, 1985, 90, 91. Mem. Colo. Soc. Profl. Journalists (sec.-treas. 1988), Denver Newspaper Guild (bd. dirs. 1998). Avocations: inventing, writing. Home: 9995 E Harvard Ave Apt 0215 Denver CO 80231-3906 Personal E-mail: dowritedenver@msn.com.

BUCKSTEIN, MARK AARON, lawyer, educator, mediator; b. NYC, July 1, 1939; s. Henry Al and Minnie Sarah (Russ) B.; children: Robin Beth, Michael Alan. BS in Math., CCNY, 1960; JD, NYU, 1963. Bar: N.Y. 1963, U.S. Dist. Ct. (so. and ea. dists.) N.Y. 1965, U.S. Supreme Ct. 1981. Assoc. Russ & Weyl, Massapequa, N.Y., 1963-64; assoc. counsel Mut. Life Ins. Co. N.Y., N.Y.C., 1964-65; assoc. Moses & Singer, N.Y.C., 1965-67, Leinwand, Maron & Hendler, N.Y.C., 1967-68; sr. ptnr. Baer Marks & Upham, N.Y.C., 1968-86; sr. v.p. external affairs, gen. counsel TWA, Inc., N.Y.C., 1986-92; exec. v.p. Am. Arbitration Assn., N.Y.C., N.J., 1992-93; exec. v.p., gen. counsel GAF Corp. and Internat. Specialty Products, Wayne, NJ, 1993-96; counsel Greenberg Traurig, Ft. Lauderdale, Fla., 1996-99, Profl. Dispute Resolution, Inc., Boca Raton, Fla., 1999—. Spl. prof. law Hofstra U. Law Sch., Hempstead, N.Y., 1981-93; adj. prof. law Rutgers U. Law Sch., Newark, 1994-96; adj. prof. Fla. Atlantic U., Grad. Sch. Bus., 2004—; bd. dirs. Bayswater Realty & Capital Corp., N.Y.C., Travel Channel Inc., N.Y.C., TWA, GAF Corp., Internat. Specialty Products, Consultis; mem. exec. com. Herzfeld & Stern, N.Y.C., 1981-84; mem. nat. arbitration and mediation com. NASD, 1998-2001. Trustee Bronx H.S. Found., 1984-96. Mem. ABA, N.Y. Bar Assn., Assn. of Bar of City of N.Y., KP (past dep. grand chancellor 1978). Jewish. Avocations: tennis, music, theater, puzzles. Home: 17064 Castlebury Ct Boca Raton FL 33496 Office: Profl Dispute Resolution 2424 N Federal Hwy Boca Raton FL 33431 Office Phone: 561-417-6602. Personal E-mail: mabresolve@aol.com.

BUCKSTEIN, STEVE, think-tank executive; b. Portland, Oreg. BS in Physics, MBA, Oreg. State U. Investment broker, Portland; pres. Cascade Policy Inst., Portland, 1991—. Founding bd. mem. Oreg. Taxpayers Union, 1978; bd. mem. Oregonians for Cost-effective Govt., 1987—88. Office: Cascade Policy Inst Ste 450 813 SW Adler Portland OR 97205

BUCKWALTER, JOSEPH ADDISON, orthopedic surgeon, educator; b. Ottumwa, Iowa, June 21, 1947; s. Joseph Addison and Carole Ann (Kelly) B.; m. Kathleen Coen, May 31, 1975; children: Jody, Andrea, Abigail. BS with high distinction, U. Iowa, 1969, MS, 1972, MD, 1974. Diplomate Am. Bd. Orthopaedic Surgery (recert., oral examiner 1988—, dir. 1990—, mem. examinations com. 1992—, chmn. examinations com. 1992-93, chmn. cert. renewal com. 1992—); lic. surgeon Iowa. Intern in internal medicine U. Iowa, Iowa City, 1974-75, resident in orthopaedics, 1975-77, 78-79, Nat. Rsch. Svc. Award rsch. fellow, 1977-78, from asst. prof. to assoc. prof. orthopaedic surgery, 1979-85, prof. orthopaedic surgery, 1985—. Mem. R&D devel. com. VA Med. Ctr. Com., 1985-88; mem. orthopaedic tumor therapy group U. Iowa Cancer Ctr., 1981—, cancer edn. subcom., 1982-90; mem. grants and fellowships adv. com. Iowa City Vets. Med. Ctr., 1983-86, chief orthopaedic surgery, 1987-91; mem. Arthritis Found. Rsch. Com., 1985-86; mem. panel NIH Consensus Devel. Confs., Bethesda, Md., 1984, 88; mem. rheumatology rsch. adv. bd. Syntex Corp., 1987-94; mem. adv. bd. WHO Multinational Collaborative Study on Predictors of Osteoarthritis, 1992; mem. sci. adv. com. Specialised Ctr. Rsch. on Osteoarthritis Rush-Presbyn.-St. Luke's Med. Ctr., Chgo., 1993—; mem. Nat. Arthritis and Musculoskeletal and Skin Diseases Adv. Coun., NIH, 1993—; disting. lectr. Hosp. Spl. Surgery, N.Y.C., 1982, Coll. Physicians and Surgeons-N.Y. Orthopaedic Hosp., 1988, U. N.Mex., 1989; guest lectr. Wilford Hall Med. Ctr., San Antonio, 1983, vis. prof., 1984; vis. prof. U. Miami, Fla., 1986, Cath. Med. Colls., Seoul, Republic of Korea, 1989, U. Pitts., 1993, Ohio State U., Columbus, 1994; vis. orthopaedic prof. U. So. Calif., L.A., 1990; Am. Orthopaedic Assn. 1991 Internat. vis. prof. Nuffield Orthopaedic Ctr., Oxford (Eng.) U., 1991, vis. prof. orthopaedics, 1991; vis. prof. orthopaedics, U. N.C., 1991; OREF Hark lectr. and vis. prof. U. Wash., Seattle, 1992; Watson Jones lectr. Royal Coll. Surgeons (Gt. Britain), 1992; A.M. Rechtman lectr. Phila. Orthopaedic Soc., 1993; Predl. guest spkr. 1993 Japanese Orthopaedic Assn. Rsch. Meeting, Matsumoto, Japan, 1993; Kelly Rsch. Award vis. prof. Mayo Clinic, Rochester, Minn., 1993; participant numerous workshops and confs. Cons. reviewer: Jour. Bone and Joint Surgery, 1979—, cons. editor for rsch., 1989—; bd. assoc. editors: Jour. Orthopaedic Rsch., 1982-85, mem. editl. adv. bd., 1985-88, co-editor-in-chief, 1993—; mem. editl. adv. bd. Orthopaedics, 1986-90; reviewer: The Lancet, 1993—; contbr. articles to profl. jours. Student rsch. fellow U. Iowa Coll. Medicine, 1970. Fellow Am. Inst. Med. and Biol. Engring. (founding), Am. Acad. Orthopaedic Surgeons (mem. com. basic scis. 1983-85, chmn. com. evaulation 1985-90, mem. at large, bd. dirs. 1988-89, mem. steering com. for devel. Musculoskeletal Conditions in U.S. 1990-92, chmn. coun. for rsch. and sci. affairs 1990-93, 94—, sec. 1993-94); mem. AAAS, Internat. Soc. Limb Salvage, Brit. Orthopaedic Assn. (companion mem.), Orthopaedic Rsch. Soc. (sec.-treas. 1985-88, bd. dirs. 1985-91, pres. 1989-90), Am. Orthopaedic Assn. (exch. fellowship com. 1989-90, chmn. internat. vis. prof. com. 1993—), Am. Orthopaedic Soc. for Sports Medicine (chmn. rsch. awards com. 1988-90, rsch. com. 1989-91), Internat. Skeletal Soc., Iowa Orthopaedic Soc., Johnson County Med. Soc., Musculoskeletal Tumor Soc., 20th Century Orthopaedic Assn., Girdlestone Orthopaedic Soc., Phi Beta Kappa, Alpha Omega Alpha. Office: U Iowa Hosps Dept Orthopaedics 200 Hawkins Dr Iowa City IA 52242-1009 Office Phone: 319-356-2595.

BUCKWALTER, KATHLEEN C., academic administrator, educator; BSN, U. Iowa; MA in Psychiatric/Mental Health Nursing, PhD in Nursing, U. Ill., Chgo. Assoc. dir. Gerontological Nursing Interventions Rsch. Ctr., dir. Ctr. on Aging U. Iowa, Found. disting. Prof., assoc. provost health scis., 1997—. Contbr. over 200 articles to profl. jours., 75 chpts. to books; editor: Nursing Diagnosis and Intervention for the Elderly (Maas, M., Buckwalter, K.C., Hardy, M.A.), 1991, Geriatric Mental Health: Current and Future Challenges, 1992, others. Mem.: IOM. Office: U Iowa Coll Nursing 101 Nursing Bldg 234 CMAB Iowa City IA 52242

BUCKWALTER, ROGER JEROME, editor, columnist; b. New Britain, Conn., Aug. 14, 1946; s. Benjamin Irving and Harriet Hoskins Buckwalter; m. Karen Ruth Adelson, June 8, 1974. BS in Broadcasting, U. Fla., 1968, MA in Journalism, Comm., 1969. Columnist The Jupiter (Fla.) Courier, 1978—, editl. page editor, 1982-2001, sr. writer, 2000-01. Guest lectr. Palm Beach C.C., Lake Worth, Fla., 1992, 98, Fla. Atlantic U. Jupiter, 2000; guest interviewer WPTV, Channel 5, West Palm Beach, Fla., 1994-99; polit. forum moderator Jupiter-Tequesta-Juno Beach C. of C., 1995—; mem. Fla. Atlantic U. Honors Coll. Adv. Bd., 1999—, com. chair, 2001—; mem. Wal-mart Scholarship Selection bd., 2000-01; mem. adv. bd. Palm Beach Atlantic Nat. Vocal Competition, 2001—, Smoke Free Workplaces Campaign, Fla., 2002. Vice chmn. Charter Rev. Com., Juno Beach, Fla., 1973-74; pres. Jupiter-Tequesta (Fla.) Unit Am. Cancer Soc., 1997-2000, chmn. com., 2000—, bd. dirs., 1996-; bd. dirs. Loxahatchee River Hist. Soc., 2003-05 v.p. for strategic planning, 2003-05, v.p. 2005—; bd. dirs. Cancer Alliance of Help and Hope, 2003—, chmn. mktg., 2003—; chmn. bd. dirs. No. Palm Beaches Cultural Alliance, 2004—. 1st lt. U.S. Army, 1969-71, Vietnam. Recipient 37 journalism awards including Best News Story award Surburban Newspapers Am., 1976 Mem. Nat. Conf. Editl. Writers, Fla. Press Assn. (Best Serious Column awards 1987, 96, Best Editl. awards 1989, 90, 93, 96), Fla. Press Club (Opinion and feature writing awards 1997). Avocations: painting, theater, writing. Personal E-mail: rogekar@aol.com.

BUCKWALTER, RONALD LAWRENCE, federal judge; b. Lancaster, Pa., Dec. 11, 1936; s. Noah Denlinger and Carolyn Marie (Lawrence) B.; m. Dollie May Fitting, May 9, 1963; children: Stephen Matthew, Wendy Susan. AB, Franklin and Marshall Coll., 1958; JD, Coll. William and Mary, 1962. Prin. Ronald L. Buckwalter, Esquire, Lancaster, 1963-71; ptnr. Shirk, Reist and Buckwalter, Lancaster, 1971-80; dist. atty. Lancaster County, Lancaster, 1978-80; judge 2nd Jud. Dist. Commonwealth Pa., 1980-90, U.S. Dist. Ct., Phila., 1990—. Sec. City Lancaster Authority, 1970; bd. dirs. Am. Cancer Soc., Lancaster, 1982, Boy Scouts Am., Lancaster, 1984, YMCA, Lancaster, 1990. 1st lt. U.S. Army NG, 1962-68. Recipient Pub. Life and Letter award Phi Sigma Alpha, 1990. Mem. Am. Judicature Soc., Fed. Bar Assn., Fed. Judges Assn., Pa. Bar Assn., Lancaster Bar Assn. (pres. 1988). Office: US Dist Ct 14614 US Courthouse 601 Market St Philadelphia PA 19106-1713 Office Phone: 215-597-3084.

BUCOLO, GAIL ANN, biotechnologist; b. Port Chester, NY, July 27, 1954; d. Joseph Anthony and Jennie (Tomassetti) B. BS in French, Oneonta State Coll., 1976; MA in French, Middlebury Coll., 1977; postgrad., Columbia U., 1981—82; MS in Biotech., Manhattan Coll., 1995. Technician NY Hosp., NYC, 1983-86; rsch. technician NYU Hosp., NYC, 1986; sr. rsch. technician Meml. Sloan Kettering, NYC, 1986-88, Columbia U., NYC, 1988-2001; tchr. Cathedral H.S., NYC, 2001—04; rsch. tech. N.Y. Meth. Hosp., Bklyn., 2004—. Corr. Scienceport, Rye, NY, 1994-96; adj. prof. Mercy Coll., Dobbs Ferry, NY, 1996—2004; summer rsch. intern Rockefeller U., 2003. Mem. AAAS, NY Acad. Scis., Sigma Xi. Roman Catholic. Achievements include work on the factor VIII inhibitor and discovery that it inhibited reverse transcriptase of HIV; work on spinal cord injury and neuronal regeneration which was implemented at the Miami Project in Fla. Home: 1025 Louise Ave Basement Apt Mamaroneck NY 10543 Office: NY Methodist Hosp Brooklyn NY E-mail: gailbucolo@aol.com.

BUCOVE, ARNOLD DAVID, psychiatrist; b. Toronto, Sept. 22, 1934; BA, Columbia U., 1956; MD, NYU, 1961. Diplomate Am. Bd. Psychiatry and Neurology. Intern Lenox Hill Hosp., N.Y.C., 1961-62; resident in psychiatry Bellevue Hosp., N.Y.C., 1962-63, St. Luke's Hosp., N.Y.C., 1963-65; chief psychiatry 36th Tactical Hosp., Bitburg, Germany, 1965-67; pvt. practice psychiatry Pleasant Valley, NY, 1967—92, Poughkeepsie, N.Y., 1992-93; pvt. practice Oneonta, N.Y., 1993-99; attending staff Craig House, Beacon, N.Y., 1977-93; asst. dir. Dutchess County Mental Health Clinic, Poughkeepsie, N.Y., 1967-68; chief psychiatry Fox Meml. Hosp., Oneonta, 1993-99, sec.-treas. med. staff, 1997-98, pres.-elect, 1998-99, pres., 1999; pvt. practice Millbrook, NY, 1967—; med. dir. Lexington Ctr. Recovery, Poughkeepsie, NY, 1999—. Cons. psychiatrist Greer Children's Cmty., Millbrook, N.Y., 1968-77; mem. courtesy staff Sharon (Conn.) Hosp., 1967-90; cons. IBM, Poughkeepsie, 1968. Contbr. articles to profl. jours. Bd. dirs. Town of Washing Civic Assn., Millbrook, 1986-93, Millbrook Music Assn., 1986-92; mem. vestry Grace Ch., Millbrook, 1971-74, mem. vestry St. Peter's Ch., Millbrook, 1989-92. Capt. USAF, 1965-67. Disting. life fellow Am. Psychiat. Assn. (pres. Mid-Hudson chpt. 1977-79); mem. Millbrook Hunt (bd. govs. 1968-71), Millbrook Golf and Tennis Club, Poughkeepsie Tennis Club. Avocations: riding, skiing, tennis.

BUCY, J. FRED, JR., retired electronics company executive; b. Tahoka, Tex., July 29, 1928; s. J. Fred and Ethel (Montgomery) Bucy; m. Odetta Greer, Jan. 25, 1947 (dec. Dec. 2000); children: J. Fred III, Roxanne, Diane. B.Physics, Tex. Tech. U., 1951; M.Physics, U. Tex., 1953; DSc (hon.), Tex. Tech U., 1994. With Tex. Instruments, Inc., Dallas, 1953-85, engr. 53-63, corp. v.p. mil. sys., 1963-67, corp. group v.p. microchips, 1967-72, exec. v.p., 1972-75, exec. v.p., chief operating officer, dir., 1974-76, pres., chief operating officer, dir., 1976-84, pres., chief exec. officer, dir., 1984-85, cons., 1985-97. Bd. dirs. Thomas Group, Inc., Optical Data Sys., Inc., Hypres, Inc., S.W. Rsch. Inst., Rectractable Tech. Inc., Intrusion Inc., Sanders Assocs., Inc., Alliant Techsystems, Inc.; cons., chmn. Tex. Nat. Rsch. Lab. Com. Patentee in field. Mem. Tech. Assessment of U.S. Congress; mem. Comptroller Gen's Panel, Pres.'s Commn. for Nat. Agenda for 80's,; comm. chmn. Nat. Rsch. Coun., Washington, Def. Sci. Bd. Dept. Def.; mem. bd. regents Tex. Tech U., Health Sci. Ctr. Tex. Tech U., 1973-91; chmn. bd. regents Tex. Tech U. and Health Sci. Ctr., 1980-82, 89-90; mem. adv. com. rsch. Tex.Higher Edn. Coordinating Bd.; external adv com. Arnold O. and Mabel M. Beckman Inst. Advanced Sci. Tech., U. Ill.; adv. coun. Woodrow Wilson Internat. Ctr. for Scholars, Washington; chmn. Tex. Sci. Adv. Coun.; nat. chmn. Enterprise Campaign Tex. Tech U.; mem. vis. com. Russian Rsch. Ctr., Harvard U.; mem. physics vis. com. MIT; mem. exec. com. marine sci. adv. coun. U. Tex., 2005 Recipient Disting. Engr. award Tex. Tech U., 1972, Disting. Alumnus award, 1991. Fellow IEEE; mem. NAE, Am. Inst. Physics, Soc. Exploration Geophysicists, Conf. Bd., Cosmos Club (Washington), Dallas Petroleum Club, Tau Beta Pi, Sigma Pi Sigma, Eta Kappa Nu (Eminent Mem.). Address: PO Box 780929 Dallas TX 75378-0929 E-mail: jfbuce@aol.com.

BUCZYNSKI, SANDY, science educator; b. Liberty, Tex., Jan. 17, 1951; d. Robert Gove and Elouise Wilson; m. Tom Buczynski, Aug. 8, 1989. BA; PhD, U. Hawaii, 2002. Tchr. Elsik H.S., Alief, Tex., 1978—88, Seaburn H.S., 1988—2002; asst. prof. U. San Diego, 2002—. Contbr. articles to profl. jours. Mem.: Nat. Assn. Biology Tchrs., Nat. Assn. Rsch. Sci. Tchg., Assn. Educators Tchrs. Sci. Avocations: quilting, hiking, hula. Office: U San Diego 5998 Alcala Park Fmt San Diego CA 92110-2492 Business E-Mail: sandyo@sandiego.edu.

BUDA, JAMES B., lawyer, manufacturing executive; b. South Bend, Ind., Mar. 9, 1947; BA, Ball State U., 1969; JD, U. Notre Dame, 1973. Bar: Ind. 1973, Ill. 1987, U.S. Ct. Appeals (7th cir.) 1987, U.S. Supreme Ct. 1987. Atty., legal dept. and other positions Caterpillar, Inc., 1987—96, assoc. gen. counsel, 1996—99; assoc. gen. counsel, legal services divsn. Caterpillar, Inc., United Kingdom, 1999—2001; v.p., legal services divsn., gen. counsel, sec. Caterpillar, Inc., Peoria, Ill., 2001—. Mem. Civil Justice Reform Group. Mem.: ATLA, ABA, Gen. Counsel Roundtable, Corp. Exec. Bd., CLO Roundtable, Assn. Gen. Counsels, Am. Soc. Corp. Secs., Internat. Assn. Def. Counsel, Fedn. Corp. and Ins. Counsel, Def. Rsch. Inst., Am. Corp. Counsel Assn., Ind. State Bar Assn., Ill. State Bar Assn. Office: Caterpillar Inc Legal Dept 100 NE Adams St Peoria IL 61629-7310 Office Phone: 309-675-4428. Business E-Mail: budajb@cat.com.

BUDA, THADDEUS J., JR., lawyer; b. Wyandotte, Mich., Apr. 9, 1943; m. Maureen A. Buda; children: Susan M., Julie A. BS, Wayne State U., 1965, JD, 1972. Bar: Mich. 1972. Sr. v.p., gen. counsel, sec. Auto-Owners Ins. Co., Lansing, Mich., 1st v.p., gen. counsel, sec., 2003—. Mem.: Mich. State Bar Assn. Office: Auto-Owners Ins Co 6101 Anacapri Blvd Lansing MI 48917

BUDALUR, THYAGARAJAN SUBBANARAYAN, chemistry professor; b. India, July 14, 1929; came to U.S., 1969, naturalized, 1977; s. Subbanarayan Subbuswamy and Parvatham (Gopalakrishnan) B.; children: Chitra, Poorna, Kartik. MA, U. Madras, 1951, M.Sc., 1954, PhD, 1956. Reader organic chemistry U. Madras, 1960-68; prof. chemistry U. Idaho, Moscow, 1968-74; prof. chemistry, dir. div. earth phys. sci. U. Tex., San Antonio, 1974-2000, emeritus prof., 2000—. Lectr. in field. Author: Mechanisms of Molecular Migrations; Selective Organic Transformations; Editorial bd. chem. jours.; contbr. articles to profl. jours.; 3 patents in field. Recipient Intra Sci. Research award, 1966 Fellow Am. Chem. Soc.; mem. Chem. Soc. London, Soc. Cosmetic Chemistry N.Y. Acad. Sci., Am. Inst. Chemists, Sigma Xi, Phi Kappa Phi. Clubs: Lions. Home: 6119 Amble Trl San Antonio TX 78249-2108

BUDD, JIM, communications manager; b. Austin, Minn. s. Stanley James and Margaret (Deutschman) B. Student, Austin State Jr. Coll. Head of CCTV dept. Northwest Camera Svc., Mpls., 1971-72; head of video svc. dept., engring., TV studio and video svc. dept. ops. Internat. Communications Svcs., Mpls., 1972-73; talent scout coord. and video cons. Wag Arts Prodns.-Talent Agy., Mpls., 1972-75; electronics dept. svc. mgr. Gordon Electric Co., Austin, 1975-78; operational ptnr. in design and mfr. of projection TV consoles with McAllister Trading Co. and ABC Electronics, Austin, 1979-84; video systems specialist The Electronics Warehouse, Inc., Rochester, Minn., 1984-85; engr., video dir., mgr. ABC Electronics & Video, Austin, 1985—; producer, dir. N.W. TV-Prodns., Austin, 1986—; mem. broadcast video staff KAAL-TV, Austin, 1997-98. Video sys. design cons. Script author, narrator of documentary videofilm: "Celebration of Hmong New Year"--Laos, 1991; producer: (video) Big Isl. Rendezvous, 1995, (video film) Olympic Torch Relay Festival, 1996. Videographer Summerset Theatre of Austin Cmty. Coll., 1987; prodn. fund vol. PBS Sta. KSMQ-TV, Austin, 1988-2002. Mem. Am. Film Inst., Am. Legion. Roman Catholic. Office: ABC Electronics Svcs 1008 5th Ave NW Austin MN 55912-2114

BUDD, LOUIS JOHN, language educator; b. St. Louis, Aug. 26, 1921; s. Vincent and Sophia (Kajszo) Budrewicz; m. Isabelle Amelia Marx, Mar. 3, 1945; children: Catherine Lou, David Harry. BA, U. Mo., 1941, MA, 1942; PhD, U. Wis., 1949; DLitt, U. Mo., 1988, Elmira Coll., 1995. Instr. U. Mo., Columbia, 1942, 46, U. Ky., Lexington, 1949-52; asst. prof. Duke U., Durham, N.C., 1952-60, assoc. prof., 1960-66, prof., 1966-83, James B. Duke prof., 1983-91, chmn. dept. English, 1973-79. Mem. vis. faculty Washington U., St. Louis, summer 1954, Northwestern U., Evanston, Ill., summer 1961; lectr. seminar Kraft div. Internat. Paper Co., summer 1959; Fulbright lectr., India, 1967, 72; vis. lectr. U. Damascus, Syria, 1978; chmn. Jay B. Hubbell Ctr. for Am. Lit. Historiography, 1976-87. Author: Mark Twain: Social Philosopher, 1962, Robert Herrick, 1971, Newspaper and Magazine Interviews with Samuel L. Clemens, 1874-1910, 1977, Our Mark Twain: The Making of His Public Personality, 1983; editor: Robert Herrick's The Web of Life and Clark's Field, 1970; (with others) Toward a New American Literary History, 1980, Critical Essays on Mark Twain, 1867-1910, 1982, 1910-80, 1983, New Essays on Adventures of Huckleberry Finn, 1985, On Mark Twain: The Best from American Literature, 1987, Mark Twain's Collected Tales, Sketches, Speeches and Essays (2 vols.), 1992, Mark Twain: The Contemporary Reviews, 1999; mem. editl. bd. A Selected Edition of W.D. Howells, South Atlantic Rev, 1978-81, U. Miss. Studies in English, 1979-95, South Atlantic Quar., 1980-87; mng. editor Am. Lit, 1979-86, chmn. editl. bd., 1986-91, Am. Lit. Realism 1870-1910, 1986—, Studies in Am. Humor, 1974—; contbr. numerous articles to profl. jours. Hon. trustee Mark Twain Meml., 1992—. 2d lt. USAAF, 1942-45. Guggenheim fellow, 1965-66; Am. Philos. Soc. grant, 1956, 70, 73; Nat. Endowment for Humanities sr. fellow, 1979-80; recipient J.H. Fisher award South Atlantic Depts. of English, 1997. Mem. MLA (Hubbell medal 1998), Am. Humor Studies Assn. (pres. 1979, 93), AAUP (pres. Duke chpt. 1971-72), Internat. Humor Studies Assn., Mark Twain Circle of Am. (founding pres. 1986-87, hon. life mem.), Phi Beta Kappa (pres. Duke Chpt. 1963-64). Home: 2753 Mcdowell Rd Durham NC 27705-5715 Office: Duke U Dept English Durham NC 27708-0015 Office Phone: 919-684-2741. Business E-Mail: budd@duke.edu.

BUDD, RICHARD WADE, academic administrator, dean, priest; b. Henderson, Md., Aug. 24, 1934; s. Bryan William and Dorothea Marie (Fouvy) B.; m. Claudia L. Wolff; children: Kimberly, Richard Wade, Janna, Eric, Gary, Stephanie. BA, Bowling Green U., 1956; MA, U. Iowa, 1962, PhD, 1964. Ordained priest Episcopal Ch., 2001. Reporter, staff writer Dayton (Ohio) Daily News, 1956-57; rsch. assoc., instr., asst. prof., dir. Inst. Comm. Studies, U. Iowa, Iowa City, 1960-71; prof., disting. prof., assoc. dean Rutgers Coll. Rutgers U., New Brunswick, N.J., chmn. dept. human comm., 1971-80, dir. Sch. Comm. Studies, 1980-83, founding dean Sch. Comm., Info. and Libr. Studies, 1983-97; v.p. for info. and technology Regent U., Virginia Beach, Va., 1997—2000, disting. scholar, 2000—; chmn. bd. Newstatements Comm. Cons., 1973-80; cons. in field.; rector Ch. of the Good Shepherd, Richmond, Va., 2002—. Author: Introduction to Content Analysis, 1964, Content Analysis of Communication, 1967, Approaches to Human Communication, 1972, Human Communication Handbook Simulations and Games, 1975, Mass Communication: Dialogue and Alternatives, 1976, Interdisciplinary Approaches to Communication, 1979, Beyond Media, 1988; assoc. editor Human Communication Research, 1974-83, Communication Quar, 1975-83; mem. editorial bd. Jour. Communication, 1976-82, Communication Yearbook, 1977-86, Mass Communications Yearbook, 1979—95. Mem. Cmty. Arts Coun. East Brunswick, 1973—80; exec. coun. East Brunswick Youth Baseball Program, 1974; active Boy Scouts Am.; priest Episcopal Diocese of So. Va., 2001; chmn. bd. dirs. Anglican Ctr. for Theology and Spirituality, Diocese of So. Va., 2003—. Lt. USNR, 1957—60. Mem. Internat. Comm. Assn. (pres. 1976-77), AAAS, Nat. Comm. Assn., Am. Assn. Public Opinion Rsch., Assn. Edn. in Journalism, ALA (com. on accrediting 1995-99), Assn. Libr. Info. Edn. Episcopalian. Home: 120 Cypress Crk Williamsburg VA 23188-7804 Office: Ch of the Good Shepherd 4206 Springhill Ave Richmond VA 23225 Office Phone: 804-233-2278. Business E-Mail: rwbudd@regent.edu.

BUDD, RUSSELL WILLS, lawyer; b. San Antonio, Tex., Mar. 9, 1954; BA cum laude, Trinity U., 1976; JD, U. Tex., 1979. Bar: Tex. 1979, U.S. Ct. Appeals, Fifth Cir. 1980, U.S. Ct. Appeals, Eleventh Cir., U.S. Dist. Ct., No. Dist. Tex. 1981, U.S. Dist. Ct., We. Dist. Tex. 1983, Mich., U.S. Supreme Ct., U.S. Ct. Appeals, Ninth Cir. 1985. Assoc. Am. Bd. Trial Advocates, 1992; state coord. Trial Lawyers for Pub. Justice, 1993; mng. shareholder Baron & Budd, Dallas. Recipient Tex. Super Lawyer, 2004. Fellow: Dallas Bar Found. (life); mem.: ABA, Trial Lawyers Care, Inc., Trial Lawyers for Pub. Justice, Am. Bd. Trial Advocates, Dallas Trial Lawyers Assn., Assn. Trial Lawyers of Am., Tex. Trial Lawyers Assn., Phi Beta Kappa. Office: Baron & Budd 3102 Oak Lawn Ave Ste 1100 Dallas TX 75219 Office Phone: 214-520-1181.

BUDD, WAYNE A., lawyer; b. Springfield, Mass., Nov. 18, 1941; married; 3 children. AB cum laude, Boston Coll., 1963; JD, Wayne State U., 1967. Pvt. practice, 1963—79; sr. ptnr. Budd, Wiley & Richlin, Boston, 1979—89; U.S. atty. Dist. of Mass., Boston, 1989—92; assoc. atty. gen. US Dept. Justice, Wash., DC, 1992—93; sr. ptnr. Goodwin, Procter & Hoar, Boston, 1993—96; group pres. Bell Atlantic-New England (now Verizon), 1996—2000; exec. v.p., gen. counsel John Hancock Fin. Svcs., Inc., 2000—. Vice-chmn. US Attys. Adv. Com. to Atty. Gen.; asst. atty. gen. Commonwealth of Mass.; trustee Boston Coll.; past lectr. Boston Coll. Sch. Law.; bd. dir. Premcor Inc., Tosco Corp., John Hancock, 1998-; dir. Bank of Boston Corp., 1993; adj. faculty mem., Boston Coll. Law Sch., 1973-1988. Asst. corp. counsel City of Boston; mem., chmn. Mass. Civil Svc. Commn., 1972-89. Recipient Salmanson Human Rels. award Anti-Defamation League of B'nai B'rith, Outstanding Achievement award Boston Edison Co. Mem. Mass. Bar Assn. (pres. 1979), Mass. Black Lawyers Assn. (pres. 1974-76). Office: John Hancock Fin Svcs Inc Legal 200 Clarendon Street PO Box 111 Boston MA 02117-0111

BUDDE, NEIL FREDERICK, publishing company executive, editor, publisher; b. Elmhurst, Ill., June 19, 1956; s. Robert Earl and Phyllis Jean (Plummer) Budde; m. Virginia Bowman Edwards, May 22, 1982. BA, Western Ky. U., 1977; MBA, U. Louisville, 1982. Copy editor Richmond (Va.) Times Dispatch, 1977—78, The Courier-Jour., Louisville, 1978—81, asst. bus. editor, 1984—86; assoc. editor Courier-Jour. Mag., Louisville, 1981—84; reporter, editor USA Today, Rosslyn, Va., 1986—87; assoc. editor Dow Jones Info. Systems, Princeton, NJ, 1987—88, dep. editl. dir., 1988—93; editor The Wall Street Jour. Interactive Edition, N.Y.C., 1993—, editor, exec. dir., 1996—98, v.p., editor, 1998—99, v.p., editor, pub., 1999—2002; pres. The Neil Budde Group, 2003—. Avocations: golf, tennis, photography. Home: 354 Myrtle Grove Ln Richmond Hill GA 31324-4413 Office Phone: 908-342-5400. E-mail: neil@neilbudde.com.

BUDELMANN, BERND ULRICH, zoologist, educator; b. Hamburg, Germany, Apr. 1, 1942; came to the U.S., 1987; s. Gunther and Minna (Siemssen) B. PhD, U. Munich, 1970; degree, U. Regensburg, 1975. Asst. prof. U. Regensburg, Germany, 1973-78, assoc. prof., 1978-87, Heisenberg fellow, 1979-84; assoc. prof. U. Tex., Galveston, 1987-93, prof., 1993—. Chief divsn. biol. marine resources, U.Tex., Galveston, 1996-2000; mem. sci. adv. bd. Stazione Zoologica Anton Dohrn, Naples, Italy, 1992-2000; exec. sec. Cephalopod Internat. Adv. Coun., 1994-2000. Contbr. articles to Nature, Philos. Transactions of Royal Soc., Jour. Comparative Physiology. Bd. dir. Galveston Symphony Orch., 1994—. Grantee Deutsche Forschungsgemeinschaft, 1979-85, NIH, 1989—, Wellcome Trust, 1991, NSF, 1997—. Mem. Am. Soc. Gravitational and Space Biology, Assn. for Rsch. on Otolaryngology, Barany Soc., Deutsche Zoologische Gesellschaft, Gesellschaft Deutscher Naturforscher und Arzte, Internat. Soc. Neuroethology, J.B. Johnson Club, Neurotological and Equilibriometric Soc., Soc. for Exptl. Biology, Soc. for Neurosci., Verband Deutscher Biologen, Rotary Club Galveston (bd. dir. 1999-2001, officer 2002—, pres. 2004-05), Sigma Xi (sec. chpt. 1988—). Lutheran. Home: 1823 Bayou Shore Dr Galveston TX 77551-4336 Office: U Tex Med Br Dept Neuroscience & Cell Biology Galveston TX 77555-1069 Office Phone: 409-772-3661. Business E-Mail: bubudelm@utmb.edu.

BUDIANSKY, STEPHEN PHILIP, writer; b. Boston, Mar. 3, 1957; s. Bernard and Nancy (Cromer) B.; m. Martha Polkey, Sept. 10, 1982; children: Rachael Elizabeth, Andrew Aaron. BS in Chemistry, Yale Coll., 1978; MS in Applied Math., Harvard U., 1979. From asst. editor to assoc. editor ES&T Mag. Am. Chem. Soc., Washington, 1979-81; science writer Am. Chem. Soc., Washington, 1981-82; corr., Washington editor Nature Mag., Washington, 1982-85; congrl. fellow Office of Tech. Assessment, Washington, 1985-86; writer, asst. mng. editor U.S. News & World Report, Washington, 1986-97, dep. editor, 1997-98. Corr. Atlantic Monthly, Boston, 1998—. Author: The Covenant of the Wild, 1992 (short-listed for Rhone-Poulenc prize sci. books 1995), Nature's Keepers, 1995 (short-listed for Rhone-Poulenc prize sci. books 1996), The Nature of Horses, 1997, If a Lion Could Talk: Animal Intelligence and the Evolution of Consciousness, 1998, Battle of Wits: The Complete Story of Codebreaking in World War II, 2000, The Truth About Dogs, 2000, Air Power, 2004, Her Majesty's Spymaster: Elizabeth I, Sir Francis Walsingham, and the Birth of Modern Espionage, 2005; contbr. articles to profl. jours. including Nature, Jour. AVMA, Cryptologia, Intelligence and Nat. Security. Grad. fellow NSF, 1978. Mem. Loudoun Hunt, Sigma Xi. Office: Black Sheep Farm 14605 Chapel Ln Leesburg VA 20176-5277*

BUDIN, WENDY C., nursing educator, researcher; m. Arnold I. Budin, June 13, 1973; children: Barri, Sarah, Jill. BSN, Adelphi U., Garden City, NY, 1973; MSN, Seton Hall U., South Orange, NJ, 1986; PhD, NYU, N.Y.C., 1996. Cert. perinatal nurse, ANCC, 2002; Lamaze childbirth educator Lamaze Internat., 1998. Assoc. prof. nursing Seton Hall U. Coll. Nursing, South Orange, NJ, 1986—2002, program dir.-Lamaze childbirth educator program, 1994—, assoc. dean grad. nursing programs and rsch., 2002—; acad. dir. online MSN program SetonWorldWide-Seton Hall U., South Orange, NJ, 2001—. Co-chair nursing/ psychosocial adv. group N.J. State Commn. on Cancer Rsch., Trenton, 1994—; cons. rsch. in nursing Excelsior Coll., Albany, NY, 1996—; med. adv. bd. North Jersey Affiliate of Susan G. Komen Breast Cancer Found., Summit, NJ, 1999—; collateral reviewer Sigma Theta Tau Internat., Indpls., 2001—. Author (co-author with j. hott): (book) Notter's Essentials of Nursing Research (Brandon/Hill Selected List of Nursing Books for Rsch., 2000)); author: (co-author with c. hoskins and j. haber) Breast Cancer: Journey to Recovery; editor (contributing editor): Journal of Perinatal Education; contbr. articles to profl. jours. Recipient Rudin Family award doctoral student achievement, NYU, 1994, Arch award, NYU Sch. Edn., 1996, Sigma Theta Tau Internat. Regional Rsch. Dissertation Award, Sigma Theta Tau Internat., 1997, NJ Gov.'s Nursing Merit award nurse rschr., NJ Dept. of Health and Sr. Svcs., 1999, N.J. Nurse of Yr. award, AWHONN, 2004, CARE award for nursing rsch., NJ State Nurses Assn., 2004, Disting. Alumnae award, NYU divsn. nursing, 2004; grantee Co-Investigator & Project Dir. Stress and Coping in Caregivers of AIDS Children, NIH - NINR, 1991, Am. Nurses Found., 1994, Co-Investigator and Nurse Interventionist for Breast Cancer: Edn., Counseling and Adjustment, AREA Grant - NINR, 1998, Fed. Nurse Traineeship, Divsn. of Nursing -Dept. of Health and Human Svcs., 2002-03; Doctoral scholarship, Sigma Theta Tau Internat., 1992, Erline P. McGriff Doctoral scholarship, NYU - Divsn. of Nursing, 1995, N.J. Breast Cancer Rsch. Vis. Scholar fellowship, N.J. Commn. on Cancer Rsch., 1996. Mem.: Oncology Nursing Soc., Assn. for Woman's Health, Obstet. & Neonatal Nursing-AWHONN, Ea. Nursing Rsch. Soc., Lamaze Internat. (certification coun.), Sigma Theta Tau (past president-gamma nu chpt.). Achievements include research in Adjustment to Breast Cancer. Office: Seton Hall Univ College of Nursing South Orange NJ 07079 Business E-Mail: budinwen@shu.edu.

BUDINGTON, WILLIAM STONE, retired librarian; b. Oberlin, Ohio, July 3, 1919; s. Robert Allyn and Mabel (Stone) B.; m. Irma Johnson BA, Williams Coll., 1940, L.H.D., 1975; BS in L.S, Columbia U., 1941, MS, 1951; BS in Elec. Engring, Va. Poly. Inst., 1946. Reference librarian Norwich U., 1941-42; librarian, engring. and phys. scis. Columbia, 1947-52; asso. librarian John Crerar Library, Chgo., 1952-65, librarian, 1965-69, exec. dir., librarian, 1969-84. Mem. U.S.-USSR Spl. Libraries Exchange, 1966; bd. dirs. Center for Research Libraries, 1970-72, chmn., 1972; mem. vis. com. on libraries Mass. Inst. Tech., 1972-77 Served with AUS, 1942-46. Fellow AAAS, Med Library Assn.; mem. ALA, Am. Soc. Info. Sci., Spl. Libraries Assn. (pres. 1964-65, Hall of Fame 1984), Am. Soc. Engring. Edn., Assn. Research Libraries (dir. 1970-74, pres. 1973), Assn. Coll. and Research Libraries (Acad. Research Librarian of Year 1982), Phi Beta Kappa, Tau Beta Pi, Eta Kappa Nu. Clubs: Caxton, Arts. Home: 211 Wood Terrace Dr Colorado Springs CO 80903-2337

BUDMAN, CATHY LINDA, psychiatrist, physician; b. Bklyn., N.Y., Mar. 15, 1957; ScB, Brown U., 1979; MD, SUNY, Buffalo, 1984. Diplomate Australian Med. Coun., Am. Bd. Neurology and Psychiatry. Intern, then resident in psychiatry U. Calif.-San Francisco Sch. Medicine, 1984-86; sr. resident in family medicine Royal Australian Coll. Family Medicine, St. Leonards, NSW, 1987-88; med. registrar drug and alcohol unit Royal Prince Alfred Hosp., Sydney, NSW, 1987-88; resident in psychiatry North Shore Hosp., Manhasset, N.Y., 1988-90, rsch. fellow neuropsychiatry, 1990-91, dir. med. student clerkship in psychiatry, 1994—; pvt. practice Manhasset, 1990—; dir. med. student edn. in psychiatry North Shore U. Hosp., Manhasset, 1994—; asst. prof. psychiatry and neurology Cornell U. Med. Coll., N.Y.C., 1993-98, NYU Sch. Medicine, N.Y.C., 1998—2001, assoc. prof. psychiatry, 2002—. Dir. Movement Disorder Clinic, 1990—; rsch. cons. dept. drug and alcohol Royal Prince Alfred Hosp., Westmead Hosp., 1986-88. Mem. APA, Nassau County Psychiat. Soc., Tourette Assn., Royal Australian Coll. Family Practitioners (assoc.). Office: North Shore Hosp Dept Psychiatry 400 Community Dr Manhasset NY 11030-3815 Office Phone: 516-562-3223.

BUDNICK, THOMAS PETER, social worker; b. Ludlow, Mass., Feb. 16, 1947; s. Henry F. and Mildred Mary (Killian) B. BS, Am. Internat. Coll., 1972, MA, 1975. Lic. cert. profl. social worker. Mailhandler U.S. Postal Svc., Springfield, Mass., 1970-72; substitute tchr. Pub. Schs. Dept., Ludlow, Mass., 1973-74; social worker Mass. Dept. Pub. Welfare, Springfield, 1975—. Pres. Am.'s Manifest Destiny Soc., Inc., West Harwich, Mass., 1979—; bd. dirs. Mass. Astronomy Club, Boston, 1988—. Contbr. numerous articles to jours. V.p. Local 509, Boston, 1989. Democrat. Home: 19 Harding Ave Ludlow MA 01056-2327

BUDNICKI, MICHAEL J., nurse; b. Perth Amboy, N.J., Aug. 1, 1957; s. Xavier and Ingrid Budnicki. Student in computer sci., 1999. LPN Jersey Shore Med. Ctr., Neptune, 1992—2002. Author: (poetry) Our Special Place, 2001, At Home on the Sea, 2005. Personal E-mail: michaelbudnicki@hotmail.com.

BUDNY, LORRAINE, freelance writer, newspaper reporter; b. Chicopee, Mass., July 18, 1917; d. Marcel Girouard and Cecile Babineau; m. J. Travers Ward, Dec. 31, 1941 (div. June 1946); m. Bernard S. Budny, Aug. 15, 1947 (dec. Aug. 1981). Student, N.Y. Theater Sch. Dramatic Art, Traphagen Sch. Fashion Design, N.Y.C. Asst. designer to Bonnie Cashin Adler & Adler, N.Y.C.; publicist Claire McCardell, N.Y.C.; dir. fashion promotion Lord & Taylor, N.Y.C., 1945-47; fashion editor Harper's Bazaar, N.Y.C., 1947-48; fashion designer Lorraine Budny Inc., N.Y.C., 1948-55; publisher, editor, writer South Kent, Conn., 1987-97; columnist, freelance writer Housatonic Publs., New Milford, Conn., 1997—. Mem. adv. com. New Milford Bank and Trust. Roman Catholic. Avocations: art museums and galleries, reading, travel, travel writing, double crostic puzzles.

BUDREVICS, ALEXANDER, landscape architect; b. Riga, Latvia, Jan. 3, 1925; arrived in Can., 1952; s. Alfred and Adele (Martinous) B.; m. Milija Vite, Apr. 8, 1948; children: Valdis, Dace, Arnis. Grad. hort. sch., Latvia, 1944; grad. landscape architect, St. Alban's (Eng.) Sch. Art, 1949, London Coll. Art, 1951. Registered landscape architect, Ont., Can. Practice landscape architecture, 1960; staff various firms, 1960; pres. Alexander Budrevics & Assocs. Ltd., Don Mills, Ont., 1965—. Ptnr. Golf Course Devel. Assn., 1969—. Designer over 3000 projects including Nat. Home Show, 1958—, CNE hort. shows, Century Sq.; contbr. articles to profl. jours. Trustee Helen M. Kippax Meml. Scholarship Fund.; chmn. exec. bd. Latvian Boy Scouts Assn.; pres. gen. assembly Latvian Nat. Fedn. Can., 1992—2000, hon. mem., 2000—; pres. Kristus Darz Home for the Aged, 1989—92, Ont. Swimming Pool Assn., Toronto, 1964; pres. cultural and edn. fund Latvian Nat. Fedn. Can., 2002—. Fellow Can. Soc. Landscape Architects (life), Am. Landscape Architects Soc., Am. Inst. Landscape Architects (internat. pres. 1969-71), Ont. Assn. Landscape Architects (emeritus, pres. 1977-78, Disting. Achievement award 1987), Can. Latvian Bus. and Profl. Assn. (pres. 1971—), Latvian Nat. Fedn. Can., (pres. 2003), Bd. of Trade Club, Empire Club of Can. Lutheran. Avocations: gardening, travel, golf. Office: Alexander Budrevics & Assoc Ltd 895 Don Mills Rd Ste 212 Toronto ON Canada M3C 1W3 Office Phone: 416-444-5201 ext. 4. Office Fax: 416-444-5208. Business E-Mail: alex@budrevics.com.

BUDUR, KUMAR, physician; b. Bellary, Karnataka, India, Feb. 4, 1971; s. Krishna and Sharada Budur; m. Kiran Gorla, Aug. 22, 2002. MBBS, Vijayanagara Inst. Med. Scis., 1995; MD, Ednl. Commn. Fgn. Med. Students, 2000. Cert. Am. Bd. Sleep Medicine, 2005. Sr. ho. officer Nat. Health Svc., Norwich, England, 1998—2000, assoc. specialist in psychiatry England, 2001; resident in psychiatry Cleve. Clin. Found., 2001—04, chief resident in psychiatry, 2003—04, fellow in sleep medicine, 2004—05, staff physician, 2005—. Mem. ednl. & grand rounds com. Cleve. Clin. Found., 2004—05; mem. selection com. Indo-Am. Psychiatry Assn., 2005—. Author: 1200 MCQS in Psychiatry, 2004; contbr. articles to profl. jours. Child sponsor Worldvision, 1997—; mem. Child Relief & You, India, 1997—, Oxfam/Help the Aged, 1998—; physician vol. Free Clinic, Cleve., 2003—. Recipient Gold medal in Physiology and Preventive Medicine, Med. Coll., Bellary, 1990, 1993, Outstanding Resident award, Indo-Am. Psychiatry Assn., 2004. Mem.: Royal Coll. Physicians, Am. Neuropsychiatry Assn., Am. Acad. Sleep Medicine, Am. Psychiatric Assn. (resident monitor 2004). Avocations: classical and Indian music, healthcare management. Office: Cleve Clinic Sleep Disorders 11203 Stokes Blvd Cleveland OH 44105

BUDZAK, STEPHEN HOWARD, tax specialist, consultant; b. N.Y.C., July 15, 1938; s. Steve and Elizabeth Katherine Budzak; m. Maria Teresa Silva, Mar. 30, 1974; children: Douglas Alan, Mike A., Jennifer E., Christopher A. AA, Glendale Coll., Glendale, Calif., 1973. Cert. Calif. Soc. Tax. Cons., Nat. Soc. Tax Profls. Revenue protection clk. U.S. Postal Svc., L.A., 1975—92, revenue protection coord., 1992—2003; tax profl. Tax Masters, Diamond Bar, Calif., 1976—. Training instr. U.S. Postal Svc., L.A., 1987—2003. Contbr. articles to profl. jours. Career day rep. YMCA, Los Angeles, 1996—97, L.A. City Sch. Dist., 2003. Mem.: Lions Club. Independent. Roman Catholic. Avocations: reading, photography, travel. Office: Tax Masters 21022 Golden Springs Dr Walnut CA 91789 Office Phone: 909-594-9926.

BUDZINSKY, ARMIN ALEXANDER, investment banker; b. Steyr, Austria, Nov. 25, 1942; arrived in US, 1951, naturalized, 1957; s. Alexander Wladimir and Maria Gisella B.; m. Pamela Plimmer, 1978 (div. 1992); children: Andrea, Natalie; m. Laura Martin, 2000 (div. 2003). AB, John Carroll U., 1964; MA. (NDEA fellow) Fulbright fellow, Rutgers U., 1969. Instr. in English Cleve. State U., 1969-72; corp. fin. cons. Citibank NA, N.Y.C., 1974-76, Dean Witter & Co., N.Y.C., 1976-77, Merrill Lynch Pierce Fenner & Smith, N.Y.C., 1977-83; v.p. corp. fin. Dunoco Corp., Houston, 1983; pres. Porcari Fearnow Capital Markets Group, Inc., Houston, 1985-86, Itec Securities Corp., Houston, 1985-86; v.p., dir. project fin., prin. Eppler, Guerin & Turner, Inc., Dallas, 1987—92; ptnr. Garland Group, 1992-93; sr. v.p., CFO Heard Energy Corp., 1993-98; pres. Archangel Diamond Corp., Vancouver, B.C., 1996-97, pres, CEO, 1997-98, chmn., 1997-98; exec. v.p., dir. United Am. eHealth Techs. Inc., Cambridge, Mass., 1998-2001; exec. v.p., CFO Decorize Inc., Springfield, Mo., 2002—04. Home: 1413 S St Marys Ave Springfield MO 65804 Personal E-mail: aab@albud.com.

BUE, CARL OLAF, JR., retired federal judge; b. Chgo., Mar. 27, 1922; s. Carl Olaf and Mabel Port (Shollar) B.; m. Mary Kathryn Waring, Dec. 27, 1948; children: Kathryn Anne, Richard Charles. AA, U. Chgo., 1942; student, U. Rome, Italy, 1945; PhB, Northwestern U., 1951; D of Jurisprudence, U. Tex., 1954. Bar: Tex. 1954. Assoc. firm Royston, Rayzor & Cook, Houston, 1954-58, mem. firm, 1958-70; U.S. dist. judge So. Dist. Tex. (Houston div.), 1970-87. Lectr. various law schs. and admiralty seminars in Tex. and other states. Contbr. articles to profl. jours. Served to capt., Adj. Gen. Dept. AUS, 1942-46, MTO. Recipient Good Citizenship medal Houston chpt. SAR, 1975, Tex. Supreme Ct. Justice Joe R. Greenhill award as outstanding jurist Mcpl. Cts. Assn., 1977, Northwestern U. Alumni Merit award for disting. profl. svc. in law, 1997; establishment at U. Tex. Sch. of Law of the Judge Carl. O. Bue Jr. Endowed Presdl. scholarship in law, 1988. Mem. Am., Fed., Tex., Houston Bar Assns., Maritime Law Assn. of U.S., Houston Philos. Soc. at Rice U., Alpha Delta Phi, Phi Alpha Delta. Republican. Lutheran. Home: 338 Knipp Rd Houston TX 77024-5044

BUECHLEIN, DANIEL MARK, archbishop; b. Jasper, Ind., Apr. 20, 1938; s. Carl and Rose (Blessinger) Buechlein. BA, St. Meinrad Coll., 1961; student, St. Meinrad Sch. Theology, 1961—64; Lic. Sacred Theology, Benedictine U. Sant' Anselmo, Rome, 1966. Ordained priest Roman Cath. Ch., 1964, consecrated bishop 1987, archbishop 1992. Asst. dean students St. Meinrad Coll., 1966—68, dir. spiritual formation, 1968—71; pres., rector St. Meinrad Sch. Theology, 1971—82, St. Meinrad Sch. Theology and St. Meinrad Coll., 1982—87; bishop Diocese of Memphis, 1987—92; archbishop Indpls., 1992—. Chmn. divsn. religion St. Meinrad Coll., 1967—71; mem. Archabbey Coun., 1967—87; formation com. Conf. of Major Superiors of Men USA, 1971—78; nat. steering com. for follow-up of Nat. Assembly Sem. Rectors and Ordinaries, 1983; com. on priestly formation Nat. Conf. Cath. Bishops, 1987—89, chmn., 1990—93, com. on marriage and family life, 1987—89, advisor doctrine com., com. on doctrine, 1989—93, adminstrv. com., 1990—93, budget com., bishop's emergency relief com., 1990—92, chmn. ad hoc com. to oversee use of Catechism of Cath. Ch., subcom. on pastoral message in abortion, 1994—, bd. dirs.; peritus Internat. Synod on Priestly Formation, Rome, 1990; bd. dirs. S.E. Regional Office for Hispanics Affairs, S.E. Pastoral Inst.; co-pres. Disciples of Christ-Roman Cath. Internat. Dialogue, 1995—. Co-author (with Bleichner and Leavitt): Preparing a Diocesan Priest: The Holistic Experience, 1987, Celibacy for the Kingdom, 1990, Commentary on a Survey of Priests Ordained Five to Nine Years, 1991; contbr. articles to profl. jours. Named Hon. chaplain, KC, Tenn., 1987. Mem.: Nat. Cath. Edn. Assn. (chmn. exec. com. sem. divsn. 1984—86), Theol. Edn. Assn. Mid-Am. (sec. 1972—74, 1980—82, v.p. 1974—76, pres. 1976—78, 1982—84), Midwest Assn. Theol. Schs. (sec.-treas. 1972—74, ptrd. 1974—75), Midwest Assn. Sem. Spiritual Dirs. (founding coord. 1971), Nat. Assn. Sem. Spiritual Dirs. (founding coord. 1972). Office: Archdiocese Indpls PO Box 1410 Indianapolis IN 46206

BUECHNER, CARL FREDERICK, minister, author; b. N.Y.C., July 11, 1926; s. Carl Frederick and Katherine (Kuhn) B.; m. Judith Friedrike Merck, Apr. 7, 1956; children: Katherine, Dinah, Sharman. Grad., Lawrenceville Sch., 1943; AB, Princeton U., 1947; BD, Union Theol. Sem., 1958; DD, Va. Episc. Sem., 1982, Lafayette U., 1984; LittD, Lehigh U., 1987, Cornell Coll., 1989; DD, Yale U., 1990, Sewanee U., 1993; LittD, Susquehanna U., Wake Forest U., 1998, Wake Forest U., 2000. Ordained minister United Presbyn. Ch. U.S.A., 1958. Tchr. English Lawrenceville Sch., 1948-53; tchr. creative writing, summer sessions N.Y.U., 1954-55; chmn. dept. religion Phillips Exeter Acad., 1958-67, sch. minister, 1960-67; William Belden Noble lectr. Harvard, 1969; Russell lectr. Tufts, 1971; Lyman Beecher lectr. Yale U., 1977; Harris lector Bangor Sem., 1979; Smyth lectr. Columbia Sem., 1981. Lectr. Trinity Inst., 1990. Author: A Long Day's Dying, 1950, The Seasons' Difference, 1952, The Return of Ansel Gibbs, 1958, The Final Beast, 1965, The Magnificent Defeat, 1966, The Hungering Dark, 1969, The Entrance to Porlock, 1970, The Alphabet of Grace, 1970, Lion Country, 1971, Open Heart, 1972, Wishful Thinking, 1973, Love Feast, 1974, The Faces of Jesus, 1974, Treasure Hunt, 1977, Telling the Truth, 1977, Peculiar Treasures, 1979, The Book of Bebb, 1979, Godric, 1980 (Pulitzer Prize finalist), The Sacred Journey, 1982, Now and Then, 1983, A Room Called Remember, 1984, Brendan, 1987, Whistling in the Dark, 1988, The Wizard's Tide, 1990, Telling Secrets, 1991, The Clown in the Belfry, 1992, Listening to Your Life, 1992, The Son of Laughter, 1993, The Longing for Home, 1996, On the Road with the Archangel, 1997, The Storm, 1998, The Eyes of the Heart, 1999, Speak What We Feel, 2001, Beyond Words, 2004. Trustee Barlow Sch., 1965-71. With AUS, 1944-46. Recipient Irene Glascock Meml. intercollegiate poetry award, 1947; O'Henry prize for story The Tiger, 1955; Richard and Hinda Rosenthal award for the Return of Ansel Gibbs, 1958 Mem. Nat. Coun. Churches (com. on lit. 1954-57), Coun. Religion in Ind. Schs. (regional chmn. 1958-63), Presbytery No. New Eng., Century Assn., Univ. Club (N.Y.C.). Presbyterian. Home and Office: 3572 State Rte 315 Pawlet VT 05761-9753

BUECHNER, JACK W(ILLIAM), lawyer, consultant, educational association administrator; b. St. Louis, June 4, 1940; s. John Edward and Gertrude Emily (Richardson) B.; children from previous marriage: Patrick John, Terrence J.; m. Nancy Chanitz; 1 child, Charles Chanitz. BA, Benedictine Coll., 1962; JD, St. Louis U., 1965. Bar: Mo. 1965, U.S. Dist. Ct. (ea. dist.) Mo. 1965, D.C., 1998, U.S. Ct. Appeals (8th cir.) 1965, U.S. Ct. Appeals (D.C. cir.) 1998. Ptnr. Buechner, McCarthy, Leonard, Kaemmerer, Owen & Laderman, Chesterfield, Mo., 1965-93; mem. 100th-102d U.S. Congresses from 2d Mo. dist., 1987-91; dep. minority whip, 1989-90; vice-chmn. Rep. study group, pres. Internat. Rep. Inst., Washington, 1991-93; prin., dir. internat. svcs. The Hawthorn Group, Arlington, Va., 1993-95; ptnr. Manatt Phelps & Phillips, Washington, 1995—2001; pres., CEO, A Presdl. Classroom for Young Americans, 2002—; of counsel Schmeltzer, Aptaker and Shepard. State rep. 94th dist. Mo. Gen. Assembly, 1972-82, minority leader, 1974-78; mem. state adv. com. U.S. Commn. on Civil Rights, 1975-82; bd. dirs. Coun. Cmty. Democracies. Lay advisor St. Louis Med. Soc., 1989-92; Mo. Tourism Commn., 1976, 82-85; prin. Coun. for Excellence in Govt.; bd. dirs. Presdl. Classroom, 2000—; bd. dirs. Goodwin House, 2005—. Recipient Meritorious Svc. award St. Louis Globe-Democrat, 1973, Legis. Achievement award St. Louis Police Officers, 1982, Pub. Svc. award Women's Polit. Caucus, Mo., Disting. Svc. award Cardinal Glennon Hosp., Mo., 1982, Nat. Security Leadership award Am. Security Coun. Found., 1988, 89, Family and Freedom award, Golden Bulldog award, 1987, 88, Guardian of Small Bus. award Nat. Fedn. Ind. Bus., 1987, 88, 90, 91, Enterprise award U.S. C. of C., 1988, 89, 90, Sound Dollar award, 1988, Eagle of Freedom award Am. Security Coun. Foun., 1990, Missourian award Mo. Heart Assn., 2003. Mem. Mo. Bar Assn., D.C. Bar Assn., Mo. Soc. Washington (pres.), Nat. Conf. State Socs. (1st v.p.), Ctr. Nat. Policy (bd. dirs. 1997-, bd. dirs. Alliance for responsible Cuba policy), The Pericles Inst. (pres. 2001-), U.S. Assn. Former Mems. Congress (pres. 2004-), The Zorig Found. (v.p.), John Marshall Club (Outstanding Atty. award 1986), Lions, Phi Delta Phi. Republican. Episcopalian. Avocations: golf, reading, travel. Home: 1303 Altamira Ct Mc Lean VA 22102-2201 Office: Presdl Classroom 119 Oronoco Alexandria VA 22314-2015 also: Schmeltzer Aptaker and Shepard 2600 Virginia Ave NW Washington DC 20037 Office Phone: 703-400-3891. Business E-Mail: jackb@presidentialclassroom.org.

BUECHNER, ROBERT WILLIAM, lawyer, educator; b. Syracuse, N.Y., Oct. 29, 1947; s. Donald F. and Barbara (Northrup) B.; m. Angela Marian Hoetker, May 28, 1978; children: Julie Marie, Robert William Jr., Leslie Ann, James Bradley. BSE, Princeton U., 1969; JD, U. Mich., 1974. Bar: Ohio, 1974, Fla. 1974, U.S. Dist. Ct. (so. dist.) Ohio 1974, U.S. Tax Ct. 1974. Assoc. Frost & Jacobs, Cin., 1974-79; pres. Buechner, Haffer, O'Connell, Meyers & Healey Co., L.P.A., Cin., 1979—. Adj. prof. Salmon P. Chase Coll. Law, No. Ky., 1975-82; instr. Cin. chpt. Chartered Life Underwriters, 1976-96; lectr. Million Dollar Roundtable, Atlanta, 1981; prodr., host TV show Greater Cin. Bus. Rev., 1993-2004. Author: (with others) Why Universal Life, 1984, Prosper Through Tax Planning, 1982, Living Gangbusters, 1986, The 8 Pathways to Financial Success, 1987, 93, 98, 2004. Mem. planning divsn. Cin. Cmty. Chest, 1978-84; trustee Cin. Venture Assn., 1994-99, pres., 1997-98; trustee Cin. Country Day Sch., 1979-93, pres., 1990-93. Recipient Alumnus of Yr. award Cin. Country Day Sch., 1985. Mem. Cin. Bar Assn. (chmn. taxation sect. 1984-85), S.W. Ohio Tax Inst. (chmn. 1981-82, 1st winner John Warrington Cmty. Svc. award 1997), Cin. Assn. (trustee 1999—, pres. 2002-03), Gyro Club (sec. 1982-83, v.p. 1999-2000), Princeton Club (pres. 1982-84), Sorta Bd. (trustee 2004—). Republican. Methodist. Avocations: golf, tennis, bridge. Office: Buechner Haffer O'Connell Meyers Healey Co LPA 105 E 4th St Ste 300 Cincinnati OH 45202-4023 Office Phone: 513-579-1500. E-mail: rhuechner@bhomh.com.

BUECHNER, THOMAS SCHARMAN, artist, museum director, retired glass manufacturing company executive; b. Sept. 25, 1926; s. Thomas Scharman and Anne Evans (Lines) B.; m. Mary C. Hawkins, Sept. 15, 1949;

children: Barbara Lines, Thomas Scharman, Matthew. Student, Princeton U., 1945, Ecole des Beaux Arts, Fontainebleau, 1946, Paris, 1947, Arts Students League, N.Y.C., 1946, 48, Institut voor Pictologie, Amsterdam, 1947. Designer Compañía de Fomento, San Juan, P.R., 1946; asst. display mgr. Met. Mus. Art, N.Y.C., 1949-51, tchr., 1949-51; dir. Corning Mus. Glass, N.Y., 1951-60, 75-80, pres., 1971-87; v.p., dir. cultural affairs Corning Glass Works, 1985-87, ret., 1987, cons., 1987—; faculty art sch. Bild-Werk, Fravenau, Germany, 1988—. Head dept. art Corning Community Coll., 1958-60; bd. dir. Bklyn. Mus.; chmn. Corning Glass Works Found., 1971-87; v.p. Steuben Glass, Corning, 1971-73, pres., 1973-82, chmn., 1982-85. Author: Glass Vessels in Dutch Painting of the 17th Century, 1952, Life and Work of Frederick Carder, 1952, Guide to the Collections of the Corning Museum of Glass, 1955, Guide to the Collections of the Brooklyn Museum, 1967, Norman Rockwell, Artist Illustrator, 1970, Arts of David Levine, 1979, Ogden Pleissner, 1984, How I Paint, 2000; portrait and landscape painter; one-man shows: Adler Gallery, N.Y.C., 1982, 84, Arnot Art Mus., 1985, 95, Heller Gallery, N.Y.c., 1989, Gallery M, Lindau, Germany, 1989, Gallery Nakama, Tokyo, 1990, 93, 96, O.K. Harris Gallery, N.Y.C., Schloss Weissenstein, Regen, Germany, 1996, Melberg Gallery, Charlotte, N.C., 2002, Principle Gallery, Alexandria, Va., 2002, West End Gallery, Corning, N.Y., 2002; represented in permanent collections Met. Mus. Art, Nat. Mus. Am. Art, Smithsonian Inst., Bklyn. Mus., Lincoln Ctr., Herbert F. Johnson Mus. Cornell U., Musée des Arts Decoratifs, Lausanne, Switzerland, Renwick Mus., Smithsonian, Washington, Corning Mus. of Glass, Corning, N.Y. Trustee Tiffany Found., Pilchuck Sch., Corning Mus. Glass, Corning Glass Works Found., Rockwell Mus., Arnot Art Mus. Arts of the Southern Finger Lakes; pres. Rockwell Mus. 1982-87, trustee 1987—. Recipient Forsythia award Bklyn. Bot. Garden, 1971, Gari Melchers medal Am. Artist fellows, 1971. Mem. Bklyn. Inst. Arts and Sci. (trustee 1971-72, pres. 1971-72), Nat. Collection Fine Arts. (commr. 1972-91). Clubs: Century Assn. Episcopalian. Studio: 10503B North Rd Corning NY 14830-3264

BUEHLER, MARTIN, hotel executive; b. Berne, Switzerland, May 24, 1947; s. Ernst Jakob and Marie (Studer) B.; m. Rosemarie Eugster, Feb. 29, 1968 (div.); children: Christiane, Mark. BBA, U. Berne, Switzerland, 1967; postgrad., Tufts U., 1978. Cert. travel agt., internat. mktg. auditor. Mgr. Tourist Info., Berne, 1972-75; exec. v.p. Inter-Europe-Hotels, Berne, 1979-84; pres. Dial Europe Inc., Miami, Fla., 1984-85; v.p. Europe Choice Hotels, Berne, 1985-88; exec. v.p. Hotel & Touristik Expert Inc., Berne, 1988-91; area pres., CEO Europe and Mid. East Park Plz. Hotels & Resorts Internat., Montreux, Switzerland, 1991-98; chmn. Boutique Hotels & Resorts Internat., Miami, 1999—, First Capital Hosp. Fin. Group, Miami, 1999—. Guest prof. Hosta, Lexsin, Switzerland, 1988-91, Ritz Hotel Sch., Switzerland, 1993, Fairleigh Dickinson U., 1994; adminstr. Internat. Jazz Festival, Berne, 1976-85. Author textbook: Hotel Marketing, 1989. Fellow Internat. Mktg. Audit Assn. Office: 1220 Washington Ave Miami FL 33139 E-mail: mbuehler@boutiquemair.com.

BUEHLER, THOMAS, psychotherapist, expressive therapist, artist; b. Zurich, Switzerland, Aug. 9, 1943; came to U.S 1989. s. Adolf and Margrit (Gredig) B.; m. Rosemarie Schiller, Apr. 19, 1995. MS, Med. Sch. U. Zurich, 1970. Cert. psychotherapist, Switzerland. Intern Accredited Swiss Hosp., 1969-75; multimedia artist Switzerland, 1973—. Psychotherapist and expressive therapist, 1979—; co-founding, training therapist Internat. Sch. of Interdisciplinary Studies, 1982-85, advisory bd. Swiss Assocs. of Psychotherapists, 1984-85; founding chmn. Cardon Found., 1991—, Cirio Found., N.Y., 1993— Author: Der Vulkan ist aufgebrochen, 1976; one man performance Roter Stadtkriecher, 1985, Red Broadway Crawler, 1985, one-man shows, New World Art Ctr., N.Y.C., 1999, The Depot Gallery, Montauk, N.Y., 1999, The Office Gallery, N.Y.C., 2001, 02, 03, 04, 05, The Broome Street Gallery, N.Y.C., 2005 Mem. Internat. Assoc. of Artist Therapists, Nat. Expressive Therapy Assn., Swiss Assoc. of Psychotherapists. Avocations: piano, guitar, travel, wilderness, foreign cultures. Home: 380 Riverside Dr 6 T/U New York NY 10025 Office: Cirio Found Ste 1004 80 8th Ave New York NY 10011

BUEHLING, CYNTHIA GWYNNE, music educator; b. Paragould, Ark., July 12, 1952; d. Edward G. and Martel M. Ross; m. Henry F. Buehling; 1 child, Louis. MusB in Edn., Ark. State U., 1975, MusM in Edn., 1977. Cert. tchr. Ark. Music tchr. Blytheville Pub. Schs., 1975—78; asst. music libr. Interlochen (Mich.) Ctr. for the Arts, 1979—80; elem. music, h.s. choir tchr. St. Francis Cath. Sch., Traverse City, Mich., 1980—81; instr. music Northwestern Mich. Coll., Traverse City, Mich., 1982—86; elem. music tchr. Pulaski County Spl. Sch. Dist., Little Rock, 1986—87, Little Rock Sch. Dist., 1987—. Childrens choir dir. Pulaski Hts. United Meth. Ch., Little Rock, 1992—2000. Named Tchr. of Yr., We. Hills Elem. Sch., 2005. Mem.: Classroom Tchrs. Assn. (sch. rep. 1990—91), Ark. Music Educator's Nat. Conf. (elem. rep. 1988—90), Music Educator's Nat. Conf., Tau Beta Sigma (life), Sigma Alpha Iota (life). Methodist. Avocations: reading, cross stitch, theater, concerts. Home: 19 Flourite Cove Little Rock AR 72212-2110 Office: Western Hills Elem 4901 Western Hills Ave Little Rock AR 72204 Office Phone: 501-447-6911. E-mail: cynthia.buehling@lrsd.org, cgbuehling@sbcglobal.net.

BUEHLMEIER, HARRY SCOTT See GORDON, SCOTT

BUEHRER, STEPHEN, state representative; b. Toledo, Ohio, Jan. 1, 1967; married; 3 children. BS in Edn., Bowling Green State U., 1989; JD, Capital U., 1997. Atty.; mem. Ohio Ho. of Reps., Columbus, 1998—, mem. criminal justice com., chair state govt. com., asst. majority fl. leader, 2001—04. Mem.: United Conservatives of Ohio, Coun. State Govt. (chmn. midwest-Can. rels. com.), Am. Legis. Exch. (state co-chair, Nat. Legislator of Yr. 2002), Ohio Twp. Assn., Fulton County Bar Assn., Ohio Bar Assn., Bowhay Legis. Leadership Inst., Ohio Right to Life, C. of C., Nat. Assn. Sports Legislators, Ohio Farm Bur., Fulton County Hist. Soc., Ducks Unlimited, Pheasants Forever. Republican. Office: 77 S High St 13th fl Columbus OH 43215-6111 Office Phone: 614-644-5091.

BUEHRLE, MARK, professional baseball player; b. St. Charles, Mo., Mar. 23, 1979; Pitcher Chgo. White Sox, 2000—. Achievements include starting pitcher, MLB All-Star Game, 2005. Office: Chgo White Sox 333 W 35th St Chicago IL 60616*

BUEL, NANCY LEE, educational association administrator; d. Truman Winthrop Eater and Jessie Alma Yearwood; m. B.G. Charles Joseph Buel, Sept. 22, 1956; children: Jeffrey Alexander, Jessie Ann, Julie Lee Butner. BA, U. of Md., College Park, 1964; MEd, U. of Okla., 1980, PhD, 1990. Asst. Dept. of Edn. Pres. U.S. Dept. of Def., Fort Sill, Okla., 1975—; instrnl. systems devel. exec. Buel, Inc., Fountain Hills, Ariz., 1984—. Mental health dir. U.S. Dept. of State, Mexico City, 1983—86. V.p. Fountain Hills Cultural Coun., 2005—; del. 2005 Dem. Conv. Ariz. Congl. Dist. 7, 2004. Recipient Molly Pitcher award, Comdt., U.S. Army F.A. Ctr., 1976. Mem.: DAR, Intergovernmental Tng. Coun., Nat. Soc. of Performance and Instrn., U.S. Distance Learning Assn., Internat. Interactive Comm. Soc., Soc. for Applied Learning Tech., Am. Soc. Tng. Developers, Phi Delta Kappa, Delta Gamma. Democrat. Episcopalian. Achievements include research in Various Training Research Projects; Implementation of the Instructional Systems Development Model in a Military Training Environment. Office Phone: 480-816-6310. Office Fax: 480-816-6312.

BUEL, RICHARD VAN WYCK, JR., retired educator, historian, editor, writer; b. Morristown, NJ, July 22, 1933; s. Richard Van Wyck Sr. and Frances Worthington (Thompson) B.; m. Joy Evelyn Margaret Day, June 5, 1964 (dec. Apr. 1987); m. Marilyn Ellman Frankel, July 18, 1992; 1 child, Margaret Alexandra. AB, Amherst Coll., 1955; A.M., Harvard U., 1957, PhD in Am. History, 1962. Tchg. fellow in history Harvard U., Cambridge, Mass., 1958-62; asst. prof. history Wesleyan U., Middletown, Conn., 1962-69, assoc. prof., 1969-75, prof., 1975—2002, emeritus prof., 2002—, chmn. history dept., 1978-81; ret., 2002. Ray A. Billington vis. prof. U.S. history Occidental Coll., 1999—2000. Author: Securing the Revolution, 1972, Dear Liberty, 1980 (Round Table of Am. Revolution award, 1981); author: (with Joy D. Buel) The Way of Duty, 1984 (Colonial Dame of Am. Book award, 1985); author: In Irons, 1998 (Fraunces Tavern Mus. Book award, 1999), America on the Brink, 2005; assoc. editor History and Theory, 1970—91; contbr. articles to profl. jours., chapters to books. Mem. Bd. Fin., Haddam, Conn., 1972—74; mem. Conn. Hist. Commn., 1996—2003, Conn. Humanities Coun., 1997—2003, Conn. Hist. Coun., 2003—; bd. dirs. No. Middlesex United Fund, Middletown, Conn., 1965—68. Fellow Charles Warren Ctr., Harvard U., 1966—67, Am. Coun. Learned Socs., 1966—67, 1974—75, NEH, 1985, Guggenheim Found., 1988; jr. humanist fellow, NEH, 1971—72, John Carter Brown fellow, 1986, Andrew W. Mellon emeritus faculty fellow, 2005—. Mem. Conn. Acad. Arts and Scis. (v.p. 1975-81), Am. Hist. Assn., Inst. Early Am. History and Culture, Soc. History Early Republic, Orgn. Am. Historians, Am. Antiquarian Soc., New Eng. Hist. Assn. (v.p. 1991, pres. 1992), Assn. Study Conn. History, Conn. Coord. Com. for Promotion History (pres. 2001—03), Pettipaug Yacht Club (rear commodore 1984-86, vice-commodore 1986-88, commodore 1988-90), Acorn Club, Phi Beta Kappa. Avocation: dinghy racing. Home: 55 N Main St Essex CT 06426-1073 Office: Wesleyan Univ Dept History Middletown CT 06459-0002 Office Phone: 860-685-2372. Business E-Mail: rbuel@wesleyan.edu.

BUELL, EDWARD RICK, II, lawyer; b. Des Moines, Jan. 28, 1948; s. Edward Rick and Betty-Jo (Heffron) B.; B.S. with high honors, Mich. State U., 1969; J.D. magna cum laude, U. Mich., 1972; children— Erica Colleen, Edward Rick III. Bar: D.C. 1973, Calif. 1975; cert. specialist in taxation law, Calif. Assoc. firm Arent, Fox, Kintner, Plotkin & Kahn, Washington, 1972-74, Brobeck, Phlegher & Harrison, San Francisco, 1974-77; ptnr. Winokur, Schoenberg, Maier & Zang, San Francisco, 1977-81; ptnr. Buell & Berner, San Francisco, 1981— . Mem. ABA, San Francisco Bar Assn., Order of Coif. Contbr. articles to legal jours. Home: 50 Stewart Dr Belvedere Tiburon CA 94920-1323

BUELL, FREDERICK HENDERSON, language educator; b. Bryn Mawr, Pa., Nov. 17, 1942; s. Clarence Adison and Marjorie (Henderson) B.; married; children: Alexander Silvano, Nicholas Mariano. BA, Yale U., 1964; PhD, Cornell U., 1970. Asst. prof. Queens Coll., CUNY, Flushing, N.Y., 1970-72, assoc. prof., 1972-78, prof., 1978—. Author: Theseus and Other Poems, 1970, W.H. Auden as a Social Poet, 1972, Full Summer, 1979, National Culture and The New Global System, 1994, From Apocalypge to Way of Life: Environmental Crisis in the American Century, 2004. Mem. Warwick (N.Y.) Valley Ctrl. Sch. Dist. Bd. Edn., 1991-97. NEA Writer's fellow, 1972, N.Y. State Coun. on Arts fellow, 1994, Nathan Cummings Contemplative Practice fellow, 1997-98, NIH Sr. Fellow, 2003. Avocations: black belt in aikido, camping, hiking. Office: CUNY Queens Coll Dept English Flushing NY 11367

BUELL, LAWRENCE INGALLS, language educator; b. Bryn Mawr, Pa., June 11, 1939; s. Clarence Addison and Marjorie (Henderson) B.; m. Phyllis Kimber; children: Denise, Deirdre. AB, Princeton U., 1961; MA, Cornell U., 1962, PhD, 1966. From asst. prof. to prof. English Oberlin (Ohio) Coll., 1966-90; prof. dept. English Harvard U., Cambridge, 1990—, dean undergrad. edn, 1992-96. Dir. Summer Inst. for High Sch. Tchrs., NEH, Oberlin, 1984-85; vis. prof. English U. Chgo., 1986; mem. faculty Bread Loaf Sch. English, 1987-88. Author: Literary Transcendentalism, 1973, New England Literary Culture, 1986, The Environmental Imagination, 1995, Writing for an Endangered World, 2001, Emerson, 2003; mem. editl. bd. Am. Quar., Phila., 1979-82, Am. Lit., Durham, N.C., 1983-86, PMLA, 1994-96. Trustee, officer Oberlin Shansi Meml. Assn., 1972-87. Woodrow Wilson Found. fellow, 1961-62; Howard Found. fellow, 1969-70; NEH Rsch. fellow, 1979-80, 2002; Guggenheim Found. fellow, 1987-88. Mem. Modern Language Assn., Am. Studies Assn. Democrat. Mem. United Ch. of Christ. Avocations: nature, sports. Office: Harvard U Dept English Cambridge MA 02138

BUELL, RODD RUSSELL, lawyer; b. Pitts., Mar. 31, 1946; s. Harold Ellsworth and Jeanne Charlotte (Russell) Buell. BS, Fla. State U., 1968; JD, U. Fla., 1970; LLM, U. Miami, 1978. Bar: Fla. 1971, U.S. Dist. Ct. (so., mid. and no. dists.) Fla. 1971, U.S. Ct. Appeals (5th and 11th cirs.) 1971. Gen. ptnr. Blackwell & Walker, P.A., Miami, 1970-95; shareholder Fleming, O'Bryan & Fleming, Ft. Lauderdale, Fla., 1995-97; pvt. practice, Coral Gables, Fla., 1997—. Mem. Dade County Def. Bar Assn. (pres. 1985-86), Def. Trial Attys. Assn. (exec. counsel 1986-88), Maritime Law Assn., Am. Bd. Trial Advs., Internat. Assn. Def. Counsel, Bath Club, Riviera Country Club, Miami Club, Univ. Club. Republican. Methodist. Home: 11883 Maidstone Dr Wellington FL 33414 Office: 228 Aragon Ave Ste C Coral Gables FL 33134 Office Phone: 561-795-5400. Personal E-mail: buelllaw@aol.com.

BUELL, WALTER F., neurologist; b. Austin, Tex., Apr. 15, 1940; s. Ralph Lewin Buell, Ruth Flynn; m. Elizabeth C. Rude; children: Jeff, Robert. BA, U. Tex., 1963, MA in Biochemistry, MD, U. Tex., 1965. Diplomate Am. Bd. Psychiatry and Neurology. Med. intern U. Pitts. Health Ctr. Hosp., 1965—66; epidemic intelligence svc. Communicable Disease Ctr., Atlanta, 1966—68; resident neurology Washington U., St. Louis, 1968—71; neurologist Neurology Clinic San Antonio, 1971—97. Clin. prof. U. Tex. Health Sci. Ctr., San Antonio, 1971—; med. cons. Tex. Rehab. Commn., Austin, 1995—; med. adv. bd. driver licensing Tex. Dept. Health, Austin; mem. Tex. Coun. on Cardiovasc. Desease and Stroke. Contbr. articles to profl. jours. Sr. asst. surgeon USPHS, 1966—68, Atlanta. Fellow: Tex. Neurol. Soc. (pres. 1980—81, Fellow 2001); mem.: AMA, Tex. Med. Assn. (chair stroke project 1997—2000), Am. Acad. Neurology, Austin Neurol. Soc. Office: PO Box 5088 Austin TX 78763-5088 Office Phone: 512-407-8251. Business E-Mail: wfbuell@pol.net.

BUENAVENTURA, MILAGROS PAEZ, psychiatrist; b. Munoz, Nueva Ecija, Philippines, Oct. 28, 1943; came to U.S., 1974; s. Lupo P. and Pilar (Paez) B.; children: Robert, Melani. AA, U. Santo Tomas, Manila, 1962, MD, 1967. Clinic physician Dr. Jose R. Reyes Meml. Hosp., Manila, 1968-71, resident in neurology and psychiatry, 1971-74; resident dept. psychiatry Milton S. Hershey Med. Ctr., Hershey, Pa., 1975-78; staff psychiat. Holy Spirit Hosp., Camp Hill, Pa., 1978-82, Harrisburg (Pa.) State Hosp., 1982—. Cons. Psychiatric Ctr., 1994—, Harrisburg, 1984—; mem. courtesy staff Harrisburg Hosp., 1987; med. dir. Helen Stevens Ctr., Carlisle, Pa., 1987-2000. Mem. Cen. Pa. Psychiat. Soc. Republican. Roman Catholic. Avocations: reading, travel, swimming.

BUENO, LOURDES, education educator; PhD, Vanderbilt U., 1995—2000. Tchg. asst. Mich. State U., 1992—95, Vanderbilt U., Nashville, 1995—2000; asst. prof. Austin Coll., Sherman, Tex., 2000—. Author: (book) Heroinas Con Voz Propia. Recipient Excellence In Rsch., Vanderbilt U., 1997, Excellence In Tchg., 1998, Rsch. award, Austin (Tex.) Coll., 2004, Faculty of Month award, 2004. Mem.: Aiso (Golden Age Internat. Assn., MLA, Casa De España In Dallas. Office: Austin College 900 North Grand Ave Ste 61645 Sherman TX 75090 Office Phone: 903-813-2259. E-mail: lbueno@austincollege.edu.

BUENO, PABLO CESAR, aeronautical engineer, educator; b. Bogota, D.C., Colombia, May 25, 1977; s. Jaime Otoniel Bueno and Lorena Restrepo. BS in Aero. Engring., The USAF Acad., Colorado Springs, Colo., 1998; MS in Engring., U. Tex., 2002. Cert. aero. engr., Consejo Profesional Nacional de Ingenierías Eléctrica, Mecánica, 1998; glider instruction pilot Colombian Civil Aero. Authority, 1999, lic. glider pilot Colombian Civil Aero. Authority, 1999, cert. tech. specialist flight instr. Colombian Civil Aero. Authority, 1999. Quality assurance dir. Aeroindustrias Leaver y Cia. S.A., Bogota, Colombia, 1998—99; lectr. dept. aero. engring. Universidad de San Buenaventura, Bogota, Colombia, 1998—99; rsch. asst. Ctr. for Aeromechanics Rsch., U. Tex.tin, Austin, Tex., 2000—; tchg. asst. dept. aeromechanics rsch. U. Tex., Austin, Tex., 2001, asst. instr. dept. aerospace engring., 2003—. Univ. liaison with Colombian Air Force and Nat. Police Universidad de San Buenaventura, Bogota, D.C., Colombia, 1999; contbg editor AIAA Student Jour., Austin, Tex., 2001—02; soaring instr. pilot - competition aerobatics team 94 Flying Tng. Squadron, USAF, Colo., 1996—98. Contbr. articles to profl. jours. Pres. and founder Colombian Student Assn. - The U. of Tex. at Austin, Austin, Tex., 2001. Cadet 1st class USAF, 1994—98. Decorated numerous mil. awards USAF. Mem.: Am. Soc. Engring. Edn. (membership coord. 2001—02, treas. 2002), Asociacion Pro-Agencia Espacial Colombiana, Am. Phys. Soc., AIAA. Avocations: flying, motorsports, soccer. Personal E-mail: bueno@mail.utexas.edu.

BUERGENTHAL, THOMAS, judge; b. Lubochna, Slovakia, May 11, 1934; came to U.S., 1951, naturalized, 1957; children: Robert, John, Alan; m. Marjorie J. Bell, 1983; stepchildren: Sebastian, Cristina. BA, Bethany Coll., 1957, LLD, 1981; JD, NYU, 1960; LLM, Harvard U., 1961, SJD, 1968; dr.jur. (hon.), U. Heidelberg, 1986; dr. jur. (hon.), Free U. of Brussels, 1997; LLD, SUNY, Buffalo, 2000, Am. U., 2002, U. Minn., 2003, George Washington U., 2004. Bar: N.Y. 1961, D.C. 1983, U.S. Supreme Ct. 1982. Instr. law U. Pa., 1961-62; from asst. prof. to prof. SUNY, Buffalo, 1962-75; vis. prof. U. Tex., Austin, 1975-76, prof., 1976-77, Fulbright and Jaworski prof., 1977-80; judge Inter-Am. Ct. Human Rights, 1979-91, pres., 1985-87; dean, prof. law Am. U., Washington, 1980-85; disting. prof. law and human rights Emory U. Sch. Law, 1985-86, I.T. Cohen prof. of human rights, 1987-89; Lobingier prof. comparative law and jurisprudence George Washington U., Washington, 1989-2000, Lobingier prof. emeritus, 2000—; judge Adminstrv. Tribunal, Inter-Am. Devel. Bank, 1989-94, pres., 1993-94. Mem. UN Human Rights Commn., 1995—99, Claims Resolution Tribunal for Dormant Accounts in Switzerland, 1998—2002, vice-chmn., 1999—2000; judge Internat. Ct. of Justice, 2000—; adv. com. Restatement (3d) of the Fgn. Rels. Law of U.S.; chmn. human rights com. U.S. Nat. Commn. for UNESCO, 1976—79; U.S. rep. UNESCO Human Rights Working Group, 1977—78; U.S. expert UN Interregional Expert Meeting on Crime Prevention and Control, 1978; mem. adv. bd. Pres. Holocaust Commn., 1978—80; v.p. UNESCO Congress on Tchg. of Human Rights, 1978; mem. UN Truth Commn. for El Salvador, 1992—93, U.S. Holocaust Meml. Coun., 1996—2001, chmn. com. on conscience, 1997—2000. Author: Law-Making in the International Civil Aviation Organization, 1969; (with L.B. Sohn) International Protection of Human Rights, 1973; (with J.V. Torney) International Human Rights and International Education, 1976, International Law and the Helsinki Accord, 1977; (with R.E. Norris) Human Rights: The Inter-Am. System, 1982; (with D. Shelton) Protecting Human Rights in the Americas, 1982, 4th edit., 1995; (with S. Murphy) Public International Law in a Nutshell, 3d edit., 2002, (with D. Shelton and D. Stewart) International Human Rights in a Nutshell, 3d edit., 2002; (with Grossman and Nikken) Manual Internacional de Derechos Humanos, 1990; (with Kiss) La Protection Internationale des Droits de l'Homme, 1991; contbr. articles to profl. jours. Recipient Pro-Humanitas Ring, West-Ost Kulturwerk, Fed. Republic of Germany, 1978, Disting. Svc. in Legal Edn. award NYU Law Sch. Assn., 1987, Wolfgang Friedmann Meml. award Columbia U. Law Sch., 1989. Mem. Am. Law Inst., Am. Soc. Internat. Law (v.p. 1980-82, hon. pres. 2001—, Goler T. Butcher medal for excellence in internat. human rights 1997, Manley Hudson medal 2002), Coun. Fgn. Rels., Inter-Am. Inst. Human Rights (pres. 1980-92, hon. pres. 1992—). Office: Internat Ct Justice Peace Palace 2517 KJ The Hague Netherlands Fax: (31-70) 302-2464. Business E-Mail: t.buergenthal@icj-cij.org.

BUESCHEL, DAVID ALAN, management consultant; b. Chgo., May 6, 1942; s. Clifford James and Dorothy Jane (Snyder) B.; m. Elizabeth Thorne Conklin, June 20, 1965; children: Andrea Conklin, Lydia Anne, Cynthia Jane. BSME, Cornell U., 1965; MBA, Stanford U., 1967. Mgmt. cons. McKinsey & Co., Inc., Chgo., 1967-75; dir. strategic planning Norlin Music Inc., 1975-76, v.p. bus. devel., 1976-77; pres. MI Fin. Co., Norlin Corp., Chgo., 1977-78; v.p., gen. mgr. Band & Orch. Group, Norlin Corp., Chgo., 1978-79; pres. Moog div. Norlin Corp., Cheektowaga, N.Y., 1979-80; v.p., gen. mgr. Austin Cons., Evanston, Ill., 1981-83; v.p. Lamalie Assocs., Inc., Chgo., 1983-86; pres. Sweeney Shepherd Bueschel Provus Harbert & Mummert, Inc., Chgo., 1986-87, prin., 1987-91; pres. Shepherd Bueschel & Provus, Inc., Chgo., 1992—. Pres. Pack It In, Ltd. Cos., 1993-97. Vice chmn., chmn. devel. com., chmn. bd. affairs com., trustee Chgo. Theol. Sem., 1987—; bd. dirs., mem. exec. com., chmn. nominating com. and pers. com. Cmty. Renewal Soc., Chgo., 1987-92; rep. Stanford Keystone Fund, Chgo., 1987-89; amb. Cornell U. Alumni, 1988—; mem. nominating com. Ill. Conf. United Ch. of Christ, 1992-95. Mem. Assn. Exec. Search Cons. (bd. dirs. 1994—, govt. affairs com. 1992-95, chmn. membership com. 1995-96, dir. regional affairs, chmn. ann. conf. commn. 1996, bd. vice chmn. 1999-2000), Stanford U. Bus. Sch. Alumni Assn. (v.p., bd. dirs. Chgo. 1988-91), Econ. Club, Univ. Club. Democrat. Avocations: skiing, sailing, golf. Office: Shepherd Bueschel & Provus Inc Ste 3020 401 N Michigan Ave Chicago IL 60611-4255 E-mail: sbp401@aol.com.

BUESCHEN, ANTON JOSLYN, physician, educator; b. Toledo, June 7, 1940; s. Robert F. and Mary J. (Joslyn) B.; m. Norma Jean McClanahan, Sept. 5, 1964; children— Anton, Elaine. Student, Va. Mil. Inst., 1958-61; MD, U. Va., 1965. Diplomate Am. Bd. Urology. Intern in surgery Vanderbilt U., 1965-66, asst. resident in surgery, 1966-67; resident in urology Ind. U., Indpls., 1969-72; practice medicine specializing in urology Birmingham, Ala., 1973—; instr. urology Tulane U. Sch. Medicine, 1972-73; asst. prof. div. urology dept. surgery U. Ala., Birmingham, 1973-75, assoc. prof., 1975-79, prof., 1979—, dir. div. urology, 1975-95, 99—; chief urology sect. Children's Hosp., Birmingham, 1978-86. Pres. U. Ala. Health Svcs. Found., 2001—. Contbr. numerous articles on urology to profl. jours. Served with M.C. U.S. Army, 1967-69. Mem. ACS, AMA (Billings Gold medal 1978), AAUP, Am. Urol. Assn. (bd. dirs., 2003—), Am. Urol. Assn. Southeastern Sect. (sec. 1997-2000, pres.-elect 2000-01, pres. 2001-2002, bd. dirs. 1994-2003), Am. Found. Urologic Disease (bd. dirs. 2000—), Am. Assn. Clin. Urologists, Soc. Univ. Urologists, Birmingham Urology Club, Jefferson County Med. Soc., Soc. for Pediatric Urology, Soc. Urologic Oncology, So. Med. Assn. (chmn. urology sect. 1987), Med. Assn. Ala. Office: U Ala Div Urology University Sta Birmingham AL 35294-0001 Personal E-mail: bueschen@bellsouth.net.

BUESSER, ANTHONY CARPENTER, lawyer; b. Detroit, Oct. 15, 1929; s. Frederick Gustavis and Lela (Carpenter) B.; m. Carolyn Sue Pickle, Mar. 13, 1954; children: Kent Anderson, Anthony Carpenter, Andrew Clayton; m. Bettina Rieveschl, Dec. 14, 1973. BA in English with honors, U. Mich., 1952, MA, 1953, JD, 1960. Bar: Mich. 1961. Assoc. Chase, Goodenough & Buesser, Detroit, 1961-66; ptnr. Buesser, Buesser, Snyder & Blank, Detroit and Bloomfield Hills, Mich., 1966-81; sole practice Birmingham, Mich., 1981—. Trustee Detroit Country Day Sch., Beverly Hills, Mich., 1970-94, chmn. bd., 1977-82, 84-87, bd. chmn. emeritus, 1987—, chmn. nominating com., 1987-94. Served with AUS, 1953-55. Recipient Avery Hopwood award major fiction U. Mich., 1953, Outstanding Alumnus award Detroit Country Day Sch., 1988. Mem. ABA, State Bar Mich., Detroit Bar Assn. (pres. 1976-77), Oakland County Bar Assn., Am. Judicature Soc., Thomas M. Cooley Club (pres. 1974-76), Alpha Delta Phi, Phi Delta Phi. Home: 756 Honey Creek Dr Ann Arbor MI 48103-1638

BUFALINO, VINCENT JOHN, hospital medical administrator; m. Joan Bufalino; 2 children. Grad. magna cum laude, Loyola U.; MD, Loyola U. Stritch Sch. Medicine, 1977. Cert. internal medicine, cardiovasc. diseases. Intern to resident, internal medicine Loyola U. Foster McGaw Hosp., fellowship to chief fellow, cardiovasc. disease; pres., CEO Midwest Heart Specialists; med. dir. Edward Heart Hosp., Naperville. Chmn. bd. Midwest Heart Found. Office: Edward Heart Hosp 4th Fl 801 S Washington St Naperville IL 60566 Office Phone: 630-527-2730.

BUFANO, RALPH A., museum executive; BS in Fine Arts, U. Minn. Dir. Exptl. Aircraft Aviation Found., Oshkosh, Wis.; pres. Kansas City (Mo.) Mus.; dir. devel. Ward Found. Mus., Salisbury, Md.; pres., CEO, The Mus. of Flight, Seattle, 1991—. Fellow: Fedn. Aeronautica Internat. (Paul Tissadier award for svcs. to aeros. and airsports), Royal Aero. Soc. Office: The Museum of Flight 9r04 E Marginal Way S Seattle WA 98108-4097

BUFE, CHARLES GLENN, geophysicist, researcher; s. Bancroft Washington and Margaret Elizabeth Bufe; life ptnr. Jacquelyn Claire Abbott, Nov. 18, 1967; children: Sierra Noel, Nathaniel Renfield children: Glennica Joy Magee. BS in Geophys. Engring., Mich. Technol. Univ., 1960, MS in Geophysics, 1962; PhD in Geology, U. Mich., 1969. Rsch. geophysicist U. Mich., Ann Arbor, 1967—69, NOAA, San Francisco, 1969—73; vis. prof. U. Wis., Milw., 1973; geophysicist U.S. Geol. Survey, Menlo Park, Calif., 1973—80, liaison to DOE and FEMA Washington, 1980—85, rsch. geophysicist Denver, 1986—; sci. advisor to U.S. govt. Joint Commn. on Econ. Cooperation, Riyadh, Saudi Arabia, 1985—86. Lt. NOAA Officer Corps, 1964—66. Fellow, NSF, 1960—62, Grove Karl Gilbert Fellowship, U.S. Geol. Survey, 1993; scholar, Nat. Merit Scholarship Corp., 1956—60. Mem.: Soc. of Exploration Geophysicists, Seismol. Soc. of Am., Am. Geophys. Union. Liberal. Achievements include research in plate tectonics,earthquake recurrence and prediction and time-varying earthquake hazard mapping; discovery of a precise, time-predictable earthquake recurrence model; development of time-to-failure analysis in nonlinear, predictive earthquake models. Avocations: photography, sailing, scuba diving, high country hiking, fly fishing. Home: 901 Miami Way Boulder CO 80305 Office: U S Geological Survey MS 966 Box 25046 DFC Denver CO 80225 Personal E-mail: cgbufe@yahoo.com. E-mail: cbufe@usgs.gov.

BUFF, EUGENE, geneticist, researcher, technologist, consultant; b. Moscow, Apr. 16, 1967; naturalized U.S. citizen, 2000; s. Michail Z. and Noemi B. (Shkundina) B.; m. Katerina Y. Sherman, Jan. 6, 1996; children: Adel Malka, Yehuda Zelig. MD, MS in Biochemistry, Pirogov Moscow State Med. Inst, 1989; postgrad., Vavilov Inst. Gen. Genetics, Moscow, 1989-90; PhD in Genetics, Russian Acad. Scis., Moscow, 1993. Rsch. asst. Inst. Gene Biology, Moscow, 1990-92, rsch. assoc., 1992-94; assoc. Howard Hughes Med. Inst., Brigham and Women's Hosp., Boston, 1994-97; rsch. fellow Mass. Gen. Hosp. Cancer Ctr., Charlestown, Mass., 1997-99; v.p., chief scientist Foresight Sci. & Tech., Inc., New Bedford, Mass., 1999—2004; cons. dir. yet2.com Inc., 2004—. Biology tchr. Migdal Ohr Jewish H.S., Moscow, 1991-94; rsch. fellow Harvard Med. Sch., Boston, 1994-99. Contbr. articles to profl. jours. Mem. AUTM, LES. Jewish. Avocations: coin collecting/numismatics, literature. Office: 17 Monsignor O'Brien Hwy Cambridge MA 02141 Business E-Mail: eugene.buff@gmail.com.

BUFF, FRANK PAUL, chemist, educator; b. Munich, Feb. 13, 1924; came to U.S., 1937, naturalized, 1944; s. Heinrich and Johanna Helene (Guggenheimer) B.; m. Iva Mary Moore, Dec. 21, 1956; children— Susan Kathleen, Marjorie Anne. AB, U. Calif., Berkeley, 1944; PhD, Calif. Inst. Tech., 1949. Jr. chemist Shell Devel. Co., Emeryville, Calif., 1946; research fellow Calif. Inst. Tech., Pasadena, 1949-50; from instr. to emeritus prof. chemistry U. Rochester, NY, 1950—; vis. prof. Inst. Theoretical Physics, Utrecht, Netherlands, 1959-60; cons. Mobil Research Corp.; summer visitor Bell Telephone Labs., 1962. Contbr.: chpt. to Handbook of Physics, 1960; mem. bd. editors Jour. Statis. Physics; contbr. articles profl. jours. Served with AUS, 1944-46. Recipient research grants NSF, Office Saline Water; AEC postdoctoral fellow, 1949-50; NSF sr. postdoctoral fellow, 1959-60 Fellow Am. Phys. Soc., Am. Inst. Chemists, A.A.A.S.; mem. Am. Chem. Soc., Phi Beta Kappa, Sigma Xi. Home: 90 Roby Dr Rochester NY 14618-2112

BUFF, IVA MOORE, librarian, musicologist; b. Port Arthur, Tex., Aug. 28, 1932; d. Thomas Richard and Iva Catherine (Smith) Moore; m. Frank P. Buff, Dec. 21, 1956; children: Susan Kathleen, Marjorie Anne. BA, MusB, U. Rochester, 1953, PhD, 1973; MA, Smith Coll., Northampton, Mass., 1954. Tchr. math. Brearley Sch., N.Y.C., 1954-55; research assoc. in musicology U. Rochester (N.Y.), 1973-75, head dept. acquisition and collection devel., 1979-91. Reader-cons. AAUW, 1989—. Author: The Chamber Duets & Trios of Carissimi, 1973, A Thematic Catalog of the Sacred Works of Giacomo Carissimi, 1979; articles Modern Music Librarianship, 1989, reviewer; asst. music rev. editor NOTES, 1986-87; assoc. editor: Am. Choral Rev., 1990-91. Fellow AAUW, 1973-75. Mem. Am. Musicol. Soc., Music Libr. Assn., Internat. Assn. Music Librs., Genesee Early Music Soc. (bd. dirs. 1990—), Mu Phi Epsilon. Avocation: photography. Home: 90 Roby Dr Rochester NY 14618-2112 Personal E-mail: imbfpb@aol.com.

BUFF, MARGARET ANNE, psychiatric nurse practitioner; b. Hanover, N.H., Nov. 2, 1955; d. Kenneth Andrew and M. Irene (Pender) Le Clair; m. James Steve Buff, Jan. 2, 1982; children: Jennifer, Steven, J. Thomas. Nursing BSN, BA in Psychology, RN, U. N.H., 1979; MA in Counselor Edn., U. N.Mex., 1985; MSN in Psychiat./Mental Health Nursing, Rivier Coll., 1997. RN, N.H., Mass.; ARNP, 1998. Staff nurse Vista Sandia Hosp., Albuquerque, 1980-81; charge nurse Los Lunas (N.Mex.) Hosp. and Tng. Sch., 1981-82; child devel. specialist Pueblo Infant Parent Edn. Project, Bernalillo, N.Mex., 1985-86; nurse, therapist Heights Psychiat. Hosp., Albuquerque, 1986-87; charge nurse Meml. Hosp., Albuquerque, 1987-88; staff nurse So. N.H. Regional Med. Ctr., Nashua, N.H., 1990-98; with Greater Lawrence (Mass.) Mental Health Ctr., 1998-2000; psychiat. nurse practioner Behavioral Health Care Svcs., Worcester, Mass., 2002—03, Prescott Health Care, 2003—. Roman Catholic. Avocation: swimming. Home: 28 Hillside Dr Brookline NH 03033-2123 Office: Amherst Psychiat Svcs 135 Rte 101A Amherst NH 03031

BUFFENBARGER, ROBERT THOMAS, labor union administrator; s. Bob and Betty Buffenbarger; m. Linda Buffenbarger; children: Amy, Andrew. Former journeyman tool and die maker General Electric, Evendale, Ohio; with Internat. Assn. Machinists and Aerospace Workers, 1986-87, exec. asst. to internat. pres., 1987-91, gen. v.p. Upper Marlboro, Md., 1991-97, internat. pres., 1997—. Co-chair. Machinists Non-Partisan Political League; mem. exec. council AFL-CIO, chmn. Com. on St. and Local Central Bodies; mem. exec. com. Internat. Metalworkers Fed.; mem. U.S. Treasury Dept. Adv. Com. to the Internat. Monetary Fund. Bd. mem. Guide Dogs of America. Office: Internat Assn Machinists and Aerospace Workers 9000 Machinists Pl Upper Marlboro MD 20772-2675 Office Phone: 301-967-4500.

BUFFENSTEIN, ALLAN S., lawyer; b. Richmond, Va., Sept. 21, 1940; m. Frona Buffenstein. BA, U. Richmond, 1962, LLB, 1965. Bar: Va. 1965. Ptnr. McCandlish Holton, Richmond. Lectr. Continuing Legal Edn., The Troubled Project, The Troubled Condominium Va. Law Found. Pres., chmn. bd. Richmond Jewish Community Ctr., 1982-84. Mem. ABA, Va. Bar Assn., Am. Bankruptcy Inst., Richmond Bar Assn. Office: McCandlish Holton 1111 E Main St PO Box 796 Richmond VA 23218-0796 Office Phone: 804-775-3803. Business E-Mail: abuffenstein@lawmh.com.

BUFFENSTEIN, DARYL R., lawyer; b. Salisbury, Zimbabwe, June 12, 1951; BA in Econs. and Comparative African Govt. and Law, U. Cape Town, South Africa, 1972; BL with honors, U. Rhodesia, 1974, LLB, 1975; LLM, U. Exeter, Eng., 1977. Bar: Ga. 1978; advocate High Ct. Zimbabwe. Ptnr. Paul, Hastings, Janofsky & Walker, Atlanta, chmn. immigration practice group. Commonwealth scholar, 1975-76. Mem. Am. Immigration Lawyers Assn. (pres. 1995—, chair Atlanta chpt. 1982-84, nat. dir. 1984-90, nat. exec. com. 1990—, gen. counsel 1999-2003), State Bar of Ga. (chmn. internat. sect. 1984-85, global p3rsonnel alliancee gen. counsel 2003—). Office: 600 Peachtree St NE Ste 2400 Atlanta GA 30308-2265 Office Phone: 404-815-2232. Office Fax: 404-685-5232. Business E-Mail: darylbuffenstein@paulhastings.com.

BUFFETT, JIMMY (JAMES WILLIAM BUFFETT), vocalist, songwriter, writer; b. Pascagoula, Miss., Dec. 25, 1946; s. James Delaney and Lorraine (Peets) B.; m. Margie Washichek, 1969 (div.), m. Jane Slagsvol, Aug. 27, 1977; children: Savannah Jane, Sarah Delaney and Cameron Marley. BS in History and Journalism, U. So. Miss., 1969. Free-lance journalist Inside Sports, Outside mag. Albums include Down to Earth, 1970, High Cumberland Jubilee, 1971, White Sport Coat and a Pink Crustacean, 1973, Living and Dying in 3/4 Time, 1974, A1A, 1974, Rancho Deluxe (film soundtrack), 1975, Havana Daydreamin', 1976, Changes in Latitudes (featuring the song "Margaritaville"), 1977, Son of a Son of a Sailor, 1978, You Had To Be There, 1978, Volcano, 1979, Coconut Telegraph, 1981, Somewhere Over China, 1981, One Particular Harbor, 1983, Riddles in the Sand, 1984, Last Mango in Paris, 1985, Songs You Know By Heart, 1985, Floridays, 1986, Hot Water, 1988, Off To See The Lizard, 1989, Feeding Frenzy, 1990, Boats, Beaches, Bars & Ballads, 1992, Before the Beach, 1993, Fruit Cakes, 1994, Barometer Soup, 1995, Banana Wind, 1996, Christmas Island, 1996, Don't Stop the Carnival, 1998, Beach House on the Moon, 1999, Buffett Live-Tuesdays, Thursdays, Saturdays, 1999, Captain America, 2002, Far Side of the World, 2002, License to Chill, 2004; author: Tales from Margaritaville, 1988, Where is Joe Merchant?, 1992, A Novel Tale, 1992, Daybreak on the Equator, 1997, Sea Level: Adventures of a Saltwater Angler, 2002, A Salty Piece of Land, 2004 (Publishers Weekly bestseller), (with Savannah Jane Buffett) The Jolly Mon, 1988, Trouble Dolls, 1990, (memoir) A Pirate Looks at Fifty, 1998; performed benefit concert for anti-nuclear legislation; film appearances include Rancho Deluxe, 1975, FM, 1978, Repo Man, 1984, Dr Duck's Super Secret All-Purpose Sauce, 1985, Hook, 1991, Cobb, 1994, Congo, 1995; TV appearances include SCTV Network 90, 1981, From the Earth to the Moon, 1998. Chmn. Save the Manatee Commn., Fla.; hon. dir. Greenpeace Found. Mem. Cousteau Soc. Democrat. Roman Catholic. Office: Margaritaville Inc Cindy Thompson 424A Fleming St Key West FL 33040 also: Mailboat Records 9200 Sunset Blvd Ste 550 Los Angeles CA 90069*

BUFFETT, WARREN EDWARD, entrepreneur, investment company executive; b. Omaha, Aug. 30, 1930; s. Howard Homan and Leila (Stahl) B.; m. Susan Thompson (dec. 2004), Apr. 19, 1952; children: Susan, Howard, Peter. Student, U. Pa., 1947-49; BS, U. Nebr., 1950; MS, Columbia, 1951. Investment salesman Buffett-Falk & Co., Omaha, 1951-54; security analyst Graham-Newman Corp., N.Y.C., 1954-56; gen. partner Buffett Partnership, Ltd., Omaha, 1956-69; chmn. & CEO Berkshire Hathaway Inc., Omaha, 1970—. Chmn. bd. Berkshire Hathaway, Inc., Nat. Indemnity Co.; bd. dirs. The Coca-Cola Co., 1989-, The Washington Post Co., 1974-86, 96-. Life trustee Grinnell Coll., 1968—, Urban Institute. Mem.: Am Acad Arts & Scis. Ranked number two on the World's Richest People list by Forbes magazine in 2001, 02, 03, 04. Office: Berkshire Hathaway Inc 1440 Kiewit Plz Omaha NE 68131*

BUFFINGTON, AUDREY VIRGINIA, elementary school educator, writer; b. Westminster, Md., Oct. 6, 1931; d. Martin Luther and Elsie Virginia (Heltibridle) Myers; m. John David Buffington, June 20, 1953 (div. 1963); 1 child, A. Virtina Buffington Hunter. BA, Western Md. Coll., 1952; MEd, Pa. State U., 1968. Cert. tchr., supr., Md., Mass. Tchr. math. Carroll County Pub. Schs., Westminster, 1952-68, supr. math., 1968-73; state math. supr. Md. Dept. Edn., Balt., 1973-79; program mgr. Ginn & Co., Lexington, Mass., 1979-81; tchr. math Wayland (Mass.) Pub. Schs., 1982-94, ret., 1994. Instr. U. Coll., Thomaston, Maine, 2002—; bd. dirs. Maine Sch. Adminstrn. Dist. 5; speaker, workshop leader numerous local and state edn. meetings. Author: Meters, Liters and Grams, 1973, textbook series Merrill Mathematics, 1985, 87, math. comic books King Features Comic Math. Libr., 1979, You are My Mommy/You are My Daddy, 1998; creator NASCO Algebra Models. Pres. Carroll County Gen. Hosp. Aux., Westminster; mem. sch. bd. Maine Sch. Adminstrv. Dist. #5. Recipient Math. Educator of Yr. award Md. Coun. Tchrs. Math., 1978, Trustee Alumni award Western Md. Coll., 1979. Republican. Lutheran. Avocations: collecting Uncle Wiggily items and works of F. Earl Christy, bridge. Home: PO Box 386 South Thomaston ME 04858-0386 E-mail: audreyb217@aol.com.

BUFFINGTON, GARY LEE ROY, safety engineer, construction executive; b. Custer, S.D., Dec. 6, 1946; s. Donald L. B. and Madge Irene (Selby) Lampert; m. Kathleen R. Treloar, Aug. 3, 1965; children: Katherine, Lowell, Gary Jr. BS in Bus. Edn., Black Hill State Coll., 1971; AA in Criminal Justice, U. S.D., 1972, MS, 1974. Cert. safety profl., EMT, law enforcement officer, mine safety and health adminstrn. instr., OSHA instr., safety exec., safety mgr., safety specialist; Canadian registered safety profl.; lic. pvt. investigator; cert. safety and health mgr. Contract miner Homestake Mining Co., Lead, SD, 1966—72; dep. sheriff, criminal investigator Pennington County Sheriff's Dept., Rapid City, SD, 1972—77; fed. mine inspector U.S. Dept. of Labor, Mine Safety and Health Adminstrn., Birmingham, Ala., 1977—79, supr., spl. investigator, 1979—81, supr., mine inspector Grand Junction, Colo., 1981—83; mgr. safety and security Black & Veatch Engrs. Stanton Energy Ctr., Orlando, Fla., 1983—87; mgr. loss control Black & Veatch Engrs. AES Thames Cogeneration Plant, Uncasville, Conn., 1987—90; mgr. loss control Trans-Mo. River Tunnel project Black & Veatch, Engrs.-Architects, Kansas City, Mo., 1990—92; mgr. safety and security, mgr. metro rail constrn. Parsons-Dillingham, L.A., 1992—95; asst. dir. constrn. safety L.A. Metro Rail Project Met. Transp. Authority, 1995—99; owner Safety Expert Witness Am. Safety Cons., L.A., 1990—; mgr. constrn. safety Parsons Constructors Inc., Pasadena, Calif., 1999—2002. Mem. ANSI A-10 Accredited Standards Com., Washington, 1984—, Mine Safety and Health Adminstrn. Standards Com., Arlington, Va., 1981-83. Named Police Officer of the Year, Sundown Optimist Club, Rapid City, 1975; recipient Meritorious Achievement award, U.S. Dept. of Labor, Arlington, 1979, Monetary Spl. Achievement award, U.S. Dept. Labor, Arlington, 1980. Mem. Am. Soc. Safety Engrs. (adminstr. mining divsn. 1998—, Safety Profl. of Yr. constrn. splty. 2000-01, Safety Profl. of Yr. mining practice splty. 2002-03), World Safety Orgn., Am. Indsl. Hygiene Assn., Am. Soc. for Indsl. Security, Nat. Safety Coun., Inst. for Safety and Health Mgmt., Nat. Fire Protection Assn., Assn. for Can. Registered Safety Profls., Moose Lodge. Republican. Lutheran. Avocations: photography, sports. Home: 20025 W Jacana Ct Santa Clarita CA 91351-5562 Office: PO Box 71017 Los Angeles CA 90071-0017 Office Phone: 213-272-7158. Personal E-mail: gbuff46@yahoo.com.

BUFFKINS, LERACHEL HAROMBE, small business owner; b. Portland, Maine, Dec. 8, 1970; d. Archie Lee Buffkins and Carol Jane Christian, Lewis Kim Christian (Stepfather); m. Tal Ricardo Valentin, Aug. 18, 1999 (div.); 1 child, Jakob Taylor. BA in Sociology, St. Mary's Coll. Md., 1992; MSW, Howard U., Washington, 1996. Cert. profl. resume writer Pa. for Resume Writers and Career Coaches, 2003, fed. job search trainer Md. Inst. for Employment and Tng. Profls., 2003. Asst. men's dept. mgr. Nordstrom Rack, Silver Spring, Md., 1992—96; tech. asst. Governor's Office for Children, Youth & Families, Baltimore, Md., 1996—97; career resource coord. Morgan State U. - Ctr. for Career Devel., Balt., 1996—97, internship/co-op coord., 1997—2003; resume writer/owner Writing For You, Inc., Laurel, Md., 2002—. Mem.: Md. Assn. for Counseling and Devel. (sec. 2004—), Nat. Resume Writers Assn., Md. Career Devel. Assn., Career Masters Inst., Nat. Assn. of Workforce Devel. Profls. (life), Nat. Career Devel. Assn. (life). R-Consevative. Avocation: flutist. Office: Writing For You Inc 14518 Cambridge Cir Laurel MD 20707 Office Phone: 301-604-2048. Office Fax: 301-604-2100. E-mail: lbuffkins@writingforyouinc.com.

BUFFLER, PATRICIA ANN, epidemiologist, educator, dean emerita; b. Doylestown, Pa., Aug. 1, 1938; d. Edward M. and Evelyn G. (Axenroth) Happ; m. Richard T. Buffler, Jan. 20, 1962; children: Martyn R., Monique L. BSN, Cath. U. Am., 1960; MPH, U. Calif., Berkeley, 1965, PhD in Epidemiology, 1973. Prof. epidemiology sch. pub. health U. Tex. Health Sci. Ctr., Houston, 1979—91; prof. U. Calif., Berkeley, 1991—, dean sch. pub. health, 1991—98, dean emerita, 1998—. Mem. expert adv. panel on occupl. health WHO, 1985—2002; mem. environment, safety and health adv. com. U.S. DOE, 1992—95; mem. bd. on water sci. and tech. NRC, 1992—94; chair, bd. dirs. Mickey Leland Nat. Urban Air Toxics Rsch. Ctr., 1994—97, Societal Inst. of Math. Scis., 1992—; mem. Nat. Commn. on Superfund, Keystone Ctr., 1992—94; mem. adv. panel on mng. nuc. materials from warheads U.S. Congress Office Tech. Assessment, 1992—93; bd. sci. counselors Nat. Inst. for Occupl. Safety and Health, 1991—93; mem. sci. adv. bd. radiation adv. com. subcom. on cancer risks associated with electric and magnetic fields U.S. EPA, 1990—93, mem. sci. adv. bd., 1996—98; mem. Nat. Adv. Coun. on Environ. Health Scis., 1995—98, NAS, Nat. Coun. Radiation Protection. Contbr. articles to profl. jours. Fellow: AAAS, Inst. Medicine of NAS, Am. Coll. Epidemiology (pres.-elect 1990—91, pres. 1991—92); mem.: APHA (epidemiology sect. 1964—), Internat. Soc. for Environ. Epidemiology (pres.-elect 1989—91, pres. 1992—94), Soc. of Toxicology, Internat. Commn. on Occupl. Health, Internat. Soc. for Exposure Assessment (charter, bd. internat. councillors 1993—98), Internat. Epidemiol. Assn., Soc. for Occupl. and Environ. Health, Am. Epidemiol. Soc., Soc. for Epidemiol. Rsch. (pres.-elect, pres., past pres. 1984—88), Collegium Ramazzini. Office: U Calif Sch Pub Health 714-F Univ Hall 140 Earl Warren Hl Berkeley CA 94720-0001

BUFFON, CHARLES EDWARD, lawyer; b. Topeka, Sept. 8, 1939; s. Merritt Woodbridge and Clare Marie (Waterfall) B.; m. Kathleen Craig Vreeland, June 6, 1964; children: Alexandra, Nathaniel Edward. AB in Internat. Rels. magna cum laude, Dartmouth Coll., 1961; LLB cum laude, Harvard U., 1964. Bar: D.C. 1965, U.S. Ct. Appeals (D.C. cir.) 1965, U.S. Ct. Appeals (6th cir.) 1966, U.S. Supreme Ct. 1971, U.S. Ct. Appeals (9th cir.) 1975, U.S. Ct. Appeals (2d cir.) 1980, U.S. Ct. Appeals (4th cir.) 1980, U.S. Ct. Appeals (3d cir.) 1981, U.S. Ct. Appeals (fed. cir.) 1982, U.S. Dist. Ct. Md. 1992, U.S. Ct. Appeals (11th cir.) 2000. Assoc. Covington & Burling, Washington, 1964-73, ptnr., 1973—, gen. counsel, 2005—. Adj. faculty U. Va. Law Sch., 1968-86, Am. U. 1988-92; lectr. in field. Contbr. articles to profl. jours. Fellow Am. Bar Found.; mem. ABA (litigation and antitrust sects.), D.C. Bar Assn. (past chmn. legal ethics com., spl. com. legal specialization, mem. steering com. sect. cts., lawyers and adminstrn. justice, D.C. rules profl. com., com. on interdisciplinary practice, Cert. Appreciation 1987, 2002), Phi Beta Kappa. Office: Covington & Burling 1201 Pennsylvania Ave NW Washington DC 20004-2401 Office Phone: 202-662-5542. Office Fax: 202-662-6291. Business E-Mail: cbuffon@rov.com.

BUFFONE, SAMUEL J., lawyer; b. New Kensington, Pa., Oct. 3, 1946; BA, Univ. Pitts., 1968; JD, Georgetown Univ., 1971. Bar: Pa. 1971, D.C. 1973, US Ct. Appeals (1st, 2d, 3d, 4th, 5th, 9th, 11th & D.C. cir.), US Supreme Ct. 1978. Law clk. Judge Francis L. Van Dusen, US Ct. Appeals 3d cir., 1971—72; ptnr. litigation dept. Ropes & Gray, Washington, 1992—, co-chmn. govt. enforcement practice group. Chmn. Practicioners Adv. Group U.S. Sentencing Commn., 1989—92. Mem.: ABA (chmn. Com. on U.S. Sentencing Commn., vice chmn. RICO Com. 1986—88, mem. White Collar Crime Com. 1984—). Office: Ropes & Gray One Metro Ctr Suite 900 700 12th St NW Washington DC 20005-3948 Office Phone: 202-508-4657. Office Fax: 202-508-4650. Business E-Mail: samuel.buffone@ropesgray.com.

BUFFORD, SAMUEL LAWRENCE, federal judge; b. Phoenix, Nov. 19, 1943; s. John Samuel and Evelyn Amelia (Rude) B.; m. Julia Marie Metzger, May 13, 1978. BA in Philosophy, Wheaton Coll., 1964; PhD, U. Tex., 1969; JD magna cum laude, U. Mich., 1973. Bar: Calif., N.Y., Ohio. Instr. philosophy La. State U., Baton Rouge, 1967-68; asst. prof. Ea. Mich. U., Ypsilanti, 1968-74; asst. prof. law Ohio State U., Columbus, 1975-77; assoc. Gendel, Raskoff, Shapiro & Quittner, L.A., 1982-85; atty. Paul, Weiss, Rifkind, Wharton & Garrison, N.Y.C., 1974-75, Sullivan Jones & Archer, San Francisco, 1977-79, Musick, Peeler & Garrett, L.A., 1979-81, Rifkind & Sterling, Beverly Hills, Calif., 1981-82, Gendel, Raskoff, Shapiro & Quittner, L.A., 1982-85; U.S. bankruptcy judge Ctrl. Dist. Calif., 1985—. Lectr. U.S.-Romanian Jud. Delegation, 1991, Internat. Tng. Ctr. for Bankers, Budapest, 1993, Bankruptcy Technical Legal Assistance Workshop, Romania, 1994, Comml. Law Project for Ukraine, 1995-96, 99, Ea. Europe Enterprise Restructuring and Privatization Project, U.S. AID, 1995-96, World Bank Global Judges Forum, 2003-04, Morocco Jud. Tng.Program; cons. World Bank Project, 2002; cons. Calif. State Bar Bd. Examiners, 1989-90; trustee Endowment for Edn.; bd. dirs. San Pedro Enterprise Cmty.; lectr. Harvard Law Sch., 2004, Nomura lectr., 2005. Sr. author: International Insolvency, 2001, editor-in-chief: Am. Bankruptcy Law Jour., 1990—94; contbr. articles to profl. jours. Younger Humanist fellowship NEH. Mem. ABA, L.A. County Bar Assn. (mem. profl. responsibility and ethics com. 1979—, chair profl. responsibility and ethics com. 1985-86, chair ethics 2000 liaison com. 1997-2002), Order of Coif. Office: US Bankruptcy Ct 255 E Temple St Ste 1582 Los Angeles CA 90012-3332

BUFORD, BARBARA FEST, retired state agency administrator; b. Camden, N.J., Mar. 26, 1941; d. Robert Eugene Fest and Helen Agnes Besso; m. Jefferson R. Taylor (div. 1972); children: Patricia A., Laurie B., Jeff Jr.; m. Rivers Henderson Buford Jr., July 15, 1976. BA in History & Criticism Art cum laude, Fla. State U., 1962. Clk. Divsn. Corrections and Sec. of State State of Fla. Govt., Tallahassee, 1962—66; clk. Fla. Legis., 1967, clk., 1970, 1972—82. Mem. Phi Beta Kappa. Episcopalian. Avocations: art, birding, calligraphy. Home: 3224 Independence Ct Tallahassee FL 32312 E-mail: barive@aol.com.

BUFORD, GREGORY, plastic surgeon; m. Krista Reiff. Degree in lit./writing, U. Calif., San Diego, 1990; MD, Georgetown U., 1994. Resident in gen. surgery Cleve. Clinic Found., 1994—99, resident in plastic surgery, 1999—2001; plastic surgeon Ctr. for Plastic & Aesthetic Surgery, Englewood, Colo., 2001—. Mem. BOTOX Cosmetic Nat. Edn. Faculty, 2002—, LipoSelection by VASER Physician Tng. Faculty, 2004—. Baker-Stuzin-Baker Cosmetic Surgery fellow, 2001. Mem.: Arapahoe Med. Soc., Colo. Med. Soc., Am. Soc. Plastic Surgery, Georgetown U. Alumni Admissions Com. Republican. Office: Ctr for Plastic & Aesthetic Surgery 125 Inverness Dr E Ste 200 Englewood CO 80112 Office Phone: 303-708-8234. Office Fax: 303-649-9694. E-mail: drbuford@newyouplasticsurgery.com.

BUFORD, JAMES A., city health department administrator; BS in Biology, Tenn. State U., 1957; MS in Ednl. Adminstrn., Ctrl. Mo. State U., 1965; MPH in Med. Care Orgn. and Adminstrn., U. Mich., 1972. Dir., dept. health and welfare City of Newark, 1972—77; adminstr., project mgr. St. Elizabeth's Hosp. Initiative, Washington, 1977—79; regional health adminstr. Dept. Health and Human Svcs., Dallas, 1979—80; dir. D.C. Dept. Human Svcs., Washington, 1980—83; pres. Buford and Assocs., Inc., Washington, 1983—85; dir. Dept. Urban Cmty. Svcs., Kansas City, Kans., 1985—86; asst. v.p. Office of Strategic Planning, N.Y.C. Health and Hosps. Corp., 1986—88; exec. dir. Kings Co. Hosp. Ctr., Bklyn., 1988—91, Divsn. of Hosp. Opers., N.Y.C., 1991—92; mgmt. cons. Human Resources Adminstrn., N.Y.C., 1992—94, U. Rsch. Corp., Bethesda, Md., 1994—99; dir. Detroit Health Dept., 1999—2002; COO D.C. Dept. Health, Washington, 2002, acting dir., 2002, dir., 2002—. Mem.: Am. Mgmt. Assn., Nat. Assn. of Health Svcs. Execs., Am. Pub. Health Assn. Office: Dept Health Govt of DC 825 N Capitol St NE Washington DC 20002

BUFORD, RONETTA MARIE, music educator; b. Kansas City, Mo., Sept. 17, 1946; d. Joseph Ronald and Violet Katheryne (Jennison) Coursey; 1 child, Frederick Kenyatta. Bachelor of Music Edn., Lincoln U. of Mo., 1968; M in Liberal Arts, Baker U., 1996. Cert. vocal and instrumental music tchr., Mo. Chmn. vocal music M.L. King Jr. High Sch., Kansas City, 1968-71; chmn. music dept. Southeast Jr. High Sch., Kansas City, 1971-75; chmn. fine arts Paseo High Sch., Kansas City, 1975-90; vocal music specialist Met. Advanced Tech. H.S., Kansas City, 1990-98, asst. girls basketball coach, asst. cross country coach, 1992-98; owner Buford's Day Care, 1996-97, Buford's Mini Univ.; TRAC music instr. Crispus Attucks Elem. Sch., 2001—02, performing arts instr., 2002—. Summer music specialist Horace Mann Elem. Sch., Kansas City, 1972; mentor Students at Risk, Kansas City, 1988; vis. lectr. Lincoln U., Jefferson City, Mo., 1980, 85, 87, NE Mo. State U., Kirksville, 1986; panelist Sta. KPRS, Kansas City, 1987; Title One mentor K.C. Mo. Sch. Dist.; min. music N.W. Mo. Conf. A.M.E. Ch., Kansas City, 1984-91, choir dir., 1985—; dir. sr. choir Ward Chapel A.M.E. Ch., KAnsas City, 1985-87; instr. of choir, band and orch. N.E. Law, Pub. Svc. and Mil. Sci. H.S., 1998-99; girl's varsity asst. basketball coach, girl's jr. varsity basketball coach, drill mistress N.E. Lady Vikings Drill Team, fine arts dept. chairperson. Author: (curricula) Junior High Learning Task, 1972, Motivating the Unmotivated, 1986. Asst. troop scoutmaster Boy Scouts Am.; spl. cons. music United Meth. Ch. Women; active NAACP; parent chaperone Kansas City Marching Cobras Drill Team, 1993—. Recipient Meritorious Service award Lincoln U. Vocal Ensemble, 1985, Outstanding Tchr. award Black Archives Mid-Am., 1987; named one of Outstanding Young Women of Am., 1983. Mem. NAACP, AAUW, MADD, Am. Choral Dirs. Assn., Am. Fedn. Tchrs., Am. Assn. Retired Persons, Music Educators Nat. Conf., Nat. Assn. Negro Women, Order Eastern Star, Order Cyrenes, Heroines of Jericho, Daus.

of Isis, Tri-M Music Honor Soc., Order Golden Circle, Nat. Coaches Assn., Bethel A.M.E. Ch. (life), Bethel Missionary Soc., Mass Choir and Parsonage Club, Licoln U. Mo. Alumni Assn., Vocat. Indsl. Clubs Am., "C" Scholarship Club, Alpha Kappa Alpha, Phi Delta Kappa, Sigma Alpha Iota. Avocation: photography. Home: 3610 E 26th St Kansas City MO 64127-4321 Office: Kansas City Sch Dist 1211 Mcgee St Kansas City MO 64106-2416

BUFORD, WILLIAM LESLIE, JR., researcher, educator; b. Aberdeen, Wash., Aug. 17, 1945; s. William L. and Hazel M. Buford; m. Elaine A. O'Sullivan, June 30, 1970; 1 child, Scarlett N.; children: Alice M. Bauder, Valerie M. Cook. BS, USAF Acad., Colo., 1968; MS, Calif. State U., Sacramento, Calif., 1976; PhD, La. State U., Baton Rouge, La., 1984. Lic. Profl. Engr., La., 1980, cert. Clin. Engr., Internat. Commn. for, 1981. Officer, instr. navigator USAF, 1968—74; capt., usaf res. Travis AFB, Calif., 1974—76; biomedical engr. Rehab. Rsch. Dept., Nat. Hansen's Disease Ctr., Carville, 1976—80; dep. chief, rehab. rsch. dept G. W. Long Hansen's Disease Ctr., Carville, La., 1980—85; chief, paul w. brand biomechanics lab Gillis W. Long Hansen's Disease, Carville, 1985—91; dir., orthopaedic biomechanics lab U. Tex. Med. Br., Galveston, Tex., 1991—99, dir., divsn. of orthopaedic rsch., 1999—. Prof., divsn. rehab. sci. U. Tex. Med. Br., Galveston, Tex., 2002—; adj., grad. faculty Univ. Tex., Austin, Tex., 1996—; adj. grad. faculty Tex. A&M U., Coll. Sta., Tex., 1992—; sr. scientist Biomedical Engring. Ctr., UTMB, Galveston, Tex., 1996—. Contbr. articles pub. to profl. jour. (Best Paper of the Issue, 1990). Capt. USAF, 1968—76, Viet Nam and CONUS. Grantee, Tex. Advanced Rsch. Program, 1996-1997, Tex. Coordinating Bd. Advanced Tech. Program, 2000-2002. Mem.: IEEE, Internat. Soc. of Biomechanics, Am. Soc. of Biomechanics. Achievements include research in Computer Simulation of Human Musculoskeletal Kinematics; patents for Co-Inventor, Hand External Fixator, 07/006, 878, 1999. Avocations: hiking, travel. Office: Univ Tex Medl Branch 301 Univ Blvd Galveston TX 77555-0174 Business E-Mail: wbuford@utmb.edu.

BUGBEE-JACKSON, JOAN, sculptor, educator; b. Oakland, Calif, Dec. 17, 1941; d. Henry Greenwood and Jeanie Lawler (Abbot) B.; m. John Michael Jackson, June 21, 1973; 1 child, Brook Bond. BA in Art, U. Calif., San Jose, 1964, MA in Art and Ceramics, 1966; student, Nat. Acad. Sch. Fine Arts, N.Y.C., 1968-72. Instr. pottery Greenwich House Pottery, NYC, 1969-71, Craft Inst. Am., NYC, 1970-72, Cordova Ext. Ctr., U. AK, 1972-79, Prince William Sound Cmty. Coll., 1979—. One-woman exhbn. in Maine, NYC, Alaska, Calif.; group exhbns. include Allied Artists Am., 1970-72, Nat. Acad. Design, 1971, 74, Nat. Sculpture Soc. Ann., 1971, 72, 73, Alaska Woman Art Show, 1987, 88, Cordova Visual Artists, 1991-96, Alaska Artists Guild Show, 1994, Am. Medallic Sculpture Nat. Travelling Exhbn., 1994-95, pres. Cordova Arts and Pageants Ltd., 1975-76; commns. include Merle K. Smith Commemorative plaque, 1973, Eyak Native Monument, 1978, Anchorage Pioneer's Home Ceramic Mural, 1979, Alaska Wildlife Series Bronze Medal, 1980, Armin F. Koernig Hatchery Plaque, 1985, Cordova Fishermen's Meml. Sculpture, 1985, Alaska's Five Gov., bronze relief, Anchorage, 1986, Reluctant Fishermen's Mermaid, bronze, 1987, Charles E. Bunnell, bronze portrait statue, Fairbanks, 1988, Alexander Baranof Monument, Sitka, Alaska, 1989, Wally Noerenberg Hatchery Plaque, Prince William Sound, Alaska, 1989, Russian-Alaskan Friendship Plaque (edit. of 4), Kayak Island, Cordova, Alaska and Vladivostok & Petropavlovsk-Kamchatskiy, Russia, 1991, Sophie-Last Among Eyak Native People, 1992, Alaska Airlines Medal Commn., 1993, Hosp. Aux. plaque, 1995, La Cirena, Mex., 1998, Alaska Vets. Monument lifesize bronze, Anchorage, 2001, Alaska R.R.: Sheffield Plaque, 2002, Joe Redington Sr., Father of the Iditarod, statue, Wasilla, Alaska, 2003, Pioneer Aviator Monument, Anchorage, 2005; also other portraits. Bd. dir. Alaska State Coun. Arts, 1991-95. Scholar, Nat. Acad. Sch. Fine Arts, 1969-72; recipient J.A. Suydam Bronze medal, 1969, Dr. Ralph Weiler prize, 1971, Helen Foster Barnet award, 1971, Daniel Chester French award, 1972, Frishmuth award, 1971, Allied Artists Am. award, 1972, C. Percival Dietsch prize, 1973, citation Alaska Legis., 1981, 82; named Alaskan Artist of Yr., 1991; Alaska Gov. Award, 2002. Fellow Nat. Sculpture Soc. Address: PO Box 374 Cordova AK 99574-0374

BUGEJA, MICHAEL JOSEPH, director, educator, writer; b. Hackensack, N.J., May 24, 1952; s. Michael Carl and Josephine (Apap) B.; m. Diane Faye Sears, Sept. 16, 1979; children: Mikayle Joseph, Shane Michael, Erin Marie BA in German, St. Peter's Coll., 1974; MS in Comms., S.D. State U., 1976; PhD in English, Okla. State U., 1985. State editor UPI, Sioux Falls, SD, 1976—79; prof. Okla. State U., Stillwater, 1979—86, Ohio U., Athens, 1986—2003, spl. asst. to pres., 1996—2003; dir. Greeniee Sch. Journalism and Comm. Iowa State U., Ames, 2003—. Hon. chancellor Nat. Fed. of State Poetry Soc. Author: Art and Craft of Poetry, 1994, Living Ethics, 1996, Guide to Writing Magazine Nonfiction, 1997, Millennium's End, 1999, Living Without Fear, 2001, Interpersonal Divide: The Search for Community in a Technological Age, 2005; mem. adv. bd. Writer's Digest, Cin., 1999, Coll. Values, 2000. Fellow Nat. Endowment for Arts, 1990, Ohio Arts Coun., 1997; NEH grantee, 1984; recipient Outstanding Tchr. award Amoco, 1985. Lutheran. Office: Iowa State U Hamilton Hall Ames IA 50010 Business E-Mail: bugeja@iastate.edu.

BUGENTAL, JAMES FREDERICK THOMAS, retired psychologist, educator; b. Fort Wayne, Ind., Dec. 25, 1915; s. Richard Francis and Hazel Jeanette (Veness) B.; m. Mary Edith Smith, Feb. 11, 1939 (div. 1967); children: James Owen, Jane Pattie Eum; m. Elizabeth Catherine Keber, June 23, 1968; 1 child, Karen Marie. BS in Edn., West Tex. State Coll., 1940; MA in Sociology, George Peabody Coll., 1941; PhD in Psychology, Ohio State U., 1948; LHD (hon.), Saybrook Inst., 1993. Diplomate Am. Bd. Examiners in Psychology. Asst. prof. psychology, counselor Ga. Sch. of Tech., 1944-45; asst. prof. psychology UCLA, 1948-54; ptnr., psychologist Psychol. Svc. Assocs., L.A., 1947-67; cons. project on future of edn. Stanford Rsch. Inst., Palo Alto, Calif., 1967-69; psychologist Palo Alto, Santa Rosa, Calif., 1967-69, San Rafael, Calif., 1967-88; cons., lectr. Disting. clinician-educator, J.F. Kennedy U., 1988, vis. scholar, U. Mont., 1988, disting. vis. prof., Calif. Sch. Profl. Psychology, Alameda, 1989-90. Author: Psychotherapy Isn't What You Think, 1999, Intimate Journeys: Stories from Life-Changing Therapy, 1990, The Art of the Psychotherapist, 1987, Psychotherapy and Process: The Fundamentals of an Existential-Humanistic Approach, 1978, The Search for Existential Identity: Patient-Therapist Dialogues in Humanistic Psychotherapy, 1976, The Search for Authenticity: An Existential Analytic Approach to Psychotherapy, 1965; editor: Challenges of Humanistic Psychology, 1967; contbr. articles to profl. jours.; editl. bd. 11 jours. Lt. USNR, 1945-46. Rockefeller scholar Calif. Inst. of Integral Studies; recipient Pathfinder award Assn. for Humanistic Psychology, 1991; fellow USPHS, Ohio State U., 1946-48. Fellow Am. Psychol. Assn. (divsn. humanistic psychology, First Rollo May award 1996; divsn. clin. psychology, cert. disting. contbn. 1986, honored career divsn. psychotherapy, 2002); mem. Assn. for Humanistic Psychology (pres. 1962-63), Calif. Psychol. Assn. (pres. 1960-61), So. Calif. Psychol. Assn. (pres. 1955-56), L.A. Soc. of Clin. Psychologists (pres. 1952-53). Democrat. Episcopalian. Avocations: friends, concerts, writing. E-mail: jeb001@pacbell.net.

BUGGE, LAWRENCE JOHN, lawyer, educator; b. Milw., June 1, 1936; s. Lawrence Anthony and Anita (Westenberg) B.; m. Mary Daly, Nov. 28, 1959 (div.); m. Elaine Andersen, Jan. 29, 1977; children: Kristin, Laura, Jill, David, Carol. AB, Marquette U., 1958; JD, Harvard U., 1963. Bar: Wis. 1963. Assoc. Foley and Lardner, Milw., Madison, Wis., 1963-70, ptnr., 1970-96, of counsel, 1996—. Pres. Nat. Conf. Commrs. on Uniform State Laws, 1989-91; adj. prof. law U. Wis. Law Sch., Madison, 1997—. Mem. Wis. Bar Assn. (pres. 1980-81), Mil. Bar Assn. (pres. 1974-75), Milw. Young Lawyers Assn. (pres. 1969-70). Home: 313 Walnut Grove Dr Madison WI 53717-1228 Office: Foley & Lardner PO Box 1497 150 E Gilman St Madison WI 53701-1497 Personal E-mail: lbugge@charter.net.

BUGGIE, FREDERICK DENMAN, management consultant; b. Toledo, Mar. 27, 1929; s. Horace and Loraine (Denman) B.; m. Betty Jo Chilcote, Sept. 7, 1951 (div. 1988); children: Martha Louise Buggie Kenney, John Chilcote Buggie; m. Debra Hingley, July 15, 1997. BA, Yale U., 1956; MBA, George Washington U., 1961. Sales engr. Alcoa, Balt. and Phila., 1956-66; pres. Gt. Lakes Rsch. Inst., Erie, Pa., 1967-69; mktg. mgr. Technicon Instruments, Tarrytown, N.Y., 1969-71; program mgr. Innotech, Norwalk, Conn., 1971-74; pres. Inomation divsn. Van Dyck Corp., Westport, Conn., 1974-76; founder, CEO Strategic Innovations Internat., Inc., Lake Wylie, SC, 1976—. Pres. SII Strategic Innovations A.G., Zurich, Switzerland; founder, chmn. Strategic Innovations Internat. Ltd., Keele, Staffordshire, Eng., Strategic Innovations B.V., Rijswijk, The Netherlands; conf. leader, lectr.; adj. prof. various univs. Author: New Product Development Strategies, 1981; contbr. over 50 articles to profl. jours. With USAF, 1950-54. Fellow Inst. Dirs.; mem. Assn. Corp. Growth, Strategic Leadership Forum, Comml. Devel. Mktg. Assn., Product Devel. & Mgmt. Assn., Yale Club (London, N.Y.C.). Home: 8 Sunrise Point River Hills Plantation Lake Wylie SC 29710 Office: Strategic Innovations Internat Inc 12 Executive Ct Lake Wylie SC 29710 E-mail: frederick.buggie.sy.51@aya.yale.edu.

BUGGS, DWAYNE ANDRE, fine arts coordinator, music educator; b. Springhill, La., Sept. 24, 1954; s. Faye Evelyn (Thomas) and Overton Joe Buggs; married. BA, La. Tech U., Ruston, 1975; MusM, So. Ill. U., Edwardsville, 1977. Cert. Lifetime K-12 Vocal Music Mo. Dept. Elem. and Secondary Edn., 1977, La. State Bd. Edn., 1975. Vocal music educator Normandy Sch. Dist., St. Louis, 1977—, k-12 coord. fine arts, 1995—. Music dir. St. James AME Ch., St. Louis, 1977—2002; choral dir. Normandy Sr. HS, St. Louis, 1985—95; organist Cote Brilliante Presbyn. Ch., St. Louis, 2003—; adj. prof. music U. Missouri-St. Louis, St. Louis, 2005—. Dir.: (mshsaa choral, solo and ensemble festiva) Choral and Vocal Competitions (Honor I - Superior Rating, 1995). Vice-chair St. Louis Legend Singers Bd. of Directors, St. Louis, Mo., 2003—05; artist-in-training co-chair Opera Theatre St. Louis Guild Bd., St. Louis, Mo., 2000—05; adv. bd. mem. E. Desmond Lee Fine Arts Collaborative, St. Louis, Mo., 1999—2005; program com. mem. Young Audiences, Inc., St. Louis, Mo., 2003—05. Recipient Outstanding Employee of Yr., Normandy Sr. HS, 1995, Outstanding Svc. award, St. James A.M.E. Ch., 1995, Eminent Educator award, Phi Delta Kappa Sorority, 1999, Apple for the Tchr., Iota Phi Lambda Sorority, 2001; fellow Grad. Minority Fellowship, So. Ill. U., Edwardsville, Ill., 1976, Summer Music Fellow, Northwestern U., Evanston, Ill., 1995. Mem.: Nat. Educators Assn., Urban Music Leadership Conf., Nat. Assn. Negro Musicians, Nat. Art Educators Assn., Assn. Theatre Arts Edn., Am. Choral Directors Assn., Music Educators Nat. Conf. (assoc.), Phi Mu Alpha Sinfonia (life). Home: 5615 Bermuda Dr Saint Louis MO 63121 Office: Normandy Sch Dist 6701 St Charles Rock Rd Saint Louis MO 63133 Office Phone: 314-493-0693. Office Fax: 314-493-0696. Personal E-mail: dwaynebuggs@sbcglobal.net. E-mail: dbuggs@normandy.k12.mo.us.

BUGHER, ROBERT DEAN, professional society administrator; b. Lafayette, Ind., Oct. 17, 1925; s. Walter Earl and Lillie Victoria (Feldner) B.; m. Patricia Jean McConnell, Sept. 7, 1945; children: Vickie Leigh, Robert James. Student, Millsaps Coll., 1943, Miami U., Oxford, Ohio, 1944; BS in Civil Engring, Purdue U., 1948; MPA, U. Mich., 1951. Staff engr. Mich. Mcpl. League, 1948-53; mgr. Mcpl. Purchasing Svc., 1951-53; sec.-treas. Mich. Mcpl. Utilities Assn., 1951-53; asst. dir. Am. Pub. Works Assn., 1953-58, exec. dir., 1958-89, exec. dir. emeritus, 1990—. Lectr. Internat. Seminar on Ekistics, Athens, Greece, 1970; chmn. nat. adv. coun. Keep Am. Beautiful, Inc., 1974-75; chmn. Nat. Conf. on Solid Waste Disposal Sites, Washington, 1971; advisor pub. mgmt. program Northwestern U., 1977-82; bd. dirs. Pub. Adminstrn. Svc., Chgo., 1958-73; trustee Nat. Acad. Code Adminstrs.; chmn. Coun. Internat. Urban Liaison, 1982-84; trustee Nat. Tng. and Devel. Svc., Am. Consortium for Internat. Pub. Adminstrn.; adv. com. internat. divsn. GAO, 1979-80. Editor: pub. works sect. Municipal Yearbook Internat. City Mgmt. Assn., 1953-58, People Making Public Works History-A Century of Progress 1894-1994, 1998; cons. editor pub. works sect., Mcpl. Pub. Works Adminstrn., 1957; chmn. adv. bd. Internat. Ctr. Acad. State and Local Govts., 1985-87. Served to 1st lt. USMCR, 1943-45. Mem. ASCE (life), Am. Pub. Works Assn. (hon.), Internat. Pub. Works Fedn. (treas. 1985-89, sec.-gen. 1990), Am. Soc. Assn. Execs., Am. Soc. Pub. Adminstrn., Internat. Union Local Authorities (pres. U.S. sect. 1977-79, v.p. 1968-70, 75-77), Internat. Solid Wastes and Pub. Cleansing Assn. (v.p. 1968-70), Internat. Fedn. Mcpl. Engrs. (treas. 1976-79), Pub. Works Hist. Soc. (hon., treas. 1975-89), Sigma Alpha Epsilon. Baptist. Office: 2345 Grand Blvd Ste 500 Kansas City MO 64108-2641 Home: 7501 E Thompson Peak Pkwy Unit 124 Scottsdale AZ 85255 Business E-Mail: rdbugher@cox.net.

BUGLIANI, ANN C., international studies educator; b. N.Y.C., Aug. 4, 1942; d. Caesar A. and Ana C. Gonzalez; m. Americo Bugliani, Jan. 1, 1961. BA, DePaul U., 1964; MA, Northwestern U., Evanston, Ill., 1966, PhD, 1973. Asst. prof. Loyola U. Chgo., 1978-82, assoc. prof., 1982-99, prof. modern lang. and lit., 1999—, chair dept. modern langs., lit., 1986-92, dir. Loyola Rome Ctr. of Liberal Arts, 2001—03. Author: Women and the Feminine Principle in the Works of Paul Claudel, 1977, The Instruction of Philosophy and Psychoanalysis by Tragedy, 1998; editor: Chairing the Foreign Language and Literature Department, 1994. Decorated Order of Les Palmes Académiques, French Republic, 1997. Mem. MLA, Assn. Depts. Fgn. Langs. (pres. 1992), Paul Claudel Soc. (pres. 1979-80), Am. Assn. Tchrs. French, Am. Assn. Tchrs. Italian, Association des Membres de L'Ordre des Palmes Academiques. Address: Via Mazzini 3 Pietrasanta Lucca 55045 Italy E-mail: abuglia@luc.edu.

BUGLIARELLO, GEORGE, academic administrator, educator; b. Trieste, Italy, May 20, 1927; arrived in U.S., 1951, naturalized, 1964; s. Federico and Spera (Gefter-Wondrich) B.; m. Virginia Upton Harding, 1960; children: Federico David, Nicholas Luigi. DEng summa cum laude, U. Padua, Italy, 1951; MSCE, U. Minn., 1954; DSc, MIT, 1959; LLD (hon.), Carnegie-Mellon U., 1986, Trinity Coll., 1997; MD (hon.), U. Trieste, 1989; EngD (hon.), Milw. Sch. Engring., 1991; LLD (hon.), Ill. Inst. Tech., 1993, EngD (hon.); LLD (hon.), Pace U., 1994, LHD (hon.); D in Arts and Humane Letters (hon.), Rensselaer Poly. Inst., 2004; DSc (hon.), U. Minn. Rsch. engr. U. Padua, 1951; from rsch. asst. to rsch. assoc. MIT, 1956-59; mem. faculty Carnegie-Mellon U., 1959-69, prof. biotech. and civil engring., 1956-69, chmn. biotechnology program, 1964-69; dean engring. U. Ill. Chgo. Cir., 1969-73; pres. Poly. U., Bklyn., 1973-94, chancellor, 1994—2003, pres. emeritus, Univ. prof., 2003—. Bd. hydraulic cons. U.S. Waterways Exptl. Sta., 1968—74; mem. sci. adv. panel Armed Forces Explosive Safety Bd., 1968—69; mem. biomed tng. engring. com. NIH, 1966—70; mem. commn. edn. Nat. Acad. Engring., 1970—73, chmn. com. ednl. sys., 1970—73, mem. tech. edn. stds. com.; chmn. bd. sci. and tech. for internat. devel. NAS, 1979—83; sci. policy reviewer Portugal OECD, 1982—83, others; U.S. rep. steering com. on sci. for stability program NATO, 1984—97, mem. steering com. on sci. for peace, 1997—2000; chair engring. adv .com. Lawrence Livermore Nat. Lab.; mem. U. Chgo. rev. com. for the decision and info. scis. divsn. Argonne Nat. Lab.; trustee William R. Kenan Jr. Inst. Engring. Tech. and Sci., Paul and Daisy Soros Fellowship for New Ams.; mem. Found. Future Bd. Advisors; bd. dirs. Lord Corp., Comtech. Corp., Keyspan Energy, Symbol Techs., Inc., Jura Corp. Author: The Biosoma-Reflections on the Syntesis of Biology, Society and Machines, 2003; co-author: (book) Computer Systems and Water Resources, 1974, The Impact of Noise Pollution, 1976, Technology, The Community and the University, 1976; editor: Bioengineering--An Engineering View, 1967, Women in Engineering, 1972, The History and Philosophy of Technology, 1979; co-editor: East-West Technology Transfer, 1996, Technology in Society; interim editor-in-chief: The Bridge; contbr. articles to profl. jours. Trustee ANSER, 1974-2000, Teagle Found., Greenwall Found., 1984-2000, Lord Found. N.C., Commn. Ind. Colls. and Universities, 1993-96; bd. visitors Duke U. Sch. Engring., 1975-2000; mem. N.Y. Partnership, 1980—, High Tech. Task Force, 1985-90, chmn., 1988-90, Mayor's Commn. Sci. and Tech., 1984-90, chmn., 1987-90; exec. com. Bd. Trustees Commn. Ind. Colls. and Univs., N.Y., 1986-89; alumni rep. MIT vis. com. for Civil Engring., 1985-91; chair, N.Y.C. Mayor's Task Force on Gramercy Park Steam Pipe Explosion, 1989-90, N.Y.C. Mayor's Adv. Coun. on Devel. of Recycling Markets and Businesses; active Nat. Medal Tech. Nomination Evaluation Com., 1987-92, chmn. 1991-92; chair Nat. Acads. Megacities Project Habitat II Conf.; mem. Nat. Acad. Sci. Com. Human Rights; mem. U.S. Nat. Acads.-Russian Acad. Sci. Com. on Terrorism Confronting the U.S. and Russia. Recipient Alza prize Biomed. Engring. Soc.; NATO sr. fellow Tech. U. Berlin, 1968; N.Y. Mayor's Awd. Excellence Sci. and Tech., 1994, N.Y. Acad. of Scis. Fellow AAAS (chair com. sci., engring. and pub. policy, 1986-89, chair panel on phys. scis. and engring. 1987-89, project 2061 1985-89), Am. Soc. Engring. Edn., ASCE (chmn. exec. com. engring. mechanics divsn. 1971-72, chmn. interdivisional task com. civil engring. in medicine and health care delivery 1969-73, Huber rsch. prize 1967), Am. Inst. Med. and Biol. Engring. (founding fellow); mem. NAE (coun. 1989-93, adv. com. tech. and the environ. 1989-92, internat. affairs adv. com. 1988-92), Internat. Assn. Hydraulic Rsch. (chmn. task com. computer langs. 1969-72), N.Y. Acad. Medicine, Nat. Assn. for Sci., Tech. and Soc. (trustee 1988—, pres. 1989-90, hon. lifetime mem.), Nat. Rsch. Coun. (bd. engring. edn. 1991-96, chair bd. on infrastructure and constructed environ. 1994-97, chair com. on alt. techs. to replace anti-pers. landmines 1999-2000, vice chair com. on army sci. and tech. for homeland def. 2002--, others), N.Y. Acad. Scis. (pres'. coun. 1990—, mem. com. human rights 1996—), Italian Soc. Advancement Sci. (hon. mem.), Sigma Xi (disting. lectr. 1996—, past pres., bd. dirs., chair ethics com.), Nat. Acad. Engring. (chair steering com.on megacities 1999--, Russ prize com. 2000, fgn. sec. 2003-), Marco Polo Soc. (pres. U.S. br.), Italian Nat. Acad. Science. Home: 5 Terrace Dr Port Washington NY 11050-3419 Office: Polytechnic U 6 Metrotech Ctr Brooklyn NY 11201-3840

BUGLIOSI, VINCENT T., lawyer; b. Hibbing, Minn., Aug. 18, 1934; s. Vincent and Ida (Valerie) B.; m. Gail Margaret Talluto, July 21, 1956; children: Wendy Suzanna, Vincent John. BBA, U. Miami, Fla., 1956; LL.B., UCLA, 1964. Bar: Calif. 1964. Dep. dist. atty., Los Angeles County, 1964-72; pvt. practice law Beverly Hills, Calif., 1972—. Prof. criminal law Beverly Sch. Law, Los Angeles, 1968-74 Author: Drugs in America, The Case For Victory, 1991; co-author: Helter-Skelter, The True Story of the Manson Murders, 1974, Till Death Us Do Part; a true murder mystery, 1978, And The Sea Will Tell, 1991, Outrage: How O.J. Simpson Got Away with Murder, 1996, No Island of Sanity: Paula Jones v. Bill Clinton: The Supreme Court on Trial, 1998,The Betrayal of America: How the Supreme Court Undermined the Constitution and Chose Our President, 2001, Candidate for dist. atty., Los Angeles County, 1972, Dem. candidate Calif. atty. gen., 1974. Served to capt. AUS, 1957. Office: 8530 Wilshire Blvd Ste 404 Beverly Hills CA 90211-3127

BUHAGIAR, MARION, editor, writer; b. N.Y.C., Oct. 27, 1932; d. George and Mae (Pietrzak) B.; 1 child, Alexa Ragozin. BA cum laude, Hunter Coll., 1953; postgrad., Mt. Holyoke Coll., 1954. Economist U.S. Dept. Commerce, 1954-57; bus. reporter Time mag., 1957-59; assoc. editor Fortune mag., 1960-73, story devel. editor, 1970-73; text editor Time-Life Books, N.Y.C., 1973-76; v.p. Boardroom Inc., 1977-84; editor Boardroom Reports, 1977-84; exec. editor Bottom Line/Personal, 1980-84; pres. Expert Connections, N.Y.C., 1994—2002; editor Street Smart Investing, 1987-89; ret., 2003. Author: How to Build a College Fund for Your Child, 1989, Battle Plan for American Business, 1992, I-Power, 1992; editor: The Book of Secrets, 1989. Adv. bd. Scientists Inst. for Pub. Info., N.Y.C. Personal E-mail: dorset2@aol.com.

BUHAIN, WILFRIDO JAVIER, medical educator; b. Bacoor, Cavite, Philippines, Oct. 12, 1940; m. Carlota Torres; children: Ronald, Edgar. AA, BS, U. Philippines, 1959, MD, 1964. Diplomate Am. Bd. Internal Medicine, Am. Bd. Pulmonary Diseases. Rsch. fellow in cardiology U. Philippines, Philippine Gen. Hosp., 1964-65; rotating intern Queens Hosp. Ctr., N.Y.C., 1965-66, resident in internal medicine, 1965-68; clin. fellow in pulmonary diseases Hosp. of U. Pa., 1968-69, chief pulmonary function lab. dept. medicine, 1971-72; rsch. fellow in pulmonary diseases Hosp. of U. Pa., VA Hosp., Phila., 1969-71; assoc. in medicine, cardiovascular-pulmonary div. med. dept. U. Pa. Sch. Medicine, 1971-72; assoc. in medicine, dept. medicine Mt. Sinai Sch. Medicine, CUNY, 1972-74; clin. instr. medicine Georgetown U., 1976-95; ret. Chief pulmonary function lab. dept. medicine Mt. Sinai Hosp. Svcs./City Hosp. Ctr. at Elmhurst, 1973-74; med. dir. respiratory therapy dept. Mt. Vernon Hosp., 1978—2003, chmn. dept. medicine, 1987-88, pres. med. staff, 1996-98; mem. exec. com. Alexandria Hosp., 1983; trustee, chmn. med. affairs coun. Inova Health Sys., 1998-99. Contbr. articles to profl. jours. Grantee, Queensborough Soc., Pa. Thoracic Soc. Fellow ACP, Am. Coll. Chest Physicians; mem. Am. Soc. Internal Medicine, Alexandria Med. Soc., Va. Med. Soc., Philippine Med. Assn. (exec. dir., past pres. Metro-Washington), Assn. Philippine Physicians in Am. (v.p.). Avocations: tennis, golf, ballroom dancing. E-mail: wbs1997@cox.net.

BUHL, CYNTHIA MAUREEN, advocate, educator; b. Los Angeles, Apr. 14, 1952; d. Albert Buhl and Dorothy Jane (Loth) Henry. BA, Lewis & Clark Coll., 1974. Dir. Resource and Counseling Ctr., Portland Youth Advs., Oreg., 1971-72; resource coordinator S.E. Youth Service Ctr., Portland Action Coms. Together, 1975-77; sec., asst. Human Rights Office Nat. Council Chs. Christ, N.Y.C., 1977-78; human rights coordinator Coalition for a New Fgn. and Mil. Policy, Washington, 1978-85; cons. Fgn. Policy Edn. Fund, Washington, 1986; nat. adv. bd. Caribbean Basin Info. Project, 1983-85; bd. dirs., legis. dir. Pax Am.'s/Priorities-PAC, 1986-90; legis. dir. Ctrl. Am. Working Group, 1990-93; dir. Indigenous Peoples Program, Bank Info. Ctr., 1994-96; legis. dir. U.S. Rep. James A. McGovern, 1997—. Author: Citizen's Guide to the Multilateral Development Banks and Indigenous Peoples: The World Bank, 1994, Spanish transl., 1995, Bahasa transl., 1996, Russian transl., 1996; co-editor: Central America 1985: Basic Information and Legislative History on U.S.-Central American Relations, 1985. Contbr. articles to various jours., mags. Co-chmn. Human Rights Working Group, Washington, 1978-81, chmn., 1982-85; chmn. Central Am. Lobby Group, 1983-85. Office Phone: 202-225-6101.

BUHLER, JILL LORIE, editor, writer; b. Seattle, Dec. 7, 1945; d. Oscar John and Marcella Jane (Hearing) Younce; 1 child, Lori Jill Moody; m. John Buhler, 1990; stepchildren: Christie Reynolds, Cathie Zatarian, Mike. AA in Gen. Edn., Am. River Coll., 1969; BA in Journalism with honors, Sacramento State U., 1973. Reporter Carmichael (Calif.) Courier, 1968-70; mng. editor Quarter Horse of the Pacific Coast, Sacramento, 1970-75, editor, 1975-84, Golden State Program Jour., 1978, Nat. Reined Cow Horse Assn. News, Sacramento, 1983-88, Pacific Coast Jour., Sacramento, 1984-88, Nat. Snaffle Bit Assn. News, Sacramento, 1988; pres., CEO Comm. Plus, Port Townsend, Wash., 1988—; bd. sec. N.W. Maritime Ctr., 2001—. Mag. cons., 1975—. Interviewer Pres. Ronald Regan, Washington, 1983; mng. editor Wash. Thoroughbred, 1989-90. Mem. 1st profl. communicators mission to USSR, 1988; bd. dirs. Carmichael Winding Way, Pasadena Homeowners Assn., 1985-87; mem. scholarship com. Thoroughbred Horse Racing's United Scholarship Trust; mem. governing bd. Wash. State Hosp. Assn., 1996-2000, mem. legis. policy com., 1999—, hosp. commr. Jefferson Gen. Hosp., 1995—, chair bd. dirs. 1997-2000, sec., 2004; mem. Jefferson County Bd. Health, 1997—, vice chmn., 1998, chmn. 2001; mem. Wash. State Health Care Leadership Com., 2003-. Recipient 1st pl. feature award, 1970, 1st pl. editl. award Jour. Assn. Jr. Colls., 1971, 1st pl. design award WCHB Yuba-Sutter Counties, Marysville, Calif., 1985, Photography awards, 1994, 95, 96. Mem. Am. River Jaycees (Speaking award 1982), Am. Horse Publs. (1st Pl. Editl. award 1983, 86), Port Townsend C. of C. (trustee, v.p. 1993, pres. 1994, officer 1996, 97, 98), Mensa (bd. dirs., asst. local sec., activities dir. 1987-88, membership chair 1988-90), Kiwanis Internat. (chair maj. emphasis program com., treas. 1992—), 5th Wheel Touring Soc. (v.p. 1970). Republican. Roman Catholic. Avocations: sailing, photography. Home: 440 Adelma Beach Rd Port Townsend WA 98368-9280 Office Phone: 360-385-9344. Personal E-mail: jillb@olypen.com.

BUHLER, LESLIE LYNN, museum director; BA in History and Art History with honors, Syracuse U., 1969; postgrad., New Sch. for Social Rsch., 1971, Am. U., 1980. Asst. for cmty. programs Met. Mus. Art, N.Y.C., 1970-72; program coord. resident assoc. program Smithsonian Instn., Washington, 1972-75; instl. devel. officer Nat. Archives and Records Svc., Washington, 1975-78; ind. cons., 1977—85; dir. devel., membership and mktg. Alban Inst., Inc., Bethesda, Md., 1985-88, dir. ops., 1988-89, exec. v.p., 1989-99, acting pres., 1994-95; exec. dir. Tudor Place Hist. House and Garden, Washington, 2000—. Grant reviewer Office of Mus. Programs, NEH, Washington, 1973-74. Bd. dirs. Mus. of City of Washington, 1980-84; vol. advisor Nat. Mus. for Bldg. Arts, Washington, 1977-79. Recipient cert. of appreciation Am. Revolution Bicentennial Adminstrn., 1976. Office: Tudor Place Found 1644 31st St NW Washington DC 20007

BUHLER, LYNN BLEDSOE, lawyer; b. Memphis, Jan. 23, 1949; d. William Stevenson and Betty (Mullins) Bledsoe; m. Jon Milton Buhler, Jan. 22, 1983. Student, Vanderbilt U., 1967-70; BA, U. Memphis, 1972, MA, 1975, JD, 1980. Bar: Tex. 1980, Tenn. 1983. Assoc. Carrington, Coleman, Sloman & Blumethal, Dallas, 1980-82, Borod & Huggins, Memphis, 1983-85; from assoc. to ptnr. Glankler, Brown, PLLC, Memphis, 1985-99, The Buhler Law Firm, Memphis, 1999—. Bd. dirs. Jr. League Memphis, Inc., 1976, 87-89, Project 1st Offender, Memphis, 1976, Memphis Speech & Hearing Ctr., 1976, Runaway House, Memphis 1976. Mem. ABA (bus. law sect., com. on fed. securities regulation 1993—, subcom. on savs. instns. 1986-88, subcom. on syndications 1990-93, subcom. on investment cos. and investment advisers 1993—), Memphis Bar Assn. (chmn. corp. counsel sect. 1994, dir. securities sect. 1997—, chmn. 1999). Episcopalian. Avocation: horseback riding. Office: The Buhler Law Firm 50 N Front St Memphis TN 38103-2126 E-mail: lbuhler@bellsouth.net.

BUHNER, BYRON BEVIS, health science facility administrator; b. Hammond, Ind., Feb. 19, 1950; s. John Colin and Betty (Bevis) B.; children: Zachery Aaron, Rebecca Bevis. AB in Comm., Ind. U., 1976, MS in Human Resource Devel., 1981. Adminstr. Ind. U., Indpls., 1976-77, instr. evaluator sch. nursing, 1981-82; tng. specialist Ayr-Way, Target Stores, Indpls., 1977-81; assoc. exec. dir. Cen. Ind. Regional Blood Ctr., Indpls., 1984-88, pres., chief exec. officer, 1988—; founding mem. Blood Ctrs. Ins. Exch., Risk Retention Group, 1993, chmn. bd. dirs., 1993-96, dir., 1996—; adminstr. Blood Rsch. and Edn. Foundn. of Ind., Inc., Indpls., 1985-89, bd. mem., 1989-94. Mem. dean's adv. coun. Ind. U. Sch. Liberal Arts, 1999—; bd. dirs. Irwin Union Bank & Trust, Hamilton County, 2000—. Producer: Multi-Image film, Focus on Transition, 1981, A Manager's Perspective, 1981; photographer: Sound, Slide program, Wearable - Arts '81. Trustee Coun. Cmty. Blood Ctrs., 1986-97, chmn. purchasing com., 1988-92, chmn. fin. com., treas., 1992-94, v.p., 1994-96, pres., 1997-99, chmn. exec. com., chmn. group svcs. com., chmn. long-range planning com. Mem. Am. Acad. Healthcare Execs. (diplomate), Ind. U. Alumni Assn. (bd. dirs. 1983-88), Am. Assn. Blood Banks, Ind. Assn. Blood Banks (bd. dirs. 1988-91), Kiwanis. Avocations: sailing, jogging, hockey, photography, coaching youth sports. Home: 11350 Idlewood Dr Fishers IN 46038 Office: Cen Ind Regional Blood Ctr 3450 N Meridian St Indianapolis IN 46208-4437 Office Phone: 317-916-5001. Business E-Mail: bbuhner@cirbc.org.

BUHOLTE, AGNESE, library director; b. Ligatne, Cēsis, Latvia, June 5, 1952; d. Jānis Dancis and Rasma (Timermane) Dance; m. Jānis Buholts, Sept. 7, 1974; children: Jānis, Inese. Diploma in lib. scis., U. Latvia, Riga, 1974. Diplomated librarian and bibliographer. Librarian Patent and Tech. Lib. of Latvia, Riga, 1974—75, chief librarian, 1975—76, head methodics dept., 1976—85, dir., 1985—. Mem. Lib. Assn. Latvia (bd. dirs. 1990—), Latvian Academic Lib. Assn. (v.p. 1998—2001, bd.dir. 2002—). Avocations: gardening, sewing, knitting, travel, music. Home: 14 Upes St Apt 11 Riga Latvia LV-1013 Office: Patent and Tech Libr of Latvia Skunu Iela 17 1974 Riga Latvia Fax: (371) 7210767. E-mail: agnese.buholte@patbib.lv.

BUHR, WALTER HEINRICH WILHELM, economics professor; b. Bremen, Germany, Aug. 27, 1938; s. Hans and Elisabeth (Gloatz) B.; m. Inge Elfriede Kaden, Apr. 12, 1967; children: Kerstin, Jan, Henning. Diploma, U. Freiburg, 1961, Dr. rer. pol., 1965; privatdozent, U. Kiel, 1972. Sci. asst. U. Kiel, 1966—72, docent of econs., 1972—73; rsch. assoc. U. Calif., Berkeley, 1968—70; prof. econs. U. Siegen, Germany, 1973—2003, prof. emeritus, 2003—. Co-author: Urban Development Models (in German) 1981; co-editor: Competition among Small Regions, 1978; contbr. articles to profl. jours. Mem. Regional Sci. Assn. Internat., Am. Econ. Assn. Home: Am Schieferberg 9 57074 Siegen Germany Office: U of Siegen Holderlinstr 3 57068 Siegen Germany E-mail: buhr@vwl.wiwi.uni-siegen.de.

BUHRMASTER, ROBERT C., manufacturing executive; b. 1947; B in Mech. Engring., Rensselaer Poly. Inst.; MBA, Dartmouth Coll. With Corning Inc., Corning, N.Y.; exec. v.p. Jostens, Inc., Mpls., 1992-93, pres., COO, 1993, CEO, 1994, chmn. bd. dirs., 1998—. Bd. dirs. Toro Corp., Nat. Alliance of Bus. Pres. Viking coun. Boy Scouts. Am.; past bd. dirs. Exec. Coun. Fgn. Diplomats, Marietta Corp. Mem. U.S. Advanced Ceramics Assn. (founding mem.). Office: 5501 Norman Center Dr Minneapolis MN 55437-1040 Office Fax: 952-897-4116.

BUHROW, WILLIAM CARL, religious organization administrator; b. Cleve., Jan. 18, 1934; s. Philip John and Edith Rose (Leutz) B.; m. Carole Corinne Craven, Feb. 14, 1959; children: William Carl Jr., David Paul, Peter John, Carole Lynn. Diploma, Phila. Coll. Bible, 1954; BA, Wheaton (Ill.) Coll., 1956, MA, 1959. Ordained to ministry Gen. Assn. Regular Bapt. Chs., 1958. Asst. pastor (Hydewood Park Bapt. Ch.), N. Plainfield, N.J., 1959-63; with Continental Fed. Savs. & Loan Assn., Cleve., 1963-81, sr. v.p., 1971-75, pres., chief exec. officer, dir., 1975-81; chmn. bd. Security Savs. Mortgage Corp., Citizens Service Corp., New Market Corp., CFS Service Corp., 1975-81; trustee Credit Bur. Cleve., 1975-81, Bldg. Expositions, Inc., 1974-84; registered rep. IDS/Am. Express, Cleve., 1982-83; gen. credit mgr. Forest City Enterprises, Inc., Cleve., 1983-85; pres. Forest City Ins. Agy., Inc., Cleve., 1983-85; asst. v.p. Mellon Fin. Services Corp., Cleve., 1985-87; exec. adminstr. The Gospel Ho. Ch. and Evangelistic Ctr., Walton Hills, Ohio, 1988—. Trustee Bapt. Bible Coll. and Theol. Sem., Clarks Summit, Pa., 1977-90; vice chmn. bd. deacons Cedar Hill Bapt. Ch., Cleveland Heights, Ohio, 1981-87; trustee, sec. and treas. Gospel House Prison Ministry Found., 1992—. Mem. Christian Bus. Men's Com. Internat., Nat. Assn. Ch. Bus. Adminstrn. Baptist. Home: 1044 Linden Ln Lyndhurst OH 44124-1051 Office: 14707 Alexander Rd Cleveland OH 44146-4924 *The supreme goal of my life is to please and honor the Lord Jesus Christ in all that I say and do. The standards, goals, and ideals outlined in the Bible, God's Holy Word, are the ones which I have adopted for my life. True happiness for me lies in the accomplishment of God's perfect will in my life and that of my family and in introducing others to Christ so they may know Him as their own personal Saviour, too. Herein lies the key to my success as a Christian administrator.*

BUI, KHOI TIEN, college counselor; b. Binh Dinh, Vietnam, Dec. 23, 1937; came to U.S., 1975; naturalized, 1982; s. Luu and Quang Thi (Tran) B.; m. Yen Kim Nguyen, Dec. 7, 1962; children: Khanh, Huy, Huan. BS in Agri., Agrl. Coll., Vietnam, 1962; BS, Law U., Vietnam, 1965; MS, Polit. and Bus. Mgmt. U., Vietnam, 1972, PhD; DLitt (hon.), London Inst. for Applied Rsch., 1991; DE (hon.), World Acad., 1997; PhD (hon.), Inst. Affairs Internat., 1997. With Ministry Agri., Republic of Vietnam, 1962-75; counselor Houston C.C., 1976—, chmn. Indochinese Culture and Refugee Info. Ctr., 1981—. Nat. Planner Tng., Taiwan, 1963, Philippines, 1965, Australia, 1968, Japan, 1970, Thailand, 1971. Author: (poetry books) America My First Feelings, 1981, 20 Poems and 1000 Thoughts, 1994; contbr. to other poetry books, novel and textbook in Vietnamese. Founder, moderator radio sta. The Voice of Free Vietnam, Houston, 1980—; chmn. Indochinese and Refugee Info. Ctr., Houston Community Coll. Decorated knight Order of Templars, officer de l'ordre des Arts et des Lettres; recipient Nat. Lit. prize Republic Vietnam, 1966, Houston's Poet Laureate award, 1984, Golden Poet award World of Poetry, 1985, Edn. award, 1985, Men of Achievement award, 1989, Medal of Honor, 1990, One-in-a-Million Medal, 1991, Most Admired Man of the Decade award, 1992, Twentieth Century award for Achievement, 1992, various medals Govt. of the Republic of Vietnam; named Man of Yr., 1990, Internat. Man of Yr., 1992, Albert Einstein medal, 1996, Literature medal, 1996. Fellow Royal Soc. Lit.; mem. Leadership Houston Assn., Pen Am. Ctr. Avocations: poetry, reading, swimming. Home: 13715 Towne Way Dr Sugar Land TX 77478-1652 Office: Houston CC 1300 Holman St Houston TX 77004-3834 E-mail: buihuyluc@hotmail.com.

BUIS, DIANNA LOVINS, elementary education educator, guidance counselor; b. Blanchester, Ohio, Jan. 23, 1961; d. Dean Edward and Mary Gethaline (Hyden) Lovins; m. Douglas Edward Buis, Sept. 2, 1983; children: Shaun Douglas, Cristopher Michael. AD in Fine Arts, Somerset (Ky.) C.C., 1980; B in Elem. Edn., U. Ky., 1983; M in Elem. Counseling, Ea. Ky. U., Richmond, 1991, postgrad., 1993. Cert. elem. guidance counselor, Ky.; rank I endorsement for individual intellectual assessment Ea. Ky. U. Tchr. Waynesburg Elem. Sch., Ky., 1982-91; elem. guidance counselor Lincoln County Bd. Edn., Stanford, Ky., 1991—2000; tchr. Eubank Elem. Sch., Eubank, Ky., 2001—; employed Pulaski County Bd. of Ed., Somerset, Ky. Asst. coach Acad. Team, Waynesburg, 1983-85; trainer, counselor-on-call Project XL-Summer Sch., Stanford, 1994; coach Olympics of the Mind, Waynesburg, 1984; individual intelligence assessment, counselor Lincoln County Sch. Sys., 1993-2000. Youth group leader for Mid./HS; youth group leader, membership com. chair Christian Ch. Mem. Ky. Assn. Sch. Adminstrn., Ctrl. Ky. Counseling Assn., Ky. Coun. on Adminstrs. of Spl. Edn., mem. Ky. Ed. Assoc., 2001-pres., Profl. Assn. Diving Instrs. Scuba Divers. Mem. Christian Ch. (Disciples Of Christ). Home: 12095 N Highway 1247 Eubank KY 42567-9005 Office Phone: 606-379-2712. Personal E-mail: dscbuis@aol.com.

BUISHAS, KRISTIN MAUREEN, elementary school educator; b. Harvey, Ill., Jan. 1, 1980; d. John Martin and Mary Louise Buishas. BA, Ea. Ill. U., 2002. Cert. elem. educator Ill., 2003. Educator St. Kieran, Chgo. Heights, Ill., 2003—. Recipient Spl. Edn. Achievement award, Ea. Ill. U., 1999. Mem.: Assn. Supervision and Curriculum Devel. (assoc.). Office: St Kieran School 700 W 195th St Chicago Heights IL 60411 Office Phone: 708-754-8999. Personal E-mail: kbuishas@hotmail.com.

BUISSONNIÈRE, MARINE, international organization administrator; physician; Korea rep. Doctors Without Borders/Médecins Sans Frontières, now sec. gen. Office: Doctors Without Borders 2nd Floor 333 7th Ave New York NY 10001-5004

BUIST, NEIL ROBERTSON MACKENZIE, pediatric educator, medical association administrator; b. Karachi, India, July 11, 1932; m. Sonia Chapman; children: Catriona, Alison, Diana. Degree with commendation, U. St. Andrews, Scotland, MB, ChB, 1956; Diploma of Child Health, London U., England, 1960. Diplomate Am. Bd. Med. Genetics, Am. Bd. Clinical Genetics. House physician internal medicine Arbroath Infirmary, 1956-57; house physician externe cardiopulmonary dept. Hosp. Marie Lannelongue, Paris, 1957; house surgeon Royal Hosp. Sick Children, Edinburgh, Scotland, 1957; commd. far east med. officer Regimental Military Svc., 1957-60; house physician Royal Infirmary, Dundee, Scotland, 1960; registrar internal medicine Maryfield Hosp., Dundee, Scotland, 1960-62; lectr. child health U. St. Andrews, Dundee, Scotland, 1962-64; rsch. fellow pediatric micro-chemistry, Sch. Health Sci. U. Colo., Denver, 1964-66; asst. prof. pediatrics, Sch. Medicine U. Oreg., Portland, 1966-70; dir. Pediatrics Metabolic Lab, Oreg. Health Sci. U., Portland, 1966-93, Metabolic Birth Defects Ctr., Oreg. Health Sci. U., Portland, 1966-98; assoc. prof. pediat. and med. genetics Oreg. Health Sci. U., Portland, 1970—76, prof. pediat. and med. genetics, 1976—98, prof. emeritus. Med. cons. Northwest Regional Newborn Screening Program, Portland, 1970—; vis. prof. WHO, China, 1988, U. Colo., 1990, Wesley Med. Ctr., Kans., 1991, Phoenix Children's Hosp., Ariz., 1991, Tucson Med. Ctr., Ariz., 1991, U. Ill., Chgo., 1991, Kapoiolani Med. Ctr., Hawaii, 1992, Shriners Hosp. for Crippled Children., Hawaii, 1992, Ark. Children's Hosp., 1993, Australasian Soc. for Human Genetics, New Zealand, 1994, LBJ Med. Ctr., Americas Samoa, 1994, Mahidol U., Bangkok, 1996, U. P.R., 1996, U. Auckland (New Zealand), 1997, Ctrl. Valley Children's Hosp., 1996-, U. Rochester, 2004, emergency disaster response physician, N.W. Med. Teams Internat., Afghanistan, 2002, Ethiopia, 2004, Sri Lanka, 2005. Author: (with others) Textbook of Pediatrics, 1973, Inherited Disorders of Amino Acid Metabolism, 1974, 1985, Clinics in Endocrinolog and Metabolism: Aspects of Neonatal Metabolism, 1976, Textbook of Pediatrics, 1978, Practice of Pediatrics, 1980, Management of High-Risk Pregnancy, 1980, Current Occular Therapy, 1980, Practice of Pediatrics, 1981, Clinics in Endocrinology and Metabolism: Aspects of Neonatal Metabolism, 1981, Textbook of Pediatrics, 1984, Disorders of Fatty Acid Metabolism in the Pediatric Practice, 1990, Birth Defects Encyclopedia, 1990, 1991, Treatment of Genetic Disease, 1991, Pediatric Clinics of North Americs Medical Genetics II, 1992, Forfar & Arneil's Textbook of Paediatrics, 1992, 97, Galactosemia New Frontiers in Research, 1993, New Horizons in Neonatal Screening, 1994, New Trends in Neonatal Screening, 1994, Alpha-1-Antitrypsin Deficiency, 1994, Diseases of the Fetus and Newborn, 1995, Inborn Metabolic Diseases: Diagnosis and Treatment, 1995; cons. editor: Inborn Metabolic Disease Text, 1995; editorial bd. mem.: Jour. of Inherited Metabolic Diseases, 1977—, Kelley Practice of Pediatrics, 1980-87, Screening, 1991-96; jour. reviewer: Am. Jour. of Human Genetics, Jour. of Pediatrics, Pediatric Rsch., Screening. Adv. com. Tri County March of Dimes, Portland, 1977—; physician Diabetic Children's Camp, 1967—. Muscle Biopsy Clinic Shriners Hosp., 1989—; bd. dirs. Mize Info. Enterprises, Dallas, 1987—. Fellow Royal Coll. Physicians Edinburgh, Fogarty Internat. Vis. Scientist, Royal Coll. Physicians Edinburgh; mem. Brit. Med. Assn., Western Soc. Pediatric Rsch. (coun. mem. 1966—), Pacific North West Pediatric Soc., Am. Pediatric Soc., Soc. for the Study of Inborn Errors of Metabolism, Soc. for Inherited Metabolic Disorders (treas. 1977-2000, pres. 2000-02), Oreg. Pediatric Soc., Oreg. Diabetes Assn., Portland Acad. Pediatrics, Internat. Newborn Screening Soc. Coun. (founding mem. 1988—). Avocations: fishing, gardening, travel. Personal E-mail: buistnrm@aol.com.

BUIST, RICHARDSON, retired corporate executive, retired banker; b. Bklyn., Aug. 8, 1921; s. George Lamb and Adelaide (Richardson) Buist; m. Jean Mackerley, Oct. 2, 1948; children: Peter Richardson, Jean Morford Buist Earle, M. Betsi Bixby. Student, Yale U. Advt. copywriter Ecloss Co., Sparta, NJ, 1946-48; advt. mgr. Sussex County Ind., Newton, NJ, 1948-50, Dover (N.J.) Advance, 1950-53; bus. mgr. N.J. Herald, Inc., Newton, 1953-70, dir., v.p., 1958-70, pub., 1967-70; dir. N.J. Press Assn., 1966-70; asst. sec., asst. treas. Morford Conservation Co., Hamburg, 1965-72, pres., 1986-95, v.p., 1995-2000, dir. emeritus, 2000—. Trust officer Midlantic Nat. Bank/Sussex & Mchts., Newton, 1971—88, Midlantic Nat. Bank, Edison, NJ, 1972—86, cons., 1986—90; dir. Newton Cemetery Co., 1989—2000, v.p., 1998—2000. Chmn. pub. rels. Morris-Sussex area coun. Boys Scouts Am., 1955—75; trustee Sussex County Music Found., 1955—75, pres., 1959—61; pres. Sussex County chpt. Am. Cancer Soc., 1956—58; mem. Morris-Sussex Area Health Facilities Planning Coun., 1965—68; v.p. Sussex County Coun. Arts, 1971—73; v.p., chmn. fin. devel. com. Newton Meml. Hosp., 1966—68, bd. govs., 1993—95, pres. bd. govs., 1968—71, chmn., 1971—73, emeritus, 1995—; founding incorporator, trustee NW Jersey Health Care, 1971—76; trustee, mem. exec. com. regional health planning coun. Health Sys. Agy., 1976—83, 1984—87, v.p., 1978—79; trustee United Way Sussex County, 1984—90, spl. gifts chmn., 1984—88, mem. allocations com., 1990—93; mem. Sussex County Arts and Heritage Coun., chmn. hist. house tour, 1993—95; mem. steering com. N.J. Highlands Coalition, 1993—; dir. N. Jersey Health Care Corp., 1988—95, asst. treas., 1991—93, dir. emeritus, 1995—; dir. Prime Care, Inc., 1989—95, chmn. bd. trustees, 1989—92. Mem.: Am. Vet. Med. Soc. Aux. (nat. chmn. legis. com. 1986—88, mem. long-range planning com. 1990—95, chmn. 1992, mem. constn. by-laws com. 1993—95), N.J. Vet. Med. Soc. Aux. (del. 1979—82, 1988—91, 2d v.p. 1990—91), Vernon Civic Assn. (dir. 1996—2000, v.p. 1997—98), Rotary (pres. 1967—68, Paul Harris fellow 1988, Above Self award 1993, Meritorious Svc. award 1998). Home: 4123 Fellowship Rd Basking Ridge NJ 07920

BUJA, L. MAXIMILIAN, pathologist, academic administrator, educator; b. New Orleans, Dec. 30, 1942; s. Louis Marcus and Fay Maxine (Kofler) B.; m. Donna Steele Kinney, Apr. 7, 1966; children: Maximilian Kinney, Evan Louis, Gregory James. BS in Biology magna cum laude, Loyola U., New Orleans, 1964; MD with honors, Tulane U., 1967, MS in Anatomy, 1968. Diplomate Am. Bd. Pathology. Resident in pathology Nat. Cancer Inst./NIH, Bethesda, Md., 1970—72; sr. investigator pathology Nat. Heart and Lung Inst./NIH, Bethesda, Md., 1972—74; asst. prof. pathology U. Tex. Health Sci. Ctr. at Dallas, 1974—77, assoc. prof. pathology, 1977—81; prof. pathology U. Tex. Southwestern Med. Ctr. at Dallas, 1981—89, acting chmn. dept. pathology, 1988—89; prof. pathology and lab. medicine U. Tex. Health Sci. Ctr. at Houston, 1989—, chmn. dept. pathology and lab. medicine, 1989—96; chmn. dept. clin. lab. scis. U. Tex.-Houston Health Sci. Ctr., 1993—96, disting. chair pathology and lab. med., 1995—, dean, 1996—2003, exec. v.p. acad. affairs, 2003—, H. Wayne Hightower disting. prof. in med. scis., 2000—04; chief of svc. clin. pathology lab. Hermann Hosp., Houston, 1989—96; pathologist-in-chief clin. pathology lab. Lyndon Baines Johnson Gen. Hosp., Houston, 1990—96; prof. lab. medicine U. Tex. Anderson Cancer Ctr., Houston, 1990—. Lectr. pathology; mem. autopsy svc.; mem. Tex. Heart Inst. St. Luke's Episcopal Hosp., Houston, 1989—, dir. Cardiovascular Pathology Rsch., 1989—95, chief cardiovasc. pathology, 2000—; 1st Chancellor's Health fellow in edn. U. Tex. System; cons. in field. Author (with Hillis and Willerson): Ischemic Heart Disease-Clinical and Pathophysiological Aspects, 1982; author: (with others) Calcium Antagonists and Cardiovascular Disease, 1984; author: Physiology and Pathophysiology of the Heart, 1984, Cardiovascular Imaging, 1991, Cardiovascular Medicine, 1995; contbg. editor: Clin. Nuc. Cardiology, 1979; mem. editl. bd. Am. Jour. Cardiovascular Pathology, 1985—95, Am. Jour. Cardiology, 1982—88, 1999—, Am. Jour. Pathology, 1980—92, Archives of Pathology and Lab. Medicine, 1985—96, Cardiovascular Pathology, 1991—, Circulation, 1983—88, Circulation Rsch., 1990—99, Lab. Investigation, 1984—, Tex. Medicine, 1984—87, Exptl. Molecular Pathology, 1999—, Jour. Am. Coll. Cardiology, 2000—04, Jour. Burns, 2001; assoc. editor: Circulation, 1993—2004; contbr. articles to profl. jours. Surgeon with USPHS, 1968-74. Recipient Joseph Diaz award Loyola U., Order of the Gold-Tipped Stethoscope award Tulane U., John Herr Musser Meml. prize; Sabbatical fellow German Sci. Found., U. Cologne, West Germany, 1988; grantee NIH, 1979, 80, 81, 84, 86-87, 89-90, 93-98, U. Tex., 1993—. Fellow: AAAS, Internat. Soc. for Heart Rsch., Am. Heart Assn. (fellow coun. on basic sci. on clin. cardiology, on atherosclerosis, on circulation, inaugural fellow basic cardiovasc. scis.), Am. Coll. Cardiology; mem.: AMA, U.S. and Can. Acad. Pathology, Tex. Soc. Microscopy, So. Soc. for Clin. Investigation, Soc. Exec. Leadership in Acad. Medicine, Histochem. Soc., Assn. Am. Med. Colls. (coun. deans 1996—2003), Am. Soc. Clin. Pathologists, Am. Soc. Clin. Investigation, Tex. Soc. Pathologists (pres. 1998, George T. Caldwell, M.D. Disting. Svc. award 2005), Tex. Med. Assn., Soc. Cardiovasc. Pathology (Merit award 1998), Internat. Acad. Pathology, Houston Soc. Clin. Pathologists (pres. 1995—96, Harlan J. Spjut award 1997), Harris County Med. Soc. (bd. dirs. 1997—), Coll. Am. Pathologists, Am. Soc. Cell Biology, Am. Fedn. Med. Rsch., Am. Coll. Healthcare Execs. (assoc.), ACP Execs., Am. Soc. Investigative Pathology, Houston Philos. Soc., Sigma Xi Sci., Beta Beta Beta, Alpha Omega Alpha. Achievements include rsch. on cardiovascular pathology; on mechanisms of cell injury, with emphasis on cell membrane integrity and intracellular electrolyte balance; on measurement of intracellular electrolytes, electron probe x-ray microanalysis and fluorescent probes; on the devel. and regenerative potential of cardiac muscle. Office: U Tex Health Sci Ctr 7000 Fannin St Ste 1715 Houston TX 77030-1501

BUJAKE, JOHN EDWARD, JR., beverage company executive; b. N.Y.C., May 23, 1933; s. John E. and Mary (Muzyka) B.; m. Gail E. Cruise, Aug. 1, 1964; children: John Edward III, Laura, Jacquelyn, William. BS, Manhattan Coll., 1954; MS, Holy Cross Coll., 1955; PhD, Columbia U., 1959; MBA, NYU, 1963. Rsch. assoc. Lever Bros., Edgewater, N.J., 1959-68; dir. R & D Foods div. Coca Cola Co., Houston, 1968-72; dir. foods R&D, Quaker Oats Co., Barrington, Ill., 1972-77, dir. R&D, 1977-78; v.p. R&D, Seven Up Co., St. Louis, 1978-87; v.p. R&D Brown-Forman Beverage Co., Louisville, 1987-98; cons., 1998—. Indsl. adv. bd. Speed Sch., U. Louisville. Mem. editl. bd. Research Mgmt, 1976-77, 97-98; contbr. articles to profl. jours. Mem. Indsl. Rsch. Inst., Am. Chem. Soc., Inst. Food Technologists, Internat. Life Scis. Inst., Calorie Control Coun. Home and Office: 5805 Round Hill Rd Louisville KY 40222-5954

BUJESE, DAVID M., diversified financial services company executive, director, accountant; b. Saddle Brook, NJ, Oct. 14, 1964; s. David P and Jean (Viglone) Bujese; m. Kathleen McNabb, Apr. 6, 1991; children: Courtney, Kyle, Nathan. BS in Acctg., Rutgers U., 1987; MBA, Boston U., 2001. CPA Conn., 1990, NJ, 1990. Audit mgr. Ernst & Young, Hartford, Conn., 1988—93; asst v.p. and contr. Conn. Surety Corp., Hartford, Conn., 1993—97; v.p., CFO Ergomedics, Inc., Burlington, Vt., 1996—97, Anocoil Corp., Rockville, Conn., 1997—2004, pres., COO, CFO, 2004—. Dir., pres. New Seasons, Inc., Manchester, Conn., 2001—. Mem.: AICPA, Conn. Soc. CPAs. Avocations: skiing, golf, carpentry. Office: Anocoil Corp PO Box 1318 60 E Main St Rockville CT 06066 Office Phone: 860-871-1200. Personal E-mail: bujese@yahoo.com. E-mail: dbujese@anocoil.com.

BUJOLD, LOIS MCMASTER, writer; b. Columbus, Ohio, Nov. 2, 1949; d. Robert Charles and Laura Elizabeth (Gerould) McMaster; m. John Fredric Bujold, Oct. 9, 1971 (div. Dec. 1992); children: Anne Elizabeth, Paul Andre. Author: (novels) Shards of Honor, 1986, The Warrior's Apprentice, 1986, Ethan of Athos, 1986, Falling Free, 1988 (Nebula award, 1989), Brothers in Arms, 1989, Borders of Infinity, 1989, The Vor Game, 1990 (Hugo award, 1991), Barrayar, 1991 (Hugo award, 1992, 1st place Locus poll, 1992), Mirror Dance, 1994 (Hugo & Locus awards, 1995), Cetaganda, 1996, Memory, 1996, Komarr, 1998 (Minn. book award, 1999), A Civil Campaign, 1999, The Curse of Chalion, 2001 (Mythopoeic award, 2002), Diplomatic Immunity, 2002, Paladin of Souls, 2003 (Hugo award, 2004, Locus award, 2004, Nebula award, 2005), The Hallowed Hunt, 2005, (novellas) The Borders of Infinity, 1987, The Mountains of Mourning, 1989 (Nebula and Hugo awards, 1990), Labyrinth, 1989 (Best Novella/Novelette Analytical Lab., 1990), Weatherman, 1990 (Best Novella Analytical Lab., 1991), Winterfair Gifts, 2004; contbr. short stories to sci. fiction mags., articles to profl. jours. Mem.: Novelists, Inc., Sci. Fiction and Fantasy Writers Am. Office: Spectrum Literary Agency 320 Central Park W Ste 1D New York NY 10025-7659 Personal E-mail: lois@dendarii.com.

BUJON DE L'ESTANG, FRANCOIS, bank executive; b. Neuilly sur Seine, France, 1940; m. Anne de Margerie; four children. Grad., Inst. Politique Paris, Ecole Nat. Adminstrn., Harvard U. Joined Ministry Fgn. Affairs, 1966, staff mem. office of the permanent sec., 1966-69, spl. advisor, dep. to pres. diplomatic advisor, 1969-73, from second to first sec. French Embassy in the U.S., 1973-75, first sec., second counselor French Embassy in London, 1975-78; advisor on internat. affairs to del. gen. for energy Ministry Industry, Paris, 1978-80; dir. internat. rels. Atomic Energy Commissariat, 1980-81; chief of staff Min. Industry, 1980—81; creator, pres., CEO COGEMA, Inc., Washington, 1982—86; sr. advisor for diplomatic affairs, def. and cooperation French Prime Min., 1986—88; amb. of France to Can. French Govt., 1989—91; sr. v.p. Compagnie de Navigation Mixte and Via Banque, Paris, 1991—92; chmn., CEO S.F.I.M., 1992; founder FBE Internat. Cons., 1992-95; amb. of France to the U.S. Washington, 1995—2002; chmn. Citigroup France, Paris, 2003—. French rep. bd. govs. Internat. Atomic Energy Agy., 1979-80; bd. dirs. Inst. Francais des Rels. Internat., Inst. Pasteur, French Space Agy., Thales. Mem. editl. bd. Revue des Deux Mondes. Pres. Harvard Bus. Sch. Club France, 1991-95. Named Officer Order of the Legion of Honor, Officer of the Nat. Order of Merit. Office: Citigroup France Office Chmn 25 rue Balzac 75008 Paris France

BUKER, ROBERT HUTCHINSON, SR., army officer, thoracic surgeon; b. Loi Mwe, Kengtung, Burma, Dec. 6, 1928; came to U.S., 1940; s. Richard S. and Minola (Hutchinson) B.; m. Ethel Hunt, Sept. 25, 1949; children: Robert Hutchinson, Traci, Nina Ruth. AB, Boston U., 1949; MS, U. Maine, 1952; MD, Columbia U., 1956; postgrad., Indsl. Coll. of Armed Forces, 1978-79. Diplomate: Am. Bd. Surgery, Am. Bd. Thoracic Surgeons. Intern Gorgas Hosp, C.Z., 1956-57; gen. surg. residency Gorgas Hosp., C.Z., 1957-60; resident in thoracic surgery Kennedy V.A. Hosp., 1962-64, Tenn. Med. Ctr., 1962-64; capt. U.S. Army, 1964, advanced through grades to maj. gen.; chief surg. cons. Pentagon, Washington, 1973-76; comdr. U.S. Army Hosp., Wuerzburg, Germany, 1976-78; dep. chief staff opns. Health Services Command, Fort Sam Houston, Tex., 1979-80; comdr. Gen. Leonard Wood

Army Hosp., Ft. Leonard Wood, Mo., 1980-81; commdr. Acad. Health Scis., Ft. Sam Houston, 1981-83; commdg. gen. Brooke Army Med. Center, Ft. Sam Houston, 1983-85; dep. Surgeon Gen. U.S. Army, Washington, 1985-89; chief surg. svcs. S.E. Kaiser-Permanente Med. Group, Atlanta, 1989-91. Chief legal medicine and risk mgmt. Kaiser-Permanente Med. Group, Atlanta, 1991-94; clin. prof. surgery Uniform U. Health Scis., Bethesda, Md., 1981—. Fellow ACS (bd. govs. 1987-89), Am. Coll. Chest Physicians, Am. Coll. Physician Execs.; mem. AMA, Soc. Thoracic Surgeons, So. Thoracic Surg. Assn., Am. Acad. Med. Dirs. Baptist. E-mail: mgrbuker@att.net.

BUKH, JENS, medical researcher; b. Flade, Mors, Denmark, Apr. 10, 1960; s. Niels and Inger Marie Bukh; m. Abelone Marup Bukh, July 3, 1994; children: Clara, Niels Johan. MD, U. Copenhagen, 1989. Attending physician U. Hosp. of Copenhagen, Copenhagen, Denmark, 1989—90; rsch. investigator NIH, Bethesda, Md., 1990—. Mem. editl. bd.: Hepatology, Jour. Clinical Microbiology; contbr. chapters to books, articles to profl. jours. Pvt. Danish Army, 1979—80. Recipient Achievement award, NIAID, 2004. Mem.: Am. Assn. Study of Liver Disease. Achievements include research in field of hepatitis C virus and related viruses. Office: NIH Bldg 50 Rm 6529 S Dr Bethesda MD 20892-8009 Office Phone: 301-594-2311. E-mail: jbukh@niaid.nih.gov.

BUKOVAC, MARTIN JOHN, horticulturist, educator; b. Johnston City, Ill., Nov. 12, 1929; s. John and Sadie (Fak) B.; m. Judith Ann Kelley, Sept. 5, 1956; 1 dau., Janice Louise. BS with honors, Mich. State U., 1951, MS, 1954, PhD, 1957; D honoris causa, U. Bonn, Germany, 1995. Asst. prof. horticulture Mich. State U., East Lansing, 1957-61, assoc. prof., 1961-63, prof., 1963; NSF sr. postdoctoral fellow Oxford U., U. Bristol, Eng., 1965-66; univ. disting. prof., 1992—. Vis. lectr. Japan Atomic Energy Rsch. Inst., 1958; adviser IAEA, Vienna, 1961; NAS exch. lectr. Coun. Acads., Yugoslavia, 1971; vis. scholar Va. Poly. Inst., Blacksburg, 1973; guest lectr. Polish Acad. Scis., 1974; disting. vis. prof. N.Mex. State U., 1976; vis. prof. Japan Soc. Promotion Sci., Osaka Prefecture U., 1977; guest lectr. Serbian Sci. Coun., Fruit Rsch. Inst., Cacak, Yugoslavia, 1979; John A. Hannah Disting. lectr. Mich. State Hort. Soc., 1980; vis. prof. U. Guelph, Ont., Can., 1982, Ohio State U., 1982, U. Zagreb, Yugoslavia, 1983, Ohio State U., 1990; collaborator Agrl. Rsch. Svc. USDA, 1982-2003; guest rschr. Hort. Rsch. Inst., Budapest, Hungary, 1983, Inst. Obstbau und Gemusebau U. Bonn, Fed. Republic Germany, 1986; Batjer Meml. lectr. Wash. State Hort. Soc., 1985; mem. agrl. rsch. adv. com. Eli Lilly Co., Indpls., 1971-88; cons. Dept. Agr.; disting. lectr. Dept. Sci. and Tech. Peoples Republic China, 1984; commencement spkr. Mich. State U., 1986; mem. internat. adv. bd. divsn. life scis. Ctr. for Nuclear Studies, Atomic Energy Commn., Grenoble, France, 1993-2000; Monselise Meml. lectr. Hebrew U., 1994; Agrl. Rsch. Svc. B.Y. Morrison Meml. lectr., 1994, Kermit Olson Meml. lectr. Univ. Minn., 1997; pres. Martin J. Bukovac Inc., 1996-2001; Donald L. Reichard Meml. lectr., Ohio State U., 1999; sci. exch. lectr. Nara (Japan) Inst. Sci. and Tech., 2000. Mem. exec. adv. bd. Ency. of Agrl. Scis., 1991-96; mem. editl. adv. bd. Ctr. for Agr. and Bioscis. Internat., 1989-2003; internat. editl. bd. Horticultural Sci., Budapest; mem. editl. bd. Ency. of Agrl. Sci., 1991-96. Pres. Okemos Music Patrons, Mich., 1973-74; bd. dirs. Mich. State U. Press, 1983-92. 1st lt. U.S. Army, 1951-53. Recipient citation meritorious rsch. Am. Hort. Soc., 1970, Disting. Faculty award Mich. State U., 1971, Disting. Svc. award Mich. Hort. Soc., 1974, Disting. Faculty award Mich. Assn. Governing Bds., 1986, Hatch Meml. Medallion award USDA, 1987, Industry Man of Yr. award Nat. Cherry Festival, 1987, Alexander von Humboldt Rsch. prize, 1995, Am. Soc. Agrl. Engrng. Outstanding Paper award, 1995, Gold Veitch Meml. medal Royal Hort. Soc., 2003, Spiridon Brusina medal Croatian Soc. for Natural Scis., 2004; Bukovac Disting. Lectr. established in his honor Mich. State Hort. Soc., 1995. Fellow AAAS, Am. Soc. Hort. Sci. (hon. life, pres. 1974-75, Joseph Harvey Gourley award 1969, 76, Marion Meadows award 1975, citation of appreciation 1975, Carroll R. Miller award 1980, Outstanding Rschr. award 1988, M.A. Blake award for disting. grad. tchg. 1975, Hall of Fame inductee 2001); mem. NAS, Am. Chem. Soc., Am. Soc. Plant Biologists (Dennis R. Hoagland award 1988), Bot. Soc. Am., Scandinavian Soc. Plant Physiologists, Japanese Soc. Plant Physiologists, Internat. Soc. Hort. Sci., Soc. Exptl. Biology, Croatian Soc. Plant Physiologists (hon.), Mich. State U. Faculty Club, Sigma Xi (pres. 1978-79 rsch. award Kedzie chpt.), Phi Kappa Phi, Gamma Sigma Delta. Home: 4428 Seneca Dr Okemos MI 48864-2946 Office: Mich State U Dept Horticulture East Lansing MI 48824 Business E-Mail: bukovacm@msu.edu.

BUKOWSKI, MARIE DIANE, artist, educator; b. Bethel Park, Pa., Sept. 21, 1970; BFA, Carnegie Mellon U., 1992; MFA, U. Pa., 2000; Cert., Jagiellonian U., Krakow, Poland, 1999. Asst. prof. art La. Tech U., Ruston, 2000—, grad. coord., 2004—. Artist-in-residence Frans Masereel Ctr., Belgium, Anchor Graphics, Chgo., Bastille, Netherlands, Tamarind Inst., Albuquerque; vis. artist, Sofia, Bulgaria. Exhibition, Trace #29 (Merit Award, 2005), Cage #3 (Prize of the Internat., 2004). Artist Mini grantee, La. Divsn. of the Arts, 2001—05, Summer Rsch. grantee, La. Tech U., 2002—04, Individual Artist grantee, Nat. Endowment for the Arts, 2003, U. Faculty fellow, La. Tech U., 2005. Mem.: Southeastern Coll. Art Conf. (assoc.), So. Graphics Coun. (assoc.), Eye Twenty Group (assoc.), Internat. Print Soc. (assoc.). Avocations: travel, reading, mathematics. Office: Louisiana Tech University School of Art PO Box 3175 Ruston LA 71272 Office Phone: 318-257-3264. Business E-Mail: bukowski@latech.edu.

BUKRY, JOHN DAVID, geologist; b. Balt., May 17, 1941; s. Howard Leroy and Irene Evelyn (Davis) Snyder. Student, Colo. Sch. Mines, 1959—60; BA, Johns Hopkins U., 1963; MA, Princeton U., 1965, PhD, 1967; postgrad., U. Ill., 1965—66, De Anza Coll., 1995—96. Geologist U.S. Army Corps Engrs., Balt., 1963; rsch. asst. Mobil Oil Co., Dallas, 1965; geologist U.S. Geol. Survey, La Jolla, Calif., 1967-84, scientist emeritus, 1996-98; geologist U.S. Minerals Mgmt. Svc., La Jolla, 1984-86, U.S. Geol. Survey, Menlo Park, Calif., 1986-96, scientist emeritus, 1998—; rsch. assoc. Geol. Rsch. Divsn. Scripps Instn. Oceanography-U. Calif., San Diego, 1970—2003. Cons. Deep Sea Drilling Project, La Jolla, 1967-87; lectr. Vetlesen Symposium, Columbia U., NYC, 1968, 3d Internat. Planktonic Conf., Kiel, Germany, 1974, Brit. Petroleum Exploration Seminar on nannoplankton biostratigraphy, Houston, 1989; shipboard micropaleontologist on D/V Glomar Challenger, 5 Deep Sea Drilling Project cruises, 1968-78; mem. stratigraphic correlations bd. NSF/Joint Oceanog. Instns. for Deep Earth Sampling, 1976-79; vis. scholar U. Calif., 2003-. Author: Leg I of the Cruises of the Drilling Vessel Glomar Challenger, 1969, Coccoliths from Texas and Europe, 1969, Leg LXIII of the Cruises of the Drilling Vessel Glomar Challenger, 1981; editor: Marine Micropaleontology, 1976-83, mem. editl. bd. Micropaleontology, 1985-90. Mobil Oil, Princeton U. fellow, 1965-67; Am. Chem. Soc., Princeton U. fellow, 1966-67. Fellow AAAS, Geol. Soc. Am., Explorers Club; mem. NSTA, Hawaiian Malacological Soc., Paleontol. Rsch. Inst., Am. Assn. Petroleum Geologists, Mars Soc., Planetary Soc., Soc. Econ. Paleontologists and Mineralogists, Internat. Nannoplankton Assn., Ecol. Soc. Am., European Union Geoscis., Oceanography Soc., U. Calif.-San Diego Ida and Cecil Green Faculty Club, San Diego Shell Club, Princeton Club No. Calif., Sigma Xi. Achievements include research in stratigraphy, paleoecology and taxonomy for 300 new species of marine nannoplankton used in ocean history studies; new study of Holocene global climate change showing Medieval Warm and Little Ice Age in nannoplankton cored in the Gulf of California. Avocations: basketball, photography, shell and mineral collecting. Office: US Geol Survey MS-910 345 Middlefield Rd Menlo Park CA 94025-3591 E-mail: dbukry@usgs.gov.

BUKTA, POLLY, state representative; b. Greenville, Pa., Apr. 3, 1937; m. Michael Bukta. BS, Mercyhurst Coll., 1962; postgrad., U. No. Iowa, 1967. Elem. tchr., Clinton, Iowa, 1967—2000; ret., 2000—; mem. Iowa Ho. Reps., DesMoines, 1997—, mem. various coms. adminstrn. and rules, edn. and transp., asst. minority leader, 2001—02, 2003—04, 2005—. Mem.: NEA, NACCP, AAUW, Clinton Area C. of C., Clinton Edn. Assn., Iowa State Tchrs. Assn., Clinton Womens Club, Delta Kappa Gamma. Democrat. Office: State Capitol East 12th and Grand Des Moines IA 50319 also: 604 S 32nd St Clinton IA 52732 Office Phone: 515-281-7331. Personal E-mail: pollyb03@msn.com.

BULAND, JOSHUA I., academic administrator, emergency medical technician; s. J. Kim and Roberta Jean Buland. BS, Briarwood Coll., 1994; BA, Alfred (N.Y.) U., 1999. Lic. EMT N.Y., 2003. EMT A.E. Crandall Hook & Ladder Co., Alfred, 1999—; asst. resident dir. Alfred (N.Y.) U., 1999; residence hall coord. SUNY, Alfred, 2000—02, coord. Greek affairs, 2000—04, coord. residence hall, 2002—; residence dir. Emerson Coll., Boston, 2002. Democrat. Jewish. Office: State University of New York 10 Upper College Drive Alfred NY 14802 Office Phone: 607-587-3214.

BULGER, BRIAN WEGG, lawyer; b. Chgo., May 27, 1951; s. John Burton and Mary Jane (Wegg) B.; m. Laura Ellen McErlean, Sept. 12, 1981; children: Burton, Kevin. AB cum laude, Georgetown U., 1972, JD, 1977. Bar: Ill. 1977, U.S. Dist. Ct. (no. dist.) Ill. 1977, U.S. Ct. Appeals (4th, 7th and 8th cirs.) 1977, U.S. Supreme Ct. 1980. From assoc. to ptnr. Pope Ballard Shepard & Fowle, Chgo., 1977-87; ptnr., dept. head Katten Muchin & Zavis, Chgo., 1987-94; founding ptnr. Meckler, Bulger & Tilson, Chgo., 1994—. Adj. prof. U. Wis. Mgmt. Inst., Milw., 1980-2000, U. Chgo. Grad. Sch. Bus., 2000—. Contbr. articles to profl. jours. Mem. ABA (former chair pub. employer labor rels. com. sect. on urban state and govt. law), Ill. State Bar Assn., Georgetown Law Alumni (bd. dirs. 1984-93). Roman Catholic. Avocations: baseball, reading, boating, skeet shooting. Office: Meckler Bulger Tilson Ste 1800 123 N Wacker Dr Chicago IL 60606

BULGER, GEORGE FRANCIS, manufacturing executive; s. George Francis and Alma Cecelia Bulger; m. Harriet Elizabeth Bianci; children: Kimberly Ann, Jennifer Louis, Allyson Lynn, Matthew James. Student, Westchester CC, Valhalla, NY, 1968—69, student, 2001—02. Mgr., designer Mode Art Jewelers, NYC, 1970—78; project mgr., buyer G.M. Crocetti, Inc., Bronx, 1979—85; owner M.T.I., Mt. Vernon, NY, 1986—95, Designs by Novello, Port Chester, NY, 1995—. Cons. Commandulli srl, Castellioni, Italy, 1987—94. Achievements include development of luster wheel; patents for inspection plate for motorcycles; caliper insert for motorcycles. Office: Novello 505 N Main St Port Chester NY 10573 Office Phone: 914-937-7711.

BULGER, ROGER JAMES, academic administrator; b. Bklyn., May 18, 1933; s. William Joseph and Florence Dorothy (Poggi) B.; m. Ruth Ellen Grouse, June 8, 1960; children: Faith Anne, Grace Ellen. AB, Harvard U., 1955, MD, 1960; postgrad., Emmanuel Coll., Cambridge (Eng.) U., 1955—56; hon. degree, Thomas Jefferson U., 1995, U. Md., Western U. Health Scis., 1998, Kirkesville U. Osteo. Medicine, 1999, Rush U., 2001. Intern, then resident in internal medicine U. Wash. Hosps., 1960—62; trainee in infectious disease and microbiology U. Wash., 1962—63; renal and metabolic diseases Boston U., 1963—64; from asst. prof. to assoc. prof. medicine U. Wash. Med. Sch., Seattle, 1966—70; med. dir. Univ. Hosp., Seattle, 1967—70; prof. cmty. health scis., assoc. dean allied health Duke U. Med. Ctr., 1970—72; exec. officer Inst. Medicine, Nat. Acad. Scis., 1972—76; prof. internal medicine George Washington U. Sch. Medicine, 1972—76; prof. internal medicine, family and community medicine, dean Med. Sch., chancellor Worcester campus U. Mass., 1976—78; pres. U. Tex. Health Sci. Ctr., Houston, 1978—88; pres., CEO Assn. Acad. Health Ctrs., 1988—. Author: Hippocrates Revisited, 1973, In Search of Modern Hippocrates, 1987, Technology, Bureaucracy and Healing, 1988, The Quest for Mercy, 1998, Philosphies and Physician, 2001, A Portrait of Leadership, 2005; also articles, chpts. in books; mem. editl. bd. various jours. Bd. dirs. Georgetown U., Rsch. Am.! Lionel de Jersey Harvard fellow, 1955-56. Fellow ACP, Acad. for Health Svcs. Rsch. (disting.); mem. Inst. Medicine, Infectious Disease Soc. Am., Nat. Acad. Social Ins. Office: Assoc Acad Health Ctrs 1400 16th St NW Ste 720 Washington DC 20036-2230 E-mail: rbulger@acadhlthctrs.org.

BULKA, MICHEAL, art critic; BFA in Sculpture, minor in Painting, Va. Commenwealth U.; MFA in studio Arts, U. Ill.-Chgo. Circle. Critic contbd. to P-Form, dialogue, C, Art in America, World Art, New Art Examiner, New City ArtNet. Mem.: Chgo. Art Critics Assn. Mailing: 1621 N Honore BF Chicago IL 60622*

BULKLEY, GREGORY BARTLETT, surgeon, research scientist, educator; b. Spokane, Wash., Apr. 28, 1943; s. George J. and Patricia (Bartlett) B.; m. Bernardine P. Healy, Aug. 13, 1967 (div. Aug. 1982); 1 child, Bartlett Anne; m. Jacqueline Ransford Graham, Oct. 9, 1993. BA with high honors, Princeton U., 1965; MD with honors, Harvard U., 1970; MD (hon.), Uppsala (Sweden) U., 1997. Diplomate Am. Bd. Med. Examiners, Am. Bd. Surgery. Rsch. fellow Harvard Med. Sch., Boston, 1967—68; intern Johns Hopkins U., Balt., 1970—71; rsch. fellow Nat. Cancer Inst., 1972—74; resident in surgery Johns Hopkins Hosp., Balt., 1971, 1974—78; asst. chief of svc. dept. surgery Johns Hopkins U., Balt., 1977—78; from instr. to assoc. prof. Johns Hopkins U. Sch. Medicine, Balt., 1977—88, dir. surg. rsch., 1985—2003, prof., 1988—, Mark M. Ravitch prof., endowed chair, 1989—; mem. faculty Johns Hopkins U. Sch. Hygiene and Pub. Health, Balt., 1991—95; faculty cellular and molecular medicine tng. program Johns Hopkins U., Balt., 1995—, dir. NIH tng. program for gastrointestinal sugeon-scientists, 1996—; mem. staff Johns Hopkins Hosp., Balt., 1970—. Vis. prof., cons. in field; GMA II study sect. NIH, Bethesda, Md., 1988-91, chmn., 1990-91, grant reviewer NIH, Med. Rsch. Coun. (Can.), VA (U.S.), mem. panel, 1989, chmn. subcom. NIH Consensus Panel, 1992; grant reviewer Med. Rsch. Coun., Australia; reviewer Med. Rsch. Coun., New Zealand; mem. consensus conf. NIH; dean's lectr. Johns Hopkins U. Sch. Medicine, 1988, professorial promotion com., 1993-99; Sigma Xi lectr. U. Kans., 1991; founder, chair SSAT, AGA, ASLD, ASGE Consensus Confs., 1996-2000; chair multiple spl. grant rev. groups NIH, 1990—. Author (,editor): (Book) Measurement of Blood Flow, 1980, Splanchnic Ischemia and Multiple Organ Failure, 1990; Former mem. editorial bd.: Med. Jours. Gastroenterology, Surgery, Free Radical Biology and Medicine, Shock, Ann. Chirugae et Gynecologie Archives of Gerontology and Geriat.; contbr. articles to profl. jours.; reviewer: New Eng. Jour. Medicine, Am. Jour. Physiology, Jour. Clin. Investigation, others. Vice chmn. FASEB Conf., 1994, chmn., 1996; nominator physiology or medicine Nobel Prize, 1990—. Lt. comdr. USPHS, 1972-74. NIH grantee, 1983—; recipient Shipley award Southern Surg. Assn., 1987, Royal Coll. medal Royal Coll. Surgeons Ireland, 1989. Fellow: ACS; mem.: Soc. Surgery Alimentary Tract (nominating com. 1995, trustee, chmn.rsch. com. 1997—2000), Soc. Internat. de Chirurgie Digestivae (trustee), Am. Gastroenterol. Assn. (chmn. subcom. program com. 1993, chmn. nominating com. 1994, chmn. subcom. program com. 1997), Am. Surg. Assn. (program com. 1995—99, chmn. 1999), Am. Physiol. Soc., Halsted Soc. (program com. 1997—99, chmn. 1999), Cosmos Club, Alpha Omega Alpha, Sigma Xi. Avocations: swimming, skiing, opera, flyfishing. Office: Johns Hopkins U Sch Medicine Blalock 685 600 N Wolfe St Baltimore MD 21287-0005 Office Phone: 410-955-8500. E-mail: gbulkley@jhmi.edu.

BULL, BERGEN IRA, retired equipment manufacturing company executive; b. Lansing, Mich., Feb. 28, 1940; s. W. Ira and Thelma (Roof) B.; m. Janet Mary Blachford, Sept. 22, 1961; children: Damon, Lauren. BA, Mich. State U., 1962; MA, Middle Tenn. State U., 1965; JD, Lewis and Clark Coll., 1969. Bar: Oreg. 1969. Acct. Hyster Co., Portland, Oreg., 1965-66, mem. credit dept., 1966-67, asst. to sec., 1967-71, asst. sec., 1971-72, sec., 1972-78, v.p., legal officer, sec., 1978-86, v.p., gen. counsel, sec., 1986-87, v.p. corp. adminstrn., gen. counsel, sec., 1987-89; v.p., gen. counsel, sec. NACCO Materials Handling Group, Inc., 1989-95, ret., 1995. Instr. bus. law Portland State U., 1971-72 Loaned exec. United Fund, 1968; mem. Diocesan Coun. and vice chancelor Episcopal Diocese of Eastern Oreg., 2000—; bd. dirs. Assoc. Oreg. Industries, 1981—96, Jr. Achievement, 1980—2001, vice-chmn., 1993, chmn., 1994; bd. dirs. Modern Group, Ltd., 1995—, Sunriver Music Festival, 1997—, treas., 1997—99, pres., 2000—03; bd. dirs. Sunriver Nature Ctr., 1998—2004, v.p., 2000, pres., 1999—2000. Mem. Oreg. Bar Assn. (inactive), Multnomah Athletic Club, Sage Springs Club & Spa, Crosswater Club. Episcopalian. Personal E-mail: bergenjan747@cmc.com.

BULL, BEVERLY JANE, piano and voice educator; b. Ogdensburg, N.Y., Apr. 18, 1927; d. David William and Mary (Coe) Cheney; m. George H. Bull, Jr., Nov. 4, 1961; 1 child, Melanie Jane Bull Byers. Student, Daynes Bus. Sch., Bath, N.Y., 1948; BA in Music, Piano and Voice, Elmira Coll., 1952; postgrad. in Voice, Cornell U., 1952-55. Sec.-receptionist Cornell U., Ithaca, N.Y., 1952-55; exec. sec. to pres. Gt. Western, Hammondsport, N.Y., 1956-58; tchr. music Avoca (N.Y.) Ctrl. Sch., 1960-61; pvt. tchr. piano, voice and oral interpretation, Homer, N.Y. Dir. adult ch. choirs and children's choirs, 1944—; tchr. music Day Care Ctr., Syracuse, N.Y., pvt. sch., Liverpool, N.Y., 1997—99. Appeared in numerous programs including poetry readings, playing and singing of sacred, classical and popular songs; soprano soloist. Vol. pianist and singer various hosps., including VA Hosp. Mem. Order Ea. Star (former dir. choir Steuben chpt.). Republican. Avocations: sewing, writing, poetry, gardening. Home: 1642 White Bridge Cir Homer NY 13077-9707

BULL, BRIAN STANLEY, pathologist, educator; b. Watford, Hertfordshire, Eng., Sept. 14, 1937; arrived in U.S., 1954, naturalized, 1960; s. Stanley and Agnes Mary (Murdoch) B.; m. Maureen Hannah Huse, June 3, 1963; children: Beverly Velda, Beryl Heather. BS in Zoology, Walla Walla Coll., 1957; MD, Loma Linda (Calif.) U., 1961. Diplomate Am. Bd. Pathology. Intern Yale U., 1961-62, resident in anat. pathology New Haven, 1962-63; resident in clin. pathology NIH, Bethesda, Md., 1963-65, fellow in hematology and electron microscopy, 1965-66, staff hematologist, 1966-67; rsch. asst. dept. anatomy Loma Linda U., 1958, dept. microbiology, 1959, asst. prof. pathology, 1968-71, assoc. prof., 1971-73, prof., 1973—, chmn. dept. pathology, 1973—, chmn. dept. pathology and human anatomy, 1993—, assoc. dean for acad. affairs Sch. Medicine, 1993-94, dean Sch. Medicine, 1994—2003. Cons. to mfrs. of med. testing devices; mem. Internat. Commn. for Standardization in Hematology, pres., 1997-99, inaugural lectr. Houwen Meml. Lectures, Internat. Soc. Lab. Hematology, 2005. Mem. bd. editors Blood Cells, Molecules and Diseases, 1995—; contbr. chpts. to books, articles to med. jours.; patentee in field; editor-in-chief Blood Cells N.Y. Heidelberg, 1985-94. Served with USPHS, 1963-67. Nat. Inst. Arthritis and Metabolic Diseases fellow, 1967-68; recipient Merck Manual award, 1961, Mosby Scholarship Book award, 1961; Ernest B. Cotlove Meml. lectr. Acad. Clin. Lab. Physicians and Scientists, 1972; named Alumnus of Yr., Walla Walla Coll., 1984, Honored Alumnus, Loma Linda U. Sch. Medicine, 1987, Humanitarian award, 1991; named Citizen of Yr., Loma Linda C. of C., 1997, President's award, Loma Linda U. Adventist Health Scis. Ctr., 2003, Disting. U. Svc. award Sch. Medicine Loma Linda U., 2003. Fellow Am. Soc. Clin. Pathologists, Am. Soc. Hematology, Coll. Am. Pathologists, FDA Panel on Hematology and Pathology Devices, Nat. Com. on Clin. Lab. Stds., N.Y. Acad. Scis.; mem. AMA, Calif. Soc. Pathologists, San Bernadino County Med. Soc. (William C. Cover Outstanding Contbn. to Medicine award 1994), Acad. Clin. Lab. Physicians and Scientists, Am. Assn. Pathologists, Sigma Xi, Alpha Omega Alpha. Seventh-day Adventist. Achievements include patents in field of blood analysis instrumentation; development of quality control algorithms for blood analyzer calibration; origination of techniques and instrumentation for the measurement of thrombosis risk and for regulation of anti-coagulation during cardiopulmonary bypass. Office: Loma Linda U Sch Medicine 11234 Anderson St Loma Linda CA 92354-2871 Office Phone: 909-558-4094. E-mail: bbull@som.llu.edu, bbullatllu@worldnet.att.net.

BULL, DAVID, fine art conservator; b. Bristol, Eng., Mar. 5, 1934; came to U.S., 1978; s. Andrew John Michael and Betty (Horler) B.; m. Janette Christine Brewer, July 26, 1955 (div. Nov. 1986); children: Victoria, Stephen, Matthew, Nicholas, Sebastian; m. Teresa Jarvis Longyear, June 3, 1989; 1 child, David Douglas John. Nat. diploma, city and guilds diploma, West of Eng. Coll. Art, 1955. Restorer of paintings City Art Gallery, Bristol, 1957-60; restorer Nat. Gallery, London, 1960-65; ptnr. David Bull and Robert Shepherd (art restorers), London, 1965-78; head painting conservation J. Paul Getty Mus., Malibu, Calif., 1978-80; dir. Norton Simon Mus., Pasadena, Calif., 1980-81; pres. Fine Art Conservation and Restoration Inc., 1981—; head of painting conservation Nat. Gallery Art, Washington, 1984-89, chmn. of painting conservation, 1990-99, sr. cons., 1999—. Bd. dirs. Save Venice, Inc. Fellow Internat. Inst. Conservation. Home and Office: 173 E 80th St New York NY 10021-0438 Office Phone: 212-439-1659. E-mail: fineartcons@erols.com.

BULL, FRANK JAMES, retired architect; b. Chattanooga, June 25, 1922; s. Louis H. and Augusta (Clausius) B.; m. Betty Frances Graham, May 7, 1949; 1 child, Birney O'Brian. BS in Architecture, Ga. Inst. Tech., 1948, BArch, 1949. Registered architect, Ga., 1951; cert. Nat. Coun. Archtl. Registration Bds. Pilot Pan Am. World Airways, NY, Fla., 1942—46; arch. Aeck Assocs. Architects, Atlanta, 1948-57; ptnr. Bull & Kenney Architects, Atlanta, 1957-88, Bull, Brown & Kilgo, Architects, Atlanta, 1988—2003; ret., 2003. Bd. dirs. Compass Environ. Inc.; cons. Fed. Republic of Germany Embassy, Washington, 1986-93; archtl. cons. for golf clubhouse Quinta do Peru, Sesimbra, Portugal and Palheiro Golfe, Funchal, Madeira Island, Portugal, 1991; lectr. in field. Co-author: Asbestos Abatement: Vol. 5 The Sourcebook on Asbestos Diseases, 1991; contbr. articles to profl. jours.; prin. works include Sanctuary for Holy Innocents Episc. Ch., Atlanta, Atlanta Speech Sch. and Clin., Hummel Hall Episc. H.S., Alexandria, Va., Jekyll Island Golf Clubhouse, McLarty Hall, Tull Hall, Turner Gymnasium, Westminster Schs., Atlanta, Dunwoody Country Club, Atlanta, East Lake Golf Clubhouse Restoration, Atlanta, others. Charter trustee Holy Innocents Episcopal Sch., Atlanta, 1962-68, chmn., 1966; founder Galloway Schs., Atlanta, 1969-75. Recipient Rambusch prize, Ecole de Beaux Arts, 1940. Mem. AIA (mem. emeritus, treas. Atlanta chpt. 1976-78, bd. dirs. Ga. assn. 1971-74), Am. Arbitration Assn. (mem. nat. panel constrn. industry arbitrators 1977-2002), Nat. Asbestos Coun. (founder, charter v.p., bd. dirs. 1983-86, 89-90, treas. 1987, exec. com. 1983-87), Cherokee Town and Country Club (charter, bd. govs. 1976-79, chmn. capital appropriations com., chmn. green com.), Omicron Delta Kappa, Tau Beta Pi, Phi Kappa Phi, Phi Eta Sigma, ANAK, Beta Theta Pi. Republican. Episcopalian. Avocations: golf, writing, lecturing. Home: 34 Willow Gln NE Atlanta GA 30342-1341 Personal E-mail: frank@addressabull.com.

BULL, GEORGE ALBERT, retired banker; b. Red Lion, Pa., May 28, 1927; s. Mervin E. and Edna May (Gohn) B.; m. Grace Kathryn Rudolph, Nov. 13, 1949; children: Donna Carol, Diana Sue, David Alan. Student, Grad. Sch. Banking, Rutgers U., 1961. From teller to cashier Citizens Nat. Bank, Front Royal, Va., 1947-64; asst. vp., cashier Monticello Nat. Bank, Charlottesville, Va., 1964; asst. cashier Nat. Bank & Trust Co., Charlottesville, 1964-80, asst. to pres., 1985-88, sr. exec. v.p., asst. to pres., 1988-89; exec. v.p., treas. Jefferson Bankshares Inc., Charlottesville, 1979-89. With U.S. Army, 1945-46. Mem. Masons. Home: 2315 Wakefield Rd Charlottesville VA 22901-1843

BULL, HENRIK HELKAND, architect; b. N.Y.C., July 13, 1929; s. Johan and Sonja (Geelmuyden) B.; m. Barbara Alpaugh, June 9, 1956; children: Peter, Nina. BArch, MIT, 1952. With Mario Corbett, San Francisco, 1954-55; pvt. practice, 1956-68; ptnr. Bull, Field, Volkmann, Stockwell, Calif., 1968-82, Bull, Volkmann, Stockwell, Calif., 1982-90, Bull Stockwell and Allen, Calif., 1990-93, Bull, Stockwell, Allen & Ripley, San Francisco, 1993-96, BSA Archs., San Francisco, 1996—. Vis. lectr. Syracuse U., 1963; mem. adv. com. San Francisco Urban Design Study, 1970-71. Works include Sunset mag. Discovery House, Tahoe Tavern Condominiums, Lake Tahoe, Calif., Snowmass Villas Condominiums, Aspen, Colo., Northstar Master Plan Village and Condominiums, Moraga Valley Presbyn. Ch., Calif., Spruce Saddle Restaurant and Poste-Montane Hotel, Beaver Creek, Colo., Bear Valley visitor ctr., Point Reyes, Calif., The Inn at Spanish Bay, Pebble Beach, Calif., Taluswood Cmty., Whistler, B.C., Jackson Gore Inn, Okemo, Vt. 1st lt.

USAF, 1952—54. Fellow AIA (pres. N. Calif. chpt. 1968, Firm award Calif. chpt. 1989). Democrat. Office: BSA Architects 501 Folsom St 4th Fl San Francisco CA 94105 Office Phone: 415-281-4720. Business E-Mail: hbull@bsaarchitects.com.

BULL, INEZ STEWART, pianist, editor, author, music educator, curator, coloratura soprano; b. Newark, Apr. 13, 1920; d. Johan Randulf and Aurora (Stewart) B. Diploma in piano, Juilliard, 1946; cert., Chautauqua Inst. Sch. Music, 1940-46; diploma, U. Oslo Grad. Sch., Norway, 1955; MusB, N.Y. Coll. Music, 1965; MA, NYU, 1972, EdD, 1979. Piano tchr. Juilliard Inst. Musical Art, NY, NY, 1942-43; chmn. music dept. Casement's Coll., Ormond Beach, Fla., 1949-50; dir. music Essex County Girls Vocat. & Tech. HS, Newark, 1953-57; dir. music, organist State of N.J. Institution for Retarded Girls North Jersey Tng. Sch., Totowa, NJ, 1953-68; spl. edn. gifted coord. Jefferson Magnet Sch. Pub. Sch. Sys., Union City, NJ, 1956-95; dir. Upper Montclair Music Sch., Montclair, NJ, 1945—, Ole Bull Music Sch., Potter County, Pa., 1952-68. Pres. N.J. Music Educators Assn. Aux. 1935-48; adjudicator Lycoming Coll., Williamsport, Pa., 1948—; conductor Whippany Symphony Orch., 1951-52; curator, builder Ole Bull Mus., Galeton, Pa., 1968—; dir. youth chorus Jefferson Sch., Union City, 1956-95; dir. Hudson County Elem. Choral Festival, 1971—; artist-in-residence, Union City; guest lectr. Columbia U., NYC, Yale U. Grad. Sch. Music, Hartford, Conn., NYU, Lycoming Coll., Williamsport, Pa., Mansfield U., Pa., Princeton U., NJ, U. Scranton, Pa., Jersey City State Coll. Author: 30 books; editor: various newsletters and mag.; author: (song) Evening Prayer, 1934, I Will Bow and Be Humble, 1954, Voice of Am., 1952; recording artist Educo Records, soloist WFMB radio sta., Daytona Beach, Fla., 1949—50, NBC, Hartford, Conn., WNJR, Union, N.J., 1952—68, WNBT-ABC, Wellsboro, Pa., 1997—2005, Norsk Rikskringkasting, Oslo, Radio and TV Francaise, Paris, recitals, France, Norway, Eng., Switzerland, S. Am., US. Choir dir. First Congl. Ch., 1940-43, Holy Trinity Luth. Ch., Nutley Luth. Ch., 1953-55; organist, choir dir. North Jersey Tng. Sch. Chapel, 1952-68; founder, dir. Ole Bull Music Festival, Galeton, Pa, 1952—; dep. gov. and mem. rsch. bd. advisors Am. Biog. Inst., Raleigh; US State Dept amb. of goodwill to Norway by order of Pres. Dwight D. Eisenhower, 1953, Norwegian Goodwill amb. to US by order of King Haakon VII, 1953. Recipient Freedom medal-Eisenhower medal, 1953, Sterling Silver plaque King Olav V of Norway, 1966, NJEA award, 1970, Performing Arts Prestige award in Edn., 1976, Olympic Gold medal Norwegian Govt., 1992, Silver medal of Honor, 1991, Gold medal of Honor, 1992, Pa. Senate Legis. citation, 1992, Outstanding Tchr. of the Handicapped in the U.S. Nat. Rsch. Coun., 1970, Woman of Distinction honorable mention award Girl Scout Coun. of Greater Essex County, 1996, Artisan award Oakeside Bloomfield Cultural Ctr., 1996, 50 Women You Should Know award Internat. YWCA, 1996, St. Olav medal King Harald V (Norway), 1999, Outstanding Woman in Arts award World History Project/Twp. of Montclair, 2000, Key to City of Renovo award, Pa., 2000, 2002, Am. Medal of Honor award Pres. of U.S., 2001, Nobel Peace prize, 2002, Congl. Medal of Merit, 2003, Congl. Medal of Excellence, 2003, Amb. of Grand Eminence, 2004, Legion of Honor medal United Cultural Conv., 2005, Spl. Alumni Svc. award NYU, 2005; Fulbright scholar U. Oslo (Norway) Grad. Sch., 1955; film made in her honor A Child is Waiting, 1963. Mem. Ole Bull Hist. Soc. (pres. 1972—), Phi Delta Kappa (pres. 1984-86, newsletter editor 1984-92), Kappa Delta Pi (pres. 1984—, newsletter editor 1984—, counselor NYU Beta Pi chpt. 1996), Pen & Brush Club, Internat. Percy Grainger Soc. (v.p.), NYU Alumnae Club Inc. (bd. dirs., rec. sec., newsletter editor, 1979—). Republican. Avocations: concert pianist, soprano, writer. Home (Summer): 79 S Cherry Springs Rd Galeton PA 16922 Office: Robert Waters Sch 2800 Summit Ave Union City NJ 07087-2329

BULL, JAMES C., poet; b. Blaine, Tenn., Mar. 20, 1945; s. James Conley and Esther F. (Hensley) Bull; m. Maret Delavallade, June 15, 1965 (div. Dec. 1967); 1 child, Maarja Esther. Author: (poetry) Spirit of Earth, 1999, Voices of Quiet, 2001, Braids of Fire, 2001, Western the Big Red, 2002, Land of the Yellowstone, 2004, A Photographic History of Fort Ringgold Texas and the Men Who Patroled the Military Trail, Circa 1900, 2002, (short story) Year of the Comet, 2004. Home: 2455 Indian Ridge Rd Blaine TN 37709-5927

BULL, MARTHA, artist, educator; d. Charles and Phyllis Smead; m. James Bull, July 28, 1973; 1 child, Caitlin. EdB in Art Edn., No. Ill. U., Dekalb, 1975, MA in Studio Art Drawing, 1986, MFA in Studio Art Drawing, 1990. Exhibitions include Harper Coll. Art Show (Hon. Mention, 1987), Elgin CC Art Show (2nd Pl., 1988), Norris Cultural Vicinity Art Shows, Elgin Bubotto Salon, 1990—95, Norris Art Shows, one-woman shows include McHenry County Coll. Grantee, Greater St. Charles Edn. Found., 2000, 2001, 2004—05. Mem.: St. Charles Edn. Assn. (assoc.), Ill. Art Edn. Assn. (assoc.), Nat. Art Edn. Assn. (assoc.). Office: Haines Mid Sch 305 S 9th St Saint Charles IL 60174

BULL, REBECCA DARLENE, music educator, musician; b. Balt., May 11, 1962; d. Elmer Leon Ledford and Nova Neavie Sherlock; m. Donald Cylburn Bull Jr., Jan. 15, 1983. BA, Towson State U., 1987, MEd, 1993. String tchr. Hereford Zone Music Program, Balt., 1988-92, Western Md. Coll., Westminster, Md., 1986-93; orch. dir. Westminster Youth Orch., Westminster, Md., 1988-93; music tchr. Cumberland County, Crossville, Tenn., 1993—; orch. dir. Children of Crossville Chamber Orch., 1996—. Author: (vocal works) Anthology, 1997-99, (orchestral work) Kumon, 1993. Cmty. Orch. Dir. Children of Crossville, 1996—, Westminster (Md.) Youth Orch., 1986-93. Named Woman of Yr., Bus. and Profl. Women's Assn., 2000, Tchr. of Yr., Crossville Elem. Sch., 1998; recipient Butterfly award, Music in Motion, 1997. Mem.: NEA, Nashville Songwriters Assn., Plateau Area Music Tchrs. Assn. (treas. 1997—), Am. String Tchrs. Assn. (Tenn. Tchr. of Yr. 2000). Avocations: songwriting, painting, reading, crafts, nature enthusiast. Home: 407 Sligo St Crossville TN 38572-3008 Office: Crossville Elem Sch 368 4th St Crossville TN 38555-4309

BULL, VIVIAN ANN, retired academic administrator, educator; b. Ironwood, Mich., Dec. 11, 1934; d. Edwin Russell and Lydia (West) Johnson; m. Robert J. Bull, Jan. 31, 1959; children: R. Camper, W. Carlson. BA, Albion (Mich.) Coll., 1956, DEcons (hon.), 1999; postgrad., London Sch. Econs., 1957; PhD, NYU, 1974; DHL (hon.), Drew U., 2003, Albion Coll., U. Portland. Economist Nat. Bank Detroit, 1955-59; with Bell Telephone Labs., Murray Hill, NJ, 1960-62; dept. econs. Drew U., Madison, NJ, 1960-92, assoc. dean, 1978-86; pres. Linfield Coll., McMinnville, Oreg., 1992—2005, ret., 2005, emeritus. Bd. dirs. Chem. Bank N.J., Morristown; trustee Africa U., Zimbabwe; treas. Joint Expedition to Caesareu Maritima Archaeology, 1971—. Author: Economic Study The West Bank: Is It Viable?, 1975. Trustee, assoc. Am. Schs. Oriental Rsch., 1982-90; trustee Colonial Symphony Soc., 1984-92, The Albright Inst. of Archaeol. Record; commr. Downtown Devel. Commn., Madison, 1986-92; mem. Univ. Sen. United Meth. Ch., 1989-96, 2000-, gen. bd. higher edn., 1988-92; mem. planning bd. Coll. Bus. Adminstrn., Africa U., Zimbabwe, 1990-91; exec. com. Nat. Assn. Commns. on Salaries, United Meth. Ch., 1986-92. Fulbright scholar, 1956, Paul Harris fellow Rotary Internat., 1988; named Disting. Alumna Albion Coll., 1979; recipient Salute to Policy Makers award Exec. Women in N.J., 1986, John Woolman Peacemaking award George Fox Coll., 1994, Equal Opportunity award Urban League of Portland, 1995. Mem. Nat. Assn. Bank Women, N.W. Assn. Colls. and Univs. (exec. com. 2000—), Phi Beta Kappa. Avocations: archaeology, travel, music. Home: 54 Prospect St Madison NJ 07940 Personal E-mail: vbull@armigerint.com.

BULLA, CLYDE ROBERT, writer; b. King City, Mo., Jan. 9, 1914; s. Julian W. and Sarah Ann (Henson) B. Columnist Tri-County News, King City, Mo., 1942-47. Author 70 books for young people including White Bird, 1966, Shoeshine Girl, 1975, A Lion to Guard Us, 1981, A Place for Angels, 1995, The Paint Brush Kid, 1999. Recipient Commonwealth Children's Book award Commonwealth Club, Calif., 1970; recipient Christopher award The Christophers, 1972, Sequoyah Book award Okla. Sch. Children, 1978, Charlie May Simon award Ark. Sch. Children, 1976, book award S.C. Sch. Children, 1980, Focal award L.A. Pub. Libr., 1991. Mem. Soc. Children's Book Writers, Authors Guild

BULLA, ROBERT, academic administrator; B in Bus., Ariz. State U. Pres., CEO Blue Cross and Blue Shield of Ariz., 1983—2001, chmn. bd. dirs., CEO, 2001—; mem. Ariz. Bd. Regents, Phoenix. Active Ariz. Econ. Roundtable, Greater Phoenix Leadership, Greater Phoenix Econ. Coun., Morrison Inst. Bd., St. Mary's Food Bank Adv. Bd. Office: Ariz Bd Regents Ste 230 2020 N Central Ave Phoenix AZ 85004

BULLARD, EDGAR JOHN, III, museum director; b. L.A., Sept. 15, 1942; s. Edgar John and Katherine Elizabeth (Dreisbach) B. BA, UCLA, 1965, MA, 1968; LHD (hon.), Loyola U., New Orleans, 1987. Asst. to dir., curator spl. projects Nat. Gallery Art, Washington, 1968-73; Montine McDaniel Freeman dir. New Orleans Mus. Art, 1973—. Alternate mem. Citizens Stamp Adv. Com., 1969-71; mem. mus. adv. panel Nat. Endowment for Arts, 1974-77. Author: Edgar Degas, 1971, John Sloan 1871-1951, 1971, Mary Cassatt: Oils and Pastels, 1972, A Panorama of American Painting, 1975. Nerdrum: The Drawings, 1994, Henry Casselli: Master of the American Watercolor, 2000, In Celebration of Light: Photographs from the Pierce Collection, 2004. Bd. dirs. La. Cultural Alliance, 1988-91, New Orleans Jazz and Heritage Found., 1974-78; trustee New Orleans Opera Assn., 2001—, Ga. Mus. Art, U. Ga., Athens, 1975-80, Kneisel Hall Chamber Music Sch., Blue Hill, Maine, 1986-02, La. Soc. for Prevention Cruelty to Animals, 1986-93, New Orleans Jazz Orch., 2003—, Haystack Mountain Sch. of Crafts, Deer Isle, Maine, 2003—; mem. adv. bd. Tulane Univ. Coll., 1999-2001; trustee Amistad Rsch. Ctr., Tulane U., 2001—. Decorated Order of Republic of Egypt, officer Am. Soc. Venerable Order St. John Jerusalem, Order of Arts and Lettres of France; Samuel H. Kress Found. fellow, 1967-68; recipient New Orleans Mayor's Art award, 1993. Mem.: Am. Assn. Mus. (bd. dirs. 1996—98), Assn. Art Mus. Dirs. Democrat. Episcopalian. Home: 1805 Milan St New Orleans LA 70115-5443 also: Greenlea Reach Rd Deer Isle ME 04627 Office: New Orleans Mus Art PO Box 19123 New Orleans LA 70179-0123 Office Phone: 504-488-2631. Business E-Mail: jbullard@noma.org.

BULLARD, ERVIN TROWBRIDGE, horticulturist; b. NYC, May 25, 1920; s. Frank Marcus and Elizabeth Trowbridge Bullard; m. Marie Jump Groo Bullard, Apr. 20, 1995; m. Madonna Jean Bullard, Sept. 4, 1948 (dec. Dec. 1, 1993); children: John Marcus, Carol Ann Rice, Ellen Sue Schedin. PhD, Purdue U., West Lafayette, IN, 1950; MS, Cornell U., Ithica, NY, 1946; BS, NC State, Raleigh, NC, 1943. Pres. Bullard Consulting, Palm Coast, Fla., 1986—; chief of party Ohio State U. in Burma, 1984—86; agr. advisor US AID, Washington, 1954—79; assoc. educator U. of Idaho, Parma, Idaho, 1950—54. Contbr. to various books on tropical horticulture. Pfc Marine Corps, 1942—44, United States. Recipient Fulbright Award, US Govt., 1951. Mem.: Interamerican Soc. for Tropical Horticulture. Presbyterian. Avocations: fishing, stamp collecting/philately. Home: 135 Cimmaron Drive Palm Coast FL 32137

BULLARD, JOHN KILBURN, educational association administrator; b. New Bedford, Mass., Aug. 21, 1947; s. John Crapo and Katharine (Kilburn) B.; m. Anne Dunbar, June 27, 1981; children: Elizabeth, Anthony, Matthew. BA magna cum laude, Harvard U., 1969; MArch, M in City Planning, MIT, 1974. Agt. Waterfront Hist. Area League (WHALE), New Bedford, 1974-85; mayor City of New Bedford, 1986-92; dir. fisheries representation New Bedford (Mass.) Seafood Co-op, 1992-93; dir. Office of Sustainable Devel. NOAA, Dept. Commerce, Washington, 1993-98; fellow Harvard Inst. Politics, 1998; dir. Family Bus. Ctr. U. Mass., Dartmouth, 1998—2002; pres. Sea Edn. Assn., 2002—. Chmn. urban econ. policy com. U.S. Conf. of Mayors, 1988-92. Photographer 3 covers for Sail mag., 1970-71. Recipient Honor Award Nat. Trust for Hist. Preservation, 1981, Preservation award Mass. Hist. Commn., 1983, Design award Mass. Gov. Michael Dukakis, 1987. Democrat. Unitarian Universalist. Avocations: sailing, tennis. Home: 19 Irving St New Bedford MA 02740-3426 Personal E-mail: jbullard@sea.edu.

BULLARD, ROGER PERRIN, artist; b. N.Y.C., July 2, 1913; s. Roger Harrington and Annie Adams (Sturges) B.; m. Georgie Genevieve Hosford, Nov. 15, 1944; 1 child, Virginia Anne. Student, Art Students League, N.Y.C., 1934-37, Universal Photographers Inc., The Bullard Haven Tech. Sch., Bridgeport, Conn., 1946. Freelance artist, Fairfield, Conn., 1937-40; machinist Heime Co., Fairfield, 1947-50, Exide Battery, Fairfield, 1950-52, Dictaphone, Bridgeport, Conn., 1952-55; draftsman Aircraft Drafting, Bridgeport, 1955-57, Sikorski Aircraft and Valve Corp., Bridgeport, 1955-56; airbrush artist Poly Photo, Bridgeport, 1957; freelance photographer Fairfield, 1958-77. Contbr. pen and ink drawings to Prof. Henry Fairfield Osborn's book, Probosidea Memoirs Mus. Natural History, N.Y.C., 1933-35. With U.S. Army, 1940-45, WWII. Republican. Episcopalian. Avocations: photography, art research, tennis, writing. Home: c/o Mary Rouseau 449 Mill Plain Rd Fairfield CT 06430-5047

BULLARD, WILLIS CLARE, JR., lawyer; b. Detroit, July 12, 1943; s. Willis C. and Virginia Katherine (Gilmore) B.; children: Willis C. III, Melissa Ann, Kaila Michelle. AB, U. Mich., 1965; JD, Detroit Coll. Law, 1971. Bar: Mich. 1971. Practice of law, Detroit, 1971-77, Troy, Mich., 1977-80, Milford, Mich., 1983—; supr. Highland Twp., Mich., 1980-82; mem. Mich. Ho. of Reps., 1983-96, Mich. Senate from 15th dist., Lansing, 1996—2002; mem. from 2d dist. County Commn., 2003—, chmn. bd., 2005—. Asst. Rep. caucus chmn., 1983-84, asst. Rep. floor leader, 1985-88, chmn. House Rep. campaign, 1987-90; chmn. House taxation com., 1993-96; chmn. task force Midwestern Legis. Conf. Coun. State Govts., 1985-86; mediator cir. and dist. cts., 1988—; chmn. bd. Mich. Ho. Reps., 2005—. Bd. dirs. Dunham Lake Property Owners Assn., 1975-78, treas., 1975-76, pres., 1976-78; mem. Dunham Lake Civic Com., 1982-87; trustee Highland Twp., 1978-80, mem. zoning bd. appeals, 1979. Named Legislator of Yr. Mich. Twp. Assn., 1984, Nat. Rep. Legislator of Yr., 2000. Mem. Oakland County Bar Assn., State Bar Mich., Oakland County Assn. Twp. Suprs. (sec.-treas. 1981), Michigamua. Clubs: U. Mich. of Greater Detroit, Highland Republican, Highland Men's (sec. 1979, pres. 1980). Republican. Home: 1849 Lakeview Dr Highland MI 48357-4817 Office Phone: 248-684-1444.

BULLARO, GRACE RUSSO, literature, film and foreign language educator, critic; b. Salerno, Italy, July 11, 1949; arrived in U.S., 1958; d. Salvatore and Carmela (Paciello) Russo; m. Frank John Bullaro, Sept. 19, 1971; children: Christian, Adrian Alexander. BA magna cum laude, CCNY, 1971; MA, SUNY, Stony Brook, 1989, PhD in Comparative Lit., 1993. Grad. tchg. asst. SUNY, Stony Brook, 1988-92; adj. asst. prof. SUNY-Nassau C.C., Garden City, 1990—, CUNY-Lehman Coll., Bronx, 1991-2000, adj. assoc. prof., 2000—02, asst. prof., 2002—; with Lincoln Ctr., NYC, 1998. Mem. acad. senate CUNY, 1997—, mem. libr. com., 1998; mem. faculty exec. com. Lehman Coll., Bronx, NY, 1999—, English dept. libr. acquisitions liaison, 2000—; mem. Tchr. of Yr. selection com.; acad. senate CUNY, Lehman Coll., 1997—99, 2001—, CUNY, 1998—, mem. Faculty Exec. Com., 1999—, liaison English Dept. Libr. Acquistions, 2000—, sec. Faculty Exec. Com., 2004—, chair English Dept. Honors Com., 2004—, faculty advisor English Honors Program, 2004—; elected sec. Exec. Com. Faculty, 2004—; chair Honors Program, English Dept., 2004—; cons. Pub. Libr. Fgn. Lang. Acquisitions, Syosset, NY, 2002—; mem. profl. adv. bd. Am. Biograph. Inst., 2002—; book reviewer in field. Author: Beyond Life is Beautiful: Comedy and Tragedy in the Cinema of Roberto Benigni, 2005; contbr. chapters to books, articles to profl. jours. Recipient Excellence in Tchg. award, Excellence in Tchg. Selection Com., SUNY, Stony Brook, 1992, Adj. Tchr. Yr. award, conferred by Tchr. Yr. Selection Com., CUNY, Lehman Coll., 2001. Mem. MLA, Popular Culture Assn./Am. Culture Assn., N.E. Modern Lang. Assn., Nat. Coun. Tchrs. English, Assn. Italian-Am. Educators, Inst. Français, Soc. Profs. Français, Phi Beta Kappa (elected sec. 2004—). Avocations: fitness trainer, tennis, travel, swimming, horseback riding. Office: CUNY Lehman Coll English Dept Bedford Park Blvd W Bronx NY 10468 Office Phone: 718-960-8362. Personal E-mail: gracerbullaro@msn.com. Business E-Mail: grace.bullaro@lehman.cuny.edu.

BULLEIT, THOMAS NELSON, JR., lawyer; b. Washington, Feb. 11, 1957; s. Thomas Nelson and Jeanne Marie (Parsley) Bulleit; m. Kristy Ann Niehaus, May 25, 2001; children: Emma Madeleine, James Vaughan. AB cum laude, Yale U., 1979; JD, U. Mich., 1985. Bar: Md. 1987, DC 1988, U.S. Supreme Ct. 1991. Law clk. to Hon. Bailey Brown U.S. Ct. Appeals (6th cir.), Memphis, 1985—86; assoc. Pierson, Ball & Dowd, Washington, 1986—89, Reed Smith Shaw & McClay, Washington, 1989—90, Hogan & Hartson, LLP, Washington, 1990—93, ptnr., 1994—. Mem. steering com. health law sect. DC Bar, 1991—94, chmn., 1994—97, chmn. coun. on sects., 1997—98. Bd. dirs. Children's Law Ctr., Washington, 1999—, chmn. bd. dirs., 2003—05. Recipient Louis Honigman award, U. Mich. Jour. Law Reform, 1985, Masters in Fraud and Abuse Law award, Nat. Health Lawyers Assn., 1996. Mem.: ABA, Am. Health Lawyers Assn. Avocations: vocal music, hiking, running. Office: Hogan & Hartson LLP 555 13th St NW Washington DC 20004 Office Phone: 202-637-8276. Business E-Mail: tnbulleit@hhlaw.com.

BULLEN, GEORGE GREGORY, music educator, composer; s. George H. and Betty L. Bullen; m. Patricia Mae Whalen, Sept. 17, 1977; 1 child, Alexis Thomas. MusB, U. Mass., 1981; MA, Smith Coll., 1983—83. Music dir. Deerfield Acad., Mass., 1984—2000; dir. of arts Bryn Mawr Sch., Balt., 2000—. Composer: (albums) Vesper Adest (award 60th Anniversary Choral Composition Competition, Va. Choral Soc., 1991), Elegy Eroica, 1994, Trio for Violin, Cello and Piano, 1993, Scherzo, 1997, The Parable of the Blind, 2000, Live'll Get You Ten, 2001. Mem.: Am. Music Ctr., Am. Choral Dir.'s Assn., Coll. Music Soc., Phi Beta Kappa. Office: Bryn Mawr Sch 109 W Melrose Ave Baltimore MD 21210 Office Phone: 410-323-8800 1670.

BULLER, CHAROLETTE ANN, elementary school educator; b. Enid, Okla., Apr. 19, 1961; d. Fobert Julius and Katherine Carrie Severin; m. Jon L. Buller, Aug. 1, 1982; children: Lukas Jon, Leah Rose, Emily Frances. BS in Edn., Ctrl. State U., Edmond, Okla., 1982, MEd, 1985. Cert. elem. edn. and reading specialist Okla. State Dept. Edn., 1985. 4th grade tchr. McCloud (Okla.) Elem. Sch., 1982—83; music tchr., chpt. I tchr. Strother Elem. Sch., Seminole, Okla., 1983—84, 1st and 2nd grade tchr., 1984—85; 3rd grade tchr. Crescent (Okla.) Elem. Sch., 1985—86, Covington (Okla.) Elem. Sch., 1986—87; 1st grade tchr. Ringwood (Okla.) Elem. Sch., 1997—98, 5th grade tchr., 1998—99, 2nd grade tchr., 1999—2002; jr. high lang. arts, acad. team coach Ringwood Schs., 2001—03, title I coord., tchr., acad. team coach, 2003—. Gifted and talented coord., title I coord., reading sufficiency coord. Ringwood Pub. Schs., 2000—. Precinct worker Major County Election Bd., Meno, Okla., 1990—97; Sunday sch. tchr. New Hopedale Mennonite Ch., Meno, Okla., 1998—2005. Recipient 1st prize statewide creative writing contest, Okla. Home Ext., 1988. Republican. Mennonite. Avocations: reading, sewing, cooking, crafts. Home: Rt 2 Box 84 Ringwood OK 73768 Office: Ringwood Pub Schs 5th and Main Ringwood OK 73768 Office Phone: 580-883-2201.

BULLER, CHRYSALIS CHABLIS, director; b. Harlan, Iowa, Jan. 31, 1979; d. Steven Lee and Anitra Kaltoft Buller. BA in Psychology, Vassar Coll., Poughkeepsie, NY, 2001; MA in Coll. Student Pers., Bowling Green State U., Ohio, 2005. Area coord. Simpson Coll., Indianola, Iowa, 2001—03; Greek affairs grad. asst. Bowling Green State U., 2003—05. Grad. advisor interfrat. coun. Bowling Green State U., 2004—05; presenter time mgmt. Greek Life. Recipient William Lanning Spirit award, Office Residence Life and Greek Affairs, 2004. Mem.: Omicron Delta Kappa (life), Gamma Sigma Alpha (life), Order of Omega (life Grad. Asst. fellow 2004), Delta Gamma Frat. (life; vol. 2004—05). Home and Office: Dean of Students Office Student Svc Bldg 387 Campus Box 2702 Normal IL 61790-2702 Office Phone: 419-372-1141, 309-438-2151.

BULLER, JEFFREY LYNN, dean; b. Milw., Sept. 9, 1954; s. Richard Martin and Marian (Stelzner) B.; m. Ruth Francis Osier, July 24, 1976 (div. Apr. 1990); m. Sandra Clemmons McClain, Aug. 24, 1996. BA, U. Notre Dame, 1976; MA, U. Wis., 1977, PhD, 1981. Asst. prof. classics Loras Coll., Dubuque, Iowa, 1981-88, assoc. prof., 1988-90; asst. dean Ga. So. U., Statesboro, 1990-93, assoc. dean, 1993—2001; v.p. acad. affairs Mary Baldwin Coll., Staunton, Va., 2001—, dean, 2001—. Chairperson Ga. Art and Sci. Deans, 1994-96. Contbr. articles to profl. jours. Fulbright fellow USIA, Washington, 1985, 97. Mem. Classical Assn. (mem. regional exec. bd. 1989-94, pres. mid. west and south 2004-05, Ovatio award 1996), Phi Beta Kappa, Phi Kappa Phi Avocations: opera, literature, travel. Office: Mary Baldwin Coll Staunton VA 24401-1000 Office Phone: 540-887-7030. Business E-Mail: jbuller@mbc.edu.

BULLERDICK, KIM H., lawyer, petroleum executive; b. Richmond, Ind., 1953; BA, Wittenberg U., 1975; JD, U. Va., 1978. Legal dept. dir. Giant Industries, Inc., Scottsdale, Ariz., 1998—2000, v.p., corp. sec., subs. officer, 1998—, gen. coun., 2000—. Office: Giant Industries Inc 23733 N Scottsdale Rd Scottsdale AZ 85255-3466

BULLIET, RICHARD WILLIAMS, historian, educator, writer; b. Rockford, Ill., Oct. 30, 1940; s. Leander Jackson and Mildred Idell (Williams) B.; m. Lucianne Cherry, June 24, 1962; 1 child, Mark Paul BA, Harvard U., 1962, MA, 1964, PhD, 1967. Instr. Harvard U., Cambridge, Mass., 1967-70, asst. prof., 1970-73; lectr. U. Calif.-Berkeley, 1973-75; assoc. prof. history Columbia U., N.Y.C., 1976-79, prof., 1979—. Author: The Patricians of Nishapur, 1972, The Camel and the Wheel, 1977 (Dexter prize), Conversion to Islam in the Medieval Period, 1979, Islam: The View from the Edge, 1993, The Case for Islam-Christian Civilization, 2004, Hunters, Herders, and Hamburgers, 2005; (novels) Kicked to Death by a Camel, 1973; The Tomb of the Twelfth Imam, 1979, The Gulf Scenario, 1984, The Sufi Fiddle, 1991; co-author: The Earth and Its Peoples, 1997; co-editor: The Encyclopedia of the Modern Middle East, 1996; editor: The Columbia History of the Twentieth Century, 1998; host-narrator: (documentary TV series) The Middle East, 1985; editor Jour. Iranian Studies, 1987-90. Guggenheim fellow, 1975-76 Mem. Mid. East Studies Assn. (exec. sec. 1977-81), Phi Beta Kappa. Avocation: painting. Home: 90 Morningside Dr New York NY 10027-7124 Office: Columbia U Mid East Inst New York NY 10027 E-mail: rwb3@columbia.edu.

BULLINGTON, GAYLE ROGERS, writer, researcher; b. Watsonville, Calif., May 17, 1923; d. Manley Duane and Gladyce Thelma (Horton) Rogers; m. Keith Charles Brown, Nov. 26, 1944 (div. Feb.4, 1963); children: Kendall Keith, Kevin Doran; m. Jack William Bullington, Dec. 23, 1978. BA, UCLA, 1949; postgrad., Northridge U., 1962; MA, Calif. Luth. U., 1974. Cert. tchr., secondary tchr. Calif. Tchr. Southgate (Calif.) Jr. H.S., 1947-48, Virgil Jr. H.S., L.A., 1948-50, North Hollywood (Calif.) H.S., 1950-52, Van Nuys (Calif.) H.S., 1953-54, Thousand Oaks (Calif.) H.S., 1963-79. Author: The Second Kiss, 1972, NAKOA's Woman, 1975—81, Gladyce With a C, 2000, Dark Corners, 2002, My Name Was Mary, 2003, Mary's Little Lamb, 2004, For Love's Sake Only, 2005. Mem. ACLU, Pub. Citizen, Common Cause, Nation Assocs. Home: 23119 19th Ave NE Arlington WA 98223-7631 Office Phone: 360-435-4622. Personal E-mail: gayle.rogers@verizon.net.

BULLIS, JO LOUISE, social services administrator, educator; d. Robert E. Bullis and Mary M. Bullis Hoyt. BS in Phys. Therapy, U. N.D., 1976, JD, 1983. Bar: N.D. 1983, Mich. 1989. Program dir. Women's Resource Ctr., Traverse City, Mich., 1992—. Adj. instr. Northwestern Mich. Coll., Traverse City, 1995—; mem. Governor's Domestic Violence Law Implementation Task Force, Lansing, Mich., 1995—96, Best Practices for Law Enforcement Tng. - Violence Against Women Tng. Inst., Lansing, 1998—99, Mich. State Planning Body - Civil Legal Services for the Poor, Lansing, 2001—, Domestic Violence Trial Manual Com. - Pros. Attorney's Assn. of Mich., Lansing, 2002—03; mem. instrs. com. Mich. Law Enforcement Acad., Lansing, 1999—; peer reviewer Mich. Domestic Violence Prevention & Treatment Bd., Lansing, Mich., 2001—; mem. adv. group Safe Haven Supervised Visitation and Safe Exch. Nat. Demonstration Project, Traverse City, 2003—. V.p., chair fin. com. Addiction Treatment Services, Inc., Traverse City, 1998—. Named Woman of the Yr., Traverse City Zonta Club, 1997, Sarah Hardy Humanitarian of the Yr., Traverse City Human Rights Commn., 2000; recipient Domestic Violence Summit III Govs. award, Mich.

Domestic Violence Prevention & Treatment Bd., 1997. Mem.: Women Lawyers Assn., Antrim-Grand Traverse-Leelanau Bar Assn., Order of the Coif, Phi Delta Phi (life Internat. Grad. of the Yr. 1983). Avocations: gardening, reading, travel, music. Office: Women's Resource Ctr Ste 2 720 S Elmwood Traverse City MI 49684 Office Phone: 231-941-1210. Business E-Mail: jbullis@wrcgt.com.

BULLOCK, ANNA MAE See TURNER, TINA

BULLOCK, BRUCE STANLEY, lawyer; b. Kissimmee, Fla., Oct. 29, 1933; s. Arthur Stanley and Athalia (Griffin) B.; m. Lydia Austill, July 8, 1960; children: Bruce Stanley Jr., Margaret Bullock Martin. BA, U. Fla., 1955, LLB, 1962, JD, 1967. Bar: Fla. 1962, U.S. Dist. Ct. (mid. and no. dists.), U.S. Supreme Ct., U.S. Ct. Appeals (11th crct.); diplomate Am. Bd. Trial Advocates; cert. crct. ct. mediator. Atty. assoc. Marks Gray Conroy & Gibbs, Jacksonville, Fla., 1962-66, atty., ptnr., 1966-73; atty., pres. Bullock & Alexander, Jacksonville, 1973-74, Bullock, Childs, Pendley & Reed, Jacksonville, 1974-95; ptnr. Bullock, Childs, Pendley & Reed, PA, Jacksonville, 1995—2003. Pres. N.E. Fla. Med. Malpractice Claims Coun. Dir., committeeman, gen. counsel Duval County (Fla.) Rep. Party, 1995-2003. Lt. USAF, 1955-59. Mem. Jacksonville Bar Assn., Jacksonville Assn. Def. Counsel (pres.), Fla. Def. Lawyers Assn., Def. Trial Lawyers Assn., Def. Rsch. Inst., U. Fla. Alumni Club (pres.), Rotary Club (v.p. S. Jacksonville chpt.), Am. Bd. Trial Advocates (pres. local chpt. 1999). Republican. Anglican. Avocations: fishing, boating, nature. Home: 2510 Hickory Bluff Ln Jacksonville FL 32223-6503 Office: Bullock Childs Pendley & Reed PA 1551 Atlantic Blvd 2d Fl Jacksonville FL 32207 Office Phone: 904-396-3007. Business E-Mail: bbullock@bcprlaw.com.

BULLOCK, CHARLES SPENCER, III, political science educator, author, consultant; b. Nashville, July 22, 1942; s. Charles Spencer and Elenor Alice (Davis) B.; m. Frances Lee Mann, Sept. 10, 1965; children— Georgia Beth, Judith Rebecca Lee. AB, William Jewell Coll., 1964; MA, Washington U., St. Louis, 1967, PhD, 1968; postgrad., Emory U., 1964-65. Asst. prof. U. Ga., Athens, 1968-72, assoc. prof., 1972-75; prof. U. Houston, 1975—77; prof. polit. sci. U. Ga., Athens, 1977—, Richard B. Russell chair polit. sci., 1980—, research fellow Inst. Behavioral Research, 1977—84, Josiah Meigs Disting. tchg. prof., 2005—. Adj. prof. U. Okla., 1987—. Co-author or co-editor: Black Political Attitudes, 1972, The New Politics, 1970, Law and Social Change, 1972, Racial Equality in America, 1975, Coercion to Compliance, 1977, Public Policy in the Eighties, 1983, PublicPolicy and Politics in America, 1978, 84, Implementation of Civil Rights Policy, 1984, Governing a Changing America, 1984, Georgia Political Almanac, 1991, Runoff Elections in the United States, 1992, Forest Resource Policy, 1993, Georgia Political Almanac, 1993-94, 1993, Georgia Political Almanac, 1995-96, 1995, David Duke and the Politics of Race in the South, 1995, New Politics of the Old South, 1998, rev. 2d edit. 2003, Open Seat Elections to the U.S. House, 2000. Mem. Ga. adv. com. to U.S. Commn. on Civil Rights; mem. Leadership Athens, 1992-93. Recipient citation for achievement William Jewell Coll., 1983, William A. Owens award for creativity in social sci. rsch., 1991, V.O. Key award for best book on so. politics, 1993, Outstanding Tchg. award, 1987, 1993, 95, 99, 2003, 05; grantee NSF, 1973-75, Nat. Inst. Edn., 1973-76. Mem. Am. Polit. Sci. Assn. (exec. coun. 1989-91), Southwestern Polit. Sci. Assn. (Outstanding Paper award 1975, Jewell Prestage Best Paper award 2003), Midwest Polit. Sci. Assn., So. Polit. Sci. Assn. (pres. 1985-86, Scott-Foresman award 1984, award for best paper on women and politics 1988-89), Ga. Polit. Sci. Assn. (pres. 2001-02), Legis. Study Group (chmn. 1983-85), Rotary. Episcopalian. Home: 1011 River Run Bishop GA 30621-1663 Office: U Ga Dept Polit Sci Athens GA 30602

BULLOCK, ELLIS WAY, JR., architect; b. Birmingham, Ala., Sept. 11, 1928; s. Ellis Way Sr. Bullock and Martha (Foute) Alexander; m. Ann Ardelia Pope, Nov. 28, 1950; children: Ellis Way III, Elbert Pope, John Howard Keith, William Frank. BArch, Auburn U., 1954. Registered architect, Fla., Ala., Ga., Miss., S.C., N.C. Apprentice architect Yonge, Look & Morrison, Pensacola, Fla., 1954-58; owner Ellis Bullock Architect, Pensacola, 1958-73; pres., CEO Bullock-Tice and Assocs. Arch., Inc., Pensacola, 1973—96. Pres. Fla. AIA, 1977, treas. AIA Rsch. Corp., Washington, 1980-81; chmn. Energy in Arch., Washington, 1980-82; mem. faculty adv. com. Auburn U. Sch. Architecture, 1980—, chmn., 1988-89; mem. Nat. Architecture Accrediting Bd., Washington, 1982-86; mem. adv. coun. U. Fla. Coll. Architecture, 1986—. Contbr. articles to profl. jours. Chmn. Pensacola Hist. Commn., 1967; chmn. City of Pensacola Archtl. Review Bd., 1968, Pensacola Bldg. Bd. of Appeals, 1970—; bd. dirs. Pensacola Symphony, 1998-2000, Fla. Bd. Architecture and Interior Design, 2002—; exec. bd. Auburn U. Coll. Architecture, Design and Constrn., 2000—; mem. Blue Ribbon Task Force on Edn., Escambia County, Fla., 1985-86; mem. adv. coun. U. Fla., 1986—; mem. sesquicentennial commn. State of Fla. 1st lt. U.S. Army, 1950-54. Recipient 1st Honor AIA-Navy, 1977, 78, Award of Merit, 1976; recipient Outstanding Design award for Air Force Systems Command Hdqrs., 1980, Gov.'s Design award, 1982, 84, Merit award for U.S. Air Force Design, 1983, Design Excellence award Air Force Regional Civil Engrs., 1984, award of merit Navy Youth Ctr., 1990, award of merit Navy Bowling Ctr. Complex, 1990; named Profl. of Yr., Pensacola News Jour., 1977. Fellow AIA (bd. dirs. 1979-82, v.p. 1981-82, jury coll. of fellows 1988-91, exec. com. coll. of fellows 1993—, bursar 1993—, vice chancellor 1994-95, chancellor 1995-96, regional rep. Fla. Caribbean 1990—, numerous awards N.W. chpt. 1974—, award of excellence Fla. N.W. chpt. 1980, 82, 86, 89, 90, Gold medal Fla. chpt. 1988, Millennium award of honor Fla. chpt. 2000), Am. Archtl. Found. (regent 1995-96, EXCOM 1995-96, task force account and reason 1988, program chmn. nat. conv. com. 1986); mem. Fla. Assn. AIA (pres. 1977, govtl. liaison com. 1984—, Gold medal 1988, gold medal noiminating com. 1990-91, balanced curriculum task force 1990, chmn. design awards jur. Ctrl. Fla. chpt. 1980, speaker ann. conf. 1997-98), Fla. Archtl. Found. (trustee 1988—, chmn. 1993), Inst. Bus. Designers (award for contractual interiors 1977), NRA, St. Andrews Soc., Rotary (Paul Harris fellow 1994). Home: 2 Hyde Park Rd Pensacola FL 32503-5830 Office: Bullock Tice Assocs 909 E Cervantes St Ste B Pensacola FL 32501-3281 E-mail: ewbjr@ewbullock.com.

BULLOCK, JOSEPH DANIEL, pediatrician, educator; b. Cin., Jan. 23, 1942; s. Joseph Craven and Emilie (Woide) B.; m. Martha Foss, June 20, 1964; children: Jennifer Zane, Sarah Harrison. BA, Wittenberg U., 1963; MD, Ohio State U., 1967, degree in pediatrics, 1969; degree in immunology, allergy, U. Calif., San Francisco, 1971. Diplomate Am. Bd. Pediat., Am. Bd. Allergy and Immunology. Clin. prof. pediatrics Ohio State U., Columbus, 1971—; pres. Midwest Allergy Assocs., Inc., Worthington, Ohio, 1971—. Contbr. articles to profl. jours. Active fund raising Wittenberg U., Springfield, Ohio, 1980-83, Columbus Sch. for Girls, 1977-86. Served to capt. USAF, 1967-71. Recipient Mead Johnson award, 1965. Fellow Am. Acad. Pediatrics, Am. Acad. Allergy, Am. Coll. Allergists (Bd. Regents 1979-82, Clemens von Pirquet award 1968, 69, 70, 71), Am. Thoracic Soc., Interasma, Ohio Soc. Allergy and Immunology (pres. 1985-87). Clubs: Columbus Country; The Golf (New Albany, Ohio); Indian Creek Country (Miami Beach, Fla.), The Surf (Surfside, Fla.). Republican. Lutheran. Home: 189 N Parkview Ave Columbus OH 43209-1435 Office: 8080 Ravines Edge Ct Columbus OH 43235-5424 Office Phone: 614-846-5944.

BULLOCK, MARY BROWN, academic administrator; m. George Bullock; children: Ashley, Graham. BA, Agnes Scott Coll., Atlanta, 1966; MA in Chinese history, Stanford U., 1968, PhD in Chinese history, 1973. Profl. assoc. Com. on Scholarly Comm. with People's Republic of China, 1973—77, dir., 1977—88; dir. Asia program Woodrow Wilson Internat. Ctr. Scholars, Washington, 1988—95; pres. Agnes Scott Coll., Decatur, Ga., 1995—. Trustee China Med. Bd. of N.Y.; dir. Nat. Com. on U.S.-China Rels., Am. Coun. Edn.; mem. adv. coun. on U.S.-China cooperation in sci., policy, rsch. and edn. NSF; chair Nat. Assn. Ind. Colls. and Univs., 2002—04, Women's Coll. Coalition; bd. dirs. Am. Coun. on Edn., Sun Trust Bank, Atlanta, Genuine Parts Co.; treas. Atlanta Regional Consortium Higher Edn. Recipient Elizabeth Luce Moore Visionary Leadership award, Dist. Svc. award, NAS; fellow, Woodrow Wilson Internat. Ctr. Scholars, Rockefeller Conf. Ctr., Bellagio, Italy; grantee, Ford Found., Henry Luce Found., Rockefeller Found., NSF. Mem.: Coun. on Fgn. Rels., Carter Ctr. Bd. of Councilors. Office: Agnes Scott Coll 141 E College Ave Decatur GA 30030 Office Phone: 404-471-6280. Business E-Mail: mbb@agnesscott.edu.

BULLOCK, SANDRA, actress; b. Arlington, Va., July 26, 1964; d. John and Helga Bullock; m. Jesse James, July 16, 2005. Attended, East Carolina U. Appearances include (TV movies) Bionic Showdown: The Six-Million Dollar Man and the Bionic Woman, 1989, Who Shot Patakango, 1989, The Preppie Murder, 1989; (TV series) Working Girl, 1990; (TV mini-series) Lucky/Chances, 1990; (feature films) Hangmen, 1987, Fire on the Amazon, 1991, Religion Inc., 1989, Love Potion #9, 1992, When the Party's Over, 1992, Who Do I Gotta Kill, 1992, The Vanishing, 1993, Demolition Man, 1993, The Thing Called Love, 1993 (also composer), Wrestling Ernest Hemingway, 1993, Speed, 1994 (Best Female Performance, Most Desirable Female MTV Movie awards), While You Were Sleeping, 1995 (Favorite Actress in a Motion Picture award People Choice Awards 1996), The Net, 1995, Two if by Sea, 1996, A Time to Kill, 1996, In Love and War, 1996, Speed 2: Cruise Control, 1997, Practical Magic, 1998, Forces of Nature, 1999, Exactly 3:30, 1999, 28 Days, 2000, Divine Secrets of the Ya-Ya Sisterhood, 2002, Crash, 2004, Loverboy, 2005; actor, dir., writer Making Sandwiches, 1996; actor, prodr. Gun Shy, 1999, Miss Congeniality, 2000, Two Weeks Notice, 2002, Miss Congeniality 2: Armed and Fabulous, 2005; actor, exec. prodr. Hope Floats, 1998, Murder By Numbers, 2002; prodr. Our Father, 1996, Trespasses, 1999; exec. prodr. (TV series) George Lopez, 2002-. Recipient Best Actress MTV's Big Picture, 1994-95, Best Actress US Mag., 1995, Favorite Actress in a Comedy/Drama Theatrical and Favorite Actress-Comedy Video awards BlockBuster Entertainment Awards, 1996, Favorite Actress People's Choice award, 1997, 1999, ShoWest Female Star of the Year, 2001, Am. Comedy Award for Funniest Female Performer in a Motion Picture, 2001.*

BULLOCK, STEVEN CARL, lawyer; b. Anderson, Ind., Jan. 19, 1949; s. Carl Pearson and Dorothy Mae (Colle) B.; m. Debra Bullock; children: Bradford, Christine, Justin, Evan. BA, Purdue U., 1971; JD, Detroit Coll., 1985. Bar: Mich. 1985, U.S. Dist. Ct. (ea. dist.) 1985, Ct. of Appeals (6th cir.) 1993, U.S. Supreme Ct. 1993. Pvt. pracitce, Inkster, Mich., 1985—. With USAF, 1971-75. Mem. Mich. Bar Assn. (criminal law sect.), Detroit Bar Assn., Detroit Founders Soc., Recorder's Ct. Bar Assn., Suburban Bar Assn., Nat. Assn. Criminal Def. Attys., Criminal Def. Lawyers of Mich., Wayne County Criminal Def. Bar Assn. Avocations: golf, travel. Office: 2228 Inkster Rd Inkster MI 48141-1811 Office Phone: 313-562-6500. E-mail: lawone123@aol.com.

BULLOCK, THEODORE HOLMES, biologist, educator; b. Nanking, China, May 16, 1915; s. Amasa Archibald and Ruth (Beckwith) B.; m. Martha Runquist, May 30, 1937; children: Elsie Christine, Stephen Holmes. Student, Pasadena Jr. Coll., 1932-34; AB, U. Calif. at Berkeley, 1936, PhD, 1940; PhD (hon.), U. Frankfurt, 1988, Loyola U., Chgo., 2000. Research assoc. Yale U. Sch. Medicine, 1942-43, instr. neuroanatomy, 1943-44; instr. Marine Biol. Lab., Woods Hole, Mass., 1944-46, head invertebrate zoology, 1955-57, trustee, 1955-57; asst. prof. anatomy U. Mo., 1944-46; asst. prof. zoology U. Calif. at Los Angeles, 1946, assoc. prof., 1948, prof., 1955-66; Brain Research Inst., U. Calif. at Los Angeles, 1960-66; prof. neurosci. Med. Sch., U. Calif. at San Diego, 1966-82, prof. emeritus, 1982—. Mem. AEC 2d Resurvey of Bikini Expdn., 1948. Author: (with G.A. Horridge) Structure and Function in the Nervous Systems of Invertebrates, 2 vols., 1965; (with others) Introduction to Nervous Systems, 1977; (with W. Heiligenberg) Electroreception, 1986 (with E. Basar) Brain Dynamics, 1989, (with E. Basar) Induced Rhythms in the Brain, 1992, How Do Brains Work?, 1993. Fellow, Ctr. Advanced Study in Behavioral Scis., Palo Alto, 1959—60; Sterling fellow zoology, Yale U., 1940—41, Rockefeller fellow exptl. neurology, 1941—42, Fulbright scholar, Stazione Zoologica, Naples, 1950—51. Fellow AAAS; mem. NAS, Am. Soc. Zoologists (chmn. comparative physiology div. 1961, pres. 1965), Soc. Neurosci. (pres. 1973-74), Internat. Soc. Neuroethology (pres. 1984-86), Am. Physiol. Soc., Soc. Gen. Physiologists, Am. Acad. Arts and Scis., Am. Philos. Soc., Internat. Brain Research Orgn., Phi Beta Kappa, Sigma Xi. Business E-Mail: tbullock@ucsd.edu.

BULLOCK, WELDON KIMBALL, health facility administrator, pathologist, educator; b. Vernal, Utah, Jan. 6, 1908; s. John Kimball and Adelaide (Arnold) B.; m. Dosia Opal Newton, Dec. 26, 1931; children: John, Jim. BA, U. Utah, 1930; MD, Northwestern U., 1934, MSc in Pathology, 1942. Diplomate Am. Bd. Pathology; lic. MD, Calif., Idaho, Utah. Intern Alameda County Hosp., 1933-34; resident in medicine Cook County Hosp., 1940-41; resident in pathology L.A. County-U. So. Calif. Med. Ctr., 1946-47; head surg. pathology LAC-U. So. Calif. Med. Ctr., 1949-69; instr. pathology Sch. Medicine U. So. Calif., 1947-48, asst. prof., 1955-62, clin. prof., 1963-74, clin. prof. emeritus, 1974—; exec. dir. Calif. Tumor Tissue Registry, various locations, 1955-95, dir. emeritus, 1995—; chief pathology svc. Orthop. Hosp., 1956-63; assoc. pathologist St. Luke Hosp., 1963-70, chief pathologist, 1970-77, assoc. pathologist, 1977-81; clin. prof. pathology Sch. Medicine Loma Linda U., 1992—. James Ewing fellow in pathology Meml. Hosp. for Cancer and Allied Disease, 1948-49; cons. Calif. Assn. Cytotechnologists, 1962—, So. Calif. Acad. Oral Pathology, 1963—, Orthop. Hosp., 1963—; mem. Am. Joint Com. Cancer Staging and End Result Reporting, 1963-69, chmn. audio-visual task force, 1966-69, mem. exec. com., 1969; mem. rev. com. clin. cancer tng. grants Nat. Cancer Inst., 1965-68; mem. cancer planning com. Calif. Regional Med. Program, Area V, U. So. Calif., 1967-69; mem. pub. health svc. spl. project rev. com. HEW, State of Calif., 1967-69; meml. lectr. Arthur Purdy Stout Soc. Surg. Pathologists, 1979. Author: Oral Cancer & Tumors of the Jaws, 1956; contbr. articles to profl. jours. Lt. Col. U.S. Army Res., 1941-45, PTO. Decorated Bronze Star. Mem. AMA, Coll. Am. Pathologists (mem. com. cancer 1965-70), Am. Soc. Clin. Pathologists, Soc. Surg. Oncology, Calif. Med. Assn., Calif. Soc. Pathologists (mem. exec. com. 1960-62, sec.-treas. 1962-65, pres.-elect 1965-66, pres. 1966-67), L.A. County Med. Assn. (chmn. com. med. examiner 1968-72), L.A. Soc. Pathologists (past pres. exec. com. 1961-62), Soc. Grad. Pathologists-L.A. County-U. So. Calif. Med. Ctr., Soc. Grad. Surgeons-L.A. County-U. So. Calif. Med. Ctr. Home: 525 N Curtis Ave # 113 Alhambra CA 91801 Office: Calif Tumor Tissue Registry 11021 Campus St # 335 Loma Linda CA 92354 Office Phone: 909-558-4788. Personal E-mail: cttr@linkline.com.

BULLOCK, WILLIAM CLAPP, JR., banker; b. Bronxville, N.Y., June 28, 1936; s. William and Elizabeth (Van Wagnen) B.; m. Edith Swain, June 21, 1958; children: Wendy, Martha, Sarah, Bill. BA, Yale U., 1958; postgrad., NYU, 1958-60. Asst. treas., asst. v.p. nat. divsn. Morgan Guaranty Trust Co., N.Y.C., 1958-69; v.p., sr. loan officer Merrill Trust Co., Bangor, Maine, 1969-71, exec. v.p., 1971-73, pres., 1973—, CEO, 1980-82, also chmn. bd. dirs.; pres. Merrill Bankshares Co., 1973—, CEO, 1980-82; exec. v.p., dir. Fleet Fin. Group, 1986-88; also chmn. bd. dirs. Merrill Bankshares Co.; pvt. practice as fin. cons., 1989—. Dir. Fed. Res. Bank of Boston, 1985-88; chmn. Merrill Mchts. Bank, 1992—. Chmn. Maine Gov.'s Task Force on Indian Land Claims, 1979-80; bd. dirs. Assoc. Industries Maine, 1978-81, Atlantic Salmon Fedn., Miramichi Salmon Assn.; bd. dirs. New England Coun., 1981—, past pres.; past treas., past trustee Maine Maritime Acad.; past trustee Maine Cmty. Found., Bangor Theol. Sem., Maine State Retirement Sys. Mem. Maine Bankers Assn. (bd. dirs., past pres.), Am. Bankers Assn., Maine C. of C. (past bd. dirs.), Yale Club, N.Y. Anglers Club. Home: 44 Bald Hill Reach Rd Orrington ME 04474-3630 Office: 201 Main St Bangor ME 04401-6402

BULLOUGH, JOHN FRANK, musician, educator; b. Washington, Oct. 15, 1928; s. John and Mabel Jean (McCalip) B.; m. Dorothy Baines, Apr. 10, 1950; children: John Frank, Lynn Diane Lazar, Patricia Ann Gibbs. BA, George Washington U., 1954; ChM choirmaster cert., Am. Guild Organists, 1956; SMM, Union Theol. Sem., 1958. Organist, asst. prof. music Hartford Theol. Sem. Found., Conn., 1958-64; from asst. prof. music to assoc. prof. to prof. Fairleigh Dickinson U., Teaneck, NJ, 1964-93, chmn. dept. fine arts, 1974-79. Music dir. Hartford Ctr. Ch., 1960-64; organist, choirmaster St. Paul's Episcopal Ch., Englewood, NJ, 1973-95; music dir., conductor The Bergen Chorale, Tenafly, NJ, 1987-91. Contbr. articles to profl. jour. V.p. bd. trustees Bergen Philharm. Orch., NJ, 1973—80; pres., bd. dirs., mem. auditions com. Rodland Found., 2002—. Mem. AAUP, Am. Guild Organists (dean Hartford chpt. 1963-64, No. Valley NJ chpt. 1975-77, chmn. region II 1984-88, convener No. NJ dist. 1991-92, dean No. NJ cpth. 1995-97), Coll. Music Soc. Episcopalian. Home: 488 Fairidge Ter Teaneck NJ 07666-2617 Personal E-mail: jbull62058@aol.com.

BULLOUGH, ROBERT VERNON, JR., educational studies professor; b. Salt Lake City, Feb. 12, 1949; s. Robert Vernon and Dolores Elaine (Clarke) B.; m. Dawn Ann Mortensen, June 18, 1976; children: Joshua Benjamin, Seth Thomas, Adam Neve, Rachel Elizabeth. BS in History, U. Utah, 1971, MEd, 1973; PhD, Ohio State U., 1976. Tchr. East High Sch., Salt Lake City, 1971-73; teaching assoc., then fellow Ohio State U., Columbus, 1973-76; asst. prof., then assoc. prof. U. Utah, Salt Lake City, 1976-89, prof. ednl. studies, 1989—99, emeritus prof., 1999—; dir. rsch. Ctr. Improvement Tchr. Edn. and Schooling and prof. tchr. edn. Brigham Young U., 1999—. Mem. Holmes Group Writing Com., 1984-86. Author: Democracy in Education: Boyd H. Bode, 1981, Human Interests in the Curriculum: Teaching and Learning in a Technological Society, 1984, The Forgotten Dream of American Education, 1988, First Year Teacher: A Case Study, 1989, Emerging as a Teacher, 1992, First Year Teacher--Eight Years Later, 1997, Becoming a Student of Teaching, 1995, 2d edit., 2001, Uncertain Lives: Children of Promise, Teachers of Hope, 2001; mem. editl. bds.; contbr. articles to profl. jours. Recipient Outstanding Writing award, AACTE, 1997. Mem. Am. Ednl. Rsch. Assn. (Outstanding Book award divsn. B 2003), Profs. of Curriculum, Phi Beta Kappa, Phi Kappa Phi, Phi Delta Kappa. Mem. Lds Ch. Avocations: book collecting, house restoration, furniture restoration, family history. Office: Brigham Young U 149 McKay Bldg Provo UT 84602 Business E-Mail: bob_bullough@byu.edu.

BULLOUGH, VERN LEROY, sexologist, nursing educator, researcher, historian; b. Salt Lake City, July 24, 1928; s. D. Vernon Bullough and Augusta Rueckert; m. Bonnie Uckerman, Aug. 2, 1947 (dec. 1996); children: David-(dec.), James, Steven, Susan, Michael; m. Gwen Brewer, Aug. 15, 1998. BSN, Calif. State U., Long Beach, 1981; BS, U. Utah, 1951; MA, U. Chgo., 1951, PhD, 1954; DSc (hon.), Buffalo State Coll., 2004. Assoc. prof. Youngstown (Ohio) U., 1954-59; from asst. prof. to prof. Calif. State U., Northridge, 1959—79; dean faculty natural and social scis. SUNY Coll., Buffalo, 1980-89, disting. prof., 1988-93, disting. prof. emeritus, 1993—. Prof. Inst. Advanced Study Sexuality, San Francisco, 1989—; adj. prof. U. So. Calif., 1994—2003, Ctr. for Sex Rsch., Calif. State U., Northridge, 1994—; fellow Ctr. for Medieval-Renaissance Studies UCLA, 1995—; founder Bonnie and Vern Bullough collection on sex and gender Oviatt Lab., Calif. State U., Northridge. Author, co-author: more than 50 books; editor (sr. editor): Free Inquiry; mem. editl. bds.: 9 jours., 2003—; contbr. more than 200 articles to profl. jours. Active in civil liberties and civil rights orgns.; founding mem. first fair housing group in U.S., 1959. With Security Agency U.S. Army, 1946—48. Named Oustanding Prof, Calif Stat Univ sys, Disting Prof, SUNY; recipient Kinsey award, John Money award, numerous other awards for rsch. into sex and gender, history, medicine, nursing and cmty. svcs. Fellow: Coun. for Sci. Medicine and Mental Health, Com. for Sci. Investigation of Claims to the Paranormal, Internat. Humanist and Ethical Union (past pres.), Acad. Humanism (laureate), Soc. Sci. Study Sex (past pres.), Am. Acad. Nursing. Office Phone: 805-449-8775. Business E-Mail: vbullough@csun.edu.

BULLY-CUMMINGS, ELLA M., police chief; b. Japan; d. Daniel Lee Bully; m. William Cummings. BA with hons. in Pub. Adminstrn., Madonna State U., 1993; JD cum laude, Mich. State U., 1998. Bar: Mich. 1998. From police officer to chief police Detroit (Mich.) Police Dept., 1977—2003, chief police, 2003—; assoc. Miller, Canfield, Paddockand Stone, PLC, 1999—2000, Foley & Lardner, 2000—02. Mem.: Mich. Assn. Chiefs Police, Nat. Orgn. Black Law Enforcement Execs., Internat. Assn. Chiefs Police, Wolverine Bar Assn., Nat. Bar Assn. Office: Detroit Police Dept 1300 Beaubien Detroit MI 48226

BULOT, JAMES JOHN, gerontologist, educator; b. New Orleans, Jan. 18, 1974; m. Lisa Potter Bulot; 1 child, Tyler Kenneth. BS, U. La., Lafayette, 1997; PhD, U. Mass., Boston, 2003. Asst. prof. gerontology U. La., Monroe, 2001—. Editor: (weekly news article on sr. heatlh) C.A.B.L.E. Connection; contbr. articles to profl. jours., newspapers. Mem. exec. com. Cmtys. Acting to Benefit La.'s Elderly, Monroe, 2001—; bd. dirs., vice chmn. N.E. La. Sr. Olympics, Monroe, 2002—; bd. dirs. N.E. La. Alzheimers Assn., 2003—. Recipient cert. of excellence, La. Bd. of Regents, 1997; grantee, Corp. for Nat. and Cmty. Svc. and Assn. of Gerontology in Higher Edn., 2002. Mem.: Am. Soc. on Aging (Outstanding Rch. Relevant to Aging and Directly Applicable to Practice award 2001), Gerontol. Soc. Am. (chair tech. and aging com. 1998—2003), Assn. for Gerontology in Higher Edn. (assoc.; faculty devel. com. 2002—), Psi Chi, Pi Gamma Mu, Blue Key, Sigma Phi Omega. Achievements include research in health information access and technology; malnutrition among community dwelling older adults; the role of health locus of control in health information access. Office: U La at Monroe Inst of Gerontology 700 University Ave Monroe LA 71209 Office Phone: 318-342-3229.

BULOVIC, VLADIMIR, engineering educator; BS in Engineering, Princeton U, 1991; MS in Electrical Engineering, Coulmbia U, 1993; MA in Electrical Engineering, Princeton U, 1995, PhD in Electrical Engineering, 1998. Grad. research, Eectrical Engineering dept. Columbia Radiation Lab, Columbia U., 1991—93, Optoelectronic Components and Materials Lab, Princeton U, 1993—98, post-doctoral research, Electrical Engineering dept., 1998—99; sr. scientist Universal Display Corp., Ewing, NJ, 1999—2000; asst. prof., dept. of Electrical Engineering and Computer Science M.I.T., 2000—. Office: c/o MIT Dept of Electrical Engineering 77 Massachusetts Ave Cambridge MA 02139

BULOW, JACK FAYE, retired library director; b. Elmira, N.Y., June 7, 1942; m. June Burwell, May 22, 1971. Associates degree, Corning (N.Y.) C.C., 1968; BA, U. Ala., Birmingham, 1971; MLS, U. Ala., Tuscaloosa, 1973. Community svcs. libr. Birmingham Pub. Libr., 1973-77, assoc. dir., 1977-93, dir., 1993—2002, ret., 2002. Developer Books-by-Mail program, Birmingham and Jefferson County, 1976; participant exec. in residence program Birmingham-So. Coll., 1987, Leadership Birmingham, 1992; elected as del. White House Conf. on Libr. and Info. Svc., Washington, 1991; elected as regional rep. White House Conf. on Libr. and Info. Svcs. Task Force, Washington, 1992; bd. dirs. Literacy Coun. Ctrl. Ala., Birmingham, 1993-2000; mem. Nat. League Cities, Washington, 1993—; mem. long range planning com. Birmingham Mus. Art, 1993-99; mem. cultural affairs com. Operation New Birmingham, 1988—; sec. Birmingham Pub. Libr. Found.; patron Cahaba River Soc. Birmingham, 1992—. With USCG, 1960-64. Recipient Forestry Recognition award Ala. Forestry Commn., 1977. Mem. ALA (chair fundraising and fin. devel. sect. 1997), Am. Hist. Print Collectors Soc., Am. Mgmt. Assn., Nat. Soc. Fund Raising Execs., Southeastern Libr. Assn., Ala. Libr. Assn. (pres. 1995, Eminent Libr. award 2000), Birmingham-So. Coll. Fine Arts Soc. Avocations: reading, golf, travel, fishing. Personal E-mail: JaBu12@aol.com.

BULOW, JEREMY ISRAEL, economist; b. N.Y.C., Jan. 30, 1954; s. Norman W. and Tova H. Bulow; m. Rhona Mahony; children: Talia, Maya, Zoe. BA, MA, Yale U., 1975; PhD, MIT, 1979. Prof. econs. Stanford (Calif.) Bus. Sch., 1979—; dir. Bur. Econs, Fed. Trade Commn., Washington, 1998—. Fellow Econometric Soc., Am. Acad. Arts & Scis. 2004; mem. ABA (vice chair antitrust sect. 1999—). Office: Stanford Bus Sch 450 Memorial Dr Stanford CA 94305-5015*

BULSON, CHRISTINE EMILY, academic librarian; b. Cooperstown, N.Y., Mar. 11, 1942; d. Emmons B. and Edith Krejci Bulson. BA, Hartwick Coll., 1964; MLS, SUNY, Albany, 1967, cert. advanced studies, 1981. Libr.

Margaretville Ctrl. Sch., 1964-66, Pleasantville (N.Y.) H.S., 1967-68; asst., sr. asst. libr. SUNY, Oneonta, 1978-91, libr., 1991—, asst. dir. for reference and circulation svcs., 1996—2002, adj. prof., 2003—. Author: Current Cookbooks, 1990, over 325 book revs. Mem. Oneonta Concert Assn. (bd. dirs. 1986—), Beta Phi Mu. Home: 232 Main St Worcester NY 12197-1903 Office: Milne Libr SUNY Oneonta NY 13820 Office Phone: 607-436-2025. Business E-Mail: bulsonce@oneonta.edu.

BULTAN, AYKUT, communications systems engineer; came to U.S., 1997; BSEE, Middle East Tech. U., Ankara, Turkey, 1986, MSEE, 1989, PhD in Elec. Engring., 1995. Rsch. and design engr. Comm. Lab. ASELSAN Corp., Ankara, 1986-89; rsch./tchg. asst. dept. elec. engring. Middle East Tech. U., Ankara, 1990—95; asst. prof. computer engring. dept. Ea. Mediterranean U., Famagusta, Cyprus, 1996-97; vis. scholar elec. and computer engring. dept. N.J. Ctr. for Multimedia Rsch., N.J. Inst. Tech., Newark, 1997-99; comms. sys. engr. Interdigital Comm. Corp., Melville, NY, 2000—. Contbr. articles to profl. jours. Undergrad. student fellow Turkish Sci. and Tech. Rsch. Assn., 1982-86. Achievements include research in time-frequency signal analysis and its applications in wireless comm; design of algorithms for third generation wireless sys., OFDM-MIMO Sys; patents in field. Avocations: skiing, scuba and skin diving, reading. Office: Interdigital Comm Corp 2 Huntington Quadrangle Melville NY 11747-4508 Office Phone: 631-622-4196. Office Fax: 631-622-0100. E-mail: aykutbultan@yahoo.com.

BUMAS, ETHAN SHASKAN, writer, educator; b. N.Y.C., Nov. 3, 1962; s. Lester Owen and Janet Marie Bumas. BA, U. Pa., 1982; MFA, Washington U., 1991, PhD, 1998. Vis. prof. U. Mo., Columbia, 1998-99; vis. writer-in-residence Ind. U., Bloomington, 1999-2000; asst. prof. Jersey City U., 2000—. Author: The Price of Tea in China, 1995 (Poets Essayists Novelists West 1996). Recipient Fulbright Rsch. award Fulbright Commn., Chile, 1996-97, Pushcart prize, 2001; Writing fellow Washington U. Writing Program, St. Louis, 1989-90, Univ. fellow Washington U. Comparative Lit., St. Louis, 1993. Mem. MLA, Poets Essayists Novelists, Associated Writing Programs. Home: 208 7th St Apt 2L Jersey City NJ 07302-2036 Office: 2039 John F Kennedy Blvd # G-303 Jersey City NJ 07305-1527 E-mail: ebumas@njcu.edu.

BUMBAUGH, DAVID EDWARD, religious studies educator, minister; b. Chambersburg, Pa., Nov. 1, 1936; s. David Edward and Julia Watson Bumbaugh; m. Beverly Ann Keplinger, June 7, 1956; children: Mark David, Geoffrey Douglas, Stephen Drew, Julia Anna Shah. BA, Wilmington Coll., 1958; BD, Meadville Theol. Sch., 1964. Min. Unitarian Universalist Cmty. Ch., Chicago Heights, Ill., 1964—69, Mt. Vernon Unitarian Ch., Alexandria, Va., 1969—84, First Universalist Ch., Syracuse, NY, 1984—88, Unitarian Ch. in Summit, NJ, 1988—98; prof. ministry Meadville Lombard Theol. Sch., Chgo., 1999—. Pres. Unitarian Universalist Hist. Soc., Boston, 2000—. Author: (theology) The Education of God, 1994, (history) Unitarian Universalism: A Narrative History, 2000; contbr. articles to profl. jours. Chair Unitarian Universalists for the Chgo. Freedom Movement, 1966—69; bd. mem. Diversity Task Force, Summit, 1995—98, St. Lawrence Unitarian Universalist Dist., Buffalo, 1986—88; pres. Metro N.Y. Unitarian Universalist Mins. Assn., Summit, 1993—95. Independent. Unitarian Universalist. Home: 5530 S Shore Dr #21C Chicago IL 60637 Office: Meadville Lombard Theological School 5701 S Woodlawn Ave Chicago IL 60637 Office Phone: 773-256-3000 ext. 229. Personal E-mail: revbev@aol.com. Business E-Mail: dbumbaugh@meadville.edu.

BUMBECK, DAVID, artist; BA, Fine Arts, Rhode Island School of Design; MA, Fine Arts, Syracuse U. Prof. Middlebury College, 1968—, prof. emeritus. Dir. Christian A. Johnson Memorial Gallery, Middlebury College, 1973—85. Exhibitions include, Dartmouth College, Everson Museum, U. of N. AZ, The Mary Ryan Gallery, prin. works include, Brooklyn Museum of Art, Library of Congress, NY Public Library, The Metropolitan Museum of Art, The Carnegie Museum of Art, The Boston Public Library. Named Academician of the National Academy of Design, 1992. Office: c/o Middlebury College Center for the Arts Route 30 South Middlebury VT 05753*

BUMGARNER, JAMES SCOTT See GARNER, JAMES

BUMGARNER, MARLENE ANNE, editor, educator, writer; b. Yorkshire, Eng., Nov. 6, 1947; arrived in U.S., 1949, naturalized, 1965; d. Rowland and May (Whittaker) Skirrow; m. John Owen Bumgarner, June 17, 1967 (div. 1982); children: Dona Ana, John Rowland; m. Robert Eltgroth, Feb. 19, 1983 (div. 1992); children: Deborah Ruth, Jamie Lynn. AA, Coll. San Mateo, 1967; BA, San Diego State Coll., 1970; MA, San Jose State Coll., 1982; EdD, Nova Southwestern U., 1992. Tech. editor electronics firms, 1967—70; coord. Peer Counseling Center, Las Cruces, N.Mex., 1970—72; tchr. elem. sch., 1974—76, 1982—84; owner, mgr. Natural Food Store Morgan Hill Trading Post, Calif., 1976—80; editor Natural Living Newsline, 1979—81; mgr. Natural Living Assocs., 1979—82; dir. Morgan Hill Country Day Sch., 1980—82; prof. child devel., chair social sci. Gavilan Coll., 1979—85, coord. child devel. programs, 1985—99, chair social sci. dept., 1999—2001, dir. & grant mgr. Tchr. & Reading Devel. Partnership, 2001—. New products editor Classroom Computer Learning mag., 1980-82. Author: Book of Whole Grains, 1976, (contbr.) The People's Cookbook, 1977, Organic Cooking for (not-so-organic) Mothers, 1980, (contbr.) Real Food Places to Eat, 1981, The New Book of Whole Grains, 1995, Working With School-Aged Children, 1999; food columnist San Jose Mercury, 1977-80, Gilroy Dispatch, 1984-86; sr. tech. writer Boole and Babbage, Inc., 1983-85; contbg. editor Mothering mag., 1981-87; contbr. articles to Mother's Manual, Baby Talk, Am. Baby, McCalls, Family Computing, PC Computing and others. Mem. Morgan Hill Libr. Commn., 1999—2001; supt. Sunday sch. St. John's Episc. Ch., 1985—85, sr. warden, 1992—94; bd. dir. Calif. Sch. Age Consortium, 1998—2003, Santa Clara Valley Red Cross (Cul-Ox chpt.), 1992—2000, YMCA (Mt. Madonna Chpt.), 1995—2000; founder, leader La Leche League of Morgan Hill, 1977—85; coord. Morgan Hill Cmty. Garden, 1982—84; participant C.C. Women Leaders for the 80's, 1987. Named Woman of Achievement, Santa Clara County, 1987, Educator of Yr., Morgan Hill C of C, 2001. Mem.: AAUW, Nat. Sch. Age Care Alliance, Nat. Assn. Edn. Young Children. E-mail: mbumgarner@gavilan.edu.

BUMGARNER, ROBERT LINVILLE, pathologist, retired military officer; b. Long Branch, Calif., Oct. 15, 1944; BS in Physics, Mich. State U., 1967, MD, 1974. Diplomate Am. Bd. in Anatomic and Clin. Pathology. Commd. ensign USN, 1967, advanced through grades to capt., 1987; intern, resident Naval Med. Ctr., Portsmouth, Va., 1975-79; chief of lab. Naval Submarine Med. Ctr., Groton, 1979-83; dir. Navy Drug Screening Lab., Jacksonville, 1983; force med. officer, commdr. submarine force U.S. Pacific Fleet, 1984-86; dir. for undersea medicine and radiation health USN, Washington, 1986-91; dir., commdg. officer Armed Forces Radiobiology Rsch. Inst., Bethesda, Md., 1991-95; dir. ancillary svcs. Naval Med. Ctr., San Diego, 1995-99; fleet surgeon U.S. Pacific Fleet, 1999—2001; prin. scientist Springfield Rsch. Facility Defense Threat Reduction Agy., Alexandria, Va., 2002—04; prin. physician Chem., Biol., Radiol., Nuclear, and High Explosives Health Effects and Response Sci. Applications Internat. Corp., Merrifield, 2004—. Expert in toxicology, radiobiology, biol. agts., 2002--. Fellow Coll. of Am. Pathologists (lead lab. accreditation inspector 1999-2001). Office: PO Box 3341 Merrifield VA 22116-3341 Office Phone: 703-676-5468. E-mail: bumgarnerr@saic.com.

BUMP, ELIZABETH BERTHA, music educator; d. Earl Harald and Lillian May Bump. BA in Music, Rivier Coll., Nashua, NH, 1978. Band dir., choir dir. Ascension Sch., Melbourne, Fla., 2002—03; recorder ensemble dir.; cantor trainer. Dir. bell choir Ascension Sch.; advisor Tri-M Nat. Music Hon. Soc., Nat. Band Acad. Nominee Disney Tchr. of Yr., 2004. Mem.: Nat. Assn. Women in Music, Schawn Keyboard Soc., Nat. Fedn. Music Clubs, Music Educators Nat. Conf., Nat. Cath. Edn. Assn. (Orlando diocesan religion com., music curriculum com.). E-mail: ebump@ascensioncatholicsch.org.

BUMPAS, STUART MARYMAN, lawyer; b. Little Rock, Oct. 7, 1944; s. Hubert Wayne Bumpas and Martha Conway (Maryman) Gaylord; m. Diane Ellen DeWare, Oct. 1, 1977. BA, Brown U., 1966; JD, U. Tex., 1969; LLM, George Washington U., 1973. Bar: Tex. 1969, D.C. 1972. Atty.-advisor Office of Chief Counsel, Washington, 1969-72; asst. to commr. IRS, Washington, 1973-74; ptnr. Locke, Purnell, Rain, Harrell, Dallas, 1974-98, Locke, Liddell & Sapp, Dallas, 1999—. Adj. prof. employee benefits Sch. Meth. U., Dallas, 1975; lectr. Washington Non-Profit Tax Conf., Am. Law Inst., Ann. Non-Profit Orgns. Inst. Contbr. articles to profl. jours. Exec. com. Meadows Sch. of Arts, So. Meth. U., Dallas; bd. dirs. Callier Ctr. for Comm. Disorders, Dallas, 1984—, Friends of Alzheimer's Dis. Ctr., Southwestern Med. Sch., Goodwill Industries, Dallas; bd. dirs., v.p. Dallas Grand Opera Assn., 1984; mem. Mayor's Commn. on Internat. Devel. Task Force on Arts and Culture, Dallas, 1988; nat. counsel Am. Heart Assn., Dallas, 1979—; trustee The Lamplighter Sch.; gen. counsel The Hockaday Sch.; gen. counsel, bd. trustees, exec. com. Dallas Mus. Art; bd. trustees Southwestern Med. Found. Mem. ABA (mem. exempt orgns. com.), Tex. Bar Assn. (former chmn. legal aspects of arts com.), Dallas Bar Assn., Bus. Adv. Com., Am. Coun. on Germany, Coun. on Fgn. Rels. Clubs: Dallas Petroleum, Brook Hollow Golf, Idlewild (Dallas); Soc. Cin. (Washington), Coral Beach and Tennis (Bermuda). Episcopalian. Home: 5306 Surrey Cir Dallas TX 75209-2427 Office: Locke Liddell & Sapp 2200 Ross Ave Ste 2200 Dallas TX 75201-6776 Office Phone: 214-740-8000. E-mail: sbumpas@lockeliddell.com.

BUMPASS, RONALD EUGENE, lawyer; b. Lubbock, Tex., Jan. 6, 1948; s. Donald E. and Edna (Pricer) B.; children: Bart, Buckley. BS in Pub. Adminstrn., U. Ark., 1970, JD, 1974. Bar: Ark. 1974, U.S. Dist. Ct. (we. dist.) Ark. 1975, U.S. Ct. Appeals (8th cir.) 1986, U.S. Supreme Ct. 1986. Pvt. practice, Fayetteville, Ark. Spl. chief justice Ark. Supreme Ct., Little Rock, 1989; arbitrator Fed. Mediation and Conciliation Svc., U.S. Dept. Labor, Am. Arbitration Assn., U.S. Postal Svc., Am. Postal Workers Union-AFL-CIO arbitration panel, Nat. Health Care Lawyers Arbitration Panel. City coun. mem. Fayetteville, Ark., 1980, chmn. police and fire commn., mem. city hall renovation com., vice mayor, 1984-88. Mem. Ark. Bar Assn. (health law com. 1990-94), Washington and Benton Counties Bar Assn., Nat. Coll. Criminal Def. Lawyers and Pub. Defenders, Nat. Health Care Lawyers, Alpha Kappa Lambda. Avocations: hunting, biking, reading, painting, horseback riding. Office: PO Box 4105 Fayetteville AR 72702-4105

BUNCH, BOB, manufacturing executive; Chmn., CEO Maverick Tube. Office: Maverick Tube Ste 700 16401 Swingley Ridge Rd Chesterfield MO 63017*

BUNCH, CHARLES E., manufacturing executive; b. 1950; BA, Internat. Affairs, Georgetown U.; MBA, Harvard U. With PPG Industries, Inc., Pitts., 1980—, mgr., European fin. and planning Paris, 1982—85, mgr. European flat glass and comml. products, 1985, mng. dir., Italian glass subs., 1986—88, corp. dir., purchasing and distbn. Pitts., 1988—92, gen. mgr., archtl. coatings, 1992—94, v.p., archtl. coatings, 1994, v.p., fiber glass, 1995—97, sr. v.p. strategic planning and corp. svcs., 1997—2000, exec. v.p., 2000—02, pres., COO, dir., 2002—05, chmn., CEO, 2005—. Bd. dirs. H.J. Heinz Co., Nat. Paint and Coatings Assoc., Nat. Assoc. Manufacturers; dir., deputy chmn. Fed. Reserve Bank of Cleveland. Bd. dirs. U. Pitts. Office: PPG Industries 1 PPG Pl Pittsburgh PA 15272*

BUNCH, CHARLOTTE, advocate; b. Ashe County, N.C., Oct. 13, 1944; d. Pardue and Marjorie Bunch. BA in History magna cum laude, Duke U., 1966; postgrad., Inst. Policy Studies, Washington, 1967-68. Founder Ctr. Women's Global Leadership Rutgers U., New Brunswick, NJ, 1989—, dir., disting. prof. women's and gender studies. Spkr. in field. Creator, editor: Quest: A Feminist Quar., 1974, 1980. Office: Ctr Womens Global Leadership Douglas Coll Rutgers U 160 Ryders Ln New Brunswick NJ 08901-8555 Office Phone: 732-932-8782. Business E-Mail: cwgl@igc.org.

BUNCH, JENNINGS BRYAN, JR., retired electrical engineer; b. Richmond, Va., Feb. 9, 1929; s. Jennings Bryan and Cora Irving (Wilson) B.; m. Dale Metcalf, Feb. 2, 1952 (dec. Nov. 1996); children: Jennifer, Pamela; m. Harriet Walton, Jan. 2, 1999. BSEE with distinction, Va. Mil. Inst., 1950; MSEE, U. Pitts., 1969. Engr. in tng. Va. Electric & Power Co., Alexandria, Richmond, 1950, 53; test engr. and mktg. assignments GE, Schenectady, N.Y., 1956-63, application engr., 1956-63, regional application engr. Pitts., Phila., 1963-73, sr. application engr., project mgr. Phila. and Schenectady, 1973-82, Malvern, Pa., 1982-91; cons. Star Design, Moorestown, N.J., 1992-96. Contbr. articles on electric utility distbn. automation systems to profl. publs. Exec. dir. Sending Experienced Ret. Vols. Everywhere (SERVE), 1993-2003. 1st lt. U.S. Army, 1950-52. Fellow: IEEE; mem.: Tau Beta Pi. Republican. Presbyterian. Avocations: hiking, astronomy.

BUNCH, MICHAEL BRANNEN, psychologist, educator; b. Miami, Fla., Oct. 19, 1949; s. Edwin Bunch and Janet (Morgan) Bradley; m. Kathryn Ann Campbell, Jan. 17, 1970; children: Melissa Anne, Amy Kathryn. BS, U. Ga., 1972, MS, 1974, PhD, 1976. Tests and measurement specialist Mountain Plains Corp., Glasgow, Mont., 1975-76; rsch. psychologist Am. Coll. Testing Program, Iowa City, 1976-78; sr. profl. NTS Rsch. Corp., Durham, N.C., 1978-82; sr. v.p. Measurement Inc., Durham, NC, 1982—. Mem. Durham Pub. Edn. Task Force, Durham, 1983-90; chmn. Durham Math. Coun., 1985-90; adj. faculty N.C. Ctrl. U., Durham, 1988-93. Mem. Am. Psychol. Soc., Am. Ednl. Rsch. Assn., Nat. Coun. Measurement in Edn., Ga. Ednl. Rsch. Assn., Sigma Xi. Home: 6 Fernwood Ct Durham NC 27713-7547 Office: Measurement Inc 423 Morris St Durham NC 27701-2128 Business E-Mail: mbunch@measinc.com.

BUNCH, RICHARD ALAN, writer, educator, poet, philosopher; b. Honolulu, June 1, 1945; s. Thornton Carlisle and DeLores (Veal) B.; m. Rita Anne Glazar, Aug. 11, 1990; children: Katharine, Richard Jr. AA in Liberal Arts, Napa Coll., 1965; student, Stanford -in-Britain, Grantham, Lincolnshire, Eng., 1966; BA in Comms., Stanford U., 1967; MA in History, U. Ariz., 1969, MDiv, 1970, DD in Religion and Theology, 1971; student in Philosophy, Vanderbilt U., 1972—75; postgrad., Temple U., 1975—76; JD, U. Memphis, 1980. Tchg. asst. philosophy Vanderbilt U., Nashville, 1973-74; instr. philosophy Belmont U., 1973-74; law clk. Cir. Ct. Shelby County, Tenn., 1979-81; atty. Horne and Peppel, Memphis, 1981-83; law clk. Tenn. Ct. Appeals, 1983; instr. philosophy Chapman U., 1986-87; instr. law Sonoma State U., 1986-87, instr. philosophy, 1990-91. Lectr. in religion U. Calif., Berkeley, 1995; adj. humanities faculty Napa Valley Coll., 1985—; instr. history and humanities Diablo Valley Coll., 1991-94, 97; adj. history and humanities faculty Solano Coll., 1988—. Author: Summer Hawk, 1991, Night Blooms, 1992, Wading the Russian River, 1993, Santa Rosa Plums, 1996, A Foggy Morning, 1996, South By Southwest, 1997, Sacred Space, 1998, Rivers of the Sea, 1998, Greatest Hits: 1970-2000, 2001, Running for Daybreak, 2004; (play) The Russian River Returns, 1999; contbr. articles to revis.; assoc. news editor, reporter, feature writer Napa Valley Times, 1985. Staff Nashville Human Rights Forum, 1974-75; chmn. Housing Authority-Bldg. Authority Bd. City of Napa, 1985-89. Recipient Grand prize Ina Coolbrith Nat. Poetry Day Contest, 1989, Jessamyn West prize in creative writing, 1990. Mem. Ina Coolbrith Cir., Poetry Soc. Am. Home: 248 Sandpiper Dr Davis CA 95616-7546

BUNCH, ROGER DALE, music educator; b. Springfield, Tenn., Sept. 21, 1944; s. Elmer Keene Bunch and Grace Virginia Poole. BS, Austin Peay State U., 1968. Band and choir educator Bransford H.S., Springfield, 1968—70, Jo Byrns H.S., Cedar Hill, Tenn., 1970—85, Greenbrier (Tenn.) H.S., 1985—2001; choir dir. Biloxi (Miss.) H.S., 2004—05. Music dir. Robertson Co. Players, Springfield, 1981—91. Fundraising program chair Am. Cancer Soc., Springfiled, 1987—97. Mem.: Miss. Choral Dir. Assn., Music Educators Nat. Conf. Democrat. Baptist. Avocations: writing, painting, cooking, travel. Home: 165 Lee St Biloxi MS 39530

BUNCHER, CHARLES RALPH, epidemiologist, educator; b. Dover, N.J., Jan. 18, 1938; BS, MIT, 1960; MS, Harvard U., 1964, ScD, 1967. Statistician Atomic Bomb Casualty Comsn., NAS, 1967-70; chief biostatistician Merrell-Nat. Labs., 1970-73, asst. prof. stats., 1970-73; prof. and dir. divsn. epidemiology and biostats. Med. Coll., U. Cin., 1973-96, prof. biostats. and epidemiology, 1973—, dir. grad. edn., 2001—. Fellow Am. Stats. Assn., Am. Coll. Epidemiology; mem. APHA, Biometrical Assn., Soc. Epidemiol. Rsch., Soc. Med. Decision Making, Soc. Clin. Trials, Tau Beta Pi. Achievements include research in cancer epidemiology; screening, diagnosis and treatment, as well as occupational and environmental epidemiology; risk analysis; statistical research; clinical trials; design of experiments; pharmaceutical research; biostatistical analysis, pharmaceutical statistics, ALS epidemiology. Office: U Cincinnati Div of Epidemiology & Biostatistics PO Box 670183 Cincinnati OH 45267-0183 Office Phone: 513-558-1410. Business E-Mail: charles.buncher@uc.edu.

BUNCKE, HARRY J., plastic surgeon, educator; Grad., Lehigh U.; MD, NY Med. Coll., 1951. With Met. Hosp., Flower and Fifth Ave. Hosp., NY Med. Coll., 1952—55; residency in plastic surgery Bronx Veterans Admin. Hosp. and NY Hosp., Cornell Med. Sch., 1954—56; Marks Fellow in plastic and maxollofacial surgery Queen Victoria Hosp., Sussex, England, 1956; sr. registrar plastic surgical and burn unit Glasgow Royal Infirmary, Scotland, 1957; mem. plastic surgery staff Mills Mem. Hosp., San Mateo, 1959—; dir. div. microsurgical replantation Ralph K. Davies Med. Ctr., San Francisco, 1975—; dir. emeritus The Buncke Clinic. Prof. surgery U. Calif., San Francisco; assoc. clin. prof. surgery Stanford U.; vis. prof. and delivered disting. lectureships at more then 50 instns. Author: 15 movies and television tapes, four books and over 400 pubs. Named Prof. Honoris Causae, French Ministry Edn.; recipient Hon. Award, Am. Assn. Plastic Surgery, 1979, Markowitz Award, Acad. Surgical Rsch., Jacobson Innovation Award, Am. Coll. Surgeons, 2004. Mem.: Japanese Soc. for Hand Surgery, Spanish Soc. Microsurgery, French Soc. Plastic and Reconstructive Surgeons, Internat. Soc. Reconstructive Microsurgery (chmn. 1977), Am. Soc. Surgery of Hand (pres. 1980), Italian Soc. Microsurgery. Achievements include first to perform toe-to-hand transplant in a rhesus monkey, 1966; the first microvascular transplant in world, 1969; the first great toe-to-thumb transplant in US, 1972; the first successful scalp replant in the US, 1976; the first four-finger replant in the US, 1976; the first latissimus seratus transplant, 1979; with Dr. Rudolf Bantic, the first successful tongue replant in the world, 1997. Office: The Buncke Clinic 45 Castro Street Ste 140N San Francisco CA 94114

BUNDA, STEPHEN MYRON, political advisor, counselor, lawyer, classical philosopher; b. Jersey City, Oct. 5, 1949; s. Stephen and Anna (Yaschak) B. BA summa cum laude, St. Peter's Coll., Jersey City, 1971; MA with honors, New Sch. Grad. Faculty, N.Y.C., 1976; JD, Rutgers Law Sch., Newark, N.J., 1987. Bar: N.J. Pol. cons. Democratic Party, N.J., 1977-92; pol. adv. Govt. of Ukraine, 1991—; counsellor-at-law Bunda & Co., Lyndhurst, N.J., 1994—. Advisor on Ukraine to U.S. Congress, Office of the Pres., Nat. Security Coun., Washington, 1991—. Mem. Nat. Honor Soc., Am. Hist. Assn., Am. Philos. Assn., Ukrainian-Am. Bar Assn., N.J. Bar Assn., Soc. for Ukrainian-Jewish Rels., Ukrainian Nat. Assn., Lawyers Com. for Human Rights. Democrat. Mem. Ukrainian Catholic Ch. Avocations: reading philosophy and history, educational travel and sight-seeing, music, art, literature, theater. Home: 691 Union Ave Lyndhurst NJ 07071-2815 Office: Stephen Myron Bunda Esquire PO Box 461 Lyndhurst NJ 07071

BUNDCHEN, GISELLE, model; b. Horizontina, Rio Grande do Sul, Brazil, July 20, 1980; d. Valdir and Vania Bundchen. Model appearing on covers of various magazines including Vogue USA, Vogue Italia GQ, Harper's Bazaar, W, Rolling Stone, marie claire, ELLE, i-D, Allure, Big, Arena, The Face; model Christian Dior, Missoni, Ralph Lauren, Celine, Victoria's Secret, ZARA, Dolce & Gabbana, Strenesse, Versace, Valentino, Gianfranco Ferre, Chloe, Forum, Alphorria, Daslu, Hering, Lycra, Cori; featured in Pirelli Calendar, 1997. Actor: (films) Taxi, 2004. Achievements include highest paid model in the world. Office: IMG Models Penthouse North 12th Fl 304 Park Ave South New York NY 10010*

BUNDI, RENEE, art director, graphic designer; b. Elmont, NY, Apr. 20, 1962; d. Anthony Joseph and Marion Rose (Graziano) B. Student, St. John's U., 1980-84. Creative dir. Coastal Comm., NYC, 1985-86; art and prodn. coord. Cahner's Pub. Co./Datamation mag., NYC, 1986-87; sr. prodn. editor CMP Publ./Var Bus. Computer Sys. News, Manhasset, NY, 1987-89, asst. art dir., 1989-91; assoc. art dir. Varbus. CMP Publ., 1991-94; sr. art dir. Info. Week Mag., 1994-2000; instr. graphic design and media arts The Gibbs Sch., 2000-01; chair web design, digital media and animation, program dir. The Gibbs Sch., Design and Animation Ctr., 2001—02; program dir. Gibbs Design and Animation Center, 2002—03; prodn. design Suede Mag., Time, Inc., 2003—. Recipient Print Design award Print mag., 1988, 91, 92, 93, 94, 95, 98, 99, 2000, Ozzie Design award Mag. Design and Prodn., 1988, 89, 90, 91, 98, 99, 2000. Mem. Graphic Artist Guild, Soc. Publ. Designers (Excellence in Design award 1987, 88, 89, 92, 93, 94, 99), ASBPE (Excellence of Design 1997, 98, 99, 2000), MacIntosh User's Group, Soc. Illustrators (Best Spot Illustration). Roman Catholic. Avocations: theater, bowling, painting, photography.

BUNDRUM, KENNETH OWEN, lawyer, writer; b. Anniston, Ala., Feb. 6, 1955; s. Cecil David Bundrum and Jessie Mae Stevenson. LLB, Roosevelt U., Zurich, 1974—78. Lawyer Nat. Bar Assn., N.Y.C., 1982—86, Nat. Lawyers Guild, N.Y.C., 2002—. Author: (book) The Fighting Stevensons: Honor and War, 1998. Candidate Ala. State Ho. Reps., Dist. 5, 1982; candidate for Ala. Atty. Gen., 2002. Recipient Legion of South Award, League of the South, 1999. Mem.: Sons of Confederate Veterans (hon. col. 1988). Republican. Roman Catholic. Home: 555 Cottaquilla Rd Jacksonville AL 36265

BUNDY, ANNALEE MARSHALL, library director; b. Chgo., Feb. 11, 1938; d. Warren Elmer and Marie Thresa (Madden) Marshall; m. John Willard Bundy, Mar. 11, 1961. BA, U. N.H., 1960; MLS, Simmons Coll., 1961. Assoc. head libr. Coll. Guam Libr., Agana, 1961-62, head libr., 1962-63; tech. libr. E.I. duPont de Nemours & Co., Maydown Works, Londonderry, No. Ireland, 1963-65; head libr. children's rm. Schenectady County (N.Y.) Libr., 1965-66; documents and periodicals libr. Grad. Sch. Pub. Affairs, SUNY, Albany, 1966-67; asst. dir. Medford (Mass.) Pub. Libr., 1967-73; dir. librs. Somerville (Mass.) Pub. Libr., 1973-78; dir. Providence Pub. Libr., 1978-88; program dir. EPA Librs. and Records Ctrs., 1990-91; exec. dir. Ames Free Libr., Easton, Mass., 1992—. Adj. faculty U. R.I. Grad. Libr. Sch.; cons. libr. bldgs., automation, govt. rels.; mem. adv. com. R.I. Sch. Design; mem. accreditation vis. team New Eng. Bd. Higher Edn.; challenge grant panelist NEH. Compiler: Alternatives in Print, II, 1972; mem. editl. bd. The Bottom Line: A Fin. Mag. for Librs.; contbr. articles to profl. jours. Mem. Mass. Cable TV Commn., 1975-79; bd. corporators Butler Hosp., 1983-2004; bd. dirs. Leadership R.I., 1984-88, R.I. Film and Video Competition. Recipient David E. Sweet award Leadership R.I., 1987, Disting. Leadership Alumni award Nat. Assn. Cmty. Leadership Orgns., 1987; Brown Humanities Inst. fellow, 1985-87. Mem. ALA (PLA/MLS sect. pres. 1981-82, chmn. Allie Beth Martin award com. 1986), New Eng. Libr. Assn., Agawam Hunt Club, Providence Art Club. Office: 53 Main St North Easton MA 02356-1496

BUNDY, BLAKELY FETRIDGE, early childhood educator, advocate; b. Chgo., Aug. 31, 1944; d. William Harrison and Bonnie Jean (Clark) Fetridge; m. Harvey Hollister Bundy III, Aug. 20, 1966; children: Harvey Hollister Bundy IV, Elizabeth Lowell, Reed Fetridge. BA cum laude, Wheaton Coll., Mass., 1966; MEd, Nat.-Louis U., 1985. Tchr. Norwich (Vt.) Kindergarten, 1966-67, Willow Wood Pre-Sch., Winnetka, Ill., 1983-93, bd. dirs., 1972-81, adv. bd., 1981-83, 93—. Bd. dirs. North Ave. Day Nursery, Chgo., 1970-76; exec. dir. Winnetka Alliance for Early Childhood, 1989—; accreditation system validator, mentor Nat. Acad. Early Childhood Programs, Washington, 1986-2004; mem. pres.'s commn. Wheaton Coll., Norton, Mass., 1987-99; trustee Brooks Sch., North Andover, Mass., 1993-2004; mem. adv. bd. Ctr. for Early Childhood Leadership, 2002—, Filene Ctr. for Work and Learning, Wheaton Coll., 1999—; cons. editor Nat. Assn. Edn. Young Children,

1991-94. Editor: Early Childhood; contbr. articles to Chgo. Tribune, Redbook, Glamour mags., Early Childhood News, Child Care Ctr. Mag., Chgo. Sun-Times, Day Care and Early Education, Young Children, other publs. Mem. Ill. Shore Coun. Girl Scouts U.S., 1981-89, World Found. for Girls Guides and Girl Scouts Friends of Our Cabana Com., Cuernavaca, Mexico, 1986-94. Mem.: Olive Baden-Powell Soc. (London), Chgo. Metro Assn. Edn. Young Children (steering com. Near North Suburban chpt. 1986—2001, commn. on salaries and working conditions 1988—92, co-chair pub. rels. com. 1992—2000, bd. dirs. 1992—, photography editor Connections 1992—, chair accreditation project mgmt. com. 1994—98, co-editor News & Views: The Accreditation Project Newsletter 1996—98, pres. 2003—05), Ill. Soc. Early Childhood Profls. (bd. dirs. 1993—96, editor newsletter), World Assn. Girl Guides and Girl Scouts, Nat. Assn. for the Edn. Young Children (photographer publs.), Ocean Reef Club (Key Largo, Fla.), Yacht Club, Stevensville Club (Mich.), Indian Hill Club (Winnetka). Episcopalian. Avocations: golf, boating. Office: Winnetka Alliance for Early Childhood 1235 Oak St Winnetka IL 60093-2168 E-mail: blakelybandy@yahoo.com.

BUNDY, CHARLES ALAN, retired foundation executive; b. Cheraw, S.C., Jan. 5, 1930; s. Jackson Corbett and Ruby Jones (Hughes) B.; m. Margaret Ellen Jackson, Feb. 27, 1954; children: Charles Alan, Robert Jackson, Dan Hughes. AB, Wofford Coll., 1951; DH (hon.), Charleston So. U. Mgr. prodn. planning J.P. Stevens & Co., Inc., Rockingham, N.C., 1951-54; mgr. Jesup (Ga.) C. of C., 1954-56, Lancaster (S.C.) C. of C., 1956-61; dist. mgr. U.S. C. of C., Birmingham, Ala., 1961-65; exec. v.p. Macon (Ga.) C. of C., 1965-71, Greg Enterprises, Lancaster, 1971-72; pres. Springs Found., Inc. and Close Found., Inc., Lancaster, 1972-97, ret., 1997; pvt. practice cons., 1997—; ret., 2004. Chmn. Diabetes Edn. Ctr.; vice chmn. Ednl. Found. at U. S.C., Lancaster. Chmn. SC Parks, Recreation and Tourism Commn., 1983—89; mem. SC Coordinating Coun. for Econ. Devel., 1986—89; mem., past chmn. S. E. Coun. on Founds.; trustee Columbia Coll., 1976—88, SC Found. Ind. Colls., 1982—93; chmn. Gov.'s Freshwater Wetlands Forum, 1989, Lancaster County Strategic Plan, 1990; trustee J. Marion Sims Found., Inc.; mem. State Govt. Reorgn. Commn., 1991; chmn. bd. 1st Meth. Ch., 1978, 1979; bd. dir. Springs Meml. Hosp. Mem. Lancaster County Higher Edn. Commn., Lancaster County C. of C. (past pres.), Rotary (past pres.). Home: 518 Briarwood Rd Lancaster SC 29720-1802

BUNDY, CHERYL LASOTA, non-profit executive, consultant; b. Kansas City, Feb. 21, 1967; d. Thomas Richard and Barbara (Miller) LaSota; m. William Paul Bundy, May 30, 1992; children: Katherine Taylor, William Paul Jr. BA, Smith Coll., 1988; MPA, NYU, 1997. Registered rep. Morgan Stanley, N.Y.C.; assoc. dir. bus. devel. OFFITBANK, N.Y.C., 1990-96, west coast rep., 1996-98; dir. centennial planning Assn. Jr. Leagues Internat., N.Y.C., 1998—2001; dir. devel. and gift planning St. James Ch., 2002—. Vol. Jr. League, N.Y.C., 1989-01, bd. dirs., 1994-96; bd. dirs. Alumnae Fund of Smith Coll., Northampton, Mass., 1993-96. Jr. League L.A., 1997-98; v.p. YWCA, N.Y.C., 2001—; vice chmn. St. Mary's Found. for Children, 2001, Bayside, N.Y., 2001—. E-mail: bundy_cheryl@hotmail.com, clb@stjames.org.

BUNDY-DESOTO, TERESA MARI, language educator, vocalist; d. Jose Jesus Avila-Carrillo and Maria del Pilar Lozano Avila; m. Glendon B. Bundy, Oct. 15, 1972 (div. May 20, 1987); children: Pete Hernandez Bundy, Angelita Dianne Bundy, Crystal Lorraine Bundy-Schwabenland, Ivan Glen Bundy; m. John B. Soto, Mar. 31, 1996. AA magna cum laude, Fresno City Coll., 1976; BA summa cum laude, Calif. State U., Fresno, 1978; Spanish and bilingual tchg. credential, Calif. State U. Fresno, 1979. Master tchr., trainer Proteus Adult Edn., Visalia, Calif., 1967—73; tchr. trainer Fresno City-County Manpower Commn., Calif., 1973—76; tchr. Spanish, mentor tchr. Ctrl. Unified Sch. Dist., Fresno, 1979—86; dept. chairperson Madera Unified Sch. Dist., Calif., 1986—89; tchr. Spanish, English Hoover H.S./Fresno Unified Sch. Dist., 1989—. Rschr., trainer Office of Edn., Washington, 1968—74; adult edn. tchr. Chavez Adult Edn. Ctr.; alt. chief examiner ofcl. GED testing ctr. Gen. Ednl. Devel. Testing Svc., 1999—; spkr. in field. Singer: recorded 2 CDs and mus. videos under stage name Luz De Luna. Profl. radio announcer Spanish Radio Stas., Fresno, 1978—96; TV model Spanish TV Univision, Fresno, 1980; judge Miss Laverkin, Utah, 1982. Recipient Miss El Futuro C.U., 1967, 1972. Mem.: Am. Coun. on Edn., Calif. Tchr. Assn. Democrat. Mem. Lds Ch. Home: 1149 E San Bruno Ave Fresno CA 93710 Office Phone: 559-225-4880. Business E-Mail: tadesot@fresno.k12.ca.us.

BUNE, KAREN LOUISE, state agency administrator; b. Washington, Mar. 6, 1954; d. Harry and Eleanor Mary (White) B. BA in Am. Studies cum laude, Am. U., 1976, MS in Adminstrn. of Justice with distinction, 1978. Diplomate in traumatic stress, cert. trauma specialist, bd. cert. in domestic violence. Case mgr. Arlington (Va.) Alcohol Safety Action Program, 1979-94; victim specialist Office of Commonwealth's Atty., Arlington, 1994—2004; cons. victim issues Dept. Justice, Office for Victims, 2001—; victim specialist, legal asst. States Attys. Office for Prince George's County, Md., 2004—. Case mgr. regional rep. of case mgmt. com. of Dirs. Assn. Commn. on Va. Alcohol Safety Action Program, Richmond, 1980-81, 84-85, 88-89, mem. subcom. studying treatment issues, 1988-94; chair career guidance subcom. alumni adv. com. Sch. Pub. Affairs Am. U., Washington, 1991-94; participant IACP Summit on Victims of Crime, 1999, nat. forum on terrorism, NCJA, 2002; adj. prof. George Mason U., Fairfax, Va., Marymount U., Arlington. Named Woman of Yr., Am. Biog. Inst., 1990; named to Outstanding Achievement in Case Mgmt. Hall of Fame; recipient Spl. Achievement award, Dept. Navy, 1973, Merit award, Arlington County, 1986, 1997, cert. Recognition Svc. to Crime Victims, 3d Ann. Neighborhood Day, 1999, cert. Appreciation, US Dept. Justice, 2000, 2004, Carl T. Earles Meml. Cmty. Svc. award, No. Va. Crime Prevention Assn., 1999, 2001, cert. Appreciation, Peddlers for Peace, 2004. Fellow: Am. Acad. Experts in Traumatic Stress (cert. in domestic violence); mem.: AAUW (nat. and Arlington, Va. chpt.), APHA, NAFE, Am. Soc. Pub. Adminstrn. (pres. No. Va. chpt. 2003—04, Kathy Hensley Disting. Svc. award No. Va. chpt. 2005), Am. Soc. Victimology, Cert. Traums Specialists Assn. Traumatic Stress Specialists, Va. Network for Victims and Witnesses of Crime, Md. Coalition Against Sexual Assault, Justice Studies Assn., Am. Criminal Justice Assn., Nat. Dist. Atty.'s Assn., Internat. Assn. Forensic Mental Health Svcs., Am. Acad. Experts in Traumatic Stress, Am. Sociol. Assn., Am. Pub. Human Svcs. Assn., Am. Profl. Soc. on Abuse of Children, Nat. Ctr. Women in Policing, Am. Probation and Parole Assn., Soc. for Study of Social Problems, Va. Assn. Female Execs., No. Va. Fraternal Order Police, No. Va. Crime Prevention Assn., Soc. Profl. Journalists, Va. Crime Prevention Assn., Internat. Narcotic Enforcement Officers Assn., Va. Sheriffs Inst., Am. Soc. Criminology, So. Criminal Justice Assn., Acad. Criminal Justice Scis., Am. Police Hall of Fame (cert. of appreciation 1985), Nat. Assn. Women Law Enforcement Execs., Nat. Ctr. Victims of Crime, Nat. Orgn. Victim Assistance, Nat. Criminal Justice Assn., Nat. Assn. Chiefs Police (award of merit 1986), Internat. Assn. Chiefs of Police (nat. adv. bd. on police-based victim response 2000—), MD Network Against Domestic Violence, World Affairs Coun., Washington Ind. Writers, Am. U. Alumni Assn. (immediate past pres. sch. pub. affairs chpt. 1994—96), Nat. Air Disaster Alliance Found., Nat. Press Club, Lambda Alpha Epsilon, Phi Delta Gamma (1st v.p. 1981—82), Phi Alpha Alpha, Phi Kappa Phi. Avocations: concerts, dance, travel, theater, writing. Home: 926 16th St S Arlington VA 22202-2606 Office Phone: 703-472-5811. Business E-Mail: kbune@gmu.edu.

BUNGAARD, ERNEST See GRAY, ALLEN

BUNGE, CHARLES ALBERT, library science educator; b. Kimball, Nebr., Mar. 18, 1936; s. Louis Herman and Leona Hazel (Cromwell) B.; m. Joanne C. VonStoeser, Aug. 20, 1960; children: Lorraine A., Jeffrey C. Stephen L. AB, U. Mo., 1959; MSLS, U. Ill., 1960, PhD, 1967. Reference libr. Daniel Boone Regional Libr., Columbia, Mo., 1960-62; Ball State Tchrs. Coll., Muncie, Ind., 1962-64; rsch. assoc. Libr. Rsch. Ctr., U. Ill., 1964-67; mem. faculty Sch. Libr. and Info. Studies U. Wis., Madison, 1967—97, prof. emeritus, 1997—. Author: Professional Education and Reference Efficiency, 1967; columnist: Wilson Library Bull, 1972-81. Mem. ALA (pres. ref. and adult svcs. divsn. 1987-88, chair com. on accreditation 1990-92, Mudge award 1983, mem. coun. 1993-96, Beta Phi Mu award 1997), Assn. Libr. and Info. Sci. Edn. (pres. 1980-81, Prof. Contribution award 1997), Wis. Libr. Assn. (pres. 1972-73, Libr. of Yr. 1983), Phi Beta Kappa, Beta Phi Mu. Home: 509 Orchard Dr Madison WI 53711-1316

BUNGE, CRYSTAL ANN, music educator; b. Carroll, Iowa, Apr. 27, 1968; d. Arlin John and Judith Ann Bunge. MusB in Edn., Morningside Coll., Sioux City, Iowa, 1990; MS in Edn., Buena Vista U., Storm Lake, Iowa, 1999. Cert. adjudicator Iowa H.S. Music Assn., 2003. K-12 vocal music and sch. newspaper advisor Graettinger Cmty. Schs., Graettinger, Iowa, 1990—94; 6-12 vocal music tchr., cheerleading coach, student advisor River Valley Cmty. Schs., Correctionville, Iowa, 1994—. Youth choir dir. Peace Luth. Ch., Wall Lake, Iowa, 2000—, accompanist, 1983—, vocalist, 1983—; cmty. chorus dir. Blackhawk Ministerial Assn., Wall Lake, 2001—; pvt. piano instr., Wall Lake, 2000—. Mem.: N.W. Iowa Choral Assn. (assoc.; v.p. 2003—04, pres. 2004—), River Valley Edn. Assn. (assoc.; v.p. 2001—02, sec. 2003—), Iowa Edn. Assn. (assoc.), NEA (assoc.), Iowa Choral Dirs. Assn. (assoc.), Am. Choral Dir. Assn. (assoc.). Home: 208 Melrose St Wall Lake IA 51466-0455 Office: River Valley Community Schools 916 Hackberry St Correctionville IA 51016-0008 Office Phone: 712-372-4656. Office Fax: 712-372-4784. Personal E-mail: cbunge@netins.net.

BUNGE, JONATHAN GUNN, lawyer; b. La Crosse, Wis., Oct. 20, 1936; s. Jonathan Clement and Anne Liddell (Gunn) Bunge; m. Gertrude Shoemaker, June 18, 1961; children: Jonathan C., Katherine E.; 1 child, William H. BA cum laude, Princeton U., 1958; JD, Harvard U., 1961. Bar: Ill. 1961, US Supreme Ct. 1968. Assoc. Lees & Bunge, Chgo., 1961—62, Keck, Mahin & Cate, Chgo., 1964—71; ptnr., 1971—95. Ross & Hardies, Chgo., 1995—2000; atty. Law Offices Jonathan G. Bunge, PC, Chgo., 2000—; of counsel Davis & Campbell, LLC, Peoria, Ill., 2004—; pres. DePaul Mgmt. Co., 1985—; instr. John Marshall Law Sch., 1968—73; mem. adv. pane. Ea.-we. Trade US Dept. Commerce, 1977—78. Served U.S. Army, 1962—64. Mem.: Maritime Law Assn., Bar Assn. 7th Cir., Ill. State Bar Assn., Internat. Bar Assn., Chgo. Bar Assn., ABA, ARC (bd. dir. Mid-Am. chpt. 1975—87, vice chmn. 1981—82, Chgo. region 1981—95, vice chmn. 1982—85, chmn. 1983—86), St. Gregory's Episcopal Sch. (mem. 1990—), Holy Comforter Ch. (vestryman Kenilworth, Ill. 1979—84, 1998—2001), Chgo. Work Ethic Corp. (bd. dir. 1988—94), Mich. Shores Club (Chgo.), Chgo. Yacht Club, Lawyers Club, Sheridan Shores Yacht Club, Econ. Club. Episc. Home: 821 Sheridan Rd Wilmette IL 60091 Office: 3014 N Racine Ste 1 Chicago IL 60657 Office Phone: 773-404-5900. Business E-Mail: jbunge@bungelaw.com.

BUNGE, MARY BARTLETT, medical educator; PhD, U. Wis., 1960. Postdoctoral fellow in neurobiology Columbia Coll. Physicians and Surgeons, N.Y.C., 1960—62; rsch. assoc. neurobiology Harvard U., Cambridge, Mass., 1968—69; rsch. assoc. anatomy Columbia U., N.Y.C., 1963—70; prof. anatomy/neurobiology Washington U., St. Louis, 1970—89; vis. rschr. MRC Cell Biophysics Unit, King's Coll., London, 1984; prof. cell biology/anatomy/neurol. surgery U. Miami, 1989—. Contbr. articles to profl. jours. Mem.: Soc. for Neurosci. Achievements include research in in the development and repair of neural tissue, particularly the cell-cell and cell-extracellular matrix interactions that occur during peripheral nerve development; during Schwann cell (SC) ensheathment and myelination and during axonal growth and regrowth. Office: Univ Miami Sch Medicine Dept Cell Biology/Anatomy 1600 NW 10th Ave Miami FL 33136

BUNGE, RUSSELL KENNETH, writer, poet, editor; b. Long Beach, Calif., Apr. 28, 1947; s. Kenneth Duncan Bunge and Mona Irene (Deleree) Coker; ptnr. Mr. Kelly A. Quiros. BA in Creative Writing, Calif. State U., Long Beach, 1972; MA in Humanities, Calif. State U., Dominguez Hills, 1985. Cert. C.C. tchr., Calif. Spl. svcs. cons. AT&T Comms., San Luis Obispo, Calif., 1973-90; info. cons. Obispo Info. Group, San Luis Obispo, 1990-95; pub. deleree com, San Luis Obispo, Calif., 1996—. Mem. adv. bd. Calif. Online Resources for Edn., Long Beach, 1993-94; edn. coord. SLONET Info. Network, 1993-95, dir., 1997-98. Author: Double Lives: Poems 1984-1985, 1985, Junction, 2001; editor: Obispo Web Digest: on the World Wide Web, 1994-96; contbr. poems to profl. publs. Founding mem. AIDS Support Network, San Luis Obispo, 1984. Mem. MLA, Assn. Study Lit. & Environ. Office: Wirewove Web Solutions PO Box 771 San Luis Obispo CA 93406-0771 E-mail: rkbunge@pacbell.net.

BUNGO, MICHAEL WILLIAM, cardiologist, educator, science administrator; b. Passaic, N.J., July 18, 1950; s. John C. and Mary Bungo; children: Elise Nicole, Jonathan Michael. BS in Chemistry, Rensselaer Poly. Inst., 1971; MD, N.J. Med. Sch., 1975. Diplomate Am. Bd. Internal Medicine, Subsplty. Bd. Cardiovasc. Diseases. Intern in internal medicine New England Deaconess Hosp., Boston, 1975-76, resident, 1976-78; asst. in medicine Peter Bent Brigham Hosp., Boston, 1976-77; cardiology fellow New England Deaconess Hosp., Harvard Med. Sch., Boston, 1978-80; head cardiovascular lab. NASA, Johnson Space Ctr., Houston, 1980-85; mem. Aerospace Medicine Bd., Houston, 1980-91; dir. Space Biomed. Rsch. Inst. NASA, Johnson Space Ctr., Houston, 1986-90; chief scientist med. scis. divsn. NASA, 1990-91; prof. medicine U. Tex., Galveston, med. dir. heart sta. divsn. cardiology, 1995—2002, vice chmn. dept. internal medicine, 1999—2002; assoc. dean U. Tex. Med. Sch., Houston, 2002—; chief of staff LBJ Gen. Hosp., Houston, 2002—. Chmn. dept. medicine St. John Hosp., Houston, 1987—89; fellowship advisor NRC, Washington, 1984—89. Editor: Results of Life Sciences Aboard the Space Shuttle, 1987; contbr. abstracts and articles to jours., chpts. to books; tech. reviewer Circulation, Aviation, Space and environ. Medicine, 1989—; mem. editl. bd. Aviation, Space and Environ. Medicine, 1997-2000. Recipient medal NASA, 1986. Fellow ACP, Am. Coll. Cardiology; mem. Am. Heart Assn., Aerospace Med. Assn. (Louis H. Bauer Founders award 1987), Tex. Med. Assn., Am. Coll. of Physician Exec., Phi Lambda Upsilon. Office: U Tex Houston Med Sch Chief of Staff LBJ Hosp 5656 Kelley St Houston TX 77026 Office Phone: 713-566-4646.

BUNIAK, RAYMOND, educational professional; b. Sao Paulo, Mar. 21, 1955; came to U.S., 1959; s. Wasyl and Katharina (Kurpita) B.; m. Karen Sue Harbecke, Apr. 28, 1957. BA in Edn., Northeastern Ill. U., Chgo., 1977; MMus, DePaul U., 1981; EdD in Curriculum and Instrn., Loyola U., 2004. Cert. tchr. K-12, 6-12 music, Ill. Profl. musician/trombone and euphonium player, condr., Chgo. metro area, 1973—; studio tchr. of brass instruments various, Chgo. metro area, 1979—; band dir. New Trier West High, Northfield, Ill., 1981-82, O.L.P.H. Sch., Glenview, Ill., 1986-94; instrnl. devel. and grants officer/tchr. Kelly H.S., Chgo., 1994—. Grant writer for tech., instrnl. program improvements, coord. Internat. Baccalaureate Program, Kelly H.S., 1997—, coord. AP program, also coord. ILCA program. Author: A 20th Century Treatise on the Trombone, 4 vols., 1984. Recipient Univ. Talent scholarship Northeastern Ill. U., 1974-77. Mem. ACDS, Francis Galpin Soc., Internat. Trombone Assn., Nat. Cath. Bandmaster's Assn., Music Educators Nat. Conf., Chgo. Fedn. of Musicians. Avocations: household renovation, auto repair, bible tchr. Home: 105 N Western Ave Bartlett IL 60103-4030 Office: Thomas Kelly High Sch 4136 S California Ave Chicago IL 60632-1817 Office Phone: 773-535-4900. E-mail: rbuniak@cps.k12.il.us, RayBuniak105@msn.com.

BUNKER, BERYL H., retired insurance company executive, volunteer; b. Chelsea, Mass., Aug. 18, 1919; d. Albert Crocker and Eva Agnes (Norris) Hardacker; m. John Wadsworth Bunker, Oct. 31, 1942. Student, Simmons Coll., 1936—38, Boston Coll. Law, 1948—49; grad., Bentley Sch. Acctg., 1958; BBA with highest honors, Northeastern U., 1962, MBA, 1967; D of Humane Svc. (hon.), Simmons Coll., 2001. CFA, CFA Inst. Legal rsch. clk. Frank Shepard Co., N.Y.C., 1938—43; cost acct. Johns Manville Corp., Pittsburg, Calif., 1943—46; studio mgr. Wheelan Studios, Boston, 1946; clerical supr. Columbian Purchasing Group, Boston, 1946—48; office mgr. Wellesley Coll., Mass., 1948—51; statistician Eastman Kodak Co., Rochester, NY, 1951—53; investment officer John Hancock Mut. Life, Boston, 1953—74; sr. v.p. John Hancock Advisers, Boston, 1974—84; ret., 1984. Mem. Ct. Women in Politics and Public Policy, Assocs. of the Boston Pub. Libr. Bd., Coll. Club Boston, 1998—, Cambridge YWCA, Neighborhood Assn. of the Back Bay; mem. world svc. coun. YWCA USA, 1992—, nat. bd. dir., 1988—94, hon. bd. dir., 1998—; pres. bd. dir. YWCA, Boston, 1985—87, active, 1977—96; bd. dir. Old South Meeting House Mus., 1989—92; mem. women's coun. Pine St. Inn, 1992—; trustee Simmons Coll., 1994—2000, chair centennial com., 1999—2000, corporator, 2000—05; chair bd. Vis. Nurses Assn. Cape Cod Found., South Dennis, 1995; mem. adv. com. On the Rise, 1997—, Boston Women's Fund, 2001—; mem. adv. com. Inst. Leadership & Change Simmons Coll., 2004—. Recipient Philanthropy award Women in Devel., 1990, Disting. Alumni award Bentley Coll., 1994; named Woman of Achievement, Cambridge YWCA, 1991, Lifetime Service to Women award, On The Rise, 1998, Lifetime Achievement award, College Club of Boston, 1998, Outstanding Alumna Northeastern U., 2000, Cmty. Cornerstone award, Woman in Devel., 2005; honoree Pine St. Inn Women's Coun., 2000. Mem. AARP, LWV, NOW, AAUW, CFA Inst., Mass. Action for Women, Mass. Women Polit. Caucus, Boston Security Analysts Soc. (treas. 1973-76), Simmons Coll. Alumnae Assn. (pres. 1989-91, Alumnae Svc. award 1984, Planned Giving award 1993), Older Women's League, Harwich Hist. Soc., Project Vote Smart, Women's Union, Friday Forum, Eire Soc., Wellesley Ctrs. for Women. Avocations: fundraising, theater, reading. Home: 790 Boylston St Apt 22F Boston MA 02199-7921 E-mail: berylb@mailstation.com.

BUNKER, DUSTY (SANDRA COBY), writer; b. Newport, R.I., Nov. 5, 1937; d. Lloyd Coby and Marjorie Louise Brown; m. A. Reid Bunker, Jr., July 1, 1958; children: April, Melanie, Matthew, Sarah. Student, U. N.H., 1955—58; Art Cert., Famous Artists' Sch., Westport, Conn., 1971. Columnist Manchester Union Leader, NH, 1972—77, Mademoiselle Mag., N.Y.C., 1994, Seacoast Scene, Hampton, 1979—80. Cons. writer Time-Life Books, Alexandria, Va., 1988; cartoonist Tree Line, 1978; lectr. in field; condr. workshops in field. Co-author (with Faith Javane): Numerology and the Divine Triangle, 1979; co-author: (with Victoria Knowles) Birthday Numerology, 1982; author: Numerology and Your Future, 1980, Numerology, Astrology and Dreams, 1987, Quintiles and Tredeciles: The Geometry of the Goddess, 1989, Dream Cycles, 1981, 2000, The Number Mysteries: One Deadly Rhyme, 2001, The Number Mysteries: The Two-Timing Corpse, 2002, The Number Mysteries: Three O'Clocks Dark Night. Mem.: Sisters in Crime, Mystery Writers of Am. Avocations: reading, movies, writing humorous skits. Home: 236 Middle Rd Brentwood NH 03833 E-mail: dusty_bunker@yahoo.com.

BUNKERS, SUZANNE LILLIAN, writer; b. Le Mars, Iowa, Apr. 20, 1950; d. Jerome Anton and Verna Mae (Klein) B.; 1 child, Rachel Susanna. BS, Iowa State U., 1972, MA, 1974; PhD, U. Wis., 1980. Tchg. asst. Iowa State U., Ames, 1972-74, Purdue U., W. Lafayette, Ind., 1974-75, U. Wis., Madison, 1975-79, lectr., 1979-80; asst. prof. Mankato (Minn.) State U., 1980-85, assoc. prof., 1985-89, prof. English, 1989—. Mem. early childhood adv. com., Mankato, Minn., 1984-85. Author: All Will Yet Be Well, 1993, In Search of Susanna, 1996, Good Earth, Black Soil, 1981; editor: The Diary of Caroline Seabury, 1991, Inscribing the Daily, 1996. Leader Troop 396 Girl Scouts Am., Mankato, Minn. 1994-97. Rsch. fellow Nat. Endowment Humanities, 1986-87, Fulbright fellow, 1988, Leadership fellow Bush Found., 1995-96. Mem. AAUW (co-chair equity com. 1994-95), YWCA, MLA (del. assembly). Avocations: writing, coaching girls' softball, travel. Home: 317 Carroll St Mankato MN 56001-2517 Office: Mankato State U Dept English PO Box 53 Mankato MN 56002-0053

BUNKER-SOLER, ANTONIO LUIS, physician; b. Caguas, P.R., Oct. 2, 1948; BS, U. P.R., Mayaguez, 1970; MD, U. P.R., San Juan, 1974. Diplomate Am. Bd. Allergy and Immunology, Am. Bd. Pediatrics. Commd. 2d lt. U.S. Army, 1973, advanced through grades to lt. col.; resident in pediatrics Brooke AMC, San Antonio, 1977; with pediatric svc. SHAPE, Belgium, 1977-79; various positions U.S. Army, Ft. Campbell, Ky., 1981-83, chief allergy-immunology svc. Frankfurt, Germany, 1989-92, various positions Ft. Hood, Tex., 1988-89, chief allergy-immunology svc. Frankfurt, Germany, 1989-92, asst. chief allergy-immunology svc. El Paso, Tex., 1992-94; various positions EAMC, Ga., 1983-88; pediatric pulmonary fellow Tex. Children's Hosp., Houston, 1994-95; pvt. practice Houston, 1995-96, Tampa, 1996—. Asst. clin. prof. MCG, Augusta, Ga., 1983-88; allergy cons. southeastern region CONUS, 1984-88, 7th MEDCOM, Europe, 1989-92, allergy cons.; presenter in field. Contbr. articles to profl. jours. Active Asthma and Allergy Support Group, Augusta, 1985-87. Decorated Army Commendation medal with oak leaf cluster, Order of Mil. Med. Merit; Allergy fellow Fitzsimons AMC, 1981. Fellow Am. Coll. Asthma, Allergy and Immunology, Tex. Med. Assn., Mil. Allergists (Dura Pharm. award 1987); mem. AMA, Am. Acad. Pediatrics, Am. Acad. Allergy and Immunology, Am. Thoracic Soc. Office: 3645 Madacahane Tampa FL 33618-2059 Home: 1421 NW 90th Ter Gainesville FL 32606-6798

BUNKIS, JURIS, plastic surgeon; b. Lubeck, Germany, Aug. 27, 1949; came to the U.S., 1974; s. Janis and Jadviga (Buzinskis) B.; m. Ruta Sternbergs, Oct. 12, 1974; children: Justin S., Jessica S. Degree, U. Toronto, 1970, MD, 1974. Intern gen. surgery Mary Imogene Bassett Hosp., Columbia U., Cooperstown, N.Y., 1974-75, jr. resident gen. surgery, 1975-76, Beth Israel Hosp., Mass. Gen. Hosp. & Shriner's Burn Inst., Harvard U., Boston, 1976-77; sr. resident gen. surgery Mary Imogene Bassett Hosp., Columbia U., Cooperstown, 1977-78, chief resident gen. surgery, 1978-79; sr. resident, chief resident plastic surgery Peter Bent Brigham & Children's Hosps., Harvard U., Boston, 1979-81; clin. instr. in surgery Harvard U., 1979-81; asst. prof. surgery divsn. plastic surgery U. Calif., San Francisco, 1981-83, asst. clin. prof. surgery, 1983-85. Asst. chief plastic surgery San Francisco Gen. Hosp. U. Calif., 1981-82, chief plastic surgery, 1983; chmn. bd. dirs., pres. Juris Bunkis M.D., Inc., Danville, Calif., 1983—; chmn. bd. dirs., pres., med. dirs. Blackhawk Surgery Ctr., Inc., Danville, 1989—; chmn. bd. dirs., pres., sec. United Bridges, Inc., 1994—; invited lectr. numerous confs. Contbr. chpts. to books and articles to med. jours. Knight, Cavalieri di San Marco (Knights of San Marco), venice, 1995. Mem. Am. Assn. Hand Surgery (mem. program com. 1983-84, socioecons. com. 84-85), Am. Soc. Plastic and Reconstructive Surgery (mem. Tel Med subcom. 1986-87), Am. Soc. Aesthetic Surgery, Calif. Med. Soc., Calif. Soc. Plastic Surgeons (mem. program com. 1984-85, mem. ethics com. 86-87, mem. newsletter com. 87-89, mem. B.M.Q.A. liaison com. 87-89), Alameda-Contra Costa Med. Assn., Lipoplasty Soc. N.Am., Internat. Soc. Aesthetic Plastic Surgery, Pan Pacific Surg. Assn., Latvian Med. and Dental Assn., Plastic Surgery Rsch. Coun., Assn. Medicorum Bohemoslovacorum J.E. Purkyne (hon.), Soc. Bohemoslovaca Chirurgiae Plasticae (hon., Prague). Avocations: golf, fly fishing. Office: United Bridges Inc 4165 Blackhawk Plaza Cir Danville CA 94506-4691

BUNKOWSKE, EUGENE WALTER, religious studies educator; b. Wecota, S.D., July 3, 1935; s. Walter Adolph and Ottille Sophie (Richter) B.; m. Bernice Bock; children: Barbara, Nancy, Walter, Joel. AA, Concordia Acad. and Jr. Coll., St. Paul, 1955; BA, Concordia Seminary, 1958, BD, MDiv, 1960; MA in Linguistics, UCLA, 1964, C Phil in Linguistics, 1968, PhD in Linguistics, 1976; LittD, Concordia Coll., 1983; DD, Christ Coll., 1991; DLitt, Concordia U., St. Paul, 1997. Missionary Luth. Ch.-Mo. Synod, Africa, 1960-82, congl. pastor, pioneer ch. planter, 1960-74, chmn. Nung Udoe dist., 1960-61, builder chs., schs., hosp., 1960-67, medical worker Ogoja Province, 1961-66, justice of peace Ogoja Province, 1962-74, chmn. Ogoja dist., 1964-69, chmn. Evang. Luth. Mission in Nigeria, 1965-67, analyzer Yala lang., orthography devel. & Bible translator, 1967-71, counselor to Yala Paramount Chief, 1969-74, fourth v.p., 1989-92, 95-98, third v.p., 1992-95; dir. mission Concordia Theol. Seminary, Ft. Wayne, Ind., 1982-88, mission prof., 1982—, mission chair prof., 1986—, grad. prof. mission, 1990—, chmn. dept. pastoral ministries, 1985-88; chmn. mission dept., 1988-90; supr. D Missiology program, chmn. Mission and Comm. Congress Concordia Theol. Seminary, Ft. Wayne, Ind., 1984—. Ling. cons. and adminstr. Luth. Bible Translators, Liberia, Sierra Leone, 1970-74; dir. Vacation Inst. for Tng. in Applied Linguistics and Bible Translation, U. Liberia, Monrovia, 1971-74; cons. United Bible Soc., 1974-80, regional translations coord., 1980-82; cons. Near West Side Cleve. Cluster, St. Paul Internat. Mission Bd. Author: Orede, 1973, Woka yi Ijona, 1974, Topics in Yala Grammar, 1976, God's Mission in Action, 1986, The Body of Christ in Mission, 1987, God's Communicators in

Mission, 1988, Receptor Oriented Gospel Communication, 1989, The State of Gospel Communication Today, 1990, Church Growth: A Biblical Perspective, 1991, The Role of the Laity in Gospel Communications, 1992, The Christian Family: Nurture and Outreach, 1993, Multicultural Outreach: Bridging Cultures - Theirs and Ours, 1995, Struggling with Change: Reaching the Lost in Changing Times, 1999, The Lutherans in Mission, 2000; translator Yala Bible, 1967-74; contbr. articles to religious and profl. publs., chpts. to books. Mem. God's Word to Nations Bible Soc. (bd. dirs., trans. and tech. cons.), World Mission Prayer League (bd. dirs.), All Nations Mission (bd. dirs., cons.), Luth. Soc. for Missiology (founding organizer). Republican. Lutheran. Avocations: travel, reading, hiking. Home: 5724 Lancashire Ct Fort Wayne IN 46825-5910 Office: Concordia Theol Seminary 6600 N Clinton St Fort Wayne IN 46825-4916

BUNN, PAUL A., JR., oncologist, educator; b. N.Y.C., Mar. 16, 1945; s. Paul A. Bunn; m. Camille Ruoff, Aug. 17, 1968; children: Rebecca, Kristen, Paul H. BA cum laude, Amherst Coll., 1967; MD, Cornell U., 1971. Diplomate Nat. Bd. Med. Examiners, Am. Bd. Internal Medicine, Am. Bd. Med. Oncology. Intern U. Calif., H.C. Moffitt Hosp., San Francisco, 1971-72, resident, 1972-73; clin. assoc. medicine br. Nat. Cancer Inst., NIH, Bethesda, Md., 1973-76; sr. investigator med. oncology br. Nat. Cancer Inst., Washington VA Hosp., 1976-81; asst. prof. medicine med. sch. Georgetown U., 1978-81; head cell kinetic sect., Navy med. oncology br. Nat. Cancer Inst., Bethesda, 1981-84; assoc. prof. medicine uniformed svcs. Univ. Health Scis., Bethesda, 1981-84; prof. medicine health scis. ctr. U. Colo., Denver, 1984—, head divsn. med. oncology, 1984-94, dir. cancer ctr., 1987—. Instl. rev. bd. NIH, Nat. Cancer Inst., 1982-84; intramural support contract rev. com. Nat. Cancer Inst., 1982-84; cancer com. U. Colo., 1984—, faculty senate health scis. ctr., 1985—, exec. com. sch. medicine, 1987—; med. bd. Univ. Hosp., 1987—; external sci. advisor cancer ctr. U. Miami, 1988-92, U. Ark., 1989-94, U. Va., 1991-94, others; oncology drug adv. com. FDA, 1992-96; sci. secretariat 7th World Conf. Lung Cancer, 1994; bd. dirs. Univ. Hosp. Resource Coun.; oncology drug adv. com. FDA, 1992-96. Author: Carboplatin (JM-8) Current Perspectives and Future Directions, 1990, Clinical Experiences With Platinum and Etoposide Therapy in Lung Cancer, 1992, (with M.E. Wood) Hematology/Oncology Secrets, 1994; assoc. editor Med. and Pediatric Oncology, 1984—, Jour. Clin. Oncology, 1991—, Cancer Rsch., 1992—, others; contbr. chpts. to books and articles to profl. jours. Bd. dirs. Colo. divsn. Am. Cancer Soc., 1989—, Leukemia Soc. Am., 1991—; bd. dirs. The Cancer Venture, 1993-94, Fair Share Colo., 1993-94; chmn. Solid Tumor Oncology Edn. Found., 1996—. With USPHS, 1973-84. Decorated Medal of Commendation; recipient Sci. of Yr. award Denver chpt. ARCS, 1992; named one of 400 Best Drs. in Am., Good Housekeeping Mag., 1991, 92; grantee Schering Plough, 1988-89, Burroughs Wellcome, 1991—, Bristol-Myers Squibb, 1993—, others. Fellow ACP; mem. AAAS, Am. Soc. Hematology (mem. sci. subcom. neoplasia 1989-92), Am. Assn. Cancer Rsch., Am. Soc. Clin. Oncology (chair program subcom. 1985-86, 90, pres.-elect 2001—), Am. Fedn. Clin. Rsch., Am. Assn. Cancer Insts. (bd. dirs. 1992—), Internat. Assn. Study Lung Cancer (bd. dirs. 1988—, pres. 1994-97), Western Assn. Physicians, S.W. Oncology Group, Lung Cancer Study Group, Alpha Omega Alpha. Office: U Colo Cancer Ctr PO Box 6511 MS 8111 Aurora CO 80045 E-mail: paul.bunn@uchsc.edu.

BUNN, RONALD FREEZE, lawyer, academic administrator; b. Jonesboro, Ark., Aug. 11, 1929; s. S. Neal and Velma (Freeze) B.; m. Rita E. Hess, Mar. 29, 1955; children: Robin Gail, Katharine Sue, Lisabeth Joann. BA, Rhodes Coll., 1951, LLD, 1973; MA, Duke U., 1953, PhD, 1956; postgrad., U. Cologne, Fed. Republic Germany, 1954-55; JD, U. Mo., 1989. Bar: Mo. 1990. Instr. U. Tex., Austin, 1956-59, asst. prof., 1960-64; asso. prof. La. State U., Baton Rouge, 1964-67, U. Houston, 1967-69; prof., dean U Houston (Grad. Sch.), 1969-74, interim dean arts and scis., 1972-74, asso. dean faculties, 1974-75, acting v.p., dean faculties, 1975-76; v.p. acad. affairs State U. N.Y. at Buffalo, 1976-80; provost U. Mo., Columbia, 1980-86, prof. polit. sci., 1986—2000; ptnr. Shurtleff, Froeschner, Bunn and Hoffman, Columbia, 1992—; adj. prof. law, 2001. Vis. lectr. Ind. U., 1962; cons. Coun. Grad. Schs. Author: Politics and Civil Liberties in Europe, 1967, German Politics and the Spiegel Affair: A Case Study of the Bonn System, 1968; News and Notes editor Jour. Politics, 1968-70; contbr. articles profl. jours. Bd. dirs. S.W. Center for Urban Research, Houston, chmn. bd., 1975-76. Fulbright predoctoral scholar, 1954-55, Fulbright rsch. scholar, 1963; NATO sr. fellow in sci., 1973. Mem. Mo. Bar Assn. (labor law com.), So. Polit. Sci. Assn. (past mem. exec. coun.), Nat. Employment Lawyers Assn., Southwestern Polit. Sci. Assn. (past v.p.), Am. Coun. on Germany, Phi Beta Kappa (pres. Mo. Alpha chpt. 1986-88), Omicron Delta Kappa. also: 25 N 9th St Columbia MO 65201-4845 Office Phone: 573-449-3874.

BUNN, TIMOTHY DAVID, newspaper editor; b. Syracuse, N.Y., Sept. 29, 1946; s. John Stewart and Katherine (Smolnycki) B.; m. Nancy Grady, May 27, 1968 BS in Journalism, Syracuse U., 1972. Pub. info. officer Central N.Y. Regional Planning Bd., Syracuse, 1972-74; met. editor Rochester Democrat & Chronicle, N.Y., 1974-79; asst. city editor Miami Herald, Fla., 1979-81; mng. editor Syracuse Post-Standard, 1981-82; exec. editor Syracuse Herald Jour., 1982-95; dep. exec. editor Syracuse Post-Std., 1995—. Served to capt. U.S. Army, 1967-71. Recipient Cmty. Svc. award NAACP, 1984, Cmty. Appreciation award Am.-Arab Anti-Discrimination Com. Mem. Am. Soc. Newspaper Editors Office: The Post-Standard Clinton Sq PO Box 4915 Syracuse NY 13221-4915

BUNN, WM. JEFFREY, secondary school educator, director; b. Havre de Grace, Md., June 25, 1974; s. Fred Lewis Bunn, II and Ramona Bunn. BA, BS, King Coll., 1996; MusM in Edn., Westminster Choir Coll., 2004; MusM, Newcastle U., 2004. Cert. tchr. Md., 2004. Asst. coodinator music minsitries Mountain Christian Ch., Joppa, Md., 1998—2001; dir. music, organist The Luth. Ch. of the Holy Comforter, Balt., 2002—04; chair music dept., organist-in-residence Mt. Carmel H.S., Essex, 2002—. Adj. instr. music Mountain Christian Ch., Joppa, Md., 1996—2001. Musician: Organ and Voice Recitals (Am. Choral Director's Assn. Nat. Student award, 1996). Recipient Eagle Scout, Boy Scouts Am., 1992, Govs. citation, State of Md., 1992. Mem.: Am. Choral Dirs. Assn. (Nat. Student award 1996), Nat. Assn. Pastoral Musicians, Gospel Music Assn., Nat. Rec. Acad. Arts and Scis., Music Educator's Nat. Conf., Am. Guild Organists, Toastmaster' Internat., Am. Numistmatist Assn. Conservative. Avocation: coin collecting/numismatics. Home: 671 Bourbon Street Havre De Grace MD 21078-3134 Office: Mt Carmel High School 1704 Old Eastern Avenue Essex MD 21221 Personal E-mail: wmjbunn@aol.com. E-mail: jbunn@olmcmd.org.

BUNNELL, GEORGE ELI, lawyer; b. Miami, Fla., Apr. 28, 1938; s. George A. and Lillian E. (Hurley) B.; Dianne Railton, Dec. 1, 1990; children: Kelley, Courtney. BA, U. Fla., 1960, LLB, 1962. Bar: Fla. 1963, U.S. Dist. Ct. (so. dist.) Fla. 1963, U.S. Supreme Ct. 1970, U.S. Ct. Appeals (11th cir.) 1982. Assoc. Nicholson, Howard & Brawner, Miami, 1963-64, Dean, Adams, George & Wood, Miami, 1964-67, ptnr., 1968-71; officer, dir. Huebner, Shaw & Bunnell, P.A., Ft. Lauderdale, Fla., 1972-77; pres., dir. Bunnell, Woulfe, Kirschbaum, Keller, McIntyre & Gregoire, Ft. Lauderdale, 1977—2004. Mem. advance staff White House, 1974-76; mem. City of Ft. Lauderdale Marine Adv. Bd., 1974-76, City of Ft. Lauderdale Civil Svc. Bd., 1977-79; bd. dirs., sec. Ft. Lauderdale Mus. Art, 1990—. Fellow Am. Coll. Trial Lawyers; mem. Internat. Assn. of Def. Counsel, Am. Bd. Trial Advs. (pres. Ft. Lauderdale chpt. 1992, nat. bd. rep. 2003—), Def. Rsch. inst., Fla. Def. Lawyers Assn., Broward County Bar Assn., Fla. Acad. of Hosp. Attys., Am. Health Lawyers Assn., Lauderdale Yacht Club. Republican. Office: Bunnell Woulfe Kirschbaum Keller McIntyre Gregoire One Financial Plaza 100 SE Third Ave Ste 900 Fort Lauderdale FL 33394 Office Phone: 954-761-8600. Business E-Mail: geb@bunnellwoulfe.com.

BUNNELL, LINDA HUNT, university chancellor; d. Byron and Bobbye Bunnell. BA in English and Comm., Baylor U., 1964; MA in English Lang. and Lit., U. Colo., 1967, PhD in English Lit., 1970. Asst. prof. English U. Calif., Riverside, 1970-77, asst. dean coll. humanities, 1972—77; from asst. dean to dean academics Calif. State U. Sys., 1977-87; vice chancellor acad. affairs Minn. State U. Sys., St. Paul, 1987-93; chancellor U. Colo., Colorado Springs, 1993—2001; sr. v.p. higher edn. Coll. Bd., 2001—02; CEO Bunnell Assocs., Colo. Springs, Colo., 2002—04; chancellor U. Wis., Stevens Point, 2004—. Active Minn. Women's Econ. Round Table, 1989-93; mem. exec. com. Nat. Coun. for Accreditation Tchr. Edn., 1996-99; bd. dirs. Aspirus Health Care, 2005-. Mem. St. Paul chpt. ARC; mem. cmty. bd. Norwest Bank, Colorado Springs, 1997—, mem. El Pomar awards for Excellence com., 1997—; mem. leadership commn. Am. Coun. Edn., 1997-2000; mem. subcom. ROTC; mem. edn. com. U.S. Army, 1998-2001. Recipient Disting. Alumni award Baylor U., 1995; named leader of yr., Colo. Springs Econ. Devel. Coun., 2001; Woodrow Wilson dissertation fellow, Univ. Colo. Avocations: gardening, baseball, cooking, sable burmese cats. Office: U Wis Stevens Point 2100 Main St Stevens Point WI 54481-3897 Office Phone: 715-346-2123. Business E-Mail: lbunnell@uwsp.edu.

BUNNELL, PETER CURTIS, retired art educator, curator; b. Poughkeepsie, N.Y., Oct. 25, 1937; s. Harold Curtis and Ruth (Buckhout) B. BFA, Rochester Inst. Tech., 1959; MFA, Ohio U., 1961; MA, Yale U., 1965. Curator of photography Mus. Modern Art, N.Y.C., 1966-72; prof. history of photography and modern art Princeton (N.J.) U., 1972—2002, prof. emeritus, 2002—. Curator of photography Art Mus. Princeton U., 1972-02, dir., 1973-78, 98-2000. Author; Clarence H. White, 1987, Minor White: The Eye That Shapes, 1989, Degrees of Guidance, 1993, Thomas Joshua Cooper, 1995, Ruth Bernhard: Photographs, 1996, Aaron Siskind: The Bond and The Free, 1997, Walter Chappell: Time Lived, 2000, Remembering Limelight, 2001, Edward Ranney: The Character of the Place, 2003, La Photographie Pictorialiste, 2004; editor: A Photographic Vision, 1980, The Art of Pictorial Photography, 1992, Photography at Princeton, 1998. Guggenheim fellow, 1979, Asian Cultural Coun. Rsch. fellow, 1984. Fellow Royal Photographic Soc. (hon.); mem. Soc. for Photog. Edn. (chmn. 1973-76), The Friends of Photography (pres. 1978-87, chmn. 1987-92), Century Assocs. Club. Office: Princeton U Dept Art And Archaelogy Princeton NJ 08544-1018

BUNNER, PATRICIA ANDREA, lawyer; b. Fairmont, W.Va., Sept. 16, 1953; d. Scott Randolph and Virginia Lenore (Keck) B. AB in History & English magna cum laude, W.Va. U., 1975, JD, 1978; postgrad., Trinity Theol. Sem., 1995—, W.Va. U., 1996—. Bar: W.Va. 1978, N.Y. 1981, D.C. 1981, U.S. Dist. Ct. (so. dist.) W.Va. 1978, U.S. Dist. Ct. (no. dist.) W.Va. 1985, U.S. Ct. Claims 1990, U.S. Supreme Ct. 1989; cert. Christian counselor, 1986—. Mem. staff Dem. Nat. Com., Washington, 1978-79; assoc. Gailor, Elias & Matz, Washington, 1979-81, N.Y. State Bankers Assn., N.Y.C., 1981-83; ptnr. Bunner & Bunner, Fairview, W.Va., 1984-94. Exec. dir. N.Y. State Consumer Mortgage Rev. Bd.; chmn. dist. VIII Consumer Mortgage Rev. Com., N.Y.C., 1982-83; cons. atty. Energy Cons. Assocs., Spring Harbor, N.Y., 1981; of counsel Monongahela (W.Va.) Soil Conservation Dist., 1985; vis. scholar Pitts. Theol. Sem., 1997—. Author: How Charley Metheney Broke the Four Minute Mile, 1971, Across the Bennefield Prong, 1973, German Anti-Semitism, Bismarck Through Weimar, 1973, N.Y. State Bankers Assn. Legis. Directory, 1983, Through a Glass Darkly, A Compendium of Film Noir, 1996, The Influence of the Seventeenth Century Scientific Revolution on Anglo-American Law, 1996, Rene Descartes, Phenomenologist, 1996, Psychology of Thomas Aquinas, 1997, John Locke's Influence on Modern Science, 1998, Conceptions of Property in Early America, 1787-1801, 1999, John Locke's Influence on Thomas Jefferson's View of Property, 1999, Thomas Jefferson as Reformer of Property Law, 1999, Plato's Influence As Seen In Environmental Traditions, 2000, Nietzches Influence on Modern Environment Thought, 2000, Islamic Cities, 2000, Newtonian Science in Colonial America, 2000, Thomas Jefferson's Land Ethic, 2000, Progress and Property, 1945-1970, 2000; presenter in field. Pres. Monongalia County Dem. Women, 1987-89; sec. Monongalia County Devel. Authority, 1984-91; pres. United Taxpayers Assn., Inc., W.Va., 1985-88; bd. dirs. W.Va. U. Morgantown, 1974-75; active W.Va. State Dem. Exec. Com., 1990, 94. Recipient WVU Canaga prize in Am. History, 1999-2000; Rilla Moran Woods fellow Nat. Fedn. Dem. Women, Washington, 1978. Mem. ATLA, ABA (vice chmn. legal econs. and new lawyers coms. 1986-87, litigation sect., 1st amendment rights and media law com., gen. practice com., corps. and banking com.), W.Va. Bar Assn. (com. econs. of law practice 1987—, com. corps. and banking 1987—), W.Va. Trial Lawyers Assn., N.Y. State Bar Assn., Monongalia County Bar Assn., Marion County Bar Assn., W.Va. Criminal Def. Lawyers Assn., Women's Info. Ctr. (founding), LWV, NAFE, W.Va. Alliance for Women's Studies (founding), Bus. and Profl. Women (bd. dirs.), Climates, Inc., Monongalia County Hist. Soc., W.Va. Brain Injury Assn., Clay-Battelle Alumni Assn., W.Va. Coll. Law Alumni Assn., Nat. Rifle Assn. (life), Nature Conservancy, Nat. Arbor Day Found., World Wildlife Fund, Am. Farmland Trust, AAUW, Sierra Club, Audobon Soc., Young Dems. Club W.Va. (sec. 1976), Phi Alpha Theta (chpt. pres. 1974-75), Phi Beta Kappa, Zeta Phi Eta, Alpha Rho (chpt. pres. 1974), History of Sci. Soc., Internat. Soc. For History, Philosophy and Soc. Study of Biology Law and Soc. Assn., Am. Legal History Soc., Phi Kappa Phi. Clubs: Woman's (bd. dirs. Morgantown chpt. 1986—). Baptist. Avocations: clothing design, cooking, creative writing, piano, swimming. Home: 15 Devine Rd Fairview WV 26570-8711 Personal E-mail: p.bunner@hotmail.com.

BUNNER, WILLIAM KECK, lawyer; b. Fairmont, W.Va., Sept. 2, 1949; s. Scott Randolph and Virginia Lenore (Keck) B. BS in Secondary Edn. magna cum laude, W.Va. U., 1970, MA in History, 1973, ABD in History, 1975, JD, 1978, postgrad., 1998—. Bar: W.Va. 1978, U.S. Dist. Ct. (so. dist.) W.Va. 1978, U.S. Dist. Ct. (no. dist.) W.Va. 1985. Tchr. Monongalia County Bd. Edn., Morgantown, W.Va., 1970-78; contract lawyer dept. fin. and adminstrn. State of W.Va., Charleston, 1978-79; pvt. practice law Fairview, W.Va., 1979-84; pres. Farm Home Svc., Inc., 1983—; ptnr. Bunner & Bunner, Morgantown and Fairview, 1984-92. Pres. Climates, 1988—; presenter Rush D. Holt History Conf., W. Va. U., 1999, ann. meeting Lawand Soc. Amm., 2003, Rocky Mountain Interdisciplinary History Conf., U. Colo., 2003. Author: Planting Churches: A Case Study of Western Monongaliu County, West Virginia, 2000, Anxiety, Alienation and Adjustment: Filmnoir and the Returning Warriorfrom WWII, 2000. Pres. Monongalia County Young Dems., 1974; parliamentarian Monongalia County Dem. Exec. Com., 1982-94; counsel, parliamentarian Young Dem. Clubs W.Va., 1974-77; bd. dirs., supr. Monongahela Soil Conservation Dist., 1982—; advisor West Run Watershed Improvement Dist., 1983—; mem. W.Va. Commn. on Rural Abandoned Mines, Rural Alliance, Monongalia County Solid Waste Auth., 1989—, also chmn., 1990-92. Mem. ABA, Monongalia County Bar Assn., Assn. Rural Conservation, Soil Conservation Soc. Am., United Taxpayers' Assn. (counsel), Monongalia County Hist. Soc., Marion County Hist. Soc., Marion County Bar Assn., W.Va. Trial Lawyers Assn, Phi Alpha Delta, Phi Alpha Theta. Democrat. Avocations: music, politics, farming, videos, regional history and genealogy. Home and Office: 15 Devine Rd Fairview WV 26570-8711 Office Phone: 304-798-3542. E-mail: Keck50@mail.westco.net.

BUNNETT, JOSEPH FREDERICK, chemist, educator; b. Portland, Oreg., Nov. 26, 1921; s. Joseph and Louise Helen (Boulan) B.; m. Sara Anne Telfer, Aug. 22, 1942; children: Alfred Boulan, David Telfer, Peter Sylvester (dec. Sept. 1972). BA, Reed Coll., 1942; PhD, U. Rochester, 1945. Mem. faculty Reed Coll., 1946-52, U. N.C., 1952-58; mem. faculty Brown U., 1958-66, prof. chemistry, 1959-66, chmn. dept., 1961-64; prof. chemistry U. Calif., Santa Cruz, 1966-91, prof. emeritus, 1991—. Erskine vis. fellow U. Canterbury, N.Z., 1967; vis. prof. U. Wash., 1956, U. Wurzburg, Germany, 1974, U. Bologna, Italy, 1988; rsch. fellow Japan Soc. for Promotion of Sci., 1979; Lady Davis vis. prof. Hebrew U., Jerusalem, Israel, 1981; mem. adv. coun. dept. chemistry Princeton (N.J.) U., 1985-89; mem. NRC com. on alternative chem. demilitarization techs., 1992-93; mem. Dept. Def. panel on Gulf War Health Effects, 1993-94; co-chmn. peer rev. com. Russian-Am. Joint Evaluation Program, 1995-96; co-chmn. NATO Advanced Rsch. Workshop on Chem. Problems Associated with Old Arsenical and Mustard Munitions, Lodz, Poland, 1996; working group chem. weapons destruction, scientific adv. bd. Orgn. Prohibition Chem. Weapons, 1999—. Co-editor: Arsenic and Old Mustard: Chemical Problems in the Destruction of Old Arsenical and Mustard Munitions, 1998; contbr. articles to profl. jours. Trustee Reed Coll., 1970-97, trustee emeritus, 1997—. Fulbright scholar, U. Coll., London, 1949—50, U. Munich, 1960—61, Guggenheim fellow, 1960—61. Fellow AAAS, Internat. Union Pure and Applied Chemistry (chmn. commn. phys. organic chemistry 1978-83, sec. organic chemistry divsn. 1981-83, v.p. 1983-85, pres. 1985-87, chmn. task force on sci. aspects of destruction of chem. warfare agts. 1991-95, chmn. com. on chem. weapon destruction 1995-2001, fellow, 2002.); mem. Am. Acad. Arts. and Scis., Am. Chem. Soc. (editor jour. Accounts of Chem. Rsch. 1966-86, Jack Flack Norris award 1992), Royal Soc. Chemistry (hon.), Pharm. Soc. Japan (hon.), Acad. Gioenia (U. Catania, hon.), Soc. Argentina de Investigaciones en Quimica Organica (hon.), Soc. Chimica Italiana (hon.). Home: 608 Arroyo Seco Santa Cruz CA 95060-3148 Office: U Calif Dept Chemistry Santa Cruz CA 95064 Office Phone: 831-459-2261. Office Fax: 831-459-2935. Personal E-mail: bunnett@cruzio.com. Business E-Mail: bunnett@chemistry.ucsc.edu.

BUNNEY, WILLIAM E, JR., psychiatrist, medical educator; b. U.S. MD. Disting. prof. dept. psychiatry U. Calif., Irvine. Mem. Nat. Sci. Adv. Bd. of Nat. Alliance of Rsch. in Schizophrenia and Depression; mem. extramural sci. adv. bd. NIMH; mem. editl. bd. The Neuroscientist, Psychiatric Annals. Editor: (books) Collegium Internationale Neuro-Pschophamacologicum, 1986; co-editor (with others): Pre & Postsynaptic Receptors, Pschopharmacology; editor: (med. jour.) Clinical Neuroscience Research. Recipient Hofheimer Rsch. award, Anna-Monika award. Mem.: CINP, Inst. Medicine, Am. Coll. Neuropsychopharmacology (pres.), West Coast Coll. Biol. Psychiatry (pres.). Office: U Calif Irvine Psychiatry Human Behavior D438 Med Scis Irvine CA 92697-1675 E-mail: webunney@uci.ed.

BUNNING, JIM, senator, former professional baseball player; b. Southgate, Ky., Oct. 23, 1931; m. Mary Catherine Bunning; 9 children. BS, Xavier U., 1953. Profl. baseball player, 1955-71; with Detroit Tigers, 1955-63, Phila. Phillies, 1964-67, Pitts. Pirates, 1968-69, L.A. Dodgers, 1969, Phila. Phillies, 1970-71; ret. profl. baseball, 1971; congressman Ky. State Senate, Frankfort, 1979-83; mem. 100th-104th Congresses from 4th Ky. dist., 1987-98; mem. budget com.; mem. ways and means com.; U.S. senator from Ky., 1999—. Mem. Spl. Com. on Aging, Com. on Energy and Natural Resources, Com. on Banking, Com. Housing and Urban Affairs. Played in eight All-Star Baseball games during career. Republican. Office: US Senate 316 Hart Senate Office Bldg Washington DC 20510-0001*

BUNTAIN, DAVID ROBERT, lawyer; b. Newport, R.I., Feb. 22, 1948; s. Robert E. and Martha Elizabeth (Deane) B.; children: Bill C., Anne S. BA, U. Nebr., 1970, JD, 1974; M in Pub. Affairs, Princeton U., 1972. Bar: Nebr. 1975, U.S. Ct. Appeals (8th cir.) 1978, U.S. Supreme Ct. 1992. Assoc. Cline, Williams, Wright, Johnson & Oldfather, LLP, Lincoln, Nebr., 1975—79, ptnr., 1980—. Instr. U. Nebr. Coll. Law, Lincoln, 1976-79; bd. dirs. Nebr. Continuing Legal Edn. Inc., 1986-89, Nebr. Human Resources Rsch. Found., 1986-90. Chair bd. advisors Nebr. Repertory Theatre, 1991—97; bd. dirs. Lincoln Symphony Orch. Assn., 2004—; pres. Pinewood Bowl Com., Lincoln, 1980—82; vice chmn. Gov.'s Commn. for Study Higher Edn., Nebr., 1984; v.p. Leadership Lincoln Inc., 1986, pres., 1987—88; mem. Nat. Dem. Com., 1992—2000. Named Outstanding Young Individual, Lincoln Jaycees, 1981. Mem.: Am. Law Inst., Lincoln C. of C. (chmn. legis. com. 1987—89, bd. dirs. 1991—94), Nebr. Bar Assn. (ho. dels. 1984—, v.p. young lawyers sect. 1980—81), Beta Theta Pi, Phi Beta Kappa, Order of Barristers, Order of Coif. Democrat. Avocations: running, sailing, musical theatre, reading. Home: 2201 Stone Creek Loop S Lincoln NE 68512 Office: Cline Williams Wright et al 233 S 13th St Ste 1900 Lincoln NE 68508-2000 Office Phone: 402-474-6900. E-mail: dbuntain@clinewilliams.com.

BUNTEN, WILLIAM DANIEL, retired banker; b. Goodland, Kans., Sept. 18, 1931; s. William Livingston and Nelle Elizabeth (Boyle) B.; m. Charlene Sue Riemen, May 23, 1954; children: Jane Denise Bunten-Hanisch, Barbara Sue Bunten Shuck, Patricia Joann Bunten-Buckner. AB, Baker U., 1953; LLB, Washburn U., 1956; MBA, U. Pa., 1958. Bar: Kans. 1956, Mich. 1959. From asst. cashier to v.p. Nat. Bank Detroit, 1957-67; from v.p. to pres. Mchts. Nat. Bank, Topeka, 1967-79; sr. exec. v.p. United Cen. Bank, Des Moines, 1979-81; from sr. v.p. to exec. v.p. United Cen. Bancshares, Des Moines, 1979-82; pres. INTRUST Bank and predecessor firm 1st Nat. Bank, Wichita, Kans., 1982-96, also bd. dirs. Vice chmn. bd. dir. INTRUST Fin. Corp. and predecessor firm 1st Fin. Corp., Wichita, Kans., 1982—96; bd. dir. Lakeway Airpark, Inc., pres., 2000—01. Bd. dirs., v.p. Jayhawk coun. Boy. Scouts Am., Topeka, 1968-78, Mid-Iowa coun., 1980-2; bd. dirs. United Way, Topeka, 1969-77, pres. 1977; bd. dirs. United Way, Des Moines, 1980-82, United Way Wichita, 1983-88, pres. 1987; bd. dirs. Topeka C. of C., 1969-74, pres. 1973; bd. dirs. Wichita C. of C., 1986-88, Greater Downtown Wichita, 1986-88, pres. 1987; bd. dirs. Downtown Action Corp., Wichita, 1988-91; bd. dirs. YMCA, Wichita, 1988-96, pres. 1992-94; sec. bd. dirs. Boys/Girls Clubs S. Cen. Kans., 1990-96; trustee Quivira coun. Boy Scouts Am., 1983-96; trustee Stormont Vail Hosp., Topeka, 1974-79, treas. 1978-79; trustee Baker U., Baldwin City, Kans., 1987-90; bd. dirs. Hospice, Wichita, 1983-84, Wichita State U. Endowment Assn., Wichita, 1984-95, dir. Health Affiliates Inc., Wichita, 1992-96. Mem. Washburn U. Alumni Assn. (bd. dirs. 1989-92, pres. 1991-92), Washburn U. Endowment Assn. (trustee 1990—), Rotary (bd. dirs. Topeka club 1977-78, treas. Wichita club 1988-89, trustee Lakeway Rotary Found. 1999, Topeka Rotary Found. 2003-04), Masons, Blue Lodge, Shriners, Washburn U. Law Sch. Alumni Assn. (trustee 2002—). Republican. Ecumenical. Avocations: flying, golf, reading, running. Home: 4000 SW Clarion Place Topeka KS 66610 Personal E-mail: bbunten@3r9.org.

BUNTING, KENNETH FREEMAN, newspaper editor; b. Houston, Dec. 9, 1948; s. Willie Freeman and Sarah Lee (Peterson) B.; m. Juliana Amy Jafvert, July 13, 1989; 1 child, Maxwell Freeman. Student, U. Mo., 1966-67; AA in Journalism, Lee Coll., 1968; BA in Journalism and History, Tex. Christian U., 1970; advanced exec. program, Northwestern U., 1996. Mgmt. trainee, reporter Harte-Hanks Newspapers Inc., Corpus Christi, Tex., 1970-71; reporter, then copy editor San Antonio Express-News, 1971-73; exec. asst. to Hon. G.J. Sutton Tex. Ho. of Reps., San Antonio, 1973-74; reporter Cin. Post, 1974-78, Sacramento Bee, 1978; reporter, asst. city editor, state capitol corr. L.A. Times, 1978-87; capitol bur. chief, city editor, dep. mng. editor, sr. editor Ft. Worth Star-Telegram, 1987-93; mng. editor Seattle Post-Intelligencer, 1993-99; exec. editor Seattle Post-Intelligence, 2000—. Journalism instr. Orange Coast Coll., Costa Mesa, Calif., 1981-82; mem. adv. bd. Maynard Inst., Oakland, Calif., 1994—. Bd. dirs. Seattle Symphony, 1995-97; mem. commn. Woodland Park Zoo, Seattle, 1995-96, 98; mem. Leadership Ft. Worth; former mem. journalism adv. bd. Tex. Christian U.; former mem. minorities task force Assn. for Edn. in Journalism and Mass Comms.; past pres. Press Club, Orange County, Calif.; past bd. dirs. Covington (Ky.) Cmty. Ctr.; past 1st v.p. Young Dems. of Tex.; past treas., mem. exec. bd. Freedom of Info. Found. of Tex.; leadership coun. ARC; bd. dirs. Alfred Friendly Press Fellowships. Mem. Nat. Assn. Black Journalists, AP Mng. Editors Assn. (mem. ethics com. 1995-96, bd. dirs. 1996-99), Am. Soc. Newspaper Editors (mem. diversity, leadership coms., chair edn. com., bd. dirs. 1999—), Soc. Profl. Journalists (bd. dirs. western Wash. chpt. 1995-96), Seattle C. of C. (mem. cmty. devel. roundtable 1994—), Alliance for Edn. (bd. dirs.), Tex. Christian U. Alumni Assn. (bd. dirs.), Freedom of Info. Found. Tex., Rainier Club, Washington Athletic Club. Unitarian Universalist. Avocations: tennis, bridge, reading. Office: Seattle-Post Intelligencer PO Box 1909 101 Elliott Ave W Seattle WA 98111*

BUNTS, FRANK EMORY, artist; b. Cleve., Mar. 2, 1932; s. Alexander Taylor and Mary (Corbin) B.; m. Norah Jean Grassle, Aug. 1, 1964. Student, Yale U., Cleve. Inst. Art; MA, Case Western Res. U., 1964. Instr. Cleve. Inst. Art, 1963-64, Ark. State U., 1965-67; mem. faculty U. Md., 1967-77, prof., 1973-77, dir. grad. art studio program, 1972-77; pres. VIA Art. One-person shows include Comara Gallery, L.A., 1967, 68, Franz Bader Gallery, Washington, 1969, 73, 75, St. John's Coll., Annapolis, Md., 1972, Deson Zaks Gallery, Chgo., 1972, Gallery 118, Mpls., 1974, NAS, Washington, 1976, Cath. U. Am., Washington, 1978, Plum Gallery, Washington, 1979, Flatiron Studio, N.Y.C., 1987, Maryanne McCarthy Fine Art, N.Y.C., 1988-89, Limelight Club, N.Y.C., 1988, Loft Lawyers, N.Y.C., 1990, 91, Roberta Wood

Gallery, Syracuse, N.Y., 1993, Effect/Cause Mail Project, 1993-95, others; group shows: San Francisco Mus. Art, 1965, Cleve. Mus. Art, 1961, 62, 63, 65, 66 (2), 67, 68, Cleve. Inst. Art, 1964, Purdue U., Lafayette, Ind., 1964-69, El Paso (Tex.) Mus. Art, 1965, Nat. Arts Club, N.Y.C., 1965, Wittenberg U., Springfield, Ohio, 1966, Pacific Luth. U., Tacoma, 1966, Scripps Coll., Clairmont, Calif., 1967, U. Detroit, 1967, U. Calif., Long Beach, 1967, Palm Springs Desert Mus., Calif., 1967, Loyola U., L.A., 1968, Salt Lake City Art Ctr., 1968, U. N.H., 1968, Brigham Young U., Provo, Utah, 1968, Ind. State U., Terre Haute, 1968, Brooks Meml. Art Gallery, Memphis, 1968, 73, Cath. U., Washington, 1969, U. Md., 1969, 70, 72, Traveling Show, 1975-76, Fine Arts Gallery San Diego, 1971, Henri Gallery, Washington, 1971, Reicher Gallery, Barat Coll., Lake Forest, Ill., 1972, Corcoran Gallery Art, 1972, Va. Poly. Inst., Blacksburg, 1973, Birmingham (Ala.) Mus. Art, 1973, Indpls. Mus. Art, 1976, Gallery K, Washington, 1978, Studio Gallery, Washington, 1976-77, Modern Mus. Art, Rijeka, Yugoslavia, 1978, Baak Gallery, Cambridge, Mass., 1978, 79, Maryanne McCarthy Fine Art, N.Y.C., 1987, 88, 89, and Southampton, N.Y., 1989, Christie's N.Y.C. Preview and Auction, 1990, Univ. Sch., Cleve., 1990, Guild Hall, East Hampton, N.Y., 1991, 92, Lillian Heidenberg Gallery, N.Y.C., 1991-92, Roberta Wood Gallery, Syracuse, 1993-96, Angel Art Pacific Design Ctr., L.A., 1993, Divine Design 95, L.A., Black and Herron Gallery, N.Y.C., 1996; Intercommunication Ctr., Tokyo Opera City, Tokyo, Japan, 1998, VIA Art Found., New York (one person exhibition), 1999—, Roberta Wood Gall., Chapel Hill, NC, 2001, Sterling Meml. Libr. Yale U., New Haven, Conn., 2005, represented in collections Mus. Art, Cleve. Mus. Art, Fine Arts Gallery, San Diego, Libr. of Congress, Corcoran Gallery Art, Washington, Cooperstown Art Assn., N.Y., Chinese Artists Assn., Beijing; artwork in the following videos: The Man from U.N.C.L.E., episode The Pop Art Affair, 1966, Callanetics, M.C.A., 1986, Portrait of an Artist by Konrad Gylfason, 1986, music video Always and Forever, Whistle C.C. Prodns., 1990, documentary video San Francisco Ctr. for Visual Studies, 1990, A Man Flies in Manhattan, 2003, Breaking Some Eggs-A Wisconsin Breakfast, 2003; work reproduced in Cleve. Mus. Art. Bull., May 1962, May 1968, Md. Art Gallery Catalog, 1969, 72, Indpl. Mus. Art catalog Painting and Sculpture Today, June 1976, Internat. Exhibition catalog Modern Mus. Art, Rijeka, Yugoslavia, 1978, The Catalog of Am. Drawings, Watercolors, Pastels and Collages Corcoran Gallery Art, Washington, 1983, N.Y. Art Rev., 1988, Millenium Art Collection, 2002, Awakener of Ramids Website, 2005. Office: VIA Art Found 15 W 24th St 7th Fl New York NY 10010-3214 E-mail: bunts@earthlink.net.

BUNTZMAN, GABRIEL FRANKLIN, investor, finance educator; b. Balt., Mar. 4, 1945; s. David and Ester Virginia Buntzman; m. Louise Daw Bailey, June 4, 1970; children: Amanda Beth Buntzman Allen, Sarah Nell. BA in Chemistry, Oakland U., 1965; MA in Geography, U. NC, 1969, PhD in Orgnl. Behavior, 1983; MBA, OH U., 1979. Prof. Western Ky. U., Bowling Green, 1983—; pres. GFB Mgmt. Group, Bowling Green, 2000—; mng. ptnr. Degma Investing LLC, LA, 2004—. Cons. Strategy Peer Group, NYC, 1985—2002; dir. Movie Devel. Group, LA, 1985—. Contbr. articles and book chpt. in field. Vol. pilot Angel Flight, Bowling Green, 2005. Mem.: Small Bus. Inst., Acad. Mgmt. Avocations: aviation, music, travel, reading, farming. Home: 1807 Ewing Frud Rd Bowling Green KY 42103

BUNZA, LINDA HATHAWAY, editor, writer, composer, director; b. Hartford, Conn., Feb. 23, 1946; m. Geoffrey J. Bunza; children: Stephen, Matthew. BA, Bates Coll., 1968; MA, The Hartford Sem. Found., 1971; PhD, Syracuse U., 1974. Editl. asst. The Harvard Ednl. Rev., Cambridge, Mass., 1974—76; mng. editor The Andover Rev., Andover, Mass., 1976—79; dir. Columbia Rsch. Inst. Arts and Humanities, Portland, Oreg., 1998—2002. Editor Renaissance Mag., Hartford, 1963—64; editl. asst. Symposium Mag., Syracuse, NY, 1973—74; editor Soc. Arts, Religion, and Contemporary Culture, N.Y., NY, 1974—78; lectr. in field. Composer: (Classical Music Composition) There is Something Still Floating, 1999, Report From A Spiral, 1998, Snow Mountain, 2000, RiverMusic, 1995, Mythology of Clouds, 1993, Sphere, 1992, Cascadia, 1989, Widmanstatten Lines, 1987, View from a Mobius Strip, 1986, Sounds from the Olympic Peninsula, 1998, Electric Night, 1984, Odalisque, 1982, Awakening Night, 1981; editor: (Book) Adventures and Misadventures of Dr. Sonjee by Dr. Prasanna Pati, Snehalata Press, 2001, (Novel) Against Parched Winds by Kanta Luthra, (Book) Art of Literary Criticism, 2000; author: Theories of Modern Art-I, 1972, Theories of Modern Art-II, 1973, Theories of Modern Art-III, 1973; author: (catalog) Blue Note: The Art of Bruce Warner, 2000, Air, 2001, Where Art Reveals Itself in Symbols, Words are Hard to Find, 2001; mem. editl. bd. Anima Mag., 1973—95. Bd. dirs. Fear No Music 20th Century Ensemble, 2000—02, Third Angle New Music Ensemble, Portland, 2000—04, Contemporary Art Coun., Portland Art Mus., 2001—04, Portland Baroque Orch., 2000—04; arts and culture com. City Club of Portland, 2000—04, arch. com., 1999—2002. Recipient Pres.'s award, Beaverton Arts Commn., 2000. Mem.: Portland Inst. Contemporary Art, European and Am. Art Coun., Portland Art Mus., Northwest Bookfest (program com.), Ancient Egypt Studies Assn., The Coll. Music Soc., Soc. Composers Internat., Friends William Stafford Assn. (life). Office: Columbia Rsch Inst Arts and Humanities PO Box 25316 Portland OR 97298 Personal E-mail: bunza@teleport.com. Business E-Mail: columbiaarts@aol.com.

BUNZEL, JOHN HARVEY, political science professor; b. N.Y.C., Apr. 15, 1924; s. Ernest Everett and Harriett (Harvey) B.; m. Barbara Bovyer, May 11, 1963; children— Cameron, Reed AB, Princeton U., 1948; MA, Columbia U., 1949; PhD, U. Calif.-Berkeley, 1954; LL.D., U. Santa Clara, 1976. Mem. faculty San Francisco State U., 1953-56, 63-70, vis. scholar Ctr. Advanced Study in Behavioral Scis., 1969-70; mem. faculty Mich. State U., East Lansing, 1956-57, Stanford U., Calif., 1957-63; pres. San Jose State U., Calif., 1970-78; sr. research fellow Hoover Inst. Stanford U., Calif., 1978—. Mem. U.S. Commn. on Civil Rights, 1983-86. Author: The American Small Businessman, 1962; Anti-Politics in America, 1967; Issues of American Public Policy, 1968; New Force on the Left, 1983, Challenge to American Schools: The Case For Standards and Values, 1985, Political Passages: Journeys of Change Through Two Decades 1968-1988, 1988, Race Relations on Campus: Stanford Students Speak, 1992; contbr. articles to profl. jours., popular mags., newspapers. Weekly columnist San Jose Mercury-News. Bd. dirs. No. Calif. Citizenship Clearing House, 1959-61; mem. Calif. Atty. Gen.'s Adv. Com., 1960-61; del. Calif. Democratic Conv., 1968; del. Dem. Nat. Conv., 1968 Recipient Presdl. award No. Calif. Polit. Sci. Assn., 1969, cert. of Honor San Francisco Bd. Suprs., 1974, Hubert Humprey Pub. Policy award Policy Studies Orgn., 1990; grantee Ford Found., Rockefeller Found., Rabinowitz Found. Mem. Am. Polit. Sci. Assn. Home: 1519 Escondido Way Belmont CA 94002-3634 Office: Stanford U Hoover Inst Stanford CA 94305

BUNZL, RUDOLPH HANS, retired manufacturing executive; b. Vienna, July 20, 1922; arrived in U.S., 1940, naturalized, 1944; s. Robert Max and Nellie Margaret (Burian) Bunzl; m. Rema R. Templeton, Apr. 6, 1947 (div.); children: Ann Mary Bunzl Kamoe, Carol Elizabeth Bunzl Showker; m. Esther R. Mendelsohn, Nov. 14, 1970. BSChemE, Ga. Inst. Tech., 1943; MA in History, U. Richmond, 1994. With Shell Chem. Co., Calif., 1943-54; v.p. Am. Filtrona Corp., Richmond, Va., 1954-59, pres., 1959-83, CEO, 1983-87, chmn. bd., 1987-95. Pres. R.E.B. Found.; trustee Richmond Symphony Found. With U.S. Army, 1944—46. Mem.: AICE. Office: 5516 Falmouth St Ste 205 Richmond VA 23230-1819

BUOCH, WILLIAM THOMAS, corporate executive; b. Atlanta, Mar. 2, 1923; m. Jean Cleste Wright; children: Steven T., David W., William Mark. Student, Ga. State U., 1946-54. Pres. Buoch Enterprises Inc., Atlanta, 1954—. Office: Buoch Enterprises Inc PO Box 90862 Atlanta GA 30364-0862

BUONAMANO, ANTHONY F., real estate agent, retired postal service worker; b. Bronx, N.Y., Nov. 22, 1924; s. Camillo and Rose DeLuca Buonamano; m. Anna J. Russo, Sept. 13, 1947; children: Diane, Maria Camille. BS Engring. Mgmt., Pacific Western Univ., La., 1993. Cert. mechanical engring. tech., Nat. Soc. of Profl. Engring. Electrician U.S. Postal Svc., N.Y., 1957—58, elevator mechanic, 1958, superintending engr., 1958—59, engr., 1959—61, supr. elevator mechanics, 1961—63, chief engr., 1963—67, plant engr., 1967—69, asst. dir. plant maintenance, 1969—71, dir. plant maintenance, 1971—73, mgr. plant maintenance, 1973—78, gen. mgr. office of plant maintenance, 1978—80, ret., 1980; lic. real state assoc. Ocean Village Realty, Ormand Beach, Fla., 1982—. Develop. internal matenance supr. promotion exam. nat. Bur. of Pers., Washington, 1965; instr. Main Post Office, San Juan, PR, 1964; acting dir. restoring vital svc. Post Office, N.Y., 1967—68. Mem. disbanded Code Enforcement Bd.; v.p. Breakaway Homeowners Assn., 1999—2001; chmn. Breakaway Trails Homeowners Assn., Ormond Beach, Fla., 2001—; v.p., chmn. edn. com. Ormond Beach Citizens Police Acad. Alumni, 1993—94; mem. Elec. Constrn. and Maintenance Elec. Idustry Evalution Panel, 1972—73, Svc. Corps. of Ret. Exec., 1988—93; pres., bd. dirs. New Brit. Homeowners Assn., 1988—93, chmn. archtl. rev. bd., 1988—94. Recipient Cert. of Appreciation, City of Ormand Beach, 1999. Mem.: Pacific Western Univ. Alumni, Daytona Bd. Realtors, Ormond Beach Police Acad. (chmn. ednl. com. citizens police acad. 1995—). Democrat. Roman Cath. Avocations: drawing, photography, writing, architectural drafting. Home: 4 Creek Br Way Ormond Beach FL 32174

BUONAMICI, APRIL GRAHAM, elementary school educator, music educator; b. Maumee, Ohio, Apr. 16, 1950; d. John and Claudine Graham; m. James Buonamici, May 31, 1975; children: Domenick, Brett, Byron. MusB, Bowling Green State U., 1972, MEd, 1973. Cert. music and elem. tchr. Ohio. Tchr. Toledo City Schs., 1972—73, Euclid City Schs., Ohio, 1973—74, Lyndhurst City Schs., Ohio, 1974—76, Colegio Internacional, Caracas, Venezuela, 1976—78, Solon City Schs., Ohio, 1978—2005. Composer: (percussion ensemble) Boredom, 1969. Pres. Christian Sci. Ch., 1983, 1986; bd. dirs. 1st Ch. of Christ, Scientist, Chagrin Falls, Ohio, 2003—05. Mem.: Solon Edn. Assn. (pres., v.p., grievance chmn., trustee 1979—2005). Christian Scientist. Avocations: skiing, piano. Home: 110 Bennett Dr Bozeman MT 59715

BUONO, LAWRENCE MICHAEL, ophthalmologist, educator, surgeon; m. Christine Speer, Sept. 27, 2003. MD, Thomas Jefferson Sch. of Medicine, Phila., 1997. Cert. Bd.in Ophthalmology Am. Bd. of Ophthalmology, 2003. Asst. prof. ophthalmology Duke U. Eye Ctr., Durham, NC, 2003—. Contbr. articles pub. to profl. jour. Neuro-ophthalmology Fellowship, Wills Eye Hosp., 2000-2001. Mem.: North Am. Neuro-ophthalmology Soc. Achievements include patents for Cataract Surgery. Office: Duke Univ Eye Center Erwin Rd Box 3802 Durham NC 27710 Office Phone: 919-681-9191.

BUONO, MAUREEN BRADY, retired elementary school educator; b. Jersey, N.J., Oct. 24, 1937; d. Lawrence Peter and Evelyn (Mauro) Brady; m. Michael Buono, July 9, 1960; children: Vincent, John. BS, Jersey City State Coll., 1958, MA, 1971. Cert. elem. tchr., reading specialist K-12, prin./supr., N.J. Tchr. first grade Palisades Park Bd. Edn., NJ, 1958—61, Fairview Schs., NJ, 1974—95, reading coord. chpt. I, 1991—92, asst. prin./reading coord., 1982—84, Number 3 Sch. and Lincoln Sch., ret., 1995. Sec. YMCA Swim Team, Hackensack, N.J., 1974-75, fund-raising chmn., 1974-77; treas. English Neighborhood Sch. PTA, Fairview, 1986-88. Recipient plaque English Neighborhood Sch. PTA, Fairview, 1988, Fellowship award Bergen County PTA, 1991, Svc. award Suburban Reading Coun., 1991. Mem. N.J. Reading Assn., (Internat. Reading Assn., state coord., pres. 1989-90, Spl. Svc. award 1991), Internat. Reading Assn. (registration chairperson 8th Ea. Regional Conf., com. reading and lang. in early childhood 1990-93), North Jersey Coun.-Internat. Reading Assn. (pres. Bergen County 1985-86, Pres.'s Club 1986, Honor Coun. 1986), Fairview Edn. Assn. (pres. 1981-83), Alpha Upsilon Alpha, Phi Delta Kappa. Independent. Roman Catholic. Avocation: swimming.

BUOTE, ROSEMARIE BOSCHEN, retired special education educator; b. Jamaica, NY, Nov. 13, 1939; d. George Frederick and Mary (Bernadick) Boschen; m. Victor Roy Buote, June 27, 1964; children: Kristine Enos, Alissa Cassidy. BA, Barrington (R.I.) Coll., 1962; MEd, R.I. Coll., Providence, 1985, Fitchburg (Mass.) State Coll., 1991. Cert. spl. edn. and elem. tchr. Elem. tchr. Town of Barrington, 1962-68, 69-70; resource rm. instructional aide Town of Rehoboth, Mass., 1983-84; spl. edn. tchr., behavior mgmt. specialist Dept. of Edn. Tri-County Dist., Ednl. Svcs. in Instnl. Schs., Taunton, Mass., 1985—2002; ret., 2002. Sec. Conservation Commn., Town of Dighton, 1971—74, Friends Taunton Libr. Bd., pres., 2004—; lay eucharistic minister Pastoral Outreach Commn., Episcopal Diocese Mass.; mem. mission and stewardship com. Episcopal Diocese Mass; bd. dirs. Gordon Coll. Alumni Bd., Wenham, Mass., 1989—92, Am. Cancer Soc. S.E. Mass. Recipient Winifred E. Curry award Excellence Edn., 2004, Winifred Curry award for Excellence in Edn., Gordon Coll. Mem.: AAUW (Mass. state v.p. for membership 2003—, sec., Taunton area br. past pres., bd. dir.), Mass. Computer Using Educators, Coun. for Children with Learning Disabilities, Coun. Children with Behavioral Disorders, Coun. Exceptional Children, Southeastern New Eng. Marine Educators, Nat. Marine Educators Assn., Ladies Tea Guild, Red Hat Soc., Dighton Garden Club (pres. 1979—82), Delta Kappa Gamma (pres. 2002—04). Avocations: reading, writing, gardening, theater. Home: 1690 Wellington St Dighton MA 02715-1000 Home Fax: 508-669-5894. Personal E-mail: Rosemariebuote@aol.com.

BURACK, ALEXANDRA, poet, educator; b. Boston, Jan. 13, 1960; d. Boris Burack, Ann Burack Penfield. BA honors, Manhattanville Coll., 1982; MFA in Writing, Sarah Lawrence Coll., 2002. Founder, exec. dir. Writing Explorations Workshops, 1982—. Founder, dir. Women's Ctr. Poetry Workshop Ea. Conn. State U., Willimantic, 1996—97. Author: On the Verge, 1997; co-founder, mng. editor: Lumina, 2002; author: numerous poems. Poetry grantee, Ludwig Vogelstein Found., 1996, Artist fellow in poetry, Conn. Commn. on Arts, 1999. Home: PO Box 99 Higganum CT 06441 E-mail: poesie@bestweb.net.

BURACK, MICHAEL LEONARD, lawyer; b. Willimantic, Conn., Oct. 10, 1942; s. Meyer and Rose Ann (Kravitz) B.; m. Maria Gallego, Oct. 20, 1978; children: Victoria Luisa, Cristina Maria. BA in physics summa cum laude, Wesleyan U., Middletown, Conn., 1960—64; postgrad. in physics, Calif. Inst. Tech., 1965; MS in Applied Physics, Stanford U., 1967, JD, 1970. Bar: Calif. 1971, D.C. 1972. Law clk. to judge U.S. Ct. Appeals for 9th Cir., San Francisco, 1970-71; assoc. Wilmer, Cutler & Pickering, Washington, 1971-77, ptnr., 1978-2000, of counsel, 2001—. Mem. staff D.C. Jud. conf. Com. on Adminstrn. of Justice under Emergency Condition, 1972-73; mem. adv. com. govt. applications of ADR of Ctr. for Pub. Resources, 1988; mem. jud. evaluation com. D.C. Bar, 1991-94. Assoc. editor Jour. Pub. Contract Law, 1988-94. Mem. ABA, Order of the Coif, Phi Beta Kappa, Sigma Xi.

BURAK, H(OWARD) PAUL, lawyer; b. NYC, July 9, 1934; s. Harry and Bette (Hauer) B.; m. Edna K. Goodman, Oct. 18, 1970; children: Hally Ann., Jason Lewis. BS, Cornell U., 1954; LLB, Columbia U., 1957. Bar: N.Y. 1958, D.C. 1967, U.S. Dist. Ct. (so. and ea. dists.) N.Y. 1967, U.S. Ct. Appeals (2d cir.) 1960, U.S. Supreme Ct. 1964. Assoc. Cadwalader, Wickersham & Taft, N.Y.C., 1957-63; dep. asst., asst. gen. counsel Agy. for Internat. Devel. U.S. State Dept., Washington, 1963-67; assoc. Rosenman Colin Kay Petschek & Freund, N.Y.C., 1967-69; ptnr. Rosenman & Colin, N.Y.C., 1969—2002, Katten Muchin Zavis Rosenman, NYC, 2002—05; of counsel Katten Muchin Rosenman, NYC, 2005—. Bd. dirs. Sony USA Found., N.Y.C. Rev. editor Columbia Law Rev., 1956-57; author pamphlets. Mem. adv. bd. N.Y.C. Ballet, 2001-04. Mem.: ABA, Assn. of Bar of City of NY, Fed. Bar Coun., NY Bar Assn., Internat. Bar Assn., Univ. Club, Birchwood Country Club. Office: Katten Muchin Rosenman LLP 575 Madison Ave New York NY 10022-2585 Office Phone: 212-940-8870. Business E-Mail: hpburak@kattenlaw.com.

BURANDT, MICHAEL CHARLES, lumber company executive, paper company executive, chemicals executive, consumer products company executive; b. Remus, Mich., July 11, 1944; s. Stanley Gerard and Frances Gertrude (Fate) B.; m. Judith Guerrero, Dec. 28, 1963 (div.); children: William, Brian; m. Margaret Ann Knapp, Mar. 6, 1971; children: Kelly, Michael, Todd. BS in Marketing, Aquinas Coll., 1966. Dir., customer relations Spartan Stores Inc., Grand Rapids, Mich., 1970—72, dir., sales promotions, 1972—76, v.p., sales, 1976—81, sr. v.p., sales and marketing, 1981—86; pres., CEO A.M. Lewis, Inc., Fla.; dir., sales, consumer products div. Georgia-Pacific Corp., Atlanta, 1988—90, gen. mgr., sales and marketing, consumer products div., 1990—94, v.p., packaged products, 1994—98, sr. v.p., packaged products, 1998—2001, pres., N. Am. consumer products, 2001—03, exec. v.p. and pres., N. Am. consumer products, 2003—. Recipient Marketer of Yr. award Am. Mktg. Assn., 1984, Telly award Nat. Assn. Advertisers, 1986. Mem. Nat. Grocers Assn. (bd. dirs. 1986—), Nat. Am. Wholesale Grocers Assn. (bd. govs. 1986—). Republican. Roman Catholic. Home: 420 S Doolin Dr Roswell GA 30076-5127 Office: Georgia-Pacific Corp 133 Peachtree St NE Atlanta GA 30303 Office Phone: 404-652-4000.

BURATTI, DENNIS P., lawyer; b. Madison, Wis., 1949; JD, U. Wis., 1973. Bar: Wis. 1973, Minn. 1973. Gen. counsel Ryan Cos., Mpls. Office: Ryan Companies Ste 300 50 S 10th St Minneapolis MN 55403

BURATYNSKI, THERESA JOAN, physician; b. Steubenville, Ohio, Apr. 21, 1964; d. Raymond Stanly and Anna Sue Buratynski; m. Peter Randall Daspit, Apr. 1, 2000. BSc, U. of Akron, 1982—86; MPH, Johns Hopkins Sch. of Pub. Health, 1998—99; MD, Case Western Res. U. Sch. of Medicine, 1990—95. Risk Sciences and Public Policy Johns Hopkins Sch. of Pub. Health, 1999. Gen. med. officer Naval Hosp. Yokosuka Japan, Yokosuka, Japan, 1996—98; dept. head of aviation medicine Med. Clinic Kaneohe Bay, Kaneohe, Hawaii, 2000—01; flight surgeon Marine Heavy Helicopter 363, Kaneohe, Hawaii, 2001—04; sr. med. officer Marine Aircraft Group 24, Kaneohe, Hawaii, 2004—. Contbr. articles to jours. Activist Kailua Neighborhood, Kailua, Hawaii, 2004—05; med. support and aid US Navy, Samoa, 2000; mem. Soroptomists Internat., Kailua, Hawaii, 2004—05. Lt. comdr. US Navy, 1996—2005, Hawaii. Decorated Navy Commendation USN, Navy Achievement medal; recipient Dr Roger Keller Jr award for Genetics and Biotechnology, U. of Akron, 1986, Daniel Lewis Raven, MD award, Case Western Res. U. Sch. of Medicine, 1995; Betty Ford Ctr. Resident in Tng. scholarship, Betty Ford Ctr., 1991, Mar. of Dimes Rsch. scholarship, Mar. of Dimes, 1991, Student fellowship in Pathology, U. Hospitals of Cleve., 1992—93, Armed Forces Health Sciences Edn. and Tng. scholarship, US Navy, 1990—95, Am. Heart Assn. Rsch. grant, Am. Heart Assn., 1986, Chattanooga Corp. grant, Chattanooga Corp., 1985, U. of Akron Honors scholarship, U. of Akron, 1982—86, Ohio Bd. of Regents scholarship, Ohio Bd. of Regents, 1982—86. Mem.: Aerospace Med. Assn., Soroptomists Internat., Phi Sigma Alpha Scholastic Hon. Soc. (life). Avocations: running, gardening, community service, reading. Home: 1286 Aulepe St Kailua HI 96734 Personal E-mail: doctjb@hotmail.com.

BURBACH, MIKE, editor; BA in Journalism and German, U. N.D. With Grand Forks (N.D.) Herald; news editor AgWeek Mag., Grand Forks; mng. editor Aberdeen (S.D.) Am. News, 1990—92; editor Minot (N.D.) Daily News, 1992—95; asst. bus. editor Detroit (Mich.) Free Press, 1995—97; v.p., exec. editor Columbus (Ga.) Ledger-Enquirer, 1997—2004; mng. editor Akron (Ohio) Beacon Jour., 2004—. Office: Akron Beacon Journal 44 E Exchange St PO Box 640 Akron OH 44309-0640

BURBAGE, TOM, aeronautical engineer; b. San Diego, Sept. 9, 1947; m. Ellen Burbage; 3 children. BS in aerospace engring., U.S. Navel Acad., 1969; MS in aeronautical systems, U. West Fla.; MS in bus. admin., UCLA. Joined Lockheed Martin, 1980, mgr. bus. devel. U.S. Govt. Progs. Burbank, Calif., v.p. Washington ops. & coord. with Dept. Defense, U.S. Congress, and Embassies of Fgn. Govts., 1987—90, v.p. bus. devel. & product support, Aeronautical Systems Marietta, Ga., 1990—92, pres., v.p., AFX Prog. mgr., 1992—94, v.p. & gen. mgr. Navy Progs., 1994, v.p. & gen. mgr., F-22 Prog., exec. v.p. consumer requirements, Aeronautical Systems, exec. v.p. & gen. mgr., Joint Strike Fighter, 2000—. Active duty USN, 1969—80, lt. comdr. USN, captain USN, ret. USNR, 1994. Recipient Aerospace Industry Personality of Yr. award, Flight Internat. Mag., 2002, Donald C. Burnham Mfg. Mgmt. Award, Soc. Mfg. Engrs., 2004. Office: Lockheed Martin 6801 Rockledge Dr Bethesda MD 20817

BURBANK, JANE RICHARDSON, historian, educator; b. Hartford, Conn., June 11, 1946; d. John and Helen Lee (West) B.; m. Frederick Cooper, Sept. 3, 1985. BA, Reed Coll., 1967; MLS, Simmons Coll., 1969; MA, Harvard U., 1971, PhD, 1981. Asst. prof. Harvard U., Cambridge, Mass., 1981-85, U. Calif., Santa Barbara, 1985-86, assoc. prof., 1986-87, U. Mich., Ann Arbor, 1987-95, prof., 1995—2002, NYU, 2002—. Reviewer Kritika, 1983, Russian Rev., 1984, 98, Am. Hist. Rev., 1988, 91, 96, Jour. Modern History, 1989, 92, 94, Slavic Rev., 1990, Harvard Ukrainian Studies, 1991; presenter in field; dir. ctr. Russian E. European studies U. Mich., 1992-95, 98. Author: Intelligentsia and Revolution: Russian Views of Bolshevism, 1917-1922, 1986, Russian Peasants Go To Court: Legal Culture in the Countryside, 2004; editor: Perestroika and Soviet Culture, 1989, Imperial Russia, New Histories for the Empire, 1998; editor Kritika, 1978-80; mem. editl. bd. Ind.-Mich. Series in Russian and East European Studies, Kritika, 1999-2001; contbr. articles to profl. jours. Fulbright-Hayes Rsch. award, 1991, Krupp Found. fellow, Ctr. for European Studies, Harvard U., 1977-78, Whiting fellow, 1980-81, Am. Coun. Learned Socs. fellow, 1983-84, Hoover Inst. Postdoctoral fellow, 1990-91; grantee NEH, 1984, 97, Harvard U., 1982-84, Internat. Rsch. and Exchs. Bd., Acad. Exch. with the USSR, 1987-88, 91, U. Mich., 1990, 91, 93, 94, 97; fellow Ctr. for Advanced Study in the Behavioral Scis., 2002-03. Mem. Am. Hist. Assn., Am. Assn. for the Advancement of Slavic Studies, Social Sci. Rsch. Coun. (joint com. on Soviet studies 1988-93), Nat. Coun. for Eurasia and East European Rsch., Phi Beta Kappa. Office: NYU 53 Washington Sq South New York NY 10012 Office Phone: 212-998-8628. Business E-Mail: jane.burbank@nyu.edu.

BURBANK, KERSHAW, writer; b. Flushing, N.Y., Jan. 1, 1914; s. Robert Abraham and Lillian Cassels (DuBose) B.; m. Elizabeth E. Hapworth, Mar. 1942 (div.); children: Kershaw Jr., Thorne Burbank Taylor; m. Sally Page Williams Crawford, May 30, 1951 (div.); m. Barbara Bennett, Dec. 16, 1961 (dec. Jan. 1985); 1 child, Bennett. BA, Yale U., 1937. Accredited pub. rels. profl. Unitman MGM Studios, Culver City, Calif., 1937-39; asst. to v.p. 20th Century-Fox Film Corp., N.Y., Calif., 1941-44; dir. nat. promotion Richard Condon Inc., N.Y.C., 1945; sr. ptnr. Burbank Assocs., N.Y.C., 1945-48; dir. pub. info. Colonial Williamsburg (Va.), Inc., 1948-51; advisor pub. affairs Office of the Rockefeller Family, N.Y.C., 1951-61; v.p., sec. Channel 13 Ednl. Broadcasting Corp., N.Y.C., 1961-65; exec. v.p., dir. Infoplan Internat., N.Y.C., 1965-69; mng. dir. Weightman Assocs., Phila., 1969-74; v.p. The Franklin Inst., Phila., 1974-79. Cons. Sleepy Hollow Restorations, Tarrytown, N.Y., 1961-64, 69-74, Palisades Interstate Pkwy., N.Y., N.J., 1961-64. Author: A Pleasant Land to See, 1973; contbr. articles to nat. mags. Trustee Elsie Lee Garthwaite Meml. Found., Rosemont, Pa., 1970—2000, CRC Found., Delray Beach, Fla., 1990-94, Woodhaven Found., Gulf Stream, Fla., 1998—2000; bd. dirs. Crossroads Club (non-profit orgn.), Delray Beach, 1988-90, Bethesda Hosp. Assn., Delray Beach, 1983-85; chmn. Coalition of Pa. Museums, 1979-80. Episcopalian. Avocations: photography, reading, travel. Home: 125 MacFarlane Dr Delray Beach FL 33483-6803

BURBANK, LYNDA A., painter; b. Burbank, Calif., Apr. 18, 1943; d. Norman Alfred and Glendora McComb Mactaggart. BA in Psychology, U. So. Calif. Prodn.designer (films) Born In East L.A., Quiet Cool, Sid And Nancy, The Wrestling Movie, Repo Man, The Slayer, Happy Birthday, Roadside Prophets, Highway To Hell, Body Rock, The Lady In Red, The Hitcher, Flicks, Losin' It, Walker, (TV Cable) True Tales, Love Kills, My Life As A Man, The Weathergirls, set decorator (TV series) Less Than Perfect, According To Jim, Geena Davis Show, Shasta Mcnasty, Mad About You, Ellen, John Ridley Pilot, Less Than Perfect Pilot, Bette Midler Pilot, Wish You Were Here Pilot, Over The Top Pilot, (TV films) The Taxman, Ride The Wind, When Love Kills, A Murderous Affair: The Carolyn Warmus Story, Running Mates, Alison Gertz Story, Keep The Change, Keeper Of The City, Call Me Anna (The Patty Duke Story), Rainbow Drive, Billy Crystal's Midnight Train To Moscow, A Summer To Remember, Doing time: Women In Prison. Home: 3205 Weldon Ave Los Angeles CA 90065

BURBANK, NELSON STONE, investment banker; b. Winchester, Mass., Sept. 16, 1920; s. Willis H. and Vivian (Casson) B.; m. Rita B. Healey, Feb. 12, 1950; children: Peter N., Nelson Stone, Jane Vivian. Student, Boston U., 1946-47. Registered rep. Vance, Sanders & Co., Inc., Boston, 1946-53; pres. Burbank & Co., Inc., Boston, 1953-83; dir., registered rep. A.G. Edwards and Sons, Inc., 1982-83; pres., bd. dirs. Colonial Investment Services, Inc., 1983-85. Bd. dirs. MassBank for Savs., Reading, ret., 1994; bd. govs. Boston Stock Exch., 1965-73, vice chmn., 1968-71, chmn., 1971-73; bd. dirs. Ag Edwards & Sons, Inc. Vice chmn. ARC, 1963-82. With AUS, 1942-45. Decorated D.F.C., Air medals. Mem. Nat. Assn. Securities Dealers (mem. bus. conduct com. 1971-73, gov. 1974-77, cons 1985-88) Home and Office: 24 Juniper Cir Reading MA 01867-1836

BURBANK, ROBINSON DERRY, crystallographer; b. Berlin, N.H., Oct. 3, 1921; s. Paul William and Hazel Louise (Robinson) B.; m. Jeannette Murielle Bisson, July 14, 1945 (div. 1975); children: Paul Robinson, Claudia Olive. BA, Colby Coll., 1942; PhD, MIT, 1950. Rsch. asst. Manhattan Project, MIT, Cambridge, 1942-45, Lab. Insulation Rsch., MIT, 1945-50; sr. physicist Gaseous Diffusion Plant, Oak Ridge, Tenn., 1950-53; group leader, crystallography Olin Industries, New Haven, Conn., 1953-55; tech. staff Bell Telephone Labs., Murray Hill, N.J., 1955-86. U.S. del. Internat. Union Crystallography, Stony Brook, L.I., N.Y., 1969, Amsterdam, 1975; mem. U.S.A. Nat. Com. Crystallography, 1968-76. Contbr. technical papers to profl. jours. Bd. dirs. Chester Twp. Taxpayers Assn., N.J., 1961-65, 70-74, pres. 1973. Mem. Am. Crystallographic Assn. (charter mem., treas. 1965-68, v.p. 1974, pres. 1975), Com. Sci. Soc. Presidents, Phi Beta Kappa, Sigma Xi. Achievements include X-ray crystallography of inorganic compounds, interhalogen compounds, noble gas compounds, phase transformations, thin films. Home: 45 Woodland Ave Summit NJ 07901-2141

BURBANK, STEPHEN BRADNER, law educator; b. NYC, Jan. 8, 1947; s. John Howard and Jean (Gedney) B.; m. Ellen Randolph Coolidge, June 13, 1970; 1 child, Peter Jefferson. AB, Harvard U., 1968, JD, 1973. Bar: Mass. 1973, Pa. 1976, U.S. Supreme Ct. 1977. Law clk. Supreme Jud. Ct. of Mass., Boston, 1973-74, Chief Justice Warren Burger, Washington, 1974-75; gen. counsel U. Pa., Phila., 1975-80, asst. prof. law, 1979-83, assoc. prof. law, 1983-86, prof. law, 1986—, Fuller prof. law, 1991-95, Berger prof. law, 1995—. Reporter 3rd Cir. Jud. Discipline Rules, Phila., 1981-82, 84, 3rd Cir. Task Force on Rule 11, Phila., 1987-89; mem. Nat. Commn. on Jud. Discipline and Removal, 1991-93; mediator, arbitrator Ctr. for Pub. Resources, NY, 1986—; cons. Dechert LLP, Phila., 1986—; mem. CPR Arbitration Commn., 1997-2000; spl. master NFL, 2002—. Mem. Com. to Visit Harvard and Radcliffe Coll., Cambridge, Mass., 1979-85; mem. adv. bd. Inst. Contemporary Art, Phila., 1982-99; charter trustee Phillips Acad., Andover, Mass., 1980-97. Mem. Am. Law Inst. (life, adviser transnat. rules of civil procedure 1997-04, adviser internat. jurisdiction and judgments 1999-05), Am. Arbitration Assn. (mem. panel of arbitrators 1985—), Am. Acad. Polit. and Social Sci. (bd. dirs. 2002-, chair 2004-), Am. Judicature Soc. (mem. exec. com. 1997-02, v.p. 1997-99), Century Assn., Phi Beta Kappa Avocations: swimming, travel, tennis. Office: U Pa Sch Law 3400 Chestnut St Philadelphia PA 19104-6204 Office Phone: 215-898-7072. E-mail: sburbank@law.upenn.edu.

BURBIDGE, E. MARGARET, astronomer, educator; b. Davenport, Eng. d. Stanley John and Marjorie (Stott) Peachey; m. Geoffrey Burbidge, Apr. 2, 1948; 1 child, Sarah. BS, PhD, U. London; Sc.D. hon., Smith Coll., 1963, U. Sussex, 1970, U. Bristol, 1972, U. Leicester, 1972, City U., 1973, U. Mich., 1978, U. Mass., 1978, Williams Coll., 1979, SUNY, Stony Brook, 1985, Rensselaer Poly. Inst., 1986, U. Notre Dame, 1986, U. Chgo., 1991. Mem. staff U. London Obs., 1948-51; rsch. fellow Yerkes Obs. U. Chgo., 1951-53, Shirley Farr fellow Yerkes obs., 1957-59, assoc. prof. Yerkes Obs., 1959-62; rsch. fellow Calif. Inst. Tech., Pasadena, 1955-57; mem. Enrico Fermi Inst. for Nuclear Studies, 1957-62; prof. astronomy dept. physics U. Calif. San Diego, 1964—89; dir. Royal Greenwich Obs. (Herstmonceux Castle), Hailsham, Eng., 1971-73; univ. prof. U. Calif., San Diego, 1984-91, prof. emeritus, 1991—, rsch. prof. dept. physics, 1990—. Lindsay Meml. lectr. Goddard Space Flight Ctr., NASA; Abby Rockefeller Mauze prof. MIT, 1968; David Elder lectr. U. Strathclyde, 1972; V. Gildersleeve lectr. Barnard Coll., 1974; Jansky lectr. Nat. Radio Astronomy Observatory, 1977; Brode lectr. Whitman Coll., 1986; Hitchcock lectr. U. Calif., Berkeley, 2001. Author (with G. Burbidge): Quasi-Stellar Objects, 1967; editor: Observatory mag., 1948—51; mem. editl. bd.: Astronomy and Astrophysics, 1969—85. Co-recipient Warner prize in Astronomy, 1959; recipient Bruce Gold medal, Astronomy Soc. Pacific, 1982, U.S. Nat. medal of Sci., 1984, Sesquicentennial medal, Mt. Holyoke Coll., 1987, Einstein medal, World Cultural Coun., 1988; fellow hon. fellow, Univ. Coll., London, Girton Coll., Lucy Cavendish Coll., Cambridge. Fellow: Royal Astron. Soc., Am. Acad. Arts and Scis., Nat. Acad. Scis. (chmn. sect.12 astronomy 1986), Royal Soc.; mem.: Internat. Astron. Union (pres. commn. 28 1970—73), Am. Astron. Soc. (v.p. 1972—74, pres. 1976—78, Henry Norris Russell lectr. 1984), Grad. Women Sci. (hon.). Office: U Calif-San Diego Ctr Astrophysics Space Scis Mail Code # 0424 La Jolla CA 92093 Office Phone: 858-534-4477. Business E-Mail: mburbidge@ucsd.edu.

BURBIDGE, GEOFFREY, astrophysicist, educator; b. Chipping Norton, Oxon, Eng., Sept. 24, 1925; s. Leslie and Eveline Burbidge; m. Margaret Peachey, 1948; 1 dau. B.Sc. with spl. honors in Physics, Bristol U., 1946; PhD, U. Coll., London, 1951. Asst. lectr. U. Coll., London, 1950-51; Agassiz fellow Harvard, 1951-52; research fellow U. Chgo., 1952-53, Cavendish Lab., Cambridge, Eng., 1953-55; Carnegie fellow Mt. Wilson and Palomar Obs., Calif. Inst. Tech., 1955-57; asst. prof. dept. astronomy U. Chgo., 1957-58, assoc. prof., 1958-62, U. Calif. San Diego, La Jolla, 1962-63, prof. physics, 1963-83, 88—; dir. Kitt Peak Nat. Obs., Tucson, 1978-84. Phillips vis. prof. Harvard U., 1968; bd. dirs. Associated Univs. Research in Astronomy, 1971-74; trustee Associated Univs., Inc., 1973-82 Author: (with Margaret Burbidge) Quasi-Stellar Objects, 1967, (with F. Hoyle and J. Narlikar) A Different Approach to Cosmology, 2000; editor Ann. Rev. Astronomy and Astrophysics, 1973-2004; sci. editor Astrophys. Jour., 1996-02; contbr. articles to sci. jours. Fellow Royal Soc. London, Am. Acad. Arts and Scis., Royal Astron. Soc., Am. Phys. Soc., Am. Assn. Adv. Sci.; mem. Am. Astron. Soc., Internat. Astron. Union, Astron. Soc. of Pacific (pres. 1974-76) Office: U Calif-San Diego 0424 Ctr Astrophysics Space Scis La Jolla CA 92093 Office Phone: 858-534-6626. Business E-Mail: gburbidge@ucsd.edu.

BURCH, BARBARA G., academic administrator; BA in English, Western Ky. U.; MA in Edn., PhD in Edn., U. Ind. Dir. curriculum devel. and rsch. Shelby County Schs., Memphis; asst. v.p. U. Memphis, acad. affairs, interim dean, assoc. dean, dir. grad. studies; dean Sch. Edn. and Human Svcs. Calif. State U., Fresno; v.p. for acad. affairs Western Ky. U., Bowling Green, 1996—, provost, 1998—. Mem.: Am. Assn. for Colls. Tchr. Edn. (pres.). Office: Provost & VP for Acad Affairs Western Ky Univ 1 Big Red Way Bowling Green KY 42101-3576

BURCH, CONNIE WEBSTER, education educator; b. Atlanta, June 20, 1955; s. Roy and Katherine Cobb Webster; m. Robert Milo Burch, Mar. 18, 1978 (dec. Feb. 1996); children: Robert Bradley, Katherine C. Turner, Brian Hamilton. BS in elem. edn., Ga. State U., 1978; MA in early childhood edn., U. Ga., 1990; MS in elem. edn., Brenau U., 1994; D in edn., Nova Southeastern U., 1997. Educator Gwinnett County Pub. Schools, Lawrenceville, Ga., 1988—2001; adj. instr. Brenau U., Gainseville, Ga., 2001—; with dept. profl. learning Gwinnett County Pub. Schools, Lawrenceville, Ga., 2001—. Exec. dir. Ga. Assn. Supervision and Curriculum, Atlanta, 2004—; chmn., exec. com. Ga. Profl. Boards Stds. Commn., 2004—. Mem. leadership Gwinnett County C. of C., 2004—05. Recipient Tchr. of the Yr., Dacula Elem. Sch., 1997. Mem.: Kappa Delta Pi Internat. Soc. Avocations: reading, travel, boating. Home: 2575 Moon Rd Loganville GA 30052 Office: Gwinnett County Pub Sch 723 Hi Hope Rd Lawrenceville GA 30043 Office Phone: 770-682-4192.

BURCH, DONALD VICTOR, lawyer; b. Niagara Falls, N.Y., Feb. 18, 1944; s. Victor James and Marva (Bogardus) B.; m. Sharron Burch, Aug. 27, 1966; children: Elizabeth Katherine, Craig Donald. BA, Vanderbilt U., 1966; JD, U. Ala., 1969. Bar: Miss. 1970. Assoc. Daniel, Coker, Horton & Bell, Jackson, Miss., 1970-76, ptnr., 1977—, shareholder. Dir. Gulf Coast Law Inst., Gulfport, Miss., 1977-81. Mem. ABA (mem. appellate practice subcom. 1981—), Miss. Bar Assn. (mem. workers compensation com. 1985-87), Hinds County Bar Assn., Def. Research Inst., So. Assn. Workers Compensation Adminstrs. Clubs: Reservoir Area Exchange (Jackson) (pres. 1987-88). Lodges: Optimists. Republican. Episcopalian. Home: 784 Benwick Dr Brandon MS 39047-8112 Office: 4400 Old Canton Rd Jackson MS 39211-5982 E-mail: dburch@danielcoker.com.

BURCH, FRANCIS BOUCHER, JR., lawyer; b. Balt., Feb. 27, 1948; s. Francis Boucher and Mary Patricia (Howe) B.; children: Sara E., Francis B. III, Michael F.; m. Elisabeth J. Harper, Sept. 29, 2002. Student, U. Fribourg, Switzerland, 1968-69; BA, Georgetown U., 1970; JD with honors, U. Md., 1974. Bar: Md. 1974, U.S. Ct. Appeals (4th cir.) 1975, U.S. Supreme Ct. 1994. Assoc. litig. dept. Piper & Marbury LLP, Balt., 1974-81, ptnr. litig. dept., 1981—91, chmn. litig. dept., 1991-94, chmn., 1994-99; co-chmn. Piper Rudnick LLP, Balt., 1999—2004; ptnr., joint CEO DLA Piper Rudnick Gray Cary (formerly Piper Rudnick LLP), Balt., 2005—. Contbr. articles to profl. jours. Bd. dirs. Greater Balt. Com., 1996—, vice-chmn., 1998—2001, chmn., 2001—03; mem. Leadership Program, 1990—, bd. dirs., 1993—98, vice-chmn., 1994—96, chmn., 1996—98, chmn. selection com., 1994—95; trustee Calvert Sch., 1989—2000, exec. com., 1991—2000, chmn., 1991—95, sec., 1991—95; trustee Western Md. Coll., 1996—2001, Johns Hopkins Health Sys. Corp., 1994—96, Johns Hopkins Hosp., 1994—96, Johns Hopkins Medicine, 1996—, Johns Hopkins U., 2005—, Balt. Mus. Art, 1990—96, 1998—2000, mem. exec. com., 1991—96, chmn. ann. giving com., 1991—93, treas., 1992—94, v.p., 1994—96, co-chmn. devel., 1994—96; bd. visitors U. Md. Sch. Law, Balt., 1993—, U. Md., 1995—; campaign cabinet, chmn. emerging markets United Way Ctrl., Md., 1994; chmn. Leadership Giving, 1999. With U.S. Army N.G., 1970—76. Fellow Am. Bar Found., Am. Coll. Trial Lawyers, Md. Bar Found.; mem. ABA, Am. Law Inst., Md. Bar Assn. (Disting. Svc. award litigation sect. 1981), Balt. City Bar Assn. (chmn. jud. appts. com. 1990-91, exec. coun. 1990-91), 4th Cir. Jud. Conf., Rule Day Club, Lawyers' Round Table Balt., Center Club, River Bend Club. Democrat. Roman Catholic. Avocations: skiing, surfing. Office: DLA Piper Rudnick Gray Cary 6225 Smith Ave Baltimore MD 21209-3600 Office Phone: 410-580-4040. Office Fax: 410-580-3001. Business E-Mail: frank.burch@dlapiper.com.

BURCH, FRANCIS FLOYD, clergyman; b. Balt., May 15, 1932; s. Thaddeus Joseph and Frances Fidelis (Greenwell) Burch. BA, Fordham U., 1956, MA, 1958; PhL, Woodstock Coll., 1957, STL, 1964; postgrad., Tronchinnes, Belgium, 1964-65; Docteur, U. Paris, Sorbonne, 1967. Joined Soc. of Jesus, 1950, ordained priest Roman Cath. Ch., 1963. Tchr. Gonzaga HS, Washington, 1957-60; from asst. prof. to assoc. prof. English St. Joseph's U., Phila., 1967—76, prof., 1976—, asst. acad. dean, 1972-74, bd. dirs., 1971-76, sec. bd. dirs., 1971-75. Artist-scholar-in-residence Millersville U., Pa., 1978. Author: Tristan Corbiere: l'orginalite des "Amours janues" et leur influence sur T. S. Eliot, 1970; editor (with P. O. Walzer): Tristan Corbiere: Ouevres completes, 1970, Sur Tristan Corbiere: lettres inedites adressees au poete et premieres critiques le concernant, 1975; translator: The Path to Transcendence: From Philosophy to Mysticism in Saint Augustine (Paul Henry), 1981, 2d edit., 2002, The Personalist Challenge: Intersubjectivity and Ontology (Maurice Nedoncelle), 1984; contbr. articles to profl. jours. Recipient Merit award, St. Joseph's U., 1980, 1983. Mem.: MLA, Internat. Soc. Neoplatonic Studies, Alpha Sigma Nu, Alpha Epsilon Delta. Home and Office: 5600 City Ave Philadelphia PA 19131-1308 E-mail: fburch@sju.edu.

BURCH, JAMES LEO, science research institute executive; b. San Antonio, Nov. 28, 1942; s. Joseph Leo Jr. and Doris Babette (Hagy) B.; m. Kathleen Marie Dowdy, Dec. 30, 1965; children: Angela Marie, Charles Joseph, Kenneth James. BS in Physics, St. Mary's U., San Antonio, 1964; PhD, Rice U., 1968; MS in Adminstrn., George Washington U., 1973. Space physicist Goddard Space Flight Ctr. NASA, Greenbelt, Md., 1971-74, space physicist Marshall Space Flight Ctr. Huntsville, Ala., 1974-77; sr. rsch. physicist S.W. Rsch. Inst., San Antonio, 1977-78, sect. mgr., 1978-80, dept. dir., 1980-85, v.p., 1985—. Prin. investigator NASA Dynamics Explorer Mission, 1978-92, Nasa Atlas Shuttle Mission, 1989-93, ESA Rosetta Comet orbiter, 1996—, NASA Image Midex mission, 1996—, NASA Magnetosphere Multiscale Mission, 2005—; mem. space sci. and applications adv. com. NASA, 1990-93; mem. NAS Space Studies Bd., 2000-04; chair NAS com. Solar and Space Physics, 2000-04. Assoc. editor Jour. Geophys. Rsch., 1977-79, 94-96, Geophys. Rsch. Letters, 1978-82, editor, 1989-90, editor-in-chief, 1990-93; contbr. numerous articles to profl. jours. Capt. U.S. Army, 1968-71. Recipient Disting. Alumnus award St. Mary's U., 1987, Van Allen Lectureship Am. Geophys. Union, 2001 Fellow Am. Geophys. Union (pres. space physics and aeronomy sect. 1996-98), Internat. Acad. Astronautics. Roman Catholic. Avocation: golf. Office: SW Rsch Inst 6220 Culebra Rd San Antonio TX 78238-5100 Business E-Mail: jburch@swri.edu.

BURCH, JOHN CHRISTOPHER, JR., investment banker; b. Nashville, Jan. 18, 1940; s. John Christopher and Frances Vivian (Harris) B.; m. Susan Marie Klein, Sept. 13, 1969; children: Frances Marie, Christina Polk, John Christopher III. BA, Vanderbilt U., 1966. Credit analyst Bank N.Y., N.Y.C., 1966-70; v.p. instl. sales Loeb Rhoades & Co., N.Y.C., 1970-75, J.C. Bradford & Co., Nashville, 1976-82; mng. dir. SunTrust Equitable Securities Corp., Nashville, 1982-2001; pres. Capital Markets Advisors LLC, Nashville, 2001—. Co-author: Capital Markets Handbook, 1999, 6th edit., 2005. With U.S. Army, 1962-65. Mem.: CFA Soc. Nashville (bd. dirs. 2005—), Nat. Assn. Security Dealers (arbitrator), Securities Industry Assn. (chmn. syndicate com. 1998—2000, bd. dirs. chair so. dist. 2001), CFA Inst., Belle Meade Country Club (Nashville). Episcopalian. Home: 705 Hillwood Blvd Nashville TN 37205-1315 Office: Capital Markets Advisors LLC Ste 228 2200 Twenty First Ave S Nashville TN 37212 Fax: 615-292-6757. Office Phone: 615-292-6323. E-mail: jburch@capitalmarketsadvisors.com.

BURCH, JOHN RUSSELL, JR., library director; b. Peoria, Ill., Mar. 22, 1968; s. John Russell and Idalia Amparo (Murgas) B.; m. Samantha Jo Bailey, July 1, 1989; children: Morgan Lourrae, Alexandra Christine, Christopher Simpson, Kayleigh Jo. BA in History, Berea (Ky.) Coll., 1990; MS in Libr. Sci., U. Ky., 1992, MA in History, postgrad., U. Ky., 2003—. Grad. asst. U. Ky. Agrl. Libr., Lexington, 1991-92; govt. documents libr. So. Ark. U., Magnolia, 1992-93; reference libr. Cumberland Coll., Williamsburg, Ky., 1993-95, pub. svcs. libr., 1995, tech. svcs. libr., 1995-2000; dir. libr. svcs. Campbellsville (Ky.) U., 2000—. Book reviewer Libr. Jour., Am. Ref. Books Ann., Choice Mag. Mem.: Phi Alpha Theta. Republican. Office: Campbellsville U Montgomery Libr 1 University Dr Campbellsville KY 42718-2799 Office Phone: 270-789-5015. Business E-Mail: jrburch@campbellsville.edu.

BURCH, JOHN THOMAS, JR., lawyer; b. Balt., Feb. 22, 1942; s. John T and Katheryn Estella (Peregoy) Burch; m. Linda Anne Shearer, Nov. 1, 1969; children: John Thomas, Richard James. BA, U. Richmond, Va., 1964, JD, 1966; LLM, George Washington U., 1971. Bar: Va. 1966, U.S. Supreme Ct. 1969, DC 1974, Mich. 1983, Md. 1993. Pvt. practice, Richmond, 1966, Washington, 1974-77; pres. Burch, Kerns and Klimek, 1977-82, Burch & Assocs., Washington, 1982-95, Burch & Bennett, P.C., Washington, 1983-85; ptnr. Alagia, Day, Marshall, Mintmire & Chauvin, Washington, 1985-90, Maloney & Burch, Washington, 1990-96; pres. Burch & Cronauer, P.C., Washington, 1995—2001, Burch & Assocs., Washington, 1982-95; with office of gen. counsel Dept. of Vets. Affairs, 2001—. Rep. committeeman City of Alexandria, Va., 1975—92; aide-de-camp brigadier gen to gov State of Va., 1976—; alt. del. Rep. Nat. Conv., 1988, 1994. Decorated Bronze Star, Meritorious Svc. medal. Mem.: VFW (dep. comdr. 1986—87), ABA (sec. pub. contract law sect. 1976—77), Va. War Meml. Found. (trustee), Nat. Vietnam and Gulf War Vets. Coalition (nat. chmn. 1983—2001), Spl. Forces Assn., Fed. Bar Assn. (nat. coun., dep. sec. 1982—83), Mil. Order of Carabou, Order St. Constantine Magna, SCV, Am. Legion, Va. Soc. SAR (pres. 1975—76, Good Citizenship award 1970, Patriots medal 1978), Soc. War of 1812, Scabbard and Blade, Knights of Malta (cheveliar order St. John Jerusalem), Phi Sigma Alpha, Phi Alpha Delta. Republican. Episcopalian. Home and Office: Burch & Cronauer PC 1015 N Pelham St Alexandria VA 22304

BURCH, JOHN WALTER, mining equipment company executive; b. Balt., July 14, 1925; s. Louis Claude and Constance (Boucher) B. m. Robin Neely Sinkler, Apr. 19, 1952; children: John C., Robert L., Charles C., Anne N. BS in Commerce, U. Va., 1951; postgrad., U.S. Coast Guard Acad., 1951. With Procter & Gamble Co., Phila., 1953-65, sales mgr., 1960-65; v.p. Warner Co., Phila., 1965-73; chmn. bd., CEO S.S. Keely Co., Phila., 1973-75; pres., chmn. bd., CEO Burch Materials Co., Inc., Wayne, Pa., 1975—; ptnr., mgr. Integrated MRO, LLC, 1998—. Dir. Eagle's Eye, Inc., Wayne; bd. dirs. Nat. Multiple Sclerosis Soc., 1970-81, v.p., exec. com., 1974-77; bd. dirs. Pa. Sports Hall of Fame, 1974—, v.p., exec. com., 1974-79; chmn. Am. Legion Tennis Tournaments for State of Pa., 1975-82; mem. U.S. Congl. Adv. Bd., 1982, bd. dirs. Eagle's Eye Lacrosse Club, 1982-87; mem. Bus. Adv. Coun., 2003, Presdl. Bus. Commn., 2004; bd. dirs. juvenile justice divsn. Cath. Social Svcs., Archdiocese Phila., 2004. With USN, 1943-46, USCG, 1951-53. Named All-Am. in lacrosse, 1949, Archdiocese of Phila. gymnasium named in honor of John Burch family, 2003. Mem. Merion Cricket Club, Merion Golf Club, Willoughby Golf Club. Republican. Roman Catholic. Office: Burch Materials Co Inc 685 Kromer Ave Berwyn PA 19312-1317 Office Phone: 610-640-4877. Business E-Mail: john@burchmaterials.com.

BURCH, LORI ANN, obstetrics nurse; b. Charleston, Ill., Jan. 27, 1967; d. Lawrence Lee and Leslie Ann (Biddle) Pedigo; m. Steven Wayne Burch, Oct. 16, 1987 (div. June 1992); 1 child, Colby Steven. Diploma, Bapt. Sch. Nursing, Springdale, Ark., 1992. RN, Ark., Mo. Staff nurse Sprindale Meml. Hosp., 1992-94; agy. RN Healthstaf, Inc., Branson, Mo., 1994-98; sch. nurse Kirbyville (Mo.) Sch. Dist., 1998—. Educator, spkr. in field. Avocations: swimming, running, travel, golf.

BURCH, MARY SEELYE QUINN, law librarian, consultant; b. Worcester, Mass., Oct. 16, 1925; d. James Henry and Mary Seelye (O'Donnell) Quinn; m. Walter Douglas Burch, Aug. 18, 1972; children: Cathi, Andrew, David, John, Joan. BS, Suny, 1976; MLS, Pratt Inst., 1979. Law libr. N.Y. Supreme Ct., Troy, 1969-82; chief law libr. Office Ct. Adminstrn., Albany, N.Y., 1982-86; libr. N.Y. State Libr., 1986-89, ret., 1989; owner Mary S. Burch Law Libr. Svc., 1983—2003. Instr. legal rsch. SUNY, 1981; selected to meet with deans of law schs. in China for improvement of legal reference materials in China. Mem. N.Y. State Bar Assn. (lectr. 1980), Ulster County Bar Assn. (cons. 1980), Am. Assn. Law Librs., Assn. Law Librs. Upstate N.Y. (pres. 1971, v.p. 1981). Roman Catholic. Avocations: pilot, swimming, sewing. Home: 312 Diamond Rock Cir Troy NY 12182

BURCH, MICHAEL IRA, public relations executive, retired federal agency administrator; b. St. Louis, June 20, 1941; s. Horatio and Iona (Anderson) B.; m. Sherilynn J. Hummel, Dec. 26, 1987; children: Paige Anne Engelson, Michelle Hummel. BA, U. Mo., 1963; postgrad., Boston U., 1965, Am. U., 1972-75. Commd. 2d lt. U.S. Air Force, 1963, advanced through grades to lt. col., 1979, served in tactical air command units, 1963-72, served at Pentagon in offices Air Force and Def. secs., 1972-83, ret., 1983; pres. Washington Communications Corp., 1983; asst. sec. for pub. affairs U.S. Dept. Def., Washington, 1983-85; v.p. communications Aerospace group McDonnell Douglas Corp., Washington, 1985-88, v.p. pub. relations St. Louis, 1988-92; sr. v.p. Burson-Marsteller, Washington, 1992-95; pres. Civitas Comm. Group, Alexandria, Va., 1995—, Nature Works, Inc., 1997—. Recipient Disting. Service medal Dept. Def., 1983, Disting. Pub. Service medal Dept. Def., 1985 Mem. Air Commando Assn., Am. Legion. Republican. Episcopalian. Avocation: sailing. Office: Nature WOrks Inc PO Box 639 Burgess VA 22432-0639

BURCH, ROBERT DALE, lawyer; b. Washington, Jan. 30, 1928; s. Dallas Stockwell and Hepsy (Berry) B.; m. Joann D. Hansen, Dec. 9, 1966; children: Berkeley, Robert Brett, Barrett Bradley. Student, Va. Mil. Inst., 1945-46; BS, U. Calif. at Berkeley, 1950, JD, 1953. Bar: Calif. bar 1954. Since practiced in, Los Angeles and Beverly Hills; ptnr. Gibson, Dunn & Crutcher, 1961—93. Lectr. U. So. Calif. Inst. Fed. Taxation, 1960, 62, 65, 75; guest lectr. U. Calif.-L.A. Law Sch., 1959; lectr. C.E.B. seminars U. Calif.; founder Robert D. Burch Ctr. for Tax Policy and Pub. Fin., U. Calif., Berkeley. Author: Federal Tax Procedures for General Practitioners; Contbr. profl. jours., textbooks. Bd. dirs. charitable founds. With AUS, 1945-47. Mem. Beverly Hills Bar Assn. (bd. govs., chmn. probate and trust com.), Law Trust, Tax and Ins. Council (past czar), Los Angeles World Affairs Council. Home: 1301 Delresto Dr Beverly Hills CA 90210-2100 Office: Gibson Dunn & Crutcher 2029 Century Park E Ste 4000 Los Angeles CA 90067-3032 also: 333 S Grand Ave Los Angeles CA 90071-1504

BURCH, THADDEUS JOSEPH, JR., physics professor, director; b. Balt., June 4, 1930; s. Thaddeus and Francis Fidelis (Greenwell) B. AB, Bellarmine Coll., 1954; MA, Fordham U., 1956, MS, 1966, PhD, 1968; STB, Woodstock Coll., 1960, STL, 1962. Ordained priest, Roman Cath. Ch., 1961. Joined S.J. Roman Cath. Ch., 1948; asst. prof. St. Joseph's Coll., Phila., 1969-72, Fordham U., N.Y.C., 1972-74; vis. assoc. prof. U. Conn., Storrs, 1974-76; assoc. prof. Marquette U., Milw., 1976-80, prof., 1980—, chmn. dept. physics, 1977-86, acting dean grad. sch., 1985-87, dean grad. sch., 1987—2003, dir. spl. projects, 2003—, acting vice provost rsch. and dean Grad. Sch., 2005—. Univ. del. Argonne (Ill.) Univs. Assn., 1977-82; mem. instl. rev. bd. Med. Coll. Wis., 1970—. Contbr. articles on physics to profl. jours. Mem. Am. Phys. Soc., Am. Assn. Physics Tchrs., Sigma Xi Home: 230 Jefferson St Leonardtown MD 20650-4800 Office: 1404 W Wisconsin Milwaukee WI 53233

BURCH, VORIS REAGAN, mediator, arbitrator, retired lawyer; b. Liberty, Tex., Feb. 10, 1930; s. Voris Reagan and Jessamae (Coffey) B.; m. Claudia Ramsland, Dec. 30, 1978; children: Melissa Burch Lively, Voris Reagan III. BBA, Tex. A&M U., 1952; JD, U. Tex., 1957. Bar: Tex. 1957. Assoc. Baker & Botts, Houston, 1957-69, ptnr., 1969-95, ret., 1995. Served to 1st lt. USAF, 1952-54. Mem. State Bar Tex. (chmn. labor law sect. 1970-71), Houston Bar Assn., Phi Delta Phi. Home and Office: 5761 Indian Cir Houston TX 77057-1302 Office Phone: 713-780-0196. E-mail: reaganburch@houston.rr.com.

BURCHAM, DAVID W., law educator; BA, Occidental Coll.; JD, Loyola Law Sch. Law clerk to Hon. Ruggero J. Aldisert Chief Judge, U.S. Ct. Appeals Third Cir.; Justice Byron R. White U.S. Supreme Ct.; atty. Dunn & Crutcher, Los Angeles; joined faculty Loyola Law Sch., 1991, assoc. dean Academic Affairs, 1999—2000, Fritz B. Burns Dean & prof law, 2000—05. Lawyer rep. Ctrl. Dist. Calif.; cons. Long Beach Unified Sch. Dist. Contbr. articles to law jours.

BURCHARD, JOHN KENNETH, retired chemical engineer; b. St. Louis, May 12, 1936; s. Kenneth Reginald and Vernora Emma (Angell) B.; m. Elizabeth Lee Suesserott, Aug. 23, 1958; children— John Christopher, Gregory Charles. BS, Carnegie Mellon U., 1957, MS, 1959, PhD, 1962. Head systems analysis group United Tech. Ctr., Sunnyvale, Calif., 1961-68; chief scientist Combustion Power Co., Menlo Park, Calif., 1968-70; lab. dir. EPA, Research Triangle Park, N.C., 1970-80; dir. chem. engring. div. Research Triangle Inst., Research Triangle Park, 1980-83; pres. Search Assocs., Inc., Chapel Hill, N.C., 1983-85; dir. Office of Research Adminstrn. U. Cen. Ark., Conway, 1985-87; asst. dir. Office Research Devel. Ariz. State U., Tempe, 1987-90; mgr. spl. projects Ariz. Dept. Environ. Quality, Phoenix, 1990-98, sr. sci. advisor, 1998-2001; vol. Tempe (Ariz.) Police Dept., 2001—. Mem. bd. sci. advisors N.C. Energy Inst. Contbr. articles to profl. jours. Served with AUS, 1963-64. Shell Oil fellow, 1958-59; NSF fellow, 1960-61 Mem. Am. Inst. Chem. Engrs., Soc. Rsch. Adminstrs., Sigma Xi, Tau Beta Pi.

BURCHELL, HOWARD BERTRAM, retired internist; b. Athens, Ont., Can., Nov. 28, 1907; s. James Edward and Edith (Milligan) B.; m. Margaret Helmholz, Aug. 14, 1942; children: Susan Burchell Profeta, Judith Burchell Bush, Cynthia Burchell Patterson, Rebecca Burchell Wilbur. MD, U. Toronto, Can., 1932; PhD., U. Minn., 1939. Intern Toronto Gen. Hosp., 1932-34; rsch. fellow U. Pitts., 1934-36; fellow in medicine Mayo Clinic, Rochester, Minn., 1936-39, cons. in medicine, 1946-68; spl. student London Hosp., 1939-40; prof. medicine U. Minn., Mpls., 1968-85, prof. emeritus, 1985—. Mem. adv. com. USAAF, 1947-40, Nat. Heart Coun., NIH, 1955-60; lectr. U.S., Can., The Netherlands, Israel. Contbr. more than 350 articles to profl. jours. Maj. USAAF, 1941-46. Fellow Am. Coll. Cardiology (master tchr. 1969, 74); mem. Am. Heart Assn. (Herrick award 1972), Assn. Am. Physicians, Am. Physiol. Soc. Mem. Unitarian-Universalist Ch. Avocation: history of medicine. Home: 3701 Bryant Ave S #412 Minneapolis MN 55409

BURCHER, HILDA BEASLEY, librarian; b. Va., June 5, 1938; d. Andrew and Virgie (Hall) Beasley; m. Eugene Stearns Burcher, June 18, 1960 (dec.); children: Eugene Andrew, Mark Eric. BA in English, U. Va., 1960; MLS, U. Md., 1967. Tchr's. profl. cert., libr's. cert. Va. Tchr. English Fairfax County Pub. Schs., Va., 1960—65, reference libr., 1969—75; head libr. St. Agnes Sch., Alexandria, Va., 1975—91; reference libr. part-time Fairfax Pub. Libr., 1987—2000; libr. St. Stephens-St. Agnes Mid. Sch., Alexandria, 1991—95; asst. libr. Alexandria City Pub. Schs., 2002, libr. media asst., 2004—. Substitute tchr. Alexandria City Pub. Schs., 1996—2001. Mem. Alexandria (Va.) Symphony League, 1987—. Mem. Va. Libr. Assn. (sch. chairperson 1994), Beta Phi Mu. Avocations: music, theater, reading, gardening.

BURCHFIEL, BURRELL CLARK, geology educator; b. Stockton, Calif., Mar. 21, 1934; s. Beryl Edward and Agnes (Clark) Burchfiel; children: Brian Edward, Brook Evans, Banjamin Clark, Halsey Royden. BS, Stanford U., 1957, MS, 1958; PhD, Yale U., 1961. Prof. geology Rice U., 1961-76, MIT, 1977-84, Schlumberger prof. geology, 1984—. Served with U.S. Army, 1958—59. Fellow Geol. Soc. Am., Am. Acad. Arts and Scis., Nat. Acad. Scis., Am. Geophys. Union, European Union Geoscis. (hon. fgn.); mem. Geol. Soc. Australia, Am. Assn. Petroleum Geologists, Chinese Acad. Scis. (fgn.). Home: 9 Robinson Park Winchester MA 01890-3717 Office: MIT 77 Massachusetts Ave # 54-1010 Cambridge MA 02139-4307 E-mail: bcburch@mit.edu

BURCHFIELD, BOBBY ROY, lawyer; b. Middlesboro, Ky., Oct. 23, 1954; s. Roy and Anna Lee (McCreary) B.; m. Teresa J. Miller, Apr. 6, 1996; 1 child, Taylor Nicole. BA, Wake Forest U., 1976; JD, George Washington U., 1979. Bar: D.C. 1980, U.S. Ct. Appeals (3rd cir.) 1981, U.S. Dist. Ct. D.C. 1982, U.S. Dist. Ct. Md. 1982, U.S. Ct. Appeals (D.C. cir.) 1982, U.S. Ct. Appeals (9th cir.) 1985, U.S. Supreme Ct. 1986, U.S. Ct. Appeals (5th cir.) 1989, U.S. Ct. Appeals (6th cir.) 1993. Law clk. to Judge Ruggero J. Aldisert U.S. Ct. Appeals (3rd cir.), Pitts., 1979-81; assoc. Covington & Burling, Washington, 1981-87, ptnr., 1987—; co-ptnr.-in-charge D.C. Office McDermott Will & Emery LLP, Washington. Gen. counsel Bush-Quayle '92, 1992; dean's adv. bd. George Washington U.; bd. trustees Wake Forest U., 2004— Editor-in-chief George Washington U. Law Rev., 1978-79. Gen. counsel Rep. Nat. Lawyers Assn., 1991—92; nat. chmn. George Washington U. Nat. Law Ctr. Ann. Fund, 1990—91, Wake Forest U. Coll. Fund, 1999—2000; mem. Wake Forest U. Alumni Coun., 1990—93, chmn., 1997—2001; vol. George Bush for Pres., Washington, 1986—88. Mem.: ABA. Republican. Office: McDermott Will & Emery LLp 600 13th St NW 12th Fl Washington DC 20005-3096 Home: 623 Potomac Ave NW Mc Lean VA 22102 Office Phone: 202-756-8003. Office Fax: 202-756-8087. Business E-Mail: bburchfield@mwe.com.

BURCHMAN, LEONARD, federal official, journalist; b. N.Y.C., Jan. 30, 1925; s. Hyman John-Hood and Edith (Speedety-Cohen) B.; m. Marilyn F. Burchman, June 11, 1950; children— Marc Harris, Corey Andrew BA, U. Denver, 1949; MA, Columbia U., 1950. Dir. press affairs N.Y. State Eisenhower presdl. campaign, 1951-52; info. officer-advance sec. labor Dept. Labor, Washington and N.Y.C., 1953-60; pres. Medigard Chem. Corp., N.Y.C., 1961; dir. integovtl. rels. Dept. Labor, Washington, 1971-78; acting asst. sec., gen. dep. asst. sect. pub. affairs HUD, Washington, 1981—. Dir. labor rels. to U.S. Senator Kenneth Keating, N.Y., 1964; pub. affairs cons. to Gov. John Lodge of Conn., 1952; sr. advisor to Coretta Scott King; chmn. Martin Luther King Jr. Fed. Holiday Commn., 1985—, commr., 1989—, treas., 1989-92. Producer Office Mgmt. Budget/NSF film: Strengthening Intergovernmental Relations between Federal and State and Local Governments, 1976. Chmn. bd. Am. Heart Assn., Washington, 1981-83; pres. Found. for Study U.S. Cabinet, 1985-89; pres. J.R.L.W., Leisure World, Md., 1994-96; chmn. FIIND, Found. to Interrupt Illegal Narcotics and Drugs To Children, 1989—; founding pres. VOTE, Voice of the Elderly, 1997—; founder nat. Consumer Watch-Out, to protect sr. citizens against Scams and Frauds, 1988—; mem. Montgomery County (Md.) Commn. on Aging, 1997-2004, States Attys. Task Force on Elder Abuse, 1997—. Recipient Disting. Svc. award Sec. HUD. Mem.: DAV (life), Am. Legion (comdr. U.S. Dept. Labor Post).

BURCK, JOSEPH RUSSELL, medical educator, consultant, minister; b. Roswell, N.Mex., Dec. 28, 1937; s. William Joseph and Leta Gladys (Menefee) Burck; m. Dorothy Antoinette Pilc, Aug. 6, 1960; children: Peter Warren, Elisabeth Varner. AB, Princeton U., 1959; BD, Princeton Theol. Sem., 1964, PhD, 1976. Ordained Presbytery of Phila., 1970, cert. pastoral counselor Am. Assn. Pastoral Counseling, 1977, chaplain supr. Assn. Clin. Pastoral Edn., 1981, chaplain Assn. Profl. Chaplains, 1998. Assoc. editor bibliography in polit. sci. Princeton Info. Tech., 1967—69; educator in pastoral care in Germany, seminaries in Lueckendorff near Zittau, Herborn, Stuttgart, Tuebingen U., Innere Mission, Berlin, 1972—74; dir. chaplaincy svcs. Larned (Kans.) State Hosp., 1976—78; asst. prof of religion and health Rush-Presbyn.-St. Luke's Med. Ctr., Chgo., 1978—85, assoc. prof. religion, health, and human values, 1985—, dir. program in ethics and ethics consultation svc., 1988—. Peer reviewer of articles Critical Care Medicine, Des Plaines, Ill., 1999—; chairperson ethics adv. com. Inst. of Medicine of Chgo., 1990—91; project dir. Clergy Ethics Study Group, 1988—90; interpreter Internat. Congress on Pastoral Care and Counseling, Arnoldshain, Germany, 1973, mem., U.S. del., Edinburgh, Scotland, 79, San Francisco, 83; outside mem. animal care and use com. U. of Ill. at Chgo., 1988—93; mem. nat. task force to prepare a brief course in ethics Assn. of Profl. Chaplains, 1993—95; chairperson com. on sr. faculty appointments and promotions, Coll. Health Scis. Rush U., 1988—92; editor, Rush ethics reporter Rush-Presbyn. St. Luke's Med. Ctr., 1991—94; bd. of dirs. representing Rush Coll. of Health Scis. Rush Geriatric Interdisciplinary Team Tng. Program, Chgo., 1997—; co-course dir. ethics in medicine Rush Med. Coll., Chgo., 1998—, course dir., clerkship, med. ethics, 1993—; vice-chair work group on governance and adminstrn. NCA accreditation rev. Rush U., Chgo., 1997; chair ethics grand rounds Rush-Presbyn.-St. Luke's, 1980—99; cons. to author of book, ethical issues, and patient rights Joint Commn. on the Accreditation of Health Care Orgns., Chgo., 1997—98; course dir. spiritual dimensions of health care Teleconference Network of Tex., Austin, 1992—97; pres. Chgo. Clin. Ethics Programs, 1994—95; lay mem., nat. ethics and peer rev. com. Am. Assn. of Electrodiagnostic Medicine, 1993—2000; marshal Rush U. graduation, representing Coll. Health Scis., 2004. Co-editor: Clergy Ethics in a Changing Society: Mapping the Terrain (10 Best Books in Ministry of the &r., 1991); author: (e-book) Is it OK to have money and still go to church?; contbr. articles, columns, essays to profl. jours., chapters to books. Adult Christian educator, instr. courses in adult Christian edn., faith and illness, theology of genetics, med. ethics, faith and money, various chs., Chgo., 1980—. Recipient Profl. Svc. award, Teleconf. Network of Tex., 1993, Rsch. award, Joint Coun. on Rsch. in Pastoral Counseling, 1988, World Coun. of Chs. fellowship, 1971—72, doctoral fellowship in theology and personality, Princeton Theol. Sem., 1964—67; grantee, Greenwall Found., 1999—2000. Mem.: Presbytery of Chgo., Assn. for Clin. Pastoral Edn., Assn. of Profl. Chaplains (nominated to White Ho. bioethics adv. commn. 1999), Inst. of Medicine of Chgo. (bd. of govs. 1990—91), Assn. for Bioethics and the Humanities. Presbyterian. Achievements include One of the first Americans teaching pastoral care in Germany, when pastoral care paradigm changed from communicating messages to listening to people; development of one of the early professionalized ethics consultation services in U.S. hospitals; Only American involved in founding of German Society for Pastoral Psychology; First online certificate of graduate study in bioethics in the U.S; development of Innovative Language For Education In Health Care Ethics; Intensive use of clinical working rounds for teaching clinical ethics; teaching about ethics in research and ethical responsibilities of scientific medicine to diagnose and treat on the basis of knowledge. Avocations: travel, photography, hiking, opera, films. Home: 1138 Clinton Ave Oak Park IL 60304-1826 Office: Rush-Presbyn-St Luke's Med Ctr 1653 W Congress Pkwy Chicago IL 60612 Office Phone: 312-942-8933. Personal E-mail: russell_burck@rush.edu.

BURCKEL, NICHOLAS C., historian, educator, school librarian, dean; b. Evansville, Ind., Aug. 15, 1943; s. Arthur J. and Anna Irene Burckel; m. Lenore M. Herriges, June 21, 1969. BA in History, Georgetown U., 1965; MA, U. Wis., 1967, PhD in History, 1971; MLS, U. Wis., Milw., 1983. Cert. archivist Acad. Cert. Archivists, 1989. Asst. archivist U. Wis., Madison, 1971—72; dir. archives and area rsch. ctr. U. Wis. Parkside, 1972—82, exec. asst. to chancellor, 1975—82, assoc. dir. libr./learning ctr., 1982—85, asst. vice chancellor, 1985; assoc. dean libr. Washington U., St. Louis, 1986—95; dean libr., assoc. prof. history Marquette U., Milw., 1995—. Pres. Midwest Archives Conf., Chgo., 1979—81; acad. libr. mgmt. intern U. Chgo., 1984—85; presdl. apppointee to commn. Nat. Hist. Publications and Records Commn., Washington, 1996—2004; bd. dirs. Ctr. Rsch. Libr., Chgo., 1998—2004; corp. coun. U. Wis. Sch. of Info. Studies, Milw., 2002—; chmn. Wis. Libr. Svcs. Bd., Madison, 2001—02. Editor: Immigration and Ethnicity, Racine: Growth and Change in a Wisconsin County (First place Coun. for Wis. Writers Scholarly Book award, 1977), Progressive Reform, Kenosha Retrospective: A Biographical Approach (State Hist. Soc. of Wis. Award of Merit, 1982); co-author: Wis. Yesterday and Today; mem. editl. bd.: Portal: Libraries and the Acad., 2000—. Recipient Disting. Alumnus, U. Wis., Milw., 2002; fellow, Ford Found., 1968—69, Palmer Sch. of Libr. and Info. Sci., 1995; scholar, Georgetown U., 1961—65. Fellow: Soc. Am. Archivists (life; pres. 1996—97); mem.: Beta Phi Mu, Libr. Honor Soc. (bd. dirs. 2000). Home: 7012 N Braeburn Ln Milwaukee WI 53209 Office: Marquette Univ 1355 W Wisconsin Ave Milwaukee WI 53201 Office Phone: 414-288-7214. E-mail: nicholas.burckel@marquette.edu.

BURCKEL, ROBERT BRUCE, mathematics professor; b. Louisville, Ky., Dec. 15, 1939; s. Arthur Joseph B. BS, U. Notre Dame, 1961; PhD, Yale U., 1968. Instr., then asst. prof. U. Oreg., Eugene, 1967-71; assoc. prof., now prof. math. Kans. State U., Manhattan, 1971—, acting chair dept. math., 1974-75. Guest prof. U. Saarlandes, Fed. Republic Germany, 1977-78, U. Erlangen-Nürnberg, Fed. Republic Germany, 1984-85, 92-93, 1999-2000. Author: Weakly Almost Periodic Functions, 1970, Characterizations of C(X), 1972, Introduction to Classical Complex Analysis, 1979; asst. editor Mathematical Intelligencer mag., 1989—. Woodrow Wilson Found./NSF, NASA fellow Yale U., 1961-66. Mem. Math. Assn. Am., Am. Math. Soc., Deutscher Mathematiker Vereinigung. Roman Catholic. Avocations: running, translations. Office Phone: 785-832-0563.

BURD, JOHN STEPHEN, retired academic administrator, music educator; b. Lock Haven, Pa., Apr. 6, 1939; s. John Wilson and Lily (Fye) Burd; m. Patricia Ayers, June 3, 1961; children: Catherine Elizabeth, Emily Susanne. B in Music Edn., Greenville Coll., 1961; MS in Sacred Music, Butler U./Christian Theo. Sem., 1964; PhD, Ind. State U., 1971. Adj. music instr. Rose Hulman Inst. Tech., Terre Haute, Ind., 1969-71; assoc. prof. Greenville (Ill.) Coll., 1971-76; prof. edn. Lindenwood Coll., St. Charles, Mo., 1976-80; v.p. acad. affairs Maryville U., St. Louis, 1980-85; pres. Brenau U., Gainesville, Ga., 1985—2004, ret., 2004; pres. emeritus, 2004—. Team evaluator Nat. Coun. Accreditation Tchr. Edn., 1979—84, 1985—; mem. exec. coun. Women's Coll. Coalition, 1989—92, NAICU Commn. State Rels. Bd., 1991—93; adv. bd. Wachovia Bank, Gainesville, 1991—. Editor: New Voices in Education, 1969—71; contbr. articles to profl. jours. V.p. Christian Arts, Inc., NJ, 1965—, pres.; choir dir. Maryville U., St. Louis, 1983—85; bd. dirs. Gainesville Symphony, 1991—94, W. Long Mus.; chair Gainesville Redevelopment Authority, Chicopee Pk. Commn.; choir dir. Ctr. Presbyn. Ch., St. Louis, 1984—85; adv. bd. N.E. Ga. Med. Ctr.; bd. dirs. Atlanta Met. Arts Fund. Recipient Outstanding Young Alumnus award, Greenville Coll., 1982, Disting. Alumnus award, 1991. Mem.: Ga. Assn. Colls. (pres. 1989—90, 2003—04), Ga. Found. Ind. Colls. (exec. bd. 1986—, vice chmn. 1993, 2002), So. Assn. Women's Colls. (pres. 1988—89), Am. Assn. Higher Edn., Am. Assn. Tchr. Edn., Gainesville C. of C. (bd. dirs.). Methodist. Avocations: tennis, travel, art. Office: Brenau Univ 500 Washington St Gainesville GA 30501-3697 Office Phone: 770-297-5952. Business E-Mail: jburd@brenau.edu.

BURD, LAWRENCE T, aerospace scientist; s. Lawrence Edward and Janet Ann Burd; m. Rebecca Ann Fritz, May 9, 1986; 1 child, Emily Nicole. BS in biochemistry, Penn State U., 1981; M in forensic sci., George Wash. U., 1989; M in adminstrn., Ctrl. Mich. U., 1989; MD, Penn State U. Coll. of Medicine, 1996; MPH, U. of Tex. Health Sci. Ctr. at Houston, 2003. Lic. Medical Doctor Pa., 1996, Board Certification in Aerospace Medicine Am. Coll. of Preventive Medicine. Systems analyst 1st Aerospace Comm. Group, Offutt AFB, Nebr., 1982—83; flight surgeon 32nd Air Refueling Squadron, McGuire AFB, NJ, 1998—2000; comdr., flight medicine flight 305th Aerospace Medicine Squadron, Fort Dix, NJ, 2000—01; grad. student Air Force Inst. of Tech., U. of Tex. Health Sci. Ctr. at Houston, San Antonio, Tex., 2001—02; resident in aerospace medicine and gen. preventive medicine USAF Sch. of Aerospace Medicine, Brooks City-Base, Tex., 2002—04; chief of aerospace medicine 436th Med. Group, Dover AFB, Del., 2004—; exec. officer 1st Aerospace Info. Systems Wing, Offutt AFB, Nebr., 1983—84; chief, contingency info. systems divsn. Aerospace Info. Systems Wing, Offutt AFB, Nebr., 1984—85; spl. agt. and chief Investigative Ops. Br., AFOSI Detachment 540, Wright Patterson AFB, Ohio, 1986—88; grad. student, air force inst. of tech. George Wash. U., Washington, 1988—89; spl. agt. and regional forensic cons. (northeastern region) AFOSI Dist. 5, Wright-Patterson AFB, Ohio, 1989—91; spl. agt. and regional forensic cons. (pacific region) Air Force Office of Spl. Investigations (AFOSI) Dist. 45, Osan AB, Korea (South), 1991—92; med. student (inactive af res.), air force health professions scholarship program Pa. State U. Coll. of Medicine, Hershey, Pa., 1992—96; resident in psychiatry 59th Med. Wing, Lackland AFB, Tex., 1996—98. Forensic cons. and expert witness AFOSI Regional Forensic Cons., Wright-Patterson AFB, Ohio, 1989—91, Osan AB, 1991—92; human factors cons. & bd. mem., air force mishap investigations 305th Med. Group, McGuire AFB, NJ, 1999—2001, 436th Med. Group, Dover AFB, Del., 2001—, cons. for aerospace, preventive, & occupl. medicine, 2004—. Lt col US Air Force, 1981, Dover AFB, DE. Recipient Honor Grad., Armed Forces Inst. of Pathology Forensic Sci. Fellowship, 1989, Jr. Officer of the Yr., Air Force Office of Spl. Investigations Dist. 5, 1987, Disting. Grad., Air Force Spl. Investigations Acad., 1986, USAF Comm. Computer Programming Course, 1982, AFROTC, Pa. State U., 1981, Honor Grad., US Army Airborne Sch., 1979, Eagle Scout, Boy Scouts of Am., 1977. Mem.: AMA, Assn. of Mil. Surgeons of the US, Soc. of USAF Flight Surgeons, Am. Coll. of Preventive Medicine, Aerospace Med. Assn., Am. Mensa, Ltd, Nat. Eagle Scout Assn., Am. Numis. Assn., Penn State Alumni Assn. Home: 400 North Dupont Highway Apt G-23 Dover DE 19901 Office: 436th Medl Group/SGP 300 Tuskegee Dr Dover DE 19902

BURD, ROBERT MEYER, hematologist, oncologist, educator; b. N.Y.C., Aug. 25, 1937; s. David and Anne (Popkin) B.; m. Alice Stoller, May 30, 1964; children: Russell J., Stephen J. AB, Columbia U., 1959, MD, 1963. Diplomate Am. Bd. Internal Medicine, Am. Bd. Hematology and Oncology. Intern Albert Einstein Med. Sch., N.Y.C., 1963-64, resident in internal medicine, 1964-66; hematology fellow Montefiore Hosp., N.Y.C., 1966-67; specializing in hematology and oncology pvt. practice medicne, Fairfield, Conn., 1969—; assoc. prof. medicine Yale U., New Haven, 1975, assoc. clin. prof. of medicine, 1975—; chief of hematology/oncology St. Vincent's Med. Ctr., 1980—; asst. prof. clin. medicine Columbia U. Coll. Physicians & Surgeons, 1998—. Chmn. hosp. com. on cancer, mng. ptnr. Med. Specialists of Fairfield, LLC, 1995—; attending physician Yale Hosp., New Haven; mem. staff Bridgeport (Conn.) Hosp.; adj. prof. medicine N.Y. Med. Coll.; med. cons. U.S. News and World Report, 1990; dir. oncology fellowship Yale-St. Vincent Hosp., 1991—96, N.Y. Med. Coll., St. Vincent's Med. Ctr., Bridgeport; adv. bd. rituxan Genentech; adv. bd. taxotere Aventis. Mem. editl. bd. (exhibitions), 1974—78. Active Leukemia Soc. Am., Hemophilia Found.; chmn. profl. edn. com. Am. Cancer Soc. Lt. comdr. USN, 1967-69. Ettinger Meml. fellow Am. Cancer Soc., 1982. Fellow ACP; mem. AMA, AAAS, Am. Soc. Hematology, Am. Soc. Internat. Medicine, Am. Soc. Clin. Oncology, N.Y. Acad. of Scis., Internat. Soc. Thrombosis and Hemostasis, Conn. Oncology Assn., Soc. Columbia Grads., Columbia U. Alumni Fedn. Coun., Columbia U. Alumni Club (pres. Fairfield Co. 1983-85, editor newsletter 1982-91), Bridgeport Med. Sco. (Physician of Yr. 1993). Office: 425 Post Rd Fairfield CT 06430-6232

BURD, STEVEN A., food service executive; b. 1949; m. Chris Burd; 2 children. BS, Carroll Coll., 1971; MA in Econs., U. Wis., 1973. With fin. and mktg. So. Pacific Transp. Co., San Francisco; with Arthur D. Little, N.Y.C., 1982-87; mgmt. cons., Safeway Stores Kohlberg Kravis Roberts & Co., 1986—91; cons. Stop & Shop Cos., Boston, 1988-89; cons., interim CEO Fred Meyer Inc., Portland, Oreg., 1991—92; pres. Safeway Inc., 1992—, CEO, 1993—, chmn., 1998—. Dir. Kohl's Corp. Office: Safeway Inc 5918 Stoneridge Mall Rd Pleasanton CA 94588-3229*

BURDE, HOWARD ALAN, lawyer; b. Phila., Nov. 5, 1962; s. Ronald Marshall and Sharon Kaplan Burde; m. Evelyn Burde, Aug. 29, 1993; children: Ariel, Simone, Jed. BA magna cum laude, Duke U., 1984; JD, U. Va., 1988. Bar: Pa. 1988, NJ 1989. Assoc., health law dept. and govt. affairs group Blank Rome LLP, Phila., 1988—92, co-chair, ptnr., health law group, 1988—92; with Alice G. Gosfield and Assoc., PC, Phila., 1992—95; chief counsel Pa. Dept. Health, Harrisburg, 1995—97; dep. gen. counsel Govs. Office Gen. Counsel, Harrisburg, Pa., 1997—2002; practice group leader, health law group Blank Rome LLP, Phila., 2002, ptnr., 2003—. Author: Health Laws of Pennsylvania, 2000; mem. editl. bd.: Jour. Health Law; contbr. chapters to books. Bd. dirs. Chisuk Emuna Synagogue, Pa. Economy League, Phila.; chmn. bd. dirs. Lower Merion Bd. Health, Lower Merion, Pa. Mem.: ABA, Pa. Economy League (bd. dirs.), Pa. Bar Assn., Pa. Futures Commn. on Justice in the 21st Century, Am. Health Lawyers Assn. Office: Blank Rome LLP One Logan Sq Philadelphia PA 19103 Office Phone: 215-569-5724. Office Fax: 215-832-5724. Business E-Mail: burde@blankrome.com.

BURDEN, CEDRIC JEROME, SR., language professor; b. Mobile, Ala., Nov. 6, 1969; s. Andrew O'Neal and Juanita (Coleman) B.; m. Teresa Ballard, Mar. 26, 1995; children: Jasmine Renee, Cedric Jerome Jr. AS, S.D. Bishop State Coll., 1989; BA, Univ. Montevallo, 1991, M, 1992. English prof. Lawson State Cmty. Coll., Birmingham, Ala., 1993—. Editing cons. Writing Voyage, 1996, Fictions, 1997, 98; author companion website Progressions, 5th edit. Sec. Alabaster Parks and Recreation Adv. Bd., 1997-98; mem. Alabaster Planning and Zoning Bd.; grad. Ala. C.C. Leadership Acad.; mem. young adv. bd. Big Bros Big Sisters Birmingham. Mem. Ala. Assn. for Developmental Edn., Nat. Assn. for Devel. Edn., Nat. Coun. of Tchrs. of Eng., Alabaster Lions Club (sec.-treas. 1997-98), Alpha Phi Alpha. Avocations: model car building, pets, playing saxophone. Home: 620 Park Forest Ln Alabaster AL 35007 Office: Lawson State Cmty Coll 3060 Wilson Rd SW Birmingham AL 35221-1717 Office Phone: 205-929-2079. Personal E-mail: cburdensr@aol.com. Business E-Mail: cburden@lawsonstate.edu.

BURDEN, JAMES EWERS, lawyer; b. Sacramento, Oct. 24, 1939; s. Herbert Spencer and Ida Elizabeth (Brosemer) B.; m. Kathryn Lee Gardner, Aug. 21, 1965; children: Kara Elizabeth Crabtree, Justin Gardner. BS, U. Calif., Berkeley, 1961; JD, U. Calif., Hastings, 1964; postgrad., U. So. Calif., 1964-65. Bar: Calif. 1965, Tax Ct. U.S. 1969, U.S. Supreme Ct. 1970. Assoc. Elliott and Aune, Santa Ana, Calif., 1965, White, Harbor, Fort & Schei, Sacramento, 1965-67, Miller, Starr & Regalia, Oakland, Calif., 1967-69, ptnr., 1969-73, Burden, Aiken, Mansuy & Stein, San Francisco, 1973-82, James E. Burden, Inc., San Francisco, 1982—; co-founder, dir., COO, sec. KineMed, Inc., Emeryville, Calif., 2001—, also bd. dirs.; founder, dir., coo Tekton Software Corp., San Francisco, 2003—. Bd. dirs. IP Floor Products, Inc., San Leandro, Calif., Denver; co-founder Gloucestershire Innovation Centre, Gloucester, Eng., EuroGen Pharmas. Ltd., Gloucester, Info4cars, Inc., Asheville, NC; underwriting mem. Lloyds of London, 1986-93; instr. U. Calif., Berkeley, Merritt Coll. 1968-74; pres., prin. Dorset Capital LLC. Contbr. articles to profl. jours. Mem.: ABA, Inst. of Dirs. (London), St. Andrews Golf Club (Fife, Scotland), Faculty Club U. Calif. Berkeley, The Univ. Club, Commonwealth Club of Calif., Claremont Country Club. Office: One Maritime Plz 4th Fl San Francisco CA 94111-3407 Office Phone: 415-421-0404. Personal E-mail: jeburden@compuserve.com.

BURDEN, JEAN PRUSSING, retired poet, editor; b. Waukegan, Ill., Sept. 01; d. Harry Frederick and Miriam (Biddlecom) Prussing; m. David Charles Burden, 1940 (div. 1949). BA, U. Chgo., 1936. Sec. John Hancock Mutual Life Ins. Co., Chgo., 1937-39, Young & Rubicam, Inc., Chgo., 1939-41; editor, copywriter Domestic Industries, Inc., Chgo., 1941-45; office mgr. O'Brion Russell & Co., Los Angeles, 1948-55; adminstr. pub. relations Meals for Millions Found., Los Angeles, 1955-65; editor Stanford Research Inst., South Pasadena, Calif., 1965-66; propr. Jean Burden & Assocs., Altadena, Calif., 1966-82; ret. Lectr. poetry to numerous colls. and univs., U.S., 1963—; supr. poetry workshop Pasadena City Coll., Calif., 1960-62, 66, U. Calif. at Irvine, 1975; also pvt. poetry workshops. Author: Naked as the Glass, 1963, Journey Toward Poetry, 1966, The Cat You Care For, 1968, The Dog You Care For, 1968, The Bird You Care For, 1970, The Fish You Care For, 1971, A Celebration of Cats, 1974, The Classic Cats, 1975, The Woman's Day Book of Hints for Cat Owners, 1980, 84, Taking Light from Each Other, 1992; poetry editor: Yankee Mag, 1955—2002; pet editor: Woman's Day Mag, 1973-82; contbr. numerous articles to various jours. and mags. MacDowell Colony fellow, 1973, 74, 76; Recipient Silver Anvil award Pub. Relations Soc. of Am., 1969, 1st prize Borestone Mountain Poetry award, 1963, Gold Crown award for lit. achievement, 1989. Mem. Poetry Soc. Am., Acad. Am. Poets, Authors Guild. Address: 1129 Beverly Way Altadena CA 91001-2517 *I think that man is constantly trying to bring down into the world of time the essences of what he dimly but intuitively feels is timeless. One of the ways in which he tries is through poetry. Without poetry, a certain kind of Reality is speechless. Or to put it a slightly different way, I believe that we inhabit two worlds at once, the world of time and the world of timelessness, and that poetry is a bridge that lets us cross over.*

BURDEN, ORDWAY PARTRIDGE, investment banker; b. N.Y.C., N.Y., Nov. 20, 1944; s. William A. M. and Margaret L. (Partridge) B.; m. Jean Poor Lynch, October 5, 1991. AB magna cum laude, Harvard U., 1966, MBA, 1968; postgrad., Harvard Law Sch., 1969-71. Gen. ptnr. William A.M. Burden Co., N.Y.C., 1966-86, dir., 1986—. Cons. on police functions Nat. Commn. for Rev. Fed. and State Laws Relating to Wiretapping and Electronic Surveillance; cons. Commn. on Rev. Nat. Policy Toward Gambling. Former mem. adv. bd. Bur. Justice Stats., Dept. of Justice; mem. nat. sponsoring com. Nat. Law Enforcement Officers Meml. Fund; v.p. Florence V. Burden Found., N.Y.C., 1990—. Mem. Internat. Assn. Chiefs Police (past mem. 5 coms.), Nat. Sheriffs Assn. (former mem. standards-ethics-edn.-devel. com.), Nat. Crime Prevention Coun. (bd. dirs.), Law Enforcement Assistance Found. (founder, pres. 1977—), Nat. Law Enforcement Coun. (founder, chmn. 1979—), Capitol Hill Club, Metropolitan Club.

BURDESHAW, WILLIAM BROOKSBANK, engineering executive; b. East Orange, N.J., Nov. 20, 1930; s. Thomas Anderson and Margaret (Villecco) B.; m. Monica Dorr, Sept. 27, 1957; children: Leath, Thomas, Anne, Alison. BS, U.S. Mil. Acad., 1953; MSEE, Ga. Inst. of Tech., 1961. Commd. 2d lt. U.S. Army, 1953, advanced through grades to brig. gen., 1975, ret., 1979; CEO, chmn. Burdeshaw Assocs., Ltd., 1979—. Cons. Def. Sci. Bd., 1985-87. Engring. mgmt. cons. co. named by INC. mag. as 121st of 500 fastest growing pvt. cos., 1985. Mem. Burning Tree Club, Congl. Country Club, George Town Club (Washington), Cripple Creek Club (Bethany Beach, Del.). Republican. Episcopalian. Office: Burdeshaw Assoc Ltd 4701 Sangamore Rd Bethesda MD 20816-2500

BURDETT, JAMES R., lawyer; b. Taylor, Pa., Sept. 29, 1951; BS, US Naval Acad., 1973; MS, George Washington U., 1981; JD, Widener U. Sch. Law, 1984. Bar: Pa. 1984, NJ 1985, Tex. 1991, DC 1998, admitted to practice: US Dist. Ct. (Dist. NJ) 1985, US Patent and Trademark Office. Ptnr., Intellectual Property Dept. and Patent Prosecution Dept. Venable LLP, Washington. LCDR USN, 1969—79. Master: Giles S. Rich Am. Inn of Ct.; mem.: Am. Intellectual Property Law Assn., ABA (Patent, Trademark and Copyright Law Sect.). Fluent in French. Office: Venable LLP 575 7th St NW Washington DC 20004 Office Phone: 202-344-4893. Office Fax: 202-344-8300. Business E-Mail: jrburdett@venable.com.

BURDETTE, BROOKS R., lawyer; b. Ga., Oct. 6, 1961; BA summa cum laude, Wofford Coll., SC, 1983; JD cum laude, Harvard Law Sch., 1986. Bar: NY 1987, registered: US Dist. Ct. (So. Dist.) NY 1987. Atty. Cravath, Swaine & Moore LLP, NYC; ptnr., pro bono dept. Schulte Roth & Zabel LLP, NYC. Dir. Harvard Legis. Rsch. Bur., 1985—86. Contbr. articles to profl. jour. Pres. Truman Scholars Assn.; v.p. Brainstorm Afterschool Inc.; trustee Harvard Law Sch. Alumni Assn., NYC. Harry Truman Scholar, Presdl. Scholar. Mem.: Fed. Bar Coun. (second cir. courts com.), NY County Lawyers Assn. (judiciary com.), ABA (co-chmn. trial evidence com.). Office: Schulte Roth & Zabel LLP 919 Third Ave New York NY 10022 Office Phone: 212-756-2272. Office Fax: 212-593-5955. Business E-Mail: brooks.burdette@srz.com.

BURDETTE, CHARLOTTE, middle school educator; b. Honolulu, June 16, 1956; d. Charles Edward and Eiko (Mizazu) Eary; m. Frederick L. Burdette; children: Kristilyn Jane Hawks Dorsey, Margaret Asley Hawks. BA in Edn., Glenville State Coll., W.Va., 1978; MA elem. edn., W. Va. Coll. of Graduate Studies, 1989. Tchr. Fayette (W.Va.) County Schs., 1985—, Collins Middle Sch., Oak Hill, W.Va., 1987—88; 4th grade tchr. Ansted (W.Va.) Elem., 1988—93, Ansted (W.Va.) Elm., 1994—2003; 3rd and 4th grade tchr. Ansted (W.Va.) Elem., 1994—2003; 3rd grade tchr. Valley Elem., Smithers, W.Va., 1993—94; tchr. Nuttall Middle Sch., Lookout, W.Va., 2003—. Mem.AFT, Fayette County Reading Assn., WV Reading Assn. Office: Nuttall Mid Sch Rte 60 P O Box 130 Personal E-mail: charlotte_burdette@yahoo.com.

BURDETTE, GARY W., music educator; b. Gallipolis, Ohio, May 31, 1980; s. Jane L and Gary J Burdette. BA in Music Edn., Marshall U., 2003. Music preK - Adult W.Va., 2003. Band dir. Pt. Pleasant (W.Va.) H.S., 2003—04, Pt. Pleasant Mid. Sch., 2004—. Com. mem. Ednl. Specifications Com., Pt. Pleasant, W.Va., 2004—05. Mem.: W.Va. Edn. Assn., Music Educators Nat. Conf., Golden Key Honour Soc. Independent. Methodist.

BURDETTE, ROBERT BRUCE, retired lawyer; b. Cin., Oct. 8, 1945; s. Lumas Carter and Myrtle Margaret (Diesel) B. AB, Columbia Coll., 1967; JD, U. Cin., 1973. Bar: Ohio 1973, U.S. Supreme Ct. 1978. Legis. atty. Libr. Congress, Washington, 1973—2003. Author: A Step Beyond The Graetz Prepayment Analysis, 1992. Mem. Mensa, St. Andrew Club, W.A.R. Goodwin Soc. Colonial Williamsburg. Methodist. Avocation: gilding and rum collecting. Home: 3672 Willowlea Ct Apt A Cincinnati OH 45208 E-mail: rburdette@fuse.net.

BURDGE, RABEL JAMES, sociology educator; b. Columbus, Ohio, Dec. 14, 1937; s. Alonzo Marshall and Mariam Francis (Prentice) B.; m. Sharon Sue Payne, June 30, 1962 (dec. June 1975); children: Stephanie, Amy, Jill; m. Joyce Loretta Piggush, Aug. 2, 1977. BS, Ohio State U., 1959, MS, 1961; PhD, Pa. State U., 1965. Asst. prof. sociology U.S. Air Force Acad., Colo., 1966-68; lectr. U. Colo., Colorado Springs, 1966-68; asst. prof. sociology U. Ky., Lexington, 1968-72, assoc. prof., 1972-76; assoc. prof. environ. sociology, rural sociology, urban and regional planning and leisure studies; dept. agrl. econs. and leisure studies U. Ill. Inst. Environ. Studies, Urbana, 1976-80, prof., 1980—96; prof. emeritus U. Ill., 1996—; prof. sociology and environ. studies Western Wash. U., Bellingham, 1996—. Vis. scholar Sch. of Australian Environ. Studies, Griffith U., Brisbane, 1982, 86, hon. prof., 1991—; vis. prof. Sch. Planning and Landscape, U. Manchester, Eng., 2002. Author: (with N. Cheek and D. Field) Leisure and Recreation Places, 1976, (with Paul Opryszek) Coping with Change: An Interdisciplinary Assessment of the Lake Shelbyville Reservoir, 1981, (with E.M. Rogers) Social Change in Rural Societies, A Rural Sociology Textbook, 3d edit., 1988, A Community Guide to Social Impact Assessment, 1998, 3d edit., 2004, A Conceptual Approach to Social Impact Assessment, 1994, 2d edit., 1998, The Concepts, Process and Methods of Social Impact Assessment, 2004; editor Jour. Leisure Rsch., 1971-74; co-editor, founder: Leisure Scis., an Interdisciplinary Jour., 1977-82, Society and Nat. Resources: An Internat. Jour., 1988-98; co-editor Longman-Cheshire Internat. Environ. Studies Series, 1990—; contbr. articles to profl. publs. Served to capt. arty. U.S. Army, 1965-68. Recipient George B. Hartzog Jr. award for environ. rsch. Clemson U., 1995. Lifetime Achievement award Internat. Assn. Society and Natural Resources, 2004. Mem. AAAS, Am. Sociol. Assn., Rural Sociol. Soc. (v.p. 1982-83, treas. 1994-2000, editor The Rural Sociologist, 1994-2000, named Disting. Rural Sociologist, 1996), Nat. Recreation and Park Assn. (Theodore/Franklin D. Roosevelt award for outstanding rsch. 1982), Internat. Assn. for Impact Assessment (pres. 1990-91, treas. 1993-96, Rose-Hulman Inst. Tech. award for contbns. to impact assessment), Acad. Leisure Scis., Sigma Xi, Phi Kappa Phi, Gamma Sigma Delta, Alpha Kappa Delta. Democrat. Methodist. Home: PO Box 4056 Bellingham WA 98227-4056 E-mail: burdge@comcast.net.

BURDI, ALPHONSE ROCCO, anatomist; b. Chgo., Aug. 28, 1935; s. Alphonse Rocco and Anna (Basilo) B.; m. Sandra Shaw, Mar. 22, 1968; children— Elizabeth Anne, Sarah Lynne. BS, No. Ill. U., DeKalb, 1957; MS, U. Ill., 1959, U. Mich., 1961, PhD, 1963; Doctorate (hon.), U. Athens, Greece, 2000. Predoctoral fellow physiology U. Ill., 1957-59; NSF summer fellow U. Mich., 1960, NIH trainee, 1960-61, NIH predoctoral research fellow, 1962, mem. faculty, 1962—, prof. emeritus cell and devel. biology, 2003—. Rsch. scientist emeritus Ctr. Human Growth and Devel., 2003; dir. integrated pre-med.-med. program U. Mich. Mem. editorial bd.: Cleft Palate Jour. 1972-88, Am. Jour. Phys. Anthropology, 1971-75, C.C. Thomas Am. Lectr. Series in Anatomy, 1971-88, Jour. Dental Research, 1977-87 . Grantee NIH. Mem. Internat. Assn. Dental Research, Am. Assn. Dental Research, Am. Cleft Palate Assn., Teratology Soc., Am. Assn. Anatomists, Am. Assn. Phys. Anthropology, Sigma Xi. Home: 2600 Page Ct Ann Arbor MI 48104-6249 Office: U Mich Dept Cell & Devel Biology Med Sci Bldg 2 Ann Arbor MI 48109-0616 Office Phone: 734-763-3265. E-mail: alburdi@umich.edu.

BURDICK, GINNY MARIE, state senator; b. Portland, Oreg., Dec. 3, 1947; BA, U. Puget Sound, 1969; M in Journalism, Oreg. U., 1973. Reporter, editor Port Angeles (Wash.) Daily News, Eugene (Oreg.) Register-Guard, AP, Bur. Nat. Affairs, Legal Times of Washington, 1969—79; environ. issues mgr. Atlantic Richfield Co., 1981—84; self-employed crisis mgmt. specialist, 1989—2004; v.p., sr. counsel Gard & Gerber Advt. and Pub. Rels., 2004—; mem., chair, senate judiciary comm. Oreg. Senate, Salem, 1996—. Democrat. Home: 4641 SW Dosch Rd Portland OR 97239-1244 Office: S 317 State Capitol Salem OR 97301 E-mail: sen.ginnyburdick@state.or.us.

BURDICK, GLENN ARTHUR, physicist, engineering educator; b. Pavilion, Wyo., Sept. 9, 1932; s. Stephen Arthur and Mary Elizabeth (McClerg) Burdick; m. Joyce Mae Huggett, July 14, 1951; children: Stephen Arthur, Randy Glenn. BS, Ga. Inst. Tech., 1958, MS, 1959; PhD, MIT, 1961. Registered profl. engr., Fla. Office mgr. Statewide Contractors, Las Vegas, Nev., 1955—56; spl. tool designer Ga. Inst. Tech., Atlanta, 1954—55, instr., 1956—59; sr. mem. rsch. staff Sperry Microwave, Oldsmar, Fla., 1961—65; prof. elec. engring. U. So. Fla., Tampa, 1965—, dean Coll. Engring., 1979—86, disting. prof. engring., 1986—, dean emeritus, 1986—; pres. Burdick Engring. and Sci., Inc., 1983—. Mem. Tampa Bay Fgn. Affairs. Com., 1981—88, Pinellas County (Fla.) High Speed Rail Task Force, 1982—91, Gov. of State of Fla. Energy Task Force, 1980—85; vice chmn. Fla. Task Force for Sci. Energy and Tech. Svc. to Industry, 1981—82. Named Engring. Faculty Mem. of Yr., State of Fla., 1986; Tex. Gulf scholar, 1957—58, Woodrow Wilson fellow, 1958—59, NSF fellow, 1958—61. Fellow: Nat. Acad. Forensic Engrs., Am. Bd. Forensic Examiners, Nat. Fire Protection Agy., Am. Assn. Forensic Sci.; mem.: IEEE (sr. Engr. of Yr. award 1980), U.S. Profl. Engrs. Edn. (vice-chmn. SE region 1986—88), N.Y. Acad. Scis., Nat. Acad. Forensic Engring., Internat. Soc. Hybrid Microelectronics (nat. pre. 1974), Fla. Engring. Soc. (Engr. of Yr. award 1981), Downtown Club, Clearwater Tennis Club (pres. Fla. chpt. 1965, 1969). Achievements include invention of underground pipeline leak detector; sail boat mast insulation. Home: 18728 Lake Iola Rd Dade City FL 33523-6117 Office: Burdick Engring and Sci Inc 18530 Lake Iola Rd Dade City FL 33523-6149

BURDICK, MARGARET SEALE (MARGE), interior designer; b. Ft. Worth, Tex., July 24, 1919; d. Walter Braton and Ivy (McCleskey) Seale; m. Donald K. Bennett (dec. May 1943); 1 child, Donald Jr.; m. William J. Walsh, Dec. 1, 1945 (div. June 1959); children: Susan S. Lynch, William J. Jr., Margaret J. Tannery; m. Lorence Connable Burdick, Oct. 21, 1961 (div. Aug. 1979); children: Michael, John, Timothy. Student, So. Meth. U., 1937-38. Interior redesigner Kalamazoo (Mich.) Country Club, 1948; interior designer Child Guidance Ctr. Jr. League (formerly Service Club), Kalamazoo, 1956, designer nearly new shop, 1955; co-owner, interior designer Red Lion Inn, Vail, Colo., 1962-80; owner MSB Designs, 1980-2001; interior designer Outstanding Homes in Vail, 1981-99. Co-organizer 1st Sch. Bd. Vail, 1963; charter bd. dirs. Vail Inst Performing Arts, 1973-84; pres. Vail Inst., 1979-84, also hon. bd. dirs. 1984-87; mem. Art Selection Com. Vail, 1981-84; bd. dirs. Gerald R. Ford Commemorative Com., Vail, 1980-85; charter mem. bd. dirs. Bravo! Colo. Music Festival, Vail and Beaver Creek, 1987-95, adv. bd., 1995-2005; bd. dirs. Betty Ford Alpine Carden Found., 1986-97, nat. adv. bd., 1997-2001; bd. dirs. Vail Religious Found. Endowment Com., 1995-2004, Bravo! Music Festival Endowment Com., 1991-98, Ctr. for the Arts Com. (now Vilar Ctr.), Beaver Creek, Vail Valley Arts Coun., 1991—, pres., 1993-97. Honoree Bravo! Colo. Music Festival, 1997. Mem.: Racquet Club (charter), Homestead Ct. Club, Vail Athletic Club (charter). Republican. Episcopalian. Home and Office: PO Box 498 Edwards CO 81632-0498 E-mail: msb@vail.net.

BURDICK, RICK L., lawyer; b. Pasos Robles, Calif., July 10, 1951; BSc cum laude, Santa Clara U., 1973; JD, Coll. William & Mary, 1976. Bar: Tex. 1976, DC 2001. Ptnr. Akin, Gump, Strauss, Hauer & Feld LLP, Houston, now ptnr.-in-charge, chair bus. transaction dept., and mem. exec. com. Washington. Bd. dir. AutoNation, Century Bus. Svcs. Inc. Contbr. William & Mary Law Review, 1975-76. Fellow Tex. Bar Found.; mem. ABA, Houston Bar Assn., Beta Gamma Sigma. Office: Akin Gump Strauss Hauer & Feld LLP Robert S Strauss Bldg 1333 New Hampshire Ave NW Washington DC 20036-1564 Office Phone: 202-887-4110. Office Fax: 202-955-7778. Business E-Mail: rburdick@akingump.com.

BURDICK, ROBERT W., newspaper editor; b. Feb. 11, 1948; m. Patty Burnett; 1 child, David. B in Polit. Sci., Fla. Atl. U., 1969. Reporter Miami Herald, Fla. Today; night city editor Palm Beach (Fla.) Post; mng. editor Palm Beach Daily News; asst. mng. editor Wichita (Kans.) Eagle; city editor/metro editor/asst. to exec. editor San Jose (Calif.) Mercury News, 1978-82; asst. mng. editor Denver Post, 1982-84; asst. mng. editor/mng. editor/editor L.A. Daily News, 1984-94; mng. editor, editor Rocky Mountain News, Denver, 1994-98, pres., 1998—2000; exec. v.p., gen. mgr. Naples (Fla.) Daily News, 2000—02, pres., pub., 2002—. Mem. Am. Soc. Newspaper Editors, Soc. Profl. Journalists, AP News Execs. Coun. (past bd. mem., past pres. Calif., Nev. chpt., past editor AP Mng. Editors News), Metro Denver C. of C. (bd. dirs.), NCCJ (bd. dirs. Denver chpt.). Avocations: skiing, hiking. Office: Naples Daily News 1075 Central Ave Naples FL 34102

BURDICK, ROGER S., state supreme court justice; BS, U. Colorado; JD, U. Idaho Sch. of Law, 1974. Bank examiner Dept. Finance, Boise, Idaho, 1970—71; atty. Webb, Pike, Burton & Carlson, Twin Falls, 1974—80; dep. prosecuting atty. Ada County; prtnr. Hart and Burdick, Jerome, 1976—80; prosecuting atty. Jerome County, 1980—81, magistrate judge, 1981—93; dist. judge Twin Falls County, 1993—2001; administrative judge Fifth Jud. Dist., 2001—03; justice Idaho Supreme Ct., 2003—. Former chmn. Juvenile Rules Com.; mem. Idaho Jud. Coun., 1990—2001; dist. judge Snake River Basin Water Adjudication, 2001—03. Mem.: Magistrate Judges Assn. (pres. 1989—91), Idaho State Bar Assn., Dist. Judges Assn. (pres. 2001—03). Office: Idaho Supreme Ct PO Box 83720 Boise ID 83720-0101

BURDICK, WILLIAM MACDONALD, biomedical engineer; b. Providence, R.I., Apr. 24, 1952; s. Franklin Pierce and Lola Alice (Cook) B. BS, Ind. U. Pa., 1975; M of Engring., Tex. A&M U., 1981; postgrad., U. Tex., 1982-86. Engring. analyst FDA, Winchester, Mass., 1988-90, reviewer neurological devices Rockville, Md., 1990-94, reviewer, gen. hosp. and personal use devices, 1994—. Inventor in field; contbr. articles to profl. jours.; contbr. poem to: Dance on the Horizon (Editor's Choice award Nat. Libr. Poetry), America at the Millennium. With USAF, 1976-78. Mem. Biomed. Engring. Soc., Humane Soc. U.S., Am. Assn. Med. Instrumentation, Nat. Multiple Sclerosis Soc. Congregationalist. Avocations: reading, writing (poetry, songs, fiction), gardening, sports. Office: 9200 Corporate Blvd Rockville MD 20850-3229 Office Phone: 301-349-1287 x171. Business E-Mail: william.burdick@fda.hhs.gov.

BURDUMY, STEPHEN T., lawyer; b. Phila., 1957; BSFS cum laude, Georgetown Univ., 1979; JD, Univ. San Francisco, 1982. Bar: Pa. 1982, NJ 1982. Ptnr. Klehr, Harrison, Harvey, Branzburg & Ellers LLP; ptnr., corp. and securities practice group Drinker Biddle & Reath LLP, Phila. Mem.: ABA, NJ Bar Assn., Pa. Bar Assn. Office: Drinker Biddle & Reath LLP One Logan Sq 18th & Cherry Sts Philadelphia PA 19103-6996 Office Phone: 215-988-2880. Office Fax: 215-988-2757. Business E-Mail: stephen.burdumy@dbr.com.

BURFEINDT, DOUGLAS GLENN, civilian military official; b. Sioux Falls, S.D., June 10, 1954; s. Raymond Ariel and Tressa Clarine Burfeindt; m. Oriela Victoria Quiros, Apr. 19, 1976; children: Douglas Glenn Jr., O. Melisa. BS, N.Y. Regents Coll., Albany, 1985; MBA, Calif. Coast U., 1996. Enlisted man U.S. Army, 1973, advanced through grades to sgt. sr. grade, intelligence specialist various locations, 1974-80; resigned, 1981; instr. U.S. Army Intelligency Sch., Ft. Huachuca, Ariz., 1980-83; intelligence ops. officer 470th M.I. Brigade, Panama, 1983-94; intelligence prodn. mgr., policy mgr. Dept. Def. IPP, U.S. So. Command, Miami, Fla., 1994—. Mem. intelligence prodrs.' coun. Dept. Def., Washington, 1994—; mem. Integrated Air Def. Study Coordinating Group, Washington, 1997—; rep. Joint Intelligence Virual Architecture Com., Washington, 1998—; owner, mgr. timberland. Mem. ASAP, Am. Legion, Fla. Internat. U. Panther Parents. Avocations: fishing, reading, photography, tree farming, conservationism.

BURFORD, JAMES, art educator; b. Vancouver, Wash., July 25, 1945; s. Jeanne Lois Swearingen and James William Burford; m. Sandra Louise Isenberg, Dec. 16, 1972; children: Elizabeth Grace, Mary Kathleen. BS, U. of Oreg., 1966—71; MFA, Carnegie Mellon, 1976—78. Instr. Carnegie Mellon, Pitts., 1976—78; assoc. prof. Mt. Vernon Coll., Washington DC, DC, 1978—2000; adj. instr. U. of Md., 2000—02, Marymount U., Arlington, Va., 2000—05, Corcoran Coll. of Art, Washington DC, DC, 2003—. Art dir. Gatehouse Gallery, Mt. Vernon Coll., Washington, 1978—99; lectr. color Hirschhorn Mus., Washington. Exhibitions include Portland Art Mus., 1971, 1972, 1973, Seattle Art Mus., 1972, Carnegie Mus. Art, 1978, 1988, 1989, 1992, 1997, Corcoran Art Gallery, 2004, 2005; actor:. Recipient Purchase award, Portland Art Mus., 1972, Coos Art Mus., 1973, U.S Steel award, Carnegie Mus., 1978, Jury award, Carnegie Mus. Art, Pitts., 1978, Rivers Arts Festival, Pitts., 1978; Arts and Humanities Found. and Workshop grantee, Mt. Vernon Coll., Washington, 1981—83, 1989—90. Mem.: Internation Artist Group, Coll. of Art Assn., Artists of Pitts. (assoc.).

BURFORD, JERRAD DALON, corporate financial executive, writer; b. Oakdale, Calif., Jan. 13, 1968; s. Dalon D. Burford and Judie M. Piscitello; m. Jeanine J. Burford, June 1, 1996; children: Grace Jane, Ava Jeanine, Jerrad Dalon Jr., Jaxon Jerrad. Degree in Agrl. Bus. and Mktg., Calif. Poly. U., 1991. Cert. fin. mgr. Merrill Lynch, 1995. Fin. advisor Merrill Lynch, Montecito, Calif., 1991—. Author: (short stories) The Storyteller (pub. in lit. jour.). Mem.: Santa Barbara (Calif.) Athletic Club, Coral Casino, Beta Theta Pi (life; treas. 1989—90). Avocations: writing, exercise, reading, travel. Office: Merrill Lynch 1482 East Valley Road 50 Montecito CA 93108 Office Phone: 805-695-7000. E-mail: jerrad_burford@ml.com.

BURFORD, PETER T., publishing executive; b. Morristown, N.J., July 29, 1955; s. Thomas M. and Betty M. Burford; m. Sherry Burford, Jan. 22, 1984; children: Sarah, Andrew. BA, Princeton (N.J.) U., 1977. Asst. editor Crown Publishers, Inc., N.Y.C., NY, 1978—82; v.p. Lyons & Burford Pub., New York, ND, 1986—97; pres., pub. Burford Books Inc., Springfield, NJ, 1997—; editor Nick Lyons Books, N.Y.C., NY, 1982—86. Office: Burford Books Inc 32 Morris Ave Springfield NJ 07081 Office Phone: 973-258-0960. Office Fax: 973-258-0113.

BURG, JOHN PARKER, electric power industry executive; b. Great Bend, Kans., Dec. 17, 1931; s. Kenneth Edwin and Viola Mae (Parker) B.; m. Ida Elizabeth Groome; children Ida Elizabeth, Clarence Oscar Edwin; m. Shirley Joan Steele, Apr. 10, 1976; children: Nathan Parker, Emily Diane, Paul Andrew. BS in Physics, BA in Math., U. Tex., 1953; MS in Physics, MIT, 1960; PhD in Geophysics, Stanford U., 1975. Asst. engr. Tex. Instruments, Inc., 1956-57, engr. Dallas, 1960; sr. rsch. geophysicist Geophys. Svc., Inc., Dallas, 1960-73; chmn. bd. dirs. Time and Space Processing, Inc., Santa Clara, Calif., 1973-83; pres. Entropic Processing, Inc., Cupertino, Calif., 1983—, also chmn. bd. dirs. Cons. oil cos., ESL, Inc., Naval Undersea Ctr., 1969-75; cons. Digicon, Inc., Houston, 1982-83; chmn. bd. dirs. Entropic Rsch. Lab., Washington, 1984-98, Entropic Geophysical, Inc., 1984-91, Entropic Speech Inc., 1984-02, Affordable Bldg. Sys., 2000—. Inventor patent predictive seismic deconvolution, multi-channel filtering. Recipient Rsch. Publication award Naval Rsch. Lab., 1984; named Life Master Am. Contract Bridge League. Fellow IEEE (contbr. to jour.). Avocation: bridge theory. Office: Durra Bldg Systems LLC 2747 State Hwy 160 PO Box 10 Whitewright TX 75491 Home: 2301 W White Ave Apt 214 Mc Kinney TX 75071 Business E-Mail: john.burg@durra.com.

BURG, RALPH, art association executive; b. Malden, Mass., Jan. 2, 1914; s. Joseph and Bessie (Meyer) B.; m. Fay E. Pristaw, Jan. 10, 1937; children: Stephen, Harvey. BA, Boston U., 19366. V.p. Beacon Musical Inst. Co., Boston, 1939-70; pres., owner Quisisana Lodge, Center Lovell, Maine, 1946-76; chmn. Edna Hibel Soc., Coral Springs, Fla., 1979-99. Editor: Hibeletter newsletter, 1979-2002. Mem. Friends for Life, B'Nai B'rith. Recipient Cultural award Minister of Culture, Flanders, Belgium, 1983. Mem. Kiwanis (various coms. Boston chpt. 1946-70), Synergistic Assn. (pres. Boston chpt. 1962-70), Edna Hibel Soc. (chmn. 1979-2002), Woodlands Country Club. Avocations: golf, tennis, writing, bridge, saxophone. Home: 4604 King Palm Dr Tamarac FL 33319-6121 Office: Edna Hibel Soc PO Box 9721 Coral Springs FL 33075-9721 Personal E-mail: maestroralph@cs.com.

BURGA, ANA MARIA, pathologist; d. Roger Enrique and Teresa Burga. BA with hons. in Spanish Lit. and Microbiology, U. Kans.; MD, U. Ill., Chgo., 1996. Lic. physician N.Y., N.J. Resident Mt. Sinai Med. Ctr., N.Y.C., 1996—2000; fellow in oncologic pathology Meml. Sloan Kettering Cancer Ctr., N.Y.C., 2000—01; fellow in breast and gynecologic pathology Armed Forces Inst. of Pathology, Washington, 2001—02; staff pathologist Englewood (N.J.) Pathologists, P.A., 2002—. Chief resident dept. pathology Mt. Sinai Hosp., N.Y.C., 1999—2000. Scholar in Oncologic Pathology, Meml. Sloan Kettering Cancer Ctr., 2000—01; chief fellow, Am. Registry Pathology, 2001—02. Fellow: Coll. Am. Pathologists; mem.: Sigma Delta Pi, Alpha Omega Alpha, Phi Beta Kappa. Office: Englewood Pathologists PA Dept of Pathology 350 Engle St Englewood NJ 07631 Office Phone: 201-892-3420. Business E-Mail: ana.burga@ehmc.com.

BURGDOERFER, JERRY, lawyer; b. Jeffersonville, Ind., May 3, 1958; s. Jerry Jack and Barbara Jean Burgdoerfer. BS, Ind. U., 1980, MBA, JD cum laude, Ind. U., 1983. Bar: Ill. 1984, U.S. Dist. Ct. (no. dist.) Ill. 1984, U.S. Tax Ct. 1984. Assoc. Adams, Fox, Adelstein, Rosen & Bell, Chgo., 1983-88, ptnr., 1988-89; assoc. Jenner & Block, Chgo., 1989-90, ptnr., 1991—; with Mori Hamada Matsumoto, Tokyo, 1991—93; co-chair corp. dept. Jenner & Block, Chgo., 1999—2002, co-chair securities practice group, 2000—, mem. mgmt. com., 2002—05; mem. State of Ill. Sec. of State Bus. Orgn. Acts Com., 2004—. Author: (book) Director and Officers Liability: Prevention, Insurance and Indemnification, 2000, Securities Law, 2003; contbr. articles to profl. jours. Vol. United Cerebral Palsy Assn., 1995—, dir., 1999—; mem. bus. orgn. acts adv. com. State of Ill. Sec. of State, 2004—; mem. exec. com. Northwestern U. Sch. Law Ann. Garrett Corp. and Securities Law Inst. Named 2d Benton, Nat. Moot Ct. Competition, 1982. Mem.: ABA, Cleve. Clin. Heart Ctr. Internat. Leadership Comm., Chgo. Coun. Fgn. Rels., Chgo. Bar Assn. (chairperson '34 Act Com. 1996—98, reporter securities com. 1997—98, vice chair 1998—99, chair 1999—2000), Ill. Bar Assn., Inter Pacific Bar Assn., Internat. Bar Assn., Japan Am. Soc. Chgo., Exec. Club Chgo., Econ. Club Chgo., Ind. U. Alumni Club Chgo. (vol. 1988—89), Phi Delta Theta (sec. chpt. 1977—78, co-founder, mem. steering com. Chgo. alumni club 1988—89), Phi Delta Phi, Phi Eta Sigma. Avocations: bicycling, water-skiing, Japanese language. Office: Jenner & Block 1 E Ibm Plz Fl 4000 Chicago IL 60611-7603

BURGDOERFER, JERRY J., marketing and distribution executive; b. Connersville, Ind., Nov. 20, 1935; s. Louis M. and Edna (Seele) B.; m. Barbara Jean Hofherr, Aug. 15, 1954; children: Steven, Jerry, Jeffrey, Stuart. BS, Ind. U., 1957. Indsl. engr. Colgate Palmolive Co., Jeffersonville, Ind., 1958-59, mktg. mgr. N.Y.C., 1959-63, Am. Can Co., Green Bay, Wis., 1953-65, dir. sales, 1966-67, v.p. Greenwich, Conn., 1968-70; pres., dir. Am. Garden Products, Inc., Boston, 1970-71; exec. v.p. Facelle Co. div. Internat. Paper Co., N.Y.C., 1971-73; v.p. worldwide mktg. Hertz Corp., N.Y.C., 1973-77, exec. v.p., dir., from 1977; pres., chief exec. officer Berkey Inc., N.Y.C., 1979-86, Carysfort Enterprises Inc., Key Largo, Fla., 1987—; v.p. corp. mktg. AT Cross Co., Lincoln, R.I., 1991—, also bd. dirs.; prin. JJB Assocs., Bracey, Va., 1996—. Bd. dirs. Avis Inc. Served with arty. U.S. Army, 1957-58. Recipient Torch of Liberty-Man of Yr. award. Mem. Acad. Alumni Fellows (Ind. U.), Phi Delta Theta, Barrington Yacht Club (bd. govs.). Office Phone: 434-636-6666.

BURGE, CATHERINE ALICE, musician, educator; b. Ann Arbor, Mich., Oct. 27, 1956; d. Furman Horace and Dorothy Louise (Anderson) Burge; m. Paul J. Schorsch, May 8, 1999. BFA, Ohio U., 1978; MusM in Piano, Clarinet, U. Idaho, 1980; postgrad., San Francisco Conservatory of Music, 1981; D in Musical Arts, U. Colo., 2003. Clarinetist, solo pianist Wash./Idaho Symphony, Pullman, Wash., 1978-80; clarinetist Spokane (Wash.) Wind Symphony, 1980; pianist Spokane Ballet, 1980; entertainer Sweet Talk, W.Va., 1981-83; with sales dept., keyboardist Roberts Music Co., Pitts., 1983-84; music therapist, coord. activities Regency Hall Nursing, Pitts., 1984-85; minister of music Cranberry Christian Ctr., Pitts., 1986-87; clarinetist, solo pianist U.S. Army Band Europe, pianist U.S. Army Jazz Combo, pianist, keyboardist U.S. Army Europe Chorus, U.S. Army Europe Quintet Heidelberg, Fed. Republic of Germany, 1987-90; vocalist, keyboardist U.S. Army Field Band, 1990-98; asst. prof. music CC Denver, 1999-2000, music dept. coord., 2000-01; music instr., choral accompanist U. Colo., Boulder, 2001—02; pianist, keyboardist Colo. Wind Ensemble, 2002—04; mem. piano faculty Front Range C.C., 2003—04; performer New Orleans Piano Inst., 2003; coord. music dept. South Fla. C.C., 2004—. Keyboardist N. Star Players, Pitts., 1985—86; instr. Abundant Life Sch., 1995—99; keyboardist, arranger Abundant Life Ch., 1999; Carnegie Hall debut with Soldier's Chorus, U.S. Army Field Band, Erich Kunzel and Pops Orch, 1997; dir. South Fla. century vocal ensemble Carnegie Hall Masterwork Festival, 2005. Singer, musician: Orchard Rd. Christian Ctr., 2000. Dir. music. Camp

Wohelo-Theater, Pa., 1985; pianist North Hills Civic Chorus, Wexford, 1985, North Star Kids, Pitts., 1986; keyboardist North Way Christian Cmty., Wexford, Pa., 1983—86; pianist Christian Servicemen's Ctr., Eppleheim, Germany, 1987—90, Tompkins Chapel, U.S. Army Europe; vocalist New Life Ch. Worship, Colorado Springs, 2003; pianist, vocal soloist Covenant Presbyn. Ch., Sebring, Fla., 2004—. Recipient Silver medal, Internat. Piano Rec. Competition Am. Music divsn.; fellow, U. Idaho; Rsch. grant, U. Colo., 2002, Enrichment grant, Music Tchrs. Nat. Assn., 2005. Mem.: Music Tchrs. Nat. Assn. (cert.). Avocations: skiing, bicycling, outdoor activities. Office: South Florida CC Music Dept 600 W College Dr Avon Park FL 33825 Office Phone: 863-784-7201. Business E-Mail: burgec@aol.com.

BURGE, CONSTANCE M., television producer; d. Phil. MFA in Playwriting, UCLA. Author: (TV series) Ally McBeal; prodr.: (TV series) Ally McBeal; author: (TV series) Boston Pub., Charmed; prodr.: (TV series) Charmed; author: (TV series) Ed; prodr.: (TV series) Savannah; author: The Power of Three: A Novelization, 1999, The Crimson Spell, 2000, Haunted By Desire, 2000, Kiss of Darkness: An Original Novel, 2000, Voodoo Moon, 2000, Whispers from the Past, 2000, Beware What You Wish, 2001, The Gypsy Enchantment, 2001, The Legacy of Merlin, 2001, Soul of the Bride, 2001, Charmed Again, 2002, Spirit of the Wolf, 2002.

BURGE, DAVID ALAN, lawyer, writer; b. Anderson, Ind., July 22, 1943; s. James Swisher and Esther M. (Sheppard) B.; m. Carolyn J. Alter, Nov. 24, 1966; children: Benjamin, Thomas. BS in Gen. Engring. with highest honors, U. Ill., 1966; JD, U. Louisville, 1970. Registered patent atty. Pres. David A. Burge Co LPA, Cleve., 1975—. Author: Patent and Trademark Tactics and Practice, 1980, 3rd edition, 1999; contbr. chpts. in books. Pres. Gen. Engring. Constituent Alumni Assn., 1984, 85. Mem.: ABA, Sigma Delta Kappa, Gamma Epsilon, Associated Locksmiths of Am., Am. Intellectual Property Law Assn., Cleve. Bar Assn., Phi Eta Sigma, Sigma Tau, Phi Kappa Phi. Avocations: antique tools, woodworking. Office: David A Burge Co LPA 2901 S Park Blvd Cleveland OH 44120-1842

BURGE, DAVID RUSSELL, concert pianist, composer, music educator; b. Evanston, Ill., Mar. 25, 1930; s. Russell David and Sylvia (Swensen) B.; m. Liliane Choney, 1993; 1 child, Russell David. MusB, Northwestern U., 1951, MusM, 1952; DMus Arts, Eastman Sch. Music, 1956; postgrad., Cherubini Conservatory, Florence, Italy, 1956-57; DFA, Bucknell U., 1980. Instr. piano Northwestern U., 1949-52; assoc. prof. music, composer-pianist in resident Whitman Coll., 1957-62; dir. MacDowell Hall Concert Series at coll., 1959-62; organist Ch. of Christ Scientist, Walla Walla, 1958-62; from asst. prof. music to prof. U. Colo., 1962-75; chmn. piano dept. Eastman Sch. Music, U. Rochester, N.Y., 1975-87, prof., 1975-93, Kilbourn prof., 1978-79; artist-in-residence U. Calif., Davis, 1975; guest prof. piano U. Stockholm, Sweden, 1981, 92, Banff Ctr., Can., 1983-84, 86, U. Auckland, New Zealand, 1988; composer-in-residence San Diego Ballet Co., 1997—. Guest prof. Odense, Denmark, 1997; guest prof. composition U. Pa., 1977; guest prof. music history U. Gothenberg, Sweden, 1980, 92; feature writer San Diego Reader; guest prof. composition San Diego State U., 2000. Rec. artist, Mercury, Advance, Candide, Nonesuch (grammy nomination 1974), CRI Records, Mus. Heritage Soc. Records, Vox Records, Proviva Records, Wergo, Albany, Capstone Records, Classico Records, Fleur de Son Classics; composer: opera Intervals, 1961; trio for violin, cello, piano, 1962; work for piano Eclipse, 1963; for flute-piano Sources I, 1964; for violin-celeste-piano Sources II, 1965; for piano Eclipse II, 1966, Sources IV, 1969; for clarinet-percussion Sources III, 1967; for soprano-piano A Song of Sixpence, 1967, Life Begins at 40, 1998; for flute-clarinet-violin-cello-piano-tape Aeolian Music, 1968; String Quartet, 1969, Twone in Sunshine, an Entertainment for Theater, 1969; for violin-orch. that no one knew, 1969, Songs of Love and Sorrow, 1989, for solo piano Go-Hyang, 1994, Sonata for Violin and Piano, 1994, Liana's Song: A Ballet in Six Parts, 1995, The Dark Journey, 12 Pieces for Dance, 1995, 24 Preludes for Piano, 1996, Luna Lunera, a Ballet in 12 Parts, 1996, Moku (Island) for three percussionists, 1998; La Loteria Ballet, 1998, The Thousand Paper Cranes, 2001, Kaleidoscope (ballet), 2001; for piano and orch. Dances of Love and Laughter, 1998, When Love Prevails for solo vibraphone, 2002, Dibujos (sketches) for violin and piano, 2003, Rainbows: A Ragtime Ballet, 2003; also songs, anthems.; contbr. over 200 articles to periodicals; columnist: Keyboard Mag., Clavier Mag., Piano Quar.; music reviewer: Music Library Assn. Notes; first major postarmistice concert, Seoul, Korea, 1953, New York debut playing all-modern program, 1961; toured, Korea, 1953-54, Europe, 1956-57, U.S.A., annually, 1960—, Eastern Europe, 1974, Far East, Australia, N.Z., 1984, 88; author: Twentieth-Century Piano Music, 1990; Vanishing Spring, 1998, Bricks and Other Stories, 2004. Served with AUS, 1952-54, Korea. Decorated by U.S. Army for cultural relations work in Korea, 1954; recipient Alumni Merit award Northwestern U., 1974, Colo. Gov.'s award, 1975, Distinguished Alumni award Eastman Sch. Music, 1975, Deems Taylor award for mus. journalism ASCAP, 1978-79; Fulbright fellow in Italy, 1956-57; Faculty Research lectr. U. Colo., 1972 Mem. ASCAP, Internat. Webern Soc. (charter), Am. Soc. Univ. Composers (founder, nat. chmn. 1970-74), Pi Kappa Lambda. Address: 5243 Caminito Apartado San Diego CA 92108-4204 E-mail: music@davidburge.net.

BURGE, JOHN WESLEY, JR., management consultant; b. Mobile, Ala., Sept. 11, 1932; s. John Wesley and Mary Jo (Guest) Burge; m. Shirley Paulette Roberts, Mar. 29, 1958; children: John, Delene, Eric, Kurt, Karen. Student, Centenary Coll., San Antonio Coll., UCLA. Engring. and mgmt. staff ITT Gilfillan, 1954-69; pres., gen. mgr. Rantec, Calabasas, Calif., 1969-71, chmn. bd. dirs.; pres., gen. mgr. electronics and space divsn. Emerson Electric Co., St. Louis, 1971-80, corp. group v.p. govt., def., 1977-89; ret., 1989; pvt. practice Pensacola, Fla., 1975—. With USAF, 1950—54. Decorated Grand Cordon Order Al-Istiqlal (Jordan). Presbyterian. Personal E-mail: jburge@cox.net.

BURGE, LARRY BRADY, artist; b. Fayetteville, N.C., Feb. 2, 1948; s. Billie Dixie and Elma Leigh (Westbrook) B.; m. Lori Jo Shepard, June 17, 1995. Student, Coll. of the Albemarle, Elizabeth City, N.C., 1972, Art Instn. sch., Mpls., 1976. One man shows include Village Smith Galleries, Winston-Salem, N.C., 1982, Kinston (N.C.) Arts Coun., 1983, Ballantyne Art Gallery, New Bern, N.C., 1984, Collector's Gallery, Raleigh, N.C., 1986, N.C. Maritime Mus., Beaufort, N.C., 1986, 91, World Art Gallery, Jacksonville, N.C., 1995, Art Masters Gallery, Beaufort, 1998, Arts and Things, Morehead City, N.C., 1999; group exhibits include Coll. of the Albemarle Art Ctr., Elizabeth City, 1972, Riverside Gallery, New Bern, 1978, Fairfield Harbor Art Exhibit, New Bern, 1978, Weyerhaeuser Art Exhibit, Grifton, N.C., 1981, 7th Ann Realist Invitational Remarque Gallery, High Point, N.C., 1983, Remarque Gallery, High Point, N.C., 1984, Spartanburg (S.C.) Arts Ctr., 1985, Snyder Gallery, Charlotte, N.C., 1987, Wilkes Art Gallery, North Wilkesboro, 1990, Mid-Town Gallery, Winston-Salem, 1993, Hampton House Gallery, Winston-Salem, 1997, N.C. Seafood Festival, Morehead, N.C., 1999, Core Sound Decon Festiveal, Harker's Island, N.C., 1999; works in corp. collections at Wachovia Bank and Trust Co., Winston-Salem, RJR Nabisco, Winston-Salem, Trotman's Gallery, Winston-Salem, Marine Fed. Credit Union, Jacksonville, N.C., Core Sound Waterfowl Mus., Harker's Island, Onslow Meml. Hosp., Jacksonville, N.C. Seafood Festival; prodr. ltd.-edit. prints of maj. paintings Salem Graphics, Inc., 1990—; listed in Ency. Living Artists, 1990, Am. Artists-A Survey of Leading Contemporaries, 1991. Home and Office: PO Box 623 927 Church St Newport NC 28570-9679

BURGE, STEVEN DONALD, city administrator; b. Omaha, Mar. 14, 1950; s. Melvin Lloyd and Mary Ann Burge. Cert. EMT, We. Iowa Tech. Coll., 1985; BS in Polit. Sci., Sociology, Wayne State Coll., 1992; MPA, U. Nebr., 1997; postgrad., S.D. State U., 1999. Cert. emergency med. technician. Mgr. housing devel., Norfolk, Nebr., 1994; city adminstr. City of Creighton, Nebr., 1995, City of Dakota City, Nebr., 1998—2000; adj. instr. intro. to sociology/sociology of deviance Wayne State Coll., Nebr., 2004—. Bd. dirs. Cardinal Devel.; pres. Northeast Nebr. Devel. Network, 1997; pres. retail Comm. Nebr. Public Power Dist., 1997; active Overall Econ. Devel. Plan, 1998. Active Knox County 911 Sys., 1995—98, Creighton Devel. Corp., 1995—98, Temporary Housing Action Team, 1994—95, Sgt Bluff Planning and Zoning, 1985—86; Sunday sch. tchr. Dakota City United Meth. Ch., 1998—2000; bd. dirs. N.E. Loess Hills Resource and Conservation and Devel., West Point, Nebr., 1998—2000; pres. Hwy. 35 Expy. Com., 1998—2000; active Pioneer Valley Days Com., 1986—87. Mem.: Nebr. Econ. Devel. Assn., Nebr. Planning and Zoning Assn.,, Midwest Sociol. Soc., Great Plains Sociol. Soc., Am. Sociol. Assn., Assn. Humanist Sociology, Jaycees (bd. dirs. Kimball County 1977—78, v.p. Kimball County 1979, v.p. Lyons 1980, regional dir. Nebr. 1981, pres. Council Bluffs 1982, pres. Sgt. Bluff 1985—87, regional dir. Iowa 1988, chmn. bd. Sgt. Bluff 1988, Iowa Hawkeye Corps 1989—2003), Alpha Kappa Delta (pres. 2000). Avocation: motorcycles/motorcycle riding. Home: 303 Spring Ave N Lake Preston SD 57249 Office Phone: 605-964-6044. E-mail: grizza@hotmail.com.

BURGE, WILLARD, JR., software company executive; b. Johnson City, N.Y., Oct. 2, 1938; s. Willard Sr. and Catherine Bernice (Matthews) B.; m. Carol Crockenberg, June 16, 1961; children: Willard III, Pennie Lynn. Registered profl. engr., Ohio. Indsl. engr. Harnischfeger Corp., Escanaba, Mich., 1966-67; sr. indsl. engr. Gen. Electric, Ladson, S.C., 1968-74, advanced mfg. engr. Mentor, Ohio, 1971-74; corp. staff engr. Eaton Corp., Willoughby Hills, Ohio, 1974-79, supr. N/C programming, 1979-80, supr. mfg. engring., 1980-82, mgr. mfg. systems engring., 1982-87; bus. unit mgr. MSC Products, Eaton Corp., Costa Mesa, Calif., 1987-91; pres., CEO CAM Software, Inc., Provo, Utah, 1991-93; chief exec. officer Key Svcs., Cypress, Calif., 1993—. Bd. dirs. CAM Software, Inc.; presenter in field. With U.S. Army, 1957. Mem. Soc. Mfg. Engrs. Republican. Avocations: photography, computers, start-up businesses. Home and Office: 1260 Oakmont Rd 53H Seal Beach CA 90740 E-mail: wburgejr@adelphia.net.

BURGE, WILLIAM LEE, retired credit manager; b. Atlanta, June 27, 1918; s. William Frederick and Leona (Payne) B.; m. Willette Richey, Feb. 27, 1937; children: Judith, William Roger. Ed., Ga. State U. Bus. Adminstrn., 1937—42; LLD (hon.), Mercer U., 1978. With Equifax Inc. (formerly Retail Credit Co.), 1936-88, br. mgr. Greensboro, N.C., 1949-51, div. mgr. Pitts., 1951-58, v.p. Atlanta, 1959-65, exec. v.p., 1964-65, pres., 1965—, CEO, 1967-83, chmn. bd., 1976-88; chmn. Equifax Inc. (Equifax Inc. affiliates), 1988, ret., 1988; chmn. emeritus Equifax Inc. (Equifax Services Ltd.), Can. Ret. dir. First Nat. Bank Atlanta Nat. Svc. Industries, Informes de Centrales of Mex.; chmn. Fernbank, Inc., 1951-57. Gen. chmn. United Way, Atlanta, 1961; chmn. United Negro Coll. Fund, 1974-75; regional chmn. Nat. Alliance of Businessmen, 1969-70; chmn. bd. regents Univ. System Ga., 1972-73; mem. coll. accreditation commn. So. Assn. Colls. and Schs.; mem. Commn. Postsecondary Edn.; trustee Atlanta Arts Alliance, YMCA; mem. bd. Central Atlanta Progress; mem. Gov.'s Adv. Council on Job Tng. Coordination, 1985-88; bd. dirs. Atlanta chpt. ARC; pres. Mus. Nat. History, 1995-96, Fernbank Mus.; chair Ga. Consortium for Fin. Literacy. Served with AUS, World War II. Named Atlanta's Young Man of Year, 1948, one of Atlanta's Leaders of Tomorrow Time mag., 1952, Alumnus of Yr. Ga. award State U., 1968, 87. Mem. Conf. Bd., Atlanta C. of C. (pres. 1966), Nat. C. of C. (panel on privacy), Jr. C. of C. (pres. 1947-48) Clubs: Kiwanis (pres. 1965). Office: Equifax Inc Ste 240 3060 Peachtree Rd Atlanta GA 30305 Office Phone: 404-760-3772. Business E-Mail: lee.burge@equifax.com.

BURGEE, G. BRENT, obstetrician, gynecologist; b. Frederick, Md., July 18, 1950; s. William Gabriel and Frances Moore Burgee; m. Terry Ann Ellis, June 9, 1973; children: Brooke, Bethany, Tyler. BA, Johns Hopkins U., 1972; MD, U. Md., 1977; student, Vt. Law Sch., 2001. Resident Williamsport (Pa.) Family Practice, 1977—80; pvt. practice in family practice Bristol, Vt., 1980—82; resident in ob-gyn. U. Mass., Worcester, 1982—85; staff physician in ob-gyn. Hitchcock Clinic, Hanover, NH, 1985—97, Gifford Med. Ctr., Randolph, Vt., 1997—. Fellow: Am. Acad. Family Physicians, Am. Coll. Ob-gyn. Address: 1201 Harlow Hill Rd Randolph VT 05060

BURGEE, JOHN HENRY, architect; b. Chgo., Aug. 28, 1933; s. Joseph Zeno and Helen (Dooley) B.; m. Gwendolyn Mary Henson, June 30, 1956; 1 son, John Gerard. BArch, U. Notre Dame, 1956, DEngr (hon.), 1983. Supt. constrn. Holabird & Root & Burgee, Chgo., 1955-56; project mgr. Naess & Murphy, Chgo., 1958-61; adminstr. design, project architect C. F. Murphy Assos., Chgo., 1961-65; assoc. ptnr. C. F. Murphy Assocs., 1965-67, ptnr., 1967; assoc. Philip Johnson (Architects), N.Y.C., 1967-68; ptnr. Johnson/Burgee, N.Y.C., 1968-82, John Burgee Architects, N.Y.C., 1982-98, Santa Barbara, Calif., 1998—. Chmn. Archtl. Rev. Bd., Bronxville, N.Y., 1974-75; chmn. Bronxville Planning Commn., 1975-77 Works include, I.D.S. Center, Mpls., Niagara Falls Conv. Center, Pennzoil Place, Houston, Crystal Cathedral, Los Angeles, AT&T Hdqrs., N.Y.C., PPG Hdqrs., Pitts., Transco Tower, Houston, Republic Bank, Houston, Nat. Center for Performing Arts, Bombay, 101 California Street, San Francisco, International Place, Boston, 190 South LaSalle Street, Chicago, IBM Headquarters, Atlanta, Mus. of Broadcasting, New York Canadian Broadcast Ctr., Toronto, Takashamya Dept. Store, N.Y., Capital Holding Ctr., Louisville, Puerto de Europa, Madrid, One Detroit Ctr., Marina Hotel and Shopping Ctr., Singapore, Ch. St. Mary, Lakeville, Conn. Pres. German-Am. Club, Bad Kreuznach, Germany, 1957-58; chmn. bldg. material sect. Met. Crusade of Mercy, Chgo., 1966-67; pres. Chgo. Br. North Montessori Sch. Bd., 1962-63, Lawrence Park Hilltop Assn., 1974-75; chmn. architecture com. Statue of Liberty/Ellis Island Centennial Commn.; mem. adv. coun. Coll. Engring. U. Notre Dame, 1982-88; bd. dirs. Lenox Hill Hosp., 1982-91, Parsons Sch. of Design, 1985-92, U. Notre Dame, 1988—, Chgo. Athenaeum, 1989-92, Music Acad. of the West, 2002-, 1st vice chmn., 2003, chmn., 2005. With U.S. Army, 1956—58. Recipient Reynolds Aluminum prize, 1978, honor award U. Notre Dame, 1981, Chgo. Architecture award. Fellow AIA, Urban Design Inst.; mem. Archtl. League N.Y. (dir.), Inst. Architecture and Urban Studies (dir. 1983, chmn., pres. 1984) Clubs: Saddle Cycle (Chgo.), Arts (Chgo.), University (Chgo.), Shenarock Shore (Rye, N.Y), Am. Yacht, Century Assn. Home: 639 Hot Springs Rd Santa Barbara CA 93108-2030 E-mail: burgeearchitect@cox.net.

BURGEE, ROBERT LARRY, financial consultant, contractor; b. Washington, July 28, 1969; s. George Larry and Virgil Kay (Smith) Burgee; m. Andrea Michelle Van Wie, June 13, 1992; children: Jonathan Robert, Kathryn Elizabeth, Ann Marie, Hannah Michelle. AA in Acctg., Prince George's C.C., Largo, Md., 1992; BS in Acctg., U. Md., 1995. Cert. fund specialist, retirement plan specialist. Auditor Washington Gas Light, 1993-95; fin. advisor Prudential Securities, Bethesda, Md., 1996; fin. advisor, pres. Lighthouse Fin. Group, Ltd., Bowie, Md., 1996—2002; owner, pres. Ranwie Home Improvements LLC, 2002—. Republican. Roman Catholic. Avocations: running, hockey, golf. Office: Ranwie Home Improvements 7601 Investment Ct Owings MD 20736 Home: 6334 North Brook Dr Dunkirk MD 20754-9110

BURGER, DELORES THERESA, historian, writer; b. St. Paul, Feb. 12, 1940; d. Arthur F. and Bessy (Latuff) Prohofsky; m. Stephen Burger, Dec. 16, 1961; children: Eric L., Linda B. Student, Bethel Coll., 1958, U. Minn., 1959. Camp conselor and hostess Union Gospel Mission, St. Paul, 1957-60; dir. group foster home Dept. Welfare, St. Paul, 1961-63; instr. Lark Workshop Handicapped, New Castle, Pa., 1965-66; historian Assn. of Gospel Rescue Missions, Kansas City, Mo., 1990—. Author: (Book) Women Who Changed the Heart of the City, 1997, Practical Religion: David Nasmith and the City Mission Movement, 2000. Vol. York (Pa.) Rescue Mission, 1967-72, Union Gospel Mission, Seattle, 1972-87 Office: Assn Gospel Rescue Missions 1045 Swift Ave Kansas City MO 64116-4127 Office Phone: 816-471-8020.

BURGER, EDMUND GANES, architect; b. Yerington, Nev., Mar. 28, 1930; s. Edmund Ganes and Rose Catherine (Kobe) B.; m. Shirley May Pratini, Jan. 21, 1968; 1 dau., Jane Lee. B.M.E., U. Santa Clara, 1951; B.Arch., U. Pa., 1959. Engr. Gen. Electric Co., 1951-52; design engr. U. Calif. Radiation Lab., 1952-57; John Stewardson fellow in architecture, 1959; architect Wurster, Bernardi & Emmons, San Francisco, 1960-63; founder Burger & Coplans, Inc. (Architects), San Francisco, 1964, pres., 1964-79; owner Edmund Burger (Architect), 1979—. Guest lectr. U. Calif., Berkeley. Important works include Acorn Housing Project, Oakland, Calif., Crescent Village Housing Project, Suisun City, Calif., Coplans residence, San Francisco, Betel Housing Project, San Francisco, Grand View Housing Project, San Francisco, Albany (Calif.) Oaks Housing, Grow Homes, San Pablo, Calif., Mariposa Housing, Dunleavy Plaza Housing, Potrero Ct. Housing, San Francisco, Lee residence, Kentfield, Calif., Burger residences, Lafayette, Calif., Oceanside, Oreg., and El Cerrito, Calif., Yamhill Valley Vineyards Winery, McMinneville, Oreg., Portico De Mar, shop and restaurant complex, Barcelona, Spain, Hendrickson residence, Newport Beach, Calif., Hamilton residence, Winters, Calif., Sanders residence, Yuba City, Calif., Strack/Villars residence, Kentfield, Calif., Breton residence, Oakland, Visitors Facilities Yosemite Nat. Park, Calif., Rogers Residence, El Cerrito, Calif, Stern Grove Outdoor Theater, San Francisco, Petersen Residence, El Cerrrito; author: Geomorphic Architecture, 1986. Recipient citation for excellence in community architecture AIA, 1969, award of merit AIA, award of merit Homes for Better Living, 1970, 79, 1st Honor award, 1973, 81, Holiday award for a beautiful Am., 1970, Honor award 4th Biennial HUD awards for design excellence, 1970, Bay Area awards for design excellence, 1969, 74, 78, Apts. of Year award Archtl. Record, 1972, Houses of Year award, 1973, Calif. Affordable Housing Competition award, 1981, HUD Building Value into Housing award, 1981, Community Design award Calif. Council AIA, 1986; design grant Nat. Endowment for Arts, 1980, HUD, 1980; constrn. grant HUD, 1981. Office: 8445 Wildcat Dr El Cerrito CA 94530 Office Phone: 510-237-8336.

BURGER, HENRY G., vocabulary scientist, anthropologist, writer; b. N.Y.C., June 27, 1923; s. B. William and Terese R. (Felleman) B.; m. Barbara G. Smith, Nov. 29, 1991. BA with honors (Pulitzer scholar), Columbia Coll., 1947; MA, Columbia U., 1965, PhD in Cultural Anthropology (State Doctoral fellow), 1967. Indsl. engr. various orgns., 1947-51; Midwest mfrs. rep., 1952-55; social sci. cons. Chgo. and N.Y.C., 1956-67; anthropologist Southwestern Coop. Ednl. Lab., Albuquerque, 1967-69; assoc. prof. anthropology and edn. U. Mo., Kansas City, 1969-73, prof., 1973-93, prof. emeritus, 1993—, founding mem. univ. wide doctoral faculty, 1974-93; founder, pub. The Wordtree, Overland Park, Kans., 1984—. Lectr. CUNY; adj. prof. ednl. anthropology U. N.Mex., 1969; anthrop. cons. U.S. VA Hosp., Kansas City, 1971—72; spkr. in field; columnist linguistic column New Times, New Verbs, 1988—. Author: Ethno-Pedagogy, 1968, 2nd edit., 1968; editor, compiler: The Wordtree, a Branching Dictionary for Solving Phys. and Social Problems, 1984, selected for exhibit at 3 insts., selected as topic Cambridge Ency. of the English Lang., 1995—, 7 time citee Oxford English Dictionary, mem. editl. bd. Coun. Anthropology and Edn., 1975—80; contbr. to anthologies, articles to profl. jours.; globally interviewed by Voice of America, 2002. Capt. AUS, 1943-46. NSF Instl. grantee, 1970. Fellow World Acad. Art and Sci., Am. Anthrop. Assn. (life), Royal Anthrop. Inst. Gt. Britain (life); mem. European Assn. for Lexicography, Internat. Assn. Semiotic Studies, English-Speaking Union (v.p. Kansas City chpt. 1995-96), Dictionary Soc. N.Am. (life, terminology com.), Kans. Acad. Sci. (life), Assn. Internationale de Terminologie, Academie Europeenne des Scis., Arts et Lettres (corr.), Columbia U. Club, Phi Beta Kappa. Achievements include discovery of the branchability of processes (corresponding, for materials, to the periodic table of elements); research on computerized causality and reasoning. Office: The Wordtree 10876 Bradshaw St Overland Park KS 66210-1148 Office Phone: 913-469-1010. Business E-Mail: burger@cctr.umkc.edu. *The computer analyzes prose information into tabulation, whence it can be re-formed diversely. Therefore computerization has revolutionized my authorship from textbooks to reference books.*

BURGER, HERBERT FRANCIS, retired advertising agency executive; b. Ligonier, Pa., Mar. 5, 1930; s. Adolph G. and Elizabeth (Johannsen) Burger; m. Jane Coulter, Oct. 1, 1966; children: Matthew F., Jennifer. BS in Econs, Thiel Coll., Greenville, Pa., 1952; MA in Journalism, Syracuse (N.Y.) U., 1955. C. Mgmt. trainee Joy Mfg. Co., 1955-56; account exec. Ketchum, MacLeod & Grove, Pitts., 1956-58, Marsteller Inc., Pitts., 1958-65; with Creamer Inc., Pitts., 1965-76; pres. Creamer Inc. (Pitts. divsn.), 1976-86; chmn., ptnr. St. George Group, Inc., Pitts., 1986-98; ret., 1998. Bd. dirs. Overly Mft. Co., Pitts., Offices of Promotion; chmn. Pitts. Media Group, Pitts. Downtown Partnership; pres. Speedwell Enterprises, 1986—. Chmn. Pitts. Downtown Plan, Pitts. Task Force. With U.S. Army, 1953—55. Mem.: Pitts. Press Club, Pitts. Advt. Club (dir.), Grove City Country Club, Longue Vue Country Club, Duquesne Club. Republican. Lutheran. Home: 301 Wildberry Rd Pittsburgh PA 15238 Office Phone: 412-903-6526.

BURGER, ROBERT MERCER, manufacturing executive, researcher; b. Frederick, Md., Feb. 14, 1927; s. William Leslie and Grace Allene (Mercer) B.; m. Marian Elizabeth Abbott, Sept. 10, 1949; children: Sharon A., Lisa A., Robert M. SB, Coll. William and Mary, 1949; ScM, Brown U., 1952, PhD, 1955. Br. chief Nat. Security Agy., Fort Meade, Md., 1955-59; fellow engr. Westinghouse Corp., Balt., 1959-62; chief scientist Research Triangle Inst., Research Triangle Park, N.C., 1962-82; v.p., chief scientist Semiconductor Research Corp., Research Triangle Park, 1982-96; cons. in field, 1982-96. Rsch. assoc. U. Md., College Park, 1955-59; adj. assoc. prof. Duke U., 1962-69; bd. vis. N.C. State U., 1992-98; prof. N.C. State U., 1995-2000. Author, editor: Fundamentals of Integrated Silicon Devices, 1965 Bd. dirs., v.p. United Fund, Durham, N.C., 1973. With USN, 1945-46. Fellow IEEE (life); mem. AAAS, Am. Phys. Soc. Republican. Presbyterian. Avocations: fishing, gardening. Home: 107 Links End Dr Cary NC 27513-5691 Office: Semiconductor Research Corp PO Box 12053 Durham NC 27709-2053 Office Phone: 919-460-9186. E-mail: rmburger@bellsouth.net.

BURGERT, DAVID LEE, lawyer; b. Kansas City, Kans., Jan. 30, 1959; s. Marion Lawrence and Barbara Jean (Marmont) B.; m. Amy Marlyse Wilson; children: Melissa Christine, Grace Josephine. BS summa cum laude, Ohio U., 1980; JD, U. Mich., 1983. Bar: Tex. 1983, U.S. Dist. Ct. (so. dist.) Tex. 1984, U.S. Dist. Ct. (we. dist.) (no. dist., 2002) Tex. 1999, U.S. Ct. Appeals (5th cir.) 1984, U.S. Tax Ct. 1993, U.S. Ct. Appeals (fed. and 8th cirs.) 1996; bd. cert. civil trial lawyer, 1990, Tex. Bd. Legal Spec. Assoc. Vinson & Elkins, Houston, 1983-86, Porter & Clements, Houston, 1986-90, ptnr., 1991-93, Porter & Hedges, Houston, 1993—. Named Tex. Superlawyer in Intellectual Property Litigation, Tex. Monthly mag., 2003—, One of Houston's Top Lawyers, Tex. Mag., 2005. Office: Porter & Hedges 1000 Main St 36th Fl Houston TX 77002-6336 Office Phone: 713-226-6668. Business E-Mail: dlburgert@porterhedges.com.

BURGESS, ANN WOLBERT, nursing educator; Van Ameringen prof. nursing U. Pa., Phila.; prof. of psychiat. and mental health nursing Boston Coll. Author: Advanced Practice Psychiatric Nursing, 1998, Psychiatric Nursing: Promoting Mental Health, 1997, Child Trauma I: Issues & Research, 1992, Community Mental Health: Target Populations, 1976, Rape: Victims of Crisis, 1974; co-editor: (with Robert K. Kessler and John E. Douglas) Sexual Homicide: Patterns and Movies, 1988, Rape and Sexual Assault II, 1985; co-author: (with Robert R. Hazelwood) Practical Aspects of Rape Investigation: A Multidisciplinary Approach, 3d edit., 1993, (with Robert Ann Prentsky) Forensic Management of Sexual Offenders, 2000, (with Robert R. Hazelwood and Park Elliott Dietz) Autoerotic Fatalities, 1983, (with Bruce A. Baldwin) Crisis Intervention Theory and Practice: A Clinical Handbook, 1981, (with Nicholas Groth and Suzanne M. Sgroi) Sexual Assault of Children and Adolescents, 1978. Mem.: Inst. Medicine, NAS. Office: Boston Coll Sch Nursing Cushing Hall 414 140 Commonwealth Ave Chestnut Hill MA 02467*

BURGESS, CHARLES ORVILLE, history professor; b. Portland, Oreg., Jan. 18, 1932; s. Rex Orville and Glendora Almanda (Sundrud) B.; m. Cora Cloepfil, June 22, 1952; children: Donna Claire Majer, Jo Dell Nicholls, Robert Charles; m. Patricia Stewart Anderson, Apr. 22, 1976; children: Marc Richard Anderson, Brian Stewart Anderson, Tricia Louise Crozier, Kristen Anne Klein. BA, U. Oreg., 1957; MS (Danforth fellow), U. Wis., 1958, PhD, 1962; Nat. Postdoctoral fellow, Harvard U., 1967-68. Asst. prof. U. Calif., Riverside, 1962-64; asst. prof. history edn. U. Wash., Seattle, 1964-66, assoc. prof., 1966-70, prof., 1970—, chmn. area ednl. policy studies, 1970-92; prof. emeritus, 1992. V.p. divsn. F Am. Ednl. Rsch. Assn., 1977-79; fgn. expert Peoples Republic of China, 1984-85. Author: The Origins of American Thought (published in China as Meiguo Sixiang Yuanyuan); 1988, (with M.L. Borrowman) What Doctrines to Embrace, 1969, Profile of an American

Philanthropist (Nettie Fowler McCormick), 1962; co-editor: (with Charles Strickland) G. Stanley Hall on Natural Education, 1965; co-author: (with Y. Yang and G. Zhu) Cultivating the World of Selfhood (published in China as Kaituo Zi Wode Shijie), 1997. Wash. com. civil rights ACLU, 1965-67; bd. dirs. Seattle Folklore Soc., 1966—. With USAF, 1950-54. Mem.: History of Edn. Soc. (pres. 1971—72), Phi Beta Kappa. Home: 14350 22nd Ave SW Burien WA 98166

BURGESS, DAVID, lawyer; b. Detroit, Nov. 30, 1948; s. Roger Edward and Claire Theresa (Sullivan) B.; m. Rebecca Culbertson Stuart, 1985 (dec. 1988); m. Catherine Mounteer, 1993; children: Jalil Riahi, Leila Riahi, Bryan Valentine, Grace Catherine. BS in Fgn. Svc., Georgetown U., 1970, MS in Fgn. Svc., JD, Georgetown U., 1978. Bar: D.C. 1978, U.S. Dist. Ct. D.C. 1979, U.S. Ct. Appeals (D.C. cir.) 1979, U.S. Ct. Appeals (fed. cir.) 1988, U.S. Ct. Internat. Trade 1988. Rsch. asst. Georgetown U. Sch. Bus. Adminstrn., Washington, 1975, asst. to dean, 1975-76; rsch. assoc., prof. Acad. in the Pub. Svc., Washington, 1976-79; asst. editor Securities Regulation Law Report, Washington; legal editor Internat. Trade Reporter Bur. Nat. Affairs, Washington, 1978-79; atty. Cadwalader, Wickersham & Taft, Washington, 1979-81; mng. editor Bur. Nat. Affairs, Washington, 1981-82; dir. U.S. Peace Corps, Niamey, Niger, 1982-84, Rabat, Morocco, 1984-85; dir. policy planning, mgmt. Peace Corps, Washington, 1985-87; dir. Bur. Human Rights and Humanitarian Affairs U.S. Dept. State, Washington, 1987-92; regional dir. Lawyers for Bush-Quayle Re-Election Campaign, 1992; chief party Rwanda Dem. and Governance Project, 1994, Russia NGO Sector Project, Moscow, 1994. Dir. democracy and civil soc. program, sr. advisor World Learning, Washington, 1995, dir. U.S. Democracy Fellows program, Washington, 1995-2002, dir. bus. devel., 2002-03; exec. v.p. Am.'s Devel. Found., Alexandria, Va., 2003-04; democracy cons., 2004—; adj. prof., Inst. World Politics, Washington, 2002—. Author: Financing Local Government, 1977, 2d edit., 1978, Preparation of the Local Budget, 2 vols., 1976, 2d edit., 1978, Local Government Accounting Fundamentals, 2d edit., 1977, Understanding Federal Assistance Programs, 2d edit., 1978, The POW/MIA Issue: Perspectives on the National League of Families, 1978; contbr. articles to publs. Mem. adv. com. Arlington County Fiscal Affairs, 1993-94; mem. pres. coun. Mary Washington Coll.; bd. mem. U.S. Selective Svc. Sys., Region II Va., 2002-. Mem. D.C. Bar Assn., Hoyas Unltd. (pres. 1992-94), Federalist Soc., Georgetown U. Alumni Assn. (bd. govs. 1975-00, class rep. 1971-91, mem. alumni senate 2000—). Republican. Roman Catholic. Home and Office: 3115 1st Pl N Arlington VA 22201-1037 E-mail: burgessdavid4@aol.com.

BURGESS, DAVID LOWRY, artist; b. Phila., Apr. 27, 1940; s. Eric Turner and Ruth Elizabeth (McNees) Burgess; m. Janet Levengood, Mar. 25, 1960; children: Kirsten Deidre, Audrey Veronica, Vashti Gabrielle. Grad., Pa. Acad. of Fine Art, U. Pa., 1961. Lectr. Phila. Coll. Art, 1964-66; arts advisor Edn. Devel. Center, 1966-68; mem. faculty Harvard U. Sch. Edn., Cambridge, Mass., 1967-68; instr. Boston U., 1969; prof. Mass. Coll. Art, 1969-89; fellow Ctr. Advanced Visual Studies M.I.T., 1971-89; dean Carnegie-Mellon U. Coll. Fine Arts, Pitts., 1989-92, A.W. Mellon prof. art, 1992—; dir. SIMLAB, 1995-97; Koopman disting. chair in art Hartford (Conn.) U. Sch. Art, 2000. Mem. Nat. Humanities faculty, 1968—80; disting. artist ECHO-UQAM, Montreal, Canada; disting. fellow Studio Creative Inquiry, Carnegie Mellon U.; mem. Ctr. for the Arts and Soc. Carnegie Mellon U.; advisor EXPO 2000, Hannover, Germany. Author: (book) Fragments, 1967, Looking and Listening, 1969, Memory, Environment, Utopia, 1973, Burgess: The Quiet Axis Trècarrè, Montreal, Canada, 1987; one-man shows include Inst. Contemporary Art, Boston, 1971, Carpetner Ctr., Harvard U., 1975, MIT, 1978, U. Que., Montreal, 1984, De Cordova Mus., Mass., 1985, 1988, Pa. Acad. Fin Arts Mus., 1987—88, exhibited in group shows at Boston Mus. Fine Arts Elements Exhbn., 1971, Multiple Interaction Team, 1972—74, CAYAC, Spain and Latin Am., 1972—74, Documenta 6, Kassel, Germany, 1977, Vienna Biennal, 1979, Sky Arts Conf, MIT, 1981—83, 1986, Ars Electronica, Austria, 1982, 1986, Kunst Acad., Germany, 1982, Artists Earthwatch, N.Mex., 1984, Monocle, Hamburg, Kunsthalle, Germany, 1985, De Cordova Mus., 1985, Pa. Acad. Fine Arts, 1987—88, Herning Kunst Mus., Denmark, 1989, Kunstverein, Karlsrahe, Germany, 1989, Contemporary Mus., Helsinki, Finland, 1989, Art Transition, 1991, Differentiel, Aix en Provence, France, 1992, Mu Gallery, Boston, 1993, MIT Mus., Cambridge, 1994, Tufts U., Mass., 1995, Pitts. Biennal, 1996, Nagoya City Mus., 1997, Fed. Res. Bank, Boston, 1998, Common Light, Cambridge, 2000, Joselott Mus. Hartford Sch. Art, 2000, Pitts. Ctr. for the Arts, 2003, Represented in permanent collections Boston Mus. Fine Arts, Houghton Libr., Harvard U., Nat. Collection Fine Arts, Washington, Smithsonian Collection, Pa. Acad. Fine Arts, Herning Kunstmuseum, Denmark, De Cordova Mus., Lincoln, Mass., SkyArt, Delphi, Greece, Mandala Pitts. Ctr. Arts, Lincoln Ctr. Galleries, NYC; appearances: (TV series) Nova, Artists in the Lab, 1982; Artists Earthwatch, KNME, 1985; Smithsonian World, 1987; New VR Techs. MSNBC, 1997; Seed of the Infinite Absolute, 2001; appearances (TV series) KQED San Francisco, 2005, Hartford Museum of Political Life, Hartford, Conn., 2002, Pitts. Ctr. for the Arts, 2002. Founding mem. exec. bd. Cambridge Arts Coun.; mem. adv. bd. Art, Edn. and Ams. Recipient Am. Acad. Arts and Letters, Nat. Inst. Arts and Letters award, 1972, Gold award, Le Devoir, Montreal, 1989; fellow Guggenheim, 1973—74; grantee Nat. Endowment Arts, 1977—78, 1984, 1986, Rockefeller Found., 1979—80, 1985—87, Mass. Coun. Arts and Humanities, 1982, 1987—88, Mass. Artists Found., 1983, Cambridge Arts Coun., 2000, Kellogg Found., 2001. Address: 1375 Cordova Rd Pittsburgh PA 15206-1430 Business E-Mail: lb30@andrew.cmu.edu.

BURGESS, EDWIN BOND, librarian, archivist; b. Amarillo, Tex., Sept. 21, 1948; s. Edwin Bond and Jean (MacTaggart) B.; m. Cynthia Ann Adelman, June 20, 1970. BA, Macalester Coll., 1970; MA, U. Minn., 1971. Intern Ft. Leonard Wood (Mo.) Libr., 1972-74; dir. SAFEGUARD, Nekoma, N.D., 1974-75; libr. Post Libr., Ft. Riley, Kans., 1975-76, Concepts Analysis Agy., Bethesda, Md., 1976-77; chief pub. svcs. U.S. Army Commmand and Gen. Staff Coll. Libr., Ft. Leavenworth, Kans., 1978-82; sys. libr. U.S. Army Tng. and Doctrine Command Libr. and Info. Network, Ft. Monroe, Va., 1982-95; archives mgr. Combined Arms Rsch. Libr., Ft. Leavenworth, 1995—2001, dir., 2001—. Reviewer Libr. Jour., 1976—, adv. bd. FL/CC, 2005-, dir Mil. Libr. Divsn. SLA, 2004-. Mem. Kans. Libr. Network Bd., Topeka, 1997-2002. Mem. Spl. Libr. Assn. (chpt. bd. dirs. 1986—), Kansas City Area Archivists. Office: Combined Arms Rsch Libr 250 Gibbon Ave Fort Leavenworth KS 66027-2314 Office Phone: 913-758-3033. E-mail: edwin.burgess@us.army.mil.

BURGESS, JAMES EDWARD, publishing executive; b. LaCrosse, Wis., Apr. 5, 1936; s. William Thomas and Margaret (Forseth) B.; m. Catherine Eleanor, Dec. 20, 1958; children: Karen E. Burgess Hardy, J. Peter, Sydney Ann, R. Curtis Student, Wayland Acad.; BS, U. Wis. Pub. Ind. Record, Helena, Mont., 1969-71, Tribune, LaCrosse, Wisc., 1971-74; v.p. newspapers Lee Enterprises, Davenport, Iowa, 1974-81, exec. v.p., 1981-84, dir., 1974-85, Madison (Wis.) Newspapers, Inc., 1975-93, pres., 1984-93; pub. Wis. State Jour., Madison, 1984-94. Chmn. Edgewood Coll., Madison, 1984—; founder Future Madison, Inc.; chmn. SAVE Commn.; chair bd. dirs. Madison Cmty. Found., U. Wis. Med. Found.; v.p. Madison Mus. Modern Art. Mem. Wis. Newspaper Assn. (past pres.), Inland Daily Press Assn. (pres., chmn. 1982-84), Wis. Assn. Lakes (bd. dirs., pres., chair). Home: 125 N Hamilton St Madison WI 53703

BURGESS, JAMES HARLAND, physics professor, researcher; b. Portland, Oreg., May 11, 1929; s. Harland F. B. and Marion U. (Burgess); m. Dorothy R. Crosby, June 10, 1951; children: Karen, Donald, Joanne. BS, Wash. State U., 1949, MS, 1951; PhD, Washington U., St. Louis, 1955. Sr. engr. Sylvania Electric Products, Mountain View, Calif., 1955-56; research assoc. Stanford U., Palo Alto, Calif., 1956-57, asst. prof. physics, 1958-62; assoc. prof. Washington U., St. Louis, 1962-73, prof., 1973-98, prof. emeritus, 1998—. Cons. in field, 1956-66. Mem. Am. Phys. Soc., Am. Assn. Physics Tchrs., Phi Beta Kappa, Sigma Xi Office: Washington U Physics Dept 1 Brookings Dr Saint Louis MO 63130-4899

BURGESS, JOHN FRANK, retired utilities executive; b. Lanett, Ala., Nov. 18, 1917; s. John Frank and Mary Catherine (Heard) B.; m. Helen Hamby, Aug. 26, 1939; children: Beverly, Barbara, Frank. BS, Auburn U.; MA, George Washington U. Commd. 2d lt. U.S. Army, 1941, advanced through grades to col., ret., 1969; regional v.p. Consol. Edison Co. of N.Y., Inc., N.Y.C., 1969-83; cons. mgmt. Melville, N.Y., 1983-85; assoc. cons. Power Mgmt. Assocs., Inc., Groton, Conn., 1985-87; Columbia, Md., 1985-89. Active bds. various civic and profl. orgns., Queens, N.Y., 1969-83. Decorated Legion of Merit with 2 oak leaf clusters; named Man of Yr. Queens County Bldg and Contractors Assn., 1977 Episcopalian. Home: 9860 Terrace Lake Pt Roswell GA 30076-3742

BURGESS, JOHN HERBERT, cardiologist, educator; b. Montreal, Que., Can., May 24, 1933; s. John Frederick and Willa Reta (McGinness) B.; m. Andrea Clouston Rutherford, May 30, 1958; children: Willa, Cynthia, Lynn, John. BSc, McGill U., Montreal, 1954, MD, CM, 1958. Med. resident Montreal Gen. Hosp., 1958-60, 62-64, dir. div. cardiology, 1973-94; Nuffield rsch. fellow U. Birmingham, Eng., 1960-62; McLaughlin rsch. fellow Cardiovascular Rsch. Inst., San Francisco, 1964-66; asst. prof. medicine McGill U., 1966-69, assoc. prof., 1969-75, prof., 1975—. Emeritus cardiologist McGill U. Health Ctr. Contbr. articles to profl. jours. Decorated Order of Can.; hon. fellow Coll. Medicine, South Africa. Master ACP; fellow Am. Coll. Cardiology, Royal Coll. Physicians and Surgeons Can. (pres. 1990-92), Royal Coll. Physicians (Edinburgh), Royal Australasian Coll. Physicians (hon.), Royal Coll. Physicians (London); mem. Can. Soc. Clin. Investigation. Avocations: cross country skiing, photography. Home: 639 Murray Hill Westmount PQ Canada H3Y 2W8 Office: Montreal Gen Hospital 1650 Cedar Ave Montreal PQ Canada H3G 1A4 Office Phone: 514-934-1934. Business E-Mail: john.burgess@muhc.mcgill.ca.

BURGESS, LARRY EUGENE, library director, historian, educator; b. Montrose, Colorado, July 18, 1945; s. Eugene Floyd and Edyth Eleanor (Faussone) B.; m. Charlotte Reid (Gaylord), Oct. 7, 1973. BA, U. Redlands, Calif., 1967; MA, Claremont Grad. Sch., 1969, PhD, 1972. Archivist A.K. Smiley Pub. Libr., Redlands, Calif., 1972-85, libr. dir., 1986—. Adj. prof. history, U. Redlands, 1972—, U. Calif., Riverside, 1979—; book reviewer Lincoln Herald, 1988—. Author: Mohonk: Its People and Spirit, 1980; (with others) A Day with Mr. Lincoln, (with others), 1994; co-author: The Hunt for Willie Boy, 1994. Vice-chmn. Calif. Heritage Preservattion Commn., 1977-84; Hist. Soc. So. Calif., L.A., pres., 2003—; bd. dirs. U. Redlands, 1987-2001. Recipient Archival Award of Excellence Calif. Heritage Preservation Commn., 1991; Preservation Merit Award Calif. Hist. Soc., 1992, Cmty. Enrichment Award Hist. Soc. So. Calif., 1994. Mem. Soc. Am. Archivists, So. Calif. Archivists (past pres.), Zamorano Club (bd. dir. 1994—, pres. 1999-2002), Rotary Club Relands (pres. 1999-2000). Avocations: travel, gardening, book collecting. Home: 923 W Fern Ave Redlands CA 92373-5877 Office: A K Smiley Pub Libr 125 W Vine St Redlands CA 92373-4728 Office Phone: 909-798-7565. E-mail: admin@aksmiley.org, admin@akspl.org.

BURGESS, LYNNE A, lawyer; B, William Smith Coll.; JD, Fordham U. Asst. gen. counsel Am. Nat. Can Co.; of counsel Colier, Shannon, Rill & Scott, Washington, 1992—94; sr. v.p., gen. counsel Entex Info. Services, 1994—2000; gen. counsel and sec. governance com. Oliver, Wyman & Co. LLC, 2001—02; v.p., gen. counsel Asbury Automotive Group, 2002—. Office: Asbury Automotive Group 622 Third Ave 37th Fl New York NY 10017

BURGESS, MARJORIE LAURA, retired protective services official; b. Whitakers, N.C., Nov. 24, 1928; d. Benjamin and Laura Lenora (Ford) Harrison; m. Bonus David Dixon, July 24, 1948 (div. Apr. 1970); children: David Kingsley (dec.), Terence David, Michael Jerome; m. William A. Burgess, June 6, 1970 (div. July 1976). AS in Correction Adminstrn., John Jay Coll. Criminal, Justice, N.Y.C., 1971; BA in Social Scis., John Jay Coll Criminal Justice, N.Y.C., 1972, postgrad., 1973-75. Correction officer N.Y. State Dept. Correction, Bedford Hills, N.Y., 1959-67, correction sgt., 1967-73, correction lt., 1973-82, 86-90, capt., 1982-86; ret., 1990. Adv. coun. divsn. sr. svcs. Bergen County, 1997. Author: (poetry) Walking on the Road of Life, 1997, Life! It's More Than A Notion, libr. of congress Watermark press, 2000. Vol. intergenerational program Martin Luther King Srs. Ctr. Mem. AAUW, Am. Correctional Assn., Alumni Assn. John Jay Coll., The Smithsonian Assocs., Retired Pub. Employees Assn., AARP. Democrat. Baptist. Avocations: writing, singing, playing scrabble, reading.

BURGESS, MICHAEL, librarian, writer; b. Fukuoka, Kyushu, Japan, Feb. 11, 1948; came to U.S., 1949; s. Roy Walter and Betty Jane (Kapel) B.; m. Mary Alice Wickizer, Oct. 15, 1976; stepchildren: Richard Albert Rogers, Mary Louise Reynnells AB with honors, Gonzaga U., 1969; MLS, U. So. Calif., 1970. Periodicals librarian Calif. State U., San Bernardino, 1970-81, chief cataloger, 1981-94, prof., 1984—2005, head tech. svcs. and collection devel., 1994—2005, emeritus, 2005—. Editor Newcastle Pub. Co., North Hollywood, Calif., 1971—92; pub. Borgo Press, San Bernardino, 1975—91, Brownstone Books, San Bernardino, 1991—99, Sidewinder Press, San Bernardino, 1991—99, Unicorn & Son, San Bernardino, 1991—99, Burgess & Wickizer, San Bernardino, 1991—99, Emeritus Enterprises, 1993—99, Starmont House, 1993—99; assoc. editor SFRA Rev., 1993—94, Millefleurs Info. Svcs., San Bernardino, 2000—. Author 96 books and short works under pen names Michael Burgess, R(obert) Reginald, Boden Clarke, and others, with occasional co-authors, including: Stella Nova, 1970, Cumulative Paperback Index, 1939-1959, 1973, Contemporary Science Fiction Authors, 1975, The Attempted Assassination of John F. Kennedy, 1976, Things to Come, 1977, Up Your Asteroid!, 1977, Science Fiction and Fantasy Literature, a Checklist, 1700-1974, 1979, The Paperback Price Guide, 1980, 2nd edit., 1983, Science Fiction & Fantasy Awards, 1981, If J.F.K. Had Lived, 1982, The House of Burgesses, 1983, 2nd edit., 1994, The Wickizer Annals, 1983, Tempest in a Teapot, 1983, A Guide to Science Fiction & Fantasy in the Library of Congress Classification Scheme, 1984, 2nd edit., 1988, The Work of Jeffrey M. Elliot, 1984, Futurevisions, 1985, Lords Temperal & Lords Spiritual, 1985, 2nd edit., 1995, The Work of Julian May, 1985, The Work of R. Reginald, 1985, The Work of George Zebrowski, 1986, 2nd edit., 1990, 3rd edit., 1996, Mystery and Detective Fiction in the Library of Congress Classification Scheme, 1988, The Work of William F. Nolan, 1988, 2nd edit., 1998, The Arms Control, Disarmament, and Military Security Dictionary, 1989, Hancer's Price Guide to Paperback Books, 3d edit., 1990, Reginald's Science Fiction and Fantasy Awards, 2nd edit., 1991, 3d edit., 1993, Reference Guide to Science Fiction, Fantasy, and Horror, 1992, Science Fiction and Fantasy Literature, 1975-1991, 1992, The Work of Robert Reginald, 2nd edit., 1992, The State and Province Vital Records Guide, 1993, The Work of Katherine Kurtz, 1993, St. James Guide to Science Fiction Writers, 1996, CSUSB Faculty Authors, Composers and Playwrights, 1996, rev. edit., 1996, BP 250, 1996, Xenograffiti, 1996, Codex Derynianus, 1998, Katydid and other Critters, 2001, The Dark-Haired Man, 2004, The Exiled Prince, 2004, Quaestiones, 2004, Murder in Retrospect, 2005; editor: Ancestral Voices, 1975, Alistair MacLean, 1976, Ancient Hauntings, 1976, Phantasmagoria, 1976, R.I.P., 1976, The Spectre Bridegroom and Other Horrors, 1976, John D. MacDonald and the Colorful World of Travis McGee, 1977, Dreamers of Dreams, 1978, King Solomon's Children, 1978, They, 1978, Worlds of Never, 1978, Science Fiction & Fantasy Book Review, 1980, Candle for Poland, 1982, The Holy Grail Revealed, 1982, The Work of Bruce McAllister, 1985, rev. edit., 1986, George Orwell's Guide Through Hell, 1986, 2nd edit., 1994, The Work of Charles Beaumont, 1986, 2nd edit., 1990, California Ranchos, 1988, The Work of Chad Oliver, 1989, The Work of Colin Wilson, 1989, The Work of Ian Watson, The Work of Reginald Bretnor, 1989, The Work of Ross Rocklynne, 1989, To Kill or Not To Kill, 1990, The Work of Dean Ing, 1990, The Work of Jack Dann, 1990, The Work of Pamela Sargent, 1990, 2nd edit., 1996, The Trilemma of World Oil Politics, 1991, The Work of Louis L'Amour, 1991, The Work of Brian W. Aldiss, 1992, Geo. Alec Effinger, 1993, Polemical Pulps, 1993, Sermons in Science Fiction, 1994, The Work of Elizabeth Chater, 1994, The Work of Jack Vance, 1994, The Work of William Eastlake, 1994, The Work of William F. Temple, 1994, The Work of Gary Brandner, 1995, The Work of Stephen King, 1996, Running From The Hunter, 1996; author of 13,000 essays, 20 short stories; editor of 1,250 books. Recipient MPPP award, 1987, Lifetime Collectors award for Contbn. to Bibliography, 1993, Pilgrim award, 1993; named title II fellow U. So. Calif., 1969-70. Mem. NEA, ACLU, Sci. Fiction and Fantasy Writers Am., Mystery Writers Am., Calif. Tchrs. Assn., Calif. Faculty Assn. (statewide librs. task force 1986-89, 93—, editor newsletter 1987-89), San Bernardino Hist. and Pioneer Soc., Internat. PEN, U.S.A. Ctr. West, Sci. Fiction Rsch. Assn., Horror Writers Am. Office: Millefleurs PO Box 2845 San Bernardino CA 92406-2845 also: Calif State U Libr 5500 University Pkwy San Bernardino CA 92407-2318

BURGESS, MICHAEL, congressman; b. Denton, Tex., Dec. 23, 1950; m. Laura Burgess; 3 children. BS, MS, North Tex. State U.; MD, U. Tex., Houston; M in Med. Mgmt., U. Tex., Dallas. Resident Parkland Hosp., Dallas; pvt. practice Ob-Gyn. Assocs., Lewisville, Tex.; chief of staff Lewisville Med. Ctr., chief obs.; mem.26th Dist. Tex. U.S. Ho. Reps. from 26th Tex. dist., 2003—; mem. transp. and infrastructure com. U.S. Ho. Reps., mem. sci. com. Mem.: Denton County Med. Soc. (pres.). Republican. Office: 1721 Longworth HOB Washington DC 20515 also: Ste 230 1660 S Stemmons Fwy Lewisville TX 75067*

BURGESS, MICHAEL PATRICK, JR., music educator, singer; b. Chgo., Aug. 3, 1965; s. Michael Patrick Burgess and Deborah Sue Dunnett; m. Andrea Gay Beute, Aug. 24, 1991; children: Olivia Joy, Mackenzie Patrick, Chloe Marie. Dr. in Musical Arts, U. Mich., 2001. Singer: O, You White Towns (premier performance) (Best of Classical Music, San Antonio Express News, 2004). Cantor, soloist, choir vocal clinician Abiding Presence Luth. Ch., San Antonio, Tex., 2002—05. Mem.: Nat. Assn. Tchrs. Singing (v.p., auditions co-chair south Tex. chpt. 2004—), Pi Kappa Lambda (Beta Sigma chpt.). Republican. Lutheran. Avocations: golf, reading, camping, guitar, landscaping/gardening. Home: 15218 Moonlit Grove San Antonio TX 78247 Office: University of Texas at San Antonio 6900 Loop 1604 West - Dept of Music San Antonio TX 78249 Office Phone: 210-458-5677. Personal E-mail: operaman_um@yahoo.com. E-mail: michael.burgess@utsa.edu.

BURGESS, RICHARD RAY, oncologist, educator, molecular biologist, researcher, biotechnologist, consultant; b. Mt. Vernon, Wash., Sept. 8, 1942; s. Robert Carl and Irene Marjorie (Wegner) B.; m. Ann Baker, June 17, 1967; children— Kristin, Andreas BS in Chemistry, Calif. Inst. Tech., 1964; PhD in Biochemistry and Molecular Biology, Harvard U., 1969. Helen Hay Whitney fellow Inst. Molecular Biology, Geneva, 1969-71; asst. prof. oncology McArdle Lab. Cancer Research U. Wis., Madison, 1971-77, assoc. prof., 1977-82, prof., 1982—, dir. Biotech. Ctr., 1984-96, James D. Watson Prof. Oncology, 2001—. Cons. in field; mem. NSF study sect. in biochemistry, 1979-84; chmn. bd. Consortium for Plant Biotech. Rsch., Inc., 1992-96. Series editor U. Wis. Biotech. Ctr. Resource Manuals; editor-in chief Jour. Protein Expression and Purification, 1990—; contbr. articles to profl. jours. Bd. dirs. Coun. Biotech. Ctrs., 1991-93; mem. Gov.'s Coun. on Biotech. Grantee NSF, 1978-80, 85-90, NIH, 1980—, Nat. Cancer Inst., 1971—; Guggenheim fellow, 1983-84; recipient medal Waksman Inst., 1999. Fellow Am. Acad. Microbiology; mem. Am. Soc. Biochemistry and Molecular Biology, Am. Chem. Soc. (Pfizer award 1982), Am. Assn. Cancer Research, Am. Soc. Microbiology, Protein Soc. Home: 10 Knollwood Ct Madison WI 53713-3479 Office: U Wis McArdle Lab Cancer Rsch 1400 University Ave Madison WI 53706-1526 Office Phone: 608-263-2635.

BURGESS, ROBERT KINGSLEY, aeronautical engineer; b. Englewood, N.J., May 27, 1929; s. Charles Leon Burgess and Nina Doris King; m. Arlene Doris Killian, June 25, 1960; children: Holly Robaczynski, Kristin Hummel. BS in Aero. Engring., Purdue U., 1951; postgrad., NYU, 1953—55, New Haven Coll., 1956—57. Registered profl. engr., Conn. Flight test engr. Sikorsky Aircraft, Stanford, Conn., 1951—62, project engr., 1962—70, chief sys. engring. ABC helicopter, 1970—74, tech. dir. internat. mktg., 1974—77, chief test ABC helicopter, 1977—78, chief competitive evaluation, 1978—79, chief engring. changes UH-60A, 1979—83, H-60 deriviative engring. mgr., 1983—85; sr. project engr. AH-64A McDonnell Douglas, Mesa, Ariz., 1985—86, project mgr. engring. change control, 1986—90, dept. mgr. product sustainment, 1990—91, dept. mgr. AH-64B, 1991—92, engring. project mgr. AH-64A/B/D, 1991—. Test pilot, cons. engr. Bridgeport (Conn.) Flight Svc., 1959; design engr. Auto Parts Mfg., Inc., Branford, Conn., 1979—81; cons. engr. Newport (RI) Offshore, Ltd., 1981—82. Contbr. articles to profl. jours. Mem.: AHS, AIAA, Aircraft Owners and Pilots Assn. Achievements include patents for electrically heated windshield wiper blade for ground vehicles. Avocation: flying. Home: 8120 E Appaloosa Tr Scottsdale AZ 85258 Office: Boeing Co 5000 E McDowell Rd Mesa AZ 85215 Office Phone: 480-891-6938. Business E-Mail: bob.burgess@boeing.com.

BURGESS, ROBERT KYLE, lawyer; b. Fairfield, Iowa, Sept. 5, 1948; s. Charles and Eleanor Pearl (Morris) B.; children: Alyssa, Kristen, Ryan; m. Michelle Wenz. BS, Northwestern U., 1970, JD, 1973. Bar: Calif. 1973, U.S. Dist. Ct. (cen. dist.) Calif. 1974, U.S. Tax Ct. 1975, U.S. Ct. Appeals (9th cir.) 1976, U.S. Ct. Appeals (5th cir.) 1977, U.S. Supreme Ct. 1977, D.C. 1980, U.S. Dist. Ct. Md. 1980, U.S. Ct. Appeals (D.C. cir.) 1981, Ill. 1982. Assoc. Latham & Watkins, Los Angeles, 1973-78, Washington, 1978-81, ptnr., 1981-82, Chgo., 1982-95; sr. v.p., gen. counsel, sec. Am. Re Corp., Princeton, N.J., 1995-97, exec. v.p., gen. counsel, sec., 1997—. Mem. Calif. Bar Assn., Ill. Bar Assn., D.C. Bar Assn. Office: Am Re Corp 555 College Rd E Princeton NJ 08540-6616

BURGESS, ROBERT RONALD, human resources executive; b. Memphis, Dec. 2, 1943; s. Doyle Eugene Burgess and Mildred Burgess (Sparks) Hamill; m. Suzie Strong, June 28, 1985; 1 child, Mary Weldon. BS in Psychology, Memphis State U., 1967, MEd, 1975, EdD (ABD), 1979. Dir. Teen Challenge, Vienna, Austria, 1971-73; religious affairs coord. Memphis State U., 1973-80; dir. human resources The Peabody, Memphis, 1980-81, GE/RCA, Memphis, N.Y.C., 1981-86; exec. dir. The Promus Companies, Memphis, 1986-99; v.p. human resources Argosy Gaming Co., Alton, Ill., 1999—. Chmn. coord. coun. Profl. Religious Assn. in Higher Edn., N.Y.C., 1978-79. Editor: Dialogue on Campus, 1978. Fund raiser WKNO Edn. T.V., Memphis, 1989, United Way, Memphis, 1988. With U.S. Army, 1969-71. Recipient Disting. Svc. award U.S. Army, Berlin, 1971. Mem. Human Resources Assn., Human Resources Planning Soc. (corp. sponsor 1989—), St. Louis Club. Avocations: antique restoration, gardening, fatherhood. Home: 50 Berkshire Dr Saint Louis MO 63117-1046 Office: Argosy 219 Piasa St Alton IL 62002-6232

BURGESS, ROBERT SARGENT, retired human services consultant; b. Providence, Oct. 19, 1916; s. Alexander Manlius and Abby (bullock) B.; m. Ruth Elizabeth Carter, Sept. 21, 1940 (dec.); children: Joan Chesebro, Marjorie Waite, Robert S. Jr., David Dyer; m. Mary Lou Hemmerling, June 4, 1999. BA, Brown U., 1938; MA, U. Chgo., 1943. Cert. social worker. Field sec. Am. Friends Svc. Com., midwest area, 1938-41; asst. dir. Ill. Bd. Welfare Commrs., Chgo., 1942-43; asst. warden RI Correctional Instns., Cranston, RI, 1943-46; sr. supr. RI Divsn. Pub. Assistance, Providence, 1946-50; exec. dir. RI Heart Assn., Providence, 1950-57; planning dir. Health & Welfare Assn., Pitts., 1957—64; exec. dir. RI Coun. Cmty. Svcs., Providence, 1964-74; ret. Spl. del. Internat. Conf. Social Welfare, The Hague, Nairobi and San Juan, 1972-75; cons. Conservation Commn., Hanover, NH, 1991-99. Author: (book) "To Try the Bloody Law" the story of Mary Dyer. Pres. RIConsumers Coop., Providence, 1947-51; 1st male mem., bd. dirs. Planned Parenthood of RI, Providence, 1968-71; chmn. RI State Coun. on Aging, Providence, 1969-71, Mass. Bd. Pub. Welfare, Boston, 1973-78, chmn., 1975-78; chmn. Providence Model Cities Coun., 1973. Mem. NASW (nat. bd. dirs. 1971-74, Robert S. Burgess Comty Svc. award), Am. Friends Svc. Com., Democratic Socialist Am., Conservation Law Found., Adult Chamber Music Players, Assn. for Statewide Health and Welfare (nat. pres. 1972-73). Socialist. Avocations: tennis, squash, square dance calling, writing, orchestra and quartet playing. Home: 80 Lyme Rd Apt 167 Hanover NH 03755-1230

BURGESS, RUTH LENORA VASSAR, speech and language educator; b. Pune, India, Aug. 6, 1939; d. Theodore R. and F. Estelle (Barnett) Vassar; m. Stanley Milton Burgess, Feb. 26, 1960; children: John Bradley, Stanley Matthew, Scott Vassar, Heidi Amanda Elizabeth, Justin David. BS in Edn., Tex. Tech. U., 1960; MA, U. Mo., 1968, PhD, 1979. Speech therapist Inkster (Mich.) Pub. Schs., 1961-62; mid. sch. tchr. Strafford (Mo.) Pub. Schs., 1962-63; speech therapist Fulton (Mo.) Pub. Schs., 1967-68; speech-lang. clinician Springfield (Mo.) Pub. Schs., 1963-66; asst. prof. Evangel Coll., Springfield, 1968-76; prof. Sch. Tchr. Edn. S.W. Mo. State U., Springfield, 1976—2005, dir. Ctr. Rsch. and Svc., 1990-97; adj. prof. Regent U., Va., 2005—. Mem. sci. adv. bd. Internat. Ctr. Enhancement of Jerusalem, Israel, 1993—; field reviewer Dept. Edn., Washington, 1993-96, U.S. Vocat. Rehab., Washington, 1993, 94, 96,99; mem. evaluation team Title I Springfield Schs., 1994. Author: The Status of the Educational Resource Teacher, 1981, Shantistan: A Peace Building Curriculum, 2005; editor The Learner in the Process, 1978-80; contbr. articles to profl. jours. Ex-officio bd. dirs. Orphanage Assn., Pune, 1968—; mem. Kodaikanal-Woodstock Alumni Assn., Atlanta, 1956—; mem. Women Issues Network, Springfield, 1993-2005. Grantee Dept. Edn., 1978-83, 90-92, Dept. Elem. and Secondary Edn., 96, Mellon Found., 1988-90. Mem. AAUW, ASCD, Am. Speech, Lang. and Hearing Assn. (cert.), Internat. Assn. for Cognitive Edn. (field editor 1990-94). Avocations: literary group, hiking, creative writing, travel, advocacy. Office: SW Mo State U 901 S National Ave Springfield MO 65804-0088 Personal E-mail: rvburgess@earthlink.net.

BURGESS, TIMOTHY M., prosecutor; b. 1956; BA, MBA, U. Alaska; JD, Northeastern U. Assoc. Gilmore and Feldman, Anchorage, 1987—89; asst. US atty dist. AK US Dept. Justice, 1989—2001, US atty. dist. AK, 2001—. Office: Fed Bldg & US Courthouse 222 W 7th Ave #9 Rm 253 Anchorage AK 99513-7567

BURGET, DEAN EDWIN, JR., plastic surgeon; b. Toledo, June 29, 1936; s. Dean E. Sr. and Marie E. (Alwine) B.; m. A. Undine Ehrman, Mar. 16, 1957 (div. Mar. 1993); children: Mark A.E., Kevin Phillips, Undine Peeples; m. Gabriella Morocz, May 14, 1993. BS, U. Toledo, 1958; MD, Yale U., 1962. Diplomate Am. Bd. Plastic Surgery. Intern surgery U. Hosps., Cleve., 1962, resident in anesthesiology, 1963; resident in gen. surgery Hahnemann Med. Coll. and Hosp., Phila., 1966-68, asst. prof., dir. divsn. plastic surgery, 1972-75; resident in plastic surgery Temple U. Hosp., Phila., 1968-70, U.S. Govt. fellow in rehab. surgery, 1970-71, instr. plastic surgery, 1970-71, Med. Coll. Pa., Phila., 1970-71, assoc. clin. prof., 1979-81; staff surgeon, cons. surgeon various cmty. hosps., 1975-85; pvt. practice Devon, Pa., 1985—. Fellow ACS; mem. Am. Soc. Plastic and Reconstructive Surgeons, Pickering Hunt Club (Phila.), Ausable Club/Adirondack Mountain Res. (St. Huberts, NY), Yale Club (NYC), Rittenhouse Club (Phila.), Penn Club, St. Nicholas Soc. City of NY, Pa. Soc. Sons Revolution, Colonial Soc. Pa., Soc. Colonial Wars Pa., Nat. Huguenot Soc., Soc. War 1812, Phila. Soc. Promoting Agr. Office: 500 Chesterbrook Blvd Wayne PA 19087 Office Phone: 610-644-8225.

BURGGRAF, FRANK BERNARD, JR., landscape architect, retired educator; b. N.Y.C., Nov. 13, 1932; s. Frank Bernard and Johanna (Verbaan) B.; m. Jane Martin Rannenberg, June 25, 1955 (div. 1997); children: Helen Marguerite, Frank Bernard, John Christian; m. Margaret Goff, Oct. 31, 1998. BS, SUNY-Syracuse, 1954; MLA, U. Pa., 1958. Registered landscape architect, N.Y. Asst. prof. U. Ga., Athens, 1958-63; assoc. prof., dir. regional planning grad. program Pa. State U., University Park, 1963-70; chief planning analyst N.Y. State Pub. Service Commn., Albany, 1970-80; cons. landscape architect, planner Delmar, N.Y., 1980-84; prof. landscape architecture U. Ark., Fayetteville, 1984-97, dir. program in landscape architecture, 1984-87, emeritus prof. landscape architecture, 1997—. Mem. N.Y. State Bd. Landscape Architecture, 1977-84, chmn., 1979-81 Contbr. articles to profl. jours. Pres. Winslow Cmty. Devel. Coun., 2002—; bd. dirs. Fayetteville Mcpl. Airport, 1997—2002. Served to lt. col. USAF, 1954—81. Fellow Am. Soc. Landscape Architects; mem. Am. Planning Assn., Elks (exalted ruler local lodge, 1990). Democrat. Home: 18665 Brentwood Mountain Rd Winslow AR 72959-9755 Personal E-mail: fburggraf@hotmail.com.

BURGHARDT, RAYMOND FRANCIS, JR., former ambassador; b. NYC, May 27, 1945; s. Raymond Francis and Marguerite (Schroeder) B.; m. Susan Day, Aug. 2, 1969; children: Helen, Caroline. BA, Columbia Coll., 1967; postgrad., Columbia Sch. Internat. Affrs., 1967-68. With U.S. Fgn. Svc., 1969—; dep. dir. Office of Vietnam, Laos and Cambodia Dept. of State, Washington, 1980-82; polit. counselor U.S. Embassy, Tegucigalpa, Honduras, 1982-84; dir. Latin Am. affairs Nat. Security Coun., Washington, 1984-85, spl. asst. to pres., sr. dir. Latin Am., 1985-87; polit. counselor U.S. Embassy, Beijing, 1987-89, dep. chief of mission Seoul, Korea, 1990-93, charge d'affaires, 1993, dep. chief of mission Manila, 1994-96, U.S. consul gen. Shanghai, 1997—99; dir. Am. Inst., Taiwan, 1999—2001; US amb. to Vietnam US Dept. State, Hanoi, 2001—04. Mem. Am. Fgn. Svc. Assn., Asia Soc. Avocations: cross country skiing, hiking, music.*

BURGHART, JAMES HENRY, electrical engineer, educator; b. Erie, Pa., July 18, 1938; s. Chester Albert and Mary Virginia (Burke) B.; m. Judith Ann Hoff, July 8, 1961; children— Jill Kathryn, Mark Alan. BS in Elec. Engring, Case Inst. Tech., 1960, MS (U.S. Steel Found. fellow 1961-63), 1962, PhD, 1965. Asst. prof., then assoc. prof. elec. engring. SUNY, Buffalo, 1969-75; prof. elec. engring. Cleve. State U., 1975—2005, chmn. dept., 1975-85, 89-97. Served as officer USAF, 1965-68. Mem. IEEE (chmn. Cleve. sect. 1980-81, sec. region 2 1989-96, profl. activities coord. region 2 1997-2000, Ohio area chair region 2 2001—2002, awards and recognition chair, 2003), Am. Soc. Engring. Edn., Sigma Xi, Eta Kappa Nu. Home: 5501 Strathaven Dr Cleveland OH 44143-1970 Office: 1983 E 24th St Cleveland OH 44115-2403 E-mail: j.burghart@ieee.org.

BURGHEIM, RICHARD, magazine editor; b. St. Louis, July 5, 1933; s. Nathaniel H. and Mary (Rudman) B. BA, Harvard U., 1955. Writer Time Mag., N.Y.C., 1960-71; dir. cable TV programming Time Inc., N.Y.C., 1972-73; editor People Mag., N.Y.C., 1974-81, 89-92; mng. editor TV-Cable Week, White Plains, N.Y., 1982-83; editor Life Mag., N.Y.C., 1984—85, Money Mag., N.Y.C., 1986-89; cons. editor Time Inc., N.Y.C., 1993—, N.Y. Times Upfront, 1999—2005. Cons. cable programming Ford Found., N.Y.C., 1972; lectr. Harvard Inst. Telecomm. and Pub. Policy, Cambridge, 1972. Bd. dirs. Children's Express, N.Y.C., 1994-97, Doe Fund, N.Y.C., 1999—, Goddard Riverside Comty. Ctr., N.Y.C., 1999—. USCG, 1956-59. Home: 230 Central Park W Apt 16D New York NY 10024-6040 Office: Time Inc Time And Life Bldg New York NY 10020

BURGHER, CEDRIC W., food service executive; BBA, U. Tex.; MBA, U. Dallas. Chartered fin. analyst. With Baker Hughes, Inc., Houston; v.p. fin. planning, treas. Enron Oil & Gas Co.; v.p. investor rels. Enron; CFO Enron Global E&P; with Halliburton, Houston, 2001, v.p. investor rels., 2002—04; exec. v.p. Burger King Corp., 2004—, CFO, 2004—, mem. exec. leadership team, 2004—. Office: Burger King Corp 5505 Blue Lagoon Dr Miami FL 33126

BURGHER, KARL E., academic administrator; married. BS with honors, Mich. Tech. U., 1980, MS in Mining Engring., 1982; BS cum laude, U. Mo., Rolla, 1984, PhD in Mining Engring., 1985, PhD (hon.) in Econs., 2003. Project mgr. Mine Waste Tech. Programs Mont. Tech. of U. Mont., 1994—2004, dir. NewMedia Group, 1998—2004; interim chair Dept. Econs. and Fin. U. Mo., Rolla, 2003—04, vis. prof. econs., mining, and engring. depts., 2003—04; vice pres. Rsch. and Contracts, interim chief tech. officer Fairmont State U. & Fairmont State Cmty. and Technical Coll., 2004—05; pres. U. Maine, Presque Isle, 2005—. Pres. Karl E. Burgher & Assocs., 1986—. Mem.: Yau Beta Pi, Sigma XI Rsch. Soc. Avocations: reading, golf, tennis, fishing. Office: U Maine at Presque Isle 181 Main St Presque Isle ME 04769-2888*

BURGIN, CHARLES EDWARD, lawyer; b. Marion, N.C., Dec. 16, 1938; m. Ellen Salsbury Burgin; children: Ellen, Lucy. BA, U. N.C., 1961; LLB, Duke U., 1964. Bar: N.C.; U.S. Supreme Ct. Law clk. to Hon. J. Braxton Craven Jr. U.S. Dist. Ct., U.S. Ct. Appeals, 1964-66; prosecuting atty. McDowell County Criminal Ct., 1966-68; sr. ptnr. Dameron, Burgin & Parker, P.A., Marion, N.C., 1968—. Bd. dirs. Shadowline, Inc.; lectr. in field. Contbr. articles to profl. jours. Bd. dirs. McDowell County Recreation Commn. 1977-87, First Union Nat. Bank 1975—; McDowell County Mountain Rescue Team 1980—; McDowell Arts and Crafts Assn. 1980—. Named Legalelite in N.C., Bus. N.C., 2004. Fellow Am. Coll. Trial Lawyers (state chmn. 1996-98, named Best Lawyers in Am. 1993—), Internat. Soc. Barristers, Am. Bar Found.; mem. ABA, N.C. Bar Assn. (pres. 1993-94), Defense Rsch. Inst., Am. Soc. Hosp. Attys., N.C. Assn. Defense Lawyers, U.S. Supreme Ct. Bar Assn. Office: Dameron Burgin & Parker PA PO Drawer 1049 26 W Court St Marion NC 28752-3906 Office Phone: 828-652-2441. E-mail: cburgin@dameronburginlaw.com.

BURGIN, GEORGE HANS, computer scientist, educator; b. Liestal, Switzerland, Feb. 13, 1930; s. Jakob and Fanny B.; m. Ulrike Franziska, July 8, 1960; children: Bernard, Claudia, Paul. Diplom ingenieur, Swiss Fed. Inst. Tech., Zurich, 1953, PhD, 1961. Cert. profl. engr., Calif. Design specialist Gen. Dynamics Corp., San Diego, 1962-64; sr. scientist Decision Sci., 1964-82; chief scientist Titan Systems, 1982-94; prin. staff engr. Titan Info. Systems, 1994-96, chief engr., 1996-98; staff engr. CommQuest Techs., 1998-99, IBM/Encinitas, 1999-2000, Triton Newtork Systems, 2000—01; sr. staff scientist Natural Selection, Inc., La Jolla, Calif., 2002—. Lectr. San Diego State U., 1979—89. Contbg. author: book Simulation, 2d edit., 1989; author: (program) Adaptive Maneuvering Logic; contbr. articles profl. jours. 1st lt. Swiss Army. Mem.: IEEE. Achievements include invention of adaptive maneuvering logic air combat simulation program; U.S. patented algorithm for a quadrature modulator precompensation. Home: 6284 Avenida Cresta La Jolla CA 92037-6505 Office: Natural Selection Inc 3333 N Torrey Pines Ct La Jolla CA 92037 Office Phone: 858-455-6449. Business E-Mail: gburgin@natural-selection.com.

BURGIN, RICHARD WESTON, writer, educator, editor; b. Brookline, Mass., Mar. 30, 1947; s. Richard and Ruth (Posselt) B.; m. Linda Kinnard Harris, Sept. 7, 1991 (div.); 1 child, Richard Daniel. BA with honors, Brandeis U., 1968; MA with highest honors, Columbia U., 1969, MPhil in Modern Am. Lit., 1980. Instr. English Tufts U., Medford, Mass., 1970-74; editor N.Y. Arts Jour., N.Y.C., 1975-80; assoc. prof. Drexel U., Phila., 1984-96; prof. St. Louis U., 1996—2005, prof. comm. and English, 2005—. Vis. lectr. U. Calif., Santa Barbara, 1981-83 Author: Ghost Quartet, 1999; (short stories) The Spirit Returns: Stories, 2000, The Identity Club: New and Selected Stories, 2005, Man Without Memory, 1989, Private Fame, 1991, Fear of Blue Skies, 1998, Conversations with Jorge Luis Borges, 1969, Conversations with Isaac Bashevis Singer, 1985, Stories and Dream Boxes, 2002; editor: Jorge Luis Borges: Conversations, 1998; editor Blvd. Mag., 1985—; composer: (CD) In All of the World, 2000, House of Sun, 2001, Doll of Dreams, 2002; contbr. articles to mags. Recipient Pushcart Press prize, 1982, 86, 98, 2002. Mem. Nat. Book Critics Cir., St. Louis Writers Workshop. Avocations: travel, sports. Office: Blvd 4579 Laclede Ave # 332 Saint Louis MO 63108-2103 Home: Apt 2N 7545 Cromwell Dr Saint Louis MO 63105-2966 Office Phone: 314-862-2643. Business E-Mail: kingd@slu.edu.

BURGIN, WALTER HOTCHKISS, JR., retired academic administrator; b. Harrisburg, Pa., Apr. 14, 1935; s. Walter Hotchkiss and Wilhelmina (Buntin) B.; m. Barbara Isabelle Waddell, June 15, 1957; children: Christine, Jennifer. AB, Dartmouth Coll., 1957; postgrad., Princeton U., 1957-59; EdM, Harvard U., 1964. Tchr. math. Phillips Exeter (N.H.) Acad., 1964-72, Mercersburg (Pa.) Acad., 1959-64, chmn. dept., 1961-64, headmaster, 1972-97; tchr. math. Sidwell Friends Sch., Washington, 1997-98; exec. dir. Edward E. Ford Found., Washington, 1998—2002; tchr. math. Maret Sch., Washington, 2002—04; ret., 2004. Mem. Pa. Bd. for Pvt. Acad. Schs., 1973—94; bd. dirs. Assist. Bd. trustees Maret Sch., Washington; hon. regent Mercersburg Acad.; bd. adv., vice-chair Edward E. Ford Found. NSF fellow, 1957-59, Shell fellow, 1964. Mem. Math. Assn. Am., Nat. Assn. Prins. Sch. for Girls, Headmasters Assn. (treas. 1993-96, v.p. 1996-97), Nat. Coun. Tchrs. Math., Nat. Assn. Ind. Schs. (bd. dirs. 1989-96, sec. 1992-96), Pa. Assn. Ind. Schs. (exec. com. 1980-90), Calif. Ct. Assn. (bd. pres.). Democrat. Mem. United Ch. of Christ. Home: 2153 California St NW Apt 402 Washington DC 20008-1845 Personal E-mail: whburgin@aol.com.

BURGIN, WILLIAM LYLE, architect; b. Colorado Springs, Colo., Apr. 30, 1946; m. Virginia Margaret Wojtul, Sept. 23, 1967; 1 child, Desdemona. BA, R.I. Sch. Design, 1972, BArch, 1973. Ptnr. Estes/Burgin Partnership, Providence, 1980-89; pres. William L. Burgin Architects, Newport, R.I., 1989—. V.p. Jamestown Hist. Soc., 1994. Recipient Preservation award Nat. Trust for Hist. Preservation, 1986, Custom Housing Selection award Builder mag., Nat. Assn. Home Builders, 1989, Design and Planning Merit award Builder's Choice, 1993, Mayor's award City of Newport, 1988-90, People's Choice award for affordable housing design R.I. Housing and Fin. Corp., 1990, AIA honor award, 1995-96, Gold medal for best new house, 1995, Housing award Fine Homebuilding mag., 1997; Rhode Island AIA Honor award Capt. Roger Wheeler Stage Beach Pavilion, 1998, Custom Home Mag. merit award Black Point House, 1999, New England AIA Honor award, 1999. Mem. AIA (citation 1993, Spl. citation for care 1987, honor award 1988, 93, RI Merit award 2005), Conanicut Yacht Club (commodore 1996-98), Nat. Tennis Club (v.p. Newport, R.I.), Jamestown Hist. Soc. (pres.). Avocations: court tennis, skiing, yachting, astronomy. Office: William L Burgin Architects Inc 150 Bellevue Ave Newport RI 02840-3230 Personal E-mail: wburgin@williamburgin.com.

BURGIO, MICHAEL, medical researcher; b. Bklyn., Sept. 20, 1942; s. John Duffy and Diega Burgio; m. Roberta Somersetin, Aug. 28, 1966 (div. July 31, 1990); children: Todd, Andera Lyn. BS, CCNY, 1963; MS in Physics, NYU, 1971. Med. rschr. Siemens Cardiac Pacemaker, Yardley, Pa., 1985—94, Home Infusion Therapy, Bklyn., 1994—97, Burgio Enterprises, Ltd., Bronx, 1995—. Lectr. in field; bd. dirs. United Medscan Corp., NJ; lectr. in field. Author: (book) Manual for Rehabilitation of Chronic Pulmonary Disease, 1989, Manual for Rehabilitation of Chronic Cardiac Disease, 1989, Training Manual for Cardiac and Pulmonary Rehabilitation, 1989, Nursing Manual of Policies and Procedures, (chpt.) Surgical Implant of A/V Pacemaker and It's Functions; co-author: (pilot study) Disc Dessication in Low Impact Injury in Young Trauma Victims; author: Burgio's Consultation Agreement, Burgio's License Agreement. Roman Catholic. Achievements include development of new method to restart heart after surgery; 9 federal copyrights in field. Home: 2440 Pearsall Ave Bronx NY 10469 Personal E-mail: burmkb@aol.com.

BURGMAN, DIERDRE ANN, lawyer; b. Logansport, Ind., Mar. 25, 1948; d. Ferdinand William Jr. and Doreen Walsh Burgman. BA, Valparaiso U., 1970, JD, 1979; LLM, Yale U., 1985. Bar: Ind. 1979, U.S. Dist. Ct. (so. dist.) Ind. 1979, N.Y. 1982, U.S. Dist. Ct. (so. dist.) N.Y. 1982, U.S. Ct. Appeals (7th cir.) 1982, U.S. Ct. Appeals (D.C. and 2d cirs.) 1984, U.S. Supreme Ct. 1985, D.C. 1988, U.S. Dist. Ct. (ea. dist.) N.Y. 1992. Law clk. to chief judge Ind. Ct. Appeals, Indpls., 1979-80; prof. law Valparaiso (Ind.) U., 1980-81; assoc. Dewey, Ballantine, Bushby, Palmer & Wood, N.Y.C., 1981-84, Cahill Gordon & Reindel, N.Y.C., 1985-92; v.p., gen. counsel N.Y. State Urban Devel. Corp., N.Y.C., 1992-95; dep. insp. gen. State N.Y., 1992-95; of counsel Vandenberg & Felieu, N.Y.C., 1995-99; cons. Salans, N.Y.C., 1999—2000, counsel, 2000—. Note editor Valparaiso U. law rev., 1978-79; contbr. articles to law jours. Mem. bd. visitors Valparaiso U. Sch. Law, 1986—95, chmn., 1989—92, mem. nat. coun., 2001—. Ind. Bar Found. scholar, 1978. Mem. ABA (trial evidence com. 1983-86, profl. liability com. 1986-89, ins. coverage litigation com. 1990-92), Assn. Bar City N.Y. (com. profl. responsibility 1988-91, com. profl. and jud. ethics 1991-95, mem. coun. jud. adminstrn. 1997-99), New York County Lawyers Assn. (com. Supreme Ct. 1987-94, chmn. 1990-93, bd. dirs. 1991-97, 2002-03, exec. com. bd. dirs. 1992-95, fin. and pers. com. 2003, mem. found., 2003-), N.Y. State Bar Assn. (mem. Ho. Dels. 1994-98, mem. com. on profl. stds. for atty. conduct 2002-). Home: 345 E 56th St Apt 5C New York NY 10022-3744

BURGOS-SASSCER, RUTH, chancellor emeritus; b. N.Y.C., Sept. 5, 1931; m. Donald Sasscer, June 14, 1958; children: Timothy, James, Julie, David. BA, Maryville (Tenn.) Coll., 1953; MA, Columbia U., 1956; PhD, Fla. State U., 1987. Mem. faculty Inter-Am. U., P.R., 1968-71; dept. chair U. P.R., Aguadilla, 1972-76, dir. non-traditional programs Cen. Adminstrn. Regional Coll., 1976-81, dir., dean, chief exec. officer Aguadilla, 1981-85; v.p. faculty and instrn. Harry S. Truman Coll., Chgo., 1988-93; pres. San Antonio Coll., 1993-96; chancellor Houston C.C. Sys., 1996-2000; sr. fellow U. Houston Law Ctr. Inst. of Higher Edn Law and Goverance, 2001—03. Bd. dirs. Nat. Postsecondary Edn. Coop., Maryville Coll. Nat. Adv. Coun., Montgomery County Coalition for Adult Literacy and ESOL. Mem. Am. Assn. C.C. Presbyterian. Home: 15115 Interlachen Dr Apt 403 Silver Spring MD 20908 Office Phone: 301-598-2288. E-mail: ruthburgossas@hotmail.com.

BURGOYNE, GRANT THOMAS, lawyer; b. Ketchikan, Alaska, Aug. 9, 1953; s. Richard Thomas and Florence Marjorie Burgoyne; m. Christina Lea Burgoyne, May 20, 1978; children: Crystal Lea, Katherine Ann. BA, U. Idaho, 1975; JD, U. Kans., 1988. Bar: Idaho 1988, U.S. Dist. Ct. Idaho 1988, U.S. Ct. Appeals (9th cir.) 1991. Intern Idaho Gov. Cecil Andrus, Boise, 1975; asst. Idaho Sec. of State, Boise, 1976-77; child support enforcement officer Idaho Dept. Health and Welfare, Boise, 1978-79; adminstrv. hearing officer Idaho Dept. Employment, Boise, 1980-86; mng. ptnr. Mauk & Burgoyne, Boise, 1996—. Adj. prof. human resources law Boise State Univ. Co-author: Idaho Employment Policies Handbook, 1998, The Idaho Tort and Insurance Law Deskbook, 1989. Bd. dirs. Human Resources Assn. of Treasure Valley, Boise, 1998-2000; chmn. Ada County Dem. Ctrl. Com., Boise, 1992-94; platform com. chmn. Idaho State Dem. Party, 1992; mem. Dem. Nat. Com., 2004—. Mem. Idaho State Bar Assn. (chmn. employment and labor law sect. 1997-98), Vandal Boosters. Democrat. Methodist. Office: Mauk & Burgoyne 515 S 6th St Boise ID 83702-7634

BURGOYNE, SUZANNE, theater educator, writer; b. St. Joseph, Mich., Oct. 25, 1946; d. Leon Edward and Betty Louise Burgoyne. Cert., Belgian Nat. Theatre Inst. (L'INSAS), Brussels, 1969; BA, Mich. State U., 1968; MA, Ohio State U., 1970; PhD, U. Mich., 1975. Vis. asst. prof. theatre N.E. Mo. State U., Kirksville, 1973—74; head dept. dramatic art So. Sem. Jr. Coll., Buena Vista, Va., 1975—77; from asst. to assoc. prof. fine and performing arts Creighton U., Omaha, 1977—89; vis. prof. directing and dramaturgy L'INSAS, Brussels, 1986—87; assoc. prof. theatre U. Mo., Columbia, 1989—97, prof. theatre, 1997—, Catherine Paine Middlebush chair fine and performing arts, 2005—. Dir.: (student-authored play) Survival Dance (show selected for performance at regional Kennedy Ctr. Am. Coll. Theatre Festival (KCACTF), 2003), (play) Oleanna (show selected for regional KCACTF-meritorious achievement award for directing (regional); Hon. Mention Award for Directing (Nat.), 1999), (and translator) La Vita Breve (by Paul Willems) (show selected for performance at regional KCACTF; Meritorious Achievement Award for Directing (regional), 1996), The Fool's Journey, 2005 (Meritorious Achievement award for directing KCACTF, 2005); co-author: Teaching and Performing: Ideas for Energizing Your Classes, revised edit.; translator: (play) Paul Willems' The Drowned Land and La Vita Breve.; translator: (of 2 of 4 plays, vol. editor) Four Plays of Paul Willems: Dreams and Reflections; contbr. articles to profl. jours., chapters to books. Recipient Author of the Month awrd, Highlights for Children Mag., 1986; Kellogg Nat. fellow, W.K. Kellogg Found., 1981—84, Summer Rsch. fellow, U. Mo. Rsch. Coun., 1992, Summer salary and travel grantee, 1994, Carnegie scholar, Carnegie Acad. for the Scholarship of Tchg. and Learning, 2000—01, NEH Summer Seminar fellow, 1979, 1985, U. Mo. Kemper fellow, 2004. Mem.: Pedagogy and Theatre of the Oppressed, Kennedy Ctr. Am. Coll. Theatre Festival (regional playwriting awards chair 1978—80), Mid-America Theatre Conf. (v.p., pres. 1991—95), Assn. for Theatre in Higher Edn. (editor, theatre topics 1993—95, v.p. for profl. devel. 1999—2003, pres. elect 2005, award as editor of Theatre Topics 1995, Outstanding Tchr. award 2003). Avocations: water aerobics, reading, gardening, swimming. Home: 103 Tracy Dr Columbia MO 65203 Office: Dept Theatre U Missouri 129 Fine Arts Columbia MO 65211 Office Phone: 573-882-0528. Personal E-mail: burgoynes@missouri.edu.

BURGUJIAN, RICHARD V., lawyer; b. NYC, Aug. 11, 1949; BS, Stevens Inst. Tech., 1971; MS, Rensselaer Polytech. Inst., 1972, Farleigh Dickinson U., 1975; JD, Rutgers U., 1984. Lic. NJ; bar: NJ 1985, NY 1987, DC 1989, lic.: US Dist. Ct. (Dist. NJ), registered: US Patent & Trademark Office. Ptnr. Finnegan, Henderson, Farabow, Farrett & Dunner LLP, Reston, Va., resident ptnr. Tokyo Office Japan, 1992—96, leader, Elec. Practice Group Reston, Va. Mem.: Am. Intellectual Property Law Assn., Inst. Elec. & Electronic Engrs., ABA, DC Bar Assn. Office: Finnegan Henderson Farabow Garrett & Dunner LLP Two Freedom Sq 11955 Freedom Dr Reston VA 20190-5675 Office Phone: 571-203-2700. Office Fax: 202-408-4400. Business E-Mail: rich.burgujian@finnegan.com.

BURGWEGER, FRANCIS JOSEPH DEWES, JR., lawyer; b. Evanston, Ill., July 5, 1942; s. Francis Dewes and Helen Theodosia (Chancellor) B.; m. Kathleen Marie Wessel, Sept. 3, 1978; children: Lauren Elizabeth, Francis Joseph Dewes III, Sherman Ward Chancellor. BA, Yale U., 1964; JD, U. Pa., 1970. Bar: Calif. 1971, N.Y. 1988, U.S. Ct. Appeals (9th cir.) 1971, U.S. Dist. Ct. (cen. dist.) Calif. 1971. Law clk. to Hon. Shirley M. Hufstedler U.S. Ct. Appeals 9th Cir., L.A., 1970-71; assoc. O'Melveny & Myers, L.A., 1971-78, ptnr., 1978-85, O'Melveny & Myers LLP, N.Y.C., 1985-97, sr. counsel, 1997—2003. Contbr. articles on environ. law. Capt. U.S. Army, 1964-67, Vietnam. Mem. Assn. of Bar of City of N.Y., N.Y. State Bar Assn., L.A. County Bar Assn. (exec. com. R.P. sect.). Avocations: books, wine, agriculture. Office: O'Melveny & Myers LLP Seven Times Sq 34th Fl New York NY 10036

BURHANS, FRANK MALCOLM, mechanical engineer; b. Hagerstown, Md., Dec. 11, 1920; s. William Humphrey Sr. and Ethel Adella (Forthman) B.; m. Jean Maria Dermott, Oct. 10, 1943; children: Stephen William, Douglas Allan, jeffrey Malcolm; m. Dorothy Olson Mutchler, July 29, 1995. BE in Mech. Engring., Johns Hopkins U., 1942; postgrad., U. Conn., 1942-43. Registered profl. engr., Wash. Design engr. Pratt & Whitney, East Hartford, Conn., 1942-55, Ford Motor Co., Dearborn, Mich., 1955-58; sr. design engr. Fairchild Engine Divsn., Deer Park, N.Y., 1958-59; sr. specialist engr. Turbine Divsn. Boeing Co., Seattle, 1959-66; prin. engr. Boeing Aircraft Engine Installations, 1967-86. Active Boy Scouts Am. Served with AC, U.S. Army, 1945-47. Recipient Silver Beaver award Boy Scouts Am. Mem. AIAA, ASME, Masons (past master/Bellevue), Lions (pres. 1996-97, zone chair 2001-02). Presbyterian (elder). Achievements include pioneering designer gas turbines and gas turbine installations.

BURHOE, BRIAN WALTER, automotive service executive; b. Worcester, Mass., Apr. 9, 1941; s. Walter De Forest and Dorothy Merrium Burhoe; m. Lynda Clayton, May 28, 1960 (div. May 1972); children: Mark S., Ty C., Scott M.; m. Joan Elaine Bredenberg, Oct. 21, 1989. Arts Baccalaureate, Clark U., Worcester, 1963, MA in History, Internat. Rels., 1971; cert. advanced mgmt. program, Northwestern U., 1985. Tchr. Orleans (Mass.) Sch. Sys., 1965-67; mgr. labor rels. Ill. Ctrl. R.R., Chgo., 1967-74, exec. asst., 1974-77; dir. human resources Midas Internat. Corp., Chgo., 1977-79, v.p. human resources, 1979-89, sr. v.p. human resources, 1989-98; pres. The Old Bookseller, Inc., 1998—. Mem.: Ill. Safety Coun. (chmn. 1992—94). Avocation: collecting out of print books. Home: 325 Nebraska St Frankfort IL 60423 Office: The Old Bookseller Inc 11 S White St Frankfort IL 60423 Office Phone: 815-464-6836.

BURI, CHARLES EDWARD, lawyer; b. Lancaster, Pa., Jan. 20, 1950; s. Karl Emerson and Verna Irene (Linville) B.; m. Susan Louise Camou, May 8, 1971; 1 child, Charles David. BS, U. Ariz., 1971, JD, 1973. Bar: Ariz. 1974,

U.S. Dist. Ct. Ariz., 1974, U.S. Ct. Appeals (9th cir.) 1977, U.S. Supreme Ct. 1980. Asst. atty Gen. Office Atty. Gen., Phoenix, 1974-83; exec. dir. Ariz. State Lottery, Phoenix, 1983-87; ptnr. Friedl, Richter & Buri, Phoenix, 1987—. Life mem. Fiesta Bown com., Phoenix, 1984—, Luke's Men, Phoenix, 1985—, Gov.'s Cabinet, Phoenix, 1983-87; trustee St. Luke's Hosp., Phoenix, 1990-91. Mem. ABA, Nat. Trial Lawyers Assn., Ariz. Trial Lawyers Assn., Ariz. Bar Assn., Maricopa County Bar Assn., Phoenix-East Rotary. Democrat. Avocations: tennis, skiing, jogging. Home: 6002 E Lafayette Blvd Scottsdale AZ 85251-3040 Office: Friedl Richter & Buri 6909 E Greenway Pkwy Ste 200 Scottsdale AZ 85254-2172

BURIAN, LAWRENCE J., lawyer; b. Bklyn., Nov. 17, 1969; s. Andrew and Ruth Yellen Burian; m. Adina Miriam Schainker, Sept. 3, 1998; children: Jonah Alec, Ethan Marc. BA in Econs., Yeshiva U., 1991; JD, Yale U., 1994. Bar: N.Y. 1995, N.J. 1996. Law clk. Justice Aharon Barak Supreme Ct. Israel, Jerusalem, 1995; assoc. Davis Polk & Wardwell, N.Y.C., 1994—2000, London, 1995; asst. gen. counsel Cablevision Sys. Corp., Bethpage, NY, 2000—02, v.p., assoc. gen. counsel, 2002—04, sr. v.p., assoc. gen. counsel bus. affairs, 2005—. Bd. dirs. Camp Morasha, 2000—04, Princeton Video Image, Inc., Lawrenceville, NJ, 2001—03, PVI Virtual Media Svcs. LLC, N.Y.C., 2003—, Safe3W, Inc., Garden City, NY, 2003—04. Dir. Young Leadership Am. Soc. for Yad Vshem, 1997. Recipient Intern award, Inst. for Pub. Affairs, 1998. Office: Cablevision Sys Corp 1111 Stewart Ave Bethpage NY 11714 Office Phone: 516-803-2300.

BURICK, LAWRENCE T., lawyer; b. Dayton, Ohio, May 15, 1943; s. Lee and Doris (Brenner) B.; m. Cynthia Joy Rosen, Aug. 31, 1969; children: Carrie R., Samuel J. BA, Miami U., 1965; JD, Northwestern U., 1968. Bar: Ohio 1968. Assoc. Smith & Schnacke, Dayton, 1969-78, ptnr., 1978-89, Thompson Hine LLP, Dayton, 1989—. Chmn. Dayton Jewish Ctr., Ohio, 1982—83, Jewish Cmty. Rels. Coun., 1980—81; pres. Jewish Fedn. Greater Dayton, Ohio, 1989—93, bd. dirs., 1977—2003; chmn. United Jewish Campaign, 1997—99; bd. dirs. Jewish Edn. in Svc. to N.Am., 1994—99, v.p., 1997—99; mem. Dayton region Nat. Conf. Cmty. and Justice, 1997—, v.p., 1999—2002, chair, 2002—04; bd. dirs. Beth Abraham Synagogue, 1997—2003. Recipient Wasserman Leadership award, Jewish Fedn. Greater Dayton, 1978. Mem. Ohio State Bar Assn., Dayton Bar Assn., Am. Bankruptcy Law Forum, Am. Bankruptcy Inst. Office: Thompson Hine LLP PO Box 8801 2000 Courthouse Plz NE Dayton OH 45401-8801 E-mail: larry.burick@thompsonhine.com.

BURINGRUD, LISA MARIE, music educator; b. Brawley, Calif., Jan. 16, 1961; d. Joseph Paul McKim and Mary Legakes-McKim; m. Joel Dean Buringrud, Nov. 30, 1991; children: Rebecca Danae, Deanna Marie. BA in Music with cert. in music therapy, Calif. State U., Long Beach, 1987; MusM in Instrumental Conducting, Calif. State U., Sacramento, 2001. Cert. profl. clear single No. subject Calif., bd. cert. music therapy Calif. Bd. Music Therapy, tchg. credential in music Calif. Music therapist, band dir. L.A. GOAL, Santa Monica, Calif., 1986—90; music therapist Fairview Developmental Ctr., Costa Mesa, Calif., 1987—90, Stockton (Calif.) Developmental Ctr., 1990; music dir. Vanden H.S., Fairfield, Calif., 1993—99; band dir. Armijo H.S., Fairfield, 1999—2000; assoc. condr. wind studies dept. Calif. State U., Sacramento, 2000—01; instrumental music dir. Mendocino (Calif.) Unified Sch. Dist., 2001—03; band dir. Calaveras H.S., San Andreas, Calif., 2003—. Prin. flutist Solano Winds, Fairfield, 1995—2001; condr., artistic dir. North Coast Wind Symphony, Mendocino, 2002—03; assoc. condr. Opera Fresca, Mendocino, 2001—03; condr. children's concert series Symphony of the Redwoods, Mendocino, 2002—. Author: (book) American Women Composers of Band Music: A Biographical Dictionary and Catalogue of Works: An Addendum and Update, 2001. Music min. St. Marks Luth. Ch., Fairfield, 2000—01; bd. dirs. St. Marks Pre-Sch., Fairfield, 1999—2001. Recipient Cert. of Appreciation for Performance, Travis AFB, 1997. Mem.: Nat. Band Dirs. Assn., Calif. Music Educators Assn. (Hon. Recognition Band Concert/Clinic Pres. 2002), Calif. Band Dirs. Assn. (Hon. Recognition Band Concert/Clinic Pres. 1999, 2003), Women Band Dirs. Internat., Am. Sch. Band Dirs. Assn., Phi Kappa Lambda. Avocations: bicycling, jogging, reading, flute performance. Office: Calaveras H S PO Box 607 San Andreas CA 95249 Office Phone: 209-754-1811. Business E-Mail: lburingrud@calaveras.k12.ca.us.

BURINI, SONIA MONTES DE OCA, apparel manufacturing and public relations executive; b. Havana, Cuba, Apr. 28, 1935; d. Francisco and Nilda (Diaz) Montes de Oca; m. Franco Burini, Apr. 5, 1959. Student, U. Havana, 1954-57, Georgetown U., 1958; BA in History cum laude, U. Miami, Coral Gables, Fla., 1971. Adminstr. Roma Fashions, Inc. D/B/A Franco B., Coral Gables, 1976-95; entrepreneur, pub. rels. exec., 1995—; dir. promotions and special events Social Mag., 2004—. Founder Nat. Parkinson Found., 1986—; v.p. Vizcayans Fund Raising Orgn., 1990—, chmn. fine arts events, 1993-95; co-chmn. 1st annual fund raising event Am. Cancer Soc. Winn-Dixie Hope Lodge Ctr.; mem. women with heart group Heart Assn. Greater Miami, Fla., 1981—; founder, bd. dirs. Cancer Link program U. Miami Comprehensive Cancer Ctr., 1987; chmn. spring fantasy luncheon Am. Cancer Soc., 1988; founding chmn. Rose Group, Am. Lung Assn., chmn. Rose Ball, 1989; amb. Mercy Hosp. Found., 1987-95; bd. dirs. Newborn program U. Miami, 1978, bd. dirs., 1982-87, amb. category years; vol. guide Viscaya Mus., Dade County, Fla., 1972-79, chmn. various coms., 1979—, found. bd. dirs., steering com., mem. com. of 100; bd. dir., Young Patroness of the Opera, 1979-87; grand patron Greater Miami Opera, 1986-95, bd. dirs., 1978—, chmn. opera gala, 1987, mem. opera guild, 1988; founding bd. mem. Ears Dears U. Miami, 1986—, chmn. 1990 gala; mem. Dade County Performing Art Ctr. Trust, 1993—; spl. chmn. fine arts events Vizcayans, 1993—; mem. sister cities com. Cities of Miami, Fla. and Nice, France, 1994—, Nat. Trust Hist. Preservation, 1997—. Named Oustanding Woman of Yr. Mayor of Dade County, 1986, Woman of Yr. Heart Assn. Greater Miami, 1986, named to Miss Charity Biscayne Bay Marriott Hotel and Marina, 1987, One of the Leading Ladies for the March of Dimes, 1998. Mem. Nat. Trust Historic Preservation, Ballet Soc. Miami (bd. dirs. 1979-80, named one of Miami's Oustanding Women 1986), Confrerie de la Chaine des Rotisseurs, NAFE, Nat. Found. Peace (bd. adv. 2001—), Opera Guild Fla. Grand Opera (bd. dirs. 2003—). Home: 5401 Collins Ave Apt 1016 Miami Beach FL 33140 Office: Roma Fashions Inc 3311 Ponce De Leon Blvd Coral Gables FL 33134-7210 Address: 4730 SW 67th Ave Miami FL 33155 Fax: 305-864-2047. Office Phone: 305-663-0473. Office Fax: 305-663-4644. E-mail: info@socialruag.com.

BURISH, THOMAS GERARD, academic administrator, psychology professor; b. Peshtigo, Wis., May 4, 1950; s. Bennie Charles and Donna Mae (Willkom) B.; m. Pamela Jean Zebrasky, June 19, 1976; children: Mark Joseph, Brent Christopher. AB summa cum laude, U. Notre Dame, 1972; MA, U. Kans., 1975, PhD, 1976. Lic. psychologist, Tenn. Asst. prof. psychology Vanderbilt U., Nashville, 1976-80, assoc. prof., 1980-86, prof., 1986—2002, dir. clin. tng., 1980-84, chair dept. psychology, 1984-86, assoc. provost, 1986—92, provost, 1992—2002; pres. Washington and Lee U., Lexington, Va., 2002—05; provost U. Notre Dame, 2005—, prof. psychology, 2005—. Mem. cancer rsch. manpower rev. com. Nat. Cancer Inst., 1991-96; co-chair Bridge task force com. Am. Cancer Soc., 1994-96; mem. breast cancer rsch. panel US Army Med. Rsch., 1995-2001. Co-editor: Coping with Chronic Disease, 1983, Cancer, Nutrition and Eating Behavior, 1985; co-author: Behavior Therapy, 1987, Health Psychology, 1991. Chmn. St. Mary's Sch. Bd., Nashville, 1982-83; participant Leadership Nashville, 1989-90; vice chair, bd. dir. Am. Cancer Soc. Fellow Am. Psychol. Assn., Am. Psychol. Soc.; mem. Acad. Behavioral Medicine Rsch., Phi Beta Kappa. Roman Catholic. Office: U Notre Dame 317 Main Bldg Notre Dame IN 46556

BURK, LINDA FAITH, music educator, director; d. Ralph John and Lucille Mary Lutz; m. Terry Timothy Burk, July 31, 1982; children: Kevin, Kelsey. MusB, Lawrence U. Conservatory Music, 1982; MusM, U. Minn., 1988. Dir. choral Totino Grace H.S., Fridley, Minn., 1982—85; dir. choral, tchr. voice Inver Hills C.C., Inver Grove Heights, Minn., 1987—89; chmn. Dept. Voice MacPhail Ctr. for Arts, Mpls., 1989—2002; tchr. music Edgewood Elem. Sch., Bklyn. Pk., Minn., 1992—2000; dir. choral North View Jr. H.S., Bklyn. Pk., 2000—. Dir. choral Angelica Cantanti, Bloomington, Minn., 1988—93; singer Dale Warland Singers, St. Paul, 1984—88; dir. choir sch. Ho. Hope Ch., St. Paul, 1993—97; presenter in field. Recipient Investment in Youth award, Dist. 279 Found., 2002. Mem.: Music Educators Nat. Conf., Am. Choral Dirs. Assn. Office: North View Junior High School 5869 69th Ave North Brooklyn Park MN 55429

BURK, MARTHA GERTRUDE, political psychologist; b. Tyler, Tex., Oct. 18, 1941; d. Ivan Lee Burk and Dorothy May (White) Dean; m. Eddie C. Talley, Sept. 2, 1960 (div. Sept. 1985); children: Edward, Mark; m. Ralph Estes, July 3, 1986. BS, U. Houston, 1962; MS, U. Tex., Arlington, 1968, PhD, 1974. Lic. psychologist, Tex. Asst. prof. mgmt. U. Tex., Arlington, 1976-79, rsch. dir. Grad. Sch. Social Work, 1974-76, ptnr. Sch. Psychology Cons., 1979-80; pres. A.U. Software, Inc., Wichita, Kans., 1981-90, Ctr. for Advancement of Pub. Policy, Washington, 1990—; now chair Nat. Coun. of Women's Organizations, Washington. Syndicated columnist. Author (software) Talley Spl. Edn. Mgmt. System, 1984, Testlab 2000, 1988, (books) Cult of Power: Sex Discrimination in Corporate America and What Can Be Done About It, 2005. Mem. Commn. Responsive Democracy, Washington, 1990, Nat. Task Force on Pay Equity, 1993—. Rsch. grantee U.S. Dept. Edn., 1989-94, named Woman of Yr., Ms Mag., 2003. Mem. NOW (nat. bd. dirs. 1988-90). Democrat. Office: Nat Coun Women's Orgns Ste 250 1050 17th St NW Washington DC 20036 Office Phone: 202-293-4505.*

BURK, RAYMOND FRANKLIN, JR., internist, educator, medical researcher; b. Kosciusko, Miss., Dec. 9, 1942; s. Raymond Franklin and Florence Annie (Davis) B.; m. Enikoe Vikor, June 17, 1967; children: Teresa Marie, Stephen Morrison. BA, U. Miss., 1963. Diplomate Am. Bd. Internal Medicine. Intern Vanderbilt Hosp., Nashville, 1968—69; resident in medicine Vanderbilt Hosp., Nashville, 1969—70; asst. prof. medicine and biochemistry U. Tex. S.W. Med. Sch., Dallas, 1975—78; assoc. prof. medicine and biochemistry La. State U. Sch. Medicine, Shreveport, 1978—80; assoc. prof. medicine U. Tex. Health Sci. Ctr., San Antonio, 1980—82, prof., 1982—87; prof. medicine Vanderbilt U., 1987—. Rschr. in field; mem. staff Vanderbilt U. Hosp., Nashville. Contbr. articles to med. jours. Maj. M.C., U.S. Army, 1970-73. Grantee NIH, 1974—. Mem. Am. Soc. Biol. Chemists, Am. Soc. Clin. Investigation, Am. Inst. Nutrition.

BURK, ROBERT S., lawyer; b. Mpls., Jan. 13, 1937; s. Harvey and Mayme (Cottle) B.; m. Eunice L. Silverman, Mar. 22, 1959; children: Bryan, Pam, Matt. BBA in Indsl. Rels., U. Minn., 1959; LLB, William Mitchell Coll. Law, 1965. Bar: Minn. 1966; qualified neutral under Rule 114 of the Minn. Gen. Rules of Practice, 1995—. Labor rels. cons. St. Paul Employers Assn., 1959-66; labor rels. mgr. Koch Refining Co., St. Paul, 1966-72, mgr. indsl. rels., 1972-75, mgr. indsl. rels., environ. affairs, 1975-77; sr. atty. Popham, Haik, Schnobrich & Kaufman, Ltd., Mpls., 1977-95, pres., CEO, 1986-90; ptnr. Burk & Seaton, P.A., Edina, Minn., 1995-2001, Burk & Landrum, P.A., Edina, 2001—. Chair bd. trustees William Mitchell Coll. Law, St. Paul, 1994-96, sec. 1991. Recipient Hon. Ronald E. Hachey Outstanding Alumnus award William Mitchell Coll. Law Alumni Assn., 1993, Disting. Svc. award William Mitchell Coll. Law, 2004. Mem. ABA (labor sect.), Minn. Bar Assn. (labor sect.). Office: Burk & Landrum PA 7400 Metro Blvd Ste 100 Edina MN 55439 E-mail: rburk@burklandrum.com. *Credibility is the only trait that marks your existence.*

BURKA, ROBERT ALAN, lawyer; b. Washington, Dec. 25, 1944; s. Fred and Louise S. (Lehmann) B.; m. Maria Eva Karpati, Dec. 22, 1968; children: Jacqueline A., Michael S., Jennifer L. AB, Dartmouth Coll., 1966; MSc in Econs., U. London, 1967; JD, Harvard U., 1970. Bar: N.Y. 1971, D.C. 1975, U.S. Supreme Ct. 1978. Law clk. to Hon. Judge Milton Pollack U.S. Dist. Ct. (so. dist.) N.Y., N.Y.C., 1971; assoc. Kaye Scholer Fierman Hays & Handler, N.Y.C., 1971-74, Bergson, Borkland, Morgolis & Adler, Washington, 1974-79; dep., then acting asst. dir. Bur. of Competition FTC, Washington, 1979-82; ptnr. LaRoe Winn & Moerman, Washington, 1982-84; pvt. practice Washington, 1984-87; ptnr. Knopf & Burka, Washington, 1987-92, Foley & Lardner, Washington, 1992—. Fulbright and Reynolds scholars, 1966-67. Mem. Phi Beta Kappa. Office: Foley & Lardner LLP 3000 K St NW Ste 500 Washington DC 20007-5143 Office Phone: 202-672-5345. Business E-Mail: rburka@foley.com.

BURKART, WALTER MARK, retired manufacturing company executive; b. Ferndale, Mich., Sept. 29, 1921; s. Michael A. and Beatrice (Pominville) B.; m. Mary Jane Hilts, Apr. 22, 1942; children: Michael Robert, Michele Sue. Student, Lawrence Inst. Tech., 1941-43. Supr. Ex-Cello Corp., Detroit, 1940-51, v.p. machine tool div., 1965-69; chief process engr. Wright Aero Co., Detroit, 1951-55; mgr. Machine Tool div. Sheffield Corp. div. Bendix, Dayton, Ohio, 1956-65; chmn. bd. Kingsbury Machine Tool Corp., Keene, N.H., 1969-98; pres. Am. Machine Tool Consortum, Tehran, 1976-77. Mem. industry sector adv. com. on capital goods for U.S.A. trade policy matters, Dept. Commerce. Active Boy Scouts Am., 1958—; mem. N.H. Gov.'s Mgmt. Rev. Bd., 1981-82. Served with USNR, 1944-46. Mem. Keene C. of C. (dir. 1971), Bus. and Industry Assn. N.H. (dir. 1980-81), Am. Mgmt. Assn., Soc. Mfg. Engrs., Nat. Machine Tool Builders Assn. Clubs: Orchard Lake (Mich.); Keene Country (N.H.); Piper's Landing Country (Fla.). Republican. Presbyterian. *It has been my managerial philosophy to give people a goal and let them choose which road to take in reaching that goal. This allows people to utilize their strengths while becoming more committed and involved. Through this participation the individual can get a greater sense of personal accomplishment. Rarely will two people go about solving a problem in the same way. While some problems do require a group solution, most simply require a solution and I believe the method is not as important as the result.*

BURKE, ALEXANDER JAMES, JR., publishing executive; b. NYC, Apr. 24, 1931; s. Alexander James and Josephine Eleanor (McGrath) B.; m. Suzanne Jeanne Gatti, June 25, 1955; children: James, Brian, Christopher, Nancy, Thomas, Matthew, Alexander John. BA cum laude, Holy Cross Coll., 1953; MA, Fordham U., 1956; MA in Scripture, Immaculate Conception Sem., 1997; PhD in Scripture, Fordham U., 2002. Prof. English Fordham U., 1953-56, 59-60; editor W.H. Sadlier Co., N.Y.C., 1959-60; mgr. Doubleday Bookstore, Manhasset, N.Y., 1952; with McGraw-Hill Book Co., N.Y.C., 1960—87, gen. mgr., 1969-70, v.p., 1970-73, exec. v.p., 1973-74, pres., 1974-82, McGraw-Hill Internat. Book Co., N.Y.C., 1983-85, exec. v.p., 1985-87; pres. Phoenix Learning Resources, 1987—; prof. English, prof. N.T., dir. pub. studies program Hofstra U., N.Y.C., 1994—. Author: The Raising of Lazarus and The Passion of Jesus in John 11 and 12, 2003. Bd. dirs. Adult Edn. Council St. Louis, 1965, Commn. on Radio and TV, Cath. Archdiocese St. Louis, 1968-72. With USAF, 1956-59. Mem. Assn. Am. Pubs. (exec. com., dir., chmn. 1978-85), Book Industry Study Group (exec. com., dir. 1976—), Am. Soc. Curriculum Devel., Nat. Coun. Tchrs. English, Cath. Bibl. Assn., Alpha Sigma Nu Roman Catholic. Home: 455 Ryder Rd Manhasset NY 11030-2761 Office Phone: 516-463-6720. Personal E-mail: ajburkejr@optonline.net.

BURKE, APRIL LEWIS, lawyer, lobbyist; b. Chgo., Apr. 5, 1952; d. Milton and Diane Lewis. Student, U. Wash., 1970-72; BA, Stanford U., 1974; JD, George Washington U., 1978. Bar: D.C. 1978, U.S. Dist. Ct. (D.C.) 1979. Asst. legis. counsel Office of Legis. Counsel, U.S. Senate, Washington, 1978-81; atty. Ballard, Spahr, Andrews and Ingersoll, Washington, 1981-83; legis. counsel Assn. Am. Univs., Washington, 1983-86, Chambers Assocs., Washington, 1987-89; v.p. Hill and Knowlton, Washington, 1990-92; prin. Lewis-Burke Assocs., Washington, 1992—. Co-chair, Coun. on Govtl. Affairs, Nat. Assn. State Univs. and Land-Grant Colls., Washington, 1994. Mem. Bd. Zoning Appeals, City of Alexandria, Va., 1990-93; commr. Alexandria Planning Commn., 1993-96. Office: Lewis-Burke Assocs 1000 Vermont Ave NW Fl 11 Washington DC 20005 Fax: (202) 289-7454. E-mail: april@lewis-burke.org.

BURKE, BERNARD FLOOD, physicist, researcher; b. Boston, June 7, 1928; s. Vincent Paul and Clare (Brine) B.; m. Jane Chapin Pann, May 30, 1953 (dec. Aug. 1993); children: Geoffrey Damian, Elizabeth Chapin, Mark Vincent, Matthew Brine; m. Elizabeth King Platt, Oct. 28, 1998. SB, MIT, 1950, PhD, 1953. Staff mem. terrestrial magnetism Carnegie Instn. of Washington, 1953-65, chmn. radio astronomy sect., 1962-65; prof. physics, Burden prof. astrophysics MIT, 1965-2001, prof. physics, Burden prof. emeritus, 2001—. Vis. prof. U. Leiden, Netherlands, 1971-72, U. Manchester, Eng., 1992-93; trustee N.E. Radio Obs. Corp., 1973-95, vice chmn., 1975-82, chmn., 1982-95; cons. NSF, NASA, Dept. Transp.; Oort lectr. U. Leiden, 1993; Karl Jansky lectr. NAt. Radio Astronomy Obs., 1998. Trustee Associated Univs., Inc., 1972-90; mem. Nat. Sci. Bd., 1990-96; commr. Marsh Conservation Dist., Cambridge, 2001—. Recipient Helen Warner prize Am. Astron. Soc., 1963; Rumford prize Am. Acad. Arts and Scis., 1971; Sherman Fairchild scholar Calif. Inst. Tech., 1984, Smithsonian Regents fellow, 1985; sr. fellow Carnegie Instn. of Washington, 1997. Fellow AAAS; mem. NAS, Am. Acad. Arts and Scis., Am. Phys. Soc., Am. Astron. Soc., Royal Astron. Soc., Internat. Astron. Union, Internat. Astron. Fedn. (Pecek lectr. 1993), Internat. Sci. Radio Union, Merle Tuve Sr. fellow Carnegie Instn. of Washington. Achievements include research on microwave spectroscopy, radio astronomy, galactic structure, antenna design, cosmology. Office: MIT Dept Physics Cambridge MA 02139

BURKE, BEVERLY J., lawyer, utilities executive; m. Gregory Saunders. BA, Brown U.; JD, George Washington U. Law clerk to Judge Norma Holloway Johnson U.S. Dist. Ct.; atty. civil litigation & appellate advocacy D.C. Govt., 1982—92; with Office Gen. Counsel Washington Gas & Light Co., 1992-96, dept. head, 1996-98, v.p., asst. gen. counsel, 1998—2001, v.p., gen. counsel, 2001—. Mediator U.S. Dist. Ct., D.C. Mem. D.C. Courts Gender Bias Task Force; bd. mem. Wash. Performing Arts Soc.; second v.p. Lafayette Elementary Home & School Assn. Mem.: ABA, D.C. Bar Assn. (Children's Initiative Com., Legal Ethics Com., Nominations Com., Screening Com.). Office: Washington Gas and Light Co 1100 H St NW Washington DC 20080-0002*

BURKE, BRIAN, professional sports team executive; Vice pres., director of hockey operations Vancouver Canucks, 1987—92; gen. mgr. Hartford (Conn.) Whalers, 1992—93; sr. v.p. and director of hockey operations NHL, 1993—98; gen. mgr. Vancouver Canucks, 1998—2004; exec. v.p., gen. mgr. Mighty Ducks of Anaheim, 2005—. Office: c/o Mighty Ducks 2695 E Katella Ave Anaheim CA 92806*

BURKE, COLIN BRADLEY, retired historian; s. Thomas James and Eva Marie Burke; m. Rosita N. Coxe, Dec. 26, 1972; 1 child, Colin Andrew. BA, San Francisco State Coll., 1962, MA, 1968; PhD, Washington U., St. Louis, 1972. Profl. musician Hungry I, ABC, Westinghouse Broadcasting, Ice Follies, San Francisco, 1954—72; history prof. U. Md., Balt., 1972—99; rsch. fellow Program on Nonprofit Orgn., Yale U., New Haven, 1999—2002; Eugene Garfield fellow Chem. Heritage Found., Phila., 2000—01; ret., 2001. Scholar in residence Nat. Security Agy., Ft. Meade, Md., 1994—95. Author: American Collegiate Populations, 1982, Information and Secrecy, 1994, The Secret in Building 26, 2004; contbr. articles to profl. publs. Advisor, mem. Howard County Bd. of Edn., Columbia, Md., 2002—03. Scholar, NEH, 1980, Ford Found., 1998, APS, 2000, NSF, 2000; Sr. Fulbright fellow, Warsaw (Poland) U., 1988—89. Office: Univ Md Dept of History 1000 Hilltop Cir Baltimore MD 21022

BURKE, BROTHER DANIEL, museum director, educator; PhD in literary criticism, La Salle U. Tchr. English West Phila. Cath. HS; v.p. academic affairs La Salle U., Phila., pres., 1969—77; founding dir. La Salle U. Art Mus., Phila., 1976—. Office: La Salle U Art Mus 1900 W Olney Ave Philadelphia PA 19141*

BURKE, DAVID, corporate chef, executive chef; b. Bklyn., Feb. 27, 1962; divorced; three children. Student, The Culinary Inst. Am. Recipient Meilleurs Ouvriers de France diploma Internat. Food Festival, Tokyo, 1988, Robert Mondavi Culinary Award of Excellence, 1996, Auggie Award Culinary Inst. Am., 1996, Five Diamond Award of Excellence, AM. Acad. Hospitality Scis., 1997; named Nat. Adv. Com. of Chefs in Am., Chef of Yr., 1991. Avocations: pinball, travel, skiing, antiquing. Office: 133 E 61st St New York NY 10021-8101

BURKE, DELTA, actress; b. Orlando, Fla., July 30, 1956; m. Gerald McRaney, May 28, 1989. Educated, London Acad. Music & Dramatic Arts. Clothing designer & mgr. Delta Burke Design, NYC. Appeared in TV movies Charleston, A Last Cry for Help, Mickey Spillane's Mike Hammer: Murder Me, Murder You, A Bunny's Tale, Where the Hell's That Gold?!!?, A Promise to Carolyn, 1996, Melanie Darrow, 1997, What Women Want, 2000; appeared in TV mini-series The Seekers, 1979; appeared in TV series The Chisholms, 1980, Filthy Rich, 1982, First and Ten, 1984; guest appearance on series Simon & Simon; regular role on series Designing Women, 1986-91; star own series Delta, 1992-93, The Women of the House, 1995; (film) Maternal Instincts, 1996; appeared on broadway Thoroughly Modern Millie, 2003, Steel Magnolias, 2005. Named Miss Fla., 1974, later competed in Miss Am. Pageant. Mailing: c/o Lyceum Theatre 247 West 44th St New York NY 10036*

BURKE, DOUG, writer; b. July 25, 1963; s. Robert Louis and Joan Mary (Rowbotham) B. BS, U. Calif., Irvine, 1986, MS, 1987, PhD in Physics, 1990; D of Sci. of Drama (hon.), Case Western Res. U., 1991. Co-author: (novel) The Dark Prophet, 1995; author: (textbook) Psychophysics and Drama, 1991, (play) Rebel King, 1995, (screenplay) Gull, 1995; actor, dir., prodr. (movie) Gull, 1998; patentee in the field of three-dimensional image creation and display systems.

BURKE, E. JAMES, lawyer, state supreme court justice; b. Wilmington, Del., June 26, 1949; s. Earl J. Burke and Elizabeth M. (Glenn) Jones; m. Michele C. Haney, Aug. 16, 1975 (div. May 1981); 1 child, Erick; m. Linda G. Matthew, Apr. 15, 1982; children: Matthew, Leanna. BS in Psychology, St. Joseph's U., Phila., 1971; JD, U. Wyo., 1977. Bar: Wyo. 1977, U.S. Dist. Ct. Wyo. 1977, U.S. Ct. Appeals (10th cir.) 1981. Ptnr. Burke, Woodard and O'Donnell, Hanes & Burke P.C., Cheyenne, Wyo., 1977—2001; judge Dist. Ct. Laramie County, 2001—04; justice Wyo. Supreme Ct., 2005—. Mem. Cheyenne-Laramie County Economic Joint Powers Bd.; founder, dean People's Law School prog. Served to 1st lt. USAF, 1971-74. Mem. Wyo. Bar Assn., Laramie County Bar Assn., Assn. Trial Lawyers Am. (state del. 1985—), Wyo. Trial Lawyers Assn. (bd. dirs. 1977—, pres. 1980), Western Trial Lawyers Assn. (bd. dirs. 1979—, pres. 1986—), Cheyenne C. of C. (leadership award 1986). Office: Wyo Supreme Ct 2301 Capitol Ave Cheyenne WY 82001

BURKE, EDMUND W., lawyer; BA in History with honors, Georgetown U., 1970, JD, 1973. Bar: DC 1973, Tex. 1985, US State Supreme Ct. V.p., Law & Govt. Affairs Burlington No. R.R., Mass.; assoc. to ptnr., litig. & transp. depts. Steptoe & Johnson lLP, Washington, 1974—, co-chmn. hiring com. Editor: Georgetown Law Jour. Mem.: Phi Beta Kappa. Office: Steptoe & Johnson LLP 1330 Connecticut Ave NW Washington DC 20036 Office Phone: 202-429-3008. Office Fax: 202-429-3902. Business E-Mail: eburke@steptoe.com.

BURKE, HARRY B., physician; m. Carole Burke; 1 child, Harry M. MD, PhD, U. Chgo., 1976—88. Assoc. prof., medicine N.Y. Med. Coll., Valhalla, 1994—2001, George Wash. U., Sch. Medicine, Washington, 2001—. Chair Com. for Molecular Biomarkers in Medicine, Washington, 2004—. Mem. rev. panel Nat. Cancer Inst., Bethesda, Md., 2005—. Grantee, NIH, 2005—. Achievements include first to develop new approaches to the discovery of molecular biomarkers. Office: George Washington U Sch Medicine 2150 Pennsylvania Ave NW Washington DC 20037 Office Phone: 202-741-2193.

BURKE, HENRY PATRICK, lawyer; b. Scranton, Pa., May 12, 1942; s. Thomas and Dorothy Maria (McCloskey) B.; m. Alyce Louise McCrone, July 5, 1975; children: Henry Patrick, Daniel. BS, U. Scranton, 1964; JD, Villanova U., 1967. Bar: Pa. 1968, U.S. Dist. Ct. (mid. dist.) Pa. 1968, U.S. Ct. Appeals (3d cir.) 1994, U.S. Ct. Appeals (fed. cir.) 2001, U.S. Ct. Internat. Trade 2001; lic. real estate broker, Pa. Law clk. Ct. Common Pleas, Lackawanna County, Pa., 1968-69; lectr. bus. law U. Scranton, 1968-69; assoc. Haggerty & McDonnell, Scranton, 1969-75; assoc. counsel Scranton Redevel. Authority, 1969-70; spl. atty. gen. and legal opinion writer Pa. State Workers' Compensation Bd., 1972-97, legal opinion writer, 1972-97; sec., gen. counsel Opportunity Products Today, Inc., 1998; assoc. Burke and Douglass, Scranton, Pa., 1975-80; co-owner Directel Inc. Wireless, 1999-2000; pvt. practice law Scranton, 1969—. Mem. exec. com. Pa. unit Am. Heart Assn., 1973-74, asst. treas. Keystone chpt., 1972; del. Dem. Nat. Conv., 1972, chmn. econ. com. Dem. Nat. Platform Com., 1972; trustee Lackawanna Jr. Coll., 1977-79, solicitor, 1979-83; mem. alumni bd. govs. U. Scranton, 1969-75, pres. Nat. Alumni Soc., 1983-85; solicitor Cath. Social Svcs., 1978-95, bd. dirs., 1978-97; pres., owner Scranton-Wilkes Barre Twins, Inc., 1993-94; pres. Atlantic Collegiate Baseball League, 1995-97. Bd. dirs. Pennsylvanians for Human Life, 2001—04, Secular Franciscan Order, 2002—; bd. dirs. Lackawanna br. Pa. Assn. for Blind, 1988—, chmn., 2003—05, pres., 2003—05. Mem. ABA, Pa. Bar Assn., Lackawanna Bar Assn., Greater Scranton Bd. Realtors, Pa. Assn. Realtors, Nat. Assn. Realtors, Intertel, Internat. Soc. Philos. Enquiry, Mensa, Alpha Sigma Nu. Democrat. Roman Catholic. Home: 319 Church St Dunmore PA 18512-1911 Office: Scranton Bank Bldg 12th Fl 108 N Washington Ave Scranton PA 18503 Office Phone: 570-344-0200.

BURKE, JAMES JOSEPH, JR., investment banker; b. Wilmington, Del., Dec. 19, 1951; s. James Joseph and Kathleen Gertrude (Nauss) B.; m. Jeanne Elizabeth Burke, Aug. 6, 1977 (div. Oct. 2002); children: James III, Jennifer, Brian. AB in Psychology, Brown U., 1973; MBA with distinction, Harvard U., 1979. 2d v.p. program JPMorgan Chase Bank, N.Y.C., 1973-77; assoc. Merrill Lynch, N.Y.C., 1979-83, v.p., 1983-85, mng. dir., 1985-94; pres., CEO Merrill Lynch Capital Ptnrs., N.Y.C., 1987-94; mng. ptnr. First Capital Ptnrs., N.Y.C., 1994—, Stonington Ptnrs., Inc. (formerly First Capital Ptnrs.), N.Y.C., 1995—. Bd. dirs. Ann Taylor Stores Corp., NYC, Lincoln Ednl. Svcs. Corp., West Orange, NJ. Trustee Seton Hall Prep. Sch., West Orange, Brown U., Providence; bd. overseers Seton Hall U. Sch. Diplomacy and Internat. Rels., Brown U. Sports Found. Office: Stonington Ptnrs 767 5th Ave New York NY 10153-0023 Business E-Mail: JBurke@stonington.com.

BURKE, JAN HELENE, author; b. Houston, Aug. 1, 1953; d. John Francis and Velda Marie Fischer; m. Timothy Edward Burke, May 28, 1988. BA, Calif. State U., Long Beach, 1978. Author: (novels) Goodnight, Irene, 1993, Hocus, 1997, Harm, 1999, Bloodlines: An Irene Kelly Novel, 2005. Recipient readers award and Macavity award for short story Ellery Queen Mystery Mag., 1994, Ellery Queen Mystery Mag. award, Agatha award. Mem. Mystery Writers Am., Am. Crime Writers League, Internat. Crime Writers Assn., Sisters in Crime. Office: PO Box 1128 Los Alamitos CA 90720-1128 Fax: 562-429-1811. E-mail: jan@janburke.com.

BURKE, JOHN, priest; b. Washington, Sept. 15, 1928; s. William Francis and Grace Allison (Logan) B. AB, Cath. U. Am., 1950, MA, 1965, STD, 1969. Joined Order Preachers, ordained priest Roman Cath. Ch., 1960. Prof. homiletics St. Stephen's Coll., Dover, Mass., 1961-64, Immaculate Conception faculty, 1964-67, 90, asst. prof., summers 1964-69, asst. prof. drama, 1968-72, dir. Preaching Workshop, 1965-67, dir. Preachers Inst., 1967-72; mem. faculty Washington Theol. Coalition, 1968-69; coord. Nat. Congress for the Word of God, 1972; founder, exec. dir. Nat. Inst. for the Word of God, Washington, 1972—; prof. Dominican House of Studies, Washington, 1990—. Author: Bible Sharing Youth Retreat Manual, 1983, Beginners' Guide to Bible Sharing, Vol. I, II, 1984, The Homilist's Guide to Scripture, Theology and Canon Law, 1987, Dominican Preaching in the Province of St. Joseph: 1832-1960, 2005; editor: Gospel Power: Toward the Revitalization of Preaching, 1978, Bible Sharing: How to Grow in the Mystery of Christ, 1979, A New Look at Preaching, 1983,A Good News Spirituality, 2000; contbr. articles to profl. jours.; producer TV film Chimbote, 1964. Mem. Radio-TV Dirs. Guild of AFTRA, Phi Beta Kappa. Roman Catholic. Address: 487 Michigan Ave NE Washington DC 20017-1584 E-mail: burkeop@aol.com. *For lasting happiness in life, one needs to experience the active presence of God.*

BURKE, JOHN EDWARD, communications editor; b. Huntington, W.Va., Aug. 10, 1942; s. Charles Joseph and Eloise Marie (Sang) B.; m. Mary Catherine Enright; children: John Lindsey, Elizabeth Ann, Caroline Catherine. BA, Marshall U., 1965; MFA, Ohio U., 1966; PhD, Ohio State U., 1971. Intern U.S. Ho. Reps., 1960-61; news writer, editor Sta. WSAZ-TV, Huntington, 1962-65; instr. Kent State U., 1966-69; dir. TV Arts dept. Cleve. Summer Sch. for Arts, 1967-68; asst. to dir. Ohio State U. Telecomms. Ctr., 1969-71; project dir. Ohio Valley Med. Microwave TV System, Columbus, 1971-73; dir., assoc. prof. biomed. comms. Ohio State U. Coll. Medicine; assoc. prof. comms. Coll. Social and Behavioral Scis., 1972-84; assoc. dean acad. affairs, prof. U. Ill. Coll. Associated Health Professions, Chgo., 1984-87; sr. mgr. sci. rels. Pharm. Products divsn. Abbott Labs., 1987-97; exec. dir., CEO Accreditation Assn. Ambulatory Health Care Inc. Adj. prof. Ohio State U., Columbus, 1989—; cons. univs., bus., industry, including U. Tenn., Nat. Med. Audio-Visual Center, Upjohn Co., N. Central Assn. Colls. and Univs., WHO, AMA. Author: History of Public Broadcasting Act of 1967, 1979; contbr. articles to profl. jours.; editor Jour. Allied Health, 1978-87; editor emeritus Jour. Allied Health, 1987—. USPHS grantee, 1972-77. Fellow Am. Soc. Allied Health Professions; mem. Health Scis. Comms. Assn., Coun. of Biology Editors, Am. Med. Writers Assn., Am. Soc. Assn. Execs., Alpha Psi Omega, Alpha Epsilon Rho. Democrat. Roman Catholic. Home: 567 Maple St Winnetka IL 60093-2335

BURKE, JOHN K(IRKLAND), JR., lawyer; b. Richmond, Va., Jan. 26, 1952; s. John Kirkland and Archer (Christian) B.; m. Miriam Smith, July 23, 1977; children: John K. III, Ruth H., B. Smith. BA in History with distinction, U. Va., 1974, JD, 1977. Bar: Va. 1977, U.S. Dist. Ct. (ea. and we. dists.) Va. 1977, U.S. Ct. Appeals (4th cir.) 1977. Law clk. to Justice George M. Cochran Supreme Ct. Va., Staunton, 1977-78; assoc. Mays and Valentine, L.L.P., Richmond, Va., 1978-84; ptnr. Mays and Valentine, Richmond, Va., 1984-2000, chmn. bus. and comml. litigation practice group; ptnr. Troutman Sanders LLP, Richmond, 2001—. Mem. City of Richmond's Human Rels. Comm., 1991-97; bd. dirs. St. Andrews Sch., Richmond, Va., 2005—. Mem. Va. Bar Assn., Bar Assn. of City of Richmond (bd. dirs. 1994-98), Soc. of the Cin. for State of Va. (asst. treas.), Va. State Bar, Country Club Va. (bd. dirs. 1999-2001). Avocations: sports, reading, music. Office: Troutman Sanders LLP PO Box 1122 Richmond VA 23218-1122 Office Phone: 804-697-1210. E-mail: john.burke@troutmansanders.com.

BURKE, JOHN MICHAEL, lawyer; b. Chgo., Oct. 9, 1941; s. John and Catherine Mary (Barrett) B.; m. Maureen Kay Fox, Oct. 5, 1968; children: Brian, Timothy, Michael. BBA, Loyola U., 1964, JD, 1965. Bar: Ill. 1965, U.S. Dist. Ct. (no. dist.) Ill. 1965, U.S. Ct. Appeals (7th cir.) 1968, U.S. Dist. Ct. (no.dist.) Ind. 1986. Assoc. Pretzel & Stouffer, Chgo., 1965—69, Shaheen, Lundberg & Callahan, Chgo., 1969—70; ptnr. Burke & Burke, Ltd., Chgo., 1970—. Sgt. U.S. Army, 1965-68. Mem. ATLA, Chgo. Bar Assn., Ill. State Bar Assn. (chmn. tort coun., svc. award 1984, civil practice com. 1997-2003, jud. evaluation com. 2002—), Ill. Trial Lawyers (bd. mgrs. 1988—), Appellate Lawyers Ill., Westmoreland Country Club (Wilmette, Ill.) Home: 2241 Kenilworth Ave Wilmette IL 60091-1523 Office: Burke & Burke Ltd 30 N LaSalle St Ste 2800 Chicago IL 60602 Office Phone: 312-726-6630. Business E-Mail: jburke@burke-burke.com.

BURKE, JOSEPH C., former university official; b. New Albany, Ind., Mar. 20, 1932; s. Dennis F. and Beatrice V. (McDevitt) B.; m. Joan Thompson, Sept. 1, 1956; children: Maura, Colleen. BA, Bellarmine Coll., Louisville, 1954; MA, Ind. U., 1958, PhD, 1965. Instr. Ohio Wesleyan U., Delaware, 1960-62; asst. prof. to prof. history Duquesne U., Pitts., 1962-70; prof. history Loyola of Montreal, 1970-73, acad. v.p., 1970-73, SUNY Coll., Plattsburgh, 1973-74, pres., 1974-85; provost, vice chancellor for acad. affairs SUNY Sys., Albany, 1985-95; pres. Rsch. Found. SUNY, Albany, 1990-95, interim chancellor, 1994; sr. fellow, dir. higher edn. prog. Nelson A. Rockefeller Inst. Govt., Albany, 1956. Cons. leadership adn planning for colls. and univs. Author books, monographs, chpts. and articles on accountability in higher edn. and performance funding and reporting. Trustee Miner Found. Rsch.; chmn. bd. Miner Agrl. Inst. Grantee Pew Charitable Trusts Luce Found., 1996—, Ford Found., 1996—. Office Phone: 518-433-5835. Business E-Mail: burkejo@rockinst.org.

BURKE, KATHLEEN B., lawyer; b. Bklyn., Sept. 2, 1948; BA, St. John's U., 1969, JD, 1973. Bar: Ohio 1973. Ptnr. Jones, Day, Reavis & Pogue, Cleve. Chair Notre Dame Coll. of Ohio, 2002—. Pres. Cleve. Skating Club, 2000-2002. Named a Woman of Achievement, Cleve. YWCA, 2004. Fellow Ohio State Bar Found. (pres. 2000); mem. Ohio State Bar Assn. (pres. 1993-94). Office: Jones Day Reavis & Pogue North Point 901 Lakeside Ave E Cleveland OH 44114-1190

BURKE, KATHRYN BRYANT, artist; b. Chattanooga, Tenn., Aug. 1, 1920; d. Louis Charlton and Mabel (Hodges) B.; John Alvin, Feb. 20, 1944; children: Kathryn Dianne, John Michael. Student, High Museum Sch. of Art, Atlanta, 1941; BFA, Atlanta Coll. of Art, 1967; postgrad., Oglethorpe U., 1967, Emory U. Grad. Sch. of Arts &, 1989. Artist designer Grizzard Advtg., Atlanta, 1941-45; freelance artist Kathryn Burke Studio, Atlanta, 1945-57; sec., treas. Art Dirs. Club, Atlanta, 1955; studio dir., instr. in painting Kathryn Burke Studio-Workshop, Atlanta. Painter: art exhibitions, solo, 1969-86. Mem. High Museum of Art, Emory U. Museum of Art and Archaeology, The Drawing Soc. Michael C. Carlos Mus. of Emory U., Metropolitan Museum of Art. Republican. Episcopalian. Avocations: reading, music, walking, nature study. Office: Kathryn Burke Studio Worksh 1300 Indian Trl NW Atlanta GA 30327-4414

BURKE, KELLY HOWARD, retired military officer, entrepreneur; b. Mobile, Ala., June 7, 1929; s. Kelly Howard and Vesta (Trussell) B.; m. Denny Ray Hosey, Dec. 30, 1951; children: Bethany, Patricia, Kelly Howard, III. BS in History, Auburn U., 1952; MS in Internat. Rels., George Washington U., 1968; postgrad., Naval War Coll., 1967-68, RAF Staff Coll., 1969-71, Indsl. Coll. Armed Forces, 1964-65. Commd. 2d lt. U.S. Air Force, 1953, advanced through grades to lt. gen., 1979; comdr. 379th Bomb Wing Wurtsmith AFB, Mich., 1973-74; comdr. 2d Bomb Wing Barksdale AFB, La., 1974-75; dep. chief of staff/plans SAC, 1975-78; dir. operational requirements Hdqrs. U.S. Air Force, Washington, 1978-79, dep. chief of staff/research, devel. and acquisition, 1979-82; ret., 1982; chmn. bd. Stafford, Burke and Hecker, Inc., Alexandria, VA, 1982. Bd. dirs. Singer Co., Tiger Internat. Inc., Flying Tigers Line Inc., Orbital Scis. Corp., OWCC Found., Children's Advocacy Ctr.; cons. White House Sci. Office, NRC, Def. Sci. Bd., Sci. Adv. Bd., others; frequent lectr. Chmn. editl. bd. Aerospace Am.; contbg. editor Armed Forces Jour.; contbr. numerous articles on nat. security issues to publd. Decorated D.S.M. with oak leaf cluster, Legion of Merit, D.F.C., Meritorious Svc. medal, Air medal with oak leaf clusters; established Burke Scholarship Endowment for 15 4-yr. coll. scholarships annually to needy students, established Burke Scholarship for outstanding AFROTC cadet, Auburn U.; named Fla. Benefactor of Yr. for this and other charitable activities, 1995. Mem. Nat. Space Club, Nat. Aviation Club Episcopalian. Home: 803 Choctaw Ln Shalimar FL 32579-2248 Office: Stafford Burke and Hecker 1006 Cameron St Alexandria VA 22314-2427 Personal E-mail: kbxel@aol.com.

BURKE, KENNETH ANDREW, advertising executive; b. Sept. 9, 1941; s. Frank Flory and Margret Anne (Tomè) B.; m. Karen Lee Burley, July 1, 1968; children: Allison Leigh Hart, Aric Jason. BSBA in Mktg., Bowling Green (Ohio) State U., 1965. Mem. Green Bay Packers Nat. Football League, Sask. Roughriders, Can. Football League; acct. exec. lang, Fisher, Stashower, Cleve., 1967-69; v.p., acct. supr. Tracy-Locke, Dallas, 1969-72; v.p. Grey Advt., N.Y.C., 1972-76, Griswold Eshleman, Cleve., 1976-79; sr. v.p., gen. mgr. Simpson Mktg., Columbus, Ohio, 1979-81; pres., CEO, chmn. Martcom Inc., Columbus, Ohio, 1981-91; chmn. ret. Ad Factory, Inc., Advt. and Mktg., Ad Factory Outlets, Columbus, Ohio, 1991-98; exec. v.p. Berkshire Product Inc., Tampa, Fla., 1983-89. Bd. dirs. Ad Factory, Newport Mktg. Svcs. Author: (children's stories) Bordini and the Black Knight, 1975. Mem. adv. bd. columbus chpt. Am. Cancer Soc., 1980-88. Recipient USN Achievement award, 1975. Mem. NRA, Am. Mktg. Assn., Columbus Advt. Fedn., NFL Alumni Assn., Columbus Numis. Soc., Am. Numis. Assn, Columbus NFL Alumni, Cleve. Advt. Club (Merit award 1968), Columbus C. of C., Upper Arlington C. of C., Theta Chi. Republican. Roman Catholic. Home: 1753 Bedford Rd Columbus OH 43212-2004 Office: Ad Factory Corp Offices 22 Gay Street Columbus OH 43215

BURKE, KEVIN CHARLES ANTONY, geologist; b. London, Nov. 13, 1929; came to U.S., 1973; s. Charles Henry and Kathleen B.; m. Angela Marion Phipps, Jan. 23, 1960; children: Nicholas, Matthew, Jane. BSc, Univ. Coll., London, 1951, PhD, 1953. Lectr. U. Ghana, 1953-56; geologist Brit. Geol. Survey, 1956-61; head geology dept. U. West Indies, Kingston, Jamaica, 1961-65; prof. geology U. Ibadan, Nigeria, 1963-71, SUNY-Albany, 1973-83; prof. U. Houston, 1983—; dir. Lunar and Planetary Inst., 1983-88; scholar in residence NRC, Washington, 1989-92. Vis. prof. U. Toronto, 1971-73, Calif. Inst. Tech., 1976, U. Minn., 1977, U. Calgary, 1979; cons. in field. NSF grantee, 1976— Fellow Geol. Soc. Am.; mem. AAAS, Am. Geophys. Union, Nigerian Mining, Geol. and Metall. Soc. (pres. internat. com. on the lithosphere 1992-95, Du Toit meml. lectr. 1995). Achievements include research in plate tectonics. Office: Univ Houston Dept Geoscis Houston TX 77204-5007 Office Phone: 713-743-3397. *There is much luck in a scientific career. I could not have known when I chose to become a geologist in 1948 that understanding of the problems I studied would be revolutionized by Plate Tectonics in 1965. To make the most of such an opportunity in geology a breadth of experience, both geographically and in different branches of geology, has proved vital.*

BURKE, LAWRENCE J., editor-in-chief; Founder, chmn., editor-in-chief Outside Mag. (now called Mariah Media Inc.), 1976—. Office: Outside Mag 400 Market St Santa Fe NM 87501

BURKE, LILLIAN WALKER, retired judge; b. Thomaston, Ga., Aug. 2, 1917; d. George P. and Ozella (Daviston) Walker; m. Ralph Livingston Burke, July 8, 1948 (dec.); 1 son, R. Bruce. BS, Ohio State U., 1947; LLB, Cleve. State U., 1951, postgrad., 1963-64; grad., Nat. Coll. State Judiciary, U. Nev., 1974. Bar: Ohio 1951. Gen. practice law, Cleve., 1952-62; asst. atty. gen. Ohio, 1962-66; mem., vice chmn. Ohio Indsl. Commn., 1966-69; judge Cleve. Mcpl. Ct., 1969-87, chief judge, 1981, 85, vis. judge, 1988-97; ret., 1997. Guest lectr. Heidelburg Coll., Tiffin, Ohio, 1971; cons. Bur. Higher Edn., HEW, 1972. Pres. Cleve. chpt. Nat. Coun. Negro Women, 1955-57; sec. East dist. Family Service Assn., 1959-60; mem. coun. human rels. Cleve. Citizens League, 1959-79; mem. Gov.'s Com. on Status of Women, 1966-67; pres. Cleve. chpt. Jack and Jill of Am., Inc., 1960-61; v.p.-at-large Greater Cleve. Safety Coun., 1969-79; mem. Cleve. Landmarks Commn., 1990-97; woman ward leader 24th Ward Republican Club, 1957-67; mem. Cuyahoga County Ctrl. Com., 1958-68; sec. Cuyahoga County Exec. Com., 1962-63; alt. del. Rep. Nat. Conv., Chgo., 1960; bd. dirs., chmn. minority div. Nat. Fedn. Rep. Women, 1966-68; life mem., past bd. dirs. Cleve. chpt. NAACP; bd. dirs. Greater Cleve. Neighborhood Ctrs. Assn., Cath. Youth Counselling Svcs.; trustee Ohio Commn. on Status of Women, 1966-70, Consumers League Ohio, 1969-75, Cleve. Music Sch. Settlement; bd. mgmt. Glenville YWCA, 1960-70; mem. project com. Cleve. Orch.; apptd. mem. City Planning Comm. Cleve., 1997-2002. Recipient achievement award Parkwood Christian Meth. Episcopal Ch., 1968, Martin Luther King Citizen's award, 1969, outstanding achievement award Ta-Wa-Si Scholarship Club, 1969, Outstanding Svc. award Morning Star Grand chpt., Cleve., 1970, award of honor Cleve. Bus. League, 1970, svc. award St. Paul AME Ch., Lima, Ohio, 1972, Woman of Achievement award Inner Club Coun., Cleve., 1973, cert. of award Nat. Coun. Negro Women, 1969, Cleve. Found. Golf Philanthropic Leadership award, 1997; named Career Woman of Yr., Cleve. Women's Career Clubs, 1969, Jewel of Yr., Women's City Club, 2002, award for hist. preservation So. African Hist. Soc., 2002, Woman of Achievement award YWCA, 2003. Mem. ABA, Nat. Assn. Investment Clubs (pres. Dynasty Investors Club 1992-96, bd. dirs. N.E. Ohio Coun. 1993-2003), Nat. Bar Assn., Ohio Bar Assn., Cuyahoga County Bar Assn., Cleve. Bar Assn., Am. Judicature Soc., Am. Judges Assn. (bd. govs. 1982-86, chmn. conv. agenda com. 1981-83), Phillis Wheatley Assn., Women Lawyers Assn. (hon. adviser), Ohio State U. Alumni Assn. (life), Cleve. Marshall Law Sch. (life), Am. Bridge Assn. (life), Women's City Club of Cleve. (life), Altrusa, Alpha Kappa Alpha. Mem. Ch. Of Christ. Home: 1357 East Blvd Cleveland OH 44106-4018

BURKE, LINDA BEERBOWER, lawyer, mining executive, metal products executive; b. Huntington, W.Va., June 19, 1948; d. William Bert and Betty Jane (Weddle) Beerbower; m. Timothy F. Burke, Jr., Aug. 26, 1972; children: Ryan Timothy, Hannah Elizabeth. BA in Govt., Coll. of William and Mary, 1970; JD, U. Pitts., 1973. Bar: Pa. 1973. Tax atty. legal dept. Aluminum Co. Am., Pitts., 1973-77, gen. tax atty. tax dept., 1977-80, mgr. legal and planning taxes, 1980-86, tax counsel, 1987-2000, asst. officer, 1992-2000, dir. taxes, 1993-2000; now v.p. Suriname Aluminum Co., Pitts., Alcoa Minerals of Jamaica, Inc., Pitts., Alcoa Steamship Co., Inc., Pitts.; with Alcoa Svc. Corp., Pitts., to 2000; v.p. Northwest Alloys, Inc., Pitts.; oper. divsn. counsel large and mid-size bus. IRS, Washington, 2000—. V.p. various Alcoa subs.; presenter on fields internat. and employee benefits taxation, IRS audit procedures, atty.-client privilege. Note editor U. Pitts. Law Rev., 1972-73. Bd. dirs. YWCA Greater Pitts., 1987-95, 97-2000, v.p., 1989-92, pres., 1993-94; Alcoa co-chmn. Taylor Allderdice-Alcoa Partnership in Edn., 1982-84, chmn., 1985-88; mem. law fellows com. U. Pitts. Law Sch., 1988—, chmn. class ann. giving fund for law sch. class, 1982-94, chmn. law fellows, 1998—; bd. dirs. Soc. Alumni Coll. William & Mary, 2000—; mem. rev. com. United Way, 1987-94; bd. dirs. Vol. Action Ctr., 1982-85; mem. pers. com. Woman's Ctr. and Shelter Greater Pitts., 1986-94; trustee St. Edmund's Acad., 1986-94, sec., 1989-90, treas., 1990-92, mem. fin. com., 1986-93, chmn. enrollment com., 1988-90, co-chmn. ann. giving, 1986-87; mem. Leadership Pitts., 1990-91, bd. dirs., 1997-2000, sec., 1999-2000; bd. trustees Am. Tax Policy Inst., 1996-2000; mem. program com. Tax Found., 1996-2000; mem. adv. group to commr. Internal Revenue, 1996-98. Recipient tribute in corp. tax Triangle Corner, 1982, Asst. Commr.'s award IRS, 1992 Mem. ABA, Allegheny County Bar Assn., Am. Corp. Counsel Assn., Pitts. Internat. Tax Soc. (program com. 1988-94), Tax Execs. Inst. (bd. dirs. Pitts. chpt. 1981-86, pres. 1985-86, nat. bd. dirs., nat. exec. com. 1988-89, 90-91, 92-95, nat. chmn. IRS adminstrv. affairs com. 1989-90, 91-92, nat. sec. 1992-93, nat. sr. v.p. 1993-94, v.p. region VI 1990-91, internat. pres. 1994-95), Pitts. Tax Club (bd. dirs. 1989-95, pres. 1993-94), Duquesne Club. Democrat. Avocations: skiing, bridge, cooking, golf.

BURKE, MARGUERITE JODI LARCOMBE, application developer, consultant; b. Pasadena, Calif. d. Richard Albert and Marguerite (Colella) L.; m. M. Theodore Jockers; children: Richard Larcombe, Sir Blair; m. Roger Eugene Burke. PhD, Columbia U. Photographers model Ford Agy., N.Y.C.; freelance writer Savannah, Ga.; pres. Jodi Larcombe Assocs., Murfreesboro, N.C., 1970—; freelance computer programmer Murfreesboro, 1981—. Exec. asst. Resinall Corp., Severn, N.C., 1981—, computer programmer, 1981-89. Author: Sailing Cookbook, 1979, others; contbr. numerous articles to mags.; dir. Shotgun Theater Prodns., 1995. Chmn. bd. dirs. Shotgun Theater Prodns., N.Y., 1996—; patron Avery Fischer Hall, N.Y.C., 1979—; mem. Mus. Art N.Y.C., 1979—. Mem. Met. Opera Oncore Soc., Am. Film Soc., Met Opera Patron Assn. (2d century cir.), Met. Opera Nat. Coun., N.Y.C. Opera, Murfreesboro Hist. Soc. Avocations: sailing, reading, sewing, travel, classical music. Home and Office: Jodi Larcombe Assocs 12 Gale Ln Ormond Beach FL 32174 Personal E-mail: galelawe@earthlink.net.

BURKE, MARIANNE KING, state agency administrator, finance company executive, consultant; b. Douglasville, Ga., May 30, 1938; d. William Horace and Evora (Morris) King; divorced; 1 child, Kelly Page. Student, Ga. Inst. Tech., 1956-59, Anchorage C.C., 1964-66, Portland State U., 1968-69; BBA, U. Alaska, 1976. CPA, Alaska. Sr. audit mgr. Price Waterhouse, 1982-90; v.p. fin., asst. sec. NANA Regional Corp., Inc., Anchorage, 1990-95; v.p. fin. NANA Devel. Corp., Inc., Anchorage, 1990-95; sec.-treas. Vanguard Industries, J.V., Anchorage, 1990-95, Alaska United Drilling, Inc., Anchorage, 1990-95; treas. NANA/Marriott Joint Venture, Anchorage, 1990-95; v.p. fin. Arctic Utilities, Inc., Anchorage, 1990-95, Tour Arctic, Inc., Anchorage, 1990-95, Purcell Svcs., Ltd., Anchorage, 1990-95, Arctic Caribou Inn, Anchorage, 1990-95, NANA Oilfield Svcs., Inc., Anchorage, 1990-95, NANA Corp. Svcs., Inc., Anchorage, 1992-95; dir. divsn. ins. State of Alaska, 1995-99; pres. Marianne K. Burke Cons., 1999—. Cons. Ins. Regulatory and Devel. Authority of India, 2002—, Superintendencia de Banca y Seguros de Peru, 2004, Ins. Supervisory Commn. Republic of Albania, 2004; cons. Bosnia and Herzegovina ins. sector Fin. Svcs. Vol. Corps, 2003; mem. State of Alaska Medicaid Rate Commn., 1985—88, State of Alaska Bd. Accountancy, 1984—87; bd. dirs. Nat. Assn. Ins. Commrs. Edn. and Rsch. Found.; chair Bd. Equalization Municipality of Anchorage, 2004—. Bd. dirs. Alaska Treatment Ctr., Anchorage, 1978, Alaska Hwy. Cruises; treas. Alaska Feminist Credit Union, Anchorage, 1979-80; mem. fund raising com. Anchorage Symphony, 1981. Mem. AICPA, Internat. Assn. Ins. Suprs. (funded mem.), Alaska Soc. CPAs, Govtl. Fin. Officers U.S. and Can., Fin. Execs. Inst. (bd. dirs.), Nat. Assn. Ins. Commrs. (bd. dirs.). Avocations: travel, reading. Home: 3818 Helvetia Dr Anchorage AK 99508-5016 Office Phone: 907-563-9790. Personal E-mail: mkburke@gci.net.

BURKE, MARY GRIGGS (MRS. JACKSON BURKE), art collector; b. St. Paul; m. Jackson Burke (dec.). BA, Sarah Lawrence Coll.; MA in Clin. Psychology, Columbia U.; postgrad., New Sch. for Social Rsch. Pvt. collector Japanese art, St. Paul, 1966—; founder The Mary & Jackson Burke Found., N.Y.C., 1972—. Mem. vis. com. Freer Gallery Art, Smithsonian Instn.; mem. Met. Mus. Art; pres. The Mary and Jackson Burke Found. Mem. nominating com., mem. membership com., mem. exec. com., mem. activities com. The Japan Soc., 1959-77, chmn. student and visitors com., 1957-63, chmn. art gallery adv. com., 1970-73, bd. dirs., 1968-77, also hon. life trustee; chmn. friend mem. Japan House Gallery, 1969-75, 87—; bd. dirs. The Cable (Wis.) Natural History Mus., 1968-92, also hon. life trustee, Sarah Lawrence Coll., Bronxville, N.Y., 1968-78, also hon. life trustee, The Internat. Crane Found., Baraboo, Wis., 1978-90, The Hobe Sound (Fla.) Nature Ctr., 1987—; mem. adv. coun. dept. art history and archeology Columbia U., N.Y.C., 1970—; mem. internat. coun. Mus. Modern Art, N.Y.C., 1970—; mem. vis. com. Freer Gallery of Art, Smithsonian Instn., Washington, 1971—, vice chmn., 1989-92; mem. vis. com. dept. Asiatic art Mus. Fine Arts, Boston, 1972-90, also friend, 1972-90; mem. vis. com. dept. Islamic art, mem. vis. com. dept. Asian art, mem. edn. com., mem. acquisitions com., bd. dirs. Met. Mus. Art, N.Y.C., 1976—, also friend Far Ea. dept., 1984—; mem. Smithsonian Assocs. nat. bd. Smithsonian Instn., Washington, 1977-83; mem. art gallery adv. com., mem. exec. com., mem. devel. com., bd. dirs. The Asia Soc., 1978-88, also hon. life trustee; friend Bklyn. Mus. Art, 1982—, Friends of Asian Art, Freer and Sackler Galleries, 1991—; William Beene fellows N.Y. Zool. Soc., 1986—. Decorated Order of The Sacred Treasure (Japan), Second Leve Gold and Silver Star (Japan), named one of top 200 collectors, ARTnews Mag., 2004. Achievements include The Mary Griggs Burke Collection of Japanese Art at Met. Mus. of Art in NY is the largest prfv. collection of Japanese art outside Japan. Avocation: collector of Japanese art. Mailing: Mary Livingston Griggs & Mary Griggs Burke Foundation 1400 Fifth Street Ctr Saint Paul MN 55101*

BURKE, MATTHEW M., lawyer; b. St. Louis, Sept. 30, 1964; BA cum laude, Holy Cross Coll., 1987; JD cum laude, Harvard Univ., 1990. Bar: Mass. 1990, US Dist. Ct. (Mass.) 1991, US Ct. Appeals 3d cir. 2001. Assoc. to ptnr. litigation dept. Ropes & Gray, Boston, 1990—, head insurance practice group. Mem.: ABA, Mass. Bar Assn., Boston Bar Assn. Office: Ropes & Gray 1 International Pl Boston MA 02110-2624 Office Phone: 617-951-7589. Office Fax: 617-951-7050. Business E-Mail: matthew.burke@ropesgray.com.

BURKE, PAUL E., JR., government agency administrator, consultant; b. Kansas City, Mo., Jan. 4, 1934; s. Paul E. and Virgnia (Moling) B.; m. Debbie Weihe; children: Anne Elizabeth, Kelly Patricia, A. Catherine, Jennifer Marie. BSBA, U. Kans., 1956. Mem. Kans. Ho. of Reps., 1972-74, Kans. Senate, 1975-97, majority leader, 1985-89, pres., 1992—96; pres., chairman/CEO Issues Mgmt. Group, Inc., Lawrence, Kans., 1996—. Chmn. Legis. Coordinating Coun., 1995; pres.-elect Nat. Conf. State Legislatures, 1990-91, pres., 1992; pres. Nat. Conf. State Legislatures Found., 1994; mem. Fed. Adv. Commn. Intergovtl. Rels., 1993-96. Councilman City of Prairie Village, Kans., 1959-63; mem. Kans. Turnpike Authority, 1965-69, chmn., 1969; mem. adv. bd. Sect. Corrections, 1973-78; mem. Gov.'s Mil. Adv. Coordinating Coun., 2002--. Capt. USAF, 1956-59; Capt. USNR, 1963-88. Mem. Kans. Assn. Commerce and Industry, Masons, Shriners, Rotary. Republican. Episcopalian. Address: 2009 Camelback Dr Lawrence KS 66047 *Personal philosophy: The reponsibility for serving in an elected capacity is one of the greatest privileges extended by one's constituents. Understanding how to convert that responsibility to the highest level of benefit for them is our greatest challenge. Service to others--rather than self--is the key.*

BURKE, PEGGY HUDGINS (MARGARET HUDGINS BURKE), auditor; b. Aug. 30, 1951; BA, U. of the South, 1973; BS, Med. Coll. Va., 1974; MBA, U. N.C., Charlotte, 1995. CPA Va., N.C. Practice mgr. MedCorp Health Sys., Columbia, SC, 1986-91; med. technologist V.A. Hosp., Columbia, SC, 1991-92, Presbyn. Hosp., Charlotte, 1992-95, fin. dir. lab., 1997-98, corp. compliance dir., 1998-2000; practice adminstr. Shelby (N.C.) Med. Assoc., 1996-97; dir. internal audit and compliance Novant Health, Inc., Charlotte, 2000—. Vestry St. Andrews Episcopal Ch., Mt. Holly, NC, 1998—99. Home: 201 Timberlane Dr Belmont NC 28012-7726 Office: 200 Hawthorne Ln Charlotte NC 28204-2515

BURKE, RAYMOND LEO, archbishop; b. Richland Center, Wis., June 30, 1948; s. Thomas F. and Marie Burke. Attended, Holy Cross Seminary, La Crosse, Wis., 1966—68, Catholic U. of Am., 1968—71, Pontifical Gregorian U., Rome, 1971—75. ordained June 29, 1975. Ordained a priest, 1975; assoc. rector Cathedral of St. Joseph the Workman, La Crosse, Wis., 1975—84; instructor of religion Aquinas High Sch., La Crosse, Wis., 1977—84; moderator of Curia and vice-chancellor Diocese of La Crosse, La Crosse, Wis., 1984, adjunct judicial vicar, 1985; visiting prof. of Canonical Jurisprudence Pontifical Gregorian U., Rome, 1985—94; bishop Diocese of La Crosse, 1994—2003; archbishop Archdiocese of St. Louis, 2004—. Bd. dirs. Nat. Catholic Rural Life Conference, 1995, bd. pres., 1996—2001; mem. Canonical Affairs Com. Nat. Conference of Catholic Bishops, 1997—99; mem. Commn. on Religious Life and Mission US Conference of Catholic Bishops, 2001—03; nat. dir. Marian Catechist Apostolate, 2000—; spiritual dir. Real Presence Assn., 2002—; mem. Vatican's Congregation for Clergy, 2003—. Office: Archdiocese of St Louis 4445 Lindell Blvd Saint Louis MO 63108*

BURKE, RICHARD A., manufacturing executive; CEO, chmn. Trek Corp., Waterloo, Wis. Bd. dir. Quad/Graphics, 1994—, chmn., 2003—. Office: Trek Corp 801 W Madison St Waterloo WI 53594-1243

BURKE, RICHARD KITCHENS, lawyer, educator; b. Helena, Ark., Aug. 21, 1922; s. James Graham and Myrtie May (Kitchens) B.; m. Bonnie Beth Byler, Jan. 21, 1946; children: Charles, Bonnie Louise. Student, U. Va., 1939-40; BA, U. Ark., 1942, LLB, 1947; PhD, Vanderbilt U., 1957. Bar: Ark. 1947, Ariz. 1959, S.D. 1974. Ptnr. Burke, Moore & Burke, Helena, 1947-52; asst. prof. polit. sci. U. Ariz., 1957-60; ptnr. Robertson, Childers, Burke & Drachman, Tucson, 1960-67; prof. polit. sci. U. Southwestern La., 1967-69; U.S. atty. Dist. Ariz., Dept. Justice, 1969-72; dep. asst. atty. gen. U.S. Dept. Justice, Washington, 1972-73; prof. law U. S.D. Sch. Law, 1973-84, dean, 1974-80; prof. law U. Ark., 1984-86, prof. emeritus, 1986—. Mem. Ariz. Rep. State Com., 1963-67; Rep. congl. candidate So. Dist. Ariz., 1962; chmn. citizen's adv. com. Ampitheater Sch. Dist., Tucson, 1964-66. With USN, 1942-45, 53-54. Decorated Air medal; Ford fellow Vanderbilt U., 1957. Mem. Am. Bar Assn., State Bar S.D., State Bar Ariz., Ark. Bar Assn. Republican. Mem. Christian Ch. Home: 13 Minentonka Dr Cherokee Village AR 72529

BURKE, ROBERT BERTRAM, lawyer, political scientist, lobbyist; b. Cleve., July 9, 1942; s. Max and Eve (Miller) B.; m. Helen Choate Hall, May 5, 1979 (div. Oct. 1983). BA, UCLA, 1963, JD, 1966; LLM, London Sch. Econs., 1967. Bar: D.C. 1972, U.S. Supreme Ct. 1977, Calif. 1978. Exec. dir. Lawyer's Com. Civil Rights Under Law, Washington, 1968-69; ptnr. Fisk, Wolfe & Burke, Paris, 1969-71; assoc. O'Connor & Hannan, Washington, 1972-74; pvt. practice Washington, 1974-79, L.A., 1978-93; contract lobbyist GCG Rose & Kindel, L.A., Sacramento, Washington, 1993—. Cons. Commonwealth Pa., Harrisburg, 1973. Chmn. So. Calif. Hollings for Pres., 1984; pres. Bldg. and Appeals Bd. City of L.A.; bd. dirs. Vols. of Am.; mem. exec. com. State Bar of Calif. pub. law sect. Mem. ABA UCLA Law Alumni Assn. (pres.). Jewish. Home: 277 S Irving Blvd Los Angeles CA 90004-3809 Office Phone: 213-624-1030. Business E-Mail: bburke@rosekindel.com.

BURKE, ROBERT HARRY, surgeon, educator; b. Cambridge, Mass., Dec. 22, 1945; s. Harry Clearfield and Joan Rosalyn (Spire) B.; m. Margaret Cauldwell Fisher, May 4, 1968; children: Christopher David, Catherine Cauldwell. Student, U. Mich. Coll. Pharmacy, 1964—67; DDS, U. Mich., 1971, MS, 1976; MD, Mich. State U., 1980. Diplomate Am. Bd. Oral and Maxillofacial Surgery, Am. Bd. Cosmetic Surgery. Pvt. practice cosmetic and reconstructive surgery, Ann Arbor, Mich. House officer oral and maxillofacial surgery U. Mich. Sch. Dentistry, U. Mich. Hosp., Ann Arbor, 1973-76; clin. asst. prof. dept. oral surgery U. Detroit Sch. Dentistry, 1976-77; adj. asst. rsch. scientist Ctr. Human Growth and Devel. U. Mich., 1976-77, adj. rsch. investigator, 1982-85; clin. asst. prof. Mich. State U., East Lansing, 1978-80, 1987—; house officer surg. emphasis St. Joseph Mercy Hosp., Ann Arbor, 1980-81; adj. rsch. investigator dept. anatomy U. Mich. Med. Sch., 1982-85; adj. clin. asst. prof. oral and maxillofacial surgery U. Mich., 1984-86, 2002-2003, adj. clin. assoc. prof. maxillofacial surgery, 2003—; lectr. U. Detroit Sch. Dentistry, 1986, assoc. clin. prof. oral and maxillofacial surgery, 1987-90; cons., lectr. dept. occlusion U. Mich. Sch. Dentistry, 1986, asst. clin. prof. dept. maxillofacial sugery, 2002, assoc. adj. clin. prof., 2002—; head sect. dentistry and oral surgery dept. gen. surgery St. Joseph Mercy Hosp., 1982-87, mem. exec. com. dept. gen. surgery, 1984-87; chmn. com. emergency care rev. Beyer Meml. Hosp., Ypsilanti, Mich., 1986, also active, 1987, 1990-2000; active staff St. Joseph Meml. Hosp.; courtesy staff Saline (Mich.) Cmty. Hosp., 1978-88; Chelsea (Mich.) Med. Ctr., 1978-88, 90-92, McPherson Cmty. Hosp., Howell, Mich., 1984-87, Herrick Meml. Hosp., 1998—, Bixby Hosp., 1998—, Annapolis Hosp., 2000-2002, Oakwood Hosp., 2000-2002; dir. Mich. Ctr. Cosmetic Surgery. Mem. editl. bd. Topics in Pain Mgmt., 1985—; contbg. editor Am. Jours. Cosmetic surgery, 1990-91; sect. editor Internat. Jour. Aesthetic and Restorative Surgery, 1992-95, 96-2000, Internat. Jour. Cosmetic Surgery and Aesthetic Dermatology, 2000—. Campaign chmn. med. and dental sects. United Way Washtenaw County, Ann Arbor, 1982, dental sect. 1983; profl. adv. com. March of Dimes Genesee County Valley Chpt., Flint, 1979; pres. Huron Pkwy. Pla. Condominium, 1984—. Fellow: Am. Acad. Aesthetic and Restorative Surgery, Am. Coll. Oral and Maxillofacial Surgeons, ACS, Internat. Coll. Surgeons; mem.: Inst. Study Profl. Risk, Washtenaw County Med. Soc., European Assn. for Cranio-Maxillofacial Surgery, Chalmers Lyons Acad. oral Surgery, European Soc. Aesthetic Surgery and Liposuction, Internat. Soc. Cosmetic Laser Surgeons, Am. Assn. Craniomaxillofacial Surgeons, Am. Assn. Cosmetic Maxillofacial Surgeons, AMA, Pres.'s Club, Victor's Club, Omicron Kappa Upsilon. Congregationalist. Office: 2260 S Huron Pky Ann Arbor MI 48104-5151 Office Phone: 734-971-0262. Business E-Mail: info@robertburke.com.

BURKE, SEAN, professional hockey player; b. Windsor, Ontario, Canada, Jan. 29, 1967; Goaltender New Jersey Devils, 1987—91, Hartford Whalers/Carolina Hurricanes, 1992—98, Vancouver Canucks, 1998, Philadelphia Flyers, 1998, Florida Panthers, 1998—99, Phoenix Coyotes, 1999—2004, Philadelphia Flyers, 2004—05, Tampa Bay Lightning, 2005—. Player NHL All-Star game, 1989, 2001, 02. Achievements include Silver Medalist with Canadian Olympic Hockey team in 1992. Office: c/o Tampa Bay Lightning 401 Channelside Dr Tampa FL 33602

BURKE, SHEILA P., federal agency administrator; b. San Francisco, Jan. 10, 1951; d. George Abbott and Mary Joan (Winfield) B.; m. David Chew, Jan. 1983; children: Daniel, Kathleen, Sarah. BSN, U. San Francisco, 1973; MA in Pub. Adminstrn., Harvard U., 1982. Staff nurse Alta Bates Hosp., Berkeley, Calif., 1973-74; dir. student affairs Nat. Student Nurses Assn., NY, 1974-75, dir. program and field svcs., 1975-77; legis. asst. Senator Bob Dole, 1977-78; profl. staff mem. Senate Com. Fin., U.S. Senate, 1979-82, dep. staff dir., 1982-85; dep. chief of staff Senate Majority Leader Bob Dole, U.S. Senate, 1985-86; chief of staff Senator Bob Dole, 1986-96; sec. U.S. Senate, Washington, 1995; undersec. Am. Mus. and nat. programs Smithsonian Instn., Washington, 2000—03, dep. sec., COO, 2004—. Adj. nursing faculty Georgetown U.; rsch. asst. J.F. Kennedy Sch. Govt., Harvard U., 1980-81, advisor to dean, 1996, exec. dean, lectr. pub. policy, 1996-2000, adj. lectr., 2000—. Republican. Address: 1323 Merrie Ridge Rd Mc Lean VA 22101-1826

BURKE, STEPHEN B., communications executive; married; 4 children. Degree with hons., Colgate U., 1980; MBA, Harvard U., 1982. Joined The Walt Disney Corp., 1985, from developer to exec. v.p., Disney Stores, 1985—92, exec. v.p. operations, Euro Disney S.A., 1992—95, pres., COO Euro Disney S.A., 1995—96, pres. ABC Broadcasting, 1996—98; pres. Comcast Cable., Phila., 1998—; from sr. v.p. to exec. v.p. Comcast Holdings Corp., 1998—2004, COO, 2004—. Mem. exec. com. C-SPAN; mem. adv. bd. Cable in the Classroom. Office: Comcast Corp 1500 Market St Philadelphia PA 19102

BURKE, THOMAS JOSEPH, JR., lawyer; b. Oct. 23, 1941; s. Thomas Joseph and Violet (Green) B.; m. Sharon Lynne Forke, Aug. 29, 1964; children: Lisa Lynne, Heather Ann. BA, Elmhurst Coll., 1963; JD, Chgo.-Kent Coll. Law, 1966. Bar: Ill. 1966, U.S. Dist. Ct. (no. dist.) Ill. 1967, U.S. Ct. Appeals (7th cir.) 1972, U.S. Supreme Ct. 1972, U.S. Ct. Appeals (11th cir.) 1994, U.S. Ct. Appeals (6th cir.) 1995. Assoc. Lord, Bissell & Brook, Chgo., 1966-74, ptnr., 1974—2003; of counsel Hall, Prangle & Schoonveld, LLC, 2004—. Fellow: Am. Coll. Trial Lawyers; mem.: Assn. Advancement Automotive Medicine, Soc. Automotive Engrs., Product Liability Adv. Coun., Ill. Assn. Def. Trial Counsel, Def. Rsch. Inst., Soc. Trial Lawyers, Chgo. Bar Assn., Mid-Day Club, Phi Delta Phi, Pi Kappa Delta. Republican. Roman Catholic. Office: Hall, Prangle & Schoonveld, LLC 225 West Washington Street, Suite 2700 Chicago IL 60606 Office Phone: 312-267-6229. Business E-Mail: tburke@hpslaw.com.

BURKE, THOMAS MICHAEL, lawyer; b. Summit, N.J., Feb. 10, 1956; s. Robert William and Eleanor Mary (Kelley) B.; m. Nancy Robin Mogab, Sept. 24, 1983; children: Colleen Margaret, Michael Thomas, Brendan Robert. BA, Notre Dame U., 1978; JD, St. Louis U., 1981. Bar: Mo. 1981, Ill. 1982, U.S. Dist. Ct. (ea. dist.) 1981. Assoc. Moser, Marsalek, Carpenter, Cleary & Jaeckel, St. Louis, 1981-86; ptnr. Noonan & Burke, St. Louis, 1986-92; prin. Thomas M. Burke, PC, St. Louis, 1992—. Bd. dirs. Legal Svcs. Ea. Mo., 1995-97. Active Vol. Lawyers program, St. Louis, St. Louis Hills Homeowner's Assn., 1984-94. Mem. Mo. Bar Assn. (bd. govs., 1998—, chair fin. com. 2002—, exec. com. 2004-05), Ill. Bar Assn., Interest On Lawyers' Trust Accounts (bd. dirs. 1997-2002, pres. 2000-01), Bar Assn. Met. St. Louis (treas. 1992-93, sec. 1993-94, v.p. 1994-95, pres.-elect 1995-96, pres. 1996-97), St. Louis Bar Found. (sec. 1993-94, treas. 1995-96), Lawyers Assn. St. Louis (exec. com. 1987-92, sec. 1992-93, treas. 1992-93, v.p. 1993-94). Office: 701 Market St Ste 1075 Saint Louis MO 63101-1886 Office Phone: 314-241-8200. Business E-Mail: tburke@burkelawfirm.com.

BURKE, THOMAS RICHARD, community college administrator; b. St. Louis, Oct. 2, 1944; s. Lloyd Richard and Frances Elizabeth (Yelton) B.; m. Sara Lou Janes, July 3, 1969; 1 child, Kimberly Ayre. BA, U. Miss., 1970, MA, 1972, PhD, 1981. Instr. Mountain Empire C.C., Big Stone Gap, Va., 1972-74, asst. prof., 1974-77, assoc. prof. history, 1977-80, acting pres., 1977, dean instrn., 1976-80; v.p. Three Rivers C.C., Poplar Bluff, Mo., 1980-86; pres. Independence C.C., 1986—, Kansas City (Kans.) C.C. Chmn. City of Poplar Bluff Hist. Commn. Served with USAF, 1965-69. Edn. Professions Devel. Act fellow, 1970-72. Mem. Am. Assn. Cmty. and Jr. Colls. (chmn. 1984-85), Kans. Assn. C.C. (chmn.), S.E. Kans. Consortium Colls. and Univs., Mo. Hist. Assn., Phi Delta Kappa, Masons, Shriners. Methodist. Office: Kansas City CC Office of Pres 7250 State Ave Kansas City KS 66112-3003

BURKE, THOMAS SEBASTIAN, JR., (JUNIOR BURKE), writer, educator; s. Colonel Thomas Burke Bishop and Anne Holderread; m. Michele Leonard, May 7, 2000; 1 child, Simone. MFA in Writing and Poetics, Naropa U., Boulder, Colo., 1996. Program dir. MFA creative writing Naropa U., Boulder, Colo., instr. summer writing program; instr. U. Denver, Tenn. State U., Nashville, 1997—98. Author: Something Gorgeous, 2005, (song cycle) Someone Else's Dream; founder, editor: Not Enough Night, 2005. Recipient Essay award, New Millenium Writing, 1997. Mem.: AAUP, Broadcast Music, Inc., Writers Guild of Am. Office: Naropa U 2130 Arapahoe Boulder CO 80302 Office Phone: 303-245-4820. Business E-Mail: jrburke@naropa.edu.

BURKE, THOMAS WILLIAM, benefits compensation analyst; b. Harmon, Ill., Aug. 1, 1947; s. John William and Mary Eileen (Long) B.; m. Mary Ellen Bosau, Nov. 27, 1970; children: Kelly, Colleen, Shannon, Tommy, Michael. BS, St. Joseph's Coll., Collegeville, Ind., 1969. CLU; ChFC; CFP; lic. ins. counselor. Asst. mgr. Conn. Gen., Chgo., 1970-77; v.p. Fin. Industries, Austin, Tex., 1977; pres. T.W. Burke Assocs., Austin, 1978-87; dir. advanced underwriting SunLife, Dallas, 1988-92; pres. Hefner Assocs., Richardson, Tex., 1992—. Tchr. continuing edn. ABA, Tex. Soc. for CPA's and Atty. CPA's, U. Tex., 1986—. Coach Little League, 1991—; bd. advisor St. Joseph's Coll. Mem. Nat. Assn. Life Underwriters, Nat. Assn. Securities Dealers, Assn. Advanced Life Underwriters, Soc. CLU's, Dallas C. of C. (govt. affairs com. 1993-94), Million Dollar Round Table. Roman Catholic. Avocations: golf, coaching baseball. Office: Hefner & Assocs 600 W Campbell Rd Ste 7 Richardson TX 75080-3388

BURKE, TIMOTHY JOHN, lawyer; b. Syracuse, N.Y., June 5, 1946; s. Francis Joseph and Alice Marie Burke; m. Denise Kay Blied, Mar. 18, 1978; 1 child, Aimee Noel; 1 child from a previous marriage, Ryan Alexander. BA with distinction, Ariz. State U., 1967, JD cum laude, 1970. Bar: Ariz. 1970, U.S. Dist. Ct. Ariz. 1970, U.S. Ct. Appeals (9th cir.) 1974. Trial atty. Antitrust divsn. U.S. Dept. Justice, Washington, 1970-72, asst. to dir. ops., 1972-74; assoc. Fennemore Craig, Phoenix, 1974—, dir., 1978—. Part-time instr. legal writing Ariz. State U., 1974-75, adj. faculty assoc. profl. responsibility Coll. of Law, 2001-03. Mem. panel rev. bd. Phoenix United Way, 1975-76; bd. dirs. Florence Crittenton Svcs., Phoenix, 1980-88, pres., 1985-87; bd. dirs. Law Soc. Ariz. State U. Coll. Law, 1991-97, 99—, pres., 2000—; bd. dirs. Valley of Sun Cmtys. in Schs., 1995-2001. Recipient spl. commendation U.s. Dept. Justice, 1973. Fellow Am. Bar Found., Ariz. Bar Found.; mem. ABA (antitrust and litigation sects., vice chmn. bus. torts and unfair competition com. 1996-98, chair 1998-2001, vice chmn. state enforcement com., 2001-04, editor Bus. Torts and Unfair Competition Newsletter 1996-98), FBA, Assn. Profl. Responsibility Lawyers (bd. dirs. 1993-98, pres. 1996-97), State Bar Ariz. (coun. antitrust sect., chmn. 1985-88, chmn. advt. com. 1992-94, ethics com. 1994-2001, chmn. 1995-2001, mem. task force on future of profession 2000, mem. case conflicts com. 2001-), mem. unauthorized practice of law adv. com., 2003-, Maricopa County Bar Assn. Office: Fennemore Craig 3003 N Central Ave Ste 2600 Phoenix AZ 85012-2913 Office Phone: 602-916-5334. Business E-Mail: tburke@fclaw.com.

BURKE, TIMOTHY MICHAEL, lawyer, educator; b. Cleve., Feb. 10, 1948; s. Ralph and Frances (Dilley) B.; m. Patricia Kathleen LaGrange, June 6, 1970; children: Nora Frances, Tara Kathleen, Michael Ralph. AB, Xavier U., Cin., 1970; JD, U. Cin., 1973. Bar: Ohio 1973, U.S. Dist. Ct. (so. dist.) Ohio 1979, U.S. Ct. Appeals (6th cir.) 1978, U.S. Supreme Ct. 1979. Legis. asst. to coun. mem. Cin. City Coun., 1971-74; spl. asst. to Congressman Tom Luken Cin., 1974, 76-77; exec. dir. Little Miami, Inc., Cin., 1975-76; prin. Manley Burke and predecessor firm, Cin., 1977—; spl. counsel to atty. gen. State of Ohio, 1978-95; law dir. Village of Lockland, Ohio, 1982—2003, Village of Evendale, Ohio, 2003—. Lectr. Xavier U., 1975-78, 81, 82-83, adj. asst. prof., 1983-85; adj. assoc. prof. U. Cin., 1977-78, 79, dir. law enforcement tech. program, 1977-78. Bd. dirs. Tri State Air Com., 1972-80, chmn., 1976-78; chmn. land use subcom. water quality adv. com. Ohio-Ky.-Ind. Regional Coun. Govts., 1975-76; bd. dirs. Lower Coun. Little Miami, Inc., 1976-82; mem. alumni bd. govs. Xavier U., 1970-76, 78-79, v.p., 1980-81, pres., 1981-82; candidate for U.S. Ho. of Reps. from 1st dist. Ohio, 1978; chmn. legal com. Cin. Zoo, bd. dirs., 1980-91; co-chmn. Zoo Tax Levy Campaign, 1982, 86; commr. Cin. Park Bd., 1991-94; participant Fgn. Policy Conf. for Young Am. Polit. Leaders, U.S. Dept. State, 1980; chmn. Hamilton County Bd. Elections, 1993—; exec. co-chmn. Hamilton County Dem. Party, 1982-86, 88-89, chmn., 1993-99, 2004—, co-chmn., 1999-2004; co-chmn. Cin. Dem. Com., 1983-89, chmn., 1989-97; 1st v.p. Ohio Dem. County Chairs Assn., 1995-99; internat. supr. Bosnia Mcpl. Elections, 1997, Elections Tng. Slovakia, 2002; team leader Law Enforcement and Justice Team, Cinti Can. Served to 1st lt. U.S. Army, 1974. Recipient svc. award Ohio River Valley Com. for Occupational Safety and Health, 1983, Leadership award Xavier U., 1984; named Ohio Dem. of Yr. Ohio Dem. Party, 1995. Mem. ABA, Am. Planning Assn. (legal sect.). Roman Catholic. Home: 3560 Mcguffey Ave Cincinnati OH 45226-1919 Office Phone: 513-721-5525. Business E-Mail: tburke@manleyburke.com.

BURKE, VICTOR LEE, sociologist, educator; b. Great Lakes, Ill., Mar. 29, 1949; s. Eugene Francis and Donna Lou Burke; m. Anna Celeste Spencer, Oct. 12, 1970; children: Victoria, Adam. BA summa cum laude, U. Ctrl. Fla., 1978; MSW, U. Mich., 1979, MA, 1982, PhD, 1989. Profl. musician various performers, 1965—70; preparation chef Walt Disney World, 1971—75; lectr. U. Mich., Sch. of Social Work, 1985—91; psychotherapist/clin. social worker Washtenaw Cmty. Mental Health Ctr., 1979—80; rsch. asst. Inst. for Social Rsch., Ctr. for Polit. Studies, U. Mich., 1979—81, Ctr. for Rsch. on Social Org., U. Mich., 1982—84; acad. counselor U. Mich. Coll. of Lit. Sciences and the Arts, 1985—91; rsch. assoc. Ctr. for Rsch. on Social Org., Dept. Sociology, U. Mich., 1985—91; asst. prof. sociology Ohio State U., 1991—97; assoc. prof. sociology, 1997—; ind. scholar U. Calif., 2001—. Lectr., dept. sociology U. Mich., 1985—91. Author: (book) The Clash of Civilizations: Warmaking and State Formation in Europe, 1997 (Ohio State U. campus award for excellence in scholarship, 1997). Bd. dirs. The Ctr., Mansfield, Ohio, 2000—03. Mem.: Internat. Inst. of Sociology, Am. Sociological Assn., La Qunita Fairways Country Club. Roman Catholic. Avocations: poker, guitar, chess, real estate, geology. Home: 5674 Tynecastle Loop Dublin OH 43106 Address: 50340 Spyglass Hill Dr La Quinta CA 92253 Office: Ohio State U Univ Drive 336 Ovalwood Hall Mansfield OH 44906 Office Phone: 419-755-4260. Business E-Mail: burke.60@osu.edu.

BURKE, WILLIAM, neurologist; b. Milw. s. Luke Wencil and Margaret Glenviev (Mineau) Burke; m. Mary Frances Roe, Oct. 15, 1977; children: Catherine Margaret, Christine Elizabeth, Erin Rose, Joseph Vincent. BS Biology, Marquette U., 1962; PhD Biochemistry, MD, St. Louis U., 1972. Cert. neurology. Asst. prof. neurology St. Louis U., 1976—83, assoc. prof. neurology, 1983—93, prof. neurology, 1993—, assoc. prof. anatomy, 1989—, assoc. prof. medicine, 1992—. Vis. scientist Cornell Med. Ctr., N.Y.C., 1971, 77, Burke Rehab. Ctr., White Plains, 1988; chmn. Mo. State Adv. Bd. for Grants in Alzheimer's and Related Disorders, 1995—97. Editor: Central Nervous System Didorder of Aging, 1987; contbr. articles to profl. jours. Expert witness Mo. Pub. Health and Safety Subcom., Jefferson City, 1992. Grantee, VA, 1978—2000, NIH, 1991—94. Fellow: Am. Acad. Neurology; mem.: AAAS, Soc. Neurosci. Roman Catholic. Avocation: golf. Home: 5517 Pinewood Forest Saint Louis MO 63118 Office: St Louis U Health Sci Ctr 3435 Vista at Grand Saint Louis MO 63110 Office Phone: 314-577-8026. Business E-Mail: burkewj@slu.edu.

BURKE, WILLIAM ROMNEY, urologist; b. Safford, Ariz., May 31, 1943; s. Ernest William and Hannah (Romney) B.; m. Mary Susan Wilkinson, June 11, 1969; children: Caroline, Kimberly, Suzanne, Brendan, Juliana, Kevin, Christopher, Kathleen, Brynn, David. AB, Stanford U., 1964; MD, Yale U., 1970. Diplomate Am. Bd. Urology. Surg. intern U. UT Med. Ctr., Salt Lake City, 1970-71, resident in surgery, 1971-72; resident in urology Yale-New Haven (Conn.) Hosp., 1972-76; instr. surgery Yale Med. Sch., New Haven, 1975—76; urologist Denver Clinic, 1976-78, Clackamas Urol. Clinic, Oreg. City, Oreg., 1978-95, The Urology Clinic, Portland, 1995-99; pvt. practice Oreg. City, Oreg., 1999—. Asst. clin. prof. urology U. Colo. Med. Ctr., Denver, 1978; chmn. dept. of surgery Willamette Falls Hosp., Oregon City, 1987-89; bd. dirs. Williamette Falls Hosp., Oregon City, Oreg. Contbr. articles to profl. jours. Mem. City of West Linn (Oreg.) Planning Commn., 1985-86; chmn. long range com. West Linn Sch. Dist., 1984, 89, mem. budget com. 1987-93. Mem.: Am. Urol. Assn. (We. sect.), N.W. Urol. Soc., Oreg. Urol. Soc., Oreg. Med. Assoc. (del. 1986—2002, trustee 2002—), Clackamas County Med. Soc. (pres. 1989, bd. dirs. 1992—). Democrat. Mem. Ch. LDS. Office: 1510 Division St Ste 10 Oregon City OR 97045-1527 Personal E-mail: wrburkefamily@hotmail.com.

BURKE, WILLIAM TEMPLE, JR., lawyer; b. San Antonio, Oct. 30, 1935; s. William Temple and Adelaide H. (Raba) B.; m. Mary Sue Johnson, June 8, 1957; children: William Patrick, Michael Edmond, Karen Elizabeth. BBA, St. Mary's U., San Antonio, JD, 1961. Bar: Tex. 1961. Practice law, Dallas; founder, pres. Burke Wright & Keiffer, PC, 1985-98; of counsel Hance/Scarborough/Wright, Dallas, 1998-2000, Hance, Scarborough, Wright, Ginsberg and Brusilow, Dallas, 2000—. Co-founder, v.p., dir. Tex. Cath. Cmty. Credit Union, 1966—69, vice-chmn. bd. dirs., 1990—91; v.p. Dallas County Hist. Survey Com., 1966; pres. Dallas Mil. Govt. Assn., 1962—63; trustee Montserrat Jesuit Retreat House, 1999—2000, treas., 1997; pres. Dallas County Small Bus. Devel. Corp., 1981—82; chmn. scout troop com. St. Patrick's Parish Roman Cath. Ch., 1976—78, chmn. fin. com., 1984—87, bldg. com., 1978—87, chmn. bd. consultors, 1978—81; vice-chmn. Cath. Commn. Appeal Diocese of Dallas, 1993—97; pres. men's club St. Patrick's Parish Roman Cath. Ch., 1963, prin. jr. H.S. Christian devel. program, 1970; bd. dirs. Dallas County War on Poverty, 1965—66, Montserrat Found., 1999—2000, DallasEcol. Found., 2004—. 1st lt. U.S. Army, 1958—60, capt. USAR, ret. Fellow Tex. Bar Found. (life), Coll. of State Bar Tex., Dallas Bar Found. (sr., life); mem. ABA, Tex. Bar Assn., Dallas Bar Assn. (co-founder, chmn. bankruptcy and comml. law sect. 1976-77, 86-87, courthouse liaison com. 1985—, lectr. 1985—, chmn. spkrs. com. 2001-02), Am. Bankruptcy Inst., John C. Ford Am. Inn Ct. (co-founder, pres. 2000-04, hon. Serjeant of the Inn 2003), Dallas Safari Club, Serra Internat. Met. Club (pres. Met. Dallas 1997-98, dist. gov. 2004—, Outstanding Mem. award 1995), Internat. Order Alhambra (exemplar 1978-95), KC (co-founder Greater Dallas chpt., coun. 799 grand knight, trustee 1964-69, dist. examplar 4th degree 1968-69, Man of Yr. award 1970), Optimists (v.p., bd. dirs. Dallas 1965-66, Man of Yr. award 1966, Pres.'s award 1968), Phi Delta Phi (life, magister 1960-61), Tau Delta Sigma (pres. 1957). Home: 9751 Larchcrest Dr Dallas TX 75238-2112 Office: 1401 Elm St Ste 4750 Dallas TX 75202

BURKE, WILLIAM THOMAS, lawyer, educator; b. Brazil, Ind., Aug. 17, 1926; JD, U. Ind., 1953; JSD, Yale U., 1959. Bar: Ind. 1953. Rsch. assoc. and lectr. Yale U., 1956-62; assoc. prof. Ohio State U., 1962-64, prof., 1964-68, U. Wash. Sch. Law, Seattle, 1968-99, prof. emeritus, 1999—. Mem. adv. com. Law of Sea Task Force, Dept. State; mem. A217 Ocean Policy Com., NAS.

Author: (with M. S. McDougal) The Public Order of the Oceans, 1962, Contemporary Legal Problems in Ocean Development, 1969, (with Legatski and Woodhead) National and International Law Enforcement in the Ocean, 1975, The New International Law of Fisheries, 1994, International Law of the Sea-Documents and Notes, 1997, 99. Office: U Wash Sch Law Gates Hall Seattle WA 98195 Office Phone: 206-543-2275. E-mail: sealaw1@comcast.net, burke@u.washington.edu.

BURKE, YVONNE WATSON BRATHWAITE (MRS. WILLIAM A. BURKE), lawyer; b. L.A., Oct. 5, 1932; d. James A. and Lola (Moore) Watson; m. William A. Burke, June 14, 1972; 1 child, Autumn Roxanne; 1 stepchild, Christine. AA, U. Calif., 1951; BA, UCLA, 1953; JD, U. So. Calif., 1956. Bar: Calif. 1956. Mem. Calif. Assembly, 1966-72, chmn. urban devel. and housing com., 1971, 72; mem. 93d-95th Congresses, 1973—79, House Appropriations Com.; chmn. Congl. Black Caucus, 1976; Los Angeles county supervisor 4th dist., 1979—80; ptnr. Jones, Dan, Reagis & Pogue, 1987—92. Dep. corp. commr., hearing officer Police Commn., 1964-66; atty., staff McCone Commn. (investigation Watts riot), 1965; past chmn. L.A. Fed. Res. Bank; U.S. adv. bd. Nestle. Vice chmn. 1984 U.S. Olympics Organizing Com.; bd. dirs. or bd. advisers numerous orgns.; former regent U. Calif., Bd. Ednl. Testing Svc.; Amateur Athletic Found.; former bd. dirs. Ford Found., Brookings Inst.; mem. bd. supr's. 2d Dist., L.A. County Bd. of Supr's., 1992—, chair, 1993-94, 97-98, 2002-03; bd. govs. L.A. Met. Transp. Authority. Recipient Profl. Achievement award UCLA, 1974, 84; named one of 200 Future Leaders Time mag., 1974, Alumni of Yr., UCLA, 1996; recipient Achievement awards C.M.E. Chs.; numerous other awards, citations.; fellow Inst. Politics John F. Kennedy Sch. Govt. Harvard, 1971-72; Chubb fellow Yale, 1972 Office: 500 W Temple St Rm 866 Los Angeles CA 90012 Office Phone: 213-974-2222. Business E-Mail: yburke@bos.co.la.ca.us.

BURKEE, IRVIN, artist; b. Kenosha, Wis., Feb. 6, 1918; s. Omar Lars and Emily (Quardokas) B.; m. Bonnie May Ness, Apr. 12, 1945; children: Brynn, Jill, Peter (dec.), Ian (dec.). Diploma, Sch. Art Inst. Chgo., 1943, postgrad., 1944-45. Owner, silversmith, goldsmith Burkee Jewelry, Blackhawk, Colo., 1950-57; painter, sculptor, Aspen, Colo., 1957-78, Cottonwood, Ariz., 1978—, Pietrasanta, Italy, 1978—. Instr. art U. Colo., 1946, 50-53, Stephens Coll., Columbia, Mo., 1947-49. Researched and created copper, silver, and bronze mural of Human History of Colorado, Colorado Historical Museum, Denver, 2002, copper, bronze and silver mural of Rocky Mountain wild birds for Aspen Ctr. Environ. Studies, Aspen, 2000; exhibited in group shows Art Inst. Chgo., Smithsonian Instn. (award 1957), Milw. Art Inst., Krannert Mus., William Rockhill Nelson Gallery, St. Louis Art Mus., Denver Art Mus., Frederik Meijer Sculpture Gardens, Grand Rapids, Mich.; represented in southwestern galleries, also pvt. collections throughout U.S.; work illustrated in books Design and Creation of Jewelry, Design through Discovery, Walls Enrichment and Ornamentation, Modernist Jewerly 1930-1960 The Wearable Art Movement. John Quincy Adams Fgn. Travel fellowship Sch. Art Inst. Chgo., 1943; Rocky Mountain Coll. Sculpture grantee, 1972. Mem. Nat. Sculpture Soc., Sedona Chamber Music Soc. (painter yearly festival poster 1989—). Address: PO Box 5361 Lake Montezuma AZ 86342-5361 E-mail: ibburkee@peoplepc.com.

BURKEMPER, DANIEL J., secondary school educator, agricultural studies educator; b. St. Charles, Mo., Jan. 29, 1976; s. Mel and Kathy Burkemper. BS in Agr., U. Mo., 1998; MS in Edn. Adminstrn., William Woods U., 2003. Instr. agr. edn. Oran (Mo.) H.S., 1981—99, Jackson (Mo.) Sr. H.S., 1999—. Mem.: Jackson (Mo.) Future Farmers Am. (adv. 1999—, hon. degree 2000). Office: Jackson High Sch 315 S Missouri Jackson MO 63755

BURKERT, ROBERT RANDALL, artist; b. Racine, Wis., Aug. 20, 1930; s. Clarence George and Margaret Ann (Sorenson) B.; m. Nancy Ekholm, Aug. 29, 1953; children: Claire, Rand. BS, U. Wis., 1952, MS, 1955. Instr. art Denison U., 1955-56; prof. drawing, printmaking, painting U. Wis., Milw., 1956-92, prof. emeritus, 1993—. One-man shows include Bradley Galleries, Milw. (8 shows), 1972-86, Rubiner Galleries, Detroit (6 shows), 1973-85, Posner Galler, Milw., 1990, 93, Retrospective, U. of Wis., Milw., 1994, Myhelan Cultural Ctr., Long Valley, Pa., 2001, others; group shows include Pratt Graphic Ctr., 1972, U.S. Cultural Ctr., Tel Aviv, 1973, Milw. Art Mus., 1975, 30 Yr. Retrospective, Wustum Mus., Racine, Wis., 1985; represented in permanent collections Tate Gallery, London, Boston Mus. Fine Arts, Met. Mus. Art, Phila. Mus., numerous others; wall mural Road to Country, 1972, wall mural Butterflies, 1986; work reproduced in Leipzig, Leipzig Proof, 1971, Compleat Printmaker, 1973, Art of the Print, 1976, 100 Years of American Printmaking, 1983, 150 Years of Wis. Printmaking, 1998; directed and produces "Colors of Change" documentary video, 1994. Former trustee Milw. Art Mus. Recipient numerous awards for prints, drawings and paintings; U. Wis. research grantee, 1969, 71, 73, 75, 77; Knapp grantee for ednl. research, 1973, Wis. Arts grantee, 1977; Fromkin grantee, 1980; recipient Gov.'s Print Commn., 1985. Home: PO Box 858 East Orleans MA 02643-0858

BURKES, LIONEL SEATON, science educator, writer, researcher; b. Hindsville, Ark., Mar. 25, 1933; s. Elmo C. and Bernie Ethel (Cook) B.; m. Pansy Lenora Hobbs Burkes, Dec. 24, 1961; children: Geoffrey Dion (dec.), Eric Kevin, Cynthia Michele, Aaron Shane, Mark Alan. BSE, U. Ark., 1960; MA in Biol. Sci., U. Mont., 1964. Cert. adminstrn. and sci., Ark., Iowa; sci. N. Mex. Instr. sci. and sociology Corona (N. Mex.) Mcpl. Schs., 1960-62; instr. sci. Albuquerque (N. Mex.) Pub. Schs., 1964-66; instr. biology and zoology U. Wis., Whitewater, 1966-69; asst. prof. edn. Mo. We. State Coll., St. Joseph, 1970-71; asst. campus dir. Southeastern Cmty. Coll., West Burlington, Iowa, 1971-75; dir. Inst. Mgmt. and Continuing Edn. Iowa Wesleyan Coll., Mt. Pleasant, 1977-78, 83-84; staff devel. specialist and tng. cert. officer La. Dept. Health and Human Resources, Office Mental Retardation, Ruston (La.) State Sch., 1982—83; instr. scis. Ft. Smith (Ark.) Pub. Schs., 1985-94; ret., 1995; rschr., writer, 1995—. Spl. rschr. Sandia Nat. Labs., Albuquerque, summers 1985-87. Contbr. articles to profl. jours. Leader U.S. delegation People to People Youth Sci. Exchange, Russia, Ukraine, 1990, China, Hong Kong, 1991, New Zealand, Australia, 1992; judge sci. fair pub. schs. N. Mex. and Ark., 1984-95; spkr. Career Days Westark C. C., Fort Smith, Ark., 1991-93. Nat. Sci. Found. Fellow U. Mont., 1961-64; recipient Nat. Security Clearance U.S. Dept. Energy, 1986, Outstanding Tchr. Proclamation Mayor of Fort Smith, Ark., 1995. Avocations: writing, reading, research, traveling abroad, hiking.

BURKET, GEORGE EDWARD, JR., retired family physician; b. Kingman, Kans., Dec. 10, 1912; s. George Edward and Jessie May (Talbert) Burket; m. Mary Elizabeth Wallace, Nov. 12, 1938; children: George Edward III, Carol Sue, Elizabeth Christine. Student, Wichita State U., 1930—33; MD, U. Kans., 1937. Diplomate Am. Bd. Family Practice (pres. 1975-1977). Intern Santa Barbara (Calif.) Gen. Hosp., 1937—38, resident, 1938—39; grad. asst. in surgery Mass. Gen. Hosp., Boston, 1955—56; practice medicine Kingman, 1939—73; preceptor in medicine U. Kans. Med. Sch., 1950—73, assoc. prof., 1973—78, clin. prof., 1978—84; ret. Bd. dirs. Kingman Savings and Loan Assn. Contbr. articles to profl. jours. Mem. Kingman Bd. Edn., 1946—58, Kans. State Bd. Health, 1960—66. Mem.: AMA, Soc. Tchrs. Family Medicine, Assn. Am. Med. Colls., Am. Acad. Family Physicians (pres. 1967—68, John Walsh Founders award 1979), Kans. Med. Soc. (pres. 1966—67), Inst. Medicine NAS (sr.), Wichita Country Club, Garden of Gods Club (Colorado Springs, Colo.), Shriners, Masons, Alpha Omega Alpha. Republican. Episcopalian. Home: Larksfield Pl V-208 7373 E 29th St N Wichita KS 67226-3405

BURKET, JOHN MCVEY, retired dermatologist; b. Des Moines, Iowa, Oct. 4, 1935; s. George Austin and Elma (McVey) B.; m. Janice Lee Feilmeyer, Dec. 29, 1956; children: Denise, Bradley, Brent, Diana, Dawn, Brian. BA, U. Iowa, 1957, MD, 1960. Diplomate Am. Bd. Dermatology, Am. Bd. Dermopathology. Resident in dermatology U. Iowa Hosp., Iowa City, 1964; chief dermatology USAF, March AFB, 1964-66; pvt. practice dermatology Medford, Oreg., 1966—. Contbr. articles to profl. jours., chpts. to books. Avocations: hunting, fishing.

BURKETT, BRADFORD CHARLES, lawyer; b. Phila., Aug. 29, 1960; s. Frederick R. and Barbara E. Burkett; m. Marcia P. Borggaard, Aug. 17, 1985; children: Gillian, Brady, Kate. BA, Rutgers U., New Brunswick, N.J., 1982; JD, Rutgers U., Camden, N.J., 1985. Bar: N.Y. 1985, N.J. 1985. Assoc. Kaye Scholer Fierman Hays & Handler, N.Y.C., 1985-94; sr. v.p., gen. counsel The Multicare Cos., Inc., Hackensack, N.J., 1994-97; sr. v.p., gen. counsel, bus. devel. Telesis Med. Mgmt., Inc., White Plains, NY, 1997-2000; CEO Physician Weblink, Inc., Englewood Cliffs, NJ, 2000—02; CEO, bd. dirs. deNovis, Inc., Lexington, Mass., 2002—05; mng. dir Scott Mason Ltd., N.Y.C., 2005—. Co-CEO CareMatrix, Inc., Newton, Mass., 2003—; bd. dirs. N. Am. Health Plans, Buffalo, 2004—, Health Edge, N.Y.C., 2005—; mng. dir. Scott-Macon Ltd., NYC. Mem. ABA, Nat. Health Lawyers Assn., Assn. Bar City N.Y., Turnaround Mgmt. Soc. Office: 17 Mayhew Ave Larchmont NY 10538 E-mail: b.burkett@att.net, burkett@gbkndvision.com.

BURKETT, DAVID INGRAM, lawyer; b. Orange, Tex., July 1, 1948; s. Jack Edward Burkett and LaVern (Ingram) Schmidt; m. Sharon Roberts, Mar. 27, 1970; children: Matthew Howard, Ashley Colleen. BA, No. La. U., 1971; JD, La. State U., 1974. Bar: La. 1975; lic. title ins. agt., La.; cert. estate planning and adminstrn. specialist. Ptnr. Brown, Erskine and Burkett, Monroe, La., 1975—. Instr. in real estate; past dir. pro bono elderly project. Chmn. St. Francis Med. Ctr. Instl. Rev. Bd.; bd. dirs., mem. exec. com. Ronald McDonald House of N.E. La.; bd. dirs. Monroe YWCA; past sec. La. Lions Eye Found. Inc., 1986-87, 1st v.p., 1988-90, pres., 1990-91, bd. dirs., mem. exec. com., chmn. fin. com.; mem. Coun. Handicapped Infants and Toddlers; past bd. dirs. La. Lions League for Crippled Children; mem. Monroe Flood Plain Mgmt. Bd., N.E. La. Cen. Corridor Com.; past pres. North La. Mental Health Assn., N.E. La. Arthritis Found.; min. edn. Forsythe Ave Ch. of Christ; mem. svc. com. ARCl past dir. Salvation Army adv. bd., Kalorama Nature Preserve; bd. dirs. Northeast La. Families Helping Families. Recipient Outstanding Cmty. Svc. award Monroe Jaycees, 1984, 100% Dist. Gov.'s award Lions Internat. Assn. Lions Clubs, 1984. Mem. ABA, La. State Bar Assn., 4th Dist. Bar Assn., Monroe C. of C. (past bd. dirs.), La. Med. Soc. (med. and legal com.), Sigma Tau Gamma (past pres.), Beta Nu. Republican. Mem. Ch. of Christ. Home: 2413 Emerson St Monroe LA 71201-2622 Office: Brown Erskine & Burkett 1216 Stubbs Ave Monroe LA 71201-5622 Office Phone: 318-388-4303. E-mail: davidb@jam.rr.com.

BURKETT, HELEN, artist; b. Washington, Feb. 15, 1942; d. Harding Theodore and Helen Louise (Torris) B.; m. J.D. Collins, Sept. 1, 1961 (Apr. 16, 1975); children: Mark W. Collins, Donna L. Collins; m. Charles Talbot Marshall, Dec. 24, 1975; 1 child, Gabrielle T. Marshall. Student, Strayer Sch. of Bus., 1960-61, Corcoran Sch. of Art, 1968-69, Md. U., 1970-73, Hilton Leech Studio-Gallery, 1976-80, Ringling Sch. Art, 1980-81. Asst. to dir. Hilton Leech Studio, Sarasota, Fla., 1975-80, workshop organizer, figure study coord., 1978-80; demonstrator, tchr., artist, owner/operator Helen Burkett Studios, Sarasota, Fla., 1975—. Juror Ann Arbor St. Art Fair, 1998; art tchr. Brevard County Watercolor Soc., Melbourne, Fla., Longboat Key Ctr. Arts, Sarasota,Fla, 2000. One person shows at Manatee Jr. Coll., 1984, Chester Art Ctr. 2001-05, Watercolor USA, 2003, Springfield Art Mus., Mo., Ctrl. Fla. C.C., Ocala, 1987, State Capitol, Tallahassee, Fla., Divsn. Cultural Affairs, Sec. State Offices, 1997; exhibited in group show at Nat. Watercolor Soc. Show, Thousand Oaks, Calif., 1999; permanent exhibits include Ctrl. Fla. C.C., Ocala, Epsom Clinic, Orlando, Fla., Orlando Sentinel, Winter Park (Fla.) Meml. Hosp., Polk Mus., Lakeland, Fla., The Disney Corp., The Ford Motor Co., The Amoco Corp., Fla. Dept. State, Hayfield Mansion, Louisville, The Former Duchess of Winsor; exhibitor numerous art festivals, 1987—; subject of periodical The Artist Mag., 1992, The Am. Artist Mag., 1996, also newspaper article Ann Arbor News, 1998. Tchr. Vis. Artist Program, Coconut Grove, Fla., 1990—. Recipient 2d prize in watercolor U. Tampa, 1991, 93, 1st prize in watercolor Lowe Art Mus./U. Miami, 1992, Purchase award Festival of the Masters-Disney Corp., 1995, Purchase award Wayne State U.-Ford Motor Co., 1995. Mem. ACLU, NOW, Am. Watercolor Soc. (assoc.), Nat. Watercolor Soc. (assoc.), Nat. Assn. Ind. Artists, Sarasota Art Assn. (bd. dirs. 1980-82), Fla. Watercolor Soc. (life, Award of Distinction 1985, 92), So. Watercolor Soc., Mich. Guild Artists. Avocations: photography, reading, hiking, bicycling. Home: Helen Burkett Studio 2988 Oak St Sarasota FL 34237-7346

BURKETT, LAWRENCE V., retired insurance company executive, lawyer; BA, U. Va., 1967, JD, 1973. Bar: Mass. 1974. V.p., assoc. gen. counsel Mass. Mut. Life Ins. Co., Springfield, 1984-88, sr. v.p., assoc. gen. counsel, 1988-92, exec. v.p., gen. counsel, 1993—. Office: Mass Mutual Life Ins Co 1295 State St Springfield MA 01111-0001

BURKETT, MARVIN D., personal computer manufacturing company executive; b. 1943; BS, MBA, U. Ariz. With semicondr. divsn. Raytheon Co., to 1972; v.p., contr., chief planning officer Advanced Micro Devices, Inc., 1972-88, sr. v.p., chief adminstrv. officer, CFO, 1989-98; exec. v.p. worldwide fin., CFO, Packard Bell NEC Inc., Sacramento, 1998—; CFO, chief adminstrv. officer Arcot Sys., Inc., Santa Clara, Calif., 2000—. Office: Arcot Sys Inc 3200 Patrick Henry Dr #200 Santa Clara CA 95054

BURKETT, ROBERT E., JR., lawyer, insurance company executive; b. Kansas City, Mo., Aug. 20, 1954; m. Molly Boso, 1981. BA, Purdue U., 1977; JD, Ind. U., 1980. Bar: Ind. 1981, Fla. 1986. Sr. v.p., legal Conseco Inc., Carmel, Ind. Office: Conseco Inc 11825 N Pennsylvania St Carmel IN 46032 Office Phone: 317-817-6100. Office Fax: 317-817-3578.

BURKETT, SUSAN L., academic administrator; b. Marion, Ind. d. Donald E. Burkett and Aileene Bateman; children: Kristin L. Dunkle, Jennifer Dunkle Parrack. BA, Juniata Coll., Huntingdon, Pa., 1970; MA, U. Utah, 1972. Cert. instr. Am. Taekwondo Assn. Dir. Carnegie Inst. Tech. Writing Ctr. Carnegie Mellon U., Pitts., 1974—85, info. mgr. Software Engring. Inst., 1985—89, assoc. provost, 1989—. Mem.: Soc. Rsch. Adminstrn., Nat. Coun. Univ. Rsch. Adminstrs., Coun. on Govt. Rels. Achievements include 4th degree black belt. Office: Carnegie Mellon U 5000 Forbes Ave Pittsburgh PA 15213 Business E-Mail: sburkett@andrew.cmu.edu.

BURKETT, TERESA MEINDERS, lawyer; b. Okarche, Okla., Aug. 3, 1959; d. Hadley Clyde and Lois Marie (Schroeder) Meinders; m. Robert Glenn Burkett, Jan. 3, 1993. BSN, U. Okla., 1982, JD, 1985. Bar: Okla. 1985. Atty. Boone Smith Davis Hurst & Dickman, Tulsa, Okla., 1985—. Pres. Hillcrest Assocs., Okla., Tulsa, Okla., 1996—98. Pres. Habitat for Humanity, Tulsa, 1993-94; v.p. Leadership Tulsa, 1995-96; bd. dirs. Cmty. Svc. Coun. Met. Tulsa, 1992—, pres., 2002-05; mem. adv. bd. The Nature Conservancy, Okla. chpt., 1998-05; bd. dirs. Life Sr. Svcs., 2005— Mem. Okla. Health Lawyers Assn. (pres. 1992-93, 2003-05, Okla. Bar Assn. (chmn. health law sect. 1996-97), Mental Health Assn. Tulsa (bd. dirs. 1998-2004 Office: Boone Smith Davis Hurst & Dickman 500 Oneok Plz 100 W 5th St Ste 500 Tulsa OK 74103-4215

BURKEY, LEE MELVILLE, lawyer; b. Beach, N.D., Mar. 21, 1914; s. Levi Melville and Mina Lou (Horner) B.; m. Lorraine Lillian Burghardt, June 11, 1938; 1 child, Lee Melville, III BA, U. Ill., 1936, MA, 1938; JD with honor, John Marshall Law Sch., 1943. Bar: Ill., 1944, U.S. Dist. Ct., 1947, U.S. Ct. Appeals, 1954, U.S. Supreme Ct.; 1983; cert. secondary tchr., Ill. Tchr. Princeton Twp. High Sch., Princeton, Ill., 1937-38, Thornton Twp. High Sch., Harvey, Ill., 1938-43; atty. Office of Solicitor, U.S. Dept. Labor, Chgo., 1944-51; ptnr. Asher, Gubbins & Segall and successor firms, Chgo., 1951-94; of counsel, 1995—. Lectr. bus. law Roosvelt Coll., Chgo., 1949—52. Contbr. numerous articles on lie detector evidence. Trustee, Village of La Grange, Ill., 1962-68, mayor, 1968-73, village atty., 1973-87; commr., pres. Northeastern Ill. Planning Commn., Chgo., 1969-73; mem. bd. dirs. United Ch. Christ, Bd. of Homeland Ministries, 1981-87; mem. exec. com. Cook County Coun. Govts., 1968-70; life mem. La Grange Area Hist. Soc.; bd. dirs. Better Bus. Bur. Met. Chgo., Inc., 1975-82, Plymouth Place, Inc., 1973-82; mem. exec. bd., S.W. Suburban Ctr. on Aging, 1993—04. Brevet 2nd Lt. Ill. Nat. Guard, 1932. Recipient Disting. Alumnus award John Marshall Law Sch., 1973, Meritorious Svc. award Am. Legion Post 1941, 1974, Honor award LaGrange Area Hist. Soc., 1987, Cmty. Svc. award S.W. Suburban Ctr. on Aging, 2000. Fellow: Coll. Labor and Employment Lawyers. (charter); mem.: SAR (state pres. 1977, Good citizenship medal 1973, Patriot medal 1977), ABA (coun. sect. labor and employment law 1982—86, governance officer 1986—96), Chgo. Bar Assn., Ill. Bar Assn. (sr. counsellor 1994), United Empire Loyalists Assn. Can., La Grange Country Club, Masons, Theta Delta Chi, Order John Marshall. Mem. First Congl. Ch.

BURKEY, MARCIA B., corporate financial executive; Degree, Macalester Coll.; M, Columbia U. Various sr. fin. positions SBC Warburg (now UBS Warburg); various exec. fin. positions including regional mgr. Bechtel Enterprises Holdings Inc., San Francisco, 1996-2000, mng. dir., CFO, 2000—. Office: Bechtel Enterprises PO Box 193965 San Francisco CA 94119

BURKHALTER, BARTON ROBERT, public health scientist; b. Toledo, July 22, 1938; s. Robert Richard and Mary Louise (Barton) B.; m. Nancy Ann Nasset, June 7, 1963 (div.); 1 child, Eric; m. Eliana Gabriela Godoy, Aug. 22, 1978; 1 child, Genevieve Divin. BS in Math. Engring. and Engring. Mechanics, U. Mich., 1961, MS in Indsl. Engring., 1962, PhD, 1964. Pres. Community System Found., Ann Arbor, Mich., 1963-72, sr. scientist, 1974-88; chmn. CSF Ltd., Ann Arbor, 1974-76; rsch. prof. cmty. medicine U. Ariz., Tuscon, 1979-88; pres. Winch Inst. Am., La Jolla, Calif., 1984-88; dir. Ctr. Internat. Health Info., Washington, 1988-91; sr. program officer Acad. Ednl. Devel., Washington, 1991-2000; dir. ops. rsch. U. Rsch. Co., Bethesda, 2000—. Adj. prof. regional planning U. Mich., Ann Arbor, 1969-76 Author: (book) Case Studies in Systems Analyses in a University Library, 1968, An Investigation of Rapidly Changing Papago Tribal Health Programs, 1979; editor: Nutrition Planning, 1977-81. Pres Washtenaw County Planned Parenthood, Ann Arbor, 1973. Mem. Hosp. Mgmt. Systems Soc. Chgo. (pres. 1974). Home: 10310 Gary Rd Potomac MD 20854-4155 Office Phone: 301-941-1846. E-mail: bburkhalter@urc-chs.com.

BURKHALTER, SUSAN SHIVELY, music educator, organist; b. Washington, Apr. 16, 1946; d. William Mays and Thelma Louise (Kanatzer) B.; m. Curtis Allen Shively, Feb. 5, 1977; children: Rachel Mirabel, Stuart William MusB, Coll. Wooster, 1970. Organist, choir dir. Olivet Episcopal Ch., Springfield, Va., 1976-77; children's choir dir. Our Savior Lutheran Ch. and Sch., Arlington, Va., 1997-1998; freelance piano tchr., organist, 1976—2005; organist, choir dir. Grace Reformed United Ch. of Christ, Washington, 2001; interim organist Kirkwood Presbyn. Ch., Springfield, 2001—02; organist Luth. Ch. of Abiding Presence, Burke, Va., 2004—05, Cameron United Meth. Ch., Alexandria, Va., 2005—. Advisor music majs. Coll. Wooster, Ohio, 1995—. Contbr. mags. and newspapers including Washington Post, American Organist, Psychology Today, and more; performer in various concerts. Vol. Carderock Springs Elem. Sch., Bethesda, Md., 1988-95, Pyle Middle Sch., 1994-2000, Walt Whitman High Sch., 1997-2005; mem. Sierra Club, ASPCA, World Wildlife Fund, African Wildlife Fund; mem. Gen. Fedn. Women's Clubs, Suburban Women's Club of Montgomery County, Md., 1999—. Mem. Music Tchrs. Nat. Assn., Am. Guild Organists. Democrat. Avocations: cats, sewing, gardening, art, poetry. Home: 7504 Hamilton Spring Rd Bethesda MD 20817-4542 Personal E-mail: scastlekep@aol.com.

BURKHARD, FRED (BUD), academic administrator; b. Jersey City, Feb. 17, 1956; s. Kenneth William and Eileen Clare Cobleigh; m. Jeannine (Nina) May Lafiner, Oct. 9, 1999; children: Rose Francis, Amanda Eileen Burkhard Kennedy. PhD, U. Wis., 1986. Assoc. prof. history Morgan State U., Balt., 1992—99; acad. dir. history U. Md. U. Coll., Adelphi, Md., 1999—. Participant wingspread conf. history curriculum Johnson Found., Am. Hist. Assn., 2005. Author: (scholarly monograph) French Marxism Between the Wars; contbr. scholarly article, and revs. Fellow Curriculum Transformation Project/Women's Studies Summer Inst., Ford Found., 1997, Summer Seminar participant, Nat. Endowment for the Humanities, 1991; grantee Rsch., Am. Coun. of Learned Societies, 1994, Schmitt Rsch. Grant, Am. Hist. Assn., 1992, rsch., Ministre des Affaires Etrangeres, France, 1987. Mem.: Nat. Women's Studies Assn., Western Soc. French History, Soc. French Hist. Studies, Am. Assn. History and Computing (pres. 2003—04), Am. Hist. Assn., Phi Alpha Theta. Office: U Md U Coll 3501 University Blvd E Adelphi MD 20783 Office Phone: 240-582-2837. E-mail: bburkhard@umuc.edu.

BURKHARDT, EDWARD ARNOLD, rail transportation executive; b. N.Y.C., July 23, 1938; s. Edward Arnold Burkhardt Sr. and Kathryn C. Dow; m. Sandra Kay Schwaegel, June 9, 1967; 1 child, Cynthia Kay. BS Indsl. Adminstrn., Yale U., 1960. Various operating positions Wabash R.R., St. Louis, 1960-64, Norfolk and Western Rlwy., St. Louis, 1964-67; asst. to gen. mgr. Chgo. Northwestern Transp. Co., 1967-68, gen. supt. transp., 1968-70, asst. v.p. transp., 1970-76, v.p. mktg., 1976-79, v.p. transp., 1979-87; bd. dirs., chmn., pres., CEO Wis. Ctrl. Transp. Corp., Chgo., 1987-99; chmn. Tranz Rail Ltd., 1993-99; bd. dirs., pres. Algoma Ctrl. Rlwy. Inc., 1995-99; bd. dirs., chmn., CEO English, Welsh and Scottish Ry. Ltd., 1995-99; bd. dirs., chmn. Australian Transport Network, 1997-99; pres./CEO Rail World, Inc., 1999—; pres. RailPolska, 1999—. Chmn. Baltic Rail Svc., 2000—, Estonian Ry. Ltd., 2001—, Montreal, Maine & Atlantic Ry. Ltd., 2003—; bd. dirs. Valeant Pharms. Internat., Costa Mesa, Calif., Poly Medica Corp., Woburn, Mass. Trustee Village of Kenilworth, Ill., 1984—93; bd. dirs. John W. Barringer R.R. Libr., St. Louis, Wheeling & Lake Erie Rlwy. Co., Lake Superior Mus. Transp., Duluth, Minn. Named Hon. consul New Zealand, Chgo. Mem.: Am. Assn. R.R. Supts., Union League Club, Western Ry. Club. Republican. Episcopalian. Office: Rail World Inc Ste 500N 8600 W Bryn Mawr Ave Chicago IL 60631-3579 Business E-Mail: eaburkhardt@railworld-inc.com.

BURKHARDT, ROGER, information technology executive; B in Physics, M in Physics, Oxford U.; MBA, NYU. With IBM Corp., 1982—97, mgr. advanced exch. sys.; v.p. Strategic Alliances Optimark Techs. Inc., 1997—2000, pres. Listed Equities, 1997—2000; chief tech. officer N.Y. Stock Exch., Inc., N.Y.C. Office: NY Stock Exch Inc 11 Wall St New York NY 10005

BURKHARDT, RONALD ROBERT, advertising executive, writer, artist; b. Jackson, Mich., July 25; s. Robert Edward and Lois Jeane (Ordway) B. AA, Jackson C.C., 1968; BBA in Advt., Western Mich. U., 1970. Copywriter, producer Campbell-Ewald Co., Detroit, 1973-75; sr. writer Cargill-Wilson & Acree/DDB, Atlanta, 1976-78; sr. v.p., creative dir. Flemister & Burkhardt, Atlanta, 1978-80; sr. writer Bozell & Jacobs, N.Y.C., 1980-81; creative supr. Young & Rubicam, N.Y.C., 1981-84; v.p., creative group head Lowe-Marschalk, N.Y.C., 1984-86; chmn., CEO, exec. creative dir., ptnr. and founder Burkhardt & Christy Advt. Inc., N.Y.C., 1986-95; CEO, creative dir., ptnr. and founder Burkhardt & Ptnrs. Ltd., N.Y.C., 1996—; co-founder, CEO, creative dir. Pillow Vision, Inc., 2001—. Pro bono cons. mayor's office, N.Y.C., Save Am. Forests, Washington; judge Clios, Internat. TV and Film Festival N.Y., CEBA Awards, Andy Awards, Stephen Kelly Awards, Addy Awards, Mercury Radio Awards, N.Y. Festivals. Exec. prodr.: (short feature film) Red, 2001; exec. prodr., creative cons. (feature film) The Mark, 2005; one-man shows include The Soho, 2001, Forbes Gallery, N.Y.C., 2002, Star Gallery, 2003, Trump Towers Art Release Galleries, NYC, 2003, Grand Havana Room Gallery, 2003, Think Art Gallery, 2003, Gallery Asto, L.A., 2004, Laguna Colony Art Gallery, Calif., 2004 (Paperworks art award BJ Spoke Gallery, 2005), One Fine Art Gallery, Chgo., 2005, Biennele Dell 'Arte Contemporanea, Florence, Italy, 2005; contbr. articles to profl. jours. including Adweek, AdAge. Exec. com. N.Y. Korean Vets. Meml. Commn.; pro-bono Riverkeeper; mem. benefit com. Edwin Gould ARTrageous Children's Svcs., Sheltering Arms Children's Svcs.; bd. dirs., branding chmn. Miss America Pageant. Recipient over 200 awards including Andy awards Advt. Club, Clio awards, Art Dirs. Club, N.Y. Internat. Festivals awards, Gold Addy award, Creativity awards, Graphics Ann. award, Mobius Gold, Black Book award, Telly Gold statues, Internat. Broadcast award Hollywood TV and Film Festival, Comm. Arts Photography Ann. award. Mem. One Club for Art and Copy (award 1976, 78, 80, 82, 84, 86, 89, 93, Comm. Arts Advt. Ann. award 1995, Effie Silver award 1997, Effie Gold award 1998, Cannes Internat. Film Festival (France) (del.). Republican. Avocations: skiing, tennis, motorcycling, baseball, Karate. Office: Burkhardt Ltd PO Box 1070 Quogue NY 11959-1070 Office Phone: 212-759-1555. Personal E-mail: ronreach@aol.com. *Intensity of purpose fuels energy, and makes life a relentless series of powerful achievements.*

BURKHART, CRAIG GARRETT, dermatologist, researcher; b. Toledo, Apr. 15, 1951; s. Garrett Giles and Mary Katherine (Egarius) Burkhart; m. Anna Kristina Jutila, Apr. 12, 1975; children: Kristina Maria, Craig Nathaniel, Heidi Rebecca. BA, U. Pa., 1972; MD, Med. Coll. Ohio, 1975; MPH, U. Toledo, 1983. Diplomate Am. Bd. Dermatology. Intern, resident, fellow U. Mich. Hosps., 1976-79; pvt. practice dermatologist, 1979—; pres. Gar-Nat Lab., Inc., 1997—. Clin. prof. medicine Med. U. Ohio; clin. asst. prof. dermatology Ohio U. Coll. Osteo. Medicine. Editor: Jour. Dermatology and Allergy, 1980—; mem. editl. bd. Jour. Current Adolescent Medicine, 1980—, mem. editl. adv. bd. Ohio State Med. Jour., 1982—, Cortlandt Forum, 1999—; contbr. chapters to books, articles to profl. jours. Mem. Toledo Zoo, Toledo Mus. Art. F. M. Douglass Found. Rsch. grantee, 1998, 2000, 2001. Mem.: AMA, Toledo Acad. Medicine (bd. dirs. 2002—), Mich. Dermatologic Assn., Ohio State Med. Assn., Ohio Dermatologic Assn. (bd. dirs. 2002—), Acad. Dermatology, Med. U. Ohio Alumni Assn., Phi Beta Kappa (pres. N.W. Ohio 1984—86). Achievements include patents in field. Home: 4556 Crossfields Rd Toledo OH 43623-2628 Office: 5600 Monroe St Ste 106B Sylvania OH 43560-2728 Office Phone: 419-885-3403. Personal E-mail: cgbakb@aol.com.

BURKHART, DAVID, music educator, director; b. Upper Darby, Pa., May 13, 1952; s. Luther and Dorothy Burkhart; m. Beth Double, Aug. 11, 1984; children: Christopher, Alexandra. BS in music edn., Mansfield U., 1970—74, MS in music, 1976—77. Band dir./music tchr. Interboro H.S., Prospect Park, Pa., 1974—. Founder So. Del. County Mid. Sch. Concert Band, Prospect Park, 1998—; founder and co-dir. Del. County H.S. All Star Big Band, Springfield, Pa., 2001—05. Baseball coach Springfield Athletic Assn., Pa., 1998—2001. Grant, Pa. Higher Edn. Assistance Agy., 1990—94. Mem.: NEA (life; treas. 1990—94), Music Educators Nat. Conf. (life), Phi Mu Alpha Sinfonia (life), Kappa Kappa Psi (life; pres. 1973—74). Avocation: jazz. Office: Interboro HS 1600 Amosland Rd Springfield PA 19064 Office Phone: 610-237-6410 115. Personal E-mail: burkhart101@comcast.net. E-mail: burkhadk@interborosd.org.

BURKHART, HAROLD EUGENE, forester, educator; b. Wellington, Kans., Feb. 29, 1944; s. Walter F. and Zelma (Lutz) B.; m. Katherine West, June 12, 1971; 1 child, Anna Katherine. BS, Okla. State U., 1965; MS, U. Ga., 1967, PhD, 1969. Asst. prof. Va. Poly. Inst. and State U., Blacksburg, 1969-73, assoc. prof., 1973-78, prof., 1978-81, Thomas M. Brooks prof., 1981-99, univ. disting. prof., 1999—. Author: Forest Measurements, 1983, 94, 2002; contbr. sci. articles to profl. jours. Sr. Rsch. fellow NRC, 1976-77; recipient Sci. Achievement award Internat. Union Forestry Rsch. Orgns., 1981, J. Shelton Horsley Rsch. award Va. Acad. Sci., 1983, Outstanding Faculty award State Coun. for Higher Edn. in Va., 1988, Disting. Agr. Alumnus award Okla. State U., 1993. Fellow AAAS, Soc. Am. Foresters (Barrington Moore Meml. award 1991); mem. Biometric Soc., Am. Forestry Assn., Sigma Xi, Phi Kappa Phi, Xi Sigma Pi. Presbyterian. Avocations: gardening, running. Office: Va Poly Inst and State U Dept Forestry Blacksburg VA 24061 Office Phone: 540-231-6952. Business E-Mail: burkhart@vt.edu.

BURKHART, JAMES EDWARD, neurologist; b. Washington, Oct. 13, 1944; s. Elder Merle and Doris (Friddle) B.; m. Marie Adele Bailey, Sept. 6, 1969; children: James, John. BA, LaSalle U., 1966; MD, Ind. U., 1970. Diplomate Am. Bd. Psychiatry and Neurology. Surg. intern N.C. Bapt. Hosp., Winston-Salem, 1970-71; resident in neurology Ind. U. Med. Ctr., Indpls., 1971-72, 75-77; flight surgeon USN, Pensacola, Fla., 1972-75; neurologist Reid Hosp., Richmond, Ind., 1977—. Lt. comdr., USN, 1972-75. Mem. Am. Neurology Assn., Ind. Neurol. Soc. Avocation: shipbuilding. Home: 2817 Northmont Ln Richmond IN 47374-1150 Office: 1712 Chester Blvd Richmond IN 47374-1669 Office Phone: 765-966-7738. Business E-Mail: hmsneuro@infocom.com.

BURKHART, JOHN ERNEST, minister, theology studies educator; b. Riverside, Calif., Oct. 25, 1927; s. Joseph Ernest and Lockie Louisa (Dryden) B.; m. Virginia Bell French, Sept. 16, 1951; children: David Aaron, Audrey Elizabeth, Deborah Ann. BA, Occidental Coll., 1949; BD, Union Theol. Sem., 1952; PhD, U. So. Calif., 1959; DD, Occidental Coll., 1964. Ordained to ministry United Presbyn. Ch., 1952. Pastor Presbyn. U. U. So. Calif., L.A., 1953-59, from instr. to prof. of Theology, 1959-1990; prof. Systematic Theology McCormick Theol. Sem., Chgo., 1990-93, prof. emeritus, 1993—. Vis. prof. Garrett Theol. Sem. Evanston, Ill., 1966, DePaul U., Chgo., 1970. Author: Kingdom, Church, and Baptism, 1959, Understanding the Word of God, 1964, Worship, 1982; contbr. articles to profl. jours. 1st lt., chaplain USAF, 1952—53. Fellow Royal Anthrop. Inst., Soc. for Values in Higher Edn.; mem. Am. Acad. Religion, Cath. Theol. Soc. of Am., N.Am. Acad. Liturgy, Am. Theol. Soc. (pres. 1969-70), Midwest Alumni Club (v.p. 1985-90), Quadrangle Club, Blue Key, Rotary, Phi Beta Kappa. Democrat. Presbyterian. Home: 569 Woodland Ridge Dubuque IA 52003 E-mail: burkhart@mchsi.com.

BURKHART, KATHERINE WEST, music educator, adult education educator; b. Roanoke, Va., Feb. 12, 1944; d. James Lemuel Wills and Kate Bradley West; m. Harold Eugene Burkhart, June 12, 1971; 1 child, Anna Katherine. BA in Music, Mary Baldwin Coll., 1966; MA in Humanities-Liberal Studies, Hollins U., 1976. Cert. basic literacy tchr. Literacy Vols. Am., ESL tchr. Literacy Vols. Am., collegiate tchr. Va. Freelance organist Va. Tech. Meml. Chapel, Blacksburg, 1964—2000, St. Luke's Anglican Ch., Rotorua, New Zealand, 1976—77; elem. sch. music tchr. Montgomery County Schs., Va., 1967—68, 1970—73; elem. music tchr. Virginia Beach (Va.) City Schs., 1968—69; ch. organist Blacksburg Presbyn. Ch., 1973—79, 1984—2000; pvt. piano tchr. Christiansburg/Blacksburg, 1973—84, 1990—; ESL program mgr. Literacy Vols. Am., Christiansburg, 1999—2000; ESL lead tchr. Rowe Furniture Co./Literacy Vols. Am., Elliston, Va., 2002—04. Tutor, cons. Literacy Vols. Am., Christiansburg, 1999—. ESL cons., com. chair Task Force on Refugee Resettlement, Blacksburg, 1999. Mem.: Va. Music Tchrs. Assn. (Highlands chpt., pres. 1993—95), Nat. Guild Piano Tchrs., Am. Guild Organists (Highlands chpt., newsletter editor 1984—86, sub-dean 1992—93, Newsletter grant 1984). Presbyterian. Avocations: reading, foreign language films, travel, tutoring. Home: 1481 Mt Tabor Rd Blacksburg VA 24060 Office: Literacy Vols Am New River Valley 195 W Main St Christiansburg VA 24073

BURKHART, MARK, real estate company executive; Cert. property mgr., real property adminstr. Property adminstr. Colliers Turley Martin Rucker, St. Louis, 1977—81, v.p., 1981—93, pres., CEO, 1993—, also bd. dirs., mem. exec. com. Office: Colliers Turley Martin Tucker Ste 500 7701 Forsyth Saint Louis MO 63105

BURKHART, WILLIAM HENRY, lawyer; b. Chgo., Jan. 3, 1931; s. Claude Albert and Mary Vern (Hall) B.; m. Rosemary Purcell, Apr. 28, 1973; 1 child, Aaron. BS Bus., Northwestern U., 1953; JD, U. Mich., 1958, MBA, 1959; LLM Taxation, NYU, 1963. Bar: Mich. 1958, N.Y. 1964, Washington 1975; CPA, Mich. Tax supr. Coopers & Lybrand, Detroit, 1960-62; assoc. atty. Cahill Gordon & Reindel, N.Y.C., 1963-72; tax ptnr. Preston, Gates & Ellis, Seattle, 1974—. Chmn. Seattle Tax Group, 1986, Seattle Internat. Tax Roundtable, 1983-85; bd. dirs. Atty. CPA Tax Clinic, Seattle. Lt. (j.g.) USN, 1953-55. Mem. Washington Athletic Club. Home: 10554 Riviera Pl NE Seattle WA 98125-6937 Office: 925 4th Ave Ste 2900 Seattle WA 98104-1158 E-mail: billb@prestongates.com.

BURKHART, WILLIAM R., lawyer; b. May 30, 1965; m. Theresa A. Burkhart. B in polit. sci., U. Fla.; JD, Harvard U., 1990. Bar: Pa. 1990. Atty. Reed Smith Shaw & McClay LLP, Pitts.; joined The Timken Co., Canton, Ohio, 1994, atty., corp. atty., legal counsel for Europe, Africa, and West Asia Colmar, France, dir. affiliations and acquistions Canton, Ohio, 1998—2000, sr. v.p., gen. counsel, 2000—. Mem. law coun. Manufacturers Alliance. Bd. dirs. Ohio C. of C.; mem. Vision Coun. Program Adv. Subcom. Ctrl. Stark County United Way, Ohio. Office: The Timken Co 1835 Dueber Ave SW Canton OH 44706-2798

BURKHOLDER, DONALD LYMAN, mathematician, educator; b. Octavia, Nebr., Jan. 19, 1927; s. Elmer and Susie (Rothrock) B.; m. Jean Annette Fox, June 17, 1950; children: Kathleen, Peter, William. BA, Earlham Coll., 1950; MS, U. Wis., 1953; PhD, U. N.C., 1955. Asst. prof. math. U. Ill., Urbana, 1955-60, assoc. prof., 1960-64, prof., 1964-98, prof. Ctr. for Advanced Study, 1978-98, prof. emeritus, 1998—. Sabbatical leaves U. Calif., Berkeley, 1961-62, Westfield Coll., U. London, 1969-70; vis. prof. Rutgers U., 1972-73; researcher Stanford U., 1961, Hebrew U., 1969, Mittag-Leffler Inst., Sweden, 1971, 82, U. Paris, 1975, Institut des Hautes Études Scientifiques, 1986, U. Edinburgh, 1986, Tel Aviv U., 1989, U. New South Wales, 1991; Mordell lectr. Cambridge U., 1986; Zygmund lectr. U. Chgo., 1988; trustee Math. Scis. Rsch. Inst., 1981-84; bd. govs. Inst. Math. and Its Applications, 1983-85, chmn., 1985. Editor: Annals Math. Statistics, 1964-67. Fellow Inst. Math. Statistics (Wald lectr. 1971, pres. 1975-76); mem. NAS, Am. Math. Soc. (mem. editorial bd. Trans. 1983-85), London Math. Soc., Am. Acad. Arts and Scis. Achievements include research in probability theory and its applications to other branches of analysis. Home: 506 W Oregon St Urbana IL 61801-4044

BURKHOLDER, ERIC ODEN, behavior analyst, consultant; b. Traverse City, Mich., Apr. 23, 1972; s. Gary Stephan and Sharon Kay Burkholder; m. Jennifer C. Fernandez. BA, Western Mich. U., 1994; MA, Ctrl. Mich. U., 1996; PhD, U. Nev., 2004. Cert. behavior analyst. Sr. clinician Spectrum Ctr. Ednl. and Behavioral Devel., Berkeley, Calif., 2001—03; behavior specialist Newark (Calif.) Unified Sch. Dist., 2003—. Ind. behavioral and autism cons., Oakley, Calif., 2002—. Contbr. articles to profl. jours. Expert providing on line consultation to parents and educators Talkautism.com, 2003—. Mem.: Assn. Behavior Analysis. Office: Newark Unified Sch Dist 5715 Musick Ave Newark CA 94560 Personal E-mail: pencil00157@aol.com.

BURKHOLDER, JOANN M., botany educator; BS in Zoology, Iowa State U., 1975; MS in Botany, U. R.I., 1981; PhD in Botany, Mich. State U., 1986. Asst. prof. dept. botany N.C. State U., Raleigh, 1986-91, assoc. prof. dept. botany, 1992—. Apptd. N.C. Marine Fisheries Commn., 1992—, Coastal Futures com., 1993-94; speaker Harvard, AAAS, Nat. Acad. Scis., NATO, Internat. Conf. on Modern and Fossil Dinoflagellates, others. Pew fellow in Conservation and Environment, 1997—; recipient Scientific Freedom and Responsibility award AAAS, 1998, Environ. Guardian award Charlotte Observer, 1996. Mem. Am. Soc. Limnology and Oceanography (chair sessions at annual meetings, bd. dirs. 1994-97), Internat. Soc. Study of Harmful Algae, Estuarine Rsch. Fedn., Phycological Soc. Am. (mem. editl. bd. 1995-97), Soc. Protozoologists, Sigma Xi. Achievements include research emphasizing in nutritional ecology of algae, hetortrophic dinoflagellates, and aquatic angiosperms, especially the effects of cultural eutorphication on both freshwater and estuarine/coastl blooms, and on seagrass disappearance; involved in discovery of a group of mixotrophic dinoflagellates resembling clay particles, which can dominate the plankton of turbid reservoirs, a severe inhibitory impact of water-column nitrite engrichment on Zostera marina, the dominant seagrass habitat species on the Atlantic Coast, a toxic dinoflagellate, Pfiesteri piscicida implicated as a major causative agent fo fish deeath and disease, with potential linkages to serious human health effects as well. Office: NC State U Dept Botany 4214 Gardner Hl Raleigh NC 27695-0001 Fax: (919) 515-3436. E-mail: burkholder@ncsu.edu.

BURKHOLDER, PETER MILLER, retired physician, educator; b. Cambridge, Mass., May 7, 1933; s. Paul Rufus and Lillian Maud (Miller) B.; m. Barbara Beers, June 3, 1956; children: Kristen Ryner, Lisanne Ryner. BS, Yale U., 1955; MD, Cornell U., N.Y.C., 1959; degree in naturopathy (hon.), S.W. Coll. Naturopathic Medicine, 2001. Intern pathology N.Y. Hosp.-Cornell Med. Ctr., 1959-60; NIH trainee in pathology Cornell U., 1960-63, instr., 1963-64, asst. prof., 1964-65, Duke U., 1965-69, asso. prof., 1969-70, U. Wis.-Madison, 1970-72, acting chmn. dept. pathology, 1971-72, prof., 1972-79, chmn. dept. pathology, 1972-74; dir. Kidney Disease Inst., N.Y. State Dept. Health, 1979-80; dep. dir. div. labs. and research N.Y. State Dept. Health, 1980-81, dir. Ctr. Lab. Scis., 1981-82; chief of staff VA Med. Ctr., Ann Arbor, Mich., 1982-84, staff pathologist, 1984-89; prof. pathology U. Mich., Ann Arbor, 1982-89; chmn. dept. pathology Maricopa Med. Ctr., Phoenix, 1989-95, asst. med. dir., 1995; clin. prof. dept. pathology U. Ariz., Tucson, 1989—. Prof. pathology Southwest Coll. Naturopathic Medicine, 1996-2000, chief acad. officer, 2000. Author: Atlas of Human Glomerular Pathology, 1974; contbg. author: Structural Basis of Renal Diseases, 1968, Pathobiology Annual, 1971, Tissue Typing and Transplantation, 1973, Glomerulonephritis Morphology Natural History and Treatment, 1973, Cornell Seminars in Nephrology, 1975; mem. editorial bd. Kidney Internat, 1970-76, Lab. Investigation, 1972-83, Exptl. Pathology, 1984-86, Clin. Nephrology, 1989-92; contbr. numerous articles to profl. jours. NIH grantee, 1961-78 Mem. AMA, Am. Soc. Exptl. Pathology, Am. Assn. Pathology, Am. Soc. Immunology, Am. Soc. Nephrology, Internat. Acad. Pathology, Internat. Soc. Nephrology, Coll. Am. Pathology, Am. Soc. Clin. Pathologist, Am. Coll. Physician Execs., Renal Path. Soc., Pluto Soc. Home: 7248 N Red Ledge Dr Paradise Valley AZ 85253-2849 E-mail: pmburk@qwest.net.

BURKHOLDER, WENDELL EUGENE, retired entomology educator, researcher; b. Octavia, Nebr., June 24, 1928; s. Elmer and Susie Burkholder; m. Leona Rose Flory, Aug. 18, 1951; children: Paul Charles, Anne Carolyn, Joseph Kern, Stephen James. AB, McPherson Coll., 1950; M.Sc., U. Nebr., 1956; PhD, U. Wis., 1967. Rsch. entomologist U.S. Dept. Agr., 1956-96; asst. prof. U. Wis.-Madison, 1967-70, asso. prof., 1970-75, prof. entomology, 1975-96; prof. emeritus, 1996—. Lectr. in field. Mem. editorial bd.: Jour. Chem. Ecology, 1980-96, Jour. Stored Products Rsch., 1992-98; contbr. chpts. to books and articles to profl. jours. Served with U.S. Army, 1951-53. NSF grantee, 1972-75, 79; Rockefeller Found. grantee, 1974-77; Nat. Inst. Occupational Safety and Health grantee, 1977-79 Mem. AAAS, Entomol. Soc. Am., Wis. Entomol. Soc., Wis. Acad. Sci. Arts, and Letters, Internat. Soc. Chem. Ecology, Sigma Xi. Achievements include patents in field. Home: 1726 Chadbourne Ave Madison WI 53726-4108 Office: U Wis Entomology Dept 237 Russell Lab Madison WI 53706-1598

BURKI, FRED ALBERT, labor union official; b. Chgo., Apr. 8, 1926; s. John and Helen (Kramer) B.; children— Bill, Ken, Scott. Student, Northwestern U., U.Ill. Started as grocery clk., 1947; pres. local 470 United Retail Workers Union, Westchester, Ill., 1951-53, rep., 1953-62, field supr., 1963-65, nat. v.p., 1966-71, nat. exec. dir., 1971-81; internat. v.p. United Food and Comml. Workers Union, AFL-CIO, 1981—; pres. local 881, 1981—. Guest lectr. labor edn., advisor U. Ill. Circle Campus, Chgo.; labor edn. adv. U. Ind., 1967—, Loyola U., 1978—; mem. Midwest Com. Labor Study in Europe; labor adv. com. Senator Charles Percy, 1977—; chmn. Westchester Bldg. Corp., 1971-83. Bd. dirs. Chgo. Regional Blood Bank/Blood Services, Blood Ctr. of No. Ill., 1983—, Midwest Assn. for Sickle Cell Anemia, 1986—; trustee United Retail Workers Union-Super-Valu Trust Fund.; mem. Ill. Detection of Deception Com., 1982—; pres. Human Services Ltd., 1984— . Served with AUS, 1943-47; battalion exec. officer, maj. Res., 1947-67, ret. Decorated Bronze Star medal; named Man of Year Combined Counties Police Assn., 1977 Mem. V.F.W. (past officer), Mil. Police Assn., Res. Officers Assn. Office Phone: 918-296-3513. Personal E-mail: FBurki@aol.com.

BURKLE, RONALD W., former food service executive, business investor; b. 1953; Pvt. practice, 1975-88; pres. Jurgensen's, Pasadena, Calif., 1986-88; prin. Yucaipa Mgmt. Co., Claremont, Calif., 1986—; chmn. Food 4 Less Supermarkets, La Habra, Calif., 1989—, Dominick's Finer Foods, Northlake, Ill., until 1998; chmn., mem. exec. com. Kroger's Foods, Inc.; CEO Smith's Food & Drug Ctrs., Inc., Salt Lake City; chmn. Fred Meyer. Majority owner (with Mario Lemieux) Nat. Hockey League, Pitts. Penguins; bd. mem. Yahoo!, Yucaipa Equity Ptnrs., L.P., Occidental Petroleum Corp., Kaufman & Broad Home Corp.; bd. mem., chmn., mem. exec. com. The Kroger Co. Mem. bd. and exec. com. Campaign Against Youth Violence; trustee J. Paul Getty Trust, 2001—, John F. Kennedy Ctr. for the Performing Arts, Nat. Urban League, L.A. County Mus. Art; chmn. bd. D.A.R.E. Am.; mem. exec. bd. for med. scis. UCLA; co-chmn. Burkle Ctr. for Internat. Rels., UCLA; mem. edn. adv. bd. RAND; founder, chmn. bd. trustees Ralphs/Food4Less Found., The Fred Meyer, Inc. Found.; bd. mem. Children's Scholarship Fund, Carter Ctr., AIDS Project L.A.; mem. e-bd. Claremont Grad. U. Named Humanitarian of Yr., AFL-CIO, Man of Yr., L.A. County Fedn. Labor; recipient Whitney M. Young award, L.A. Urban League.

BURKMAN, ERNEST, JR., education educator; b. Detroit, Oct. 4, 1929; s. Ernest and Rose (Emmehizer) B.; m. Nancy Barron, Mar. 11, 1953; children: Laura, Linda, Jan, Patricia. BS, Ea. Mich U., 1952; MS, U. Mich., 1955, MA, 1958, EdD, 1961. Sci. tchr. Edsel Ford High Sch., Dearborn, Mich., 1955-60; from asst. prof. to prof. Fla. State U., Tallahassee, 1960—. Co-dir. Turkish Nat. Sci. Lise Project, Ankara, 1961-66; dir. Intermediate Sci. Curriculum Study, 1966-72, U.S. and nationwide, Individualized Sci. Instruction System Project, U.S. and nationwide, 1972-81; cons. over 35 agys., U.S. and 15 countries, 1961—. Author: Current Trends in Science Education, 1966, The Natural World, 1975-88; co-author, editor: Individualized Science Instructional System, (25 vol. book series), 1981-88; contbr. articles to profl. jours. Fellow AAAS; mem. Nat. Sci. Tchr. Assn., Am. Ednl. Rsch. Assn. Office: Fla State U Coll Edn Tallahassee FL 32306

BURKOFF, JOHN MICHAEL, law educator; b. Louisville, Nov. 16, 1948; s. Stanley Thomas and Joyce Ann (Switow) B.; m. Nancy Mammen, Aug. 17, 1969; children: Amy Nicole, David Michael. AB, U. Mich., 1970, JD, 1973; LLM, Harvard U., 1976. Bar: Mich. 1974, Pa. 1979. Law clk. to justice Mich. Supreme Ct., Detroit, 1973-75; adj. prof. law Wayne State U., Detroit, 1974-75; instr. law Boston U., 1975-76; asst. prof. U. Pitts., 1976-79, assoc. prof., 1979-82, prof., 1982—, assoc. dean, 2000—04. Of counsel Marcus & Shapira, Pitts., 1976-2000; mem. faculty Pa. Coll. of Judiciary, 1983—; reporter Prosecution Function and Def. Function Stds. Task Force, ABA, 1988-93. Author: Criminal Offenses and Defenses in Pennsylvania, 1984, 5th edit., 2004, Criminal Defense Ethics: Law and Liability, 1986, 2d edit., 2002, Search Warrant Law Desk Book, 1987, Ineffective Assistance of Counsel, 1993, Readings in Criminal Law, 1998, Criminal Procedure: Cases, Problems and Exercises, 2000, 2d edit, 2004, Criminal Law: Cases, Problems and Exercises, 2002, 2d edit., 2005, Principles of Criminal Procedure, 2004; editor: Search and Seizure Law Report. Del. Dem. Nat. Conv., N.Y.C., 1980; chair Pitts. Citizens Police Rev. Bd., 1997-99. Named Hon. Chief Police City of Louisville, 1980; Ford Found. fellow, 1976. Mem. ABA (chair trial judge standards task force 1997-2000), ACLU, Pa. Bar Assn., Assn. Am. Law Schs. (chair criminal justice sect. 1980, exec. coun. 1977-82), U.S. Supreme Ct. Hist. Soc. Democrat. Jewish. Home: 6104 Kentucky Ave Pittsburgh PA 15206-4213 Office: U Pitts Sch Law Pittsburgh PA 15260 Business E-Mail: burkoff@pitt.edu.

BURKS, A. WESLEY, pediatrics educator; b. Marshall, Ark., Apr. 21, 1954; m. Jan Getty; children: Chris, Sarah, Collin. BS in Biology and Chemistry, U. Cen. Ark., 1976; MD, U. Ark., 1980. Diplomate Am. Bd. Pediatrics, Am. Bd. Allergy and Immunology. Fellow in allergy/immunology/pulmonary diseases dept. pediatrics Duke U. Med. Ctr., Durham, N.C., 1983-85; intern in pediatrics Ark. Children's Hosp./U. Ark. for Med. Scis., Little Rock, 1980-81, resident in pediatrics, 1981-83, chief resident, 1983; prof. pediatrics U. Ark. for Med. Scis., 1996—2003; prof. pediatrics Med. Sch. Duke U., Chapell Hill, SC, 2003—. Mem. rsch. coun. U. Ark. for Med. Scis., 1989-2003; co-dir. pediatric clin. rsch. unit Ark. Children's Hosp., 1990-2003, dir. HLA tissue typing lab., 1991-2003. Mem. editorial bd., ad hoc reviewer Jour. Allergy and Clin. Immunology; ad hoc reviewer Pediatrics, Jour. Pediatrics, Pediatric Allergy and Immunology; contbr. numerous articles to sci. jours. Bd. dirs. Food Allergy Network, 1992, Ark. Regional Organ Recovery Agy., 1992. Named one of Outstanding Young Men of Am., 1981. Mem. AMA, Am. Acad. Allergy and Immunology (chmn. adverse reactions fo foods com. 1992), Am. Acad. Pediatrics, Ark. Acad. Pediatrics, Soc. for Pediatric Rsch., So. Soc. Pediatric Rsch. (rsch. councilor 1990-91), Clin. Immunology Soc., Southeastern Allergy Soc., Alan Cazort Allergy Soc., Alpha Chi (chpt. pres. 1975-76). Presbyterian. Avocations: soccer, baseball, basketball, youth coaching. Home: 306 Faison Rd Chapel Hill NC 27517-5667 Office: Duke Univ Med Sch Box 3530 DUMC Durham NC 27710 Office Phone: 919-681-2949. Business E-Mail: wesley.burks@duke.edu.

BURKS, DAVID BASIL, academic administrator, educator; b. Ava, Mo., May 13, 1943; m. Leah Ann Gentry; children: Bryan, Stephen, Marleah. BA, Harding Coll., 1965; MBA, U. Tex., 1966; PhD, Fla. State U., 1974. CPA, Tex. Mem. internal audit staff Exxon Inc., Houston, 1966-67; dir. placement, bus. instr. Harding Coll., Searcy, Ark., 1967-71, dean sch. bus., 1974-87, dir. Am. Studies program, 1982, pres., 1987—. Deacon Coll. Ch. of Christ, Searcy, 1985, elder, 1996, chmn. bd. dirs. Camp Wildwood, Searcy, 1975-79. Author: The Christian Alternative for Business, 1978; creator computerized bus. game Strategic Management Simulation, 1974. Mem. Kiwanis, Searcy Club. Republican. Office: Harding U Office of Pres 900 E Center Ave Stop 12256 Searcy AR 72149-0002

BURKS, JACK D., investment executive; b. San Antonio, Apr. 1, 1951; s. D.C. and Inez M. (Lyons) B.; m. Pamela Kay Bowen. BA, Ind. U., 1972, MBA, 1979. V.p. Pitts. Nat. Bank, 1973-84; mgr. dir. Offitbank, N.Y.C., 1984—. Bd. dirs. Alzheimers Assn., N.Y.C., 1994-98. Avocations: travel, military history, wine.

BURKS, ROCKY ALAN, disability access coordinator, consultant; b. San Bernardino, Calif., June 12, 1952; s. Lloyd Jackson and Vivian Elnora B.; m. Nikki Ann Stone (div. 1974); 1 child, Gannon Leroy; m. Lydia Ann Deatherage, Aug. 20, 1983. BA in Social Welfare, BA in Sociology, Calif. State U., Chico, 1979. Instrument flight instr. USAF, Del Rio, Tex., 1971—75; dir. outreach and recruitment, Office of Vets. Affairs Calif. State U., Chico, 1976—81; exec. dir. Easter Seal Soc. of Butte County, Chico, 1981—82, No. Calif. Ind. Living Program, Chico, 1982—85; soc. worker Butte County (Calif.) Welfare Dept., 1985—87; exec. dir. Ind. Living Svcs. of No. Calif., Inc., Chico, 1988—2004; disability access coord. supr. County of Marin, 2003—. Bd. dirs. Calif. Coalition of Ind. Living Ctrs., Sacramento, pres., 1991-94; bd. dirs. Pub. Interest Ctr. on Long-term Care, Sacramento, treas., 1994-98; mem. disability access adv. bd. Divsn. of the State Arch., Sacramento, 1995-99, Disabled Access Bd. of Appeals, Butte County Building Divsn., Oroville, 1994-2003; disability access code adv, com, Calif. Bldg. Stds. Commn., 1999—; bldg., fire and other codes adv. com., 2002—; mem. DRA fund, adv. and distbn. com. The San Francisco Found., 1999—; universal design adv. bd., Divsn. State Architect, 2002-03; disability access regulations advisory com. Nat. Fire Protection Assn., 2004—; mem. ADA adv. com. Butte County Bd. Suprs. 2002-03; bd. dirs. Marin Ctr. for Ind. Living, 2004—; mem. disability access regulations adv. com. Nat. Fire Protection Assn., 2004—. Editor: (newsletter) Independent Life, 1988—2004, Voice, 1976—81. Transp. adv. commn. Butte County Assn. Govts., Oroville, 1992-2004; mem. Californians for Disability Rights, Coalition of Disability Access Profls.; bd. dirs. Marin Ctr. Ind. Living, 2004— Recipient Cert. of Congl. Recognition, Congressman Wally Herger, Chico, 1993, 96, Disability Advocate award Calif. Assn. Persons with Handicaps, 1994, Region IX Disability Advocate award Nat. Coun. Ind. Living, 1998, Master Instr. award Air Tng. Command, USAF, 1975; named citizen Chickasaw Indian Nation. Mem. Am. Legion, Nat. Fire Protection Assn. (adv. com. disability access regulations 2004—), Vietnam Vets. Am., Masons, Shriners, Scottish Rite, Chico Breakfast Lions (pres. 1991-92, Lion of Yr. award 1990, Melvin Jones fellow), Lions Eye Found. Calif. and Nev. (life). Avocations: scuba diving, boating, reading, art. Home: 7476 Maximillian Pl Rohnert Park CA 94928 Office: County of Marin 3501 Civic Ctr Dr Rm 404 San Rafael CA 94903 Office Phone: 415-499-7002. Business E-Mail: rburks@co.marin.ca.us.

BURLEIGH, A. PETER, ambassador; b. L.A., Mar. 7, 1942; s. Ralph Wendell and Margaret (McKenney) B. AB, Colgate U., 1963; postgrad., U. Pa., 1965-66. Vol. Peace Corps, Nepal, 1963-65; joined Fgn. Svc., 1967;

various positions Dept. State, Washington, 1967-85, dir. No. Gulf Affairs, 1985-87, dep. asst. sec. for Near Eastern and South Asian Affairs, 1987-89, dep. asst. sec. for intelligence and rsch., 1989-91, coord. for counter-terrorism, amb., 1991-92, dep. asst. sec. for pers., 1992-95; amb. Dem. Socialist Republic Sri Lanka, Republic Maldives, 1995-97; dep. U.S. rep. to UN, 1997-99; ret. Vis. disting. prof., amb.-in-residence U. Miami, 2004—. Recipient Presdl. Svc. award U.S. Govt., 1990, 93, Disting. Svc. award Sec. of State, Washington, 2000, Presdl. Disting. Svc. award, 2000. Office: 2300 Riverlane Ter Fort Lauderdale FL 33312-4762 Personal E-mail: apburl@bellsouth.net.

BURLEIGH, LEWIS ALBERT, lawyer; b. Augusta, Maine, May 15, 1940; s. Lewis A. and Ursula (Maher) B.; m. Rinda H. Burleigh, June 22, 1963; children: Lewis A. IV, Jennifer, Erica. AB cum laude, Harvard U., 1962, JD, 1965. Bar: N.Y. 1966, Mass. 1973,Calif. 1982, Pa. 1985. Assoc. Dewey Ballantine Bushby Palmer & Wood, N.Y.C., 1965-72; ptnr. Csaplar & Bok (name changed to Gaston & Snow), Boston and San Francisco, 1973-91, Day Berry & Howard, Boston, 1991—2001, Dechert LLP, Boston, 2001—. Fellow Am. Coll. Investment Counsel; mem. ABA, N.Y. State Bar Assn., Calif. Bar Assn., Am. Soc. Internat. Law, Harvard Club. Avocation: flying. Office: Dechert LLP 200 Clarendon St Fl 27 Boston MA 02116 Office Phone: 617-654-8601. Business E-Mail: lewis.burleigh@dechert.com.

BURLEIGH, WILLIAM ROBERT, newspaper executive; b. Evansville, Ind., Sept. 6, 1935; s. Joseph Charles and Emma Bertha (Wittgen) B.; m. Catherine Anne Husted, Nov. 28, 1964; children: David William, Catherine Anne, Margaret Walden. BS, Marquette U., Milw., 1957; LLD (hon.), U. So. Ind., 1979. From reporter to editor, pres. Evansville Press, 1951-77; editor Cin. Post, 1977-83; v.p., gen. editl. mgr. Scripps-Howard Newspapers, Cin., 1984-86, sr. v.p. newspapers and publs., 1986-90, exec. v.p., 1990-94, pres., COO, 1994-96, pres., CEO, 1996-99; chmn., CEO E.W. Scripps Co., Cin., 1999-2000, chmn., 2000—. With AUS, 1957-58. Mem. Queen City Club, Cin. Lit. Club, Cin. Country Club, Cin. Comml. Club, Alpha Sigma Nu. Roman Catholic. Office: E W Scripps 312 Walnut St Cincinnati OH 45202-4024*

BURLESKI, JOSEPH ANTHONY, JR., information technology executive; b. Poughkeepsie, N.Y., June 30, 1960; s. Joseph Anthony, Sr. and Fredeline (Cyr) Burleski; m. Judith Ann Lezon, June 10, 1989; children: Joseph Anthony III, Jessica Ann. BSBA, Marist Coll., 1982; MBA Mktg., U. Phoenix, 1992; grad. in human rels. and effective speaking, Dale Carnegie, 1990. Cert. project mgmt. profl. Project Mgmt. Inst., exec. project mgr. IBM. Computer operator IBM, Poughkeepsie, 1982-83, lead/sr. computer operator, 1983-84, systems programmer, 1984-85, assoc. systems programmer, 1985-86, mgr. offshift computer ops., 1986-87, mgr. info. processing Boulder, Colo., 1987-88, mgr. MVS systems programming, 1988-91; mgr. location and field svcs. devel. Integrated Systems Solutions Corp. subs. IBM, Boulder, 1991-93, mgr. location and field svc. devel. ind. test, 1992-93; mgr. VM/VSE svcs. Integrated Sys. Solutions Corp. subs. IBM, Boulder, 1993-94, account mgr., 1994-96; delivery project exec. IBM Global Svcs., Boulder, 1997-98, delivery exec. St. Louis, 1998—2000, sr. delivery project exec., 2001—; bd. dirs. IBM Cert. Bd., 2000—. Mem. IBM Data Processing Ops. Coun., Poughkeepsie, 1983—92, Project Mgmt. Inst., 1995—. Coach Spl. Olympics, 1987—98; asst. cubmaster Boy Scouts Am., 2002—03, 2005—, cubmaster, 2003—05, Cub Scout roundtable chmn., 2004—, asst. boy scout scoutmaster, 2005—, mem. scout tng. com., 2005—. Mem.: Am. Assn. Individual Investors, Marist Coll. Alumni Assn. (contbr.), Nat. Eagle Scout Assn., KC (Ascension Coun. # 11139), Order of Arrow (chpt. sec., editor 1976—77, chpt. pres. 1977—78, chpt. treas. 1980—81), Vigil Nat. Honor Soc. Roman Catholic. Avocations: running, reading, camping, hiking, raising tropical fish. Office: Bldg 302-3E MD S306-2182 325 JS McDonnell Blvd Hazelwood MO 63042 Office Phone: 314-252-6069. Business E-Mail: burleski@us.ibm.com.

BURLETT, HELEN MARIE, elementary school educator; b. Dunkirk, NY, Jan. 8, 1941; d. Maurice J. and Anna M. (Carpenter) Waite; m. James R. Burlett, May 12, 1962; 1 child, Amanda Julia. BS in Legal Studies, SUNY Fredonia, 1996. Substitute tchr. various sch. dists., NY, 1996—. Sec. No. Chautauqua Landlord's Assn., Dunkirk, 1996—. Mem. AAUW (1st v.p. 1998—, chmn. book sale 1998, pres. 2000-2002), VFW Auxillary, DAR (past chaplain 1973), Mayflower Soc., Magna Carta Soc., Fredonia Preservation Soc., Daughters of Am. Colonist, Soc. Descandents of Valley Forge. Meth. Home: 4616 W Lake Rd Dunkirk NY 14048-9609

BURLEY, JOHN M, music educator; b. Lincoln, Nebr., Oct. 3, 1946; s. Alvin M Burley and V Ilene BUrley; m. Barbara Ann Burley, June 8, 1969; children: John Christian, Erin Elizabeth. M in Music Edn., Ft. Hays State U., 1969, U. Ill., 1970, EdD in Music Edn., 1979. Prof. music Centennial H.S., Champaign, Ill., 1970—74, dir. music, 1975—77; asst. dir. sch. music U. Ill., 1979—83; prof. music, dir. jazz studies Scottsdale Coll., Ariz., 1983—. Music curriculum cons. and adj. various coll., 1983—. Contbr. articles to profl. jours. Avocations: painting, trumpet. Office: Scottsdale Coll 9000 E Chaparral Rd Scottsdale AZ 85256 Home: 10918 E Kalil Scottsdale AZ 85259 Business E-Mail: j.burley@sccmail.maricopa.com.

BURLING, JAMES C., lawyer; b. 1950; AB, Grinnell Coll., 1972; JD, Harvard Univ., 1976. Bar: Mass. 1977, US Supreme Ct. Atty. FTC, 1976—78, Hale & Dorr, 1978—2004, past chmn. exec. com.; ptnr., co-chmn. Antitrust & Competition dept., mem. Litigation dept. Wilmer Cutler Pickering Hale & Dorr, Boston, 2004—. Contbr. articles to profl. jours. Bd. dir. Ctr. for Pub. Representation, New Eng. Ctr. for Children. Named a Mass. Super Lawyer, Boston Mag., 2004. Fellow: Mass. Bar Assn.; mem.: ABA (past vice chmn., Intellectual Property com.), Boston Bar Assn., Phi Beta Kappa. Office: Wilmer Cutler Pickering Hale & Dorr 60 State St Boston MA 02109 Office Phone: 617-526-6416. Office Fax: 617-526-5000. Business E-Mail: james.burling@wilmerhale.com.

BURLINGAME, ALMA LYMAN, chemist, educator; b. Cranston, R.I., Apr. 29, 1937; s. Herman Follett Jr. and Rose Irene (Kohler) B.; children: Mark, Walter; m. Marilyn F. Schwartz, Feb. 14, 1993; 1 stepchild, Corey Schwartz. BS, U. R.I., 1959; PhD, MIT, 1962. Asst. prof. U. Calif., Berkeley, 1963-68, assoc. chemist, 1968-72, rsch. chemist, 1972-78, prof. San Francisco, 1978—, Univ. Coll., London, 1996—2002. Vis. prof. Ludwig Inst. for Cancer Rsch., London, 1993-94. Editor: Topics in Organic Mass Spectrometry, 1970, Mass Spectrometry in Health and Life Science, 1985, Biological Mass Spectrometry, 1990, Mass Spectrometry in the Biological Sciences, 1995, Mass Spectrometry in Biology and Medicine, 2000; dep. editor Molecular and Cellular Proteomics, 2002—; contbr. articles to profl. jours. With USAR, 1954-62. Guggenheim Found. fellow, 1970. Fellow AAAS. Office: U Calif Dept Pharm Chemistry San Francisco CA 94143-0001 Office Phone: 415-476-5641. Business E-Mail: alb@cgl.ucsf.edu.

BURLINGAME, EDWARD LIVERMORE, book publisher; b. N.Y.C., Jan. 21, 1935; s. Anson and Elizabeth Harlow (Hussey) B.; m. Perdita Remony Plowden, May 18, 1963; children: Remony Elizabeth, Phyllida Anne, Roger Anson. BA, Harvard U., 1957; AMP, Harvard Bus. Sch., 1982. Editor MacGibbon & Kee, Ltd., London, 1959-61; sr. editor New Am. Library, N.Y.C., 1961-65; v.p., editor-in-chief Walker & Co., N.Y.C., 1965-68; sr. v.p., editor-in-chief trade div. J.B. Lippincott Co., Phila. and N.Y.C., 1968-78, dir., 1970-78; v.p., pub. Lippincott & Crowell, N.Y.C., 1979-80; v.p., editor-in-chief, pub. trade group Harper & Row, Pubs., Inc., N.Y.C., 1980-87; pub. Edward Burlingame Books (an imprint of HarperCollins Pubs.), 1987-93; pres. The Adventure Libr., 1993—2003. Mem. Eastern regional panel Pres.'s Commn. on White House Fellowships, 1982-84; mem. vis. com. New Sch. for Social Rsch., 1991-95; trustee North Salem Lib. Served to lt. (j.g.) USNR, 1957-59. Mem. Assn. Am. Pubs. (copyright com. 1976-77, internat. freedom to publish com. 1977-80, exec. council gen. pub. div. 1981-88, vice chmn. 1984-85, chmn. 1985-86), PEN (treas., exec. bd. 1970-73). Clubs: Century Assn. Personal E-mail: edwardb@pobox.com.

BURLINGAME, GARY ALFRED, environmental scientist; b. Phila., May 12, 1958; s. John W. and Betty J. Burlingame; m. Deborah Ann McCanney, June 6, 1981; children: Laura E., Christopher J., Corey D. BS in environ. Sci., Drexel U., 1981, MS in environ. Sci., 1983. Rsch. asst. Drexel U., Phila., 1979—82; aquatic biologist Phila. (Pa) Water Dept., 1982—89, lab. program scientist, 1989—95, supr. water quality rsch., 1995—2003, admin. scientist, 2003—. Adj. assoc. prof. Drexel U., 1982—2003; adv. bd. Am. Water Works Assn. Rsch. Found., Denver, 1995—; com. mem. Nat. Rsch. Coun., Pub. Water Distribution Sys., Wash., DC, 2004—06. Contbr. articles various profl. jours. Recipient Golden Spigot award, Am. Water Works Assn., 2000, Opflow Pub. award, 2001. Mem.: Internat. Water Assn. (sec. of specialist group 2003—), Water Environ. Fed., Am. Water Works Assn. Presbyn. Avocations: photography, creative writing, poetry. Office: Phila Water Dept 1500 E Hunting Pk Ave Philadelphia PA 19124 Office Phone: 215-685-1417. Office Fax: 215-743-5594. E-mail: gary.burlingame@phila.gov.

BURLINGAME, MARK WAYNE, cardiothoracic surgeon; b. St. Paul, Oct. 8, 1950; s. Charles Frank and Patricia Ann (Meyer) B.; m. Anine Marie Davidson, Apr. 18, 1975; children: Patrick, Kathleen, Julia, Ross. BA in Biology, Northwestern U., 1971; MD cum laude, Creighton U., 1975. Diplomate Am. Bd. Surgery, Am. Bd. Thoracic Surgery; lic. surgeon, Ala., Wis., Mich., Pa. Quality control microbiologist Allergan Pharms., 1971; extern Tex. Heart Inst. Baylor U., 1974; intern U. Ala. Hosps., Birmingham, 1975-80; resident in cardiothoracic surgery Med. Coll. Wis. Hosps., Milw., 1980-82; pvt. practice Pontiac, Mich., 1982-83, Lancaster, Pa., 1983—; active staff Lancaster Gen. Hosp., 1983—. Dir. critical care Lancaster Gen. Hosp., 1993—, chmn. dept. surgery, 1997-2000, chief divsn. of cardiothoracic surgery, 2000—; courtesy staff Lancaster Regional Med. Ctr., 1983—, Cmty. Hosp. Lancaster, 1983—. Contbr. articles to profl. jours. Rsch. fellow NSF, 1969, 70, Argonne Nat. Lab./U.S. Atomic Energy Commn., 1970; Summer fellow Creighton U., 1972. Fellow ACS, Am. Coll. Cardiology, Am. Coll. Chest Physicians, Soc. Thoracic Surgeons; mem. Pa. Med. Soc., Pa. Assn. Thoracic Surgery, Lancaster City and County Med. Soc., Beta Beta Beta, Alpha Omega Alpha. Avocations: piano, golf, gourmet food, wine. Office: Cardiothoracic Surgeons Lancaster 555 N Duke St Lancaster PA 17604-3555 Home: 39 Deer Ford Dr Lancaster PA 17601-5642 Office Phone: 717-544-4995. E-mail: CTSL@cardiacsurgeons.com.

BURMASTER, ELIZABETH, school system administrator; b. Balt., July 26, 1954; m. John Burmaster; 3 children. B in Music Edn., U. Wis., 1976, M in Edn1. Adminstrn., 1984. Vocal music and creative dramatics dir. Longfellow Elem. and Sennett Middle Sch., Madison, Wis., 1976—78; choral and drama dir. East H.S., Madison, 1978—85; asst. prin. Marquette Middle Sch., Madison, 1985—88; fine arts coord. Madison Sch. Dist., 1988—90; prin. Hawthorne Elem., Madison, 1990—92, Madison West H.S., 1992—2001; state supt. pub. instrn. State of Wis., Madison, 2001—. Mem. Govs. Econ. Growth Coun., Coun. Chief State Sch. Officers, chair task force on early childhood learning, bd. dirs.; chair-elect Nat. Ctr. for Learning and Citizenship. Mem. bd. regents U. Wis.; mem. Edn. Commn. of the States, Wis. Tech. Coll. Sys. Bd., Ednl. Comms. Bd., Very Spl. Arts Wis., Gov.'s Work-Based Learning Bd.; bd. dirs. TEACH Wis. Mem.: Coun. of Chief State Sch. Officers, SAI-Music Assn., Tempo Internat., Assn. Wis. Sch. Adminstrs. Mailing: Wis Dept Pub Instrn PO Box 7841 Madison WI 53707-7841

BURMEISTER, JOHN LUTHER, chemistry professor, consultant; b. Fountain Springs, Pa., Feb. 20, 1938; s. Luther John and Frieda May (Tielmann) B.; m. Doris Aileen Crawford, June 25, 1960; children: Lisa Anne, Jeffrey Scott. BS in Chemistry, Franklin and Marshall Coll., 1959; PhD in Chemistry, Northwestern U., 1964. Instr. chemistry U. Ill., Urbana, 1963-64; asst. prof. chemistry U. Del., Newark, 1964-69, assoc. prof., 1969-73, prof., 1973-93, alumni disting. prof., 1993—, assoc. chmn. dept., 1974—, NCAA faculty athletic rep., 1982—. Pres. Covered Bridge Farms Maintenance Corp., Newark, 1977-79; chmn. chemistry editl. rev. bd. Control Data Corp., Mpls., 1981-85. Mem. editl. bd. Inorganica Chimica Acta, Padua, Italy, 1967-88, Synthesis and Reactivity Inorganic Metal-Organic Chemistry, NYC, 1970-98; contbr. numerous articles to profl. jours. Ruling elder Head Christiana Presbyn. Ch., Newark, 1969—. Recipient Excellence Tchg. award Lindback Found. Del. Alumni Assn., 1968, 79, award Excellence chemistry Tchr., Chem. Mfrs. Assn., Washington, 1981, faculty recognition award Mortar Bd., 1984, Prof. Yr. award Coll. Arts Sci., 1985, Del. Prof. Yr. award Carnegie Found., 1994, Advancement Tchr. Cun. Advancement Support Edn., 1994, Disting. Del. Scientist award, 1994, Excellence Tchg. award Alpha Lambda Delta, 1997, Coll. Arts Sci. Disting. Alumni Prof. award, 1997. Mem. Am. Chem. Soc. (sec.-treas. inorganic divsn. 1975-77, alt. councillor, 1977-79, assoc. nat. com. chem. edn. 1983-84, councillor Del. sect. 1987-89), Sigma Xi, Phi Lambda Upsilon, Phi Kappa Phi (v.p. Del. chpt. 1979-80, pres. 1980-81), Omicron Delta Kappa. Republican. Office: U Del Dept Chemistry-Biochemistry Newark DE 19716 Office Phone: 302-831-1130. Business E-Mail: jlburm@chem.udel.edu.

BURMEISTER, PAUL FREDERICK, farmer; b. Great Bend, Kans., June 11, 1938; s. Ferdinand Frederick Adam and Gertrude Nellie (Hanson) B. BA in Chemistry and Agr., Ft. Hays State U., 1960; postgrad., U. Kans., 1961. Farmer, Claflin, Kans., 1952-61, 64—. Farmer coop. Kans. Agrl. Experiment Sta., Ft. Hays Br. Sta., Hays, Kans., 1970, Kans. Rural Ctr., Whiting, 1991-92; panel mem. Kans. Sustainable Agr. Conf., Great Bend and Salina, 1991-92; mem. Kans. Natural Resource Coun., Topeka, 1975—, Nat. Resources Def. Coun., NYC, 1975—; participant U. Akron Nat. Energy Forum, 1976, Nat. Low-Level Radioactive Waste Mgmt. Strategy Rev. Workshop, Washington, 1981, Office Radiation Programs, EPA, Denver, 1978; guest spkr., Rapid City, S.D., 1993; mem. farmer adv. com. Sunshine Farm Project, The Land Inst., Salina, 1995-2001. Contbr. articles to environ. and agrl. jours. Vol. Am. Peace Corps, Ludhiana, India, 1961-63; local organizer campaign Union of Concerned Scientists, Cambridge, Mass.; lobbyist on environ. protection and conservation issues, Topeka, 1976-80; mem. Renew Am., Washington, 1980—; mem. The Menninger Found., Topeka, 1989—, Environ. Action, 1982—; lay mem. ad hoc task force on ecology Christian lifestyle United Ch. of Christ, 1977-78, commn. on outreach Kans.-Okla. conf., 1988-96, 98-99, network environ. and econ. responsibility; del. to 23rd Gen. Synod meeting of United Ch. of Christ, Kansas City, Mo., 2001; mem. Kans.-Okla. Conf. Coun. United Ch. Christ, 1999-2003; participant Kans. Citizens Forum Com. for Humanities, Topeka, 1987; bd. trustees Clara Barton Hosp. Found., Hoisington, Kans., 2005-. With USNG, 1963—69. Recipient Bankers award Banks of Barton County, Kans. and U.S. Soil Conservation Svc., 1990. Mem. Nat. Wildlife Fedn. (life), Nat. Coun. Returned Peace Corps Vols., Nat. Arbor Day Found., World Wildlife Fund (charter), Am. Wind Energy Assn., Am. Solar Energy Soc. (life), Heartland Renewable Energy Soc., Midwest Renewable Energy Assn., 1998—, Kans. Assn. Wheat Growers, Kans. Farmers Union, Kans. Organic Prodrs., Inc., Friends of the Earth, Cousteau Soc. (founding yr. mem.), Kans. State Hist. Soc. (life), Kans. Wildlife Fedn., Sierra Club (life), Native Forest Coun., Ducks Unltd. Inc., Environ. Def., Wilderness Soc., Friends of India, Rainforest Alliance, Nat. Parks Conservation Assn., Nature Conservancy, Tau Kappa Epsilon (sec. 1958-59, scholar 1959), Phi Eta Sigma (historian 1958-59), Phi Kappa Phi, Delta Epsilon. Avocations: photography, hiking, exploring. Address: 1332 NE 180th Rd Claflin KS 67525-9219 Office Phone: 620-587-3919.

BURNER, CLARA MILLER, librarian; b. Gettysburg, Pa., May 27, 1943; d. Herbert and Ruth (Myers) Miller; m. Emory C. Bogle, March 21, 1970 (div. March 1991); 1 child, Andrew Miller Ibrahim Bogle; m. Robert Henry Burner, Aug. 20, 1995 (dec.). BA in Spanish, Pa. State U., 1965; MLS, Pratt Inst., 1968. Reference libr. Richmond (Va.) Pub. Libr., 1970-76, branch libr., 1977-85, deputy city libr., 1985—, acting city libr., 1996-97. Mem. Am. Libr. Assn. (Va. chapt.). Methodist. Office: Richmond Public Library 101 E Franklin St Richmond VA 23219-2107

BURNES, KENNETT FARRAR, chemical company executive; b. Washington, Feb. 23, 1943; s. Richard M. and Ruth (Carney) B.; m. Barbara Jackson; children: Jennifer, Nathaniel, Lisa, Alison. AB, Harvard U., 1965, LLB, 1968. Ptnr. Choate, Hall & Stewart, Boston, 1968-87; v.p., gen. counsel Cabot Corp., Waltham, Mass., 1987-88, exec. v.p. Boston, 1988-95, pres., COO, 1995—2001, chmn., pres., CEO, 2001—. Bd. dirs. Neozyme Corp., Renaissance Properties Inc., Boston, White Flower Farm, Inc., Litchfield, Conn., Cabot Corp. Chmn. bd. Park Sch., Brookline, Mass., 1971-82. Office: Cabot Corp 75 State St Ste 13 Boston MA 02109-1806*

BURNETT, ARTHUR LOUIS, SR., judge; b. Spotsylvania County, Va., Mar. 15, 1935; s. Robert Louis and Lena Victoria (Bumbry) B.; m. Ann Lloyd, May 14, 1960; children: Darnellena, Arthur Louis II, Darryl, Darlisa, Dionne. BA summa cum laude, Howard U., 1957; LLB, NYU, 1958; grad., Fed. Exec. Inst., 1978. Bar: D.C. 1958, U.S. Dist. Ct. Md. 1963, U.S. Supreme Ct. 1964. Atty. Gen.'s Honor Program atty. fraud sect. criminal divsn. U.S. Dept. Justice, Washington, 1958, atty. to acting dep. chief gen. crimes sect., 1960-65; spl. asst. U.S. atty., Balt. and East St. Louis, Ill., 1961-63; asst. U.S. atty. D.C., 1965-68; legal adviser, gen. counsel D.C. Dept. Met. Police, 1968-69; U.S. magistrate U.S. Dist. Ct., Washington, 1969-75; asst. gen. counsel legal adv. divsn. U.S. CSC, 1975-78; assoc. gen. counsel Office of Personnel Mgmt., 1979-80; U.S. magistrate U.S. Dist. Ct. D.C., 1980-87; judge Superior Ct. D.C., 1987-98, sr. judge, 1998—; faculty Fed. Jud. Center, 1970—, Nat. Jud. Coll., 1974—; nat. exec. dir. Nat. African Am. Drug Policy Coalition, 2004—. Judge-in-residence Children's Def. Fund, 1998—; program chmn. ann. meeting Nat. Conf. Spl. Ct. Judges, Washington, 1973, chmn. elect, acting chmn., 1974-75, chmn., 1975; program chmn. ann. meeting Nat. Council U.S. Magistrates, Williamsburg, Va., 1974, pres., 1983-84; program participant D.C. Circuit Jud. Conf., 1974, U.S. Ct. Claims Jud. Conf., 1979; adj. prof. Columbus Sch. Law, Cath. U. Am., 1997—, Cath. U., 1997—, Sch. Law Howard U., 1998—. Mem. NYU Law Rev., 1957-58; editor Directory of Minority Judges of U.S., 1997—. Bd. dirs. Fellowship of Christian Athletes, Washington, 2000, Nat. Assn. for Children of Alcoholics, 2000—. Recipient Founders Day award NYU, 1958, Sustained Superior Performance award U.S. Atty. Gen., 1963, Disting. Service award CSC, 1978, Meritorious Service award U.S. Office of Personnel Mgmt., 1980, Jud. award of excellence Washington Met. Trial Lawyers Assn., 1999, award of excellence Nat. Conf. State Trial Judges, 1999, Outstanding Disting. Service award Fed. Bar Assn., 1983. Mem. ABA (Franklin N. Flashner jud. award as outstanding judge on ct. of spl. jurisdiction 1985, coun. adminstrv. law and regulatory practice sect. 1987-90, liaison rep. of adminstrv. law and regulatory practice sect. to adminstrv. conf. of U.S. 1990-94, JAD task force on improving opportunities for minorities 1988-2004, judge Edward R. Finch Law Day USA speech award 1991, asst. sec. 1991-93, chair civil right and employment discrimination com. 1992-95, sec. adminstrv. law and regulatory practice 1993-95, chmn. CJS com. on criminal rules and evidence 1993-97, standing com. on substance abuse 1995-99, standing com. unmet legal needs of children 2003—, co-chmn. editl. bd. Criminal Justice Mag. 1997-2000, adv. com. and standing com. on pro bono and pub. svc. 2001-, State Justice Initiatives award 2002, Spirit of Excellence award 2005), Fed. Bar Assn. (sect. coord. 1987-88, chmn. fed. litigation sect. 1984-85, chmn. standing com. on U.S. magistrates, dep. chmn. sect. adminstrn. of justice 1983-84, chmn. standing com. on U.S. magistrate, chmn. sect. adminstrn. of justice 1983-84, 95-97, pres. DC chpt. 1984-85, chmn. profl. ethics com. 1991-93, chmn. audit com. 1999—, Disting. Svc. award 1978, Pres.'s award 1994, Earl Kintner award 2002, Spirit Excellence award 2005), Washington Bar Assn. (chmn. jud. com. 2000-01, Ollie Mae Cooper award 1997), Nat. Bar Assn. (chmn. cmty. and youth action com. jud. coun. 1995—, chmn. profl. ethics com., jud. coun. asst. sec., The Pres.'s award 1996, Raymond Pace Alexander award, 2004, E. Francis Stradford award, 2004), Bar Assn. DC, DC Unified Bar, Am. Judicature Soc., Am. Judges Assn. (sec-treas. Prettyman-Leventhal Inn of Ct. Washington 1991-94, pres. 1994-95), Phi Beta Kappa, Omega Psi Phi. Office: Howard U Sch Law Holy Cross Hall Rm #318 2900 Van Ness St NW Washington DC 20008 Office Phone: 202-806-8211. Personal E-mail: albsr2alb@aol.com, aburnettsr@aol.com.

BURNETT, CALVIN, artist, educator; b. Cambridge, Mass., July 18, 1921; s. Nathan Lowe and Adelaide (Waller) B.; m. Torrey Milligan, Aug. 20, 1960; 1 child, Tobey. BS in Education, Mass. Coll. Art, 1951; M.F.A., Boston U., 1960, BFA (hon.), 1993, postgrad., 1960-71. One-person shows: Northeastern U., Boston, 1980; Franklin-Pierce Coll., N.H., 1981; Mass. Coll. Art, Boston, 1982, Boston Public Lib., 1993, Nat. Ctr. African-Am. Artists, Boston, 1995; exhibited in group shows Smithsonian Travling, 1980-84; Atlanta Life Ins. Co.; Studio Mus., Harlem, N.Y.; represented in permanent collection FOGG, Cambridge, Mass.; Mus. Fine Arts, Boston; Bazalel Mus., Israel; Dusable, Chgo.; Oakland, Calif.; instr. Elma Lewis Sch., Roxbury, Mass., 1951-53; instr., illustrator Decordova Mus., Lincoln, Mass., 1952-56; illustration prof. emeritus Mass. Coll. Art, Boston, 1956-87; cons., juror Nat. Ctr. Afro Am. Artists, Roxbury, 1981. Author, designer, illustrator: Objective Drawing Techniques, 1966. Recipient Disting. Service award Mass. Coll. Art, 1979. Mem. Mass. Coll. Art Faculty Assn., NEA, Mass. Tchrs. Assn., Friends of Schomburg Collection, Mus. Afro Am. History, Boston Afro Am. Artists Assn. (co-founder 1961). Democrat. Baptist. Avocations: pianist, clarinetist. Home: 87 Fisher St Medway MA 02053-2232

BURNETT, CAROL, actress, comedienne, singer; b. San Antonio, Apr. 26, 1933; d. Jody and Louise (Creighton) B.; m. Joseph Hamilton, 1963 (div.); children: Carrie Louise, Jody Ann, Erin Kate; m. Brian Miller, 2001. Student, UCLA, 1952-54. Introduced comedy song I Made a Fool of Myself Over John Foster Dulles, 1957; Broadway debut in Once Upon a Mattress, 1959; regular performer in Garry Moore TV show, 1959-62; appeared several CBS-TV spls., 1962-63; star Carol Burnett Show, CBS-TV, 1966-77, Carol & Co., 1990-91; appeared on Broadway, Once Upon a Mattress, 1960, Plaza Suite, 1970, I Do, I Do, (musical) 1973, Same Time Next Year, 1977, Moon Over Buffalo, 1995 (Tony nomination), co-wrote play (with Carrie Hamilton), Hollywood Arms, 2001; films include Who's Been Sleeping in My Bed, 1963, Pete 'n' Tillie, 1972, Front Page, 1974, A Wedding, 1977, Health, 1979, Four Seasons, 1981, Chu Chu and the Philly Flash, 1981, Annie, 1982, Noises Off, 1992, Moon Over Broadway, 1997, Get Bruce, 1999, The Trumpet of the Swan (voice), 2001; TV movies Friendly Fire, 1978, The Grass is Always Greener Over the Septic Tank, 1979, The Tenth Month, 1979, Life of the Party, 1982, Between Friends, 1983, Hostage, 1988, Men, Movies, and Carol, 1994, Seasons of the Heart, 1994, The Marriage Fool, 1998 (American Comedy award, 1998), Grace, 1998, Once Upon a Mattress, 2004; club engagements, Harrah's Club, The Sands, Caesar's Palace, MGM Grand; TV specials Julie and Carol: Together Again, 1989, Happy Birthday Elizabeth: A Celebration of Life, 1997, Putting it Together, 2000, Carol Burnett: Show Stoppers, 2001; TV series Mad About You, 1996-1998; TV miniseries Fresno, 1986, A Century of Women, 1994; dir., writer The Universal Story, 1995, also prodr. Southern Star: Portrait of Atlanta, 1996; prodr. Fred Astaire: Puttin' On His Top Hat, 1980, Fred Astaire: Change Partners and Dance, 1980, Bacall on Bogart, 1988, Fred Astaire Songbook, 1991, Southern Star: A Portrait of Atlanta, 1996, others. Recipient outstanding comedienne award Am. Guild Variety Artists, 5 times; Emmy award for outstanding variety performance Acad. TV Arts and Scis., 5 times; Emmy award for best supporting actress in a comedy series for Mad About You, 1997; TV Guide award for outstanding female performer, 1961, 62, 63; Peabody award, 1963; Golden Globe award for outstanding comedienne of year Fgn. Press Assn., 8 times; Woman of Year award Acad. TV Arts and Scis.; 12 People's Choice awards; 1st ann. Nat. TV Critics Circle award for outstanding performance, 1977; San Sebastian Film Festival award for best actress for A Wedding, 1978; 1st Ace award Best Actress Between Friends, 1983, Horatio Alger award Horatio Alger Assn. Disting. Ams., 1988; named One of 20 Most Admired Women Gallup Poll, 1977. Address: ICM 8942 Wilshire Blvd Fl 2 Beverly Hills CA 90211-1934*

BURNETT, CLAIRE CONKLIN, music educator; b. Huntington, N.Y., Feb. 15, 1954; d. Roger Bedell and Marjorie (Driscol) C.; m. Robert W. Burnett, Oct. 6, 1990. BS in Music Edn., West Chester U., 1976; MME, U. Conn., 1988. Substitute tchr. Northport (N.Y.) Pub. Schs., 1976-77; tchr. Canaan (Vt.) Meml. High Sch., 1977-81; instrumental tchr. Lake Region Schs., Orleans, Vt., 1981-82; choral dir. Rocky Hill (Conn.) High Sch., 1982—. Choral chmn. Charter Oak Conf. Music Festival, Conn., 1984-90, 97, No. Region Jr. High Music Festival, New Britain, Conn., 1984-85; mem. scholarship com. Suffield (Conn.) Arts Coun., 1988-90. Author: K-12 Music

Curriculum, 1980. Dir. Northernaires Community Chorus, Colebrook, N.H., 1978-81, North Country Community Band, Canaan, 1979-81; mem. Friends of Suffield, 1987-88; mem. St. James Episopal Ch., West Hartford, Conn.; mem. Hartford Chorale, 1988 Guest conductor North Country Music Festival, Newport, Vt., 1979. Mem. NEA, Music Educators Nat. Conn., Conn. Music Educators Assn. (pub. rels. co-chmn. 1986-88, 82-90), Vt. Music Educators Assn., Am. Choral Dirs. Assn. (Conn. chpt. exec. sec. 1988-89, pres. 1991-93, v.p. 1993—, chair divsn. sr. high R&S, 1994-96), New Eng. Music Festival Assn., Concora (bd. dirs. 1995—, v.p. 1996—), Concora (v.p. bd. dirs., 1997—). Republican. Avocations: bicycling, skiing, golf, tennis, cooking, gardening, art. Office: Rocky Hill High Sch 50 Chapin Ave Rocky Hill CT 06067-2300 Office Phone: 860-258-7721 x 34. E-mail: burnettc@comcast.net.

BURNETT, E. C., III, judge; b. Spartanburg County, SC, Jan. 26, 1942; s. E. C., Jr. and Lucy (Byers) Burnett; m. Jami Grant, 1963; children: Curry, Sharon, Jeffrey. AB, Wofford Coll., 1964; JD, U. S.C., 1969. Bar: S.C. 1969. Pvt. practice atty., Spartanburg; mem. SC Ho. of Reps., 1973-74; probate judge Spartanburg County, 1976-80; judge family ct., 1980-81, Seventh Jud. Cir., 1981-95; assoc. justice SC Supreme Ct., 1995—. Elder Mt. Calvary Presbyn. Ch. Maj. USAR, 1964—66. Mem.: Spartanburg County Bar Assn., S.C. Bar Assn. Home: 200 Burnett Rd Pauline SC 29374-2610 Office: State Supreme Court PO Box 11330 Columbia SC 29211

BURNETT, ELIZABETH B., lawyer; b. 1955; married; 2 children. BA, Brown U., 1976; JD cum laude, U. Mich., 1979. Bar: Mass. 1979, US Dist. Ct. (Dist. Mass.), US Ct. Appeals (1st Cir.). Ptnr., chair, Litig. Sect. Mintz Levin Cohn Ferris Glovsky & Popeo PC, Boston. Founding bd. mem. Jane Doe Safety Fund.; bd. dir. NewFund, Brown U. Sports Found., Greater Boston YMCA. Named a Super Lawyer, Boston Mag. Office: Mintz Levin Cohn Ferris Glovsky & Popeo PC One Financial Ctr Boston MA 02111 Office Phone: 617-348-1613. Office Fax: 617-542-2241. Business E-Mail: eburnett@mintz.com.

BURNETT, GEORGE A., directory publishing executive; BA, MBA, Dartmouth Univ. With D'Arcy Masius Benton and Bowles advt. agy.; pres. local svcs, gen. mgr. card, operator svcs. AT&T; pres., CEO, mass mkt. retail group Am. Elec. Power, Columbus, Ohio; chief mktg. officer Qwest Comm.; pres., CEO Dex Media Inc. (subs. Qwest Comm.), Englewood, Colo., 2002—. Bd. dir. Dex Media Inc.; chmn. bd. dir. Yellow Pages Assn. Bd. dir. Spl. Olympics Colo. Office: Dex Media Inc 198 Inverness Dr W Englewood CO 80112 Office Phone: 303-784-2900.*

BURNETT, HENRY, lawyer; b. NYC, Feb. 24, 1927; s. Lucien Dallam and Ruth (Hinkle) B.; m. Florence Stewart, July 19, 1952; children: Marian Starr, Betsy Callaway, Henry Stewart. BA, U. Va., 1947, LLB, 1950. Bar: Va. 1950, Fla. 1951. Ptnr. Fowler, White, Burnett, Miami, Fla., 1957—93, pres., 1957—93, ptnr., 1993—. Bd. dirs. Dade County Citizens Safety Council, Travelers Aid, United Family and Children's Services. Served with USNR, 1945-46. Fellow Am. Coll. Trial Lawyers; mem. Am., Fla., Dade County bar assns., Fla. Def. Lawyers Assn. (pres. 1967-68), Dade County Def. Bar Assn. (pres. 1966-67), Internat. Assn. Def. Counsel (exec. com. 1972-74, pres. 1976-77), Riviera Country Club. Episcopalian. Home: 8871 SW 68th Ave Miami FL 33156 Office: Espirito Santo Bldg 1395 Brickall Ave 14th Fl Miami FL 33131 Office Phone: 305-789-9206. E-mail: hburnett@fowler-white.com.

BURNETT, IRIS JACOBSON, corporate communications specialist; b. Bklyn., Nov. 14, 1946; d. Milton and Rose (Dubroff) Groman; m. Allan Jacobson; 1 child, Seth Jacobson; m. David Burnett, Jan. 29, 1984; 1 child, Jordan Burnett. BS, Emerson Coll., 1968, MS in Commn. Theory, 1971. Instr. Boston U., 1971-73; dir. press and pub. rels. Dept. Parks and Recreation, Boston, 1975-77; dir. internat. visitors U.S. Dept. State, Washington, 1977-80; dir. security Dem. Nat. Conv., N.Y.C., 1980; sr. v.p. Arrive Unltd., Washington, 1980-84; pres. In Advance, Arlington, 1984-87; asst. prof. Am. U., Washington, 1987-90; pres. Sound Remarks, Arlington, 1990-92; exec. dir. Debates '92, Washington, 1992; chief staff USIA, Washington, 1993-96; sr. v.p. for corp. comm. USA Network, N.Y.C., 1997-99; prof. Am. U. Sch. Comm., 1999—. Co-founder, co-chair, pres. Count Mein for Women's Econ. Ind., 2002; pres. Kai Prodns. Author: Hart for Pres., 1984, Nat. Surrogate Schedule, 1984, Inauguration, Transition: Clinton Gore Campaign, 1992, (novels) Schlepper! A Mostly True Tale of Presidential Politics, 2004; prodr.: (documentary) The Gefilte Fish Chronicles. Active McGovern presdl. campaign, Boston, 1972; mem. nat. staff Udall for Pres., Washington, 1974-76, Carter-Mondale '76, 1976-77; bd. dirs. Tap Am. Project, 1994—; official del. 4th World Conf. on Women; bd. gov.'s USO.; founder Broad Confidence in Chair Women; bd. dirs. Erase the Hate Found.; mem. Bretton Woods Com. Named Presdl. appt. to Bd. Govs. USO. Mem. Women's Fgn. Policy Group, Emily's List, Nat. Jewish Dem. Coalition.

BURNETT, JEAN B. (MRS. JAMES R. BURNETT), biochemist; b. Flint, Mich., Feb. 19, 1924; d. Chester M. and Katheryn (Krasser) Bullard; B.S., Mich. State U., 1944, M.S., 1945, Ph.D. (Council fellow), 1952; m. James R. Burnett, June 8, 1947. Research assoc. dept. zoology Mich. State U., East Lansing, 1954-59, dept. biochemistry, 1959-61, acting dir. research biochem. genetics, dept. biochemistry, 1961-62, assoc. prof., asst. chmn. dept. biomechanics, 1973-82, prof. dept. anatomy, 1982-84, prof. dept. zoology, Coll. Natural Sci. and Coll. Osteo. Medicine, 1984—; assoc. biochemist Mass. Gen. Hosp., Boston, 1964-73; prin. research assoc. dermatology Harvard, 1962-73, faculty medicine, 1964-73, also spl. lectr., cons., tutor Med. Sch.; vis. prof. dept. biology U. Ariz., 1979-80. USPHS, NIH grantee, 1965-68; Gen. Research Support grantee Mass. Gen. Hosp., 1968-72; Ford Found. travel grantee, 1973; Am. Cancer Soc. grantee, 1971-73; Internat. Pigment Cell Conf. travel grantee, 1980; recipient Med. Found. award, 1970. Mem. AAAS, Am. Chem. Soc., Am. Inst. Biol. Sci., Genetics Soc. Am., Soc. Investigative Dermatology, N.Y. Acad. Scis., Sigma Xi (Research award 1971), Pi Kappa Delta, Kappa Delta Pi, Pi Mu Epsilon, Sigma Delta Epsilon. Home: PO Box 805 Okemos MI 48805-0805

BURNETT, KEITHA DENISE, social studies educator; b. Tarboro, N.C., July 26, 1961; d. Allen and Roxie (Hinton) L.; m. Michael David Burnett, Nov. 9, 1996; 1 child, Melanie. BA, U. N.C., 1982; MPA, U. N.D., 1985; PhD, Fla. Internat., 1995. Tchr. Miami-Dade Pub. Schs., 1985—. Evaluation com. State of Fla., Daytona, 1996-97. Mem. PTA, Miami, 1991—. Named Social Studies Tchr. of Yr. Dade County Coun. for Social Studies, 1996, Outstanding Svc. award Alumni at Bethune Cookman Coll., 1997. Mem. NAACP, Am. Soc. Pub. Adminstrn. (bd. dirs. south Fla. chpt. 1995—), Nat. Writer's Assn., Local Coun. for Social Studies, Nat. Coun. for Social Studies, Alpha Kappa Alpha, Phi Delta Kappa. Democrat. Baptist. Avocations: reading, writing, travel, family gathering/reunions. Office: Coral Reef Sr High 10101 SW 152nd St Miami FL 33157-1603 E-mail: mkbur293@aol.com.

BURNETT, LONNIE SHELDON, obstetrics and gynecology educator; b. Saratoga, Tex., Aug. 2, 1927; s. Lonnie and Lois (Swift) B.; m. Betty Pearle Scruggs, Dec. 22, 1950; children: Anne Julian, Michael Julian. BS, U. Tex., 1948; MD, U. Tex., Galveston, 1953. Diplomate Am. Coll. Obstetricians and Gynecologists (chmn. Tenn. sect. 1988-91, mem. com. on sci. program 1988-91). Intern Henry Ford Hosp., Detroit, 1953-54; resident in internal medicine Mayo Clinic, Rochester, Minn., 1954-55; resident in ob-gyn. Johns Hopkins Hosp., Balt., 1957-62, fellow in microbiology, 1962-64; asst. prof. microbiology Johns Hopkins U., Balt., 1964-67, asst. prof. ob-gyn., 1964-70, assoc. prof., 1970-76; chmn. dept. ob-gyn. Vanderbilt U., Nashville, 1976-95, prof. ob-gyn., 1976—, Frances and John C. Burch prof. ob-gyn., 1995—. Mem. ob-gyn. text com. Nat. Bd. Med. Examiners, 1988-91. Co-author: Novak's Textbook of Gynecology, 11th edit., 1988; contbr. articles to profl. jours. Capt. USAF, 1955-57. Macy scholar Josiah Macy Jr. Found., 1965-70. Mem.: Nashville Acad. Medicine (pres. 1999—2000), Tenn. Ob-Gyn. Soc. (pres. 1988—90). Republican. Episcopalian. Avocation: photography. Home: 78 Concord Park W Nashville TN 37205-4707 Office: Vanderbilt Med Ctr N Dept Ob-Gyn 1611 21st Ave S Nashville TN 37212-3103 Office Phone: 615-322-7358. Business E-Mail: lonnie.burnett@vanderbilt.edu. E-mail: lsburnett@comcast.net.

BURNETT, MARK, television producer; b. London, July 17, 1960; 2 children. Founder Mark Burnett Productions. Creator: (televised annual adventure race) Eco-Challenge, 1995— (Sports Emmy award for Outstanding Program Achievement for Eco-Challenge: Morocco, 2000, Banff Rockie award in the Sports Program Category, Banff Rockie Awards Festival, 2000); creator, exec. prodr.: (TV series) Survivor, 2000— (Favorite Reality Based Television Program, People's Choice Award, 2001, 2002, 2003, 2004, Special Recognition award, Gay & Lesbian Alliance Against Defamation, Emmy award for Outstanding Non-Fiction Program, 2001); exec. prodr.: (TV series) Combat Missions, Boarding House: North Shore, 2003; creator, exec. prodr.: (TV series) The Apprentice, 2003—; exec. prodr.: The Restaurant, 2003—04, The Casino, 2004, The Contender, 2005—, Rock Star: INXS, 2005—; author: Dare to Succeed: How to Survive and Thrive in the Game of Life, 2002, Jump In! Even if You Don't Know How to Swim, 2005. Bd. dirs. Elizabeth Glaser Pediatric Aids Found. Served with British Army Paratroop Regiment, N. Ireland and Falkland Islands. Named to 100 Most Influential People list, Time mag., 2004; recipient Philanthropist of the Year award, Reality Cares Found. Mem.: Nat. Academy of Television Arts and Sciences, British Academy of Film and Television Arts, LA (two elected terms, bd. dirs.). Avocations: scuba diving, skydiving.

BURNETT, MICHAEL BRUCE, benefits compensation analyst; b. Arlington, Va., Jan. 5, 1950; s. Arden Louis and June Elizabeth Burnett; m. Julie Ann Ophaug, Apr. 18, 1953; children: Kylie Marie, Lindsey Arden. BS in Bus. Edn. and Secondary Edn., U. N.D., 1976. Cert. phlebotimist Nat. Bd. of Lab. Profl. Technicans, 2000; Stephens' min. Holy Trinity Luth. Ch., Va., 1988; counselors Cert. Rehab. Provider of Va., 2004, vocational case mgr. Workers' Compensation Commn., Md., 2004. Sr. vocat. case mgr. CorVel Corp., Fairfax, Va., 1997—. Cons. mgmt. tng. Intelligent Solutions, Inc., Fairfax, Va., 1994—96. Editor sales manual-vocational counselors, author return to work program for fed. govt. Bd. dirs. Holy Spirit Luth. Ch., Centreville, Va., 2000—01. Recipient Achievement award, Travelers Ins. Co.-Conservco, Student Tchr. of the Yr. award, Lake Area Vocat. Tech. Ctr., 1975-1976. Mem.: Nat. Assn. of Rehab. Profls. in Pvt. Sector, Nat. Rehab. Assn., Toastmasters (cert.). Baptist. Avocation: counselor for men's anger. Home: 5806 Waterdale Ct Centreville VA 20121 Office: CorVel Corp Ste 11350 Random Hills Rd Fairfax VA 22030 Personal E-mail: mburnett3@cox.net. Business E-Mail: michael_burnett@corvel.com.

BURNETT, RALPH GEORGE, lawyer; b. Milw., Apr. 13, 1956; s. Ralph G. and Joan T. Burnett; m. Eileen M. Gallagher, May 31, 1980; children: Christopher, Jessica, Thomas, Sarah, Andrew. BA, Marquette U., 1978; JD, U. Wis., 1981. Bar: Wis. 1981, U.S. Dist. Ct. (ea. and we. dists.) Wis. 1981, U.S. Ct. Appeals (7th cir.) 1981, U.S. Dist. Ct. (we. dist.) Mich. 1997, U.S. Ct. Appeals (6th cir.) 1997. Law clk. to Hon. Judge Harlington Wood U.S. Ct. Appeals 7th Cir., Chgo., 1981-82; lawyer Smith & O'Neil, Milw., 1983-84, Trowbridge, Planert & Schaefer, Green Bay, Wis., 1985-86, Liebmann, Conway, Olejniczak & Jerry, S.C., Green Bay, Wis., 1986—. Officer Robert J. Parins Inn of Ct., Green Bay, 1997—. Co-author: Wisconsin Trial Practice, 1999. Mem. allocations com. United Way N.E. Wis., Green Bay, 1988-91; bd. mem. paralegal program N.E. Wis. Tech. Coll., Green Bay, 1993-2000; bd. mem. parish coun. St. Mary's Ch., De Pere, 1997-2003; bd. mem. Cerebral Palsy, Green Bay, 1989-92; bd. mem. steering com. Notre Dame Sch., De Pere, 1998. Fellow Am. Coll. Trial Advocates, Am. Coll. Trial Lawyers, Am. Bar Found., Wisc. Bar Found.; mem. ABA, State Bar Wis. (bd. dirs., chmn. litigation sect. 1996-99, pres-elect 2003, pres. 2003-04), Wis. Acad. Trial Lawyers (bd. dirs. 1995-2000; amicus commuter, constitutional challenge com., exec. com., regional dir. N.E. Wis. chpt., pres.-elect 2002-03). Avocations: woodworking, athletics. Office: Liebmann Conway Olejniczak & Jerry SC 231 S Adams St PO Box 23200 Green Bay WI 54305 Business E-Mail: RGB@lcojlaw.law.

BURNETTE, ADA M. PURYEAR, retired educational association administrator; b. Darlington, S.C. d. Theodore and Floia (King) Peoples; m. Paul Lionel Puryear, March 27, 1954 (div. 1975); children: Paul Lionel, Jr., Paula Lynn. BA in Math., Talladega Coll., 1953; postgrad., Chgo. State U., 1954-56; MA in Reading, U. Chgo., 1958; PhD, Fla. State U., 1986; postgrad., Fla. A&M U., 1994, Oxford U., 2005. High sch. math tchr., Winston-Salem, N.C., 1953-54; elem. tchr. Chgo. Pub. Schs., 1954-58; reading clinician U. Chgo., 1958; dir. reading clinic, asst. prof. Norfolk State U., 1958-61, Tuskegee Inst., 1961-66; coord. freshman math., asst. prof. math. Fisk U., 1966-70; adminstr. early childhood basic skills and elem. edn. State of Fla. Dept. Edn., Tallahassee, 1973-88; assoc. prof., program dir., grad. studies dir. Bethune-Cookman Coll., Daytona Beach, Fla., 1988-90; dir., supt. Fla. A&M U. Devel. Rsch. Pub. Sch. Dist., Tallahassee, 1990-93; coord., prof., dept. chmn., dir. PhD program devel. Fla. A&M U., 1993-98, coord., prof., 1998—2003, prof., dir. Robert H. Anderson Ednl. Leadership Libr., 1998—2003, prof. emerita, 2003—; coord. off campus program Baldesta State U., 2005—. Hostess radio talk show, 1977—79; sec.-treas. Afro-Am. Rsch. Assocs., 1968—74; tutor, diagnostician, lectr., cons., planner, 1958—; cons. Job Corps, N.C. Advancement Sch., pub. co.; lectr. univ. classes; trustee Fla. A&M U., 2003, pres. faculty senate, 1999—2003, trustee, 2003, adj. prof., 2003—. Regular columnist profl. jours., 1974—; writer grants proposals; weekly columnist Capital Outlook, 1991-97; contbr. articles to profl. publs. Pres. PTA, 1975—76, v.p., 1983—84; edn. commentator Sta. WFSU, 1993—94; mem. United Fund com., Leon County 4C Bd.; pres. Norfolk Women's Interracial Coun., 1960; del. state Dem. women's meeting, Fla., 1978, 1979; mem. Dem. Exec. Com. Leon County, 1981—88, 1991—93; deacon Presbyn. Ch., 1981—2004, AME ch. grief chmn., 2004—. Mem.: AAUW (regional dir. 2003—, pres. Tallahassee chpt. 2005—, FLAAUW dir. 2005—), Am. Acad. Cert. Pub. Mgmt., Fla. Assn. Cert. Pub. Mng. NF (bd. dirs. 2004—), Nat. Assn. African Am. Studies (coord. 1999—), Fla. Soc. Cert. Pub. Mgrs. (newsletter bd., pres. North Fla. chpt. 2004, pres. North Fla. chpt. 2004—, state bd. 2004—), Am. Assn. Sch. Adminstrs., Socs. Docta Inc. (sec. 1987—93), So. Assn. Colls. and Schs. (elem. and mid. sch. commn.), Assn. Childhood Edn. Internat., Leon Assn. Children Under Six (pres. 1977), So. Assn. Children Under Six, Fla. Assn. Children Under Six, Nat. Assn. Edn. Young Children, Nat. Assn. Elem. Sch. Prins., Internat. Reading Assn. (pres. Concerned Educators Black Students 1983—86, nat. early childhood com., nat. textbook com., libr./media com., nat. med. com., nat. awards com., nat. media com.), Fla. ASCD (regional dir. policy rev. jour. editl. bd. 1995—), Alliance of Black Sch. Educators, Assn. State Cons. on Early Childhood Edn., Fla. State Reading Assn., Fla. Coun. Elem. Edn., Fla. Assn. Suprs. and Adminstrs., The Holidays (nat. sec. fin. 1993—97, nat. v.p. 1997—2001, nat. pres. 2001—, chpt. pres.), Drifters (nat. membership chmn. 1977—79, Nat. Now Black Woman 1984, historian, reporter 1992—94, pres. 1994—99, cluster coord. 2000—), FAMU Ladies Art and Social Club (pres.), Alpha Kappa Alpha (treas., summer sch. dir., undergrad. adv., parliamentarian, sec.), Pi Lambda Theta, Phi Kappa Phi (pres. 1985—86, v.p. pub. rels. chair), Phi Delta Kappa (advisor 2004—). Home: PO Box 38543 Tallahassee FL 32315-8543 Office: Fla A&M U Gore Edn Ctr C-204A Tallahassee FL 32307 Office Phone: 850-561-2670. Personal E-mail: draburnette@wmconnect.com. *Never do anything illegal or immoral as you strive for excellence and do your best in all you do in your journey to make this world a better place.*

BURNETTE, CHARLES GALYON, protective services official; b. Tampa, Fla., Nov. 20, 1958; s. Charles Galyon Burnette and Eugenia Sue Fowler; m. Pamela Lea Cannon, Sept. 5, 1981; children: Autumn Lea, Heather Miranda. AA in Criminal Justice, Okaloosa-Walton Jr. Coll., 1978, BA in Criminal Justice with honors, 1980. Patrol officer St. Petersburg Police Dept., 1982-85, burglary detective, 1985-88, acting sgt., 1988-89, sgt. patrol divsn., 1989-90, 92-99, sgt. field tng., 1990-92, detective sgt. divsn. vice and narcotics, 1999—. Mem. task force St. Petersburg's Crime Prevention through Environ. Design, 1998—. Loaned exec. United Way, St. Petersburg, 1998, mem. Keel Club, 1998-2000, 2002. Recipient Herman Goldstein Internat. award for Individual Problem Solving in Policing, 1996. Mem. NRA, Fla. Narcotics Officer's Assn., Alpha Phi Sigma, Lambda Alpha Epsilon, Phi Kappa Phi. Avocation: reading. Home: 8273-101 Court N Seminole FL 33777 Office: St Petersburg Police Dept 1300-1 Ave N Saint Petersburg FL 33705

BURNETTE, HARRY FORBES, lawyer; b. Chattanooga, Sept. 28, 1947; s. Harry G. and Ruth (Forbes) B.; m. Carolyn G. Gash, Sept. 5, 1970; children: Harry Eric, Chad Forbes, Heather Carolyn. BA, Maryville Coll., 1970; JD, U. Tenn., 1973. Bar: Tenn. 1973, U.S. Dist. Ct. (ea. dist.) Tenn. 1973, U.S. Ct. Appeals (6th cir.) 1977. Assoc., then ptnr. Humphrey, Hutcheson & Mosley, Chattanooga, 1973-78; ptnr. Robinson, Stanley & Burnette, Chattanooga, 1978-83, Burnette Dobson and Hardeman, Chattanooga, 1983—. Mem. ABA, ATLA, Tenn. Trial Lawyers Assn. (bd. govs. 1989-91), Chattanooga Trial Lawyers Assn. (bd. dirs. 1981-85, 2001—), Fed. Bar Assn. (pres. Chattanooga chpt. 1979-80), Nat. Employment Lawyers Assn. (Tenn. dir. 1988-89, state v.p. and dir. 2002-03). Democrat. Presbyterian. Home: 5117 Mountain Creek Rd Chattanooga TN 37415-1605 Office: Burnette Dobson & Hardeman 713 Cherry St Chattanooga TN 37402-1910 Office Phone: 423-266-2121. Business E-Mail: hburnette@bdhlaw.com.

BURNETTE, MARY MALISSA, lawyer; b. Morven, NC, May 23, 1950; d. Harvey Lorraine and Mary Malissa (Ratliff) B. BA, U. SC, 1971, JD, 1977. Bar: S.C. 1977, U.S. Dist. Ct. S.C. 1978, U.S. Ct. Appeals (4th cir.) 1978, U.S. Supreme Ct. 1998; cert. specialist in employment and labor law. Dir. Richland/Lexington Sr. Citizens Ctr., Columbia, SC, 1973-74; atty. SC Gov.'s Office, Columbia, SC, 1977-78; dep. lt. gov. State of S.C., Columbia, SC, 1979-82; ptnr. Gergel, Burnette, Nickles, Grant & Leclair, Columbia, SC, 1982-96, Burnette & Leclair, Columbia, SC, 1996—2005, Burnette & Rothstein, P.A., Columbia, SC, 2005—. Disting. alumni spkr. U. S.C., 1995—. Co-author (editor): Labor and Employment Law for South Carolina Lawyers, 1999, 2nd edit, 2004. Campaign mgr. Medlock for Atty. Gen., Columbia, 1982; bd. dirs. Family Svc. Ctr., 1985-89, Men's Resource Ctr., 1987-89, The Nurturing Ctr., 2002—04; chmn. adv. bd. S.C. Crime Victims, 1984-89; chmn. bd. visitors Columbia Coll., 1989-90; coun. on ministries Washington St., United Meth. Ch., 1988-89, chmn. adminstrv. bd., 1990-93, chmn. staff-parish rels. com., 1997-98; pres. Greater Columbia Cmty. Rels. Coun., 1995—96; chair Gov.'s Task Force on Domestic Violence, 2000. Named one of Best Lawyers in Am., 2005-; recipient Ten for the Future award Columbia Record, 1978, Career Woman award Columbia YWCA, 1980. Mem. ATLA, S.C. Bar (various coms. 1977—, chair quality of life com. 1994, chair jud. qualifications com. 1999-2001, resolution of fee disputes bd. 2005—), S.C. Trial Lawyers (chair employment law sect. 1990-95, 2001-04), S.C. Bus. and Profl. Women (Career Woman award 1987, S.C. Young Career Woman 1979), S.C. Women Lawyers Assn. (pres. 2001). Democrat. Avocations: travel, softball, baseball. Office: Burnette & Rothstein PA 2322 Devine St Columbia SC 29205-2404 Office Phone: 803-251-0202. Personal E-mail: mmburnette@mindspring.com.

BURNETTE, OLLEN LAWRENCE, JR., historian; b. Bethel, N.C., Sept. 30, 1927; s. Ollen Lawrence and Eva E. (Highsmith) Burnette; m. M. Elizabeth Tull, Aug. 25, 1951 (div. 1995); children: Ollen L. III, Elizabeth B. Newsome-Cousins, Graham T., John H., William N.; m. Jeanne A. MacRitchie, June 10, 2000. BA in History, U. Richmond, 1945; MA in History, U. Va., Charlottesville, 1948, PhD in History, 1952; LLD, Southwestern Adventist Coll., 1989. Instr. history Petersburg (Va.) HS, 1948-49, VMI, Lexington, 1951-53, asst. to supt., 1981—86; editor Charles Scribner's Sons, N.Y.C., 1953-57; dir. publs. State Hist. Soc. Wis., Madison, 1957-63; rsch. prof. history, dept. chmn. Birmingham (Ala.)-So. Coll., 1963-72; dean of faculty, rsch. prof. history Stratford Coll., Danville, Va., 1972-74; vis. prof. history N.C. State A&T U., Greensboro, 1974-75; exec. dir. West Piedmont Planning Commn., Martinsville, Va., 1975-80; pres. Timber Ridge Enterprises, Ltd., Lynchburg, 1980—, Around Again, LLC, Cons., Lillian, 1996—. Author: Beneath the Footnote: A Guide to the Use of American Historical Documentation, 1970, A Syllabus of American History, 1959, Wisconsin Witness to F. J. Turner, 1958; editor: Life in America, 1972, A Soviet View of the American Past, 1962, Coastal Kingdom: A History of Baldwin County, Alabama, 2001, Readings on the Development of the American Constitution, 2005, From the Heart: Poems, 2005—. Elder Timber Ridge Presbyn. Ch., Lexington, 1980—; moderator Shenandoah Presbytery, 1988; bd. dirs. Stonewall Jackson Hosp., Lexington, 1980—83. Mem.: Orgn. Am. Historians, Am. Hist. Assn., Am. Inst. Cert. Planners, Nat. Assn. Rev. Appraisers (sr.), Va. Highlands Scottish Soc. (bd. dirs. 1989—), Phi Beta Kappa, Omicron Delta Kappa. Avocations: photography, hiking, travel. Home and Office: 34231 Kathryn Dr Lillian AL 36549-5105

BURNETTE, SUSAN LEATHERS, music educator; b. Conway, S.C., July 9, 1941; d. William Warren and Bessie Louise (Thackston) Leathers; m. Thurman Everett Burnette, Aug. 24, 1963; children: Susan Elisabeth, Zackary Everett. BA, Meredith Coll., 1963. Tchr. music Granville County Schs., Creedmoor, N.C., 1963-65, Hyde County Schs., Swan Quarter, N.C., 1965-68, Wake County Schs., Raleigh, N.C., 1968-72; presch. tchr. music Creedmoor Bapt. Presch., Raleigh, 1976-90, Sertoma Arts Ctr., Raleigh, 1991—; pvt. piano tchr., Raleigh, 1976—. Precinct committeewoman Wake County Dem. Com., Raleigh, 1980—; Sunday sch. tchr., deacon, organist Creedmoor Road Bapt. Ch., Raleigh, 1968-90; bd. dirs. Sanderson Band Boosters, Raleigh, 1987-90, Sanderson H.S. PTA, 1987-94; trustee Meredith Coll., Raleigh, 1997—, mem. exec. com., 1999-2000. Mem. Nat. Music Tchrs. Assn., N.C. Music Tchrs. Assn., Raleigh Piano Tchrs. Assn. (sec.-treas. 1990-94, v.p. 1994-96, pres. 1996-98, bd. dirs. 1999—), Meredith County Alumnae Assn. (pres. Wake County chpt. 1973-74). Avocations: walking, reading, sewing. Home: 6504 Ben Bur Rd Raleigh NC 27612-2302

BURNETTE, TAMARA NABORS, elementary school educator; d. William P. and Thelma Byars Nabors; m. Robert A. Baldwin; children: William Bradley, Jennifer Lea. BA in Edn., Presbyn. Coll., 1980; MEd in Elem. Edn., Lander U. Tchr. M.S. Bailey Elem. Sch. Laurens Dist. 56, Clinton, SC, 1981—2003, tchr. Clinton (S.C.) Elem. Sch., 2003—. Grantee, S.C. ETA, 1995. Mem.: ADK (pres. 1996—98, v.p. 1994—96, treas. 1990—94). Avocations: gardening, horseback riding, reading, swimming, bicycling. Home: 116 Reeder St Joanna SC 29351

BURNEY, RHETT D., lawyer; b. Charlotte, NC, Mar. 13, 1970; s. D.F. and Joy Burney. BA, Presbyn. Coll., Clinton, SC, 1992; JD, U. SC, 1995. Bar: SC 1995, U.S. Dist. Ct. SC 1996, cert.: (domestic mediator). Ptnr. Turner and Burney, PC, Laurens, SC, 1995—. Atty. to assist disciplinary counsel SC Bar, Columbia, 1999—. Elder 1st Presbyn. Ch. Laurens, 2000—; bd. dirs. YMCA, Laurens, 1998—2001, Hospice, Laurens, 2002—. Mem.: Laurens County Bar (pres. 1997—). Office: Turner & Burney PC 105 W Public Sq Laurens SC 29360 E-mail: rdburney@backroads.net.

BURNHAM, ALBERT DAVID, education educator, researcher, historian, consultant; b. Salem, Mass., June 8, 1950; s. Harry Warren and Mildred Louise Burnham. BS, Minot State Coll., Minot, N.D., 1976; MA, Univ. N.D., Grand Forks, N.D., 1982, ArtsD, 1986. Asst. prof. Univ. Minn., Duluth, Minn., 1986—96; instr. history Fond du Lac Cmty. Coll., Cloquet, Minn., 1987—94; adj. prof. Viterbo Univ., LaCrosse, Wis., 1998—2004; instr. history El Paso CC, Tex., 2004—. Cons. rschr. St. Louis County Hist. Soc., Duluth, Minn., 1996, Bason Elec. Power Coop., Williston, ND, 1983; cons. writer Minn. Dept. of Nat. Resources, Bemidii, Minn., 1988. Contbr. articles pub. to profl. jour. Mem.: Fronter Army of the Dakotas, Ft. Abraham Lincoln Found., Am. Hist. Assn., Duluth African Drumming Ensemble, Duluth Animal Allies, Phi Alpha Theta. Christian. Achievements include won first amendment lawsuit in the U.S. 8th Circut Ct. of Appeals. Avocations: history, canoeing, hiking, kayaking, travel. Home: 3254 Arrambide St El Paso TX 79936 Office Phone: 915-831-2274. E-mail: docdakota1875@yahoo.com.

BURNHAM, BRYSON PAINE, retired lawyer; b. Chgo., Oct. 11, 1917; s. Raymond and Patti (Paine) B.; m. Frances Katherine Burns, Feb. 8, 1941; children: Janice Young, Stephanie Paine. BA, U. Chgo., 1938, JD, 1940. Bar:

Ill. 1940, Colo. 1983. Assoc., then ptnr. Mayer, Brown & Platt, Chgo., 1940-83; of counsel Shand, McLachlan and Newbold, Durango, Colo., 1985-93. Bd. dirs. Fort Lewis Coll. Found., 1986-2002. Home: 315 Highland Hill Dr Timberline View Estates Durango CO 81301

BURNHAM, CHRISTOPHER BANCROFT, international organization official, former federal agency administrator; b. N.Y.C., Sept. 28, 1956; s. Alexander O. and Joan B.; m. Courtney Burnham; 1 child, George Emerson. BA, Washington & Lee, 1980; MPA, Harvard U., 1992. Mem. N.Y. Futures Exch., N.Y.C., 1983-85; rep. Conn. Gen. Assembly, Hartford, 1987-92; banker First Boston, N.Y.C., 1990-93, Advest Corp. Fin., Hartford, 1993-95; state treas. State of Conn., Hartford, 1995—97; chmn, CEO InviteUSA.com, 2000—02; CFO, asst. sec. for resource mgmt. US Dept. State, Washington, 2002—05, acting under sec. for mgmt., 2005; under-sec. gen. mgmt. UN, NYC, 2005—. Maj. USMCR, Persian Gulf War. Republican. Episcopalian. Office: UN Secretariat Bldg New York NY 10017

BURNHAM, CLIFFORD WAYNE, geology educator, director; b. Murietta, Calif., Oct. 24, 1922; AB magna cum laude, Pomona Coll., 1951; MS in Geology, Calif. Inst. Tech., 1953, PhD in Geochem., 1955. Geologist Riverside Cement co., 1951; asst. prof. econ. geology Pa. State U., 1955-59, assoc. prof. geochem., 1959-65, prof. geochem., 1965-86, prof. emeritus, 1986—, head dept. geoscis., 1974-85. Adj. prof. U. Ind., 1987—. Ariz. State U., 1992—. Contbr. articles to profl. jours. Lt. USN, 1942-46. Fellow Am. Geophys. Union, Geol. Soc. Am. (Roebling medal 1998), Mineralogical Soc. Am.; mem. AAAS, Geochem. Soc. (pres. 1974), Soc. Econ. Geologists, Phi Beta Kappa, Sigma Xi.

BURNHAM, DAVID BRIGHT, writer, educator; b. Boston, Jan. 24, 1933; s. Addison Center and Dorothy (Moore) B.; m. Sophy Tayloe Doub, Mar. 12, 1960 (div. 1984); children: Sarah Tayloe, Molly Bright; m. Joanne Omang, 1985. BA, Harvard, 1955; DHL (hon.), John Jay Coll., CUNY, 2003. Reporter UPI, Washington, 1959-61, Newsweek mag., Washington, 1961-63; writer CBS, NYC, 1963-65; asst. dir. Pres.'s Commn. Law Enforcement and Adminstrn. of Justice, Washington, 1965-67; reporter NY Times, 1967-86; journalist/writer Aspen Inst. Humanistic Studies, 1980-82. Co-dir., co-founder Transactional Records Access Clearinghouse, 1989—; assoc. rsch. prof. S.I. Newhouse Sch. Pub. Communications, Syracuse U.; mem. adv. bd. EPIC. Author: The Rise of the Computer State, 1988, A Law Unto Itself: Power, Politics and the IRS, 1989 (Best Investigative Book Investigative Editors and Reporters 1990), Above The Law: Secret Deals, Political Fixes, and other Misadventures of the U.S. Dept. of Justice, 1996. Recipient George K. Polk award, 1968, Silurians award, 1968; NY Newspaper Guild award, 1968; Gold Typewriter award for investigative reporting NY Reporters Assn., 1972; named fellow Alicia Patterson Found., 1987, Rockefeller Found. scholar, Bellagio, Italy, 1992. Office: Transactional Records Access Clearinghouse 1718 Conn Ave NW Ste 200 Washington DC 20009 Office Phone: 202-518-9000. Business E-Mail: dburnham@syr.edu.

BURNHAM, DAVID HENDERSON, management consultant; b. Quincy, Mass., Mar. 4, 1942; s. Roger Appleton and Phyllis Katherine (Kline) B.; m. Frances Margarita Parry, Feb. 15, 1964; children: Amery Appleton, Hugh Tebault Ramseyer. BA, Northeastern U., 1964; MBA, Harvard U., 1969. With U.S. Peace Corps, Ethiopia, 1964—66; assoc. Sterling Inst., Boston, 1969; v.p., treas. McBer & Co., Boston, 1970-72, pres., 1972-77, David H. Burnham and Assocs., orgn. devel. cons., Boston, Singapore, Sydney, London, 1977-91; dir. strategic planning Interaction Assocs., Cambridge, Mass., 1992-94; ptnr. Burnham Rosen Group, Boston, 1994—. Proprietor Boston Athaeneum, 2000—. Producer film Motives Moving Business (Am. Film Festival award 1975); contbr. articles to profl. jours. Treas., v.p. Children's Mus., Boston, 1972-81, pres., CEO, 1981-83, chmn., 1984-86, hon. trustee, 1988—; pres. Cavalier King Charles Spaniel Club, Louisville, 1972-78; bd. dirs. Children's Mus., London, 1984-86, Mental Health Found., U.K., 1987-88, Drive for Youth Programme, U.K., 1986-91; mem. com. Derby Acad. Coun., Hingham, Mass., 1974-81; mem. vestry St. Stephen's Episcopal Ch., Cohasset, 2001-2005. Honoree Boston Coun. for Arts for svc. to Boston Pub. Libr., 2000; recipient McKinsey award Harvard Bus. Rev., 1976. Mem.: ASTD, OD Network, Greater Boston Assn. Tng. and Devel. (dir. 1997—2000), New England Hist. and Genealogical Soc. (dir. 1999—2005, coun. 2005—), Assn. Mgmt. Edn. and Devel. (Eng.), Harvard Bus. Sch. Assn., Bostonian Soc. (life), Colonial Soc. Mass. (life; bd. dirs. 2003—), Cohasset Yacht Club, Cohasset Golf Club, Harvard Club (Boston and NY), Somerset Club (Boston). Home: 30 Atlantic Ave Cohasset MA 02025-1803 Office: Burnham Rosen Group 88 Broad St Boston MA 02110 Office Phone: 617-350-6100. Business E-Mail: dburnham@burnrose.com.

BURNHAM, HAROLD ARTHUR, pharmaceutical executive, physician; b. Boston, Nov. 6, 1929; s. Howard Rowland and Edna Adelaide (Teachout) B.; m. Lucienne Jeanne Seas, June 28, 1952; children: Philippe Henri, Isabelle Jeanne BS, Union Coll., 1951; MA, Middlebury Coll., 1952; postgrad., Albany State Tchrs. Coll., 1953-54, Adelphi U., 1958-59, Nassau Community Coll., 1961-62; MD, U. Md., 1966. Diplomate Am. Bd. Med. Examiners, Am. Bd. Family Practice (charter). Tchr. sci., French and track team coach South Glens Falls Cen. High Sch., N.Y., 1952-54; med. rep., hosp. salesman Upjohn Co., Bklyn., 1956-62; intern South Baltimore Gen. Hosp., 1966-67; resident in family practice Glen Cove Community Hosp., N.Y., 1967-69; practice family medicine Glen Cove, 1969-75; assoc. med. dir. Winthrop Labs. div. Sterling Drug Inc., N.Y.C., 1975-76, med. dir. Glenbrook Labs. div., 1977, v.p. med. affairs, sr. v.p. Winthrop Product Inc., 1977-80, N.J., 1977-80, Sydney Ross Co. and Sterling Products Internat., N.Y.C., 1977-80; v.p., med. dir. Glenbrook Labs. div. Sterling Drugs, Inc., N.Y.C., 1980; med. dir. Choay Labs. Inc., N.Y.C., 1980-82; asst. med. dir. L.I. State Vets. Home, Stony Brook, 1993-94; primary care physician ambulatory care clinics Nassau County Dept. Health, Mineola, N.Y., 1995-96; physician, English transl. cons. hematology dept. Hotel Dieu Hosp., Paris, 2001—. Spl. cons. Labs. Choay, S.A., Paris, 1982—; asst. med dir. United Presbyn. Residence, Woodbury, N.Y., 1983-93; instr. Sch. Practical Nursing, Glen Cove Community Hosp., 1970-75; instr. geriatrics in coop. with Glen Cove Community Hosp. Family Practice Residency Program, 1983-93; cons., clinician in medicine Nassau County Pub. Health Dept., 1975-76, mem. long term health care com., 1989-96; med. cons. Webb Inst. Naval Architecture and Marine Design, Glen Cove, N.Y., 1970-96; clin. asst. prof., SUNY, 1993-94; attending physician infectious diseases HIV Clinic, Nassau County Med. Ctr., East Meadow, N.Y., 1995-96; preceptor family practice program North Shore U. Hosp. at Glen Cove, 1999—, hon. staff dept. family practice, 2003—. N.Am. corr. weekly Internet French med. publ. Expression Médicale, 1998—. Scoutmaster Boy Scouts Am., Glens Falls, N.Y., 1953-54, com. mem., 1968—, merit badge counsellor for first aid, pub. health emergency care, chemistry and mammals for Sagamore dist., 1968—; mem. Clan Gordon, 1983—, bagpiper Highlanders Pipes and Drums Band, Locust Valley, N.Y., 1982—, chmn., 1986—; lay reader St. John's of Lattingtown Episcopal Ch., N.Y., 1968—, vestryman, 1983—, clk. of vestry, 1986—, 7-8th gr. Sunday Sch. tchr., 1967—; mem. search com. for new rector, 1993, 2004, jr. high Sunday sch. tchr., 1967-; trustee Hawley Found., 1984—, v.p. bd., 1991-99, v.p. emeritus, 1999—; Rep. election site inspector Nassau County, 1997—; del. to 120th conf. Episcopal Diocese of L.I.; vol. primary care physician Project U.S.A., Rural Indian Health Svc. Ctrs., Oneida (N.Y.) Iroquois Reservation and Owyhee (Nev.) Indian Hosp., 1995—; bd. edn. election inspector, Glen Cove, 2001-. Named hon. chieftain, Annual Scottish Games, Old Westbury Gardens, 2004; recipient Alvin H. Toffler award, North Shore U. Hosp. Class of 2002. Fellow Am. Acad. Family Physicians (charter); mem. AMA (life; 14 continuing edn. awards), Pan Am. Med. Soc., N.Y. State Med. Soc. (life), Nassau County Med. Soc. (life), L.I. Scottish Clans Assn. (trustee 1984—, piper to chief 1986—, hon. Cheiftain annual Scottish games, 2004), Nu Sigma Nu. Episcopalian. Office: 18 Purdue Rd Glen Cove NY 11542-2009 E-mail: haburnham@earthlink.net.

BURNHAM, J. V., retired sales executive; b. Pascagoula, Miss., May 23, 1923; s. George Luther and Eli Vashti (Hough) B.; m. Patti Lauri Latham, May 18, 1946; children: James Steven, Jon Douglas, Richard Scott, Bruce Edward, Vernon Alan. AA, Jones County (Miss.) Jr. Coll., 1946; AS, Rochester Inst. Tech., 1948; BS, U. Houston, 1951, MEd, 1963. Mgr. The Progress-Item, Ellisville, Miss., 1948-50; asst. prof., asst. mgr. U. Houston Journalism and Printing Plant, 1950-57; estimator, product supt. purchasing Chas. P. Young Co., Houston, 1957-67, asst. sec.-treas., 1967-69, v.p. sales, 1969-91, sr. v.p., 1991—2001, ret., 2001. Assoc. editor Am. Oceanography, 1968-71; southwest corr. Inland Printer and Nat. Lithographer, 1952-60. Founding mem. Am. Air Mus. in Britain; pres. Printing Industries of Gulf Coast, Houston, 1971—73; chmn. emeritus, bd. dirs. Tex. Printing Edn. Found., Houston; active The Heritage Found., The Concord Coalition, Adm. Nimitz Found., St. Joseph Found., Hist. Mt. Vernon, Young America's Found., Rep. Presdl. Task Force, Nat. Rep. Senatorial Com. Order of Merit, Nat. Rep. Congl. Com.; life, chmns. adv. bd. Rep. Nat. Com.; active Rep. Party of Tex., Rep. Nat. Candidate Trust, George Bush Pres. Libr. & Mus., Reagan Pres. Found., Young Am. Found., Judicial Watch. Lt. USNR, 1943—46. Recipient Scouters award Boy Scouts Am., 1960, Scouters Key award, 1965, Wood Badge award, 1964; named Man of Yr., Houston Graphics Soc., 1968, Printing Industry of Gulf Coast, 1970. Mem.: BAMPAC, Rochester Inst. tech. Alumni Assn., Tex. Police Officers Assn., Pres's. Club of Chas. P. Young Co. (charter, Outstanding Sales Achivement award), Mt. Vernon Ladies Assn., Juvenile Diabetes Found., Am. Diabetes Assn., Am. Kidney Found., High Frontier, Hummel Collectors Club (Houston), Crime Stoppers of Houston (gold cir. member), Ducks Unltd., U.S. Navy Meml. Found., Naval Aviation Mus. Found., Houston Public TV, United Srs. Assn., WWII Meml. Found., Claremont Inst., U.S. Hist. Soc. (life), Nat. Eagle Scout Assn. (life), Tex. State Rifle Assn. (life), Naval Airship Assn. (life), Am. Legion (life), U. Houston Alumni (life), Jones County Jr. Coll. Alumni (life), U.S. Navy Pub. Affairs Alumni Assn. (life), VFW (life), NRA (life), PGA Ptnrs. Club (life; charter), Am. Fedn. Police, Gun Owners Am., Second Amendment Found. (charter), USS Constitution Mus. Found., Houston Lithographic Club, Rep.-Presdl. Legion of Merit, U.S. Golf Assn., Houston Golf Assn., Citizens Against Govt. Waste, NRA Whittington Ctr. Founders Club, Braeburn Country Club, 100 Club Houston, Houston Craftsmens Club (hon.; life, past pres., Ben Franklin award 1971), Nat. Home Gardening Club (life), Santa Fe Trail Gun Club (life). Republican. Methodist.

BURNHAM, JOHN CHYNOWETH, historian, educator; b. Boulder, Colo., July 14, 1929; s. William Allds and Florence (Hasbrouck) B.; m. Marjorie Ann Spencer, Aug. 31, 1957; children: Leonard, Abigail, Peter, Melissa. BA, Stanford U., 1951, PhD, 1958; MA, U. Wis., 1952. Lectr. Claremont Men's Coll., Calif., 1956-57; mem. faculty Stanford U., 1956, 57-58; postdoctoral fellow Founds. Fund for Research in Psychiatry, New Haven, 1958-61; asst. prof. San Francisco State Coll., 1961-63; from mem. faculty to rsch. prof. history Ohio State U., Columbus, Ohio, 1963—2002, rsch. prof. history, 2002—. Sr. Fulbright lectr. U. Melbourne, Australia, 1967, U. Tasmania, Australia, 1973, U. New Eng., Australia, 1973; Tallman vis. prof. history and psychology Bowdoin Coll., Brunswick, Maine, 1982; fellow Robinson Coll., U. Cambridge, 2002-2003; cons. panelist NEH, 1974—, dir. nat. seminar for professions, 1975, 76, 79; assoc. area adv. Coun. on Internat. Exch. of Scholars, 1975-78; mem. spl. study sect. NIH, 1978-79, 84-85, 92. Author: Psychoanalysis and American Medicine 1894-1918, 1967, Jelliffe: American Physician and Psychoanalyst, 1983, How Superstition Won and Science Lost: Popularizing Science in the United States, 1987, Paths into American Culture: Psychology, Medicine, and Morals, 1988, Bad Habits: Drinking, Smoking, Taking Drugs, Gambling, Sexual Misbehavior, and Swearing in American History, 1993, How the Idea of Profession Changed the Writing of Medical History, 1998, What is Medical History?, 2005; (with Buenker and Crunden) Progressivism, 1977; editor: Science in America-Historical Selections, 1971; editor Jour. of History of Behavioral Scis., 1997-2000. Recipient Publ. award Ohio Acad. History, 1993. Fellow AAAS, APA; mem. Am. Assn. for History of Medicine (v.p. 1988-90, pres. 1990-92), Orgn. Am. Historians, Am. Hist. Assn., History of Sci. Soc., Midwest History of Sci. Junto (pres. 1982-83), Cheiron Internat. Soc. for History of Behavioral and Social Scis. (presiding officer 1977-78) Home: 4158 Kendale Rd Columbus OH 43220-4136 Office: Ohio State U Dept History 230 W 17th Ave Columbus OH 43210-1367

BURNHAM, JOHN LUDWIG, agent; b. L.A., Mar. 1, 1953; s. Jerome Ludwig and Linda (Benjamin) B.; m. Andrea Buckland Feldstein, Aug. 12, 1989; 1 child, Daisy. BA, UCLA, 1976, JD, 1980. Agt. Kohnner Levy, L.A., 1979-81, ICM, L.A., 1981-84, William Morris Agy., Beverly Hills, Calif., 1984—, co-head, sr. v.p. movie dept., 1991—. Office: William Morris Agy Inc 1 William Morris Pl Beverly Hills CA 90212 Office Phone: 310-859-4000. Office Fax: 310-859-4462.

BURNHAM, LEM, psychologist, think-tank executive; b. Winter Haven, Fla., Aug. 30, 1947; s. John L. and Lillie Belle B.; m. Barbara J. Mackin, Sept. 8, 1981; children: Shannon LeeAnne, Lewis, Kara, Bryan. Diploma, N.Am. Sch. Conservation, Irvine, Calif., 1969; BA in Psychology, U.S. Internat. U., 1974; MS in Counseling Psychology, Minn. State U., 1978; PhD in Psychoednl. Processes, Temple U., 1984. Diplomate Am. Bd. Forensic Examiners, Am. Bd. Psychol. Specialties, Am. Psycholtherapy Assn.; cert. forensic clin. psychology, psychol. assessment, evaluation and testing, substance abuse psychology. Profl. football player World Football League, Honolulu, 1974-75, Can. Football League, Winnipeg, Can., 1976, NFL Phila. Eagles, 1977-80; cross-cultural community planner City and County of Honolulu, 1975; sr. counselor Pa. Prison Soc., Phila., 1982; pres. bd. Career Transition Inst., Inc., Phila., 1981-83; psychologist, health care adminstr. West Jersey Health System, 1984-87; pvt. practice cons., 1988—92; pres. and CEO ANTIS Mgmt., LLC, 2003—. Vice chmn. Digital Champions, LLC, 2003—; pres., chief exec. officer Athletic Motivation, Inc., 1989-92; team psychologist for Balt. Orioles, 1989-94, Phila. Eagles, 1988-92, Phila. 76ers, 1986-92; lectr. in field; dir. and v.p. player devel. NFL, 1992-2002; bd. dirs. YMCA of Greater N.Y., 1991-2001. Mem. Nat. Adv. Coun. on Violence Against Women, chmn. sports subcom., 1995—; bd. dirs. Corp. Alliance to End Ptnr. Violence, 1995-2002. Served with USMC, 1965-69, Vietnam. Decorated Vietnamese Service award, Vietnamese Commendation award; recipient cert. of appreciation Kiwanis Club, Ramon, Calif., 1979, Del. Valley Med. Ctr., Phila., 1980, Community Service award Com. on Alcohol and Drug Abuse Crozer Chester Hosp., 1981. Mem. Am. Psychotherapy Assn., Am. Psychol. Soc., Am. Coll. Forensic Examiners, NFL Alumni Assn. (bd. dirs. Phila. Eagles chpt. 1986-98), Maxwell Football Club (life, v.p. community rels. 1990—, bd. govs.). Office: ANTIS Mgmt LLC 109 Muirfield Moorestown NJ 08057-9754 Office Phone: 856-608-9753. E-mail: drlemburnham@antiscorp.com.

BURNHAM, NOEL CHARLES, lawyer; b. Detroit, June 27, 1946; s. David Clark and Mary Margaret Burnham; m. Lindsey Davis, Aug. 8, 1996; children: Matthew Clark, Andrew charles, Kendall Margaret. BA, Johns Hopkins U., 1969; JD, Boston U., 1972. Bar: N.Y. 1973, U.S. Dist. Ct. (no. dist.) N.Y. 1973, U.S. Tax Ct. 1973, Del. 1996, Pa. 1997, U.S. Dist. Ct. Del. 1997, U.S. Dist. Ct. S.D., N.Y., 2005. Trust officer Nat. Comml. Bank and Trust Co., Albany, N.Y., 1972-76; v.p. Wilmington (Del.) Trust Co., 1976-2001; sec., gen. counsel Brandywine Fin. Corp., Wilmington, 1985-2001; atty. Montgomery, McCracken, Walker & Rhoads, Phila., 2001—. Mem. Del. Adv. Com. Credit Ins. Vol. Habitat for Humanity New Castle County, Wilmington, 1999—. With USN, 1965-70. Mem. Fed. Bar Assn., Del. State Bar Assn., Delvacca. Presbyterian. Avocations: golf, boating, boat building, yacht design. Office: Montgomery McCracken Walker & Rhoads 300 Delaware Ave Ste 750 Wilmington DE 19801 Office Phone: 302-504-7890. Business E-Mail: nburnham@mmwr.com.

BURNHAM, PATRICIA WHITE, consultant, advocate, writer, business executive; b. Omaha, July 30, 1933; d. William Max and Berniece Irene (Shockey) Orr; m. William L. White, June 18, 1955 (div. Nov. 1979); children: Lucinda, Christopher, Duncan; m. Robert A. Burnham, Feb. 23, 1980. BA in English, DePauw U., Greencastle, Ind., 1955; MA in English, Ill. State U., 1966, PhD in Adminstrn., 1977. Tchr. Morton Grove (Ill.) and Evansville (Ind.) pub. schs., 1955-60; instr. Ill. State U., Normal, 1963-71, dir. Nat. Student Exchange, 1971-74, acad. advisor and continuing edn. coord., 1974-76, asst. dean, 1976-79; assoc. dir. Ill. Bd. Higher Edn., Springfield, 1979-80; assoc. vice provost Ohio State U., Columbus, 1980-81; specialist bus. ins. Nationwide Ins. Co., Columbus, 1981-83; v.p. pvt. banking Chase Manhattan Bank, N.A., N.Y.C., 1983-88; pres. Transitions Group, Inc., East Burke, Vt., 1986—. Adj. prof. U. Vt., 1997—. Author: Life's Third Act, 1994; contbr. articles to publs. and seminars on successful aging, adult policies and programs. Pres. Cmty. Vt. Elders, 1994—99; mem. Vt. Health Resource Allocation Adv., 2004—; bd. dirs. Northeastern Vt. Hosp., St. Johnsbury, 1997—, bd. chair, 2000—04; bd. dirs. Vt. Cmty. Loan Fund, Vt. Assn. Non-Profit Orgns., 1998—2000, Dartmouth Hitchcock Alliance, 2004—. Mem. Phi Beta Kappa, Phi Delta Kappa. Congregationalist. Avocations: hiking, literature, writing. Office: Transitions Assocs PO Box 43 Lower Waterford VT 05848 Home: 391 Copenhagen Road Waterford VT 05819 Office Phone: 802-748-2979.

BURNHAM, STEPHEN JOHN, civil engineer; b. Springfield, Mass., June 13, 1948; s. Orvis Samuel, Jr. and Shirley Nairne (Turnwall) B.; m. Marjorie Elizabeth Viken, Feb. 14, 1970; children: Sandra Janice, Lisa Jennifer, Todsaporn Soonthorn. BSCE, U. Calif., Davis, 1970. Registered profl. engr., Minn., Ariz. With Fed. Hwy. Adminstrn., Washington, 1970—, planning and rsch. engr. Lincoln, Nebr., 1986—. Fin. officer CAP, Phoenix, 1983, Fairfax, Va., 1984-86, Lincoln, 1986-89, squadron comdr., 1991-92; treas. SDA Ch., Fairfax, 1986; life master Am. Contract Bridge League (sec. treas. unit 184, 1994-2000). Mem. Am. Mensa (life mem., pres. Lincoln chpt. 1992-93, regional vice chair 1997-2003). Democrat. Office: Fed Hwy Adminstrn 100 Centennial Mall N Rm 220 Lincoln NE 68508-3803

BURNHAM, WALTER DEAN, political science professor; b. Columbus, Ohio, June 15, 1930; s. Alfred Huntington Jr. and Gertrude Elinor (Hamburger) B.; m. Patricia Ann Mullan, June 7, 1958; children: John Patrick, Anne More. BA, Johns Hopkins U., 1951; AM, Harvard U., 1958, PhD, 1962; LittD (hon.), Rutgers U., 1982. Instr. polit. sci. Boston Coll., 1958-61; asst. prof. Kenyon Coll., Gambier, Ohio, 1961-64, Haverford (Pa.) Coll., 1964-66; from assoc. to full prof. Washington U., St. Louis, 1966-71; prof. MIT, Cambridge, Mass., 1971-88, Ruth and Arthur Sloan prof. polit. sci., 1984-88; Frank C. Erwin Jr. Centennial prof. govt. U. Tex., Austin, 1988—94, prof. emeritus, 1994—. Vis. scholar Phi Beta Kappa, 1995—. Author: Presidential Ballots, 1955, 2d edit., 1976, Critical Elections, 1970, The Current Crisis in Am. Politics, 1982, Democracy in the Making, 1983, 2d edit., 1986. With U.S. Army, 1953-56. Fellow Social Sci. Rsch. Coun., 1963, Guggenheim Found., 1974, Ctr. Advanced Study in Behavioral Sci., 1979. Fellow Am. Acad. Arts and Scis.; mem. Am. Polit. Sci. Assn. (mem. coun. 1984-86, pres. organized sect. on politics and history 1993-94), Phi Beta Kappa (vis. scholar 1995-96). Avocation: opera. Office: U Tex Dept Govt Burdine Hall # 536 Austin TX 78712 Home: 4203 Greenridge Pl Austin TX 78759

BURNIM, KALMAN AARON, theatre educator emeritus; b. Malden, Mass., Mar. 7, 1928; s. Jack K. and Sadie (Levy) B.; m. Verna Ruth Lesser, June 6, 1928; children: Ira, Judith, Esther Burnim Ouray. BA in Drama magna cum laude, Tufts U., 1950; MA in Theater, Ind. U., 1951; PhD, Yale U., 1958. Mng. exec. New England Adding Machine Co., Boston, 1951-55; asst. prof. Valparaiso (Ind.) U., 1958-59, U. Pitts., 1959-60, Tufts U., Medford, Mass., 1960-61, assoc. prof., dir. theater, 1961-65, prof. drama, 1965, chmn. dept. drama, exec. dir. theater, 1966-75, Fletcher prof. oratory and drama, 1971-87, emeritus prof., 1987—. Rsch. prof. English George Washington U., Washington, 1975-76, 85-86; mem. nat. screening com. for theater Fulbright Commn., Washington, 1985-89; mem. exec. com. Internat. Fedn. for Theatre Rsch., 1979-83, 91-95; cons. Folger Shakespeare Libr., 2002-05; panelist, del. various confs. Author: David Garrick, Director, 1961; co-author: The Prompter, An Eighteenth Century Theatrical Paper, 1966, The Biographical Dictionary of Actors, Actresses, Dancers, Managers, and Other Stage Personnel in London Stage, 1660-1800, 16 vols., 1973-93, (George Freedley Meml. award Theatre Library Assn. 1979, 94), Pictures in the Garrick Club. A Catalogue, 1997, (with P.H. Highfill Jr.) John Bell, Patron of Theatrical Portraiture, 1998, (with Andrew Wilton) The Richard Bebb Collection in the Garrick Club, 2001; editor: The Letters of Sarah and William Siddons to Hester Lynch Thrale Piozzi, 1969, The Complete Plays of George Colman the Elder, 6 vols., 1983, (with John Baskett) Brief Lives, Sitters and Artists in the Portraits in the Garvick Club, 2003; assoc. editor Ednl. Theatre Jour., 1968-70; contbr. articles to profl. jours. Guggenheim fellow, 1964-65, Folger Library fellow, 1957-58, 69, 71; Sterling fellow Yale U., 1957-58; Am. Council for Learned Socs. grantee, 1966, 71; NEH grantee, 1967-68, 70, 74-76, 85-86; Tufts faculty research grantee, 1960-81. Mem. Am. Soc. for Theatre Rsch. (pres. 1985-91, mem. exec. com. 1960-63, 64-69, 72-75, 83-86, program chmn. 1963-65, 76, chmn. publs. com. 1975-76, 79-82, del. to Am. Coun. Learned Socs. 1976-82, spl. citation 1994), Brit. Soc. for Theatre Rsch., Am. Soc. for Eighteenth-Century Studies, IREX (chmn. commn. on Am.-Soviet theatre exchs. 1988-91), Coll. Fellows Am. Theatre, Phi Beta Kappa (pres. Tufts chpt. 1983-85), Garrick Club. also: 22 Cranmore Ln Melrose MA 02176-1507 Business E-Mail: kburnim@aya.yale.edu.

BURNINGHAM, KIM RICHARD, educational association administrator, former state legislator; b. Salt Lake City, Sept. 14, 1936; s. Rulon and Margie (Stringham) Burningham; m. Susan Ball Clarke, Dec. 19, 1968; children: Christian, Tyler David. BS, U. Utah, 1960; MA, U. Ariz., 1967; MFA, U. So. Calif., 1977. Cert. secondary tchr., Utah. Tchr. Bountiful (Utah) High Sch., 1960-88; mem. Utah Ho. of Reps., Salt Lake City, 1979-94; cons. Shipley Assocs., Bountiful, 1989-94, Franklin Covey, 1994—. Gubernatorial appointee as exec. dir. Utah Statehood Centennial Commn., 1994-96; mem. Utah State Bd. Edn., 1999-2000, vice chmn., 2000-01, chmn., 2001-; bd. dirs. Nat. Assn. State Bds. Edn., 2000-01, pres.-elect, 2004, pres. 2005—. Author dramas for stage and film, also articles; columnist, Davis County Clipper, 2000—. Mem. state strategic planning com. Utah Tomorrow, 1989-2003 Recipient Carl Perkins Humanitarian of Yr. award, ACTE, 2002. Mem. NEA, PTA (life), Utah Edn. Assn., Davis Edn. Assn., Nat. Forensic League. Mem. Lds Ch. Avocations: gardening, history. Home: 932 Canyon Crest Dr Bountiful UT 84010-2002 E-mail: krb84010@aol.com.

BURNISON, BOYD EDWARD, lawyer; b. Arnolds Park, Iowa, Dec. 12, 1934; s. Boyd WIlliam and Lucile (Harnden) B.; m. Mari Amaral; children: Erica Lafore, Alison Katherine. BS, Iowa State U., 1957; JD, U. Calif., Berkeley, 1961. Bar: Calif. 1962, U.S. Supreme Ct. 1971, U.S. Dist. Ct. (no. dist.) Calif. 1962, U.S. Ct. Appeals (9th cir.) 1962, U.S. Dist. Ct. (ea. dist.) Calif. 1970, U.S. Dist. Ct. (ctrl. dist.) Calif. 1992. Dep. counsel Yolo County, Calif., 1962-65; assoc. Steel & Arostegui, Marysville, Calif., 1965-66, St. Sure, Moore & Hoyt, Oakland, Calif., 1966-70; ptnr. St. Sure, Moore, Hoyt & Sizoo, Oakland and San Francisco, 1970-75; v.p. Crosby, Heafey, Roach & May, P.C., Oakland, 1975-2000, also bd. dirs.; pres. Boyd E Burnison A Profl. Law Corp., Walnut Creek, Calif., 2001—05, Diablo, 2005—. Advisor Berkeley YMCA, 1971—, Yolo County YMCA, 1962—65, bd. dirs., 1965; trustee, sec., legal counsel Easter Seal Found., Alameda County, 1974—79, hon. trustee, 1979—; trustee Alameda County Law Libr., 2001—, v.p., 2003—05, pres., 2005—; bd. dirs. Easter Seal Soc. Crippled Children and Adults of Alameda County Calif., 1972—75, Moot Ct. Bd., U. Calif., 1960—61, East Bay Conservation Corps, 1997—2000, treas., 2000. Named Vol. of Yr., Berkeley YMCA, 1999. Fellow: ABA Found. (life); mem.: ABA (labor rels. and employment law sect., equal employment law com. 1972—), Sproul Assoc. Boalt Hall Law Sch. U. Calif. Berkeley, Indsl. Rels. Rsch. Assn., Contra Costa County Bar Assn. (labor law sect.), Bar Assn. San Francisco (labor law sect.), Yuba Sutter Bar Assn., Yolo County Bar Assn. (sec. 1965), Alameda County Bar Found. (bd. dirs. 1993—95), Alameda County Bar Assn. (chmn. memberships and directory com. 1973—74, 1980, chmn. law office econs. com. 1975—77, assn. dir. 1981—85, pres. 1984, vice chmn. bench bar liaison com. 1983, chmn. 1984, Disting. Svc. award 1987), State Bar Calif. (spl. labor counsel 1981—84, labor and employment law sect. 1982—), Nat. Conf. Bar Pres.'s, Rotary (Paul Harris fellow), Round Hill Country Club, Iowa State Alumni Assn., Order Knoll, Phi Delta Phi, Pi Kappa Alpha. Democrat. Home: PO Box 743 2704 Caballo Ranchero Dr Diablo CA 94528-0743 Office: Boyd E Burnison A Profl Law Corp PO Box 743 Diablo CA 94528 Office Phone: 925-855-9032. Office Fax: 925-855-9332. E-mail: bburnison@sbcglobal.net.

BURNLEY, JAMES HORACE, IV, lawyer; b. High Point, N.C., July 30, 1948; s. James Horace and Dorothy Mary (Rockwell) B. BA magna cum laude, Yale U., 1970; JD, Harvard U., 1973. Bar: NC 1973, DC 1989. Assoc. Brooks, Pierce, McLendon, Humphrey & Leonard, 1973-75; ptnr. Turner, Enochs, Foster, Sparrow & Burnley, P.A., 1975-81; dir. VISTA, 1981-82; assoc. dep. atty. gen. Dept. Justice, Washington, 1982-83; gen. counsel Dept. Transp., Washington, 1983, dep. sec., 1983-87, sec., 1987-89; ptnr. Shaw, Pittman, Potts & Trowbridge, Washington, 1989-92, Winston & Strawn, Washington, 1993—; ptnr., legis. & govt. affairs dept. Venable LLP, Washington. Trustee Jamestown Found., Intercollegiate Studies Inst.; bd. dirs. Reagan Alumni Assn., Freedom Works; chmn., Roe Inst. Adv. Com. Heritage Found. Republican. Office: Venable LLP 575 7th St NW Washington DC 20004 Office Phone: 202-344-4054. Office Fax: 202-344-8300. Business E-Mail: jhburnley@venable.com.

BURNLEY, JUNE WILLIAMS, secondary school educator; b. St. Augustine, Fla., Mar. 13, 1936; d. Marcellus Henry Gilford and Ella (Broadus) Williams. BS, N.C. Agrl. and Tech. U., 1958; MA, Villanova U., 1975, St. John's Coll., Annapolis, Md., 1993; student, Oxford U., London, 1995. Cert. English tchr., counseling psychologist. Grade sch. tchr., 1958-59; lang. arts supr. Wharton Ctr., Phila., 1967-68; English/French lang. tchr. Hatch. Jr. H.S., Camden, N.J., 1962-68; English tchr. George Washington H.S., Phila., 1968-93, secondary counseling intern, 1975. Mem. Pa. State Coun. English Tchrs., 1968-93, Educators to Africa, Phila., 1993-97; tutor Temple-New Career Ladders, 1975-76. Mem. Germantown Civic League, Phila., 1993, West Mt. Airy Neighbors, Phila., 1968—, Social Action Com., Phila., 1993-95, Germantown Hist. Soc., Unitarian Soc. Germantown; vol. guide in tng. Phila. Mus. Art, 1996—. Pa. State Bd. Edn. fellow, 1985, Arco & Exxon fellow, 1991, St. John's Coll. fellow, 1992-93. Fellow Commonwealth Partnership; mem. Nat. Coun. English Tchrs. (Svc. award 1972), Eleanor Trailor Readers (co-founder), Literary Group (founder), Literati (founder), Amnesty Internat., Phi Delta Kappa, Delta Sigma Theta. Avocations: reading, knitting, sewing, word games, travel. Home: 700 Elkins Ave Apt E3 Elkins Park PA 19027-2315 Personal E-mail: alithaevol@aol.com.

BURNS, ALTON JAY, plastic surgeon; b. Garland, Tex., Apr. 16, 1955; BS magna cum laude, Baylor U., Waco, Tex., 1977; MD, U. Tex. Southwestern Med. Sch., Dallas, 1981. Cert. Tex. State Bd. Med. Examiners, 1981, Am. Bd. Surgery, 1987, Am. Bd. Plastic Surgeons, 1990. Intern, gen. surgery U. Utah Sch. Medicine, Salt Lake City, 1981—82, resident, gen. surgery, 1982—86; resident, plastic surgery U. Tex. Southwestern Med. Sch., Dallas, 1986—88; fellow, vascular anomalies Boston Children's Hosp., 1988; asst. prof., plastic surgery U. Tex. Southwestern Med. Ctr., Dallas, 1988—. Contbr. articles to profl. journals. Fellow: ACS; mem.: AMA, Dallas County Medical Soc., Am. Soc. for Aesthetic Plastic Surgeons (chair, facial surgery com.), Am. Soc. for Laser Medicine and Surgery, Plastic and Cosmetic Surgeons of Dallas, Am. Soc. Plastic Surgeons, Tex. Soc. Plastic Surgeons, Dallas County Med. Soc., Tex. Med. Assn. Office: Univ Texas Southwestern Med Ctr Dept Plastic Surgery Bldg G8239 5323 Harry Hines Blvd Dallas TX 75390-9132*

BURNS, ARNOLD IRWIN, lawyer; b. N.Y.C., Apr. 14, 1930; s. Herman Leon and Rose (Lauterstein) B.; m. Felice Bernstein, June 17, 1951; children: Linda Susan, Douglas Todd. AB, Union Coll., Schenectady, 1950; LL.B., Cornell U., 1953; postgrad., Parker Sch. Internat. Law, 1960; JD, Hofstra U., 1986. Bar: N.Y. 1953, D.C. 1977. Ptnr. Burns Summit Rovins & Feldesman (and predecessors), N.Y.C., 1960-86; assoc. atty. gen. U.S. Govt., Washington, 1986; dep. atty. gen. U.S. Dept. Justice, Washington, 1986-88; mem. Proskauer Rose LLP, N.Y.C., 1988-99; mng. dir. Natexis Bleichroeder Inc., N.Y.C., 1999—2003; chmn. The QuanStar Group, LLC, 2004—. Bd. dirs., mem. exec. com. New Valley Corp.; mem. exec. com. Econ. Devel. Corp of City of NY. Note editor: Cornell Law Quar, 1952-53. Former chmn., life trustee Union Coll., Schenectady; former chmn., now chmn. emeritus bd. dirs. Freedom Found., Valley Forge, Pa.; emeritus chmn. nat. bd. govs. Boys and Girls Clubs Am.; mem. adv. com., co-chmn. nat. capital campaign Cornell Law Sch., Ithaca, N.Y.; bd. dirs., mem. exec. com. Econ. Devel. Corp., City N.Y.; former chmn. N.Y.C. Commn. on Youth Empowerment Svcs.; former mem. N.Y.C. Commn. to Monitor Police Corruption; former chmn. Nat. Ctr. for Victims of Crime; chmn. Internat. Ctr. for Missing and Exploited Children; vice chmn. Nat. Ctr. for Missing and Exploited Children; bd. dirs. Vis. Nurse Svc., N.Y.; dir. YES Newtork; chmn. emeritus Coun. for Unity; active Nat. Prison Indsl. Task Force. Capt. U.S. Army, 1953—57. Mem. Anti-Defamation League (life; nat. com.), Fed. Bar Coun., Cornell Law Assn., Met. Club, Army Navy Club, N.Y. Athletic Club, Friars Club, Rockefeller Club, Order of Coif, Phi Kappa Phi, Kappa Nu, Alpha Phi Omega. Republican. Jewish. Home: 25 Sutton Pl S Apt 11F New York NY 10022-2462 Office Phone: 212-956-3037. E-mail: aburns@quanstar.com.

BURNS, ARTHUR LEE, architect; b. Indpls., July 5, 1924; s. Charles Raymond and Dorothy Frances (Young) B.; m. Dorothy Maxine Kingsland, Oct. 26, 1946 (dec.); children— Stephen Robert (dec.), Melody Lee; m. Frances C. Mathers, Jan. 12, 1988. BS in Architecture, U. Cin., 1949. Archtl. draftsman Foster Engring. Co., Ltd., Indpls., 1941-42; archtl. draftsman Albert V. Walters (Architect), Cin., 1946-48; chief draftsman Arend & Arend (Architects), Cin., 1948-49; architect The McGuire & Shook Corp., Indpls., 1949-84, v.p., 1964-71, sec.-treas., 1972-73, pres., 1974-75, exec. v.p., 1976-77, v.p., 1978-79, sec.-treas., 1980-84; archtl. cons., 1984—. Bd. dirs. Friends of Winter Haven Pub. Libr., 1995—2001, 2002—, pres., 1997—98. Served with USAF, 1943—46. Fellow AIA (sec.-treas. Indpls. chpt. 1965-66, v.p. 1967, pres. 1968, mem. documents bd. 1973-85, chmn. 1978-79); mem. Ind. Soc. Architects (bd. dirs. 1968-69, v.p. 1971, pres. 1972, Edward D. Pierre medal 1972), Constrn. Specifications Inst. (v.p. Indpls. chpt. 1966-67, pres. 1967-68), Broad Ripple Sertoma Club Indpls. (v.p. 1973-74, pres. 1974-75, Gold Honor Club), Cypress Gardens Sertoma Club Winter Haven (bd. dirs. 1991-99, 2000-02). Republican. Methodist. Home: 2987 Plantation Rd Winter Haven FL 33884-1235

BURNS, BERNARD JOHN, III, public defender; b. Alexandria, Va., Apr. 28, 1956; s. Bernard John and Mary Theresa (O'Malley) B.; m. Pamela Sue Endres, June 9, 1990; 1 child, Kristie Keener. BA in Journalism, U. Iowa, 1982, JD with distinction, 1984. Bar: Iowa 1985, U.S. Dist. Ct. (so. dist.) Iowa 1987, U.S. Supreme Ct. 1989, U.S. Ct. Appeals (8th cir.) 1992. Asst. appellate defender Iowa Appellate Defender, Des Moines, 1985-94; asst. pub. defender Des Moines Adult Pub. Defender, 1994-99; asst. fed. defender Office of Fed. Defender, Des Moines, 1999—. Author: 4A Iowa Practice: Criminal Procedure. Bd. dirs. Met. Arts Alliance Greater Des Moines, 1996-2003, pres., 2000; bd. dirs. Drama Workshop, 2004-05; mem. Iowa Criminal and Juvenile Justice Planning Commn., 1993-99; chmn. Jazz in July Planning Com., Des Moines, 1997-2003; keyboard player Goodnight Dallas. Named Outstanding Sr., Iowa Sch. Journalism, 1982. Mem. Nat. Assn. Fed. Defenders, Iowa Pub. Defenders Assn. (pres. 1991-99), Chopin Soc. (v.p. 1982), Blackstone Inn of Ct., Am. Mock Trial Assn., Judges Hall of Fame, Friends of Iowa Civil Rights, Inc. (Spl. Recognition award), Phi Beta Kappa. Avocations: composer, actor, writer and producer, tae kwon do instructor, musician. Office: Fed Defender 400 Locust St Ste 340 Des Moines IA 50309-2258 Business E-Mail: bjohnb@mchsi.com.

BURNS, BRIAN PATRICK, lawyer; b. Cambridge, Mass., July 12, 1936; s. John Joseph and Alice (Blake) B.; m. Sheila Ann O'Connor, June 23, 1962; children: Sheila Ann, Brian Patrick, Sean Richard, Roderick O'Connor. BA, Holy Cross Coll., 1957; LLB, Harvard U., 1960. Bar: Mass. 1960, N.Y. 1961, Calif. 1965. Law clk., spl. asst. to regional adminstr. New York Regional Office, SEC, 1958-59; asso. Webster, Sheffield, Fleischmann, Hitchcock & Brookfield, N.Y.C., 1960-64; ptnr. Cullinan, Hancock, Rothert & Burns, San Francisco, 1965-74; sr. ptnr. Cullinan, Burns & Helmer, San Francisco, 1975-78; firm Burns & Whitehead, San Francisco, 1978-86; chmn., chief exec. officer, chmn. exec. com. Boothe Fin. Corp., San Francisco, 1981-87, also bd. dirs.; chmn. Robert Half Internat. Inc., 1987-88; chmn., CEO BF Enterprises Inc., 1987—. Dir. U.S. Banknote Corp., N.Y.C., from 1967, chmn. exec. and fin. coms., 1973-76; dir. Coca Cola Bottling Co., N.Y., 1974-86, chmn. exec. com., 1979-86; dir. Kellogg Co., 1979-89, chmn. fin. com. 1984-89; dir. Calif. Jockey, 1980-89; dir., chmn. audit com. Flexi-Van Corp., N.Y.C., 1984-85; dir., chmn. exec. com. Pinnacle Petroleum Corp., The Woodlands, Tex., 1983-85; dir., chmn. ops. review com. Brink's Inc., Chgo., 1976-78; dir., chmn. acquisition com. Pacific Holding Corp., Los Angeles, 1972-78; dir., mem. exec. com. Beverly Wilshire Hotel, Beverly Hills, Calif., Calif., 1967-86; dir., chmn. exec. com. USR Industries, The Woodlands, 1980-83; dir., chmn. audit com. ROCOR Internat., Palo Alto, Calif., 1976-82; underwriting mem. Lloyds of London, 1978-89; lectr. continuing edn. of bar U. Calif., 1969, 74, 76, advanced bus. seminar, 1971; seminar on investment opportunities in wine industry McGraw Hill Coll., N.Y., 1973, Legal Edn. Inst., 1976. Bd. dirs. Boys Club of San Francisco, 1971-80, Am. Irish Found., 1978-87, Am. Ireland Fund, 1987—; trustee Holy Cross Coll., 1978-89. Mem. ABA (mem. small bus. com. corp. bus. and banking sect. 1972-76), State Bar Cal. (vice chmn. com. on corps. 1971-75), Bar Assn. San Francisco (chmn. com. on corp. banking and bus. law 1968-69), Calif. Jockey Club (dir. San Mateo, Calif. 1988-89). Clubs: Royal Dublin Soc.; Bohemian, Burlingame Country, Family, Olympic, Sky, N.Y. Athletic, Les Ambassadeurs, Mil. and Hospitaller Order St. Lazarus of Jerusalem (comdr. companion). Roman Catholic. Office: BF Enterprises Inc 100 Bush St Ste 1250 San Francisco CA 94104-3914

BURNS, CARROLL DEAN, insurance company executive; b. Chattanooga, Dec. 22, 1932; s. William Thomas and Lillis (Gill) B.; m. Jean Baird, Aug. 29, 1954; children: Randy, Lori. BS, U. Tenn., 1954. C.P.A., Tenn., Ohio. With Provident Life and Accident Ins. Co., Chattanooga, 1957-63, mgr. data processing, 1960-63; with Union Central Life Ins. Co., Cin., 1963-79, exec. v.p., comptr., bd. dirs., 1974-79; pres., CEO Life Ins. Co. Ga., Atlanta, 1979-94; exec. v.p. Georgia US Corp., Atlanta, 1989-94; ret., 1995. Pres., COO Southland Life Ins. Co.; bd. dirs. Union Cen. Life Assurance Corp., Life Ins. Co. Ga., First of Ga. Ins. Group, Assoc. Drs. Ins. Co., Southland Ins. Co.; former chmn. Civil Svc. Bd., Fairfield, Ohio. Former trustee Better Bus. Bur. Cin. Served with USAF, 1955-57. Mem. BEta Alpha Psi, Atlanta Country Club, Georgian Club, Sugarloaf Country Club. Baptist. Home: 2075 Sugarloaf Club Dr Duluth GA 30097-4098 Personal E-mail: cdburns@charter.net.

BURNS, CASSANDRA STROUD, prosecutor; b. Lynchburg, Va., May 22, 1960; d. James Wesley and Jeanette Lou (Garner) Stroud; m. Stephen Burns; children: Leila Jeanette, India Veronica. BA, U. Va., 1982; JD, N.C. Cen. U., 1985; MBA candidate, Regis U., 2005. Bar: Va. 1986, N.J. 1986, U.S. Dist. Ct. (ea. dist.) Va. 1987, U.S. Ct. Appeals (4th cir.) 1987, U.S. Bankruptcy Ct. (ea. dist.) Va. 1987; cert. in criminal law. Law clk. Office Atty. Gen. State of Va., Richmond, summer 1984; law intern Office Dist. Atty. State of N.C., Durham, 1985; staff atty. Tidewater Legal Aid Soc., Chesapeake, Va., 1987-89; asst. atty. Commonwealth of Va., Petersburg, 1989-90; assoc. atty. Bland and Stroud, Petersburg, 1990; asst. pub. defender City of Petersburg, 1990-91, Commonwealth's atty., 1991—; adj. prof. Va. Commonwealth U., 2003, Va. State U., 2004—. Founder BED Task Force on Babies Exposed to Drugs, 1991, Buddies of Petersburg Program, 1997—. Sec. Chesapeake Task Force Coun. on Youth Svcs., 1987-89; ch. directress and organist; mem. NAACP; chair Petersburg-Dinwiddie Cmty. Criminal Justice Bd.; bd. dirs. Mary Carter Beacon House, 2004—; mem. leadership coun. United Way, 2004—. Mem. Va. Bar Assn. (mem. coun. 1993-99), Old Dominion Bar Assn., Va. Assn. Commonwealth Attys. (bd. dirs., mem. coun. 1993-2000), Legal Svcs. Corp. Va. (bd. dirs.), Nat. Bd. Trial Advocacy (cert.), Nat. Dist. Attys. Assn., Southside Va. Legal Aid Soc. (bd. dirs.), Petersburg Bar Assn., Nat. Black Prosecutors Assn. (regional dir.), Petersburg Jaycees, Order Eastern Star, Peterburg C. of C., Kiwanis, Internat., Buddies Club, Phi Alpha Delta, Alpha Kappa Alpha. Democrat. Baptist. Avocations: piano, organ, volleyball, needlework, pets. Home: 326 N Park Dr Petersburg VA 23805-2442 Office: Commonwealth's Atty 150 N Sycamore St Petersburg VA 23803 Office Phone: 804-861-8899. E-mail: bossyda@aol.com.

BURNS, C(HARLES) PATRICK, hematologist, oncologist; b. Kansas City, Mo., Oct. 8, 1937; s. Charles Edgar and Ruth (Eastham) B.; m. Janet Sue Walsh, June 15, 1968; children: Charles Geoffrey, Scott Patrick. BA, U. Kans., 1959, MD, 1963. Diplomate Am. Bd. Internal Medicine, subsplty. bds. hematology, med. oncology. Intern Cleve. Met. Gen. Hosp., 1963-64; asst. resident in internal medicine Univ. Hosps., Cleve., 1966-68, sr. resident in hematology, 1968-69; instr. medicine Case Western Res. U., Cleve., 1970-71; asst. chief hematology Cleve. VA Hosp., 1970-71; asst. prof. medicine U. Iowa Hosps., Iowa City, 1971-75, assoc. prof. medicine, 1975-80, prof., 1980—, dir. sect. med. oncology, co-dir. divsn. hematatol./oncology, 1980-85, dir. div. hematology, oncology, blood marrow transplantation, 1985-99. Vis. scientist Imperial Cancer Rsch. Fund Labs., London, 1982-83; cons. U.S. VA Hosp.; mem. study sect. on exptl. therapeutics NIH, Cancer Ctr. Support Rev. Commn. Nat. Cancer Inst., NIH, NIH Cancer Clin. Investigation Rev. Com., Com. H Nat. Cancer Inst., VA Med. Rsch. Svc. Career Devel. Com.; mem. external adv. com. U. Oreg. Cancer Ctr., 1994-2000; mem. oncology group external adv. com., ACS, 2004-; cons. Irish Rsch. Bd., Dublin, 2000— Mem. bd. assoc. editors Cancer Rsch., 1988-2000, rsch. and publs. on hematologic malignancies, tumor lipid biochemistry, leukemia and oncology, role of oxidation in cancer treatment. Served to capt. M.C., AUS, 1964-66. Am. Cancer Soc. fellow in hematology-oncology, 1968-69, USPHS fellow in medicine, 1969-70; USPHS career awardee, 1978; Outstanding Paper Presentation, Am. Oil Chemists Soc., 1992. Fellow ACP; mem. AAAS, Am. Bd. Internal Medicine (subsplty. bd. hematology test writing com. 1992-98, com. on recent advances in hematology, 2002-), Am. Soc. Hematology, Am. Assn. Cancer Rsch., Internat. Soc. Hematology, Ctrl. Soc. Clin. Rsch., Am. Soc. Clin. Oncology, Soc. Exptl. Biology and Medicine, Oxygen Soc., Royal Soc. Medicine, Am. Fedn. Clin. Rsch., Internat. Soc. for the Study of Fatty Acids and Lipids, Phi Beta Pi, Lambda Chi Alpha, Alpha Omega Alpha. Home: 2046 Rochester Ct Iowa City IA 52245-3246 Office: U Iowa Univ Hosps Dept Medicine Iowa City IA 52242 Office Phone: 319-356-2038. Business E-Mail: c-burns@uiowa.edu.

BURNS, CHESTER RAY, medical educator; b. Nashville, Dec. 5, 1937; s. Leslie Andrew and Margaret (Drake) B.; m. Ann Christine Griffey, Aug. 31, 1962; children: Christine, Derek. BA, Vanderbilt U., 1959, MD, 1963; PhD, Johns Hopkins U., 1969. Asst. prof. history medicine U. Tex. Med. Br., Galveston, 1969-71, James Wade Rockwell asst. prof. history medicine, 1971-75, James Wade Rockwell assoc. prof., 1975-79, James Wade Rockwell prof., 1979—. Cons. Nat. Ctr. for Health Svcs. Rsch., Washington, 1976-78; mem. nat. bd. cons. NEH, Washington, 1978-83. Editor: Humanism in Medicine, 1973, Legacies in Ethics and Medicine, 1977, Legacies in Law and Medicine, 1977; co-editor: Philosophy of Medicine and Bioethics: A Twenty Year Retrospective and Critical Appraisal, 1997; co-editor: Proceedings of the 37th International Congress on the History of Medicine, 2002, Saving Lives, Training Caregivers, Making Discoveries A Centennial History of the University of Texas Medical Branch at Galveston, 2003, Practicing the Medical Humanities, 2003; author numerous essays. Bd. dirs. The Grand 1894 Opera House, Galveston, 1986—88. Mem. Am. Assn. for History of Medicine (exec. coun. 1972-75), Soc. for Health and Human Values (pres. 1975-76), Am. Osler Soc. (bd. govs. 1984-87, 2002—, pres. 2004—), Internat. Soc. for History of Medicine (treas. 1991—2003), Tex. State Hist. Assn. (exec. coun. 1993-97), Rotary (pres. Galveston club 1980-81, gov. Dist. 5910, 1993-94). Democrat. Methodist. Avocations: swimming, photography. Office: U Tex Med Br Ashbel Smith Bldg Rm 2 Galveston TX 77555-1311 Office Phone: 409-772-9389. E-mail: cburns@utmb.edu.

BURNS, CONRAD RAY, senator; b. Gallatin, Mo., Jan. 25, 1935; s. Russell and Mary Frances (Knight) B.; m. Phyllis Jean Kuhlmann; children: Keely Lynn, Garrett Russell. Student, U. Mo., 1952-54. Field rep. Polled Hereford World Mag., Kansas City, Mo., 1963-69; pub. rels. Billings (Mont.) Livestock Com., 1969-73; farm dir. KULR TV, Billings, 1974; pres., founder No. Ag-Network, Billings, 1975-86; commissioner Yellowstone County, Billings, 1987-89; senator from Montana U.S. Senate, 1989—. Mem. Aging Com., Small Bus. Com., chmn. Appropriations Subcom. of Mil. Constrn., chmn. Com. Sci. and Transp. Subcom. of Comms., chmn. Energy and Nat. Resources With USMC, 1955-57. Mem. Nat. Assn. Farm Broadcasters, Am. Legion, Rotary, Masons, Shriners. Republican. Lutheran. Avocation: football officiating. Office: US Senate 187 Dirksen Senate Off Bldg Washington DC 20510-0001*

BURNS, DAN W., manufacturing executive; b. Auburn, Calif., Sept. 10, 1925; s. William and Edith Lynn (Johnston) B.; 1 child, Dan Jr. Dir. materials Menasco Mfg. Co., 1951-56; v.p., gen. mgr. Hufford Corp., 1956-58; pres. Hufford div. Siegler Corp., 1958-61; v.p. Siegler Corp., 1961-62, Lear Siegler, Inc., 1962-64; pres., dir. Electrada Corp., Culver City, Calif., 1964; pres., chief exec. officer Sargent Industries, Inc., L.A., 1964-85, chmn. bd. dirs., 1985-88. Now chmn. bd. dirs., CEO Arlington Industries, Inc.; bd. dirs. Gen. Automotive Corp., Dover Tech. Internat., Inc., Kistler Aerospace Corp. Bd. dirs. San Diego Aerospace Mus., Smithsonian Inst., The Pres.'s Cir., Nat. Acad. Scis., Atlantic Coun. of U.S., George C. Marshall Found.; bd. overseers Hoover Instn., Stanford U. Capt. U.S. Army, 1941-47; prisoner of war Japan; asst. mil. attache 1946, China; adc to Gen. George C. Marshall 1946-47. Mem. OAS Sports Com. (dir.), L.A. Country Club, St. Francis Yacht Club, Calif. Club, Conquistador del Cielo, Cosmos Club Washington, Pacific-Union Club (San Francisco). Home: 7400 Bryan Canyon Rd Carson City NV 89704-9588

BURNS, DANIEL HOBART, management consultant; b. Atlanta, Jan. 26, 1928; s. Hobart H. and Florence (Kuhn) B.; B.A., U. Ala., 1949; grad. Armed Forces Staff Coll., 1966, Air Command and Staff Coll., 1969, Air War Coll., 1972; postgrad. U. S.C., 1975, Regent Coll., U. B.C., 1978-79, Trinity Episcopal Sch. for Ministry, 1979-80; m. Barbara Ann Grimsley, Jan. 15, 1949 (div. July 1974); children: Eric Grimsley, Daniel Hobart, Barbara Bennett, Arlene Chester; m. Ann Lyn Horrell, Sept. 28, 1979 (div. Mar. 1997); children: Jessica Florence, Stephen John. Account exec. Sta. WCOS, Columbia, S.C., 1949-51; sales mgr. sta. WIS, Columbia, 1951-57; ins. agt. Aetna Life Ins. Co., Columbia, 1957-60; propr. Daniel H. Burns Co., mgmt. cons., broker, Columbia, 1960—; pres., dir. Nat. Search, Inc., 1966—, Indsl. Surveys, Inc., 1968—; Alliance Bldg. Industries, 1971-84; cons., Ednl. TV Network, govts. of Israel, Greece, W. Ger., Fed. Grants Projects, S.C. Ednl. TV Network; guest lectr. U. S.C.; cons. sales mgmt. and market analysis, analytical and conceptual problem solving; owner Western Rare Books-Fine Art, 1983—, Internat. Galleries, Empire Gallery, Empire Pub. Co.; bd. dir. Boulder Sch. of Massage Therapy. Pres., Schneider Sch. PTA, 1963-66; supr. registration City of Columbia, 1962-69; asst. project dir., statewide law enforcement edn. through TV, 1966-69; cons. Pitts. Leadership Found., 1980-81; dist. commr. Boy Scouts Am.; pres., committeeperson Boulder County Rep. Party; pres., bd. dirs. Internat. Communications Resources Found.; bd. dirs. Travelers Aid Assn. Am., Nat. Council USO; Columbia Sch. Theology for Laity; bd. dirs., exec. com. Consol. Agys. of United Funds; Richland County chpt. Nat. Found. Served with USAAF, 1943-46; lt. col. USAF ret. Mem. S.C. Football Ofcls. Assn., Columbia Real Estate Bd., Air Force Assn., Am. Y-Flyer Yacht Racing Assn., AAUP, Am. Mgmt. Assn., Nat. Assn. Ednl. Broadcasters, Soc. for Advancement Mgmt., Am. Soc. Real Estate Appraisers, Interprofl. Cons. Council, Nat. Assn. Security Dealers, Soc. Am. Archivists, Nat. Hist. Soc., Internat. Platform Assn., Hist. Columbia Found., S.C. Press Assn., Columbia C. of C., Am. Soc. Personal Adminstrn., Sierra Club, Columbia Lyric Opera, Internat. Christian Leaders, Fellowship Christian Athletes, English Speaking Union, N. Am. Yacht Racing Union, Sigma Phi Epsilon. Episcopalian/Anglican. Clubs: Charleston (S.C.) Yacht; Yachting of Am., Workshop Theatre, First Nighters, Columbia Squash Racquets, Town Theatre, Masons (Shriner), Rotary. Author publs. in field. Home: 7425 Empire Dr Boulder CO 80303-5007 Office: 7425 Empire Dr Boulder CO 80303-5007 E-mail: empgal@earthlink.net.

BURNS, DAVID MITCHELL, writer, retired diplomat, musician; b. Pineville, Ky., Dec. 1, 1928; s. Judge and Louise (Cooke) B.; m. Sandra Dunlop, June 8, 1955; children: David A., Patrick C. BA, Princeton U., 1953; student, Sch. Advanced Internat. Studies, Johns Hopkins U., 1957, 60, Howard U., 1957, 60, Fgn. Service Inst., Tangier, Morocco, 1967-69. Advt. trainee Gen. Electric Co., 1953; instr. English, U. Kans., 1954-55; asst. cultural affairs officer Am. embassy, Damascus, Syria, 1955-56, Beirut, 1956; dir. Iran-Am. Soc., Isfahan, 1957; information officer Am. consulate general Salisbury, Fedn. Rhodesia and Nyasaland, 1957-59; pub. affairs officer Am. embassy, Bamako, Mali, 1960-62, cultural affairs officer Tunis, Tunisia, 1962-63; cultural policy officer Africa, USIA, 1963-67; pub. affairs officer Am. interests sect. embassy of Switzerland, Algiers, Algeria, 1969-72; dir. sci. and tech. programs USIA, 1972-77; dir. climate project AAAS, Washington, 1978-90. Author: Gateway: Dr. Thomas Walker and the Opening of Kentucky, Quests; CD's as leader of Hot Mustard Quintet include Swing Song, Don't Postpone Joy, Nothing Loved Is Ever Lost, Rainbow Room, 1975—; contbr. articles to newspapers and mags., 1953—. Fulbright grantee U. Lille and Salzburg Seminar in Am. Studies, 1953-54; recipient award of merit Ky. Hist. Soc., 2001. Mem. Nat. Assn. Sci. Writers, Nat. Book Critics Cir., Jazz Journalists Assn. Clubs: Cosmos, Dacor (Washington). Office: 1712 19th St NW Washington DC 20009-1606 E-mail: davesand@comcast.net.

BURNS, DIANN, newscaster; m. Marc Watts; 1 child. BA in Politics and Mass Comm., Cleve. State U., Ohio; MA, Columbia U. Grad. Sch. of Journalism, N.Y. Gen. assignment reporter Cleve. Plain Dealer; sports editor, photographer and reporter Cleve. Call and Post; field prodr. and reporter Ind. Network News of N.Y.; reporter to weekend anchor WLS-TV, Chgo., 1985—94, co-anchor 5pm and 10pm news, 1994—2003; co-anchor 5pm, 6pm and 10pm news WBBM-TV, Chgo., 2003—. Spokesperson Pediatric AIDS Chgo.; hon. co-chair Ricky Byrdsong Mem. Race Against Hate. Office: WBBM-TV 630 N McClurg Ct Chicago IL 60601

BURNS, DRUSILLA LORENE, microbiologist; b. Manhattan, Kans., Feb. 14, 1953; BS in Chemistry, Tulane U., 1975; PhD, U. Calif., Berkeley, 1980. Fellow lab cellular metabolism NIH, 1980-84; from sr. fellow to rsch. chemist FDA Ctr. for Biologics Evaluation and Rsch., Bethesda, 1984-94, chief lab. pertussis, 1994-99, chief lab. respiratory and spl. pathogens, 1999—. Ad hoc reviewer in field. Mem. editl. bd. Infection and Immunity, 1989-98, Jour. Biol. Chemistry, 1995-2000; editor Infection and Immunity, 1998—; contbr. articles to profl. jours. Recipient Am. Inst. Chemists award, 1975, DA Commrs. Spl. Citation, 1989. Mem. AAAS, Am. Acad. Microbiology, Am. Soc. Microbiology (internat. activities com., pub. and sci. affairs bd. 1989-92, councilor divsn. B 1999), Phi Beta Kappa. Achievements include patents for process for isolation of the B oligomer of pertussis toxin; process for the purification of a 69,000 da outer membrane protein of Bordetella pertussis. Office: Ctr for Biologics Eval 8800 Rockville Pike Bldg 29 Bethesda MD 20892-0001 Business E-Mail: burns@cber.fda.gov.

BURNS, EDWARD J., JR., actor, film director; b. Valley Stream, N.Y., Jan. 29, 1968; s. Edward Sr. and Molly Burns; m. Christy Turlington, June 7, 2003; 1 child. BA, Hunter Coll. Entrepreneur Irish Twin Prodn. Co. Actor, dir., writer (films) The Brothers McMullen, 1995 (Jury Spl. prize Deauville Film Festival, 1995, Ind. Spirit award, 1995, Nova award, 1995, Grand Jury prize Sundance Film Festival, 1995), She's the One, 1996, No Looking Back, 1998, Sidewalks of New York, 2001; actor: (films) Saving Private Ryan, 1998, Any Given Sunday, 1999, 15 Minutes, 2001, Life or Something Like It, 2002, Confidence, 2003, The River King, 2005, A Sound of Thunder, 2005; actor, dir. (films) Looking for Kitty, 2004, writer, actor, prodr., dir. Ash Wednesday, 2002, writer, prodr. (TV series) The Fighting Fitzgeralds, 2001, writer (films) Flight of the Phoenix, 2004. Recipient ShoWest award for Screenwriter of Yr., 1996.*

BURNS, EDWARD MORTON, II, lawyer; b. Waynesboro, Va., Aug. 19, 1947; s. Edward Morton and Sara Frances (Lafferty) B.; m. Gale Hiserman, June 21, 1971 (div. Oct. 1991); children: Kelly, Gregory; m. Sherrie Lee Cupp, June 19, 1993; children: Matthew, Grayson. BA with high honors, U. Va., 1969, JD, 1972. Bar: Ga. 1972, Va. 1974. Assoc. Sutherland, Asbill & Brennan, Atlanta, 1972-74; ptnr. Poindexter, Burns & Marks, Waynesboro, 1974-89; pvt. practice, Waynesboro, 1989—. Mem. adv. bd. Suntrust Bank, Staunton, Va. Chmn., mem. Waynesboro Area Com., 1976—. Mem. Va. State

Bar, Va. Trial Lawyers Assn., Augusta County Bar Assn. (pres. 1994-95), Kiwanis (past pres., bd. dirs. Waynesboro). Democrat. Baptist. Office: 2611 W Main St Ste 5 Waynesboro VA 22980-1600 E-mail: burnsp@cfw.com.

BURNS, SISTER ELIZABETH MARY, hospital administrator; b. Estherville, Iowa, Mar. 3, 1927; d. Bernard Aloysius and Viola Caroline (Brennan) B. Diploma in Nursing, St. Joseph Mercy Sch. Nursing, Sioux City, Iowa, 1952; BS in Nursing Edn, Mercy Coll., Detroit, 1957; M.Sc. in Nursing, Wayne State U., 1958; Ed.D., Columbia U., 1969. Joined Sisters of Mercy, Roman Cath. Ch., 1946; nursing supr. Mercy Med. Center, Dubuque, Iowa, 1952-55; supr. orthopedics and urology St. Joseph Mercy Hosp., Sioux City, 1955-56; dir. Sch. Nursing, 1958-63; chmn. dept. nursing Mercy Coll. of Detroit, 1963-73; dir. health services Sisters of Mercy, Province of Detroit, 1973-77; pres., chief exec. officer Marian Health Center, Sioux City, 1977-87; sabbatical leave, 1988. Coord. life planning Sisters of Mercy, 1989-90, mem. province adminstrv. team, 1990-98; cons. Trinity Health, 2001—. Bd. dirs. Mercy Sch. Nursing of Detroit, 1968-77, Mercy H.S., Farmington Hills, Mich., 2000—; mem. exec. com. Greater Detroit Area Hosp. Coun., 1973-77; trustee St. Mary Coll., Omaha, 1981-82, Briar Cliff Coll., Sioux City, 1981-87, Battle Creek Health Sys., 1998-2000, 02-04, Mercy Med. Ctr., Sioux City, Iowa, 2001—; chmn. Mercy Health Adv. Coun., 1978-80. Mem. Western Iowa League for Nursing (pres. 1960-62), Nat. League for Nursing, Sisters of Mercy Shared Svcs. Coordinating Com., Cath. Hosp. Assn. (trustee 1977-80), Sisters of Mercy Health Corp. (trustee 1988-90, governance coord. 1998-2001), Mercy Health Svcs. (chair bd. 1990-95, membership bd. 1995-98, historian 1998-2004). Address: 28554 Eleven Mile Farmington MI 48336-1507 Business E-Mail: eburns@mercydetroit.org.

BURNS, ELIZABETH MURPHY, media executive; b. Superior, Wis., Dec. 4, 1945; d. Morgan and Elizabeth (Beck) Murphy; m. Richard Ramsey Burns, June 24, 1984. Student, U. Ariz., 1963-67. Promotion and programming sec. Sta. KGUN-TV, Tucson, 1967-68; programming and traffic sec. Sta. KFMB-TV, San Diego, 1968-69; owner, operator Sta. KKAR, Pomona, Calif., 1970-73; co-owner, pres. Evening Telegram Co. (parent co. Murphy Stas.); pres. Morgan Murphy Stas., Madison, Wis., 1976—. Bd. dirs. Nat. Guardian Life Ins. Co., Republic Bank, Nat. Assn. Broadcasters, various media stas. and corps. Mem. Wis. Broadcasters Assn., Madison Club, Northland Country Club (Duluth), Boulders Country Club (Carefree, Ariz.), Bishop's Bay Country Club, Silverleaf Golf Club (Scottsdale, Ariz.). Roman Catholic. Avocations: golf, travel. Home: 180 Paine Farm Rd Duluth MN 55804-2609 Office: Sta WISC-TV 7025 Raymond Rd Madison WI 53719-5053 Personal E-mail: emb@embtv.com.

BURNS, FRANCIS RAYMOND, medical association administrator, researcher; b. Ogden, Utah, Oct. 13, 1935; s. Gerald Eugene and Lucy Marie (Sargent) B.; m. Marilyn McDonald, Feb. 15, 1959 (div. Sept. 1968); children: Lawrence R., John W.; m. Lucia Esperanza Gaitan, Sept. 19, 1993; 1 child, Francis Leonard. AA, San Francisco City Coll., 1961; BA, San Francisco State U., 1968, postgrad., 1968-72; MA, Calif. State U., 2001. Dir. Biofeedback Clinic Noogenesis Inc., San Francisco, 1968—, dir. clinic, head R&D, 1968—, dir., pres., 1968—. Inventor in field. Vol. coord. San Francisco Neighborhood Renovation Group, 1972-74. With USN, 1953-56. Nominated Fulbright fellow, 2001. Avocations: gardening, camping, travel, innovative research, reading. Office: Noogenesis Inc Ste 102 1301 Ignacio Valley Rd Walnut Creek CA 94598

BURNS, GEORGE FRANKLIN, archivist, retired English language educator; b. Milan, Aug. 17, 1921; s. George Franklin Burns and Pearle Barbee Katherine; m. Mary John Wade, Aug. 24, 1968 (dec. 1999); 1 stepchild, Scott Lockwood II. BA, Cumberland U., 1942, JD, 1944; MA, George Peabody Coll., 1967; PhD, Vanderbilt U., 1973. Reporter Wilson County News, Lebanon, Tenn., 1942—43; assoc. editor Lebanon Dem., 1943—66; staff corr. Nashville Banner, 1948—65; reviewer lit. page The Tennessean, Nashville, 1962—77, columnist, 1980—81; prof. English and pub. rels. dir. Cumberland U., Lebanon, 1959—63, 1966—74; faculty Tenn. Technol. U., Cookeville, 1974—90; emeritus prof. Cumberland U., Lebanon, 1989—, English archivist, 1991—. Historian, editor Tenn. Commn. for Commemoration of 50th Anniversary of 2d Army Tenn. Maneuvers, 1993—95; founder Vol. State Athletic Conf., 1947. Author: (critical book) Mr. Faulkner in Tennessee, 1986, 5 books on Tenn. history; contbr. Tennessee Encyclopedia, 1998. Cir. Dem. Nat. Com., 1999—; chair Wilson County Libr. Bd., 1956; sec. Regional Planning Commn., 1950—60. Recipient Disting. Svc. award, Jaycees, 1952, C. of C., 1958. Mem.: MLA (life), History Assocs. (past pres.), Rotary (Paul Harris award), Sigma Alpha Epsilon. Democrat. Presbyterian. Avocations: photography, travel. Home: 1809 Andover Dr Garland TX 75041 Office: Cumberland U Archives PO Box 1415 Lebanon TN 37088

BURNS, GLENN RICHARD, dentist; b. Marietta, Ohio, Mar. 23, 1951; s. Alphas Gale Burns and Elma June (Sayres) George; m. Linda Edith Bailey, June 10, 1978; children: Geoffrey William, Katharine May. BS in Zoology, Ohio U., 1973; DDS, Ohio State U., 1980. Gen. practice dentistry, Lancaster, Ohio, 1980—. Bd. dirs. Lancaster YMCA, Fairfield County, 1985-91; Presbyn. elder. Served to sgt. U.S. Army, 1973-77. Fellow Acad. Gen. Dentistry, 1991. Fellow Pierre Fauchard Acad.; mem. ADA, Ohio Dental Assn., Hocking Valley Dental Soc. (chmn. children's dental health month 1983-86, v.p. 1991, pres. 1993), Acad. Gen. Dentistry, Christian Dental Soc., Aircraft Owners and Pilots Assn., Flying Dentist Assn., Am. Bonanza Soc., Pilots for Christ Internat., Lifeline Pilots, Kiwanis (v.p. 1988, 1st v.p. 1989, pres. 1990), Xi Psi Phi (v.p. 1984-88, pres. 1988-92). Republican. Avocations: golf, reading, flying, photography. Home: 3931 Mudhouse Rd NE Lancaster OH 43130-8716 Office: 208 N Columbus St Lancaster OH 43130-3005

BURNS, GRANT FRANCIS, librarian, editor; b. Owosso, Mich., June 18, 1947; s. Francis M. and Marie A. (Olsen) B.; m. Stephanie Winston Voight, Feb. 4, 1972; children: Andrea, Steven. BA in Social Sci., Mich. State U., 1969; AM in English, U. Mich., 1973, MLS, 1976. Ref. libr. U. Mich., Flint, 1977—, asst. dir. Thompson Libr., 2001—. Author: The Atomic Papers, 1984, The Sports Pages, 1987, Affordable Housing, 1989, The Nuclear Present, 1992, Librarians in Fiction, 1998, Email User's Handbook, 2002, Railroad in American Fiction, 2005; contbr. articles to profl. jours. Avocations: reading, gardening. Home: 621 Kedzie St East Lansing MI 48823-3535 Office: Thompson Libr U Mich Flint MI 48502 E-mail: gfburns@umich.edu.

BURNS, HEATHER LEE, management consultant; b. Worcester, Mass., Jan. 11, 1951; d. Harry Warren and Priscilla (Howard) B. BA with distinction, magna cum laude, Colby Coll., 1973; M in Community Planning, U. R.I., 1975. Jr. planner then sr. planner Met. Area Planning Coun., Boston, 1975-77; from cons. to sr. v.p. Booz, Allen and Hamilton, Bethesda, 1977—; COO, Women's Way, Phila., 1992-93. Adj. instr. U. Pa. Fels Ctr. of Govt. Contbr. articles to profl. jours. Avocations: foreign languages, athletics, music.

BURNS, H(ERBERT) MICHAEL, health care executive, director; b. Toronto, Ont., Can., June 19, 1937; s. Charles Folwer Williams and Janet Mary (Wilson) B.; m. Susan P. Cathers, Dec. 23, 1980; children: Charles F.M., Janet Michelle. Student, Cornell U., Trinity Coll. Sch., Port Hope, Can. With Nesbitt Burns (and predecessor cos.), 1958-77; dep. chmn., bd. dirs. Extendicare Inc. Pres., treas. Kingfield Investments Ltd. and assoc. subs.; bd. dirs. Algoma Ctrl. Corp., Landmark Global Fin. Inc. Past pres. Royal Agrl. Winter Fair; bd. trustees Trinity Coll. Sch., Olympic Trust Can.; chancellor Renison Coll., U. Waterloo, Can.; chmn. adv. bd. Can. Fedn. for AIDS Rsch. Mem. Toronto Club, Kappa Alpha. Avocations: recreation, farming. Home: 1314 King Vaughan Rd Maple ON Canada L6A 2A5 Office: Extendicare Inc 3000 Steeles Ave E Ste 300 Markham ON Canada L3R 9W2

BURNS, IKUKO KAWAI, artist; b. Tokyo, Jan. 1, 1936; came to U.S., 1959, naturalized, 1965; d. Ichiro and Asa (Sato) Kawai; m. Padraic Burns, Oct. 19, 1959; children: Kenneth C., Amelia P., Margaret A. BA, Yamagata U., 1958; postgrad., Sch. Mus. Fine Arts, 1961-64. Announcer Hokkaido Broadcasting Co., Sapporo, Japan, 1958-59; instr. Japanese Yale U., New Haven, 1960; rsch. assoc. Harvard U. Edwin Reischauer Inst., 1998—. Foundry asst. David Phillips Bronze Art Casting, Somerville, Mass., 1980—; lectr. U. Mass., Boston, 1982-83. Exhibited Gallery 355, Bentley Coll. Gallery, 1979, Copley Soc. Boston, 1980, 95, Fed. Res. Bank, John Hancock, Boston City Hall, 1981, Yamagata Matsuzakaya Gallery, 1985, Japan Soc. Boston, Inc., 1985, City Hall Gallery, Sapparo, Japan, 1987, Wako Gallery, Ginza, Tokyo, 1987, 90, Fed. Res. Bank Gallery, Boston, 1988, Art Complex Mus., Duxbury, Mass., 1990, Chinese Cultural Inst., Boston, 1991, (group show) Mass. Hort. Soc., 1992, Seibu Dept. Store, Akarenga Hall, Japan, 1993, Hera Gallery, R.I., 1994, Ohnuma Fine Arts Gallery, Japan, 1996, Gallery Okuda Internat., Washington, 1997, Honen-in, Kyoto, Japan, 2005; prin. works include Hopkins Meml. plaque Dartmouth Coll., Hanover, NH, standing figure Pres. Vigdis Finrbogadottir, Reykjavik, 1992, Yamagata City Hall, Japan, Meml. plaque Kagashka, Can., Tobishima Design, NY, Hironaka Inst., Tokyo, 1993, Yamagata Old State House, Japan, 1994, Honenin, Kyuto, Tokyo, 2005. Mem. Copley Soc. Boston, Asian-Am. Artist Assn., Japanese Assn. Greater Boston, Japan Soc. Boston (bd. dirs. 1980-), Mass./Hokkaido Sister Assn. (v.p. 1998-). Home: 9 Downing Rd Brookline MA 02445-2114 Studio: 9 Downing Rd Brookline MA 02445-2114 Business E-Mail: padburns@bu.edu.

BURNS, IVAN ALFRED, grocery products and industrial company executive; b. Leamington Spa, England, Jan. 18, 1935; s. Cecil Ivan and Dorothy Constance (Mote) B.; m. Angela Loeffel, May 16, 1959; children: Pauline Cecile, Charla Cheyney, Claudine. BS, Coventry Coll., 1958. Various positions Deere & Co., Moline, Ill., 1969-73; dir. internat. ACF Industries Inc., N.Y.C., 1973-75, v.p., 1975-81, pres., COO, 1981-84, chmn., CEO, 1983-90; dir. CPC Internat. Inc., Englewood Cliffs, NJ, 1985-87, pres. corn refining divsn., 1987-90, exec. v.p. adminstrn., 1987—; pres., dir. Picca Enterprises, Inc., New Canaan, Conn., 1984-96. Bd. dirs. Continental Corp., N.Y.C. Patentee valve, 1980. Bd. dirs. United Way, New York, 1984-85; mem. bus. adv. bd. Northwestern U., 1983-92. Mem. Conf. Bd. Republican. Mem. Ch. of England. Avocations: horse breeding, collecting netsukes, martial arts. Home and Office: 57 Deer Park Rd New Canaan CT 06840

BURNS, JAMES MILTON, retired educator; b. Coal City, Ind., Feb. 22, 1922; s. Ray L. and N. Eugenie (Pickett) B.; m. Thomasina Ciofalo, Aug. 22, 1970. MusB, Manhattan Sch. Music, 1949, MusM, 1953; EdD, Fairleigh Dickinson U., 1984. Tchr. music Atlantic City Bd. Edn., 1968-92. Researcher acoustics of band instruments.

BURNS, JAMES W., academic administrator, researcher, consultant; s. Wesley and Zelda Burns; m. Suzanne M. Barnell. Masters, No. Ariz. U., 1985, Doctorate, 1990. Dir. grad. studies MNU, Olathe, Kans., 1995—2001; dir. grad. sch. Calif. State U., Turlock, 2002—04, dean grad. sch., 2004—. Tchr. edn. reform task force US Dept. Edn., Nat. Assn. Colls. Tchr. Edn., Topeka; moderator Olathe Unified Sch. Bd. Candidate Debates, 1996; mem. Policy and Procedures com. Kans. State Bd. Edn., Topeka, 1998—2001, mem. Tchr. of Yr. Selection com., 1998—2001; exec. com. Kans. Assn. Colls. Tchr. Edn., Topeka, 1998—2001. Named Alumnus of Yr., MidAm. Nazarene U., 1996; Internat. Program Devel. grantee, Henry Luce Found., 2000, Program Planning and Implementation grantee, Ford Found., 2003—05, Devel. grantee, Alfred P. Sloan Found., 2003—05. Mem.: Coun. Grad. Schs. (Program Devel. grants 2003—05), Western Assn. Grad. Schs., Phi Kappa Phi (life; sec., treas. 2004). Avocations: music, art, travel, photography. Office: Calif State U 801 W Monte Vista Ave Turlock CA 95382

BURNS, JAMES WILLIAM, financial executive; b. Winnipeg, Man., Can., Dec. 27, 1929; s. Charles William and Helen Gladys (Mackay) B.; children: James F.C., Martha J., Alan W. B in Commerce, U. Man., 1951; MBA, Harvard U., 1953, LLD (hon.), 1988. With Great-West Life Assurance Co., 1953—, dir., 1970, pres., CEO, 1971-79, chmn., 1979—92; pres. Power Corp. Can., 1979-86, dep. chmn., 1986—2002; chmn., CEO Power Fin. Corp., 1986-90. Bd. dirs. Investors Group Gt.-West Life Assurance Co., Gt.-West Lifeco, Inc., Gt.-West Life and Annuity Ins. Co., London Life Ins. Co., London Ins. Group, Inc.; dir. emeritus Power Corp. Can., Power Fin. Corp. Founding dir. Man. Mus. Man and Nature, Coun. Bus. & Arts; past chmn. Conf. Bd. Can.; mem. Gov.'s Coun., Shaw Festival. Named Officer of the Order of Can.; Hon. col. Queen's Own Cameron Highlanders of Can. Mem. St. Charles Country Club, Man. Club, Toronto Club, Mount-Royal Club. Office: Power Corp Can 2600 One Lombard Pl Winnipeg MB Canada R3BOX5

BURNS, JOHN JOSEPH, pharmacology educator; b. Flushing, NY, Oct. 8, 1920; s. Thomas F. and Katherine (Kane) B. BS, Queens Coll., 1942; MA, Columbia U., 1948, PhD, 1950. With lab. chem. pharmacology Nat. Heart Inst., 1950-60, dep. chief lab., 1957-60; head sec. clin. pharmacology, also adj. asst. prof. biochemistry NYU research service Goldwater Meml. Hosp., Welfare Island, N.Y., 1950-57; dir. research pharmacodynamics div. Wellcome Research Labs., Burroughs Wellcome & Co. (U.S.A.) Inc., Tuckahoe, N.Y., 1960-66; v.p. for research Hoffmann-LaRoche Inc., Nutley, N.J., 1967-84. Vis. prof. pharmacology Albert Einstein Coll. Medicine, 1960-68, Cornell U. Med. Coll., 1996—; adj. prof. Cornell U. Med. Coll., 1969-84, Rockefeller U., 1984-94; adj. mem. Roche Inst. Molecular Biology, 1984-96; cons. pharmacology and toxicology programs NIH; chmn. com. problems drug safety Drug Rsch. Bd., 1965-72. Contbr. articles to profl. jours. Served with AUS, 1944-46. Fellow Am. Inst. Chemists; mem. Inst. Medicine, Nat. Acad. Scis., N.Y. Acad. Scis. (v.p. 1964-65), Am. Soc. Pharmacology and Exptl. Therapeutics (pres. 1972-73), Am. Soc. Biol. Chemists, Am. Inst. Nutrition, Am. Coll. Neuropsychopharmacology, Internat. Union Pharmacology (pres. 1975-78) Achievements include research in metabolism drugs, vitamins and carbohydrates. Home: 331 Lansdowne Westport CT 06880-5651

BURNS, JOHN JOSEPH, JR., financial and insurance holding company executive; b. Cambridge, Mass., June 27, 1931; s. John Joseph and Alice (Blake) Burns; m. Barbara Ann Miller, Oct. 18, 1958; children: John J. Burns III, Christine, Gregory, Timothy, Jennifer. BS in Fin., Boston Coll., 1953; MBA, Harvard U., 1955. Asso. buying dept. and arbitrage dept. Goldman Sachs & Co., 1957-63; assoc. N.Y. Securities, 1963-67, gen. ptnr., 1968; v.p. fin., dir. Alleghany Corp., NYC, 1968-77, pres., dir., 1977—, mem. exec. com., 1977—, CEO, 1992—, vice chmn., dir., 2005—. With USN, 1955-57. Mem.: Links Club. Roman Catholic. Office: Alleghany Corp 161 Cherry St New Canaan CT 06840 E-mail: jburns@alleghany.com.

BURNS, JOSEPH ARTHUR, planetary science educator; b. N.Y.C., Mar. 22, 1941; s. John Driscoll and Genevieve Mary (McCarthy) B.; m. Judith Ann Klein, July 1, 1967; children: Patrick M., Caitlin M. BS, Webb Inst., Glen Cove, N.Y., 1962; PhD, Cornell U., 1966. Asst. prof. Cornell U., Ithaca, NY, 1966-67, 68-74, assoc. prof., 1974-81, prof., 1981-94; Irving Porter Church prof. engring. and astronomy, 1994—; chmn. theoretical and applied mechs. Cornell U., Ithaca, NY, 1987-93, vice provost phys. scis. and engring., 2003—; NRC rsch. assoc. NASA Goddard Space Ctr., Greenbelt, Md., 1967-68; NAS exch. fellow Inst. Geophysics, Moscow, 1973; sr. scientist NASA Ames Rsch. Ctr., Mountain View, Calif., 1975-76, 82-83. Astronome titulaire Observatoire de Paris, France, 1979, 84; vis. prof. astronomy U. Calif., Berkeley, 1982-83; vis. prof. planetary sci. U. Ariz., Tucson, 1989-90; mem. space and earth scis. adv. com. NASA, 1983-87, solar sys. exploration com., 1988-92, NAS space studies bd., 1989-95, chair NAS com. planet exploration, 1992-95, mem. solar sys. decadal panel NRC, 2001-02. Author 160 rsch. articles, 1966—; editor: Planetary Satellites, 1977, Satellites, 1986; editor Icarus-Internat. Jour. of Solar Sys. Studies, 1979-97; bd. rev. editors Sci., 2000—. Recipient various rsch. awards and grants NSF, 1976-86, 97, NASA, 1976—, NATO, 1998-2000, N.Y. Coun. Arts, 1972, NASA Sci. Achievement awards, 1997, 98, 2000. Fellow AAAS, Am. Geophys. Union; mem. Internat. Acad. Astronautics, Russian Acad. Sci., Am. Astron. Soc. (chmn. planetary scis. 1983-84, chmn. dynamical astronomy 2000-2001, v.p. 2001-04, Masursky Prize 1994), Internat. Astron. Union (mem. solar sys. com. 1986-89, v.p. solar system 1996-99, v.p. celestial mechanics 2003—). Office: Cornell U Kimball Hall Dept Astronomy Ithaca NY 14853 E-mail: jab16@cornell.edu.

BURNS, JOSEPH M., economist; b. N.Y.C., N.Y., Aug. 2, 1938; s. Arthur F. and Helen (Bernstein) B.; m. Ellen N. Herbst, Sept. 3, 1992; children: Stephen Juran, Rebecca Anne. AB, Swarthmore Coll., 1960; MA, U. Chgo., 1961, PhD, 1967. Economist rsch. dept. Fed. Reserve Bank N.Y., N.Y.C., 1961-62; asst. prof. dept. econs. UCLA, 1966-71; assoc. prof. dept. econs. Rice U., Houston, 1971-74; sr. economist, dep. dir. monetary rsch. office asst. sec. for internat. affairs U.S. Dept. Treasury, Washington, 1974-76; sr. economist, assoc. dir. rsch. div. econs. and edn. Commodity Futures Trading Commn., Washington, 1976-79; sr. economist antitrust div. U.S. Dept. Justice, Washington, 1979-2000. Vis. assoc. prof. dept. econ. Stanford U., Calif., 1973—74; professorial lectr. fin. dept. Georgetown U. Sch. Bus., Washington, 1979, 84. Author: Acctg. Standards and Internat. Fin., 1976, A Treatise on Markets, 1979; contbr. articles to profl. jours. Fellow, Earhart Found, 1960—61, 1963—65, Ford Found., 1965—66, Hoover Instn., 1973—74. Mem.: Am. Econ. Assn. (census adv. com. 1972—75). Personal E-mail: jmburns88@msn.com.

BURNS, JURATE, library director; b. Schwabisch Gmund, Bavaria, Mar. 24, 1948; arrived in US, 1949; d. Leonardas and Emilija Montvidas Kutkus; m. Matthew Wallace Burns, Dec. 21, 1968; children: Matthew Jr., Jeffrey. BA in theatre, Mich. State U., 1969; MLS, U. Ala., 1975. English reading tchr. Anne Arundol County, Md., 1970—72; speech, English tchr. Tuscaloosa, Ala., 1972—75; real estate broker Destin, Fla., 1981—99; libr. dir., 1999—2004. Bd. pres. Panhandle Libr. Access Network, Panama City Beach, 2004. Mem. Choctawhatchee Basin Alliance, 2000—01. Mem.: ALA, Pub. Libr. Assn., Fla. Libr. Assn., Beta Phi Mu. Roman Catholic. Office: Destin Libr Destin FL 32541 Office Phone: 850-837-8572. Office Fax: 850-837-5248. E-mail: jburns@cityofdestin.com.

BURNS, KENNETH LAUREN, filmmaker, historian; b. Bklyn., July 29, 1953; s. Robert Kyle and Lyla Smith (Tupper) B.; children: Sarah, Lilly. BA, Hampshire Coll., 1975; LHD (hon.), Bowdoin Coll., 1991; LittD (hon.), Amherst Coll., 1991; LHD (hon.), U. N.H.; DFA, Franklin Pierce Coll.; LittD (hon.), Notre Dame Coll., Manchester, N.H.; HHD (hon.), Coll. of St. Joseph, Rutland, Vt.; LHD (hon.), Springfield Coll. Ill., Pace U.; PhD (hon.), CUNY. Pres., owner Florentine Films, Walpole, N.H., 1975—. Films include Brooklyn Bridge, 1981 Christopher award 1963, Erik Barnouw prize Hist. Films), The Shakers: Hands to Work, Hearts to God, 1984 (CINE Golden Eagle award 1984), Huey Long, 1985 (Silver Baton award Dupont-Columbia Journalism 1988), The Statue of Liberty, 1985 (Christopher award 1987, CINE Golden Eagle award, Acad. award nomination 1986), Thomas Hart Benton, 1988 (CINE Golden Eagle award 1988, Golden Apple award Nat. Ednl. Film Festival 1989), The Congress, 1988 (CINE Golden Eagle award 1989, Red Ribbon Am. Film Festival 1989), The Civil War, 1990 (Emmy award for outstanding information series 1991, for outstanding individual achievement, writing 1991, CINE Gold Eagle award, Lincoln prize Gettysburg Coll. 1991, Dartmouth Film award 1990, Bell I. Wiley award Civil War Round Table, N.Y., 1991, D.W. Griffiths award, Christopher award, Peabody award 1990, Gabriel award 1991, People's Choice award 1991, Humanitas award 1991, Charles Frankel prize NEH 1991, Grammy award (2) 1992, numerous others), Radio Pioneers, 1981, Baseball (Outstanding Informational Series Emmy award), The West, 1996 (Erik Barnouw prize 1997), Thomas Jefferson, 1997, Lewis and Clark: The Journey of the Corps of Discovery, 1997, Frank Lloyd Wright, 1998, Not for Ourselves Alone: The Story of Elizabeth Cady Stanton & Susan B. Anthony, 1999, Jazz, 2000, Mark Twain, 2001, Horatio's Drive: America's First Road Trip, 2003; Unforgivable Blackness: The Rise and Fall of Jack Johnson, 2004 (Emmy nom., outstanding directing for nonfiction programming, 2005); author: (with others) Centennial, 1986, (with Amy Stechler Burns) The Shakers: Hands to Work, Hearts to God, 1987, (with Geoffrey Ward and Ric Burns) The Civil War: An Illustrated History, 1990, Empire of the Air, 1992: retrospectives Smithsonian Instn., 1991, Walker Arts Ctr., Mpls., 1991, Pub. Broadcasting Svc., 1991-92, (with Geoffrey C. Ward) Baseball, 1994, (with Dayton Funcan) Lewis & Clark: The Journey of the Corps of Discovery, 1998. Trustee Hampshire Coll., Amherst, Mass., 1992—, N.H. Humanities Coun.; bd. dirs. MacDowell Colony, Peterborough, N.H. Mem. Acad. Motion Picture, Arts and Scis., Soc. Am. Historians, N.H. Humanities Coun. (trustee), Mass. Hist. Soc. (corr.). Home and Office: Maple Grove Rd P O Box 613 Walpole NH 03608*

BURNS, KEVIN J., computer software services executive; b. 1949; m. Nancy Burns. BA, Ohio State U.; MA, U. Colo., 1973. With Cincom Syss., Inc., Cin., 1972-79; founder, pres., CEO Intersolv, Inc. (formerly Sage Software), Rockville, Md., 1982—96, chmn. bd., 1996. Bd. dirs. NFR Security, interim CEO, 2002—03; bd. dirs. Vocus, Managed Objects, Cyveillance, APTSoft, Panacya, Intellitactics. Office: Lazard Technology Partners 48th Fl 30 Rockefeller Plz New York NY 10020 Office Phone: 212-632-6000. Office Fax: 212-332-8677.

BURNS, KEVIN MICHAEL, video editor; b. Boston; s. William Leslie and Frances Mary Burns; m. Marie Kashan, Nov. 15, 1991 (div.);1 child, M. Reneé; stepchild, Catherine Ann Taylor; life ptnr. Isabel Taylor. AS in Surg. Tech., Baylor U., 1969; BA, Bridgewater State Tchrs. Coll., 1976; MS (hon.), Yale U., 1977. Sr. employment interviewer Mass. Divsn. Employment Security, Quincy, 1978; owner Trackside Restaurant, ME; vocat. rehab. counselor Mass. Rehab. Commn., Hyannis, Mass., 1978-79; mktg. cons. Stephi-Volt Corp., Chambersburg, PA, 1989-1996; local dir. Save Children Found., Louisville, 1999-2000; assignment editor Sta. WHAS-TV, Louisville, 2000—. Mem. U.S. Civil Def. Org., Hull, Mass., 1976-79. Sgt. USMC, 1969-70. Decorated Purple Heart, Bronze Star; recipient Emmy, 1999. Mem. Ky. Cols. (hon.). Democrat. Roman Catholic. Avocations: biking, swimming, sailing. E-mail: marine01usa@hotmail.com.

BURNS, LAWRENCE D., automotive executive; B in Mech. Engring., GM Inst.; M in Engring, Pub. Policy, U. Mich.; PhD in Civil Engring., U. Calif., Berkeley. Rsch. devel. staff GM Corp., 1969—, v.p. rsch., devel. and strategic planning, 1998—. Mem. GM Automotive Strategy Bd., Automotive Strategy Bd. Mem.: U. Mich. Ctr. Hearing Problems (bd. mem.), Deafness Rsch. Found. (bd. mem.). Office: GM Corp 300 Renaissance Ctr PO Box 300 Detroit MI 48265-3000*

BURNS, LESLIE KAYE, artist; b. Columbus, Miss., Sept. 21, 1953; d. Fayette Charles Jr. and Mary Theo (Wright) B. BFA in Printmaking/Advt. Art cum laude, Miss. U. for Women, 1975; MFA in Photography/Printmaking, U. Ala., 1978. Multi-image prodr., photographer Pitluk Group Advt. Agy., San Antonio, 1981-87; dir. media prodn. Inst. Texan Cultures U. Tex., San Antonio, 1987-2001. Artist: From a Girl to a Woman: Necole's Fifteenth Birthday, 1999 (47th Ann. Columbus Internat. Film and Video Festival honoree, Assn. Women in Comms. San Antonio Profl. chpt. award of merit for outstanding achievement in field of comms. 1999), Tex. Folklife Festival: 30 Pub. Svc. Announcement (Tex. Festivals and Events Assn. Mktg. award for pub. svc. ad or ad 2000). Recipient mktg. award Tex. Festivals and Events Assn., 1998. Mem. Am. Assn. Museums. Avocation: collecting folk and fine art.

BURNS, M. MICHELE, energy executive, former air transportation executive; B in bus. adminstrn. summa cum laude, M. Accountancy, U. Ga. Mgmt. Arthur Anderson, 1981-84, mgr., 1984-91, ptnr., 1991-99; v.p. corp. taxes, treas. Delta Airlines, 1999, sr. v.p. fin., treas., 2000, exec. v.p., CFO, 2000—04, Mirant Corp., Atlanta, 2004—. Mem. bd. dirs. Wal-Mart Stores Inc., Cisco Systems Inc., Ivan Allen Co., Atlanta Symphony Orch. Office: Mirant Corp 1155 Perimeter Ctr W Atlanta GA 30338-5416

BURNS, MARCELLINE, retired psychologist, researcher; BA in Psychology, San Diego State U., 1955; MA, Calif. State U., L.A., 1969; PhD, U. Calif., Irvine, 1972. Co-founder So. Calif. Rsch. Inst., LA, 1973—2003, ret., 2003. Cons., expert witness alcohol and drug effects on performance, FSTs, HGN, and drug recognition; lectr. in field. Contbr. articles to profl. jours.

Recipient Public Svc. award U.S. Dept. Trans., 1993. Achievements include research on alcohol and drug effects, field sobriety tests and drug recognition. Office Phone: 805-382-4696. Business E-Mail: mburns4430@adelphia.net.

BURNS, MARVIN GERALD, lawyer; b. L.A., July 3, 1930; s. Milton and Belle (Cytron) B.; m. Barbara Irene Fisher, Aug. 23, 1953; children: Scott Douglas, Jody Lynn, Bradley Frederick. BA, U. Ariz., 1951; JD, Harvard U., 1954. Bar: Calif. 1955. Mem. Inner City Arts for Inner City Children. With AUS, 1955-56. Mem.: Beverly Hills Tennis, Sycamore Park Tennis. Home: 10350 Wilshire Blvd Ph 4 Los Angeles CA 90024-4734 Office: 9107 Wilshire Blvd Ste 800 Beverly Hills CA 90210-5533 Office Phone: 310-278-6500. Business E-Mail: mburns@lurie-zepeda.com. E-mail: burns5401@aol.com. *I believe that hard work in its time and place, play in its time and place, love, understanding and practice of the golden rule at all times, in all places, a firm belief in truth and honesty and that there is no better land, no better system, no better life than our imperfect, necessary to improve, America, leads to personal fulfillment and a better life for all.*

BURNS, MAX, former congressman; b. Millen, Ga., Nov. 8, 1948; m. Lora Dean Black, 1972; children: Andrew, Nathan. B in Indsl. Engring., Ga. Tech. U., 1973; M in Bus. Info. Sys., Ga. State U., 1977, PhD in Bus. Adminstrn., 1987. Mgr. Oxford Industries, N.Am. Mission Bd. So. Bapt. Conv.; prof. info. sys. Ga. So. U. Coll. Bus. Adminstrn., Statesboro; congressman 12 Dist. Ga. U.S. Ho. Reps., 2003—05. Instr., Australia, New Zealand, Republic of Korea; cons. Gulfstream Aerospace and Grinnell Corp. Mem. CSRA Regional Devel. Ctr.; former chmn. regional 1 adv. coun. Ga. Dept. Industry, Trade, and Tourism; mem. Screven County Commn., 1993—98, chmn., 1997—98; deacon Jackson Bapt. Ch.; bd. dirs. Screven County Livestock Assn., Cmty. Christian Sch. Bd., Ga. Limousin Assn. 1st lt. USAR. Republican.

BURNS, MELINDA, journalist; BA in English, Harvard U.; MS in Education, U. Southern Calif. Reporter L.A. Times, 1984—85; with Santa Barbara News Press, 1985—, sr. writer, regional affaris, housing, transportation, Latino issues. Recipient Science Journalism award, AAAS, 2004. Achievements include several awards for reporting on farm-workers and the environment. Office: Santa Barbara News Press 715 Anacapa St Santa Barbara CA 93101 Address: Santa Barbara News Press PO Box 1359 Santa Barbara CA 93102 Office Phone: 805-564-5262. Office Fax: 805-966-6258. Business E-Mail: mburns@newspress.com.

BURNS, MICHAEL FELIX, lawyer; 3 children. BA in History, Calif. State U., Long Beach, 1979; JD, Whittier Coll., 1982. Bar: Calif. 1983, U.S. Dist. Ct. (ctrl. dist.) Calif. 1983, U.S. Ct. Appeals (9th cir.) 1983, U.S. Supreme Ct. 1992. Dep. dist. atty. Riverside County Dist. Atty.'s Office, Riverside, Calif., 1984-89. Asst. mng. editor Whittier Law Rev., 1982. Mem. Sigma Alpha Epsilon. Office: 3842 Myers Rd Riverside CA 92503

BURNS, MICHAEL J., automotive executive; b. Monticello, Ind., Mar. 1, 1952; B of Mech. Engring., Kettering U., 1975; MBA, U. Pa., 1979. Ops. mgr. Delco electronics GM Corp., Singapore, 1981—85, from treas. office staff to dir. overseas fin. analysis NY, 1985—87, from head hybrid electronics ops. to v.p. vehicle sys. bus. unit Delco electronics Singapore, 1988—93, v.p. Delphi Harrison thermal sys. Lockport, NY, 1994—95, v.p., gen. mgr. Delphi Delco electronics sys., 1996—98, group v.p., pres. Europe divsn. Zurich, Switzerland, 1998—2004; chmn. pres. & CEO Dana Corp., Toledo, 2004—. Supervisory bd. Adam Opel AG; bd. dirs. Saab Automobile AB; key exec. Wharton Sch.-U. Pa. Mem.: European Automobile Mfrs. Assn. (bd. dirs.), Soc. Automotive Engrs., Swiss-Am. C. of C. (bd. dirs.). Office: Dana Corporation 4500 Dorr St Toledo OH 43615*

BURNS, MICHAEL JOSEPH, operations and sales-marketing executive; b. Passaic, NJ, Feb. 18, 1943; s. Michael Joseph and Ellen Kathryn B.; m. Emma Anne, Dec. 19, 1964; children: Michael, Jeffrey, Tricia, Stephen. BA in English, William Paterson Univ., Wayne, N.J., 1964; JD, Seton Hall U., Newark, 1975. Bar: NJ 1975. Purchasing analyst Am. Brands Co., 1972-75; div. purchasing mgr. Dutch Boy Paints, NL Industries, 1975-76; v.p. purchasing Dutch Boy, Inc., 1977-78; pres., gen. mgr. Dutch Boy, Inc. (Dutch Boy coatings div.), 1978-80; pres., CEO Kroehler Mfg. Co., Naperville, Ill., 1980-88; pres., COO Rymer Co., Rolling Meadows, Ill., 1983-88; pres. Emerald Group, Lake Forest, Ill., 1989-90; pres., CEO Designer Foods, Inc., Wilmington, Del., 1990-91; chmn., pres., CEO SeaWatch Internat., Ltd., Easton, Md., 1991-99; pres., CEO Pioneer Human Svcs., Seattle, 1999—. Bd. dirs. Second Chance, 1999-, Eastside Acad., 2001-. Served to capt. USMCR, 1964-67, Vietnam. NJ State scholar; recipient Disting. Alumni award Wm. Paterson Univ. Mem. ABA, Am. Arbitration Assn. Presbyterian. Office: 7440 W Marginal Way S Seattle WA 98108-4141 Office Phone: 206-768-1990. Personal E-mail: mike.burns@p-h-s.com.

BURNS, MICHAEL THORNTON, historian, educator, farmer; b. NYC, Dec. 30, 1947; s. Frank Xavier Burns and Mary Lou DeWeese; m. Elizabeth Topham Kennan, June 8, 1986; 1 stepchild: Frank Alexander Kennan. BA summa cum laude, UCLA, 1976, MA, 1977; PhD, Yale U., 1981. Tchg. fellow Yale U., New Haven, 1978-79; vis. dir. d'etudes Ecole des Hautes Etudes, Paris, 1991; from asst. to assoc. prof. Mt. Holyoke Coll., South Hadley, Mass., 1981-93, prof. of modern European history, Dana faculty fellow, 1993—2002, prof. emeritus, 2002—; affiliate scholar Centre Coll., Danville, Ky.; owner, operator Cambus-Kenneth cattle and Thoroughbred Horse Farm, Danville, Ky., 2000—. Adv. editor Blackwell's New Perspectives, Oxford, Eng., 1995-2001, Ency. of French-Am. Rels., 2001-; cons. WGBH Western Traditions, Boston, 1986-87, The Jewish Mus., Dreyfus Affair, N.Y.C., 1987; awards panel mem. Phi Beta Kappa, Washington, 1994-95. Author: Rural Society and French Politics, 1984, Main Trends in History (rev. of G. Barraclough) 1991, Dreyfus: A Family Affair, 1992 (Phi Alpha Theta Best Book award 1993, Prix Bernard LeCache 1994), France and the Dreyfus Affair 1999. Vol. Holyoke Therapeutic Riding, Holyoke, Mass., 1992-93; bd. dirs. Five Coll. Pub. Sch. Ptnrship, Amherst, Mass., 1988-92, Bluegrass Conservancy, Lexington, Ky., 2002-, Ky. Ctr. Arts, Louisville, 2004—. Fellow Woodrow Wilson Internat. Ctr. for Scholars, Washington, 1992-93, Rockefeller Found. Humanities, N.Y., 1983-84, Tocqueville award French-Am. Found., N.Y.C., 1979-80, Fulbright award, 1979-80. Mem. Thoroughbred Club of Am., Thoroughbred Owners and Breeders, Phi Beta Kappa. Episcopalian. Avocations: horseback riding, historical preservation and land conservation. Office: Mt Holyoke Coll 50 College St South Hadley MA 01075

BURNS, MICHAEL VINCENT, assistant principal; m. Susan I. Burns, July 1, 1972; 1 child, Maureen. BS in Phys. Edn., Butler U., 1973; MS in Liberal Studies, SUNY, Stonybrook, 1978; SAS in Adminstrn., Dowling Coll., 1995. Tchr. phys. edn. East Hampton (N.Y.) Sch. Dist., 1974—2000, dean of students, 2000—01, asst. prin., 2001—. Sgt. U.S. Army, 1968—70, Vietnam. Decorated Bronze star, Purple Heart. Mem.: N.Y. State Sch. Adminstrn. Assn., Nat. Strength and Conditioning Assn., N.Y. State Assn. for Health, Phys. Edn., Recreation and Dance, East Hampton Coaches Assn. (pres.), East Hampton Tchrs. Assn. (v.p.). Democrat. Roman Catholic. Avocations: exercise, bicycling, kayaking, weightlifting. Home: 37 Eisenhower Dr East Quogue NY 11942 Office: East Hampton Unified Sch Dist 2 Long Ln East Quogue NY 11942

BURNS, NED HAMILTON, civil engineering educator; b. Magnolia, Ark., Nov. 25, 1932; s. Andrew Louis and Ila Mae (Martin) B.; m. Martha Ann Fontaine, June 11, 1955; children: Kathryn Jane, Stephanie Ann, Michael Everett. BS, U. Tex., 1954, MS, 1958; PhD, U. Ill., 1962. Registered profl. engr., Tex. Instr. U. Tex., Austin, 1957-59, asst. prof., 1962-65, assoc. prof., 1965-70, prof. civil engring., 1970-83, Zarrow Centennial prof. engring., 1983—; assoc. dean engring. for acad. affairs, 1989-93; dir. Ferguson Structural Engring. Lab., 1994-97. Rsch. asst. U. Ill., Urbana, 1959-62. Author: (with T. Y. Lin) Design of Prestressed Concrete Structures, 1981 (McGraw Hill Book of Month 1982), S.I. Version-Design of Prestressed Concrete Structures, 1982, Legend of Post-Tensioning, 2005; contbr. articles to profl. jours. With U.S. Army, 1955—57. Recipient Gen. Dynamics Tchg. award U. Tex. Coll. Engring., 1965, AMOCO Tchg. award, 1983, Martin P. Korn award for outstanding jour. paper, 1993, Blunk Meml. Professorship Tchg. award U. Tex., 1996-97; named Disting. Grad. U. Tex., 2005. Fellow: Post-Tensioning Inst. (bd. dirs. 1975, Legends award, 2005), Am. Soc. Civil Engrs.(com. chmn. 1975—, T. Y. Lin award 1994), Prestressed Concrete Inst. (com. mem. 1968-, Martin Korn award for best paper 1993, Disting. Educator award 2000); mem. NAE, NSPE (chpt. pres. 1970), Am. Concrete Inst. (bd. dirs. 1983-87, Joe Kelley award for contbns. to engring. edn. 1990, Structural Rsch. award 2005), Tex. Soc. Profl. Engring. (Young Engr. of Yr. award 1970, Travis chpt. Engr. of Yr. award 1987). Democrat. Baptist. Home: 3917 Rockledge Dr Austin TX 78731-2921 Office: U Tex Dept Civil Engring Austin TX 78712

BURNS, PADRAIC, physician, psychiatrist, psychoanalyst, educator; b. Des Moines, Aug. 31, 1929; s. Charles and Ethel P. (Bentz) B.; m. Ikuko Kawai, Oct. 19, 1959; children: Kenneth, Amelia, Margaret. BA, U. Chgo., 1948; postgrad., NYU, 1949-51; MD, Yale U., 1955. Diplomate Am. Bd. Psychiatry, 1965, Am. Bd. Child Psychiatry, 1967. Asst. prof. psychiatry Boston U., 1969-72, assoc. prof. psychiatry, 1972—. Capt. U.S. Army, 1957-59. Fellow Am. Acad. Child Psychiatry; mem. Am. Psychiat. Assn., Mass. Psychiat. Soc., Boston Psychoanalytic Soc. and Inst. Home: 9 Downing Rd Brookline MA 02445-2114 Office: 7 Orchard Rd Brookline MA 02445-2119

BURNS, PATRICK JOSEPH, writer, editor, language arts and music educator; b. Albuquerque, N.Mex., Aug. 8, 1952; s. Raymond George and Jessica E. Burns; m. Stephanie S. Gooch, May 25, 1984; children: Chanda Szalay, Corrina Jessica, Christopher Marcel, Graham Carlton. BA, U. N.Mex, Albuquerque, 1975; Post Bacc. Tchrs. Lic., U. N.Mex, Albuquerque, N. Mex., 1993; cert. univ., U. Cervera (Spain) de Lerida, 1975. Tchr. Pub. Schs., Pojoaque, Los Alamos, Taos, Santa Fe, N.Mex., 1993—; lang. arts, music and tech. tchr. Editor (annotator): In the Shadow of Los Alamos: Selected Writings of Edith Warner (Pub. by U. N.Mex Press, 2001); contbr. chpt. to book (Pub.: Frank Waters Found., Taos, 2003); composer: (songs) Indian Summer (Voted best single of the yr., N.Mex Music Industry Coalition, 1989), Honky Tonk Girls (1st Pl. N.Mex Songwriters Showcase, 1992). Mem.: Broadcast Music Inc., Nat. Assn. for Music Edn., SW Writers (assoc.).

BURNS, PATRICK OWEN, venture capital company executive; b. Yonkers, N.Y., Aug. 6, 1937; s. Edward Dermott and Anne L. (Gallagher) B.; m. Barbara Hope Van Riper, Nov. 4, 1967; children: Patrick Owen, Elizabeth Willett. AB, Dartmouth Coll., 1959; LLB cum laude, Harvard U., 1962. Bar: N.Y. 1964, U.S. Dist. Ct. (so. dist.) N.Y. 1965. Legal advisor Dept. Coops., Lesotho, 1962-63; assoc. Milbank, Tweed, Hadley & McCloy, N.Y.C., 1963-69; nat. dep. dir. Interracial Coun. for Bus. Opportunity, N.Y.C., 1969-75, acting nat. exec. dir., 1972-74; exec. v.p. Minority Equity Capital Co., Inc., N.Y.C., 1971-78, dir., 1974-85, pres., 1978-85; ptnr. Consumer Venture Group, 1985; v.p. R&D Funding Corp., 1986-97; v.p., 1st v.p., sr. v.p. Prudential Securities, 1986-97; sr. advisor Early Stage Enterprises, 1997—2002, AcrossFrontiers Internat., Inc., 1999—2002, Pharmalab, Sydney, Australia, 2002—. Bd. dirs., vice chmn. Euclid Sys. Corp.; bd. dirs. Progen Inds., Ltd., FirmView, Inc.; chmn. StablEyes, Inc.; cons. Warren Commn., 1964; mem. exec. com. SEC Govt. Bus. Forum on Small Bus. Capital Formation, 1983—85; chmn. Task Force State Capital Formation, 1984. Contbr. articles to profl. jours. Regent L.I. Coll. Hosp., 1976—, vice chmn. bd., 1981—97; trustee Continuum Health Ptnrs., Inc., 2001—, St. Luke's-Roosevelt Hosp. Ctr., 2001—, Beth Israel Med. Ctr., 2001—, Beth Israel Found., 2001—, New Cmty. Found., 1998—, Continuum Hospice Care, 2003—; pres. Friends of Bushnell-Sage Libr., Sheffield, Mass., 2002—; candidate N.Y.C. City Coun., 1969; bd. dirs. Resources for Children with Spl. Needs., Inc., 1990—, pres., 1994—; bd. dirs. Cobble Hill Health Ctr., 1976—, Nat. Ctr. Social Entrepreneurs, 1985—2002, Heights & Hill Cmty. Coun., Inc., 1992—, pres., 1999—2002; dir. New Cmty. Devel. Loan Corp., 2002—. Class of '26 fellow Dartmouth Coll. Mem. Am. Assn. Minority Enterprise Small Bus. Investment Cos. (dir. 1979-85, chmn. bd. 1983-85), Coun. Fgn. Rels., N.Y. Venture Capital Forum, Nat. Assn. Small Bus. Investment Cos. (gov. 1983-85), Sheffield (Mass.) Hist. Soc. (fin. com. 1999—). Democrat. Home: 22 Sidney Pl Brooklyn NY 11201-4607 Office: 2776 Towerview Rd Herndon VA 20171 Office Phone: 718-246-7007. Office Fax: 718-246-5964. Personal E-mail: pburns64@aol.com.

BURNS, PAUL YODER, forester, educator; b. Tulsa, Okla., July 4, 1920; s. Paul Patchin and Mary Emily (Knowles) B.; m. Kathleen Iola Chase, Dec. 4, 1942; children: Virginia B. Belland, Margaret B. Feierabend, Nancy B. McNeill. BS, U. Tulsa, 1941; M in Forestry, Yale U., 1946, PhD, 1949. Asst., assoc. prof. U. Mo., Columbia, 1948-55; prof. forestry La. State U., Baton Rouge, 1955-86, prof. emeritus of forestry, 1986-96. Dir. sch. forestry La. State U., Baton Rouge, 1955-76; commr. La. Forestry Commn., Baton Rouge, 1955-76. Editor: Forest Management in Plan & Practice, 1956, Southern Forest Soils, 1959; co-editor: Southern Forestry in Practice, 1977, Christmas Tree Production & Marketing, 1983. Pres. bd. dirs. La. State U. YMCA-YWCA, Baton Rouge, 1957-59; mem. La. Conf. Ch. Bd., Baton Rouge, 1967-73; pres. La. Coun. Human Rels., Baton Rouge, 1987-89; chair bd. dirs. The FISH Good Samaritans, Baton Rouge, 1996. Recipient Disting. Alumnus award U. Tulsa, 1974, Humanitarian award Baton Rouge Coun. Human Rels., 1984, Peacemaking award, Bienville House Ctr. for Peace, Baton Rouge, 1991, Brotherhood award Baton Rouge chpt. NCCJ, 1995. Fellow Soc. Am. Foresters, La. Soc. Am. Foresters (chmn. 1990, Disting Svc. to Forestry 1989), Phi Kappa Phi, Sigma Xi, Xi Sigma Pi. Presbyterian. Avocations: tennis, piano. Home: 2137 Cedardale Ave Baton Rouge LA 70808-2810 Office: La State Univ Sch Renewable Natural Resources Baton Rouge LA 70803-0001 Office Phone: 225-578-4204. Personal E-mail: pyburns@lycos.com.

BURNS, PETER C., science educator, engineering educator; b. Fredericton, New Brunswick, Can., Oct. 17, 1966; came to U.S., 1995; s. Carman George Burns and Ruth Joyce Linden; m. Tammy E. Chesley, 1992; children: Kelson O., Sarah V. BSc with honors, U. New Brunswick, Can., 1988; MSc in Geology, U. Western Ont., Can., 1990; PhD in Geology, U. Man., Can., 1994. Rsch. fellow U. Cambridge, England, 1994-95; post doctoral fellow U. N.Mex., 1995-96; vis. asst. prof. U. Ill., Urbana-Champaign, 1996-97; from asst. prof. to assoc. prof., dir. grad. studies U. Notre Dame, 1997-99, assoc. prof., 1999—2002, prof., 2002—, Massman chair dept. civil engring. and geol. sci., 2002—. Contbr. articles to profl. jours. Recipient Donath medal Geol. Soc. Am., 1999, award Mineral. Soc. Am., 2001. Fellow: Mineral. Soc. Am. (life MSA award 2001); mem.: Am. Chem. Soc., Mineral. Assn. Can. (councillor 1997—2005, Young Scientist medal 1998, Hawley medal 1997). Achievements include research in mineralogy and crystallography, mineralogy of nuclear waste disposal, environmental mineralogy, mineral crystal structures and crystal chemistry, mineral structure energetics, mineral paragenesis. Office: U Notre Dame 160 Fitzpatrick Engring Notre Dame IN 46556 E-mail: pburns@nd.edu.

BURNS, R. NICHOLAS (ROBERT NICHOLAS BURNS), federal agency administrator, former ambassador; b. Buffalo, Jan. 28, 1956; m. Elizabeth Baylies; 3 children. BA in European History summa cum laude, Boston Coll., 1978; MA in Internat. Econs. and Am. Fgn. Policy with distinction, Johns Hopkins Sch. Advanced Internat. Studies, 1980. Intern U.S. Embassy Nouakchott, Mauritania, 1980-81; program officer A.T. Internat., 1981-82; vice consul and staff asst. to the Amb. in Cairo, Egypt, 1983-85; polit. officer Am. Consulate Gen., Jerusalem, 1985-87; staff officer dept. ops. ctr. and secretariat US Dept. State, 1987-88, spl. asst. to the counselor of the dept. Soviet & Ea. European Affairs, 1989-90, White House dir. Soviet affairs, 1990-93, sr. dir. for Russian, Ukraine & Eurasia affairs & spl. asst. to the Pres., 1993-95, sr. fgn. svc. officer, nat. security coun. staff at the White House, 1991—, spokesman for Sec. of State, acting asst. sec. pub. affairs, 1995-97, US amb. to Greece Athens, 1997-2001; US permanent rep. NATO, Brussels, 2001—05; under sec. for polit. affairs US Dept. State, Washington, 2005—. Mem. Phi Beta Kappa. Office: US Dept State 2201 C St NW Rm 7240 Washington DC 20520

BURNS, RED, academic administrator; 4 children. Joined, co-founder, interactive telecomms. program Tisch Sch. Arts NYU, 1979—, chair, interactive telecomms. program Tisch Sch. Arts, 1981—, Tokyo Broadcasting System Prof. Communications, 1997—. Bd. dirs. Media Lab Europe, The Visual Media Task Force, The Convergent Media Group; mem. adv. bd. The N.Y. Times Digital Company; juror On-Line Journalism Awards, Nat. Mag. Awards, Webby Awards; prin. investigator three on-going rsch. programs funded by Interval Rsch., Intel and Microsoft. Creator CD-ROM on chaos theory, Electronic Neighborhood. Bd. dirs. The Charles H. Revson Found.; ProBono.net; Ivrae Inst.; mentor The Ross Sch. Named one of 100 top leaders of N.Y.'s economy, Crain's N.Y., top 100 most influential women in bus., Top 25 Influential People on the Net, Newsweek's 50 for the Future, N.Y. Cyber Sixty, N.Y. Mag.; named to Silicon Alley's 100; recipient Matrix award, 1997, All-Star Educator award, Crain's, Award of Excellence in Sci. and Tech., Mayor of N.Y.C., Spl. Educator award, Art Dir. Club, Chrysler Design Award, 2002. Mem.: N.Y. New Media Assn. (founding mem.). Office: NYU Tisch Sch Arts 721 Broadway 4th Fl New York NY 10003-6807

BURNS, RICHARD, telecommunications industry executive; b. Louisville, Ky. Mgmt. asst. BellSouth Corp. (formerly South Ctrl. Bell), Atlanta, 1976; v.p. Network Ops. for Tenn. and Ky. BellSouth Corp., Atlanta, exec. Telecom. Network Ops. for Ga., pres. broadband and internet svcs., v.p. process and cost mgmt., 2002—. Vol. United Way, Jr. Achievement. Office: BellSouth Corp 1155 Peachtree St NE Atlanta GA 30309-3610

BURNS, RICHARD DEAN, historian, educator, writer; b. Des Moines, June 16, 1929; s. Richard B. and Luella (Everling) B.; m. Frances R. Sullivan, Jan. 14, 1950 (dec. July 1993); 1 son, Richard Dean; m. Glenda F. Burns, Sept. 21, 1996; stepchildren: Scott E. Burns, Kent C. Burns, Dana Burns Mayadag. BS with honors, U. Ill., 1957, MA, 1958, PhD, 1960. Prof. emeritus Calif. State U., L.A., 1960-92, prof., 1970-92, chmn. dept., 1969-72, 86-92. Pubr./pres. Regina Books, 1980—; vis. lectr. L.A. City Coll., Whittier Coll., U. Minn., Mpls., 1964-65, UCLA, U. So. Calif.; program cons., lectr. Western Ctr., NEH, 1973-75. Author: (with W. Fisher) Armament and Disarmament, 1964, (with D. Urquidi) Disarmament in Historical Perspective, 4 vols, 1969, (with E. Bennett) Diplomats in Crisis, 1975; (with L. Brune) The Quest for Missile Defenses: 1944-2003, 2004, Chronology of the Cold War, 2005; editor: An Arms Control and Disarmament Bibliography, 1977, Guide to American Foreign Relations Since 1770, 1982, (with M. Leitenberg) The Wars in Vietnam, Cambodia, and Laos, 1945-82, 1984, Harry S. Truman: A Bibliography of His Times and Presidency, 1984, Herbert Hoover: A Bibliography of His Times and Presidency, 1991, Encyclopedia of Arms Control and Disarmament, 3 vols., 1993, (with A. DeConde, F. Logevall) Encyclopedia of American Foreign Policy, 3 vols., 2002, (with Lester Brune) Chronological History of U.S. Foreign Relations, 3 vols., 2002; bibliographer, series editor: War/Peace Bibliographies, 1973—; contbr. articles to profl. jours. Served with USAF, 1947-56. Named Univ. Outstanding Prof., 1978-79; Social Sci. Rsch. Coun. fellow, 1959-60; grantee NEH, 1978-79, U.S. Inst. Peace, 1991-92. Mem. Conf. on Peace Rsch. (nat. coun. 1970-72), Soc. Historians Am. Fgn. Rels. (nat. coun. 1986-89), Phi Kappa Phi, Phi Alpha Theta. Office: Regina Books PO Box 280 Claremont CA 91711-0280

BURNS, RICHARD GORDON, retired lawyer, writer, consultant; b. Stockton, Calif., May 15, 1925; s. Earl Gordon and Alberta Viola (Whale) Burns; m. Eloise Estelle Beil, June 23, 1951 (div. May 25, 1985); children: Kenneth Charles, Donald Gordon. AA with honors, U. Calif., Berkeley, 1948; AB, Stanford U., 1949, JD, 1951. Atty. Clausen & Burns, San Francisco, 1951—61; cons. Wyo. Pacific Oil Co., LA, 1956—; pvt. practice Corte Madera, Calif., 1961—86; pub. Good Book Pub., Kihei, Hawaii, 1991—. Bd. dirs. Clean Fuels Hawaii, G.O.A.L. Project, Pitts.; advisor God's Way Ministry, Inc., 1997—; cons. Uniti, Honolulu, 2000—; bd. dirs. Freedom Ranch Maui, Inc., 2003, Global Outreach in Addiction Rsch., 2005. Coauthor (with Bill Pittman): Courage To Change, 1998; author (as Dick B.): New Light on Alcoholism: God, Sam Shoemaker and A.A., 1999; author: The Akron Genesis of Alcoholics Anonymous, 1998, Anne Smith's Journal, 1998, Dr. Bob and His Library, 1998, The Good Book and The Big Book: AA's Roots in the Bible, 1998, The Oxford Group and Alcoholics Anonymous, 1998, That Amazing Grace, 1996, The Books Early AAs Read for Spiritual Growth, 1999, Good Morning!Quiet Time, Morning Watch, Meditation, and Early A.A., 1998, Turning Point: A History of Early A.A.'s Spiritual Roots and Successes, 1997, Utilizing A.A.'s Spiritual Roots for Recovery Today, 1999, The Golden Text of A.A., 1999, By the Power of God, 2000, Why Early A.A. Succeeded: The Good Book in Alcoholics Anonymous Yesterday and today, 2001, Making Known the Biblical Roots of A.A., 2002, God and Alcoholism: A Growing Opportunity in the 21st Century, 2002, Hope!: The Story of Geraldine Owen Delaney, Alina Lodge and Recovery, 2002, Cured! A Proven Solution for Alcoholics and Addicts, 2003, Comments at First Nationwide AA History Conference, 2003;: Twelve Steps for You, 2003, When Early AAs Were Cured and Why, 2003, Henrietta B. Seiberling: Ohio's Lady With A Cause, 2004, The James Club and the Orginal A.A. Program's Absoulte Essentials, 2005, The Original P.A. Program and Absolute Essentials, 2005; editor: Stanford Law Rev., 1950. Pres. Almonte Improvement Club, Mill Valley, Calif., 1960; dir. Almonte Sanitary Bd., Marin County, Calif., 1962—64; pres. C. of C., Corte Madera, 1972, Corte Madera Ctr. Merchant Co., 1975, Redwoods Retirement Ctr., Mill Valley, 1980, Cmty. Ch., Mill Valley, 1971. Sgt. U.S. Army, 1943—46. Mem.: Global Outreach for Addiction Leadership, Orgn. Am. Historians, Rsch. Soc. Alcoholism, Internat. Substance Abuse and Addiction Coalition, Assn. Med. Edn. and Rsch. Substance Abuse, Christian Assn. Psychol. Studies, Maui Writers Guild, Am. Hist. Assn., Coalition Prison Evangelists, Alcohol and Drugs History Soc., Stanford Alumni Assn., Phi Beta Kappa, Phi Delta Phi, Delta Tau Delta. Avocations: travel, Bible study, swimming, walking. Office: PO Box 837 Kihei HI 96753-0837 Office Phone: 808-874-4876. Personal E-mail: dickb@dickb.com.

BURNS, RICHARD RAMSEY, lawyer; b. Duluth, Minn., May 3, 1946; s. Herbert Morgan and Janet (Strobel) B.; Jennifer, Brian; m. Elizabeth Murphy, June 15, 1984. BA with distinction, U. Mich., 1968, JD magna cum laude, 1971. Bar: Calif. 1972, U.S. Dist. Ct. (no. dist.) Calif. 1972, U.S. Ct. Appeals (9th cir.) 1972, Minn. 1976, U.S. Dist. Ct. Minn. 1976, Wis. 1983, U.S. Tax. Ct. 1983. Assoc. Orrick, Herrington, Rowley & Sutcliffe, San Francisco, 1971-76; ptnr. Hanft, Fride, P.A., Duluth, 1976—. Gen. counsel Morgan Murphy Stas., Madison, Wis., 1982—. Chmn. Duluth-Superior Area Cmty. Found., 1988-90; chair United Way of Greater Duluth, Inc., 1998-99; bd. dirs. Northland Coll., Ashland, Wis. Fellow Am. Coll. Trust and Estate Counsel (state chair); mem. Calif. Bar Assn., Wis. Bar Assn., Minn. Bar Assn. (past. exec. com., past chmn. probate and trust coun.), 11th Dist. Bar Assn. (past pres., past chmn. ethics com.), Arrowhead Estate Planning Coun. (pres. 1980), Northland Country Club (pres. 1982), Boulders Club, Silverleaf Golf Club and Spa, Kitchi Gammi Club (bd. dirs.) Republican. Avocations: travel, golf, reading, fishing. Home: 180 Paine Farm Rd Duluth MN 55804-2609 Office: Hanft Fride PA 1000 First Bank Pl 130 W Superior St Ste 1000 Duluth MN 55802-2056 Office Phone: 218-722-4766. Business E-Mail: rrb@hanftlaw.com.

BURNS, ROBERT, JR., retired architect, painter; b. Jackson, Miss., Jan. 29, 1936; s. Robert Sr. and Grace Hortense (Inmon) B. BS in Architecture, Ga. Inst. Tech., 1959, BArch, 1960. Registered architect emeritus, Miss. Architect Overstreet, Ware, Ware & Lewis, Jackson, 1961-70, Ware, Lewis & Eaton, Jackson, 1970-71, Jones & Haas, Jackson, 1971-74, Leon Burton & Assocs., Jackson, 1974-75, Glenn Albritton Designer, Jackson, 1975-83, Breland & Farmer, Jackson, 1983-84, The Plan House, Jackson, 1984-86; part-time tchr. art dept. Miss. Coll., 1987; architect Johnny Wynne & Assocs., Ltd., Jackson, 1995-96; ret., 1996. Author: numerous poems, (short stories) My Antique, It Isn't Nice, Marie and Me, Rich Folk Have Roaches, Too, The Snake and Mr. D.; Represented in permanent collections Miss. Mus. Art (Mrs. Horace Hammond award, 1965), Miss. Coll., Hinds Jr. Coll., others, one-man shows include, Miss., Ga., Fla. Tenor soloist 1st Bapt. Ch., Jackson, 1967-68, 1st Christian Ch., Jackson, 1968-71, Covenant Presbyn. Ch., Jackson, 1971-74, Galloway Meml. United Meth. Ch., 1989-91, Northminster Bapt. Ch.,

Jackson, 1995-97, St. Luke's United Meth. Ch., Jackson, 1991-94, song leader, 1991-94; tenor soloist Woodland Hills Bapt. Ch., Jackson, 98-00; mem. Friends of the Gallery, Mcpl. Art Gallery, Jackson, 1981-93; mem. rev. panel Arts Alliance of Miss., 1989. Sgt. USAR, 1961-67. Mem. Am. Hemerocallis Soc., Inc. Republican. Baptist. Avocations: art, writing, music, growing daylilies and flowers. Home: 609 Broadway Ave Jackson MS 39216-3206

BURNS, ROBERT PASCHAL, architect, educator; b. Roxboro, N.C., Dec. 7, 1933; s. Robert Paschal and Majorie Dearing (Lacy) B.; m. Norma DeCamp, Dec. 4, 1973; children— Emily Carter, Robert Adam, Linda Paige B. Arch., N.C. State U., 1957; M.Arch., MIT, 1962; postgrad., Ecole Des Beaux Arts, France, 1957-58. Archtl. designer Eduardo Catalano, Architect, Cambridge, Mass., 1962-65; asst. prof. architecture N.C. State U., Raleigh, 1965-67, assoc. prof., 1967-70, prof., 1970—, head dept., 1967-74, 83-91, assoc. dean Sch. of Design, 1984-90; prin. Envirotek, Inc., Raleigh, 1972-74, Burnstudio Architects, Raleigh, 1978—. Exhbn. curator Matthew Nowicki: Sketches and Visions, N.C. State U. Visual Arts Ctr., 1993. Author, editor: 100 Courthouses, 1978; prin. works include Chatham County Law Enforcment Ctr., Lenoir County Courthouse Bd. dirs. The Cinema, Raleigh, 1966-79. Served with U.S. Army, 1959 Recipient Paris prize Nat. Inst. for Archtl. Edn., 1957, AIA Sch. medal N.C. State U., 1957, Book award, 1957, Alexander Quarles Holloday medal for excellence, 1995, cert. N.C. State Bar, 1979, William Henley Dietrick Svc. medal, 2004, various awards for archtl. design; Graham Found. grantee, 1994. Fellow AIA; mem. Assn. Collegiate Schs. Architecture (pres. 1979-80, Disting. Prof. award 1995), Phi Kappa Phi (Nat. Artist award 1998—). Democrat. Avocations: book collecting, cooking. Home: 750 Washington St Raleigh NC 27605-1298 Office: NC State U Sch of Design PO Box 7701 Raleigh NC 27695-0001 Office Phone: 919-515-8357. Business E-Mail: robert_burns@ncsu.edu.

BURNS, ROBERT PATRICK, law educator; b. NYC, Mar. 23, 1947; s. Frances William and Helen (Moskol) B.; m. Mary Elizabeth Griffin, June 7, 1975; children: Matthew, Elizabeth. AB, Fordham U., 1969; JD, U. Chgo., 1974, PhD, 1982. Bar: Ill. 1974, U.S. Dist. Ct. (no. dist.) Ill. 1974, U.S. Ct. Appeals (7th cir.) 1977, U.S. Supreme Ct. 1978. Litigation atty. Legal Assistance Found., Chgo., 1974-79, dir. atty. training, 1979; gen. counsel Ill. Legis. Commn., Springfield, 1979-80; prof. law Northwestern U., Chgo., 1980—. Tchr. Nat. Inst. Trial Advocacy, South Bend, Ind., 1981—. Author: A Theory of the Trial, 1999, Problems and Materials in Evidence and Trial Advocacy, 2001, exercises and Problems in Professional Responsibility, 2001, Evidence in Context, 2001; contbr. articles to profl. jours. Bd. dirs. Evanston Dems., Ill., 1984. Kent fellow Danforth Found., 1974, NSF fellow, 1970. Mem. ABA, Soc. for Values in Higher Edn. Roman Catholic. Office: Northwestern U Sch Law 357 E Chicago Ave Chicago IL 60611-3059 E-mail: r-burns@law.northwestern.edu.

BURNS, SARAH ELLEN, law educator; b. Ponca City, Okla., June 13, 1949; d. John William and Sarah Elizabeth (Phillips) Burns BA magna cum laude, U. Okla., 1971, MA, 1972, Stanford U., 1976; JD, Yale U., 1979. Bar: DC 1979, NY 1989, US Supreme Ct., US Ct. Appeals DC, 4th, 10th, 11th Cirs., US Dist. Ct. DC, US Dist. Ct. So. and Ea. Dists. NY. Assoc. Covington & Burling, Washington, 1979-82, Patterson, Belknap, Webb & Tyler, Washington, 1982-83; coord. atty. ERA Legis. History Project, Washington, 1983; fellow Women's Law and Pub. Policy Program, Washington, 1983-84; asst. dir. sex discrimination clinic Georgetown U., Washington, 1984-86; legal dir. NOW Legal Def. and Edn. Fund, NYC, 1986-90; asst. prof. clin. law NYU Sch. Law, 1990—93, assoc. prof., 1993—96, prof., 1996—. Schefelman disting. lectr. U. Wash. Law Sch., 1990. Named Dyson Disting. Lectr. Pace U. Sch. Law, 1989. Mem. Phi Beta Kappa. Office: NYU Sch Law 245 Sullivan St 5th Fl New York NY 10012 Office Phone: 212-998-6464. E-mail: burns@juris.law.nyu.edu.*

BURNS, SCOTT, columnist; b. Cambridge, Mass., Nov. 9, 1940; s. Robert Milton Clark Burns and Joanne (Mahoney) Blasius; m. Allegra Wendy Eames, Dec. 11, 1965 (div. Sept. 1990); children: Jasper Bayard (dec.), Oliver Byron; m. Carolyn Jo Schroeder, Jan. 2, 1995. BS, MIT, 1962. Columnist, editor Boston (Mass.) Herald Am., 1977-83; columnist Dallas (Tex.) Morning News, 1985—; syndicated columnist, 1980—. Author: Squeeze It Til The Eagle Grins, 1972, Home, Inc., 1975; co-author: The Coming Generational Storm, 2004. Office: Dallas Morning News Communications Ctr PO Box 655237 Dallas TX 75265-5237 Home: 50 Calle Sin Sonte Santa Fe NM 87507 Office Phone: 214-977-8915. Business E-Mail: sburns@dallasnews.com.

BURNS, SCOTT PATRICK, lawyer; b. Balt., 1964; BA with honors, Johns Hopkins U., 1986; JD, U. Pa., 1989. Bar: Md. 1989, U.S. Ct. Appeals Md., U.S. Ct. Appeals (fourth cir.), U.S. Dist. Ct. Md. Ptnr. Tydings & Rosenberg LLP, Balt. Editor: The Defense Line, 1995—99. Named one of Top 20 Lawyers in the next Generation, Balt. Mag., 2003. Mem.: Def. Rsch. Inst., Md. Def. Counsel (mem. exec. com. 1995—2003, pres. 2001—02). Office: Tydings & Rosenberg LLP 100 E Pratt St 26th Fl Baltimore MD 21202 Office Phone: 410-752-9743. Office Fax: 410-727-5460. E-mail: sburns@tydingslaw.com.

BURNS, SHELLY LEAH, elementary school educator; b. Evansville, Ind., Jan. 10, 1973; d. Norman C. and Ada L. Burns. BS, Ball State U., 1996. Tchr. elem. music Troup County Schs., LaGrange, Ga., 1996—2004, tchr. 2d grade, 2004—05. Dir. Troup County Elem. Chorus, 2003; mem. choir Advent Luth. Ch., LaGrange, 1992—2005, youth leader, tchr., 2004—05, co-chair Woman of Evangel. Ch. Am., 2004—05. Mem.: Music Educators Nat. Conf. Avocations: piano, reading.

BURNS, STEPHANIE A., chemicals executive; PhD in Organic Chemistry, Iowa State Univ.; post-doctoral study, Univ. Languedoc-Rousillon, France. Rschr. Dow Corning, Midland, Mich., 1983—87, prod. devel. mgr., 1987—94, dir., women's health, 1994—97, sci., tech. dir., Europe Brussels, 1997—99, industry dir, life sciences, Europe to European elec. industry dir., 1999—2000, exec. v.p. Midland, Mich., 2000—03, pres., 2003—, COO, 2003—04, CEO, 2004—. Bd. dir. Dow Corning, 2000—, Manpower Inc., Chem. Bank Midland area, Mich. Molecular Inst. Adv. bd. Chem. & Engring. News. Bd. trustees Midland Cmty. Ctr. Named Mich. Woman Exec. of Yr., 2003; named one of 100 Most Powerful Women in World, Forbes Mag., 2005. Mem.: Am. Chem. Coun. (bd. dir.), Am. Chem. Soc. Office: Dow Corning PO Box 994 Midland MI 48686-0994 Office Phone: 989-496-7881. Office Fax: 989-496-6731.*

BURNS, STEPHEN GILBERT, lawyer; b. N.Y.C., Apr. 29, 1953; s. Gilbert Leo and Ellen (Scully) B.; m. Joan Louise Wallace, Aug. 6, 1977; children: Christopher, Allison. Student, U. Vienna, Austria, 1974; BA, Colgate U., 1975; JD, George Washington U., 1978. Bar: D.C. 1978, U.S. Ct. Appeals (D.C. cir.) 1980. Atty. Nuclear Regulatory Commn., Washington, 1978-83, dep. chief counsel regional ops. and enforcement, 1983-86, legal asst. to commr., 1986-89, exec. asst. to chmn., 1989-91, dir. Office of Commn. Appellate Adjudication, 1991-94, assoc. gen. counsel, 1994-98, dep. gen. counsel, 1998—. Recipient Disting. Svc. medal, Nuclear Regulatory Commn., 2001. Mem. ABA. Presbyterian. Office: US Nuclear Regulatory Commn Office Of Gen Counsel Ms 15B21 Washington DC 20555-0001 Office Phone: 301-415-1740.

BURNS, STEPHEN L., lawyer; b. Tulsa, Okla., Mar. 3, 1965; BBA, Univ. Okla., 1987; JD, Univ. Tex., Austin, 1990. Bar: NY 1991. Assoc. Cravath Swaine & Moore LLP, NYC, 1990—98, ptnr., corp., 1998—. Office: Cravath Swaine & Moore LLP Worldwide Tower 825 Eighth Ave New York NY 10019-7475 Office Phone: 212-474-1146. Office Fax: 212-474-3700. Business E-Mail: sburns@cravath.com.

BURNS, SUZETTE GASKIN, elementary school educator; b. Ligonier, Pa., July 31, 1953; d. William Joseph and Florence May Gaskin; m. Kevin Lawrence Burns; children: Seth Adam, Kirk Richard. BS in Edn., Clarion U. of Pa., 1975. Cert. instrnl. II Pa., master's equivalency Pa. Classroom tchr. Ligonier Valley Sch. Dist., Ligonier, 1975—80, 1990—. Pub. rels. specialist R. K. Mellon Elem., Ligonier, 2004—. Mem.: NEA, Pa. State Edn. Assn. Home: 437 Schultz Ave Latrobe PA 15650 Office: R K Mellon Elem 559 Bell St Ligonier PA 15658

BURNS, TERRENCE MICHAEL, lawyer; b. Evergreen Park, Ill., Mar. 2, 1954; s. Jerome Joseph Burns and Eileen Beatrice (Collins) Neary; m. Therese Porucznik, Mar. 24, 1979; children: David, Steven, Theresa, Daniel. BA, Loyola U., Chgo., 1975; JD, DePaul U., 1978. Bar: Ill. 1978, U.S. Dist. Ct. (no. dist.) Ill. 1978, U.S. Ct. Appeals (7th cir.) 1979, U.S. Supreme Ct. 1985, U.S. Dist. Ct. (no. dist.) Ind. 1989. Asst. state's atty. Cook County, Chgo., 1979-85; ptnr. Dykema Gossett Rooks Pitts, Chgo., 1985—. Mem. inquiry bd. Ill. Supreme Ct. Atty. Registration and Disciplinary Commn., Chgo., 1986-90, chair hearing bd., 1990—; mem. coun. regents Loyola U., Chgo., 2002—. Mem. ABA (ann. meeting adv. com.), Chgo. Bar Assn. (treas. 1997-99, 2d v.p. 1999-2000, 1st v.p. 2000-01, pres. 2001-2002, bd. mgrs. 1995-97, chair fin. com. 1997-99, criminal law com. 1979-83, jud. candidate evaluation com. 1981-86, 87-95, chmn. investigation divsn. evaluation com. 1991-92, chmn. hearing divsn. evaluation com. 1992-93, gen. chmn. 1993-95, ct. liaison com. 1993-95, tort reform subcom. 1997), Chgo. Bar Found. (bd. dirs. 1999-2000). Roman Catholic. Office: Rooks Pitts & Poust 10 S Wacker Dr Ste 2300 Chicago IL 60606-7407

BURNS, THEODORE WEBER, gastroenterologist; b. New Iberia, La., Apr. 15, 1944; s. James Patout and Mary T. (Weber) B.; m. Linda Ann Cox, Aug. 29, 1970 (dec.); children: Theodore W. Jr., David D., William J., Jennifer L. DDS, Loyola U., New Orleans, 1968; MD, La. State U., 1972. Diplomate Am. Bd. Internal Medicine, Am. Bd. Gastroenterology. Intern, then resident U. Fla., Gainesville, 1972-75, fellow in gastroenterology, 1975-77; asst. prof. medicine Uniformed Svcs. Sch. Medicine, Bethesda, Md., 1977-79; staff physician, ptnr., dir. gastrointestinal rsch. Ochsner Clinic, New Orleans, 1979-86; ptnr., physician Digestive Disease Assocs., Gainesville, 1986—. Contbr. articles to profl. jours. Vol. United Way, Gainesville, 1990. Lt. comdr. USN, 1977-79. NIH rsch. svc. grantee U. Fla., 1976-77. Fellow ACP, Am. Coll. Gastroenterology; mem. Am. Soc. for Gastrointestinal Endoscopy, Alpha Omega Alpha. Roman Catholic. Avocation: water sports. Office: Digestive Disease Assocs 6400 W Newberry Rd Ste 302 Gainesville FL 32605-6604

BURNS, THOMAS DAVID, lawyer; b. Andover, Mass., Apr. 4, 1921; s. Joseph Lawrence and Catherine (Horne) Burns; m. Sylvia Lansing, Sept. 14, 1946 (div. 1982); children: Wendy Tilghman, Lansing, Diane Longley, Lisa; m. Marjorie Andrew Brown, Mar. 12, 1983. Student, Brown U., 1938—41; LLB, Boston U., 1943. Bar: Mass. 1944, U.S. Dist. Ct. 1948, U.S. Ct. Appeals 1951, U.S. Supreme Ct. 1957. Assoc. Friedman, Atherton, King & Turner, Boston, 1946-50, ptnr., 1950-60; sr. and founding ptnr. Burns & Levinson, Boston, 1960—. Chmn. com. jud. selection Joint Com. Boston and Mass. Bar, 1970—75; mem. jud. coun. Com. of Mass., 1973—77; mem. Mass. Spl. Legis. Commn. Malpractice, 1975—, Mass. Jud. Nominating Commn., 1979—83; spl. counsel to Boston City Coun., 1981. Co-editor: Recollections of World War II Phillips Andover, 1938; contbr. articles to profl. jours. Chmn. Planning Bd. Appeals, Andover, 1956—57; trustee Stratton Mountain Vt. Civic Assn., Mus. Am. Textile History, 1992—; bd. dirs. Birch Hill Corp., Stratton, Vt.; trustee, clk. Pike Sch., Andover; mem. Mass. Hist. Soc., Western Front Assn.; mem. adv. bd. PBS channel II WGBH, Boston; chmn. Andover Rep. Fin. Com., 1953—57; mem. alumni coun. and devel. com. Phillips Andover Acad. Lt. USNR, 1943—46, PTO, ETO. Fellow: ABA, Mass. Def. Lawyers Assn. (dir.), Nat. Assn. R.R. Trial Counsel, Internat. Assn. Def. Counsel, Boston Bar Found., Boston Bar Assn. (mem. exec. coun.), Mass. Bar Assn. (mem. exec. com.), Am. Coll. Trial Lawyers (state chmn. 1968, bd. regents 1970—76, treas. 1974—77), Mass. Bar Found. (trustee), Am. Bar Found., Boston Vis. Nurses Assn., Fed. Ins. and Corp. Counsel, Boston U. Law Sch. (mem. alumni coun. and devel. com., alumni award, Disting. Profl. Svc. award 1996), Boston City Club, Coral Beach Club (Bermuda), North Adnover Country Club, The Country Club (Brookline), Duxbury Yacht Club, Delta Kappa Epsilon; mem.: Am. Coll. Trial Lawyers Found. (dir.). Office: Burns & Levinson 125 Summer St Ste 602 Boston MA 02110-1616 Office Phone: 617-345-3000. E-mail: tburns@b-l.com.

BURNS, THOMAS SAMUEL, history professor; b. Michigan City, Ind., June 7, 1945; m. Carol Ann Morris, June 29, 1968; 1 child, Catherine Elizabeth. AB, Wabash Coll., 1967; postgrad., Am. Sch. Classical Studies, Athens, summer 1967; MA, U. Mich., 1968, PhD, 1974. Asst. prof. history Emory U., Atlanta, 1974-80, assoc. prof., 1980-85, Samuel Candler Dobbs prof. history, 1985—, chmn. dept. history, 1989-92. Dir. summer seminar for sch. tchrs. NEH, 1985, 88; adj. prof. U. Windsor, Ont., summer 1978, 79; vis. research prof. Kommission für alte Geschichte und Epigraphik des deutschen archäologischen Instituts in München, spring 1982; vis. research prof. Römisch-Germanische Kommission des deut. arch. Instituts, Frankfurt, spring 1982; Gastprof. Universität Augsburg, 1986. Author: The Ostrogoths: Kingship and Society, 1980, A History of the Ostrogoths, 1984, (with B.H. Overbeck) Rome and the Germans as Seen in Coinage, 1987, Barbarians within the Gates of Rome, 1994, (with J.W. Eadie) Urban Centers and Rural Realities, 2000, Rome and the Barbarians 100 B.C.-A.D. 400, 2003; co-dir. of Archaeological excavations in Passau, Germany, 1978-79, Manching, Germany, 1985, Pecs, Hungary, 1998; contbr. articles to profl. jours. With U.S. Army, 1969-71. Recipient Emory Williams Disting. Teaching award Emory U., 1982, Thomas Jefferson award Emory U., 2004; Fulbright fellow Fed. Republic Germany, 1986, Boak fellow in ancient history U. Mich., 1971-74; Disting. Vis. scholar-in-residence U. Adelaide, Australia Mem. Medieval Acad. Am. (nominating com. 1987-88), Ga. Classical Assn., AAUP (pres. Emory U. chpt. 1983-84), Phi Beta Kappa, Omicron Delta Kappa. Avocations: camping, fishing, wilderness canoeing, travel. Home: 2405 Dooley Dr Apt BP03 Decatur GA 30033 Office: Emory U Dept History Atlanta GA 30322-0001 Office Phone: 404-727-6555. Business E-Mail: histsb@emory.edu.

BURNS, TONI ANTHONY, artist; b. L.A., Sept. 6, 1937; d. Earle Francis and LaVerne Myrtle (Holmberg) Anthony; m. George Orin Burns, May 14, 1965; children: Robert Anthony, James Randolph. BFA, Calif. State U. Long Beach, 1959, postgrad., 1960. Cert. secondary tchr. Calif. Interior decorator Ruth Connor Interiors, Downey, Calif., 1960—62; tech. illustrator N.Am. Rockwell Corp., Downey, 1962—64, McDonnell-Douglas Aircraft, Long Beach, 1964—65; graphic layout artist Beckman Instruments, Fullerton, Calif., 1968—70; owner, creator Original Art Rock Owls, San Juan Capistrano, Calif., 1970—78; custom jewelry designer Jewelry by Toni Burns, San Juan Capistrano, 1979—98; jewelry designer, ptnr. SuperNatural Art, San Juan Capistrano, 1999—; prin., owner Silver Dolls, San Juan Capistrano, 2003—. Wholesale exhibitor L.A. Gift Show, 1971-78, Beckman Handcrafts, L.A., 1982. Juried shows include Village West Gallery, Laguna Beach, Calif., summers 1971-75, Art-A-Fair Festival, Laguna Beach, 1984-86, Downey Art Mus., 1992, Fine Arts Pavillion, 1993. Recipient 1st pl. San Clemente Art Gallery, 1984, 99. Mem. Am. Craft Coun., Metal Arts Soc. So. Calif. Avocations: family genealogy, travel, photography. Office Phone: 949-388-4309. Business E-Mail: sales@supernaturalart.com.

BURNS, URSULA M., printing company executive; b. NYC, Sept. 20, 1958; m. Lloyd Bean; 2 children. BS, Polytech. Inst., 1980; MS in Mech. Engring., Columbia U., 1981. Joined as mechanical engr., held several positions in engring., including product develop. and planning Xerox Corp. 1980; exec. asst. to chmn. & CEO Paul A. Allaire Xerox Corp., 1991, lead several bus. teams, 1992—2000, sr. v.p. corp. strategic svc., 2000—, pres. bus. group ops. Stamford, Conn., 2002—. Bd. dirs. Hunt Corp., Banta Corp., U. Rochester Med. Sch., Am. Express, Boston Scientific Corp., FIRST, Nat. Assn. Mfrs., PQ Corp., Rochester Bus. Alliance. Mem.: Nat. Assn. Mfr. (bd. dirs.), Indsl. Mgmt. Coun. Rochester (bd. dirs.). Office: Xerox 800 Long Ridge Rd Stamford CT 06904

BURNS, VIRGINIA, social worker; b. Boston, June 10, 1925; d. Thomas Patrick and Katherine Louise (Dempsey) Burns. AB in Sociology, Boston U., 1946, MSW, 1951; EdD honors, Wheelock Coll., 1994. Group work specialist Boston Children's Svc. Assn., 1951-58; group work cons. East London Family Svc. Units, 1958-59; assoc. exec. sec. group work coun. Welfare Fedn. Cleve., 1959-62; sr. staff mem. Office Juvenile Delinquency & Youth Devel. U.S. Dept. Health, Edn. and Welfare, Washington, 1962-67, asst. to asst. sec. cmty. svcs., 1967-69; sr. assoc. youth involvement study New Transcentury Found., Washington, 1969-70; assoc. prof., dir. social svc. project U. Chgo., Sch. Social Svc. Adminstrn., 1970-73; dir. cmty. svc., divsn. drug rehab. Dept. Mental Health, Boston, 1973-76; dir. cons. & edn. program Mass. Mental Health Ctr., Boston, 1976-82; lectr. mental health Harvard Med. Sch., Boston, 1978-82; dir. advocacy, Boston Children Svc. Assn. Mass. Soc. Prevention of Cruelty Children, Boston, 1983-94; instr. social welfare, coord. cmty. projects Smith Coll. Sch. Social Work, Northampton, Mass., 1994-99; instr. social welfare policy Salem (Mass.) State Coll. Sch. Social Work, 1993-99. Cons. in field. Contbr. articles to profl. jours., chpts. in books. Founding chair Children's Advocacy Network Mass., 1984—93, Latchkey Children's Coalition Mass., 1988—92; v.p. Mass. Human Svc. Coalition, 1984—99; legis. liaison Mass. Working Group on Women in Prison, 2000—; bd. dirs. Hispanic Office Planning and Evaluation, 1990—97, Here House, 1989—90, Parents Helping Parents, 2001—02, Inst. Health and Recovery, 2003—05; bd. advisors Aid to Incarcerated Mothers, 2002—05; active United Fair Economy, Boston, 1994—99, Tax Equity Alliance Mass., 1990—99; mem. adv. com. Wheelock Coll., 1999—2005. Named Alumna of Yr., Boston U. Sch. Social Work, 1968; scholar, Fulbright, 1958—58. Mem.: NASW (chair polit. action com. Mass. chpt. 1984—2001, award for greatest contbn. to social policy and change 1990, Lifetime Achievement award 2003—04), Boston U. Alumni Assn. (Disting.). Avocations: gardening, bicycling, cooking, flower arranging. Home: 41A Cushing St Cambridge MA 02138-4581 E-mail: Burns472@aol.com.

BURNS, WARD, textile company executive; b. New Bedford, Mass., May 31, 1928; s. Frederick Lloyd and Pauline (Ward) B.; m. Cynthia A. Butterworth, Dec. 19, 1964; children: Helen Abby, David Ward, Walton Lloyd. BA, Amherst Coll., 1950; MBA, Harvard U., 1952; spl. student, NYU, 1955-57; LLD (hon.), Phila. Coll. Sci., 1984. CPA, N.Y. Mgr. Price Waterhouse & Co. (C.P.A.s), N.Y.C., 1954-62; assoc. Laurence S. and David Rockefeller, Brussels, Belgium, 1962-65; with J.P. Stevens & Co., Inc., N.Y.C., 1965-88, controller, 1969-78, group v.p., 1978-80, pres., 1980-86, vice chmn., 1987-88. Also dir., mem. exec. com.; bd. dirs. Stevens Graphics, Inc., Atlanta, 1972-92; cons. ARS, Milan, Italy, HVL, Brussels, ARCO, Florence and Milan, 1963-65 Mem. editorial adv. bd.: Jour. Accountancy, 1969-72. Treas., dir. Internat. Sch. Brussels, 1963-65; bd. dirs. Internat. Sch. Brussels Found., N.Y.C., 1965—, pres. 1967-97; pres. Friends New Cavell Hosp. Inc.; bd. dirs., 1972-78; trustee Daniel Webster Coll., Nashua, N.H., 1995—, chmn., bd. trustees, 1997-99; vice chmn. Friends of the Amherst Coll. Libr., 1978—. Served as capt. USAF, 1952-53. Mem. AICPA, N.Y. State Soc. CPAs, Fin. Execs. Inst., St. Andrews Soc., Univ. Club, Links Club, Econs. Club N.Y.C., The Pilgrims, Sky Club, Chappaquiddick Beach Club, Edgartown Yacht Club, Clove Valley Rod and Gun Club, Amherst Club (N.Y.), Harvard Club (Boston), Phi Alpha Psi, Phi Kappa Psi. Office Phone: 212-994-9317.

BURNS, WILLIAM GLENN, lawyer; b. Shreveport, La., Jan. 13, 1949; s. Carrol and Doris Yvonne (Broadway) B.; m. Linda Roach, Aug. 14, 1971 (div. 1981); m. Marilyn Waites, Oct. 28, 1982 (div. 1992); 1 child, Brandon Nicholas; m. Marianne Everard, Aug. 15, 1992. BS, La. State U., 1971, JD, 1973. Bar: La. 1973, U.S. Ct. Appeals (5th cir.) 1974, U.S. Dist. Ct. (ea. dist.) La. 1976, U.S. Ct. Appeals (11th cir.) 1981, U.S. Dist. Ct. (mid. dist.) La. 1985, U.S. Supreme Ct. 1986. Asst. atty. gen. La. Dept. Justice, New Orleans, 1973-76; assoc. Murray & Murray, New Orleans, 1976-80; asst. U.S. atty. U.S. Dept. Justice, New Orleans, 1980-85; ptnr. Monroe & Lemann, New Orleans, 1985-91; spl. counsel Hoffman, Sutterfield, New Orleans, 1992; ptnr. Hailey, McNamara, New Orleans, 1993—. Fellow Inst. of Politics Loyola U., 1978; adj. faculty Tulane U. Law Sch., 1997—. Editor: Consumer Relations and Bank Holding Companies, 1972. Del. Nat. Dem. Mid-Term Conf., La., 1978; mem. bd. devel. Mercy Hosp., New Orleans, 1979, mem. met. area com., 1988-91, curriculum com. 1988, 89. Mem. ABA, La. Bar Assn. Republican. Baptist. Avocations: sports, Am. history, La. polit. history. Office: Hailey McNamara Hall Larmann Papale 1 Galleria Blvd Metairie LA 70001-2082

BURNS, WILLIAM JOSEPH, ambassador, former federal agency administrator; b. Ft. Bragg, NC, Apr. 4, 1956; m. Lisa Carty, 2 children. BA in History, LaSalle U., 1978; M Internat. Rels., Oxford U., PhD, 1981. With U.S. Fgn. Svc., 1982—, polit. officer Amman, Jordan, 1982—84, staff mem. Bur. Near East Affairs, staff mem. Office of Dep. Sec. State; spl. asst. to Pres., sr. dir. Near East, South Asian Affairs NSC; acting dir., prin. dep. dir. policy planning staff US Dept. State; minister-counselor for polit. affairs U.S. Fgn. Svc., Moscow; exec. sec. and spl. asst. to sec. US Dept. State, US amb. to Kingdom of Jordan Amman, 1998—2001, asst. sec. Bur. Near Eastern Affairs Washington, 2001—05, interim under sec. for polit. affairs, 2005, US amb. to Russian Fedn. Moscow, 2005—. Author: Economic Aid and American Policy Toward Egypt, 1955-1981, 1985. Recipient Disting. Honor award State Dept., James Clement Dunn award, others; Marshall scholar, 1978-81. Office: US Embassy 5430 Moscow Pl Washington DC 20521

BURR, BROOKS MILO, zoology educator; b. Toledo, Aug. 15, 1949; s. Lawrence E. and Beverly Joy (Herald) B.; m. Patti Ann Grubb, Mar. 5, 1977 (div. July 1987); 1 child, Jordan Brooks. BA, Greenville Coll., 1971; MS, U. Ill., 1974, PhD, 1977. Cert. scuba diver Nat. Assn. Underwater Instrs. Lab. instr. dept. biology Greenville (Ill.) Coll., 1971-72; rsch. asst. Ill. Natural History Survey, Champaign, 1972-77, affiliate scientist Ctr. for Biodiversity Urbana, 1989—; from asst. prof. to prof. dept. zoology So. Ill. U., Carbondale, 1977—. Mem. adv. panel U.S. Fish and Wildlife Svc., 1990—; adj. prof. dept. biology U. N.Mex., Albuquerque, 1991—; adj. prof. dept. ecology, ethology and evolution U. Ill., 1993—. Co-author: A Distributional Atlas of Kentucky Fishes, 1986, A Field Guide to Fishes, North America North of Mexico, 1991 (selected as one of Outstanding Acad. Books of 1992 by Choice Mag.); contbr. more than 120 articles to profl. jours. Recipient Paper of Yr. award Ohio Jour. Sci., 1986, Coll. Sci. Rsch. award, So. Ill. Univ., 2001; Phi Kappa Phi Outstanding scholar So. Ill. U., 2002. Mem. AAAS, Am. Soc. Ichthyologists and Herpetologists (sec., mem. exec. com. 1990-94, pres.-elect 2000, pres. 2001—), Soc. Systematic Zoology, Biol. Soc. Washington, Assn. Systematic Collections, Sigma Xi (Leo M. Kaplan award 1990), Phi Kappa Phi (Scholar of Yr. 2002). Achievements include the discovery and description of 10 species of fish new to science from North American fresh waters. Home: 203 S Wedgewood Ln Carbondale IL 62901-2147 Office: So Ill Univ Dept Zoology Carbondale IL 62901-6501 Office Phone: 618-453-4112. Business E-Mail: burr@zoology.siu.edu.

BURR, DAVID BENTLEY, anatomy educator; b. Findlay, Ohio, June 28, 1951; s. Willard Bentley and Dorothy Eleanor (Beiler) B.; m. Lisa Marie Pedigo; children: Kathryn Lise, Michael David, Erik Johan. BA, Beloit Coll., 1973; MA, U. Colo., 1974, PhD, 1977. Instr. anatomy U. Kans. Med. Ctr., Kansas City, 1977-78, asst. prof. anatomy, 1978-80; asst. prof. anatomy and orthop. surgery W.Va. U., Morgantown, 1980-83, assoc. prof., 1983-86, prof., 1986-90; chmn. dept. anatomy and cell biology, prof. anatomy, bioengring. and orthopedic surgery Ind. U., Indpls., 1990—. Mem. adv. bd. dirs. Primate Found. Am., Tempe, Ariz., 1978—; cons. County Med. Examiner, Morgantown, 1983-89; mem. Adv. Group for the Treatment Human Remains, USDA, Monongahela Nat. Forest Svc., 1989; cons. NASA, 1990-91, Am. Inst. Biol. Sci., NAS, 1990—, U.S. Congress Office Tech. Assessment, 1990; mem. biochemistry study sect. Arthritis found., 1992-95; spl. grants rev. com. NIH,

1996-2000. Author: Structure, Function & Adaptation of Compact Bone, 1989, Skeletal Tissue Mechanics, 1998, Musculoskeletal Fatigue and Stress Fracture, 2001, Bridging the Gap Between Dental and Orthopaedic Implants, 2002; mem. editl. bd. Bone, 1993-2003, Jour. Bone and Mineral Metabolism, 1994-, Jour. Biomech., 1999-, Calcif. Tiss. Int., 2000-; assoc. editor Bone, 2004-, Jour. Musculoskeletal Neuronal Interactions, 2004-; contbr. articles to profl. jours. Pres. First Ward Sch. PTA, Morgantown, 1987—88; sec. Cub Scout Pack Com., 1989; chmn. troop com. Boy Scouts Am., 1993—95; linesman Morgantown Soccer League, 1988; sec. Classic Ragtime Soc., 1997—98; clk. witness and svc. First Friends Meeting, 1999—2001; mem. adminstrv. bd. Epworth United Meth. Ch., Indpls., 1992—93. Rsch. grantee NIH, 1988—, Orthopedic Rsch. and Edn. Found., 1985-86. Mem.: Internat. Soc. for Musculoskeletal and Neuronal Interactions (bd. dirs. 1999—2000, 2002—), Assn. Anatomy, Cell Biology and Neurobiology Chairpersons (pres. 2001—02), Am. Anatomy Assn. (exec. com. 1998—2001, chmn. jour. trust fund com. 2002—04, sec.-treas. 2004—05, pres.-elect 2005—), Orthop. Rsch. Assn. (chmn. membership com. 2002—03, program chair 2005—), Internat. Soc. Bone Mineral Rsch., Am. Soc. Bone Mineral Rsch. Avocations: piano, softball, racquetball, stamps, reading. Office: Ind U Sch Medicine Dept Anat & Cell Biology 635 Barnhill Dr Indianapolis IN 46202-5126 Office Phone: 317-274-7496. Business E-Mail: dburr@iupui.edu.

BURR, JOAN ANN, artist, educator; b. NYC; d. John Joseph and Vivian (Monroe) Schneider; m. Raymond Aaron Burr, Feb. 14, 1956; children: Jesse, Jody, David, Donna, Terri. AA, Rose Coll., 1977; student, La. Tech., 1980, Scottsdale Artists Sch., 1982, 83, Norton Gallery of Art, West Palm Beach, Fla. Freelance artist, 1970—. Art instr. pvt. classes, 1975-90. One person shows include Sakura, Stuart, Fla.; exhibited in group shows at Okla. Festival of Arts Invitational, 1971-84, Arts Festival Cultural Ctr., Stuart, 1990, 92-93, 1st Nat. Bank of Palm City Fla., 1993, Phippen Mus., Prescott, Ariz., 1995, Taos (N.Mex.) Watercolor Soc. Show, 1995, others; represented in pvt. collections including Gov.'s Mansion, Oklahoma City, Liberty Nat. Bank, Oklahoma city, Babbitt Trading Post, Ariz., Cordell (Okla.) Nat. Bank; featured in publs. Okla. Art Gallery Mag., Ency. of Living Artists in Am., Sunshine Artists Mag., Splash 6. Recipient David Gale award Western Fedn. Artists, 1st pl. award Lake Worth Nat. Art Exhbn., 1993, Grumbacher Gold medal award Ariz. Watercolor Show, 1st pl. award Sedona Ann., 1st pl. award Winslow Arts Assn., Best of Show award Crossroads Show, 1st pl. award Guthrie Ann. Mem.: Internat. Soc. Exptl. Artist (signature mem.), No. Ariz. Art Assn., Am. Watercolor Assn. (assoc.). Avocations: collecting Native Am. arts, dolls, camping, photography. Home: PO Box 286 Joseph City AZ 86032-0286

BURR, RICHARD M., senator, former congressman; b. Charlottesville, Va., Nov. 30, 1955; m. Brooke Fauth; children: Tyler, William. BA in Comm., Wake Forest U., 1978. Nat. sales mgr. Carswell Distributing, 1978-94; state co-chmn. N.C. Taxpayers United, 1993-98; mem. U.S. Ho. of Reps. from 5th N.C. dist., 1995—2005; U.S. senator from NC, 2005—. Mem. Senate Energy & Nat. Resources Comm., 2005—, Senate Health, Edn., Labor & Pensions Comm., 2005—, Senate Indian Affairs Comm., 2005—, Senate Vet. Affairs Comm., 2005—. Co-chmn. Partnership for Drug Free NC; bd. dirs. Brenner Children's Hosp. Recipient Award for Mfg. Legis. Excellence, Nat. Assn. Mfrs., 1999, Jefferson award, Citizens for a Sound Econ., 2001, Legislator of the Year, Biotechnology Industry Org., 2002. Republican. Presbyn. Office: US Senate 217 Dirksen Senate Office Bldg Washington DC 20510 Office Phone: 202-224-3154.*

BURR, RONALD EDWIN, publisher; b. Chgo., Oct. 5, 1949; m. My Hanh Duong-Tran. AB in Polit. Sci., Ind. U., 1972, MBA in Fin., 1976. Circulation mgr. The Am. Spectator, Bloomington, Ind., 1970—75, bus. mgr., 1975—79, sr. pub., 1979—80, gen. mgr., 1980—81, pub. Arlington, Va., 1981—97; pres. Red Line Mktg. LLC, Vienna, Va., 1979—; COO CHQ website, 1999—2001; pres. Burr Media Group LLC, Vienna, Va., 2003—. Mng. ptnr. Lemley Yarling & Co., Chgo., 1976—; bd. dirs., Launchspace Publs. Mem. Ind. Hist. Soc., Cath. Press Assn. Roman Catholic. Office: Red Line Mktg LLC PO Box 156 Vienna VA 22183-0156 E-mail: Ronaldeburr@hotmail.com.

BURR, SCOTT ALLEN, lawyer; s. Walter B. III and Patricia (Lord) Rothenberger. BA, Albright Coll., 1985; JD, The Dickinson Sch. Law, 1988; LLM in Internat. Law, Georgetown U., 1994; LLM in Trial Advocacy, Temple U. Law Sch., 1999. Bar: Pa. 1988, U.S. Dist. Ct. (ea. dist.) Pa. 1988, N.J. 1988, U.S. Dist. Ct. N.J. 1988. Sr. assoc. Spector, Gadon & Rosen, Phila., 1994—2000; sr. counsel Astigarraga Davis, Miami, 2002—. V.p. Nite & Day Mag., Ltd., Phila., 1990—. Author: (published law review article) 15 U. Pa. J. Int'l. Bus. L. 221 (1994), 6 Dick. J. Int.'l L. Active 237, 1987, ACLU, Phila., 1989—. Scholar, Albright Coll., 1985. Mem. ABA (internat. law sect., litigation and ins. and torts sect.), Fla. Bar Assn. (vice chair corp. and banking litigation), Dade County Bar Assn. Democrat. Lutheran. Avocations: sailing, equestrian riding, body building, water-skiing. Office: Astigarra Davis 701 Brickell Ave Ste 1650 Miami FL 33131 E-mail: sburr@astidavis.com.

BURR, TIMOTHY FULLER, lawyer; b. New Bedford, Mass., Oct. 18, 1952; s. John Thayer and Joan (Ames) B.; m. Marguerite Conti, Feb. 28, 1981; children: Emily Ames, Lisa Conti, David Thayer. AB, Harvard U., 1975; JD, U. Miami, 1979. Bar: La. 1979, Tex. 1993, Fla. 1996, U.S. Supreme Ct., U.S. Cir. Ct., U.S. Dist. Ct. Admirality and litigation atty. Galloway, Johnson, Tompkins, Burr & Smith, New Orleans, Houston, Lafayette, Gulf Breeze, 1979—, mng. dir. firm New Orleans, Gulf Breeze, 1987—. Past chmn. St. Tammary Parish Zoning Bd.; mem. Gulf Breeze Devel. Rev. Bd., 2003-04; pres. Optimist Club Gulf Breeze, Fla., 2001-02. Mem. La. Bar Assn., Tex. Bar Assn., Fla. Bar Assn., Maritime Law Assn. U.S., Tammany Yacht Club, Pensacola Yacht Club. Republican. Home: 281 Plantation Hill Rd Gulf Breeze FL 32561-4050 Office: 1101 Gulf Breeze Pky Ste 2 Gulf Breeze FL 32561-4468 Office Phone: 850-934-3800.

BURR, TOM, artist; b. New Haven, 1963; Update 1992, 1992—93, Tom Burr, 1995—96, Stainless, 1996—97, Parasite, 1997—98, Slung Low, Kunstverein Braunschweig, 2000, Deliberate Living, Greene Naftali Gallery, NY, 2001, Deep Purple, Whitney Mus. Am. Art, 2002—03, Whitney Biennial Am. Art, 2004, It's All An Illusion. A Sculpture Project., Migros Mus. fur Gegenwartskunst, Zurich, 2004, The Future Has a Silver Lining-Genealogies of Glamour, 2004. Office: c/o American Fine Arts Co 22 Wooster St New York NY 10013*

BURR, TRACY L., food products executive; BS, U. Utah; M in Accountancy, Utah State U. CPA Tex., Calif., Utah. N.Am. corp. contr. Albert Fisher N.Am.; ptnr. Ernst & Young LLP, Deloitte & Touche; exec. v.p., CFO Schwan Food, Marshall, Minn., 2002—. Office: Schwan Food 115 W College Dr Marshall MN 56258

BURR, WINTHROP AMES, psychiatrist; b. Boston, Jan. 3, 1943; s. John T. and Joan A. Burr; m. Barbara H. Hertz, June 27, 1967; children: Valentine A., Adam T. MD, Harvard Med. Sch., 1969. Diplomate Am. Bd. Psychiatry Neurology. Intern Strong Meml. Hosp., Rochester, NY, 1969—70; resident in adult psychiatry Mass. Mental Health Ctr., Boston, 1970—73; pvt. practice Cambridge, Mass., 1975—; staff psychiatrist V.A. Outpatient Clinic, Boston, 1976—84; dir. tng. mental health svc. Harvard U. Health Svcs., Cambridge, Mass., 1984—. Corr. sec. Friends of Blue Hills, Canton, Mass., 1999—. Asst. surgeon USPHS, 1973—75, Atlanta. Mem.: Am. Psychiat. Assn. Office: Harvard Univ Health Svcs 75 Mt Auburn St Cambridge MA 02138 Office Phone: 617-495-2049. E-mail: wburr@uhs.harvard.edu.

BURRELL, CALVIN ARCHIE, minister; b. Fairview, Okla., June 22, 1943; s. Lawrence Lester and Lottie Edna (Davison) B.; m. Barbara Ann Mann, May 29, 1966; children: Debra, Darla, Donna. BS, Northwestern State U., 1965; MA, So. Nazarene U., Bethany, Okla., 1978. Ordained to ministry Ch. of God, 1966. Tchr., prin., dean boys Spring Vale Acad., Owosso, Mich., 1964-76; pastor Ch. of God (Seventh Day), Ft. Smith, Ark., 1970-73, Shawnee, Okla., 1976-78, Denver, 1978-88, Galena Park, Tex., 1996—2004; pres. gen. conf. Ch. of God, Denver, 1987-97; editor Bible Advocate Mag., Denver, 1997—, dir. ministries tng. sys., 2002—. Instr. Summit Sch. Theology, Denver, 1978-95; officer Bible Sabath Assn., 1983-. Office: Ch of God 330 W 152d Ave PO Box 33677 Denver CO 80233-0677 Office Phone: 303-452-7973.

BURRELL, E. WILLIAM, retired university adminstrator, educator; b. Providence, Apr. 28, 1927; s. Edward John and Helene Agnes (Kelly) B.; m. Barbara Mary O'Connor, Apr. 18, 1953; children: Jason Edwin, Mary Elizabeth. Student, Providence Coll., 1945-47; AB, Fordham U., 1949; MA, Boston U., 1959; EdD, Harvard U., 1964; HLD honoris causa, Salve Regina U., 1996. Tchr. Providence Sch. Dept., 1957-65; prof. English and edn. Salve Regina U., Newport, R.I., 1965-96, chmn. dept. edn., 1967-73, dean of coll., 1974-77, v.p., dean of faculty and grad. studies, 1977-95, emeritus prof., 1996—. Mem. accreditation team, sometime chmn. New Eng. Assn. Schs. and Colls., Winchester, Mass., 1975-86. Mem. allocations panel United Way Southeastern New Eng., Providence, 1976-93; bd. dirs. Samaritans of R.I., Providence, 1985-90. Mem. R.I. Coun. Tchrs. English (life; founder 1959, pres. 1965-67), Barnard Club (pres. 1971-72), Phi Delta Kappa.

BURRELL, ORVILLE RICHARD (SHAGGY), popular musician; b. Kingston, Jamaica, Oct. 22, 1968; arrived in Bklyn., 1986; 2 children. Albums Pure Pleasure, 1993, Boombastic, 1995 (Grammy award, best reggae album, 1996), Midnite Lover, 1997, Hot Shot, 2000, Mr. Lover Lover: The Best of Shaggy Part 1, 2002, Hot Shot Ultramix, 2002, Lucky Day, 2003, Boombastic Hits, 2004, Essential Shaggy, 2004, Clothes Drop, 2005. Served with USMC, 1988—92, Operation Desert Storm, Persian Gulf War. Office: c/o Geffen Records 2220 Colorado Ave Santa Monica CA 90404

BURRELL, PAMELA, actress; b. Tacoma, Aug. 4, 1945; d. Donald A. and Mickey Rose (Curtiss) B.; m. Monty Silver, July 18, 1965 (div. 1978); children: Deirdre Paige, Emily Beth; m. Peter J. Gatto, Apr. 21, 1979. Studies with Sandy Miesner; student, San Francisco Ballet, N.Y.C. Ballet. Actress: (stage prodns.) Arms and the Man, 1967 (Theatre World award 1968), Where's Charley?, 1974, Berkeley Square, 1976, The Boss, 1976, Tatyana Repina, 1978, Biography, 1979, Strider, 1979, Sunday in the Park with George, 1985, also numerous regional stage appearances, 1967-86, (feature films) Da Duva, 1967, Popeye, 1980, (TV series) The Catlins, 1984-85, (TV episodes) Search for Tomorrow, Ryan's Hope, Spencer for Hire, 1986. Mem. Actors' Equity Assn., Screen Actors Guild, AFTRA.

BURRI, BETTY JANE, research chemist; b. San Francisco, Jan. 23, 1955; d. Paul Gene and Carleen Georgette (Meyers) B.; m. Kurt Randall Annweiler, Dec. 1, 1984. BA, San Francisco State U., 1976; MS, Calif. State U., Long Beach, 1978; PhD, U. Calif. San Diego, La Jolla, 1982. Research asst. Scripps Clinic, La Jolla, 1982-83, research assoc., 1983-85; research chemist Western Human Nutrition Rsch. Ctr., USDA, San Francisco, 1985-99, Davis, Calif., 1999—; adj. prof. nutrition dept. U. Nev., 1993-98, U. Calif., 2000—; leader crisis rsch. Davis, Calif., 2003—. Mem. steering com. Carotenoid Rsch. Interaction Group, 1994-97. Co-editor Carotenoid News, 1995-99; contbr. articles to profl. jours. Grantee NIH, 1982, 85, USDA, 1986-2002, Spinal Cord Rsch. Found., 1998, Am. Chem. Soc., 1998-2002; affiliate fellow Am. Heart Assn., 1983, 84. Mem. Assn. Women in Sci. (founding dir. San Diego chpt.), N.Y. Acad. Sci., Carotenoid Rsch. Interaction Group, Internat. Carotenoid Soc., Am. Chem. Soc. Office: Western Human Nutrition Rsch Ctr 229 Creuss Hall 1 Shields Ave Davis CA 95616 Business E-Mail: bburri@whnrc.usda.gov.

BURRIDGE, MICHAEL JOHN, veterinarian, educator, research director; b. St. Albans, Eng., Apr. 27, 1942; came to U.S., 1973; s. Arthur Wilfred Bailey and Georgina Augusta (Davis) Burridge; m. Desree Margaret Wiggins, Aug. 13, 1973 (div. Sept. 1981); m. Karen Maureen Bengtsson, Jan. 1, 1983; 1 child, Christina Michelle. BVM&S, U. Edinburgh, Scotland, 1966; MPVM, U. Calif., Davis, 1974, PhD, 1976. Rsch. asst. East African Trypanosomiasis Rsch. Orgn., Tororo, Uganda, 1966; vet. practitioner Grant and Arnold, Woking, Eng., 1967-68; animal health officer Food & Agr. Orgn., Kabete, Kenya, 1968-73; grad. rsch. asst. U. Calif., Davis, 1973-76; assoc. prof. U. Fla., Gainesville, 1976-82, prof., 1982—, chmn. dept., 1984-93. Mem. com. on animal health NAS, Washington, 1980-83; cons. World Bank, Zaire, 1982, USAID, India, 1987, 91; cons. vet. medicine Williams & Wilkins, Balt., 1982-99; bd. dirs. Internat. Laveran Found., Annecy, France, 1991-94. Editor: Impact of Diseases on Livestock Production in the Tropics, 1984. Grantee US AID, 1985-2005 Achievements include co-invention of attractant decoy for tick control, self-medicating applicators for parasite control, and diagnostic tests and vaccines for rickettsial diseases. Home: 10021 SW 67th Dr Gainesville FL 32608-6304 Office: U Fla Dept Pathobiology PO Box 110880 Gainesville FL 32611-0880 Office Phone: 352-392-4700 x3131. Business E-Mail: burridgem@mail.vetmed.ufl.edu.

BURRILL, KATHLEEN R. F. (KATHLEEN R. F. GRIFFIN-BURRILL), language educator; b. Canterbury, U.K., Mar. 8, 1924; d. William Henry and Ruby Amy (Webber) Griffin; children: Anne Ruth, Jane Ruth. AM, Columbia U., 1957, PhD, 1964; cert., Mid. East Inst., Columbia U, 1959. Officer of Brit. Coun., Ankara, Turkey, U.K., 1947-55; lectr. to prof. Middle East and Asian langs. and cultures Columbia U., N.Y.C., 1957-2000, prof. emerita, 2000—. Author: The Quatrains of Nesimi, Fourteenth-Century Turkic Hurufi Poet; co-editor Archivum Ottomanicum, 1984-95; contbr. articles to profl. jours. and encys. Recipient rsch. and travel award, Coun. Rsch. Humanities, 1966—67; fellow, Columbia U., 1957—59, Ford Found., 1959—60, Am. Rsch. Inst. in Turkey, summers, 1967, 1975. Fellow: Mid. East Studies Assn. (dir. 1974—76, founding fellow); mem.: Am. Assn. Tchrs. Turkic Langs. (pres. 1986—2002, hon. pres. 2003—), Mid. East Inst. (Washington), Brit. Soc. Mid. East Studies, Inst. Turkish Studies (governing bd. 1995—2001, founding assoc.), Turkish Studies Assn. (dir. 1974—76).

BURRIS, BOYD LEE, psychiatrist, psychoanalyst, physician, educator; b. Knoxville, Tenn., Jan. 28, 1930; s. Fred Roosevelt and Mildred Blanche Burris. BS, U. Tenn., Knoxville, 1951; MD, U. Tenn., Memphis, 1952. Diplomate in psychiatry Am. Bd. Psychiatry and Neurology; cert. in psychoanalysis. Tng. and supervising analyst Balt.-Washington Inst. for Psychoanalysis, Washington, 1974—, co-dir., 1980-86; clin. prof. psychiatry and behavioral scis. George Washington U. Sch. Medicine, Washington, 1983—; clin. prof. psychiatry Georgetown U. Sch. Medicine, Washington, 1990—; mem. bd. trustees Ctr. for Advanced Psychoanalytic Studies, Princeton, N.J., Aspen, Colo., 1982—, pres. bd. trustees and dir., 1994—2003; pvt. practice psychiatry and psychoanalysis Washington, 1960—. Active staff George Washington U. Hosp., 1963-96; cons. Potomac Found. for Mental Health, Bethesda, Md., 1969-78, St. Elizabeth's Hosp., Washington, 1969-88. Contbr. chpt. to book, articles to profl. jours. Lt. comdr. M.C., USN, 1954-56. Mem. Am. Psychiat. Assn. (chair tellers com. 1987-88), Am. Psychoanalytic Assn. (bd. on profl. standards 1982-86, 2000-2002), Balt./Washington Soc. for Psychoanalysis (pres. 1978-79). Home: 3100 Rolling Rd Chevy Chase MD 20815-4038 Office: 4545 42nd St NW Ste 310 Washington DC 20016-4623 Office Phone: 202-244-5500.

BURRIS, CRAVEN ALLEN, retired college administrator, educator; b. Wingate, N.C., Sept. 11, 1929; s. Craven Cullom and Virginia Neulin (Currie) B.; m. Jane Russell Burris, June 19, 1955; children: Christa Cullom, David Allen. AA, Wingate Coll., 1949; BS, Wake Forest U., 1951; BDiv, Southeastern Bapt. Sem., Wake Forest, N.C., 1958; MA, Duke U., 1959, PhD, 1964. Prof. history and govt. Gardner-Webb U., Boiling Springs, N.C., 1958-66; prof. history, govt. and interdisciplinary studies St. Andrews Presbyn. Coll., Laurinburg, N.C., 1966-69; v.p., dean of coll., prof. history and politics Meredith Coll., Raleigh, N.C., 1969-98, ret., 1998, acting pres., 1971. Vis. lectr. in politics N.C. State U., Raleigh, 2003, tchr. ENCORE Program, 2000—04. Contbr. articles to profl. jours. Precinct ofcr. State Conv. del., N.C. Dem. Party, 1969, 71; pres., dir. Tammy Lynn Found./Retarded Children, Raleigh, 1980—; chmn. Raleigh Hist. Dists. Commn., 2000-2001. Lt. USNR, 1951-55, Italy and Atlantic Fleet. Recipient Disting. Alumni award Wingate U., 1983, Fulbright Study Trip, U.S. Govt., Pakistan, 1973, Study Trip USSR, 1988, Rsch. Brit. Mus. and Libr., 1963, 97. Mem. Civitan Internat. (v.p. bd. dirs. 1970—), Lions Club (editor 1965), Masons. Baptist. Avocations: choral singing, tennis, racquetball, golf, sailing, gardening. Home: 1322 Duplin Rd Raleigh NC 27607-3721 Office: Meredith Coll 3800 Hillsborough St Raleigh NC 27607-5237

BURRIS, JAMES FREDERICK, federal healthcare administrator, educator; b. Mauston, Wis., Apr. 15, 1947; s. James Duane and Margaret Katherine (Jones) B.; m. Christine Tuve, July 3, 1971; 1 child, Cameron William Tuve. AB, ScB, Brown U., 1970; MD, Columbia U., 1974. Diplomate Am. Bd. Internal Medicine, Subspecialty Bd. Geriatrics, Am. Bd. Clin. Pharmacology. Intern Roosevelt Hosp., N.Y.C., 1974-75; resident in internal medicine Georgetown U. Med. Ctr., Washington, 1977-79; fellow in hypertension VA Med. Ctr., Washington, 1979-81; asst. prof. Sch. Medicine, Georgetown U., Washington, 1981-86, assoc. prof., 1986-91, coord. MD/PhD program, 1988-94, prof., 1991-97; clin. prof., 1997—; asst. dean Sch. Medicine, Georgetown U., Washington, 1987-90; assoc. dean Sch. Medicine Georgetown U., 1990-97, dir. continuing profl. edn., 1994-97; dep. chief R&D officer Vets. Health Adminstrn., U.S. Dept. Vets Affairs, Washington, 1997—2003; chief cons. Geriatrics and Extended Care, Vets. Health Adminstrn, US Dept. Vets. Affairs, Washington, 2003—. Bd. dirs. Inst. for Clin. Rsch., Washington, 1989-92; bd. regents Am. Bd. Clin. Pharmacology, 1992-98, 2002—; rsch. adminstr. cert. coun.; rsch. assoc. hypertension unit VA Med. Ctr., Washington, 1981-92; vis. investigator Centre Hospitalier, U. Vaudois, Lausanne, Switzerland, 1982-83; dir. clin. rsch. Cardiovasc. Ctr. No. Va., Falls Church, 1988-92; under-sec. health's exec. performance award U.S. Dept. of Vet. Affairs, 1999, 2000, Commendation award, 2003-. Mem. editl. bd. Jour. Clin. Pharmacology, Jour. Am. Geriat. Soc., Clin. Pharmacology and Therapeutics; contbr. over 250 articles to profl. jours. Cubmaster Boy Scouts Am., 1995-98, asst. scoutmaster, 1998—. Lt. comdr. USPHS, 1975-77 (active duty), 1977- (inactive reserve). Recipient svc. award ARC, 1970, outstanding svc. citation DAV, 1987, meritorious svc. award Am. Heart Assn., 1994, Cubmasters award Boy Scouts Am., 1998, James E. West award, 1997, Scouter's Tng. Key award, 2000, Vicennial medal Georgetown U., 2000; commd. officer student tng. and extern program scholar USPHS, 1973-74; rsch. fellow Found. for Rsch. of Cardiovascular Diseases, Lausanne, 1983. Fellow: ACP, Am. Coll. Cardiology, Am. Coll. Clin. Pharmacology (bd. regents 1990—95, 1998—2003, hon. regent 2003, sec. 2004—, Disting. Svc. award 1992), Am. Coll. Preventive Medicine, Am. Geriatrics Soc.; mem.: AMA (physician's recognition award 1982, 1985, 1988, 1991, 1994, 1997, 2001), Am. Heart Assn. (chmn. rsch. peer rev. com. 1992—94, rsch. com. 1994—96, bd. dirs. Nation's Capital affiliate 1994—97, v.p. 1995—96, fellow couns. on high blood pressure rsch., circulation, epidemiology, coun. clin. cardiology), Sigma Xi. Achievements include education and research in hypertension, hyperlipidemia, preventive cardiology and clinical pharmacology; grants and contracts management and regulatory affairs and technology transfer administration; direction of continuing professional education programs; federal research and healthcare policy development and program implementation. Office: Vets Health Adminstrn (114) Dept VA 810 Vermont Ave NW Washington DC 20420-0001 E-mail: james.burris@va.gov.

BURRIS, JOHN EDWARD, academic administrator, biologist, educator; b. Feb. 1, 1949; s. Robert Harza and Katherine (Brusse) Burris; m. Sally Ann Sandermann, Dec. 21, 1974; children: Jennifer, Margaret, Mary. AB, Harvard U., 1971; postgrad., U. Wis., 1971—72; PhD, U. Calif., San Diego, 1976. Asst. prof. biology Pa. State U., University Park, 1976—83, assoc. prof. biology, 1983—85, adj. assoc. prof., 1985—89, adj. prof., 1989—2001; pres. Beloit College, Beloit, Wis., 2000—. Dir. bd. biology NRC, Washington, 1984—89; exec. dir. Commn. Life Scis., 1988—92, mem., 1993—97; dir., CEO Marine Biol. Lab., Woods Hole, Mass., 1992—2000; pres.-elect Am. Inst. Biol. Scis., 1995, pres., 96; chmn. adv. com. student sci. enrichment program Burroughs Wellcome Fund, 1995—2002; life and microgravity scis. and applications adv. com. NASA, 1997—2001; trustee Krasnow Inst., 1999—2002; bd. dirs. Radiation Effects Rsch. Found. Mem.: AAAS (bd. dirs. 2002—), Naples Stazione Zoologica, Consiglio Sci., Phi Beta Kappa. Office: 700 College St Beloit WI 53511 Office Phone: 608-363-2201. Business E-Mail: burrisj@beloit.edu.

BURRIS, JOHNNY CLARK, law educator; b. Paris, Ky., May 21, 1953; s. John Curtis and Ada (Sargent) B.; m. Jane Wright, July 1975 (div. Sept. 1980); m. Cathy Jackson, Mar. 1981 (div. Feb. 1984); m. Nancy Nevius, Aug. 6, 1985; 1 child, Sarah Nevius. BA, U. Ky., 1975; JD, No. Ky. U., 1978; LLM, Columbia U., 1984. Bar: Ky. 1978, U.S. Ct. Appeals (6th cir.) 1978, Ohio 1979, U.S. Dist. Ct. (ea. dist.) Ky. 1979, U.S. Ct. Appeals (11th cir.) 1987. Law clk. to presiding justice Ky. Supreme Ct., Frankfort, 1978—79; asst. atty. Commonwealth Atty. Kenton County, Covington, Ky., 1979; asst. dean Nova Southeastern U. Shepard Broad Law Ctr., Ft. Lauderdale, Fla., 1979—84, asst. prof. law, 1981—87, assoc. prof. law, 1987—89, prof. law, 1989—. Mem. No. Ky. Law Rev., 1976-78. Mem. ABA, Ky. Bar Assn., Fed. Bar Assn., Fla. Bar Assn. (affiliate), Omicron Delta Kappa. Office: Nova Southeastern U Shepard Broad Law Ctr 3305 College Ave Fort Lauderdale FL 33314-7721 Office Phone: 954-262-6176. Business E-Mail: burrisj@nsu.law.nova.edu.

BURRIS, ROBERT HARZA, biochemist, educator; b. Brookings, SD, Apr. 13, 1914; s. Edward T. and Mabel T. (Harza) Burris; m. Katherine Irene Brusse, Sept. 12, 1945; children: Jean Carol, John Edward, Ellen Louise. BS, S.D. State Coll., 1936, D.Sc., 1966; MS, U. Wis., 1938, PhD, 1940. NRC fellow Columbia U., 1940—41; faculty U. Wis., Madison, 1941—, prof., 1951—84; chmn. biochemistry Coll. Agr., 1958—70, W.H. Peterson prof. biochemistry, 1976—84, prof. emeritus, 1984—. Recipient Charles Thom award, Soc. Indsl. Microbiology, 1977, Nat. Medal of Sci., 1980, Carty award, NAS, 1984, Wolf award in Agr., 1985; fellow Guggenheim Found., Cambridge U., 1954. Mem.: NAS, AAAS, Am. Soc. Plant Physiologists (pres. 1960, Stephen Hales award 1968, Charles Reid Barnes award 1977), Indian Nat. Sci. Acad. (fgn. assoc.), Am. Soc. Microbiology, Biochem. Soc., Am. Philos. Soc., Am. Soc. Biochemistry and Molecular Biology, Am. Chem. Soc. (Spencer award 1990). Home: 6225 Mineral Point Rd Madison WI 53705 Business E-Mail: burris@biochem.wisc.edu.

BURRIS, STEVEN MICHAEL, lawyer; b. LA, Dec. 30, 1952; s. Michael Victor and Patricia (McNeer) Burris; m. Melanie Schultz, Oct. 29, 1983; 1 child from previous marriage, Michael Steven. AB with distinction, Stanford U., 1975; JD with honors, U. So. Calif., 1978. Bar: Nev. 1978, Calif. 1978, U.S. Dist. Ct. Nev. 1978, U.S. Ct. Appeals (9th cir.) 1982. Assoc. Rogers, Monsey, Woodbury et al, Las Vegas, Nev., 1978—81; ptnr. Sacco & Burris, Las Vegas, 1981—84; pres. Burris & Thomas, Las Vegas, 1984—. Tchr. Clark County CC, Las Vegas, 1979—80. Author: (booklet) Your Personal Injury Case, 1982; co-author: (manual) Trial Advocacy in Nevada, 1991, Trying the Auto Injury Case in Nevada, 1992; editor-in-chief: The Advocate, 2000—. Bd. dirs. Sr. Citizens Mobile Home Pk. Found., Las Vegas, 1981—84; vice chmn. Coun. Ministries Fellowship Bapt. Ch., Las Vegas, 1988. Recipient Am. Jurisprudence award, Bancroft Whitney's Pubs., 1977, Pres.'s award, U.S. Jaycees, 1981. Mem.: ATLA, Clark County Bar Assn. (cert. of Merit 1987—88), Nev. Bar Assn., Nev. Trial Lawyers Assn. (bd. govs. 1992—, pres. 1997), Gideons (pres.). Democrat.

BURRIS, TERRY EUGENE, ophthalmologist, corneal specialist; b. Enid, Okla., Jan. 26, 1952; s. Wiley Eugene and Elizabeth B.; m. Tima Burris; 4 children. BS, MD, Pitts. State U., 1974. Diplomate Am. Bd. Ophthalmology. Dir. corneal and external disease svcs., dept. ophthalmology Naval Hosp., Oakland, Calif., 1982-86; cons. corneal and external diseases, dept. ophthalmology Pacific Med. Ctr., San Francisco, 1984-86; chief and founder Cornea and External Disease Svc. Devers Eye Inst., Portland, Oreg., 1986-90; med./surg. dir. Lions Eyebank of Oreg., Devers Eye Inst., Portland, 1986-90; dir., founder Lions Eyebank of Oreg., Eyebank Rsch. Lab., 1986-90; pres. we. region Eyebank Assn. of Am., 1989-91, mem. eyebank accreditation bd., 1990—; assoc. clin. prof. ophthalmology Casey Eye Inst./Oreg. Health Sci. U., Portland, 1998—; founding ophthalmologist Northwest Corneal Svcs.,

Portland, 1990—. Cons. sci. medicine adv. bd. Keravision, Inc., 1987—2001; tech. cons. Chiron Ophthalmics, 1988—98; prin. investigator Intrastromal Corneal Ring for Phase II and III Protocol Keravision, Inc., 1995—2002. Comdr. M.C., USNR. Avocations: collecting minerals, writing music. Office: Northwest Corneal Svcs 6950 SW Hampton St Ste 150 Portland OR 97223-8380 E-mail: nwcornea.com.

BURROUGHS, HAROLD R., lawyer; BA cum laude, Middlebury Coll., 1982; JD cum laude, U. Mich., 1990. Bar: Mo 1990. Ptnr., group dep. Banking, Bus. and Pub. Fin. Bryan Cave LLP, St. Louis. Office: Bryan Cave LLP One Metropolitan Square 211 N Broadway, Ste 3600 Saint Louis MO 63102 Office Phone: 314-259-2706. E-mail: hrburroughs@bryancave.com.

BURROUGHS, MARGARET TAYLOR GOSS, artist, former museum director; b. St. Rose, La., Nov. 1, 1917; d. Alexander and Octavia (Pierre) Taylor; m. Bernard Goss, 1937; 1 child, Gayle; m. Charles Burroughs, 1949; 1 adopted child, Paul. BA in Edn, Art Inst. Chgo., 1946, MA, 1948; LHD (hon.), Lewis U., 1972; DHL (hon.), Chgo. State U., 1983. Tchr. art Chgo. Public Schs., 1944-68; prof. humanities Kennedy King Coll., Chgo., 1969-79; exec. dir., founder DuSable Mus. African Am. History, Chgo., 1961-84, dir. emeritus, 1984—; group shows include: LA County Mus., 1976, Corcoran Gallery, 1980; mem. Chgo. Council Fine Arts, 1976-80, Nat. Commn. Negro History and Culture, 1981—; founder Nat. Conf. Artists, 1959. Fellow NEH, 1968. Office: DuSable Museum 740 E 56th Pl Chicago IL 60637-1495 Office Phone: 312-742-4737.

BURROUGHS, THOMAS, JR., media consultant; b. Columbia, S.C., Mar. 7, 1943; s. Thomas Burroughs, Sr. and Marie (Bell) Burroughs; m. Levonne Cummings, Oct. 22, 1994; children: Arlisa Monique Dailey, Thomas Robert. Student, Allen-Benedict Coll., Ind. U., U. Ghana. Prodr./asst. cameraman Ind. U. audio-visual dept., Bloomington, 1970—73; libr. Rare Book Libr., Bloomington, 1971; freelance photographer Cin., 1976—79; photo tech. Qualex/Kodak, Cin., 1978—2003. Photo cons. Qualex/Kodak, Cin., 1982—89. Photographer (cover) Tommy Scott-Young Poems, 1978, (magazine) Downbeat Internat. Jazz Magazine, 1978, (collection) Cincinnati Photographers, 1979. Mem. Woodlawn PTO, Ohio, 2002; degreed Mason Prince Hall Grand Lodge of Ohio Free and Accepted Mason, 2001—03. Recipient Best Of Show, Art Consortium, 1980. Mem.: Sierra Club. Achievements include many photographic projects including brochures, exhibitions, group shows, annual reports, copyrighted Poster-of-the-Year Blackervisions. Avocations: bicycling, gardening, fly fishing. Home: 1238 Timberland Drive Cincinnati OH 45215

BURROW, DAVID MICHAEL, mathematics professor, academic administrator; b. Moline, Ill., Oct. 11, 1962; s. George Irving and Elizabeth Zane (Miller) B. BA with high honors, No. Iowa U., 1983; MEd with highest honors, So. Miss. U., 1992; TAG Cert., Morningside Coll., 1995. Cert. tchr., Iowa. Tchr., broadcasting sponsor, speech dir., student coun. moderator, quiz bowl coach Bishop Garrigan H.S., Algona, Iowa, 1983—; gifted/talented coord., 1993—. Instr. Iowa Lakes C.C., Algona, 1993—, Iowa Lakes CC, Alguna, 1993—; evaluator; pvt. tutor, 1990—. Bd. dirs. First Congl. Ch., Algona, 1988—. Gov's award for Volunteerism, 2003. Mem. Math. Assn., Am., Nat. Coun. Tchrs. Math., Iowa Coun. Tchrs. Math., Nat. Cath. Edn. Assn., Nat. Fedn. Interscholastic Activities, Phi Delta Kappa. Democrat. Avocations: internet, travel, reading, hiking, music. Office: Garrigan High Sch 1224 N Mccoy St Algona IA 50511-1299

BURROW, GERARD NOEL, internist, educator; b. Boston, Jan. 9, 1933; s. William and Noelle Elvira (Money) B.; m. Ann Huntington Rademacher, June 22, 1956; children: Peter Noel, Elisabeth Huntington, Sarah Rogers. BA, Brown U., 1954; MD, Yale U., 1958. From asst. prof. to prof. Yale U. Sch. Medicine, New Haven, 1966-76; prof. dept. medicine U. Toronto, Canada, 1976-81, Sir John and Lady Eaton prof. medicine, 1981-88, chmn. dept., 1981-88; vice-chancellor for health scis., dean U. Calif. Sch. Medicine, San Diego, 1988-92; dean Yale U. Sch. Medicine, New Haven, 1992-97; David Paige Smith prof. medicine Yale U., New Haven, 1997—2002; dean emeritus Yale U. Sch. Medicine, 2002—; pres., CEO Sea Rsch. Found., Mystic, Conn., 2002—. Author: The Thyroid Gland in Pregnancy, 1972, A History of Yale's School of Medicine: Passing Torches to Others, 2002; editor: (with Ferris) Medical Complications During Pregnancy, 1975, 82, 88, 94, 99 (with Duffy) 2004. Chmn., bd. dirs., U. Conn. Health Ctr.; chmn., bd. dirs., trustee U. Conn Fellow ACP, Royal Coll. Physicians (Can.); mem. Assn. Am. Physicians, Am. Thyroid Assn., Inst. Medicine of NAS. Office: Sea Rsch Found 55 Coogan Blvd Mystic CT 06355-3289 Office Phone: 860-572-5955.

BURROW, HAROLD, retired gas industry executive; b. Navasota, Tex., Dec. 1, 1914; s. Benjamin Donald and Minnie (Weaver) B.; m. Vassa Woodley; children: Larry W., Harry W., Janice K. With Tenneco, Inc., Houston, 1943-66, pres., mem. exec. com., 1960-66; chmn. bd., mem. exec. com. Colo. Interstate Gas Co., Colorado Springs, 1974—, also bd. dirs.; vice chmn. bd., mem. exec. com. Coastal Corp. (formerly Coastal States Gas Corp.), Houston, 1974—2001; chmn. bd., CEO Coastal Natural Gas Co., 1995-2001. Mem. exec. bd., bd. dirs., mem. exec. com. Am. Nat. Resources, Detroit. Mem. Petroleum Club (Houston), Ramada-Tajas Club (Houston). Methodist.

BURROW, PAUL IRVING, secondary school educator; b. Iowa City, Iowa, Aug. 16, 1955; s. George Irving and Elizabeth Zane (Miller) B.; m. Nancy Kay Rader, Sept. 8, 1979; children: Rachel, Timothy. BA, Drake U., 1976, MA, 1981. Tchr. Spanish, social studies Adair (Iowa) -Casey Schs., 1977-78, Oskaloosa (Iowa) Sr. H.S., 1978—. Bd. dirs. Iowa State Employee's Benefits Assn., chmn. 2002—; exec. bd. Crisis Intervention Svcs., Oskaloosa, 1996-2000; mem. coun. Boy Scouts Am., Oskaloosa, 1988-95; pastor Kirkville United Meth. Ch., 1999—, Hispanic Ministries, Central United Meth. Ch., Oskaloosa, 2001—. Mem. Am. Coun. Tchrs. Fgn. Langs., Iowa Fgn. Lang. Assn. (pres. 1985-87, Secondary Tchr. of Yr. 2004), Iowa Edn. Assn. (exec. bd. 1997—), Oksaloosa Edn. Assn. (spokesperson 1985-2000, grievance chair 1998—, Tchr of Yr. 1992). Democrat. Methodist. Avocations: computers, genealogy, camping, travel. Home: 2212 Lynndale Rd Oskaloosa IA 52577-9129 Office: 1816 N 3rd St Oskaloosa IA 52577

BURROWES, CARL PATRICK, communications educator; b. Monrovia, Liberia, Oct. 29, 1952; came to U.S., 1980; s. Cecil Augustus and Hyacinth Aletha (Campbell) B.; m. Adjoa Deborah Jackson, Sept. 26, 1981; children: Kassahun, Hyacinth Bendu. BA in Journalism, Howard U., 1976; MA in Comm., Syracuse U., 1979; PhD in Comm., Temple U., 1994. Corr. West Africa, Monrovia, Liberia, 1979-80, New African, Monrovia, 1979-80; instr. U. Liberia, Monrovia, 1979-80, Hampton (Va.) Inst., 1980-81; asst. prof. Calumet Coll., Whiting, Ind., 1981-84, Glassboro (N.J.) State Coll., 1984-90; assoc. prof. Calif. State U., Fullerton, 1990—. Exec. dir. Liberia Rsch. & Info. Project, Glassboro, 1984-90; bd. mem. Assn. Constl. Democracy in Liberia, Washington, 1988-90. Mng. editor Lone Star Newsletter, Fullerton, 1994—. Mem. Soc. Profl. Journalists, Assn. Edn. in Journalism and Mass Comm., Liberia Studies Assn., Frederick Douglass Soc.

BURROWES, ROBERT ARTHUR, transportation consultant, travel-tour operator; b. Bozeman, Mont., Dec. 26, 1919; s. Douglas Henry and Florence May Burrowes; m. Dorthalee Vervil, Aug. 14, 1945 (div. 1956); children: James Douglas, Harold Leslie; m. Annie May Mortimore, Aug. 28, 1958. Clk. exec. dept. East Bay Transit Co., Oakland, Calif., 1938-42; with traffic dept. Bamberger Electric R.R., Salt Lake City, 1942-43; traffic mgr. Pacific Greyhound Lines, San Francisco, 1943-51, Yosemite Gray Line, San Francisco, 1951-61; owner, mgr. Lincoln Bus Line, Stockton, Calif., 1961-72; dir. transp. Culver City (Calif.) Mcpl. Bus. Line, 1972-77; exec. dir. Humboldt Transit Authority, Eureka, Calif., 1977-85; transit cons., Calif., 1985—. Contbr. articles to motor bus mags. Mem. Lyon County Mus. Soc., chmn., 1974-80; mem. State Transp. Com., Carson City, Nev., 1986—. Mem. Am. Sunbathing Assn. (life), Nev. Hist. Soc., Motor Bus Soc., Pacific Bus Mus., Profl. Car Soc., Bay area Electric Railway Assn. (life). Republican. Avocation: yerington senior citizens. Home: 500 Fairview St Yerington NV 89447-3231

BURROWS, BERTHA JEAN, retired academic administrator; b. Brush, Colo., June 15, 1930; d. John and Marie Pabst; m. Leslie R. Burrows, Sept. 2, 1951; children: Paul Eric, Amy Susan, Julie Diane, David Arthur. BA in Bus., U. Colo., 1952. Sec. Dental Found. Colo., Denver, 1969—70, John Boswick, MD, Denver, 1970—72; adminstrv. cons. dept. contg. edn. U. Colo. Sch. Dentistry, Denver, 1975—76; asst. dir. vol. svcs. U. Colo. Health Sci. Ctr., 1977—80; sec. Denver Neurosurg. Assn., Denver, 1981—83; ret., 1983. Bookkeeper Clark & Co., Denver, 1981—83; com. mem. U. Colo. Hosp., Denver, 1999—. Vol. U. Colo. Hosp., Denver, 1970—; treas., asst. mgr. U. Colo. Hosp. Gift Shop, 1997—, bd. mgrs., 1987—. Mem.: Colo. Assn. Healthcare Auxilians and Vols. (treas. 2000—01, chmn. gift shop 2002—03, pres.-elect 2003—04, pres. 2004—05), U. Colo. Srs. Assn. (pres. 2002—). Home: 6911 E Iliff Place Denver CO 80224

BURROWS, BRIAN WILLIAM, retired research and development company executive, retired manufacturing executive; b. Burnie, Tasmania, Australia, Nov. 15, 1939; came to U.S., 1966; s. William Henry and Jean Elizabeth (Ling) B.; 1 child, Karin; m. Penny Nathan Kahan, 1998. BSc, U. Tasmania, 1960, BSc with honors, 1962; PhD, Southampton U., 1966. Staff scientist Tyco Labs., Inc., Waltham, Mass., 1966-68; lectr. Macquarie U., Sydney, Australia, 1969-71; chef de sect. Battelle-Geneva, Switzerland, 1971-75; group leader Inco, Ltd., Mississauga, Ont., Can., 1976-77; program mgr., lab. dir. Gould, Inc., Rolling Meadows, Ill., 1977-86; v.p. rsch. and tech. USG Corp., Chgo., 1986—2005, ret., 2005. Contbr. articles to tech. jours.; patentee in field. Fellow: AAAS; mem.: Am. Chem. Soc., Union League Club. Home: 927 Longmeadow Ct Barrington IL 60010-9391

BURROWS, DONALD ALBERT, artist, painter, photographer, dean; b. Chgo., June 26, 1937; s. Charles Fredrick and Bertha Lillian (Olesen) B.; m. Philomena Durkin, Mar. 3, 1962 (div. 1983); children: Jennifer Maria, Charles Fredrick, Quentin Connor; m. Charlyn Butterfield, Apr. 2, 1995. BFA, Sch. of the Art Inst. of Chgo., 1961, MFA, 1963. Dir. Mobile (Ala.) Art Mus., 1964-66, Ft. Worth Art Mus., 1966-67, Ctr. for Creative Studies, Detroit, 1967-68; prof. humanities City Colls. of Chgo., 1968-83; assoc. dean Harrington Inst., Chgo., 1974-84; acad. dean Ray Coll. of Design, Chgo., 1986-93; prin. artist, designer Misaine/Chaleur, Inc., Gardena, Calif., 1990—, Modern Classic Artworks, Lexington, Ky., art dir.; pres., CEO ChyCogo and Co., Ltd., Willowbrook, Ill., 1987—. One-man shows include Hansen Gallery, Chgo., 1986, Elmhurst (Ill.) Coll., 1986, Galleria Renata, Chgo., 1988. Mem. Am. Soc. Interior Designers, Alumni Assn. Sch. of Art Inst. Chgo., Alumni Assn. U. Chgo., Art Inst. Chgo. (Ryerson Fgn. Traveling fellow, 1961-63). Home: 717 Maplewood Ct Unit D Willowbrook IL 60527-7539

BURROWS, EDWIN GLADDING, retired broadcaster, writer, poet; b. Dallas, July 23, 1917; s. Millar Burrows, Irene B. (Gladding); m. Gwenyth Lemon, 1940 (div. 1971); children: Edwin Gwynne, Daniel William, David John; m. Beth Elpern, Dec. 7, 1973. BA, Yale U., 1938; MA, U. Mich., 1940. Program dir. Sta. WWJ-FM, Detroit, 1940-43, Sta. WPAG, Ann Arbor, Mich., 1946-48; program dir., mgr. Stas. WUOM-WVGR, U. Mich., Ann Arbor, 1948-70, exec. prodr., 1973-82; dir. Nat. Ctr. for Audio Experimentation, U. Wis., Madison, 1970-73; ret., 1982. Condr. poetry readings through Mich., 1965—82; poetry readings State of Wash., 1986—; helped charter radio divsn. Nat. Ednl. Radio of Nat. Assn. Ednl. Broadcasters, former region III dir., chmn. bd., 1965; chmn./mem. bd. network adv. com. Nat. Assn. Ednl. Broadcasters; lobbyist for inclusion of radio in Pub. Broadcasting Act of 1967. Author: (poetry) The Arctic Tern and Other Poems, 1957, Man Fishing, 1970, Kiva, 1976, Properties: A Play for Voices, 1979, The House of August, 1985, (chapbooks) The Crossings, 1976, On the Road to Bailey's, 1979, Handsigns for Rain, 1989, The Birds Under the Earth, 1997, Sailing As Before, 2001; contbr. poetry to anthologies including Anthology of Magazine Verse, 1984, A Centennial Sampler of Edmonds Writing, 1989, ORL 50th Anniversary Anthology, 1993, The Age of Koestler: Practices of the Wind, 1994, The Sumac Reader, poems to over 150 jours. including Atlantic Monthly, Ascent, Am. Poetry, Black Warrior, Blue Mesa, Chariton, Cream City, Gettysburg, Hawaii, Iowa, Mass., Mich. Quar., Paris, Seattle, and Va. Quar. revs., Confluence, Epoc. Lt. USN, 1943—46. Recipient Ohio State awards, 1953, 1954, 1955, 1956, 1971, 1974, Borestone Mountain poetry award, 1964, 1st ann. poetry award Ascent, 1987, donated his papers to U. Md. at College Park Librs., 1991; fellow Yaddo Found., 1963, 1966.

BURROWS, ELIZABETH MACDONALD, religious organization executive, educator; b. Portland, Oreg., Jan. 30, 1930; d. Leland R. and Ruth M. (Frew) MacDonald. Certificate, Chinmaya Trust Sandeepany, Bombay; PhD (hon.), Internat. U. Philosophy and Sci., 1975; ThD, Christian Coll. Universal Peace, 1992. Ordained to ministry First Christian Ch., 1976. Mgr. credit Home Utilities, Seattle, 1958, Montgomery Ward, Crescent City, Calif., 1963; supr. Oreg. dist. tng. West Coast Tele., Beaverton, 1965; pres. Christ Ch. of Universal Peace, Seattle, 1971—, prof. religion, also bd. dirs.; pres. Archives Internat., Seattle, 1971—; v.p. James Tyler Kent Inst. Homeopathy, 1984-95; sec. Louis Braille Inst. for the Blind, 1995—. Author: Crystal Planet, 1979, Pathway of the Immortal, 1980, Odyssey of the Apocalypse, 1981, Harp of Destiny, 1984, Commentary for Gospel of Peace of Jesus Christ According to John, 1986, Seasons of the Soul, 1995, Voyagers of the Sand, 1996, The Song of God, 1998, Hold the Anchovies, 1996, Pilgrim of the Shadow, 1998, Maya Sangh and the Valley of the White Ones, 2001, The Secret Jesus Scroll, 2002, Poetry Chapbook, 2002, Visions, 2002, Maya Sangh and the Valley of the White One, Eat to Heal, 2002, Mystil Voyage, 2004, Htrae, 2005, Psalms Solemnis, 2005. Recipient Pres. award for literary excellence CADER, 1994, 95, 97, Diamond Homer award Famous Poets Soc., 1998, Pub.'s Choice award Poets of the New Era, 2002. Mem. Internat. Speakers Platform, Internat. New Thought Alliance, Cousteau Soc., Internat. Order of Chivalry, The Planetary Soc. Home: 10529 Ashworth Ave N Seattle WA 98133-8937 Office Phone: 206-362-4134. Personal E-mail: starbase2001@earthlink.net. *Oneness with God is mankind's ultimate vision. This results in a profound journey which covers strange and wonderful worlds beyond mortal boundaries. To reach oneness is to achieve more than anyone can imagine, or more than anyone has ever dreamed.*

BURROWS, HENRY PETER, III, secondary school educator; b. Selma, Ala., Jan. 26, 1944; s. Henry Peter Jr. and Josepine (Porter) B.; m. Dinah Shore, Aug. 26, 1983. BA in English, U. Del., 1967; BS in Edn., Auburn U., Montgomery, Ala., 1996; MA in History, U. Ala., 1986. Cert. tchr., Ala.; cert. airline trasnport pilot, command pilot. Commd. 2d lt. USAF, 1967, advanced through grades to lt. col., 1986, fighter pilot/staff officer worldwide, 1967-88, ret., 1988; airline pilot Pan Am. World Airways, Miami, Fla., 1989-91; tchr. math. Autauga County Bd. Edn., Prattville, Ala., 1996—. Contbr. articles and short stories to mags.; mem. editl. bd. Ala. Jour. Math., Montgomery, 1996—. Decorated DFC, Air medal; Chancellor's scholar Auburn U., 1996. Mem. NEA, Ala. Edn. Assn., Math. Assn. Am., Phi Kappa Phi, Kappa Delta Pi, Phi Alpha Theta. Avocations: coin collecting/numismatics, photography, jogging, reading. Office: Prattville Jr HS 1135 N Chestnut St Prattville AL 36067 Home: 102 Jordon Crossing Prattville AL 36067

BURROWS, JAMES, television and motion picture director, producer; b. L.A., Dec. 30, 1940; s. Abe Burrows. BA, Oberlin Coll.; MFA, Yale U. Off-Broadway prodns.: dir. (motion picture) Partners, 1982, (TV film) More Than Friends, 1978, (TV pilots) Lou Grant, Dear John, Night Court, Wings, Roc, Frasier, Friends, Newsradio, Third Rock from the Sun, Caroline in the City, Stark Raving Mad, Madigan Men, The Weber Show/ Cursed, Dexter Prep; co-creator, (TV series) The Mary Tyler Moore Show, 1976-76, The Bob Newhart Show, 1975-77, Taxi, 1978-82; co-creator, co-exec. producer, dir. Cheers, 1982-93, exec. producer, dir. Will & Grace, 1998-. Recipient Dirs. Guild Am. award for comedy direction, 1984, 91, 94, 99, Emmy awards NATAS for dir. in comedy series Taxi, 1979-80, 81-82 seasons, Cheers, 1982-83, 90-91 seasons; Emmy award as co-producer Cheers, 1982-83, 83-84, 89-90, 90-91 seasons; Emmy award as director of a Comedy Series for Fraiser, 1994, American Comedy award for Lifetime Achievement, 1996. Office: care Paramount TV Prodns 5555 Melrose Ave # Bungl Los Angeles CA 90038-3112

BURROWS, KENNETH DAVID, lawyer; b. Bklyn., Mar. 26, 1941; s. Selig S. and Gladys (Spatt) B.; m. Erica Jong, Aug. 5, 1989. BA, Brown U., 1967; JD, Fordham U., 1970. Bar: N.Y. 1971, Conn. 1973, U.S. Dist. Ct. (so. dist.) N.Y. 1972, U.S. Dist. Ct. Conn. 1993, U.S. Supreme Ct. 1973. Assoc. Phillips, Nizer, Benjamin, Krim & Ballon, N.Y.C., 1970-77; ptnr. Kleinberg, Kaplan, Wolff, Cohen & Burrows, N.Y.C., 1977-79, Burrows & Poster, N.Y.C., 1980-89, Burrows & Franzblau, N.Y.C., 1990-91; arbitrator small claims ct. City of N.Y., 1975-95; lectr. Practising Law Inst., 1996—; spl. master Supreme Ct. State of N.Y., N.Y. County, 1980-89; arbitrator U.S. Dist. Ct. (ea. dist.) N.Y., 1994—; mediator U.S. Dist. Ct. (so. dist.) N.Y., 1994—; ptnr. Bender Burrows & Rosenthal LLC, NYC, 2003—. Mem. Appellate Divsn. 1st Dept. Com. on Law Guardians. Served with USCGR, 1960-68. Mem. ABA, N.Y. State Bar Assn., Assn. Bar City N.Y., Am. Acad. Matrimonial Lawyers, N.Y. County Lawyers Assn., Am. Arbitration Assn. (mem. nat. arbitrators panel 1973-97), Internat. Acad. Matrimonial Lawyers. Office: Bender Burrows and Rosenthal 451 Park Ave S Fl 8 New York NY 10016 Office Phone: 212-725-7111. E-mail: kburrows@pipeline.com.

BURROWS, MICHAEL DONALD, lawyer; b. Oak Park, Ill., May 23, 1944; s. Milford Denton and Helen Jean (Spitali) B.; m. Sandi Miller, Feb. 6, 1982; 1 child, Matthew Denton. BA, Williams Coll., 1967; JD, N.Y. Law Sch., 1973. Bar: N.Y. 1974, U.S. Dist. Ct. (ea. and so. dists.) N.Y. 1974, U.S. Ct. Appeals (2d cir.) 1978, U.S. Supreme Ct. 1981. Assoc. Baker & McKenzie, N.Y.C., 1973-80, ptnr., 1980-95, of counsel, 1995-99, mem. internat. exec. com., 1986-88; ptnr. Winston & Strawn, N.Y.C., 1999—2004, exec. com., chmn. N.Y. Litigation dept., 2004; shareholder Greenberg Traurig, 2004—. Co-author: The Practice of International Litigation, 1992. With USMC, 1968-70. Mem. ABA, Assn.of Bar of City of N.Y. Office: 160 E 89th St New York NY 10128 Office Phone: 212-801-6757. Business E-Mail: burrowsm@gtlaw.com.

BURRUS, CHARLES ANDREW, JR., retired research physicist; b. Shelby, N.C., July 16, 1927; s. Charles Andrew and Velma (Martin) B.; m. Barbara Ione Dunlevy, May 4, 1957; children— Charles Andrew III, Barbara Jean, John Alan BS cum laude in Physics, Davidson Coll., 1950; MS in Physics, Emory U., 1951; PhD in Physics (Tex. Co. fellow, Shell Co. fellow), Duke U., 1955. Rsch. assoc. dept. physics Duke U., Durham, N.C., 1954-55; tech. staff AT&T Bell Labs., Holmdel, N.J., 1955-1996, ret., 1996. Cons. Lucent Technologies Bell Labs., 1996—. Contbr. articles on millimeter and submillimeter-wave spectroscopy, techniques and semicondr. devices for lightwave communications, long-wavelength photoemitters and high-speed photodetectors, quantum-well devices, and optical fibers for lightwave communications to tech. jours. Served with USNR, 1945-46. Named Disting. Mem. Tech. Staff AT&T Bell Labs., 1982, fellow, 1988. Fellow AAAS, Am. Phys. Soc., IEEE (life), Optical Soc. Am. (David Richardson medal 1982). Methodist. Home: 62 Highland Ave Fair Haven NJ 07704-3641 Office: Lucent Technologies Bell Labs Crawford Hill Lab 791 Holmdel Keyport Rd Holmdel NJ 07733-0400 E-mail: cburrus@lucent.com.

BURRUS, CHARLES SIDNEY (SIDNEY BURRUS), electrical engineering educator; b. Abilene, Tex., Oct. 9, 1934; s. Charles Hooker B. and Aleta (Hunter) Hoffman; m. Mary Lee Powell, June 7, 1958; children: Mary Virginia, Charles Stephen. BA, Rice U., 1957, BSEE, 1958, MS, 1960; PhD, Stanford U., 1965. Registered profl. engr., Tex. Lectr. Stanford U., Calif., 1964-65; asst. prof. elec. engring. Rice U., Houston, 1965-70, assoc. prof., 1970-74, prof., 1974—, chmn. dept. elec. engring., 1984—92, dir. Computer and Info. Tech. Inst., 1992—, Maxfield and Oshman Prof. Elec. and Computer Engring., dean George R. Brown Sch. Engring., 1998—. Vis. prof. Universitaet Erlangen-Nürnberg, Germany, 1975, 79, MIT, 1989-90; vis. fellow Trinity Coll., Cambridge, Eng., 1984.cons. IBM, Tex. Instruments, VA Hos., 1975— Author: Algorithms for DSP, 1984, Digital Filter Design, 1987; contbr. articles to profl. jours. Served to lt. USN, 1958-62. Recipient Humboldt Award, 1975, Signal Processing Soc. Award, 1995; Sr. Fulbright Fellowship, 1985. Fellow IEEE (Sr. Paper award 1974, Tech. Achievement award 1985); mem. Am. Soc. Elec. Engring., Sigma Xi, Tau Beta Pi Democrat. Baptist. Office: Rice U Dept Elec Engring PO Box 1892 Houston TX 77251-1892 Office Phone: 713-348-5484.

BURRUS, ROBERT LEWIS, JR., lawyer; b. Richmond, Va., Sept. 16, 1934; s. Robert Lewis and Bessie (Hart) Burrus; m. Ann Williams, Aug. 1, 1964; children: David Curran, Peter Tandy, Lewis Graves BA, U. Richmond, 1955; LLD, Duke U., 1958. Bar: Va. 1958. Assoc. McGuire Woods LLP, Richmond, Va., 1959-63, ptnr., 1963—, chmn., 1990—. Bd. dirs. CSX Corp., Richmond, Smithfield Foods, Smithfield, Va., S&K Famous Brands, Richmond, Amvest Corp., Charlottesville, Va. Trustee U. Richmond, presdl. search com. chmn., 1997-98, rector, 1998-2002; bd. visitors Duke U. Law Sch., Durham, NC; dir. R.E.B. Found., Richmond, Va.; bd. dirs. Va. Mus. Fine Arts Found.; past trustee Va. Mus. Fine Arts, Va. Hist. Soc., Richmond Children's Mus.; past chmn. State Coun. Higher Edn. for Va.; past dir., chmn. exec. com. Richmond Renaissance; past bd. dirs. Circuit City Found.; past mem. Gov.'s Commn. Intercollegiate Athletics, 1991-92; past pres. St. Christopher's Sch. Found., Richmond. Recipient Charles S. Rhyne Award Duke U., 1998, Alumni of Yr. Award U. Richmond, 1998, Trustees Disting. Svc. Award, 2002, Silver Hope Award Nat. Multiple Sclerosis Soc., 2000, Humanitarian Award Nat. Conf. for Cmty. and Justice, 2001. Fellow Am. Bar Found., Va. Law Found.; mem. ABA, Va. Bar Assn. (chmn. corp. law com. 1975-77, chmn. bus. sect. 1976-77), Richmond Bar Assn., Commonwealth Club, Chgo. Club, Country Club Va., Bull and Bear Club, Kinloch Golf Club, Forum Club, Omicron Delta Kappa. Episcopalian. Office: McGuireWoods LLP One James Ctr 901 E Cary St Richmond VA 23219-4030 Office Phone: 804-775-4306. Office Fax: 804-698-2023. Business E-Mail: rburrus@mcguirewoods.com.

BURRUS, WILLIAM HENRY, labor union administrator; b. Wheeling, W.Va. s. William and Gertrude Burrus; m. Ethelda Burrus; 4 children. Attended, W.Va. State Coll. Pres. Am. Postal Workers Union, Cleveland, 1974—80, exec. v.p., 1980—2001, nat. pres., 2001—. Bd. mem. Fed. Adv. Coun. Occupl. Safety and Health; dir. research edn. Ohio State Postal Workers. Bd. mem. Nat. Black Coll. Alumni Hall Fame, Nat. Coalition Black Voter Participation, Ohio Adv. Bd. US Civil Rights Commn., 1979—81, A. Philip Randolph Inst., v.p., 1982—, Black Trade Labor Union, 1977. With 101st Airborne Divsn. U.S. Army, with 4th Armored Tank Divsn. U.S. Army. Recipient Frederick O'Neal award, 1981, Philip Randolph Achievement award, 1982, Disting. Svc. award, Martin Luther King Ctr., 1989. Office: Am Postal Workers Union 1300 L St NW Washington DC 20005 Office Phone: 202-842-4200, 202-842-8500.

BURRUSS, TERRY GENE, architect; b. Dec. 30, 1950; s. Alvin Eugene and Fern (Pelton) B.; m. Merilyn Kloss, Dec. 20, 1981; children: Mamie Christine, Gracie Aline. BArch, BA, U. Ark., 1973. Registered architect, Ark. Intern architect firm Robinson and Wassell, Inc., Little Rock, Ark., 1973-75; practice architecture Evo-Tech Prodn., Little Rock, Ark., 1976-78, I.D.E.A., Eureka Springs, Ark., 1976-78; architect Store Planning Assocs., San Francisco, 1978; assoc. Design 3, Architects, Little Rock, 1979; v.p., divsn. mgr. Mehlburger, Tanner, Renshaw and Assocs., Little Rock, 1980-84; v.p. Mehlburger, Tanner, Robinson & Assocs., Little Rock, 1984-87; pres. Terry Burruss Architects, Little Rock, 1987—. Instr. Hatha Yoga Community Edn. Program, 1976-77, St. Francis House, Little Rock, 1978, Parapsychology Ctr., 1978-79; vis. prof. constrn. mgmt. program U. Ark., Little Rock, 1999-2002; mem. Ark. Environ. Barriers Coun. Author: Flow Gently Sweet Alpha, 1972, Inflatables, an Alternative to the Deflated Classroom, 1973, Accessibility Guidelines for Meeting and Lodging Facilities, 1981, Housing for the Developmentally Disabled, 1986. Chmn. ministerial rels. Unity Ch. of Little Rock, 1986-87, pres. bd. dirs., 1987; pres. Montessori Children's Ctr. Parent

Tchrs. Orgn., 1986-87; pres. Unity Ch., 1987, Ctrl. High Neighborhood Assn., 1989-90; chmn. Gov.'s Mansion Area, 1998-2000; mem. bd. adjustment City of Little Rock, 2003—. Mem. AIA (state chmn. 1981), U. Ark. Alumni Assn., Little Rock Jaycees (dir. 1981-83, sec. 1982-83, chmn. TV auction 1982), Alpha Phi Omega, Pi Kappa Alpha. Home: 12 Tallyho Ln Little Rock AR 72227-2416 Office: 1202 Main St Ste 230 Little Rock AR 72202-5076 Office Phone: 501-376-3676. E-mail: tbartichoke@aristotle.net.

BURSEY, MAURICE M., retired chemistry professor; b. Balt., July 27, 1939; s. Reginald Price and Edna Frances (Moyer) B.; m. Joan Marie Tesarek, Dec. 28, 1970; children— John Thomas Kieran, Sara Helen Moyer. BA, Johns Hopkins U., 1959, MA, 1960, PhD, 1963. Lectr. Johns Hopkins U., Balt., 1963-64; asst. prof. Purdue U., Lafayette, Ind., 1964-66; asst. prof. chemistry U. N.C., Chapel Hill, 1966-69, assoc. prof., 1969-74, prof., 1974-96, prof. emeritus, 1996—. Editor Mass Spectrometry Revs., 1990-93; contbr. articles to profl. jours. Recipient various research grants. Fellow Am. Inst. Chemists, Royal Soc. Chemistry; mem. Am. Chem. Soc. (council, 1976-2001, bd. dirs. 1993-2001), Am. Soc. Mass Spectrometry, Alpha Chi Sigma (Grand Master Alchemist nat. pres. 1986-88). Democrat. Roman Catholic. Home: 101 Longwood Pl Chapel Hill NC 27514-9584 Personal E-mail: mauricebursey@aol.com.

BURSHTAN, JOHN WILLIS, television producer; b. Cedar Rapids, Iowa, July 4, 1958; s. Alvin and Ann Carol (Lichtenstein) B.; children: Eduard (Erik), Maria. BS in Mass. Comm., Miami U., Oxford, Ohio, 1980. Prodr./dir. WKEF TV, Dayton, Ohio, 1978-81, QUBE Interactive TV/Warner Cable Comm., Cin., 1981-85, promotions mgr., 1985-87; prodr., dir., writer Paradise Prodrs. Group, Inc., L.A., 1987-91; prodr./dir. mktg. and devel. Rocky Mountain PBS, Denver, 1991-95, exec. prodr. sta. and cultural affairs, 1995—. Recipient Nat. Cable TV Assn. Ace award for Swordquest, 1983, Emmy award Gov.'s Trophy for Vietnam: We Remember, 1984, Heartland Emmy awards, 1992, 93, 94, 95, 96, 97, 98, 99, 2000, 01, 02, 03, NEA award for Really Short Shows, 1994, Gold plaque, Chgo. Internat. Film Festival, 1994,CINE Golden Eagle award for Klondike and Snow: A Tale of Twin Polar Bears, 1997, others, Wrangler Award for Spirit of Colo. Cowboys, 2002. Mem. Writers Guild of Am. West,. Office: Rocky Mountain PBS 1089 Bannock St Denver CO 80204-4067

BURSKY, HERMAN AARON, lawyer; b. Bklyn., Jan. 16, 1938; s. Abraham S. and Anna R. (Polstein) B.; m. Dolores Kelner, Sept. 3, 1961; children: Daniel Jay, Jennifer Dina. BA, B in Hebrew Lit., Yeshiva U., 1959; LLB, Cornell U., 1962. Bar: N.Y. 1963. Assoc. Levin & Weintraub, N.Y.C., 1963-69; atty. CIT Fin. Corp., N.Y.C., 1969-70; assoc. Otterbourg, Steindler, Houston & Rosen, P.C., N.Y.C., 1970-71; ptnr. Shea & Gould, N.Y.C., 1971-91, Rosenman & Colin, N.Y.C., 1991-98; counsel Fischbein, Badillo, Wagner and Harding, 2000—. Contbg. author: Practical Guide to Bankruptcy and Debtor Relief, 1964. Served as pvt. U.S. Army, 1962-63. Mem. ABA, N.Y. State Bar Assn., Fed. Bar Council, Assn. Comml. Fin. Attys., N.Y. County Lawyers Assn. (bankruptcy com. 1973-80). Clubs: Inwood Country (N.Y.). Jewish. Home: 25 Muriel Ave Lawrence NY 11559-1810 Office: Fischbein Badillo Wagner Harding 909 3rd Ave Fl 18 New York NY 10022-4731 Office Phone: 212-453-3901. Business E-Mail: hbursky@fbwhlaw.com.

BURSLEY, KATHLEEN A., lawyer; b. Washington, Mar. 20, 1954; d. G.H. Patrick and Claire (Mulvany) B. BA, Pomona Coll., 1976; JD, Cornell U., 1979. Bar: N.Y. 1980, U.S. Dist. Ct. (ea. and so. dists.) N.Y. 1980, U.S. Ct. Appeals (5th and 11th cirs.) 1981, Fla. 1984, U.S. Dist. Ct. (mid. dist.) Fla. 1984, Tex. 1985, Mass. 1995. Assoc. Haight, Gardner, Poor & Havens, N.Y.C., 1979-81; counsel Harcourt Brace Jovanovich, Inc., N.Y.C. and Orlando, Fla., 1981-85, v.p. and counsel San Antonio and Orlando, 1985-92; assoc. gen. counsel pub. Harcourt Gen., Inc., Chestnut Hill, Mass., 1992—; gen. counsel Harcourt, Inc., Chestnut Hill, Mass., 1992—; v.p. Harcourt Gen., Inc., 1998—. Mem. Maritime Law Assn. (proctor). Address: 4018 E Massachusetts St Long Beach CA 90814-2825 E-mail: kbursley@harcourtgeneral.com.

BURSMA, ALBERT, JR., publishing company executive; b. Holland, Mich., May 19, 1937; s. Albert and Jessica (Van Wieren) B.; m. Phyllis Joan Brink, June 27, 1959; children: Jane Elizabeth, James Mark. BA, Hope Coll., 1959; MA, U. Redlands, 1961; postgrad., U. Wis.-Madison, 1963. Tchr. pub. schs., Long Beach, Calif., 1960-61, Madison, 1961-63; salesman McGraw-Hill, N.Y.C., 1963-70; dir. mktg. D.C. Heath, Lexington, Mass., 1970-79, sr. v.p., gen. mgr., 1979-86, pres. sch. pub. divsn., 1986-95; exec. v.p. Houghton Mifflin Co., Boston, 1995—. Mem. Assn. Am. Pubs. (chmn. sch. divsn. exec. com. 1984-85, 93-94). Home: 258 Willis Rd Sudbury MA 01776-1330 Office: Houghton Mifflin Co 222 Berkeley St Fl 7 Boston MA 02116-3764

BURSON, BETSY LEE, librarian; b. Olney, Tex., Dec. 16, 1942; d. James Hollis and Lora Elizabeth (Talbott) B.; m. Winston Rabb Henderson, June 26, 1976. BS in Edn., Kans. State Tchrs. Coll., 1964; MLS, Tex. Woman's U., 1967, PhD in Libr. Info. Studies, 1987. With Phoenix Pub. Libr., 1967-74; libr. dir. Glendale (Ariz.) Pub. Libr., 1974-75; project archivist Phoenix History Project, 1975-77; adj. faculty U. Ariz., Tucson, 1979, Tex. Woman's U., Denton, 1980; libr. cons. La. State Libr., Baton Rouge, 1982-85; libr. dir. El Paso (Tex.) Pub. Libr., 1987-90, Arlington (Tex.) Pub. Libr., 1990—. Named Librarian of the Yr. Tex. Library Assn., 1995. Office: Tx Dept of Health Genetic Screening 1100 W 49th St Austin TX 78756-3101

BURSON, CHARLES W., former federal official, former state attorney general, lawyer; b. Memphis; m. Marion 1971; children: Clare, Kate. BA, U. Mich., 1966; MA, Cambridge U., England, 1968; JD, Harvard U., 1970. Assoc. Burson & Burson and Burson & Walkup, Memphis; ptnr. Wildman, Harrold, Allen, Dixon, & McDonnell, Memphis, 1981-88; atty. gen. State of Tenn., Nashville; counsel to v.p. Office of V.P., Washington, 1993-99, chief of staff to v.p., 1999—2001; exec. v.p., sec., gen. counsel Monsanto Co., 2001—. Del. Tenn. Constl. Conv., 1977, (chmn. State Spending Limitation Com.). Mem. Nat. Assn. Attys. Gen. (pres. 1994-95, chair FTC working group, mem. exec. com. securities group, chair consumer protection com. 1990-91, vice chair securities working group, Wyman award 1994), Tenn. Bd. Law Examiners (past pres.). Office: Off of Gen Counsel Monsanto Co Ste 450E 1300 I St NW Washington DC 20005

BURSON, HAROLD, public relations executive, director; b. Memphis, Feb. 15, 1921; s. Maurice and Esther (Bach) Burson; m. Betty Ann Foster, Oct. 30, 1947; children: Scott, Mark. BA, U. Miss., 1940; DHL (hon.), Boston U., 1988. Corr., reporter Memphis Comml. Appeal, 1938—40; dir. Ole Miss News Bur., Oxford, Miss., 1939—40; dir. pub. rels. H.K. Ferguson Co., N.Y.C., 1941—43; chmn. Burson-Marsteller, N.Y.C., 1953—; bd. dirs., mem. exec. com. Young & Rubicam, N.Y.C.; pub. affairs adviser to Pres. Ronald Reagan, 1989—94; mem. adv. coun. Emory U. Bus. Sch., Medill Sch. Journalism Northwestern U., U. So. Calif. Sch. Journalism; trustee Ab. Fortas Meml. Fund, Kennedy Ctr.; hon. prof. Fudan U., Shanghai, 1999; vis. prof. Leeds Met. U., Yorkshire, 2001; exec.-in-residence U. Ky. Coll. Commn., 2000. Harold Burson chair pub. relations Boston U., 2002. Chmn. bd., mem. exec. com. Nat. Coun. on Econ. Edn.; bd. dirs., exec. com., v.p. pub. info. Nat. Safety Coun., 1968—76; bd. dirs. Kennedy Ctr. Prodns., Washington, Catalyst Inc., 1978—89; former trustee World Wildlife Fund, 1979—81, Found. for Pub. Rels. Rsch. and Edn.; trustee Hackley Sch., Tarrytown, NY, 1968—76; chmn. pvt. sector pub. rels. com. USIA; mem. Fine Arts Commn., 1981—85; exec. com. Young Astronauts Coun., 1984—88; adv. bd. Bus. Coun. for Internat. Understanding; pres. coun. N.Y. Acad. Sci.; trustee World Environ. Ctr. Named Pub. Rels. Profl. of Yr., Pub. Rels. News, 1977, 1989, Most Influential Person in Pub. Rels. in 20th Century, PR Week, 1999, to U. Miss. Hall of Fame, 1980; named to Hall of Fame, Internat. Coun. Consulting Orgs., 2003; recipient Gold Anvil award, Pub. Rels. Soc. Am., 1980, Horatio Alger award, 1986, Arthur Page award, 1990, Lifetime Achievement award, Inside PR, 1993, Alexander Hamilton award for lifetime achievement in pub. rels., Inst. Pub. Rels. Mem.: Horatio Alger Assn., N.Y. Acad. Med. (trustee 2003), Am. Philatelic Soc., N.Y. Soc. Security Analysts, Internat. Pub. Rels. Assn., Am. Pub. Rels. Assn., Blue Key Club, Econ. Club N.Y. (exec. com.), Scarsdale Golf Club, Overseas Press Club, Mid-Am. Club, Omicron Delta Kappa. Office: Burson-Marsteller 230 Park Ave S New York NY 10003-1513 Office Phone: 212-614-4444. Business E-Mail: harold_burson@nyc.bm.com.

BURSON, SCOTT FOSTER, labor lawyer; b. N.Y.C., May 28, 1952; s. Harold and Bette Anne (Foster) B.; m. Wendy Faith Liebow, Aug. 12, 1979; children: Allison Liebow, Esther Miriam Liebow. BA, Wesleyan U., Middletown, Conn., 1974; JD, U. Chgo., 1977; M. Law Libr., U. Wash., 1981. Bar: Mass. 1977, U.S. Dist Ct. Mass. 1978, U.S. Ct. Appeals (1st cir.) 1978, (9th cir.) 1991, U.S. Dist Ct. R.I. 1980, Wash. 1981. Assoc. Palmer & Dodge, Boston, 1977-80; law clk. to judge U.S. Dist. Ct., Providence, 1980; document librarian law libr. U. Wash., Seattle, 1982-84, head reference librarian law libr., 1984-87; field atty. NLRB, Seattle, 1987-93, supervisory atty. Boston, 1993—. Adj. prof. law U. Wash., Seattle, 1987. Contbr. articles to Legal Reference Svcs. Quar., 1984, Law Libr. Jour., 1987. Mem. Solid Waste Adv. Com., Seattle, 1988, 90-93; town meeting mem. Lexington, 1998—, sch. chmn., 2000—. Mem. Beta Phi Mu, Phi Beta Kappa. Democrat. Jewish.

BURSON, THOMAS DANIEL, retired aerospace executive; b. Hartselle, Ala., Jan. 7, 1936; s. Daniel Webster and Ardia (Starks) B.; m. Mary Frances Wilson, June 7, 1958; children: Kelly Frances, Robyn Elizabeth, Thomas Scott. BME with high honor, Auburn U., 1958; MBA, U. So. Calif., 1969. Asst. mgr. contract adminstrn. Hycon Co., Monrovia, Calif., 1961-63, mgr. customer contracts, 1963-66, asst. to pres., 1966-67, dir. mktg., 1967-71, v.p., 1969-71; dir. contracts and pricing Actron Divsn. McDonnell Douglas Corp., Monrovia, 1971-76, v.p. fiscal mgmt., 1976-79, v.p., gen. mgr., 1979-83; v.p. ops. McDonnell Douglas Astronautics Co., Huntington Beach, Calif., 1983-84, v.p. fiscal mgmt., 1984-87, v.p., dep. gen. mgr., 1987-88, v.p., gen. mgr. Space Transp. Divsn., 1989-96; ret., 1996. Chmn. comml. space transp. adv. com. to Sec. Transp., 1996. With USN, 1958—61. Mem. AIAA (George M. Low Space Transp. award 1996), ASME, Nat. Contract Mgmt. Assn., Phi Kappa Phi, Tau Beta Pi, Pi Tau Sigma, Beta Gamma Sigma, Kappa Alpha. Home: 19731 Seashore Cir Huntington Beach CA 92648-3037

BURSTEIN, ELIAS, physicist, researcher; b. N.Y.C., Sept. 30, 1917; s. Samuel and Sarah (Plotkin) B.; m. Rena Ruth Benson, Sept. 19, 1943; children— Joanna Bliss, Sandra Joy, Miriam Stephanie. AB, Bklyn. Coll., 1938; A.M., U. Kans., 1941; postgrad., MIT, 1941-43, Cath. U., 1946-48; DTech (hon.), Chalmers U. Tech., Göteborg, Sweden, 1982; DSc (hon.), Bklyn. Coll., 1985, Emory U., 1994, Ohio State U., 1999. Physicist Crystal br. U.S. Naval Research Lab., 1945-58, head semiconductor br., 1958; prof. physics U. Pa., Phila., 1958-82, Mary Amanda Wood prof. physics, 1982-88, emeritus, 1988—. Jubilee vis. prof. physics Chalmers U. Tech., Goteborg, 1981; mem. solid state scis. adv. panel NRC-NAS, 1971-80, chmn., 1977-79, condensed matter physics adv. com. Internat. Ctr. for Theoretical Physics, 1990-96, Trieste; com. on sci. and the arts, Franklin Inst., 1994—; Miller Inst. vis. rsch. prof. physics U. Calif., Berkeley, 1996. Founding editor Solid State Comms., 1963, sec. bd. editors, 1963-69, editor-in-chief, 1969-1992; co-editor Comments on Solid State Physics, 1971-93; patentee in field. Recipient Navy Civilian Meritorious Service award, 1957; John Price Wetherill medal Franklin Inst., 1979; Guggenheim fellow, 1980; Alexander Von Humboldt Sr. U.S. Scientist award, 1988-90, 92-93. Fellow AAAS, Am. Phys. Soc. (sec.-treas. div. solid state physics 1956-61, Isakson prize 1986), Optical Soc. Am.; mem. Nat. Acad. Scis., Phi Beta Kappa, Sigma Xi. Office: U Pa Dept Physics and Astronomy Philadelphia PA 19104 Business E-Mail: burstein@physics.upenn.edu.

BURSTEIN, HAROLD JOHN, oncologist; m. Mary Mullen; children: Ellen, Katherine. AB, Harvard U., 1986; MD, PhD, Harvard U., Boston, 1994. Diplomate Am. Bd. Internal Medicine, Am. Bd. Oncology. Intern, resident Mass. Gen. Hosp., Boston, 1994—96; oncology fellow Dana-Farber Cancer Inst., Boston, 1996—99, oncologist, 1999—. Asst. prof. medicine Harvard Med. Sch., 2002—. Office: Dana-Farber Cancer Inst 44 Binney St Boston MA 02115 Office Phone: 617-632-3800.

BURSTEIN, HARVEY, lawyer, educator; b. St. Louis, Jan. 3, 1923; m. Morris and Rachel (Johannes) B.; m. Ina Bebchick, Sept. 25, 1947. LLB, Creighton U., 1948. Bar: Nebr. 1948, U.S. Supreme Ct. 1953, Mass. 1954, N.Y. 1963. Spl. agt. FBI, 1948-53; chief fgn. and domestic investigations, surveys and phys. security U.S. Dept. State, 1953-54; pvt. practice, 1954—61; 1978—79; security officer M.I.T., Cambridge, 1956-61; v.p. and gen. counsel Norman Co., Inc., Valley Stream, N.Y., 1961-73; pres. Harvey Cons. Corp., Valley Stream, 1961-73; corp. security dir. Sheraton Corp., Boston, 1973-74; dir. security and safety New Eng. Mut. Life Ins. Co., Boston, 1975-78; corp. dir. safety and security, staff atty. Data Gen. Corp., Westboro, Mass., 1979-90. Guest lectr. Ind. U., Mich. State U., Wellesley Coll., Babson Coll.; adj. asst. prof. Coll. Liberal Arts Fordham U.; adj. prof. Grad. Sch. Bus. Adminstr. Fordham U.; vis. prof. Sch. Hotel Adminstrn. Cornell U.; adj. assoc. prof. Coll. Criminal Justice Northeastern U., vis. prof., 1990-95, David B. Schulman prof. security, 1995-2005, prof. emeritus, 2005—; arbitrator Civil Ct. NYC, 1971-73, 95-05. Author: 10 books on security mgmt.; contbr. articles on security mgmt. and investigations to profl. jours. Liaison with aux. police for Chief of Police, Brookline, Mass., 1955—61; mem. bd. overseers Spaulding Rehab. Hosp., Boston, 2003—; mem. Citizens Com. Better Law Enforcement, Town of Mamaroneck, NY, 1971—73. With AUS, 1942—46. Recipient Big Pi award Pi Lambda Phi, 1981. Mem.: Boston Bar Assn., Am. Soc. for Indsl. Security, Soc. of Ex-FBI Agts., Am. Judicature Soc., Masons, Pi Lambda Phi. Democrat. Jewish. Home: 19 Linden Sq Wellesley MA 02482-4717 Office: Coll Criminal Justice Northeastern U Boston MA 02115 Office Phone: 617-373-3057. Business E-Mail: harveybchs@verizon.net. E-mail: H.Burstein@neu.edu.

BURSTEIN, MICHAEL CLIFFORD, enterprise integration consultant; s. Edward Marion and Ethel Kaplan Burstein; m. Laurel Douglass Crooks, Dec. 20, 1973; 1 child, Adam. BA in Math. (Concentration), Johns Hopkins U., 1964; MS in Ops. Rsch., George Wash. U. Sch. Engring. and Applied Scis., 1969; PhD in Managerial Econ. & Decision Scis., Northwestern U., 1977. Cert. enterprise integrator Soc. Mfg. Engrs., 2000, cert. engring. mgr. Soc. Mfg. Engrs., 2004, registered rep. Nat. Assn. Securities Dealers, 2002. Asst. prof. indsl. engring. and ops. rsch. Sch. Engring. U. Mass., Amherst, 1980—85; prin. scientist Indsl. Tech. Inst., Ann Arbor, Mich., 1985—88; vis. assoc. prof. ops. mgmt. U. Mich., Sch. Mgmt., Ann Arbor, 1989—90; adj. assoc. prof. ops. mgmt. Yale U., Sch. Mgmt., New Haven, 1991—92; assoc. prof. ops. mgmt., dir. Ctr. Bus. Competitiveness U. Wis., Milw., 1992—96, dir. Ctr. Bus. Competitiveness, 1992—95; cons. Milw., 1996—97; CEO, pres. T.I.P.E., Inc., Belchertown, Mass., 1998—. Fellow Yale U., Jonathan Edwards Coll., New Haven, 1991—92. Co-editor and contbr. (book) Manufacturing Strategy: The Research Agenda for the Next Decade, 1990; assoc. editor: Mgmt. Sci., 1985—90, Internat. Jour. Flexible Mfg. Sys., 1986—2000, IIE Transactions, 1986—90; editl. bd. Engring. Economist, 1986—89; contbr. articles and chapters to books and jour. Mem. Planning Bd., Pelham, Mass., 1982—85; chair Cub Scout Pack Com., Dexter, Mich., 1986—87, asst. scout master, 1989—91; mem. Zoning Bd. Appeals, Westhampton, Mass., 2001—04. With U.S. Army, 1965—70. Mem.: Soc. Mfg. Engrs. (chair product and process design and mgmt. cmty. 2001—, mem. cert. oversight and appeals com. 2003—), Soc. Concurrent Product Devel. (Boston chpt. bd. mem. 2000—, Outstanding Contributor 2002), CAMI Consortium (academic rev. panelist, cost mgmt. sys. program 1986—88), Omicron Delta Epsilon, Alpha Pi Mu, Tau Beta Pi. Judaism. Achievements include development of methodology for integrating multi-generational technology planning with replacement and capacity decision-making (first applied at Harley Davidson, 1993); strategy-based approach for the identification of technology opportunities and threats (first applied through the Michigan Modernization Service, 1986); coordinated the development of the Video-instructional MS in Engineering Management Program at the University of MA (Amherst) and then worldwide via the National Technological University (1984). Avocations: hiking, cross country skiing, snowshoeing, bicycling, swimming. Home and Office: TIPE Inc 632 Warrenwright Rd Belchertown MA 01007 Office Phone: 413-237-3359. E-mail: mcb.tipe@att.net.

BURSTEIN, RICHARD JOEL, lawyer; b. Detroit, Feb. 9, 1945; s. Harry Seymour and Florence (Rosen) B.; m. Gayle Lee Handmaker, Dec. 21, 1969; children: Stephanie Faith, Melissa Amy. Grad., U. Mich., 1966; JD, Wayne State U., 1969. Bar: Mich. 1969, U.S. Ct. Appeals (ea. dist.) Mich. 1969. Ptnr. Smith Miro Hirsch & Brody, Detroit, 1969-81, Honigman Miller Schwartz & Cohn, Detroit, 1981—. Bd. dirs. Sandy Corp., Troy, Mich.; bd. dirs. Met. Affairs Corp., Detroit; co-chmn. Artrain. Mem. Am. Coll. Real Estate Lawyers. Office: Honigman Miller Schwartz & Cohn 32270 Telegraph Rd Ste 225 Bingham Farms MI 48025

BURSTEIN, SHARON ANN, corporate communications specialist, designer; b. Schenectady, N.Y., July 18, 1952; d. Harold Edward and Lois Ida (Hesner) Rieck; m. Richard Lyle Burstein, Sept. 8, 1985; 1 child, Alexandra Blaire. BA, Nat. Lewis U., 1974; postgrad., Russell Sage Coll., 1974-78, Union Coll., 1980. Cert. tchr., N.Y. Elem. tchr. Saratoga Springs (N.Y.) Schs., 1974-80; ednl. cons. Whitcomb Assocs., Boston, 1980-81; ednl. mktg. specialist Monroe Sys. for Bus., Newington, Conn., 1981-83; nat. mktg. mgr. Victor Techs., Hartford, Conn., 1983, Exclusives, Boston, 1984-85; dir. pub. rels. Lawrence Group, Albany, N.Y., 1985-87, dir. corp. comm., 1987-88, v.p., 1988-89, v.p investors rels. N.Y.C., 1987-89; pres. S.A. Burstein & Assocs., Albany, 1989—, Neswick Ct., 1994-99. Adj. prof. Russell Sage Coll., Troy, N.Y., 1994-99; exec. prodr. Carmine's Television Show-NBC; cons. N.Y. Assn. Bus. Ofcls., 1982-83; trustee Nat. Lewis U., 2005—. Editor: Helpline newspaper, 1985, 87; co-prodr. Playing It Safe, 1986 (Nori award 1987), To Be As Independent As You Can be (Nori award 1989), Cookbook Capital Connoisseur (Nori award 1989), Camp Ever Young (Nori award 1993); acted in TV comml., 1981 (Addy award 1982); prodr. Carmine's Table TV Show (NBC); exec. prodr. A Place With a Heart, 2004 (Comm. award). Bd. dirs. Multiple Sclerosis Soc., Albany, 1986, Mohawk Pathways Girl Scouts U.S.; active N.Y. Spl. Olympics, 1987; v.p. bd. dirs. Capital Repertory Theater Guild, 1999—. Recipient Disting. Alumni award, Nat. Lewis U., 2004. Mem. Nat. Investor Rels. Inst., Am. Mgmt. Assn., Assn. Profl. Communicators, Nat. Assn. Investment Clubs, Tennis Industry Assn., Albany C. of C. (women's bus. coun.), Steuben Club, Women's Press Club, Kappa Delta Pi. Democrat. Avocations: writing, tennis, golf, skiing, reading. Home: 4 Birch Hill Rd Loudonville NY 12211-2004

BURSTELL, ED, personal care industry executive; Former buyer cosmetics and fragrance Bloomingdale's; former assoc. buyer color and treatment Bonwit Teller; cosmetics and fragrance buyer Henri Bendel, Inc. divsn. of Ltd. Brands, Inc., 1991—97, v.p. and gen. mgr., 1998—2002, pres. and gen. mgr., 2003—. Mailing: Henri Bendel Inc 712 5th Ave New York NY 10019

BURSTEN, STUART LOWELL, physician, biochemist; b. L.A., Jan. 19, 1953; s. Leo and Goldie (Zeff) B.; m. Colleen Sue Thompson, May 4, 1980; children: Elisa Michelle, Shawna Mariel, Tiana Marie; m. Lesley Domino, Mar. 26, 2000. BS in Biology, AB Psychology, Stanford U., 1975; MD, Yale U., 1980. Diplomate Am. Bd. Internal Medicine, Am. Bd. Nephrology. Intern Boston City Hosp., 1980-81; resident internal medicine U. Wash., Seattle, 1981-83, fellow nephrology, 1983-85, postdoctoral rsch. fellow, nephrology, 1985-86; acting instr. U. Wash. Sch. Medicine, 1986-88, asst. prof. medicine, 1988-92, clin. asst. prof. medicine, 1992-94, clin. assoc. prof. medicine, 1994-2001; co-dir., second messenger protein chemistry divsn. Cell Therapeutic, Inc., Seattle, 1992-95, prin. scientist, lipid biology and biochemistry, 1995-2000; prin. cons., rsch. dir. Inst. Lipid Studies, 2000—. Contbr. articles to profl. jours.; patentee. Rsch. dir. Friends of Snoqualmie Valley, Wash., 1986-89. Nat. Merit Found. scholar 1971, Nat. Grocers Assn. scholar, 1971, S&H Green Stamps Assn. scholar 1971; grantee NIH, 1975-78; recipient Northwest Kidney Found. Rsch. award, 1988-89, Nat. Inst. Arthritis, Diabetes, Digestive, and Kidney Diseases fellowship, 1985-86, others. Fellow: ACP; mem.: AAAS, Am. Stats. Assn., Am. Chem. Soc., Am. Soc. Nephrology, N.Y. Acad. Scis., Am. Fedn. Med. Rsch., Am. Heart Assn. Achievements include discovering that theobromine-based alkyl chains with patentable substitutions result in modulation of fatty acid and lipid peroxidative metabolism in mammalian cells, which in turn results in profound protection against acute inflammation and oxidant injury - this has introduced or is introducing an entire new class of compounds for treatment of a broad range of human diseases, incuding renal and liver disease, and protection against acute immune damage and the side effects of radiation; in addition, related compounds have been found to have potent anti-tumor activity based on interaction with lipid-directed enzymes. Office: Inst Lipid Studies 22287 Mulholland Hwy #325 Calabasas CA 91302 Office Phone: 707-252-8407. Business E-Mail: lpaatbaby@msn.com.

BURSTON, RICHARD MERVIN, marketing executive; b. Brookline, Mass., Oct. 31, 1924; s. Mark and Anita (Andrews) B.; m. Phoebe Harvey Hopkins, Aug. 29, 1958; children: Abby Lyn, Seth Hopkins, Joshua Craig, Mark Andrews, Amanda Lee. BA, Bowdoin Coll., 1949; MBA, Harvard U., 1952. Mgr. beauty dept. Kendall Co., Boston, 1953-58; regional sales mgr. M. Pier Co., Ft. Lauderdale, Fla., 1958-59; nat. sales mgr. Ozon Products, Inc., Bklyn., 1959-63; v.p., co-founder Burston/Larkin Assocs., Stamford, Conn., 1964-88; pres., CEO Excalibur, Inc., Stamford, 1981-88; founder, pres. Burston Inc., Stamford, 1987-98, cons., 1999—. Dir. Nat. Beauty and Barber Reps. Assn., N.Y.C., 1973-74, Louv Yacht Yard, Norwalk, Conn., 1969-73; cons. Ruckel Mfg., Inc., N.Y.C., 1969-87. Dir. Roxbury-Riverbank Little League, Stamford, 1971-82; fundraiser Bowdoin Coll., Brunswick, Maine, 1983-90, mem. alumni coun., 1994-98, pres., 1997-98. Lt. USNR, 1943-46, PTO. Recipient Man of Yr. award United Beauty Supply Corp., Bridgeport, Conn., 1983. Mem. Beauty and Barber Supply Inst., Am. Beauty Assn., Kents Hill Sch. Alumni Assn. (bd. dirs. 1994-2000, trustee 1994-2004, hon. trustee for life 2004), Miramichi Rod and Gun Club Inc. (pres. 2002), High Head Yacht Club (dir. 1997-2000). Republican. Jewish. Avocation: fly fishing. Home: 408 High Head Rd Harpswell ME 04079-2917 Office: Burston Inc 45 Church St Stamford CT 06906-1711 Business E-Mail: dpburst@suscom-maine.net.

BURSTYN, JOAN NETTA, education educator; b. Leicester, Eng., Mar. 6, 1929; d. David Edward and Nellie (Wachman) Jacobs; m. Harold L. Burstyn, Aug. 19, 1958; children: Judith, Gail, Daniel. BA with honors, U. London, 1950, cert. of edn., 1952, acad. diploma in edn., 1958, PhD, 1968. Tchg. fellow edn. Harvard U., Cambridge, Mass., 1959—64; lectr. U. Pitts., 1967; lectr. psychology and edn. Carnegie Mellon U., Pitts., 1967—68, instr., 1968, asst. prof., 1969—74, dir. tchr. edn., 1970—74; assoc. prof., chairperson dept. edn. Douglass Coll. Rutgers U., New Brunswick, NJ, 1974—81, prof. edn. Douglass Coll., 1981—85, dir. women's studies program Douglass Coll., 1981—85; dean sch. edn. Syracuse U., NY, 1986—89, prof. cultural founds. of edn. and history, 1986—2003, prof. emeritus, rsch. prof. edn., 2003—. Co-dir. Fund for Improvement of Post-Secondary Edn. Grant, 1983-85; vis. prof. Monash U., Australia, summer 1989; Emens disting. prof. Ball State U., 1996; dir. pilot grant NEH, 1980-82; prin. investigator grant subcontract U.S. Dept. Justice, 1998-2002; mem. adv. bd. Women Transcending Boundaries, 2004— Author: Song Cycle, 1976, Victorian Education and the Ideal of Womanhood, 1980, Waiting for the Lame Horse, 1987; co-author: Preventing Violence in Schools: A Challenge to American Democracy, 2001; editor: Preparation for Life?, 1986, Desktop Publishing in the University, 1991, Educating Tomorrow's Valuable Citizen, 1996; editor-in-chief Past and Promise: Lives of New Jersey Women, 1990, assoc. editor Signs: Jour. of Women in Culture and Soc., 1980—89; mem. editl. bd.: Signs: Jour. Women in Culture and Soc., 1980—89, History of Edn. Quar, 1982—86, History of Higher Edn. Ann., 1989—, Issues in Edn., 1983—87, Syracuse U. Press, 1991—94, Ednl. Founds., 2000—03, Jour. Sch. Violence, 2001—, mem. editl. bd.:; contbr. articles to profl. jours. Mem. adv. bd. nurse-midwifery ednl. program U. Medicine and Dentistry N.J., 1978-83; bd. dirs. Children's Sch. Sci., Woods Hole, Mass., 1977-80; assoc. dir. N.E. Council Women in Devel., 1981-82; mem. joint com. Am. Hist. Assn. and Can. Hist. Assn., 1978-81. Recipient grant-in-aid John F. Kennedy Sch. Govt. and Bunting Inst.,

1964-65; Marion Talbot fellow AAUW, 1965-66; recipient Faculty Merit award Rutgers U., 1977, 81. Fellow AAAS; mem. AAUW, Am. Hist. Assn., Am. Ednl. Rsch. Assn. (com. on freedom of inquiry and human rights 1984-86, pubs. com. 1986-89), History of Edn. Soc. U.S. (pres. 1985-86), Am. Ednl. Studies Assn. (chmn. publs. com. 1984-85, pres. 1995-96,). Office: Syracuse U Sch Edn 303 Huntington Hl Syracuse NY 13244-0001 Business E-Mail: jburstyn@syr.edu.

BURSTYN, MIKE LAWRENCE, actor; b. NYC, July 1, 1945; s. Paul Pesach'ke and Lillian (Lux) Burstein; m. Edti Pupisky; children: Peter, Adam. Actor Parents' Yiddish Theatre, world tour, 1952-62; pres. Kit Prodns. Ltd., Scarsdale, NY, 1986—. Guest lectr., Harvard U. Actor in Broadway prodns: Barnum, 1981-82, The Megilla, Inquest, The Prisoner of Second Ave., 1989, The Rothschilds, 1990, On Second Avenue, 2005; Overseas Stage: The Dutch Production of Barnum, 1988-89; television performer, The Mike Burstyn Show, Israel and Holland, 1978-81, Israel Culture Line WNYC-TV, NYC, 1990; entertainer concert stages and nightclubs, worldwide, 1975—; performer Kennedy Ctr. Honors, CBS-TV, 1981, Royal Variety Show Palladium, London, 1979; recording artist, CBS Records, Israel, 1964—; guest star numerous dramatic, variety and game shows on US and internat. TV. Bd. dirs. Variety Club Israel, Tel Aviv, 1980; hon. pres. Israeli Cystic Fibrosis Orgn., Tel Aviv, 1986-. With Israeli Def. Forces, 1967-. Recipient Kinor David award, Israeli Acad. Motion Pictures, 1966, 76. Mem. AFTRA, Actors Equity Assn., Screen Actors Guild, Hebrew Actors Union, Israel Union Performing Artists. Avocations: golf, scuba diving, sailing. Office: Kit Prodns Ltd 401 E 34th St # 530A New York NY 10016-4914*

BURT, ALLEN DANIEL, artist; b. Owensboro, Ky., Aug. 17, 1930; s. Harold Allan and Catherine Eleanor (Coulter) B.; m. Anne Warren, May 31, 1935; 1 child, Barbara. Student, Kansas. State Coll., 1949, 50, Trinity U., 1955, 56, S.W. Tex. State U., 1965. Artist, 1949—. Tchr. watercolor numerous workshops; painting instr. Hill Country Arts Found., Artists and Craftsmen Associated-Dallas, Brownsville Art League, Watercolor Art Soc. Ft. Worth, Midland Art Assn., Tex., So. Ariz. Watercolor Guild, Tucson, Ardmore Art Guild, Okla., Amarillo Art Assn., Tex., No. Ariz. Watercolor Soc., Sedona, Watercolor Soc. Ind., Indpls. Exhibited in group shows at Nat. Acad. Galleries, N.Y., Knickerbocker Artists, N.Y. (Argmari/Arches/Rives Paper award 1991, Gold Medal Honor award 1992), Hudson Valley Art Assn., White Plains, N.Y., Salmagundi Club, N.Y., Nat. Arts Club, N.Y., Audubon Artists, N.Y. (Alice Melrose award 1990, Winsor & Newton award 1993, Silver Medal Honor award 1994)), Rocky Mountain Nat. Watermedia, Golden, Colo.(The Colorist award 1995, Vance Kirkland Meml. award 1997), La. Watercolor Soc., New Orleans, Watercolor West, Glendale, Calif. (Founders award 1991, Juror's award 1994), Midwest Watercolor Soc., Green Bay, Wis. (Mcpl. Art League Chgo. award 1991), Nat. Watercolor Soc., Brea, Calif. (Jurors award, St. Cuthbert's Paper Mill award 1995, Combined Donors award 1997), Am. Watercolor Soc., N.Y. (Clara Stroud Meml. award 1993), S.W. Watercolor Soc., Coppini Acad. Fine Arts, Tex. Watercolor Soc. (Midland Arts Assn. award 1997), La. Watercolor Soc., Nat. Acad. Design, others. Sgt. U.S. Army, 1951-54. Recipient Excellence award We. Fedn. Watercolor Socs., 1988, 90, 92, David Gayle Meml. award 1997, El Cajon Art Assn. award 12th Ann. San Diego Watercolor Soc. Award Exhbn., 1991, Best of Show award 1997, Jack Richeson award 18th Ann. Exhbn., 1995, others. Mem. Am. Watercolor Soc., Nat. Watercolor Soc., Allied Artists Am. (Gold Medal Honor award 78th Ann. Exhbn. 1991, Jane Peterson Meml. award 80th Ann. Exhbn. 1994, David Wu and Elsie Vect-Key award 82d Ann. Exhbn. 1996), Audubon Artists, Knickerbocker Artists, SW Watercolor Soc. (tchr.). Avocations: travel, reading, teaching. Home and Office: 109 St Andrews Loop Kerrville TX 78028-6442

BURT, ALVIN MILLER, III, anatomist, educator, cell biologist, writer; b. Bridgeport, Conn., Aug. 14, 1935; s. Alvin Miller and Esther Louise (Carey) B.; m. Dorothy Hanlin, July 15, 1961 (div.); children: Constance Walker, Carolyn Marie; m. Judith Nath, July 13, 1991; 1 stepchild, Stephen Jacob Nath. BA, Amherst Coll., 1957; PhD (USPHS fellow 1960-61), U. Kans., 1962. Asst. prof. anatomy Med. Coll. Va., Richmond, 1962-63; instr. Yale U. Med. Sch., 1963-66; mem. faculty Vanderbilt U. Med. Sch., 1966—, prof. anatomy, 1974-85, prof. cell biology, 1985-2000, prof. cell biology emeritus, 2000—; prof. cell biology Nursing Sch. Vanderbilt U., Nashville, 1994-2000, prof. cell biology in nursing emeritus, 2000—; sole proprietor Creative Manuscripts and CM Web Graphics, Hendersonville. Vis. scientist Agrl. Rsch. Coun., Inst. Animal Physiology, Babraham, Cambridge, Eng., 1972-73; bd. dirs. Trinity Health Svcs., LLC Author: Textbook of Neuroanatomy, 1993; contbr. articles to profl. jours. Vestryman Episcopal Ch. of Advent, Brentwood, Tenn., 1977-81, sr. warden, 1979-81, lay reader, chalice bearer, 1975-87, tchr. adult classes, mem. diocesan lay ministry com., 1981-85; lay reader, chalice bearer St. Philips Episcopal Ch., Donelson, Tenn., 1989-92, vestryman, 1991-92, mem. diocesan total ministry com., 1990-93; mem. Stephen Ministry Diocese of Tenn., 1991—; dir. pastoral care St. Ann's Episcopal Ch., Nashville, 1993-96, lay reader, 1994—, chalice bearer, 1996—, vestryman, 2002-05; mem. steering com. Interfaith AIDS Ministry, 1994-96; vol. ombudsman rep. Mid Cumberland Human Resources Ctr., 2001—. Recipient Research Career Devel. award USPHS, 1968-73 Mem. Am. Assn. Anatomists, Am. Soc. Neurochemistry, Human Anatomy & Physiology Soc., Internat. Soc. Neurochemistry, Internat. Brain Rsch. Orgn., Soc. Neurosci., Tenn. Outdoor Writers Assn. (v.p. 1985-86, pres.-elect 1986-87, pres. 1987-88, chmn. bd. dirs. 1988-89), Southeastern Outdoor Press Assn. (Webmaster 2002-2005), Bass Anglers Sportsmens Soc., Tenn. Spoonplugging Club (bd. dirs. 1980-88, editor newsletter 1980-85), Sigma Xi. Home and Office: 149 Bay Dr Hendersonville TN 37075-4040

BURT, ALVIN VICTOR, JR., journalist; b. Oglethorpe County, Ga., Sept. 11, 1927; s. Alvin Victor and Mabel (Sorrow) B.; m. Gloria White. BA in Edn, U. Fla., 1949. With U.P., 1949-50, Atlanta Jour., 1950-51, Jacksonville (Fla.) Jour., 1951-55; with Miami (Fla.) Herald, 1955-66, Latin Am. editor, 1962-66, assigned Washington, 1962, editorial writer, 1967-73, columnist, 1973-96; editor Hartwell (Ga.) Sun, 1966-67. Co-author: Papa Doc, 1969; author: Florida A Place in the Sun, 1974, Becalmed in the Mullet Latitudes, 1983, Al Burt's Florida, 1997, The Tropic of Cracker, 1999. Recipient Ernie Pyle award for newspaper writing, 1961, State award A.P. for feature writing, 1964, citation Fla. Legislature, 1965, Scripps-Howard award for best interviews in nation, 1966, Editorial Writing award Fla. Soc. Newspaper Editors-Fla. Press Assn., 1973, Overseas Press award, 1974, J.C. Penney spl. award U. Mo., 1980, Outstanding Journalist award Fla. Audubon Soc., 1984, First Ann. AL Burt award for extraordinary lifelong commitment 1000 Friends of Fla., 1989, Commentator of Yr. award Fla. Wildlife Fedn., 1990, Patrick Smith Lit. award Fla. Hist. Soc., 1998, LeRoy Collins Lifetime Chievement award Leadership Fla., 2004; inducted into Ind. Alligator Hall of Fame, 1998; named Alumnus of Distinction U. Fla. Coll. of Journalism and Comms., 1999. Office: PO Box 17 Melrose FL 32666-0017

BURT, FRANK DAVIES, lawyer, real estate company executive; b. Washington, Sept. 19, 1958; s. William Charles and Margery (Davies) B.; m. Carol Hackett, Sept. 3, 1988. BA, Brown U., 1980; JD, U. Pa., 1983. Bar: Mass. 1983. Assoc. Nutter, McClennan, Fish, Boston, 1983-86; sr. v.p., gen. counsel Boston Properties, Inc., 1986—. Mem. Moot Ct. Bd. U. Pa., Phila., 1982. Mem. Boston Bar Assn., Assn. Corp. Coun., New Eng. Corp. Counsel Assn., Phi Beta Kappa. Democrat. Avocation: skiing. Office: Boston Properties Inc 111 Huntington Ave Boston MA 02199

BURT, GWYNNE ELAYNE, minister, theology studies educator; b. Hackensack, NJ, June 28, 1962; s. Eugene Marshall Sr. and Hortense Marshall. BS in adminstr. and Mgmt., LaRoche Coll., 1984. Personnel asst. Kmart Apparel, North Bergen, NJ, 1984—87; recruiter JJT, Tab Richards, Anython Ryan Assoc., NJ, 1988—92; tchr. Hackensack Pub. Schs., Hackensack, NJ, 1992—95, Plaza Sch. of Tech., Paramus, NJ, 1994—99; sr. rsch. editor Lexis-Nexis, New Providence, NJ, 1999—2001; min. Mt. Calvary Bapt. Ch., Englewood, NJ, 2000—05; tchr. St. James Preparatory Sch., Newark, 2002—04. Contbr. articles various profl. jours. Bapt. Achievements include ministered in Nairobi, Kenya, Italy, Switzerland, Mexico, Jamica and throughout the U.S. Avocations: writing, singing, dance. Home: 119 Poplar Ave Hackensack NJ 07601 E-mail: prophetGB@aol.com.

BURT, JEFFREY AMSTERDAM, lawyer; b. Phila., Apr. 27, 1944; s. Samuel Matthew and Esther (Amsterdam) B.; m. Sandra Cass, Dec. 17, 1967; children: Stephen, Daniel, Jonathan, Andrew. BA, Princeton, 1966; LLB, Yale U., 1970; MA in Econs., 1970. Bar: Md. 1971, DC 1971. Law clk. to judge U.S. Ct. Appeals (4th cir.), Balt., 1970-71; assoc. Arnold & Porter, Washington, 1971-77; ptnr., 1978—. Adj. prof. law Georgetown U., 1987-95; frequent lectr. Pres., Green Acres, Inc. Ind. Sch., Rockville, Md., 1984-86. Author: (with others) International Joint Ventures, 1986, 2nd edit., 1992; co-editor: Joint Ventures with Internat. Ptnrs., 1997. Mem. ABA (co-chairperson NIS Law Com. Sect. Internat. Law and Practice 1992-98), Russian Am. C. of C. (dir., sec.). Office: Arnold & Porter 555 12th St NW Washington DC 20004-1206

BURT, JOHN HARRIS, bishop; b. Marquette, Mich., Apr. 11, 1918; s. Bates G. and Emily May (Bailey) B.; m. Martha M. Miller, Feb. 16, 1946; children: Susan, Emily, Sarah, Mary. BA, Amherst Coll., 1940, D.D. (hon.), 1960; BA, Va. Theol. Sem., 1943, B.D., 1967; D.D., Youngstown U., 1958, Kenyon Coll., 1967. Boys worker Christodora House, N.Y.C., 1940-41; ordained to ministry Episcopal Ch., 1943; canon Christ Ch. Cathedral; rector St. Paul's Ch., St. Louis, 1943-44; chaplain to Episc. students U. Mich., 1946-50; rector St. John's Ch., Youngstown, Ohio, 1950-57, All Saints Ch., Pasadena, Calif., 1957-67; bishop coadjutor Ohio, 1967-68; Episc. bishop of Ohio, 1968-84. Pres. So. Calif. Council Chs., 1962-65; mem. bd. Ch. Soc. Coll. Work, 1964-71; chmn. clergy deployment bd. Episc. Ch., 1971-73 Co-author: World Religions and World Peace, 1969, Joy in the Struggle - Memoirs of Ecumenical Dialogue, 1993; author: Economic Justice and the Christian Conscience, 1987. Pres. Youngstown Coordinating Coun., 1953-56, Pasadena Cmty. Coun., 1964-66; trustee Pomona Coll., 1963-66, Va. Theol. Sem., 1967-72, Colgate-Rochester Div. Sch., 1968-84, Kenyon Coll., 1967-84; bd. dirs. United Way L.A., 1964-67, Cleve. Urban Coalition, 1968-70, Ams. for Energy Independence, 1975-85; bd. dirs. Nat. Com. Against Censorship, 1974—; chmn. bd. dirs. St. John's Home for Girls, Painesville, Ohio, 1968-84; governing bd. Nat. Coun. Chs., 1970-81; mem. Com. on Ch. Order, Consultation of Ch. Union, 1980-88; chmn. com. on theology Episc. Ch. House Bishops, 1973-80; chmn. Urban Bishops Coalition, 1977-93, Faith and Order Commn. Ohio Coun. Chs., 1970-74; bd. dirs. Episcopal Ch. Pub. Co., 1985-92, pres., 1990-92; chmn. commn. ecumenical rels. Episc. Ch., 1973-79, also chmn. commn. mid. judicatories, cons. on ch. union, 1975-79; chmn. com. human affairs and health Episc. Ch., 1982-85; chmn. Bishops Com. Nat. and Internat. Affairs, 1982-85; chmn. Ecumenical Gt. Lakes Project on Econ. Crisis, 1983-89; chmn. Presiding Bishop's Com. Christian-Jewish Rels., 1986-91; pres. Nat. Christian Leadership Conf. on Israel, 1988-99; mem. ch. rels. com. U.S. Holocaust Meml. Coun., 1989-96; mem. Ecumenical Consultation on New Religions Movements, 1985-87; bd. dirs. Ams. for Med. Progress, Inc., 1992-95. Chaplain USNR, 1943-46. Recipient Arvona Lynch Human Relations award Youngstown, 1956; Rissica Human Relations award Jewish War Vets., 1966; Pasadena Community Relations award, 1967; Cleve.'s Simon Bolivar award, 1972; Pitts.'s Thomas Merton award, 1978; Human Rights award Ohio br. ACLU, 1980; Ecumenical Leadership award Christian Ch. (Disciples of Christ), 1986, Am. Jewish Com. award, 1991. Mem. Phi Gamma Delta. Episcopalian. Home: Middle Island Point Rd # 25 Marquette MI 49855-9726

BURT, MARVIN ROGER, financial advisor, investment manager; b. LA, Mar. 5, 1937; s. Henry Howard Burt and Iris Faith (Green) Welton; m. Joy Lee Rougk, July 20, 1958; children: Sandra Marie, Scott Marvin. BA, UCLA, 1958; MPA, George Washington U., 1965, D in Pub. Adminstrn., 1969. CFP. Mgmt. trainee Bank Am., LA, 1961—62; program analyst Dept. Def., Washington, 1962—65, Exec. Office Pres., Washington, 1965—66; mem. sr. rsch. staff Resource Mgmt. Corp., Bethesda, Md., 1966—67; sr. cons. Peat Marwick Mitchell, Washington, 1967—68; cons. Potomac, Md., 1968—69; mem. sr. staff Urban Inst., Washington, 1969—72; pres. Burt Assocs., Inc., Bethesda, 1972—2002, Inst. Human Resources Rsch., Bethesda, 1973—82; asst. v.p. Sci. Applications Internat., McLean, Va., 1982—85; chmn. bd. Burt Assocs., Inc., Bethesda, 1972—. Cons. Govt. Agys., Washington, 1965—82. Author: Options for Improving the Care of Neglected and Dependent Children, 1971, Policy Analysis, 1974, A Comprehensive Emergency Services System for Neglected and Abused Children, 1977, Drug Abuse, 1979, Children of Heroin Addicts, 1980; contbr. articles to profl. jours. Mem. Cmty. Coordinated Child Care, Bethesda, 1976—77, Montgomery County Drug. Abuse Adv. Com., 1990—92; chmn. coun. on ministries North Bethesda (Md.) United Meth. Ch., 1975—76, 1981—82, chmn. bd. dirs., 1977—78, bd. dirs., 1986—92, lay del. to ann. conf., 1989, chmn. staff-parish rels. com., 1990—92, chmn. fin. com., 2001—; bd. dirs. Mental Health Assn. Montgomery County, 2002—03. Grantee, USPHS, 1977—82. Fellow: AAAS; mem.: Registry Fin. Planning Practitioners, Inst. Cert. Fin. Planners (dean mid-atlantic conf. 1995), Internat. Assn. Fin. Planning (v.p. nat. capital chpt. 1987—89), Ops. Rsch. Soc. Am. (chmn. tech. sect. 1979—80), Avenel Commn. Assn. (pres. 1998—2000, bd. dirs. 1996—2001), Bethesda/Chevy Chase C. of C. (chmn. small bus. com. 1990—91, v.p. small bus., bd. dirs. 1991—93), Potomac Rotary (pres. 1991—92, bd. dirs. 1987—93, pres. Potomac Rotary Charities, Inc. 1992). Avocations: hiking, golf. Home: 5 Willow Gate Ct Bethesda MD 20817-4110 Office: Burt Assocs Inc 6010 Executive Blvd Ste 900 Rockville MD 20852 Office Phone: 301-770-9880. Personal E-mail: mburt@comcast.net. Business E-Mail: mburt@burtassociates.com.

BURT, RICHARD, lawyer; V.p. fin. and devel. Sandoz Corp., 1978—89, v.p., gen. counsel, sec., 1978—89; v.p. legal affairs ABB subs. Asea Brown Boveri Ltd., NY, 1989; sr. v.p., gen. counsel, sec. ABB Inc. N.Am. subs. ABB Group, Zurich, Switzerland; sr. v.p., gen. counsel Bechtel, San Francisco, 2002—. Mem.: Am. Corp. Counsel Assn. (Westchester/So. Conn. chpt.). Office: Bechtel 50 Beale St San Francisco CA 94105-1895

BURT, ROBERT AMSTERDAM, lawyer, educator; b. Phila., Feb. 3, 1939; s. Samuel Matthew and Esther (Amsterdam) B.; m. Linda Gordon Rose, June 14, 1964; children: Anne Elizabeth, Jessica Ellen. AB, Princeton U., 1960; BA in Jurisprudence, Oxford (Eng.) U., 1962, MA, 1968; JD, Yale U., 1964, MA (hon.), 1976. Bar: D.C. 1966, Mich. 1973, U.S. Supreme Ct. 1971. Law clk. to chief judge U.S. Ct. Appeals D.C., 1964-65; asst. gen. counsel Office President's Spl. Rep. Trade Negotiations, 1965-66; senatorial legis. asst., 1966-68; assoc. prof. law U. Chgo. Law Sch., 1968-70; assoc. prof., then prof. law U. Mich. Law Sch., 1970-76; prof. law in psychiatry U. Mich. Med. Sch., 1973-76; Southmayd prof. Yale U. Law Sch., 1976-93, Alexander M. Bickel prof., 1993—. Spl. master U.S. Dist. Ct. Conn., 1987-92, 95. Author: Taking Care of Strangers, 1979, Two Jewish Justices: Outcasts in the Promised Land, 1988, Constitution in Conflict, 1992, Death Is That Man Taking Names: Intersections of American Medicine, Law and Culture, 2002. Bd. dirs. Benhaven Sch. Autistic Persons, New Haven, 1977—, chmn., 1983-96; bd. dirs. Judge David L. Bazelon Ctr. for Mental Health Law, 1985—, chmn., 1990-2000; mem. adv. bd. Project on Death in Am., Open Soc. Inst., 1994-2004; bd. dirs. Slifka Ctr. for Jewish Life at Yale, 1996—. Rockefeller fellow, 1976, John Simon Guggenheim fellow, 1997—98. Mem.: NAS, Inst. Medicine. Democrat. Jewish. Home: 66 Dogwood Cir Woodbridge CT 06525-1254 Office: Yale U Sch Law PO Box 208215 127 Wall St New Haven CT 06511-6636 Office Phone: 203-432-4960. Business E-Mail: robert.burt@yale.edu.

BURT, THOMAS WILLIAM, lawyer; b. Spokane, Wash., Jan. 24, 1955; s. Jack Wallace and Peggy (Windes) B.; m. Ann Darling, Apr. 2, 1989; children: Trevor D. Welling, Griffin D., Caroline D. AB in Human Biology, Stanford U., 1976; JD, U. Wash., 1979. Bar: Wash. 1979, U.S. Ct. Appeals (9th cir.) 1979, U.S. Dist. Ct. (we. dist.) Wash. 1980. Law clk. to judge Ozell Trask U.S. Ct. Appeals (9th cir.), Phoenix, 1979-80; ptnr., atty. Riddell, Williams, Bullitt & Walkinshaw, Seattle, 1980-95; sr. corp. atty. litig. Microsoft Corp., Redmond, Wash., 1995—2003, corp. v.p., dep. gen. counsel, 2003—. Bd. dirs. Bainbridge Island (Wash.) Land Trust, 1990-91. Mem. ABA, Wash. Bar Assn., Seattle-King County Bar. Avocations: sports car racing, skiing, sailing. Office: Microsoft Corp One Microsoft Way Redmond WA 98052 Office Phone: 425-703-6323. Business E-Mail: tburt@microsoft.com.

BURT, WALLACE JOSEPH, JR., insurance company executive; b. Burlington, Iowa, Apr. 1, 1924; s. Wallace Joseph and Lel (Catlow) Burt; m. Alice Olmsted, June 22, 1946; children: Lockwood, David, Virginia. Student, Iowa State Coll., 1942, U. Wis., 1945. V.p., dir. 1st Ins. Fin. Co., Des Moines, 1946—50, Northea. Ins. Co., Hartford, Conn., 1950—59; pres., owner Hail Reins. Mgmt., Inc., Ormond Beach, Fla., 1960—89; chmn. Burt & Scheld, Inc., Ormond Beach, 1961—89; chmn. U.S. br. Hamburg Internat. Reins. Co., 1976—81; chmn. 1st N.Y. Syndicate Corp., 1979—89, W.J. Burt Mgmt., Inc., N.Y.C., 1979—89; pres. Ormond Reins. Co., 1976—92, Oceanside RE Group, Inc., 1989. Dir., v.p. Barnett Bank, Ormond Beach; underwriting mem. Lloyd's of London; dir. N.Y. Ins. Exch., 1983—84. Trustee, pres. Ormond Beach Meml. Hosp. Served to 1st lt. USAAF, WWII. Decorated D.F.C., Purple Heart, Air medal with 5 oak leaf clusters. Home: 222 Riverside Dr Ormond Beach FL 32176-6504 Office: 140 S Atlantic Ave Ormond Beach FL 32176-6689 Office Phone: 386-615-9175.

BURTI, CHRISTOPHER LOUIS, lawyer; b. Muroc, Calif., Oct. 15, 1950; s. Louis Burti and Johanna Renate (Schmidt) Landa; m. Linda Carol Pipkin, Sept. 15, 1973; children: Christopher Louis Jr., Erika Pipkin. BSBA, E. Carolina U., 1975; JD, U. N.C., 1979. Bar: N.C. 1979, U.S. Dist. Ct. (ea. dist.) N.C. 1983. Assoc. Lewis, Lewis & Lewis, Farmville, N.C., 1979-82; ptnr. Lewis & Burti, Farmville, 1982-94; v.p., legal counsel Statewide Title, Inc., Greenville, N.C., 1994—. Atty. Town of Farmville, NC, 1982—84, Town of Falkland, 1989—. Cubmaster Farmville Troop 25 Boy Scouts Am.; bd. dirs. Farmville Child Devel. Ctr., 1983—84, 2000—, Farmville Cmty. Arts Coun., 1983—84, 2000, 2002, Farmville Charitable Svcs., 1987—89; pres. N.C. Land Title Assn., 2002—. With U.S. Army, 1970—72. Mem.: Pitt County Bar Assn., N.C. Mcpl. Attys. Assn. (bd. dirs. 1988—89, chmn. cable comm. com. 1991), N.C. Bar Assn., Farmville C. of C. (bd. dirs. 1982—83), Farmville Country Club, Masons (past master, past dist. dep. grand master), Phi Sigma Pi, Beta Gamma Sigma, Phi Kappa Phi. Democrat. Episcopalian. Avocations: sailing, skiing, woodworking, photography. Office: Statewide Title Inc 110 E Arlington Blvd Greenville NC 27858-5012 Business E-Mail: chris@statewidetitle.com.

BURTLESS, GARY THOMAS, economist, consultant; b. Cayuga County, N.Y., Apr. 11, 1950; s. Charles Bernie and Patricia Ann (MacCone) B.; m. Elise Kathe Bruml, Nov. 27, 1976; children: Andrew B., Matthew B. BA, Yale U., 1972; PhD, MIT, 1977. Economist Office Sc., HEW, Washington, 1977-79, U.S. Dept. Labor, Washington, 1979-81; John D. and Nancy C. Whitehead chair in econ. studies Brookings Instn., Washington, 1981—. Vis. prof. pub. affairs U. Md., College Park, 1993; cons. various orgns., 1981—, U.S. Dept. Lab., 1985—, World Bank, Washington, 1990-97. Author: Can America Afford To Grow Old, 1989, Growth With Equity: Economic Policymaking for the Next Century, 1993, Globaphobia: Confronting Fears about Open Trade, 1998; co-editor Jour. Human Resources, 1988-96, Brookings-Wharton Papers on Urban Affairs, 2003—, A Future of Lousy Jobs?, 1990, Five Years After: Long Term Effects of Welfare-to-Work Programs, 1995, Does Money Matter? Effect of School Resources, 1996, Work, Health and Income Among the Elderly, 1997, Aging Societies: The Global Dimension, 1998; mem. editl. bd. Jour. Policy Analysis and Mgmt., 1999—; contbr. articles to profl. jours. Commn. mem. panel on fin. adequacy Trustees Social Security, 1989; mem .tech. panel Adv. Coun. on Social Security, 1994—95; mem. com. on health and safety needs of older workers NAS, 2001—04. Recipient Leontief prize Ea. Econ. Assn., 1978. Mem.: Assn. Pub. Policy Analysis & Mgmt., Nat. Acad. Social Ins. (commn. mem. panel on Social Security notch 1988, panel on privatizing Social Security 1997—98), Am. Econ. Assn. Avocations: history, hiking. Office: Brookings Instn 1775 Massachusetts Ave NW Washington DC 20036-2103 Office Phone: 202-797-6000. Personal E-mail: brookinfo@brookings.edu. Business E-Mail: communiations@brookings.edu.

BURTLEY, CALVIN, art director; b. Cairo, Ill., Feb. 28, 1945; s. Brooks Jr. and Gustava (Robinson) B. Cert., Famous Artist Sch., Conn., 1973; AA, L.A. Trade Tech. Coll., 1982; BFA, U. So. Calif., 1992. Ordained elder, Presbyn. of Pacific. Graphic artist U. So. Calif., L.A., 1982-92; art cons. L.A., 1992-95; pub. rels. adminstr. Cultural Affairs, L.A., 1995-96; pres. Burtley Fine Arts, L.A., 1997—; tchr. Jr. Art Ctr., L.A., 1999. Exhbns. include Palms Westminster Presbyn. Ch., L.A., 1995, L.A. Mcpl. Art Gallery, 1996, St. Andrews Abbey, Valyermo, Calif., 1997, The Presbytery of the Pacific, L.A., 1997, Hollywood Digital, L.A., 1998, City of Brea Gallery, 1998, Palos Verdes Art Ctr., 1999, Nat. Art Program City of L.A., 1999. V.p. Palms Westminster Presbyn. Ch., L.A., 1996—; mem. Cmty. Coalition, L.A., 1999; vol. Cir. of Friends, Easter Seals, After Sch. Programs, L.A., 1999. With USN, 1965-69. Named Person of Yr., Palms Westminster Woman's Assn., 1996. Mem. Am. Legion. Democrat. Avocations: painting, reading, languages, classical music. E-mail: artbrush@email.com.

BURTNETT, JANE S., public relations consultant; b. Mt. Vernon, NY, June 6, 1956; d. Robert Claus and Joan Arleen Burtnett. BA, Ariz. State U., 1978. Graphic designer St. Joseph's Hosp. & Med. Ctr., Phoenix, 1979-81; editor World Assn. Girl Guides & Girl Scouts, London, 1981-83; calligrapher Pengraphics, Phoenix, 1984-85; pub. rels. specialist Ariz. Cactus Pine Girl Scout Coun., Phoenix, 1985-90, mem. mgmt. team, 1990-94; pres., prin. Blue Corn Cons., Scottsdale, Ariz., 1984—; asst. to pres. LemmonTree Enterprises, Tempe, Ariz., 1996-98; info. specialist coord. undergrad. admissions Ariz. State U., Tempe, 1998—2005, strategic mktg. and comms. specialist, 2005—. Presenter in field. Editor, author (newsletter) The Listening Post, 1985-90, Citation, 1995—; publ., editor (newsletter) The Cheap Living in Tough Times, 1995-97; contbr. articles to mags. Vol. Leukemia and Lymphoma Soc. Am., 1993—. Mem.: Am. Mktg. Assn., Internat. Assoc. of Bus. Comm. (Phoenix Copper Quill Merit award 2000, 2003, Phoenix Copper Quill Excellence award 2003), Desert Bot. Garden, Toastmasters Internat. (Humorous Speech award 2000), Scottsdale Leadership Class XIV, Ariz. Yoga Assn., Am. Volkssporters Assn., World Assn. Girl Guides and Girl Scouts, Pi Alpha Alpha, Phi Kappa Phi. Democrat. Avocations: world travel (visiting all 7 continents before age 40), walking, gardening, birding, dance.

BURTON, AL, television producer, television director, writer; b. Chgo. s. D. Chester and Isabelle (Olenick) G.; m. Sally Lou Lewis, Jan. 8, 1956; 1 dau., Jennifer. BS cum laude, Northwestern U. Exec. v.p. creative affairs Norman Lear-Embassy Communications, Inc., 1973-83; exec. producer-cons. Universal TV, 1983-92; exec. prodr., v.p. syndication Castle Rock Entertainment, 1992-95; pres. Al Burton Prodns., Beverly Hills, Calif., 1995—. Bd. dirs. Pilgrim Group Funds; adv. bd. Samantha Smith Found. Producer Johnny Mercer's Mus. Chairs, 1952-55, Oscar Levant Show, 1955-61; creative producer Teen-Age Fair, 1962-72; exec. producer Charles in Charge, CBS-TV, 1984-85, Tribune Entertainment, 1986-91, Together We Stand, CBS-TV, 1986-87, Nothing Is Easy, 1987-88, The New Lassie, The Family Channel, 1989-92 (Outstanding Family Classic award Youth in Film 1994), Out of the Blue, Tribune Entertainment, 1995-96, Win Ben Stein's Money, Disney, Comedy Ctrl., 1997— (Cable Ace nomination, Emmy nomination 1998, 99, 2001, shared 2 Emmys, 1998, Emmy award for Outstanding Game Show 1999); creative supr. Mary Hartman, Mary Hartman, Fernwood 2Night, America 2Night; prodn. supr. One Day At a Time, Facts of Life, Silver Spoons, The Jeffersons, Square Pegs, Different Strokes; composer-lyricist theme songs for Facts of Life, Different Strokes, Charles in Charge, The New Lassie (Genesis award, 1992), Together We Stand, Nothing Is Easy; cons. Domestic Life CBS-TV, 1983-84, Alan King Show, 1986. Shared Emmy honors for outstanding comedy series All in the Family, 1978-89, Producers award Nat. Coun. for Families and TV, 1984, Jackie Coogan award for Oustanding Contbn. to Youth through Entertainment, 1991; honored for Different Strokes, NCCH, 1979-80; honored by Calif. Gov.'s Com. for employment of the handicapped for Facts of Life, 1981-82, for Charles in Charge, 1988; recipient Youth in Film award Charles in Charge, 1990, The

New Lassie, 1994, Genesis award for portrayal animal issues The New Lassie, 1992; spl. commendation Entertainment Industries Coun. for The New Lassie and Charles in Charge, 1990. Mem. AFTRA, Chmn.'s Coun. of Caucus for Producers, Writers and Dirs., Dirs. Guild Am., Writers Guild Am., Acad. TV Arts and Scis., Acad. Magical Arts. Home: 555 Laurel Ave San Mateo CA 94401 Office Phone: 650-348-3463. Personal E-mail: alburton22@aol.com. *I believe that, in order to achieve success, one should make an occupation of his or her hobby.*

BURTON, ALAN HARVEY, city official; b. Chgo., Mar. 26, 1952; s. Harvey C. and Lois (Fitzpatrick) B.; (div. Oct. 1987); children: Douglas Alan, Marla Joy. BS, We. Ill. U., 1974, MS, 1986. Cert. Nat. Accreditation for Ormand Beach Leisure Svc. 2003. Recreation supr. Park Ridge Park Dist., Ill., 1974—75; dir. parks and recreation York Ctr. Park Dist., Lombard, Ill., 1975—78, City of Berwyn, Ill., 1978—82, adminstr., 1982—86; dir. parks and recreation Norridge Park Dist., Ill., 1986—93; recreation bur. chief City of Orlando, Fla., 1993—96; dir. leisure svcs. City of Ormond Beach, Fla., 1996—. Chmn. Berwyn Bus. Commn., 1984-86; cons. Berwyn Devel. Corp., 1986-88. Active Suburban Cook County Spl. Olympics, Franklin Park, Ill., 1983; hon. EMT Ill. Dept. Pub. Health, 1984; mem. at large Boy Scouts Am., La Grange, Ill., 1986, chmn. dist. nominating com.; rep. West Cen. Mcpl. Conf., Western Springs, Ill., 1987; pres. United Way of Harwood Heights (Ill.)/Norridge, 1990; active Fla. Conservation Corps., 1994, Birthplace of Speed Centennial Com., 2000; bd. dirs. Ormond Art Mus., Ormond Meml. Art Mus., Fla. Pk. and Recreation Found. Recipient Arbor Day award Ill. Assn. Park Dists., 1977, Individual Merit award, 1986, Gold Medal finalist Nat. Sporting Goods Found., 1991, 92, 93, 2002. Mem. Nat. Park and Recreation Assn. (U.S. del. to Japan, youth at risk sect., program chair SE regional coun.), Nat. Soc. Fundraising Execs., Fla. Recreation and Park Assn. (Agy. Excellence award 2003), Ill. Park and Recreation Assn. (issues com., long-range planning com., Meritorious Svc. award 1990, Facility Showcase award for skatebd. design), Northeastern Ill. Planning Commn. (open space com. 1991-92), Fla. Park and Recreation Assn. (chmn. fin. taskforce, chmn. adminstrn. sect., Faculty award 1999, Al Monaco Cmty. Svc. award, Agy. Excellence award 2003), West Suburban Spl. Recreation Assn. (bd. dirs. 1991), Jackson Hole Conservation Alliance, Berwyn Hist. Soc., Kiwanis Club of Ormond Beach (bd. dirs., Internat. George F. Hixson fellow, v.p., pres.-elect). Lutheran. Avocations: bowling, theater, genealogy, biking, science fiction. Home: 915 Ocean Shore Blvd Apt 707 Ormond Beach FL 32176-8307 Business E-Mail: burton@ormondbeach.org.

BURTON, BERNARD OTTWAY, lawyer; b. Axton, Va., Mar. 12, 1916; BS in Commerce, U. N.C., 1941; Indsl. Adminstr. Degree, Harvard U., 1943; JD, U. N.C., 1945. Bar: N.C. 1945, U.S. Dist. Ct., 1948. Counsel Randolph County Airport Commn., Asheboro, N.C., 1948-50; spl. right-of-way N.C. Hwy. Commn., Asheboro, N.C., 1965-68; sole-practice Ottway Burton PA, Asheboro, N.C., 1945—. Dir. N.C. R.R. Co., 1964-68. With Med. Svc. Corps., 1934-37. Mem.: ABA, N.C. Bar Assn., Shriners, Masons. Democrat. Methodist. Avocations: gardening, photography, golf, history. Office: 838 Westmont DR Asheboro NC 27205-4262

BURTON, BETTY JUNE, retired pastor; b. Muskegon, Mich., June 11, 1923; d. Bernard J. and Louise Ella (Weaver) Mulder; m. Harold Ver Berkmoes, June 4, 1943 (div. 1966); children: Suzanne, James, Michael, William, Judith, David (dec.); m. Eldon Franklin Burton, June 27, 1971 (dec. May 8, 2003). Student of music, psychology and religion, Hope Coll., 1941-45; student, Garrett Evang. Theol. Sem., 1984-85. Ordained to ministry United Meth. Ch., 1986. Librarian Vassar Hosp. Sch. Nursing, Poughkeepsie, N.Y., 1958-60, Hackley Pub. Library, Muskegon, 1960-64, Boyne City (Mich.) Pub. Library, 1972-74; reporter Ludington (Mich.) Daily News, 1975-81; caseworker Aid to Dependent Children Mich. Dept. Social Services, Hart, 1974-78; pastor various Meth. Chs., Norwood, Barnard and Charlevoix, Mich., 1981-83, Mears (Mich.) United Meth. Ch., 1985, 86; assoc. pastor United Meth. Centenary, Pentwater, Mich., 1986-90; pastor First Congl. Ch. of Central Lake, Mich., 1990-92, Thompsonville (Mich.) Congl. Church, 1982—83. Guest preacher, spkr. various chs. Sec. Pentwater Planning Commn., 1985; vol. chaplain Grand Tranverse Pavilions Nursing Home. Mem. NAFE, Internat. Platform Assn., Am. Platform Assn., Am. Assn. Christian Counselors, Nat. Christian Counselors Assn., Nat. Trust Hist. Preservation, Am. Mus. Natural History, Nat. Audubon Soc., Am. Acad. Ministry, Hist. Soc. Mich., Oceana County Hist. Soc., Kappa Beta Phi (pres. 1943), Xi Gamma Beta (sec. 1970). Clubs: Women's of Pentwater (v.p. 1986—), Garden of Pentwater (pres. 1986—), Sierra. Republican. Avocations: writing, fishing, gardening, birding, travel. Home and Office: 3848 Silver Lake Rd Apt 108 Traverse City MI 49684-7005

BURTON, B.J. (BETTY JANE), playwright; d. Robert Ellis and Barbara Elizabeth (Williams) Burton. BA in theatre, U. Mo., 1973; attended, Am. Conservatory Theatre, 1978; grad. in theatre, Villanova U., 1997; student MFA in creative writing, Rosemont Coll., 2003—. Author: (plays) Hunting Season, 1990, Buddy, 1992, Lunch on the Fifth, 1993, Lobelia Lodge, 1995, Pizza Again, 1996, Green Benches, 2000, Marjorie and Helen, 2000, Room For Love, 2002, Newsroom, 2004. Recipient Pa. Playwriting award, Theatre Assn. Pa., 1994, Playwriting award, 1994; fellow, Pa. Coun. Arts, 1990, 2000. Mem.: AFTRA, SAG, Actors Equity Assn., The Dramatists Guild. Avocations: painting, photography. Office: PO Box 445 Wayne PA 19087 Personal E-mail: bj_burton@hotmail.com.

BURTON, BRETT R., music educator, minister; b. Madisonville, Ky., July 13, 1971; s. Bobby G. and Mollie Jane Burton; m. Laura Grace Patterson, Nov. 14, 1998. MusB Edn., Murray State U., Murray, Ky., 1995, MusM Edn., 1999. Music dir. Ballard County Schs., Barlow, Ky., 1995—98; dir. choral activities Madisonville-North Hopkins H.S., Madisonville, Ky., 1999—. Founder/dir. Children's Chorus of Madisonville, Madisonville, Ky., 2003—; bi-vocational music min. Grapevine Bapt. Ch., Madisonville, Ky., 1999—2003. Actor(music director): (plays) The Music Man, Oklahoma!. Music com. Little Bethel Bapt. Assn., Madisonville, Ky., 2002—05. Mem.: Music Educators Nat. Conf. (MENC), Am. Choral Dirs.Assn., Ky. Music Educators Assn. (festival commn. 1999—2005, Second Dist. H.S. Music Tchr. of the Yr. 2005), Phi Mu Alpha Sinfonia Music Frat. (music dir. 1992—93). Bapt. Avocations: model railroading, railfanning, travel, music. Home: 527 North Seminary St Madisonville KY 42431 Office: Madisonville-North Hopkins H S 4515 Hanson Rd Madisonville KY 42431 Office Phone: 270-825-6017 271. Office Fax: 270-825-6045. Personal E-mail: bburton@hopkins.k12.ky.us.

BURTON, BRUCE ARTHUR, education educator; b. Newark, N.J. s. Donald Lawrence and Alice Beatrice Burton; m. Jamie Ann Crowl, June 4, 1967; children: Bruce Harold, William Trahern. BA, Bowdoin Coll., Brunswick, Maine, 1967; MLitt, Univ. Edinburgh, Edinburgh, Scotland, 1969. Tchr. Scarborough Sch., Briarecliff Manor, NY, 1969—70; prof. Castleton State Coll., Castleton, Vt., 1970—96. Editor Turtle Quarertly, Niagara Falls, NY, 1988—. Author: (novels) Hail! Nene Karenna The Hymn, 1981, Japanese translation, 1988, In the Valley of the Shadow: The Story of David Jones and Jane McCrea; contbr. numerous essays to profl. jour. Past chair Zoning Bd. of Adj., Castleton, Vt., 1972, Planning Commn., Castleton, Vt., 1972. Mem.: Writers Guild of Am. Achievements include patents for inlaid brick walkway bed leveler pat. no. 6053659; heating and ventilating air conditioning workers servicing cart pat. no. 6619065. Avocations: anthropology, camping, gardening, nature study. Personal E-mail: bruceburton@aol.com.

BURTON, CATHERINE MARIE, lawyer; b. Houston, Sept. 17, 1964; d. Charles Lee and Norma Jean (Welch) B. BA in Polit. Sci., U. Okla., 1987, JD, 1990. Bar: Okla. 1990, U.S. Dist. Ct. (we. dist.) Okla. 1990. Asst. pub. defender Okla. County Pub. Defender, Oklahoma City, 1990-96; ptnr. Coyle & McCoy, Oklahoma City, 1996—2003, Burton & Goodman, Oklahoma City, 2003—. Bd. dirs. Okla. Coalition to Abolish Death Penalty, Oklahoma City, 1995-2000; active Amnesty Internat., Oklahoma City, 1996-2003; active ACLU, Oklahoma City, 1997, bd. dirs., 1999-2001 Recipient Cert. of Appreciation, Nat. Assn. Criminal Def. Lawyers, Santa Monica, Calif., 1996. Mem. Okla. Criminal Def. Lawyers Assn. (bd. dirs. 1998, 99, 2d v.p. 1999-2000, v.p. 2000-01), Okla. County Bar Assn. (vol. law related edn. 1998); master Am. Inn. Ct. Democrat. Roman Catholic. Avocations: reading, singing, volunteer work, talking, cooking. Office: Burton & Goodman PMC 500 N Walker Ste B Oklahoma City OK 73102 Office Phone: 405-236-2221. Business E-Mail: cb@burtongoodmanlaw.com.

BURTON, CHARLES VICTOR, neurosurgeon; b. N.Y.C., Jan. 2, 1935; s. Norman Howard and Ruth Esther (Putziger) B.; m. Joy Burton; children—Matthew, Timothy, Andrew, Dawn, Stacy, Chad. Student, Johns Hopkins U., Balt., 1952-56; MD, N.Y. Med. Coll., 1960. Diplomate Am. Bd. Neurol. Surgery, Nat. Bd. Med. Examiners, Am. Bd. Forensic Medicine, Am Bd. Spinal Surgery. Intern surgery Yale U. Med. Ctr., 1961-62; asst. resident neurol. surgery Johns Hopkins Hosp., Balt., 1962-66, chief resident, 1966-67; assoc. chief surgery, chief neurosurgery USPHS Hosp., Seattle, 1967-69; vis. research affiliate Primate Ctr., U. Wash., 1967-69; asst. prof. neurosurgery Temple U. Health Scis. Ctr., Phila., 1970-73, assoc. prof., 1973-74, neurol. research coordinator, 1970-74; dir. dept. neuroaugmentive surgery Sister Kenny Inst., Mpls., 1974-81, med. dir. Low Back Clinic, 1978-81; med. dir. Inst. for Low Back Care, Mpls., 1981-96; sr. med. dir. Inst. Low Back and Neck Care, Mpls., 1996—2004; dir. Ctr. Restorative Spine Surgery, Mpls., 2003—. Biomed. Instrumentations Internat., Ltd., 1988-92; co-chmn. Joint Neurosurg. Com. on Devices and Drugs, 1973-77; chmn. adv. panel on neurologic devices FDA, 1974-77, Internat. Standards Orgn., 1974-76; mem. U.S. Biomed. Instrumentation Del. to Soviet Union, 1974; co-chmn. Am. Bd. Spine Surgery. Editor Neuroorthopedics jour., 1987-1998, editor The Burton Report; editor-in-chief www.burtonreport.com, 2000—. Named Top Surgeon, Consumers Rsch. Coun. Am., 2004—; rsch. fellow, Nat. Polio Found., 1956, HEW, 1958, neurosurg. fellow, Johns Hopkins Hosp., 1960—61, 1962—67, 1969—70. Fellow ACS (exec. com. Minn. chpt. 1989-92); mem. Congress Neurol. Surgeons (chmn. com. materials and devices 1972-79), Am. Assn. Neurol. Surgeons, Minn. Neurosurg. Soc., AAAS, ASTM (chmn. com. materials 173-78), Internat. Soc. Study of Lumbar Spine (exec. com. 1986-89), N.Am. Spine Soc. (exec. com. 1987-91, chmn. com. on profl. conduct 1991-92, dir. coun. mem. affairs 1992-94, bd. dirs. 1990-94), Am. Nat. Standards Inst. (med. device tech. adv. bd. 1973-78), Am. Bd. Spine Surgery (bd. dirs. 1997—, vice chair 2002—, chair ethics com. 1998—), Philadelphia County Med. Soc. (med.-legal com. 1970-74), Minn. Med. Assn. (Gold medal award for best sci. presentation at 1975 meeting, subcom. on med. testimony 1978—), Hennepin County Med. Soc. (med.-legal com. 1975—), Mpls. Acad. Medicine, Cor et Manus Soc., Profl. Assn. Diving Instrs. (underwater photography splty. diver), Am. Back Soc., Twin Cities Spine Soc. (pres. 1994-95), Back Pain Assn. Am. (hon. chmn. 1995—), Am. Bd. Spine Surgery (bd. dirs. 1997, chmn. ethics com., v.p. 2002—, chmn. med.-legal com., co-chmn. 2002—), Johns Hopkins U. Alumni Assn. (pres. Minn. chpt. 1988-92), Yale Surg. Soc., Alpha Epsilon Delta. Achievements include patents for surgical devices, operating room fiberoptic headlights, clinical therapy systems and techniques. Home: 148 W Lake St Excelsior MN 55331-1744 Office: Ctr Restorative Spine Surgery Ste 402 2800 Chicago Ave Minneapolis MN 55407-1382 Office Phone: 612-879-8084. Business E-Mail: cburton@restorativespinesurgery.com.

BURTON, CHARLES WILLIAM, lawyer; b. Port Arthur, Tex. BA in Journalism, Univ. Ark., Little Rock, 1986, JD with high honors, 1989. Bar: Tex. 1990, Ark. 1990. Journalist Texarkana newspaper, Ark.; editor and publisher newspaper, Hope, Ark.; editor Assoc. Press.; dep. asst. to President of US, staff dir. for Chief of Staff the White House, Washington, 1993—94; dir. US Enrichment Corp., 1996—98; ptnr., chair, energy industry practice worldwide Jones Day, Houston. Former mem. Nat. Petroleum Coun, program adv. bd. mem. Energy Coun.; bd. dir. Inst. for Energy Law; energy policy coord. Clinton Gore campaign, 1991—92; del. Democratic Nat. Conv., Tex., 1992. Assoc. editor Law Rev., 1989; editor: ABA nat. law student mag. Mem.: TIPRO (Tex. affiliate), IPAA. Office: Jones Day Ste 3300 717 Texas Houston TX 77002-2712 Business E-Mail: bburton@jonesday.com.

BURTON, CHERYL, newscaster; b. Chgo. BS in Psychology and Biology, U. Ill., Champaign. Host Minority Bus. Report WGN-TV, Chgo., 1989; reporter WMBD-TV, Peoria, Ill., 1990; weekend anchor KWCH-TV, Wichita, Kans., 1990—92, host Viewpoint, 1990—92; weekend co-anchor and reporter WLS-TV, Chgo., 1992—2003, co-anchor and contbg. anchor 5 pm news, 2003—. Vol. Boys and Girls Club of Am., Rush-Presbyn./St. Luke's Fashion Show; motivational spkr. Chgo. Pub. Sch.; bd. mem. City Yr., Chgo. Recipient Kizzy Image and Achievement award, 1998, Phenomenal Woman award, Expo Today's Black Woman, 1997. Mem.: Nat. Assn. of Black Journalists, Chgo. Assn. of Black Journalists ((now named Russ Ewing award) 1996, 2003), Life with Lupus Guild, Delta Sigma Theta. Office: WLS-TV 190 N State St Chicago IL 60601

BURTON, DAN L., congressman; b. Indpls., June 21, 1938; m. Barbara Jean Logan, 1959; children: Kelly, Danielle Lee, Danny Lee II. Mem. Ind. Ho. Reps., Indpls., 1967-68, 77-80, Ind. State Senate, 1969-70, 81-82; owner ins. and real estate firm, 1968—; mem. U.S. Congress from 5th Ind. dist. (formerly 6th), 1983—. Mem. internat. rels. com.; chmn. govt. reform and oversight com. Pres. Vols. of Am.; pres. Ind. Christian Benevolent Assn., Com. for Constl. Govt., Family Support Ctr. Served with U.S. Army, 1957-58. Republican. Office: US Ho of Reps 2185 Rayburn Ofc Bldg Washington DC 20515-1406

BURTON, DAVID K., lawyer; b. Phila., July 11, 1970; s. Kenneth Burton and Georgia May Peters; m. Tyler Katherine Bradford, Dec. 28, 1993; children: Joshua David, Alexander Bradford. BA, Ithaca Coll., 1993; JD, Georgetown U., 1996. Bar: Pa. 1996, N.J. 1996, U.S. Tax Ct. 1997. Atty. Morgan, Lewis & Bockius LLP, Phila., 1996—2000; tax counsel leasing and M&A GE Comml. Fin., Stamford, Conn., 2000—. Contbr. articles to profl. jours. Dailey scholar, Georgetown U. Law Ctr., 1994. Mem.: ABA (tax sect.), Equipment Leasing Assn. (fed. tax com.), Phi Kappa Phi. Office: GE Comml Fin 260 Long Ridge Rd Stamford CT 06927 Office Phone: 203-357-3485.

BURTON, DONALD JOSEPH, chemistry professor; b. Balt., July 16, 1934; s. Lawrence Andrew and Dorothy Wilhelmina (Koehler) B.; m. Margaret Anna Billing, June 21, 1958; children— Andrew, Jennifer, David, Julie, Elizabeth. BS, Loyola Coll., Balt., 1956; PhD, Cornell U., 1961; postgrad., Purdue U., 1961-62. Asst. prof. chemistry dept. U. Iowa, Iowa City, 1962-67, assoc. prof., 1967-70, prof., 1970—, Roy Carver/Ralph Shriner prof. chemistry, 1989—. Recipient Gov.'s Sci. Medal for Sci. Achievement, 1988; Japanese Soc. for Promotion Sci. fellow, 1979 Mem. Am. Chem. Soc. (chmn. fluorine divsn. 1978, award for creative work in fluorine chemistry 1984, Midwest Chemistry award 1990, ACS divsn. Fluorine Chemistry Disting. Svc. award 2003), Chem. Soc. London, Sigma Xi, Alpha Chi Sigma. Home: 105 Notting Hill Ln Iowa City IA 52245-9217 Office: U Iowa Dept Chemistry Iowa City IA 52242 Business E-Mail: donald-burton@uiowa.edu.

BURTON, EVA ELLA MARY, primary school educator; b. Gillette, Wyo., Sept. 12, 1925; d. Evart Rae Potts and Hazel Jemima Tharp; m. Edwin Harry Wells, Jan. 25, 1945 (dec.); children: Virginia, John, Harry, Valerie, Edella, Donna; m. Howard Dale Burton, June 7, 1990. Student, U. Wyo., 1942—45. Tchr. Dist. II of Campbell County, Weston, Wyo., 1945—46, Dist. of Crook County, 1946—47, Dist. of Shasta County, Redding, Calif., 1949—50; sub. tchr. Dist. I of Sheridan County, Sheridan, Wyo., 1964—70; ins. sales Royal Neighbors of Am., Rock Island, Ill., 1984—91. Ins. counseling Royal Neighbors of Am., Sheridan and Glendo, Wyo., 1999—. Author: (book) Wyoming Legacy Little Powder School, 2000, Mystery in History; Legends of Currant Creek Ranch with Butch Cassidy and William H. Gottsche, 2004. Mem.: Royal Neighbors of Am., Am. Legion Aux. (pres. 2001—04). Republican. Avocations: singing, reading, tutoring, horseback riding. Home and Office: 1408 So Glendo Hwy PO Box 261 Glendo WY 82213 Office Phone: 307-735-4564.

BURTON, GEORGE AUBREY, JR., accountant; b. Texarkana, Ark., June 21, 1926; s. George Aubrey Burton and Theo Marvis Simmons-Burton; m. Joan Cunningham, July 31, 1947 (dec. Oct. 2002); children: George Aubrey Burton, III, Sandra Burton-Batten. BS, Centenary Coll., 1947—50. CPA, State Bd. Of Acctg./La., 1953. Reporter Dun & Bradstreet, Shreveport, La., 1947—49; acct. Opferkuch, Mc Guirt, Watts & West CPA's, Shreveport, La., 1949—53. Ptnr. Opferkuch, McGuirt, Watts & West CPA's, Shreveport, 1953, Burton & Penn CPA'S, Shreveport, 1964—74; CPA George A. Burton, Jr., Shreveport, 1953—64, George A. Burton, Jr. CPA, Shreveport, 1978—; commr. fin. City Of Shreveport, 1971—78. Treas. Jaycees, Shreveport, 1953—54, exec. v.p., 1955—56, pres., 1956—57; regional v.p. La. Jaycees, 1958—59, exec. v.p., 1959—60; mem. Shreveport Airport Authority; chmn. Caddo Parish Exec. Com., La.; pres. Caddo Parish Bd. Election Suprs., 1978—; exec. com. La. State Fair, Shreveport, 1971—78; dir. Shreveport C. of C., 1956—57. Seaman 1/c Navy Seabees, 1943—46, Central Pacific. Recipient JCI Life Mem., Jr. C. of C., 1973. Mem.: La. CPA Soc. (state committe), Jr. ROTC Parents Club (life). Home: 770 Delaware Shreveport LA 71106 Office: George A Burton Jr CPA 1300 Grimmett Dr Shreveport LA 71107 Office Phone: 318-222-7555. Personal E-mail: gburton@worldnet.att.net.

BURTON, GLENN WILLARD, geneticist; b. Clatonia, Nebr., May 5, 1910; s. Joseph Fearn and Nellie (Rittenburg) Burton; m. Helen Maurine Jeffryes, Dec. 16, 1934; children: Elizabeth Ann Fowler, Robert Glenn, Thomas Jeffryes, Joseph William, Richard Bennett. BS, U. Nebr., 1932, DSc (hon.), 1962; MS, Rutgers U., 1933, PhD, 1936, DSc (hon.), 1955. With USDA and U. Ga. at Tifton Exptl. Sta., 1936—, prin. geneticist, 1952—, chmn. div. agronomy, 1950—64; Univ. Found. prof. U. Ga., 1957. Mem. Tift County Bd. Edn., 1953—58. Recipient 1st Ann. Agrl. award, So. Seedsman Assn., 1950, Sears-Roebuck Rsch. award, 1953, 1960, Superior Svc. award, USDA, 1955, 1st Ford Almanac Crops and Soils Rsch. award, 1962, Disting. Svc. award, 1980, Pres.'s award for Disting. Fed. Civilian Svc., 1981, Nat. Medal of Sci., 1983, named Man of Yr., So. Agriculture Progressive Farmer, 1954, named to Hall of Fame, USDA ARS, 1987, numerous other awards and citations. Fellow: Am. Soc. Agronomy (v.p. 1961, pres. 1962, Stevenson award 1949, John Scott award 1957); mem.: Nat. Acad. Sci., Am. Soc. Range Mgmt., Am. Genetic Assn., Gamma Sigma, Alpha Zeta, Sigma Xi. Home: 421 10th St W Tifton GA 31794-3917 Office: USDA Coastal Plain Experimental Station Tifton GA 31794*

BURTON, JANET RUTH WISNER, music educator; b. Ft. Payne, Ala., Nov. 25, 1955; d. Robert Thurston and Mary Lou (Garrett) Wisner; m. David Lee Malone (div.); 1 child, Mara Ruth Malone; m. O.E. "Buddy" Burton, Oct. 18, 1991. AA in Music, Nat. Sch. Music, Roanoke, Ala., 1979; Assoc., N.E. State Jr. Coll., Rainsville, Ala., 1990; BSE, Athens State Coll., 1992; MusMA, Jacksonville (Ala.) State U., 2004. Cert. tchr. Ala., Tenn. Substitute tchr. Catawba County Schs., Maiden, NC, 1992—94; music dir. Cornerstone Ch., Maiden, NC, 1992—95; tchr. Lincolnton (NC) H.S., 1994—95; music dir. Gault Ave. Bapt. Ch., Ft. Payne, Ala., 1995—96; substitute tchr. Lake Travis Schs., Austin, Tex., 1995—99; tchr. Hilltop Acad., Cedar Park, Tex., 1997—99; program dir. Hilltop Bapt. Ch., Cedar Park, Tex., 1997—99; band interium Geraldine (Ala.) H.S., 1999—2000; music tchr. K-6 Plainview H.S., Rainsville, Ala., 2000—01, Huntland (Tenn.) H.S., 2004—05. Owner, prodr. (TV show) Gospel Music Time with Buddy & Janet Burton, 2002—05; composer: numerous songs, 1980—2000; author, instr. Do Re Mi's of Music. Named Miss Congeniality, DeKalb County Jr. Miss, Ft. Payne, 1974; recipient Ballroom Dance award, Fred Astaire Studios, 1985, Leadership award, Omicron Delta Kappa, 2003; grantee, Ala. Arts Coun., 1995. Mem.: Tenn. Tchrs. Edn. Assn., Nat. Assn. Music Educators, C.C. Rainsville. Avocations: painting, reading, nature walks, movies, musical instruments. Home: PO Box 8 Rainsville AL 35986 Office: Huntland HS 300 Gore St Huntland TN 37345 Office Phone: 256-638-6591. Personal E-mail: buddy@fumcscottsboro.org.

BURTON, JEANETTE RICKMAN, elementary school educator; b. Richmond, Va., Apr. 22, 1959; m. Douglas A. Burton; children: Laura M., Thomas D. BS, James Madison U., 1980. Tchr. Richmond (Va.) Pub. Schs., Va., 1983—. Methodist. Home: 10939 Rickey Ct Glen Allen VA 23060 Office: Richmond Pub Schs 2300 Hanover Ave Richmond VA 23220

BURTON, JEFF, race car driver; b. June 29, 1967; m. Kim Burton; children: Kimberle Paige, Harrison. Named Orange County Speedway champion, 1987, South Boston Most Popular Driver, Va., 1988, 4-time winner, NASCAR Busch Grand Nat. Divsn. series, 1989—92, qulified, 6th NASCAR Winston Cup, London, N.H., 1993, NASCAR Rookie of Yr., 1994, 3 top-10 finishes, 6th NASCAR Winston Cup, London, N.H., 1994, 2 top-10 finishes, 1995, 6 top-10 finishes, 1996, winner, Winston Cup, Tex., 1997, Winston Cup, London, Va., 1997, Winston Cup, Martinsville, Va., 1997, 13 top-10 finishes, Winston Cup, 1998, 18 top-5 finishes, 1998, winner, InterState Batteries 500, 1997, Hanes 500, 1997, Jiffy Lube 300, 1997, 1998, 1999, DuraLube/KMart 500, 1999, Exide NASCAR 400, 1998, Las Vegas 400, 1999, Transsouth Fin. 400, 1999, Coca-Cola 600, 1999, Pepsi So. 500, 1999, Pop Secret 400, 1999, CarsDirect.com 400, 2000, 21-time winner, NASCAR Winston Racing Series. Avocations: basketball, boating.*

BURTON, JENNIFER J., music educator; b. Neenah, Wis., Aug. 5, 1954; d. Clifford Euclid and Esther Emma Burton. B in Music Edn., U. Wis., Eau Claire, 1976, postgrad., 1992; M in Mus Edn. with Suzuki emphasis, U. Wis., Stevens Point, 1977. Suzuki violin specialist Am. Suzuki Talent Edn. Ctr., U. Wis., Stevens Point, 1977-93; Suzuki violin specialist, adminstrv. dir. Suzuki Inst. Dallas, 1993—2003, dir., 1993—2003, Burton Suzuki Studio, Dallas, 2003—. Clinician summer camp Am. Suzuki Inst., Stevens Point, 1977—, Intermountain Suzuki Inst., Salt Lake City, 1996, Colo. Suzuki Inst., Aspen, 1996—, Mont. Suzuki Inst., 1998, Santa Fe Suzuki Inst., 2002, DFW WOW Suzuki Inst., 2003; dir. summer Suzuki camp Tex. Christian U., Ft. Worth, 1998—2000. Contbr. articles to profl. jours. Vol. Spl. Olympics, Dallas, 1994—96; mem. orch. bd. Cathedral of Hope, Dallas, 1998—; concert mistress, string chair Cathedral of Hope Orch., Dallas, 1995—; bd. dirs., prin. II violin Ctrl. Wis. Symphony Orch., Stevens Point, 1983—93; mem. Japanese tour group Tex. Commn. Arts, 1994. Grantee Hickman, Wis. Arts Bd., 1990. Mem.: Dallas Music Tchrs. Assn. (string asst. 1994—), Tex. Music Tchrs. Assn., North Tex. Suzuki Assn. (founding mem., sec. 2001—03, pres. 2003—), Suzuki Assn. Ams. (nat. bd. dirs. 1995—98), Dallas Arboretum, Phi Kappa Phi. Democrat. Avocations: writing, walking, paper making, travel, softball.

BURTON, JEREMY, information technology executive; B in info. systems engring., U. Surrey. Customer support, presales, product mgmt., engring. positions Oracle, 1995—2002, sr. v.p. product and svcs. mktg.; sr. v.p., chief mktg. officer VERITAS Software Corp., Mountain View, Calif., 2002—. Founder Oracle Tech. Network. Office: VERITAS Software Corp 350 Ellis St Mountain View CA 94043

BURTON, JOE BOB, music educator; s. Joe Earl and Wilma Jeanne Burton; children: Nathan Kyle, Joseph Robert. BA, Southeastern Okla. State U., 1972. Band dir. Comanche (Okla.) Pub. Schs., 1973—80, Okmulgee (Okla.) Pub. Sch., 1981—93, Broken Arrow (Okla.) Schs., 1994—. Named Tchr. of Yr., Okmulgee Schs., 1992.

BURTON, JOHN BRYAN, music educator; b. Lubbock, Tex., Nov. 10, 1948; s. John Clark and Geraldine (Wolf) B. B in Music Edn., West Tex. State U., 1970; MA, Western State Coll. Colo., 1973; D in Music Edn., U. So. Miss., 1986. Dir. bands, humanities Jal (N.Mex.) Schs., 1978-79; dir. bands, gen. music Bronte (Tex.) Schs., 1979-80; dir. bands Comfort (Tex.) Schs., 1980-82; dir. high sch. band, music coord. Kirbyville (Tex.) Ind. Schs., 1982-84; grad. asst. U. So. Miss., Hattiesburg, 1984-86; asst. prof. music, dir. bands, music theatre dir. Frostburg (Md.) State U., 1986-91; prof. music edn. West Chester (Pa.) Univ., 1991—, coord. grad. studies, 1997—, dir. post baccalaureate tchr. cert. program, 2001—. Panelist Symposium on Native

Am. Musics, Coll. Music Soc. 33d Nat. Meeting, Washington, 1990; curriculum cons. Prince Georges County Schs., Upper Marlboro, Md., 1991, other Mid-Atlantic schs.; guest condr. Allegany County Honor Band, Tri-State Honor Band, 1986-87, Allegany County Band, Bedford County Band, Mineral County Band, 1987-88, Allegany Solo and Ensemble Festival Harford County Intermediate Bands Festival, 1990-91; cons. Native Am. music, 1993, 94, nat. chair, editor Social Scis. Rsch. Group Soc. for Rsch. in Music Edn., 1994-96; edit. adv. bd. mem. Tchg. Music, 1996-98; vis. prof. U. Washington, 1995, Ga. State U., 1995, Trenton State Coll., 1996, U. Okla., 1996, U. Nebr., 1997, U. Sioux Falls, 1997, Rider U., 1998; presenter, lectr. in field. Assoc. editor: Scholars, 1994-2003; author: moving Within the Circle: Contemporary Native American Music and Dance, 1993, Music of the Minority Nationalities of the People's Republic of China, 1989, When the Earth Was Like New: Songs and Stories of the Western Apache, 1994, Songs of A Living Apache Tradition: The Musical Life of Chesley Goseyun Wilson, 1994, (with Maria P. Kreiter) Voices of the Wind: Native American Flute Music, 1997; co-author: Welcome to Mussomeli: Italian Children's Songs, 1999; contbg. author: Multicultural Perspectives in Music Education, 2d edit., 1996, Getting Started with Teaching Multicultural Music, 1996, Making Connections: Multicultural Traditions and the National Standards in Music Education, 1996, Strategies for Teaching: General Music K-4, 1996, Strategies for Teaching: General Music 5-8, 1996, Strategies for Teaching: General Music 9-12, 1996, Strategies for Teaching: Beginning and Middle Level Band Grades 5-8, 1996, Strategies for Teaching: High School Band, 1996, Strategies for Teaching: College Methods Class, 1996, Strategies for Teaching: High School Chorus, 1996, Many Seeds, Different Flowers--The Music Education Legacy of Carl Orff, 1997, On the Sociology of Music Education, 1997; mem. editl. bd. Music Edn. Internat., 2001--; contbr. songs to World of Children's Song, 1993, lessons and photographs to The Music Connection, 1995, songs and lessons to Share the Music, 1995, World Music and Music Education: Facing the Issue, 2002, Making Music (classroom music texttbook series), song transcriptions to OAKE Multicultural Songs, Dances and Games, 1995, online instrl. manual, Music in South India, 2003, Music of West Africa, 2004, Music in East Africa, 2004; contbr. articles to profl. jours. Mem. Internat. Soc. Music Edn.(commn. cmty. music activity, Durban, South Africa, 1998, mem. exec. bd.), Nat. Band Assn., Music Educators Nat. Conf. (presenter nat. meeting 1992, 94, 96, 98, 2000, 02, 04), Australia Soc. Music Educators, Pa. Music Educators Assn., Coll. Band Dirs. Nat. Assn., Coll. Music Soc., Soc. for Ethnomusicology (chair edn. com. 1999—), Soc. Music Tchr. Edn. (ea. rep. 1998—), Associated Photographers Internat., Audubon Soc., Amnesty Internat., Phi Mu Alpha, Alpha Chi, Kappa Delta Pi, Kappa Kappa Psi. Avocations: photography, travel, gardening. Home: 441 Webb Rd Chadds Ford PA 19317-9125 Office: West Chester U Sch Music West Chester PA 19383-0001 E-mail: jburton3@wcupa.edu.

BURTON, JOHN CAMPBELL, university dean, educator, consultant; b. N.Y.C., Sept. 17, 1932; s. James Campbell and Barbara (French) B.; m. Jane Garnjost, Apr. 6, 1957; children: Eve Bradley, Bruce Campbell. BA, Haverford Coll., 1954; MBA, Columbia U., 1956, PhD, 1962. C.P.A., N.Y. Staff acct. Arthur Young & Co., N.Y.C., 1956-60; prof. acctg. and fin. Grad. Sch. Bus. Columbia U., N.Y.C., 1962-72, Ernst & Young prof. acctg. and fin., 1978—, dean Grad. Sch. Bus., 1982-88. Chief acct. SEC, Washington, 1972-76; dep. mayor fin. City of N.Y., 1976-77; bd. dirs. Scholastic Inc.; dir., chmn. audit com. Commerce Clearing House Inc., 1979-95, First Pa. Corp.-First Pa. Bank, 1982-85; mem. adv. and valuation com. Warburg-Pincus Venture Capital Funds; mem. U.S. Comptroller Gen. Cons. Panel, 1978-95; bd. dirs. Accts. for Pub. Interest, 1978-85. Editor: Corporate Financial Reporting: Conflicts and Challenges, 1969, Corporate Financial Reporting: Ethical and Other Problems, 1972, (with Russell Palmer and Robert Kay) Handbook of Accounting and Auditing, 1981, The International World of Accounting: Challenges and Opportunities, 1981; co-mng. editor Acctg. Horizons, 1989-91; author: Accounting for Business Combinations, 1970, (with W.T. Porter) Auditing: A Conceptual Approach, 1971, and others; contbr. articles to profl. jours. Pres., trustee Millbrook Sch. (N.Y.), 1958-88; trustee ex officio Am. Assembly, 1982-88. Recipient Disting. Scholar award Hofstra U., 1975; Ford Found. fellow, 1961-62 Mem. AICPA (coun. 1980-83), Am. Acctg. Assn. (acad. v.p. 1980-82), Am. Fin. Assn., Am. Econ. Assn., Fin. Execs. Inst., Assn. Govtl. Accts., Nat. Assn. Securities Dealers (pub. gov. 1990-94), Met. Club (N.Y.C.), Lake Sunapee Yacht Club (N.H.). Clubs: Metropolitan (N.Y.C.); Lake Sunapee Yacht (N.H.). Home: 130 East End Ave Apt 12A New York NY 10028-7553 E-mail: jburton996@aol.com.

BURTON, JOHN WILLIAMS, retired physics professor, computer scientist; b. Atlanta, Ga., Apr. 15, 1937; s. Joe Wright and Lula Grace (Williams) B.; m. Patricia A. Wilson, Sept. 5, 1959; children: Rebecca, Timothy, Amy, Mark. BS, Carson-Newman Coll., 1959; MS, U. Ill., 1961, PhD, 1965; MS, U. Tenn., 1978. Prof. physics Carson-Newman Coll., Jefferson City, Tenn., 1964—2002, chair dept. physics, 1964-76, dir. computer ctr., 1978-89. Adj. prof. Walter State C.C., Morristown, Tenn., 1974-75, U. Tenn., Knoxville, 1975-78; cons. Oak Ridge (Tenn.) Nat. Lab., 1965-75. Computer programmer numerous ednl. programs; writer, prodr., performer several religious monologues. Advisor Sigma Pi Sigma, Jefferson City, 1970-1996; co-pres. PTA, Jefferson City, 1969-70. Mem. Am. Assn. Physics Tchrs., Knoxville Choral Soc. and Soloist, Blue Key Nat. Honor Soc., Sigma Xi, Phi Mu Epsilon. Baptist. E-mail: jburton@cn.edu.

BURTON, JOSEPH RANDOLPH, lawyer; b. Houston, Sept. 10, 1951; s. Joseph Milburn and Lee (Hillegeist) B.; m. Regina Helen O'Brien, Mar. 13, 1982; children: Cara Eileen, Ross Andrew. BS, Yale U., 1974; JD, South Tex. Coll., Houston, 1982. Bar: Tex. 1983, U.S. Dist. Ct. (so. and ea. dists.) Tex. 1983, U.S. Supreme Ct. 1996. Asst. dist. atty. Harris County Dist. Atty's Office, Houston, 1984-87; litigation assoc. Kennedy, Sanford, Kuhl & Hackney, Houston, 1987-90; ptnr. Moerer & Burton, Houston, 1990—. Contbr. articles to profl. jours.; featured on TV shows, including ABC News Prime Time Live, 20/20, HBO, Discovery Channel, Donahue, Good Morning Am. Founder, spokesperson Justice for Children, Houston, 1987—, Citizens Response Group; bd. dirs. Houston Area Women's Ctr., 1987-89, Aid to Victims of Domestic Abuse, 1987, Children's Trust Fund of Tex. Coun., 1994-98; child advocate mem. Tex. Child Fatality Rev. Com. Recipient AIA Pres.'s award, 1998, Victims' Resource Inst. with U. Houston Kim Houston award, 1999; named Outstanding Young Lawyer of Houston, Houston Young Lawyers' Assn., 1987-88, Mayor's award Outstanding Vol. Svc., 1998, e-town Achievement award, 2002; finalist 5 Outstnding Young Houstonians, Houston Jr. C. of C., 1988. Fellow Tex. Bar Found.; mem. ABA, Houston Bar Assn., South Tex. Coll. of Law Alumni Assn., Garland Walker Inns of Ct. Democrat. Avocation: golf. Home: 18418 Snowwood Dr Spring TX 77388-5100 Office: The Burton Law Firm 440 Louisiana St Ste 1300 Houston TX 77002-1634 Office Phone: 713-222-6262.

BURTON, LAVON D., education educator; b. Abilene, Tex., Sept. 5, 1957; d. Floyd Lewis and Jane Evelyn Duncan; m. Brian Keith Burton; children: Tyler, Briana. BS inEdn., Abilene Christian U., 1981, MEd, 1997. Cert. profl. tchg. Tex., edn. agy. adminstrn. Tex. Tchr. Abilene (Tex.) Ind. Sch. Dist., 1981—86, instr. acad. advance, 1987—94, acad. advance program dir., 1994—. Troop leader Girl Scouts of Am., Abilene, 1996—2002; vol. in pub. schs., orgn. mem. Abilene Ind. Sch. Dist., 1992—2002; youth adv. team mem. Hillcrest Ch. of Christ, Abilene, 1999—2002, Bible class tchr., 1979—2002, drama writer, dir., 1997—2002; Chair bd. dirs. Paramount Theater Children's Performing Arts Series, Abilene, 1997—2002; mem., soloist Hillcrest Singers, Abilene, 1986—2002; PTA exec. bd. dirs. Taylor Elem. Sch., Abilene, 1994—2002, Franklin Mid. Sch., Abilene, 1998—2001. Named Vol. of the Yr., Abilene Cultural Affairs Coun., 1999. Mem.: Big Country Coun. of Tchrs. Math. and Sci., Nat. Coun. Tchrs. of Math. Church Of Christ. Avocations: piano, singing, sewing, reading.

BURTON, LAWRENCE DEVERE, agriculturist, educator; b. Afton, Wyo., May 27, 1943; s. Lawrence VanOrden and Maybell (Hoopes) B.; m. Arva Merrill, Nov. 20, 1967; children: LauraLee, Paul, Shawn, Renee, Kaylyn, Kelly, Brett. BS, Utah State U., 1968; MS, Brigham Young U., 1972; PhD, Iowa State U., 1987. Agr. tchr. Box Elder County Sch. Dist., Brigham City, Utah, 1967-68, Morgan County Sch. Dist., Morgan, Utah, 1968-70, Minidoka County Sch. Dist., Rupert, Idaho, 1972-79, Cassia County Sch. Dist., Declo, Idaho, 1979-84; instr. Iowa State U., Ames, 1984-87; area vocat. edn. coord. Idaho State Div. Vocat. Edn., Pocatello, 1987-88, state supr. agrl. sci. and tech. Boise, 1988-97; dir. rsch. Idaho State Divsn. Vocat. Edn., Boise, 1997-99; mem. telecomm. coun. Idaho State Bd. Edn., 1997-98, mem. coun. acad. affairs and programs, 1997—; instrnl. dean Coll. So. Idaho, Twin Falls, 2000—05. Biochem. cons. rep. Ctr. for Occupational Rsch. and Devel., Waco, Tex., 1989-94; chmn. Nat. Task Force, Agrl. Edn. Ind. Study Honors program, 1993, mem. tech. commn.; mem. Nat. Task Force, Environ. Edn., 1996. Author: Agriscience and Technology, 1991, 97, Ecology of Fish and Wildlife, 1995, 2d edit., 2003, Introduction to Forestry Science, 1998, Agriscience, Fundamentals and Applications, 2000, 2d edit., 2004; contbr. articles to profl. jours. Vice-chmn. Minidoka County Fair Bd., Rupert, Idaho, 1977-80. Mem. Am. Vocat. Assn., Am. Vocat. Info. Assn., Nat. Vocat. Agrl. Tchrs. Assn., Idaho Vocat. Agrl. Tchrs. Assn. (pres. 1981-82, Adminstr. of Yr. 1989), Am. Vocat. Info. Assn., Nat. Assn. Suprs. Agrl. Edn. (western v.p. 1990-91, nat. pres. 1993-94), Gamma Sigma Delta, Alpha Zeta. Mem. Lds Ch. Home: 802 Sunrise Blvd N Twin Falls ID 83301-4247 Office: Coll So Idaho PO Box 1238 Twin Falls ID 83303-1238 Office Phone: 208-732-8123. Personal E-mail: ldevereb@yahoo.com. Business E-Mail: dburton@csi.edu.

BURTON, LESLIE ANNE, psychologist; b. N.Y.C. BA, Queens Coll., 1977; MS, U. Chgo., 1983, PhD, 1985. Lic. psychologist, N.Y., Calif. Intern Columbia U. Coll. Physicians and Surgeons, N.Y.C., 1983-84; fellow in psychology Cornell U. Med. Coll., 1984-86; asst. prof. psychology in neurosci. Cornell U. Med. Coll./Burke Rehab. Hosp./N.Y. Hosp., White Plains, 1986-90; asst. prof. psychology Fordham U., Bronx, NY, 1994—, assoc. prof. psychology, 1999—. Adj. assoc. prof. psychology in neurosci. Cornell U. Coll. N.Y. Hosp., N.Y.C., 1995—. Contbr. articles to profl. jours. Mem. APA, Internat. Neuropsychol. Soc., Nat. Acad. Neuropsychology, Cognitive Neurosci. Soc., N.Y. Acad. Scis. Office: Fordham U Psychology Dept 441 E Fordham Rd Bronx NY 10458-9993

BURTON, MARY LOUISE HIMES, information technology executive; b. Altoona, Pa., Oct. 4, 1948; d. Paul Silas and Clara Marie (Bettwy) Himes; m. Carl Hansel Burton, Aug. 28, 1983; children: Michael, Edward, Carla. AA, Mt. Aloysius Jr. Coll., 1968; BS in Edn., Slippery Rock U., 1970; MLS magna cum laude, U. Pitts., 1982. Cataloguer Slipper Rock (Pa.) U., 1968-70; cataloguer, children's librn. Altoona Area Pub. Libr., 1970-71; dir. libr. svcs. Altoona Hosp., 1971-83; project coord. Coll. of Physician of Phila., 1983-84; med. libr. VAMC, Coatesville, Pa., 1984-85, acting chief libr. svc., 1985-86, chief libr. svc., 1986-94; asst. chief IRM, 1994-96, computer specialist, 1996—. Mem. Nat. Adv. Group for Info. Security, 1991-2001, vice chmn., 1996-98; security officer Automated Info. Sys., 1988—; local resource libr. Mideastern Regional Med. Libr. Program, Phila., 1976-82, Greater Northeastern Regional Med. Libr. Program, N.Y.C., 1983-93; master instr. MS office, 2000. Mem. United Ch. of Christ. Mem. Spl. Librs. Assn., Pa. Libr. Assn. (chmn. spl. librs. divsn. and bd. dirs. 1980-82, 85-86, 89-90), Med. Libr. Assn., Acad. Health Info. Profls. (sec. DV-MUG 1996), VFW Aux., Assn. Health Info. Profls., Consortium Health Info. (pres. 1990-93). Avocations: vocalist, organist, pianist. Home: 5495 Highview Dr Gap PA 17527-9553 Office: VAMC 1400 Blackhorse Hill Rd Coatesville PA 19320-2096 Office Phone: 610-384-7711 ext. 4561. Personal E-mail: chmlburton@comcast.net. Business E-Mail: marylou.burton@med.va.gov.

BURTON, MICHAEL LADD, anthropology educator; b. Long Beach, Calif., June 6, 1942; s. Warren Nathan Burton and Dorothy Brent (Braden) Asquith; children: Melissa, Christopher; m. Ellen Greenberger, Aug. 26, 1979. BS in Econs., MIT, 1964; PhD in Anthropology, Stanford U., 1968. Rsch. fellow Harvard U., 1968-69; asst. prof. U. Calif., Irvine, 1969-76; rsch. fellow U. Nairobi, Kenya, 1973-74; assoc. prof. U. Calif., Irvine, 1976-83, prof., 1983—, chmn., dept. anthropology, 1986-91, 2003—. Contbr. articles to profl. jours. NSF grantee, 1981-89, 91-93. Mem. Am. Anthropol. Assn., Soc. for Cross-Cultural Rsch., Soc. Econ. Anthropology, Soc. Applied Anthropology, Assn. Social Anthropology of Oceania. Home: 10 Morning Sun Irvine CA 92603-3715 Office: U Calif Dept Anthropology Irvine CA 92697-5100 Office Phone: 949-824-7208. Business E-Mail: mlburton@uci.edu.

BURTON, PAUL FLOYD, social worker; b. Seattle, May 24, 1939; s. Floyd James and Mary Teresa (Chovanak) B.; m. Roxanne Maude Johnson, July 21, 1961; children: Russell Floyd, Joan Teresa. BA, U. Wash., 1961, MSW, 1967. Juvenile parole counselor Divsn. Juvenile Rehab. State of Wash., 1961-66; social worker VA, Seattle, 1967-72; social worker, cons. Work Release Program, King County, Wash., 1967-72; supr., chief psychiatry sect. Social Work Svc. VA, Topeka, 1972-73; pvt. practice Topeka and L.A., 1972—; chief social work svc. VA, Sepulveda, Calif., 1973-98; assoc. dir. Cmty. Care Svcs., VA Greater L.A. Healthcare System, 1998—2001, dir. cmty. residential care, 2001—. EEO coord. Med. ctr., 1974-77. Named VA Social Worker of Yr., U.S. Dept. VA Social Work Leadership Coun., 2002; recipient Va. Social Work Pioneer award, 2004. Mem. NASW (newsletter edito Puget Sound chpt. 1970-71), Acad. Cert. Social Workers, Ctr. for Studies in Social Functioning, Soc. Social Svc. Leaders Healthcare, Assn. Va. Social Workers (founder 1979, charter mem. and pres. 1980-81, newsletter editor 1982-83, 89-91, pres. elect 1993-95, pres. 1995-97, newsletter editor 2000-2002, treas. 2003). Home: 14063 Remington St Arleta CA 91331-5359 Office: 16111 Plummer St Sepulveda CA 91343-2036 Office Phone: 818-895-9596.

BURTON, PEGGY, advertising and marketing executive; b. N.Y.C. BSBA, NYU, 1960. Freelance TV producer, N.Y.C., 1964-67; TV producer Young & Rubicam, N.Y.C., 1967-69; sr. acct. exec. Daniel & Charles, N.Y.C., 1969-74; ptnr., v.p. Bruderer Hartnett Advt. Agy., N.Y.C., 1974-76; dir. Comm. Am. Express Co., N.Y.C., 1976-83; pres. advt. Dreyfus Corp., N.Y.C., 1983-95; pres. Burton Commns. Multi Media, N.Y.C., 1995—. Vol. Met. Mus. Art; bd. dirs. Nat. Sch. Com. Econ. Edn., Mallon Fund. Mem. Internat. Advt. Assn., N.Y. New Media Assn., Fin. Women's Assn., Fgn. Policy Assn., Bus. Execs. for Nat. Security, NYU Gallatin Arts Com., N.Y. Athletic Club, Nat. Arts Club. Address: 220 Central Park S New York NY 10019-1417 Office Phone: 212-581-4592. E-mail: pegbur@aol.com.

BURTON, RICHARD IRVING, orthopedist, educator; b. Providence, Sept. 18, 1936; s. Kenneth Gould and Edith Irving (Vayro) B.; m. Margaret Ann Leaman, Apr. 5, 1961; children: Thomas Kenneth, Douglas Leaman. BA, Amherst Coll., 1958; MD, Harvard U., 1962. Diplomate Am. Bd. Orthopaedic Surgery (examiner 1980—, bd. dirs. 1989-98). Intern U. Rochester, N.Y., 1962-63, resident in surgery, 1963-64; resident in orthopedic surgery Harvard U., 1966-70; fellow in hand surgery Roosevelt Hosp., N.Y.C., 1970-71; asst. prof. Cleve. Clinic Found., 1971-72, head sect. surgery of hand, 1971-74, assoc. prof., 1973-74; mem. faculty U. Rochester Med. Sch., 1974—, head sect. surgery of hand, 1974—2003, prof. orthopedics, 1979—, Marjorie Strong Wehle prof. orthopedics, 1995-2000, dean's prof., 2000—02, assoc. chmn. dept. orthopedics, 1981-88, chmn., 1988—2000, acting chmn. dept. neurol. surgery, 2000—02, sr. assoc. dean for acad. affairs, 2002—; sr. assoc. orthopedist Strong Meml. Hosp., Rochester, 1974-79, orthopedist, 1979—; sr. assoc. dean for acad. affairs U. Rochester Med. Sch., 2002—. Chmn. cert. of added qualifications com. Am. Bd. Orthopaedic Surgery, 1994-98. Assoc. editor Jour. Hand Surgery, 1980-84; contbr. articles to profl. jours., chpts. to books. Mem. exec. com. Monroe County chpt. Am. Arthritis Found., 1983-86; elder Presbyn. Ch. Buswell Disting. Svc. fellow, U. rochester, 1980-81. Recipient Exec. of Yr. award, Profl. Secs. Internat., Flower City chpt., 1981. Mem. ACS, AAAS, Am. Acad. Orthopedic Surgeons (chmn. hand and wrist com. 1986-89, orthopedic resources com. 1989-91), Am. Bd. Orthop. Surgery (dir. 1988-98), Am. Bd. Med. Specialties (voting rep. 1995-98), Am. Soc. Surgery of the Hand (coord. divsn. edn. 1982-85, coun. 1985-89, chmn. membership com. 1991, v.p. 1990, pres.-elect 1991, pres. 1992), Am. Orthopedic Assn. (exec. com. 1986, resident rsch. conf. com. 1987-89, chair 1989, membership com. 1989-92, chmn. 1992, exec. com. 1992, forward planning com. 1996-99), Interurban Orthopedic Soc., Eastern Orthopedic Assn., Monroe County Med. Soc., N.Y. State Med. Soc., Rochester Acad. Medicine, Rochester Orthopedic Soc., Soc. N.Y. State Orthopedic Surgeons, Littler-Eaton Soc., Amherst Alumni Assn Office: U Rochester Med Ctr Deans Office Box 706 601 Elmwood Ave Rochester NY 14642-0001

BURTON, RICHARD JAY, lawyer; b. NYC, May 4, 1949; s. Melvin F. Burton and Shirley (Burton) Silber; m. Truly Demetra Dourdis, June 11, 1972; 1 child, Marc Aaron. BA, George Washington U., 1971; JD, U. Miami, 1974. Bar: Fla. 1974, D.C. 1976, U.S. Supreme Ct. 1979. Founder Med. Commn. on Human Rights, Washington, 1969-71; adminstrv. aide Fla. Legis., 1973-74; gov. affairs liaison Dade County Fla. Legis., 1974; assoc. Richard H.W. Maloy and Assocs., Coral Gables, Fla., 1974-76; atty., advisor FAA, Washington, 1976-77; assoc. Pompan, Rumizen & Reynolds, Washington, 1978-79, Donald M. Murtha and Assocs., Washington, 1978-79; ptnr. Schoninger, Siegfried, Kipnis, Burton & Sussman PA, Miami, Fla., 1979-82; sole practice Miami, 1982—; gen. counsel Rexall Sundown Inc., 1982-90. Guest lectr. U. Miami Sch. of Law, Coral Gables, 1982. Mem. constrn. law panel Am. Arbitration Assn., 1974—; mem. legis. com. Builders Assn. South Fla., 1980—; mem. Builder Industry Polit. Action Com.; fire commr. Met. Dade County, 1988, 92, vice chmn. fire commn., 1989-90. Mem. ABA, DC Bar Assn., Fed. Bar Assn., Fla. Bar Assn. (constr. law com.), Phi Alpha Delta. Democrat. Jewish. Avocations: skiing, scuba diving, tennis. Office Phone: 305-705-0888. E-mail: RB@Burtons.net.

BURTON, ROBERT GENE, printing company executive; b. Pontiac, Mich., Apr. 4, 1939; s. Earl R. and Verna L. Burton; m. Paula M. Suwanski, May 26, 1972; children: Robert Gene Jr., Michael, Joseph. BS, Murray (Ky.) State U., 1962; MA, U. Tenn., 1964; postgrad., U. Chgo., 1964, U. Ala., 1965—67; D (hon.), Murray State U., 1968, U. Conn., 2000. From salesman to nat. sales dir. SRA/IBM Corp., Dallas and Chgo., 1967—76; from midwest dir. to mktg. dir. CBS, Chgo. and N.Y.C., 1976—78, v.p. mktg., 1978—79, v.p. ops. N.Y.C., 1978—79; v.p. pub. ABC, N.Y.C., 1980, pres. leisure mags., 1980—81, group v.p. spl. interest pub., 1981, pres., 1981—91; v.p. Capital Cities/ABC, Inc., 1991; chmn. bd., pres., CEO World Color Press Inc., 1991—99; pres., CEO Moore Corp., 2000—01, chmn., pres., CEO, 2001—02, Burton Mgmt. Group., LLC, 2003—. Mem. adv. bd. NYU Bus. Press. Trustee Eagle Hill Sch., Greenwich, Conn.; mem. bd. overseers U. Conn. Sch. Bus. Adminstrn.; past trustee Murray State U., Boy Scouts Am. Nat. Mus., Murray; former chmn. Nat. Bible Week/Laymen's Nat. Bible Assn.; former pub. industry chmn. Juvenile Diabetes Found.; bd. dirs. Cancer Care of Conn.; bd. advisors Breast Cancer Alliance; bd. dirs. Kentuckians of N.Y., Burton Charitable Found., NYU, past pres. adv. bd.; bd. dirs. Murray State U. Coll. Bus. and Pub. Affairs, past dean's adv. coun. Named to Murray State Football Hall of Fame, Printing Industry Hall of Fame; recipient award, Spl. Achievement Soc. and Athletic Hall of Fame, West Frankfort, Ill., Oak award, Ky. Advocates for Higher Edn. Mem.: Assn. Bus. Pubs. (past chmn.), Greenwich (Conn.) Country Club, Washington Nat. Press Club. Republican. Baptist. E-mail: info@burtonmg.com.

BURTON, ROBERT LYLE, accounting firm executive; m. Lee Sanders; 2 children. Diploma, Kinman Bus. U. CPA. With LeMaster & Daniels, Spokane, Wash., 1963-86, mng. ptnr., 1986-97, sr. advisor, 1997—. Adv. bd. acctg. dept. U. Wash.; chmn. The Am. Group of CPA Firms. Trustee Econ. Devel. Coun.; past chmn. Samaritan Hosp. Found., Moses Lake, Wash. Mem. AICPA (agri-bus. com., adv. group B), Washington Soc. CPAs (former dir., v.p., com. chmn., legis. com.), Spokane Club, Inland Empire Fly Fishermen, Moses Lake Golf and Country Club, Rotary. Office: LeMaster and Daniels PLLC 601 W Riverside Ave Ste 700 Spokane WA 99201-0622

BURTON, SCOT, finance educator; b. Houston, Feb. 24, 1953; s. William James and Mary (Tilley) B.; m. Jana Louise Keller, Apr. 3, 1982. BBA, U. Tex., 1974, MBA, 1976; PhD, U. Houston, 1985. V.p. consumer research Tex. Commerce Bank, Houston, 1977-81; fellow, research asst. U. Houston, 1982-85; assoc. prof. mktg. La. State U., Baton Rouge, 1986-92; prof., Wal-Mart chair in mktg. U. Ark., Fayetteville, 1993—. Cons. in field. Contbr. articles to profl. jours. Mem. Am. Mktg. Assn., Assn. Consumer Rsch., Acad. Mktg. Sci. Office: U Ark Dept Mktg Badm # 302 Fayetteville AR 72701

BURTON, SEAN MICHAEL, performing company executive, conductor; b. Hartford, Conn., July 9, 1978; s. Thomas Russell and Kathleen Ann Durkin Burton; m. Shannon Marie Salyards, Aug. 21, 2004. MusB, U. Hartford, 2000; MusM, Boston U., 2004. Pre-K-12 vocal and instrumental music cert. Conn. State Bd. Edn., 2000. Asst. condr., bass sect. leader First Ch. of Christ in Hartford, 1998—2000; condr. Concordia Chorale Conn. Conservatory Performing Arts, New Milford, 2000—01; choral and orch. dir. Weston H.S., Weston, 2000—02; music dir., condr. Boston U. Choral Soc., 2002—04; music dir. Tabernacle Congl. Ch., Salem, Mass., 2002—03; asst. condr., bass sect. leader Marsh Chapel at Boston U., 2003—04; founder, artistic dir. Boston Orpheus Ensemble, 2004—; program adminstr., choral dir. Met. Opera Guild, Boston, 2004—; asst. condr. The Masterworks Chorale, Lexington, Mass., 2004—. Condr., treble choir New Eng. Music Camp, Sydney, Maine, 2004—05; condr., mid. sch. all-county choir Tompkins-Seneca Music Educators Assn., Newfield, NY, 2005; condr., jr. high all-county choir Oswego County Music Educators Assn., Central Square, NY, 2002; condr., inst. madrigal ensemble Hartwick Coll. Summer Music Festival & Inst., Oneonta, NY, 2000, condr., women's choir, 1998—99; chorus master Conn. Concert Opera, West Hartford, Conn., 1999; guest condr. Waltham (Mass.) Philharm. Orch., 2003. Contbr. articles to profl. jours. Bldg. rep. Weston Tchrs. Assn., 2001—02. Recipient Excellence in Choral Conducting award, The Hartt Sch., U. Hartford, 1998, Excellence in Choral Music award, 1999, Regents' Honor Award, U. of Hartford, 1999, Dept. Honors, Boston U., 2004; grantee, Weston Edn. Found., 2000—01; scholar, Boston U., 2002—04. Mem.: Coll. Music Soc., Nat. Assn. for Music Edn., Internat. Fedn. for Choral Music, Chorus Am., Am. Symphony Orch. League, Am. Choral Dirs. Assn., Pi Kappa Lambda, Alpha Chi. Office Phone: 617-216-2951.

BURTON, TED J., secondary school educator, music educator; b. La Mesa, Calif., Nov. 26, 1957; s. Teddy Joe Burton and Inez Joe Holdaway; m. Nancy Christine Austin, July 21, 1984; children: Matthew Austin, Taylor Michael, Alex Christopher. AA, Imperial Valley Coll., 1979; BA in Music, Cal Poly U., 1982; MEd in Music, So. Oreg. U., 2000. Lic. tchr. Oreg., 1992. Band dir. St. Don Bosco H.S., Rosemead, Calif., 1982—86, Azusa High, Pilot Butte Mid. Sch., Bend, Oreg., 1992—2001, Ctrl. Oreg. C.C., 1995—97, Mountain View H.S., 2001—. Mem.: Music Educators Nat. Conf., Oreg. Music Educators Assn. (dist. 5 chair 2003—05). Home: 1967 NE Red Rock Ln Bend OR 97701 Office Phone: 541-383-6400.

BURTON, THOMAS LEE, school psychologist; b. Balt., Oct. 18, 1948; s. Wilbur Darwin Burton Jr. and Katherine Irby Burton; m. Barbara Moe Fimey, Oct. 14, 1948; children: Morgan L., Laurel M. Morgan. BS, Union Coll., 1973; MEd, Lunchburg Coll., 1976; EdS, James Madison U., 1988. Tchr., Campbell County, Va., 1975—80; dental tech. Chevrolet, Charlottesville, 1982—84; sch. psychologist Queen Anne's County Pub. Sch., Centerville, Md., 1988—. Mem. North Health Adv. Bd., Centerville, 1991—96. Mem.: NEA, Nat Assn. Sch. Psychologists, Md. Sch. Psychologists Assn. Avocations: writing, singing, guitar, cooking. Home: 100 Tolion Ln Stevensville MD 21666 Office: Queen Annes County Bd Edn 202 Centerfield Ave Centreville MD 21617

BURTON, THOMAS M., journalist; BA in history, Dartmouth Coll.; LLD, Georgetown U. Law Ctr. With Dallas Times Herald; investigative and assoc. counsel NY State Assembly's Office Legis. Oversight and Investigation, NYC, 1975—76; reporter Balt. Sun, 1976—78; investigative reporter Phila. Bulletin, 1978—81, Chgo. Sun Times, 1981—85, Chgo. Tribune, 1985—89; gen. assignment reporter Wall St. Jour., 1990—91, med. reporter, 1991—. Co-recipient first place, special projects category, Nat. Assn. Agrl. Journalists, 1996, Gerald Leob award for disting. bus. and fin. journalism, 1996; recipient Peter Lisagor award, bus. journalism category, Chgo. Headline Club, 1993,

Peter Lisagor award, bus./wire svc. category, 1995, Pulitzer Prize for explanatory reporting, 2004. Mem.: Investigative Reports & Editors Inc. Office: Wall Street Jour 200 Liberty St New York NY 10281

BURTON, TIM (TIMOTHY WILLIAM BURTON), film director; b. Burbank, Calif., Aug. 25, 1958; m. Lena Gieseke, Feb. 24, 1989 (div. Dec. 31, 1991); engaged Lisa Marie, 1992-2001; engaged Helena Bonham Carter, 2001-, c. Billy Ray. Student Calif. Inst. Arts (Disney Fellowship), 1979—80. Cartoon artist Disney Prodn., apprentice animator. Animator: The Fox and the Hound, 1981; Dir.: (films) Vincent, 1982, Frankenweenie, 1984, Pee-Wee's Big Adventure, 1984, Beetlejuice, 1988, Batman, 1989, Sleepy Hollow, 1999, Planet of the Apes, 2001, Big Fish, 2003, Charlie and the Chocolate Factory, 2005, Corpse Bride, 2005; prodr. The Nightmare Before Christmas, (also production designer) 1993, Cabin Boy, 1994, Batman Forever, 1995, James and the Giant Peach, 1996, others; dir., prodr.: (films) Stalk of the Celery, 1979, Edward Scissorhands,(also screenwriter) 1990, Batman Returns, 1992, Ed Wood, 1994, Mars Attacks!, 1996, The World of Stainboy, 2000; dir.: (TV films) Hansel and Gretel, 1982; exec prodr.: (TV films) Lost in Oz, 2000; exec. prodr.: (TV series) Beetlejuice, 1989-91, Family Dog, 1992; author: My Art & Films, 1993, The Melancholy Death of Oyster Boy and Other Stories, 1997. Named one of 50 Greatest Directors of All Time, Entertainment Weekly, Tropopkin's Top 25 Most Intriguing People. Office: Chapman Bird & Grey 1990 S Bundy Dr Ste 200 Los Angeles CA 90025-5240*

BURTON, WARD, professional race car driver; b. South Boston, Va., Oct. 25, 1961; married; m. Tabitha Burton; children: Sarah, Jeb. Student, Elon Coll. Race car driver NASCAR Busch Series Grand Nat. Divsn., 1990, Bill Davis Racing, High Point, NC. Achievements include winner Winston Cup, 1995; 23 top 5 career starts; 37 top 10 stars in 148 races; career finishes include 5 top 5 finishes and 24 top 10 finishes in 146 races; winner N.C. Motor Speedway, 1995; AC Delco 400, 1995; Mall.com 400, 2000. Avocations: wildlife conservation, hunting. Office: c/o Bill Davis Racing 301 Old Thomasville Rd High Point NC 27260-8190 Mailing: Ward Burton Enterprises PO Box 519 Halifax VA 24558*

BURTON, WILLIAM JOSEPH, engineering executive; b. Gaffney, S.C., Mar. 22, 1931; s. Emory Goss and Olivia (Copeland) B.; m. Joan Holland Burton, Sept. 26, 1987. BSME, U. S.C., 1957, MSME, 1964; PhDME, Tex. A&M U., 1970. Registered profl. engr., Tenn., Fla. Sr. dynamics engr. Lockheed-Ga. Co., Marietta, 1957-62; sr. project engr. Allison div. GM Corp., Indpls., 1964-67; asst. prof., researcher Tex. A&M U., College Station, 1968-70; asst. prof. U. Tenn., Knoxville, 1970-74; projects mgr. Tenn. Valley Authority, Chattanooga, 1974-79; program mgr. Dept. Navy, Washington, 1979-94; chair equal employment opportunity com. Chesapeake divsn. Naval Facilities Engring. Command, Washington, 1982—83; cons. engr. Ocean and Power Applications, Lakeland, Fla., 1993—. Lectr. in field nat. and internat. audiences; adj. prof. mech. and aerospace engring., energy conversion tech. U. Tenn., Knoxville, 1974—75; spkr. and presenter, various venues and topics. Author: On the Heating Surface Effects of Nucleate Boiling Data Correlation, 1964, The Effects of Surface Roughness on the Wave Forces on a Circular Cylindrical Pile, 1970; author more than 50 articles on ocean engring., power and propulsion, aircraft structures, planning and economics, ethics. Secretary, mem. hospitality com. Exch. Club, Knoxville, 1975, bd. dirs., 1976; coord. charitable campaign Naval Facilities Engring. Com., Washington, 1982; mem. Heritage Found., Rep. Nat. Com. With U.S. Army, 1951-53. Recipient Occupation medal, 1952, Nat. Def. Svc. medal U.S. Army, 1953, Antarctic Svc. medal U.S. Dept. of Navy, 1962, Wisdom award of honor, 2000; Eminent Wisdom fellow Scroll of Wisdom Hall of Fame, 2000. Fellow ASME (organizer, chmn. tech. sessions for internat. confs. 1982-87, chmn. exec. com. ocean engring. divsn. 1985, mem.-at-large energy resources bd. 1986-92, chmn. com. honors & awards energy resources bd. 1992-98, com. on tech. planning coun. on engring. 1992-94, fellow peer rev. bd. 1992-97, rep. energy resources bd. to nat. nominating com. 1998—, Golden Cert. ocean engring. divsn. 1989), Va. Soc. Profl. Engrs. (no. Va. regional coun. 1988); mem. AAAS, NSPE (pres.-elect Fairfax chpt. 1988), Soc. Mfg. Engrs., Soc. Naval Architects and Marine Engrs., S.C. Hist. Soc., Nat. Trust for Historic Preservation, Polk County (Fla.) Hist. Assn., VFW, Marine Tech. Soc., U. S.C. Alumni Assn. (life), U. South Caroliniana Soc., Heritage Found.; lifetime affiliate Tau Beta Pi Scholastic honorary Enging. Soc. SC Beta, 1958, Rep. Nat. Com., Sigma Xi, Tau Beta Pi Hon. Engring. Soc. (life), Texas A&M U. Assn. or Former Students Bronze Level. Baptist. Avocations: travel, bicycling, classic guitar, golf, tennis. Home: 307 Miramar Dr Lakeland FL 33803-2633 Office: Naval Facilities Engring Svc Ctr East Coast Detachment 901 E M St SE 218 Wash Navy Yard Washington DC 20374-0001 Office Phone: 863-687-4365. E-mail: wmburton@hotmail.com.

BURTON-MISKELL, HELEN, retired librarian; b. Clark County, Ark., Feb. 20, 1923; m. Francis Anthony Miskell, Nov. 15, 1946 (dec. 1971); children: Susan Marie Miskell, Kevin Francis Miskell. BA with honors, U. No. Tex., 1947; MLS, U. Tex., 1976. Cert. Tex. Edn. Agency State of Tex., 1955, State of Tex., 1947. Tchr. Ganado HS, Ganado, Tex., 1949—50, Austin Pub. Sch., Austin, Tex., 1955—72; lib. Thorndale Pub. Sch., Thorndale, Tex., 1978—80, Roosevelt Elem. Sch., McAllen, Tex., 1980—81, Fredericksburg HS, Fredericksburg, Tex., 1981—82, Pace HS, Brownsville, Tex., 1982—84; ret., 1984. Author: (poems) Homeplace and Other Poems, 1995, Petals in the Wind, 1997, A Walk in the Sun, 1998, Wind in the Pines, 2000. Mem.: Sierra Club. Avocations: reading, writing, genealogy.

BURTT, ANNE DAMPMAN, special education educator; b. Phila., Nov. 22, 1950; d. Elmer and Anne (Scott) Dampman; m. James Burtt, Aug. 5, 1972. BS in Edn. cum laude, Duquesne U., 1972; MEd, U. Pitts., 1976, Temple U., 1985. Cert. spl. edn., elem. tchr., reading specialist. Tchr. Pitts. Pub. Schs., 1972-77; tchr. Montgomery County (Pa.) Intermediate Unit, 1997—2000, Archdiocese of Phila. Schs., 2000—; archdiocese Phila. Schs., 2000—. Mem. PTO, 1972—, Chpt. Attention Deficit Disorders, 1989—, CHADD Bux-Mont. Divsn., Behavioral Disorders/Learning Disorders. Recipient Pius X award Archdiocese Phila., Most Successful Grad. 25th Yr. Reunion West Phila. Cath. Girls' H.S. Mem. Pa. State Edn. Assn., Coun. for Exceptional Children, Behavior Disorders and Learning Disabilities. Home: 131 Maple Ave Willow Grove PA 19090-2902

BURTT, LARICE ANNADEL ROSEMAN, artist; b. Phila., June 22, 1928; d. Milo A.J. Roseman and Anna Sterling; m. James C. Burtt, June 25, 1960; childen, James M., Kyleann S. BS in Biology, Bucknell U., 1950; MS in Nursing, Yale U., 1955; studied art with Dr. Selma Burke, studied with William A. Smith; cert., Katherine Gibbs Sec. Sch., 1951. Med. clinical instr. Jefferson Hosp., Phila., 1956-57; med. surgical instr. Rowan Meml. Hosp., Salisbury, N.C., 1958-59. Workshop leader Yale, New Haven Hosp. Pain Mgmt. Ctrs., New Haven, Ct., 1996, Attleboro Nursing Home, Langhorne, Pa., Chandler Hall, Newtown, Pa.; demo instr. Delaware Valley Schs., Pa., 1979—; profl. demonstrator in field, 1977—. Painter (3 dimensional stone painting), many locations, 1976-99; one person shows include Arnot Art Mus., Elmira, N.Y., 1987, Cannon Bldg., Washington, DC 1995, Yale Univ. Sch. Nursing, New Haven, Conn., 1996, Abington Art Ctr., Pa., Upstairs Gallery, Buckingham, Pa.; exhibited in group shows at Immaculata Coll., Accent and Images Gallery, Lahaska, Pa., Nova, 1990-2004, Jane Anthony Gallery, Newtown, Pa., 2000, Abington (Pa.) Art Ctr., Wilson Sch. Mt. Lakes Gallery Show, 2001-04, Galleria Vermese, New Orleans, La., 2005, many area group exhbns., 1977—; represented in permanent collection Grand Canyon Nat. Pk. Mus. Mem. AAUW, Northhampton Hist. Soc., Middletown Grange, Bucks County Guild Craftsman (exhbn. at Franklin and Marshall Coll. 1979-96), James Michener Art Mus., Doylestown (Pa.), Doylestown Art League, Pa. Guild. Avocations: tennis, piano, visual/performing arts, community affairs, service art shows. Home: 31 Beth Dr Richboro PA 18954-1901 Personal E-mail: lariceburtt@aol.com.

BURWELL, ANTHONY SCOTT, manufacturing engineer; b. Seward, Nebr., Jan. 27, 1974; s. Scott Evan Burwell and Glenda Sue Bushek; m. Kara Lynn Earnest, Oct. 16, 2004; 1 child, Gracie Lynn. AAS in Mfg. Engring., Southeast C.C., 1993. Prod. engring. drafter Square D Co., Lincoln, Nebr., 1994, engring. lab. tech., 1994—2001, sr. quality assurance tech., 2001—03; quality control tech. Kawasaki Motors Mfr., 2003—05, quality assurance engr., 2005—. ISO mgmt. rep. Kawasaki Motor Mfg., 2005—. Mem.: Am. Soc. Quality. Lutheran. Avocations: drums, writing, bicycling, rafting, camping. Home: 626 S 48th St Lincoln NE 68510 Office: Kawasaki Motors Mfg 6600 NW 27th St Lincoln NE 68524

BURWELL, ROBERT LEMMON, JR., chemist, educator; b. Balt., May 6, 1912; s. Robert Lemmon and Anne Hume (Lewis) B.; m. Elise Frank, Dec. 23, 1939 (dec. Nov. 2001); children: Mary Elise, Augusta Somervell. AB, St. John's Coll., Annapolis, Md., 1932; PhD (Procter fellow), Princeton U., 1936. Instr. chemistry Trinity Coll., 1936-39; instr. Northwestern U., 1939-45, asst. prof., 1946, asso. prof., 1946-52, prof., 1952—, Ipatieff prof. chemistry, 1970-80, Ipatieff prof. emeritus, 1980—, chmn. dept. chemistry, 1952-57; Humboldt sr. scientist Tech. U. Munich, 1981; vis. prof. U. Pierre et Marie Curie, Paris, 1982. Dir. Internat. Congress Catalysis, 1956-65; chmn. Gordon Research Conf. Catalysis, 1957; sec. Council Internat. Congress Catalysis, 1968-72, v.p., 1972-76, pres., 1980-84; cons. Amoco Corp., 1949-92. Served as lt. USNR, 1942-45. Mem. Am. Chem. Soc. (chmn. div. phys. chemistry 1958-59, mem. council policy com. 1969-72, Kendall award in colloid and surface chemistry 1973, Lubrizol award in petroleum chemistry 1983, Langmuir award 1985), Catalysis Soc. (dir. 1977-81, pres. 1973-77, First Burwell lectr. 1983), Internat. Union Pure and Applied Chemistry (titular mem. colloid and surface chemistry commn. 1969-77). Achievements include research in heterogeneous catalysis and surface chemistry. Office: Dept of Chemistry Northwestern Univ Evanston IL 60208-0001 Home: 1141 Eastham Road Cuttingsville VT 05738 E-mail: rburl@widomaker.com.

BURZYNSKI, JAMES BRADLEY, state legislator; b. Christopher, Ill., July 13, 1955; m. Judy Burzynski; 2 children. AA, Rend Lake CC; BA, Ill. Wesleyan Coll. Tchr. Pinckneyville Mid. Schs.; farm bur. mgr. Clark, Clinton counties; govtl. affairs dir. DeKalb County Farm Bur.; chmn. DeKalb County Rep. Com.; mem. Ill. State Ho. Reps., 1990—93, Ill. State Senate Dist. 35, 1993—. Chair licenced activities com.; mem. state govt. ops. com.; mem. exec. edn. and higher edn. appropriations com.; senate rep. caucus chmn., 2003—. Adv. bd. DeKalb Salvation Army. Mem.: C. of C. Rockford, C. of C. Belvidere, C. of C. Rochelle, C. of C. Dekalb, Midwest Higher Edn. Commn., C. of C. Sycamore, Sycamore Kiwanis. Address: 505 Dekalb Ave Sycamore IL 60178-1719 Office Phone: 815-895-6318. E-mail: info@senatorbrad.com.

BURZYNSKI, NORMAN STEPHEN, editor; b. Pitts., Nov. 21, 1928; s. Ladislaus and Eleanor Marie B.; m. Ann Louise Adams, June 11, 1951; children: Michael Derek, Stephanie Ann, Eric Adams, Karen Ruth, John Kerstan, Joan Lorraine. BA in Journalism, U. Pitts., 1953; MS in Bus. Adminstrn., George Washington U., 1971; A. Applied Sci. summa cum laude in Aviation Tech.— Airport Mgmt., No. Va. Community Coll., Manassas, 1977, A. Applied Sci. summa cum laude in Aviation Tech.— Air Traffic Control, A. Applied Sci. magna cum laude in Comml. Art, 1982. Editor corporate publs. PPG Industries, Pitts., 1958-72, pub. relations rep., 1972-73; air res. forces liaison officer Office of Info., U.S. Air Force, Washington, 1968-72; chief Office of Info., U.S. Air Force Res., 1973-76; editor The Officer, Res. Officers Assn. U.S., Washington, 1976-95. Editor Civil War Camera, Luray, Va., 1998—. Served to lt. U.S. Army, 1951-52; to col. USAF, 1968-76. Mem. Res. Officers Assn., Air Force Assn., Aircraft Owners and Pilots Assn., Exptl. Aircraft Assn., Aviation and Space Writers Assn. Home: 4 Jackson Dr Luray VA 22835-9606 E-mail: nsb@shentel.net.

BURZYNSKI, STANISLAW RAJMUND, internist; b. Lublin, Poland, Jan. 23, 1943; came to U.S., 1970; s. Grzegorz and Zofia Miroslawa (Radzikowski) B. MD with distinction, Med. Acad., Lublin, 1967, PhD, 1968. Tchg. asst. Med. Acad., 1962-67, intern, resident, 1967-70; rsch. assoc. Baylor U., 1970-72, asst. prof., 1972-77; pvt. practice specializing in internal medicine Houston, 1977—; pres. Burzynski Clinic, 1979—. Dir. Burzynski Rsch. Lab., 1977-83; pres. Burzynski Rsch. Inst., Inc., 1983-2002. Contbr. articles to profl. jours. Nat. Cancer Inst. grantee, 1974, West Found. grantee, 1975. Mem. AMA, AAAS, Am. Assn. Cancer Rsch., Harris County Med. Soc., Polish Nat. Alliance (pres. Houston chpt. 1974-75), Soc. Neurosci., Soc. Neuro-oncology, Tex. Med. Assn., Sigma Xi. Roman Catholic. Achievements include discovery of antineoplastons components of biochem. def. system against cancer; described structure of Ameletin, 1st substance known to be responsible for remembering sound in animal's brain; invented new treatment for cancer, AIDS, viral infections, autoimmune diseases, neurofibromatosis, and Parkinson's disease; gene silencing theory of aging. Home: 20 W Rivercrest Dr Houston TX 77042-2127 Office: 9432 Old Katy Rd Ste 200 Houston TX 77055-6330 Office Phone: 713-335-5697. Business E-Mail: info@burzynskiclinic.com.

BURZYNSKI, SUSAN MARIE, newspaper editor; b. Jackson, Mich., Jan. 1, 1953; d. Leon Walter and Claudia (Kulpinski) B.; m. James W. Bush, May 22, 1976 (div. 1989); children: Lisa M., Kevin J.; m. George K. Bullard, Jr., Mar. 21, 1992. AA, Jackson C.C., 1972; BA, Mich. State, 1974. Reporter Saratogian, Saratoga Springs, N.Y., 1974, Gongwer News Svc., Lansing, Mich., 1975, The State Jour., Lansing, 1975-79; Metro editor Port Huron (Mich.) Times Herald, 1979-82, mng. editor, 1982-86; asst. city editor Detroit News, 1986-87, Sunday news editor, 1987, news editor, 1988-91, asst. mng. editor/news, 1991-96, asst. mng. editor, recruiting and tng., 1996-98, asst. mng. editor, adminstr., 1998-2000, assoc. editor, 2000—04, mng. editor, 2004—. Roman Catholic. Avocations: swimming, tennis, biking, knitting, knitting. Office: Detroit News 615 W Lafayette Blvd Detroit MI 48226-3197 Office Phone: 313-222-2772. Business E-Mail: sburzynski@detnews.com.

BUS, JAMES STANLEY, toxicologist; b. Kalamazoo, Mich., June 27, 1949; s. Charles J. and Sena (Wolthuis) B.; m. Gerda W. Hekman, Apr. 20, 1974; children: Sara E., Timothy J., Brian M. BS in Medicinal Chemistry, U. Mich., 1971; PhD in Pharmacology, Mich. State U., 1975. Diplomate Am. Bd. Toxicology (v.p., pres. 1985-87). NIH predoctoral trainee Dept. Pharmacology, Mich. State U., East Lansing, 1971-75; asst. prof. environ. health U. Cin., 1975-76; scientist I (biochem. toxicologist) Chem. Industry Inst. Toxicology, Research Triangle Park, N.C., 1977-84, scientist II (biochem. toxicologist), 1984-86; assoc. dir. pathology/toxicology, dir. drug metabolism rsch. The Upjohn Co., Kalamazoo, 1986-89; toxicology rsch. lab. Dow Chem. Co., Midland, Mich., 1989-91, project mgr., 1992-93, rsch. mgr., tech. dir., 1994—2001, dir. external tech., 2001—. Adj. assoc. prof. curriculum in toxicology U. N.C., Chapel Hill, 1984-88; adj. prof. pharmacology/toxicology Mich. State U., East Lansing, 1987—; toxicology expert Am. Conf. for Govtl. Indsl. Hygienists, Cin., 1993-2002; safety assessment bd. advisors Merck, Sharp & Dohme Lab., West Point, Pa., 1985-86; mem. bd. sci. counselors EPA, 1996-2003, mem. sci. adv. bd., 2003—; mem. sci. adv. bd. NTP, 1997-2001. Co-editor: Patty's Industrial Hygiene and Toxicology, Vol. 3B, 1995; assoc. editor Toxicology and Applied Pharmacology, 1989-92, speciality editor, 2003—; editl. bd. Reproductive Toxicology, 1986-96; contbr. articles to profl. jours. Trustee Covenant Coll., Lookout Mountain,. Ga., 1984-87. Recipient Robert A. Scala award, Environ. Occupl. Health Sci. Inst., Rutgers U., 1999, Disting. Alumni award, Mich. State U. Dept. Pharmacol. Toxicology, 2001. Mem. Soc. Toxicology (pres. 1996-97, Achievement award 1987), Am. Soc. for Pharmacology and Exptl. Therapeutics, Teratology Soc., Am. Conf. Govt. Indsl. Hygiene (mem. chem. substances threshold limit value com. 1993-2002), Nat. Acad. Scis. (emerging issues and data on environ. contaminants com. 2002—). Republican. Achievements include research dealing with mechanisms of chemical toxicity, including oxidant and glutathione mediated toxicities. Office: Dow Chemical Co Toxicology Rsch Lab 1803 Bldg Midland MI 48674-0001 Office Phone: 989-636-4557. Business E-Mail: jbus@dow.com.

BUS, ROGER JAY, lawyer; b. Kalamazoo, Mich., 1953; s. Charles J. and Sena Bus; m. Lida Margaret Sell, Aug. 27, 1977; children: Emily Lynn, Stephen Charles. Student, Calvin Coll., 1971-73; BA, U. Mich., 1975; JD, U. Toledo, 1979. Bar: Mich. 1979, U.S. Dist. Ct. (we. dist.) Mich. 1979. Law clk. to presiding justice Kalamazoo Cir. Ct., 1978; intern Toledo Legal Aid, 1979; staff atty. Legal Aid Bur. SW Mich., Kalamazoo, 1979-81; assoc. Stanley, Davidoff & Gray, Kalamazoo, 1981-83; owner, atty. Debt Relief Law Ctr., Kalamazoo, 1983—. Deacon Ref. Bapt. Ch., Kalamazoo, 1983-85; precinct del. Kalamazoo County Reps., 1986-88; bd. dirs., atty. Kalamazoo Gospel Mission, 1983-86, v.p., 1997-98, bd. dirs., 1996-2003, chmn. bd., 2000-02; adult Sunday sch. tchr. Calvary Bible Ch., elder, 1988-98, elder clk., 1989-91, 97-98, missions coun., 1999-2003; mem. missions team Richland Bible Ch., 2000-03, adult Sunday Sch. tchr., 2001-04, elder, 2002-04; team mem. Operation Mobilization, Grenada, 2002. Fellow Christian Magicians (lectr. 2005); mem. Fed. Bar Assn. (lectr. western dist. Mich. bankruptcy div. 1990-92, 97, 2001, spkr. we. dist. Mich. 2001), Am. Bankruptcy Inst., Mich. Bar Assn., Kalamazoo County Bar Assn., Nat. Assn. Chpt. 13 Trustees, Nat. Assn. Consumer Bankruptcy Attys., Soc. Am. Magicians, Internat. Brotherhood Magicians. Avocations: global missions, reading, religious book collecting, Gospel magic, evangelism. Home: 5330 Stoney Brook Rd Kalamazoo MI 49009-3850 Office: Debt Relief Law Ctr 903 E Cork St Kalamazoo MI 49001-4875 Office Phone: 269-342-1116. Personal E-mail: busmagic@aol.com.

BUSBY, DAVID, lawyer; b. Ada, Okla., Jan. 29, 1926; s. Orel and Hope B.; m. Mary Beth Baker, June 9, 1962; children: Helen Hope Busby Burleigh, Alison Sears Busby Vareika, Robert David, John Orel. BA, 1948; LL.B., Okla. U., 1951. Bar: Okla. 1950, D.C. 1959, N.Y. 1959, U.S. Supreme Ct. 1959. Assoc. Busby, Harrell & Trice, Ada, 1951-55; counsel Subcom. on Automobile Mktg. Practices, Com. on Interstate and Fgn. Commerce, U.S. Senate, Washington, 1955-58, Subcom. Fgn. Commerce, 1958; ptnr. Hays, Busby & Rivkin, N.Y.C., 1958-77, Busby, Rehm & Leonard, 1977-87; of counsel Dorsey & Whitney, Washington, 1988—2004. Trade advisor Ministry of Fin., Republic of Latvia, 1996; lectr., Moscow, Kiev, Chisinev, Kampala, 1995-98; mem. accountability rev. bd. terrorist attack on U.S. Embassy, Dar Es Salaam, 1998-99. Mem. Nat. Motor Vehicle Safety Adv. Coun., 1966-68; pres. League Young Dems. of Okla., 1951; city judge, Ada, 1952-53; bd. dirs. Legal Aid Soc. D.C.; mem. Washington Nat. Cathedral chpt., 1984-91. Served with USNR, 1944-46. Mem. ABA (chmn. standing com. on customs law 1973-76), Fed. Cir. Bar Assn. (bd. dirs.), Customs and Internat. Trade Bar Assn. (bd. dirs.), Nat. Cathedral Assn. (bd. trustees 1992-96), Met. Club. Episcopalian. Office: Dorsey & Whitney Ste 4005 1001 Pennsylvania Ave NW Washington DC 20004 Office Phone: 202-442-3512. Business E-Mail: busby.david@dorseylaw.com.

BUSBY, EDWARD OLIVER, retired dean; b. Macomb, Ill., June 22, 1926; s. Lynn John and Pauline (Hoebel) B.; m. Lois E. Tehan, June 17, 1950; children: Thomas L., John E., Paula L. BS, U. Wis., 1950, MS, 1962, PhD, 1971. Resident engr. Wis. Hwy. Commn., 1950-51; asst. city engr. City of LaCrosse, Wis., 1951-53; sales engr. Wis. Culvert Co., 1953-59; lectr. civil engring. U. Wis., Madison, 1959-66; dean Coll. Engring. U. Wis.-Platteville, 1966-84, dean emeritus, 1985—. Mem. Wis. Examining Bd. for Profl. Engrs., 1981-84; v.p. Platteville Area Indsl. Devel. Corp., 1977-80; vis. prof. U. Tenn., 1984-85; treas. U. Wis.-Platteville Found., 1989-95. Contbr. articles in field to profl. jours. Served with U.S. Navy, 1944-46 NSF fellow, 1970-71 Fellow ASCE (chmn. profl. registration com. 1985-86); mem. Wis. Soc. Profl. Engrs. (pres. 1972-73), Nat. Soc. Profl. Engrs. (nat. dir. 1976-81, vice chmn. engrs. edn. 1971-73) Republican. Home: 7628 Widgeon Way Madison WI 53717-1805

BUSBY, JAY RICHMOND, protective services official, consultant; b. Corpus Christi, Tex., July 29, 1969; s. James Robert and Pamela Lynn Busby; m. Theresa Ann Stifflemire, Feb. 14, 1992; children: Trenton Mead Linebaugh, Taylor Deon Linebaugh, Jakeb Reece. BS in Criminal Justice, Columbia So. U. Cert. Master Peace Officer State of Tex., 1999. State police officer Lower Colo. River Authority, Austin, Tex., 1990—. Cons. Counter-Terrorism Assn. Am., Tex., 2000—; owner TravelSpire.com, Leander, Tex., 2004—. Head coach Cedar Country Youth Soccer Assn., Cedar Park, Tex., 1995—2000; pres. Liberty Hill Jaycees, Tex., 1998—2001. Ssgt. Tex. Guard, 1998, ssgt. mil. police Tex. Guard, 1999—. Recipient Meritorious Svc. award, Tex. State Guard, 2004, Terrorism Campaign award, 2004. Mem.: Nat. Assn. Marine Patrol Officers, Nat. Assn. EMTs, Tex. Tactical Police Officer Assn., Nat. Assn. Ind. Travel Agents, Cruise Line Industry Am., Nat. Counter-Terrorism Officers Assn. R-Conservative. Episcopalian. Home: PO Box 1244 Leander TX 78646 Office: Lower Colorado River Authority 3200 Lake Austin Blvd Austin TX 78753

BUSBY, MARJEAN (MARJORIE JEAN BUSBY), retired journalist; b. Kansas City, Mo., Jan. 31, 1931; d. Vivian Eric and Stella Mae (Lindley) Phillips; m. Robert Jackson Busby, Apr. 11, 1969 (dec. Feb. 1989). B.J., U. Mo., 1952. With Kansas City Star Co. (Knight Ridder purchased 1997), 1952-2000, editor women's news, 1969-73, assoc. Sunday editor, People Sect. editor, 1973-77, fashion editor, 1978-81, feature and home writer, 1981-2000; ret., 2000. Mem. Fashion Group (1st recipient Kansas City appreciation award 1978), LSV, Mortar Board, Soc. Profl. Journalists, Friends of Art, Belle of Am. Royal Orgn., Kappa Alpha Theta (pres. Alpha Mu chpt. 1951-52) Presbyterian. Home: 9804 Mercier St Kansas City MO 64114-3860

BUSBY, MORRIS D., former ambassador; b. Memphis; married; 2 children. BA, Marshall U.; MS, George Washington U.; postgrad., U.S. Naval Destroyer Sch., Def. Intelligence Sch., Naval War Coll. With USN, various locations including Vietnam, 1971-73; mem. staff Office of Coord. of Ocean Affairs, dir. Office Oceans and Polar Affairs, dep. asst. sec. ocean affairs, amb. oceans and fisheries affairs Dept. of State, 1973-81, alt. rep. to conf. on disarmament Geneva, Switzerland, 1981-83, dep. chief of mission Mexico City, 1984-87, founder, office head assistance program for Nicaraguan resistance, 1987-88, prin. dep. asst. sec. inter-Am. affairs, 1987-88, spl. envoy to C.Am., sr. dep., 1988-89; head counter-terrorism Dept. State, 1989-91; amb. to Colombia Dept. of State, Bogota, 1991-94; pres. BGI, Internet. Cons. Svcs., 1994—. Decorated Bronze Star; recipient 3 Presdl. Meritorious Svc. awards Govt. Colombia Gran Cruz de Boyaca. Office: Buzz Corp PO Box 1189 Mathews VA 23109-1918

BUSBY, NITA JUNE, small business owner; b. Pitts., Aug. 28, 1932; d. William Frederich and Monica (Vinciunes) Guidotti; m. Michael Petrunio (div.); children: Michele, Donna, David, Elizabeth, William; m. Harry Leslie Busby BA in English, Calif. State U., Fullerton, 1973, MLS, 1976. Health sci. libr. Whittier Hosp., Calif., 1978-82; owner, gen. mgr. Resumés, Etc., Orange, 1982—. Sec. Orange County chpt. Calif. Staffing Profls., 2000—04. Mem. Nat. Assn. Women Bus. Owners (pres. Orange county chpt. 1991-92), Women in Mgmt. (pres. Orange County chpt. 1984-85), Profl. Assn. Resumé Writers (author monthly book revs. 1992-93), Assn. Profl. Cons., Calif. State U. Libr. Sci. Alumni Assn. (pres. 1976-77, 89-90, 90-91) Republican. Roman Catholic. Avocations: reading, walking, vegetable gardening. Office: Resumés Etc 438 E Katella Ave Ste G Orange CA 92867-4857 Office Phone: 714-633-2783. Personal E-mail: resumes100@aol.com. Business E-Mail: nbusby@resumesetc.net.

BUSCEMI, PETER, lawyer; b. Bklyn., Sept. 25, 1950; s. Vincent and Ilse (Griesser) Buscemi; m. Judith Ann Miller, June 27, 1981. BA, Columbia U., 1969, JD, 1976; MA, Princeton U., 1971. Bar: N.Y. 1977, D.C. 1979, U.S. Supreme Ct. 1980, U.S. Dist. Ct. (D.C. dist.) 1981, U.S. Ct. Appeals (D.C. cir.) 1981, U.S. Dist. Ct. (so. dist.) N.Y. 1982, U.S. Ct. Appeals (5th and 11th cirs.) 1982, U.S. Ct. Appeals (2d cir.) 1985, U.S. Ct. Appeals (fed. cir.) 1986, U.S. Ct. Appeals (3d and 4th cirs.) 1990, U.S. Ct. Appeals (6th cir.) 1993, U.S. Ct. Appeals (1st cir.) 1994, U.S. Ct. Appeals (7th cir.) 1995, U.S. Ct. Appeals (10th cir.) 1998. Law clk. to Hon. Carl McGowan U.S. Ct. Appeals (D.C. cir.), Washington, 1976—77; asst. to solicitor gen. U.S. Dept. Justice, Washington, 1977—81; spl. asst. U.S. atty. U.S. Atty.'s Office, Alexandria, Va., 1980; assoc. Paul, Weiss, Rifkind, Wharton & Garrison, Washington, 1981—86, Morgan, Lewis & Bockius, LLP, Washington, 1986—87, ptnr., 1987—, mem. litig. practice group. Mem.: D.C. Prisoner's Legal Svcs. Project (bd. dirs.), D.C. Bar Assn.-litig. sect., criminal law sect., cts. lawyers & adminstrn. justice sects., ABA-antitrust& criminal law sects., ABA-litig. adminstrv. sect.,

Lifeline (bd. dirs.). Office: Morgan Lewis & Bockius LLP 1111 Pennsylvania Ave NW Washington DC 20004 Office Phone: 202-739-5190. Office Fax: 202-739-3001. Business E-Mail: pbuscemi@morganlewis.com.

BUSCEMI, STEVE, actor; b. Bklyn., Dec. 13, 1957; m. Jo Andres, 1987; 1 child, Lucian. Student, Lee Strasberg Inst., N.Y.C. Fireman; stand-up comedian N.Y.C. Appeared in films Parting Glances, 1986, Sleepwalk, 1986, Kiss Daddy Good Night, 1987, Vibes, 1988, Heart of Midnight, 1989, Slaves of New York, 1989, Mystery Train, 1989, The Grifters, 1990, Miller's Crossing, 1990, King of New York, 1990, Zandalee, 1991, Barton Fink, 1991, Billy Bathgate, 1991, Criscross, 1992, In the Soup, 1992, Reservoir Dogs, 1992, Me and the Mob, 1992, Twenty Bucks, 1993, The Hudsucker Proxy, 1994, Airheads, 1994, Pulp Fiction, 1994, Floundering, 1994, Desperado, 1995, Things to Do in Denver When You're Dead, 1995, Fargo, 1996, Black Kites, 1996, Kansas City, 1996, Search for One-Eye Kimmy, 1996, Escape from LA., 1996, The Real Blonde, 1997, Divine Trash, 1997, Con Air, 1997, The Big Lebowski, 1998, The Wedding Singer, 1998, Louis et Frank, 1998, Armageddon, 1998, The Impostors, 1998, Big Daddy, 1999, 28 Days, 2000, Ghost World, 2000, Monsters Inc., 2001 (voice), Domestic Distrubance, 2001, The Laramie Project, 2002, Mr. Deeds, 2002, Spy Kids 2: Island of Lost Dreams, 2002, Deadrockstar, 2002, Spy Kids 3-D: Game Over, 2003, Big Fish, 2003, Home on the Range (voice), 2004, Who's the Top?, 2005, The Island, 2005, others; producer, dir. films What Happened to Pete?, 1993; dir. film Trees Lounge, 1996; appeared in Tales from the Crypt, 1993, also Miami Vice, L.A. Law, The Sopranos, 2004; other TV appearances include Lonesome Dove, The Last Outlaw.*

BÜSCH, ANNEMARIE, retired mental health nurse; b. Ger. d. Jurgen Julius and Anna (Stark) B. RN, Anschar Sch. Nursing, Kiel, Fed. Republic Germany, 1954; student, Traverse City State Hosp., Mich., 1959, Wayne State U., 1962, Colby-Sawyer Coll., New London, N.H., 1981. Lic. nurse, N.H., Vt., Fed. Republic Germany. Asst. head nurse Univ. Eye Inst., Kiel, 1954-56; nurse aide, grad. nurse Ontario Hosp., London, Can.; staff nurse, charge nurse Grace Hosp., Receiving Hosp., Detroit, 1962-67; coll. health nurse Wayne St. U., Detroit, 1967-70; staff nurse Mary Hitchcock Meml. Hosp., Hanover, 1970-71, nurse mental health dept., 1978-82; charge nurse Dartmouth Coll. Health Svc., Hanover, N.H., 1971-77; staff nurse, charge nurse Hanover Health Terrace; staff nurse Temporary Nurses, Inc., Hanover, Vis. Nurse Alliance of Vt. and N.H., White River Junction, Vt.; ret., 1997. Camp nurse Nat. Music Camp InterLochen, Mich.

BUSCH, ANNIE, library director; b. Joplin, Mo., Jan. 6, 1947; d. George Lee and Margaret Eleanor (Williams) Chancellor; 1 child, William Andrew Keller. BA, Mo. U., 1969, MA, 1976. Br. mgr. St. Charles (Mo.) City Coun. Libr., 1977-84, Springfield/Greene County (Mo.) Libr., 1985-89, exec. dir., 1989—. Exec. bd. Mo. Libr. Network Corp., St. Louis, 1991-96. Adv. bd. Springfield Pub. Sch. Found., 1992—94, St. John's Health Sys., Boys and Girls Town, Good Cmty. Task Force, 1999—2002; pres. Ozarks Regional Info. On-Line Network, Springfield, 1993—98; mem. Gov.'s Commn. on Informational Tech., Cmty. Task Force, Springfield, 1993—98, Cmty. Partnership of the Ozarks, 1998; exec. bd. Mo. Rsch. and Edn. Network, pres., 1996—97; task force Mo. Goals 2000, Mo. Census 2000 Complete Count Com., 1999—2000; coord. com. Springfield Vision 20/20; chair Sec. of State Adv. Coun., 2001—; adv. com. S.W. Mo. State U. Coll. Humanities and Pub. Affairs; trustee Mayor's Commn. for Children; bd. dirs. Ozarks Pub. TV, 1994—2000, Every Kid Counts, Wilson's Creek Nat. Battlefield Found., Mayors Commn. for Children, 2005—; bd. trustees Forest Inst. Profl. Psychology. Mem.: Mo. Libr. Assn. (exec. bd. 1990—94, pres. 1993—94), Springfield Area C. of C. (bd. dirs.), Springfield Rotary (pres. 1998—99). Office: Springfield-Greene Cty Libr PO Box 760 Springfield MO 65801-0760 Office Phone: 417-847-8120 ext 5. E-mail: annie@mail.sgcl.org.

BUSCH, ARTHUR ALLEN, lawyer; b. Flint, Mich., July 25, 1954; s. William Allen and Anna Elizabeth (York) B.; m. Bernadette Marie-Therese Regnier, Aug. 28, 1982. BA, Mich. State U., 1976, MLIR, 1977; JD, T.M. Cooley Law Sch., 1982. Bar: Mich. 1982, U.S. Dist. Ct. (ea. dist.) Mich. 1984. Supr. pers. Nat. Gypsum Co., Gibsonburg, Ohio, 1977-78; instr. Mich. State U., East Lansing, 1980-82; pvt. practice Flint, 1982-92; instr. C.S. Mott C.C., Flint, 1978—. Counsel Flint City Coun., 1982-84; cons. labor atty. City of Flint, 1984; prosecutor Genesee County, 1993—. Commr. Genesee County, 1986-92, mem. planning com., pks. and recreation; active Valley Area Agy. on Aging. Mem. Mich. Bar Assn., Genesee County Bar Assn. Democrat. Baptist. Office: 200 Courthouse Flint MI 48502

BUSCH, AUGUST A., IV, food products executive; BS, MS in Bus. Adminstrn., St. Louis U.; degree, Internat. Brewing Inst., Berlin. Line foreman Anheuser-Busch, Inc., St. Louis, exec. asst. to brewing v.p., with mktg. dept., 1989, brand dir., 1991, v.p. brand mgmt., 1994, v.p. mktg., 1996—2000, v.p. mktg. and wholesale ops., 2000—02, pres., 2002—, mgmt. com., bd. dirs.; v.p., group exec. Anheuser-Busch companies Inc., St. Louis, 2000—; strategy com. mem. Anheuser-Busch Companies Inc., St. Louis. Chmn. Beer Inst.; bd. mem. FedEx Corp., Memphis, 2003—. Bd. mem. Muscular Dystrophy Assn., Loyola Inst., St. Louis, The BackStoppers; mem. adv. bd. Am. Paralysis Assn., General Henry Hugh Shelton Leadership Initiative, NC State U.; bd. fellows Claremont U. Ctr. and Grad. Sch.; bd. govs. Cardinal Glennon Hosp., St. Louis; gen. co-chmn. St. Louis Am. Found. Awards program. Named Corp. Mktg. Exec. of Yr., Delaney Report, 1999, Lew Wasserman Spirit of Democracy Man of Yr., 2003; named to Am. Advt. Fedn. Hall of Achievement, 2000; recipient Advertiser of Yr., 48th Cannes Internat. Advt. Festival, 2001, Intrepid Salute Award, Gerald S. Snyder Heart Award, Larry King Cardiac Found. Office: Anheuser-Busch Companies Inc One Busch Place Saint Louis MO 63118*

BUSCH, AUGUST ADOLPHUS, III, brewery executive; b. St. Louis, June 16, 1937; s. August Anheuser and Elizabeth (Overton) Busch; m. Susan Marie Hornibrook, Aug. 17, 1963 (div. 1969); children: August Adolphus IV, Susan Marie II; m. Virginia L. Wiley, Dec. 28, 1974; children: Steven August, Virginia Marie. Student, U. Ariz., 1957—58, Siebel Inst. Tech., 1960—61. With Anheuser-Busch, Inc., St. Louis, 1957—2002, pres., 1974—75, CEO, 1975—2002, chmn. bd. dir., 1977—. Bd. dir. Southwestern Bell Tel. Co., 1980—83, SBC Comm. Inc., 1983—, Emerson Electric Co., Grupo Modelo SA de CV. Exec. bd. St. Louis Boy Scouts Am.; bd. dirs. United Way Greater St. Louis. Mem.: Log Cabin Club, St. Louis Country Club. Office: Anheuser-Busch Cos Inc 1 Busch Pl Saint Louis MO 63118-1852*

BUSCH, BEVERLY GAIL, English language educator, literature educator, instructional resource center administrator; b. Boston, Oct. 27, 1948; d. Andrew Earl Thompson and Martha Bartlett; m. Peter Raymond Busch, Apr. 15, 1972; children: Cheyenne J., Carin S., Luke W. BA, U. Mass., 1970; MA, Middlebury Coll., 1978; MPhil, Drew U., 1981, PhD, 1986. Cert. English tchr. Mass., NJ. Adj. faculty mem. Coll. St. Elizabeth, Madison, N.J., 1981-83, Centenary Coll., Hackettstown, N.J., 1981-83; coord. ministries program Phillipsburg (N.J.) Alliance Ch., 1995-99; adj. prof. English Warren County Cmty. Coll., Washington, N.J., 1995-99; prof. English Somerset Christian Coll., Zarephath, NJ, 1999—, dir. Instructional Resource Ctr., chmn. Dept. Gen. Edn., 1999—. Author poetry and inspirational articles; mem. editl. adv. bd.: Collegiate Press, 2002—04, Rowman & Littlefield Pubs., Inc., 2004—05. Mem. Greenwich Twp. Bd. Edn., Stewartsville, N.J., 1995-99; pres. Greenwich Twp. Parent Tchr. Orgn., 1989-92, Parents On Site, 1994-96. Mem.: MLA, Acad. Am. Poets, NJ Coun. Tchrs. English, Nat. Coun. Tchrs. English, Evangel. Theol. Soc., Drew U. Alumni Assn., Middlebury Coll. Alumni Assn., U. Mass. Alumni Assn. Republican. Avocations: walking, biking, crafts. Home: 113 Kennedy Mill Rd Stewartsville NJ 08886 Office Phone: 732-356-1595 x1126. Business E-Mail: bbusch@somerset.edu.

BUSCH, DANIEL ADOLPH, geologist, educator; b. St. Paul, May 31, 1912; s. Karl George Adolph and Lulu Elizabeth Busch; m. Emilie Louise Finch; children: Daniel Andrew(dec.), David Arthur. BSc, Capital U., 1934; MA, Ohio State U., 1936, PhD, 1939; DSc (hon.), Capital U., 1960. Instr. U. Pitts., 1938—42; with Pa. Geol. Survey, Pitts., 1943—44, Huntley & Huntley Petroleum Cons., Pitts., 1944—46; sr. rsch. geologist Carter Rsch. Lab., Tulsa, 1946—51; chief geologist Zephyr Petroleum Co., Tulsa, 1951—54; petroleum geology cons. Tulsa, 1955—89; ret., 1989. Vis. prof. geology U. Okla., Norman, 1964—74; lectr. Oil & Gas Cons., Internat., Tulsa, 1967—89; lectr. in field; cons. in field. Author: (book) Stratigraphic Traps in Sandstones - Exploration Techniques, 1974 (Robert Dott Best Publ. award, 1975), Exploration Methods for Sandstone Reservoirs, 1985. Fellow: Geol. Soc. Am. (sr.); mem.: Am. Assn. Petroleum Geologists (hon.; v.p. 1966—67, pres. 1973—74, Matson award 1959, Leverson award 1971, Sidney Powers medal 1982, Monroe Cheney award 2003, Am. Registry of Outstanding Profls. 2003—), Sigma Xi. Avocations: travel, gardening, investments. Home: 3757 S Wheeling Ave Tulsa OK 74105

BUSCH, ESTELLE WINSTON, theater director; b. NYC, Aug. 30, 1914; d. Max and Eva Weinberg; m. Ben Busch, Dec. 30, 1942 (dec.); children: Mark, Carolann Carter. Grad., Group Theatre, NY, 1935. Founder Pact Theatre, LA, 1965—70; adminstr. Theatre Alliance, LA, 1972—78; founder, v.p. Women in Theatre, LA, 1978—2004; adminstr. Synthaxis Theatre, LA, 1978—2004, dir., 1984—2004; co-chair MidValley Neighborhood Coun. Theatre, North Hollywood Valley, Calif., 2003—04. Tchr. Valley Store Front, North Hollywood, 2002—03; dir. Collage Improvization Show, 1978—2004. One-woman shows include Edinburgh Theatre Art Festival, 1979—80; dir.: (plays) Emergence of Mel, 2002. Conv. del. AFTRA, LA, 1970—80; active C. of C. North Hollywood, 1993—2003; founder Women in Theater, 1978, bd. dirs., v.p., liaison to AFTRA, SAG, Actors Equity, 1978—81; L.A. rep. Edinburgh Art Festival, 1979; mem. women's coms. SAG, AFTRA, Actors Equity, 1969—79; founder Equity Waiver Theatre Scene, L.A., 1969, Valley Theatre League, 1993; mem. No-Ho Theatre Com., 1994—2004; del. AFTRA conv., 1969—79; co-chair theatre com. Neighborhood Coun. North Hollywood, 2003; advocate women's issues Dem. Party, Calif., 1993—2003; bd. dirs. San Fernando Arts Coun., 1982—85. Named 4th dist. Pioneer Woman of Yr., Councilman Tom LaBonge, 2003; named one of 10 Women of Yr., Commn. on Status of Women, 1999; recipient Juanine Clay Life Achievement award, Valley Theatre League, 1979—2000, proclamation of appreciation, L.A. City Coun., 1979—2003, honor, NO-HO News, 1994, certs. of appreciation, State Sen. Richard Alarcon, State Contr. Helen Connor, U.S. Sen. Barbara Boxer, Dist. Atty. Gil Garcetti, letter of congratulation, Pres. Bill Clinton, 1999—2001, Red Carpet award, Women in Theatre, 2004, proclamation in honor of 90th birthday, L.A. City Coun., 2004. Avocations: travel, dance. Home: 6310 Whitsett Ave #4 North Hollywood CA 91606 Office Phone: 818-382-2904.

BUSCH, FREDERICK MATTHEW, writer, educator; b. N.Y.C., Aug. 1, 1941; s. Benjamin and Phyllis (Schnell) B.; m. Judith Burroughs, Nov. 29, 1963; children: Benjamin, Nicholas. BA, Muhlenberg Coll., Allentown, Pa., 1962, LittD (hon.), 1980; MA, Columbia U., 1967. Writer for mags., N.Y.C., and Greenwich, Conn., 1963—66; from instr. to prof. Colgate U., Hamilton, N.Y., 1966-87, Fairchild prof. lit., 1987—2003. Acting dir. Program in Creative Writing U. Iowa, Iowa City, 1978-79. Author: 27 books including Sometimes I Live in the Country, 1986, Absent Friends, 1989, Harry and Catherine, 1990, Closing Arguments, 1991, Long Way From Home, 1993, The Children in the Woods: New and Selected Stories, 1994 (PEN/Faulkner award nomination, 1995), Girls, 1997, (essays) A Dangerous Profession, 1998, (novel) The Night Inspector, 1999 (PEN/Faulkner award nomination, NBCC award nomination, 2000); editor: (anthology) Letters to a Fiction Writer, 1997, (stories) Don't Tell Anyone, 2000, A Memory of War, 2003, (novel) North, 2005; numerous other essays and short stories. Recipient Nat. Jewish Book award for fiction, Jewish Book Coun., 1986, Fiction award, AAAL, 1986, PEN/Malamud, 1991, Award of Merit, AAAL, 2001; fellow, Guggenheim Found., 1981—82, Ingram Merrill Found., 1981—82. Mem.: PEN, Am. Acad. Arts and Scis., Authors Guild Am.

BUSCH, J. HERBERT, electrical contractor, writer; b. Cleve., Mar. 16, 1920; s. Edward A. and Anna Busch; m. Ruth Singer Busch, June 14, 1942; children: Pamela Friedman, Sheryl Pariser(dec.). Grad., Glenville H.S., Cleve., 1938. Contractor Discount Electric of Va., Inc., Fairfax. Tchr. Elec. Trade Sch., Parma, Ohio. Author: numerous books, more than 1,000 poems, stories, and songs. Capt. signal corps U.S. Army, 1942—46. Jewish.

BUSCH, JOHN ARTHUR, lawyer; b. Indpls., Mar. 23, 1951; s. John L. and Betty (Thomas) B.; m. Barbara Ann Holt, June 23, 1973; children: Abigail, Elizabeth, Amanda, Rachel. BA, Wabash Coll., 1973; JD, Duke U., 1976. Bar: Wis. 1976, U.S. Dist. Ct. (ea. we. dists.) Wis., U.S. Ct. Appeals (5th and 7th cirs.) 1976. Assoc. Michael, Best & Friedrich, Milw., 1976-83, ptnr., 1983—; chmn. litigation dept. Michael Best & Friedrich, Milw., 1990-95, mgmt. com., 1995-2001, mng. ptnr. Milw. office, 2003—04. Mem. ad hoc com. on alternative dispute resolution Milw. Cir. Ct., ad hoc com. on multidisciplinary practices State Bar, mem. bd. govs., 2001-03. Treas. North Shore Rep. Club, Milw., 1984-85, vice chmn., 1985-86, chmn., 1987-89; del. Rep. State Conv., Milw., 1986; mem. local rules adv. com. Ea. dist., Wis.; mem. com. Fed. Bench Bar; mem. bd. dir. Mich. Maritime Mus., New Am. Policy Inst. Master: Am. Inns of Ct.; mem.: ABA, Wis. Bar Assn., Milw. Bar Assn. Home: 1025 E Lyon St Milwaukee WI 53202 Office: Michael Best & Friedrich 100 E Wisconsin Ave Ste 3300 Milwaukee WI 53202-4108 Office Phone: 414-225-4977. Business E-Mail: jabusch@michaelbest.com.

BUSCH, JONATHAN CARL, music educator; b. Lansing, Mich., Nov. 26, 1957; s. Henry Lowell and Barbara June Busch; m. Anne Marie Boven, Aug. 6, 1983; children: Kenaniah James, Bethany Marie, Hannah Christine. MusB, Grand Rapids Bapt. Coll., 1980; MusM, U. of Mich., 1984; postgrad., Oakland U., Rochester, Mich., 2004. Cert. tchr. Mich. Music dir. Grace Bible Christian Acad., Ann Arbor, Mich., 1982—87, Grace Bible Ch., Ann Arbor, 1984—87, Southfield (Mich.) Christian Sch., 1987—; interim music dir., worship leader Highland Pk. Bapt. Ch., Southfield, 1994; worship leader Calvary Bapt. Ch., Waterford, Mich., 2004—; instr. jr. high summer arts camp Oakland U., Rochester, Mich., 2004. Asst.-substitute condr., worship leader Highland Pk. Bapt. Ch., Southfield, 1988—2004. Mem. choir and orch. Highland Pk. Bapt. Ch., Southfield, 1987—2004; mem. Farmington Cmty. Band/Jazz Band, Farmington, 2004—05. Mem.: Music Educators Nat. Conf., Mich. Sch. Vocal Music Assn. (state bd. rec. sec. 2004—05), Mich. Sch. Band and Orch. Assn. (dist. corr. sec. 2004—05). Republican. Achievements include Initiated School participation in Michigan School Vocal Music Association; Addition of Band Blast and Bands Alive group band programs to performance curriculum. Avocations: music, photography, frisbee. Office: Southfield Christian Sch 28650 Lahser Rd Southfield MI 48034 Office Phone: 248-357-3660. Office Fax: 248-357-5271. Personal E-mail: joncbusch@isp.com. E-mail: jbusch@southfieldchristian.org.

BUSCH, KURT, race car driver; b. Las Vegas, Nev., Aug. 4, 1978; s. Tom and Gaye Busch. Race car driver Roush Racing, Concord, NC. Named NASCAR Hobby Stock Rookie of Yr., Champion, 1996, Featherlite S.W. Series Rookie of the Yr., 1998, Featherlite S.W. Series Champion, 1999, Craftsman Truck Series Rookie of the Yr., 2d in points, 2000. Office: Roush Racing 7050 Aviation Blvd Concord NC 28027-8196

BUSCH, KYLE, race car driver; b. Las Vegas, Nev., May 2, 1985; Driver, Craftsman Truck Series Billy Ballew Motorsports, 1985—; driver, Nextel Cup Series and Busch Series Hendrick Motorsports, 2003—. Named Busch Series Rookie of Yr., 2004; finished runner-up in Busch Series; 5 Busch Series victories. Winner of the 2005 Sony HD 500, NASCAR Nextel Cup Series in Fontana, California; youngest driver ever to win a race in the Nextel Cup history.*

BUSCH, MICHAEL, state legislator; b. Balt., Jan. 4, 1947; BS, Temple U., 1970. Tchr., coach St. Mary's H.S., 1973-79; adminstr. youth athletics Anne Arundel County, Md., 1979—; del. dist. 30 Md. State Delegation, 1987—, spkr. ho., 2003—. Mem. numerous coms. including most recently Md. State Delegation, chmn. econ. matters com., 1994—, mem. legis. policy com., 1994—, mem. rules and exec. nominations com., 1994—. Chmn. Anne Arundel County Delegation, 1992-93; mem. St. Mary's Sch. Bd., 1992—; bd. trustees The Md. Hist. Trust, 1995. Named Coach of the Yr., 1978, Man of Yr., Anne arundel County Lacrosse Assn., 1982, Legislator of Yr., Anne Arundel County Nurses Assn., 1989; recipient Presdl. Citation, Md. Recreation and Parks Assn., 1989; named to Sports Hall Fame, Anne Arundel County, 2003, Legis. of Yr., Annapolis and Anne Arundel County C. of C., 2005. Office: State House H 101 Annapolis MD 21401

BUSCH, MILDRED MOORMAN, music educator; b. Dallas, Jan. 8, 1920; d. Cull Cade Moorman and Lila Love; m. Theodore Norman Busch, June 3, 1946 (div. 1954); 1 child, Kathryn Anne Busch Garcia. MusB, BA, Baylor U., 1940; MA, West Tex. A&M U., 1954. Cert. piano and music theory. Head piano dept. San Marcos (Tex.) Acad., 1940—41; tchg. fellow in piano Baylor U., 1942—43; piano instr. Conservatory of Musical Arts, Amarillo, Tex., 1943—52; freelance piano instr. Amarillo, 1952—54; pub. rels. Betty Smith Assoc., NYC, 1954—55; freelance piano instr. Amarillo, 1955—. Composer piano teaching pieces. Vol. N.W. Tex. Hosp., Amarillo, USO, Amarillo; pianist Amarillo Little Theatre; vol. Meals on Wheels, Amarillo. Mem.: Amarillo Music Tchrs. Assn., Friends of Planned Parenthood (life), Magna Charta Dames and Barons. Presbyterian. Avocations: doll collecting, cats, charity work, church activities. Home and Office: 6717 Adirondack Trail Amarillo TX 79106

BUSCH, NANCY ELIZABETH, artist, educator; b. Manitowoc, Wis., Sept. 7, 1944; d. Edgar Wilhelm and Dorothy Janette (Blust) Putz; m. Charles Nels Busch, Aug. 21, 1965; 1 son, Alexander. BA in Journalism, U. Mich., 1966; student, Birmingham Bloomfield Art Assn, 1978-88, Ctr. for Creative Studies, 1985; postgrad., U. Mich., 1987-88; MFA, Wayne State U., 1990. Sales rep. Grosse Pointe News, Mich., 1966-68; pres. Nels Advt. Co., Birmingham, Mich., 1968-75, Busch & Morris, Birmingham, 1975-80, Busch & Assocs., Birmingham, 1980-88; prof. Instituto Federico Brandt, Caracas, Venezuela, 1991-93; artist, tchr. MFA program U. Vt., 2003. Cons. U. Mich. Devel. Bd., Ann Arbor, 1973-80. One-woman shows include Wayne State U., Mich., 1990, Sala Mendoza, Caracas, 1991, 93, Galeria Diners, Bogota, 1993-94, Galeria Ruth Benzacar, Buenos Aires, 1996, Centro Cultural Borges, Buenos Aires, 1996, Joseph Borges Museo, Caracas, Venezuela, 1998; group shows include Creative Arts Ctr., Pontiac, Mich., 1990, Wayne State U., Mich., 1990, Willis Gallery, Detroit, 1990; pvt. collections include Aco Corp. Collection, Caracas, Univ. de los Andes, Bogota, Columbia, Museo de Arte Contemporaneo, Bogota. Recipient award of Excellence Nat. Pub. Rels. Soc. am., 1975-80, Design awared Internat. Graphics, 1980. Mem. Econs. Club of Detroit, Adcraft Club of Detroit, Am. Mktg. Assn., Southeastern Mich. Hosp. Assn. (awards for concept and creative devel. in reports, brochures and other collateral materials 1975-80), Am. Hosp. Assn., Mich. Hosp. Assn. (awards for reports, brochures and othe materials 1975-80).

BUSCH, ROBERT HENRY, geneticist, researcher; b. Jefferson, Iowa, Oct. 22, 1937; s. Henry and Lena Margaret (Osterman) B.; m. Mavis Ann Bushman, Nov. 23, 1958; children: Shari Lynne, Todd William. BSc, Iowa State U., 1959, MSc, 1963; PhD, Purdue U., 1967. Asst. prof. N.D. State U., Fargo, 1967-72, assoc. prof., 1973-77, prof., 1977-78; rsch. geneticist USDA-ARS/U. Minn., St. Paul, 1978—. Cons. Nat. Hail Ins. Coun., Ill. and Colo., 1969-75, Internat. Atomic Energy Agy., UN. Developer 9 wheat varieties; contbr. chpts. to books, articles to profl. jours. Recipient Dedicated Svc. award Polk County Crop Improvement Assn., East Grand Forks, Minn., 1984; named Premier Seedsman Minn. Crop Improvement Assn., St. Paul, 1985. Fellow Crop Sci. Soc. Am. (editor 1976-78, com. chair 1988-90, bd. dirs. 1989-90), Am. Soc. Agronomy (Achievement award, Midwest Sr. Sci. 1998). Methodist. Avocations: sailing, fishing. Home: 2485 Galtier Cir Saint Paul MN 55113-3609 Office: U Minn Dept Agronomy Saint Paul MN 55108

BUSCH, ROBERT KURT, music educator; b. Anchorage, Aug. 27, 1975; s. Larry Wayne Busch and Patricia Gail Dean; m. Christina Marie Fore. B in Music Edn., Valdosta State U., Ga., 1997; M in Adminstrn. and Supervision, Mid. Tenn. State, 2004. Profl. Educators Lic. Tenn., 2001, Beginning Administrators Licenses Tenn., 2004. Music educator Highland Pk. Elem. Sch., Columbia, Tenn., 1998—. Music dir. Highland Pk. Voices, Columbia, Tenn., 1998—. Actor: (musical theater) Oklahoma; dir., dir., dir., dir., dir.: Music in the Parks Competition, (Superior Rating (First Pl.), 2002), (cd and dvd project) A Tribute To Our Soldiers. Abc assoc. dir. Columbia Am. Bowling Congress, Tenn., 2001—02; football coach E.A. Cox Mid. Sch., 2002—05. Mem.: ASCD (assoc.), Am. Bowling Congress, Alpha Lambda Delta (pres. 1994—95). Home: 401 4th Ave Columbia TN 38401 Office: Highland Park Elem Sch 1606 Highland Ave Columbia TN 38401 Office Phone: 931-388-7325.

BUSCHBACH, THOMAS CHARLES, geologist, consultant; b. Cicero, Ill., May 12, 1923; s. Thomas Dominick and Vivian (Smiley) B.; m. Mildred Merle Fletcher, Nov. 26, 1947; children— Thomas Richard, Susan Kay, Deborah Lynn BS, U. Ill., 1950, MS, 1951, PhD, 1959. Geologist, structural geology, stratigraphy, underground storage of natural gas Ill. Geol. Survey, 1951-78; coordinator New Madrid Seismotectonic Study, U.S. Nuclear Regulatory Commn., 1976-85; research prof. geology St. Louis U., 1978-85; geologic cons. Champaign, Ill., 1985—. Served to lt. comdr. USNR, 1942-47 Fellow Geol. Soc. Am. Home: 604 Park Lane Dr Champaign IL 61820-7631 Office: PO Box 1608 Champaign IL 61824-1608 Office Phone: 217-356-3667. E-mail: tcbusch@aol.com.

BUSCHE, LEON FRANK, secondary school educator; b. Elgin, Ill., Jan. 5, 1945; s. Leonard Herman and Hilda Loretta (Lamp) B.; m. Alice Eileen Morrison, Aug. 7, 1976; children: Karen Eileen, Susan Leigh. BA, The Am. U., 1967. Cert. tchr., Md. Intern Office of Vice Pres. Hubert Humphrey, Washington, 1964-65; tchr. T.W. Pyle Jr. High Sch., Bethesda, Md., 1967-72, 73-75, The Am. Sch. in London, 1972-73; tchr., dept. head Ridgeview Jr. High Sch., Gaithersburg, Md., 1973-88, Quince Orchard High Sch., Gaithersburg, 1988—2001; supr. student tchr. Hood Coll., 2002—. Active North Potomac (Md.) Citizens Assn., 1989—; mem. pastoral coun. Mother Seton Parish, 1987-90, chair, 1987-88, 89-90, vice chair 1988-89, Visitation Parish, chair liturgy com., 1990-94, chair pastoral coun., 1994-2002. Recipient Agnes Meyer Outstanding Tchr. award, Washington Post, 2001, Order of Merit, Archdiocese of Wash., 2003. Mem. Am. Fedn. Tchrs., Nat. Coun. for the Social Studies, Md. Coun. for the Social Studies, Montgomery County Social Studies tchrs. orgn. (sec. 1984-85, pres. 1985-87), Mary of Nazareth Elem. Sch. (mem., adv. bd., 1993-94). Democrat. Roman Catholic. Home: 12185 Hidden Brook Ter North Potomac MD 20878-3321

BUSCHKE, HERMAN, neurologist; b. Berlin, Oct. 15, 1932; came to U.S., 1934, naturalized, 1945; s. Franz Julius and Ruth Helen (Minkowski) B.; children: Thomas, Katherine; m. Bertelle Selig, 1993. BA, Reed Coll., 1954; MD, Western Res. U., 1958. Diplomate: Am. Bd. Psychiatry and Neurology. Intern Bronx (N.Y.) Mcpl. Hosp. Center, 1958-59, resident in neurology, 1959-62; asst. instr. neurology Albert Einstein Coll. Medicine, Bronx, N.Y., 1961-62, asso. prof., 1969-74, prof., 1974—, prof. neurosci., 1974—; practice medicine specializing in neurology Bronx, N.Y., 1969—. Staff mem., attending neurologist Hosp. of Albert Einstein Coll. of Medicine; instr. medicine Stanford U., 1962-63, asst. prof., 1963-69 Named Lena and Joseph Gluck Disting. Scholar in Neurology, 1973. Office: Albert Einstein Coll Medicine Saul R Korey Dept Neurology 50 E 89th St New York NY 10128 Office Phone: 718-430-2460. Business E-Mail: buschke@aecom.yu.edu.

BUSCHMANN, SIEGFRIED, manufacturing executive; b. Essen, Germany, July 12, 1937; s. Walter and Frieda Maria (von. Stamm) B.; m. Rita Renate Moch, May 7, 1965; children: Verena, Mark. Diploma, Wilhelms U. Various exec. positions Thyssen AG, Duesseldorf, Germany, 1964-82; pres. Thyssen Holding Corp., Troy, Mich., 1982-99; chmn. ThyssenKrupp USA, Inc., 1999—; sr. v.p. The Budd Co., Troy, 1982-83, sr. v.p., CFO, 1983-86, vice chmn., CFO, 1986-89, chmn., CEO, 1989—2001, chmn. bd., 2001—02. Chmn. exec. bd. Thyssen Budd Automotive GmbH, Essen, Germany,

1997—99; v.chmn., exec. bd. Thyssen Krupp Automotive AG, Bochum, Germany, 1999—2001, mem. supervisory bd., 2001—. Avocation: golf. Office: Thyssenkrupp USA Inc PO Box 5084 3155 W Big Beaver Rd Troy MI 48007-5084

BUSCHMANN, WALDEMAR G., lawyer; b. Lewiston, Maine, June 25, 1944; s. August and Elizabeth Lowe King) B.; m. Cynthia C. Cooper, Dec. 25, 1973; children: Christina, Erich. BA, Dartmouth Coll., 1966; JD, Northeastern U., 1972. Bar: Maine 1972, U.S. Dist. Ct. Maine 1972, U.S. Supreme Ct. 1974. Asst. atty. gen. State of Maine, Augusta, 1972-87; ptnr. Weeks & Hutchins, Waterville, Maine, 1987—. Chmn. planning bd. Town of Sidney, Maine, 1978-84; bd. dirs. Maine Children's Home, Waterville, 1992—, Maine Civil Svc. Appeals Bd., Augusta, 1988-97; bd. trustees Inland Hosp., Waterville, 1990—; bd. dirs. Gob. Baxter Sch. for the Deaf, 1998—. Mem. Maine Bar Assn., Maine Trial Lawyers Assn., Waterville Bar Assn. (v.p. 1995, pres. 1995-97), Kennebec County Bar Assn., Rotary. Republican. Office: Weeks & Hutchins PO Box 417 Waterville ME 04903-0417

BUSCH-ROSSNAGEL, NANCY ANN, psychology professor, dean; b. Denver, May 29, 1951; d. Edwin J. and Eleanor (Edison) Busch; m. Stephen Mark Rossnagel, Aug. 24, 1978; children: Amy Margaret, Philip Kenneth. BA, Scripps Coll., 1972; postgrad., Merrill-Palmer Inst., 1972-73; MS, Wayne State U., 1973; PhD, Pa. State U., 1979. Lectr. U. Guelph, Ont., Can., 1973-77; from asst. to assoc. prof. Colo. State U., Ft. Collins, 1979-84; from assoc. prof. to prof. Fordham U., Bronx, N.Y., 1986—, from asst. chair to chair dept. psychology, 1987-96, assoc. dean Grad. Sch. Arts and Scis., 1997-2000, dean, 2000—. Vis. lectr. Fordham U., N.Y.C., 1983-85; project dir. Hispanic Rsch. Ctr., Bronx, 1984-86; cons. N.Y.C. Bd. Edn., 1987—, Office of Substance Abuse Prevention, N.Y.C., 1991-92. Co-editor: Individuals as Producers of Their Development, 1981; editor Research Monographs in Adolescence, 1990-2000; cons. editor Jour. Personality and Social Psychology, 1989-91; mem. editl. bd. Applied Devel. Sci., 1996—; contbr. articles to profl. jours., chpts. to books. Grantee Bur. for Edn. Handicapped, 1978, Colo. State U., 1980-83, Fordham U., 1987-90, Nat. Inst. Child Health and Human Devel., 1993-97, Ford Found., Coun. Grad. Sch., 2004, Sloan Found., Coun. Grad. Sch., 2004. Mem. APA, Soc. for Rsch. on Child Devel., Internat. Soc. for Study of Behavioral Devel., Am. Psychol. Soc., Assn. Grad. Schs. in Cath. Colls. and Univs. (exec. com.). Office: Fordham U Grad Sch Arts and Scis 441 E Fordham Rd Bronx NY 10458-9993 Business E-Mail: gsasdean@fordham.edu.

BUSDICKER, GORDON G., retired lawyer; b. Winona, Minn., Oct. 12, 1933; s. Harry John and Edna Mae (Rogers) B.; m. Noreen Decker; children— Karla E., Pamela J., Alison G., Neal A. BA, Hamline U., St. Paul, 1955; JD, Harvard U., 1958. Bar: Minn. Atty. Aluminum Co. of Am., Pitts., 1958-61; assoc. Faegre & Benson, Mpls., 1961-67, ptnr., 1967-99, ret., 1999. Trustee Hamline U., St. Paul, 1973—. Mem. ABA, Minn. Bar Assn., Interlachen Golf Club. Republican. Congregationalist. Avocations: boating, genealogy. Home: 3833 Abbott Ave S Minneapolis MN 55410-1036 Office Phone: 612-925-2091. Personal E-mail: busdick1@mn.rr.com.

BUSECK, PETER R., geochemistry educator; s. Paul M. and Edith G. (Stern) Buseck; m. Alice E. Bien, June 20, 1960; children: Lori, David, Susan, Paul. AB, Antioch Coll., 1957; MA, Columbia U., 1959, PhD, 1962. Fellow Geophys. Lab. Carnegie Inst., Washington, 1961-63; mem. faculty depts. chemistry and geology Ariz. State U., Tempe, 1963—, Regents' prof., 1989—. Vis. prof. geology Oxford (Eng.) U., 1970-71, Stanford (Calif.) U., 1979-80, U. Paris, 1986-87; spl. asst. to dir. NSF, 1994-95; mem. sci. staff Office of Sci. and Tech. Policy, White House, 1994-95, vis. scholar, Dept. Earth & Planetary Scis., Harvard U., 2001-04. Contbr. articles to profl. jours. Fellow, NSF, 1970—71. Fellow AAAS, Geol. Soc. Am., Meteorite Soc., Mineral Soc. Am.; mem. Am. Geophys. Union, Geochem. Soc., Microbeam Soc., Can. Mineral Soc., Microscope Soc. Am. Office: Ariz State U Dept Geol Scis Tempe AZ 85287-1404 Office Phone: 480-965-3945. E-mail: pbuseck@asu.edu.

BUSELMEIER, BERNARD JOSEPH, insurance company executive; b. Detroit, Feb. 10, 1956; s. Bernard August and Rita Mathilda (Cook) Buselmier; m. Carolyn Diane Karamon, Mar. 22, 2003; 1 child, Andrew Joseph. BBA in Acctg., U. Detroit, 1980, MBA, 1990. Various fin. positions ins. group Auto Club Mich., Dearborn, Mich., 1974-81; various fin. positions Motors Ins. Corp., Detroit, 1981-89, treas., 1989-98, v.p., treas., 1993-98; exec. v.p., CFO, Integon Corp., Winston-Salem, N.C., 1998-99; CFO GMAC Ins. Personal Lines, St. Louis, 1999—. Office: GMAC Ins Personal Lines 13736 Riverfort Dr Ste 700 Maryland Heights MO 63043

BUSER, CAROLYN ELIZABETH, correctional educator; b. St. Paul, June 14, 1946; d. Jerome Alfred and Ella Caroline (Anderson) B.; m. Richard John Ward, Sept. 17, 1977; children: John Jerome Buser Ward, Carl Alfred Buser Ward. BA in English, Carleton Coll., 1968; MS in Spl. Edn., U. Md., 1985, PhD in Ednl. Policy and Adminstrn., 1996. Correctional tchr. Md. Div. Correction, Hughesville, 1970-74, Balt., 1974-76; correctional edn. supr. Md. Dept. Edn. Md. Penitentiary, Balt., 1976-80, Md. Correctional Instn., Jessup, 1980-88; correctional edn. supr. Md. Dept. Edn., Md. correctional pre-release program Md. Correctional Instn. for Women, Jessup, 1988-94; field coord. correctional edn. Md. Dept. Edn., 1994-2001, dir. correctional edn., 2001—. Cons. Am. Correctional Assn., Laurel, Md., 1980; Md. state dir. Correctional Edn. Assn., Laurel, 1988-90; program supr. Prison Literacy, Nat. Inst. Corrections, Washington (designated exemplary program, 1986). Mem. editl. rev. bd. Jour. Correctional Edn., 2002—. Fellow Edn. Behaviorally Disordered Students, U. Md., 1985. Mem.: Md. State Use Indus. Coun., Md. Assn. Adult Cmty. and Continuing Edn., Correctional Edn. Assn. (region II sec. 1986, edit. bd. Jour. Correctional Edn. 2002—), Phi Kappa Phi. Office: Md State Dept Edn 200 W Baltimore St Baltimore MD 21201-2595 Office Phone: 410-767-0458. Business E-Mail: cbuser@msde.state.md.us.

BUSER, ROSE M., elementary school educator; b. Port Washington, Wis., Oct. 2, 1948; d. Arthur Leo and Louise Angela Buser; children: Hajira, Rabiah, Joshua. BS in Edn., U. Wis., Whitewater, 1971, MS in Tchg., 1973; postgrad., Ohio State U., 1978—81. Lic. tchr. Dept. of Pub. Instrn., Wis., 1999. Tchr. Abbott Acad., Santo Domingo, Dominican Republic, 1972; instr. Briam Instituto de Idiomas, Madrid, 1973—74; Spanish tchr. Yellow Springs (Ohio) Schs., 1978—81; instr. U. Houston, 1981—82; immersion tchr. Milw. Pub. Schs., 1990—91; bilingual tchr. Christian Day Sch., San Juan, PR, 1991—92; ESL tchr. Oshkosh Area Sch. Dist., Oshkosh, Wis., 1995—. Coord., family cmty. ctr. Oshkosh Area Sch. Dist., 1999—; pub. spkr, Bhopal, India, 1983; bd. dirs. EvenStart Program, Oshkosh, Wis., 2002—, Lao Hmong Assn., Oshkosh, Wis., 2003—; diversity chairperson AAUW, Oshkosh, Wis., 2001—; at risk restructuring bd. Oshkosh Area Sch. Dist., 2003—; cooperating tchr. U. of Wis., Oshkosh, 2001—; vol. tchr. Newman Club, Chimayo, N.Mex., 1967—69, Orphanage La Esperanza, Mexico City, 1970; bilingual sec. Agencia Antillana, Santo Domingo, Dominican Republic, 1972. Recipient Tchr. of the Yr. award, Target Found., 1998; Healthy Nurturing grantee, Aurora Found., 2003, Assisting Endangered Langs. grantee, Alce Cozzi Found., 2003. Mem.: AAUW (diversity chair 2001—), Tchrs. of English to Speakers of Other Langs. (assoc.), Wis. Tchrs. of English to Speakers of Other Languages (assoc.), Wis. Edn. Assn. (assoc.), Delta Pi. Democrat. Roman Catholic. Office: Webster Stanley Elem Sch 745 Hazel St Oshkosh WI 54901 Office Phone: 920-424-0460. E-mail: busers@mac.com.

BUSEY, ROXANE C., lawyer; b. Chgo., June 15, 1949; BA cum laude, Miami U., 1970; MAT, Northwestern U., 1971, JD, 1975. Bar: Ill. 1975. Ptnr. Baker & McKenzie, Chgo. Mem. ABA (chair health com., antitrust sect. 1989-92, antitrust sect. coun. 1992-95, officer 1995-03, chair antitrust sect. 2001-02, chmn. task force antitrust modernization 2004-), Ill. State Bar Assn. (chair antitrust coun. 1984-85), Chgo. Bar Assn. (chair antitrust sect. 1990-91). Office: Baker &McKenzie LLP 1 Prudential Plz 130 E Randolph Dr Ste 3500 Chicago IL 60601 Office Phone: 312-569-1354.

BUSFIELD, ROGER MELVIL, JR., retired trade association executive, educator; b. Ft. Worth, Feb. 4, 1926; s. Roger Melvil and Julia Mabel (Clark) B.; m. Jean Wilson, Mar. 26, 1948 (div. Oct. 1960); children: Terry Jean, Roger Melvil III, Timothy Clark; m. Virginia Bailey, Dec. 1, 1962 (dec. July 1991); 1 child, Julia Lucille; m. Addie Howard Davis, June 17, 1995. Student, U. Tex., 1943, 46; BA, Southwestern U., 1947, MA, 1948; PhD, Fla. State U., 1954. Asst. prof. Southwestern U., 1947-49; instr. U. Ala., 1949-50, Fla. State U., 1950-54; asst. prof. speech Mich. State U., 1954-60; editl. svcs. specialist Oldsmobile divsn. Gen. Motors Corp., Lansing, Mich., 1960; gen. publs. supr. Consumers Power Co., Jackson, Mich., 1960-61; assoc. dir. Mich. Hosp. Assn., Lansing, 1961-73; exec. dir. Ark. Hosp. Assn., Little Rock, 1973-81, pres., 1981-94, pres. emeritus, 1994—. Adj. prof. health svcs. mgmt. Webster U., 1979-97. Author: The Playwright's Art, 1958, Arabic transl., 1964, (with others) The Children's Theatre, 1960; editor Theatre Arts Bibliography, 1964; contbr. articles to profl. jours.; author profl. motion picture scenarios. Trustee Ctrl. Mich. U., 1967-73, chmn., 1970; mem. Mich. Gov.'s Commn. on Higher Edn., 1972-74; mem. Ark. Gov.'s Emergency Med. Svcs. Adv. Coun., 1975-94, chmn., 1978-84; mem. Ark. Gov.'s Task Force on Rural Hosps., 1988-89, Ark. Dept. of Health Long Range Planning Com., 1988-89; chmn. AIDS adv. com. Ark. Dept. Health, 1990-97; mem. Ark. Gov.'s Task Force Health Care Reform, 1993-96; chmn. Health Data Task Force, Ark. Resources Comm., 1994-95; mem. adv. bd. Ark. Pediat. Facility, 1995-96. Served with USMC, 1943-46. Named Tex. Outstanding Author, Theta Sigma Phi, 1958; recipient Disting. Alumnus award Southwestern U., 1971, Senate-House Concurrent Resolution of Tribute, Mich. Legis., 1973, Bd. Trustees award Am. Hosp. Assn., 1994, Merit award Ark. Hosp. Assn., 1994. Mem. Am. Soc. Assn. Execs., Ark. Soc. Assn. Execs. (pres. 1981-82), Pub. Rels. Assn. Mich. (pres. 1966), Speech Comm. Assn., Am. Coll. Health Care Execs., State Hosp. Assn. Exec. Forum (sec., treas. 1989, pres. 1991), Am. Hosp. Assn. (coun. legis. 1975-77, coun. allied and govtl. rels. 1983-86), San Gabriel Writers League (pres. 2000-01), Rotary (Little Rock). Methodist. Home: PO Box 2267 Georgetown TX 78627-2267 Office Phone: 512-930-1396. Personal E-mail: busfield@cox-internet.com.

BUSFIELD, TIMOTHY, actor; b. Lansing, Mich., June 12, 1957; divorced; 1 child, Willy; m. Jennifer; children, Daisy and Samuel. From apprentice to mem. Actors Theatre of Louisville; mem. Circle Repertory Co., N.Y.C.; founder Fantasy Theatre, Sacramento. Appeared in theater prodns. including Robin Goodfellow (children's version of A Midsummer Night's Dream), Getting Out, Actors Theatre, A Life, Long Wharf Theatre, Broadway prodn. Brighton Beach Memoirs (understudy), TV prodns. Reggie, After M.A.S.H., Paper Chase; TV series include Trapper John, M.D. (role as J.T.), thirtysomething (Emmy award as Outstanding Supporting Actor in a Drama Series, 1991), Byrds of Paradise, 1994, In the Line of Duty Kidnapped, 1995, In the Shadow of Evil, 1995, Champs, 1996, The Unspeakable, 1996, The West Wing, 1999-2000, 2002-03; television movies include Strays, 1991, Calendar Girl, Cop Killer?, The Bambi Bembrenek Story, 1992, When Secrets Kill, 1997, Trucks 1997, When Secrets Kill, 1997, Buffalo Soldiers, 1997, The Darklings, 1999, Stuck In the Middle with You, 2003; films include Stripes, 1981, Revenge of the Nerds, 1984, Revenge of the Nerds II: Nerds in Paradise, 1987, Field of Dreams, 1989, Sneakers, 1992, Little Big League, 1994, Quiz Show, 1994, First Kid, 1996, Wanted, 1999, Time at the Top, 1999, National Security, 2003. Address: care William Morris Agency 151 S El Camino Dr Beverly Hills CA 90212-2704

BUSH, BARBARA PIERCE, former First Lady of the United States, volunteer; b. Rye, N.Y., June 8, 1925; d. Marvin and Pauline (Robinson) Pierce; m. George Herbert Walker Bush, Jan. 6, 1945; children: George Walker, Pauline Robin (dec.), John Ellis, Neil Mallon, Marvin Pierce, Dorothy Walker. Student, Smith Coll., 1943-44; hon. degrees, Stritch Coll., Milw., 1981, Mt. Vernon Coll., Washington, 1981, Hood Coll., Frederick, Md., 1983, Howard U., Washington, 1987, Judson Coll., Marion, Ala., 1988, Bennett Coll., Greensboro, N.C., 1989, Smith Coll., 1989, Morehouse Sch. Medicine, 1989. First Lady of the U.S., Washington, 1989—93;per. & facilities div. Dept. Administration, Washington, 1992. Author: C. Fred Story, 1984, Millie's Book, 1990, Barbara Bush: A Memoir, 1994, Reflections: Life After the White House, 2003. Hon. chair adv. bd. Reading is Fundamental; hon. mem. Bus. Coun. for Effective Literacy; mem. adv. coun. Soc. of Meml. Sloan-Kettering Cancer Ctr.; hon. mem. bd. dirs. Children's Oncology Svcs. of Met. Washington, The Washington Home, The Kingsbury Ctr.; hon. chmn. nat. adv. coun. Literacy Vols. of Am., Nat. Sch. Vols. Program; sponsor Laubach Literacy Internat.; nat. hon. chmn. Leukemia Soc. of Am.; hon. mem. bd. trustees Morehouse Sch. of Medicine; hon. nat. chmn. Nat. Organ Donor Awareness Week, 1982-86; pres. Ladies of the Senate, 1981-88; mem. women's com. Smithsonian Assocs., Tex. Fedn. of Rep. Women, life mem., hon. mem.; hon. chairperson for the Nat. Com. on Literacy and Edn. United Way, Barbara Bush Found. for Family Literacy, 1989-, Washington Parent Group Fund, Girls Clubs of Am., 10th anniversay Harvest Nat. Food Bank Network; hon. chmn. Nat. Com. for the Prevention of Child Abuse and Childhelp U.S.A.; hon. pres. Girl Scouts U.S; hon. chair Nat. Com. for Adoption; mem. bd. trustees Mayo Clinic Found.; hon. chair Read Am., Boarder Baby Project; mem. bd. visitors M. D. Anderson Cancer Ctr.; hon. chair Leukemia Soc. Am., Children's Literacy Initiative; hon. mem. Reading is Fundamental; ambassador at large Americares; honorary mem. Barbara Bush Found. for Family Literacy. Recipient Nat. Outstanding Mother of Yr. award, 1984, Woman of Yr. award USO, 1986, Disting. Leadership award United Negro Coll. Fund 1986, Disting. Am. Woman award Mt. St. Joseph Coll., 1987, Free Spirit award Freedom Forum, 1995. Mem. Tex. Fedn. Rep. Women (life), Internat. II Club (Washington), Magic Circle Rep. Women's Club (Houston), YWCA. Episcopalian.

BUSH, BETTY J., music educator, elementary school educator; d. Calvin and Etherine Bush; children: Patrick A., Jean A. BS, Wiley Coll., 1969; MEd, Tex. A&M U., 1974, adminstrv. cert., 1992. Substitute tchr. Marshall Ind. Sch. Dist., Tex., 1970; choral dir. Gilbert Elem. Sch., North Las Vegas, Nev., 1970—71; choral dir., tchr. English J.B. Hood Mid. Sch., Dallas, 1971—78; tchr. talented & gifted B. Jordan Sch., 1978—79; choral dir. T.W. Browne Mid. Sch., 1979—2005. Mem. supt. adv. bd. Dallas Ind. Sch. Dist., 2003—05, chair supt. adv. bd., 1999—2002. Mem.: Dallas Music Educators Assn. Avocations: piano, music.

BUSH, BILLY, television personality; s. Jonathan and Jodi Bush; m. Sydney Bush; children: Josephine, Mary Bradley. B in internat. studies and govt., Colby Coll., 1994. Host afternoon show WLKZ-FM, NH; host midday show WARW-FM, DC; host "Billy Busy and the Bush League Morning Show" WWZZ-FM, DC, 1997—2001; East coast corr. Access Hollywood, 2001—04, co-anchor, 2004—; host Let's Make a Deal, NBC, 2003. Contbr. The Today Show, NBC; co-host Miss USA, 2003, 04, Miss Universe, 2003. Office: Access Hollywood NBC Studios 3000 W Alamea Ave Burbank CA 91523 Office Phone: 818-526-7000.

BUSH, CRYSTAL REED, lawyer; b. Chgo., Dec. 14, 1957; d. Alonzo and Elmethra (Luster) Reed. BA in History, Roosevelt U., 1979; JD, DePaul U., 1995. Tchr. Chgo. Bd. Edn., 1979-90; pvt. practice Chgo., 1990—; pres. Buree Assocs., Chgo., 1991-96. Fin. editor The Leguenet, 1991; contbr. articles to jours. Treas., chair program com. Women's Entrepreneur Network, Chgo., 1990-91; treas. League of Black Women, Chgo., 1991-92. Recipient Exceptional Contbn. award to Afro-Am. Cmty. AT&T, 1991-93. Mem. ABA, Nat. Assn. Women Bus. Owners (Chgo. chpt.), Chgo. Bar Assn. (dir. young lawyers sect., past co-chair client devel. and firm econs. com., past legislation liaison estate planning com.). Office: Ste 2215 400 N Mcclurg Ct Chicago IL 60611-4343

BUSH, DEBRA W., occupational health nurse; b. Salem, Ill., Dec. 22, 1952; d. Merle D. and Georgia Lee (Johnson) Anderson; m. Thomas E. Howarth, June 16, 1973 (div. Sept. 1979; 1 child, Michael T.; m. Gene Bush, Feb. 14, 2004. Diploma in Practical Nursing, Vo-Tech Teche Area, New Iberia, La., 1972; ADN, Miss. Delta Jr. Coll., Moorhead, 1975. LPN, La.; cert. occupl. health nurse. LPN in ICU Iberia Gen. Hosp., New Iberia, 1972-73, head nurse ICU, 1979-81; charge nurse infection control Bolivar County Hosp., Cleveland, Miss., 1973-79, dir. long-term care, 1981-89; sr. indsl. nurse Baxter Healthcare Corp., Cleveland, 1989-96, Tampa, Fla., 1996—. Mem.: Miss. Assn. Occupl. Health Nurses, Am. Assn. Occupl. Health Nurses. Republican. Baptist. Avocations: reading, singing, cross-stitch, exercise. Office: Baxter Healthcare Corp 7511 114th Ave Largo FL 33773-5129 Office Phone: 727-548-2770. Business E-Mail: debbie_bush@baxter.com.

BUSH, ELLEN D., music educator; b. Orange County, Calif., Aug. 8, 1942; d. David Moy Bush and Mary Ellen Morgan; m. Lewis Dale Norwood, July 27, 1960 (div. Dec. 1990); children: N. Jayne Klossner, Angela Ellen Norwood. *Daughter, Nola Jayne Klossner, summa cum laude, is an administrative nursing director and has recently completed a nursing textbook. She has done volunteer work and community theater. Sister, Laura Bell Sisk, magna cum laude, is an educator who has taught elementary school and art. She has published four books, led divorce and rape recovery seminars, and currently creates college workbooks on tragedy and anger prevention. Brother, Wilson Ellsworth Boatwright, has taught high school and currently works for Human Services. He is an artist and a member of the American Truck Historical Society.* D of Naturopathy, Trinity Coll. Natural Health, Warsaw, Ind., 1999. Instr. piano pvt. practice. Mem.: Tex. Music Tchrs. Assn., Cypress Tchrs. Assn., Music Tchrs. Nat. Assn. (founder campaign tolerance, mediator world peace 1987—). Office Phone: 281-374-9303.

BUSH, EUGENE NYLE, pharmacologist, researcher; b. McKeesport, Pa., Apr. 14, 1952; s. Nyle E. and Rosalia M. (Merlino) B.; m. Janet Rosemary Ruscitto, May 7, 1977; children: Stephen Michael, Rebecca Renee, Timothy George. BS in Pharmacy, U. Pitts., 1977, PhD in Pharmacology, 1981. Registered pharmacist, Pa., Ill. Tchg. asst. U. Pitts., 1978—81; staff pharmacist We. Pa. Hosp., Pitts., 1977—81; pharmacologist II Abbott Labs., 1981—84, pharmacologist I, 1984—87, sr. rsch. scientist Abbott Park, Ill., 1986—88, rsch. investigator, 1988—89, group leader, endocrine pharmacol., 1989—91, sr. group leader endocrine pharmacol., 1991—97, assoc. Volwiler rsch. fellow, 1996—. Co-author numerous publs.; contbr. articles to profl. jours. Mem.: Am. Coll. Clin. Pharmacy, Am. Diabetes Assn., Am. Pharm. Assn., Endocrine Soc., Nat. Eagle Scout Assn., Sigma Xi. Republican. Roman Catholic. Avocations: gardening, photography, computers, bicycling. Home: 816 Bedford Ct Libertyville IL 60048-3002 Office: Abbott Labs R47M Bldg AP13A/2 100 Abbott Park Rd North Chicago IL 60064-6126 Office Phone: 847-937-4599. E-mail: gene.bush@abbott.com.

BUSH, FREDERICK MORRIS, federal official; b. Newport News, Va., Feb. 6, 1949; s. Morris and Dorothy Montony B.; m. Catherine Marie Murphy, Sept. 10, 1977; children— Alexander Murphy Morris, Taylor McGrath, Channing Barbara and Margaret Montony (twins). BA, U. Colo., 1971; MA in Internat. Studies, Am. U., 1974. Clk. Republican policy com. U.S. Senate, 1971-73; legis. asst. Ho. of Reps., 1973; asst. to fin. chmn. Rep. Nat. Com., 1973-74; dep. fin. dir. Pres. Ford Com., 1975-77; nat. fin. dir. George Bush for Pres., 1979-80; asst. sec. commerce for tourism; dep. Chief of Staff to v.p.; pres. Bush & Co.; commr. gen. U.S.A. Universal Expn., Seville, Spain, 1991-92; U.S. amb., commr. gen. Expo 92, Seville, 1992—; assoc. dir. Woodrow Wilson Internat. Ctr. for Scholars, Washington. Founder Rep. Assocs. Chgo.; trustee Am. Ctr. Internat. Leadership; dep. fin. chmn. for George Bush for Pres.; fin. chmn. San Diego host com. Rep. Nat. Conv.; fin. chmn. Reps. Abroad; fin. chmn. Washington bdi. com. 2012 Olympic Games, 1998—; assoc. dir. Woodrow Wilson Internat. Ctr. for Scholars, 1998—. Republican. Home: 8208 Kerry Rd Chevy Chase MD 20815-4808 Business E-Mail: bushfred@wwic.si.edu.

BUSH, GAIL, school librarian, educator; b. Chgo., May 2, 1952; d. George William and Norma T. Fish; m. Robert K. Bush, Sept. 7, 1978; children: Matthew Thomas, Claire Anne. BA in Anthropology magna cum laude, U. Ill., 1973, MLS, 1977; PhD in Ednl. Psychology, Loyola U., Chgo., 2001. Cert. libr. media, Ill. Head libr. Nat. Coll. Edn. (now Nat.-Louis U.), Chgo., 1977—79; mgr. corp. libr. Heidrick & Struggles, Chgo., 1979—82; instr. grad. rsch., reference libr. Nat. Coll. Edn., Wilmette, Ill., 1982—92; curriculum libr. Maine Twp. H.S. West, Des Plaines, Ill., 1992—2002; dir. sch. libr. media program Dominican U., River Forest, Ill., 2002—, assoc. prof., 2002—. Adv. com. Ill. State Libr., 2003—; edits. adv. bd., ALA, 2002—, Tchr. Libr. Adv. Bd., 2002—; goals 2000 cons. Loyola U. Chgo., 1997-2000, lectr., 1998—; pub. cons. Greenwood Press, Westport, Conn., 2000-2002; info. lit. cons. Great Plains Network, Lincoln, Nebr., 1999-2000; mem. adv. bd. Knowledge Quest, 2003—. Author: The School Buddy System: the Practice of Collaboration; mem. editl. bd. Am. Assn. Sch. Librs., 1997-2000; contbr. articles to profl. jours. including Ednl. Leadership, Knowledge Quest, Sch. Libr. Jour., NASSP Bull., tchr.-libr. Voice Youth Advocates, Ill. Reading Coun. Jour. Named Sch. Libr. of Yr. North Suburban Libr. Sys., 1999; Shoah Visual History Found. fellow, 2001—02. Mem. ALA, ASCD, Am. Assn. Sch. Librs. (Nat. Sch. Libr. Media Program of Yr. 1996), Internat. Reading Assn., Am. Ednl. Rsch. Assn., Freedom to Read Found., Beta Phi Mu, Phi Delta Kappa Office: Dominican Univ 7900 W Division St River Forest IL 60305 Office Phone: 708-524-6541. Business E-Mail: gbush@dom.edu.

BUSH, GEORGE HERBERT WALKER, 41st President of the United States; b. Milton, Mass., June 12, 1924; s. Prescott Sheldon and Dorothy (Walker) B.; m. Barbara Pierce, Jan. 6, 1945; children: George W., John E., Neil M., Marvin P., Dorothy W. Koch. BA in Econs., Yale U., 1948; numerous other hon. degrees. Co-founder Bush-Overbey Oil Devel. Co., 1951; Co-founder, dir. Zapata Petroleum Corp., Midland, 1953-59; pres. Zapata Off Shore Co., Houston, 1956-64, chmn. bd., 1964-66; mem. 90th-91st Congresses from 7th Dist. Tex., 1967-71, Ways and Means com.; U.S. amb. to UN, 1971-73; chmn. Rep. Nat. Com., 1973-74; chief U.S. Liaison Office Peking, People's Republic China, 1974-75; dir. CIA, 1976-77; v.p. served under Pres. Ronald Reagan U.S., 1981-89; President of the U.S., 1989-93; spl. envoy for tsunami reconstruction UN, 2005—. Bd. visitors M.D. Anderson Cancer Ctr., Houston. Co-author: A World Transformed, 1998; author: All The Best, George Bush: My Life and Other Writings, 1999. Del. Rep. Nat. Conv., 1964, 69; Rep. candidate U.S. senator from Tex., 1964, 70. Lt. (j.g.), pilot USN, WWII. Decorated D.F.C., Air medals (3). Republican. Office: 10000 Memorial Dr, Ste 900 Houston TX 77024-3422

BUSH, GEORGE WALKER, 43rd President of the United States; b. New Haven, Conn., July 6, 1946; s. George Herbert Walker and Barbara (Pierce) Bush; m. Laura Lane Welsh, Nov. 5, 1977; children: Barbara, Jenna. BA in History, Yale U., 1968; MBA, Harvard U., 1975. CEO Bush Exploration, Midland, Tex., 1975—83; chmn., CEO Spectrum 7 Energy Corp., Midland, Tex., 1983—87; dir. Harken Energy Corp. (formerly Spectrum 7 Energy Corp.), Midland, Tex., 1986; sr. advisor George Herbert Walker Bush Presidential campaign, 1988; mng. gen. ptnr. Tex. Rangers (baseball franchise), 1989—94; gov. State of Tex., Austin, 1994—2000; pres. US, Washington, 2001—. Co-author (with Karen Hughes): A Charge to Keep, 1999. Pilot Texas Air Nat. Guard, 1968—70. Named Person of the Year, Time mag., 2004; named one of most influential people, 2005; recipient Big D award, Dallas All Sports Assn., 1989. Mem.: Delta Kappa Epsilon (pres. 1965—68). Republican. Achievements include first Governor in Texas history to be elected to two consecutive four-year terms; won re-election as Pres. in 2004. Office: The White House 1600 Pennsylvania Ave NW Washington DC 20500*

BUSH, HARRY LEONARD, JR., surgery educator; b. Auburn, Ala., July 11, 1942; m. Ellen Parker; children: Alexander, Charles, Scott. BS, Princeton U., 1964; MD, Columbia U., 1968. Diplomate Am. Bd. Surgery; cert. gen. vascular surgeon. Surgical intern Presbyn. Hosp., N.Y.C., 1968-69, fellow, dept. surgery, 1969-70, resident gen. surgery, 1973-76; instr. surgery Columbia U., N.Y.C., 1975-76, Boston U. Sch. Medicine, 1976-77; asst. prof. surgery Tufts U. Sch. Medicine, Boston, 1979-86, assoc. prof. surgery, 1986-87, Cornell U. Med. Coll., N.Y.C., 1987—. Dir. surg. ICU Boston VA Med. Ctr, 1983-84, staff surgeon 1979-87, asst. dir. transplant svc. 1979-87, chmn. animal studies subcommittee 1980-85, chmn. R & D com. 1983-84; assoc. staff surgeon New Eng. Med. Ctr., Boston, 1979-83, staff surgeon 1983-87; asst. dir. organ preservation lab. New Eng. Organ Bank, Boston,

1979-87, trustee 1984-87; chief div. vascular surgery N.Y. Hosp., 1988—, assoc. attending surgeon 1987—, dir. non-invasive vascular lab 1987—, chief divsn. vascular surgery, 1988-97; asst. dir. transplant svc. Tufts New Eng. Med. Ctr., Boston, 1979-87; chief surg. svc. Lemuel Shattuck Hosp., Boston, 1984-87; cons. med. rsch. svc. Va. Cen. Office, Washington, 1985-86; vice-chmn. dept. surgery Presbyn. Hosp., 1997—. Author (with others): Complications of Thoracic and Cardiovascular Surgery, 1979, Peripheral Vascular Diseases, 1987, Common Problems in Vascular Surgery, 1989, Aortic Surgery, 1989, Current Critical Problems in Vascular Surgery, 1989, Current Therapy in Vascular Surgery, 1991; contbr. over 70 articles to profl. jours. Mem. Am. Heart Assn., 1976—. With U.S. Navy, 1970-73. Westchester Heart Assn. Rsch. fellow, 1969-70; co-prin. investigator VA Merit Rev. Program, 1980-82; prin. investigator, VA Merit Rev. Program, 1983-86, 86-89; co-investigator NIH, 1982-84; prin. investigator NIH, 1988-91, Wyeth-Ayerst Labs., 1989-90. Fellow Am. Coll. Surgeons; mem. Internat. Cardiovascular Soc., Internat. Soc. for Applied Cardiovascular Biology, New Eng. Soc. for Vascular Surgery, New Eng. Surg. Soc., N.Y. Soc. for Cardiovascular Surgery, N.Y. Surg. Soc., N.Y. Clin. Soc., Boston Surg. Soc., Ea. Vascular Soc., Assn. for Acad. Surgery, Soc. Critical Care Medicine, Soc. for Vascular Surgery, Coun. on Cardiovascular Surgery, Soc. Univ. Surgeons, Stroke Coun., Sigma Xi. Achievements include research in arterial blockage, cardiology, drug and surgical treatment for arterial and cardiological therapy, limb salvage, vein grafts, kidney transplantation, renal transplantation. Office: NY Presbyn Weill Med Ctr Dept Surgery 525 E 68th St Payson 708A New York NY 10021-4870

BUSH, HOLLY NEWSOM, management consultant; BBA in Acctg., Tex. Christian U., 1984, MBA in Fin., 1990. CPA Tex. Auditor Coopers & Lybrand, Ft. Worth, 1984-86; sr. auditor McCaslin Wright & Greenwood, Ft. Worth, 1986-88; sr. cons. Andersen Consulting, Dallas, 1990-93; prin. Booz Allen & Hamilton, Dallas, 1993—. Mem.: AICPA, Tex. Soc. CPAs. Avocations: reading, bicycling, horseback riding, piano. Office: Booz Allen and Hamilton 1401 Bellefonte Ln Colleyville TX 76034 Fax: 214-712-6660.

BUSH, JANICE, principal; b. Detroit, Oct. 23, 1947; d. James and Annie Bush. BA, Western Mich. U., 1968; MA, Wayne State U., 1972, EdD, 1997. Cert. tchr. Mich. Tchr. Detroit Pub. Schs., 1969—78, tchr., coord., 1979—84, instr. specialist, 1985, asst. prin., 1985—95, prin., 1975—. Editl. bd. Profl. Women's Network, Detroit, 1988—89; bd. govs. Wayne State U., Coll. of Edn., Detroit, 1988—89; bd. dirs. IN Site, Detroit, 1992. Recipient Golen Apple award, State of Mich., 2000. Mem.: Delta Sigma Theta Sorority (exec. bd. 1966—). Avocations: travel, reading, investment club.

BUSH, JEB (JOHN ELLIS BUSH), governor; b. Midland, Tex., Feb. 11, 1953; s. George Herbert Walker and Barbara Pierce Bush; m. Columba Garnica Gallo, Feb. 23, 1974; children: George, Noelle, John Jr. BA in Latin Am. Affairs, U. Tex., 1974. V.p. Tex. Commerce Bank, Caracas, Venezuela, 1974—79; co-founder Codina Bush Group, Miami, Fla., 1981—93; pres., COO Codina Group, Miami, Fla., 1995—98; sec. commerce State of Fla., Tallahassee, 1987—88, gov., 1999—. Chmn., Dade County Rep. Party, 1984-86; bd. dirs. Safecard Services, 1995-96. Co-author (with Brian Yablonski): Profiles in Character, 1996. Chmn. Miami-Dade County Beacon Coun., 1990-91, vol. Miami Children's Hosp., United Way of Dade County, Dade County Homeless Trust; founder Found. for Fla.'s Future, 1995; co-founder Liberty City Charter Sch., 1995, trustee, Heritage Found., 1995 Republican. Roman Catholic. Office: Office of the Governor The Capitol Tallahassee FL 32399-0001 E-mail: fl_governor@eog.state.fl.us.

BUSH, KAREN LEE, lawyer; b. Denville, NJ, May 29, 1958; BA with honors in English, cum laude, Bucknell U., 1980; JD with honors, George Washington U., 1984. Bar: Calif. 1984, DC 1988, Md. 1996. Assoc. Rutan & Tucker, 1985—86; dep. city atty. Signal Hill & Laguna Beach, Calif., 1985—86; ptnr. Anderson Kill Orlick & Oshinsky LLP, Washington, 1986—, co-chmn. diversity com./quality of life com. Mem.: Md. State Bar Assn., DC Bar. Office: Dickstein Shapiro Morin & Oshinsky 1201 L St NW Washington DC 20037-1526 Office Phone: 202-955-6601. Office Fax: 202-887-0689. Business E-Mail: BushK@dsmo.com.

BUSH, LAURA WELCH, First Lady of United States; b. Midland, Tex., Nov. 4, 1946; d. Harold Bruch and Jenna Louise (Hawkins) Welch; m. George Walker Bush, Nov. 5, 1977; children: Jenna, Barbara. BS in Edn., So. Meth. U., 1968; MLS, U. Tex., Austin, 1973. Tchr. Longfellow Elem. Sch., Dallas, 1968—69, John F. Kennedy Elem. Sch., Houston, 1969—72; libr. Houston Pub. Lib., 1973—74, Dawson Elem. Sch., Austin, 1974—77; First Lady State of Tex., 1995—2001; First Lady of the U.S., 2001—. Established Adopt-A-Caseworker programs, Tex., Rainbow Rooms, Tex.; launched National Book Festival, 2001; speaker Republican Nat. Convention, NYC, 2004. Named one of Most Powerful Women, Forbes mag., 2004, 2005. Republican. Address: The White House 1600 Pennsylvania Ave NW Washington DC 20500

BUSH, LAUREN, model; b. 1984; d. Neil and Sharon. Student, Princeton U. Appeared in fashion mag. including Town and Country, Vogue; model Abercrombie & Fitch, Tommy Hilfiger clothing line, 2002—. Hon. spokesperson World Food Program, UN, 2004—. Office: Elite Modeling Agy 111 E 22nd St New York NY 10010

BUSH, LYNN JEANNE, federal judge; b. Little Rock, Ark., Dec. 30, 1948; d. John E. Bush III and Alice Saville B.; 1 child, Brian Bush Ferguson. BA, Antioch Coll., 1970; JD, Georgetown U., 1976. Assoc. Steptoe and Johnson, Washington, summer 1975; part-time law clk. Nat. Labor Rels. Bd., Washington, 1976; trial atty. comml. litigation br. US Dept. Justice, Washington, 1976-87; sr. trial atty. Naval Facilities Engring. Command, Dept. of Navy, Alexandria, Va., 1987-89, counsel engring. field activity, 1989-96; adminstr. judge Bd. of Contract Appeals US Dept. Housing & Urban Devel., Washington, 1996-98; judge US Ct. Fed. Claims, Washington, 1998—. Mem. Nat. Bar Assn., Nat. Assn. Women Judges, Bd. of Contract Appeals Judges Assn., Bd. of Contract Appeals Bar Assn., Sr. Exec. Assn.*

BUSH, MARGARET EVELYN, elementary school educator; b. Cocoa Solo, Panama Canal Zone, Sept. 10, 1949; d. Grover Freeman Garey and Margaret Elizabeth Fogland, Dick V. Fogland (Stepfather); m. George B. Bush, Mar. 14, 1970 (div. Dec. 1991); children: Cammie Webster, Dawn Hage, Selby. BS magna cum laude, Cameron U., 1996. Nat. bd. cert. tchr. Okla., 2004. With U.S. Civil Svc., 1967—90; religious edn. dir. Ft. Huachuca, Ariz., 1986—91; elem. tchr. Lawton (Okla.) Pub. Schs., 1997—. Religious edn. tchr. Holy Family Cath. Ch., Lawton, 2004—. Mem.: Phi Kappa Phi. Republican. Home: 346 NW 65th ST Lawton OK 73505 Office: Almer West Elem Sch 6092 SW Delta Ave Lawton OK 73505

BUSH, MARJORIE EVELYNN TOWER-TOOKER, media specialist, librarian, educator; b. Atkinson, Nebr., Mar. 12, 1925; d. Albert Ralph and Vera Marie (Rickover) Tower-Tooker; m. Louis T. Genung, Feb. 2, 1944 (dec. Jan. 1982); 1 child, Louis Thompson; m. Laurence Scott Bush, Sept. 22, 1984; 1 stepchild, Roger A. Student, U. Nebr., 1951, Wayne State Coll., 1942-47; BA, Colo. State Coll., 1966, U. No. Colo., 1970; postgrad., Doane Coll., 1967-68, U. Utah, 1973-74, PhD (hon.), 1973; MA in Tchg., Hastings (Nebr.) Coll., 2000. Elem. tchr. Atkinson Pub. Schs., 1958-69; adminstr. librs. and audiovisual comm. Clay County Dist. I-C, Fairfield, Nebr., 1972-81; media specialist Albion (Nebr.) City Schs., 1981—. Mem. Neb. Gov.'s White House Conf. on Libraries. Chmn. edn. adminstrv. bd. Park Hill United Meth. Ch., Denver, also pres.; sec. Denver Symphony Guild, Colo. Symphony Guild, 1990-96. Mem. NEA (life), ALA, AAUW, ASCD, Nat. Coun. Tchrs. English, Nebr. Edn. Assn., Colo. Edn. Assn., Nebr. Libr. Assn., Nebr. Ednl. Media Assn., Mountain Plain Libr. Assn., Assn. Childhood Edn. Internat., Assn. Ednl. Comm. & Tech., Internat. Visual Literacy Assn., Nat. Coun. Exceptional Children, Alumni Assn. U. No. Colo. (life charter), Women Educators Nebr., United Meth. Women (pres.), Am. Legion Aux., Nebr. Lay Citizens Assn. (exec.), Am. NAt. Cowbelles, Nebr. Cowbelles, Internat. Platform Assn., LWV, Women's Soc. Christian Svc., Ak-Sar-Ben, Windsor Gardens Club (Denver), Opti-Mrs. Club (pres.), Optimists Internat., Columbine Optimists (pres. 1987-88), Ea. Star. Address: 1003 E 9th St Hastings NE 68901-4140

BUSH, MARK ROBERT, physician; b. San Mateo, Calif., July 4, 1962; s. Paul Robert and Roberta Sue (Penninsten) B.; m. Christine Stephanie Smith, Aug. 6, 1988; children: Cameron Michael, Alexis Victoria. BA in Biology, U. Calif., Berkeley, 1985; MD, Georgetown U., 1991. Diplomate Nat. Bd. Med. Examiners. Resident in ob-gyn William Beaumont AMC, El Paso, Tex., 1991-95; assoc., attending faculty dept. ob-gyn Duke U. Med. Ctr., Durham, N.C., 1995-98; chief divsn. reproductive endocrinology and infertility Madigan AMC, Tacoma, 1998—; clin. asst. prof. dept. ob-gyn. U. Wash. Sch. Medicine, Seattle, 1998—. Guest rschr. LMC, NIEHS, NIH, Research Triangle Park, N.C., 1997—. Contbr. articles to profl. jours. Maj. Med. Corps., U.S. Army. Mem. AMA (Physician's Recognition award 1994-97, 97-2000), ACOG (Oustanding Scientific Paper award 1993, Best Scientific Paper award 1996), Am. Soc. Reproductive Medicine, Soc. for Gynecol. Investigation (assoc.), Soc. Reproductive Endocrinology and Infertility (assoc.). Home: 4 Redbud Ct Potomac MD 20854-3731 E-mail: maj_mark_bush@smtplink.mamc.amedd.army.mil.

BUSH, MICHAEL, architectural firm executive; Assoc. Tsoi/Kobus & Assoc., Inc., Cambridge, Mass., 1992—99, assoc. prin., 1999—2002, prin., v.p., 2002—. Office: Tsoi/Kobus & Assoc Inc One Brattle Sq PO Box 9114 Cambridge MA 02238-9114

BUSH, NEIL, management executive; b. Midland, Tex., Jan. 22, 1955; s. George Herbert Walker and Barbara (Pierce) Bush; m. Sharon Smith, 1980 (div. 2002); children: Lauren, Pierce; m. Maria Manass, 2004; 1 child, Ashley. BA in Internat. Rels., Tulane U., 1977, MA in Bus., 1979. With Interlink Mgmt. Corp., Houston, 1994—99; founder, chmn. Ignite! Inc., Austin, Tex., 1999—. Office: Ignite Inc 4030 W Braker Ln #175 Austin TX 78759 Office Phone: 512-697-7085. Business E-Mail: nbush@ignitelearning.com.

BUSH, NORMAN, research and development company executive; b. N.Y.C., Dec. 10, 1929; s. Louis and Ida (Trembola) B.; m. Audrey Faith Blumberg, Dec. 28, 1952; children: Stewart Alan, I. Jeffrey, Ellen Gail Dash. BBA, CUNY, 1951, MBA, 1952; PhD, N.C. State U., 1962. Statistician Army Chem. Ctr., Edgewood, Md., 1952-56, RCA Svc. Co., Patrick AFB, Fla., 1956-58, DBA and ICF, Melbourne, Fla., 1962-64, Pan Am Airlines, Patrick AFB, Fla., 1964-72; div. mgr. ENSCO Inc., Melbourne, Fla., 1972-83, pres., chief oper. officer Springfield, Va., 1983-94, chmn. bd., 1989-95. Contbr. articles to statis. jours. With U.S. Army, 1952-54. Mem. Am. Statis. Assn. Republican. Avocation: travel.

BUSH, RAYMOND T., accountant, architectural firm executive; b. Providence, R.I., Sept. 7, 1939; s. Raymond F. and Regina C. (Pearl) B.; m. Barbara Ann Cormier, May 31, 1962; children: Laura Jean, Raymond F., Matthew T., James J., Michael. BS in Acctg. and Fin., Bryant Coll., 1960. CPA, R.I. Auditor USDA, Providence, 1960-66; audit supr. KPMG Peat Marwick LLP, Providence, 1966-69; mgr. system and audit Ludlow Corp., Needham Heights, Mass., 1969-71, asst. treas., 1971-73, v.p., gen. mgr., 1973-80; pres. Recticel Foam Corp., Needham Heights, 1980-83; sr. v.p. fin. and adminstrn. Maguire Group Inc., Providence, 1983—. Dir. Ocean State Bus. Devel.; pres. East Atlantic Casualty Co. Ltd.; cons. Bryant Coll. Small Bus. Devel. Ctr. Mem. R.I. Indsl. Recreational Bldg. Authority; trustee Providence Pub. Libr. Fellow R.I. Soc. CPA's; mem. Am. Inst. CPA's. Roman Catholic. Home: 3 Hayfield Ln Cumberland RI 02864-4114 Office: Maguire Group Inc 33 Commercial St Foxboro MA 02035-2885 Office Phone: 508-543-1700.

BUSH, SANDI TOKOA, elementary school educator; b. Albany, Ga., Aug. 1, 1953; d. Charlie and Beauty (Miller) Bush; 1 child, Allen. BS, Barry U., Miami, 1983; MS, Nova U., 1987; PhD, Union Inst. and U., U. Cin., 2001. Cert. tchr. Fla. Counselor Health and Rehab. Svcs., Miami, Fla., 1979-86; tchr. Dade County Pub. Schs., Miami, 1986—. Tchr., tutor Ind. Children's Group, Miami, 1987—; co-chmn. Hall of Fame Dade County Sch. Bd., 1986—, world difference, 1987—; Miami tchg. fellow Miami-Dade Sch. Sys. Author: (book) World of Poetry Anthology The Sun, 1991; co-author: Experiences with Discrimination: From Deep Within, 1998; contbr. articles to profl. jours.; author: Does the Infusion of Conflict Resolution Intervention Strategies Into a School's Curriculum Effectively Reduce or Extinguish Violent or Aggressive Behavior in At-Risk Students. Miami Tchg. fellow. Mem.: Nova U. Assocs., Nova U. Alumni Assn. (mem. recruitment com. 1987—88, Recognition award 1988), Smithsonian Assocs. (Recognition award 1988), Am. Mus. Natural History (assoc.). Avocations: reading, classical music, walking, jogging, tennis. E-mail: sbush33050@yahoo.com.

BUSH, SARAH LILLIAN, historian; b. Kansas City, Mo., Sept. 17, 1920; d. William Adam and Lettie Evelyn (Burrill) Lewis; m. Walter Nelson Bush, June 7, 1946 (dec.); children: William Read, Robert Nelson. AB, U. Kans., 1941; BS, U. Ill., 1943. Clk. circulation dept. Kansas City Pub. Library, 1941-42, asst. librarian Paseo br., 1943-44; librarian Kansas City Jr. Coll., 1944-46; substitute librarian San Mateo County Library, Woodside amd Portola Valley, Calif., 1975-77; various temporary positions, 1979-87; owner Metriguide, Palo Alto, Calif., 1975-78. Author: Atherton Lands, 1979, rev. edition 1987. Editor: Atherton Recollections, 1973. Pres., v.p. Jr. Librarians, Kansas City, 1944-46; courtesy, yearbook & historian AAUW, Menlo-Atherton branch (Calif.) Br.; asst. Sunday sch. tchr., vol. Holy Trinity Ch., Menlo Park, 1955-78; v.p., membership com., libr. chairperson, English reading program, parent edn. chairperson Menlo Atherton High Sch. PTA, 1964-73; founder, bd. dirs. Friends of Atherton Community Library, 1967-2002, oral historian, 1968-2002, chair Bicentennial event, 1976; bd. dirs. Menlo Park Hist. Assn., 1979-82, oral historian, 1973-2002; bd. dirs. Civic Interest League, Atherton, 1978-81; mem. hist. county commn. Town of Atherton, 1980-87; vol. Allied Arts Palo Alto Aux. to Children's Hosp. at Stanford, 1967—, oral historian, 1978—, historian, 1980—; vol. United Crusade, Garfield Sch., Redwood City, 1957-61, 74-88, Encinal Sch., Menlo Park, Calif., 1961-73, program dir., chmn. summer recreation, historian, sec.; vol. Stanford Mothers Club, 1977-81, others; historian, awards chairperson Cub Scouts Boy Scouts Am.; founder Atherton Heritage Assn. 1989, bd. dirs., 1989-2004, dir., 1989-94; mem. Guild Gourmet, 1971—, Mid Peninsula History Consortium, 1993-95; oral historian St. Andrew's Ch., Saratoga, Calif., 2003—; vol. Los Gatos Meadows, Calif.; family hist. rschr. for writer. Recipient Good Neighbor award Atherton Civic Interest League, 1992. Mem. PTA (life). Episcopalian. Avocations: gourmet cooking, entertaining, reading.

BUSH, SPENCER HARRISON, metallurgist, consultant; b. Flint, Mich., Apr. 4, 1920; s. Edward Charles and Rachel Beatrice (Roser) B.; m. Roberta Lee Warren, Aug. 28, 1948; children: David Spencer, Carl Edward. Student, Flint Jr. Coll., 1938-40, Ohio State U., 1943-44, U. Mich., 1946-53. Registered profl. engr., Calif. Asst. chemist Dow Chem. Co., 1940-42, 46; assoc. Engring. Rsch. Inst., U. Mich., 1947-53; research asst. Office Naval Rsch., 1950-53, instr. dental materials, 1951-53; metallurgist Hanford Atomic Products Operation, Gen. Electric Co., 1953-54, supr. phys. metallurgy, 1954-57, supr. fuels fabrication devel., 1957-60, metall. specialist, 1960-63, cons. metallurgist, 1963-65; cons. to dir. Battelle Pacific N.W. Labs., Richland, Wash., 1965-70, sr. staff cons., 1970-83, sr. staff scientist, 1985-2000; pres. Rev. & Synthesis Assocs., cons., 1983—. Lectr. metall. engring. Ctr. for Grad. Study U. Wash., 1953-67, affiliate prof., 1967-78; chmn., mem. com. study group on pressure vessel materials Electric Power Rsch. Inst., 1974-78; cons. U. Calif. Lawrence Livermore Labs., 1975-79, Integral Fast Reactor U. Chgo., 1984-94; chmn. com. on reactor safeguards U.S. AEC, 1971; mem. Wash. Bd. Boiler Rules, 1972-85; mem. spec. adv. com. for Argonne Nuc. Tech. Pgm., U Chgo. 1994-2002; chmn. piping design com. Joint NRC/Pressure Vessel Rsch. Coun., 1982-90, PVRC Peer Rev. on ASME Code Simplification, exec. com., 1982—, mem. steering com. on fatigue, 1992—, hon. emeritus mem., 1999; mem. nuclear safety rsch. rev. com. NRC, 1988-94; mem. high level waste structural integrity panel Dept. Energy Brookhaven Nat. Lab., 1992-97. Contbr. tech. articles to profl. jours. Served with U.S. Army, 1942-46. Recipient Silver Beaver award Boy Scouts Am.; Am. Foundrymens Soc. fellow, 1948-50; Regents prof. U. Calif., Berkeley, 1973-74 Fellow ASME (hon., bd. nuc. codes and stds. 1983-2000, chmn. sec. XI 1985-90, hon. mem. subcom. XI 1995, exec. bd. NDE divsn. 1984-90, chmn. 1987-88, nat. nominating com. 1988-90, Langer award 1983, Melvin R. Green Codes & Stds. medal 1997), ASM (life, chmn. program coun. 1966-67, trustee 1967-69, chmn. fellow com. 1968, trustee found. 2004—), Am. Nuc. Soc. (adv. editl. bd. nuc. applications 1965-77, bd. dirs. 1984-87, Thompson award 1987); mem. AIME (chmn. ann. seminar com. 1967-68), ASTM (Gillette lectr. 1975), Am. Soc. Nondestructive Testing (Mehl lectr.), Nat. Acad. Engring., Sigma Xi, Tau Beta Pi, Phi Kappa Phi. Home and Office: 630 Cedar Ave Richland WA 99352-3632 Office Phone: 509-943-0233. E-mail: shb2544@bossig.com.

BUSH, THOMAS NORMAN, lawyer; b. Lancaster County, Va., Nov. 13, 1947; s. T. Edwin and Willie Ann (Landman) B.; m. Carolyn Sue Brown; children: Jason, Jennifer. BS in Acctg., Va. Tech, 1970; JD, U. Richmond, 1977. Bar: Va.; CPA, Va. Staff acct. KPMG Peat Marwick, Richmond, Va., 1970-71; sr. auditor U.S. Army, Frankfurt, Germany, 1972-74; pvt. practice acctg. Richmond, 1974-77; tax mgr. PricewaterhouseCoopers, Richmond, 1977-81; v.p., tax counsel Fort James Corp., Richmond, 1981-98, Deerfield, Ill., 1999—2000; chief advisor tax audits Ga. Pacific Corp., Deerfield, 2000—. V.p. Fort James Found., 1993-2000; chmn. corp. matching gift U. Richmond Annual Fund steering com., 1996-97; mem. dept. acctg. adv. bd. Va. Tech., 1991—; mem. steering com. Ctr. for Leadership, Govt. and Global Econs., 1995-99. Mem. ABA, AICPA, Va. State Bar, Internat. Fiscal Assn., Am. Forest and Paper Assn. (tax com. 1986-94), Tax Execs. Inst. (pres. Va. chpt. 1989-90, regional v.p. 1995-96, bd. dirs. 1993-96, nominating com. 1996-97, vice chair IRS adminstrv. affairs com. 1997-99, mem. IRS customer satisfaction task force 1998-99), Tax Found. (program com. 1996—), Va. Soc. CPAs, Va. Mfrs. Assn. (tax com. 1988-99), Civitan (pres. West End Richmond 1982). Methodist. Avocations: coaching, baseball, travel. Home: 5912 Midnight Pass Rd Sarasota FL 34242-8708 Office: Ga Pacific Corp 1919 S Broadway Green Bay WI 54304-4905 E-mail: norm.bush@gapac.com.

BUSH, WES, science administrator; B in Elect. Engring., MSEE, MIT; grad., UCLA. With engring. staff Aerospace Corp.; corp. v.p., pres. space tech. Comsat Labs; from. sys. engr. to v.p., gen. mgr. telecomm. programs divsn. TRW Aero. Sys., 1987—99, pres., CEO, 2001—03; v.p., gen. mgr. TRW Ventures, 2000—01; corp. v.p., pres. space tech. Northrop Grumman Corp, LA, 2003—. Office: Northrop Grumman Corp 1840 Century Park E Los Angeles CA 90067-2199

BUSH, WILLIAM ARDEN, federal agency administrator; b. Ogallala, Nebr., Feb. 1, 1948; s. James L. and Phyllis M. (Sullivan) Bush; m. Carol L. Jensen, June 14, 1970; 1 child, Daniel Arden. A in Bus. Adminstr., Northeastern Jr. Coll., 1969; BSBA, Kearney State Coll., 1972, MBA, 1981; MS in Acct., Okla. City U., 1987. CPA Okla. Gen. mgr., contr. Sullivan-Bush Dept. Store, Ogallala, 1972-73, ptnr., 1973-79; grad. tchg. asst. in acctg. Kearney (Nebr.) State Coll., 1980-81; job office mgr. South Prairie Constrn. Co., Oklahoma City, 1981; agt. IRS, Enid, Oklahoma City, 1981-87, supr. Oklahoma City, 1987—99, agent, 1999—. Pres. W.A. Bush Investment Advisor, Ogallala, 1974—75; instr. supplemental acctg. Rose State Coll., 1990—99; adj. prof. Rose State Jr. Coll., 1990—99. Wrestling coach Ogallala Jaycees, 1975; leader Cub Scouts Am., Ogallala, 1976; chmn. bd. trustees Congl. Ch., Ogallala, 1974. Mem.: Big Mac Sports (Ogallala) (chmn. com. 1978—79), Masons, Rotary (1st v.p. 1979). Republican. Avocations: studying, reading, travel. Home: 11321 N Shannon Ave Oklahoma City OK 73162-2149 Office: IRS 55 N Robinson Ave Ste A Oklahoma City OK 73102-9237

BUSH, WILLIAM GLENN, manufacturing company executive, engineer; b. Lakeland, Fla., Nov. 28, 1937; s. William Baker and Lois (Collins) B.; m. Ruby Joyce King, June 10, 1960; children: Wesley Glenn, William Stuart, Brian Lewis. B in Indsl. Engring., Ga. Inst. Tech., 1960. Registered profl. engr., Calif. Indsl. engr. Procter & Gamble, Perry, Fla., 1960-61, FMC Corp., Lakeland, 1961-62, shop foreman, 1962-63, supr. mfg. engring., 1963-65, mgr. prodn. control, 1966-70, mgr. mfg., 1970-72, gen. mgr. ops. Riverside, Calif., 1972-75, div. gen. mgr. Fairmont, W.Va., 1975-79, corp. dir. bus. planning Chgo., 1979-80, group exec., 1980-81, corp. v.p., 1981-89; chief engr. Durand Machinery, Woodbury, Ga., 1965-66; dir. engring. Mark Industries, Brea, Calif., 1990-92; dir. product engring. Indsl. Dynamics Inc., Torrance, Calif., 1992-1999; cons. engr., 1999—. Bd. govs. mfrs. div. Am. Mining Congress, 1976-78; chmn. bd. dirs. BS&B Engring., 1985-86. Mem. agrl. adv. com. U. Calif., Riverside, 1974-75; mem. adv. bd. Ga. Inst. Tech., 1988-91; bd. dirs. Riverside C. of C., 1973-75, United Way, Riverside, 1973-75, Fairmont C. of C., 1977-79. Mem.: SAR, Soc. Descendants Wash.'s Army Valley Forge, Sons of the Revolution, Nat. Soc. Sons Am. Colonists. Republican. Presbyterian. Home and Office: 201 Ocean Ave # 1502B Santa Monica CA 90402

BUSH, WILLIAM MERRITT, lawyer; b. Long Beach, Calif., June 23, 1941; s. Lloyd Merritt and Barbara Ann (Bufkin) B.; m. Dorothy Irene Vasvary, June 25, 1966; children: Steven Merritt, Amy Elizabeth. BA, Stanford U., 1963; JD, U. Calif., Hastings, 1966. Bar: Calif. 1967, U.S. Dist. Ct. (ctrl. dist.) Calif. 1967, U.S. Dist. Ct. (so. dist.) Calif. 1976. Assoc. Dannemeyer & Tuohey, Fullerton, Calif., 1967, Miller, Bush & Minnott, Fullerton, Calif., 1967-69, ptnr., 1970-88; pvt. practice Fullerton, Calif., 1989—. Human rels. commr., City of Fullerton, 1971-77; mem. site coun., Fullerton H.S., 1986-88. Fellow Am. Acad. Matrimonial Lawyers; mem. Orange County Bar Assn. (dir. 1982-85), Calif. State Bar (mem. family law cons. group, family law sect. 1979, mem. family law adv. commn. 1979-85, chmn. commn. 1982-85, bd. legal specialization 1982-89, chmn. 1987-88). Republican. Methodist. Avocations: computers, walking, body surfing. Office: 110 E Wilshire Ave Ste 210 Fullerton CA 92832-1945 Office Phone: 714-992-0800, 714-992-0800. Business E-Mail: wmbushesq@lawbush.com.

BUSHEE, WARD, III, newspaper editor; b. Redding, Calif., 1949; m. Claudia Bushee; children: Ward Gardiner, Mary Standish. BS in History, San Diego State U., 1971. Sports editor Gilroy (Calif.) Dispatch, 1973—75; asst. city editor/sports editor/reporter/copy editor The Californian, Salinas, Calif., 1975—79; sports editor Marin County (Calif.) Ind. Jour., 1979—82; asst. content editor sports USA Today, Arlington, Va., 1982—85; asst. mng. editor sports Westchester (N.Y.) Suburban Newspapers, 1985—86; exec. editor Argus Leader, Sioux Falls, SD, 1986—90; editor Reno (Nev.) Gazette-Jour., 1990—99, Cin. (Ohio) Enquirer, 1999—2002, Ariz. Republic, Phoenix, 2002—, v.p. news, 2002—. Named Editor of Yr., 1992, 97, Gannett Co., Inc., Pres.'s Ring winner 1992-97, 99-2001, 04. Mem. Nev. Press Assn. (pres. 1993, 94, API discussion leader 1996). Office: The Arizona Republic 200 E Van Buren St Phoenix AZ 85004

BUSHEY, ALAN SCOTT, retired insurance holding company executive; b. Peoria, Ill., Apr. 16, 1930; s. Leo James and Luella Frederica (Brunnenmeyer) B. BA, Augustana Coll., Rock Island, Ill., 1952; MBA, Stanford U., 1954. Asst. prof. mktg. and stats. San Jose State Coll., Calif., 1958-59; dir. econ. and mktg. rsch. Continental Casualty Co., Chgo., 1959-68; asst. v.p. CNA/Ins., Chgo., 1968-72; v.p. CNA Fin. Corp., Chgo., 1972-74, USLIFE Corp., N.Y.C., 1974-84, sr. v.p., 1984-88, exec. v.p., 1988-97. Bd. dirs. Ecumenical Inst., Chgo., 1963-74. Served to lt. (j.g.) USNR, 1954-57 Mem. Nat. Assn. Bus. Economists (coun. 1973-76), Life Ins. Mktg. Rsch. Assn. (chmn. mkt. rsch. com. 1985-87, vice chmn. rsch. coun. 1994, chmn. adv. svcs. coun. 1995), Am. Statis. Assn. (bd. dirs. Chgo. chpt. 1965-67), LOMA (strategic mgmt. com. 1987-93), Brit. Schs. and Univs. Found. (bd. dirs. 1993—, hon. sec. 1995-97, pres. 1997-2001, chmn. 2001—), Caledonian Found. USA (trustee 2000—), Sarasota Yacht Club. Republican. Lutheran. Home: 340 S Palm Ave # 122 Sarasota FL 34236-6741 E-mail: a.scottbushey@verizon.net.

BUSHINSKY, JAY (JOSEPH MASON), journalist, news correspondent; b. Buffalo, N.Y., Dec. 8, 1932; s. Joshua M. and Malka (Coralnik) B.; m. Dvora Apte, Dec. 30, 1952; children: Shay, Aviv, Dahlia. BA, Queens Coll., 1955; MS in Edn., Yeshiva U., N.Y.C., 1959; MS in Journalism, Columbia U., 1963. Mcpl. reporter Times Herald/Record, Middletown, N.Y., 1963-64; copy editor Miami (Fla.) Herald, 1964-66; spl. corr. Chgo. Daily News Fgn. Svc., 1966—73; corr. Westinghouse Broadcasting Co., 1967—69; Tel Aviv bur. chief Westinghouse Broadcasting Co. (now Infinity), 1969—; corr. Chgo. Sun-Times, Tel Aviv, 1978-85, Middle East bur. chief, columnist, 1986-96; Jerusalem bur. chief Cable News Network, 1980-85; corr. Independent News Network, 1985-87, WWOR-TV, N.Y.C., 1987, Sta. WPIX-TV, N.Y.C., 1991-94, Global TV Network (Can.), 1993—95, Toronto Sun, 1994—, Fox TV Network, 1995—, Boston Herald, 1998-99; diplomatic corr. The Jerusalem Post, 1997-98. Tchr. social studies L.I. City (N.Y.) H.S., 1958-59, William C. Bryant H.S., N.Y.C., 1959-62; lectr. journalism Tel Aviv U., 1966-70, Bar Ilan U., 1993-2004; asst. prof. journalism U. Mo., 1976-1981; columnist The Daily Herald, 1996-2000; columnist Toronto Sun, 1994—, Jewish Chronicle, Pitts., 1990—, Intermountain Jewish News, 2005—. Served with AUS, 1955-57. Chgo. Newspaper Guild award for investigative reporting for expose of Nazi war criminals in U.S., 1978; co-recipient Media award for econ. understanding Amos Tuck Sch. Bus. Adminstrn., Dartmouth Coll., 1979; named to Chgo. Journalism Hall of Fame, 2002. Mem. Fgn. Press Assn. in Israel (chmn. 1968-71), Overseas Press Club Am. (award for Best Radio Spot News Reporting from Abroad to Group W Foreign News Service for coverage of Yom Kippur War in Mideast, Joint citation 1974). Home and Office: Rehov Hatsafon 5 Savyon 56530 Israel

BUSHKIN, MERLE JEROME, investment banker; b. Dayton, Ohio, Mar. 21, 1935; s. Charles D. and Eva (Flegel) B.; m. Leone Edricks, Aug. 6, 1961; children: Elizabeth Bushkin Schnitzer, Nancy Louise. AB, Harvard U., 1956, MBA, 1960. Mgmt. cons. Cresap, McCormick & Paget, N.Y.C., 1960-64; planning and mktg. positions Mobil Oil Corp., N.Y.C., 1964-70; fin. v.p., treas., corp. sec. Wollensak, Inc., Rochester, N.Y., 1970-71; v.p., mgr. mergers and acquisitions CBWL-Hayden Stone Inc. (predecessor of Smith Barney and Lehman Bros. Inc.), N.Y.C., NY, 1971—72; pres. Bushkin Assocs., Inc., 1972—. Lectr. in field. Mem.: Harvard Club NY, Woodstock Country Club. Home: 86 Caterson Ter Hartsdale NY 10530-2605 also: PO Box 639 Brownsville VT 05037 Office: Bushkin Assocs Inc PO Box 111 White Plains NY 10602-0111 Office Phone: 914-761-3024. E-mail: mbushkin@bushkin.com.

BUSHKOVA, JULIA, violinist, educator; d. Robert Bushkov and Zoria Schikhmoorzayeva; 1 child, Tioma Bushkov. MusM, Moscow Conservatory, 1985. Instr. of violin Interlochen Arts Acad., Interlochen, Mich., 1988—2000; prof. of violin Coll. of Music, U. of North Tex., Denton, 2000—; faculty/performer Internat. Sch. for Mus. Arts, Niagara-on-the-Lake, Canada, 2000—, Interlochen Arts Camp, Interlochen, Mich., 1995—2000; violin faculty Internat. Sch. for Musical Arts, Niagara-on-the-Lake, Canada, 2000—, Weathersfield Music Festival, Ludlow, Vt., 2001—02, Yellow Barn Music Festival, Putney, Vt., 1997. Musician: (recitals, concerti, chamber concerts) Concerts at: Weill Recital Hall at Carnegie Hall, NYC; BargeMusic Festival, NYC; International Festivals in Italy and Canada; Chamber Music International, Dallas and Fort-Worth, TX; Soloist with various symphony orchestras (Gt. reviews, Radio broadcasts, 2004), (solo recitals, soloist with orchestras) Numerous recitals and concerti throughout Midwest, including: Ann Arbor, Grand Rapids, Detroit; musician: (U.) Performances abroad include: London, Edinburgh, Oxford, Bath, Birmingham, U.K.; Balingen, Bisingen, Frankfurt, GERMANY; New York City, NY; Pittsburgh, PA; Veneto, ITALY, etc.; musician: (violinist) (solo performances) radio and TV broadc performances: WRR-FM (Tex.), NPR's Performance Today, WGVU-TV, Grand Rapids; WBLV, Grand Rapids/Muskegon, MI; WFMT, Chicago, IL; KOTM-FM and KGRS-FM (Iowa), WRUV-FM (Vermont), CBC Radio (Canada). Named Outstanding Tchr., Interlochen Arts Acad., 1990; recipient, 1995. Mem.: Am. String Tchrs. Assn., Chamber Music Am. Office: University of North Texas College of Music PO Box 311367 Denton TX 76203 Office Fax: 940-565-2002. Business E-Mail: jbushkova@music.nnt.edu.

BUSHMAN, JOSEPH CHARLES, artist; b. Grand Rapids, Mich., May 21, 1954; s. Charles Joseph and Francis Clair (Jost) B. AAS in Comml. Art, Ferris State Coll., 1975. With Granny's Kitchen, Grand Rapids, 1970-72, Oven Fresh Bakery, Grand Rapids, 1972-74; artist, camera technician Diocesan Pubs., Inc., Grand Rapids, 1975-79, Unigraphics, Inc., Grand Rapids, 1980; film technician, processor Corp. Color, Grand Rapids, 1981-84; camera man, stripper Forrest Printing, Holland, Mich., 1984-85; dark rm. technician II Amway Corp., Ada, Mich., 1985; lic. residential builder Cambridge Devel. Co., Grand Rapids, 1987-88; with art dept. Ace High Screen Printing Co., Grand Rapids, 1992—. Mem. Astron. Soc. of the Pacific, Grand Rapids Amateur Astron. Assn., Nat. Geographic Soc., Planetary Soc., Cath. Order of Forresters (rec. sec. 1970). Roman Catholic. Home and Office: 1538 32d St SW Grand Rapids MI 49509-2718

BUSHMAN, RICHARD LYMAN, history educator, writer, consultant; b. Salt Lake City, June 20, 1931; s. Ted and Dorothy (Lyman) B.; m. Claudia Lauper, Aug. 19, 1955; children: Clarissa, Richard Jr., Karl, Margaret, Serge, Benjamin. AB, Harvard U., 1955, MA, 1960, PhD, 1961. From asst. prof. to assoc. prof. Brigham Young U., Provo, Utah, 1960-63, 1965-68; postdoctoral fellow Brown U., Providence, 1963-65; prof. Boston U., 1968-77, U. Del., 1977-89, Columbia U., NYC, 1989—, now Gouverneur Morris Prof of History emeritus. Chmn. history dept. U. Del., 1977-83; pres. Mormon History Assn., 1985-86. Author: From Puritan to Yankee, 1967 (Bancroft award), King and People in Provincial Mass., 1985, Joseph Smith and the Beginnings of Mormonism, 1984, The Refinement of America, 1992, Joseph Smith: Rough Stone Rolling, 2005. Guggenheim fellow Guggenheim Found., 1976, Regents fellow Smithsonian, 1984; recipient Bancroft prize Columbia U., 1968, Evans Biography prize Brigham Young U., 1985. Mem. Am. Hist. Assn., Am. Antiquarian Soc., Orgn. of American Historians, Mass. Hist. Soc., Mormon History Assn. Mem. L D S Ch.

BUSHNELL, CANDACE, columnist, writer; b. Conn., 1959; d. Calvin Camille Bushnell; m. Charles Askegard, July 4, 2002. Attended, Rice U. Writer Ladies' Home Journal, Good Housekeeping, Self, Mademoiselle, Cosmo Beauty and Fitness, Family Circle, GQ, Vogue; columnist New York Observer, 1994—98. Author: (short stories) Four Blondes, 2000, (novels) Sex and the City, 1996, Trading Up, 2003, Lipstick Jungle, 2005. Achievements include collection of columns for New York Observer, "Sex and the City", was made into HBO series of same name, 1998-2004. Office: c/o Atlantic Monthly Press 841 Broadway New York NY 10003 Mailing: c/o Heather Schroder ICM 40 West 57th St New York NY 10019*

BUSHNELL, DAVID SHERMAN, psychologist, consultant; b. Whittier, Calif., Jan. 7, 1927; s. David Sherman and Lillian Dudley Bushnell; m. Susan Ratner, Jan. 1, 1984; children: Beckie Lynn Krantz, Kimberlie Anne Laderriere, Karen Jo McCarthy, Douglas Scott. PhB, U. Chgo., Chgo., 1947, MA, 1950. Asst. study dir., survey rsch. ctr. U. Mich., Ann Arbor, Mich., 1953—55; pres. Bushnell and Assoc., Potomac, Md., 1995—; mgmt. comm. cons. I.B.M., N.Y.C., 1955—61; rsch. social psychologist Stanford Rsch. Inst., Menlo Pk., Calif., 1961—64; rsch. dir. U.S. Office of Edn., Washington, 1964—69; v.p. devel. Human Resources Rsch. Orgn., Alexandria, Va., 1971—74; rsch. dir. Am. Assn. of Cmty. and Jr. Colleges, Washington, 1974—78; rsch. prof., ctr. dir. Am. U., Washington, 1979—83, George Mason U., Fairfax, Va., 1983—90; ctr. dir. Human Resources Rsch. Orgn., Alexandria, Va., 1990—95. External evaluator Bowie State U., Bowie, Md., 1995—; bd. mem. Meridian Pub. Charter Sch., Washington, 2001—; fellow Battelle Meml. Inst., Columbus, Ohio, 1969—70, Am. Sociol. Soc., Washington, 1953—89; chmn. Network of Quality and Productivity Ctrs., Gary, Ind., 1990—91; editl. bd. mem. Jour. of Human Resources, Madison, Wis., 1966—70; bd. mem. DC Chpt. Am. Sociol. Assn., Washington; assoc. editor Jour. of Tech. Transfer, Indpls., 1988—95. Co-author: (text book) Planned Change in Education; author: Organizing for Change: New Priorities for Community Colleges, (a model for evaluating tng.) Training and Development Journal (Cited one of best articles, 1991); co-author: (millennium review of productivity trends) National Productivity Review (Millennium Edit. of NPR, 2000); contbr. over 20 articles to profl. jour. Bd. mem. Meridian Pub. Charter Sch., Washington. 3rd class petty officer USN, 1945—46, San Francisco. Recipient Disting. Svc. Award, Bowie State U., 2001, Gold Medal Educator of the 70's, Edn. Mag., 1971, Phi Kappa Delta Sociology Hon., Am. Sociol. Assn., 1952; scholar Honor Entrance Scholarship, U. Chgo., 1943-1947. Mem.: Am. Edn. Rsch. Assn. (hon.; bd. mem. 1972—74), Rochester Pers. Assn. (assoc.; pres. 1959), Ea. Evaluation Rsch. Soc. (assoc.), Am. Assn. of Higher Edn. (assoc.). Achievements include chief arch.and leader, ednl. systems for the 70's; grad. fellowship awarded by the Batelle Meml. Inst. Avocations: tennis, fishing. Office: Bowie State Univ 14000 Jerico Pk Rd Bowie MD 20715 Office Phone: 301-860-3885. Business E-Mail: dbushnell@bowiestate.edu.

BUSHNELL, GEORGE EDWARD, III, lawyer; b. Detroit, Feb. 18, 1952; s. George Edward Jr. and Elizabeth (Whelden) B.; m. Eileen Mary Maguire, Sept. 16, 1989; children: Ann-Elizabeth, Emily Spears, George Edward. BA, Bucknell U., 1974; JD, Emory U., 1981. Bar: Ga. 1981, D.C. 1983, N.Y. 1986. Vol. U.S. Peace Corps, Burkina Faso, 1974-76, tng. dir., 1976-77; staff asst. to hon. Lucien Nedzi U.S. Ho. of Reps., Washington, 1977-78; assoc. Duncan, Allen and Mitchell, Washington, Ivory Coast, Congo, 1981-85, Shearman & Sterling, N.Y.C., 1985-91; corp. counsel Joseph E. Seagram & Sons, Inc., N.Y.C., 1991-2001; sr. v.p., dep. gen. counsel Vivendi Universal S.A., N.Y.C., 2001—. Mem.: ABA, N.Y. State Bar Assn. Home: 1075 Park Ave Apt 2A New York NY 10128-1003 Office: Vivendi Universal 800 3rd Ave New York NY 10022-7604 Office Phone: 212-572-7855.

BUSHNELL, PRUDENCE, diplomat, former management consultant, trainer; b. Washington, Nov. 26, 1946; d. Gerald Sherman and Bernice Edna (Duflo) B.; m. Richard Alan Buckley, Oct. 26, 1979. BA, U. Md., 1969; MS, Russell Sage Coll., 1980. Bi-lingual sec. Embassy of Morocco, Washington, 1969-70; chief sec. U. Md., College Park, 1970-72; tng. mgr. Legal Svcs. Tng. Program, Washington, 1972-76; dir. Cultural Learning Concepts, Dallas, 1976-81; mgr. adminstrv. ops. U.S. Consulate Bombay, U.S. Embassy, Dakar, 1982-86; dir. exec. devel. Fgn. Svc. Inst., Washington, 1986-89; dep. chief mission U.S. Embassy Dakar, Dept. State, Washington, 1989-92; dep. asst. sec. for African affairs Dept. State, Washington, 1993-96; U.S. amb. to Kenya Dept. of State, Nairobi, 1996-99, U.S. amb. to Guatemala, 1999—2002, dean Leadership and Mgmt. Sch., Fgn. Svc. Inst., 2002—. Avocations: gardening, walking, writing. Office: US Dept State 2201 C St NW Washington DC 20520

BUSHNELL, RODERICK PAUL, lawyer; b. Buffalo, Mar. 6, 1944; s. Paul Hazen and Martha Atlee Bushnell; m. Suzann Yvonne Kaiser, Aug. 27, 1966; 1 child, Arlo Phillip. BA, Rutgers U., 1966; JD, Georgetown U., 1969. Bar: Calif. 1970, U.S. Supreme Ct. 1980.; cert. Civil Trial Advocate, Nat. Bd. Trial Advocates. Atty. dept. water resources, Sacramento, 1969-71; ptnr. Bushnell, Caplan & Fielding, San Francisco, 1971—. Adv. bd. dirs. Bread & Roses, Inc., Mill Valley, Calif. Mem. ATLA, ABA (labor and employment sects.), San Francisco Bar Assn. (labor and employment sects.; arbitrator), San Francisco Superior Ct. (arbitrator), Fed. Ct. Early Neutral Evaluator, Calif. Bar Assn. (labor and employement sects.), Consumer Attys. Calif., San Francisco Trial Lawyers Assn., Nat. Employment Lawyers Assn., Calif. Employment Lawyers Assn. Office: Bushnell Caplan & Fielding 221 Pine St Ste 600 San Francisco CA 94104-2705 Office Phone: 415-217-3800. Personal E-mail: rbushnell@sprynet.com.

BUSHOR, MARK ELDON, pastor, writer, consultant; b. St. Louis, Aug. 22, 1954; PhD, Southwestern Bapt. Theol. Sem., Ft. Worth, 1998. Pastor Crossroads Ch., Cleburne. Office: 110 N Caddo Cleburne TX 76031

BUSKIRK, ELSWORTH ROBERT, physiologist, educator; b. Beloit, Wis., Aug. 11, 1925; s. Ellsworth Fred and Laura Ellen (Parman) B.; m. Mable Heen, Aug. 28, 1948; children: Laurel Ann Buskirk Wiegand, Kristine Janet Buskirk Hallett. Student, U. Wis., 1943; BA, St. Olaf Coll., Northfield, Minn., 1949; MA, U. Minn., 1951, PhD, 1954. Lab. and tchg. asst. Lab. Physiol. Hygiene, U. Minn., 1951-53; rsch. fellow Life Inst. Med. Rsch. Fund, 1953-54; physiologist Environ. Rsch. Ctr., Natick, Mass., 1954-57, Nat. Inst. for Arthritis, Metabolic and Digestive Diseases, NIH, Bethesda, Md., 1957-63; prof. applied physiology Pa. State U., University Park, 1963-92, dir. Lab. Human Performance Rsch., 1963-92, Marie Underhill Noll prof. Human Performance, 1988-92, emeritus, 1992—. Mem. sci. adv. com. Pres.' Coun. on Phys. Fitness, 1959-61; mem. applied physiology study sect. divsn. rsch. grants NIH, 1964-68, 76-80; mem. com. on interplay of engring. with biology and medicine NAS-NAE, 1968-74, 82-88; mem. rsch. com. Pa. Heart Assn., 1970-73, 82-86, 87-89, 90-95; mem. Pa. Gov.'s Coun. on Phys. Fitness and Sports, 1978-82; mem. com. on mil. nutrition rsch. NAS/NRC, 1982-90; mem. clin. scis. study sect. divsn. rsch. grants NIH, 1989-92, spl. reviewer, 1992-99; mem. Def. Women's Rsch. Com. IOM, NAS-NRC, 1995. Sect. editor Jour. Applied Physiology, 1974-78, assoc. editor, 1978-84; co-editor Sci. and Medicine in Sports and Exercise, 1974, editor, 1973-75; editor-in-chief, 1984-88, cons., editor, 1989-94; mem. editl. bd. Physician and Sports Medicine, 1974-85, Jour. Cardiopulmonary Rehab., 1980-2000, Underseas and Hyperbaric Medicine, 1988-95, Am. Jour. Clin. Nutrition, 1982-92, Jour. Gerontology, 1982-92, Exptl. Gerontology, 1989-98; also over 250 articles on physiology, revs. to sci. jours. Bd. visitors Sargent Coll., Boston U., 1976-92; bd. dirs. Ctr. Cmty. Hosp., Pa., 1966-70, sec., 1971-72, v.p., 1973, pres., 1974-75. With U.S. Army, 1943—46, with ETO, 1943—46, mem. 3rd Army commd. 2d lt. infantry, France, Germany. Recipient Disting. Alumni award St. Olaf Coll., 1969, Daggs Svc. award Am. Physiol. Soc., 2000; rsch. grantee NIH, 1963-92, U.S. Olympic Com., 1965-68, USAF, 1965-69, Pa. Dept. Health, 1966-67, Pa. Heart Assn., 1966, 76-80, NSF, 1968-70, Nat. Inst. Occupl. Safety and Health, 1969-74; NATO sr. fellow in sci., 1977; named to Athletic Hall of Fame, St. Olaf Coll., 2000. Mem. AAAS, AAPHERD, ASHRAE, Aerospace Med. Assn., Am. Acad. Phys. Edn., Am. Coll. Sports Medicine (citations 1973, 75, Honor award 1984, editl. award 1989, 93, Mid-Atlantic regional chpt. Svc. award 1991), Am. Inst. Nutrition, Am. Physiol. Soc. (pres. environ. and exercise sect. 1987-91, com. on coms. 1988-92, Honor award environ. exercise physiology sect. 1993, Daggs award 2002), Am. Heart Assn. (coun. on epidemiology), N.Y. Acad. Scis., NIH Alumni Assn., Pa. Heart Assn. (rsch. com. 1988-94), Am. Diabetes Assn., Coun. Biology Editors (Healthy Am. Fitness Leaders award 1992), Centre Hills Country Club; fellow Am. Soc. Nutrition. Lutheran. Home: 216 Hunter Ave State College PA 16801-6947 Office: Pa State U 119 Noll Lab University Park PA 16802-6900

BUSKIRK, RUSSELL L., small business owner; b. Huntington, W. Va., Aug. 17, 1954; s. George Thomas (Tom) and Betty Jane (Harris) Buskirk. Degree, U. Mass., 1999, Campbell Ctr., 2003, U. NC, 2004. Mgr., carpenter Advair Construction, Lexington, Ky., 1979—84; restorator, mgr. Beckfords of Charleston, Charleston, SC, 1987—94; owner Buskirk Restorations, Inc., Charleston, 1994—. Spkr., tchr. Charleston Antique Symposium, Charleston, 1999—2004; vettor, spkr. Winter Antique Show, N.Y.C., 2004—05; mem., adv. bd. MESDA, Winston Salem, NY, 2004—. Contbr. articles various profl. jours. Recipient Samual Gillard Stoney award, 1999. Mem.: Friends of Colial Williamsburg, Am. Inst. Conservation, Preservation Soc., Johns Island Park Com. Avocation: surf and white water kayaking. Office: Buskirk Restorations 413 Fleming Rd 12 Charleston SC 29403 Office Phone: 843-406-9861. E-mail: russellbuskirk@msn.com.

BUSNER, PHILIP H., retired lawyer, judge; b. Bklyn., Mar. 26, 1927; s. Joseph and Ray (Grajewer) B.; m. Naomi Marcia Greenfield, June 24, 1951; children: Joan Alexandra, Carey Elizabeth. BA cum laude, NYU, 1949; LLB, Harvard U., 1952. Bar: N.Y. 1953, U.S. Dist. Ct. (so. dist.) N.Y. 1956, U.S. Dist. Ct. (ea. dist.) N.Y. 1958, U.S. Ct. Appeals (2d cir.) 1956, U.S. Supreme Ct. 1974. Assoc. Rein, Mound & Cotton, N.Y.C., 1953, Hess, Mela, Segall, Popkin & Guterman, N.Y.C., 1954-55, Carroad & Carroad, N.Y.C., 1955-72; ptnr. Young, Sonnenfeld & Busner, N.Y.C., 1972-75, Sonnenfeld & Busner, N.Y.C., 1976-78, Sonnenfeld, Busner & Weinstein, N.Y.C., 1978-85, Sonnenfeld, Busner & Richman, N.Y.C., 1986-88; pvt. practice Great Neck, N.Y., 1989-97; ret., 1998. Trustee Asthmatic Children's Found. N.Y., 1978-87; adminstrv. judge N.Y.C. Dept. Transp., 1989-93; arbitrator N.Y.C. Civil Ct., 1990-92, Nassau County Dist. Ct., 1990-95, Suffolk County Dist. Ct., 1990-93. With USAAF, 1945-47. Mem. Am. Arbitration Assn. (arbitrator 1990-92), Phi Beta Kappa. Home: One Todd Dr Sands Point NY 11050

BUSQUET, ANNE M., Internet company executive; BS in Hotel Adminstrn., Cornell U.; MBA, Columbia U. Mktg. mgr. Am. Express, 1978, sr. v.p., gen. mgr. Optima card divsn., 1988—92, sr. .vp., gen. mgr. mdse. svcs. bus., 1992—93, exec. v.p. consumer card group, 1993—95, pres. relationship svcs. divsn., 1995—2000, pres. interactive svcs. and new bus. divsn., 2000—01; pres. AMB Advisors, LLC; sr. advisor InterActiveCorp, 2003—04, CEO local svcs., 2004—. Office: InterActive Corp 152 West 57th St 42nd Fl New York NY 10019

BUSQUETS, JOSE M., physician; b. Ponce, PR, Sept. 29, 1973; s. Antonio R. Busquets and Emma H. Ferriol; m. Ginette M. Pales, June 4, 1999; children: Daniela I., Miguel J. MD, U. P.R., San Juan, 1995—99. Otolaryngology-head and neck surgery resident U. P.R., San Juan, 1999—2004; rhinology fellow, clin. instr. Oreg. Health and Sci. U., Portland, 2004—. Scholar, Harvard U., 1991—95, Nat. Hispanic Scholar Soc., 1991. Mem.: Am. Acad. Facial Plastic and Reconstructive Surgery, Am. Acad. Otolaryngic Allergy, Am. Rhinologic Soc., Am. Acad. Otolaryngology-Head and Neck Surgery.

BUSQUETS, MIGUEL ANTONIO, ophthalmologist; b. Hyannis, Mass., July 14, 1971; s. Miguel Salvador and Anne Healy Busquets; m. Gretchen Elizabeth Gruener; children: Talia children: Marisa. BA magna cum laude, Harvard U., 1992; MD, Duke U., 1996. Med./surg. intern Carilion Roanoke (Va.) Meml. Hosps., 1996—97; ophthalmology resident Washington U., St. Louis, 1997—2000; vitreoretinal fellow Barnes Retina Inst., St. Louis, 2000—02; vitreoretinal specialist/cons. Assocs. in Ophthalmology, Pitts., 2002—. Lectr. in field. Contbr. articles to profl. jours. Recipient Rosenbaum Rsch. award, Washington U., 1999; grantee Lawrence grant, Retina Rsch. Found., 1999. Mem.: AMA, Allegheny Councy Med. Soc., Pa. Med. Soc., Mo. Soc. Eye Physicians and Surgeons, Assn. for Rsch. in Vision and Ophthalmology, Am. Acadamy Ophthalmology. Achievements include research in photodynamic therapy for choroidal neovascularization. Avocations: marathon running, swimming. Office: 500 Lewis Run Rd Ste 218 Pittsburgh PA 15122 Personal E-mail: MGMBusquets@aol.com.

BUSS, DANIEL FRANK, environmental scientist; b. Milw., Jan. 13, 1943; s. Lynn Charles and Pearl Elizabeth (Ward) B.; m. Ann Makal, Jan. 22, 1977; children: Jessica, Jonathan. BS, Carroll Coll., 1965; MS in Biology, U. Wis., 1972, MS in Environ. Engring., 1977, P.D.D. in Environ. Engring., 1985. Registered profl. engr., Wis. Dir. limnological studies Aqua-Tech, Inc., Waukesha, Wis., 1969-72; project mgr. environ. studies Point Beach Nuclear Plant, Two Creeks, Wis., 1972-76; assoc., dir. aquatic studies environ. sci. div. Camp Dresser & McKee, Inc., Milw., 1977—, dir. indsl. service, 1978-90, office mgr., coord. for environ. assesments Milw., 1990—; mgr. Buss Environ. Cons. LLC, Milw. Lectr. on nuclear power and environ., environ. auditing; mgr. hazardous waste superfund projects, dredge disposal planning projects; asbestos insp., mgmt. planner EPA, 1988, nat. accounts mgr. for performance of environ. site assessments for property trans.; instr. environ. site assments according to domestic and internat. stds. with consideration of bus. environ. risk for real property. Author: An Environmental Study of the Ecological Effects on Lake Michigan of the Thermal Discharge from the Point Beach Nuclear Plant, 1976, Environmental Auditing-- A Systematic Approach, 1984; contbr. articles to profl. jours, chpts. to books Mem. ASCE (chmn. site constrn. and remediation implementation manual task com.),Am. Nuclear Soc. (sec.-treas. Wis. sect., program mgr. waste disposal studies, program mgr. for remedial programs involving jet fuel and deicer contamination at Gen. Mitchell Internat. Airport), Midwest Soc. Electron Microscopists, Internat. Soc. Theoretical and Applied Limnology and Oceanography, Internat. Assn. Gt. Lakes Rsch., Am. Indsl. Hygiene Soc., Nat. Assn. Environ. Profls., Fed. Water Pollution Control Adminstrn., Cons. Engrs. Coun. (chmn. liaison com. Ill. and Chgo. Bar Assn., mem. com. for devel. site investigation manual ASCE, sec. ASCE com. to develop remedial design, feasibility study manual), Am. Assn. Environ. Engrs. (diplomate 1990, cert. hazardous materials mgr. 1988, hazard control mgr. 1988), Program mgr. design, construction mgmt., oper. UV/Oxidation system (used for treating herbicide contaminated ground water in Wisconsin), Am. Acad. Environ. Engrs. (Wis. state rep.), Glendale Wis. Econ. Devel. Com. and Bus. Coun., Sigma Xi. Home: 5543 N Shasta Dr Milwaukee WI 53209-4924 Office Phone: 414-559-8808. E-mail: danbuss@wi.rr.com.

BUSS, EMILY, law educator; b. 1960; BA in English, Yale Univ., New Haven, Conn., 1982; JD, Yale Law Sch., New Haven, Conn., 1986. Bar: Pa. 1988, Md. 1989, Ill. 1997. Law clk. to Hon. Louis H. Pollack US Dist. Ct. Ea. Dist. Pa., 1986—87; law clk. to Justice Harry A. Blackmun US Supreme Ct., Washington, 1987—88; staff atty. child advocacy unit Legal Aid Bur., Inc., Balt., 1989—90; staff atty. Juvenile Law Ctr., Phila., 1990—93, dep. dir., 1993—96; asst. prof. law U. Chgo. Law Sch., 1996—2001, prof., 2001—, faculty dir. academic affairs, 2001—03, Kanter Dir. Chgo. Policy Initiatives. Mem. U. Chgo. Athletic Bd., Chgo., 1998—2001, Local Sch. Coun., Blair Early Childhood Ctr., Chgo., 1999—2000, pres., 2000—02; mem. Chgo. Bd. Student and Campus Life Subcommittee on Athletics, Chgo., 2001—02, chmn., 2002. Office: U Chgo Law Sch 1111 E 60 St Chicago IL 60637 Office Phone: 773-834-0007. E-mail: e-buss-doss@uchicago.edu.

BUSS, JEANIE, professional sports team executive; d. Jerry Buss; m. Steve Timmons, Feb. 14, 1990 (div. 1993). Grad., U. So. Calif. Owner, gen. mgr. L.A. Strings, 1981—93; owner, pres. L.A. Blades, 1994—97; pres. Sports Forum Inc.; pres., dir. booking Great Western Forum, L.A., 1995—99; exec. v.p. bus. ops. L.A. Lakers, 1999—. Bd. dirs. L.A. Sports Coun., 1995—. Office: LA Laker Great Western Foru 555 N Nash St El Segundo CA 90245-2818

BUSS, KATHLEEN E., music educator; b. Boulder, Colo., May 31, 1957; d. Frank F. Priest and Charlee M. Amis; m. Harry Dean Buss, June 19, 1980; 1 child, Charles Harlan. MusB in Piano Pedagogy, U. Colo., 1979. Tchr. aid Mountain Shadows Montessori, Boulder, Colo., 1979—80, 1991—92; adminstrv. asst. Haddock Ins. Agy., Boulder, 1980—84; pvt. lic. day care provider Boulder and Niwot, 1984—90; child care referral svc. staff City of Boulder, 1990—91; part-time pvt. piano tchr. Kathy's Piano Studio, Boulder and Niwot, 1976—, full time pvt. piano tchr. Niwot, 1992—. Recipient award, Nat. Guild Piano Tchrs., 1975, Paderewski Gold medal, 1975. Mem.: Boulder Area Music Tchr. Assn. (2nd v.p. 1993—95), Nat. Federated Music Tchrs. (festival chair 1997, pres. 2001—02), Music Tchrs. Nat. Assn. Lutheran. Avocations: running, hiking, skiing, snowshoeing, antiques. Home and Office: PO Box 342 Niwot CO 80544 Office Phone: 303-652-3115.

BUSSACCO, PATRICK L., reading specialist; b. Pittston, Pa., Mar. 17, 1949; s. Archie and Romilda Bussacco. BS, Bloomsburg (Pa.) State Coll., 1971, MEd, 1974; cert. reading specialist, reading supr., Bloomsburg State (Pa.) Coll., 1974. Reading specialist K-12 Old Forge (Pa.) Sch. Dist., 1975—. Lector St. Cecilia Ch., Exeter, Pa., 1990—. Mem.: NEA, Old Forge Edn. Assn. Democrat. Roman Catholic. Avocation: computers. Office: Old Forge Jr H S 300 Marion St Old Forge PA 18518-1693

BUSSARD, JANICE WINGEIER, retired secondary school educator; b. Lowell, Mich., Mar. 2, 1925; d. Carl L. and E. May (Velzy) Wingeier; m. James W. Bussard, June 15, 1947; children: Jane, Jody, Jiselle, Jill. BS, Western Mich. U., 1946. Cert. secondary edn. tchr., Mich. Tchr. bus. edn. Spring Lake H.S., Mich., 1965—86; inventor Spring Lake, 1987—97. Achievements include 10 issued patents in U.S. and 1 in Canada in the field of holography. Mfr. holographic labels for security, authentication and decoration for applications to any substrate. Home: 201 N Fruitport Rd Spring Lake MI 49456-0193 Office Phone: 616-842-5626. Personal E-mail: hologirl25@hotmail.com.

BUSSE, EILEEN ELAINE, special education educator; b. Green Bay, Wis., Oct. 16, 1957; d. Ervin F. Dohl and Elaine I. (Behnke) Richmond; m. John F. Busse, July 5, 1980; children: Jessica Lynn, Jeremy John. BS in Elem. and Spl. Edn., U. Wis., Eau Claire, 1979; MS in Spl. Edn., U. Wis., Whitewater, 1985. Cert. tchr. elem. and spl. edn. Tchr. spl. edn.-mentally retarded Ithaca (Wis.) Pub. Schs., 1979-80; spl. edn. tchr. Walworth County CDEB, Whitewater, Wis., 1980—, Lakeview Elem. Sch., 1991-2000, Whitewater H.S., 2000—. Coop. tchr. U. Wis., Whitewater, 1988—; summer sch. tchr. St. Thomas U., St. Paul, Minn., 2003-2005. Author: Student Owned Spelling, 1991, II, 1992, III, 1994. Mem. First English Luth. Ch. edn. com., Whitewater, 1990-95, 98-2005, chmn. edn. com., 1993-95, mem. ch. coun., 1993-94, 97-2005; active Girl Scouts U.S.A., 1992-2000; advisor sr. high youth 1st English Luth. Ch., 1998-2005. Recipient Excellence in Edn. award U.S. Dept. Edn., 1984-85, Recognized spl. educator, 1998. Mem. Coun. for Exceptional Children, Wis. Assn. Children with Behavioral Disorders, Milw. (Wis.) County Zool. Soc., Delta Kappa Gamma. Avocations: reading, travel, gardening. Home: 455 Ventura Ln Whitewater WI 53190-1548 Office: Whitewater HS 534 S Elizabeth St Whitewater WI 53190 Office Phone: 262-472-8203. Personal E-mail: bussee@charter.net. Business E-Mail: ebusse@wwusd.org.

BUSSE, KEITH, manufacturing executive; BA business, U Saint Francis; MBA, In. U, 1978. Division controller to v.p. Nucor Corp., 1972—93; founder Steel Dynamics, 1993, chmn., pres., CEO, 1993—. Named Entrepreneur of the Yr., Ernst & Young, 1997; named one of the top 10 entrepreneurs in the U.S., Business Week, 1997, the best 5 Undiscovered CEO's, Investor Magazine, 1999; recipient Distinguished Alumnus Award, Indiana University, 1991. Office: c/o Steel Dynamics 6714 Pointe Inverness Way Fort Wayne IN 46804*

BUSSE, LEONARD WAYNE, banker, financial consultant; b. Chgo., June 29, 1938; s. Edward William and Elsie Helen (Weidner) B.; m. Gretchen Guam Beal, Sept. 7, 1963; children: Whitney Lee, Carter Douglas. BS, Purdue U., 1960; postgrad., Northwestern U., 1964-67. CPA, Ill. With Continental Ill. Corp., Chgo., 1963-88, v.p., 1973-81, sr. v.p., 1981-85, head internat. banking dept., 1985; exec. v.p. Continental Bank, Chgo., 1985-88; cons. The Busse Group, Vail, Colo., 1989-93; pres., CEO, bd. dirs. The Pacific Bank, San Francisco, 1993-94; CEO, bd. dirs. First Citizen Bank Ltd., Port of Spain, Trinidad, 1994-96; CFO, bd. dirs. Worldbridge Broadband Svcs., Denver, 1998-2000; v.p. fin. Open Access Broadland Network, Denver, 1999-2001; sr. advisor Headwaters MB, Denver, 2001—. Bd. dirs. Exabyte Corp., Boulder, Colo. Bd. dirs. McGraw Wildlife Found., Elgin, Ill., 1982-92, Vectra Banking Corp., Denver, 1993-94. Mem. AICPA. Republican. Lutheran. Avocations: skiing, hunting, biking, fishing.

BUSSGANG, JULIAN JAKUB, electronics engineer, consultant; b. Lwow, Poland, Mar. 26, 1925; came to U.S., 1949, naturalized, 1954; s. Joseph and Stephanie (Philipp) B.; m. Fay Rita Vogel, Aug. 14, 1960; children: Jessica Edith, Julia Claire, Jeffrey Joseph. B.Sc. in Engring., U. London, 1949; S.M. in Elec. Engring., MIT, 1951; PhD in Applied Physics, Harvard U., 1955. Mem. tech. staff Lincoln Lab., MIT, Lexington, 1951-55; mgr. applied rsch. RCA, Burlington, Mass., 1955-62; pres. Signatron, Inc., Lexington, 1962-87; pvt. practice cons. Lexington, 1988—. Vis. lectr. Harvard U., 1964; lectr. Northeastern U., Boston, 1962-65; mem. Mass. del. White House Conf. on Small Bus., 1980. Assoc. editor: Radio Sci., 1976-78; translator: The Last Eyewitnesses: Children of the Holocaust Speak, Vol. 1, 1998, Vol. 2, 2005; contbr. chpts. to books, also articles; patentee in field. Mem. Town Mtg., Lexington, 1975-93; mem. alumni coun. MIT, 1965-72; bd. overseers Mus. of Sci., Boston, 1989-95; vol. exec. Internat. Exec. Svc. Corps., 1993, 94, 95. With Free Polish Forces, 1942-46. Fellow IEEE (life fellow, chmn. Boston sect. 1994-95, vice chmn. life members com. 2005). Home and Office: 2 Forest St Lexington MA 02421-4911 *I was a child-refugee, an adolescent-soldier, a student-immigrant, a young engineer and an adult entrepreneur. In every phase of my life I was blessed with the friendship and support of many wonderful people from various walks of life. Even in the darkest moments I had faith that each of us could improve the world a little.*

BUSSIERE, BRUCE EMILE, protective services official; b. Holyoke, Mass. s. Emile Oscar Jr. and Beverly Ann B.; m. Lyn Madlyn, Nov. 29, 1981; children: Heather Ann, Zachary Joseph, Courtney Lyn, Brittney Marie. AS, Springfield Tech. C.C., 1990. Correctional officer Conn. Dept. Corrections, Somers, 1981-87, lt., shift supr., 1982-90, lt. ops. Enfield, 1990-93, capt., staff comdr. Windsor Locks, 1993-95, capt. ops. Somers, 1995-96, chief tactical ops. Wethersfield, 1996—. Head coach Agawam (Mass.) Youth Football, 1996—; coach Agawam Little League, 1994-2002; asst. coach Agawam High Sch. Football, 1996—. Mem. U.S. Correctional Tactical Officers Assn. (pres. 1999-2001), Am. Football Coaches Assn., Nat. Youth Sports Coun. Republican. Roman Catholic. Avocations: reading, football, baseball, hockey. Home: 30 Elbert Rd Agawam MA 01001 Office: Conn Dept Corrections 24 Walcott Hill Rd Wethersfield CT 06109 E-mail: bruce.bussiere@po.state.ct.us.

BUSSIERE, EMILE R., lawyer; b. Manchester, N.H., May 16, 1932; s. Joseph and Emere (Gagnon) B.; m. Joan H. Blais, Aug. 16, 1969; children—Jaqueline, Denise, Emile R., Michelle, Christine. J.D., Boston Coll., 1954. Bar: N.H. 1954. U.S. commr. U.S. Dist. Ct. N.H., 1959-63; county atty. County of Hillsborough (N.H.), 1963-68; practice law, Manchester. Democratic nominee for Gov. N.H., 1968. Served to pfc. U.S. Army, 1956-58. Mem. N.H. Bar Assn. Roman Catholic. Office: 15 North St Manchester NH 03104-3016

BUSSINO, MELINDA HOLDEN, human services administrator; b. Boston, Apr. 20, 1946; d. Sharon Virtulan and Grace (Fitzgerald) Holden; m. Louis Logue Doyle, Feb. 14, 1974 (dec. Oct. 1980); children: Sarah, Joseph; m. Fred John Bussino, Sept. 22, 1998 (dec. Jan. 2000). BA in Psychology, U. N.H., 1968. Dir. outreach and tng. Stratford County Cmty. Action, Somersworth, N.H., 1968-73; trainer, cons. New Eng. Regional Commn., Boston, 1971-73; office mgr. Beacon Banjo Co., Westminster, Vt., 1980-88; asst. to pastor United Meth. Ch., Brattleboro, Vt., 1985-89; exec. dir. Brattleboro Area Drop In Ctr., 1989—; cons. Putney, Vt., 1994—. Chmn. Brattleboro Human Resource Coun., 1990—; bd. dirs., past pres. Vt. Affordable Housing Coalition, 1990—, Vt. Campaign to End Child Hunger, 1991-99; vice chair Windham Regional Commn., Brattleboro, 1995—; organizer, bd. dirs. N.H. Low Income Advocacy Coun., 1972-73, Operation Low Income People, N.H., 1969-73; adv. coun., bd. dirs. Vt. Protection Advocacy, Montpelier, Vt., 1995-2001; vice chair Westminster (Vt.) Planning Commn., 2003—. Recipient Vt. Woman of Distinction award, 1996, Humanitarian award Brattleboro Pastoral Counseling Ctr., 2001. Democrat. Methodist. Avocations: gardening, cooking, grandchildren, skiing. Home: PO Box 387 Putney VT 05346-0387 Office: Brattleboro Area Drop In Ctr PO Box 175 Brattleboro VT 05302-0175 Office Phone: 800-852-4286 x103. Business E-Mail: badicmelinda@together.net.

BUSSY, CARVEL DE, retired military officer, educator; b. Champaign, Ill., Oct. 29, 1919; s. Martin Kaucher Busey and Raye Hanley; m. Elisabeth de Bussy, Oct. 9, 1968 (dec. Oct. 1998); m. Shirley de Bussy, Aug. 31, 1999; children: Bruce, Armand, Yvonne. BA, Ohio State U., 1940, MA, 1942; PhD, Cath. U., 1969. Commd. 2d lt. U.S. Army, 1942, advanced through grades to lt. col., ret.; mil. attaché Am. Embassy, Saigon, Indochina, 1954-56; prof. D.C. Tchrs. Coll., Washington, 1967-79, Cath. U., Washington, 1980—, Georgetown U., Washington, 1997—. Translator, editor East European Monographs, Columbia U. Press, Bradenton, Fla., 1987—, Return to the Center, 1993, Crime at Mayerling, 1995; adv. bd. Am. Biog. Inst., Raleigh, N.C., 1995—; comms. commn. Interallied Confederation of Res. Officers, Brussels, 1978—. Author: Prague Sunset, 1998. Chmn., divsn. fgn. langs. D.C. Tchrs. Coll., Washington, 1974-79. Named Officier Acad. Palsm Rep. of France, 1991, Chevalier, 1983. Mem. MLA (life), Res. Officers Assn. (commn. mem. 1978—), Union Interalliée (diplomatic), Diplomatic and Consular Officers (ret.), Officers Club, German Studies Assn. (sect. chmn.), Rocky Mountain Modern Lang. Assn. (sect. chair 1980—), Phi Beta Kappa, Phi Alpha Theta, Eta Simga Phi, Phi Eta Sigma. Avocations: music, piano, equitation. Home: 3901 Connecticut Ave NW Washington DC 20008 Office: Met Coll Cath U of Am Michigan Ave NE Washington DC 20064

BUSTAMANTE, CRUZ M., lieutenant governor; b. Dinuba, Calif., Jan. 4, 1953; s. Cruz and Dominga Bustamante Jr.; m. Arcelia De La Pena; children: Leticia, Sonia, Marisa. BA, Fresno State U. Past intern for Congressman B.F. Sisk, Washington; formerly with Fresno employment and tng. commn. City of Fresno, past program dir. summer youth employment tng. program, 1977—83; past dist. rep. Congressman Rick Lehman and Assemblyman Bruce Bronzan State of Calif.; mem. Calif. State Assembly, 1993, spkr. of assembly, 1996-98; lt. gov. State of Calif., 1998—. Mem. U.S. Census Monitoring Bd. Trustee Calif. State U.; regent U. Calif.; chair State Lands Commn.; vice chair Aerospace States Assn. Named Legislator of Yr. Assn. Mexican Am. Educators, U. Calif. Alumni Assn.; recipient True Am. Role Model award Mexican Am. Polit. Assn., Calif. Coastal Hero award, Pres.'s award NAACP, Friend of Labor award Mexican Am. Polit. Assn. Democrat. Office: State Capitol Rm 1114 Sacramento CA 95814 also: 300 S Spring St Ste 12702 Los Angeles CA 90013 Address: 2550 Mariposa Mall Rm 5006 Fresno CA 93721 also: 701 B St San Diego CA 92101 Office Phone: 916-445-8994. Business E-Mail: Cruz.Bustamante@ltg.ca.gov.

BUSTAMANTE, NESTOR, lawyer; b. Havana, Cuba, Apr. 20, 1960; came to the U.S., 1961; s. Nestor and Clara Rosa (Sanchez) B.; m. Marilyn Gonzalez, Sept. 20, 1986; children: Tiffany Alexandra, Nestor C. AA, U. Fla., 1980, BS in Journalism, 1982, JD, 1985. Bar: Fla. 1986, U.S. Dist. Ct. (so. dist.) Fla. 1989, U.S. Supreme Ct. 1991. Asst. state atty. State Atty.'s Office 11th Cir., Miami, 1986-88; juvenile serious offender prosecutor State Atty.'s Office, Miami, 1987-88, spl. prosecutor, gang prosecutor, 1987-88; asst. divsn. chief State Atty.'s Office-11th Jud. Cir., Miami, 1987-88; of counsel Fernandez-Caubi, Fernandez & Aguilar et al., Miami, 1988-89; atty. Ferencik, Libanoff, Brandt, Bustamante and Williams PA, Ft. Lauderdale, Fla., 1989—, ptnr., 1996—. Mem. code and rules of evidence com. The Fla. Bar, 1989—90, jud. evaluation com., 2000; vice chmn. Dade County Constrn. Trades Qualifying Bd.; adj. faculty dept. constrn. mgmt. Fla. Internat. U. Contbr. articles to newsletters. Vice chmn. Miami-Dade Constrn. Trades Qualifying Bd. Named Hon. mem. Quien es Quien Publs., Inc., N.Y.C., 1990. Mem. ATLA (scoring judge nat. finals student trial advocacy competition 1994, 95), Fed. Bar Assn., Dade County Bar Assn. (mem. juvenile divsn. com. 1988-92, mem. media and pub. rels. com. 1989-91, mem. constrn. law com. 1990-91), Phi Delta Phi, U. Fla. Alumni Assn. Office: Ferencik Libanoff Brandt Bustamante & Williams PA 150 S Pine Island Rd Ste 400 Fort Lauderdale FL 33324-2667 Office Phone: 305-949-8003. Business E-Mail: nbustamante@flbbwlaw.com. E-mail: flbbnb@mindspring.com.

BUSTER, CHAROLETT ANN, minister, medical/surgical nurse; b. Pocahontas, Ark., June 18, 1946; d. Charles Edward and Mary Jewel (Milliron) Clatterbaugh; m. Franklin Dee Buster, July 23, 1964 (dec.); children: Janet, Kirk, Patricia, Matthew. AA in Nursing, Shasta Coll., 1987. RN Calif., cert. coronary care, critical care nurse, Calif. Tchr., prin. h.s. Enterprise Christian Sch., Redding, Calif., 1979—89; relief charge nurse Redding Med. Ctr., 1987—97; minister, fgn. missionary to Asia United Pentecostal Ch. Internat., Hazelwood, Mo., 1997—. Home: 1560 Cordova St Anderson CA 96007

BUSTER, JOHN EDMOND, obstetrician, medical researcher; b. Oxnard, Calif., July 18, 1941; s. Edmund B. and Beatrice (Keller) B. Student, Stanford U., 1959-62; MD, UCLA, 1966. Diplomate Am. Bd. Obstetrics and Gynecology. Intern Harbor UCLA Med. Ctr., Torrance, Calif., 1966-67, resident, 1967-71, rsch. fellow, 1971-73, faculty, 1975—; prof. ob-gyn. UCLA Sch. Medicine, 1983, U. Tenn., Memphis, 1987-94; prof. ob-gyn., dir. divsn. reproductive endocrinology Baylor Coll. Medicine, Houston, 1994—; div. divsn. reproductive endocrinology UCLA Sch. Medicine. Examiner Am. Bd. Ob-Gyn. Contbr. articles to profl. jours. Served to lt. col. U.S. Army, 1973-75. Mem. Am. Gynecologic and Obstet. Soc., Soc. for Gynecologic Investigation. Presbyterian. Office: Baylor Coll Medicine 6550 Fannin St Ste 801 Houston TX 77030-2739 E-mail: jbuster@bcm.tmc.edu.

BUSTIN, EDOUARD JEAN, political scientist, educator; b. Hollogne aux Pierres, Belgium, Apr. 9, 1933; came to U.S., 1961; s. Maurice and Mariette (De Graeve) B.; m. Francine Lekeu, Apr. 13, 1957 (dec. 1984); children: Denis, Olivier; m. Marisol Maura, Nov. 16, 1991. Cand.Phil., U. Liege, 1953, D. en Droit, 1956, Lic.Sc. Diplomat., 1957. Asst. in pub. law and adminstrn. U. Liege, 1956-59; atty. in Liege, 1956-59; sr. lectr., then vis. prof. U. Officielle du Congo, 1959-71; vis. lectr. polit. sci. UCLA, 1961-63; mem. faculty Boston U., 1963—, prof. polit. sci., 1970—, chmn. dept., 1977-82, 86-87, asso. African Studies Ctr., 1963—. Dir. Francophone Africa Rsch. Group, 1993—; vis. prof. U. de Bordeaux, 1996-97. Author: Lunda Under Belgian Rule: The Politics of Ethnicity, 1975; co-author: Five African States: Responses to Diversity, 1963. Decorated officer Palmes Académiques (France). Mem. African Studies Assn., Centre d'Etudes d'Afrique Noire, Inst. Africain. Office: 270 Bay State Rd Boston MA 02215-1403 E-mail: ebustin@bu.edu.

BUSTIN, GEORGE LEO, lawyer; b. Perth Amboy, N.J., Feb. 10, 1948; s. George and Agnes W. (Bulvanoski) B.; m. Halina Orestovna Kaniuka, July 9, 1979; children: Michael G., Alexander G. AB summa cum laude, Princeton U., 1970; JD magna cum laude, Harvard U., 1973. Bar: N.Y. 1973, U.S. Dist. Ct. (so. dist.), U.S. Ct. Appeals ((2nd cir.), 1974. Assoc. Cleary, Gottlieb, Steen & Hamilton, N.Y.C., 1973-81, ptnr., 1982-84; vis. prof. Princeton (N.J.) U., 1991; ptnr. Cleary, Gottlieb, Steen & Hamilton, Brussels, 1984-90, 1992—; chair Brussels chpt. Internat. divsn. N.Y. State Bar Assn., 1996—. Chair Princeton Alumni Schs. Com., Belgium, 1998—; dir. Sabre Found. (Europe) S.p.r.l. Author: Business Transactions with the USSR, 1975, International Business Transactions, 1980, International Financial Law Review, 1990, Insights, 1990. Mem. ABA (vice chair European law com. 2003—, co-chair fall meeting of sect. internat. law and practice 2003, Spl. Achievement award 2004), Cercle Gaulois Artistique et Litteraire, Harvard Law Sch. Assn. (sec. Brussels 1989-92), N.Y. State Bar Assn., Assn. Bar City N.Y. (co-chair coms. on rels. with European bars 2001—04), Ordre Francais du barreau de Bruxelles, Brussels Sports Assn. (bd. dirs. 1996-98). Home: 39 Rue de La Gendarmerie 1380 Lasne Belgium Office: Cleary Gottlieb Steen & Hamilton 57 Rue de La Loi 1040 Brussels Belgium Office Phone: 322 287 2000. Business E-Mail: gbustin@cgsh.com.

BUSTOS, CRYSTL, softball player; b. Canyon Country, Calif., Sept. 8, 1977; Student, Palm Beach Cmty. Coll., Lake Worth, Fla. Profl. softball player Orlando Wahoos, WPSL, 1998, Akron Racers, WPSL, 1999; softball player US Women's Elite Team, 2002; mem. U.S.A. Women's Softball Team, Athens Olympics, Greece, 2004. Named two-time first team All-American, Nat. Jr. Coll. Athletic Assn., 1998, two-time Player of Yr., 1998, MVP, WPSL, 1998; recipient Gold medalist, Olympic Games, Sydney, 2000, Pan Am. Games, 2003. Achievements include member of the Orlando Wahoos WPSL Championship Team in 1998; member of the U.S.A. Women's Softball Gold Medal Team at the Sydney Olympics in 2000.

BUSTOS, RUDOLPH R., health facility administrator; s. Maria T. and Jose R. Bustos; 1 child, Alan Otto-Raymond. BA, Westfield State Coll., 1968; MEd, Springfield Coll., 1971; PhD, Capella U., 2001—. LCSW Mass., 2002; cert. sch. psychologist Mass., 1974, S.C., 2001. Supr. Mass. Dept. Social Svcs., South Yarmouth, 1980—98; coord. psychoeducational svcs. High Plains Mental Health Ctr., Hays, Kans., 2001—. Lectr. Petach Tikvah Day Care Ctr. for Elderly, Israel, 2000—00; adj. prof. Limestone Coll., Gaffney, SC, 2000—01, Ft. Hays State U., Hays, 2001—; presenter in field. Actor: (plays) Jesus Christ Superstar. Grant writer Cherokee County ARC, Gaffney, 2000—01, Cherokee Suicide Intervention Ctr., 2000—01, Cape Cod Therapeutic Riding Ctr., Brewster, Mass., 1998—2000; sixth degree black belt U.S. Karate Assn., Sagamore, Mass., 1996. With U.S. Army, 1968—70. Mem.: AAUP (assoc.), Coun. Exceptional Children (assoc.), Am. Ednl. Rsch. Assn. (assoc.), U.S. Karate Assn. (life). Achievements include development of Virtual Course: Teaching Young Hispanic CHildren with Special Needs; research in Survey research about MIT's OpenCourseWare; Distance Education in the Military; Presidential Sports Award in Karate, 1994; Black Belt in Karate 1987. Office: Fort Hays State U 600 Park St Hays KS 67601 Business E-Mail: rbustos@fhsu.edu.

BUSTREO, FLAVIA, epidemiologist; b. Padua, Italy, Aug. 17, 1961; d. Lino and Maria Bustreo. Grad. in Communicable Disease Epidemiology, London Sch. of Hygiene and Tropical Medicine, 1994; grad., CUAMM Coll., Padova, Italy, 1993; postgrad. in sports medicine & rehab., U. Padova, Italy, 1990, grad. in Medicine and Surgery with honors, 1987. Clinician Italian Assn. of Physicians, 1987. Clinician in internal medicine Inst. Gris, Treviso, Italy, 1990—91; sports medicine and rehab. physician Ctr. di Medicina Dello Sport, Venice, Italy, 1990—93; clinician rschr. Regional U. Ctr. of Sports Medicine, Padova, Italy, 1990—93; med. officer in the integrated program on communicable diseases WHO, Copenhagen, 1994—95, med. officer in the global tb program Geneva, 1995—97, med. officer in child health Khartoum, Sudan, 1997—99; sr. pub. health specialist World Bank Hdqs., Washington, 1999—; dep. dir. Child Survival Partnership, NYC, 2004—. Presenter in field. Contbr. articles to profl. jours. Sec. of Venice sect. Interat. Physicians forPrevention of Nuc. War, Venice, 1990—2005; vol. Italian NGOs, Padova, 1992—93, Rijeka, Croatia, 1991—93; mem. of del. to Iraq to assess the situation of children in the country after the war and the sanctions Internat. Physicians for the Prevention of Nuc. War, Italy, 1992. Recipient Bank award for Capacity Bldg. for Sr. WHO and World Bank Staff, World Bank, 2000, Bank award for Senegal Cmty. Nutrition Project, 2002, Bank award for Preparation of the Healthy Start in Life Conf., 2002; scholar 3 Yr. Scholarship For Postgrad. Med. Studies, Italian Ministry of Universities and Sci. Rsch., 1988-1990. Avocation: languages. Office Phone: 202-458-2175. Personal E-mail: fbustreo@worldbank.org.

BUSWELL, ARTHUR LEE, psychiatrist; b. Okla. City, Nov. 13, 1951; s. Arthur Wilcox and Loleta JoAnn Buswell; m. Catherine Margaret Cotton, Nov. 10, 1995. BA in History, U. Okla., 1974, BA in German, 1975, MD, 1987. Bd. cert. Am. Bd. Psychiatry and Neurology, 1997. Intern residency in psychiatry Tulane U., New Orleans, 1987—91, fellow geriatric neuropsychiatry, 1992; pvt. practice Enid, Okla.; med. dir. Generations Geriatric Psychiatry, 1993—98, Child and Adolescent Residential Ctr., Meadow Lake, 1996; staff psychiatrist N.W. Okla. Behavioral Health Ctr., Woodward, Okla., 1993—94. Cons. psychiatrist Ponca Tribal Health Ctr., Ponca City, Okla., 2000—03, No. Okla. Resource Ctr., Enid, 1993—2003. ILT field arty. U.S. Army, 1975—78, Italy. Mem.: Am. Assn. for the Advancement of Sci., Math. Assn. of Am., Am. Psychiatric Assn. Independent. Avocations: reading, writing, languages, statistical analysis. Office: PMB 154 1610 S 31st St Ste 102 Temple TX 76504 Home: 5200 Indian Springs Dr Temple TX 76502-6518 Office Phone: 254-778-4811. Business E-Mail: arthur.buswell@med.va.gov.

BUSWELL, ARTHUR WILCOX, physician, surgeon; b. Oklahoma City, Jan. 6, 1926; s. Albert Currier and Enid May (Scott) Buswell; m. Loleta JoAnn Sherrill, June 11, 1950; children: Arthur Lee, Robert Joseph, Barbara JoAnn, Brian A., Gayla, Richard; m. Jane Marie Fuksa, Mar. 1, 1969. Intern Fitzsimons Army Hosp., Aurora, Colo., 1952—53; surg. resident Wesley Hosp., Oklahoma City, 1954—55; practice medicine and surgery Hennessey, Okla., 1955—63; dep. surgeon Ft. Wainwright and Yukon Command, 1963—65; chief staff Kingfisher Cmty. Hosp., 1956—57; supt. health Kingfisher County, 1960—61; chief profl. svc. Bassett Army Hosp., 1963—65; div. surgeon 1st Armored Div., Ft. Hood, Tex., 1965—67; 1st Inf. Div. Vietnam, 1967—68; med. project officer U.S. Army Combat Devels. Command Experimentation Command, Ft. Ord, Calif., 1968—72; also chief human factors div. and chief experimentation div. of experimentation command; chief profl. svcs. Reynolds Army Hosp., Ft. Sill, Okla., 1972—73; comdr. med. dept. activities Ft. Stewart, Ga., 1973—77; chief profl. svcs. Kenner Army Hosp., Ft. Lee, Va., 1977—78; comdr. med. dept. activities Alaska, 1979—83. Adj. asst. prof. med. scis. Baylor U., 1973—. Mem. Kingfisher Meml. Libr. Bd.; pres. Ft. Stewart Sch. Bd., 1977; bd. dirs. Ft. Stewart Fed. Credit Union, 1977, Chisholm Trail Mus., 1986—, Friends of Librs. in Okla., 1987—; pres. Friends of Libr. for Kingfisher County, 1984—88. Served with AUS, 1944—46, 1st lt. U.S. Army, 1952—54, maj. to col. U.S. Army, 1961—83. Decorated Legion of Merit with 2 oak leaf clusters, Soldier's medal, Bronze Star for Valor with oak leaf cluster, Meritorious Service medal, Air medal with 3 oak leaf clusters, Army Commendation medal, Gallantry cross with palm, Honor medal 1st class (both Vietnam); named Citizen of Yr., Kingfisher C. of C., 1988; named to Kingfisher H.S. Hall of Fame, 1987. Fellow: Royal Soc. Health; mem.: AMA, Garfield-Kingfisher County Med. Soc., Assn. Mil. Surgeons U.S., Army Aviation Med. Assn., Aerospace Med. Assn., Okla. State Med. Assn. Home: PO Box 703 Kingfisher OK 73750-0703

BUTCHER, BOBBY GENE, retired military officer; b. Mineral Wells, W.Va., Apr. 30, 1936; s. John Franklin and Anna Pearl (Hersman) B.; m. Patricia Maureen O'Keefe, Dec. 15, 1961 (dec. Dec. 1996); 1 child, Lisa Lee Butcher Clardy. BS, W.Va. U., 1958; grad., USN Flight Sch., 1960; postgrad., USMC Amphibious Warfare Sch., 1966-67, USMC Command and Staff Coll., 1973-74. Commd. 2d lt. USMC, 1959, advanced through grades to maj. gen., 1989; officer in charge USMC Officer Selection Office, Phila., 1971-73; ops. officer Marine Attack Tng. Squadron 102, Yuma, Ariz., 1974, exec. officer, 1974-76, comdg. officer, 1976-77; ops. officer Marine Corps Air Sta., Yuma, 1977-79; ops. plans officer 3d Marine Div., Camp Courtney, Okinawa, 1979-80; comdg. officer Marine Aviation Weapons and Tactics Squadron One, Yuma, 1980-82; participant Dept. State Sr. Seminar, Arlington, Va., 1982-83; asst. chief staff, plans and policy, comdr. Naval Striking and Support Forces, So. Europe, Naples, Italy, 1983-86; asst. wing comdr. 3d Marine Aircraft Wing, El Toro, Calif., 1986-87; comdg. gen. 6th Marine Expeditionary Brigade, Camp Lejeune, N.C., 1987-89; dir. ops. U.S. Pacific Command, Honolulu, 1989-91; comdg. gen. Landing Force Command, Coronado, Calif., 1991-92. Cons. specializing in Marine Corps and joint mil. matters. Decorated Def. D.S.M., D.S.M., Def. Superior Svc. medal, Legion of Merit, DFC, Bronze Star with combat V, Air medals (15); recipient various other unit and personal medals and ribbons. Mem. The Ret. Officers Assn. (nat. bd. dirs.), Flying Leatherneck Hist. Found. (chmn. bd. dirs.), USS Midway Mus. (bd. dirs.), The Early and Pioneer Naval Aviators' Assn. (Golden Eagles). Republican. Methodist. Home: 110 Carob Way Coronado CA 92118-2433 E-mail: thunderBGB@san.rr.com.

BUTCHER, C. PRESTON, real estate company executive; b. Roswell, N.Mex., 1939; BEE, U. Tex., 1962. With Lincoln Property Co. N.C. Inc., 1968—72; pres., CEO Lincoln Property Co., 1972—99; founder Legacy Ptnrs., Foster City, Calif., 1999—, CEO, 1999—. Bd. dir. Charles Schwab Corp., BRE Properties Inc.; co-founder Calif. Housing Coun., dir.; co-founder Nat. Multi Housing Coun.; mem. policy adv. bd. U. Calif., Berkeley, Calif. Mem. Bay Area Coun. Econ. Forum; bd. dir. Bridge. Office: Legacy Partners 4000 E Third Ave Ste 600 Foster City CA 94404

BUTCHER, EDWARD BERNIE, state senator; b. Lewistown, Mont., July 20, 1943; m. Pamela Butcher; children: Trevis, Ross, Becky. BA, Ea. Mont. State, 1965; MA, U. Mont., 1967; postgrad., U. Colo., 1967, N.D. State U., 1969. Asst. prof. Valley City State U., 1968-71; owner Rolling Hills Ranch, 1972—; lectr. Am. studies U. Great Falls, 1974-79; nat. sales dir. Evans Bio Corp, 1987-88; sr. regional mgr. Attco Assocs., 1988—; Rep. senator dist. 47 Mont. State Senate, 2000—05; Mont. State Ho. of Reps, 2005—. Mem. exec. com. Gov.'s Agr. Adv. Bd., 1980-84; chair Montanans for Term Limits, 1992;

chmn. House Agriculture com., 2005-. Mem. Mont. Bd. Crime Control, 1976-80; chair Fergus County Review Commn., 1994-96. Lutheran. Office: PO Box 89 800 Butcher Rd Winifred MT 59489

BUTCHER, FRED R., biochemistry professor, university administrator; b. Rochester, Pa., Aug. 11, 1943; s. Goble S. and Monnie (Gibson) B.; children: Allen Ray, Amy Jo. BS, Ohio State U., 1965, PhD, 1969. Postdoctoral fellow U. Wis., Madison, 1969-71; asst. prof. Brown U., Providence, 1971-76, assoc. prof., 1976-78; prof. W.Va. U., Morgantown, 1978—, chmn. dept. biochemistry, 1981-84, assoc. dean Sch. Medicine, 1984-89, dir. MBR Cancer Ctr., 1989-2000, sr. assoc. v.p., 1993—; exec. dir. Blanchette Rockefeller Neurosics. Inst., Morgantown, 1998—2000. Home: Rt 1 Box 325 Bruceton Mills WV 26525 Office Phone: 304-293-1536. Business E-Mail: fbutcher@hsc.wvu.edu.

BUTCHER, JACK ROBERT (JACK RISIN), manufacturing executive, film producer, actor; b. Akron, Ohio, Dec. 10, 1941; s. William Hobart and Marguerite Bell (Dalton) Butcher; m. Gloria Jean Hartman, June 1, 1963 (dec. July 1995); children: Jack R. II, William H.(dec.), Charlotte Jean. BA in Math., Jacksonville U., 1964; cert. in mgmt. consulting, Akron U., 1979; cert. in paralegal, CCT Inst., 1990; cert. in radio broadcasting, Chaffey Coll., 1994. Pres. Portableacher Corp., Hesperia, Calif., 1977—; v.p. Nice Day Products, Hesperia, 1980—85; pres. Mark Profl. Mgmt. and Design Co., Hesperia, 1983—, Nice Day Products, Hesperia, 1985—; owner Movie Funding Without Risk Co., 1996—; pres. Vallivue Prodns., Phelan, Calif., 2000—; co-owner Rizinn Consolidated Holdings Corp., 2001—. Co-owner JB Scale Co., Hesperia, 1991—. Actor, voice-overs and commls.: Film Industry Workshop Sch. Acting, 1995—99; author: (poems) Something Good, 1978, Forever My Valentine, 1996. Mem.: SAG, Internat. Platform Assn. (bd. govs. 1996—, Silver Bowl award 1995), Royal Order of Jesters, Shriners, Masons. Achievements include patents in field. Avocations: hunting, travel, designing, acting, commercial voice-overs. Home and Office: 577 Colchester Ct Akron OH 44319 Personal E-mail: jrbutcher5@yahoo.com.

BUTCHER, KAREN A., lawyer; b. Dec. 30, 1966; BS, U. Va, 1988; JD, U. Va. Sch. Law, 1993. Bar: Va. 1993, D.C. 1994. Ptnr. Morgan, Lewis & Bockius LLP, Washington, asst. leader intellectual property trademark/copyright practice group. Mem.: Internat. Trademark Assn.-Info. Resources Com. Office: Morgan Lewis & Bockius 1111 Pennsylvania Ave NW Washington DC 20004 Office Phone: 202-739-5526. Office Fax: 202-739-3001. Business E-Mail: kbutcher@morganlewis.com.

BUTCHER, LARRY L., neuroscientist, educator; b. Richmond, Ind., Feb. 21, 1940; s. Frederick L. Butcher and Ellen E. Jennings; m. Nancy J. Woolf, Dec. 24, 1983; children: Lawson, Ashley. BA, U. Mich., 1962, MS, 1964, PhD, 1967; postgrad., U. Goteborg, Sweden, 1967—69. Prof. UCLA, 1969—, dir., gerontology minor program, 1997—. Cons. Pilgrim Sch., L.A., 2000—. Contbr. scientific papers to profl. jours. Mem.: Sigma Xi. Office: UCLA 405 Hilgard Ave Los Angeles CA 90095-1563 Business E-Mail: butcher@psych.ucla.edu.

BUTCHER, RUSSELL DEVEREUX, writer, photographer; b. Bryn Mawr, Pa., Feb. 8, 1938; s. Devereux and Mary Frances (Taft) B.; m. Pamela Richards, Apr. 12, 1967 (div. 1993); children: Pamela Marie (dec.), Neill Devereux, Wendy Nan; m. Karen T. Black, Nov. 29, 1997. BA, U. Colo., 1960; postgrad., U. Mich., 1960-61. Rsch. editor Sierra Club, San Francisco, 1961-65; editl. writer N.Y. Times, 1963-79; publicity writer Save-the-Redwoods League, San Francisco, 1963-65; conservation specialist Nat. Audubon Soc., N.Y.C., 1965-66; chief pub. rels. and publs. Mus. of N.Mex., Santa Fe, 1967-69; freelance writer, photographer, author, 1969-80. Conservation zoning cons. Town of Mount Desert, Maine, 1978-79, S.W. and Calif. rep. Nat. Parks and Conservation Assn., 1980-90, Pacific S.W. regional dir., 1990-93. Author: Maine Paradise, 1973, New Mexico: Gift of the Earth, 1975, The Desert, 1976, Field Guide to Acadia National Park, Maine, 1977, rev. edit., 2005, Exploring Our National Parks and Monuments, 9th edit., 1995, Exploring Our National Historic Parks and Sites, 1997, America's National Wildlife Refuges: A Complete Guide, 2003; author, compiler: Guide to National Parks (8 regional guides), 1999; mem. editl. bd. Audubon mag.; manuscript editor KC Publs., 1985-88; contbr. articles to profl. jours. Mem. Ariz. Strip Dist. adv. coun. U.S. Bur. Land Mgmt., 1983—90; bd. dirs. Friends Saguaro Nat. Park, 1997—2002, Rincon Inst., 2002—. Nat. Parks and Conservation Assn. fellow, 1993-99. Mem. Save-the-Redwoods League (life), Nat. Parks and Conservation Assn., Maine Audubon Soc. (pres. Down East chpt. 1978-80, trustee 1979-80), Friends of Lake Dist. Eng. (life), Sierra Club (life). Episcopalian (Vestryman 1978-81). Address: 5948 N Misty Ridge Dr Tucson AZ 85718-3438

BUTCHKO, HARRIETT HAYS, physician; b. Athens, Ga., Mar. 31, 1950; d. William Jackson and Carolyn Ross Hays; m. Gregory Michael Butchko, July 8, 1972; children: Karin Hayston, Jeffrey Maston. Student, Canal Zone Coll., Balboa, 1968—69; BS, U. Ga., 1972; MD, Northwestern U., 1982. Diplomate Nat. Bd. Med. Examiners, 1984. Intern, resident Northwestern U., 1982—85; assoc. dir. clin. rsch. G.D. Searle & Co., Skokie, Ill., 1985—86, The NutraSweet Co., Skokie, 1986—91, dir. clin. rsch. and regulatory affairs Deerfield, Ill., 1991—97, v.p. med. and sci. affairs and chief med. officer Chgo., 2000—03; sr. dir. global regulatory coordination Monsanto Co., Skokie, 1997—2000; prin. scientist Exponent, Inc., Wood Dale, Ill., 2003—. Editor: (book) The Clinical Evaluation of a Food Additive: Assessment of Aspartame; contbr. chapters to books, articles to profl. jours. Fellow: Am. Coll. Nutrition; mem.: AMA, Am. Soc. Nutrition Scis., Am. Soc. Clin. Nutrition, Am. Acad. Neurology (assoc.), Internat. Soc. Regulatory Toxicology and Pharmacology, N.Am. Assn. for Study of Obesity, Phi Beta Kappa. Republican. Avocations: creating stained glass windows, collecting American brilliant cut glass, collecting antiques. Office Phone: 630-274-3221. E-mail: hbutchko@exponent.com.

BUTENHOFF, SUSAN G., public relations executive; b. N.Y.C., Jan. 13, 1960; BA in Internat. Rels. with hons., Sussex U., Eng.; MPhil, Wolfson Coll., Cambridge U., Eng. Account exec. Ellen Farmer Prodns., 1984-85, Ketchum Pub. Rels., N.Y.C., 1988-90, v.p., account supr., 1990-91; prin., CEO Access Pub. Rels., San Francisco, 1991—, pres., CEO. Mem. Pub. Rels. Soc. Am. Office: Access Comm 101 Howard St Fl 2D San Francisco CA 94105-1629

BUTERA, ANN MICHELE, consulting company executive; b. Bayside, N.Y., Apr. 27, 1958; d. Gaetano Thomas and Josephine (Inserro) B. BA, L.I. U., 1979; MBA, Adelphi U., 1982. Dept. mgr. Abraham & Straus Stores, Huntington, N.Y., 1978-80; mgmt. cons. Chase Manhattan Bank N.A., Lake Success, N.Y., 1980-83, Nat. Bankcard Corp., Melville, N.Y., 1983-84; pres. Whole Person Project, Inc., Elmont, N.Y., 1984—. Bd. dirs. Nassau County coun. Girl Scouts U.S., 1985-95. Recipient Bus. Achievement award Women on the Job, 1990. Mem. NAFE, ASTD, Fin. Women Internat., L.I. Networking Entrepreneurs (pres. 1984-91), Inst. Internal Auditors, Assn. Govt. Auditors, L.I. Ctr. for Bus. and Profl. Women, World Futurists Soc. Republican. Roman Catholic. Avocations: tennis, dance, gardening. Home and Office: Whole Person Project Inc 82 Cerenzia Blvd Elmont NY 11003-3631 Office Phone: 516-354-3551. E-mail: annbutera@cs.com.

BUTHMAN, MARK A., retail executive; m. Tammy Buthman; 3 children. Fin. assoc. in corp. acctg. and procedures and controls Kimberly-Clark, Neenah, Wis., 1982, from project analyst to sr. strategic analyst, dir. corp. strategic analysis, 1984—95, cost analyst Memphis, 1983, v.p. strategic planning and analysis Dallas, 1997—2001, v.p. fin. Irving, Tex., 2001—. Office: Kimberly Clark Corp 351 Phelps Dr Irving TX 75038

BUTHOD, MARY CLARE, school administrator; b. Tulsa, Aug. 20, 1945; d. Arthur Paul and Mary Rudelle (Dougherty) B. MA in Teaching, Tulsa U., 1969; M Christian Spirituality, Creighton U., 1981. Joined Order of St. Benedict. Asst. tchr. HeadStart, Tulsa, 1966; tchr. Madalene Parish Sch., Tulsa, 1968-69, Monte Cassino Pvt. Sch., Tulsa, 1969-79; prin. Monte Cassino Elem. Sch., Tulsa, 1979-86; dir. Monte Cassino Sch., Tulsa, 1986—. Mem. convent coun. Benedictine Sisters, Tulsa, 1975-88, dir. formation programs, 1983—; examiner Okla. Quality Found. Mem. State Congl. Ednl. Com., Tulsa, 1989-90; co-chair for edn. and human devel. Tulsa Coalition Against Illegal Use of Drugs, 1990-91; mem. adv. com. Okla. State Schs. Attuned, 2002—. Recognized for Excellence in Edn. U.S. Dept. Edn., 1993-94. Mem. Tulsa Reading Coun. (sec. 1975-77), Nat. Cath. Edn. Assn., Delta Kappa Gamma. Home: 2200 S Lewis Tulsa OK 74114-3117 Office: Monte Cassino Sch 2206 S Lewis Ave Tulsa OK 74114-3109 Office Phone: 918-746-4112. Business E-Mail: smc@montecasino.org.

BUTKI, BRIAN DAVID, psychologist, educator; b. Dearborn, Mich., May 18, 1970; s. Alice Mary Gibson and Julius Jerome Butki; m. Erin Rae Chandler, Aug. 9, 1997; children: Camden Grace children: Alisha Rae. BS, U. Wyo., Laramie, 1988—92, MSEd, 1992—93; PhD, U. N.C., Greensboro, 1994—98. Asst. prof. So. Ill. U., Edwardsville, 1998—2003; therapeutic recreation dir. Youth Focus, Inc., Greensboro, NC, 1998—99; dir. youth sport camps, asst. prof. Colo. State U., Ft. Collins, 2004—. Owner and dir. P.E.A.K. Performance Cons., Ft. Collins, 1998—. Tng. dir. Spl. Olympics of Ill., Highland, 1999—; dir. Metro East Humane Soc., Edwardsville, Ill., 2000—. Recipient Greensboro Grad. Award, State of N.C., 1994—98. Mem.: ASPCA, Am. Alliance of Health, Phys. Edn., Recreation, and Dance, Soc. of Behavioral Medicine, Assn. for the Advancement of Applied Sport Psychology, Phi Beta Kappa. Avocations: bicycling, travel, music, reading, hiking. Office: Colo State U PO Box 1582 Fort Collins CO 80523 Personal E-mail: bbutki13@yahoo.com.

BUTKIEWICZ, JAMES LEON, economics educator, researcher, consultant; b. Kingston, Pa., Sept. 8, 1949; s. Joseph Leon and Anne (Lawlor) B.; m. Mary Ellen Fischer, Aug. 14, 1971; children: Erica, Lauren. BA, Wilkes Coll., 1971; PhD, U. Va., 1977. Asst. prof. econs. U. Del., Newark, 1976-82, assoc. prof., 1982-94, prof. econs., 1994—, assoc. dean Coll. Bus. and Econs., 1984-88, 91-96, chmn. dept. econs., 1996—2001; dir. grad. studies U. Del., Dept. Econ., 2003—04. Asst. prof. U. Va., Charlottesville, 1975; econ. cons., Newark, 1978—; guest lectr. Am. Coll, Bryn Mawr, Pa., 1985-89; cons. Office Tech. Assessment, Washington, 1988-89; vis. prof. U. Lyonn, France, 2001commentator weekly radio program, 1980-82; econ. analyst local TV and radio stas., 1980-82 Editor: Keynes Economic Legacy, 1986; acting editor Ea. Econ. Jour., 2004-05, mem. editl. bd., 2001—; contbr. articles to profl. jours. Mem. Cecil County (Md.) Comprehensive Planning Com., 1988-90; mem. Del. Ins. Commr.'s Task Force of the Future of Del. Agts. and Agys., 1991-92, Cecil County Econ. Devel. Com., Bus. Retention and Fin. SubCom., chair 2000— Recipient 1st place for teaching Joint Coun. on Econ. Edn., 1988; Rsch grant U. Del., 1989, Del. Dept. Devel. grant, 1988 Mem. Am. Econ. Assn., Econ. History Assn., So. Econ. Assn., Phi Kappa Phi (pres. U. Del. chpt. 1986-91). Republican. Roman Catholic. Avocations: skiing, basketball. Office: U Del Dept Econs Newark DE 19716 Office Phone: 302-831-1891. Business E-Mail: butkiewj@lerner.udel.edu.

BUTLER, BRETT, comedienne, actress; b. Montgomery, AL, 1958; d. Roland Decatur Anderson, Jr. and Carol; adoptive parent Bob Butler; m. Charles Wilson, 1978 (div. 1981); m. Ken Ziegler, 1987. Waitress, Houston, 1981-82; stand-up comedian, 1982—. Star, exec. prodr. TV series Grace Under Fire, 1993-98; appeared on TV in It's Just A Ride, 1994; in film Bruno, 1999; TV film It's Just a Ride, 1994.

BUTLER, CHARLES RANDOLPH, JR., federal judge; b. NYC, Mar. 28, 1940; BA, Washington and Lee U., 1962; LLB, U. Ala., 1966. Assoc. Hamilton Butler Riddick and LaTour, Mobile, Ala., 1966-69; asst. pub. defender Mobile County, 1969-70, dist. atty., 1971-75; ptnr. Butler and Sullivan, Mobile, 1975-84, Hamilton Butler Riddick Tarlton and Sullivan P.C., Mobile, 1984-88; dist. judge US Dist. Ct. (so. dist.) Ala., Mobile, 1988-94, 2003—, chief dist. judge, 1994—2003, sr. dist. judge., 2005—. Adj. prof. criminal justice program U. So. Ala., 1972-76; mem. jud. coun. 11th cir., 1994-2003, jud. conf. com. on criminal law, 1993-99, jud. conf. com., 1999-2002; past liaison mem. to long-range planning com. of the AO; past mem. program and adminstrn. subcom., planning for the future and automation subcom., probaton and pretrial umbrella group; mem. exec. com. Jud. Conf. of U.S., 1999-2002. Lst lt. USAR, 1962-64. Recipient Jud. award of merit Ala. State Bar, 2003; named One of Outstanding Young Men of Am., Mobile County Jaycees, 1971. Office: US Dist Ct 113 Saint Joseph St Mobile AL 36602-3683 Office Phone: 251-690-2175.

BUTLER, CHRISTOPHER DAVID, mathematician, educator; b. Cleve., July 18, 1961; s. Thomas Albert and Mary Jo Frum Butler; m. Jennifer Lynne Ehrlinger, Aug. 4, 1990; children: Michael James, Erin Elizabeth. BS with honors, Case We. Res. U., 1983, MS, 1985. Instr. math. Case We. Res. U., Cleve., 1985—. Recipient Meritorius Svc. award, Case Alumni Assn., 2003. Mem.: Golden Key (hon.). Lutheran. Avocations: swimming, racquetball. Home: 1007 Bryan Dr South Euclid OH 44121 Office: Case Western Res U 10900 Euclid Ave Cleveland OH 44106 E-mail: chris@case.edu.

BUTLER, COLETTE M., minister; b. Chgo., Mar. 26, 1959; d. Eugene Rivers and Constance Bateman; m. Daryl Lee Butler, July 15, 1993; children: Natasha, Cynthinia, Lanina, Angeline, Darrell, Kimberly. Cert. of completion, Midwest Bible Coll., 1999; cert. of ordination, Holy Trinity, 2001. Cashier/payroll Burt's Shoe Store, Chgo., 1975—80; data entry First Nat. Bank/Bank One, Chgo., 1980—85; customer svc., receptionist Preferred Care Network, Chgo., 1986—90; customer svc. Culinary, Chgo., 1991—94; owner Mr. B's Auto Repair, Chgo., 1995; sec. Bank of Am., Chgo., 1999—2000; founder, pres., shepherd All Nations Kingdom of God, Chgo., 1997. Pharmacy advisor Healthstar, Chgo., 1989—90; fundraiser cons. Corner Stone, Chgo.; ministerial bd. Lighthouse, Chgo., 1999—2000. Author: Bone of His Bone, 2001; contbr. articles to profl. jours. Organizer Mind, Body & Spirit Ministries, Chgo., 2001, recovery shepherd, 2001, feeding & clothing adminstr., 2002, pres., 1999—2003, founder. Avocations: sewing, crocheting, reading. Office: All Nations Kingdom of God PO Box 368603 Chicago IL 60609 E-mail: allnationskingdomofgod@netzero.net.

BUTLER, DAVID, lawyer; b. St. Paul, June 11, 1930; s. Francis David and Alida (Bigelow) B.; m. Diana Dodge Duffy, Aug. 29, 1952 (div. 1957); children: Anne, Lawrence David; m. Barbara Williams Clark, July 12, 1958; children: Molly Elizabeth, Peter, Katherine BA, Princeton U., 1952; LLB, Harvard U., 1957. Bar. Colo. 1958, U.S. Dist. Ct. Colo. 1958. Assoc. Holland & Hart, Denver, 1957-63, ptnr., 1963-95, chmn. mgmt. com., 1990-95; of counsel, 1996—. Gen. counsel 1st Interstate Bank Denver, 1984-86; bd. dirs. UMB Bank Colo., Denver. Mem. bd. editors Harvard Law Rev., 1955-57. Chmn. lawyers adv. com. United Way, Denver, 1989—94; trustee Graland Country Day Sch., Denver, 1971—79, Legal Aid Found., Colo., 1991—97, chmn., 1993—97. Colo. Planning Group for Legal Svcs. to the Poor, 1995—2002; bd. dirs. Met. Denver Legal Aid Soc., 1971—74; trustee Colo. Lawyers Trust Account Found., 2000—; chmn. Colo. Access to Justice Commn., 2003—04, sec., 2005—. 1st lt. U.S. Army, 1952—54. Mem. ABA, Colo. Bar Assn. (chmn. tax sect. 1970, Jacob V. Schaetzel pro bono award 2002), Denver Bar Assn. Office: Holland & Hart 555 17th St Ste 2900 Denver CO 80202-3979

BUTLER, DAVID J., newspaper editor; b. Taylorville, Ill., June 19, 1950; s. Donald and Jeanie B.; m. Kathryn Lee, Nov. 2, 1991. BS in Journalism and Photography, Southern Ill. U., 1972. Metro editor, reporter The Southern Illinoisan, Carbondale, Ill., 1972-78; asst. city editor The Sun-Sentinel, Fort Lauderdale, Fla., 1978; mng. editor The Messenger-Inquirer, Owensboro, Ky., 1978-81, Jacksonville (Fla.) Jour., 1981-83; asst. mng. editor Rocky Mountain News, Denver, 1983-88; editor New Haven Register, New Haven, 1988-96, LA Daily News, 1997—2005; and v.p. LA Newspaper Group; editor, pub. Detroit News, 2005—. Office: Detroit News 615 W Lafayette Blvd Detroit MI 48226 Office Phone: 313-222-2300.*

BUTLER, DOUGLAS JOHN, physician; b. Greensboro, N.C., Nov. 23, 1954; s. John C. and Jeannette Douglas. BA magna cum laude, Miami Univ., 1975; MD, Ohio State, 1978. Diplomate Am. Bd. Family Practice. Family medicine resident Moses Cone Hosp., Greensboro, 1978-81; attending physician, pvt. practice Ashe Meml. Hosp., Jefferson, NC, 1981-93, chief staff, 1982—83; emergency dept. physician Lake Norman Reg. Medical Ctr., Mooresville, NC, 1993; emergency dept. medical dir. Alexander Cmty. Hosp., Taylorsville, NC, 1993-2000, chief staff, 1999; locum tenens physician Indian Health Svc., 2000—; attending physician Old Fort Med. Clinic/McDowell Hosp., Marion, NC, 2001—02. Author: Ashe County Discovering the Lost Province, 1993; contbr. articles to profl. jours. Chmn. Ashe County EMS Coun., Jefferson, 1986—91. Mem.: Am. Heart Assn. (pres. Ashe County chpt. 1986—91), Jefferson Rotary. Avocations: photography, mountain climbing, travel.

BUTLER, FREDERICK GEORGE, retired drug company executive; b. Greenwich, Conn., Mar. 25, 1919; s. Harold Nassau and Rosa (Rhinhart) B.; m. Sarah Lou Allred, Sept. 23, 1945; children: Pamela Sue, Frederick Houston (dec.). AB, Middlebury (Vt.) Coll., 1941; MBA, Columbia U., 1947. CPA, N.Y. With Price Waterhouse & Co., 1941—42, 1947—49, McKesson & Robbins, Inc., N.Y.C., 1949—63, asst. comptr., 1952—61, comptr., 1961—63; contr. Bristol-Myers Co., N.Y.C., 1963—66, v.p., contr., 1966—69, v.p. ops., 1970—76; ret., 1976. Pioneered developement of bar code (compatible universal product code and nat. drug code) for supermarket automated checkout scanning and inventory control. Village mayor, Briarcliff Manor, N.Y., 1969-71. Served to comdr. USNR, 1942-46, 51-52. Mem. Fin. Execs. Inst., Pres.'s Club, Hillsdale (Mich.) Coll., Chi Psi. Methodist. Home: 6825 Davis Blvd Apt 219 Naples FL 34104-5325 Personal E-mail: fbutler@swfla.rr.com.

BUTLER, GLORIA SINGLETON, state legislator; children: Felicia, Leslie. AS in Bus. Adminstrn., Perimeter Coll. Fiscal acctg. asst. Health Scis. Ctr., Emory U., Atlanta; mem. Ga. State Senate, Atlanta, 1999—, sec. pub. safety com., mem. edn., retirement and transp. coms. Leg. asst. to U.S. Congresswoman Cynthia McKinney, Washington, 1992; mem. USIA Speaker program, South Africa, Zimbabwe, Swaziland, 1994; asst. to dir. AmeriCorps Team for Nat. Svc., 1996 Olympics and paralympics; dir. operation Big Vote, Coalition for Black Voter participation, 4th Congrl. Dist., DeKalb County, 1996; pub. rels. dir. Martin Luther King Jr. March com., 1997; mem. exec. staff, staff of intergovtl. rels. Office DeKalb County Sheriff. Mem. NOW, NAACP (exec. bd. DeKalb County chpt.), Nat. Coun. Negro Women, DeKalb Women's Polit. Caucus, Nat. Women's Polit. Caucus. Democrat. Office: Ste 420D State Capitol Atlanta GA 30334-9003

BUTLER, GRACE CAROLINE, medical researcher; b. Lima, Peru, Dec. 19, 1937; (parents Am. citizens); d. Everett Lyle and Mary Isabella (Sloatman) Gage; m. William Langdon Butler, Dec. 28, 1961; children: Mary Dyer, William Langdon Jr. AA, Stephens Coll., 1957; BS in Nursing, Columbia U., 1960; postgrad., Union County Coll., 1984. Head nurse N.Y. State Psychiat. Inst., N.Y.C., 1960-61; clin. instr. Columbia U., N.Y.C., 1960-61; staff nurse, educator Vis. Nurse Service, Summit, N.J., 1962-63; health adminstr. Eagle Island Girl Scout Camp, Tupper Lake, N.Y., 1964; evening supr. Ashbrook Nursing Home, Scotch Plains, N.J., 1968-72; teaching asst. Scotch Plains-Fanwood (N.J.) Sch. System, 1975-78; staff nurse Westfield (N.J.) Med. Group, 1980-82, head nurse, 1982-83, supr., 1983-84; office adminstr. Harris S. Vernick, MD, PA, Westfield, 1984-86, corp. v.p., office adminstr., 1986-88, Assocs. in Medicine, Westfield, 1988-90; pvt. researcher, 1990—. Diabetes instr. Boehringer Manneheim Diagnostics, 1984—, Eli Lilly and Co., Indpls., 1984—; microbiologist tester Med. Technol. Corp., Somerset, NJ, 1984—; computer advisor Cordis Corp., Miami, 1985—. Asst. leader Girl Scouts U.S., Fanwood, 1970—73; bd. dirs. PTA, Scotch Plains, Fanwood, 1973—79; religious instr. All Sts. Episcopal Ch., Scotch Plains, 1967—82, 1995—, mem. altar guild, 1994—, mem. vestry, 1999—2005, lay eucharistic min., 2001—. Mem.: Am. Soc. Notaries, League Ednl. Advancement RNs, Columbia U./Presbyn. Hosp. Sch. Nursing Alumni Assn. Republican. Episcopalian. Avocations: sewing, water sports, gardening, wood refinishing. Home: 125 Russell Rd Fanwood NJ 07023-1063

BUTLER, GREGORY B., utilities executive, lawyer; b. Cazenovia, NY; m. Nancy Butler; children: Liza, Sarah. BA in History, SUNY, Stony Brook, 1980; JD, Union U., 1988. Bar: N.Y., U.S. Ct. Appeals (9th cir.). Assoc. counsel N.Y. State Assembly, 1988—90; sr. atty. advisor legal policy U.S. Dept. Justice, 1990—92; sr. counsel Niagara Mohawk Power Corp., 1992—95; v.p. fed. affairs New Eng. Elec. System, 1995—96, v.p. govtl. affairs, 1997—2001; v.p., gen. counsel, sec. Northeast Utilities, Hartford, Conn., 2001—03, sr. v.p., gen. counsel, sec., 2003—. Bd. adv. Govt. Law Ctr. Albany Law Sch.; bd. parole State of Conn., 1998—2004. Bd. dirs. Northeast Utilities Found., New England Legal Found., 2004—. Mem.: Energy Bar Assn. Office: Northeast Utilities PO Box 270 Hartford CT 06141-0270 also: Northeast Utilities 107 Selden St Berlin CT 06037

BUTLER, JACK FAIRCHILD, electric power industry executive; b. El Centro, Calif., July 18, 1933; s. Jack Orval and Dorothy (Marsh) B.; m. Colette Alice Guerard, Sept. 6, 1959; children— Alice, Jack, Michael, Patricia. Student, San Jose State Coll., 1951-54; BS, U. Calif., Berkeley, 1959, MS, 1960, PhD, 1962. Research staff mem. Mass. Inst. Tech., Lincoln Lab., Lexington, Mass., 1962-68; staff scientist Gen. Dynamics Corp., Pomona, Calif., 1968-71; sr. staff mem. Arthur D. Little, Inc., Cambridge, Mass., 1971-74; co-founder, co-owner, dir., pres. Laser Analytics, Inc., Lexington, 1974-81; founder, owner, dir., pres. Butler Research and Engring., Inc., 1981-85; co-founder, co-owner, dir., pres. San Diego Semicondrs., Inc., 1985-91, Aurora Techs. Corp., 1991-95; co-founder, co-owner, pres. Digirad (formerly Aurora Techs. Corp.), 1995-98; ret., 1998. Contbr. articles to sci. jours. Served with USMC, 1954-57. Mem. IEEE (life), AAAS, Am. Inst. Physics (life), Gen. Soc. Mayflower Descs. (life).

BUTLER, JAMES NEWTON, chemist, educator; b. Cleveland, Ohio, Mar. 27, 1934; s. Clyde Henry and Margaret (Manor) B.; m. Nancy Elizabeth Close, Aug. 31, 1957 (div.); 1 son, Christopher J.; m. Rosamond Hatch Bee, Dec. 10, 1966; stepchildren: Alden G. Bee, Kenneth M. Bee. BS, Rensselaer Poly. Inst., 1955; PhD, Harvard U., 1959. Staff scientist NACA Lewis Lab., Cleve., summers 1952-57, MIT Lincoln Lab., summer 1958; instr. U. B.C., Vancouver, 1959-61, asst. prof., 1961-63; sr. scientist Tyco Labs., Inc., Waltham, Mass., 1963-66, dept. head, 1966-71; from lectr. to prof. emeritus Harvard U., Cambridge, Mass., 1970—2000, prof. emeritus, 2000—; cons. Tyco Labs., Inc., Waltham, Mass., 1962-63, 71-73. Mem. steering com. co-author report Petroleum in the Marine Environment, Nat. Acad. Scis.—NRC, 1973-75, 80-82; mem. tech. panel, report drafting com. Com. on Environ. Decision-Making, 1975-77; chmn. com. on effectiveness of oil spill dispersants, NRC, 1985-89; cons. EPA, 1978—, NOAA, 1981—. Author: Ionic Equilibrium, 1964, rev. edit., 1998, Solubility and pH Calculations, 1964, The Calculus of Chemistry, 1965, Problems for Introductory University Chemistry, 1967, Pelagic Tar from Bermuda and the Sargasso Sea, 1973, Carbon Dioxide Equilibria and Their Applications, 1982, reprinted, 1991, Studies of Sargassum and the Sargassum Community, 1983, Using Oil Spill Dispersants on the Sea, 1989, The Exxon Valdez Oil Spill: Fate and Effects in Alaskan Waters, 1995; also articles. Trustee Bermuda Biol. Sta., 1972-97, v.p., 1985-86, 89-93, pres., 1986-89, life trustee, 1997—. NSF Faculty Sci. fellow, 1977; Alumni scholar Relsselaer Poly. Inst., 1955, NSF fellow, GE fellow Harvard U., 1959. Mem. Am. Chem. Soc., AAAS, Am. Soc. Limnology and Oceanography, Internat. Soc. Electrochemistry, Electrochem. Soc. N.Y. (chmn. Boston sect.), Gordon Research Conf. on Electrochemistry (chmn.), Assn. Harvard Chemists (pres.), Sigma Xi, Phi Lambda Upsilon. Business E-Mail: butler@deas.harvard.edu.

BUTLER, JOHN LOWE, IV, psychiatrist, educator; b. Acequia, Idaho, Nov. 5, 1920; s. John Lowe III and Bertha Malvina (Thurber) B.; m. Marjorie Lu Call, Aug. 12, 1945; children: Kenneth Lee, Janet Sue Westwood, John Lowe V. BS in Edn., U. Idaho, 1942; MD, Johns Hopkins U., 1946. Acting supt. Kooskia (Idaho) Pub. Schs., 1942-43; Carnegie postdoctoral fellow, Sch. of

Indsl. & Labor Rels. Cornell U., Ithaca, N.Y., 1950-52; indsl. psychiatrist Mut. Security Agy., Paris, 1952-53, The Hague, The Netherlands, 1954-55; dir. mental health Idaho State Bd. of Health, Boise, 1956-58; prof. psychiatry Oreg. Health Scis. U., Portland, 1958—2003; pvt. practice Portland, 1959-92; prof. emeritus Oreg. Health Scis. U., Portland, 2003. Cons., writer, 1958—; vis. prof. psychology U. Idaho, 1950—; staff mem. Guidance & Counseling Inst., Oreg. State Sys. of Higher Edn., Portland, 1960-68; co-dir. Pastoral Leadership & Counselor Tng. Inst., Portland, 1960-75; cons. tng. in human rels. improvement, 1952—. Contbr. articles to profl. jours. Mem. various coms. City Club of Portland, 1969—. Lt. (j.g.) USN, 1943-50. Recipient Career Tchr. grant U.S. Nat. Inst. Mental Health, 1959-61; named to Hall of Fame Alumni Assn. U. Idaho, 1997 (Disting. 2003). Life fellow Am. Psychiat. Assn. (pres. Oreg. Dist. br. 1977-78), North Pacific Soc. of Neurology & Psychiatry (bd. dirs. 1976-78); mem. Johns Hopkins Med. and Surg. Soc. (pres. Oreg. chpt. 1970-71), Oreg. Med. Assn. (life), Phi Beta Kappa. Democrat. Unitarian/Universalist. Home: 2229 SW Kings Ct Portland OR 97205-1121

BUTLER, JOHN MUSGRAVE, financial consultant; b. Bklyn., Dec. 6, 1928; s. John Joseph and Sabina Catherine (Musgrave) Butler; m. Ann Elizabeth Kelly, July 9, 1955; children: Maureen, John, Ellen, Suzanne. BA cum laude, St. John's U., 1950; MBA, NYU, 1951. CPA N.Y., Ill. Sr. acct. Lybrand, Ross Bros. & Montgomery (CPAs), N.Y.C., 1953-59; sr. auditor ITT Corp., N.Y.C., 1959-62; asst. to contr. Dictaphone Corp., Bridgeport, Conn., 1962-63, contr. Bridgeport, Rye, NY, 1964—68; v.p. acctg. Chgo. & North Western Ry. Co., 1968-69, v.p. fin. and acctg., 1969-72, Chgo. and North Western Transp. Co., 1972-79, sr. v.p. fin. and acctg., 1979-89, dir., 1976-89, trustee, 1978-82, acting sr. v.p. fin. and acctg., 1994; sr. v.p. fin. and acctg., dir. CNW Corp., 1985-89; cons. in fin. and acctg. for bus., 1989—; instr. fin. DePaul U., Chgo., 1989—2001. Dir. Cath. Med. Mission Bd., N.Y.C., 1998—2000. With USCGR, 1951—53. Mem.: Fin. Execs. Inst. Roman Catholic. Office: 119 E Palatine Rd Ste 206 Palatine IL 60067-5132

BUTLER, JOHN WILLIAM, JR., lawyer; b. Detroit, Feb. 18, 1956; s. John William Sr. and Lucille Elmira (Miller) B. AB magna cum laude, Princeton U., 1977; JD, U. Mich., 1980. Bar: Mich. 1980, US Dist. Ct. (ea. and we. dist.) Mich. 1981, US Ct. Appeals (6th cir.), Ill. 1992. Assoc. Honigman, Miller, Schwartz and Cohn, Detroit, 1980-81; ptnr. Butzel, Keidan, Simon, Myers & Graham, Detroit, 1981-90; ptnr., co-leader corp. restructuring Skadden, Arps, Slate, Meagher & Flom, LLP, Chgo., 1990—. Chmn. bd. gov. Comml. Fin. Assn. Edn. Found.; co-chmn. INSOL 2005 World Congress; dir. Am. Bd. Certification, 1993—2003; group of Thirty-Six INSOL Internat., 1995—; chmn. Am. Bd. Certification, 1997. Contbr. chapters to books. Bd. gov. Hugh O'Brian Youth Leadership, 1998—; mem. exec. adv. council Children Affected by AIDS, 2003—; co-chair Renaissance American/BeardGroup Corp. Reorganizations Conf., 1999—, Healthcare Transactions Conf., 2000—. Named leader in the corp. restructuring and insolvency field, Chamber's Global, Chambers USA; named one of Top Dozen Restructuring Lawyers in Am., Turnarounds & Workouts, Top Ten Worldwide Restructuring Lawyers, Global Counsel, 2002, "Dealmakers of the Yr.", The American Lawyer, 2004; named to Client Svc. All Star Team, BTI Consulting Group, 2004; recipient Chairman's award, Turnaround Mgmt. Assn., 2001. Fellow, Am. Coll. Bankruptcy, 1997, Internat. Solvency Inst., 2002. Mem. ABA, Am. Bankruptcy Inst.(dir. 1992-98), Comml. Law League Am., Fed. Bar Assn., Mich. Bar Assn., Oakland County Bar Assn., Detroit Bar Assn., Turnaround Mgmt. Assn. (dir. 1991-99 & 2001-, chmn. 1996-97, chmn. award 2001, chmn. anniversary conventions, 10th (1998) and 15th (2003)); assoc. gen. counsel, Commercial Fin. Assn., 1998-2002. Republican. Presbyterian. Avocation: officiate HS and Coll. football teams. Office: Skadden Arps Slate Meagher & Flom 333 W Wacker Dr Chicago IL 60606 Office Phone: 312-407-0730. Office Fax: 312-407-8501. Business E-Mail: jbutler@skadden.com.

BUTLER, JON TERRY, computer engineering educator, researcher; b. Balt., Dec. 26, 1943; s. Herbert Harriss and Vera Esse (Buck) B.; m. Susan Beth Wood, Feb. 24, 1968 (div. Aug. 1996); 1 child, Anne Elizabeth; m. Fujiko Sakaguchi, Jan. 31, 1998. BEE, Rensselaer Poly. Inst., 1966, M in Engring., 1967; PhD, Ohio State U., 1973. Registered profl. engr., Ohio. NRC postdoctoral assoc. Air Force Avionics Lab., Wright-Patterson AFB, Ohio, 1973-74; sr. postdoctoral assoc. Naval Postgrad. Sch., Wright-Patterson AFB, Ohio, 1980-81; assoc. prof. Northwestern U., Evanston, Ill., 1974-87; prof. Naval Postgrad. Sch., Monterey, Calif., 1987—, Navalex Chair prof., 1985-87. Editor: Multi-Valued Logic in VLSI, 1991; contbr. articles to profl. jours. Capt. USAF, 1967—70. Recipient Faculty Performance award Naval Postgrad. Sch., 1990-93. Fellow IEEE; mem. IEEE Computer Soc. (chmn. multiple-valued logic com. 1980-81, Disting. vis. 1982-86, press editor 1986-90, editor-in-chief Computer mag. 1991-92, editor-in-chief Computer Soc. Press 1993-97, chmn. Computer Soc. fellows evaluation com. 1999, chmn. Computer Soc. transactions ops. com. 1998-99, chmn. Computer Soc. Press ops. com. 2000—, Meritorious Svc. award 1988, 92, TAB Pioneer award 1989, cert. appreciation 1982, 89, 91, 95, 96, 99, 2000, Disting. Svc. award 1995, Third Centennial medal 2000, bd. govs. 1991-97). Presbyterian. Office: Naval Postgrad Sch Dept Elec Computer Engring Code EC-BU Monterey CA 93943-5121 Office Phone: 831-656-3299. E-mail: Jon_Butler2@redshift.com.

BUTLER, JONATHAN PUTNAM, architect; b. Portchester, N.Y., June 6, 1940; s. Jonathan Fairchild and Mary Elizabeth (Putnam) Butler; m. Deborah Day Rogers, Mar. 18, 1967; children: Jonathan Rogers, Pauline Washburn, Benjamin Putnam, Cynthia Day. BA, Princeton U., 1962, MFA, 1965; MArch, Columbia U., 1966. Designer, programmer, planner Skidmore, Owings & Merrill, Architects, N.Y.C., 1968—71; ptnr. Rogers, Butler, Burgun & Shahine, N.Y.C., 1971—79; pres. Butler, Rogers & Baskett, N.Y.C., 1979—2003; pvt. practice Jonathan P. Butler AIA LLC, Niantic, Conn., 2003—. Bd. dirs. Woodlawn Cemetery, Bronx, N.Y. Mem AIA, Nat. Coun. Archl. Registration Bds. (cert.), Union Club. Home: 14 West Ln Niantic CT 06357-3716 Office: Jonathan P Butler AIA LLC 14 West Ln Niantic CT 06357 Office Phone: 860-739-9180. Business E-Mail: jonb@butlerarch.com.

BUTLER, JOSEPH EDWARD, marketing executive, consultant; b. Portland, Aug. 1, 1945; s. Joseph Edward and MaryAnne Butler; m. Catherine Mary Cormier, Apr. 16, 1982; 1 child, Christie Regina. BS in Engring. Physics, Merrimack Coll., Mass., 1967; MA in Physics, Williams Coll., Mass., 1969; MBA, Northeastern U., 1974. Certified Electromagnetic Compatibility Engineer, Natiional Assn. of Radio and Telecommunication Engineers, 1988. Engr. RCA, Burlington, Mass., 1967—71; sr. engr., sect. mgr. Raytheon, Bedford, Mass., 1971—81; mgr. of corp. stds. GenRad, Concord, Mass., 1981—86; mktg. mgr., new bus. devel. Chomerics, Woburn, Mass., 1986—. Town travel soccer dir. Hamilton Wenham Youth Soccer, Mass., 1994—2005; pres. Hamilton Wenham Edn. Fund, 1997—2003; fundraising Hamilton Wenham Regional H.S. Sports and Activities Alliance, 2004—. Recipient IEEE Millenium award, IEEE, 2000. Mem.: IEEE EMC Standards Bd. (bd. of dirs. 1990—2003), Soc. of Automotive Engrs., Assn. for the Advancement of Med. Instrumentation, IEEE Electromagnetic Compatibility Soc. (life; pres. 2001—02). Home: 78 Old Cart Rd South Hamilton MA 01982 Office: Chomerics Divsn Parker Hannifn 77 Dragon Ct Woburn MA 01901 Office Phone: 781-939-4267. Home Fax: 978-468-2515; Office Fax: 781-939-4213. Personal E-mail: jbemc@aol.com. E-mail: jbutler@parker.com.

BUTLER, KATHERINE E., lawyer; BA, Smith Coll; JD, Suffolk U.; LLM, Boston U. Bar: Mass. 1980. Lead legal counsel Software Internat. Corp., Andover, Mass.; atty. GE, 1981—98; lead counsel GE Info. Svcs. Europe; sr. counsel GE Info. Svcs., Rockville, Md.; sr. v.p., gen. counsel Software AG, Inc. (USA), Reston, Va., 1998—. Avocation: bicycling. Office: Software AG Inc 11190 Sunrise Valley Dr Reston VA 20191-5453*

BUTLER, KERRY, actress; Actor: (Broadway plays) Les Miserables, 1987—2003, Blood Brothers, 1993—95, Beauty and the Beast, 1994—95, Hairspray, 2002—03, Little Shop of Horrors, 2003— (nominated best actress Outer Critics Cir.), The Man in the White Suit, 2005, (regional stage shows) Prodigal, Le Passe Muraille, Bat Boy The Musical, The "I" Word, The Folsom Head, Bright Lights, Big City, Oklahoma. Office: Abrams Artists Agy 26th Fl 275 Seventh Ave New York NY 10001 Office Phone: 646-486-4600. Office Fax: 646-486-0100.*

BUTLER, KEVIN M., electronics executive; B in Psychology, U. Notre Dame, 1977, M in Psychology, 1979. Various pos., including prodn. supr., plant pers. mgr., sr. adminstr. classified employee complensation, mgr. exec. compensation GM Chevrolet Motor Divsn., 1976—89; dir. human resources GM Hydramatic divsn., Ypsilanti, Mich., 1989—91; dir. GM Health Care Plans, 1991—95; gen. dir. GM Health Care initiative staff, 1995—97; gen. dir. human resources Delphi Corp., Troy, Mich., 1997—2000, v.p. human resource mgmt., 2000—, mem. strategy bd., exec. champion pers. team. Exec. com. Midwest Bus. Group on Health. Adv. bd. Ind. U., Kokomo, Xavier U. Health Adminstrn.; bd. dirs. Am. Soc. Employers. Office: World Hdqrs Delphi Corp 5725 Delphi Dr Troy MI 48098-2815 Office Phone: 248-813-2000. Office Fax: 248-813-2670.*

BUTLER, LOUIS BENNETT, JR., state supreme court justice, lawyer; b. Chgo., Feb. 15, 1952; s. Louis Bennett and Gwendolyn (Prescott) B.; m. Irene Marianne Hecht, Aug. 30, 1981; children: Jessica Marianne, Erika Nicole. BA, Lawrence U., 1973; JD, U. Wis., Madison, 1977. Bar: Ill. 1978, Wis. 1979, U.S. Dist. Ct. (no. dist.) Ill. 1978, U.S. Dist. Ct. (ea. dist.) Wis. 1979, U.S. Ct. Appeals (7th cir.) 1979, U.S. Supreme Ct. 1983. Teaching asst. legal writing U. Wis. Law Sch., Madison, 1974-76; patient rights adv. Bur. Mental Health, Madison, 1976; hearing examiner, 1976-77; legal intern Prisoner's Legal Assistance, Chgo., 1977-78; atty. Independence Bank, Chgo., 1978-79, appellate atty. Office State Pub. Defender, Milw., 1979-92, judge, Milw. Mcpl. Ct., 1992-2002, Milw. Cty. Circuit Ct., 2002-04; justice, Wis. Supreme Ct., 2004-; Active South Shore Community Orgn., Chgo., 1978; pres. adv. bd. Adaptive Behavior Ctr., Chgo. Reed Mental Health Ctr., 1978; mem. faculty Nat. Jud. Coll., Reno, Nev., 2001-04; adj. prof. Marquette U., 1991-92; bd. dirs. criminal law sect. State Bar Wis., individual rights and responsibilities sect. Mem. Wis. Bar Assn., Ill. State Bar Assn., Wis. Black Lawyer's Assn. (treas. 1984-85, bd. dirs. 1984—, pres. 1985-86), NAACP. Democrat. Roman Catholic. Office: Wisc Supreme Ct PO Box 1688 Madison WI 53701-1688 Office Phone: 608-266-1884. Business E-Mail: louis.butler@wiscourts.gov.

BUTLER, LUTHER DALE, writer; b. Alamosa, Colo., Nov. 14, 1929; s. David H. and Linnie A. (Jenkins) B.; m. M. Jo Branton; 1 child, Luther D. Jr. BA, Ea. N.Mex. U., 1953; BD, So. Bapt. Theol. Sem., Louisville, 1960; MA in English, Tarleton State U., 1986. With El Paso Natural Gas, Farmington, N.Mex., 1952; dir. Boyce Bapt. Ctr., Louisville, 1956-61; various positions Tex. Dept. Agr., Stephensville, 1962-84. Author: Preacher, 1993, Mysterious Valley, 1993, Red Heifer, 1998, County Dublin and Blood on the Moon, 1999, Amite County and Mississippi Woman, 1999, Indians and Soldiers and Ranchers and Rustlers, 1999, Homesteaders and Sheepherders, 1999, I Knew an Man who had Six Sons and Squash Blossom, 1999, Mysterious Valley, 1999, Aids: No Place to Die, Apostate, Bastard, Bucaneer, Catfish Charlie, 2002, Curse of God, 2002, Death Rode a White Horse, 2002, books 1 and 2, The Deluge, 2002, Man Named Job and the Navahos, 2002, Shark Bait, 2002, Woman in the Attic Window, 2002, Tuck, 2002; author numerous poems in anthologies. With USN, 1952—55. Home and Office: 1310 N Wildwood Dr Stephenville TX 76401-2330 Office Phone: 254-968-3282. E-mail: lbutler@evath.net.

BUTLER, MANLEY CALDWELL, retired lawyer; b. Roanoke, Va., June 2, 1925; s. W.W.S. Butler Jr.; m. June Nolde, June 26, 1950; children: Manley, Henry, James, Marshall. AB, U. Richmond, 1948; JD, U. Va., 1950; LLD (hon.), Washington & Lee U., 1978. Bar: Va. 1950. Mem. Va. Ho. Dels., 1962-72, minority leader; mem. 92d-97th Congresses from 6th Va. dist., Judiciary Com., Com. on Govt. Ops., Woods, Rogers & Hazlegrove, P.L.C., 1983—99; ret., 1999. Mem. Nat. Bankruptcy Rev. Commn., 1995-97. Fellow Am. Bar Found., Am. Coll. Bankruptcy, Va. Law Found.; mem. ABA, Va. Bar Assn., Va. State Bar Assn., Roanoke Bar Assn., Am. Bankruptcy Inst., Raven Soc., Order of Coif, Phi Beta Kappa, Tau Kappa Alpha, Omicron Delta Kappa, Pi Delta Epsilon, Phi Gamma Delta. Episcopalian. Home: Unit 202 4434 Pheasant Ridge Rd Roanoke VA 24014-5279 Office Phone: 540-989-1915. Personal E-mail: nuniepapa@cox.net.

BUTLER, MARGARET KAMPSCHAEFER, retired computer scientist; b. Evansville, Ind., Mar. 7, 1924; d. Otto Louis and Lou Etta (Rehsteiner) Kampschaefer; m. James W. Butler, Sept. 30, 1951; 1 child, Jay. AB, Ind. U., 1944; postgrad., U.S. Dept. Agr. Grad. Sch., 1945, U. Chgo., 1949, U. Minn., 1950. Statistician U.S. Bur. Labor Statistics, Washington, 1945-46, U.S. Air Forces in Europe, Erlangen and Wiesbaden, Germany, 1946-48, U.S. Bur. Labor Statistics, St. Paul, 1949-51; mathematician Argonne (Ill.) Nat. Lab., 1948-49, 51-80, sr. computer scientist, 1980-92; dir. Argonne Code Ctr. and Nat. Energy Software Ctr. Dept. Energy Computer Program Exch., 1960-91; spl. term appointee Argonne Nat. Lab., 1993—. Cons. AMF Corp., 1956—57, OECD, 1964, Poole Bros., 1967. Author: Careers for Women in Nuclear Science and Technology, 1992; editor Computer Physics Communications, 1969-80; contbr. (chpt.) The Application of Digital Computers to Problems in Reactor Physics, 1968, Advances in Nuclear Sci. and Technology, 1976; contbr. articles to profl. publs. Treas. Timberlake Civic Assn., 1958; rep. mem. nomination com. Hinsdale (Ill.) Caucus, 1961-62; coord. 6th dist. ERA, 1973-80; elected del. Rep. Nat. Conv., 1980; bd. mgr. DuPage dist. YWCA Met. Chgo., 1987-90; computer and info. sys. adv. bd. Coll. DuPage, 1987-95; industry adv. bd. computer sci. dept. Bradley U., 1988-91; vice chair Ill. Women's Polit. Caucus, 1987-90; chair voters svc. LWV, Burr-Ridge-Willowbrook, 1991-93; vol. Morton Arboretum, 1996—, Friends of Indian Prairie Pub. Libr., 2000-02; mem. LaGrange Park Friends Libr., 2002-; bd. dirs. Plymouth Place Residents Coun., 2003-05, treas., 2004—, mem. spl. fin. and program coms, 2005—. Recipient cert. of leadership Met. YWCA, Chgo., 1985, Merit award Chgo. Assn. Technol. Socs., 1988; named to Fed. 100, 1991; named Outstanding Woman Leader of DuPage County Sci., Tech. and Health Care, 1992. Fellow Am. Nuclear Soc. (mem. publs. com. 1965-71, bd. dirs. 1976-79, exec. com. 1977-78, chmn. bylaws and rules com., 1979-82, profl. women in ANS com. 1991-93, reviewer for publs., spl. award math. and computer divsn. 1992); mem. Assn. Computing Machinery (exec. com., sec. Chgo. chpt. 1963-65, publs. chmn. nat. conf. 1968, reviewer for publs.), Assn. Women in Sci. (pres. Chgo. area chpt. 1982, nat. exec. bd. 1985-87), Nat. Computer Conf. (chmn. Pioneer Day com. 1985, tech. program chmn. 1987). Independent. Home: 107 Brewster Lane La Grange Park IL 60526-6003 *My goal is the removal of barriers restricting individuals from achieving their full potential and the furtherance of individual rights.*

BUTLER, MARILYN KATHARINE, school librarian, social studies educator; b. Colony, Kans., Feb. 3, 1953; d. Andy James and Virginia Anabelle Bauer; m. Scott Alan Butler, Apr. 17, 1999. AA, Allen County Cmty. Jr. Coll., Iola, Kans., 1973; B in Secondary Edn., Emporia State U., 1975, MLS, 1976. Dist. libr. Offerle Elem. Sch./Kinsley Jr./Sr. HS, Kans., 1976—; social studies tchr. Kinsley (Kans.) Jr./Sr. H.S., 2001—. V.p. Family and Consumer Sci. Com., Kinsley, 2001—; com. mem. Edwards County Exec. Bd., Kinsley, 2001—. Blood donor ARC, Kinsley, Kans., 1979—; home deliverer Meals on Wheels, Kinsley, 1993—95; fair supt. Edwards Country Fair, Kinsley, 1997—; mem. Offerle United Meth. Ch., 2000—05. Named Grand Champion in Horticulture, Edwards County Fair, 2004, Jan. Employee of Month, 2005. Mem.: NEA (assoc.), Kans. Assn. Sch. Librs. (assoc.), Kinsley-Offerle Tchrs. Assn. (assoc.; sec., treas. 1980—, acting pres. 2003—). Methodist. Avocations: reading, hand stitchery, gardening, travel. Home: 211 N Main Offerle KS 67563 Office: Kinsley Jr/Srr HS 716 Colony Kinsley KS 67547 E-mail: mbutler@usd347.org.

BUTLER, MARK WILLIAM, religious organization administrator; b. Columbus, Ohio, Sept. 20, 1973; s. James Frederick and Melinda Lee Butler; m. Susan Elizabeth Tracy, Aug. 21, 1993; children: Anna Marie, Mary Kathryn, Andrew Thomas. BA, Berea Coll., 1995; M of Theol. Studies, Meth. Theol. Sch. Ohio, 1999. Cert. youth min. Diocese of Columbus, Ohio, 2004, Catechist Diocese of Columbus, Ohio, 1999. Cons. Dept. Religious Edn., Columbus, Ohio, 1998—2000; dir. Office Youth and Young Adult Ministry, 2000—. Chair Advocacy Mgmt. Com. (Nat. Fedn. Cath. Youth Ministry), Washington, 2004—; mem. Cath. Schs. Adv. Commn. (Diocese of Columbus), 2000—; chair Youth Forum Planning Com. (Columbus Coalition Against Family Violence), 2004—; bd. dirs. Disciples Now Ministries, Balt. Editor (webmaster): (web page: www.cdeducation.org/oym) Office of Youth and Young Adult Ministry Web Page. Chair, advocacy mgmt. com. Nat. Fedn. Cath. Youth Ministry, Washington, 2004—04; mem. Parish Advocates for Persons with Disabilities Adv. Commn. (Diocese of Columbus), 2002—04, Inclusion Com. (Diocese of Columbus), 1998—2004. Recipient Nat. Youth Ministry award, Nat. Fedn. Cath. Youth Ministry, 2002, Bronze Pelican award, Cath. Com. Scouting, Columbus, 2003, St. Anne award, Cath. Com. Girl Scouts and Camp Fire, Columbus, 2003. Mem.: Diocesan Assn. Religious Educators (assoc.). Roman Catholic. Office: Office Youth and Young Adult Ministry 197 East Gay St Columbus OH 43215 Office Phone: 614-241-2565. E-mail: mbutler@cdeducation.org.

BUTLER, MERLIN GENE, physician, medical geneticist, educator; b. Atkinson, Nebr., Aug. 2, 1952; s. Garold Melvin and Berdena June (Sandall) B.; m. Ranae Ilene Kisker, Oct. 2, 1976; children: Michelle Ranae, Brian Gene. BA with very high distinction, Chadron State Coll., 1974, BS with very high distinction, 1975; MD, U. Nebr., Omaha, 1978; MS, U. Nebr., Lincoln, 1980; PhD, Ind. U., Indpls., 1984. Supervising physician Med. Info. Svcs., Omaha, 1978-80; rsch. assoc. dept. biology U. Notre Dame, South Bend, Ind., 1983-84; med. dir. North Ctrl. Ind. Regional Genetics Ctr., South Bend, 1983-84; dir. cytogenetics Meml. Hosp., South Bend, 1983-84; NIH postdoctoral fellow dept. med. genetics Sch. Medicine Ind. U., Indpls., 1980-83, adj. asst. prof. dept. med. genetics Sch. Medicine, 1984; asst. prof. dept. pediatrics Sch. Medicine Vanderbilt U., Nashville, 1984-90, dir. regional genetics program Sch. Medicine, 1984-98, dir. Cytogenetics Lab. dept. pediatrics Sch. Medicine, 1989-98, assoc. prof. dept. pediatrics, 1990-98, assoc. prof. dept. pathology, 1991-98, investigator John F. Kennedy Ctr. Rsch. on Edn. and Human Devel., Peabody Coll., 1987-98; assoc. dir. Inst. Behavior and Genetics; assoc. prof. dept. orthopedics Vanderbilt U., 1994-98. Adj. assoc. prof. dept. pediatrics Meharry Med. Coll., Nashville, 1988-98; genetics cons. Baptist Hosp., Nashville, 1985-98, Westside Hosp., Nashville, 1985-98, Nashville Gen. Hosp., 1985-98, chief, section of Med. Genetics and Molecular Medicine, Children's Mercy Hosp., Kansas City, Mo., 1998—, William R. Brown prof., chmn., 1998—, prof. dept. pediats., U. Mo.-Kansas City Sch. Medicine; mem. epidemiology genetic diseases subcom. Ind. State Bd. Health, 1983-84; faculty interviewer Vanderbilt U., 1987; peer reviewer Am. Jour. Human Genetics, Am. Jour. Med. Genetics, Clin. Genetics, Am. Jour. Diseases of Children, Dysmorphology and Clin. Genetics, Am. Jour. Mental Retardation, Jour. Pediatrics, So. Med. Jour., Human Mutations, Cancer Genetics and Cytogenetics, Pediatrics, Genomics, Prader-Willi Perspectives; mem. ad-hoc grant review com. NIH, 1990—, craniofacial assessment team Vanderbilt U., 1992-98; lectr., presenter in field. Author: Fragile X Syndrome: A Major Cause of X-Linked Mental Retardation, 1988, 1989; author: (with others) Genetics for the Medically Oriented, 1983, Novak's Textbook of Gynecology, 11th edit., 1988, Birth Defects Encyclopedia, 1990, Prader-Willi Syndrome and Other Chromosome 15q Deletion Disorders, 1992, Human Genetics: New Perspectives, 1994, 1992 International Fragile X Conference Proceedings, 1992, Prader-Willi and Angelman Syndromes Examples of Genetic Imprinting in Man, 1994, Prader-Willi Syndrome: A Guide for Parents and Physicians, 1995, Prader-Willi Syndrome: Clinical and Genetic Findings, 2000' editor: Genetics of Developmental Disabilities, 2005, Management of Prader-Willi Syndrome, 2005; mem. editl. bd. Prader-Willi Perspectives, 1992—; contbr. numerous articles to profl. jours. including Nature and New England Jour. Medicine. Grant reviewer March of Dimes Birth Defects Found., 1985—. Recipient Disting. Svc. award Chadron State Coll., 1986, Teaching award Osler Inst., 1989; grantee Univ. Rsch. Coun., 1985, 92-93, Tenn. Dept. Mental Health and Mental Retardation, 1986-91, Clin. Nutrition Rsch. Unit, 1986-88, Joseph P. Kennedy, Jr. Found., 1988, Clin. Rsch. Ctr. Meharry Med. Coll., 1989-98, Dept. Pathology, 1992-93, Orthopedic Rsch. Edn. Found., 1993-95, NIH, 1995—; Cancer Rsch. grantee Ind. U. Med. Ctr., 1980, Biomed. Rsch. Support grantee, 1985, 88, 89—, Clin. Rsch. grantee March of Dimes Birth Defects Found., 1987, 88, 90-92, Lyle V. Andrews Meml. scholar, 1974. Fellow Am. Coll. Med. Genetics (founder, diplomate, lab. practice subcom. 1993); mem. AMA (Physician Recognition award 1984, 87, 00), AAAS, Am. Bd. Med. Genetics (cert. clin. genetics and clin. cytogenetics), Am. Genetics Assn., Am. Soc. Human Genetics (cytogenetics resource com. 1992-97), Am. Fedn. Clin. Rsch., Coll. Am. Pathologists (cytogenetics resource com. 1992-97, molecular pathology resource com. 1993-97), So. Med. Assn., Davidson County Pediatric Soc., Metro. Med. Soc., Prader-Willi Syndrome Assn. (med. rsch. task force 1985—, diagnostic task force 1991—, sci. adv. bd. 1991—, chair 2000—), N.Y. Acad. Scis., Sigma Xi, Phi Chi. Avocations: gardening, camping, fishing, collecting sports memorabilia. Home: 6410 Hillside St Shawnee KS 66218-9070 Office: Children's Mercy Hosp 2401 Gillham Rd Kansas City MO 64108-4698 E-mail: mgbutler@cmh.edu.

BUTLER, MICHAEL FRANCIS, lawyer; b. Pitts., Aug. 17, 1935; s. Frank J. and Mary M. (Montgomery) B. BA magna cum laude, Harvard U., 1957; LLB, Yale U., 1960. Bar: Pa., D.C. Mem. Kirkpatrick & Lockhart, Pitts., 1960-69; asst. gen. counsel for domestic and internat. bus., then dep. gen. counsel U.S. Dept. Commerce, Washington, 1969-73; v.p., gen. counsel Overseas Pvt. Investment Corp., Washington, 1973-75; gen. counsel Fed. Energy Adminstrn., Washington, 1975-77; ptnr. Andrews & Kurth, Washington, 1977-92. Bd. dirs., chmn. audit com. Three Rivers Bancorp, Inc., Three Rivers Bank & Trust Co.; mem. adv. com. Fagan & Co.; mem. panel of arbitrators Dispute Settlement Ctr., Internat. Energy Agy., Paris; past mem. or chmn. U.S. dels. to OECD coms., Berne Union, Adminstrv. Conf. of U.S. Contbr. articles to profl. publs. Past vice chmn. class spl. gifts com. Harvard Coll. and Yale Law Sch.; past bd. dirs., sec. Three Rivers Arts Festival, Pitts.; past bd. dirs. Bryce Harlow Found. Fellow Am. Bar Found. (life); mem. ABA (past chmn. com. on fgn. investment in U.S. internat. law sect.), Am. Arbitration Assn. (mem. comml. panel of arbitrators), Pa. Bar Assn., D.C. Bar Assn., Allegheny County Bar Assn., Am. Law Inst., Am. Judicature Soc., Am. Soc. Internat. Law, Internat. Bar Assn., Washington Fgn. Law Soc., Inter-Am. Bar Assn., Harvard Club West Pa. (past. sec.), Harvard Club of D.C. (past bd. dirs.), Met. Club, Rolling Rock Club (Ligonier, Pa.), Harvard-Yale-Princeton Club (Pitts.). Republican. Presbyterian. Home and Office: 2214 Massachusetts Ave NW Washington DC 20008-2812

BUTLER, MICHAEL WARD, economics professor; b. Great Bend, Kans., June 11, 1939; s. George Ward and Mary Jane (Lambert) B.; m. Regina Ann Hammond, Sept. 8, 1995; 1 child, Alexander Ward. BSBA, Fort Hays State U., 1963, MS in Econs., 1964; PhD in Econs., U. Ark., 1974. Diplomate Am. Bd. Forensic Examiners. Data processing sales rep. IBM, Wichita, Kans., 1964-66; instr. econs. Butler County C.C., El Dorado, Kans., 1964-70; asst. prof. econs. U. North Ala., Florence, 1973-75, assoc. prof. econs., 1975-78, prof. econs., 1978-97, dean coll. bus., 1997-2001; dean Coll. Bus. and Profl. Studies, Angelo State U., San Angelo, Tex., 2001—. Referee Jour. Forensic Econs., Kansas City, Mo., 1988—; editl. adv. Ark. Bus. Econs. Rev., Fayetteville, Ark., 1976-99; editl. bd. Am. Bd. of Forensic Examiners, Springfield, Mo., 1995-98; mem. mgmt. adv. com. Wise Alloys, L.L.C., 1999-2001; pres. Region 3, Assn. of Collegiate Bus. Schs. and Programs, 1999-2000; bd. dirs. Wells Fargo Cmty. Bank; chmn. Concho Valley Ctr. for Entrepreneurship. Editor: Jour. Legal Econs., 1991—2005. Bd. govs. Soc. Litig. Economists, 2000-02. Recipient Outstanding Achievement award Am. Higher Ed., 1985; Disting. Svc. award Ala. C. of C., Montgomery, 1976. Mem. Assn. Collegiate Bus. Schs. and Programs (pres. region 3 1999-2000), Nat. Assn. Forensic Economists, Am. Coll. Forensic Examiners, Am. Rehab. Econs. Assoc. (adv. bd. 1992-94), MidSouth Acad. Econs. and Fin. (pres.

85-86), Am. Acad. Econ. Fin. Experts (pres. 1994-96, svc. award 1995), Am. Econs. Assn., San Angelo C. of C. Avocations: wine collecting, boating. Home: 3101 Clearview Dr San Angelo TX 76904 Office: Angelo State U PO Box 11030 University Station San Angelo TX 76909 Office Phone: 325-942-2337. Business E-Mail: michael.butler@angelo.edu.

BUTLER, OCTAVIA ESTELLE, writer; b. Pasadena, Calif., June 22, 1947; d. Laurice and Octavia Margaret (Guy) B. AA, Pasadena City Coll., 1968; student, Calif. State U., Los Angeles, 1969—. Free-lance writer, Los Angeles, 1975—. MacArthur fellow, 1995. Author: Patternmaster, 1976, Mind of My Mind, 1977, Survivor, 1978, Kindred, 1979, Wild Seed, 1980, Clay's Ark, 1984, Dawn, 1987, Adulthood Rites, 1988, Imago, 1989, Parable of the Sower, 1993 (Nebula award winner), Bloodchild, 1995, Parable of the Talents, 1998, Fledgling, 2005; also sci. fiction short stories. Mem. adv. bd. Science Fiction Mus. and Hall of Fame. Recipient fifth prize Writer's Digest Short Story Contest, 1967, Creative Arts Achievement award L.A. YWCA, 1980, Sci. Fiction (Hugo) Best Novelette award World Sci. Fiction Conf., 1985, Best Short Story award World Sci. Fiction Conv., 1984, Nebula Best Novelette award Sci. Fiction Writers Am., 1985, Locus Best Novelette award, 1985, Best Novelette award Sci. Fiction Chronicle Reader, 1985, Nebula award for Best Novel, Sci. Fiction and Fantasy Writers Am., 2000; fellow John D. and Catherine T. MacArthur Found., 1995. Mem. Sci. Fiction Writers Am., Nat. Writers Union. Address: PO Box 25400 Seattle WA 98165-2300*

BUTLER, ORTON CARMICHAEL, climatologist; b. Millersburg, Ohio, June 9, 1923; s. Maxon Henry Butler and Atossa Ruth Carmichael; m. Betty Ellen Johnson, Sept. 15, 1951; children: Marilyn Jean, Kathryn Ellen. BA, Oberlin Coll., 1948; MA, Clark U., 1951; PhD, Ohio State U., 1969. Rsch. analyst, China specialist U.S. Army Engr. Strategic Intelligence, Washington, 1951-60; prof. Memphis State U. (now U. Memphis), 1960-81; prof. emeritus U. Memphis, 1981. Author: (book) An Introductory Soils Laboratory Handbook, 1979, other publs. Cpl. U.S. Army, 1942-46, PTO. Mem. Masons. Republican. United Ch. of Christ. Avocations: tree farming, gardening, golf.

BUTLER, PAM, artist; b. NYC, Jan. 12, 1955; d. Arthur D. and Kathleen (Lehman) Butler. Student, SUNY, Buffalo, 1976-78; BS in Fine Arts, Empire State Coll., 1982; MFA, Sch. Visual Arts, 1990. Guest lectr. Trinity Coll., Hartford, Conn., 1991; tchr. PS 87 After Sch. Art Program, N.Y.C., 1992-93; guest lectr. Internat. Ctr. for Photography, 1994, Empire State Coll., 1994, 95. Mem. adv. bd. PS 122 Gallery, N.Y.C., 1995—; Nat. Endowment for Arts outreach resident Va. Ctr. for Arts, 1997. Work exhibited at Adam L. Gimble Gallery, 1982, Visual Arts Gallery, 1990, Milkie Way Gallery, 1991, PS 122 Gallery, 1992, 95, Muranushi Lederman, Inc., 1992 Horodner Romley Gallery, 1992, Doley Le Cappellaine, 1992 (all N.Y.C.), Delta Axis Ctr. for Contemporary Art, Memphis, 1992, Art in General, N.Y.C., 1993, Artists Space, N.Y.C., 1993, Hallwalls, Buffalo, N.Y., 1993, 95, FDR Gallery, N.Y.C., 1994, Russet Lederman, N.Y.C., 1994, Contemporary Art Ctr. (catalogue), Moscow, 1994, White Columns, N.Y.C., 1994, 95, Scotland Street Mus., Glasgow, 1995, Collett Art Gallery, Ogden, Utah, 1996, Eich Space Gallery, N.Y.C., 1997, Jorgensen Gallery, N.Y.C., 1998, Tribes Gallery, N.Y.C., 1998, Gramercy Art Fair, N.Y.C., 1999, White Columns, N.Y.C., 1999, Jean Deaux Gallery, Bklyn., 2000, 31 Grand St. Gallery, Bklyn., 2000, Cheryl Pelavin Gallery, N.Y.C., 2001, Gerber-Seid Visual, N.Y.C., 2002; pub. projects include (installed posters) Good Girl Project, N.Y.C., 1994-96, Memphis, 1994, Buffalo, 1995, (billboard) Art Belongs to the People, Moscow, 1994, (performance and posters) The Win Project, N.Y.C., 1994—. Fellow N.Y. Found. for Arts, 1997. Office: Good Girl Project 250 Moore St # 209 Brooklyn NY 11206

BUTLER, PATRICIA CLAIRE, history educator; b. N.Y.C., Jan. 16, 1935; d. John Joseph Butler and Genevieve Katherine Vanderbilt. BSM, Manhattanville Coll., 1970; postgrad., St. John's U., 1970; MSEd, L.I. U., 1973. Cert. tchr. NY. Educator grades 1-6 Diocese of Rockville Centre, NY, 1955—63, music educator grades K-8, 1970—75; educator grades 1-8 Diocese of Bklyn., 1963—75; music educator Molloy Coll., Rockville Centre, 1970—75; educator history and religion Corpus Christi Sch., Mineola, NY, 1976—89, Sacred Heart Sch., Highland Falls, NY, 1993—2005. Dir. agenda com. Corpus Christi Sch., Mineola, 1976—89; dir. chorus and choirs, accompanist Diocese of Rockville Centre, 1955, Diocese of Bklyn. Mem.: Fedn. Cath. Tchrs. Republican. Roman Catholic. Avocations: reading, politics, ice skating, classical music, walking. Home: PO Box 641 Fort Montgomery NY 10922 Office: Sacred Heart Sch 7 Cozzens Ave Highland Falls NY 10928

BUTLER, PATRICIA E., mathematician, educator; d. Michael J. and Edith J. Clifford; m. Jeffry A. Butler, June 13, 1985; children: Kevin M., Kathryn F. M in Gifted Edn., No. Ill. U., 1982. Cert. Tchr. Math. 9-12 Ill., 1974. Tchr., chair math. dept. West Aurora H.S., Ill., 1974—. Recipient Edyth Mae Slythe award, Am. Math. Assn., 2001. Office: West Aurora High School 1201 W New York St Aurora IL 60506 Business E-Mail: pebutler@sd129.org.

BUTLER, RANDALL EDWARD, lawyer; b. Houston, Sept. 11, 1954; m. Katherine Ann Simmons, Aug. 25, 1973; children: Lauren Elizabeth, Mary Katherine. BA magna cum laude, Houston Bapt. U., 1976; postgrad., Southwestern Bapt. Theol. Sem., 1976-77; JD cum laude, U. Houston, 1980. Bar: Tex. 1980, Fed. Bar 1981. Briefing atty. 14th Ct. of Civil Appeals, Houston, 1980-81; assoc. Fulbright & Jaworski, Houston, 1981-89, ptnr., 1989-91, Cook & Wallace PC, 1992, Cook & Butler LLP, 1992-96, Cook Butler & Doyle LLP, Houston, 1996-98; pres. Butler Mediation Services, 1999—, Butler Enterprises L.L.C., 2001; gen. ptnr. Butler Online Mediation L.P., 2001. Instr. Houston Bapt. U., 1980—81; adj. prof. med. malpractice U. Houston Law Ctr.; mediation tng. Atty.-mediator inst., 1995; with Advanced Mediator Tng., Atty. Mediator Inst., 1995—, Harvard Negotiation Workshop, 1997, Conciliator Tng., Inst. for Christian Conciliation, 1999, Advanced Practicum Inst. for Christian Conciliation, 2000; lectr. on conflict resolution ROM Leadership Develop. & Peace Project, Fuzine, Croatia, 2002—; adj. prof. Internat. Conflict Resolution course, U. St. Thomas, 2003—. Contbr. articles to profl. jours. Bd. dirs. UBA Ctr. for Counseling, 1989-91, mem. pres.'s coun. Houston Bapt U., 1989-91, bd. trustees, 1990-92. Recipient Pres.'s award Houston Bapt. U., 1976; Riverside scholar, 1976; grantee Houston Bapt. U. Edn. Found. Fellow Houston Bar Found.; mem. ABA, State Bar of Tex. (ADR sect.). Achievements include patents pending for created online sys. for mediating mass litigation, 2001. Avocations: skiing, hiking, history, landscape gardening. Office: Butler Mediation Svcs 5300 Memorial Ste 800 Houston TX 77007 Fax: 713-626-9836. E-mail: randall@butlermediation.com.

BUTLER, RAYMOND ARCHIBALD, cartographer; b. Windsor, Va. s. J. Butler and Odie Underwood; m. Phyllis Jane Holden, June 1942; children: David Holden, Pamela Rae Butler Chryst, Keith Underwood, Melanie Butler Post. Student, Syracuse U., 1932—36. Asst. to Admiral Byrd, 1939—41; chief of Arctic Unit Aero Med. Lab., Wright Field; cartographer of Antarctic Projects Rsch. Ctr., Washington. Recipient Spl. Medal of Honor, Rear Adm. Richard E. Byrd, 1947, Mountain named in his honor at South Pole. Democrat. Baptist. Avocations: birdwatching, hiking, camping, painting oil landscapes. Home: 5433 Pigeon Hill Rd Spring Grove PA 17362

BUTLER, REX LAMONT, lawyer; b. New Brunswick, N.J., Mar. 24, 1951; s. Ekker and Beatrice (Curry) B.; m. Stephanie Butler; children: Nijel Jaibrun, Vikteria Lamontra, Octavia Reneè Lamontra, Synclaire Lamontra. AA with honors, Fla. Jr. Coll., 1975; BA, U. North Fla., 1977; JD, Howard U., 1983. Bar: Alaska 1983, U.S. Dist. Ct. Alaska 1983, U.S. Ct. Appeals (9th cir.) 1984, U.S. Ct. Appeals (D.C. cir.) 1984, U.S. Supreme Ct. 1996. Assoc. M. Ashley Dickerson, Inc., Anchorage, 1983-84; profl. legis. asst. State of Alaska, Juneau, 1984, asst. atty. gen. Anchorage, 1984-85; pvt. practice Anchorage, 1985—; owner Rex Attys. Video, Inc. (RAV, Inc.), 2000. Adj. prof. law Anchorage C.C., 1985, U. Alaska, Anchorage, 1990—; mem. State Ct. Criminal Pattern Jury Instructions Com., 1997; chmn. lawyer rep. com. Alaska 9th Cir. Judicial Conf., 1997-98; law analyst for the news. Pres. Alaska Black Caucus, Anchorage, 1986, bd. dirs., 1987-88; gen. counsel NAACP, Anchorage, 1985-87, life mem., v.p. Anchorage branch, 2002-04; commr. Anchorage Telephone Utility, 1985-87; trustee Anchorage Sr. Ctr., Inc., 1985-87, Shiloh Missionary Bapt. Ch., Anchorage, 1985-87; bd. dirs. Ctr. Drug Problems, Anchorage, 1985-86, Alaska Civil Liberties Union, 1987-88; active fin. com. Dem. Cen. Com. Alaska; founder Rights Advocacy Project, Inc. (RAP, Inc.), 2004. With USN, 1969-73. Named one of Outstanding Young Men Am., 1984; recipient Cert. Appreciation, African Relief Campaign, 1985. Mem. ABA, Nat. Bar Assn., Nat. Assn. Criminal Defense Lawyers, Alaska Bar Assn., Assn. Trial Lawyers Am., Anchorage Bar Assn., Alaska Trial Lawyers Assn., Lions Internat., Omega Psi Phi (dist. counselor 1995-96, 98-2002). Democrat. Home: PO Box 200025 Anchorage AK 99520-0025 Office: 745 W 4th Ave Ste 300 Anchorage AK 99501-2157 Fax: 907-276-3306. Office Phone: 907-272-1497. Business E-Mail: rexattys@alaska.net.

BUTLER, RICHARD J., federal agency administrator, consultant; m. Mindiann Reisman, Dec. 26, 1981; children: Eric Phillip, Andrew Francis, Matthew Jared. BS in Polit. Sci., U. Md., 1992. Commd. 2d lt. US Army, 1988—2001; mil. expert, war crimes analyst Internat. Criminal Tribunal for Former Yugoslavia, The Hague, Netherlands, 1997—2003; intelligence rsch. specialist US Immigration and Customs Enforcement, Atlanta, 2004—. Mem.: Assn. US Army, Am. Soc. Internat. Law. Achievements include prosecution military expert in landmark Srebrenica genocide and war crimes conviction of Gen. Radislav Krstic at the International Criminal Tribunal for the Former Yugoslavia (1999-2004). Avocation: military history. Office: US Immigration and Customs Enforcement 1691 Phoenix Blvd Atlanta GA 30349 Office Phone: 770-994-4193. Business E-Mail: richard.butler@dhs.gov.

BUTLER, ROBERT CARLYLE, III, lawyer; b. Tulsa, Okla., Mar. 1, 1973; s. Robert Carlyle and Mary Virginia Butler; m. Erin Sutherland, May 30, 2000. BA, U. Tulsa, 1996, JD, 2000. Bar: Okla. 2000, U.S. Dist. Ct. (no. dist.) Okla. 2000, U.S. Ct. Appeals (10th cir.) 2000. Counsel Wagner & Grandy LLP, Tulsa, Okla., 2000—02; counsel, owner Butler Law Office PLLC, Tulsa, 2002—. Bd. dirs. Comml. Bank, Tulsa. Author: Pre and Post Nuptial Agreements, 2001. Mem.: ABA, Tulsa County Bar Assn., Okla. Bar Assn. Republican. Avocations: tennis, coaching Pop Warner, German language, Big Brothers and Big Sisters. Office: 5508 S Lewis Tulsa OK 74105

BUTLER, ROBERT OLEN, writer, educator; b. Granite City, Ill., Jan. 20, 1945; s. Robert Olen Sr. and Lucille Frances (Hall) B.; m. Carol Supplee, Aug. 10, 1968 (div. Jan. 1972); m. Marylin Geller, July 1, 1972 (div. July 1987); 1 child, Joshua Robert; m. Maureen Donlan, July 21, 1987 (div. Mar. 1995); m. Elizabeth Dewberry, Apr. 23, 1995. BS summa cum laude in Oral Interpretation, Northwestern U., 1967; MA in Playwriting, U. Iowa, 1969; postgrad., New Sch. Social Rsch., 1979-81; LHD, McNeese State U., 1994. Editor-in-chief Energy User News, N.Y.C., 1975-85; assoc. prof. fiction writing McNeese State U., Lake Charles, La., 1985—93, prof., 1993—2001; Francis Epps prof. Fla. State U., 2001—. Summer faculty Iowa Summer Writing Festival U. Iowa, Port Townsend (Wash.) Writers Conf., New Orleans Writers' Conf., Southampton Writers' Conf., Long Island U., N.Y., Hofstra U. Summer Writing Conf., Hempstead, N.Y., others, 1988—. Author: The Alleys of Eden, 1981 (also wrote screenplay 1991-92), Sun Dogs, 1982, Countrymen of Bones, 1983, Fragments, 1984, On Distant Ground, 1985, Wabash, 1987, The Deuce, 1989, (short story collection) A Good Scent from a Strange Mountain, 1992 (Pulitzer Prize for fiction 1993, Richard and Hinda Rosenthal Found. award Am. Acad. Arts & Letters 1993, nominee PEN/Faulkner award 1993, Notable Book 1993 Notable Books Coun. Am. Libr. Assn.), They Whisper, 1994, Tabloid Dreams, 1996, The Deep Green Sea, 1998, Mr. Spaceman, 2000, Silver Rose Anthology: Award-Winning Short Stories, 2001, 2002, Fair Warning, 2002, From Where You Dream: The Process of Writing Fiction, 2005; author numerous short stories; works translated to 12 langs.; contbr. articles, book reviews to jours., newspapers, screenplays. Sgt. U.S. Army, 1969-72, Vietnam. Recipient Emily Clark Balch award best work fiction, 1990 Va. Quar. Rev., 1991, TuDo Chinh Kien award outstanding contbns. Am. culture by Vietnam vet. Vietnam Vets. Am., 1987, Medal of Merit, Lotos Club, 1996; grantee NEA, 1994; fellow John Simon Guggenheim Found., 1993. Mem. PEN, WGAWest. Office: English Dept Fla State U 411 Williams Bldg Tallahassee FL 32306-1580 E-mail: rbutler@english.fsu.edu.

BUTLER, ROBERT THOMAS, retired advertising executive; b. Westmont, N.J., Feb. 22, 1925; s. John T. and Kathryn M. (Donehower) B.; m. Eleanore MacIndoe, May 4, 1950; children— R. Mark, Kathryn J., Elizabeth Anne. BS, Temple U., Phila., 1951. Market research mgr. James Lees Carpet Co., 1951-53; v.p. N.W. Ayer, Phila., 1953-74; pres. Gray & Rogers, Phila., 1975-90. Served with USCG, 1943-46. Mem.: St. David's (Pa.) Golf, Merion Cricket (Haverford, Pa.). Republican. Episcopalian.

BUTLER, RUSSELL, artist; b. N.Y.C., Mar. 7, 1949; s. Milton W. and Dorothy Ann (Adams) B. BFA, U. Buffalo, 1971; postgrad., San Francisco Art Inst., 1977. Art dir. Anneliesees Sch., Laguna Beach, Calif., 1977—90, Willowbrook, Calif., 1987-88; owner Russ Butler Sch. of Art, Laguna Beach, 1981-84; artist Stein/Brief Corp., Newport Beach, Calif., 1983, Xerox, San Francisco, 1985, City of Laguna Beach, 1986, Transamerica Corp., Los Angeles, 1987, U. Calif. Irvine Med. Ctr., Orange, Calif., 1987-88. Co-founder Henry T. Ncholas and Henry Samueli Home Design and Murals, Broadcom Corp. Prin. works include (commemorative murals) Legend of the Waters, 1988, Delusions of Grandeur, 1987, Dreamer, 1983, 5 major paintings U. Calif. Irvine Med. Ctr., painting Am. Cancer Soc., 1994, mural Chas. Gibson, 1996, mural Dr. Richard Ellenbogen, 1997, mural French 75 Restaurant, Laguna Beach, Calif., mural Mariott Hotel, Dana Pt., Calif., 1998, mural Dr. Henry Samueli, 2000-2003, mural and design, Patrick Mahoney, 2004; exhibited at L.A. Art Expo, 1988, 90, Sheraton Rosemead, Magic Internat., 1989; one-man exhbns. Fortuny Gallery, Laguna Beach, Calif., 1990, Arnold & Mabel Beckman Ctr. of Am. Acads. Sci. & Engring., 1992; lobby paintings include San Clemente Corp. Ctr., 1990, Greater L.A. World Trade Ctr., 1992; also exhibited at The Naked Truth exhbn. Costa Mesa, L.A., 1991, The Artist's Ball exhbn., Costa Mesa, Calif.; designer/muralist pvt. homes; creative designer 2001 Opera Pacific Ball, Santa Ana, Calif., Sta. KOCE-TV Awards Show, Festa Italiana, 2002, Opera Pacific Ball, 2003. Mem. Aliso Artists Alliance (pres. 1981-84). Avocations: wildlife photography, body building, horticulture, mystical studies, music. Home: 128 W Avenida Lobos Marinos San Clemente CA 92672 Office Phone: 949-463-2896. Personal E-mail: russbutler@cox.net.

BUTLER, SAMUEL COLES, lawyer; b. Logansport, Ind., Mar. 10, 1930; s. Melvin Linwood and Jane Lavina (Flynn) B.; m. Sally Eugenia Thackston, June 28, 1952; children: Samuel Coles, Leigh F., Elizabeth J. AB magna cum laude, Harvard U., 1951, LLB magna cum laude, 1954. Bar: D.C. 1954, Ind. 1954, N.Y. 1957. Law clk. to Justice Minton U.S. Supreme Ct., 1954; assoc. Cravath, Swaine & Moore, N.Y.C., 1956—60, ptnr., 1961—2003, sr. counsel, 2004—. Trustee Vassar Coll., 1969-77, NY Pub. Libr., 1979—, chmn. bd., 1999—2004; trustee Am. Mus. Natural History, 1989-93, The September 11 Fund, 2001-04; chmn. Harvard Coll. Fund, 1977-85; bd. overseers Harvard U., 1982-88, pres. bd., 1986-88; bd. dirs. Culver Ednl. Found., 1981-2001, v.p. bd. 1985-2001. With U.S. Army, 1954-56. Mem. Coun. Fgn. Rels. Home: 1220 Park Ave New York NY 10128-1733 Office: Cravath Swaine & Moore LLP 825 8th Ave New York NY 10019-7475

BUTLER, SHEILA MORRIS, occupational health nurse; b. Paducah, Ky., Sept. 12, 1944; d. Edwin Morris and Beatrice Aileen (Hobbs) Word; m. Benjamin Edward Butler, Dec. 4, 1976; 1 child, Michelle Renee. ADN, Paducah Jr. Coll., 1966. Cert. occupational health nurse, Am. Bd. Occupational Health, occupational hearing conservationist. Staff nurse Marshall County Hosp., Benton, Ky., 1966-67; shift nursing supr. Parkview Hosp., Dyersburg, Tenn., 1967-69, obstet. nursing supr., 1969-72; clin. nursing instr. State of Tenn. Dept. of Edn., Nashville, 1968-69; charge nurse Dravo-Groves-Newberg, Hamlettsburg, Ill., 1972-74; surg. nurse Western Bapt. Hosp., Paducah, Ky., 1974-76; ophthalmic asst. Dr. Harry Abell, Jr., Paducah, Ky., 1976-83; occupational health cons. self-employed, Paducah, Ky., 1983-86; plant nurse Air Products & Chemicals, Inc., Calvert City, Ky., 1986—. Bd. dirs. Nat. Nurses Soc. on Addiction, 1983-84; bd. dirs. Am. Bd. Occupational Health Nurses, 1994-2001, treas., 1997-99, chair Cohn adv. bd., 1999-2000; sec. Jackson Purchase Oper. Nurses, Paducah, 1975-76; cmty. asst. panel Agy. for Toxic Substance and Disease Registry of CDC, Atlanta, 1991-94; pres. Jackson Purchase Occupational Health Nurse, 1993-96. Mem. Nat. Arbor Day Found. Named Student Nurse of Yr., Circle K-Paducah Jr. Coll., 1966, Ky. Col., Gov. Louie B. Nunn, 1971—; recipient Chem. Group Recognition award Air Products & Chems., 1990, 91. Mem. NAFE, Am. Assn. Occupational Health Nurses (pres. Jackson Purchase sect. 1993-95), Civil Def. of McCracken County, Order of Ea. Star, Esther # 5 Ruth, Daus. of the Nile Neith Temple, Chinese Shar-Pei Club of Am. Democrat. Baptist. Avocations: bicycling, swimming, gardening, needle work. Home: 248 Hayes St Benton KY 42025-6649 Office: Air Products & Chemicals PO Box 97 Calvert City KY 42029-0097 Office Phone: 270-395-2256. Business E-Mail: butlersw@airproducts.com. E-mail: swb912@mchsi.com.

BUTLER, TERRENCE LAMONT, lawyer; b. N.Y.C., Oct. 22, 1957; s. John Lewis and Fay Winifred Butler. BA, Columbia U., 1980; JD, Howard U., 1984. Bar: N.Y. 1997. Law clk. John Butler, Esq., Bklyn., 1984-90; pvt. practice Bklyn., 1990—. Counsel RELCO Corp./T Prodns., Bklyn., 1990—; computer cons. RelTub Corp., Bklyn., 1997. Author, prodr. CD Sing A Song, 1997. Mem. Kings County Criminal Bar Assn., Bklyn. Bar Assn., Met. Black Bar Assn. Avocations: martial arts, jogging, puzzles, creative writing, acting. Office: 78 Ralph Ave Ste 200 Brooklyn NY 11221-4118 Office Phone: 917-443-1691.

BUTLER, THOMAS WILLIAM, retired health and social services administrator; b. Aiken, SC, Aug. 29, 1933; s. Eddie and Lillie Mae B.; BA, Adelphi U., 1958; MS in Social Work, Columbia U., 1964; MPA, NYU, 1970; children: Kathi Susan, Thomas William, Michael David. Case supr. Nassau County (NY) Dept. Social Svcs., 1959-67; exec. asst. Joint Legis. Com. on Problems of Public Health Svcs., Medicare, Medicaid and Compulsory Health Ins., N.Y. State, 1967-69; dir. cmty. affairs NYC Health and Hosps. Corp., 1969-72; with div. alcohol, drug abuse and mental health Public Health Service, Dept. Health and Human Svc., NYC, 1972-95, regional cons. for mental health, 1972-79, regional supr. substance abuse and mental health, 1979-81, co-acting dir. Region II, NYC, 1981, chief health services, 1981-85, chief primary care health services, 1985-86, chief planning, evaluation and data mgmt. services, 1986-95, acting dir. grants mgmt., 1987-88, dep. dir., Divsn. of Health Svcs. Delivery, 1992-95, ret., 1995; guest lectr. NYU, 1977, Grad. Sch. Mgmt. and Urban Professions, New Sch. for Social Rsch., 1977-95. Mem. alumni bd. Columbia U., 1964-67, 76-78, 81-84, Columbia U. Sch. of Social Work rep. Alumni Fedn., 1975-78; bd. dirs. NCCJ, NYC, 1978-80, 80-. Served with U.S. Army, 1954-56; ETO. Recipient Internat. Service award Salvation Army, 1978; univ. athletic scholar, 1952-54, 56-58, univ. acad. scholar, 1952-54. Mem. NASW, NY U. Alumni, Adelphi Alumni, Acad. Cert. Social Workers, Am. Legion. Author: Community Organization: A Case Study, 1970; contbr. articles to profl. jours.; inventor in field. Home and Office: 14 N Ferndale Pl Montauk NY 11954 also: 52 Udall Dr Great Neck NY 11020-1530

BUTLER, TIMOTHY W., business educator; b. Tietonville, Tenn., Nov. 20, 1954; s. Perry Miller and Tennessee Tipton Butler; m. Beverly Jane Goodale, May 19, 1984; children: Timothy Wynn Jr., Rebecca Joy. AA, Emory at Oxford, 1975; BBA, U. Memphis, 1978, MBA, 1981; PhD, U. S.C., 1989. Lectr. Wayne State U., Detroit, 1987—89, asst. prof., 1989—96, assoc. prof., 1996—, chair faculty senate Bus. Sch., 2004—. Mem. editl. bd. Internat. Jour. Integrated Supply Mgmt., 2004—, Health Care Mgmt. Sci., 2005—. Reader to blind and reading impaired Detroit Radio Info. Svc., 2004—05; Sunday sch. tchr. Grosse Pointe (Mich.) Meml. Ch., 2004—05. Mem.: Decision Scis. Inst., Inst. Operations Rsch. and Mgmt. Sci. (mem. health tech. sect./coun. 2000—03), Detroit Econ. Club, Beta Gamma Sigma. Avocations: baseball, reading, travel, music. Office: Wayne State U Sch Bus Adminstrn 5201 Cass Ave Detroit MI 48202-3930

BUTLER, VINCENT PAUL, JR., internist, educator; b. Jersey City, Feb. 16, 1929; s. Vincent Paul and Ruth Eilene (Lynch) B. AB, St. Peter's Coll., 1949; MD, Columbia U., 1954. Intern Presbyn. Hosp., N.Y.C., 1954-55, resident, 1955-56, 58-59, asst. physician, 1963-68, asst. attending physician, 1968-71, asso. attending physician, 1971-74, attending physician, 1974—2004; trainee clin. immunology U. Rochester Med. Center, 1959-61; research fellow immunochemistry dept. microbiology Columbia U., 1961-63, asst. prof. medicine, 1963-70, assoc. prof., 1970-74, prof., 1974-98, prof. emeritus, 1999—, spl. lectr., 1999—. Asst. vis. physician 1st med. div. Bellevue Hosp., N.Y.C., 1963-68, Harlem Hosp., N.Y.C., 1968-88; mem. VA Merit Rev. Bd. in Immunology, 1974-77, chmn., 1976-77; mem. immunol. sci. study sect. NIH, 1979-83, chmn., 1980-83 Mem. rsch. com. Arthritis Found., 1986-91, chmn., 1989-91; bd. trustees St. Peter's Prep. Sch., Jersey City, 1985-93, chmn., 1991-93. Lt. M.C. USN, 1956-58. Helen Hay Whitney Found. fellow, 1960-63; Arthritis Found. investigator, 1963-68; Josiah Macy, Jr. Found. scholar dept. zoology Univ. Coll., London, 1979-80; recipient Research Career Devel. award NIH, 1968-73; Joseph Mather Smith prize Columbia U. Coll. Physicians and Surgeons, 1973; Irma T. Hirschl Charitable Trust Career Scientist, 1973-78 Fellow AAAS; mem. Assn. Am. Physicians, Am. Soc. Clin. Investigation, Am. Assn. Immunologists, Am. Soc. Pharmacology and Exptl. Therapeutics, Am. Heart Assn., N.Y. Heart Assn., Am. Fedn. Med. Research, Harvey Soc. Roman Catholic. Home: 66 Tulip St Summit NJ 07901 Office: 630 W 168th St New York NY 10032-3702 Office Phone: 212-305-4059. Business E-Mail: vpb2@columbia.edu.

BUTLER, WILLIAM BLAINE, dean, dental educator; b. Huntingdon, Tenn., Apr. 8, 1947; s. Hugh L. and Virgie L. (Parker) B. Student, U. Pitts., 1965-66; BS, Tenn. State U., Nashville, 1969; DDS, Meharry Med. Coll., 1973; MS, U. Mich., 1977. Diplomate Am. Bd. Prosthodontics, Tenn. Bd. Prosthodontics. Asst. prof. U. Mich. Sch. Dentistry, Ann Arbor, 1978—79; instr. Meharry Med. Coll. Sch. Dentistry, Nashville, 1973-74, asst. prof., 1979—84, asst. prof., chmn. dept. prosthodontics, 1984-86, assoc. prof. to prof., chmn. dept. prosthodontics, 1986—99, prof., assoc. dean academic affairs, 1999—2000, prof., dean, 2000—; pvt. practice prosthodontics Butler Dental Clinic, Nashville, 1981—. MARC faculty fellow Nat. Inst. Gen. Med. Sciences, 1974—77. Contbr. articles to profl. jours. Co-chmn. bldg. task force Met. Interdenominational Ch., Nashville, 1986-87, mem. eccles. coun., 1986-90; charter mem. 18th Ave Cmty. Ctr., Nashville, 1991. Fellow: Am. Coll. Prosthodontists, mem: ADA, Nat. Dental Assn., Am. Acad. Fixed Prosthodontics, Mich. Prosthodontic Soc., Capital City Dental Soc. (pres. 1993-95), Francis B. Vedder Soc. Crown and Bridge Prosthodontics, Omicron Kappa Upsilon (past pres.), Alpha Phi Alpha. Avocations: birding, including wildlife habitat for birds, photography, fishing, landscape gardening. Office: Meharry Med Coll Sch Dentistry Office of Dean 1005 Dr DB Todd Jr Blvd Nashville TN 37208-3599

BUTLER, WILLIAM JOSEPH, lawyer, educator; b. Brighton, Mass., Mar. 22, 1924; s. Patrick Lawrence and Delia (Conley) B.; m. Jane Hays, Dec. 22, 1945; children: Arthur Hays, Patricia. Student, Harvard U., 1946, NYU, 1949; DHL (hon.), U. Cin., 1988. Bar: N.Y. 1950. Assoc. Hays, St. John, Abramson & Schulman, N.Y.C., 1949-53; ptnr. Butler, Jablow & Geller, N.Y.C., 1953—. A founder Arthur Garfield Hays Civil Liberties program NYU Sch. Law, 1958; spl. counsel in landmark case on school prayer tried in Supreme Ct. ACLU, DC, 1962; lectr. Practicing Law Inst., 1966; sec., dir., gen. counsel Walco Nat. Corp., FAO Schwartz, N.Y.C., 1961—85; internat. legal observer to South African Elections, 1994; mem. faculty Salzburg Seminar, Austria, 1989, UN Devel. Program, Poland, 1992, Woodrow Wilson Sch. of Pub. and Internat. Affairs, Princeton U., 2000—01; spl. regional adv. for N.Am. on human rights UN High Commr. Mary Robinson, 1998. Author: Human Rights and the Legal System in Iran, 1976, The Decline of Democracy in the Phillipines, 1977, Human Rights in United States and United Kingdom Foreign Policy, Guatemala, a New Beginning, 1987, Palau; A Challenge to the

Rule of Law in Micronesia, 1988, The New South Africa - The Dawn of Democracy, 1994; contbr. papers to U. Cin. Law Libr., articles to profl. jours. Mem. commn. urban affairs Am. Jewish Congress, 1965-70; dir. emeritus N.Y. Civil Liberties Union, Internat. League for Human Rights; exec. com. League to Abolish Capital Punishment; standing com. human rights World Peace Through Law Ctr., Geneva; chmn. adv. com. Morgan Inst. Human Rights, U. Cin. Sch. Law; internat. legal observer Internat. Human Rights Orgn., Internat. Criminal Tribunal for Former Yugoslavia in the Hague, The Netherlands, 1996—, others; faculty Salzburg (Austria) Seminar, 1989; UN Devel. Prog. to Poland, 1992. With U.S. Merchant Marine Svc., 1942—45. Recipient Spl. Citation for contbn. to cause of religious freedom, 1962, William J. Butler Human Rights medal, Urban Morgan Inst. Human Rights, U. Cin., 1999—, Florinda Lasker Civil Liberties award, 2004. Mem. Internat. Commn. Jurists (Geneva) (chmn. exec. com. 1975-90, pres., dir. Am. Assn., UN rep.), Coun. on Fgn. Rels., ABA, Assn. Bar City N.Y. (bd. dirs. Ctr. Internat. Policy, chmn. com. internat. human rights), Inter-Am. Assn. Democracy and Freedom, Internat. Law Assn. (Am. br.), Am. Soc. Internat. Law, Harvard Club (N.Y.C.), U. Club Dublin. Office: 280 Madison Ave New York NY 10016-0801

BUTLER, WILLIAM THOMAS, academic administrator, physician, educator; b. Boston, Aug. 10, 1932; s. Albert Quigg and Elizabeth West (Visknìskki) B.; m. Marilou Beutel, Apr. 26, 1957; children: Marilyn West, Thomas Charles, Robin Eileen; m. Carol Ann Pike, Nov. 23, 1977. AB, Oberlin Coll., 1954; MD, Western Res. U., 1958; grad. program for health systems mgmt., Harvard U., 1974, A.M.P., 1979. Intern and asst. resident in internal medicine Mass. Gen. Hosp., Boston, 1958—61, clin. fellow in medicine, 1960—61, resident in internal medicine, 1964—65; research fellow in bacteriology and immunology Harvard Med. Sch., 1960—61; clin. assoc. Lab. Clin. Investigations, Nat. Inst. Allergy and Infectious Diseases, NIH, Bethesda, Md., 1961—62, chief clin. assoc., 1962—63, clin. investigator, 1963—64, acting head clin. immunology sect., 1965—66; asst. prof. Baylor Coll. Medicine, Houston, 1966—68, assoc. prof., 1968—71, prof. microbiology and immunology, prof. internal medicine, 1971—, asso. dean, 1973—74, dean admissions, 1974—77, acting exec. v.p., 1976—77, exec. v.p., dean, 1977—79, pres., 1979—96, chancellor, 1996—2004, chancellor emeritus, 2004—. Mem. spl. med. adv. group VA, 1981-91, chmn., 1984-91; bd. dirs. Lyondell Chem. Co., chmn. bd., 1997—; mem. Am. Quality and Productivity Ctr., 1991-2004, chmn. S.W. CEO Coun., 1997-98, mem., 1994—. Mem. forward planning com. Tex. Med. Ctr., 1981-96; bd. dirs. South Main Ctr. Assn., exec. com., 1980-94, chmn., 1989-91, coun. advisors, 1994—; past assoc. chmn. key group United Way Campaign, Flagship Divsn., group chmn., 1990; mem. Houston Econ. Summit Host Com., 1990; bd. dirs. Blvd. Oaks Civic Assn., 1982-85, Sci. Engring. Fair of Houston, 1985—, United Way Tex. Gulf Coast, trustee, 1993-99, exec. com. 1998-99; nat. bd. dirs. Points of Light Found., 1995-2004; mem. coordinating bd. Tex. Coll. and Univ. System, Health Professions Edn. Adv. Com., 1984-95, chmn., 1988-95, rsch. adv. com., 1987-90; mem. The Houston Forum, 1981—, bd. govs., 1983-92, 1996-2004; mem. Tex. Sesquicentennial Celebration Com., 1984-86; mem. bd. edn. blue ribbon com. Houston Ind. Sch. Dist., 1986; adv. bd. Covenant House Tex., 1987-90; HISD City-Wide Com., 1987; vice-chmn. health svcs., 1990 U.S. Savs. Bond Program. Mem. AMA, Am. Assn. Immunologists, Am. Soc. Clin. Investigation, N.Y. Acad. Scis., Infectious Diseases Soc. Am., Inst. Medicine, Nat. Acad. Scis. (membership com. 1992-96, sect. 12 1992—, vice chmn., 1992-94, chmn. 1994-96, com. on prevention and control of sexually transmitted diseases 1995-96, chmn. 1995-96), Assn. Acad. Health Ctrs., Assn. Am. Med. Colls. (chmn. coun. deans 1987-89, adminstrv. bd. 1983-90, exec. coun. 1984-92, mgmt. edn. programs planning com. 1986-96, chmn.-elect 1989-90, chmn. 1990-91, project 3000x2000 implementation com. chmn. 1991-2002, nominating com. chmn. 1982), Harris County Med. Soc., Houston Acad. Medicine, Tex. Med. Assn. (adv. coun. med. edn.), Houston C. of C. (bd. dirs. 1981-82, 83-89), Greater Houston Partnership, Inc. (bd. dirs. 1989, 92-99, co-chair healthcare task force 1994-97, bus. issues adv. com. 1994-99, govtl. rels. adv. com. 1995-97), Houston Mus. Nat. Sci. (ex officio 1989-94), River Oaks Country Club, Doctors' Club (bd. govs. 1980-84, pres. 1982), Harvard Bus. Sch. of Houston Club, Sigma Xi, Alpha Omega Alpha. Methodist. Achievements include research numerous publs. on infectious disease and immunology. Office: Baylor Coll Medicine 1 Baylor Plz Ste 177A Houston TX 77030-3498

BUTLER YANK, LESLIE ANN, artist, writer, editor; b. Salem, Oreg., Nov. 19, 1945; d. Marlow Dole and Lala Ann (Erlandson) Butler; m. Howard Dennis Yank, July 4, 2001. Student, Lewis and Clark Coll., 1963-64; BS, U. Oreg., 1969; postgrad., Portland State U., 1972-73, Lewis and Clark Coll., 1991. Creative trainee Ketchum Advt., San Francisco, 1970-71; asst. advt. dir. Mktg. Systems, Inc., Portland, Oreg., 1971-74; prodn. mgr., art dir., copywriter Finzer-Smith, Portland, 1974-76; copywriter Gerber Advt., Portland, 1976-78; freelance copywriter Portland, 1983-84, 83-85; copywriter McCann-Erickson, Portland, 1980-81; copy chief Brookstone Co., Peterborough, N.H., 1981-83; creative dir. Whitman Advt., Portland, 1984-87; prin. L.A. Advt., 1987—; portrait artist. Author: The Dream Road and Other Tales From Hidden Hills, 1997; editor (arts and antiques): Living mag.; designer of fence featured in Better Homes & Gardens, 2000; one-woman shows include Ocean Lodge, Cannon Beach Oreg., 2004, Fifth Ave. Stes., Porland, 2004, Lawrence Gallery, Portland, 2004, City Hall, 2005, exhibitions include Rhodes Stingfellow Gallery, Cannon Beach, Oreg., 2004—, Brodrick Gallery, Portland, 2004—, Sikta Art Invitational, Porland, 2003, 2004, Associated Arts Regional Juried Fine Arts Show, Ocean Shores, Wash., 2005, Coos Art Mus., Richland, Wash., 2005, exhibitions include many others, Represented in permanent collections George and Barbara Bush, Houston, Rue McClanahan, Bevelry Hills, Michael Jackson, Hollywood, Gary Maffei and Marc Linter, Portland. Spokeswoman Nat. Alopecia Areata Found., San Rafeal, Calif., 2004; Co-founder, v.p., newsletter editor Animal Rescue and Care Fund, 1972—81; mem. Friends of the Performing Arts Ctr., Portland Art Mus., Oreg. Humane Soc.; pres. OMSI; bd. dirs. Portland Opera Assn., 2000—02, Oreg. Humane Soc., 2002—. Recipient Internat. Film and TV Festival N.Y. Finalist award, 1985, 86, 87, 88, Internat. Radio Festival of N.Y. award, 1984, 85, 88, Hollywood Radio and TV Soc. Internat. Broadcasting award, 1981, TV Comml. Festival Silver Telly award, 1985, TV Comml. Festival Bronze Telly, 1986, AVC Silver Cindy, 1986, Los Angeles Advt. Women LULU, 1986, 87, 88, 89 Ad Week What's New Portfolio, 1986, N.W. Addy award Seattle Advt. Fedn., 1984, Best in the West award, 1985, Portland Advt. Fedn. Rosey Finalist award, 1986, Nat. winner Silver Microphone award, 1987, 88, 89. Mem.: Portland Art Mus., Portland Inst, Contemporary Art, Nat. Oil and Acrylic Painters Soc., People for Ethical Treatment of Animals. E-mail: labartist@aol.com.

BUTNEV, VIKTOR YURIEVICH, research scientist; MD, N.I.Pirogov Moscow State Med. Sch., 1975—81; PhD, Inst. for Exptl. Endocrinology and Hormone Chemistry, 1981—86. Therapeutist State Exam. Bd. of N.I.Pirogov Moscow State Med. Sch., 1981. Jr. rsch. scientist Inst. for Exptl. Endocrinology and Hormone Chemistry, Moscow, 1981—88, sr. rsch. scientist, 1988—94; postdoctoral fellow dept. biol. scis. Wichita State U., Kans., 1994—98; protein hormone biochemist Nat. Hormone and Pituitary Program, Rsch. and Edn. Inst., Harbor-UCLA Med. Ctr., Torrance, Calif., 1998—99; postdoctoral fellow dept. physiology and biophysics U Iowa, Iowa City, 1999—2002; scientist Genzyme Glycobiology Rsch. Inst., Oklahoma City, 2002—. NIH grantee, 1999—2002. Mem.: AAAS, Soc. for Study of Reprodn., Endocrine Soc. Achievements include discovery, isolation, and characterization of glycosylated prolactin and its carbohydrate moiety. Office: Genzyme Glycobiology Rsch Inst 800 Research Pkwy Ste 200 Oklahoma City OK 73104 Personal E-mail: butnev@aol.com. E-mail: viktor.butnev@genzyme.com.

BUTO, KATHLEEN A., health products executive; BA, Rutgers U.; MPA, Harvard U. With Health Care Financing Adminstrn., 1982—2000; sr. health advisor Congl. Budget Office, 2000—02; v.p. for health policy, govt. affairs Johnson & Johnson, Washington, 2002—. Office: Johnson & Johnson 1350 Eye St NW #1210 Washington DC 20005 Office Phone: 202-589-1000.

BUTORAC, FRANK GEORGE, librarian, educator; b. Crosby, Minn., Feb. 12, 1927; s. Frank and Mary (Paun) B.; m. Mary Regis McGowan Ratigan, Apr. 8, 1972; stepchildren: Helen Elizabeth, Nicholas. AB, U. Mich., 1950, AM, 1956, AMLS, 1958; postgrad., Cornell Law Sch., 1950-51, Harvard U., 1953; postgrad. in philosophy, U. Notre Dame, 1959, 60-62; postgrad. in theology, Holy Cross Coll., 1962-66; postgrad., Cath. U., 1963, Georgetown U., 1965, NYU, 1968-70, 79-81, Cambridge U., 1975, postgrad., 2005, Oxford U., 1989, postgrad., 1995, postgrad., 2003, Trinity Coll., Dublin, 1990. With exec. tng. program U.S. Rubber, Mishawaka, Ind., 1952-53; tchr. 6th grade Jefferson Sch., Wayne, Mich., 1953-54; tchr. social studies Slauson Jr. H.S., Ann Arbor, Mich., 1954-55; supervising tchr. social studies Lincoln Consol. H.S., Ea. Mich. U., Ypsilanti, 1955-57; circulation libr., engring. libr. U. Mich., Ann Arbor, 1958-59; joined Congregation of Holy Cross, 1959; postulant U. Notre Dame, 1959; seminarian and temporary profession, 1959-66; novice Sacred Heart Novitiate, Jordan, Minn., 1959-60; registrar Mercer C.C., Trenton, N.J., 1966-68, asst. dir. cmty. and ext. svcs., 1968-70, dir. evening and ext. ops., 1970-71, dir. spl. programs, 1971-74, dir. libr. svcs., 1974-84, chmn. libr. tech. program, 1974-84, dir. libr. devel., 1984-87, libr., 1987—. Cons. libr. edn., libr. mgmt. Pres. U. Mich. Clubs Coun. 2d Dist., 1991-93; chmn. U. Mich. Newman Ctr. Fund Drive, 1958; professed Secular Franciscan Order Monastery of St. Clare, Bordentown, N.J., 1984, 3d Order Dominican, 2003—; ann. participant Yale U.-Hopkins summer seminar program, 2000—. Bd. dirs. U. Mich. Alumni Assn., 1995-98; chmn. Anna B. Stokes Found., Trenton, 1972; dean's adv. com. Cornell Law Sch., 1972-73; mem. N.J. State Adv. Com. on Aging, 1971; mem. Mich. State Ctrl. Com. Young Democrats, 1949-50. Served with USN, 1944-47. Recipient Tall Cedars of Lebanon award for Cmty. Svc., Trenton, 1974. Mem. ALA, N.J. Libr. Assn. (exec. bd. 1977-78), Purnell Sch. Parents Assn., Cornell Law Assn., Bennington Coll. Parents Assn., Pine Manor Coll. Parents Assn., U. Mich. Ctrl. N.J. (pres. 1987-91), Mensa, English Speaking Union, Nassau Club (Princeton, N.J.), Princeton Club (N.Y.C.), Trenton Lions Club (pres. 1972), Trenton Torch Club (pres. 1972), Cornell Club Ctrl. N.J. (pres. 1977-78), Marines' Meml. Club (San Francisco), Cath. Alumni Club Trenton (pres. 1968), Theta Delta Chi, Phi Delta Phi, Phi Delta Kappa, Kappa Delta Pi, Alpha Phi Omega. Republican. Roman Catholic. Home: 6 Mercer St Princeton NJ 08540-6808 Office: 1200 Old Trenton Rd Princeton Junction NJ 08550-3407 Office Phone: 609-586-4800. Personal E-mail: butoracf@yahoo.com.

BUTOW, ROBERT JOSEPH CHARLES, historian, educator; b. San Mateo, Calif., Mar. 19, 1924; s. Frederick W.C. and Louise Marie B.; m. Irene Elkeles; 1 child, Stephanie Cecile. BA magna cum laude, Stanford U., 1947, MA, 1948, PhD, 1953. Instr. history Princeton U., 1954—59, asst. prof., 1959—60, rsch. assoc. Ctr. of Internat. Studies, 1954—60; assoc. prof. East Asian history and internat. studies U. Wash., Seattle, 1960—66, prof., 1966—90, prof. emeritus, 1990—. Mem. Inst. for Advanced Study, 1962-63. Author: Japan's Decision to Surrender, 1954, 67, Tojo and the Coming of the War, 1961, 69, The John Doe Associates: Backdoor Diplomacy for Peace, 1941, 1974. 2d lt. U.S. Army, 1943-46. Grantee Social Sci. Rsch. Coun., 1956-57, Rockefeller Found., 1956-57, Eleanor Roosevelt Inst., 1977-78; Guggenheim fellow, 1965-66, 78-79, fellow Woodrow Wilson Ctr., 1987-88, Japan Found., 1987-88. Mem. Assn. of Mems. of Inst. for Advanced Study, Soc. Historians of Am. Fgn. Rels., World War Two Studies Assn. Office: U Wash Box 353650 Seattle WA 98195-3650 Office Phone: 206-543-4370. E-mail: rbutow@u.washington.edu.

BUTOWSKY, DAVID MARTIN, lawyer; b. Phila., Aug. 14, 1936; s. Hyman and Pearl (Berks) B.; children: Michael, Ellen, Edward, Erica; m. Fredda Butowsky. AB, Temple U., 1958; LL.B., George Washington U., 1962. Bar: Md. 1962, N.Y. 1971. Practice law, N.Y.C., 1971—; chief enforcement atty. SEC, Washington, 1962-70; assoc. Breed Abbott & Morgan, N.Y.C., 1970-71; ptnr. Butowsky Schwenke & Devine, N.Y.C., 1971-75, Gordon Altman Butowsky Weitzen Shalov & Wein, N.Y.C., 1975-99, Mayer, Brown & Platt, N.Y.C., 1999—. Lectr. to orgns. Contbr. articles to profl. publs. Mem. Am., Fed., N.Y. County bar assns., City Bar Assn. N.Y. Home: 360 E 72nd St Apt C-3202 New York NY 10021-4766

BUTT, EDWARD THOMAS, JR., lawyer; b. Chgo., Oct. 27, 1947; s. Edward T. and Helen Kathryn (Guy) B.; m. Leslie Laidlaw Hilton, Oct. 20, 1972; children: Julie Guy, Andrew McNaughton. BA, Lawrence U., 1968; JD, U. Mich., 1971. Bar: Ill. 1971, U.S. Dist. Ct. (no. dist.) Ill. 1971, Wis. 1975, U.S. Dist. Ct. (ea. dist.) Wis. 1978, U.S. Ct. Appeals (7th cir.) 1978, U.S. Ct. Claims 1982, U.S. Ct. Appeals (6th cir.) 1986, U.S. Ct. Appeals (6th cir.) 1987, Mich. 1997. Assoc. Wildman, Harrold, Allen & Dixon, Chgo., 1971-75, 76-78, ptnr., 1979-94, Lund & Butt, S.C., Minocqua, Wis., 1975-76; of counsel Swanson, Martin & Bell, Chgo. and Lisle, Ill., 1994—. Bd. dirs. Constl. Rights Found., Chgo. Mem. ABA, State Bar Wis., State Bar Mich., Def. Rsch. Inst., Crystal Lake Yacht Club, Crystal Downs Country Club. Avocations: distance running, sailing, golf. Home: Michabou Shores 1006 Tiba Rd Frankfort MI 49635-9216 Office: Swanson Martin & Bell 2525 Cabot Dr Ste 204 Lisle IL 60532

BUTT, MOHAMMAD ZAMAN, internist, geriatrician, researcher; b. Gujrat, Pakistan, Feb. 19, 1964; arrived in U.S.A., 1994; s. Anayat Ullah and Parveen Akhtar; m. Shumaila Zaman Butt, Oct. 22, 1993; children: Ummia, Ushnaa. BSc, Punjab U., 1984; MBBS, King Edward Med. Coll., 1989. Diplomate in internal medicine Am. Bd. Internal Medicine, 1998, in geriatric medicine Am. Bd. Internal Medicine, 2002, lic. physician N.Y., N.J., D.C. Surgeon Mayo Hosp., Lahore, Pakistan, 1990—91, physician, 1991; med. officer Omar Hosp., Lahore, 1992, Ittefaq Hosp., Lahore, 1993—94; resident internal medicine Brookdale U. Hosp., Bklyn., 1995—98; fellow geriatric medicine George Washington U. Hosp., Washington, 1999—2000; geriatrician Brookdale U. Hosp., 2001—03, Shorefront Jewish Geriatric Ctr., Bklyn., 2001—. Reviewer Geriatric Medicine Bd. Am. Bd. Internal Medicine, 2003; mem. staff Met. Jewish Health Sys., Bklyn., 2001—; healthcare provider Am. Heart Assn., Bklyn., 2002—. Host ednl. programs on TV:. Avocations: painting, travel, music, stamp collecting/philately, coin collecting/numismatics. Home: 2665 Homecrest Ave Apt 2S Brooklyn NY 11235 Office: Shorefront Jewish Geriatric Ctr 3015 West 29th St Brooklyn NY 11224

BUTT, P. LAWRENCE, lawyer; b. Indpls., 1941; BBA, U. Cinn., 1964; JD, Ind. U., 1968. Bar: 1968. With Marsh Supermarkets, Inc., Indpls., 1977—, v.p., counsel, sec., 1992—97, sr. v.p., counsel, sec., 1997—. Bd. dirs. Marsh Supermarkets, Inc. Office: Marsh Supermarkets Inc 9800 Crosspoint Blvd Indianapolis IN 46256-3350 Office Phone: 317-594-2100. Office Fax: 317-594-2704.

BUTT, SAMEER, filmmaker, writer; s. Khalida and Yusuf Butt. Mem./market maker Am. Stock Exch., N.Y.C., 1996—99; dir. of prodn. IndiePlanet/Urban Box Office, N.Y.C., 1999—2000. Pres. NY Spice Film Co., N.Y.C., 2000—. Actor: (films) Atomic Tabasco (Acad. Award, 1998); prodr.(writer): (documentary news spl.) Islamabad: Rock City; dir.(co-producer): (documentary) Becoming Muslim: Submitting to Allah in Am.; contbr. comedy The Daily Show; dir.: (documentary) Dollars and $ex; creator, writer: (situation comedy) New York Spice. E-mail: sameerybutt@hotmail.com.

BUTTARO, LUCIA, language educator, consultant; b. Bklyn., May 21, 1963; d. Giuseppe Buttaro and Maria Christina Vuotto-Buttaro. BS Inst. de Enseranza Superior Daguerre, Buenos Aires, 1986; MS in edn., Fordham U., NYC, 1996, PhD, 1999. Instr. English High Lyceum of English Culture, Buenos Aires, 1982—85, Cambridge Inst., Buenos Aires, Aeon Eng. Conversation Sch., Toyahoshi, Japan, 1990—91, Alpha English Sch., Toyahoshi, Japan, 1991—92; GED lectr. Spanish Bronx Coll. CUNY, 1992—98; adj. prof. Baruch Coll. CUNY, 1995—; literacy cons. NYC Dept. of Edn., Bklyn., 2001—; asst. prof. Fordham U., NYC, 1999—, Kingsborough Coll. CUNY, Bklyn., 1999—. Del. Acad. Scholars Program, Shanghai, 2002—03; ESL med. instr. Action for Russian Immigrants, Bklyn., 1994—; mem. writing across the curriculum com. CUNY; mem. com. on admissions Kingsborough Coll. CUNY, mem. academic standing com. Contbr. articles to profl. jours., presentations to profl. conferences, 2000. Recipient PSC CUNY Rsch award program, 2002—03; grantee Fulbright Tchr. and Adminstr. Exch. Program, 2002—03. Mem.: ENLACE (bd. dir. 1999—), Phi Delta Kappa. Democrat. Roman Catholic. Avocations: travel, photography. Home: 1395 E Second St Brooklyn NY 11230 Personal E-mail: drbuttaro@aol.com.

BUTTE, AMY S., stock exchange executive; BA in Polit. Sci. and Psychology, Yale U.; MBA, Harvard U. Various positions Andersen Consulting, Merrin Fin., Bridge Trading Co., Inc., Merrill Lynch; sr. mng. dir. Bear Stearns, 1999—2002; CFO, chief strategist fin. svcs. divsn. Credit Suisse First Boston, 2002—03; exec. v.p. NY Stock Exch. Inc., NYC, 2004, CFO, 2004—. Active NY Women's Found.; mem. corp. adv. bd. NYC Ballet; participant World Econ. Forum's Young Global Leader Program. Office: NY Stock Exch Inc 11 Wall St New York NY 10005

BUTTENWIESER, LAWRENCE BENJAMIN, lawyer; b. N.Y.C., Jan. 11, 1932; s. Benjamin Joseph and Helen (Lehman) B.; m. Ann Harriet Lubin, July 13, 1956; children: William Lawrence, Carol Helen Sharp, Jill Ann Schloss, Peter Lubin BA, U. Chgo., 1951, MA, 1955; JD, Yale U., 1956; DHL (hon.), Yeshiva U., 1974. Bar: N.Y. 1956. Assoc. Rosenman & Colin, NYC, 1956-66, ptnr., 1966—2002; counsel KMZ Rosenman, 2002—. Chmn. bd. dirs. Gen. Am. Investors Co., Inc., N.Y.C. Past pres., trustee Associated YM-YWHAs of Greater NY; past v.p., dir. Citizens Housing and Planning Coun. of NY; past treas., dir. City Ctr. of Music and Drama, Inc.; past dir. Coun. on Social Work. Edn.; past trustee Dalton Sch.; past. hon. chmn. bd., trustee, past pres. Fedn. Jewish Philanthropies NY; past chmn. bd., trustee Montefiore Med. Ctr.; past gen. campaign chmn. United Neighborhood Houses NY; past trustee, NY Acad. Sci.UJA/Fed. Joint Campaign; past chmn., past trustee Am. Jewish World Svc.; past chmn., trustee Citizens Budget Commn.; dir. Playwrights Horizons Inc.; trustee U. Chgo. Mem. Assn. Bar City N.Y. Office: KMZ Rosenman Fl 21 575 Madison Ave Fl 21 New York NY 10022-2511 Office Phone: 212-940-8560. E-mail: lawrence.buttenwieser@kattenlaw.com.

BUTTERBRODT, JOHN ERVIN, real estate executive; b. Beaver Dam, Wis., Feb. 14, 1929; s. Ervin E. and Josephine M. (O'Mare) B.; m. June Rose Bohalter, Sept. 27, 1952; children— Claire, Daniel, Larry. U. Agriculture short course, 1946-47. Cert. tchr. real estate, rental weatherization inspector, real estate appraiser, sr. profl. appraiser; internat. cert. farm appraiser; cert. gen., lic. appraiser, Wis. Vice-pres. Pure Milk Assn., 1967-69; pres. Asso. Milk Producers, Inc. Chgo., 1969-75, State Brand Creameries, Madison, Wis., 1970—, Wis. Real Estate Co., Wis. Real Estate of Burnett Inc., 1978—, Sunset Hills Golf & Supper Club Inc., 1979—; chmn. bd. Realty World-Wis. Real Estate, Inc., 1985—; treas. Real Estate Cons., 1983—. Dir. Town Mut. Ins. Co., Central Milk Sales, Central Milk Producers Coop. Pres. Sch. Bd., 1968; Bd. dirs. Nat. Milk Producers Fedn., Central Am. Coop. Fedn., World Dairy Expo. Recipient Am. Farmer degree Future Farmers of Am., 1949, hon. degree, 1973; Outstanding Wis. Farmer award, 1965; Outstanding Wis. 4-H Alumni award, 1973; named Realtor of Yr., 1979 Mem.: United Dairy Industry Assn. Republican. Office: 1708 N Spring St Beaver Dam WI 53916-1106 Office Phone: 920-887-1733. Business E-Mail: johnb@wisreal.com.

BUTTERFIELD, ALEXANDER PORTER, government agency administrator, air transportation executive; b. Pensacola, Fla., Apr. 6, 1926; s. Horace Bushnell and Susan A. (Alexander) B.; m. Charlotte Mary Maguire, Sept. 9, 1949 (div. Jan. 1985); children: Leslie Carter (dec.), Alexander Porter Jr., Susan Carter Holcomb, Elisabeth Gordon Buchholz. BS, U. Md., 1956; MS, George Washington U., 1967; MA, U. Calif., 2005; PhD (hon.), Embry-Riddle U., 1973. Commd. 2d lt. USAF, 1949, advanced through grades to col., 1966, fighter pilot, fighter-gunnery instr., weapons officer, mem. Skyblazers (U.S. jet aerobatic team Europe), 1949-53; aide to comdr. 4th Allied Tactical Air Force NATO, 1954-55; ops. officer interceptor squadron, 1955-56; asst. prof. USAF Acad., 1957-59; sr. aide to comdr.-in-chief U.S. Pacific Air Forces, 1959-62; comdr. fighter squadron Okinawa, 1962-63; comdr. tactical reconnaissance task forces S.E. Asia, 1963-64; tactical air warfare policy planner USAF hdqrs., 1964-65; mil. asst. to spl. asst. sec. def., 1965-66; student Nat. War Coll., 1966-67; sr. U.S. mil. rep., comdr. in chief Pacific rep. Australia, 1967-69; retired, 1969; dep. asst. Pres. Richard M. Nixon, 1969-73; sec. to Cabinet, 1969-73; adminstr. FAA, 1973-75; lectr. Ethics in Govt. Am. Program Bur., 1975-76; exec. v.p., chief oper. officer, dir. Internat. Air Svc. Co. Ltd., 1977-79; pres., chief oper. officer, dir. Calif. Life Corp., 1979-80. Chmn. GMA Corp., Global Network Inc., 1981—82; chmn., CEO Armistead & Alexander, Inc., 1983—94. Contbr. articles to profl. jours. and nat. mags.; mem. editorial bd. L.A. County Mus. Natural History mag. Terra, 1983-86. Presidentially apptd. mem. Nat. Armed Forces Mus. adv. bd. Smithsonian Instn., 1970—76; mem. mil. sci. expediton to South Pole, 1988; leader of U.S. govt. industry del. to Moscow for ministerial leval talks on tech. and trade, 1973; key witness U.S. senate select com.'s hearings on Watergate, 1973, and before U.S. Ho. of Reps. Jud. Com. during deliberations on impeachment of Pres. Richard Nixon, 1974; chmn. Chancellor's Assocs. U. Calif., San Diego; bd. dirs. Internat. Flight Safety Found., L.A., 1976—81, County Mus. Natural History, 1981—85. Decorated Legion of Merit, DFC, Air medal with 3 bronze oak leaf clusters, Bronze Star. Mem.: SAG, Air Force Assn., Tailhook Assn., Coun. for Excellence in Govt., Am. Film Inst., Thunderbird Alumni Assn., Bel-Air Country Club (L.A.), Univ. Club (San Diego). Home: 5340 Toscana Way # 416 San Diego CA 92122

BUTTERFIELD, ANDREA CHRISTINE, psychology educator, educational association administrator; Student study abroad program, U. Md., Munich, Germany, 1973; BA in Childhood Edn., U. Fla., 1975; MEd in Reading, Beaver Coll., 1977; postgrad. reading supr. cert. program, Millersville U., 1985; DEd in Adult Edn., Pa. State U., 1995. Cert. supervisory I supr. reading, instrnl. II reading specialist-elem., Pa., supervisory II, Shippensburg U., 2003. Reading specialist Lauderdale Lakes Middle Sch., Fla., 1977-78; coord., oper. individual title I Roman Cath. H.S. for Boys Sch. Dist. of Phila., 1978-85; supr. of reading specialist interns and grad. instr., clin. practicum reading clinic Millersville U., Pa., 1985-86; reading specialist Ebenezer Elementary Sch. and Cedar Crest Middle Sch., Cornwall-Lebanon Sch. Dist., Lebanon, Pa., 1985—. Adj. instr. Camden County Coll., N.J., 1980; cons. to ednl. orgns., 1994—; part-time faculty ednl. psychology Pa. State U., Harrisburg, 1995—. Speaker in field. Planning commr., bd. officer Derry Township, Hershey, Pa., 1992—, design rev. bd. mem., 1994—. Mem. ASCD, PASCD (pres. elect so. region, chmn. so. region spring conf. planning com.), Internat. Reading Assn., Phi Kappa Phi, Phi Kappa Delta. Home: 440 Leearden Rd Hershey PA 17033-2140 Personal E-mail: acbutterfield@yahoo.com.

BUTTERFIELD, BENJAMIN PARRISH, lawyer; b. Orlando, Fla., Feb. 4, 1960; s. Robert Latta and Barbara (West) B. BA, Covenant Coll., 1982; JD, Stetson U., 1986. Bar: Fla. 1986, U.S. Dist. Ct. Fla. 1986. Assoc. Maguire, Voorhis & Wells, P.A., Orlando, Fla., 1986-93, ptnr., 1993-96; gen. counsel Hughes Supply, Inc., Orlando, 1996—; gen. counsel, sec. Lennar Corp., Miami, Fla. Bd. dirs. Orange County Hist. Soc., Orlando, 1995-96, Boys and Girls Clubs of Ctrl. Fla., 1996-97. Mem. Orange County Bar Assn. (chmn. bus. law sect. 1994-95), Univ. Club. Republican. Presbyterian. Avocations: hunting, fishing, scuba. Office: Hughes Supply Inc 20 N Orange Ave Ste 200 Orlando FL 32801-4646

BUTTERFIELD, BRUCE SCOTT, publishing, communications and education executive, consultant; s. Richard and Mary; m. Karin; children: Elizabeth, Timothy. BA cum laude, Amherst Coll.; MA, Harvard U.; MBA, U. Conn.; advanced cert. in journalism and creative fiction, Newspaper Inst. Am. Mng. editor, adminstr. Golden Press/Western Pub. Co., N.Y.C., 1972-77; v.p., pub. Scholastic Inc., N.Y.C., 1978-83; pres. Longman-Addison Wesley Pub. Group/Pearson PLC, White Plains, N.Y., 1984-93, Prentice Hall Regents/Simon & Schuster/Viacom Inc., Upper Saddle River, NJ, 1993-97; CEO, pres. VirtualEd, Inc., 2002—. Author: Fantasy and the Free School Thought: E.B. White and His Literature for Children; Our Real Work Can't Be Drudgery; editor various books including: ABC's Wide World of Sports,

Buccaneers; Book of the Mysterious, Chroma-Schema, Calculator Games; Children's Bible Stories, Oh Heavenly Dog, The Watcher in the Woods. Named Most Valuable Semi-Pro Pitcher, Bergen Highlanders, All New Eng. Baseball Pitcher, All Am. Baseball Pitcher, named to U. Conn. Bus. Sch. Hall of Fame; recipient Wall St. Jour. Achievement award; Nat. Fedn. Music award; J.F. Kennedy Brotherhood Essay award; Gardener Fletcher fellow; St. Clair Meml. fellow; Amherst Coll. fellow. Mem. Beta Gamma Sigma, Phi Delta Kappa, Phi Delta Sigma.

BUTTERFIELD, CHARLES EDWARD, JR., educational consultant; b. Urbana, Ill., Mar. 31, 1928; s. Charles E. and Bessie J. (Winters) B.; m. Gayle Coberley, Jan. 27, 1952; children: Jeffrey M., Carey J. BS in Biology, Chemistry, Physics, Psychology, Edn., U. Ill., 1951, MS, 1953; postgrad., Duke U., 1958, No. Ill. U., 1958—59, Mich. State U., 1959, postgrad., 1964—65, postgrad., 1972, Knox Coll., 1962, Fla. State U., 1969, U. Colo., 1970. Field exec. Nottawa Trails Coun. Boy Scouts Am., Battle Creek, Mich., 1953—54; instr. sci. Gardner-South Wilmington Twp. H.S., Ill., 1954—59; pub. rels. cons., ednl. cons. Dresden Nuc. Power Plant Consol. Edison, Braidwood, Ill., 1958—60; biology coord. Lake Park H.S., Medinah, Ill., 1959—65; sr. sci. project editor Singer/Random House Pub. Co., N.Y.C., 1965—68; sci. supr. K-12 Ramsey Pub. Schs., NJ, 1968—82; sci. edn. cons., 1981—; pres., CFO, Shield Cons., 1977—. Instr. radiation physics N.W. Cmty. Hosp., Arlington Heights, Ill., 1963-65; cons. Rand McNally Pubs., 1972-80; peer reviewer NSF proposals, 1979-84; mem. sci. adv. bd. Raintree Publs., Milw., 1981-86; assoc. Thomas A. Edison Found., 1981-88; condr. various workshops for sci. tchrs., 1965—. Contbg. author: NSSA Sourcebook for Science Supervisors, 2d edit., 1976, 3d edit., 1988. Pres. Bd. Edn., Gardner, Ill., 1956-57, Foxwood Village Fedn. Mfrd. Home Owners of Fla., 1988-90; co-project dir., fin. officer suprs. programs NSF/NSSA/PEEC, 1979-83; pres., treas., bd. dirs. Highland Fairways Property Owners Assn., 1993-96, 99-2002, fin. cons., 1996—; judge Seiko Youth Challenge, 1994, 95. With USN and USMC, 1946-48. Recipient Allendale (N.J.) Cmty. Lifesaving award, 1976; NSF/AAAS fellow Mich. State U., 1964-66, fellow 1st Southeastern NASA Aerospace Conf., 1961. Fellow AAAS; mem. NEA, ACLU, Nat. Sci. Ednl. Leadership Assn. (exec. com. 1974-80, pres. 1977-78, sr. staff various other confs. U. Calif. at San Diego, 1979, U. Iowa 1979-80, supr. nat. elections 1982-2000, editl. adv. bd. 1986-91, Outstanding Svc. award 1990, 98, 1st hon. lifetime exec. bd. award for outstanding svc. 2000—), NSTA (exec. bd. 1977-78, Disting. Svc. Sci. Edn. citation 1981), Am. Humanist Assn., N.J. Sci. Tchrs. Assn., N.J. Sci. Suprs. Assn. (Disting. Svc. award 1982), Ramsey Suprs. Assn. (founding pres. 1980-81), Bergen County Sci. Suprs. Assn. (pres. 1971-73, Outstanding Svc. award 1974, 78), Sch. Sci. and Math. Assn., Am. Inst. Biol. Scis. (cons. biol. sci. curriculum study 1965—), Nat. Assn. Biol. Tchrs., Coun. Elem. Sci. Internat., Assn. Edn. Tchrs. Sci., N.J. Prins. and Suprs. Assn., Am. Assn. Notaries, Nat. Notary Assn., U. Ill. Alumni Assn., Fla. So. Coll. Sixth Man Club, Cmty. Assns. Inst., 1st Marine Divsn. Assn., Fleet Marine Force Combat Med. Pers. Assn., Am. Legion, USN Meml. Found., Lakeland (Fla.) C. of C., Mensa, Masons, DeMolay Internat. (chevalier), Order Ea. Star, Humanist Assn. West Ctrl. Fla. (charter), Norwalk H.S. Alumni Assn., U. Ill. Alumni Assn., Psi Chi. Office: 22 Spring Ave Oakland NJ 07436-1930 Personal E-mail: chargayb2@earthlink.net.

BUTTERFIELD, DEBORAH KAY, sculptor; b. San Diego, May 7, 1949; m. John Buck; 2 children. BA, U. Calif., Davis, 1971, MFA, 1973; DFA (hon.), Mont. State U., 1998, Rocky Mountain Coll., Billings, Mont., 1997, Whitman Coll., Walla Walla, Wash., 2004. Asst. prof. sculpture U. Wis., Madison, 1975-76, Mont. State U., Bozeman, 1979-81, adj. prof., 1981-84. One-man shows include Lowe Mus. Art U. Miami, Coral Gables, Fla., 1992, San Diego Mus. Art, 1996, Yellowstone Art Mus., Billings, Mont., 2003-04, The Contemporary Mus. Art, Honolulu, 2004, Appleton Mus. Art, Ocala, Fla., 2004, U. Art Mus., U. La., Lafayette, 2005, Neuberger Art Mus., Purchase N.Y., 2005, Norton Mus. Art, West Palm Beach, Fla., 2005; exhibited in groups shows U. Mus. Berkeley, Calif., 1974, Whitney Mus. Am. Art, N.Y., 1979, Albright-Knox Gallery, Buffalo, 1979, Israel Mus., Jerusalem, 1980, Arco Ctr. Visual Art, 1981, Walker Art Ctr., Mpls., 1982, Dallas Mus. Fine Arts, 1982, Oakland, 1983, Chgo., 1985, Contemporary Art Ctr., Honolulu, 1986, Whitney Mus., 1988, Contemporary Art Mus., Honolulu, 1993, Seattle Mus. Art, 1994, The White House, Washington, Yale U., New Haven, 1997; represented in permanent collections Whitney Mus. Am. Art, N.Y., San Francisco Mus. Contemporary Art, Israel Mus., Jerusalem, Walker Art Ctr., Mpls., Met. Mus. Art, N.Y., Hirshhorn Mus., Washington, Seattle Art Mus., UCLA Sculpture Garden, L.A. Mus. Contemporary Art; commd. Copley Square, Boston, Portland (Oreg.) Airport, Denver Art Mus., Kansas City (Mo.) Zoo, White House, Washington, 2000, Monte Carlo, Monaco, 2000, Smithsonian Instn., Washington, San Francisco Internat. Airport. Nat. Endowment Arts grantee, 1977, 80, Guggenheim grantee, 1980; Commission Portland Internat. Airport.

BUTTERFIELD, GEORGE KENNETH, JR., congressman, former state supreme court justice; b. Wilson, N.C., Apr. 27, 1947; s. G. K. and Addie (Davis) Butterfield; children: Valeisha Monique, Jenetta Lenai. BS, NC Central U., 1971, JD, 1974. Sr. ptnr. Butterfield, Fitch & Wynn, 1974—88; resident judge NC Superior Ct Dist 7B, 1989—2001; assoc. justice Supreme Ct. N.C., 2001—02; spl. judge NC Superior Ct., 2002—04; mem. U.S. Ho. of Reps. from 1st N.C. dist., 2004—, mem. agriculture com., armed svc. com., mem. subcom. on dept. ops., oversight, nutrition and forestry & subcom. on livestock and horticulture. U.S. Army, 1968—70. Mem.: NC Bar Assn. (v.p. 2003—). Democrat. Office: US Ho of Reps 413 Cannon Ho Office Bldg Washington DC 20515-3301 also: Dist Office 415 E Blvd Ste 100 Williamston NC 27892*

BUTTERFIELD, SAMUEL HALE, retired federal official, writer; b. Moscow, Idaho, Nov. 8, 1924; s. Rolston Samuel and Leone (Hamilton) Butterfield; m. Lois Herrington, Feb. 10, 1948; children: Charles Oliver, Stephen Crandall, Susan Hale Waite. Student, U. Idaho, 1942-43, 46-47; BS in Fgn. Service, Georgetown U., 1949, MA in Am. History, 1953. Retail salesman, 1949-50; labor economist Dept. Labor, 1950-53; examiner, fiscal economist, internat. div. Bur. Budget, 1953-58; with AID and predecessors, 1958-80; dir. Office E. and So. Africa, 1960-62; dep. dir. Mission to Tanganyika, 1962-64, Mission to Sudan, 1964-65; dir. Mission to Tanzania, 1966-68; mem. sr. seminar in fgn. policy Dept. State, 1968-69; assoc. asst. adminstr. for tech. assistance AID, 1969-76; dir. Mission to Nepal, 1976-80; affiliate prof. U. Idaho, Moscow, 1981-89; sr. advisor on nat. conservation strategy Internat. Union Conservation Nature (IUCN), Govt. Botswana, 1985-87; environ. planning cons. Nepal, 1990; ret., 1990. Author: U.S. Development Aid-A Historic First, Achievements and Failures in the Twentieth Century, 2004; contbr. articles to profl. jours. Pres. Wash.-Idaho Symphony Assn., 1992—95. With USAAF, 1943—46. Named Disting. Vol., Wash.-Idaho Symphony Assn., 1996; named to alumni Hall of Fame, U. Idaho, 1999; recipient Outstanding Career Achievement award, U.S. AID's, 1981. Mem.: ACLU, Soc. Internat. Devel. (pres. Palouse chpt. 1982—83), Forestry Assn. Botswana, Am. Fgn. Svc. Assn., Sr. Seminar Alumni Assn., Beta Theta Pi. Personal E-mail: butterfield@lentilland.com.

BUTTERKLEE, NEIL HOWARD, lawyer; b. Bklyn., Mar. 17, 1958; s. Samuel and Edith (Uday) B.; m. Arlene Marie Eberle, July 5, 1982. BA, SUNY, Stony Brook, 1980, MS, 1982; MBA, Adelphi U., Garden City, N.Y., 1987; JD, N.Y. Law Sch., 1992. Bar: Conn. 1992, N.Y. 1993, D.C. 1994, U.S. Dist. Ct. (ea. and so. dists.) N.Y. 1993, U.S. Ct. Appeals (D.C. cir.) 1997, U.S. Supreme Ct., 1997. Tech. writer Consolidated Edison Co. N.Y. Inc., N.Y.C., 1982-83, analyst, 1983-89, sr. analyst, 1989-93, atty., 1993-95, staff atty., 1995-99, sr. staff atty., 1999—2002, sr. atty., 2002—. Editor: Law Review. Recipient Scholarship N.Y. Law Sch., N.Y.C., 1988-92; nationally ranked fencer U.S. Fencing Assn., 1984-88. Mem. ABA, N.Y. State Bar Assn., Conn. Bar Assn., Assn. Bar City N.Y., Energy Bar Assn. Avocations: golf, writing. Office: Consolidated Edison Co NY 4 Irving Pl Rm 1815 New York NY 10003-3598 E-mail: butterklee@coned.com.

BUTTERMAN, JAY RONALD, lawyer; b. NYC, June 15, 1958; s. Louis and Ellen (Schmeltzer) B. BA, Vassar Coll., 1983; JD, Yeshiva U., 1988. Bar: N.J. 1988, N.Y. 1989, U.S. Dist. Ct. (so. dist.) N.Y. 1991, U.S. Dist. Ct. (ea. dist.) N.Y. 1996, U.S. Dist. Ct. N.J. 1988, U.S. Supreme Ct. 2002. Assoc. Hoffinger Friedland Dobrish Bernfeld & Hasen, N.Y.C., 1988-91; sole practitioner N.Y.C., 1991-95; mng. ptnr. Law firm of Jay R. Butterman, N.Y.C., 1995-99; sr. ptnr. Butterman, Kahn & Gardner, LLP, 1999—. Recipient Outstanding Acad. Achievement award Acad. Am. Matrimonial Lawyers, 1988. Mem. ABA, ATLA, N.Y. State Bar Assn., Assn. Bar City N.Y. Democrat. Avocations: oriental art, antiquarian books. Office: 425 Park Ave 27th Fl New York NY 10022 Office Phone: 212-308-7697.

BUTTERMORE, JOHN R., automotive executive; BS, U.S. Naval Acad., 1973; MA, U. Rochester, 1984; post grad., Harvard Bus. Sch. Mgmt., 1989, Am.Grad. Sch. Internat. Mgmt., 1996. Mfg. engr. GM Corp. Rochester Products Div., NY, 1978—86; chief engr. GM Corp., 1986—87; plant mgr. GM Corp. Operations, Grand Rapids, Mich., 1987—89; dir. product engring. GM Corp. Allison Transmission, Indpls., 1989—93; dir. mfg. engring. GM Corp. Powertrain, Pontiac, Mich., 1994—96; mfg. mgr. GM Corp. Engine Plants, 1996—2000, GM North Am. Vehicle Assembly Plants, 2000—02; v.p GM North America, 2002—. With USN. Mem.: GM North Am. (stragety bd. mem.).

BUTTERS, RONALD RICHARD, language educator; b. Cedar Rapids, Iowa, Feb. 12, 1940; s. Richard Orton and Dorothy Mae B.; children: Rebecca, Catherine, Rachel. BA, U. Iowa, 1962, PhD, 1967. Asst. prof. English Duke U., Durham, N.C., 1967-74, assoc. prof. English, 1974-90, prof. English, 1990—2005, prof. Anthropology, 2000—. Editor Am. Speech Jour. Am. Dialect Soc., 1981-95; vis. scholar Ctr. Applied Linguistics, Washington, 1988-89; mem. editl. adv. bd. New Oxford American Dictionary. *Extensive experience as chair of the Duke English Department, the Duke Program in Linguistics, and as co-director of the Duke-North Carolina State Doctoral Program in English Linguistics (currently serving in all three positions). Over 15 years experience as a legal consultant in linguistics and expert witness specializing in the interpretation of statutes, contracts, and product warnings, the role of the linguist in American death-penalty appeals, and semiotic and linguistics issues in trademark litigation.* Author: The Death of Black English, 1989; co-author: Displacing Hompohobia, 1989 (CEW best spl. issue award 1989); chief editor Am. Dialect Soc. publs., 1996—. Recipient Rsch. grant NEH, 1973-74. Mem. Am. Dialect Soc. (v.p. 1997-99, pres. 2000-02), Internat. Assn. Forensic Linguists, Linguistic Soc. Am., Southeastern Conf. Linguistics (pres. 1983), Law and Soc. Assn., Dictionary Soc. N.Am. Office: Duke U PO Box 90015 Durham NC 27708-0015 Home: 1000 Lamond Ave Durham NC 27701-2021 Office Phone: 919-684-2741. Personal E-mail: ronbutters@aol.com.

BUTTERWORTH, ROBERT ROMAN, psychologist, researcher, media therapist; b. Pittsfield, Mass., June 24, 1946; s. John Leon and Martha Helen (Roman) B. BA, SUNY, 1972; MA, Marist Coll., 1975; PhD in Clin. Psychology, Calif. Grad. Inst., 1983. Asst. clin. psychologist N.Y. State Dept. Mental Hygiene, Wassaic, 1972-75; pres. Internat. Trauma Assocs., L.A. and Downey, Calif., 1976—. Cons. L.a. County Dept. Health Svc.; staff clinician San Bernardino County Dept. Mental Health, 1983-85; staff psychologist State of Calif. Dept. Mental Health, 1985—; media interviews include PA, L.A. Times, N.Y. Times, USA Today, Wall St Jour., Washington Post, Redbook mag., London Daily Mail and many others; TV and radio interviews include Larry King Live, CBA, NBA and ABC networks, Oprah Winfrey Show, CNN Newsnight, Can. Radio Network, Mut. Radio Network and many others. Served with USAF, 1965-69. Mem. Am. Psychol. Assn. for Media Psychology, Calif. Psychol. Assn., Nat. Accreditation Assn. Psychoanalysis. Office: PO Box 76477 Los Angeles CA 90076-0477 Office Phone: 213-487-7339. Business E-Mail: robert@drbutterworth.net.

BUTTERWORTH, S. KENDALL, lawyer; d. Charles Kenneth and Sue (Anderson) Butterworth. BA with honors, U. Va., 1991; JD cum laude, U. Ga. Sch. Law, 1994. Bar: Ga. 1994, U.S. Dist. Ct., no. dist., Ga. 1994, U.S. Ct. Appeals (11th cir.) 1994. Assoc. Kilpatrick Stockton LLP, Atlanta, 1994—97; atty. Bellsouth Telecomm., 1997—98, Bellsouth Cellular Corp., 1999—2000; litigation counsel Bellsouth Corp., 2001, sr. litigation counsel, 2001—. Mem. advisory bd. Atlanta Legal Aid Soc., 2002—; spl. asst. to chair Supreme Ct. Commn. on Indigent Def., Atlanta, 2001—04. Recipient Up and Comer Under 40, Atlanta Bus. Chronicle, 2004—05. Mem.: Ga. State Bar (mem. bd. govs. 1999—, pres. Young Lawyers divsn., Atlanta 2000—01), ABA (mem. Ho. of Dels., Chgo. 2000—04, mem. jury commn. 2004—05, named Star of the Quarter 1999, 2004, 2005), Atlanta Bar Assn. Avocations: running, travel, music. Office: Bellsouth Corp 1155 Peachtree St Ste 1700 Atlanta GA 30309 Office Phone: 404-249-3388. Office Fax: 404-249-2118. Business E-Mail: kendall.butterworth@bellsouth.com.

BUTTERWORTH, WILLIAM EDMUND, III, (W.E.B. GRIFFITH), writer; b. Newark, Nov. 10, 1929; s. William Edmund and Gladys Schnable Butterworth; married; 3 children. PhD in Mil. Fiction (hon.), Norwich U. Author: The Brotherhood of War Book I, The Lieutenants, 1982 (Ala. Author's award Ala. Libr. Assn., 1982), BookThe Brotherhood of War Book II, The Captains, 1982, The Brotherhood of War Book III, The Majors, 1983, The Brotherhood of War Book IV, The Colonels, 1983, The Brotherhood of War Book V, The Berets, 1984, BookThe Brotherhood of War VI, The Generals, 1986, The Brotherhood of War Book VII, The New Breed, 1987, The Brotherhood of War Book VIII, The Aviators, 1988, The Brotherhood of War Book IX, Special Ops, 2002, The Corps Book I, Semper Fi, 1986, The Corps Book II, Call to Arms, 1987, The Corps Book III, Counterattack, 1990, The Corps Book IV, Battleground, 1991, The Corps Book V, Line of Fire, 1992, The Corps Book VI, Close Combat, 1993, The Corps Book VII, Behind the Lines, 1996, The Corps Book VIII, In Danger's Path, 1999, The Corps Book IX, Under Fire, 2002, The Corps Book X, Retreat Hell!, 2004, Badge of Honor Book I, Men in Blue, 1991, Badge of Honor Book II, Special Operations, 1991, Badge of Honor Book III, The Victim, 1991, Badge of Honor Book IV, The Witness, 1992, Badge of Honor Book V, The Assassin, 1993, Badge of Honor Book VI, The Murderers, 1995, Badge of Honor Book VII, The Investigators, 1998, Badge of Honor Book VIII, Final Justice, 2003, Honor Bound Book I, Honor Bound, 1994, Honor Bound Book II, Blood and Honor, 1997, Honor Bound Book III, Secret Honor, 2000, Men At War Book I, The Last Heroes, 1997, Men At War Book II, The Secret Warriors, 1998, Men At War Book III, The Soldier Spies, 1999, Men At War Book IV, The Fighting Agents, 2001, By Order of the President, 2004. With U.S. Army, 1946—47, with U.S. Army, 1951—53. Mem.: Spl. Ops. Assn. (hon.), Marine Raider Assn. (life), Marine Combat Correspondants (life).

BUTTIGIEG, JOSEPH J., bank executive; BBA, U. Notre Dame; JD, Mich. State U. Coll. Law. Various to sr. v.p. Manufacturer's Bank, Detroit, 1972-89, exec. v.p., 1989-91; exec. v.p. global corp. banking Comerica, Inc., Detroit, 1995-99, vice-chmn. bus. bank, 1999—. Office: Comerica Inc Comerica Twr/500 Woodward A Detroit MI 48226

BUTTINGER FEDELI, CATHARINE SARINA CAROLINE, psychiatrist; b. Bruchsal, Fed. Republic Germany, July 23, 1951; came to U.S., 1982; d. John Levine and Juliana Magdalena Buttinger; m. Roger L. M. Dunbar, Oct. 7, 1982; 1 child, Emma Magdalena; m. Mario Fedeli, Dec. 2, 1994; 1 child, Alberto Julius. Abitur, Schuldorf-Bergstrasse, Germany, 1973; MD, U. Heidelberg, Germany, 1980, Med.Sc.D., 1982; postgrad., Columbia U., 1985-88. Neurosurgeon U. Hosp. Heidelberg, 1980-82; rschr. Albert Einstein Coll. Medicine, N.Y.C., 1982-83, intern, 1984-85; rschr. NYU, N.Y.C., 1983-84; psychiatrist Columbia U. Coll. Physicians and Surgeons, N.Y.C., 1985-88; rsch. fellow eating disorders Columbia U., N.Y.C., 1988-90; candidate Columbia U. Ctr. for Psycho-Analytic Tng. and Rsch., 1985-92; pvt. practice, 1988—. Faculty Columbia U. Coll. Physicians and Surgeons. Ginsburg fellow Group for Advancement of Psychiatry, 1986-88. Mem. AMA, Am. Psychiat. Assn., German Med. Assn. Home and Office: 40 Club House Ln Scarsdale NY 10583-3146 Office: 275 Central Park W New York NY 10024-3015 Office Phone: 212-580-8187. E-mail: CFedeli@aol.com.

BUTTLAR, RUDOLPH OTTO, retired college dean; b. Chgo., Dec. 31, 1934; s. Otto Robert and Lucille Ann (Blasnig) B.; m. Lois Jacqueline Mercier, June 5, 1955; children— Michael Robert, Andrew Scott, John David. BS in Chemistry, Wheaton (Ill.) Coll., 1956; PhD in Inorganic Chemistry, Ind. U., 1962. Mem. faculty Kent (Ohio) State U., 1962-96, asso. prof. chemistry, 1971-96; dean Kent (Ohio) State U. (Coll. Arts and Scis.), 1975-96. Adminstrv. cons., 1996—. Mem. Am. Chem. Soc., Am. Sci. Affiliation. Baptist. Home: 5936 Horning Rd Kent OH 44240-4140 E-mail: rbuttlar@neo.rr.com.

BUTTNER, JEAN BERNHARD, diversified financial services company executive; b. New Rochelle, NY, Nov. 3, 1934; d. Arnold and Janet (Kinghorn) Bernhard; m. Edgar Buttner, Sept. 13, 1958 (div.); children: Janet, Edgar Arnold, Marianne. BA, Vassar Coll., 1957; cert. bus. adminstrn., Harvard-Radcliffe program, 1958; Montessori diploma, Coll. Notre Dame, Belmont, Calif., 1967; D Bus. Administrn. (hon.), U. Bridgeport, 1994. Past v.p. Buttner Cos., Oakland, Calif.; pres. Value Line Inc. (subs. Arnold Bernhard & Co., Inc.), N.Y.C., 1985; chmn., pres. Vanderbilt Advt., Inc., 1988—; chmn., pres., CEO Value Line Inc. (subs. Arnold Bernhard & Co., Inc.), N.Y.C., 1988—; chmn., pres. Compupower, 1988—, Value Line Securities, Inc., 1988—90, Value Line Pub., Inc., 1990, Value Line Distbn. Ctr., Inc., 1994—; chmn., CEO, pres. AB Properties, Inc., 1999. Chmn., pres. Value Line Mut. Funds. Editor-in-chief Value Line Investment Survey. Past trustee Skidmore Coll.; past pres. Piedmont Sch. Bd.; past dir. Berkeley Montessori Sch.; past mem. NYC Partnership, Com. of 200; past mem. adv. coun. Stanford Bus. Sch.; past mem. Presdl. Roundtable; past vis. com. for bd. overseers Harvard Bus. Sch.; past bd. dirs. Harvard Bus. Sch. Club Greater N.Y.; past west coast admissions rep. Vassar Coll.; past trustee Radcliffe Coll., Williams Coll., Emma Willard Sch., Coll. Prep. Sch. Com. for Econ. Devel.; trustee Choate Rosemary Hall. Named one of N.Y.'s 75 Most Influential Women in Business, Crain's, 1996, One of N.Y.'s 100 Most Influential Women in Business, Crain's, 1999; recipient Alumni Achievement award, Harvard U. Grad. Sch. Bus. Adminstrn., 1995, Alumnae award Choate Rosemary Hall, Wallingford, Conn., 1995, Emma Lazarus award Associated Builders and Owners of N.Y., Inc., 1996; Life Achievement award Emma Willard Sch., 1998. Republican. Congregationalist. Avocations: reading, swimming, biking, tennis, skiing. Office: Value Line Inc 220 E 42nd St Fl 6 New York NY 10017-5891 E-mail: jbb@valueline.com.

BUTTON, CHARLES E., environmental scientist, educator; b. North Bend, Pa., July 5, 1964; s. Jane L. and John M. Button; m. Beth Caruso; children: Sky, River. BA in Geography, Mansfield U. Pa., 1987; MS in Geoenvironmental Studies, Shippensburg U. Pa., 1989; PhD, U. Cin., 2003. Planning dir. East Buffalo Twp., Lewisburg, Pa., 1989—90; watershed storm water mgmt. planner Union County, 1989—90; environ. scientist, planner Herbert, Rowland & Grubic, Harrisburg, Pa., 1990—91; environ. programs dir. U. NC, Chapel Hill, NC, 1991—96; solid waste mgmt. dir. Macon County, Franklin, NC, 1996—98; water resources rsch. fellow US EPA, Cin., 1999—2003; adj. prof. U. of Cin., 2003—04; prof. Ctrl. Conn. State U., New Britain, 2004—. Co-founder, bd. mem. Nat. Coll. & U. Recycling Caucus, Washingtonton, 1991—97. Recipient Recycling Merit award, NC Recyclers' Assn., 1992. Mem.: Assn. of Am. Geographers. Office: Ctrl Conn State Univ Diloretto Hall New Britain CT 04010 Office Phone: 860-832-2788. Business E-Mail: buttonche@ccsu.edu.

BUTTON, DONALD D., electrical engineer; b. Summit, N.J., Mar. 19, 1957; s. Donald Demarest and Marea Button; m. Daisy Tavares de Almeida, Sept. 30, 2000; 1 child, Amanda Almeida. BSEE, U. Del., Newark, Delaware, 1980. Lic. Residential Electrical Inspector, Internat. Code Coun., 2004, registered profl. engr., Ga. Antenna design engr. Raytheon Co., Wayland, Mass., 1980—83; sr. antenna design engr. Sanders Assoc., Inc., Nashua, NH, 1983—86; microwave antenna design mgr. Gabriel Electronics, Inc., Scarborough, Maine, 1986—94; staff elec. engr. EMS Technologies, Inc., Norcross, Ga., 1994—2003; dir. forensic elec. engring. Forensic and Sci. Testing, Inc., Atlanta, 2003—. Contbr. scientific papers to profl. publs. Deacon United Ch. of Christ, Windham, Maine, 1988—92. Mem.: IEEE, NSPE, Am. Soc. Testing of Materials (forensic engring. com., electrical conductor com.), Nat. Fire Protection Assn., Internat. Assn. Arson Investigators, Nat. Acad. of Forensic Engrs. (corr.), Am. Radio Relay League (life), Eta Kappa Nu (life; chpt. pres. 1979—80). Achievements include patents for stacked biconical omnidirectional antenna. Avocations: classical piano, photography, amateur radio. Home: 4503 Prather Pass Dr Loganville GA 30052 Personal E-mail: dondb99@bellsouth.net.

BUTTON, RENA PRITSKER, public relations executive; b. Providence, Feb. 15, 1925; d. Isadore and Esther (Kay) Pritsker; m. Daniel E. Button, Aug. 16, 1969; children by previous marriage: Joshua, Bruce, David Posner. Student, Pembroke Coll., 1942—45; BS, Simmons Coll., 1948; postgrad., Union U., 1968—69. Spl. asst. to U.S. Rep., 1967-69; spl. projects coord. United Jewish Appeal, 1971-74; exec. dir. Nat. Coun. Jewish Women, Inc., N.Y.C., 1974-76; pres. Button Assos., N.Y.C., 1976—; exec. v.p. Catalyst, N.Y.C., 1980-82; pres. Button & Button, Albany, N.Y., 1982—. Adv. coun. N.Y. State Senate Minority, 1980—; exec. dir. N.Y. State Coun. on Alcoholism and Other Drug Addictions, 1990-93; pres., founder Two Together, A Pilot Reading Program for Young People, 1997-2003. Co-producer, moderator: TV pub. affairs program Speak For Yourself, Albany, N.Y., 1963-66. Chair pub. affairs com. Marymount Manhattan Coll.; past bd. dirs. Albany YWCA, Albany Coun. Chs. Devel. Corp., World Affairs Coun., Planned Parenthood Assn. Albany; trustee Jerusalem Women's Seminar, Citizens for Family Planning, N.Y. Com. Integrated Housing, Hist. Albany Found. Ctr. for Counseling, Town of Bethlehem Pub. Libr., 1999; pres. Sr. Svc. Ctr. Albany Area, Two Together, 1997; bd. dirs. Com. Modern Cts.; exec. dir. N.Y. Head Injury Assn., 1993-96; candidate N.Y. State Assembly 102d Dist., 1996; trustee Albany Symphony Orch., 2002—. Mem. Siasconset Casino Club, Univ. Club. Clubs: Siasconset Casino (Siasconset, Mass.), Univ. (Albany). Home and Office: 16 Spruce Ct Delmar NY 12054-2614 E-mail: rbutton96@aol.com.

BUTTON, RICHARD TOTTEN, television producer, ice skater; b. Englewood, N.J., July 18, 1929; s. George and Evelyn Bunn Totten B.; children: Edward Totten, Emily Rada. BA, Harvard U., 1952, LLB, 1956; LHD (hon.), Buena Vista Coll., 1988. Dir. Decorative Arts Trust, 1979-80. Commentator ABC Sports; creator The Superstars sports competitions, The World Profl. Figure Skating Championships; prodr. Broadway shows: Sweet Sue, 1987, Artist Descending a Staircase, 1989; nat. spokesperson Brain Injury ASsn. Am., 2003. Author: Dick Button on Skates, 1955, Instant Skating, 1964; contbr. articles to various mags. Pres. Richmondtown Restoration, Inc., 1968-77. U.S. figure skating champion, 1946-52; world figure skating champion, 1948-52; European figure skating champion, 1948; Olympic gold medalist, 1948, 52; recipient James E. Sullivan award, 1949, Emmy award for outstanding sports personality-analyst, 1980-81; named to U.S. Olympic Hall of Fame. Mem. Bar Assn. D.C., Skating Club N.Y., Skating Club Boston, Phila. Skating Club.

BUTTON, STEVEN D., music educator; b. Hamilton, N.Y., May 19, 1963; s. Merville James and Martha Button; m. Ilze Brink, Apr. 1, 1989; children: Hannah Louisa, Lucas James. BA in Music, Ithaca Coll., N.Y., 1988; MA in Music Edn., Crane Sch. Music, Potsdam, N.Y., 1994. Cert. tchr.-permanent N.Y. State. Instr. instrumental music South African Coll. Schs., Cape Town, 1988—89, Stamford (N.Y.) Ctrl. Schs., 1989—90, Oneonta City Schs., 1990—95, Canastota (N.Y.) Ctrl. Schs., 1995—. Instr. instrumental music summers Hartwick Coll. Music Festival, Oneonta, NY, 1999—2003. Mailing: 1105 Sunnycrest Rd Syracuse NY 13206-3160

BUTTREY, DONALD WAYNE, lawyer; b. Terre Haute, Ind., Feb. 6, 1935; s. William Edgar and Nellie (Vaughn) B.; children: Greg, Alan, Jason; m. Karen Lake, Mar. 23, 1985. BS, Ind. State U., 1956; JD, Ind. U., 1961. Bar: Ind. 1961, U.S. Dist. Ct. 1961, U.S. Ct. Appeals (7th cir.) 1972, U.S. Tax Ct. 1972, U.S. Supreme Ct. 1972. Law clk. to chief judge Steckler, U.S. Dist. Ct. So. Dist. Ind., 1961-63; mem. McHale, Cook & Welch, P.C., Indpls.,

1963—2001, pres., 1986-93, chmn., 1993—2001; of counsel Wooden & McLaughlin, LLP, 2001—. Chmn. Ctrl. Region IRS-Bar Liaison Com., 1984; jud. nominating com. Marion County Mcpl. Ct., 1993-96; mem. Estate Planning Coun. Indpls., 1990—. Note editor Ind. Law Jour., 1960-61. Trustee Ind. State U., 1992-2000, v.p. bd., 1997-2000; bd. dirs. Ind. State U. Found., 1991—. With AUS, 1956-58, Korea. Fellow Am. Coll. Tax Counsel, Am. Bar Found., Ind. State Bar Found., Indpls. Bar Found. (pres. 1993-96, Buchanan award 1999); mem. ABA (taxation, real property, probate and trust sect., liaison IRS-Bar Liaison com., taxation sect. 1995-96), Ind. State Bar Assn. (bd. govs. 1994-96, taxation, real property, probate and trust sect., chmn. taxation sect. 1982-83), Indpls. Bar Assn. (pres. 1990, mem. probate, taxation sects.), Highland Golf and Country Club, Columbia Club, Univ. Club (bd. dirs. 1997-2000). Presbyterian. E-mail: dbuttrey@woodmaclaw.com.

BUTTRICK, HAROLD, architect; b. Bryn Mawr, Pa., Jan. 2, 1931; s. Charles Edgar and Constance (La Boiteaux) B.; m. Ann Octavia White, Sept. 3, 1955; children: John Ward, Jerome Chanler, Mary Constance, Sarah Elizabeth, Catherine. Student, The Sorbonne, Paris, 1950-51; AB, Harvard U., 1953, MArch, 1959. Cert. NCRB. Prin. Harold Buttrick & Assocs., N.Y.C., 1963-75, Smotrich Platt & Buttrick, N.Y.C., 1975-76, Buttrick White & Burtis, N.Y.C., 1976-97, Murphy Burnham & Buttrick, N.Y.C., 1998—. Prin archtl. works include Corpus Christi Monastery, Nairobi, Kenya, 1967, Green Vale Sch., Iselin Ctr., Glen Head, N.Y., 1971, Trans World Airlines 747 Hangar, John F. Kennedy Airport, 1971, Carter Giraffe House, Bronx Zoo, 1981, 42 Tower Records Stores, 1982-94, St. Thomas Choir Sch., N.Y.C., 1987, Central Park projects, Loeb Boathouse, 1986, Ballplayers Refreshment Stand, 1990, restoration of the Pulitzer Fountain and Grand Army Plz., 1990, The Charles A. Dana Discovery Ctr., 1993, Outdoor Performance Stage, Bushnell Park, Hartford, Conn., 1995, Battery Park City Authority Offices, 1996, Trinity Mid. Sch., NYC, 1998, St. Bartholomew's Ch., Master Plan, NYC, 2004. Bd. dirs. N.Y. Soc. Libr., 1989-93. Recipient Preservation League of N.Y. State awards, 1990-91, 96, City Club of N.Y. Bard awards Loeb Boathouse, 1986, St. Thomas Choir Sch., 1990, Ballplayers Refreshment Stand, 1992. Fellow AIA (Brick in Architecture award 1991, 95), NY State Assn. Archs.; mem. Century Assn., New Yorkers for Parks (mem. bd. NY 2000—). Office: Murphy Burnham & Buttrick 48 W 37th St New York NY 10018 Office Phone: 212-768-7676.

BUTTS, CAROL HENDERSON, human resources specialist, consultant; b. Anniston, Ala., Feb. 11, 1946; d. William Edward and Mary (Hill) Henderson; m. Robert Russell Butts, Feb. 12, 1976 (div. Mar. 1989); children: Jabe Bowden, Deborah Ann Miller. BA, Jacksonville State U., 1970. From pers. counselor to tng. dir. Norrell, Inc., Atlanta, 1971-77; creative dir. TV Tempo Stevens County, Toccoa, Ga., 1978-82; gen. mgr. Niermann Pers. Svcs., Atlanta, 1983-87; dir. tng. and continuing edn. KOT Pers., Atlanta, 1987-90; gen. mgr., v.p. med. divsn. Prestige Pers. Svcs., Norcross, Ga., 1990-94; dir. med. divsn. MedPro Pers., Atlanta, 1994-95; pres. MedStat, Inc., Alpharetta, Ga., 1995—. Pres. Habitat for Humanity, 1996—97. Recipient Editor's Choice award, Internat. Libr. Poetry, 2001—02, Poet of Merit award, 2002. Fellow: Nat. Assn. Pers. Cons., Am. Biog. Inst.; mem.: NOW, NAFE (pres. 1996—97), NAUW (pres. 1996—97), Ga. Assn. Pers. Cons. (chair, Disting. Cons. of Yr. 1978), Jacksonville State U. Alumni Assn. (Alumni fo the Yr. nominee 1997), Sigma Tau Alpha, Alpha Xi Delta. Avocations: reading, writing, poetry, fishing, water sports. Office Phone: 770-993-6838. Personal E-mail: cdearbutts@aol.com.

BUTTS, EDWARD PERRY, civil engineer, environmental consultant; b. Ukiah, Calif., July 29, 1958; s. Edward Oren Butts and Orvilla June (Daily) Hutcheson; m. JoAnne Catherine Zellner, Aug. 14, 1978; children: Brooke C., Adam E. Cert. continuing studies in Irrigation Theory and Practices, U. Nebr., 1980. Registered profl. civil and environ. engr., Oreg., Wash., cert. water rights examiner, Oreg., sprinkler irrigation designer, Irrigation Assn. Oreg., control sys. engr., Oreg., registered gen. contractor, Oreg., Wash., lic. pump installation contractor, Oreg., diplomate, Am. Bd. Engring. and Tech., Am. Coll. Forensic Examiners, Am. Acad. Environ. Engrs., cert. plant engr., Assn. Facilities Engring., Assoc. Facilities Engring., pump installer, Nat. Groundwater Assn., bd. cert. environ. and forensic engr. Technician Ace Pump Sales, Salem, Oreg., 1976, Stettler Supply Co., Salem, 1976-78, assoc. engr., 1978-86, chief engr., 1986—90, v.p. engring., 1990-97, pres., 1997—2003, chief engr., 2003—04; owner 4B Engring. Consulting, 2004—. Profl. engr. exam. question reviewer Nat. Coun. Engring. Examiners, Clemson, SC, 1989—; profl. engr. exam. supr. Oreg. State Bd. Engring. Examiners, Salem, 1986—96; mem. Marion County Water Mgmt. Coun., 1994—2000, Oreg. Drinking Water Adv. Com., 1999—; mem. blue ribbon com. Oreg. Dept. Environ. Quality, 2003—05; mem. Oreg. State Bd. Examiners Engring. and Land Surveying, 2003—; editl. adv. bd. Pumps & Systems mag., 2001; mem. Oreg. Groundwater Adv. Com., 2001—03; mem. ANSI vertical turbine and centrifugal pump standards com. Hydraulic Inst., 2000—02. Contbg. editor: Pumps and Systems Mag., 2001; contbr. and author of over 60 papers and articles to profl. jours. including Jour. Pub. Works Mag., AWWA Opflow, Pumps and Sys.; columnist Water Well Jour. Coach Little League Cascade Basketball Leage, Turner, Oreg., 1990-94; vol. Jr. Achievement; presdl. bus. commn. Nat. Rep. Congrl. Com., 2002—. Recipient Merit award Am. City and County Mag., 1990, Cmty. Vol. citation City of Keizer, Oreg., 1993, Cert. of appreciation Oreg. State Bd. Engring. Examiners, 1996, Commendation letter City of Salem, 1996, Application Design award Spraying Systems Co., 1996, Apex award Most Improved Jour.,Oreg. Republican of Yr., 2001, Meritorius Svc. medal Nat. Rep. Congl. Com., 2001-02, Presdl. Bus. Commn., 2002, Businessman of Yr., Congl. Order of Merit Nat. Rep. Congl. Com., 2003. Fellow ASCE; mem. ASME, NSPE, IEEE, Am. Pub. Works Assn., Assn. Groundwater Scientists and Engrs., Am. Acad. Environ. Engrs. (Oreg. gov., mem. nat. bd. trustees 2004-, mem. water and wastewater subcom.), Nat. Ground Water Assn. (nominee equipment design award, 2003), Oreg. Groundwater Assn., Profl. Engrs. Oreg. (mid-Willamette chpt. v.p. 1990-91, pres. 1992-93, state v.p. 1993-95, state pres.-elect 1995-96, state pres. 1996-97, nat. dir. 1999-2000, Young Engr. of Yr. award 1993-94, President's award, 2004), Am. Water Works Assn., Oreg. Assn. Water Utilities (bd. dirs. 1998—, Friend of Rural Water award 2002, del. Nat. Water Rally, 2001-03). Republican. Achievements include devel. of system used to install multiple pumps in water wells. Office: 3000 Market St NE Ste 528 Salem OR 97301 E-mail: epbpe@juno.com, epbpe@4bengineering.com.

BUTTS, HERBERT CLELL, retired dentist, educator; b. Dover, Tenn., Aug. 24, 1924; s. Sidney Lewis and Georgia (Sawyer) B.; m. Quay Coker; children: Marla Lyce, April Chyrese, Dawn Denise, Sidney Coker. Student, U. Tenn. Jr. Coll., 1942-43, Memphis State U., 1946-47; DDS, U. Tenn., 1950; MS, U. Iowa, 1966. Pvt. practice dentistry, Memphis, 1950-58; mem. faculty Coll. Dentistry, U. Tenn., Memphis, part-time 1950-58, 58-60, assoc. dean acad. affairs, 1978-81, spl. advisor to dean, 1986-2000; ret., 2000; fgn. svc. officer, dental edn. advisor State Dept. Fgn. Aid program, San Salvador, El Salvador, 1960-64; assoc. prof. St. Louis U. Sch. Dentistry, 1966-67; prof., chmn. dept. operative dentistry Coll. Dental Medicine, Med. U. S.C., Charleston, 1967-70, asst. dean for admissions and student affairs, 1970, 72-74, acting dean, 1971; editor-in-chief ADA, Chgo., 1974-77; dean Sch. Dental Medicine So. Ill. U., Alton, 1981-86. Editor U. Tenn. Coll. Dentistry Bull., 1990-2000. With USNR, 1943-46. Recipient Outstanding Alumnus award U. Tenn. Coll. Dentistry, 1975. Mem. ADA, Tenn. Dental Assn. (fellowship award 1993), Memphis Dental Soc., Am. Coll. Dentists (pres. Tenn. sect. 1994, sec.-treas. Tenn. sect. 1995-98), Internat. Coll. Dentists, Am. Assn. Dental Schs., Ala. Dental Assn. (hon.), Am. Assn. Women Dentists (hon.), Omicron Kappa Upsilon. Home: 1360 Peabody Ave Memphis TN 38104-3636

BUTTS, HUGH FLORENZ, physician, psychiatrist, psychoanalyst; b. N.Y.C., Dec. 2, 1926; s. Lucius Cornelius and Edith Eliza Butts; m. June Dobbs, June 9, 1953 (div. Dec. 1971); children: Lucia Irene, Florence, Eric Hugh; m. Clementine Riggsbee, Dec. 11, 1971; children: Sydney Clementine, Samantha Florenz, Heather Marguerita. BS, CCNY, 1949; MD, Meharry Med. Coll., 1953. Diplomate Am. Bd. Psychiatry and Neurology. Intern Morrisania Hosp., 1956; resident Bronx VA Hosp., 1958; psychiatry instr. Columbia U., N.Y.C., 1962-65, assoc. prof. psychiatry, 1965-67, asst. clin. prof. psychiatry, 1967-74; mem. faculty Columbia Psychoanalytic Clinic, N.Y.C., 1962-87, supervising and tng. analyst, 1968-87; lectr. Columbia Coll., N.Y.C., 1969-71; instr. Seek program CCNY, N.Y.C., 1972-74. Prof. psychiatry Albert Einstein Coll. Medicine, Bronx, 1974-81; cons. Altanta U. Sch. Social Work, 1970-74; vis. prof. psychiatry Meharry Med. Coll., Nashville, 1980-82; dir. Bronx Psychiat. Ctr., 1974-79; 1st dept. commr. N.Y. State Office Mental Health, Albany, N.Y., 1975-76; chmn. adv. bd. The Med. Herald, 1991-2002. Pres., founder Clementine Pub. Co., 1989, Lit. Mind Assocs., 1989; author Racism and Post traumatic Stress Disorder, 2005; contbr. more than 200 articles to profl. jours. With USAAF, 1944-45. Recipient Spl. Merit award Assn. for Psychoanalytic Medicine, 1967; travel fellow Ford Found., 1972. Fellow: NY Acad. Scis., Am. Psychiat. Assn. (Disting. Life fellow 2003); mem.: Am. Psychoanalytic Assn. Avocations: gardening, fishing, antique collecting, playing the violin, writing. Office: 350 Central Park W New York NY 10025-6547 Office Phone: 212-864-6191. E-mail: hfbuttsmd@aol.com.

BUTTZ, CHARLES WILLIAM, outdoor advertising executive; b. Aberdeen, SD, Aug. 8, 1932; s. Ward Leland and Mary Baker (Eddy) B.; m. Teresa Margarita Castro, July 28, 1956; children: Jean, Teresa, Charles, William, James. BCE, Rensselaer Polytech Inst., 1956; MBA, U. Conn., 1974. Registered profl. engr. N.Y., N.J. Chief engr. Kuala Lumpur Transp. Study, Malaysia, 1963—64; project mgr. Tippetts Abbett McCarthy Stratton Engrs., N.Y.C., 1956—65; mgmt. cons. Booz, Allen and Hamilton, N.Y.C., 1965—67; dir. Knight, Gladieux and Smith Cons., N.Y.C., 1967—74; group mgr. Boeing Computer Svcs. Cons., N.Y.C., 1974—76; v.p. Middlesex Rsch. Ctr., Washington, 1976—77; pres. Ea. Shelter-All Inc., Mountainhome, Pa., 1977—, N.J. Shelter-All Inc., Columbia, 1980—, Regional Shelter-All Inc., Buck Hill Falls, Pa., 1985—. Instr. mktg. U. Conn., Stamford, 1975-76. Pres. St. Paul's Housing Corp., Norwalk, Conn., 1974-77; com. mem. Alfred Dater Coun. Boy Scouts Am., Stamford, 1970-77; v.p., camp chmn. Darien (Conn.) United Way, 1974; v.p., sec. Darien Young Mens Christian Assn., 1974-77; dir. United Way Monroe County, Tannersville, Pa., 1984-97. Maj. USAR, 1956-70. Scholar, Wall St. Jour., 1974. Mem. ASCE, Pa. Soc., Inst. Transp. Engrs., Am. Legion, Army and Navy Club. Episcopalian. Home: Cottage 266 Buck Hill Falls PA 18323 Office: Ea Shelter-All Inc PO Box 152 Mountainhome PA 18342

BUTZ, GENEVA MAE, pastor; b. Emmaus, Pa., May 11, 1944; d. Edwin F. and Arlene E. (Engler) B. BA, Hood Coll., 1966; MRE, Union Theol. Sem., 1968; D Divinity (hon.), Ursinus Coll., 1994. Ordained clergywoman United Ch. of Christ, 1972. Dir. Christian edn. United Ch. of Christ, Palos Verdes, Calif., 1968-72; mng. editor Youth mag., United Ch. Bd. for Homeland Ministries, Phila., 1972-75; affiliate rep. Ecumenical Community of Taizé, France, New Zealand, Australia, Indonesia, India and others, 1975-77; parish worker Temple Presbyn. Ch., Phila., 1978-83; pastor Old First Reformed Ch., United Ch. Christ, Phila., 1984—2003; assoc. conf. minister Pa. SE Conf. United Ch. Christ, 2003—. Bd. dirs. Met. Christian Coun. of Phila., 1985-96, 98—; chair Ch. and Ministry Com., Phila. Assn. United Ch. Christ, 1983-86; cons. Auburn Theol. Sem., N.Y., 1988-89; coord. 5-Day urban seminar for incoming students Lancaster Theol. Sem., 1986-93, The Small Ch. and Cultural Change, Bangor Theol. Sem., 1988; mem. adv. com. on evangelism and membership growth priority United Ch. Christ, 1989=90; team chair Toward the 21st Century, A Church-wide Planning Process for the United Ch. Christ, 1990-93; spkr. Faith Journey, consultation XVI in Parish Ministry for United Ch. Christ Clergy, Orlando, Fla., 1991; guest preacher Nat. Cathedral, Washington, 1993; commencement spkr. Lancaster Theol. Sem., 1996; sabbatical visitor to ch. in Indonesia through Common Global Mission Bd. (Disciples of Christ/United Ch. Christ), 2001. Author: Color Me Well, 1986, Christmas Comes Alive, 1988, Christmas in All Seasons, 1995; contbr. Women Pray, Karen Roller, Ed, 1986. Bd. dirs. Bethesda Project, Inc., Phila., 1986-98, Phila. Religious Leadership Devel. Fund, 1988-98, Maternity Care Coalition, Phila., 1999—; del. Gen. Synod-United Ch. Christ, Cleve., Ft. Worth, Providence, Kansas City, 1987-89, 99-2001; ecumenical del. Gen. Assembly Presbyn. Ch. (USA), 1989; adv. bd. Seamen's Ch. Inst., Phila., 1992-2003; trustee Lancaster Theol. Sem., 1992—; 2d v.p. Met. Christian Coun. Phila., 1998—. Named One of 85 People to Watch, Phila. Mag., 1985, One of 7 Clergy Leading U.S. Constl. Bicentennial Parade, 1987, Valiant Woman of Yr., Ch. Women United, 1991; recipient Human Rels. award, NCCJ, Phila., 1985; fellow Merrill fellow, Harvard Div. Sch., 1993. Mem. Nat. Orgn. of Women, Ch. Women United of Greater Phila., Old Phila. Clergy, Assn. United Arts and Religion, Phila. Assn. (ministrial standing). Democrat. Office: Pa SE Conf United Ch of Christ 505 S 2d St Collegeville PA 19426 E-mail: gbutz@psec.org. *Being religious is so simple that as adults we find it hard to achieve. Children do it easily. We need to work with children so we don't destroy their natural religious inclination. The future of the faith lies in our ability to evoke the innate religious sensitivity in all people.*

BUTZ, GLORIA K., elementary school educator; b. Salem, Oreg., Aug. 29, 1951; d. Mary Carolyn (Davis) Mann; m. Loren O. Butz, Aug. 18, 1973; children: Janiess Dielle, Karel Trevor. BA Music Edn., Seattle Pacific U., 1973, MEd, 1981. Cert. elem./secondary tchr., Wash.; profl. cert. Assn. Christian Schs. Internat. Music tchr., grades K-6 Auburn (Wash.) Sch. dist. #408, 1973-75, tchr. sixth grade, 1975-77; reading tutor Valley Christian Sch., Auburn, 1983-84, elem. tchr., fifth/sixth grades, 1984—; head tchr. Valley Christian Mid. Sch., Auburn, 2000—03, prin., 2003—. Mem. sch. bd. Valley Christian Sch., 1982-84; young author's camp staff mem., Seattle Pacific U., Wash., 1981-83. Dir. Vacation Bible Sch., Auburn Free Meth. Ch., 1987, 89, 92, 94. Mem. Internat. Reading Assn., Washington Orgn. for Reading Devel. Republican. Avocations: piano, flute, travel, gardening, sewing. Home: 1505 24th St SE Auburn WA 98002-7837

BUTZ, NORBERT LEO, actor; b. St. Louis, Jan. 30, 1967; m. Sydney Butz; children: Clara Virginia, Maggie Lou. BFA, Webster U.; MFA, Ala. Shakespeare Theatre. Actor: (Broadway plays) Rent, 1996; (Broadway plays, nat. tour) Cabaret (Helen Hayes award, outstanding actor in a musical); (Broadway plays) Thou Shalt Not, 2001, Wicked, 2003, Dirty Rotten Scoundrels, 2005 (Tony award, best performance by a leading actor in a musical, 2005, Drama League award, disting. performance, 2005, Outer Critics Circle award, outstanding actor in a musical, 2005, Drama Desk award, oustanding actor in a musical, 2005); (plays, off-broadway) Buicks, The Last Five Years, 2002 (Drama League award, outstanding actor in a musical); (plays) Juno and the Paycock, Saved; (films) Went to Coney Island on a Mission from God...Be Back by Five, 1998, (voice) Looking for an Echo, 2000, Noon Blue Apples, 2002, West of Here, 2002.

BUTZNER, JOHN DECKER, JR., retired federal judge; b. Scranton, Pa., Oct. 2, 1917; BA, U. Scranton, 1939; LLB, U. Va., 1941. Bar: Va. 1941. Pvt. practice law, Fredericksburg, 1941—58; judge 15th and 39th Jud. Cir. of Va., 1958—62; U.S. judge Ea. Dist. Va., 1962—67; cir. judge U.S. Ct. Appeals (4th cir.), Richmond, Va., 1967—98; judge for appointment of ind. counsel U.S. Ct. Appeals for D.C. Cir., 1988—98. With USAAF, 1942—45.

BUVANENDRAN, ASOKUMAR, medical educator, anesthesiologist; arrived in U.S., 1995; MD, 1989. Cert. Am. Bd. Anesthesiology, 1999. Resident, pain fellow Rush U., 1999, assoc. prof. Chgo., 2000—. Contbr. articles to profl. jours. Grantee, Rush U., 2004. Office: Rush Univ Med Ctr # 550 1725 W Harrison St Chicago IL 60612 Office Phone: 312-942-6449. Office Fax: 312-942-8858.

BUX, WILLIAM JOHN, lawyer; b. Wadsworth, Ohio, Nov. 10, 1946; s. William J. and Helen M. (Sybelnik) B.; m. Linda Alice Zenar, Feb. 13, 1971. BSME, Ohio State U., 1969, MS, 1970; JD cum laude, So. Meth. U., 1977. Bar: Tex. 1977, U.S. Dist. Ct. (so. dist.) Tex. 1978, U.S. Ct. Appeals (5th cir.) 1978, U.S. Dist. Ct. (no. dist.) Tex. 1980, U.S. Dist. Ct. (ea. and we. dists.) Tex. 1981, U.S. Ct. Appeals (11th cir.) 1981, U.S. Supreme Ct. 1982; cert. Labor & Employment Law Tex. Bd. Legal Specialization. Assoc. Vinson & Elkins, Houston, 1977-85; ptnr. Hughes & Luce, Dallas, 1985-93; shareholder Locke Purnell Rain Harrell, Dallas, 1994-97; ptnr. Liddell, Sapp, Zivley, Hill & La Boon, Houston, 1997-98, Locke, Liddell & Sapp, Houston, 1999—. Author: Developing and Enforcing Drug and Alcohol Abuse Work Rules: A Primer for Texas Employers, 1984. Sec. So. Meth. U. Law Sch. Alumni Council, Dallas, 1986-88. Capt. USAF, 1971-74. Mem. ABA, Tex. Bar Assn. (chmn. labor and employment law sect. 1992-93), Houston Bar Assn., 5th Cir. Bar Assn. (named Tex. Super Lawyer 2003-05), Order of the Coif. Republican. Roman Catholic. Home: 2511 Westgate St Houston TX 77019-6609 Office: Locke Liddell & Sapp 600 Travis St 3400 JP Morgan Chase Twr Houston TX 77002-3095 Office Phone: 713-226-1275.

BUXBAUM, RICHARD M., lawyer, educator; b. 1930; AB, Cornell U., 1950, LLB, 1952; LLM, U. Calif., Berkeley, 1953; Dr. (hon.), U. Osnabrück, 1992, Eötvös Lorand U., Budapest, Hungary, 1993. Bar: Calif. 1953, N.Y. 1953. Practice law pvt. firm, Rochester, N.Y., 1957-61; prof. U. Calif., Berkeley, 1961—, dean internat. and area studies, 1993-99. Hon. prof. U. Peking, 1998. Editor-in-chief Am. Jour. Comparative Law, 1987-2004. Property commn. mem. Found. for Responsibility, Remembrance, and the Future, Germany, 2001—. Recipient Humboldt prize, 1991, German Order of Merit, 1992, Officier Arts et Lettres, France, 1997, Order of Rio Branco, Brazil, 1998. Mem. AAAS, Am. Law Inst., Internat. Acad. Comparative Law, German Soc. Comparative Law (corr.), Coun. on Fgn. Rels. Office: U Calif Sch Law 888 Simon Hall Berkeley CA 94720-0001 Office Phone: 510-642-1771. Business E-Mail: bux@berkeley.edu.

BUXBAUM, ROBERT C(OURTNEY), internist; b. Milw., Dec. 16, 1930; s. Edwin C. and Lillian (Tousman) B.; m. Ann S. Shocket, Dec. 26, 1955; children: Laura, Carl, Paula, Margaret. AB, Harvard U., 1952; MD, U. Pa., 1956. Diplomate Am. Bd. Internal Medicine, Am. Bd. Hospice and Palliative Medicine. Intern Henry Ford Hosp., Detroit, 1956-57; officer USPHS, San Carlos Apache Res., Ariz., 1957-59; resident, rsch. fellow U. Wis. Hosp., Madison, 1959-63; from rsch. assoc. to instr. Harvard Med. Sch., Boston, 1963-69, asst. prof. medicine, 1969—2004, clin. assoc. prof. medicine, 2004—. Internist Harvard Cmty. Health Plan (now Harvard Vanguard Med. Assocs.), Boston, 1969—; cons. health policy; founding mem. Mass. Compassionate Care Coalition, 1999—, pres., 2003—. Author: Sports for Life, 1979; contbr. articles to profl. jours. V.p. Mass. Compassionate Care Coalition, 2000—03, pres., 2003—; chmn. Gov.'s Com. on Fitness, Mass., 1975—80. Fellow ACP. Mem. Am. Acad. Hospice and Palliative Medicine. Avocations: playing oboe, swimming, skiing. Office: Harvard Vanguard Med Assocs Faultner Hosp 1153 Centre St 6th Fl Boston MA 02130 Office Phone: 617-838-5437. Business E-Mail: robert_buxbaum@hms.harvard.edu.

BUXTON, DOUGLAS FRANCISCO, ophthalmologist, educator; b. N.Y.C., Nov. 5, 1952; s. Jorge Norman and Amalia (Gonzalez) B. BA, Yale U., 1975; postgrad., Columbia U., 1977; MD, Cornell U., 1982. Diplomate Am. Bd. Ophthalmology, Nat. Bd. Med. Examiners; diplomate in cataract/implant surgery, penetrating keratoplasty, and laser in situ keratomileusis Am. Bd. Eye Surgery. Intern St. Vincent's Hosp. and Med. Ctr., N.Y.C., 1982—83; resident N.Y. Eye and Ear Infirmary, N.Y.C., 1983—86, fellow in cornea and external disease, 1986—88, attending surgeon, 1986—; asst. attending surgeon dept. ophthalmology Manhattan Eye, Ear and Throat Hosp., N.Y.C., 1988—; clin. assoc. prof. ophthalmology N.Y. Med. Coll., 1991—. Contbr. articles to profl. jours. Fellow Am. Acad. Ophthalmology; mem. Am. Coll. Eye Surgeons, Am. Soc. Cataract and Refractive Surgeons, Castroviejo Cornea Soc., N.Y. Intra-Ocular Lens Implant Soc., Pan Am. Assn. Ophthalmology, N.Y. Keratorefractive Soc. Office: NY Eye and Ear Infirmary 310 E 14th St Ste 403 New York NY 10003-4201 Fax: (212) 353-5772. Office Phone: 212-979-4410. Business E-Mail: dbuxton@nyee.edu.

BUXTON, MARGARET ROSE, human resources specialist, director; m. Bobby Lee Buxton, Feb. 23, 1980; children: Johnathan Martin, Justin Marcellous. BS, Hampton U., Va., 1972, EdM, 1987; EdD, George Wash. U., Washington, 1998. Tchr. Va. Beach Pub. Sch., Va., 1982—89, asst. prin., 1989—90, human resource specialist, 1990—2003; human resources dir. Portsmouth Pub. Sch., 2003—. Cons. JONJUS Diversity Consultants, Portsmouth, Va., 2000—. Chair Dept. of Behavioral Health Svcs., 1997—. Recipient President's award, PTA, 1995, Human Rights award, Human Rights Commn., 1999, 2001. Mem.: ASCD, Links, Inc., Jack and Jill of Am., Inc. (v.p. and sec. 1994—98, cert. of Appreciation 1998). Roman Catholic. Achievements include research in diversity for educators. Avocations: reading, youth mentor, jogging, travel, family. Home: 308 Dinwiddie St Portsmouth VA 23704 Office: Portsmouth Pub Sch PO Box 998 Portsmouth VA 23704 E-mail: margaret.buxton@pps.k12.va.us.

BUXTON, ZANE KELLY, pastor; b. Austin, Minn., Apr. 4, 1946; s.Harry Lee Buxton and Kathryn Martha (Miller) LaDue; m. Karol Kay Kelly, June 3, 1967; 1 child Kristin Kelly. BA in History, Bethel Coll., 1968; BD, Fuller Theological Seminary, 1971; ThM, Princeton Theol. Sem., 1989. Pastor E Friesland Presbyn. Ch., Rushmore, Minn., 1971-75; assoc. pastor North Shore Presbyn. Ch., Shorewood, Wis., 1975-81, Westminster Presbyn. Ch., Des Moines, 1981-85; pastor Community Presbyn. Ch., Clarendon Hills, Ill., 1985-93; mgr. jud. process Presbyn. Ch. (U.S.A.), Louisville, 1994—2001; synod exec. Synod of the Rocky Mountains, Denver, 2002—. Pres. North Shore Neighbors, Shorewood, 1983-84. Mem. Milw. Mental Health Cons., Milw. Broadcast Ministry, Chgo. Presbytery (moderator 1991). Democratic. Avocations: reading, cabinet-making, bicycling, canoeing. Home: 3501 Whitford Dr Highlands Ranch CO 80126-8056 Office: Synod of the Rocky Mountains Ste 206 3025 W 37th Ave Denver CO 80211 Office Phone: 303-477-9070. Personal E-mail: zbuxton@att.net.

BUYANOVSKY, SOPHIA, linguist, educator; b. Moscow, Nov. 17, 1956; d. Michael and Lubor Yakobishvili; m. Lev Buyanovsky, Aug. 27, 1977; children: Michael, Paul, Daniel. BA, MA, Moscow State U. Tchr. of Russian S.I. Tech. H.S., N.Y.C., 1989—. Home: 16850 Collins Ave #128 Sunny Isles Beach FL 33160-4238

BUYER, STEVEN EARLE, congressman, lawyer; b. Rensselaer, Ind., Nov. 26, 1958; m. Joni Geyer; children: Colleen, Ryan. BS in Bus. Adminstrn., The Citadel, 1980; JD, Valparaiso U., 1984. Officer Med. Svc. Corps U.S. Army, 1980, spl. asst. to U.S. Atty., 1984-87; dep. atty. gen. Ind., 1987-88; atty., 1988—92; legal counsel 22nd Theater Army, Saudi Arabia, 1990-91; legal advisor U.S Armed Forces/Western Enemy Prisoner of War Camps/War Crimes Interrogations, Saudi Arabia, 1991; mem. U.S. Congress from 4th Ind. Dist., 1993—. Mem. com. on energy & commerce, U.S. Ho. of Reps.; mem. health, Energy and Air quality, environment & hazardous materials subcoms.; mem. com. on vet.'s affairs, chmn. subcom. oversights & investigations. Natl. Gaurd and Reserve Components Caucus Decorated Bronze Star. Republican. Office: US Ho Reps 2230 Rayburn HOB Washington DC 20515-1405*

BUYERS, JOHN WILLIAM AMERMAN, agribusiness and specialty foods company executive; b. Coatesville, Pa., July 17, 1928; s. William Buchanan and Rebecca (Watson) B.; m. Elizabeth Lindsey; children: Elsie Buyers Viehman, Rebecca Watson Buyers-Basso, Jane Palmer Buyers-Russo. BA in History cum laude, Princeton U., 1952; MS in Indsl. Mgmt., MIT, 1963. Div. ops. mgr. Bell Tel. Co. Pa., 1953-66; dir. ops. and pers. Gen. Waterworks Corp., Phila., 1966-68, pres., CEO, 1971-75; v.p. adminstrn. Internat. Utilities Corp., Phila., 1968-71; pres., CEO, dir. C. Brewer and Co., Ltd., Honolulu, 1975—, chmn. bd., 1982—; chmn., CEO D. Buyers Enterprises, LLC, 2001—. Chmn. Calif. and Hawaiian Sugar Co., 1982-84, 86-90; pres., chmn. bd. Buyco, Inc., 1986—; mem. Hawaii Joint Coun. Econ. Edn., Japan-Hawaii Econ. Coun.; bd. dirs. BancWest, First Hawaiian Bank, John B. Sanfilippo & Sons, Inc., ML Macadamia Orchards, L.P. Trustee U. Hawaii Found., 1986—; chmn. bd. dirs. Hawaii Visitors Bur., 1990-91; mem. Gov.'s Blue Ribbon Panel on the Future of Healthcare in Hawaii; bd. dirs. Hawaii Sports Found., 1990-95; mem. adv. group to U.S. Dist. Ctr. With USMC, 1946-48. Sloan fellow MIT, 1962-63. Mem. Hawaiian Sugar Planters Assn. (chmn. bd. dirs. 1980-82, dir.), C. of C. Hawaii (chmn. bd. dirs. 1981-2004), Nat. Alliance Bus. (chmn. Hawaii Pacific Metro chpt. 1978), Cap and Gown Club (Princeton), Hilo Yacht Club, Oahu County Club, Pacific Club, Waialae

County Club, Prouts Neck (Maine) County Club, U.S. C. of C. (mem. food and agr. com. 1991—), Beretania Tennis Club. Presbyterian. Office: D Buyers Enterprises LLC 26-238 Hawaii Belt Rd Hilo HI 96720 Office Phone: 808-969-8181. Business E-Mail: JWABuyers@dbuyers.com.

BUYSE, MARYLOU, pediatrician, geneticist, medical association administrator; b. N.Y.C., June 27, 1946; d. George J. and Barbara M. (Sauer) B.; m. Carl N. Edwards, Jan. 22, 1982. AB, Hunter Coll., 1966; MD, Med. Coll. Pa., 1970; MS in Med. Adminstrn., U. Wis., 1993. Diplomate Am. Bd. Med. Genetics. Intern U. Mich., 1970-71; resident in pediatrics L.A. County-U. So. Calif. Med. Ctr., 1971-73, fellow, 1973-75, U. So. Calif. Sch. Medicine, 1975-84, asst. prof. pediatrics, 1973—75, Tufts U., 1976-84; coord. Myelodysplasia Clinic Tufts-New Eng. Med. Ctr., Boston, 1976-79; dir. Cystic Fibrosis Clinic, staff pediatrician Ctr. for Genetic Counseling and Birth Defects Evaluation, 1975-82; med. dir. Ctr. for Birth Defects Info. Service, 1978-82, dir. center, 1982-94; pres. Medx Ltd., 1985-94, Ctr. for Birth Defects Info. Scis., Inc., 1985-94; dir. clin. genetics Children's Hosp., Boston, 1985-86; mem. med. adv. bd. Mass. Cystic Fibrosis Found., 1977-79; med. dir. Fernald State Sch., 1988—94; assoc. med. dir. MassPRO, 1993-95; mem. Mass. Bd. Registration in Medicine, 1994-95; assoc. med. dir. Care Advantage Health Sys., Inc., med. dir., 1996-97, United Health Care of New England, 1997-98, consulting physician advisor, 1998-99, v.p. health affairs, 1999-2001; pres., CEO Mass. Assn. Health Plans, 2001—. Chair R.I. Folic Acid Coun., R.I. March of Dimes, 1999-2001; cons. in field. Assoc. editor Birth Defects Compendium, 2d edit., 1979; assoc. editor Syndrome Identification Jour., 1977-82, editor, 1982; editor Jour. Clin. Dysmorphology, 1982-86, Dysmorphology and Clinical Genetics, 1986-94; editor-in-chief Birth Defects Encyclopedia, 1990. Recipient Physicians Recognition award AMA, 1975, Alumni Achievement award Med. Coll. Pa., 1987; named to Alumni Hall of Fame, Hunter Coll., 1998. Fellow Am. Acad. Pediatrics, Mass. Med. Soc. (asst. sec.-treas. 1991-94, trustee 1991-2000, sec.-treas. 1994-96, v.p. 1996-97, pres.-elect 1997-98, pres. 1998-99); mem. Am. Med. Women's Assn. (pres. Mass. br. 39 1986-91), Am. Mgmt. Assn., Am. Soc. Human Genetics, AAAS, Am. Med. Writers Assn., Soc. Craniofacial Genetics (pres. 1986), Am. Coll. Physician Execs., Teratology Soc., Charles River Dist. Med. Soc. (pres. 1993-95), Alpha Omega Alpha. Office: Ctr Birth Defects Info Svcs Inc Box 1776 Dover MA 02030

BUYSMAN, ANGELA ROCHELLE, music educator; b. Columbia, S.C., Dec. 22, 1971; d. Ronald Gene and Jackie Ann Brunson; m. Lon Lee Buysman, June 15, 1996; 1 child, Joan Joanie Ann. MusB Edn., Newberry Coll., Newberry, S.C., 1994. Cert. music edn., instrumental K-12 S.C., 1994. Band and choral dir. Whitmire H.S., Whitmire, SC, 1994—95; orch. tchr. Union County Schs., Union, SC, 1995—99, Laurens Sch. Dist. 55, Laurens, SC, 1998—. Violin coach Laurens Dist. 55 strings camp, 2000—; intern S.C. Gov.'s Sch. of the Arts, Greenville, SC, 1998; camp counselor Brevard Music Ctr., Brevard, NC, 1994; musician cmty. and sch. functions. Actor: (musical) Joseph and the Amazing Technicolor Dreamcoat. Recipient Champion-Womens Class-Enduros, Southeastern Enduro and Trailriders Assn., 2001—02; grantee Spl. Project grantee, S.C. Dept. of Edn., 2004. Mem.: SC. Music Educators Assn., Music Educators Nat. Conf., Greenville Enduro Riders Assn., Cardinal Key, Alpha Xi Delta (chaplin 1993—94). Christian. Avocation: racing off-road motorcycles. Home: 1621 Wham Lawn Rd Gray Court SC 29645 Office: Laurens School District 55 West Main St Laurens SC 29360 Office Phone: 864-984-3568. Personal E-mail: buysmanzoom@yahoo.com. E-mail: abuysman@laurens55.k12.sc.us.

BUYSSE, PAUL HENRI MARIA, manufacturing executive; b. Mar. 17, 1945; s. Eugene and Germain (Van Hecke) Buysse; children: Frank, Pia, Ann, Sophie, Thomas. Various mktg. and sales positions Ford Motor Co., 1966; dep. mng. dir. British Leyland Credit N.V., 1976; gen. mgr. car sales and mktg. British Leyland Belgium N.V., 1976; exec. dir. Tenneco Belgium, 1980; mng. dir. J.I. Case Benelux, 1980; gen. mgr. Europe North J.I. Case, Internat. Harvester and Poclain, 1984; group mng. dir. Hansen Transmissions Internat., 1988; group chief exec. BTR Automotive and Engring. Group, 1989, BTR Engring. and Dunlop Overseas, 1991; exec. dir. BTR plc, London, 1992; CEO Vickers plc, London, 1998; chmn. Bakaert, 2000. Group chief exec. BTR Industries Ltd., 1989, regional chief exec., 1994—98; dir. BTR Internat. Ltd., 1991; CEO Vickers plc, 1998—2000; chmn. Bekaert N.V., 2000, Vidiobank; bd. dirs. Winterthur, Fortis Bank Zone North-Ctr.; chmn. Prince Philippe Found., Coll. Censors Nat. Bank of Belgium. Named a Knight, Order of Leopold, Belgium, 1988, Cmdr., 2001, Cmdr. of the Brit. Empire, 1997, Baron, King Albert II of Belgium, 1998; named an Officer in the Order of Orange-Nassau, The Netherlands, 1994, Hon. Dean of Labour, Belgium, 1994, Officer in the French Nat. Order of Merit, 1996. Mem.: Royal Automobile Club Belgium (bd. dirs.). Home: Sparrendreef 104 8300 Knokke Belgium Office: Bekaert N V Diamant Bldg A Reyerslaan 80 1030 Brussels Belgium Office Phone: 32 2 706 84 54. E-mail: paul.buysse@bekaert.com.

BUZACOTT, JOHN ALAN, engineering educator; b. Sydney, N.S.W., Australia, May 21, 1937; emigrated to Can., 1967; s. Alan Ernest and Jean Elizabeth (Bingle) B.; m. Ursula Schulmerich, Sept. 7, 1963; children: Alan J., Kimberly A. BSc, U. Sydney, 1957, BE, 1959; MSc, U. Birmingham, Eng., 1962, PhD, 1967; Dr. honoris causa (hon.), Tech. U. Eindhoven, 2001. Engr. Associated Elec. Industries, Rugby, Eng., 1959-61; ops. research systems officer A.E.I. Hotpoint Ltd., London, 1963-64; asst. prof. U. Toronto, 1967-71, assoc. prof., 1971-77, prof., 1977-83, U. Waterloo, Ont., Can., 1984-91, York U., North York, 1991—2002, prof. emeritus, 2002—. Author: Scale in Production Systems, 1982, Stochastic Models of Manufacturing Systems, 1993; corr. editor: Canadian Jour. Info. Processing and Ops. Research, 1974-78. Mem. Can. Operational Rsch. Soc. (pres. 1983-84), Inst. for Ops. Rsch. and Mgmt. Sci., Prodn. and Ops. Mgmt. Soc. (pres. 1999). Home: 68 Divadale Dr Toronto ON Canada M4G 2P2 Office: York U Schulich Sch Bus North York ON Canada M3J 1P3 Business E-Mail: jbuzacot@schulich.yorku.ca.

BUZARD, A. VINCENT, lawyer; b. Sullivan, Ind., June 7, 1942; BA, Wabash Coll., 1964; JD cum laude, Univ. Mich., 1967. Corp. counsel, Rochester, NY, 1971—73; founder A.Vincent Buzard Law Firm (merged with Harris Beach & Wilcox), 1980—97; ptnr. Harris Beach & Wilcox, Rochester, 1997—. Recipient Adolph J. Rodenbeck award. Mem.: ABA (ho. dels. 1993, 2004—), NY State Trial Lawyers Assn., Assn. of Trial Lawyers of Am., Monroe County Bar Assn. (pres. 1993—94), NY State Bar Assn. (v.p. 1997—2001, pres.-elect 2004, mem., Ho. of Del.), NY State Head Injury Assn. (bd. dir., sec. 1984—88, pres. 1990—92). Office: Harris Beach LLP 130 E Main St Rochester NY 14604 Office Phone: 585-419-8605.

BUZARD, KURT ANDRE, ophthalmologist; b. Lakewood, Colo., Apr. 9, 1953; s. Donald Keith and Sonja Marie (Vik) B. BA in Math. and Physics, Northwestern U., 1975; MA in Applied Physics, Stanford, U., 1976; MD, Northwestern U., 1980. Diplomate Am. Bd. Ophthalmology, Nat. Bd. Med. Examiners. Intern medicine L.A. County-U. So. Calif. Med. Ctr., 1980-81; resident Jules Stein Eye Inst. UCLA, 1982-85; fellow cornea/refractive surgery Richard C. Troutman, MD, 1985-86; ophthalmologist, corneal specialist Las Vegas, Nev., 1986—. Staff physician Rancho Los Amigos Hosp., 1981-82; clin. asst. prof. div. ophthalmology dept. surgery U. Nev. Sch. Medicine, 1988—; clin. asst. prof. dept. ophthalmol. medicine Tulane U. Med. Ctr., New Orleans, 1991; med. dir. S.W. Eye Procurement Ctr., Las Vegas, 1989—; affiliate Humana Hosp.-Sunrise, 1989—, Las Vegas Surg. Ctr., 1989—, Las Vegas Surg. Ctr., Med. Ctr. So. Nev., 1989—; assoc. staff Valley Hosp., Las Vegas, 1986—; mem. med. adv. bd. Donor Orgn. Referral Svc.; internat. hon. advisor Tung Wah Ea. Hosp., Hong Kong, 1999-2003. Author: (with Richard Troutman) Corneal Astigmatism: Etiology, Prevention and Management, 1992, (with Miles Friedlander and Jean Luc Febbraro) The Blue Line Incision and Refractive Phacoemulsification, 2000; mem. editorial bd. Refractive and Corneal Surgery, 1992—; contbr. articles to profl. jours. Mem. Las Vegas C. of C., 1989. Recipient Rsch. award Jules Stein Inst., L.A., 1985. Fellow Am. Acad. Ophthalmology (Honor award 1999), Am. Coll. Surgeons; mem. Am. Soc. Cataract and Refractive Surgery, AMA, Assn. for Rsch. in Vision and Ophthalmology, Castroviejo Soc., Colombian Soc. Ophthalmology (corr.), Eye Bank Assn. of Am.-Paton Soc., Internat. Soc. for Eye Rsch., Internat. Soc. Refractive Keratoplasty (long-range planning com., alternative rep. to Am. Acad. Ophthalmology, bd. dirs. 1992-94), Pan Am. Assn. Ophthalmology, Pan Am. Implant Assn., Phi Eta Sigma, Phi Beta Kappa. Avocations: computers, photography. Office: 7135 W Sahara Ave Las Vegas NV 89117-2828

BUZBEE, RICHARD EDGAR, retired newspaper editor; b. Fordyce, Ark., Aug. 16, 1931; s. Edgar Andrew and Helen Koester (Darling) B.; m. Marie Palmer, Apr. 16, 1955; children: Robert Edgar, William Bruce, James Palmer, John Richard. B.J., BA, U. Mo., 1954. Mgmt. intern Harris Newspaper Group, Chanute (Kans.) Tribune, Burlington (Iowa) Hawk-Eye, also Olathe (Kans.) News, 1957-63; editor, pub. Olathe News, 1963-79, Hutchinson (Kans.) News, 1979-93; ret. Hutchinson Pub. Co., 1993. Hon. chmn. bd. dirs. Hutchinson Pub. Co., 1993—; ptnr. Radine Enterprises, Olathe. Trustee William Allen White Found.; pres. Olathe C. of C., 1969, Olathe United Way, 1968, Johnson County chpt. ARC, 1978-79; chmn. Johnson County Scholarship Found., 1968; mem. Olathe Public Bldg. Commn. 1, 1964-65, 2, 1978-79; co-chmn. Olathe Home-for-Christmas from Vietnam Project, 1969-72; mem. bd. Hutchinson Public Library, 1980-87, chmn., 1982-83; bd. dirs. Hutchinson Symphony Assn., 1980-88, pres. 1987. Served to lt. (j.g.) USNR, 1954-57. Mem. Greater Hutchinson C. of C. (chmn. 1988), Rotary (bd. dirs. 1981-83), Phi Beta Kappa. Clubs: Rotary. (dir. 1981-83). Republican. Methodist. Home: 4 Crescent Blvd Hutchinson KS 67502-5541 Personal E-mail: dick@buzbee.net.

BUZBEE, SALLY STREFF, news correspondent; b. Walla Walla, Wash. d. Eldyn and Monica Streff; m. John Buzbee; children: Margaret, Emma. BA in Journalism, U. Kans., 1988; IEMBA, Georgetown U., 1997. Joined AP, Topeka, 1988, bus. writer Kansas City, Kans., 1988—92, with L.A., 1992—93, correspondent in charge of San Diego bur., 1993—95, with Washington bur., 1995—2004, reporter, Washington bur., 1995—96, news editor, 1996, world svcs. supr., Washington bur., asst. chief, bur. for news, Washington bur., 2003—04, chief of Mid. East news Cairo, 2004—. Office: Associated Press 2021 K St NW 6th fl Washington DC 20006-1082

BUZZARD, JAMES A., manufacturing executive; BS in Pulp and Paper Tech., N.C. State U.; MBA in Fin., U. Pa. From Comptroller's Dept. to pres. MeadWestvaco Corp., Stamford, Conn., 1978—2003, pres., 2003—. Mem.: Web Offset Assn. (mem. supplier adv. bd.). Office: MeadWestvaco 100 High Ridge Park Stamford CT 06905

BUZZARD, STEVEN RAY, lawyer; b. Centralia, Wash., May 22, 1946; s. Richard James and Phylis Margaret (Bevington) B.; m. Joan Elizabeth Merrow, Nov. 11, 1967; children: Elizabeth Jane, Richard Wolcott, James Merrow. BA, Cen. Wash. State Coll., 1972; postgrad., U. Wash., 1973; JD, U. Puget Sound, 1975. Bar: Wash. 1975, U.S. Dist. Ct. (we. dist.) Wash. 1976, U.S. Supreme Ct. 1979, U.S. Tax Ct. 1983. Assoc. Shires, Kruse, Wallace, Roper & Kamps, Port Orchard, Wash., 1975-77; ptnr. Buzzard & O'Connell, Centralia, 1978-80, Buzzard & Tripp, Centralia, 1980-94, Buzzard & Assoc., Centralia, 1994—. City atty. Mossyrock, Wash., 1979-94, Vader, Wash., 1989-96, Bucoda, Wash., 1989-99; judge Centralia, 1980-84, Winlock, Wash., 1983—; sec. Consol. Enterprizes Inc., Centralia, 1986-88; judge Chehalis (Wash.) Mcpl. Ct., 1998—, Winlock Mcpl. Ct., 1983—, Napavine Mcpl. Ct., 2001—, Vader Mcpl. Ct., 2001—; past pres. Reliable Enterprises, Inc. Chmn. bd. dirs. Lewis County Cmty. Svcs., Chehalis, Wash., 1981-84; bd. dirs. Lewis County United Way, 1993-95; mem. adv. bd. Centralia Sch. Dist., 1995—; founding mem., trustee, treas. Dollars for Scholars, Scholarship Found., 1997-2002. Mem. ABA (rural judges com. 1986), Wash. State Bar Assn. (ct. rules com. 1992-), Lewis County Bar Assn. (past pres.), Assn. Trial Lawyers Am., Wash. State Trial Lawyers Assn., Wash. State Govt. Lawyers Bar Assn. (former trustee), Wash. State Dist. and Mcpl. Ct. Judges Assn. (dist. and mcpl. rural judges com.), Wash. Bd. Jud. Adminstrn. (best practices com. 2001—, ct. improvement com., 2001-), Dist. and Mcpl. Judges Assn. (dist. and mcpl. rural judges com., ct. improvement com., long range planning com.), Kiwanis (pres.-elect 1991, pres. 1992-93, Disting. Past Pres. award 1994), Elks (trustee Centralia 1981—). Avocations: running, boating, hiking, biking, fishing. Office: Buzzard & Assoc 314 Harrison Ave Centralia WA 98531-1326 Fax: (360) 330-2078. Office Phone: 360-736-1108.

BUZZELLI, CHARLOTTE GRACE, special education educator; b. Mar. 21, 1947; d. Edmund Albert and Sarah Agnes (Russo) Buzzelli. BS, U. Akron (Ohio), 1969, MS in Edn., 1976. Tchr. St. Anthony Sch., Akron, 1969-76; program coord., tchr. Akron Montessori Sch. Continuing Edn. Program, Eastwood Ctr., Akron, 1976-77; dir. edn. Fallsview Psychiat. Hosp., Ohio Dept. Mental Health, Cuyahoga Falls, 1977-92, developer job tng. partnership grant program and spl. needs handicapped grant program, 1992-97; tng. coord. N.E. regional & program educator children svcs. Ohio Dept. Mental Health State Operated Svcs., 1992—97. Spl. edn. svcs. developer and educator cmty svcs. divsn. North Coast Behavioral Healthcare Sys., Ohio Dept. Mental Health, 1997-2002; tchr. adult basic lit. edn. program Akron City Sch. Dist., 1992—; developer Akron City Schs. Project Rise Homeless Youth Family Learning Literacy Program, 2001—; cons. in field; pioneered first spl. edn. program in Ohio for adult state psychiat. hosp.; developed 1st cmty.-based adult basic edn. program in state instn. in Ohio; program cons. state operated svcs. State of Ohio; participant U. Hawaii Study Tours Rsch. Projects, Internat. Edn. and East Asia Pi Lambda Theta Orient Study Tour, Manoa campus, 1990, spl. edn. rsch. U. Akron, 1976. Developer literacy evaluation program Project Rise Homeless Youth, Akron, 2000—; supr. Ctr. for Literacy, U. Akron Students Svs. Learners Program, Homeless Shelters Akron Pub. Schs. programs; supr. dept. ctr. lit. U. Akron; mem. gospel meets Symphony chorus Akron Symphony Orch. Gospel Choir, 1996—; mem. choir Diocese of Cleve., St. John's Cathedral, Mass of Jubilee Gospel Choir, 1998, 2000. Named Ohio Tchr. of Yr., 1979; recipient A Key award, U. Akron, Urban Light award for outstanding svc., 2001, Cmty. Svc. Achievement award, Italian Am. Soc., Cmty. Collaboration award, Summit County Housing Network, 2003, 2004. Mem. CEC (coun. pres.), ASCD, Assn. Children with Learning Disabilities, Internat. Reading Assn., U. Akron Alumni Assn. (Disting. Edn. award 2004), Univ. Club, Akron Women's City Club, Coll. Club of Akron, Pi Lambda Theta (pres.), Phi Delta Kappa, Delta Kappa Gamma, Gamma Beta (pres.), Kappa Kappa Iota. Avocations: pet therapy to children and adults with disabilities, reading, travel, writing, singing. Home: 662 Dayton St Akron OH 44310-2301 Office: Adult Basic Literacy Edn Profl Devel Acad 785 Carnegie Ave Akron OH 44314

BUZZI, RUTH, comedienne; b. Westerly, R.I., July 24, 1936; d. Angelo Peter and Rena Pauline (Macchi) B.; m. Kent Perkins, Dec. 10, 1979. Grad., Pasadena Playhouse Coll. of Theatre Arts, 1957. Appeared on Broadway in Sweet Charity; appeared in off-Broadway theater prodns. including Misguided Tour, A Man's a Man; network TV appearances include Garry Moore Show, Rowan and Martin's Laugh-In, Dean Martin Roasts, Trapper John, M.D., Medical Center, Alice, The Entertainers, Carol Burnett and Friends, Flip, Donnie and Marie, The Dean Martin Comedy Hour, Tony Orlando and Dawn, Day of Our Lives, Passions, 2003, The Jamii Foxx Show, Diagnosis Murder, The Muppet Show, Sesame Street, That Girl, The Monkees, Saved By the Bell, Love Boat, The Munsters Today, Masquerade, Adam 12, Major Dad, Here's Lucy; films include Freaky Friday, 1972, Skatetown, U.S.A., 1977, The Apple Dumpling Gang Rides Again, 1979, The Villain, 1979, The North Avenue Irregulars, 1979, Surf II, 1984, Bad Guys, 1986, Dixie Lanes, 1988, Diggin Up Business, 1990; TV movies In Name Only, 1969; featured commedienne in 19 mus. revues; filmed numerous TV and radio commls. for various sponsors; recorded hundreds of voice overs for cartoon series including Linus the Lionhearted, Pound Puppies and Berenstein Bears; club acts at MGM Grand Hotel and Sahara Hotel, Las Vegas. Recipient Golden Globe award, Image award NAACP; named to R.I. Hall of Fame; inducted into Broadcasting Hall of Fame; nominee 5 Emmy awards. Mem. DAR (hon.). Address: c/o AMR Ste 438 5042 Wilshire Blvd Los Angeles CA 90036

BYARS, MERLENE HUTTO, accountant, artist, writer; b. West Columbia, SC, Nov. 8, 1931; d. Gideon Thomas and Nettie (Fail) Hutto; m. Alvin Willard Byars, June 10, 1950 (dec.); children: Alvin Gregg, Robin Mark, Jay C., Blaine Derrick; m. Fred W. Klutzow, Dec. 10, 1999. Student, Palmer Coll., Midlands Tech., U. S.C., 1988—; diploma in Journalism, Internat. Corr. Sch., 1995, Longridge Writers Group, 1995. Acct. State of SC, 1964-93; ret., 1993; pres. Merlene Hutto Byars Enterprises, Cayce, 1993—. Designer Collegiate Licensing Co., US Trademark, 1989—; mem. Thinktank for Ret. Employees, U. SC Edn. Found., 1998—2003. Pub. Lintheads, 1986, Olympia-Pacific: The Way It was 1895-1970, 1981; Did Jesus Drive a Pickup Truck, 1993, Fate, Faith and Fortitude, 2003; The Plantation Era in South Carolina; pub., produr. (play) Lintheads and Hard Times, 1986; creator quilt which hung in SC State Capital for bicentennial celebration, 1988; designer Saxe Gotha Twp. Flag, 1993; author: The State of South Carolina Scrap Book, Orangeburg District, 1990, A Scrap Book of SC, Dutch Fork, Saxe Gotha, Lexington County, 1994, The Plantation Era of SC, 1996, Colonization, Plantations and More in South Carolina, 2004, A History of St. Luke's Lutheran Church within the Olympia-Pacific Community Columbia, South Carolina, 2004; exhibited art at Oxford (Eng.) U., 1997, Internat. Congress on Arts and Comm., 1997, Sonesta Hotel, New Orleans, 1998—; exhibited art and book From My Scrap Book of the State of SC; Xlibris publ. new book, 2003, Fate, Faith and Fortitude, Life of F.W. Klutzow, MD., Four Seasons, The Ritz, 1999—; exhibited genealogy and art work St. John's Coll., Cambridge U., 2001. Life mem. Women's Missionary Soc., United Luth. Ch., 1954—; mem. edn. found. U. SC, 1969-93; treas. Airport HS Booster Club, 1969-76; sec. Saxe Gotha Hist. Soc., Lexington County, 1994-96; mem. USC Edn. Found., Think-Tank for 2001 fundraising campaign/ret. faculty and staff, 1998-2001; rep. Cayce Hist. Com. at Am. Biographical Inst./Internat. Biographical Ctr. Congress, New Orleans, 1998. Recipient numerous awards for quilting SC State Fair, 1976—, Cert. for rose rsch. test panel Jackson and Perkins, 1982, Foremost Women in Comm. award, 1969-70, Cayce Amb. award, City of Cayce, 1994. Fellow Internat. Biog. Assn. (dep. dir. gen. 1999—), U.S.C. Caroliniana Soc., U.S.C. Thomas Cooper Libr. Soc.; mem. Cayce Mus. History (contbr. books, award for contribution 1987), SC State Mus., Town and Country Assn., Kiwanis Internat. Club (sec. Cayce West Columbia chpt. 2003—). Avocations: history, geneologist, reading, sewing, travel. Home: PO Box 3387 West Columbia SC 29171-3387 Office Phone: 803-794-6288. E-mail: needle1@msn.com.

BYARS, T DOUGLAS, JR., veterinarian, consultant; b. San Francisco, Sept. 20, 1943; s. Tandy Douglas and Ruby Jane Byars; m. Susan Elizabeth Arnett-Byars, May 17, 1968; children: Carrie Rebecca, Jeremy Douglas. AA, Modesto (Calif.) Jr. Coll., 1965; BS, Calif. State Poly. U., 1968; DVM, U. Calif., Davis, 1974. Diplomate Am. Coll. Veterinary Internal Medicine 1981, Am. Coll. Veterinary Emergency Critical Care 1997. Intern U. Ga., Athens, 1974—75; practitioner Ocala, Fla., Logandale, Nev., 1975—77; assoc. prof. U. Ga., Athens, 1977—83; medicine dir. Hagyard-Davidson-McGee, Lexington, Ky., 1983—2004; pvt. practice Byars Equine Advisory, Georgetown, Ky., 2004—. Internat. spkr. in field. Contbr. articles to profl. jours., chapters to books. Bd. mem. Ky. Horse Coun., 1995—98. Recipient Equus award, Am. Assn. Equine Practitioners, 1998. Mem.: Am. Coll. Veterinary Internal Medicine (credentials com. 1981—83), Ctrl. Ky. Equine Practitioners (pres. 1993—94). Avocations: raising horses, farm and ranch work. Office: Byars Equine Advisory 2183 Iron Works Rd Georgetown KY 40324 Office Phone: 502-867-7299. E-mail: tdbyarseqa@aol.com.

BYARS, WALTER RYLAND, JR., lawyer; b. Birmingham, Ala., Oct. 5, 1928; s. Walter Ryland and Essie (Hopper) B.; m. Mildred Lucile Rhodes, Dec. 22, 1950; children: Debra Leigh Byars Patterson, Walter Ryland III, Rebecca Lynn Byars Pradat, John Baxter. BS, U. Ala., 1948, LLB, 1952, JD, 1969. Bar: Ala. 1952, U.S. Ct. Appeals (5th and 11th cirs.), U.S. Dist. Ct. (no., mid. and so. dists.) Ala., U.S. Supreme Ct. Pvt. practice, Troy, Ala., 1953-57; atty. legal dept. So. Bell. Tel. & Tel. Co., Atlanta, 1957-59, gen. atty. Birmingham, 1959-68; ptnr. Steiner, Crum & Baker, 1968—; city atty. Montgomery, Ala., 2002—; ptnr. Steiner, Crum & Byars, PC, Montgomery, 2003—. Bd. editors Ala. Law Rev., 1951-52. Lt. (j.g.) USNR, 1952-53. Fellow Am. Bar Found., Ala. Bar Found., Internat. Soc. Barristers (gov. 1977-83, sec.-treas. 1979-80, 2d v.p. 1980-81, 1st v.p. 1981-82, pres. 1982-83), Am. Coll. Trial Lawyers; mem. ABA (Young Lawyers past mem. exec. council, com. chmn.), Ala. Bar Assn. (pres.-elect 1983-84, pres. 1984-85, past pres. Young Lawyers, past sect. chmn., past com. chmn.), Pike County Bar Assn. (past pres.), Birmingham Bar Assn. (past com. chmn.), Montgomery County Bar Assn. (past com. chmn., bd. dirs. 1976-79, v.p. 1978, pres. 1979), Ala. Law Inst. (coun.), Montgomery Area Com. of 100, Masons, Sigma Chi, Phi Alpha Delta. Methodist. Home: 1744 Fairforest Dr Montgomery AL 36106-2602 Office: Regions Bank Bldg PO Box 668 Montgomery AL 36101-0668 Office Phone: 334-832-8800. Business E-Mail: wbyars@steinercrum.com.

BYBEE, JAY SCOTT, federal judge, former federal agency administrator; b. Oakland, Calif., Oct. 27, 1953; s. Rowan Scott and Joan (Hickman) B.; m. Dianna Jean Greer, Feb. 15, 1986; children: Scott, David, Alyssa, Ryan. BA, Brigham Young U., 1977, JD, 1980. Bar: D.C. 1981, U.S. Ct. Appeals (4th cir.) 1983, U.S. Supreme Ct. 1985, U.S. Ct. Appeals (5th cir.) 1986, U.S. Ct. Appeals (2d, 9th, 10th and D.C. cirs.) 1987. Law clk. to Hon. Donald Russell U.S. Ct. Appeals (4th cir.), 1980-81; assoc. Sidley & Austin, Washington, 1981-84; atty., Office of Legal Policy U.S. Dept. Justice, Washington, 1984—86, atty. civil divsn., 1986—89; assoc. counsel to Pres. The White House, Washington, 1989-91; prof. law La. State U., Baton Rouge, 1991-98, U. Nev., Las Vegas, 1999—2001; asst. atty. gen. Office Legal Counsel U.S. Dept. Justice, Washington, 2001—02; judge U.S. Ct. Appeals (9th cir.), San Francisco, 2003—. Contbr. articles to profl. jours. Missionary Mormon Ch., Santiago, Chile, 1973-75. Edwin S. Hinckley scholar, Brigham Young U., 1976-77. Mem. Phi Kappa Phi. Avocations: piano, all sports, reading. Office: US Ct Appeals Lloyd B George US Courthouse Ste 3099 333 Las Vegas Blvd Las Vegas NV 89101*

BYBEE, RODGER WAYNE, science administrator; b. San Francisco, Feb. 21, 1942; s. Wayne and Mary Genevieve (Mungon) B.; m. Patricia Ann Brovsky, May 28, 1966. BA, Colo. State Coll., 1966; MA, U. No. Colo., 1969; PhD, NYU, 1975. Tchr. sci. Greeley (Colo.) Pub. Schs., 1965-66; instr. sci. U. No. Colo., Greeley, 1966-70; teaching fellow NYU, N.Y.C., 1970-72; instr. edn. Carleton Coll., Northfield, Minn., 1972-75, asst. prof., 1975-81, assoc. prof., chmn. dept., 1981-85; assoc. dir. Biol. Scis. Curriculum Study, Colorado Springs, 1986-95, acting dir., 1992-93; exec. dir. Ctr. Sci., Math. and Engring. Edn. NRC, Washington, 1995-99; exec. dir. BSCS, Colorado Springs, Colo., 1999—. Mem. adv. bd. for sci. assessment Nat. Assessment Ednl. Progress, Princeton, N.J., 1987-89, 92-93, 95-96; mem. adv. bd. Social Sci. Edn. Consortium, Boulder, Colo., 1987-90; chairperson working group on curriculum NRC project on Nat. Sci. Ednl. Stds., 1993-95; chmn. Sci. Framework 2006, Orgn. Econ. Coop. and Devel., Paris, France. Author: numerous books; contbr. numerous articles to profl. jours. NSF grantee, 1986—. Fellow AAAS (mem.-at-large 1987-90, chair sect. Q 1993-94, coun. del.), Nat. Assn. Rsch. Sci. Teaching (rsch. coord. 1986-89). Home: PO Box 563 Frisco CO 80443-0563 Office: BSCS 5415 Mark Dabling Blvd Colorado Springs CO 80918-3842 E-mail: rbybee@bscs.org.

BYE, JAMES EDWARD, lawyer; b. Thief River Falls, Minn., May 2, 1930; s. Morris and Ida Mathilda (Dahl) B.; m. Patricia Ann Nadolski, Dec. 27, 1952; children: David Stanley, Anne Elizabeth. BBA with distinction, U. Minn., 1951; LLB cum laude, Harvard U., 1956. Bar: Colo. 1957, U.S. Tax Ct., U.S. Ct. Appeals (10th cir.), U.S. Supreme Ct. 1992. Assoc. Holme Roberts & Owen, Denver, 1957-61; ptnr. Holme, Roberts & Owen LLP, Denver, 1961—. Editor Harvard U. Law Rev. Chmn. continuing legal and jud. edn. Colo. Supreme Ct., Denver, 1977-78; chmn. Alexis de Tocqueville Soc. Met. Denver, 1986-89, Met. Denver GIVES, 1986-91; trustee Loretto Hts. Coll., Denver, 1977-88, Regis. Coll., 1988-92, U. Colo. Found., The Two Percent Club, 1991, Children's Hosp., 1993-95; chmn. urban emphasis program, Denver Area coun. Boy Scouts Am., 1992—, The Spot, 1996—; Tointon Inst. Adv. Bd., 2000—, Latin Am. Rsch. & Svc. Agy., 2000, U.

Denver Grad. Sch. Internat. Studies, U. Colo. Found., Piton Found., Mexican Cultural Ctr., Minoru Yasui Com. Denver Found., Summer Scholars, 2000—, Hispanics in Philanthropy, 2000—; bd. dirs. Mex. Cultural Ctr. & Ctr. Affordable Housing, Urban Peak, Alliance Health Quality Partnership, 2002-. Recipient Silver Beaver award, 1996, Disting. Svc. to Humanity award Vols. of Am., 1996, Pub. Svc. award U. Colo. Grad. Sch. Pub. Affairs, 1996, Alex de Tocqueville Soc. award United Way, Reconocimiento Ohtli award Sec. of Fgn. Rels. of Mex., 1998, William Funk award Colo. Assn. Nonprofit Orgns., 1998, Ally award Women's Vision Found., 1999, Whitney M. Young Jr. Svc. award Boy Scouts Am., 1999, Maverick Thinker's award Urban Peak, 2001. Fellow Am. Bar Found. (life), Colo. Bar Found.; mem. ABA (natural resources com. tax sect.), Colo. Bar Assn., Denver Bar Assn., Am. Coll. Tax Counsel, Denver Estate Planning Coun., Greater Denver Tax Counsel Assn. Avocation: golf. Office: Holme Roberts & Owen LLP 1700 Lincoln St Ste 4100 Denver CO 80203-4541 E-mail: jim.bye@hro.com.

BYE, KERMIT EDWARD, federal judge, lawyer; b. Hatton, N.D., Jan. 13, 1937; s. Kermit Berthrand and Margaret B. (Brekke) Bye; m. Carol Beth Soliah, Aug. 23, 1958; children: Laura Lee, William Edward, Bethany Ann. BS, U. N.D., 1959, JD, 1962. Bar: N.D. 1962, U.S. Dist. Ct. N.D. 1962, U.S. Ct. Appeals (8th cir.) 1969, U.S. Supreme Ct. 1974, Minn. 1981. Dep. securities commr. State of N.D., 1962—64, spl. asst. atty. gen., 1964—66; asst. U.S. atty. U.S. Atty.'s Office, Dist. N.D., 1966—68; ptnr. Vogel Brantner Kelly Knutson Weir & Bye, Fargo, ND, 1968—2000; judge U.S. Ct. Appeals (8th cir.), Fargo, 2000—. Mem. editl. bd.: N.D. Law Rev., 1961—62. Chmn. Red River Human Svcs. Found., 1980—83; S.E. Mental Health and Retardation Ctr., Inc. Fellow: Am. Bar Found.; mem.: ABA (state del. 1986—95, bd. govs. 1999—2001, state del. 2002—), Minn. Bar Assn., Cass County Bar Assn., N.D. State Bar Assn. (pres. 1983—84). Lutheran. Office: 655 1st Ave N Ste 330 Fargo ND 58102 Office Phone: 701-297-7270. E-mail: zhanna@ce8.uscourts.gov.

BYE, RAYMOND ERWIN, JR., academic administrator; b. Mobile, Ala., Feb. 22, 1944; s. Raymond Erwin and Frances (Bain) Bye; m. Katherine Jackson, Dec. 28, 1971; children: Philip Jackson, Eleanor Ashley. BA, Rhodes Coll., Memphis, 1966; MA, Kent State U., 1968, PhD, 1974. Resident dir., 1966-68; area residence dir. Kent (Ohio) State U., 1968-69, asst. to pres., 1969-71, asst. to vice pres. student affairs, 1971-72; asst. to dir., deputy head, head congl. affairs NSF, Washington, 1973-83, dir. office of legis. and pub. affairs, 1983-94; assoc. v.p. rsch. Fla. State U., Tallahassee, 1994-98, v.p. rsch., 1999—2003, dir. fed. rels., 2004—. Adv. bd. Knight Found., 2002—; bd. dirs. Tallahassee Chamber, 1995—2005, Econ. Devel. Commn., 1995—98, TMH Hosp., 1998—2001, Oak Ridge Assn. Univs., 2001—03, Coun. Gov. Affairs, DC, pres., 1998—2000, Fla. State U. Rsch. Found., 1998—2003; bd. dirs. Nat. Assn. State Univ. Land Grant Coll.s, 1999—2000, chair coun. govt. affairs, 1999—2001; bd. govs. Oak Ridge Nat. Lab., 2000—03. Recipient Disting. Svc. award, NSF, 1989, Pres. Meritorious Exec. award, 1991. Mem.: AAAS, Acad. Mgmt., So. Polit. Sci. Assn., Fla. Econ. Club (bd. dirs. 2002—). Office: Fla State U Westcott Bldg Tallahassee FL 32306-1330 Office Phone: 850-645-1410. E-mail: rbye@mailer.fsu.edu.

BYEARS, LATASHA, professional basketball player; b. Aug. 12, 1973; Student, N.E. Okla. A&M Jr. Coll., 1992—94; grad., DePaul U., 1996. Basketball player Faenza, Italy, 1996—97, Beskijas, Turkey, 1996—97; basketball player Sacramento Monarchs Women's NBA, 1997—2000; basketball player LA Sparks WNBA, 2000—. Vol. Meals on Wheels. Office: Los Angeles Sparks Ste 100 2151 E Grand Ave El Segundo CA 90245

BYEFF, PETER DAVID, hematologist, oncologist; b. Nov. 27, 1948; s. Herbert Isaac and Ruth Helen (Wolfe) B.; m. Gail Schneider, Apr. 2, 1982. BA, U. Pa., 1970; MD, Johns Hopkins U., 1974. Diplomate Am. Bd. Internal Medicine (subcert. in med. oncology and hematology), Nat. Bd. Med. Examiners. Intern Georgetown U. Hosp., Washington, 1974-75, resident in internal medicine, 1975-77; vis. fellow in hematology and oncology Columbia-Presbyn. Med. Ctr., N.Y.C., 1977-81, Damon Runyon-Walter Winchell oncology fellow, 1977-81. Instr. Coll. Physicians and Surgeons, Columbia U., N.Y.C.; assoc. prof., attending physician U. Conn.; attending physician Bradley Meml. Hosp., Southington, Conn., New Britain (Conn.) Gen. Hosp., med. dir. George Bray Cancer Ctr.; sr. investigator Gynecologic Oncology Group; prin. investigator Eastern Cooperative Oncology Group, Nat. Surg. Bowel and Breast project. Office: Bradley Med Bldg 55 Meriden Ave Ste 1-a Southington CT 06489-3237 also: 40 Hart St New Britain CT 06052-1743 Office Phone: 860-621-9316.

BYER, DIANA, performing company executive; b. Trenton, NJ, Aug. 31, 1946; d. Fred and Norma (Handis) B. Student, Juilliard Sch., 1964—66. Soloist Manhattan Festival Ballet, N.Y.C., 1972, Les Grands Ballet Canadiens, Montreal, Can., 1975; dir. Ballet Sch. of N.Y., N.Y.C., 1978—, N.Y. Theatre Ballet, 1978—. Dir., founder Project LIFT scholarship program for children living N.Y.C. homeless shelters, 1989—. Helen Weiselberg scholar Nat. Arts Club, 1988, 90, 93 Achievements include being subject of Lincoln Ctr. presentation Dreams on a Shoestring, 1992. Office: NY Theatre Ballet 30 E 31st St New York NY 10016-6825 Office Phone: 212-679-0401. Business E-Mail: dianabyer@nytb.org.

BYER, THEODORE SCOTT, accountant; b. Trenton, NJ, Oct. 2, 1957; s. Fred and Norma (Handis) B.; m. Marcy Pam Steier, Aug. 8, 1981; children: Sarah, Tara, Hallie. BA, Muhlenberg Coll., 1979; MBA, Rider Coll., 1986. CPA, CFP. Auditor State of N.J., Trenton, 1979-80; staff acct. Louis H. Linowitz and Co., Trenton, 1980-82; supr. Amper, Politzner & Mattia, Flemington, N.J., 1982-88; tax mgr. Price Waterhouse, N.Y.C., 1988-90; sr. mgr. Salomon & Co., P.C., N.Y.C., 1990-94; ptnr. Mintz, Rosenfeld & Co., Fairfield, N.J., 1994—. Co-author: Taxation of Foreign Nationals in the United States, 1990; editor: Selecting and Installing Medical Practice Computer Software, 1996. Fellow N.J. State Soc. CPAs (co-founder Hunterdon-Warren chpt.); mem. AICPA, N.Y. State Soc. CPAs. Avocations: avid reader, music, computers. Home: 87 Cedar Ln Berkeley Heights NJ 07922-2400 Office: Mintz Rosenfeld & Co 60 Route 46 E Fairfield NJ 07004-3007 Office Phone: 973-882-1100. Business E-Mail: tbyer@mintzrosenfeld.com.

BYERLEIN, ANNE P., human resources specialist, food products executive; Various positions PepsiCo., v.p. corp. human resources, 1988—96; v.p. human resources Yum Brands, Inc. (formerly Tricon Global Restaurants), Louisville, 1997—2002; chief people officer KFC, 2000—02, Yum Brands, Inc., Louisville, 2002—. Past pres. Leadership Palm Beach County. Office: Yum Brands Inc 1441 Gardiner Ln Louisville KY 40213 Office Phone: 502-874-8300. Office Fax: 502-874-8790.*

BYERLY, CARL WESLEY, music educator, academic administrator; b. Columbus, Ohio, Apr. 6, 1960; s. Donald Byerly and Patricia Ann Shank; m. Thayer Jeannine Simar, Oct. 22; children: Carl Weston, Neiman Christian. BA in Ch. Music, Jackson Coll. Ministries, Jackson, Miss., 1981; B in Music Edn., Miss. Coll., Clinton, 1983; MA in Music, U. Tex., Tyler, 1985; PhD in Choral Conducting, Clayton U., Mo., 1987. Cert. music tchr. Mich. Music dir. South Flint Tabernacle, Mich., 1991—97, Tabernacle Christian Acad., Mich., 1991—97; prof. music Mott C.C., Flint, Mich., 1991—93; founder, coord. Midwest Music Ministry Encounter, Pontiac, Mich., 1991—2001, Mich. Charter Sch. Fine Arts Camp, Grand Blanc, Mich., 2000—; adminstr. fine arts Woodland Park Acad., Grand Blanc, 1997—; prof. music U. Mich., Flint, 1993—. Chmn. music divsn. Spring Fest Arts Festival, Grand Blanc, 2000—03; head choral dir. Music In the Parks/Flint Symphony Orch., 1992—; bd. dirs., music dept. Grand Blanc Arts Coun., 1999—; pianist for Pres. Gerald Ford, 1976; dir. U. Mich. Gospel Choir, Flint; numerous nat. TV performances. Dir.(exec. prodr.): (recording CD) Colorblind/U. Mich. Flint Gospel Choir, 2001 (nomination outstanding choir Nat. Gospel Truth Mag. Music awards, Las Vegas, 2002), Come On Home, 1996; musician: (recording) Make a Joyful Noise, 1978 (Grammy award nomination, 1979); performer: Nat. Stellar Awards, 2002. Hon. bd. dirs. Gospel Music Workshop of Am., Flint, 1998—2002. Recipient Drum Major award, Mayor of Flint, 1996. Mem.: Mich. Elem. and Mid. Sch. Prins. Assn. Republican. Apostolic. Avocations: fishing, hunting, antiques. Home: 1459 Wiggins Rd Fenton MI 48430 Office: Woodland Park Acad 9127 S Saginaw Rd Grand Blanc MI 48439

BYERLY, GARY R., geophysics educator, department chairman; b. Paducah, Ky., Apr. 13, 1948; s. Chester Raymond and Lillie Joyce Byerly; m. Maud M. Walsh; children: Zachary D., Benjamin L. PhD, Mich. State U., 1974. Fellow Smithsonian Mus. Natural History, Washington, 1974—76; NRC fellow US Geol. Survey, Reston, Va., 1975—77. Chair dept. geology and geophysics La. State U., Baton Rouge, 1995—99, assoc. dean Coll. Basic Sciences, 2003—. Author: Geologic Evolution of the Barberton Greenstone Belt, South Africa. Mem.: Am. Geophys. Union, Geol. Soc. Am., Sigma Xi. Achievements include research in Awarded LSU Alumni Professorship. Office: LSU Geology and Geophysics E235 Howe-Russell Baton Rouge LA 70803 Office Phone: 225-578-5318.

BYERLY, RADFORD, JR., science administrator; b. Houston, May 22, 1936; s. Radford and Garvis N. (Cook) B.; m. Kathryn Jester, May 13, 1960 (div. 1980); children: Laura, Hamilton, Charles; m. Carol Ann Ries, Apr. 10, 1987. BA, Williams Coll., 1958, MA, 1960; PhD, Rice U., 1967. Sr. engr. No. Rsch. & Engring. Co., Cambridge, Mass., 1961-63; postdoctoral fellow U. Colo., Boulder, 1967-69, dir. Ctr. for Space and Geoscis. Policy, 1987-91, vis. scholar Ctr. for Sci. and Tech. Policy Rsch., 2001—; physicist, mgr. Nat. Bur. Standards, Washington, 1969-75; mem. profl. staff com. on sci. and tech. U.S. Ho. of Reps., Washington, 1975-87, chief of staff, com. on sci. and tech., 1991-93; v.p. pub.policy U. Corp. for Atmosphere Rsch., Boulder, 1993-94; dir. Roberts Inst., Boulder, 1993-94. Mem. space sta. adv. com. NASA, 1988-91, space sci. adv. com., 1987-91, 93-98; mem. adv. com. on space launch industry OTA, 1993-95; mem. bd. assessment NIST NAS, 1993-2000, mem. NAS com. on Dept. Energy peer rev. 1997-98, mem. com. environ. R&D, 2000-01, mem. com. on staged respository strategies, 2001-03; mem. NAS Space Studies Bd., 2001—; hon. lectr. Mid-Am. State Univs. Assn., 1988-89. Editor Space Policy Reconsidered, 1989, Space Policy Alternatives, 1991, Prediction: Science, Decision Making, and the Future of Nature, 2000; contbr. articles to profl. jours. NSF fellow, 1963-67. Fellow AAAS (com. on sci. engring. and pub. policy 1998—); mem. AIAA (chmn. civil space subcom. 1988-89), Assn. Univs. Rsch. in Astronomy (bd. dirs. 1998—2004, pers. policy com. 2002-2004), Am. Phys. Soc., Phi Beta Kappa, Sigma Xi (pres. U. Colo. chpt. 1995-97). Avocations: skiing, hiking, gardening. Home: 3870 Birchwood Dr Boulder CO 80304-1419 E-mail: hrbyerly@comcast.net.

BYERLY, STEVEN LEE, educational consultant; s. Jerry Sterling Byerly and Betty Jean Basile; m. Dora Jean Chriss, June 14, 1968; children: David, John. BA, Azusa Pacific Coll., Calif., 1970; MA, Calif. State U., San Bernardino, 1986; PhD, U. Calif.-Riverside, 1995. Asst. prin. Hesperia H.S., Calif., 1991—95; prin. Marysville H.S., Kans., 1995—97, Pierce H.S., Arbuckle, Calif., 1997—2000, San Jacinto H.S., San Jacinto, Calif., 2000—01; dir. curriculum and instrn. Sutter Union H.S. Dist., Sutter, Calif., 2001—. Adj. instr. Azusa Pacific U., 1990—91. Author: Poestricks, 1989, Linking Classroom Instruction to the Real World, The Kappan, 2001; contbr. columns in newspapers. Mem. CIF Realignment Com. of No. Calif., 1999; pres. Sacramento Valley League of No. Calif., 1998—2000; chair Sch. Bond Com., Hesperia, 1990, Affirmative Action Planning Com., Hesperia, 1993. Named History Tchr. of the Yr., DAR, 1991. Mem.: Am. Ednl. Rsch. Assn. Avocations: theater, quarter horses, model trains. Office Phone: 530-822-5161 234.

BYERRUM, RICHARD UGLOW, college dean; b. Aurora, Ill., Sept. 22, 1920; s. Earl Edward and Florence (Uglow) B.; m. Claire Somers, Apr. 3, 1945; children: Elizabeth, Mary, Carey. AB, Wabash Coll., 1942, D.Sc. (hon.), 1967; PhD, U. Ill., 1947. Teaching asst. U. Ill., 1942-44; research asso. U.S. Chem. Corps, toxicity dept. U. Chgo., 1944-47; faculty Mich. State U., East Lansing, 1947—, prof. biochemistry, 1957-91, prof. emeritus, 1991—; acting dir. Mich. State U. (Inst. Biology and Medicine), 1961-62; dean Mich. State U. (Coll. Natural Sci.), 1962-86. Author: (with others) Experimental Biochemistry, 1956; Editorial bd.: (with others) Phytochemistry, 1961-81; Contbr. (with others) numerous articles to profl. jours. Mem. Project Hope, 1961—; Trustee Mich. Health Council, 1961—, pres., 1966. Travel grantee Internat. Congress Biochemistry, Vienna, 1958; Travel grantee Internat. Congress Biochemistry, Montreal, 1959 Mem. Am. Chem. Soc. (lectr. vis. scientist program, awards com., visitor for com. profl. tng.), N. Central Assn. Colls. and Secondary Schs., A.A.A.S., Am. Soc. Plant Physiologists (trustee, exec. com.), Am. Soc. Biol. Chemists, Soc. Exptl. Biology and Medicine, Mich. Acad. Arts, Sci. and Letters, Phi Beta Kappa (pres. local chpt. 1962), Sigma Xi (awards com., Jr. Research award Mich. State U. chpt. 1958), Phi Kappa Phi (pres. 1968-69), Phi Lambda Upsilon, Alpha Chi Sigma, Beta Theta Pi. Achievements include patent in cancer tumor inhibiting material. Home: 2407 Sapphire Ln East Lansing MI 48823-7264

BYERS, ALTON CLAIR, geographer; b. Washington, Feb. 7, 1952; s. Alton Clair and Margaret Agnes Byers; m. Elizabeth Andrews, Mar. 19, 1983; children: Daniel, Barbara Lee. BA in Geography, U. Colo., 1975, PhD in Geography, 1987; MA in Geography, Syracuse U., 1979. Conservation officer South-East Consortium for Internat. Devel., Chapel Hill, NC, 1980—82; chief of party Ruhenger: Resources Anaylsis and Mgmt. project SE Consortium for Internat. Devel., Rwanda, 1988—89; program dir. Mountain Inst., Washington, 1990—. Applied mountain rsch. Nat. Geog. Soc., others, Washington, 1990—. Contbr. photographic exhibits on Himalaya, Andes; dir.: (mountain studies curriculum devel.) Mountains: A Global Resource, Exploring Our Living Mountain Laboratory. Adv. bd. mem. Mountain Studies Inst., Silverton, Colo., 2003—05; regional editor Mountain R & D, Berne, Switzerland, 2002—05; adv. com. dept. of geography Va. Inst. Tech., Blacksburg. Finalist Cyrus R. Vance award for Internat. Edn. in W.Va., Cyrus R. Vance Found., 2004, awards program, Nat. Wetlands Found., 2004; recipient Mountain Conservation award, W. Va. chpt. Nature Conservancy, 2000; grantee, Nat. Geog. Soc., 1995, 2001, 2004, $10 Million + In Devel., Edn., And Rsch. Grants, U.S. govt. and foundations, 1995 to present; fellow Mountain Hazards Mapping Project, UN U., Nepal, 1984. Mem.: Assn. Am. Geographers (assoc. Disting. Career award 2004), Am. Alpine Club (assoc.), Explorers Club (assoc.), Am. Alpine Club (assoc.). Achievements include research in contemporary landscape change analyses in the Himalaya, Andes, and other mountain regions of the world; long term field research leading to the conservation and restoration of alpine ecosystems in the Himalaya and Andes; co-developer of models for mountain protected areas and buffer zones worldwide; promotion of mountain environments and people through research, education, and advocacy. Avocations: mountain climbing, mountain trekking, nature study, writing. Home: 107 Westridge Dr Elkins WV 26241 Office: Mountain Inst 100 Campus Dr LA 108 Elkins WV 26241 Office Phone: 304-637-1223. Office Fax: 304-673-1988. Personal E-mail: abyers@mountain.org.

BYERS, FRANKLIN HAYS, II, lawyer; b. Rantoul, Ill., June 1, 1952; s. Franklin Hays and Florence Aileen (Nichols) B.; children: Franklin Hays, III, Barrett Jameson. BS, U. Ill., 1974, JD, 1977. Bar: Ill. 1977, U.S. Ct. Appeals (7th cir.) 1985, U.S. Supreme Ct., 1986. Pvt. practice, Decatur, Ill., 1977—. Mem. Ill. State Bar Assn. (assembley mem., 1988-90). Office: 3769 N Woodford St Decatur IL 62526-2717 Office Phone: 217-875-3301.

BYERS, GEORGE WILLIAM, retired entomology educator; b. Washington, May 16, 1923; s. George and Helen (Kessler) B.; m. Martha Esther Sparks, Feb. 25, 1945 (div. 1953); children: George William, Carolyn Sylvia; m. Gloria B. Wong, Dec. 16, 1955; children: Bruce Alan, Brian William, Douglas Eric. BS, Purdue U., 1947; MS, U. Mich., 1948, PhD, 1952. Asst. prof. dept. entomology U. Kans., Lawrence, 1956-60, curator Snow Entomol. Mus., 1956-83, dir., sr. curator, 1983-88, assoc. prof., 1960-65, prof. entomology, 1965-88, prof. dept. systematics and ecology, 1969-88, chmn. dept. entomology, 1969-72, 84-87, ret., 1988. Vis. prof. Mountain Lake Biol. Sta. U. Va., alt. summers, 1961-92, U. Minn. biol. sta., 1970. Author: several book chpts.; contbr. articles to profl. jours. With U.S. Army, 1942-46, 53-56, WWII and Korea; lt. col. M.S.C., USAR, ret. Rackham fellow U. Mich., 1952-53; NSF grantee, 1958-87, 97-99. Mem. Entomol. Soc. Am. (editl. bd. Annals 1967-72, chmn. 1971-72), Entomol. Soc. Can., Ctrl. States Entomol. Soc. (pres. 1958-59), Entomol. Soc. Washington, Soc. Systematic Biology (editor Syst. Zool. jour. 1963-66), Phi Beta Kappa, Phi Kappa Phi, Sigma Xi. Avocations: invertebrate paleontology, photography, ornithology. Home: 909 Holiday Dr Lawrence KS 66049-3006 Office: U Kans Entomology Divsn Natural History Mus Lawrence KS 66045-7523 Office Phone: 785-864-4538. Business E-Mail: ksem@ku.edu.

BYERS, JOHN RAOUL, III, food products executive, conservationist; b. Rochester, NY, Nov. 24, 1931; s. John Raoul Byers, Jr. and Dorothy Lynwood Bishop; m. Sharon Lynne Schlag, Feb. 24, 1968; children: John Winston, James William. AB, Cornell U., 1954; MBA, NYU, 1960. Internat. cocoa merchant Gill & Duffus, Inc., N.Y.C., 1956—78, v.p., 1966-80; pres., dir. Gill & Duffus Svcs., Inc., N.Y.C., 1980-81; prin. Byers Co., Inc., Scarsdale, N.Y., 1982-87; mgr. Machado & Co. Inc., N.Y.C., 1987-91; v.p. Westway Merkuria divsn. Amerop Sugar Corp., N.Y.C., 1991-94; cocoa grader Bd. of Trade City of N.Y., 1992—. Deacon Hitchcock Presbyn. Ch., Scarsdale, 1996—98; pres., dir. Garth Woods Conservancy on the Bronx River Pkwy., Inc., Scarsdale, 1997—2004; dir. Bronx River Pkwy. Reservation Conservancy, White Plains, NY, 2000—02. With U.S. Army, 1954—56. Avocations: reading and writing history, economics and biography. Home and Office: 187 Garth Rd Scarsdale NY 10583-3973

BYERS, KEITH THOMAS, librarian, educator; b. Laurel, Miss., Nov. 13, 1952; s. Theodore Kenneth and Alma Gladys B. ABA, Orangeburg-Calhoun Tech. Coll., 1973; BS in Mech. Engring., S.C. State U., Orangeburg, 1980, MEd in Maths., 1988; M in Libr. and Info. Scis., U. S.C., 1999; MDiv in Ministry, Erskine Theol. Seminary, 1997. Cert. tchr., S.C., cert. librarian S.C. Libr. Bd. Security guard Pinkerton's Inc., Orangeburg, 1973-80; devel. mech. engr. Bell Telephone Labs., Norcross, Ga., 1980-84; libr. asst. Erskine Coll. and Sem., Due West, S.C., 1997, Luth. Theol. So. Sem., Columbia, S.C., 1998-99; libr. intern S.C. State U., Orangeburg, 1999; reference dept. Orangeburg Co. Pub. Libr., 2000—. Contbr. articles to Christian Observer; inventor test probe, hand tool. Mem.: ALA, S.E. Libr. Assn., Travelers Protective Assn., S.C. Libr. Assn., Am. Theol. Libr. Assn., Am. Forestry Assn. (life), Clowns of Am. (life), Alpha Kappa Mu. Presbyterian. Avocations: electronics, fishing, gardening, mechanics, woodworking. Home: 1635 Central St Orangeburg SC 29115-3321

BYERS, MATTHEW T(ODD), lawyer, educator; b. Ridley Park, Pa., May 30, 1963; s. Richard Lynn and Joyce Ann (Ralston) B.; m. Lori Byers; children: Amanda Michelle, Amber, Helen, David, Saren, Loren. BA, U. N. Mex., 1985, JD, 1990. Bar: N.Mex. 1990, U.S. Dist. Ct. N.Mex. 1991, U.S. Ct. Appeals (10th cir.) 1991, U.S. Tax Ct. 1991, Pa. 1997. Staff Los Alamos (N.Mex.) Nat. Lab., 1989—90; assoc. Marek, Francis & Byers, P.A., Carlsbad, N.Mex., 1990—2001, ptnr., 1998—2001; assoc. Forry, Ullman, Ullman & Forry, Reading, Pa., 1997; pvt. practice Carlsbad, 2001—03; assoc. McCormick, Caraway, Tabor & Riley, Carlsbad, 2003—. Assoc. editor N. Mex. U. Law Review, 1990. Bd. dirs. United Way of Carlsbad, 1990-93. Recipient Cert. of Achievement Renaissance Program, Carlsbad, 1991. Mem. ABA, State Bar Assn. N.Mex., Eddy Cty. Bar Assn. (pres. 1993, 2003), George L. Reese Jr. Inn of Court, Pa. Bar Assn. Democrat. Baptist. Avocations: softball, music, reading. Office: 112 N Canyon Carlsbad NM 88220

BYERS, NINA, physics professor; b. LA, Jan. 19, 1930; d. Irving M. and Eva (Gertzoff) B.; m. Arthur A. Milhaupt, Jr., Sept. 8, 1974 (dec.). BA in Physics with highest honors, U. Calif., Berkeley, 1950; MS in Physics, U. Chgo., 1953, PhD, 1956; MA, U. Oxford, Eng., 1967. Research fellow dept. math. physics U. Birmingham, Eng., 1956-58; research assoc., asst. prof. Inst. Theoretical Physics and dept. physics Stanford, 1958-61; asst. then assoc. prof. physics UCLA, 1961-67, prof. physics, 1967—. Mem. Sch. Math., Inst. Advanced Studies, Princeton, N.J., 1964-65; ofcl. fellow Somerville Coll., Oxford, 1967-68, Janet Watson vis. fellow, 1968-74; faculty lectr., mem. dept. theoretical physics Oxford U., 1967-74, sr. vis. scientist, 1973-74; official fellow and tutor in physics, Somerville Coll. John Simon Guggenheim Meml. fellow, 1964-65, Sci. Rsch. Coun. fellow Oxford U., 1978, 85. Fellow AAAS (mem-at-large physics sect., com. on freedom and responsibility 1983-86), Am. Phys. Soc. (councillor-at-large 1977-81, panel pub. affairs 1980-83, vice-chmn. forum on physics and soc. 1981-82, 2002--, chmn. 1982-83, vice-chmn. forum on history of physics 2002-03, chair-elect, 2003-04, chair 2004-05); mem. Fedn. Am. Scientists (nat. coun. 1972-76, 78-80, exec. com. 1974-76, 78-80). Achievements include research in theory of particle physics and superconductivity; history of physics; contributions of 20th century women to physics. Office: U Calif Dept Physics Los Angeles CA 90095-0001

BYERS, WALTER, athletic association executive; b. Kansas City, Mo., Mar. 13, 1922; s. Ward and Lucille (Hebard) B.; children: Ward, Ellen, Frederick. Student, Rice U., 1939-40, U. Iowa, 1940-43. News reporter United Press Assn. (later U.P.I.), St. Louis, 1944, U.P.I., Madison, Wis., 1945, sports editor Chgo., 1945, asst. sports editor N.Y.C., 1946-47; also fgn. sports editor; dir. Big Ten Conf. Service Bur., Chgo., 1947-51; exec. asst. NCAA, Chgo., 1947-51, exec. dir., 1951-52, Kansas City, Mo., 1952-73, Shawnee Mission, Kans., 1973-87, exec. dir. emeritus, 1988-90. Pres. Byers Seven Cross Ranch, Inc., Emmett, Kans., 1974—, Ironwood Seven Cross Ranch, Inc., Hatfield, Mo., 1992-2002, Volland, Kans., 2002—, Byers Land and Cattle Co., Mission, Kans., 1996—; mgr. Byers Ranches, Limited Liability Co., 1997-. With M.C. AUS, 1944. Home and Office: PO Box 96 Saint Marys KS 66536

BYERS, WILLIAM D, chemicals executive; BS in Chem. Engring., Ohio State U., 1973; MBA, U. of Oreg., 1982. With CH2M Hill, 1982—, v.p. and dir., mgmt. systems, 1990—. Dir. Inst. of Chem. Engr. (pres. 2004), 1997—; diplomat Am. Acad. of Environ. Engrs. Office: VP Mgmt Sys 9191 S Jamaica St Englewood CO 80112 also: Pres Am Inst of Chem Engrs 3 Park Ave New York NY 10016-5991

BYERS-PEVITTS, BEVERLEY, college administrator, educator; b. Ohio County, Ky., Aug. 15, 1939; d. Stanley Beveridge and Vera Elizabeth (Amos) Byers; m. Robert Richard Pevitts, June 12, 1966; 1 child, Robert Stanley. BA, Ky. Wesleyan Coll., 1961; MA, So. Ill. U., 1967, PhD, 1980. Dir. theatre and faculty Dept. English, Speech, Drama Young Harris (Ga.) Coll., 1966-69; dir. theatre and asst. prof. speech and theatre arts Western Carolina U., Cullowhee, N.C., 1969-71; coord. supplementary progr., asst. prof. Eng. and drama Pfeiffer Coll., Misenheimer, N.C., 1972-74; dir. and prof. speech and theatre Ky. Wesleyan U., Owensboro, 1974-86; chair theatre arts U. Nev., Las Vegas, 1986-89, prof. and dir. grad. studies in theatre arts, 1986-90; dean coll. of humanities and fine arts, prof. U. No. Iowa, Cedar Falls, 1990-95; v.p. acad. affairs Tex. Woman's U., Denton, 1995—2001; Pres., Park U., Parkville, Mo., 2001—. Lectr. in field; conductor workshops in field. Editor: Theatre Topics, 1990-93; contbr. articles to profl. jours.; author: (plays) Reflections in a Window, 1982, rev., 1983, Beauty and the Beast, 1982, Time and the Rock, 1981, Family Haven, 1979, Take Courage, Stand Beside Us, 1977, A Strange and Beautiful Light, 1976-77; co-author: Epilogue to Glory, 1966. Bd. dirs. Waterloo/Cedar Falls Symphony Orch., 1990-94, Iowa Citizens for the Arts, 1991-94; coord. spl. drama programs WeCan, Inc., Las Vegas, 1986; tchr. Elderhostel Program; program coord. NOW. NEH Seminar grantee U. Wis.-Milw., 1983, NYU, 1977; recipient Outstanding Alumni award Ky. Wesleyan Coll., 1983; named Disting. Woman Am. Theatre Assn., 1977; grantee Ford Found., Exxon Corp.; elected to Nat. Theatre Conf., 1992—. Mem. Assn. for Theatre in Higher Edn. (founding pres. 1986-87, bd. govs. 1986-89), Assn. for Communication Adminstrn. (exec. com. 1988-91), Univ. and Coll. Theatre Assn. of Am. Theatre Assn. (pres. 1985-86), League Profl. Theatre Women N.Y., Internat. Coun. of Fine Arts Deans, Coun. of Colls. of Arts and Scis., Order of Oak and Ivy, Alpha Psi Omega. Avocations: gourmet cooking, travel, collecting antiques. Office: Park University 8700 NW River Park Dr Kansas City MO 64152

BYFIELD, BERT A., conservative humanitarian novelist; b. Lansing, Mich., Mar. 9, 1943; s. Virgil Albert and Frances Mary Pitts; m. Theresa Anne Baldassare, Dec. 2, 1972 (div. Dec. 1996); children: Cyndee, Maria, Catherine, Charity; m. Barbara Lloyd Scott, May 16, 1998. Author Caravela Books, Henrietta, N.Y., 1995—. Author: Rage of the Bear, 1995, Scream of the Eagle, 1999, Last Stand at Perekop, 2001, Father Gregory, 2003, Koba, 2003. Organizer Computer People for Peace, 1968-70. With USN, 1960-64. Russian Orthodox. Avocations: computer programming, computer games. Office: Caravela Books 134 Goodburlet Rd Henrietta NY 14467-9503 E-mail: bbyfieldww@caravelabooks.com.

BYLER, LOWELL J., retired music educator; b. Goshen, Ind., Mar. 26, 1929; s. Clarence R. and Ida E. Byler; m. Miriam Ruth Kauffman, June 9, 1950; children: Susan Bamesberger, Lori Reethof. BS in Edn., Goshen Coll., 1951; MusM, U. Mich., 1955; DMA, Northwestern U., 1959. Prof. music Hesston (Kans.) Coll., 1951—53, 1955—58, 1959—73, Millsaps Coll., Jackson, Miss., 1958—63, Ea. Mennonite U., Harrisonburg, Va., 1973—77, Sterling (Kans.) Coll., 1979—82, Livingston (Ala.) U., 1985—86, Tougaloo Coll., Jackson, 1986—87; ret., 1987. Founding dir. Jackson Choral Soc., 1960—63; 1st trumpet Jackson Symphony, 1959—60. Mem.: Nat. Assn. Tchrs. Singing, Am. Choral Dirs. Assn. Avocations: gardening, bowling. Home: 1261 Lincolnshire Dr Harrisonburg VA 22802 E-mail: ljbyler@adelphia.net.

BYLINSKY, GENE MICHAEL, magazine editor; b. Belgrade, Yugoslavia, Dec. 30, 1930; s. Michael Ivan and Dora (Shadan) B.; m. Gwen Gallegos, Aug. 14, 1955; children: Tanya, Gregory. BA in Journalism, La. State U., 1955. Staff reporter Wall St. Jour., Dallas, 1957-59, San Francisco, 1959-61, N.Y.C., 1961; sci. writer Nat. Observer, Washington, 1961-62, Newhouse Newspapers, Washington, 1962-66; bd. editors Fortune Mag., N.Y.C., 1966—2001, contbg. writer, 2002—. Author: The Innovation Millionaires, 1976, Mood Control, 1978, Life in Darwin's Universe, 1981, Silicon Valley, High Tech Window on the Future, 1985. Served with AUS, 1956. Recipient 21st Ann. Albert Lasker Med. Journalism award, 1970, Deadline award Sigma Delta Chi, 1970, 72, 79, spl. commendation AMA, 1967, 68, 72, Journalism award, 1974, Claude Bernard Sci. Journalism award Nat. Soc. Med. Rsch., 1973, 74, James T. Grady award for interpreting chemistry to pub. Am. Chem. Soc., 1976, Am. Space Writers Assn. award, 1976-79, Bus. Journalism award U. Mo.-Columbia, 1984, Journalism award Am. Assn. Engring. Socs./Engring. Found., 1995, hon. mention award, 1970, 71, hon. mention award AAAS-Westinghouse Corp., 1975, 76, 77, hon. mention award Overseas Press Club, 1988. Mem. Nat. Assn. Sci. Writers, N.Y. Acad. Scis. Mem. Russian Orthodox Ch. Office: Fortune Magazine Time and Life Bldg Rockefeller Plz New York NY 10020-2002

BYNES, AMANDA, actress; b. Thousand Oaks, Calif., Apr. 3, 1986; d. Rick and Lynn Bynes. Actor: (films) Big Fat Liar, 2002, What a Girl Wants, 2003, Lovewrecked, 2005, (voice) Robots, 2005,: (TV series) All That, 1996—2000 (nominee Cable Ace award, 1997), The Amanda Show, 1999—2002, (voice) Rugrats, 2002—04, What I Like About You, 2002—, (voice): (videos) Charlotte's Web 2: Wilbur's Great Adventure, 2003—; appeared as herself/guest panelist (TV series) Figure It Out, 1997—2000. Recipient Favorite TV Actress, Kid's Choice Awards, 2001, 2002, 2003, Favorite Movie Actress, 2003. Achievements include discovered at age 10 at a kid's comedy showcase at the Laugh Factory, LA and signed immediately by Nickelodeon for TV series All That. Office: Endeavor Talent Agy 9701 Wilshire Blvd 10th Fl Beverly Hills CA 90212*

BYNES, FRANK HOWARD, JR., physician; b. Savannah, Ga., Dec. 3, 1950; s. Frank Howard and Frenchye (Mason) B.; m. Janice Ratta, July 24, 1987; children: Patricia, Frenchye. BS, Savannah State Coll., 1972; MD, Meharry Med. Coll. Resident gen. surgery Staten Island (N.Y.) Hosp., 1978-82; resident internal medicine N.Y. infirmary Beekam Downtown Hosp., N.Y.C., 1983-86; dir. medicine USAF Sheppard Regional Hosp., Sheppard AFB, Tex., 1986-87; pvt. practice internal medicine N.Y.C., 1987-90; attending physician Bronx (N.Y.) Lebanon Hosp., 1990-93; pvt. practice internal medicine Savannah, Ga., 1994—. Maj. USAF, 1986-87. Mem. AMA, AAAS, ACP, N.Y. Acad. Scis., Assn. Mil. Surgeons of U.S., Alpha Phi Alpha. Office Phone: 912-354-0899.

BYNUM, MAGNOLIA VIRGINIA WRIGHT, retired secondary school educator; b. Waynesboro, Ga., Jan. 10, 1934; d. George and Edith Arilee (Williams) Wright; m. Marvin Bynum, Sept. 17, 1955 (dec. Oct. 1977). BS in Bus. Edn., N.C. A&T State U., Greensboro, N.C., 1956; postgrad., NYU, 1964—65; MS in Edn., CUNY, Bklyn., 1985, Adv. Cert. Guidance & Counseling, 1986. Enging. adminstr. Radio Receptor Co., Bklyn., 1957—59; data processing staff NYU, N.Y.C., 1959—64; tchr., dean, counselor Lincoln H.S., Jersey City, 1964—92; ret., 1992. Adj. prof. CUNY, Bklyn., 1986—90; asst. to Congressman Edolphus Towns, 10th Congl. Dist., Bklyn., 1982—90; counselor incentive program dept. human resources Bklyn. Coll., 1992—93; cons. Parent Advocacy, Medgars Evers Coll., Bklyn., 1984—85. Editor-in-chief (newsletter) Cornerstone Torch, 1993—97. Mem. Cmty. Coalition for Edn., Greensboro, NC, NAACP; spearheaded Hard of Hearing campaign, Bklyn.; women's day chairperson New Zion Missionary Bapt. Ch., Greensboro, NC; chairperson bd. dirs. Chama Child Devel., Bklyn., 1983—91, Cornerstone Day Care Ctr., Bklyn., 1991—97. Named to Faculty Achievement Hall of Fame, Lincoln H.S., 1981; recipient Outstanding Cmty. Svc. award, Bklyn. Coll. Grad. Students, 1984, citations, Congl. Record, 1990, 1997; scholar Myers Jacob Guidance & Counseling scholar, 1984. Mem.: Alpha Kappa Alpha, Phi Delta Kappa, Kappa Delta Pi. Baptist. Avocations: reading, travel, singing. Home: 563 Summerwalk Rd Greensboro NC 27455

BYNUM, SARAH SHUN-LIEN, writer, educator; b. Feb. 14, 1972; married. BA, Brown U.; MS in Fiction Writing, Iowa Writers Workshop. Tchr. English & Am. Hist. Berkeley Carroll Sch., Bklyn.; v.p., sr. cons. Goodale Assocs., N.Y.C., 2000—. Author: Madeleine Is Sleeping (Nat. Book Award finalist, 2004); contbr. articles to profl. jours. Mem.: Phi Beta Kappa. Office: Goodale Assocs 509 Madison Ave Ste 1112 New York NY 10022

BYNUM, TERRELL WARD, humanities educator, consultant; s. Terrell Waltham and Elizabeth Bynum; m. Aline W. Bynum, June 22, 1965; children: Timothy H., Andrew J. BS in Chemistry with honors and distinction, BA in Philosophy with honors and distinction, U. Del., Newark, 1963; MA in Philosophy, Princeton U., N.J., 1966; MPhil, PhD in Philosophy, Grad. Sch. CUNY, N.Y.C., 1986. Asst. prof. philosophy Am. U., Washington, 1967—68, SUNY, Albany, NY, 1968—74, Ramapo Coll., Mah Wah, NJ, 1974—75, Dutchess Coll. of SUNY, Poughkeepsie, NY, 1975—78, assoc. prof. philosophy, 1978—87, So. Conn. State U., New Haven, 1987—89, prof. philosophy, 1989—. Exec. dir. Am. Assn. of Philosophy Tchrs., 1978—82, pres., 1984—86; dir. rsch. ctr. on computing & soc. So. Conn. State U., New Haven, 1987—; organizer and co-director Nat. Conf. on Computing and Values, New Haven, 1988—92; chair, com. on profl. ethics Assn. for Computing Machinery, N.Y.C., 1993—96; chair com. on philosophy and computing Am. Philos. Assn., Newark, 1994—97; organizer internat. confs. on computer ethics. Translator (biographer and editor): Gottlob Frege, Conceptual Notation and Related Articles (Oxford U. Press Classic, 2002); co-editor (and author): Computer Ethics and Profl. Responsibility; co-editor: (with James H. Moor) Cyberphilosophy: The Intersection of Philosophy and Computing, The Digital Phoenix: How Computers Are Changing Philosophy; founder and editor-in-chief Metaphilosophy, 1968—94, host and assoc. prodr. What Is Computer Ethics?; contbr. articles to profl. jours. Fellow, Woodrow Wilson Found., 1963-1965, Danforth Found., 1963-1967, Andrew Mellon Found., 1982-1983; grantee Computer Ethics Rsch., NSF, 1989, 1991, 1992, 1993; Fulbright Fellow in Eng., US Govt., 1963-1964, Dartmouth Coll. Humanities Rsch. Fellowship, 1998. Mem.: Internat. Soc. for Ethics and Info. Tech., Internat. Assn. for Computing and Philosophy (bd. mem. 2001), Assn. for Computing Machinery, Am. Philos. Assn., Computer Profls. Social Responsibility (life). Achievements include development of computer ethics as a field of scholarly research and teaching. Avocations: travel, bird watching, walking, poetry writing, science reading. Office: So Conn State U 501 Crescent St New Haven CT 06515 Office Phone: 203-392-6790. Business E-Mail: bynumt2@southernct.edu.

BYRD, ALICIA D., minister, sociologist; d. William Lee and Myrtice Ernestine Byrd. BA, Wheaton Coll., Ill., 1975; MA, U. Ill., Springfield, 1977; MDiv, Howard U., Washington, 1985; PhD, Am. U., Washington, 1988. Assoc. dean of students Gordon Coll., Wenham, Mass., 1977—79; sophomore counselor Boston U., 1979—82; assoc. dean of students Cath. U. of Am., Washington, 1982—85; dir. of theol. edn. Congress of Nat. Black Chs., Washington, 1987—97; vis. prof. Nazareth Coll., Rochester, NY, 1997—99; exec. dir. St. Stephens Econ. Devel. Corp, Elkridge, Md., 1998—; pastor St. Stephens AME Ch., Elkridge, 1988—; assoc. organizer Interfaith Action Communities, Seat Pleasant, Md., 2001—03; adj. prof. Wesley Sem., Washington, 2002—, Prince George's C.C., Landover, Md., 2003—. Cons. Coun. on Founds., Washington, 1987—95, Nat. Congress of Cmty. Econ. Devel., Washington, 1988—90, Lilly Endowment, Indpls., 1992—94, Ford Found., N.Y.C., 1995—97. Editor: (devotional bible) African American Devotional Bible, (book) Restoring Broken Places and Rebuilding Communities, Philanthropy and the Black Church. Chair St. Stephens Econ. Devel. Corp, Elkridge, Md., 1998—2003. Mem.: Alpha Kappa Alpha. Home: PO Box 8242 Elkridge MD 21075 Office: St Stephens AME Church 7741 Mayfield Ave Elkridge MD 21075 Personal E-mail: olivia_1953@yahoo.com.

BYRD, AMY CONNOR, secondary school educator; b. New Brunswick, N.J., Apr. 15, 1949; d. Parker Ewan Jr. and Amy (Sadler) Connor; m. William Greaner Neal, July 10, 1971 (div. July 1976); m. Harry Clifton Byrd III, Sept. 7, 1978; children: Parker Talmadge, Pierce Katherine. BA in English, Coker Coll., 1971. Cert. tchr. English. Free-lance photographer, Culpeper, Va., 1971-79; English tchr. Culpeper (Va.) County High, 1979—. Creator The Phoenix Project, 1994. Recipient 1st place award in creative photography Va. Press Assn., 1977. Mem. Va. Edn. Assn. (presenter 1993), Va. Tchrs. English. Presbyterian. Avocations: reading, creative teaching. Home: 13240 Windmill Way Culpeper VA 22701-5136 Office: Culpeper County High Sch 12402 Achievement Dr Culpeper VA 22701 Office Phone: 540-727-0092. E-mail: amybyrd6@aol.com.

BYRD, ANDREW WAYNE, investment company executive; b. Nashville, Apr. 16, 1954; s. Benjamin F. and Allison (Caldwell) B.; m. Marianne Menefee; children: Marianne, Valere, Andrew Jr. BA, Vanderbilt U., 1976, JD, 1979; LLM, Georgetown U., 1981. Bar: Tenn., 1979, U.S. Dist. Ct. (mid. dist.) Tenn. 1979, U.S. Supreme Ct. 2001. Atty. Stokes & Bartholomew, Nashville, 1981-84; exec. v.p. Gen. Cap Am. Inc., 1987-94, Gen. Capital Corp., Nashville, 1984-89, pres., 1989-94, Andrew W. Byrd & Co., LLC, 1994—. Chmn., bd. dirs. Multi-Link, Inc., Lexington, Ky., Albertville (Ala.) Quality Foods, Inc., Precision Boilers, Inc., Morristown, Tenn., So. Quality Meats, Inc., Pontotoc, Miss. Mem. Leadership Nashville, 1984-85; deacon 1st Presbyn. Ch., 1982-92, elder, 200—; bd. dirs. Tenn. divsn. Am. Cancer Soc., 1982-88, 92-97, Cheekwood, 1987-93; bd. dirs. Boy Scouts of Am., Mid. Tenn. Coun., 1995—, v.p. manpower, 2002-04, treas., 2005—; bd. dirs. Exch. Club Charities, 2003-05; bd. dirs. Vanderbilt Children's Hosp., 1987-93, chmn., 1991-93. Mem. ABA, Tenn. Bar Assn., Nashville Bar Assn., Nashville Area C. of C. (bd. dirs. 2003-), Exch. Club (pres. 1993-94). Democrat. Avocations: tennis, gardening, travel. Home: 4419 Harding Pl Nashville TN 37205-4530 Office: Andrew W Byrd & Co LLC 201 4th Ave N Ste 1250 Nashville TN 37219-2092 Office Phone: 615-256-8061.

BYRD, BETTY RANTZE, writer; b. Oklahoma City, July 8, 1949; d. Rolande Brown and Mary Louise Haner; m. Gordon Peter Rantze (div.); 1 child, Elizabeth Chase Rantze; m. William James Byrd, Sept. 16, 1995. BA, U. Ariz., 1974; legal asst. cert., Capital U., 1975. Society editor The Spectator Newspaper, Columbus, Ohio, 1974—75; paralegal Paul Bran-Pub. Defender, Lewisburg, Pa., 1976—77. Author: Trinity's Daughter, 2002; actor: appeared in numerous commls., films, TV. Vol. Salvation Army, Meals-on-Wheels, San Diego, Spl. Olympics, San Diego, Family Recovery Ctr., San Diego. Mem.: AFTRA, SAG, Rancho Santa Fe Literary Soc., Nat. Charity League. Avocations: photography, golf, travel, walking, scrapbooks. Home and Office: PO Box 2593 Rancho Santa Fe CA 92067

BYRD, CHRISTINE WATERMAN SWENT, lawyer; b. Oakland, Calif., Apr. 11, 1951; d. Langan Waterman and Eleanor (Herz) Swent; m. Gary Lee Byrd, June 20, 1981; children: Amy, George. BA, Stanford U., 1972; JD, U. Va., 1975. Bar: Calif. 1976, U.S. Dist. Ct. (ctrl., so. no., ea. dists.) Calif., U.S. Ct. Appeals (9th cir.). Law clk. to Hon. William P. Gray U.S. Dist. Ct., L.A., 1975-76; assoc. Jones, Day, Reavis & Pogue, L.A., 1976-82, ptnr., 1987-96; asst. U.S. atty. criminal divsn. U.S. Atty.'s Office, Ctrl. Dist. Calif., L.A., 1982-87; ptnr. Irell & Manella, L.A., 1996—. Mem. Calif. Law Revision Commn., 1992-97. Author: The Future of the U.S. Multinational Corporation, 1975; contbr. articles to profl. jours. Fellow: Coll. Comml. Arbitrators, Am. Coll. Trial Lawyers; mem.: ABA (vice chmn. ADR Advocacy in Litig. 2003—), Assn. Bus. Trial Lawyers (bd. govs. 1996—99), 9th Jud. Cir. Hist. Soc. (bd. dirs. 1986—, pres. 1997—2002), Century City Bar Assn. (bd. govs. 2001—05), Stanford Profl. Women L.A. County, Am. Arbitration Assn. (large and complex case panel 1992—, nat. energy panel 1998—, bd. dirs. 1999—), Women Lawyers Assn. L.A. County, L.A. County Bar Assn., Calif. State Bar (com. fed. cts. 1985—88), Stanford U. Alumni Assn. Republican. Office: Irell & Manella LLP 1800 Ave Of Stars Ste 900 Los Angeles CA 90067-4276 Office Phone: 310-277-1010. Business E-Mail: cbyrd@irell.com.

BYRD, EVA WILSON, communications executive; Dir. media Bates Health World, New York, NY, 1994—, v.p., dir. media. Office: Girgenti Hughes Butler & McDowell Fl 8 100 Ave of the Americas New York NY 10013-1687

BYRD, GARY ELLIS, lawyer; b. Dothan, Ala., Mar. 8, 1957; m. Emily Marie Reid; children: Elizabeth, Virginia and Victoria (twins). BS in Pre-Law and Am. History summa cum laude, Troy State U., 1979; JD, U. Ala., 1982. Bar: Ga. (no. and middle dists.) 1983, U.S. Dist. Ct. (no. and so. dists), Ga., U.S. Ct. Appeals. Ptnr. Bishoff & Byrd, Talbotton, Ga., 1982-86; assoc. Bunn & Kirby, Hamilton, Ga., 1993—, 1993-96; ptnr. Bunn & Byrd, Hamilton, Ga., 1996—2000; city atty. Woodland, Ga., 1986—, Geneva, Ga., 1988—, Shiloh, Ga., 1994—; ptnr. Bunn, Byrd, Newsom & Hix, 2001—, city atty. Junction City, Ga., 2002; pvt. practice, 2003—. Chmn. bd. dirs. Talbot County Law Libr., Talbotton, 1992-2004, 2001-2002; bd. dirs. Harris County Law Libr., Hamilton, 1998-2004. Contbr. numerous articles to newspapers and profl. jours., chpt. to book; author City of Woodland city code, 1986, City of Geneva charter, 2000, City of Shiloh charter, 2001. Bd. dirs. Chattahoochie-Flint RESA, Americus, Ga., 1986-87, Pine Mountain Regional Arts Coun., Manchester, Ga., 1986-88; pres., chmn. exec. com. Talbot County 2000 Group, Talbotton, 1987-88; coach debate team dept. social studies Manchester (Ga.) H.S., 1982; chmn. appropriations com. Harris County YMCA, Hamilton, 1994-2000, 2002-03, bd. dirs. 1994-2000, 2002-03; mem. budget com. City of Talbotton, 1989-92, councilman, 1985-92, mem. policy adv. com., 1986-92, vol. fireman, 1982-93; ct. apptd. adminstr. City of Geneva, Ga., 1992; mem. adv. com. Am. Security Coun., Washington, 1976-82; dir. Harris County Indigent Def. Program, 1999-2004. Recipient Outstanding Svc. award Talbot County Jaycees, 1983, Mem. Ga. Bar Assn., Ga. Mcpl. Assn. (atty.'s sect.), Talbot County C. of C. (chmn. membership com. 1992-93, bd. dirs. 1993), Harris County C. of C. (bd. dirs. 2000-02), Troy State U. Alumni Assn. (membership com. East Ala./West Ctrl. Ga. chpt. 1993-99, Rotary (chmn. internat. svc. com. 2002-04), Phi Kappa Phi, Phi Alpha Theta (State Hist. Rsch. award 1979). Author, City of Geneva, GA Charter, 2000; Author, City of Shiloh, GA Charter, 2001. Avocations: model trains, stock car racing. Home: PO Box 119 Hamilton GA 31811-0119 Office: 103 N College St PO Box 489 Hamilton GA 31811-0489 Office Phone: 706-628-5511. E-mail: byrdgary@msn.com.

BYRD, HARRY FLOOD, JR., publishing executive, retired senator; b. Winchester, Va., Dec. 20, 1914; s. Harry Flood and Anne Douglas (Beverley) B.; m. Gretchen B. Thomson, Aug. 9, 1941 (dec. Oct. 1989); children: Harry, Thomas Thomson, Beverley. Student, Va. Mil. Inst., 1931—33, U. Va., 1933—35, LLD, LHD, D in Internat. Svc., U. Va. Editor Winchester Evening Star, 1935—81; pub. Harrisonburg (Va.) Daily News-Record, 1937—2000; pres., dir. Rockingham Pub. Co., 1946—; dir. AP, 1950-66; v.p., mem. exec. com., mem. Va. Senate, 1947-65; mem. U.S. Senate from Va., 1965-83, chmn. subcom. on taxation. Author Va. automatic tax reduction law. Mem. Va. Dem. Ctrl. Com., 1940-66. Served to lt. comdr. USNR, 1942-46. Recipient Honor medal Freedoms Found.; named to Va. Comm. Hall of Fame. Mem. VFW, Va. Press Assn. (Man of Yr.), Am. Legion, Masons (33d degree, insp. gen. hon.), Rotarian Club, National Press Club, Army-Navy Club. Office: Rockingham Pub Co Inc 2 N Kent St Winchester VA 22601-5038 Office Phone: 540-662-7745.

BYRD, HENRY STEPHENSON (STEVE), plastic surgeon, educator; BA with honors, North Tex. State U., 1968; MD with honors, U. Tex., Galveston, 1972. Diplomate Am. Bd. Surgery, 1978, Am. Bd. Plastic Surgery, 1980, lic. Tex., Utah. Surg. intern U. Tex. Southwestern Med. Ctr., Dallas, 1972—73, resident plastic surgery, 1977—79, prof., vice chair plastic surgery, 1979—; resident gen. surgery U. Utah Med. Ctr., Salt Lake City, 1973—77; chief pediat. plastic surgery sect. Children's Med. Ctr., Dallas, 1979—. Sec.-treas., bd. mem. Selected Readings in Plastic Surgery, 1980—; treas. Rhinoplasty Soc.; chmn. Bd. Pediat. Surg. Alliance; bd. mem. Health Tex. Provider Network; sec. Preferred Surg. Specialist Tex.; attending staff Parkland Meml. Hosp., Dallas, U. Med. Ctr., Dallas; assoc. staff Presbyn. Hosp., Dallas, Med. Arts Hosp., Dallas; assoc. tchg. staff St. Paul Med. Ctr., Dallas; dir. plastic surgery svc., mem. cleft lip-craniofacial team Children's Med. Ctr., Dallas; chief plastic and reconstructive surgery svc. Baylor U. Med. Ctr., Dallas, 1996—. Fellow: ACS; mem.: Plastic Surgery Ednl. Found. (bd. mem. 1993—, chmn. in-svc. exam com. 1989—91, mem. long range planning task force 1991, mem. mktg. com. 1991, bd. dirs. 1996—98, mem. select com. on forward planning 1996—), Dallas County Med. Soc., Dallas Soc. Plastic Surgeons (sec.-treas.), Tex. Soc. Plastic Surgeons, Tex. Med. Assn., Am. Cleft Palate Assn., Am. Soc. for Aesthetic Plastic Surgery (mem. edn. commn.), Am. Assn. Plastic Surgeons, Am. Soc. Plastic and Reconstructive Surgeons (mem. sci. program com. 1991, James Barrett Brown award 1984), Alpha Omega Alpha, Blue Key Honor Soc. Office: Dallas Plastic Surgery Inst 411 N Washington Ave Ste 6000 LB 13 Dallas TX 75246 Office Phone: 214-821-9662. Office Fax: 214-828-2609. Business E-Mail: info@drstevebyrd.com.*

BYRD, ISAAC BURLIN, retired biologist; b. Canoe, Ala., Mar. 14, 1925; s. Isaac Britt and Mary Adline (Wright) B.; m. Marjorie Fé Elmore, Sept. 24, 1949; children— Cathy Ann, Teresa Carol, Gary Curtis. BS, Auburn U., 1948, MS, 1950. Chief fisheries sect. Ala. Dept. Conservation, 1951-65; fed. aid coordinator fisheries research and devel. Bur. Comml. Fisheries, Dept. Interior, 1965-70; chief div. state-fed. relationships, fisheries research, devel. and mgmt. Nat. Marine Fisheries Service, St. Petersburg, Fla., 1970-85, asst. regional dir. S.E. Region, 1985-91, ret., 1991. Adminstr. Internat. Fisheries Agreement (for U.S. shrimp fishermen to fish Brazilian coastal waters), 1975-76; mem. adv. com. to organize 1st fishery mgmt. councils and to develop initial fed. policies under Fisheries Conservation and Mgmt. Act 1976 (for marine fisheries in fisheries conservation zone of U.S.); chmn. Gulf of Mexico State/Fed. Fisheries Mgmt. Bd., 1985-86, 88-89; chmn. South Atlantic State/Fed. Fisheries Mgmt. Bd., 1990-91 Contbg. author: McCanes Standard Fishing Ency., Internat. Angling Guide, 1965; contbr. articles to sci. jours. Served with USAAF, 1943-46. Recipient Gov. Ala. award outstanding tech. accomplishments conservation, 1964 Fellow Am. Inst. Fishery Research Biologists; mem. Am. Fisheries Soc. (pres. So. div. 1958, pres. 1965-66, asso. editor trans. 1955-58), World Mariculture Soc. (dir. 1972-73), Internat. Assn. Fish and Wildlife Agys., Gulf and Caribbean Fisheries Inst., Inland Comml. Fisheries Assn., Phi Kappa Phi, Omicron Delta Kappa, Gamma Sigma Delta, Alpha Zeta, Alpha Gamma Rho. Methodist. Achievements include initiating the 1st fisheries mgmt. and fisheries research program in state for Ala. Dept. Conservation. Home: 11105 7th St E Treasure Island Saint Petersburg FL 33706

BYRD, ISAAC KENITH, JR., lawyer; b. Shaw, Miss., Feb. 3, 1952; BA Polit. Sci./Sociology magna cum laude, Tougaloo Coll., 1973; JD, Northwestern U., 1976. Staff atty. Swift & Co. Legal Dept., Chgo., 1976-78; assoc. Banks & Nichols, Jackson, Miss., 1978-80, ptnr., 1980-81, Owens & Byrd, Jackson, 1982-86; pvt. practice Byrd & Assocs., Jackson, 1986—. Part-time instr. polit. sci. Tougaloo Coll., 1980, bd. trustees, 1987—; bd. dirs. Miss. Dept. Corrections, 1984-88, vice-chmn., 1986-88; apptd. Chancery Ct. judge Hinds County, Miss., 1989. First black Chancery judge in Miss. Bd. dirs. Arts Alliance, New Stage Theater, Ballet Miss.; campaign coord. former gov. William Winter, 1979; active Miss. Mus. Art-Rembrandt Soc., Hinds County Dem. Exec. Com., 1980-85; campaign mgr. Shirley Watson for Jackson City Commr., 1984; gen. counsel Miss. State Conf. of the NAACP. Recipient Miss. Outstanding 4-H Leadership award, 1969, Father Walter Legal scholarship, Indianola, Miss., 1973, 74, NAACP State Vernon Dahmer award, 1985, Thelma Sanders Milestone award Jackson Minority Bus., 1992, Faces of Courage award Medgar Evers Statue Fund, 1992; named Hinds County Trial Lawyers Assn. Outstanding Trial Lawyer, 1984, Tougaloo Coll. Alumnus of Yr., 1984, Tugaloo Coll. Hall of Fame, 2003; named to Am.'s Top Black Lawyers, Black Enterprise mag., 2003. Mem. ABA, Nat. Bar Assn., Miss. Bar Assn. (vice-chmn., state bar disciplinary adv. com.), Assn. Trial Lawyers Am. (bd. govs. 1992, publs. com., standing com., birth trauma litigation group, minority caucus del., sexual abuse litigation group, M Club), Miss. Trial Lawyers Assn. (bd. mem., Pres.'s Club, exec. com. ATLA del.), Magnolia Bar Assn. (legis. com., platinum circle mem., continuing legal edn. chmn. 1992-93), NAACP (life), ACLU Miss. (bd. mem.), Alpha Phi Alpha. Democrat. Baptist. Avocations: jogging, reading, antique collecting. Office: Byrd & Assoc 427 East Fortification St PO Box 19 Jackson MS 39205 Office Phone: 601-714-4226. Office Fax: 601-354-1254.

BYRD, JAMES EVERETT, lawyer; b. Cin., Aug. 1, 1958; BS, U. Dayton, Ohio, 1980, JD cum laude, 1984. Law clk. U.S. Dist Ct. (so. dist.), Ohio, 1983; assoc. Smith & Schnacke, Dayton, 1984-89; v.p., gen. counsel Internat. Cargo Svcs., Virginia Beach, Va., 1989-91; assoc. Beale, Balfour et al., Richmond, Va., 1991-92; corp. counsel Huffy Corp., Dayton, 1992-94; ind. corp. legal cons., 1994-95; assoc. gen. counsel Lexis Nexis divsn. Reed Elsevier, Inc., Dayton, 1995—. Pres. Condominium Owners Assn., Dayton, 1995-99. Mem. ABA, Ohio Bar Assn., Va. Bar Assn. Office: Lexis Nexis 9443 Springboro Pike Miamisburg OH 45342-4425 E-mail: james.e.byrd@lexisnexis.com.

BYRD, KATHRYN SUSAN, psychologist, educator; d. George Washington Byrd and Josie Beth Mayes. BA, Centenary Coll., Shreveport, La., 1974; MS, Northwestern State U., Natchitoches, La., 1977; PhD, U. Tex, Richardson, 1995. Cert. mediator Tex., 2004. Coord. of academic advising, communication arts & tech. divsn. Eastfield Coll., Mesquite, Tex., 2001—, adj. faculty, 2001—. Acad. adv. Eastfield Coll., Mesquite, Tex., 1999—; apptd. to district-wide ednl. improvement coun. Garland Ind. Sch. Dist., 2004—05. Mem. of class of 2002, Eastfield Coll. rep. Leadership Garland, Mesquite, Tex., 2002. Mem.: APA, Romance Writers Am., Bluebonnet Bebes Doll Collectors Club. Republican. Southern Baptist. Office: Eastfield College 3737 Motley Dr Mesquite TX 75150 Office Phone: 972-860-7671. Business E-Mail: ksb4323@dcccd.edu.

BYRD, LARRY DONALD, behavioral pharmacologist; b. Salisbury, N.C., July 14, 1936; s. Donald Thomas and Mildred (Gardner) B.; m. Corrinne Williams, Dec. 23, 1961; children: Kay, Lynn, Renee, Andrew. AB, E. Carolina U.; Greenville, N.C., 1962; MA, E. Carolina U., 1964; PhD, U. N.C., 1968; postgrad., Harvard U., 1967-70. Faculty E. Carolina U., 1962-64; tchg. and rsch. asst. exptl. psychology U. N.C., Chapel Hill, 1964-67; rsch. fellow pharmacology, instr. psychobiology Harvard Med. Sch., 1967-70; assoc. scientist Lab. Psychobiology New Eng. Reg. Primate Rsch. Ctr., 1969-74;

psychobiologist, chmn. divsn. primate behavior Yerkes Primate Rsch. Ctr., Emory U., Atlanta, 1974-79, assoc. rsch. prof., chmn. divsn. primate behavior, 1979-80, lectr. dept. psychology, 1974-81, assoc. rsch. prof., chief divsn. behavioral biology, 1980-82, prof., chief divsn. behavioral biology, 1982-97, prof. dept. pharmacology, 1995-97; prof. emeritus, 1998. Adj. prof. dept. psychology Emory U., 1981-97; cons. Dept. Pharmacological and Physiol. Scis. U. Chgo., 1973, MIT Press, Cambridge, 1975, Nat. Ctr. for Toxicological Rsch. FDA, Jefferson, Ark., 1976-77, S.W. Found. for Rsch. and Edn., San Antonio, 1977, Naval Aerospace Med. Rsch. Lab. U.S. Naval Air Sta., Pensacola, Fla., 1977, G.D. Searle and Co., Skokie, Ill., 1986, Battelle Meml. Inst., Columbus, Ohio, 1989-94; mem. spl. rev. com. Contract Rev. Unit Nat. Inst. on Drug Abuse, Lexington, Ky., 1979-81, mem. spl. rev. com. biomed. rsch. rev. com., 1981-82, spl. rev. cons. clin., behavioral and psychosocial rsch. rev. com., 1981-82, mem., 1982-85, chmn., 1984-85, others; spl. rev. cons. dept. medicine and surgery VA, Washington, 1983, NSF, Washington, 1984, div. of rsch. resources NIH, Washington, 1983, mem. spl. study sect. div. rsch. grants, 1984, panel mem. Workshop on Implemenation of Pub. Health Svc. Policy on Humane Care and Use of Lab. Animals, 1989, others; panel mem. USPHS Animal Welfare Forum Alcohol, Drug Abuse and Mental Health Adminstrn., 1985; active numerous other career related orgns. Editorial bd. Jour. Exptl. Analysis of Behavior, 1969-79, 87-91; assoc. editor Jour. Exptl. Analysis of Behavior, 1970-76; cons. editor Am. Jour. Primatology, 1980-83; editor Psychopharmacology Newsletter, 1976-82; editorial advisor Jour. Pharmacology and Exptl. Therapeutics, Jour. Exptl. Analysis of Behavior, others; contbr. numerous articles to profl. jours. Mem. sci. adv. com. Nat. Families in Action, 1991—95. Recipient Outstanding Alumnus award, E. Carolina U., 1977, Disting. Alumnus award, U. N.C., 1987. Fellow AAAS, Am. Psychol. Assn. (exec. com. psychopharmacology divsn. 1976-95, neurobehavioral toxicity test standards com. 1980-97, coord. Young Psychopharmacologist award 1985-95, bd. sci. affairs com. on animals in rsch. and ethics 1990-93); mem. Assn. for Assessment and Accreditation Lab. Animal Care (trustee 1990-98, exec. com. 1991-98, sec. 1993, vice chmn. 1994-96, chmn. 1996-98), Am. Soc. Pharmacology and Exptl. Therapeutics, Nat. Families in Action (sci. adv. com. 1991-95), Am. Soc. Primatologist, Behavioral Pharmacology Soc. (pres. 1984-86), Soc. Exptl. Analysis of Behavior (v.p. 1975-76, bd. dirs. 1970-78), European Behavioral Pharmacology Soc., Southeastern Pharmacology Soc., Am Pub. Health Assn., Behavioral Toxicology Soc., Southeastern Assn. for Behavior Analysis, Internat. Study Group Investigating Drugs as Reinforcers, Emory Neurosci. Group, Phi Sigma Pi. Home: 2730 Camp Branch Rd Buford GA 30519-4455 Business E-Mail: lbyrd@emory.edu.

BYRD, LLOYD GARLAND, retired civil engineer; b. Atlanta, May 6, 1923; s. Lloyd Porter and Gladys Ardee (Daniell) B.; m. Jeanne Mae Parkhurst, Jan. 23, 1943; children: Gary Daniell, Donna Jeanne, Jeffrey Alan, Julie Anne. BCE, Ohio State U., 1950. Staff engr. Ohio Dept. Hwys., Columbus, 1949-52; maintenence engr. Ohio Turnpike Commn., Berea, 1952-60; assoc. editor Pub. Works Publs., Ridgewood, N.J., 1960-63; ptnr. Byrd, Tallamy, MacDonald & Lewis, Falls Church, Va., 1963-72; sr. v.p., mgr. Byrd, Tallamy, MacDonald & Lewis div. Wilbur Smith & Assocs., Falls Church, 1972-84; interim dir. Strategic Hwy. Rsch. Program, Washington, 1984-86; pvt. practice Washington, 1986-99; ret. Chmn. group 3 coun. Transp. Rsch. Bd., Washington, 1972-76, chmn. overview com.; ex-officio governing bd. NRC, Washington, 1989-95; mem. bd. cons. Eno Found., Westport, Conn., 1986-89; mem. report rev. com. NRC, 1997—. Co-author: Street and Highway Maintenance Manual: American Public Works Association, 1985; assoc. editor: Handbook of Highway Engring., 1975; chmn. pub. affairs coun. Am. Assn. Engring. Socs., 1992. Chmn. Fairfax County (Va.) Human Rights Commn., 1978-79; pres. Fairfax County C. of C., 1975-76; bd. dirs. Hospice of Carolina Foothills, Inc. Recipient Disting. Alumnus award Ohio State U. Coll. Engring., 1978, Roy W. Crum award Transp. Rsch. Bd., Washington, 1986, P.D. McLean Meml. award Road Gang, Washington, 1989, Disting. Lectr. award, 1998, Transp. Rsch Bd. Fellow ASCE (pres. nat. capital sect. Washington 1976-77, nat. bd. dirs. N.Y.C. 1979-82, Wilbur S. Smith award 1985, Francis C. Turner Lecture award 1995); mem. NAE, Am. Pub. Works Assn., Univ. Club (Washington), Tryon (N.C.) Country Club, Rotary Club. Republican. Congregationalist. Avocations: golf, bridge. Personal E-mail: lgbyrd@alltel.net.

BYRD, LORELEE, state treasurer; b. Bassett, Nebr., Apr. 14, 1956; m. Scott Byrd, 1976 (div.); children: Amy, Ryan. Auditor Mut. Protective Ins. and Mut. Ins.; aide to state and fed. lawmakers; unclaimed property admin., 1995; dep. state treas., 1995—2001; state treas., 2001—. Past mem. Rep. State Ctrl. Com., Douglas County Rep. Ctrl. Com.; past pres. Metro Right to Life; past mem. bd. dirs. Nebr. Right to Life; aide to Senator Sharon Beck Omaha; aide to Owen Elmer Indianola; aide to U.S. rep. Doug Bereuter Nebr. Office: PO Box 94788 Lincoln NE 68509-4788 E-mail: lbyrd@treasurer.org.

BYRD, MARC ROBERT, display designer; b. Flint, Mich., May 14, 1954; s. Robert Lee and Cynthia Ann (Poland) B.; m. Bonnie Jill Berlin, Nov. 25, 1975 (div. June 1977). Student, Ea. Mich. U., 1972-75; grad., Am. Floral Sch., Chgo., 1978; BS, U. Redlands, 2002, MA in Mgmt., 2004. Gen. mgr., dir. floral shops; designer Olive Tree Florist, Palm Desert, Calif., 1978-79, Kayo's Flower Fashions, Palm Springs, 1979-80; owner, designer Village Florist, Inc., Palm Springs, 1980-85; pres. Mon Ami Florist, Inc., Beverly Hills, 1986-87; gen. mgr. Silverio's, Santa Monica, 1987; gen. mgr., hotel florist, creative dir. Four Seasons Hotel, Beverly Hills, 1988-90; pres. Marc Fredericks, Inc., Beverly Hills, 1990-97; event florist Marc Byrd of Floral Works, L.A., 1997—2002, Marc Byrd Holiday Decor, 2002—. Author: Celebrity Flowers, 1989. Del., Dem. County Conv., 1972, Dem. County Conv., 1972, Dem. State Conv., 1972, Dem. Nat. Conv., 1972. Mem. Soc. Am. Florists, So. Calif. Floral Assn., Desert Mus., Robinson's Gardens, U. Redlands Alumni Assn. (bd. dirs.), Whitehead Leadership Soc. (bd. dirs.) Democrat. Episcopalian. Avocations: skiing, tennis, community service. Office Fax: 323-962-9275. Personal E-mail: marcbyrd@earthlink.net.

BYRD, MICKEY JOE, secondary school educator, singer, composer; b. Vienna, Mo., May 8, 1957; s. Curtis Roy and Martha Priscilla Byrd; m. Deborah Gwenn Richardson, Dec. 29, 1979; children: Elizabeth Kaye, Curtis Glendon. BA in social studies summa cum laude, Sch. Ozarks, 1980. Tchr., coach Maries R-1 HS, Vienna, Mo., 1980—. Musician: (albums) No Frills, 1995 (Billboard Songwriting Achievement award, 1995), singer recorded 6 CD's songs. Vol. coach girls softball and basketball, Vienna, 1981—; vol. remodeler Friends of Maries County Libr., 1996. Named Most Influential Tchr., U. Mo., Columbia, 1991—92; recipient Tchr. Appreciation award, Mo. Scholars Acad., 1991. Mem.: Nashville Songwriters Assn. Internat., Mo. State Tchrs. Assn. Achievements include recorded 6 CD's including CD single "The Chance/Gentle Souls" to benefit Spl. Olympics Mo. Home: 503 N Main Vienna MO 65582 Office: Maries R-1 HS Hwy 42 E Vienna MO 65582 Office Phone: 573-422-3363.

BYRD, MILTON BRUCE, academic administrator; b. Boston, Jan. 29, 1922; s. Max Joseph and Rebecca (Malkiel) B.; m. Susanne J. Schwerin, Aug. 30, 1953 (dec. 2005); children: Deborah, Leslie, David. AB cum laude, Boston U., 1948, MA, 1949; PhD, U. Wis., 1953; postgrad. (fellow), U. Mich., 1961-62. Teaching asst. English U. Wis., 1949-53; instr., asst. prof. English Ind. U., 1953-58; asst. prof., assoc. prof. humanities So. Ill. U., 1958-62, head div. humanities, 1958-60, supr. acad. advisement, 1959-60, asso. dean, 1960- 62; v.p. acad. affairs No. Mich. U., 1962-66; pres. Chgo. State U., 1966-74; provost Fla. Internat. U., 1974-78; pres. Adams State Coll., Alamosa, Colo., 1978-81; v.p. corp. devel. Frontier Cos., Anchorage, 1981-85; pres. Charter Coll., 1985—. Bd. dirs Chgo. Council for Urban Edn., Union for Experimenting Colls. and Univs., Am. Assn. State Colls. and Univs., Resource Devel. Council Alaska, Alaska Commn. Econ. Edn.; v.p. Common Sense for Alaska, Inc.; former pres. Alaska Support Industry Alliance; pres. Alaska World Affairs Coun. Author: (with Arnold L. Goldsmith) Publication Guide for Literary and Linguistic Scholars, 1958; contbr. to profl. jours. Vice chmn. Alaska Commn. on Postsecondary Edn. Served with USAAF, 1943—46. Mem. MLA, Nat. Council Tchrs. English, Coll. English Assn., Am. Studies Assn., AAUP, Fla. Assn. Univ. Adminstrs. (former pres.), Rocky Mountain Athletic Conf. (former pres.), Assn. for Higher Edn., Pub. Relations Soc. Am., NEA, Alaska Press Club, Mich. Edn. Assn., Phi Beta Kappa, Phi Delta Kappa. Clubs: Rotary. Office: # 120 2221 E Northern Lights Blvd Anchorage AK 99508-4143 Business E-Mail: mbyrd@chartercollege.edu.

BYRD, ROBERT CARLYLE, senator; b. N. Wilkesboro, NC, Nov. 20, 1917; s. Cornelius Sale and Ada (Kirby) B.; m. Erma Ora James, May 29, 1937; children: Mona Carole (Mrs. Mohammad Fatemi), Marjorie Ellen (Mrs. John Moore). Student, Beckley Coll., Concord Coll., Morris Harvey Coll., 1950-51, Marshall U., 1951-52, BA in Polit. sci., 1994; JD cum laude, Am. U., 1963. Mem. W.Va. Ho. of Reps., 1947-50, 83d-85th Congresses from 6th W.Va. dist., W.Va. Senate, 1951-52; U.S. senator from W.Va., 1959—; senate majority leader, 1977-80, 87-88; senate minority leader, 1981-86. Mem. appropriations com., armed svcs. com., rules and adminstrn. budget com., senate Dem. steering and coord. com. Author: The Senate, 1789-1989, 4 vols., 1989-94, The Senate of the Roman Republic: Addresses on the History of Roman Constitutionalism, 1995, Losing America, 2004; contbr. articles to profl. jours. Recipient Disting. Svc award Radio and TV News Dirs. Assn. 1986; named Most Influential Mem. U.S. Senate, U.S. News and World Report Poll, 1979, Legislator of Yr. Nat. Coal Assn., 1986, West Virginian of the 20th Century, 2001. Mem. Country Music Assn. (hon.) Lodges: Masons (33 degree). Democrat. Baptist. Office: US Senate 311 Hart Senate Ofc Bldg Washington DC 20510-0001 also: 300 Virginia St Ste 2630 Charleston WV 25301*

BYRD, STEPHEN FRED, human resource consultant; b. Charleston, S.C., June 12, 1928; s. Paul Fred and Dorothy B.; m. Margaret A. McAulay, Apr. 15, 1955; children: Owen, Susan. Student, CCNY, 1945-48; LLB, N.Y. Law Sch., 1951. Bar: N.Y. 1951. Corp. indsl. rels. rep. Pan Am. Airways, 1957-62, Sinclair Oil Corp., 1962-64; v.p. employee rels. indsl. chems. div. Allied Chem. Corp., 1964-68; v.p. indsl. rels. and pers. Internat. Nickel Co., Ltd., 1968-72; sr. v.p. human resources Schering-Plough Corp., Madison, N.J., 1973-88; cons. Right Assocs., Parsippany, N.J., 1988-90. Author: Front Line Supervisors Labor Relations Handbook, 1962, Management Strategy in Collective Bargaining, 1964. Bd. dirs. United Fund Morris County, N.J., Big Bros. Morris County, Morristown YMCA, 1962-63; chmn. Madison council Boy Scouts Am., 1975-76; trustee Drew U., Madison, N.J., 1976-80. With AUS, 1952-53, Korea. Mem. Indsl. Relations Research Assn., N.Y. Law Sch. Alumni Assn. Home and Office: 23 Academy Rd Madison NJ 07940-2001 Office Phone: 973-822-0507. E-mail: byrd@pmbstudio.com.

BYRD, THOMAS RUSSELL, medical educator; b. Palo Alto, Calif., Mar. 9, 1942; s. Oliver Erasmus and Jennie Christine (Sonnichsen) B.; children: Patrick, Kristina, Jaime Lynn, Jenna. AA, Menlo Coll., 1961; BS in Health Sci., Calif. State U., San Jose, 1963; MA in Health Edn., Stanford U., 1965. Cert. state c.c. tchg. credential Calif. Tchr. Palo Alto (Calif.) Unified Sch. Dist., 1966-68; prof. De Anza Coll., Cupertino, Calif., 1968—2002. Mem. free med. treatment teams Interplast (Stanford U.), 1976—80, fundraiser, 1976—86; mobile tng. instr. Transp. Security Adminstrn., 2002—04. Author: Medical Readings on First Aid, 1971, Medical Readings on Counseling and Psychological Services, 1971, Medical Readings on Family Life, 1971, Medical Readings on Vision, Speech and Hearing, 1971, Medical Readings on Nutrition, 1971, Medical Readings on Heroin, 1972, Medical Readings on the Heart, 1973, Medical Readings in Health Sciences, 1974, In Case of Emergency, 1976, Preventive Health Concepts, 1976, Health Sciences: Selected Medical Readings, 1979, Addictive Awareness, 1990, Lives Written in Sand, 1997. Vol. instr., trainer in lic. oxygen adminstrn., AED, bio/hazard protection, CPRFPR and emergency response ARC, 1966—; vol. health caregiver live-in, 1995—2003. Mem.: Calif. Assn. Alcohol and Drug Abuse Educators (lic. educator), U.S. Masters Swimming (nat. champ long distance open water swim Capitola to Santa Cruz 6 mile 1998, All Am. honours for long distance open water swimming competition 1998). Democrat. Avocations: landscaping, gardening, open water swimming, writing. Home: 1533 Madrono Ave Palo Alto CA 94306-1016 E-mail: t.byrd@sbcglobal.net.

BYRD, WARREN EDGAR, II, lawyer; b. Bogalusa, La., Dec. 28, 1950; s. H. Warren and Martha Helen (Conner) B.; m. Arlene Dianne Calcote, June 16, 1974; children: Lauren Elizabeth, Matthew Warren. BS, La. State U., 1973, JD, 1978. Bar: La. 1978, U.S. Dist. Ct. (mid., ea. and we. dists.) La. 1978, U.S. Ct. Appeals (5th cir.) 1978. Law clk. Judge E. Gordon West U.S. Dist. Judge, Baton Rouge, La., 1978-80; assoc. Due, Dodson & de Gravelles, Baton Rouge, 1980-81, Wray, Robinson & Kracht, Baton Rouge, 1981-83; asst. atty. gen. La. Dept. Justice, Baton Rouge, 1983-88; assoc. Adams and Reese, Baton Rouge, 1988—, ptnr., 1992—. Speaker Nat. Bus. Inst., Baton Rouge, 1991-92, Fed. Publs. Seminar, New Orleans, 1993, Exec. Enterpriser Seminar, New Orleans, 1994, environ. law seminar La. State U., Baton Rouge, 1997. Bd. dirs. Audubon Coun. Girl Scouts, Baton Rouge, 1986-94, 3d v.p. 1990-91 (Thanks Badge 1990, honor award 1990, Vol. award 1997); soccer referee USSF, NISOA, LHSAA. Named to, La. State U. Track and Field Ofcls. Hall of Fame. Mem. Fed. Bar Assn. (Baton Rouge chpt. treas. 1980-86), La. State Bar Assn. (environ. law sect. coun. 1997, v.p. 2003—), Baton Rouge Bar Assn. (ADR com. 1990—, chmn. com. 1993-95), La. State U. Track and Field Ofcls. Assn., Greater Baton Rouge C. of C. (govtl. fiscal affairs com.). Avocations: running, soccer referee, weightlifting, track. Office: Adams and Reese Bank One Ctr N Twr 19th Fl 451 Florida St Baton Rouge LA 70801-1700

BYRD, WYATT, microbiologist, researcher; b. Panama City, Fla., June 23, 1958; s. Elizabeth and Isaac Byrd; m. Dagmar Beinert, Sept. 18, 1962; children: Lewis, Fiona. PhD, U. of Ga., 1985—91. Rsch. asst. Walter Reed Army Inst. of Rsch., Silver Spring, Md., 1998—; rsch. assoc. Miami U., Oxford, Ohio, 1993—97. Mem.: Am. Soc. for Microbiology (assoc.). Home: 20144 Timber Oak Lane Germantown MD 20874 Office: Walter Reed Army Inst Rsch 503 Robert Grant Ave Silver Spring MD 20910 E-mail: wyatt.byrd@na.amedd.army.mil.

BYRD-BENNETT, BARBARA, school system administrator; m. Bruce Bennett; 1 child, Nailah Bennett. BA in English, L.I. U.; M in English Lit., NYU; MEd, Pace U.; Doctorate (hon.), John Carroll U., Notre Dame Coll. Elem. sch. tchr., Manhattan and Bronx, NY, 1965—75; adj. assoc. prof. Coll. of New Rochelle, 1975—91; spl. asst. to Manhattan Supt. for Curriculum, 1982—84; priin. PS 36, Manhattan, NY, 1984—92; adj. assoc. prof. CCNY, 1989—93; dep. exed. dir. for instrn. and profl. devel. N.Y.C. Schs., 1992—94; supt. Chancellor's Dist., N.Y.C. Sch. Sys., 1996—98; CEO Cleve. Mcpl. Sch. Dist., 1998—. Apptd. to edn. com. States Nat. Ctr. for Ednl. Accountability; apptd. to vis. com. Mandel Sch. Applied Scis. Recipient Cleve. Bus. Woman of Yr., 2001. Mem.: Urban Supts. Assn. Am. (v.p.), Internat. Women's Forum. Office: Cleve Mcpl Sch Dist 1380 E Sixth St Cleveland OH 44114

BYRKETT, GARY LEE, information technology manager; b. Indianapolis, Aug. 21, 1950; s. Robert Harry and Betty Lou Byrkett; m. Sharon Kay Arvin, Oct. 20, 1984. BS in Interdisciplinary Engring., Purdue U., 1972. Plant mgr. St. Francis Hosp. and Health Ctrs., Beech Grove, Ind., 1975—. Chmn. Ind. Coun. on Ind. Living, Indpls., 1996—99; co-chmn. Accessing Tech. Through Awareness Ind., Indpls., 1991—92; pres. Ctrl. Ind. chpt. Muscular Dystrophy Assn., Indpls., 1981—85; bd. mem. Indpls. Resource Ctr. For Independant Living, 1990—97. Recipient Outstanding Achievment ward, Muscular Dystrophy Assn., 1997. Mem.: ASME, Assn. of Energy Engineers, Assn. of Facility Engineers, Nat. Fire Protection Assn. Methodist. Avocations: motor sports, jazz. Office: St Francis Hospl and Health Ctrs 1600 Albany Beech Grove IN 46107 E-mail: gary.byrkett@ssfhs.org.

BYRNE, CAROL ANN, librarian, secondary school educator; b. N.Y.C., June 2, 1947; d. Charles P. and Agnes M. (Wise) Byrne; m. Peter A. Greenbaum, Feb. 10, 1968 (div. 1996); children: Peter A., James B. AAS, Suffolk County Community Coll., 1983; BA, SUNY, Stony Brook, 1984; MLS, CW Post U., 1989. Cert. tchr., libr. Libr. Islip (N.Y.) Pub. Libr., 1987-89, Deer Park (N.Y.) Pub. Libr., 1989—; libr., tchr. Deer Park Schs., 1989—. Pub. libr. Half Hollow Hills Libr., Dix Hills and Melville, N.Y., 1991-95; liaison mem. Bd. Coop. Ednl. Svcs. Libr., Lindenhurst, N.Y., 1989—, mem. coun., 1992—; workshop leader Libr. Conf., 1992; presenter in field. Co-author: Secondary School Library Media Curriculum, 1990; contbr. articles to libr. jours. Active W.K. Vanderbilt Hist. Soc., Oakdale, N.Y., 1979—; mem. restoration com. Dowling Coll., Oakdale, 1986—; high sch. coord., chmn. Human Understanding and Growth Seminar. Mem. ALA, N.Y. Libr. Assn., L.I. Sch. Media Assocs., Inc., Sch. Libr. Media Specialists, Suffolk County Libr. Assn., Suffolk South Shore Lions Club (rec. sec. 1999—), Phi Theta Kappa, Alpha Beta Gamma. Democrat. Home: 171 Irish Ln Islip Terrace NY 11752-2109 Office: Deer Park High Sch 30 Rockaway Ave Deer Park NY 11729-3298

BYRNE, GABRIEL, actor; b. Dublin, May 12, 1950; m. Ellen Barkin, 1988 (div. 1993); children: Jack, Romy. Actor: (films) On a Paving Stone Mounted, 1978, The Outsider, 1979, Excalibur, 1981, The Keep, 1983, Hannah K., 1983, Defence of the Realm, 1985, Gothic, 1985, Lionheart, 1987, Hello, Again, 1987, Siesta, 1987, Julia and Julia, 1988, A Soldier's Tale, 1988, The Courier, 1988, Miller's Crossing, 1990, Shipwrecked, 1991, Dark Obsession, 1991, Cool World, 1992, Point of No Return, 1993, A Dangerous Woman, 1993, A Simple Twist of Fate, 1994, Trial by Jury, 1994, Little Women, 1994, The Usual Suspects, 1995, Frankie Starlight, 1995, Past into Present, 1996, Mad Dog Time, 1996, Dr. Hagard's Disease, 1996, Somebody is Waiting, 1996, The End of Violence, 1997, Smillas Sense of Snow, 1997, The Man in the Iron Mask, 1998, Polish Wedding, 1998, Enemy of the State, 1998, This Is the Sean, 1998, Quest for Camelot (voice), 1998, The Brylcreem Boys, 1998, Stigmata, 1999, End of Days, 1999, Madigan Men, 2000, Ghost Ship, 2002, Shade, 2003, Vanity Fair, 2004, P.S., 2004, El Puente de San Luis Ray, 2004, Assault on Precinct 13, 2005; (TV movies) Wagner, 1983, Reflections, 1983, Mussolini: The Untold Story, 1985, Christopher Columbus, 1985, Buffalo Girls, 1995, (TV series) The Riordan's, Bracken; actor, co-exec. prodr. Spider, 2002; actor, assoc. prodr.: (films) Into the West, 1993; co-exec. prodr.: (films) In the Name of the Father, 1993; actor, exec. prodr. Last of the High Kings, 1996, Smilla's Sense of Snow, 1997, Weapons of Mass Destruction, 1996, Toby's Story, 1998, Polish Wedding, 1998, This is the Sea, 1998, The Man in the Iron Mask, 1998, (voice) Quest for Camelot, 1998, An Ideal Husband, 1999; dir. End of Violence, 1996, The Lark in the Clear Air, 1996; actor, writer Draiocht, 1996; narrator Irish Cinema: Ourselves Alone?, 1997; author: (book) Pictures in My Head, 2001. Office: United Talent Agy 9560 Wilshire Blvd Ste 500 Beverly Hills CA 90212*

BYRNE, GEORGE MELVIN, physician; b. Aug. 1, 1933; s. Carlton and Esther (Smith) B.; m. Joan Stecher, July 14, 1956; children: Kathryne, Michael, David; m. Margaret C. Smith, Dec. 18, 1982; m. Barbara Barrett, May 19, 2001. BA, Occidental Coll., 1958; MD, U. So. Calif., 1962. Intern Huntington Meml. Hosp., Pasadena, Calif., 1962-63, resident, 1963-64; family practice So. Calif. Permanente Med. Group, 1964-81; physician-in-charge Pasadena Med. Office, 1966-81; asst. dir. family practice residency Kaiser Found. Hosp., L.A., 1971-73; clin. instr. emergency medicine Sch. Medicine U. So. Calif., 1973-80; v.p. East Ridge Co., 1983-84, sec., 1984; dir. Alan Johnson Porsche Audi, Inc., 1974-82, sec., 1974-77, v.p., 1978-82. Bd. dirs. Kaiser-Permanente Mgmt. Assn., 1976-77; mem. regional mgmt. com. So. Calif. Lung Assn., 1976-77; mem. pres.'s cir. Occidental Coll., L.A. Drs. Symphony Orch., 1975-80; mem. profl. sect. Am. Diabetes Assn. Fellow Am. Acad. Family Physicians (charter); mem. AMA, Calif. Med. Assn., L.A. County Med. Assn., Calif. Acad. Family Physicians, Internat. Horn Soc., Quarter Century Wireless Assn., Am. Radio Relay League (Pub. Svc. award), Sierra (life), So. Calif. Dx Club. Home: 528 Meadowview Dr La Canada Flintridge CA 91011-2816 Personal E-mail: GMByrne@aol.com.

BYRNE, GERARD ANTHONY (GERRY), publishing company executive; b. N.Y.C., Apr. 27, 1944; s. Thomas Edward and Eileen (Reilly) B.; m. Elizabeth Julia Daly, Dec. 6, 1969; children: Megan, Gavin. BA in Econs., Fordham U., 1966. Advt. sales rep. N.Y. Daily News, N.Y.C., 1969-73, Advt. Age, N.Y.C., 1973-77, internat. sales dir., 1977-80, ea. sales mgr. N.Y.C., 1980-82; pub., v.p. Electronic Media, N.Y.C., 1982-84; v.p./pub. Crain's N.Y. Bus., N.Y.C., 1984-87; v.p., dir. corp. communications Crain Communications, N.Y.C., 1987-88; sr. v.p. corp. planning and internat. devel. Act III Pub., N.Y.C., 1988-89; pub. Variety, N.Y.C., 1990-92, v.p., dir. pub. ops., 1993-95; group v.p., pub. Daily Variety and Weekly Variety, N.Y.C., 1996—2000; v.p., group pub. Variety, Inc., N.Y.C., 1997—2000; pres., CEO Stagebill Media, 2000—02; CEO Gerry Byrne Media Ptnrs. LLC, 2002—. Sr. advisor Parade Mag. Bd. dirs. African Med. Relief Found., Operation Smile Internat., Cath. Youth Orgn., N.Y.C., Am. Mus. Moving Image, The Intrepid Mus. Found., The Westhampton Beach Performing Arts Ctr., Am. Friend of the Nat. Film and TV Sch., London, Fisher House Found., Vets. Advantage, Reisenbach Found., NYC Police Mus., Armory Found., Creative Coalition; chmn. Quills Literacy Found. Capt. USMC, 1966-69, Vietnam. Recipient combat action ribbon, Navy achievement medal, Show East Salah Hassanein Humanitarian award, 1996. Mem. Internat. Radio and TV Soc., N.Y. Athletic Club, VFW, Friendly Sons of St. Patrick. Roman Catholic. Avocations: fishing, tennis, photography, skiing, golf. Home: 6 Peter Cooper Rd New York NY 10010-6701 Office Phone: 212-450-7063. E-mail: gerrybyrnemp@aol.com.

BYRNE, GRANVILLE BLAND, III, lawyer; b. San Antonio, Jan. 26, 1952; s. Granville Bland and Mary (Dowling) B.; divorced; children: Peyton Smith, Fulton Buckner; m. Monique Renée Wise, 1999; 1 child, Monique Renée-Christienne. AB, U. N.C., Chapel Hill, 1974; JD, Harvard U., 1978. Bar: Ga. 1978, U.S. Dist. Ct. (no. dist.) Ga. 1978, U.S. Ct. Appeals (5th cir.) 1978, U.S. Ct. Appeals (11th cir.) 1981. Assoc. Swift, Currie, McGhee & Hiers, Atlanta, 1978-84, ptnr., 1984-94; prin. Byrne, Eldridge, Moore & Davis, P.C., Atlanta, 1994—99, Byrne, Moore & Davis, PC, Atlanta, 1999—2002, Byrne & Davis, PC, Atlanta, 2003, Byrne, Davis & Hicks, PC, Atlanta, 2003—. Bd. dirs. Cagle's, Inc. Elder, mem. session 1st Presbyn. Ch. Atlanta, 1993-96, 99-2002. Mem. ABA, Ga. Bar Assn., Atlanta Bar Assn. Democrat. Presbyterian. Home: 3555 Castlegate Dr NW Atlanta GA 30327-2601 Office: Byrne Davis & Hicks PC 3340 Peachtree Rd NE Atlanta GA 30326-1000 Office Phone: 404-266-7260. Personal E-mail: gbb3@bellsouth.net.

BYRNE, JAMES FREDERICK, banker; b. Fairmont, N.C., July 30, 1931; m. Daphne Martin, July 22, 1955; children— Paula Jean, Daphne Ann, Laura BS, Wake Forest U., 1953; MBA, U. N.C., 1959. Ptnr. Byrne-Floyd Realty, Fairmont, N.C., 1961-80; v.p., city exec. So. Nat. Bank, Fairmont, 1963-69, mgr. master charge Lumberton, N.C., 1969-71, v.p., dir. mktg., 1971-77, sr. v.p., dir. customer services, 1977-83, exec. v.p., 1983, exec. v.p., dir. retail banking, 1985-89, sr. exec. v.p., chief adminstrv. officer, 1989-94. Mem. endowment bd. Pembroke State U., NC, 1985—87, chmn. libr. bd., NC, 1995—96. Pres. Am. Lung Assn. of N.C., Wilmington, 1971, Raleigh, 1972, N.C. rep. dir., N.Y., 1977-89; nat. v.p. Am. Lung Assn., 1989. Recipient Vol. of Yr. award, Am. Lung Assn. of N.C., 1972—90, Nat. Humanitarian award, 1993. Mem. Bank Mktg. Assn., N.C. Bankers Assn., Shrine Club (pres. 1996-97), Rotary (pres. 1968), Masons. Home: 905 Dogwood Dr Fairmont NC 28340-2115

BYRNE, JOHN EDWARD (JEB BYRNE), retired federal official; b. N.Y.C., Jan. 15, 1925; s. Harry Theodore and Mary Elizabeth (Whelen) B.; m. Beverly Ann McKinley, Mar. 31, 1951; children— Peter J., David F., John P., Michael T. BA, Marquette U., 1949; MA, George Washington U., 1973, PhD, 1987. News service corr. UPI, Milw., 1949-50, Albany, N.Y., 1951, Portland, Maine, 1951-56, Augusta, Maine, 1956-58; gov.'s press sec., state promotion ofcl. State of Maine, Augusta, 1959-60; exec. GSA, Washington, 1961-80; dir. fed. register Nat. Archives and Records Adminstrn., Washington, 1980-88. Fulbright scholar Alexander Turnbull Libr., Wellington, New Zealand, 1989. Served to 2d lt. USAAF, 1943-45 Roman Catholic. Home: 2104 Marthas Rd Alexandria VA 22307-1823

BYRNE, JOHN MICHAEL, energy and environmental engineering educator; b. Chgo., Nov. 2, 1949; s. Michael Thomas and Mabel Victoria (Cranford) B.; m. Elizabeth Maria Garey, Aug. 9, 1975; children: Brian, Tara. BA in Econs., U. Del., 1971, MA, 1973, PhD in Urban Affairs and Pub. Policy,

1980. Asst. prof. Coll. Urban Affairs and Pub. Policy, U. Del., Newark, 1982-86, assoc. prof., 1986-92, prof., 1992—2004, dist. prof. of public policy, 2004—, dir. Energy Policy Rsch. Group, 1981-84, dir. Ctr. for Energy and Environ. Policy, 1984—, chair Urban Affairs and Pub. Policy grad. program, 1992-96. Apptd. environ. policy advisor Korea Nat. Assembly, 1998—; co-exec. dir. Joint Inst. for a Sustainable Energy and Environ. Future, 1999—. Co-editor: Energy and Cities, 1985, The Politics of Energy R&D, 1988, Energy and Environment: The Policy Challenge, 1992, Governing the Atom: The Politics of Risk, 1996, Environmental Justice, 2002, Energy Revolution, 2004, Bull. Sci., Tech., and Soc., 1995—; contbg. author: 2d and 3d Assessment Reports of the Intergovtl. Panel on Climate Change, 1995—. Bd. dirs. Urban Environ. Ctr., Environ. Market Solutions, Inc., Internat. Solar Cities Initiative. Grantee ESMAP/World Bank, 1990-91, U.S. Dept. Energy/Nat. Renewable Energy Lab., 1991-2001, UNIDEL Found., 1992, U.S. EPA, 1994, 97-2001, Asia Found., 1995, Inst. Internat. Edn., 1996-97, W. Alton Jones Found., 1997-2002, U.S. Dept. Energy, 2002—, Blue Moon Fund, 2003—, Beyond Petroleum Found., 2004—; recipient Fulbright Sr. Lectr./Rschr. award, 1995. Mem.: Internat. Assn. Sci., Tech. and Soc. (bd. dirs.), Nat. Assn. Sci., Tech. and Soc. (adv. bd. 1991—), IEEE Social Implications of Tech. Affiliate. Avocations: music, woodworking, hiking. Office: U Del Ctr Energy & Environ Policy Newark DE 19716-7381 Office Phone: 302-831-8405.

BYRNE, JOHN VINCENT, higher education consultant; b. Hempstead, NY, May 9, 1928; s. Frank E. and Kathleen (Barry) B.; m. Shirley O'Connor, Nov. 26, 1954; children: Donna, Lisa, Karen, Steven. AB, Hamilton Coll., 1951, JD (hon.), 1994; MA, Columbia U., 1953; PhD, U. So. Calif., 1957. Research geologist Humble Oil & Refinery Co., Houston, 1957-60; assoc. prof. Oreg. State U., Corvallis, 1960-66, prof. oceanography, 1966—, chmn. dept., 1968-72, dean Sch. Oceanography, 1972-76, acting dean research, 1976-77, dean research, 1977-80, v.p. for research and grad. studies, 1980-81, pres., 1984-95; adminstr. NOAA, Washington, 1981-84; U.S. commr. Internat. Whaling Commn., 1982—85; pres. Oreg. State U., 1984-95; higher edn. cons. Corvallis, 1996—. Program dir. oceanography NSF, 1966-67; exec. dir. Kellogg Commn. on Future of State and Land Grant Univs., 1996-2000; dir. Harbor Br. Ocean Inst., Oregon Coast Aquarium. Recipient Carter teaching award Oreg. State U., 1964. Fellow AAAS, Geol. Soc. Am.; mem. Geol. Soc. Am., Am. Geophys. Union, Sigma Xi, Chi Psi. Home: 3190 NW Deer Run St Corvallis OR 97330-3107 Office: Autzen House 811 SW Jefferson Ave Corvallis OR 97333-4506 Office Phone: 541-737-3542. Business E-Mail: john.byrne@oregonstate.edu.

BYRNE, KATHARINE CRANE, lawyer; b. Chgo., Dec. 31, 1958; d. William Patrick and Jane M. (Burke) B.; 1 child, William Byrne Vogt. BA, St. Mary's Coll., Notre Dame, Ind., 1980; JD, Loyola U., 1988. Bar: Ill. 1988, U.S. Dist. Ct. (no. dist.) Ill. 1988, U.S. Ct. Appeals (7th cir.) 1991, Fed. Trial Bar (no. dist.) Ill. 1992. Event planner Gaper's Caterers, Chgo., 1980-84; coord. Jane Byrne Campaign Com., Chgo., 1985-87; law clk. Cooney & Conway, Chgo., 1987-88, atty., 1988—. Lectr. Andrews 8th Ann. Asbestos Litigation Conf., 1996, 97, 99, 02. Author: Premises Liability, 1994. Lectr. Ill. Inst. for Continuing Legal Edn., Chgo., 1991; pres. Beautiful Chgo. (Ill.) Commn., 1994. Mem. ATLA, Ill. Trial Lawyers Assn. (lectr. seminar 1995, 97, 98, 00, 01, 02, 03, 04, 05, bd. mgrs. 1998—), Celtic Lawyers. Democrat. Roman Catholic. Home: 550 E Pearson St Chicago IL 60611-2051 Office: Cooney & Conway 120 N La Salle St Chicago IL 60602-2424 Office Phone: 312-236-6166. Business E-Mail: kbyrne@cooneyconway.com.

BYRNE, MICHAEL JOSEPH, manufacturing executive; b. Apr. 3, 1928; s. Michael Joseph and Edith (Lueken) Byrne; m. Eileen Kelly, June 27, 1953; children: Michael Joseph, Nancy, James, Thomas, Patrick, Terrence. BSC in mktg., Loyola U., Chgo., 1952. Sales engr. Emery Industries, Inc., Cin., 1952—59; with Pennsalt Chem. Corp., Phila., 1959—60; pres. Oakton Cleaners, Inc., Skokie, Ill., 1960—70, Datatax Inc., Skokie, Ill., 1970—74, Midwest Synthetic Lubrication Products, 1978—, Pure Water Sys., 1984—, Superior Tax Svc., 1984—. With U.S. Army, 1946—48. Mem.: AIM, Toastmasters Internat., VFW, Alpha Kappa Psi. Home: PO Box 916 Prospect Heights IL 60070-0916 Personal E-mail: mypaintlid@comcast.net.

BYRNE, NOEL THOMAS, sociologist, educator; b. San Francisco, May 11, 1943; s. Joseph Joshua and Naomi Pearl (Denison) B.; m. Dale W. Elrod, Aug. 6, 1989. BA in Sociology, Sonoma State Coll., 1971; MA in Sociology, Rutgers U., 1975, PhD in Sociology, 1987. Instr. sociology Douglass Coll., Rutgers U., New Brunswick, N.J., 1974-76, Hartnell Coll., Salinas, Calif., 1977-78; from lectr. to assoc. prof. dept. mgmt. Sonoma State U., Rohnert Park, Calif., 1978-94, chmn. dept. of mgmt., 1990-91, from. assoc. prof. to prof. sociology dept., 1994—, chmn. dept. sociology, 1997—2002; cons. prof. Emile Durkheim Inst. for Advanced Study, Grand Cayman, B.W.I., 1990-93. Chair of faculty Sonoma State U., 2002—03, chair acad. senate, 2002—03. Contbr. articles and revs. to profl. lit. Recipient Dell Pub. award Rutgers U. Grad. Sociology Program, 1976, Louis Bevier fellow, 1977-78. Mem. AAAS, Am. Sociol. Assn., Pacific Sociol. Assn., N.Y. Acad. Sci., Soc. for Study Symbolic Interaction (rev. editor Jour. 1980-83), Soc. for Study Social Problems, Commonwealth Club. Democrat. Home: 4773 Ross Rd Sebastopol CA 95472-2114 Office: Sonoma State U Dept Sociology Rohnert Park CA 94928 Office Phone: 707-664-2517. Business E-Mail: noel.byrne@sonoma.edu.

BYRNE, RICHARD HILL, counselor, educator; b. Lancaster, Pa., Aug. 3, 1915; s. Jacob Hill and Mary Deborah (Allwein) B.; m. Magdalene Antoinette Wardell, June 12, 1954; children— Christopher, Mary, Matthew, Peter AB, Franklin and Marshall Coll., 1938; MA, Columbia U., 1947, Ed.D., 1952. Tchr. several sch. systems, Lancaster County, Pa., 1939-42; counselor Allegany County Schs., Cumberland, Md., 1949-50; state guidance supr. State of N.H., Concord, 1950-51; assoc., then prof., chmn. counseling dept. U. Md., College Park, 1951-82, prof. emeritus, 1983—, resident grad. prof. Upper Heyford, Eng., 1982-84, Boston U., Germany, 1984-86. Cons. U.S. Dept. Labor, Washington, 1964-68; cons. in guidance numerous sch. systems, Md., Pa., Va., 1951-82; dir. interprofl. research ctr. on pupil services, College Park, Md., 1963-68 Author: The School Counselor, 1963, Guidance: A Behavioral Approach, 1977, Becoming a Master Counselor, 1994. Served to capt. U.S. Army, 1942-46, ETO Mem. Am. Psychol. Assn., Md. Personnel and Guidance Assn. (1st pres. 1957-58) Home: 1390 Ventnor Ave Tarpon Springs FL 34689-2731

BYRNE, SUSAN M., investment company executive; Asst. treas. GAF Corp.; founder, chmn., CEO Westwood Mgmt. Group, Dallas, 1983—. Investment advisor, pres. The Gabelli Westwood Funds; bd. mem. U. Tex. Investment Mgmt. Co.; trustee City Dallas Employees Retirement Fund, Southwestern Med. Found.; chair investment com. First Presbyn. Ch. Dallas Found.; mem. Tex. Govs. Bus. Coun.; mem., former bd. mem. Com. of 200. Mem.: Dallas Soc. Securities Analysts, N.Y. Soc. Securities Analysts, Internat. Women's Forum (bd. mem. Dallas chpt.). Office: Westwood Holdings Group Inc Ste 1300 300 Crescent Ct Dallas TX 75201

BYRNE, WILLIAM ANDREW, education educator, historian; b. Valparaiso, Fla., Jan. 19, 1944; s. William Andrew Byrne and Ramonde Ruckel Williams; m. Ute Johanna Byrne, Nov. 27, 1964; children: Drew, Sean. BA, Fla. State U., 1968, MA, 1971, PhD, 1979. Adj. asst. prof. Okaloosa Walton C.C., Niceville, Fla., 1982—85; adj. assoc. prof. U. of West Fla., 1986—94; assoc. prof. Norfolk State U., 1994—2000, prof. and chair, 2000—03, asst. dean, sch. of liberal arts, 2003—. Strategic planning com. Norfolk State U., 2002, budget com., 1998, adv. com., 2003. Contbr. articles to jours. Mem. Chrysler Mus., 1995, Va. Symphony, 1995, Norfolk Botanical Garden, 1995. Pers. specialist SP4 E4 U.S. Army, 1962—65, Germany. Mem.: Georgia Hist. Soc., Southern Hist. Assn., Org. of Am. Historians, Phi Kappa Phi, Phi Alpha Theta. Democrat. Avocation: golf. Home: 1209 Willow Creek Ct Chesapeake VA 23321 Office: Norfolk State U 700 Park Ave Norfolk VA 23504 Office Phone: 757-823-2082. Business E-Mail: wabyrne@nsu.edu.

BYRNE-DEMPSEY, CECELIA (CECELIA DEMPSEY), journalist; b. L.A., Aug. 7, 1925; d. John Joseph and Margaret Agnes (Frakell) B.; m. John Dempsey, Mar. 25, 1951 (dec. June 1981); children: Margaret, Elizabeth, John, Cecelia, Cathrine, Patricia, Bridget, Charles, Mary Teresa. Student, Immaculate Heart Coll., 1944; BA in Psychology, Calif. State U., Northridge, 1975, BA in Journalism, 1978, MA in Mass Comm., 1992. Staff Lockheed Aircraft Corp., Burbank, Calif., 1943—, Office Naval Rsch., San Francisco, 1947—; with Sisters of Mercy, Burlingame, Calif., 1945—, Sisters of Presentation, San Francisco, 1949—; mem. staff Calif. State U., 1976—. Rschr., journalism historian early Am. newspapers, 1978—. Author: The Meaning Index: A Model for Early American Newspaper Indexing: a research guide, 1992. Mentor 4-H Club; past mem. Urban Corp., L.A Mem. Mensa, Kappa Gamma Delta. Republican. Jewish. Avocations: poetry, gardening, philosophical meditation.

BYRNES, BRUCE L., manufacturing executive; b. Columbus, Ohio, Mar. 29, 1948; BA in Philosophy of Religion, Princeton U., 1970. Brand asst. Procter & Gamble, Cin., 1970—71, sales trainee, 1971—72, asst. brand mgr., 1972—74, brand mgr., 1974—78, assoc. advt. mgr. paper products divsn., 1978—82, advt. mgr. coffee divsn., 1982—84, advt. mgr. packaged soap and detergent divsn., 1984—86, mgr. packaged soap and detergent divsn., 1986—87, v.p. packaged soap and detergent divsn., 1987—90, v.p. No. Europe, 1990—91, pres. paper and beverage products, Procter & Gamble Europe, group v.p., 1991—95, pres. paper products-U.S., Procter & Gamble N.Am., group v.p., 1995—96, pres. health care products-U.S., Procter & Gamble N.Am., group v.p., 1996—97, pres. health care products-N.Am., Procter & Gamble N.Am., group v.p., 1997—99, pres. global health care and corp. new ventures, 1999—2000, pres. global beauty care and global health care, 2000—02, vice chmn. bd. dirs., pres. global beauty, global feminine and global health care, 2002—. Mem. steering coun. Success by 6, 2002—; trustee Cin. Art Mus., 1996—; maj. firms chair 1999 Fine Arts Fund Campaign, 1998—99. Office: The Procter & Gamble Co 1 Procter & Gamble Plz Cincinnati OH 45202

BYRNES, CHRISTOPHER IAN, engineering educator; b. NYC, June 28, 1949; s. Richard Francis and Jeanne (Orchard) Byrnes; children: Kathleen, Alison, Christopher; m. Gwendolyn Renee Byrnes, Feb. 14, 2005. BS in math., Manhattan Coll., 1971; MS in math., U. Mass., 1973, PhD in math., 1975; D of Tech. (hon.), Royal Inst. Tech., Stockholm, 1998. Instr. U. Utah, Salt Lake City, 1975-78; asst. prof. Harvard U., Cambridge, Mass., 1978-81, assoc. prof., 1981-85; rsch. prof. Ariz. State U., Tempe, 1985-89; prof. Washington U., St. Louis, 1989—, chmn. dept. systems sci. and math., 1989—91, dean Sch. Engring. and Applied Sci., 1991—. Adj. prof. Royal Inst. Tech., Stockholm, 1985—90; cons. Sci. Sys., Inc., Cambridge, 1980—84, Sys. Engring., Inc., Greenbelt, Md., 1986; sci. advisor Sherwood Davis & Geck, 1996—98, Cernium Inc., 2002—, Midwest Bank Ctr., 2002—; mem. NRC; bd. dirs., chmn. nominating and governance com. Belden Inc.; chmn. bd. dirs. Ctr. for Emerging Techs., 1993—2003; pres., bd. dirs. WUTA, Inc. Editor: (book series) Progress in Systems Control, 1988—01, Foundations of Systems and Control, 1998—2001; Nonlinear Synthesis, 1991, 13 other books; contbr. numerous articles to profl. jours., book revs. Recipient Best Paper award, IFAC, 1993. Fellow: IEEE (Geroge Axelby award 1991, 2003), Acad. Sci. St. Louis, Japan Soc. for Promotion Sci.; mem.: AAAS, Regional Chamber for Growth Assn. (vice chmn. tech., chmn. Tech. Gateway Alliance 2000—03), Royal Swedish Acad. Engring. Sci. (fgn.), Am. Math. Soc., Soc. Indsl. Applied Math. (program com. 1986—89, Reid prize 2005), Tau Beta Pi, Sigma Xi. Avocations: cooking, fishing, travel. Office: Washington U Sch Engring and Applied Sci 1 Brookings Dr Saint Louis MO 63130-4899 Office Phone: 314-935-5363.

BYRNES, DAVID J., museum administrator; s. Ervine George and Norine Connell Byrnes; m. Martha Joan Miller, Apr. 23, 1982; children: Kevin Miller, Erin Claire, Sarah Marie. BA, George Wash. U., 1977; MA, Tex. Tech U., 1979. Fund Raising Techniques W.Va. U., Morgantown, WV, 1979, Institutional Develop. for Non-Profit Organizations, The Graduate C Hartford, CT, 1983. Program dir. Ft. New Salem, Salem Coll., W.Va., 1979—81; exec. dir. Lockwood-Mathews Mansion Mus., Norwalk, Conn., 1981—93; dir. of corp. and found. rels. Sacred Heart U., Fairfield, Conn., 1993—96; exec. dir. Rye Hist. Soc., Rye, NY, 1996—98; pres. Midway Village & Mus. Ctr., Rockford, Ill., 1999—. Treas. Assn. of Midwest Mus. Bd., St. Louis, 2002—; pres. Kiwanis Internat., Norwalk, Conn., 1986—87; chmn. Cub Scout Pack Com., Pack 170, Newtown, Conn., 1995—96; cub master, pack 8 Pk. City Magnet Sch., Bridgeport, Conn., 1994—95, den leader, pack 8, 1992—94; chmn. All Mus. Mktg. Com., Rockford, Ill., 2003—; mem. Rotary Internat., Rockford, Ill., 2000—; commr. Conn. Tourism Industries Com., Norwalk, Conn., 1987—94, chmn., 1993—94; grant reviewer Inst. of Mus. and Libr. Services, Washington, 1982—90, Washington, 2001—; spkr. Large Estate Seminar, Detroit, 1985; bd. of dir. Darien Hist. Soc. Home: 941 Thickett Trail Roscoe IL 61073 Office: Midway Village & Mus Ctr 6799 Guilford Rd Rockford IL 61107 Office Phone: 815-397-9112 103. Office Fax: 815-397-9156. E-mail: daveb@midwayvillage.com.

BYRNES, JAMES BERNARD, museum director, consultant; b. N.Y.C., Feb. 19, 1917; s. Patrick J.A. and Janet E. (Geiger) B.; m. Barbara A. Cecil, June 10, 1946; 1 son, Ronald L. Student, N.A.D., 1936-38, Am. Artist Sch., 1938-40, Art Students League, 1940-42, U. Perugia, Italy, 1951, Inst. Meschini, Rome, 1952. Art tchr. mus. activity program N.Y.C. Bd. Edn., 1936-40; indsl. designer Michael Saphier Assos., N.Y.C., 1940-42; audio visual specialist USNR, 1944—45; with L.A. County Mus., 1946-47, assoc. curator modern contemporary art, 1947-48, curator, asst. to dir., 1948-53; dir. Colorado Springs Fine Arts Center, 1954-55; from assoc. dir. to dir. N.C. Mus. Art, 1956-60; dir. New Orleans Mus. Art, 1961-71, dir. emeritus, 1989—; dir. Newport Harbor Art Mus., Newport Beach, Calif., 1972-75. Vis. lectr. U. Fla., 1961, Newcomb Coll., Tulane U., 1963; art cons. Author: Masterpieces of Art, W.R. Valentiner Memorial, 1959, Tobacco and Smoking in Art, 1960, Fetes de la Palette, 1963, Edgar Degas, His Family and Friends in New Orleans, 1965, Odyssey of an Art Collector, 1966, Art of Ancient and Modern Latin America, 1968, The Artist as Collector of Primitive Art, 1975, also numerous mus. catalogs. Decorated knight Order Leopold II (Belgium); recipient Isaac Delgado Meml. award, New Orleans Mus. of Art, 1998. Mem. Am. Soc. Interior Design (hon. life), Am. Soc. Appraisers (sr.), Appraisers Assn. Am. Office: James B Byrnes and Assocs 7820 Mulholland Dr Los Angeles CA 90046-1223 Personal E-mail: jasbyrn@earthlink.net.

BYRNES, MARTIN ANDREW, English and language arts professor; b. New Brighton, Pa., Feb. 7, 1973; s. William Andrew and Helen Tasevich Byrnes. BA in English, U. of Dayton, 1991—95. English/lang. arts tchr. Hopewell H.S., Aliquippa, Pa., 1996—. H.s. soccer coach Beaver Area Sr. H.S., Beaver, Pa., 1998—. Fellow: Western Pa. Writing Project. Office: Hopewell High School 1215 Longvue Avenue Aliquippa PA 15001 Office Phone: 724-378-8565.

BYRNES, MICHAEL FRANCIS, podiatrist; b. Chgo., Aug. 11, 1957; s. Edward and Dorothy Franchi; m. Debra Michelle Moody, July, 31, 1982. BA, Loyola U., Chgo., 1979; D in Podiatry Medicine, Ill. Coll. Podiatry Med., 1984. Diplomate Am. Bd. Podiatric Surgery. Practice medicine specializing in podiatrics Ridgeland Foot Clinic., Chgo., 1984—. Surgeon Mercy Surg. Ctr., Justice, Ill., 1984—, Holy Cross Hosp., 1987—, Palos Cmty. Hosp., 1997—; assoc. prof. Dr. Scholl Coll. Podiatric Medicine; mem. sci. and med. staff Mercy Hosp. and Med. Ctr. Contbr. case reports to Jour. Foot Surgery, 1985. Bd. dirs. Animal Welfare League, Chgo., 1993—, chief fin. officer, 1998-99, 2000-01. Precinct capt. 49th Dem. Ward., Chgo., 1976-80. Winner state skating championship, 1980; recipient commendation Oaklawn Police Dept., 1995, VFW award Oaklawn Post, 1995, Courage award The Wizard of Oz on Ice, TNT Prodns., 1995, Clark Oil award, 1995. Fellow Am. Coll. Foot Surgeons; mem. Am. Podiatric Med. Assn., Ill. Podiatric Med. Assn. (co-chmn. legis. com. 1985-86, del.), Am. Acad. Podiatric Sports Medicine. Roman Catholic. Avocation: skating. Home: 203 Kenmare Dr Burr Ridge IL 60527-5299 Office: 9941 Southwest Hwy Oak Lawn IL 60453-3767 E-mail: mbyrnes@pol.net.

BYRNES, WILLIAM JOSEPH, lawyer; b. Bklyn., Apr. 11, 1940; s. William James and Margaret Mary (English) B.; m. Catherine Belle Rollings, Aug. 15, 1970 (dec. 2002); children: Jennifer, Suzanne. BS, Fordham U., 1961; JD, Yale U., 1964. Bar: NY 1965, DC 1970, Va. 1992. Atty. AEC, Washington, 1964-68; internat. mgr. Comm. Satellite Corp., Washington, 1968-70; ptnr. Haley, Bader & Potts, Arlington, Va., 1970-95; of counsel Irwin Campbell & Tannenwald, Washington, 1995-96; pvt. practice, McLean, Va., 1997—; v.p. Shared Spectrum Co. Author: Telecom. Regulation: Something Old and Something New in the Comm. Act: A Legis. History of the Major Amendments, 1934-1996, 1999; co-author: The Common Carrier Provisions--A Product of Evolutionary Devel. in A Legis. History of the Comm. Act, 1989, Decency Redux: The Curious History of the New FCC Broadcast Indecency Policy, 1989, A New Telecom. Paradigm, 1993; actor: various local theater companies. Candidate Fairfax County Bd. Suprs., 1995; v.p., bd. dirs. McLean Citizens Assn., past pres.; v.p. Great Falls Players. Recipient cert. U.S. AEC, 1967. Mem. Fed. Comm. Bar Assn., Va. State Bar, DC Bar Assn. Avocations: acting, videography. Office: 7921 Old Falls Rd Mc Lean VA 22102-2414

BYROM, FLETCHER LAUMAN, chemical manufacturing company executive; b. Cleve., July 13, 1918; s. Fletcher L. and Elizabeth (Collins) B.; m. Marie L. McIntyre, Feb. 17, 1945; children: Fletcher Lauman, Carol A. Byrom Conrad, Susan J. Byrom Evans. BS in Metallurgy, Pa. State U., 1940. Sales engr. Am. Steel & Wire Co., Cleve., 1940-42; procurement and adminstrv. coord. Naval Ordnance Lab., also Bur. Ordnance and Research Planning Bd., Navy Dept., 1942-47; from asst. to gen. mgr. Tar Products divsn. Koppers Co., Inc., Pitts., 1947-82, pres., 1960—70, chmn., 1970—82; mgr. Micasu Tungsten LLC, 2000—. Mem. Pitts. br. Fed. Res. Bd. Cleve., 1962-68, chmn., 1966-68, N.Y. Stock Exch., 1980-86; mem. bd. govs. Com. Devel. Am. Capital, 1989-2004; bd. dirs. Purecycle Corp., 1988-2004, pres., bd. dirs. Micasu Corp. Bd. dirs. Allegheny Conf. on Cmty. Devel., v.p., 1970-83; chmn. Hershey Med. Ctr. Subcom., 1970-73; chmn. Pres.'s Export Coun., 1974-79, Pub. Edn. Fund, 1980-85; chmn. bd. trustees Presbyn.-Univ. Hosp., 1972-83, Kiskiminetas Springs Sch., 1971-82; trustee Carnegie Mellon U., 1975-81, Allegheny Coll., 1969-79, Pa. State U., 1970-73; former trustee, Inst. Advanced Study, Inst. for Future Mem., Hudson Inst., Keystone Ctr.; trustee Conf. Bd., 1962-82, lifetime chancellor, 1968—; mem. pres.'s circle NAS, chmn., 1999-2000; trustee Com. for Econ. Devel., chmn. bd. dirs., 1978-84, lifetime trustee. Recipient Disting. Civilian Service award U.S. Navy Dept., Disting. Alumnus Pa. State U., David Ford McFarland award Pa. State U., 1979, Alumni Achievement award Harvard U. Bus. Sch., 1981, William Metcalf award West Pa. Engring. Soc., 1985; Woodrow Wilson Edn. Found. vis. fellow, Pa. State U. fellow. Mem. Pa. State U. Alumni Assn. (pres. 1965-66), Coun. Retired CEO's, Duquesne Club (Pitts.), Links Club (N.Y.C.), Phi Kappa Psi. Presbyterian. Home and Office: 305 Village Heights Dr Apt 328 State College PA 16801 Office Phone: 814-278-1200. Personal E-mail: fmicasu3@aol.com.

BYRON, BEVERLY BUTCHER, retired congresswoman; b. Balt., July 27, 1932; d. Harry C. and Ruth Butcher; m. Goodloe E. Byron, 1952 (dec.); children: Goodloe E. Jr., Barton Kimball, Mary McComas; m. B. Kirk Walsh, 1986. Student, Hood Coll., 1962-64. Mem. 96th-102nd Congresses from 6th Md. dist., 1979-93; Presdl. appt. to base closing and realignment commn., 1993. Bd. dirs. McDonnell Douglas, Constellation Energy Group, Blue Cross/Blue Shield, UNC Corp., Farm and Mech. Nat. Bank, LMI, Def. Adv. Commn. on Women in the Mil.; exec. panel Chief of Naval Ops.; adv. bd. NASA, A.F. Meml. Found. State treas. Md. Young Dems., 1962, 65; bd. assocs. Hood Coll.; bd. visitors USAF Acad., 1980-87; trustee Mt. St. Mary's Coll.; bd. dirs. Frederick County chpt. ARC; sec. Frederick Heart Assn., 1974-79; mem. Frederick Phys. Fitness Commn.; chmn. Md. Phys. Fitness Commn., 1979-89; mem. Frederick County Landmarks Found.; bd. dirs. Am. Hiking Soc.; bd. dirs. Adventure Sports Inst., 1992—; bd. advisors Internat. Studies Frostburg State U., 1990—, Am. Volkssport Assn., 1991—; mem. bd. vis. U.S. Naval Acad., 1995—, chair, 1997-2002; chair TedCo. Recipient Pres.'s medal John Hopkins U. Democrat. Episcopalian. Home: 306 Grove Blvd Frederick MD 21701-4813

BYRON, ERIC HOWARD, sculptor, museum researcher and administrator; b. NYC, Jan. 14, 1948; s. Melville and Ruth (Levine) Byron. BA, Beloit Coll., 1970; postgrad., Hunter Coll., 1972-75, YIVO Inst./Columbia U., 1972-76; MA, Goddard Coll., 1979; postgrad, NYU, 1985. Founder, dir. The Synagogue Rescue Project, Inc., N.Y.C., 1974-85; mus. technician South St. Seaport Mus., N.Y.C., 1992-93, Statue of Liberty Nat. Monument/Ellis Island Immigration Mus, N.Y.C., 1993—. Lectr. sr. citizens N.Y. Tech. Inst., 1982; coord. oral history project Brookdale Ctr. on Aging, Hunter Coll., N.Y.C., 1982, discography project Ellis Island Mus. Immigration, 1997—. Exhibited in group shows at Ward-Nasse Gallery, 1975-76, Detail, N.Y.C., 1989, Nathaniel's Music Box, N.Y.C., 1989, Civilization, 1989, Am. Craftsman, 1989-90, Dinosaur Hill, N.Y.C., 1990, Mus. Am. Folk Art, N.Y.C., 1990, Mark Milliken Gallery, N.Y.C., 1990, Faith Nightengale Gallery, San Diego, 1991-92, Whitney Mus., N.Y.C., 1992; sculpture, performer Washington Sq. Pk., 1989-2001; featured on PBS Channel 13 City Arts, 1998, also on Nat. Pub. Radio, 1999. Fellow Brookdale Ctr. on Aging, N.Y.C., 1985; recipient archeology award Profl. Archeologists N.Y.C., 1997. Mem.: N.Y. State Archaeol. Assn. (Met. chpt.), Nat. Steroscopic Assn., Nat. Trust Historic Preservation. Home: 411 E 10th St Apt 15F New York NY 10009-4212 Office: Statue of Liberty Nat Mus Liberty Island New York NY 10004-1467 Office Phone: 212-363-3206 153. Business E-Mail: ericbyron@earthlink.net.

BYRON, FREDERICK WILLIAM, JR., physicist, educator, university vice chancellor; b. Manchester, N.H., July 8, 1938; s. Frederick William and Anna (Muir) B.; m. Edith Iselin, June 23, 1961; children: Kenniston, Alexander deNeufville. AB, Harvard U., 1959; PhD, Columbia U., 1963. Acting asst. prof. U. Calif., Berkeley, 1963-65, asst. prof., 1965-66, U. Mass., Amherst, 1966-69, assoc. prof., 1969-74, prof., 1974—, head dept. physics and astronomy, 1975-79; dean U. Mass. (Faculty Natural Scis. and Math.), Amherst, 1979-93; coordinating dean U. Mass. (Coll. of Arts and Scis.), Amherst, 1989-91; vice chancellor rsch. and econ. devel. U. Mass., Amherst, 1994—. Bd. dirs. Reg. Tech. Corp., 2003—. Author: (with Robert W. Fuller) The Mathematics of Classical and Quantum Physics, 1970; contbr. articles to profl. jours. Alfred P. Sloan Found. fellow, 1965-67; Fulbright research scholar, 1973-74 Fellow Am. Phys. Soc. Office: U Mass 512 Goodell Bldg Amherst MA 01003 E-mail: byron@resgs.umass.edu, fredbyron@yahoo.com.

BYRON, WILLIAM JAMES, minister, retired academic administrator, finance educator; b. Pitts., May 25, 1927; s. Harold J. and Mary I. (Langton) B. AB in Philosophy, St. Louis U., 1955, Ph.L., 1956, MA in Econs, 1959; S.T.B., Woodstock Coll., 1960, S.T.L., 1962; PhD in Econs, U. Md., 1969; cert., Harvard U. Inst. Edml. Mgmt., 1974. Joined S.J., 1950, ordained priest Roman Cath. Ch., 1961. Tchr. math. Scranton (Pa.) Prep. Sch., 1956-58; manpower rsch. fellow Dept. Labor, 1965-66; asst. prof. econs. Loyola Coll., Balt., 1967-69; assoc. prof. social ethics, rector Woodstock Coll., Woodstock Jesuit Community, 1967-73; dean Coll. Arts and Scis. Loyola U., New Orleans, 1973-75; pres. U. Scranton, 1975-82, Cath. U. Am., Washington, 1982-92; rsch. assoc. Georgetown U., 1992-93, Disting. prof. mgmt. Sch. of Bus. Washington, 1993—2000; rsch. prof. Sellinger Sch. Bus., Loyola Coll. in Md. Author: Toward Stewardship: An Interim Ethic of Poverty, Pollution and Power, 1975, Quadrangle Considerations, 1989, Take Your Diploma and Run, 1992, Finding Work Without Losing Heart, 1995, The 365 Days of Christmas, 1996, Answers from Within, 1998, Jesuit Saturdays, 2000; editor: Causes of World Hunger, 1982; contbr. numerous articles to profl. jurs. Bd. dirs. Fed. City Coun., Joint Commn. on Accreditation Healthcare Orgns., U. San Francisco, Loyola Coll. in Md., Balt. With U.S. Army, 1945-56. Mem. Am. Econs. Assn., Am. Soc. Christian Ethics, Assn. Cath. Colls. and Univs., Phi Beta Kappa, Alpha Sigma Nu Mailing: 4603 Millbrook Rd Baltimore MD 21212 Office Phone: 410-617-2121. Business E-Mail: wbyron@loyola.edu.

BYRUM, EDITH WARD, retired music educator; d. Cecil Thomas Ward, Sr. and Nora Lee (Rountree) Ward; m. James Lee Byrum, Jr., Dec. 18, 1960 (div. Sept. 1992); children: Steven Ward, Susan Yvonne. BS in Music Edn., Longwood Coll., 1960. Tchr. Deep Creek H.S., Chesapeake, Va., 1960—61, Rena B. Wright Elem., Chesapeake, 1967—70, G.W. Carver Elem., Chesapeake, 1970, Sparrow Rd. Elem., Chesapeake, 1971—77; tchr. music G.A. Treakle Elem., Chesapeake, 1977—86, Crestwood Elem., Chesapeake, 1986—97, Deep Creek Elem., Chesapeake, 1996—2004, Deep Creek Intermediate, Chesapeake, 2001—03, Grassfield Elem., Chesapeake, 2003—04, Hickory Mid., 2004; ret. Pianist, organizer New Horizon Gospel Quartet, Chesapeake, 1993—97; Sunday sch. tchr. Deep Creek Bapt. Ch., Chesapeake, 1972—83, pianist, organist, 1975—98, fin. com., 1966—67, 1975—76. Mem.: Va. Music Educators Assn., PTA (life), Sigma Alpha Iota. Avocations: cooking, gardening, travel. Home: 620 Brisa Ct Chesapeake VA 23322

BYSIEWICZ, SUSAN, state official; b. New Haven, Conn. m. David Donaldson; 3 children. BA magna cum laude, Yale Coll., 1983; JD, Duke U., 1986. Corp. atty. White & Case, N.Y., 1986-88, Robinson & Cole, Hartford, Conn., 1988-92; with law dept. Aetna Life and Casualty, 1992-94; state rep. 100th dist. judiciary com. State of Conn., 1992-98, chair govt. adminstrn. and elections com., 1995-98, Sec. of State, 1998—. Author: Ella: A Biography of Governor Ella T. Grasso, 1984. Conn. Bar Assn., N.Y. Bar Assn. Democrat. Address: Rm 104 State Capitol Hartford CT 06106 E-mail: susan.bysiewicz@po.state.ct.us.

BYSTRYN, JEAN-CLAUDE, dermatologist, educator; b. Paris, May 8, 1938; arrived in U.S., 1949, naturalized, 1958; s. Iser and Sara Bystryn; m. Marcia Hammill, May 14, 1972; children: Anne, Alexander. BS, U. Chgo., 1958; MD, NYU, 1962. Diplomate Am. Bd. Deratology, Am. Bd. Immunodermatopathology. Intern Montefiore Hosp., N.Y.C., 1962-63, resident in medicine, 1963-64; resident in dermatology NYU Sch. Medicine, N.Y.C., 1966-69, USPHS postgrad. tng. fellow in immunology, 1968-72, asst. prof. clin. dermatology, 1971—72, assoc. prof., 1976-84, prof., 1984—. Asst. dispensary physician Albany Med. Coll., 1964—66; asst. attending physician Univ. Hosp., N.Y.C., 1969—; asst. vis. dermatologist Bellevue Hosp. Ctr., N.Y.C., 1969—; dir. melanoma program NYU Kaplan Cancer Ctr., N.Y.C.; dir. Immunofluorescence Lab. NYU Med. Sch., N.Y.C. Contbr. articles to profl. jours. Mem. adv. bd. Skin Cancer Found., Vitiligo Found., Nat. Alepecia Areata Found., Am. Skin Assn., Nat. Pemphigus Found. Lt. comdr. USPHS, 1964—66. Recipient Irma T. Hirschl Rsch. Career award, AOA; Ford Found. fellow, 1954—58, NIH grantee, 1970—. Mem.: N.Y. Dermatol. Soc. (dir.), Soc. Investigative Dermatology, Am. Assn. Cancer Rsch., Am. Assn. Immunologists, Am. Acad. Dermatology, Am. Dermatology Assn. Office: NYU Med Ctr U Hosp 530 1st Ave New York NY 10016-6402 Office Phone: 212-889-3846.

BYUN, SUNG HUN, research scientist; b. Pusan, Republic of Korea, Mar. 20, 1962; s. Haksoo Byun and Youngsook Woo, Oak-ja Um (Stepmother). BS, Korea Aviation U., 1985; MS, Korea Advanced Inst. of Sci. and Tech., 1987; PhD, U. of Tex., 1998. Rsch. staff Jet Propulsion Lab., Pasadena, Calif., 1999—. Recipient Spot award, Jet Propulsion Lab., 2004, Tech. award, NASA, 2004. Mem.: Inst. of Nav., Tau Beta Pi Engring. Honor Soc. Achievements include research in Developed satellite precise orbit determination method using Global Positioning System in a kinematic mode. Avocations: sailing, skiing. Home: 105 South El Molino Ave Pasadena CA 91101 Office: Jet Propulsion Lab 4800 Oak Grove Dr Pasadena CA 91109-8099 Office Phone: 818-393-5452. Office Fax: 818-393-5452. Personal E-mail: byun@caltech.edu. E-mail: sung.h.byun@jpl.nasa.gov.

BYYNY, RICHARD LEE, academic administrator; b. South Gate, Calif., Jan. 6, 1939; s. Oswald and Essa Burnetta (McGinnis) B.; m. Jo Ellen Garverick, Aug. 25, 1962; children: Kristen, Jan, Richard. BA in History, U. So. Calif., 1960, MD, 1964. Intern and resident in internal medicine Columbia Presbyn. Med. Ctr., N.Y.C., 1964-66, chief resident, 1968-69; fellow in endocrinology Vanderbilt U., Nashville, 1969-71; asst. prof. medicine U. Chgo., 1971-74, head div. internal medicine, 1972-77, assoc. prof., 1975-77; prof. internal medicine U. Colo., Denver, 1977—, head divsn. internal medicine, 1977-94, vice-chmn. dept. medicine Health Scis. Ctr., 1977-85, exec. vice chancellor, 1994-95, v.p. acad. affairs, 1995-97, chancellor Boulder, 1997—2005; exec. dir. Ctr. for Health Policy, U. Colo. Hosp., 2005—. Med. dir. ambulatory care, 1990-92; mem. Coun. on Econ. Devel., Boulder, Colo., mem. Rocky Mtn. Regional Adv. Bd. Inst. of Internal Edn., 2004-. Author: A Clinical Guide in the Care of Older Women, 1990, 95; contbr. numerous articles to profl. jours., chpts. to textbooks, monographs. Pres. Ill. Council Continuing Med. Edn., Ill., 1976-77; bd. dirs. Denver affiliate Am. Heart Assn., 1987-98 (pres. 1994-95), Boulder Com. Hosp., 1997—, Bank of Boulder, Boulder Econ. Coun., arm of Boulder C. of C., U.S. Coun. on Competitiveness Big 12 Conf. Served to capt. USAF, 1966-68. Recipient Merck award U. So. Calif., 1964; Am. Coun. Edn. fellow, 1992-93. Fellow ACP; mem. AAAS, Soc. for Gen. Internal Medicine (pres. 1979-80), Am. Soc. Hypertension, Western Soc. Clin. Investigation, Endocrine Soc., Am. Fedn. for Clin. Rsch., Am. Coun. Edn. (commn. leadership instl. effectiveness), Alpha Omega Alpha (bd. dirs. 1996—). Clubs: U. Club Denver; Arapahoe Tennis (Englewood, Colo.), Boulder Country Club. Avocations: tennis, skiing, running, surfing, sailing. Home: 2900 Park Lake Dr Boulder CO 80301-5139 Office: Univ Colo Hosp Ctr for Health Policy PO Box 6508 Aurora CO 80045 Business E-Mail: richard.byyny@udsc.edu.

BZDELL, SUSAN ROSENBLUM, archivist, educator; b. Huntsville, Ala., May 21, 1952; d. Fred O. and Valtena Gibbs Rosenblum; m. Stephen S. Bzdell, Jr., Aug. 13, 1988. BA, U. Ala., Huntsville, 1971—82; MA, Fla. State U., Tallahasse, 1987—89. Picture framer, artifact display, Huntsville, Ala., 1971—86; contractor, cons. Elkmont, Ala., 1988—91; asst. archivist Limestone County Commn., Athens, Ala., 1991—95; archivist Morgan County Commn., Decatur, Ala., 1995—. Cons. Athens State Archives, Ala., 1999—2001. Author: Heritage of Morgan County, 1998, South of the River, 2003. Bd. mem. Old State Bank, Decatur, Ala., 2002—05, Main St., Decatur, Ala., 2003—05. Mem.: Morgan County Hist. Soc., Morgan County Genealogical Soc., Nat. Assn. Govt. Activists and Record Adminstrs., Am. Assn. State and Local History, Assn. County Commns., Soc. Ala. Archivist. Avocations: reading, painting, sewing, crafts. Home: 23651 Pepper Farm Ln Elkmont AL 35620 Office: Morgan County Archives 624 Bank St Decatur AL 35601

BZOCH, KENNETH RUDOLPH, speech and language educator, department chairman; b. Chgo., Nov. 6, 1927; s. Rudolph and Mildred (Novotny) B.; m. Lorrayne M. Cali, Oct. 29, 1950; children: Kathleen Marie, Kevin Jude. BA, DePaul U., Chgo., 1951; MA, Northwestern U., 1952, PhD, 1956. Cert. clin. competence-speech pathology, CCC-audiology; lic. speech pathologist, Fla. Asst. prof. Loyola U., Chgo., 1953-57, Northwestern U., Chgo., 1957-59; assoc. prof. U. Fla., Gainesville, 1960-64, prof., chair, 1964-96. Program dir. Communicative Disorders and Craniofacial Ctr., Shands Hosp., U. Fla.; researcher in field. Author: Communicative Disorders Related to Cleft Lip and Palate, 5th edit., 2004, Receptive-Expressive Language Test: A Method of Assessing Language Skills in Infancy, 3d edit., 2004, How Babies Learn To Talk: A Book for New Parents and Grandparents, 2004. Cpl. USMC, 1946-47. Fellow Am. Cleft Palate Assn. (past pres.), Fla. Cleft Palate Assn. (hon., past pres.), Fla. Speech Lang. and Hearing Assn. (hon., past pres.). Home and Office: 640 NW 57th St Gainesville FL 32607-6103 Office Phone: 352-331-7171. Personal E-mail: bzoch@aol.com.

BZYMEK, ZBIGNIEW MARIAN, engineering educator; b. Warsaw, Aug. 5, 1935; came to U.S., 1981; s. Stefan and Stefania (Turek) Bzymek; m. Danuta Jaworska, Oct. 22, 1966; children: Malgorzata, Dorota, Zbigniew Wojciech. MS in Engring., Politechnika Warszawska, Warsaw, Poland, 1959, PhD in Engring. Sci., 1967; MS in Engring., U. Mich., 1961. Asst. Politechnika Warszawska, 1961, sr. asst., 1961-67, adj. prof., 1967-73, docent, 1973-81; assoc. prof., dir. CAD & CAM, Expert Sys. Lab. U. Conn., Storrs, 1981—. Cons. Head Mgmt. Ctr. for Hwy. Data Processing, 1978-81; designer bridge sect. Transproject, Warsaw, 1961-63. Author: (Hungarian and Polish) Application of Computers in Structural Analysis, 1966, others; translator (from Russian): Structural Analysis by Means of Digital Computers, 1970; sect. editor (monthly) Drogownictwo, 1977-81; head editor Rsch. Reports on Automatization of Structural Design, 1974-81; contbr. numerous articles to profl. jours. Recipient 1st Prize for Design Competition Soc. of Transp. Engrs., 1974, Hon. mention, 1974. Mem. ASME (2nd Nat. Design award), Internat. Orgn. for Sci. and Tech. (chmn. CAD/CAM com. 1987-92), N.Y. Acad. Scis., Assn. for Computers Machinery (spl. interest group graphics 1982), Polish Acad. of Sci. (mem. civil engring. com., computer graphics pioneer, award 1976), Soc. of Bldg. Engrs. (Stefan Bryla award 1977). Achievements include research in computer graphics, structural analysis, bridge and machine design and theory of engineering design and problem solving; introduced multithickness and multicolor computer graphics representation in structural analysis systems; introduced principles of miniaturization, nanotechnology and biotechnology in problem solving in engineering. Avocations: tennis, skiing, sailing, coin collecting/numismatics. Home: 260 Codfish Falls Rd Storrs Mansfield CT 06268-1407 Office: U Conn U-3139 ME 191 Auditorium Rd Storrs Mansfield CT 06269-9012 Office Phone: 860-486-2275. Business E-Mail: bzymek@uconnvm.uconn.edu.

CAAN, JAMES, actor, director; b. N.Y.C., Mar. 26, 1939; s. Sophie and Arthur Caan; m. Linda Stokes, 1995; children: James Arthur, Jacob Arthur; m. Ingrid Hayjek, 1990 (div. 1994); 1 child, Alexander; m. Sheila Ryan, 1976 (div. 1977); 1 child, Scott; m. Dee Jay Mathis, 1960 (div. 1966); 1 child, Tara. Student, Hofstra Coll., Mich. State U. Actor: (off-Broadway play) La Ronde, 1961; (films) Lady in a Cage, 1964, The Glory Guys, 1965, Red Line 7000, 1965, El Dorado, 1966, Games, 1967, Countdown, 1968, Journey to Shiloh, 1968, Submarine X-1, 1968, Rain People, 1969, Rabbit, Run, 1970, T.R. Baskin, 1971, The Godfather, 1972, Slither, 1972, Cinderella Liberty, 1973, Freebie and the Bean, 1974, The Gambler, 1974, The Godfather-Part II, 1974, Funny Lady, 1975, Rollerball, 1975, The Killer Elite, 1975, Gone with the West, 1976, Harry and Walter Go to New York, 1976, Silent Movie (as himself), 1976, A Bridge Too Far, 1977, Another Man, Another Chance, 1977, Comes a Horseman, 1978, Chapter Two, 1979, Hide in Plain Sight, 1980, Thief, 1981, Bolero, 1981, Kiss Me Goodbye, 1982, Gardens of Stone, 1987, Alien Nation, 1988, Dick Tracy, 1990, Misery, 1990, For The Boys, 1991, Honeymoon in Vegas, 1992, The Program, 1993, Flesh and Bone, 1993, A Boy Called Hate, 1996, North Star, 1996, Bottlerocket, 1996, Eraser, 1996, Bulletproof, 1996, This is My Father, 1998, Mickey Blue Eyes, 1999, The Yards, 2000, Way of the Gun, 2000, Luckytown, 2000, Viva Las Nowhere, 2001, In the Shadows, 2001, City of Ghosts, 2002, Dogville, 2003, Dallas 362, 2003, This Thing of Ours, 2003, Jericho Mansions, 2003, Elf, 2003; dir. Hide in Plain Sight, 1980; (TV films) Brian's Song, 1971, Superstunt, 1978, Poodle Springs, 1998, Warden of Red Rock, 2001, Lathe of Heaven, 2002, Blood Crime, 2002; (TV series) Las Vegas, 2003-; numerous TV appearances. Director (films) Hide in Plain Sight, 1980. Office: Endeavor care Fred Specktor 9701 Wilshire Blvd Fl 10 Beverly Hills CA 90212-2010

CABALQUINTO, LUIS CARRAZCAL, freelance writer; b. Magarao, Camarines Sur, Philippines, Jan. 31, 1935; came to U.S., 1968; s. Geminiano and Irene (Carrazcal) C. BA in Journalism, U. Philippines, 1967; postgrad., Cornell U., 1968—71, NYU, 1982—84. Editor Office Philippine Pres., Manila, 1960—66; editor, instr. U. Phillipines, Los Baños, 1966—75; customer svc. rep. Pfizer Inc., N.Y.C., 1980—90; pvt. practice N.Y.C., 1990—. Author: The Dog-eater and Other Poems, 1989, The Ibalon Collection, 1991, Dreamwanderer, 1992, Bridgeable Shores, 2001, Moon Over Magarao, New and Selected Poems, 2003, Manahatta Mahal, 2004. Recipient Dylan Thomas Poetry award New Sch. Social Rsch., 1979, Poetry prize Acad. Am. Poets, 1985, fiction prize Philippine Graphic Mag., 1992; fellow N.Y. Found. Arts, 1989. Mem. Poetry Soc. Am., Poets Writers, Writers Cmty., Am. PEN. Avocations: fishing, movies, gardening, photography, travel. Home: 1 Stuyvesant Oval MF New York NY 10009-2101 Office: PO Box 618 P Stuyvesant Sta New York NY 10009-0618 Office Phone: 212-254-4514. Personal E-mail: DonLuisC@aol.com.

CABANA, ROBERT D., aerospace transportation executive, astronaut; b. Mpls., Jan. 23, 1949; m. Nancy Joan Shimer; children: Jeffrey, Christopher, Sarah. BS in Math., U.S. Naval Acad., 1971; grad., Naval Flight Officer Tng., Pensacola, Fla., 1972, U.S. Naval Test Pilot Sch., 1981. Commd. ensign USMC, advanced through grades to col., ret., 2000; bombardier/navigator Marine Air Wings, Cherry Point, NC and Iwakuni, Japan; naval aviator 2d Marine Aircraft Wing, Cherry Point; project mgr., X-29 advanced then. demonstrator project officer, test pilot Naval Air Test Ctr., Patuxent River, Md.; asst. ops. officer Marine Aircraft Group Twelve, Iwakuni, Japan; flight software coord Astronaut Office Space Shuttle, NASA, 1985—86, dep. chief aircraft ops. Johnson Space Ctr. Houston, 1986—89, lead astronaut Shuttle Avionics Integration Lab., spacecraft communicator, chief astronaut appearances, chief Astronaut Office, dep. dir. flight crew ops., mgr. internat. ops. Internat. Space Sta. Program, dir. Human Space Flight Programs, Russia, 2001—02, dir. Flight Crew Ops. Directorate, 2002—04, dep. dir., Johnson Space Ctr. Houston, 2004—. NASA lead rep. Russian Aviation and Spacy Agy. Decorated DFC, Def. Superior Svc. medal, Def. Meritorious Svc. medal, Meritorious Svc. medal; recipient award, DAR, 1976, De La Vaulx medal, Fedn. Aeronautique Internat., 1994, Nat. Intelligence Medal of Achievement. Mem.: Assn. Space Explorers, Soc. Exptl. Test Pilots (assoc.). Achievements include four space flights; logged over 1,010 hours in space; pilot on STS-41 Discovery (Oct. 6-10, 1990), STS-53 Disco (Dec. 2-9, 1992); mission comdr. STS-65 Columbia (July 8-23, 1994) and STS-88 Endeavour (Dec. 4-15, 1998). Avocations: jogging, softball, sailing, woodworking, bicycling. Office: Astronaut Office/CB NASA Johnson Space Ctr Houston TX 77058

CABANISS, DALE, government agency administrator; BA, U. Georgia; JD, Columbus Sch. Law at Catholic U. Legislative asst. and dir. to Sen. Frank Murkowski; chief counsel Senate Govt. Affairs Subcommittee on Post Office and Civil Service; staff member Senate Appropriations Subcommittee; chmn. Federal Labor Relations Authority, 2001—. Office: FLRA 607 14th St NW Washington DC 20424

CABAY, ROBERT JOHN, physician, dentist; s. John A. and Irene M. Cabay; m. Gina Grace Angela Bill, Aug. 8, 1993. BS in Gen. Studies, Northwestern U., 1979—95; DDS, Loyola U. of Chgo., 1982—86; MPH, U. of Ill. Sch. of Pub. Health, 1990—91; MD, U. of Ill. Coll. of Medicine, 2000—04. Diplomate Am. Bd. of Quality Assurance and Utilization Rev. Physicians, 1992. Gen. dentist Charles J. Zasso, DDS, FAGD and Assocs., Ltd., Schaumburg, Ill., 1986—. Dental cons., 1999—. Children of Veterans scholarship, U. of Ill., 2000—04, Fellow, Acad. of Gen. Dentistry, 1999. Fellow: Acad. of Gen. Dentistry; mem.: ADA, AMA, Chgo. Dental Soc., Ill. State Dental Soc., Am. Soc. for Clin. Pathology, Chgo. Med. Soc., Ill. State Med. Soc., Alpha Sigma Nu. Office: Charles J Zasso DDS FAGD & Assocs Ltd 2 Woodfield Mall Schaumburg IL 60173-5012 Home: 2530 Nelson Sq Westchester IL 60154-5028

CABELA, RICHARD N., retail executive; b. Nebr. m. Mary A. Cabela; 9 children. Student, Regis Coll., 1956—58. Chmn., dir. Cabela's Inc. direct mktg. Exec. com. Direct Marketing Ednl. Found. Regent Regis Univ., 1994—, bd. trustees. Recipient Small Businessman of the Yr. award, 1970, Nebr. Hall of Fame award, 1994, Alumni Achievement award, Regis Univ., 2003. Roman Catholic. Office: Cabela's One Cabela Dr Sidney NE 69160 Office Phone: 308-254-5505. Office Fax: 308-254-4800.*

CABELL, ELIZABETH ARLISSE, psychologist; b. Bryan, Tex., Apr. 14, 1947; d. John David Kernodle and Jeanne Forrest (McCluer) Riley; m. Kent E. Johnson, Dec. 23, 1967 (div. May 1972); m. Donald Allen Cabell, May 19, 1978; children: Ryan, Andrew. BA with honors, U. Tex., 1968; MA, U. Colo., 1973, PhD, 1977. Lic. sch. psychologist. Vocat. trainer Mary Lee Sch. Spl. Edn., Austin, Tex., 1968-69; employment counselor Colo. Div. Employment, Denver, 1971-73; sch. psychologist Aurora (Colo.) Mental Health Ctr./Aurora Pub. Schs., 1974-76, Douglas County Schs., Castle Rock, Colo., 1976-77, Jefferson County Schs., Lakewood, Colo., 1977-80, Denver Pub. Schs., 1980-82; coord. spl. learning support program/learning disabled adult Community Coll. of Denver, 1983-89; sch. psychologist Denver Pub. Schs., 1989—. Mem. faculty part-time Met. State Coll., Denver, 1984-86; mem. grad. faculty part-time U. Colo., Denver, 1977-81, 86-89; presenter in field. U.S. Dept. Edn. grantee, 1987-89. Mem. APA, Colo. Soc. Sch. Psychologists (treas. 2002-04), Colo. Assn. for Gifted and Talented, Autism Soc. Am. (bd. dirs. Colo. chpt. 1996-2001), Littleton Assn. for Gifted and Talented (bd. dirs. 1996-98), Nat. Kidney Found. (living donor 2001). Democrat. Home: 4271 E Links Pwky Littleton CO 80122 Personal E-mail: betsy_cabell@dpsk12.org.

CABELL, FREDRICK, JR., lawyer; b. Hazleton, Pa., Nov. 8, 1961; s. Frederick William Cabell and Tomasina Marie Nilo Leanza; m. Laurie Ann Cunningham, July 27, 1985; children: Jane E., James F. BS in BA, Susquehanna U., 1984; JD, Cath. U., 1988. Bar: Pa. 1988, D.C. 1990. Jud. law clk. Hon. Terrence W. Boyle, U.S. Dist. Ct. for Ea. Dist., Elizabeth City, N.C., 1988-89; assoc. Crowell & Moring, Washington, 1989-91, Frumkin, Shralow & Cerullo, P.C., Pottsville, Pa., 1991—. Recipient Am. Jurisprudence award (2) Lawyers Coop. Pubrs., 1988. Mem. Pa. Bar Assn., Schuykill County Bar Assn., Federalist Soc., KC. Republican. Roman Catholic. Home: 3909 Brisban St Harrisburg PA 17111-2230 Office: Frumkin Shralow & Cerullo Second St & Laurel Blvd Pottsville PA 17901

CABEZAS, HERIBERTO, chemical engineer, researcher; b. La Esperanza, Las Villas, Cuba; arrived in U.S., 1967, naturalized, 1974; s. Heriberto and Ana Rosa C.; m. Isaura Vazquez. BSChemE, N.J. Inst. Tech., Newark, 1980; MSChemE, U. Fla., 1981, PhD in Chem. Engring., 1985. Asst. prof. chem. engring. U. Ariz., 1985-93; leader simulation and design team, sustainable tech. divsn. EPA Nat. Risk Mgmt. Rsch. Lab., Cin., 1994-2000; chief sustainable environ. br. sustainable tech. div. EPA Nat. Risk Mmgt. Rsch. Lab., Cin., 2000—. Cons. Nat. Inst. Stds. and Tech., Gaithersburg, Md., 1986-93, rschr. biotech. divsn., 1993-94. Contbr. numerous articles to profl. jours. Mem. AIChE, AAAS, Tau Beta Pi, Omega Chi Epsilon. Roman Catholic. Achievements include development of Paris II solvent design software, waste reduction war algorithm for chemical process design, sustainable systems theory. Office: US EPA 26 W Martin Luther King Dr Cincinnati OH 45268-0001 Business E-Mail: cabezas.heriberto@epa.gov.

CABIALLAVETTA, MATHIS, insurance company executive; Joined Union Bank of Switzerland, 1971—, CEO; vice chmn. Marsh & McLennan Co., Inc., NYC, 1998—99; chmn. Marsh & McLennan Co. Europe, 1999—. Bd. dirs. Philip Morris Cos., 2002—, Altria Group, Inc., HBM BioVentures AG, Swiss Am. Chamber of Commerce. Office: Marsh & McLennan Co Inc 1166 Ave of the Americas New York NY 10036-2774*

CABLE, CHARLES ALLEN, mathematician; b. Akeley, Pa., Jan. 15, 1932; s. Elton Thomas and Margaret (Fox) C.; m. Mabel Elizabeth Yeck, Dec. 19, 1955; children: Christopher A., Carolyn E. BS, Edinboro State Coll., 1954; M.Ed., U. N.C., 1959; PhD in Math., Pa. State U., 1969. Instr. math. Interlaken High Sch., N.Y., 1954-55, Tidioute High Sch., Pa., 1957-58; asst. prof. math Juniata Coll., Huntingdon, Pa., 1959-67; assoc. prof. dept. math. Allegheny Coll., Meadville, Pa., 1969-75, prof. dept. math., 1975-96, chmn. dept., 1970-90. Editorial reviewer: Math. Mag., 1975-80; assoc. editor: Focus, 1981-85. Served with AUS, 1955-57. Gen. Elec. fellow, 1958; NSF fellow, 1959, 61, 68, 73; NDEA fellow, 1969 Mem. Am. Math. Soc., Math. Assn. Am. (chmn. Allegheny Mountain chpt. 1973-75, bd. govs. 1981-84, mem. newsletter editorial com. 1981-85, com. on student chpts. 1987-93, publs. com. 1983-86), AAUP. Republican. Presbyterian. Office: Allegheny Coll N Main St Meadville PA 16335

CABLE, JOHN FRANKLIN, lawyer; b. Hannibal, Mo., Dec. 22, 1941; s. John William and Dorothy (Stanley) C.; m. Leslie Gibbs, Apr. 5, 1965; children: Coventry, Tory, John. AB, Stanford U., 1964; LLB, Harvard U., 1967. Bar: Oreg. 1967. Assoc. Miller, Nash, Wiener, Hager & Carlsen, Portland, Oreg., 1967-73, ptnr., 1973—. Office: Miller Nash LLP 111 SW 5th Ave Fl 35 Portland OR 97204-3604 Office Phone: 503-205-2508. E-mail: frank.cable@millernash.com.

CABOT, ANTHONY N. (TONY), lawyer; BA summa cum laude, Univ. Cleve., 1978; JD cum laude, Ariz. State Univ., 1981. Bar: Ariz. 1981, Nev. 1982. Ptnr., chair, gaming practice Lionel Sawyer & Collins, Las Vegas, Nev.; ptnr., govt. rels., adminstrv. law practice group Lewis & Roca LLP, Las Vegas, Nev. Adj. prof., internat. gaming inst. Univ. Nev., Las Vegas, 1994—; distance learning prof., hospitality law Univ. Houston, Tex. Co-editor-in-chief Gaming Law Rev., editorial bd. Gaming Rsch. & Rev. Jour.; author: (reference books) on gaming law, internet gambling. Mem.: State Bar Ariz., Internat. Assn. Gaming Attys. (past gen. counsel), Nev. Gaming Attys. Assn. (pres. 1992—94), State Bar Nev. (exec. coun. gaming law sect. 1993), Internat. Masters Gaming Law (pres., founding mem.), Casino Mgmt. Assn. (chmn., bd. dir.). Office: Lewis & Roca LLP 6th Fl 3993 Howard Hughes Pkwy Las Vegas NV 89109 Office Phone: 702-949-8280. Office Fax: 702-949-8367. Business E-Mail: acabot@lrlaw.com.*

CABOT, HUGH, III, painter, sculptor; b. Boston, Mar. 22, 1930; s. Hugh and Louise (Melanson) C.; m. Olivia P. Taylor, Sept. 8, 1967. Student, Boston Mus., 1948, Ashmolean Mus., Oxford, England, 1960, Coll. Ams., Mexico City, 1956, San Carlos Acad. Portrait, landscape painter. Author (illustrator): Korea I (Globe); one-man shows include U.S. Navy Hist. and Records Dept., U.S. Navy Art Gallery, The Pentagon, Nat. War Mus., Washington, La Muse de la Marine, Paris, exhibited in group shows at Tex. Tri-State, 1969, Represented in permanent collections Starmont Vail Med. Ctr., Topeka, Kans., Tucson Med. Ctr., Harwood Found., Taos, N.Mex., Washburn U., Topeka, U. Ariz., Tucson, Chandler (Ariz.) Ctr. Arts, Booth Western Mus. Art, Cartersville, Ga.; Ofcl. artist for Korean War. With USN, Korean War. Named Artist of Yr., Scottsdale, Ariz., 1978, 30th ann. Mem. Salmagundi Club (N.Y.C.). Office Phone: 520-398-2721.

CABOT, LEWIS PICKERING, manufacturing company executive, art consultant; b. Sept. 6, 1937; s. John Moors and Elizabeth (Lewis) C.; m. Judith Ogden, July 1, 1960 (div. 1974); children: Elizabeth Lewis, Edward Ogden, Timothy Pickering; m. Susan Knight, July 15, 1978; children: James Eliot, Alexander Lee. AB, Harvard U., 1961, MBA, 1964. Trainee F.S. Moseley & Co., Boston, 1961-62; analyst John P. Chase, Inc., Boston, 1964-68; prin. Gardner & Preston Moss, Boston, 1968-73; chmn., pres. Artcounsel, Inc., Portland, Maine, 1973—; chmn., CEO Southworth Internat. Group, Inc., Portland, Maine, 1977—; pres. ZY-AX Realty, Portland, Maine, 1977—. Chmn. Shellback Corp., 1984-93; pres., chmn. Maine Art Leasing, 1988—; bd. dirs. Material Handling Roundtable; trustee NE Pooled Common Fund, Princeton, N.J., 1972-94. Trustee, pres. Soc. Arts and Crafts, Boston, 1962-66; trustee Phila. Maritime Mus., 1963-68, Mus. Fine Arts, Boston, 1966-90, Mus. Am. Folk Art, N.Y.C., 1973-77, Maine Coll. Art, 1982-91, Portland (Maine) Mus. Art, 1994—, Storm King Art Ctr., Mountainville, N.Y., 1961-72, Maine Maritime Mus., 1997—. Mem. com. Harvard U. Art Mus., Cambridge, Mass., 1982-88; bd. dirs. Maine State Music Theater, 1996-2001. Mem. Met. Club (Washington), Somerset Club (Boston), N.Y. Yacht Club (N.Y.C.). Office: Southworth Internat Group 11 Gray Rd Falmouth ME 04105-2027 Office Phone: 207-878-0700 x4204. Business E-Mail: lcabot@southworthproducts.com.

CABOT, LOUIS WELLINGTON, foundation trustee; b. Boston, Aug. 3, 1921; s. Thomas Dudley and Virginia (Wellington) C.; m. Mabel Hobart Brandon, 1997. AB, Harvard U., 1943, MBA, 1948; LLD (hon.), Norwich U., 1961. With Cabot Corp., 1948-96, pres., 1960-69, chmn. bd., 1969-86; chmn. Brookings Instn., Washington, 1986-92, hon. trustee; chmn. Cabot Wellington, LLC; trustee Cabot Family Trust, VWC Found. Bd. dirs. Owens-Corning Fiberglas Corp., 1961-91, Wang Labs Inc., 1982-91, New Eng. Tel. & Tel., 1965-82, R.R. Donnelley & Sons Co., 1965-91; bd. dirs. Fed. Res. Bank Boston, 1970-78, chmn., 1975-78; U.S. rep. 15th Plenary Session UN Econ. Commn. for Europe, 1960; mem. bus. ethics adv. coun. Dept. Commerce, 1961-63; dir., New Eng. chmn. Nat. Alliance Businessmen, 1970-72, Boston chmn., 1968-69; chmn. Sloan Commn. on Govt. and Higher Edn., 1977-80;

mem. Pres.'s Blue Ribbon Commn. on Def. Mgmt., 1985-86; mem. Def. Sec.'s Commn. on Base Realignment and Closure, 1988; dir. Nat. Coun. for U.S.-China Trade, 1978-82. Mem. bd. overseers Harvard U., 1970-76; chmn. Harvard Coll. Fund Coun., 1963-65; pres. Beverly (Mass.) Hosp., 1958-61; chmn. Com. Corp. Support Pvt. Univs., 1977-83; trustee Norwich U., 1952-77, Mus. of Sci., Boston; corp. mem. MIT; trustee Woods Hole Oceanographic Inst., Northeastern U Conservation Internat. & Island Inst. Fellow: Am. Acad. Arts and Scis. (v.p.); mem.: NAS (pres. cir., co-chmn. 1992—95), Coun. Fgn. Rels., NY Yacht Club, Met. Club, Comml. Club (Boston) (pres. 1970—72), Somerset Club, Harvard Club, Sigma Xi, Phi Beta Kappa. Office: Cabot-Wellington LLC 70 Federal St Boston MA 02110-1906 Office Phone: 617-451-1744.

CABRAL, CYRIL, JR., engineer, researcher; s. Cyril Cabral, Sr. and Phyllis Rose Cabral. BS in Physics and Math., Pace U., 1988; BSEE, Manhattan Coll., 1989; MSEE, Poly. U., 1992. Engr. Thomas J. Watson Rsch. Ctr. IBM, Yorktown Heights, N.Y., 1989—2002, rsch. staff mem. Thomas J. Watson Rsch. Ctr., 2002—. Adj. lectr. Pace U., Pleasantville, N.Y., 1993—2001. Recipient Outstanding Innovation, Internat. Bus. Machine, 2000, Corp. award, 2001. Achievements include holder of 58 U.S. patents.

CABRAL, SAM A., protective services official, labor union administrator; Student, Defiance Coll., U. Toledo; AA in Criminal Justice, Ohio State U.; degree, Nat. FBI Acad., 1978; student, George Meany Ctr. Labor Studies. Chief union steward Campbell Soup, 1961—64; from policeman to detective sgt. Defiance Police Dept., 1965—73, detective sgt., 1973—91, ret., 1991; pres. Internat. Union Police Assns., Alexandria, Va., 1995—. Mem. commn. crime control Congress, 1994. Office: Internat Union Police Assns 1421 Prince St Ste 400 Alexandria VA 22314

CABRANES, JOSÉ ALBERTO, judge; b. Mayagüez, P.R., Dec. 22, 1940; s. Manuel and Carmen López Cabranes; m. Kate Stith, Sept. 15, 1984; children: Alejo, Benjamin José;children from previous marriage: Jennifer Ann, Amy Alexandra. AB, Columbia U., 1961; JD, Yale U., 1965; MLitt in Internat. Law, Cambridge (Eng.) U., 1967; LLD (hon.), Colgate U., 1988, other univs. Bar: N.Y. 1968, D.C. 1975, U.S. Dist. Ct. Conn. 1976. Assoc. Casey, Lane & Mittendorf, N.Y.C., 1967—71; assoc. prof. law sch. Rutgers U., Newark, 1971—73; spl. counsel to gov. P.R., head Office Commonwealth P.R., Washington, 1973—75; gen. counsel Yale U., New Haven, 1975—79; judge U.S. Dist. Ct. Conn., New Haven, 1979—94, chief judge, 1992—94; judge U.S. Ct. Appeals (2nd cir.), 1994—. Mem. Pres.'s Commn. White House Fellowships, 1993—96, Pres.'s Commn. Mental Health, 1977—78; U.S. del. Conf. Security and Coop. in Europe, Belgrade, 1977—78; founding mem. P.R. Legal Def. and Edn. Fund, 1972, chmn. bd., 1977—80; cons. to sec. Dept. State, 1978; mem. Fed. Cts. Study Com., 1988—90; instr. history P.R. Colegio San Ignacio de Loyola, Rio Piedras, PR, 1962; supr. in internat. law Queens' Coll., Cambridge U., 1966—67. Author: Citizenship and the American Empire, 1979; co-author (with Kate Stith): Fear of Judging: Sentencing Guidelines in the Federal Courts, 1998 (Cert. of Merit, ABA); author: articles on law and internat. affairs. Trustee Yale U., 1987—99, Yale-New Haven Hosp., 1978—80, 1984—87, Colgate U., 1981—90, Century Found., N.Y.C., 1983—2000, Columbia U., 2000—, Fed. Jud. Ctr., 1986—90; mem. Coun. on Fgn. Rels.; bd. dirs. Aspira of NY, chmn., 1971—73; bd. dirs. James Madison Meml. Fellowship Found., 1995—2003. Recipient Life Achievement award, Nat. P.R. Coalition, 1987, John Jay award, Columbia Coll., 1991, Life Achievement award student divsn., Nat. Hispanic Bar Assn., 1991, Learned Hand medal for excellence in fed. jurisprudence, Fed. Bar Coun., 2000; Kellett rsch. fellow, Columbia Coll. at Cambridge U., 1965—67. Fellow: ABA, Mex.-Am. Lawyers Assn. (Spl. Recognition award 1994); mem.: Nat. Hispanic Bar Assn., Am. Law Inst., Conn. Bar Assn. (Naruk Jud. award 1993). Roman Catholic. Office: US Ct of Appeals US Courthouse 141 Church St New Haven CT 06510-2030

CABRASER, ELIZABETH JOAN, lawyer; b. Oakland, Calif., June 23, 1952; AB, U. Calif., Berkeley, 1975; JD, U. Calif., 1978. Bar: Calif. 1978, U.S. Dist. Ct. (no., ea., cen. and so. dists.) Calif. 1979, U.S. Ct. Appeals (2d, 3rd, 5th, 6th, 9th, 10th, and 11th cirs.) 1979, U.S. Tax Ct. 1979, U.S. Dist. Ct. Hawaii 1986, U.S. Dist. Ct. Ariz. 1990, U.S. Supreme Ct. 1996. Ptnr. Lieff, Cabraser, Heimann & Bernstein LLP, San Francisco, 1978—. Contbr., editor California Causes of Action, 1998, Moore's Federal Practice, 1999, editor-in-chief California Class Actions Practice and Procedures, 2003; contbr. articles to law jours. Named one of Top 100 U.S. Lawyers, 1997, 2000, Top 50 Women Lawyers, Nat. Law Jour., 1998, Top Ten Lawyers in Bay Area, San Francisco Chronicle, 2003; recipient Presdl. Award of Merit, Consumer Attys. Calif., 1998, Matthew O. Tobriner Public Service Award, Legal Aid Soc., 2000, Disting. Jurisprudence Award, Anti-Defamation League, 2002, U. Calif., Berkeley Sch. Law Citation Award, 2003. Mem. ABA (tort and ins. practice sect., sect. litig. com. on class action and derivative skills, chair subcom. on mass torts), ATLA, Coun. Am. Law Inst., Calif. Constn. Rev. Commn., Nat. Ctr. for State Cts. (mass tort conf. planning com.), Women Trial Lawyer Caucus, Consumer Attys. Calif., Calif. Women Lawyers, Assn. Bus. Trial Lawyers, Nat. Assn. Securities and Comml. Attys., Bay Area Lawyers for Individual Freedom, Bar Assn. San Francisco (v.p. securities litig., bd. dirs.). Office: Lieff Cabraser Heimann & Bernstein LLP Embarcadero Ctr W 30th Fl 275 Battery St San Francisco CA 94111-3305 E-mail: ecabraser@lchb.com.*

CABRERA, ANGEL, dean, finance educator; b. Madrid, Aug. 5, 1967; came to U.S., 1991; s. Angel and Virtudes (Izquierdo) C.; m. Elizabeth Jean Frazer, Mar. 19, 1994. Degree in telecommunication engring., Univ. Politecnica, Madrid, 1990; MS in Psychology, Ga. Inst Tech, 1993, PhD in Psychology, 1995. Rsch. engr. Univ. Politecnica, Madrid, 1990-91, asst. prof., 1990-91; mgr. Accenture, 1995-96; vis. prof. Carlos III U., 1997-98; prof. Instituto de Empresa, Madrid, 1998—2004, dir. human resource dept., 1999-2000, dean, 2001—04; pres. Thunderbird, Garvin Sch. of Internat. Mgmt., Glendale, Ariz., 2004—. Contbr. articles to profl. jours. Goethe Inst. scholar DAAD, 1989, Fulbright scholar, 1991-95. Mem. APA, European Soc. Cognitive Psychology, Cognitive Sci. Soc. Office: President of Thunderbird Garvin Sch of Internat Mgmt 5620 W Thunderbird Rd Ste F1 Glendale AZ 85306

CABRERA, QUINCY RODOLFO, minister, educator; b. Lingle, Wyo., Feb. 14, 1943; s. Pedro Cabrera and Sarah Garcia; m. Ruth Estrada, Nov. 4, 1966 (dec. 1980); children: Pablo, Juan, Sarai; m. Maria Esther, July 26, 1985; children: Rodolfo, Esther, Caleb, Joshua. MEd, L.A. State U., 1965; PhD, U. Autonoma de Mex., 1968; DD, Fuller Theol. Seminary, 1994. Tchr., missionary Assemblies of God Bible Sem., Tijuana, Baja, tchr. theology L.A., 1990—92; pastor New Life Christian Ctr., L.A., 1992—. Dir. Abundant Life Theol. Ctr., 2005. Author: The Holy Trinity, 1980, Essentials of Preaching, 1986. Pres. Mex. Am. Political Assn., L.A., 1982-87; mem. Police commn., L.A., 1997, L.A. City Council, 1998; bd. edn. L.A. Unified Sch. Dist., 1998-2000; bd. mem. YMCA, L.A., 2001. Recipient Latino of Yr. award Hispanic Mag., 1995. Democrat. Avocations: mountain climbing, boating. Home: 1410 Perez Lane Los Angeles CA 90033 Office: El Adalid Ministries PO Box 432399 San Diego CA 92143-2399

CABRERA, RICARDO, music educator, choral director; b. Neptune, N.J., Apr. 28, 1951; s. Lillian Gladys Rios and Ismael Cabrera; m. Dolly U. Garcia, Oct. 18, 1961; m. Flor Rosina Mattos, Nov. 3, 1949 (div. Dec. 22, 1996); children: Marcos Ivan, Gabriel Armando. M of Music Edn., Fla. State U., 1980. Cert. tchr. Dept. of Edn., P.R., 1983. Tchr. music Dept of Edn., Bayamon, PR, 1980—86, supr. music San Juan, PR, 1986—87; prof. Interam. U. of P.R., San German, PR, 1989—, choral dir., 2005—. Min. of music, choral dir. Sion Luth. Ch., Bayamon, PR, 1980—86; pres. P.R. Choral Dir. Assn., San Juan, 1983—85; theory and flute instr. San Juan's Children's Choir, PR, 1985—86; adjudicator and advisor for selection of proposals on cultural projects Cultural Inst. of P.R., San Juan; choral arranger; mus. dir. Drama Danza Mus. Theatre and Dance Co. of P.R., San Juan; music dept. dir. Interam. Univ. of P.R., San German, 2000—01. Dir.: (choral orchestral work) Mozart Requiem Performance, (music theatre - stage performance) Carmina Burana, (choral work) Handel's Messiah, (choral orchestral work) Schubert Mass in G, Mozart's Coronation Mass. Adjudicator for numerous choral festivals and competitions, San German, PR, 1985—2005. With U.S. Army, 1971—73. Mem.: Choral Soc. of P.R. (assoc.). Lutheran. Avocations: reading, travel, music, jogging. Home: B-16 Calle 2 Mans de San German San German PR 00683 Office: Interam Univ of PR PO Box 5100 C-38 San German PR 00683 Office Phone: 787-264-1912.

CABROL, NATHALIE AGNES, research scientist; b. Bagneux, France, Aug. 30, 1963; d. Jean Cabrol and Michele Marcelle Quatre-Sols; m. Edmond Antoine Grin, Apr. 15, 2000. PhD in Planetary Scis., Sorbonne U., Paris, 1985—91. Fellow NASA Ames Rsch. Ctr., Space Sci. Divsn., Moffett Field, Calif., 1996—98; prin. investigator SETI Inst., NASA Ames Rsch. Ctr., Space Sci. Divsn., Moffett Field, Calif., 1998—. Contbr. chapters to books, articles to profl. jours. Recipient Silver Medal for Rsch. Work, Obs. of Triel (France), 1992, Medal for Edn. and Pub. Outreach, City of Triel, France, 1994, Gold medal Internat. Water and Sci. award, Unesco, European Parliament, Bronze Medal for Edn. and Pub. Outreach, Ecole des Mines de Douai (France), 1996, Silver Medal, Societe d'Encouragement au Progres, 1997, ASIP, 2004, Women of Discovery: Air and Space Award, World Wings Quest, 2005; grantee Mars Exploration Rover Mission Participating Scientist, NASA, 2002—, NASA Ames Rsch. Ctr., 2002—03, NASA Astrobiology Inst., 2003—, NASA Astrobiology Sci. and Tech. for Exploring Planets, 2003—; Carey Fellow, Wings World Quest, 2005. Achievements include research in exploring the highest lakes on Earth as analogs to ancient Martian lakes in order to understand their potential for life inception and survival and study the limits of life on Earth; the Gusev crater as a landing site for the Mars Exploration Mission; first to free dive(without oxygen tanks) in high-altitude lakes (5, 916 m or 18, 500 ft) to study human physiological response and adaptation to high altitude; develop science exploration strategies for automated robotic vehicles (rovers) to search for habitable environments and life on Mars; being a member of the Mars Exploration Rover Science Team. Office: NASA Ames Rsch Ctr/SETI Inst Space Science Divsn MS 245-3 Moffett Field CA 94035 Office Phone: 650-604-0312. Home Fax: 650-967-6981; Office Fax: 650-604-6779. Business E-Mail: ncabrol@mail.arc.nasa.gov.

CACALANO, NICHOLAS ANTHONY, research scientist, educator; b. Yonkers, N.Y., July 14, 1963; PhD, Columbia U., 1992. Postdoctoral rsch. scientist DNAX Rsch. Inst., Palo Alto, Calif., 1996—2001; asst. prof. UCLA Sch. of Medicine, L.A., 2001—. Recipient STOP Cancer award, STOP Cancer Orgn., 2002—. Mem.: AACR (assoc.). Home: 10644 Eastborne Ave Los Angeles CA 90024 Office: UCLA Sch Medicine 10833 LeConte Ave Los Angeles CA 90095 Office Phone: 310-267-2803. Home Fax: 310-206-1260; Office Fax: 310-206-1260. Personal E-mail: ncacalano@mednet.ucla.edu.

CACAYORIN, EDWIN D., medical association administrator, neurologist; b. Philippines, Apr. 21, 1947; m. Donna Lee Miller; children: Edward Ross Corrin, Laura Jean Corrin. MD, Far Ea. U. Inst. of Medicine, Philippines, 1971. Cert. Added Qualification (CAQ) in Neuroradiology Am. Bd. of Radiology, 1996, diplomate Radiology Am. Bd. of Radiology, 1978. Radiologist, spl. procedures Western Pa. Hosp., Pitts., 1977—79; asst. prof. of radiology SUNY Health Sci. Ctr., Syracuse, NY, 1980—82, chief of neuroradiology, 1982—92, prof. of neurosurgery, 1989—92; med. dir. and neuroradiologist Ctrl. Tex. Imaging Ctr., St. David's Med. Ctr., Austin, Tex., 1992—98; diagnostic, interventional neuroradiology Allegheny Gen. Hosp., Pitts., 1993—94; prof., chief of neuroradiology St. Louis U. Hosp., St. Louis, 1998—2001, U. Tex. Health Sci. Ctr., Hermann Hosp., Houston, 2001—. Reviewer Am. Jour. of Neuroradiology, 1987—97; exec. com. appointment, dept. of radiology SUNY Health Sci. Ctr. at Syracuse, 1988—92; reviewer Radiographics, 1990—95; pres. Capital Imaging Assn., Austin, Tex., 1994—95; reviewer Radiology, 2003—; fellowship neuroradiology U. Pittsburgh under Charles Kerber and Arthur Rosenbaum, 1980. Lecturer (various scientific presentations); contbr. chapters to books Neurological Surgery, Imaging of Athletic Injuries, Microsurgical Carotid Endarterectomy, articles various profl. jours. Recipient Physician's Recognition award, AMA, 1980, Cert. of Merit, Am. Roentgen Ray Soc., 1981, Legislative Resolution, Senatorial Commendation, SUNY, NY State Senate, 1987, Outstanding Tchr. award, St. Louis U. Radiology Residents, 1999-2000, Summa Cum Laude award on stroke, ASNR, Vancouver, CA, 2002. Mem.: Am. Soc. of Neuroradiology, Radiol. Soc. of N.Am. Achievements include research in embolization of vascular lesions of the central nervous system with n-butyl cyanoacrylate. Clinical trial sponsored by Tri-Point Medical LP (completed); balloon dilitation of cerebral vessels in spasm. Clinical trial sponsored by Interventional Therapeutics Corp. (completed); currently involved in innovative endovascular treatment of strokes and intracranial aneurysms. Avocations: travel, music. Office: UT Health Sci Ctr Houston TX

CACCIATORE, RONALD KEITH, lawyer; b. Donaldsville, Ga., Feb. 5, 1937; s. Angelo D. and Myrtice E. (Williams) C.; children: Rhonda, Donna, Rex. Student, Spring Hill Coll., 1955-56; BA, U. Fla., 1960; JD, 1963. Bar: Fla. 1963, U.S. Supreme Ct. 1969. Asst. state atty. 13th Jud. Cir., 1963-65; pvt. practice Tampa, Fla., 1967. Lectr. criminal law; mem. 13th Jud. Cir. Jud. Nominating Commn., 1976-80, chmn., 1980; mem. Fed. Judiciary Adv. Commn. Fla., 1987—. Trustee Hillsborough C.C., 1979-83, chmn., 1982-83. Recipient Jack Edmund award for civility and excellence in the practice of criminal law. Fellow Am. Coll. Trial Lawyers; mem. Hillsborough County Bar Assn. (pres. 1975-76, chmn. trial lawyers sect. 1983-85, Herbert G. Goldburg Meml. award 1991), Fla. Bar Assn. (chmn. criminal law sect. 1977-78), Fla. Coun. Bar Pres.'s (chmn. 1979-80), Fed. Bar Assn. (pres. Tampa Bay chpt. 1985-86, fed. jud. nominationcom. Fla. 1999—, George C. Carr Meml. award Tampa Bay chpt. 1996), Master of the Bar, White-Ferguson Inn, Herbert G. Goldburg Criminal Law Am. Inn of Ct. (pres. 2000—), Am. Inns of Ct., Palma Ceia Golf and Country Club, University Club.

CACCIATORE, S. SAMMY, lawyer; b. Tampa, Fla., Aug. 2, 1942; s. Sam and Margarita C.; m. Carolyn Michels, Aug. 10, 1963; children: Elaine Michel, Sammy Michel. BA, JD, Stetson U., DeLand, Fla., 1966. Bar: Fla. 1966, U.S. Ct. Appeals (5th cir.) 1967, U.S. Supreme Ct. 1971, U.S. Ct. Appeals (11th cir.) 1981, U.S. Dist. Ct. (mid. dist. 1966) Fla. Asst. public defender 9th jud. cir. State of Fla., State of Fla., 1966; assoc. firm Orlando, Fla., 1966-67; pvt. practice Melbourne, Fla., 1967—; ptnr. Nance, Cacciatore, Hamilton, Barger, Nance & Cacciotore, Melbourne, Fla., 1970—. Mem. 5th Dist. Appellate Nomination Commn., 1979-83; mem. Fla. Med. Malpractice Adv. Com., 1982; mem. jud. nominating commn. Fla. Supreme Ct. 1986-90, mem. Supreme Ct. Jury Instrn. Com., 2001—; bd. overseers Stetson U. Coll. Law, 1995—; trustee Stetson U., 2000—; lectr. in field. Contbr. articles to profl. jour., chpt. to books. Trustee A. Max Brewer Meml. Law Libr., Brevard County, Fla., 1972-76, chmn., 1972-75. Mem. ABA, ATLA, Am. Law Inst., Internat. Acad. Trial Lawyers, Am. Bd. Profl. Liability Lawyers, Am. Bd. Trial Advocates, Nat. Bd. Trial Advocacy, Acad. Fla. Trial Lawyers (bd. dir. 1970—, pres. 1984-85, Pres.'s award 1983), Internat. Acad. Trial Lawyers Assn. (adminstrn. of justice com. 1989), Fla. Bar (bd. govs. 1994-99, exec. com. 1995-99, vice chmn. advt. task force 1995-97, budget com. 1994-97, chmn. 1996, mem. exec. com. trial lawyer sect. 1975, chmn. constl. revision com. 1997—, mem. legis. com. 1995-99, chmn. 1998-99, mem. jury instrn. com. Fla. Supreme Ct., 2001—), So. Trial Lawyers Assn., Stetson Lawyers Assn. (1st v.p. 1992-93, pres.-elect 1994-95, pres. 1995-96), Brevard County Bar Assn. (bd. dir., Pres.'s award 1975), Vassar Carlton Inn of Ct. (emeritus), Eau Gallie Yacht Club (gov., vice commodore 1981-82, commodore 1983-84). Democrat. Roman Catholic. Office: 525 N Harbor City Blvd Melbourne FL 32935-6837 Office Phone: 321-777-7777. Business E-Mail: sammy@nancelaw.com. *The law is a living, growing institution of our lives. Lawyers need to remember this and nurture its development as one would a child. It should grow straight and strong for the benefit of the people.*

CACCIATORE, SHAREN WENDY, educational administrator; b. Boston, Mass., Feb. 18, 1960; d. Frederick Everett Robertson and Doris Marie McLean; m. Carmelo Cacciatore, Mar. 19, 1978; children: John, Carmelo, Alfonso, Catherine. BA Humanities, Stonehill Coll., Easton, MA, 1999; MA Edn., Harvard U., Cambridge, MA, 2000. Founder / dir. / pres. The Story Train, Inc., Middleboro, Mass., 1994—; treas. / adminstrv. officer Cacciatore Bros., Inc., Middleboro, Mass., 1985. Dir. The Story Train Literacy Ctr., Middleboro, Mass., 2000—. Contbr. articles to profl. publs. Recipient Hon. Award Recognition, The Nat. Dean's List, 1999. Fellow: Internat. Reading Assn., Religious Studies and Philos. Assn., The Am. Philos. Assn., Nat. Coun. Teachers English, Phi Delta Kappa Internat. Achievements include patents for 501C-3 non-profit status awarded, US IRS, The Story Train, Inc., 1995; Service Mark awarded from US Patent and Trademark Office: The Story Train website, 1997. Avocations: creative writing, volunteering. Office: The Story Train Literacy Center 353 West Grove Street Middleboro MA 02346 E-mail: stytrain@ici.net.

CACCIOTTOLO, NEIL JOSEPH, media specialist; b. Chgo., Nov. 9, 1954; s. Neil Joseph Sr. and Marie Grace (Colella) Cacciottolo. BA in Comms., Omega Sch. Comms., 2004. Drep. dir. Sunset Promotions, Chgo., 1984—2001, dir. media, 2002—; pub. rels. cons. City of Chgo., 2001—02. Prodn. cons. Sunset Media, Chgo., 1991—, music educator ea. divsn., 1995—. Prodr.: (CD) Reunion of the Nashville "A" Team, 2004; author: The Do's and Don'ts of the Music Industry, 1990. Named Prodr. Yr., Country Music Assn. Am., 1992, Record Co. of Yr., 1992. Mem.: Chg. Music Ptnrs. (bd. dirs. 2004), City Club Chgo. Democrat. Avocations: cooking, golf, reading, intergovernmental affairs. Home and Office: 3638 West 111th St Box 557934 Chicago IL 60655 Office Phone: 708-371-9533. E-mail: sunsetpromogrp@comcast.net.

CACERES, FRANKLIN THOMAS, writer; b. N.Y.C., July 8, 1946; s. Frank Caceres and Louise Caamano; m. Magali Zayas; children: Anthony Caceres, German Gomez, Zaira Gomez. BBA, Manhattan Coll., 1969; MA, U. South Fla., 1998; PhD, Clayton Coll. Natural Health. Regional credit mgr. Carrier Air Conditioners, Inc., Clearwater, Fla., 1988—94; asst. acad. dean Hillsborough C.C., Mac Dill AFB, Fla., 1994—96; mgmt. sys. analyst Hillsborough County Bd. Commrs., Tampa, Fla., 1996—. Cons. Hispanic Bus. Initiative Fund, Tampa, 1996—. Author: (novels) Because They Were, 2002, Chronic Nights, 2003, By Reason of Privilege, 2005; contbr. articles to profl. jours. and newsletters. Mem. So. Poverty Law Ctr., Montgomery, 2000—, Hillsborough Alliance for Citizens with Disabilities, Tampa, 1996—, Nat. Coun. La Raza, Washington, 2000—. With U.S. Army, 1969—71. Mem.: Paralyzed Vets. Am., Mystery Writers Am., Nat. Multiple Sclerosis Soc., Tampa Writers' Alliance (treas.), League United Latin Am. Citizens, Phi Kappa Phi. Roman Catholic. Avocation: woodworking. E-mail: caceresf@hotmail.com.

CACERES, HERNAN MARCELO, composer, educator; b. Santiago, Chile, Mar. 20, 1966; s. Hugo Hernan Caceres and Edith Noemi Larrondo; m. Viviana Sara Insunza, Nov. 19, 1989; children: Marcelo Ivan, Paola Sara. BMus in Piano performance, Cath. U. of Chile, Santiago, 1995; MMus in Piano performance, Andrews U., Berrien Springs, Mich., 2003. Performer, lectr. Ministry of Edn., Santiago, Chile, 1985—89; prof. music Adventist U. of Chile, Chillan, 1990—96; chair music dept. Adventist U. of Colombia, Medellin, Colombia, 1997—2000; pianist, organist, choir dir. First Presbyn. Ch., Benton Harbor, Mich., 2001—; univ. singers piano accompanist Andrews U., Berrien Springs, Mich., 2001—, adj. instr. piano, 2001—; prof. piano The Salvation Army Cmty. Ctr., Benton Harbor, Mich., 2002—. Piano soloist, chamber music and condr. prestigious Chilean music instns., 1980—96; piano concerto Santa Cecilia Chamber Orch., Chillan, Chile, 1992, Cath. U. of Chile, Santiago, 1995; solo recital Linda Vista U., Pueblo Nuevo, Chiapas, Mexico, 1997; orchestra and hand bell choir condr. Adventist U. of Colombia, Medellin, 1997—2000; orch. asst. condr. Andrews U., Berrien Springs, Mich., 2002; piano concerto Sinfonia-Chamber Orch. of P.R., San Juan, 2002; solo recital First Presbyn. Ch., Benton Harbor, Mich., 2003; piano performance Howard Performing Arts Ctr. Dedication Concert, Berrien Springs, Mich., 2003. Composer: (piano compositions) several pieces performed in Chile, Colombia and U.S.A. Recipient Young Artist Competition award, Andrews U., 2002, First Pl. award, 16th Luis A. Ferre Internat. Piano Competition, 2002; Piano scholarship, Amigos del Teatro Mcpl. Corp., 1986, 1987. Mem.: Internat. Adventist Musicians Assn., Phi Kappa Phi. Office: Andrews Univ 100 US Hwy 31 Berrien Springs MI 49103 Office Phone: 269-471-3555. Business E-Mail: caceres@andrews.edu.

CACHIA, PIERRE JACQUES, Middle East languages and culture educator, researcher; b. Fayoum, Egypt, Apr. 30, 1921; came to U.S., 1975; s. François and Anna Rachel (Axler) C.; m. Phyllis Barbara Oyston, Mar. 20, 1953; children: Susan Margaret, Philip Greville, Helen Frances; m. Merle McNeill Dalziel, Sept. 26, 1992. BA, Am. U., Cairo, 1942; PhD, U. Edinburgh, 1951. Mem. faculty Am. U., Cairo, 1946-48, U. Edinburgh, Scotland, 1949-75; prof. Arabic lang. and lit. Columbia U., N.Y.C., 1975-91, chmn. dept. Middle East langs. and cultures, 1980-83, prof. emeritus, 1991—. Author: Taha Husayn, 1956, Popular Egyptian Narrative Ballads, 1989, An Overview of Modern Arabic Literature, 1990, The Arch Rhetorician: A Handbook of Late Arabic Badi', 1998, Arabic Literature - An Overview, 2002; co-author: History of Islamic Spain, 1965, 1977, 1992, 1996, Land-locked Islands: two alien lives in Egypt, 1999; translator (by Tawfiq al-Hakim): The Prison of Life, 1992; translator: (by Yahya Haqqi) Blood and Mud, 1999; compiler The Monitor-Arabic Grammatical Terms, 1973; editor: The Book of the Demonstration by Eutychius, Vol. 1, 1960, Vol. 2, 1961; co-editor: Islam: Past Influence and Present Challenge, 1979, Jour. Arabic Lit., 1970—96; contbr. encys., Orientalist jours., Great Lit. of Ea. World, African Writers, Life Writing. Grantee NEH, 1977; grantee Smithsonian Instn., 1979; fellow Am. Research Ctr. in Egypt, Cairo, 1982; fellow Woodrow Wilson Ctr., Washington, 1991-92. Mem.: Union Européenne d'Arabisants et d'Islamisants, Brit. Soc. Middle Eastern Studies, Am. Assn. Tchrs. Arabic, Middle East Studies Assn., Am. Oriental Soc. E-mail: pjc1@columbia.edu.

CACHOPO, PATRICIA ANN, music educator; b. San Jose, Calif., Sept. 21, 1939; d. Joseph James and Lauretta Catherine (Scholes) Romani; m. Ronald Louis Cachopo; children: Ronald Patrick, Todd Anthony, Patrick Joseph. BA in creative arts, San Jose State U., 1982. Owner, tchr. Patricia Cachopo Piano Studio, Santa Clara, Calif., 1973—. Tchr. Presbyn. Music Sch., Sunnyvale, Calif., Marilyn Cartein's Music Sch., San Jose, Calif. Letterwriting activist Sierra Club, HSUS, NRDC, Calif., 1983—2005; signature collector Pro Paw Prop 4 Initiative, Calif., 1997—98; donator Amnesty Internat., Ocean Conservancy, Calif., 1995—2005; vol. St. Justins Ladies Guild, The Music Tchrs. Assn. of Calif., O'Connor's Hosp. Recipient Nat. Honor Roll, Nat. Piano Playing Auditions, 1979. Mem.: Music Tchrs. Assn. of Calif. (newsletter editor 1982—84), Nat. Guild Piano Tchrs. Democrat. Cath. Avocations: running, walking, weightlifting, yoga, drawing. Home: 2337 Harriston St Santa Clara CA 95050 Office Phone: 408-248-5992.

CACIOPPO, CURTIS PAT, composer, pianist; b. Ravenna, Ohio, Sept. 23, 1951; s. Joseph Pat and Nancy Jane Cacioppo; m. Christine Lynne Carlson, Nov. 23, 1973; children: Charles Alexander, Nicholas Immanuel. MusB, Kent State U., 1973; MA, NY U., 1976, Harvard U., 1979; PhD, Harvard U., Cambridge, Mass., 1977—80. Asst. prof., lectr. Harvard U., Cambridge, Mass., 1979—83; Ruth Marshall Magill prof. of music Haverford Coll., Pa., 2000—. Composer: (string quartet) Nayénĕzgani (Monsterslayer). Co-founder, Native Am. Fund Haverford Coll., Pa. Recipient Lifetime Achievement award, Am. Acad. Arts and Letters, 1997; Howard Found. Fellow, Brown U., 1990—91. Mem.: Rowfant Bibliophilic Soc. Avocations: antique autos, history, travel. Office: Haverford Coll 370 Lancaster Ave Haverford PA 19041 Office Phone: 610-896-1008.

CACIOPPO, JOHN TERRANCE, psychologist, educator, medical researcher; b. Marshall, Tex., June 12, 1951; s. Cyrus Joseph and Mary Katherine (Kazimour) Cacioppo; m. Barbara Lee Andersen, May 17, 1981 (div. 1998); children: Christina Elizabeth, Anthony Cyrus; m. Wendi L. Gardner, Sept. 8, 2001. BS in Econs., U. Mo., Columbia, 1973; MA in Psychology, Ohio State U., 1975, PhD in Psychology, 1977. Asst. prof. psychology U. Notre Dame, Ind., 1977-79, U. Iowa, Iowa City, 1979-81, assoc. prof., 1981-85, prof. psychology, 1985-89, Ohio State U., 1989-98, Univ. chaired prof. psychology, 1998-99; Tiffany-Margaret Blake disting. svc. prof. U. Chgo., 1999—. Vis. faculty Yale U., 1986, U. Hawaii, 1990, U. Chgo., 1998—99; tng. grant dir. NIMH Social Psychology, 1993—98; co-dir. Inst. for Mind and Biology, 1999—2004; dir. Social Psychology Program, 1999—; dir. Ctr. Cognitive and Social Neurosci. U. Chgo., 2004—. Author, editor: 10 books; editor: Psychophysiology, 1994—97; mem. editl. bd.: various prof. jours.; contbr. over 300 articles to profl. jours. Active John D. and Catherine T. MacArthur Found. Network on Mid-Body Integrations, 1995-98; bd. dirs. Ohio State U. Rsch. Found., 1993-98 Recipient Early Career Contbn. award Psychophysiology, 1981, Troland Rsch. award NAS, 1989, Disting. Sci. Contbr. Psychophysiol., Soc. Psychophysiol. Rsch., 2000; NSF grantee, 1979—, Campbell award Soc. Personality and Social Psychology, 2000. Fellow: APA (past pres. 2 divsns., Disting. Sci. Contbn. award 2002), Acad. Behavioral Medicine Rsch., Am. Psychol. Soc. (keynote spkr. ann. meeting 2002, bd. dirs. 2002—); mem.: AAAS, Am. Acad. Arts and Scis., Soc. Exptl. Psychologists, Soc. Exptl. Social Psychology, Soc. Personality and Social Psychology (pres. 1995), Soc. Psychophysiol. Rsch. (bd. dirs. 1985—88, officer 1991—94, pres. 1992—93, bd. dirs. 1998—2000), Sigma Xi (nat. lectr. 1996—98). Office: U Chgo Dept Psychology Chicago IL 60637

CADA, GLENN FRANCIS, fisheries biologist; b. Columbus, Nebr., Nov. 2, 1949; s. Jerome John and Blanche Ann (Polodna) C.; m. Phyllis Marie Brabec, Aug. 19, 1972: children: Michael, Suzanne, Holly. BS, U. Nebr., 1971; MS, Colo. State U., 1973; PhD, U. Nebr., 1977. Rsch. staff mem. Oak Ridge Nat. Lab., Oak Ridge, Tenn., 1977—. Fellow Am. Inst. Fishery Rsch. Biologists; mem. Am. Fisheries Soc. (cert. fisheries biologist). Avocations: music, photography, travel, hiking. Office: Oak Ridge Nat Lab PO Box 2008 Oak Ridge TN 37831-6036

CADDELL, FOSTER, artist; b. Aug. 2, 1921; s. Foster and Clara (Bamford) C.; m. June A. Kaufmann, Apr. 10, 1943 (dec. Feb. 1989); m. Gail L. Marchant, Feb. 14, 1993. Student, R.I. Sch. Design, 1940-43; pvt. study with, Peter Helck, Robert Brackman, Guy Wiggins. Artist Providence Lithograph Co., R.I., 1939-52; freelance illustrator, 1951-65; owner, instr. Foster Caddell's Art Sch., Voluntown, Conn., 1958—. One-man shows Providence Art Club, 1948, 63, South County (R.I.) Art Assn., 1967, Slater Mus., Norwich Acad., 1976, Heritage Plantations of Sandwich, 1985; group shows include Springfield Mus. Fine Arts, 1962-77, Am. Watercolor Soc., 1973, NAD, 1973, Am. Artists Profl. League (awards 1953, 71, 72, 89, 90, 91), Acad. Artists Am. (awards 1968, 73, 75), Slater Mus., Norwich Acad., 1975-80, Providence Art Club (award 1978, 79, 92), Nat. Arts Club, 1978, Internat. Soc. Artists (award 1978), Soc. des Pastellists de France, 1987, The Monmouth (N.J.) Mus., 1994, Brown U. Libr., Providence, 1995, Pastel Soc. No. Fla. (award 1996), Pastel Soc. Am. (elected Hall of Fame 1998), Beijing Acad. Fine Arts, 1997, others; specialist in portraiture, 1965—; author: Keys to Successful Landscape Painting, 1976, Keys to Successful Color, 1979, Keys to Painting Better Portraits, 1982, Oil Painting Techniques, 1983, Landscape Painting Techniques, 1984, Foster Caddell's Keys to Successful Landscape Painting, 1993, Pastel Interpretations, 1993, The Art of Pastel Portraiture, 1996, Best Pastels II, 1998, Best of Sketching and Drawing, 1998, Pastel Jour. 2000, Pastel Artists Internat. 2001; work on display at pastelsocietyofamerica.org, artshow.com, Conn. Soc. Portrait Artists, ctpastelsociety.com; artist ofcl. portraits of father and son, U.S. Sen. Thomas J. Dodd, 1965, and U.S. Sen. Christopher J. Dodd, 2004. Served as artist USAAC, WWII. Recipient award, Norwich Acad., 1947, Ogunquit Art Ctr., 1949, Conservative Painters R.I., 1962, Salmagundi Club, 1973, 1980, No. Fla. Pastel Soc., 1996, Award of Excellence, Mystic Seaport Maritime Gallery, 1996, Best of Show award Mystic Art Assn., 1997, award, Conn. Pastel Soc., 1990—94, 1998, 1999, Honor award, 2001, 2002, 2003, 2004. Mem. Oil Painters of Am., Washington Soc. of Portrait Artists (award 1998), Lyme Art Assn., Providence Art Club, Am. Artists Profl. League, Acad. Artists Am., Am. Soc. Portrait Artists, Salmagundi Club, Pastel Soc. Am. (award 1990, 91, 92, 93, 94, 98, 99), Internat. Soc. of Portrait Artists (award 2004), Conn. Soc. Portrait Artists (Best of Show 2003, Lifetime Achievement award 2005). Address: 47 Pendleton Hill Rd Voluntown CT 06384-1920 Office Phone: 860-376-9583. Personal E-mail: fcaddell@sbcglobal.net.

CADDELL, JOHN A., lawyer; b. Tuscumbia, Ala., Apr. 23, 1910; s. Thomas Arthur and Florence Lee (Huff) C.; m. Lucy Bowen Harris, Sept. 1, 1935; children— Thomas A., Lucinda Lee, Henry Harris and John A. (twins). AB, U. Ala., 1931, LLB, 1933, LLD (hon.), 1982. Bar: Ala. bar 1933. Since practiced in, Decatur. Sec., dir. Southeastern Metals Co., Inc., Birmingham, 1946-68; chmn. bd. First Nat. Bank Decatur, 1976-81; City atty., Decatur, 1936-59; counsel com. investigating campaign expenditures U.S. Ho. of Reps., 1944; bd. commrs. Ala. State Bar, 1939-54, Jud. Council Ala., 1946-58; mem. bd. Bar Examiners Ala., 1949, 50 Mem. Ala. Democratic Exec. Com., 1938-50; Trustee U. Ala., 1954-79, also pres. pro tem, 1974-78. Fellow Am. Coll. Trust and Estate Counsel, Am. Coll. Trial Lawyers, Am. Bar Found.; mem. ABA, Ala. Bar Assn. (pres. 1951-52), Morgan County Bar Assn., U. Ala. Alumni Assn. (pres. 1953), Decatur C. of C. (pres. 1943-44), Ala. Acad. Honor, Pi Kappa Alpha, Omicron Delta Kappa, Phi Delta Phi. Democrat (mem. Ala. exec. com. 1938-50). Presbyn. (elder). Clubs: Athletic, U. Alabama, Decatur Kiwanis (pres. 1939). Home: PO Box 2688 Decatur AL 35602-2688 Office: 214 Johnston St SE Decatur AL 35601-2516 Office Phone: 256-340-8002. Personal E-mail: jcaddell2200@aol.com.

CADDY, EDMUND H.H., JR., architect; b. NYC, Apr. 17, 1928; s. Edmund Harrington Homer and Glenna Corinne (Garratt) C.; m. Mary Audrey Ortiz, Dec. 22, 1951; children— Edmund Harrington Homer III, Mary Elizabeth. BA, Princeton, 1952, M.F.A. (grad. sch. fellow), 1955. With Louis E. Jallade, N.Y.C., 1949-53, Eggers & Higgins, N.Y.C., 1953-55; dir. design Dalton-Dalton Assocs., Cleve., 1955-60; assoc. Raymond & Rado, N.Y.C., 1960-68; gen. ptnr. Raymond & Rado and Ptnrs., N.Y.C., 1968-72, Raymond, Rado, Caddy & Bonington, P.C., N.Y.C., 1972-80, pres., 1980-83; project mgr. Robinson, Mills & Williams, San Francisco, 1983-87, McCue, Boone, Tomsick, San Francisco, 1987-88, O'Brien-Kreitzberg, San Francisco, 1988-90; Sverdrup Corp., 1990-94; archtl. design cons., 1994—. Apptd. by Pres. John F. Kennedy to adv. com. arts John F. Kennedy Ctr. Performing Arts, 1963-70; mem. archtl. adv. commn. N.Y.C. C.C., CUNY, 1979-83. Works include Suburban Hosp, Cleve., 1957, J.M. Smucker Co, Salinas, Cal., 1957, Brookpark (Ohio) City Hall, 1959; Cleve. Transit System addition, 1959, adminstrn. bldg., Met. Water Treatment System, Saigon, 1960, Franklin D. Roosevelt High Sch, N.Y.C., 1963, Crown Heights Intermediate Sch, N.Y.C., 1966, engring. complex design, Stony Brook Campus, State U. N.Y., 1970, Sibley's dept. stores, Syracuse, N.Y., 1973, Rochester Downtown Devel. Study, 1975, R.H. Macy & Co. dept. store, Stamford, Conn., 1979; project mgr. Main Postal Facility, San Francisco, 1985, Univ. Ctr., U. Calif., Irvine, 1987, Santa Clara (Calif.) County CourtHouse, Ft. Mojave Resort Devel., 1991-94. Pres. bd. trustees Montclair (N.J.) Cmty. Hosp., 1973-80. Served with USMC, 1946-48, USMCR, 1948-53. Mem. AIA, Tower Club (Princeton), Racquet and Tennis Club (N.Y.C.) Home: 1999 Baldwin Way Bolingbrook IL 60490-6551

CADDY, MICHAEL DOUGLAS, lawyer; b. Long Beach, Calif., Mar. 23, 1938; s. Frank Edward and Tabitha (Miles) C. BS in Fgn. Svc., Georgetown U., 1960; JD, NYU, 1966. Bar: DC 1970, Tex. 1979. Practiced in, Washington and, Tex.; exec. dir. com. on pub. affairs McGraw-Edison Co., N.Y.C., 1960-61; asst. to lt. gov. State of N.Y., 1962-65; asst. to exec. v.p. NAM, N.Y.C., 1966-67; Washington liaison Gen. Foods Corp., 1968-70; assoc. Gall, Lane, Powell & Kilcullen, 1970-74; legis. counsel Nat. Assn. Realtors, Washington, 1975-76; atty. Office Tex. Sec. of State, Austin, 1980-81. Author: The Hundred Million Dollar Payoff, 1974, How They Rig Our Elections, 1975, Understanding Insurance, 1984, Legislative Trends in Insurance Regulation, 1985, Exploring America's Future, 1987. Mem. Rep. County Com., N.Y.C., 1965-66; nat. dir. Young Ams. for Freedom, 1960-62. Scholar Intercollegiate Studies Inst., 1957-59. Mem.: FBA, ACLU, ABA, ATLA, Nat. Lesbian and Gay Law Assn., Nat. Trust Hist. Preservation, People for Am. Way, Supreme Ct. Hist. Soc., Nat. Coun. Crime and Delinquency, Internat. Platform Assn., Am. Acad. Polit. and Social Sci., Am. Econ. Assn., Assn. Former Intelligence Officers, Am. Judicature Soc., Stonewall Lawyers Assn. Houston, Houston Bar Assn., Tikkun Cmty. Office: 7941 Katy Fwy Ste 296 Houston TX 77024-1924 E-mail: douglascaddy@justice.com.

CADE, JAMES ROBERT, medical educator; b. 1927; Asst. prof. medicine U. Fla., Gainesville, 1961, prof. medicine. Achievements include invention of Gatorade sports drink. Office: U Fla Dept Medicine PO Box 100204 Gainesville FL 32610-0204

CADE, WALTER, III, artist, actor, musician, vocalist; b. NYC; s. Walter Cade and Helen (Henderson) Brehon. Student, Arts Students League, Inst. Modern Art. Appeared in (plays) Amen Corner, Hatful of Rain, Jim Pavone & the Buzz Bomb, Mary Mary, Don't Bother I Can't Cope, Harlequinade, The Story of Ulysses, Mateus, Which Way America, Poetry Now Subway Cinema, (films) Cotton Comes to Harlem, Education of Sonny Carson, Claudine, Now, Angel Heart, The Wiz, FX, (T.V.) Joe Franklin Show, Positively Black, Soul, Sammy Davis Telethon, June Rolands, Musical Chairs, Big Blue Marble; one man shows include: Ocean County Coll., 1977, Jackson State U., 1980, Phoenix Gallery, Atlanta, 1982, Olin Mus. Art, Bates Coll., Maine, 1993, U.S. Nat. Tennis Ctr., Arthur Ashe Stadium, U.S. Open, NY, 1997, 98, 99, Sande Webster Gallery, Pa., 2000, others; 2-man shows include: Lewiston-Auburn Coll., Maine, 1993, others; 3 man shows include: Suffolk CC, 1987; group shows include Whitney Mus., 1971, Corcoran Gallery, 1972, Black Expo, NYC, 1973, Miss. Mus. Fine Art, 1991, Roanoke (Va.) Mus. Fine Art, 1982, Tampa Mus., 1982, Hunter Mus. Art, 1983, Tucson Mus. Art, 1983, New Eng. Fine Arts Inst., Maine, 1993, Lewiston-Auburn Coll., 1994; represented in permanent collections Fine Arts Mus. South, Bruce Mus., Virginia Beach Art Mus., Rockefeller Found., Peter A. Juley and son Collection, Smithsonian Inst. Nat. Mus. Am. Art, others. Recipient Best in show award Las Olas Art Festival, 1980, Arts Festival Atlanta, 1981, Bruce Mus., 1983-84, 94, 1st prize Fine Arts Mus. South, 1982, others. Mem. SAG, Artists Equity. Home: 17203 119th Ave Jamaica NY 11434-2261

CADE, WILLIAM TODD, research scientist, physical therapist; b. Trenton, NJ, May 30, 1969; s. William Louis and Janice Bowser Cade; m. Ashley Elizabeth Williams, May 24, 2003. BS, U. of Md., 1988—91; MS, U. of Miami, 1992—94; PhD, U. of Md., 1997—2002. Cert. physical therapist Mo. State Bd. of Healing Arts, 2002. Staff phys. therapist Veterans Adminstrn. Med. Ctr., Balt., 1995—97, MedStar Home Health Care, White Marsh, Md., 1995—2002; rsch. fellow Wash. U. Sch. of Medicine, Saint Louis, Mo., 2002—; rsch. asst. U. of Md. Sch. of Medicine. Recipient Young Scientist award, 4th Internat. Workshop on Adverse Drug Reactions and Lipodystrophy in HIV, 2002, Mid-Atlantic Regional Chpt. Presidents award, Am. Coll. of Sports Medicine, 2001, Health Scholarship award, US Veterans Adminstrn.; Ruth L. Kirschstein Individual Nat. Rsch. Svc. award, NIH, 2003—. Mem.: Am. Diabetes Assn. Christian. Home: 3529 Hartford St Saint Louis MO 63118 Office: Washington Univ Sch of Medicine 660 South Euclid Ave Saint Louis MO 63110 Office Phone: 314-362-7637. Personal E-mail: tcade@im.wustl.edu.

CADENA, ALVARO, manufacturing executive; b. Bucaramanga, Santander, Colombia, Nov. 8, 1943; came to U.S., 1965; s. Gonzalo and Eva (Uribe) C.; m. Martha Mendez, Jan. 22, 1966; children: Alvaro, Jorge, Sylvia. BME, NYU, 1973; M in Engring., Rochester Inst. Tech., 1976. Mgr. internat. sales Graham Mfg. Co., Inc., Batavia, NY, 1980-83, v.p. internat. sales, 1983-86, exec. v.p., 1986—98; pres., CEO Graham Mfg. Co., Inc. (now Graham Corp.), Batavia, NY, 1998—. Named Outstanding Alumnus 1987, Rochester Inst. Tech. Mem. ASME. Office: Graham Corp PO Box 719 Batavia NY 14021-0719

CADENA, FREDERICO EDUARDO, finance company executive; b. Mexico City; s. Frederico Marquez Cadena and Francis Carol Samame; m. Elizabeth Ann Kopplin, Dec. 14, 2002; 1 child, Samuel Joseph. BA in Econs., Rochville U., 2003; postgrad. in Fin., Heriot Watt U., Edimburgh, Scotland, 2004—. Registered rep. Series 7 Nat. Assn. of Securities Dealers, 2002, securities prin. Series 24 Nat. Assn. of Securities Dealers, 2004, options prin. Series 4 Nat. Assn. of Securities Dealers, 2004. Ops. mgr. Global Rsch. and Recovery, El Paso, Tex., 1997—99; svc. mgr. Excell Agt. Svcs., Las Cruces, N.Mex., 1999—2001; sales mgr. Providian Fin., El Paso, Tex., 2001—02; investment rep. Edward Jones Investments, El Paso, Tex., 2002—04; v.p. risk and margin OptionsXpress, El Paso, Tex., 2004—. Chmn. El Paso County Parks Bd., El Paso, Tex., 1998—99; v.p. Associacion de Lidres Mexicanos-Americanos, El Paso, Tex., 1999—99; dir. of club devel. Tex. Young Rep. Fedn., 1998—99; exec. dir. El Paso County Rep. Party, Tex., 1996—98; vestry mem. All Saints Episcopal Ch., El Paso, Tex., 2002—04. Recipient Vol. of the Yr. award, Rep. Party of Tex., 1998. Mem.: Profl. Risk Mgr.'s Internat. Assn., Global Assn. of Risk Profls. R-Consevative. Episcopal. Avocations: investing/trading, cooking, fitness, wine tasting, travel. Home: 2109 Sun Country Dr El Paso TX 79938 Office: OptionsXpress 4725 Ripley St El Paso TX 79922 Office Phone: 312-267-6482. Personal E-mail: fred@fredcadena.com. Business E-Mail: fcadena@optionsxpress.com.

CADENHEAD, ALFRED PAUL, lawyer; b. LaGrange, Ga., Oct. 14, 1926; s. Roy E. and Omie (Bishop) C.; m. Sara Davenport, Oct. 14, 1945; children: Steven Paul, David James. Jr. coll. certificate, W. Ga. Coll., 1944; LLB, Emory U., 1949. Bar: Ga. 1949. Sr. counsel, ptnr. Hurt, Richardson, Garner, Todd & Cadenhead, Atlanta; with Hurt, Richardson, 1977-92; of counsel Fellows, Johnson & La Briola, Atlanta, 1993—. Pres. Atlanta Legal Aid Soc., 1958. Pres. Met. Atlanta Mental Health Assn., 1964-65, Ga. Assn. Mental Health, 1968; past trustee Queens Coll., Charlotte, N.C.; lifetime trustee West Ga. Found. Served with paratroops U.S. Army, 1944-46. Recipient West Ga. Coll. Disting. Svc. award, 1993, Emory U. Law Sch. Disting. Alumnus award, 1996, Ben F. Johnson Pub. Svc. award Ga. State U., 1999, Founders award State U. West Ga., 2001. Fellow ABA, Am. Acad. Matrimonial Lawyers, Am. Coll. Trial Lawyers, Internat Soc. Barristers; mem. State Bar Ga. (past bd. govs.), Atlanta Bar Assn. (pres. 1970-71, Charles E. Watkins award for disting. and sustained svc. 1992, Leadership award 2000, Professionalism award, 2004), Atlanta Estate Planning Coun. (pres. 1976). Presbyterian. Home: 6305 Riverside Dr NW Atlanta GA 30328-3646 Office: South Tower Peachtree Ctr Ste 2300 225 Peachtree St NE Atlanta GA 30303-1731 Office Phone: 404-586-2027.

CADES, STEWART RUSSELL, lawyer, communications executive; b. Phila., Jan. 16, 1942; s. Ralph E. and Lillian G. (Mann) C. BS in Econs., U. Pa., 1964, LLB, 1967; MEd, Temple U., 1971. Bar: Pa. 1971. Sole practice, Phila. and Bala-Cynwyd, Pa., 1971—; chmn. bd. Porcupine Communications Co., Phila., 1971—. Pres. Nairn U.S. Holdings divsn. Stewart Nairn Group P.L.C., 1980-86; bd. dirs. Cloche Assocs., Inc., Andrews & Leith, Ltd., ACM Worldwide, Ltd.; mng. dir. Overseas Strategic Consulting, 1992—; chmn. bd. dirs. Towne Met., Inc., 1985-92, pres. Election judge Montgomery County, Pa., 1975—77; ct. vol. probation dept. Ct. Common Pleas Phila. County, 1972—74; vice-chmn. Montgomery County Planning Commn., 1980—95; bd. dirs. Southeastern Pa. Transit Authority, 1991—97, trustee, 1991—97, pension com., 1991—97, chmn. real estate com., 1991—97; mem. adv. bd. City of Phila. Airport, 1994—, mem. exec. com., 2000—01; bd. dirs. Friends of Phila. Mus. Art, 1985—91, vice chmn., 1987—89; bd. dirs. Juvenile Law Ctr., 1983—98, pres., 1986—90; bd. dirs. SEPTA Transit Mus.; assocs. adv. bd. Phila. Mus. Art, 2001—, co-chairperson assoc. adv. bd., 2004—, trustee, 2004—, Pa. Acad. Fine Arts, 1992—2002; bd. dirs. Found. Arch., 1999—2002, Conservation Ctr. Art and Hist. Artifacts, 2000—; sec., sch. chmn. alumni undergrad admissions U. Pa., 1978—2001, alumni pres. Class of '64, 1975—90; v.p. Fabric Workshop and Mus., 1992—. Mem.: ABA, Montgomery County Bar Assn., Phila. Bar Assn. (ct. house & detention facilities com. 1983—86), Pa. Bar Assn., Print Club (bd. govs. 1978—98, hon. bd. 1999—). Office: 1500 Walnut St Philadelphia PA 19102

CADET, PATRICK, biology professor, researcher; Ph.D., U. Tex., Galveston, 1998. Post-doctoral rschr. SUNY/Coll. at Old Westbury, 1999—2004, asst. prof., 2004—. Mem. L.I. Sch. Music and Art Found., Albertson, NY, 2003—05. Grantee, Nat. Inst. Drug Abuse, 1999—. Mem.: SUNY/Coll. at Old Westbury Alumni Assn. (life; bd. of directors 2000—05, Excellence in Sci. 2000). Democrat. Achievements include patents for identification of a novel mu3 opiate receptor. Office: SUNY/College at Old Westbury 223 Store Hill Rd Old Westbury NY 11568 Office Phone: 516-876-2739. E-mail: patcad@sunynri.org.

CADIEUX, ROGER JOSEPH, geriatrics services professional; b. Bay Shore, NY, Feb. 7, 1945; m. Kathryn Cadieux; children: Kevin, Kristin, Brooke, Michael. BS, Northwestern State U., 1973; MD, La. State U., 1977. Cert. geriatric psychiatrist, RN anesthetist. Intern, then resident in psychiatry Coll. Medicine Pa. State U., Hershey, 1977-81, psychogeriatric fellow, instr. Coll. Medicine Milton S. Hershey Med. ctr., 1980-81, asst. prof. dept. psychiatry, 1981-93, assoc. prof. psychiatry, 1993-99; clin. prof. psychiatry, 1999—; dir. geriatric assessment program Pa. State U. Coll. Medicine, 1992-98; psychiat. cons. Jewish Home of Harrisburg, 1985—, Homeland Ctr. of Harrisburg, 1993—; program dir. Pa. Dept. Aging, 1986—, physician cons., 1987—; pres. Commonwealth Affiliates, P.C., 1992—. Contbr. articles to profl. jours. Fellow Am. Bd. Psychiatry and Neurology (disting., diplomate); mem. Am. Psychiat. Assn., Am. Geriatric Soc., Am. Assn. for Geriatric Psychiatry, Acad. Sleep Disorders Medicine, Alpha Omega Alpha. Office: 2215 Forest Hills Dr Ste38 Harrisburg PA 17112-1099 Office Phone: 717-540-5353. Personal E-mail: rjcpsy@aol.com.

CADMAN, EDWIN CLARENCE, dean, health facility administrator, medical educator; b. Bandon, Oreg., May 14, 1945; s. Edwin Herbert Cadman and Gloria (Ranellie) Wilson; children: Tim, Kevin, Brian. AB, Stanford U., 1967; MD, U. Oreg., 1971. Intern in internal medicine Stanford (Calif.) U. Hosp., 1971-74; fellow in oncology Yale U., New Haven, 1974-76, asst. prof. medicine, 1976-79, assoc. prof. medicine, 1979-83, prof., chmn. medicine, 1987-94, prof., 1994—99; prof. medicine, dir. Cancer Rsch. Inst. U. Calif., San Francisco, 1983-87, vice chmn. dept. medicine, 1985-87; chief of staff, sr. v.p. med. affairs Yale New Haven Hosp., 1994—99; dean John A. Burns Sch. of Med. Univ. of Hawaii, 1999—. Prof. Am. Cancer Soc., 1985-87. Contbr. over 300 articles to profl. jours. Basketball coach Novato (Calif.) Park and Recreation, 1985. Capt. USNG, 1972-78. Recipient Gold Headed Cane award U. Oreg. Med. Sch., 1971. Fellow AAAS, ACP; mem. AFCR (pres. 1984-86), ASCI, AAP, ASCO/AACR, AOA. Avocations: running, fishing, reading. Office: John A Burns Sch Med 1960 E West Rd Honolulu HI 96822

CADMAN, WILSON KENNEDY, retired utilities executive; b. Wichita, Kans., Sept. 7, 1927; s. Wilson K. and Ethel Louise (Wheeler) C.; m. Mary Roslyn Rowley, Nov. 22, 1950; children: Elizabeth Louise, Cadman Haywood, Robert Wilson. AB, Wichita State U., 1951, postgrad., 1953, Okla. State U., 1965. With Kans. Gas & Electric Co., Wichita, 1951-92, mgr. Wichita divsn., 1967-70, v.p., 1970-79, pres., 1979-92, chief exec. officer, 1981-92, also chmn. bd. dirs.; ret., 1992. Sr. advisor Barr Devlin & Assocs. Investment Bankers, N.Y.C.; bd. dirs. Bank IV of Wichita, El Paso (Tex.) Electric Co., Columbia Energy Group, Herndon, Va., Clark/Bardes Inc., Dallas, Broadbande2e.com, Newport Beach, Calif., Ponca Products Mfg., Wichita, Kans. Bd. govs. Wichita State U. Endowment Assn.; bd. dirs. Wichita State U. Athletic Scholarship Orgn.; mem. Gov.'s Task Force on High Tech. Devel., Mayor's Econ. Adv. Council, Kans. Water Resources Council. Served with USN, 1945-46. Mem. Edison Electric Inst., Wichita Area Devel. (exec. com.), Wichita State U. Endowment Assn., Wichita Club, Wichita Country Club, Univ. Club, Crestview Country Club, Kiwanis, Phi Lambda Psi. Home: The Cloisters 8905 E Douglas Wichita KS 67207 also: PO Box 160-583 33 Hidden Village Big Sky MT 59716

CADY, DENNIS VERN, painter, printmaker, sculptor; b. Portland, Oreg., Nov. 10, 1944; s. Clyde Edward and Lucille Leoney Cady. Attended, Portland State U., 1963—66, attended, 1968, Pratt Graphics Art Ctr., 1977; studied with Reuben Town, Bklyn. Mus. Art Sch., 1969—71; BS, NY Empire State Coll., 1976. One-man shows include Gallery Hunter Mountain, 1994, Libr. Jacques Mattarasso, 1995, Heritage Studio, 1998, Spring St. Studio, 2000, Crosby Painting Studio, 2000, The Karpeles Mann Script Mus., 2003, Queens Coll., 2004, Represented in permanent collections Mus. Modern Art, Newark Pub. Libr., NY Pub. Libr., US Dept. State, U. Toronto, Citibank, Delbitte, NY Times, IBM, Merrill Lynch, Mobile Oil Co., UPS. E4 German Army, 1966—69. Recipient Purchase award, Queensborough CC, 1996. Mem.: NW Print Council.

CADY, DUANE MAYNARD, surgeon; b. Endicott, N.Y., 1934; m. Joyce Cady; 5 children. BS in Chem., Atlantic Union Coll., Mass.; MD, Loma Linda U., 1959. Diplomate Am. Bd. Surgery. Intern SUNY-Syracuse Med. Ctr., 1959-60, resident in surgery, 1960-64, clin. assoc. prof. surgery; pvt. practice N.Y.C. Apptd. chair N.Y. State Medicaid Managed Care Adv. Coun.; mem. N.Y. State Pub. Health Couns. Task Force on Pain Mgmt.; mem. med. staff pres., chair dept. surgery, bd. trustees St. Joseph's Hosp., Syracuse. Captain & army surgeon Medical Corps U.S. Army. Fellow Am. Coll. Surgeons; mem. AMA (coun. med. svc., bd. trustees, pres. AMA Found., 2004-), Med. Soc. of the State of NY (past pres. & chmn.), Am. Soc. Gen. Surgeons. Mailing: PO Box 137 La Fayette NY 13084

CADY, ELWYN LOOMIS, JR., legal association administrator, educator; b. Ames, Iowa, Feb. 21, 1926; s. Elwyn Loomis Sr. and Annabel (Lacey) C.; m. Jane Carolyn Elliott, Jan. 27, 1964 (dec. Dec. 1989); children: James Anson, Kathryn Anne; stepchildren: Martin Norman Jensen III, Paul Elliott Jensen. JD, Tulane U., 1951; BS in Medicine, U. Mo., 1955. Bar: Mo. 1951, U.S. Supreme Ct. 1965. Sci. comml. tchr., athletic dir. and coach Vermillion (Kans.) Rural H.S., 1948-49; pvt. practice Kansas City, St. Louis, Independence, Mo., 1951—; dir. law-medicine program U. Kansas City, 1951-56; asst. dir. Law-Sci. Inst. U. Tex., Austin, 1956-57, sec. Law-Sci. Acad. Am., 1956-57; of counsel Koenig & Dietz, St. Louis, 1959-74; gen. counsel Elliott Oil, Inc., Independence, 1966—2004, Overland Park Dry Cleaners, Inc. Mem. com. on mgmt. Ea. Jackson County Planned Parenthood Clinics, Independence, 1970-75. Author: (book) Law and Contemporary Nursing, 1961, 1st. rev. edit., 1963; author: (with others) Immediate Care of the Acutely Ill and Injured, 1974, Cardiac Arrest and Resuscitation, 1958, 4th rev. edit., 1974, West's Federal Practice Manual, 1960, rev. 2d edit., 1989, Gradwohl's Legal Medicine, 1954; book reviewer sci. books and films. Legal Counsel Friends of the Truman Campus, U. Mo.-Kansas City, Independence, 1987-97, Cmty. Assn. for the Arts, Independence, 1991—; charter mem. Friends of Nat. Frontier Trails Ctr., Independence, 1990—, Independence Hist. Trails City Com., 1991—. With U.S. Army, 1944-45, ETO. Fellow Harry S. Truman Libr. Inst. for Nat. and Internat. Affairs (hon.), Am. Acad. Forensic Sci. (ret.); mem. AAAS (life), Nat. Geog. Soc. (life), Am. Legion (past comdr., judge adv., chaplain, chmn. state blood donor program, chmn. dist. oratorical contest), Mo. Writers' Guild (past pres., historian), Soc. Mayflower Descs. (gov. Heart of Am. colony), Phi Alpha Delta (life), Phi Beta Pi, Tau Kappa Epsilon. Home and Office: 1919 Drumm Ave Independence MO 64055-1836 Office Phone: 816-252-2219.

CADY, JOSEPH HOWARD, management consultant; b. Dallas, Feb. 2, 1959; BS, San Diego State U., 1981, MBA, 1988. Cert. mgmt. cons. Coord. project Mitsubishi Bank of Calif., Escondido and L.A., 1979—82; ind. mgmt. cons. San Diego, 1985—87; sr. cons. Deloitte & Touche, San Diego, 1989—90; mng. ptnr. C S Cons. Group, San Diego, 1990—. Guest lectr. U. San Diego, 1987-97, Southwestern Coll., Chula Vista, Calif., 1990; instr. San Diego State U., 1996-98; spkr. in field. Contbr. articles to profl. jours. Mem. Cons. Roundtable of San Diego. Avocations: reading, sports, flying. Office: C S Cons Group 11491 Raedene Way San Diego CA 92131

CADY, MARK S., state supreme court justice; b. Rapid City, SD, July 12, 1953; married; 2 children. Undergrad. degree, Drake U., JD, 1978. Law clk. 2d Jud. Dist. Ct., 1978-79; asst. Webster County atty.; with law firm Ft. Dodge; dist. assoc. judge, 1983—86; dist. ct. judge, 1986—94; judge Iowa Ct. Appeals, 1994—98, chief judge, 1997—98; justice Iowa Supreme Ct., 1998—. Author: (book) Curbing Litigation Abuse and Misuse: A Judicial

Response. Chmn. Supreme Ct. Task Force on Ct.'s and Cmty.'s Response to Domestic Abuse. Mem.: Webster County Bar Assn., Iowa State Bar Assn. Office: Iowa Supreme Ct 1111 E Ct Ave Des Moines IA 50319 E-mail: MarkS.Cady@jb.state.ia.us.*

CAESAR, GODFREY WRENSFORD, biologist, educator; b. Georgetown, Guyana; Student, Queen's Coll., Georgetown; DSc, DePaul U., 1977. Pvt. practice, NYC. Presenter in field. Contbr. articles to profl. jours. Avocations: dance, jogging, cooking. Address: 209 W 137th St New York NY 10030-2406

CAETANO, RAUL, psychiatrist, educator; b. São Paulo, Brazil, May 5, 1945; came to U.S., 1978; s. Silvestre Vieira and Vera Vieira (Barbosa) C.; m. Patrice Vaeth, Sept. 30, 1995; children: Izabel, Lauren, Helena. MD, U. Rio de Janeiro, 1969, diploma in Psychiatry, 1971; MPH, U. Calif., Berkeley, 1979, PhD, 1983. Psychiatrist Pinel Hosp., Rio de Janeiro, 1969-73; asst. prof. State U., Rio de Janeiro, 1969-73; rsch. psychiatrist Inst. Psychiatry U. London, 1973-76; asst. prof. Inst. Psychiatry, Rio de Janeiro, 1976-78; vis. scholar Alcohol Rsch. Group, Berkeley, 1978-83, assoc. scientist to sr. scientist, 1983-94, dir., 1992—. Adj. prof. Sch. Pub. Health, U. Calif., Berkeley, 1991-98; assoc. dir. Calif. Pacific Med. Ctr. Rsch. Inst., San Francisco, 1992-93; prof., regional dean Sch. Pub. Health, U. Tex., 1998—. Contbr. articles to profl. jours. WHO fellow, 1973-76; rsch. grantee Nat. Inst. Alcohol Abuse and Alcoholism, 1985—. Mem. APHA, Am. Coll. Epidemiology, Rsch. Soc. Alcoholism. Roman Catholic. Office: V8112 5323 Harry Hines Blvd Dallas TX 75390-9128 Office Phone: 214-648-1080. Business E-Mail: raul.caetano@utsouthwestern.edu.

CAFFEE, VIRGINIA MAUREEN, executive assistant; b. Kansas City, Mo., Feb. 25, 1948; d. Frederick Arthur Gladden and Ethel Elizabeth (Keithly) Courier; m. Marcus Pat Caffee, May 31, 1975; 1 child, Katheryn Elizabeth. Student, Ctrl. Mo. State U., 1966-73, Okla. State U., 1977-78; BBA in Bus. Edn., Sam Houston State U., 1985. Cert. profl. sec., 1975. Land abstractor Johnson County Title Co., Warrensburg, Mo., 1967-68; dept. sec., bus. placement office Ctrl. Mo. State U., Warrensburg, 1968-69; exec. sec. European Exchange System, Giessen, Germany, 1969-70; confidential sec. Consolidated Freightways, Kansas City, 1972-73; exec. sec. Behring Internat., Houston, 1974-75; sr. sec. Tenneco Oil Co.-E&P, Houston, 1979-84; exec. sec. St. Petersburg (Fla.) Hilton & Towers, 1989-90; adminstrv. mgr. Tampa Bay Engring., Clearwater, Fla., 1990-92; office mgr., WP trainer Marcus Caffee, Consulting, Largo, Fla., 1992-95; sr. adminstrv. asst. BMH Inc., Dallas, 1995-97; exec. sec. GTE Comms. Corp., Irving, Tex., 1997-2000, mem. Internet coun., 1999—2000; exec. asst. Verizon-ESG, 2000—02, human resources bus. ptnr., 2001—. Ad hoc instr. St. Petersburg (Fla.) Jr. Coll., 1993, Profl. Secs. Internat. chpt. liaison for CPS rev. course, 1993-94; presenter in field. Editor (performance programs) Suncoast Singers, 1991-94 (Cmty. Svc. award Arts Coun. Co-op 1993), Clearwater Cmty. Chorus, 1993-95, Ft. Worth Civic Chorus, Fall 1995, (newsletters) Clearwater Sparkler, 1992-93 (1st pl. award 1993), Fla. Divsn. The Secretariat, 1993-94; editor: Livin, Lovin, Laughin, 1995, Texana Newsletter, 1997-98; webmaster T-L Divsn., 1997—. Sec. Montgomery County Choral Soc., Conroe, Tex., 1986-88, publicity co-chmn., 1987-89; pres. Anona Meth. Ch. Choir, Largo, 1990-91; mem. adv. bd. Mountain View C.C., Dallas, 1999. Named Sec. of Yr. Profl. Secs. Internat. Inc. Clearwater chpt., 1994; recipient Mo. State Tchrs. scholarship Mo. Congress Parents and Tchrs., 1966. Mem. CPS Acad., Internat. Assn. Adminstrv. Profls. (chmn. secs. week, sec. Clearwater chpt. 1992-93, pres. 1994, chmn. seminar and v.p. Clearwater chpt. 1992-93, workshop spkr. Fla. divsn. 1993, program spkr. St. Petersburg chpt. 1993, alt. del. to internat. conv. 1993, 96, 98, del. to internat. conv. 1999, alt. del. to divsn. meeting 1993, 94, del. dist. conv. 1994, 98, Sec. of Yr. 1994-95, del. Fla. divsn. meeting 1995, program spkr. Trinity chpt. 1996, del. Tex.-La. meeting 1996, 97, 98, 99, divsn. treas. Tex.-La. divsn. 1996, v.p. 1997-98, pres.-elect 1998-99, pres. 1999-00, workshop spkr. internat. conv. Chgo. 2000), CPS Soc. Tex. (roster chmn. 1983-85); Soc. Human Resource Mgmt., Women's Assn. Verizon Employees. Republican. Methodist. Avocations: choral singing, sewing, movies, ensemble singing performances. Home: 218 Oakmont Dr Trophy Club TX 76262-5472 E-mail: gcaffee@mccinternet.com.

CAFFERTY, PASTORA SAN JUAN, education educator; b. Cienfuegos, Las Villas, Cuba, July 29, 1940; arrived in US, 1947; d. Jose Antonio and Hortensia (Horruitiner) San Juan; m. Michael Cafferty, Apr. 13, 1971 (dec. 1973); m. Henry P. Russe, Aug. 18, 1988 (dec. 1991). BA, St. Bernard Coll., 1967; MA, George Washington U., 1969, PhD, 1971; DHC, Columbia Coll., 1987. Instr. George Washington U., Washington, 1967-69; asst. to sec. U.S. Dept. Transp., Washington, 1969-70, U.S. HUD, Washington, 1970-71; asst. prof. U. Chgo., 1971-76, assoc. prof., 1976-83, prof., 1983—. Bd. dirs. Kimberly-Clark Corp., Dallas, Peoples' Energy Corp., Chgo., Waste Mgmt. Inc., Houston, Harris Fin. Corp., Chgo. Author: The Politics of Language: The Dilemma of Bilingual Education for Puerto Ricans, 1981, Backs Against The Wall, 1983, The Dilemma of American Immigration, 1983, Hispanics in the U.S.A., 1985, 2d edit., 1992, Hispanics: An Agenda for 21st Century, 1999, 2d edit., 2002. Bd. dirs. Lyric Opera Assn., Chgo., 1990—, Rush Univ. Med. Ctr., 1993— White House fellow U.S. Govt., 1969-70. Mem. Chgo. Yacht Club. Democrat. Roman Catholic. Office: U Chgo 969 E 60th St Chicago IL 60637-2677 Office Phone: 773-702-8959. Business E-Mail: p_caffert@uchicago.edu.

CAFFEY, H. DAVID, music educator; b. Austin, Tex., June 2, 1950; s. Howard Lee and Dorothy May (Mangum) Caffey; m. Linda Kay Larson, June 13, 1970; children: Heather Leigh, Sean Efraim. BMus, U. Tex., 1972, MMus, 1974; postgrad., Calif. State U., Northridge, 1973; cert. in exec. leadership, Claremont Grad. U., 2000. Asst. prof. music So. Oreg. State Coll., Ashland, 1974—76; dir. jazz studies, instr. Sam Houston State U., Huntsville, Tex., 1976—79; asst. prof. music U. Denver, 1979—83, assoc. prof., 1983—84; asst. prof. music Calif. State U., L.A., 1984—86, assoc. prof., 1986—91, prof., 1991—2001, chmn. dept., 1993—2001; assoc. dean, prof. music, Coll. of Letters, Arts & Social Scis. Calif. State Poly. U., Pomona, 2001—05; prof. music, dir. U. No. Colo., 2005—. Mem. adv. bd. Luckman Fine Arts Ctr., L.A., 1993—96; bd. dirs. Friends of Music, Calif. State U., L.A., 1993—2001; mem. adv. bd. L.A. County H.S. of Arts, 1993—98; mem. bd. advisors Calif. Inst. for Preservation Jazz, Calif. State U., Long Beach, 1996—2001; mem. adv. bd. cultural arts coun. Mt. San Antonio Coll., 1996—98; music program adv. com. Riverside C.C., 2003—. Composer over 40 published compositions, 1975—; prodr. 9 record albums, 1979-90; contbr. articles to profl. jours. Mem.: ASCAP (award for composition 1981—85, 2001—04), Nat. Assn. Schs. Music (inst. rep. 1993—2001, regional vice chair 1995—97, 1999—2000, inst. rep. 2005—), Am. Fedn. Musicians, Music Educators Nat. Conf., Comml. Music Educators (nat. bd. 1992—96), Internat. Assn. Jazz Educators (Calif. state pres. 1991—96, U.S. rep. internat. exec. bd. 1998—2002, pres.-elect 2002—04, pres. 2004—06, winner composition contest 1978). Avocations: golf, reading, travel. Office: Sch Music Univ Northern Colorado Greeley CO 80639 Office Phone: 970-351-1924, 970-351-1924. Personal E-mail: david.caffey@unco.edu.

CAFFEY, HORACE ROUSE, academic administrator, agricultural company executive; b. Grenada, Miss., Mar. 24, 1929; s. C. Horace and Anna Belle (James) C.; m. Lois (Granger) Stevens, Mar. 13, 1999; children: Brenda, Jerry, Belle, Rex. BS, Miss. State U., 1951, MS, 1955; PhD, La State U., 1959. Agronomist in charge rice project Miss. Agrl. Exptl. Sta., Stoneville, 1958-62; supt. La. State U. Rice Sta., La. Agrl. Exptl. Sta., Crowley, 1962-70; assoc. dir., prof. La. State U., La. Agrl. Exptl. Sta., Baton Rouge, 1970-79; vice-chancellor adminstrn. La. State U. Agrl. Ctr., 1979-80, vice-chancellor internat. programs, 1980-81; chancellor La. State U. Agr. Ctr., 1984-97, La. State U., Alexandria, 1981-84; pres., CEO Caffey Internat. Inc., 1997—; interim v.p. for acad. affairs La. Coll., Pineville, 2005—. Internat. rice cons. AID, World Bank, other orgns., 1965—; mem. pub. health study team Nat. Acad. Sci., Washington, 1973-74; mem. adv. bd. Regents Masters Plan Higher Edn., Baton Rouge, 1977; Nat. co-chair joint coun. for Food and Agr., 1989-94, Internat. Sci. and Edn. Coun., 1986-90; chmn. Nat. Assn. State Univs. and Land Grant Colls. divsn. Agr. Budget Com., 1989. Contbr. articles to profl. jours., chapters to books. Pres. Internat. Rice Festival, Crowley, 1968; bd. dirs. Boy Scouts U.S.A., United Way, others. Served to 1st lt. U.S. Army, 1951-54. Recipient Internat. award of Merit Gamma Sigma Delta, 1970, 81; honoree Internat. Rice Festival, 1974; named Man of Yr. Crowley C. of C., 1969-70, Progressive Farmer Man of Yr. in Svc. to La. Agr., 1986, Outstanding Alumnus Coll. Agr. of La. State U., 1992, Alumnus of Yr., La. State U., 1993, Outstanding Alumnus of Yr., Coll. Agr., Miss. State U., 1993. Mem. Sigma Xi, Gamma Sigma Delta, Phi Delta Kappa, Omicron Delta Kappa, Phi Delta Phi, Phi Zeta. Lodges: Masons; Rotary. Democrat. Baptist. Home: 10471 Barry Dr Baton Rouge LA 70809-3265 Office: Chancellor Emeritus La State U 4560 Essen Ln Baton Rouge LA 70809-3424 Office Phone: 225-763-3997. E-mail: hrcaffey@agctr.lsu.edu, hrcaffey@aol.com.

CAFFREY, LYNN REGINA, education educator; b. Queens, NY, May 31, 1961; d. Charles Daniel and Clare (Carney) Mailley; m. Robert Dennis Caffrey, Apr. 26, 1986; children: Katelyn Rose, Anna Leigh, Emily Joy. AA, Nassau C.C., 1982; BS in Edn., SUNY, Cortland, 1984; MS, St. John's Univ., 1989. Adminstrv. asst. Grumman Data Sys., N.Y.C., 1984-85; 1st grade tchr. Waverly Park Elem., Lynbrook, NY, 1985-88; reading specialist St. John's U., Jamaica, NY, 1988-90; instr. Tomlinson Coll., Cleveland, Tenn., 1990-92, Cleveland State Coll., 1990-92; instr., supr. student tchrs. Lee Coll., Cleveland, 1991-92; asst. prof., supr. student tchr. York (Pa.) Coll., 1993—2004; instr. focused master's program Penn State York, 2004—05; children's ministries specialist Praise Cmty. Ch., York, 2004—. Mem. edn. policies bd. Christian Sch. York, 1993—. Recipient Excellence Edn. Tchg. award, N.Y. State Edn. Dept., 1986—87, Adj. Tchr. of the Yr. award, York Coll., 2002. Mem.: ASCD. Office: Praise Community Ch 705 S Ogontz St York PA 17403

CAFIERO, JENNIFER ANNETTE, academic administrator, educator; b. Bklyn., Jan. 8, 1975; d. Pasquale and Annette Rosemary Cafiero. Master's degree, Pace U., 2000. Cert. tchr. N.Y. Exec. asst. Pace U., N.Y.C., 1997—98, coord. of enrollment rsch., 1998—2000, dir. of enrollment planning and reporting, 2000—. Adj. prof. math. Pace U., N.Y.C., 2002—. Mem.: Assn. for Instl. Rsch., Am. Motorcyclist Assn. Avocations: motorcycling, home improvement, travel, boating. Home and Office: Pace Univ 1 Pace Plz New York NY 10038 E-mail: jcafiero@pace.edu.

CAFRITZ, PEGGY COOPER, communications executive; b. Mobile, Ala., Apr. 7, 1947; d. Algernon Johnson and G. Catherine (Mouton) C.; married; 2 children. BA in Polit. Sci., George Washington U., 1968, JD, 1971. Bar: D.C. 1972. Founder Workshops for Careers in Arts, Washington, 1968; developer, chmn. bd. Duke Ellington Sch. Arts., Washington, 1968-84; dir. Arrowstreet, Architects and Planners Inc., Cambridge, Mass., 1972-74, Washington, 1972-74; spl. asst. to pres. Post-Newsweek Stas. Inc., Washington, 1974-77; programming exec., producer documentary films Sta. WTOP-TV, Washington, 1974-77. Cons. arts critic pub. TV show Around Town, 1986—. Cultural arts critic (PBS TV show) Around Town, 1986—. Mem. exec. com. D.C. Commn. Arts and Humanities, 1970-75, chmn., 1979-87, chmn. emeritus, 1987—; trustee Am. Film Inst., 1972-74, Pratt Inst., 1991; bd. govs. Corcoran Gallery Art, Washington, 1972-74; exec. dir. gt. issure program D.C. Bicentennial Commn., 1974; bd. dirs. Washington Performing Arts Soc., 1983—, Kennedy Ctr. Performing Arts, 1986—, Women's Project, 1987—, Nat. Guild Community Schs. of Arts, 1976-80, Pennsylvania Ave. Devel. Corp., Washington, 1979-87, Atlanta U., 1983-86, Washington, Am. Place Theater, N.Y.C.; co-chmn. Mayor's Blue Ribbon Task Force on Cultural and Econ. Devel., 1987-88; mem. exec. bd. Nat. Assembly State Arts Agys., 1979-86, planning com., 1986-87; mem. conv. staff Dem. Nat. Com., 1972, 76; mem. steering com. Carter-Mondale, Washington, 1976; mem. nat. panel Arts, Edn. and Ams., 1975-79; mem. internat. com. UNICEF, 1976-79; chair Smithsonian Cultural Edn. Com., 1989—; co-chair Smithsonian Cultural Equity Com., 1988—; mem. African-Am. Instnl. study adv. com. Smithsonian Instn., 1990— pres., D.C. St. Bd. of Education, 2001-. Fellow Woodrow Wilson Internat. Ctr. for Scholars, 1971; recipient John D. Rockefeller III award, 1972, George F. Peabody award U. Ga., 1976, Emmy award, 1977, 27th Ann. Broadcast Media award, 1977, Zeta Phi Beta award for outstanding contbn. in the arts, 1974, N.Y. Black Film Festival award, 1976, Women's Achievement award Pub. TV, 1984, Brava award for Outstanding Contbn. to Arts in Washington, 1988, Mayor's Art award for excellence in svc. to arts, 1991, 20th Malcolm X DayAnniversary award Arts Advocacy, 1991, Ann. Cultural Alliance award, 1992; named Washingtonian of Yr. Washingtonian mag., 1972, Woman of Yr. Mademoiselle mag., 1973, and numerous other awards. Mem. ABA, D.C. Bar Assn. Home and Office: 3030 Chain Bridge Rd NW Washington DC 20016-3410 *Growing up black in the fully segregated city of Mobile, Alabama, instilled in me a youthful passion "to become the wind and not the blown." This passion, from which flows the energy that drives me to achieve has never abated; it has broadened: I do hope that I have done and will continue to do much to help others so that they too can become the wind.*

CAGAPTAY, SONER, historian, researcher, political organization worker, director; arrived in U.S., 1996; BA, Marmara U., Turkey, 1993; MA, Bilkent U., Turkey, 1995; MPhil, Yale U., 2000, PhD, 2003. Tchg. asst. Dept. History Yale U., New Haven, 1997—2002; sr. fellow Washington (D.C.) Inst. Near East Policy, 2002—, dir. Turkish Rsch. Program, 2002—; vis. prof. Princeton U., Princeton, NJ, 2005. Lectr. Yale U., 2002—03; adj. asst. prof. Georgetown U., Washington, 2005. Contbr. articles to profl. jours. Mem.: Assembly Turkish-Am. Assns. (pres. bd. 2002—04). Office: The Washington Inst Near East Policy 1828 L Street NW Ste 1050 Washington DC 20016 Office Phone: 202-452-0650.

CAGE, ALLIE M., communications executive; b. Memphis, Feb. 2, 1953; d. Ernest Hampton Sr. and Robie Lee (Bynum) Cage. BS, Cornell U., 1975; MBA, Tenn. State U., 1986. Pres., owner Profl. Svc., Inc., Memphis, 1981-83; dir. tutorial ctr. Tenn. State U., Nashville, 1984-85; rsch. assoc. Inst. African Affairs, Nashville, 1986-88; ptnr. Cage, Smith & Assocs., Nashville, 1988-91; mktg. dir. So. Colour, Inc., Brentwood, Tenn., 1994—; owner, pres. Cage Comm. Co., Madison, Tenn., 1988—. Bd. dirs. So. Colour, Inc. Author: (weekly publ.) Rap Sheet, 1983—86; co-author: (pub., cassette rec.) Arbitration, 1975; freelance reporter various newspapers, 1986—. Bd. dirs. Rainbow Coalition Davidson County, Tenn., 1984—, Nat. Coalition to Save Black Colls., Nashville, 1986—; pres. Lit. Soc., 1991—; publicity coord., vol. coord. Unity Build Habitat for Humanity, project dir. Ecumenical Build 2002; publicity coord., vol. coord. Unity Build Bldg. Together for Christ, 1999—; min. in tng. St. Luke CME Ch., Nashville, min. Named to So. Women in Pub. Svc., Stennis Ctr. Pub. Svc. and Miss. U. for Women, 1992. Mem.: NAACP (life), Am. Mgmt. Assn., Nat. Hook-Up Black Women. Democrat. Avocations: travel, reading, tennis, volleyball, music. Office: 510 Heritage Dr Unit 25 Madison TN 37115-6001 E-mail: amcage@msn.com.

CAGE, JACK HAYS, executive search consultant; b. San Francisco, Mar. 15, 1953; s. James Gilliam and Audrey (Shade) C.; children: Catherine, Anna. BS, U.S. Mil. Acad., 1975; MA, Columbia U., 1981, PhD, 1982. Commd. 2d lt. U.S. Army, 1975, advanced through grades to Col., 1995, ret., 1997; mng. dir. Sullivan & Co., N.Y.C., 1997-99; ptnr. Heidrick & Struggles, N.Y.C., 1999—, co-head global ins. tech. practice. Ptnr. Fin. Svcs. Info. Tech., N.Y.C., 1997—; CIO, chief tech. officer Ins. Tech. Practice. Recipient Bronze Star U.S. Army, 1989, 3 Legion of Merit awards U.S. Army. Mem. Assn. Exec. Search Cons. Avocations: personal investment, information systems, travel.

CAGE, NICOLAS (NICOLAS COPPOLA), actor; b. Long Beach, Calif., Jan. 7, 1964; s. August Coppola and Joy Vogelsang; m. Patricia Arquette, Apr. 8, 1995 (div. May 18, 2001); m. Lisa Marie Presley, Aug. 10, 2002 (div. May 16, 2004); m. Alice Kim, July 30, 2004; 1 child. Grad., UCLA; DFA (hon.), Calif. State Fullerton, 2001. Actor: (feature films) Fast Times At Ridgemont High, 1982, Valley Girl, 1983, Rumble Fish, 1983, Racing with the Moon, 1984, Birdy, 1984, The Boy in Blue, 1986, The Cotton Club, 1984, Peggy Sue Got Married, 1986, Raising Arizona, 1986, Moonstruck, 1988, Vampire's Kiss, 1989, Never on a Tuesday, 1989, Tempo di Uccidere, 1989, Fire Birds, 1990, Wild at Heart, 1990, Zandalee, 1991, Honeymoon in Vegas, 1992, Time to Kill, 1992, Amos & Andrew, 1993, Red Rock West, 1993, Deadfall, 1993, Guarding Tess, 1994, It Could Happen to You, 1994, Trapped in Paradise, 1994, Kiss of Death, 1995, Leaving Las Vegas, 1995 (Best Actor award L.A. Film Critics 1995, Best Actor award N.Y. Film Critics 1995, Golden Globe award for best actor 1996, Acad. award for best actor 1996), The Rock, 1996, The Funeral, 1996, Con Air, 1997, Face Off, 1997, Welcome to Hollywood, 1998, Snake Eyes, 1998, City of Angels, 1998, 8MM, 1999, Bringing Out the Dead, 1999, Gone in 60 Seconds, 2000, Family Man, 2000, Captain Corelli's Mandolin, 2001, Windtalkers, 2002, Adaptation, 2002, Matchstick Men, 2003, National Treasure, 2004; actor, prodr.: (films) Sonny (also dir.), 2002, Lord of War, 2005; prodr.: (films) Shadow of the Vampire, 2000, The Life of David Gale, 2003. Office: Saturn Films 9000 W Sunset Blvd Ste 911 West Hollywood CA 90069-5809 also: Creative Artists Agy 9830 Wilshire Blvd Beverly Hills CA 90212-1804*

CAGGIANO, JOSEPH, advertising executive; b. NYC, Oct. 22, 1925; s. Daniel Joseph and Lucia (Gaudiosi) C.; m. Catherine Marie Gilmore, Aug. 28, 1948; children— Cathleen, Mary Yvonne. BBA, Pace Coll., 1953. Chief accountant Criterion Advt. Co., N.Y.C., 1947-57; treas. Emerson Foote, Inc., N.Y.C., 1957-67; became sr. v.p. Bozell & Jacobs, Inc. (now Bozell, Jacobs, Kenyon & Eckhardt Inc.), N.Y.C., 1967, exec. v.p. finance and adminstrn. Omaha, 1971-91, vice chmn. bd., chief financial officer, 1991-97; vice chmn. bd. dirs. emeritus Bozell, Jacobs, Kenyon & Eckhart Inc., 1991—, ret., 1998. Bd. dirs. St. Mary's Coll., Omaha Zool. Soc. Served with USNR, 1943-46, ETO, PTO. Mem. N.Y. Credit and Financial Mgmt. Assn., Omaha Zool. Soc. (dir.) Home: 9731 Fieldcrest Dr Omaha NE 68114-4932 *Luck in business is best defined as preparation meeting opportunity while always keeping a positive attitude. Dedication and fairness to a cause is mandatory. There are few short cuts to success in business or meaningful relationships with family and friends; and still fewer gray areas. It would have been impossible to achieve any degree of success without the help and understanding of my wife and family.*

CAGINALP, AYDIN S., lawyer; b. Ankara, Turkey, Aug. 2, 1950; AB, Ind. U., 1972; JD, Tulane U., 1974; LLM in Taxation, NYU, 1975. Bar: N.Y. 1976, U.S. Dist. Ct. (so. and ea. dists.) N.Y. 1976, U.S. Tax Ct. 1976. Ptnr., mem. ptnrs. com. Alston & Bird LLP, N.Y.C. Bd. editors Tulane U. Law Rev., 1973-74. Address: Alston & Bird LLP 90 Park Ave New York NY 10016-1387 Office Phone: 212-210-9414. Office Fax: 212-210-9444. Business E-Mail: acaginalp@alston.com.

CAGINALP, GUNDUZ, mathematician, educator, researcher; b. Ankara, Turkey, July 20, 1952; came to US, 1959; s. Nejat Tahsin and Munire Feyma (Deniz) C; m. Eva Keller, Aug. 14, 1992; children: Carey Allen, Reginald Jarrett, Ryan Lee. AB cum laude with distinction in all subjects, Cornell U., l973, MA, l976, PhD, l978. Postdoctoral fellow Cornell U., Ithaca, NY, 1978; rsch. assoc. Rockefeller U., NYC, 1978-80; Zeev Nehari rsch. asst. prof. Carnegie-Mellon U., Pitts., 1980-83, vis. asst. prof., 1983-84; asst. prof. math. U. Pitts., Pitts., 1984-85, assoc. prof., 1985-90, prof., 1990—, group leader applied math., 1988-90. Mem. bd. advisers Internat. Found. for Rsch. in Exptl. Econ., 2002-. Editor Jour. Psychology and Fin. Markets, 2000-02, Jour. Behavioral Fin., 2003-04; mem. editl. bd. Applied Math. Fin.; contbr. articles to profl. jour. Grantee, NSF, 1980—2000, Nat. Inst. of Standards and Tech., 1990—92; Grad. fellow, Cornell U., 1973, Fred Maytag Family Found. scholar, 2001. Mem. Am. Math. Soc., Am. Phys. Soc., Soc. for Indsl. and Applied Math., Econ. Sci. Assn., Nat. Inst. Stds. and Tech., Phi Beta Kappa. Achievements include proof of theorems on existence and properties of surface free energy; studied connections between statis. mechanics and quantum field theory; developed phase field methods for studying free boundary problems; rsch. on applying renormalization group methods to differential equations; analyzed experimental econ. using differential equations and time series; established that price patterns in finan. markets have predictive value. Home: 12 Rosemont Ln Pittsburgh PA 15217-3161 Office: U Pitts Dept Math Pittsburgh PA 15260 Business E-Mail: caginalp@pitt.edu.

CAGLE, AMANDA CAROL, music educator; b. Atlanta, Nov. 23, 1979; d. Randall Cagle, Debra Cagle. A in Music, Reinhardt Coll., 2000. Pvt. piano tchr., Alpharetta, Ga., 1996—2000.

CAGLE, MELINDA REEVES, editor; d. Harry Tillman Reeves and Lillie Mae Dunn; m. Carrol Dean Cagle, June 2, 1968; children: Jeffrey, Thomas, Andrew, David, Sarah, Caroline, Anne, John. Student, Tex. Tech. U., 1967—68; BFA, U. Houston, 1975; postgrad., No. Ill. U., 1976—77. Mem. history coun. Bapt. Gen. Conv. Tex., Dallas, 2003—. Editor: (history jour.) The Herald, 2003—. Historian, ch. coun. First Bapt. Ch., Woodlands, Tex., 1998—. Mem.: Jr. League Houston, Inc. (chmn. The Goldfarb Project 1988—90), Montgomery County Geneal. and Hist. Soc. (bd. mem. 2000—, Vol. of Yr. 2003). Avocations: piano, painting, genealogy. Home: 18 W Shaker Ct The Woodlands TX 77380

CAGLE, WILLIAM REA, retired librarian; b. Hollywood, Calif., Nov. 15, 1933; s. Howard Clinton and Eunice (Colcord Althouse) C.; m. Terry Lucinda Conrad, Jan. 17, 1975; children by previous marriage: Michael Stewart, Chantal Gabrielle, Mark Christopher, Monique Antoinette. AB in English, UCLA, 1956, MLS, 1962; postgrad., Oxford U., 1959-60. Asst. to librarian Henry E. Huntington Library and Art Gallery, San Marino, Calif., 1960-62; librarian for English Ind. U. Libraries, Bloomington, 1962-67, asst. Lilly librarian, 1967-75, acting Lilly librarian, 1975—77, Lilly librarian, 1977-97. Dir.'s acad. adv. com. Harry Ransom Humanities Rsch. Ctr. U. Tex.; mem. adv. bd. U. S.C. Ctr. for Literary Biography; adv. bd. Maine Women Writers Collection U. New England. Author: A Matter of Taste, 1990, revised and enlarged, 1999, Two Hundred and Fifty Years of the British Novel: 1740-1989, 1990, American Books on Food and Drink, 1998, 150 Years of the American Short Story, 1998, Lit Check: The Center for Literary Biography Online Checklist, University of South Carolina, www.cla.sc.edu/engl/litcheck/litcheck.html; contbr. to Printing and the Mind of Man, 1967; editor Ind. U. Bookman, 1966-89; mem. adv. bd. Dictionary Lit. Biography, Cambridge edit. Joseph Conrad, Bibliography of United States Literature, Chadwyck-Healey American Poetry Full-Text Database; mem. editl. bd. Pitts. Series in Bibliography; contbr. articles to profl. jours. Trustee Carver Meml. Libr., Searsport, Maine, Camden Pub. Libr.; mem. collection adv. bd. Kinsey Inst. Sex, Gender and Reprodn. With U.S. Army, 1956—59. Mem.: Assn. Internat. de Biliophilie, Benjamin Franklin Guild (bd. govs.), Baxter Soc., Lincoln Soc., Caxton Club (Chgo.), Grolier Club (N.Y.C.), Century Club. Home: 56 Mountain St Camden ME 04843 E-mail: caglet@adelphia.net.

CAGLE, YVONNE DARLENE, astronaut; b. West Point, N.Y., Apr. 24, 1959; BA in Biochemistry, San Francisco State U., 1981; PhD in Medicine, U. Wash., 1985. Cert. ACLS instr.; flight surgeon. Intern Highland Gen. Hosp., Oakland, Calif., 1985; resident in family practice Ghent FP Ea. Va. Med. Sch., 1992; dep. project mgr. Kelsey-Seybold Clinics NASA-JSC Occupl. Health Clinic, 1994—96; tech. astronaut office ops. planning br. NASA Johnson Space Ctr., 1996—. Clin. asst. prof. U. Tex., Galveston; cons. in field. Active Boys and Girls Club Am.; vol. family practice clinical faculty U. Calif., Davis; active Third Bapt. Ch. With USAF. Named one of Outstanding Young Women of Am.; recipient Disting. Scientist award, Nat. Tech. Assn., Commendation award, Marin County Bd. Supr., Novato Sch. Bd. Mem.: Aerospace Med. Assn., Am. Acad. Family Physicians. Avocations: jigsaw puzzles, juggling, skating, hiking, music. Office: NASA Johnson Space Ctr Mailcode JA Houston TX 77058

CAGNEY, LAWRENCE K., lawyer; b. Feb. 2, 1957; AB, Fordham U., 1978; JD, Gerogetown U., 1981. Bar: NY 1982. Asst. counsel Warner Lambert, 1985—86; assoc. Milbank, Tweed, Hadley & McCloy, 1981—84, Debevoise & Plimpton LLP, NYC, 1986—90, ptnr., 1990—, chair Exec. Compensation and Employee Benefits Practice Groups. Mem.: ABA, Assn. Bar of City NY. Office: Debevoise & Plimpton LLP 919 Third Ave New York NY 10022 Office Phone: 212-909-6909. Office Fax: 212-909-6836. E-mail: lkcagney@debevoise.com.

CAGNEY, NANETTE HEATH, lawyer; b. Norfolk, Va., Oct. 3, 1957; d. Thomas Patrick and Phyllis L. (Heath) C. BA in Social Work, Loyola U. of the South, New Orleans, 1976-78; JD, Tulane U., 1982. Bar: La. 1983, U.S. Dist. ct. (we. dist.) La. 1985. Social work asst. VA Psychiat. Hosp., Gulfport, Miss., summer 1977; child care worker Cath. Charities, Metairie, La., 1976-78; elegibility worker family svc. La. Dept. Health and Human Resources, Gretna, 1978-79; landman ARCO Exploration Co., Lafayette, La., 1982-85; staff atty. TXO Prodn. Co., Dallas, 1985-86; pvt. practice Lafayette, 1986-88; ptnr. Beard & Cagney, P.C., Lafayette, 1988-91; law clk. to dist. ct. judge U.S. Dist. Ct., Western Dist. La., Lake Charles, 1992—. Hearing coord. CASA Teen Ct., Lafayette, 1988-90, exec. dir., 1988-90; vice chair Lafayette Bd. Zoning Adjustments, 1988-91; bd. dirs. S.W. La. AIDS Coun., 1993-97, Faith Temple, Sulphur, La., 1995-99; pres. Quota Internat. of Lake Charles, 1996-97; state bd. Aglow Internat., 1993-99; steering com. State Bar Assn. Com. on Alcohol and Drug Abuse, 1989—; state ethics com. Bar Assn., 1989-95, ad hoc disciplinary com., 1989-93. Mem. La. Bar Assn., Lafayette County Bar Assn., Acadiana Assn. Women Attys. (community liaison chair 1986-88, pres. 1988-89), Assn. Trial Lawyers Am., Acadiana Assn. Women Bus. Owners (treas. 1986-87, pres. 1987-88), Zeta Tau Alpha (sec. Lake Charles alum 1992—). Democrat. Avocations: sailing, fishing, gardening. Office: 611 Broad St Ste 328 Lake Charles LA 70601-4380 Office Phone: 318-437-3880.

CAGNEY, WILLIAM ROBERT, psychologist; b. Pitts., Oct. 7, 1937; s. Edward Patrick and Pearl Barbara (Sebastian) C.; m. Vivian Antoinette Tartaglia, June 26, 1965; children: Lori Anne, Julie Alissa, Melissa Beth. BS, Duquesne U., 1960, MA, 1965, PhD, 1968. Lic. psychologist, Pa.; cert. Nat. Register Health Svcs.; cert. profl. qualification in psychology Assn. State and Provincial Psychology Bds.; diplomate in clin. hypnotherapy NBCCH, Nat. Bd. cert. clin. Hypnotherapists. Psychology intern, staff psychologist Dixmont State Hosp., Glenfield, Pa., 1962-68; staff psychologist South Hills Child Guidance Ctr., Pitts., 1968-69; asst. dir., psychol. svcs. Woodville State Hosp., Carnegie, Pa., 1968-70; chief psychologist Counseling Ctr. of South Hills, Pitts., 1970-72; clin. dir. Chartiers MH/MR Ctr., Bridgeville, Pa., 1972-79; pvt. practice Pitts., 1971—. Cons. Outreach South, Mt. Lebanon, Pa., 1976-2004, South Hills Interfaith Ministries, Bethel Park, Pa., 1969-2003, Crisis Addiction Recovery Edn., Inc., Washington, Pa., 1984-88, YMCA South Hills, Pitts., 1977-78; field supr. dept. psychology U. Pitts., 1970-73, W.Va. U., Morgantown, 1973-78; resident psychologist Sta. KDKA-TV Pitts. Today, 1978-79; presenter seminars and workshops to profl. and cmty. groups, 1972—. Cons. Twp. Upper St. Clair Adminstrn., Police, Schs., Family Resource Program, Upper St. Clair, Pa., 1986-89. Fellow Pa. Psychol. Assn.; mem. APA, Greater Pitts. Psychol. Assn., Am. Group Therapy Assn. Avocations: fitness activities, art and music appreciation. Office: 1725 Washington Rd Ste 509 Pittsburgh PA 15241-1207 Office Phone: 412-833-9250. E-mail: cagsfive@aol.com, cagstive@adelphia.net.

CAGUIAT, CARLOS JOSE, health facility administrator, priest; b. N.Y.C., Jan. 23, 1937; s. Carlos C. and Carmen C.; m. Julianna Skomsky, Aug. 29, 1958; children: Stephen D., Jonathan J., Sarah E. Caguiat Borthwick. BA, CCNY, 1958; MDiv, Gen. Theol. Sem., 1965; MPA, NYU, 1976. Ordained priest Episcopal Ch., 1965. Curate St. Christopher Chapel, N.Y.C., 1965—68; vicar St. Christopher's Chapel, N.Y.C., 1968—71; exec. dir. project for human comm. Episcopal Diocese of N.Y., N.Y.C., 1971-73; project mgr. ambulatory care/cmty. rels. N.Y.C. Health and Hosps. Corp., 1973-76, regional coord. for adminstrn./ops. 1975-76; assoc. dir. adminstrn./ops. Morrisania Neighborhood Family Care Ctr., Bronx, N.Y., 1976-78, adminstr., 1978-81; adminstrv. dir. Clin. Ctr., Mich. State U., East Lansing, 1981-90; regional v.p. St. Francis Acad., Lake Placid, NY, 1990—2002, strategic planning and ventures v.p. Saranac Lake, NY, 1999—2002. Chair decentralized unit of several parishes, N.Y.C.; mem. Diocese of N.Y. Pension Bd., Ecumenical Commn., Budget Com., 1967-81; vice chair North Country Behavioral Health Devel. Corp., 1997-98, chair, 1999-2002. Chair Two Bridges Settlement Housing Corp.; bd. dirs. Settlement Housing Fund., 1969-73; pres. Mid-Mich. South Health Sys. Agy., 1985-88; bd. trustees Adirondack Med. Ctr., 2004—; bd. dirs. Med. Ctr. Infantry and Intelligence Officer, U.S. Army, St. Francis Acad., 2002— Fellow Am. Coll. Health Care Execs., Lake Placid Rotary (bd. dirs., v.p., 2002, pres. 2003-04, sec. 2004—), Lakeside House (bd. dirs. 2003—) Home: 20 Oakwood Place Saranac Lake NY 12983 Personal E-mail: CarlosC@st-francis.org. Business E-Mail: carlosc@capitol.net.

CAHALANE, MICHAEL JOHN, surgeon, medical educator; b. Cambridge, Mass., Oct. 1, 1952; s. Michael John and Mary Evangeline Cahalane; m. Nancy Linda Morse, July 17, 1977; children: Michael John, Kristen Lynn. MD, Boston U. Sch. Medicine, 1980. Diplomate Am. Bd. Surgery. Surgeon Beth Israel Deaconess Med. Ctr., Boston, 1987—. Dir. undergraduate med. edn. Beth Israel Deaconess Med. Ctr., 2005. Recipient Humanism in Medicine award, Healthcare Found. NJ, S. Robert Stone award excellence in tchg., Beth Israel Hosp., Faculty award excellence in tchg., Harvard Med. Sch., 1998, Peter Reizenstein prize, Internat. Jour. Quality Health Care, 2001. Mem.: Alpha Omega Alpha. Independent. Roman Catholic. Avocations: travel, reading. Home: 22 Anis Rd Belmont MA 02478 Office: Beth Israel Deaconess Med Ctr 110 Francis St Boston MA 02115 Office Phone: 617-632-9786. Personal E-mail: corkcelt@msn.com. E-mail: mcahalan@bidmc.harvard.edu.

CAHAN, CORA, not-for-profit developer; m. Bernard Gersten. Dancer; co-founder, exec. dir. The Feld Ballet, N.Y.C.; co-founder, v.p. Joyce Theater, N.Y.C., 1979—98; pres., dir. The New 42nd St., Inc., N.Y.C., 1990—. Trustee emeritus Joyce Theatre. Recipient All-Star 2001 award, Crain's N.Y. Bus. mag., Ernie award, Dance/USA, 2002. Office: The New 42nd St Inc 10th Fl 229 West 42nd St New York NY 10036-7299

CAHILL, CATHERINE FRANCES, environmental scientist, educator; b. Woodland, Calif., July 30, 1968; d. Thomas Andrew and Virginia Arnoldy Cahill. BS in Applied Physics, U. Calif., 1990; MS in Atmospheric Scis., U. Wash., 1994; PhD in Atmospheric Scis., U. Nev., 1996. Fulbright fellow U. Coll. Galway, Galway, Ireland, 1996—97; vis. asst. rsch. prof. Desert Rsch. Inst., Reno, 1997—98; prof. U. Alaska Fairbanks, Alaska, 1998—. Program chair for atmospheric sci. program U. Alaska Fairbanks, Alaska, 2000—01. Contbr. articles pub. to profl. jour. Mem. U.S. China Polar Sci. Panel. Fellow Fulbright Fellowship, Coun. for the Internat. Exch. of Students, 1996-1997. Mem.: Amerian Geophys. Union, Am. Chem. Soc. (chair alaska sect. 2000—01), Sigma Pi Sigma, Sigma Xi. Democrat-Npl. Achievements include research in long-range transport of aerosols to the Arctic. Avocations: travel, reading. Office: Univ Alaska Fairbanks 900 Yukon Dr Rm 182 Fairbanks AK 99775 Office Phone: 907-474-6905. Office Fax: 907-474-5640. Business E-Mail: ffcfc@uaf.edu.

CAHILL, CHARLES L., retired academic administrator, chemistry educator; b. El Reno, Okla., Feb. 23, 1933; m. Dorotha Ann Cleek, Feb. 14, 1954; children: Steven Charles, Terri Ann, Susan Beth. AB in Chemistry, Okla. Bapt. U., 1955; MS in Biochemistry, U. Okla., 1957, PhD in Biochemistry, 1961. Rsch. asst., biochemist Vets. Hosp., Sch. Medicine, U. Okla., Oklahoma City, 1955-57; NIH predoctoral fellow Sch. Medicine, U. Okla., Oklahoma City, 1957-60; clin. chemist med. arts labs. Oklahoma City U., 1960-61, asst. prof. chemistry, 1961-63, asst. prof., chmn. dept., 1963-67, assoc. prof., chmn. dept., assoc. dean Coll. Arts and Sci., 1967-69, prof. chemistry, assoc. dean, dir. rsch., 1970-71; vice chancellor for acad. affairs U. N.C., Wilmington, 1971—92, provost, vice chancellor acad. affairs, 1992-2000, prof. emeritus, 2000—; ret. Mem. Rotary. Avocations: bass fishing, hunting, golf.

CAHILL, EILEEN MARY, secondary school educator; b. Norwich, N.Y., Nov. 3, 1950; d. Kevin Tracey and Martha Sue (Eckard) C. BA, D'Youville Coll., Buffalo, 1972; MA, U. Toronto, 1974; PhD, SUNY, Buffalo, 1987. Cert. tchr., N.Y. English tchr. North Collins (N.Y.) Ctrl. Sch., 1972-85; curator of lit. Rosenbach Mus. and Libr., Phila., 1988-89; instr. English Temple U., Phila., 1987-88, Bryn Mawr (Pa.) Coll., 1987-88; English tchr. Marlborough Sch., L.A., 1989-96; dir. studies Salem Acad., Winston-Salem, N.C., 1998—. Mem. Stanford (Calif.) Ctr. for Rsch. on Women, 1990-94. Author articles. Coun. for Basic Edn. Nat. fellow for ind. study in humanities, 1993. Mem. MLA, Am. Conf. for Irish Studies, Irish Am. Cultural Inst. Democrat. Avocations: writing, travel, photography. Home: 7825 Fair Oaks Dr Clemmons NC 27012-8407 Office: Salem Acad 500 E Salem Ave Winston Salem NC 27101-5386 Office Phone: 336-917-5506.

CAHILL, GEORGE FRANCIS, JR., physician, educator; b. NYC, July 7, 1927; s. George Francis and Eva Marion (Wagner) C.; m. Sarah Townsend duPont, Dec. 20, 1949; children: Colleen Cahill Remley, Peter duPont, George Francis III, Sarah Rhett Cahill Zuckerman, Eva Wagner Cahill Georgaklis, Elizabeth Anglin Cahill Tiedemann. BS, Yale, 1949; MD, Columbia U., 1953; MA, Harvard U., 1966. Intern Peter Bent Brigham Hosp., Boston, 1953-54, resident, 1954-55, 57-58; rsch. fellow biol. chemistry Harvard U. Med. Sch., 1955-57; assoc. in medicine Peter Bent Brigham Hosp., 1962-65; practice medicine specializing in metabolism Boston, 1965-78; sr. physician Peter Bent Brigham Hosp., 1983—94; prof. medicine Harvard U., 1970-90, prof. emeritus, 1990—; prof. biol. scis. Darmouth Coll., Hanover, NH, 1990—97. Prin. cons. endocrinology, metabolism VA, 1972-75; investigator Howard Hughes Med. Inst., 1962-68, dir. rsch., 1978-85, v.p. sci. edn. and devel., 1985-89, sr. scientist, 1989-90, cons., 1991-1994; mem. rsch. tng. coms. NIH. Contbr. articles to profl. jours. Chmn. bd. dir. Greenwall Found., 1992-96; v.p. trustees Hotchkiss Sch., 1992-97; overseer Dartmouth Med. Sch. and the Everett C. Koop Inst., 1990-95. With USNR, 1945-47. Recipient Banting medal U.S., 1971, Banting medal Eng., 1974, J.P. Hoet award Belgium, 1973, Gairdner Internat. award Can., 1979. Fellow AAAS, Am. Acad. Arts and Scis.; mem. Am. Diabetes Assn. (pres. 1975, Lilly award 1965), Endocrine Soc. (Oppenheimer award 1963), Nat. Commn. on Diabetes, Am. Soc. Clin. Investigation, Assn. Am. Physicians, Am. Clin. Climatol. Assn., Am. Physiol. Soc. Home: PO Box 367 Stoddard NH 03464

CAHILL, HARRY AMORY, diplomat, educator; b. N.Y.C., Jan. 10, 1930; s. Harry Amory and Elaine Olga (Loumena) C.; m. Angelica Margarita Ravazzoli, Dec. 12, 1956; children— Alan, Daniel, Sylvia, Irene, Madeleine, Steven BA, Manhattan Coll., N.Y.C., 1951; postgrad., Johns Hopkins U., 1964-65; MS, George Washington U., Washington, 1972. Sales exec. Johns Manville Corp., N.Y.C., 1954-56; fgn. service officer U.S. Dept. of State, Washington, 1956-59, Oslo, 1959-61, Warsaw, 1961-64, Belgrade, Yugoslavia, 1965-68, Montevideo, Uruguay, 1968-71, Lagos, Nigeria, 1975-78, Colombo, Sri Lanka, 1979-81; dir. comml. service U.S. Dept. Commerce, 1982-83; U.S. consul gen. Dept. of State, Bombay, 1983-87; U.S. Mission to UN, dep. U.S. rep. UN Econ. and Social Coun., N.Y.C., 1987-89; pres. Amory Assoc., Inc., McLean, Va., 1990—, World of Film Found., N.Y.C. Prof. Pepperdine U., 1992—, Georgetown U., 1995; cons. U.S. Dept. State, 1991—, U.S. Dept. Def., 1999—. Author: The China Trade and U.S. Tariffs, 1973. Pres. Hinduja Found., NYC, 1993—2002. Woodrow Wilson Nat. Fellowship found. fellow, 1990-93. Mem. Am. Fgn. Svc. Assn. Roman Catholic. Avocation: photography. Office: 1240 Daleview Dr Mc Lean VA 22102-1539

CAHILL, JOAN, nun, educator; d. John Francis and Catherine Adele Cahill. BA in English, St. Francis Coll., 1967; MS in Early Childhood, LI U., 1980; MS in Religious Edn., Fordham U., 1994. Cert. adminstrn./supervision, 1989. Tchr. St. Aloysius Elem., Bklyn., 1956—66, St. Joseph Elem., LI City, 1966—69; prin. St. Aloysius Elem., Bklyn., 1969—76; tchr. St. Nicholas Elem., 1976—80; prin. St. Margaret Elem., Middle Village, 1980—94; participant sabbatical program Weston Sch. Theology, Cambridge, Mass., 1994—95; regional superior Sisters St. Dominic, Amityville, 1995—2001; tchr. adult edn. GED SUNY, Hempstead, 1999—2002; tchr. ESL Lawrence Sch. Dist., Lawrence, 2001—02; campus ministry Kingsborough CC, Bklyn., 2002—. Lobbyist Leadership Conf. Religious Women, Albany, NY, 2000. Mem.: Spiritual Dirs. Internat., Campus Ministry Assn. Avocations: cooking, baking, counted cross stitch, knitting, sewing. Office: Kingsborough Cmty Coll 2001 Oriental Blvd Long Beach NY 11561 Office Phone: 718-368-5391.

CAHILL, JOHN T., consumer products company executive; AB in Econs., MBA in Bus. Adminstrn., Harvard U. CFO RKO Pictures; v.p. corp. fin., asst. treas. PepsiCo, 1989—93, sr. v.p., treas., 1997—98; sr. v.p. fin., CFO KFC, 1993—96; sr. v.p., CFO PepsiCo N.Am., 1996—97; exec. v.p., CFO Pepsi Bottling Group, 1998—2000, pres., COO, 2000—01, pres., CEO, 2001—03, chmn. & CEO, 2003—. Bd. dirs. U.S.-Russia Bus. Coun., Woodward/White Pub. Co. Mem.: Grocery Mfrs. Am. (industry affairs coun.), Nat. Soft Drink Assn. (chmn.). Office: Pepsi Bottling Group Inc 1 Pepsi Way Somers NY 10589-2201*

CAHILL, LAWRENCE R., lawyer; b. Syracuse, N.Y., Apr. 17, 1947; BA, U. Rochester, 1969; JD, U. Chgo., 1972. Bar: Ill. 1973, Mass. 1977. Comml. real estate develop., Chgo.; atty. Goodwin, Procter & Hoar, Boston; ptnr., real estate group Goodwin Procter LLP, Boston, mem. diversity com.; chair, hiring ptnr. legal hiring com. Address: Goodwin Proctor LLP Exchange Pl 53 State St Boston MA 02109-2803 Office Phone: 617-570-1411. Office Fax: 617-523-1231. Business E-Mail: lcahill@goodwinprocter.com.

CAHILL, MICHAEL R., psychologist; b. Decatur, Ill., Feb. 14, 1953; s. Bernard R. and Hilda P. Cahill; m. Connie J. Leamon, June 14, 1975; children: Joycelyn, Amber. BS magna cum laude in Tng. and Devel., U. Tex., 1992; MS in Spl. Edn., Tex. A&M U., 1995; MA in Pupil Personnel, Azusa Pacific U., 2001. Cert. elem. tchg. Calif., Ariz., Tex., spl. edn. Calif., Ariz., Tex., sch. counselor Calif., Ariz., sch. psychologist Calif., Ariz. Spl. edn. tchr. Celesta (Tex.) Ind. Sch. Dist., 1992—93, Lancaster (Tex.) Ind. Sch. Dist., 1993—94, Stanfield (Ariz.) Elem. Sch. Dist., 1994—95; resource specialist Moreno Valley (Calif.) Unifed Sch. Dist., 1995—2001, Riverside County Office Edn., Calif., 2001—03; sch. psychologist Palo Vendell Sch. Dist., Blythe, Calif., 2003—. Mem.: Ariz. Assn. Sch. Psychologists, Calif. Assn. Sch. Psychologists, Nat. Assn. Sch. Psychologists, Phi Theta Kappa, Alpha Chi. Pentacostal. Home: 16277 W Jackson St Goodyear AZ 85338 Office: Palo Verde Unified Sch Dist 811 @ Chandway Blythe CA 92225

CAHILL, RICHARD ANDERSON, medical educator; b. Washington, Sept. 3, 1939; s. George Joseph and Lucille Anderson Cahill; m. Cathleen Elizabeth Wichman, June 11, 1971; children: William Dylan, Maragaret Elizabeth. BS, St. Louis U., 1963, MD, 1967. Diplomate Am. Bd. Pediat., cert. Sub-bd. Pediatric Hematology/Oncology. Assoc. prof. of pediat. All Children's Hosp., U. Soth Fla., St. Petersburg, 1997—2001, St. Louis U. Sch. of Medicine, 2001—03; assoc. clin. prof. of pediat. Pediatric Rsch. Inst., St. Louis, 2003—. Head, stem cell transplant Cardinal Glennon Children's Hosp., St. Louis, 2001—03; assoc. prof. of pediat. Allergy/Immunology All Children's Hosp., St. Petersuburg, Fla.; asst. prof. of pediat. Georgetown U. Sch. of Medicine, Washington. Capt. USN, 1972—96. Mem.: Am. Soc. of Hematology. Democrat. Roman Catholic. Achievements include research in replacement of mesenchymal/stromal cells. Avocations: biking, swimming, reading, cooking, hiking. Home: 4620 Pershing Pl Saint Louis MO 63108 Office: Pediatric Rsch Inst/CGCH 3662 Park Ave Saint Louis MO 63110-2512 Office Phone: 314-577-5623 6134. Office Fax: 314-577-5398. Personal E-mail: cahillcathleen@hotmail.com. Business E-mail: cahillra@slu.edu.

CAHILL, RICHARD FREDERICK, lawyer; b. Columbus, Nebr., June 18, 1953; s. Donald Francis and Hazel Fredeline (Garbers) C.; m. Helen Marie Girard, Dec. 4, 1982; children: Jacqueline Michelle, Catherine Elizabeth, Marc Alexander. Student, Worcester Coll., Oxford, 1973; BA with highest honors, UCLA, 1975; JD, U. Notre Dame, 1978. Bar: Calif. 1978, U.S. Dist. Ct. (ea. dist.) Calif. 1978, U.S. Dist. Ct. (cen. dist.) Calif. 1983, U.S. Dist. Ct. (so. dist.) Calif. 1992, U.S. Dist. Ct. (no. dist.) Calif. 2002, U.S. Ct. Appeals (9th cir.) 1992. Dep. dist. atty. Tulare County Dist. Atty., Visalia, Calif., 1978-81; staff atty. Supreme Ct. of Nev., Carson City, 1981-83; assoc. Acret & Perochet, Brentwood, Calif., 1983-84, Thelen, Marrin, Johnson & Bridges, L.A., 1984-89; ptnr. Hammond Zuetel & Cahill, Pasadena, Calif., 1989-98, Pivo, Halbreich, Cahill & Yim, Irvine, Calif., 1999—2003; mng. sr. counsel Tenet Health Sys., Santa Ana, Calif., 2003—. Mem. Pasadena Bar Assn., Los Angeles County Bar Assn., Assn. So. Calif. Defense Counsel, Notre Dame Legal Aid and Defender Assn. (assoc. dir.), Am. Health Lawyers Assn., Phi Beta Kappa, Phi Alpha Delta (charter, v.p. 1977-78), Pi Gamma Mu, Phi Alpha Theta (charter pres. 1973-74), Phi Eta Sigma, Sigma Chi. Republican. Roman Catholic. Avocation: tennis. Home: 201 Windwood Ln Sierra Madre CA 91024-2677 Office: Tenet Health Sys Law Dept 3 Imperial Promenade Ste 740 Santa Ana CA 92707 Office Phone: 714-428-6713. E-mail: rich.cahill@tenethealth.com.

CAHILL, THOMAS ANDREW, physicist, researcher; b. Paterson, NJ, Mar. 4, 1937; s. Thomas Vincent and Margery (Groesbeck) C.; m. Virginia Ann Arnoldy, June 26, 1965; children: Catherine Frances, Thomas Michael. BA, Holy Cross Coll., Worcester, Mass., 1959; PhD in Physics; NDEA fellow, U. Calif., Los Angeles, 1965. Asst. prof. in residence U. Calif., Los Angeles, 1965-66; NATO fellow, research physicist Centre d'Etudes Nucleaires de Saclay, France, 1966-67; prof. physics U. Calif., Davis, 1967-94; acting dir. Crocker Nuclear Lab., 1972, dir., 1980-89. Dir. Inst. Ecology, 1972-75; cons. NRC of Can., Louvre Mus. UN Global Atmospheric Watch, 1990—; mem. Internat. Com. on PIXE and Its Application, Calif. Atty. Gen., Nat. Audubon Soc., Mono Lake Com. Author: (with J. McCray) Electronic Circuit Analysis for Scientists, 1973; editor Internat. Jour. Pixe, 1989—; contbr. articles to profl. jours. on physics, applied physics, hist. analyses and air pollution. Prin. investigator IMPROVE Nat. Air Pollution Network., 1987-97; co-dir. Crocker Hist. and Archeol. Projects; head U. Calif. Delta Group, Davis, 1997-. OAS fellow, 1968, Japanese Nat. Rsch. fellow, Kyoto, 1992. Mem. Am. Phys. Soc., Air Pollution Control Assn., Am. Assn. Aerosol Rsch., Sigma Xi Democrat. Roman Catholic. Home: 1813 Amador Ave Davis CA 95616-3104 Office: U Calif Dept Applied Sci One Shields Ave Davis CA 95616 Business E-Mail: tacahill@ucdavis.edu.

CAHILL, VERNA ELEANORE, writer; b. Nashua, N.H., Mar. 20, 1916; d. Edward Nazairre Dufault; m. Albert Pressey, Aug. 1936 (div. Oct. 1958); m. George Cahill (dec. Sept. 15, 1983). Student, Holy Cross Coll., 1973—79, U. N.H., 1958—60. Asst. editor Ins. mag., 1961—70. Editor: (poetry column) Sunday Union Leader; contbr. articles to numerous mags. and anthologies; author: But To The Hungray Soul Grant from Mass, 1985; host Edit, Talk Show, 1986. Mem.: Poetry Soc. N.H. (v.p., rec. sec., editor soc. publ., historian, bd. dirs., pres. 1964—). Avocations: interior decorating, landscaping, classical music.

CAHIR, JOHN JOSEPH, meteorologist, educator, educational administrator; b. Scituate, Mass., Oct. 8, 1933; s. Jeremiah Francis and Mary Eleanor (Duggan) C.; m. Mary Anne Louise Schrott, Dec. 1, 1962; children: Ellen, William, Kathryn, Barton. BS in Meteorology, Pa. State U., 1961, PhD, 1971. Meteorologist trainee, meteorologist U.S. Weather Bur., 1956-64; instr. meteorology Pa. State U., University Park, 1965-70, asst. prof., 1971-74, assoc. prof., 1975-79, prof., 1980—2002, prof. emeritus, 2002—; assoc. dean Coll. Earth and Mineral Scis., Pa. State U., University Park, 1980-93; vice provost, dean for undergrad. edn. Pa. State U., University Park, 1993—2002. Vis. prof. St. Augustine's Coll., Va. State Coll.; cons. in field; mem. Commn. Atmospheric Scis., World Meteorol. Orgn. (UN), 1986-97, alt. prin. U.S. del. to 9th session, Sofia, Bulgaria, 1986, del. to 10th session, Offenbach, Fed. Republic Germany, 1990, 11th session, Geneva, 1994; mem. com. on info. sys. for ports and harbors Marine Bd., NRC, 1985; Earth Sci. Adv. com. U. Space Rsch. Assn., 1987-93, convenor, 1992-93; mem. policy adv. com. Coop. Program for Meteorol. Edn. and Tng. (COMET), U. Corp. Atmospheric Rsch., 1988-92, chair, 1996-99, mem. adv. panel, 1996-00, vis. scientist, 2003—; instnl. mem. The Coll. Bd., 1993-02, Boro State Coll. Planning Com., 2003-, vice chair, 2004-. Co-author: Principles of Climatology, 1969, The Atmosphere, 1975, 78 81; editor: Monthly Weather Rev., 1977-80; contbr. papers, research reports to profl. publs. Bd. dirs. Pa. Coll. Tech., Williamsport, 1994—, Standards for Success, Washington, 2001-02. Served with USN, 1958-60. Recipient McKay Donkin award svc. faculty Pa. State U., 2003; Nat. Ctr. Atmospheric Rsch. fellow 1974. Fellow Am. Meteorol. Soc. (chmn. com. on weather forecasting and analysis 1979-80, seal of approval for TV weathercasting, nat. councillor 1986-89, chmn. com. on undergrad. awards 1986, nominating com. 1990-91, chmn. 1991, investment com. 1997—, chair 1999—); mem. Royal Meteorol. Soc., Am. Geophys. Union, Nat. Weather Assn. (pres. 1981-82, Svc. award 1979), Am. Assn. Univs. (task force on Undergrad. Edn. 1999-02). Office: 617 Walker Bldg University Park PA 16802-1505 Business E-Mail: jjc2@psu.edu.

CAHN, JAMES, lawyer, martial arts educator; b. Cleve., Apr. 16, 1946; s. Sherman D. and Barbara Cahn; m. Jean A. Johnson, May 20, 1978; children: Rachel, Lucy. BA, U. Pa., 1968; JD, Ohio State U., 1973; 7th Degree Black Belt, Oriental Martial Arts Coll., 2003. Bar: Ohio 1973. Assoc. Calfee, Halter & Griswold, Cleve., 1973-75; pvt. practice Cleve., 1975-77; ptnr. Hermann, Cahn & Schneider, Cleve., 1977—. Instr., Master Oriental Martial Arts Coll., Cleve. and Columbus, Ohio, 1975—; legal counsel U.S. Taekwondo Union, Colorado Springs, Colo., 1977-81, 85-86; lectr. Ohio Jud. Coll., others. Founding mem. Ctr. for Principled Family Advocacy, pres., 2002. Fellow Am. Acad. Matrimonial Lawyers (pres. Ohio chpt. 1997-98); mem. ABA, Ohio State Bar Assn., Cuyahoga County Bar Assn. (chair family law sect. 1990-91), Cleve. Bar Assn. (family law sect.), US Taekwondo Aliance (officer), Chmont Country Club Office: Hermann Cahn & Schneider 1301 E 9th St Ste 500 Cleveland OH 44114-1876

CAHN, JEFFREY BARTON, lawyer; b. NYC, Jan. 1, 1943; s. Harold Leon and Vivian (Loewy) C.; m. Miriam Epstein, Jan. 22, 1965; children: Lauren Samantha, Vanessa Shari. BA, Ind. U., 1964; JD, Rutgers U., 1967. Bar: N.J. 1967, U.S. Dist. Ct. N.J. 1967, U.S. Ct. Appeals (3d cir.) 1971, U.S. Supreme Ct. 1971, U.S. Tax Ct. 1973, U.S. Ct. Appeals (D.C. cir.), 1979, N.Y. 1980, U.S. Ct. Appeals (9th cir.) 1981, U.S. Claims Ct. 1981, U.S. Dist. Ct. (so. dist.) N.Y. 1992, U.S. Dist. Ct. (ea. dist.) N.Y. 1994, U.S. Ct. Appeals (2nd cir.) 1998. Law clk. to sr. presiding judge Appellate Div. N.J. Superior Ct., Trenton, N.J., 1967-68; assoc. Schapira, Steiner & Walder, Newark, 1968-72; ptnr. Sills, Cummis, Radin, Tischman, Epstein & Gross, Newark, 1972—. Author: (with others) New Jersey Transaction Guide, Vol. 12, 1993, The Use of Another's Trademark: A Review of the Law in The United States, Canada, and Western Europe, 1997; co-author, editor: Trademark Law Basics Coursebook, 2001; rsch. editor: Rutgers Law Rev., 1966-67; cons. editor Trademark Administration, 1999; contbr. articles to profl. jours. Mem. ATLA, ABA, N.J. State Bar Assn., Essex County Bar Assn., Internat. Trademark Assn. (publs. bd., 2002, projects editl. bd. 2001-), N.Y. State Bar Assn. (sect. intellectual property, chair copyright law com.), Am. Intellectual Property Law Assn., N.J. Intellectual Property Law Assn., Phi Delta Phi (Outstanding Grad. 1967). Jewish. Home: 72 Winged Foot Dr Livingston NJ 07039-8229 Office: Sills Cummis Epstein & Gross Legal Ctr 1 Riverfront Plz Fl 13 Newark NJ 07102-5401 Office Phone: 973-643-5858. Business E-Mail: jcahn@sillscummis.com.

CAHN, JOHN WERNER, metallurgist, educator; b. Germany, Jan. 9, 1928; arrived in U.S., 1939, naturalized, 1945; s. Felix H. and Lucie (Schwarz) C.; m. Anne Hessing, Aug. 20, 1950; children: Martin Charles, Andrew Blender, Lorie Selma. BS, U. Mich., 1949; PhD, U. Calif. at Berkeley, 1953; DSc (hon.), Northwestern U., 1990, U. d'Evry, France, 1996. Instr. U. Chgo., 1952-54; with research lab. Gen. Electric Co., 1954-64; prof. metallurgy MIT, 1964-78; ctr. scientist Nat. Inst. Standards and Tech. (formerly Nat. Bur. Standards), 1978—, sr. fellow, 1984—. Vis. prof. Isreli Inst. Tech., Haifa, 1971—72, 1980; cons. in field, 1986—; chmn. Gordon Conf. Phys. Metallurgy, 1964; affil. prof. physics U. Wash., Seattle, 1984—; rsch. fellow Japan Soc. Promotion of Sci., 1981—82. Research and articles on surfaces and interfaces, thermodynamics, phase changes, quasicrystals. Recipient Dickson prize, Carnegie Mellon U., 1981, Gold medal, U.S. Dept. Commerce, 1982, Von Hippel award, Materials Rsch. Soc., 1985, Stratton award, Nat. Bur. Stds., 1986, Michelson-Morley prize, Case Western Res. U., 1991, William Hume-Rothery award, Minerals, Metals and Materials Soc., 1993, Harvey prize, Israel Inst. Tech., 1995, Nat. Medal of Sci., 1998, Bakhuis-Roozeboom medal, Netherlands Acad. Sci., 1999, Heyn medal, German Materials Soc., 2001, Bower award, Franklin Inst., 2002; fellow Guggenheim Found., 1960.

Fellow: Am. Soc. Metals Internat. (Saveur award 1989), Am. Inst. Metallurg. Engrs., Am. Acad. Arts and Scis.; mem.: Japan Inst. Metals (gold medal 1994), Indian Materials Rsch. Soc. (hon.), Am. Ceramics Soc. (hon.), NAE, NAS. Home: 6610 Pyle Rd Bethesda MD 20817-5454 Office: Nat Inst Standards And Tech Gaithersburg MD 20899-8555

CAHN, STEVEN MARK, philosopher, educator; b. Springfield, Mass., Aug. 6, 1942; s. Judah and Evelyn (Baum) C.; m. Marilyn (Ross), May 4, 1974. AB, Columbia U., 1963, PhD, 1966. Vis. instr. Dartmouth Coll., 1966; vis. prof. U. Rochester, NY, 1967; asst. prof. philosophy Vassar Coll., Poughkeepsie, NY, 1966-68, NYU, N.Y.C., 1968-71, assoc. prof., 1971-73, dir. grad. studies, 1972, dir. under grad. studies, 1971-73; prof., chmn. dept. philosophy U. Vt., Burlington, Vt., 1973-80, adj. prof. philosophy, 1980-83; dean grad. studies, prof. philosophy Grad. Sch. and Univ. Ctr., CUNY, 1983—, provost, v.p. for acad. affairs, 1984-92, acting pres., 1991; program officer Exxon Edn. Found., N.Y.C., 1978-79; assoc. dir. Rockefeller Found., N.Y.C., 1979-81, acting dir. humanities, 1981-82; dir. div. gen. programs NEH, Washington, 1982-83. Pres. John Dewey Found., 1983—; cons., panelist NEH, 1975—82. Author: Fate, Logic, and Time, 1967, 1982, 2004, A New Introduction to Philosophy, 1971, 1986, 2004, The Eclipse of Excellence: A Critique of American Higher Education, 1973, 2004, Education and the Democratic Ideal, 1979, 2004, Saints and Scamps: Ethics in Academia, 1986, rev., 1994, Philosophical Explorations: Freedom, God and Goodness, 1989, Puzzles & Perplexities: Collected Essays, 2002, God, Reason, and Religion, 2005; editor (with Frank A. Tillman): Philosophy of Art and Aesthetics: From Plato to Wittgenstein, 1969; editor: The Philosophical Foundations of Education, 1970, Philosophy of Religion, 1970, Classics of Western Philosophy, 1977, 6th edit., 2002, New Studies in the Philosophy of John Dewey, 1977, Scholars Who Teach: The Art of College Teaching, 1978, 2004; editor: (with David Shatz) Contemporary Philosophy of Religion, 1982; editor: (with Patricia Kitcher and George Sher) Reason at Work: Introductory Readings in Philosophy, 1984, 3d edit., 1995; editor: Morality, Responsibility and the University: Studies in Academic Ethics, 1990, Affirmative Action and the University: A Philosophical Inquiry, 1993; editor: (with Joram G. Haber) Twentieth Century Ethical Theory, 1995; editor: The Affirmative Action Debate, 1995, 2d edit., 2002, Classic and Contemporary Readings in the Philosophy of Education, 1997, Classics of Modern Political Theory: Machiavelli to Mill, 1997; editor: (with Peter Markie) Ethics: History, Theory, and Contemporary Issues, 1998, 3d edit., 2005; editor: Classics of Political and Moral Philosophy, 2002; editor: (with David Shatz) Questions About God, 2002; editor: (with Tziporah Kasachkoff) Morality and Public Policy, 2003; editor: (with Maureen Eckert and Robert Buckley) Knowledge and Reality, 2003; editor: Philosophy for the 21st Century: A Comprehensive Reader, 2003, Ten Essential Texts in the Philosophy of Religion: Classics and Contemporary Issues, 2004, Political Philosophy: The Essential Texts, 2004, Exploring Philosophy: An Introductory Anthology, 2d edit., 2005; editor: (with Maureen Eckert) Philosophical Horizons: Introductory Readings, 2005; gen. editor: Issues in Acad. Ethics, 1994—, Critical Essays on the Classics, 1997—, Blackwell Philosophy Guides, 2001—, Blackwell Readings in Philosophy, 2001—. Chmn. standing com. on tchg. philosophy Am. Philos. Assn., 1985-90, del. Am. Coun. Learned Socs., 1998-2002. Home: 100 W 57th St New York NY 10019-3302 Office: CUNY Grad Sch U Ctr 365 5th Ave New York NY 10016-4334 Business E-Mail: scahn@gc.cuny.edu.

CAHOON, ROBERT STRANGE, lawyer; b. Plymouth, N.C., Dec. 25, 1915; s. Louis Clyde and Minnie Harrison Cahoon; m. Ermah Yelverton Cahoon, July 5, 1941; children: Marilyn, Robert S. Cahoon, Jr.(dec.). LLB, Waike Forest U., 1941. Bar: N.C., U.S. Dist. Ct. (mid. dist.) N.C., U.S. Ct. Appeals (4th cir.), U.S. Supreme Ct. Pvt. practice, Wilmington, NC, 1941—44, Greensboro, NC, 1944—; ptnr. Cahoon, Edgerton, Alspaugh, Greensboro, 1954—61, Cahoon & Swisher, Greensboro, 1961—. Cpl. U.S. Army, 1944—46. Mem.: Greensboro Criminal Def. Attys. (1st pres. 1972—), Greensboro Bar Assn., N.C. Bar Assn., N.C. State Bar. Democrat. Methodist. Avocations: horses, gardening. Home: 213 W Avondale Dr Greensboro NC 27403

CAHOUET, ANN P., lawyer; b. Annapolis, Md., Sept. 7, 1957; BA in comparative lit., Scripps Coll., 1980; JD, U. Pitts., 1991. Bar: Pa. 1991. Positions in book pub. and advt.; joined Reed Smith LLP, Pitts., 1991, named dir. pro bono and cmty. svc., 1996, now dir. cmty. support. Mentor Career Literacy for African Am. Youth program, Duquesne U. Recipient Children's Voice Award, Allegheny County Ct. Apptd. Spl. Advocates, 2002, Caritas Award for Pub. Svc., Cath. Charities of Pitts., 2003. Mem.: Allegheny County Bar Assn. (mem. adoption com.), Pa. Bar Assn., ABA. Office: Reed Smith LLP 435 Sixth Ave Pittsburgh PA 15219 Office Phone: 412-288-4198. Office Fax: 412-288-3063. Business E-Mail: acahouet@reedsmith.com.

CAI, LEI, music educator, pianist; b. Shanghai, Nov. 27, 1973; arrived in U.S., 1992; s. Shi-Chun Cai and Ya-De Zhang. MusD, Fla. State U., Tallahassee, 2002. Asst. prof. of piano Ouachita Bapt. U., Arkadelphia, Ark., 2001—. Author: The Chinese Piano Sch. Named So. Divsn. Collegiate Artist, Music Teachers Nat. Assn., 1998; recipient Young Chang Artist, Tenn. Music Teachers Assn., 1999, Young Artist award, Oak Ridge Symphony, 1999, Tallahassee Music Guild award; Performing Arts scholarship, Liberace Scholarship found., 1996, Nat. Piano Scholarship Competition, U. Tenn., Knoxville. Mem.: Music Teachers Nat. Assn., Nat. Fedn. of Music Clubs, Alpha Chi, Pi Kappa Lambda. Office: Ouachita Baptist Univ Divsn of Music Box 3771 Arkadelphia AR 71998 Office Phone: 870-245-5140. E-mail: cai-pianist@yahoo.com.

CAI, MING ZHI, chemist, researcher, film producer; b. Changsha, China, Feb. 22, 1935; arrived in U.S., 1986; d. Xian Cai and Xian Jiao Du; m. Jing Yi Jin, Apr. 18, 1958; children: Ge Jin, Jun Jin. BS with hons. in Chemistry, Wu Han U., 1957. Tchr. polymer sci. U. Sci. and Tech. China, 1958—73; tchr. Raman spectroscopy Ctr. Instrumental Analysis Tsing Hua U., 1973—86; surface rschr. enhanced Raman spectroscopy UCLA, 1991—93. Rschr. Micro-Raman spectroscopy Sch. Chemistry Ga. Inst. Tech., Atlanta, 1986—89, rschr. Ultra Violet resonance Raman spectroscopy dept. chemistry, 1989—90. Prodr.: (video series for TV stas.) Local Conditions and Customs of America, 1998—; (films, TV stas.) The Stories of Chinese Americans, 2001—; (documentaries) Teacher of Ballet, 2003—, Gymnastic Coaches, 2003—, Mongolia Doctor in LA, 2003—, World Basketball Invitational Tournament for Chinese, 2003—, Joys of Spring, 2004—, Paradise on the Sea, 2004—, The Coast Cities of Mexico, 2004—, I Love You China, 2004—, Kentucky Derby, 2004—, Magical Photographer, 2004—, At Xmas Eve, 2004—, Antique Cars, 2004—, The Tournament of Roses Parade, 2005—, Celebrate Lunar New Year, 2005—, One Hundred Years of Las Vegas, 2005—, sci. and edn. films, —. Mem.: Internat. Artist Photographer Soc., Assn. Rsch. Vision and Opthalmology, Microbeam Analysis Soc., Internat. Soc. Eye Rsch., Sci. and Tech. Soc. China, Instrumental Measurement Soc. China, Chem. Soc. China, Nat. Mus. Women in Arts. Avocations: painting, photo design, film editing, travel, organic agriculture. Personal E-mail: mingzhicai@yahoo.com.

CAI, WEIZHONG (WILL), electronics engineer, researcher, physicist; b. Shanghai, June 28, 1969; arrived in U.S., 1994; s. Xin-fang Cai and Ding-zhen Chen; m. Jenny Zheng; 1 child, Katelyn. BS in Physics, Fudan U., 1991; PhDEE, Pa. State U., 2000. Rschr., asst. to dir., editor-in-chief NSPL Ann. Report Nat. Surface Physics Lab. of China, Shanghai, 1991—94; grad. rschr. Pa. State U., University Park, 1994—2000; sr. semicondr. rschr. ON Semicondr. Corp. (former divsn. Motorola), Phoenix, 2000—04; Jazz Semicondr., 2004—. Mem. 21st Internat. Conf. on the Physics of Semiconductors Local Orgn. Com., Shanghai, 1992, mem. 4th Internat. Conf. on the Surface of Semicondrs., 93; tech. reviewer Am. Vacuum Soc., Research Triangle Park, NC, 1999—; invited lectr. Fudan U., China, 2001. Editor: III-V Semiconductor Heterostructures: Physics and Devices, 2003, (book) Transworld Rsch. Publ.; contbr. chapters to books, over 35 articles to profl. jours. Recipient Judge award, Pa. Jr. Acad. Sci, 1997, Grad. Travel award, 39th Electronic Material Conf., Ft. Collins, Colo., 1997, Pandalai Mem. Award of Excellence, 2004; grantee with Prof. D. L. Miller, Tyco Internat. Co., 1998—2000. Mem.: IEEE, The Electrochemical Soc., Surface Analysis Soc. Japan, Inst. Physics U.K. (assoc.), Sigma Xi. Achievements include invention of a new passivation technique for GaAs surfaces; 2 patents in field. Mailing: Mail Drop H109 4321 Jamboree Rd Newport Beach CA 92660

CAIAZZO, NICHOLAS R., lawyer; b. Bklyn., Jan. 28, 1963; BA, NYU, 1985; JD, St. John's U., 1988. Bar: NY 1988, NJ 1988. Ptnr. Wilson, Elser, Moskowitz, Edelman & Dicker LLP, NYC. Mem.: ABA, Def. Rsch. Inst., NY State Trial Lawyers Assn., NY State Bar Assn. Office: Wilson Elser Moskowitz Edelman & Dicker LLP 23rd Fl 150 E 42nd St New York NY 10017-5639 Office Phone: 212-490-3000 ext. 2121. Office Fax: 212-490-3038. Business E-Mail: caiazzon@wemed.com.

CAIAZZO, TOM A, political scientist, educator; b. Bronx, N.Y., Sept. 11, 1966; s. Lena Mary and Felice Phil Caiazzo; m. Janet M Gladden, Dec. 11, 1992; 1 child, Dante Phillip-Thomas. PhD in Polit. sci., Clark U., Atlanta, Ga., 1996. Prof. polit. sci. Collin County C.C., Plano, Tex., 1995—2003; prof. polit. sci. Gulf Coast C.C., Panama City, Fla., 2003—. Mem. Rep. Party, Plano, Tex., 1996—2003. Fellow Grad. Tchg. Assistantship, Clark Atlanta U., 1994-1995; grantee Rsch. Grant, United We Stand Am., Inc., 1993-1994. Mem.: Kiwanis (assoc.). R-Liberal. Achievements include Canidate for U.S. Congress. 2002. Office: Gulf Coast Comty Coll 5230 West Highway 98 Panama City FL 32401-1058 Office Phone: 850-769-1551 (1)2831.

CAILLÉ, ANDRÉ, public service company executive; b. Saint-Luc, Que., Can., Sept. 11, 1943; s. Jean-Paul C. BSc, U. Montreal, 1965, MSc, 1966, PhD in Phys. Chemistry, 1968. Dir. Canada/Quebec Com. on St. Lawrence River, Quebec, 1975-77, Environ. Protection Services, Quebec, 1978-79, dep. minister, 1980-82; v.p. planning and pub. affairs Gaz Metro, Montreal, 1982—83, sr. v.p. adminstrn. and pub. affairs, 1983-85, exec. v.p., COO, 1985-87, 1987—96; pres., CEO Hydro-Quebec, Montreal, 1996—. Chmn. bd. Noverco Inc.; chancellor U. Montreal; pres. Conseil des Gouverneurs De La Federation Quebecoise pour le Saumon Atlantique; chmn.-elect World Energy Coun.; bd. dirs. Hydro-Que. Internat., Conf. Bd. Can., Montreal Heart Inst. Rsch. Fund. Office: Hydro-Que 75 René-Levesque Blvd W Montreal PQ Canada H2Z 1A4 Fax: 514-289-5238. Office Phone: 514-289-3132. E-mail: caille.andre@hydro.qc.ca.

CAIN, ALBERT CLIFFORD, psychologist, educator; b. Chgo, July 19, 1933; s. Edward Arthur and Fae Anita (Shafton) C.; m. Barbara Strean, Nov. 15, 1959; children: Steven, Kenneth. BA, U. Mich., 1954, PhD, 1962. From asst. prof. to assoc. prof. dept. psychology and psychiatry U. Mich., Ann Arbor, Mich., 1962-69, prof. dept. psychology, 1969—, chmn. dept. psychology, 1981-91; chief psychologist Child. Psychiat. Hosp., Ann Arbor, Mich., 1964-69. Mem. rev. com. Ctr. for Studies of Suicide Prevention NIMH, 1969-72. Editor: Survivors of Suicide, 1972; contbr. articles to profl. jour. Recipient Young Contributor award Am. Assn. Suicidology, 1973. Fellow APA, Am. Orthopsychiatric Assn. (bd. dir. 1978-81, editor jour. 1983-88); mem. Phi Beta Kappa. Home: 1927 Hampton Ct Ann Arbor MI 48103-4521 Office: U Mich Dept Psychology 2251 East Hall 525 E University Ave Ann Arbor MI 48109-1109

CAIN, BEVERLY LYNN, library director; b. Barberton, Ohio, Aug. 5, 1959; d. Norwood Wayne and Mildred Marie Cain. MusB, U. Akron, 1981; MLS, Kent State U., 1986. Reference libr. Medina County Libr., Medina, Ohio, 1986-88, reference mgr., 1988-92; br. mgr. Upper Arlington (Ohio) Libr., 1992-97; dir. Portsmouth (Ohio) Pub. Libr., 1997—. Mem. Portsmouth Cmty. Orch., 1997—. Libr. Svcs. Constrn. Act grantee State Libr. Ohio, 1989, 90. Mem. ALA, Ohio Libr. Coun. (asst. coord. N.E. chpt. 1999—, Diana Vescelius Meml. award 1992), Portsmouth C. of C., Rotary (bd. dirs. 1999—). Avocations: music, antiques, animal welfare. Office: Portsmouth Pub Libr 1220 Gallia St Portsmouth OH 45662-4217 E-mail: cainbe@oplin.lib.oh.us.

CAIN, BRUCE EDWARD, political science professor, consultant; b. Boston, Nov. 28, 1948; s. Arthur James and Ruth Elizabeth (Osterberg) Cain; children: Timothy, Andrew. BA, Bowdoin Coll., 1970; BPhil, Oxford U., 1972; PhD in Polit. Sci., Harvard U., 1976. Asst. prof. Calif. Inst. Tech., Pasadena, 1976—82, assoc. prof., 1983—86, prof. polit. sci., 1986—89, U. Calif., Berkeley, 1989—, acting dir. Inst. Govtl. Studies, 1997—99, dir. Inst. Govtl. Studies, 1999—, dir. Washington Ctr. Washington, 2005—. Cons. Calif. State Assembly, 1981-82, L.A. City Coun., 1986, Fairbank and Assocs., L.A., 1985-86, L.A. Times, 1986-89, Ariz. State Legis. Redistricting, 2002; polit. analyst KTVU, 1998—; expert witness N.Y. State Bd. Elections, 2004. Author: The Reapportionment Puzzle, 1984, The Personal Vote, 1987, Congressional Redistricting, 1990; co-author (with Elizabeth R. Gerber): Voting at the Political Fault Line: California's Experiment with the Blanket Primary, 2002; contbr. articles to profl. jours. Rhodes scholar Oxford U., 1970-72. Mem.: Am. Polit. Sci. Assn., Am. Acad. Arts and Scis. Office: U Calif Washington Ctr 1608 Rhode Island Ave NW Washington DC 20036 Office Phone: 510-642-1474. E-mail: bruce.cain@ucdc.edu.

CAIN, BURTON EDWARD, retired chemistry professor; b. Batavia, NY, Sept. 11, 1942; s. Burton Leo and Bettie S. (Williams) C. BA, SUNY, Binghamton, 1964; PhD, Syracuse U., 1971. Biochemist Onondaga County (NY) Pub. Health Labs., Syracuse, 1971-72, O'Brien & Gere Cons. Engrs., Inc., Syracuse, 1972-74; asst. prof. chemistry Nat. Tech. Inst. Deaf, Rochester, NY, 1974-80, assoc. prof. dept. chemistry, 1980—84, prof., 1984—2005; asst. chemistry dept. head Rochester Inst. Tech., 1981—87, 1988—2003, assoc. chemistry dept. head, 2003—05; prof. emeritus, 2005—; ret., 2005. Reader Advanced Placement chemistry exams. Ednl. Testing Svc., June 1987, 88, 89, 90, 91, 92. Author: The Basics of Technical Communicating, 1988; contbr. articles to profl. jours. Reviewer grant proposals coll. sci. instrument program NSF, 1987, instrumentation and lab. improvement program NSF, 1992. Recipient Eisenhart Outstanding Tchr. award, 1980. Mem. Am. Chem. Soc., AAAS, AAUP, NSTA, Nat. Assn. Deaf, Conf. Am. Instrs. for Deaf, Registry of Interpreters for Deaf, Sigma Xi, Phi Lambda Upsilon, Gamma Epsilon Tau (Tchr. of Yr. award 1983). Home: 200 East Ave Apt 1105 Rochester NY 14604-2633

CAIN, COLEEN W., writer, educator; b. Birmingham, Iowa, Sept. 2, 1916; d. Marida Irwin Cain and Effie Lavina Walters; m. James Cazort McClurkin, Feb. 5, 1937 (dec. Jan. 1938); m. James Robert Cazort, Dec. 24, 1942 (div. Oct. 1970); 1 child, Sidney Cain; m. Eugene Everett Bauer, Nov. 3, 1974 (div. Feb. 1983). BA in Journalism, U. Ark., 1938. Cert. real estate agt. Wash., 1946, Ark., 1948. Tech. writer Manpower, Inc., Huntsville, Ala., 1966—69; editor, arts reviews Huntsville Times, 1969—70; fgn. news corr. Beijing PRC Jour. Am., Bellevue, Wash., 1980—83; instr. Beijing Fgn. Langs. Inst., 1981—83; lectr. Continuing Edn. Bellevue & South Seattle C.C., 1983—88; pres., owner Cain-Lockhart Press, Issaquah, Wash., 1985; instr. Issaquah Cmty. Ctr., 1996, North Bellevue Cmty. Sr. Ctr., 1997—; pres., owner Grazel-Pierce Pubs., 2004. Spkr. in field. Author: 115 Jet Stories for Your Briefcase, 2001, 2d edit., 2003, Beth Bauer's Enjoy China More, 1985, Wild Blue, 1st of WWII Trilogy, 2002, 2d edit., 2005, Glory After the War, 2d of WWII Trilogy, 2005. Singer Seattle Symphony Chorale, New Orleans Opera Soc., Cascadian Chorale, Huntsville Cmty. Chorus; mem. 41st dist. Democrats, Bellevue, 1972; alt. del. King County Democrats, Seattle, 1992; election judge Westlake Precinct, Issaquah, 1991—98; mezzo soloist in choirs, chorales. Recipient cert. of excellence, City of Bellevue Parks and Cmty. Svcs. Dept., 2001. Mem.: Book Pub. Northwest, Pub. Mktg. Assn., Seattle Free Lances (treas. 1997—98, adviser 2001), Pacific Northwest Writers Assn. (critique editor 1995—99, 3rd place nonfiction award 1976). Democrat. Presbyterian. Avocation: music. Home: 19510 S E 51st St Issaquah WA 98027-9327 Office Phone: 425-392-0508. Personal E-mail: cwcain@peoplepc.com.

CAIN, DAVID, lawyer; b. Findley, Ohio, Nov. 1, 1963; s. William Cain; life ptnr. Timothy Lauer. JD, New Eng. Sch. Law, Boston, 1990. Bar: Hawaii 1990. Pvt. practice law, Wailuku, Hawaii, 1990—. Named to Grand Jury Counsel, Hawaii Supreme Ct., 1999; recipient Gov.'s Kilohana Aaard, Gov.'s Office Hawaii, 2000, Appreciation of Pro Bono Svc. award, Legislature State of Hawaii, 2001. Mem.: Hawaii State Bar Assn., Am. Bankruptcy Inst., Rotary (bd. dirs. 1999—2001). Mailing: Law Offices of David W Cain, LLC 1923A E Vineyard St Wailuku HI 96793 Business E-Mail: dave@cain.net.

CAIN, DAVID H., lawyer, former state legislator; b. Pampa, Tex., Nov. 13, 1947; s. Don and Betty Anne C.; m. Sally Anne Haenelt; children: David, Jennifer. BA in History, McMurry Coll., 1970; JD, U. Tex., 1973. Bar: Tex. 1973. Assoc. Crowder & Mattox, Dallas, 1973-78; ptnr. Bennett & Cain, Dallas, 1979-82; pvt. practice Dallas, 1982-86; assoc. Burleson, Pate, and Gibson, Dallas, 1986—; mem. Tex. Ho. of Reps., Austin, 1977-95, chmn. transp. com., 1983-95; mem. Tex. Senate, Austin, 1995—2002, vice chmn. econ. devel. com., 1997-99, chmn. Senate subcom. on infrastructure, 1999, vice chmn. spl. com. on electric utility restructuring, 1999. Chair Tex. Sunset Adv. Commn., 1991-93, transp. com. So. Legis. Conf., 1991-93. Founder Clean Dallas East; mem. Parents as First Tchrs. Recipient Friend of Bus. award Tex. C. of C., 1993; named Outstanding Young Man of Am. by Jaycees, 1978, 81, Legis. Crime Fighter of Yr. by Greater Dallas Crime Commn., 1993, One of Ten Best Legislators by Tex. Monthly Mag., 1993. Mem. State Bar of Tex., Dallas Bar Assn., East Dallas Bar Assn., Nat. Conf. State Legislatures, Greater Dallas C. of C. Democrat. Methodist. Avocations: running, travel. Office: Burleson, Pate & Gibson 2414 N Akard Suite 700 Dallas TX 75201

CAIN, DAVID PAUL, art educator; b. Idpls., Oct. 14, 1928; s. Cecil Jordan and Carol Catherine Cain; BA, Earlham Coll., 1950. Art tchr. Am. HS, Mexico City, 1954—55; illustrator, photo. Freelance, N.Y.C., NY, 1955—70; art, photo tchr. Grove Sch., Madison, Conn., 1970—74; art tchr. Lincoln HS, San Jose, Costa Rica, 1975; photo. tchr. Guilford Art Sch., Guilford, Conn., 1976—77; artist, photo. Freelance, Hamden, Conn., 1978—; art tchr. Meriden Art Gallery, Meriden, Conn., 1978—, Hamden Arts Commn., Hamden, Conn., 1978—. Exhibitions include, Mexico City, Munich, Germany, N.Y.C., Collingswood, NJ, Albuquerque, N. Mex., Idpls., Meriden, Conn., Hamden, Conn, Hartford, Conn, Old Saybrook, Conn, Branford, Conn, North Haven, Conn., Old Lyme, Conn., Essex, Conn., one-man shows include, Munich, Germany, Earlham Coll., Ind., Alden House, Mass., Yale U., Conn., Madison, Conn., Guilford, Conn., Hamden, Conn., Harftford, Conn., North Haven, Conn., Branford, Conn., Old Saybrook, Conn. Cpl. U.S. Army, 1951—53, Germany. Mem.: Mt. Carmel Art Assn., North Haven Art Guild, Clinton Art Soc., Guilford Art League, The Brownstone Group, Arts and Crafts Assn., Conn. Pastel Soc. Avocation: photography.

CAIN, DONALD EZELL, retired judge; b. San Marcos, Tex., Oct. 8, 1921; s. Erie Montclair and Betty Belle (Howell) C.; m. Betty Anne Culberson, June 14, 1952; children: David, Dale Cain Husen, Donald Ezell, Randolph. A.S., North Tex. Agrl. Coll., 1941; BBA, U. Tex., 1943, LL.B., 1948; postgrad., Nat. Jud. Coll., Reno, 1974, 78, 82. Bar: Tex. 1948. With contracts dept. Convair, Ft. Worth, 1948-50; pvt. practice law Pampa, Tex., 1951-76; county atty. Gray County, Tex., 1955-68; county judge, 1971-77; dist. judge 223rd Dist. Ct. Tex., 1977-91; sr. dist. judge State of Tex., 1991—, ret. Pres. Adobe Walls coun. Boy Scouts Am., 1957-59; bd. dirs. Pampa United Fund, 1956-60. Served from ensign to lt. USNR, 1943-46; as lt., 1950-51. Recipient Silver Beaver award Boy Scouts Am., 1958 Fellow Tex. Bar Found.; mem. ABA, Tex. Bar Assn., Gray County Bar Assn. (pres. 1968), Am. Judicature Soc., Tex. Judges and Commrs. Assn., Panhandle County Judges and Commrs. Assn. (pres. 1975), Pampa C. of C. (dir. 1959-60), Phi Alpha Delta. Clubs: Masons, Rotary (pres. 1958-59), Pampa Country. Democrat. Baptist. Home: 2321 Chestnut Dr Pampa TX 79065-2910

CAIN, DOUGLAS MYLCHREEST, lawyer; b. Chgo., Sept. 8, 1938; s. Douglas M. Jr. and Louise C. (Coleman) C.; m. Constance Alexis Adams Moffit, Apr. 18, 1970; children: Victoria Elizabeth Moffit, Alexandra Catherine Moffit. AB, Harvard U., 1960; JD with distinction, U. Mich., 1966; LL.M., N.Y. U., 1970. Bar: Colo. 1966, U.S. Ct. Appeals (10th cir.) 1972, U.S. Supreme Ct. 1972. Assoc. Sherman & Howard, L.L.C., Denver, 1966-72, ptnr., 1972-93; equity mem., 1993—; chmn. policy council Sherman & Howard, Denver, 1984-87; adj. prof. law U. Denver, 1972-78. Mem. Rocky Mountain Estate Planning Council, pres., 1976-77 Assoc. editor: Mich. Law Rev, 1964-66; contbr. articles to profl. jours. Bd. dirs. Craig Hosp. Found., 1980-86, v.p., 1984-85, pres., 1986-87, 88-89; bd. dirs. Colo. Jud. Inst., 1990-96, chmn., 1992-93; bd. dirs. Colo. chpt. Am. Diabetes Assn., 1993, Breathe Better Found., 1993—, Colo. Coun. Econ. Edn., 1996-98, Fortune Found., 1998—; mem. Estate Planning Seminar Group. With USN, 1960—63. Fellow Am. Coll. Tax Coun., Am. Coll. Trust and Estate Counsel; mem. ABA, Colo. Bar Assn. (gov. 1980-82), Greater Denver Tax Coun. Assn. (v.p. 1987, pres. 1988), Assn. Harvard Alumni (regional dir. 1978-81), Rocky Mountain Harvard Club (pres. 1977-78, 92-93), Denver Country Club, Mile High Club, Rotary. Home: 1960 Hudson St Denver CO 80220-1459 Office: Sherman & Howard LLC 633 17th St Ste 3000 Denver CO 80202-3665 Office Phone: 303-299-8122. Business E-Mail: dcain@sah.com.

CAIN, GEORGE HARVEY, lawyer, legal association administrator; b. Washington, Aug. 3, 1920; s. J. Harvey and Madeleine (McGettigan) C.; m. Patricia J. Campbell, Apr. 23, 1946 (div.); children: George Harvey, James C., John P., Paul J.; m. Constance S. Collins, Aug. 10, 1985 BS, Georgetown U., 1942; JD, Harvard U., 1948. Bar: N.Y. 1949, Ohio 1972, Conn. 1977, U.S. Supreme Ct. 1995. Practiced law, N.Y. State, 1949-71, 73-76; pvt. practice, 1972-73; sec., gen. counsel Nat. Carloading Corp., 1949-54; mem. firm Spence & Hotchkiss, 1954-55; gen. atty., asst. sec. Cerro Corp., 1955-68, sec., gen. atty., 1968-72; v.p., gen. counsel Pickands Mather Co., Cleve., 1971-73; v.p., sec., gen. counsel Flintkote Co., White Plains, N.Y., 1973-76, Stamford, Conn., 1976-80; spl. counsel Day, Berry & Howard, Hartford and Stamford, Conn., 1980-82, ptnr. Stamford, 1983-90, of counsel, 1991—. Sec. Cerro Sales Corp., 1955-71; bd. dirs., sec. Leadership Housing Sys., Inc., 1970-71; bd. dirs., gen. counsel Atlantic Cement Co., Inc., 1962-71; bd. dirs. Hajoca Corp., 1975-79, Polymer Bldg. Sys., Inc.; adj. prof. U. Bridgeport Law Sch., 1983-86. Author: Turning Points: New Paths and Second Careers for Lawyers, 1994, Law Firm Partnership: Its Rights and Responsibilities, 1995, 2nd edit., 1999, Law Partnership Revisited, 2002. Served to 1st lt. USAAF, 1942-46; to capt. USAF, 1951-52. Fellow Am. Bar Found.; mem. ABA (chair sr. lawyers divsn. 2002—), N.Y. State Bar Assn., N.Y.C. Bar Assn., Ohio Bar Assn., Conn. Bar Assn., Am. Law Inst., Am. Soc. Corp. Secs., Georgetown U. Alumni Assn. (mem. Alumni senate), Harvard Club N.Y., Dutch Treat Club. Office: Day Berry & Howard City Place I Hartford CT 06103-3499 Office Phone: 860-676-8535.

CAIN, HARRY P., II, health science association administrator; m. Elizabeth Maury Bethea; 3 children. Grad., Stanford Univ.; PhD, Brandeis Univ. Dir., Office of Policy Devel. and Planning Dept. HEW, asst. dir., Nat. Inst. of Mental Health; exec. dir. Am. Health Planning Assn., 1978—82; exec.v.p. bus. alliances Blue Cross and Blue Shield Assn., Chgo., sr. v.p., fed. programs. Mem.: Inst. Medicine. Office: Blue Cross & Blue Shield Assn 233 N Michigan Ave Chicago IL 60601-7689

CAIN, JAMES NELSON, arts school and concert administrator; b. Arcadia, Ohio, Jan. 6, 1930; s. Alfred Ray and Gladys Eliza (Cruikshank) C.; m. Marthellen Jones, June 12, 1950; children— Nelson, Jennifer, Richard, Elizabeth. AB, Ohio State U., Columbus, 1955. Dir. Prestige Concerts, Inc., Columbus, 1948-62; exec. dir. Music Assos. Aspen, Inc., Colo., 1962-68; from asst. mgr. to mgr. St. Louis Symphony Orch., 1968-80; v.p. St. Louis Conservatory and Schs. Arts, 1980-94. Home: 2 Nantucket Ln Saint Louis MO 63132-4111 Personal E-mail: JNCain@prodigy.com.

CAIN, JAMES P., ambassador, lawyer; BA cum laude, Wake Forest U., JD cum laude, 1984. Bar: NC 1984. Atty., co-founder Kilpatrick Stockton, LLP, Raleigh, NC, 1985—2000, ptnr., 2002—05; pres., COO Carolina Hurricanes

NHL/Gale Force Holdings, 2000—02; U.S. amb. to Denmark US Dept. State, Copenhagen, 2005—. NC vice chair Bush-Cheney campaign, 2004; mem. Rep. Nat. Com. Office: 5280 Copehagen Pl Washington DC 20521*

CAIN, JEFFREY J., physician; s. James L. and Darlene L. Cain. MD, Oreg. Health Sciences U., 1985. Diplomate Am. Bd. Family Practice. Asst. dir. family medicine residency St. Anthony Hosp., Denver, 1993—2000; chief family medicine Children's Hosp., Denver, 2001—. Founder and pres. Nat. Tar Wars, Colo., 1993—2000. Chmn. pub. policy and advocacy com. Amputee Coalition of Am., Knoxville, Tenn., 2003—05; chmn. Colo. Coalition of Working Amputees, Denver, 1999—2005. Fellow: Am. Acad. Family Medicine (del. 2004—05, Pub. Health award 1995); mem.: Soc. Teachers of Family Medicine (Advocacy award 2004). Avocations: flying, skiing. Office: Children's Hosp 1056 E 19th Ave B085 Denver CO 80209 Office Phone: 303-861-3980. E-mail: cain.jeffrey@tchden.org.

CAIN, JUDITH SHARP, mathematics educator, consultant; d. Sturdy O. and Erna E. Sharp; children: Jason Charles, Crystal Heather, Jeffrey Ronald. MEd, U. La., Lafayette, 1989. Cert. tchr. 1-8, secondary math., mid. sch. math. La., supr. of instrn. La., adminstr. La. Estimator Sellers, Dubroc & Assoc., Inc., Civil Engrs., Lafayette, 1972—81; tchr. mid. sch. math. Lafayette Parish Sch. Bd., Cathedral Carmel Sch., 1986—97; lead tchr., connected math. project Lafayette Parish Sch. Bd., Lafayette, La., 1999—, presenter workshops and inservices, 1997—. Math. workshop cons./tchr. trainer various sch. districts, La., 1999—; mem. com. grade level expectations and textbook adoption, intern rev. LEAP range finding, iLEAP rev. com., LAA2 com., LEAP item rev. com. La. Dept. of Edn., 2003—05. Author: An Evaluation of the Connected Math. Project. Active St. Anne's Cath. Ch., Youngsville, La. Named Outstanding Tchr., Diocese of Lafayette, 1993—94, Tchr. of Yr., Lafayette Parish, 2000. Mem.: NEA, ASCD, Nat. Coun. Suprs. Math., La. Tchrs. Math., Nat. Coun. Tchrs. Math. Office: Lafayette Parish Sch Bd 805 Teurlings Dr Lafayette LA 70501 Office Fax: 337-289-1997. Personal E-mail: judycain@excite.com. E-mail: cain.judy@gmail.com.

CAIN, LINDA JOANNE, academic administrator; b. Oakland, Calif., Aug. 5, 1943; d. John Gunnar and Virginia Helen (Johnson) Lyle; m. Mark E. Cain, Mar. 15, 1985. A.B. in History, U. Calif., Berkeley, 1965; A.M.L.S., U. Mich., 1967. Supr. microform reading room, periodicals reading room, interlibrary loan unit at grad. libr. U. Mich., 1967-69, U. Calif., Berkeley, 1969-78, reference, coll. devel. librarian Moffitt Undergrad. Libr., 1969-72, coord. pub. svcs. Moffitt Undergrad. Library, 1972-75, adminstrv. asst. to assoc. univ. librarian for pub. svcs., 1977-78, instr. bibliography I, 1971, 74-75; head librarian reference svcs., acting asst. dir. pub. svcs. U. Tex., Austin, 1978-80, assoc. dir. pub. svcs., 1980-84, assoc. dir., 1984-87; dean and libr. U. Cin., 1987-90, assoc. provost, 1990—2004, orientation to learning instr., 2003-04; Mem. editl. bd. Jour. Acad. Librarianship, 1980-88; contbr. articles to profl. jours. Council Libr. Resources acad. library mgmt. intern, 1975-76. UCLA sr. fellow, 1985. Mem. ALA, ALAO, AHE, Educause. Office: U Cin Adminstrn PO Box 210097 Cincinnati OH 45221-0097 Business E-Mail: linda.cain@uc.edu.

CAIN, MARCENA JEAN BEESLEY, retail executive; b. Kingman, Kans., May 1, 1935; d. Albert Eugene and Stella Wanda (Ruthowski) Beesley; m. Kenneth B. Cain, Aug. 4, 1951 (dec. Aug. 17, 2000); children: Kenneth Thomas, David Raymond. With AMVETS Thrift Stores, Washington, 1971—, asst. dir., 1971—87, exec. adminstr., 1987—; pres., asst. dir. AMVETS Value Village Thrift Stores, Balt. Ptnr. Bank St. Joint Venture Realty, Del-Mar Realty, Oakland Ctr. Partnership Ltd., 1987; pres. Familty Thrift Ctr., Inc.; v.p. 4 corps; chmn. bd. dirs. Alamo II Thrift Stores, 1993. DC area rep. PTA Valley Forge Mil. Acad. Named Woman of the Yr., Balt.'s Best BPW, 1981; recipient Disting. Citizen's citation, Howard Co., 1987, Gov.'s citation, State of Md., 1987, Dedicated Svc. award, Seat Pleasant, Md., 1987, Congl. cert. Merit, 1991, 1992, AMVETS Dept. Md. Freestate award, 1994, Silver Helmet Spl. award for cmty. svc., 2003, Nat. Amvet's Silver Helmet award. Mem.: DAV Aux. (past nat. historian), Affiliated Mchts. Assn. Balt. (past pres.), Govanstown Mchts. Assn. (rec. sec.), Highlandtown Mchts. Assn. (bd. dirs. 1980, pres. 1981, 1983—84, chmn. bd. dirs. 1982, 1984—85), Highlandtown Businessmen Assn., Bus. and Profl. Women's Club, Kiwanis. Republican. Christian Scientist. Office: 3424 Eastern Ave Baltimore MD 21224-4121

CAIN, RUSSELL M., psychiatrist, educator, administrator; b. Pitts., Aug. 31, 1940; s. Ralph H. and Lillian (Noon) C.; m. Nancy Napier, Oct. 23, 1965; 1 child, Christine Elizabeth. BS, Ohio State U., 1962; postgrad., Coll. de France, Paris, 1962-63, Inst. de Neurophysiologie Gen.; MD, Ohio State U., 1967. Diplomate Am. Bd. Psychiatry and Neurology. Intern U. Wis., Madison, 1967-68, resident in psychiatry, 1968-71, fellow in family therapy, 1970—71; with U. Rochester, NY, 1973—2004, prof. emeritus, 2004. Lt. comdr. M.C., USN, 1971-73. Recipient Recognition award Commn. on Accreditation Rehab. Facilities; gen. Univ. scholar in medicine Ohio State U., 1963-67; NIMH fellow in psychiatry, 1968-71. Fellow Am. Psychiat. Assn. (disting. life fellow, Falk fellow 1969-70); mem. Rochester Acad. Medicine, Med. Soc.of Monroe County, Genesee Valley Psychiat. Assn. (pres. 1995-97), U.S. Naval Inst., Genesee Conservation League, Marines Meml. Assn., U. Wis. Alumna Assn., The Oxford Alumni Assn. Avocations: sailing, photography, music, reading, travel. Personal E-mail: rmcain@frontiernet.net.

CAIN, TIM J., lawyer; b. Angola, Ind., July 12, 1958; s. Nancy J. (Nichols) C.; m. Debra J. VanWagner, Feb. 28, 1976; children: Christine M., Stephanie L., Katherine S., Jennifer A. BA in Polit. Sci. with honors, Ind. U., 1980; JD, Valparaiso U., 1984; MBA, Ind. Wesleyan U., 1991; LLM in Internat. Bus. and Trade with honors, John Marshall Law Sch., 2001. Bar: Ind. 1984, U.S. Dist. Ct. (no. and so. dists.) Ind. 1984, U.S. Supreme Ct., 2002. Assoc. Hartz & Eberhard, LaGrange, Ind., 1984-85; pub. defender LaGrange Cir. Ct., 1985-86; sr. assoc. Eberhard & Assocs., LaGrange, 1985-86; chief dep. to Pros. Atty.'s Office, LaGrange, 1986-87; ptnr. Eberhard & Cain, LaGrange, 1986-89; pvt. practice LaGrange, 1989-95; pros. atty. La Grange (Ind.) County, 1991—2002; ptnr. Williams and Cain, Ft. Wayne, Ind., 2002—. Asst. atty. La Grange County, La Grange; atty. Town of Shipshewana, Ind., 1984-93. Coach Orland (Ind.) Little League, 1977-79, Prairie Hts. Baseball, LaGrange, 1986-90; pres. Prairie Hts. H.S. Dollars for Scholars, LaGrange, 1989; active LaGrange County Coun. on Aging, 1989-91, Prairie Hts. At-Risk Students Com., 1989—, LaGrange County 4-H Fair Assn., 1993-97. Mem.Ind. Bar Assn., LaGrange County Bar Assn. (sec.-treas. 1986-87, v.p. 1987-89, pres. 1990-93). Clubs: Exchange (pres. 1988-89). Republican. Home: 360 S 900 E Lagrange IN 46761-9529 Office: 110 W Berry Ste 1910 Fort Wayne IN 46802 Office Phone: 260-420-3100. E-mail: tim@williams-cain.com.

CAIN, VERNON, retired diversified financial services company executive; b. Bisbee, Ariz., Jan. 5, 1947; BS, No. Ariz. U., 1969; MBA with honors, Roosevelt U., 1984. Pres. U.S. holdings Dawson Holdings PLC, Oregon, Ill., 1985-96, CEO, mng. dir. info. svcs. group, 1996-2000. Mem. Am. Libr. Assn. Home: 4505 W Sunset Dunes Pl Tucson AZ 85743-8345 Office Phone: 520-743-4696. Personal E-mail: verncain@aol.com.

CAIN, WILLIAM STANLEY, experimental psychologist, educator, researcher; b. NYC, Sept. 7, 1941; s. William Henry and June Rose (Stanley) Cain; m. Claire Murphy, Oct. 30, 1993; children: Justin, Alison stepchildren: Michael, Jennifer, Courtney. BS, Fordham U., 1963; MSc, Brown U., 1966, PhD, 1968. From asst. fellow to fellow John B. Pierce Lab., New Haven, 1967-94; from instr. to assoc. prof. dept. epidemiology, pub. health, and psychology Yale U., New Haven, 1967-84, prof., 1984-94; prof. otolaryngology U. Calif., San Diego, 1994—. Mem. sensory disorders study sect. NIH, Bethesda, Md., 1991—95; mem. sci. adv. bd. Ctr. Indoor Air Rsch., Linthicum, Md., 1991—99. Mem. editl. bd. Chem. Senses, 1985—94, mem. editl. adv. bd. Indoor Air, 1990—2000, 2005—, Physiology and Behavior, 1995—96; editor: 5 books, 1971—; contbr. articles to profl. jours. Recipient Jacob Javits/Claude Pepper award, NIH, 1984, Sense of Smell Rsch. award, Fragrance Rsch. Fund, 1986. Fellow: ASHRAE (Crosby Field award 1984), APA, Acad. Indoor Air Rsch.; mem.: N.Y. Acad. Scis. (pres. 1986), Assn. Chemoreception Scis. (exec. chmn. 1983—84). Home: 4459 Nabal Dr La Mesa CA 91941-7168 Office: U Calif Dept Surgery 9500 Gilman Dr Rm Mc957 La Jolla CA 92093-0957 Office Phone: 858-622-5831. Business E-Mail: wcain@ucsd.edu.

CAINE, EDWARD PETER, religious organization administrator; b. N.Y.C., Mar. 5, 1951; s. Stuart and Doris Caine; m. Jill Barbara Winkleman, Sept. 10, 1978; children: Ilysse Brooke, Jennifer Anne. BS in Engring., BA in History, Lehigh U., 1973; MBA, Temple U., 1977. CPA Pa. Chief fin. analyst Girard Bank, Pa., 1973—77; mgr. Arthur Andersen & Co., Pa., 1977—81, sr. mgr., 1983—85; 2nd v.p. Chase Manhattan, NY, 1981—83; v.p. of fin., treas. Berger Holdings, Pa., 1985—90; CFO, chief adminstrv. officer ECC Mgmt. Svcs., Pa., 1990—96; sr. mgr. MAXIMUS, Reston, Va., 1996—2002; chief adminstrv. officer Union for Reform Judaism, N.Y.C., 2002—. Mem. Pres. Clinton's Round Table on Race Rels. Past treas. Ithan Mills Homeowner's Assn., Bryn Mawr, Pa.; advisor RJ Health and Welfare Trust; past regional v.p. Union of Am. Hebrew Congregations, Phila.; past pres. Main Line Reform Temple, Wynnewood, Pa.; bd. dirs. Reform Pension Bd., N.Y.C., URJ Press Bd., N.Y.C.; staff pension bd. URJ; bd. dirs. 633 Condo Bd., N.Y.C.; bus. cons. RJ Mag., N.Y.C.; past pres. Temple U. Bus. Sch. Alumni Assn., Phila. Recipient Membership, Beta Alpha Psi - Nat. Acctg. Frat. Mem.: Nat. Assn. Temple Adminstrs. (bd. dirs.), AICPA, Religious Conf. Mgmt. Assn., Profl. Conf. Mgmt. Assn., N.Y. Soc. Assn. Execs., Pa. Inst. CPAs (past. chmn. BGE com.), Am. Soc. Assn. Execs., Golden Slipper Club. Democrat. Home: 16 Stonecreek Ln Bryn Mawr PA 19010 Office: Union for Reform Judaism 633 Third Ave New York NY 10017 E-mail: ecaine@urj.org.

CAINE, FRANKLYN A., aerospace transportation executive; b. Plainfield, N.J., Mar. 1950; B in Chem. Engring., Princeton U., 1971; MBA in fin., internat. bus., U. Chicago, 1976. Mgmt. RCA Corp., Penn Central Corp., Exxon Corp.; sr. v.p. controller, dir. corp. devel. United Techs. Corp., Hartford, Conn.; exec. v.p., CFO Wang Global, 1994-99; sr. v.p., CFO Raytheon Co., Lexington, Mass., 1999—2002; dir. Phase Forward. Office: Phase Forward 880 Winter St Waltham MA 02451*

CAINE, JONATHAN SAUL, geologist, researcher; BA in geology, SUNY, 1986, MA in geology, 1991; PhD in geology, U. Utah, 1999. Cons. hydrogeologist Mohonk Preserve, New Paltz, NY, 1989—92; rsch. asst. U. Utah, Dept. Geology and Geophysics, Salt Lake City, 1993—99; post doctoral rsch. fellow U.S. Geological Survey, Denver, 1999—2000; rsch geologist Crustal Imaging and Characterization Team, U.S. Geological Survey, Geologic Divsn., Denver, 2000—. Contbr. articles various profl. jours. Invited lectr. various profl. venues. Mem.: Soc. for Values in Higher Edn., Nat. Assn. of Geoscience Tchrs., Geological Soc. of Am., Am. Geophysical Union. Office: US Geological Survey PO Box 25046 MS964 Denver CO 80225-0046 E-mail: jscaine@usgs.gov.

CAINE, MARTIN LAWRENCE, lawyer; Bar: N.Y. 1962. Atty. pvt. practice, Westbury, NY. Office: 675 Old Country Rd Westbury NY 11590-4503 also: 217 Broadway New York NY 10007

CAINE, MICHAEL, actor; b. London, Mar. 14, 1933; s. Maurice and Ellen Frances Marie Micklewhite; m. Patricia Haines, 1954; children: Dominique, Natasha; m. Shakira Baksh, 1973. Asst. stage mgr. Westminster Repertory, Horsham, England, 1953; actor Lowestoft Repertory, 1953-55, Theatre Workshop, London, 1955. Actor: What's It All About?: An Autobiography, 1993, (numerous TV appearances):, 1957—63,: (plays) Next Time I'll Sing for You, 1963; (films) A Hill in Korea, 1956, How to Murder a Rich Uncle, 1958, Zulu, 1964, The Ipcress File, 1965, Alfie, The Wrong Box, Gambit, 1966, Hurry Sundown, 1967, Woman Times Seven, 1967, Deadfall, 1967, The Magus, 1968, Battle of Britain, 1968, Play Dirty, 1968, The Italian Job, 1969, Too Late the Hero, 1970, The Last Valley, 1971, Get Carter, 1971, Zee & Co., 1972, Kidnapped, 1972, Pulp, 1972, Sleuth, 1973, The Black Windmill, 1974, Marseilles Contract, 1974, The Wilby Conspiracy, 1974, Fat Chance, 1975, The Romantic Englishwoman, 1975, The Man Who Would Be King, 1975, Harry and Walter Go to New York, 1975, The Eagle Has Landed, 1976, A Bridge Too Far, 1976, Silver Bears, 1976, The Swarm, 1977, California Suite, 1978, Beyond the Poseidon Adventure, 1979, Dressed to Kill, 1980, The Island, 1980, The Hand, 1981, Victory, 1981, Deathtrap, 1982, Educating Rita, 1983, Beyond the Limit, 1983, The Jigsaw Man, 1984, The Holcroft Covenant, 1984, Blame It On Rio, 1984, The Whistle Blower, 1985, Hannah and Her Sisters, 1986 (Acad. award for best supporting actor, 1987), Water, Sweet Liberty, 1986, Mona Lisa, 1986, Half Moon Street, 1986, Jaws The Revenge, Surrender, 1987, Without a Clue, 1988, Dirty Rotten Scoundrels, 1988, Shock to the System, 1989, Bullseye!, 1990, Jekyll and Hyde, 1990, Mr. Destiny, 1990, Noises Off, 1991, The Muppets Christmas Carol, 1992, On Deadly Ground, 1994, Bullet to Beijing, 1995, Blood and Wine, 1996, Curtain Call, 1997, Blue Ice, 1993, Little Voice, 1998 (Golden Globe), Debtors, 1999, Cider House Rules, 1999 (Acad. award for best supporting actor), Quills, 1999, Shiner, 2000, Get Carter, 2000, Miss Congeniality, 2000, Last Orders, 2001, Quicksand, 2001, The Quiet American, 2002 (Acad. award nomination, 2002), Austin Powers 3, 2002, The Actor, 2003, Secondhand Lions, 2003, The Statement, 2003, Around the Bend, 2004, The Weatherman, 2005, Batman Begins, 2005, Bewitched, 2005; actor, exec. prodr.: (films) The Fourth Protocol, 1987; actor: (TV miniseries) Jack the Ripper, 1988, World War II: When Lions Roared, 1994 (Emmy nominee for Lead Actor in a Miniseries, 1994). Named Companion of Order of the Brit. Empire, 1992, Sir Michael Caine, 2000. Knight, Queen of Eng., 2000. Office: care Pam PR Inc 4401 Wilshire Blvd Los Angeles CA 90010-3728 also: Chelsea Harbour London England

CAINE, PAUL JASON, publishing executive; b. NYC, Apr. 21, 1964; s. Donald Ray and Pearl Jane (Silberstein) C. BA, Ind. U., 1986. Asst. media planner J. Walter Thompson Co., NYC, 1986, media planner, 1987—89; assoc. pub., Teen People Time Warner Inc., NYC, 1997—2001, assoc. pub., advt. sales, People mag., 2001—02, pub., Teen People, 2002—03, pub., Entertainment Weekly, 2003—, pub., People mag., 2004—. Chmn. com. Union Bd. Concert. Named to Advertising Hall of Achievement, 2004. Mem. Tau Kappa Epsilon (pres. alumni chpt.). Avocation: piano. Office: Entertainment Weekly 1675 Broadway New York NY 10019*

CAINE, RAYMOND WILLIAM, JR., retired public relations executive; b. Fall River, Mass., June 30, 1932; s. Raymond W. and Emma (Gardella) C.; m. Sharon G. Henry, Nov. 10, 1956; children: Karen, Kimberly, Patrick, Peter. BS, Providence Coll., 1956. Sr. v.p. advt., pub. relations Creamer, Dickson, Basford, N.Y.C. and Providence, 1966-74; v.p. pub. rels. Blue Cross (Blue Shield), Providence, 1974-80; v.p. corp. communications Textron, Inc., Providence, 1980-94; ret. Contbr. articles to profl. jours. Bd. dirs. R.I. Commodores, 1987—, Newport Preservation Soc., Newport Hist. Soc.; trustee The Miriam Hosp. Recipient Bell Ringer award Publicity Club Boston, 1971, 72. Mem. Pub. Rels. Soc. Am. (bd. dir. 1971-73), Newport Reading Rm. Avocations: golf, home remodeling.

CAINE, STANLEY PAUL, college administrator; b. Huron, SD, Feb. 11, 1940; s. Louis Vernon and Elizabeth (Holland) C.; m. Karen Anne Mickelson, July 11, 1964; children: Rebecca, Kathryn, David. BA, Macalester Coll., 1962; MS, U. Wis., 1964, PhD, 1967; LLD, Hanover Coll., 2000; LittD, MacMurray Coll., 2003. Asst. prof. history Lindenwood Coll., St. Charles, Mo., 1967-71; from asst. to assoc. prof. history DePauw U., Greencastle, Ind., 1971-77; prof. history, v.p. for acad. affairs Hanover (Ind.) Coll., 1977-89; pres. Adrian (Mich.) Coll., 1989—. Bd. dirs. NCAA Coun., 1995-96, vice chair mgmt. coun. divsn. III, 1997-99, pres.'s coun., 1999-2002; cons., evaluator North Ctrl. Assn., 1984—. Author: The Myth of a Political Reform, 1970; contbr. to book The Progressive Era, 1974; co-editor: Political Reform in Wisconsin, 1973. Bd. dirs. Nat. Assn. Schs., Colls. and Univs. of United Meth. Ch., 1994-97, 2000—, pres., 2002-03; mem. Lenawee Tomorrow, Adrian, 1989—. Recipient D.C. Everest prize Wis. State Hist. Soc., 1968; Woodrow Wilson fellow, 1962-63, Nat. Presbyn. fellow Presbyn. Ch. U.S., 1963-65 Mem. Orgn. Am. Historians, Nat. Assn. Ind. Colls. Univs. (bd. dirs. 1997-2000), Rotary. Methodist. Avocations: sports, reading. Office: Adrian Coll Office of Pres 110 S Madison St Adrian MI 49221-2518 Business E-Mail: scaine@adrian.edu.

CAINE, STEPHEN HOWARD, data processing executive; b. Washington, Feb. 11, 1941; s. Walter E. and Jeanette (Wenborne) C. Student, Calif. Inst. Tech., 1958-62. Sr. programmer Calif. Inst. Tech., Pasadena, 1962-65, mgr. sys. programming, 1965-69, mgr. programming, 1969-70; pres. Caine, Farber & Gordon, Inc., Pasadena, 1970—; gen. mgr. Gatekeeper Systems, Pasadena, 1995—. Lectr. applied sci. Calif. Inst. Tech., Pasadena, 1965-71, vis. assoc. elec. engring., 1976, vis. assoc. computer sci., 1976-84; dir. San Gabriel Valley Learning Ctrs., 1992-95. Mem. Pasadena Tournament of Roses Assn., 1976—, vice chmn. com., 1996—2000, chmn. com., 2000—, bd. dirs., 2004—. Mem. AAAS, IEEE, Nat. Assn. Corrosion Engrs., Am. Ordnance Assn., Assn. Computing Machinery, Athanaeum Club (Pasadena), Houston Club. Home: 77 Patrician Way Pasadena CA 91105-1039

CAINE, VIRGINIA A., city health department administrator; BS, Gustavus Adolphus Coll., Minn., 1973; MD, N.Y. Upstate Med. Ctr., Syracuse. Resident U. Cin.; resident, infectious diseases U. Wash., Seattle; assoc. prof., medicine Ind. U. Sch. Medicine; dir. Marion Co. Health Dept., Indpls., 1993—. Mem., com. credentialing for pub. health workforce CDC, mem., bioterrorism and emergency preparedness com. Co-dir. Indpls. Campaign for Healthy Babies Initiative; bd. mem. Damien AIDS Ctr.; bd. mem., substance abuse Fairbanks Hosp.; bd. mem. Ind. AIDS Fund, Indpls. Alliance for Health Promotion, Ind. State Women's Health Com.; mem. Cmty. Drug Summit, Mayor's Commn. on Family Violence, City of Indpls. Mayor's Emergency Preparedness Task Force; mem. adv. bd. Women's Fund of Ctrl. Ind. Named one of Influential Women in Indpls., Indpls. Bus. Jour., The Ind. Lawyer; recipient Superstar award, Ind. AIDServe, 1998, Outstanding Svc. award, Indpls. Bus. Jour. Mem.: Ind. Pub. Health Assn., Nat. Med. Assn. (chair, infectious diseases, co-chair, AIDS sect., Internist of Yr. 1999), Nat. Assn. of County and City Health Officials, Am. Pub. Health Assn. (pres. 2004—, New Leadership award). Office: Marion Co Health Dept 3838 N Rural St Indianapolis IN 46205-2930

CAIRNS, DIANE PATRICIA, motion picture executive; b. Fairbanks, Alaska, Mar. 2, 1957; d. Dion Melvin and Marsha Lala (Andrews) C. BBA, U. So. Calif., 1980, MFA, 2003. Literary agt. Sy Fischer Agy., L.A., 1980-85; sr. v.p. Internat. Creative Mgmt., L.A., 1985-96; sr. v.p. prodn. Universal Pictures, L.A., 1996-97, Cairns Co., L.A., 2004—. Mem. NOW, Acad. Motion Picture Arts and Scis., Women's Action Coun., Amnesty Internat., L.A. County Mus. of Art Home and Office: 8231 Tuscany Ave Playa Del Rey CA 90293-7825

CAIRNS, ELTON JAMES, chemical engineering professor; s. James Edward and Claire Angele (Larzelere) C.; m. Miriam Esther Citron, Dec. 26, 1974; 1 dau., Valerie Helen; stepchildren: Benjamin David, Joshua Aaron. BS in Chemistry, BSChemE, Mich. Tech. U., Houghton, 1955; PhD in Chem. Engring., U. Calif., Berkeley, 1959. Phys. chemist GE Rsch. Lab., Schenectady, NY, 1959-66; group leader, then sect. head chem. engring. divsn. Argonne (Ill.) Nat. Lab., 1966-73; asst. head electrochemistry dept. GM Rsch. Labs., 1973-78; assoc. lab. dir., dir. energy and environment divsn. Lawrence Berkeley (Calif.) Nat. Lab., 1978-96, head Energy Conversion and Storage Program, 1982—98, head Berkeley Electrochemical Rsch. Coun., 1982—, C.D. Hollowell meml. lectr., 1996; prof. chem. engring. U. Calif., 1978—. Cons. in field; mem. numerous govt. panels. Author: (with H.A. Liebhafsky) Fuel Cells and Fuel Batteries, 1968; mem. editl. bd. Advances in Electrochemistry and Electrochem. Engring., 1974—; divsn. editor Jour. Electrochem. Soc., 1968-91; regional editor Electrochimica Acta, 1984-99, editor, 2000-04; contbr. articles to profl. jours.; patentee in field. Recipient IR-100 award, 1968, Centennial medal Case Western Res. U., 1980, R & D 100 award, 1992, Melvin Calvin medal of distinction Mich. Technol. U., 1998; named Croft lectr. U. Mo., 1979, McCabe lectr. U. NC, 1993; grantee DuPont Co., 1956; Dow Chem. Co. fellow, univ. fellow, NSF fellow, Std. Oil Co. Calif. grantee, U. Calif., Berkeley. Fellow Am. Insts. Chemists, Electrochem. Soc. (chmn. phys. electrochem. divsn. 1981-84, v.p. 1986-89, pres. 1989-90, Francis Mills Turner award 1963); mem. AIChE (chmn. energy conversion com. 1970-94), AAAS, Am. Chem. Soc., Internat. Soc. Electrochemistry (chmn. electrochem. energy conversion divsn. 1977-85, U.S. nat. sec. 1983-89, v.p. 1984-88, pres. 1999-2000), Intersoc. Energy Conversion Engring. Conf. (steering com. 1970-2003, gen. chmn. 1976, 90, 97, program chmn. 1983, co-chair internat. meeting on lithium batteries 2002), Sigma Xi (pres. Berkeley chpt. 2002-03). Home: 239 Langlie Ct Walnut Creek CA 94598-3615 Office: Lawrence Berkeley Nat Lab 1 Cyclotron Rd Berkeley CA 94720-0001 Office Phone: 510-486-5028. E-mail: ejcairns@lbl.gov, cairns@cchem.berkeley.edu.

CAIRNS, JAMES DONALD, lawyer; b. Chelsea, Mass., Aug. 7, 1931; s. Stewart Scott and Kathleen (Hand) C.; m. Alice Crout Cairns, June 18, 1988; children from previous marriage: Douglas S., Timothy H., Pamela S., Heather M. AB, Harvard U., 1952; JD, Ohio State U., 1958. Bar: Fla. 1974, Ohio 1958, U.S. Dist. Ct. (no. dist.) Ohio 1975, U.S. Tax Ct. 1963, Supreme Ct., 2000. Ptnr. Squire, Sanders & Dempsey, Cleve., 1958-95, Spieth, Bell, McCurdy & Newell, Cleve., 1995—. Served to lt. (j.g.) USNR, 1952-55. Mem. ABA, Am. Coll. Trust and Estate Counsel, Fla. Bar Assn., Ohio State Bar Assn., Bar Assn. Greater Cleve., Union Club, Edgewater Yacht Club, Shoreby Club. Democrat. Episcopalian. Office: Spieth Bell McCurdy Newell 2000 Huntington Bldg 925 Euclid Ave Cleveland OH 44115-1408 Office Phone: 216-696-4700. Personal E-mail: dcairns@att.net. Business E-Mail: dcairns@spiethbell.com.

CAIRNS, JAMES ROBERT, mechanical engineering educator; b. Indpls., Feb. 4, 1930; s. John Joseph and Agatha Bertha (Krebs) C.; m. Catherine I. DiCicco, Feb. 6, 1954; children: James Robert, Steven J., Michael P., Daniel F., Timothy E., Robert B. BS in Mech. Engring, U. Detroit, 1954; MS in Engring, U. Mich., 1959, PhD, 1963. Registered profl. engr., Mich. cert. energy mgr. Instr. U. Detroit, 1954-57, U. Mich., Ann Arbor, 1957-63, asst. prof. Dearborn, 1963-65, asso. prof., 1965-68, prof. mech. engring., 1968—, chmn. engring. div., 1964-73, acting dean, 1973-75, dean, 1975-81. Cons. and expert witness in product liability litigation. Contbr. articles to profl. jours. Ford Faculty fellow, 1960-63 Mem. ASME, ASHRAE, Assn. Energy Engrs., Am. Soc. Engring. Edn., Common Cause, Tau Beta Pi, Pi Tau Sigma. Roman Catholic. Home: 836 Dover Dr Dearborn Heights MI 48127-4144 Office: 4901 Evergreen Rd Dearborn MI 48128-2406 Business E-Mail: b.cairns@core.com.

CAIRNS, ZACHARY ALLAN, music educator; b. Champaign, Ill. s. Scott Neil and Virginia Akers Cairns; m. Whitney Carlisle Simpson. BS in music edn., Penn State U., 2002, MA, 2000. Sr. band dir. Northwestern Lehigh H.S., New Tripoli, Pa., 2003—04. Music composer/arranger various H.S., Pa., 2001—04. Mem.: Music Educators Nat. Conf., Percussive Arts Soc., Soc. Music Theory. Home: 1339 N 14th St Apt 19 Whitehall PA 18052

CAIRO, ARMON ANTHONY, physician; b. Steelton, Pa., Jan. 5, 1925; s. Salvatore A. and Josephine (Priete) C.; m. Laura Irene Jones, Oct. 25, 1933; children: Michael, Richard, Susan, Catherine, James. BS, Franklin & Marshall Coll., 1945; MD, Georgetown U., 1948. Bd. cert. in internal medicine and neurology and psychiatry. Intern Georgetown U. Hosp., Washington, 1948-49; medical resident Mt. Alto VA Hosp., Washington, 1950-52, Georgetown U. Hosp., Washington, 1952; instr. in medicine Georgetown U. Med. Sch., Washington, 1954-56, asst. prof. medicine, 1956-60; fellow in psychiatry George Washington U., Washington, 1960-64; pvt. practice Chevy Chase, Md., 1964—. Cons. hearing and appeals bd. Social Security Adminstrn., Arlington, Va., 1958—; commr. mental health Superior Ct., Washington, 1983—; clin. assoc. prof. psychiatry Georgetown U., Washington, 1964—. Contbr. articles to profl. jours. Lt. USN, 1952-54, Korea. Citation for Merit

Eastern Psychoanalytic Assn., Washington, 1976. Fellow Am. Psychiat. Assn., Am. Soc. Physician Analysts (pres. 1975-76); mem. Montgomery County Med. Soc., Med. and Chirurgical Faculty State Md. Republican. Roman Catholic. Avocations: golf, italian classes, bridge. Home: 6002 Corewood Ln Bethesda MD 20816-2302 Office: 5480 Wisconsin Ave Bethesda MD 20815-3530 Office Phone: 301-657-8090.

CAIRO, JIMMY MICHAEL, physiologist, educator; b. New Orleans, Jan. 8, 1952; s. John August and Mary Evelyn (Peterson) C.; m. Rhonda Lynn Philmon, Jan. 24, 1986; children: Brooke Cambre, Allyson Marie. BS, U. Southwestern La., 1974; MS, Tulane U., 1977; PhD, La. State U., 1986. Instr. cardiopulmonary scis. La. State U., New Orleans, 1978-85, asst. prof., 1985-88, assoc. prof., 1988-94, head dept. cardiopulmonary sci., 1989—, prof., 1994—; dean La. State U., Sch. Allied Health Professions, New Orleans, 2004—. Adj. assoc. prof. Tulane U., New Orleans, 1991—; cons. pulmonary Children's Hosp., New Orleans, 1988—; sec. Joint Rev. Com. for Respiratory Therapy Edn., 1996-97, chmn. Com. on Accreditation for Respiratory Care, 1998; bd. dirs. Nat. Bd. for Respiratory Care. Author: Introduction to Respiratory Care, 1990, Mosby's Respiratory Care Equipment, 7th edit., 2004; contbr. articles to profl. jours. Mem. AAAS, Am. Thoracic Soc., Am. Assn. Respiratory Care. Office: La State U Health Scis Ctr 1900 Gravier St New Orleans LA 70112-2232 Business E-Mail: jcairo@lsuhsc.edu.

CAIVANO, ERNESTO, artist; b. Madrid, 1972; BFA, The Cooper Union, 1999; MFA, Columbia U., 2001. Exhibitions include Group, Intercontinental Gallery, Montreal, Can., 1999, Part 01, Wallach Gallery, NYC, 2000, Thesis Exhbn., Columbia U., NYC, 2001, Medium, Roy Neiman Gallery, NYC, 2001, Miami Ambassador, Fredric Snitzer Gallery, Miami, Fla., 2002, Shallow Interiors, Rivington Arms Gallery, NYC, 2002, Amenities, Gershwin Hotel, NYC, 2002, My Sources Say Yes, Guild & Greyshkul, NYC, 2003, Terrarium, Bronx River Art Ctr., NY, 2003, Druid Wood as a Superconductor, Space 101, Bklyn., 2003, Game Over, Grimm/Rosenfeld, Munich, 2003, New Topography, Georffrey Young Gallery, Great Barrington, Mass., 2003, Group Show, Grant/Selwyn Fine Art, LA, 2003, St. Valentine's Day Massacre, 85 Chambers, NYC, 2003, Placemakerk Gallery, Miami, 2004, PS 1 Contemporary Art Ctr., LI, 2004, Whitney Biennial, Whitney Mus. Am. Art, 2004, Summer Drawing Exhbn., David Zwirner Gallery, NYC, 2004, one-man shows include Arboreal, 31 Grand Inc., Bklyn., 2003, Mating Grounds, Richard Heller Gallery, LA, 2004. Recipient Joan Sovern award, 2000, 2001, Hayward prize, Am. Austrian Found., 2001, 2002; Cmty. Found. Grant, 1996—2001, Salzburg Kunstakademie Fellowship, 2002. Home and Office: 48 Eldridge St #6E New York NY 10002*

CAJORI, CHARLES FLORIAN, artist, educator; b. Palo Alto, Calif., Mar. 9, 1921; s. Florian Anton and Marion (Haines) C.; m. Barbara Grossman, June 23, 1967; children: Marion, Nicole. Student, Colo. Coll., 1939—40, Cleve. Art Sch., 1940—42, Columbia U., 1946—48, Skowhegan Sch., 1947, student, 1948. Instr. Notre Dame of Md., Balt., 1950-56, Cooper Union, N.Y.C., 1956-59, 60-65; vis. artist U. Calif., Berkeley, 1959; instr. N.Y. Studio Sch., N.Y.C., 1964—69, 1985—; prof. Queens Coll., N.Y.C., 1965-86; instr. Yale U., Hew Haven, 1989. Co-founder Tanager Gallery, N.Y.C., 1952, N.Y. Studio Sch., N.Y.C., 1964; one-man shows include Howard Wise Gallery, N.Y.C., 1963, Bennington (Vt.) Coll., 1969, Landmark Gallery, N.Y.C., 1974, 81, Ingber Gallery Ltd., N.Y.C., 1976, Am. U., Washington, 1977, 88, Gross McCleaf Gallery, Phila., 1983, 85, N.Y. Studio Sch., N.Y.C., 1988, Cen. Conn. State U., New Britain, Conn., 1992, Dartmouth Coll., N.H., 1996, N.Y. Studio Sch., 2000, Paessagio Gallery, West Hartford, Conn., 2002, Wright State U., Daytona, Ohio, 2004, Lohin Geduld Gallery, N.Y.C., 2004,David Findlay Jr. Gallery, N.Y.C., 2005; exhibited in numerous group shows including Chgo. Art Inst., 1964, Whitney Mus., N.Y.C., 1965, Artists Choice, 1977, 3-man show, Loeb Ctr., NYU, N.Y.C., 1970, Wadsworth Atheneum, Hartford, Conn., 1983, Bruce Mus., Greenwich, Conn., 1989, New Britain Mus., 1990, Nat. Acad., N.Y.C., 2003, 04, Inst. Arts and Letters, 2001, Frye Mus., 2002; represented in permanent collections including Am. U., Washington, Del. Art Ctr., Wilmington, Met. Mus. Art, N.Y.C., Mitchner Collection, Austin, Tex., NYU, N.Y.C., U. N.Mex., Albuquerque, Walker Art Ctr., Mpls., Whitney Mus., Geigy Chem. Corp. Ardsley, N.Y., Snite Mus., U. Notre Dame, Ind., Honolulu Art Acad., Hirshhorn Mus., Washington, Met. Mus. Art, N.Y.C., Ark. Art Ctr., Little Rock, Denver Art Mus. Served with USAAF, 1942-46. Recipient Distinction in Arts award Yale U., 1959, purchase awards Longview Found., 1962, purchase awards Ford Found., 1963, purchase awards Childe-Hassam, 1975, 76, 80, award for painting Inst. Arts and Letters, N.Y.C., 1970, Louis Comfort Tiffany award, 1979, Altman Figure prize Nat. Acad., 1983, 87, 94, 2000; Guggenheim fellow, 2001; Fulbright grantee, 1952-53, Nat. Endowment Arts grantee, 1981. Mem. NAD, Coll. Art Assn. Home: 2338 Litchfield Rd Watertown CT 06795-1005 Office: NY Studio Sch 8 W 8th St New York NY 10011-9002

CAKONI, FIORALBA, mathematics professor; b. Elbasan, Albania, Aug. 14, 1964; arrived in U.S., 2000; d. Halil and Andush Cakoni; m. Astrit Isufi, July 30, 1987; 1 child, Annie Isufi. PhD, Tirana U./Patras U., 1996. Rschr. U. Del., Newark, 2000—02, asst. prof., 2002—. Presenter, rschr. in field. Author: Solution Methods in Inverne Scoktering Theory, 2005. Alexander von Humboldt fellow, U. Stuttgart, Germany, 1998—2000. Office: U Del Dept Math Sci Newark DE 19711

CALABRESE, EDWARD J., toxicologist; b. Aug. 10, 1946; BA, State Coll. Bridgewater, Mass., 1968, MA in biology, 1972; PhD in physiology/toxicology, U. Mass., Amherst, 1973, EdD in sci. edn., 1974. Bd. cert. Toxicological Scis., 1976. Asst. prof. environment/occupl. medicine Sch. Pub. Health, U. Ill., 1974—76; prof. toxicology Sch. Pub. Health, U. Mass., Amherst, 1976—. Dir. Northeast Regional Environ. Pub. Health Ctr., U. Mass.; chmn. BELLE Adv. Com. Author: Principles of Animal Extrapolation, Nutrition and Environmental Health, Vols. I & II, Ecogenetics, Safe Drinking Water Act: Amendments, Regulations and Standards, Soils Contaminated by Petroleum: Environmental & Pub. Health Effects, Petroleum Contaminated Soils, Vols. I & II, Ozone Risk Communication and Management, Hydrocarbon Contaminated Soils, Vols. I, II, III, Hydrocarbon Contaminated Soils and Groundwater, Vols. I, II, III, Multiple Chemical Interactions, Air Toxics and Risk Management, Alcohol Interactions with Drugs and Chemicals, Regulating Drinking Water Quality, Biological Effects of Low Level Exposure to Chemicals and Radiation, Contaminated Soils: Diesel Fuel Contamination, Risk Assessment and Environmental Fate Methodologies, Principles and Practices for Petroleum Contaminated Soils, Performing Ecological Risk Assessments; contbr. Mem.: Agency for Toxic Substances and Disease Registry (ATSDR) (mem. bd. scientific counselors), NATO Counties Safe Drinking Water Com., U.S. Nat. Acad. Scis. Achievements include research in the area of host factors affecting susceptibility to pollutants. Office: NE Regional Environ Pub Health Ctr U Mass Amherst Morrill Science 1 N344 Amherst MA 01002 E-mail: edwardc@schoolph.umass.edu.

CALABRESE, JOSEPH A., lawyer; b. Paterson, NJ, 1956; BA summa cum laude, Boston Coll., 1978; JD cum laude, Cornell U., 1981. Bar: Calif. 1981, US Dist. Ct. (Central Dist. Calif) 1981. Chair, entertainment and media practice group O'Melveny and Myers LLP, LA, mng. ptnr., office head (Century City office). Spkr. in the field. Staff mem. Cornell Internat. Law Jour., 1979—80, articles editor, 1980—81. Dir. Educate the Children Found., Constitutional Rights Found. Mem.: Independent Film and Television Alliance (arbitrator), Century City Bar Assn., Am. Film Mktg. Assn. (mem., arbitration panel), ABA (task force on alternative dispute resolution in entertainment industry). Office: O'Melveny & Myers LLP 1999 Avenue of the Stars 7th Fl Los Angeles CA 90067-6035 Office Phone: 310-246-6743. Office Fax: 310-246-6779. Business E-Mail: jcalabrese@omm.com.

CALABRESE, MICHAEL RAPHAEL, lawyer, consultant; b. Atlantic City, May 28, 1956; s. Angelo William and Sally (Snyder) C.; m. Kitty R. Calabrese. BS in Fgn. Service, Georgetown U., 1978; JD, U. Va., 1982. Law clk. to cir. judge U.S. Ct. Appeals (4th cir.), Washington, 1982-83; assoc. Mudge, Rose et al, Washington, 1983-84, Finley, Kumble et al, Washington, 1984-86, Morgan, Lewis & Bockius, Washington, 1986-92; ptnr. McKenna & Cuneo, Washington, 1992-95; asst. gen. counsel Lockheed Martin Corp., Bethesda, Md., 1995-99; ptnr. Coudert Bros., Washington, 1999—2003. Mem.: Columbia Country Club, Univ. Club, Army and Navy Club, Phi Beta Kappa. Republican. Home: 19051 West Pinnacle Circle Baton Rouge LA 70810

CALABRESE, PHILIP GEORGE, mathematician, researcher, small business owner; s. George Vincent Calabrese; children: Adam Philip, Trinity Maria, Christopher Michael, Daniel Terry(dec.). BS, Ill. Inst. of Tech., 1963, MS, 1965, PhD, 1968. Owner, sole propr. Data Synthesis, San Diego, 1979—; sr. scientist U.S. Navy (SSC-SD), San Diego, 1999—2004, Data Synthesis, San Diego, 2004—. Math. rsch. U.S. Navy, San Diego, 1990—. Contbr. articles various profl. jours. Study group leader, author Fellowship of Readers Urantia Bk., San Diego. Recipient Sr. Rsch. Assoc., NRC, 1990-1993. Mem.: Am. Math. Soc. (assoc.). Democrat-Npl. Achievements include research in boolean fractions, conditional events. Avocations: cosmology, classical piano, gardening, racquetball. Home: 2919 Luna Ave San Diego CA 92117 Personal E-mail: pc@datasynthesis.org.

CALABRESE, ROSALIE SUE, management consultant, writer; b. N.Y.C., Feb. 17, 1938; d. Julius and Florence (Tuck) Hochman; m. Anthony J. Calabrese, June 15, 1960 (div.); 1 child, Christopher. BA in Journalism, CCNY, 1959. Asst. news editor Electronic News, N.Y.C., 1960; asst. to publicist Abner Klipstein, N.Y.C., 1963; asst. to producer Leonard Field, N.Y.C., 1964; mgr. Am. Composers Alliance, N.Y.C., 1969-85, exec. dir., gen. mgr., 1985-94; dir. Rosalie Calabrese Mgmt., N.Y.C., 1983—. Music advisor Phyllis Rose Dance Co., N.Y.C., 1987—, also bd. dirs.; sec. bd. dirs. Am. Composers Orch., N.Y.C., 1987-93; pres., bd. dirs. 1st Ave. Ensemble, 1993—, Golden Fleece Ltd., 1994—; bd. dirs. Friends Am. Composers, treas., 1991-94; adv. bd. Downtown Music Prodns., 1991—, Joan Miller's Dance Players, N.Y.C., 1991-94, Copland House, 1996-97; mem. editl. adv. bd. New Music Connoisseur Mag., 2002-05; mem. music com., Estate Project for Artists with AIDS, 2001-03. Author, lyricist: (musicals) A Hell of An Angel, Simone, Not in Earnest, Murdering Macbeth, Pop Life, Does Anyone Here Speak Arabic?, Friends and Relations, Double-Play, C-R; assoc. prodr., treas. box office: (play) Courtyard, 1959, The Mime and Me; co-prodr.: various plays at White Lake (N.Y.) Playhouse, also packaged tours for Prodn. Assocs.; dir. The Bagel Baker's Daughter, 1999, night club acts for Florence Hayle; contbr. short stories and poetry to lit., nat. mags. and anthologies. Mem.: Poetry Soc. Am., Poets and Writers, Broadcast Music Inc., Dramatists Guild. Office: Rosalie Calabrese Mgmt PO Box 20580 New York NY 10025-1521

CALABRESI, GUIDO, federal judge, law educator; b. Milan, Oct. 18, 1932; s. Massimo and Bianca Maria (Finzi Contini) C.; m. Anne Gordon Audubon Tyler, May 20, 1961; children: Bianca Finzi Contini, Anne Gordon Audubon, Massimo Franklin Tyler BS in Analytical Econs., Yale U., 1953, LLB, 1958, MA (hon.), 1962; BA in Politics, Philosophy and Econs., Oxford U., 1955, MA in Politics, Philosophy and Econs., 1959; LLD (hon.), Notre Dame U., 1979, Villanova U., 1984, U. Toronto, 1985, Boston Coll., 1986, Cath. U. Am., 1986, U. Chgo., 1988, Conn. Coll., 1988, Chgo.-Kent-I.T.T., 1989, William Mitchell Coll. Law, 1992, Princeton U., 1992, Detroit Mercy Sch. Law, 1994, Seton Hall U., 1995, Albertus Magnus Coll., 1995, Lewis and Clark Coll., 1996, St. John's U., 1997, Pace U., 1998, Iona Coll., 1998, Roger Williams U., 1999, Hofstra U., 1999, N.Y. Law Sch., 1999, Skidmore Coll., 2000, Colby Coll., 2001, U. San Diego, 2001; Dott. Ius SD (hon.), U. Turin, Italy, 1982; JD (hon.), U. Pavia, Italy, 1987, U. Stockholm, 1993; PhD (hon.), U. Haifa, Israel, 1988; DPhil, U. Tel Aviv, 1998; LHD (hon.), U. New Haven, 1989, Williams Coll., 1991, Quinnipiac Coll., 1993; DSc in Politics (hon.), U. Padua, Italy, 1990; Dott. Jur. (hon.), U. Bologna, Italy, 1991, U. Milan, 1998. Bar: Conn. 1958. Asst. instr. dept. econs. Yale U., New Haven, Conn., 1955-56; law clk. to Hon. Hugo Black U.S. Supreme Ct., Washington, 1958-59; asst. prof. Yale U. Law Sch., 1959-61, assoc. prof., 1961-62, prof., 1962-70, John Thomas Smith prof. law, 1970-78, Sterling prof. law, 1978-95; prof. emeritus, lectr. Yale U., 1995—; dean Yale U. Law Sch., 1985-94, Sterling prof. law emeritus, lectr. New Haven, 1995—; judge U.S. Ct. Appeals 2d cir., New Haven, 1994—. Fellow Timothy Dwight Coll., 1960—; vis. prof. Harvard U. Law Sch., 1969-70, Japan Am. Studies Seminar, Kyoto-Doshisha Univs., summer 1972, European U. Inst., Florence, Italy, 1979; Arthur L. Goodhart prof. legal sci. Cambridge U., also fellow St. John's Coll., 1980-81. Author: The Costs of Accidents: A Legal and Economic Analysis, 1970; (with P. Bobbitt) Tragic Choices, 1978; A Common Law for the Age of Statutes, 1983 (ABA citation of merit, Order of Coif Triennial Book award); Ideals, Beliefs, Attitudes and the Law: Private Law Perspectives on a Public Law Problem (Silver Gavel award ABA), 1985; contbr. articles to profl. jours. Hon. trustee Hopkins Grammar Sch., pres. 1976-80; trustee St. Thomas More Chapel, Yale U.; vice-chmn. bd. trustees Carolyn Found., Minn. Rhodes scholar, 1953; named one of Ten Outstanding Young Men Am., U.S. Jaycees, 1962; recipient Laetare Medal, U. Notre Dame, 1985, Marshall-Wythe medal Coll. William and Mary, 1985, award for outstanding rsch. in law and govt. Fellows of Am. Bar Found., 1998, Thomas Jefferson medal in law Jefferson Found./U. Va. Law Sch., 2000. Fellow Am. Acad. Arts & Scis., Associazione Italiana di Diritto Comparato, Brit. Acad. (corr.), Royal Swedish Acad. Scis. (fgn.), Nat. Acad. dei Lincei (fgn.), Acad. delle Sci. di Torino (fgn.); mem. Conn. Bar Assn., Assn. Am. Law Schs. (exec. com. 1986-89), Am. Philos. Soc. Home: 639 Amity Rd Woodbridge CT 06525-1206 Office: US Ct Appeals 2d Cir 157 Church St New Haven CT 06510-2100*

CALABRESI, STEVEN G., law educator; BA cum laude, Yale U., 1980, JD, 1983. Law clk. to Hon. Ralph K. Winter US Ct. Appeals (2nd cir.), New Haven, 1983—84; to Hon. Robert H. Bork US Ct. Appeals, DC cir., 1984—85; spl. asst. to atty. gen. US Dept. Justice, 1985—87; spl. asst. to asst. to Pres. for Domestic Affairs The White House, 1987; law clk. to Hon. Antonin Scalia US Supreme Ct., 1987—88; rsch. assoc. Am. Enterprise Inst. for Pub. Policy Rsch., 1988—90; speechwriter to Vice President Dan Quayle The White House, 1990; asst. prof. law Northwestern U. Sch. Law, Chgo., 1990—93, assoc. prof., 1993—96, prof., 1996—, George C. Dix prof. constitutional law, 1998—2001, 2004—. Contbr. articles to profl. jours. Office: Northwestern U Sch Law 357 E Chicago Ave Chicago IL 60611 Office Phone: 312-503-7012. E-mail: s-calabresi@law.northwestern.edu.*

CALAMAR, GLORIA, artist; b. NYC, Sept. 7, 1921; d. Louis B. and Dina (Cotter) Calamar; m. R.L. Redgate, Aug. 22, 1950 (div. 1972); children: Chris James, Steven Clay, Michael Cotter. Cert., Otis Art Inst., L.A., 1943; student, Art Students League, N.Y.C., 1944-45; BA in Art History, State Univ. Coll. N.Y. at New Paltz, 1970. Instr. art history and painting Orange County (N.Y.) Community Coll., 1964-69; instr. art history Mt. St. Mary Coll., Newburgh, N.Y., 1968-69; instr. painting Santa Barbara City Coll., 1975-80. Judge Hallmark Art Contest, N.Y., 1968; lectr. Woodstock (N.Y.) Sch. Art, 1994; color slide lectr. throughout world. Artist in water color, oil, pen and ink, 1946—; one woman shows include Georgetown U., 1974, Portland (Oreg.) C.C., 1973, Willamette U., 1972, U. Oreg., 1971-72, U. Calif. at Berkeley, 1969, Santa Barbara (Calif.) Mus. Art, 1950, Musèe d'Art Moderne de la Ville de Paris, 1967, Galèrie de la Madeleine, Brussels, Belgium, 1964, Landau Gallery, Beverly Hills, Calif., 1953, Parnassus Sq., Woodstock, N.Y., 1978, Ibiza, Balearic Islands, Spain, 1978, Santorini, Greece, 1980, Beaux Arts Ctr., Tunis, Tunisia, 1981, Alkamal Gallery, Jerusalem, Israel, 1981, Jaisalmer, India, 1984, Women's Cmty. Bldg., Santa Barbara, 1986, Jewish Cmty. Ctr., San Francisco, 1986; group shows include Delgado Mus., New Orleans, 1950, San Francisco Art Assn., 1953, L.A. County Mus. Art, 1954, Bertrand Russell Centenary Invitational, London, 1972-73, Woodstock Art Assn., 1978, Faulkner Gallery Santa Barbara, 1992, 93; curated Santa Barbara Visual Artists League Exhbn., 1993, 94; book, video Tar Pits Park Landmark Proposal, Portola Sycamore Tree Landmark Proposal, Carpinteria Airport Landmark Proposal, Juarez-Hosmer Adobe Landmark Proposal, Leaping Greyhound Bridge Landmark Proposal, Los Clavelitos Landmark Proposal, Los Cruces Adobe Landmark Proposal, De la Cuesta Adobe Landmark Proposal; painted the facade of Wells Cathedral, 1999-00; producer video TV program; author: Traveling Artist, 1995; prodr. TV video series Traveling Artist; contbr. articles to publs; prodr. (video) The Traveling Artist, 1996—. Curator Visual Artists League Exhbn., Santa Barbara, 1992, 93, 94, 95; mem. Santa Barbara County Hist. Landmark Adv. Commn. Nat. Endowment for Arts grantee, 1980-81; recipient Calif. Gov.'s Historic Preservation award Santa Barbara County Hist. Landmark Adv. Commn., 1999. Mem. Woodstock (N.Y.) Art Assn. (life), Alumni Assn. Otis Art Inst. (L.A.), Art Students League N.Y. (life), Santa Barbara Visual Artists League. *Many people have told me that I am a strong painter and add in the same breath— like a man. Others have asked me which comes first— my work or my children. I wonder how many male artists have been evaluated or interrogated in the same way. To the former I say thank you for the evaluation of strength but to be a woman artist does not preclude this ingredient. To the latter (I say) one interest supports the other and each is given priority at different times. Much in the same way that food and drink are necessary to the whole person and each is given priority at different times.*

CALAMARO, RAYMOND STUART, lawyer; b. Cairo, May 28, 1944; came to U.S., 1947, naturalized, 1960; s. Albert and Charlotte (Golub) C.; m. Jaana Pirinen; 1 child, Alexander M. AB, Cornell U., 1966; JD, NYU, 1969. Bar: N.Y. State 1970, U.S. Supreme Ct. 1975, D.C. 1976. Legis. dir. Sen.Gaylord Nelson, Washington, 1973-75; exec. dir. Com. for Pub. Justice, N.Y.C., 1975-76; adj. faculty New Sch. Social Rsch., N.Y.C., 1976; staff profl. Carter/Mondale Transition Team, Washington, 1976-77; dep. asst. atty. gen. Office Legis. Affairs, Dept. Justice, Washington, 1977-79; pvt. practice Washington and Brussels, 1979-95; team leader Clinton-Gore Transition Team, 1992-93; ptnr. Hogan & Hartson, Washington, 1995—. U.S. vice-chmn. U.S.-Korea Com. on Bus. Coop., 1997-99. Recipient Royal Order of Polar Star King Carl XVI Gustav, Sweden, 1989. Mem. Met. Club (Washington), St. Albans Tennis Club (Washington). Home: 5073 Lowell St NW Washington DC 20016-2616 Office: Hogan & Hartson 555 13th St NW Ste 800W Washington DC 20004-1109 also: rue de l'Industrie 26 1040 Brussels Belgium E-mail: RSCalamaro@HHLaw.com.

CALAME, KATHRYN LEE, microbiologist, educator; b. Leavenworth, Kans., Apr. 23, 1940; d. Jay O. and Marjorie B.; m. Byron Edward Calame, June 9, 1962; children: Christine Lee, Jonathan David. BS, U. Mo., 1962; MS, George Washington U., 1965, PhD, 1975. Asst. prof. biol. chemisty UCLA, 1980-85, assoc. prof., 1985-88, prof., 1988; prof. microbiology Coll. Physicians and Surgeons Columbia U., N.Y.C., 1988—. Mem. sci. rev. bd. Howard Hughes Med. Inst., 2002—. Exec. editor: Nucleic Acids Rsch., 1992-98; mem. bd. rev. editors: Sci. Mag., 1988-2000; assoc. editor Jour. Clin. Investigation; contbr. articles to profl. jours. Trustee Leukemia Soc. Am., N.Y.C., 1992—2001, chair grant rev. com., 1992-96; mem. bd. sci. counselors Nat. Inst. Child Health and Devel., 1999—2004. Recipient Stohlman award Leukemia Soc. Am., 1989, Faculty Alumni award U. Mo., Columbia, 1996; disting. lecture in basic sci., Columbia Physicians and Surgeons, 1998. Fellow: AAAS, Am. Acad. Arts and Sci.; mem.: Am. Assn. Biochemistry and Molecular Biology (chair pub. com. 1992—93). Democrat. Avocations: cooking, gardening, reading, antiques. Office: Columbia U Dept Microbiology 701 W 168th St New York NY 10032-2704 Business E-Mail: klc1@columbia.edu.

CALAMOS, JOHN PETER, SR., brokerage house executive; b. Aug. 28, 1940; s. Peter and Mary (Kyriakopoulos) C.; m. Jackie Calamos, Aug. 15, 1962; children: John Peter Jr. and Laura Lynn. BS in Econs., Ill. Inst. Tech., 1963, MBA in Fin., 1965. Registered rep. DuPont Walston Co., Chgo., 1971-74, Loeb Rhoades Co., Chgo., 1974, Bache & Co., Chgo., 1974-75, Hornblower-Weeks Co., Chgo., 1975-76; sr. v.p. Woodlard & Co., Chgo., 1976-77; pres., mng. dir. Calamos Asset Mgmt., Inc., Oak Brook, Ill., 1977—, also CEO. Pres. Calamos Convertible Income Fund, Oak Brook, 1985—. Author: Investing in a Convertible Securities: A Guide to Their Risks and Rewards, 1988; contbr. articles to profl. jours. Served as maj. USAF, 1965-70, Vietnam. Mem. Internat. Assn. Fin. Planners, Chgo. Assn. Commerce and Industry, Assn. Investment Mgmt. Sales Execs., Inst. Investment Mgmt. Cons., Investment Mgmt. Cons. Assn. Clubs: Sky Haven (Aurora, Ill.) (pres.). Avocations: airplanes, tennis. Office: Calamos Asset Mgmt Inc 1111 E Warrenville Rd Naperville IL 60563-1405*

CALAMOS, NICK P., diversified financial services company executive; BS in Econs., So. Ill. U.; MS in Fin., No. Ill. U. Cert. fin. analyst. From fin. analyst to sr. exec. v.p. Calamos Investments, Naperville, Ill., 1983—2003, sr. exec. v.p., 2003—, head investments, 2003—, CIO, 2003—. Author: Convertible Arbitrage: Insights and Techniques for Successful Hedging, 2003. Mem.: Investment Analysts Soc. Chgo. Office: Calamos Investments 1111 E Warrenville Rd Naperville IL 60563-1405

CALAMUNCI, ANTHONY JOSEPH, lawyer; b. Jamestown, N.Y., Feb. 2, 1968; s. Augusta Joseph and Dianne Easter (Colera) C.; m. Kathleen Mary Cross, June 20, 1992; children: Anthony Joseph Jr., Jacob George. BA, Alfred U., 1990; JD, Ohio Northern U., 1994. Bar: Ohio 1994, U.S. Dist. Ct. (no. dist.) Ohio 1995, U.S. Ct. Appeals (6th cir.) 1996. Assoc. Philip R. Joelson, Atty. at Law, Toledo, 1994; pvt. practice Toledo, 1994-96; asst. prosecutor Lucas County Prosecutor's Office, Toledo, 1995-97; ptnr. Calamunci, Joelson Manore, Fatah and Silvers LLP, Toledo, 1997. Mem. NIASH, Lucas County, Ohio, 1997. Republican. Roman Catholic. Home: 5141 Shadywood Ct Sylvania OH 43560-4609 Office: Calamunci Joelson et al 1776 Tremainsville Rd Toledo OH 43613-4039

CALARCO, VINCENT ANTHONY, specialty chemicals company executive; b. NYC, May 29, 1942; s. George Michael and Madeline J. Calarco; m. Linda Joyce Maniscalco, Apr. 10, 1971; children: David V., Christopher G. BS, Polytech. U. N.Y., 1963; MBA, Harvard U., 1970. With Crompton & Knowles Corp., N.Y.C., pres., CEO, 1985—2004, chmn. bd., 1986—. Bd. dirs. Newmont Mining, Con Edison, The Hosp. of St. Raphael. Trustee Poly. U. With U.S. Army, 1966—68. Mem.: Chem. Heritage Found. (vice chmn., trustee, exec. com.), Nat. Found. for History of Chemistry (trustee, exec. com.,), Am. Chemistry Coun. (chmn. bd. internat. com., chmn. Office of Chem. Industry Trade Advisor), Am. Soc. Chem. Industry (chmn. Am. sect. 1998—99, pres. 1998—2000), Am. Chem. Soc., Harvard Bus. Sch. Club.

CALATCHI, RALPH FRANKLIN, investment banker, writer; b. Alpes-de-Haute Provence, France, Apr. 18, 1944; came to U.S. 1969; s. Mony and Odette (Calef) C.; children: Sophie C., Rafaela C., Ralph C. M in Econ., U. Law and Econs., Paris, 1970; MBA, Columbia U., N.Y.C., 1970; PhD in Econ., U. Paris, 1973; degree in Chinese Lang., Cambridge U., 1980, Bejing U., 1982. Head new bus. sect. Kuhn Loeb & Co., N.Y.C., 1970-72; mgr. The Nikko Securities Co., Ltd., Tokyo, Paris, 1973-75; dir., chmn.'s alt. Sociedad Financiera Union C.A., Caracas, Venezuela, 1975-83; chmn. and chief exec. officer Wood Gundy Calatchi China Investments, Ltd., Shanghai, Toronto, Hong Kong, 1984-87, Calatchi Investments Ltd., London, 1987-89; pres. Calatchi Capital Corp., Ft. Lauderdale, 1990—; spl. advisor to bd. dirs. Banco Union S.A., Caracas, Venezuela, 1994—95. Author, editor: Property Finance: An International Perspective, 1992; co-founder, editor: The Action Letter Inc., 1993—94; chief editor: World Property Finance Atlas: Comparing and contrasting commercial real estate in 25 countries, 1997. Founding mem., chmn. adv. com. Cmty. Redevel. Agy., 2002—04; founding mem., chmn. Budget Rev. Com., 1995—2004; mem. adv. bd. Sand and Spurs Equestrian Park, 1995—2003; candidate mayor City of Pompano Beach, 2004; adv. bd. Charter Amendment, 2003—04. Avocations: golf, flying, skiing. Home: 4116 W Palm Aire Dr Apt 161B Pompano Beach FL 33069-4145 Office Phone: 954-973-6303. Personal E-mail: calatchi@comcast.net.

CALATRAVA, SANTIAGO, architect, structural engineer, artist; b. Valencia, Spain, July 28, 1951; Degree, Inst. Architecture, Valencia, 1974, Fed. Inst. Tech., Zürich, 1979; D of Tech. Sci., Fed. Inst. Tech., 1981; D (hon.), Poly U., Valencia, 1993, U. Seville, Spain, 1994; LittD in Environ. Studies (hon.), Heriot-Watt U., Edinburgh, Scotland, 1994; DSc (hon.), U. Coll. Salford, Eng., 1995, U. Strathclyde, Glasgow, Scotland, 1995—97, U. Tech., Delft, The Netherlands, 1995; D (hon.), Milw. Sch. Engring., Wis., 1995—97;

D of Civil Engring. (hon.), U. degli Stugi di Cassino, Italy, 1999; D of Tech. (hon.), Lund U., Sweden, 1999; D (hon.), Technion, Israel, 2004. Lic. structural engr., Ill., profl. engr., Calif. Pvt. practice, Zurich, 1981—, Paris, 1989—, Valencia, Spain, 1991—. Prin. works include Stadelhofen Rlwy. Sta., Zürich, Switzerland (City of Zürich award, 1991, Brunel award, 1992), Alamillo Bridge and La Cartuja Viaduct, Seville, Spain, Campo Volantin Footbridge, Bilbao, Spain, Sondica Airport, Bilbao, 2000, Alameda Bridge and Underground Sta., Valencia, City of Arts and Sci. Valencia, Oriente Sta., Lisbon, Portugal, Lyon Airport Sta., Lyon, Turning Torso Tower, Malmö, World Trade Ctr. Transp. Hub, N.Y.C., Milw. Art Mus. expansion, Milw., 2001, Tererife Auditorium, Canary Islands, exhibitions include Jamileh Weber Gallery, Zürich, 1985, Mus. of Architecture, Basel, Switzerland, 1985, traveling exhbn., NY, St. Louis, Chgo., LA, Toronto, Montreal, 1985, Suomen Rakennustaiteen Mus., Helsinki, Finland, 1991, Mus. of Design, Zürich, Switzerland, 1991, Dutch Inst. Architecture, Rotterdam, Holland, 1992, Royal Inst. Brit. Architects, London, Eng., 1992, ArkitekturMuseet, Stockholm, Sweden, 1992, Deutsches Mus., Munich, Germany, 1993, Mus. Modern Art, NYC, NY, 1993, La Lonja Mus., Valencia, Italy, 1993, Pavilion Overbeck Soc., Lübeck, Germany, 1993, Architecture Ctr., Gammel Dok, Copenhagen, Sweden, 1993, Bruton St. Gallery, London, Eng., 1994, Mus. Applied and Folk Art, Moscow, Russia, 1994, Ma Gallery, Tokyo, Japan, 1994, Arqueria de los Nuevos Ministerios, Madrid, Spain, 1994, Sala de Arte La Recova, Santa Cruz de Tenerife, 1994, Mus. of Design, Zürich, Switzerland, 1995, Ctr. Cultural de Belem, Lisbon, Portugal, 1995, Navarra Mus. Pamplona, 1995, Archivo Floral, Bilbao, 1995, Palazzo della Raggione, Padova, Italy, 1995, Dept. of Bldg., Basel, Switzerland, 1995, Milw. Art Mus., 1995, Britannic Tower, London, 1995, Israel Nat. Mus. of Sci., Haifa, 1995, Palazzo Strozzi, Florence, 2000—01, Met. Mus. Art, N.Y.C., 2005. Named Global Leader for Tomorrow, World Econ. Forum, Davos, Switzerland, 1993, Gold Master of the High Direction Forum, Madrid, 1995; named one of Time Mag. 100 Most Influential People, 2005; recipient Auguste Perret prize, Internat. Union Architects, 1985, Art prize, City of Barcelona, 1985, Press Assn. award, Valencia, 1985, prize, Internat. Assn. Bridge and Structural Engring., 1985, Fomento de las Artes y del Diseño, Spain, 1985, Fritz Schumacher prize for urbanism, architecture and engring., Hamburg, Germany, 1985, Silver medal for rsch. and technique, Found. Acad. Architecture, Paris, 1990, European Glulam award, Munich, 1991, Gold medal, Inst. Structural Engrs., London, 1992, II Honor prize, City of Pedreguer, 1993, Urban Design award, City of Toronto, 1993, medal of honor, Fundación Garcia Cabrerizo, Madrid, 1993, award for good bldg., Canton of Lucerne, Switzerland, 1995, Gold medal, Ministry of Culture, Granada, Spain, 1995, European award for steel structures, Berlin, 1995, art prize, Louis Vuitton-Moet Hennessy, Paris, 1995, Principe de ASTURIAS award for the arts, 1999, Gold medal, AIA, 2005, Eugene McDermott award in the arts, MIT, 2005, Gold Medal, Am. Inst. Architects, 2005; fellow Fazlur Rahman Khan Internat. for architecture and engring., 1985. Fellow: Royal Incorporation of Architects (Scotland) (hon.); mem.: Royal Swedish Acad. Engring. Scis., Order of Arts and Letters (Paris), European Acad. (Cologne, Germany), Real Acad. Bellas Artes de San Carlos, Internat. Acad. Architecture, Union of Swiss Architects, Real Acad. Bellas Artes de San Fernando (hon.), Coll. Architects Mexico City (hon.), Royal Inst. Brit. Architects (hon.), Union of German Architects (hon.). Office: Santiago Calatrava SA Parkring 11 8002 Zurich Switzerland*

CALDEN, DIANE DOROTHY, reading educator; b. Oakland, Calif., Sept. 11, 1959; d. Willard Herbert and Dorothy Rose-Lentz Kirckof; m. John Willard Calden, Sept. 13, 1986; children: Grace, Walker, Isaac. BS in Corrections and Sociology, Monkato State U., 1983; MA in Spl. Edn., U. No. Colo., 1989. Lic. profl. tchr. Colo. Spl. edn. tchr. Van Buren Elem. Sch., Loveland, Colo., 1990—93, Estes Park (Colo.) Mid. Sch., 1993—2001; reading tchr. Estes Park (Colo.) Elem. Sch., 2001—. Democrat. Avocations: hiking, beadwork, knitting, skiing, bicycling. Office: Estes Park Elem Sch 650 Community Dr Estes Park CO 80517

CALDENTEY, RENE A., engineering educator; b. Concepcion, Chile, Dec. 1, 1970; s. Mateo Caldentey and Monica Morales; m. Carola Saba, Dec. 29, 2001. PhD, MIT, Cambridge, Mass., 1997—2001. Asst. prof. U. Chile, Santiago, 1995—97, NYU, N.Y.C., 2001—. Business E-Mail: rcaldent@stern.nyu.edu.

CALDER, IAIN WILSON, publishing company executive; b. Scotland, Feb. 27, 1939; arrived in U.S., 1967, naturalized; s. William and Charlotte G. (West) C.; m. Jane Brownlea Bell, Apr. 17, 1965; children: Douglas William, Glen Robert Bell. Student pub. schs., Falkirk, Scotland. Reporter Falkirk Sentinel, 1955-56, Stirling Jour., 1956, Falkirk Mail, 1956-60, Glasgow Daily Record, 1960-64; London bur. chief Nat. Enquirer, 1964-67, articles editor, 1967-73, exec. editor, 1973-75, editor, 1975-91, pres. Lantana, Fla., 1976-95, editor-in-chief, 1991-95, editor emeritus, 1995-97; exec. v.p. pub. Am. Media Inc., 1994-97. Dir. Am. Media, Inc./Nat. Enquirer; Disting. lectr Fla. Atlantic U. Bd. dirs. Bethesda Hosp. Found., 1997—.

CALDER, JAMES J., lawyer; b. NYC, Apr. 5, 1954; BA, U. Va., 1974, JD, 1977. Bar: NY 1978, US Ct. Appeals, 2nd and 3rd Cir., US Dist. Ct., Ea. and So. Dists. NY, US Supreme Ct. Ptnr. Katten Muchin Zavis Rosenman, NYC. Mem.: ABA, Assn. Bar of City NY, Phi Beta Kappa. Office: Katten Muchin Zavis Rosenman 575 Madison Ave New York NY 10022 Office Phone: 212-940-7035. Office Fax: 212-940-3817. E-mail: james.calder@kmzr.com.

CALDER, KENT EYRING, political science professor, federal agency administrator; b. Salt Lake City, Apr. 18, 1948; s. Grant H. and Rose (Eyring) C.; m. Toshiko Matsuura; children: Mari, Ryan. BA with honors, U. Utah, 1970; AM, Harvard U., 1972, PhD, 1979. Staff mem. U.S. Ho. of Reps., Washington, 1968-69; tchg. fellow Harvard U. Dept. of Govt., Cambridge, Mass., 1972-74; rsch. economist U.S. Fed. Trade Commn., Washington, 1974-78; vis. fellow U. Tokyo, 1977—78; exec. dir. U.S.-Japan Program Harvard U., Cambridge, 1979-80, lectr., 1979-83; asst. prof. Woodrow Wilson Sch., Princeton (N.J.) U., 1983—89, tenured faculty, 1989—2003, dir. U.S.-Japan program, 1990—2003; Edwin O. Reischauer prof. East Asian Studies Johns Hopkins U., Washington, 2003—, dir. Reischauer Ctr. East Asian Studies Washington, D.C., 2003—. Internat. adv. bd. Japanese Ministry of Fin., Inst. of Fiscal and Monetary Policy, Tokyo, 1987-96; Japan chair Ctr. for Strategic and Internat. Studies, Washington, 1989-91, 96; spl. advisor to U.S. Amb. to Japan, 1996-2001; mem. Bretton Woods Com., 2001—; mem. nat. U.S. adv. bd. Japan Found., 2003—; vis. prof. Seoul (Rep. Korea) Nat. U., 2005—. Author: Crisis and Compensation, 1988 (Ohira and Arisawa Meml. prizes 1990), Japan's Changing Role in Asia, 1992, Strategic Capitalism, 1993, Pacific Defense, 1996 (Mainichi Asia-Pacific Grand prize 1997); co-author: The Eastasia Edge, 1982; mem. editl. bd. Asian Security, 2005—. Instr. Japan Soc. U.S.-Japan Leadership Program, N.Y.C., 1988-91, U. Pa. Wharton Sch. Internat. Forum, 1990—; trustee Princeton in Asia, 1987-95; mem. Coun. on Fgn. Rels., 1990—, internat. adv. bd. Waseda U. Sch. Asia-Pacific Studies, 1998—, World Econ. Forum East Asia Summits, 1998—, Bretton Woods Com., 2001—. 1st lt. U.S. Army, 1975-76. Named Fulbright Faculty Fellow and Doctoral Fellow, 1985-86, 75-76, Faculty Research Fellow The Japan Found., 1984, Graduate Prize Fellow Harvard U., 1970-74. Mem. Am. Polit. Sci. Assn., Assn. for Asian Studies, Phi Beta Kappa, Phi Kappa Phi (Sparks Fellow 1970-71, Gibbs Fellow 1970), OECD Tide 2000 Club. Avocations: stamp collecting/philately, collecting classic African musical instruments, tennis. Home: 197 Shadybrook Ln Princeton NJ 08540-4135 Office: Sch Adv Internat Studies 1619 Mass Ave NW Washington DC 20036-1984 Office Phone: 202-663-5889. Business E-Mail: kcalder@jhu.edu.

CALDER, ROBERT AUSTIN, preventive medicine physician, administrator; b. Beloit, Wis., May 21, 1954; s. John T. and Rosemary A. (Austin) C.; m. Daphne R. Calder, Aug. 17, 1979; children: Heather, Joseph. BS, U. Wis., 1979; MD, Med. Coll. Wis., 1982; MS, U. Wis., Milw., 1984. Diplomate Am. Bd. Preventive Medicine. Chief, preventive medicine U.S. Army, Ft. Sill, Okla., 1985-87; epidemiologist Fla. Dept. Health, Tallahassee, 1987-90; assoc. dir. Merck & Co., Inc., West Point, Pa., 1990-91, dir., 1992-93, sr. dir., 1993-98, exec. dir., 1999—. Capt., U.S. Army, 1985-87. Eagle Scout, 1970. Fellow Am. Coll. Preventive Medicine. Roman Catholic. Avocation: sailing. Home: 905 Farwell Dr Madison WI 53704-6035 Office: Merck & Co Inc 4 Westbrook Corp Ctr Westchester IL 60154 Business E-Mail: robert_calder@merck.com.

CALDERA, LOUIS EDWARD, academic administrator, former federal official; b. El Paso, Tex., Apr. 1, 1956; s. Benjamin Luis and Soledad (Siqueiros) C.; m. Eva Orlebeke Caldera. BS, U.S. Mil. Acad., 1978; JD, MBA, Harvard U., 1987. Bar: Calif. 1987. Commd. 2nd lt. U.S. Army, 1978, advanced through ranks to capt., 1982, resigned commn., 1983; assoc. O'Melveny & Myers, L.A., 1987-89, Buchalter, Nemer, Fields & Younger, L.A., 1990-91; deputy county counsel County of L.A., 1991-92; mem. Calif. State Assembly, 46th Dist., L.A., 1992-97, chmn. banking and fin. com.; mng. dir., COO Corp. for Nat. Svc., Washington, 1997-98; Sec. of the Army Washington, 1998—2001; vice chancellor, univ. advancement Calif. State U., 2001—03; pres. Univ. New Mexico, Albuquerque, 2003—. Democrat. Roman Catholic. Office: 1 Univ New Mexico Albuquerque NM 87131

CALDERHEAD, WILLIAM JOHN, special education educator, researcher; b. White Plains, NY, May 10, 1955; s. William Lamar and Margaret Elizabeth Calderhead. BA in History, Johns Hopkins U., 1977; MA in History, U. Va., Charlottesville, 1982; BS in Math Edn., U. Md., College Park, 1986, MEd in Spl. Edn., 1990; PhD in Spl. Edn., U. Oreg., Eugene, 2003. Spl. edn. tchr. Montgomery County Pub. Schs., Rockville, Md., 1992—2000; adj. asst. prof. U. Oreg., Eugene, 2004; asst. prof. U. Ky., Lexington, 2004—. Jr. rschr. Ariz. site visit team ABT Assocs., Bethesda, Md., 2001. Philip Francis DuPont fellow, U. Va., 1977—79. Mem.: Am. Ednl. Rsch. Assn., Coun. for Exceptional Children, Assn. for Behavior Analysis (assoc.). Avocations: bicycling, swimming, hiking. Office: University of Kentucky 229 Taylor Education Building Lexington KY 40506-0001 Office Phone: 859-257-7689. Office Fax: 859-257-1325. E-mail: wjcald2@uky.edu.

CALDERO-FIQUEROA, ANA JHANILCA, language educator; b. San Juan, P.R., Jan. 14, 1963; d. Jose Luis Caldero and Maria Mercedes Fiqueroa. BA in Spanish Lang., U. Ctrl. Fla., 1984; MA in Spanish Lit., U. Wis., 1988. Fgn. lang. prof. Valencia C.C./West, Orlando, Fla., 1989—. Faculty advisor Valencia Internat. Students, Orlando, 2001—. Prodr.: (Hispanic heritage theater celebration) Garcia Lorca: Homage to the Spanish Poet, (Hispanic heritage celebration) Homage to Jose Marti, Homage to Spanish Poets/Generation of 98, (homage to the music of Cuba & P.R.) Two Islands in a Sea of Music, (Hispanic heritage celebration) Women in Arts; author: (short story) From the Distance (3d pl. short story competition, 1990), The Dream Searcher (hon. mention short story category, 1992). Avocations: travel, reading, writing. Office: Valencia CC-West Campus 1800 S Kirkman Rd PO Box 3028 Orlando FL 32811 E-mail: acaldero@valenciacc.edu.

CALDERON, BRENDA F., language educator, interpreter; b. Kitchener, Ont., Canada, July 9, 1948; arrived in U.S., 1972; d. Howard Wilfrid and Marjorie Priscilla Hessenaur; m. Juan Antonio Calderon, Apr. 21, 1973; children: Victoria, Rachel. BA with honors, U. Western Ont., 1970; MA, U. Toronto, 1972. Prof. Spanish Oral Roberts U., Tulsa, 1972—, leader 16 study trips to Spain, 1972—. Scholar, Ciber U. S.C., Columbia, 2000. Republican. Avocation: water-skiing.

CALDERON, ERNEST, lawyer; b. Morenci, Ariz., Oct. 24, 1957; BS, No. Ariz. U., 1979; JD, U. Ariz., 1982. Bar: Ariz. 1983, U.S. Dist. Ct. Ariz. 1983, U.S. Ct. Appeals (9th cir.) 1984, U.S. Ct. Appeals (D.C. cir.) 1984, U.S. Supreme Ct. 1986. Law clk. to Judge Walter E. Craig, U.S. Dist. Ct., 1982—84; atty. Jennings, Strouss & Salmon, PLC, Phoenix. Fellow: Ariz. Bar Found.; mem.: Am. Bar Found., Am. Law Inst., State Bar Ariz. (pres. 2002—03).

CALDERON, JAIME A., psychologist, educator; b. Guayaquil, Ecuador, Apr. 24, 1944; s. Jaime B. Calderón and Isabel Romoleroux; m. Jane E. Calderón, Jan. 20, 1974; children: Jaime, Joshua, Joanna. Lic. Sch. Psychologist. Sci. tchr. Houston I.S.D.; spl. edn. tchr. Alief I.S.D., Tex.; head master Am. Sch. Guayaquil, Ecuador; sch. psychologist Tomball I.S.D., Tex., Galena Pk. I.S.D., Tex., Okecchobee County Schs., Fla., Seminole County Schs., Sanford, Fla. Lectr. U. Loza, Ecuador, 2002. Contbr. articles to profl. jours. in field. Mem.: APA, Fla. Assn. Sch. Psychologists, NASP. Republican. Avocations: walking, reading, writing. Home: 555 Estates Pl Longwood FL 32779

CALDERON, RONALD, state official; b. Montebello, Calif., Aug. 12, 1957; m. Ana Calderon; children: Jessica, Zachary. Student, Western State U. Law; BA, UCLA, 1980. Owner fin. svcs. sales and mktg. firm; mgr. mfg. industry; mortgage banker; real estate agt.; chief of staff Assemblyman Ed Chavez; state assembly mem. Dist. 58 Calif. State Assembly, 2002—. Mem. appropriations com.; mem. banking and fin. com.; mem. govtl. orgn. com.; mem. ins. com.; mem. utilities and commerce com. Mem. La Merced Elem. Sch. PTA, 1998—; bd. dirs. L.A. Econ. Devel. Corp., 1998—, N.E. Cmty. Clinic, 1999—; mem. Gangs Out of Downey, 2001—. Democrat. Mailing: Rm 2179 PO Box 942849 Sacramento CA 94249 Office: Ste 100 400 N Montebello Blvd Montebello CA 90640

CALDERON, SILA MARIA, former governor; b. San Juan, Sept. 23, 1942; 3 children. B in Polit. Sci. with honors, degree, Manhattanville Coll.; MPA, U. P.R.; degree (hon.), Boston U., New School U., Hunter Coll., Rutgers U. Worked for Sec. of Labor; spl. asst. econ. devel. and labor for Gov. Hernández Colón, 1974; chief of staff Gov. Hernández Colón, 1985, sec. interior, sec. state, 1988; mayor City of San Juan, 1996—2000; gov. PR, San Juan, 2001—05. Bd. dirs. Banco Popular P.R. Named Outstanding Woman of Yr., PR C. of C., 1975, 1985, 1987, Puerto Rican Products Assn., 1986, PR chpt. Am. Assn. Pub. Works, 1988; recipient Harvard Found. award, Golden Plate award, Acad. Achievement. Mem.: Sister Isolina Ferré Found. Democrat.

CALDERONE, BOB, business owner, chef; m. Susan Finegold. Mem. staff Panache (now 798 Main St.), Cambridge, Mass., 1979—88; chef Lafayette Hotel, Boston, Copley Plz., Boston, Dedham Hilton, Boston; owner Anago Bistro (formerly 798 Main St.), Boston, 1992, Anago, Lenox Hotel, Boston.

CALDERONE, DANA, primary school educator, reading specialist; b. Phila., Oct. 22, 1976; d. Robert Francis and Rose Ann Severino; m. Michael Joseph Calderone, July 12, 2003. BS in Edn., Cabrini Coll., Radnor, Pa., 1998, MS in Edn. and Reading, 2002. Cert. elem. educator Pa., 1998, early childhood educator Pa., 1998, reading specialist Pa., 2002. Third grade tchr. St. Andrew Sch., Drexel Hill, Pa., 1998—2002; reading specialist for grades k-6, instrnl. support tchr. William Penn Sch. Dist. East Lansdowne Basics Sch., Pa., 2002—04; kindergarten reading specialist Garnet Valley Sch. Dist., Concord Elem. Sch. and Bethel Springs Elem. Sch., Glen Mills, Pa., 2004—. Pvt. reading tutor, Pa., 1997—; after sch. counselor St. Andrew's Sch., Drexel Hill, 1998—2002; sr. summer camp counselor Jewish Cmty. Ctr. Greater Phila., Wynnewood, Pa., 1996—2002. Patience Cavanagh McFadden scholar, Cabrini Coll., 1997. Mem.: Pa. State Edn. Assn., Keystone State Reading Assn., Del. Valley Reading Assn., Internat. Reading Assn., Kappa Delta Pi. Roman Catholic. Avocations: reading, swimming, baking, walking, travel. Office Phone: 610-579-6112.

CALDERONE, JOSEPH DANIEL, campus ministry director, educator; b. Bryn Mawr, Pa., Feb. 26, 1948; s. Joseph Albert and Sara Jane (Giangiulio) C. B.A. in Social Scis. Villanova U., 1970, M.A. in Counseling, 1973. M.A. in Theology, Washington Theol. Union, 1975; Cert. Advanced Grad. Study in Higher Edn. Adminstrn., Northeastern U., 1976, Ed.D. in Higher Edn. Adminstrn., 1982. Ordained priest Roman Catholic Ch., 1973. Campus minister Villanova U., Pa., 1973-74; assoc. dir. campus ministry Merrimack Coll., North Andover, Mass., 1974-76, dir. campus ministry, 1976-78; diocesan dir. campus ministry, Orlando and Winter Park, Fla., 1978—; prof. mgmt. and counseling theory St. Leo Coll., St. Leo, Fla., 1984—; prof. bus. ethics Rollins Coll., Winter Park, Fla., 1983— . Mem. Nat. Assn. Diocesan Dirs. Campus Ministry (sec., treas. 1984—), Nat. Assn. Coll. and Univ. Chaplains (mem. at large 1985—). Democrat. Home and Office: 430 E Lyman Ave Winter Park FL 32789-4416

CALDERONI, ROBERT M., software company executive; BS in Acctg. and Fin., Fordham U. CPA, Calif. Various fin. mgmt. positions IBM, Apple Computers, 1996-97; sr. v.p. fin., CFO Avery Dennison, Pasadena, Calif., 1997—2001; CFO Ariba, Inc., Sunnyvale, Calif., 2000—01, exec. v.p., CFO, 2001, pres., 2001—04, CEO, 2001—, chmn., 2003—. Bd. dirs. Ariba, Inc.; bd. dir. Juniper Networks, Inc. Office: Ariba Inc 807 11th Ave Sunnyvale CA 94089 Office Phone: 650-390-1000.

CALDWELL, ANN B., music educator; b. Anniston, Ala., July 12, 1947; d. Byron Brenford and Bernice New Boyd; m. John Harold Harmon, Mar. 22, 1969 (div. Sept. 28, 1983); children: Heather, John Harold II; m. Bobby Ted Caldwell, Aug. 14, 1987. MusB in Edn., Birmingham (Ala.) So. Coll., 1969; MusM in Edn., Jacksonville (Ala.) U., 1975. Music tchr. elem. sch. Auburn (Ala.) City Schs., 1969; choral dir. Oxford (Ala.) HS, 1969—74; instr. music So. Union State C.C., Wadley, Ala., 1974—89, dir. music, 1989—. Choir dir. First United Meth. Ch., Wedowee, Ala., 1999—; exec. dir. Miss. So. Union Scholarship Pageant, Wadley, 1984—; mem. nat. forum advisors Mid-Am. Prodns., Inc., N.Y.C., 1996—97. Dir.: (choral group) The So. Union Sound, Carnegie Hall, NYC, 1993—2003. Mem.: Wedowee Music Club (past pres.), Delta Kappa Gamma, Kappa Delta Epsilon, Delta Zeta. Methodist. Avocations: music, reading, crossword puzzles. Home: 524 Conty Road 29 Wedowee AL 36278 Office: Southern Union State Cmty Coll PO Box 1000 Wadley AL 36276-1000

CALDWELL, ANN WICKINS, academic administrator; b. Rochester, N.Y., Dec. 3, 1943; d. Ralph Everett and Constance Ann (McCoy) Wickins; m. Herbert Cline Caldwell, Sept. 17, 1966; children: Constance Haley Blacklow, Robert James. BA in English Lit., U. Mich., 1965. Reporter Democrat & Chronicle, Rochester, 1961-64; asst. to dean Harvard Grad. Sch. of Edn., Cambridge, Mass., 1965-70, editor alumni quarterly, 1968-71; freelance editor, writer Harvard U. and Radcliffe, Cambridge, 1971-73; assoc. sec. Philips Acad., Andover, Mass., 1973—80; v.p. for planning and resources Wheaton Coll., Norton, Mass., 1980-90; assoc. dir. Mus. Fine Arts, Boston, 1990-91; v.p. for devel. Brown U., Providence, 1991-97; pres. MGH Inst. Health Professions, Boston, 1997—. Chair bicentennial com. Newburyport, Mass., 1974—76; citizens adv. com. Pub. Sch., Newburyport, 1979—80; bd. dirs. Am. Laryngological Voice Rsch. & Edn. Found.; trustee Women's Edn. and Indsl. Union, Boston, 1988—91, John Hope Settlement Ho., Providence, 1997—, Jr. Achievement of Ea. Mass., 2004—. Mem.: Women in Devel. Boston (founder, pres. 1984—86), Coun. for Advancement and Support of Edn. (trustee, sec. dist. 1 1985—87, trustee, sec. nat. 1987—89), Boston Club, Chilton Club, Phi Delta Kappa. Avocations: sailing, skiing, travel, reading. Office: Charlestown Navy Yard 36 First Ave Boston MA 02129-4724 Business E-Mail: acaldwell@mghihp.edu.

CALDWELL, BARRETT SCOTT, industrial engineering educator; b. Phila., Sept. 25, 1962; s. Shirl C. and Jacqueline H. (Horsey) C.; m. Shanta Wilson Hartsough, Sept. 1, 1986 (div.); children: Piers Hartsough C., Kyrie Eleison Hartsough C. BS in Aero. & Astronautics, BS in Humanities, MIT, 1985; MA in Psychology, U. Calif., Davis, 1987, PhD in Social Psychology, 1990. Grad. student lectr. U. Calif., Davis, 1985-90; asst. prof. U. Wis., Madison, 1990-97, assoc. prof., 1997—2000, Purdue U., West Lafayette, Ind., 2000—. Author: (book) Social Processes in Isolated Groups of U.S. Park Service Rangers, 1990; contbr. articles to Behavior and Info. Tech. and Human Factors. Mem. ministry and counsel Madison Quakers Monthly Meeting, 1992-94; dir., Ind Space Grant Consortium, 2001—. Recipient Minority Rsch. Initiation award NSF, Madison, 1994, grad. fellowship NSF, Davis, 1985, Ameritech Faculty fellowship, Madison, 1991. Mem. Human Factors and Ergonomics Soc. (chair tech. program com.). Avocation: rowing. Office: Purdue U-Sch of Indsl Engring 315 N Grant StRm 228D Lafayette IN 47907-2023 E-mail: bscaldwell@purdue.edu.

CALDWELL, BILLY RAY, geologist; b. Newellton, La., Apr. 20, 1932; s. Leslie Richardson and Helen Merle (Clark) C.; m. Carolyn Marie Heath; children: Caryn, Jeana, Craig. BA, Tex. Christian U., 1954, MA, 1970; PhD, Cambridge Grad. Sch., 2004. Cert. petroleum geologist, profl. geologist; lic. geoscientist, Tex. Geologist Geol. Engring. Svc. Co., Ft. Worth, Tex., 1954-60; sci. tchr. Ft. Worth and Lake Worth Sch. Dists., 1960-63; mgr. Outdoor Living, 1963-71; instr. geology Tarrant County Coll., Ft. Worth, 1971—. Petroleum and environ. geologist cons., Ft. Worth, 1971—. Bd. dirs. Ft. Worth and Tarrant County Homebuilders Assn., 1973; mem. Ft. Worth Environ. Coun. Named Dir. of Yr. Ft. Worth Jaycees, 1966-67. Mem. Am. Inst. Profl. Geologists, Am. Assn. Petroleum Geologists, Geol. Soc. Am., Ft. Worth Geol. Soc. Republican. Baptist. Avocations: travel, church work, enrichment lecturing on cruise ships. Home: 305 Bodart Ln Fort Worth TX 76108-3804 Office: PO Box 150989 Fort Worth TX 76108-0989 Office Phone: 817-246-5477. Personal E-mail: bcgeology@aol.com.

CALDWELL, CHARLES M., federal judge; b. 1954; BS, Evansville U., 1976; JD, Northwestern U., 1979. Asst. U.S. trustee U.S. Dist. Ct. (so. dist.) Ohio, 1988-93; staff atty. bankruptcy divsn. Adminstrv. Office U.S. Cts., Washington, 1986-88; bankruptcy judge U.S. Bankruptcy Ct., Columbus, 1993—. Office: US Bankruptcy Ct 170 N High St Columbus OH 43215-2403 Office Phone: 614-469-6638. E-mail: charles_caldwell@ohsb.uscourts.gov.

CALDWELL, CINDY SUE, mathematician, educator; d. Clifton Floyd and Verna Mildred Caldwell. AA, Rend Lake Coll.; BA in Secondary Edn., McKendree Coll.; MS in Curriculum and Instrn., So. Ill. U. Cert. tchr. 1985. Staff Spokesman Pub. Co., Christopher, Ill., 1982, 1983; chpt. 1 math. tchr. grades 7-9 Harlan (Ky.) Ind. Sch. Dist., 1984—86; jr. HS math. tchr. Chester (Ill.) Cmty. Unit 139, 1986—87; math. tchr. Ramsey (Ill.) HS, 1987—95, Southeastern Ill. Coll., Harrisburg, 1995—97, John A. Logan Coll., Carterville, Ill., 1996—2000, Rend Lake Coll., Ina, Ill., 1996—. Presenter in field. Mem.: So. Ill. Coun. Tchrs. Math., Ill. Math. Assn. C.C., Ill. Coun. Tchrs. Math., Math. Assn. Am., Nat. Coun. Tchrs. Math. Baptist. Avocations: golf, keyboards, logic puzzles, contemporary Christian music.

CALDWELL, COURTNEY LYNN, lawyer, real estate consultant; b. Washington, Mar. 5, 1948; d. Joseph Morton and Moselle (Smith) Caldwell. Attended, Duke Univ., 1966-68, U. Calif., Berkeley, 1967, 1968-69; BA, U. Calif., Santa Barbara, 1970, MA, 1975; JD (hon.), George Washington Univ., 1982. Bar: DC, Wash. 1986, Calif. 1989. Jud. clk. U.S. Ct. Appeals for 9th Cir., Seattle, 1982-83; assoc. Arnold and Porter, Washington, 1983-85, Perkins Coie, Seattle, 1985-88; dir. western ops. Edn. Real Estate Svc., Inc., Irvine, Calif., 1988-91, sr. v.p., 1991-98; ind. cons., Orange County, Calif., 1998—. Bd. dir. Univ. Town Ctr. Assn., 1994; bd. dir. Habitat for Humanity, Orange County, 1993-94, chair legal com., 1994. Named Nat. Law Ctr. Law Rev. scholar, 1981—82. Mem.: Calif. Bar Assn. Avocation: fgn. languages. Home and Office: 140 Cabrillo St 15 Costa Mesa CA 92627 Office Phone: 949-650-8170. Personal E-mail: clcaldwell@earthlink.net.

CALDWELL, DALE GILBERT, state official; b. Boston, July 6, 1960; s. Gilbert Haven and Grace Estelle (Dungee) C.; m. Sharon Marie Richards, Aug. 16, 2003; 1 child, Ashley Marie. BA in Econs., Princeton U., 1982; MBA in Fin., U. Pa., 1988. Cert. fin. planner; cert. mgmt. cons.; cert. tennis tchg. profl. Sr. mgr., mgmt. cons. divsn. Deloitte & Touche, Parsippany, NJ, 1988—99; exec. dir. Newark Alliance, 1999—2002; dep. commr. N.J. Dept. Cmty. Affairs, Trenton, 2002—. Author of poems. Pres., bd. dirs. Middlesex County Ednl. Svcs. Commn., 1999-; bd. dirs. New Brunswick Bd. Edn., 1998-, Ea. sect. USTA, 2004-; bd. commrs. Asbury Park Housing Authority, 2003-. Avocations: Hymn writing, coin collecting/numismatics, nationally ranked tennis player, nationally ranked triathelete, nationally ranked duathelete. Office: 101 S Broad St Trenton NJ 08625-0800 Office Phone: 609-292-9111. Business E-Mail: dcaldwell@dca.state.nj.us. E-mail: dalegcaldwell@aol.com.

CALDWELL, DAVID ORVILLE, retired physics professor; b. Los Angeles, Jan. 5, 1925; s. Orville Robert and Audrey Norton (Anderson) C.; m. Miriam Ann Planck, Nov. 4, 1950 (div. Apr. 1978); children: Bruce David, Diana Miriam; m. Edith Helen Anderson, Dec. 29, 1984. BS in Physics, Calif. Inst. Tech., 1947; postgrad., Stanford U., 1947-48; MA in Physics, UCLA, 1949, PhD in Physics, 1953. From instr. to assoc. prof. physics MIT, Cambridge, 1954-63; vis. assoc. prof. physics Princeton U., N.J., 1963-64; lectr. physics dept. U. Calif., Berkeley, 1964-65, prof. physics Santa Barbara, 1965—, now prof. emeritus. Cons. U. Calif. Radiation Lab., Berkeley, 1957-58, 64-67, Am. Sci. and Engring., Boston, 1959-60, Inst. Def. Analyses, Washington, 1960-67; dir. U. Calif. Intercampus Inst. for Rsch. at Particle Accelerators, 1984-95, assoc. dir. U. Calif. Inst. for Nuc. and Particle Astrophysics and Cosmology, 1995—. Contbr. numerous articles to profl. jours. Served to 2d lt. USAAF, 1943-46. Recipient von Humboldt Sr. Disting. Sci. award, 1987; rsch. grantee Dept. Energy, 1966—; Ford Found. fellow, 1961-62, NSF fellow 1953-54, 1960-61, Guggenheim fellow, 1971-72. Fellow Am. Phys. Soc.; mem. Phys. Soc. (exec. com. 1976-78). Democrat. Avocations: tennis, skiing. Office: U Calif Physics Dept Santa Barbara CA 93106

CALDWELL, ELEANOR, artist; b. Kansas City, Mo., May 1, 1927; d. Earl Kendrick and Etta (Clark) Caldwell. BS in Edn., Southwest Mo. State U., 1948; MA, Columbia U. Tchrs. Coll., 1953, EdD, 1959. Tchr. art h.s. in Mo. and Iowa, 1948—52; instr. art Southwest Mo. State U., 1953—54; asst. prof. Ft. Hays State U., Kans., 1954—57; instr. Columbia U. Tchrs. Coll., N.Y.C., 1957—59; prof., chmn. art dept. N.W Mo. State Coll., Maryville, 1959—60; assoc. prof. Edinboro State Coll., Pa., 1960—62, Pa. State U., Collegeville, 1962—63, No. Ill. U., De Kalb, 1963—64, Fort Hays State U., Kans., 1964—67; prof. art No. Ill. U., De Kalb, 1967—83, prof. emeritus, 1983—. Supr. children's art carnival Mus. Modern Art, 1957—59; lectr. art edn. Queens Coll., Bklyn., 1957—59; dir. Oakbrook Inviational Craftes Exhbn., 1968—84; consulting tchr. Arrowmont Sch. Arts and Crafts, Gatlinburg, Tenn., 1974. Represented in permanent collections Denver Pub. Schs., Colo. Women's Coll., Ft. Hays State Coll., No. Ill. U., Sheldon Meml. Art Mus., Lincoln, Nebr., Arrowmont Sch. Arts and Crafts; editor: Contemporary Jewelry, 1970. Mem. Fine Arts bd. U. Ariz., 1999—; bd. trustees Tucson, 1996—2002. Recipient Pub. Svc. award, Ill. Sesquicentennial Commn., 1968; grantee, No. Ill. U., 1968, 1970, 1974—80. Mem.: Ariz. Designer Craftsmen, Am. Crafts Coun., Soc. N. Am. Goldsmiths, Delta Kappa Gamma, Kappa Delta Pi, Pi Lambda Theta. E-mail: savont31@msn.com.

CALDWELL, ELWOOD FLEMING, food scientist, educator; b. Gladstone, Man., Can., Apr. 3, 1923; s. Charles Fleming and Frances Marion (Ridd) C.; m. Irene Margaret Sebille, June 13, 1949; children: John Fleming, Keith Allan; m. Florence Annette Zar, June 23, 1979. BS, U. Man., 1943; MA in Food Chemistry, U. Toronto, 1949, PhD in Nutrition, 1953; MBA, U. Chgo., 1956. Chemist Lake of the Woods Milling Co., Can., 1943-47; research chemist Can. Breweries Ltd., Toronto, Ont., 1948-49; chief chemist Christie, Brown & Co. div. Nabisco, Toronto, 1949-51; research assoc. in nutrition U. Toronto, 1951-53; with Quaker Oats Co., Barrington, Ill., 1953-72, dir. research and devel., 1969-72; prof., head dept. food sci. and nutrition U. Minn., St. Paul, 1972-86, exec. assoc. to dean Coll. Agr., 1986-88; dir. sci. svcs. Am. Assn. Cereal Chemists, 1988-94, analysis svcs. coord., 1994-98; exec. editor Cereal Foods World, 1986-91; chmn. bd. Dairy Quality Control Inst., Inc., St. Paul, 1972-88, R. & D. Assocs. for Mil. Food & Packaging, Inc., San Antonio, 1970-71; chmn. evening program in food sci. Ill. Inst. Tech., Chgo., 1965-69. Contbr. articles to sci. jours. Chmn. North Barrington (Ill.) Bd. Appeals, 1966-69, mayor, 1969-72; vice-chmn. Barrington Area Council Govts., 1972; bd. dirs. Family Guidance Barrington, 1971-72. Recipient cert. of appreciation for civilian service U.S. Army Materiel Command, 1970. Fellow Am. Assn. Cereal Chemists (Geddes Meml. award 1996), Inst. Food Technologists (Chmn.'s Svc. award Chgo. sect. 1975, Chmn.'s award Minn. sect. 1977, Calvert L. Willey Disting. Svc. award 1991); mem. Am. Assn. Family and Consumer Scis., AOAC Internat. (Reference Material Achievement award 2002), Kiwanis, Phi Tau Sigma (nat. pres. 1980-81), Gamma Sigma Delta (award of merit 1988), Phi Upsilon Omicron. Republican. Lutheran.

CALDWELL, GAIL, book critic; b. Amarillo, Tex., Jan. 20, 1951; d. Bill M. and Ruby C. BA, U. Tex., 1978, MA in Am. Studies, 1980. Instr. U. Tex., Austin, to 1981; staff writer, critic Boston Globe, 1985—, book editor, 1992—95. Judge Radcliffe Bunting Fiction Fellowship; nominator Irish-Times/Aer Lingus Internat. Fiction Prize; mem. Pulitzer jury fiction, 1991 (chmn. of jury 1995 & 1997). Recipient Pulitzer Prize for criticism, 2001. Mem. PEN New Eng. (bd. dirs.), Nat. Book Critics Circle. Office: The Boston Globe PO Box 2378 135 Morrissey Blvd Boston MA 02125-3338

CALDWELL, GARNETT ERNEST, lawyer; b. Houston, July 2, 1934; s. William Ernest and Ethel Leona (Jones) C. BA, U. Houston, 1957, JD, 1959. Bar: Tex. 1958. Pvt. practice law, Houston, 1959-64; ptnr. Ginther, Erwin, Dillard & Caldwell, Houston, 1964-65, Prappas, Caldwell & Moncure, Houston, 1965-77, Caldwell & Baggott, Houston, 1977-82, Caldwell, Wallis, Pruitt & Baggott, Houston, 1982; pvt. practice Houston, 1982-85, 87-90, Houston and Galveston, 1990—; ptnr. Caldwell & Lareau, 1985-87. Lectr. govt. U. Houston, 1961—62. 2d lt. U.S. Army, 1957, lt. col. Res., 1977—. Decorated knight and knight comdr. Royal Yugoslavian Order St. John of Jerusalem. Mem. Galveston County Bar Assn., Houston Bar Assn., Houston Sr. Lawyers Forum, Houston Bankruptcy Conf., Res. Officers Assn., Houston Early Music Soc., K.C., Delta Theta Phi. Roman Catholic. Home and Office: 1619 Post Office St Galveston TX 77550-4813 Office Phone: 409-762-3500.

CALDWELL, GUY ALEXANDER, biology professor, biomedical researcher; b. Upper Montclair, N.J., Dec. 15, 1962; s. Marc Guy and Victoria Rustamova Caldwell; m. Kim A. Neifer, Feb. 21, 1966. BS in Biology, Wash. & Lee U., 1986; Ph.D. in Cell and Molecular Biology, U. Tenn., 1996. Rsch. intern Burroughs-Wellcome Co., Rsch. Triangle Pk., NC, 1986—87; postdoctoral fellow Columbia U., N.Y.C., 1995—99; asst. prof. biol. sciences U. Ala., Tuscaloosa, 1999—. Adj. asst. rsch. prof. neurology U. Ala. Birmingham Med. Sch., 2004—. Author: Biotechnology: A Laboratory Course. Nominee Carnegie/CASE U.S. Professor of Yr., 2005; recipient Career award, NSF, 2003; grantee, Dystonia Med. Rsch. Found., 2000, Nat. Parkinson Found., 2002, Parkinson's Disease Found., 2002, Michael J. Fox Found. Parkinson's Rsch., 2003, Bachmann-Strauss Dystonia and Parkinson Found., 2004; Basil O'Connor scholar, March of Dimes Birth Defects Found., 2001. Mem.: AAAS, Movement Disorders Soc., Am. Epilepsy Soc., Soc. Neuroscience, Genetics Soc. Am., Am. Soc. Cell Biology, Golden Key (hon.). Achievements include research in molecular basis of neurological disorders including Parkinson's disease, dystonia, and epilepsy. Office: U Ala Box 870344 Tuscaloosa AL 35487-0344 Office Phone: 205-348-9926.

CALDWELL, IAN, writer; b. Washington, 1976; BA in History, Princeton U., 1998. Co-author: (novels) (with Dustin Thomason) The Rule of Four, 2004 (Publishers Weekly bestseller list, 2004, NY Times bestseller list, 2004, San Francisco Chronicle bestseller list, 2004, Boston Globe bestseller list, 2004, New York Post bestseller list, 2004). Mem.: Phi Beta Kappa. Office: c/o Dial Books 375 Hudson St New York NY 10014

CALDWELL, JOAN MARIE, artist, educator; b. Lancaster, Pa., Dec. 17, 1927; d. George Joseph and Doris (Fay) Brouillette; m. Richard Holmes Caldwell, Dec. 24, 1970 (div. Jan. 8, 1987); children: Toni Lauren, Wendy Ann, Andrea Joy, Richard Blake, Spencer Edward. Diploma, Mus. Fine Arts Sch., Boston, 1949; BA magna cum laude, U. Calif., San Diego, 1988; MFA in Studio Painting, Calif. State U., Fullerton, 1993. Tchr. Sch. Organic Edn., Fairhope, Ala., 1950-52, Mobile (Ala.) H.S., 1952, Monteverde Sch., Costa Rica, 1955-60; instr. Calif. State U., Fullerton, 1993; artist, 1952—. Exhbns. include Orlando Gallery, Tarzana, Calif., 1993-, Downey Art Mus., 1995, Self Help Graphies, 1995, Miracosta Coll., 1996, San Diego (Calif.) Mus. Art, 1998, S.W. Coll., 1999, Oceanside Mus. Art, 2003. Avocations: writing, photography. Home: 4410 41st St San Diego CA 92116 Office Phone: 619-283-0154. E-mail: jocaldwell@mac.com.

CALDWELL, JOE R., lawyer; b. Jackson, Miss., Mar. 27, 1949; BA with distinction, Syracuse U., 1971; JD, Rutgers U., 1974; LLM, Georgetown U., 1984; MPA, Harvard U., 1985. Bar: NJ 1974, DC 1978, U.S. Ct. Appeals (2d, 4th and 5th cir.), U.S. Supreme Ct. Dep atty. gen. Divsn. Criminal Justice, NJ, 1974—75; legal officer U.S. Supreme Ct., 1980—82, counsel, asst. to Chief Justice Warren E. Burger, 1982—84; chief of staff, legal counsel to Mayor Sharon Pratt Kelly Washington, 1991; ptnr. Baker Botts LLP, Washington. Faculty mem. Georgetown U., 1992—; vice chmn. dean's Alumni adv. coun. Harvard U., 2002—; spkr. in field. Mem. legal def. and edn. fund NAACP; bd. dirs., past pres. Big Brothers Big Sisters Nat. Capital Area. Fellow: Am. Coll. Trial Lawyers; mem.: ABA, NJ State Bar Assn., DC Bar Assn. Office: Baker Botts LLP The Warner 1299 Pennsylvania Ave NW Washington DC 20004-2400 Office Phone: 202-639-7788. Office Fax: 202-585-1074. E-mail: joe.caldwell@bakerbotts.com.

CALDWELL, JOHN ALVIS, JR., experimental psychologist; b. New Orleans, June 16, 1955; s. John Alvis and Patsy Ruth (Richardson) C.; m. Jo Lynn Woodard, July 18, 1981. BA cum laude, Troy State U., 1976; MS in Psychology, U. South Ala., 1979; PhD in Psychology, U. So. Miss., 1984. Psychologist II Eufaula (Ala.) Adolescent Adjustment Ctr., 1979-80, coord. drug-free clinic, 1980-81; asst. dir. behavioral med. lab. Children's Hosp. Nat. Med. Ctr., Washington, 1984-86; rsch. psychologist U.S. Army Aeromed. Rsch. Lab., Ft. Rucker, Ala., 1986—2002; vis. scientist NASA Ames Rsch. Ctr., Moffett Field, Calif., 2001—02; prin. rsch. psychologist Air Force Rsch. Lab., Brooks AFB, Tex., 2002—. Sec., chief edn. working group 19 NATO Adv. Group R&D, 1991-94; math. and sci. adv. com. mem. Troy State U., 1992-2002; adj. faculty U.S. Army Sch. Aerospace Medicine, 1996—, USAF Sch. Aerospace Medicine, 2004—; mem. spkrs. bur. Nat. Sleep Found., 1996—, mem. sci. coun., 1999—; instr. Army Aviation Psychology course, Ft. Rucker, 1998—; instr. U.S. Army Aviation Pre-Command Course, 1997-2002; chmn. sci. rev. com. U.S. Army Aero. Rsch. Lab., 1996-2000; sci. cons. sustained ops. rsch. and policy groups, 1999-2001; prepared and distributed unique ednl. brochures on aviator fatigue; sleep expert USA Today/Nat. Sleep Found. 1999 Hotline; lead sci. cons. on pharmacol. fatigue mgmt. USAF Sustained Ops. Working Group, 1999-2002; mem. com. metabolic monitoring techs. for mil. field application Inst. Medicine, Nat. Acads., 2003-04, fatigue mgmt. cons. for NASA Engring. and Safety Ctr., 2003-. Spl. guest editor Biol. Psychology, Amsterdam, 1994; jour. referee Aviation Space and Environ. Medicine, 1992—, mem. editl. rev. bd., 2001-03; referee Jour. Exptl. Psychology, 1998-99; contbr. articles to profl. jours., authored and co-authored one book and two book chpts. Dir. ch. choir St. John Cath. Ch., Enterprise, Ala., 1991-97; vol. counselor Wiregrass Emergency Pregnancy Svc., Daleville, Ala., 1992; mem. Enterprise cmty. choir, 1991, St. Luke's Meth. Ch. Christmas choir, Enterprise, 1995-97; mem. U.S. Army Aeromed. Rsch. Lab. Choir, Ft. Rucker, 1992-93; mem. spl. choir Enterprise Ch. LDS, 1993-94; mem. ch. choir St. Columba Cath. Ch., Dothan, Ala., 1998; mem. Dothan (Ala.) Cmty. Choir, 1999-2000, Enterprise Cmty. Choir, 1999; music leader Our Lady of Loretto Cath. Ch., Ft. Rucker, Ala., 1999. Recipient writing award, U.S. Army Aviation Med. Assn., 1996. Mem. AAAS, Aerospace Med. Assn., Sigma Xi, Psi Chi, Aircraft Owners and Pilots Assn. Republican. Roman Catholic. Achievements include conducting the first aviator performance study of the new stimulant modafinil in helicopter pilots and in F-117 pilots, the first controlled study of performance sustaining effects of dextroamphetamine in helicopter pilots, first in-flight helicopter pilot evaluation of the chem. def. antidote atropine sulfate, first studies on the feasibility of monitoring helicopter pilot brain activity during actual flight conditions, first controlled study on the effects of fatigue in F-117 pilots. Home: 7430 Legend Point San Antonio TX 78244 Office: Air Force Rsch Lab AFRL/HEPF 2485 Gillingham Dr Brooks City-Base TX 78235 Office Phone: 210-536-8251. Business E-Mail: john.caldwell@brooks.af.mil. E-mail: airspeed669@hotmail.com.

CALDWELL, JOHN THOMAS, JR., communications executive; b. Sewickley, Pa., July 30, 1932; s. John Thomas and Helen Olive (Sheats) C.; m. Margery Eleanor Hill, Dec. 31, 1971. AB, U. Pitts., 1955; postgrad., Mich. State U., U. Mich., Harvard U. Sch. Bus. Mem. prodn. staff Sta. WKAR-TV, East Lansing, Mich., 1955-56, dir., 1957, prodr., 1958, prodn. mgr., 1959-62; distbn. mgr. Nat. Ednl. TV, Inc., Ann Arbor, Mich., 1962-64; v.p. distbn. and ops., 1964-66; ops. mgr. Sta. WGBH, Boston, 1966-70; gen. mgr. Sta. WGBY-TV, Springfield, Mass., 1971-79; pres., gen. mgr. Sta. WTVS-TV, Detroit, 1979-83; dir. electronic communication, corp. pub. affairs Ford Motor Co., Dearborn, Mich., 1983-86, dir. internal comm., pub. affairs, 1986-94; v.p. bus. comm. planning Convergent Media Systems, 1995-98; pres. The Caldwell Co., Grosse Pointe, Mich., 1998—. Bd. dirs. Public Broadcasting Service, 1977-81, Sta. WTVS-TV, 1979-92. Bd. dirs. Detroit Symphony Orch., 1979—87, Mich. Cancer Found., 1980—96, Boys and Girls Clubs Mich., 1981—84, Springfield (Mass.) Symphony Orch., 1975—79; mem. U. Mich. Cmty. Adv. Bd., 1979—88, Mich. State Film, TV and Rec. Arts Adv. Coun., 1984—86; bd. dirs. Karmanos Cancer Inst., 1986, Mich. Info. Tech. Network, 1995—2001, Karmanos Cancer Found., 2002—. Woodrow Wilson fellow, 1981 Mem. Nat. Acad. TV Arts and Sci., Mich. Corp. Public Broadcasting (dir. 1979-83), Internat. TV Assn., Economic (Detroit) Club, Grosse Pointe Yacht Club, Skyline Club, Marina Club at Jonathon's Landing, Jupiter, Fla. Home: 874 Lake Shore Rd Grosse Pointe Shores MI 48236-1273 Office Phone: 313-886-1800.

CALDWELL, L. SCOTT, actress; b. Chgo., Apr. 17; Mem. Milw. Repertory Theatre, 1981-82. Mem. Negro Ensemble Co. Appeared in The Daughters of the Mock, 1978, A Season to Unravel, 1979, Old Phantoms, 1979, Plays from Africa, 1979, Home, 1979, 80, Boesman and Lena, 1981, Colored People's Time, 1982, About Heaven and Earth, 1983; other theater appearances include A Raisin in the Sun, Buffalo, 1982, A Play of Giants, 1984, Come and Gone, New Haven, 1985, Boston, 1986, N.Y.C., 1988 (Antoinette Perry award for best featured actress in a play, 1988), Proposals, A Month of Sundays, N.Y.C., 1987, Going to St. Ives, 2005 (Obie award, Village Voice, 2005); appeared in films Without a Trace, 1983, Exterminator 2, 1984, Up Against the Wall, 1991, Dutch, 1991, The Fugitive, 1993, The Switch, 1993, Soweto Green, 1995, The Net, 1995, Devil in a Blue Dress, 1995, Graham's Diner, 1999, Mystery, Alaska, 1999, Dragonfly, 2002; TV movies: God Bless the Child, 1988, Dangerous Passion, 1990, Love, Lies and Murder, 1991, Baby of the Bride, 1991, Extreme Justice, 1993, Darkness Before Dawn, 1993, For the Love of My Child: The Anissa Ayala Story, 1993, Down Came a Blackbird, 1995. Twilight Man, 1996, Dying to Be Perfect: The Ellen Hart Pena Story, 1996, Weapons of Mass Distraction, 1997, Intimate Betrayal, 1999, The Last Man On Planet Earth, 1999; TV series The Outsiders, 1990, Queens Supreme, 2003, recurring role in Judging Amy. Mailing: c/o Primary Stages 59 East 59th St New York NY 10022*

CALDWELL, LESLIE RAGON, lawyer; b. Pitts., Aug. 30, 1957; BA in economics summa cum laude, Pa. State U., 1979; JD with honors, George Washington U., 1982. Bar: NY 1983. Assoc. Cadwalader, Wickersham & Taft LLP, NYC, 1984—87; asst. US atty. US Atty.'s Office Ea. Dist. NY, Brooklyn, 1987—98, dep. chief Narcotics Sect., dep. chief General Crimes Sect., chief Violent Criminal Enterprises Sect., 1994—97, sr. trial counsel, 1997—98; asst. US atty. US Atty.'s Office No. Dist. Calif., San Francisco, 1998—2002, dep. chief Criminal Divsn., chief Econ. Crimes Unit, chief Securities & Fraud Sect., chief Criminal Divsn., 2001—02; dir. Enron Task Force US Dept. Justice, 2002—04; ptnr. Morgan Lewis & Bockius LLP, NYC, 2004—. Adj. faculty NY Law Sch. Recipient Henry L. Stimson Medal, Assn. Bar City NY, 1994, John Marshall Award for Trial of Litig., Atty. Gen., Award for Fraud Prevention, Spl. Achievement Award, US Dept. Justice. Office: Morgan Lewis & Bockius LLP 101 Park Ave New York NY 10178-0060

CALDWELL, LOUISE PHINNEY, historical researcher, community volunteer; b. Dallas, Sept. 19, 1938; d. Carl Lawrence and Louise (Snow) Phinney; m. Josef Caldwell, Sept. 8, 1962; children: Mattie Caldwell Roberts, Jane Barron Caldwell Jackson, Josef Caldwell Jr., Charles Phinney Caldwell. Grad., The Hockaday Sch., 1956; student, Sweet Briar Coll., 1956-57. Owner retail bus., Dallas, 1965-75; project chmn. Mus. of Dallas History, 1985—95; interim dir. Dallas Hist. Soc., 1990, chmn., 1991-93, pres., 1987-91, life trustee, 1991, exec. com., 2005—; bd. Friends of the Dallas Publ. Libr., 2003. Membership chair trustee com. Tex. Assn. Mus., Austin, 1986-88; mem.-at-large Women's Coun. Dallas County, 1991—; adv. 36th Inf. Divsn. Mus. Com., Camp Mabry, Austin, Tex.; v.p., treas. Hist. Inquiry, Inc., 1992—. Author rsch. project 150 Years of Lone Star Cuisine, 1986. Mem. Dallas County Hist. Commn., 1989-90; chmn. Awards for Excellence in Cmty. Svc., Dallas, 1983-89; founding co-chmn. Jubilee Dallas! Celebrating 150 Years, 1990-91; mem. charter bd. dir. Friends of Fair Park, Dallas, 1985-91; mem. Crystal Charity Ball Com.; chmn. Festival Shakespeare, 1994. Recipient Heritage award Dallas County Heritage Soc., 1982. Fellow Dallas Hist. Soc. (chmn. Fellows 1982-84), Mayflower Soc., Nat. Soc. of Colonial Dames, Daus. of Republic of Tex. (chpt. v.p. 1991-92), Dallas Woman's Club, Dallas Garden club, Charter 100 Club, Belterling Found. Democrat. Episcopalian. Avocations: collects & catalogues, antique glass trade beads, folk art of Hispanic southwest.

CALDWELL, LYNTON KEITH, social scientist, educator; b. Montezuma, Iowa, Nov. 21, 1913; s. Lee Lynton and Alberta (Mace) C.; m. Helen A. Walcher, Dec. 21, 1940; children: Edwin Lee, Elaine Lynette. PhB, U. Chgo., 1935, PhD, 1943; MA, Harvard U., 1938; LLD (hon.), Western Mich. U., 1977. Asst. prof. govt. Ind. U., South Bend, 1939-44, dir. advanced studies in sci., tech. and public policy Bloomington, 1965—, Arthur F. Bentley prof. polit. sci., 1971-84, prof. pub. and environ. affairs, 1970—; dir. research and publs. Council of State Govts., 1944-47; faculty U. Chgo., 1945-47; prof. polit. sci. Syracuse U., 1947-54; dir. Pub. Adminstrn. Inst. for Turkey and Middle East, UN, Ankara, 1954-55; prof. polit. sci. U. Calif., Berkeley, 1955-56. Mem. environmental adv. bd. C.E., 1970—; mem. Sea Grant adv. panel NOAA, 1971—; panel mem. Office Tech. Assessment, 1977—; cons. U.S. Senate Com. on Interior and Insular Affairs, 1969—, UN, 1973-74, UNESCO, 1975—, Army Environ. Policy Inst., 1991—, Nat. Com. on New Directions for Nat. Wildlife Refuge System, 1990—; mem. Nat. Commn. on Materials Policy, 1971—, Nat. Acad. Scis. Com. on Internat. Environ. Programs, 1970—; chmn. com. internat. law, policy and adminstrn. IUCN, 1969-77; mem. Internat. Coun. Environ. Law, 1985—; mem. sci. adv. bd. Internat. Joint Commn., 1984-91; Franklin lectr. Auburn U., 1972; Disting. Profl. lectr. U. Ala., 1981, William and Mary, 1991, U. Houston, 1992. Author: Administrative Theories of Hamilton and Jefferson, 1944, 2d edit., 1988, Environment: A Challenge to Modern Society, 1970, In Defense of Earth, 1972, Environmental Policy and Administration, 1975, Citizens and the Environment, 1976, Science and the National Environmental Policy Act, 1982, International Environmental Policy: From the 20th to the 21st Century, 1984, 3d edit., 1996, Biocracy: Public Policy and the Life Sciences, 1987, Perspectives on Ecosystem Managment for the Great Lakes, 1988, Between Two Worlds: Science, The Environmental Movement and Policy Choice, 1990, (with K. Schrader-Frechette) Policy for Land: Law and Ethics, 1993, Ecologia: Ciencia y politica medioambiental, 1993, Environment as a Focus for Public Policy, 1995, The National Environmental Policy Act: An Agenda for the Future, 1998; co-editor: Environmental Policy: Transnational Issues and National Trends, 1997, The National Environmental Policy Act: Agenda for the Future, 1999; mem. bd. editors Environ. Conservation Jour., 1973-93, Natural Resources Jour., 1973—, Sci., Tech. and Soc., 1979-91, Environ. Profl. Jour., 1981-89, Politics and the Life Scis., 1982-96, Colo. Jour. Internat. Environ. Law and Policy, 1990—, Ambiente y Recursos Naturales (Argentina), 1985—, Environmental Awareness (India), 1989—, Duke U. Law and Policy Forum, 1991—, Environ., 1993-95, Global Environ. Politics, 1999—. Bd. govs. The Nature Conservancy, 1959-65, Shirley Heinze Environ. Fund., Global Environ. and Energy in the 21st Century, 1988—. Recipient Sagamore of Wabash award State of Ind., 1980, H. and M. Sprout award Internat. Studies Assn., 1985, Global 500 award UN Environ. Programme, 1991, Disting. Svc. award Ind. U., 2001, Spirit of Philanthropy award Ind. U. Press, 2001; grantee Conservation Found., 1968-69, NSF, 1963—, Conservation and Research Found., 1969-70, U.S. Office Edn., 1973; guest fellow Woodrow Wilson Internat. Ctr. for Scholars Smithsonian Instn., 1971-72, East-West Ctr. fellow, 1981; named to Royal Order of Crown Thailand. Fellow AAAS; mem. Am. Soc. Pub. Adminstrn. (William Mosher award 1966, Laverne Burchfield award 1972, Marshall E. Dimock award 1981), Nat. Acad. Pub. Adminstrn., Royal Soc. Arts, Nat. Acad. Law and Social Scis. (hon. Cordoba, Argentina chpt.), Internat. Assn. for Impact Assessment (Rose Hulman Inst. Tech. award for outstanding achievement 1989), Am. Polit. Sci. Assn. (John M. Gaus award 1996), Natural Resource Coun. of Am. (Nat. Environ. Quality award 1997), Policy Studies Orgn. (Aaron Wildavsky book award 1996). Office: Indiana Univ Sch Pub & Environ Affairs Bloomington IN 47405 Home: 2735 Silver Creek Dr Bloomington IN 47401-4582 E-mail: lkcaldwe@indiana.edu.

CALDWELL, MARY PERI, counseling psychologist, educator; b. Cleve., Aug. 21, 1935; d. Francesco and Gerlanda (Gagliano) Peri; m. Robert Joseph Caldwell, 1956 (div. 1962); children: Deborah Ann, Thomas Robert (dec.). BS in Edn., Kent State U., 1961; MA in Counseling Psychology, Alfred Adler Inst., Chgo., 1981. Diplomate Am. Psychotherapy Assn.; cert. clin. mental health counselor; lic. mental health counselor, Fla., clin. counselor, Ohio. Tchr. various sch. systems, Cleve., 1957-85; pvt. practice as counseling psychologist Brunswick, Ohio, 1980-87, Coral Springs, Fla., 1987—; mem. faculty, dir. Cleve. Inst. Adlerian Studies, 1983—, exec. sec., 1978-82, pres., 1982-84. Mem. med. staff Care Unit, Coral Springs, FairOaks Hosp., Delray, Fla.; mem. mental health profl. staff Univ. Pavillion Hosp., Tamarac, Fla.; lectr. U.S. and Can. Author: Stress/Distress/Burnout: Resolving the Puzzle of Stress, 1983, also Post Vention Manual Listner's Program for Broward County Mental Health Assn.; author parent edn. workbook for adolescents; editor: Adlerian Psychology Bull., 1983-86; contbr. articles to profl. jours. Leader various parent edn. groups, 1981—; bd. dirs. Kids In Distress, Inc., Henderson Mental Health Ctr., Inc., Nova Southeastern U. Lunch Forum; bd. dirs., pres. Kids In Distress Aux. West. Jennings Found. grantee, 1979; recipient Disting. Service award N.E. Ohio Tchrs. Assn., 1983, Nat. Disting. Svc. award Registry Counseling and Devel., 1990, Woman of the Yr. award, 1995, 1000+ Club award of the Am. Cancer Soc. Mem. AACD, N.Am. Soc. Adlerian Psychology (clin. mem., assembly del., Outstanding Woman award 1980), Am. Mental Health Counselors Assn., Fla. Assn. Counseling and Devel., Broward County Mental Health Assn. (adv. bd., bd. dirs. Kids in Distress Aux. West), Exec. Women Coral Springs, Am. Bus. Women's Assn., Fla. Speakers Assn., Broward County Assn. Counseling and Devel. (mem. exec. bd.), Coral Springs C. of C., Rotary, Gamma Phi Beta (pres. 1967-70). Avocations: tennis, travel, piano, watercolor painting. Office: 4653 N University Dr Coral Springs FL 33067-4620 Home: 12545 NW 57th Pl Coral Springs FL 33076-3468

CALDWELL, NAOMI RACHEL, library and information scientist, educator; b. Providence, Mar. 31, 1958; d. Atwood Alexander II and Juanita (Johnson) Caldwell; 1 child, William Earl Wood. BS, Clarion State Coll., 1980; MSLS, Clarion U. Pa., 1982; postgrad., Tex. A&M U., 1986—87, Providence Coll., 1990—92; PhD in Libr. and Info. Studies, U. Pitts., 2002. Cert. tchg. libr.; cert. libr. media specialist. Asst. dir., adult svcs. libr. Oil City (Pa.) Pub. Libr., 1984—85; microtext reference libr. Sterling C. Evans Libr., Tex. A&M U., College Station, 1985—87; libr. media specialist Nathan Bishop Mid. Sch., Providence, 1987—92; libr. sci. doctoral fellow dept. libr. sci. Sch. Libr. and Info. Sci. U. Pitts., 1992—94; sch. library media specialist Feinstein H.S. for Pub. Svc., Providence, 1994—99; asst. prof. U. R.I. Grad. Sch. Libr. Info. Studies, 2002—. Mem. discovery award com. U.S. Bd. on Books for Young People, 1994; mem. com. R.I. Children's Book Award, 1990—92, R.I. Read-Aloud, 1990—92; participant Native Am. and Alaskan Native Pre-Conf. to White House Conf. on Librs. and Info. Scis., Washington, 1991, George Washington U. Nat. Indian Policy Ctr. Forum on Native Am. Librs. and Info. Svcs., Washington, 1991; participant, del., spkr. Internat. Indigenous Librs. Forum, Auckland, New Zealand, 1999, Santa Fe, 2003;

hon. del. White House Conf. on Libr. and Info. Svcs., Washington, 1991; bd. dirs. Ocean State Freenet; mem. exec. bd. R.I. Ednl. Media Assn., 1996—97; cons. Am. Coll. Testing, 1995—; mem. exec. bd. Native Am. child literacy program If I Can Read, I Can Do Anything, 2001—; mem. Coalition Libr. Advocates, 2002—; del., spkr. Internat. Indigenous Libr. Forum, Santa Fe, 2003; presenter in field. Mem. editl. adv. bd., reviewer: Multicultural Rev., 1991—; mem. adv. bd. Native Ams. Info. Dir., 1992, OYATE, 1992—, Gale Ency. Multicultural Am., Native N.Am. Ref. Libr.; mem. exec. bd.: OYATE, 2001—; reviewer Clarion Books, Greenwood Press, Random House, Harcourt Brace Trade Divsn., Browndeer Press, Oryx Press; contbr. articles to profl. jours. Mem. State of R.I. Libr. Bd., 1996-97, Spl. Presdl. Adv. Com. on Libr. of Congress, 1996-97; mem. nominating com. R.I. chpt. Girl Scouts of Am., 1998-99; enrolled mem. Ramapough Lenape Tribe; bd. dirs. Tomaquaq Indian Mus., 2005—. Mem.: ALA (councilor-at-large 1992—96, chmn. com. on status of women in librarianship 1995—97, nominating com. 1996—97, legis. assembly 1996—98, councilor-at-large 1996—2000, assembly on planning and budget 1998—99, presdl. task force spectrum program, com. on coms. 1999—2000, spectrum jury com. 2001—02, com. on diversity 2001—04, pres.'s adv. com. 2003—04), R.I. Coalition of Libr. Advs. (sec. 2003), Native Am. N.E. Librs., Worcraft Cir. Native Writers and Storytellers, Windwalker Coalition, Libr. Adminstrn. Mgmt. Assn., Spl. Librs. Assn., Am. Assn. Sch. Librs., Am. Indian Libr. Assn. (new mems. round table publicity com. 1986, new mems. round table minority recruitment com. 1986—88, OLOS libr. svcs. for Am. Indian people subcom. 1986—88, ALCTS micropub. com. 1988—90, OLOS libr. svcs. for Am. Indian people subcom. 1990—91, pres. 1990—94, mem. coun. com. on minority concerns 1991—92, chmn. 1992—94, sec. 1994—96, mem. coun. com. on minority concerns 1994—96, chair book award task force 2004, chair youth book award com. 2005—). Home: 475 Sowams Rd Barrington RI 02806-2745 Office: U RI Grad Sch Libr and Info Studies 11 Rodman Hall Kingston RI 02881 Office Phone: 401-874-2278. E-mail: inpeacencw@aol.com.

CALDWELL, PAULETTE M., law educator; b. 1944; BS, Howard U., 1966, JD, 1969. Bar: NY 1972. Atty. Patterson, Belknap, Webb & Tyler, NYC, 1969-72, 1974-79; asst. counsel The Ford Found., NYC, 1972-74; asst. prof. NYU Sch. Law, 1979-80, assoc. prof., 1980-84, prof., 1984—. Office: NYU Sch Law Vanderbilt Hall Rm 318 40 Washington Sq S New York NY 10012-1099 Office Phone: 212-998-6192. E-mail: paulette.caldwell@nyu.edu.*

CALDWELL, PETER C., history professor; b. Ashland, Oreg., Oct. 11, 1965; s. Peter R. and Susan Havens Caldwell; m. Lora J. Wildenthal, July 27, 1996; 1 child, Vera Rebecca Margaret. BA, NYU, 1987; MA, Cornell U., 1989, PhD, 1993. Prof. Dept. of History, Rice U., Houston, 2003—, chair, dept. of history, 2003—. Author: (book) Popular Sovereignty and the Crisis of German Constitutional Law: The Theory and Practice of Weimar Constitutionalism, Dictatorship, State Planning, and Social Theory in the German Democratic Republic; editor: From Liberal Democracy to Fascism: Legal and Political Thought in the Weimar Republic. Recipient Charles Duncan award for Outstanding Acad. Achievement, Rice U., 2003, Faculty Tchg. and Mentoring award, Grad. Student Assn., Rice U., 2001; fellow Rsch. award, Alexander-von-Humboldt Stiftung, 2001—02; Postdoctoral fellow, Ctr. for German and European Studies, 1995—96, Doctoral fellow, DAAD, 1990—91. Atheist. Avocation: cooking. Office: Dept History Rice Univ 6100 Main St Houston TX 77251-1892 Office Phone: 713-348-4947. Office Fax: 713-348-5207. E-mail: caldwell@rice.edu.

CALDWELL, PHILIP, retired automobile manufacturing company executive, retired finance company executive; b. Bourneville, Ohio, Jan. 27, 1920; s. Robert Clyde and Wilhelmina (Hemphill) C.; m. Betsey Chinn Clark, Oct. 27, 1945; children: Lawrence Clark, Lucy Hemphill Caldwell-Stair (Mrs. Thomas O. Stair), Désirée Caldwell Armitage (Mrs. William F. Armitage, Jr.). BA in Econs., Muskingum Coll., 1940, HHD (hon.), 1974; MBA, Harvard U., 1942; DBA (hon.), Upper Iowa U., 1978; LLD (hon.), Boston U., 1979, Ea. Mich. U., 1979, Miami U., 1980, Davidson Coll., 1982, Ohio U., 1984, U. Mich., 1984, Lawrence Inst. Tech., 1984. Served to lt. USNR, 1942-46; civilian Navy Dept., 1946-53, dep. dir. procurement policy div., 1948-53; with Ford Motor Co., 1953-90, v.p., gen. mgr. truck ops., 1968-70; pres., dir. Philco-Ford Corp. subs., 1970-71, v.p. mfg. group N.Am. automotive ops., 1971-72; chmn., CEO Ford of Europe, Inc., 1972-73, exec. v.p. internat. automotive ops., 1973-77; dir. Ford of Europe Inc., Ford Latin Am., Ford Mideast and Africa, Ford Asia Pacific, 1973-85; vice chmn. bd. Ford Motor Co., 1977-79, dep. CEO, 1978-79, pres., 1978-80, CEO, 1979-85, chmn. bd. dirs., 1980-85, dir., 1973-90, Ford Motor Credit Co., Ford of Can., 1977-85; mem. Ford European Adv. Coun., 1976-88, chmn., 1987-88; sr. mng. dir. Lehman Bros. Inc., N.Y.C., 1985-98. Bd. dirs. Mettler-Toledo, Inc., 1998-2005, chmn., 1996-98, The Mex. Fund., Castech Aluminum Group, Inc., 1994-96, Chase Manhattan Corp., Chase Manhattan Bank NA, 1982-85; Digital Equipment Corp., 1980-95, Federated Dept. Stores Inc., 1984-88, Russell Reynolds Assocs., Inc., 1984-2005, The Kellogg Company, 1985-92, Shearson Lehman Bros. Holdings, 1985-93, Specialty Coatings Grp. Inc., 1991-93, Zurich Am. Ins. Group, 1987-99, Zurich Reinsurance Ctr. Holdings, 1993-97, Waters Corp., 1994-2005, Mettler-Toledo, Inc. 1998-2005; mem. policy com. The Bus. Roundtable, 1980-85, Bus. Coun., 1980-2001, Com. for Econ. Devel., 1979—, Conf. Bd., 1979—, Trilateral Commn., 1979-86; mem. U.S. Trade Rep. Adv. Com. for Trade Negotiations, 1983-85; mem. Pres.'s Export Coun., 1985-89; mem. Mex.-U.S. Bus. Com., 1985—; mem. adv. bd. Russell Reynolds Assocs, Inc., 2005—; adv. coun. Japan-U.S. Econ. Rels., 1981-85; dir. Japan Soc., 1983-89, vice chmn., chmn. exec. com. 1987-89; mem. motor truck com. Automobile Mfg. Assn., 1964-70; mem. transp. com. U.S. C. of C., 1968-77; mem. U.S. coun. Internat. C. of C., 1973-77, U.S. Coun. for Internat. Bus., 1977-85; mem. internat. adv. com. Chase Manhattan Bank, 1979-85; mem. Coun. Fgn. Rels., 1985—; mem. Zurich Fin. Svcs. Group U.S. Adv. Bd., 1999-2001. Trustee Muskingum Coll., 1967—, Winterthur Mus. and Gardens, 1986-2000; dir. Harvard Bus. Sch. Assocs., 1977-93; dir. Inst. Europeen de Adminstrn. des Affaires (INSEAD), 1978-81, chmn. U.S. adv. bd., 1979-84, mem. internat. coun., 1983-2002; bd. advisors The Jerome Levy Econs. Inst., 1988-2001; bus. adv. coun. Kent State U., 1968-70; mem. Merrill-Palmer Inst., 1971-81, New Detroit, Inc., vice-chair, 1977-85, Detroit Renaissance, 1979-85, dir. Detroit Symphony Orch., 1974-85; charter mem. Bus. Higher Edn. Forum, 1979-84; dir. Citizens Rsch. Coun. of Mich., 1980-85; hon. bd. mem. Plan Internat. USA, 1989—; dir. Econ. Club of Detroit, 1977-86. Recipient 1st William A. Jump Meml. award, 1950, Meritorious Civilian Svc. awardUS Navy Dept., 1953, Disting. Svc. Alumni award Muskingum Coll., 1978, Internat.Exec. of Yr. award Sch. Mgmt. Brigham Young U., 1983, Bus. Statesman of Yr. award Harvard Bus. Sch. Club Greater N.Y., 1984, Businessman of Yr. award Harvard Bus. Sch. Club Columbus, Ohio, 1984, Alumni Achievement award Harvard Bus. Sch.,1985; named Automotive Industry Leader of Yr. Automotive Hall of Fame, 1984; Harvard Bus. Sch. Philip Caldwell Professorship of Bus. Adminstrn. named in his honor, 1990; named Statesman of Yr. Harvard Bus. Sch. Club Detroit, 1991; elected laureate Nat. Bus. Hall of Fame, 1995. Mem. The Links, River Club (N.Y.C.). Office: Ford Motor Co W Bldg 225 High Ridge Rd Stamford CT 06905-3000 Fax: 203-357-8241.

CALDWELL, RICHARD H., lawyer; b. Pine Bluff, Ark., 1939; BS cum laude, U. Houston, 1960; LLB, Harvard Law Sch., 1963. Bar: Tex. 1963, US Ct. Appeals (5th Cir.), US Ct. Appeals (11th Cir.), US Dist. Ct. (No. Dist.) Tex., US Dist. Ct. (So. Dist.) Tex., US Dist. Ct. (Ea. Dist.) Tex., US Dist. Ct. (We. Dist.) Tex., US Supreme Ct. Ptnr., co-chmn. Litig. Sect. Andrews Kurth LLP, Houston, mem. mgmt. com. Bd. dir. U. Houston Law Sch. Found. Fellow: Internat. Acad. Trial Lawyers, Houston Bar Found., Tex. Bar Found.; mem.: State Bar Tex., ABA, Phi Kappa Phi, Omicron Delta Kappa. Office: Andrews Kurth LLP Ste 4200 600 Travis St Houston TX 77002-3090 Office Phone: 713-220-4712. Office Fax: 713-238-7361. Business E-Mail: rcaldwell@andrewskurth.com.

CALDWELL, STOKELY G., JR., lawyer; m. Julie Caldwell; 2 children. BA, Hampden-Sydney Coll., 1978; JD summa cum laude, Washington and Lee U., 1986. Bar: NC 1986. Banking officer Dominion Bankshares Corp., 1978—82, Bank of Boston, 1982—84; ptnr. Robinson, Bradshaw, & Hinson, P.A., Charlotte, NC, bd. dirs. Note and comment editor Washington and Lee Law Review. Com. mem. Found. Fighting Blindness; bd. dirs. Lakewood Preschool Cooperative, 2000—05, chmn., 2003, Charlotte Preschool Partnership, 2004. Mem.: Sports Lawyers Assn. (bd. dirs.), NC Bar Assn. (bd. gov., chair sports and entertainment law section), Order of Coif, Omicron Delta Kappa. Office: Robinson Bradshaw & Hinson PA 101 N Tryon St Ste 1900 Charlotte NC 28246-1900 Office Phone: 704-377-2536. Business E-Mail: scaldwell@rbh.com.

CALDWELL, SUSAN HAVENS, art educator; b. Clinton, Okla., June 9, 1938; d. Charles Hayes and Mary Jane (Oberer) Havens; m. Peter Richard Caldwell, Aug. 30, 1961; children: Margaret Elizabeth Caldwell Mesander, Peter Charles. BA, Washburn U., 1961; PhD, Cornell U., 1974. Asst. prof. art history dept. art Boise (Idaho) State U., 1974-76; asst. prof. Sch. Art U. Okla., Norman, 1976-81, assoc. prof., 1981—2004, prof., 2004—, asst. dir. MA program in art history. Author (co-prodr.): (films) And They Sang a New Song: 24 Musical Elders at Santiago de Compostela, 1989; contbr. articles to profl. jours.; author: (exhbn. catalog) Art of the Sixties, 2002, (monograph) Queen Sancha's Persuasion: A Regenerated Leon Symbolized in San Isidero's Pantheon and its Treasures, 2000. Recipient Arts and Edn. award, Gov. Okla., 1994, Irene and Julian J. Rothbaum Presdl. Prof. of Excellence in Arts award, Okla. U. Coll. Fine Arts, 2003; fellow, Samuel H. Kress Found., 1968—69; grantee, U.S.-Spanish Joint Com. Cultural Coop., 1986—87. Mem.: NOW, Soc. Hispanic Art Hist. Studies U.S., Internat. Ctr. Medieval Art, Coll. Art Assn. Am. Democrat. Office: Univ Okla Sch of Art 520 Parrington Oval Norman OK 73019-3010 Office Phone: 405-325-3252. Personal E-mail: shcaldwell@ou.edu.

CALDWELL, WESLEY STUART, III, lawyer, lobbyist; b. Teaneck, NJ, June 3, 1946; s. Wesley S. Jr. and Helen Skrek C.; m. Theresa Hale, Apr. 20, 1970 (div. Jan. 1988); children: Ashley Hale, Ferris Elena; m. J.R. Dillenback, May 27, 1988. BA in Liberal Arts, Fairleigh Dickinson U., 1968; JD, Rutgers U., 1975. Bar: N.J. 1975, U.S. Dist. Ct. N.J. 1975, U.S. Supreme Ct. 1992. Dep. atty. gen. N.J. Atty. Gen.'s Office, Trenton, 1975-78; assoc. gen. counsel Prudential Reins. Co., Newark, 1978-79; v.p. Am. Ins. Assn., N.Y.C., 1979-86; ptnr. LeBoeuf, Lamb, Greene & MacRae, Newark, 1986-95, Caldwell Megna & Brewster, Trenton, 1995-97, Caldwell Megna, Trenton, 1997—2001; ins. regulatory atty. Wesley S. Caldwell III Law Offices, Trenton, 2002—. Regulatory counsel AFLAC, Columbus, Ga., 1991—, Clarendon Ins., N.Y.C.; others. With U.S. Army, 1969-72. Mem. N.J. Bar Assn. (past chmn. ins. law sect.). Avocations: golf, pocket billiards. Home: 180 Aqueduct Rd Washington Crossing PA 18977 Office: 224 W State St Trenton NJ 08608-1002 Office Phone: 609-396-2000. Business E-Mail: wscaldwell@inslawcaldwell.com.

CALDWELL-SMITH, GAETANA LEE, writer; d. Ennis Combs Caldwell and Maria Esperanza Ilya-Salituri Sanchez Hill; children: Roark Smith, Terrence Smith, Douglas Smith. BA cum laude, San Francisco State U., 1994. Comml. ins. underwriter Fireman's Fund Ins. Co., San Francisco, 1978—84; account rep. Marsh & McLennan Ins. Co., San Francisco, 1984—97; theatre writer Socialist Action Newspaper, San Francisco, 1998—2002. Author: (solo performance plays) The Cynthia Trilogy: Part I, The Sign, 1996 (1st prize Dominican Players, San Rafael, Calif., 1998); actor: (solo perfornace) The Cynthia Trilogy: Part I, The Sign, 1996 (2nd prize Dominican Players, San Rafael, Calif., 1998). Mem.: Wild Plum (writer 2001—02), San Francisco Bay Area Theatre Critics Cir. (theatre writer 2001—02). Avocations: swimming, bicycling, hiking.

CALE, CHARLES GRIFFIN, lawyer, real estate analyst; b. St. Louis, Aug. 19, 1940; s. Julian Dutro and Judith Hadley (Griffin) C.; m. Jessie Leete Rawn, Dec. 30, 1978; children: Whitney Rawn, Walter Griffin, Elizabeth Judith. BA, Principia Coll., Elsah, Ill., 1961; LLB, Stanford U., 1964; LLM, U. So. Calif., 1966. Bar: Calif. 1965. Pvt. practice, L.A., 1965—81, 1985—90; ptnr. Adams, Duque & Hazeltine, L.A., 1970—81, Morgan, Lewis & Bockius, L.A., 1985—90. Bd. dirs., co-chmn., CEO World Cup USA 1994, Inc., L.A., 1991. Group v.p. sports L.A. Olympic Organizing Com., 1982-84; assoc. counselor U.S. Olympic Com., 1985, spl. asst. to pres., 1985-89, asst. to pres, dir. olympic del., 1989-92; bd. dirs. Century 21 Real Estate-Can. Ltd., 1995-97, Rapattoni Corp., 2001—, Foresters Equity Svcs. Corp., 2001—. Trustee St. John's Hosp. and Med. Ctr., Santa Monica, Marymount H.S.; asst. chief de mission U.S. Olympic Team, 1988; bd. dirs. Hallum Prevention of Child Abuse Fund, 1976-96. Recipient Gold medal of Youth and Sports, France, 1984. Mem.: State Bar Calif., Ind. Order Foresters (bd. dirs. 1993—2001), Eagle Springs Golf Club, The Beach Club, L.A. Country Club, Calif. Club. Office: PO Box 688 Pacific Palisades CA 90272-0688

CALE, WILLIAM GRAHAM, JR., environmental sciences educator, university administrator, researcher; b. Phila., Dec. 10, 1947; s. William Graham and Kathryn (Rowland) C.; m. Betty Jean Byrd, June 8, 1974. B.S., Pa. State U., 1969; Ph.D. in Zoology, U. Ga., 1975. Asst. prof. ecology and environ. scis. U. Tex.-Dallas, Richardson, 1975-80, assoc. prof. environ. scis., 1980-87, full prof. 1987-89, assoc. dean Sch. Natural Scis. and Math., 1983-85, 87-89, chmn. dept. environ. scis., 1984-89; dean Coll Natural Scis. and Math. Ind. Univ. Pa., 1989-94; exec. v.p. for acad. affairs Lamar U., Beaumont, Tex., 1994—; vis. sci. Oak Ridge Nat. Lab., 1981, 84, 85. Mem. NSF grant adv. panel, 1985-88, Dept. Energy grant rev. panel, 1989-90; contbr. articles to profl. jours. NSF grantee, 1978, 81, 83, 85. Mem. Ecol. Soc. Am., Am. Inst. Biol. Scis., Internat. Assn. for Ecology, Internat. Soc. for Ecol. Modelling, Sigma Xi. Democrat. Avocations: tournament bridge, golf. Office: Lamar U PO Box 10002 Beaumont TX 77710-0002

CALEGARI, MARIA, ballerina; b. NYC, Mar. 30, 1957; d. Richard A. and Marion (Gentile) C. Student, DuPons Dance Studio, Queens, 1960-66, Ballet Acad., 1966-71, Sch. Am. Ballet, 1971-74. Mem. corps de ballet N.Y.C. Ballet, 1974-81, soloist, 1981-83, prin., 1983-94; guest artist Richmond Ballet, 1996—; artistic dir. dance Conn. Conservatory of the Performing Arts, New Milford, 2002—; artistic dir. The Maria Calegari Schl of Ballet, New Milford, Conn., 2003—. Artist-in-residence Richmond Ballet, Richmond Ctr. for Dance, State Ballet of Va., 1997—98, Conn. Cons. of Performing Arts, New Milford, 1999—. Dancer in N.Y.C. Ballet's Balanchine Celebration, 1993, Celebrating Balanchine, Kennedy Ctr., 1995. Repétiteur George Balanchine Trust, Robbins Rights Trust. Recipient Alumni award Profl. Children's Sch., 1986. Address: 404 Richardsville Rd Carmel NY 10512-3771 E-mail: mcale50064@aol.com.

CALELLO, PAUL, banker; b. N.Y.C., Feb. 14, 1961; BA, Villanova (Pa.) U., 1983; MBA, Columbia U., 1987. With global mktgs. divsn. Bankers Trust Co., N.Y.C., 1986, 87; v.p., sr. risk mgr. equity derivatives products (Asia) Derivative Products of Asia/Bankers Trust Internat., Tokyo, 1987-90; dir./mng. dir., head derivatives products trading Asia Credit Suisse First Boston (Japan) Ltd./Credit Suisse Fin., Tokyo, 1990-92; mng. dir., head N.Am. fixed income, global equities trading Credit Suisse Fin. Products, London, 1992-94; mng. dir., mem. global equity operating com. CS First Boston, N.Y.C., 1994-95; pres. CSFP Capital Inc., N.Y.C., 1994-99; mng. dir., mem. exec. bd., mgmt. co., co-head trading Credit Suisse Fin. Products, N.Y.C., 1994-99, head mktg. for the Ams., 1994-99; mem. fixed income and equity mgmt. com. Credit Suisse First Boston, N.Y.C., 1997, mng. dir., global head equity derivatives/convertibles, 1997—2002, mem. global oper. com. and firms exec. bd., 2000—, chmn. and CEO, Asia Pacific region, 2002—. Bd. dirs. CSFB Long Term Capital Ptnrs., N.Y.C., 1998—. Trustee charitable contbns. Credit Suisse First Boston Found., N.Y.C., 1999—. Office: Credit Suisse First Boston 11 Madison Ave Fl 3D New York NY 10010-3629

CALENDAR, RICHARD LANE, biochemistry educator; b. Hackensack, N.J., Aug. 2, 1940; s. Howard L. and Jean (Wappler) C.; m. Gunilla Viola Jansen, Jan. 6, 1969 (div. Sept. 1983); children: Hugo Raphael, Johanna Magdalena. BS in Chemistry, Duke U., 1962; PhD in Biochemistry, Stanford U., 1967. Helen Hay Whitney fellow Karolinska Inst., Stockholm, 1966-68; mem. faculty dept. cell and molecular biology U. Calif., Berkeley, 1968—, asst. prof. to prof., 1968—76. Alexander von Humboldt fellow, Munich, 1973, Guggenheim fellow, Stockholm, 1979-80. Home: 940 Euclid Ave Berkeley CA 94708-1436 Office: U Calif 401 Barker Hall Berkeley CA 94720-3208

CALETTI, DEB L., writer; b. San Rafael, Calif., June 16, 1963; d. Paul Albert Caletti and Evelyn Ann Siler; m. Elliott Wolf, 2004 (div. July 1999); children: Samantha Bannon, Nicholas Bannon. BA in Journalism, U. Wash., 1985. Mem. adv. bd. Bellevue (Wash.) C.C. Ctr. for Liberal Arts; spkr. and lyricist. Author: The Queen of Everything, 2002, Honey, Baby, Sweetheart, 2003 (Nat. Book Award finalist, 2004, Pacific N.W. Bookseller Assn. award, 2005, Best Books of 2004 award, Calif. Young Reader medal finalist, 2005, Internat. Reading Assn. Notable Children's Book award, 2005, Soc. of Sch. Librs. Internat. Book Awards Honor Book), Wild Roses, 2005. Literary fellow, Artist Trust-Wash. State Arts Commn., 2001. Mem.: PEN USA, Amnesty Internat. Avocations: painting, writing.

CALEVAS, HARRY POWELL, management consultant; b. Williamsburg, Va., Nov. 18, 1918; s. Gus and Elizabeth (Powell) C.; m. Betty Nicoolette Chronaker, July 4, 1939 (wid. Nov. 1989); children: Philip H., Stanley P.; m. Jenny Steele. Diploma in mech. engring., Case Sch. Applied Scis., Cleve., 1939; MBA, Pacific Western U., 1980, DBA, 1985. Lic. real estate broker, real estate property mgr., Fla. Real Estate Commn. V.p., gen. mgr. Radisson Hotel, Mpls., 1949-53; v.p. Banker Life & Casualty, Chgo., 1953-63; pres. Fla. Bd. Trade, Ft. Lauderdale, 1963-95. Author: Condominium Management Handbook, 1985, The Wandering Moon, 1994, Positive Way to Profit, 1965; author twelve cookbooks/internat. food recipes. Capt. Merchant Marines, ATO. Mem. Am. Legion, SAR, Decendants George Washington, Optimist Club (bd. dirs. 1990-96). Republican. Baptist. Avocations: writing, golf, travel, tennis. Home: 1010 S Ocean Blvd Apt 803 Pompano Beach FL 33062-6630 Fax: 954-782-2023.

CALFEE, ROBERT CHILTON, psychologist, educator; b. Lexington, Ky., Jan. 26, 1933; s. Robert Klair and Nancy Bernice (Stipp) C.; m. Nel Pearl Little, June 30, 1991. BA, UCLA, 1959, MA, 1960, PhD, 1963. Asst. prof. psychology U. Wis., 1964-66, assoc. prof., 1966-69; assoc. prof. edn. Stanford U., 1969-71, prof., 1971-98, prof. emeritus, 1998—; assoc. dean research and devel., dir. Center for Ednl. Research, 1976-80; with Sch. Edn. U. Calif., Riverside, 1998—. Cons. and speaker in field; vice-chmn. State of Calif. Commn. for Establishment of Acad. Content and Performance Stds., 1996-2002; mem. com. on equivalancy and linkage of ednl. tests NRC/NAS, 1998-2000, Energy and Edn. Task Force, 2005-; mem. ednl. adv. bd., Leapfrog Edn., 1997-. Author: Human Experimental Psychology, 1975, Cognitive Psychology and Educational Practice, 1982, Experimental Methods in Psychology, 1985, Handbook of Educational Psychology, Teach Our Children Well, 1995, (with Marilyn J. Chambliss) Textbooks for Learning, 1999; editor: Jour. Ednl. Psychology, 1984-90, Ednl. Assessment, 1992-2002. Trustee Palo Alto (Calif.) Sch. Dist., 1984-88; vice chair Calif. Commn. for Ednl. Stds. NCO USAF, 1953—57. Guggenheim Meml. fellow, 1972; fellow Center for Advanced Study in Behavioral Scis., 1981-82 Fellow AAAS, APA; mem. Am. Ednl. Rsch. Assn., Internat. Reading Assn. (named to Hall of Fame), Nat. Conf. Rsch. in English, Psychonomic Soc., Nat. Coun. Tchrs. English, Nat. Soc. Study of Edn. (bd. trustees), Sigma Xi. Home: 215 Bathurst Rd Riverside CA 92506-6129 Office: U Calif Sch Edn 1207 Sproul Hall Riverside CA 92521-0001 Office Phone: 951-827-5802. Office Fax: 951-533-0034. Business E-Mail: robert.calfee@ucr.edu.

CALHOUN, CRAIG JACKSON, social scientist, educator; b. Watseka, Ill., June 16, 1952; s. Jay Robert and Audrey Thelma (Jackson) C.; m. Pamela Frances DeLargy, Aug. 2, 1980. BA, U. So. Calif., 1972; MA, Columbia U., 1974, U. Manchester (Eng.), 1975; D Phil, Oxford U. (Eng.), 1980. Rsch. assoc. Columbia U., N.Y.C., 1972-74; instr. U. N.C., Chapel Hill, 1977-80, asst. prof. sociology, 1980-85, assoc. prof., 1985-89, prof. sociology and history, 1989-96; prof. NYU, 1996—, chair dept. sociology, 1996-99; pres. Social Sci. Rsch. Coun., N.Y.C., 1999—. Tech. advisor U.S. AID, Govt. of Sudan, 1984-86; dir. program in social theory and cross-cultural studies U. N.C., 1989-95, office of internat. programs 1990-93, chmn. curriculum in internat. studies, 1990-93, dir. Univ. Ctr. for Internat. Studies, 1993-96; vis. prof. dept. sociology, U. Oslo, 1991-97; vis. fellow Swedish Collegium for Advanced Study in Social Scis., 1994; rsch. fellow Ctr. for Transcultural Studies-Ctr. for Psychosocial Studies, Chgo., 1983; Irene Flecknoe Ross lectr., UCLA, 1994-5; Harry Bridges lectr. U. Wash., 1995, Howard W. Beers lectr. U. Ky., 1997, Benjamin J. Meaker Disting. vis. prof. U. Bristol, 2000. Author: The Question of Class Struggle, 1982; co-author: Sociology, 1988, Neither Gods Nor Emperors: Students and the Struggle for Democracy in China, 1995, Critical Social Theory: Culture, History, and the Challenge of Difference, 1995, Nationalism, 1997; editor: The Anthropological Study of Education, 1976: Habermas and the Public Sphere, 1992, Sociological Theory, 1994-99, Hannah Arendt and the Meaning of Politics, 1997, Dictionary of the Social Science, 2002, Understanding September 11, 2002; contbr. numerous articles to profl. jours. Recipient Kellogg Found. fellow, 1982-85; R.J. Reynolds Fund award U. N.C. 1985, Disting. Contrbn. to Scholarship award Am. Sociol. Assn. Fellow Royal Anthrop. Inst.; mem. Am. Sociol. Assn. (chair sect. comparative hist. sociology 1984-85, chair com. on internat. sociology 1988-92, chair sect. on theoretics of sociology, 1991-92; coun. mem. 2000—), Sociol. Rsch. Assn., Soc. for Comparative Rsch. Address: SSRC 810 7th Ave New York NY 10019-5818 Office: NYU Dept Sociology 269 Mercer St New York NY 10003-6633 E-mail: craig.calhoun@nyu.edu.

CALHOUN, DAVID L., manufacturing executive; Grad., Va. Poly. Inst., 1979; completed the GE Fin. Mgmt. program. Joined the GE corp. audit staff Gen. Electric Co., 1981, mgr. of programs and planning GE corp. audit staff, 1986, apptd. staff exec. at the GE Corp. Exec. office, 1989; mgr. of mktg. for the Americas GE Plastics, 1989; v.p. of audit staff Gen. Electric Corp.; pres. of the Pacific region GE Plastics, 1994—95; pres.,CEO GE Trans. Sys., 1995—97; pres., CEO GE Lighting, 1997—99; named pres., CEO GE Employers Reinsurance Co., 1999—2000; pres., CEO GE Aircraft Engines, 2000—03, GE Transp., 2003—05; vice chmn. GE Infrastructure, 2005—. Office: General Electric Co 3135 Easton Turnpike Fairfield CT 06828*

CALHOUN, JIM, college basketball coach; m. Patricia McDevitt; children: James, Jeffrey. BA in Sociology, Am. Internat. Coll., 1968. Asst. basketball coach Am. Internat. Coll., 1966-68; head coach basketball Old Lyme H.S., Conn., 1969, Westport (Mass.) H.S., 1970, Dedham H.S., Mass., 1971-72; head coach Northeastern U., U. Conn., 1986—. Author: (novels) Dare to Dream: Connecticut Basketball's Remarkable March to the National Championship, 1999. Past chair Ronald McDonald Houses, We. New England; hon. chmn. Conn. chpt. Am. Cancer Soc.; hon. chmn. New Haven Pub. Edn. Fund; mem. adv. staff we. region Big. Bros./Big Sisters; mem. nat. adv. bd. Ctr. for the Study of Sports in Soc.; hon. chmn. Conn. Sports Mus. and Hall of Fame, greater Hartford chpt. Juvenile Diabetes Found. Named Coach of the Yr.,1990, Big East Coach of the Yr., 1990, 1994, 1996, 1998; winner NCAA Big East Title, 1999; NCAA Divsn. I champs 1999, 2004; NIT Champions, 1988. Mem. Nat. Assn. Basketball Coaches (mem. nom. com. Hall of Fame), Big East Conf. Coaches Assn. (pres.). Office: Univ of Connecticut 2095 Hillside Rd Storrs Mansfield CT 06269-9017

CALHOUN, JOHN ALFRED, social services administrator; b. Phila., Dec. 1, 1939; s. John Alfred and Helen Fordham (Webster) C.; m. Ottilia Klenota, May 29, 1971; children: Byron, Hollis. BA, Brown U., 1962; M in Div., Episcopal Div. Sch., Cambridge, Mass., 1965; MPA, Harvard U., 1986; DHL (hon.), Heidelberg Coll., 2001. Tchr. Phila. pub. schs., 1965-66; program adminstr. Action for Boston Community Devel., 1966-70; v.p. Tech. Devel. Corp., Boston, 1970-73; exec. dir., founder Justice Resource Inst., Boston, 1973-76; commr. Mass. Dept. of Youth Svcs., Boston, 1976-79, U.S. Adminstrn. for Children, Youth and Families, Washington, 1979-81; v.p., dir. Ctr. for Govtl. Affairs Child Welfare League, Washington, 1981-83; pres., CEO Nat. Crime Prevention Coun., Washington, 1983—. V.p. Internat. Ctr.

for the Prevention of Crime; bd. dirs. Ctr. for Internat. Leadership, D.C., The Nat. Assembly of Voluntary Health and Social Welfare Ags., Childrens Trust Neighborhood Initiative; assoc. in edn. Harvard U., 1978; moderator Aspen Inst., 1980—; founder Pre-trial Diversion Programs, Mass., Urban Ct. Mediation Cmty. Sentencing, Mass., Cmty. Responses to Drug Abuse, 10 Sites Across the U.S.; mem. U.S. Atty. Gen.'s Coordinating Coun. on Juvenile Justice; founder Youth as Resources., Mass. and Ind., Ctr. for Faith and Svc., Teens, Crime and the Cmty.(nationwide); adv. bd. Nat. League of Cities Children and Youth subcom. Author: What, Me Evaluate?, 1986; editor: Crime in Urban Communities, 1986, Making a Difference, 1985, Reaching Out: School-based Community Service Programs, Teen Crime and the Community, National Service and Public Safety: Partnerships for Safer Communities, Taking the Offensive: How Seven Cities Did It, Changing Communities Through Faith in Action:Crime Prevenation in the New Millenium, Philanthropy and Faith; contbr. articles to profl. jours. Coach McLean (Va.) Youth; tchr. confirmation class Louisville Presbyn. Ch., McLean; state chmn. Mass. Adolescent Task Force, 1978; chmn. Mass. State of the Family Task Force, 1979; pres. Franklin Flaschner Found., 1978; treas. Met. Beaverbrook Area Mental Health Bd.; bd. advisors U. Mass. Coll. Cmty. Pub. Svc., 1979; bd. dirs. Edna Stein Acad., Boston, Pekinese Island Sch., Woods Hole, Mass.; mem. adv. bd. Va. Dept. for Children, 1990-94, Operation Kids, Advertising Council Inc. Littauer fellow Harvard U. Kennedy Sch. of Govt., 1986; recipient award of Recognition Am. Arbitration Assn., 1978, award of Recognition, U.S. Office Juvenile Justice and Delinquency Prevention, 1998, Spirit of Crazy Horse award Reclaiming Youth Internat., 2002. Mem. Am. Probation/ Parole Assn. (prevention com.). Democrat. Presbyterian. Avocations: photography, tennis, gardening, coaching, skiing. Home: 921 Mackall Ave Mc Lean VA 22101-1617 Office: Nat Crime Prevention Coun Office Pres & CEO 13th Fl 1000 Connecticut Ave NW Washington DC 20036-5302 E-mail: hopematters@cox.net.

CALHOUN, JOHN C., JR., academic administrator; b. Betula, Pa., Mar. 21, 1917; s. John C. and Martha (Rowe) C.; m. Ruth Elizabeth Huston, June 10, 1941; children: John, Emily, Mary Beth, Ruth Ellen. BS in Petroleum and Natural Gas Engring., Pa. State U., 1937, MS, 1941, PhD, 1946; DSc (hon.), Ripon Coll., 1975. Research asst., instr. petroleum and natural gas engring. Pa. State U., 1937-46, prof., head dept. petroleum and natural gas engring., 1950-55; assoc. prof., then prof. Sch. Petroleum Engring., U. Okla., 1946-50, chmn., 1948-50; dean Sch. Engring. Tex. Agrl. and Mech. Coll., College Station, 1955-57; dir. Engring. Expt. Sta., Engring. Ext. Service Tex. Agrl. and Mech. U., College Station, 1955-57, v.p. engring., 1957-59, vice chancellor for engring., 1959-60, vice chancellor for devel., 1960-63, v.p. programs, 1965-71, Disting. prof. petroleum engring., 1965-83, dir. Office Sea Grant Programs, 1968-72, dean geoscis., 1969-71, v.p. acad. affairs, 1971-77, exec. vice chancellor for programs Tex. A&M U. System, 1977-80, dep. chancellor for engring., 1980-83; dir. Crisman Inst. Petroleum Reservoir Mgmt., 1984-87; dep. chancellor for engring. emeritus Tex. A&M U. Sys., College Station, 1983—; asst., sci. advisor to sec. Dept. Interior, Washington, 1963-65. Vice chmn. Engring. Coll. Rsch. Coun., 1959-62; mem. Fed. Coun. for Sci. and Tech., 1963-65, Presdl. Task Force on Oceanography, 1969, Nat. Adv. Coun. on Oceans and Atmosphere, 1971-72, Tex. Coastal and Marine Coun., 1972-83; acting dir. Office Water Resources Rsch., 1964; mem. environ. pollution panel Pres.'s Sci. Adv. Com., 1964-66; chmn. com. on oceanography NAS, 1967-70, chmn. ocean sci. affairs bd., 1970-72; chmn. Pres.'s Santa Barbara Oil Spill Panel and Panel on Union Oil Lease, 1969; mem. adv. panel Internat. Decade Ocean Exploration, NSF, 1970-72; mem. nat. adv. coun. on minorities in engring. Nat. Acad. Engring., 1973-74; mem. naval studies bd. Nat. Acad. Scis., 1974-79; bd. dirs. Inst. Nautical Archeology, 1976-86; dir. Tex. Petroleum Rsch. Com., 1978-82; cons. So. Regional Edn. Bd., 1953-54, Pa. Dept. Forests & Waters, 1955, World Bank, 1978-85, Coun. Internat. Edn. Exch., 1988-92; mem. rsch. coordination panel Gas Rsch. Inst., 1977-82; mem. adv. com. on mining and mineral resources rsch. Dept. Interior, 1987-94. Author: Fundamentals of Reservoir Engineering, 1953; contbr. articles to profl. jours. Chmn. Coll. Sta. United Fund, 1961; trustee U. Corp. for Atmospheric Rsch., 1969-71, chmn. bd., 1968-71; trustee Tex. Agrl. and Mech. Rsch. Found., 1961-82, Tex. Inst. for Rehab. and Rsch., 1981-82; bd. dirs. EDUCOM, 1966-69, Houston Area Rsch. Ctr., 1982-83; exec. dir., pres. Gulf Univs. Rsch. Corp., 1966-69. Recipient 15th Sea Grant award Sea Grant Assn., 1984, Lifetime Achievement award Dwight Look Coll. Engring., Tex. A&M U., 2001; alumni fellow Pa. State U., 1976. Fellow AAAS, Marine Tech. Soc. (pres. 1975-76), Am. Soc. Engring. Edn. (v.p., dir. 1968-72, pres. 1974, Centennial medallion 1993, Collins award 1996); mem. Nat. Acad. Engring., Engrs. Coun. Profl. Devel. (bd. dirs. 1964-67), Engrs. Joint Coun. (bd. dirs. 1972-77), AIME (hon.), Soc. Petroleum Engrs. (pres. 1964, DeGolyer medal 1982, Anthony F. Lucas Gold medal 1997), Am. Assn. Engring. Socs. (mem. exec. com. internat. affairs coun. 1980-81), Sigma Xi, Tau Beta Pi, Sigma Gamma Epsilon, Phi Kappa Phi, Tau Kappa Epsilon. Presbyterian. Home: 1106 Ashburn Ave College Station TX 77840-2502

CALHOUN, JOHN R., lawyer; m. Elizabeth Calhoun; four children. BA in Polit. Sci., U. Iowa, 1956, JD, 1958. Bar: Iowa, 1958, Calif. 1960, U.S. Ct. Appeals (9th cir.) 1987, U.S. Ct. Appeals (fed. cir.) 1997, U.S. Dist. Ct. (cen. dist.) Calif. 1960, U.S. Supreme Ct. 1963, U.S. Ct. Mil. Appeals 1963. Commd. 2d lt. U.S. Army Res., 1958, advanced through grades to col., JAG Corp., ret., 1988; atty. U.S. Securities and Exch. Commn., 1960, Automobile Club of So. Calif., 1960-61; dep. dist. atty. L.A. Dist. Atty.'s Office, 1961-62; dep. city prosecutor Long Beach (Calif.) City Prosecutor's Office, 1962-67; dep. city atty. Long Beach City Atty.'s Office, 1967-78, asst. city atty., 1978-85, city atty., 1985-98; commr., pres. Long Beach Harbor Commn., 1999—2005. Decorated Legion of Merit, Meritorious Svc. medal. Mem. Calif. Bar Assn., Long Beach Bar Assn. (bd. govs. 1974-75, 87-88), Rotary, Res. Officers Assn., Long Beach Area C. of C., Phi Delta Phi, Phi Delta Theta. Home: 4011 Chestnut Ave Long Beach CA 90807-3207

CALHOUN, JOSEPH PATRICK, economics professor, researcher; b. Elgin, Ill., Oct. 30, 1967; s. William Patrick Calhoun and Violet Lucille Mihevc; m. Kimberly Rose Rasmussen, Apr. 27, 1996; children: Tayla Rose, Savannah May, Kendra Miriam Joy. BS, Ill. State U., 1990; MBA, DePaul U., 1997; PhD, U. Ga., 2003. Underwriter The Travelers Ins. Co., Naperville, Ill., 1990—93; cons. Deloitte & Touche, San Francisco, 1993—94; sr. underwriter BlueCross BlueShield Ill., Chgo., 1994—97, United HealthCare, Schaumburg, Ill., 1997—99; grad. student instr. U. Ga., Dept. Econ., Athens, Ga., 1999—2005; lectr., asst. dir. Stavros Ctr. for Econ. Edn., Fla. State U., Tallahassee, 2005—. Asst. dir. Stavros Ctr. for Econ. Edn., Tallahassee, 2004. Recipient Grad. Tchg. award, U. Ga., 2003. Mem.: Nat. Assn. Econ. Educators (assoc.), Nat. Coun. Econ. Edn. (assoc.), Assn. for Instl. Rsch. (assoc.), Assn. for Study of Higher Edn. (assoc.), Am. Econ. Assn. (assoc.). Conservative. Methodist. Avocations: landscaping, construction, biking. Home: 2804 Shamrock St N Tallahassee FL 32309 Office: Fla State U 250 S Woodward Ave Tallahassee FL 32306 Office Phone: 850-644-7723. Home Fax: 850-644-7795. E-mail: jcalhoun@fsu.edu.

CALHOUN, LAWRENCE, psychology educator; b. Lavras, Brazil; came to U.S., 1963; BA, St. Andrews Presbyn. Coll., 1967; MA, Xavier U., Cin., 1969; PhD, U. Ga., 1973. Psychology educator Univ. N.C., Charlotte, 1973—. Author: Dealing With Crisis, 1976, Psychology and Human Reproduction, 1980, Trauma and Transformation, 1995, Facilitating Posttraumatic Growth, 1999; contbr. articles to profl. jours. Office: U NC Psychology Dept Charlotte NC 28223

CALHOUN, NOAH ROBERT, oral maxillofacial surgeon, educator; b. Clarendon, Ark., Mar. 23, 1921; s. Noah and Della (Sherman) Calhoun; m. Cecelia Christopher, Oct. 19, 1950; children: Stephen Marc, Cecelia Noel. DDS, Dental Sch., Howard U., 1948; M.Dental Sci., Tufts Med. and Dental Sch., 1955. Oral surgeon VA Hosp., Tuskegee, Ala., 1950—52, Kessler AFB, Biloxi, Miss., 1952—53; chief dental service VA Hosp., Tuskegee, Ala., 1955—57, oral surgeon, asst. chief dental surgeon Washington, 1964—74; chief dental service, oral surgeon VA Med. Center, Washington, 1974—; prof. oral surgery Dental Sch., Howard U., Washington, 1966—92, Georgetown U., Washington, 1975—93; prof. emeritus Dental Coll. Howard U., 1992—. Dir. Tuskegee Red Cross, Ala., 1962—64; chmn. Nat. Concerned VA Dentists, 1975, Inst. Medicine-NAS, 1975. Sect. editor Current Lit. in Internat. Oral/Maxillofacial Surgery, 1986, mem. editl. bd. Jour. Oral and Maxillofacial Surveys, 1993; contbr. articles to profl. jours. Mem. fin. com. St. Michael Ch., Silver Spring, Md. Mem.: NAACP (trustee D.C. chpt.), ADA, Inst. Medicine of NAS, Am. Coll. Dentistry, Internat. Coll. Dentistry, Am. Soc. Oral and Maxillofacial Surgeons (Audio Visual award 1978), Bridge Masters Washington (pres.), Omicron Kappa Upsilon. Roman Catholic. Office: Dental Coll Howard U Washington DC 20001 Office Phone: 202-882-1846. Personal E-mail: ncalh@aol.com.

CALHOUN, RAMONA, human services administrator, academic administrator, consultant; b. Akron, Ohio, Sept. 2, 1950; d. Howell and Rebecca (Hammonds) C.; m. William J. Webb, Sept. 1969 (div. 1973); 1 child, Forrest J. Webb. BS, U. Akron, 1980; MS, SUNY, Oswego, 1988; PhD, Walden U., 2001. Sales corr./sec. Monsanto Co., Akron, Ohio, 1973-77; student instr./career guide U. Akron; instr. SUNY Delhi Coll., Delhi, 1980-82; Dept. chair-bus. SUNY Morrisville Edn. Opportunity Ctr., Syracuse, 1983-88; dir. program opns., Job Tng. Partnership Agy. City of Syracuse, 1988—91; dir., student svcs, grants Ivy Tech State Coll., 1991—95; acad. dir. Ctr. Ohio Tech Coll. Artist charcoal sketch Portrait in Bronze (Best of Show, 1990); writer-poet Rain Dance, 1979; contbr. poetry to African Am. Jour. Bd. dirs. YWCA of Syracuse and Onandaga, 1990-92, City/County Youth Bd., 1989-91; com. mem. N.Y. State Task Force on the Older Worker, Albany, 1990-91, N.Y. State Task Force for Career Pathways for Youth. Recipient Leadership award, SUNY Oswego, 1988. Mem. N.Y. Assn. Tng. and Employment Profls., Partnership for Employment and Tng. Avocations: reading, writing (short stories, poetry, novels), painting.

CALHOUN-MCKEON, MARIANNE, elementary school educator, home economist, educator; b. N.Y., Mar. 1, 1957; d. James Joseph and Mary Ellen Calhoun; m. Peter Gerard McKeon, Apr. 20, 1985. BS in Family and Consumer Studies, CUNY, 1980, MS in Home Econs., 1990. Cert. Am. Assn. Family and Consumer Scis., 1987. Editl. asst. H.W. Wilson Pubs., Bronx, NY, 1980—85; tchr. Inwood Intermediate Sch., N.Y., 1986—. Photographer: Teens in Action, 1989, Exploring Life Skills, 1991, Work and Family Life Newsletter, 1994, 1996. Recipient N.Y. State Mid. Sch. Recognition award, N.Y. State Mid. Sch. Assn., 1996. Mem.: Assn. Career and Tech. Edn., Am. Ednl. Rsch. Assn., Assn. Childhood Edn., Assn. Family and Consumer Scis., N.Y. State Assn. Career and Tech. Edn., N.Y. State Assn. Family and Consumer Sci. Educators (area coord. 1995—, in svc. trainer 1995—, team mem. goals 2000 profl. devel. assessment pilot 2000, presenter, contbr. newsletter 1996—, mem. planning com. and selections for scholarship N.Y.C. chpt. 1996—2003, named N.Y. State Tchr. of Yr. 2000), Internat. Fedn. Home Econs. (rep. N.Y. state U.S. Devel. Fund 2004—, mem. com. 2004—, participant congresses), UN Devel. Fund Women. Avocations: travel, photography, interior decorating, reading, writing. Home: 1346 Lohengrin Pl Bronx NY 10465-1326 Office: Inwood Intermediate Sch 52 650 Academy St New York NY 10034

CALIGIURI, JOSEPH FRANK, retired engineering executive; b. Columbus, Ohio, Feb. 13, 1928; s. Frank and Angeline Josephine (Gentile) C.; m. Barbara Jane Delaney, June 15, 1948 (dec. 1996); children: Mark, Timothy, Jeffrey, Anderw; m. Tanya Alberta Condon, June 24, 1998. BSEE, Ohio State U., 1949, MSEE, 1951. Chief engr. Sperry Gyroscope Co., Great Neck, NY, 1966-69; v.p. engring. Guidance and Control Sys. divsn. Litton Industries, Inc., Woodland Hills, Calif., 1969-71, pres., 1971-77, v.p. parent co., 1974-77, sr. v.p., group head Beverly Hills, Calif., 1977-81, exec. v.p., head advanced electronics group, 1981-93; ret., 1993. Bd. dirs. Titan Corp., Phillip Mark Cos. Home: 1353 Oak Grove Pl Westlake Village CA 91362-4248

CALINESCU, ADRIANA GABRIELA, curator, art historian; b. Bucharest, Romania, Dec. 30, 1941; came to U.S., 1973; d. Nicolae and Tamara Gane; m. Matei Alexe Calinescu, Apr. 29, 1963; children: Irena, Matthew. BA, Cen. Lyceé, Bucharest, 1959; MA in English, U. Bucharest, 1964; MLS, Ind. U., 1976, MA in Art History, 1983. Asst. prof. Inst. Theater and Cinema, Bucharest, 1967-73; rsch. assoc. Ind. U. Art Mus., Bloomington, 1979-83, Thomas T. Solley curator ancient art, assoc. scholar, 1992—. Vis. assoc. mem. Am. Sch. Classical Studies, Athens, Greece, 1984. Author: The Art of Ancient Jewelry, 1994, Egypt After Alexander, 2005; author, co-editor: Ancient Art from the V. G. Simkhovitch Collection, 1988; editor: Ancient Jewelry and Archaeology, 1996. NEA fellow, 1984; grantee Salzburg Seminar, 1970, NEA, 1987, 93, Kress Found., 1991, Internat. Rsch. and Exchanges Bd., 1991. Mem. Am. Inst. Archaeology, Classical Art Soc., Beta Phi Mu. Office: Ind U Art Mus E 7th St Bloomington IN 47405 Office Phone: 812-855-1033.

CALINGAERT, MICHAEL, non-profit organization executive; b. Detroit, Sept. 17, 1933; s. George and Dorothy C.; m. Efrem Funghi, June 20, 1962; children: Alexander, Daniel, Nicholas. BA, Swarthmore Coll., 1955; post-grad., U. Cologne, Fed. Republic Germany, 1955-56, U. Calif., Berkeley, 1963-64. Commd. fgn. svc. officer Dept. State, 1956, intelligence rsch. specialist Washington, 1957-58; vice consul Am. consulate gen. Mogadiscio, Somalia, 1959—61; econ. officer Am. consulate gen. Bremen, Germany, 1961-63; econ. officer Am. Embassy, Colombo, Sri Lanka, 1964-68; chief food policy div. Dept. State, Washington, 1968-72; econ. counselor Am. Embassy, Tokyo, 1972-75, econ./comml. min. Rome, 1975-79; dep. asst. sec. for internat. resources and food policy Dept. State, 1979-83; econ. min. Am. Embassy, London, 1983-87; vis. sr. fellow Nat. Planning Assn., Washington, 1987-89, sr. fellow, 1993-97; non-resident sr. fellow Atlantic Coun. U.S., 1989; dir. of European ops. Pharm. Mfrs. Assn. (U.S.), Belgium, 1989-93; dir. The Monnet-Madison Inst., Brussels, 1994-97; exec. dir. Coun. for U.S. and Italy, 1997—2003, exec. v.p., 2003—. Rsch. fellow Inst. for European Studies, Free U. Brussels, 1994-98, mem. polit. sect., 1998—2002; guest scholar The Brookings Inst., 1996-2004, vis. scholar Ctr. for the U.S. and Europe, 2004—. Author: The 1992 Challenge from Europe: Development of the European Community's Internal Market, 1988, European Integration Revisited: Progress, Prospects, and U.S. Interests, 1996; contbr. numerous articles to profl. jours. Recipient Meritorious Honor award Dept. State, 1971, Superior Honor award, 1981 Mem. Am. Fgn. Svc. Assn., Royal Inst. Internat. Affairs, Inst. Affari Internat. Office: The Brookings Inst 1775 Massachusetts Ave NW Washington DC 20036-2103 Office Phone: 202-797-6135.

CALINGER, RONALD STEVE, historian; b. Aliquippa, Pa., Apr. 6, 1942; s. Thomas H. and Mary (Blicha) Calinger; m. Betty Jeanne Mikulecky, Dec. 21, 1974; children: John Michael, Anne Sun Nyeo. AB summa cum laude, Ohio U., 1963; MA, U. Pitts., 1964; PhD, U. Chgo., 1971. Assoc. editor scis. A.N. Marquis Publ. Co., Chgo., 1966-68; mem. faculty Rensselaer Poly. Inst., Troy, NY, 1969-85, assoc. prof. history, 1975-85, chmn. dept. history and polit. sci., 1977-82, dean Undergrad. Coll., 1982-85; dean sch. arts scis. Cath. U. Am., Washington, 1985-87, assoc. to ordinary prof. history, 1987—. Author: (book) Gottfried Wilhelm Leibniz, 1976, A Contextual History of Mathematics: Up to Euler, 1999, (electronic book) A Study Guide for a Contextual History of Mathematics, 2001; co-author: Dictionary of Twentieth Century World Politics, 1993; editor: (book) Classics of Mathematics, 1982, Classics of Mathematics, rev. edit., 1995, Vita Mathematica, 1996, The Johns Hopkins University History of Mathematics Series, 2004—, The John Zeender Festschrift, 2005; contbr. Dictionary Sci. Biography, 1971—74, Dictionary Am. Biography, 1977; sect. editor: History and Pedagogy of Math. newsletter, 1989—98; contbr. articles and revs. to scholarly jours. Recipient Henry Schuman Prize, 1968, Austrian Cross Scis. & Arts 1st Class, 1996, Foley Outstanding Educator of the Yr. award, Nat. Bd. Dir. Aplha Delta Gamma, 2001, Dornan Meml. Tchr. of Yr. award, Cath. U., 2005; grantee German Marshall Fund, 1987, 1989, NSF, 1995, 1996, 1998, Hitachi, Internat. Virtual Inst. Hist. Studies Math., 1998—2001. Mem.: Math. Assn. Am. (hist. maths. com.), Atlantic Coun. (acad. assoc.), History Sci. Soc. (Washington rep. 1991—2001), Am. Hist. Assn., The Euler Soc. (chancellor 2001—), Phi Beta Kappa. Roman Catholic. Achievements include research in the history of mathematics; biographies of Leonhard Euler and Gottfried Leibniz; development of Newtonian science and competing Leibnizian and Wolffian thought in 18th century Brandenburg-Prussia and Russia; the University of Berlin Mathematics Seminar under Kummer-Weiestrass, and Imperial Austria. Home: 12806 Lacy Dr Silver Spring MD 20904-2916 Office Phone: 202-319-5484. E-mail: calinger@cua.edu.

CALIO, ANTHONY JOHN, research scientist, operations research specialist; b. Phila., Oct. 27, 1929; s. Antonio and Mary Emma (Cappuccio) C.; m. Jenanne L. Murphy. BA, postgrad., U. Pa., 1953, Carnegie Inst. Tech., 1959; ScD (hon.), Washington U., St. Louis, 1974; postgrad. (Sloan fellow), Stanford U., 1974-75. With Westinghouse Electric Corp., Pitts., 1956-59; chief nuclear physics sect. Am. Machine & Foundry Co., Alexandria, Va., 1959-61; v.p. Mt. Vernon Rsch. Co., 1961-63; electronic rsch. task group NASA Hdqrs., Washington, 1963-64; chief rsch. engring. NASA (Electronics Rsch. Ctr.), Boston, 1964-65; chief instrumentation and systems integration br. NASA Hdqrs., Washington, 1965-67, asst. dir. planetary exploration, 1967-68; dir. sci. and applications NASA Johnson Space Ctr., Houston, 1969-75; dep. assoc. adminstr. office space scis. NASA Hdqrs., Washington, 1975-77, assoc. adminstr. Office of Space and Terrestrial Applications, 1977-81; dep. adminstrn. NOAA Dept. Commerce, 1981-84, under sec. for oceans and atmosphere, 1984-87; sr. v.p. Planning Rsch. Corp., McLean, Va., 1987-90; from exec. v.p. to sr. v.p. Hughes Info. Tech. Corp., Reston, Va., 1991-97; sr. v.p. Hughes Info. Tech. Sys., 1996-97; pres. Space Sys., 1996-97, Hughes Info. Tech. Sys., 1997-99; ret., 1999. With U.S. Army, 1954-56. Recipient Group Achievement award (2) NASA, 1969, Exceptional Service medal, 1969, Apollo Achievement award, 1970, Exceptional Sci. Achievement medal, 1971, Lunar Sci. Team award, 1973, Disting. Service medal, 1973, 81, presdl. rank of Disting. Exec., 1980 Fellow AIAA, Am. Astron. Soc.; mem. Am. Geophys. Union. Home: 4920 Scurlock Rd Freeland WA 98249-9632

CALIO, NICHOLAS E., diversified financial services company executive; b. Jan. 10, 1953; m. Lydia Keller; 3 children. BA, Ohio Wesleyan U., 1975; JD, Case Western U., 1978. Assoc. Santarelli & Gimer, 1978—81; of counsel Santarelli & Bond, 1981—84; litig. counsel Washington Legal Found., 1981—84; sr. v.p. govt. rels., exec. dir. wholesaler-distbr. polit. action com. Nat. Assn. Wholesaler-Distbrs., 1984—89; v.p. Duberstein Group, Inc., Washington, 1991—92; asst. to pres. for legis. affairs Pres. George H.W. Bush, 1992—93; ptnr. O'Brien & Calio, 1993—2001; asst. to pres. for legis. affairs Pres. George W. Bush, Washington, 2001—03; sr. v.p. global govt. affairs Citigroup, N.Y.C., 2003—. Bd. trustee Ohio Wesleyan Univ., Georgetown Visitation Preparatory Sch. Office: Citigroup Inc 399 Park Ave New York NY 10043*

CALIP, ROGER, writer, educator; b. Manila, Sept. 19, 1941; came to U.S. 1968; s. Generoso and Paula (Echalar) C. LittB in Journalism, U. Santo Tomas, Manila, 1961; Lic. Es Lettres, U. Paris, 1968; MA in Sociology, U. Conn., 1972, MA in French, 1977. Proofreader Robinson & Cole, Hartford, Conn., 1986-90; contbg. editor The Business Times, East Hartford, Conn., 1986-88; contbg. writer The Hartford News, Hartford, 1988-90; tchr. of writing Manchester (Conn.) C.C., 1988-98, West Hartford Continuing Edn., 1999—; freelance bus. writer Hartford Courant, Conn., 2001—03. Adj. instr. sociology Tunxis C.C., Farmington, Conn., 1992-94; adj. instr. French Mitchell Coll., New London, Conn., 1998-99 Contbr. articles and essays to mags. and newspapers. Recipient Rank 14 Top 100 Articles Writer's Digest, 1980, 2d Pl. short story Hartford Advocate, 1996. Mem.: Assn. Writers and Writing Programs. Roman Catholic. Avocation: reading. Home and Office: 19 Fennbrook Rd West Hartford CT 06119-2205 Personal E-mail: rcalip2265@aol.com.

CALISE, NICHOLAS JAMES, lawyer; b. N.Y.C., Sept. 15, 1941; s. William J. and Adeline (Rota) C.; m. Mary G. Flannery, Nov. 10, 1965; children: James R., Lori K. AB, Middlebury Coll., 1962; MBA, LLB, Columbia U., 1965. Bar: N.Y. 1965, Conn., 1974, Ohio, 1986, Colo. 2000. Assoc., ptnr. Olvany, Eisner & Donnelly, N.Y.C., 1969-76; corp. staff atty. Richardson-Vicks Inc., Wilton, Conn., 1976-82, div. counsel, dir. planning and bus. devel. home care products div. Memphis, 1982-84; staff v.p., sec., asst. gen. counsel The B.F. Goodrich Co., Akron, Ohio, 1984-89, v.p., sec., assoc. gen. counsel, 1989-99. Mem. Flood and Erosion Control Bd., Darien, Conn., 1976, Rep. Town Meeting, Darien, 1977-78; chmn. Zoning Bd. Appeals, Darien, 1978-82; Justice of the Peace, Darien, 1982. Served to lt. USN, 1965-68, capt. JAGC, USNR, 1984-96, ret. Mem.: ABA, Ohio Bar Assn., Colo. Bar Assn., N.Y. State Bar Assn., Am. Corp. Counsel Assn., Am. Soc. Corp. Secs. (bd. dirs. 1990—93, pres. 1991—92, chmn. nat. conf. com. 1997, mem. various coms.), U.S. Naval Inst., Navy League (life), Naval Res. Assn. (life), Judge Advs. Assn. (life), Res. Officers' Assn. (life), Club Cordillera (pres. 2004—, bd. dirs., pres. 2003—), Country Club of Hudson (bd. trustees 1996—99, sec. 1997—99, Bracebridge H. Young Disting. Svc. award 2001), Am. Legion. Roman Catholic. Home: 731 Forest Trail Edwards CO 81632 E-mail: caliselaw@yahoo.com.

CALISE, WILLIAM JOSEPH, JR., lawyer; b. N.Y.C., May 22, 1938; s. William Joseph and Adeline (Rota) C.; m. Kathryn A. Varner; children: Kimberly Elizabeth, Andrea Elizabeth. BA, Bucknell U., 1960; MBA, JD, Columbia U., 1963. Bar: N.Y. 1963, D.C. 1981. Assoc., then ptnr. Chadbourne & Parke, NYC, 1967—94; sr. v.p., gen. counsel, sec. Rockwell Automation, Inc. (formerly Rockwell Internat.), Milw., 1994—2004. Bd. dirs. Henry St. Settlement, N.Y.C., 1977-94, Jr. Achievement Inc., 1999-2004; mem. Allendale (N.J.) Sch. Bd., 1977-80. Capt. U.S. Army, 1964-66. Mem. Assn. Bar N.Y.C., Assn. Gen. Counsel. Roman Catholic. Office Phone: 805-564-1888. Personal E-mail: casacalise@cox.net.

CALKINS, BENJAMIN, lawyer; b. Boston, Jan. 20, 1956; s. Evan and Virginia (Brady) C.; m. Lindsay Noble, July 4, 1981; children: Sarah Noble, Bradley Phillips, Patricia Noble, Haley McCormick. AB, Harvard U., 1978; JD, U. Mich., 1981. Bar: D.C. 1982, U.S. Dist. Ct. (ea. dist.) Mich. 1982, Ohio 1983, U.S. Dist. Ct. (no. dist.) Ohio 1983, U.S. Ct. Appeals (6th cir.) 1986, N.Y. 1990. Law clk. to presiding justice U.S. Dist. Ct. (ea. dist.) Mich., Detroit, 1981-83; assoc. Squire, Sanders & Dempsey, Cleve., 1983-89; ptnr. Benesch, Friedlander, Coplan & Aronoff, Cleve., 1989—, Spieth, Bell, McCurdy & Newell Co., L.P.A., Cleve., 1996—. Founder and pres., New Farm Markes, 1999—. Assoc. editor U. Mich. Law Rev., 1979-80, sr. editor, 1980-81; contbr. articles to profl. jours. Sustaining mem. Rep. Nat. Com., Washington, 1985—; mem. ballot issues com. Citizens League Greater Cleve., 1989-93, mem. task force on edn. governance, 1991-92; mem. fin. com. Ga. County Rep. Cen. and Exec. Coms., 1990—; mem. strategic planning com. West Geauga Sch. Dist., 1990-91; founder Newbury Ednl. Found.; treas. Friends of Newbury Schs., 1993—; grad. Leadership Geauga, 2002; chair mktg. com., livestock sales com. Geauga County Jr. Fair, 2000—; trustee Geauga County Far Bur., 2003—, chair policy devel. com., 2004—, treas., 2005—. Mem. ABA (corp., banking and bus. law sect.), Ohio Bar Assn. (mem. corp. law com.), Cleve. Bar Assn. (securities law sect., corp. banking and bus. law sect.), D.C. Bar Assn., Greater Cleve. Internat. Lawyers Group (sec. 1991-92, v.p. 1992—, membership chmn. 1992-2000), Assn. for Corp. Growth, Ohio Venture Assn. (v.p. 1996—, chmn. programs 2001-04, pres. 2004—), Union Club, Harvard Club (trustee 1985-88, 94—, v.p. 1988-90, pres. 1990-94). Presbyterian. Avocations: sports, animal husbandry. Home: 11510 Music St Newbury OH 44065-9565 Office: Spieth Bell McCurdy & Newell Co LPA 2000 Huntington Bldg 925 Euclid Ave Cleveland OH 44115-1408 Office Phone: 216-535-1025. Business E-Mail: bcalkins@spiethbell.com.

CALKINS, CARROL OTTO, retired entomologist, researcher, educator; b. Sioux Falls, SD, June 4, 1937; s. Glenn Keeler and Nell (Olson) C.; m. Janice Marie McGuire, Oct. 3, 1959; children: Debra Diane, Lori Lynn. BS, SD State Coll., 1959, PhD, 1974; MS, U. Nebr., Lincoln, 1964. Cert. in ecology, behavior, agrl. entomology Am. Registry Profl. Entomologists. Entomologist, Agrl. Rsch. Svc., US Dept. Agr., Lincoln, Nebr., 1960-64; rsch. entomologist Agrl. Research Service, U.S. Dept. Agr., Brookings, SD, 1964-72, rsch. leader, Gainesville, Fla., 1972-77, 80-93, Yakima, Wash., 1993-2002, ret., 2002; head entomology sect. Seibersdorf Lab., IAEA, Vienna, Austria, 1977-80; instr. U. Nebr., 1961-64, SD State U., 1964-72; with U.S. Dept. Agr.,

Gainesville, Fla., 1980—, collaborator Wis. Dept. Agr., 2002—; assoc. prof. U. Fla., Gainesville, 1981—93; prof. Wash. State U., 1993-2002. With Air N.G., 1960-66. Mem. Entomol. Soc. Am., Ecol. Soc. Am., AAAS, Fla. Entomol. Soc., Sigma Xi, Alpha Zeta, Gamma Sigma Delta. Roman Catholic. Lodge: Elks (Brookings, Elk of Year 1971). Contbr. articles to profl. jours. Personal E-mail: jcottocar@aol.com. Business E-Mail: ccalkins@yarl.ars.usda.gov.

CALKINS, DAVID ROSS, physician, medical educator; b. Kansas City, Kans., May 27, 1948; s. Leroy Adelbert and Emily Virginia (Kyger) C.; m. Susan Spalding Rice, Sept. 22, 1989; 1 child, Christopher Ross. AB, Princeton (N.J.) U., 1970; MD, MPP, Harvard U., 1975. Diplomate Am. Bd. Internal Medicine. Intern U. Wash., Seattle, 1975-76; resident in medicine Beth Israel Hosp., Boston, 1976-78, from asst. to assoc. in medicine, 1981-96; fellow White House, Washington, 1978-79; spl. asst., dep. exec. sec. HHS, Washington, 1979-81; from instr. to asst. prof. medicine Harvard Med. Sch., Boston, 1981-96; from instr. to asst. prof. Harvard Sch. Pub. Health, Boston, 1985-96, dir. profl. programs dept. health policy and mgmt., 1985-96; chief div. gen. internal medicine, med. dir. ambulatory svc. New Eng. Deaconess Hosp., Boston, 1991-96; assoc. dean for primary care U. Kans. Sch. Medicine, Kansas City, 1996-98, from assoc. prof. to prof. internal and preventive medicine, 1996-99, sr. assoc. dean for edn., 1998-99; assoc. prof. medicine Harvard Med. Sch., Boston, 1999—, assoc. dean for clin. programs, 1999—2003; sr. fellow Inst. Healthcare Improvement, Cambridge, Mass., 2003—. Office: 50 Staniford St Ste 300 Boston MA 02114 Office Phone: 617-724-8065. Business E-Mail: dcalkins@partners.org.

CALKINS, DIANE KAY, retired elementary school educator, musician, golfer; b. Vinton, Iowa, Oct. 9, 1946; d. Lloyd James and Ruth Lorraine Sheffler; m. David Lee Calkins. BS in Edn., Wartburg Coll., Waverly, Iowa, 1969; MEd, U. Cin., 1970. Tchr. Norwood Sch., Ohio, 1970—2000; ret.; organist Immanuel Presbyn. Ch.; medalist Women's US Amateur Qualifier, 1979; winner Ohio State Stroke Play Championship, 1984, 1985, 1994; qualified Women's US Open Golf Championship, 1987; runner-up Ohio State Championship, 1992; winner Cin. Sr. City Championship, 2003. Avocations: golf, music.

CALKINS, EVAN, physician, educator; b. Newton, Mass., July 15, 1920; s. Grosvenor and Patty (Phillips) C.; m. Virginia McC. Brady, Sept. 9, 1946; children: Sarah Calkins Oxnard, Stephen, Lucy McCormick, Joan, Benjamin, Hugh, Ellen Rountree, Geoffrey, Timothy. Grad., Milton Acad., 1939; AB, Harvard U., 1942, MD, 1945. Intern, asst. resident medicine Johns Hopkins, 1946-47, 48-50; chief resident physician Mass. Gen. Hosp., 1951-52, mem. arthritis unit, 1952-61; NRC fellow med. scis. Harvard, 1950-51, instr., asst. prof. medicine, 1952-61; practice medicine, specializing in rheumatology Boston, 1951-61, Buffalo, 1961—; prof. medicine SUNY, Buffalo, 1961-94, prof. emeritus, 1994—, chmn. dept. medicine, 1965-77; head dept. medicine Buffalo Gen. Hosp., 1961-68; dir. medicine E.J. Meyer Meml. Hosp., 1968-78; head gerontology sect. Buffalo VA Med. Ctr., 1978-90; head div. geriatrics/gerontology SUNY-Buffalo, 1978-90. Founder, pres. Network in Aging of Western N.Y., Inc., 1980-83; cons. Nat. Inst. Arthritis and Metabolic Diseases Tng. Grants Com., 1958-62, Program Project Com., 1964-68, Nat. Instn. Spl. Study Sect. for Health Manpower, 1969-77, for Behavioral Medicine, 1978-79; mem. acad. awards com. Nat. Inst. on Aging, 1979-80, mem. nat. adv. coun., 1985-88; dir. Western N.Y. Geriatric Edn. Ctr., 1983-88, co-dir., 1988-90; dir. Multidisciplinary Ctr. on Aging SUNY-Buffalo, 1989-90, prof. family medicine, 1987-94; sr. physician and coord. geriatric programs Health Care Plan, 1990-97; ptnr. Promedicus Health Group, 1998-2001; co-dir. WNY/Rochester Osteoporosis Ednl. Resource Ctr., 1999; pvt. practice rheumatology and geriatrics, 2001—. Author: Yesterdays: Memoir from Six Generations of an American Family 175202004, 2004; editor: Handbook of Medical Emergencies, 1945, Geriatric Medicine, 1983, Practice of Geriatrics, 1986, 2d edit., 1991, New Ways to Care for Older People: Building Systems Based on Evidence, 1998, contbr. articles to profl. jours. Pres. Nat. Assn. Geriatric Edn. Ctrs., 1992-93. Capt. M.C. AUS, 1943-45, 46-48. Recipient Presdl. citation for Community Service, 1983 Fellow ACP (master 1989, Laureate award N.Y. Upstate chpt. 1998), Am. Coll. Rheumatology (founder, pres. 1967-68, master 1986), Gerontol. Soc. Am. (chair clin. med. sect. 1989, Freeman award 1991), Am. Geriatrics Soc. (Milo D. Leavitt award 1986); mem. Am. Clin. and Climatological Assn. (v.p. 1987), Am. Soc. Clin. Investigation, Assn. Am. Physicians, Soc. Medicine Argentina (hon.), Argentine Soc. Gerontology and Geriatrics (hon.), Soc. Fellows John Hopkins U., Alpha Omega Alpha. Home: 3799 Windover Dr Hamburg NY 14075-6338 Office: Village Rheumatology 17 Long Ave Ste 110 Hamburg NY 14075-6388 Office Phone: 716-646-5188.

CALKINS, HUGH, foundation executive; b. Newton, Mass., Feb. 20, 1924; s. Grosvenor and Patty (Phillips) C.; m. Ann Clark, June 14, 1955; children: Peter, Andrew, Margaret, Elizabeth. AB, LLB, Harvard U., 1949, D (hon.) in Law, 1985. Bar: Ohio 1950. Law clk. to presiding judge U.S. Ct. Appeals (2d cir.), N.Y.C., 1949-50; law clk. to justice Felix Frankfurter U.S. Supreme Ct., Washington, 1950-51; from assoc. to ptnr. Jones, Day, Reavis & Pogue, Cleve., 1951-90; tchr. elem. schs. Cleve. City Sch. Dist., 1991-94. Contbr. articles on fed. income tax to profl. jours. Mem. Cleve. Bd. Edn., 1965-69; assoc. dir. Pres.'s Commn. on Nat. Goals, Washington, 1960; mem., pres., fellow Harvard U., 1968-85; mem. task forces Cleve. Summit on Edn., 1990-94; v.p., trustee Initiatives in Urban Edn., 1991—. Capt. USAF, 1943-46. Mem. ABA (chmn. tax sect. 1985-86), Am. Law Inst. (coun.), City Club, Cleve. Skating Club, Rowfant Club, Phi Beta Kappa. Democrat. Unitarian Universalist. Home and Office: 3345 N Park Blvd Cleveland OH 44118 Office Phone: 316-397-9749. Personal E-mail: calk2@earthlink.net.

CALKINS, MONICA E., psychology professor; b. Paoli, Pa. BA cum laude, Temple U., Phila., 1991; PhD, U. Minn., Mpls., 2002. Post-doctoral fellow U. Pa., Phila., 2002—04, asst. prof. psychology, 2004—. Contbr. entries to ency., articles to profl. jours. Recipient Harrison Gough Travel award, Dept. Psychology U. Minn., 2000, Grad. Rsch. Partnership Program award, U. Minn., 2001, Harrison Gough Rsch. Travel award, 2002, Young Investigator award, Internat. Congress on Schizophrenia Rsch., 2005; fellow, U. Minn., 1994—95, 2000—01, in Neuropsychiatry, NIMH, 2002—04, Scottish Rite, 2002—04; grantee, NIMH, 1996—98, 2003, NSF and Assn. Practical and Profl. Ethics, 1999—2000, U. Minn., 2001. Mem.: APA, Schizophrenia Internat. Rsch. Soc., Golden Key, Psi Chi, Eta Sigma Phi, Alpha Lambda Delta. Office: U Pa 10 Gates 3400 Spruce St Philadelphia PA 19104 Office Phone: 215-662-4678. Office Fax: 215-662-7903. E-mail: mcalkins@bbl.med.upenn.edu.

CALKINS, RALPH NELSON, retired economics professor; b. Albuquerque, Apr. 28, 1926; s. Fred Myron and Luella (McDonald) C.; m. Ruth J. (Thatcher) Calkins, Jan. 8, 1949; children: Alison, Paul, Patricia. BBA, U. N.Mex., 1947, MA, 1949; PhD, Columbia U., 1963. Instr. econs. Bloomfield (N.J.) Coll., 1949-53, dean, 1953-67; assoc. prof. U. Alaska, Fairbanks, 1967-68; prof. dept. econs. and bus. adminstrn. Hanover (Ind.) Coll., 1968-91, prof. emeritus, 1991. Author: The Gradual Encroachment-Capitalism As We Know It, 2003. With USN, 1944-46. Mem. AAAS, Am. Econ. Assn., Am. Solar Energy Soc., Union of Concerned Scientists (sponsor), Ind. Acad. Social Scis. (bd. dirs. 1985-88). Democrat. Home: 7424 Edith Blvd NE Albuquerque NM 87113-1202 Personal E-mail: ralphntuth@aol.com.

CALKINS, STEPHEN, lawyer, educator; b. Balt., Mar. 20, 1950; s. Evan and Virginia (Brady) C.; m. Joan Wadsworth, Oct. 18, 1981; children: Timothy, Geoffrey, Virginia. BA, Yale U., 1972; JD, Harvard U., 1975. Bar: N.Y. 1976, D.C. 1977, U.S. Dist. Ct. D.C. 1979. Law clk. to FTC commr. S. Nye, Washington, 1975-76; assoc. Covington & Burling, Washington, 1976-83; assoc. law prof. Wayne State U., Detroit, 1983-88, prof., 1988—, dir. grad. studies, 2004—; gen. counsel FTC, Washington, 1995-97; of counsel Covington & Burling, Washington, 1997—, program dir. conf. bd. antitrust conf., 2001—. Vis. assoc. prof. law U. Mich., Ann Arbor, 1985, U. Pa., Phila., 1987; vis. prof. law U. Utrecht, Netherlands, 1989; chair career devel. Wayne State U., 1990-91. Author: (with Gellhorn and Kovacic) Antitrust Law and Economics in a Nutshell, 5th edit., 2004; editor: Antitrust Law Developments, 1984, 86, 88; editor legal book revs. The Antitrust Bull., 1986—; articles editor Antitrust, 1991-95. Co-chair Yale Alumni Fund, 1972; counsel Ind. Commn. on Admissions Practices in Cranbrook Sch., Detroit, 1984-85; mem. Northville Zoning Bd. Appeals, 1987-95; rep.-at-large Assn. Yale Alumni Assembly, 1989-92; bd. dirs. yale Alumni Assn. of Mich., 2002—; elder First Presbyn. Ch. of Northville, 1989-92. Rsch. fellow Wayne State U., 1984; USAID grantee, 1999-2004; recipient FTC award disting. svc., 1997. Fellow: ABA (counsel to com. on FTC 1988—89, coun. antitrust sect. 1988—91, 1997—2000, coun. adminstrv. law sect. 1999—2002, Antitrust sect. 50th anniversary pub. award 2002), Am. Bar Found., Am. Antitrust Inst. (sr.); mem.: Am. Assn. Law Schs. (sec. antitrust sect. 1987—91, chair-elect 1991—93, chair 1993—95), Am. Law Inst., Northville Swim Club, Yale Club (Detroit) (bd. dirs. 2002—), Harvard Club. Avocations: reading, skiing, rollerblading. Home: 317 W Dunlap St Northville MI 48167-1404 Office: Wayne State U Law Sch 471 W Palmer Detroit MI 48202 Office Phone: 313-577-3945. Business E-Mail: calkins@wayne.edu.

CALKINS, SUSAN W., state supreme court justice; Grad., U. Colo.; JD, U. Maine. Staff atty., exec. dir. Pine Tree Legal Assistance; judge Maine Dist. Ct., 1980-90, chief judge, 1990—94; judge Maine Superior Ct., 1995—98; justice Maine Supreme Ct., 1998—. Ct. liaison Bd. of Bar Examiners, Jud. Ethics Com., Advisory Com. on Rules of Evidence. Fellow: Maine Bar Foundation; mem.: ABA (mem. Judges' Advisory Com. on Ethics & Professional Responsibility). Office: Maine Supreme Ct 142 Federal St PO Box 368 Portland ME 04112-0368*

CALKINS, SUSANNAH EBY, retired economist; b. Bucyrus, Ohio, Jan. 16, 1924; d. Samuel L. and Mae (McClure) Eby; m. G. Nathan Calkins, Nov. 19, 1949 (dec.); children: Helen E. (dec.), Margaret S. Van Auken, Sarah A. (dec.), Abigail Calkins Aguirre. AB, Goucher Coll., 1945; MS in Econs. (Univ. scholar 1946-47), U. Wis., 1947. Fiscal analyst U.S. Bur. Budget, 1945-50; economist U.S. Council Econ. Advisors, 1950-51, U.S. Office Price Stabilization, 1951-53, U.S. Bur. Budget, 1953-55; cons. U.S. Adv. Commn. on Intergovtl. Rels., Washington, 1972-73, 74-75, cons. on counter-cyclical aid programs, 1977-78, sr. analyst, 1979-87, exec. asst. to dir., 1987-89. Cons. revenue sharing Brookings Instn., Washington, 1973—74. Author (with R. Nathan and A. Manvel): Monitoring Revenue Sharing, 1975. Sponsor S.S. Goucher Victory, Balt., 1945; bd. dirs. Bread for the City, 1994—2002. Mem. Am. Econs. Assn., George Towne Club (Washington), Phi Beta Kappa. Presbyterian. Home: 6504 Dearborn Dr Falls Church VA 22044-1115

CALL, DENISE HODGINS, curator, artist, freelance/self-employed writer; b. Philadelphia, Pa., Oct. 27, 1942; d. James Francis Hodgins and Catherine C. Whitney-Lear; m. Stephen M. Call, Jan. 22, 1994; m. Edward J. Gilhooly, July 16, 1966 (div.); children: Caitlyn Gilhooly Parker, Mairin Gilhooly Kuligowski, Edward J. Gilhooly, III, Bevin J. Gilhooly. BA in English with honors, Cabrini Coll., 1960—64; Grad. studies, University of Pa., 1964—66. Assoc. curator NJ. Ctr. for Visual Arts, Summit, NJ, 2000—; artist and freelance writer DHC Enterprises, Morristown, NJ, 1998—; jet fuel sales Exxon Co. Internat., Florham Park, NJ, 1980—97; v.p. of mktg. BA Internat., Morristown, NJ, 1984—86; tchr. of english Marylawn of the Oranges, South Orange, NJ, 1978—80; reader svc. editor Chilton Co./Food Engring., Philadelphia, Pa., 1960—66. Dir. Artemis Group, Morristown, NJ, 1990—98. Mem.: Somerset Art Assn. Avocations: cross country skiing, hiking. Home: 20 Raven Dr Morristown NJ 07960 Office: New Jersey Center for Visual Arts 68 Elm St Summit NJ 07901 Office Phone: 908-273-9121. Personal E-mail: dhcall@aol.com.

CALL, GREGORY S., academic administrator, mathematics professor; AB in Math. summa cum laude, Dartmouth Coll.; MA, PhD, Harvard Univ. Prof. math. Amherst (Mass.) Coll., 1988—, dean new students, 2003—05, interim dean faculty, 2003—05, dean faculty, 2005—. Office: Dean of the Faculty Amherst Coll PO Box 5000 Amherst MA 01002-5000 Office Phone: 413-542-2334. Office Fax: 413-542-2621.

CALL, MERLIN WENDELL, lawyer; b. Long Beach, Calif., Nov. 25, 1931; s. True and Bernice (Johnson) C.; m. Kathryn J. Gage, Dec. 22, 1956 (div.); children: Christopher, Lori. AB, Stanford U., 1951, JD, 1953. Bar: Calif. 1953. Assoc. Tuttle & Taylor, L.A., 1955-60, ptnr., 1960-2000; sr. counsel Shapiro, Borenstein & Dupont, Santa Monica, Calif., 2000—02. Bd. visitors Stanford Sch. Law, 1987-90. Chmn. bd. trustees Westmont Coll., Santa Barbara, Calif., 1988—94, The Fuller Found., Pasadena, Calif., 1987—94, Mission Aviation Fellowship, Redlands, Calif., 1974—78, Gospel Broadcasting Assn., 1967—78, De Pree Leadership Ctr., 2001—; mem. Town Hall Calif., L.A., 1958—; trustee Fuller Theol. Sem., Pasadena, 1963—78, 1983—, chmn., 2001—; trustee China Connection, 2001—, Westmont Coll., Santa Barbara, Calif., 1984—, The Fuller Found., 1987—, Mission Aviation Fellowship, Redlands, Calif., 1963—78. Mem. Phi Beta Kappa, Order of Coif. Home: 1660 La Loma Rd Pasadena CA 91105-2158 Office: 225 S Lake Ave Ste 300 Pasadena CA 91101- E-mail: mwcall@earthlink.net, mwcalllaw@polarisnet.net.

CALL, NEIL JUDSON, manufacturing executive; b. Detroit, June 15, 1933; s. Judson Francis and Glennys Jean (Amluxen) C.; m. Jane E. Rathslag, Feb. 4, 1956; children: Laura, Keith; m. Eleanor Ann King, Nov. 23, 1978. BBA, U. Mich., 1955, MBA, 1956. C.P.A., Mich. With Hogan Juengel & Harding (C.P.A.'s), Detroit, 1956-61, Ford Motor Co., Dearborn, Mich., 1961-65; with Ford Motor Credit Co., Dearborn, 1965-67, Gulf & Western Industries Inc., N.Y.C., 1968-86, v.p., 1970-79, sr. v.p., 1979-83, exec. v.p., 1983-84, D.F. King & Co., Inc., N.Y.C., 1986-89, Dewe Rogerson Inc., N.Y.C., 1990-92, Mackenzie Ptnrs., Inc., N.Y.C., 1992—. Bd. dirs. Sona Bank. Bd. dirs. Lower Fla. Keys Hosp. Dist., 2000—. Served with U.S. Army, 1956-58. Home: 1500 Atlantic Blvd Apt 307 Key West FL 33040-5071 Office: Mackenzie Ptnrs Inc 105 Madison Ave New York NY 10016-7002 Office Phone: 212-929-5804. Personal E-mail: nandecall@aol.com.

CALLAGHAN, JOHN WILLIAM, JR., information technology manager, retired military officer; b. Frankfurt, Germany, Nov. 20, 1953; s. John William and Virginia Timberman Callaghan; m. Vivian Anne Simmons, Apr. 20, 1957; children: John William III, Virginia Keyes, Samuel Brooks. BS in Math and Physics, Campbell U., N.C., 1979; MA in Security Mgmt., Webster U., St. Louis, 1996; EdD, George Wash. U., Washington, D.C., 2001—. Comptrollership, U.S. Dept. of Def., 1988; Counter Terrorism U.S. Dept. of Def., 1989. Army officer inf. and counter terrorism Various Units to include Army Rangers, SF Detachment Delta (planning HQ), 82d Airborne Div, 2d Inf. Div Korea, Dep. J-3 Haiti Op Uphold Democracy, U.S. and Korea, 1979—97; sr. program analyst Ballistic Missile Def. Orgn., Sr. Budget Analyst, Pentagon, Futron Corp., Arlington, Va., 1997—99; sr. sys. integrator Discoverer II, Joint Space Based Radar Intelligence Program, Pentagon, SRS Technologies Corp., Arlington, Va., 1999—2000; site mgr., sr. program analyst Joint Urban Warfare & Counter Terrorism, Joint Chiefs of Staff, Pentagon- SRS Technologies Corp., Arlington, Va., 2000—01; sr. program mgr. Anti- Terrorism, Homeland Security, U.S. Dept. of Interior, Veridian, Fairfax, Va., 2001—03; sr. bus. area mgr. Counter Terrorism & Intelligence Ops. Support Svcs. Harris Corp, Alexandria, Va., 2003—. Vice nat. comdr. Korean Veteran's of Am., Washington, 1999—2003. Maj. U.S. Army, 1972—97. Scholar George Wash. U. Excellence in Edn., Dept. of Higher Edn., 2001—03. Mem.: The Ret. Officer Assn. (assoc.). Conservative. Roman Catholic. Achievements include Vice Nat. Comdr. Korean Def. Veteran's of Am. (U.S. Congressionally approved Vet. organization). Avocations: running, reading history, outdoor work. Home: 8211 Greeley Blvd Springfield VA 22152 Office: Harris Corp 1201 E Abingdon Ste 500 Alexandria VA 22314 E-mail: john.callaghan@harris.com.

CALLAHAM, MICHAEL L., emergency physician, educator; MD, U. Calif., 1970. Resident emergency medicine U. So. Calif. L.A. County/U. So. Calif. Med. Ctr., 1974; prof. clin. medicine Med. Ctr. at U. Calif., San Francisco, 1990—, chief divsn. emergency medicine. Editor: Controversies in Trauma Management, 1984; author: Current Therapy in Emergency Medicine, 1987, Decision Making in Emergency Medicine, 1990, Current Practice of Emergency Medicine, 1991; dep. editor: Annals Emergency Medicine, editor in chief:, 2002—, peer reviewer: New Eng. Jour. Medicine, Jour. AMA, Jour. Am. Coll. Cardiology. Recipient Edn. award, Am. Coll. Emergency Physicians Calif. chpt., 2000. Mem.: Coun. Sci. Editors (chmn. editl. policy com.), World Assn. Med. Editors (chmn. ethics com. 2002—). Office: Univ Calif San Francisco Med Ctr Emergency Medicine 505 Parnassus Ave San Francisco CA 94122

CALLAHAN, ALSTON, physician, author; b. Vicksburg, Miss., Mar. 16, 1911; s. Neil and Effie (Alston) C.; m. Eivor Holst, Feb. 23, 1941; children: Kristina Alice, Patrick Alston, Michael Alston, Timothy Alston, Karin Eivor, Kevin (dec. 1961). AB, Miss. Coll., 1929; MD, Tulane U., 1933, MS in Ophthalmology, 1936; RSM, Tulane U., London, 1990. Diplomate Am. Bd. Ophthalmology. Intern Charity Hosp., New Orleans, 1933-35, resident in ophthalmology, 1936-37; hon. mem. emeritus Eye Found. Univ. Hosps., Birmingham, Ala., 1959—; also founder Callahan Eye Found. Hosp., Birmingham, Ala., 1964; co-developer Rsch. and Profl. Office Bldg. E.F. Hosp., 1985-87; founder Internat. Retinal Rsch Found., Inc., Birmingham, 1997. Author: Surgery of the Eye, Injuries, 1950, Surgery of the Eye, Diseases, 1956, Reconstructive Surgery of the Eyelids and Ocular Adnexa, 1966, (with M. Callahan) Ophthalmic Plastic Surgery, 1979; contbr. articles to profl. jours. Served to capt. M.C., AUS, 1944-46 Recipient award Ala. Acad. Honor, 1996; named Tulane Alumnus of Yr., 1997, to Ala. Healthcare Hall of Fame, 1998. Fellow ACS, Royal Australian Coll. Ophthalmology (hon.); mem. Am. Acad. Ophthalmology, So. Med. Assn. (emeritus), Am. Soc. Ophthal. Plastic Surgery, Alpha Omega Alpha, Sigma Alpha Epsilon. Clubs: Mountain Brook, The Club, Metropolitan, Explorers. also: Internat Retinal Rsch Found Inc 700 18th St S Ste 511 Birmingham AL 35233-3802 Office: 1720 University Blvd Birmingham AL 35233-1816

CALLAHAN, BILL, college football coach; b. Chicago, July 31, 1956; m. Valerie Callahan; 4 children. Offensive line coach Northern Arizona U., 1987—88; offensive coord. So. Ill. Univ., 1989; offensive line coach Univ. Wis., 1990—94, Phila. Eagles, 1995—97, Oakland Raiders, 1997—2000, tight ends coach, 1998, offensive coordinator, 1998—2002, head coach, 2002—03, Univ. Neb., Lincoln, 2004—. Office: Univ Neb 103 S Stadium Lincoln NE 68588

CALLAHAN, CONSUELO MARIA, federal judge; b. Palo Alto, Calif., June 9, 1950; married; 2 children. BA, Leland Stanford Jr. Univ., 1972; JD, McGeorge Sch. Law, Univ. Pacific, 1975; LLM, Univ. Va., 2004—. Bar: Calif. 1975. Dep. city atty. City of Stockton, Stockton, Calif., 1975—76; dep. dist. atty. Dist. Atty. Office, San Joaquin County, Calif., 1976—82, sup. dist. atty., 1982—86; ct. comm. Mcpl. Ct. of Stockton, Stockton, Calif., 1986—92; judge San Joaquin County Superior Ct., San Joaquin, Calif., 1992—96; Assoc. judge Ct. of Appeal, State of Calif., Calif., 1996—2003; judge, U.S. Court of Appeals (9th. cir.), 2003—. Recipient Award for Criminal Justice Programs, Gov., Susan B. Anthony Award for Women of Achievement, Stockton Peacemaker of the Yr., 1997, Mexican-Am. Hall of Fame, San Joaquin County, 1999. Office: US Ct Appeals 95 Seventh St San Francisco CA 94103*

CALLAHAN, DANIEL J., lawyer; b. Chgo., Sept. 13, 1949; children: Caitlin, Michael. BA magna cum laude, Western Ill. U., 1976; JD with honors, U. Calif., 1979. Bar: Calif. 1980, Hawaii 1980, U.S. Supreme Ct. 1997. Editor U. Calif. at Davis Law Rev., 1978; founder, mng. ptnr. Callahan & Blaine, Santa Ana, Calif., 1984—. Sponsor Elizabeth Glaser Pediatric Aids Found., YMCA, Orange County, Braille Inst., CHOC found. Children & Good Sheppard Luth. Charities. Named Trial Lawyer of Yr., OCTLA, 2000, Calif. Bus. Litig. Trial Lawyer of Yr., Calif. Lawyer Mag., 2003, Trial Lawyer of Yr., Orange County, 2004; named one of Hot 25, OC Metro Mag., 2000, Nation's Top Ten Trial Lawyers, Nat. Law Jour., 2004; recipient Pres. Pro Bono award, Calif. State Bar, 1994. Mem.: Orange County Bar Assn. (chair Law Practice Mgmt. Sect. 1993—95, chair Bus. Litigation Sect. 1996, voted Top Gun 2000). Achievements include obtained $934 million verdict in 1993, the higheste in Orange County history and in the state of Californa in 2003. Office: Callahan & Blaine Ste 900 3 Hutton Centre Dr Santa Ana CA 92707 Office Phone: 714-241-4444.

CALLAHAN, DANIEL JOHN, biomedical researcher; b. Washington, July 19, 1930; s. Vincent Francis and Anita (Hawkins) Callahan; m. Sidney Cornelia de Shazo, June 5, 1954; children: Mark Sidney, Stephen Daniel, John Vincent, Peter Thorn, Sarah Elisabeth, David Lee. BA, Yale U., 1952; MA, Georgetown U., 1957; PhD, Harvard U., 1965; DSc (hon.), U. Medicine and Dentistry of N.J., 1981; DHL (hon.), U. Colo., 1990, Williams Coll., 1992, Oreg. State U., 1997. Exec. editor The Commonweal, N.Y.C., 1961—68; staff assoc. Population Council, 1969—70; co-founder, pres. The Hastings Ctr., 1969—96, dir. internat. programs, 1997—; resident scholar Aspen Inst. Humanistic Studies, 1975. Vis. asst. prof. religion Temple U., 1964; vis. asst. prof. religious studies Brown U., 1965; vis. prof. theology Marymount Coll., 1966; vis. prof. U. Pa., 1970; sr. fellow Harvard Ctr. for Population and Devel. Studies, 1996; cons. med. ethics, jud. coun. AMA, 1972—82, ACP, 1979—86; spl. cons. Commn. on Population Growth and Am. Future, 1970—71, NEH, 1979; hon. prof. Charles U. Med. Sch., Prague, 1997—; sr. fellow Harvard Med. Sch., 1998—; sr. rsch. scholar Yale U., 2004—. Author: The Mind of the Catholic Layman, 1963, Honesty in the Church, 1965, The New Church, 1966, Abortion: Law, Choice and Morality, 1970, Ethics and Population Limitation, 1971, The Tyranny of Survival, 1973, The Teaching of Ethics in the Military, 1982, Setting Limits: Medical Goals in an Aging Society, 1987, What Kind of Life: The Limits of Medical Progress, 1990, The Troubled Dream of Life: Living with Morality, 1993, False Hopes: Why America's Quest for Perfect Health is a Recipe for Failure, 1998, What Price Better Health: Hazards of the Research Imperative, 2003; also essays, articles:; co-editor: Christianity Divided: Protestant and Roman Catholic Theological Issues, 1961, Ethical Issues in Human Genetics, 1973; editor: Federal Aid and Catholic Schools, 1964, Secular City Debate, 1966, The Catholic Case for Contraception, 1969, The American Population Debate, 1971, Science, Ethics and Medicine, 1976, Knowledge, Value and Belief, 1977, Morals, Science and Sociality, 1978, Knowing and Valuing, 1979, Ethics Teaching in Higher Education, 1980, Ethical Issues in Population Aid, 1980, The Roots of Ethics, 1981, Ethics in Hard Times, 1981, Ethics, the Social Sciences and Policy Analysis, 1983, Abortion: Understanding Differences, 1984, Applying the Humanities, 1985, Representation and Responsibility, 1985, A World Growing Old, 1995, What Price Mental Health?, 1995, Promoting Healthy Behavior, 2000, The Role of Complementary and Alternative Medicine, 2002, What Price Better Health, 2003; mem. editl. adv. bd.: Tech. in Soc., 1981—, mem. adv. bd.: Ency. of Life Scis., 1982, Sci., Tech. and Human Values, 1979—, Bus. and Profl. Ethics, 1981, Criminal Justice Ethics, 1982, Environ. Ethics, 1982, Jour. Bioethics, 1985—96. Mem. nat. adv. bd. Health Promotion Program, Henry J. Kaiser Family Found., 1987—91, N.Y. Panel and HIV Screening, 1987; adv. com. to dir. Ctr. for Disease Control, DHHS; mem. N.Y. Coun. for Humanities, 1975—79, Nat. Book Award Com., 1975, N.Y. State Health Adv. Coun., 1975—76; selection com. Ford-Rockefeller Program in Population Policy, 1975—78, Rockefeller Found. Program in Humanities, 1980; elector Nat. Medal for Lit., 1979—83; pub. mem. Am. Bd. Med. Specialties, 1982—87, N.Y. Sci. Policy Assn., 1985—91; mem. N.Y. Task Force on Life and Law, 1985—87; trustee U. Pa. Med. Ctr., 1987—91; mem. adv. com. on sci. integrity HHS, 1991—93. Named one of 200 Outstanding Young Men Leaders, Time mag., 1974; recipient Thomas More medal, 1970, Career Achievement award, Soc. Bioethics and Med. Humanities, 2001, Daryl J. Mase Disting. Leadership award, 1987, Book of Yr. award, Am. Jour. Nursing, 1987, Henry Knowles Beecher award, The Hastings Ctr., 1989, James H. Hamilton Book award, Am. Coll. Health Care Execs., 1990, Pres. Cabinet award, U. Tex., 1995, Scientific Freedom and Responsibility award, AAAS, 1995, Joseph Leiter award, Nat. Libr. of Medicine, 1999, ARCHON award, Sigma Theta Tau Internat. Honor Soc. of Nursing, 1999, Washington Irving Book award for

Fals Hopes, 1999, Thomas More medal, 1970, Career Achievement award, Soc. Bioethics and Med. Humanities, 2001, Daryl J. Mase Disting. Leadership award, 1987, Book of Yr. award, Am. Jour. Nursing, 1987, Henry Knowles Beecher award, The Hastings Ctr., 1989, James H. Hamilton Book award, Am. Coll. Health Care Execs., 1990, Pres. Cabinet award, U. Tex., 1995, Scientific Freedom and Responsibility award, AAAS, 1995, Joseph Leiter award, Nat. Libr. of Medicine, 1999, ARCHON award, Sigma Theta Tau Internat. Honor Soc. of Nursing, 1999, Washington Irving Book award for False Hopes, 1999, Movison prize for sci. and society, MIT; fellow nat. fellow, Bus. Enterprise Trust, 1989—95, nat., 1989—95; scholar Tekolste scholar, Ind. Hosp. Assn., 1986, Tekolste, 1986. Fellow: AAAS (Sci. Freedom and Responsibility award 1996); mem.: Soc. for Study Social Biology (bd. dirs. 1987—95), Inst. Medicine of NAS, Am. Assn. for Advancement Humanities, Harvard Grad. Soc. (coun. 1989—92, sr. scholar 1994—). Home: PO Box 260 Ardsley On Hudson NY 10503-0260 Office: The Hastings Ctr 21 Malcolm Gordon Rd Garrison NY 10524-5555

CALLAHAN, DEBRA JEAN, not-for-profit organization executive; b. Burbank, Calif., June 4, 1958; d. Robert Bascom and Betty Jean Callahan; m. Kenneth A. Cook. Student, Calif. State Poly. U., San Luis Obispo, 1976-79; BA magna cum laude, U. Calif., Santa Barbara, 1981. Legal asst. Loo, Merideth & McMillan, L.A., 1982-83; field staff Mondale for Pres., Washington, 1984; dep. state campaign mgr. Mondale-Ferraro Com., Kansas City, Mo., 1984; regional polit. dir. League of Conservation Voters, Portsmouth, N.H., 1985-86; dep. campaign mgr. Kent Conrad for U.S. Senate, Bismarck, N.D., 1986; exec. asst. to Senator Kent Conrad, Washington, 1986-87; dep. nat. polit. dir. Gore for Pres., Washington, 1987-88; exec. dir. Ams. for the Environment, Washington, 1988-90; campaign mgr. Re-election Rep. Howard Wolpe (D-Md.), 1990; policy cons. Nat. Toxics Campaign, 1991—; program dir. W. Alton Jones Found., 1992-95; exec. dir. Brainerd Found., Seattle, 1995-96; pres. League of Conservation Voters, Washington, 1996—. Polit. cons. League of Conservation Voters, 1988. Field dir. Hands Across Am., St. Louis, 1986; bd. dirs. World Resources Inst., 1998—, Earth Day Network, 1999-2003. U. Calif. Dept. Environ. Studies scholar, Santa Barbara, 1981, Alumni award, 1998. Avocations: travel, reading, scuba diving, bicycling, music. Office: League of Conservation Voters 1920 L St NW Ste 800 Washington DC 20036-5045

CALLAHAN, DENNIS S., insurance company executive; BA in Math., NYU. V.p. global ops. and tech. Goldman, Sachs & Co., NYC, 1971—91; chief info. officer Wellington Mgmt. Co., Boston, 1991—95; sr. v.p. Fidelity's Asset Svcs. Group, Boston, 1995—97; chief info. officer Am. Internat. Group, NYC, 1997—2000; sr. v.p., chief info. officer Guardian Life Ins. Co. Am., NYC, 2000—. Office: Guardian Life Ins Co 7 Hanover Sq New York NY 10004-2616

CALLAHAN, EDWARD WILLIAM, chemical engineer, retired manufacturing executive; b. NYC, July 17, 1930; s. William Patrick and Clara (Schultz) C.; m. Barbara Jane Willmarth, Nov. 23, 1985; children: Susan Lynne, Kevin Foster. B.Ch.E., Cornell U., 1953. Engr. Solvay div. Allied Chem. Corp., Syracuse, N.Y., 1953-65, dir. comml. devel., 1965-66; asst. to pres. Allied Signal Corp., N.Y.C., 1966-70, gen. mgr. environ. services Morristown, N.J., 1970-78, v.p. health, safety and environ. scis., 1978-95; ret. Bd. dirs. Am. Cancer Soc., Morristown, 1982-84; trustee Ind. Coll. Fund. of N.J., 1988-94. Mem.: Chem. Mfrs. Assn. (chmn. environ. mgmt. com. 1978—82), Am. Indsl. Health Coun. (dir. 1978—91), Chem. Industry Inst. Toxicology (dir. 1974—91, Conf. Bd. environ. com. chmn. 1994—95), World Environ. Ctr. (bd. dirs. 1992—98), Internat. Environ. Forum (chmn. 1986—94), Quantuck Beach Club, Quogue Field Club, Shinnecock Yacht Club, Union Club, F & AM (Holland Lodge No. 8). Home: 389 S Lake Dr Apt 4C Palm Beach FL 33480

CALLAHAN, JAMES MICHAEL, physician, educator; b. Ilion, N.Y., July 24, 1959; s. Joseph R. and Eileen R. Callahan; m. Irene G. Gazetos, June 26, 1982; children: Peter J., Katherine E., Christine S. BS, St. Lawrence U., Canton, N.Y., 1977—81; MD, SUNY Upstate Med. U., Syracuse, 1981—85. Diplomate Am. Bd. Pediat., 1989, in Pediat. Emergency Medicine Am. Bd. Pediat., 1994. Clin. asst. prof., pediat. U. Pa. Sch. Medicine, Phila., 1995—96; asst. prof., pediat. Ohio State U. Coll. Medicine, Columbus, 1996—97; asst. prof., emergency medicine and pediat. SUNY Upstate Med. U., Syracuse, 1997—2002, assoc. prof., emergency medicine and pediat., 2002—, dir. pediatric emergency medicine fellowship program, 2005—. Office: SUNY Upstate Med Univ 750 E Adams St Syracuse NY 13210 Office Phone: 315-464-6210. Office Fax: 315-464-6229. Personal E-mail: callahaj@upstate.edu.

CALLAHAN, JEAN M., personnel administrator; d. John Martin Hildebrandt and Catherine Mary Dore; m. Gerald Francis Callahan, July 11, 1969; 1 child, Christopher. BS, CUNY, 1967, MEd, 1969; MA in Labor studies, SUNY, 1981; MS in Spl. Edn., Adelphi U., N.Y., 1983; diploma in adminstrn., Long Island U. CW Post, N.Y., 1989. Cert. home and careers, elem. edn. and spl. edn. N.Y. Tchr. home and careers various schs., Long Island, NY, 1971—83; consumer tchr. Ea. Suffolk Bd. Cooperative Svcs. Edn., Long Island, NY, 1985; spl. edn. tchr. Miller (N.Y.) Pl. Union Free Sch. Dist., 1985—96, adminstr. pupil personnel adminstr., 1994—. Chairperson spl. edn. Miller (N.Y.) Pl. Union Free Sch. Dist., 1994—96; ednl. cons. ACCES Partnerships, Long Island, NY, 1993—96, N.Y. Dirs. Com., 2001—. Mem.: Coun. Exceptional Children, Coun. Adminstrs. Spl. Edn. (Long Island Chpt.) (treas. 2000—). Avocations: exercise, swimming, reading. Office: Miller Pl Union Free Sch Dist 275 Rte 25A Miller Place NY 11764 E-mail: jcallaha@millerplace.k12.ny.us.

CALLAHAN, J(OHN) WILLIAM (BILL CALLAHAN), judge; b. Rockville Centre, N.Y., Feb. 8, 1947; s. Peter Felix and Catherine L. C. BA, Mich. State U., 1971, JD cum laude, 1974. Atty. Bank of Commonwealth, Detroit, 1974-76; assoc. Hoops & Hudson, P.C., Detroit, 1976-79, Tyler & Canham, P.C., Detroit, 1979-80, Stark & Reagan, P.C., Troy, Mich., 1980-81; pvt. practice Farmington Hills, Mich., 1981-86; mem. Plunkett & Cooney, P.C., Detroit, 1986-96; judge Wayne County Cir. Ct., Detroit, 1996—. Bd. dirs. Vietnam Vets. Am. Chpt. 9, Detroit, 1981-85. With USMC, 1967-69, Vietnam. Mem. Detroit Bar Assn. Office: 1813 City-County Bldg Detroit MI 48226

CALLAHAN, LEANDRES, finance educator; b. Waukegan, Ill., Feb. 22, 1971; s. Sylvester Alvin and Dorethia Mary Callahan; m. Tasha Renee Callahan, Mar. 24, 1992; children: Nayyirah, Elyaas. Psychol. advisor African Am. Cultural, North Chicago, Ill., 1993—2002. Served with Air N.G., 1988—98. Home: 1931 Greenfield Ave North Chicago IL 60064 Home Fax: 847-689-4384.

CALLAHAN, MICHAEL JOHN, lawyer; BS, Georgetown U., 1990; JD with honors, U. Conn. Atty. Skadden, Arps, Slate, Meagher & Flom, LLP, 1995—99; mgr. bus. devel., corp. counsel electronics Electronics for Imaging Inc., 1999; corp. counsel Yahoo!, Inc., Sunnyvale, Calif., 1999—2000, sr. corp. counsel, 2000, assoc. gen. counsel, 2000—01, dep. gen. counsel, asst. sec., 2001—03, gen. counsel, sec., 2003—. Office: Yahoo Inc 701 First Ave Sunnyvale CA 94089 Office Phone: 408-349-3300. Office Fax: 408-349-3301.

CALLAHAN, MICHAEL R., lawyer; b. NYC, Apr. 11, 1953; BA, No. Ill. U.; JD, DePaul U., 1979. Bar: Ill. 1979. Law clerk to Justice Daniel P. Ward Ill. Supreme Ct., 1979—81; ptnr. head Health Care Practice group Katten Muchin Zavis Rosenman, Chgo. Adj. prof. DePaul Coll., Masters in Health Law Prog. Mem.: ABA, Am. Health Lawyers Assn., Ill. Assn. of Hosp. Attys., Chgo. Bar Assn. Office: Katten Muchin Zavis Rosenman 525 W Monroe St Chicago IL 60661 Office Phone: 312-902-5634. Office Fax: 312-577-8945. E-mail: michael.callahan@kmzr.com.

CALLAHAN, MICHAEL THOMAS, arbitrator, consultant, construction executive, writer; b. Kansas City, Mo., Oct. 7, 1948; s. Harry Leslie and Venita June (Yohn) Callahan; m. Stella Sue Paffenbach, Mar. 21, 1970; children: Molly Leigh, Michael Kroh. BA, U. Kans., 1970; JD, U. Mo., 1973, LLM, 1979; postgrad., Temple U., 1976-77. Bar: Kans. 1973, N.J. 1975, Mo. 1977. V.p. T.J. Constrn., Inc., Lenexa, Kans., 1973-74; sr. cons. Wagner-Hohns-Inglis, Inc., Mt. Holly, NJ, 1974-77, v.p. Kansas City, Mo., 1977-86; exec. v.p. CCL Constrn. Cons., Overland Park, Kans., 1986-88, pres., 1988—. Adj. prof. U. Kans., Iowa State U.; arbitrator; lectr. in field; chmn. CCL Pacific Corp.; pres. Handcrafted Wines Kans., Inc. Home: 9011 Delmar St Shawnee Mission KS 66207-2343 Office: CCL Constrn Cons 4600 College Blvd Ste 104 Overland Park KS 66211-1606 Office Phone: 913-491-8626 ext 8626. Business E-Mail: cclcon@ix.netcom.com.

CALLAHAN, PATRICIA R., bank executive; BSME, M in Mgmt. and Fin., MIT. Various mgmt. positions Crocker Nat. Bank, 1977—84, sr. v.p., mgr. corp. svcs., 1984—93; dir. human resources Wells Fargo & Co., 1993—97, exec. v.p. wholesale banking sys. fin. and ops., 1997—98, exec. v.p., dir. human resources, 1998—. Bd. dirs. United Way Bay Area; bd. trustees Dominican U. Calif. Office: Wells Fargo & Co 420 Montgomery St San Francisco CA 94163*

CALLAHAN, ROBERT EDWARD, lawyer; b. N.Y.C., Aug. 17, 1949; s. John Francis and Helen M. (Jones) C.; m. Terry Aune Callahan, Sept. 30, 1989. BA, U. Calif., Santa Barbara, 1971; JD, U. Santa Clara, Calif., 1975. Bar: Calif. 1975, U.S. Dist. Ct. (cen., ea. and so. dists.) Calif. 1976, U.S. Ct. Appeals (9th cir.) 1991. Ptnr. Virtue and Scheck, Newport Beach, Calif., 1978-84, Paone, Callahan, McHolm & Winton, Irvine, Calif., 1984-2000; pvt. practice Newport Beach, 2000—. Pres. U. Calif. Irvine Athletic Found., 1984-86, bd. dirs., 1983-94; bd. dirs. U. Calif. Irvine Found., 1995-2001, Hoag Hosp. Found., 1999—; bd. dirs. Orange County Youth Sports Found., 1990—, pres., 1992-95, Orange County Youth Sports Found., 1991, mem. exec. com., 1993-96. Mem. Newport Harbor Area C. of C., Newport Beach Athletic Club, Ctr. Club, Hoag Hosp. 552 Club (bd. dirs. 1991-97, pres. 1995-96), Commodores Club (exec. com. 1993, pres. 1996-97), Newport Beach Country Club. Office: 4041 MacArthur Blvd Ste 350 Newport Beach CA 92660 E-mail: rcallahan@rcallahanlaw.com.

CALLAHAN, ROBERT JOHN, JR., lawyer, arbitrator; b. St. Louis, July 3, 1923; s. Robert John and Elizabeth Mae Deck (Gentner) C.; m. Dorothy Foley, Apr. 18, 1958 (dec. Nov. 1980); m. Barbara Kelsall Couture, May 22, 1982. Grad., Chaminade Coll., 1941; BS in Bus. Adminstrn., Washington U., 1944; JD cum laude, Notre Dame U., 1948. Bar: Mo. 1948, U.S. Ct. Appeals (fed. cir.) 1951, U.S. Supreme Ct. 1955, U.S. Ct. Mil. Appeals. Ptnr. Callahan and Callahan, St. Louis, 1948-56; sole practice St. Louis, 1956—. Contbr. articles to legal jours. Candidate for judge St. Louis County Cir. Ct., 1960. Served with FBI and USCGR, 1944-45; former liaison officer USAF Acad. Served to capt. JAGC, USAFR. Coro fellow. Mem. ABA, Lawyers Assn. of St. Louis, St. Louis Bar Assn., Am. Assn. Trial Lawyers, Notre Dame U. Law Assn., U. Notre Dame Alumni Assn., Nat. Panel Consumer Arbitrators, Ret. Air Force Officers Assn., Phi Delta Theta. Republican. Roman Catholic. Office: 32 Normandy Dr Lake Saint Louis MO 63367-1502 Office Phone: 636-625-8584.

CALLAHAN, SONNY (H.L. CALLAHAN), former congressman; b. Mobile, Ala., Sept. 11, 1932; m. Karen Reed; children: Scott, Patrick, Shawn Cushing, Chris, Cameron (dec.), Kelly Thomas. Grad., McGill Inst. Pres., chmn. bd., chief exec. officer Finch Cos., Mobile and Montgomery, Ala., 1964-84; mem. Ala. Ho. of Reps., 1970-78, chmn. Mobile County delegation; mem. Ala. Senate, 1978-82, U.S. Congress from 1st Ala. dist., 1985—2002; mem. appropriations com.; chmn. subcom. on energy and water devel.; pres. Sonny Callahan and Assoc. Served with USN, 1952-54 Mem. Mobile Area C. of C., Ala. Movers Assn., Ala. Trucking Assn., Kiwanis, Optimists, Ala. Port Authority Bd. Republican. Office: Sonny Callahan and Assoc

CALLAHAN, THOMAS JAMES, lawyer; b. Cleve., Jan. 21, 1957; s. Thomas Joseph and Lucille Dorothy (DeVries) C.; m. Laura Jean Schwartz, Oct. 13, 1979; children: Thomas, Michael. BS cum laude in Acctg., Duke U., 1979; JD cum laude, Case Western Reserve U., 1985. Bar: Ohio 1985, U.S. Ct. Appeals (6th cir.) 1987, U.S. Tax Ct. 1987, U.S. Dist. Ct. (no. dist.) Ohio 1987, U.S. Ct. Fed. Claims 1987, U.S. Ct. Appeals (fed. cir.) 2000, U.S. Supreme Ct. 2000; CPA, Ohio 1981. Staff st. acct. Price Waterhouse, Cleve., 1979-82, mgr., 1985-86; assoc. Thompson Hine LLP, Cleve., 1986-96, ptnr., 1997—, leader tax practice. Vice chair allocations com. United Way Svcs., Cleve., 1992-96; mem. arbitration com. Cuyahoga Ct. Common Pleas, Cleve., 1989—. Mem.: AICPA, ABA (tax sect., chair adminstrv. practice com.), Am. Coll. Tax Counsel (regent), Cleve. Tax Inst. (exec. com. 1999—2005, chair 2001, 2004), Cleve. Bar Assn. (spkr. 1994—, chmn. gen. tax com. 1999), Tax Club Cleve. (bd. dirs. 2000, treas. 2001, v.p. 2002—03, pres. 2004). Office: Thompson Hine LLP 3900 Key Ctr 127 Pub Sq Cleveland OH 44114-1216 Office Phone: 216-566-5612. E-mail: tom.callahan@thompsonhine.com.

CALLAHAN, TIMOTHY T., real estate company executive; BA, Notre Dame (Ind.) U.; student in Bus. Adminstrn., NYU. Sr. v.p. Chem. Realty Corp., 1974—88; from dir. devel to v.p. fin. Edward J. DeBartolo Corp., Youngstown, Ohio, 1988—92; sr. v.p. EGI, 1992—95; pres., CEO Equity Office Properties Trust, 1996—2002; pres. Trizec Properties, Inc., Chgo., 2002—, CEO, 2002—, bd. dir. Office: Trizec Properties Inc 233 S Wacker Dr Ste 4600 Chicago IL 60606

CALLAHAN, VINCENT FRANCIS, JR., state legislator, publishing executive; b. Washington, Oct. 30, 1931; s. Vincent Francis and Anita (Hawkins) C.; m. Dorothy Helen Budge, Aug. 27, 1960 (dec. Jan. 5, 2005); children: Vincent Francis III, Elizabeth Lauren, Anita Marie, Cynthia Helen, Robert Bruce. BS in Fgn. Svc., Georgetown U., 1957; LHD (hon.), No. Va. C.C., 1997. Pres. Callahan Publs., 1957-2000; mem. Va. Hos. of Dels., 1968—, minority leader, 1982-85, chmn. appropriations com. Author eight books including: Missle Contracts Guide, 1958, Space Guide, 1959, Underwater Defense Handbook, 1963, Military Research Handbook, 1963. Candidate for lt. gov. Va., 1965; state fin. chmn. Rep. Party of Va., 1966-68; candidate for U.S. Congress, 1976; chmn. No. Va. Cmty. Found.; co-chmn. Jamestown-Yorktown Found. With USMC, 1950-53; as lt. USCGR, 1959-63. Mem. U.S. Naval Inst., Nat. Press Club, Kiwanis (past pres. McLean, Va.). Republican. Roman Catholic. Office: PO Box 1173 Mc Lean VA 22101-1173 Personal E-mail: dcalla5475@aol.com.

CALLAN, CLAIR MARIE, physician, laboratory director, educator; b. Sleaford, Lincolnshire, Eng., May 18, 1940; d. Joseph Edward and Margaret Mary (Hart) Mills; m. John Patrick Callan, Apr. 4, 1964; children: Eoin, Grainne, Colm, Maeve. M.B., B.Surgery, B. in Art of Obstetrics, Univ. Coll., Dublin, Ireland, 1963, MBA U. Phoenix, 1993. Intern Mater Hosp., Dublin, 1963-64, resident in anesthesia, 1964-65; staff physician State of Conn., Middletown, 1966-68; anesthesiologist St. Francis Hosp., Hartford, Conn., 1972-76; med. dir. Dept. of Income Maintenance, State of Conn., Hartford, 1978-84; v.p. med. and regulatory affairs, dir. med. affairs Abbott Labs., Abbott Park, Ill., 1985-92, venture head, 1992-93, v.p. med. and regulatory affairs and advanced rsch. hosp. products divsn., 1993—; clin. asst. prof. med., Chgo. Med. Sch./U. Health Scis., 1987—; CEO Callan Consulting, 2004—; sr. fellow Nat. Alliance for Health Info. Tech. Contbr. articles to profl. jours. Pres. PTA, Wethersfield, Conn., 1974, Capitol Region Assn. of Pvt. Swim Clubs, Hartford, 1978. Mem. Am. Med. Women's Assn. (pres. 1984-85, councillor 1981-83), AMA (pres. Conn. aux. 1979-81, v.p. sci. quality and pub. health 1999-2004, interim sr. v.p. profl. stds.), Am. Acad. Med. Dirs. Republican. Roman Catholic. Avocations: tennis; golf; needlework. Home: 1835 W North Pond Ln Lake Forest IL 60045-4819

CALLAN, EDWARD THOMAS, language educator; b. Ballina, Ireland, Dec. 3, 1917; s. Owen and Ellen (O'Connor) C.; m. R. Claire Wegner, Aug. 6, 1955; children: Joseph Mark, Ruth Ann. BA, Witwatersrand U., 1947; MA, Fordham U., 1953; DPhil, U. South Africa, 1959. Instr. in English Fordham U., N.Y.C., 1952-54, Loyola U., Chgo., 1954-57; assoc. prof. English Western Mich. U., Kalamazoo, 1957-63, prof. English, 1964-83, Disting univ. prof., 1982-83, Disting. univ. prof. emeritus, 1983—. Vis. prof. English U. Mich., Ann Arbor, 1968; nat. panel of spkrs. Ministry for Info., London, 1950-52; external examiner Rhodes U., South Africa, 1968-72, U. Toronto, 1975-76; lectr. Oxford U., 1974. Author: Auden, 1983, Yeats on Yeats, 1981, Alan Paton, 1968, 2d edit., 1982, (play) I Am of Ireland, 1988, Molly's Only Playboy, 2000, (video film) I Am of Ireland, 2001. Bd. dirs. New Vic Theatre, Kalamazoo, 1974-79. With South African Artillery, 1941-46. Carnegie grant Oxford U., 1960-61. Mem. MLA (life), Oxford Soc. Roman Catholic. Avocation: tennis. Home: 2012 Quail Cove Dr Kalamazoo MI 49009-1868 E-mail: ecallan@aol.com.

CALLAN, JOHN GARLING, management consultant; b. N.Y.C., Oct. 12, 1946; s. Andrew Thomas and Virginia Garling (Wheatley) C.; m. Linda Ferguson Adkinson, Aug. 28, 1978. BA in Russian Lang., U. N.C., 1969. Pres. Alex Nichols Agy., Inc., L.A., 1971-73; pres., founder Calico Air Courier Svc., L.A., 1973-79; v.p. mktg. DHL Worldwide Express, Burlingame, Calif., 1979-82; pres. TNT Skypak, Inc., Burlingame, Calif., 1982-83; sr. v.p. mktg. and sales Purolator Courier Corp., Basking Ridge, N.J., 1983-84, sr. v.p. internat., 1984-85; pres. Callan Assocs., Mendham, N.J., 1985-87; dir. entertainment imaging Polaroid Corp., Cambridge, Mass., 1987-93, dir. new bus. devel., 1993-95; COO Milestone Sys., Inc., Lexington, Mass., 1995-97; founder, owner ePicture.com, Essex, Conn., 1998—; prin. John G. Callan, Cons., 1997—2002; founder, prin. Ursa Major Assocs., LLC, Essex, Conn., 2002—. Contract cons. PriceWaterhouse Coopers, Arlington, Va., 1997—; bd. dirs. ImageWare Sys., Inc., San Diego. V.p. Washington Valley Cmty. Assn., Mendham, 1986; bd. govs. The Gore Pl. Soc., Waltham, Mass., 1993-96; lay Eucharistic min. St. Peter's Episcopal Ch., Weston, 1995—; bd. trustees Hurricane Island Outward Bound Sch., 2001—; bd. mgrs. Boston Cannons, Maj. League, Lacrosse, 2001-03. Morehead scholar U. N.C., Chapel Hill, 1965-69. Mem. Air Courier Conf. Am., Inc. (sec. 1981-82, dir. 1979-82), Travel Industry Assn. Am. (bd. dirs. 1987-92), Parcel Shippers Assn (bd.dirs., 2003—).

CALLAN, JOSI IRENE, museum director; b. Yorkshire, Eng., Jan. 30, 1946; came to U.S., 1953; d. Roger Bradshaw and Irene (Newbury) Winstanley; children: James, Heather, Brett Jack; m. Patrick Marc Callan, June 26, 1984. BA in Art History summa cum laude, Calif. State U., Domingues Hills, 1978, MA in Behavioral Scis., 1981. Dir. community rels./alumni affairs Calif. State U., Dominguez Hills, adminstrv. fellow office chancellor Long Beach, assoc. dir. univ. svcs. office chancellor, 1979-85; dir. capital campaign, assoc. dir. devel. Sta. KVIE-TV, Sacramento, 1985-86; dir. project devel. Pacific Mountain Network, Denver, 1986-87; dir. mktg. and devel. Denver Symphony Orch., 1988-89; assoc. dir. San Jose (Calif.) Mus. Art, 1989-91, dir., 1991-99, Mus. of Glass, Tacoma, Wash., 1999—. Asst. prof. sch. social and behavioral scis. Calif. State U., Dominguez Hills, 1981—; mem. adv. com. Issues Facing Mus. in 1990s JKF U., 1990-91. Mem. com. arts policy Santa Clara Arts Coun., 1990-92; chair San Jose Arts Roundtable, 1992-93; active ArtTable, 1992—, Community Leadership San Jose, 1992-93, Am. Leadership Forum, 1994, bd. dirs., 2000—; mem. adv. bd. Bay Area Rsch. Project, 1992—; mem. Calif. Arts Coun., Visual Arts Panel, 1993-95, Santa Clara Arts Coun. Visual Arts Panel, 1993; bd. dirs. YWCA, 1993—. Recipient Leadership award Knight Found., 1995; Women of Vision honoree Career Action Ctr., 1998; fellow Calif. State U., 1982-83. Mem. AAUW, Am. Assn. Mus., Nat. Soc. Fund Raising Execs. (bd. dirs. 1991), Colo. Assn. Fund Raisers, Art Mus. Devel. Assn., Assn. Art Mus. Dirs., We. Mus. Assn., Calif. State U. Alumni Coun. (pres. 1981-83), Rotary Internat. Office: Museum of Glass 1801 E Dock St Tacoma WA 98402-3217

CALLAND, ALBERT M., III, federal agency administrator; Grad, US Naval Acad., 1974; MS, Indsl. Coll. of Armed Forces. Assoc. dir. ctrl. intelligence for military support USN, 1987—92, comdr. SEAL Team One, 1992—95, comdr. Naval Spl. Warfare Devel. Group, 1997—99, comdr. SOCCENT, 2000, joint forces spl. ops. component command Operation Enduring Freedom, 2001; comdr. naval spl. warfare command, 2002—04; assoc. dir. ctrl. intelligence for military support CIA, 2004—05, acting dep. dir., 2005, dep. dir., 2005—. Decorated Disting Svc. Medal, Superior Svc. Medal (two awards), Legion of Merit, Bronze Star Medal, Def. Meritorious Svc. Medal (two awards), Meritorious Svc. Medal (five awards), Navy Comendation Medal, others. Office: CIA Office Dep Dir Washington DC 20505*

CALLANDER, BRUCE DOUGLAS, journalist, freelance writer; b. Malone, NY, Dec. 23, 1923; s. Douglas Newton and Blanche Keller (Redfield) C.; m. Imogene A. O'Malley, Nov. 23, 1979; children by previous marriage—Richard Scott, John Byron AB with cert. in Journalism, U. Mich., Ann Arbor, 1948. Indsl. editor Kaiser Frazer Co., Willow Run, Mich., 1948-50; pub. relations officer U.S. Air Force, Ohio, Md., 1951-52; assoc. editor Air Force Times, Washington, 1952-67, mng. editor, 1967-72, editor Springfield, Va., 1972-85; freelance writer, mil. historian Mullett Lake, Mich., 1986—. Served to capt. USAF, 1942-45, 51-52; Italy. Recipient Hopwood awards U. Mich., 1945, 48; Freedom Found. award, 1982. Mem.: St. Andrews Soc. (Washington). Avocations: painting, sculpting, woodworking, playing the flute. Personal E-mail: brucal@hmo.net.

CALLANDER, KAY EILEEN PAISLEY, business owner, retired education educator, writer; b. Coshocton, Ohio, Oct. 15, 1938; d. Dalton Olas and Dorothy Pauline (Davis) Paisley; m. Don Larry Callander, Nov. 18, 1977. BSE, Muskingum Coll., 1960; MA in Speech Edn., Ohio State U., 1964, postgrad., 1964-84. Cert. elem., gifted, drama, theater tchr., Ohio. Tchr. Columbus (Ohio) Pub. Schs., 1960-70, 80-88, drama specialist, 1970-80, classroom, gifted/talented tchr., 1986-90, ret., 1990; sole prop. The Ali Group, Kay Kards, 1992—. Coord. Artists-in-the Schs., 1977-88; ednl. cons. Innovation Alliance Youth Adv. Coun., 1992—; cons., presenter in field. Producer-dir., Shady Lane Music Festival, 1980-88; dir. tchr. (nat. distbr. video) The Trial of Gold E. Locks, 1983-84; rep., media pub. relations liason Sch. News., 1983-88; author, creator Trivia Game About Black Americans; presenter for workshop by Human Svc. Group and Creative Edn. Coop., Columbus, Ohio, 1989. Benefactor, Columbus Jazz Arts Group; v.p., bd. dirs. Neoteric Dance and Theater Co., Columbus, 1985-87; tchr., participant Future Stars sculpture exhibit, Ft. Hayes Ctr., Columbus Pub. Schs., 1988; tchr. advisor Columbus Coun. PTAs, 1983-86, co-chmn. reflections com., 1984-87; mem. Columbus Mus. Art, Citizens for Humane Action, Inc.; upt.'s adv. coun. Columbus Pub. Schs., 1967-68; presenter Young Author Seminar, Ohio Dept. Edn., 1988, Illustrating Methods for Young Authors' Books, 1986-87; cons. and workshop leader seminar/workshop Tchg. About the Constitution in Elem. Schs., Franklin County Ednl. Coun., 1988; sponsor Minority Youth Recognition Awards, 1994. Named Educator of Yr., Shady Lane PTA, 1982, Columbus Coun. PTAs, 1989, winner Colour Columbus Landscape Design Competition, 1990; Sch. Excellence grantee Columbus Pub. Schs.; Commendation Columbus Bd. Edn. and Ohio Ho. of Reps. for Child Assault Prevention project, 1986-87; first place winner statewide photo contest Ohio Vet. Assn., 1991; recipient Muskingum Coll. Alumni Disting. Svc. award, 1995. Mem. ASCD, AAUW, Assn. for Childhood Edn. Internat., Ohio Coun. for Social Studies, Franklin County Ret. Tchrs. Assn., Nat. Mus. Women in the Arts, Ohio State U. Alumni Assn., U.S. Army Officers Club, Navy League, Liturgical Art Guild Ohio, Columbus Jazz Arts Group, Columbus Mus. Art, Nat. Coun. for Social Studies, Columbus Art League, Columbus Maennerchor (Damen sect.). Republican. Avocations: painting, photography, swimming, golf, playing piano and organ. Home: 9131 Indian Mound Rd Pickerington OH 43147 Personal E-mail: pais16091@aol.com. E-mail: paiscallander@earthlink.net.

CALLAR, DONNA HOWE, counseling administrator, educator; b. Moundsville, W.Va., June 29, 1940; d. Chester Ray and Freda Marie Howe; m. Donald Evan Callar, Nov. 19, 1972 (dec. Sept. 1996). BA, West Liberty State Coll., 1962; MEd, W.Va. U., 1965, MEd, 1968; PhD, Union Grad. Sch., 1987. Lic. profl. counselor Va., cert. clin. mental health counselor Nat. Bd. Cert. Counselors, Inc. Tchr. elem., prin., jr. high counselor Marshall County

Schs., Moundsville, 1962—70; counselor elem. Berkeley County Schs., Martinsburg, W.Va., 1970—72; sch. social worker Fairfax County Schs., Va., 1973—90; counselor elem. Loudoun County Schs., Leesburg, Va., 1990—. Adj. prof. Bowie State U., Md., 1980—, U. Va., Fairfax, 1980—. Author: Those Dynamite Years--Teenagers, 1987; author: (pamphlet) Introducing Elementary Guidance, 1969. Named Woman of Yr., Annandale chpt. Bus. and Profl. Women, 1980; recipient Excellence in Edn. award, Fairfax Cmty. Action, 1990. Mem.: NEA, Va. Edn. Assn., Am. Sch. Counselors (W.Va. coord.), Alpha Delta Kappa. Avocations: flying, reading, sewing, antiques. Home: 1334 W Washington St Harpers Ferry WV 25425

CALLARD, DAVID JACOBUS, investment company executive; b. Boston, July 14, 1938; s. Henry Hadden and Clarissa Cooley (Jacobus) C.; m. Deborah Winston, 1960 (div. 1982); children: Owen Winston, Francis Jacobus, Anne Lloyd, Elizabeth Hadden, Samuel Porter; m. Mary R. Morgan, July 14, 1990. AB, Princeton U., 1959; postgrad., Union Theol. Sem., 1964-65; JD, NYU, 1969. With Morgan Guaranty Trust Co., N.Y.C., 1959-61, asst. v.p., 1965-69, v.p., 1970-72; gen. ptnr. Alex Brown & Sons, Balt., 1972-84; mng. dir., 1984-89; bd. dirs. Alex Brown Inc., Balt., 1984-89; pres. Wand Ptnrs. Inc., N.Y.C., 1991—; chmn. Pelican Investment Mgmt., Inc., Boston, 2002—. Bd. dirs. Fulcrum Analytics, Inc., Seedworks, Inc., ACSIS, Inc., 2002—. Chmn. bd. dirs. Union Theol. Sem., N.Y.C.; dep. exec. dir. Pres.'s Commn. on All Vol. Armed Forces, 1969-70. Lt. USMC, 1961-64. Boothe Ferris fellow, 1964-65 Mem. Union Club, Knickerbocker Club, Elkridge (Balt.). Democrat. Episcopalian. Office Phone: 212-949-1936.

CALLAWAY, BEN ANDERSON, journalist; b. Oakland, Calif., Mar. 16, 1927; s. Owen M. and Aulis (Anderson) C.; m. Patricia Hurd, Apr. 7, 1951; children: Randall Owen, Karen Callaway Franks. Student, Stanford, 1946-47; BA, Denison U., 1950. Sports writer, wildlife editor Denver Post, 1950-57; with Phila. Daily News, 1957-80, sports editor, 1961-70, outdoor columnist, 1961-80; outdoor editor Phila. Inquirer, 1980-91, editor fishing reports, 1992—2000; outdoor columnist Courier-Post, 1992—2001. Exec. editor Metro East Outdoor News, 1973-77; co-editor Penn-Jersey Outdoor Sportsman, 1976-77; free-lance mag. writer-photographer; commentator Sta. KYW, 1972-95. Sports chmn. Phila. United Fund, 1966-70; active local Boy Scouts Am., Eagle, 1942. Served with USNR, 1945-46. Recipient Henshall award Am. Fishing Tackle Mfrs. Assn., 1964, Old Salt award N.J. Resort Assn., 1967, Johnson Deep Woods award, 1977; gold medal Pa. Fish and Game Protective Assn., 1978; McCulloch Outdoor Writing award, 1978 Mem. Phila. Sports Writers Assn. (pres. 1968-70), Denver Sports Writers and Broadcasters Assn. (pres. 1957), Outdoor Writers Am. (dir. 1976-79, 89—92, Pa. Outdoor Writers, Boating Writers Internat. (dir. 1976-85), Met. N.Y. Rod and Gun Editors, N.J. Outdoor Writers Assn. (v.p. 1982-86, pres. 1988-91), Blue Key, Beta Theta Pi, Pi Delta Epsilon, Omicron Delta Kappa. Presbyn. (elder) and Meth. Address: 146 Buckingham Dr Southampton NJ 08088

CALLAWAY, CLIFFORD WAYNE, physician; b. Easton, Md., May 28, 1941; s. Charles Herschel and Anna Agnes (Stradley) C.; 1 child, David Wayne; m. Jackie Chalkley. BA, U. Del., 1963; MD, Northwestern U., 1967. Diplomate Am. Bd. Internal Medicine, Am. Bd. Endocrinology, Diabetes and Metabolism, Am. Bd. Nutrition. Resident in internal medicine Northwestern U. Med. Ctr., Chgo., 1967—69, Mayo Grad. Sch. Medicine, Rochester, Minn., 1971—73, advanced clin. resident in endocrinology, 1973—75; assoc. cons. Mayo Clinic, 1975—78, cons. endocrinology, 1978—85, dir. nutrition and lipid clinics, 1980—85; rsch. assoc. Harvard Med. Sch., Boston, 1976—78; dir. ctr. clin. nutrition George Washington U., Washington, 1986—88; sr. sci. cons. Food & Nutrition Bd., NRC/NAS, Washington, 1987—88; pvt. practice Washington, 1988—. Author 4 books; contbr. articles to profl. jours. Acting exec. sec. nutrition coordinating office HHS, Washington, 1980. Mayo Found. scholar, 1976-78. Mem. Am. Soc. Clin. Nutrition (treas. 1988), Am. Bd. Nutrition (bd. dirs. 1983-89, 95-98, sec.-treas. 1984-86, v.p. 1986-88), Am. Inst. Nutrition (chair and various coms.), Am. Dietetics Assn. (hon.), Am. Osler Soc. (bd. dirs.), Am. Assn. Clin. Endocrinologists (bd. dirs. 1992-95), Ctrl. European Ctr. for Health and Environment (bd. dirs.), Wash. Acad. Medicine. Achievements include development and writing of dietary guidelines for Americans (USDA/DHHS). Office: 2311 M St NW Ste 301 Washington DC 20037-1468 Office Phone: 202-331-3336. Personal E-mail: cwcallaway@aol.com.

CALLAWAY, HOWARD HOLLIS, resort executive; b. La Grange, Ga., Apr. 2, 1927; s. Cason Jewell and Virginia (Hand) C.; m. Elizabeth Walton, June 11, 1949; children: Elizabeth Callaway Considine, Howard Hollis Jr., Edward Cason, Virginia Callaway Martin, Ralph Walton. Student, Ga. Inst. Tech., 1944-45; BS, U.S. Mil. Acad., 1949. Commd. 2d lt. AUS, 1949, advanced through grades to 1st lt., 1952; resigned, 1952; mem. 89th Congress from 3d Ga. dist.; U.S. sec. Army Washington, 1973-75; campaign mgr. Pres. Ford Com., 1975-76; dir. Crested Butte (Colo.) Mountain Resort, 1975—. Pres. Nat. 4-H, svc. com.; former chmn. bd. trustees Ida Cason Callaway Found., Pine Mountain, Ga., Freedoms Found. at Valley Forge; former bd. regents U. Sys. Ga.; Rep. candidate for gov. of Ga., 1966; candidate Rep. primary for U.S. Senate from Colo., 1980; chmn. Colo. Rep. Com., 1981-87, chmn. GOPAC, 1987-93; mem. Def. Base Realignment and Closure Commn., 1992; active com. Ga. Dept. Industry, Trade and Tourism, 2001--. 1st lt. inf. U.S. Army, 1949-52. Mem. World Pres.' Orgn. (past pres.), Young Pres.' Orgn. (past pres.), Chief Execs. Orgn., Capital City Club (Atlanta), Piedmont Driving Club (Atlanta), Bohemian Club (San Francisco), Phi Delta Theta, Phi Kappa Phi. Episcopalian. Home: PO Box 1326 Pine Mountain GA 31822 Office Phone: 706-663-5075. Business E-Mail: bocallaway@callawaygardens.com.

CALLAWAY, STEPHEN V., federal judge; b. Olney, Ill., 1947; m. Marilyn Williams; two children. BA, La. State U., 1970, JD, 1973. Ptnr. Burnett, Sutton, Walker & Callaway, 1973-86; bankruptcy judge U.S. Dist. Ct. (we. dist.) La., Shreveport, 1986—, chief bankruptcy judge, 2005—. With USMCR. Office: US Dist Ct (we dist) La Rm 4400 300 Fannin St Ste 4400 Shreveport LA 71101-3124 Fax: (318) 676-4241.

CALLEN, JAMES DONALD, plasma physicist, nuclear engineer; b. Wichita, Kans., Jan. 31, 1941; s. Donald Dewitt and Bonnie Jean (Walton) C.; m. Judith Carolyn Chinn, Aug. 26, 1961; children: Jeffrey Scott, Sandra Jean. BS in Nuclear Engring., Kans. State U., 1962, MS in Nuclear Engring., 1964; PhD in Nuclear Engring., MIT, 1968. Postdoctoral fellow Inst. for Advanced Study, Princeton, N.J., 1968-69; asst. prof. aeros. and astronautics MIT, Cambridge, 1969-72; mem. rsch. staff fusion energy divsn. Oak Ridge (Tenn.) Nat. Lab., 1972-74, group leader, 1974-75, head plasma theory sect., 1975-79; prof. nuc. engring. and physics U. Wis., Madison, 1979-86, D.W. Kerst prof. engring. physics and physics, 1986—. Mem. editor. bd. Nuc. Fusion Jour., 1978-97; assoc. editor divsn. plasma physics Phys. Rev. Letters Jour., 1980-85; contbr. over 165 articles to profl. jours. Recipient Dept. of Energy Disting. Assoc. award, 1988, Disting. Career award Fusion Power Assocs., 2002; named to Coll. Engring. Hall of Fame, Kans. State U., 1991; Fulbright fellow Tech. Hogesch., Eindhoven, Netherlands, 1962-63; Guggenheim fellow, 1986. Fellow Am. Phys. Soc. (chmn. divsn. plasma physics 1986), Am. Nuc. Soc.; mem. NAE, AAAS. Office: U Wis 1500 Engineering Dr 521 ERB Madison WI 53706-1609 Business E-Mail: callen@engr.wisc.edu.

CALLEN, JEFFREY PHILLIP, dermatologist, educator; b. May 30, 1947; s. Irwin R. and Rose P. (Cohen) C.; m. Susan B. Manis, Dec. 21, 1968; children: Amy, David. BS, U. Wis., 1969; MD, U. Mich., 1972. Diplomate Am. Bd. Internal Medicine, Am. Bd. Dermatology. Intern, resident in internal medicine U. Mich., Ann Arbor, 1972-75, intern, resident in dermatology, 1975-77; from asst. clin. prof. to dir. residency tng. program U. Louisville Sch. Medicine, 1977-84, dir. residency tng. program, 1984-88; chief dermatology svc. Louisville VA Hosp., 1984-93, prof., chief dermatology divsn., 1988—. Author: Manual of Dermatology, 1980, Cutaneous Aspects of Internal Disease, 1981, Neurology Clinics North America, 1987, Dermatologic Signs of Systemic Disease, 1988, 3d edit., 2003, Color Atlas of Dermatology, 1993, 2d edit., 2000, Current Practice of Dermatology, 1995; editor: Clinics in Rheumatic Disease, 1982, Dermatologic Clinics, 1985, 89, 2002, Medical Clinics of North America, 1982, 84, 86, 89; editor-in-chief Dermavision video program; mem. editl. bd. Internat. Jour. Dermatology, 1990-95; asst. editor Internat. Jour. Dermatology, 1993-95, Jour. Am. Acad. Dermatology, 1995-2003; assoc. editor Archives Dermatology, 2003— Bd. dirs. Actor's Theater of Louisville, 1982-98, 2000—, sec., 1986-87, Ky. Arts and Crafts Found., 1991-97; bd. govs. JB Speed Art Mus., 1995-2003 Fellow ACP, Am. Acad. Dermatology (chmn. audio/visual edn. com., task force therapeutic agts., internal med. symposium 1978-83, chmn. sci. and tech. exhibits 1986-89, dir. various symposiums, mem. coun. sci. assembly 1993-98, chair 1997-98, chair com. to evaluate ann. meeting, 1999-2003, vice chair coun. on edn. 2002-2003, chair coun. on edn. 2003—, v.p.-elect 2003-2004, v.p. 2004-2005, bd. dirs. 1995-99, mem. exec. com. 1997-99, 2003-2005, co-chair program for 21st century 1999-2000, chair psoriasis edn. conf. 2002, chair unity summit), Am. Coll. Rheumatology (founder, chair skin disease study group 1996-98, 2000-02); mem. AMA, Am. Fedn. Clin. Rsch., Am. Dermatol. Assn., Dermatology Found. (trustee 1984-90), Louisville Theatrical Assn. (bd. dirs. 1999-2002). Achievements include research on condition in which systemic disease has cutaneous manifestations, lupus erythematosus, psoriasis, dermatomyositis. Office: U Louisville Dept Dermatology 310 E Broadway Ste 200 Louisville KY 40202-1745 Office Phone: 502-583-1749.

CALLENBACH, ERNEST, writer, editor; b. Williamsport, Pa., Apr. 3, 1929; m. Christine Leefeldt, May 19, 1978; children: Joanna, Hans. Ph.B., U. Chgo., 1949, MA, 1953. Editor Film Quar., U. Calif. Press, Berkeley, 1958-91, editor books, 1958-91. Author: Living Poor With Style, 1971, rev. as Living Cheaply With Style, 2000, Ecotopia, 1975, Ecotopian Ency. for the Eighties, 1981, Ecotopia Emerging, 1981, Publisher's Lunch, 1989, Earth's Ten Commandments, 1990, Bring Back the Buffalo!, 1995, Ecology: A Pocket Guide, 1998; co-author: The Art of Friendship, 1979, Citizen Legislature, 1985, Humphrey the Wayward Whale, 1986, EcoManagement, 1993. Mem. Nat. Writers Union. Address: care Banyan Tree Books 1963 El Dorado Ave Berkeley CA 94707-2441

CALLENDER, CLIVE ORVILLE, surgeon; b. NYC, Nov. 16, 1936; s. Joseph and Ida (Burke) C.; m. Fern Irene Marshall, May 25, 1968; children: Joseph, Ealena, Arianne. AB, Hunter Coll., 1959, DSc (hon.), 1998; MD, Meharry Med. Coll., 1963. Diplomate Am. Bd. Surgery, 1970. Intern U. Cin., 1963-64; asst. resident Harlem Hosp., N.Y.C., 1964-65, Howard U. and Freedmans Hosp., Washington, 1965-66, 67-68, chief resident, 1968-69, instr. dept. surgery, 1969-71; asst. resident Meml. Hosp. for Cancer and Allied Diseases, N.Y.C., 1966-67; cons. surgery Port Harcourt Gen. Hosp., Nigeria, 1970, 71; med. officer D.C. Gen. Hosp., 1970-71; NIH postdoctoral rsch. and clin. transplant fellow U. Minn., 1971-73; asst. prof. surgery Howard U. Med. Coll., Washington, 1973-76, assoc. prof., 1976-81, prof. surgery, 1981—, vice-chmn. dept. surgery, 1980-95, chmn. dept. surgery, 1996—, LaSalle D. Leffall, Jr. prof. surgery, 1996—, dir. transplant ctr., 1973—. Transplantation cons., Bermuda, 1977, V.I., 1978, 82-86; cons. Ethiopian Surg., Amenity Med. Sch., 1984; G.P.A. Ford Meml. lectr., 1978; mem. task force on organ procurement and transplantation HEW, 1984; testifier com. on labor and human resources U.S. Senate, 1983; mem. end stage renal disease study com. Inst. Medicine, 1989-90, com. on xenograft transplantation: ethical issues and pub. policy Inst. of Medicine, 1995-96, to the Sec. Health, 1990-94; mem. Inst. of Medicine Com. on Non-Heart-Beating Organ Transplantation II, 1999; fellowship in liver transplantation Pitts. U., 1986-87; founder, prin. investigator Nat. Minority Organ and Tissue Transplant Edn. Program, 1991—. Mem. editl. adv. bd. New Directions, 1974-91, Contemporary Dialysis and Nephrology Jour., 1993-95, Clin. Transplant Proceedings, 1998—, Am. Jour. Kidney Disease, 2001—); contbr. articles to med. jours. Testified for Ho. of Reps. Com. on Appropriation, U.S. Congress, 1992, others; councillor Soc. Organ Sharing, 1993, sec., 1995; chmn. tissue com. D.C. chpt. ARC, 1993-95; trustee Hunter Coll. Found., 2000. Recipient Hoffman LaRoche award, 1961, Charles Nelson Gold medal, 1963, Hudson Meadows award, 1963, Charles R. Drew Rsch. award, 1969, Daniel Hale Williams award, 1969, William Alonzo Warfield award, 1977, Howard U. Faculty Outstanding Unit award, 1982, 1st Humanitarian award Cmty. of Caring Ctr., 1990, Disting. Svc. award Surg. Sect. Nat. Med. Assn., 1990, Howard U. Health Affairs Disting. Svc. award, 1984, Outstanding Svc. award Dialysis and Transplant Support, Inc., 1993, Howard U. Legacy of Leadership in Health award, 1995, 11th ann. Minds in Motion award Sci. Skills Ctr., 1993, Edler Garnet Hawkins Humanitarian award Bronx Urban League, 1993; appreciation plaque for 1st renal transplant in V.I., Gov. St. Thomas, 1983, plaque for outstanding contbns. V.I. Legislature, 1984; named to Hunter Coll. Hall of Fame, 1989, Practitioner of Yr., Nat. Med. Assn., 1989, Scroll of Merit, Nat. Med. Assn., 1998, 1 of 10 Outstanding African Am. Male, WHMM-TV, Washington, 1994, 1 of 133 Gifts to the World Alumni Achievers, CUNY, 1995, Pearl Watson Meml. award for excellence in health care delivery Caribbean Am. Intercultural Orgn., Inc., 1995, Pioneer in Edn. award Inst. for Ind. Edn., 1995, Kidney Patients medal of Excellence 2nd Am. Assn., 1997, Leadership Edn. award Shiloh Bapt. Ch., 2002, Humanitarian Svc. award Julia West Hamilton League, 2005, others. Fellow ACS (LaSalle D. Leffall, Jr. award 1998, Mary McLeod Bethune Legacy award, 2000), Am. Coll. Surgeons (bd. govs. 1994-00); mem. D.C. Med. Soc. (past vice chmn., chmn. surg. sect. 1994—, bd. trustees 1995), Internat. Soc. Organ Sharing (sec. 1993—), Transplantation Soc., Am. Soc. Transplantation Surgeons (chmn. membership com. 1986, organ placement com. 1991, mem. ethics com. 1995-97), N.Y. Acad. Medicine, Am. Assn. Kidney Patients (bd. dirs. 1998), Nat. Assn. Former Foster Care Children Am. (bd. dirs. 1998-99), Nat. Kidney Found. (nat. bd. dirs. 1991-94, nat. capital area 1977-90), Am. Surg. Assn., Am. Coun. on Transplantation (bd. dirs.), Nat. Med. Assn., Soc. Surg. Assn., Inst. Cellular Therapeutics (adv. bd.), United Network of Organ Sharing (vice-chair 1996-98, chair 1998-00), Soc. Black Acad. Surgeons (pres. elect 1998-01, pres. 2001—), Alpha Omega Alpha, Alpha Phi Omega, Alpha Phi Alpha. Office: 2041 Georgia Ave NW Washington DC 20060-0001 Office Phone: 202-865-1441. E-mail: ccallender@howard.edu.

CALLENDER, JOHN FRANCIS, lawyer; b. Jacksonville, Fla., May 3, 1944; s. Francis Louis and Ethel (McLean) C.; m. Susan Carithers, June 13, 1969; children: John Francis Jr., Susanna McLean. AB cum laude, Davidson Coll., 1966; MA, U. N.C., 1969; JD with distinction, Duke U., 1976. Bar: Fla. 1976, U.S. Supreme Ct. 1982, bd. cert. civil trial lawyer: Fla. Bar. Asst. states atty. State of Fla., Jacksonville, 1980-81; ptnr. Turner, Ford & Callender, P.A., Jacksonville, 1981-84; pvt. practice Jacksonville, 1984—. Pres. Mental Health Clinic Jacksonville, Inc., 1985; bd. dirs. Vol. Jacksonville, Inc., 1981-84, AANR Edn. Found., Inc., 2003—, FANR, 2004—. Served with U.S. Army, 1970-73. Fellow Am. Soc. Papyrologists, 1969. Mem.: ATLA, ABA, Jacksonville Bar Assn., Fla. Bar, Acad. Fla. Trial Lawyers, Phi Beta Kappa Alumni Assn. N.E. Fla. (treas. 1996—99, pres. 1999—2000), Am. Mensa Ltd., Fla. Yacht Club, Rotary Club (pres. 1997, asst. dist. gov. 1999—2002, dist. sec. 2002—03). Democrat. Episcopalian. Avocations: sailing, windsurfing, fishing, tennis, swimming. Home: 1745 Woodmere Dr Jacksonville FL 32210-2233 Office: 1301 Riverplace Blvd Ste 2105 Jacksonville FL 32207-9027 Office Phone: 904-398-8833. E-mail: jcallend@fdn.com.

CALLENDER, NORMA ANNE, psychology educator, counselor; b. Huntsville, Tex., May 10, 1933; d. C.W. Carswell and Nell Ruth (Collard) Hughes Bost; m. B.G. Callender, 1951 (div. 1964); remarried 1967 (div. 1973); children: Teresa Elizabeth, Leslie Gemey, Shannah Hughes, Kelly Mari; m. E Purfurst, June 1965 (div. Aug. 1965). BS, U. Houston, 1969; MA, U. Houston at Clear Lake, 1977; postgrad., U. Houston, 1970, Tex. So. U., 1971, Lamar U., 1972-73, U. Houston-Clear Lake, 1979, 87, 89-93, St. Thomas U., 1985, 86, Aerospace Inst., NASA, Johnson Space Ctr., 1986, U. Houston-Clear Lake, summer 98, San Jacinto Coll., 1988—99, postgrad., 1994, postgrad., 2001—03. Cert. profl. reading specialist, Tex.; lic. profl. counselor. Tchr. Houston Ind. Schs., 1969-70; co-counselor, instr. Ellington AFB, Houston, 1971; tchr. Clear Creek Schs., League City, Tex., 1970-86; owner, dir. Bay Area Tutoring and Reading Clinic, Clear Lake City, Tex., 1970—. Bay Area Tng. Assocs., 1982-98, Bay Area Family Counseling, 1995—; cons., LPC intern Guidance Ctr., Pasadena (Tex.) Ind. Sch. Dist., 1993-95; prin. Gateway Foods USA, 2005—. Instr. San Jacinto Coll., Pasadena, 1980-81, 91-93; adj. instr. U. Houston, Clear Lake, 1986-91; founder, editor BATA Books Pub., 1997—; cons. in field. Author: numerous poems. State advisor U.S. Congl. Adv. Bd., 1985-87; vol., bd. dirs. Family Outreach Ctr., 1989-92; vol. Bay Area Coun. on Drugs and Alcohol, Nassau Bay, Tex., 1993-94; bd. dirs. Ballet San Jacinto, 1985-87; adv. bd. Cmty. Ednl. TV, 1990-92. Recipient Franklin award U. Houston, 1965-67; Delta Kappa Gamma/Beta Omicron scholar, 1967-68, PTA scholar, 1973, Berwin scholar, 1976, Mary Gibbs Jones scholar, 1976-77, Found. Econ. Edn. scholar, 1976, Insts. Achievement Human Potential scholar, Phila., 1987. Mem.: ACA, The NET: Bay Area Mental Health Providers Network, Internat. Reading Assn., Clear Creek Educators Assn. (past, honorarium 1976, 1977, 1985), Leadership Clear Lake Alumni Assn. (charter, program and projects com. mem. 1986—87, edn. com. 1985), U. Houston Alumni Assn. (life), Phi Theta Kappa, Phi Delta Kappa, Kappa Delta Pi, Psi Chi (life), Phi Kappa Phi (life). Mem. Life Tabernacle Ch. Office: Ste R 1234 Bay Area Blvd Houston TX 77058-2538

CALLEO, DAVID PATRICK, history professor, political scientist; b. Binghamton, N.Y., July 19, 1934; s. Patrick and Gertrude (Crowe) C.; m. Avis Thayer Bohlen. BA, Yale U., 1955, MA, 1957, PhD, 1959. Instr. polit. sci. Brown U., Providence, 1959-60; from instr. to asst. prof. polit. sci. Yale U., New Haven, 1961-67; rsch. fellow Nuffield Coll., Oxford U., 1966—67; cons. to undersec. for polit. affairs U.S. Dept. of State, Washington, 1967-68; prof., dir. European studies Nitze Sch. Advanced Internat. Studies Johns Hopkins U., Washington, 1968—, Dean Acheson chair Nitze Sch. Advanced Internat. Studies, 1988—, Univ. prof., 2001—; sr. Fulbright lectr. Fed. Republic Germany, 1975; assoc. fellow Jonathan Edwards Coll, Yale U., New Haven, 1972—; v.p. Lehrman Inst., N.Y.C., 1972-87; project dir. The Twentieth Century Fund, N.Y.C., 1981-85. Project dir. The 20th Century Fund, N.Y.C., 1993-99; assoc. Centre d'Etudes et de Rsch. Internat., 1993-94; enseignant invité Inst. d'études politiques de Paris, 1993-94; invited prof. Inst. U. de hautes études Internat., Geneva, 1999; fellow Am. Acad., Berlin, 2005 Author: America and the World Political Economy, 1973 (Gladys M. Kammerer award Best Book Analyzing Am. Nat. Policy, Am. Polit. Sci. Assn. 1973), The German Problem Reconsidered, 1978, The Imperious Economy, 1982, Beyond American Hegemony, 1987, The Bankrupting of America, 1992, Rethinking Europe's Future, 2001. Trustee, Jonathan Edwards Trust, 1972—. Guggenheim fellow, 1966-67. Mem. Am. Polit. Sci. Assn., Coun. on Fgn. Rels., Brooks' (London), Met. Club Washington, Century Assn. (N.Y.C.), Internat. Inst. for Strategic Studies, Literary Soc. (Washington); fellow Am. Acad. in Berlin, 2005 Avocations: gardening, squash, opera. Office Phone: 202-663-5796. Business E-Mail: dcalleo@jhu.edu.

CALLERY, T. GRANT, lawyer; b. White Plains, NY, Oct. 12, 1946; s. Thomas Ricker and Jean Grant Callery; m. Jacqueline Ann Machan, May 11, 1949; children: Megan Elizabeth-Callery Peluso, Brian Matthew. BS, Marietta Coll., 1968; JD, Georgetown U., 1973. Bar: DC 1973, U.S. Supreme Ct., U.S. Ct. Appeals (D.C. cir.), U.S. Tax Ct., U.S. Dist. Ct. D.C. Atty. US CSC, Washington, 1973—74; assoc. Winkelman & Delaney, 1974—79; various NASD, 1979—93, exec. v.p., gen. counsel, 1993—. Trustee Marietta Coll., Ohio, 2003—. Contbr. articles to profl. jours., chapters to books. With U.S. Army, 1969—71, Vietnam. Decorated Bronze Star medal US Army, Good Conduct medal. Mem.: ABA, Fed. Bar Assn. (chair young lawyers divsn. 1977—78). Avocations: boating, photography. Office: NASD Inc 1735 K St NW Washington DC 20006 Office Phone: 202-728-8285.

CALLETON, THEODORE EDWARD, lawyer, educator; b. Newark, Dec. 13, 1934; s. Edward James and Dorothy (Dewey) C.; m. Elizabeth Bennett Brown, Feb. 4, 1961; children: Susan Bennett, Pamela Barritt, Christopher Dewey.; m. Kathy E'Beth Conkle, Feb. 22, 1983; 1 child, James Frederick. BA, Yale U., 1956; LLB, Columbia U., 1962. Bar: Calif. 1963, U.S. Dist. Ct. (so. dist.) Calif. 1963, U.S. Tax Ct. 1977. Assoc. O'Melveny & Myers, L.A., 1962-69, Agnew, Miller & Carlson, L.A., 1969, ptnr., 1970-79; pvt. practice L.A., 1979-83; ptnr. Kindel & Anderson, L.A., 1983-92, Calleton & Merritt, Pasadena, Calif., 1992-99, Calleton & Trytten, Pasadena, 1999—2002; pvt. practice Pasadena, 2002—. Academician Internat. Acad. Estate and Trust Law, 1974—; lectr. Calif. Continuing Edn. Bar, 1970—96, U. So. Calif. Tax Inst., 1972, 76, 91, Calif. State U., L.A., 1974—93, Practicing Law Inst., 1976—86, Am. Law Inst., 1985; bd. dirs. UCLA/Continuing Edn. of Bar Estate Planning Inst., 1979—; adj. prof. Golden Gate U. Law Sch., 1997—2000, Loyola U. Sch. Law, 2002—. Author: The Short Term Trust, 1977, A Life Insurance Primer, 1978, Calleton's Wills and Trusts, 1992—2003; co-author: California Will Drafting Practice, 1982, Tax Planning for Professionals, 1985, California Estate Planning, 2002; contbr. articles to profl. jours.; co-author: Drafting California Revocable Trusts, 2003. Chmn. Arroyo Seco Master Planning Commn., Pasadena, Calif., 1970-71; bd. dirs. Montessori Sch., Inc., 1964-68, chmn., 1966-68, Am. Montessori Soc., N.Y.C., 1967-72, chmn., 1969-72; trustee Walden Sch. of Calif., 1970-86, 90-94, chmn., 1980-86; trustee Episc. Children's Home of L.A., 1971-75; bd. dirs. L.A. Master Chorale Assn., 1989-94, San Gabriel Valley Coun., Boy Scouts of Am., 2002-2004. Lt. USMC, 1956-59. Fellow Am. Coll. Trust and Estate Counsel; mem. L.A. County Bar Assn. (chmn. taxation sect. 1980-81, chmn. probate and trust law sect. 1981-82, Dana Latham Meml. award 1996), Aurelian Honor Soc., Elihu, Beta Theta Pi, Phi Delta Phi. Home: 301 Churchill Rd Sierra Madre CA 91024-1354 Office: 200 S Los Robles Ave Ste 678 Pasadena CA 91101-4600 Office Phone: 626-395-0860. Business E-Mail: ted@calletonlaw.com.

CALLEY, JOHN, former motion picture company executive, film producer; b. N.J., 1930; m. Olinka Schoberova, 1972 (div.); m. Meg Tilly, 1995 (div.); stepchildren: Emily, David, Will, Sabrina. Dir. nighttime programming, dir. programming sales NBC, 1951-57; prodn. exec. and TV producer Henry Jaffe Enterprises, 1957; v.p. radio and TV Ted Bates Advt. Agy., 1958; exec. v.p., film producer Filmways, Inc., 1960-69; with Warner Bros., Inc., Burbank, Calif., 1969-87, exec. v.p. world-wide prodn., 1969-75, pres., 1975-80, vice chmn. bd., 1977-80, cons., 1980-87; independent film prodr., 1987—93; pres., COO, United Artists Pictures, 1993-96; pres., CEO, Sony Pictures Entertainment, Inc., Culver City, Calif., 1996—98, chmn., CEO, 1998—2003. Prodr. (films): Face in the Rain, 1963, The Loved One, 1965, Eye of the Devil, 1967, Don't Make Waves, 1967, Ice Station Zebra, 1968, Castle Keep, 1969, Catch-22, 1970, Fat Man and Little Boy, 1989, Postcards from the Edge, 1990, The Remains of the Day, 1993, Closer, 2004.*

CALLIER, MARIA CECILE, actress, writer; BA in English Edn., U. No. Colo., 1979; MA in Info. Tech., Capella U. Cert. secondary tchr. English. Broadcast journalist and prodr. various TV and pub. radio sta. programs, Colo., 1983—2005; reporter Free Speech Radio News, N.Y.C.; freelance writer Colo., 1993—; pub. rels. dir. and grantwriter Grand River Hosp. Dist., Rifle, Colo., 1997-98; pub. rels. writer Colo. Mountain Coll., Glenwood Spring, Colo., 1997—2001; prepaid legal svcs. assoc. and group benefits cons. Westminster, Colo., 1995—98, 2001—; reporter Free Speech Radio News, N.Y.C., 2005—. Tchr. various schs. in Denver area and Roaring Fork Valley, 1979-96; sales and mktg. rep. various radio stas. and newspapers, Colo., 1986—; local coord. and cmty. counselor, Acad. Yr. Am., Am. Inst. Foreign Study, 1991—, Au Pair in Am., 1992-97; local coord. Multiple Sclerosis Walk, Glenwood Springs, Colo., 1998. Appeared in (films) Christmas Vacation '95, Murder in High Places, He's Still There, Endangered Species; (TV shows) Unsolved Mysteries, Sky Merchant Home Shopping Program; provides voiceover and narration for various TV and radio commls.; publicist, ghostwriter Glenwood Springs Ctr. for the Arts, 2000—. Mem. SAG, NAFE, Nat. Writer's Union. Home and Office: 1180 Opal St #104 Broomfield CO 80020 Office Phone: 720-252-8759. E-mail: mariacecile@aol.com.

CALLIES, DAVID LEE, lawyer, educator; b. Chgo., Apr. 21, 1943; s. Gustav E. and Ann D. Callies; m. Laurie Breeden, Dec. 28, 1996; 1 child, Sarah Wayne Callies. AB, DePauw U., 1965; JD, U. Mich., 1968; LLM, U. Nottingham, England, 1969. Bar: Ill. 1969, Hawaii 1978, U.S. Supreme Ct. 1974. Spl. asst. states atty., McHenry County, Ill., 1969; assoc. firm Ross, Hardies, O'Keefe, Babcock & Parsons, Chgo., 1969-75, ptnr., 1975-78; prof. law Richardson Sch. Law, U. Hawaii, Honolulu, 1978—; Benjamin A. Kudo prof. law U. Hawaii, Honolulu, 1995—. Mem. adv. com. on planning and growth mgmt. City and County of Honolulu Coun., 1978-88, mem. citizens adv. com. on State Functional Plan for Conservation Lands, 1979-93. Author: (with Fred P. Bosselman) the Quiet Revolution in Land Use Control, 1971 (with Fred P. Bosselman and John S. Banta) The Taking Issue, 1973, Regulating Paradise: Land Use Controls in Hawaii, 1984, (with Robert Freilich and Tom Roberts) Cases and Materials on Land Use, 1986, 4th edit., 2004, Preserving Paradise: Why Regulation Won't Work, 1994 (in Japanese 1994, in Chinese 1999), Land Use Law in the United States, 1994; editor: After Lucas: Land Use Regulation and the Taking of Property Without Compensation, 1993, Takings: Land Development Conditions and Regulatory Takings After Dolan and Lucas, 1995, (with Hylton, Mandelker and Franzese) Property Law and the Public Interest, 1998, 2nd edit., 2003 (with Kotaka) Taking Land, 2002, (with Curtin and Tappendorf) Bargaining For Development: A Handbook, 2003; co-editor Environ. and Land Use Law Rev., 2000—. Named Best Prof., U. Hawaii Law Sch., 1990-91, 91-92; Mich. Ford Found. fellow U. Nottingham (Eng.), 1969, life mem. Clare Hall, Cambridge U., 1999. Fellow: Am. Inst. Cert. Planners; mem.: ABA (chmn. com. on land use, planning and zoning 1980—82, coun. sect. on state and local govt. 1981—85, sec. 1986—87, exec. com. 1986—90, chmn. 1989—90, coun. sect. on state and local govt. 1995—), Internat. Bar Assn. (coun. Asia Pacific Forum 1993—96, co-chair Acads. Forum 1994—96, chair 1996—98), Ill. Bar Assn., Am. Bar Found., Coll. Am. Real Estate Lawyers, Am. Assn. Law Schs. (chair, state & local gov. sect. 2004), Hawaii State Bar Assn. (chair, real property and fin. svc. sect. 1997), Am. Planning Assn., Am. Law Inst., Lambda Alpha Internat. (pres. Aloha chpt. 1989—90, internat. v.p. Asia-Pacific region 2001—, Internat. Mem. of Yr. 1994). Home: 4620 Sierra Dr Honolulu HI 96816 Office: U Hawaii Richardson Sch Law 2515 Dole St Honolulu HI 96822-2328 Office Phone: 808-956-6550. Business E-Mail: dcallies@hawaii.edu.

CALLIGAN, WILLIAM DENNIS, retired life insurance company executive; b. Hibbing, Minn., Mar. 21, 1925; s. Raymond George and Ann Matilda (Olson) C.; m. Aletha E. Cornelius, Dec. 21, 1949; children— Ann M., Timothy M. BA, Yankton (S.D.) Coll., 1949. With N.Y. Life Ins. Co., 1953—, dir. mass market products N.Y.C., 1963-77, v.p. pensions, 1977-87. Mem. Internat. Found. Employee Benefit Plans, Inc. Served with USMC, World War II. Home: 66 Noe Ave Madison NJ 07940-2835

CALLINAN, TOM, editor; Corr. St. Cloud (Minn.) Daily Times, 1975; various positions Little Falls (Minn.) Daily Transcript, 1977—83; from asst. city editor to mng. editor Argus Leader, Sioux Falls, Minn., 1983—86; editor Lansing (Mich.) State Jour., 1986—91; exec. editor Fort Myers News-Press, 1991—94; editor Dem. and Chronicle and Times-Union, Rochester, NY, 1994—2000, v.p. news, 1994—2000; editor The Ariz. Republic, Phoenix, 2000—02, Cin. (Ohio) Enquirer, 2002—, v.p. news, 2002—. Named Gannett's Editor of Yr., 1997; recipient six Gannett Pres.'s Rings in News. Office: Cincinnati Enquirer 312 Elm St Fl 18 Cincinnati OH 45202-2724

CALLIS, CLAYTON FOWLER, research chemist; b. Sedalia, Mo., Sept. 25, 1923; s. Edward J. and Mary L. (Fowler) C.; m. Sara R. Steele, Apr. 9, 1949 (dec.); children: Joanne, Judy. BA, Ctrl. Meth. Coll., Fayette, Mo., 1944; MS, U. Ill., 1946, PhD, 1948; DS (hon.), Ctrl. Meth. Coll., 2000. Rsch. chemist Gen. Electric Co., Richland, Wash., 1948-51, Monsanto Co., Anniston, Ala., 1951-52, Dayton, Ohio, 1952-57, St. Louis, 1957-85; dir. R & D inorganic div., St. Louis, 1969-70; dir. R & D detergents and phosphates div. Monsanto Co., St. Louis, 1971-75; dir. environ. ops. and tech. planning Monsanto Indsl. Chems. Co., St. Louis, 1975-83; dir. environ. ops. Monsanto Fibers & Intermediate Co. Monsanto Co., St. Louis, 1983-85; ret., 1985; v.p. Chelan Assocs., 1985-89, pres., 1990-91; dir. ad interim Chem. Abstracts Svc. div. Am. Chem. Soc., 1991-92, cons., 1992—. Mem. exec. com. sci. adv. bd. EPA, 1984-86. Mem. editorial bd. Jour. Am. Chem. Soc., 1963-72; author: (with Ray R. Irani) Particle Size, Measurement, Interpretation and Application, 1963; contbr. articles to profl. jours.; patentee. Trustee Mt. Mercy Coll., 1979—; bd. curators Ctrl. Meth. Coll., 1983-91, 92-2000. Recipient Disting. Alumni award Central Meth. Coll., 1970, U. Ill. Alumni Achievement award, 1997. Mem. Am. Chem. Soc. (dir.-at-large 1977-87, chmn. bd. 1982, 83, pres.-elect 1988, pres. 1989, St. Louis award 1971, Henry A. Hill award 1990, Heroes of Chemistry award 1997, Disting. Svc. award 2000), Soap and Detergent Assn. (steering com. 1975), Am. Inst. Chemists (mems. and fellows award 1984), Sigma Xi, Alpha Chi Sigma, Phi Kappa Phi, Phi Lambda Upsilon, Sigma Epsilon Pi. Republican. Presbyterian. Home: 7215 Shaftesbury Ave Saint Louis MO 63130-3042 E-mail: cfcallis@swbell.net.

CALLISON, JAMES W., retired lawyer, air transportation executive; b. Jamestown, N.Y., Sept. 8, 1928; s. J. Waldo and Gladys A. C.; m. Gladys I. Robinson, Oct. 3, 1959; children: Sharon Elizabeth, Maria Judith, Christopher James. AB with honors, U. Mich., 1950, JD with honors (Overbeck award 1952, Jerome S. Freud Meml. award 1953), 1953. Bar: D.C. 1954, Ga. 1960, U.S. Supreme Ct., 1961. Atty. Pogue & Neal, Washington, 1953-57; with Delta Air Lines, Inc., Atlanta, 1957-93, v.p. law and regulatory affairs, 1974-78, sr. v.p., gen. counsel, 1978-81, sr. v.p., gen. counsel, corp. sec., 1981-88; sr. v.p. legal and corp. affairs, sec. Delta Air Lines Inc., 1988-90; sr. v.p. corp. and external affairs Delta Air Lines, Inc., 1990-91, sr. v.p. corp. affairs, 1991-93; ret., 1993. Contbr. articles to legal jours.; asst. editor: Mich. Law Rev, 1952-53. Bd. dirs. St. Joseph's Mercy Found. (chmn. planned giving com.). Recipient Papal Pro Ecclesia Et Pontifice award, 1966. Mem. State Bar Ga. (chmn. corp. counsel sect. 1989-90, mem. emeritus), Atlanta Bar Assn. (life), Atlanta Athletic Club, Order of Coif. Home: 2034 Dunwoody Club Way Dunwoody GA 30338-3024

CALLO, JOSEPH FRANCIS, writer; b. NYC, Dec. 16, 1929; s. Joseph Francis and Mary Ellen (Brennan) C. (Mary Walsh C. stepmother); m. Susan Catherine Jones, June 10, 1952 (div. Nov. 1978); children: Joseph Francis III, James D., Mary Ellen, Kathleen E., Patricia A.; m. Sally Chin McElwreath, Mar. 17, 1979; 1 stepson, Robert Joseph McElwreath. BA, Yale U., 1952. Account exec. firm Joseph F. Callo Inc., N.Y.C., 1952-58; v.p. Potts-Woodbury Inc., N.Y.C., 1958-60, also dir., 1958-60; pres. Callo & Carroll Inc., N.Y.C., 1960-74; chmn. bd. dirs., creative dir. Callo Berger Albanese Inc., N.Y.C., 1974-75; TV prodr. NBC-TV, also PBS, 1976-78; exec. v.p. Albert Frank/FCB, Inc., N.Y.C., 1978-81; sr. v.p. Grey Advt., 1981-83, Muir Cornelius Moore, Inc., 1983-84. Ptnr. Leeward Islands Yacht Charters, 1980-83; adj. assoc. prof. comm. arts St. John's U., N.Y.C., 1965-78; mem. mktg. rev. group USN, 1973-74. Author: Legacy of Leadership: Lessons from Admiral Lord Nelson, 1999, Nelson Speaks, 2001, Nelson in the Caribbean, 2002. Bd. advisors Nat. Maritime Hist. Soc. Served with USNR, 1952—54, rear adm. Res. Mem.: Soc. Nautical Rsch. (Gt. Britain), Surface Navy Assn. (founding pres. greater NY chpt.), The Naval Club (London), Yale Club of N.Y. Home: 330 E 38th St Apt 25A New York NY 10016-2727 Office Phone: 212-972-8651. Personal E-mail: jfc1952@aol.com.

CALLON, MARGARET JOANN, writer, minister; b. Brown County, Ind., Aug. 30, 1946; d. Sanford Sherman Marshall and Essie Rosemary Jacob; m. Ralph Stephen Callon, Sept. 14, 1964; children: Steven, Carolyn, Roy. Lic. minister Ind., 1982. Activity coord. Welcome Nursing Facility, Franklin, Ind., 1977—88; prin., owner Variety Gift Shop, Nashville, 1988—92; nursing asst. Brown County Cmty. Care, Nashville, 9202; song writer Hilltop Records, Hollywood, Calif., 2002—; minister Gospel Revelation, Inc., Connersville, Ind., 1982—. Author: Guardian Angel In The Midst Of Life's Tempest, 2000, (songs) Little Angels God Has Lent, 2000, I See Love Written Everywhere, 2001, Praying God's Way, 2002, God's Healing Way, 2003. Avocations: hiking, bowling, visiting elderly. Home and Office: 7815 SR 135 N Morgantown IN 46160

CALLOW, ALLAN DANA, surgeon; b. W. Somerville, Mass., Apr. 9, 1916; s. Edward Rol and Carrie (Fowles) C.; m. Eleanor Magee (dec. 1986); children: Beverly Ann Callow Nelson, Susan Diane Callow Moseley, Allan Dana Jr.; m. Una Scully Ryan, May 26, 1989; stepchildren: Tamsin Smith, Amy Ryan. BS, Tufts U., 1938, MS, 1948, PhD in Physiology, 1952; MD, Harvard, 1942, DSc (hon.), 1987. Intern Boston City Hosp., 1942-43; rsch. fellow, resident in gen. and vascular surgery Tufts New Eng. Med. Ctr., Boston, 1947-51, vice chmn. dept. surgery, 1966-82; cons. vascular surgery, dir. Vascular Surgery Rsch. Group, TNEMC, 1982-90; prof. surgery vascular div. Washington Univ Sch Medicine, St. Louis, 1990-94; rsch. prof. medicine, surgery Boston U. Med. Ctr., 1995—. Mem. Whitaker Inst. Advanced Cardiovascular Rsch.; spl. fellow vascular diseases Mayo Clinic, Rochester, Minn., 1948-49; instr. to prof. surgery Tufts U. Sch. Medicine, Boston, 1948-64; cons. to surgeon gen. Med. Corps, U.S. Navy, also civilian community hosps.; mem. study com. div. med. scis. NRC, 1969-72 Author: Carotid Surgery, 1996; editor: Vascular Surgery, 1995; assoc. editor Jour. Vasc. Surgery, 1969—; contbr. articles on vascular surgery, gen. surgery, med. edn. to profl. jours. Trustee Tufts U., 1971—, chmn. bd., 1977-87; trustee Civic Edn. Found., Lincoln Filene Center; chmn. bd. deacons Wellesley Congl. Ch., 1962-66. With M.C. USNR, 1943-46, PTO; rear adm. Res. (ret.). Decorated Legion of Merit; recipient award Hellenic Internat. Red Cross, Predl. medal Tufts U. Mem. Internat. Cardiovascular Soc. (sec.-gen. 1967-77, pres. 1977-79, pres. N.Am. chpt. 1974-75), A.C.S. (gov. 1974—, pres. Mass. chpt. 1973), New Eng. Surg. Soc., AMA (ho. dels. 1966-70), New Eng. Soc. Vascular Surgery (pres. 1977-78), Soc. Vascular Surgery (pres. 1986), Soc. Biomaterials (Clemson award 1988), Boston Surg. Soc. (pres. 1978), Mass. Med. Soc., Mass. Soc. Med. Rsch. (pres. 1988—), Am. Surg. Assn., European Soc. Vascular Surgery, So. Vascular Assn., Assn. Med. Consultants to Armed Forces, Navy Inst., Navy League, Navy Res. Officers Assn., Phi Beta Kappa, Sigma Xi, Delta Upsilon, Alpha Omega Alpha; hon. mem. Hellenic, Mexican, Argentine socs. angiology, Italian, Belgian surg. socs., European Soc. Cardiovascular Surgery. Clubs: Union (Boston), Wardroom (Boston). Home: 329 Hammond St Chestnut Hill MA 02467-1207 Office: Boston U Med Ctr 80 E Concord St Boston MA 02118-2307 Office Phone: 617-638-5692. Personal E-mail: allancallow@peoplepc.com.

CALLOW, WILLIAM GRANT, retired judge; b. Waukesha, Wis., Apr. 9, 1921; s. Curtis Grant and Mildred G. C.; m. Jean A. Zilavy, Apr. 15, 1950; children: William G., Christine S., Katherine H. PhB in Econs, U. Wis., 1943, JD, 1948. Bar: Wis.; cert. for Fla. mediation. Asst. city atty., Waukesha, 1948-52; city atty., 1952-60; county judge Waukesha, 1961-77; justice Supreme Ct. Wis., Madison, 1978-92; ret. Asst. prof. U. Minn., 1951-52; mem. faculty Wis. Jud. Coll., 1968-75; Wis. commr. Nat. Conf. Commrs. on Uniform State Laws, 1967—; arbitrator Wis. Employment Rel. Commn.; arbitrator-mediator bus. disputes; arbitration and mediation nat. and internat. res. judge, 1992—. With USMC, 1943-45; with USAF, 1951-52, Korea. Recipient Outstanding Alumnus award U. Wis., 1973 Fellow Am. Bar Found.; mem. ABA, Dane County Bar Assn., Waukesha County Bar Assn. Episcopalian. E-mail: justicehi@aol.com.

CALLOWAY, MARK T., lawyer, former prosecutor; married. Grad. in Polit. Sci., N.C. State U., 1980; JD, Campbell Univ., 1983. Bar: N.C. 1983, U.S. Dist. Ct. (we., mid., ea. dists.) N.C., U.S. Ct. Appeals (4th cir.), U.S. Supreme Ct. Rsch. asst. to Hon. Jack L. Cozort N.C. Ct. Appeals; law clk. to Hon. Robert D. Potter U.S. Dist. Ct. (we. dist.) N.C.; assoc., then ptnr./shareholder James, McElroy & Diehl, P.A., Charlotte, NC, 1987-94; U.S. atty. for we. dist. N.C. U.S. Dept. Justice, Charlotte, 1994—2001; ptnr., govt. investigations, compliance group Alston & Bird, LLP, Charlotte, NC, 2001—. Office: Alston & Bird LLP Bank Amer Plz Ste 4000 101 S Tryon St Charlotte NC 28280 Office Phone: 704-444-1089. Business E-Mail: mcalloway@alston.com.

CALLSEN, CHRISTIAN EDWARD, health products executive; b. 1938; married. AB, Miami U., 1959; MBA, Harvard U., 1966. With Cole Nat. Corp., Cleve., 1966-87, various mgmt. and v.p. positions, 1966-87, exec. v.p., 1983-87; pres. Hyatt Legal Svcs., Cleve., 1987-90, Profl. Vet. Hosps., Detroit, 1991, Profl. Med. Mgmt., Cleve., 1992—2000, Applied Med. Tech., Cleve., 1993-96; chmn., CEO Allen Med. Sys., Cleve., 1995-99; pres. Polymer Concepts, Inc., 1999; dir. Sight Resources Corp.; chmn. TAGA Med. Techs., Inc., 2000. Lt. USN, 1959-64. Home: 235 College St Hudson OH 44236-2908 Office: 7561 Tyler Blvd Ste 8 Mentor OH 44060-4867 Office Phone: 440-953-9605. Personal E-mail: cec235@aol.com.

CALLUM, MYLES, magazine editor, writer; b. Lynn, Mass., Apr. 4, 1934; s. Abraham Edward and Ann Edith (Caswell) C.; m. Suzanne Connellis, Apr. 22, 1967 (div. 1974); children— Deborah, Jennifer. Student, U. Conn., 1951-53, N.Y. U., 1958-61. Pvt. investigator, Stamford, Conn., 1958-59; assoc. editor Leisure mag., N.Y.C., 1959-60; asst. editor Good Housekeeping mag., N.Y.C., 1961-63, assoc. editor, 1963-69, dir. spl. publs. divsn., 1969-70; mng. editor Better Homes and Gardens, Des Moines, 1971-75; assoc. editor TV Guide, Radnor, Pa., 1977-86, sr. editor., 1986-91, sr. writer N.Y.C., 1991-96, contbg. editor, 1996-97. White Ho. cons., writer Fed. health programs, 1968; constructor crossword puzzles, 1998—. Author: Body-Building and Self-Defense, 1961, Body Talk, 1972, also articles. Served with CIC AUS, 1955-57. Home: 2367 Julio Ln Santa Rosa CA 95401-5725

CALMAN, CRAIG DAVID, actor, writer; b. Riverside, Calif., June 11, 1953; Student, Pacific U., Forest Grove, Oreg., 1971-72, U. de Querétaro, Mex., 1972-73; BA in Motion Picture/TV, UCLA, 1975. Sr. admitting worker UCLA Med. Ctr., 1974-76; actor/playwright Old Globe Theatre, San Diego, 1977-78, Off Broadway and regional, N.Y.C. and East Coast, 1979-86; exec. asst. various film/TV studios and law firms, L.A., 1986-89, Orion Pictures Corp., L.A., 1989-90; dir. staged readings L.A., 1991—, The Transcription Co., 1998—. Actor with starring roles (TV and film) ADP Industrial, Teamwork, Macbeth, Flesteron in Amazonia, co-starring roles in Commercial Break, Sullivan's Travels; actor with co-starring/lead roles (theatre) in Book of the Dead, Dark Lady of the Sonnets, Hamlet, Rosencrantz and Guildenstern are Dead, Much Ado About Nothing, Too True to be Good, Henry V, Richard III, The Rivals, Merchant of Venice, A Day for Surprises, The Tavern, The Earrings of Madame De..., The Firebugs, and others; columnist World Wide Web mag. FilmZone, 1995-97. Author play/screenplays: The Turn of the Century, Strangled Nocturne, Skidoo Ruins, Life Without Father, Patterns Woven In A Park; author: The Turn of the Century; author one-act plays, screenplays, full-length plays, poetry; writer asst. Hal Roach, Bel Air, Calif., 1987-88. Vol. book reader Recording for the Blind, L.A., 1991—. Recipient Old Globe Theatre Atlas award for best actor in a comedy role for Too True to be Good, 1977-78; Helene Wurlitzer Found. of N.Mex. Writers Residency grantee, 1988; finalist Walt Disney fellowship program, 1992, Chesterfield Film Writers Project, 1997. Mem. SAG, Actors Equity Assn., Actors Studio West (playwright/dir. unit 2000—), Mark Rydell's Directory Unit, 2003-04. Office: 6632 Lexington Ave PMB # 77 Los Angeles CA 90038-1306 Office Phone: 323-906-8886. Personal E-mail: craigcalman@earthlink.net.

CALMAN, ROBERT FREDERICK, mining executive; b. Mineola, N.Y., May 14, 1932; s. William Arthur and Ida (Albersworth) C.; m. Susan Jean Raphael, June 20, 1959 (div. 1978); children: Andrew Frederick, Camille, Matthew Alexander; m. Doris Sumerson, June 9, 1979. BA, Yale U., 1954; MS, MIT, 1967. With Chase Manhattan Bank, N.Y.C., 1954-61, asst. treas., 1961; with Mobil Oil Corp., N.Y.C., 1961-70, treas. N.Am. div., 1964-68, treas. Internat. div., 1968-69; v.p. finance, treas. IU Internat. Corp., Phila., 1970-72, group v.p. devel., 1972-74, exec. v.p., 1974-78, vice chmn., 1978-85, chmn. fin. com., dir., 1986-88; chmn., dir. Echo Bay Mines Ltd., Edmonton, Alta., Can., 1981-96. Bd. dirs. Corp. Cons. Group, Ltd., Bank of N.Y. Trust Co. of Fla., The Gold Inst., Am. Mining Congress; lectr. NYU, 1968-69. Author: Linear Programming and Cash Management/Cash Alpha, 1968. Pres., Phila. chpt. Nat. Found. for Ileitis and Colitis, Inc., 1974-75; pres., mem. bd. govs. Soc. Alfred P. Sloan Fellows; dir. alumni fund, mem. corp. devel. com. Mass. Inst. Tech. Served to 1st lt., arty. AUS, 1955-57. Recipient E.P. Brooks prize Mass. Inst. Tech., 1967. Mem. Phi Beta Kappa, Phi Gamma Delta. Republican. Christian Scientist. Office: 241 S 6th St Apt 2302 Philadelphia PA 19106-3736 E-mail: BobCalman@cs.com.

CALOGERO, PASCAL FRANK, JR., state supreme court justice; b. New Orleans, Nov. 9, 1931; s. Pascal Frank and Louise (Moore) C.; children— Deborah Ann Calogero Applebaum, David, Pascal III, Elizabeth, Thomas, Michael, Stephen, Gerald, Katie, Chrissy. Student, Loyola U., New Orleans, 1949-51, JD, 1954; LLM in Jud. Process, U. Va., 1992; LLD (hon.), Loyola U., New Orleans, 1991. Bar: La. Law clerk Civil Dist. Ct.; ptnr. Landrieu, Calogero & Kronlage, 1958-69, Calogero & Kronlage, 1969-73; gen. counsel La. Stadium and Expn. Dist., 1970-73; assoc. justice Supreme Ct. La., New Orleans, 1973-90, chief justice, 1990—. Mem. La. Democratic State Central Com., 1963-71; mem. subcom. on del. selection La. Dem. Party, 1971; del. Dem. Nat. Conv., 1968; bd. directors Conference Chief Justices, 1997-; lecturer U. New Orleans, Harvard Law Sch., Loyola Sch. of Law. Served to capt. U.S. Army, 1954—57. Recipient Disting. Jurist award La. Bar Founds., 1991; Judge Bob Jones Meml. award, Am. Judges Assn., 1995, Justice Albert Tate, Jr. award La. Assn. Criminal Defense Lawyers, 1997, Outstanding Jud. award Victims & Citizens Against Crime, Inc., 1999. Mem. ABA, La. Bar Assn., New Orleans Bar Assn., Greater New Orleans Trial Lawyers Assn. (v.p. 1967-69), Order of the Coif. Office: Supreme Ct La 400 Royal St New Orleans LA 70130 E-mail: icaloger@lasc.org.*

CALOGERO, RACHEL MARIE, psychologist; b. Oneida, NY, Oct. 26, 1976; MA, Coll. of William and Mary; PhD, Syracuse U. Exercise coord. The Renfrew Ctr., Philadelphia, Pa., 2001—03, rsch. coord. Phila., 2000—03. Office Phone: 315-443-2762.

CALOHAN, SHANNON LEIGH, elementary school educator; b. Kansas City, Mo., July 13, 1968; d. Michael Stephen and Kathryn Arlene (Hart) Calohan. BA in Edn., U. Mo., Kansas City, 1990, MA in Edn., 1999. Cert. lifetime educator State of Mo. Tchr. DeLaSalle Edn. Ctr., Kansas City, 1994—97, Liberty Acad., Mo., 1997—. Recipient Excellence in Edn. Tchg. award, Northland C. of C., 2003. Mem.: Mo. Nat. Edn. Assn., Alpha Delta Pi (advisor U. Mo. Kansas City 1991—2002). Home: 9 Victory Dr Liberty MO 64068

CALORE, PAUL, writer, retired government agency administrator; b. Providence, Apr. 5, 1938; s. Enrico and Ida Calore; m. Cecelia Ferreira, Apr. 18, 1964; children: Vickie Noel, Stephen, Cheryl Calore-Abatacola. BA magna cum laude, Johnston & Wales U., 1976. Ops. br. chief Def. Logistics Agy., Needham, Mass., 1981—93. Author: Land Campaigns of the Civil War, 2000, Naval Campaigns of the Civil War, 2002. Mem.: Civil War Ctr., Civil War Preservation Trust. Avocations: collecting Civil War memorabilia, travel. Personal E-mail: paulcalore1@wmconnect.com.

CALVA, ROBERT BARAQUIEL, music educator; b. Witchita, Sept. 15, 1959; s. Erma Mae and Robert Calva. Cert. Musicians Inst., Hollywood, 1992, Svc. Calif., 2002. Music instr. Delian Music, Culver City, Calif.; git instr. Musicians Inst., Hollywood, Calif.; instr. music Atscocita Sch. Music, Humble, Tex. Musician The Missing Links, LA. Author: (book) Texas Blues Guitar, Blues - Rock Soloing for Guitar. Mem. Berachah Ch., Houston, 1980—2005. Conservative. Avocations: reading, exercise, natural healing, history, movies. Office: Musicians Inst 1655 McCadden Pl Hollywood CA 90028 Home: 12300 Sherman Way # 164 North Hollywood CA 91605 Personal E-mail: rbcalva@aol.com. E-mail: robertc@mi.edu.

CALVANI, TERRY, lawyer; b. Carlsbad, N.Mex., Jan. 29, 1947; s. Torello Howard and Mary Virginia (Hawkins) C.; m. Mary Virginia Anderson, May 3, 1969; m. Judith Thompson, Aug. 28, 1980; children: Dominic Mario, Torello Howard; m. Sarah Holter Hill, June 19, 2003. BA, U. N.Mex., 1969; JD with distinction, Cornell U., 1972. Bar: N.Mex. 1972, Calif. 1972, Tenn. 1978, D.C. 1992, U.S. Dist. Ct. N.Mex. 1972, U.S. Dist. Ct. (no. dist.) Calif. 1972, U.S. Dist. Ct. (mid. dist.) Tenn. 1978, U.S. Dist. Ct. D.C. 1994, U.S. Ct. Appeals (9th cir.) 1972, U.S. Ct. Appeals (6th cir.) 1977, U.S. Ct. Appeals (5th cir.) 1981, U.S. Ct. Appeals (11th cir.) 1981, U.S. Ct. Appeals (D.C. cir.) 1994, U.S. Supreme Ct. 1985. Tchg. fellow Stanford U. Law Sch., 1972-73; asst. prof. law Vanderbilt U. Sch. Law, Nashville, 1974—77, assoc. prof., 1977—80, prof., 1980—83; assoc. Pillsbury, Madison & Sutro (now Pillsbury Winthrop LLP), San Francisco, 1973-74, ptnr., 1990—2002; mem. The Competition Authority Republic of Ireland, 2002—05; of counsel Freshfields Bruckhaus Deringer, Washington, 2005—. Vis. prof. law U. Va., Charlottesville, 1981—82; of counsel Haksell Slaughter & Young, Birmingham, 1980—83; commr. U.S. F.T.C., 1983—90, acting chmn., 1985—86; lectr. Harvard U. Sch. Law, 1998—2002, Trinity Coll., Dublin, 2005; sr. lecturing fellow Duke U. Sch. Law, 2000. Author: (with John Siegfried) Economic Analysis and Antitrust Law, 1979, 2d edit., 1988; mem. editl. bd. Antitrust Bull., 1982—, Bur. Nat. Affairs RICO Report, 1986-96. Mem.: ABA (chmn. spl. com. to study antitrust penalties and damages antitrust sec 1979—82, chmn. Robinson-Patman com. antitrust sect. 1981—83, coun. mem. 1985—86), Am. Law Inst. (coun. mem. 1990—93), 6th Jud. Conf. (life), Lagunitas Country Club (Ross), Stephen's Green Club (Dublin), Richland Country Club (Nashville), Pacific Union Club (San Francisco), The Club (Birmingham), G.C. Club Tenn. (Nashville), Colonnade Club (Charlottesville), Olympic Club (San Francisco), Malahide Tennis and Croquet Club (Dublin County), Order of the Coif. Roman Catholic. Office: Freshfields Bruckhaus Deringer Ste 600 701 Pennsylvania Dr Washington DC 20004 Office Phone: +353 0 1 804 5432. Fax: +353 1 804 5401. E-mail: tc@tca.ie.

CALVANO, LINDA SUE LEY, insurance company executive; b. Franklin, Ind., Nov. 27, 1949; d. Jiles Rex and Naomi Katherine (Van Horn) Riggs; m. Thomas Alan Ley Calvano, Feb. 28, 1987. BS in Edn. with distinction, Ind. U.-Purdue U., 1971, MS in Edn. with highest distinction, 1975. Cert. paralegal; lic. life, accident, health, property and casualty ins. agt., Ind.; cert. total quality mgmt.; project mgmt. profl. designation. Elem. tchr. Indpls. Pub. Schs., 1972-74, Center Grove Community Schs., Greenwood, Ind., 1974-81; dir. adminstrn. Brougher Agy., Inc., Greenwood, 1981-84; mgr. claims/customer svc. The Associated Group, Inc., Indpls., 1984-89; v.p. team ops. Key Benefit Adminstrs., Inc., Indpls., 1989-92; regional mgr. ops. & rev. projects Anthem Blue Cross Blue Shield, Indpls., 1992-97, quality assurance dir., 1997—. Mem. cotillion com. Humane Soc. Indpls., 1991; vol. Riley Run for Children, Indpls., 1985-92. Recipient Good Girl Citizenship award Women's Aux. of Am. Legion, 1968. Mem. Am. Mgmt. Assn., Nat. Assn. Life Underwriters, Nat. Assn. Health Underwriters, Inst. Internal Auditors, Indpls. Paralegal Assn., Project Mgmt. Inst., Toastmasters Internat. Republican. Episcopalian. Home: 6358 Bluff Acres Dr Greenwood IN 46143-9037 Office: Anthem Blue Cross Blue Shield 220 Virginia Ave Indianapolis IN 46204 Office Phone: 317-287-8160.

CALVANO, PHYLLIS, publishing executive; BBA in Acctg., Iona Coll., 1978; MBA, NYU, 1986. CPA N.Y. From controller Times Books, WQXR and Edn. Enrichment Materials to v.p., controller The N.Y. Times The N.Y. Times Co., 1982—2004, v.p., 2004—, controller The N.Y. Times, 2004—. Office: The NY Times 229 W 43rd St New York NY 10036

CALVAR, JOSE, III, (PEPPIE CALVAR), music educator, church musician; s. Jose and Carmen Maria Calvar. MusB in Music Edn., East Carolina U., Greenville NC, 2002—02; MusM, Ga. State U., Atlanta, 2004. Music dir. Corpus Christi Cath. Ch., Stone Mountain, Ga., 2003—04; choral dir. NW Sch. of the Arts, Charlotte, NC, 2004—; dir. of youth music Myers Pk. United Meth. Ch., Charlotte, NC, 2004—. Dir.: (choral/orch. concert) A Concert of Joys and Sorrows; composer: (orchestral) Glorionga, (choral octavo) Ave Maria, O Nata Lux, (extended work for chorus and big band) Mass of Reconciliation. Scholar, Ga. State U., 2002-2004, East Carolina U., 1999-2002. Mem.: MENC, ACDA. Office: NW Sch Arts 1415 Beatties Ford Rd Charlotte NC 28216 Office Phone: 980-343-5500. Personal E-mail: theorycomp@alltel.net. E-mail: jose.calvar@cms.k12.nc.us.

CALVARESE, MICHELLE, geographer, educator; b. Norristown, Pa., Sept. 2, 1970; d. Annunzio and Rose Calvarese. BA, Villanova (Pa.) U., 1992; MA, West Chester (Pa.) U., 1995; PhD, Tex. A&M U., 2001. Asst. prof. Calif. State U., Fresno, Calif., 2000—. Mem.: Calif. Geog. Soc., Nat. Coun. Geographics Edn., Am. Assn. Am. Geographers, Fresno (Calif.) Hist. Soc. Office: LSU Fresno 2225 E San Ramon 5669 Fresno CA 93740

CALVER, RICHARD ALLEN, retired college dean; b. Chillicothe, Ohio, Feb. 16, 1939; s. Robert K. Calver and Catherine Mae (Roush) Bryan; m. Susan Jane Yost, Oct. 9, 1988; children: Mark R. Fortney, Sherry Sue Skinner, Alan D. Fortney. Student, U. Hawaii, 1959-61; BSBA, W.Va. U., 1963; MS in Bus., Va. Commonwealth U., 1970; C.A.G.S.E., Va. Tech. U., 1983, EdD in C.C. Edn., 1984. Mgmt. trainee Sears Roebuck & Co., 1963, Reuben H. Donnelley Corp., 1963-64, state publs. and customer rels. mgr., 1964-68; state job analyst Va. Divsn. pers., Richmond, 1968-70; dean adminstrv. svcs. S.W. Va. C.C., Richlands, 1970-88, Thomas Nelson C.C., Hampton, Va., 1988—2002, interim pres., 1994-95, spl. asst. to pres., 2002—05. Mem. accreditation teams So. Assn. Colls. and Schs., 1976-95, Mid. States Assn., 1983-94. Mem. Lebanon (Va.) Town Coun., 1978-82; mem. spl. edn. adv. com. Russell County Sch. Bd., 1984-88, Va. Peninsula Inst. Leadership Inst. Program, 1989; mem. Greater Williamsburg Area Crossroads planning com., 1999—. With USAF, 1957-61. Mem. Nat. Assn. Coll. and Univ. Bus. Officers, Nat. Coun. C.C. Bus. Officers (Regional Outstanding Bus. officer 1990, nat. bd. dirs. 1985-94), So. Assn. Coll. and Univ. Bus. officers, Ea. Assn. Coll. and U. Bus. Officers, Coll. and Univ. Pers. Assn., Lions (pres. Lebanon club 1976-77), Shriners (pres. club 1974-75), Scottish Rite (32d degree), Masons, Delta Tau Delta, Phi Kappa Phi, Phi Theta Kappa (hon.). Methodist. Home: 5509 N Mallard Run Williamsburg VA 23188-9415

CALVERT, CLYDE EMMETT, former state agency administrator; b. Lexington, Ky., Feb. 24, 1937; s. Emmett I. and Minnie (Hall) C.; m. Violet Stafford, Sept. 22, 1962; children: Emmett Bradford, Eric Brandon. BS in Commerce and Acctg., U. Ky., 1959. Rsch. asst. U. Ky., Lexington, 1959; from auditor to audit mgr. Ky. Revenue Cabinet, Lexington, 1959-87, sec. Frankfort, 1987-91. Bd. dirs. Ky. Housing Corp., Frankfort, Ky. Workers Compensation Funding Commn., Frankfort, State Property and Bldg. Commn., Frankfort, Commonwealth Venture Fund, Ky. Employees Deferred Compensation System, Frankfort, 1991-94. Mem. tax com. Ky. Farm Bur., Louisville, 1991; vol. non-profit schs., Lexington; coach, league ofcl. various sport orgns., Lexington, 1975-86. Recipient Cert. of merit, Office Vocat. Rehab., 1990. Mem. Southeastern Assn. Tax Adminstrs., Fedn. Tax Adminstrs., Lexington Yacht Club. Democrat. Presbyterian. Avocations: boating, woodworking, brick laying. Home: 3536 Castlegate Wynd Lexington KY 40502-7701 E-mail: emmettcalvert@insightbb.com.

CALVERT, DELBERT WILLIAM, retired energy executive; b. Bosworth, Mo., Jan. 29, 1927; s. William McKinley and Ruby Leona (Berrier) Calvert; m. Mary Lee Brown, Feb. 10, 1947 (div. Mar. 1971); children: Gary D., Danial L.; m. Melva Allen Hurst, Sept. 4, 1971; stepchildren: Holly Hurst, Allen Hurst. BSCE, U. Mo., 1952. Asst. mgr. supply and transp. divsn. Phillips Petroleum Co., Bartlesville, Okla., 1952-63; asst. to v.p. Tex. Ea. Transmission Corp., Houston, 1963-65; mgr. diversification dept. No. Natural Gas Co., Omaha, 1965-68; pres. Williams Bros. Pipe Line Co., Tulsa, 1968-71; exec. v.p. The Williams Cos., Tulsa, 1971-85, also bd. dirs.; chmn. bd. Williams Energy Co., 1975-79, also bd. dirs.; chmn., CEO, Agrico Chem. Co., Tulsa, 1977-85, also bd. dirs. Pres. Wiliams Techs., Inc., 1992—97; chmn. bd. dirs. Black Mesa Pipeline Co., 1996—97, adv. dir., 1997—98. Apptd. to gov.'s agroindustry policy commn., 1987—; mem. exec. bd. Indian Nations coun. Boy Scouts Am., 1969—, pres., 1974—76; mem. U. Mo. Devel. Fund, 1969—, chmn., 1972—73; bd. dirs. Goodwill Industries Tulsa. With AUS, 1945—47. Mem.: Potash and Phosphate Inst. (dir. 1982—85), Fertilizer Industry Assn. (chmn. bd.), Am. Petroleum Inst. (gen. com. div. transp. 1971), Okla. Petroleum Coun. (dir. 1968—, pres. 1977—78), Mo. U. Civil Engring. Acad. Disting. Alumni (Pipe Liner of Yr. 1998), Garden of Gods Club (Colorado Springs, Colo.), Univ. Club (Columbia, Mo.), Waikoloa (Hawaii) Village Golf Club, Pi Mu Epsilon, Chi Epsilon, Tau Beta Pi. Home: PO Box 384690 Waikoloa HI 96738 E-mail: tinkanbill@aol.com.

CALVERT, GORDON LEE, retired legal association executive; b. Wardensville, W.Va., Sept. 2, 1921; s. Aaron Lee and Ada (Brill) C.; m. Margaret James, June 9, 1945; children— Gordon R., Roger L., Walter R. BA with distinction, George Washington U., 1943, JD with distinction, 1945. Bar: D.C. 1946. Assoc. firm Covington & Burling, Washington, 1944-46; with Investment Bankers Assn. Am., Washington, 1946-71, exec. dir., gen. counsel, 1966-71; exec. v.p., gen. counsel Securities Industry Assn., 1972; v.p., gen. counsel N.Y. Stock Exchange, Washington, 1973-76; exec. dir. comml. collection agy. sect. Comml. Law League Am., Washington, 1976-92. Author: Fundamentals of Municipal Bonds, 1959, Digest of Investments of State Pension Funds, 1960, Digest of State Laws Regulating Debt Collection Agencies, 1977, 81. Mem. ABA, Order of Coif, Pi Kappa Alpha, Phi Delta Phi, Omicron Delta Kappa, Met. Club (Washington), Columbia Country Club (Chevy Chase, Md.). Presbyterian. Home: 3100 N Leisure World Blvd Apt 526 Silver Spring MD 20906

CALVERT, JACK GEORGE, atmospheric chemist, educator; b. Inglewood, Calif., May 9, 1923; s. John George and Emma (Eschstruth) C.; m. Doris Arlene Breimon, Nov. 8, 1946; children: Richard John, Mark Steven. BS in Chemistry, UCLA, 1944, PhD, 1949. Mem. faculty Ohio State U., 1950-81, prof. chemistry, 1960-81, Kimberly prof. chemistry, 1974-81, prof. emeritus, 1981—, chmn. dept., 1964-68; sr. scientist Nat. Ctr. Atmospheric Rsch., Boulder, Colo., 1982-94, sr. rsch. assoc., 1994—2002, sr. scientist emeritus, 2002—. Vis. scientist Oak Ridge (Tenn.) Nat. Lab., Environ. Scis. Divsn., 2002—; cons. air pollution tng. com. USPHS, 1964-66; cons. World Innovation Found., 2001—; mem. Nat. Air Pollution Control Manpower Devel. Com., 1966-69, chmn., 1968-69; bd. dirs. Gordon Rsch. Confs., 1969-71; mem. air pollution control rsch. grants com. EPA, 1970-72, chmn., 1971-72, mem. chemistry and physics adv. com., 1973-75; chmn. air pollution com. Conservation Found., 1968-70; mem. air conservation commn. Am. Lung Assn., 1973-75; chmn. EPA environ. chemistry/physics grants rev. panel, 1979-83; mem. State of Colo. Air Quality Control Commn., 1987-90, Disting. Acad. Adv. Group of Auto/Oil Air Quality Improvement Rsch. Program, 1989-96; mem. panel on atmospheric effects of aviation NRC/NAS, 1995-98, mem. com. on ozone potential of reformulated gasoline, 1997-99; atmospheric chemistry tech. implementation panel Am. Chem. Coun., 1998-2004. Author: (with J. N. Pitts, Jr.) Photochemistry, 1966, Graduate School in the Sciences, 1972; also articles. Ensign USNR, 1944-46. Named Honor Prof. of Year Coll. Arts and Scis., Ohio State U., 1957; recipient Alumni award for disting. tchg., 1961, Disting. Rsch. award, 1981; fellow NRC Can., 1949; Guggenheim fellow, 1977-78 Fellow Ohio Acad. Sci., Am. Inst. Chemists, Am. Geophys. Union; mem. AAUP, Am. Chem. Soc. (award for creative rsch. in environ. sci. and tech. 1981, Columbus sect. award 1981), Air Pollution Control Assn. (Chambers award 1986), Phi Beta Kappa, Sigma Xi, Pi Mu Epsilon, Phi Lambda Upsilon, Alpha Chi Sigma. Achievements include research on photochemistry, reaction kinetics, atmospheric chemistry, mechanisms free radical reactions. Personal E-mail: jgcalvert@tds.net. Business E-Mail: calvert@ucar.edu, calvertj@ornl.gov.

CALVERT, JAY H., JR., lawyer; b. Charleston, S.C., Mar. 19, 1945; m. Ann E., June 14, 1969; children: Amanda, Emily, Sarah. BA, Amherst (Mass.) Coll., 1967; JD, U. Va., 1970. Bar: Pa. 1970, U.S. Dist. Ct. (ea. dist.) Pa. 1970, U.S. Ct. Appeals (3d cir.) 1971, U.S. Dist. Ct. (mid. dist.) Pa. 1973, U.S. Ct. Appeals (2d cir.) 1980, U.S. Ct. Appeals (8th cir.) 1987, U.S. Supreme Ct. 1989, U.S. Dist. Ct. Ariz. 1994, U.S. Dist. Ct. (we. dist.) Pa. 2000. Assoc. Morgan, Lewis & Bockius LLP, Phila., 1970—78, ptnr., 1978—, exec. ptnr., 1987—90; mem. firm governing bd. Morgan Lewis & Bockius LLP, Phila., 1989—94; mng. ptnr. Morgan, Lewis & Bockius LLP, Phila., 1990—94, mem. exec. com., 1997—98, sr. ptnr. litigation sect., 1990—, mgr. litigation sect., 1996—99. Trustee Agnes Irwin Sch., Rosemont, Pa., 1988-94; pres., bd. dirs. St. David's Nursery Sch., Wayne, Pa., 1980-94; mem. ann. fund campaign com. Inglis House, 1998-04 Mem. ABA, Pa. Bar Assn., Phila. Bar Assn., Lawyers Club Phila., Leukemia and Lymphoma Soc. Am. (trustee Phila. chpt. 1982—, pres. bd. dirs. 2005—), Phila. Zool. Soc. (chmn. devel. com. 1993-96, chmn. facilities, exhibits and safety com., 1997-01, bd. dirs., 1992—, vice-chmn. bd. dirs., 1994-96, 04—), Pyramid Club (mem. bd. govs. 2004—) Avocations: biking, gardening, hiking, horseback riding, animal husbandry. Office: Morgan Lewis & Bockius LLP 1701 Market St Philadelphia PA 19103-2903 Office Phone: 215-963-5462. Business E-Mail: jcalvert@morganlewis.com.

CALVERT, KEN, congressman; b. Corona, Calif., June 8, 1953; AA, Chaffey Coll., 1973; BA Econs., San Diego State U., 1975. Corona/ Norco youth chmn. for Nixon, 1968, 82; county youth chmn. rep. Vesey's Dist., 1970, 43d dist., 1972; congl. aide to Rep. Vesey, Calif., 1975-79; gen. mgr. Jolly Fox Restaurant, Corona, Calif., 1975-79, Marcus W. Meairs Co., Corona, Calif., 1979-81; pres., gen. mgr. Ken Calvert Real Properties, Corona, Calif., 1981—; Reagan-Bush campaign worker, 1980; co chmn. Wilson for Senate Campaign, 1982, George Deukmejian election, 1978, 82, 86, George Bush election, 1988, Pete Wilson senate elections, 1982, 88, Pete Wilson for Gov. election, 1990; mem. U.S. Congress from 43rd Calif. dist., 1993—2003, U.S. Congress from 44th dist., 2003—; mem. armed svcs., resources, sci. com. Former v.p. Corona/ Norco Rep. Assembly; chmn. Riverside Rep. Party, 1984-88, County Riverside Asset Leasing; bd. realtors Corono/ Norco Exec. bd. Corona Community Hosp. Corp. 200 Club; mem. Corona Airport adv. commn.; adv. com. Temescal/ El Cerrito Community Plan. Mem. Riverside County Rep. Winners Circle (charter), Lincoln Club (co-chmn., charter, 1986-90), Corona Rotary Club (pres. 1991), Elks, Navy League Corona Norco, Corona C. of C. (pres. 1990), Noroco C. of C., Monday Morning Group, Corona Group (past chmn.), Econ. Devel. Ptnrship., Silver Eagles (March AFB support group, charter). Republican. Office: US Ho of Reps 2201 Rayburn Ho Office Bldg Washington DC 20515-0001 also: Office of Ken Calvert 3400 Central Avenue Suite 200 Riverside CA 92506

CALVERT, WALTER RANDOLPH, lawyer; b. Takoma Park, Md., Jan. 7, 1958; s. Gordon Lee and Margaret (James) C.; m. Cynthia Thomas, Apr. 22, 1989. BS in Commerce, U. Va., 1980; JD, Coll. William & Mary, 1983. Bar: Md. 1983, DC 1989, admitted to practice: US Dist. Ct. (Dist. Md.) 1984, US Ct. Fed. Claims 1993, US Ct. Appeals (Fed. Cir.) 1994, US Tax Ct. 1994. From assoc. to sr. assoc. Semmes, Bowen & Semmes, Balt., 1983—; ptnr., Taxation Dept. Venable LLP, Balt. Lectr. in field. Contbr. articles to mags. Eagle scout Boy Scouts Am., 1976. Recipient Mero Award, Md. State Bar Assn. (Taxation Sect.). Mem. ABA (Taxation Sect., State & Local Govt. Law Sect., Bus. Law Sect.), Md. State Bar Assn. (chmn. taxation sect. publs. and state legis. coms. 1984-90), Nat. Assn. Bond Lawyers. Office: Venable LLP 1800 Mercantile Bank & Trust Bldg 2 Hopkins Plz Baltimore MD 21201 Office Phone: 410-244-7726. Office Fax: 410-244-7742. Business E-Mail: wrcalvert@venable.com.

CALVERT, WILLIAM PRESTON, radiologist; b. Warrensburg, Mo., July 2, 1934; s. William Geery and Elizabeth (Spaulding) C.; m. Mary Kay Kersh, Apr. 4, 1976. BS, MIT, 1956; MD, U. Pa., 1960. Diplomate Am. Bd. Nuclear Medicine, Am. Bd. Radiology. Intern Pa. Hosp., Phila., 1960-61, resident in medicine, 1961-62, 64-66, chief med. resident, chief resident physician, 1965-66; resident in gastroenterology U. Miami, 1966-67, NIH fellow in gastroenterology, 1967-68, resident in radiology, 1968-71; radiologist Meml. Hosp., Hollywood, Fla., 1971-72; chief dept. radiology Larkin Gen. Hosp., South Miami, Fla., 1972-80, radiologist, 1980-89, Jackson Meml. Hosp., U. Miami, 1989-93, Univ. Hosp., Tammarac, Fla., 1993-95; part-time radiologist Northern Navajo Med. Ctr., Shiprock, N.Mex., 1995-2000; ret., 2000. Clin. instr. radiology U. Miami Sch. Medicine, 1971-76, clin. asst. prof. radiology, 1984-88, clin. assoc. prof. radiology, 1988-94. Bd. dirs. Wediko Farms Children's Svcs., Carbondale, Ill. Served with M.C., USAF, 1962-64. Mem. AMA, Fla. Med. Assn., Fla., Greater Miami radiol. socs., Soc. Nuclear Medicine, Radiol. Soc. N.Am., Explorers Club.

CALVEY, KEVIN, lawyer, state representative; b. Milw., Wis., July 13, 1966; s. Harry and Mary Jane Calvey; children: Chance, Chelsey. BA, U. Dallas, 1988; JD, Georgetown U., 1993. Bar: Okla. Rep. Ho. Reps., State of Okla., Okla. City, 1999—, chmn. revenue and tax com., mem. energy & utology regulatory, jud. coms. Asst. minority fl. leader Okla. Ho. Reps., Okla. City, 1999—, mem. subcom. on select agys, to com. of appropriations and budget, 1999—, mem.commerce, industry and labor, revenue and taxation, and tourism and recreation coms., 1999—. Mem. civil justice task force Am. Legis. Exchange Coun.; mem. adv. bd. S. Okla. City Coun. of Neighborhoods; mem. Okla. Acad. for State Goals, Leadership Okla., Leadership Okla. City; mem. adv. bd. Mid-Del Tech. Ctr.; mem. Eagle Ridge/Crooked Oak Prevention Coalition, Mid-Del Com. Schs. for Healthy Lifestyles; grad. Sixth Del City Citizen' Police Acad.; chmn. Okla. County Rep. Conv., 2003; Sunday sch. tchr. St. Paul Ch, Del City, Okla. Named Legislator of Yr., Okla. Assn. Drug and Alcohol Counselors., 2000, 2002, 2004, Friend of Accuracy, Libertarian Party Okla., 2002, Guardian of Small Bus., Nat. Fedn. Ind. Bus., 2000, 2002; recipient Cert. of Recognition, Okla. Assn. Realtors, Authority to People award, State C. of C., Cert. of Recognition, Am. Legion Post 73, Award citation, VFW Post 9969 & Ladies Aux., Scouting Spirit award, Boy Scouts Am. Troop 60, 1999. Mem.: Rotary. Republican. Roman Catholic. Office: 2399 N Lincoln Blvd Rm 508 Oklahoma City OK 73105 Home and Office: 4416 SE 39th St Del City OK 73115 Office Phone: 405-557-7370. E-mail: kevincalvey@okhouse.gov.

CALVIN, ALLEN DAVID, psychologist, educator; b. St. Paul, Feb. 17, 1928; s. Carl and Zelda (Engelson) C.; m. Dorothy VerStrate, Oct. 5, 1953; children: Jamie, Kris, David, Scott. BA in Psychology cum laude, U. Minn., 1950; MA in Psychology, U. Tex., 1951, PhD in Exptl. Psychology, 1953. Instr. Mich. State U., East Lansing, 1953-55; asst. prof. Hollins Coll., 1955-59, assoc. prof., 1959-61. Dir. Britannica Ctr. for Studies in Learning and Motivation, Menlo Park, Calif., 1961; prin. investigator grant for automated tchg. fgn. langs. Carnegie Found., 1960; USPHS grantee, 1960; pres. Behavioral Rsch. Labs., 1962-74; prof., dean Sch. Edn., U. San Francisco, 1974-78; Henry Clay Hall prof. orgn. and leadership, 1978—; prof. Pacific Grad. Sch. Psychology, 1984-2001. Author textbooks. Served with USNR, 1946-47. Mem. Am. Psychol. Assn., AAAS, Sigma Xi, Psi Chi. Home: 1645 15th Ave San Francisco CA 94122-3523 Office: Pacific Grad Sch Psychology 935 E Meadow Dr Palo Alto CA 94303-4233 Office Phone: 650-843-3402. Business E-Mail: a.calvin@pgsp.edu.

CALVIN, DONALD LEE, stock exchange official; b. Mount Olive, Ill., Nov. 10, 1931; m. Louise Elinor Peterson, Mar. 28, 1952; children: Jane Calvin Palasek, Sally Anne Calvin Salvaterra. Student, Ea. Ill. U., 1950-54, LLD, 1990; LLB, U. Ill., 1956. Bar: Ill. 1956. Atty. Office Sec. of State of Ill., Springfield, 1957-58, securities commr., 1959-62; syndicate mgr. A.C. Allyn & Co., Chgo., 1962-63; atty. F.I. DuPont & Co., Chgo., 1963-64; exec. asst. civic and govt. affairs NY Stock Exch., NYC, 1964-65, v.p., 1966-77, sr. v.p., 1977—86, exec. v.p., 1986—87; chmn. Internat. Bus. Enterprises, Inc., NYC, 1987—. Advisor to chmn. Chgo. Bd. Options Exch., Geneva Stock Exch., 1987—96; advisor to pres. Fedn. Internat. des Bourses de Valeurs, Paris, 1989—98, Kuala Lampur Stock Exch., 1991—2000, São Paulo (Brazil) Stock Exch., 1993—98, Stock Exch. of Hong Kong, 1995—98, Cairo and Alexandria, Egypt Stock Exchs., 1997—; bd. dirs. Internat. Fin. Ctr. and Exch. of Curacao, bd. dirs. SEC Hist. Soc.; bd. dirs. Nat. Coun. on Econ. Edn.; chmn. Nat. Stock Exch., Chgo., 2002—. With USMCR, 1951-56. Mem. ABA, Internat. Bar Assn., Ill. State Bar Assn., Chgo. Bar Assn., Am. Law Inst., Met. Club NYC, Stock Exch. Luncheon Club, Manhasset Bay Yacht Club (Port Washington, NY). Home: 4 Knolls Ln Manhasset NY 11030-1630 Office Phone: 212-832-2525. Personal E-mail: calvindonaldl@aol.com.

CALVIN, DOROTHY VER STRATE, computer company executive; b. Dec. 22, 1929; d. Herman and Christina (Plakmyer) Ver Strate; m. Allen D. Calvin, Oct. 5, 1953; children: Jamie, Kris, Bufo, Scott. BS magna cum laude, Mich. State U., 1951; MA, U. San Francisco, 1988, EdD, 1991. Mgr. data processing Behavioral Rsch. Labs., Menlo Park, Calif., 1972-75; dir. Mgmt. Info. Sys. Inst. for Profl. Devel., San Jose, Calif., 1975-76; sys. analyst, programmer Pacific Bell Info. Sys., San Francisco, Calif., 1976-81, staff mgr., 1981-84; mgr. applications devel. Data Architects Inc., San Francisco, Calif., 1984-86; pres. Ver Strate Press, San Francisco, Calif., 1986—. Instr., Downtown C.C., San Francisco, 1980-84, Cañada C.C., 1986-92, Skyline Coll., 1988-92, City Coll. of San Francisco, 1992—; mem. computer curriculum adv. coun. San Francisco City Coll., 1982-84. V.p. LWV, Roanoke, Va., 1956-58. Pres. Bulliss Purissima Parents Group, Los Altos, Calif., 1962-64; bd. dirs. Vols. for Israel, 1986-87. Mem. IEEE Computer Soc., Assn. Sys. Mgmt., Assn. Women in Computing, Phi Delta Kappa. Democrat. Avocations: computing, gardening, jogging, reading. Office: Ver Strate Press 1645 15th Ave San Francisco CA 94122-3523 Personal E-mail: dcalvin2@aol.com.

CALVIN, JAMES WILLARD, thoracic and vascular surgeon; b. Oakland, Calif., Dec. 7, 1929; s. George Fairchild and Mary Norris Calvin; m. Claudine Deprez (div. 1971); m. Carrie Carman, 1973; children: Carolyne, Frances, Sophie. BA, Stanford U., 1951; MD, MChir, McGill U., 1955. Diplomate Nat. Bd. Med. Examiners, Am. Bd. Surgery, Am. Bd. Thoracic Surgery spl. qualifications gen. vascular surgery. Intern Stanford (Calif.) U., 1955-56, resident dept. surgery, 1959-63, chief resident dept. surgery, 1963-64; group practice Sansum Med. Clinic, Santa Barbara, Calif., 1964-66; pvt. practice Thoracic and Cardiovascular Med. Group, Inc., Ventura, Calif., 1966—95. Bd. dirs. Rehab. Inst. Santa Barbara, bd. trustees; scientific adv. coun. Ramus Med. Technologies, Carpinteria, Calif., 1996-2001; hosp. staff Cmty. Meml. Hosp., Ventura; chief staff Cmty. Meml. Hosp., Ventura, 1994. Contbr. articles to profl. jours. Quality of care reviewer Medicare, 1985—95; bd. dirs. Friends of the Libr., La Quinta, Calif., 1999—. With USAF, 1956—58. NIH rsch. fellow, 1960-61. Fellow ACS (rep. hosps. of Ventura County 1980-87), Am. Coll. of Chest Physicians; mem. AAAS, AMA, Am. Cancer Soc. (Ventura county chpt., bd. dirs. 1969-72), Am. Heart Assn. (coun. on cardiovascular diseases), Am. Lung Assn., Am. Thoracic Soc., Calif. Med. Assn., Internat. Cardiovascular Soc. (N.Am. chpt.), N.Am. Soc. for Pacing and Electrophysiology, Samson Thoracic Surg., Soc. for Clin. Vascular Surgery, Soc. for Thoracic Surgeons, So. Calif. Vascular Surg. Soc., Ventura County Heart Assn. (pres. 1965), Ventura County Med. Soc. (pres. 1979, bd. govs. 1975-81). Home: 47-515 Via Florence La Quinta CA 92253 E-mail: jcalvin@dc.rr.com.

CALVIN, JAMIE DUIF, retired interactive designer; b. Lansing, Mich., July 28, 1954; d. Allen David and Dorothy Viola Calvin; m. Craig Aaron Tovey, Mar. 23, 1980 (div. Oct. 1994); children: Kendl, David, Leo. BBA in Computer Info. Sys., Ga. State U., 1990. Pres. Strategy, Inc., Atlanta, 1982-94; sr. designer Jade River Designs, Atlanta, 1994-98; sr. tech. cons. interactive media IBM, Atlanta, 1998-99; v.p. global retail practice Scient, San Francisco, 1999—, ret. Author: 6 Myths of Web Marketing, 1996, Marketing Manager's Plain English Guide to the Internet, 1998; columnist Chess Life Mag., 1996-97. Mem. ACM, Assn. Internet Profls., HTML Writers Guild (governing bd. 1998), U.S. Chess Fedn. (publs. com. 1996-97, Top 50 U.S. Women Chessplayers). Avocation: chess. Office: Scient One Market Spear Tower 36th Fl Ste 3646 San Francisco CA 94105- E-mail: dcalvin@scient.com.

CALVO, ROQUE JOHN, professional society administrator; b. Allentown, Pa., Sept. 26, 1958; s. Rocco John and Ruth Hattie (Zimpfer) C.; m. Marianne Willever, Feb. 27, 1982; children: Amy Elizabeth, Roque John. BS, Lebanon Valley Coll., 1980; MBA, Rider U., 1986. Acctg. supv. Electrochem. Soc., Inc., Pennington, N.J., 1980-82, asst. exec. dir., 1982-91, exec. dir., 1991—. Adv. bd. Fedn. Materials Socs., Washington, 1991—; meeting adv. bd. Starwood Hotels and Resorts Worldwide. Mem. Am. Soc. Assn. Execs., Coun. Engring. and Sci. Society Execs. (bd. dirs. 1995-2002, pres. 2000-01), N.J. Soc. Assn. Execs. Avocations: golf, basketball, reading. Office: Electrochemical Soc Inc 65 S Main St Pennington NJ 08534-2827 Office Phone: 609-737-1902. E-mail: rcalvo12@aol.com, roque.calvo@electrochem.org.

CAMACCI, MICHAEL A., commercial real estate broker, development consultant; b. Youngstown, Ohio, Feb. 6, 1951; s. Martin B. and Viola F. (Conti) C.; m. Susan Hawkins, Oct. 18, 1985; 1 child, Michael Philip. BBA, Youngstown Coll., 1974. Cert. bus. analyst. Acct. U.S. Steel Corp., Youngstown, 1969-80; mgr. sales Soc. Realty, Boardman, Ohio, 1980-81; dir. sales Pop-ins Maid Services, Columbiana, Ohio, 1981-82; bus. broker Franco Assocs., Girard, Ohio, 1982-86; pres. JMC Realty, Inc., Youngstown, 1986-99; pres., broker Camacci Real Estate, 1986—; pres. Hillview Nursing Home, 1988-99, Valley View Nursing Home, 1990-99, Pyramid Printing, Inc., 1991-99; dir. Crestview Nursing & Rehab. Facility, 1999—2002; CEO Van Fossan & Assoc., 2000—. Pres. Wedgewood Property Mgmt., Inc., 4682 North, LLC, 55 West, LLC, 1997-2002, 19th Hole Investments, 1997-2002; pres. CRE Holding Corp., 1996; pres. 20 West, LLC, 1998—, Goldco Internat., 1997—, Downtown Partners, Landmark Real Estate Svcs, Inc., 1998—, CPR, LLC, 2003-; mgr. 48 North, LLC; broker, mgr. LandQuest Comml. Real Estate, LLC Mem. Youngstown-Warren Regional Growth Alliance; v.p. Austintown Growth Found., 1994-96. Served with U.S. Army, 1971-77. Mem. BBB, Am. Health Care Assn., Ohio Health Care Assn., Nat. Assn. Printers and Lithographers, Internat. Coun. Shopping Ctrs., Youngstown-Warren Area C. of C., Columbiana Area C. of C., Mahoning County Home Builders Assn., Downtown Ptnrs. Democrat. Roman Catholic. Office: Camacci Real Estate Inc 5533 Mahoning Ave Youngstown OH 44515-2316 E-mail: broker8400@landmarkohio.com.

CAMACHO, FELIX PEREZ, governor; b. Camp Zama, Japan, Oct. 30, 1957; s. Carlos G. and Lourdes Perez Camacho; m. Joann Gumataotao Garcia Camacho; children: Jessica Lourdes, Felix James, Maria Amparo. BBA in Fin., Marquette U., 1980. Ins. mgr. property casualty divsn. Pacific Fin. Corp.; account adminstr. IBM; senator, Guam; gov., 2002—. Mem.: Nat. Coun. State Legislators, Asian Pacific Parliamentarian Union. Republican. Roman Catholic. Office: Office of the Governor PO Box 2950 Hagatna GU 96932

CAMACHO, MARGARITA TICZON, cardiothoracic surgeon, educator; b. N.Y.C., Dec. 31, 1955; d. Augusto M. and Consorcia (Ticzon) C. BA in Chemistry, Vassar Coll., 1978; MD, N.Y. Med. Coll., 1994. Diplomate Am. Bd. Surgery, Am. Bd. Thoracic Surgery. Resident and resident in gen. surgery Lenox Hill Hosp., N.Y.C., 1984—89; resident in cardiothoracic surgery Albert Einstein Coll. Medicine, Bronx, NY, 1989—91, asst. prof. dept. cardiothoracic surgery, 1994—2002, clin. assoc. prof., 2002—; hon. clin. vis. fellow U. Leicester, England, 1992; clin. assoc. dept. thoracic and cardiovasc. surgery Cleve. Clin. Found., 1993—94; attending surgeon Montefiore Med. Ctr., Bronx, 1994—2003, dir. cardiothoracic ICU, 1995—2003; attending surgeon dept. cardiovasc. and thoracic surgery North Shore Univ. Hosp., Manhasset, NY, 2003—. Clin. asst. prof. Cardiothoracic Surgery NYU, 2003—. Contbg. author: Management of Acute Myocardial Infarction, 1994, (films) Everting Stapled Closures of Bronchus, Pulmonary Vessels, and Parenchyma in Pulmonary Lobectomies and Parenchymal Reactions, 1989, The Use of Goretex Surgical Membranes as a Pericardial Substitute, 1992, Left Ventricular Outflow Obstruction, 1992, Congenital Sub-Aortic Stenosis: A Spectrum of Surgical Entities, 1993; contbr. chpts. in books and articles to profl. jours. Recipient Charles H. Bryan award for Clin. Excellence in Thoracic and Cardiovasc. Surgery, Cleve. Clin. Found., 1994. Fellow ACS (assoc., pres. Bronx chpt. 2003-06); mem. AAUW, Soc. Thoracic Surgeons, Soc. Women in Thoracic Surgery (bd. dirs., v.p. 2003-04, pres. 2005—), Internat. Soc. Heart and Lung Transplantation, Heart Failure Soc. Am., Vassar Club N.Y (bd. dirs., chair membership com. 2004—) Home: 332 National Ct Roslyn NY 11576 Office: North Shore Univ Hosp Dept Cardiovasc Surgery 300 Community Dr Manhasset NY 11030

CAMARA, JORGE DE GUZMAN, ophthalmologist, humanitarian, researcher, educator; b. Ann Arbor, Mich., May 21, 1950; s. Augusto A. and Feliciana (de Guzman) C.; m. Virginia Valdes, June 23, 1977; 1 child, Augusto Carlos. BS in Pre-Medicine, U. Philippines, 1972, MD cum laude, 1976. Diplomate Am. Bd. Ophthalmology. Surg. intern U. Tex, Houston, 1977-78; resident in ophthalmology Baylor Coll. Medicine, Houston, 1978-81, fell in ophthalmic plastic and reconstructive surgery, 1981-82; ophthalmologist Straub Clinic and Hosp., Honolulu, 1982-88; pvt. practice, Honolulu, 1988—; assoc. prof. U. Hawaii Sch. Medicine, Honolulu, 1982—. Cons. Tripler Army Hosp., Honolulu, 1982—; chmn. dept. ophthalmology and otorhinolaryngology, bd. dirs. St. Francis Med. Ctr.; bd. dirs. Am. Savs. Bank, Hawaiian

Electric Industries. Bd. dirs. Aloha Med. Mission, Honolulu, 1988—. Fellow Am. Acad. Ophthalmology, Am. Soc. Ophthalmic Plastic and Reconstructive Surgery; mem. AMA, Hawaii Ophthal. Soc. (pub. rels. officer 1984-85, pres. 1992, chmn. com. for indigent svcs. 1994—), Philippine Med. Assn. Hawaii (pres. 1988—), Assn. Philippine Ophthalmologists in Am. (pres.-elect 2000). Roman Catholic. Avocations: tennis, piano. Office: 2226 Liliha St Ste 407 Honolulu HI 96817-1651 E-mail: jordegcam@msn.com.

CAMARA, VINCENT ANTONIN REGINALD, mathematician, educator, statistician, researcher; arrived in U.S., 1992; s. Athanase and Lucie Camara; m. Gislhaine Claire P. Soivilus. BSc in Math., U. Dakar, 1984, MS in Pure Math., 1986; MS in Applied Math., U. North Fla., 1994; PhD in Math. and Option Statis., U. South Fla., 1997. Educator stats. U. NC, Charlotte, NC, 1997—98; educator math. and stats. U. South Fla., Tampa, 1998—2001, St. Leo U., Largo, Fla., 2001—. Assoc. dir., rschr. Rsch. Ctr. for Boyesian Applications, Inc., 2003—; presenter in field. Contbr. articles to profl. jours.; mem. editl. bd.: Jour. Modern Applied Statis. Methods. Mem.: The Risk Analysis Soc., The Bayesian Statis. Soc., Am. Statis. Assn., Phi Kappa Phi, Pi Mu Epsilon. Home: 8799 Bardmoor Boulevard Unit 201 Largo FL 33777 Personal E-mail: gvcamara@ij.net. Business E-Mail: vincent.camara@saintleo.edu.

CAMARDA, CHARLES J., astronaut; b. Queens, NY, May 8, 1952; s. Jack and Ray Camarda; m. Melinda Miller; 4 children. BS in Aerospace Engring., Poly. Inst. Bklyn., 1974; MS in Engring. Sci., George Washington U., 1980; PhD in Aerospace Engring., Va. Poly. Inst. and State U., 1990. Rsch. scientist thermal structures br., divsn. structures and materials Langley Rsch. Ctr., NASA, Hampton, Va., 1974—89, head structures and materials tech. maturation team, Nat. Aero-Space Plan program, 1989—94, head thermal structures br., 1994—96; astronaut, mission specialist NASA, Johnson Space Ctr., Houston, 1996—. Assigned tech. duties in the Astronaut Office Spacecraft Systems/Ops. Br.; served on Expedition-8 back-up crew; mission specialist 5 (MS-5), STS-114 (Discovery) Return to Flight mission NASA, 2005. Recipient NASA Cert. Recognition (12), Sustained Superior Performance awards (2), Spl. Achievement awards (2), Technology Commercialization awards(2), Space Station Program Team Excellence award, NASA Group Achievement award, NASA Superior Accomplishment award, NASA Honor award, Rsch. and Devel. 100 award for one of the top Tech. Innovations, Indsl. Rsch. Mag., 1983. Fellow: AIAA (assoc.). Achievements include Holds 7 Patents; development of heat-pipe-cooled sandwich panel. Avocations: racquetball, running, weightlifting, boxing. Office: Astronaut Office/CB NASA Johnson Space Ctr Houston TX 77058*

CAMARDO, MICHAEL F., engineering company executive; BS in econ., Villanova Univ. With RCA Service Company (merged w/ GE), 1964—90; pres. GE Government Svc. (merged w/ Martin Marietta), 1990—93, Martin Marietta Services Group (merged w/ Lockheed Martin), 1993—95, Lockheed Martin Services Group (now Technology Services Group), 1995—99; exec. v.p., info., tech. svcs. Lockheed Martin Corp, 1999—. Bd. of dir. exec. advisory council, Rutgers Univ. Bd. of dir. American Red Cross. Office: Lockheed Martin Tech 6801 Rockledge Dr Bethesda MD 20817

CAMBARERI, ROBIN LOUISE, music educator; d. John LeRoy and Catherine Jean Burnett; m. Joseph Patrick Cambareri; children: Gabriella Louise, Nicholas Joseph. MusB in edn., Crane Sch. Music, 1992; MSc in edn., State U. of NY at Oswego, 2000. Music tchr. Red Creek Ctrl. Sch., NY, 1993—95; vocal music tchr. Syracuse City Sch. Dist., NY, 1995—97; instrumental music tchr. Waterloo Ctrl. Sch., NY, 1997—2001; vocal music tchr. Geneva City Sch. Dist., NY, 2000—. Mus. dir. Seneca Cmty. Players, NY, 1996; music dept. chmn. Geneva City Sch. Dist., 2002—; adv. for broadway bound Syracuse City Sch. Dist., 1996—97. Recipient Give Them a Hand award, Geneva Sch. Dist. Adminstrn., 2004. Mem.: Nat. Edn. Assn., Geneva Teacher's Assn. Avocations: reading, dance, singing, piano, crafts. Home: 65 Green St Seneca Falls NY 13148 Office: Geneva City Sch Dist 400 North St Geneva NY 14456

CAMBER, DIANE WOOLFE, museum director; b. Miami Beach, Fla. m. Isaac Camber. BA in Art History, Barnard Coll.; postgrad., Columbia U., Mass. Coll. Art; MEd in Arts Edn., Boston State Coll. Mus. lectr., pub. rels. specialist Albright-Knox Art Gallery, Buffalo, 1962—64; mus. educator De Cordova and Dana Mus., Lincoln, Mass., 1967—68; mus. lectr. Mus. Fine Arts, Boston, 1968—69; art specialist L.A. Pub. Schs., 1970—77; instr. Ft. Lauderdale (Fla.) Art Inst., 1978—79; assoc. dir. Miami (Fla.) Design Preservation League, 1978—80; acting dir. Bass Mus. Art, Miami, 1980—82, exec. dir., chief curator, 1982—. Co-author: Frank Lloyd Wright: Decorative Objects, Prints, Drawings, Florida Projects, 1984. Campaigned to place Miami's Art Deco Dist. on the Nat. Register of Historica Places; bd. dirs. Chaim Gross Found., NY. Recipient Chevalier des Arts et Lettres, French Govt., 1989. Mem.: Fla. Art Mus. Dirs. Assn. (v.p. 1984—86, pres. 1986—), Mus. Trustees Assn. (mem. adv. coun. dirs.), Am. Assn. Art Mus. Dirs. Office: Bass Mus Art 2121 Park Ave Miami Beach FL 33139

CAMBLIN, RON E., youth and education minister; b. Lawrence, Kans., May 24, 1954; s. Glenn E. Camblin and Betty N. (Jordan) Handley; m. Barbara Sue Thompson, May 31, 1975; children: Justin Ryan and Ashley Brooke. Student, Ozark State Coll., 1972-75; BS, Fla. Christian Coll., 1982. Youth min. Villa Heights Christian Ch., Joplin, Mo., 1973-75; min. Dadeville (Mo.) Christian Ch., 1975-78; youth min. 1st Christian Ch., Wauchula, Fla., 1978-80, Pine Hills Christian Ch., Orlando, Fla., 1980-92, 1st Christian Ch., Largo, Fla., 1982-88, Westwood-Cheviot Ch. of Christ, Cin., 1988-89; min. of youth and edn. Harborside Christian Ch., Safety Harbor, Fla., 1989-93; sr. pastor Woodford Christian Ch., Versailles, Ky., 1993-97, Eastside Christian Ch., Lexington, Ky., 1998—. Pres. Fla. Christian Youth Conv., 1973-74; cons. Standard Pub. Co., Cin., 1987—. Recipient Ch. Growth award Nat. Ch. Growth Rsch. Ctr., 1981. Mem. Fla. Christian Coll. Alumni Assn. (pres. k1982-83), Nat. Network Youth Mins. Republican. E-mail: www.eastsidecc.org. Office: Eastside Christian Ch PO Box 55349 Lexington KY 40555-5349

CAMBON, ELISE MURRAY, music educator, musician; b. New Orleans, Feb. 27, 1917; d. Maurice Cornelius Cambon and Marie Camilia Murray. BA, Tulane U., 1939, PhD, 1975; postgrad., Benedictine Abbey of Solesmes, France, 1955; MusM, U. Mich., 1947. Organist, music dir. St. Louis Cathedral, New Orleans, 1941—; instr. music Ursuline Coll., New Orleans, 1949—51, Ursuline Acad., New Orleans, 1942—49, McGhee Sch., New Orleans, 1951—61; prof. music Loyola U., New Orleans, 1959—82, founding chmn. dept. liturgical music Coll. Music. Condr. St. Louis Cathedral Choir in Europe, England and Ireland. Coord. choirs and brass choir One Shell Sq. La. Philharm. Orch., New Orleans, 1989—. Recipient 1st prize musicol. rsch., Mu Phi Epsilon, 1975—76, Order of Chevalier des Arts et Lettres, French Govt., 1983; grantee, Schlieder Found., 1959, for concert tours, Archdiocese of New Orleans and St. Louis Cathedral, 1987—98; Fulbright scholar, Hochschule Musik in Frankfurt-am-Main, Germany, 1951—53. Mem.: Bach Oratorio Soc. (founding mem.), Am. Guild Organists (founding mem., dean). Roman Catholic.

CAMBONE, STEPHEN A., federal agency administrator; BA in Polit. Sci., Cath. U., 1973; MA in Polit. Sci., Claremont Grad. Sch., 1977, PhD in Polit. Sci., 1982. Staff mem. office of dir. Los Alamos Nat. Lab., 1982—86; dep. dir. strategic analysis SRS Techs. (Washington Ops.), 1986—90; dir. for strategic def. policy Office of Sec. Def., 1990—93; sr. fellow in polit.-mil. studies Ctr. for Strategic and Internat. Studies, 1993—98; staff dir. Commn. to Assess the Ballistic Missile Threat to U.S., 1998; dir. rsch. Inst. for Nat. Strategic Studies, Nat. Def. U., 1998—2000; staff dir. Commn. to Assess U.S. Nat. Security Space Mgmt. and Orgn., 2000—01; spl. asst. Sec. and Dep. Sec. Def., 2001; prin. dep. under Sec. Def. for Policy Dept. of Def., Washington, 2001—02, dir of program analysis and evaluation, 2001—03, under sec of defense for intelligence, 2003—. Office: Dept of Defense 2100 Defense Pentagon Washington DC 20301-2000

CAMBOU, BERTRAND, information technology executive; Engring. Degree, Supelec, Paris; D in Elec. Engring., Paris XI U. With Motorola, 1984—99; COO, co-pres., bd. dirs. Gemplus; mng. dir., bd. dirs. Ingenico, 1999—2002; exec. v.p., pres., CEO Spansion, Advanced Micro Devices, Sunnyvale, Calif., 2002—. Achievements include patents in field. Office: Advanced Micro Devices One AMD Pl PO Box 3453 Sunnyvale CA 94088-3453

CAMBRIA, CHRISTOPHER C., lawyer; b. July 1958; CPA. Assoc. Cravath, Swaine & Moore, 1986—93, Fried, Frank, Harris, Shriver & Jacobson, 1993—97; sr. v.p., sec., gen. counsel L-3 Communications Holdings Inc., 1997—. Office: L-3 Communications Holdings Inc 600 3rd Ave New York NY 10016 Office Phone: 212-697-1111. Home Fax: 212-867-5249.

CAMBRICE, ROBERT LOUIS, lawyer; b. Nov. 23, 1947; s. Eugene and Edna Bertha (Jackson) Cambrice; m. Christine Jackson, Jan. 7, 1972; children: Bryan, Graham. BA cum laude, Tex. So. U., 1969; JD, U. Tex., 1972. Bar: Tex. 1973, U.S. Dist. Ct. (so. dist.) Tex. 1975, U.S. Ct. Appeals (5th cir.) 1975, U.S. Ct. Appeals (11th cir.) 1981, U.S. Supreme Ct. 1981. Asst. atty. City of Houston, 1974-76, 1986—, sr. trial atty. legal dept., 1990-92, chief def. litigation dept., 1992—; pvt. practice Houston, 1976-81; asst. atty. Harris County, Tex., 1981-85; asst. atty. Legal Dept. City Houston, 2005—. Earl Warren fellow, 1969—72. Mem.: NAACP, ABA, Nat. Bar Assn., Alpha Kappa Mu. Roman Catholic. Business E-Mail: Robert.Cambrice@cityofhouston.net.

CAMBY, MARCUS D., professional basketball player; b. Hartford, Conn., Mar. 22, 1974; B.Edn., U. Mass., 1996. Forward Toronto Raptors, 1996-98, N.Y. Knicks, 1998—2002, Denver Nuggets, 2002—. Tutor math. and English to pub. sch. students. Named to 1996-97 NBA All-Rookie First Team. Office: c/o Denver Nuggets 1000 Chopper Circle Denver CO 80204

CAMELO, DIANNE M., lawyer; b. Bronx, N.Y., Apr. 9, 1960; AB cum laude, Colgate U., 1982; JD, Fordham U., 1985. Bar: N.J., U.S. Dist. Ct., Dist. of N.J. 1985, N.Y., U.S. Dist. Ct., So. and Ea. Dists. of N.Y. 1986. Ptnr. Levy, Stopol & Camelo, LLP, Uniondale, NY; of counsel Audiovox Corp., Hauppauge. Mem.: N.Y. State Bar Assn., Nassau County Bar Assn. Office: Levy, Stopol & Camelo, LLP 1425 EAB Plaza Uniondale NY 11556-1425 Office Phone: 516-802-7007.

CAMERA, NICHOLAS J., lawyer; b. NYC, Jan. 12, 1947; s. Anthony Joseph and Cecile Elizabeth (Merritt) C.; m. Barbara Danko, July 10, 1971 (div. 1986); children: David Merritt, Lauren Anne; m. Susan Salorio, June 30, 2001. BS, Wagner Coll., Staten Island, N.Y., 1969; JD, Bklyn. Law Sch., 1972; MBA, Fordham U., 1980; MA, Columbia U., 1997. Bar: N.Y. 1973, U.S. Dist. Ct. (so. and ea. dists.) N.Y. 1973, U.S. Ct. Appeals (2d cir.) 1973. Assoc. Bigham, Englar, Jones & Houston, NYC, 1972-78; gen. atty. Phelps Dodge Industries, Inc., NYC, 1978-82; asst. gen. counsel Congoleum Corp., Kearney, NJ, 1982, Avon Products, Inc., NYC, 1982-91; sr. v.p., gen. counsel, sec. Interpub. Group of Cos., NYC. Mem. ABA, Assn. of Bar of City of N.Y., Am. Soc. Corp. Secs. Office: Interpub Group of Cos 1114 Avenue Of The Americas Fl 19 New York NY 10036

CAMERIUS, JAMES WALTER, marketing educator, corporate researcher; b. Chgo., June 14, 1939; s. Wilbert Albert and Violet Elna (Johnson) C. BS, No. Mich. U., 1961; MS, U. N.D., 1963; postgrad., U. Okla., 1974-77. From instr. to assoc. prof. No. Mich. U., Marquette, 1963-90, prof. mktg., 1990—. Lectr. in field; adv. bd. S.E. Advanced Tech. Edn. Consortium. Mem. editl. bd. Bus. Case Jour., Jour. SMET Edn. Cir. lay rep. Luth. Ch.-Mo. Synod, 1987-89; pres. Redeemer Luth. Ch., Marquette, 1989-90, sec. to ch. coun., 1990-92, bd. elders, 1993-98, v.p., 2000-2001, pres. 2001-02; mktg. track chair N.Am. Case Rsch. and Mktg. Assn., 1997-2003. Recipient MAGB Disting. Prof. award, 1995; Rsch. grantee Direct Selling Edn. Found., 1987-2002, Walker L. Cisler Sch. No. Mich. U., 1990, Filene Rsch. Inst., 1994; named Outstanding Case Reviewer, Case Rsch. Jour., 1998. Fellow Acad. Mktg. Sci.; mem. Am. Mktg. Assn., Soc. Case Rsch. (v.p. 1990-91, case workshop dir. 1999, pres.-elect 2000, pres. 2001-02, archivist), N.Am. Case Rsch. Assn. (bd. dirs. 2003—, newsletter editor), World Assn. for Case Method Rsch. and Application (case colloquium dir. 1997—, adv. bd.), Econ. Club, Alpha Kappa Psi (Alumni award). Democrat. Home: 171 Lakewood Ln Marquette MI 49855-9543 Office: No Mich U Mktg Dept Marquette MI 49855 Business E-Mail: jcameriu@nmu.edu.

CAMERO, CALDWELL AUSTIN, lawyer; b. LA, Aug. 6, 1975; d. Raymond Cesar and Leslie Austin Camero; m. Joel Frederic Pace, July 17, 1999. BA cum laude, Providence Coll., 1997; JD, William Mitchell Coll. Law, 2001. Bar: Minn. 2001, Wis. 2002, U.S. Dist. Ct. (we. dist.) Wis. 2003, U.S. Dist. Ct. Minn. 2003. Corp. counsel Menard, Inc., Eau Claire, Wis., 2001. Vol. bus. assistance program State Bar Wis., Madison, 2004—; vol. Eau Claire Regional Arts Ctr., 2003—; mem. emerging leaders divsn. adv. coun., co-chair cmty. svc. com. United Way Greater Eau Claire, 2003—04; bd. mem. Greater Chippewa Valley Boys and Girls Club, 2005—. Recipient Excellence for the Future award, Ctr. for Computer-Assisted Legal Instrn., 2001, Achievement in Vol. Pub. Svc. award, Minn. Justice Found., 2001. Mem.: ABA (intellectual property law sect. 2002—, young lawyers divsn. 2002—), Am. Intellectual Property Law Assn. (trademark law and litigation coms. 2004—, women in intellectual property law com. 2004—, young lawyers com. 2004—), Hennepin County Bar Assn., Minn. State Bar Assn., Eau Clair County Bar Assn. (treas., cmty. svc. com. 2004—, meetings programs socl. subcom. 2005—), Wis. State Bar Assn. (intellectual property law sect. 2002—, young lawyers divsn. 2002—), Jr. League Eau Claire (bd. dirs., v.p. 2004—). Avocations: running, travel, biking, water-skiing, baking. Personal E-mail: caldwellcamero@hotmail.com.

CAMERON, ALASTAIR GRAHAM WALTER, astrophysicist, educator; b. Winnipeg, Man., Can., June 21, 1925; came to U.S., 1959, naturalized, 1963; s. Alexander Thomas and Airdrie Edna (Bell) C.; m. Elizabeth Aston MacMillan, June 11, 1955. B.Sc., U. Man., 1947; PhD, U. Sask., 1952, D.Sc. (hon.), 1977; A.M. (hon.), Harvard U., 1973. Asst. prof. physics Iowa State Coll., Ames, 1952-54; asst., assoc. and sr. research officer Atomic Energy Can., Ltd., Chalk River, Ont., 1954-61; sr. research fellow Calif. Inst. Tech., Pasadena, 1959-60; sr. scientist Goddard Inst. Space Studies, N.Y., 1961-66; prof. space physics Yeshiva U., 1966-73; prof. astronomy Harvard U., Cambridge, Mass., 1973-97, Donald H. Menzel prof. astrophysics, 1997-99, Donald H. Menzel rsch. prof. astrophysics, 1999—2004, Donald H. Menzel prof. astrophysics emeritus, 2004—; sr. rsch. scientist Lunar and Planetary Lab., U. Ariz., 2000—. Chmn. Space Sci. Bd., 1976-82, Nat. Acad. Scis. Contbr. articles to profl. jours. Recipient J. Lawrence Smith medal NAS, 1988, Disting. Pub. Service medal NASA, 1983. Mem. NAS, AAAS, Am. Phys. Soc., Am. Geophys. Union (Harry H. Hess medal 1989), Am. Astron. Soc. (Russell lectr. 1997), Internat. Astron. Union, Meteoritical Soc. (Leonard medal 1994). Office: Lunar and Planetary Lab 1629 E University Blvd 527A Tucson AZ 85721 Business E-Mail: acameron@lpl.arizona.edu.

CAMERON, ALEX BRIAN, accountant, educator; b. Fresno, Calif., Nov. 20, 1943; s. Alexander Archer and Francette (Maize) C.; m. Judy Lea Helphrey, June 7, 1969; children: Michelle, Michael. BA, Eastern Wash. U., 1969, MBA, 1970; PhD, U. Utah, 1982. cert. in mgmt. acctg. Mgr. prodn. planning Bunker Hill Mining Co., Kellog, Idaho, 1970-77; asst. prof. Wash. State U., Pullman, 1978-79; assoc. prof. Eastern Wash. U., Cheney, 1981-87, prof., 1987—, chmn. dept. acctg., 1988-89, assoc. dean, 1990-97, interimm v.p. bus. and fin., 1998-99, interim dean Coll. Bus. and Pub. Adminstrn., 1999-2001. Contbr. articles to profl. jours. Avocations: sailing, golf, volleyball. Home: 15212 Pinnacle Ln Veradale WA 99037-9163 Office: 668 N Riverpoint Blvd Spokane WA 99202-1677 Office Phone: 509-358-2260. Business E-Mail: acameron@ewu.edu. E-mail: jcameron52@comcast.net.

CAMERON, CARL (KARL LAMBERG-KARLOVSKY), political correspondent; b. New Haven, Conn., Sept. 22, 1961; s. C.C. and Martha Lamberg-Karlovsky; m. Pauline Lamberg-Karlovsky, Oct. 10, 1987; children: Kyle, Ryan. With Sta. WFEA, Manchester, NH, 1985, Sta. WZID, Manchester, NH, 1985; polit. dir. Sta. WMUR-TV, Manchester, NH; chief congl., polit. corr. FOX News Channel, Washington, 1996—2005, chief White House corr., 2005—. Recipient numerous AP awards, 1987-95, Assn. of Broadcasters awards, 1987-99. Office: FOX News Channel 400 N Capitol St NW Ste 550 Washington DC 20001 E-mail: cameron@foxnews.com.*

CAMERON, DONALD B., JR., lawyer; BA, Kenyon Coll., 1971; JD, Vanderbilt U., 1974; LLM, Vrije Universiteit Brussels, 1975. Bar: DC 1979, US Ct. Internat. Trade, Ct. Appeals, Fed. Cir. Ptnr. litig., co-chair Internat. Trade Group Kaye Scholer LLP, Washington, DC. Mem.: ABA. Office: Kaye Scholer LLP McPherson Bldg 901 Fifteenth Street, NW, Ste 1100 Washington DC 20005 Office Phone: 202-682-3630. E-mail: dcameron@kayescholer.com.

CAMERON, DORT, electronics executive; b. 1945; m. Elizabeth Cameron. Grad., Middlebury Coll. With Drexel Burnham Comml. Paper, Inc., Dallas, 1966—84, pres.; with Investment Ltd. Partnership, Greenwich, Conn., 1984—99, mng. gen. ptnr.; chmn. Entex Info. Svcs., Rye Brook, NY, 1993—99; trustee emeritus Middlebury Coll. Bd. mem. Rippowan Cisqua Sch. Westchester Land Trust; dir. First Marblehead Corp. Office: Airlie Group 115 E Putnam Ave Greenwich CT 06830-5643*

CAMERON, DOUGLAS E., lawyer; b. Wheeling, W.Va., Feb. 19, 1959; BA in economics/acctg. summa cum laude, Bethany Coll., W.Va., 1981; JD magna cum laude, U. Pitts., 1984. Bar: Pa. 1984, US Ct. Appeals 2nd Cir., US Ct. Appeals 3rd Cir., US Ct. Appeals 7th Cir., US Ct. Appeals Fed. Cir., US Dist. Ct. We. Dist. Pa., US Dist. Ct. Mid. Dist. Pa., US Dist. Ct. Ea. Dist. Pa., Supreme Ct. Pa., Supreme Ct. Appeals W.Va., US Supreme Ct. Assoc. Reed Smith LLP, Pitts., 1984—93, ptnr., 1993—; practice group leader ins. coverage group, 2003—. Office: Reed Smith LLP 435 Sixth Ave Pittsburgh PA 15219 Office Phone: 412-288-4104. Office Fax: 412-288-3063. Business E-Mail: dcameron@reedsmith.com.

CAMERON, DUKE EDWARD, cardiac surgeon, educator; b. Miami, Fla., Mar. 9, 1952; s. Edward John and Joanne (Abbott) C.; m. Claudia Oppenheim; children: Danielle, Nicole. AB, Harvard Coll., 1974; MD, Yale U., 1978. Resident gen. surgery Yale-New Haven Hosp., 1978-84, resident cardiothoracic surgery, 1984-87; prof. surgery, dir. pediatric cardiac surgery Johns Hopkins Hosp., Balt. Fellow ACS; mem. Soc. Thoracic Surgeons, So. Thoracic Surg. Assn., Am. Assn. Thorac Surg. Home: 2209 South Rd Baltimore MD 21209-4437 Office: Johns Hopkins Hosp Blalock 618 600 N Wolfe St Baltimore MD 21287 Office Phone: 410-955-2698. Business E-Mail: dcameron@jhmi.edu.

CAMERON, HEATHER ANNE, publishing executive; b. Montreal, Quebec, Can., Mar. 12, 1951; came to U.S., 1981; d. Douglas George and Jeanne Sutherland (Thompson) C.; m. Ward Eric Shaw, Dec. 20, 1980; 1 child, Geoffrey Cameron. BA, Queen's U., Kingston, Ont., Can., 1973; MLS, McGill U., Montreal, 1977. Head reference and bibliography sect. Nat. Libr. Can., Ottawa, 1977-80; head editl. dept. Librs. Unltd., Inc., Denver, 1981-86; v.p. acquisitions and editl. devel. ABC-CLIO, Inc., Santa Barbara, Calif., 1986-92, pres., pub. Santa Barbara, Denver and, Eng., 1992-97; v.p., gen. mgr. Westgroup, San Francisco, 1997—. Bd. dirs. Friends of Librs. U.S.A., v.p., 1996, pres., 1997—. Mem. ALA (com. chair 1993—), Friends of Librs. USA (dir. 1994—, pres. 1997-2000), Amnesty Internat., Phi Beta Mu. Office: Thomson-West 425 Market St San Francisco CA 94105 Office Phone: 415-344-5010. Business E-Mail: heather.cameron@thomson.com.

CAMERON, JAMES, film director, screenwriter, producer; b. Kapuskasing, Ont., Can., Aug. 16, 1954; s. Philip and Shirley Cameron; m. Sharon Williams, 1974 (div. 1985); m. Gale Ann Hurd, 1985 (div. 1989); m. Katheryn Bigelow, 1989 (div. 1991); m. Linda Hamilton, 1997 (div. 1999); 1 child: Suzy Amis. Grad. in Physics, Calif. State U., Fullerton. Head Lightstorm Entertainment, Burbank, Calif., 1992—; CEO Digital Domain, 1993—. Art dir. Battle Beyond the Stars, 1980, prodn. designer Galaxy of Terror, 1981, creator spl. effects Escape from New York, 1981; dir.: (films) Piranha II: The Spawning, 1981, Terminator 2 3-D, 1996; (TV films) Earthship, 2001; screenwriter Rambo: First Blood Part II, 1985, Strange Days, 1995, exec. prodr. Point Break, 1991, dir., screenwriter Xenogenesis, 1978, The Terminator, 1984, Aliens, 1986, The Abyss, 1989, dir., prodr., editor (films) Titanic, 1997 (Academy award for Best Picture and Best Dir., 9 others, 1997), dir., prodr. Ghosts of the Abyss, 2002, (TV) Expedition Bismarck, 2002, dir., prodr., screenwriter Terminator II: Judgement Day, 1991 (6 Academy award nominations, Ray Bradbury award for dramatic screenwriting, 5 Saturn awards Acad. Sci. Fiction, 5 MTV Movie awards, People's Choice award), True Lies, 1994, writer, exec. prodr. (TV series) Dark Angel, 2000—; author (films): Terminator 3: Rise of the Machines, 2003; prodr.(films): Volcanos of the Deep Sea, 2003. Mem. adv. bd. Science Fiction Mus. and Hall of Fame. Office: Lightstorm Entertainment 919 Santa Monica Blvd Santa Monica CA 90401-2704

CAMERON, JEFFREY M., lawyer; b. June 1970; Assoc. Vinson & Elkins LLP, 1996—2004; v.p., legal counsel, sec. Group 1 Automotive, 2004—. Office: Group 1 Automotive 950 Echo Ln Ste 100 Houston TX 77024 Office Phone: 713-647-5700. Office Fax: 713-647-5800. Business E-Mail: jcameron@group1auto.com.

CAMERON, JOHN CLIFFORD, lawyer, health science association administrator; b. Phila., Sept. 17, 1946; m. Eileen Duffy, July 12, 1975; children: Christopher, Meghan. BA, U. Pitts., 1969; MBA, Temple U., 1972; JD, Widener U., 1976; LLM, NYU, 1980. Bar: Pa. 1977, N.J. 1977, Md. 1995. Asst. adminstr. Phila. Psychiatric Ctr., 1972-76; jud. clk. to presiding justice N.J. Superior Ct., Newark, 1976-77; asst. adminstr. St. Elizabeth Hosp., Elizabeth, NJ, 1977; v.p. corp. legal affairs Methodist Hosp., Phila., 1978-94; legal cons. North Penn Hosp, Lansdale, Pa., 1994-95; counsel, legal adminstr. Hodes, Ulman, Pessin & Katz, P.A., Towson, Md., 1995-96; asst. to pres. Temple U. Health Sys., Phila., 1996—; asst. sec. Neumann Med. Ctr., Phila., 1997—2002, Jeanes Hosp., Phila., 1997—, Northwood Nursing Home, Phila., 1997—2002, Temple Physicians, Inc., Phila., 1997—, Temple Univ. Hosp., Phila., 1997—, Lower Bucks Hosp., Bristol, Pa., 1997—2002, Episcopal Hosp., Phila., 1997—, Temple U. Children's Med. Ctr., Phila., 1997, Northeastern Hosp., Phila., 1997—, Temple Continuing Care Ctr., Phila., 1997—2002. Sec. Suthbrelt Properties, Ltd., Phila., 1981-94, Asbury Corp., Wilmington, Del., 1982-94, Healthmark, Inc., Moorestown, N.J., 1982-94, Meth. Hosp. Nursing Ctr., Phila., 1983-94; asst. sec. various hosps. and nursing homes, 1997—, instr. Grad. Sch. Mgmt., Pa. State U., 1991—; instr. mgmt. dept. Neumann Coll., 1991-96; instr. bus. divsn. Rosemont Coll., 1995-96. Contbr. articles to profl. jours. Mem. campaign United Way, Phila., 1979-94; mem. health and welfare com. United Meth. Eastern Pa. Conf., 1978-94; advisor Explorer Post, Boy Scouts Am., 1988-94; mem. steering com. Golden Cross, Phila., 1984-94; sec. Tredyffrin Twp. Park and Recreation Bd., 1987-95; alumni rep. Widener U.; mem. environ. adv. com. and open space task force Tredyffrin Twp., 1991-95. Fellow Am. Coll. Healthcare Execs. (chmn. bylaws com. 1995-96); mem. ABA, N.J. Bar Assn., Pa. Bar Assn., Phila. Bar Assn., Am. Hosp. Assn., Hosp. Assn. Pa., Swedish Colonial Soc. (bd dirs. 1992—, gov. 1993-95), Sons of Union Vets. of Civil War, SAR. Avocations: swimming, music. Home: 1410 Church Rd Malvern PA 19355-9714

CAMERON, JOHN M., nuclear scientist, educator, science administrator; b. Aug. 9, 1940; BSc, Queens U., Ireland, 1962; MSc, UCLA, 1965, PhD, 1967. Tech. asst. U.K. Atomic Energy Authority, Eng., 1962-63; asst. prof. UCLA, 1967-68; rsch. assoc. U. Wash., Seattle, 1968-70; asst. prof. to prof. U. Alta., 1970-87; dir. Cyclotron Facility, prof. dept. physics Ind. U., Bloomington, 1987—. Asst. dir. initial ops. TRIUMF, Vancouver, 1973-74; vis scientist U.

Paris, SIN Switzerland, 1977-78; staff scientist Nat. Saturne Lab., France, 1981-82; dir. Nuclear Rsch. Ctr., U. Alta., 1985-87. Fellow Am. Phys. Soc. Office: IN Univ Bloomington Cyclotron Facility 2401 Milo Sampson Ln Bloomington IN 47408-1368 Office Phone: 812-855-3316.

CAMERON, KAY, conductor, composer; b. Robbins, N.C. d. Joe and Gladys Cameron. MusB, U. N.C., 1972, MusM, 1973. Music dir. Kennedy Ctr. For the Performing Arts, Washington, 1994—; condr. Words and Music, Musicals in Concert; music supr. Sondheim Celebration. Tchr. Richmond Pub. Schs., Va., 1973-77; music dir., condr. broadway and nat. tours, N.Y., 1978-1996; arranger, orchestrator musicals and TV, 1979-1996; vis. lectr. U. N.C., Wilmington, 1997-98; condr. concert featuring Cy Coleman, Kennedy Ctr. Opera House Orch. Music dir., condr. State Fair, The Will Rogers Follies, Phantom, The King and I, On The 20th Century, Sugar Babies, Showboat, The Sound of Music, Salute To The Broadway Composer, The Sound Of Rodgers And Hammerstein, New Moon, La Cage Aux Folles (opera) Amelia Goes To The Ball, Candide, Die Fledermaus, Hansel and Gretel, The Medium, Madama Butterfly, The Telephone, others; arranger, orchestrator Show Boat on PBS, United Nations 40th Anniversary, Herman & Soundheim Together, (compositions) A Christmas Carol, Heroes, others. Mem. Am. Fedn. Musicians. Home: 121 Loder Ave Wilmington NC 28409 E-mail: kcameron@kennedy-center.org.

CAMERON, KIRK MACGREGOR DRUMMOND, statistician; b. Glendale, Calif., Oct. 27, 1962; s. Paul Drummond and Virginia May (Rusthoi) C.; m. Kelly Mitchell, May 21, 1994; chilre: Kaitlyn Gray, Kit MacGregor, Kyle Henry, Kristyn Virginia. BS in Math., U. Nebr., 1984; MS in Statis., Stanford U., 1989, PhD in Statis., 1990. Statis. cons. Family Rsch. Inst., Colorado Springs, Colo., 1983—; sr. statis. Sci. Applications Internat. Corp., McLean, Va., 1990-95; pres., statis. cons. Macstat Cons., Colorado Springs, 1995—. Bd. dirs. Family Rsch. Inst., editor, 1995—; cons. and nat expert on groundwater monitoring optimization to USAF, EPA, and Dept. Edn. Contbr. articles to profl. jours.; contbr. scientific papers. Youth counselor McLean Bible Ch., 1991-94; Sunday sch. leader Village Seven Presbyn., Colorado Springs, 1995—2002, 2005—; county del. El Paso County Rep. Conv., Colorado Springs, 1998. NSF Grad. fellow, 1984, Pew Found. Teaching fellow, 1990. Mem. Am. Statis. Assn., Inst. Math. Stats., Rand Alumni Assn., Phi Beta Kappa. Avocations: rock collecting, guitar, hiking, camping, tennis. Office Phone: 719-532-0453. E-mail: kcmacstat@qwest.net.

CAMERON, LUCILLE WILSON, retired dean; b. Nashua, N.H., Dec. 21, 1932; d. Hugh Alexander and Louise Perham (Baldwin) C.; m. James Robert Doris, Aug. 19, 1976; children: Glenn A. Browning, Gail W. Browning, Valerie B. Cruickshank. BA, U. R.I., 1964, MLS, 1972. Social case worker R.I. Dept. Pub. Assistance, Providence, 1964-70; asst. circulation libr. U. R.I. Libr., Kingston, 1970-72, reserve libr., 1972-73, reference/bibliographer, 1973-88, head reference unit, 1983-86, chair pub. svcs., 1988-89, interim dean, 1989-90, dean, 1990—, dean emerita. Bd. trustees North Scituate (R.I.) Pub. Libr., 1995, pres., 1996. Co-author: Labor and Industrial Relations Journals and Serials, 1989; contbr. articles to profl. jours. Bd. trustees North Scituate (R.I.) Pub. Libr., 1995—, pres., 1996—. Recipient Computerized Intergrated Libr. System award Champlin Founds., Providence, 1989, 90, 91, Coll. Tech. Libr. Program award U.S. Dept. Edn., Washington, 1990, Disting. Alumna award Grad. Sch. Libr. and Info. Studies, U. R.I., Kingston, 1991. Mem. ALA, Assn. Coll. and Rsch. Librs., Consortium R.I. Acad. and Rsch. Librs., Higher Edn. Libr. Info. Network (chair), Univ. Press New England (gov.), North Scituate (R.I.) Pub. Libr. Assn. (bd. trustees 1995—, pres. 1996—), Alpha Kappa Delta.

CAMERON, NICHOLAS ALLEN, manufacturing executive; b. Phila., Jan. 6, 1939; s. Nicholas Guyot and Katherine (Rogers) C.; m. Leslie Wood, Dec. 14, 1974; children: Christopher Wilson, Pamela Wilson. BS, Yale U., 1960. Treas. Allied Corp., Morristown, N.J., 1979-81, v.p. and treas., 1981-82, v.p. fin., 1982-83, v.p. planning and devel., 1983-85; sr. v.p. planning, devel. and adminstrn. Allied-Signal Inc., Morristown, N.J., 1985-86; sr. v.p. tech. and bus. devel. Bendix Aerospace-Allied-Signal, Inc., Arlington, Va., 1986-87; group pres. Allied-Signal Aerospace, 1988; sr. v.p. ops. svcs. Allied-Signal, Inc., Morristown, N.J., 1988-90, sr. v.p., gen. mgr. chem. intermediates, 1990-95. Bd. dirs. Morristown Meml. Health Found., 1996—2001, United Way of Morris County, Morristown, N.J., 1980-86, 90-98, campaign chmn., 1991, chief vol. officer, 1993-95, bd. chmn., 1996-98; bd. dirs. Morris 2000, 1990-97, 99-2003, chmn., 1993-96; mem. adv. bd. Morristown Hosp., 1998—; pres. Morris County Park Commn., 1999-2004 Mem. Morris County C. of C. (bd. dirs. 1975-86, 1990-98), Tau Beta Pi. Clubs: St. Elmo Soc. (New Haven); Morris County Golf. Republican. Episcopalian. Home and Office: 27 Kitchell Rd Morristown NJ 07960 Office Phone: 973-683-0344. Personal E-mail: ncame1639@aol.com.

CAMERON, PAUL DRUMMOND, health facility administrator; b. Pitts., Nov. 9, 1939; s. Nelson Drummond and Veronica (Witco) C.; m. Virginia May Rusthoi BA, L.A. Pacific Coll., 1961; MA, Calif. State U., L.A., 1962; PhD, U. Colo., 1966. Asst. prof. psychology Stout State U., Menomonie, Wis., 1966-67, Wayne State U., Detroit, 1967-69; assoc. prof. psychology U. Louisville, 1970-73, Fuller Grad. Sch. Psychology, Pasadena, Calif., 1976-79; assoc. prof. marriage and family U. Nebr., Lincoln, 1979-80; pvt. practice psychologist Lincoln, 1980-83; chmn. Family Rsch. Inst., Washington, 1982-95, Colo. Springs, 1995—. Reviewer Am. Psychologist, Jour. Gerontology, Psychol. Reports; presenter, witness, cons. in field. Author: Exposing the AIDS Scandal, 1988, The Gay 90's, 1993; contbr. articles to profl. jours. Mem. Ea. Psychol. Assn., Nat. Assn. for Rsch. and Treatment of Homosexuality. Republican. Lutheran. Achievements include investigation of health effects of second-hand tobacco smoke; investigation of first comprehensive national random sample of sexuality; documented abbreviated lifespan of homosexuals; documented poorer parenting by homosexuals. Office: Family Rsch Inst PO Box 62640 Colorado Springs CO 80962-2640

CAMERON, RITA GIOVANNETTI, writer, publishing executive; b. Washington; d. Joseph Angelo and Adeline Katherine (Fochett) C. BS with honors, U. Md., 1957; MEd, Am. U., Washington, 1962; DEd, Nova U., 1978. Tchr. D.C. pub. schs., Washington, 1959-64; prin. Prince George's County (Md.) Pub. Schs., 1964-73, 76-84; supr. instrn. K-12 Prince George's County pub. schs., 1973-76; free-lance writer ednl. materials Media, Materials Inc., Balt., 1965-75, Learning Well, Balt., 1995, World Class Learning Materials, Inc., Balt., 2000—; free-lance writer travel articles AAA, Washington, 1978-83; owner, pub. Sch. House Global Enterprises, Fort Washington, Md., 1980—. Presenter, cons. to sch. systems and ednl. orgns., 1985—. Author: Let's Learn About Maryland and Prince George's County, 1970, Let's Learn About Maryland, 1972, 95, Super Sub! Or How to Substitute Teach in Elementary School, 1974, AAA Travel articles and Traffic Safety Teacher Guide Grades 4-6, 1982, 83; author, pub.: The Master Teacher's Plan and Record Book, 1985, The School House Encyclopedia of Educational Programs and Activities, 1991; author, publisher and nat. marketer of 88 social studies and sci. ednl. materials for students grades 4-10; developer/owner School House Global Enterprises Pub. Co. Food preparer So Others Might Eat, Washington, 1985—, food preparer for Missions of Charity Home for AIDS Victims, Washington, 1992—, sponsor Christian Found. for Children and Aging, 1998—. Recipient Outstanding Citizenship award DAR, 1954, Nat. Tchr. award Expedition Nat. Tchr. Awards Program, 1960-61, Outstanding Tchr. Sci. award D.C. Coun. Engring. and Archtl. Soc. and Washington Acad. Scis., 1964, Outstanding Educator of Yr. award Prince George's County Bd. Edn., 1982-83, Am. Hist. award DAR, 1987, Outstanding Contbn. to Bicentennial Leadership Project award Couns. for Advancement of Citizenship, 1989. Mem.: Kennedy Ctr. Stars, Ford Theater, Smithsonian Assocs., Phi Kappa Phi. Roman Catholic. Avocations: art, music, theater, antiques, travel. Office: Sch House Global Enterprises PO Box 441028 Fort Washington MD 20749-1028 Office Phone: 301-292-8877. Business E-Mail: dawn@schoolhouseglobalenterprises.com. *In one form or another, I have been a teacher all my life. It's been an enormous responsibility, matched only by enormous satisfaction. The knowledge, skills, love for learning, and feelings of self-worth given to students are among the finest gifts they will ever receive.*

CAMERON, SCOTT, music educator, tubist; b. Cleve., Feb. 8, 1967; s. Bruce Cameron and Thomasine Marie Newuan; m. Andrea Marie Callery, Aug. 3, 1997; children: Connor Charles, Thomas Patrick, Hannah Marie. B of Music Edn., Ind. U., 1993; MusM, U. Md. Tubist The U.S. Army Field Band, Md., 1994—; dir. band Am. U., Washington, 2003—. Performer: (CD) The Legacy of Aaron Copland, 1999, The Legacy of John Paynter, 2001. With USAF, 1994—. Mem.: Music Educators Nat. Conf., Kappa Kappa Psi (hon.). Democrat. Episcopalian. Avocations: golf, poker, running, travel.

CAMERON, THOMAS WILLIAM LANE, investment company executive; b. Newton, Mass., Feb. 19, 1927; s. Percy G. and Mary W.D. (Mitchell) C.; m. Carol Louise Soliday, June 17, 1950; children: Helen Delone, Thomas Mitchell (dec.). AB cum laude, Harvard, 1948, MBA, 1951. With sales dept. Procter & Gamble, Boston, 1951-53; with Hopper, Soliday, & Co., Inc., Phila., 1953-66, ptnr., 1961—, pres., 1966-72, chmn., 1972-83; dir. Hopper, Soliday & Co., Inc., 1983-86; sr. v.p. Interstate/Johnson Lane, Johns Island, SC, 1986—99; chmn. Sovereign Investors Inc., 1979-91; vice chmn. John Hancock Sovereign Investors, 1991-96; chmn. Cameron & Assocs., Inc., 1999—, Rising Dividend Growth Fund, 2004—. Chmn. Phila.-Balt.-Washington Stock Exch., 1970-74, bd. govs., 1963-75; chmn. Dividend Growth Advisers, 2004—. Bd. mgrs. Franklin Inst., 1970-90, chmn., 1978-81; bd. dirs. Holling Cancer Ctr., Med. U. S.C., 1992—2002. Served with USNR, 1944-46. Mem.: Waynesborough Country (Paoli, Pa.) (pres. 1965-67); Harvard (Phila.) (pres. 1965-66), Harvard Bus. Sch. (Phila.) (pres. 1962-64). Home: PO Box 4051 Ladys Island SC 29907 Office: Cameron & Assocs Inc 1894 Andell Bluff Blvd Johns Island SC 29455-8222

CAMERON, TIMOTHY G., lawyer; b. Auckland, New Zealand, May 6, 1971; B.Com., LLB, Univ. Auckland, 1994, M.ComLaw, 1997; LLM, Univ. Chgo., 1998. Bar: New Zealand 1994, NY 1999, lic.: US Tax Ct. 2003. Assoc. Russell McVeagh McKenzie Bartleet & Co., Auckland, New Zealand, 1994—97, Cravath, Swaine & Moore LLP, NYC, 1998—2005, ptnr., litig., 2005—. Mem.: ABA, NY State Bar Assn., Auckland and New Zealand Dist. Law Societies. Office: Cravath Swaine & Moore LLP Worldwide Plz 825 Eighth Ave New York NY 10019-7475 Office Phone: 212-474-1120. Office Fax: 212-474-3700. Business E-Mail: tcameron@cravath.com.

CAMERON, W. BRUCE, writer; b. Petoskey, Mich., 1956; 3 children. Grad., Westminster Coll. Freelance writer; various positions, including salesman, collection mgr., dir. of ops., chief knowledge officer; host, online humor column, 1995; columnist Rocky Mountain News, 1998—2001; syndicated columnist Creator's Syndicate, 2001—. Public speaker. Author: 8 Simple Rules for Dating My Teenage Daughter, 2001 (NY Times Bestseller), How to Remodel a Man, 2004. Mailing: c/o St Martin's Press 175 Fifth Ave New York NY 10010 Office Phone: 212-674-5151. Personal E-mail: bruce@wbrucecameron.com.*

CAMEROS, ALAN LEE, finance company executive; b. Rochester, N.Y., May 24, 1935; s. Maurice and Alice Cameros; m. Nancy Jean Sonner, Aug. 1967; children: Cynthia, Brian. BA, Cornell U., 1957; LLB, U. Va., 1960. Bar: Va. 1960, N.Y. 1960. V.p. Gen. Home Furnishings, Rochester, 1960-72, CEO, 1972—. Bd. dirs. Meml. Art Gallery, Rochester, Ctr. for Govtl. Rsch., Rochester, Inst. Competitive State Govt., Rochester. Chmn. Mus. Trustee Assn., Washington, 1990-93, Nathaniel Rochester Soc., 1998-2000. Fellow Corning Mus. Glass; mem. Genesee Valley Club, Country Club Rochester, Inst. Fellows, Rochester Inst. Tech. Avocations: golf, squash, skiing, sailing, writing. Office: Gen Home Furnishings 3300 Monroe Ave Ste 205 Rochester NY 14618-4622

CAMERY, JOHN WILLIAM, computer engineer; b. Cin., Feb. 5, 1951; s. Donald Otis and Mary Lynne (Edgington) C. *In July, 1997, using his frequent flyer miles, he organized the family vacation. His parents, well known in amateur radio and Army MARS, his Aunt Emily Leslie, his sisters, Amy Sue and Marianne, their husbands, Moussa Abdallah and John Meyer, and their children, Kristen, Matthew, John and Mary Elizabeth flew to Hawaii, staying at Puamana, Maui and the Imperial. They traversed the islands, up Haleakela and Diamond Head and even underseas courtesy of his friend Maily Schara at Atlantis Submarines. Kristen and Matthew snorkeled at Hanauma Bay and learned to train dolphins at Sea Life Park. Matthew learned to surf.* BA, U. Cin., 1972; MS, Carnegie-Mellon U., 1974. Mathematician U.S. Army Material Systems Analysis Agy., Aberdeen Proving Grounds, Md., 1973; student asst. engring. spectrum analysis task force Fed. Comms. Commn., Park Ridge, Ill., 1974; mathematician U.S. Army Comms. Electronics-Engring. Agy., Washington, 1975-83; computer specialist U.S. Army Mgmt. Systems Analysis Agy., Washington, 1983; mathematician Def. Comms. Agy., Washington, 1983-86; programmer, analyst Gen. Scis. Corp., Laurel, Md., 1986-87; software engr. Sygnetron Protection Systems, Timonium, Md., 1987-88, Automation Cons., Inc., Balt., 1988-89, RDA Logicon, Leavenworth, Kans., 1989-2001; application sys. analyst Battle Commd. Tng. Ctr. Anteon Corp., Schofield Barracks, Hawaii, 2001—. Cons. Martin Marietta Ocean Systems Ops., Glen Burnie, Md., 1988—. *He was instrumental in designing the system to consolidate the "genser" message traffic centers for the Pentagon. During the pre-INF Treaty period, he supported the software maintenance effort on the Theater Mission Planning System and Mission Data Preparation System for TLAM-N and GLCM. He has collected data for the FCC to evaluate their Automated Frequency Assignment Model, enhanced the Data Systems Dynamic Simulator for NASA at Goddard Space Flight Center, developed the communication software for the Global Telemetered Seismograph Network and provided technical support for the "Corps Battle Simulation" warfighter exercises world-wide for the Battle Command Training Program.* Carnegie-Mellon U. fellow, 1972—73. Mem. Am. Math. Soc., Societe Mathematique de France, IEEE Computer Soc., European Math. Soc., Imperial Hawaii Vacation Club, Greater Cin. Amateur Radio Club. Republican. Mem. Christian Ch. Avocations: music, dance, swimming, electronics, travel. Home: 94-647 Kauakapuu Loop Mililani HI 96789-1832 Office: Anteon Corp PO Box 861563 Wahiawa HI 96786-1563 Office Phone: 808-656-3501. Personal E-mail: jcamery@anteon.com. Business E-Mail: cameryjw@hawaii.army.mil.

CAMHI, REBECCAANN, librarian; b. Montgomery, W.Va., Nov. 23, 1949; d. Shelborn W. and Margie F. (Woodson) Cale; m. Alan S. Camhi, July 3, 1977; children: Liza, Jonathan. BA, Marietta Coll., 1974; MLS, SUNY, Buffalo, 1978. Libr. City of Tonawanda (N.Y.) Schs., 1978-80, Lockport (N.Y.) City Schs., 1981-84, Newfane (N.Y.) Schs., 1985-86, Kenmore (N.Y.) Tonawanda Schs., 1987—. Presenter N.Y. State Whole Lang. Conf. 1992. Contbr. articles to profl. jours. Mem. Sch. Librs. Assn. of Western N.Y., Phi Beta Mu. Home: 6 Foxcroft Ln Buffalo NY 14221-3202 Office: Hoover Elem Sch 199 Thorncliff Rd Buffalo NY 14223-1278

CAMHY, SHERRY WALLERSTEIN, artist; b. N.Y.C., Nov. 12, 1940; d. Abraham and Irene Kronen Wallerstein; children: Abraham, Caroline. M of Art Edn., Columbia U., 1970; postgrad., NYU. Med. sch. tchr. anatomy Montclair Art Mus., Montclair, N.J., 1987, 88; tchr. painting and drawing Rockland Ctr. for the Arts, N.Y., 1989-93; tchr. Tisch Sch. Arts N.Y. Univ., 1998—; tchr. anatomy Sch. of Visual Arts, N.Y.C., 1999—; tchr. anatomy and life drawing Art Students League, N.Y.C., 1999—. Author: The Art of the Pencil, 1997; one-person shows Pace U., N.Y.C., 1993, Nat. Arts Club, N.Y.C., West Hampton Beach Libr., L.I.; groups shows include Santa Barbara Mus. of Natural History, 1990, Frank Caro Gallery, Santa Barbara, Calif., 1992, Nat. Art Club, 1996, Faculty Sch. of Visual Arts and Art Students League, 1994-97, Prince Street Gallery, 1994, Hammond Mus., 1993, So. Allegheniess Mus. Art, Aldrich Mus. Ridgefield, 1999, Eleanor Etinger Gallery, 2001, Sherry French Gallery, 2002—, Salander-O'Reilly Gallery, 2004, Katonah Mus., 2005, Israel Mus., New Orleans Mus. Fine Art, So. Allegenies Mus. Mem. Nat. Arts Club. Office: Studio 819 West Chelsea Art Ctr 526 W 26th St # W New York NY 10001-5517 Office Phone: 212-741-9183. Personal E-mail: sherrycamhy@godaddy.com.

CAMI, RUSSELL, lawyer; b. Bronx, NY, Apr. 26, 1967; BA cum laude, Harvard Univ., 1989; JD, Rutgers Univ., Newark, 1993. Bar: NY 1994. Law clk., Hon. Kevin Thomas Duffy US Dist. Ct., So. Dist. NY; assoc. Cravath, Swaine & Moore LLP, NYC & London, 1994—2001, ptnr., corp. NYC, 2001—. Sr. articles editor Rutgers Law Rev. Mem.: Order of Coif. Office: Cravath Swaine & Moore LLP Worldwide Plz 825 Eighth Ave New York NY 10019-7475 Office Phone: 212-474-1048. Office Fax: 212-474-3700. Business E-Mail: rcami@cravath.com.

CAMILLERI, LOUIS C., consumer goods company executive; Grad. econ. and bus. adminstrn., Lausanne University, 1976. Bus. analyst W.R. Grace and Co., Laussane, Switzerland; with Philip Morris, 1978—, various postiions in Europe, 1978—95, sr. v.p. corp. planning, 1995, pres., CEO Kraft Foods Internat., 1995—96; sr. v.p., CFO Philip Morris Companies Inc., 1996—2002; pres., CEO Altria Group (formerly Philip Morris Companies Inc.), 2002—; chmn. bd. of dir. Kraft Foods Inc.; bd. of dir. SABMiller plc. Office: Altria Group 120 Park Ave New York NY 10017-5592*

CAMILLERI, MICHAEL, lawyer, educator; b. N.Y.C., July 16, 1953; s. Joseph and Lena (Calatozzo) C.; m. Debralyn Fisher, Aug. 5, 1989; children: Bryan, Brandon, Brooke. BA, L.I. U., 1974; JD, Fordham U., 1977. Bar: N.Y. 1978. Sr. v.p., gen. counsel Nat. Coun. Compensation Ins., N.Y.C., 1978-91; ptnr. Adorno & Zeder, Miami, Fla., 1991-99; pres. AmTrust Ins. Group, Boca Raton, Fla.; prin. Preferred Ins. Capital Cons., Boca Raton, 2001—; pres. Newport Star Reins. Co., Columbia, SC, 2003—. Pres. Ins. Data Resources, 1997-2000; cons. Family Counseling Ctr., Bklyn., 1980-85; adj. prof. law Coll. Ins., N.Y.C., 1981-91; arbitrator civil ct., N.Y.C., 1983-91. Author: Matthew Bender's Accident and Health Law, 1989; editor: Werbel's N.Y. Worker's Compensation Law, 1986-94. Mem. ABA, N.Y. State Bar Assn., D.C. Bar Assn., Profl. Bowlers Assn. Office: PICC Ste 415 2101 NW Corporate Blvd Boca Raton FL 33431

CAMINITI, DONALD ANGELO, lawyer; BA magna cum laude, Rutgers U., 1973, JD, 1976. Bar: N.J. 1976, D.C. 1977, N.Y. 1980; cert. civil trial atty. N.J. Supreme Ct., cert. trial lawyer Nat. Bd. Trial Advocacy. Ptnr. Breslin & Breslin, P.A., Hackensack, N.J., 1977—; counsel Housing Authority of Bergen County, 1977—; asst. counsel Twp. of River Vale, 1977-80; counsel Housing Devel. Corp. Bergen County, 1978—, North Bergen Rent Leveling Bd., 1980—, North Bergen Housing Authority, 1980-84, Englewood Housing Authority, 1991—, Fort Lee Housing Authority, 1993—; spl. counsel Dept. Housing and Urban Devel., N.J., 1990—; counsel Guttenberg Housing Authority, 1995—. Master Morris Pashman Inns Ct., 1998—; speaker in field. Co-author: (with others) Recreation and Sports Equipment Products Liability Practice Guide, 1988. With USAF, 1966-70. Mem.: ATLA (parliamentarian N.J. chpt. 1984—85, seminar com. chmn. 1984—87, chmn. edn. com. 1990—91, v.p. 1990—91, 2d v.p. 1991—92, 1st v.p. 1992—93, pres.-elect 1993—94, pres. 1994—95, bd. govs. 2001—), ABA, Bergen County Bar Assn., N.Y. Bar Assn., D.C. Bar Assn., N.J. Bar Assn., Phi Beta Kappa. Office: Breslin and Breslin PA 41 Main St Hackensack NJ 07601-7087 Home: 7 Parkwood Ln Mendham NJ 07945-2201 Office Phone: 201-342-4014.

CAMINKER, EVAN H., dean, law educator; BA summa cum laude, UCLA; JD, Yale Law Sch. Faculty mem. UCLA, 1991—99; prof. U. Mich. Sch. Law, Ann Arbor, 1999—, assoc. dean, 2001—03, dean, 2003—. Clerk for Justice William J. Brennan U.S. Supreme Court; for Judge William A. Norris Ninth Cir. Ct. of Appeals; atty. Ctr. for Law in Pub. Interest, Los Angeles, Wilmer, Cutler & Pickering, Washington, DC; dep. asst. atty. gen. Office of Legal Coun., U.S. Dept. Justice, 2000—01. Sr. editor Yale Law Jour.; contbr. articles to law jours. Recipient Benjamin Scharps Prize, Disting. Profs. Award for Civil Liberties Edn., ACLU; Coker Fellow. Office: U Mich Law Sch 324 Hutchins Hall 625 S State St Ann Arbor MI 48109-1215 Office Phone: 734-764-0514. Office Fax: 734-763-1055. Business E-Mail: caminker@umich.edu.

CAMMACK, ANN, librarian, secondary school educator; b. Akron, Ohio, Sept. 24, 1947; d. Matthew John and Anna (Maxim) Klinovsky; m. Robert Floyd Cammack, Sept. 27, 1969; children: Lisa Ann, Holly Ann, Noël Ann, Monica Ann. BA, Youngstown State U., 1969; MLS, Tex. Woman's U., 1995, PhD, 2001. Cert. tchr. secondary sch. Ohio, elem. and secondary sch., Tex. English tchr. Struthers (Ohio) City Schs., 1969-83; asst. cataloger Amon Carter Mus., Ft. Worth, 1997, 2000—01; libr. asst. spl. collections U. Tex., Arlington, 2005. Life mem. Tex. Parent Tchrs. Assn., historian Arlington, 1991-92. Doctoral fellow Tex. Woman's U., 1996. Mem. AAUW, ALA, Ladies Aux. VFW, Tex. Libr. Assn., Youngstown State U. Alumni Assn., Beta Phi Mu. Avocation: golf.

CAMMAKER, SHELDON IRA, lawyer; b. N.Y.C., Apr. 26, 1939; s. Jack Robert and Anne (Benjamin) C.; children: Joshua, Meredith. BA magna cum laude, Brandeis U., Waltham, Mass., 1961; JD cum laude, Harvard U., 1964. Bar: N.Y. 1965, U.S. Dist. Ct. (so. dist.) N.Y. 1961. Assoc. Botein Hays & Sklar, N.Y.C., 1964-70, ptnr., 1971-87; exec. v.p., gen. counsel Emcor Group, Inc., Norwalk, Conn., 1987—. Office: Emcor Group Inc 301 Merritt Seven Norwalk CT 06851-6214 Office Phone: 203-849-7831. Business E-Mail: scammaker@emcorgroup.com.

CAMMARATA, BERNARD, retail company executive; b. 1940; Mdse. mgr. J. W. Mays, N.Y.C., 1962-67, Wilmington (Del.) Dry Goods, 1967-70; v.p., gen. mdse. mgr. Marshalls Dept. Store, Woburn, Mass., 1976; founder TJ Maxx, 1976; pres., CEO TJX Operating Cos., 1976-89, TJX Cos., Inc., Framingham, Mass., 1989—2000, chmn. bd., 1999—. Dir. Heritage Property Investment Trust Inc. With U.S. Army, 1959—62. Office: TJX Companies Inc 770 Cochituate Rd Framingham MA 01701*

CAMMARATA, JOAN FRANCES, Spanish language and literature educator; b. Bklyn., Dec. 22, 1950; d. John and Angelina Mary (Guarnera) Cammarata; m. Richard Montemarano, Aug. 9, 1975. BA summa cum laude, Fordham U., 1972; MA, Columbia U., 1974, MPhil, 1977, PhD, 1982. Preceptor Columbia Coll., N.Y.C., 1974—82; adj. instr. Fordham U., N.Y.C., 1980—81; adj. asst. prof. Iona Coll., New Rochelle, NY, 1982—84; asst. prof. Manhattan Coll., Riverdale, NY, 1982—90, assoc. prof., 1990—96, prof., 1996—. Author: Mythological Themes in the Works of Garcilaso de la Vega, 1983; editor: Women in the Discourse of Early Modern Spain, 2003; mem. editl. bd. Modern Lang. Studies; editl. reviewer D.C. Heath; contbr. articles and revs. to profl. jours. Fellow arts and sci. Columbia U., 1972-75; grantee Manhattan Coll., 1985, 91, NEH, 1987, 88, Spain's Min Edn. Culture, 1997—; Rsch. Fellowship grantee NYU Faculty Seminars, 1992, 94; named univ. assoc. Faculty Resources Network Program NYU, 1985—; Andrew Mellon Found. vis. scholar, 1990; scholar-in-residence NYU, 1991-92, 97-98. Mem.: MLA (del. assembly), N.Y. State Assn. Fgn. Lang. Tchrs., Am. Assn. Tchrs. Spanish and Portugese, Assn. Internat. de Hispanistas, Renaissance Soc. Am., Inst. Internat. de Lit. Iberoamericana, South Atlantic, South Ctrl. and Midwest MLA, N.E. MLA (rsch. fellow 1991, v.p. 1997—98, pres. 1998—), Am. Coun. Tchg. of Fgn. Langs, Cervantes Soc. Am., Hispanic Inst. Roman Catholic. Avocations: piano, gardening, writing, needlecrafts. Office: Manhattan Coll Bronx NY 10471 Business E-Mail: joan.cammarata@manhattan.edu.

CAMMARATA, RICHARD JOHN, financial advisor; b. Boston, June 29, 1950; s. Dominic Joseph and Anna Mary (Masone) C. BA, Stonehill Coll., 1972. Mgr. Ace Fence Co., South Boston, 1972-83; fin. advisor, investor self-employed Randolph, Mass., 1983—. Mem. Am. Security Coun., Nat. Adv. Bd., Boston, Va., 1988—. Mem. Rep. Presdl. Task Force, Washington, 1987—, Rep. Nat. Com., Washington, 1984—, GOPAC, Washington, 1984—. Mem. N.Y. Acad. Scis., AAAS. Republican. Roman Catholic. Home and Office: 47 Eugenia St Randolph MA 02368-1950

CAMMISA, FRANK P., JR., surgeon, educator; b. Waterbury, Conn., Jan. 18, 1956; m. Gail McGovern; children: Anne Katherine, Frank P. III, John Patrick. BS summa cum laude, Tufts U., 1978; MD, Columbia U., 1982. Diplomate Nat. Bd. Med. Examiners, Am. Bd. Orthopaedic Surgery. Resident in gen. surgery The Presbyn. Hosp., Columbia-Presbyn. Med. Ctr., N.Y.C., 1982-83; resident in orthopaedic surgery The Hosp. for Spl. Surgery, N.Y.C., 1983-87; fellow in spinal surgery U. Miami (Fla.)-Jackson Meml. Med. Ctr., 1987-88; asst. scientist rsch. divsn. The Hosp. for Spl. Surgery, N.Y.C., 1988-99, asst. attending surgeon, 1988-99, chief spine svc., 1995—, assoc. scientist rsch. divsn., assoc. attending surgeon, 2000—, dir. spine care Inst., 1999—. Vis. clin. fellow surgery Coll. of Physicians and Surgeons, Columbia U., N.Y.C., 1982-83; clin. assoc. surgery Cornell U. Med. Coll., N.Y.C., 1983-87, instr. orthopaedic surgery, 1988-89, asst. prof. orthopaedic surgery, 1990-99, assoc. prof. clin. orthopaedic surgery, 2000—; attending surgeon VA Hosp., Miami, 1987-88; asst. attending surgeon The N.Y. Hosp., N.Y.C., 1988-99; attending surgeon spinal cord injury svc. Burke Rehab. Ctr., White Plains, N.Y., 1988—; attending surgeon VA Hosp., Bronx, N.Y., 1988—; assoc. attending surgeon N.Y. Presbyn. Hosp., 2000—; presenter in field; cons. Meml. Sloan Kettering Cancer Ctr., N.Y.C., 1988—; spinal cons. St. John's U. Athletic Teams, 1988—, N.Y. Knights World League of Am. Football, 1991-92, Phoenix Alliance, 1993, N.Y. Racing Assn., 1993. Editorial bd.: Orthopaedic Product News, 1990-91; contbr. chpts. to books and articles to profl. jours. Grantee The Hosp. for Spl. Surgery, 1986, Acromed Corp., 1988, Orthopaedic Rsch. and Edn. Found., 1991-92; recipient Harvard Book prize Harvard Club So. Conn., 1974, Tufts Psychology Soc. Rsch. award Tufts U., 1978, Resident award N.Y. Acad. Medicine, Sect. Orthopaedic Surgery, 1986, 87, Lewis Clark Wagner award Hosp. for Spl. Surgery, N.Y.C., 1986; N.Am. Traveling fellowship Am. Orthopaedic Assn., 1989; Ofcl. citation Gen. Assembly State of Conn., 1992. Mem. ACS, ACP, Am. Acad. Orthopaedic Surgeons, Internat. Coll. Surgeons, Am. Coll. Spine Surgery; mem. AMA, N.Am. Spine Soc., Am. Spinal Injury Assn., Internat. Soc. for Study of Lumbar Spine, Cervical Spine Rsch. Soc., Scoliosis Rsch. Soc., Med. Soc. State N.Y., N.Y. State Soc. Orthop. Surgeons, N.Y. County Med. Soc., Alumni Assn. The Hosp. for Spl. Surgery, Assn. of the Alumni, Coll. Physicians and Surgeons, Columbia U., The Irish-Am. Orthop. Soc., Ea. Orthop. Assn. (Fellow scholar award 1988, Spinal Rsch. award 1989), Groupe Internat. Cotrel-Dubousset, N.Y. Athletic Club, Winged Foot Golf Club, Phi Beta Kappa, Psi Chi, Alpha Omega Alpha, Delta Tau Delta. Office: Hosp for Spl Surgery 535 E 70th St New York NY 10021-4898

CAMMUSE, JERRY DWAINE, publishing executive, musician; b. Madison, Tenn., Feb. 8, 1950; s. Calvin Arthur and Gladace Virginia (Simmons) C.; m. Louise Clayton, Oct. 17, 1970 (div. Nov. 1975); children: Becky Diane, Crystal Dawn, Valarie Susan; m. Freda Lavern Garner, Dec., 17, 1976 (dec. Sept. 1998); children: India Necole, Tanya Cheyenne, Rachel Marie, Laurie Marie. Student, Duke U., 1970-72, Union U., 1999—. Owner, founder Dwaine Madison Music, Madison, Tenn., 1966—; band leader Wondering Cowboys, Madison, Tenn., 1964-67, Wanderers, Madison, Tenn., 1970-89, Gospelaires, Only, Tenn., 1991—; CEO, pres. Inkwell Printing and Pub., Nashville, 1976—. Exec. dir. Jerry Reed Thompson Station Congregation, Brentwood, Tenn., 1982—; 1st vice comdr. Am. Legion Post 105, Madison, Tenn., 1973-75. Author numerous songs including Springtime, 1966, Sunshine, 1975, My Eternity, 1998, Down on My Knees Lord (In Prayer), Last Night I Saw an Angel, Lord Hear Our Prayers, If My Heart Were a Window, Asking for a Miracle, God Bless the Little Children, The Tears, Hands of the Lord, God's Eternal Home, Jesus Oh Jesus, Holy Trinity, 2004. 1st lt. USMC, 1967-70, Vietnam Mem. ASCAP, Nashville Songwriters Assn. Internat., Nashville Assn. Musicians, Country Music Assn., Gospel Music Assn., Broadcast Music Inc. Avocations: ministry assistance to the poor, underprivileged, and aged. Office: Rt # 1 Only TN 37140

CAMNER, HOWARD, author, poet; b. Miami, Fla., Jan. 14, 1957; s. Edward I. and Ida (Puldy) C.; m. Susan Clara Camner, July 29, 2000; 2 children. BA in English, Fla. Internat. U., 1982; LittD (hon.), London Sch. Applied Rsch., 1995. Cert. English tchr., Fla. Editor Southwind Mag., Miami, Fla., 1976-78; performance poet Writers' Exch., N.Y.C., 1979-81; freelance writer various publications, Miami, 1982-84; screenwriter Harris Prodns., L.A., 1985-89; TV prodr., host Century Cable, L.A., 1986-88; writing instr. Dade County Schs., Miami, 1990—. Author: (poems) Notes from the Eye of a Hurricane, 1979, Transitions, 1980, Scattered Shadows, 1980, Road Note Elegy, 1980, A Work in Progress, 1981, Poetry from Hell to Breakfast, 1981, Midnight at the Laundromat, 1983, Hard Times on Easy Street, 1987, Madman in the Alley, 1989, Stray Dog Wail, 1991, Banned in Babylon, 1993, Jammed Zipper, 1994, Bed of Nails, 1995, Brutal Delicacies, 1996, Hiss, 2000; co-author: Southern Gothic, Taj Mahal Review: Florida in Poetry, 1995, also over 100 lit. collections. Recipient Literary award, MiPo, 2004. Mem. Nat. Writers Assn., Acad. of Am. Poets, Poets and Writers, Inc., Poetry Soc. of Am., So. Fla. Poetry Inst., Authors Guild. Home: 10440 SW 76th St Miami FL 33173-2903 Personal E-mail: hcamner@aol.com.

CAMOUGIS, GEORGE, health, safety and environmental consultant; b. Concord, Mass., May 10, 1930; s. Charles George and Angeliki (Georgekopoulou) C.; m. Irene Andreson, Nov. 18, 1961; children: Caroline A., Elizabeth M., Sarah A. BS magna cum laude, Tufts U., 1952; MA, Harvard U., 1957, PhD, 1958. Asst. prof. physiology Clark U., 1958—62, assoc. prof., 1962—64, affiliate prof., 1964—79; sr. neurophysiologist Astra Pharm. Products, Inc., Worcester, Mass., 1964—66, head sect. neuropharmacology, 1966—68; pres., rsch. dir., dir. New Eng. Rsch., Inc., Worcester, 1968—88; sr. cons. New Eng. Indsl. Waste, Inc., 1988—89; 19v.p., compliance officer Am. Reclamation Corp., 1989—96. Cons. Bd. Radioactive Waste Mgmt. NAS, 1987-92, numerous state and fed. agys. including Army C.E., Fed. Hwy. Adminstrn., U.S. Dept. Interior, EPA; cons. Mass. Dept. Mental Health, 1997—; affiliate prof. Worcester Poly. Inst., 1970-82; adj. prof. toxicology Tufts U. Sch. Vet. Medicine, 1981-84; panelist NSF; mem. corp. Bermuda Biol. Sta. for Rsch., 1968-85; lectr. in field, U.S., Can.; mem. Worcester Sci. Ctr. Planning Com., 1963. Author: Nerves, Muscles and Electricity, 1970, Environmental Biology for Engineers, 1981; contbr. numerous articles to profl. jours., 1959—; patentee drug; cons. editor Acad. Press, Inc., 1978; mem. editl. adv. bd. Hazardous Waste Mgmt., 1983-90. Bd. dirs. Worcester Children's Friend Soc., 1968-92, v.p. 1978-84, pres. 1984-87. With USNR, 1952-54, Korea. Virginia B. Gibbs scholar, 1954-55; E.L. Mark fellow, 1956, USPHS fellow, 1957-58; NIH grantee, 1962-64, Office Naval Rsch. grantee, 1963-64; recipient Sci. Achievement award Worcester Engring. Soc., 1985. Mem. AAAS, Biophys. Soc., Am. Physiol. Soc., N.Y. Acad. Scis., ASTM, Soc. Environ. Toxicology and Chemistry, Harvard Club (Boston), Phi Beta Kappa, Sigma Xi. Republican. Greek Orthodox. Home and Office: 7 Wheeler Ave Worcester MA 01609-1707 Office Phone: 508-798-0047.

CAMP, CLAY STEPHEN, psychologist; b. Lake Charles, La., Sept. 3, 1966; s. John Clayton and Mary Joan (Thibodeaux) Camp; m. Lisa Karen Miller, June 6, 1987; 1 child, Courtney. BA, Wake Forest U., Winston-Salem, NC, 1988; MA, Appalachian State U., Boone, NC, 1992. Lic. Psychol. Assoc. NC Bd. Psychology. Staff psychologist New River Mental Health, Wilkesboro, NC, 1992—96, Foothills Sexual Abuse Intervention Svcs., Morganton, NC, 1996—97, Crossroads Behavioral Healthcare, Statesville, NC, 1997—. Counselor Our Father's Pl., Statesville, 2004—, Character Builders, Statesville, 2004—. Mem. NC Assn. for the Mgmt. and Treatment of Sexual Offenders, 2004—; youth dir. Jefferson United Meth. Ch., 1989—91. Democrat. United Methodist. Avocations: chess, computer games. E-mail: claycamp@skybest.com.

CAMP, CLIFTON DURRETT, JR., retired publishing executive; b. Trenton, Ky., Aug. 2, 1927; s. Clifton Durrett and Virginia (McElwain) C.; m. Mary Jane Peters, June 9, 1950; children: Daniel Durrett, Thomas Clifton, Pamela Jane, Emily Ann. BS, U. Ky., 1950. Sr. acct. Sheldon, Curry and Masterson, St. Petersburg, Fla., 1950-54; asst. contr. Times Pub. Co., St. Petersburg, 1954-57, contr., 1957-71, treas., 1960-73, v.p. adminstrn., 1967-73, sec., 1969—73, bus. mgr., 1974-82, sr. v.p., 1982-88, also bd. dirs.; owner, pub. Sumter County Times, Bushnell, Fla., 1973-76, Wildwood Herald Express, Bushnell, 1973-76. Bd. dir. Poynter Inst. for Media Studies, St. Petersburg; sec. Mod. Graphic Arts, St. Petersburg, 1976-87, also bd. dirs.; pres. Fla. Trend, Inc., St. Petersburg, 1984-87; bd. dirs. Fla. Press Ctr., Tallahassee, 1980-87, pres., 1984; bd. dirs. Congl. Quar., Inc., Washington, 1986-88; bd. dir. Poynter Libr. U. South Fla. Treas. United Way, St. Petersburg, 1965-68; bd. dirs. Salvation Army Adv. Bd., 1970-78, Bayfront Med. Ctr., 1981-87, St. James United Meth. Ch., Tampa, 1995—. With USN, 1945-46. Mem. Fla. Press Assn. (bd. dirs. 1982-87), Internat. Newspaper Fin. Execs. (bd. dirs. 1964-70), Hunters Green Country Club (Tampa).

CAMP, DAVID LEE, congressman, lawyer; b. Midland, Mich., July 9, 1953; m. Nancy Keil, Sept. 10, 1994; children: Andrew, David, Lauren. BA magna cum laude, Albion (Mich.) Coll., 1975; JD, U. San Diego, 1978. Bar: Mich., Calif., DC, admitted to practice: US Supreme Ct., US Dist. Ct. (Ea. Dist.) Mich., US Dist. Ct. (So. Dist.) Calif. With Riecker, Van Dam, Looby & Barker, 1978-90; spl. asst. atty. gen. Mich., 1980-84; adminstrv. asst. to Congressman Bill Schuette, 1985-87; state rep. 102nd Dist. Mich., 1989-91; mem. U.S. Congress from 10th (now 4th) Mich. dist., 1991—, mem. ways and means com., asst. minority whip, mem. select com. on homeland security. Chmn. Spkrs. Correction Day Com. Mem.: Midland County Bar Assn., ABA. Republican. Office: US Ho of Reps 137 Cannon Bldg Washington DC 20515-2204*

CAMP, DELPHA JEANNE, counselor; b. Yakima, Wash., Apr. 20, 1937; d. George Emerson and Emilie Loraine (Rivard) Stevens; m. George Ernest Mills, Aug. 13, 1960 (dec. 1975); children: Adriene Phillips, Stacey Harcus, Ryan, Tiffany; m. James Clell Camp, June 24, 1978 (dec. 2004); children: Catherine Thompson (dec.), Wayne (dec.), Darla Coolman, John, Janna Barnes. BEd, Gonzaga Univ., 1959; MS, Univ. Oreg., 1977. Lic. profl. counselor; cert. in death, dying and bereavement. Tchr. Riverside Sch. Dist., Milan, Wash., 1959-61, Cheney (Wash.) Sch. Dist., 1968-70; asst. prof. Univ. Oreg., Eugene, 1979-92; pvt. practice Eugene, 1992—. Mem. faculty Marylhurst (Oreg.) U., 1992—2002. Mem. Assn. for Death Edn. and Counseling (bd. dirs. 1990-93, co-chair conf. 1994, 2002, 1st v.p. 1998-99, pres. 1999-00, Svc. award 1990), Am. Mental Health Counselors Assn., Oreg. Mental Health Counselors Assn. Avocations: reading, classical music. Home: 440 E 39th Ave Eugene OR 97405-4722 Office: 317 W Broadway Ste 217 Eugene OR 97401-2890 Office Phone: 541-485-3175. E-mail: deljcamp@aol.com.

CAMP, DONALD EUGENE, experimental photographer, educator; b. Meadville, Pa., July 28, 1940; s. Ira Guy and Martha Gladys (Irving) C.; m. Marie Josephé Dumont, Nov. 26, 1966; children: Stephanie Martha Helené, Dorothea Rae. BFA, Tyler Sch. Art, Phila., 1987; MFA, Tyler Sch. Art, 1989. Staff photographer Phila. Bulletin, 1972-81; asst. prof. Tyler Sch. of Art, Phila., 1989-91, Slippery Rock (Pa.) U., 1992—. Dir. Future Faculty Fellowship program Temple U., Phila., 1990—91; vis. asst. prof. Ursinus Coll., Collegeville, Pa., 2000—, artist in-residence, vis. asst. prof. art, 2002—; mem. bd. overseers Inst. Contemporary Art, U. Pa., 2002—. One person exhbns. include Nat. Mus. The Gambia, 2000, Smithsonian, 2000, Anacostia Mus. and Ctr. for African Am. History and Culture, 2000, Reflections In Black. 1840-Present, 2000, The Chemistry of Color, Sorgenti Collection Pa. Acad. Fine Art, 2005; photographs have appeared in many popular magazines including Ebony, News Week, People; represented in numerous pub. collections including ARCO collection, Phila. Mus. Art, and Schaumberg Ctr. for Black Culture, N.Y.C., Pa. Conv. Ctr., U. Mich. Mus. of Art; appeared in Face to Face Exhbn. Nat. Jewish Am. Mus. in Phila., U. Mich. Mus. Art, 1998, Inst. Contemporary Art, U. Pa., 1999. Mem. Spiritual Assembly of Bahais of Phila., 2003—, Interfaith Support Group, Phila., 1989-92. Recipient Future Faculty fellowship Temple U., Phila., 1988, Eugene Feldman award The Print Club, 1983; named Pa. Visual Artist fellow, 1990, Smithsonian Am. Artist Oral History, 1991, PEW Charitable Trust resident artist to the Am. Acad. in Rome, 1994; John Simon Guggenheim Found. fellow, 1995-96, fellow NEA, Pew Charitable Trust fellow, Pa. Coun. for the Arts fellow. Mem. Soc. Photographic Educators (bd. dirs. 1990-94, chmn., founder multicultural caucus, 1990-93), Recherche. Avocations: baha'i promotion, magic. Home: 4511 Spruce St Philadelphia PA 19139-4526 Business E-Mail: doncamp@cartel.net.

CAMP, JEFFERY MARK, web site designer, military officer; b. Glens Falls, N.Y., Dec. 14, 1964; s. Leroy Phillip and Karen Gray Camp; m. Andrea Marie Gallo, Sept. 11, 1999. AS, City Colls. Chgo., 1989; BS, Siena Coll., 1993; postgrad., DePaul U., 1999—. IBM cert. AS/400 solutions sales; IBM cert. RS/6000 solutions sales; IBM cert. AS/400 solutions design; IBM cert. RS/6000 SP sales. Sr. AS/400 sales specialist IBM Corp., Atlanta, 1995-2000, sr. Web server specialist Chgo., 2000—. Capt. U.S. Army, 1983-2001. Republican. Roman Catholic. Avocations: marathons, travel. Home: 1415 W Cuyler Ave Chicago IL 60613 Office: 1801 S Meyers Rd Ste 300 Villa Park IL 60181-5237 Home Fax: 773-529-3987. E-mail: jeffcamp@us.ibm.com, jcamp@flashcom.net.

CAMP, JOHN See SANFORD, JOHN

CAMP, JOHN BLISS, journalist, television producer; b. Nashville, Nov. 2, 1935; s. William Eledge and Lena Marie Camp; m. Cecile Annette Giles, Dec. 13, 1986. Student, Columbia Coll., L.A., 1960. Dir. investigative reporting Sta. WCKT-TV, Boston, 1976—82; investigative prodr., reporter Sta. WBRZ-TV, Baton Rouge, 1982—89; sr. investigative corr. Cable News Network (CNN), Atlanta, 1989—2000; ind. reporter, prodr. Atlanta, 2000—. Freelance reporter, prodr., Baton Rouge. Prodr., reporter (TV documentary) Give Me That Big Time Religion (George Foster Peabody award Columbia Dupont, 1984), (investigative documentary) The Best Insurance Commissioner Money Can Buy (George Foster Peabody award Columbia Dupont, 1988), Mafia Influence on South Florida (George Foster Peabody award, 1976). Founder O'Brien Ho., Baton Rouge, 1971—2004. With USAF, 1957. Recipient Nat. Headliners award, 1983, 1985, 1990, SDX Excellence in Journalism award, Soc. Profl. Journalists, 1984, 1988. Mem.: Investigative Reporters and Editors, Inc., Baton Rouge Press Club (pres. 1972—73). Democrat. Avocation: golf. Home: 32 Beechgrove Ln The Bluffs LA 70748 Office: John Camp Prodns 643 St Charles St Baton Rouge LA 70802 Office Phone: 225-343-4974. Home Fax: 225-634-9948; Office Fax: 225-343-5136. Personal E-mail: jblisscamp@aol.com.

CAMP, JOSEPH SHELTON, JR., film producer, director, writer; b. St. Louis, Apr. 20, 1939; s. Joseph Shelton and Ruth Wilhelmena (McLaulin) C.; m. Andrea Carolyn Hopkins, Aug. 7, 1960; children: Joseph Shelton III, Brandon Andrew. BBA, U. Miss., 1961. Jr. account exec. McCann-Erickson Advt., Houston, 1961-62; owner Joe Camp Real Estate, Houston, 1962-64; account exec. Norsworthy-Mercer, Dallas, 1964-69; dir. TV commls. Jamieson Film Co., Dallas, 1969-71; founder, pres., writer, producer, dir. feature films Mulberry Square Prodns., Inc., Dallas, 1971-90, Gulfport, Miss., 1991-94, Chapel Hill, N.C., 1994—. Producer, dir., writer films including Benji, 1974, Hawmps, 1976, For the Love of Benji, 1977, The Double McGuffin, 1979, Oh Heavenly Dog, 1980, Benji The Hunted, 1987; TV spls. The Phenomenon of Benji, 1978, Benji's Very Own Christmas Story, 1978, Benji at Work, 1980, Benji (Takes a Dive) at Marineland, 1981; TV series Benji, Zax and the Alien Prince, 1983; author: Underdog, 1993. Bd. trustees Piney Woods Country Life Sch., Warren Wilson Coll.; adv. bd. N.C. Sch. of Arts, Sch. of Film Making. Mem. Dir.'s Guild Am., Writer's Guild Am. Office: 29067 Aerie Rd Valley Center CA 92082-5728 *I hope that I have been able to help people in a troubled time to lose themselves for a moment in a piece of entertainment and, when it's over, to feel better for having done so, to have a new respect for persistence in achieving objectives and a new feeling of hope and happiness in their lives. I hope to inspire others to follow their dreams with passion and persistence, to reach further than they might have otherwise.*

CAMP, KIMBERLY N., museum administrator, artist; b. Camden, N.J., Sept. 11, 1956; d. Hubert E. and Marie (Dimery) C.; m. Seydou Coulibaly, Apr. 1997 (div. Feb. 2001). BA, U. Pitts., 1978; MS, Drexel U., 1986. Dir. artistic design project City Camden, 1984-86; program dir. Pa. Coun. on Arts, Harrisburg, 1986-89; dir. exptl. gallery Smithsonian Instn., Washington, 1989-94; pres. Charles H. Wright Mus. African Am. History, Detroit, 1994-98; pres., CEO Barnes Found., Merion, Pa., 1998—2005. Evaluator Am. Assn. Mus., Washington, 1994—; panel chair Nat. Endowment for Arts, Washington, 1991-92; vice chair, bd. dirs. Assn. Am. Cultures, Washington, 1987-89. One-woman shows include Clifton Art Ctr., N.J., Glouchester County Coll., Deptford Township, N.J., Passaic Count C.C., Paterson, N.J., Diggs Gallery, Winston-Salem, N.C., Galerie Francois, Washington, Banneker Douglass Mus., Annapolis, Md., 3d Bienniel Nat. Black Arts Festival, Atlanta, Manchester Craftsmen's Guilde, Pitts., Caribbean Cultural Ctr., N.Y.C., Jr. Black Acad. Arts and Letters, Dallas, Walt Whitman Ctr. Arts and Humanities, Camden, Longwood Gardens, Kennett Square, Pa., Art Mus. Western Va., Raonoke, Harrison Mus. African Am. Culture, Roanoke, 1994; represented in permanent collections J.B Speed Art Mus., Manchester Craftsmen's Guild, Reader's Digest, Camden Hist. Soc.; mng. editor Nat. Conf. Artists Phila. Chpt. newsletter, 1980-84. Bd. dirs. Bus. Vols. for Arts, 1994-97. Recipient Nat. Svc. award Nat. Conf. Artists, 1984, Arts Achievement award City of Camden, 1984, Cmty. Svc. award Assn/ Negro Bus. and Profl. Women, 1985, Builders of Cmty. award Camden County Cultural and Heritage Commn., 1986, Purchase award J.B. Speed Art Mus., 1988, Spirit of Detroit award Detroit City Coun., 1994; Arts Internat. grantee Ctr. Internat. Exch. Scholars, 1994, Roger L. Stevens Nat. Arts award Carnegie Mellon U. H. John Heinz Sch. Mgmt., 1999; fellow Kellogg Nat. Leadership Program, 1994-97. Mem. Assn. Am. Cultures (bd. dirs. 1989—), Am. Assn. Museums (bd. dirs. 1995-97), Links, Inc., N.J. Coun. on Arts. Address: 1202 Yarmouth Rd Wynnewood PA 19096 Office Fax: 610-658-0944. Business E-Mail: kcamp911@msn.com.

CAMP, RICHARD J., ecologist, statistician, researcher; b. Anchorage, Dec. 6, 1965; s. Chester V. and Yvonne E. Camp; m. J. Kiko Camp, 2002. BS, U. Minn., 1991; MS, Colo. State U., 1995. Cert. in conservation biology Program in Ecol. Studies, Colo. State U. Rsch. assoc. Colo. State U., Ft. Collins, 1991-97; quality assurance specialist New Belgium Brewing Co., Inc., Ft. Collins, 1997-98; devel. coord. Obsessive-Compulsive Found., Inc., New Haven, 1998-99; computer/biol. technician Colo. Natural Heritage Program, Ft. Collins, 1999; rsch. project coord. Rsch. Corp., U. Hawaii, Hawaii National Park, 1999—. Mem. ornithol. adv. com. Hawaii Heritage Program, 2000-2002; adv. mem. Hawaii Forest Bird Recovery Team, U.S. Fish and Wildlife Svc., 1999-2002; grad. student rep. faculty coun. internat. program Colo. State U., Ft. Collins, 1992-93. Contbr. articles to sci. jours. Named Regional Rep. Hugh O'Brian Youth Leadership, 1982, Outstanding Sophomore, 1982, Mem. of Yr., Future Farmers of Am., 1984; student fellow Concordia Coll., 1984. Mem. Am. Ornithologists' Union, Am. Soc. Naturalists, Soc. for Conservation Biology (sci. presentation selector ann. meeting 1995, 2001), Pacific Conservation Biology, Western N.Am. Naturalist, Hawaii Audubon Soc., Big Island Road Runners Club (newsletter editor), Xeries Soc., Xi Sigma Pi. Avocations: long-distance running, cooking, longboard surfing, travel. Home: PO Box 281 Volcano HI 96785 Office: Pacific Island Ecosystem Rsch Ctr Bldg 344 PO Box 44 Hawaii National Park HI 96718 E-mail: rick_camp@usgs.gov.

CAMP, THOMAS EDWARD, retired librarian; b. July 12, 1929; s. Charles Walter and Annie Laura (Brazzel) C.; m. Elizabeth Anne Sowar, Sept. 4, 1952; children: Anne Winifred, Thomas David. BA, Centenary Coll., Shreveport, 1950; MLS, La. State U., 1953. Binding asst. La. State U. Library, Baton Rouge, 1951-53; circulation librarian Perkins Sch. Theology Bridwell Libr., So. Meth. U., Dallas, 1955-57; librarian Sch. Theology, U. of South, Sewanee, Tenn., 1957-93. Assoc. univ. librarian, 1976-93, acting univ. librarian, 1981-82. C-author: Using Theological Libraries and Books, 1963; contbr. articles to profl. jours. Pres. Franklin County Assn. for Retarded, 1971-72. Served with AUS, 1953-55. Mem. ALA, Am. Theol. Library Assn. (exec. sec. 1965-67), Tenn. Library Assn. Democrat. Episcopalian. Home: 209 Carruthers Rd PO Box 820 Sewanee TN 37375-0820 Personal E-mail: ecamp@sewanee.edu.

CAMP, THOMAS HARLEY, economist; b. Charlotte, N.C., Aug. 13, 1929; s. Thomas Franklin and Agnes Mae (Davis) C.; m. Frances Ann Rogers, Mar. 20, 1953 (dec. Feb. 1998); children: Thomas Harley Jr., Landon G.; m. Sheila M. Schell, Apr. 24, 1999. BSc, U. N.C., 1956; postgrad, Am. U., 1965-67. Industry econ. USDA, Washington, 1959-70, location leader Austin, Tex., 1970-74, rsch. leader College Station, Tex., 1974-86, program leader Weslaco, Tex., 1986-88, agrl. mktg. specialist Lane, Okla., 1988-90; cons. Georgetown, Tex., 1990—. Author, co-author 44 sci. publs.; contbr. articles to profl. jours. Cubmaster Boy Scouts Am., Springfield, Va., 1965-69, asst. scoutmaster, 1966-70, scoutmaster, Round Rock, Tex., 1970-72, asst. scoutmaster, Austin, 1972-74. With USN, 1946-51, Korea. Mem. Am. Soc. Agrl. Engrs., Animal Air Transp. Assn., Food Distbn. Rsch. Soc., Transp. Rsch. Forum, Masons. Presbyterian. Avocations: photography, boating. Home and Office: 1005 Fountainwood Dr Georgetown TX 78628-1906

CAMPAGNOLO, MARY FRANCES, physician; b. Teaneck, N.J., 1956; MD, George Washington U., 1982. Diplomate with qualification in geriat. Am. Bd. Family Practice. Intern Overlook Hosp., Summit, NJ, 1982—83, resident in family practice, 1983—85; staff physician Virtua-Meml. Hosp. of Burlington County, Mt. Holly, NJ, 1987—; chief dept. family practice Virtua-Meml. Hosp. Burlington County, 1993—. Named one of Top Drs. 2003, N.J. Monthly Mag., Del. Valley Consumer, Top Drs. for Women, N.J. Living, Top Drs. 2004, Phila. Mag., Top Drs. 2005, South Jersey Mag., 2005. Mem.: N.J. Acad. Family Physicians (Lifetime Achievement Chair award 2005). Office: Ashurst Family Physicians PA 1561 Rte 38 Ste 6 Lumberton NJ 08048 Office Phone: 609-267-2100. Business E-Mail: mcampagnolo@ashurstfp.com.

CAMPAIGNE, ERNEST EDWARD, chemistry educator; b. Chgo., Feb. 13, 1914; s. John Herbert and Nellie (Daufel) C.; m. Jean Hill White, Jan. 1, 1941; children: David Alan, Claudia Jean, Barbara Naomi. BS, Northwestern U., 1936, MS, 1938, PhD in Biochemistry, 1940. Instr. Bowdoin Coll., Brunswick, Maine, 1940-41; research assoc. Northwestern U., Evanston, Ill., 1941-42; assoc. biochemist M.D. Anderson Hosp. for Cancer Research, Galveston, Tex., 1942-43; mem. faculty dept. chemistry Ind. U., Bloomington, 1943—, prof. chemistry, 1953-84. Vis. prof. UCLA, 1954-55; cons. NIH, 1960-64, 72-76; cons. in field Author: (with J. C. Muhler and C. H. Rohrer) Introduction to Chemistry, 1972, Elementary Organic Chemistry, 1962. Hon. mem. Ind. Acad. Fellow N.Y. Acad. Scis., Ind. Acad. Sci. (pres. 1986-88); mem. AAAS, Am. Chem. Soc., Chem. Soc. (London), Internat. Union Pure and Applied Chemistry (chmn., convenor medicinal chemistry sect. organic div. 1969-75, U.S. del. Munich 1973) Research on synthesis of drugs, antihistamines, anticonvulsant drugs for treatment of epilepsy, molecular dimensions of drugs to interpret their optimum dimensions and nature of receptor sites. Home: 935 Juniper Pl Bloomington IN 47408-1285

CAMPAIGNE, LINDA MARY, special education educator; b. Niagara Falls, N.Y., Dec. 17, 1948; d. Howard Albert and Mary Ellen (Eckel) C. BA, Tarkio Coll., 1973. Tchr. spl. edn. Brownsville (Tex.) Ind. Sch. Dist., 1980-81, 1985-89; program asst. Retama Manor, Brownsville; case mgr. Lancaster (Tex.) Residential Ctr., 1989-90; tchr. spl. edn. Wilmer-Hutchins Ind. Sch. Dist., Dallas, 1990-95. Author of poems. Recipient Assn. Retarded Citizens Vol. award, 1979, Inst. Achievement Human Potential citation, 1974. Avocations: reading, swimming, bowling, crafts, needlecrafts. Home: 5303 Bryan St Dallas TX 75206-7892 Personal E-mail: lcampaigne@hotmail.com.

CAMPANA, GABRIEL J., ambassador, elementary school educator; BS in Elem. Edn. magna cum laude, Bloomsburg U., 1987; MS in Edn. magna cum laude, Wilkes U., 1991; postgrad., Harvard U., 2002; DSc in Edn., U. Sarasota summa cum laude, 2003. Curriculum participant Williamsport Sch. Dist., Pa., 1988—; 5th grade educator Thaddeus Stevens Elem. Sch., 1998—; ambassador, tchr. Senaca Nat. Reserve, NY, 2004; team mem. Pa. Gov. Achievement Gap Com., 2004—. Vis. prof., diversity trainer Various Colls throughout Pa., NJ, and NY. Author: Project SMART, 2004. Founder online multicultural student newsletter SMART (Students Making All Races Tolerant); city councilman Williamsport, Pa., 1996—. Mem.: Nat. Coun. Soc. Studies, Nat. Assn. for Multicultural Edn., Assn. for Supervision and Curriculum Devel., Asia Soc., Kappa Delta Pi.

CAMPANELLI, JOHN RICHARD, composer; b. Hartford, Conn., May 9, 1949; B of Music Composition, U. Mo., Kansas City, 1974; MusM, U. Hartford, 1979; D in Musical Arts, U. Mich., 1983. Part time faculty in theory and composition Hartt Sch. Music, U. Hartford, 1979—80; adj. asst. prof. composition and theory Sch. Music, Bowling Green State U., Ohio, 1984—85; adj. asst. prof. music composition Sch. Music, U. Mich., 1986—87; freelancer Ann Arbor, Mich. Prodr. concerts Contemporary Music Forum, Washington, 1988—90. Composer: Piano Trio #1, 1987, The Queen of Air and Darkness, 1992, Of Nights Both Blue & Haunted, 1993 (Marimolin prize, 1993). Recipient Holtkamp prize, 1979; grantee, Meet the Composer, 1994; Charles Ives fellow, Am. Acad. Arts and Letters, 1984, Goddard Lieberson fellow, 1996. Mem.: ASCAP (awards 1981—), Am. Music Ctr. Home and Studio: 3453 Rhea St Ann Arbor MI 48103

CAMPANELLI, MICHELE WALLACE, writer; b. Melbourne, Fla., Oct. 24, 1971; d. Robert E. and Fontaine M. Wallace; m. Louis Vincent Campanelli III, Aug. 8, 1998. Legal Studies, Keiser Coll. Novel Writing Writers Digest Sch. Author: (short stories) Chicken Soup for the Teenage Soul III, Chocolate for a Mother's Heart, Charity Red Rock Press, Chocolats pour le Bonheur d'une Femme, Chocolate for a Teen's Heart, Chocolate for a Woman's Blessings, Chocolate for a Teen's Soul, Chicken Soup Living Your Dreams (10 Yr. Anniversary Edit., 2003), Stories for a Teen's Heart III, Chocolate for a Woman's Spirit, Chicken Soup Christmas Treasury, Writers Net, Book of Prose (Best Short Stories Collection, 2003), Chicken Soup for Nascar, Chocolate for a Teen's Dreams, Chicken Soup for the Christian Teenage Soul, Cup of Comfort for Christmas, Chicken Soup Working Woman's Soul, Chicken Soup Bride's Soul, Chocolate for a Mother's Heart, National Best-selling Book, Chicken Soup for the Grandparent's Soul, Chicken Soup for the Teacher's Soul (#1 NY Times Nat. Best-selling Book), Chicken Soup Christmas Treasury for Kids (Nat. Best-selling Book, USA Today, 2002), Chicken Soup for the Romantic Soul (Nat. Best-selling Book, USA Today, 2003), (novels) Keeper of the Shroud, Jamison, Margarita, The Case of the Numbers Kidnapper, Sports Girls, Taker of the Shroud, Monsters of the Ice, The Great American, Black Widow, Caddies & Condos, The Artist Novel, (audio book) Chicken Soup for the Teenage Soul III (#1 NY Times Best-selling Book), Keeper of the Shroud, (columnist) United Ch. Christ; contbr. articles. Mem. United Meth. Ch. Recipient Story of the Month, PetsOnline.Org, 2003, Michele Wallace Campanelli, Woman spreads 'Soul' into Millions of Books, Fla. Today Newspaper Featured Article Palm Bay Bull., Sept 10, 2003, Pictured in Woman's World Mag., 2004. Achievements include 2 #1 New York Times Best-selling Stories, 9 stories in Nat. Best-selling book list, 28 Short Story Books in 36 languages, 2 Audiobooks, 4 e-books and Paperback Novels.

CAMPANELLI, RICHARD M., federal agency administrator; m. Shannon Campanelli; 3 children. BS in Economics, U. Va.; JD, U. Va. Law Sch. Trial atty., Spl. Litigation Section of the Civil Rights Divsn. U.S. Dept. Justice; mem., S. Africa Working Group U.S. Dept. State, sr. spl. asst. to atty. gen., 1987—89; atty. Gammon & Grange, PC, McLean, Va., 1989—2002; adj. prof. George Mason U.; dir., Office of Civil Rights U.S. Dept. Health and Human Svcs., 2002—. Office: Office for Civil Rights US Dept Health and Human Svcs 200 Independence Ave SW Rm 515F HHH Bldg Washington DC 20201

CAMPASINO, ELLEN MARIE, elementary school educator; b. Titusville, Pa., Aug. 30, 1950; d. Frank and Helen (Lowicki) Campasino. BS in Elem. and Early Childhood Edn., Edinboro U., 1972, cert. in elem. and early childhood edn., 1978. 1st grade tchr. St. Titus Sch., Titusville, 1975-76, 4th grade tchr., 1976-77, 3rd grade tchr., 1977—. Coaching tchr. St. Titus Tchr. Induction Program, Titusville, 1989—90, asst. to prin., 1993—. Mem. ministry tng. program Diocese of Erie; min. hospitality St. Walburga Parish, Roman Cath. Ch., Titusville. Recipient Svc. award, Diocese of Erie, 1988, 1990, 1996, 25 Yrs. of Svc. award, 2000—01. Avocations: reading, doll collecting, embroidery. Office: St Titus Sch 528 W Main St Titusville PA 16354-1598

CAMPBELL, ABE WILLIAM, music educator; b. St. Louis, Jan. 22, 1950; s. Thomas Edward and Dorothy Caroline (Strauss) C.; m. Joanne Marie Hutchinson, June 19, 1971; children: Bob, Amy, Anne, Molly. B of Music Edn., So. Ill. U., 1972. Dir. band & choir Mercy High Sch., St. Louis, 1972-76, Pattonville R-3 Dist., St. Louis, 1976-80; tchr. music, social studies Immaculate Heart of Mary, St. Louis, 1981-83, Little Flower Sch., St. Louis, 1983-86; tchr. St. Louis Prep Sem., 1986-87; tchr. 6th grade Our Lady Lourdes, St. Louis, 1987-88; substance abuse counselor St. Clare Hosp., Alton, Ill., 1988-91; tchr. music St. Gregory Sch., St. Louis, 1991—96, asst. prin., 1993—96, JFK H.S., 1996—97, St. Thomas Aquinas-Mercy H.S., 1997—. Mem. sch. bd. Little Flower Cath. Sch., St. Louis, 1981-83; mem. parish coun. Little Flower Ch., St. Louis, 1987-90. Mem. NAt. Cath. Edn. Assn., Nat. Mid. Sch. Assn., Music Educators Nat. Conf. Roman Catholic. Avocations: acting, gardening, bowling. Home: 1131 Ralph Ter Richmond Heights MO 63117-1528

CAMPBELL, ADDISON JAMES, JR., writer; b. Dilliner, Pa., Dec. 16, 1933; s. Addison James Campbell and Nora Lee (Marshall) Reynolds; m. Fumie Murashige, Oct. 13, 1962; 1 child, Gary Clark Campbell. Pres. Action Bolt Corp., Houston, 1965-72. Author: Nanci's World, Ukelele Lil of Lihue, The Object; co-author: Fumie Murashige Campbell, 1994; contbr. numerous articles and research papers to profl. jours. Sgt. USMC, 1952-55. Recipient recognition award for Adult Correction Officer for Island of Kauai, State of Hawaii, 1987, 88.

CAMPBELL, ALAN, actor; b. Homestead, Fla., Apr. 22, 1957; s. Edward John and Audrey Carolyn (Griner) C. BBA, U. of Miami. Performer Urban Arts Corps, New York, NY, 1982; founding member H.O.L.A. (Heart of Los Angeles) Youth Theater, Los Angeles, CA. Stage appearances include: I Love My Wife (Coconut Grove Theatre, FL), Boogie-Woogie Rumble of Dream Deferred (Urban Arts Corp), On Shiloh Hill (Ford Theatre, Wash. DC) The Nerd (Birmingham Theatre, Detroit, MI), Sunset Boulevard (L.A. and Broadway - Tony nomination, Lead Actor in a Musical, 1995), Contact, 2000, Beauty and the Beast, 2005; TV appearances include: (series) The Facts of Life, Throb, B.J. and the Bear, Counterattack: Crime in America, 1982, Three's a Crowd, 1984-85, Jake and the Fatman, 1987-92, Matlock, Another World, (movie) Red Flag: The Ultimate Game, 1981; film appearances include: Smokey and the Bandit II, 1980, The Final Terror, 1983, Weekend Warriors, 1986, Hollywood Air Force Base. Office: J Michael Bloom & Assoc 233 Park Ave S Fl 10 New York NY 10003-1606*

CAMPBELL, ALLAN MCCULLOCH, bacteriology educator; b. Berkeley, Calif., Apr. 27, 1929; s. Lindsay and Virginia Margaret (Henning) C.; m. Alice Del Campillo, Sept. 5, 1958; children— Wendy, Joseph. BS in Chemistry, U. Calif. at Berkeley, 1950; MS in Bacteriology, U. Ill., 1951; PhD, 1953; PhD hon. degree, U. Chgo., 1978, U. Rochester, 1981. Instr. bacteriology U. Mich., 1953-57; research asso. Carnegie Inst., Cold Spring Harbor, N.Y., 1957-58; asst. prof. biology U. Rochester, N.Y., 1958-61, assoc. prof., 1961-63, prof., 1963-68; prof. biol. sci. Stanford (Calif.) U., 1968—, Barbara Kimball Browning prof. humanities and scis., 1992—. Author: Episomes, 1969; co-author: General Virology, 1978; editor Gene, 1980-90, mem. editl. bd., 1990—; assoc. editor Virology, 1963-69; assoc. editor Ann. Rev. Genetics, 1969-84, editor, 1984—; spl. editor Evolution, 1985-88; editl. bd. Jour. Bacteriology, 1966-72, Jour. Virology, 1967-75, New Biologist, 1989-92. Served with AUS, 1953-55. Recipient Research Career award USPHS, 1962-68 Mem. Nat. Acad. Scis., Am. Acad. Arts and Scis., Am. Soc. Microbiology (Abbott Lifetime Achievement award 2004), Soc. Am. Naturalists, Genetics Soc. Am., AAAS, Am. Acad. Microbiology. Democrat. Home: 947 Mears Ct Stanford CA 94305-1041 Office: Stanford U Dept Biol Scis Stanford CA 94305 Business E-Mail: AMC@stanford.edu. *I've always thought that each individual has some contribution to human knowledge that he is uniquely suited to make. So I try to be organized and to avoid doing things that I expect will get done. anyway, by others. And, of course, everything worthwhile requires hard work.*

CAMPBELL, ALMIRA TAYLOR, retired librarian; b. Hyde Park, Mass., May 26, 1920; d. Arthur Balcom and Mildred Victoria (Fuller) Taylor; m. Vincent Alexander Douglas Argyle Campbell, June 26, 1953 (dec. 1985); 1 child, Faith Campbell Bacastow. AA, Colby Jr. Coll., 1940; BA, Mt. Holyoke Coll., 1942; BS Sch. Libr. Sci., Simmons Coll., 1943. Acquisitions asst. Yale Law Sch. Libr., New Haven, 1943-45; prof. asst. accessions dept. Williston Meml. Libr./Mt. Holyoke Coll., South Hadley, Mass., 1945-48; head libr. Mt. Hermon (Mass.) Sch., 1948-53; head libr., tchr. French Stoneleigh Prospect Hill Sch., Greenfield, Mass., 1961-70; cataloguer F.L. Boyden Libr./Deerfield (Mass.) Acad., 1970-79; now ret. Vol. Ormond Beach (Fla.) Pub. Libr., 1983-89. Vol. Meml. Hosp., Ormond Beach, 1981-2000, Halifax Humane Soc., Ormond Beach, 1988-2000; Circle leader, mem. choir Christ Presbyn. Ch., Ormond Beach, 1986-2000; leader Alzheimer Support Group, Daytona Beach, Fla., 1987-92. Mem. AAUW. Republican. Avocations: singing, dance, swimming, walking, bridge. Home: 8820 Walther Blvd Apt 1614 Parkville MD 21234-9041

CAMPBELL, ANDREW, manufacturing executive; V.p. fin., CFO Duplex Products, Inc., 1994—95, pres., bd. dirs., 1995—96; sr. v.p. fin., CFO Safety Kleen Corp., 1997—98; exec. v.p. fin. and adminstrn., CFO Dominick's Supermarkets, Inc., 1998; acting CFO Foamex Internat., Inc., 1999; v.p., CFO Pactiv Corp., Lake Forest, Ill., 1999—2001, sr. v.p., CFO, 2001—. Office: Pactiv Corp 1900 W Field Ct Lake Forest IL 60045

CAMPBELL, ANDREW CHRISTOPHER, director; b. West Palm Beach, Fla., Jan. 16, 1977; s. Alice Elizabeth Campbell. BS in Indsl. Engring., U. Ctrl. Fla., Orlando, 1999, MPA, 2002. Resident asst. U. Ctrl. Fla., Orlando, 1997—99, grad. asst. residence life, 1999—2003; area coord. residence life U. North Fla., Jacksonville, 2003—. Residence hall assn. adviser U. North Fla., Jacksonville, 2003—. Mem.: Southeastern Assn. Housing Officers, Am. Coll. Pers. Assn., Nat. Assn. Student Pers. Adminstrs. Avocation: jogging. Office Phone: 904-620-4676. E-mail: acampbel@unf.edu.

CAMPBELL, ANDREW WILLIAM, immunotoxicology physician; b. Beirut, Apr. 3, 1948; s. William Alexander and Gisela (Landes) C.; children: Denia Giselle, Michelle Elise, Colin Alexander, Ian William. BA in Pre-med., Psychology, Franklin Piere Coll., Rindge, N.H., 1970; MD, U. Autonoma de Guadalajara, Mex., 1974. Diplomate Am. Bd. Family Practice, Am. Bd. Forensic Examiners, Am. Bd. Forensic Medicine. Intern Pediat. Hosp. Infantil, Ob-gyn., Clin. Santa Monica, Guadalajara, Mex., 1974-75, Pub. Health Dept., Guadalajara, Mex., 1975-76; resident gen. surgery Orlando (Fla.) Regional Med. Ctr., 1977-78; resident family practice Med. Coll. Ga., Augusta, 1978-81; pvt. practice family physician Two Physician Practice, Sarasota, Fla., 1981, with former chief surgeon Eisenhower Med. Ctr., Augusta, Ga.; pvt. practice Augusta, Wrens and Louisvlle, Ga., 1983-84, Houston, 1985—; med. dir. Med. Ctr. for Immune and Toxic Disorders, Houston, 1993—. Staff mem. Meml. City Med. Ctr., Spring Branch Med. Ctr.; chmn. dept. family practice Sam Houston Meml. Hosp., Houston, 1987, chmn. credentials com., 88, exec. com., 1987—89; lectr. and spkr. at Artificial Implants and Toxic Exposure Symposia; faculty U. Tex. Sch. Medicine, 1993—98; cons., presenter in field. Author (with others): Health Effects of Toxic Chemicals, 1994, Textbook of Nephrology (2 vols.), 1995; co-editor: Internat. Jour. Occupl. Medicine and Toxicology, 1992—95; mem. editl. bd.: Toxicology and Indsl. Health, 1994—96; contbr. chapters to books, articles to profl. jours. Founder Clinic for the Indigent, St. John Vianney Ch., Houston, 1987; bd. trustees Sam Houston Meml. Hosp., 1987-93. Recipient Consumer's Choice award Am. Nurses in Bus. Assn., Houston, 1994. Fellow: Am. Acad. Family Physicians; mem.: AMA, AAAS, Am. Assn. Immunologists, Indoor Air Quality Assn. of Tex., Tex. Med. Assn., Am. Bd. Forensic Examiners, Harris County Med. Soc., Soc. Mucosal Immunology, Internat. Soc. Neuroimmunology, Am. Acad. Clin. Toxicology, Am. Coll. Occupl. and Environ. Medicine, Tex. Acad. Family Physicians. Republican. Avocations: golf, collecting pipes, collecting pens. Office Phone: 281-681-8989. Business E-Mail: md@immunotoxicology.com.

CAMPBELL, ARTHUR ANDREWS, retired federal agency administrator; b. Bklyn., Feb. 8, 1924; s. Arthur Monroe and Jo Ethel (Andrews) C.; m. Nancy Elizabeth Pyle, Jan. 28, 1961; children— Julia, Tay. AB, Antioch Coll., 1948; postgrad., Columbia U., 1947-50. Editorial clk. Met. Life Ins. Co., N.Y.C., 1950-52; statistician U.S. Bur. of Census, Washington, 1952-56; asso. research prof. Scripps Found. for Research in Population Problems, Miami U., Oxford, Ohio, 1956-64; chief natality stats. br. Nat. Center for Health Stats., Washington, 1964-68; dep. dir. Center for Population Research, NIH, Bethesda, Md., 1968-94; ret., 1994. Co-author: Family Planning, Sterility, and Population Growth, 1959, Fertility and Family Planning in the U.S, 1966, Trends and Variations in Fertility in the U.S, 1968, Manual of Fertility Analysis, 1983. Served with USN, 1943-46. Recipient Meritorious Service award U.S. Dept. Commerce, 1957; Dir.'s award NIH, 1976 Fellow Am. Statis. Assn.; mem. Population Assn. Am. (pres. 1973-74), Internat. Union for Sci. Study Population.

CAMPBELL, ARTHUR J., music educator; b. Sydney, Nova Scotia, Canada, Oct. 26, 1967; arrived in U.S., 1990; MusB, Mount Allison U., 1990; MusM, Northwestern U., Evanston, Ill., 1991, Mus D, 1995. Clarinetist Symphony Nova Scotia, Halifax, 1995—96; prof. clarinet Grand Valley State U., Allendale, Mich., 1996—. Concert soloist: over 40 concerts annually worldwide, performer extensive recordings of contemporary and traditional music for clarinet. Recipient Am. Artist Abroad award, Internat. Clarinet Assn., Internat. Recording Project award, Top Clarinet award, Nat. Music Festival Canada, 1988. Office: Grand Valley State U 1 Campus Dr Allendale MI 49401-9401 Fax: 616-331-3100. E-mail: campbela@gvsu.edu.

CAMPBELL, AUDREY LEIGH, communications professional; b. Cleve., Oct. 30, 1959; d. Odis E. and Winnie R. Campbell. BS in Journalism, Ohio U., Athens, 1982; MBA in Internat. Mgmt., Baldwin-Wallace Coll., Berea, Ohio, 1999. TV announcer and news reporter WOUB-TV, Athens, Ohio, 1980—81; radio sta. sec. WQAL-FM, Cleve., 1981—82, radio sta. adminstrv. asst., sec., 1981—82; radio advt. traffic WJW-AM, Cleve., 1982—85, adv. traffic dir., 1983—86; media rels. rep., news editor Bus. Wire, Cleve., 1985—2001; billing supr. WWWE-AM-WDOK-FM, 1985—86; news editor Bus. Wire, Cleve., 1986—88, newsroom supr., sr. editor, 1988—90, media rels. rep., 1990—2001; sr. assoc. corp. comm. Convergys Corp., Cin., 2001—02, nat. media rels. specialist, 2002—05, pub. rels. and exec. comm. specialist, 2005—. Instr. Warrensville Heights (Ohio) Adult Edn. Dept., 1985-94. Author: Campbell Family Photos, 1994. Mem. Internat. Assn. Bus. Comm., Nat. Assn. Black Journalists (bd. mem., rec. sec. 1998), Press Club Cleve. (bd. dirs.). Baptist. Avocations: piano, bowling, travel, reading. Office: Convergys Corp PO Box 1638 Cincinnati OH 45201-1638 Personal E-mail: alcambell@aol.com.

CAMPBELL, BALLARD CROOKER, JR., historian, educator; b. East Orange, N.J., Nov. 30, 1940; s. Ballard Crooker and Ruth A. (Boman) Campbell; m. Wendy E. Kent, Dec. 26, 1965 (div. May 1980); children: Cynthia Ann, Erica Lynn; m. Eugenie F. Benoit, Oct. 15, 1988. BA in Polit. sci., Northwestern U., 1962; MA in History, Northeastern U., 1964; PhD of History, U. Wis., 1970. From instr. to assoc. prof. Northeastern U., Boston, 1969—82, prof. history, law, policy and soc. PhD Program, 1982—. Author: Representative Democracy, 1980, Growth of American Government, 1995; editor: The Human Tradition in the Gilded Age and Progressive Era, 2000, American Presidential Campaigns and Elections, 2003; contbr. articles to profl. jours. Fellow, Am. Coun. Learned Socs., 1982, Charles Warren Ctr. Harvard U., 1976—77; grantee, Am. Philos. Soc., 1971, 1982. Mem.: Soc. Historians of Gilded Age and Progressive Era (pres. 2002—04), Social Sci. Hist. Assn. (exec. com. 1996—99), Orgn. Am. Historians, Am. Hist. Assn. Office: Northeastern Univ History Dept 360 Huntington Ave Boston MA 02115 Office Phone: 617-373-4448. Business E-Mail: campbell@neu.edu.

CAMPBELL, BEBE MOORE, writer; b. Phila. m. Ellis Gordon Jr.; 2 children. BS in Elem. Edn., Univ. Pitts. Author: (memoir) Sweet Summer, Growing Up With and Without My Dad, 1989, (novels) Your Blues Ain't Like Mine, 1992 (NY Times Notable Book of Yr., NAACP Image award for Lit.), Brothers and Sisters, Singing in the Comeback Choir, 2000 (NY Times Bestseller list), What You Owe Me, 2001 (NY Times Bestseller list, LA Times Best Book, 2001), 72 Hour Hold, 2005, (non-fiction) Successful Women, Angry Men: Backlash in the Two-Career Marriage, 2000, (children's books) Sometimes My Mommy Gets Angry, 2003 (Nat. Alliance for Mentally Ill Outstanding Lit. award, 2003); contbr. articles to NY Times Mag., Washington Post, LA Times, Essense, Ebony, Black Enterprise, others; regular commentator on NPR's Morning Edition. Mem. Nat. Alliance for Mentally Ill (NAMI); founding mem. NAMI-Inglewood, Calif. Mailing: c/o Gordon/Barash Assoc Inc Ste 1501 3255 Wilshire Blvd Los Angeles CA 90010-1418*

CAMPBELL, BEN NIGHTHORSE, former senator; b. Auburn, Calif., Apr. 13, 1933; s. Albert and Mary Vierra Campbell; m. Linda Aline Price, 1966; children: Colin Lee, Shanan Lee. BA, Calif. U., San Jose, 1957; spl. rsch. student, Meiji U., Tokyo, 1960—64. Educator Sacramento Law Enforcement Agy.; mem. Colo. Gen. Assembly, 1983-86, U.S. Ho. Reps., 1987-93; US senator from Colo., 1993—2005. Chair, Com. on Indian Affairs, 2001; rancher, jewelry designer, Ignacio, Colo. Chief No. Cheyenne Tribe. Served in USAF, 1951—54. Named Outstanding Legislator Colo. Bankers Assn., 1984, Man of Yr. LaPlata Farm Bur., Durango, Colo., 1984; named one of Ten Best Legislators Denver Post/Channel 4, 1986. Mem. Am. Quarter Horse Assn., Am. Brangus Assn., Am. Indian Edn. Assn. Republican. Avocation: silversmithing, jewelry-making.

CAMPBELL, BRUCE ALAN, corporate communications specialist; b. Washington, Jan. 19, 1944; s. Albert Angus and Jean Lorraine (Winter) C.; m. Jennifer Lee Drew, May 3, 1968 (div. Dec. 1986); children: Kirsten, Robert; m. Lorna Marion Wise Ekholm, Aug. 21, 1993. BA, Oberlin Coll., 1966; MA, U. Mich., 1968, PhD, 1971. Asst. prof. to assoc. prof. U. Ga., Athens, 1971-83, dir. survey rsch. ctr., 1981-83; v.p. Marktrend Mkt. Rsch., Vancouver, Canada, 1983-84; pres., CEO Campbell Goodell Traynor Consul, Vancouver, Canada, 1984—2000; sr. cons. CGT Rsch. Internat. (formerly named Campbell Goodell Traynor Consul), Vancouver, Canada, 2000—02; v.p. Corp. Insights, Inc., Vancouver, 1992-96; pres. Argus Strategies, Ltd., Vancouver, 1988—. Dir. Downtown Vancouver Assn., 1989-96, pres., 1994-96, mem. adv. bd., 1996—; dir. Parking Corp. of Vancouver, 1992-2000, v.p., 1994-96, chmn. bd., 1996-98; bd. dir s. Downtown Vancouver Bus. Improvement Assn., 1994-96; mem. Vancouver Econ. Devel. Commn., 1996. Author: The American Electorate, 1979, profl. jours. Avocations: musical theatre, minor hockey officiating. Office: Argus Strategies Ltd 2224 W 15th Ave Vancouver BC Canada V6K 2Y7 Office Phone: 604-732-8865.

CAMPBELL, BRUCE CRICHTON, hospital administrator; b. Balt., July 21, 1947; s. James Allen and Elda Shaffer (Crichton) C.; m. Linda Page Cottrell, June 28, 1969; children: Molly Shaffer, Andrew Crichton. BA, Lake Forest Coll., 1969; M.H.A., Washington U., St. Louis, 1973; DPH, U. Ill., 1979. Adminstrv. asst. Passavant Meml. Hosp., Chgo., 1970-71; adminstrv. resident Albany (N.Y.) Med. Center Hosp., 1972-73; adminstrv. asst. Rush-Presbyn.-St. Luke's Med. Center, Chgo., 1973-75, asst. adminstr., 1975-77, asst. v.p., 1977-79, v.p. adminstrv. affairs, 1979-83; chmn. dept. health systems mgmt. Rush U., Chgo., 1977-81, dean Coll. Health Scis., 1981-83; exec. dir. U. Chgo. Hosps. and Clinics, 1983-85; lectr. Grad. Sch. Bus., U. Chgo., 1983-85; pres. Campbell Assocs., Chgo., 1985-92; exec. v.p. Ill. Masonic Med. Ctr., Chgo., 1993, pres., 1993-2000, Advocate Luth. Gen. Hosp., Park Ridge, Ill., 2000—. W.K. Kellogg Found. fellow, 1977; Leadership Greater Chgo. fellow, 1984-85 Fellow Am. Coll. Healthcare Execs.; mem. Young Adminstrs. Chgo. (pres. 1977), Assn. Univ. Programs in Health Adminstrn., Am. Hosp. Assn., Ill. Hosp. Assn., Chgo. Hosp. Council. Office: Advocate Luth Gen Hosp 1775 Dempster St Park Ridge IL 60068

CAMPBELL, BYRON CHESSER, publishing company executive; b. Evanston, Ill., Feb. 6, 1934; s. Chesser Milburn and Hallie (Calhoun) C.; m. Barbara Mace, Aug. 16, 1958 (div. Apr. 1982); children: Evan Chesser, Aimee Campbell Wood; m. Meta Pierce, Aug. 13, 1983; stepchildren: Marc Wise, Meier Wise, Matthew Wise, Miles Wise. BA, Yale U., 1955; MBA, Harvard U., 1959. Various positions Burlington (Vt.) Free Press, 1959-61; prodn. engr., asst. labor rels. mgr. Chicago Tribune, 1961-68, prodn. mgr., 1970-73; bus. mgr. Chicago Today, 1968-70; asst. to pres. Tribune Co., 1973-75; pres., gen. mgr. Area Publs. Corp., Merrill Printing Co., Chgo., 1975-77; pres., chief exec. officer News and Sun-Sentinel Co., Ft. Lauderdale, Fla., 1977-83; pres., pub. L.A. Daily News; pres., chief exec. officer Tribune Newspapers West, Inc., L.A., 1983-87; pres., pub. The Record, Hackensack, N.J.; v.p. Macromedia Inc., Hackensack, 1988-91. Bd. dirs. Home News Pub. Co., New Brunswick, N.J., Newspapers of New Eng., Concord, N.H., George W. Prescott Pub. Co., Quincy, Mass., Journal-Star Printing Co., Lincoln, Nebr., Freedom Comm., Inc., Irvine, Calif. Bd. dirs. Lyric Opera Chgo., Newberry Libr. Chgo., Sta. WPBT, Miami, Fla., Rush-Presbyn.-St. Luke's Med. Ctr., Chgo.; bd. dirs., campaign chmn. United Way of Bergen County, 1989-91; adv. bd. Bergen 2000; bd. dirs., pres., campaign chmn. United Way of Broward County, Fla.; bd. dirs., chmn. San Fernando Valley Cultural Found., L.A.; bd. dirs., pres.,Chgo. Youth Ctrs., Broward Community Blood Ctr.; bd. dirs., exec. com. Broward Workshop; bd. dirs. United Way, L.A., campaign chmn. San Fernando Valley; bd. dirs., 1st v.p. Ft. Lauderdale Symphony. Lt. USN, 1955-57. Mem. AP (nominating com.), Am. Newspaper Pubs. Assn. (govt. affairs com., newsprint com. 1989-92), Am. Press Inst. (bd. dirs. 1984-93), Inland Press Assn. (pres., bd. dirs.), Greater L.A. C. of C. (bd. dirs.), Econ. Club (Chgo.), Yale Club (Chgo., bd. dirs., pres.), Lotos Club (N.Y.C.), Univ. Club (Chgo., bd. dirs., admissions com.), Saddle and Cycle Club (Chgo., bd. dirs., admissions com.), Lauderdale Yacht Club (Ft. Lauderdale, Fla.), Ristigouche Salmon Club (Matapedia, Que.). Avocations: tennis, wine, fly fishing, travel, golf. E-mail: bccampbell@webtv.net.

CAMPBELL, CARL LESTER, banker; b. Sunbury, Pa., Apr. 10, 1943; s. Claude L. and Viola W. Campbell; m. Mary E. Bingaman, June 5, 1965; children: Carla L., Craig L. BS, Susquehanna U., 1965; postgrad., Stonier Grad. Sch. Banking, 1978. Br. mgr. asst. v.p. Tri-County Nat. Bank, Middleburg, Pa., 1965-72; asst. v.p. adminstrn. Pa. Nat. Bank, Pottsville, 1972-74, adminstrv. v.p., 1974-80, sr. v.p., 1980-81, exec. v.p., 1981-82, pres. chief exec. officer, 1982-86; pres., chief exec. officer Keystone Fin., Inc., Harrisburg, Pa., 1986-98, chmn., CEO, 1998-2000; vice chmn. M&T Bank, Harrisburg, 2000—. Office: M and T Bank 3607 Derry St Harrisburg PA 17111-1900

CAMPBELL, CATHERINE LYNN, elementary school educator; b. Lynchburg, Va., Mar. 16, 1961; d. Tomie Eawell Campbell and Barbara (Arthur) McCraw. BA, Sweet Briar Coll., 1983; MEd in Adminstrv. and Supervision, U. Va., 2003. Cert. elem. tchr., NK-8 tchr. VA. Tchr. Amherst (Va.) County Pub. Schs., 1984—. Mem. Va. Real Estate Bd. Common Interest Properties. Mem.: ASCD, Va. Edn. Assn., NEA, Nat. Honor Soc. Avocations: horseback riding, raising quarter horses. Home: 139 Cedar Crest Dr Ste 107 Madison Heights VA 24572-2366 Office: Amherst County Pub Schs Amherst VA 24521 Office Phone: 434-846-1307. Personal E-mail: ccampbell@amherst.k12.va.us, ccamp74205@aol.com.

CAMPBELL, CECIL DEAN, academic administrator, educator; b. Washington, D.C., Sept. 18, 1969; s. Lloyd George Cecil and Lynette Yvonne Campbell; m. Dalila C. Treminio, Apr. 27, 2002; children: John Anthony children: Margaret Mendoza, Marilyn Mendoza, Daniela Marie. BA, Yale U., 1991; MA, Boston Coll., 1999; EdD, U. So. Calif., L.A., 2004. Sales and bus.

cons. Mobil Oil Corp., Fairfax, Va., 1991—92; mktg. analyst EG&G Dynatrend, Arlington, Va., 1993—95; program mgr. UCLA, 2000—02; rsch. asst. Ctr. for Higher Edn. Policy Analysis, L.A.; dir. Office of the Provost U. So. Calif., L.A., 2004—. Asst. adj. prof. U. So. Calif., L.A., 2004—. Adminstrv. fellow, Lynch Sch. Edn., Boston Coll., 1997, 1998, Dauterive scholar, Rossier Sch. Edn., U. So. Calif., 1999. Mem.: Am. Ednl. Rsch. Assn., Assn. for the Study Higher Edn. Office: Univ Southern California 3601 Watt Way GFS 227 Los Angeles CA 90089-1695 Office Phone: 213-740-8702. Office Fax: 213-740-9757.

CAMPBELL, CHAD, professional golfer; b. Andrews, Tex., May 31, 1974; Degree, UNLV, 1996. Winner The Tour Championships, 2003, Bay Hill Championships, 2004. Mem. Ryder Cup Team, 2004. Named Rookie of Yr. (Hooters Tour), 1997, First Team Jr. Coll. All-Am. Achievements include three time Hooters Tour player of the yr. Avocation: hunting. Office: c/o PGA Tour 112 PGA Tour Blvd Ponte Vedra Beach FL 32082

CAMPBELL, CHESTER DOUGLAS, writer; b. Nashville, Nov. 30, 1925; s. James Carl and Maude Logue Campbell; m. Sarah Anne Scott, Sept. 4, 1999; m. Alma Beatrice Miracle, May 4, 1953 (dec. Feb. 13, 1998); children: Stephen Douglas, Mark Alan, Sarah Anne, Carrie Elizabeth. BS, U. Tenn., 1949. Cert. Assn. Exec. Am. Soc. of Assn. Execs., 1975. Reporter The Knoxville (Tenn.) Jour., 1947—51; intelligence officer U. S. Air Force, 1951—53; newspaper reporter The Nashville Banner, 1954—59; pub. rels. exec. Metcalfe Pub. Rels., Nashville, 1961—62; editor Nashville Mag., 1963—69; advt. copywriter Noble-Dury and Assocs., Nashville, 1969—70; exec. v.p. Tenn. Assn. of Life Underwriters, Nashville, 1971—89. Author: (novels) Secret of the Scroll, 2002 (Bloody Dagger award, 2003), Designed to Kill, 2004, Deadly Illusions, 2005. Adminstrv. bd. mem. City Rd. Chapel United Meth. Ch., Madison, Tenn., 1992—2001, ch. historian, 1995—2001; sec., v.p., pres. Tenn. Soc. of Assn. Execs., Nashville, 1983—85; assn. execs. adv. coun. Nat. Assn. of Life Underwriters, Washington, 1980—83. Capt. USAF, 1952—53, Korean War, lt. col. USAF, 1953—71. Mem.: The Authors Guild, Tenn. Mountain Writers, Tenn. Writers Alliance, Sisters in Crime, Mystery Writers of Am. (rep. west area S.E. chpt. 2005), Am. Soc. of Assn. Execs. (life; membership com. 1975—77). Office: Village Properties PO Box 281 Madison TN 37116-0281 Office Phone: 615-868-3011. Personal E-mail: campbellcd@mindspring.com. Business E-Mail: chester@chesterdcampbell.com.

CAMPBELL, CHRISTIAN LARSEN L., lawyer; b. Chgo., Nov. 21, 1950; s. William Joseph and Marie Agnes (Cloherty) C.; m. Heather Gilchrist, Mar. 7, 1987; children: Christian Jr., Brent, Amelia. BA, MA in Econ., Northwestern U., 1972; JD, Harvard U., 1975. Bar: Ill. 1975, U.S. Dist. Ct. (no. dist.) Ill. 1975, U.S. Ct. Appeals (7th cir.) 1975, U.S. Ct. Appeals (5th cir.) 1980, U.S. Supreme Ct. 1980. Assoc. Sidley & Austin, Chgo., 1975-83, ptnr., 1983—90; v.p., gen. counsel, sec. Nalco Chem. Co., Naperville, Ill., 1990—94; sr. v.p., gen. counsel, sec. Owens Corning, 1995—97, Yum! Brands, 1997—, chief franchise officer, 2003—. Mem. ABA, Ill. State Bar Assn., Ky. Bar Assn., Chgo. Bar Assn., Louisville Bar Assn., Am. Mgmt. Assn. (lectr.1976—). Clubs: Barclay (Chgo.). Avocations: tennis, jogging. Office: Yum! Brands 1441 Gardiner Ln Louisville KY 40213-1914 Office Phone: 502-874-2467.*

CAMPBELL, COLIN, obstetrician, gynecologist, dean; b. Washington, June 24, 1927; s. Colin and Margaret (Kingsland) Masters C.; m. Catherine Marian Hayden, Aug. 20, 1952; children: Catherine, Janet, Philip. AB, Stanford U., 1949; MD, CM, McGill U., 1953; EdM, Temple U., 1967; DHL, U. Akron, 1991. Diplomate Am. Bd. Ob-Gyn. Intern George Washington Hosp., Washington, 1953-54; asst. resident in pathology U.S. VA Hosp., Coral Gables, Fla., 1954; gen. practice resident Dade County Hosp., Kendall, Fla., 1955; gen. practice medicine Perrine, Fla., 1955-57; asst. resident, resident in ob-gyn. Hosp. for the Women of Md., Balt., 1957-60; practice medicine specializing in ob-gyn. Balt., 1960-61; instr. ob-gyn. Temple U., Phila., 1961-64; asst. prof. ob-gyn. U. Mich., Ann Arbor, 1964-67, assoc. prof., 1967-71, prof., 1971-78, asst. dean Med. Sch., 1972-76, assoc. dean, 1976-78; prof. ob-gyn., dean U. Ala. Sch. Primary Med. Care, Huntsville, 1978-83; prof. ob-gyn., pres., dean Northeastern Ohio Univs. Coll. Medicine, Rootstown, 1983-92, pres., dean emeritus, 1992—. Contbr. numerous articles to profl. jours. Fellow ACOG. Home: 4741 Mint Dr Memphis TN 38117-4010 Office: Northeastern Ohio Us Coll Medicine 4209 State Route 44 Rootstown OH 44272-9698

CAMPBELL, COLIN GOETZE, foundation president; b. N.Y.C., Nov. 3, 1935; s. Joseph and Marjorie (Goetze) C.; m. Nancy Nash, June 20, 1959; children: Elizabeth, Jennifer, Colin, Blair. AB, Cornell U., 1957; JD, Columbia U., 1960; LLD (hon.), Amherst Coll., 1972, Williams Coll., 1973, Dickinson Coll., 1982, U. Hartford, 1983, Wesleyan U., 1989, Conn. Coll., 1990, Fairfield U., 1999; DHL (hon.), Trinity Coll., 1981, Georgetown U., 1984; PhD in Pub. Sci. (hon.), Cedar Crest Coll., 1997. Bar: Conn. 1961. Atty. Cummings & Lockwood, Stamford, Conn., 1960-62; asst. to pres. Am. Stock Exch., N.Y.C., 1962-63, sec., 1963-64, v.p., 1964-67; adminstrv. v.p. Wesleyan U., Middletown, Conn., 1967-69, exec. v.p., 1969-70, pres., 1970-88, pres. emeritus, 1988—; pres. Rockefeller Bros. Fund, 1988-2000; chmn., pres. Colonial Williamsburg (Va.) Found., 2000—. Bd. dirs. Pitney Bowes, Sysco Corp. Bd. dirs. Rockefeller Fin. Svcs. Mem. Am. Acad. Arts and Scis., Coun. on Fgn. Rels., Century Assn., Knickerbocker Club, Psi Upsilon, Phi Delta Phi. Episcopalian. Home: Coke-Garrett House 465 E Nicholson St Williamsburg VA 23185 Office: Colonial Williamsburg Found PO Box 1776 Williamsburg VA 23187-1776 Office Phone: 757-220-7200. E-mail: ccampbell@cwf.org.

CAMPBELL, COLIN HERALD, former mayor; b. Winnipeg, Man., Can., Jan. 18, 1911; s. Colin Charles and Aimee Florence (Herald) C.; m. Virginia Paris, July 20, 1935; children: Susanna Herald, Corinna Buford, Virginia Wallace. BA, Reed Coll., 1933. Exec. sec. City Club of Portland, 1934-39; alumni sec., dir. endowment adminstrn. Reed Coll., 1939-42; exec. sec. N.W. Inst. Internat. Rels., 1940-42; supr. contract, engr. Kaiser Co., Inc., 1942-45; asst. pers. dir. Portland Gas & Coke Co., 1945-48; dir. indsl. rels. Pacific Power & Light Co., Portland, 1948-76. Mem. Oreg. Adv. Com. on Fair Employment Practices Act, 1949-55; trustee, chmn., pres. Portland Symphonic Choir, 1950-54; trustee Portland Civic Theater, 1941-54; bd. dirs. Portland Symphony Soc., 1957-60, Cmty. Child Guidance Clinic, 1966-68; active United Way, 1945-75; bd. dirs. Contemporary Crafts Assn., 1972-76, treas., 1975-76; bd. dirs. Lake Oswego Corp., 1961-65, 71-73, 74-76, corp. sec., 1964, pres., 1973-74, treas., 1975-76; mem. Com. on Citizen Involvement, City of Lake Oswego, 1975-77; chmn. Bicentennial Com., Lake Oswego, 1975-76; sec.-treas. Met. Area Comms. Commn., 1980-85; treas. Clackamas County Cmty. Action Agy., 1980-82, chmn., 1982-85; fin. adv. com. West Clackamas County LWV, 1974-76, 78-80; councilman City of Lake Oswego, 1977-78, mayor, 1979-85, chmn. libr. growth task force, 1987-89, chmn. hist. rev. bd., 1990-92; chmn. energy adv. com. League Oreg. Cities, 1982-84; adv. bd., chmn. fin. com. Lake Oswego Adult Cmty. Ctr., 1985-88; pres. Oswego Heritage coun., 1992-95, sec., 1995-96, treas., 1997-99, dir., 2000, dir. emeritus, 2001—; mem. County Blue Ribbon Com. on Law Enforcement, 1987-89; fee arbitration panel Oreg. State Bar Assn., 1995-2000; mem. resident coun. Mary's Woods CCRC, 2001— Mem. Edison Electric Inst. (exec. com.), N.W. Electric Light and Power Assn., Lake Oswego C. of C. (v.p. 1986-87, chmn. land use com. 1990-91), Nat. Trust for Hist. Preservation, Hist. Preservation League Oreg., Oreg. Hist. Soc., McLoughlin Meml. Assn., Oswego Heritage Coun. (pres. 1992-94, 95-96, treas. 1997-99, editor 1992-2003), Clackamas County Hist. Assn., Rotary (treas. Lake Oswego chpt. 1990-93). Republican. Presbyterian. Home: Apt 306 17440 Holy Names Dr Lake Oswego OR 97034-5143 Personal E-mail: colinhc@comcast.net.

CAMPBELL, COLIN KYDD, electrical and computer engineering educator, researcher; b. St. Andrews, Fife, Scotland, May 3, 1927; s. David Walker and Jean (Hutchison) C.; m. Vivian Gwyn Norval, Apr. 17, 1954; children—Barry, Gwyn, Ian B.Sc. in Engring. with honors, St. Andrews U., 1952; S.M., MIT, 1953; PhD, St. Andrews U., 1960; D.Sc., U. Dundee, 1984. Registered profl. engr., Ont. Communications engr. Fgn. Office and Diplomatic Wireless Service, London, Eng., 1946-47; communications engr. Brit. Embassy, Washington, 1947-48; electronics engr. Atomic Instrument Co., Cambridge, Mass., 1954-57; asst. prof. elec. and computer engring. McMaster U., Hamilton, Ont., Can., 1960-63, assoc. prof. elec. and computer engring., 1963-67, prof. elec. engring., 1967-89, prof. elec. and computer engring., 1989—, prof. emeritus. Vis. scholar Ctr. for Power Electronic Sys., Va. Poly. Inst. and State U., Blacksburg, 2000, 02. Author: Surface Acoustic Wave Devices and Their Signal Processing Applications, 1989, Surface Acoustic Wave Devices for Mobile and Wireless Communication, 1998; contbr. numerous articles to profl. jours. Served with Brit. Army, 1944-46 Recipient The Inventor insignia Can. Patents and Devel. Ltd., 1973, invitation fellow Japan Soc. for Promotion of Sci., 1995, rsch. fellow Rand Afrikaans U., South Africa, 1995. Fellow Royal Soc. Can. (Thomas Eadie medal 1983), Engring. Inst. Can., Royal Soc. Arts London, IEEE (life); mem. Sigma Xi Mem. Ch. of England. Club: Royal Canadian Mil. Inst. (Toronto) Avocation: fishing. Home: 160 Parkview Dr Ancaster ON Canada L9G 1Z5 Office: McMaster U Elec Computer Engring 1280 Main St W Hamilton ON Canada L8S 4K1 Business E-Mail: colin.kydd.campbell@sympatico.ca.

CAMPBELL, CONSTANCE RUTH, education educator; b. Hondman, Ky. d. Floyd Tidsworth, Jr. and Mary Ida Campbell Tidsworth. BA, Okla. Bapt. Univ., Shawnee, Okla., 1981; MS, Univ. Ky., Lexington, Ky., 1983; PhD, Fla. State, Tallahessee, Fla., 1992. Dir. counseling Union Coll., Baranville, Ky., 1983—87; prof. Ga. Sothern Univ., Statesboro, Ga., 1992—. Women's/gender studies adv. bd. Ga. Southern Univ., Stateboro, Ga., 1992—2003, latino outreach adv. bd., 2001, cons., 1995—. Mem. C. of C., Stateboro, Ga., 2001—. Recipient Tchg. award, Coll. of Bus. Adminstrn., 2001, Svc. award, 2001. Mem.: Southern Mgmt. Assn., Acad. of Mgmt. Avocations: piano, travel, walking.

CAMPBELL, DAVID GEORGE, research ecologist, writer, educator; b. Decatur, Ill., Jan. 28, 1949; s. George Robert and Jean Blossom C.; m. Karen S. Lowell; 1 child, Tatiana Claire Lowell-Campbell. BA, Kalamazoo Coll., 1971; MS, U. Mich., 1973; PhD, Johns Hopkins U., 1984. Exec. dir. Bahamas Nat. Trust, Nassau, 1974-77; ecologist N.Y. Bot. Garden, Bronx, 1984-88, leader Amazon Expdns., 1974-92, research fellow, 1989—; prof. biology, chair environ. studies Grinnell (Iowa) Coll., 1989—, Henry R. Luce prof. nations-global environ., 1989—2000. Adj. prof. U. Nanjing, China, 1993—; prof. Semester at Sea, 1997; prof. Grinnell-in-London, 1999; cons. Internat. Union for Conservation of Nature, 1978-79, leader Maya forest project, Belize, 1993—; biologist and lectr. M.V. World Discoverer in Amazon and Antarctic, 1981-87, L.B. Yamal to North Pole, 1995; biologist Brazilian Antarctic Expdn., 1987-88. Author: The Ephemeral Islands, 1978, The Crystal Desert, 1992, Islands in Space and Time, 1996, A Land of Ghosts, 2004; editor: Floristic Inventory of Tropical Countries, 1989; contbr. articles to profl. jours. Recipient Fulling award Soc. Econ. Botany, 1987, Houghton Mifflin Lit. fellow, 1992, Pen/Martha Albrand award for nonfiction, 1993, John Burroughs medal, 1994; Guggenheim fellow, 1989. Fellow Linnean Soc. London, Royal Geog. Soc. London, Explorers Club Office: Grinnell Coll Dept Biology Grinnell IA 50112 Office Phone: 691-269-3172. E-mail: campbell@grinnell.edu.

CAMPBELL, DAVID GWYNNE, petroleum executive, geologist; b. May 2, 1930; s. Lois Raymond Henager and La Vada (Ray) Henager Campbell; m. Janet Gay Newland, March 1, 1958; 1 child, Carl David. BS, Tulsa U., 1953; MS, U. Okla., 1957. Geologist Lone Star Producing Co., Oklahoma City, 1957-65; dist. geologist, geol. cons. Tenneco Oil Co., Oklahoma City, 1965-77; exploration mgr. Leede Exploration, Oklahoma City, 1977-80; pres. Earth Hawk Exploration, Inc., Oklahoma City, 1980—. Divsn. exploration mgr. PetroCorp., Inc., Oklahoma City, 1983-92, divsn. gen. mgr. 1992-96; cons. Jr. Achievement, Oklahoma City, 1996—; active U. Okla. Sch. Geology and Geophysics Alumni 1985—, bd. dirs. adv. coun. 1988-90, sec. 1990-91, vice chmn., 1991-92, chmn., 1992-93, life mem., 1994, centennial com., 2000-01, U. Okla. Trailblazer award com., 2003—. Contbr. articles to Jour. Cherokee Studies. Active Last Frontier Coun. Boy Scouts Am., 1960-73, edn. chmn. Eagle Dist. 1963-67; gubernatorial appointee Native Am. Cultural and Edn. Authority, 2002—; Okla. Cultural Coalition Gala com., 1999. Recipient cert. of appreciation, Nat. Exch. Club, Oklahoma City, 1999, Okla. Gov.'s Arts award for cmty. svc., 2003. Mem. AAAS, Internat. Assn. Energy Economists, Soc. Ind. Profl. Earth Scientists (pres. Okla. chpt. 1988, chmn. 1989, chmn. polit. affairs com. 1991), Soc. Profl. Well Log Analysts, Am. Assn. Petroleum Geologists (hon. mem. 1995, chmn. house of dels. 1981-82, house of dels. mem.-at-large 1982—, exec. com. 1981-82, 90-91, found. trustee assoc. 1983—, corp. mem. Am. Assn. Petroleum Geologists Found. 1996—, mem. adv. coun. 1984-87, councillor mid-continent sect. 1984-87, nominating com. 1984-85, 86-87, astrogeology com. 1984-2004, honors and awards com. 1984-85, 85-86, adv. bd. Treatise of Petroleum Geology 1986-91, nat. membership adv. coun. 1987-90, membership com. chmn. mid-continent sect. 1987-90, Disting. Svc. award 1989, nat. v.p. 1990-91, cand. nat. pres.-elect. 2000-2001, mid-continent councillor energy minerals divsn. 1992-94, chmn. com. of coms. 1992-98, mem. com. of coms. 1992-2004, charter mem. divsn. Environ. Geoscis. 1992), Okla. City Geol. Soc. (hon. life mem. 1992, pub. rels. chmn. Spkrs. Bur. 1963-64, chmn. stratigraphic code com. 1967-68, presdl. appointee 1969-70, advt. mgr. Shale Shaker 1969-71, rep. to AAPG Ho. of Dels. 1980-86, bylaws and incorp. rev. com. 1986), Okla. City Geol. Found. (founding pres. 1993-98, bd. dir. 1993-2001), Ind. Petroleum Assn. Am. (Okla. chpt. regulatory affairs com. 1991-93), Okla. City Assn. Petroleum Landmen, Houston Geol. Soc., Tulsa Geol. Soc., Petroleum Exploration Soc. Great Britain, Okla. City Petroleum Club (bd. dir. 1987-90, 1995-98, sec. 1989, 2d v.p. 1990, chmn. membership com. 1988-90), Geol. Soc. Moscow, N.Y. Acad. Scis., Okla. City C. of C., Okla. Hist. Soc., Cherokee Nat. Hist. Soc. (devel. com. 1987-95, bd. trustees nat. soc. 1983-96), Ctr. Am. Indian (bd. dir. 1988-92), Red Earth Indian Ctr. (bd. dir. 1992—, co-founder Red Earth Amb. of Yr. award, chmn. auction 1993, v.p. 1994-97, pres. 1997-98, Spirit award, 1999), Nat. Mus. Am. Indian, Am. Indian Cultural Soc., Houston Mus. Fine Arts, Okla. Pilots Assn., Exptl. Aircraft Assn., Aircraft Owners and Pilots Assn., First Families of Twin Ters., Clan Campbell of N. Am., Sigma Xi, Pi Kappa Alpha. Home: 6109 Woodbridge Rd Oklahoma City OK 73162-3220 Office: Earth Hawk Exploration Inc PO Box 2396 Oklahoma City OK 73101-2396 Office Phone: 405-236-3030. Personal E-mail: earthhawk1@sbcglobal.net.

CAMPBELL, DAVID KELLY, theoretical physicist, engineering educator; b. Long Beach, Calif., July 23, 1944; s. S. Kelly and Elizabeth (Platt) C.; m. Ulrike Bibl, Aug. 30, 1967; children: Jean-Pierre N., Michael C. BA in chemistry and physics, Harvard U., 1966; PhD in theoretical physics and applied math., Cambridge U., Eng., 1970. Instr. and rsch. assoc. U. Ill., Urbana, 1970-72; mem. Inst. for Advanced Study Princeton U., 1972-74; J.R. Oppenheimer Fellow Los Alamos Nat. Lab., 1974—77, staff mem., 1977—92, dir. Ctr. for Nonlinear Studies, 1987—92; prof., head. dept. physics U. Ill., 1992—2000; dean Coll. Engring. Boston U., 2000—, interim provost, 2004—. Editor: Order in Chaos, 1981, Interactive Electrons in Reduced Dimensions, 1989, Chaos/XAOC: Soviet-American Perspectives in Nonlinear Science, 1990—. Named Disting Lectr. Assn. Western U., Dept. Energy, 1989-90, Dept. Edn., Peoples Republic China, 1986; Eminent scholar State of N.Mex., 1989. Fellow AAAS, Am. Phys. Soc. Office: Boston U Coll Engring 44 Cummington St Boston MA 02215

CAMPBELL, DEMAREST LINDSAY, artist, writer, interior designer; d. Peter Stephen III and Mary Elizabeth (Edwards) C.; m. Dale Gordon Haugo, 1978. BFA in Art History, MFA in Asian Art History, MFA in Theatre Design. Designer murals and residential interiors Demarest Campbell Art and Interiors, San Francisco, 1975—; chargeman scenic artist Am. Conservatory Theatre, 1976—. Designed, painted and sculpted over 250 prodns. for Broadway, internat. opera, motion pictures. Mem. NOW, Asian Art Mus. Soc., San Francisco. Mem. NOW, Internat. Alliance of Theatrical Stage Employees, Art Dirs. Guild and Scenic, Title and Graphic Artists (Local 800), Sherlock Holmes Soc. London, Amnesty Internat., Nat. Trust for Hist. Preservation (Gt. Britian and U.S.A. chpt.), Fine Arts Mus. Soc. San Francisco, Shavian Malthus Soc. (charter Gt. Britian chpt.), Humane Soc. of U.S. (millennium mem.). Avocations: medical history, pre-twentieth century military history.

CAMPBELL, DENNIS MARION, academic administrator, educator, theologian; b. Dalhart, Tex., Aug. 23, 1945; s. Francis Marion and Margaret (Osterberg) C.; m. Leesa Heydenreich, June 13, 1970; children: Margaret Heyden, Robert Trevor. AB, Duke U., 1967, PhD, 1973; BD, Yale U., 1970; DD (hon.), Fla. So. U., 1986. Ordained to ministry United Meth. Ch., 1974. Min. Trinity United Meth. Ch., Durham, N.C., 1973-74; chmn. dept. religion Converse Coll., Spartanburg, S.C., 1974-79; dir. continuing edn. Div. Sch. Duke U., Durham, 1979-82, prof. theology, 1982—, dean. Div. Sch., 1982-97; headmaster Woodberry Forest (Va.) Sch., 1997—; trustee The Duke Endowment, Charlotte, NC, 2004—. Mem. Oxford (Eng.) Inst. Theol. Studies, 1982, 87, 92, Denver, 1996; gen. conf. United Meth. Ch., Balt., 1984, St. Louis, 1988, Louisville, 1992; del. World Meth. Coun., Nairobi, Kenya, 1987, World Coun. Chs. 7th Assembly, Canberra, Australia, 1991. Author: Authority and the Renewal of American Theology, 1976, Doctors, Lawyers, Ministers: Christian Ethics in Professional Practice, 1982, The Yoke of Obedience: The Meaning of Ordination in Methodism, 1988, Who Will Go For Us?, 1994. Chmn. Protection of Human Subjects Com.; bd. dirs. Family Health Internat., Research Triangle Park, 1986—, Internat. Coalition Boys Schs; bd. visitors Perkins Sch. Theology So. Meth. U., Dallas, 1987—; overseers com. Harvard U., 1992—. Mem. Am. Theol. Soc., Am. Acad. Religion, Soc. Christian Ethics, Assn. Theol. Schs. (accrediting com. 1986—), Phi Beta Kappa, Omicron Delta Kappa. Methodist. Home: PO Box 48 Woodberry Forest VA 22989-0048 Office: The Residence Woodberry Forest VA 22989-0048

CAMPBELL, DONAL, state official; b. Lewisburg, Tenn., May 1, 1951; B of Criminal Justice, Tenn. State U., 1981. Youth dormitory attendant, supr. Mid. Tenn. Reception and Guidance Ctr.; psychiat. technician State of Tenn. Mental Health Dept.; correctional officer, local warden of security, adminstr. Deberry Correctional; former commr. Corrections Dept., State of Tenn., Nashville; now commr. Corrections Dept., State of Ala., Montgomery, Ala. Mem. Am. Corrections Assn. (bd. commn. for accreditation, 1998-2000), Tenn. Corrections Assn., Assn. State Correctional Adminstrs., So. States Correctional Assn. Office: Ala Dept Corrections 101 S Union St Montgomery AL 36130

CAMPBELL, DOUGLAS G., art educator; b. Syracuse, N.Y., Nov. 7, 1946; s. Laurence R. Campbell and Kathryn B. Gourley; m. L. Rebecca Propst, July 23, 1948; children: Joshua Samuel Campbell-Propst, Ian Nathanael Propst-Campbell. BA, Fla. State U., 1968; MFA, Pratt Inst., Bklyn., 1972; PhD in Comparative Arts, Ohio U., 1979. Prof. of art George Fox U., Newberg, Oreg., 1990—. Dir. Donald H. Lindgren Gallery George Fox U., Newberg. Ink drawing, Atlanta Review, acrylic painting, Mars Hill Review; contbr. articles, essays, poetry to profl. jours.; author: Seeing: When Art and Faith Intersect, 2002. With USN, 1968—70. Recipient Purchase Prize, Art About Agr. Exhibit, Oreg. State U., 1990; grantee Humanities Study grantee, NEH, 1995, Summer Seminar grantee, 1981, Faculty Rsch. grantee, George Fox U., 1991, 1996, 2000, 2003; scholar Ctr. for Peace Learning scholar, 1999—2000. Mem.: Coll. Art Assn. of Am. (assoc.), Christians in the Visual Arts (assoc.). Christian. Avocations: tae kwan do, hiking. Office: George Fox Univ 414 N Meridian St #6021 Newberg OR 97132 Office Phone: 503-554-2635. E-mail: dcampbell@georgefox.edu.

CAMPBELL, EARL DUNCAN, computer consultant; b. Berkeley, Calif., Sept. 5, 1946; s. Thomas S. and Mary (Hanlon) Campbell; m. Kathleen L. Gavin, Aug. 17, 1968 (div. May 1985); children: Kelly Lora, Heather Marie; m. Janice M. Holl, Oct. 31, 1992. AA in Philosophy, Monmouth U., W. Long Branch, N.J., 1970, BS in Acctg., 1972; MBA, Baruch U., N.Y.C., 1974. Cert. sys. analyst IBM, 1969. With Johnson & Johnson, New Brunswick, NJ, 1974—79; pres. SMS Consulting, Woodbridge, NJ, 1979—95, Campbell & Rathsam, Matawan, NJ, 1995—2003. Bus. and computer cons., Chgo., San Francisco, N.Y.C., 1979—2003. Sgt. USAF, 1964—68. Named N.J. Businessman of Yr., Bus. Adv. Coun., 2002. Mem.: Benevolent and Protective Order of Elks (exalted ruler 1982—83). Office: Campbell and Rathsam Inc 11 Morganville Rd Matawan NJ 07747 Office Phone: 732-583-8340. E-mail: earlcampbell@msn.com.

CAMPBELL, EDWARD JOSEPH, retired machinery company executive; b. Boston, Feb. 21, 1928; s. Edward and Mary (Doherty) C.; divorced; children: Gary, Kevin, Diane. BSME, Northwestern U., 1952, MBA, 1959. With Am. Brakeshoe Co., 1952-58, Whirlpool Corp., 1958-65; gen. mgr. Joy Mfg. Co., 1965-67; exec. v.p. J.I. Case Co. subs. Tenneco, Inc., 1968-78; pres., chief exec. officer Newport News Shipbuilding & Dry Dock Co. subs. Tenneco, Inc., Va., 1979-91; pres. J.I. Case Co. subs. Tenneco Inc., Racine, Wis., 1992-94. Bd. dir. Global Marine, Zurn Industries, Titan Internat., ABS Group; chmn. Campbell Enterprises. Mem. bd. and adv. coun. Webb Inst., Northwestern U., William & Mary Coll., U. Wis. Vet. Medicine Sch., Hampden & Sydney Coll.; chmn. Navy League US Found., elected ato NAE 1986 (Nat. Acad. of Engrng., With USNR, 1946-48. Home: 1 Deepwood Dr Unit A1 Racine WI 53402-2868 Office: PO Box 8 Racine WI 53401-0008

CAMPBELL, EDWARD WALLACE, nutritionist; b. Elizabeth, N.J., June 29, 1939; s. Edward Wallace Sr. and Dorothy Mae (Fairchild) C.; m. Phyllis A. Vecere, Sept. 27, 1959 (div. 1985); children: Diane Theresa, Christina Marie. PhD, Am. Coll., 1988; DLitt, Wellington U., 1990; MD, Open Internat. U., 1991, DSc, 1992; diploma, Lyons Med. Lab. Sch. Diplomate Internat. Coll. Acupuncture, Am. Coll. Manipulation and Nutrition, Inst. for Human Biomechanics, Am. Bd. Nutrition and Clin. Nutrition; cert. wellness counselor; Australian postgrad. cert. in acupuncture. Pvt. practice, 1974-94; dean of students Nat. Nutrition Inst., Oak Park, Ill., 1988-92; exec. dir. Am. Bd. Nutritional and Naturopathic Cert., Toms River, N.J., 1989-92; dir. R & D Vitagenics Rsch., Brick, N.J., 1990-95; dir. rsch. World AIDS Rsch. Inc., 1995—. Spkr. Nat. Health Fedn., 1987-93; prof. Open Internat. U. Author: Orthomolecular Protocol for Morbid Obesity with Adjunctive Congestive Heart Failure, 1987, Orthomolecular Protocols for the Physician, 1988, The Etiology of Hyperlipoproteinemia, 1990, Nutritional Management of Peripheral Vascular Diseases, 1991; contbg. editor: Am. Nutrition Cons. Assn. Jour., 1988-93. Assoc. mem. Am. Mus. Nat. History; mem. Lighthouse at Community Med. Ctr., Nat. Arbor Day Found., Rep. Nat. Com., Washington, 1980—; del. Rep. Party Platform Planning Com., Washington 1991-92, Presdl. Trust, Washington, 1992; campaign trustee Rep. Presdl. Task Force, Washington, 1987, 93. Fellow Found. for Complementary Medicine, Commonwealth (U.K.) Inst. Natural Medicine, Medicina Alternativa Sci. Soc., The Homeopathic Found.; mem. AARP (ret. tchrs. divsn.), Internat. Assn. Holistic Health and Medicine, Am. Nutrition Cons. Assn., Nat. Health Fedn., Am. Assn. of Nutritional Cons., Wilson Ctr. Assocs., Homeopathy and Homotoxicology Symposium, Va. Sheriffs Inst., Law Enforcement Alliance Am., Am. Legion, Senators Club, Clan Campbell Soc. Methodist. Avocations: hunting, fishing, chess, numismatism. ***One's achievements are of no importance when accomplished without regard for morality and ethics.***

CAMPBELL, EDWIN DENTON, educational association administrator, consultant, accountant; b. Boston, June 25, 1927; s. William Edwin and Mildred (Altmiller) C.; m. Crystal Cousins, 1973; children: Geraldine, Linda, David, Sean, Jennifer. Grad., Bentley Coll., Boston, 1948; CAS, Harvard U., 1971; EdD, 1975. CPA, Mass. Mgr. Arthur Andersen & Co. (C.P.A.s), Boston, 1948-53; v.p. Lab. for Electronics, Inc., Boston, 1953-62, also dir.; exec. v.p. Itek Corp., Lexington, Mass., 1962-70, dir., 1962-83; pres. Edn. Devel. Ctr., Newton, Mass., 1971-76, trustee, 1971—2004; pres. Gulf Mgmt. Inst. div. Gulf Oil Corp., Boston, 1976-83; on loan as exec. v.p. Nat. Alliance of Bus., Washington, 1983-86; dean sch. bus. Adelphi U., Garden City, N.Y., 1986-87; trustee Ednl. Testing Svc., Princeton, N.J., 1983-87, v.p., 1987-89; exec. dir. Coalition of Essential Schs., Annenberg Inst. for Sch. Reform, Brown U., Providence, 1990-96; prin. Padanaram Assocs., Inc., 1996—2001. Interim exec. dir. Plimoth Plantation, 1997; bd. dirs. Artworks!, 1993-2003; mem. faculty Bentley Coll., Boston, 1956-58. Cons. editor: Change, 1980-98. Trustee Bentley Coll., 1963—, New Bedford Whaling Mus., 1996—2003,

Friends Acad., 1996—2002, Ptnrs. in Edn., Inc., 1997-99; v.p. Mass. Assn. Mental Health, 1965-68, bd. dirs., 1962-73; mem. Mass Commn. Vocat. Rehab., 1966-68, Coll. Bd. Commn. on Pre-coll. Counseling, 1984-86; mem. vis. com. Harvard Sch. Edn., 1977-83; mem. fin. com. Town of Carlisle, Mass., 1965-68; trustee Boston Urban Found., 1969-75, Mass. Taxpayers Found., 1962-68, Fenn Sch., 1970-75, OSTI, Inc., 1971-76, Lesley Coll., 1972-76, Mass. Advocacy Ctr., 1975-76. Served with USMC, 1943-45, PTO. Mem. Assn. Industries Mass. (pres. 1967-69, now dir.), Harvard Club Boston, Cosmos Club Washington (D.C.), New Bedford Yacht Club.

CAMPBELL, EILEEN M., oil industry executive; married; 2 children. Bachelor's, U. Md. Lobbyist Gov. NJ; with Nat. Assn. Mfrs.; lobbyist United Gas Pipe Line Co.; mgr. govt. affairs Marathon Oil Corp., Houston, 1991—98, v.p. human resources, 2000—; dir. state govt. affairs USX, 1998—2000. Office: Marathon Oil Corp Hdqrs 5555 San Felipe Rd Houston TX 77056-2723*

CAMPBELL, FENTON GREGORY, academic administrator, historian; b. Columbia, Tenn., Dec. 16, 1939; s. Fenton G. and Ruth (Hayes) C.; m. Barbara D. Kuhn, Aug. 29, 1970; children: Fenton H., Matthew W., Charles H. AB, Baylor U., 1960; postgrad., Philipps U., Marburg/Lahn, Germany, 1960-61; MA, Emory U., 1962; postgrad., Charles U., Prague, Czechoslovakia, 1965-66; PhD, Yale U., 1967; postgrad., Harvard U., 1981. Rsch. staff historian Yale U., New Haven, 1966-68, spl. asst. to acting pres., 1977-78; asst. prof. history U. Wis., Milw., 1968-69; asst. prof. European history U. Chgo., 1969-76, spl. asst. to pres., 1978-87, sec. bd. trustees, 1979-87, sr. lectr., 1985-87; pres., prof. history Carthage Coll., Kenosha, Wis., 1987—. Fellow Woodrow Wilson Internat. Ctr. for Scholars, Smithsonian Instn., Washington, 1976-77; participant Japan Study Program for Internat. Execs., 1987; bd. dirs. Thrivent Mut. Funds, Johnson Family Mut. Funds., Prairie Sch., United Health Systems, Wis., Nat. Assn. Independent Colleges and Univs. Author: Confrontation in Central Europe, 1975; joint editor Akten zur deutschen auswartigen Politik, 1918-1945, 1966-96; contbr. articles and revs. to profl. jours. Fulbright grantee, 1960-61, 73-74; Woodrow Wilson fellow, 1961-62; U.S.A.-Czechoslovakia Exch. fellow, 1965-66, 73-74, 85. Mem. Mid-Day Club (Chgo.), Coun. on Fgn. Rels. (NYC), Phi Beta Kappa, Omicron Delta Kappa. Office: Carthage Coll Kenosha WI 53140-1360 Office Phone: 262-551-5858. Business E-Mail: poc@carthage.edu.

CAMPBELL, FINLEY ALEXANDER, geologist, consultant; b. Kenora, Ont., Can., Jan. 5, 1927; s. Finley McLeod and Vivian (Delve) C.; m. Barbara Elizabeth Cromarty, Oct. 17, 1953; children— Robert Finley, Glen David, Cheryl Ann. B.Sc., Brandon Coll., U. Man., Can., 1950; MA, Queen's U., Kingston, Ont., 1956; PhD, Princeton U., 1958. Exploration and mining geologist Prospectors Airways, Toronto, 1950-58; asst. and asso. prof. geology U. Alta., Can., Edmonton, 1958-65; prof., head dept. geology U. Calgary, Alta., 1965-69, v.p. capital resources, 1969-71, v.p. acad., 1971-76, prof. geology, 1976-84, v.p. priorities and planning, 1984-88, prof. emeritus, 1988—; geol. cons., 1988—. Bd. dirs., vice chmn. Can Energy Research Inst. Contbr. articles on geol. topics to profl. jours. Bd. dirs. Calgary Olympic Devel. Assn.; mem. minister's adv. bd. Tyrrell Mus. Palaeontology. Decorated Queen's Jubilee medal Can.; recipient Commemorative medal for 125th Anniversary of Can., Geology medal Brandon U. Honor Soc.; Sir James Dunne fellow, 1955-56; Princeton Alumni fellow, 1957-58. Fellow Royal Soc. Can.; mem. Assn. The Univ. of Calgary (pres. emeritus), Geol. Assn. Can., Mineral Assn. Can., Soc. Econ. Geologists, Assn. Profl. Geologists Alta., Am. Mineral Soc. Royal Soc. Can., Can. Inst. Mining and Metallurgy, Brandon Univ. Alumni Assn. (reg. dir., Disting. Svc. award Hockey Hall of Fame 1994), Glenmore Yacht Club, Silver Springs Golf and Country Club, Clearwater Bay Yacht Club. Home: 3408 Benton Dr NW Calgary AB Canada T2L 1W8 Office: U Calgary Dept Geology and Geophysics Calgary AB Canada T2N 1N4 Office Phone: 402-220-7110. Business E-Mail: campbelf@ucalgary.ca.

CAMPBELL, FRANCES HARVELL, educational association administrator; b. Goldston, N.C. d. George Henry and Evelyn (Meggs) Harvell. BS magna cum laude, U. Md., 1982; postgrad., Fla. State U., 1997—99. Asst. to Congressman Claude Pepper U.S. Ho. of Reps., 1966-80, staff dir., 1980-89; exec. dir. Claude Pepper Ctr., 1996—2004; dir. Claude Pepper Found., 1986—2004. Exec. dir. Franklin D. Roosevelt Meml. Commn., 1988-92. Del. White House Conf. on Aging; v.p. Dem. Women of Capitol Hill, 1982—83; bd. dirs. Fla. State U. Found., 1995—2001, Nat. Com. to Preserve Social Security and Medicare, 1994—2004, v.p., 2004; bd. dirs. Econ. Club Fla., 1993—99, Fla. Assn. Non-profit Orgns., Zonta, 1998—2002, Killearn Homeowners Assn., 2001—03; v.p. LWV, 2002—04, dir., 2001—. Mem. ACLU, AAUW, Tiger Bay Club, Zonta, Economic Club of Fl., Phi Kappa Phi, Alpha Sigma Lambda. Avocations: orchid culture, reading, travel, the Arts. Home: 3943 Leane Dr Tallahassee FL 32309-2210 E-mail: francescampbell6@aol.com.

CAMPBELL, FRANCIS JAMES, retired chemist; b. Toledo, Ohio, July 29, 1924; s. Herbert J. and Florence E. (Kelch) C.; m. Elizabeth P. Savage, Aug. 21, 1948; children: Nancy, MaryLou, Joan, Kathryn, Janice, James, Daniel. BS in Chem. Engring., U. Toledo, 1948. Cert. profl. chemist. Chemist Dow Chem. Co., Midland, Mich., 1948-53; chemist Dow Corning Corp., Midland, 1953-58, Naval Rsch. Lab., Washington, 1958-93; retired, 1993. Chmn. radiation effects on elec. insulation com. Internat. Electrotech. Commn., Geneva, 1974-85 House com. mem. Ind. Living for Handicapped, Inc., Washington, 1983-92; No. Va. chmn. Joint Bd. on Sci. and Engring. Edn., Washington, 1965-92. With U.S. Army, 1943-45. Recipient Research Publs. award Naval Research Lab., 1982, USN Meritorious Civilian Svc. award, 1997; decorated D.F.C., Air medal with 2 oak leaf clusters, Asiatic-Pacific Theater ribbon, WWII victory medal; inducted into Edward Drummond Libbey High Sch. Hall of Fame, Toledo, 1996; inducted as hon. fellow Washington Acad. Scis., 1999. Fellow IEEE (life); mem. IEEE Dielectrics and Elec. Insulation Soc. (Eric O. Forster award for Disting. Svc. 1992), Am. Chem. Soc., Am. Legion, Sigma Xi. Achievements include patents on thermal control coatings and battery packaging to prolong satellite life; research in thermal aging and multi-factor effects on reliability of electrical insulation of wire and cable, radiation curing of polymer matrix composites and adhesives, and in radiation damage in organic materials; in identifing the failure mechanisms in Kapton insulated wires that were responsible for a high number of electrical fires in Naval aircraft. Home: 2412 Crest St Alexandria VA 22302-2715

CAMPBELL, FREDERICK HOLLISTER, retired lawyer, historian; b. Somerville, Mass., June 14, 1923; s. George Murray and Irene Ivers (Smith) C.; m. Amy Holding Strohm, Apr. 14, 1951; 1 child, Susan Hollister. AB, Dartmouth Coll., 1944; JD, Northwestern U., 1949; postgrad., Indsl. Coll. Armed Forces, 1961-62; MA in History, U. Colo., 1984, PhD in History, 1993. Bar: Ill. 1950, U.S. Supreme Ct. 1967, Colo. 1968. Joined USMCR, 1942, USMC, 1953, advanced through grades to lt. col., 1962; assoc. editor Callaghan and Co., Chgo., 1949-50; pvt. practice Colorado Springs, Colo., 1968-88; ptnr. Gibson, Gerdes and Campbell, 1969-79; pvt. practice, 1980-88; gen. counsel 1st Fin. Mortgaage Corp., 1988-96; vice-chmn., corp. sec. 1st Fin. Mortgage Corp., 1993-96, ret., 1996; hon. instr. history U. Colo., Colorado Springs, 1986—99. Judge adv. USMC, Camp Lejeune, N.C., Korea, Parris Island, S.C., 1950-67, El Toro, Calif., Vietnam, Washington, 1950-67; vis. instr. Colo. Coll., 1993-95, asst. prof., 1996-97. Author: John's American Notary and Commissioner of Deeds Manual, 1950; contbr. articles to profl. jours. Mem. Estate Planning Coun., Colorado Springs, 1971—81, v.p., 1977—78; trustee Frontier Village Found., 1971—77; precinct committeeman Rep. Party, 1971—86; del. Colo. State Conv., 1972, 1974, 1976, 1980; bd. dirs. Rocky Mountain Nature Assn., 1975—2001, pres., 1979—92; bd. dirs. Rocky Mountain Nat. Park Assocs., 1986—2001, v.p., 1986—92, sec., 1992—95; bd. dirs. Colorado Springs Symphony Assn., 2002—03. 1st lt. USMC, 1952. Mem. Colo. Bar Assn., El Paso County Bar Assn. Am. Arbitration Assn., Marines Meml. Club, Phi Alpha Theta. Congregationalist.

CAMPBELL, GAVIN ELLIOTT, real estate investor and developer; m. Diana McClain, May 31, 1997; 2 children. BA in Polit. Philosophy magna cum laude, Yale U., 1982; MBA in Fin., U. Chgo., 1989. Analyst internat. trade Ill. Dept. Agr., Springfield, 1982—83; asst. to gov. State of Ill., Springfield, 1983—85; dep. dir. Civic Com., Chgo., 1985—90; assoc. acquisitions LaSalle Investment Mgmt., Inc., Chgo., 1990—92; v.p. acquisitions LaSalle Investment Mgmt., Chgo., 1992—93, exec. v.p. acquisitions, 1994—95, prin., acquisitions, 1996—98, mng. dir., acquisitions, 1999—; pres. Fla. Office Property Co., 1998—. Mng. prin. Steelbridge Capital, 2004—. Pres. Latino Chgo. Theater Co., Chgo., 1990-96, Leadership Fellows Assn., Chgo., 1996-98; dir. Yale Coll. Alumni Schs. Com., Chgo., 1991-95; com. rep. A.N. Pritzker Local Sch. Coun., 1993-98; co-founder, mem. exec. com. Young Leader's Fund, 1994-96; bd. dirs., chmn. Landmarks Preservation Coun. Ill., 2004—. Gov.'s fellow, Springfield, 1982, fellow Leadership Greater Chgo., 1987. Mem.: Economic Club Chgo. Avocation: historic building restoration. Office: Steelbridge Capital 4064 N Lincoln Ave Ste 178 Chicago IL 60618 E-mail: gcampbell@steelbridgecapital.com.

CAMPBELL, GEORGE, JR., physicist, medical association administrator; s. George Washington and Lillian (Britt) C.; m. Mary Schmidt Campbell, Aug. 24, 1968; children: Garikai, Sekou, Britt. BS in Physics, Drexel U., 1968; PhD in Theoretical Physics, Syracuse U., 1977; postgrad., Yale U., 1988; D (hon.), Drexel U., 2000, Coe Coll., 2002, Syracuse U., 2003. Sr. faculty Nkumbi Internat. Coll., Kabwe, Zambia, 1969-71; staff scientist AT&T Bell Labs., Holmdel, NJ, 1977-83, third level mgr., 1983-89; pres., CEO Nat. Action Coun. for Minorities in Engring., Inc., NYC, 1989-2000; Porth disting. lectr. U. Mo.-Rolla, 1993, 99; pres. Cooper Union for the Advancement of Sci. and Art, NYC, 2000—, engring. adv. coun. Adv. bd. US Sec. of Energy, Washington, 1990-93, NRC Com. on Women in Sci. and Engring., 1991-95, Coll. Engring. Cooper Union, Sta. WGBH-TV Discovering Women series, 1993-94, Merck Inst. Sci. Edn., 1993-99; mem. nat. commn. Ill. Inst. Tech., 1994; pres. Coalition for Equity and Access to Sci., Tech., Engring. and Math., 1996-97; regular guest commentator, PBS-TV Nightly Bus. Report; serves on Morella Commn., US Congress, mem. adv. bd., US Sec. of Energy, NYC Chancellor's Task Force on Sci. Edn (chmn.). Co-editor: Access Denied: Race, Ethnicity and the Scientific Enterprise, 2000, contbr. chpts. to books, articles to profl. jours. including Phys. Rev. D, Jour. Math. Physics, Issues in Sci. and Tech., Procs. IEEE Globecom, Black Issues in Higher Edn., Black Collegian, Chronicle of Higher Edn., NACME Rsch. Letter, AAAS Sci. and Tech. Policy Yearbook, 1995; commentator Nightly Bus. Report, 1993-2000. Bd. dirs. NY Hall of Sci., 1994—, Oak Ridge Assoc. Univs., 1993-99, Crossroads Theater Co., 1990-95, Consolidated Edison, Inc., 2000—, Montefiore Med. Ctr., 2001-; mem. NSF adv. bd. Comprehensive Regional Ctr. for Minorities, NY chmn., 1990-93; trustee, mem. exec. com. Rensselaer Poly. Inst., Troy, NY, 1991—, Woodrow Wilson Nat. Fellowship Found., 2004—, Commn. on Ind. Colls. and Univs., 2004—,; chmn. NYC Chancellor's Task Force on Sci. Edn., 1992-93; task force on minorities in sci. Nat. Inst. Environ. Health Scis., 1994; bd. govs. All Nations Alliance for Minority Participation in Sci. and Engring., 1995-2000; trustee Poly. U., Bklyn., 1997-2000, Consolidated Edison, Inc., NY, Commission on Independent Colleges and Universities (cIcu), 2004-; mem. Pres.' Info. Tech. Adv. Com. Socio-Econ. and Workforce Panel, 1998—; mem. Congl. Commn. on Advancement of Women and Minorities in Sci. and Tech., 1999-2000. Recipient George Arents Pioneer medal in physics Syracuse U., 1993, Drexel U. Centennial medal, 1992, Presdl. award for excellence in math., sci. and engring. mentoring, 1996, EPIC award US Dept. Labor, 1998, Disting. Svc. award for sci. and tech. Poly. U., 1999, Leon J. Obermeyer award, City Phila. Bd. Edn.; named Black Achiever in Industry, YMCA, NYC, 1987; Simon Guggenheim scholar Guggenheim Found., Phila., 1963-67. Fellow AAAS (com. on sci., engring. and pub. policy 1990-96), NY Acad. Scis. (pres. coun. 1991—),; mem. Am. Phys. Soc. (pres. cir. 1997-2002), Nat. Acad. Scis., Nat. Acad. Engring. and Inst. Medicine, Nat. Acad. Engring. (steering com. on engr. of 2020), Sigma Pi Sigma. Achievements include extending bootstrap model to SU(4)-symmetric strong interaction physics; responsible for third generation satellite 3 power system development. Office: The Cooper Union for the Advancement of Sci and Art Cooper Sq New York NY 10003-7120 E-mail: campbell@cooper.edu.

CAMPBELL, GEORGE EMERSON, lawyer; b. Piggott, Ark., Sept. 23, 1932; s. Sid and Mae (Harris) C.; m. Anna Claire Janes, June 22, 1960 (dec. Mar. 1971); children: Dianne, Carole; m. Joan Stafford Rule, Apr. 7, 1973. JD, U. Ark., Fayetteville, 1955. Bar: Ark. 1955, U.S. Supreme Ct. 1971. Law clk. to judge Ark. Supreme Ct., 1959-60; mem. Rose Law Firm, P.A., Little Rock, 1960—; Del. 7th Ark. Constl. Conv., 1969-70; regional v.p. Nat. Mcpl. League, 1974-86. Mem. Ark. Ednl. TV Commn., 1976-92, chmn., 1980-82, 88-91. Chmn. bd. Pulaski County Law Libr., 1980—; bd. dirs. Ark. Arts Ctr., 1991-95, sec. 1992-93), Ark. Symphony Orch. Soc., 1982-87, Ark. Capital Corp., pres. 2001-03, chmn. 2003-05; bd. dirs. Ark. Cert. Devel. Corp., Downtown Partnership, 1978-2002, Youth Home Inc., 1986-92, pres., 1991-92; bd. dirs. Ark. Ednl. TV Found., 1984-92, chmn., 1988-91. With USNR, 1955-77, comdr. ret. Fellow Am. Bar Found.; mem. ABA, Ark. Bar Assn., Pulaski County Bar Assn., Am. Law Inst. (life mem.), Nat. Assn. Bond Lawyers Office Fax: 501-375-1309. E-mail: gcampbell@roselawfirm.com.

CAMPBELL, GILBERT SADLER, surgeon, educator; b. Toronto, Ont., Can., Jan. 4, 1924; s. Gilbert S. and Ellen (Thorson) C.; m. Dorothy Jean Nugent, Sept. 18, 1947 (div. 1960); children: Kathryn Ellen, Rebecca Sadler, Thomas Kim, William Riley; m. Joan Louise Hancock, Sept. 28, 1961; children: Susan Muffin, John Gilbert. Student, Hampden Sydney Coll., 1939-40; BA, U. Va., 1943, MD, 1946; MS, U. Minn., 1949, PhD, 1954. Intern U. Minn. Hosps., Mpls., 1946-47, tchg. asst., 1947-49, researcher Am. Cancer Soc., 1951-53, sr. surgery resident, 1953-54; instr. physiology U. Minn., Mpls., 1948-49, instr. surgery, 1954-55, asst. prof., 1955-58; prof. surgery U. Okla., Oklahoma City, 1958-65; prof. surgery and thoracic surgery U. Okla. Med. Ctr., Oklahoma City, 1958-65; prof. surgery, chief thoracic surgery U. Ark. for Med. Scis., Little Rock, 1965-90; cons. surgery Little Rock VA Hosp, 1965-90, Ark. Children's Hosp., Little Rock, 1973-90; mem. courtesy staff Ark. Bapt. Med. Ctr., Little Rock, 1972-90; prof. emeritus, 1990—. Contbr. articles in field to med. jours. Served to capt. U.S. Army, 1949-51. Decorated Purple Heart, Bronze Star with oak leaf cluster, Silver Star with oak leaf cluster U.S. Army; Mary R. Markle scholar, 1954-59; recipient Horsley prize U. Va., 1954; named Surgery Alumnus of Yr. U. Minn., 1983; named to U. Ark. Medicine Hall of Fame. Mem. Am. Assn. Thoracic Surgery, AMA (ho. of dels. 1976-82), Am. Physiol. Soc., Am. Surg. Assn., Halsted Soc. (pres. 1978), Internat. Cardiovascular Soc. (v.p. N. Am. Chpt. 1973), Societe Internationale de Chirurgie, Soc. Thoracic Surgeons, Soc. Univ. Surgeons, Soc. Vascular Surgery, So. Surg. Assn. (1st v.p. 1981), Western Surg. Assn., S.W. Surg. Congress (pres. 1980), Raven Soc., Alpha Omega Alpha Home: 66 River Ridge Rd Little Rock AR 72227-1526

CAMPBELL, HENRY CUMMINGS, librarian; b. Vancouver, BC, Can., Apr. 22, 1919; s. Henry and Margaret (Cummings) C.; m. Sylvia Woodsworth, Sept. 13, 1943; children— Shiela (Mrs. David Macrae), Bonnie, Robin. BA, U. B.C., 1940; BLS, U. Toronto, 1941; MA, Columbia U., 1949. Librarian, film producer Nat. Film Bd., Can., Ottawa, 1941-46; with Secretariat UN, N.Y., 1946-48, UNESCO, Paris, 1949-56; chief librarian Toronto (Can.) Pub. Library, 1956-78; gen. mgr. Cinfolink Svcs., Toronto, 1994—. Lectr. U. Toronto Sch. Libr. Sci., 1970-71; cons. on info. systems and libr. svcs. Canadian Govt. Social Sci. Rsch. Coun. Can., UNESCO; active State Sci. and Tech. Commn., Beijing, China, 1991—, China Internet Info. Svcs., 1997—. Author: How To Find Out About Canada, 1967, Canadian Libraries, 1972, rev. edit., Early Days on the Great Lakes, 1971, The Public Library in the Urban Metropolitan Setting, 1973, Development of Public Library Systems and Services, 1982, Computer Information Systems in the People's Republic of China, Cinfolink Directory of Information Services in China and Hong Kong, 1993-94, 1993, Cinfolink Annual Review of Information Services in China, 1995-96, 1996, Looking for Harrison, 1993, Cinfolink China Internet Directory, 2002, (with Joachim Wieder) IFLA: A History 1927-2002, 2002. Recipient Prof. Kawla award for Library and Info. Sci., 1984 Fellow IFLA (hon.); mem. Internat. Assn. Met. City Librs. (pres. 1971-74), Canadian Libr. Assn. (pres. 1973-74), Ont. Continuing Edn. Assn. (pres. 1966), Fedn. Can.-China Friendship Socs. (pres. 1985-88), Ex Libris Assn. (pres. 2002—).

CAMPBELL, IAN DAVID, opera company director; b. Brisbane, Australia, Dec. 21, 1945; came to U.S., 1982; m. Ann Spira; children: Benjamin, David. BA, U. Sydney, Australia, 1967. Prin. tenor singer The Australian Opera, Sydney, 1967-74; sr. music officer The Australia Council, Sydney, 1974-76; gen. mgr., stage dir. The State Opera of South Australia, Adelaide, 1976-82; asst. artistic adminstr. Met. Opera, N.Y.C., 1982-83; gen. dir. San Diego Opera, 1983—. Guest lectr. U. Adelaide, 1978; guest prof. San Diego State U., 1986—; cons. Lyric Opera Queensland, Australia, 1980-81; bd. dirs. Opera Am., Washington, 1986-95, 1997-2001, 2004—, chmn., 2001-04; chmn. judges Met. Opera Auditions, Sydney, 1989, Masterclasses, Music Acad. of the West, 1993-96. Producer, host San Diego Opera Radio Program, 1984-2001, At the Opera with Ian Campbell, 2001--; stage director La Bohème, 1981, 2005 (San Diego Opera), The Tales of Hoffmann, 1982 (both in South Australia), Falstaff (San Diego Opera), 1999, Cavalleria Rusticana/Pagliacci (Santa Barbara Grand Opera), 1999, Il Trovatore (San Diego Opera), 2000, Tosca (San Diego Opera), 2002, Katya Kabanova (San Diego Opera), 2003, La Traviata (San Diego Opera), 2004. Mem., bd. dirs. San Diego Conv. and Visitors Bur., 1997-2002. Recipient Peri award Opera Guild So. Calif., 1984; named Headliner of Yr., San Diego Press Club, 1991, Father of Yr., San Diego, 1997. Fellow: Australian Inst. Mgmt.; mem.: Rotary, San Diego Press Club. Avocation: golf. Office: San Diego Opera 1200 3rd Ave Fl 18 San Diego CA 92101-4112 E-mail: ian.campbell@sdopera.com.

CAMPBELL, JACQUELINE GLASS, history professor; arrived in US, 1984; d. Gerald and Sylvia Mildred Glass; children: Stephanie F. Bindman, Justin A. Bindman, Daniel G.L. Bindman. BA summa cum laude, U. South Fla., Tampa, 1992; MA, Duke U., Durham, NC, 1995, PhD, 2000. Prof. history U. Conn., Storrs, 2001—. Author: (book) When Sherman Marched North from the Sea: Resistance on the Confederate Home Front, 2003. Mem.: Am. Hist. Assn. Office: Univ Connecticut Dept History 241 Glenbrook Rd U 2103 Storrs CT 06269

CAMPBELL, JACQUELYN C., community health nurse; b. Camden, NJ, Aug. 2, 1946; d. Joseph and Dorothy (Cutler) Bowman; 1 child, Christina, Bradley. BSN, Duke U., 1968; MSN, Wright State U., 1980; PhD in Nursing, U. Rochester, 1986. RN, Mich. Instr. Sinclair Community Coll., Dayton, Ohio, 1976-79, Wayne State U. Coll. Nursing, Detroit, 1980-82, mem. faculty, 1984—, assoc. prof., 1988—; teaching asst. U. Rochester (N.Y.) Sch. Nursing, 1982-84; Anna D. Wolf Endowed Prof., Sch. Nursing Johns Hopkins U., associate dean for the Ph.D. program and res., Sch. Nursing. Bd. dirs. Family Violence Prevention Fund, House of Ruth; mem. violence rev. panel NIMH, Washington. Co-author: Nursing Care of Victims of Family Violence, 1984 (AJN Book of Yr.); author: To Have & To Fix, Cultural Perspectives on Wife Beating, 2d edit., 1999, Assessing Dangerousness: Violence by Sexual Offenders, Batterers and Child Abusers, 1994, Ending Domestic Violence: Changing Public Perceptions/Halting the Epidemic, 1997, Empowering Survivors of Abuse: Health Care for Battered Women and their Children, 1998, Family Violence and Nursing Practice, 2003, Nursing Care Survivors of Family Violence 2d edit., 1993; mem. editorial bd. to sci. jours.; contbr. articles to profl. jours. V.p., bd. dirs. Women's Justice Ctr., Ann Arbor, Mich., 1987—; pres. Coun. on the Status of Women, Detroit, 1988-92; support group facilitator My Sister's Place, Detroit, 1989-92; mem. adv. bd. Wayne County Adv. Bd. Interpersonal Violence, Detroit, 1991-92, adv. panel Robert Wood Johnson Found., Princeton, N.J., 1990-92; prin. investigator NIH, NCNR, 1990—; mem. Dept. Defense Task Force on Domestic Violence. Recipient First ward NIH, 1987-92; W.K. Kellogg Found., 1990-93. Mem. ANA (chair task force on violence 1991-92), APHA, Am. acad. Nursing, a.A.N. award 1988), Inst. Medicine, Midwest Nursing Rsch. Soc. (Helen Werley new investigator 1992), Nursing Rsch. Consortium on Violence and Abuse, Nursing Network on Violence Against Women. Democrat. Avocation: tennis. Office: Johns Hopkins Univ Sch Nursing 525 N Wolfe St Baltimore MD 21205-2110

CAMPBELL, JAMES L., military career officer; b. Ft. Benning, Ga., Aug. 16, 1949; m. Carol Anderson; children: Scott, Casey. Grad., U. Mo.; BS in Phys. Edn., 1971; MS in Phys. Edn., U. Ill.; MA in Nat. Security & Strategic Studies, Naval War Coll.; grad., U.S. Army Command & Gen. Staff, Naval War Coll. Commd. 2nd lt. US Army, advanced through grades to lt. gen.; dir. instrn. dept. phys. edn. US Mil. Acad.; with 15th Battalion, 4th combat support tng. brigade US Army, Ft. Jackson, SC, co. comdr. 1st Battalion, 32d Infantry, 2nd Infantry Divsn. Camp Casey, rifle platoon leader, reconnaissance platoon leader, comdr. 4th Bn., 27th Inf., 25th Inf. Divsn. (Light) Schofield Barracks, Hawaii, 1984—89, ACofS, G3, 9th Inf. Divsn. (Motorized) Ft. Lewis, Wash., dep. chief staff I Corps, chief of staff, comdr. 1st Brigade, 10th Mountain Divsn., exec. officer to the chief of staff, comdr. UN Quick Reaction Force, dir., multinational force staff, comdr., multinational divsn. (North), comdr. Joint Task Force-Full Acctg., asst. divsn. comdr., 25th Inf. Divsn. (Light), asst. divsn. comdr. (ops.), 25th Inf. Divsn. (Light), 1996—99, commdg. gen. 10th Mountain Divsn. (Light) Fort Drum, NY, 1999—2002, comdr., Pacific (USARPAC) Fort Shafter, Hawaii, 2002—04, exec. officer, army staff, Off of the Chief of Staff Wash., DC, 2004—. Decorated Def. Superior Svc. medal with oak leaf cluster, Legion of Merit with 2 oak leaf clusters, Bronze star, Meritorious Svc. medal with 3 oak leaf clusters, Army Commendation medal, Army Achievement medal. Office: Office Army Chief of Staff 1500 Army Pentagon Washington DC 20310-1500

CAMPBELL, JAMES P., utilities executive; b. New York, N.Y., Sept. 14, 1957; BS in Mktg., St. John's U.; MBA, Hofstra U. Sales/mktg. rep. GE Appliances, 1981, mgr. microwave cooking products Louisville, 1992—99; v.p. sales/mktg. GE, 1999—2001; pres., CEO GE Appliances, 2001—02; CEO GE Consumer Products, 2002—.

CAMPBELL, JAMES R., transportation executive; b. July 16, 1941; s. Ray E. and Anne Louise (Wooten) Campbell. BS, U. Houston, 1965; postgrad., Case Western Res. U., 1967-68, Yale U., 1990. Personnel asst. The Standard Oil Co., Cleve., 1966-68; dir. equal opportunity programs Turner Constrn. Co., Cleve., 1968-73; employment project dir. Nat. Assn. Drug Abuse Problems, N.Y.C., 1973-74; exec. dir. The Cuyahoga Plan Ohio, Cleve., 1974-77; dir. EEO compliance and cmty. activities the continental Group, Inc., Stamford, Conn., 1978-85; cons. human resources James Campbell & Assocs., Inc., 1985-88; asst. v.p. strategic human resource planning MTA N.Y.C. Transit, Bklyn., 1990—93, acting dep. v.p. employee resources, 1993—96, asst. v.p. employee resources, 1988—90; v.p. adminstrn. MTA Long Island Bus, Garden City, NY, 1996—. Expert witness HUD, 1970, U.S. Ho. of Reps. subcom., 1972. Contbr. Chmn. task force, mem. steering com. Cleve. Fedn. Cmty. Devel. Manpower Planning & Devel. Commn., 1971—73; mem. cmty. adv. bd. Cleve. Press, 1972; mem. Pres.'s com. Employment of People With Disabilities, 1985—91. With USAF, 1958—62, Japan. Recipient Key to City, Cleve., 1970, Outstanding Cmty. Svc. award, Urban League Cleve., 1972. Mem.: ASTD, Nat. Tartan Day Com., N.Y. Human Resources Planning Soc., Pers. Accreditation Inst., Soc. Human Resources Mgmt. (life-time profl. cert. advanced level), Human Resource Assn. N.Y., St. George's Soc. N.Y., St. Andrew's Soc. N.Y. State, Clan Campbell Edn. Found. (trustee 2000—), Clan Campbell Soc. (dep. commr. N.Y.C. 1998—2000, trustee 2000—, N.Am. chpt.), N.Y. Caledonian Club (chieftain 1999, trustee 2000—02, chief 2001—02, dir. 2004—), Omicron Delta Kappa (circle v.p. 1965, Gold Key 1965). Home: 504 W 110th St Apt 8-d New York NY 10025-2008 Office: MTA LI Bus 700 Commercial Ave Garden City NY 11530-6410 Personal E-mail: jamesrcampbell1@rcn.com.

CAMPBELL, JAMES ROBERT, retired bank executive; b. Rochester, Minn., May 24, 1942; s. Donald William and Alice Marie (Gray) Campbell; m. Carmen Dawn Starkson, July 11, 1964; children: Peter Ian, Kathryn Ann. BS in Bus, U. Minn., 1964. Comml. banking officer Norwest. Nat. Bank Mpls., 1964-67, asst. v.p., 1967-71, sr. v.p. nat. dept., 1976-79, pres., COO,

1984-86; pres., dir. Lease N.W., Inc., Mpls., 1971-75, Norwest Bank Omaha N.A., 1979-82; regional pres. Norwest Corp.-Norwest Banks, 1982-84; pres., CEO Wells Fargo Bank, Mpls., 1986-95, chmn. bd. dirs., 1995—2002; chmn. bd. Norwest Bank Minn. N.A., Mpls., 1995-98; ret., 2002; interim dean Carlton Sch. Mgmt., U. Minn. Group exec. v.p. Wells Fargo & Co., 1998—2002; exec. v.p. Norwest Corp.; bd. dirs. Allianz U.S. A., Marvin Lumber & Cedar Co., Cretex Cos. Inc., Lifetouch, Inc., Forsythe Appraisals, Inc. Chmn. The Itasca Project; bd. dirs. Mpls. Inst. Arts, U. Minn. Found. Mem.: World Pres. Orgn., Minn. Exec. Orgn., Royal Poinciena Golf Club, Bay Colony Golf Club, Spring Hill Golf Club, Mpls. Club, Minikahda Club. Presbyterian. Home: 5521 Woodcrest Dr Edina MN 55424-1651 Office Phone: 612-667-9141. Business E-Mail: James.r.campbell@wellsFargo.com.

CAMPBELL, JAMES ROBERT (BOB CAMPBELL), reporter; b. Amherst, Tex., Oct. 19, 1946; s. Howard Norman and Joyce Greathouse Campbell; m. Ruth Ann Friedberg, Apr. 25, 2004; children: Colin, Casey, Paige. BA, West Tex. A&M U., 1970, postgrard., 1995—96. Secondary cert. Tex. Edn. Agy. Reporter Amarillo (Tex.) Globe-News, Grand Junction (Colo.) Daily Sentinel, 1969—74, Abilene (Tex.) Reporter-News, Lubbock (Tex.) Avalanche-Jour., 1974—85, Snyder Daily News, Lamesa Press-Reporter, Tex., 1987—91; English tchr. Littlefield and Lubbock Ind. Schs. Dists., 1995—97; editor Colorado City (Tex.) Record, 1998—2002; reporter Odessa (Tex.) Am., 2002—04, Midland (Tex.) Reporter-Telegraph, 2004—. Author: (poetry) Billy the Kid's Last Dance, 2002; musician: The Midnight Ramblers, 1979—84, Texas-Born Man, 2001; columnist Lubbock Mag., 1997—98; contbr. poetry to Caprock Sun. Recipient 1st pl. award for photography, West Tex. Press Assn., 1989. Mem.: Tex. Press Assn., Sheriffs Assn. Tex. Democrat. Mem. Ch. Of Christ. Avocations: guitar, songwriting, writing poetry and prose, running, weightlifting.

CAMPBELL, JANE LOUISE, mayor; b. May 19, 1953; d. Paul and Joan (Brown) C.; m. Hunter Morrison, Dec. 8, 1984; children: Jessica Elizabeth, Catherine Joanna. BA in History, U. Mich., 1974; MS in Urban Studies, Cleve. State U., 1980. Mem. State of Ohio Ho. of Reps. 11th dist., Columbus, 1984—92, majority whip, 1992—2000; mayor City of Cleve., 2001—. Apptd. mem. Nat. Com. on Welfare Reform; mem. Cuyahoga County Plan Commn., Fin. and Appropriations Com., Ways and Means Com., Aging and Housing Com.; active Nat. Coun. State Legislators, vice-chair Human Svcs. Com., Children, Families and Youth Com., past pres. Women's Network, mem. Federal Budget and Taxation Com.; chair Abused, Neglected Children Oversight Com.; vice-chair Select Com. on Child Abuse and Juvenile Justice, 1989; mem. gov. task force on Adolescent Sexuality and Pregnanacy, 1986, com. to Study Ohio's Sch. Found. Program Distribution of State Funds to Sch. Dists., 1991; exec. dir. Friends of Shaker Square, 1982-84; nat. field dir. ERAmerica, 1979-82; founding dir. Womenspace, 1975-79. Elder Heights Christian Ch. Recipient Legislative Leadership award Ohio Psychological Assn., 1986, Legislative award Ohio Hunger Task Force, 1987, Recognition award Ohio Primary Care Assn., 1987, Dean's Disting. Alumni award Cleve. State Univ., 1987, Hall of Fame award Nat. Senior Citizens, 1988, State Public Official of the Year award Ohio Chpt. Nat. Assn. of Social Workers, 1988, Found. award Ohio Chpt. ACLU, 1988, Legislative award Ohio Assn. of Counseling and Devel., 1989, Ohio Assn. of County Bds. of Mental Retardation/Developmental Disabilities award, 1989, Cancer Fighter award Ireland Cancer Ctr., 1990, Legislative award Ohio Human Svcs. Dirs. Assn., 1990, Hosephine Irwin award Womenspace, 1991, Spcl. Recognition award Providence House, 1991, Citizen award Ohio Assn. for the Edn. of Young Children, 1991, Legislator of the Year award Greater Cleve. Nurses Assn., 1991, Legislative award Nat. Assn. of Sch. Psychologists, 1992, Outstanding Svc. award Public Children's Svcs. Assn., 1992., numerous others. Democrat. Office: Cleveland City Hall 601 Lakeside Ave Rm 202 Cleveland OH 44114 Office Phone: 216-664-3990. Business E-Mail: mayorcampbell@city.cleveland.oh.us.

CAMPBELL, JANE TURNER, retired realtor, retired secondary school educator, retired adult education educator, retired real estate broker; b. Macon, Mo., July 8, 1931; d. Thomas Freeman and Rena Ellen (Vandiver) Turner; m. Duard Ray McDonald, Aug. 25, 1952 (div. 1955); m. Ian MacCallum Campbell, Mar. 28, 1958; children: Colin Turner, Clay Ian. BS in Edn., U. Mo., 1953; postgrad., San Diego State Coll., 1955-57, UCLA, 1958. Cert. secondary sch. tchr. Calif., Ill., N.J., lic. real estate salesperson, broker N.J., Pa., Mo., real estate broker N.J., Pa. Tchr. Hallsville (Mo.) HS, 1953-54; co-owner McDonalds' Clothiers, Wewoka, Okla., 1954-55; tchr., class advisor Imperial (Calif.) HS, 1955-58, Temple City (Calif.) HS, 1958-59; prof. Coll. San Mateo, Calif., 1965-70, McHenry County Coll., Crystal Lake, Ill., 1972-76, Waubonsee Coll., Aurora, Ill., 1976-79; tchr., adminstr. Purnell Sch., Pottersville, NJ, 1980-86; realtor Sig Kuhne Realtors, Milford, NJ, 1986-89, Burgdorff Realtors, Inc., Pittstown, NJ, 1989-94, ret., 1994. Co-founder Audio, Verbal and Tutorial Ctr. McHenry County Coll., Crystal Lake, Ill., 1975—77. Author: Shorthand I, Shorthand II, Shorthand III, Office Procedures I, Bookkeeping I, Bookkeeping II, Bookkeeping III, Medical Secretary, Legal Secretary, Office Procedures II, Business Law, Office Machines I, Office Machines II for AVT. Chair Holland Twp. (N.J.) Hist. Preservation Commn., 1989—95; chairperson Delaware Valley Autumn Antique Show, Milford, NJ, 1988—93; chair Christmas Project, Hunterdon County, NJ, 1988—94. Mem.: N.J. Assn. Realtors, Hunterdon County Bd. Realtors (Cmty. Svc. award 1988), Golden Talents (pres., v.p., trustee 1988—91), Holland Twp. Women's Club (chairperson Clarence Carter Night 1988), Pi Beta Phi (province pres.). Republican. Episcopalian. Avocations: swimming, boating, antiques, genealogy. Fax: 435-946-3508. Personal E-mail: Ianjane1@aol.com.

CAMPBELL, JANET CORAL, architect; b. Albuquerque, Nov. 24, 1953; d. Ovid Sylvester Campbell II and Evelyn Grace (Kistler) London; m. Rodney Lee Pope, June 12, 1977 (div. 1991). BS, Ga. Inst. Tech., 1975, MArch, 1977; MS in Real Estate, Ga. State U., 1989. Registered architect, Ga. Assoc. planner Metro Atlanta Rapid Transp. Authority, 1977-78; project designer Toombs, Amisano & Wells, Atlanta, 1978-80; project arch., designer Thompson, Ventielett & Steinback, Atlanta, 1980-84; project arch. Dimery, Corbet & West, Atlanta, 1984; arch., renderer Dan Harmon & Assocs., Atlanta, 1984-85; pres. Chantilly Properties, Inc., Atlanta, 1985-91; prin. Campbell Pope & Assocs., Atlanta, 1985-91; arch. J.D. & Assocs., Burlingame, Calif., 1991; sr. arch. U. Calif., San Francisco, 1991—99; prin. Campbell and Assoc., San Francisco, 1992—; arch. Skidmore, Owings & Merrill, 2002, Soga and Assoc., 2003—. Exhibitions include High Mus., Atlanta, 1982. Central com. 12th dist. Rep. Party, San Francisco, 2005—. Recipient Nat. Inst. for Arch. Edn. award, 1975. Mem. AIA (bd. dirs. Ga. chpt. 1989-91, Excellence of Studies award 1977), Midwestern Roofing Contractors Assn. (assoc.). Republican. Mem. Plymouth Brethren Ch. Avocations: painting, reading. Home: 2 Parker Ave # 302 San Francisco CA 94118-2659 Office Phone: 415-261-2613. E-mail: campbellarchitec@aol.com.

CAMPBELL, JEFFREY C., pharmaceutical executive; b. July 16, 1960; m. Susan Campbell; children: Grace, Eric, Patrick. BA in Econ., Stanford U., 1985; MBA, Harvard U., 1990. Cert. pub. acct. Deloitte Haskins & Sells, 1986—88; sr. analyst, fin. Am. Airlines, 1990—92, mgr., fin. planning, 1992—93, mng. dir., internat. planning, 1993—95, mng. dir., corp. fin. and banking, 1995—98, v.p., corp. devel., treas., 1998—2000, v.p., Europe, 2000—02, sr. v.p., fin., CFO, 2002—03; sr. v.p., CFO McKesson Corp., San Francisco, 2004—. Office: McKesson Corp One Post St San Francisco CA 94104

CAMPBELL, JOAN VIRGINIA LOWEKE, secondary school educator, language educator; b. Detroit, Nov. 8, 1942; d. George Paul and Lolamae (Weians) L.; m. James Bachelder Campbell, July 26, 1975; 1 child, James Bachelder Loweke. *Parents George Paul and Lolamae Weians Loweke, whose families came to America as farmers and small business entrepreneurs, were of German and Scandinavian decent. Both were self-made individuals, from families of seven children, supported their families throughout the early twentieth century disasters, and dedicated their lives to education. Lolamae Weians was an elementary and secondary teacher, and George Paul retired as professor emeritus in engineering and celestial mechanics at Wayne State University in Detroit, Michigan. He is credited as the initiator, in the 1950's, of the first aerospace program in the United States.* BA in German, French, Hope Coll., 1965; student, U. Cologne (Germany), 1964, U. Salzburg (Austria), 1968, U. Stuttgart (Germany), 1970-71, Sampere Inst., Madrid, 1982, Millersville (Pa.) State U., 1983, 84, 90, Va. Poly. Inst. and State U., 1976-77, 80-84, U. Va., 1996-97, 98-99. Cert. secondary tchr., Mich., Kans., Va. Tchr. French and German I, II Grand Haven (Mich.) Jr. H.S., 1965-69; asst. instr. elementary and intermediate German U. Kans., Lawrence, 1969-70, 71-72; tchr. German I, II Ctrl. Jr. H.S., Lawrence, Kans., 1972-74; tchr. French I, II, sr. English Oskaloosa (Kans.) H.S., 1974-75; tchr. German I-IV Highland Park H.S., Topeka, 1975-76; tchr. French I-V, Spanish I and II Blacksburg (Va.) H.S., 1977—. Tchr. French, Spanish YMCS, YMCA evening courses, Blacksburg, Va., 1976-80; mem. audio visual com. Montgomery County Fgn. Lang. Collaborative Group, Blacksburg, 1984-87; chaperone Am. Inst. Fgn. Study, Germany, France, Spain, 1968-82, area adminstr. summer and winter programs abroad, Western Mich., 1968-69; chaperone Ednl. Adventures, Quebec City, Montreal, 1984, 90-91, 93-94, 98, Montgomery County Schs.; presenter in field. Author: The Gothic Cathedral, 1995. Mem. Internat. Host Family Orgn. Va. Poly. Inst. and State U., Blacksburg, 1977— Fulbright exch. fellow U. Kans., 1970-71, Fulbright fellow Goethe Insts., 1976, Rockefeller fellow Rockefeller Assn. and Nat. Endowment Humanities, 1986, NDEA fellow, 1966; recognized as Va. Gov.'s Sch. Outstanding Educator, 1990. Mem. Am. Assn. Tchrs. French (state and region IV U.S. Recognition effort, dedication and high scores on nat. French exams, 1988, 96, 97, founder La Soc. Hon. de Français for Outstanding Students in French Blacksburg chpt. 1977, state com., dist. adminstr. Le Grand Concours-Nat. French Exams 1980—), Am. Assn. Tchrs. Spanish and Portuguese, Am. Assn. Tchrs. German (life, Va. exec. com. sec. 1977-83, co-chmn. nat. German exams Va. chpt. 1984-87, state nominating com. 1984-87, chmn. 1984-85, life), Nat. Assn. Edn. (Blacksburg H.S. rep. 1980-82), Va. Assn. Edn., Montgomery County Assn. Edn., Assn. Supervision and Curriculum Devel., Fgn. Lang. Assn. Va. (life) Republican. Presbyterian. Avocations: gardening, hiking, travel, classical music, art history. Home: 3003 Mclean Ct Blacksburg VA 24060-8110 Office: Blacksburg HS 520 Patrick Henry Dr Blacksburg VA 24060-3106 Personal E-mail: jayhawk@vt.edu.

CAMPBELL, JOHN, ambassador; b. Washington, 1944; BA, MA, U. Va.; PhD, U. Wisconsin, 1970. Prof. British and French History Mary Baldwin Coll., Staunton, Va., 1970—75; foreign service officer US Dept. State, 1975—, political counselor Lagos, Nigeria, 1988—90, political counselor Pretoria/Cape Town, South Africa, 1993—96, deputy asst. sec., Bureau of Human Resources, US amb. to Nigeria, 2004—. State Dept. sr. fellow Woodrow Wilson Sch., Princeton U., 1990—91. Office: US Dept State 8300 Lagos Pl Washington DC 20521-8300 Office Phone: 234-9-523-0960. Office Fax: 234-9-523-0353.*

CAMPBELL, JOHN MICHAEL, lawyer; b. N.Y.C., Nov. 18, 1954; s. John Erin and Margaret Domenica Campbell; m. Karen Sue Ralstin, Mar. 13, 1976; children: Michael Aaron, Matthew Everett, Rebekah Michelle, Benjamin David. BS, U. Notre Dame, 1976; JD, Calif. Western Sch. Law, 1979. Bar: Calif. 1979, U.S. Dist. Ct. (so. dist.) Calif. 1979, U.S. Tax Ct. 1980, Fla. 1986, U.S. Dist. Ct. (mid. dist.) Fla. 1986, U.S. Ct. Mil. Appeals 1980. Asst. counsel U.S. Dept. Def., Orlando, Fla., 1985-87; assoc. gen. counsel Sea World, Inc., Orlando, 1987-92; sr. assoc. Holland & Knight, Orlando, 1992-94; ptnr. Campbell & Heavener, P.A., Casselberry, Fla., 1994-99; dep. gen. counsel Sunterra Corp., 2000—. Bd. dirs. Lake Eola Charter Sch., Orlando, 1997-98, Shepherd Care, Orlando, 1990-98. Maj. U.S. Army, 1980-85. Mem. Corp. Counsel Assn. Ctrl. Fla. (v.p. 1991-92). Republican. Baptist. Avocations: photography, scuba diving. Home: 5691 Pond Pine Pt Oviedo FL 32765-9441 Office: Sunterra Corp 1781 Park Center Dr Orlando FL 32835 Fax: 407-532-1140. E-mail: jcampbell@sunterra.com.

CAMPBELL, JOHN MORGAN, retired chemical engineer; b. Virden, Ill., Mar. 24, 1922; s. John M. and Ione Marie (Whittler) C.; m. Gwendolyn Thompson, Aug. 27, 1945; children: John Morgan, Robert, Charles. BS in Chem. Engring, Iowa State U., 1943; MS, U. Okla., 1948, PhD, 1951. Devel. engr. and supr. E.I. duPont de Nemours & Co., Inc., 1943-46; spl. instr. chem. engring. U. Okla., 1946-50; tech. adviser to v.p. Black Sivalls and Bryson, Oklahoma City, 1951-54; mem. faculty U. Okla. Sch. Petroleum Engring., 1954-69, chmn. dept., 1956-63, Erle P. Halliburton prof., 1963-69, dir., 1969, Petroleum Research Center, 1964-69. Pres. John M. Campbell & Co. (engring. counselors, mgmt. consultants), 1968-82; chmn. bd. Petrotech Ltd., Petroleum Learning Programs Ltd. Author: Oil Property Evaluation, 1959, Effective Technical Communications, 1969, Decision Methods For Petroleum Investments, 1969, Gas Conditioning and Processing, 2 vols., 1970, 6th edit., 2000, The Professional - From Puberty to Senility, 1970, Effective Communication for the Technical Man, 1972, Petroleum Reservoir Property Evaluation, 1973, Mineral Property Economics (3 vols.), 1978, Petroleum Evaluation for Financial Disclosures, 1983, Analysis and Management of Petroleum Investments, 1987, Successful Communication Strategies and Practices, 2000, Analysis and Management of Risky Investments, 2001; also numerous articles, chpts. in books. Recipient Hanlon award Gas Processors Assn., 1987, Disting. Achievement award Iowa State U., 1988, Disting. Grad. award Okla. U. Mem. NAE, AIME (hon. mem. 1994, exec. com. coun. edn., mineral industries econs. award 1989), Soc. Petroleum Engrs. (hon. mem. 1994, J.F. Caril award 1978, Arps award 1989), Am. Arbitration Assn. (arbitration panel), Internat. Petroleum Inst. (pres. 1968-82), Sigma Alpha Epsilon, Phi Lambda Upsilon, Pi Epsilon Tau. Clubs: Lion. Home: 6 Rustic Hills St Norman OK 73072-7411

CAMPBELL, JOHN RICHARD, pediatric surgeon; b. Pratt, Kans., Jan. 16, 1932; s. John Ross and Laura (Harkrader) C.; m. Susan Charlotte Baker, June 9, 1962; children: Kathryn, John Richard, George Ridgway. BA, U. Kans., 1954, MD, 1958. Diplomate Am. Bd. Surgery with cert. of spl. qualifications in pediatric surgery. Rotating intern Hosp. U. Pa., 1958-59; resident in gen. surgery U. Kans. Hosp., 1959-63; resident in pediatric surgery Children's Hosp. of Phila., 1965-67; asst. instr. U. Pa. Med. Sch., 1965-67; mem. faculty U. Oreg. Health Scis. Ctr., Portland, 1967—, prof. surgery emeritus, 2000, prof. surgery and pediatrics emeritus, 2000—, chief pediatric surgery, prof. emeritus surgery and pediats., 2000—; surgeon-in-chief Doernbecher Children's Hosp., Portland, 1967-99. Cons. VA, Shriners Crippled Children's hosps., Alaska Native Med. Ctr., Anchorage. Served to lt. comdr. M.C. USNR, 1963-65. Mem. A.C.S., Soc. Acad. Surgeons, Am. Acad. Pediatrics, Am. Pediatric Surg. Assn., Pacific Assn. Pediatric Surgeons, North Pacific Pediatric Soc., North Pacific Surg. Assn., Pacific Coast Surg. Assn., Portland Acad. Pediatrics, Portland Surg. Soc. Presbyterian. Office: Oreg Health Scis Univ 745 SW Gaines St # Cdw7 Portland OR 97239-2901 Office Phone: 503-494-7764. Business E-Mail: campbell@ohsu.edu.

CAMPBELL, JON R., diversified financial services company executive; b. Byron, Minn., Feb. 14, 1955; m. Susan Campbell. BSB, U. Minn., 1977. With Norwest Corp., 1977—98, regional credit trainee Omaha, 1977—79; from comml. banking officer to sr. level positions Norwest Bank, St. Paul, 1979—86; v.p., chief credit officer Twin Cities Cmty. Banking, 1986—87; sr. regional credit officer Minn. Cmty. Banking, 1987—88; regional mgr. Twin Cities Cmty. Banking, 1988—90; regional pres. for Ill. & Ind. Norwest Corp., 1990—93; pres. Norwest Bank, Ariz., 1993—98; (Norwest Corp. merged with Wells Fargo & Co., 1998); regional pres. Wells Fargo & Co., Phoenix, 1998—2000, Mpls., 2000—02, regional pres. Great Lakes region, 2002—; pres., CEO Wells Fargo Bank, Minn., 2002—. Exec. com. Minn. Bus. Partnership. Chmn. adv. bd. Grow Minn.!; bd. dirs. Greater Twin Cities United Way, Capital City Partnership, Minn. Orchestral Assn.; bd. trustees Mpls. Found.; bd. overseers Carlson Sch. Mgmt., U. Minn. Office: Wells Fargo & Co 90 S 7th St Minneapolis MN 55479*

CAMPBELL, JOSEPHINE ANNE CONRAD, news service executive; b. Evansville, Ind., Jan. 31, 1927; d. Owen McIntyre and Josephine Anne (Greene) C.; m. Donald Herman Campbell, Mar. 15, 1946 (dec. Mar. 3, 1988); children: Kathleen Mary, Carolyn Margret, Deborah Jean. Cub reporter Daytona Beach (Fla.) News-Jour., 1944-45; copy boy Washington Post, 1945-46; copy editor World Report Mag., Washington, 1946-47; mem. pub. rels. staff AMVETS, Washington, 1952-53; pub. rels. person Govt. Pakistan, Washington, 1953-55; Washington and UN corr. Daily NAWA-I-WAQT, Lahore, Pakistan, 1955-56; writer, editor USIA, 1956-86; founder, CEO Ecotopics Internat. News Svc., Ocean City, Md., 1986-98, Willits, Calif., 1998—. Columnist Prince George's Jour., 1994-2000. Chair White House/Justice Dept. Task Force on Sex Discrimination USIA Press Svc.; active Gov.'s Task Force to Examine State Pension Investment in South Africa, 1987; v.p. Am. Fedn. Govt. Employees, AFL-CIO, Local #1812, 1969—78, del. nat. conv., 1974—76; del. founding conf. Coalition Labor Union Women, 1974; exec. com. Prince George's County NCCJ, 1980—84; rep. Ocean City State Coastal and Watershed Resources adv. Com., 1991—98; steering com., commr. Worcester County Commn. for Women, 1995—98; active Friends of Ocean City Libr., 1988—, Friends of Willits Libr., 1999—; citizen's adv. bd. Willits News, 1999—2000, op-ed writer, 1999—. Jefferson fellow, George Washington U., 1980—81. Mem. NAACP (3d v.p. Worcester County 1992-98; Sonoma County, Calif. br. 1999—), ACLU (Prince George County exec. bd. 1975-81, chair, 85-88, Mendocino County exec. bd. 2003—), Nat. Writers Union Local 3, Nat. Press Club, Dog Writers Assn. Am., Women's Inst. Freedom of Press, Conservation Voters, Worldwatch, Nat. Resources Def. Coun., Mendocino County Nat. Women's Polit. Caucus, Women's Club Ocean City (2d v.p. 1996), Marine's Meml. Club. Democrat. Roman Catholic. Avocations: photography, poetry writing, political activism. Fax: 707-456-0713. Office Phone: 707-456-0841.

CAMPBELL, JUDITH E., retired insurance company executive; BA, Chestnut Hill Coll., 1969. With Chem. Bank, N.Y., sr. v.p. consumer sales and svc. delivery, head ops. and adminstrn. consumer banking, sr. v.p., 1991—92; with Consumer Banking, 1992—97; sr. v.p., chief info. officer, bd. dirs. N.Y. Life Ins. Co., NYC, 1997—. Bd. trustees Drew U. Office: NY Life Ins Co 51 Madison Ave New York NY 10010-1603

CAMPBELL, KARLYN KOHRS, speech educator; b. Blomkest, Minn., Apr. 16, 1937; d. Meinhard and Dorothy (Siegers) Kohrs; m. Paul Newell Campbell, Sept. 16, 1967 (dec. Mar. 1999). BA, Macalester Coll., 1958; MA, U. Minn., 1959, PhD, 1968; LHD (hon.), Mich. State U., 2004. Asst. prof. SUNY, Brockport, 1959-63; with The Brit. Coll., Palermo, Italy, 1964; asst. prof. Calif. State U., L.A., 1966-71; assoc. prof. SUNY, Binghamton, 1971-72, CUNY, 1973-74; prof. comms. studies U. Kans., Lawrence, 1974-86, dir. women's studies, 1983-86; prof. comms. studies U. Minn., Mpls., 1986—, dept. chair, 1993—96, 1999—2005. Inaugural Gladys Borchers lectr. U. Wis., Madison, 1974; vis. prof Dokkyo U., Tokyo, 2005-. Author: Critiques of Contemporary Rhetoric, 1972, rev. edit., 1997, Form and Genre, 1978, The Rhetorical Act, 1982, rev. edit. 2002, The Interplay of Influence, 1983, rev. edit., 2005, Man Cannot Speak for Her, 2 Vols., 1989, Deeds Done in Words, 1990, editor: Women Public Speakers in the United States, 1800-1925: A Bio-Critical Sourcebook, 1993, Quar. Jour. Speech, 2001-04; co-editor: Guilford Revisioning Rhetoric series, 1995-2000; mem. editl. bd. Comm. Monographs, 1977-80, Quar. Jour. Speech, 1981-86, 92-94, editor, 2001—, Critical Studies in Mass Comm., 1993-99, Rhetoric and Pub. Affairs, 1997-2000, Philosophy and Rhetoric, 1988-93; contbr. articles to profl. jours. Recipient Woolbert Rsch. award, 1987, Winans-Wichelns Book award, 1990, Ehninger Rsch. award, 1991, Elizabeth Andersch award, U. Ohio, 2004; Tozer scholar Macalester Coll., 1958, Tozer fellow, 1959; fellow Shorenstein Barone Ctr., JFK Sch. of Govt., Harvard, 1992; Disting. Woman scholar U. Minn., 2002. Mem. Nat. Comm. Assn. (disting. scholar award 1992, Francine Merritt award for significant contbns. to the lives of women in comm. 1996 Women's Caucus), Ctrl. States Speech Comm. Assn., Rhetoric Soc. Am., Phi Beta Kappa, Pi Phi Epsilon. Office: U Minn Dept Comm Studies 225 Ford Hall 224 Church SE Minneapolis MN 55455 Business E-Mail: campb003@umn.edu.

CAMPBELL, KATHERINE MARIE LANGREHR, elementary and secondary education educator; b. N.Y.C., Dec. 4, 1947; d. Anton A. and Katherine (Batky) Langrehr; m. Frederick Augustus Campbell, Nov. 4, 1967; children: Julie Ann, Alicyn Katherine. BA in History, U. Bridgeport, 1970; MS in Lang. Arts Edn., Ctrl. Conn. State U., 1992. Tchr. grades 3 and 5 Holy Rosary Parochial Sch., Bridgeport, Conn., 1968-71; outreach worker Migratory Children's Program Vernon (Conn.) Bd. Edn., 1980-81; sales rep. Procter & Gamble, Wilton, Conn., 1982-86; reading/math tutor Bennet Jr. H.S., Manchester, Conn., 1986-87; tchr. lang. arts Elisabeth M. Bennet Mid. Sch., Manchester, Conn., 1987-96, dept. head lang. arts, 1994-96; tchr. grade 5 Verplanck Elem. Sch., Manchester, 1996—2005; tchr. grade 4 Buckley Elem. Sch., Manchester, 2005—. Mem. content validation com. Nat. Bd. Profl. Teaching Stds., 1996; presenter in field. Mem. Gifted & Talented Bd. Vernon Bd. Edn., 1992-93; dir. Planning Bd. Emergency Shelter, Vernon, 1984-85; scout leader Girl Scouts Am., Vernon, 1979-80; treas., bd. dirs. PTO Vernon Elem. Sch., 1976-80. Recipient Celebration of Excellence award State of Conn., 1992; Conn. Writing Project fellow, 1989; nominee Heroes in Edn. award Readers Digest, 1992, Am. Tchrs. award Disney, 2001. Mem.: Internat. Reading Assn. Office: Buckley Elem Sch 250 Vernon St Manchester CT 06040

CAMPBELL, KEVIN P., oil industry executive; B in Computer Sci., Tex. A&M U. With Atlantic Richfield Co.; dir. info. sys. Tex. Industries, Inc.; v.p., CIO Hunt Oil, Dallas, 2002—. Mem.: Am. Heart Assn. (nat. info. tech. expert panel), Dallas/Ft. Worth Soc. Info. Mgmt. (chmn. exec. bd.), Nat. Eagle Scout Assn. (life). Office: Hunt Oil 1445 Ross at Field Fountain Place 1 Dallas TX 75202

CAMPBELL, KEVIN PETER, physiology and biophysics educator, researcher; b. Bklyn., Jan. 19, 1952; s. Miller Jerome and Anna L. (Telesco) C.; m. Anna A. Derragon, Jan. 5, 1974; children: Colleen, Kerry, David. BS in Physics, Manhattan Coll., 1973; MS, U. Rochester, 1976, PhD, 1979. Grad. fellow U. Rochester (N.Y.), 1973-77, teaching asst., 1976-78; Elon Huntington Hooker fellow dept. radiation biology and biophysics, U. Rochester (N.Y.), 1977-78; Med. Rsch. Coun. postdoctoral fellow U. Toronto, Ont., Can., 1978-81; asst. prof. dept. physiology and biophysics U. Iowa, Iowa City, 1981-85, assoc. prof., 1985-88, prof., 1988—, Found. Disting. prof., 1989—, Howard Hughes Med. Inst. investigator, 1989—. Mem. editorial bd. Jour. Biol. Chemistry, Circulation Rsch., Cell Calcium; reviewer for Nature, Jour. Clin. Investigation, Jour. Cell Biology, Proc. NAS, Archives Biochem. and Biophysics, Molecular Pharmacology, Biophys. Jour.; contbr. numerous articles and abstracts to profl. jours. Patentee immunogen conjugates and use; co-patentee in field. Grantee NIH, NSF, NATO, Muscular Dystrophy Assn., 1981—; recipient Amgen award Am. Society Biochemistry and Molecular Biology, 1994, Internat. Albert Fleckenstein award, G. Conte prize, Elsevier Sci. award. Mem. AAAS, Biophys. Soc. (officer 1988—), N.Y. Acad. Scis., Soc. Gen. Physiologists, Am. Physiology Soc., Am. Soc. Cell Biology, Am. Soc. Biochem. Chemists, Am. Heart Assn. (established investigator, coun. high blood pressure rsch., cell transport and metabolism rsch. study com. 1989—), Inst. Medicine, NAS, Sigma Xi (Bendix award), Phi Beta Kappa. Roman Catholic. Office: U Iowa HHMI 400 Eckstein Med Rsch Ctr Iowa City IA 52242

CAMPBELL, LEONARD M., lawyer; b. Denver, Apr. 12, 1918; s. Bernard Francis and May (Moran) C.; m. Dot J. Baker, Sept. 23, 1944; children: Brian T., Teri Pat, Thomas P. AB, U. Colo., 1941, LLB, 1943. Bar: Colo. 1943. With Gorsuch, Kirgis, 1948-88, sr. ptnr., 1951-88; city atty. Denver, 1951-53; of counsel Gorsuch, Kirgis LLC, 1989—2004. Cons. pub. utility matters Colo. Mcpl. League. Mem. Denver Charter Com., 1947; mgr. Safety and Excise for Denver, 1947-48; chmn. Denver Com. Human Relations, 1954; mem. Denver Planning Bd., 1950-51; mem. Bd. Water Commrs., Denver, 1965-70, pres., 1968-69; mem. Gov.'s Com. on Jud. Compensation, 1972; chmn. U. Colo. Law Alumni Devel. Fund, 1962. Served with USAAF, 1943-46. Mem. ABA, Colo. Bar Assn. (pres. 1978-79, Award of Merit 1967), Denver Bar Assn. (pres. 1969), Am. Coll. Trial Lawyers, Cath. Lawyers Guild Denver (pres. 1962, St. Thomas More award 1978), Nat. Inst. Mcpl. Law Officers (v.p.

1952), Colo. Judicial Inst. (Chancellor Chester Alter award 1987), Denver Athletic Club (sec. 1960-61, pres. 1962). Democrat. Roman Catholic. Home and Office: 3447 S Birch St Denver CO 80222-7212

CAMPBELL, LESLIE CAINE (CAINE CAMPBELL), writer, historian; b. New Orleans, June 5, 1932; s. George Alexander and Nell Ruble C.; m. Bettye Bryan, June 10, 1961; children: Cathryn Campbell Jordan, Roxane Campbell Rose. BS in Bus., Miss. State U., 1954; MA in History, U. Miss., 1964, PhD in History, 1967. Chmn. div. humanities Ark. Coll., Batesville, 1967-68; assoc. dean Sch. Arts and Scis. Auburn (Ala.) U., 1968-86, dean Coll. Liberal Arts, 1986-88, prof. history and journalism, 1988-92. Hartman lectr. U. Miss., 1983. Author: Two Hundred Years of Pharmacy, 1976 (Am. Inst. History of Pharmacy award 1977), A Reminder of Stones, 2001, Mickey, Do You Hear Them Singing?, 2004; contbg. author: Research Institutions and Learned Societies, 1982, Foundations, 1984; contbg. editor Nat. Forum, 1987-92; newsman NBC News-TV and Radio, 1962-66. With USN, 1955—58. NSF fellow, 1966; Challenge grantee NEH, 1980. Mem. Am. Assn. Univ. Adminstrs. (bd. dirs. 1987-90), Assn. Ala. Coll. Adminstrs. (pres. 1988). Office: 126 Summerhill Hoschton GA 30548

CAMPBELL, LEVIN HICKS, federal judge; b. Summit, NJ, Jan. 2, 1927; s. Worthington and Louise (Hooper) Campbell; m. Eleanor Saltonstall Lewis, June 1, 1957; children: Eleanor S., Levin H., Sarah H. AB cum laude, Harvard U., 1948, LLB, 1951; postgrad., Nat. Coll. State Judiciary, 1970; LLD (hon.), Suffolk U., 1975; LLD (hon.), Colby Coll., 1982. Bar: D.C. 1951, Mass. 1954. Assoc. firm Ropes & Gray, Boston, 1954—64; mem. Mass. Ho. of Reps., 1963—64; asst. atty. gen. State of Mass., 1965—66, spl. asst. atty. gen., 1966—67, 1st asst. atty. gen., 1967—68; assoc. justice Superior Ct. of Mass., 1969—72; judge U.S. Dist. Ct. Mass., Boston, 1972, U.S. Ct. Appeals (1st cir.), Boston, 1972—, chief judge, 1983—90, sr. judge, 1992—. Fellow Inst. of Politics J.F. Kennedy Sch. Govt. Harvard U., 1968—69, study group leader, 1980; faculty chmn. law sessions Salzburg Seminar in Am. Studies, 1981. Pres. Cambridge 9 Neighborhood Assn., 1960—62; treas. Cambridge Ctr. for Adult Edn., 1961—64; campaign chmn. Cambridge United Fund, 1965; mem. bd. overseers Boston Symphony Orch., 1969—75, 1977—80; pres. bd. overseers Shady Hill Sch., 1969—70; mem. vis. com. Harvard U. Press, 1958—64; v.p. Cambridge Cmty. Svcs.; corp. mem. SEA Ednl. Assn., 1982—; trustee Colby Coll., Waterville, Maine, 1981—90, 1991—99, Asheville (N.C.) Sch., 1987—98; overseer U.S. Constn. Mus. 1st lt. (j.g.) U.S. Army, 1951—54, Korea. Mem.: ABA, Mass. Hist. Soc. (coun. 1993—96, v.p. 1996—99, pres. 2000—02, coun. 2003—), U.S. Jud. Conf. (ct. adminstrn. com. 1975—83, chmn. subcom. on supporting pers. 1980—83, exec. com. 1985—90, ad hoc com. study jud. conf. 1987, fed. ct. study com. 1988—90, chmn. com. to rev. cir. coun. conduct and disability orders 1989—94, nat. commn. on jud. discipline and removal 1991—93), Boston Bar Assn., Mass. Bar Found. (long range planning com. 1999—2000), Am. Bar Found., Am. Law Inst. Office: US Ct of Appeals US Courthouse 1 Courthouse Way Ste 6720 Boston MA 02210-3008*

CAMPBELL, LEWIS B., aerospace technology executive; b. 1946; BS in Mech. Engrng., Duke U. Various mgmt. positions Gen. Motors, 1968-88, v.p., gen. mgr. Flint automotive divsn. Buick-Oldsmobile-Cadillac group, 1988-91, v.p., gen. mgr. GMC truck divsn., 1991-92; exec. v.p. Textron Inc., 1992-94, COO, 1992—98, pres., 1994-98, 2001—, CEO, 1998—, chmn., 1999—. Office: Textron Inc 40 Westminster St Providence RI 02903

CAMPBELL, LINZY LEON, molecular biology researcher, educator; b. Panhandle, Tex., Feb. 10, 1927; s. Linzy Leon and Eula Irene (McSpadden) C.; m. Alice P. Dauksa, Feb. 7, 1953. BA in Bacteriology and Chemistry, U. Tex., 1949, MA, 1950, PhD, 1952. Rsch. scientist U. Tex., 1947-51; predoctoral rsch. fellow NIH, 1951-52; postdoctoral rsch. fellow Nat. Microbiol. Inst., U. Calif. at Berkeley, 1952-54; asst. prof., then assoc. prof. Wash. State U., 1954-59; assoc. prof. Western Res. U. Sch. Medicine, 1959-62; sr. rsch. fellow USPHS, 1959-62; prof. microbiology U. Ill. at Urbana, 1962-72, head dept., 1963-71, dir. Sch. Life Scis., 1971-72; prof. microbiology, provost and v.p. acad. affairs U. Del., Newark, 1972-88, univ. rsch. prof. molecular bioscis., 1988-89, Hugh M. Morris rsch. prof. molecular bioscis., 1989—. Editorial bd.: Jour. Bacteriology, 1961-65; editor, 1964-65, editor-in-chief, 1965-77; Contbr. articles to profl. jours. Served with USNR, 1944-46. Fellow AAAS; mem. Am. Soc. Microbiology (chmn. publ. bd. 1965-80, councilor at large 1962-64, v.p. 1972-73, pres. 1973-74), Am. Soc. Biochemistry and Molecular Biology. Office: U Delaware Dept Biology 400 Morris Library Newark DE 19717 Office Phone: 302-831-6767. Business E-Mail: campbell@udel.edu.

CAMPBELL, LOUIS LORNE, mathematics professor; b. Winnipeg, Man., Can., Oct. 20, 1928; s. Elgin Smith and Jonina Solveig (Johnson) C.; m. Eha Johanson, June 12, 1954; children: Ian, Barry, Barbara. BSc, U. Man., 1950; MS, Iowa State U., 1951; PhD, U. Toronto., 1955. Def. sci. officer Def. Rsch. Bd., Ottawa, Ont., Can., 1954-58; asst. prof., then assoc. prof. U. Windsor, Ont., Can., 1958-63; assoc. prof., then prof. Queen's U., Kingston, Ont., Can., 1963-96, prof. emeritus, 1996—, head dept. math and stats., 1980-90. Contbr. articles to profl. publs. Fellow IEEE; mem. Can. Math. Soc. (treas. 1982-85), Can. Statis. Soc., Am. Math. Soc. Home: 153 Byron Crescent Kingston ON Canada K7M 1J2 Office: Queens U Dept Math and Stats Kingston ON Canada K7L 3N6 E-mail: campblll@mast.queensu.ca.

CAMPBELL, M. TRANT, lawyer; b. Norfolk, Va., Feb. 14, 1949; s. Allan Adams and Thirza (Trant) C.; m. Mary Kane; children: K. Thirza, Margaret E. BA in Eng. Lit., U. Va., 1971; JD, U. Conn., 1974. Bar: Mass. 1975, U.S. Dist. Ct. Mass. 1975. Assoc. Appleton, Kubicek, Rice & Mitchell, Springfield, Mass., 1974-77, ptnr., 1977-79, Allen & Fitzgerald, Springfield, 1979-80; sole practitioner Gordon and Campbell, Springfield, 1980-81; atty. Law Offices of Norris E. Dibble & M. Trant Campbell, Springfield, 1981-86; ptnr. Dibble, Campbell & Barba, Springfield, 1987-93; prin. Welch, Campbell & Barba, P.C., Springfield, 1993—. Gen. counsel Wilbraham Cmty. Assn. Inc., 1988—, Wilbraham Cares About Teens Inc., 1993—. Co-author, co-editor: Prosecutors Handbook, 1975. Chmn. Hampden County Probate Ct. mediation project, 1993-95, Hampden County Probate Ct. bench-bar com., 1995-1997; dir. Child and Family Svcs., Springfield, 1981-94, exec. com., 1984-94, pres. 1991-93; dir., trustee Oak Grove Cemetery, Springfield, 1976—, clk. 1979-84, pres. 1984-94; dir. Western Mass. Radio Reading Svc. Inc., 1985-87; overseer Bay State Health Systems, 1977—, med. edn. com. 1978; instr. Sexton Ednl. Ctr., 1981-82; chmn. Wilbraham Council on Aging, 1984-84; mem. Wilbraham Planning Bd., 1987-89, Wilbraham Commn. on Parks and Recreation, 1996-2002. Mem. Hampden County Bar Assn. (exec. com. young lawyers sect. 1978-82). Home: 7 Inwood Dr Wilbraham MA 01095-2025 Office: Welch Campbell & Barba 1500 Main St Springfield MA 01115-5608 E-mail: mtcampbell@welchcampbellbarba.com.

CAMPBELL, MARIA BOUCHELLE, lawyer, consultant; b. Mullins, S.C., Jan. 23, 1944; d. Colin Reid and Margaret Minor (Perry) C. Student, Agnes Scott Coll., 1961-63; AB, U. Ga., 1965, JD, 1967. Bar: Ga. 1967, Fla. 1968, Ala. 1969. Pvt. practice law, Birmingham, Ala., 1968-94; law clk. U.S. Cir. Ct. Appeals, Miami, Fla., 1967-68; assoc. Cabaniss, Johnston and Gardner, 1968-73; sec., counsel Ala. Bancorp., Birmingham, 1973-79; sr. v.p., sec., gen. counsel AmSouth Bancorp., 1979-84, exec. v.p., gen. counsel, 1984-94, AmSouth Bank, 1984-94; exec. asst. to rector Parish of Trinity Ch., N.Y.C., 1994-99; lawyer, mediator Sirote & Permutt, 1999-2001; cabinet ofcl., supt. of banks State of Ala., Montgomery, 2001—03; chmn. fin. svcs. SC& B Strategic Solutions, Montgomery, 2003—; of counsel Steiner Crum & Byars, Montgomery, 2003—. Bd. trustees Ptnrship for Women's Health Columbia U., 1996-2000; bd. dirs. Leake and Watts Childrens Svcs., Inc., 1997-99; lectr. continuing legal edn. programs; cons. to charitable orgns. Exec. editor Ga. Law Rev, 1966-67. Bd. dirs. St. Anne's Home, Birmingham, 1969-74, chancellor, 1969-74; bd. dirs. Children's Aid Soc., Birmingham, 1970-94, 1st v.p., 1988-90, pres., 1990-92; trustee Canterbury Cathedral Trust in Am., 1992—, Discovery 2000 Children's Mus., 1991-94, Soc. for Propagation of Christian Knowledge, 1991-93; bd. dirs. NCCJ, 1985-94, 99-2002, state chair, 1990-93; bd. dirs. Positive Maturity, 1976-78, Mental Health Assn., 1978-81, YWCA, 1979-80, Op. New Birmingham, 1985-87, pers. com., 1987-90, v.p., 1990-94; bd. dirs. Soc. for the Fine Arts U. Ala., 1986-89, Baptist Hospital Found. of Birmingham Inc., 1994-95, Alliance for Downtown N.Y., 1995-99, chair affordable housing initiative region 2020, 2000-01, Habitat for Humanity of Birmingham, 2000-02; commr. Housing Authority, Birmingham Dist., 1980-85, Birmingham Partnership, 1985-86, Leadership Birmingham, 1986—, program com., 1989-90, co-chair program com., 1990-91, mem.'s coun., 1999-2002; mem. pres. adv. coun. Birmingham So. Coll, 1988-92, chair bd. overseers Masters Program, 1990-94; mem. pres.'s cabinet U. Ala., 1990-95; trustee Ala. Diocese Episcopal Ch., 1971-72, 74-75, mem. canonical revision com., 1973-75, 89-91, liturg. commn., 1976-78, treas., chmn. dept. fin., 1979-83, 2000-03; mem. coun., 1983-87, chancellor, 1987-91, cons. on stewardship edn., 1981-94, dep. to gen. conv., 1985, 88, 91; mem. Standing Commn. on Constn. and Canons, 1988-94, mem. investment com., 2000—, vice chmn., 2003—; vestryman St. Luke's Episcopal Ch., 1991-94; bd. advisors So. region of Am. Soc. Corp. Secs., pres., 1992-94; cmty. advisor Jr. League Birmingham, 1992-93; mem. adv. bd. Cahaba River Soc., 1991-94; trustee St. Andrew's Sewanee Sch., 1998—; commr. Ala. Securities Commn., 2001-03; bd. dirs. Ala. Agrl. Commn., 2001-03; bd. dirs. Ala. Housing Fin. Authority, 2001-03; bd. regents Univ. of the South, 2002—; bd. dirs. Housing Enterprise Ctrl. Ala., 2003—, Fin. Investors of South, 2003—04, Associated Long Term Care Ins. Co., 2004—. Named One of Top 10 Women in Birmingham, 1989, One of Top 5 Women in Bus., 1993. Mem. ABA, State Bar Ga., Fla. Bar, Ala. Bar Assn., Birmingham Bar Assn., Am. Corp. Counsel Assn. (bd. dirs. Ala. 1984-89), Assn. Bank Holding Cos. (chmn. lawyers com. 1986-87), Greater Birmingham C. of C. (bd. dirs. 1988-94, exec. com. 1992-94, vice chmn., gen. counsel 1993-94), Kiwanis, The Church Club N.Y., Order of St. John of Jerusalem, Summit Club. Office: PO Box 668 Montgomery AL 36101 Office Phone: 334-956-6800. Personal E-mail: mcampbell@scbstrategic.com.

CAMPBELL, MARTA SMITH, librarian; b. Buffalo, June 25, 1941; d. Frank Lawrence Jr. and Alice (Bement) Smith; m. Harry William Campbell Jr., 1964 (div. 1981); children: Marta Christine, Jennifer Leigh. BA in English Lit., Bucknell U., Lewisburg, Pa., 1963; MLS, So. Conn. State U., New Haven, 1983. Libr. and head of collection mgmt. Westport (Conn.) Pub. Libr., 1983—. Democrat. Congregational. Home: 10 Bauer Pl Westport CT 06880 Office: Westport Pub Libr Westport CT 06880 Office Phone: 203-291-4842. Business E-Mail: mcampbell@westportlibrary.org.

CAMPBELL, MARTHA MADISON, educational administrator; b. Glen Ridge, N.J., May 9, 1941; d. Kenneth and Margaret Bruce (Macon) C.; m. Morton Park Iler, May 30, 1964 (div. July 1988); children: Douglas Gordon, Janet Madison, Bruce Campbell; m. David Malcolm Potts, March 25, 1995. BS, Wellesley Coll., 1963; MA, U. Colo., 1989, PhD, 1994. Statis. analyst A.C. Nielsen Co., N.Y.C., 1963; founder, dir. Population Speakout, Denver, 1988-93; mktg. cons. Specialized Comm., Denver, 1989-93; sr. program officer population David and Lucile Packard Found., Los Altos, Calif., 1994-99; lectr., co-dir. Ctr. Entrepreneurship Internat. Health & Devel., Sch. Pub. Health U. Calif., Berkeley, 2000—. Vis. scholar U. Calif. Berkeley, 1994; cons. Planned Parent Fedn. Am., 1990-91. Contbr. articles to profl. jours. Pres., founder Venture Strategies Health and Devel. Avocations: music, reading, hiking. Office: U Calif Sch Public Health 310 Warren Hall Berkeley CA 94720-7360 E-mail: mcbell@berkeley.edu.

CAMPBELL, MARY MARTHA GRIGGS, writer, public relations specialist, realtor; b. Chattanooga, June 12, 1946; d. Erick and Josephine (Davis) Griggs; 1 child, Martha Josephine. BA, U. Tenn., 1971. Staff writer News-Free Press, Chattanooga, 1972—74; editor publs. Provident Life & Accident Ins. Co., Chattanooga, 1975—80; dir. pub. rels. The McCallie Sch., Chattanooga, 1980—84; pub. rels. specialist Chattanooga-Hamilton County Bicentennial Libr., 1984—90; mgr. pub. rels. Siskin Hosp./Found., Chattanooga, 1990—96; dir. devel. Alpha Delta Pi Found., Atlanta, 1996—99; dir. devel. rsch. Columbia Coll., SC, 1999—2003; dir. Saluda Shoals Found., 2005—. Mem. Eastminster Presbyn. Ch.; bd. dirs. Moccasin Bend Coun. Girl Scouts U.S.A., Chattanooga, 1978—83, Dance Theatre Workshop, Chattanooga, 1980—81, Chattanooga Ballet, 1985—. Mem.: Coun. for Advancement and Support Edn., Internat. Assn. Bus. Communicators (chpt. pres. 1981), Greater Columbia C. of C. Office: 5705 Bush River Rd Columbia SC 29212 Office Phone: 803-213-2015.

CAMPBELL, MARY SCHMIDT, dean; b. Phila., Pennsylvania, Oct. 21, 1947; d. Harvey Nathaniel and Elaine Juanita (Harris) S.; m. George Campbell, Jr., Aug. 24, 1968; children: Garikai, Sekou, Britt Jackson. BA in Eng. Lit., Swarthmore Coll., 1969; MA in Art Hist., Syracuse U., 1973, PhD Humanities, 1982; ArtsD (hon.), Pace U., 1991; DFA (hon.), CCNY, 1992; PhD (hon), Colgate U., 1994; PhD (hon.), Coll. of New Rochelle, 2001. Art editor Syracuse New Times, NY, 1973—77; guest curator, curator Everson mus., Syracuse, 1974—76; exec. dir. Studio Mus. in Harlem, N.Y.C., 1977—87; commr. cultural affairs City of N.Y., 1987—91; dean Tisch Sch. Arts, NYU, N.Y.C., 1991—. Bd. mgrs. Swarthmore (Pa.) Coll., 1987-99; mem. fine arts vis. com. bd. overseers, Harvard Coll., Harvard U., Cambridge, Mass., 1991-95; mem. Tony nominating com., 1996-98, 2000-2002. Co-author: Harlem Renaissance: Art of Black America, 1987, Memory & Metaphor, 1991; prodr. (film) Sembene: A Biography, 1994. Mem. N.Y.C. Mayor's Adv. Commn. on Culture, 1991-94; co-chmn. subcom. on culture Dem. Nat. Conf., N.Y.C., 1992; bd. dirs. N.Y. Shakespeare Festival, 1993—, Harlem Sch. Arts, 1997-2001; bd. trustees Am. Acad. in Rome, 1999—, Bklyn. Mus. Art, 1999-2002, mem. bd. trustees, United Nations Internat. Sch., 2001-. Recipient George Arents award Syracuse U., 1993, Project of Yr. award N.Y. Coun. on Humanities; Tisch Sch. fellow Am. Acad. Arts & Scis. Democrat. Baptist. Avocations: jogging, writing. Office: NYU Tisch Sch of the Arts 721 Broadway 12th Flr New York NY 10003-6862

CAMPBELL, MARY STINECIPHER, retired chemist; b. Chattanooga, Feb. 26, 1940; d. Jesse Franklin and Florence Gladys (Marshall) S.; m. John David Fowler Jr. (div. Mar. 1979); children: John Christopher, Jesse David; m. Billy M. Campbell, Jan. 1995. BA, Earlham Coll., 1962; PhD, U. N.C., 1967. Cert. organic fruit grower. Postdoctoral researcher Research Triangle Inst., Research Triangle Park, N.C., 1966-68, 74-76; staff Los Alamos (N.Mex.) Nat. Lab., 1976—2004; ret., 2004. Adj. prof. organic, inorganic and phys. chemistry U. N.Mex. Grad. Ctr., Los Alamos, 1989—; instr. chemistry lab., 1989; vis. scientist AFOSR (AFATL), Eglin AFB, Fla., 1980-81. Contbr. articles to profl. jours.; inventor ammonium nitrate explosive systems and other explosive salts. Commr. Acequia Sancochada Cmty. ditch; mem. Habitat for Humanity. Mem. Am. Chem. Soc., N.Mex. Network Women in Sci. and Engring. (v.p. 1985-86, pres. 1986-87, No. chpt. pres. 1999), Toastmasters Internat. (pres. 1988, 98, 696 Club), Bio-Integral Rsch. Ctr., N.Mex. Apple Coun. Democrat. Unitarian Universalist. Avocations: skiing, dog training, hiking, singing, gardening. Personal E-mail: bmcampbell@newmexico.com.

CAMPBELL, MICHAEL L., recreational facility executive; Co-founder Premiere Cinemas Corp., 1982—89; founder, CEO Regal Cinemas, 1989—; and chmn., CEO Regal Entertainment Group, Knoxville, Tenn. Bd. dir. Fandango, Inc. Mem.: Nat. Assn. Theatre Owners (exec. com., bd. dir.). Office: National CineMedia 9110 E Nichols Ave Ste 200 Englewood CO 80112 also: Regal Entertainment Group 7132 Regal Ln Knoxville TN 37918

CAMPBELL, MICHAEL RAY, music educator; b. Charleston, W.Va., June 18, 1954; s. Cledith Vernon and Barbara Ann Campbell. MA, Marshall U., Huntington, W. Va., 1984. Cert. tchg. Ky., 1976. Music specialist Greenup County Schs., Greenup, Ky., 1976—87; choral dir. Fairview H.S., Ashland, Ky., 1987—97; dir. of choirs Paul Blazer H.S., Ashland, Ky., 1997—. Organist St. Andrew's Episcopal Ch., Barbourville, Ky., 1996—. Named Ky. Music Educators Dist. 8 H.S. Tchr. of the Yr., KMEA - Dist. 8, 1989-90, Ky. Music Educators Dist. 8 Elem. Sch. Tchr. of the Yr., 1988-89. Mem.: Ky. Edn. Assn., Ky. Music Educators Assn. (dist. 8 choral chairperson 1993—95). Home: 526 Monroe Ave Huntington WV 25704 Office: Paul Blazer H S Blazer Blvd Ashland KY 41102 Personal E-mail: vze23sxp@verizon.net.

CAMPBELL, MILDRED CORUM, business owner, nurse; b. Warfield, Va., Feb. 24, 1934; d. Oliver Lee and Hazel King (Young) Corum; m. Hugh Stuart Campbell, Dec. 2, 1972. BSN, U. Va., 1956. Head nurse plastic surgery U. Va. Med. Ctr., Charlottesville, 1956-58, head nurse cardio-surg., 1958-61; staff nurs operating rm. NIH Heart Inst., Bethesda, Md., 1961-62; supr. operating and recovery rms. Med. Univ. of S.C., Charleston, 1962-64; head nurse cardio operating rms. Meth. Hosp., Tex. Med. Ctr., Houston, 1964-67; supr. operating and recovery rms. Cedars of Lebanon Med. Ctr., L.A., 1967-68; product-nurse cons. Ethicon, Inc., Somerville, N.J., 1968-69; nurse cons. Johnson & Johnson, New Brunswick, N.J., 1969-70; gen. mgr. Ariz. Heart Inst., Phoenix, 1970-72; owner, pres., bd. dirs. Highland Packaging Labs., Inc., Somerville, 1983—2002; ret., 2002. Mem., moderator Nat. Ass. Operating Rm. Nurses, Denver, 1963-76; pres. Aux. Orgn., Muhlenberg Hosp., Plainfield, N.J., 1979-80; chmn. Assn. for Retarded Citizens Fund Raising Ball, Somerset County, N.J., 1982. Mem. Inst. Packaging Profls. Home: 29 Lambert Dr Princeton NJ 08540-2304 E-mail: hs.cam@verizon.net.

CAMPBELL, MONNA KAY, music educator; d. D. F. and Mona Belle McNabb; m. D. Paul Campbell, June 20, 1970; children: Ladd, Beau, Mandy, Lyndsey. MusB, NSU, 1970. Music tchr. La Plata Elem. Sch., Mo., La Plata HS. Recipient Tchr. of Yr., Catoosa Pub. Schs., 2004. Mem.: NEA.

CAMPBELL, NANCY DUFF, lawyer; b. 1943; BA, Barnard Coll., 1965; JD, NYU, 1968. Bar: DC 1968. Atty. Ctr. Social Welfare Policy and Law; prof. Cath. U. Sch. Law, Georgetown U. Law Ctr.; founder, co.-pres. Nat. Women's Law Ctr. Mem. US Commn. on Child and Family Welfare. Author: jour. articles on women's legal issues. Bd. dir. Women Law & Devel. Internat.; bd. adv. Community Tax Law Report, Alliance Nat. Def., Inst. Women's Policy Rsch.; mem. Nat. Conf. State Legis. Child Care Adv. Comm., Campaign Family Leave Income Adv. Comm. Named Women of Genius, Trinity Coll.; named one of 25 Heroines, Working Woman mag.; recipient Lifetime Achievement award, US Dept. Health and Human Svcs. Fellow: ABA; mem.: D.C. Bar (bd. gov. & exec. comm., William J. Brennan award). Office: Nat Womens Law Ctr Ste 800 11 DuPont Cir Washington DC 20036

CAMPBELL, NEAL FRANKLIN, music educator; b. Pittsboro, N.C., Jan. 27, 1953; s. Owen Riley and Aline Grey (Mangum) C.; m. Gwynn McLaurine Callis, May 13, 1996. MusB, Manhattan Sch. Music, 1983, MusM, 1985, D of Mus. Arts, 1996. Asst. organist All Saints' Ch., Chevy Chase, Md., 1973-76; organist, choirmaster St. Peter's Ch., Phila., 1976-77, St. George's By the River, Rumson, N.J., 1977-80, Christ Ch., Bloomfield, N.J., 1980-85, St. Stephen's Ch., Richmond, Va., 1985—; adj. asst. prof. music U. Richmond, 1997—. Author: Music and Life of Harold Friedell, 1996; performer recordings, radio and TV. Recipient Bronson Ragan award Manhattan Sch. Music, 1983. Mem. Am. Guild Organists (dean 1989-90, chair recital com. 1995-96, nat. coun. 2000—), Assn. Anglican Musicians, Organ Hist. Soc., Royal Coll. Organists (London), Ch. Club N.Y. Episcopalian. Office: 6000 Grove Ave Richmond VA 23226-2601 Office Phone: 804-288-3318. Business E-Mail: ncampbel@richmond.edu. E-mail: nealcampbell@ststephensch.org.

CAMPBELL, NEVE, actress; b. Guelph, Ont., Can., Oct. 3, 1973; m. Jeffrey Colt, Apr. 1995 (div. 1997). Student, Nat. Ballet Sch. Can. Actress (films) Scream, 1996 (Saturn award for Best Actress, MTV Movie award nomination, MTV Movie award for Best Female Performance), The Craft, 1996, Scream 2, 1997 (Blockbuster Entertainment award for Favorite Actress-Horror, MTV Movie award for Best Female Performance), 54, 1998, Wild Things, 1998, Three to Tango, 1999, Scream 3, 2000, Drowning Mona, 2000, Hairshirt, 2001, Investigating Sex, 2001, Lost Junction, 2003, Blind Horizon, 2004; writer, actor (films): the Company, 2003. Named one of 50 Most Beautiful People, People mag., 1998. Office: Creative Artists Agy 9830 Wilshire Blvd Beverly Hills CA 90212-1825

CAMPBELL, NORMAN M., music educator; b. Sayre, Pa., Dec. 22, 1949; s. Frank D. and Eleanor E. Campbell; m. Sharon A. Campbell; children: Vicki Bradeen, Susan, Patrick, Kathi Aiello. BS in Music Edn., Mansfield (Pa.) State Coll., 1971. Music educator Athens (Pa.) Area Sch. Dist., 1972—88; music chair, dir. choirs Abington Heights Sch. Dist., Clarks Summit, Pa., 1988—. Dir. choirs, vocal music tchr. Marywood U. Summer Music Camp, Scranton, Pa., 1975—; choir dir. Athens United Meth. Ch., 1985—88; educator vocal workshops Marywood U., Scranton, 1990, Mansfield U., 1980. Served with U.S. Army N.G., 1971—77. Mem.: NEA, Abington Heights Edn. Assn., Pa. Music Educators Assn. (advisor Dist. 9 Choral Festival 1972—2002, 25-Yr. Contbn. to Music Edn. award 1997). Methodist. Avocations: vocal coaching, music arranging, singing, bowling, travel. Home: 124 Maple Ave Clarks Summit PA 18411-2239 Office: Abington Heights HS 222 Noble Rd Clarks Summit PA 18411 Personal E-mail: tennore1@aol.com.

CAMPBELL, PAUL, JR., lawyer; b. Chattanooga, Dec. 23, 1915; s. Paul and Margaret Douglas (Meriwether) C.; m. Nelson Chambliss Whitaker; children: Nelson Douglas, Paul III, Michael Ross, Douglas Meriwether. BA, Union Coll., 1937; LLB, George Washington U., 1940. Bar: Tenn. 1940, U.S. Dist. Ct. Tenn. 1942, U.S. Ct. Appeals (6th cir.) 1942, U.S. Supreme Ct. 1964. Pvt. practice, Chattanooga, 1941-42, 46-96; spl. agt. FBI, Phila. and Buffalo, 1942-44; ptnr. Campbell & Campbell, Chattanooga, 1996—. Served to lt., USNR, 1944-46. Mem. ABA, Tenn. Bar Assn., Am. Judicature Assn., Am. Bed. Trial Advocates, Am. Coll. Trial Lawyers, Chattanooga Bar Assn., Tenn. Bar Found., Fed. Bar Assn., U.S. Sixth Cir. Jud. Conf. (life). Methodist. Office: 1200 James Bldg Chattanooga TN 37402 Office Phone: 423-266-1108.

CAMPBELL, PAUL, III, lawyer; b. Chattanooga, Feb. 1, 1946; children: Paul IV, Kolter M. BA, Vanderbilt U., 1968; MA, Middlebury Coll., 1972; postgrad., So. Meth. U., 1971-72, Emory U., 1972-73; JD, U. Tenn., 1975. Bar: Tenn. 1976, Ga. 1977. Tchr. English St. Mark's Sch., Dallas, 1968-72; ptnr. Campbell & Campbell, Chattanooga, 1976-98; mem. Witt, Gaither & Whitaker, Chattanooga, 1998—2002, Shumacker Witt Gaither & Whitaker, Chattanooga, 2002—. Adj. prof. English, U. Tenn., Chattanooga, 1976, adj. prof. law, 1979-81, adj. prof. pre-trial litigation, Knoxville, 1996, adj. prof. pol. sci., 2002-; mem. Tenn. Ct. of Judiciary, 1995-2003; mem. Tenn. Jud. Evaluation Guidelines Commn., 1994-95. Author: Tennessee Admissibility of Evidence in Civil Cases, 1987; co-author: Tennessee Automobile Liability Insurance, 1986, 95, 96, 99, 2002; editor-in-chief Tenn. Law Rev., 1975; contbr. articles to profl. jours. Bd. mgrs. YMCA Youth Residential Ctr., 1977-80; mem. McCallie Sch. Alumni Coun., 1987-93, U. Tenn. Dean's Alumni adv. coun. law coll., 1979—; trustee, Harbison Found., 1994-96; bd. Cmty. Found. Greater Chattanooga, 2002-. Recipient Am. Jurisprudence award U. Tenn., 1974, U. Ten. Coll. Law Pub. Svc. award, 1995; Alumni Achievement award McCallie Sch., 1994. Mem. ABA (ho. del. 2002—), Am. Bar Found., Tenn. Bar Assn. (bd. govs. 1985-94, pres. 1992-93), Tenn. Bar Found., Chattanooga Bar Found., Chattanooga Bar Assn. (bd. govs. 1983-85), State Bar Ga., Fed. Bar Assn. (dir. chpt. 1983-88), Fed. Defense and Corp. Counsel, Def. Rsch. Inst., Internat. Assn. Def. Counsel, Order of Coif, Phi Kappa Phi. Office: Shumacker Witt Gaither & Whitaker 736 Market St Ste 1100 Chattanooga TN 37402-4856

CAMPBELL, PAUL GARY, lawyer; b. Lancaster, Pa., Aug. 2, 1965; s. Guy Erb and Daisy Marie (Sellers) C.; m. Melinda Kay Breidenbaugh, May 28, 1988; children: Faith Ann, Gregory Paul, Joy Melinda, Hope Marlene. BA in Polit. Sci., Millersville U. Pa., 1986; JD, Widener U., 1989. Bar: Pa. 1989. Law clk. to Hon. Richard H. Horn, York County Ct. Common Pleas for 19th Jud. Dist., York, Pa., 1989-90; assoc. Law Offices D. Patrick Zimmerman, Lancaster, 1991-93, Law Offices Michael J. Rostolsky, Lancaster, 1993-96; pvt. practice, Holtwood, Pa., 1997—. Photographer, firefighter, fin. sec. Pequea (Pa.) Vol. Fire Co., 1991-97; supr. Martic Twp., Pequea, 1992-98. Mem. Lions (pres. Tucquan, Pa. 1994-95). Republican. Avocations: hunting, sports, woodworking, reading. Home: 168 Pinnacle Rd W Holtwood PA 17532-9673 Office: PO Box 148 Holtwood PA 17532-0148 Office Phone: 717-284-5944. Personal E-mail: odreksuh@netzero.net.

CAMPBELL, REGAN HELEN, engineer; b. Hershey, Pa., Apr. 26, 1975; d. James Reynolds, Jr. and Roberta Long Campbell. BS in Aero. sci., Embry-Riddle Aero. U., Daytona Beach, Fla., 1997; MS in Engring. Physics, Ga. Inst. Tech., Atlanta, 2000, PhD in Engring. Psych., 2003. Accident investigator Nat. Trans. Safety Bd., Atlanta, 1997—2002; knowledge engr. Applied Sys. Intelligence, Roswell, Ga., 2000—02; human factors engr. Naval Air Warfare Ctr., Patuxent River, Md., 2002—03, Naval Surface Warfare Ctr., Panama City, Fla., 2003—. Contbr. chapters to books, articles to profl. jours. Presdl. fellow, Ga. Inst. Tech., 1999—2002. Mem.: APA, Human Factors & Ergonomics Soc. Avocations: flying, scuba diving, reading, dance, hiking. Office: Naval Surface Warfare Ctr 110 Vernon Ave Panama City FL 32407

CAMPBELL, RENEA, director, consultant; b. Griffin, Ga., Oct. 25, 1964; d. Landon D. Smith and Mattie R. Brisco-Smith; children: Jerrod Lane Smith, Jamie Elyce, Jennifer Renea, Jason Joseph. AA, Lee Coll., 1984; BA, U. Houston Clear Lake, 1986, MS, 2001. Cert. Secondary English Tchr. Tex. State Bd. Educator Certification, 1988, Secondary History Tchr. Tex. State Bd. Educator Certification, 1988, Secondary Lang. Arts Tchr. Tex. State Bd. Educator Certification, 1994, Secondary Social Studies Tchr. Tex. State Bd. Educator Certification, 1994, Secondary Prin. Tex. State Bd. Educator Certification, 2001. English, history faculty mem. Crosby HS, Tex., 1989—91; english, social studies faculty mem. Sterling HS, Baytown, Tex., 1991—97; spl. populations coord. Galveston Ind. Sch. Dist., Tex., 1997—99; dir. k-12 partnerships Coll. of Mainland, Texas City, 1999—. Cons. Career Edn., League City, Tex.; design developer Collegiate HS Petrochemical Careers. Author: Tech Prep is Best, NTPN Connections. Recipient Tech. Prep. Excellence award, Tex. Gulf Coast Tech. Prep. Consortium, 2001, 2003. Mem.: ASCD, Career and Tech. Assn. Tex., Tex. Assn. Coll. Tech. Educators, Assn. Career and Tech. Edn., Nat. Tech. Prep. Network. Office: Coll of Mainland 1200 Amburn Rd Texas City TX 77590

CAMPBELL, RICHARD BRUCE, lawyer; b. Phila., Jan. 5, 1947; s. George B. and Edith (Neithammer) C.; m. Patricia Ann James, Mar. 7, 1981; children: Ron Martin, Rebecca Joi. BA, U. S.C., 1968, JD, 1974. Bar: U.S. Dist. Ct. S.C. 1975, U.S. Ct. Appeals (4th cir.) 1976, U.S. Ct. Appeals (5th cir.) 1983, Colo. 1985, U.S. Dist. Ct. Colo. 1986, U.S. Ct. Appeals (fed. cir.) 1989, Fla. 1989, U.S. Dist. Ct. (mid. dist.) Fla., U.S. Ct. Appeals (11th cir.) 1992. Law clk. to presiding justice U.S. Dist. Ct., Columbia, S.C., 1975; ptnr. Henderson & Salley, Aiken, S.C., 1975-80; atty. TVA, Knoxville, 1980-85; ptnr. Wells, Love & Scoby, Boulder, Colo., 1986-89; shareholder Carlton Fields PA, Tampa, Fla., 1989—2005; of counsel Carey, O'Malley, Whitaker and Manson PA, Tampa, 2005—. Lectr. in field. Contbr. articles to profl. jours. Served to capt. USAF, 1968—72. Mem. ABA, Am. Arbitration Assn. (panelist), Fla. Bar Assn., Colo. Bar Assn., Hillsborough County Bar Assn. Avocations: travel, skiing, photography. Office: Carey O'Malley Whitaker and Manson PA 712 S Oregon Ave Tampa FL 33606 Business E-Mail: rcampbell@cowmpa.com.

CAMPBELL, ROBERT, architect, writer; b. Buffalo, Mar. 31, 1937; s. R. Douglas and Amy (Armitage) C.; m. Janice Jaye Gold, Feb. 2, 1969 (div. 1990); 1 child, Nicholas. AB magna cum laude with highest honors, Harvard U., 1958, MArch, 1967; MS in Journalism, Columbia U., 1960. Registered architect, Mass. Writer, editor Parade mag., 1960-63; designer Benjamin Thompson Assocs., 1968-69; assoc. Sert Jackson & Assocs., 1967-75; architecture critic Boston Globe, 1973—; pvt. practice architecture Cambridge, Mass., 1975—. Cons. Am. Acad. Arts and Scis., Whitehead Inst., Boston Symphony Orch., Isabella Stewart Gardner Mus., Mayors Inst. for City Design, City of San Francisco; lectr. in field; mem. vis. faculty U. N.C. Sch. Architecture, Charlotte, 1979-94; Sam Gibbons Eminent scholar U. South Fla., 1993-2002; vis. scholar MIT, 1991-94; Max Fisher vis. prof. U. Mich., 2002; artist-in-residence Am. Acad. Rome, 1997. Author: Cityscapes of Boston: An American City Through Time; contbg. editor Architectural Record mag., Preservation mag.; contbr. articles to profl. jours.; published poet, photographer. Mem. Mid-Cambridge Neighborhood Assn.; propr. Boston Athenaeum. Recipient Francis Kelley prize, 1967, Pulitzer Prize for Criticism, 1996; named Julia Amory Appleton traveling fellow, 1967, Nat. Endowment for Arts design fellow, 1975; Nat. Arts Journalism Program sr. fellow Columbia U., 2003; grantee Graham Found., 1991, 2003. Fellow AIA (nat. design com., medal for criticism 1980), Am. Acad. Arts and Scis.; mem. Boston Archtl. Ctr. (hon. life), Boston Soc. Architects (award of honor 2004), Cambridge Club, St. Botolph Club, Tavern Club, Examiner Club, Century Assn. (N.Y.C.), Saturday Club, Phi Beta Kappa. Democrat. Address: 54 Antrim St Cambridge MA 02139-1102 Fax: 617-576-4784. E-mail: Robert@RCampbell.net.

CAMPBELL, ROBERT AYERST, accounting company executive; b. Montreal, Que., Can., July 15, 1940; s. James Kenneth and Doris Victoria (Ayerst) C.; m. Cynthia Abbey, Aug. 17, 1963; children: Colin Ayerst, David Arthur, Sarah Reid. BBA, Clarkson U., 1961; MBA, U. Colo., 1966. CPA. Staff acct. Touche Ross, Montreal, 1961-63, mgr. Rochester, N.Y., 1968-75; ptnr.-in-charge Touche Ross Internat., Tokyo, 1975-78; audit ptnr.-in-charge Touche Ross, Milw., 1978-82, mng. ptnr. Dallas, 1982-90; exec. dir. internat. Deloitte & Touche LLP U.S., Wilton, Conn., 1990-95; Asia Pacific regional mng. ptnr. Deloitte Touche Tohmatsu Internat., 1995—, exec. com., 1995—. Bd. dirs. Deloitte & Touche LLP U.S.A., Deloitte Touche Tohmatsu, Deloitte Touche Tohmatsu Hong Kong, Deloitte Touche Tohmatsu China; asst. dir. admissions Clarkson U., Potsdam, N.Y., 1963-65, instr. acctg., 1966-68. Treas., dir. Am. Sch. in Japan, Tokyo, 1976-78 Mem. AICPA, Conn. Soc. CPAs, Beta Gamma Sigma, Beta Alpha Pi, Hong Kong Club, Genessee Valley Club. Republican. Presbyterian. Home: 37 Granite Way Grantham NH 03753-0482 Office: 1400 Wing On Centre 111 Connaught Rd Ctrl Hong Kong Hong Kong E-mail: bobcampell@deloitte.com.hk.

CAMPBELL, ROBERT CHARLES, minister, theology studies educator; b. Chandler, Ariz., Mar. 9, 1924; s. Alexander Joshua and Florence (Betzner) C.; m. Lotus Idamae Graham, July 12, 1945; children: Robin Carl, Cherry Colleen. AB, Westmont Coll., 1944; BD, Eastern Baptist Theol. Sem., 1947, ThM, 1949, ThD, 1951, DD (hon.), 1974; MA, U. So. Calif., 1959; postgrad., Dropsie U., 1949-51, U. Pa., 1951-52, NYU, 1960-62, U. Cambridge, Eng., 1969; DLitt (hon.), Am. Bapt. Sem. of West, 1972; HHD (hon.), Alderson-Broaddus Coll., 1979; LHD (hon.), Linfield Coll., 1982; LLD (hon.), Franklin Coll., 1986. Ordained to ministry Am. Bapt. Ch., 1947; pastor 34th St. Bapt. Ch., Phila., 1945-49; instr. Eastern Bapt. Theol. Sem., Phila., 1949-51; asst. prof. Eastern Coll., St. Davids, Pa., 1951-53; assoc. prof. N.T. Am. Bapt. Sem. of West, Covina, Cal., 1953-54, dean, prof., 1954-72; gen. sec. Am. Bapt. Chs. in U.S.A., Valley Forge, Pa., 1972-87; pres. Eastern Bapt. Theol. Sem., Phila., 1987-89, ret. Vis. lectr. Sch. Theology at Claremont, Calif., 1961-63, U. Redlands, Calif., 1959-60, 66-67, Fuller Theology Seminary, Calif., 1992-97; Bd. mgrs. Am. Bapt. Bd. of Edn. and Publ., 1956-59, 65-69; v.p. So. Calif. Bapt. Conv., 1967-68; pres. Am. Bapt. Chs. of Pacific S.W., 1970-71; Pres. N.Am. Bapt. Fellowship, 1974-76; mem. exec. com. Bapt. World Alliance, 1972-90, v.p., 1975-80; mem. exec. com., gov. bd. Nat. Council Chs. of Christ in U.S.A., 1972-87; del. to World Council of Chs., 1975, 83, mem. central com., 1975-90. Author: Great Words of the Faith, 1965, The Gospel of Paul, 1973, Evangelistic Emphases in Ephesians, Jesus Still Has Something To Say, 1987. Baptist. Home: 1763 Royal Oaks Dr No Apt D20 Bradbury CA 91015

CAMPBELL, ROBERT DAVID, manufacturing executive, metal products executive; b. Teaneck, N.J., May 5, 1947; s. Robert Wesley and Phyllis May Julich; m. Elizabeth I. Young, June 15, 1978; 1 child, Ariel. BS, Syracuse U., 1969. Trader C. Tennant Sons & Co., N.Y.C., 1969—73, Cargill, N.Y.C., 1974—75; mng. dir. Amalgamated Metal Corp., Zug, Switzerland, 1975—80; pres. Amalgamet Inc., N.Y.C., 1978—80; v.p. Samincorp Inc., N.Y.C., 1980—84; pres. RST Resources, Inc., N.Y.C., 1984—93; pres., CEO Global Minerals & Metals Corp., N.Y.C., 1993—. Mem.: Cannon Point South (bd. dirs. 1983—95), Metropolitan Club, NY Copper Club. Avocations: tennis, scuba, sailing, skiing. Home: 45 Sutton Pl S New York NY 10022-2444

CAMPBELL, ROBERT EMMETT, retired health products executive, medical association administrator; b. Passaic, N.J., Oct. 24, 1933; Grad., Fordham U., 1955, Rutgers U., 1962; PhD (hon.), Fordham U., U. Medicine & Dentistry of NJ. Joined Johnson & Johnson, New Brunswick, NJ, 1955, corp. gen. controller & assist. treasurer, 1971—75, v.p. finance, 1975—76, bd. mem., treasurer, 1976—80, v.p. finance, 1980—83; vice chmn. exec. com. IMPATH, 1985—; vice chmn., dir. Johnson & Johnson, New Brunswick, NJ, 1989—95, ret., 1995. Mem. advisory council U. Notre Dame Coll. Sci.; bd. mem. Parker Memorial Home; mem. bd. of overseers Robert Wood Johnson Med. Sch.; bd. chmn. New Brunswick Affiliated Hospitals. Chmn. bd. trustees Fordham U., 1992-98, Robert Wood Johnson Found., 1999—; chmn. bd. dirs. Cancer Inst. N.J., 1995—. Served USAF. Address: Robert Wood Johnson Found Rte 1 & College Rd E PO Box 2316 Princeton NJ 08543-2316

CAMPBELL, ROBERT H., retired oil company executive; b. Pitts., June 11, 1937; m. Nancy Wertz, Feb. 27, 1976; children: R. Douglas, Heather. B in ChemE, Princeton U., 1959; M in ChemE, Carnegie Mellon U., 1961; M in Mgmt., MIT, 1978. Various engring. positions Sun Co., Phila., 1960—75, mgr. refinery ops. Corpus Christi, Tex., 1975—77; v.p. human resources Sun Ship, Inc., Chester, Pa., 1978—80, pres., 1980, Sun Refining and Mktg. Co., Phila., 1983—89; exec. v.p. Sun Co. Inc., Radnor, Pa., 1988—91, pres., CEO, 1991, CEO, chmn., 1991—2000, also chmn. bd.; ret., 2000. Bd. dirs. Phila. Nat. Bank, Elwyn Insts. Cigna Corp. Apptd. mem. Dep. Sec. of Energy W. Henson Moore Alternative Fuels Coun., 1990. Mem.: Am. Petroleum Inst. (bd. dirs. 1988). Republican. Office: c/o Sunoco 1801 Market St Philadelphia PA 19103-1699*

CAMPBELL, ROBERT HEDGCOCK, investment banker, lawyer; b. Ann Arbor, Mich., Jan. 16, 1948; s. Robert Miller and Ruth Adele (Hedgcock) C.; m. Katherine Kettering, June 17, 1972; children: Mollie DuPlan, Katherine Elizabeth, Anne Kettering. BA, U. Wash., 1970, JD, 1973. Bar. Wash. 1973, Wash. State Supreme Ct. 1973, Fed. 1973, U.S. Dist. Ct. (we. dist.) Wash. 1973, Ct. Appeals (9th cir.) 1981. Assoc. Roberts & Shefelman, Seattle, 1973-78, ptnr., 1978-85; sr. v.p. Lehman Bros., Inc., Seattle, 1985-87, mng. dir., 1987—. Bd. dirs. Pogo Producing Co., 1999—; dir., treas. Nat. Assn. Bd. Lawyers, Hinsdale, Ill., 1982-85; pres., trustee Wash. State Soc. Hosp. Attys., Seattle, 1982-85; mem. econs. dept. vis. com. U. Wash., 1995-97; mem. Law Sch. dean's adv. bd. U. Wash., 1999—. Contbr. articles to profl. jours. Trustee Bellevue (Wash.) Schs. Found., 1988-91, pres., 1989-90; nation chief Bellevue Eastside YMCA Indian Princess Program, 1983-88; trustee Wash. Phikeia Found., 1983-91, Sandy Hook Yacht Club Estates, Inc., 1993-98; mem. Wash. Gov.'s Food Processing Coun., 1990-91. Mem. U. Wash. Varsity Swimming Alumni Bd. Republican. Avocations: skiing, wind surfing, bike riding, physical fitness, golf. Home: 8604 NE 10th St Medina WA 98039-3915 Office: Lehman Bros Bank of America Tower 701 5th Ave Ste 7101 Seattle WA 98104-7016 Office Phone: 206-344-5888. Personal E-mail: ibe2ski@msn.com. Business E-Mail: rhcampbe@lehman.com.

CAMPBELL, ROBERT MURRAY, JR., surgeon, researcher; b. Nashville, May 7, 1951; s. Robert Murray and Betty Ann (Kennedy) Campbell; m. Corey Le Campbell, Mar. 31, 2001; children: Abigail Le, Noah Robert. Studied, Vanderbilt U., Nashville, 1969—71; BA, Johns Hopkins U., Balt., 1971—73; MD, Georgetown U., 1973—77. Diplomate Nat. Bd. Med. Examiners, 1978, cert. in Orthopedics Am. Bd. Orthopedic Surgery, 1982. Resident, orthopedic surgery Fitzsimmons Army Med. Ctr., Denver, 1978—81; orthopedist U.S. Army, Fort Meade, Md., 1981—85; fellow, pediatric orthops. A.I. Dupont Inst., Wilmington, Del., 1985—86; pvt. practice, pediatric orthops. San Antonio, 1986—92; asst. prof., orthops. U. Tex. Health Sci. Ctr., San Antonio, 1992—96, assoc. prof., orthops., 1996—2002, prof., orthops., 2003—. Cons. U.S. Consumer Product and Safety Commn., 2000; mem., med. adv. com. Nat. Orgn. of Rare Disorders, 2000—; dir. Thoracic Inst., Christus Santa Rosa Children's Hosp., San Antonio, 2001—. Cons., reviewer Jour. of Bone and Joint Surgery, 1987—; contbr. articles to profl. jours. Participant Orthop. Edn. in Third World Countries, 1999—. Maj. U.S. Army, 1983—85. Recipient Imagineer Award, Mind Sci. Found. of San Antonio, 1993, Miracle Maker Award, A.H. Robins/Wyeth Pediat., 1994, Therapeutic Achievement award, Nat. Org. Rare Diseases, 2005, Endowed Chair in Pediat. Orthopedics, Dielmann Pres. Coun., 2005; grantee, Nat. Orgn. Rare Disorders, 1992—93, FDA Office Orphan Products Devel., 1994—2000. Fellow: Scoliosis Rsch. Soc. (chmn., growing spine com. 2002); mem.: Pediatric Orthop. Soc. of N.Am. (edowed chair, pres. coun. 2004), Clin. Orthop. Soc. (pres. 2005). Achievements include invention of the verticle expandable prosthetic titanium rib and the FDA approval of this device as a humanitarium use device; the apparatus and method for effecting surgical incision through use of a fluid jet; the co-invention of the bioabsorbable intramedullary rod implant system. Avocations: white-water rafting, biking, running. Office: Dept Orthops UTH-SCSA Mailcode 7774 7703 Floyd Cir San Antonio TX 78229 Office Phone: 210-567-5125, 210-704-2988. Business E-Mail: campbellr@uthscsa.edu, rcampbell.thoracic.institute@christushealth.org.

CAMPBELL, RONALD NEIL, retired graphics designer; b. Morristown, NJ, Mar. 7, 1926; s. Carroll Francis and Emily Ruth (Peters) C.; m. Jule Gallina, Sept. 22, 1956; 1 son, Bruce G. B.F.A., R.I. Sch. Design, 1951. With Fortune mag., N.Y.C., 1952-82, art dir., 1974-82; ret. Freelance writer Sports Illustrated, CASE Currents, Graphis mag.; freelance graphic designer, lectr., 1951—; mem. adv. bd. Internat. Editorial Design Forum; design cons. Harvard Mag., 1985-95, Harvard Bus. Rev., 1987-90. Served with USNR, 1944-46. Recipient merit awards Art Dirs. Club N.Y., merit awards Comm. Arts Mag., merit awards Art Direction Mag., Page One award Am. Newspaper Guild, 2 Silver awards Editl. Design Forum, N.J. State Disting. Svc. medal, 2003. Mem. Soc. Illustrators (Gold and Silver medals), Am. Inst. Graphic Arts (merit awards), Soc. Publ. Designers (hon. bd. dirs., merit awards), Univ. and Coll. Designers Assn., U.S.S. Bon Homme Richard Assn. Home: 37 Barton Hollow Rd Flemington NJ 08822-5929 Office: 136 Waverly Pl Apt 8A New York NY 10014-6822 Office Phone: 212-924-1953.

CAMPBELL, SANDRA KAY, librarian; b. Warren, Ark., July 17, 1956; d. Erie Ingram; m. Bobby Campbell; 1 child, David Dupree Russell. BA, U. Ark., 1978; MLS, Atlanta U., 1979. Intern Pub. Libr. of Columbus (Ohio) and County of Franklin, 1979-80; dir. libr. County of Bradley, Warren, 1980-81; specialist Southeast Ark. Regional Libr., Monticello, 1982-83; instr. U. Ark., Pine Bluff, 1982, asst. libr. Monticello, 1984—2001; dir. U. Ark. Monticello Libr., 2001—. Bd. dirs. Delta Counseling, Monticello, 1981, Ark. Endowment for Humanities, Little Rock, 1986-89; vol. pub. rels. com. Bradley County Civic League, Warren, 1980-82. Mem.: Ark. Libr. Assn., Monticello Book Club, Beta Phi Mu, Phi Kappa Delta. Democrat. Methodist. Avocations: backgammon, cross-stitch, latch hook. Home: PO Box 312 Monticello AR 71657-0312 Office: U Ark PO Box 3599 Monticello AR 71656-3599

CAMPBELL, SCOTT ROBERT, lawyer, former food products executive; b. Burbank, Calif., June 7, 1946; s. Robert Clyde and Jenevieve Anne (Olsen) C.; Patricia Marie Bovan, Dec 30, 2003; 1 son, Donald Steven. BA, Claremont Men's Coll., 1970; JD, Cornell U., 1973. Bar: Ohio 1973, U.S. Dist. Ct. (so. dist.) Ohio 1974, Minn. 1976, Calif. 1989, U.S. Dist. Ct. (no. dist.) Calif. 1989, U.S. Ct. Appeals (9th cir.) 1989, U.S. Dist. Ct. (cen. and so. dists.) Calif. 1990, U.S. Ct. Appeals (5th cir.) 1991, U.S. Tax Ct. 1991, U.S. Ct. Appeals (fed. cir.) 2001. Assoc. Taft, Stettinius & Hollister, Cin., 1973-76; atty. Mpls. Star & Tribune, 1976-77; sr. v.p., gen. counsel, sec. Kellogg Co., Battle Creek, Mich., 1977-89; ptnr. Furth Fahrner Mason, San Francisco, 1989-2000, Zelle, Hofmann, Voelbel, Mason & Gette, LLP, San Francisco, 2000—. U.S. del. ILO Food and Beverage Conf., Geneva, 1984; participant, presenter first U.S.-USSR Legal Seminar, Moscow, 1988; speaker other legal seminars. Mem. ABA, Ohio Bar Assn., Minn. Bar Assn., Calif. Bar. Assn. Office: Zelle Hofmann Voelbel Mason & Gette LLP 44 Montgomery St Ste 3400 San Francisco CA 94104 Office Phone: 415-633-1903. Personal E-mail: srclaw@ix.netcom.com. Business E-Mail: scampbell@zells.com.

CAMPBELL, STEWART FRED, foundation administrator, consultant; b. St. Louis, June 29, 1931; s. Archibald Stewart and Charlotte (Ehrmann) C.; m. Ann Abbey Hudson, Dec. 18, 1954; children: Karen Ann, Deborah Ann. BS, Lehigh U., Bethlehem, Pa., 1954; MBA, NYU, 1961. With Mfrs. Hanover Trust Co., N.Y.C., 1958-64, asst. sec., 1962-64; with Duke Endowment, N.Y.C., 1964-79, asst. treas., 1967-73, treas., 1973-79; sec.-treas. Alfred P. Sloan Found., N.Y.C., 1979-86, fin. v.p., sec., 1986—2004. Treas. Doris Duke Trust, 1973-79, Angler B. Duke Meml., Inc., 1973-79, Nanaline H. Duke Fund, 1973-79; asst. treas. Duke Power Co., 1968-75; bd. dirs. Skytop Lodge, Inc., 1992—, v.p., 1993-95, chmn. bd., 1995-2000. Treas. Essex unit N.J. Assn. Retarded Children, 1967-72, trustee, 1966-74; trustee Meml. Home of Upper Montclair, 1987-96, pres., 1990-95. Mem. Delta Phi. Clubs: Montclair Golf, Skytop (Pa.). Home: 3 Wendover Rd Montclair NJ 07042-3031 E-mail: campbell@sloan.org.

CAMPBELL, SUSAN ELAINE, director; d. Bill and Dixie Campbell. BS in Psychology, La. State U.; MS in Higher Edn. and Student Affairs, Ind. U.; PhD in Higher Edn., Pa. State U. Residence hall dir. Austin Coll., Sherman, Tex., 1988—91; coord. womens' residence halls U. Tex., Austin, 1991—93; grad. rsch. asst. Pa. State U., University Park, 1993—99; program evaluator Legislative Office of Edn. Oversight, Columbus, Ohio, 1999—2003; policy rsch. assoc. Bd. Regents, U. Sys. Ga., Atlanta, 2003—. Mem.: Am. Edn. Rsch. Assn., Assn. for Instl. Rsch., Assn. for the Study Higher Edn., Pi Lambda Theta, Phi Kappa Phi, Phi Delta Kappa. Home: 3181 Sprucewood Dr Decatur GA 30033

CAMPBELL, SYLVIA JUNE, secondary educator; b. Dyersburg, Tenn., Jan. 13, 1957; d. Ernest Martin and Shoko (Okuyama) Stanley; m. Paul Timothy Campbell, June 14, 1980; 1 child, Colin Blair. B Music Edn., Baylor U., 1979. Cert. tchr. instrumental music, all levels, Tex. Band dir. Edward H. White Mid. Sch., San Antonio, 1979-80, Richfield HS, Waco, 1980-83, Midway Ind. Sch. Dist., 1987-88, Lake Air Mid. Sch., 1988-90, China Spring (Tex.) Ind. Sch. Dist., 1990-92, band dir. Mid. Sch., 1997—; band dir. Waco (Tex.) H.S., 1996—97, China Spring Mid. Sch., 1997—. Asst. condr. Waco (Tex.) Symphony Youth Orch. Charter mem., exec. bd. prin. flutist/piccoloist Waco (Tex.) Cmty. Band, 1981—. Mem. Tex. Music Educators Assn., Tex. Bandmasters Assn. United Methodist. United Meth. Avocations: gardening, singing, outdoor activities, reading. Home: 4228 Mitchell Rd Waco TX 76710-2140

CAMPBELL, TERRI GWEN GILL, epidemiology coordinator; b. Pampa, Tex., Dec. 26, 1962; d. Terry Lewis Gill and Sarah Ladon Gill-Northcutt; m. Mark G. Campbell, July 29, 1987. BSN, West Tex. State U., 1982—85. Cert. in Infection Control Certification Bd. for Infection Control, 2000; RN, Tex., 1986, Nat. Certification Corp., 1988. Staff devel. specialist NW Tex. Healthcare Sys., Amarillo, Tex., 1990—96, case mgr., 1996—98, epidemiology coord., 1998—. Mem. City Steering Com. for Weapons of Mass Destruction, Amarillo, 2000—; chmn., bioterrorism planning com., surveillance subcommittee City of Amarillo, 2000—02; chmn., bioterrorism planning com. City of Amarillo, Tex., 2002—. Chief of health and safety Potter County Fire Rescue, Amarillo, Tex., 2002—. Mem.: Assn. for Professionals in Infection Control and Epidemiology. Avocations: crafts, rappelling. Office: Northwest Texas Healthcare System 1501 S Coulter Amarillo TX 79106

CAMPBELL, THOMAS DOUGLAS, lawyer, consultant; b. N.Y.C., Jan. 5, 1951; s. Edward Thomas and Dorothy Alice (Moore) C.; m. Mary Anne Mahin, Dec. 22, 1978; 1 child, Kristen Anne. BA, U. Del., 1972; JD, U. Pa., 1976. Bar: Del. 1977. Law clk. Law Offices Bayard Brill & Handleman, Wilmington, Del., 1974-77; govt. affairs rep. Northeastern U.S. Standard Oil Co. Ind., 1977-78; Washington rep. Std. Oil Co., Ind., 1978-85; pres. Thomas D. Campbell and Assocs., Inc., Alexandria, Va., 1985—; chmn. bd. dirs. Compressus, inc., 2001—. With U.S. Army, 1968-69, Del. Air N.G., 1969-77. Elected to Wall of Fame, U. Del., 2000; recipient US Congress Congressional Leadership award, 2003, Presdl. Call to Svc. award, 2004. Mem. ABA, Del. Bar Assn., Congl. Awards Found. (chmn. bd. dirs. 1995-2003), Duke of Edinburgh's Internat. Award Assn. (internat. trustee 2001-03), Phi Beta Kappa, Phi Kappa Phi, Omicron Delta Epsilon, Omicron Delta Kappa. Republican. Episcopalian. Office: 6215 Ventnor Ave C2 Ventnor City NJ 08406 Home: PO Box 37 Cruz Bay St John VI 00831

CAMPBELL, TOM, former congressman, dean; b. Chgo., Aug. 14, 1952; s. William J. and Marie Campbell; m. Susanne Martin. BA, MA in Econs. with highest honors, U. Chgo., 1973, PhD in Econs. with highest dept. fellowship, 1980; JD magna cum laude, Harvard U., 1976. Law clk. to Judge George E. MacKinnon U.S. Ct. Appeals (D.C. cir.), 1976-77; law clk. to Justice Byron R. White U.S. Supreme Ct., Washington, 1977-78; assoc. Winston & Strawn, Chgo., 1978-80; White Ho. fellow Office Chief of Staff, Washington, 1980-81; exec. asst. to dep. atty. gen. Dept. Justice, Washington, 1981; dir. Bur. Competition FTC, Washington, 1981-83; mem. 101st, 102nd, 104th, 105th, 106th Congresses from Calif. 12th Dist., 1989—93; mem. com. on sci., space and tech., com. on judiciary, banking, fin. and urban affairs; mem. Calif. State Senate, 1993-95, 104th-106th Congresses from Calif. 15th Dist., 1995-2001; mem. com. internat. rels., com. on banking, joint econ. com.; dean Haas Sch. Bus. U. Calif., Berkeley, 2002—. Prof. Stanford Law Sch., 1983-2002; bd. dirs., DEMOS. Referee Jour. Polit. Economy, Internat. Rev. Law and Econs. Nat. adv. bd. Haas Ctr. Pub. Svc., Stanford U. Mem. ABA (antitrust sect., coun. 1985-88, program chmn. 1983-84), Coun. on Fgn. Rels., World Affairs Coun. No. Calif. (chair 2003-). Republican.

CAMPBELL, VANCE ALEXANDER, information technology educator; b. Bayonne, N.J., Sept. 28, 1969; s. Doreen Yambo; m. Beata Turel-Campbell, Mar. 11, 1969; 1 child, Kassandra. MEd in Adminstrn. & Supervision, St. Peter's, 2003. Ccnai Cisco, 2004. Cisco instr. Roselle Cisco Acad., Roselle, NJ, 2000—05; program dir. Union County Workforce Invetsement Bd., Elizabeth, 2004—05. Mem.: KC (Grand Knight 2004—05), Phi Alpha Theta. Libertarian. Roman Catholic. Avocations: bicycling, swimming, weightlifting, computer gaming. Office: Roselle Bd Edn 122 EAst 6th Ave Roselle NJ 07203 Office Phone: 908-298-2026. Personal E-mail: vcampbell@roselleschools.org.

CAMPBELL, WILLIAM HENRY, JR., financial consultant, former federal agency administrator; b. Quincy, Mass., Mar. 12, 1947; s. William Henry and Alice Elizabeth (Cleary) C.; m. Pamela Jeanne Beall, Mar. 29, 1974; children: Jennifer Anne, John Matthew. BS in Engring., Mass. Maritime Acad., 1967; Dipl. Mgmt., Indsl. Coll. Armed Forces, Washington, 1984; MS in Tech. Mgmt., Johns Hopkins U., Balt., 1987. Chief engr. U.S. Merchant Marine, 1967-73; chief main propulsion br. George G. Sharp, Inc., Hyattsville, Md., 1973-75; sr. mech. engr. USCG, Washington, 1975-77, chief sys. tech. div., 1980-85; investigator-in-chg. Nat. Transp. Safety Bd., Washington, 1977-80; dep. comdr. engring. quality Naval Supply Sys. Command, Washington, 1985-91; chief procurement mgmt. and sr. competition advocate USCG, 1991—2000; dep. asst. sec. for finance, dep. CFO US Dept. Veterans Affairs, Washington, 2000—02, asst. sec. mgmt., CFO, 2002—05, acting asst. sec for human resources & adminstr., 2003—05; v.p. Aon Consulting, Chgo., 2005—. Contbr. articles to profl. jours. Recipient Engring. award Brotherhood of Marine Officers, 1967, Disting. Svc. award Nat. Transp. Safety Bd., 1980, Equal Opportunity award U.S. DOT, 1983, Superior Civilian Svc. medal USN, 1991. Mem. Mass. Maritime Acad. Alumni Assn., Indsl. Coll. Armed Forces Alumni Assn., Johns Hopkins U. Alumni Assn. Democrat. Avocations: history, philosophy, economics. Office: Aon Consulting 200 E Randolph St Chicago IL 60601

CAMPBELL, WILLIAM J., lawyer; b. Grand Junction, Colo., Feb. 10, 1945; s. Timothy Samuel and Narcissa Cooke C.; m. Marsha Logan Campbell, June 16, 1979; children: John Bradford Geiger, Elizabeth Weir

Zeiger, Anne Wentworth Campbell, Amy Logan Campbell. BA cum laude, Colo. Coll., 1967; JD, U. Colo., 1971. Bar: Colo. 1971, U.S. Dist. Ct. Colo. 1971. Shareholder Bradley, Campbell, Carney & Madsen, P.C., Golden, Colo., 1971-95; ptnr. Faegre & Benson LLP, Denver, 1995—. Mem. U. Colo. Law Rev., 1970-71. Bd. trustees Colo. Colo.; bd. dirs. World Trade Ctr., Denver. Named Outstanding Young Lawyer, First Jud. Dist. Bar Assn., 1982; Boettcher scholar Boettcher Found., 1963-67; Grad. fellow Rotary Found., 1969. Mem. Colo. Bar Assn., Colo. Assn. Corp. Counsel, Phi Beta Kappa. Republican. Episcopalian. Avocation: golf. Home: 6781 Lupine Cir Arvada CO 80007 Office: Faegre & Benson LLP 3200 Wells Fargo Ctr 1700 Lincoln St Denver CO 80203 Office Phone: 303-607-3500.

CAMPBELL, WILLIAM J., JR., lawyer; b. Nov. 5, 1948; BA, U. Chgo., 1970; JD, U. Mich., 1973. Bar: Ill. 1973, U.S. Dist. Ct. (no. dist.) Ill. 1973, U.S. Ct. Appeals (7th cir.) Calif. 1974, U.S. Dist. Ct. (ctrl. dist.) Calif. 1974, U.S. Ct. Mil. Appeals 1976, U.S. Supreme Ct. 1978, U.S. Dist. Ct. (ctrl. dist.) Ill. 1979, U.S. Ct. Appeals (2nd, 5th and 9th cirs.) 1980, U.S. Dist. Ct. (no. dist.) Calif. 1983. Ptnr. Rudnick & Wolfe, Chgo.; ptnr., comml. litig. DLA Piper Rudnick Gray Cary, Chgo. Lt. USN, 1973-76; JAGC, USNR, 1970-82. Office: DLA Piper Rudnick Gray Cary 203 N La Salle St Ste 1900 Chicago IL 60601-1210 Office Phone: 312-368-7050. Office Fax: 312-236-7516. Business E-Mail: william.campbell@piperrudnick.com.

CAMPBELL, WILLIAM O'NEAL, retired physician; b. McCaysville, Ga., May 22, 1928; s. Martin Hoyt Campbell and Pauline Kimsey; m. Reba Kathern Hughes, June 14, 1961; 1 child, Martin Lee. AA, Tenn. Wesylan Coll., 1948; MD, U. Tenn. Memphis, 1962. Diplomate Am. Acad. Family Physicians. Resident Carraway Meth. Hosp., Birmingham, Ala., 1965; family physician Copperhill, Tenn., 1965—77; staff physician Tenn. Valley Authority, Chattanooga, 1977—94; ret., 1994. Cons. U. So. Ala. Med. Mus., Mobile, Med. Mus., Foley, Ala. Mem.: AMA, Med. Collectors Assn., Chattanooga and Hamilton County Med. Soc., Alpha Omega Alpha, Alpha Epsilon Delta. Home: 4900 Bal Harbor Dr Chattanooga TN 37416

CAMPBELL, WILLIAM STEEN, publishing executive, writer; b. New Cumberland, W.Va., June 27, 1919; s. Robert N. and Ethel (Steen) C.; m. Rosemary J. Bingham, Apr. 21, 1945 (dec. Dec. 1992); children: Diana J., Sarah A., Paul C., John W. Grad., Steubenville (Ohio) Bus. Coll., 1938. Ordained minister Progressive Universal Life Ch., 2002. Cost acct. Hancock Mfg. Co., New Cumberland, 1938-39; cashier, statistician Weirton Steel Co., W.Va., 1939-42; travel exec. Am. Express Co., N.Y.C., 1946-47; adminstr., account exec. Good Housekeeping mag., 1947-55; pub. Cosmopolitan mag., 1955-57; asst. dir. circulation Hearst Mags., N.Y.C., 1957-61; gen. mgr. Motor Boating mag., 1961-62; v.p., dir. circulation Hearst Mags., 1962-85; pres. Internat. Circulation Distbrs., 1978-81, Mags., Meetings, Messages, Ltd., 1986—. With Periodical Pubs. Svc. Bur. subs. Hearst Corp., Sandusky, Ohio, 1964-85, v.p., chief exec., 1964-69, pres., chief exec., 1970-85; dir. Audit Bur. Circulations, 1974-86, Nat. Mag. Co., Ltd., London, Randolph Jamaica Ltd., Omega Pub. Corp. Fla., Hearst Can. Ltd., 1964-85; former chmn. Ctrl. Registry, Mag. Pubs. Assn.; chmn. bd trustees Hearst Employees Retirement Plan, 1971-85; mem. pres.'s coun. Brandeis U., 1974-81; chmn. nat. corp. and found. com. U. Miami, 1979-85; dir. Broadway Assn., 1985-90, v.p., 1988-90; keynote spkr. Fifth Ann. Hospitality Industry Luncheon, Santa Barbara, Calif., 1996. Bd. dirs. Santa Barbara Rep. Club, 1993-94, Lobero Theatre Found., 1994-96, v.p., 1995-96. Lt. col. USAF, 1942-46, ETO. Recipient Lee C. Williams award Mag. Fulfillment Mgrs. Assn., 1974, Torch of Liberty award Anti-Defamation League, 1979. Mem. Campbell Clan Soc., Mil. Order of World Wars (chaplain), Masons, Cosmopolitan Club (chaplain). Home and Office: Apt 309 1150 Coast Village Rd Santa Barbara CA 93108-2722

CAMPBELL, WILLIAM V., computer company executive; b. Pitts. married; 1 son. BS in Econs., MS in Econs., Columbia U. V.p. J. Walter Thompson, N.Y.C.; dir. mktg. film divsn. Eastman Kodak Co.; v.p. mktg. Apple Computer Inc., 1983, v.p. sales, 1984, v.p. distgn. svc. and support, exec. v.p., 1984, group exec. of U.S.; founder, pres., CEO Claris Corp. (purchased by Apple Computer), 1990; pres., CEO GO Corp., 1990-94, Intuit, 1994-98, 1999—2000, chmn. bd., 1998—. Bd. dirs. Great Plains Software, SanDisk, Apple Computer Inc. Dir. Nat. Football Found. and Hall of Fame. Named to InfoWorld's Top 25 CTOs, 2004. Office: Intuit Inc 2535 Garcia Ave Mountain View CA 94043-1111

CAMPEAU, RICHARD JOHN, JR., internal medicine and radiology educator; b. New Orleans, Mar. 30, 1944; s. Richard John Campeau Sr. and Shirley Claire Lequay; m. Erin E. Boh, Aug. 1, 1980 (div. Oct. 1986); m. Nathalie Jacqueline DuBois, Oct. 16, 1996; 1 child, Anastasia. BS, La. State U., 1966, MD, 1969. Diplomate Am. Bd. Internal Medicine, Am. Bd. Nuclear Medicine. Intern Tulane U., 1969-70, resident in internal medicine, 1970-72; fellow in nuclear medicine Johns Hopkins Hosp., 1972-73; asst. chief nuclear medicine svcs. VA Med. Ctr., Miami, Fla., 1973-74; asst. prof. radiology U. Miami, 1974-76, asst. prof. radiology, chief imaging divsn., 1975-76; dir. sect. nuclear medicine Tulane U., 1976—, assoc. prof. clin. radiology, 1976-92, assoc. prof. clin. internal medicine, 1982-92, prof. clin. radiology and internal medicine, 1992—. Cons. in nuclear medicine VA Med. Ctr., New Orleans, 1976-86, staff physician, 1986—; med. dir. nuclear medicine tech. program Delgado C.C., New Orleans, 1991—; cons. staff physician Our Lady of the Lake Regional Med. Ctr., Baton Rouge, La., 1998—. Mem. edit. bd. Clin. Nuclear Medicine, 1987—; contbr. numerous articles to profl. jours. Mem. Am. Heart Assn., Am. Soc. Nuclear Cardiology, European Assn. Nuclear Medicine, Inter Am. Coll. Radiology, Am. Telemedicine Assn., Am. Coll. Nuclear Medicine, Soc. of Chefs of Acad. Nuclear Medicine Sects., Assn. Univ. Radiologists, Am. Inst. Ultrasound in Medicine, Soc. Nuclear Medicine, Am. Coll. Nuclear Physicians, Musser-Burch Soc., Alpha Omega Alpha, Phi Delta Epsilon. Democrat. Avocations: music, wine collecting, physical fitness, backgammon, cooking. Office: Dept Radiology SL-54 1430 Tulane Ave New Orleans LA 70112 E-mail: richard.campeau@tulane.edu.

CAMPELLO, FLORENCIO LENNOX, artist, art critic; b. Guantanamo, US Naval Base, Cuba, Sept. 6, 1956; s. Florencio and Ana Olivia Campello; m. Catriona Trafford Fraser; 1 child, Callum Fraser-Sharp; m. Mary Bridgett Strasser (div. Sept. 8, 1993); children: Vanessa, Elise. BS Art, U. Wash. Sch. Art, 1981; MS, Naval Postgrad. Sch., Monterey, Calif., 1987. Art critic Dimensions Mag., Norfolk, Va., 1994—99, Visions Mag. for the Visual Arts, Virginia Beach, Va., 1995—2000, Crier Media, Alexandria, Va., 1999—, Washington Post.com, 2001—, Culturefllux Mag., 2001—04, DC One Mag., 2002—04, Art Krush, 2003, Pitch Mag., City Beat, Manassas Jour.; info. warfare advisor KSI, Arlington, Va., 1997—. Advisor D.C. Arts & Humanities Commn., Washington, 1999—2005; guest curator Athenaeum, Alexandria, Va., 2001, Greater Reston Arts Ctr., Reston, Va., 1997, Gallery West, Alexandria, Va., 1997, League of Fairfax Artists, Fairfax, Va., 2000; assoc. dealer Sothebys.com; curator From Here and From There: A Survey of Contemporary Cuban Art Fraser Gallery, Bethesda, Md., 2003; curator Seven: A Survey of Artists; mem. Wash. Project for the Arts, 2005. Artwork, Body of Works, 1970 (Our Lady of Loretto Art Medal, 1970), original artwork, America Desnuda, 1981 (Prix de Peinture de Raymond Duncan Musee des Duncan. Paris, France, 1981), drawing, 1981 (Silver Medal, Salon of the 50 States. Musee des Duncan. Paris, France, 1981), watercolor, Road Near Memmuir, Scotland, 1990 (Most Popular Award. 42nd North Wynd River Art Show. Wyoming, 1990), etching, Mujertrees, 1980 (First Prize (Printmaking). Whipple Gallery National. Marshall, MN., 1980), watercolors, Edzell Castle, 1991 (First Prize (Watercolors). Montana Art Society. Billings, Montana, 1991), charcoal drawing, Feral Mermaid, 1995 (Best of Show. 20th Princess Anne Art Show. Virginia Beach, VA, 1995), Female Nude, 1996 (Best of Show. Festival in the Park. Roanoke, Virginia., 1996), one-man shows include The Hub Gallery, 1979, Arts Northwest Gallery, Wash., 1981, Galeria Sevillana, Spain, 1984, Warehouse Gallery, Scotland, 1992, Chevrier's Presidio Gallery, Calif., 1993—94, Fraser Gallery, Washington, D.C., 1996—2005, 2001, 49 West, Md., 1997, Eklektikos Gallery, Washington, D.C., 2000, represented by, Fraser Gallery, exhibitions include McManus Mus., Scotland, Brusque Mus., Brazil, San Bernardino County Art Mus., Calif., Musee des Duncan, France, Frick Mus., OH, Meadows Mus. Art, Shreveport, La., Hunter Mus., Tenn., Sacramento Fine Arts Ctr., Calif., Rock Springs Art Ctr., Wyo. Decorated Meritorious Svc. medal USN, Navy Commendation Medal (4), Navy Achievement Medal (2); recipient second prize, Bellgrade Art Festival, 1997, 1998. Mem.: Art Dealers Assn. of Greater Washington.

CAMPER, FRED, freelance writer, educator; b. Chgo., 1947; BS in Physics, MIT, 1971; attended, NYU, Dept. Cinema Studies. Lab technician for a company specializing in environ. measurements of radioactivity; tchr. asst. NYU, 1972, instr., 1973; tchr., film-making and film history Sch. Art Inst. Chgo., 1976—82, chmn. film-making dept., 1977—81, tchr. American Melodrama, 2000. Lectr. on art, photography, and film for college and universities in NY, NJ and Ill.; lectr. in the field; tchr., reading course in art issues U. Ill. at Urbana-Champaign; co-founder, mem. a film by, 2003—. Freelance writer, publisher (film articles for a variety of periodicals, catalogues and books), 1968—, writer on film Chicago Reader, 1976, 1986—, writer on art, 1989—, writer (of reviews of art and photgraphy exhibits and interviews with artists), 1993—. Recipient Lisagor award, 1999, Film Preservation Honor, Anthology Film Archives, 2001, Best DVD award, Cinemarati, Exceptional Achievement in Criticism award, 2004. Mem.: Nat. Writers Union, Internat. Assn. of Art Critics, Chgo. Art Critics Assn. (co-founder, mem.). Avocations: travel, art, music. Address: PO Box A3866 Chicago IL 60690-3866 E-mail: f@fredcamper.com.*

CAMPER, JOHN JACOB, reporter, academic administrator; b. Toledo, Sept. 8, 1943; m. Cleraine Uguccioni, Mar. 27, 1971 (div. May 1981); 1 child, Sarah; m. Mary C. Galligan, Jan. 9, 1988; 1 child, Joseph. BA, Kenyon Coll., 1964. Reporter Detroit News, 1965-68; reporter, critic Chgo. Daily News, 1968-78; editorial writer Chgo. Sun-Times, 1979-84; dept. head external relations Regional Transp. Authority, Chgo., 1984-85; media coord. Chgo. World's Fair Authority, 1985; reporter Chgo. Tribune, 1985-90; assoc. chancellor for pub. affairs U. Ill., Chgo., 1990-97; dep. press sec., speech writer Mayor of Chgo., 1997—; v.p. Chgo. Pub. Rels. Forum, 1995-97, pres., 1997-98. Bd. dirs. Family Svc. Mental Health Ctr. of Oak Park and River Forest, 1990-97. Recipient Peter Lisagor award Chgo. Headline Club, 1983, UPI award, Chgo., 1983, Stick-O-Type, Chgo. Newspaper Guild, 1983, Nat. Assn. Black Journalists award, 1987. Home: 1846 W Newport Ave Chicago IL 60657-1024 Office: 502 City Hall 121 N Lasalle St Chicago IL 60602-1202 E-mail: jcamper@cityofchicago.org.

CAMPER, NYAL DWIGHT, plant physiology educator; b. Lynchburg, Va., May 12, 1939; s. Herbert Nyal and Grace Irene (Leedy) C.; m. Margaret Jane Bratton; children: Shea Lynn, Britney Dawn. BS, N.C. State U., 1962, PhD, 1967. Asst. prof. dept. plant pathology and physiology Clemson (S.C.) U., 1966-71, assoc. prof., 1971-77, prof., 1977—. Contbr. chpts. to books and articles to profl. jours. Named endowed prof. S.C. Commn. Higher Edn.; grantee in field. Mem. Am. Soc. Plant Physiologists, Am. Chem. Soc., Weed Sci. Soc. Am., Internat. Assn. for Plant Tissue Culture, S.C. Acad. Sci. (pres. 1998-99, 2003-2004), Sigma Xi. Office: Dept Entomology Soils and Plant Sci Clemson U Clemson SC 29634-0315 Office Phone: 864-656-5743. E-mail: dcamper@clemson.edu.

CAMPHAUSEN, FRED HOWARD, retired physicist; b. L.A., Aug. 23, 1933; s. Fred Henry and Eloise (Ingebretsen) C.; m. Martina Simon, Apr. 2, 1956 (div.); children: Raymond Thomas, Karin Maria; m. Marianna P. Dembinski, Aug. 2, 1980. BA in Physics, U. Calif., 1961. With Naval Weapons Cen., China Lake, Calif., 1961-88; physicist, project mgr. electronic warfare test/evaluation, 1980-88; owner, mgr. Mountain High West, 1980—. Contbr. articles to profl. jours. With U.S. Army Security Agy., 1953-56. Mem. Am. Legion, Mono Lake Com., Yosemite Assn., Death Valley Nat. History Assn., Am. Alpine Club, Sierra Club Republican. Roman Catholic. Home and Office: 2765 Sierra Vista Way Bishop CA 93514-3046

CAMPHOR, JAMES WINKY, JR., educational administrator; b. Balt., Mar. 16, 1927; s. Emma Rosetta (Lewis) Butler; m. Lillie Mae Gilliard (div. Sept. 1976); children: Yvonne, Michael, Yolande; m. Florine Alston Camphor, Aug. 10, 1980. BS, Coppin Coll., 1951; MA, Coppin State Coll., 1971. Tchr. Dept. Edn., Balt., 1951-53, Dept. Juvenile Svcs., Chettenham, Md., 1953-75, demonstration tchr., 1972-75; behavior specialist Dept. Health and Mental Hygiene, Montgomery County, Md., 1975-87, ednl. supr., 1987—. Cons. Fantastic Buddies Travel, Balt., 1980-94. Co-author: (study) Social Studies in the Training School, 1963. Mem. adv. bd. Foster Grandparents Assn., Prince George County, Md., 1991—94, Nat. Assn. Sickle Cell Disease, Balt., 1984—94, chmn. Walk-A-Thon, 1991; pres. Am. Fedn. State County Mcpl. Employees Assn., Assn. State County Employees Montgomery County, 1991; mem. adv. com. capital campaign Coppin State Coll., 1998—2002, mem. cmty. fundraising coalition, 2002—, pres. nat. alumni assn., 2002—; supt. Sunday sch. Emmanuel Cmty. Ch., Balt., 1945. Recipient Comty. Svc. award Nat. Assn. Sickle Cell Disease, 1988, Presdl. citation Nat. Assn. in Higher Edn., 1992, Gov.'s Citation award William Donald Shafer, Annapolis, Md., 1994, Commitment to Edn. award City Coun. of Balt., 1994. Mem. Black Profl. Men Inc., Bus. and Profl. Coun. (pres. 1989-94), Comty. Men (comty. mem., bus. mgr. 1985-92), Lucky Ten Inc. (charter, pres. 1990-94), Elks, Phi Beta Sigma (pres. 1990-94). Democrat. Avocations: reading, tutoring, travel, collecting pipes, singing. Home: 3308 Lauri Rd Baltimore MD 21244-1324 Office: Dept Health and Mental Hygiene 3100 Gracefield Rd Silver Spring MD 20904-1870

CAMPHOUSE, MARK DAVID, music educator, composer, conductor; b. Oak Park, Ill., May 3, 1954; s. William Henry and Esther C.; m. Elizabeth Ann Curtis, June 20, 1982; children: Elizabeth Curtis Camphouse, Briton Curtis Camphouse. B in Music, Northwestern U., 1975, M in Music, 1976. Vis. instr. music U. Okla., Norman, 1976-77, St. Cloud (Minn.) State U., 1977-78; asst. prof. music Blackburn Coll., Carlinville, Ill., 1980-84; music dir. and conductor N.Mex. Music Festival, Taos, 1978-82; assoc. prof. music Radford (Va.) U., 1984-99; prof. music, 2000—; assoc. dir. Va. Govs. Sch. Arts, Radford, 1986-89; acting dean music New World Sch. Arts, Miami, Fla., 1998-99. Author: Composers on Composing for Band; composer: 15 published works for symphonic bands. Recipient Outstanding Faculty award, State Coun. Higher Edn. Va., 2002. Mem. Nat. Band Assn. (1st Prize music composition 1991, bd. dirs. 1998—), Am. Bandmasters Assn., Music Edn. Nat. Conf., Am. Symphony Orch. League, Coll. Band Dir. Nat. Assn. Republican. Methodist. Avocations: racquetball, flag collecting. Home: 106 Hidden Valley Dr Radford VA 24141-3912 Office: Radford U Dept Music PO Box 6968 Radford VA 24142-6968 E-mail: mcamphou@radford.edu.

CAMPION, EDMUND JOSEPH, composer, educator; b. Dallas, Tex., July 9, 1957; s. James Timothy Campion and Mary Louise Kucera; m. Danielle De Gruttola. BA, U. Tex., 1984; MA, Columbia U., 1987, DMA, 1993. Assoc. prof. music U. Calif., Berkeley, 1996—. Composer in residence Ctr. New Music and Audio Technologies, Berkeley, 1996—. Composer: Losing Touch, 1994, Domus Aurea, 2000, L'Autre (The Other), 2000. Recipient Lili Boulonger Composition award, U. Mass., 1993, Rome prize, Am. Acad. in Rome, 1995, Hinrichsen award, Am. Acad. of Arts and Letters, 1999. Achievements include works published by Billaudot Editions and Henry Lemoine, Paris, Peters Editions, N.Y. Avocations: computers, music. Office: U Calif Dept Music #1200 104 Morrison Hall Berkeley CA 94720-1200 Fax: 510-642-7918. E-mail: campion@cnmat.berkeley.edu.

CAMPION, JANE, film director, screenwriter; b. Wellington, New Zealand; d. Richard and Edith Campion. BA in Anthropology, Victoria U., Wellington, 1975; Diploma of Fine Arts, Chelsea Sch. Arts, London, 1979; degree, Sydney Coll. Arts, 1979; Diploma in Direction, Australian Film and T.V. Sch., Sydney, 1984; DLitt (hon.), Victoria U., 1999. Adj. prof. Sydney Coll. Arts, 2000. Dir., screenwriter Peel: An Exercise in Discipline, 1982 (also editor, Palme d'Or short film category Cannes Internat. Film Festival 1986, Diploma of Merit Melbourne Film Festival, 1983, finalist Greater Union awards, Australian Film Inst. awards 1983-84), A Girl's Own Story, 1983 (with Gerard Lee, Rouben Mamoulian award 1984, Best overall short film Sydney Film Festival 1984, Unique Artist Merit Melbourne Film Festival 1984, Best Direction, Best Screenplay, Best Cinematography Australian Film Inst. 1984, First Prize Cinestud Amsterdam Film Festival, 1985, Best Film Cinestud 1985, First Prize Festival and Press prize), writer/dir. Mishaps of Seduction and Conquest, 1984-85, Passionless Moments (also prodr., dir., writer, with Gerard Lee and dir. photography, Unique Artist Merit Melbourne Film Festival 1984, Best Exptl. Film Australian Film Inst. 1984, Most Popular Short Film Sydney Film Festival 1985), screened at Cannes Un Certain Regard, 1986, After Hours, 1984 (XL Elders award Best Short Fiction, Best Short Fiction Melbourne Internat. Film Festival 1985), Dancing Daze (TV series), 1985, (TV movie) Two Friends, 1986 (Golden Plaque TV category Chgo. Internat. Film Festival 1987, Best Dir., Best Telemovie, Best Screenplay Australian Film Inst. awards 1987, screened at Cannes in Un Certain Regard, 1986, Edinburgh Film Festival, Sydney and Melbourne Film Festival, 1986), Sweetie, co-writer, dir. 1988, (Georges Sadoul prize Best Fgn. Film, Best Dir., Best Actress, Best Film Australian Critics awards 1990, New Generation award L.A. Film Critics, 1990, Best Fgn. Film Spirit of Independence awards 1990), An Angel at my Table, 1990 (Byron Kennedy award Australian Cinema 1990, Spl. Jury prize, Elvira Notari award Best Woman Dir., Agia Scuola Italian Min. Culture, Best Film Si presci award Panel Internat. Critics, Best Film O.C.I.C. award Christian journalists, Best Film for Young Audiences Cinema e Ragazzi Italian film critics prize, Critics award Toronto Film Festival, Most popular film in the Forum, Otto Debelius prize Berlin Film Festival, Best Fgn. Film, Spirit of Independence Awards, Venice Film Festival, World Premiere, 1990); writer, dir. The Piano, 1993 (Palme d'Or Cannes Internat. Film Festival 1993, Academy Award Best Original Screenplay 1994, Best Picture, Best Dir., Best Cinematography nominations, Acad. Awards, Australian Film Inst. awards, Australia Film Critics, Southeastern Film Critics Assn., others, Best Fgn. Film Chgo. Film Critics, Caesar awards (2000 WIN award, Wimfemme Film Festival Women's Image Network); composer: Feel the Cold, 1983, (play) The Portrait of A Lady, 1996, Holy Smoke, 1998-99 (Best Film Francesco Pasinetti award, pres. Internat. jury Mostra Internat. Art Cinematography Festival Venice Film Festival, 1997, Nat. Union Film Journalists, nominated Best Costume Acad. awards 1997, nominated Best Supporting Actress Acad. awards 1997; dir. In the Cut, 2002-03. Office: HLA Mgmt Pty Ltd 87 Pitt St Redfern NSW 2016 Australia also: PO Box 1536 Strawberry Hills NSW 2012 Australia

CAMPION, ROBERT THOMAS, manufacturing executive; b. Mpls., June 23, 1921; s. Leo P. and Naomi (Revord) C.; m. Wilhelmina Knapp, June 8, 1946; 1 son, Michael. Student, Loyola U., Chgo., 1939-41, 46-48. C.P.A., Ill. With Alexander Grant & Co., Chgo., 1946-57, ptnr., 1954-57; with Lear Siegler, Inc., Santa Monica, Calif., 1957—, pres., 1971-85, chief exec. officer, dir., 1971-86, chmn., 1974-86; pvt. investor, 1987—. Served with AUS, 1942-46. Mem. AICPA, Ill. Soc. CPAs, Bel Air Country Club, Jonathan Club, La Quinta Country Club. Republican. Office: Blair House # 406 10490 Wilshire Blvd Los Angeles CA 90024-4646

CAMPION, THOMAS FRANCIS, lawyer; b. Bklyn., Aug. 15, 1935; s. Thomas Francis and Genevieve Agnes (Schantz) C.; m. Virginia Grosscup, Aug. 21, 1965; children: Caroline, Michael. AB, Fordham U., 1957; LLB, Cornell U., 1961. Bar: N.J. 1961, U.S. Dist. Ct. N.J. 1961, U.S. Ct. Appeals (3d cir.) 1965, U.S. Supreme Ct. 1966, U.S. Dist. Ct. D.C. 1970, N.Y. 1988. Law clk. to judge Appellate Div.-Superior Ct. N.J., 1961-62; assoc. Shanley & Fisher, Newark and Morristown, NJ, 1962-67, ptnr. Morristown, 1968-99, Drinker, Biddle & Shanley, LLP, Florham Park, NJ, 1999—2002; ptnr., litig. Drinker, Biddle & Reath, LLP, Florham Park, NJ, 2003—, and co-head, profl. liability claims practice group. Bd. on trial atty. cert. N.J. Supreme Ct., 1982—89, chmn., 1987—89, chmn. disciplinary oversight com., 1994—2001, vice chmn. commn. on rules of profl. conduct, 2001—03. Contbr. articles to profl. jours. Mem. N.J. Gov.'s Mgmt. Commn., 1970. 1st lt. USAR, 1957-61. Fellow Am. Bar Found., Am. Coll. Trial Lawyers; mem. ABA, N.J. Bar Assn. (past chmn. jud. and county prosecutor appointments com., civil cts. task force), Essex County Bar Assn., Morris County Bar Assn., Assn. Fed. Bar N.J. (pres. 1980-82), Univ. Club (N.Y.C.). Office Phone: 973-549-7300. Business E-Mail: thomas.campion@dbr.com.

CAMPLIN, PETER M., SR., entrepreneur, writer; b. Buffalo, June 11, 1943; s. Kenneth William and June (Tefft) Camplin; m. Cynthia W. Watson, July 24, 1965; children: Peter M. II, Brett W. BA, Colby Coll., 1965. Cert. notary pub. State of Maine, 2004. Pres. Down East Properties, Inc., York, Maine, 1970—80, Peter Camplin & Co., York, Maine, 1980—91, Camplin & Rozelle, CabinetMakers, York, Maine, 1985—91, Renaissance Devel. Corp., York, Maine, 1985—91; v.p. Camplin/Marino Properties, Inc., Portland, Maine, 1989—; pres. Sea Dog Brewing Co., Camden, Maine, 1992—2000; mng. ptnr. WWN Group, LLC, Jensen Beach, Fla., 2000—. Instr. So. Maine Vocat. Inst., South Portland, 1979—80. Author: (novel) Cleopatra's Return; brewer (beer) Sea Dog Penobscot Pilsener (Gt. Am. Beer Festival gold medal, 1995). Mem. Hist. Soc., York, Maine, 1986—87. Mem.: Master Brewers Assn. (cert. master brewer), Maine Writer's Alliance (assoc.), Island Dunes Golf and Tennis Club. Independent. Methodist. Achievements include restoration and rehabilitation of numerous historically significant buildings. Avocations: reading, kayaking, tennis, travel, sailing. Office Phone: 772-229-7435. Personal E-mail: oldefrothingslosh@hotmail.com.

CAMPO, DAVE, professional football coach; b. July 18, 1947; m. Kay Campo; 6 children. Student, Ctrl. Conn. State. Football coach various Colls., 1971-89; asst. coach to head coach Dallas Cowboys, 1989—2002; defensive coord. Cleve. Browns, 2003—04; asst. head coach/secondary coach Jacksonville Jaguars, 2005—. Office: Jacksonville Jaguars 1 Alltel Stadium Pl Jacksonville FL 32202

CAMPO, RICHARD J., real estate company executive; Degree, Oreg. State U., 1976. CPA AICPA. Chmn. Camden Property Trust, Houston, 1993—, bd. trust mgrs., 1993—, CEO, 1993—. Mem. Oreg. State U. Found., Greater Houston (Tex.) Partnership; bd. dirs. Nat. Multifamily Housing Coun., exec. com. Mem.: Harris County-Houston Sports Authority. Office: Camden Property Trust 3 Greenway Plaza Ste 1300 Houston TX 77046

CAMPO, TODD RUSSELL, principal, law enforcement educator; b. Dansville, N.Y., Oct. 25, 1953; s. Frank James and Shirley May (Mothorpe) C.; m. Jo Ann Marie Rocco; children: Christy Ellen, Todd Russell Jr., Joshua James, Mathew Ryan. BS in Edn., SUNY, Oswego, 1976; MA in Religion magna cum laude, Liberty U., 1989; MA summa cum laude, Simon Greenleaf Sch. Law, 1991; PhD summa cum laude, Trinity Theol. Sem., 1997; grad. Internat. Inst. Human Rights, U. Strasbourg (France), 1990; honor grad., L.A. Police Acad., 1998. Prof. Chafer Theol. Sem., Huntington Beach, Calif., 1989—; prin. Hawthorne (Calif.) Christian Sch., 1990-96. Apologist Reasons to Believe, Pasadena, Calif., 1989-91; minister of edn. Hawthorne Christian Sch., 1990-96; elder, min. Grace Ch., Fountain Valley, 1990—. Sponsor World Vision, 1988—, Wycliff Bible Translators, 1992—. Capt. USMC, 1976-83. Named A.A.U. Nat., North Am. and World Bench Press Champion, 1998, U.S. Nat. Champion, 2000, N. Am. Champion, 2000. Mem. Assn. for Christian Schs. Internat., Christian Leadership Assn., Grace Evang. Soc., Am. Legion. Republican. Mem. Christian Ch. Avocations: family, reading, systematic theology, philosophy, pilot. Home: 1529 Beechwood St Santa Ana CA 92705-6906 Office: LA Police Dept 1358 Wilcox Ave Los Angeles CA 90028-8195

CAMPOFRANCO, SALVATORE, real estate company executive; married; 2 children. BS in Acctg., St. John's U., N.Y., 1980. CPA N.Y. Mgr. Kenneth Leventhal Real Estate Group, NY; sr. v.p. fin. and ops. Towermarc Corp.; sr. v.p., mng. dir. Westchester and Conn. divsn. Reckson Assocs. Realty Corp., 1996—2003, exec. v.p., COO Melville, NY, 2003—. Trustee St. Luke's Sch., New Canaan, Conn. Recipient Westchester County Bus. Leader of Yr. award, 2000. Mem.: Westchester County Assn. (trustee, mem. exec. com.). Office: Reckson Assocs Realty Corp 225 Broadhollow Rd Melville NY 11747-4833

CAMPOLETTANO, THOMAS ALFRED, international contract manager; b. Long Island City, NY, Feb. 13, 1946; s. Barney and Mary (Felner) C.; m. Kathy Lee Clemons, Mar. 19, 1989; 1 stepchild, Christopher; children by previous marriage: Lisa, Jennifer, Tricia. AAS, Nassau Coll., 1971; BA, U. South Fla., 1977; postgrad., Am. Grad. U., 1980-85, Touro Coll., 1980-85; internat. contracting cert., George Washington U., 1998. Cert. profl. contract mgr. Cost/price analyst Grumman Aero. Corp., Bethpage, N.Y., 1963-70; sr. cost/price analyst Potter Instrument Co., Plainview, N.Y., 1970-73; prin. fin. analyst, govt. liaison Space Systems div. Honeywell, Inc., Clearwater, Fla., 1973—, sr. contracts mgr. Honeywell Aerospace and Electronics, 2002—. Prof. Honeywell Fed. Contracting Tng. program Author: Profit Proposal Initiatives, 1990; co-author: Weighted Guidelines Profit, 1984. With USN, 1963-66, Vietnam, 7th Fleet Flag Commendation, Combat Air Ops., 1965. Recipient Apollo Space Program commendation, NASA, 1969, Honeywell Fin. Achievement award, 1992 Mem. Nat. Contract Mgmt. Assn., Fin. Exec. Inst. (mem. com. on govt. bus. 1985), Def. Industry Offset Assn. Republican. Roman Catholic. Avocation: golf. Office: Honeywell Inc 13350 Us Highway 19 N Clearwater FL 33764-7290 Personal E-mail: bulltmp@aol.com. Business E-Mail: tom.a.campolettano@honeywell.com.

CAMPOS, FERNANDO, editor-in-chief; b. Santiago, Dominican Republic, May 30, 1934; came to U.S., 1949; s. Manuel DeJesus and Luz (Navarro) C. Grad. high sch., Commerce, N.Y. Trademark and patent clk. Haseltine & Lake, N.Y.C., 1953-55; gen. clk. Everywoman's Mag., N.Y.C., 1955-56, Rexall, L.A., 1956-57; legal rsch. libr. U.S. Army, Ft. Dix, N.J., 1957-59; legal clk. Lucke & Lucke, N.Y.C., 1959-62; mgr. list dept. St. John Assocs., N.Y.C., 1962-68; feature writer Temas Mag., N.Y.C., 1968-77; editor-in-chief Canales Mag., N.Y.C., 1977—2000; entertainment editor La Voz Hispana, 2000—. Fgn. corres. Cinema Mag., Havana, Cuba, 1956-57, El Redondel, Mexico City, 1985-87. Translator: 1001 Ideas of Interior Decoration, 1969; illustrator several pubs. Recipient Hispanic Columnist of Yr. award, Record World Mag., 1977, Press award, Inst. Puerto Rico, 1978, Media award Latin Exch., 1979, Silver medal Arts-Scis.-Lettres, Paris, 1979, Outstanding Dominican award, 2003. Mem. Assn. Hispanic Critics (founder 1967, pres. 1976-78, 81-83, hon. pres. 1983—). Avocation: travel. Home and Office: Canales Mag Apt 8E 215 W 92nd St New York NY 10025-7444 E-mail: ace215@hotmail.com.

CAMPOS, LUIS, puzzle writer; arrived in U.S., 1948; s. Manuel de Jesus Campos and Luz Navarro; 1 child, Larry. Grad., Benjamin Franklin H.S., N.Y.C., 1952. Mem. adv. and inventory staff House of Fabrics, Inc., Sherman Oaks, Calif., 1963—82; puzzle creator United Feature Syndicate, N.Y.C., 1983—. Editor: (magazine) VOL.NO. Poetry Mag., 1983. With U.S. Army, 1952—54. Roman Catholic. Achievements include patents in field; has published over 10,000 puzzles. Avocations: poetry, drawing. Mailing: PO Box 15866 North Hollywood CA 91615-5866 Office Phone: 818-768-5053. E-mail: poempoema@aol.com.

CAMPOS-ORREGO, NORA PATRICIA, lawyer, consultant; b. Lima, Peru, Sept. 3, 1959; d. Victor M. Campos and Ofelia A. Orrego. BA, Cath. U. Peru, 1979, LLB, 1983, Lawyer, 1984; JD magna cum laude, InterAm. U. P.R., San Juan, 1989. Bar: PR 1989, Peru 1984, U.S. Supreme Ct. 2003. Legal asst. women's affairs commn. P.R. Gov.'s Office, San Juan, 1988-89, lawyer women's affairs commn., 1989-93, P.R. Gov.'s Office/Immigration Law Practice, Miami, Fla., 1993-94; women's discrimination cons. San Juan, P.R., 1994-95; pvt. practice specializing in immigration law Miami, 1996—. Editor: Law Sch. Mag., 1988—89. All Am. scholar U. P.R., 1988-89. Mem. ABA, FBA, Am. Immigration Lawyers Assn., P.R. Bar Assn., Peru Bar Assn. Roman Catholic. Avocations: sightseeing, reading, dance, walking. Address: Apostolic Mission Christ 261 NE 23 St Miami FL 33137 Office Phone: 305-951-8737. E-mail: nora2003@bellsouth.net.

CANADA, MARY WHITFIELD, retired librarian; b. Richmond, Va., June 13, 1919; d. Waverly Thomas and Ruth Bradshaw (Smith) C. BA magna cum laude, Emory and Henry Coll., 1940; MA in English, Duke U., 1942; BS in LS, U. NC, 1956. Asst. circulation dept. Duke U. Libr., 1942-45, undergrad. libr., 1945-55, reference libr., 1956-85, asst. head reference dept., 1967-79, head dept., 1979-85, ret., 1985. Contbr. articles to profl. jours. Mem. exec. com. Friends of Duke U. Libr. Duke U. grantee Can., 1979, 81. Mem. ALA (life; initiated performance evaluation discussion group), Southeastern Libr. Assn. (sec. coll. and univ. sect., chmn. nominating com. reference svcs. divsn., also chmn. divsn.), NC Libr. Assn. (chmn. nominating com., chmn. newspaper com., chmn. coll. and univ. sect.), Alumni Assn. Sch. Libr. Sci. U. NC (pres.), Va. Hist. Soc. (life), Va. Geneal. Soc., DAR (chpt. regent), Friends of Va. State Archives, Campus club (Duke U.), Planning Adv. Com. North Ctrl. Durham, Va. Mus. Beta Phi Mu. Methodist. Home: 1312 Lancaster St Durham NC 27701-1132

CANADAY, RICHARD A., lawyer; b. Alton, Ill., Aug. 26, 1947; AB, Stanford U., 1969; JD, U. Calif., 1973. Bar: Oreg. 1973, Wash. 1987. Ptnr. Miller Nash LLP, Portland, Oreg. Mem. ABA, Oreg. State Bar, Wash. State Bar Assn. Office: Miller Nash LLP 111 SW 5th Ave Ste 3500 Portland OR 97204-3638 Office Phone: 503-205-2512. E-mail: rich.canaday@millernash.com.

CANADY, ALEXA IRENE, pediatric neurosurgeon; b. Lansing, Mich., Nov. 7, 1950; d. Clinton Jr. and Hortense (Golden) C.; m. George Davis, June 18, 1988. BS, U. Mich., 1971, MD cum laude, 1975; DHL (hon.), Marygrove Coll., 1994; DHL (hon.) (hon.), U. Detroit, 1997; DSc (hon.), Ctrl. Mich. U., 1999, U. So. Conn., 1999. Diplomate Am. Bd. Neurol. Surgery. Intern in surgery Yale U., New Haven, 1975-76; resident in neurosurgery U. Minn., Mpls., 1976-81; fellow in pediatric neurosurgery Children's Hosp. Pa., Phila., 1981-82; instr. neurosurgery U. Pa., Phila., 1981-82; staff neurosurgeon, instr. neurosurgery Henry Ford Hosp., Detroit, 1982-83; asst. dir. neurosurgery Children's Hosp. Mich., Detroit, 1986-87, chief of neurosurgery, 1987-97; assoc. prof. neurosurgery Wayne State U., Detroit, 1988-91, vice chmn. neurosurgery, 1991—2001; prof. neurosurgery, 1997—2001. Clin. instr. neurosurgery Wayne State U. Sch. Medicine, 1985, mem. internal rev. com. dept. anatomy, 1988, chmn. search com. dept. neurosurgery, 1989, internal rev. com. dept. neurology, 1991-92, 125th anniversary celebration com., 1992, internal rev. com. dept. pediat., 1993, chmn. search com. dept. ophthalmology, 1992-93, internal rev. com. dept. neurosurgery, 1994; chmn. neurobil. devices panel, FDA; vis. prof. Med. Coll. S.C., 1990; cons. neurol. devices panel Med. Devices Adv. Com., FDA, 1994; mem. surg. com. Children's Hosp. Mich., chmn. operating room subcom. surg. com., intensive care unit com., med. record com., med. exec. com.; mem. med. staff Children's Hosp. Mich., William Beaumont Hosp, Royal Oak and Troy, Mich., Harper-Grace Hosps., Detroit, Hutzel Hosp., Detroit, Sinai Hosp., Detroit, Huron Valley Hosp., Milford, Mich., Crittenton Hosp., Rochester Hills, Mich., St. John Hosp. and Med. Ctr., Detroit; presenter various profl confs. in U.S. and internat. Contbr. chpts. to books. Mem. Mich. Head Injury Alliance, Mich. Myelodysplasia Assn.; bd. dirs. Inst. Am. Bus., 1986-88. Recipient Citation Women's Med. Assn., 1975, Candace award Nat. Coalition 100 Black Women, N.Y., 1986, Golden Heritage award, 1989, Leonard F. Sain Esteemed Alumni award U. Mich., 1990, Disting. Alumni award Everett H.S., Pres.'s award Am. Med. Women's Assn., 1993, Variety Heart award for Med., Sci. and Tech. Variety Club, 1994, Shining Star award Colgate-Palmolive Co./Starlight Found., 1994, Golden Apple award Roeper Sch., 1995, Athena award Alumni Assn. U. Mich., 1995; named Outstanding Young Woman in Am., 1977, Top 100 Bus. & Profl. Women of Am., 1985, Woman of Yr. Detroit Club Nat. Assn. Negro Bus. & Profl. Women's Club, Inc., 1986; named to Mich. Woman's Hall of Fame, 1989; grantee Am. Cancer Soc., 1979, Minn. Med. Found., 1979, Am. Cancer Soc., 1981-82, Widman Found. Early Intervention Treatment and Follow-Up of Infants with Post-hemorrhagic Hydrocephalus, 1984-85, Neuropsychol. Recovery and Family Adaptation to CHI Children's Hosp. Mich., 1987-88, Hydrocephalus Induced Endocrinopathies: Morphologic Correlates Children's Hosp. Mich., 1989, 91. Mem. AMA, ACS, Am. Assn. Neurol. Surgeons, Congress Neurol. Surgeons, Am. Soc. Pediatric Neurosurgery, Nat. Med. Assn. Detroit Med. Soc., Mich. Assn. Neurol. Surgeons (sec. 1992-93, v.p. 1994-95, pres. 1995-96), Transplantation Soc. Mich. (adv. bd. 1993-94), Mich. State Med. Soc. (child abuse and neglect divsn. 1986), Southeastern Mich. Surg. Soc. (sec. 1986-87), Soc. Crit. Care Medicine, Wayne County Med. Soc. (ethics com., pub. affairs com., law com.), U. Mich. Med. Ctr. Alumni Soc., Delta Sigma Theta. Office: 6064 Forest Green Rd Pensacola FL 32505 Office Phone: 850-416-7101. Business E-Mail: alexacanady@aol.com.

CANADY, RICHARD WARREN, lawyer; b. Boone, Iowa., Dec. 7, 1934; s. Cecil M. and Myra N. (Shurtz) C.; m. Carol Jean Canady, Feb. 1, 1960; children— Michael Warren, Kelly Lynn. B.S.C., Iowa U., 1956, J.D. with distinction, 1959; LL.M., Georgetown U., 1962. Bar: Iowa 1959, Calif. 1962. Legal specialist Office of Navy JAG, 1960-62; law clk. to judge U.S. Ct. Appeals 9th Cir., 1962-63; assoc. White, Froehlich & Peterson, San Diego, 1963-64; ptnr. Howard, Rice, Nemerovski, Canady, Falk & Babkin, San Francisco, 1968-86, mng. ptnr., 1968-74, 86—. Trustee, v.p. Iowa Law Sch. Found. Served with USNR, 1959-62. Mem. ABA, State Bar Calif., Iowa Bar Assn., San Francisco Bar Assn., Order of Coif. Presbyterian. Clubs: Olympic, San Francisco Golf; Palm Valley Country Club (Palm Desert, Calif.). Home: 8 St Bernard Ln Belvedere Tiburon CA 94920-1819 Office: 3 Embarcadero Ctr San Francisco CA 94111-4003

CANADY, TIMOTHY W., music educator; b. Seward, Nebr., Sept. 17, 1965; s. Don R. and Pam S. Canady; m. Teresa K. Harter, July 18, 1998; children: Lauren, Grace. BME, Emporia State U., 1989. Cert. music tchr. Kans. Choral music tchr. Labette County H.S., Altamont, Kans., 1989—92, Ulysses (Kans.) H.S., 1993—99, Hutchinson (Kans.) H.S., 1999—. Staff mem. Kans. Ambassadors of Music, Wichita, 1998—; mem. Wichita Chamber Chorale, 2000. Bd. mem. Reno County, Reno County Choral Soc., Hutchinson, 2002—02. Mem.: Music Educators Nat. Conf., Kans. Music Educators Assn., Am. Choral Dirs. Assn. Personal E-mail: tcanady@cox.net.

CANALES, JAMES EARL, JR., foundation administrator; b. San Francisco, Nov. 6, 1966; s. James Earl Canales Sr. and Maritsa M. (Solorzano) Espinoza. BA, Stanford U., 1988, MA, 1989. English tchr., class dean San Francisco Univ. H.S., 1989-91, dir. admissions, 1991-93; program assoc. The James Irvine Found., San Francisco, 1993-95, program officer, spl. asst. to pres., 1995-97, chief adminstrv. officer, corp. sec., 1997-99, v.p., corp. sec., 1999—2003, pres, CEO, 2003—. Bd. dirs. Nat. Ctr. for Nonprofit Bds., Washington, 1996-03; vice-chmn. bd. dirs. KQED, Inc.; bd. regents, St. Ignatius Coll. Preparatory, 2001-03. Chair, bd. dirs. Larkin St. Youth Ctr., San Francisco, 1992-99; bd. dirs., Nat. Assn. for Cmty. Leadership, Indpls., 1994-97, Nat. Ctr. for Nonprofit Bds., Washington, 1996-03; trustee San Francisco Day Sch., 1996-99. Andrew W. Mellon Edn. Found. fellow, 1988-89. Mem. Stanford Alumni Assn. (bd. dirs. 1997—, vice chmn. 2001-03, chmn. 2003--). Democrat. Roman Catholic. Home: 21 Carmel St San Francisco CA 94117-4332 Office: 575 Market St Ste 3400 San Francisco CA 94105 E-mail: jcanales@irvine.org.

CANAPARY, HERBERT CARTON, insurance company executive; b. Bklyn., Dec. 1, 1932; s. Edward Paul and Alice G. (Brennan) C.; m. Mary E. Dolan, May 6, 1961; children: Patrick, Ellen, Ann, Jennifer Henriksen. BBA, Manhattan Coll., 1954; MS in Fin., Columbia U., 1957. With Manhattan Life Ins. Co., N.Y.C., 1957-80, asst. sec., 1961-70, 2d v.p., 1970-79, v.p., treas., 1974-80; v.p. investments Union Labor Life Ins. Co., Washington, 1981—, MRCo., 2000—, GBL Holdings, Inc., 2000. Roman Catholic. Home: One Goshen Ct Gaithersburg MD 20882 Office: 111 Massachusetts Ave NW Washington DC 20001-1461 also: 1300 Market St Wilmington DE 19801

CANARY, LEURA GARRETT, prosecutor; m. William J. Canary; children: William James, Margaret Garrett. Grad., Huntington Coll.; JD, U. Ala. Asst. atty. gen State of Ala., 1981—90; trial atty. civil divsn. US Dept. ustice, 1990—94; asst. U.S. atty. (mid. dist.) Ala. US Dept. Justice, 1994—2001, U.S. atty. (mid. dist.) Ala., 2001—. Office: Office of US Atty One Ct Sq Ste 201 Montgomery AL 36104

CANARY, NANCY HALLIDAY, lawyer; b. Cleve., Apr. 21, 1941; d. Robert Fraser and Nanna (Hall) Halliday; m. Sumner Canary, Dec. 1975 (dec. Jan. 1979). BA, Case Western Res. U., 1963; JD, Cleve. State U., 1968. Bar: Ohio 1968, Fla. 1972, U.S. Dist. Ct. (no. dist.) Ohio 1975, U.S. Supreme Ct. 1974, U.S. Dist. Ct. (so. dist.) Fla. 1994. Law clk. to presiding judge Ohio Ct. Appeals, Cleve., 1968—69; ptnr. McDonald, Hopkins & Hardy, Cleve., 1969—83; ptnr. managing Palm Beach office Thompson, Hine, LLP, Cleve., 1984—2002; sole practitioner Palm Beach, Fla., 2003—. Trustee Beck Ctr. for Cultural Arts, Lakewood, Ohio, 1980—90, Ohio Motorists Assn., 1989—95, Ohio Chamber Orch.; trustee, mem. devel. adv. com. Fairview Gen. Hosp., Cleve., 1980—96; chairperson Sumner Canary Lectureship com. Case Western Res. U. Law Sch.; sec. bd. govs. Churchill Ctr., Washington, 2000—02; bd. dirs. Comerica Bank & Trust Co., F.S.B., 1993—2000. Mem. Ohio State Bar Assn., Cleve. Bar Assn., Palm Beach County Bar Assn., Estate Planning Coun. Cleve., Estate Planning Coun. Palm Beach County, Gulf Stream (Fla.) Golf Club, Westwood Country Club (Cleve.). Republican. Avocations: music, horseback riding, collecting Churchill books. Home: Unit 1806 12500 Edgewater Dr Cleveland OH 44107-1677 also: 200 N Ocean Blvd Delray Beach FL 33483-7126 Office: 125 Worth Ave # 117 Palm Beach FL 33480 Office Phone: 561-833-5900, 216-226-7466.

CANAVAN, CHRISTINE ESTELLE, state legislator; b. Dorchester, Mass., Jan. 25, 1950; m. Paul Canavan; 2 children. Grad., Massasoit C.C., 1983; BS summa cum laude, U. Mass., 1988. RN. Mem. Mass. Ho. of Reps., Boston, 1993—, chair second fl. divsn., spl. legis. com. on foster care. Mem. Brockton (Mass.) Sch. Com., 1990-94, vice chmn., 1992-2000, Brockton (Mass.) Libr. Found. Mem. Polish White Eagles, Brockton (Mass.) Hist. Soc. Democrat. Roman Catholic. Home: 29 Mystic St Brockton MA 02302-2825 Office: Mass Ho of Reps Mass State House Rm 122 Boston MA 02133 Office Phone: 617-722-2006. Business E-Mail: rep.christinecanavan@hou.state.ma.us.

CANAVAN, THOMAS GERARD, television executive; b. Teaneck, N.J., Dec. 5, 1953; s. Robert Vincent and Catherine Patricia (Farinella) C.; children: Christopher Andrew, Evan Michael. BA, U. Notre Dame, 1976. Pres. A.F. Assocs., Inc. subs. Ascent Media Group, Northvale, NJ, 1977—2003, Video Rentals, Inc., Northvale, N.J., 1992—; pres. systems and product group Video Svcs. Corp., Northvale, N.J., 1997—; exec. v.p. sys. and tech. svcs. Ascent Media Network Svcs. Mem.: Audio Engring. Soc., Soc. Motion Picture and TV Engrs. Avocations: audio, music. Office: Ascent Media Network Svcs 100 Stonehurst Ct Northvale NJ 07647-2487 Home: 852 Zibold Ct Westwood NJ 07675-6142 Office Phone: 201-750-3001.

CANBACK, STAFFAN, corporate advisor; s. Owe and Ulla Canback; m. Charlotte Heyden, Jan. 26, 2002; children: Simon, Rasmus, Daniel. MSc, Royal Inst. of Tech., 1975—79; MBA, Harvard Bus. Sch., 1981—83; DBA, Brunel U., 2002. Mng. dir. Canback Dangel, Boston; systems devel. engr. ABB, Vasteras, Sweden, 1980—81; ptnr. McKinsey & Co, Stockholm, 1984—94, Monitor Co., Cambridge, Mass., 1994—2002. Scholar, Fulbright Commn., 1981, Marcus Wallenberg, 1994. Office: Canback Dangel 10 Derne St Boston MA 02114

CANBY, WILLIAM CAMERON, JR., federal judge; b. St. Paul, May 22, 1931; s. William Cameron and Margaret Leah (Lewis) Canby; m. Jane Adams, June 18, 1954; children: William Nathan, John Adams, Margaret Lewis. AB, Yale U., 1953; LLB, U. Minn., 1956. Bar: Minn. 1956, Ariz. 1972. Law clk. U.S. Supreme Ct. Justice Charles E. Whittaker, 1958—59; assoc. firm Oppenheimer, Hodgson, Brown, Baer & Wolff, St. Paul, 1959—62; assoc., then dep. dir. Peace Corps, Ethiopia, 1962—64, dir., 1964—66; asst. to U.S. Senator Walter Mondale, 1966; asst. to pres. SUNY, 1967; prof. law Ariz. State U., 1967—80; judge U.S. Ct. Appeals (9th cir.), Phoenix, 1980—96, sr. judge, 1996—; chief justice High Ct. of the Trust Ter. of the Pacific Islands, 1993—94. Bd. dirs. Ariz. Ctr. Law in Pub. Interest, 1974—80, Maricopa County Legal Aid Soc., 1972—78, D.N.A.-People's Legal Svcs., 1978—80; Fulbright prof. Makerere U. Faculty Law, Kampala, Uganda, 1970—71. Author: American Indian Law, 2004; note editor: Minn. Law Rev., 1955—56; contbr. articles to profl. jours. Precinct and state committeeman Dem. Party Ariz., 1972—80; bd. dirs. Ctrl. Ariz. Coalition for Right to Choose, 1976—80. 1st lt. USAF, 1956—58. Mem.: Maricopa County Bar Assn., State Bar Ariz., Order of Coif, Phi Beta Kappa. Office: Sandra Day O'Connor US Courthouse 401 W Washington St SPC 55 Phoenix AZ 85003-2156 Office Phone: 602-322-7300.

CANCE, WILLIAM GEORGE, surgery educator; b. Waterbury, Conn., June 14, 1957; MD, Duke U., 1982. Diplomate Am. Bd. Surgeons. Intern Barnes Hosp., Washington U., St. Louis, 1982-83, resident in gen. surgery, 1983-84, 86-88; fellow in surg. oncology Meml. Sloan Kettering Cancer Ctr., 1988-90; asst. prof. surgery U. N.C., Chapel Hill, 1990-95, chief sect. surg. oncology, 1993—2002, assoc. prof. surgery, 1995-99, prof. surgery, 1999—2002, James F. Newsome M.D. Endowed term prof. in surg. oncology, 1998—2002, Hector MacLean disting. prof. cancer rsch., 2002; prof., chair dept. U. Fla., Gainesville, 2003—. Mem. staff U. N.C. Hosps., 1990—. Fellow ACS (George H.A. Clowes Jr. Meml. Rsch. Career Devel. award 1994); mem. Assn. Acad. Surgery, Soc. Surg. Oncology, Soc. Univ. Surgeons, Am. Surg. Assn., Soc. Clin. Surgery. Office: Univ Fla Dept Surgery PO Box 100286 1600 SW Archer Rd Rm 6172 Gainesville FL 32610-3001 E-mail: cance@surgery.ufl.edu.

CANCELLARO, JOSEPH JAMES, composer, educator; b. Bayshore, N.Y., Jan. 10, 1967; s. Joseph James and Katherine Marie Cancellaro; m. Monika Anna Zeromska, June 8, 1996; children: Nastazja Barbara, Joseph James, Julia Katherine. MusB, Berklee Coll. Mujsic, Boston, 1989; MusM, New Eng. Conservatory of Music, Boston, 1992; PhD, U. of Edinburgh, Scotland, 1997. Prof. Columbia Coll., Chgo., 2000—. Author: (textbook) Sound Design for Interactive Media; composer: (piano concerto) Piano Concerto No.1, (composition) Surface Geometry, String Quartet No. 2, (oratorio for highland pipes) Oratorio for Highland Pipes, Choir and Orchestra. Recipient Boston Symphony Youth Concerts award, Boston Symphony Orch., 1989. Mem.: IGDA (assoc.). Office: Columbia College Chicago 600 South Michigan Ave Chicago IL 60605 Office Phone: 312-344-7063.

CANCELLIERI, CARMELA R., psychiatrist; b. N.Y., 1951; d. Remo and Charlotte (Leverich) Cancellieri. BA, Fordham U., Bronx, N.Y., 1968—72; MD, SUNY, Bklyn., 1974—78. Pvt. practice, Bronx, NY, 1984—98, Bronxville, NY, 1998—. Cons., geriatric psychiatry Sarah Neuman Nursing Home, Mamaronek, NY, 2002—03, Providence Rest Home. Fellow: Am. Psychiat. Assn.; mem.: AMA, Am. Assn. Geriatric Psychiatry. Office: Carmela Cancellieri MD One Stone Pl Ste 302 Bronxville NY 10708

CANCIAMILLA, JOSEPH, state legislator; b. Pittsburg, Calif., Apr. 19, 1955; m. Laura Canciamilla. BA, St. Mary's Coll., 1978; JD, John F. Kennedy Sch. Law, 1986. Mem. sch. bd. Pittsburg Sch. Dist., 1973—87; lawyer, 1986—; mayor, councilman City of Pittsburg, 1987—96; county supr. Contra Costa County, 1996—2000; mem., dist. 11 Calif. State Assembly, 2000—. Co-owner Pittsburg Funeral Chapel, 1992—; mem. Aging and Long-Term Care Com., Revenue and Taxation Com., Vet. Affairs Com., Jobs Econ. Devel. and the Economy Com. Mem.: State Bar Calif., NAACP (life), Young Mens Inst., Italian Am. Club. Democrat. Mailing: PO Box 942849 Rm 2141 Sacramento CA 94249-0011 Office: 815 Estudillo St Martinez CA 94553 Office Phone: 916-319-2011.

CANCIO, MARGARITA R., infectious disease physician; b. Pinar del Rio, Cuba, Sept. 29, 1959; d. Jose and Maria Cabrera; m. Derry H. Cancio, June 6, 1982. BS magna cum laude, U. South Fla., 1979; MD. Am. Bd. Internal Medicine, Infectious and Tropical Medicine. Clin. assoc. prof. dept. internal medicine USF Coll. Medicine, 2001—; chief of staff dept. internal medicine Tampa Gen. Hosp.; epidemiologist Town & Country Meml., Vencor, Tampa and Saint Petersburg. Served numerous med. staff coms. at area hosps.; lectr. in field. Founder, med. dir. Internat. Traveelr's Clinic, Infectious Disease Assocs. Tampa Bay, Kidcare; mem. comty. Hillsborough County AIDS Coordination Coun., Suncoast AIDS Network Fla., Shadow program coll. medicine students, USF and USF-HRS AIDS Patient Care Clinic. Named physician of Yr. Tampa Bay Latin Am. Med. Soc., 1997, Hispanic Woman of Yr., 1998. Fellow ACP; mem. AMA, Hillsborough County Med. Assn., Infectious Disease Soc. Am. (pres. 1989—), Soc. Hosp. Epidemiology, Am. Soc. Microbiology, Fla. Infectious Disease Soc., Fla. Health Sci. Bd. (trustee), USF (trustee), Alpha Omega Alpha. Office: Infectious Disease Assoc 4 Columbia Dr # 820 Tampa FL 33606 Fax: (813) 254-6414. Office Phone: 813-251-8444. Business E-Mail: cfalcon@travelerclinic.com.

CANCRO, ROBERT, psychiatrist, educator; b. NYC, Feb. 23, 1932; s. Joseph and Marie E. (Cicchetti) C.; m. Gloria Costanzo, Dec. 8, 1956; children: Robert, Carol. Student, Fordham U., 1948-51; MD, SUNY, 1955. Intern Kings County Hosp., Bklyn., 1955-56, resident in psychiatry, 1956-59; attending staff Gracie Sq. Hosp., N.Y.C., 1959-66; clin. instr. SUNY Downstate Med. Ctr., Bklyn., 1959-66; staff psychiatrist Menninger Found., Topeka, Kans., 1966-69; cons. Topeka State and VA Hosps., 1967-69; prof. dept. psychiatry U. Conn. Health Ctr., Farmington, 1970-76; prof., chmn. dept. psychiatry NYU Med. Ctr., 1976—; dir. N.S. Kline Inst. Psychiat. Research, 1982—. Cons. psychiat. edn. br. NIMH; biol. scis. sect. NIMH. Editor 10 books.; Contbr. articles on schizophrenia to profl. jours. Recipient Freida Fromm-Reichmann award, 1975, Strecker award, 1978, Dean award, 1981, Lehmann award, 1992. Fellow A.C.P., Am. Coll. Psychiatrists, Am. Psychiat. Assn.; mem. Am. Psychol. Assn., Assn. Am. Med. Colls., Am. Assn. Social Psychiatry (pres. 1984-86), N.Y. Acad. Scis., AAAS, AMA. Home: 118 Mclain Rd Mount Kisco NY 10549-4932 Office: NYU Med Ctr 550 1st Ave New York NY 10016-6402 Office Phone: 212-263-5744. Business E-Mail: robert.cancro@med.nyu.edu.

CANDAGE, HOWARD EVERETT, insurance management consultant, agent, broker; b. Blue Hill, Maine, Sept. 23, 1952; s. Aubrey Llewellyn and Evelyn Edsley (Carter) C.; m. Jeri-Lynn Moore, Nov. 3, 1979; children, Chelsea Alyssa, Curran Aubrey. CPCU, cert. assoc. in marine ins. mgmt., cert. ethics trainer, Inst. for Global Ethics. Ind. comml. fisherman, Blue Hill, Maine, 1970-79; ins. agt. J.T. Rosborough, Inc., Ellsworth, Maine, 1979-80, W.C. Ladd & Sons, Inc., Rockland, Maine, 1980-86, br. mgr. Damariscotta, Maine, 1986-89, resident v.p., 1988-90; ptnr. Cole-Harrison Agy. of Maine, Inc./Atlantic Yacht Insurers, Ltd., Kennebunk, 1990-93; mktg. mgr. Hanover Ins. Co. Maine, Scarborough, 1993-96; owner Ins. Resources, Gorham, Maine, 1996-98; pres. H.E. Candage, Inc., Portland, Maine, 1998—. Pres., Maine Marine Industry Assocs., Freeport, 1982-83; appointed adj. faculty Ctrl. Maine Tech. Coll., 1998—; dean sch. bus. Ind. Ins. Agts. Am. Virtual U.; underwriting mem. comml. fishing vessel safety adv. coun. USCG, 2003—. Recipient Chmn.'s award Am. Assn. Mng. Gen. Agts., 1992. Mem. Am. Soc. Appraisers, Am. Mgmt. Assn. (cert.), Soc. Chartered Property and Casualty Underwriters (treas. Maine chpt. 1990-92, v.p. 1992-93, pres.-elect 1993-94, pres. 1994-95), Nat. Soc. of Chartered Property and Casualty Underwriters (nat. chpt. affairs com.), Ind. Ins. Agts. Assn. Maine (chmn. com. 1983-84, 91-92, bd. dirs. 1990-93, Young Agt. of Yr. 1987), Soc. Ins. Rsch., Soc. Ins. Counselors (cert.), Am. Soc. Appraisers. Avocations: woodworking, travel, photography. Home: 6 Meadow Crossing Dr Gorham ME 04038-2058 Office: Marine Trade Ctr 2 Portland Fish Pier Ste 214 Portland ME 04101-4698 E-mail: howard@candage.com, hcandage@insurancemergers.com.

CANDIB, MURRAY A., retail executive, consultant; b. Chelsea, Mass., Sept. 16, 1915; s. Jacob and Fannie (Einbinder) C.; m. Claudette Aggie, Oct. 8, 1972 (dec. Dec. 1991); children: Nancy, Rachel, David, Caroline; m. Maureen Davis, July 30, 1995. BA, Boston U., 1950. Founder King's Dept. Store Inc., 1949; pres. Canco Enterprises, Worcester, Mass. Credited with being the pioneer of self-service dept. stores; subject of articles in Fortune Mag., Harvard Bus. Rev. and profl. jours. Founder, life trustee, soc. mem. Mt. Sinai Hosp., Miami Beach, Fla.; benefactor Miami Heart Inst.; charter mem. Rep. Presdl. Task Force, 1981-, U.S. Senatorial Club, 1981-, Nat. Rep. Senatorial Com.; mem. Fla. Victory Com. Brandeis U. fellow, 1966; recipient

Human Relations award Am. Jewish Com., Nat. Community Service award Jewish Theol. Sem. of Am., 1965, Man of Yr. award Mental Health Clinic, Mt. Sinai Hosp., N.Y.C., Man of Yr. award Boys Wear Industry of N.Y., Hall of Fame award U. Mass. Mem. Am. Heart Assn., Shriners, Masons, Westview Country Club Miami. Avocations: tennis, golf, painting, boating. Office: 306 Main St Worcester MA 01608-1550 Personal E-mail: maggsmom@aol.com.

CANDIDO, A. MICHAEL, contracting company executive, real estate manager; b. Falls Church, Va., June 23, 1953; s. Albert Babbitts and Rose Marie (Naturale) C.; m. Joyce Mary Baratta, Sept. 27, 1975; children: Rosalie, Elizabeth, Jacqueline, Allison. BA in Acctg., William Paterson U., 1975. Office mgr. J. Moore & Co., Livingston, N.J., 1973-79, v.p., 1979-95, pres., 1995—, Essex Realty Co., Cedar Grove, N.J., 1991—. Adj. prof. Kean U. N.J., Union, 1988-93. Mem. Essex Fells Zoning Bd., NJ, 1995—, MCA Legis Com., 2000—; elected mem. Essex County Rep. Com., NJ, 2004; vice-chmn. Essex Fells Zoning Bd., NJ, 2001—; trustee Steamfitters Local 475, Warren, NJ, 1995—; chmn. bldg. and grounds com. Notre Dame Ch., No. Caldwell, NJ, 1997—; chmn. MCAA Industry Fund, Washington, 2004—. Recipient Man of Yr. award, ACE Mentoring Program, 2003. Mem.: ASHRAE, Mech. Contracting Industry Coun. (treas. 2004—), Mech. Contractors Assn. NJ (treas. 1998—2000, v.p. 2000—02, pres. 2002—04), Mech. Contractors Assn. (treas. polit. action com. 1998, mem. legis. com. 2000—, Mentoring Program Man of Yr. award 2003), Internat. Soc. Pharm. Engrs., Essex County Rep. Com., Bay Head Hist. Soc., Essex Fells Country Club. Roman Catholic. Avocations: golf, photography, books, music. Office: J Moore & Co 118 Naylon Ave Livingston NJ 07039-1006 E-mail: mikecandido@jmoore.com.

CANDIDO, ARTHUR ALDO, publishing and distribution company executive; b. Corona, Queens, N.Y., June 6, 1960; BA, CUNY, 1982. Ops. mgr. Scholium Internat. Inc., Port Washington, N.Y., 1982-91, pres., 1991—. Mem. Spl. Librs. Assn., Am. Booksellers Assn. Office: Scholium Internat Inc PO Box 1519 Port Washington NY 11050-7519 Business E-Mail: artcandido@cs.com.

CANDIOTI, BEATRIZ AZUCENA, artist; b. Buenos Aires, Aug. 1, 1935; came to U.S., 1965; d. Romulo and Sara (Remon) Candioti; children: Patricia B. Kelly LeBienvenu, Martin G. Kelly, Andrea Kelly Smethurst. BA in Art, U. Louisville, 1981; postgrad., U. Ky., 1987-90. Exhibited in solo shows at Coffeetrees Gallery, Louisville, 1984, Chase Gallery, Paris, Ky., 1988, Swearingen Gallery, Louisville, 1984-91, Fredonia (Kans.) Arrs Cou., 1993, In Vivo, Indpls., 1996, NationsBank, Boca Raton, Fla., 1998-99, B. Deemer Gallery, Louisville, 1992-2000, others; group shows include Sherbrooke Internat. Painters Salon, Que., Can., Little Gallery, Douglas, Ariz., La. Art Ctr., Baton Rouge, Pine Tree Gallery, Troy, Ala., Malton Gallery, Cin., J. B. Speed Art Mus., Louisville, A.R.T.S., Nashville, Kathryn A. Todd Fine Arts Gallery, Indpls., Indpls. Mus. Art, Consul Gen. of Spain, Boca Raton, Ryals Gallery, Boca Raton, Lagerquist Gallery, Atlanta, B. Deemer Gallery; represented in collections at Nat. Mus. Am. Art/Smithsonian Instn., Monastery of St. Bernard de Clairvaux, Miami, A.B. Chandler Med. Ctr./U. Ky., Ky. Horse Park, Louisville, Dillingham and Murphy, San Francisco, others including pvt. collections. Recipient numerous awards for art. Address: 316 Benson St Naples FL 34113-8505

CANDLAND, D. STUART, lawyer; b. Madison, Wis., Sept. 6, 1942; s. Don Charles and Dorothy Jane (Nelson) C.; m. Evelyn McComber, Dec. 3, 1982; children: Ashley, Tara Lynn, Brett. BA with honors, Brigham Young U., 1967; JD, U. Calif., Berkeley, 1970. Bar: Calif. 1971, U.S. Dist. Ct. (no. dist.) Calif. 1971, U.S. Ct. Appeals (9th cir.) 1971. Dep. atty. gen. State of Calif., San Francisco, 1970-73; dep. dist. atty. Solano County Dist. Atty.'s Office, Fairfield, Calif., 1973-75; assoc. Law Offices of M. Craddick, Walnut Creek, Calif., 1976-78; ptnr. Craddick, Candland & Conti, Danville, Calif., 1979—. Asst. prof. law Armstrong Sch. Law, Berkeley, 1971-77. Mem. ABA, Assn. Def. Counsel, Contra Costa County Bar Assn. (Calif. med-legal com.). Office: Craddick Candland & Conti Ste 260 915 San Ramon Valley Blvd Danville CA 94526-4021 Business E-Mail: scandland@ccclawfirm.com.

CANDLAND, DOUGLAS KEITH, psychology professor; b. Long Beach, Calif., July 9, 1934; s. Horace George and Erma Louise (Downing) C.; m. Mary Homrighausen, June 18, 1959; children: Kevin, Christopher, Ian. AB, Pomona Coll., 1956; PhD, Princeton U., 1959. Rsch. fellow U. Va., 1959-60, Delta Primate Ctr., 1967-68, Pa. State U., 1968-69, U. Stirling, Scotland, 1972-73, Cambridge (Eng.) U., 1977-78; Fulbright fellow U. Mysore (India), 1983; asst. prof. psychology Bucknell U., 1960-64, assoc. prof., 1964-67, prof., 1967—85, prof. animal behavior, 1985—2002, Presdl. prof., 1973-80, head program in animal behavior, 1968—2002, pres. div. teaching of psychology, 1976-77, head dept. psychology, 1970-75, Class of 1956 lectr., 1971, Homer P. Rainey prof. emeritus psychology and animal behavior, 2004—. Vis. scholar U. Calif., Berkeley, 1996-97. Author: Exploring Behavior, 1961, Psychology: The Experimental Approach, 1968, 2d edit., 1978, Emotion, Bodily Change, 1961, Emotion, 1979, Feral Children and Clever Animals, Reflections on Human Nature, 1993, Handbook of Comparative Psychology, 1998, The Psychology of Mental Fossils, Toward an Archeo-Psychology, 2005; editor: Rev. Gen. Psychology, 2002—; contbr. chpts. to profl. books; editor The Primates, 1968-78, Animal Behavior, 1979-89; assoc. editor Animal Learning and Behavior, 1976-84, Teaching of Psychology, 1976-84, Am. Jour. Primatology, 1980-84; cons. editor Jour. Comparative Psychology, 1988-94; documentary film featured scientist: The Boy Who Was Raised With Monkeys, 1999, The Rise of Animal Rights, 2001, Le Compagnie Taxi Brousse Artes, French TV, 2005, Sci. and Insight, Russian State TV, 2005. Bd. dirs. Wildlife Preservation Trust Internat. (chmn. conservation 1989-94), Pa. Cinema Register, 1976-79, 86-89. Recipient award Lindback Found., 1971; Harriman award Bucknell U., 1979 Fellow Am. Psychol. Assn. (award for disting. contbn. to edn. 1978); mem. Brit. Psychol. Assn., Psychonomic Soc., Internat. Soc. Primatologists, Animal Behavior Soc. (chmn. policy and planning, Disting. Contbn. to Edn. award 1999). Home: 125 Stein Ln Lewisburg PA 17837-1742 Office: Bucknell U Lewisburg PA 17837 Office Phone: 570-577-1431. Business E-Mail: dcandlan@bucknell.edu.

CANDLER, FAXON DAVID, small business owner; b. Reidsville, N.C., Oct. 13, 1934; s. Faxon Douglas Candler and Inez Levenior Echols. *My father was born in Candler's Mountain in Lynchburg, Virginia. He was very smart in mechanical things. After his death in 1947, my aunts became my mentors; they were also mentors before his death. My mom also put much into my education. My great uncle had several automation inventions that were used at the American Tobacco Company. He would also be a mentor and helped me learn about electronics in the mornings before school. Thomas Edison and Henry Ford also had much to do with my education choices. This last year I have become involved in statistics and probability.* Student, Presbyn. Jr. Coll., Maxton, N.C., 1953, Guilford Coll., 1961. Draftsman, machinist Newman Machine Co., Greensboro, 1961; owner Candler Instruments, Greensboro, NC, 1962; with ECT, Salisbury, NC, 1963—94; owner Lab Links Engring. Lab, Salisbury, 1994—. Composer: Fantasy Impromptu, 1953. Vol. VA Med. Ctr., Salisbury, 1995—; mem. Rep. Nat. Com., Washington, 1976—78; Rep. Nat. Com. Washington, 1978. With Signal Corp U.S. Army, 1954—57. Baptist. Achievements include patents pending in field. Avocation: piano. Home and Office: 517 N Cedar St Salisbury NC 28144 Personal E-mail: kindman7@bellsouth.net.

CANDLER, JAMES NALL, JR., lawyer; b. Detroit, Jan. 25, 1943; s. James Nall and Lorna Augusta (Blood) C.; m. Jean Ward McKinnon, Mar. 8, 1974; children: Christine, Elizabeth, Anne. AB, Princeton U., 1965; JD, U. Mich., 1970. Bar: Mich. 1970. Assoc. Dickinson Wright PLLC, Detroit, 1970-77, ptnr., 1977—. Adj. prof. real estate planning U. Detroit Sch. of Law, 1975-80. Bd. dirs. Detroit Inst. Ophthalmology Grosse Pointe Park, Mich., 1983—, chmn., 1994—. Lt. USNR, 1965-67. Mem. Internat. Assn. Attys. and Execs. in Corp. Real Estate, State Bar Mich. (chmn. real property law sect. 1998-99), Am. Coll. of Real Estate Lawyers, Grosse Pointe Club (chmn. 1987-89), Country Club of Detroit. Republican. Avocations: sailing, golf, platform tennis. Home: 211 Country Club Dr Grosse Pointe Farms MI 48236-2901 Office: 500 Woodward Ave Ste 4000 Detroit MI 48226-3425 Office Phone: 313-223-3513. E-mail: jcandler@dickinson-wright.com.

CANDLIN, FRANCES ANN, psychotherapist, social worker, educator; b. Phila., July 18, 1945; d. Francis Townley and Wilma (David) C. BA magna cum laude, Loretto Heights Coll., 1967; MSW with honors, St. Louis U., 1971. Diplomate Am. Bd. Clin. Social Work; cert. social worker; lic. clin. social worker, Colo. Trainee recreational therapist Jewish Hosp., St. Louis, 1970—71; trainee social worker Jefferson Barracks VA Hosp., St. Louis, 1970—71; social worker Adams County Juvenile Probation, Brighton, Colo., 1972—74, Boulder County Social Svcs., Colo., 1974—75; sch. social worker Adams County Sch. Dist. #50, Westminster, Colo., 1975—80; workshop presenter Human Enrichment Cons., Denver, 1980—90; pvt. practice Denver, 1980—; dir. Madison St. Counseling Ctr., Denver, 1991—97; founder, dir. Women's Mysteries Tour Co., 1993, Enneagram Ctr. of Colo., 1997—. Cons. Mountain Plains Regional Ctr., Denver, 1981-85, Dept. Edn., Topeka, 1981-87, Dept. Spl. Edn., Nebr., Colo., Mo., N.Mex., Utah, 1982-86. Bd. dirs. Denver Sch. for Gifted, 1982-86, Weaver Found., 1985-86, St. Mary's Acad., Englewood, Colo., 1985-88. Recipient stipend NIMH, 1969, VA Social Work Trainee, 1970. Mem. NASW, NOW, Acad. Cert. Social Workers, Internat. Enneagram Assn., Assn. Transpersonal Psychology, Colo. Assn. Clin. Social Workers, Vajra Soc. (bd. dirs. 1990—). Avocations: world travel, women's issues, spiritual devel. Office: Enneagram Ctr Colo PO Box 933 Glenwood Springs CO 81602

CANDLISH, MALCOLM, manufacturing executive; b. Liverpool, Eng., Aug. 23, 1935; came to U.S., 1963; s. Norman Dennis and Jane Jefferson (Grieves) C.; m. Jasmine Rosemary Cresswell, Apr. 15, 1963; children: Fiona, Vanessa, Sarah, John. BSc, London Sch. Econs., 1956. Mgr. mktg., asst. mgr. prodn. Beecham Products, Brazil, Eng., 1958-63; product mgr. Colgate Palmolive, N.Y.C., 1963-65; prin. McKinsey and Co., N.Y.C., Cleve., Toronto, Melbourne and Sydney, Australia, 1965-77; pres., sr. v.p. mktg. Wilson Sporting Goods, Chgo., 1977-83; pres. Samsonite Corp., Denver, 1983-89; chmn., CEO Sealy, Inc. (formerly Ohio Mattress Co.), Cleve., 1989-92, First Alert, Inc., Aurora, IL, 1992-98. Bd. dirs. Mile High United Way, Denver, 1985-89. Lt. British Army, 1956-58. Mem. Luggage and Leather Goods Mfrs. Am. (bd. dirs. 1984-89), Econ. Club (founding mem.). Avocations: literature, philosophy, sports. Personal E-mail: candlish@aol.com.

CANDOCIA, FRANK, computer engineer, educator; s. Francisco and Borja Candocia; m. Yudit Candocia, Aug. 7, 1993; children: Noah, Adrian. BSEE, Fla. Internat. U., 1990, MSEE, 1993; PhD in Elec. and Computing Engring., U. Fla., 1994. Sr. systems devel. engr. Raytheon Systems Co., Bedford, Mass., 1998—2000; prof. Fla. Internat. U., Miami, Fla., 2000—. Sci. jour. reviewer Signal Processing; presenter numerous conf.; session chair IEEE Internat. Conf.; design leader of search and acquisition functionality of x-band radar Raytheon Systems Co.; rsch. asst. M.I.T. Lincoln Lab., Lexington, Mass., 1998. Scholar NHSF Recipient, Nat. Hispanic Scholarship Fund, 1995-1996; Summer fellow, Motorola, 1995. Mem.: IEEE. Achievements include design of search and acquisition portion of the X-band radar for Raytheon Systems Company under the multi-billion dollar U.S. Govt. NMD/LSI initiative; development of first optimally constrained deconvolution algorithm for magnetic force microscopy resolution increase; research in seminal contributions to comparametric image processing; development optimal approaches for the joint spatial and tonal registration of images; extension of joint registration work to allow for multiple and simultaneous image registration; development of general solution to Dr. Steve Mann's (Ph.D. MIT) comparametric formulation that allows any camera's response function to be estimated to arbitrary accuracy; research in contributions to learned super-resolution image processing with spatially varying filters. Office: Fla Internat U 10555 W Flagler St EC 3915 Miami FL 33174 Office Phone: 305-348-3017. Office Fax: 305-348-3707. E-mail: candocia@fiu.edu.

CANDOTTI, FABIO, geneticist, pediatrician; MD summa cum laude, U. Brescia, Italy, 1987. Diplomate in pediats. and pediat. allergy and immunology; lic. physician, Italy. Med. staff fellow dept. pediatrics U. Brescia, Italy, 1988-89; enlisted Italian Army Sch. of Medicine, Florence, 1989; resident in pediatrics U. Brescia, 1989-92, staff mem. Bone Marrow Transplantation Unit, 1990-91, postdoctoral fellow Lab. of Biotechnology, 1991-92; postdoctoral fellow Metabolism Br. NCI, NIH, Bethesda, Md., 1992-94; postdoctoral fellow Clin. Gene Therapy Br. NHGRI/NIH, Bethesda, 1994-96. Lectr. Italian Nat. Health Svc. Nursing Sch., Brescia, 1991-92; asst. prof. dept. pediatrics U. Brescia, 1996-97; tenure-track investigator NHGRI/NIH, Bethesda, 1998—2004, sr. investigator, 2004-; mem. animal care and use com. NHGRI, 1998-2002, vice chair animal care and use com., 2003-, head NIH gene therapy interest group, 1998—, NHGRI liaison to NIH Office of Biotech. Activities, 1999—; attending physician dept. pediatrics Brescia City Hosp., Italy, 1996-97, Clin. Ctr., NIH, Bethesda, 1998—; investigator in field. Co-author: (book) The Child: Health and Disease, 1993; mem. editl. bd. Exptl. Hematology; contbr. articles to profl. jours., books, and publs. Physician, lt. Italian Army, 1988—. Recipient fellowship Italian Nat. Health Svc., 1988, Assn. for Child with Cancer, Brescia, 1990-91, Fondazione Golgi, Brescia, 1992-94; recipient awards nat. Ctr. for Human Genome Rsch. Scientific Retreat, Airlie, Va., 1995, 96, NIH Merit award, 1999, others; grantee in field. Mem. Internat. Soc. for Exptl. Hematology, Italian Soc. Pediatrics, Working Group on Human Genetics, Italian Soc. Pediatric Immunology and Allergy, European Soc. Gene Therapy, Am. Assn. Immunologists, Am. Soc. Gene Therapy (hematopoietic cell gene therapy com. 2004—), European Soc. Immunodeficiencies, Pan Am. Group for Immunodeficiency, Clin. Immunology Soc. (membership com. 2004-), Am. Soc. Clin. Investigation, Am. Soc. Hematology, Am. Soc. Hematology. Office: 49 Convent Dr 49/3A20 Bethesda MD 20892 Business E-Mail: fabio@nhgri.nih.gov.

CANDRIS, LAURA A., lawyer; b. Frankfort, Ky., Apr. 5, 1955; d. Charles M. and Dorothy (King) Sutton; m. Aris S. Candris, Dec. 22, 1974. AB with distinction in polit. sci., Transylvania Coll., 1975; postgrad., U. Pitts., 1975-77, U. Fla., 1977-78; JD, U. Pitts., 1978. Bar: Fla. 1978, U.S. Dist. Ct. (mid. dist.) Fla. 1978, U.S. Ct. Appeals (4th cir.) 1980, Pa. 1981, U.S. Dist. Ct. (we. dist.) Pa. 1982, U.S. Ct. Appeals (3d cir.) 1983. Assoc. Coffman, Coleman, Andrews & Grogan, Jacksonville, Fla., 1978-80, Manion, Alder & Cohen, Pitts., 1981-85, Eckert, Seamans, Cherin & Mellott, Pitts., 1985-86, ptnr., 1987-96, vice chmn. labor and employment law dept, mem. practice mgmt. com., mem. strategic planning com.; ptnr. Meyer Unkovic & Scott, LLP, Pitts., 1996—, chair labor, employment law and employee benefits sect., mem. litigation and transactions depts. Contbr. over 30 articles to profl. jours. including Compensation and Benefits Rev., Forum Reporter, Employment Law Inst. manuals, Ref. Manual for the 34th Ann. Mid-West Labor Law Conf. Dynamic Bus. Mem. O'Hara Twp. Coun., 1986—90, O'Hara Twp. Planning Commn., 1990; pres. Big Bros. & Big Sisters Greater Pitts., 2004—; bd. dirs. Tri-State Employers Assn., 1991—93, Parent and Child Guidance Ctr., 1991—2001, v.p., 1998—99, mem. exec. com., 1998—2001, pres., 1999—2000, sec., 2000—01; treas., mem. exec. com. SMC Bus. Couns., 1993—94, bd. dirs., 1993—96, Big Bros. & Big Sisters Greater Pitts., 1998—, v.p. planning, 2001—02, mem. exec. com., 2001—, v.p. adminstrn., 2003—, pres., 2004—; bd. dirs. The Whale's Tale, 2000—01; bd. dirs., mem. exec. com. FamilyLinks, 2000—01. Nat. Merit Found. scholar 1972-75; named Ky. Col., 1974. Mem.: ABA (EEO com. labor sect., labor and employment law com. litigation sect.), Allegheny County Bar Assn. (coun. on professionalism 1990—2000, mem. employment sect. fed. cts. sect. 2003—, newsletter editor 2003—, coun. mem. 2003—, vice chmn. 2004—05, chair-elect 2005—, women in the law div., hqrs. com. and pers. subcom.), Pa. Bar Assn. (employment sect.), Fla. Bar Assn. Republican. Avocations: skiing, travel, bicycling, reading. Office: Meyer Unkovic & Scott LLP 1300 Oliver Bldg Pittsburgh PA 15222 Office Phone: 412-456-289'. Business E-Mail: lac@muslaw.com.

CAÑEDO, MARION, school system administrator; b. Marion, Man., Can. m. Angel Canedo; children: Eric Vosburgh, Dana Vosburgh. BE, Geneseo State Coll.; M, Cert. Advanced Studies in Curriculum and Supervision, Buffalo State Coll. Tchr. Buffalo Pub. Schs., 1968, prin., dir. early childhood ctrs. and acads., dir. reading, asst. supt. stds. and tchg. effectiveness, assoc. supt. curriculum, 1999—2000, interim supt., 2000—. Founder Invention Conv.; lectr. in critical and creative thinking, Egypt, 2000. Author: Inventive Thinking Curriculum Guide. Named N.Y. State Tchr. of Yr., 1979; named to We. N.Y. Women's Hall of Fame, 2001; recipient Nat. Excellence Edn. award, 1994, NCCJ Brotherhood/Sisterhood award in edn., 2002.

CANELLOS, GEORGE PETER, hematologist, educator, oncologist; b. Boston, Nov. 1, 1934; s. Peter and Pota C. (Coronios) C.; m. Jean H. Speare, July 27, 1958; children: Peter, George, Andrew Phillip. AB, Harvard U., 1956; MD, Columbia U., 1960; Doctor Honoris Causa, Nat. and Kapodestrian U. Athens, Greece, 1997. Diplomate Am. Bd. Internal Medicine, 1967, Am. Bd Internal Medicine, Hematology, 1972, Am. Bd. Internal Medicine, Medical Oncology, 1973; lic. Mass., 1962. Intern surgery Mass. Gen. Hosp., 1961—62, asst. resident medicine, 1962—63, sr. resident medicine, 1965—66, clin. rsch. fellow medicine, 1962, physician in medicine, 1966—, attending physician, hematology-oncology svc., 1997—; rsch. fellow Royal Postgraduate Med. Sch., London, 1966—67; active staff Children's Hosp. Med. Ctr., Boston, 1978—96, attending physician, 1977—78; clin assoc., medicine branch Nat. Cancer Inst., Bethesda, Md., 1963—65, sr. investigator, 1967-74, attending physician, medicine branch, 1967—75, clin. dir. Bethesda, Md., 1974-75; chief divsn. med. oncology Sidney Farber Cancer Inst./Dana-Farber Cancer Inst., Boston, 1975—95; med. dir. for network devel. Dana-Farber/Partners CancerCare, 1995—2004; attending physician Dana-Faber Cancer Inst., 1975—; cons. physician medicine Georgetown U. Hosp., Wash., 1971—75; sr. assoc. medicine Peter Bent Brigham Hosp., Boston, 1975—82; rsch. fellow medicine Harvard Med. Sch., 1962—63, assoc. prof. medicine Boston, 1975-83, prof., 1983-88, William Rosenberg prof. medicine, 1988—; physician Beth Israel Hosp., Boston, 1988—; attending physician, medical svc. Brigham and Women's Hosp., Boston, 1976—78, sr. physician, 1983—, physician, 1982—83, attending physician, hematology-oncology svc., 1997—. Asst. clin prof. med. Georgetown U. Sch. Medicine, Wash., 1971—74, assoc. clin. prof. medicine, 1974—75; assoc. prof. medicine Harvard Med. Sch., 1975—83, prof. medicine, 1983—88; sr. investigator and attending physician, medicine branch Nat. Cancer Inst., Bethesda, Md., 1967—73, head sect. on hematology investigations and asst. chief medicine branch, 1973—74, acting clin. dir., acting assoc. dir. for med. oncology, divsn. cancer treatment, 1974—75; oncologic drugs adv. com. Food and Drug Adminstrn., Wash., DC, 1984—88; vis. prof. U. Colo., 1976, Mayo Clinic, 1977, UCLA, 1978, Wadsworth VA Ctr., 1978, U. Fla., 1979, St. Bartholomew's Hosp., London, 1980, U. Rochester, 1981; Shenson vis, prof. Stanford U., 1992; several other vis, prof. positions; prin. investigator Dana-Farber Cancer Inst., 1982—, mem. lymphoma com., 1982—, chair, lymphoma com., 1998—2003. Editor: Neoplastic Diseases of the Blood, 1985, 2d edit., 1991; editor in chief Jour. Clin. Oncology, 1988-2001; editl. bd. European jour. of Cancer and Clin. Oncology, 1983-, Jour. Internal Medicine, 1989-, Current Opinion in Oncology, 1989-, Hematology/Oncology Clinics N.Am., 2004-Am. Cancer Soc. Trust, Inc., 1986—; external review com. Wash. U. Cancer Ctr., St. Louis, 1996—; Med. Oncology Fellowship Selection Dana-Farber Cancer Inst./Dana-Farber Ptnrs. CancerCare, 1975—; Internat. Adv. Com. Specialty Care Exec. Com. Partners HealthCare Sys., 1997—; Clin. Rsch. Coordinating Com. Dana-Farber/Ptnrs. Cancer Care, 2001—. Recipient Achievement award, Nat. Conf. of Christians and Jews, 1984, Hippocratic award, AHEPA, 1985, Disting. Physician award, Hellenic Med. Soc. NY, 1988, Leonideion award, Pan-Laconian Fedn. US and Can., 1993, Disting. Svc. award for Sci. Achievement, Am. Soc. Clin. Oncology, 1996, Disting. Sci. award, HSCO, 1996, Lifetime Achievement award, Alpha Omega Coun., 1999, Key to the Cure award, Cure for Lymphoma Found., 1999, George Papanicolaou award, Nwe England Hellanic Med. and Dental Soc., 2000, Ellis Island Medal of Honor, NECO, 2004. Fellow ACP, Royal Coll. Physicians London and Scotland; mem. Am. Soc. for Clin. Investigation, Assn. Am. Physicians, Am. Soc. Clin. Oncology (pres. 1993-94), Am. Assn. Cancer Rsch., Am. Fedn. for Clin. Rsch., Am. Soc. Hematology, Mass. Soc. Clin. Oncology. Office: Dana-Farber Cancer Inst 44 Binney St Boston MA 02115-6084 Office Phone: 617-632-3470.

CANELLOS, PETER CONSTANTINE, lawyer; b. N.Y.C., Mar. 24, 1944; s. Constantine and Helen (Demetracopoulos) C.; m. Connie Salaoutis, Dec. 28, 1969; children: Sophia, Eleni. BA summa cum laude, Columbia U., 1964, LLB magna cum laude, 1967. Bar: N.Y., 1967. Law clk. Judge Charles D. Breitel, N.Y.S. Ct. Appeals; assoc. Cravath, Swaine & Moore, N.Y.C., 1969-77; ptnr. Wachtell, Lipton, Rosen & Katz, N.Y.C., 1977—, chmn. tax dept. Editor (in chief): Columbia Law Rev.; contbr. articles to profl. jours. Fulbright scholar Univ. Amsterdam, The Netherlands, 1968-69. Mem. Am. Law Inst., N.Y. State Bar Assn. (chair tax sect.), Assn. of Bar of City of N.Y, Phi Beta Kappa. Office: Wachtell Lipton Rosen & Katz 51 W 52nd St Fl 29 New York NY 10019-6150 Office Phone: 212-403-1241. Office Fax: 212-403-2241. Business E-Mail: pcanellos@wlrk.com.

CANEPA, MARK A., information technology executive; BEE, MEE, Carnegie-Mellon U.; completed Advanced Mgmt. Program, Wharton Sch., U. Pa. Former gen. mgr. workstation divsn. Hewlett-Packard; v.p., gen. mgr. workgroup server product group Sun Microsystems, Santa Clara, Calif., 1996—2000, mem. internet desktop and server products group, 2000—01, exec. v.p. network storage products group, 2001—. Office: Sun Microsystems Inc 4150 Network Cir Santa Clara CA 95054 Office Phone: 650-960-1300, 800-555-9786. Office Fax: 408-276-3804.

CANER, EMIN DAVID, lawyer; b. N.Y.C., June 27, 1960; s. Ali Riza and Anjela Josephine Caner; m. Eva Chovancakova, May 19, 2002; stepchildren: Michaela Chovancakova, Pavlina Chovancakova. AS, McHenry County Coll., Crystal Lake, Ill., 1983; AAS, Ind. Vocat. Tech. Coll., Evansville, 1988; BA, Calif. State U., LA, 1992; JD, Thomas M. Cooley Law Sch., 1998. Bar: Ill. 1999, U.S. Dist. Ct. (no. dist.) Ill. 1999. Data entry clk. Can. Nat./Ill. Ctrl. R.R., Chgo., 1999—2000; pvt. practice Chgo., 2000—. Metros scholar, Sixty Plus Elderlaw Clinic, Lansing, Mich., 1997. Mem.: ABA, Ill. State Bar Assn., Chgo. Bar Assn. Avocations: walking, bicycle riding. Office: Law offices of E David Caner 442 Ela St Apt 3N Barrington IL 60010-3369 Business E-Mail: david_caner@attymail.com.

CANES, BRIAN DENNIS, benefits compensation analyst; b. London, July 14, 1945; arrived in U.S., 1982; s. Jules Joel C. and Freda Rica (Gavronsky) C; m. Melanie Maxine Segal, June 29, 1969; 1 child, David. BSc, U. Witwatersrand, Johannesburg, South Africa, 1967; student, Inst. Actuaries, London. Systems mgr. Shepley & Fitchett Consulting Actuaries, Johannesburg, 1968-75; asst. v.p. William M. Mercer Ltd., Toronto, Canada, 1975-80, contr., 1980-82; prin. Mercer Consulting, N.Y.C., 1982—87; sr. systems cons. Watson Wyatt Worldwide, N.Y.C., 1987—93; asst. dir. systems Ernst & Young ABC, N.Y.C., 1993-96; sr. mgr. Ernst & Young Mgmt. Cons., 1996-99; v.p., RetireMentor, product mgr. Golden Retirement Resources, N.Y.C., 1999—2004; sr. v.p. Actuarial & Econs., 2005—. Office: Golden Retirement Resources Inc 500 5th Ave Fl 48 New York NY 10110 E-mail: brian@canes.net.

CANESTRARI, RONALD J., state legislator; b. Cohoes, NY, May 22, 1943; BS, Fordham Coll., 1965; JD, Fordham Univ., 1968. Atty. US Army, Fed. Govt.; mayor City of Cohoes, 1976—89; assemblyman dist. 106 NY State Assembly, 1989—. With U.S. Army, 1969—71. Mem.: NY State Bar Assn. Democrat. Address: 717 Legislative Office Bldg Albany NY 12248-0001 Office Phone: 518-455-4474. Office Fax: 518-455-4727. E-mail: Canestr@Assembly.State.NY.US.

CANES-WRONE, BRANDICE, political scientist, educator; b. Washington, Jan. 25, 1971; d. Michael and Mary Pat Canes; m. David A. Wrone. PhD, Stanford U., 1998; AB, Princeton Univ., 1993. Asst. prof. of polit. sci. MIT, Cambridge, Mass., 1998—2002; vis. asst. prof. of polit. sci. Calif. Inst. of

Tech., Calif., 2001—02; assoc. prof. of polit. sci. Northwestern U., Ill., 2002—. Editl. bd. mem. Presdl. Studies Quar. Author: (scholarly articles) American Political Science Review, American Journal of Political Science, Journal of Politics, among other journals (Patrick J. Fett Award, 1997). Fellow EPA Sci. to Achieve Results Fellowship, EPA, 1997—98. Mem.: Midwest Polit. Sci. Assn., Am. Polit. Sci. Assn. Office: Northwestern Univ 601 University Pl Scott Hall Evanston IL 60208

CANFIELD, ANDREW TROTTER, lawyer, writer; b. N.Y.C., Apr. 30, 1953; s. Edward Francis and Janet Powell (Trotter) C.; m. Marguerite Southworth Dove, May 30, 1987; children: Augusta Phillips, Lilian Sinclair. BA in History, U. Va., 1976; JD, Am. U., 1991. Bar: Pa. 1991, D.C. 1993. Rsch. assoc. Planning Rsch. Corp., McLean, Va., 1977-79; legal asst. Casey, Scott and Canfield P.C., Washington, 1979-88, law clk., 1988-91, assoc., 1991-93, Canfield and Smith, Washington, 1993-94, of counsel, 1994—. Technical and legal writer on solar energy, environ. law, manufactured housing, computer products liability and govt. timber contracts, 1976—. Republican. Episcopalian. Avocations: history, audio, photography, poetry, skiing. Home: PO Box 819 1117 Webster Rd Shelburne VT 05482

CANFIELD, CHERYL LUCAS, epidemiologist; d. Paul Keith and Joanne Bissonette Lucas; m. Raymond Gordon Canfield; 1 child, Raymond Gordon Jr. BA, SUNY, Buffalo, 1983, MS in Epidemiology, 1988. Epidemiologist Ecology and Environment, Lancaster, NY, 1991—95; corp. compliance officer Ind. Health Assn., Williamsville, NY, 1995—. Strategic planner Univ. Heights Cmty. Devel. Assn., Buffalo, 2000—03; pres. West Main Block Club, Buffalo, 1996—2003. Mem.: Health Care Compliance Assn. Avocations: international travel and cultures, pen and ink rendering, rollerblading, community activism. Office: Ind Health Assn 511 Farber Lakes Dr Williamsville NY 14221 Address: 9660 High St Clarence Center NY 14032

CANFIELD, CINDY KAY RAUP, elementary school educator; b. Bethlehem, Pa., Oct. 4, 1955; d. Paul Dixon Raup and Norma Louise (Haas) Hagman. AAS in Advt. Art, Northampton County C.C., Bethlehem, 1975; BA in Art Edn., Kutztown U., 1977, MEd in Art Edn., 1990. Cert. art edn. K-12, Pa. Tchr. art. Floyd Schaeffer Elem. Sch./Nazareth (Pa.) Area Sch. Dist., 1977-78, Ritter Elem. Sch./Allentown Sch. Dist., 1978-84; instr. fine arts Union Terr. Elem. Sch./Allentown Sch. Dist., 1981-84, Hiram W. Dodd Elem. Sch./Allentown Sch. Dist., 1984—. Coop. tchr. Kutztown U., 1981—; fine arts instr. Baum Sch. Art, 1986-87; mem. Getty Grant Consortium, 1986-87; mem. adj. faculty Muhlenberg Coll., Allentown, 1987—; observer Getty Inst. for Educators on the Arts, L.A., 1987; facilitator, participant discipline based art edn. inst., Allentown Sch. Dist., 1988, curriculum writer, 1990, 91, asst. coord., chair dist. and staff meetings, dist.-wide elem. art exhibit; mem. art. edn. adv. bd. Allentown (Pa.) Art Mus., 1992—. Vol. ball decorating com. Musikfest, 1990-93. Mem. Nat. Art Edn. Assn. (Outstanding Ea. Elem. Art Educator award 1992), Pa. Art Edn. Assn. (Outstanding Art Educator award 1991). Avocations: art, reading, gardening, home renovation. Office: Hiram W Dodd Elem Sch 1944 Church Rd Allentown PA 18104-1606

CANFIELD, CINDY SUE, art educator; b. Farmington, Mo., June 22, 1960; d. Lee Roy and Dale Collins; m. John M. Canfield II, Aug. 2, 1987; children: Clara Seleena, Johnell Mckinlee, Macarthur. B in Art Edn., Coll. Ozarks, 1983; post grad., Drury, 1984; post grad, U. Va., 1992. Cert. tchg. Mo. Weaver Coll. Ozarks, Point Lookout, 1978—83; tchr H.S. art Steelville Pub. Schs., 1983—85, Miller Pub. Schs., 1985—86, Strafford Pub. Schs., 1986—92; educator elem. art Hollister Pub. Schs., Mo., 1992—. Arts basic program site coord. Hollister Pub. Schs., Taney County, 1992—, dir. cmty. art events, Hollister, 1992—, new sch. com. bond organizer, 1994—95; dir. pub. rels. Sch. Bond Issue, 1994—. Author: Southwest Arts Reference Directory, 1991, K-12 Sequential Art Curriculum Guide, 1991. Active Taney County Character Edn. Bldg. Team, 2005. Recipient Nat. Tchr. Inst. Excellence award, Robert Rauschenburg, 1994, Arts Alliance grant, Getty Found., 1992—94, Conservation award, Soil Water Co., 2001. Mem.: PTA, S.W Dist. Art Tchrs. Assn., Nat. Art Educator's Assn. Avocations: reading, writing, painting, sculpting, swimming. Home: 295 Quincy Rd Kirbyville MO 65679 Office: Hollister Pub Schs 1798 State Hwy Hollister MO 65672 Office Phone: 417-334-5112. Business E-Mail: blcny922cancun@wmconnect.com.

CANFIELD, EDWARD FRANCIS, lawyer, legal association administrator; b. Phila., Apr. 7, 1922; s. Frank James and Eunice C. (Sullivan) C.; m. Janet Powell Trotter, 1952 (div. 1991); children: Andrew Trotter, Janet Powell; m. Margaret Harvey O'Brien, 1993. BA, St. Joseph's U., 1943; JD, U. Pa., 1949. Bar: Pa. 1949, D.C. 1972. Practice in, Phila., 1949-51; with RCA, 1953-60, Philco-Ford Corp., 1960-69, corp. dir. govt. planning and mktg., 1961-69; pres. Leisure Time Industries, Inc., 1969; mng. ptnr. Casey, Scott & Canfield, 1971-93; ptnr. Canfield & Smith, Washington, 1993—. Lt. comdr. USNR, ret. Mem. Fed. Bar Assn., D.C. Bar Assn., Phila. Bar Assn., Congl. Country Club (Bethesda, Md.), Overbrook Golf Club (Bryn Mawr, Pa.), Atlantic City (N.J.) Country Club. Home: 1 Andover Rd Haverford PA 19041-1002 Office: Canfield & Smith 910 17th St NW Ste 800 Washington DC 20006 also: 117 S 17th St Philadelphia PA 19103-5025 Office Phone: 202-833-4020.

CANFIELD, JACK, writer, speaker, trainer; b. Ft. Worth, Aug. 19, 1944; s. Elmer Elwyn and Ellen Waterhouse (Taylor) C.; m. Judy Ohlbaum, 1971 (div. Nov. 1976); children: Oran, Kyle; m. Georgia Lee Noble, Sept. 9, 1978 (div. dec. 1999); 1 child, Christopher. BA, Harvard U., 1966; MEd, U. Mass., 1973; PhD, U. Santa Monica, 1981. Educator Clinton (Iowa) Job Corps Ctr., 1968-69; dir. edn. W.C. Stone Found., Chgo., 1969-70; co-dir. New Eng. Ctr., Leverett, Mass., 1971-77; instr. U. Mass., Amherst, 1978-80; dir. ednl. svcs. Insight of Tng. Seminars, Santa Monica, Calif., 1981-83; pres. Self-Esteem Seminars, Culver City, Calif., 1983—, Santa Barbara, Calif., 1983—; CEO Chicken Soup for the Soul Ent., Santa Barbara, 1998—. Pres. Inst. Holistic Edn., Amherst, 1975-81; mem. adv. bd. The Wyland Found., Laguna, Calif., 1997—. Author: Personalized Learning: Confluent Processes in the Classroom, 1976, Self-Esteem and Peak Performance: A Transcript, 1991, Los Angeles Dodgers Team Esteem Program: A Self-Esteem Curriculum Guide, 1992; co-author: (with H.C. Wells) About Me: A Curriculum for a Developing Self, 1971, Japanese edit., 1977, 100 Ways to Enhance Self-Concept in the Classroom: A Handbook for Teachers and Parents, 1976, rev. edit., 1993, (with others) Self-Esteem in the Classroom: A Curriculum Guide, 1986, (with A. Mecca, et al) Toward A State of Esteem: The Final Report of the California Task Force to Promote Self-Esteem and Personal and Social Responsibility, 1990, (with. F. Siccone) 101 Ways to Develop Student Self-Esteem and Responsibility in the Classroom, Vol. II: The Power to Succeed in School and Beyond, 1992, vol. I, 1994, (with M.V. Hansen) Chicken Soup for the Soul: 101 Stories to Open the Heart and Rekindle the Spirit, 1993, large print edit., 1996, various translations (Abby award Am. Booksellers Assn. 1995, other awards, #1 N.Y. Times Best Seller List over 2 years, #1 Pubs. Weekly Best Seller List over 2 years, others), Dare to Win, 1994, various translations, 1996—, (with K. Goldberg) Follow Your Dreams: A Goals Setting Workbook, 1994, (with M.V. Hansen) A 2nd Helping of Chicken Soup for the Soul: 101 More Stories to Open the Heart and Rekindle the Spirit, 1995, large print edit., 1996, various translations (various awards), The Aladdin Factor: How to Ask for and Get Everything You Want in Life, 1995, various translations, (with M.V. Hansen and D. Von Welanetz Wentworth) Chicken Soup for the Soul Cookbook: Stories and Recipes from the Heart, 1995, (with M.V. Hansen) A 3rd Serving of Chicken Soup for the Soul: 101 More Stories to Open the Heart and Rekindle the Spirit, 1996, (with J. Miller) Heart at Work: Stories and Strategies for Building Self-Esteem and Reawakening the Soul at Work, 1996, various translations, (with M.V. Hansen) The Chicken Soup for the Soul Journal, 1996, (with M.V. Hansen, P. Aubery, and N. Mitchell) Chicken Soup for the Surviving Soul: 101 Stories of Courage and Inspiration from Those Who Have Survived Cancer, 1996, various translations, (with M.V. Hansen and B. Spilchuk) A Cup of Chicken Soup for the Soul, 1996, (with M.V. Hansen and P. Hansen) Condensed Chicken Soup for the Soul, 1996, Chicken Soup for the Kid's Soul, 1998, (with M.V. Hansen, M. Shimoff, and J. Hawthorne) Chicken Soup for the Woman's Soul: 101 Stories to Open the Heart and Rekindle the Spirits of Women, 1996, various translations, Chicken Soup for the Mother's Soul: 101 Stories to Open the Hearts and Rekindle the Spirits of Women, 1997, (with M.V. Hansen, M. Rutte, M. Rogerson, and T. Clauss) Chicken Soup for the Soul at Work: 101 Stories of Courage Compassion and Creativity in the Workplace, 1996, (with M.V. Hansen, H. McCarty, and M. McCarty) A Fourth Course of Chicken Soup for the Soul: 101 Stories to Open the Heart and Rekindle the Spirit, 1997, (with M.V. Hansen and K. Kirberger) Chicken Soup for the Teenage Soul: 101 Stories About Life, Love and Learning, 1997, (with M.V. Hansen and P. Aubery) Chicken Soup for the Christian Soul: 101 Stories to Open the Hearts and Rekindle the Spirits of Christians, 1997, (with M.V. Hansen) A Little Sip of Chicken Soup for the Soul: Inspiring Stories of Self-Affirmation, 1997, Another Sip of Chicken Soup for the Soul: Heartwarming Stories of the Love Between Parents and Children, 1997, A Fifth Portion of Chicken Soup for the Soul: 101 Stories to Open the Heart and Rekindle the Spirit, 1998, (with M.V. Hansen, M. Becker, DVM, and C. Kline) Chicken Soup for the Pet Lover's Soul: 101 Stories to Open the Hearts and Rekindle the Spirits of Pet Lovers, 1998, (with M.V. Hansen and R. Camacho) Chicken Soup for the Country Soul: 101 Stories Served up Country Style and Straight from the Heart, 1998, (with M.V. Hansen, P. Hansen and I. Dunlap) Chicken Soup for the Kid's Soul, 1998, (with M.V. Hansen, M. Shimoffand J. Hawthorne) A 2nd Chicken Soup for the Woman's Soul, 1998, (with M.V. Hansen and K. Kirberger) Chicken Soup for the Teenage Soul II, 1998, Chicken Soup for the Teenage Soul Journal, 1998, (with M.V. Hansen, M.& C. Donnelly and B. DeAngelis) Chicken Soup for the Couple's Soul, 1999 (with M.V. Hansen, J. Aubery and M.& C. Donnelly) Chicken Soup for the Golfer's Soul, 1999, (with M.V. Hansen, Ki. Kirberger and D. Clark) Chicken Soup for the College Soul, 1999 (with M.V. Hansen and H. McNamara) Chicken Soup for the Unsinkable Soul, 1999, (with M.V. Hansen, M. Shimoff and J. Hawthorne) Chicken Soup for the Single Soul, 1999, (with M.V. Hansen, M. Becker and Carol Kline) Chicken Soup for the Cat and Dog Lover's Soul, 1999 (with M.V. Hansen and Don Dible) Chicken Soup for the Dental Soul, 1999, (with P. Meyer, B. Chesser, M.V. Hansen and A. Seeger) Chicken Soup for the Golden Soul, 2000, (with Janet Switzer) The Success Principles: How to Get From Where You Are to Where You Want to Be, 2005, (with M.V. Hansen, P. Aubery and N. Autio) Chicken Soup for the Christian Family Soul, 2000. Named Outstanding Young Man of Am., U.S. Jaycees, 1978; recipient So. Calif. Book Publicist of the Yr. award, L.A., 1995, Body Mind Spirit Book award Body Mind Spirit Mag., 1996, Chancellor's Medal, U. Mass., 1998, Promise to the Earth award Nat. Arbor Day Found., 1998, Oprah's Angel Network award, 1999. Mem. Nat. Coun. for Self-Esteem (founder, bd. dirs. 1986-98, adv. bd. 1986—, Nat. Leadership award 1993), Nat. Spkrs. Assn. (Cert. Speaking Profl. award 1989). Democrat. Avocations: tennis, travel, guitar. Office: Chicken Soup for the Soul Enterprises Inc 929 Via Fruteria Santa Barbara CA 93110-2321

CANGANELLI, VINCENT GUGLIELMO, retired psychiatrist; b. Indpls., Sept. 3, 1927; s. Benedetto Antonio and Mary Ethel Canganelli; m. Beverly Janice Neal (div.); children: Michael Antonio, Patrick William, Theresa Ann, Joanne Leah, Janice Maria, Mark Angelo, Monica Louise. MD, Ind. U., Indpls., 1952. Lic. psychiatrist Ind. Intern St. Vincent's Hosp., Indpls., 1953; psychiatrist Ind., 1952—69, 1969—77, 1977—83, 1983—89, 1989—93, 1996—97, 1994—95, 1995—96; ret., 1997. Cons. in field. With USN, 1946. Mem.: Am. Psychiat. Assn. (life). Roman Catholic. Avocation: writing. Home: 1151 Park Ave Apt 1016 Valparaiso IN 46385

CANGEMI, JOSEPH PETER, psychologist, consultant, educator; b. Syracuse, N.Y., June 26, 1936; m. Amelia Elena Santaló, Oct. 6, 1962; children: Michelle, Lisa Ann. BS, SUNY, Oswego, 1959; MS, Syracuse U., 1964; EdD, Ind. U., 1974; LittD (hon.), William Woods U., 1996; DHC (hon.), Moscow State U., 2001. Diplomate Am. Bd. Vocat. Experts, Am. Bd. Forensic Examiners, Am. Coll. Counselors; diplomate in profl. counseling Internat. Acad. Behavioral Medicine, Counseling and Psychotherapy; cert. sch. psychologist, counselor, N.Y. Instr. Syracuse Pub. Schs., 1959-60, vocat. rehab. coord., rsch. assoc., 1961-65; instr., asst. dir. Carol Morgan Sch., Santo Domingo, Dominican Republic, 1960-61; asst. head basketball coach SUNY C.C., Syracuse, 1962-63, lectr., chmn. dept. psychology evening-extension divsn., 1962-65, vis. lectr., 1966; supr. edn. Orinoco Mining divsn. U.S. Steel Corp., Ciudad Piar, Venezuela, 1965-66, supr. tng. and devel. Puerto Ordaz and Ciudad Piar, Venezuela, 1966-68; asst. prof. psychology Western Ky. U., Bowling Green, 1968-75, assoc. prof., 1975-79, prof., 1979—; dir. Inst. Leadership, Inc., Inst. for Creative Leadership Strategies, Inc., 1970—. Project dir. U. Los Andes, Merida, Venezuela, Inter-Am. Devel. Bank, Washington, Western Ky. U., 1975-77; cons. R.R. Donnelley & Sons, Coca Cola, Gould Corp., Eaton Corp., Firestone Tire and Rubber Co., Uniroyal/Goodrich Tire and Rubber Co., Gen. Tire and Rubber Co., Jefferson Smurfit, Std. Products, Tyson Foods, others; host Conversation program Western Ky. U. Divsn. Radio, TV Film, 1968-71. Author: Higher Education and the Development of Self-Actualizing Personalities, 1977, La Administracion Participativa, 1983, (with Casimir Kowalski) Perspectives in Higher Education, 1983, Higher Education in the United States and Latin America, 1983, (with George Guttschalk) Effective Management, 1980, (with Casimir Kowalski and Jeffrey Claypool) Participative Management: Employee Management Cooperation, 1985, Chinese edit., 1990, (with Mario Noronha) Marketing Y Venda, Portuguese edit., 1992, (with Casimir Kowalski) Andersonville Prison, Lessons in Organizational Failure, 1993, (with Carl Kreisler) Raymond C. Gibson-Distinguished Kentuckian, Renowned Educator and Statesman: An Anthology, 1996, (with Mario Noronha, Casimir Kowalski, George Guttschalk) Falhas Organizaciones, Portuguese edit., 1996, (with Tatyana Ushakova and Casimir Kowalski) Leadership for the 21st Century, Russian edit., Russian Academy of Sciences, (with Casimir Kawalski and Habib Khan) Leadership Behavior, 1998, (with R. Miller, C. Kowalski, T. Hollopeter) Developing Trust in Organizations, 2005; editor: Educator's Svc. Bull., 1971-72, Psychology and Edn.: An Interdisciplinary Jour., 1977—, Jour. Human Behavior and Learning, 1983-90, Orgn. Devel. Jour., 1983-89; mem. editl. bd. Archivos Panamenos de Psicologia, 1968-88, Coll. Student Jour., 1973-2004, Faculty Rsch. Bull. of Western Ky. U., 1977-88, Jour. Instructional Psychology, 1977-90, Counseling and Values, 1979-84, Technol. Horizons in Edn. Jour., 1979-92 Edn., 1976—, Jour. Fgn. Psychology, Russia, 1996—, Forensic Examiner, 1998-2004; contbr. over 400 articles, chpts. to profl. publs. Trustee William Woods U., 1988—; past bd. dirs. COCITE (Cooperativa de Ensino Superior de Technicas Avancadas de Gestao e Informatica) Technol. U., Lisbon; past mem. House of Goa, Lisbon, Portugal, 1996-97. Recipient certs. and awards U.S. Army Armor Sch., 1974; Eaton Corp., 1974, 76, Nat. Autonomous U. Nicaragua, 1976, ICETEX, Colombia, 1977, Colombian Nat. Assn. Indsl. Engrs., 1977, Decreto award City of Bucaramanga, Colombia, 1976, 77, Quality Control Assn., 1979, Decreto award State of Santander, Colombia, 1977, Excellence in Productive Tchg. award Western Ky. U. Coll. Edn., 1979, 91, 99, Firestone Tire and Rubber Co. award, 1978, 81, Profl.-Tech. Socs. award, 1983, Coll. Student Jour. and Models of Excellence award, 1983, Disting. Pub. Svc. award Western Ky. U., 1983, Excellence in Pub. Svc. award Coll. Edn., 1983, Disting. Alumnus award SUNY, Oswego, 1983; award from Uniroyal-Goodrich Tire and Rubber Co., 1986, Excellence in Rsch. and Creativity award Coll. Edn., Western Ky. U., 1987, United Rubber Workers/Internat. Brotherhood Elec. Workers and Firestone Tire & Rubber Co. award, 1991; featured personality Orgn. Devel. Jour., 1989, Jour. Edn. award, Project Innovation, 1992 (featured on cover in summer issue); Bridgestone-Firestone award Valencia, Venezuela, 1994, Outstanding Contbn. award Southea. divsn. Redman Industries, 1996; dreated awards at several univs. Mem. ACA (regional chmn. com. internat. edn. 1976 life), Nat. Vocat. Guidance Assn. Profl., Internat. Coun. Psychologists (past area chmn. Ky.), Assn. Specialists in Group Work (charter), Panamanian Psychol. Assn. (hon.), Ky. Acad. Arts and Scis. (life), Internat. Assn. Edn. and Vocat. Guidance, Nat. Assn. Gifted (bd. dirs. 1973), Colombian Nat. Soc. Indsl. Engrs. (hon.), Romanian Acad. Scis. (hon.), Internat. Registry Orgn. Devel. Profls., RODP, InterAm. Soc. Psychology, Acad. Mgmt., Soc. Psychology in Mgmt., Capitol Arts Assn., Alumni Assn. SUNY-Oswego, Ind. U. Alumni Assn. (life), Bowling Green Country Club, Gold Key, Pi Kappa Delta, Psi Chi, Sigma Delta Psi, Sigma Tau Delta, Phi Delta Kappa. Home: 1409 Mt Ayr Cir Bowling Green KY 42103-4708 Office: Western Ky U Dept Psychology Bowling Green KY 42101 Office Phone: 270-842-3436. Business E-Mail: joseph.cangemi@wku.edu, joseph.cangem@insight.bb.

CANGEMI, MICHAEL PAUL, accountant, author, consultant; b. Bklyn., May 5, 1948; s. Ignatius and Mary (Chimento) C.; m. Maria D. Ruscitti, Nov. 23, 1974; children: Michael Jason, Marc Ignatius. BBA, Pace U., 1970. CPA, NY; cert. info. sys. auditor. Asst. to v.p. ops. Blair & Co., NYC, 1966—70; prin. Arthur Young & Co., NYC, 1970—80; v.p. Phelps Dodge Corp., NYC, 1980—88; ptnr., nat. dir. EDP auditing BDO Seidman, 1988—92; sr. v.p., CFO, CEO Etienne Aigner Inc., Edison, NJ, 1992—2000; pres., CEO, bd. dirs. Etienne Aigner Group, Edison, 2000—04; founder, pres. MC Comm., 2004—. Lectr. field. Author: Managing the Audit Function-A Corporate Audit Department Procedures Guide, 1993, 3d edit., 2003, Managing the Audit Function Chinese lang. edit., 2005; contbg. author: The Handbook for EDP Auditing, 1986; co-author: Auditing in an EDP Environment; contbr. articles to profl. jours. Bd. mem. N.J. Reads, Inc., 2003—. Recipient Alumni Achievement award, Pace U. Lubin Sch. Bus., 2003. Mem. AICPA, NY State Soc. CPA (data processing com. 1979-80, computer usage and data processing com. 1980-82), EDP Auditors Assn. (internat. bd. dirs. 1982-89, trustee 1982-89, v.p. edn. 1982-84, exec. v.p. 1984-85, assn. found. pres. 1985-86, pres. NY chpt. bd. dirs. 1978-86, 2d v.p., 1979-80, 1st v.p. 1983, nominating com. 1982-86, conf. site selection com. 1981-82, editor Info. Sys. Control Jour., 1987—, editor-in-chief, 1992-94, assoc. editor EDPACS newsletter, The EDP Audit, Control and Security, 1988-94, J.J. Wasserman award 1987, Eugene M. Frank award 1989, Michael P. Cangemi best article-best book award, 1996), Fin. Execs. Inst., Inst. Internal Auditors (program devel. com. for 1986 conf. 1984-86, bd. govs. NY chpt. 1986-92, bd. rsch. advisors 1987-93, pres. NY chpt. 1989-90, trustee rsch. found. 1994-2000), Soc. Info. Sys. Quality (bd. dirs. 1987-88), Arthur Young Businessmen's Assn. (bd. dirs. 1982-89, v.p. 1985-89), Metuchen (NJ) Golf Country Club. Roman Catholic. Home: 18 Fishel Rd Edison NJ 08820-3217 Office: Info Systems Audit & Control Assn Ste 1010 3701 Algonquin Rd Rolling Meadows IL 60008-3124

CANHAM, ANDREA, artist; b. Watertown, N.Y., Sept. 21, 1956; d. Alan Tracey and Hazel (Baker) C.; m. Jonathan Lang, 1980 (div. 1983); m. Richard Lavrito, Aug. 14, 1988. BFA, Syracuse U., 1980. Artist in residency Oneida County, 1987; bd. dirs. Mohawk Valley Ctr. for the Arts, Little Falls, N.Y., 1989-96; with Artist's at Work Cmty Projects, Utica, N.Y., 1995; panel mem. Decentralization Panel of Ctrl. N.Y., 1995-97; teaching artist Art in Edn. Inst. Ctrl. N.Y. Cmty Art Coun., 1995-97; artist. Exhbns. include Women in the Arts Festival, Syracuse, N.Y., 1980, Charlotte Printmakers 4th Annual Eastern U.S. Print Exhbn., 1980, SUNY Region Art Show, 1985, 86, 88, Women's Caucus for the Arts Regional Show, 1988, National '90' Scholararie Arts Coun., 1990, Gallery 17 N.Y. State Mus., Albany, 1990, Fresh Impressions Gallery 53, Cooperstown, N.Y., 1992, Art in the Sun, Pompano Beach, Fla., 1992, Cornhill Arts Festival, Rochester, N.Y., 1992, An Occasion for the Arts, Williamsburg, Va., 1993, Mannyunk Arts Festival, Phila., 1993, Three Rivers Arts Festival, Ft. Lauderdale, Fla., 1993, Los Olas Mus. Art Festival, Pompano Beach, Fla., 1993, 97, 98, Old Town Art Fair, 1993-2002, Chgo. II, Festival of Arts, St. Louis, 1994-95, Port Clinton Art Festival, Highland Park, Ill., 1994-97, Ctrl. Pa. Festival of Arts, State Coll., 1993-96, Ann Arbor Street Art Fair, 1992, 94, 99, Springfest, Charlotte, N.C., 1995-97, Uptown Art Festival, Mpls., 1996, Naples Nat. Art Festival, Fla., 1995, 2000-02, Paradise City Arts Festival, 2002, Coconut Grove Festival of Art, Miami, 2002; one and two man exhbns. include Hanover Gallery, Syracuse, N.Y., 1980, Payne Hall gallery, Mohawk Valley C.C., Utica, N.Y., 1989, Elm Tree Art Gallery, Albany, N.Y., 1990, Canastota Mus., N.Y., 1991, South Shore Arts, Little Falls, N.Y., 1990, 92. Docent guide Ft. Lauderdale Mus. Art, docent coun., 2002. Named Best in Show, Canal Celebration, Little Falls, N.Y., 1990,91, Best in Category, Art in the Sun, Pompano, Fla., 1992; recipient Hon. Mention, WCNY Art Auction, 1994, Award of Distinction, St. Augustine Festival of the Arts, 1994, Award of Merit, Ctrl. Pa. Festival of the Arts, 1994, Best in 2-Dimensional Art, Port Clinton Art Festival, Highland Park, Ill., 1994, Second Pl., Festival of the Arts, St. Louis, 1994, Summerfest, Charlotte, N.C., 1995, First Pl. Painting, Beaux Arts Festival, Coral Gables, Fla., 1997. Home: 1124 North B St Lake Worth FL 33460

CANHAM, PRUELLA CROMARTIE NIVER, music educator; b. Statesboro, Ga., Dec. 4, 1924; d. Esten Graham and Mary Lee (Jones) Cromartie; m. Robert G. Niver June 4, 1946 (div. 1965) m. David L. Canham July 26, 1985; 1 child, Peddy Niver Hayhurst Moran. BS in Bus. and Music, Ga. So. U., 1944; postgrad., various univs. tchr. voice, piano, chorus and bus. career maths. North Ft. Myers H.S., Fla.; former sec. Statesboro Air Base, Ga., Warner Robbins Air Base, Macon, Ga.; former tchr. Westside Sch., Bulloch County, Ga., Southside Sch., Opelika, Ala. Mem. Singers Club of L.I.; guest spkr., panelist various cultural orgns. in Fla. and so. states; soloist various chs. and schs.; music cons. local theater groups; mem. Fla. State Secondary Music Instructional Materials Coun. Nominee Gannett Found. Heart of Gold Humanatarian award, 1981; named Vocal Solo. Lit. Music Specialist State of Florida, Lee County Florida Tchr. of the Year, 1987, nominee Nat. Tchr. Hall of Fame, 1998; recipient Nat. Libr. Poet's Editor's Choice award, 1994; cert. Appreciation Nat. Park Trust, 1995, Lee County Sch. Dist. Fla., 1991, numerous awards in 2002, including: ABI Hall of Fame, Poet of Year, Internat. Poet Merit and Honored Mem., Living Legions, Worlds Lifetime Achievement award, Companion of Honor, Internat. Peace Prize, Am. Medal of Honor; Nobel Prize for Oustanding Achievement and Contbr. to Humanity, 2002; recipient Congl. Medal of Excellence, 2004. Mem. AAAS, Am. Ch. Dirs. Assn., Fla. Music Educator Assns., Music Educators Nat. Conf., Lee County Alliance of the Arts (charter), Fla. Vocal Assn. (past coord., state bd.), Nat. Assn. of Tchrs. of Singing in Am. and Cand., So. Fla. Symphony and Chorus Assn., Am. Guild of Organists, Fla. League of the Arts (past pres. and bd. dirs., hon. life, 1998—), Lee County Ret. Tchrs. Assn., Fla. Vocal Assn., Am. Choral Assn., Internat. Soc. Poets (disting. mem. 1994, merit award, 1995), Profl. Women's Adv. Bd., others. Home: 1271 Burtwood Dr Fort Myers FL 33901-8711

CANIER, CAREN R., painter, educator; b. N.Y.C., Mar. 25, 1953; d. Samuel and Frances Canier; m. Langdon C. Quin, III; children: Langdon C. Quin IV, Adrian F. Quin. BFA, Cornell U., Ithaca, N.Y., 1974; MFA, Boston U., 1976. Prof., art Rensselaer Polytech. Inst., Troy, NY, 1978—. One-woman shows include Robert Schoelkopf Gallery, N.Y., 1985, 1991, Bowery Gallery, 2001, Boston U. Galleries, 2002. Fellow, Am. Acad. in Rome, 1977—78, N.Y. Found. for the Arts, 1985, 1990; grantee, Ingram Merrill Found., 1986, Pollock/Krasner Found., 1990. Office: Arts Dept Rensselaer Polytech Inst Troy NY 12180 Office Phone: 518-276-2675. Business E-Mail: caniec@rpi.edu.

CANIPAROLI, VAL WILLIAM, choreographer, dancer; b. Renton, Wash., Sept. 12, 1951; s. Francisco and Leonora (Marconi) C. Student, Wash. State U., 1969—71, San Francisco Ballet Sch., 1971—72. Dancer San Francisco Opera, 1973, San Francisco Ballet, 1973—; co-dir. OMO, San Francisco, 1985; resident choreographer San Francisco Ballet, 1983—, Ballet West, 1993—97, Tulsa Ballet, 2001—. Choreographer (ballets) Street Song, 1980, Pacific Northwest Ballet, Seattle, 1980, 91, The Bridge, 1998, Love-lies-Bleeding, 1982, Aria, 1998, Slow, 1998, Ciao Marcello, 1997, Hamlet and Ophelia, 1985, In Perpetuum, 1990, Aubade, 1985 (Isadora Duncan award 1986), Narcisse, 1987, Ririe Woodbury Dance Co., 1988, Ritual, 1990, A Door is Ajar, 1990, Jacob's Pillow Dance festival, 1990, Pulcinella, 1991, Concerto Grosso, 1992, Seeing Stars, 1993, Lady of the Camellias, 1993, Ballet West, 1994, Lambarena, 1995, Capriccio, Chgo. Lyric Opera, 1994, Bow Out, 1995, San Francisco Symphony Pops, 1995-96, Prawn Watching, 1996, Djangology, 1997, Open Veins, 1998, Book of Alleged Dances, 1998, Going for Baroque, 1999, Attention Please, 1999, The Nutcracker, 2001, Torque, 2001, Jaybird Lounge, 2001, Death of a Moth, 2001, Unspoken, 2002, No Other, 2002, boink!, 2002, Gustave's Rooster, 2003, Vivace, 2003, Sonata for Two Pianos and Percussion, Boston Ballet, 2004, A Doll's House, San Francisco, 2004, others. Recipient Isadora Duncan award, 1987, 97, 2001, Choo-San Goh and H. Robert Magee Found. award for choreography, 1994, 97; Nat. Endowment Arts fellow, 1981-88. Fellow Calif. Arts Coun. Choreographers. Avocations: music, theater, dance. Home: 355 First St 602 San Francisco CA 94105 Office: San Francisco Ballet 455 Franklin St San Francisco CA 94102-4471

CANIZARES, CLAUDE ROGER, astrophysicist, educator; b. Tucson, June 14, 1945; s. Orlando and Stephanie (Bolan) C.; children: Kristen, Alexander. BA, Harvard U., 1967, MA, 1968, PhD, 1972. Postdoctoral fellow MIT, 1971—74, prof., 1974—84, Bruno Rossi prof. exptl. physics, 1984—, dir. Ctr. for Space Rsch., 1990—2002, assoc. provost, 2002—. Assoc. dir. NASA-Chandra X-ray Obs. Ctr.; chair NRC Space Studies Bd., 1994-2000; chair space sci. adv. com. NASA, 1993-94, mem. Space Earth Sci. Adv. Com., Washington, 1986-88; mem. adv. coun. NASA, 1992-2000; mem. astron. and astrophysics survey com. NRC, Washington, 1989-91; trustee Assoc. Univs., Inc., 1997—; mem. Air Force Sci. Adv. Bd., 1999—; mem. bd. on physics and astronomy NRC, 2001—. Contbr. articles over 170 to profl. jours. Royal Soc. vis. fellow, Cambridge, Eng., 1981-82, Alfred P. Sloan Found. fellow, 1980-84; NASA grantee, 1975—. Fellow Am. Phys. Soc., Am. Acad. Arts & Sci. 2004; mem. NAS (mem. governing coun. 2005-), AAAS, Am. Astron. Soc., Internat. Astron. Union, Internat. Acad. Astronautics, Phi Beta Kappa, Sigma Xi. Achievements include first implementation of studies in x-ray spectroscopy and plasma diagnostics of supernova remnants, clusters of galaxies. Office: MIT 77 Massachusetts Ave 3-234 Cambridge MA 02139-4309 E-mail: crc@mit.edu.*

CANJAR, PATRICIA MCWADE, psychologist; b. Pitts., Mar. 14, 1932; d. Robert Malachai McWade and Lillian Kathryn (Seidenstricker) Robb; m. Lawrence N. Canjar, Aug. 4, 1951 (dec. Nov. 1972); 1 son, R. Michael; m. James M. McDonald, Sept. 24, 1977. A.A., Carlow Coll., 1951; B.A., U. Detroit, 1973, M.A., 1975. Lic. psychologist, Mich. Psychologist, Robinwood Clinic, Detroit, 1973-77, Psychol. Resources, Birmingham, Mich., 1977-80, Realistic Living Ctr., Warren, Mich., 1983-85, Behavior Ctr., Birmingham, 1980-84; with Eastwood Cmty. Clinic, Big Beaver, Mich., 1984-94; ret. 1994. Mem. Nat. YWCA Spl. Commn., Boston, N.Y.C. and Washington, 1967; bd. dirs. YWCA, Pitts., 1961-65, Detroit, 1965-67; asst. coordinator United We Sing, Pitts. Music Festival, 1955-65; pres. Carnegie Mellon Women's Club, Pitts., 1963-65, U. Detroit Faculty Wives' Club, 1968-70; mem. State of Mich. Fair Campaign Practices Commn., 1968-70; treas. Grandview Beach Assn., 1982-84, pres., 1984-87. Fellow Am. Psychol. Assn.; mem. Mich. Assn. Profl. Psychologist, Mich. Assn. Alcohol and Drug Abuse Counselors. Democrat. Roman Catholic.

CANLAS, LUZANO PANCHO, SR., writer, researcher; b. La Paz, Tarlac, The Philippines, July 4, 1940; came to U.S., 1988; s. Juan Patio and Baltazara (Pancho) C.; m. Rosario Supan, Mar. 4, 1966; children: Luzano Jr., Richard, Jenny. Student, U. of East, Manila, 1957-61. Land adminstr., Philippines, 1961—87; writer, researcher, 1967—. Author: Concise History of The Philippines, 1991, (med. guide) What You Need to Know about Arthritis and Rheumatism, 1991, (Solomon's proverbs) Book of Wisdom, 1991, (Internat. proverbs) 1001 Proverbs-Guide for a Better Life, 1991, (med. guide) Hypertension-The Silent Killer, 1991, (med. guide) What You Need to Know about Your Heart and 34 Other Related Topics, 1992, 10 other books. Pres. Ch. of Christ Youth Orgn., The Philippines, 1964-66, Ch. of Christ Parents Orgn., 1966—. Recipient Most Prolific Writer/Researcher, Lira Pampanguena, 1985. Mem.: Wash. Independent Writer, Am. Med. Writers Assn. Avocation: reading. Home: 8811 Bismarck Dr Fort Washington MD 20744 Office Phone: 301-839-2434.

CANN, SHARON LEE, retired health science librarian; b. Ft. Riley, Kans., Aug. 14, 1935; d. Roman S. and Cora Elon (George) Foote; m. Donald Clair Cann, May 16, 1964. Student, Sophia U., Tokyo, 1955-57; BA, Calif. State U., Sacramento, 1959; MSLS, Atlanta U., 1977; EdD, U. Ga., 1995. Cert. health scis. libr. Recreation worker ARC, Korea, Morocco, France, 1960-64; shelflister Libr. Congress, Washington, 1967-69; tchr. Lang Ctr., Taipei, Taiwan, 1971-73; libr. tech. asst. Emory U., Atlanta, 1974-76; health sci. libr. Northside Hosp., Atlanta, 1977-85, libr. cons., 1985-86; libr. area health edn. ctr., learning resource ctr. Morehouse Sch. Medicine, 1985-86; edn. libr. Ga. State U., 1986-93; dir. libr. svcs. Ga. Bapt. Coll. Nursing, 1993-99, ret., 1999. Author: Life in a Fishbowl: A Call To serve, 2003; editor Update, publ. Ga. Health Scis. Libr. Assn., 1981; contbr. articles to profl. jours. Chmn. Calif. Christian Youth in Govt. Seminar, 1958. Named Miss Far East Air Force, 1957, Alumni Top Twenty, Calif. State U., Sacramento, 1959; recipient Miss Meiji Bowl Tokyo, 1957. Mem. ALA, Med. Libr. Assn. (hon. life; bookkeeper So. chpt. 1996-98, credentialing com. 1996-2000, 05, nursing and allied health sect. continuing edn. chair 1998-2000), Spl. Libr. Assn. (dir. South Atlantic chpt. 1985-87), Ga. Libr. Assn. (spl. libr. divsn. chmn. 1983-85), Ga. Health Scis. Libr. Assn. (hon. life, chmn. 1981-82), Atlanta Health Sci. Libr. (chmn. 1979, 95), Am. Numis. Assn., ARC Overseas Assn., Audubon Soc., Women in Mil. Svc. for Am., Suncity Hilton Head Computer Club (v.p. 2003). Home: 69 Plymouth Ln Bluffton SC 29909-5062 E-mail: sharoncann@aol.com.

CANNAVALE, BOBBY (ROBERTO CANNAVALE), actor; b. Union City, NJ, May 3, 1971; m. Jenny Lumet, 1994 (div. 2003); 1 child, Jacob. Mem. Circle Repertory Theatre, Lab Theatre Co. Actor: (films) I'm Not Rappaport, 1996, Night Falls on Manhattan, 1997, Gloria, 1999, The Bone Collector, 1999, The Devil and Daniel Webster, 2001, 3 A.M., 2001, Washington Heights, 2002, The Guru, 2002, The Station Agent, 2003, Fresh Cut Grass, 2004, Haven, 2004, Shall We Dance, 2004, The Breakup Artist, 2004, Happy Endings, 2005, Romance & Cigarettes, 2005; (TV films) When Trumpets Fade, 1998, The Exonerated, 2005; (TV series) Third Watch, 1999—2001, 100 Centre Street, 2001, (TV mini series) Kingpin, 2003; guest appearances include Trinity, 1998—99, Sex and the City, 2000, Law & Order: Special Victims Unit, 2002, Ally McBeal, 2002, Law & Order, 2002, Oz, 2003, Law & Order: Criminal Intent, 2003, Will & Grace (several episodes), 2004—05 (Creative Arts Primetime Emmy award for guest actor in a comedy series, 2005), Six Feet Under, 2004.*

CANNELL, JOHN REDFERNE, lawyer; b. Cambridge, Mass., Apr. 3, 1937; s. John and Thyra (Larson) C.; m. Elizabeth Ann May, May 28, 1960; children: John R. Jr. (dec.), James C., William H. AB, Princeton U., 1958; LLB, Columbia U., 1961. Bar: NY 1961. Assoc. Simpson Thacher & Bartlett, NYC, 1961-70, ptnr., 1970-95, ret., 1996—. Gov. Am. Bus. Coun., Singapore, 1982-85, vice chmn., 1984-85; dir. Mattapoisett Casino, 2002-04. Trustee Kessler Inst. for Rehab., West Orange, NJ, 1986-97, vice chmn., 1989-92, chmn., 1992-95; trustee Henry H. Kessler Found., 1992—, chmn., 1996-99; trustee Marcus Ward Home, Maplewood, NJ, 1996—; dir. Kessler Rehab. Corp., 1992—2003, Kessler Med. Rehab. Rsch. and Edn. Corp., 1997—; bd. dir. New Alternatives for Children, Inc., 1996—. Mem. Montclair Golf Club (trustee 2001—), Univ. Club, Bay Club (Mattapoisett). Episcopalian. Avocations: squash, golf. Office: Simpson Thacher & Bartlett 425 Lexington Ave Fl 17 New York NY 10017-3903

CANNISTRACI, DIANE FRANCES, sales executive; b. Bronx, N.Y., Jan. 9, 1950; d. John and Dorothy (Romano) C. Student, Orlando (Fla.) Jr. Coll., 1968-70, Teiko Post Coll., 1991-92. Ea. regional sales mgr. Kierulff Airline/Internation Supply, 1979-86; western regional sales mgr. C & K Unimax, Wallingford, Conn., 1989-90; sales and mktg. rep. U.S. C. of C., 1990-91; store mgr. Petite Sophisticate, Manchester, Conn., 1991-92; internat. and airline mktg. Richey Cypress Electronics, Wallingford, 1992-96; sales account exec. Midway Indsl. Electronics, Plainview, NY, 1996—2000; Rep. coord. Suffolk County Bd. Election, 2000—. Committeewoman Rep. Party, Huntington, N.Y.; fund raiser Am. Heart Assn., Rocky Hill, Conn., Am. Diabetes Assn., Rocky Hill; vol. Hartford (Conn.) Hist. Soc., With USNG, 1981-86. Recipient All Around Womanhood award PTA, Huntington Station, N.Y., 1968. Mem.: Air Carrier Purchasing. Republican. Roman Catholic. Home: 345 Depot Rd Huntington Station NY 11746-3339

CANNIZZARO, RUSS B., art educator, department chairman; s. John Joseph and Rose Cannizzaro; m. Carol S. Lisonbee, Jan. 10, 1986; children: Greg Hawley, Chris Hawley, Justin Hawley, Breanne Hawley. AA, Mesa C.C., 1995; BA, Ottawa U., Tempe, Ariz., 1997; M in Edn., Ariz. State U., 1999. Chmn. dept. fine arts Tempe Union H.S. Dist., 1997—2005. Recipient Excellence in Edn. Award, Tempe Diablos, 1999, Microsoft Tech. Grant, 1999. Mem.: NEA, Ariz. Arts Edn. Assn., Art Renewal Ctr. Home and Office: Russ Cannizzaro Fine Arts 865 West 8th Place Mesa AZ 85201 Office Phone: 480-833-8094. E-mail: russcannizzaro@yahoo.com.

CANNOM, DAVID SHEFVELAND, cardiologist, director; b. Kans. City, May 24, 1940; s. C. Wesley and Esther Shefveland Cannom; m. Phyllis Monroe, Oct. 26, 1974; children: Rebecca Robinson Fong, Elizabeth Reed Fong, Hannah Lynn; m. Sally Reed (div. July 1, 1973). BA, DePauw U., 1962; MD, U. Minn., 1967. Diplomate Am. Bd. Internal Medicine, Cardiology, 1975. Fellow in cardiology Sch. Medicine Stanford U., Palo Alto, Calif., 1971—73; dir. Cardiac Care Unit Yale-New Haven (Conn.) Hosp., 1971—73; clin. cardiologist San Pedro (Calif.) Peninsula Hosp., 1976—85; med. dir. cardiology Good Samaritan Hosp., L.A., 1985—. Co-founder, pres. Cardiac Arrhythmia Rsch. and Edn. Found., Irvine, Calif., 1995—98. Contbr. over 230 articles to profl. jours. Active Chadwick Sch., Palos Verdes, Calif., 1984—95. Lt. comdr. Pub. Health Svc. U.S. Army, 1971—73. Recipient Michele Mirowski award, Guidant, 2005. Mem.: Am. Heart Assn. (pres. 1989—90, Eugene Drake M.D. award 2004), Heart Rhythm Soc. Found. (chmn. bd. 2005), N.Am. Soc. Pacing and Electrophysiology (pres. 2000—01), Am. coll. Cardiology (pres. Calif. chpt. 1999—2000), The Sunset Club, The Beach Club, The Calif. Club, Alpha Omega Alpha. Republican. Episc. Avocations: tennis, running. Office: Los Angeles Cardiology Associates 1245 Wilshire Blvd 703 Los Angeles CA 90017 Office Phone: 213-977-0419, publish. Office Fax: 213-977-0225. E-mail: dcannom@lacard.com.

CANNON, ALICE GRACE, counselor; b. Greenville, N.C., Nov. 3, 1949; d. Carl William Hannah and Lula Estelle Briley; children: Mary Alice Cannon Blankenship, Laren Jay. PhD, DD, Progressive Universal Life Ch., 2000. Commd. 2d lt. USAF, 1973, advanced through ranks to staff sgt., 1980, ret., 1993; clk. U.S. Postal Svc., Norfolk, Va., 1994—97, ret.; min. Progressive Universal Life Ch., Sacramento, 2000—, counseling practitioner, 2001—, min., 2000; counselor practioner, 2001. Staff sgt. USAF, 1983, Grenada Invasion, staff sgt. USAF, 1991—92, Desert Storm. Mem.: AARP, Air Force Meml. Assn., Disabled Vets. Assn. Avocations: Black Belt in Tae Kwan Do, reading, museums, travel, music. Home: 2618 Summitt Ridge Loop Morrisville NC 27560-6974 E-mail: snowy777@msn.com.

CANNON, CARL N., publishing executive; b. Ga. Grad., U. Ga., 1965. Advt. mgr. Morris Comm., Augusta, Ga., advt. dir. Lubbock, Tex., gen. mgr. Amarillo, Tex., mgr. corp. group Augusta, publ. Jacksonville, Fla., 1990—; v.p. Morris. Comm., Fla. Group, Augusta, Ga., 1990—; pub. The Fla. Times-Union, Jacksonville, Fla., 1995—. Avocations: golf, fishing, pro sports. Office: Fla Times-Union PO Box 1949 Jacksonville FL 32231-0053

CANNON, CHRISTOPHER BLACK, congressman, lawyer; b. Salt Lake City, Utah, Oct. 20, 1950; m. Claudia Fox, 1978; 8 children. BS, Brigham Young U., 1974; attended, Harvard Bus. Sch., 1975—76; JD, Brigham Young U., 1980. Bar: Utah 1980. Apptd. asst. assoc. solicitor Dept. Interior, 1983—84, assoc. solicitor, 1984—86; cons. to Asst. Sec. Productivity, Tech. and Innovation Dept. Commerce, 1986—87; co-owner Geneva Steel, Orem, Utah, 1987—90; owner Cannon Industries, Inc., 1990—95; Utah fin. chmn., 1995—96; mem. nat. fin. com. Lamar Alexander for Pres., 1995—96; mem. US Congress, 3rd Utah dist., 1996—, chmn. subcom. on commercial and adminstrv. law, mem. com. on govt. reform. Mem. Resources, Judiciary, and Sci. coms. Mem. nat. fin. com., Utah fin. chmn. Pres. George Bush Re-election Campaign, 1991—92; del. Rep. Nat. Conv., 1992, 1996; fin. chmn. Utah Rep. Party, 1991—92. Republican. Office: Dist Office 51 S Univ Ave Ste 317 Provo UT 84606 also: US Ho of Reps 2436 Rayburn House Off Bldg Washington DC 20515-4403 Business E-Mail: cannon.ut03@mail.house.gov.*

CANNON, DAVID C., mechanical engineer, consultant; b. Raleigh, N.C., Sept. 27, 1937; s. Doyle L. and Katherine C. (Coker) Cannon; m. Patsy Sturgeon, Feb. 12, 1977; children: Patricia, Mary, Ann, Katherine, John, Ben. BSME, Clemson U., 1959; MSME, Case Inst., 1965. Registered profl. engr., S.C. Sr. project engr. Sonoco Products Co., Hartsville, SC, 1965-87; pres. Edisto Shrimp Co., Edisto Island, SC, 1987-92, Edisto Seafarms, Inc., Edisto Island, 1993—2001; contract engr., pres. Prodn. Engring., LLC, 2002—. Pres. Edisto Beach Property Owners Assn., 2002—05. 1st lt. Ordnance Corps U.S. Army, 1960—68. Mem.: ASME, S.C. Shrimp Growers Assn., S.C. Aquaculture Assn., World Aquaculture Soc. Methodist. Achievements include patents for square column form; die cutter feeder; disposable beer keg. Home and Office: PO Box 370 Edisto Island SC 29438 E-mail: dccannon@earthlink.net.

CANNON, DAVID JOSEPH, lawyer; b. Milw., Aug. 6, 1933; s. George W. and Florence (Dean) c.; m. Carol Nevins, Mar. 10, 1962; children: Charles, Courtney. BS, Marquette U., 1955, JD, 1960. Bar; Wis. 1960, U.S. Dist. Ct. (ea. dist.) Wis. 1960, U.S. Ct. Appeals (7th cir.) 1969, U.S. Ct. Appeals (8th cir.) 1976, U.S. Dist. Ct. (we. dist.) Wis. 1976, U.S. Ct. Appeals (5th cir.) 1978, U.S. Ct. Appeals (4th cir.) 1997. Atty. Cannon & Cannon, Milw., 1960-66; asst. dist. atty. Milw. County Dist. Atty., 1966-68, dist. atty., 1968; U.S. atty. Dept. Justice Ea. Dist. Wis., Milw., 1969-73; ptnr. Michael, Best & Friedrich, Milw., 1973—. Home: 1520 Sunset Dr Elm Grove WI 53122-1629 Office: Michael Best & Friedrich 100 E Wisconsin Ave Ste 3300 Milwaukee WI 53202-4108 Office Phone: 414-225-4978.

CANNON, DYAN, actress; b. Tacoma, Jan. 4, 1937; m. Cary Grant (div.); 1 dau., Jennifer; m. Stanley Fimberg, 1985 (div. 1990). Student, U. Wash.; studied with Sanford Meisner. Former model; TV appearances include Diane's Adventure, Harlequin's Diamond Girl, 1998; Broadway appearances include Ninety-Day Mistress; with road company How to Succeed in Business Without Really Trying; motion pictures include Bob and Carol and Ted and Alice, 1969 (Acad. award nomination), Le Casse, 1970, The Anderson Tapes, 1971, The Love Machine, 1971, Such Good Friends, 1971, Doctors' Wives, 1971, The Last of Sheila, 1973, Shamus, 1973, Child Under a Leaf, 1974, Revenge of the Pink Panther, 1978, Heaven Can Wait, 1978 (Golden Globe award Best Supporting Actress), Coast to Coast, 1980, Honeysuckle Rose, 1980, Author, Author, 1982, Deathtrap, 1982, Caddyshack II, 1988, The End of Innocence (also dir. and prod. screenwriter), 1990, The Pickle, 1993, One Point of View, That Darn Cat, 1997, Out to Sea, 1997, 8 Heads in a Duffel Bag, 1997, Drop Dead, 1998, Kiss of a Stranger, 1999, Kangaroo Jack, 2003; appeared in TV movies Virginia Hill Story, 1974, Lady of the House, 1978, Having It All, 1983, Master of the Game, 1984, Arthur the King, 1985, Jenny's War, 1985, Rock and Roll Mom, 1988, Jailbirds, 1991, Christmas in Connecticut, 1992, Based on an Untrue Story, 1993, A Perry Mason Mystery: The Case of the Jealous Jokester, 1995, The Rockford Files: If the Frame Fits..., 1996, The Sender, 1997, Allie & Me, 1997, Beverly Hills Family Robinson, 1998, Diamond Girl, 1998, Black Jaq, 1998, My Mother, the Spy, 2000; appeared in TV series Ally McBeal, 1997, Three Sisters, 2001; dir., writer, prodr. short live action film Growing Pains: Number One, 1976 (Acad. award nomination). Named Best Actress of Yr., Nat. Assn. Theater Owners. Address: Agy for the Performing Arts 12th Fl 9000 Sunset Blvd Los Angeles CA 90069

CANNON, FRANK See MAYHAR, ARDATH

CANNON, GARLAND, linguist, educator; b. Fort Worth, Dec. 5, 1924; m. Patricia Richardson, 1947; children— Margaret, India, Jennifer, William. BA in English, U. Tex., 1947, PhD in English Linguistics, 1954; MA in English, Stanford U., 1952. Instr. U. Hawaii, Honolulu, 1949-52; instr. U. Tex., Austin, 1952-54, U. Mich., Ann Arbor, 1954-55; asst. prof. speech U. Calif.-Berkeley, 1955-56; acad. dir. Am. U. Lang. Ctr., Bangkok, 1956-57; asst. prof. English U. Fla., Gainesville, 1957-58; vis. prof. linguistics U. P.R., 1958-59; asst. prof. linguistics Columbia U., N.Y.C., 1959-62; dir. English lang. program for Afghanistan, Kabul, 1960—62; assoc. prof. Northeastern Ill. U., Chgo., 1962-63, Queens Coll., CUNY, 1963-66; assoc. prof. English Tex. A&M U., College Station, 1966-68, prof. English, 1968—; vis. prof. humanities U. Mich., 1970-71; vis. prof. linguistics Kuwait U., 1979-81. Vis. prof. linguistics Inst. Teknologi Mara, Kuala Lumpur, 1987; vis. summer prof. Cambridge U., 1980, Oxford U., 1974, MIT, 1969, U. Wash., 1967; lectr. throughout world Author: Sir William Jones, Orientalist: A Bibliography, 1952, Biography, 1964, A History of the English Language, 1972, An Integrated Transformational Grammar of the English Language, 1978, Sir William Jones: A Bibliography of Primary and Secondary Sources, 1979, Historical Change and English Word-Formation, 1987, Oriental Jones: The Life and Mind of Sir William Jones, 1990, Arabic Loanwords in English, 1994, (with A. Pfeffer) German Loanwords in English, 1994, Japanese Loanwords in English, 1996, (with A. Kaye) Persian Loanwords in English, 2001; editor: The Letters of Sir William Jones, 1970 (Book of Yr. Sunday London Telegraph 1970); editor: The Collected Works of Sir William Jones, 1993, Objects of Enquiry: The Life and Influences of Sir William Jones, 1995; contbr. numerous articles to profl. jours. Recipient Disting. Achievement award Tex. A&M U., 1972; Indian Govt. grantee, 1984; Linguistic Soc. Am./Am. Council Learned Socs. grantee, 1984; Am. Philos. Soc. grantee, Eng., 1964, 66, 74 Mem. MLA (exec. com. gen. linguistics discussion group 1982-85, chmn. 1984, 85, exec. com. present-day-English 1986-89, 94-97, exec. com. lexicography 1986-89, chmn. 1989, rep. to del. assembly 1985-88), Am. Dialect Soc. (exec. coun. 1989-93), Dictionary Soc. N.Am., South Asian Lit. Assn. (pres. 1979-85). Office: Tex A&M U Dept English College Station TX 77843-0001

CANNON, GAYLE ELIZABETH, lawyer; b. Dallas, May 12, 1941; d. Harry Feldman and Rosalie Bertha (Fischl) Lack; m. Joe D. Goldstrich, Dec. 23, 1962 (div. July 1977); m. Charles B. Cannon, Oct. 29, 1978; children: Josh, Marc, Jeremy. Student. U. Tex., 1959-60; BA, So. Meth. U., 1961, JD, 1965. Bar: Tex. 1965. Asst. gen. counsel Pizza Inn Inc., Dallas, 1977-88, v.p., sec., gen. counsel, 1986-88; of counsel Thompson & Knight LLP, 1995—. Spkr. franchising seminars ABA Forum on Franchising, State Bar of Tex., Dallas Bar, Southwestern Legal Found., Internat. Franchising Assn. Bd. dirs. Shakespeare Festival of Dallas, past pres.; bd. dirs. Children's Cancer Fund. Named, one of Best Lawyers in Dallas and Fort Worth, 1997—2005, named in top 200 Dallas Lawyers Best Lawyers in America, Woodwar/White, Inc., 1998—2004, named Super Lawyer, Texas Monthly, 2002—05. Mem.: ABA. Democrat. Office Phone: 214-969-1700. E-mail: gayle.cannon@tklaw.com.

CANNON, GEORGE W., JR., magistrate judge; Atty. priv. practice, St. Croix; magistrate judge V.I. Dist. Ct., St. Croix Div., 2004—. Office: VI Dist Ct St Croix Div Almeric L Chritian Fed Bldg 3013 Estate Golden Rock St Croix VI 00820 also: PO BOX 1548 Frederiksted VI 00841-1548 Office Phone: 340-773-1601, 340-773-2743.

CANNON, GRACE BERT, retired immunologist; b. Chambersburg, Pa., Jan. 29, 1937; d. Charles Wesley and Gladys (Raff) Bert; m. W. Dilworth Cannon, June 3, 1961 (div. 1972); children: Michael Quayle Cannon, Susan Radcliffe Cannon Antolin, Peter Bert Cannon. AB, Goucher Coll., 1958; PhD, Washington U., St. Louis, 1962. Fellow Columbia U., N.Y.C., 1962-64, Columbia U. Coll. Physicians and Surgeons, N.Y.C., 1964-65; staff fellow NIH Nat. Cancer Inst., Bethesda, Md., 1966-67; cell biologist Litton Bionetics, Inc., Kensington, Md., 1972-80, head immunology sect., 1980-85; dir. sci. ImmuQuest Labs., Inc., Rockville, Md., 1985-88; pres. Biomedical Analytics, Inc., Rockville, Md., 1988-2001; mgr. ATLIS Fed. Svcs., Inc., Rockville, Md., 1991-95, dir. Silver Spring, Md., 1995-97; sr. assoc. United Info. Sys., Inc., Bethesda, Md., 1998—2000; ret., 2000. Mem. contract rev. coms. Nat. Cancer Inst., 1983-87. Contbr. articles to profl. jours. Mem. Pub. Svc. Health Club, Bethesda, Md., 1984—, sec., 1990-2000. Grantee USPHS, 1959-65, NSF, 1959. Mem. AAAS, Am. Assn. for Cancer Rsch., N.Y. Acad. Sci., Sigma Xi. Home and Office: 1908 Nero Ct Walnut Creek CA 94598

CANNON, HERBERT SETH, investment banker; b. Bklyn., Dec. 3, 1931; s. Joseph and Gertrude (Kimmel) C.; m. Edith Marks, June 20, 1954; children: Naomi Sue, Nina Louise. BA, Washington and Jefferson Coll., 1953; student, Cornell U. Law Sch., 1953—54; LLB, Fordham U., 1960. Salesman Manhattan Scalloping & Embroidery Co., N.Y.C., 1956-57; stock broker Hirsch & Co., N.Y.C., 1956-61, Wineman, Weiss & Co., N.Y.C., 1961-62; pres. Weis, Voisin, Cannon, Inc., N.Y.C., 1963-70; chmn. bd. Elgin Nat. Industries, Inc., N.Y.C., 1967-70; chmn. bd., pres. Cannon, Jerold & Co., Inc., 1970-73; chmn. bd. PUD Industries, Inc., 1971-83, CitiWide Capital Corp., 1984-88, CitiWide Securities Corp., 1984-88; pres. Cannon Enterprises Inc., real estate devel., investment bankers and fin. cons., Boca Raton, Fla., 1975-93; chmn. bd. Holistic Svcs. Corp., 1979-83; pres. HSC Consulting, Inc., 1997—. Past trustee Washington and Jefferson Coll. Served with AUS, 1954-56. Mem. Young Pres. Orgn., World Bus. Coun., Metro Pres. Orgn. Home and Office: 6530 Las Flores Dr Boca Raton FL 33433 Office Phone: 561-212-4678. E-mail: hsc0039@aol.com. *Make it happen.*

CANNON, HUGH, lawyer; b. Albemarle, N.C., Oct. 11, 1931; s. Hubert Napoleon and Nettie (Harris) C.; m. Jo Anne Weisner, Mar. 21, 1988. AB, Davidson Coll., 1953; BA, Oxford U., 1955, MA, 1960; LLB, Harvard U., 1958. Bar: N.C. 1958, D.C. 1978, S.C. 1979. Mem. staff U. N.C. Inst. Govt., Chapel Hill, 1959; mem. firm Sanford, Phillips, McCoy & Weaver, Fayetteville, N.C., 1960; asst to Gov. of N.C., Raleigh, 1961; dir. adminstrn. State of N.C., 1962-65, state budget officer, 1963; mem., mng. ptnr. Sanford, Cannon, Adams & McCullough, Raleigh, 1965-79; pvt. practice Charleston, S.C., 1979—; mem. Everett, Gaskins, Hancock and Stevens attys., Raleigh, 1990—; v.p. gen. counsel Palmetto Ford, Inc., Charleston, 1979—. Author: Cannon's Concise Guide to Rules of Order, 1992. Parliamentarian NEA, 1965—; mem. nat. adv. coun. Am. Inst. Parliamentarians; pres. Friends of Coll., Raleigh, 1963; alt. de. Dem. Nat. Conv., 1964, chief parliamentarian, 1976, 80, 84, 88, 92, 96; bd. govs. U. N.C., 1972-81; trustee Davidson Coll., 1966-74, N.C. Sch. Arts, 1963-72; mem. sch. bd. Charleston County, 2000—. Rhodes scholar, 1955. Mem. Phi Beta Kappa, Omicron Delta Kappa, Phi Gamma Delta. Episcopalian. Home: PO Box 31820 Charleston SC 29417-1820 Office: 1625 Savannah Hwy Charleston SC 29407-2236 Office Phone: 803-571-4801.

CANNON, JAMES WASHINGTON, JR., lawyer; b. Ft. McClellan, Ala., Sept. 21, 1951; s. James Washington and Bessie Inez (Ponds) C.; m. Susan Lefler, Sept. 23, 1986 (div. Feb. 1988); m. Sandra Bishop, Nov. 23, 1988. BA, Bowling Green State U., 1973; MA, Webster U., 1978; JD, U. Tex., 1982. Bar: Tex. 1983, U.S. Dist. Ct. (we. dist.) Tex. 1987, U.S. Ct. Appeals for Fed. Cir., U.S. Supreme Ct. Assoc. O'Haire, Fiore & Oaley, Fed. Republic Germany, 1982-84; asst. atty. gen. State of Tex., Austin, 1984-85; asst. atty. City of Austin, 1985-86; assoc. O'Haire, Fiore & Daley, Austin, 1986-89, Akin, Gump, Strauss, Hauer & Feld, Austin, 1989; ptnr. Cray Cary Ware & Freidenrich LLP, Austin; atty., intellectual property litig. Baker Botts LLP, Austin, 2002—. Mem. Task Force on Revision of Tex. Rule of Civil Procedure, Tex. Supreme Ct. Panel on Health Care Discovery; dir. Trial Advocacy U. Tex. Sch. Law. Mem. Seton Forum, Austin, 1987. Capt. U.S. Army, 1973-79. Named a Tex. Super Lawyer, Tex. Monthly and Law & Politics Mag., 2003, 2004; named one of Best Lawyers in Austin, Austin Mag., 2002; named to Am. Top Black Lawyers, Black Enterprise Mag., 2003. Mem.: ABA, Tex. Bar Found., Fed. Cir. Bar Assn., Austin Intellectual Property Law Assn., Am. Intellectual Property Law Assn., Am. Bd. Trial Advocates, Am. Soc. Law, Medicine & Ethics, Internat. Acad. Trial Lawyers, Nat. Order Barristers, Tex. Assn. Def. Counsel, Travis County Young Lawyers Assn., Assn. Trial Lawyers Am., Phi Alpha Delta. Democrat. Roman Catholic. Office: Baker Botts LLP 1500 San Jacinto Ctr 98 San Jacinto Blvd Austin TX 78701-4039 Office Phone: 512-322-2653. E-mail: jim.cannon@bakerbotts.com.

CANNON, JOE LOUIS, retired orthodontist; b. Jan. 27, 1929; MS, DDS, U. Tenn., 1957. Pvt. practice orthodontist, Memphis, 1957—98; ret., 1998. Col. USAF, 1949—53, Korea. Decorated Purple Heart, Legion of Merit, Disting. Flying Cross, Air Medal with three oak leaves. Home: 4834 Fleetview Ave Memphis TN 38117-3225

CANNON, JOHN, III, lawyer; b. Phila., Mar. 19, 1954; s. John and Edythe (Grebe) Cannon. BA, Denison U., 1976; JD, Dickinson Sch. Law, 1983. Bar: Pa. 1983, Hawaii 1986, U.S. Dist. Ct. (ea. dist.) Pa. 1983, U.S. Ct. Appeals

(3d cir.) 1985. Account exec. PRO Services, Inc., Flourtown, Pa., 1976-79, br. officer mgr. Pitts., 1979-80; law clk. Montgomery County Ct. of Common Pleas, Norristown, Pa., 1983-84; assoc. Rawle & Henderson, Phila., 1984-88; comml. litigation counsel CIGNA Corp., Phila., 1988-90; counsel fin. svcs. divsn. CIGNA Internat., Phila., 1990-93, sr. counsel, 1993-95, v.p., sr. counsel, 1995-97, sr. v.p., chief counsel, 1997-2000, CIGNA Healthcare, Bloomfield, Conn., 1999—2003, Conn. Gen. Life Ins. Co., Bloomfield, Conn., 1999—2003; sr. v.p. pub. affairs, assoc. gen. counsel CIGNA Corp., Phila., 2003—. V.p. Life Ins. Co. N.Am.; trustee U.S.-China Legal Coop. Fund, Washington, 1998—. Comments editor Dickinson Internat. Law Ann., 1983. Pres. CIGNA Found., Phila., 2003—. Mem. ABA, Pa. Bar Assn., Hawaii State Bar Assn., Greater Phila. C. of C. (bd. dirs. 2003—), Kappa Sigma (pres. 1975-76), Gamma Xi (v.p., trustee 1982-86). Republican. Episcopalian. Office: Cigna Corp 1650 Market St Philadelphia PA 19192

CANNON, JONATHAN Z., lawyer, educator; m. Alice P. Cannon; children: Ariel, Maia A., Benjamin Z. BA summa cum laude, Williams Coll., 1967; postgrad., Oxford U., 1967-68; JD cum laude, U. Pa., 1974. Law clk. U.S. Ct. Appeals (D.C. cir.), 1974-75; assoc. Beveridge & Diamond, P.C., 1975-80, ptnr., 1980-86; dep. gen. counsel, litigation and regional ops. Office Gen. Counsel, U.S. EPA, Washington, 1987; dep. asst. adminstr. Office Enforcement and Compliance Monitoring, U.S. EPA, Washington, 1987-88, Office Solid Waste and Emergency Response, U.S. EPA, Washington, 1988-89, acting asst. adminstr., 1989; ptnr. Beveridge & Diamond, P.C., 1990-92; dir. Gulf of Mexico Program U.S. EPA, Washington, 1992-93, acting asst. adminstr. Office Policy, Planning & Evaluation, 1993, acting dep. adminstr., spl. advisor to adminstr., 1993, asst. adminstr., CFO, Office Adminstrn. and Resource Mgmt., 1993-95, gen. counsel, 1995-98; prof. U. Va. Sch. Law, Charlottesville, 1998—, dir. Ctr. Environ. Studies. Lectr. environ. law U. Va. Sch. Law, 1983-87, 97-98; adj. prof. environ. law Washington and Lee Law Sch., 1982-83. Office: U Va Sch Law 580 Massie Rd Charlottesville VA 22903-1738 Office Phone: 804-924-3819. E-mail: jzc8j@virginia.edu.

CANNON, L. KINDER, III, lawyer; b. Tallahassee, Oct. 19, 1942; BA, Duke U., 1964; JD, U. Fla., 1966. Bar: Fla. 1967. Gen. counsel Holland & Knight, Jacksonville, Fla. Exec. editor U. Fla. Law Review, 1966. Mem. ABA, Fla. Bar, Fla. Bar, Jacksonville Bar Assn., Fla. Bar Examiners (mem. 1990-95, chmn. 1995), Fla. Bar Grievance Com.; Fellow Am. Bar Found. Office: Holland & Knight LLP 50 N Laura St Ste 3900 Jacksonville FL 32202-3622 Office Phone: 904-798-5477. Business E-Mail: kinder.cannon@hklaw.com.

CANNON, LENA FERRARA LEE, retired education educator; b. Morgantown, W.Va., Oct. 12, 1918; d. Emil and Philomena (Purificato) Ferrara; m. Robert Young Cannon, June 10, 1948; children: Emilie, Robert Y. Jr., Leigh. BS, W.Va. U., 1940, MS, 1944; postgrad., U. Wis., 1945-48. Tchr. Osage (W.Va.) Jr. High Sch., 1941-45; rsch. asst. U. Wis., Madison, 1945-48; asst. prof. Auburn (Ala.) U., 1948-70, asst. producer, host Ala. Pub. TV, 1955-84, specialist in foods nutrition, 1970-84; ret., 1984. Weekly TV program PBS-TV, 1955-84, weekly columns Montgomery Adv., 1979-84, Columbus Enquirer, 1960-65. Author: Today's Home, Vols. 1-3, 1953-84, Southern Living's Quick and Easy Cookbook, 1979, Menu Celebrations; contbr. articles to profl. jours. Bd. dirs. Commn. Aging, Montgomery, Ala., 1981-83, Apobonna Commn. Aging, 1979-83; adv. bd. Auburn U. Theatre. Mem. Internat. Platform Assn., Am. Home Econs. Assn., Am. Women Radio TV, Women in Communications, Phi Upsilon Omicron. Roman Catholic. Avocations: cooking, dance, entertaining, bridge, reading.

CANNON, LOUIS SIMEON, journalist, writer; b. N.Y.C., June 3, 1933; s. Jack and Irene (Kohn) C.; m. Virginia Oprian, Feb. 2, 1953 (div. 1983); children: Carl, David, Judy, Jack; m. Mary L. Shinkwin, Sept. 7, 1985. Student, U. Nev., 1950-51, San Francisco State U., 1951-52. Reporter Lafayette Sun, Calif., 1957; editor Newark (Calif.) Sun, 1957-58, Merced Sun Star, Calif., 1958-60, Contra Costa Times, Calif., 1960-61, San Jose (Calif.) Mercury News, Calif., 1961-69; Sacramento corr. San Jose Mercury News, Calif., 1965-69; Washington corr. Ridder Pubs., Washington, 1969-72; reporter The Washington Post, 1972-96, spl. corr., 1997-99. Author: Ronnie and Jesse, 1969, The McCloskey Challenge, 1972, Reporting: An Inside View, 1977, Reagan, 1982, President Reagan: The Role of a Lifetime, 1991, rev. and updated 2000, Official Negligence: How Rodney King and the Riots Changed Los Angeles and the LAPD, 1998, The Presidential Portfolio: Ronald Reagan, 2001, Governor Reagon: His Rise to Power, 2003. Recipient Gerald R. Ford prize Gerald Ford Libr., 1988, Merriman Smith award White House Corrs. Assn., 1986, Aldo Beckman award, 1984, Washington Journalism Rev. award, 1985, Disting. Reporting of Pub. Affairs award Am. Polit. Sci. Assn., 1968, Lifetime Achievement award Ctr. for Calif. Studies at Calif. State U., Sacramento, 2001. Mem. Soc. of Profl. Journalists, Authors Guild. Home: PO Box 436 Summerland CA 93067-0436 Personal E-mail: cannonlou@hotmail.com.

CANNON, MAJOR TOM, retired special education educator; b. Anniston, Ala., Nov. 11, 1932; s. Thomas Albert and Sallie Mae (James) C. BA in Liberal Arts, Samford U., 1961; postgrad., So. Bapt. Theol. Sem., 1961-62, Tulane U., 1962-63, Auburn U., 1963-64; MEd in Counseling, U. Ga., 1968; postgrad., U. S.C., 1971, 81, 84, Francis Marion Coll., 1979—80, Western Md. Coll., 1980, S.C. State Coll., 1981-85, U. Charleston, 1993, The Citadel, Charleston, S.C., 1996-97, Charleston So. U., Francis Marion Coll., 2000, postgrad., 2003. Cert. prin., guidance counselor, spl. edn. tchr., psychology, S.C. English tchr. North Whitfield H.S., Dalton, Ga., 1964-65, Savannah (Ga.) H.S., 1965-66; guidance counselor Savannah Pub. Schs., 1966-79; dir. spl. svcs. Marlboro County Sch. Dist., Bennettsville, S.C., 1979-80, coord. programs for handicapped, 1980-81; tchr. trainable mentally retarded Edisto Mid. Sch., Orangeburg, S.C., 1981-86; tchr. learning disabled Norman C. Toole Mid. Sch., Charleston, S.C., 1986-88, Berkeley Mid. Sch., Moncks Corner, S.C., 1988-97, chmn. dept. spl. edn., 1991-94; specialist learning disabilities Berkeley County Sch. Dist., Moncks Corner, 1995-97; resource C.E. Murray H.S., Greeleyville, 1997—2004; ret. Labor resources technician City of Savannah, 1979; presenter in field; mem. Strategic Planning Com. for Berkeley County Sch. Dist., 1993-97, Sch. Improvement Coun., 1996-97. Contbr. poetry to Great Poems of the Western World, 1990, Our World's Favorite Gold and Silver Poems, 1991, Perceptions, 1994, Am. Poetry Annual, 1994; author resource manuals and videotaped lessons. Charter Rep. Nat. Com., 1992—, Rep. Presdl. Task Force, 1989—, Rep. Nat. Commn. on Am. Agenda, 1996, Nat. Rep. Senatorial Com., 1990—; at-large del. Rep. Party Platform Planning Com.; mem. Ga. Com. on Children and Youth, 1968. With USN, 1953-57. Recipient Nat. Def. Edn. award U.S. Office of Edn., 1966-67, GE Found. award, 1971, Rep. Presdl. Legion of Merit, 1992-2001, Rep. Presdl. award, 1994, Rep. Presdl. Order of Merit, 1997. Mem. ASCD, ASPCA, AARP, Acad. Am. Poets, Nat. Authors Registry, Coun. for Exceptional Children, Am. Pers. and Guidance Assn., Am. Sch. Counselors Assn. (Ga. coord.), Nat. Assn. Sch. Counselors, Am. Legion, VFW (life), Ga. Assn. Educators, Ga. Pers. and Guidance Assn., Palmetto Tchrs. Assn., Sierra Club, Nature Conservancy, Nat. Resources Def. Coun., World Wildlife Soc., Defenders of Wildlife, Rainforest Alliance, Ocean Conservancy, Nat. Trust for Hist. Preservation, Civil War Preservation Trust, Environ. Def., Heritage Found., Nat. Pks. Conservancy Assn., Humane Soc. U.S., Phi Delta Kappa, Kappa Delta Pi. Republican. Baptist. Avocations: coin collecting/numismatics, philately, pets, scientific experiments, historical studies. Home: 324 Tulane Dr Ladson SC 29456-6235 Office: 207-A E Brooks St Kingstree SC 29556-3441 Office Phone: 843-382-7511.

CANNON, MARK WILCOX, retired government official; b. Salt Lake City, Aug. 29, 1928; s. Joseph Jenne and Ramona (Wilcox) C.; m. Ruth Marian Dixon, Dec. 28, 1956 (div. Jun. 1992); children: Lucile, Mark, Kristen Cannon Brown. m. Betty Ann Schomann, June 25, 1993. Student, Deep Springs Coll., 1944-46; BA, U. Utah, 1949; MA, Harvard U., 1954, MPA, 1955, PhD, 1961. Missionary Ch. Jesus Christ of Latter-Day Saints, Argentina, 1949-52; rsch. analyst Utah Found., 1953; sec. Utah Sch. Merit Study Com., 1954; instr. Brigham Young U., 1955, chmn. dept. polit. sci., 1961-64; mem. staff U.S. Senator W.F. Bennett, 1961, 62-63; adminstrv. asst. to U.S. congressman Henry A. Dixon, 1956-61; mem. staff Inst. Pub. Adminstrn., N.Y.C., 1964-72, dir. urban devel. program Venezuela, 1964-65, dir. internat. programs N.Y.C., 1965-68, dir., 1968-72; adminstrv. asst. to chief justice of U.S., 1972-85; staff dir. Commn. on Bicentennial of U.S. Constn., 1985-88; vice chmn., bd. dirs. Geneva Steel; exec. v.p. Geneva Devel., 1988-89; vice chair Cannon Industries, 1989-96. Venture capitalist, 1989—; guest scholar Woodrow Wilson Internat. Ctr. for Scholars, 1989. Author: (with R. Joseph Monsen) The Makers of Public Policy: American Power Groups and Their Ideologies, 1965; (with others) Partnership for Progress: Atlanta-Fulton County Consolidation, 1969, Urban Government for Valencia, 1973, Views From The Bench: The Judiciary and Constitutional Politics, 1985; contbg. author: Development Administration in Latin America, 1973; contbr. articles to profl. jour.; mem. editorial bd. Judicature, 1975-76. Trustee Inst. Pub. Adminstrn. Recipient ann. award Western Polit. Sci. Assn., 1963 Mem. Nat. Acad. Pub. Adminstrn., Internat. Studies Assn. (sec. 1962-63). Home: 8360 Greensboro Dr Apt 917 Mc Lean VA 22102-3543 Office Phone: 703-790-5134. E-mail: mwcannon@erols.com. *Much of my motivation, orientation, and values stem from a conviction of the masterful leadership of a perfect personal God who is exemplary in His knowledge and utilization of eternal laws to promote the eternal progress and happiness of each human being, partially by providing a complicated earthly learning environment and by permitting people to deal freely with individual and social problems, thereby providing laboratory opportunities for the flourishing of character, knowledge, and wisdom.*

CANNON, MICHAEL R., electronics executive; b. 1953; BA Mech. Engr., MI State U.; attended, Harvard Bus. Sch. Various positions in engring. & mgmt. Boeing Co.; v.p. S.E. Asia ops. Imprimis Tech.; sr. v.p. Syquest Tech. Inc.; various positions including v.p. mobile & desktop bus. unit IBM, v.p. product design, v.p. worldwide ops.; pres., CEO Maxtor, 1996—2003; pres., CEO, dir. Solectron, 2003—. Bd. dirs. Adobe Systems, Silicon Valley Mfg. Group., Maxtor Corp. Office: Solectron 847 Gibraltor Dr Milpitas CA 95035*

CANNON, PATRICK FRANCIS, public relations executive; b. Braddock, Pa., Mar. 2, 1938; s. Peter J. and Kathleen (Donnelly) C.; children by previous marriage: Patrick F. Jr., Elizabeth Kathleen; m. Jeanette Krema, Nov. 22, 1986. BA, Northwestern U., 1969. Ops. mgr. Compact Industries, Albert Lea, Minn., 1968-72; pub. info. dir. Dept. Pub. Works, Chgo., 1970-72; acct. exec. Humes & Assocs., Chgo., 1972-77; freelance journalist, cons. Oak Park, Ill., 1977-79; mgr. pub. rels. and prodn. Lions Clubs Internat., Oak Brook, Ill., 1979-2001; pvt. comms. cons., writer, 2001—. Editor: Water in Rural America, 1973, Wastewater in Rural America, 1974, We Serve: A History of the Lions Clubs, 1991; contbr. articles to profl. jours. and mags.; exec. producer, writer (pub. TV documentaries) With Very Little...Blindness Prevention in Developing Countries, 1991, The Search for Light, 1993, A Dangerous Time for Kids, 1997. Exec. dir. Civic Arts Coun. Oak Park, 1977-79; vol. svc. com. Frank Lloyd Wright Preservation Trust, 1988-94, pub. programs com., 1995-96, chmn. Wright Plus Housewalk, 1996, tour com., 2004—, endorcement com., 2005—; bd. adv. U.S. Internat. Film and Video Festival; internat. bd. adv. World Media Festival; mktg. and pub. rels. com. Oak Park Area YMCA. Named PR All Star 1996, Inside PR Mag.; recipient awards Publicity Club of Chgo., PRSA, Internat. Assn. of Bus. Comms., U.S. Film and Video Festival, others. Mem. Lions (pres. 1983-84). Roman Catholic. Avocations: history, horse racing. Home and Office: 243 Iowa St Oak Park IL 60302-2347 Office Phone: 708-383-0579. E-mail: patnette@comcast.net.

CANNON, ROBERT EUGENE, library director; b. Dec. 20, 1945; s. Wendell Eugene and Louise Marie (Bredehoeft) C.; m. Miriam Ruth Hillson, May 25, 1974; 1 child, Alexander. BA in Music, Calif. State U., L.A., 1967; postgrad., Ariz. State U., 1967-68; MS in Lib. Sci., U. So. Calif., 1970; M in Pub. Adminstrn., San Diego State U., 1978. Adult svcs. libr. Tucson Pub. Libr., 1969-70, Altadena Libr. Dist., 1970-71; head tech. processing, regional coord. San Diego County Libr., 1971-76; asst. dir. Tulare County Libr., Visalia, Calif., 1976-78; dir. Kern County Libr., Bakersfield, Calif., 1978-86; exec. dir. Pub. Libr. of Charlotte and Mecklenburg County, 1986—2003; dir. Broward County Libr., Ft. Lauderdale, Fla., 2003—; exec. bd. Southeast Libr. Info. Network, 2003—; bd. dirs. Broward County Libr. Found., 2003—. Bd. dirs. Mecklenburg County Law and Govt. Libr., Inc., 1992-2003; sec., treas. Pub. Libr. Charlotte and Mecklenburg County, 1986-2003; sec. Mus. New South, 1991-93, bd. dirs., 1991-97. Former mem. Leadership Charlotte; founder Novello Festival of Reading, 1991—2003, ProSearch Info. Svc., 1991—96, Internat. Bus. Libr., 1994—2003, Virtual Libr., 1995—2000, Virtual Village Comm. Ctr., 2000—03, BizLink, 1998—2003, (websites) Readers Club, 1999—2003, StoryPlace, 2000—03, Brarydog.net, 1999—2003, BookHive, 1999—2003; co-founder Charlotte's Web, 1995—2000; bd. vis. Sch. Info. and Libr. Sci. U. N.C., Chapel Hill; bd. vis. Johnson C. Smith U., 2002—03; mem. steering com. Charlotte Alliance Info. Referral Svcs., 1995—97; mem. Internat. Network Pub. Librs. Bertelsman Found., Germany, 1996—2003; mem. leadership group Charlotte Reads, 2001—03; mem. steering com. Leave a Legacy, 1998—2003; mem. Leadership Cir. United Way of Ctrl. Carolinas, 1997—2003; co-founder Novello Festival Press, 2000—03, ImaginOn: The Joe and Joan Martin Ctr., 2003; founder ImginOn.org, 2003; bd. dirs. Smart Start of Charlotte Mecklenburg, 2000—03. Named N.C. Libr. Dir. of Yr., N.C. Pub. Libr. Dirs. Assn, 1995, Local Hero, Creative Loafing newspaper; recipient Pegasus award, Pub. Rels. Soc. Am., 1998, Bridge Builders award, Partnerships for Livable Cmtys., 2003. Mem. ALA, Fla. Libr. Assn., Charlotte/Mecklenburg Coalition for Literacy, 1988-89, Kern County Hist. Records Commn. (vice chmn. 1978-86), Southeastern Libr. Assn. (treas., chmn. conf. com. 1993-95), Mecklenburg Hist. Assn., Cultural Edn. Collaboration (bd. dirs. 1998-2000). Achievements include development and completion of various libraries and branches across the country. Office: Broward County Libr 100 S Andrews Ave Fort Lauderdale FL 33301-1830

CANNON, ROBERT HAMILTON, JR., aerospace engineering educator; b. Cleve., Oct. 6, 1923; s. Robert Hamilton and Catharine (Putnam) C.; m. Dorothea Alta Collins, Jan. 4, 1945 (dec. Apr. 1988); children: Philip Gregory, Douglas Charles, Beverly Jo, Frederick Scott, David John, Joseph Collins, James Robert; m. Vera Berlin Crie, May 27, 1989. BS, U. Rochester, 1944; Sc.D. (du Pont fellow), MIT, 1950. Rsch. engr. Baker Mfg. Co., Evansville, Wis., 1946-50; instr. MIT, 1949-50; research engr. Bendix Aviation Research Labs., Detroit, 1950-51; with Autonetics div. N.Am. Aviation Inc., Downey, Calif., 1951-57, supr. automatic flight control systems, 1951-54, systems engr. inertial nav. instruments and systems, 1954-57; assoc. prof. mech. engring. MIT, 1957-59; mem. faculty Stanford U., 1959-74, prof. aeros. and astronautics, 1962-74, founder Guidance and Control Lab., 1960—69; chief scientist USAF, 1966-68; asst. sec. U.S. Dept. Transp. Washington, 1970-74; chmn. div. engring. and applied sci. Calif. Inst. Tech., Pasadena, 1974-79; Charles Lee Powell prof. aeronautics and astronautics Stanford U., 1979—, chmn. dept., 1979-90, founder aerospace robotics lab., 1980—97, dir. emeritus, 1997—; chmn. sci. adv. com. to CEO GM, 1979-84. Mem. Draper Corp., 1975—; vice chmn. sci. adv. bd. USAF, 1968-70; chmn. assembly engring. NRC, 1974-75, chmn. energy engring. bd., 1975-81, com. on nuclear and alt. energy sources, 1975-78, aeros. and space engring. bd., 1975-79, 85-92, governing bd., 1976-78, ocean studies bd., 1991-94; chmn. Gen. Electric Space Sta. Adv. Bd., 1985-87; chmn. Pres.'s Com. on Nat. Medal of Sci., 1984-88; chmn. NASA Flight Telerobotic Servicer Commn., 1987-91; tech. adv. coun. Boeing Corp., 1984-94, R.R. Donnelley, 1984-89, Comsat, 1985-87, United Techs. Corp., 1989-92; commn. underwater vehicles Marine Bd. Author: Dynamics of Physical Systems, 1967; also articles. Served to lt. (j.g.) USNR, 1944-46. Fellow AIAA (dir. 1968-70), Am. Acad. Arts and Scis., Internat. Acad. Astronautics; mem. Nat. Acad. Engring. (councillor 1975-81), Sigma Xi, Theta Chi (chpt. pres. 1943-44), Tau Beta Pi. Presbyterian. Achievements include devel. hydrofoil boats, automatic flight control, inertial guidance instruments and systems, space vehicle control, drag free satellite, gyro test of gen. relativity, tech. assessment of climatic impact of stratospheric flight, wave-actuated upwelling pump, flexible robot and space robot control systems, underwater free-flying robots, automonous task-commanded helicopter, nat. energy alternatives. Office: Stanford U Dept Aeronautics & Astronautics Durand Bldg Rm 357a Stanford CA 94305-8468

CANNON, WILLIAM BERNARD, retired academic administrator; b. Cascade, Iowa, Nov. 10, 1920; s. Charles Bernard and Irma (White) C.; m. Jeanne Adair Ketchum, Aug. 16, 1944; children: Julia, Dominic, William, Robert. Ph.B., U. Chgo., 1947; MA, 1949. Budget examiner Bur. Budget, 1951-54, 59-62; asst. v.p. U. Chgo., 1954-59, v.p. programs and projects, 1968-74; dean Lyndon B. Johnson Sch. Pub. Affairs, U. Tex. at Austin, 1974-75; v.p. bus. and fin. U. Chgo., 1976-83, prof., 1976-89, prof. emeritus, 1989—. Asst. chief, office legis. reference for health, edn. and welfare programs Bur. Budget, 1962-65, chief edn., manpower and sci. div., 1965-67; dep. chmn. Nat. Endowment for the Arts, 1968 Mem. selection com. Rockefeller Pub. Service Awards, 1976-81; mem. Midwest selection com. H.S. Truman Scholarship Program, 1977-87. Served with AUS, 1943-46. Mem. Phi Beta Kappa. Home: Apt 148 4401 Spicewood Springs Austin TX 78759 E-mail: 73003.544@compuserve.com.

CANO, KRISTIN MARIA, lawyer; b. McKeesport, Pa., Oct. 27, 1951; d. John S. and Sally (Kavic) C. BS in Biochemistry, Pa. State U., 1973; MS in Forensic Sci., George Washington U., 1975; JD, Southwestern U., 1978; LLM in Securities Regulation, Georgetown U., 1984. Bar: Calif. 1978, U.S. Dist. Ct. (cen., no. and so. dists.) Calif. 1984, U.S. Dist. Ct. Ariz., 1988, U.S. Supreme Ct. 1988, U.S. Ct. Appeals (9th cir.) 1992. Assoc. Yusim, Cassidy, Stein & Hanger, Beverly Hills, Calif., 1979-81, Walker and Hartley, Newport Beach, Calif., 1981-82, Milberg, Weiss, Bershad, Spethrie & Lerach, San Diego, 1984; pvt. practice Newport Beach, 1984—. Bd. dirs., v.p. Sandcastle Community Assn., Corona del Mar, Calif., 1987-97; active Leadership Tomorrow Class of 1994. Mem. Orange County Bar Assn., Balboa Bay Club. Democrat. Roman Catholic. Avocations: ballet, ice skating, bicycling, photography, golf. Office: 1 Corporate Plaza Dr Ste 110 Newport Beach CA 92660-7924 Office Phone: 949-759-1505. Business E-Mail: cano@securities-law.com.

CANO-BALLESTA, JUAN, Spanish language educator; b. Murcia, Spain, Mar. 12, 1932; s. José Cano and Marcelina Ballesta; m. Mercedes Cano, Sept. 12, 1969. PhD, Ludwig Maximilian U., Munich, 1961. Lektor U. Göttingen, Germany, 1962-65; asst. prof. Spanish Yale U., New Haven, 1966-71; assoc. prof. Boston U., 1971-75; prof. U. Pitts., 1976-83; Commonwealth prof. U. Va., Charlottesville, 1983—2001, acting chmn. dept. Spanish and Italian, 1984-85, prof. emeritus, 2001—. Author: La Poesia de Miguel Hernández, 1962, La poesia española entre pureza y revolución, 1972, 2d edit. 1996, Literatura y tecnologia; las letras españolas ante la revolución industrial, 1981, 2d edit., 1999, Las estrategias de la imaginacion, 1994; editor: Poesia y prosa de guerra de Miguel Hernández, 1977, En torno a Miguel Hernández, 1978, Articulos sociales, politicos y de critica literaria de Mariano J. de Larra, 1982, El rayo que no cesa de Miguel Hernández, 1988, Viento del pueblo de Miguel Hernández, 1989, Nuevas amistades de J. Garcia Hortelano, Poesía española reciente (1980-2000), 2001, La mentira de las sombras, critica cinematografica de Juan Gil-Albert, 2003. Fellow Morse Research Soc. Yale U., 1968-69, Am. Council Learned Socs., Madrid, 1975-76, Ctr. for Advanced Studies U. Va., 1983-84. Mem. MLA, Internat. Assn. Hispanists, Southeastern Medieval Assn., Am. Assn. Tchrs. Spanish and Portugese. Office: 115 Wilson Ct Charlottesville VA 22901-2941

CANONERO, MILENA, costume designer; b. Turin, Italy; m. Marshall Bell. Costume designer: (films) A Clockwork Orange, 1971, (with Ulla-Britt Soderlund) Barry Lyndon, 1975 (Academy award best costume design 1975), Midnight Express, 1978, The Shining, 1980, Chariots of Fire, 1981 (Academy award best costume design 1981, British Academy award best costume design 1982), The Hunger, 1983, The Cotton Club, 1984, Give My Regards to Broad Street, 1984, Out of Africa, 1985 (Academy award nomination best costume design 1985, British Academy award nomination best costume design 1986), Haunted Summer, 1988, Tucker: The Man and His Dream, 1988 (Academy award nomination best costume design 1988), Dick Tracy, 1990 (Academy award nomination best costume design 1990), The Godfather, Part III, 1990, Damage, 1992, (with Elisabetta Beraldo) Camilla, 1993, The Life Aquatic, 2004, Oceans Twelve, 2004, (TV series) Miami Vice, 1986-89; costume designer, visual cons.: (films) Barfly, 1987; assoc. prodr.: (films) Good Morning Babylon, 1987, Mamba, 1988; costume design cons.: (films) Lost Angels, 1989, Reversal of Fortune, 1990. Recipient Coty Am. Fashion Critics' award 1984, Career Achievement award in Film from Costume Designers Guild, 2001. Office: care Marc H Glick Glick and Weintraub 1501 Broadway New York NY 10036-5601 Home: Los Angeles

CANONI, JOHN DAVID, lawyer; b. Newton, Mass., May 11, 1939; s. John Joseph and Olga Elizabeth (Mangini) C.; m. Katherine Ariadna Bryant, Aug. 18, 1962; children: Lisa Ann, Peter Christopher, John Charles, Scott Francis. BA cum laude, Amherst Coll., 1960; LLB, Yale U., 1963. Bar: NY 1964, U.S. Ct. Appeals (2d cir.) 1966, US Ct. Appeals (3d cir.) 1967, US Ct. Appeals (4th cir.) 1968, US Ct. Appeals (1st cir.) 1969, US Supreme Ct. 1971, US Ct. Appeals (7th cir.) 1972. Assoc. Townley & Updike, NYC, 1963-71, ptnr., 1971-95, Nixon Peabody LLP, NYC, 1995—. Mem. Lt. Gov.'s Task Force on Plant Closings, NY, 1984-85. Mem. ABA, NY State Bar Assn. (chmn. labor & employment law sect. 1983-84), CPR Inst, Dispute Resolution, Yale Club. Republican. Roman Catholic. Home: 20 High Meadows Mount Kisco NY 10549-3847 Office: Nixon Peabody LLP 437 Madison Ave New York NY 10022-7001 Office Phone: 212-940-3169. Office Fax: 866-947-2320. Personal E-mail: jcanoni@aol.com. Business E-Mail: jcanoni@nixonpeabody.com.

CANSECO, JOSE, retired professional baseball player; b. Havana, Cuba, July 2, 1964; m. Esther Haddad (div. 1991); m. Jessica Sekely (div. 1999). With Oakland (Calif.) Athletics, 1982—92, 1997, Tex. Rangers, 1992-94, Boston Red Sox, 1994-96, Toronto Bluejays, 1998, Tampa Bay Devil Rays, 1999—2000, NY Yankees, 2000, Chgo. White Sox, 2001. Appeared in instructional video, Jose Canseco's Baseball Camp, 1989; author: Juiced: Wild Times, Rampant 'Roids, Smash Hits and How Baseball Got Big, 2005. Named Am. League Rookie of the Yr., 1986, Am. League Most Valuable Player, 1988; named to Am. League All-Star team, 1986, 1988—90, 1999; recipient Am. League Silver Slugger Award, 1988, 1990—91, 1998. Mem. Am. League All-Star Team, 1986, 88, 89, 90, 92. Achievements include first player to have 40 home runs and 40 stolen bases in same season, 1988; mem. World Series Champion, Oakland Athletics, 1989, New York Yankees, 2000; led Am. League in Home Runs (42), 1988, (44), 1991, RBI's (124), 1988. Office: Regan Books HarperCollins 10 E 53rd St New York NY 10022*

CANSLER, LESLIE ERVIN, retired newspaper editor; b. Hickory, N.C., Sept. 16, 1920; s. Leslie Ervin and Mabel Pearl (Braswell) C.; m. Marie Muriel Olwell, Aug. 19, 1944 (div.); children: David, Robert, James.; m. Elizabeth Marie Walters (dec.); 1 dau., Leslie Anne. BA, Wake Forest U., 1941. News editor Daily Advance, Elizabeth City, N.C., 1941; reporter Raleigh (N.C.) Times, 1941-42, 46, city editor, 1946-47; with News-Jour. Co., Wilmington, Del., 1947-88, day mng. editor, 1966-68, mng. editor, 1968-76, assoc. Sunday editor, 1976-79, Sunday editor, 1979-80, assoc. editor, 1980-89. Served with USNR, 1942-45. Mem. Sigma Phi Epsilon. Republican. Episcopalian. Home: 11 Bristol Way New Castle DE 19720-3906

CANTARELLA, PAOLO, former automotive executive; b. Vercelli, Italy, 1944; Grad., Turin Polytechnic. With Fiat S.p.A, Turin, Italy, 1977—2002, asst. to the CEO, 1980—83; mng. dir., Comau, 1983; dir., supply & distribution Fiat Auto, 1989—90, gen. mgr., 1990, CEO, 1990—96; pres., CEO Fiat S.p.A., Turin, Italy, 1996—2002. Pres. European Automobile Mfrs. Assn., 2000; bd. dirs. Polaroid Group, 2003—. Office: Polaroid Corp Corp Hdqts 1265 Main St Bldg W3 Waltham MA 02451

CANTELLA, VINCENT MICHELE, securities trader, director; b. Boston, Oct. 27, 1917; s. Michele and Josephine (Sapienza) C.; m. Josephine R. Castanien, Nov. 19, 1944; children: Betsy Ann, David V., Steven M. BS, Boston U., 1939. Mng. ptnr. Cantella & Co., Boston, 1952-74; ptnr. Josephthal & Co., Boston, 1974-78, 1974-78; pres. Cantella & Co. Inc., 1979, 1979-97, chmn., 1997—. Mem. Boston Stock Exch., 1953—2005, bd. govs., mem. exec. com., 1963—74, 1979—91, chmn. exec. com., 1971—73, chmn. bd. govs., 1973—74; pres. Boston Stock Exch. Clearing Corp., 1964—68; mem. Midwest Stock Exch., 1965—72, Pacific Coast Stock Exch., 1965—78, N.Y. Stock Exch., 1969—78, Detroit Stock Exch., 1963—76, P.B.W. Stock Exch., 1970—73, Am. Stock Exch., 1972—75. Ret. Maj. USMC, World War II. Mem.: The N.Y. Stock Exc. Luncheon Club, Boston Athletic Club. Home: 635 Lewis Wharf Boston MA 02110-3924 Office: 2 Oliver St Boston MA 02109-4901 Office Phone: 617-521-8630.

CANTELON, JOHN EDWARD, retired university chancellor; b. Warroad, Minn., June 20, 1924; s. Arthur Edward and Georgia (Turnbull) C.; m. Joy Elizabeth Norton, Aug. 16, 1953; children: Barbara Jean, Charles Norton. Student, U. Man., 1941-42; BA, Reed Coll., 1948; PhD, Oxford U., 1951; D.H.L., Hebrew Union Coll.-Jewish Inst. Religion, 1972. Ordained to diocese of Oreg., 1952; pastor Fairmont Presbyn. Ch., Eugene, Oreg., 1952-53; mem. staff Christian Assn., U. Pa., 1953-57; asso. sec. div. higher edn. United Presbyn. Ch., Phila., 1957-60; univ. chaplain, asso. prof. U. So. Calif., 1960-67; prof. U. So. Calif. Sch. Relgion, 1967-70; vice provost, dean U. So. Calif. Coll. Letters, Arts and Scis., 1972-76; v.p. undergrad. studies U. So. Calif. (Coll. Letters, Arts and Scis.), 1972-76, Bicentennial prof., 1976; provost, v.p. for acad. affairs Central Mich. U., Mt. Pleasant, 1976-86, prof., 1976-89, provost emeritus, 1986; v.p. for acad. affairs Walden U., 1991-94, chancellor, 1995-99, chancellor emeritus, 1999—. Pres. Middle Mich. Devel. Corp. Author: Higher Education and the Campus Revolution, 1969, Terrorism and the Moral Majority, 1984. Served with AUS, 1943-46. Recipient Gov. Gen.'s medal acad. excellence Neepawa Collegiate Inst., 1941 Mem. Newcomen Soc., Univ. Club, Phi Beta Kappa, Phi Kappa Phi, Blue Key, Skull and Dagger, Sigma Iota Epsilon. Home: Portland Plz # 1201 1500 SW 5th Ave Portland OR 97201-5458 E-mail: jcantelo@teleport.com.

CANTELON, PHILIP LOUIS, historian; b. Ft. Wayne, Ind., Nov. 7, 1940; s. Philip Eccles and Marie (Gehrke) C.; m. Eileen S. McGuckian, Feb. 14, 1989. AB, Dartmouth Coll., 1962; MA, U. Mich., 1963; PhD, Ind. U., 1971. Asst. prof. Williams Coll., Williamstown, Mass., 1968-77; Fulbright prof. Kyushu Nat. U./Seinan Gakuin U., Fukuoka, Japan, 1978-79; pres., CEO, History Assocs. Inc., Rockville, Md., 1980—. Adj. prof. Cath. U., 2002; exec. sec. Nat. Coun. Pub. History, Washington, 1979-81; sec.-treas. Soc. History in Fed. Govt., Washington, 1979-80, pres., 1995-96; chmn. Montgomery County Hist. Preservation Commn., 1985-91; pres. Montgomery County Hist. Soc., Rockville, 1991-95, Peerless Rockville Historic Preservation, Ltd., 1996-2002. Author: Crisis Contained, 1980, The History of MCI, 1993, The Roadway Story, 1996, Never Stand Still: The History of Consolidated Freightways and CNF Transportation Inc., 1999, The History of Mere Point: 1878-2003, 2003; editor: The American Atom, 1989, Corporate Archives and History, 1993. Recipient Franklin D. Roosevelt award, Soc. for History of Fed. Govt., 2004. Mem.: Oral History Assn., Orgn Am. Historians (chmn. com. on rsch. and access to his. documentations 1999), Cosmos Club (admissions com. 1993—94, chair bd. mgmt. 1995—99, v.p. 1999—2000, pres. 2000—01, bd. mgmt. 2001—02). Home: 11807 Dinwiddie Dr Rockville MD 20852-4459 Office: History Assocs Inc 300 N Stonestreet Ave Rockville MD 20850 E-mail: pcantelon@historyassociates.com.

CANTERBURY, CHARLES, protective services official, labor union administrator; 2 children. BA, Coastal Carolina U. From Patrol Divsn. to mgr. Ops. Bur. Horry County Police Dept., Conway, SC, 1978, mgr. Ops. Bur. From founder local lodge to pres. Fraternal Order Police, Washington, 1984—2003, pres., 2003—.

CANTERO, RAOUL G., III, state supreme court justice; b. Madrid, Aug. 1, 1960; m. Ana Maria Cantero; children: Christian, Michael, Elisa. BA in English and Bus., Fla. State U.; JD cum laude, Harvard U. Bd. cert. in appellate practice:. Law clk. to Hon. Edward B. Davis U.S. Dist. Ct. (so. dist.) Fla.; shareholder, head appellate divsn. Adorno & Yoss, Miami; justice Fla. Supreme Ct., Tallahassee, 2002—. Lectr. in field. Contbr. articles to legal jours., short stories to anthologies; author: Certifying Questions to the Florida Supreme Court: What's So Important?, 2002, Changes to the Florida Rules of Appellate Procedure, 1997, Discovery from Medical Experts: How Much is Too Much?, 1997, Non-Final Review of Insurance Coverage Issues: Wading through the Quagmire, 1995. Mem. planning and zoning bd. City of Coral Gables, 1993—2001; mem. pastoral coun. St. Augustine Ch., 1990—97, chmn., 1997—2001, head Men's Retreat Ministry, 1994—2000; bd. dirs. Legal Svcs. of Greater Miami, Inc., 1991—95. Mem.: Dade County Bar Assn. (mem. appellate ct. com. 1998—99), Fla. Bar Assn. (mem. appellate rules com. 1993, sec. 1997—99, treas. appellate practice sect. 1999—2000, vice-chair 2001—02, sec. appellate practice sect. 2000—01, mem. 11th jud. cir. jud. nominating commn. 2001—02). Office: Fla Supreme Ct 500 S Duval St Tallahassee FL 32399*

CANTILLI, EDMUND JOSEPH, safety engineer, educator, translator, writer, consultant; b. Yonkers, N.Y., Feb. 12, 1927; s. Ettore and Maria (deRubeis) C.; m. Nella Franco, May 15, 1948; children: Robert, John, Teresa. AB, Columbia U., 1954, BS, 1955; cert., Yale Bur. Hwy. Traffic, 1957; PhD in Transp. Planning and Engring., Poly. Inst. Bklyn., 1972; postgrad. in urban planning and pub. safety, NYU, 1968-71. Registered profl. engr., N.Y., N.J., Calif.; profl. planner, N.J.; bd. cert. safe ty profl. (BCSP); bd. cert. planner (AICP); bd. cert. forensic engr. (BCFE). Supervising engr. safety rsch. and studies Port Authority of N.Y. & N.J., 1955-69; prof. transp. and safety engring. Poly. U., N.Y.C., 1969-90, prof. emeritus, 1990—; pres. Urbitran Assocs., 1973-81; exec. dir., chmn. bd. Internat. Inst. for Safety Trans., Inc., 1977—; pres. EJC Safety Assocs., Inc., 1989—. Tchr. Italian, algebra, traffic engring., urban planning, transp. planning, urban and transp. geography, land use planning, aesthetics, environment, indsl., traffic and transp. safety engring., human factors engring., ethics for engrs.; cons. transp. and traffic safety engring., community planning, traffic engring., transp. planning, accident reconstrn., environ. impacts, 1969—; vis. prof. transp. safety engring. Inst. Superior Técnico, Lisbon, 1987-97; advisor to doctorate students Poly. U., CUNY, 1969-94, Politecnico di Milano, U. Trieste, Italy, 1980-98; consulting forensic engr., accident reconstructionist, expert witness transp. accident litigation including hwy. traffic, railroad, rail rapid transit, pedestrian accidents, 1969—. Translator (Italian-English autobiog. Joseph Tusiani): The Difficult Word; The New Word; The Ancient Word, 1988; author: Programming Environmental Improvements in Public Transportation, 1974, Transportation and the Disadvantaged, 1974, Transportation System Safety, 1979; editor: Transportation and Aging, 1971, Pedestrian Planning and Design, 1971; editor, contbr.: Traffic Engineering Theory and Control, 1973; editor and calligrapher There Is No Death That Is Not Ennobled by So Great A Cause, 1976; contbr. over 200 articles to profl. jours. and trade jours.; developer daylight running lights, methods of severity evaluation of accidents, identification, priority-setting and treatment of roadside hazards, transp. system safety methodology; expert systems for improving traffic safety; introduced diagrammatic traffic signs, collision energy-absorption devices. With U.S. Army, 1945-49, 50-51. Fellow ASCE, Inst. Transp. Engrs., Nat. Acad. Forensic Engrs.; mem. NSPE, Am. Planning Assn. (charter), Am. Inst. Cert. Planners (cert.), Am. Soc. Safety Engrs., N.Y. Acad. Scis., Nat. Assn. Profl. Accident Reconstrn. Specialists, Internat. Assn. for Accidents and Traffic Medicine, Human Factors Soc., N.Y. Acad. Scis., System Safety Soc., Sigma Xi. Home: 134 Euston Rd West Hempstead NY 11552-1024 Office: PO Box 63 Franklin Square NY 11010-0063 E-mail: ejcsafety@aol.com, insafetran@aol.com, cantoxxv@aol.com.

CANTLEY, KEVIN RILOUS, architectural firm executive; b. North Hollywood, Calif. married. BArch with highest honors, MArch, Ga. Inst. Tech.; postgrad., L'Ecole des Beaux-Arts, Paris. Cert. NCARB. Joined Cooper Carry Inc., Atlanta, 1980, prin., 1986, v.p., 1989, COO, 1990, pres., CEO, 1995—. Program dir. Coll. Arch., Ga. Inst. Tech., Atlanta; spkr. in field. Mem.: AIA (dir.), Archs. Found. Ga., Nat. Assn. Indsl. and Office Pks., Urban Land Inst. Office: Cooper Carry Inc Ste 200 3520 Piedmont Rd NE Atlanta GA 30305-1595

CANTLIFFE, DANIEL JAMES, horticulture educator; b. N.Y.C., Oct. 31, 1943; s. Sarah Lucretia Keesler C.; m. Elizabeth F. Lapetina, June 5, 1965; children: Christine, Deanna, Danielle, Cheri. BS, Delaware Valley Coll., Doylestown Pa., 1965; MS, Purdue U., 1967, PhD, 1971. Asst. prof. horticulture U. Fla., Gainesville, 1974-76, assoc. prof., 1976-81, prof., 1981—, asst. chair dept., 1983-84, acting chair dept., 1984-85, chmn. dept., 1985-92, acting chair dept. fruit crops, 1991-92, chair dept. hort. scis., 1992—. Vis. prof. U. Hawaii, Honolulu, 1979-80; sci. cons. Sun Seeds Genetics, Hollister, Calif., 1987, Pillsbury Co., 1987—, Teltech Inc., Bloomington, Minn., 1988—, DNAP, Monsanto, Seed Dynamics, Ball Seed Co., Sybron Chem., Dow Agro Scis. Contbr. articles to profl. jours. and conf. procs., chpts. to books. Recipient rsch. award Fla. Fruit and Vegetable Assn., Orlando, 1986, Alumni Achievement award Delaware Valley Coll., Doylestown, 1990, Distinguished Agrl. Alumni award Purdue Univ., 1999. Fellow: Crop Sci. Soc. Am. (pres. 1991—92, Seed Sci. award 1997), Am. Soc. Hort. Sci. (v.p. rsch. 1991—92, pres.-elect 1993—94, pres. 1994—95, chmn. 1995—96, Outstanding Grad. Educator award 1991, Best Paper Vegetable Sect. 1992, Membership Recruitment award 1996, Outstanding Rsch. award 1997, vegetable publ. award 1997, So. Region Leadership and Adminstrn. award 2000); mem.: Plasticulture Soc. Am., N. Am. Strawberry Growers Assn., Bot. Soc. Am., Internat. Soc. Tropical Horticulture, Am. Soc. Agronomy, Fla. State Hort. Soc. (hon.; v.p. vegetable sect. 1984—85, pres. 1991—92, chmn. exec. com. 1992—93, best paper vegetable sect. 1990, 1992, 1993, profl. execellence program award 1996, USDA Group Hon. award for Excellence 1997, best paper vegetable sect. 2001, 2003, 2004, 2005), Am. Soc. Plant Physiologists, Internat. Soc. Horticulture, Fla. Seed Assn., Crop Sci. Soc. Am., Internat. Soc. Hort. Sci. (chair sect. of vegetables 1998—), Phi Beta Delta, Gamma Sigma Delta (Disting. Leadership award 2003, Dist. Svc. Africa award 2005), Phi Kappa Phi, Delta Tau Alpha, Sigma Xi. Office: U of Fla Hort Scis Dept PO Box 110690 1251 Fifield Hall Gainesville FL 32611-0690 Office Phone: 352-392-1928. Business E-Mail: djc@ifas.ufl.edu.

CANTONA, JOSEPH CHRISTIAN, director; b. Queens, NY, Sept. 18, 1973; s. Joseph Michael and Karen Ann Cantona. BS in Computer Mgmt., Ea. Ill. U., 1996; MS in Coll. Student Pers. Adminstrn., Ctrl. Mo. State U., 1998. Residence hall dir. U. Wis., La Crosse, 1998—2002; assoc. dir. residential life Emporia State U., Kans., 2002—. Mem.: Assn. Coll. and U. Housing Officers (media tech. com. chair 2000—02). D-Liberal. Office: Emporia State Univ 1200 Commercial St Campus Box 4009 Emporia KS 66801 Office Fax: 620-341-6228. Business E-Mail: cantonaj@emporia.edu.

CANTONI, LOUIS JOSEPH, retired psychologist, sculptor, poet; b. Detroit, May 22, 1919; s. Pietro and Stella (Puricelli) Cantoni; m. Lucile Eudora Moses, Aug. 7, 1948; children: Christopher Louis, Sylvia Therese. AB, U. Calif., Berkeley, 1946; MSW, U. Mich., 1949, PhD, 1953. Personnel mgr. Johns-Manville Corp., Pittsburg, Calif., 1944-46; social caseworker Detroit Dept. Pub. Welfare, 1946-49; counselor Mich. Div. Vocat. Rehab., Detroit, 1949-50; conf. leader, tchr. psychology, coordinator family and community relations program Gen. Motors Inst., Flint, Mich., 1951-56; from assoc. prof. to prof., dir. rehab. counseling Wayne State U., Detroit, 1956-89. Author books and monographs including: The 1939-1943 Flint Michigan Guidance Demonstration, 1953, Marriage and Community Relations, 1954; (with Mrs. Cantoni) Counseling Your Friends, 1961, Supervised Practice in Rehabilitation Counseling, 1978, Writings of Louis J. Cantoni, 1981, Essays, Theses and Projects in Rehabilitation Counseling, 1989; (with Mrs. Cantoni) Theoretical Underpinnings of Practice in Family Service Agencies, 1990; (poetry) With Joy I Called to You, 1969, Gradually The Dreams Change, 1979, A Festival of Lanternes, 1994; editor: Placement of the Handicapped in Competitive Employment, 1957; poetry editor Cathedral Digest, 1973-75; co-editor: Preparation of Vocational Rehabilitation Counselors Through Field Instruction, 1958; prin. editor: (poetry) Golden Song Anthology, 1985; editor jours. Mich. Rehab. Assn. Digest, 1961-63, Grad. Comment, 1963-64; bibliography, books and reprints placed in Reuther Libr. Archives Wayne State U., Detroit; contbr. articles, revs., poems, comments, abstracts, and illustrations to jours. Judge Mich. regional and nat. essay and poetry contests, 1965-77; bd. dirs. Mich. Rehab. Assn., 1962-64, 78-79, Mich. Rehab. Conseling Assn., 1985-87. 2d lt. AUS, 1942-44. Recipient award for leadership and service Mich. Rehab. Assn., 1964, Mich. Rehab. Counseling Assn., 1985, 87, 88, Outstanding Service award Mich. State Bd. Edn., 1989, South and West ann. poetry award, 1970, Meritorious Service award Wayne State U., 1971, 81, 86, 87, 89, Excellence in Poetry award Pig's Wing Press, 1997, Edizioni Universum Author of the Yr. award, 2000. Fellow AAAS; mem. AAUP, APA, Coun. of Rehab. Counselor Educators (sec. 1957-58, chmn. 1965-66), Nat. Rehab. Assn., Nat. Congress of Orgns. of the Physically Handicapped, Nat. Assn. of the Physically Handicapped, Nat. Alliance for the Mentally Ill, Am. Inst. Econ. Rsch., Poetry Soc. Am., Mich. Rehab. Assn. (pres. 1963-64), Detroit Rehab. Assn. (pres. 1958), Mich. Counseling Assn., Mich. Career Devel. Assn., Mich. Assn. for Humanistic Edn. and Devel. (Outstanding Svc. award 1997), Mich. Employment Counselors Assn., Mich. Assn. for Marriage and Family Counseling, Internat. Inst. Met. Detroit, World Poetry Soc. (Edwin A. Falkowski Meml. award 1990), Acad. Am. Poets, Detroit Inst. Arts, Friends of Detroit Pub. Libr., Friends of Marshall M. Fredericks Sculpture Gallery, Soc. for Study of Midwestern Lit., U.S. Hist. Soc., Italic Studies Inst., USN Meml., Internat. Sculpture Ctr., Nat. Sculpture Soc., Sculptors Guild Mich., Lladro Collectors Soc., Birmingham-Bloomfield Art Ctr., Psychology and the Arts, Poetry Soc. Mich. (Outstanding Svc. award 1984), Detroit Film Soc., Detroit Zool. Soc., Poetry Resource Ctr. Mich., Univ. Club, Scarab Club (Detroit), Phi Kappa Phi, Phi Delta Kappa. Democrat. Episcopalian. Achievements include research in theory and practice of counseling and psychotherapy, psychosocial aspects of disabling conditions, therapeutic and vocational counseling with disabled persons; workplace accommodation for the disabled, vocational rehabilitation of the severely disabled. Home: 2591 Woodstock Dr Detroit MI 48203-1062 *His destination, when he set out, was pure poetry, although he did not recognize it. He came to cherish the gifts of sun, rain, a walk in the woods, a brightening smile. His wife radiates the clear beauty of mature women. His children, albeit circuitously, took on his values. He feels near to man and God and views death as another beginning. He has reached his destination many times and welcomes sunset as well as sunrise, conflict as well as calm. He knows now that much of his life has been pure poetry.*

CANTOR, ALAN BRUCE, management consultant, application developer; b. Mt. Vernon, NY, Apr. 30, 1948; s. Howard and Muriel Anita C.; m. Judith Jolanda Szarka, Mar. 1, 1987; 1 child, Alec Brandon. BS in Social Scis., Cornell U., 1970; MBA, U. Pa., 1973. Mgmt. cons. M & M Risks Mgmt. Svcs., N.Y.C., 1974-78; nat. svcs. officer spl. projects divsn. Marsh & McLennan Risk Mgmt. Svcs., L.A., 1980-81; sr. v.p. sr. cons. prin. Warren, Mc Veigh & Griffin, Inc., 1981-82; founder, pres. Cantor & Co., 1982—; founder, ptnr., mng. dir. Beacon Health Informatics, LLC, 2002—. Co-mgr. Air Travel Rsch. Group, NYC, 1977-79; instr. risk mgmt. program Am. Mgmt. Assn.,; lectr. Risk and Inst. Mgmt. Soc. Conf., 1975-87, Med. Edn. Spkrs. Bur. So. Calif., 1990--; seminars How to Use Spreadsheets in Risk Mgmt., 1986-89, How to Use Computers in Risk Mgmt., 1989-93. Contbr. articles to profl. jours. Cons., vol. Urban Cons. Group, N.Y.C.; elder Beverly Hills Presbyn. Ch., 1991—; co-project dir. East European Orphans Toy Ministry, 1999—. Mem. Cornell Alumni Assn. N.Y.C. (bd. govs., program chmn.), Cornell Alumni Assn. So. Calif., Wharton Bus. Sch. Club (N.Y.C., chmn., mem. adv. com. L.A.), L.A. Athletic. Achievements include design of airline industry model; development of Riskmap risk mgmt. software products; Riskmap Windows version, Exposure Base Mgmt. Sys., patient care monitoring sys., Med. Quality Mgmt. Sys. Plus, Med. Quality Mgmt. Sys. Plus Windows version, MQMS Plus; Qualworx. Office: Cantor & Co Beacon Health Informatics 9100 Wilshire Blvd Beverly Hills CA 90212-3415 Office Phone: 310-859-7277.

CANTOR, ARNOLD, labor relations official; b. Rochester, N.Y., Jan. 4, 1927; s. Samuel Abraham and Bessie (Brightman) Cantor; m. Meriam Renee Teichner; children: Nadine, Duane, Paul, Glenn, Erica. BMusic, U. Rochester, N.Y., 1949; M in Music, U. Rochester, 1953; MA in Sociology, CCNY, 1995; PhD in Sociology, 1997. Cert. clarinet performer Eastman Sch. of Music. Tchr. instrumental music Rochester Pub. Schs., NY, 1949—57, dean of students, 1957—62, v. prin. h.s., 1962—68, prin., 1968—70; exec. dir. Profl. Staff Congress CUNY, 1970—95. Adj. asst. prof. Baruch Coll. CUNY, 1996—. Mem.: AAUP (mem. exec. com. 1969—), N.Y. State United Tchrs. (bd. dirs. 1961—70, pres. Rochester tchrs. assn 1963—65), Am. Fedn. Tchrs. (Disting. Svc. award 1994). Democrat. Jewish. Achievements include Led Rochester Tchrs. Assn. to 1st collective bargaining contract agreement in N.Y. state outside of N.Y.C. Avocations: music, photography. Home: 122 Philip Pl Hawthorne NY 10532-2108

CANTOR, BERNARD JACK, lawyer; b. N.Y.C., Aug. 18, 1927; s. Alexander J. and Tillie (Henzeloff) Cantor; m. Judith L. Levin, Mar. 25, 1951; children: Glenn H., Cliff A., James E., Ellen B., Mark E. BME, Cornell U., 1949; JD, George Washington U., 1952. Bar: DC 1952, U.S. Patent Office 1952, Mich. 1952, registered: U.S. (patent atty.), Can. Examiner U.S. Patent Office, Washington, 1949-52; pvt. practice Detroit, 1952-88; ptnr. firm Harness, Dickey & Pierce, Troy, Mich., 1988—. Lectr. in field. Contbr. articles to profl. jours. Mem. nat. bd. govs. Am. Jewish Com.; mem. exec. coun. Detroit area Boy Scouts Am., 1972—. With U.S. Army, 1944—46. Recipient Ellsworth award patent law, George Washington U., 1952, Shofar award, Boy Scouts Am., 1975, Silver Beaver award, 1975, Disting. Eagle award, 1985. Fellow: Mich. State Bar Found.; mem.: ABA, Am. Technion Soc. (nat. bd. regents), Cornell Engring. Soc., Am. Arbitration Assn. (arbitrator), Am. Intellectual Property Law Assn., Mich. Patent Law Assn., Oakland Bar Assn., Detroit Bar Assn., Mich. Bar Assn. (dir. econs. sect., arbitrator State of Mich. grievance com.), Beta Sigma Rho, Phi Delta Phi, Pi Tau Sigma. Home: 5685 Forman Dr Bloomfield Hills MI 48301-1154 Office: Harness Dickey & Pierce 5445 Corporate Dr Troy MI 48098-2683 Office Phone: 248-641-1600. Business E-Mail: cantor@hdp.com.

CANTOR, CHARLES ROBERT, biochemistry professor; b. Bklyn., Aug. 26, 1942; s. Louis and Ida Dianne (Banks) C. AB summa cum laude, Columbia U., 1963; PhD, U. Calif., Berkeley, 1966. Asst. prof. chemistry Columbia U., NYC, 1966-69, assoc. prof. chemistry and biol. scis., 1969-72, prof., 1972-81, prof., chmn. genetics and devel., dep. dir. Comprehensive Cancer Ctr. Coll. Physicians and Surgeons, 1981-89; dir. Human Genome Ctr. Lawrence Berkeley Lab, 1988-90; prof. molecular biology U. Calif., Berkeley, 1989-92; prof. biomed. engring. Boston U., 1992—, chmn., 1994-98, dir. Ctr. for Advanced Biotech., 1992—, prof. pharmacology, 1995—; prin. scientist human genome project Dept. Energy, 1990-92; chief sci. officer Sequenom, Inc., 1998—; also bd. dirs., 2000—. Sherman Fairchild vis. scholar Calif. Inst. Tech., 1975-76; mem. biophysics and biophys. chemistry study sect. NIH, 1971-75; mem. cell and molecular basis of disease rev. com. Nat. Inst. Gen. Med. Scis., 1977-81, coun. mem., 1986-89; mem. ozone update com. NRC, 1983, mem. rsch. opportunities in biology com., 1985-89, com. on the human genome, 1986-89, com. on bits of power, 1995-96; trustee Cold Spring Harbor Lab., 1977-83; mem. proposal rev. panel Stanford Sychrotron Radiation Lab., 1976-88; mem. U.S. Nat. Commn., Internat. Union Pure & Applied Biophysics, 1986-94, vice chmn., 1988-91, chmn., 1991-94; sci. adv. bd. Hereditary Disease Found., 1987-89; mem. coun. Human Genome Orgn., 1989-92, v.p. 1990-92, pres. America's, 1991-98; chmn. Department of Energy Human Genome Coordinating com., 1989-92; adv. com. Searle Scholars program, 1987-93, chair, 1993-94, mem. adv. com. program in parasite biology MacArthur Found., 1990-93; mem. sci. adv. coun. Roswell Park Cancer Inst. 1992-98; sci. adv. com. European Molecular Biology Lab., 1989-94; bd. sci. counselors Nat. Ctr. for Biotechnology Info., Nat. Libr. Medicine, 1990-95; cons. Incyte Pharm. Inc., 1992-98, Genelabs, Inc., 1988-, Samsung Advanced Inst. Tech., 2000-; mem. coun. Internat. Union Pure and Applied Biophysics, 1993-99; vis. com. biology Brookhaven Nat. Lab., 1986-89; bd. dirs. and chair sci. adv. com. Avitech Diagnostics, Inc. (formerly ATGC Inc.), 1992-1997; mem. nomenclature com. IUBMB, 1989-; chair adv. com. European Bioinformatics Inst., 1993-94; mem. USDA Genome Adv. Com., 1992-98; co-chair biotech. adv. coun. Fisher Sci., 1994—; mem. biology adv. com. Lawrence Livermore Nat. Lab., 1995-; chair 2000-04; chair sci. adv. com. Sequenom, Inc., Sequenom Instruments GmbH, 1995-, mem. sci. adv. com., Aclara, Inc., 1996-2003, Caliper, Inc., 1996-; bd. dirs. ExSar, Inc. (formerly Carta, Inc., formerly Thermaphore, Inc.), 1999-2004, SIGA Inc. (formerly Plexus Inc.), The Molecular Scis. Inst., Selectx-pharmaceuticals, 2003-2004(chair sci adv. bd., 2003-); mem. sci. adv. com., Odyssey Inc., 2002-; pres. Biochemist, Inc., 2001-2002; mem. FASEB consensus conf. on fed. funding, 1995-2000; quest scholar Quest Diagnostics, Inc., 1997-99; mem. biotech. coun. Dept. of Energy, 1996-99; mem. unconventional pathogen countermeasures adv. com. DARPA (Def. Advanced Projects Rsch. Agy., 1996-2000; adj. prof. biomed. engring., U. Calif., San Diego, 2002-. Author: (with Paul R. Schimmel) Biophysical Chemistry, I, II, III, (with Cassandra L. Smith) Genomics; assoc. editor Ann. Rev. Biophysics, 1983-93. Trustee Assoc. Univs. Inc., 1999-2000; bd. dirs. Keystone Confs., 1999-. Recipient Fresenius award Phi Lambda Upsilon, 1972; Eli Lilly award in biol. chemistry Am. Chem. Soc., 1978; Alfred P. Sloan fellow, 1969-71; Guggenheim fellow, 1973-74; Nat. Cancer Inst. outstanding investigator grantee, 1985, Analytica prize, 1988; ISCO prize, 1989, Sober prize ASBMB, 1990. Fellow AAAS, Biophys. Soc. (mem. coun. 1977-81, Emily Gray prize 2000, fellow 2000); mem. Am. Acad. Arts and Scis., NAS, Am. Soc. Biol. Chemists, Am. Chem. Soc., Soc. Analytical Cytology, Harvey Soc., Am. Soc. Human Genetics, Biomed. Engring. Soc., Japanese Biochem. Soc. (hon.). Home: 526 Stratford Ct Apt E Del Mar CA 92014-2767 Office: Sequenom Inc 3595 John Hopkins Ct San Diego CA 92121 E-mail: ccantor@sequenom.com.

CANTOR, CLIFFORD A., lawyer; s. Bernard J. and Judith L. Cantor; m. Pauline N. Ota, Dec. 31, 1979; children: Rebecca L., Clara E., Daniel L. BS, MIT, 1975; MS, U. Colo., 1977; JD magna cum laude, Harvard U., 1987. Bar: Alaska 1987, Wash. 1988, U.S. Ct. Appeals (2nd cir.) 1999, U.S. Ct. Appeals (9th cir.) 1991, U.S. Ct. Appeals (7th cir.) 1996, U.S. Supreme Ct. 2005. Clk. Alaska Supreme Ct., Anchorage, 1987—88; pvt. practice Sammamish, Wash., 1998—. Dir. Goose Island Barge Line, Inc., Bethel, Alaska, 1983—85; mem. King County Citizen Adv. Com., East Lake Sammamish, 1990—93. Author: Fiduciary Liability in Emerging Health Care, 1997. Fireman Bethel Vol. Fire Dept., 1977—84, EMT, 1981—84. Mem.: ABA. Achievements include patents for Fishing Net Hanging Jig. Avocations: hiking, canoeing. Office: Law Offices of Clifford A Cantor PC 627 208th Avenue SE Sammamish WA 98074-7033 Office Phone: 425-868-7813. Office Fax: 425-868-7870.

CANTOR, ERIC I., congressman, lawyer; b. Richmond, Va., June 6, 1963; m. Diana Marcy Fine; children: Evan, Jenna, Michael. BA, George Washington U., 1985; JD, Coll. William & Mary, 1988; MS, Columbia U., 1989. Mem. Va. State Legis., 1992-2001, co-chair claims. com., 1992-2001, mem. cts. of justice, 1992-2001, mem. gen. laws com., 1992-2001, mem. corp. ins. & banking com., 1992-2001, mem. sci. & tech. com., 2000-2001; mem. U.S. Congress from 7th Va. dist., 2001—; mem. fin. svcs. com., internat. rels. com.; house asst. majority whip, 2001—; chmn. congress. task force on terrorism and warfare, 2001—. Republican. Jewish. Office: 329 Cannon House Office Bldg Washington DC 20515-4607*

CANTOR, HERBERT I., lawyer; b. N.Y.C., Dec. 10, 1935; s. David and Ethel C.; m. Lynn Hardie, July 8, 1972; children: David, Susan. BA in Chemistry, NYU, 1965; JD, Cath. U. Am., 1970. Bar: Md. 1970, U.S. Dist. Ct. Md. 1970, D.C. 1971, U.S. Dist. Ct. D.C. 1971, U.S. Ct. Appeals (5th, D.C. and fed. cirs.) 1971, U.S. Supreme Ct. 1974, U.S. Ct. Appeals (4th cir.) 1981, U.S. Ct. Claims 1987. Patent examiner U.S. Patent Office, Washington, 1965-67; agt. Jacobi, Davidson & Jacobi, Washington, 1967-68; pvt. practice Washington, 1968-70; with Kraft, Cantor & Singer, Cantor & Lessler, Washington, 1971-85; ptnr. Cantor & Lessler, Washington, 1982-85, Wegner, Cantor, Mueller & Player, Washington, 1985-94; Evenson, McKeown, Edwards & Lenahan, Washington, 1994-2001; Crowell & Moring, 2001—.

Adj. prof. Law Ctr. Georgetown Univ., Washington, 1988-89. Assoc. editor Cath. U. Law Rev., 1969-70. Mem. Am. Chem. Soc., Fedn. Internat. des Conseils Propriete Industrielle, Am. Intellectual Property Assn. Office: Crowell & Moring 1001 Pennsylvania Ave NW Washington DC 20004 Office Phone: 202-624-2500. E-mail: hcantor@crowell.com.

CANTOR, JAMES ELLIOT, lawyer; b. Detroit, Mar. 14, 1958; s. Bernard J. and Judith (Levin) C.; m. Susan Elaine Finger, Dec. 26, 1983; children: Tilly Samantha, Brian Alexander. BS in Natural Resources, U. Mich., 1980; JD, Cornell U., 1986. Bar: Alaska 1986. Assoc. Perkins Coie, Anchorage, 1986-91; asst. atty. gen. environ. sect. Alaska, Atty. Gen.'s Office, Anchorage, 1991-98, supervising atty. transp. sect., 1998—, chief asst. atty. gen., 2003—. Mem. Eagle River (Alaska) Pk. and Recreation Bd. of Suprs., 1989-95, chmn., 1991-92; dir. Anchorage (Alaska) Trails and Greenways Coalition, 1994-97; commr. Municipality of Anchorage, The Municipality of Anchorage Heritage Land Bank Adv. Commn., 1999—, chmn., 2002-03. Mem. Anchorage Inn of Ct. Avocation: dog sled racing. Office: Atty Gen Office 1031 W 4th Ave Ste 200 Anchorage AK 99501-5903

CANTOR, LINDA C., retired history educator; b. N.Y.C., Nov. 25, 1947; d. Henry and Sylvia (Pepper) C. BA in History, Bklyn. Coll., 1968; MA in History, U. Ill., Urbana, 1969; MLS, Queens Coll., 1973. Tchr. history Sarah J. Hale H.S., Bklyn., 1969—99, ret., 1999; staff developer N.Y.C. (N.Y.) Bd. Edn., 1999—2002. Program chair S.J. Hale H.S., Bklyn., 1976—99. Editor: (newsletter) LINEAGE (Jewish Genealogy Soc. L.I.), 1995-99. Mem. Jewish Genealogy Soc. L.I. (bd. dirs. 1988-90, sec. 1990-91, pres. 1992-94, past pres. 1995), Jewish Genealogy Soc. N.Y. (mem. exec. coun., 1999-2001, sec. 2001-), Assn. Jewish Genealogical Socs. (dir. 1995-97, co-chair 26th Internat. Conf. on Jewish Genealogy). Avocation: genealogy. Home: 205 W End Ave Apt 6L New York NY 10023-4818

CANTOR, MELVYN LEON, retired lawyer; b. Boston, Aug. 13, 1942; s. Manuel and Adeline (Raffel) C.; m. Susan Gershen, June 7, 1964 (div. Jan. 1981); children: Matthew, Douglas; m. Kathryn Gabler, Jan. 3, 1982; 1 child, Joanna. BA, U. Vt., 1964; LLB magna cum laude, U. Pa., 1967. Bar: N.Y. 1969, U.S. Dist. Ct. (so. and ea. dists.) N.Y. 1971, U.S. Ct. Appeals (2nd cir.) 1971, U.S. Ct. Appeals (3d cir.) 1974, U.S. Ct. Appeals (5th cir.) 1986, U.S. Supreme Ct. 1987. Law clk. to Hon. Stanley A. Weigel U.S. Dist. Ct., San Francisco, 1967-68; assoc. Simpson, Thacher & Bartlett, N.Y.C., 1968-74, ptnr., 1974-97; of counsel, 1998—. Adj. prof. Yeshiva U. Benjamin Cardozo Sch. Law, N.Y.C., 1977-81, lectr. in law, Columbia U. Contbr. numerous articles to profl. jours. Fellow Am. Coll. Trial Lawyers; mem. Bar Assn. of City of NY Office: Simpson Thacher & Bartlett 425 Lexington Ave Fl 14 New York NY 10017-3903

CANTOR, NANCY, academic administrator; b. NYC; m. Steven Brechin; children: Maddy, Archie. AB, Sarah Lawrence Coll., 1974; PhD in Psychology, Stanford U., 1978. Faculty, chair dept. psychology Princeton (NJ) U., 1991—96; dean Horace H. Rackham Sch. Grad. Studies, vice provost for acad. affairs U. Mich., Ann Arbor, 1996—97, provost, exec. v.p. acad. affairs, 1997—2001; chancellor U. Ill.-Urbana-Champaign, 2001—04; chancellor, pres. Syracuse U., NY, 2004—. Mem. adv. bd. NSF; mem. com. on nat. needs in biomed. and behavioral sci. rsch. NRC, mem. com. on women in sci. and engring. Co-author (or co-editor): 3 books; contbr. 50 articles to profl. jours., chpts. to books. Recipient Woman of Achievement award, Anti Defamation League. Fellow: Soc. for Personality and Social Psychology, APA (Disting. Sci. award for early career contbn. in psychology), Am. Psychol. Soc.; mem.: Am. Assn. for Higher Edn. (vice chair bd. dirs.), Am. Acad. Arts and Sci., Inst. of Medicine of NAS. Office: Syracuse U 300 Tolley Adminstrn Bldg Syracuse NY 13244-1100 E-mail: cancellor@syr.edu.*

CANTOR, RICHARD IRA, physician, corporate health executive; b. N.Y.C., Jan. 25, 1944; s. Jacob Alvin and Sarah Cantor; m. Patricia Ann Honeycutt, June 7, 1970. AB, NYU, 1965; MD, Med. Coll. Va., 1970; postgrad., Bellevue Hosp. Ctr., N.Y.C., 1970-73. Diplomate Am. Bd. Internal Medicine. Intern Bellevue Hosp. Ctr., N.Y.C., 1970-71, resident, 1971-73; internist N.Y. Med. Group, N.Y.C., 1973-76; asst. med. dir. substance abuse programs Bellevue Hosp., 1973-76, med. dir. substance abuse programs, 1976-79; med. dir. Med Plan, N.Y.C., 1979-84; employee health unit Equitable Life Assurance Soc. U.S., N.Y.C., 1984-87; v.p., dir. health and med. svcs. Citibank, N.Y.C., 1988-89, v.p., dir. health, med. and staff svcs., 1989-91, v.p., corp. med. dir., 1991-98, Citigroup, N.Y.C., 1998—. Teaching asst. in medicine N.Y.U. Med. Ctr., N.Y.C., 1970-73, asst. prof. clin. medicine, 1983—; attending physician Cabrini Med. Ctr., N.Y.C., 1973-76, Bellevue Hosp. Ctr., 1973—; chmn. policy adv. bd. N.Y.C. Methadone Maintenance Treatment Programs, 1976-77; med. cons. Am. Fedn. State, County, and Mcpl. Employees, N.Y.C., 1979-84. Columnist Ask Your Med Plan Doctor, Pub. Employee Press, 1980-84. NIH trainee in endocrinology Med. Coll. Va., 1968. Mem. ACP, AMA, Am. Coll. Occupl. and Environ. Medicine, Royal Soc. Medicine (London), Am. Coll. Physician Execs., N.Y. Occupl. Med. Assn. (exec. com. 1997), Med. Execs., Med. Soc. County N.Y., Med. Soc. State N.Y., Nat. Corp. Med. Assocs., Internat. Soc. Travel Medicine, Med. Dirs. Forum, Phi Beta Kappa, Alpha Omega Alpha, Sigma Zeta. Office: Citibank 399 Park Ave New York NY 10022-4699 Office Phone: 212-559-0032.

CANTOR, SAMUEL C., lawyer; b. Phila., Mar. 11, 1919; s. Joseph and Miryl (Ginzberg) C.; m. Dorothy Van Brink, Apr. 9, 1943; children: Judith Ann Stone, Barbara Ann Palm. BSS, CCNY, 1940; JD, Columbia, 1943. Bar: N.Y. 1943, U.S. Dist. Ct. (so. and ea. dists.) N.Y. 1951, U.S. Supreme Ct 1969, D.C. 1971. Asst. dist. atty., N.Y.C., 1943-48; legislative counsel N.Y. State Senate; counsel N.Y.C. Affairs Com. N.Y. State Senate, 1949-59; mem. firm Newcomb, Woolsey & Cantor, Newcomb & Cantor, N.Y.C., 1951-59; 1st dep. supt. ins. State of N.Y., 1959-64, acting supt. ins., 1963-64; 2d v.p., gen. solicitor Mut. Life Ins. Co. N.Y., 1964-66, v.p., gen. counsel, 1967-72, sr. v.p., gen. counsel, 1973-74, sr. v.p. law and external affairs, 1974-75, sr. v.p. law and corp. affairs, 1975-78, exec. v.p. law and corp. affairs, 1978-84; counsel Rogers & Wells, 1984-89. Bd. dir. Mut. Life Ins. Co N.Y., Mony Reins. Corp., Monyco, Inc., Key Resources, Inc., Mony Advisors, Inc.; chmn. exec. com. N.Y. Life Ins. Guaranty Corp., 1974-84; mem. spl. com. on ins. holding holding cos. N.Y. Supt. Ins., 1967, N.Y. State select com. pub. employee pensions, 1973 Contbr. articles to Golf and other mags., legal and ins. jours. Fellow Am. Bar Found.; mem. Ins. Fedn. N.Y. (pres. 1967-68), Am. Bar Assn., N.Y. State Bar Assn., Am. Life Conv. (v.p. N.Y. State 1965-70), Am. Coun. Life Ins. (chmn. legal sect. 1977, chmn. legis. com. 1977-78, N.Y. State v.p. 1977-84), Health Ins. Assn. Am. (chmn. govt. rels. com. 1975, chmn. health care com. N.Y. State 1974-80), Assn. Life Ins. Counsel (dir.), Am. Judicature Soc., Bar Assn. City N.Y., N.Y. Law Inst., Nat. Attys. Assn., N.Y. State Dist. Attys. Assn., Union Internationale des Avocats, Columbia U. Law Sch. Alumni Assn. (dir.) Clubs: Mason. (N.Y.C.), University (N.Y.C.); Met., Univ. (Washington); Fort Orange (Albany, N.Y.); Sawgrass Country, Marsh Landing, Ponte Vedra (Fla.); La Costa Country (Carlsbad, Calif.); Confrérie des Chevaliers du Tastevin; Fairview Country (Greenwich, Conn.); Royal Dornoch Golf (Scotland), Am. Seniors Golf Assn., U.S. Golf Assn. (committeeman). Home: 10 Audubon Ln Greenwich CT 06831-2501 also: 34 Little Bay Harbor Dr Ponte Vedra Beach FL 32082-3707

CANTRELL, CAROL HOWE, municipal administrator; b. Martins Ferry, Feb. 10, 1947; d. Ferd A. and Geraldine (Hayne) Howe; m. William O. Cantrell, Dec. 29, 1968 (div. Oct. 1997); children: David, Paul, Emily. BS in Acctg. magna cum laude, U. Rio Grande, Ohio, 1982. Formerly cost analyst Holzer Med. Ctr.; formerly tax adminstr. Rio Grande, Ohio; adminstr. mcpl. income tax and ins. Village of Middleport, Ohio, 1988—. Vol. in orgns. that supprot children and teenagers; mem. First united Presbyn. Ch., Gallipolis. Mem. Greater Ohio Assn. Tax Adminstrs. Presbyterian. Home: 662 4th Ave Gallipolis OH 45631-1231 Office: Tax Dept 237 Race St Middleport OH 45760-1054

CANTRELL, DUANE L., retail executive; Degree in econs., Kans. State U., 1978; postgrad., U. Va. From merchandiser to exec. v.p. ops., sr. v.p. retail ops., sr. v.p. merchandise distbn. and planning Payless ShoeSource, Inc., Topeka, 1978—99; exec. v.p. retail ops. Payless ShoeSource, 1999—2002, pres., dir., 2002—. Trustee Kansas State U. Found.; chmn. adv. bd. Coll. Bus. Adminstrn. Kans. State U., mem. Mike Ahearn adv. bd. Office: Payless ShoeSource Inc 3231 SE 6th Ave Topeka KS 66607-2207

CANTRELL, JOSEPH SIRES, chemistry professor; b. Parker, Kans., July 31, 1932; s. Joseph Sires and Alta Fern (Collins) C.; m. Margaret Joyce Herr, Aug. 17, 1958; children: Mark Alan, Kenneth Aaron, Keith Floyd. AB, Emporia (Kans.) State U., 1954; MS, Kans. State U., 1958, PhD, 1961. Scientist, chemist Procter and Gamble Co., Cin., 1961—65; asst. prof. chemistry Miami U., Oxford, Ohio, 1965—68, assoc. prof., 1968—80, prof., 1980—2002, emeritus prof., 2002—. Cons. Mound Lab., EG and G, Miamisburg, Ohio, 1982—, Lawrence Livermore (Calif.) Nat. Lab., 1984—. Contbr. numerous articles to profl. jours. Cubmaster pack 937, Boy Scouts Am., Hamilton, Ohio, 1978-80, com. chmn. troop 956, 1980-86, scoutmaster troop 930, Oxford, 1986-89, dist. commr. Dan Beard coun., 1970—. Sgt. U.S. Army, 1954-56. Fellow Ohio Acad. Sci., 1981, Inst. Environ. Sci., 1988. Mem. AAAS, Am. Chem. Soc. (chmn. Cin. sect. 1983-84), Electrochem. Soc. (Masons (master Oxford 1969, 76), Sigma Xi (pres. Miami U. chpt. 1980-81). Methodist. Avocations: camping, hiking, stamp collecting/philately, painting. Home: 1364 Morman Rd Hamilton OH 45013-4366

CANTRELL, LANA, actress, lawyer, singer; b. Sydney, Australia, Aug. 7, 1943; d. Hubert Clarence and Dorothy Jean (Thistlethwaite) C. JD, Fordham Law Sch., 1993. Bar: N.Y. 1994. Former of counsel Ballon Stoll Bader & Adler, N.Y.C.; assoc. Sendroff & Assocs. PC, N.Y.C., 1996—. Singer supper clubs, TV programs, Australia, 1958-62; U.S. debut: TV show The Tonight Show, NBC, 1962; rec. artist RCA and Polydor Records, 1967— (Grammy award as Most Promising New Female Artist, Nat. Assn. Rec. Arts and Scis. 1967); recs. include Lana!, Act III, And Then There Was Lana, The Now of Then! Pres. Thrush, Inc.; U.S. rep. Internat. Song Festival, Poland, 1966, UN Internat. Women's Year Concert, Paris, France, 1975. Decorated Order of Australia, 2003; recipient 1st prize Internat. Song Festival Poland, 1966; 1st Internat. Woman of Yr. award Feminist Party, 1973 Office: 300 E 71st St New York NY 10021-5234

CANTRELL, ROBERT WENDELL, otolaryngologist, head and neck surgeon, educator; b. Neosho, Mo., Apr. 25, 1933; s. Lloyd L. and Ruby R. (Moffett) Cantrell; m. Young Hi Lee, Feb. 6, 1964; children: Mark L., Elizabeth L., Victoria L., Robert Wendell, Jr. Student, U.S. Naval Acad., 1952—55; AB, George Washington U., 1956, MD, 1960. Diplomate Am. Bd. Otolaryngology 1969. Intern N.Y. Hosp-Cornell U., 1960—61; resident in otolaryngology Nat. Naval Med. Center, Bethesda, Md., 1965—69; chmn. dept. otolaryngology Naval Regional Med. Center, San Diego, 1969—76; Fitz-Hugh prof. dept. otolaryngology-head and neck surgery U. Va., Charlottesville, Va., 1976—; acting v.p., provost U. Va. Health Scis. Ctr., Charlottesville, Va., 1995—96, v.p., provost, 1996—2001; dir. Va. Health Policy Ctr., Charlottesville, Va., 2001—04. Bd. dirs. Am. Bd. Otolaryngology, 1980—98, exec. v.p., 1990—98. Mem. editl. bd. Laryngoscope, 1976—88, Annals of Otology, Rhinology and Laryngology, 1977—88, Am. Jour. of Otolaryngology, 1978—82, Archives of Otolaryngology, 1979—88; contbr. articles to profl. jours. Mayor City of Oakmont, Md., 1968—69. Capt. USN, 1961—76, capt. USNR, 1976—91. Recipient Huron W. Lawson prize, 1960; fellow, Am. Heart Assn., 1959. Mem.: Am. Otol. Soc., Am. Laryngol. Assn. (coun. 1988—90, treas. 1990—95, pres.-elect 1995, pres. 1996—97), Am. Broncho-Esophagological Assn. (pres. 1988—89), Soc. Univ. Otolaryngologists (pres. 1982), Am. Soc. Head and Neck Surgery (pres. 1985—86), Triological Soc. (v.p. So. sect. 1989—90, Mosher award 1974), Am. Acad. Facial Plastic and Reconstructive Surgery (v.p. So. sect. 1980—83), Am. Acad. Otolaryngology-Head and Neck Surgery (pres. 1987), AMA, Alpha Omega Alpha. Home: 1925 Owensville Rd Charlottesville VA 22901-8824

CANTRELL, SCOTT, newspaper music critic; b. Ft. Smith, Ark., Nov. 14, 1949; s. Bert Thomas and Elizabeth Winstel (Scott) C. BFA, So. Meth. U., 1971; MS, Rensselaer Poly. Inst., 1974. Prodr., announcer Sta. WMHT, Schenectady, N.Y., 1973-86; music critic Times Union, Albany, N.Y., 1981-87, Rochester, N.Y., 1987-90; classical music editor Kansas City (Mo.) Star, 1990-99; music critic Dallas Morning News, 1999—. Freelance contbr. N.Y. Times, High Fidelity, Musical Am., Ovation, Classical and various other publs., 1973—; organist, choirmaster various chs., Albany, 1971-87. Recipient Deems Taylor award ASCAP, 1987, 89. Mem. Am. Guild of Organists, Music Critics Assn. N.Am. (exec. bd. 1989-2001, pres. 1993-97). Episcopalian. Avocations: travel, art, architecture, reading, cuisines. Office: The Dallas Morning News PO Box 655237 Dallas TX 75265-5237 E-mail: scantrell@dallasnews.com.

CANTRELL, SHARRON CAULK, principal; b. Columbia, Tenn., Oct. 2, 1947; d. Tom English and Beulah (Goodin) Caulk; m. William Terry Cantrell, Mar. 18, 1989; 1 child, Jordan; children from previous marriage: Christopher, George English, Steffenee Copley. BA, George Peabody Coll. Tchrs., 1970; MS, Vanderbilt U., 1980; EdS, Mid. Tenn. State U., 1986. Tchr. Ft. Campbell Jr. High Sch., Columbia, Tenn., 1970-71, Whitthorne Jr. High Sch., Columbia, Tenn., 1977-86, Spring Hill (Tenn.) High Sch., 1986—. Mem. NEA, AAUW (pres. Tenn. divsn. 1983-85), Maury County Edn. Assn. (pres. 1983-84), Tenn. Edn. Assn., Assn. Preservation Tenn. Antiquities, Maury Alliance, Friends of Children's Hosp., Rotary (bd. dirs.), Phi Delta Kappa. Mem. Ch. of Christ. Home: 5299 Main St Spring Hill TN 37174-2495 Office: Spring Hill High Sch 1 Raider Ln Columbia TN 38401-7346

CANTRILL, THOMAS H., lawyer; b. Springfield, Mo., Apr. 5, 1948; BBA with honors, So. Meth. U., 1970; JD with honors, U. Tex., 1973. Bar: Tex. 1973. Shareholder Jenkens & Gilchrist, P.C., Dallas, firm leader estate planning practice group, firm pres. & chmn., 2004—. Fellow Tex. Bar Found.; mem. ABA, Am. Coll. Trusts and Estate Counsel, Tex. State Bar Assn., Dallas Bar Assn., Internat. Acad. Estate and Trust Law, Order Coif, Beta Alpha Psi, Beta Gamma Sigma. Office: Jenkens & Gilchrist PC 1445 Ross Ave Ste 3200 Dallas TX 75202-2799 Office Phone: 214-855-4324. Office Fax: 214-855-4300. Business E-Mail: tcantrill@jenkens.com.

CANTU, JOSE FRANCISCO, retired postal worker; b. San Antonio, Tex., Nov. 26, 1938; s. Francisco Martinez Cantu and Josephine d'Antin; m. Irene Trevino, Apr. 8, 1958; children: Cathy Lynn Cantu-Ott, Joseph Dwayne, Joel Chris. BA, St. Mary's U., 1967—72; M of mgmt. and supervision adminstrn., Ctrl. Mich. U., 1974—75; MPA, Nova U., 1975—77, D of pub. adminstrn., 1977—78. Postmaster US Postal Svc., Pleasanton, Calif., 1984—98, dist. mgr., mktg. & sales Oakland, Calif., 1998—99. Customer svc. rep. US Postal Svc., San Antonio, 1958—73; mgmt. edn. specialist Postal Svc. Tng. & Devel. Inst., Oak Brook, Ill., 1973—74, Bethesda, Md., 1974—77. Author: (poetry) A Chorus of Christmas Carols, Vale of Dreams, (novels) Francisco Ducias: The Deadeye Deuce. Pres. Lodi Writers' Assn., Lodi, Calif., 2003—04, v.p., 2005. Sgt e-5 US Army, 1960—62, Ft. Gordon, GA.

CANTÚ, NORMA V., law educator, former federal official; b. Brownsville, Tex., Nov. 2, 1954; BS summa cum laude, Pan Am. U., 1973; JD, Harvard U., 1977. Bar: Tex. 1978, U.S. Dist. Ct. (so. dist.) Tex. 1979, U.S. Dist. Ct. (we. dist.) Tex. 1981, U.S. Ct. Appeals (5th and 11th cirs.) 1982, Calif. 1985, U.S. Ct. Appeals (10th cir.) 1986, U.S. Dist. Ct. (no. dist.) Tex. 1992. Tchr. English, Brownsville, 1974, San Antonio, 1979; intern Office of Atty. Gen. Tex., 1977-78; atty. Mex. Am. Legal Def. and Ednl. Fund, 1979—93, regional counsel, 1985-93; asst. sec. for civil rights Office for Civil Rights U.S. Dept. of Edn., Washington, 1993—2001; prof. law and edn. U. Tex., Austin, Tex., 2001—. U.S. rep. OAS Commn. on Children, 1999—2001. Officer Avance Parent Child Tng. Program, 1990; bd. dirs. Hispanic Health Policy Devel. Program, 1992, MALDEF, 2001—02, Mex. Am. Leadership Coun., 2002—, Leadership San Antonio, 1992—. Named to San Antonio Women Hall of Fame, Women in Sports Edn. Hall of Fame. Office: U Tex at Austin Sch Law Townes Hall Rm 3118M 727 E Dean Keeton St Austin TX 78705 Home: 140 Twinleaf Ln San Antonio TX 78213 Office Phone: 512-232-7111.

CANTUS, H. HOLLISTER, marketing consultant, government relations consultant; b. N.Y.C., Nov. 16, 1937; s. Howard J. and Eleanor (Hollister) C.; m. Barbara Jane Park, Feb. 7, 1961; children: Charles Hollister, Jane Scott. BA, Williams Coll., 1959. Mem. prof. staff Com. on Armed Services U.S. Ho. Reps., Washington, 1970-74; dep. asst. sec. def. U.S. Dept. Def., Washington, 1974-75; dir. congl. relations U.S. Energy Research and Devel. Adminstrn., Washington, 1975-77; group v.p. bldg. systems United Technologies Corp., Washington, 1977-87; assoc. adminstr. NASA, 1987-88; group v.p. missiles and space Lockheed Corp., Washington, 1988-94; sr. v.p. ICF Kaiser Internat., Inc., Fairfax, Va., 1994-99; CEO The ILEX Group, McLean, Va., 1997—. Bd. dirs. European Aeronautics Space and Def. Supplies and Svcs., Inc., Tioga Holdings, Inc., Applied Knowledge Group, Inc., No. Va. Regional Partnership, Inc. Capt. USNR, 1961-83. Fellow AIAA (assoc.); mem. Georgetown Club, Farmington (Va.) Country Club. Republican. Office: The ILEX Group 11951 Freedom Dr 13th Fl Reston VA 20190 E-mail: bjilex@aol.com.

CANTWELL, CHRISTOPHER WILLIAM, artist; b. Atwater, Calif., Dec. 24, 1960; s. Donald Byron and Ann Louise Cantwell; m. Susan Rebecca Moore, Sept. 19, 1982 (div. 1997); children: Claire Elyse Moore, Katie Lynn Moore. Owner, artist Christopher W. Cantwell Woodworks, Modesto, Calif., 1979-82, Oakhurst, Calif., 1982—. Cons. Internat. Union for conservation of Natural Resources, Cambridge, Eng., 1991—. Contbr. art book Jewelry Boxes, 1996; one-man shows include Houston Ctr. for Contemporary Craft, 2004; exhibited at Del Mano Gallery, 1990, 98, 99, Furniture Soc. Conf., San Francisco, 1998, Del Mano, 1999, Laguna Art Mus., 1999, Orange County Mus. Art, 2000, OXO Tower, London, England, 2001, Collins Gallery, Glasgow, Scotland, 2002, Jeffrey Weiss Gallery, 2003, L.I. Beach Mus. Art, 2003; represented in permanent collections Irving Lipton Collection, Robert Bohlen Collection, White House Ornament Collection. Youth advisor Oakhurst Luth. Ch., 1992-96. Mem. Am. Craft Coun., World Wildlife Fund, Program for Belize, Good Wood Alliance (CITES Liaison 1994—), Box Art Soc. (pres. 1999—). Democrat. Avocations: rock climbing, skiing, surfing. Home and Office: PO Box 1736 Oakhurst CA 93644-1736

CANTWELL, DON, artistic director; b. Charleston, S.C., July 10, 1935; s. James Richard Jr. and Helen (Thompson) C.; m. Patricia Downs; children: Kimberly S., Dewey C. Jr., Joshua Paul. Grad. high sch., Charleston. Dir. Charleston Ballet Sch., 1969—; artistic dir. Charleston Ballet Theatre, 1969—. Mem. Southeastern Ballet Assn. (v.p. 1981-82, 85-86, pres. 1983-84, 86-87, chmn. bd. 1984-85, 87-88). Office: Charleston Ballet Theatre 477 King St Charleston SC 29403-6231 Office Phone: 843-723-7334.

CANTWELL, JOHN WALSH, advertising executive; b. Fall River, Mass., July 16, 1922; s. William J. and Esther (Walsh) C.; m. Evelyna Dyson; children from previous marriage: Sharon, Peter, Paul. BS in Econs., Holy Cross Coll., 1944; MA, Georgetown U., 1945; postgrad., Columbia U., 1949-50. Asst. sales mgr. Internat. Milling Co., 1947-48; v.p. mgmt. supr. Compton Advt., N.Y.C., 1948-60; sr. v.p. mgmt. supr. Sullivan, Stauffer Colwell & Bayles, N.Y.C., 1960-65; pres., CEO Pritchard, Wood (advt.), N.Y.C., 1965-68, Parkson Advt. Agy., Inc., 1968-69; sr. v.p. J.B. Williams Co., Inc., 1968-69; pres. Jack Cantwell, Inc., 1970—; chmn., CEO Dolphin Med. Acoustics, Ltd., 1997-99; CEO Byrd Walsh Internat. LLP, 2004—. Office: Essex Towers 340 Sunset Dr Ste 1405 Fort Lauderdale FL 33301-2653

CANTWELL, MARIA E., senator; b. Indpls., Oct. 13, 1958; d. Rose and Paul Cantwell. BA Public Policy, Miami U. of Ohio. State repr. Dist. 44, Wash., 1987—92; mem. 103rd Congress from 1st Wash. dist., Washington, 1993—95; v.p. Progressive Networks, 1995—97; sr. v.p. Real Networks, 1997—2000; U.S. senator from Wash., 2001—. Democrat. Office: 717 Hart Senate Bldg Washington DC 20510*

CANTWELL, WILLIAM CASEY, church musician; b. Ft. Worth, Nov. 18, 1960; s. Albert Lee and Geraldine Cantwell. MusB in Organ Performance, Centenary Coll. La., 1984. Organist Noel United Meth. Ch., Shreveport, La., 1979—84; organist, music assoc. First United Meth. Ch., Wichita Falls, 1984—89; assoc. organist, dir. music Boston Ave. United Meth. Ch., Tulsa, Okla., 1989—99, organist, 1999—2001; assoc. organist, dir. comm. Trinity Episcopal Ch., Tulsa, 2001—04, organist, dir. music, 2004—. Mem.: Assn. Anglican Musicians, Am. Choral Dir. Assn., Am. Guild Organists (mem. nat. coun. 1998—2004, dean, sub-dean). Democrat. Episcopalian. Avocations: travel, reading, theater, opera. Home: 1434 S Frisco Tulsa OK 74119 Office: Trinity Episcopal Ch 501 S Cininnati Tulsa OK 74103 Office Phone: 918-582-4128. Business E-Mail: ccantwell@trinitytulsa.org.

CANTY, DAWN M., lawyer; b. Chgo., June 21, 1964; AB, U. Chgo., 1986; JD, U. Mich., 1989. Bar: Ill. 1989. Ptnr. Katten Muchin Zavis Rosenman, Chgo. Mem.: ABA, Am. Bar Assn., Trial Bar of No. Dist. of Ill. Office: Katten Muchin Zavis Rosenman 525 W Monroe St Chicago IL 60661 Office Phone: 312-902-5253. Office Fax: 312-577-8607. E-mail: dawn.canty@kmzr.com.

CANUMALLA, SRIDHAR, mechanical engineer; b. Hyderabad, Andhra, India, 1967; BTech, Jawaharlal Nehru Technol. U., Hyderabad, 1989; PhD, Pa. State U., 1995. Rsch. asst. Pa. State U., University Park, Pa., 1989-95; stress analysis cons. Motorola, Schaumburg, Ill., 1995; staff scientist Sonoscan, Inc., Bensenville, Ill., 1995—. Contbr. articles to profl. jours. Judge Pa. State Jr. Sci. Competition, University Park, 1993. Mem. ASME, IEEE, Am. Soc. Metals. Achievements include contbns. to the field of composites and to non-destructive inspection of electronic packages using acoustic microscopy. Office: Sonoscan Inc 2149 Pratt Blvd Elk Grove Village IL 60007-5914

CANUPP, ROGER S., biologist; s. Alfred G. and Virginia K. Canupp; m. Patty L. Canupp, June 3, 1967; children: Leigh A. Cristales, John J. BS in Biology, Pikeville Coll., Kentucky, 1964—68; MS in Adminstrn., Ctrl. Mich. U., 1986—89. Biology tchr. Amanda-Clearcreek Local Schs., Amanda, Ohio, 1968—71; sr. exec. therapeutic specialist GlaxoSmithKline, Columbus, 1980—. Adj. asst. prof. clin. pharmacy practice U. Toledo Coll. of Pharmacy, 1992—99. Bd. dirs. The Open Shelter, Columbus, Ohio, 1990—95. With Med. Svc. Corps. U.S. Army, 1971—73. Mem.: Am. Coll. Clin. Pharmacology. Achievements include design of lab. procedures for Schistasome rsch. Office Phone: 614-354-8335.

CANZONIER, WALTER JUDE, shellfish aquaculturist; b. New Brunswick, NJ, Feb. 6, 1936; s. Joseph V. and Mary M. (Patterson) C. BS, St. Peter's Coll., Jersey City, 1957; postgrad., Rutgers U., 1957-64. Teaching asst. dept. zoology Rutgers U., New Brunswick, N.J., 1958-59, rsch. asst. dept. oyster culture, 1960-67, rsch. assoc., 1968-71, 81-87; rsch. fellow Inst. Marine Biology, CNR, Venice, Italy, 1971-77; dir. Coastal Resources Applied Rsch. Lab., Venice, 1977-80; dir. R & D, Aquarius Assocs., Port Noris, N.J., 1987—. Mem. tech. coms. Italian Ministry Sanità and Ministry Merchant Marine, 1974-80, Interstate Shellfish Sanitation Conf., 1980—; cons. on marine sci. UNESCO, France, 1978—. Contbr. articles to profl. jours. Organizer, treas. Point Pleasant Beach (N.J.) Taxpayers Assn., 1963-70; bd. dirs. N.E. Regional Aquaculture Ctr., 1992—, mem. exec. com., 1993-96, 2001-05; mem. N.J. Taskforce for Revitalization of Shellfish Industry, 1997, N.J. Aquaculture Adv. Coun., 2000-04. Recipient numerous grants from pub. agys. in N.Am. and Europe, 1971—. Mem. Nat. Shellfisheries Assn., Soc. Invertebrate Pathology, World Aquaculture Soc. N.J. Aquaculture Assn. (trustee 1989—, pres. 1991—). Achievements include development of shellfish sanitation guidelines and regulations for state and national health agencies in North America and Europe; design of marine research and aquaculture facilities in Asia, Europe and North America; advocacy for legis. to promote comml. aquaculture devel. Home: 44 Cowart Ave Manasquan NJ 08736-3102 Office: Aquarius Assocs PO Box 662 Port Norris NJ 08349-0662 Office Phone: 856-785-0402. Personal E-mail: garugala@att.net.

CAO, JUNWEI, research scientist; arrived in U.S., 2004; s. Guilan Gao; m. Yu Han, Oct. 5, 1998. BSc, Tsinghua U., Beijing, China, MSc, 1998; PhD, U. Warwick, Coventry, UK, 2001. Rsch. fellow U. Warwick, Coventry, 2001—02; rsch. scientist NEC Europe Ltd., Bonn, Germany, 2002—04, MIT, Cambridge, 2004—. Proposal evaluator European Commn., Brussels, 2003—03; invited spkr. Poznan Supercomputing and Networking Ctr., Poznan, Poland, 2003—03, Vanderbilt U., Nashville, 2002—02, Ohio State U., Columbus, Ohio, 2002—02. Co-author: Object-oriented Modeling, Analysis and Design of Complex Systems, 2002, Multi-Agent Systems: Theories, Methods and Applications, 2004; contbr. articles pub. to profl. jour. Recipient TOP TEN Student Candidates, Tsinghua U., 1997, Best Gradute Students, 1996, Golden for Social Works, Tsinghua Univ., 1994; scholar Spl. Rsch. Studentship, Univ. Warwick, 1999-2001. Mem.: ACM, IEEE, Open Sci. Grid Consortium, IEEE Computer Soc. Achievements include first to Resource mgmt. for Grid Computing; Multi-agent systems for Grid Computing; Workflow mgmt. for Grid Computing; QoS support for Grid Computing; Performance prediction for Grid Computing; development of ARMS: an agent-based resource mgmt. systems for grid computing; ARMSim: a modeling and simulation environment for agent-based Grid Computing; GridFlow: workflow management for grid computing; MACIP: Mfg. Application Computer Integrated Platform. Office: Mass Inst of Tech 77 Mass Ave Cambridge MA 02139-4307 Business E-Mail: caoj@mit.edu.

CAO, LI, social studies educator; s. Changming Cao and Huazhi Peng; m. Grace Xiang Li, Dec. 26, 1984; 1 child, Jennifer Jianqin. PhD, McGill U., Montreal, QC Canada, 2001. Asst. prof. St. Mary's U. Minn., Mpls., 2000—01; asst. prof. ednl. psychology State U. West Ga., Carrollton, Ga., 2001—. Sr. rsch. assoc. AXDEV Corp., Brossard, Quebec, Canada, 1997—99. Recipient Dean's awards, Queen's U., Kingston, Ont. Can., 1994, Grad. awards, Queen's U. Kingston, Ont. Can., 1995; fellow Royal Bank fellowship, Royal Bank, 1997; grantee Rsch. grant, Found. for Info. and Rsch. Que., 1997; scholar Guang Hua scholarship, Guang Hua Found., 1991. Mem.: AAUP, Can. Soc. Study of Edn., Ea. Region of Ednl. Rsch. Assn., Am. Ednl. Rsch. Assn. Avocations: running, travel, reading. Office: State U West Ga 1600 Maple St CEPD Carrollton GA 30118 Personal E-mail: lcao@westga.edu.

CAO, XINHUA, medical researcher; b. Suzhou, Anhui Province, China, Sept. 30, 1957; arrived in U.S., 1998; s. Xianzhi Cao and Wenshu Zhang; m. Wei Xiong, Nov. 28, 1957; 1 child, Yifan. BSEE, Xi'an (China) Jiaotong U., 1982, MSEE, 1989, PhD, 1996. Assoc. prof. Xi'an Jiaotong U., Xi'an, China, 1989—98; rsch. fellow, vis. scholar U. of Calif. at San Francisco, San Francisco, 1998—2003; rsch. scientist Harvard Med. Sch., Boston, 2003—. Recipient Silver Medal, Beijing Internat. Invention Exhbn. Fair, 1996, First-grade Award of Sci. & Tech. Progress, Nat. Edn. Com. of China, 1991. Mem.: IEEE. Achievements include patents for a digital x-ray radiography imaging device with a scanning table; a stereo display and stereo observation device for medical imaging. Office: Harvard Medical School 220 Longwood Avenue Boston MA 02115

CAOUETTE, DAVID PAUL, public relations executive; b. Sanford, Maine, Aug. 6, 1960; s. Paul Henry and Barbara (Stackpole) C. BA with distinction, U. Maine, Orono, 1983. Editor employee communications Union Mutual Life Ins. Co., Portland, Maine, 1981-84, pub. rels. acct. exec., 1984-85; mgr. employee communications UNUM Life Ins. Co., Portland, 1985-87; v.p., mgr. communications Integrated Resources, Inc., N.Y.C., 1987-89; asst. dir. corp. communications Fin. Guaranty Ins. Co., N.Y.C., 1989—; a.v.p. corp. comms. GE Capital/FGIC, N.Y.C., 1989-94; corp. comms. dir. AT&T Capital, Morristown, N.J., 1994-98; fin. comm. dir. AT&T Corp., Basking Ridge, NJ, 1998—2001; v.p. corp. media rels. and fin. comms. AT&T Wireless Svcs. Corp., Redmond, Wash., 2001—05; v.p. corp. commn. The Walt Disney Co., Burbank, Calif., 2005—. Ptnr., co-founder Interactive Communications, Inc., Merrick, N.Y., 1989—. Recipient Grand award ARC awards, 2002, Best of Show NIRI, Seattle, 2002, 2003, Nicholson Annual Report award, 2004 Mem. Internat. Assn. Bus. Communicators, Pub. Rels. Soc. Am., Nat. Investor Rels. Inst. Democrat. Roman Catholic. Home: 803 197th Ave SE Sammamish WA 98075-7499 Office: The Walt Disney Co 500 S Buena Vista St Burbank CA 91521 E-mail: david.caouette@disney.com.

CAPALBO, CARMEN, theater director, theater producer; b. Harrisburg, Pa., Nov. 1, 1925; s. Joseph and Concetta (Riggio) C.; m. Patricia McBride, July 9, 1950 (div. June 1961); children: Carla, Marco. Student, Yale Sch. Drama. Prodns. include: dir., co-prodr. (plays) Juno and the Paycock, Shadow and Substance, Dear Brutus, Awake and Sing!, The Threepenny Opera, The Potting Shed, A Moon for the Misbegotten, The Cave Dwellers, The Rise and Fall of the City of Mahagonny; dir. (opera) The Good Soldier Schweik, (plays) A Connecticut Yankee, Seidman and Son, The Strangers, Enter Solly Gold, Slowly, By Thy Hand Unfurled; original dir.: The Sign in Sidney Brustein's Window, The Chosen; also TV prodn. The Power and the Glory; story cons.: Studio One, 1951-52; cons. The Bronx: After the Fires, Conversation with Eddie, 1983; prodn. mgr. Emlyn Williams as Charles Dickens, 1952-53, Jean-Louis Barrault-Madeleine Renaud Co., 1952; dir., prodr., writer 200 radio plays. Served with U.S. Army, 1944—45. Decorated Bronze Star, Purple Heart; recipient spl. Tony award 1956, Obie award 1956. Mem. League N.Y. Theatres, Dirs. Guild Am., Soc. Stage Dirs. and Choreographers, Dramatists Guild, League OffBroadway Theatres (co-founder 1958, exec. bd. 1958-60). Address: 500 2nd Ave New York NY 10016-8606

CAPALDI, ELIZABETH ANN DEUTSCH, psychological sciences professor; b. NYC, May 13, 1945; d. Frederick and Nettie (Tarasuck) Deutsch; m. Egidio J. Capaldi, Jan. 20, 1968 (div. May 1985) AB, U. Rochester, 1965; PhD, U. Tex., 1969. Asst. prof. dept. psychol. scis. Purdue U., West Lafayette, Ind., 1969-74, assoc. prof., 1974-78, prof., 1979-86, asst. dean Grad. Sch., 1982-86, head dept. psychol. scis., 1983-88, sec.-treas. council of grad. dept. psychology, 1986-88; prof. U. Fla., Gainesville, 1988-2000, provost, v.p. acad. affairs, 1996-99; provost SUNY, Buffalo, 2000—04, vice chancellor, chief of staff, 2004—. Spl. asst. to pres., U. Fla., 1991-96. Author: Psychology, 1989, 4th edit., 1996; cons. editor Jour. Exptl. Psychology, 1991-96; assoc. editor Psychonomic Bull. Rev., 1993-98; contbr. articles to profl. jours. NIMH grantee, 1984-94, NSF grantee, 1995-98. Fellow AAAS, APA, Am. Psychol. Soc. (mem. governing bd. 1991-96, pres. 1999); mem. Psychonomic Soc. (mem. governing bd. 1992-97), Midwestern Psychol. Assn. (sec.-treas. 1988-90, pres. 1991), Sigma Xi. Office: SUNY State University Plz T-9 Albany NY 12246 Office Phone: 518-443-5538. Business E-Mail: betty.capaldi@suny.edu.

CAPALDINI, MARK LAURENCE, investment banker, information services executive; b. Bluefield, West Virginia, Feb. 10, 1954; s. Louis Aloysius and Marie Pia (Frigo) C.; m. Laura Jane (Hotchkiss), June 25, 1983. BS in Engring. Sci., Yale U., 1975; MBA, Harvard U., 1979. Sr. cons. Arthur Andersen and Co., N.Y.C., 1975—77; asst. to the pub. The Washington Post, 1979—80, asst. controller, 1980—82, asst. to the dir. circulation, 1982, zone mgr. home delivery, 1983, mgr. circulation ops., 1983—86; acct. exec. Claritas, Inc., Alexandria, Va., 1986—87, v.p. media, 1987—91, sr. v.p. mktg., 1991—92, exec. v.p., 1992—94; pres. LEGI-SLATE, Inc., Washington. 1994—97; pres., CEO Congl. Information Svc., Inc., Bethesda, Md., 1997—99, PC Data Inc., Reston, Va., 2000; pres. Curiosita, Reston, Va., 2000—01; mng. dir. MCG Capital Corp., Arlington, Va., 2001—02; ptnr., CMO Focus Enterprises, Inc., Washington, 2003—. Bd. dir. Yale Alumni Fund, New Haven, 1985-90, Information Industry Assn., 1995-1997, Found. for Independent Higher Edn., 1998-2000, Washington. Mem.: Assn. for Corp. Growth, Potomac Officers Club, World Pres. Orgn. (Chesapeake br. 2004—). Office: Focus Enterprises Inc 1150 Connecticut Ave N W Washington DC 20036 Office Phone: 202-470-1963. Personal E-mail: markcapaldini@foodsenterprises.com.

CAPANNA, ALBERT HOWARD, neuroscientist, neurosurgeon, lawyer; b. Utica, N.Y., May 12, 1947; m. Dawn McLouth; children: Christine, Alicia, Albert II, Danielle, Gabriella, Guy, Brianna, Gianna, Beau, Bianca. BA, U. Tex., 1970; MD, Wayne State U., 1974; JD, U. Nev., 2001. Med. intern St. John Hosp., Detroit, 1974, resident in gen. surgery, 1974-75; resident in neurosurgery Wayne State U., Detroit, 1975-79; fellow in microneurosurgery U. Zurich, 1979; stereotactic fellow U. Paris, 1980; fellow in pediatric neurosurgery Hosp. for Sick Children, Toronto, 1980; pvt. practice Las Vegas, Nev., 1980—; clin. asst. prof. neurosurgery sch. medicine U. Nev., 1983—. Chief staff Sunrise Hosp., Las Vegas, 1993-94; chief neurosurgery Univ. Med. Ctr., Las Vegas; clin. prof. U. Nev. Sch. Medicine, 1991—. Mem.: Rocky Mountain Neurosurg. Soc. (sec. 1998—2001, pres. 2002—03). Office: Internat Neurosci Cons 716 S 6th St Las Vegas NV 89101 Office Phone: 702-382-1960. Personal E-mail: acapanna@aol.com.

CAPAR, SOPHIA A., music educator; b. Munich, Nov. 24, 1947; arrived in U.S.A., 1949; d. Antony and Irena Kochanewycz Capar; m. George Kalman, Sept. 12, 1970 (div. Sept. 1989); children: Christina, Mark. BA, Rutgers U., 1969; MA, Montclair State U., 1970. Cert. English as Second Lang. Montclair State U., Supr. Montclair State U. Music tchr. Escambia County Bd. of Med., Pensacola, Fla., 1970; instr. Tidewater C.C., Va. Beach, Va., 1975—76; music tchr. Paterson Bd. Edn., Paterson, NJ, 1987—90, South Orange Maplewood Bd. Edn., S. Orange, NJ, 1990—91, Clifton Bd. Edn., Clifton, NJ, 1991—. Trustee Clifton Libr. Bd., Clifton; mem. Women's Edn. Com., Trenton, NJ. Vol. N.J. Performance Art Ctr., Newark. Mem.: NEA, Am. Choral Dir. Assn., N.J. Edn. Assn. (Women in Edn. com.), Ukranian Nat. Women's League Am. (numerous positions 1987—). Ukranian Cath. Home: 5 Chittenden Rd Clifton NJ 07013-4203

CAPAROTTA, KEVIN JON, musician; b. New Orleans, July 1, 1970; s. Joseph and Marcia Durand Caparotta; m. Kimberly Ann Marocco, May 14, 1994; 1 child, David Patrick. MusB, Loyola U., New Orleans, 1992. Prin. accompanist New Orleans Children's Chorus, New Orleans, 1988—; organist St. Catherine of Siena Ch., Metairie, La., 1994—2004. Composer: (choral music) May The Road Rise To Meet You. Mem.: La. Music Educators Assn., Music Educators Nat. Conf., Am. Choral Directors Assn. Office: Brother Martin High School 4401 Elysian Fields Avenue New Orleans LA 70122 Office Phone: 504-283-1561 3091. Office Fax: 504-286-8462. Personal E-mail: kcaparotta@cox.net.

CAPARRO, JAMES, information technology executive, former record company executive; b. Bklyn., Dec. 26, 1951; s. Vincent and Clara (Curran) C.; m. Mary Judith Senna; children: Daniel, James Michael, Kristin. BA, William Paterson Coll., 1973; postgrad., Garden State U., New Sch. for Social Research. With Sony Music, 1973; several sales and mktg. positions Epic Records; with CBS Records, N.Y.C., 1973-79, sales rep., 1979-80, sales mgr., 1980-83, Mid Atlantic, 1983-87; v.p. sales CBS Records, N.Y.C., 1987-88; with PolyGram Group Distbn., N.Y.C., 1988—98, exec. v.p., 1990-92, pres., CEO, 1992—98; chmn., CEO Island Def Jam Music Group (divsn. of Universal Music Group), 1998—2001; CEO WEA Corp., 2002—03; pres., CEO Atari Inc., 2004—05; founder, pres., CEO Entertainment Distbn. Corp. (divsn. of Glenayre Technologies Inc.), 2005—. Bd. dirs. Atari Inc., 2002—, Prana Found., T.J. Martell Found. Originator, exec. in charge prodn. (TV spl.) Michael Jackson-The Magic Returns, 1987. Active PTA, Rockville, Md., 1983-86. Recipient Masterworks Branch of Yr. award CBS Records, N.Y., 1984, Columbia Branch of Yr. CBS Records, N.Y., 1985; named CEO of Yr., S.I.N. Mag., 2001. Mem. Country Music Assn., Nat. Assn. Rec. Merchandisers (bd. dir., recipient Distributor of Yr., 1993-97). Republican. Roman Catholic. Avocations: golf, reading, music, jogging.

CAPASSO, FEDERICO, physicist; b. Rome, June 24, 1949; came to U.S., 1976; D in Physics summa cum laude, U. Rome, 1973; D in Electronic Engring. (hon.), U. Bologna, Italy, 2003. Rschr. Fondazione Bordoni, Rome, 1974-76; vis. scientist Bell Labs., Holmdel, NJ, 1976-77, mem. tech. staff, Lucent Techs. (formerly AT&T), Murray Hill, NJ, 1978-87, head quantum phenomena and device rsch. dept., 1987-97, head semiconductor physics rsch. dept., 1997-2000, v.p. phys. rsch., 2000—02; Robert L. Wallace prof. applied physics, Vinton Hayes sr. rsch. fellow elec. engring. Harvard U., 2003—. Co-chmn. Internat. Semiconductor Device Rsch. Symposium, Charlottesville, Va., 1995; chmn. Internat. Conf. on Advances in Semiconductors and Superconductors, Newport Beach, 1988, 90; program co-chmn. Picosecond Electronics and Optoelectronics Conf., Lake Tahoe, 1987; program com., mem. of 20 internat. confs.; invited lectr. at over 160 internat. confs. Editor 4 books; mem. editl. bd. Il Nuovo Cimento, Applied Physics Letters, Semiconductor Sci. and Tech.; holder 46 U.S. patents, more than 50 fgn. patents; contbr. over 300 articles to profl. jours. Recipient award N.Y. Acad. Scis., 1993, Gold medal Heinrich Welker Meml., 1994, Vinci Excellence award LMVH, 1995, medal Materials Rsch. Soc., 1995, Electronics Letters Premium award Inst. of Elec. Engrs. (London), 1995, Bell Labs. fellow award, 1997, John Price Wetherill medal Franklin Inst., 1997, Rank prize, 1998, Capitolium prize, 1998, Alessandro Volta Meml. medal, 1999, Willis Lamb medal in laser physics, 2000, Tommassoni Internat. prize U. Roma, 2004, King Faisal Internat. prize Sci., 2005; named hon. mem. Franklin Inst., 1997, Goff Smith Prize, U. of Mich., 2003. Fellow AAAS (Newcomb Cleveland prize 1995), Am. Acad. Arts and Scis., IEEE (David Sarnoff award 1991, W. Streifer Sci. Achievement award 1998, Edison Medal 2004), Am. Phys. Soc. (Arthur Schawlow prize in laser sci. 2004), Optical Soc. Am. (Robert Wood prize 2001), Internat. Soc. for Optical Engring., Inst. of Physics (Duddell medal 2001); mem. NAE, NAS, European Acad. Sci. Business E-Mail: capasso@deas.harvard.edu.

CAPDEVILLE, ALEX, academic administrator; PhD. CEO Helena Coll. Tech., 1978—2000; chancellor Mont. State Univ., Northern, Havre, 2000—. Mailing: Montana State Univ Northern PO Box 7751 Havre MT 59501*

CAPE, JAMES ODIES E., fashion designer; b. Detroit, Nov. 18, 1947; s. Odies E. and Juanita K. (Brandon) C. Student, Henry Ford C.C., 1973-75, Am. Acad. Dramatic Arts, N.Y.C., 1975-76, Pace U., 1977-78. Trapeze artist Mills Bros. Circus, 1962; skater Ice Capades, 1971-72; creator, dir., instr. skating program City of Southfield, Mich., 1972, 73; haute couture designer James E. Cape & Assocs., Dearborn, Mich., 1986—. Mem. Marji Kunz scholarship award com. Wayne State U., Detroit. Film reviewer Times-Herald Newspapers, 1989-90; clothing designs pub. in various mags. and newspapers; creations for TV and stage including the Emmys, The Am. Music Awards, Dick Clark-ABC Prodns., Showtime Spl. Aretha, Trump Castle, Atlantic City, The Chgo. Theater, Kennedy Ctr., Washington, Radio City Music Hall; co-prodr. Eartha Kitt, A Night in Paris; spl. commd. designs various celebrities; spl. publicity creations for Detroit Inst. Arts, Am. Lung Assn.; producer, host TV show "Town Talk." Recipient Pre-silver, bronze medals U.S. Figure Skating Assn., 1969, Citation award City of Dearborn, 1994, Wayne County (Mich.) Resolution award, 1993, Spl. Tribute award State of Mich. Ho. of Reps., 1994, Page award Herald Newspapers, 1999-2000. Mem. AFTRA, Actors Equity, Soc. for Cinephiles. Home: James E Cape & Assocs 500 N Rosevere Dearborn MI 48128 E-mail: JamesECape@aol.com.

CAPECCHI, MARIO RENATO, genetics educator; b. Verona, Italy, Oct. 6, 1937; BS, Antioch Coll., 1961; PhD in Biophysics, Harvard U., 1967. Soc. fellows, jr. fellow biophysics Harvard U., 1966-69, from asst. prof. to assoc. prof. biochemistry med. sch., 1969-73; prof. Biology U. Utah, 1973-88; prof. human genetics U. Utah Sch. Medicine, Salt Lake City, 1989—; investigator Howard Hughes Inst./U. Utah, Salt Lake City, 1988—; disting. prof. human genetics Howard Hughes Inst./U.Utah, 1993—. Mem. bd. sci. counselors Nat. Cancer Inst. Recipient Biochemistry award, Am. Chem. Soc., 1969, Intrnat award, Gairdner Found., Can., 1990, Alfred P. Sloan Jr. prize, Gen. Motors Corp., 1994, Molecular Bioanalytics prize, 1996, Kyoto Prize in Basic Schs., 1996, Franklin medal, Franklin Inst., 1997, Baxter award, AAMC, 1988, Horace Mann Disting. Alumni award, Antioch Coll., 2000, Premio Phoenix-Anni Verdi award, Associazione Anni Verdi, 2000, 33d Jimenez-Diaz prize, Fundacion Concita Rabago de Jiminez-Diaz, 2001, Albert Lasker award Basic Med. Rsch., 2001, Laureate of the Nat. Medal of Sci. award, 2001, Utah Gov.'s Medal of Sci. and Tech. award, 2002, Wolf prize in Medicine, 2002—03, Pezcollar Found. Internat. Cancer Rsch. award, Am. Assn. Cancer Rsch., 2003, March of Dimes prize in devel. biology, 2005. Mem. NAS, Am. Biochem. Soc., Am. Soc. Biol. Chemistry, Am. Soc. Microbiology, Molecular Med. Soc., N.Y. Acad. Sci., Soc. Devel. Biology, Internat. Genome Soc., Genetics Soc. Am., Am. Acad. Microbiology, European Acd. Scis. Achievements include research in gaining an understanding of how the information encoded in the gene is translated by the cell, elucidating the mechanism of genetic recombination in mouse embryo-derived stem (ES) cells, developing gene targeting in the mouse, gaining an understanding of embryonic and neuronal mammalian development through the use of gene targeting. Office: Howard Hughes Med Inst Univ Utah 15 N 2030 E Rm 5100 Salt Lake City UT 84112-5331 Office Phone: 801-581-7096. Business E-Mail: mario.capecchi@genetics.utah.edu.

CAPEHART, BARNEY LEE, industrial engineer, systems engineer, educator; b. Galena, Kans., Aug. 20, 1940; s. Samuel Alfred and Mary Jane (Bliss) Capehart; m. Lynne Carol Fowler, Sept. 2, 1961; children: Thomas David, Jeffrey Donald, Cynthia Diane. BSEE, U. Okla., 1961, MEE, 1962, PhD, 1967. Instr. elec. engring. U. Okla., Norman, 1965—67; mem. tech. staff Aerospace Corp., San Bernardino, Calif., 1967—68; asst. prof. indsl. and sys. engring. U. Fla., Gainesville, 1968—72; assoc. prof. indsl. engring. U. Tenn., 1972—73; assoc. prof. indsl. and sys. engring. U. Fla., Gainesville, 1973—79, prof., 1979—, asst. chmn., 1987—88. Cons. Martin Marietta Corp., U.S. Naval Tng. Device Ctr., State of Fla., Hicks and Assocs., Casazza, Schultz & Assocs., U.S. Dept. Energy, Dep. Ass. Sec. Bldg. Techs., Washington, 1989—90; nat. lectr. Assn. Energy Engrs.; expert witness in energy and safety cases; chmn. Regional Energy Action Com., 1977—79; mem. Region IV adv. group appropriate tech. Dept. Energy, 1978—80; mem. Local Energy Action Program, 1980—81. Author: books in field; editor: Internat. Jour. Energy Sys., 1985—88; contbr. articles to profl. jours. Pres. Fla. League Conservation Voters, 1984—86; dir. Energy Analysis and Diagnostic Center U. Fla., Fla., dir. Indsl. Assessment Ctr., 1995—99; grad. leadership Gainesville, 1984. Decorated USAF Commendation medal; named May 26, 1987, Barney Capehart Day in his honor, Alachua County, Fla.; named to Assn. Energy Engrs. Hall of Fame; recipient Palladium medal, Am. Assn. Engring. Socs., 1988. Fellow: IEEE (mem. energy com. 1988—90), AAAS, Inst. Indsl. Engrs. (dir. energy mgmt. divsn. 1986—87); mem.: Assn. Energy Engrs., Fla. Conservation Found., Audubon Soc. (Fla. chpt. Conservationist of the Yr. 1987), Sigma Xi, Fla. Blue Key, Eta Kappa Nu, Tau Beta Pi, Alpha Pi Mu, Sigma Tau. Home: 1601 NW 35th Way Gainesville FL 32605-4846 Office: U Fla Dept Indsl & Systems Engring 303 Weil Hall Gainesville FL 32611-2083 Office Phone: 352-392-1464 x2008. Business E-Mail: capehart@ise.ufl.edu.

CAPELLAS, MICHAEL D., telecommunications industry executive; b. Aug. 19, 1954; m. Marie Capellas; 2 children. BBA Kent St. U., 1976. With Republic Steel Corp., 1976—81; corp. dir. for info. systems, contr. and treas. of Asia Pacific ops. Schlumberger Ltd., 1981—96; founder, mng. ptnr. Benchmarking Partners, Cambridge, Mass., 1996; dir. supply chain mgmt. SAP Am., 1996—97; sr. v.p., gen. mgr. for global energy bus. Oracle Corp., 1997—98; chief info. officer Compaq Computer Corp., Houston, 1998-99, acting COO, 1999, pres., CEO, chmn., 1999—2002; pres. Hewlett-Packard Co., 2002; CEO, chmn WorldCom Inc. (now MCI), 2002—04; pres., CEO MCI, Inc., Ashburn, Va., 2004—. Mem. of the bd. of gov. Boys and Girls Clubs of America; mem. bd. trustee Am. U., Washington; supports City Year. Recipient Hope Technology Award, ctr. for Missing and Exploited Children. Mem.: bd. of Trustees of American University in Wash. DC. Avocations: travel, golf, running, music. Office: MCI 22001 Loudoun County Pky Ashburn VA 20147 Office Phone: 703-886-5600. Office Fax: 212-885-0570.

CAPELLE-FRANK, JACQUELINE AIMEE, writer; b. Fond du Lac, Wis., Dec. 23, 1935; d. Ira Richard and Aimee Cecilia (Dignin) Capelle; divorced; children: P. Malachi, Tamara, Daria Frank-Weber. AA, Edison C.C., Naples, Fla., 1986; cert., U. Cambridge, Eng., 1991, U. Oxford, 1992, Paris Am. Acad., 1992; BA, Fla. Internat. U., 1994. Part-time instr. Internat. Coll., 1999. Author: (children's book) What's a Library, 1974, (anthologies) Poetic Voices of America, 1996, 97. Mem. adv. bd. Greater Naples Leadership, Inc., 1999—. Mem. AAUW, Nat. Mus. Women, Collier County Hist. Soc. (bd. dirs. 1994—, pres. 1997-2001), Nat. Trust for Hist. Preservation, Mus. Trustee Assn., Cooperstown Art Assn. Republican. Presbyterian. Avocations: reading, travel, country walks, gardening, swimming. Home: 143 4th Ave N Naples FL 34102-8421

CAPELLI, JOHN PLACIDO, nephrologist, educator; b. Hammonton, N.J., May 23, 1936; s. John L. and Marie C.; m. Patricia Ann Verna, Nov. 4, 1961; children: John L., Elizabeth Ann, David S. BS in Biology, Villanova U., 1958; MD, Jefferson Med. Coll., 1962. Diplomate: Am. Bd. Internal Medicine (Nephrology). Intern Michael Reese Hosp., Chgo., 1962-63; resident Thomas Jefferson U. Hosp., 1963-65, NIH fellow in nephrology, 1965-67, Martin E. Rehfuss chief resident internal medicine, 1967-68; practice medicine specializing in nephrology Haddonfield, N.J., 1968—; clin. prof. medicine U. Medicine and Dentistry N.J., 1995—; pres. Lourdes Med. Assn., P.A. and Health Mgmt. Svcs. Orgn., Inc., 1995—, Nephrology Network for N.J., P.C., 1995—. Dir. div. clin. pharmacology Jefferson Med. Coll., Phila., 1968-69; dir. hemodialysis unit Our Lady of Lourdes Med. Ctr., Camden, N.J., 1969—, dir. div. nephrology and transplantation, 1974—, chief of staff, 1980-86, v.p. med. affairs, 1987-2001, sr. v.p. med. affairs, 2002—; clin. prof. medicine Thomas Jefferson U., Phila., 1974—; mem. chronic renal disease adv. com. N.J. Dept. Health, 1969-79, chmn., 1971-73, 74-75; pres. Health Mgmt. Svcs. Orgns., Inc., 1995—, N.J. Renal Mgmt., 1996—. Discovered extra-renal source of renin in uterus, 1968; contbr. articles to med. jours. Named to Order of Knights St. Gregory, 1995. Mem. Am. Soc. Nephrology, Internat. Soc. Nephrology, Renal Physicians Assn. (pres. 1977-79), AMA, Med. Soc. N.J., Am. Soc. Artificial Internal Organs, Southeastern Organ Procurement Found., Nat. Kidney Found. Roman Catholic. Office: Haddon Renal Med Specialists 35 Kings Hwy E Haddonfield NJ 08033-2009 Office Phone: 856-757-3903. Personal E-mail: jpcapelli@aol.com.

CAPELOS, THERESA, political scientist, researcher; b. Athens, Greece, Mar. 26, 1974; d. Ioannis Capelos and Angeliki Karakastsanis. PhD in Polit. sci. and Polit. Behavior, SUNY-Stony Brook, 2002. Post-doctoral rsch. assoc. Ctr. Survey Rsch. SUNY, Stony Brook, 2002—04. Office: SUNY Ctr Survey Rsch, Polit Science Stony Brook NY 11794

CAPEN, CHARLES CHABERT, veterinary pathology educator; b. Tacoma, Sept. 3, 1936; s. Charles (Kenneth) and Ruth (Chabert) C.; m. Sharron Lee Martin, June 27, 1968. DVM, Wash. State U., 1960; MS, Ohio State U., 1961, PhD, 1965. Instr. dept. vet. pathology Ohio State U., Columbus, 1962—65, asst. prof. dept. vet. pathology, 1965—67, assoc. prof., 1967—70, prof., 1970—, prof. endocrinology Coll. Medicine, 1972—, chmn. dept. vet. pathobiology, 1981—94, chmn., 1982—94, interim chmn. dept. bioscis., 1994—97; chmn., 1997—2002. Israel Doniach Meml. lectr. Brit. Endocrine Soc. meeting, Manchester, 1989; plenary lectr. Italian Soc. Endocrinology Congress, Pisa, 1995. Editor: (series) Animal Models of Human Disease, 1979—96; mem. editl. bd.: Lab. Investigation, 1988—; Vet. Pathology, 1986—87; Am. Jour. Pathology, 1984—88; Exptl. and Toxicologic Pathology, 1990—; Food and Chem. Toxicology, 1993—; Drug and Chem. Toxicology, 1994—; Toxicology and Ecotoxicology News, 1993—; Handbook on Rat Tumor Pathology WHO/IARC, 1991—96. Mem. Opera Columbus, 1982—, Columbus Symphony Assn., 1972—. Named Disting. U. prof., Ohio State U., 2001; recipient Disting. scholar award, 1993, Dean's Tchg. Excellence award for grad. edn., Coll. Vet. Medicine, 1993, Disting. Vet. Alumnus award, Wash. State U., 1997, Career Achievement award in canine rsch., Am. Vet. Med. Found., 1997. Mem.: AVMA (Nat. Borden rsch. award 1975, small animal rsch. award 1984, Gaines rsch. award 1987, excellence in canine rsch. award 1995, George Scott Meml. award of Toxicology Forum 1997), Am. Assn. Clin. Chemistry (Outstanding Contbns. Animal Clin. Chemistry award 2004), Soc. Toxicol. Pathologists (pres. 1997—98), U.S. Can. Acad. Pathology (coun. 1989—92), Inst. Medicine/NAS, Am. Coll. Vet. Pathologists (coun. 1975—81, pres. 1978—79, diplomate, disting. mem.).

Avocations: travel, wildlife and nature photography. Office: The Ohio State U Dept Vet Bioscis 1925 Coffey Rd Columbus OH 43210-1005 Office Phone: 614-247-6206. Business E-Mail: capen.2@osu.edu.

CAPENER, REGNER ALVIN, electronics engineer, writer; b. Astoria, Oreg., Apr. 18, 1942; s. Alvin Earnest and Lillian Lorraine (Lehtosaari) C.; divorced; children: Deborah, Christian, Melodie, Ariella; m. Della Denise Melson, May 17, 1983; children: Shelley, Danielle, Rebekah, Joshua. Student, U. Nebr., 1957-58, 59-60, Southwestern Coll., Waxahachie, Tex., 1958-59, Bethany Bible Coll., 1963-64; BA Sales and Mktg., Gen. Motors Inst., 1968; student Greek and Hebrew studies, Fuller Theol. Sem., 1974—75; EE diploma, Panasonic's Elec. Engring. Inst., 1983. Ordained minister Full Gospel Assembly Ch., 1971. Rsch. engr. Lockheed Missiles & Space Corp., Palo Alto, Calif., 1962-64; engr., talk show host Sta. KHOF-FM, Glendale, Calif., 1966-67; youth min. Bethel Union Ch., Duarte, Calif., 1966-67; pres. Intermountain Electronics, Salt Lake City, 1967-72; assoc. pastor Full Gospel Assembly, Salt Lake City, 1968-72, Long Beach (Calif.) Christian Ctr., 1972-76; v.p. Refuge Ministries, Inc., Long Beach, 1972-76; pres. Christian Broadcasting Network-Alaska, Inc., Fairbanks, 1977-83; gen. mgr. Action Sch. of Broadcasting, Anchorage, 1983-85; pres., pastor House of Praise, Anchorage, 1984-93; chief engr. KTBY-TV, Inc., Anchorage, 1988-93; pres. R & DC Engring., Anchorage, 1991—; chief engr. KTLM-TV, McAllen, Tex., 1999—2003; pres. R & DC Ministries, 2005—; sr. pastor House of Praise and Worship, 2005—. Area dir. Christian Broadcasting Network, Virginia Beach, 1977-83; cons., dir. Union Bond and Trust Co., Anchorage, 1985-86; author, editor univ. courses, 1984-85; dep. gov. Am. Biog. Inst. Rsch. Assn., 1990—. Author: Spiritual Maturity, 1975, Spiritual Warfare, 1976, The Doctrine of Submission, 1988, A Vision for Praise, 1988, Ekklesia, 1993, For the Marriage of the Lamb Has Come, 1996, Open Letters to the Ekklesia, 1997, Another Coffee Break, 2005; author, composer numerous gospel songs; creator numerous broadcasting and electronic instrument inventions. Sec., Christian Businessmen's Com., Salt Lake City, 1968-72; area advisor Women's Aglow Internat., Fairbanks, 1981-83; local co-chmn. campaign Boucher for Gov. Com., Fairbanks, 1982; campaigner for Boucher, Anchorage, 1984, Clark Gruening for Senate Com., Barrow, Alaska, 1980; TV producer Stevens for U.S. Senate, Barrow, 1978; fundraiser City of Refuge, Mex., 1973-75; statewide rep. Sudden Infant Death Syndrome, Barrow, 1978-82; founder Operation Blessing/Alaska, 1981; mem. resch. bd. advisors Am. Biog. Inst., 1990—; advisor Anchorage chpt. Women's Aglow Internat., 1990-91, bd. dirs., v.p., 2001-04, Hidalgo County Children's Adv. Ctr.; candidate for U.S. Ho. of Reps., 2003-04; mem. Coun. Nat. Policy, 2004—. Mem. IEEE, Soc. Broadcast Engrs. (sec. Rio Grande Valley chpt. 2001—, Anchorage chpt. 1989, 90, CBNT cert.), Internat. Soc. Classical Guitarists (sec. 1967-69), Nat. Assn. Broadcasters, Tex. Assn. Broadcasters (coun. nat. policy 2005—), McAllen C. of C. Republican. Avocations: musician, languages, history. Office: R & DC Ministries 3 25 Mi N Shuerbach Rd RR-15 Box 6180 Mission TX 78574-9589 Office Phone: 956-571-3520. E-mail: capener@aol.com, r_capener@msn.com. *The word "impossible" need never be a part of the vocabulary of one whose life is intertwined with the Lord Jesus Christ. I have learned that there are no problems in life which do not have clear and definitive solutions when approached from the standpoint of a personal relationship with Jesus Christ.*

CAPERS, ALBERTA A., secondary school educator; b. Phila., Jan. 21, 1966; d. Charles Agustus and Alberta Alto Lloyd; m. Gregory Capers, June 26, 1999; children: George Bush, Christina Bush, Anthony Burns. BA, Heath Mission Coll., Phila., 2000, MA, 2002. Cert. completion Strengthening Families Program, Phila., 1999. Crisis youth worker Voyage Ho., Inc., Phila., 1982—85; asst. tchr. R.W. Brown Cmty. Ctr., Phila., 1987—89; crisis worker Peoples Emergency Ctr., Phila., 1989—93; residential counselor Interim Ho. West, Phila., 1994—96, asst. tchr., 1996—98; tchr. English Delaware Valley Charter H.S., Phila., 1999—. Chair, Words of Hope Delaware Valley Charter H.S., 2000—. Democrat. Full Gospel Ch. Avocations: creative writing, reading, perfume bottles, decorating. Home: 6740 Old York Rd Philadelphia PA 19126 Office: Delaware Valley Charter High Sch 5538 B Wayne Ave Philadelphia PA 19144 Office Phone: 267-336-2730. E-mail: GregAlberta@verizon.net.

CAPERS, DOMINIC, professional football coach; b. Cambridge, Ohio, Aug. 5, 1950; BS in Psychology and Phys. Edn., Mount Union Coll.; MA in Adminstrn., Kent State U. Grad. asst. Kent State U., 1972-74, U. Wash.; defensive backs coach U. Hawaii, 1975, defensive coach, 1976; defensive asst. coach San Jose State, 1977, U. Calif., 1978-79; defensive backs coach U. Tenn., 1980-81, Ohio State, 1982-83, Phila. Stars (USFL), 1984, Balt. Stars (USFL), 1985, New Orleans Saints, 1986-91; defensive coord. Pitts. Steelers, 1992-94; head coach Carolina Panthers, 1995-98; defensive coord. Jacksonville Jaguars, 1999-2001; head coach Houston Texans, 2001—. Named NFC Coach of the Yr., 1996.

CAPERS, GREGG, secondary school educator, musician; b. Bronx, N.Y., Jan. 21, 1961; s. Joe Simon and Evelyn Delores Capers; m. Alberta Amber Lloyd, Jan. 21, 1966; children: George Steven Bush, Christina Lillian Bush, Anthony Tony Burno. MusB, Bowie State U., 1983; Assoc. Degree, Comml. Programming Unlimited, N.Y.C., 1985; cert., Trident Tech. Coll., Charleston, S.C., 1988. Min. praise and worship God's Positive Minds, Phila., 1998—2003; tchr. Del. Valley Charter H.S., Phila., 1999—. Musical and choir dir. Inspirational Words for Life, Phila., 1999—. Min. music Ministers of Praise, Phila. Recipient John Phillip Sousa Award For Music Excellence, USMC, 1980. Democrat. Home: 6740 Old York Rd Philadelphia PA 19126 Office: Inspirational Words Of Life 6740 Old York Rd Philadelphia PA 19126 Office Phone: 215-424-7003. Personal E-mail: greg.alberta@verizon.net.

CAPICE, PHILIP CHARLES, broadcast executive; b. Bernardsville, N.J., June 24, 1931; s. Philip Joseph and Angelina Mary (Togno) C. BA, Dickinson Coll., 1952; M.F.A., Columbia U., 1954. Production supr., assoc. program dir. Benton & Bowles Inc., N.Y.C., 1954-64, Vice pres. in charge program devel., 1965-69; dir. spl. programs CBS-TV Network, N.Y.C., 1969-74; sr. v.p. creative affairs Lorimar Prodns., Burbank, Calif., 1974-78; pres. Lorimar TV, Burbank, Calif., 1978-79; ind. producer Lorimar Productions, Culver City, Calif., from 1979; pres., chief exec. officer Raven's Claw Productions, Los Angeles, Calif. Since 1974, exec. producer Dallas, Eight Is Enough, The Blue Knight, Two Marriages, Helter Skelter, Sybil (Emmy Award, 1977, Peabody Award, 1977), Green Eyes (Peabody Award, 1978, Humanitas Prize, 1978), Eric, Widow, Studs Lonigan, A Man Called Intrepid, The Runaways, The Prince of Central Park, A Question of Guilt, Some Kind of Miracle (Christopher Award, 1978), Returning Home, Conspiracy of Terror, Hunter, Married: The First Year, The Rivermen, Mary and Joseph: A Love Story, The Stranger Within, A Matter of Life and Death, Bunco, Some People Like Us, Private Sessions, others. Trustee Dickinson Coll. Recipient Emmy award, 1977, Peabody award, 1977, 78. Mem. Acad. TV Arts and Scis., The Caucus for Producers, Writers and Dirs.

CAPITAN, WILLIAM HARRY, university president emeritus; b. Owosso, Mich., Feb. 7, 1933; s. Harry and Anthe (Sarris) C.; m. Dolores Marie Randolph, Sept. 19, 1959; children: Rita, Edwin. BA, U. Mich., 1954; postgrad., Queens U.; postgrad. (Ulster Am. fellow), 1954-55; MA, U. Minn., 1958, PhD, 1960. Registered mediator 2001, lic. Capt. USCG, auxiliary USCG, 2001, comdr. flotilla, 2005. Instr. philosophy U. Minn., 1959-60, U. Md., 1960-62; asst. prof., assoc. prof., chmn. dept. Oberlin (Ohio) Coll., 1962-70; dean fine arts, v.p. acad. affairs, acting pres. Saginaw Valley State U., U. Ctr., Mich., 1970-74; v.p. acad. affairs, dean faculty, acting pres. W.Va. Wesleyan Coll., Buckhannon, 1974-79; pres. Ga. Southwestern U/, Americus, 1979-95; pres. emeritus Ga. Southwestern Coll., Americus, 1996—. Adj. prof. U. Ga., 1996. Author: Introduction to the Philosophy of Religion, 1972, Speak For Yourself, 1987; editor: (with D.D. Merrill) Metaphysics and Explanation, Art, Religion, and Mind, 1967, The Ethical Navigator, 2000. Trustee Charles L. Mix Meml. Fund, Inc., 1979—96; pres. Americus Sumter County C. of C., 1985; v.p. Hellenic-Am. C. of C., Atlanta; lay reader Episcopal Ch., Americus, Ga.; bd. dir. Saginaw Symphony Orch., 1970—74; Project Save; Buckhannon C. of C.; Sumter County United Way. Am. Council Lerned Socs. fellow Paris, 1967-68 Mem. Am. Soc. Aesthetics, Am. Philos. Assn., Rotary (pres. 1990-91), Beta Theta Phi, Omicron Delta Kappa, Phi Kappa Phi, Phi Delta Kappa. Episcopalian. Office: GA Southwestern State U Americus GA 31709 *Clarity of objectives, persistence, and Christian respect for persons have guided me in whatever of value I have accomplished. My failures came when I wasn't very clear about what I was doing. America rewards, supports, and buoys up those with initiative. This is why my parents were able to go from "rags to riches" and I from illiterate to lettered. We Americans help one another, and we shape our institutions to help, too. May we ever remain so.*

CAPITO, SHELLEY MOORE, congresswoman; b. Glen Dale, WV, Nov. 26, 1953; m. Charles L. Capito, Jr.; children: Charles, Moore, Shelley. BS in zoology, Duke U., 1975; MEd, U. Va., 1976. Career counselor West Va. State Coll.; dir. Ednl. Info. Ctr. West Va. Bd. Regents; mem. West Va. House of Delegates, 30th dist., 1996—2000, U.S. Ho. of Reps. from 2nd WV dist., 2001—; minority chair health and human resources committee; mem. judiciary committee., banking commitee, insurance committee. Mem. 107th Congress House Banking and Fin. Svcs. com., House Transportation and Infrastructure com., House Small Bus. com. Mem. YWCA (past pres.), Cmty. coun., Kanawha Valley, West Va. Interagency Coun. Early Intervention. Republican. Mem. First Presbyn. Ch. Office: US House of Rep 1431 Longworth House Office bldg Washington DC 20515-4802*

CAPIZZI, MICHAEL ROBERT, prosecutor; b. Detroit, Oct. 19, 1939; s. I.A. and Adelaide E. (Jennelle) C.; m. Sandra Jo Jones, June 22, 1963; children: Cori Anne, Pamela Jo. BSBA, Ea. Mich. U., 1961; JD, U. Mich., 1964. Bar: Calif. 1965, U.S. Dist. Ct. (so. dist., cent. dist.) Calif. 1965, U.S. Ct. Appeals (9th cir.) 1970, U.S. Supreme Ct. 1971, U.S. Ct. Fed. Claims 2001, U.S. Dist. Ct. (east. dist.) Calif. 2004. Dep. dist. atty., Orange County, Calif., 1965-68; head writs, appeals and spl. assignments sect., 1968-71; asst. dist. atty., dir. spl. ops., 1971-86; legal counsel, mem. exec. bd. Interstate Organized Crime Index, 1971-79, Law Enforcement Intelligence Unit, 1971-95, chief asst. dist. atty., 1986-90, dist. atty., 1990-99. Instr. criminal justice Santa Ana Coll., 1967-76, Calif. State U., 1976-87. Commr. City Planning Commn., Fountain Valley, Calif., 1971-80, vice chmn. 1972-73, chmn. 1973-75, 79-80; candidate for Rep. nomination Calif. Atty. Gen., 1998. Fellow Am. Coll. Trial Lawyers; mem. Nat. Dist. Attys. Assn. (bd. dirs. 1995-96, v.p. 1996-99), Calif. Dist. Attys. Assn. (outstanding prosecutor award 1980, v.p. 1995, pres. 1996), Calif. Bar Assn., Orange County Bar Assn. (chmn. cts. com. 1977, chmn. coll. of trial advocacy com. 1978-81, bd. dirs. 1977-81, sec.-treas. 1982, pres. 1984). Office: PO Box 1938 Santa Ana CA 92702-1938 Office Phone: 714-283-1878. E-mail: mrclaw@socal.rr.com.

CAPLAN, ALLAN HART, lawyer; BA, U. Manitoba, 1966; JD, William Mitchell Coll. Law, 1974. Bar: Minn. 1974, Wis. 1988, Fed. Ct. Former asst. atty., Hennepin County; former pub. defender; ptnr. Allan Hart Caplan and Assocs. P.A., Minn., 1983—. Spkr. in field. Named Minn Super Lawyer Criminal Def., Mpls.-St. Paul Mag., Minn. Law and Politics. Mem.: NACDL (life), Minn. State Bar Assn., Hennepin County Bar Assn. Office: Allan Hart Caplan and Assocs PA 525 Lumbar Exchange Bldg 10 S 5th St Minneapolis MN 55402 Office Phone: 612-341-4570. Office Fax: 612-341-0507. E-mail: acaplan@crimdefense.com.

CAPLAN, ARTHUR, university program director, educator; b. Boston, Mar. 21, 1950; s. Sidney and Natalie (Fluke) C.; m. Margaret Brennan; 1 child, Zachary. BA, Brandeis U., 1971; MA, Columbia U., 1973, PhD in history and philosophy of sci., 1979; six degrees (hon.), from coll. and med. sch. Staff assoc. in ethical issues in sci. and medicine The Hastings Ctr., 1975-76, assoc. for humanities, 1977-84, assoc. dir., 1984—87; instr. Sch. of Pub. Health Columbia U., N.Y.C., 1977-78, assoc. for social medicine, 1978-81; prof. philosophy, surgery; dir. Ctr. for Biomedical Ethics U. Minn., Mpls., 1987-94; Emmanuel and Robert Hart prof. bioethics, chair dept. med. ethics, dir. Ctr. Bioethics U. Pa., Phila., 1994—. Vis. prof. U. Pitts., 1986: adv. bd. Poynter Inst., Nat. Marrow Donor Program, ARC; chair adv. com. UN on Human Cloning, Dept. Health and Human Svcs. on Blood Safety and Availability; mem. Presdnl. Adv. Com. on Gulf War Illnesses; mem. spl. adv. com. Internat. Olympic Com. on Genetics and Gene Therapy, Am. Chem. Coun.; spl. adv. panel Nat. Inst. Mental Health on Human Experienentation on Vulnerable Subjects; mem. biotechnology adv. panel Dupot; columnist MSNBC.com; frequent guest and commentator Nat. Pub. Radio, CNN, MSNBC, NY Times, Washington Post, Phila. Inquiror, and others; cons. in field. Author: Moral Matters, 1995, Prescribing Our Future: Ethical Challenges in Genetic Counseling, 1993, If I Were a Rich Man Could I Buy a Pancreas and Other Essays on Medical Ethics, 1992, When Medicine Went Mad: Bioethics and the Holocaust, 1992, Everyday Ethics: Resolving Dilemmas in Nursing Home Life, 1990, Beyond Baby M, 1990; contbr. articles to profl. jours.; lectr., commentator in field. Mem. Clin. Health Care Task Force, Wash. (vice chmn. ethics working group 1993-94); cons. Office of Tech. Assessment U.S. Congress, Minn. Dept. Health, Am. Found. for AIDS Rsch., NIH, Dept. Health and Human Svcs., Nat. Marrow Donor Program, Lifesource-Organ Procurement Org., Nat. Acad. Scis.-Inst. Medicine, state legis. Pa., Minn., N.Y., N.J. Recipient Commr.'s award Dept. Health and Human Svcs., 1993, McGovern Medal, Am. Med. Writers Assn.; named Person of Yr., USA Today, 2001; named one of Fifty Most Influential People in Am. Health Care, Modern Health Care Mag., Ten Most Influential People in Am. in Biotechnology, Nat. Jour. Fellow Hastings Ctr., NY Acad. Medicine, Coll. Physicians of Phila., Am. Assn. Advancement Sci.; mem. Am. Assn. Bioethics (pres. 1993-95), Ctrl. Soc. for Clin. Rsch. Avocation: tennis. Office: U Pa 3401 Market St Philadelphia PA 19104-3318 E-mail: caplan@mail.med.upenn.edu.

CAPLAN, BYRON CRAIG, fine arts educator; b. Frederick, Md., July 31, 1954; s. Reuben Norman Caplan and Bonnie Dale Weddel. MFA, Yale U., 1979. News videographer, editor KYW-TV, Phila., 1980—92; asst. prof. Ithaca Coll., Ithaca, NY, 1993—97; free-lance prodr. Bc Productions, Brunswick, Maine, 1997—2005; asst. prof. Robert Morris Univ., Moon, Pa., 2005—. Prodr. Maine Pub. Tv, Lewiston, Maine, 1995—97. Prodr.: (ednl. televisionn series) Quest: Investigating The World We Call Maine (Boston/New Eng. Emmy Award, 1997), (documentary) Three Small Town American Celebrations (1st Pl., documentary category, broadcast edn. assocaiton prodn. competition, 2001), (experimental video) sketch #3 Carlsbad (hon. mention, black maria film festival, 2001). Document living history Ithaca Hist. Soc., Ithaca, NY. Pendleton Grant, Ithaca Coll., 2003. Mem.: Assn. Of Ind. Video And Filmmakers, U. Film and Video Assn., Broadcast Edn. Assn. Mailing: 421 N Cayuga St Sewickley PA Personal E-mail: byroncaplan@netzero.net.

CAPLAN, EDWIN HARVEY, retired dean, retired finance educator; b. Boston, Aug. 24, 1926; s. Henry and Dorothy (Nathanson) C.; m. Ramona Hootner, June 20, 1948; children— Gary, Dennis, Jeffrey, Nancy BBA, U. Mich., 1950, MBA, 1952; PhD, U. Calif., 1965. CPA, Calif., Mich. Ptnr. J.J. Gotlieb & Co., CPAs, Detroit, 1953-56; prof. acctg. Humboldt State U., 1956-61, U. Oreg., 1964-67; prof. U. N.Mex., Albuquerque, 1967-91, assoc. dean Sch. Mgmt., 1982-83, dean Sch. Mgmt., 1989-90, prof. emeritus, 1991—. Cons. in field. Contbr. articles to profl. jours. 1st lt. U.S. Army, 1944-46. Mem. AICPA, Am. Acctg. Assn., Inst. Mgmt. Accts. Home: 8201 Harwood Ave NE Albuquerque NM 87110-1517 Business E-Mail: ecaplan@unm.edu.

CAPLAN, LOUIS ROBERT, neurologist, educator; b. Balt., Dec. 31, 1936; s. Carl Clarence and Bess Pauline (Cohen) C.; m. F. Brenda Fields, Nov. 28, 1963; children: Laura, Daniel, Jonathan, David, Jeremy, Benjamin. BA cum laude, Williams Coll., 1958; MD summa cum laude, U. Md., 1962. Diplomate Am. Bd. Internal Medicine, Am. Bd. Psychiatry and Neurology. Intern to jr. asst. resident Boston City Hosp., 1962-64; resident Harvard Neurol. Unit, Boston, 1966-69; cerebrovascular fellow Mass. Gen. Hosp., Boston, 1969-70; neurologist Beth Israel Hosp., Boston, 1970-78; asst. prof. Harvard Med. Sch., Boston, 1970-78, prof. neurology, 1999; chief neurologist Michael Reese Hosp., Chgo., 1978-84; prof. neurology U. Chgo., 1980-84; chief neurologist New England Med. Ctr., Boston, 1984-97; prof., chmn. dept. neurology Tufts U., Boston, 1984-97, prof. medicine, 1989-97; neurologist Beth Israel Deaconess Med. Ctr., Boston, 1998—; prof. neurology Harvard Med. Sch., 1999—. Author: stroke: A Clinical Approach, 1986, 3rd edit., 2000, Consultations in Neurology, 1987, The Effective Clinical Neurologist, 2nd edit., 2001, Vertebrobasilar Arterial Disease, 1993; author: (with others) Cerebral Small Artery Disease, 1993; author: Management of Persons with Stroke, 1993, Brainstem Localization and Function, 1993, Intercerebral Hemmorhage, 1994, Family Guide to Stroke, 1994, Brain Ischemia-Basic Concepts and Clinical Relevance, 1995, Stroke Syndromes, 2nd edit., 2001, Posterior Circulation Disease, 1996, Neurologic Disorders: Course and Treatment, 1996, 2d edit., 2003, Primer on Cerebrovascular Diseases, 1997; author: (with others) Clinical Neurocardiology, 1999; author: Uncommon Causes of Stroke, 2001, Striking Back at Stroke--A Doctor-Patient Journal, 2003; contbr. over 500 articles to profl. jours.; contbr. more than 500 articles to profl. jours. Bd. dirs. Solomon Schecter Day Sch., Boston, 1977-78, Chgo., 1983-85. Capt. U.S. Army, 1962-64. Recipient House Officer Teaching prize Michael Reese Hosp., 1980. Fellow Am. Acad. Neurology, Am. Neurol. Assn., Stroke Coun. Am. Heart Assn. (chmn. 1987-89, sci. adv. com. 1990—), Royal Soc. of Medicine; mem. Coun. Med. Specialties Socs. (rep. 1982-90), Chgo. Neurol. Soc. (chmn. 1984-85), Boston Soc. Neurology and Psychiatry (pres. 1988-89), Chgo. Heart Assn. (chmn. stroke com. 1979-84), Australian Neurol. Soc. (hon.), German Neurol. Assn. (hon.), Phi Beta Kappa, Alpha Omega Alpha. Democrat. Jewish. Office: Beth Israel Deaconess MC Dept Neurology 330 Brookline Ave Palmer 127 Boston MA 02215-5400 Office Phone: 617-632-8911. Business E-Mail: lcaplan@bidmc.harvard.edu.

CAPLAN, MITCHELL H., diversified financial services company executive; b. Va; AB, Brandeis U., 1979; MBA, JD, Emory U. Assoc. Shearman & Sterling, 1985—90; with Strategic Devel. Dept. Telebanc Fin. Corp., 1990—2000; from chief fin. products officer, mng. dir. to CEO E*Trade Fin. Corp., Menlo Pk., Calif., 2000—03, CEO, 2003—. Bd. dirs. Juvenile Diabetes Found. Capitol Charter, The Am. Com. Weizmann Inst. Sci. Office: ETRADE Financial Corp 671 Glebe Road N 11th Fl Arlington VA 22203*

CAPLAN, RONALD MERVYN, obstetrician, gynecologist; b. Montreal, Dec. 12, 1937; came to U.S., 1971; s. Philip and Betty (Gamer) C.; m. Marilyn Gail Amdur, Dec. 23, 1962; children: Randy Sue, Gordon. BSc, McGill U., Montreal, 1958, MD CM, 1962. Resident Royal Victorial Hosp., Montreal, 1963-67; instr. ob-gyn McGill U., 1968-71; practice medicine specializing in ob-gyn Montreal, 1968-71, N.Y.C., 1971—; mem. attending staff Royal Victoria Hosp., Montreal, 1968-71; asst. attending physician in ob-gyn N.Y. Hosp., N.Y.C., 1971, now assoc. attending physician. Clin. assoc. prof. ob-gyn NY Weill Cornell Med. Coll. Editor: (with William J. Sweeney, III) Advances in Obstetrics and Gynecology (Williams, Wilkins), 1978, Principles of Obstetrics, 1982. Fellow ACS, Am. Coll. Obstetricians and Gynecologists, Royal Coll. Surgeons (Can.); mem. AMA, N.Y. Med. Soc., Soc. Reproductive Surgeons, Griffis Faculty Club of Cornell U. Office: 955 Old Quaker Hill Rd Pawling NY 12564

CAPLES, RICHARD JAMES, performing company executive, lawyer; b. Balt., June 7, 1949; s. Delphin Delmas and Louise Skinner (Leigh) C. BA, Yale U., 1971; MA, Johns Hopkins U., 1974; JD, Cornell U., 1977. Bar: N.Y. 1978, U.S. Dist. Ct. (so. and ea. dists.) N.Y. 1978. Assoc. Donovan Leisure Newton & Irvine, N.Y.C., 1977-81, Shearman & Sterling, N.Y.C., 1981-83; exec. dir. Santa Fe Festival Theater, 1983-84, Lar Lubovitch Dance Co., N.Y.C., 1984—; dir. Doug Varone and Dancers, N.Y.C., 1995—, Dance/USA, Washington, 1995—2002, also sec. bd., 1998-2000, treas., 2000—02, dir., 2004—, vice chmn., 2004—; sec.-treas. Project Ballet Theater, 2000—. With Park 58 Corp., N.Y.C., 1989—, pres., 1994-2004; bd. dirs. Artists Cmty. Fed. Credit Union, 2003—, sec., 2004, asst. treas., 2005—. Mem. Am. Soc. Internat. Law, N.Y. State Bar Assn., Assn. Bar City of N.Y. (com. on copyright 2002—, com. on art law, 2003—), Am. Coun. on Germany, Johns Hopkins Alumni Assn. (bd. dirs. N.Y.C. chpt. 1988-92), Univ. Club, Yale Club, Johns Hopkins Club (Balt.) Episcopalian. Home: 470 Park Ave New York NY 10022-1903 Office: Lar Lubovitch Dance Co 229 W 42d St 8th Fl New York NY 10036-7299 Office Phone: 212-221-7909. Personal E-mail: DickCaples@aol.com. Business E-Mail: Lubovitch@aol.com.

CAPLICE, CHRISTOPHER, engineering educator; BS in Civil Engring., Va. Military Inst.; MS in Civil Engring., U. Tex.; PhD, Mass. Inst. Tech., 1996. V.p. product mgmt. and profl. svcs. Logistics.com, Burlington, Mass.; v.p. transp. planning Chainalytics; prin. rsch. assoc. ctr. transp. and logistics Mass. Inst. Tech., exec. dir. master engring. in logistics program. Contbr. articles to profl. jours. including Jour. Bus. Logistics, Internat. Jour. Logistics Mgmt., Transportation Rsch. Capt. Army Corps Engrs. Office: Mass Inst Tech 77 Massachusetts Ave Bldg E40-363 Cambridge MA 02139-4307 Office Phone: 617-258-7975. Business E-Mail: caplice@mit.edu.

CAPLICE, SISTER MARY PATRICIA, religious studies educator; b. N.Y.C., Mar. 7, 1936; d. Michael Joseph and Mary Aloysius Caplice. B of Social Sci., Fairfield U., 1964; MA in History, Hunter Coll., 1968. Tchr. grades 3 and 7 Notre Dame Acad., SI, NY, 1955—58, chmn. social studies dept., 1964—68, Ridgefield, Conn., 1968—72, 1976—88; tchr. social studies Waterbury (Conn.) Cath. High Sch., 1958—64; chmn. social studies dept. Stamford Cath. High Sch., 1972—80; mem. coun. religious cmty. Congregation Notre Dame, Ridgefield, 1996—; prin. LF Sch., 1989—96; supt. Diocese Pensacola-Tallahassee, Fla., 1996—2005; province leader Congregation Notre Dame, Ridgefield, Conn., 2005—. Mem. fed. assistance adv. com. U.S. Conf. Cath. Bishops, Washington, 2000—05; mem. adv. coun. John Paul II Cath. High Sch., Tallahassee, 2000—05, Pensacola Cath. High Sch., 1996—2005, St. Michael Inerparochal Sch., 1996—2005; mem. Diocesan Commn. Cath. Schs., 1996—2005. Mem. Sch. Readiness Coalition, Escambia County, Fla., 2001—04. Grantee, U.S. Dept. Edn., 1972. Mem.: Edn. Found., Chief Adminstrs. Cath. Edn., Nat. Cath. Ednl. Assn. Roman Catholic. Avocations: reading, cooking, walking. Office: 30 Highfield Rd Wilton CT 06897 Office Phone: 203-762-4310.

CAPLICE, NOEL M., cardiologist, researcher; s. James M. and Margaret B. Caplice; m. Katie M. Kearney, May 25, 1990; children: Ross J., Samuel K. MB, BCh, Nat. U. of Ireland, 1986. Lic. Minn. Licensure Bd., 1999. Author: (med. rsch.) Growth factors released after angioplasty (Young Investigator award, Australian Cardiac Soc., 1996). Fellow Coll. of Physicians, Royal Australian Coll. of Physicians, 1996, Royal Coll. of Physicians, Ireland, 2001. Achievements include discovery of Stent for cell-based gene delivery.

CAPLIN, JERROLD LEON, health physicist; b. Phila., Jan. 25, 1930; s. Samuel Harry and Katherine (Socloff) C.; children: Sally C. Daniels, Patricia Graham Reed. AB, Temple U., 1951, postgrad., 1952—53. Supervisory health physicist U.S. Army C.E., Ft. Belvoir, Va., 1959—61; health physicist radiation protection stds. AEC, U.S. Nuc. Regulatory Commn., Washington, 1961—81, project mgr. repairstor R&D, nuc. reactor environ. assessments, 1961—81; ret., 1981; cons., 1981—. Guest lectr. radiation sci. Georgetown U. Grad. Sch., 1987-97; sr. scientist Advanced Sys. Tech., Inc., 1993-97; photographer, newspaper editor, sci. writer, 1983—; sr. tech. editor Advanced Technologies and Labs. Internat., Inc., 2000-03. Co-author, editor Manual Respiratory Protection Against Airborne Radioactive Materials, 1976. Active Nat. Mus. of Women in Arts, Friends of the Nat. Zoo, Friends of the Kennedy Ctr. Lt. USNR, 1953-58. AEC Radiol. Physics fellow, Vanderbilt U., Oak Ridge Nat. Lab., 1951—52. Mem. AAAS, ASTM, Am. Nat. Stds. Inst., Am. Conf. Gov. Indsl. Hygienists (chmn. com. 1977-83), Am. Assn. Physics Tchrs., Am. Film Inst., Nat. Ctr. Sci. Edn. (assoc.), Internat. Radiation Protection Assn., U.S. Naval Inst., Nat. Wildlife Fedn., Nat. Geog. Soc., Nat. Trust for Hist. Preservation, Health Physics Soc., Smithsonian Instn. (resident assoc. 1970—), Wilderness Soc., Libr. Congress Assocs., Com. Sci. Investigation of Claims of the Paranormal Assoc. Home and Office: 9 Goodport Ln Gaithersburg MD 20878-1001 Personal E-mail: jcaplin001@aol.com.

CAPLIN, MORTIMER MAXWELL, lawyer, educator; b. N.Y.C., July 11, 1916; s. Daniel and Lillian (Epstein) C.; m. Ruth Sacks, Oct. 18, 1942; children: Lee Evan, Michael Andrew, Jeremy Owen, Catherine Jean. BS, U.

Va., 1937, LLB, 1940; JSD, NYU, 1953; LLD (hon.), St. Michael's Coll., 1964. Bar: Va. 1941, N.Y. 1942, D.C. 1964. Law clk. to Hon. Armistead M. Dobie U.S. Ct. Appeals (4th cir.), Richmond, 1940-41; assoc. Paul, Weiss, Rifkind, Wharton & Garrison, N.Y.C., 1941-42, 45-50; prof. law U. Va., Charlottesville, 1950-61, vis. prof. law, 1965-87, prof. emeritus, 1988—; ptnr. Perkins, Battle & Minor, Charlottesville, 1952-61; U.S. commr. IRS, Washington, 1961-64; sr. ptnr. Caplin & Drysdale, Washington, 1964—. Mem. Pres.'s Task Force on Taxation, 1960; bd. dirs. Danaher Corp., Washington, Fairchild Corp., McLean, Va., Presdl. Realty Corp., White Plains, N.Y., Environ. and Energy Study Inst.; mem. pub. rev. bd. Arthur Andersen & Co., Chgo., 1980-88; reorgn. trustee Webb & Knapp, Inc., 1965-72. Author: Proxies, Annual Meetings and Corporate Democracy, 1953, Doing Business in Other States, 1959; editor-in-chief Va. Law Rev., 1939-40; contbr. numerous articles on tax and corp. matters to profl. jours. Past chmn. bd. dirs. Nat. Civic Svc. League, Am. Coun. on Internat. Sports; past chmn. nat citizens adv. com. Assn. Am. Med. Colls.; trustee Arena Stage, U. Va. Law Sch. Found., Wolf Trap Found. Performing Arts, Shakespeare Theatre, Washington, Arena Stage, Washington, Peace Through Law Found., Washington; bd. overseers U. V.I.; chmn. adv. bd. Hospitality and Info. Svc., Washington; hon. chmn. Coun. for Arts, U. Va.; past pres. Atlantic Coast Conf.; emeritus trustee George Washington U.; mem. bd. visitors U. Va., 1992-97; pres., bd. dirs. Indigent Civil Litigation Fund; mem. governing coun. U. Va. Miller Ctr. Pub. Affairs. Decorated mem. initial landing force Normandy Invasion USN; recipient, Va. State Bar and Va. Soc. CPAs award, 1960, Achievement award, Tax Soc. of NYU, 1962, Judge Learned Hand Human Rels. award, Am. Jewish Com., 1963, Pub. Svc. award, VFW, 1963, Judge Learned Hand Human Rels. award, Am. Jewish Com., 1993, Alexander Hamilton award, U.S. Treasury Dept., 1964, Disting. Svc. award, Tax Execs. Inst., 1964, medal in law, U. Va. Thomas Jefferson Found., 2001. Fellow Am. Bar Found. (bd. dirs. 2003—), Am. Tax Policy Inst., Am. Coll. Tax Counsel; mem. ABA (ho. of dels. 1980-92, mem. fed. jud. com. 1993-96, ALI-ABA com. continuing profl. edn. 1997-2000, chair DC Fellows), Nat. Conf. of Lawyers and CPAs, Am. Law Inst. (life), N.Y. State Bar Assn., Va. Bar Assn., D.C. Bar Assn., Am. Bar Fedn. (bd. dirs. 2003-), D.C. Bar Found. (adv. com.), Univ. Club (Washington), Fed. City Club (bd. govs.), Colonnade Club (Charlottesville), Order of Coif, Phi Beta Kappa, Phi Beta Kappa Assocs., Omicron Delta Kappa. Democrat. Jewish. Avocations: swimming, tennis, hiking. Home: 5610 Wisconsin Ave Apt 18E Chevy Chase MD 20815-4415 Office: One Thomas Circle NW Washington DC 20005-5802 Office Phone: 202-862-5050. E-mail: mmc@capdale.com.

CAPLOE, ROBERTA, magazine editor; b. Framingham, Mass., Mar. 24, 1962; d. Robert Coleman and Jeanne Adele (Goldburg) Caploe. BA, Barnard Coll., 1984. Sr. prodr. Phone Programs Inc., N.Y.C., 1985—88; exec. editor Soap Opera Digest Presents, N.Y.C., 1988—89; West Coast editor Soap Opera Digest, L.A., 1989—95; exec. editor Seventeen mag., N.Y.C., 1997—2000; editor-in-chief Youth Entertainment Group, Primedia, 2000—03; exec. editor Ladies Home Jour., N.Y.C., 2003—. Co-author (with Jamie Caploe): Melrose Confidential. Assoc. mem. Acad. TV Arts and Scis. Avocation: tennis. Office: Ladies Home Jour 20th Fl 125 Park Ave New York NY 10017

CAPLOW, THEODORE, sociologist, educator; b. N.Y.C., May 1, 1920; s. Samuel Nathaniel and Florence (Israel) C.; m. Margaret Mary Pettit, 1981. AB, U. Chgo., 1939; PhD, U. Minn., 1946; LLD, Ball State U., 2003. Mem. faculty U. Minn., 1945-60; prof. sociology Columbia U., 1961-70; chmn. dept. sociology U. Va., Charlottesville, 1970-78, 84-86, Commonwealth prof., 1973—2005. Vis. prof. U. Bordeaux, France, 1950, U. Aix-Marseille, France, 1951, U. Utrecht, Netherlands, 1954-55, Stanford, 1957, P.R., 1959, U. Bogota, Colombia, 1962, Sorbonne, Paris, France, 1968-69, Institut d'Etudes Politiques, Paris, 1983, U. Rome, 1984, U. Oslo, 1986; pres. Mendota Research Group Inc., 1957-65 Author: Sociology of Work, 1954, Principles of Organization, 1964, Two Against One, 1968, L'Enquête Sociologique, 1970, Toward Social Hope, 1975, Peace Games, 1989, American Social Trends, 1991, Perverse Incentives, 1994; sr. author: The Academic Marketplace, 1957, The Urban Ambience, 1964, Middletown Families, 1982, All Faithful People, 1983, Recent Social Trends in the United States, 1960-90, 1991, Systems of War and Peace, 1995, Sociologie Militaire, 2000, The First Measured Century, 2001, Leviathen Transformed, 2002. With AUS, 1943-45, PTO. Decorated Purple Heart. Mem. Tocqueville Soc. (pres. 1979-83), Am. Sociol. Assn. (sec. 1983-86), Farmington Hunt Club, Albemarle Yacht Club,(Charlottesville), Century (N.Y.C.), Tarratine Club (Dark Harbor, Maine). E-mail: tc@virginia.edu.

CAPO-CHICHI, LUDOVIC JOSEPH ANATOLE, research scientist, consultant, agricultural engineer, consultant; s. Remy August and Pauline Capo-chichi; m. Pelagie Adjoua Adonde; children: Axel Giraud Francky, Matania Patricia Dona, William Michael Enangnon. Degree in agrl. engring., Nat. U. of Benin, 1988; MS, Auburn U., 1997, PhD, 2002. Agrl. engr. Group of Rsch. and Action for the Promotion of Agr. and Devel., Cotonou, Benin, 1988—94; rsch. asst. Auburn (Ala.) U., 1994—97, grad. rsch. asst., 1998—2002, postdoctoral fellow, 2002—03, rsch. fellow, 2003—; cons. Internat. Plant Genetics Resources Inst., Cotonou, 1997—98. Cons., supr., advisor Auburn U., 2002—. Prayer group host, Auburn, 2001—05. Grantee The Rockefeller Found., 2002; travel grantee, Auburn U., 2000, 2001. Mem.: Crop Sci. Soc. Am., Am. Soc. Agronomy (corr. winner poster presentation 2003), Gamma Sigma Delta. Achievements include first to map two important genes that govern pod and pubescence colors of Mucuna pruriens; research in dinitroaniline-induced genetic changes in Bermudagrass; effect of genotypes and environment on L-Dopa doncentration in Mucuna's Seeds at different latitudes in the world; use of molecular markers to study genetic diversity of velvetbean; Amplify Fragment Length Polymorphism (AFLP) assessment of genetic variability of velvetbean (Mucuna sp.) accessions; demonstration that the founder source of the invasive species Imperata cylindrica in the southeastern USA contains the lowest genetic diversity using molecular markers; demonstration that anthropogenic dispersal is one of the powerfull agents for local dispersal of the invasive species Imperata cylindrica using molecular markers. Office: Auburn U 202 Funchess Hall Auburn AL 36849 Office Phone: 334-844-3988. E-mail: cludovic@acesag.auburn.edu.

CAPODILUPO, ELIZABETH JEANNE HATTON, public relations executive; b. McRae, Ga., May 3, 1940; d. Lewis Irby and Essee Elizabeth (Parker) Hatton; m. Raphael S. Capodilupo, Jan. 21, 1967. Grad., Dale Carnegie Inst., 1976. Sec. A.R. Clark Acct., Fernandina Beach, Fla., 1958-59; receptionist, girl Friday Sta. WNDT-TV, N.Y.C., 1960-62, Coy Hunt and Co., N.Y.C., 1962-69; clk. Woodlawn Cemetery, Bronx, N.Y., 1969-71, historian, cmty. affairs coord., 1971-84, editor newsletter, 1979—, asst. to pres., 1984-99, dir. pub. rels., 1984; grad. asst. Dale Carnegie Inst., 1977-78. Rschr. Woodlawn Cemetery's Hall of Fame; contbr. articles to Collier Encyclopedia, 1985; contbr. articles to profl. jours. Chmn. ann. Adm. Farragut Honor Ceremony, Bronx, 1976—; founder, chmn. Toys for Needy Children, 1983-97; bd. dirs. Bronx Mus. Arts, v.p., 1983-84; pres. Bronx Coun. Arts, 1987-90, Network Orgn. Bronx Women, 1997-98; adv. bd. Salvation Army, 1985, Bronx Arts Ensemble, 1985; bd. mgrs. Bronx YMCA, 1985, vice-chmn., 1989—; bd. dirs. Bronx Urban League, 1985, Bronx Coun. on Arts, 1985, pres. 1987-90; active Bronx Landmarks Task Force, 1994—. Recipient award citation VFW, 1976, Voice of Democracy Program judge's citation, 1980, Disting. Community Svc. award N.Y.C. Council, Il Leone di Sanmarco award Italian Heritage & Culture Com. Bronx, 1989, Lifetime Achievement Humanitarian award Bronx Coun. on Arts, 1999-2000; named Woman of Yr., YMCA, Bronx, 1986, Network Orgn. Bronx Women, 1986, Jeanne and Ray Capodilupo named as Mr. & Mrs. Bronx 1989-90 proclaimed by Borough Pres., named Pioneer of the Bronx, 1992, Citizen of Yr. Bronx Club, 1995; recipient cert. appreciation Dale Carnegie Inst., 1977, Outstanding Citizenship award Bronx N.E. Kiwanis Club, 1981, Service to Youth award YMCA of Bronx, 1983; recipient proclamation City Council of N.Y., Italian Heritage and Culture Com. of the Bronx, 1989; Outstanding Cemeterian award Am. Cemetery Assn., 1987-88; Citation of Merit Bronx Borough Pres.'s Office, 1988; Spl. Hons. for Outstanding Vol. Work Ladies Aux. Our Lady of Mercy Med. Ctr.; named Hon. Grand Marshall Bronx Columbus Day Parade, 1987-89, Bronx Meml. Day Parade, 1989; apptd. to commn. celebrating 350 yrs. of the Bronx by Borough Pres., recipient Pioneer award for Women's History Month for Outstanding Humanitarian Svcs., 1991, Lifetime Achievement award Bronx YMCA, 1999-2000, Role Model award Columbus Alliance, 2000; Jeanne Hatton Capodilupo Day proclaimed by Bronx Borough Presdl. Proclamation, 1999. Mem. Bronx County Hist. Soc., Network Orgn. Bronx Women (pres. 1997-99), Women in Communication, Bronx C. of C. (sec. 1988), YMCA (life mem.), N.Y. Press Club, Italian Big Sisters Club, Women's City Club, Order Eastern Star. Methodist. Office: 371 Scosdale Rd Yonkers NY 10707 Personal E-mail: smilerjean@aol.com.

CAPOLARELLO, JOE R., photojournalist; b. Bklyn., Sept. 6, 1961; s. Carmelo and Grace (Auditore) Capolarello. Cert. in news prodn. and tech., Inst. New Cinema Artists, N.Y.C., 1981; cert. in TV news video workshop, U. Okla., Norman, 1986; cert. in TV news feature workshop, Internat. Film & TV Workshops, Rockport, Maine, 1987; cert. in leadership in broadcast photojournalism, Poynter Inst. Media Studies, St. Petersburg, Fla., 1992. Photojournalist, videotape editor, field producer W.Va. Jour. Sta. WSWP-TV, Beckley, W.Va., 1982-83; photojournalist Eyewitness News Sta. WABC-TV, N.Y.C., 1983; photojournalist Bus. Times, ESPN, N.Y.C., 1984, Broadcast News Svc., N.Y.C., 1984, Cable News Network, Inc., N.Y.C., 1984—, Entertainment Tonight, Paramount Pictures Corp., N.Y.C., 1988-91, Fox News at Seven, Ten O'Clock News, Sta. WNYW-TV, N.Y.C., 1988-91, USA Today: The Television Show, Grant Tinker/Gannett East Prodns. Inc., N.Y.C., 1988-89, Preview: the best of the new, TV Program Enterprises, N.Y.C., 1990; photojournalist Personalities Twentieth Century Fox Film Corp., N.Y.C., 1991. Mem.: Nat. Press Photographers Assn., TV and Radio Working Press Assn., Nat. Hon. Broadcasting Soc., Acad. TV Arts and Scis. Democrat. Avocation: travel. Home: 1 Liberty St Little Ferry NJ 07643-2303 Office: Cable News Network 1 Time Warner Ctr New York NY 10019-8012 Office Phone: 212-275-7835. Personal E-mail: JoeCapolarello@hotmail.com.

CAPON, EDWIN GOULD, retired religious organization administrator, minister; b. Boston, Apr. 1, 1924; s. Gould and Helen (Wood) C.; m. Norma Jean Wilcoxson (div. Jan. 1971); children: Peter Lawrence, Jonathan Edwin; m. Esther Constance Nicastro, Sept. 5, 1975. AB, Harvard U., 1947; STM, Andover-Newton Theol. Sem., 1949. Ordained to ministry Swedenborgian Ch., 1949. Min. Bridgewater (Mass.) New Ch., 1948-51, Elmwood (Mass.) New Ch., 1949-55, Detroit New Ch., Royal Oak, Mich., 1977-79; v.p. Swedenborg Sch. Religion, Cambridge, Mass., 1953-55, pres. Cambridge and Newton, Mass., 1955-77; pastor San Francisco Swedenborgian Ch., 1979-90; interim min. St. Paul Swedenborgian Ch., 1991-92, min., 1992-94; pres. The Swedenborgian Ch., Newton, 1992-98, chmn. coun. mins., 1956-67. Trustee Urbana (Ohio) U., 1966-80, 92-99; v.p. Mass. Coun. Chs. Mem. Swedenborgian Ch. Avocations: hiking, mountain climbing in new england.

CAPONE, LUCIEN, JR., management consultant, former naval officer; b. Bristol, R.I. s. Lucien and Louise Dolores (Malafronte) C.; m. Charlotte Loretta Lammers, July 22, 1950; children: Lucien, Judith Ann. BS, U.S. Naval Acad., 1949; grad., Naval Postgrad. Sch., 1955, Indsl. Coll. Armed Forces, 1967; MS in Bus. Adminstrn, George Washington U., 1967, postgrad., 1970—71. Commd. ensign USN, 1949, advanced through grades to rear adm., served on destroyers Atlantic Fleet, 1949-54, mem. staff Office Chief Naval Ops. Dept. of Navy, 1955-57, exec. officer U.S.S. Huse, 1957-59, staff, comdr. Mid. East Force Persian Gulf, 1959-61, head plans, programs, and requirements br. Naval Comm. Sys. Hdqrs. Washington, 1961-63; comdg. officer U.S.S. Hammerberg, 1963-64; dep. chief of staff Def. Comm. Agy., Washington, 1964-66; comdg. officer U.S.S. Dahlgren, 1967-69; asst. comdr. plans, programs, requirements Naval Telecom. Command USN, Washington, 1969-72; comdg. officer U.S.S. Richmond K. Turner, 1972-74; dep. dir. nat. mil. command sys. tech. support Def. Comm. Agy., Washington, 1974-76, dir. command and control tech. ctr., 1976-78; dep. dir. command and control Def. Comm. Agy. USN, 1976-78; dir. Inter-Am. Def. Coll., Washington, 1978-79; exec. Booz, Allen & Hamilton, Inc., McLean, Va., 1979-97, v.p., 1983-88, sr. v.p., 1988-97, bd. dirs., oper. coun., 1988-97; cons., 1997—. Decorated Legion of Merit, Def. Superior Svc. medal with oak leaf cluster. Mem. IEEE, AIAA, Armed Forces Comm. and Electronics Assn. (past pres. DC chpt.). Office: Booz Allen & Hamilton Inc Ste 700 8283 Greensboro Dr Mc Lean VA 22102-3838 E-mail: capone_luke@bah.com.

CAPONE, MARYANN, financial planner; b. Bklyn., July 25, 1952; d. Pasquale and Dorothy (Rizzo) Capone; m. Donald Walter Huebner, June 7, 1975; 1 child, Melissa Lauren. BA, Queens (N.Y.) Coll., 1974; MBA, St. John's U., Queens, 1980. Cert. financial planner, enrolled agent for the IRS 2001. Asst. to head rsch. F. Eberstadt, N.Y.C., 1975-78; asst. v.p. Merrill Lynch, N.Y.C., 1978-81; v.p. Integrated Resources, N.Y.C., 1981-84, Mid-Island Equities, Wesbury, N.Y., 1984-85, Am. Savs. Bank, N.Y.C., 1985-86; 1st v.p. Greater N.Y. Savs. Bank, N.Y.C., 1986-97; prin. MCH Fin. Planning, Massapequa, N.Y., 1997—; enrolled agt. IRS. Adj. prof. acctg. Molloy Coll., Rockville Centre, 2003. Instr. religious edn. St. James Roman Cath. Ch., Seaford, N.Y., 1988—, mem. adv. bd. religious edn., 1996—; bd. dirs. Fin. Planning Assn. L.I., 2004—, Women Fin. Group, 2004. Roman Catholic. Home and Office: MCH Fin Planning & Tax Svc 433 N Atlanta Ave North Massapequa NY 11758 Office Phone: 516-752-4178. E-mail: mcapone7@optonline.net.

CAPONEGRO, NANCY, retired elementary school educator; b. Elizabeth, N.J., July 10, 1940; d. Charles and Mary (Bryden) McCarron; m. John Edward Caponegro, Aug. 21, 1965; children: Cheryl Ayn, John Charles. BS, Ball State U., 1962; MA, NYU, 1965. Cert. elem. tchr., N.Y., art tchr. kindergarten-12, N.Y. Tchr. art Sachem Cen. Schs., Holbrook, N.Y., 1962-67, Smithtown (N.Y.) Schs., 1969—98; ret. Named Woman of Yr., St. James Times, 1988; N.Y. State Coun. of Arts grantee, 1988. Mem. Smithtown Stitchers Guild (winner Hoffman fabric challenge 1990-91, 91-92, 92-93). Episcopalian. Avocations: quilting, music, silk painting. Home: 7 Woodhollow Rd Smithtown NY 11787-3721

CAPONIGRO, JEFFREY RALPH, public relations counselor; b. Kankakee, Ill., Aug. 13, 1957; s. Ralph A. and Barbara Jean (Paul) C.; m. Ellen Colleen Kennedy, Oct. 15, 1982; children: Nicholas J., Michael J. BA, Ctrl. Mich. U., 1979. Sports reporter Observer and Eccentric newspaper, Rochester, Mich., 1974-75, Mt. Pleasant (Mich.) Times, 1975-77, Midland (Mich.) Daily News, 1977-79; acct. exec. Desmond & Assocs., Oak Park, Mich., 1979-80; v.p. Anthony M. Franco, Inc., Detroit, 1980-84; chmn., pres., CEO Shandwick USA (formerly Casey Comm. Mgmt., Inc.), Southfield, 1984—95; founder & CEO Caponigro Public Relations Inc., Detroit, 1995—. Contbr. author: Best Sports Stories, 1978. Mem. Pub. Rels. Soc. Am. (accredited, Detroit chpt., nat. accrediation bd.). Home: 5790 Springbrook Dr Troy MI 48098-5352 Office: #1750 4000 Town Ctr Southfield MI 48075-1411

CAPORALE, D. NICK, lawyer; b. Omaha, Sept. 13, 1928; s. Michele and Lucia Caporale; m. Margaret Nilson, Aug. 5, 1950; children: Laura Diane Stevenson, Leland Alan. BA, U. Nebr.-Omaha, 1949, M.Sc., 1954; JD with distinction, U. Nebr.-Lincoln, 1957. Bar: Nebr. 1957, U.S. Dist. Ct. Nebr. 1957, U.S. Ct. Appeals 8th cir. 1958, U.S. Supreme Ct. 1970. Judge Nebr. Dist. Ct., Omaha, 1979—82, Nebr. Supreme Ct., Lincoln, 1982—98; of counsel Baird Holm Law Firm, 1998—. Lectr. U. Nebr., Lincoln, 1982—84, Lincoln, 2000—03. Pres. Omaha Community Playhouse, 1976. Served to 1st lt. U.S. Army, 1952—54, Korea. Decorated Bronze Star; recipient Alumni Achievement U. Nebr.-Omaha, 1972; Disting. Alumni Award, U. Nebr. Coll. Law, 2004. Fellow Am. Coll. Trial Lawyers, Internat. Soc. Barristers; mem. Order of Coif. Office: Baird Holm Law Firm 1500 Woodmen Tower Omaha NE 68102 Office Phone: 402-344-0500. Business E-Mail: dncaporale@bairdholm.com.

CAPORIZZO, A. WILLIAM, lawyer; b. 1960; BS magna cum laude, Univ. Pa., 1982; JD magna cum laude, Boston Univ., 1985. CPA; bar: Mass. 1985, Conn. 1992. Ptnr., co-chmn. Tax dept., mem. Joint Venture & Fund Formation group Wilmer Cutler Pickering Hale & Dorr, Boston. Mem.: ABA, Mass. Bar Assn., Boston Bar Assn. Office: Wilmer Cutler Pickering Hale & Dorr 60 State St Boston MA 02109 Office Phone: 617-526-6411. Office Fax: 617-526-5000. Business E-Mail: william.caporizzo@wilmerhale.com.

CAPOUYA, EMILE, writer; b. N.Y.C. Student, Columbia U., Oxford U. Asst. prof. English Bard Coll., Annandale-on-Hudson, N.Y.; lectr. comparative lit. New Sch. Soc. Rsch., N.Y.C.; assoc. prof. English Bernard M. Baruch Coll., CUNY, N.Y.C., 1971—. Faculty mem. Julliard Sch., 1971—; literary editor Nation, 1970-76; editor New Am. Rev., 1979—; editorial dir. Hippocrene Books, 1980—; exec. dir. Funk & Wagnalls; pub. New Amsterdam Books. Editor: (with Keitha Tompkins) The Essential Kropotkin, 1975; author: From Rebellion to Responsibility, 1965, In the Sparrow Hills, 1993 (Sue Kaufman prize for first fiction Am. Acad. Arts and Letters 1994). Guggenheim fellow, 1964-65. Office: Bernard M Baruch College CUNY Dept of English 17 Lexington Ave Dept Of New York NY 10010-5518

CAPOZZI, LOU, public relations executive; Formerly with Hill & Knowlton, 1968; pres., CEO Manning, Selvage & Lee (subs. Publicis Groupe), NYC, 1995—2005; exec. chair Publicis PR and Corp. Comm. Group, NYC, 2005—. Chmn. Coun. PR Firms. Office: Publicis Group PR & Corp Comm 1675 Broadway New York NY 10019

CAPP, DAVID A., former prosecutor; Criminal divsn. chief U.S. Atty.'s Office, Dyer, 1988-91, 1st asst. atty., U.S. Atty, no. dist Ind, 1999—2001. Office: US Attys Office 5400 Federal Plz #1500 Hammond IN 46320-1843

CAPP, MICHAEL PAUL, pediatrician, educator; b. Yonkers, NY, July 1, 1930; s. Michael and Mary (Bybel) Capp; m. Constance Whitehead, Jan. 4, 1989; children: Marianne, Michael, Steven, John. BS, Roanoke Coll., Salem, Va., 1952; MD, U. N.C., 1958. Diplomate Am. Bd. Radiology. Lab. instr. physics Roanoke Coll., 1952; tchg. asst. Grad. Sch. Physics, Duke U., 1952—54; intern in pediat. Duke U. Med. Ctr., 1958—59, resident in radiology, 1959—62, assoc. in radiology, 1962, asst. prof., 1963—66, assoc. prof., 1966—70, dir. diagnostic divsn., dept. radiology, 1967—70, asst. prof. pediat., 1968—70, radiologist in charge pediatric cardiology, 1962—70; dir. Duke U. Med. Ctr. (Pediatric Radiology Program), 1965—70, Duke Med. Center (Med. Students Teaching Program Diagnostic Radiology), 1965-66; prof., chmn. dept. radiology U. Ariz. Coll. Medicine, Tucson, 1970—93, prof. emeritus, 1993—; chief of staff Ariz. Med. Ctr., Univ. Hosp., 1971—73; exec. dir. Am. Bd. of Radiology, Tucson, 1993—2001. Mem. NRC com. on Radiology James Picker Found., 1972. Contbr. articles to profl. jours. Mem.: NAS, AMA, Inst. Medicine, Soc. for Chmn. Acad. Radiology Depts. (pres. 1977), Soc. for Pediatric Radiology, Eastern Radiol. Soc. (sci. program chmn. 1967, v.p. 1973—), Pima County Med. Soc., N.Y. Acad. Scis., N.Am. Soc. Cardiac Radiologists (pres. 1975), Radiol. Soc. N.Am. (chmn. sci. exhibits com. 1976—79), Am. Bd. Radiology (treas. 1982—85, v.p. 1985, pres. 1987—89, exec. dir. 1993—), Am. Heart Assn. (pres. coun. on cardiovasc. radiology 1976—78), Am. Assn. Univ. Radiologists (exec. com. 1970, Gold medal 1988), Am. Roentgen Ray Soc. (pres. 1990), Am. Coll. Radiology, Sigma Pi Sigma. Office: U Arizona Coll Med 1501 N Campbell Ave PO Box 245017 Tucson AZ 85724

CAPPARELL, LORRAINE SUSAN, artist, sculptor, painter; b. Rochester, N.Y., July 26, 1947; d. Edmond Seth and Ruth Myrtle (Goettel) Spencer; m. James Capparell, Aug. 23, 1969 (div. 1995); m. Lars Speyer, July 26, 1997. BS, Cornell U., 1969. Exec. trainee McCurdy's, Rochester, 1969-70; prodn. artist Coakley-Heagerty, San Jose, Calif., 1971-73; freelance graphic designer Palo Alto, Calif., 1974—; photographer, 1978—; sculptor, painter, 1980—. Artist, creator Hands, 1982, The Three Ages of Women, 1986, Five Women: Tree of Life, 1994, Erato, 1995, Observer, 1996, Yin and Yang, 1997, Abhaya, 2001, Mahapajapati, 2002. Bd. dirs. Cult. Odyssey San Francisco, 1985—, Women's Caucus for the Arts, Palo Alto, 1986—. Mem. Kappa Kappa Gamma. Buddhist. Avocations: meditation, travel, writing, cooking, tai chi. Home: 698 Kendall Ave Palo Alto CA 94306-2723

CAPPEL, CONSTANCE, educational consultant, writer; b. Dayton, Ohio, June 22, 1936; d. Adam Denison and Mary Louise (Henry) C.; m. R.A. Montgomery Jr., June 16, 1962 (div. Apr. 1980); children: Raymond A. Montgomery III, Anson Cappel Montgomery. BA, Sarah Lawrence Coll., 1959; MA, Columbia U., N.Y.C., 1961; PhD, Union Inst. & Univ., Cin., 1991. Editor Newsweek, N.Y.C., 1961—63, Vogue, N.Y.C., 1964—66; mem. faculty Pine Manor Coll., Chestnut Hill, Mass., 1968—72, prof.; grad. prof. Goddard Coll., Plainfield, Vt., 1975—80; founder, CEO, pub. Vt. Crossroad Press, Waitsfield, 1972—82; comml. realtor Investmark, Dayton, 1983—85; prin., founder, CEO Cappel Cons., San Francisco, 1986—94; bus. advisor U.S. Peace Corps, Lodz, Poland, 1994—96; mgr. Price Waterhouse Real Estate, Warsaw, 1996—97; dir. devel. Conflict Resolution Catalysts, Montpelier, Vt., 1997; tchr. trainer U.S. Peace Corps., Kazakhstan, 1998; pres. Newport (N.H.) Earth Inst., 1999; faculty Norman Rockwell Mus., 2000—02. Adj. faculty PhD program Union Inst. and U., 2002—05. Author: Hemingway in Michigan, 1966, paperback 1977, 99, Vermont School Bus Ride, 1977, Utopian Colleges, 1999, Sweetgrass and Smoke, 2002, A Stairwell in Lodz, 2004; editor: A Union of Voices: Accounts of the Union Institute & University, 2004. Editor, founder Women's Rights Project/ACLU, Vt., 1973-74; grad. alumni/ae bd. The Union Inst. & Univ., 1992-94, 99—, sec., 1993; v.p. bd. Chief Andrew Blackbird Mus., bd. dirs. 2002—, pres. 2004—; bd. dirs. Harbor Springs Hist. Soc., trustee, 2002—. McDowell Colony fellow, Peterborough, N.H., 1972, 1974. Mem.: Petoskey Audabon Soc., New Eng. Antiquities Rsch. Assn., Archaeol. Conservancy, Mich. Hemingway Soc., Great Lakes Lighthouse Keepers Assn., PEN Am. Ctr., Ernest Hemingway Soc., Audubon Soc., Harbor Springs Womens Club. Democrat. Radhi Suami. Office: 524 Pine St Harbor Springs MI 49740

CAPPELLANO, ROSEMARIE ZACCONE, small business owner; b. Council Bluffs, Iowa, Apr. 1, 1952; d. Carl Paul and Marianna (Urbano) Zaccone; m. Al Cappellano, June 23, 1940; children: Marco, Mario. Degree in bus., U. Nebr., 1978. Owner Al's Angels and Gifts, Omaha, 1996—. Spkr. in field; exhibitor An Event With Angels. Named Columbus Day Queen, Sons of Italy, 1976. Mem.: Cath. Daus. Democrat. Roman Catholic. Avocations: travel, gourmet cooking, music, movies. Office: Al's Angels and Gifts 12291 W Center Rd Omaha NE 68144 Office Phone: 402-330-1333. Office Fax: 402-333-4325. E-mail: alsangels291@aol.com.

CAPPELLAZZO, AMY, art appraiser, writer; BA in Fine Arts, NYU; MA in Urban Design and City Planning, Pratt Inst., NYC. Dir. Rubell Family Collection & Found., Miami; internat. co-head, post-war and contemporary art dept. Christie's, NYC. Bd. dir. LA Contemporary Exhbns.; lectr. in field. Co-editor In Company: The Collaborations of Robert Creeley, 1999. Bd. dir. Miami Light Project. Office: Christie's/NY 20 Rockefeller Plz New York NY 10020 Office Phone: 212-636-4932. Office Fax: 212-636-4932. Business E-Mail: acappellazzo@christies.com.*

CAPPELLO, EVE, speaker, trainer, author; b. Sydney, Australia; d. Nem and Ethel Shapira; children: Frances Soskins, Alan Kazdin. BA, Calif. State U., Dominguez Hills, 1974; MA, Pacific Western U., 1977, PhD, 1978. Singer, pianist, L.A., 1956—76; profl. devel. and mgmt. staff tng. Calif. Inst. Tech., 1977—; instr. Calif. State U., St. Mary's Coll., U. So. Calif., Loyola Marymount U.; founder, pres. A-C-T Internat.; founder WIN Internat. Invited speaker World Congress Behavior Therapy, Israel, Melbourne U., Australia; newspaper columnist, 1976—. Author: Let's Get Growing, 1979, The Professional Touch, 1988, 3d edit., 2000, Dr Eve's Garden, 1984, Act, Don't React, 4th edit. 2000, The Game of the Name, 1985, The Perfectionist Syndrome, 1990, Why Aren't More Women Running the Show?, 1994, Great Sex After 50, 2d edit., More Great Sex After 50, 2003; contbr. articles to profl. jours. Named to Internat. Hall of Fame, Bus. and Profl. Women, 1994. Mem. Internat. Platform Assn. (bd. dirs., affirmative action com., bd. govs.), Toastmasters, DTM (area gov.), Alpha Gamma. Office Phone: 626-794-4076. Personal E-mail: dreve@earthlink.net.

CAPPETO, MICHAEL ARNOLD, university dean; b. Union, N.J., Dec. 17, 1947; s. James J. and Constance (Conza) C.; m. Beverlee A. Johnson, Dec. 19, 1970; children: Christine, Jennifer. BA, James Madison U., 1970, MS, 1971; EdD, Va. Poly Inst., 1977. Asst. dir. student affairs Va. Mil. Inst., Lexington, 1971-74; asst. dean students Washington and Lee U., Lexington, 1975-78, assoc. dean students, 1978-86; dean of students Harvey Mudd Coll., Claremont, Calif., 1986-92; dean of coll. Colgate U., Hamilton, N.Y., 1992—. Evaluator career planning program, counselor edn. dept. Coll. Edn. U. Va., 1980-81; chmn. on-campus eval. com. Coll. Placement Council, 1984-85. Chmn., Rockbridge County Cmty. Svcs. Bd., Lexington, 1984-85; v.p. Boy Scouts Am. Old Baldy Coun., Calif., 1989-92. Mem. Va. Assn. Student Personnel Adminstrs. (pres. 1983-84, Outstanding Student Personnel Profl. award 1985), Nat. Assn. Student Personnel Adminstrs. (dir. membership recruitment and orientation for Va. 1978-80, chmn. So. Calif. exec. com. 1990-92, editl. bd. NASPA Jour. 1992-98), Nat. Assn. Campus Activities (southeastern unit chmn. 1973-74). Roman Catholic. Office: Colgate U Office of Dean Coll Hamilton NY 13346

CAPPIELLO, ANGELA, program manager; b. New Hyde Park, N.Y., July 6, 1954; d. Augustine and Angela (Tamburello) C. Cert. meeting and conv. mgmt., NYU, 1988, cert. assn. mgmt., cert. food and beverage mgmt., NYU, 1989, cert. travel mgmt., 1990, cert. hotel and motel mgmt., 1991, cert. in fin. controls, 1992, cert. mgmt. practices, 1998. Cert. meeting profl., assn. exec. Mgr. meetings and convs. N.Y. Libr. Assn., N.Y.C., 1987-89; conf. coord. ASCE, N.Y.C., 1989; mgr. meetings and confs. Coun. Cons. Orgns., N.Y.C., 1990-91; asst. to pres. Goodstein Devel. Corp., N.Y.C., 1991-93; asst. meetings mgr. Nat. Episcopal Ch., N.Y.C., 1993-96, dir. grants program, 1996-99; mgr. meetings SCP Comm./Cliggott Pub., N.Y.C., 1999—2004; program mgr. Curry Rockefeller Group, Tarrytown, NY, 2004—; dir. membership devel. and spl. events Bldg. Owners and Mgrs. Assn. Greater NY, NYC, 2004—. Mem. Meeting Profls. Internat. (bd. dirs. N.Y. chpt. 1991-93). Home: 36 New Hyde Park Rd New Hyde Park NY 11040-4935 Office: Bldg Owners and Mgrs Assn Greater NY Ste 1000 11 Penn Plz New York NY 10001 E-mail: apcmeetings@worldnet.att.net.

CAPPIELLO, FRANK ANTHONY, JR., investment advisor; b. Trenton, N.J., Jan. 5, 1926; s. Frank A. and Rose Marie (Clapis) C.; m. Marie Therese Rhodes, June, 1954; children: Frank Rhodes, Annmarie, Elaine. AB, U. Notre Dame, 1949; postgrad., Cornell U. Law Sch., 1949-50; MBA, Harvard U., 1954. Supr. rate research Va. Electric and Power Co., Richmond, 1954-61; mgr. research dept. Alexander Brown & Sons, 1961-67; v.p. Securities Monumental Life Ins. Co., 1968-74; fin. v.p. Monumental Corp., 1970-80; pres. Monumental Capital Mgmt., Inc., Balt., 1974-80, Dowbeaters, Inc., Summit, N.J. and Balt., 1981-83, McCullough, Andrews and Cappiello, Inc., Balt. and San Francisco, 1983—2003; founder, dir. Bank of Md., 1985-90; chmn. Cappiello-Rushmore Mutual Funds, Bethesda, Md., 1993—2000; chmn., mng. dir. Montgomery Bros., Cappiello, LLC, 2003—. TV panelist Wall St. Week, 1970—; disting. visiting prof. fin. Loyola Coll., Balt., 1986—; mem. adv. investment com. Md. State Retirement Systems. Author: Finding the Next Super Stock, 1982, From Main Street to Wall Street, 1988. Trustee Balt. City Pension System; mem., commr. Md. State Econ. and Community Devel. Commn., 1977-80. Served with U.S. Marine Corps, 1950-52. Mem. Fin. Analysts Fedn. (chmn., dir.), Balt. Security Analysts Soc. Clubs: Univ., Harvard (N.Y.C.); Hamilton Street (Balt.). Roman Catholic. Home: 19 Buchanan Rd Baltimore MD 21212-1013 Office: 10751 Falls Rd Ste 250 Lutherville Timonium MD 21093-4552 Office Phone: 410-337-2255. E-mail: cappiello@aol.com.

CAPPITELLA, MAURO JOHN, architect; b. NYC, July 11, 1934; s. Gaetano and Maria (D'Errico) Cappitella; m. Christine Wilhelmine Otte, Oct. 11, 1964; children: Mark, Christina Cappitella-Bartels, Nicole Cappitella-Snyder. *Parents Maria and Gaetano left Melfi, Italy in 1920 and 1921, respectively. They met, married and settled in New York, where they worked as a seamstress and steelworker. Brother, Joseph, became a New York City police officer. Paternal grandfather, Mauro Cappitella, was a stone mason and worked on the City College of New York.* BS in Architecture, CCNY, 1956; postgrad., Columbia U., 1960-62; M in Urban Planning, NYU, 1967. Registered arch., N.Y., N.J., lic. Nat. Coun. Archtl. Registration Bds., profl. planner, N.J. Designer Garfinkel & Marenberg, N.Y.C., 1956-57; arch. Western Electric Co., Inc., N.Y.C., 1957-68. Cons. arch., Norwood, NJ, 1968—76, Upper Saddle River, NJ, 1976—; arch. project mng. cons. The Ives Group Architects and Planner, Fair Lawn, NJ, 1991—. Garfinkel and Marenberg schs. and shopping ctrs., U.S. Army Officers Club, U.S. Army Mus. for 3d Inf. Divsn., Wurzburg, Germany, Western Elec. shop, warehouse, office, med. facilities, mgmt. tng. ctrs., Bell Labs., Holmdel, N.J. and Naperville, Ill., Port Authority, N.Y., N.J., Newark Airport redevel. program, Kennedy Airport, LaGuardia Airport. Served to 1st lt. U.S. Army, 1957—59. Mem.: AIA (N.J. liaison rep. to N.J. State Bd. Archs. 1997), West Point Mil. Acad. (supt. office vol.), Archs. League No. N.J. (bd. dirs. 1980—83, sec. 1984—85, v.p. 1985, 1st v.p. 1986, pres.-elect 1987, pres. 1988, bd. dirs. 1989—91, pres. 1993, bd. dirs. 1994—96, Dir. of the Yr. award 1980, 1981, Anton Vegliante award 1993), N.J. Soc. Archs. (bd. dirs. 1983—84, 1987—89, 1993—96), Saddle River Valley Investment Club (pres. 2003—05), Soc. 3d U.S. Inf. Divsn. U.S. Army, Saddle River Tennis Club (dir. 1984—2005), Rotary. Republican. Roman Catholic. Achievements include Port Authority NY/NJ Path Rail Facilities developed under station improvement program; design of first racially integrated manufacturing facility in Winston-Salem, NC. Office: 332 E Saddle River Rd Upper Saddle River NJ 07458-2108 Office Phone: 201-327-4064. Personal E-mail: baron332@optonline.net.

CAPPO, JOSEPH C., journalist, writer; b. Chgo., Feb. 24, 1936; s. Joseph V. and Frances (Maggio) Cacioppo; m. Mary Anne Cappo, May 7, 1967; children: Elizabeth, John. BA, DePaul U., 1957. Reporter Hollister Publs., Wilmette, Ill., 1961-62, Chgo. Daily News, 1962-68, bus. columnist, 1968-78; columnist Crain's Chgo. Bus., 1978—, pub., 1979-89, editor at large, 2003—; v.p. Crain Comm., Inc., 1981-89, sr. v.p., 1989-95, sr. v.p. internat., 1996—2003; pres. Crain Comms. of Mex., 2001—02. Pub. Advt. Age, 1989—92, publishing dir., 1992—99; dir. Assn. Area Bus. Publs., 1982—88, pres., 1985—86. Author: Future Scope: Success Strategies for the 1990's and Beyond, 1990, The Future of Advertising: New Clients, New Media, New Consumers in the Post Television Age, 2003. Bd. dirs. Off the Street Club, Chgo., 1981—, Chgo. Advt. Fedn., 1987-93, Mus. Broadcast Comm., 1984-90, Ill. Coun. on Econ. Edn., 1990-95. With U.S. Army, 1959-61. Recipient award Ill. Press Assn., 1962, (with other Daily News staffers) Nat. Headliner award, 1966, Disting. Alumni award DePaul U., 1975, Page One award Chgo. Newspaper Guild, 1978, Peter Lisagor award Sigma Delta Chi, 1978, Outstanding Achievement award in comm., Justinian Soc. Lawyers, 1979, Champion award YWCA of Met. Chgo., 1984, Media Svc. award Chgo. Lung Assn., 1990, Dante award Joint Civic Com. Italian-Ams., 2003. Mem.: Bus. and Econ. Writers (bd. govs. 1984—89), Econ. Club (Chgo.), Internat. Advt. Assn. (world bd. 1994—, sr. v.p. 1996—98, world pres. 1998—2000), Delta Mu Delta (hon.). Roman Catholic. Office: Crain Communications Inc 360 N Michigan Ave Chicago IL 60601-3806

CAPPS, DAVID EDWARD, JR., assistant dean; b. Atlanta, Nov. 1, 1946; s. David Edward Capps Sr. and Mary Elinor (Tyner) Roberts; m. Jamie Renee Gibson, Dec. 28, 1982. AA, Clarke Meml. Coll., 1967; BS, U. So. Miss., 1969, MS, 1977. Resident hall dir. Ga. So. U., Statesboro, 1977-80; asst. dir. student activities Embry-Riddle Aero. U., Daytona, Fla., 1980-83; summer youth counselor C.E.T.A., Crystal River, Fla., 1983; admissions specialist Pasco Hernando C.C., New Port Richey, Fla., 1984-85, continuing edn. specialist, 1985-86, asst. dean of students Brooksville, Fla., 1986—. With USN, 1969-73. Mem. Fla. Assn. C.C.'s, Rotary. Baptist. Avocations: jazz, movies, good restaurants, quality time with wife. Home: 20119 Back Nine Dr Boca Raton FL 33498

CAPPS, ETHAN LEROY, retired oil industry executive; b. Sherman, Tex., Dec. 2, 1924; s. Ethen Daniel and Anne Mae (Anderson) C.; m. Emily Ann Tyson, Sept. 8, 1951; children— Richard LeRoy, Nancy Elizabeth. BS, Tex. A&M U., 1948; grad., Advanced Mgmt. Program, Harvard U., 1965. C.P.A., Tex. With Tenn. Gas Transmission Co., Houston, 1948-59, asst. treas., budget dir., 1960-61; chief acct. Midwestern Gas Transmission Co., Houston, 1959; v.p. Tenneco Corp., Houston, 1961-63; adminstrv. v.p., controller Tenneco Oil Co., Houston, 1963-73; v.p., treas. Tenneco Inc., 1974-84, v.p. fin. mgmt. devel. and ins. and loss control, 1984-86, ret., 1986. Elder First Presbyn. Ch., Houston. Mem.: Petroleum (Houston), Racquet (Houston). Home: 4718 Hallmark Dr Apt 501 Houston TX 77056

CAPPS, JAMES LEIGH, II, lawyer, military officer; b. Brunswick, Ga., 1956; s. Thomas Edwin Sr. and Betty Marie C.; m. Nancy Ann Fisher, 1978; children: Bonnie Lynn, James Leigh III. AA, Seminole C.C., Sanford, Fla., 1976; BA in History, U. Cen. Fla., 1981; JD, U. Fla., 1987. Bar: Fla. 1987, U.S. Ct. Mil. Appeals 1988, Colo. 1990, U.S. Ct. Appeals (4th cir.) 1997. Enlisted USAF, 1976, advanced through grades to maj., 1995, med. svc. specialist MacDill AFB, Fla., 1977-79, air weapons dir. Germany, 1982-84, claims officer Homestead AFB, Fla., 1987-88, area def. counsel, 1988-90, dep. staff judge adv. Onizuka AFB, Calif., 1990-93; atty. office of state atty. 18th Jud. Ct., Sanford, Fla., 1994; assoc. Dominick Salfi Law Offices, Maitland, Fla., 1993-94; res. judge adv. Moody AFB, Ga., 1993-99; of counsel Dominick Salfi Law Offices, Maitland, Fla., 1994—; pvt. practice, 1996—; res. judge adv. Patrick AFB, Fla., 2000—; civilian contract specialist for Naval Air Warfare Ctr. USN, Orlando, Fla., 1999—; contract specialist Flight Sch. XXI Simulation Svcs. Assigned to 16th Air Force Hdqs., Aviano AFB, Italy, Operation Joint Endeavor, 1996; implementation force Dayton Peace Accords UN. Atty. Vietnam Vets. Ctrl. Fla., 1998—99. Maj. USAFR. Recipient McCarthy award for legal svc. Air Combat Command, 1995. Mem.: VFW, DAV, Am. Legion. Democrat. Office: Law Office of James Capps PO Box 2551 Sanford FL 32773 Personal E-mail: cappslegal@aol.com.

CAPPS, JOSEPH MICHAEL, music educator, director; b. Goldsboro, N.C., Sept. 16, 1976; s. Terry Michael Capps and Sheree Rigdon Mumblow; m. Erin Florence Capps, Nov. 26, 1977. MusB in Music Edn. and Performance, Elon Coll., 1999. Instr. Music And Arts Ctr., Burlington, NC, 1998—; dir. bands A.l. Stanback Mid. Sch., Hillsborough, NC, 2000—. Chmn. hons. band audition Ctrl. Dist., NC, 2004—. Dir. benefit concert Relay for Life; active Ctrl. Dist. Menc, NC, 2005. Mem.: Internat. Assn. Jazz Edn., Music Educators N.C. (bd. dirs. ctrl. dist. 2005, nominee Band Dir. of Yr. award 2000). Office: A L Stanback Middle School 3700 Nc Hwy 86 South Hillsborough NC 27278 Office Phone: 919-644-3200 242. E-mail: michael.capps@orange.k12.nc.us.

CAPPS, LARRY LYNN, school librarian; b. Liberal, Kans., Aug. 27, 1950; s. Charles Andrew and Mary Edna Capps; m. Janet Sue Smith, Jan. 9, 1971; children: Heather Lynn, Larry Lynn Capps II. BA in Edn., Northeastern State U., 1972; MLS, U. Okla., 1980. Tchr. H.S. French and English Weleetka (Okla.) Pub. Schs., 1972—73; tchr. H.S. English, libr. Bowlegs (Okla.) Pub. Schs., 1973—83; libr., yearbook, acad. bowl teams Dale (Okla.) Pub. Schs., 1983—. Mem.: NEA, Okla. Jr. Acad. Bowl Assn. (treas., membership chmn. 1997—), Okla. Acad. Coaches Assn., Okla. Edn. Assn. Republican. Baptist. Avocations: stamp collecting/philately, coin collecting/numismatics, television, movies, music. Office: Dale Pub Schs 300 Smith Ave Dale OK 74851 Office Phone: 405-964-5514. Home Fax: 405-878-0546.

CAPPS, LOIS RAGNHILD GRIMSRUD, congresswoman, former school nurse; b. Ladysmith, Wis., Jan. 10, 1938; d. Jurgen Milton and Solveig Magdalene (Gullixson) Grimsrud; m. Walter Holden Capps, Aug. 21, 1960 (dec.); children: Lisa Margaret, Todd Holden, Laura Karolina. BSN with honors, Pacific Luth. U., 1959; MA in Religion, Yale U., 1964; MA in Edn., U. Calif., Santa Barbara, 1990. RN, Calif.; cert. sch. nurse, Calif.; jr. coll. instr., Calif. Asst. instr. Emanuel Hosp. Sch. Nursing, Portland, Oreg., 1959-60; surgery flr. nurse Yale/New Haven Hosp., 1960-62, head nurse, out patient, 1962-63; staff nurse Vis. Nurse Assn., Hamden, Ct., 1963-64; sch. nurse Santa Barbara Sch. Dists., Calif., 1968-70, 77-98; dir. teenage pregnancy and parenting project Santa Barbara, 1985-86; mem. U.S. Congress from 23rd Calif. dist., Washington, 1998—; mem. Budget com. and Energy and Commerce com. Mem. commerce com., former mem. sci. com., internat. rels. com; mem U.S. Congress, campaign finance reform task force, budget task force, Calif. ISTEA task force, congrl. caucus women's issues, congrl. task force tobacco and health, diabetes caucus, congrl. caucus on the arts, House com. on the budget; instr. Santa Barbara City Coll., 1990—. Bd. dirs. Am. Heart Assn., Santa Barbara, 1989—, The Adoption Ctr., Santa Barbara, 1986-90, Family Svc. Agy., Santa Barbara, 1994—, Stop AIDS Now, Santa Barbara, 1994—, Santa Barbara Women's Polit. Com., 1991—; instr. CPR, first aid, ARC, Santa Barbara, 1985—; bd. dirs. Pacific Luth. Theol. Sem. Democrat. Lutheran. Office: US House of Reps 1707 Longworth Ho Office Bldg Washington DC 20515-0001 Home: 1216 State Street Ste 403 Santa Barbara CA 93101 Fax: 202-225-5632. E-mail: lois.capps@mail.house.gov.

CAPPS, PHILLIP LEWIS, music educator; b. Greenville, SC, Nov. 13, 1951; s. Furman Lewis and Edna Capps; m. Kathryn Coad, Nov. 22, 1978; 1 child, Grace Kathryn. BA, Lander Coll., 1977; MA in Edn., The Citadel, 1990. Cert. tchr. Edn. Dept. SC, 1978. Music educator Pickens (S.C.) Schs., 1978—79, Berkeley S.C. County Sch. Dept., Moncks Corner, 1980—90, math educator, 1990—91, band educator, 1992—. Mem.: SC Music Educators (assoc.), Low Country Winds (assoc.). Office: Sangaree Intermediate School 201 School House Ln Summerville SC 29483

CAPPS, RICHARD HENRY, retired minister; b. Columbia, SC, June 22, 1944; s. Henry Eddie and Maude Cecile (Simpson) Crapps; m. Joyce Dianne Wood, Aug. 2, 1968; children: Richard Henry (Hank) Jr., Elizabeth Cecille. AA, North Greenville Coll., 1965; BA, Furman U., 1967; ThM with honors, New Orleans Bapt. Theol. Sem., 1970, DMin, 1978. Ordained min. So. Bapt. Ch., 1965. Pastor Fairfield Bapt. Ch., Winnsboro, SC, 1964-68, Soc. Hill Bapt. Ch., Oakvale, Miss., 1969-71, First Bapt. Ch., Gaston, SC, 1971-79, interim pastor Cheraw, SC, 1968; sr. pastor Laurel Bapt. Ch., Greenville, SC, 1979-82; dir. missions South Roanoke Bapt. Assn., Greenville, 1982-93, Liberty Bapt. Assn., Thomasville, NC, 1993-98; area dir. Piedmont/Western NC Prison Fellowship, Winston-Salem, 1999; min. missions and outreach Forsyth Park Bapt. Ch., Winston-Salem, 2000, sr. pastor, 2000—03; sr. pastor, missions min. Marketplace Ministries Fellowship, SBC, Winston-Salem, 2003—; agy. monitor Second Harvest Food Bank N.W. NC, Winston-Salem, 2004—. S.S. enlargement campaign cons. SC Bapt. State Conv., 1981-82; PACT cons. N.Am. Mission Bd., Atlanta, 1988-95; state disaster relief coord. NC Bapt. Min., Cary, 1989-93; ch. growth cons. Bapt. State Conv. of NC, Cary, 1996-98. Contbr. articles to profl. publs. Bd. dirs. Greenville Boys Choir, 1986-90, Transplant Recipient Suport Sys., Pitt County Meml. Hosp., Greenville, 1991-93; mem. Greenville Choral Soc., 1990-93; mem. religion in schs. task force Pitt County Schs., Greenville, 1993; vice chmn. chaplains bd. Davidson Correction Ctr., Lexington, NC, 1996-98; vol. greeter ARC, 2000—; bd. dirs. Davidson County Smart Start, 2004—, Svcs. for Deaf and Hard of Hearing, Davidson County, Lexington, 2005. Recipient Am. Legion award, 1965; named Vol. of Yr., Davidson Correctional Ctr., 1997, Northwestern NC chpt. ARC, 2000. Mem. Dir. of Missions Conf. (pres. 1986-87, treas. 1987-98), Thomasville C. of C., Lexington Ministerial Assn., Gaston Ruritan Club (chaplain 1973-77), Am. Numis. Assn., Nat. Probation and Parole Assn., Sierra Club. Democrat. Avocations: African violets, roses, antiques/collectibles, walking, collecting stamps and coins. Home: 198 Creekside Dr High Point NC 27265-9209 Office: PO Box 5808 Winston Salem NC 27113-5808 Office Phone: 336-749-3222.

CAPPS, THOMAS EDWARD, utilities company executive, lawyer; b. Wilmington, N.C., Oct. 31, 1935; s. Edward S. Jr. and Agnes (Rhodes) C.; m. Jane Paden, Sept. 13, 1963; children: Ashley R., Leigh C. AB, U. N.C., 1958, JD, 1965. Bar: Fla. 1975, N.C. 1966. Sr. counsel Carolina Power & Light Co., Raleigh, N.C., 1970-74; v.p., gen. counsel Boston Edison Co., 1974-75; sr. ptnr. Steel Hector & Davis, Miami, Fla., 1975-84; exec. v.p. Va. Power, Richmond, 1984-86; pres. Dominion Resources, Inc., Richmond, 1986—2003, chief exec. officer, 1990—, chmn. bd. dirs., 2001—. Bd. dirs. Amerigroup Corp., Assoc. Elec. & Gas Ins. Svc. Bd. dirs. Va. Blood Svcs., 1986. Lt. USCG, 1959-62. Mem. ABA, Bd. of Bar Overseers, N.C. Bar Assn., Fla. Bar Assn., Mass. Bar Assn. Episcopalian. Office: Dominion Resources Inc PO Box 26532 Richmond VA 23261-6532*

CAPPS, THOS E., energy executive; b. 1935; B, JD, U. N.C., Chapel Hill. Sr. counsel Carolina Power and Light Co., 1970; v.p., general counsel Boston Edison Co., 1974—75; atty. Steel Hector and Davis, 1975; v.p. Va. Power, 1984—86; pres. Dominion Resources, Richmond, 1986—89, COO, 1989—90, CEO, chmn., 1992—, chmn., pres., CEO, 2001—03. Chmn., bd. dirs. Va. Electric and Power Co., Consolidated Natural Gas Co.; bd. dirs. Amerigroup Corp., Associated Electric and Gas Insurance Svc. Office: Dominion Resources Inc 120 Tredegar St Richmond VA 23219-4306*

CAPPS, W. LEE, III, retail executive; BBA in Acct., Midwestern State U., 1974. CPA. Acct. KPMG PeatMarwick, 1974—85; CFO Am. Recreation Products Kellwood Co., St. Louis, 1988—96, dir. corp. develop., 1996—98, v.p., 1998, pres., operating services div., 1999—2000, CFO, 2000—, sr. v.p. finance, 2002, exec. v.p. finance, 2003—05, COO, 2005—. Bd. dir. Make A Wish Found., St. Louis. Office: Kellwood Co 600 Kellwood Pkwy Saint Louis MO 63178*

CAPPUCCIO, PAUL T., lawyer, communications executive; b. West Peabody, Mass., June 5, 1961; AB, Georgetown U., 1983; JD, Harvard U., 1986. Bar: Ohio 1989, DC 1990. Law clk. to Hon. Alex Kozinski U.S. Ct. Appeals (9th cir.), 1986—87; law clk. to Hon. Antonin Scalia U.S. Supreme Ct., 1987—88, law clk. to Hon. Anthony M. Kennedy, 1989; assoc. Jones, Day Reavis & Pogue, 1989—91; assoc. dep. atty. gen. U.S. Dept. Justice, 1991—93; ptnr. Kirkland & Ellis, 1993—99; sr. v.p., gen. counsel Am. Online, Inc., 1999—2001; exec. v.p., gen. counsel, sec. Time Warner Inc., NYC, 2001—. Adj. prof. U. Calif., Berkeley, 1990, 91, Georgetown U. Law Ctr., Washington, 1991, 93, Columbia U. Sch. Law, N.Y.C., 1996, 97. Bd. dirs. Washington Scholarship Fund, 1997—, Inst. Jud. Adminstrn., NYU Sch. Law. Office: Time Warner Inc Law Dept One Time Warner Ctr New York NY 10019

CAPPY, RALPH JOSEPH, state supreme court justice; b. Pitts., Aug. 25, 1943; s. Joseph R. and Catherine (Miljus) C.; m. Janet Fry, Apr. 19, 1985; 1 child, Erik. BS in Psychology, U. Pitts., 1965, JD, 1968. Bar: Pa. 1968, U.S. Dist. Ct. (we. dist.) Pa. 1968, U.S. Supreme Ct. 1975. Law clerk to president judge Ct. of Common Pleas of Allegheny County, 1968—70; atty. civil and family court litigation priv. practice, 1968—78; trial defender, first asst. homicide atty., dep. dir. Office of Public Defender of Allegheny County, 1970—75; public defender Allegheny County, 1975—78; judge Family and Juvenile Ct. Ct. of Common Pleas, Allegheny County, 1978—89, judge criminal div., 1979—85, judge civil div., 1985—86, presiding admin. judge civil div., 1986—90; justice Pa. Supreme Ct., 1989—. Lectr. constl. law U. Pitts., 1970-72; instr. criminal law and trial tactics City of Pitts. Police Acad., Allegheny County Police Acad., 1970-74; liaison justice to Supreme Ct. Appellate Procedural Rules Com., 1990-94, Minor Judiciary of Pa., 1990-94, Pa. Bd. of Law Examiners, 1990-94, First Jud. Dist., 1990-94, Supreme Ct. Civil, Domestic Relations & Orphans' Ct. Procedural Rules Com., 1994-96, Pa. Bd. of Law Examiners, 1994-96, Civil Procedural Rules Com., Pa. Bd. of Law Examiners, Pa. Continuing Legal Education Bd., 1996-. Mem. Pitts. Health and Welfare Planning Agy., 1984—; mem. jud. ethics com. Pa. Law Jour., 1980-82; trustee U. Pitts., 1992—, bd. visitors, 1992—. Named Man of Yr., Sons of Italy; recipient Acad. of Trial Lawyers award, Citation of Merit, Mothers Against Drunk Driving, Man of Yr., Italian Am. Heritage Found., Pa. State Police, Pa. Fraternal Order of Police. Fellow Am. Bar Found.; mem. ABA, Pa. Bar Assn. (Jud. award 1997), Allegheny Bar Assn., Pa. Conf. State Trial Judges (legis. and planning com. 1978-83, legis. com., zone rep. 1984—, chmn. edn. com. 1985-88), Pa. Coll. Judiciary (lectr. 1983—, treas. 1987—, sec. 1988—), NACCP (life), Pitts. Athletic Assn. Office: Pa Supreme Ct 1 Oxford Ct Ste 3130 Pittsburgh PA 15219-1407

CAPRARO, FRANZ, accountant; b. Uder-Eichsfeld, Thuringia, Germany, Nov. 19, 1941; came to U.S., 1959; s. Ernst Capraro and Lia (Loeschmann) Baeuscher; m. Daniela DiPauli, Dec. 26, 1964; 1 child, Monica L. BBA cum laude, U. Miami, 1964. CPA Fla. Ptnr. Deloitte Haskins & Sells (name now Deloitte & Touche), Miami, 1966-84; exec. v.p. The Wolfson Initiative Corp., Miami, 1984-95; v.p. The Novecento Corp., Miami, 1984-95, Washington Storage Co., Miami, 1984-95, The Foundlings, Inc., Miami Beach, 1984-95, The Hampton Roads, Inc., Miami Beach, 1984-95; pvt. practice acctg. Davie, Fla., 1995-96; ptnr. Grau & Co., P.A., Miami, 1996—. Treas. The Jour. of Decorative and Propaganda Arts, Miami, 1986-98; attended Nat. Security Forum, U.S. Air War Coll., Montgomery, Ala., 1993. Mem. exec. com. U. Miami Citizens Bd., Coral Gables, 1987—; treas. Mitchell Wolfson Family Found., Miami, 1985—; bd. dirs. Louis Wolfson II Media History Ctr., Miami, 1987-95; trustee Greater Miami Opera Fin. Com., 1991-96. 1st lt. U.S. Army Fin. Corps, France, 1965-66. Recipient Certificate of Appreciation City of Miami Beach, 1987; named Honorary Conch City of Key West, 1987. Mem. AICPA, Fla. Inst. CPAs, Schlaraffia Costa Aurea (treas. 1986-87), U.S. Air War Coll. Alumni Assn. (life). Roman Catholic. Avocations: reading, travel. Home: 2821 SW 116th Ave Fort Lauderdale FL 33330-1418 Office: Grau & Company PA PH 2 1110 Brickell Ave Miami FL 33131

CAPRIATI, JENNIFER MARIA, professional tennis player; b. N.Y.C., Mar. 29, 1976; d. Stefano and Denise (Deamicis) Capriati. Profl. tennis player, 1990—. Mem. U.S. Wightman Cup Team, 1989, U.S. Fed Cup Team, 1990—91, 1996, 2000. Winner: (jr. singles) French Open, 1989, U.S. Open, 1989, (jr. doubles, with McGrath) Italian Open, 1989, Wimbledon, 1989, Championships: Roland Garros, 2001, Australian Open, 2001, 02, Gold medal, U.S. Women's Singles, Barcelona Olympic Games, 1992, Espy award as Comback Athlete of Yr., 2002; named Comback Player of Yr., WTA, 1996, Female Athlete of Yr., AP, 2001, Singles Champion of Yr., Internat. Tennis Fedn., 2001, Sportswoman of the Year by US Olympic Comm., 2001. Avocations: dance, swimming, reading, music, golf. Office: Internat Mgmt Group care Barbara Perry 22 E 71st St New York NY 10021-4975 Address: Ste 1500 One Progress Plaza Saint Petersburg FL 33701

CAPRIO, ANTHONY S., academic administrator; b. Providence, Apr. 12, 1945; s. Salvatore and Esther (Iafrati) C. BA, Wesleyan U., 1967; MA, Columbia U., 1969, PhD, 1973; BA (hon.), Western New Eng. Coll., 2000. Asst. prof. langs. and fgn. studies Lehman Coll., CUNY, Bronx, 1971-76; assoc. prof. Cedar Crest Coll., Allentown, Pa., 1976-80; prof., adminstr. Am. U., Washington, 1980-89; provost Oglethorpe U., Atlanta, 1989-96; pres. Western New Eng. Coll., Springfield, Mass., 1996—. Corporator Hampden Bank, 2004—; mem. Nat. Humanities Faculty, 1977—. Author: Reflets de la femme, 1973, En Français, 1976, 3d edit., 1985; contbr. over 100 articles to profl. jours., chpts. to books. Trustee Willie Ross Sch. for the Deaf, 1999—, Springfield Symphony Orch., 1998-2004; bd. dirs. Springfield Adult Edn. Coun., 1999-2002, Greater Springfield Convention and Visitors Bur., 1999—, Pioneer Valley Econ. Devel. Coun., 2000—, Springfield Sch. Vols., 2000—, Tuition Exch. Inc., 1994—, Mass. Mentoring Partnership, 2001—; exec. com. Assn. Ind. Colls. and Univs. in Mass., 1999-2002; mem. cabinet Cmty. United Way of Pioneer Valley, 1998—; co-chair Leadership Coun. of Springfield Mentoring Partnership, 1998—2004; corporator Springfield Libr. and Mus. Assn., 1998—; task force on workforce devel. Pioneer Valley Planning Commn., 1998—2003; pres. Cooperating Colls. of Greater Springfield, 2000—; accreditation com. ABA, 2002—. Recipient Adminstr.-Faculty award Am. U., 1984, Disting. Adminstr. and Educator award Greater Washington Assn. Fgn. Lang. Educators, 1986. Mem. Am. Translators Assn., Am. Assn. Higher Edn., Am. Assn. Univ. Adminstrs., Soc. Coll. and Univ. Planning, Phi Beta Kappa, Omicron Delta Kappa, Phi Beta Delta, Phi Beta Kappa (fellow), others. Office: Western New Eng Coll Office of President 1215 Wilbraham Rd Springfield MA 01119-2612 Office Phone: 413-782-1243. Business E-Mail: acaprio@wnec.edu.

CAPRON, ALEXANDER MORGAN, lawyer, educator; b. Hartford, Conn., Aug. 16, 1944; s. Willaim Mosher and Margaret (Morgan) Capron; m. Barbara A. Brown, Nov. 9, 1969 (div. Dec. 1985); 1 child, Jared Capron-Brown; m. Kathleen West, Mar. 4, 1989; children: Charles Spencer West Capron, Christopher Gordon West Capron, Andrew Morgan West Capron. BA, Swarthmore Coll., 1966; LLB, Yale U., 1969; MA (hon.), U. Pa., 1975. Bar: D.C. 1970, Pa. 1978. Law clk. to presiding judge U.S. Ct. Appeals, Washington, 1969—70; lectr., rsch. assoc. Yale U., 1970—72; asst. prof. law U. Pa., 1972—75, vice dean, 1976, assoc. prof., 1975—78, prof. law and human genetics, 1978—82; exec. dir. Pres.'s Commn. for Study of Ethical Problems in Med. and Biomedical and Behavioral Rsch., Washington, 1980—83; prof. law, ethics and pub. policy Law Ctr. Georgetown U., Washington, 1983—84, inst. fellow Kennedy Inst. Ethics, 1983—84; Topping prof. law, medicine and pub. policy U. So. Calif., LA, 1985—89, Univ. prof., 1989—, prof. medicine and law, 1991—, Henry W. Bruce prof. equity, 1991—; co-dir. Pacific Ctr. for Health Policy and Ethics, LA, 1990—; dir. ethics and health WHO, 2002—03, dir. ethics, trade, human rights and health law, 2003—. Mem. bd. advisors Am. Bd. Internal Medicine, 1985—95, chmn., 1991—95; cons. NIH, mem. subcom. on human gene therapy, 1984—92, mem. recombinant DNA adv. com., 1990—95; chmn. Congrl. Biomedical Ethics Adv. Commn., 1987—91; mem. Joint Commn. on Accreditation of Healthcare Orgns., 1994—, mem. ethics adv. com., 1984—85; mem. Nat. Bioethics Adv. Commn., 1996—2001. Author (with Katz): Catastrophic Diseases: Who Decides What?, 1976; author: (with others) Genetic Counseling: Facts, Values and Norms, 1979, Law, Science and Medicine, 1984, supplements, 1987, 1989, 2d edit., Treatise on Health Care Law, 1991; contbr. articles to profl. jours. Bd. mgrs. Swarthmore Coll., 1982—85; bd. trustees The Century Found. Fellow: AAAS, Hastings Ctr. (bd. dirs. 1975—98, Inst. Soc., Ethics and Life Scis.), Am. Coll. Legal Medicine (hon.); mem.: AAUP (exec. com. Pa. chpt.), Internat. Assn. Bioethics (mem. bd. 1992—96, 2001—, v.p. 2003—05, pres. 2005—), Am. Soc. Law, Medicine and Ethics (pres. 1988—89), Inst. Medicine of NAS (bd. dirs. 1985—90), Swarthmore Coll. Alumni Soc. (v.p. 1974—77). Office: SDE/ETH WHO Avenue Appia 20 1211 Geneva 27 Switzerland Office Phone: +41 22 791-1439. Business E-Mail: caprona@who.int.

CAPRONI, VALERIE E., lawyer, federal agency administrator; BA in Psychology magna cum laude, Tulane U., New Orleans, 1976; JD summa cum laude, U. Ga., 1979. Clk. Hon. Phyllis Kravitch, U.S. Ct. Appeals, 11th cir., 1979—80; assoc. litigation dept. Cravath, Swaine & Moore, N.Y.C., 1980—85; asst. U.S. atty. Criminal divsn. U.S. Atty.'s Office, Ea. Dist. N.Y., 1985—89; gen. counsel N.Y. State Urban Devel. Corp., 1989—92; chief of spl. prosecutions, chief organized crime and racketeering sect. U.S. Atty.'s Office, 1992—94, chief criminal divsn., 1994—98; regional dir. Pacific Regional office SEC, L.A. and San Francisco, 1998—2001; counsel Simpson Thacher & Bartlett, N.Y.C., 2001—03; gen. counsel Office of Gen. Counsel, FBI, Washington, 2003—. Office: FBI J Edgar Hoover Bldg 935 Pennsylvania Ave NW Washington DC 20535-0001

CAPSHAW, KATE (KATHY SUE NAIL), actress; b. Ft. Worth, Nov. 3, 1953; m. John Capshaw (div.); 1 child: Jessica; m. Steven Spielberg, Oct. 12, 1991; children: Theo, Sasha, Sawyer, Mikaela, Destry. Student, U. Mo. Actress: (feature films) A Little Sex, 1982, Indiana Jones and the Temple of Doom, 1984, Best Defense, 1984, Dreamscape, 1984, Windy City, 1984, Power, 1986, Spacecamp, 1986, Ti Presento un'Amica, 1988, Black Rain, 1989, Love at Large, 1990, My Heroes Have Always Been Cowboys, 1991, Love Affair, 1994, Just Cause, 1995, How to Make an American Quilt, 1995, Duke of Groove, 1995, The Locusts, 1997, Life During Wartime, 1997, No Dogs Allowed, 1996; (TV series) The Edge of Night, Black Tie Affair, 1993, (TV movies) Missing Children: A Mother's Story, 1982, The Quick and the Dead, 1987, Her Secret Life, 1987, Internal Affairs, 1988, Next Door, 1994, Due East, 2002; (TV miniseries) A Girl Thing, 2001; actress, prodr.: The Love Letter, 1999. Mem. Screen Actors Guild, AFTRA. Office: Creative Artists Agy care Kevin Huvane 9830 Wilshire Blvd Beverly Hills CA 90212-1804

CAPSHAW, TOMMIE DEAN, judge; b. Oklahoma City, Sept. 20, 1936; m. Dian Shipp; 1 child, Charles W. BS in Bus., Oklahoma City U., 1958; postrad., U. Ark., 1958-59; JD, U. Okla., 1961. Bar: Okla. 1961-2000, Wyo. 1971, Ind. 1975. Assoc. Looney, Watts, Looney, Nichols and Johnson, Oklahoma City, 1961-63, Pierce, Duncan, Couch and Hendrickson, Oklahoma City, 1963-70; trial atty., v.p. Capshaw Well Service Co., Liberty Pipe and Supply Co., Casper, Wyo.; adminstrv. law judge Evansville, Ind., 1973-75, 96-99; hearing office chief adminstrv. law judge, 1975—96; acting regional chief adminstrv. law judge Chgo., 1977—78; sr. adminstrv. law judge, 1999—. Acting appeals coun. mem., Arlington, Va., 1980, acting chief adminstrv. law judge, 1984; mem. faculty U. Evansville, 1977, So. Ill. U. Sch. Law, 1988—, So. Ind. U., 1990; lectr. in field. Author: A Manual for Continuing Judicial Education, 1981, Practical Aspects of Handling Social Security Disability Claims, 1982, Judicial Practice Handbook, 1990, A Quest for Quality, Speedy Justice, 1991; contbr. numerous articles to profl. jours., chpt. to textbook. Adv. coun. Boy Scouts Am., scoutmaster, den leader, 1969—2003, Nat. Jud. Coll. U. Nev.; bd. dirs. Casper Symphony, 1972-73, Casper United Fund, 1972-73, Midget Football Assn., Casper, 1972-73, German Twp. Water Dist., 1984-85; pres. Evansville Unitarian Universalist Ch., 1984-86; performer Evansville Philharm. Orch., 1986-98; bd. dirs. German Twp. Vol. Fire Dept., 1998-2003, vol. Hospice, 2000—. Recipient Kappa Alpha Order Ct. of Honor award, 1962, Silver Beaver award Boy Scouts Am., 1980, presentation for vol. svc. contbg. betterment of cmty. Office Hearings and Appeals, 1992, presentation outstanding jud. mentor tng. Supreme Ct. Iowa, 1992, presentation disting. mentor tng. Fla. Jud. Ctl., 1992, Robert V. Pagant award Nat. Jud. Coll., 2002. Mem. Okla. Bar Assn., Okla. County Bar Assn. (v.p. 1967), Wyo. Bar Assn., Evansville Bar Assn. (jud. rep. 1986-87, James Bethel Gresham Freedom award 1988), Young Lawyers Assn., Assn. Adminstrv. Law Judges HHS (bd. dirs. 1979-82, Tic Vickery award 1998), Oklahoma City U. Alumni Assn. (bd. dirs. 1965). Home: 6105 School Rd # 6 Evansville IN 47720

CAPUANO, MICHAEL EVERETT, congressman, lawyer; b. Somerville, Mass., Jan. 9, 1952; s. Andrew and Rita (Garvey) C.; m. Barbara Teebagy, 1974; children: Michael, Joseph. BA in Psychology, Dartmouth Coll., 1973; JD, Boston Coll., 1977; postgrad., Boston U. Bar: Mass. 1977. Former atty. Mass. Legislative Aide; Alderman Ward 5 Somerville, 1977-79; alderman-at-large, 1985-89; mayor, 1990-99; congressman 8th Dist. Mass., 1999—. Mem. Ho. Dem. Leadership team (regional whip), com. fin. svcs., subcoms. on Captial Mkts., Securities and Govt. Sponsored Enterprises, banking subcom. housing and cmty. mem. Ho. Dem. steering and policy com., com. transp. and infrastructure, subcom. allocation, hwys. and transit and aviation. Democrat. Office: US Ho of Reps 1530 Longworth House Office Bldg Washington DC 20515-2108 also: Dist Office 110 First St Cambridge MA 02141*

CAPUTE, COURTNEY G., lawyer; b. Granville, Ohio, Sept. 20, 1977; BA, Ohio Wesleyan U., 1977; JD, U. Md., 1986. Bar: Md. 1987. Ptnr., Real Estate Dept, Comm. Dept. Venable LLP, Balt., compensation com., assoc. evaluation com., chiar, partnership selection com. Notes & comments editor Md. Law Rev., 1985—86. Pres. Turnaround Inc., Balt.; pro bono counsel Manna House, Balt. Mem.: ABA, Md. State Bar Assn., Bar Assn. Balt. City. Office: Venable LLP 1800 Mercantile Bank & Trust Bldg 2 Hopkins Plz Baltimore MD 21201 Office Phone: 410-244-7531. Office Fax: 410-244-7742. Business E-Mail: cgcapute@venable.com.

CAPUTO, ANNE SPENCER, knowledge and learning programs director; b. Eugene, Oreg., Jan. 14, 1947; d. Richard J. and Adelaide Bernice (Marsh) Spencer; m. Richard Philip Caputo, July 15, 1977 (dec. Sept. 1997); 1 child: Christopher Spencer Caputo. BA in History, Lewis and Clark Coll., Portland, Oreg., 1969; MA, U. Oreg., 1971; MALS, San Jose State U., 1976. Librarian San Jose State U., Calif., 1972-76; online instr. DIALOG Info. Svcs., Palo Alto, Calif., 1976-77, chief info. scientist Washington, 1977-85, mgr. classroom instrn. program, 1986-89, dir. acad. programs, 1990-96; sr. dir. prof. devel. Knight-Ridder Info., Arlington, Va., 1996-97; sr. dir. acad. and profl. market devel. The Dialog Corp., Arlington, 1998; dir. info. pro and acad. programs Factiva, Washington, 1998—. Asst. prof. info. sci. Cath. U. Am., Washington, 1978—2000; online cons. Nat. Com. Library-Info. Sci., Washington, 1980—82; adj. prof. U. Md. Coll. Info. Studies, 2000—. Author: Brief Guide to DIALOG Searching, 1979; contbr. articles to profl. jours. Named Info. Sci. Tchr. of Yr. Catholic U. Am., 1983; recipient Rose Vormelker award, 2004. Mem.: ALA, Am. Assn. Sch. Librarians, D.C. Library Assn., Am. Soc. for Info. Sci. (chair Potomac Valley chpt. 1985—86, officer), Spl. Library Assn. (pres. 2002, bd. dirs. 2005—, Rose Vormalker award 2004). Episcopalian. Avocation: photographing architectural details on national trust buildings. Home: 4113 Orleans Pl Alexandria VA 22304-1618 Office: Factiva Ste 300 1600 K St NW Washington DC 20006 E-mail: anne.caputo@factiva.com.

CAPUTO, DANIEL VINCENT, psychologist; b. N.Y.C. s. Pasquale and Hortense C. AB, Bklyn. Coll., 1954; PhD, U. Ill., 1961. Registered psychologist, Nat. Register of Health Providers in Psychology; lic. psychologist, N.Y. Prof. med. psychology Wash. U., St. Louis, 1959-64; prof. psychology Queens Coll., CUNY, Flushing, 1964—, prof. emeritus, 1998—, chair dept. psychology, 1974-77; rsch. assoc. St. Vincent's Med. Ctr., S.I., N.Y. Pvt. practice clin. psychology, 1973—. Contbr. to Infants Born at Risk, 1979, Pre-term Birth: Relevance to Optimal Psychological Development, 1981, Multivariate Analysis of the Type A Personality, 1981. Rsch. grantee NIMH, 1963. Fellow N.Y. Acad. Scis.; mem. APA, Eastern Psychol. Assn., N.Y. State Psychol. Assn. (rep. exec. com. 1981-83), Biofeedback Soc. Am. (cert.). Roman Catholic. Office: 16-07 150th St Whitestone NY 11357-2545 also: Queens Coll Dept Psychology Kissena Blvd Flushing NY 11367 Office Phone: 718-746-5868. Personal E-mail: drdvcaputo@nyc.rr.com.

CAPUTO, DAVID ARMAND, academic administrator, political scientist, educator; b. Brownsville, Pa., Aug. 30, 1943; s. Armand and Marie E. (Smalstig) C.; m. Alice M. Glotfelty, June 27, 1964; children— Christopher, Elizabeth, Jeffrey. BA, Miami U., Oxford, Ohio, 1965; MA, Yale U., 1967, MPhil, 1968, PhD, 1970. Mem. faculty Purdue U., 1969—, prof. polit. sci., 1977—, head dept., 1978-87, dean Sch. Liberal Arts, 1987-95; pres. Hunter Coll., CUNY, N.Y.C., 1995-2000, Pace U., N.Y.C., 2000—. Author: Urban America: The Policy Alternatives, 1976; co-author: Urban Politics and Decentralization, 1974; editor: Politics of Policy-Making in America, 1977. Trustee Madison Ave. Presbyn. Ch., N.Y.C., 2000—03; ruling elder Ctrl. Presbyn. Ch., Lafayette, Ind., 1981—87. Woodrow Wilson nat. fellow, 1965-66; NSF faculty fellow, 1977; Fulbright fellow, Italy, 1985; Lilly fellow, 1985; Bologna chair Fulbright sr. fellow, Italy, 1993. Mem. Am. Polit. Sci. Assn., Am. Soc. Public Adminstrn., Midwest Polit. Sci. Assn., So. Polit. Sci. Assn., Phi Beta Kappa, Omicron Delta Kappa. Office: Pace Univ One Pace Plz New York NY 10038 Office Phone: 212-346-1097. Business E-Mail: president@pace.edu.

CAPUTO, GREGORY MICHAEL, internist, educator; b. May 18, 1954; s. Joseph Vincent and Mary (Pisapia) C.; m. Leesa, June 10, 1978; children: Jennifer, Michael. BA in Biol. Sci., U. Del., 1976; MD, U. Md., 1980. Diplomate Am. Bd. Internal Medicine, Am. Bd. Infectious Disease. Intern Thomas Jefferson U. Hosp., Phila., 1980-81, clin. asst. prof. dept. medicine, 1987-90; resident Milton S. Hershey Med. Ctr., Pa. State U. Coll. Medicine, Hershey, Pa., 1981-83, fellow divsn. infectious diseases, 1983-84; from asst. prof. to prof. medicine Pa. State U., Hershey, 1990-98, prof., 1998—; chief divsn. gen. internal medicine Milton S. Hershey Med. Ctr., Hershey, Pa., 1996—2004, vice-chair dept. medicine, 2002—04, interim chiaR dept. emergency medicine, 2004—. Mem. staff Med. Ctr. Del., Wilmington, 1990—95, Alfred I. duPont Med. Ctr., 1990—, med. dir. diabetes amputation prevention program, 1993—99; dir. Cecil County Lyme Disease Clinic, Elkton, 1988—90; cons. Assn. Acad. Health Ctrs., Am. Lyme Disease Found., 1992—; vis. scholar Johns Hopkins Ctr. Preventive Cardiology, 2001—02; lectr. in field. Author: (chpt.) Comprehensive Textbook of Pulmonary Medicine, 1991, The Foot in Diabetes, 2d edit., 1994; co-author: (chpt.) Comprehensive Textbook Pulmonary Medicine Update, 1995, (computer program) The Prevention Guides for Clinicians and Patients, 1996; co-editor: Medical Consultation, 1997; reviewer New Eng. Jour. Medicine, Internal Medicine Jour., Clin. Infectious Diseases, Diabetes Care; contbr. articles to profl. jours. Recipient Fletcher Brown award, 1975, Disting. Physician award, 1995; Harvard Med. Sch. fellow, 1984-85, C. Everett Koop Inst. fellow Dartmouth Coll., 1996, 97; Ellis scholar, 1976, vis. scholar Johns Hopkins Med. Instns., 2001-02. Fellow ACP; mem. Am. Soc. Microbiology, Soc. Gen. Internal Medicine, Am. Diabetes Assn., Phi Beta Kappa, Phi Kappa Phi, Beta Beta Beta, Alpha Omega Alpha. Avocations: music, tennis, hiking. Office: Milton S Hershey MC Divsn Gen Int Med MC HU15 500 University Dr Hershey PA 17033

CAPUTO, KATHRYN MARY, paralegal; b. Bklyn., N.Y., June 29, 1948; d. Fortunato and Agnes (Iovino) Villacci; m. Joseph John Caputo, Apr. 4, 1976. AS in Bus. Adminstrn., Nassau C.C., Garden City, N.Y., 1989. Legal asst. Jacob Jacobson, Oceanside, NY, 1973—77; legal asst., office mgr. Joseph Kaldor, P.C., Franklin Square, 1978—82, William H. George, Valley Stream, 1983—89; exec. legal asst., office adminstr. Katz & Bernstein, Westbury, 1990—93; sr. paralegal and office adminstr. Blaustein & Weinick, Garden City, NY, 1993—2004, Mark R. Blaustein, P.C., 2004—. Instr. adult continuing edn. legal sec. procedures Lawrence (N.Y.) H.S., 1992—. Spl. events coord. Bklyn.-Queens Marriage Encounter, 1981, 82, 83, 85, 86; mem. Lynbrook Civic Assn., St. Raymond's R.C. Ch. Pastoral Coun., 1999-2002, sec. 2000-02, Renew 2000, mem. rev. bd.; mem. St. Vincent DePaul Soc., sec., 2001—. Mem. L.I. Paralegal Assn. Avocations: travel, reading, theater, gardening. Office: Mark R Blaustein PC 1205 Franklin Ave Garden City NY 11530-1629 Office Phone: 516-248-5800. E-mail: kacapbwparalgl@hotmail.com.

CAPUTO, LISA M., finance company executive; b. Wilkes-Barre, Pa. d. A. Richard and Rosemary (Shea) C. BA in French and Polit. Sci. magna cum laude, Brown U., 1986; MS in Journalism with highest honors, Northwestern U., 1987. Press sec., fed. grants coord. U.S. Rep. Bob Traxler, Washington, 1987-89; press sec. nat. issues Dukakis-Bentsen Campaign, Boston, 1988; press sec. U.S. Senator Tim Wirth, Washington, 1989-92; dir. vice presdl. media ops. Dem. Nat. Conv., N.Y.C., 1992; press sec. to Hillary Rodham Clinton Clinton-Gore Campaign and Presdl. Transition, Little Rock, 1992; dep. asst. to Pres., press sec. to First Lady The White House, Washington, 1993-96; v.p. corporate comm. CBS, 1996—98; v.p., global comm. and synergy Disney Pub. Worldwide, 1998—99; pres., CEO, Women and Co. Citigroup Inc., 2000—, mng. dir., bus. ops. and planning, global consumer div., 2003—05; sr. mng. dir. bus. ops. and planning Globe Consumer Group, 2005—. Contbg. editor George Mag., 1997—2000; co-host, Crossfire CNN; co-host, Equal Time CNBC, MSNBC; mem. Coun. Foreign Relations, Fin. Women's Assn. Office: Citigroup Inc 399 Park Ave New York NY 10022

CAPUTO, LUCIO, trade company executive; b. Monreale, Italy, May 22, 1935; arrived in U.S., 1967; s. Giuseppe and Gioacchina C.; m. Maria Luisa Mayr, Oct. 5, 1967; 1 child, Giorgio. Law degree, Palermo U., 1957, journalism degree, 1958, degree in polit. sci., 1960, postgrad. in econs., 1961. Bar: Italy, 1961. Journalist, Italy, 1950—65; assoc. Studio Legale Caputo-Orlando, Palermo, Italy, 1960—62; ofcl. Italian Fgn. Trade Inst., 1962—82; market rschr. Libya, Cyprus, 1963; dep. trade commr. London, 1964—67; dir. study mission S.E. Asia, 1967; Italian trade commr. Phila., 1967—71, N.Y.C., 1972—82; founder Italian Wine Promotion Ctr., N.Y.C., 1975—, Italian Tile Ctr., N.Y.C., 1979—, Italian Fashion Ctr., N.Y.C., 1980—, Italian Shoe Ctr., N.Y.C., 1981—, ITAL Trade Ctr., N.Y.C., 1981—. Pres. Ital Trade USA Corp., 1982-86, Italian Wine and Food Inst., 1984—; organizer ann. Italian Week on 5th Ave., NYC; pres., bd. dirs. Gruppo Esponenti Italiani, 1974—. Signer agreement between Italy and People's Republic of China, 1967; editor trade mags.: Italy Presents, Quality (English, French, Spanish, German), 1962-64; contbr. articles to popular mags. and newspapers. Adv. bd. mem. Italy-Am. C. of C., 1972-82; U.S. rep. Verona Fair Orgn., 1980—; chmn. Internat. Trade Ctr., Inc., 1987—; exec. dir. Gruppo Ristoratori Italiani, 1988-90; vice-chmn., bd. dirs. Nat. Wine Coalition, 1990-95; chmn. bd. dirs. European Wine Coun., 1993—, chmn. bus. adv. coun. for gov., 1996—; adv. coun. Princeton U.; Lt. Italian Air Force, 1959-61. Named Cavaliere Ufficiale nell'Ordine al Merito della Republica Italiana, 1972, Commendatore, 1981, Grande Ufficiale, 1996, Cavaliere di Gran Croce, 2003. Mem. Sommelier Soc. Am., Italian Sommelier Soc., Italian Bar Assn., Italian Journalist Assn., Fgn. Consular Assn. Phila., Soc. Fgn. Consuls NY, Am. Soc. Italian Legions of Merit (chmn. bd. dirs.), Assn. Pres. of Maj. Italian-Am. Orgns. (sec., bd. dirs.), NIAF (bd. dirs., 2005—). Office: Lincoln Bldg 60 E 42d St Ste 1341 New York NY 10165 Mailing: PO Box 789 New York NY 10150 Office Phone: 212-867-4111. Office Fax: 212-867-4114. Business E-Mail: iwfi@aol.com.

CAPUTO, PHILIP JOSEPH, writer, journalist; b. Chgo., June 10, 1941; s. Joseph and Marie Ylonda (Napolitan) C.; m. Jill Esther Ongemach, June 21, 1969 (div. 1982); children: Geoffrey Jacob, Marc Antony.; m. Marcelle Lynn Besse, Oct. 30, 1982 (div. 1985); m. Leslie Blanchard Ware, June 4, 1988. BA in English, Loyola U., Chgo., 1964. Mem. staff Chgo. Tribune, 1968-72; fgn. corr. Europe, Middle East, USSR, 1972-77; freelance writer, 1977—. Author: A Rumor of War, 1977, Horn of Africa, 1980, Del Corso's Gallery, 1983, Indian Country, 1987, Means of Escape, 1991, Equation for Evil, 1996, Exiles, 1997, The Voyage, 1999, Ghosts of Tsavo, 2002, Acts of Faith, 2005, 13 Seconds: A Look Back at the Kent State Shootings, 2005; contbr. to N.Y. Times, L.A. Times, Boston Globe, Nat. Geog. Adventure, others. Served with USMCR, 1964-67, Vietnam. Recipient award Ill. AP, Ill. United Press award, Green Gavel award ABA, Overseas Press Club award, Pulitzer prize, Sidney Hillman award, others. Mem. Authors Guild. Democrat. Roman Catholic. Address: care Aaron Priest Lit Agy 708 3rd Ave New York NY 10017-4201*

CARABALLO, BEATRICE MARIA, preservationist; b. Camden, NJ, Aug. 11, 1969; d. Antonio Juan and Maria Antonia Sanabria; m. Edgardo Lopéz (dec.); children: Daniel E. Lopéz, Christina M. Lopéz; m. Juan Antonio Caraballo, Feb. 26, 1991; 1 child, Crystal A. Ambassador South Performing Arts Ctr.; producer, co-host Radio Unika 1270AM. Cons. PNS Corp.; coord. Regional Puerto Rican Festivals & Parades Conf., 2005. Author: (books) Reminiscences of Camden Roots, New Jersey Safe Deposit & Trust Co. Confidential aide Camden City Council, NJ, Woodlynne City Council, Woodlynne; mem. South Jersey Minority C. of C. Recipient Proclamation, Cumberland County, Senator Asselta Citation, Assembly Commendation. Mem.: Legacy Landmarks, Latino Profl. Network. Democrat. Achievements include preservation of the New Jersey Safe Deposit & Trust Co. offshore performance association. Avocation: poetry. Home: 103 Cedar Ave Camden NJ 08101 Office: San Juan Bautista Parade Inc PO Box Camden NJ 08101

CARABALLO, DIMAS J., music educator; b. Habana, Cuba, Oct. 3, 1962; arrived in U.S., 1967; s. Jose Caraballo and Marta Suarez. AA in piano performance, Broward Cmty. Coll.; BA in piano performance, U Miami; MusM, U Mich. Vis. assoc. prof. of Dance in the Dance Dept. U Mich., Ann Arbor, 1996—99; Master Instr. Piano Pvt. Practice. Adjudicator, The Northe Am. Internat. Invitational Piano Competition, The Mich. Music Tchr. Assoc. Piano Examinations, The Vivace Piano Competition, The Nat. Fedn. of Music Clubs Piano Solo Div., The Margaret Denise Scholarship Competition; guest artist to raise money for Nat. Philippino Nurses Assn. Annual Scholarship Fund; guest artist Plymouth Symphony, Plymouth, Mich. Co-dir.: (ballets) The Netherlands Dance Co. - Jiri Kylian, Master, The Gyori Ballet Gyori Nenzeti Szinhaz Theatre Annual Concert, The Dance Theater of Harlem, The Am. Ballet Theater of N.Y. Recipient First Place, Southeast Fla. Chopin Competition, Annual Fort Lauderdale Piano Concerto Competition, Mich. Music Tchr. Assn. Collegiate Level State Competition, Germania Piano Concerto Competition, Finalist, Young Keyboard Artist Competition. Master: Am. Music Guild; mem.: Music Nat. Tchr. Assn. (assoc.), Mich. Music Tchr. Assn. (assoc.). Home: 44105 Lee Ann Lane S Canton MI 48187

CARABIAS LILLO, JULIA, government official; b. Mexico City, Mex., 1954; BA, MA, Nat. Autonomous, 1981. Sec. Environ., Natural Resources & Fisheries, Mexico, 1998—2000. Prof. sci. Nat. Autonomous U., 1981, U. Coun. UNAM, 1989-93, 2000—; pres. Nat. Ecol. Inst.; mem. Coun. Nat. Solidarity Program; mem. adv. coun. Nat. Conservation Fund. Recipient 23rd Annual J. Paul Getty Wildlife Conservation prize, WWF, 2001, Internat. Cosmos prize, 2004. Office: Nat Autonomous U Mexico Av Universidad 3000 Circuito Escolar Ciu 04510 Mexico

CARACO, VIRGINIA, artist; b. Gloversville, N.Y., Aug. 31, 1951; d. Fred Ernest and Evelyn Eve (Franko) Marshall; m. Joseph Charles Caraco, Oct. 16, 1970; 1 child, Donald Joseph cert. indsl. drafting, cert. archtl. drafting, Trident Tech. Coll., 1970. Edn. coord. Hist. Camden (S.C.) Revolutionary War Site, artist in residence, herbalist on site. Exhbns. include Fine Art Ctr. of Kershaw County, 1985-2005, Canty Bldg. S.C. State Fair, 1994-99, Sumter Galley of Art, 1981-85, Nations Bank, Aug., 1985. Chmn. NBSC Oil Painter's Invitational, Sumter Gallery Art, 1983-86; exhbn. com. chmn. Fine Art Ctr., Camden, S.C., 1986-89; pres. Sumter Art Guild, 1983-84, v.p., 1984-85; chmn. Congl. Art Comp., 1983; chmn. Iris Festival, Fine Arts Swan Lake Gardens, Sumter, 1984. Named Artist of Month, Sumter Art Gallery, 1985. Mem. Camden Art Assn. (v.p. 1986-87, pres. 1994-95), Colored Pencil Soc. Am., S.C. Watercolor Soc., Trenholm Art Guild, Artist Attic Coop. Gallery, Camden Art Assn. (v.p., corr. sec. 2004-05). Avocations: needlepoint design, writer, gardener. Home: Cedar Cottage 200 Poplar Ln Camden SC 29020-1612 Office Phone: 808-432-9841. E-mail: caracov@yahoo.com.

CARALEY, DEMETRIOS JAMES, political science professor, writer; b. NYC, June 22, 1932; s. Christopher and Stella (Psaras) C.; children (from previous marriage): James Christopher (dec.), David Andrew, Anne Leslie; m. Vilma Mairo Bornemann; 1 child, Lisa Anne. BA summa cum laude, Columbia U., 1954, MPhil, PhD, 1962. Mem. faculty Barnard Coll. and Columbia U., N.Y.C., 1959—, prof. polit. sci., 1968—, Janet H. Robb prof. social scis., 1980—; editor Polit. Sci. Quar., 1973—; dir. Grad. Program in Pub. Policy and Adminstrn. Columbia U., 1978-85, chmn. Barnard dept. polit. sci., 1965-95; pres. Acad. Polit. Sci., 1992—. Vis. scholar Russell Sage Found., 1995-96. Author: Politics of Military Unification, 1966, New York City's Deputy Mayor & City Administrator, 1966, Party Politics and National Elections, 1966, (with R. H. Connery) Governing the City, 1969, City Governments and Urban Problems, 1977, American Political Institutions in the 1970's, 1976, (with M.A. Epstein) The Making of American Foreign and Domestic Policy, 1978, Doing More With Less, 1982, (with R. H. Connery) National Security and Nuclear Strategy, 1983, The President's War Powers, 1984, Volatilities in the New World Politics, 1993, Critical Issues for Clinton's Domestic Agenda, 1994, (with B.B. Hartman) American Leadership, Ethnic Conflict, and the New World Politics, 1997, The New American Interventionism, 1999, September 11, Terrorist Attacks and US. Foreign Policy, 2002, American Hegemony: Preventive War, Iraq, and Imposing Democracy, 2004; contbr. American Politics and Public Policy, 1978, Urban Policymaking, 1979. Mem. North Tarrytown Zoning Bd. Appeals, 1970-71; mem. North Tarrytown Bd. Trustees, 1971-73, dep. mayor and acting mayor, 1972-73; chmn. North Tarrytown Planning Bd., 1977-79. Served with USNR, 1954-56. Mem. Am. Polit. Sci. Assn., Acad. Polit. Sci. (bd. dirs., pres. 1992—), Phi Beta Kappa. Club: University (N.Y.C.). Democrat. Office: Columbia Univ Barnard Coll Dept Polit Sci New York NY 10027 also: Acad Polit Sci/Polit Sci Quar 475 Riverside Dr Ste 1274 New York NY 10115-1299 Office Phone: 212-870-2500. Business E-Mail: dc121@columbia.edu. E-mail: editors@psgonline.org.

CARAM, DOROTHY FARRINGTON, educational consultant; b. McAllen, Tex., Jan. 14, 1933; d. Curtis Leon and Elena (Santander) Farrington; m. Pedro C. Caram, June 7, 1958 (dec. Aug. 2000); children: Pedro M., Juan D., Hector L., Jose M. BA, Rice U., 1955, MA, 1974; EdD, U. Houston, 1982; postgrad., U. Madrid, 1957. Tchr. Houston Ind. Sch. Dist., 1955-56, 56-60, St. Mark's Episcopal Ch., Houston, 1964-65; substitute tchr. St. Vincent De Paul Cath. Sch., Houston, 1965-68; mgr. med. office Houston, 1983; dir. Fed. Home Loan Bank, Little Rock, 1976-82; pres. Inst. Hispanic Culture, Houston, 1983, 93, chmn. bd., pres., 1984; with Houston Ednl. Excellence Program, 1980. Mem. task force Tex. Edn. Agy., 1981-83; adv.

coun. Nat. Inst. Neurol. and Communicative Disorders and Stroke, 1972-76; pres. IDM Satellite Comm. of Tex. Divsn., Inc., 1990, chmn. bd., 1998—99 asst. to pres. U. Houston, 1991-94, ret., 1994. Mem. coun. Miller Theater, Houston, 1976—, adv. bd. emeritus, 2000-; bd. dirs. Houston Pops, 1983-87, United Way Tex., 1991-94; mem. task force Quality Integrated Edn., Houston, 1972; bd. dirs. United Way Tex., Gulf Coast, 1989-95, exec. bd., sec.; mem. Civil Commn. Houston, 1983-85; bd. mgrs. Harris County Hosp. Dist., 1988-90, emeritus, 2005; founder, bd. dirs. Houston Hispanic Forum, 1985, pres., 1989-90; chmn. bd. Teatro Bilingue de Houston, 1989-90; pres. Mexican Cultural Inst. Houston, Inc., 1997; bd. dirs. Southmain Ctr. Assn., 1998-2005, Harris County Hosp. Dist. Found., 1997—, Houston Ind. Sch. Dist. Found., 1996-2002, chmn. peer com. magnet and vanguard schs., 1996-2002; adv. bd. Theater Under Stars, Career and Recovery, Jobs for Progress of Tex. Gulf Coast, Inc., AAMA; bd. dirs. Majestic Seas Aquarium, 1998-99, Houston CC Found., 2004—, U. St. Thomas, 2004—; bd. dirs., treas. Colonial Homes Found. for Youth, 1999; mem. Mil. and Hospitler Order of St. Lazarus of Jerusalem, 1982-; pres. Braes Rep. Women, 2002-2003, precinct judge, 1998—; v.p. edn. bd. Houston Grand Opera, 2001-05; commr. Commn. of Arts State of Tex., 2004—; rice alumni 50th graduation com., 2001-05, alumni council U. Houston, 2003. Recipient Willie Velasquez Outstanding Hispanic Citizenship award, 1994, Dorothy F. Caram Leadership award Blueprint-United Way Tex. Gulf Coast, 2000-02, Woman of Vision award Delta Gamma Found., 2003; named Vol. of Yr., United Way Tex. Gulf Coast, 1992, Outstanding Alumnus, Coll. Edn. U. Houston, 2000, Rice U., 2005; decorated Lady in Court of Isabel La Catolica by King Carlos (Spain), 1984; Oustanding Sr. fellow Am. Leadership Forum, 2004. Mem. Cedars Club (pres. 1978). Roman Catholic. Home: 2603 Glen Haven Blvd Houston TX 77025-2132 Personal E-mail: dcaram@worldnet.att.net.

CARAM, EVE LA SALLE, language educator, writer; b. Hot Springs, Ark., May 11, 1934; d. Raymond Briggs and Lois Elizabeth (Merritt) La Salle; m. Richard George Caram, Apr. 19, 1965 (div. Apr. 1978); 1 child, Bethel Eve. *Mother, Lois Merritt La Salle, pianist, with Gov. Tom Terrell and singer Ruth Stearns, opened the first radio station in Arkansas on New Year's Eve, 1921. Daughter, Bethel Eve, actress/writer, living in New York City with partner Neil Potter, writes and performs in their comedy shows, most recently, "The Grey Area."* BA, Bard Coll., 1956; MA, U. Mo., 1977. English instr. Stephens Coll., Columbia, Mo., 1974,79-82; fiction writing grad. instr. Sch. Profl. Writing U. So. Calif., L.A., 1982-87; English lit. and writing instr. Calif. State U., Northridge, 1983—; sr. fiction writing instr. The Writers' Program UCLA, 1983—. Fiction contest judge Calif. State U., Long Beach, 1992, 94, writer's conf. spkr., 1985-87, 94; spkr., mem. panel Tex. Am. Studies Assn., Wichita Falls, 1998. *Forthcoming publications include a novel, The Blue Geography, a novella, Looking for Johnny, and a story collection, Eight Stories. She is preparing another novel for publication entitled Rushes From Girlhood, which was written in her youth. She has also begun writing a memoir about her reading.* Author: Dear Corpus Christi, 1991, 2d edit., 2000, Wintershine, 1994, Rena, A Late Journey, 2000; editor: Palm Readings, Stories from Southern California, 1998; fiction editor West/Word, 1991. Mem.: AAUP, Assn. Calif. State Profs., Nat. Assn. Tchrs. English, Poets and Writers, PEN Ctr. U.S.A. West, Inst. Noetic Scis., Green Peace. Democrat. Avocations: swimming, beach walks, outdoors. Home: 3400 Ben Lomond Pl Apt 121 Los Angeles CA 90027-2952 Office: UCLA Ext The Writers' Program 10995 Le Conte Ave Los Angeles CA 90095-3001 also: Calif State U English Dept 1811 Nordoff Northridge CA 91330-0001 E-mail: ecaram1@earthlink.net.

CARAMAZZA, ALFONSO, psychology professor; b. Aragona, Agrigento, Italy, June 22, 1946; arrived in U.S., 1971; s. Carmelo and Emma (Zammuto) C.; children: Pierre, Simone, Francesca. BA in Psychology, McGill U., Montreal, Can., 1970; MA, Johns Hopkins U., 1972, PhD, 1974; Doctor (hon.), U. Catholique de Louvain, Belgium, 1993. From asst. prof. to assoc. prof. Johns Hopkins U., Balt., 1974-81, prof., 1981-93, chair, 1987-92; David T. McLaughlin Disting. prof. Dartmouth Coll., Hanover, N.H., 1993-95; prof. Harvard U., 1995—, Daniel and Amy Starch prof. psychology, 2002—. Lectr. in field. Author: (with E. Zurif) The Acquisition and Breakdown of Language: Parallels and Divergencies, 1978, Cognitive Neuropsychology and Neurolinguistics in Models of Cognitive Function and Impairment, 1990, Issues in Reading Writing and Speaking: A Neuropsychological Perspective, 1991; mem. editl. bd. Cognitive Neurosci., 1998, Cognitive Brain Rsch., 1991, Cortex, 1981, others; contbr. articles to profl. jours., chpts. to books. Recipient Javits Neuroscience Investigator award NIH, J.L. Signoret Prize in Biology. Home: 28 Marshall St Brookline MA 02446-5468 Office: Harvard Univ Dept Psychology William James Hall Cambridge MA 02138

CARAPEZZI, WILLIAM R., JR., lawyer; BA acctg., Fairfield U., 1979; JD, Western New England Sch. Law; LLM taxation, NYU Sch. Law. Conn. pub. acct. Tax mgr. Arthur Andersen & Co., Hartford, Conn., 1983—89; treas. AT&T, sr. tax atty., 1989—98; v.p., Global Tax & Trade Lucent Technologies Inc., sr. v.p., gen. counsel, corp. sec., 1998—. Conn. Bar Assn., ABA, Conn. Society CPA's. Office: Lucent Technologies Inc 600 Mountain Ave New Providence NJ 07974-0636

CARASSO, ALFRED SAM, mathematician; b. Alexandria, Egypt, Apr. 9, 1939; arrived in US, 1962; s. Samuel and Renee (Ades) Carasso; m. Beatrice Kozak, June 12, 1964; children: Adam Leonard, Rachel Lisa. BSc in Physics, U. Adelaide, Australia, 1960; PhD in Math., U. Wis., 1968. Meteorologist Bur. Meteorology, Adelaide, 1960-62; rsch. asst. grad. sch. U. Wis., Madison, 1962-68; asst. prof. math. Mich. State U., East Lansing, 1968-69, U. N.Mex., Albuquerque, 1969-72, assoc. prof., 1972-76, prof., 1976-81; mathematician Nat. Inst. Standards and Tech., Gaithersburg, Md., 1982—. Vis staff mem Los Alamos Nat Lab, N.Mex., 1972—81; cons. Inst Def Analyses's Ctr Computing Scis, 1996—2003. Contbr. articles to profl jours. Mem.: Soc Indust and Applied Math, Am Math Soc, Cosmos Club. Jewish. Achievements include significant contributions to the deconvolution problem; and to such related areas of mathematical analysis as ill-posed continuation, time-reversed parabolic equations, holomorphic semigroup theory, and first kind integral equations; invention of slowly divergent schemes and backward beam formalism for solving inverse diffusion equations; invention of APEX and BEAK methods in blind image deconvolution; development of slow evolution constraint for extensive class of ill-posed PDE problems; creation of singular integral method in Lipschitz space characterization of non smooth imagery; applications in system identification, nondestructive evaluation, inverse heat transfer, image reconstruction; discovery of useful property of heavy-tailed Lévy stable laws in blind deconvolution of wide classes of images, including Hubble space telescope, Landsat, and electron microscope imagery, MRI and PET brain scans; patented image reconstruction procedures. Office: Nat Inst Stds and Tech Math & Computational Scis Gaithersburg MD 20899-0001 E-mail: alfred.carasso@nist.gov.

CARAVAN, RONALD L., music educator, composer; b. Pottsville, Pa., Nov. 20, 1946; s. Vincent R. and Isabelle Slater Caravan; m. Nancy Carol Nelsen, June 28, 1989; children: Michelle, Adrienne, Lisa. BS in music edn., State U. of NY, 1968; MA in music theory, Eastman Sch. of Music, 1973, MusD in music edn., 1974. Cert. clarinet performance NY, 1974. Music prof. State U. NY, Potsdam, NY, 1975—76, Oswego, NY, 1977—78, Fredonia, NY, 1978—79, Syracuse U., Syracuse, NY, 1980—; writer, editor The Valley News, Fulton, NY, 1974—. Pres. No. Am. Saxophone Alliance, 1986—88, jour. editor, 1978—84; woodwind review editor NY State Sch. Music Assn., 1986—. Contbr. articles various prof. jour.;, composer mus. compositions, pedagogic collections, and music arrangements. With U.S. Army, 1968—70. Recipient Amy Writing award, The Amy Found., 2000, 2001. Mem.: NY Press Assn. Home: PO Box 376 Phoenix NY 13135 Office: Syracuse U Setnor Sch of Music Syracuse NY 13244 Office Phone: 315-598-6397. E-mail: rlcarava@syr.edu.

CARAVATT, PAUL JOSEPH, JR., communications executive; b. New Britain, Conn., Dec. 13, 1922; s. Paul Joseph and Bessie (Avery) C.; m. B. Laura Bennett, June 22, 1946; children— Cynthia Diane, Suzanne Laura. AB, Dartmouth, 1945, MBA, 1947. With Nat. Dairy Assn., 1947-49, Young & Rubicam, 1949-50; advt. mgr. Hunting and Fishing mag., 1950-52, Biow Co., 1952-56; v.p. Ogilvy, Benson & Mather, 1956-59; sr. v.p. Foote, Cone & Belding, 1960-64, LaRoche, McCaffrey & McCall (advt. agy.), N.Y.C., 1964-66; pres. Carl Ally, Ind. (advt. agy.), N.Y.C., 1966-67; chmn. bd., chief exec. officer Marschalk Co., Inc. (mem. Interpublic Group of Cos.), N.Y.C., 1967-69; sr. v.p., dir. Interpub. Group Cos., N.Y.C., 1970-72; pres., chief exec. officer, dir. Caravatt Communications, 1971-86, Newtel World Communications, N.Y.C., 1971-86; pres., chief exec. officer Caravatt Mktg., Wilton, Conn., 1986—; pres. Caravatt Mktg. Group, 1998—. Exec. dir. Vision Fund, The Lighthouse, 1994—97. Mem. SAR, Spl. Interest Video Assn. (pres., exec. dir. 1988-97), Newcomen Soc., Univ. Club (N.Y.C.), Ednl. Found. of Spl. Interest Marketers and Prodrs. (pres. 1997—), Zeta Psi. Congregationalist. Home: 512 Burr Rd Southbury CT 06488 Office Phone: 203-762-0162. Personal E-mail: caramktg@sbcglobal.net.

CARBAUGH, JOHN EDWARD, JR., lawyer; b. Greenville, S.C., Sept. 4, 1945; s. John Edward and Mary Lou (McCarley) C.; m. Mary Middleton Calhoun: children: John, Martha, Leacy, Miller. BA, U. of South, 1967; JD, U. S.C., 1973, postgrad., 1967-69, Georgetown U., 1977-79. Bar: S.C. 1973, U.S. Ct. Appeals (4th cir.) 1982, U.S. Supreme Ct. 1982. With White House Staff, Washington, 1969-70; campaign dir. re-elect Thurmond campaign Washington, 1970-73; legis. asst. U.S. Senate, Washington, 1974-82; pvt. practice Washington, 1982—. Bd. dirs. Westech. Internat., Inc., Washington Watch, Inc., Splty. Materials and Mfg., Inc., Tech. Holdings, Inc., The Stealth Corp., Inc.; mem. Pres. Commn. on Econ. Justice, Washington, 1985-87 Author: The Revisionists, 1991, We Need Each Other: U.S.-Japan Relations Approach the 21st Century, 1992; co-author: A Program for Military Independence, 1980; contbr. articles to profl. jours. Rep. Nat. Platform Staff, 1976, 80, 84, 88, 92, 96; Presdl. Transition Team, 1980-81. Sgt. USAR, 1969-77. Mem. Met. Club. Republican. Presbyterian. Avocations: tennis, travel, horticulture. Address: 1300 N 17th St Ste 1100 Arlington VA 22209

CARBINE, JAMES EDMOND, lawyer; b. Scotts Bluff, Nebr., June 3, 1945; s. Edmond Horace Carbine and Mabel (Porterfield) Hukle; m. Marianne Lemly, Aug. 5, 1972; 1 child, Matthew. BA, Mich. State U., 1967; JD, U. Md., 1972. Bar: Md. 1972. Assoc. Weinberg and Green, Balt., 1972-79, ptnr., 1980-96, chmn. litigation dept., 1985-95; pvt. practice Balt., 1996—. Panel mem. Nat. Press Club Symposium, 1974. Reporter Govs. Landlord Tenant Commn., Md., 1973-76; mem. Mayor's Bus. Roundtable, Balt., 1983-85; bd. dirs. Greater Homewood Community Corp., Balt., 1980-82; trustee Roland Park Found., 1986-87; bd. dirs. Md. Vol. Lawyers Svc., 1991-2002. With U.S. Army, 1968-70. Named one of Outstanding Young Men Am., Jaycees, 1977. Mem. ABA (computer litigation com., corp. coun. com., co-chair trial practice com. 1994-97), Md. Bar Assn., Balt. City Bar Assn., Nat. Press Club (panelist 1974). Avocation: outdoor sports. Office: 111 S Calvert St Ste 2700 Baltimore MD 21202-6143 Office Phone: 410-385-5300. Business E-Mail: jcarbine@trialaw.com.

CARBINE, SHARON, lawyer; b. Bryn Mawr, Feb. 14, 1950; d. Thomas Joseph and Mary Teresa (Loftus) Carbine. BA, Temple U., 1972, JD, 1974, LLM in Taxation, 1977. Bar: Pa. 1974, Tex. 1981; CPA, Tex. Atty. Altemose Cos., Ctr. Square, Pa., 1974-75; law clk. to presiding justice Ct. Common Pleas, Phila., summer, 1975; tax atty. Provident Mut. Life Ins. Co., Phila., 1975-77, Emhart Corp., Farmington, Conn., 1977-78; tax sr. Peat Marwick Mitchell & Co., Phila., 1978-79; legal counsel to gov.'s chief energy advisor Tex. Energy and Natural Resources Adv. Coun., Austin, 1979-80; tax atty. Sun Co., Inc., Dallas, 1980-82; pvt. practice law Haverford, Pa., 1982-83; tax atty. Ebasco Svcs., Inc., N.Y.C., 1983-84; pvt. practice law King of Prussia, Pa., 1985-88; asst. treas., mgr. corp. taxation PQ Corp., Valley Forge, Pa., 1988-89; law clk. to presiding judge Superior Ct. Pa., Bala Cynwyd, 1989-90; tax atty. Fidelity Mut. Life Ins. Co., Radnor, Pa., 1991; ins. agent Sun Fin Group, Radnor, Pa., 1992-93; dir. regional mktg. Gen. Am. Life Ins. Co., Plymouth Meeting, Pa., 1993-94. V.p., gen. counsel Commonwealth Trust Co., Wilmington, Del., 1995—; software trainer Rsch. Inst. Am. Group, 1996-97; sr. info. tech. analyst VWR Corp., 1998; tech. writer LegalEdge Software, 1999, CB Techs., Inc., 1999-2000; pres. Carbine Creative Consulting, Inc., 2000—. Vol. Rep. Party, 1964—; mem. Jaycees, Phila., 1978-79, Austin, Tex., 1979-80; bd. dirs. Rep. Women of the Main Line, Bryn Mawr, Pa., 1983, 93. Mem. Brehon Law Soc., Internet Bus. Alliance, Network Women Computer Tech. Roman Catholic. Home: 515 Plymouth Rd, # Q-6 Plymouth Meeting PA 19462

CARBO, TONI (TONI CARBO BEARMAN), information scientist, educator; b. Middletown, Conn., Nov. 14, 1942; d. Anthony Joseph and Theresa (Bauer) Carbo; m. David A. Bearman, Nov. 14, 1970 (div. Nov. 1995); 1 child, Amanda Carole Bearman Rochon; m. Clark Coolidge, July 7, 1962 (div. Apr. 1966). AB, Brown U., 1969; MS, Drexel U., 1973, PhD, 1977. Bibliog. asst. Am. Math. Soc., Math. Revs., 1962-63; supr. Brown U. Phys. Scis. Library, Providence, 1963-66, 67-71; subject specialist U. Wash. Engring. Library, Seattle, 1966-67; teaching and research asst. Drexel U., Phila., 1971-74; exec. dir. Nat. Fedn. Abstracting and Info. Svcs., Phila., 1974-79; cons. for strategic planning and new product devel. Instn. Elec. Engrs., London, 1979-80; exec. dir. U.S. Nat. Commn. on Libraries and Info. Sci., Washington, 1980-86; prof. U. Pitts. Sch. Info. Sci., 1986—, dean, 1986—2002. Adv. com. U.S. Dept. Commerce, Patent and Trademark Office, 1987—90; trustee Engring. Info., Inc., 1985—87; Lazerow lectr. U. Ind., 1984, U. Toronto, 1999; Schwing lectr. La. State U., 1988; lectr. No. Ohio Am. Soc. Info. Spl. Librs. Assn., 1990; lectr. Beta Phi Mu, Phila., 1992; Sigma chpt. lectr. Drexel U., Phila.; U.S. adv. coun. Nat. Info. Infrastructure, 1994—96; U.S. del. G-7 Info. Soc. Conf.; bd. dirs. Pa. Info. Hwy. Consortium; Miles Conrad lectr. Nat. Fedn. Abstracting & Info. Svcs., 1997; Biennial Srygley lectr. Fla. State U., 1997; Nasser Sharify lectr. Pratt U., 1997; mem. Nat. Conf. Lawyers and Scientists of the AAAS and ABA, 2000—; Cunningham lectr. Vanderbilt U., 2002; lectr. in field; jury mem. Senator John Heinz Award for Technology, the Economy and Employment, 1998—2003, chair, 2001. Co-editor: Internat. Info. and Libr. Rev., 1989—92; editor, 1993—; mem. editl. bds. profl. jours.:; contbr. articles to profl. jours. Mem. presdl. adv. com. Carnegie Libr. Pitts.; mem. adv. coun. Girls and Women's Found. Western Pa., 2004—; chair Bd. Policy Archive, 2004—; bd. dirs. Greater Pitts. Literacy Coun. Named Disting. Dau. Pa., Gov. Penn. Edward Rendell, 2004; recipient Disting. Alumni award, Drexel U. Coll. Info. Studies, 1984, 100 Most Disting. Alumni award, 1992, 100th Anniversary medal, Drexel U., 1992, Silver Anniversary award, U.S. Nat. Commn. Librs. & Info. Sci., 1996, Leadership award in Sci. and Tech., YWCA Greater Pitts., 2000; fellow Madison Coun., Libr. Congress, 2002—03. Fellow: AAAS (chmn. sect. T 1992—93, coun. 1997—99), Spl. Librs. Assn. (rsch. com. 1987—92, internat. rels. com. 1991), Inst. Info. Scientists, Nat. Fedn. Abstracting and Info. Svcs. (hon.); mem.: ALA (coun. 1988—92, 50th Anniversary Honor Roll 1996), Internat. Women's Forum Western Pa., Assn. Libr. and Info. Sci. Edn. (bd. dirs. 1996—2000, pres. 1997—98, chair conf. planning com. 1997—98, 1999—2000, co-chair 2004, governance com. 2005, Profl. Contbn. to Libr. and Info. Sci. Edn. award 2002, 2005), Internat. Fedn. Info. and Documentation (co-chair U.S. nat. com. 1990—2000, chair global info. infrastructure and superhighways taskforce 1993—96, mem. coun., chair info. structures and policies com. 1997—2000), Nat. Info. Stds. Orgns. (bd. dirs. 1987—90), Pa. Libr. Assn. (adv. bd. Pa. Gov.'s Conf. libr. and info. svcs. 1996, Disting. Svc. award 1996), Am. Soc. Info. Sci. and Tech. (chmn. networking com., chmn. 50th ann. conf., pres. 1989—90, chmn. planning and nominations com. 1990—91, SIG III cabinet rep. 2003—, Watson Davis award 1983), 3 Rivers Connect (bd. dirs., exec. com. 1998—2004, vice chair 1999—2004, interim chair 2003), Ctr. Democracy and Tech. (bd. dirs. 1996—2005, chair 1999—2002), Laurel Initiative (bd. dirs. 1990—93). Home: 263 Maple Ave Pittsburgh PA 15218-1523 Office: 135 N Bellefield Ave Pittsburgh PA 15213-2609 Office Phone: 412-624-9310. Business E-Mail: tcarbo@mail.sis.pitt.edu.

CARBONE, ANTHONY J., chemicals executive; m. Patricia; children: Christopher, Carolyn. BS in Mech. Engring., Yale U.; MBA, Ctrl. Mich. U. Various tech. svc. and devel. positions Dow Chem. Co., Midland, Mich., 1962-67, sect. head, 1967-69, group mgr. TS&D, 1969-70, product sales mgr. laminated and coated products, 1970-72, mktg. mgr. laminated and coated products, 1972-74, group v.p. Dow Plastics, Chems., Plastic bus. group, 1993-95; also bd. dirs., mem. exec. com.; mktg. dir. Dow Lat. Am., Coral Gables, Fla., 1974-76; bus. mgr. STYROFOAM brand functional products adn sys. dept. Dow U.S.A., Midland, 1976-80, dir. mktg. functional products and sys., 1980-83, gen. mgr. coatings and resins dept., 1983-87, gen. mgr. separation sys. dept., 1983-86, v.p. Dow Plastics, 1987-91; group v.p. Dow Plastics Dow N.Am., 1991-93; exec. v.p. Dow Chem. Co., Midland, 1996—2000, vice chmn., 2000—. Bd. dir. Rockwell Collins. Mem. adv. coun. Heritage Found. Mem. Am. Plastics Coun.(mem. bd., exec. com.), Am. Chem. Soc., Soc. Plastic Industries. Office: The Dow Chem Co 2030 Dow Ctr Midland MI 48674

CARBONE, DAVID PAUL, oncologist; b. Albany, N.Y., Aug. 8, 1955; MD PhD, Johns Hopkins, Balt., Md., 1988. Cert. Med. Oncolog Am. Bd. of Internal Medicine, 1988. Prof. medicine and cancer biology Vanderbilt U., Nashville, 1996—. Office: Vanderbilt Cancer Ctr 2200 Pierce Ave Nashville TN 37064 Office Phone: 615-936-3524. Office Fax: 615-936-3322. Business E-Mail: d.carbone@vanderbilt.edu.

CARBONELL, JOAQUIN R., III, telecommunications industry executive, lawyer; b. Camaguey, Cuba, 1952; arrived in US, 1961; BA summa cum laude, Boston Coll.; JD, Duke U.; MS in mgmt., Stanford U., 1989. Bar: Fla. 1978. Joined BellSouth Enterprises Inc., 1980; gen. atty. BellSouth, Fla., 1986—90, named gen. atty. DC office, 1990; v.p. Latin Am. BellSouth Internat., pres. Latin Am.; pres. BellSouth Europe; v.p., group counsel wireless svcs. BellSouth Enterprises, Inc.; exec. v.p., gen. counsel of regulatory and legal Cingular Wireless, 2001—04; exec. v.p., gen. counsel Cingular Wireless (after merger with AT&T Wireless), 2004—. Alfred P. Sloan Fellow, 1989. Mem.: Phi Beta Kappa. Office: Cingular Wireless Glenridge Highlands Two 5565 Glenridge Connector Atlanta GA 30342

CARBONELL, JOSEFINA G., federal agency administrator; b. Cuba; 1 child, Alfredo. Student, Fla. Internat. U. With Little Havana Activities and Nutrition Ctrs., Dade County, Fla., 1972—, pres., CEO, 1982—2001; asst. sec. for adminstrn. on aging Dept. HHS, Washington, 2001—. Recipient Citizen of Yr. award, Miami, 1992, Charles Whited Spirit of Excellence award, Miami Herald, 1993, Cmty. Svc. award, Nat. Alliance for Hispanic Health, 1995, Monsignor Bryan Walsh Outstanding Human Svc. award, United Way, 1997, Commrs. Team award, Social Security Adminstrn., 1997, Claude Pepper Cmty. Svc. award, 2001; fellow in health mgmt., John F. Kennedy Sch. Govt., Harvard U. Office: US Dept HHS 1 Massachusetts Ave NW Washington DC 20201

CARBONI, STEFANO, curator; Assoc. curator dept. Islamic art Met. Mus. Art, NYC. Author: Glass From Islamic Lands: The al-Sabah Collection, 2001; co-author (with David Whitehouse): Glass of the Sultans: Twelve Centuries of Islamic Masterworks, 2001; Co-curator (with Linda Komaroff) (exhibitions) The Legacy of Genghis Khan: Courtly Art and Culture in Western Asia, 1256-1353 (Alfred H. Barr Jr. Award for exhbn. catalogue, Coll. Art Assn., 2004). Office: Met Mus Art 1000 Fifth Ave New York NY 10028-0198*

CARBULLIDO, F. PHILIP, territory supreme court justice; b. Tamuning, Guam, Feb. 5, 1953; s. Francisco Chaco and Maria Salas (Castro) Carbullido; m. Fay Diana Lizama Garrido; children: Brandon Philip, Kristina Joy, Adam Philip, Steven Philip. BS in Polit. Sci., U. Oreg., 1975; JD, U. Calif., Davis, 1978. Intern to asst. atty. gen. Office Atty. Gen.; assoc. Arriola and Lamorena, Arriola & Cowan, ptnr., Carbullido & Pipes, P.C., 1983—97, Carbullido Bordallo & Brooks, LLP, 1997, Carbullido & Brooks LLP; justice Guam Supreme Ct., Hagåtña, 2000—; chief justice Supreme Ct. Guam, Hagåtña, 2003—. Recipient award of Merit, Pacific Jaycees, 1983; Profl. Tech. scholar, Govt. of Guam. Office: Supreme Ct Guam Jud Ctr Ste 300 120 W O'Brien Dr Hagatna GU 96910 Business E-Mail: justice@guamsupremecourt.com.*

CARCATERRA, LORENZO GABRIEL, writer; b. N.Y.C., Oct. 16, 1954; s. Mario and Raffaela Carcaterra; m. Susan J. Toepfer, May 16, 1981; children: Katherine Marie, Nicholas Gabriel. BS, St. John's U., 1976. News editor, copyboy, clk., reporter N.Y. Daily News, N.Y.C., 1976—83; sr. writer Time, Inc., N.Y.C., 1983—84; freelance writer, 1984—88; mng. editor CBS-Grosso/Jacobson Prodns., Top Cops, N.Y.C., 1990—94; freelance writer N.Y.C., NY, 1990—, L.A., 1990—. CEO One Punch Prodns., N.Y.C., 1997—. Author: A Safe Place, 1993, Sleepers, 1995, Apaches, 1997, Gangster, 2000, (novels) Street Boys, 2002, Paradise City, 2004, Chasers, 2005, (screenplays) Street Boys, 2002, Dreamer, 1996, Doubt, 1997, Ringers, 1998, The Force, 1999, Law & Order, 2003—04, The Ghost, 2005. Recipient Leone Di San Marco award, Lehman Coll., Bronx, N.Y., 1994. Mem.: Mystery Writers Am., Authors Guild, Writers Guild Am. East, Internat. Nat. Assn. Crime Writers. Republican. Roman Catholic. Avocations: running, weight-lifting, travel, book collecting, sports.

CARCIERI, DONALD L., governor; b. RI, Dec. 16, 1942; s. Nicola and Marguerite Carcieri; m. Suzanne Owren; children: Matthew, Alison, Jill, Sarah. Degree in Internat. Rels., Brown U. Tchr.; various positions including exec. v.p. Old Stone Bank; head West Indies ops. Cath. Relief Svcs., Kingston, Jamaica, 1981—83; various positions including CEO Cookson Am., RI, 1983, joint mng. dir. Cookson Group Worldwide; gov. State of RI, 2002—. Mem. Cath. Relief Svcs. Leadership Coun.; former chair R.I. Math./Sci. Edn. Coalition; co-founder Acad. Children's Sci. Ctr., East Greenwich; dir. Providence Ctr., RI. Republican. Roman Catholic. Office: Office of the Gov State House Rm 115 Providence RI 02903

CARD, ANDREW HILL, JR., federal official; b. Brockton, Mass., May 10, 1947; s. Andrew Hill and Joyce (Whitaker) C.; m. Kathleene Marie Bryan; children: Tabetha, Rachel, Drew. BS in Engring., U. S. C., 1971; MA, LLD (hon.), Mount Ida Coll. and Assumption Coll.; MA, DPA (hon.), Curry Coll.; postgrad., Mass. Maritime Acad. Structural design engr. Maurice Reidy Engrs., Inc., 1971-72, David M. Berg, Inc., 1972-75; held several elected and appointed offices Holbrook, Mass., 1971-82; rep. Gen. Ct. of Commonwealth of Mass., 1975-82; v.p. CMIS Corp., Vienna, Va., 1983; spl. asst. to Pres. Ronald Reagan for Intergovtl. Affairs The White House, 1983-87; N.H. campaign mgr. for George Bush, 1987-88; dep. asst. to Pres., dir. Office of Intergovernmental Affairs The White House, Washington, 1988, asst. to Pres. and dep. chief of staff, 1989-92; sec. U.S. Dept. Transp., Washington, 1992—93; pres., CEO Am. Automobile Mfrs. Assn., Washington, 1992—98; v.p. govt. relations GM, 1999—2000; chief of staff The White House, Washington, 2000—. Mem. adv. commn. on intergovtl. relations, 1988; head of task force Federal relief effort Hurricane Andrew So. Fla., 1992. Candidate for gov., Mass., 1983. With USN, 1965-67. Named one of Nation's Outstanding Legislators, Nat. Rep. Legislators' Assn., 1982. Office: Chief of Staff 1600 Pennsylvania Ave NW Washington DC 20502*

CARD, DEBORAH FRANCES, orchestra administrator; b. Pottstown, Pa., Sept. 30, 1956; d. Marshall Anthony and Winifred (Hitz) R. BA, Stanford U., 1978; MBA, U. So. Calif., 1985. Orch. mgr. L.A. Philharm., 1978-86; exec. dir. L.A. Chamber Orch., 1986-92, Seattle Symphony, 1992—. Bd. dirs. AIDS project L.A., 1985-92; active Jr. League L.A., 1982-92. Mem. Am. Symphony Orch. League, Assn. Calif. Symphony Orchs. (pres. 1988-91), Assn. N.W. Symphony Orchs. (bd. dirs. 1993—), Chamber Music Soc. L.A. (bd. dirs. 1987-92), Ojai Festival (pres.'s coun.). Democrat. Episcopalian. Avocations: skiing, tennis, gardening, reading. Office: Seattle Symphony Ctr House PO Box 21906 Seattle WA 98111-3906 Home: 1536 W Nelson St Chicago IL 60657-3104

CARD, ORSON SCOTT (BYRON WALLEY), writer; b. Richland, Wash., Aug. 24, 1951; s. Willard Richards and Peggy Jane (Park) C.; m. Kristine Allen, May 17, 1977; children: Geoffrey, Emily, Charles, Zina, Erin. BA in Theater, Brigham Young U., 1975; MA in English, U. Utah, 1981. Editor Brigham Young U. Press, Provo, Utah, 1974-76; assoc. editor Ensign mag., Salt Lake City, 1976-78; sr. editor Compute! Publs., Greensboro, N.C., 1983; game design cons. Lucasfilm Games, 1989-92. Instr. Brigham Young U., U.

Utah, U. Notre Dame, Appalachian State U., Clarion West Writer's Workshop, Cape Cod Writers Conf., Antioch Writers Workshop; columnist "You Got No Friends in This World", Science Fiction Review, 1979-86, "Book to Look For", Fantasy and Science Fiction, 1987—, "Gameplay", Compute!, 1988—. Author: (fiction) Capitol, 1978, Hot Sleep, 1978, A Planet Called Treason, 1979, Songmaster, 1980 (Hamilton/Brackett award 1981), Unaccompanied Sonata and Other Stories, 1980, Hart's Hope, 1982, The Worthing Chronicle, 1983, A Woman of Destiny, 1983, Ender's Game, 1985 (Nebula award 1985, Hugo award 1986, Hamilton/Brackett award 1986), Speaker For The Dead, 1986 (Nebula award 1986, Hugo award 1987, Locus award 1987), Hatrack River, 1986 (Hugo award nomination 1986, World Fantasy award 1987), Wyrms, 1987, Seventh Son, 1987 (Locus award best fantasy 1988, Hugo award nomination 1988, World Fantasy award nomination 1988), Cardography, 1987, Eye for Eye, 1987 (Hugo award 1988, Locus award nomination 1988), Treason, 1988, Red Prophet, 1988 (Locus award 1989), Prentice Alvin, 1989, Folk of the Fringe, 1989, The Abyss, 1989, Maps in a Mirror, 1990, The Worthing Saga, 1990, Xenocide, 1991, The Memory of Earth, 1992, Lost Boys, 1992, The Call of Earth, 1992, The Changed Man, 1992, Flux, 1992, Cruel Miracles, 1992, Monkey Sonatas, 1993, The Ships of Earth, 1993, A Storyteller in Zion, 1993, Earthfall, 1994, (with David Dollahite) Turning Hearts, 1994, (with Kathryn H. Kidd) Lovelock, 1994, Earthborn, 1995, Alvin Journeyman, 1995 (Locus award 1996), Pastwatch: The Redemption of Christopher Columbus, 1996, Children of the Mind, 1996, Treasure Box, 1996, Stone Tables, 1997, Homebody, 1998, Heartfire, 1998, Enchantment, 1999, Ender's Shadow, 1999, Magic Mirror, 1999, Sarah, 2000, Shadow of the Hegeman, 2001, Rebekah, 2001, Shadow Puppets, 2002, The Crystal City, 2003, First Meetings: in the Enderverse, 2003, Shadow of the Giant, 2005 (Publishers Weekly Bestseller list), Magic Street, 2005; (nonfiction) Listen, Mom and Dad, 1978, Saintspeak, 1981, Ainge, 1982, Characters and Viewpoint, 1988, How to Write Science Fiction and Fantasy, 1990 (Hugo award for non-fiction 1991); (plays) The Apostate, 1970, In Flight, 1970, Across Five Summers, 1971, Of Gideon, 1971, Stone Tables, 1973, A Christmas Carol, 1974, Father, Mother, Mother, and Mom, 1974, Liberty Jail, 1975, Rag Mission, 1977, Fresh Courage Take, 1978, Elders and Sisters, 1979, Wings, 1982; editor: Dragons of Darkness, 1981, Dragons of Light, 1983; author numerous audio and videoplays; contbr. short stories and essays to Fantasy & Sci. Fiction, Windows Sources and other mags. Recipient John W. Campbell award World Sci. Fiction Conv., 1978, Hugo award nominations World Sci. Fiction Conv., 1978, 79, 80, Nebula award nominations Sci. Fiction Writers of America, 1979, 80, Utah State Inst. of Fine Arts prize, 1980. Mem. Sci. Fiction Writers Am., Authors Guild. Democrat. Mem. Lds Ch. Address: c/o Tor Books 175 5th Ave Fl 14 New York NY 10010-7703 also: Barbara Bova Lit Agy PO Box 770365 Naples FL 34107*

CARDAMONE, RICHARD J., federal judge; b. Utica, N.Y., Oct. 10, 1925; s. Joseph J. and Josephine (Scala) Cardamone; m. Catherine Baker Clarke, Aug. 28, 1946. BA, Harvard U., 1948; LLB, Syracuse U., 1952. Bar: N.Y. 1952. Pvt. practice, Utica, 1952—62; judge N.Y. State Supreme Ct., 1963—71, judge appelate divsn. 4th dept., 1971—81; judge U.S. Ct. Appeals (2nd cir.), Utica, 1981—93, sr. judge, 1993—. Pres. NY State Assn. Supreme Ct. Justices, 1977—78. Lt. (j.g.) USNR, 1943—46. Mem.: Oneida County Bar Assn., N.Y. State Bar Assn., Am. Law Inst. Roman Catholic. Office: US Ct Appeals 10 Broad St Utica NY 13501-1233

CARDENAS, BRENDA EILEEN, literature and language professor, poet; d. Joseph Robert and Diane Irene Cardenas. BA in English, U. Wis., Milw., 1987; MFA in Creative Writing, U. Mich., Ann Arbor, 1995. Cert. tchr. U. Wis., 1989. English tchr. Menomonee Falls H.S., Wis., 1990—93; adj. prof., English U. Mich., Ann Arbor, 1995—98, Wayne State U., Detroit, 1996, 1998; creative writing instr. Mex. Fine Arts Ctr. Mus., Chgo., 1998—2001, youth initiatives coord., 1999—2001; prof., English Wilbur Wright Coll., Chgo., 2001—. Adv. bd. mem. Movimiento Artistica Chicano, Chgo., 1998—; bd. dirs. The Guild Complex, Chgo., 2000—03. Editor: Between the Heart and the Land, 2001; contbr. articles to profl. jours.; author: (poetry) From the Tongues of Brick and Stone, 2005. Fellow in Lit., NEH, 1993. Mem.: Nat. Coun. Tchrs. English, Assn. Writers & Writing Programs. Avocations: reading, camping, hiking, bicycling. Office Phone: 773-481-8589. Business E-Mail: bcardenas@core.com.

CARDENAS, DIANA DELIA, physician, educator; b. San Antonio, Tex., Apr. 10, 1947; d. Ralph Roman and Rosa (Garza) C.; m. Thomas McKenzie Hooton, Aug. 20, 1971; children: Angela, Jessica. BA with highest honors, U. Tex., 1969; MD, U. Tex., Dallas, 1973; MS, U. Wash., 1976, MHA, 2001. Diplomate Nat. Bd. Med. Examiners, Am. Bd. Phys. Medicine & Rehab., Am. Bd. Electrodiagnostic Medicine. Asst. prof. dept. rehab. medicine Emory U., Atlanta, 1976-81; instr. dept. rehab. medicine U. Wash., Seattle, 1981-82, asst. prof. dept. rehab. medicine, 1982-86, assoc. prof. dept. rehab. medicine, 1986-92, prof. rehab. medicine, 1992—. Med. dir. rehab. medicine clinic U. Wash. Med. Ctr., Seattle, 1982—99; project dir. N.W. Regional Spinal Cord Injury Sys., Seattle, 1990—; mem. Accreditation Coun. for Grad. Med. Edn. Residency Rev. Com., 1995—96; chief of svc. rehab medicine U. Wash. Med. Ctr., 2002—. Editor: Rehabilitation & The Chronic Renal Disease Patient, 1985, Maximizing Rehabilitation in Chronic Renal Disease, 1989; acad. editor Archives of Phys. Medicine and Rehab., 1997-99; contbr. articles to profl. jours. Co-chairperson Lakeside Sch. Auction Student Vols., Seattle, 1991; bd. dirs. CONSEJO Counseling & Referral Svc; elected to Inst. Medicine of Nat. Acad., 2004. Mem.: Inst. of Medicine Nat. Acad. Sci. (com. on assessing rehab. sci. and engring. 1996—97, com. on injury prevention and control 1997—99), Nat. Inst. Child Health and Human Devel. (rsch. subcom. 1996—99), Am. Assn. Electrodiagnostic Medicine, Am. Congress of Rehab. Medicine (chairperson rehab. practice com. 1981—83, bd. govs. 2003, Ann. Essay Contest winner 1976), Am. Acad. Phys. Medicine and Rehab. (chairperson rsch. adv. and advocacy com. 1997—99), Am. Spinal Injury Assn. (chairperson rsch. com. 1990—94, bd. dirs. 1994—2000, co-chair internat. rels. com. 1995—98, chair internat. rels. com. 1999—, chair mktg. com. 2000—03), Assn. Acad. Physiatrists (chair awards com. 1993—99). Avocations: art collecting, sewing, painting. Office: Univ Wash Dept Rehab Med Box 356490 1959 NE Pacific St Seattle WA 98195-0001

CARDENAS, RENE F., nuclear medicine physician, oncologist; arrived in U.S., 2003; s. Felipe G. Cardenas and Evangelina T. Valdes; m. Rosalia Duran; children: Helena Eva, Raul Rene. Postgrad., U. San Juan, P.R., 1958; MD, Havana U., Cuba, 1960; postgrad., Cathedra Radiology, Sch. Medicine, Moscow, 1961—62, Inst. Boris Kidric, Belgrade, Yugoslavia, 1966; specialist in Oncology, first degree, Havana (Cuba) U., 1967; postgrad., U. Montevideo, Uruguay, 1967, Inst. Cancer Jean Perrin, Clermont Ferrand, France, 1970; PhD, Karlovy U., Prague, Czechoslovakia, 1984. Head nuc. medicine dept. Nat. Inst. Oncology, Havana, 1962—77, 1980—93, mem. sci. coun., 1980—2003; titular prof. Sch. Medicine, U. Havana, 1985—93, mem. sci. coun., 1989—2003; head nuc. medicine dept. Nat. Inst. Oncology (SOLCA), Guayaquil, Ecuador, 1993—2003. Pres. sci. com. Nat. Inst. Oncology, Havana, 1982—88; mem. sci. com. Sec. Nuc. Affairs, Havana, 1984—93, Sch. Medicine, Havana U., 1988—93; sci. adviser to the gen. dir. Ecuadorian Commn. Atomic Energy. Contbr. articles to profl. jours. Pres. nat. group nuc. medicine Ministry Pub. Health, Havana, 1982—93. Named Honor Guest of Guayaquil, Mayor of Guayaquil, 1994; recipient medal and cert. for 25 years of achievements in rsch., Acad. Sci. Cuba, 1987; fellow, Internat. Atomic Energy Agy., Vienna, 1980; grantee, 1969—74. Mem.: Soc. Nuc. Medicine, Soc. Oncology Ecuador (hon.), Soc. Cardiology Ecuador (sr.). Roman Catholic. Achievements include patents for software of PC coupled to gamma camera; development of synthesis of several radiopharmaceuticals for nuclear medicine; formulation of several kits of radiopharmaceuticals. Avocation: painting. Home: 265 SW 49th Ave Miami FL 33134 Personal E-mail: rcardenas1@yahoo.com.

CARDENES, ANDRES JORGE, musician, educator; b. Havana, Cuba, May 2, 1957; came to U.S., 1958; s. Andres Manuel and Arlene (Cuevas) C. Student, Ind. U., 1975-80; diploma, Meisterkurse Zurich, Switzerland, 1977. Asst. prof. music Ind. U., Bloomington, 1980-82; prof. music Espoo Festival, Helsinki, Finland, 1982; prof. U. Utah, Salt Lake City, 1982-85; prof. music U. Mich., 1987-89. Mem. artistic com. Utah Symphony, Salt Lake City, 1983-85; cons. in field; bd. dirs. Intermountain-West Music Festival, Salt Lake City, 1984-88; artistic dir. Strings in the Mountains Chamber Music Festival, Steamboat Springs, Colo.; prof. violin studies Carnegie Mellon U., 1989—. Concertmaster Utah Symphony, Salt Lake City, 1982-85, San Diego Symphony, 1985-86, Pitts. Symphony, 1987—; concert violin soloist, 1981—; 1985-86; editor: Concerto by Ramiro Cortes, 1983; performer worldwide Nuclear Arms Freeze, 1980—. Cultural amb. UNICEF, 1980—; chmn., co-founder Underprivileged Arts Student San Diego Soc.; cultural chmn. Make-a-Wish Found. of Pitts. Recipient Bronze medal Queen Elizabeth Internat. Violin Competition, Brussels, 1980, Bronze medal Sibelius Internat. Violin Competition, Helsinki, 1980, Bronze medal Tchaikovsky Internat. Violin Competition, Moscow, 1982, Bronze medal Internat. Violin Competition, Indpls., 1986, Pitts. Classical Artist of Yr., 1998, Starling Found. endowed chair Carnegie-Mellon U., 1998, Shalom awrd Kollell Found. Mem. Young San Diegans Soc. (bd. dirs.). Clubs: Machista (Bloomington) (pres. 1978—). Roman Catholic. Office: Pittsburgh Symphony Orch Heinz Hall 600 Penn Ave Ste 1 Pittsburgh PA 15222-3259

CARDER, PAUL CHARLES, retired advertising executive; b. Oak Park, Ill., Jan. 27, 1941; arrived in Can., 1967; s. Lawrence E. and Irene (Zahler) C.; children from previous marriages: Greg Lawrence, Tracy Allison, Leigh Rebecca Kamping-Carder, Amanda Rachel Kamping-Carder. BA, U. Mich., 1962; MBA, Harvard U., 1964. Account exec. Ogilvy & Mather, N.Y.C., 1964-65; v.p. Ogilvy & Mather Can., Ltd., Toronto, Ont., Can., 1966-73; v.p., dir. client svcs. Doyle Dane Bernbach, Toronto, 1974-77; sr. v.p., mng. dir. Vicker & Benson, Ltd., Toronto, 1978-83; pres., CEO Carder Gray Advt., Inc., Toronto, 1983-90, DDB Needham Worldwide, Toronto, 1990-94; ret., 1994; dean, faculty Bus. and Creative Arts George Brown Coll., Toronto, 1999—2002. Adj. prof. Queen's U. Sch. Bus., 1995—96; prin. Paladin Co.; dir. mktg. and bus. devel. Davies, Ward, Phillips & Vineberg, 2003—. Bd. dirs. Nat. Ballet Can., Toronto, 1984-90, Thousand Islands Playhouse, 1995—, Heart and Stroke Found. of Ont., 1997—, Toronto Cmty. Found., 2000—. Mem. Inst. Can. Advt. (dir., treas. 1988-90), dir. Harvard Bus. Sch. Club of Toronto. Liberal party of Ontario. Avocations: tennis, skiing. Office: Davies Ward Phillips & Vineberg 44th Fl 1 First Canadian Pl Toronto ON Canada M5X 1B1 Personal E-mail: pcarder@sympatico.ca. Business E-Mail: pcarder@dwpv.com.

CARDIERI, ALEXANDER M., music specialist, music educator; b. Brooklyn, NY, May 9, 1953; s. Alexander Sr. and Mary Cardieri; m. Filis A. DeRodio, Jan. 14, 1978; children: George, Alexis. MusB, Manhattan Sch. of Music, New York, NY, 1976, MusM, 1980. Cert. Eng. as a second lang. Tchr. (min. of music) Bklyn. Diocese, Bklyn., 1979—84, Queens, NY, 1979—84; tchr. (music) St. Joseph HS, Bklyn., 1981—84, Patagonia Sch., Patagonia, Ariz., 1985—95, tchr. (band dir.), 1985—95; music specialist Nogales Ltd. Sch. Dist., Nogales, Ariz., 1995—96, Sunnyside Ltd. Sch. Dist., Tucson, 1996—; adj. music instr. Pima Comm. Coll., Tucson, 1996—. Pianist Anthony's In the Catalinas Restaurant, Tucson, 1989—. Author: (Thesis) An Anthology and Approach to Ear Training Through the Use of Familiar Tunes, 1979. Recipient Who's Who Among Am. Tchr., 1990, O.M. Hartsell Excellence in Tchg. Music award, 2003; grantee tech. grant, Sunnyside Found./ AZ, 2002. Mem.: MENC: The Nat. Assoc. for Music Ed. Republican. Roman Catholic. Achievements include General Music Curriculum co-writer; Sunnyside Ltd. Sch. Dist. Career Ladder Level III tchr. Avocations: computers, hiking, aerobics. Home: 12770 E Wentworth Ct Vail AZ 85641 E-mail: alexc@sunnysideud.k12.az.us.

CARDIFF, ROBERT DARRELL, pathology educator; b. San Francisco, Dec. 5, 1935; s. George Darrell and Helen (Kohfield) C.; m. Sally Joan Bounds, June 23, 1962; children: Darrell, Todd, Shelley. BS, U. Calif., Berkeley, 1958, PhD, 1968; MD, U. Calif., San Francisco, 1962. Intern King's County Hosp., Bklyn., 1962-63; resident in pathology U. Oreg., Portland, 1963-66; NIH fellow U. Calif., Berkeley, 1966-68, mem. faculty med. sch. Davis, 1971—, prof. pathology Med. Sch., 1977—, chair dept. pathology, 1990-96; dir. Ctr. for Med. Informatics U. Calif. Davis Healthcare Sys., 1996-98, faculty Ctr. for Comparative Medicine; chair Med. Informatics Grad. Group, 2002—. Mem. sci. adv. bd. Contra Costa Cancer Fund, Walnut Creek, Calif., 1985-99; mem. Univ.-Wide AIDS Task Force, Berkeley, 1984-87; vis. prof. Sun-Yat Sen U. Med. Sci., Peoples Republic of China, 1985, 93, Harvard Med. Sch., 1990, U. Calif. San Diego, 1998-99. Mem. editl. bd. Human Pathology, 1992—, Tumor Markers, 1992—, Internat. Jour. Oncology, 1992—, Jour. Mamgland Biol. and Neoplasia, 1998—; contbr. articles to profl. jours. Lt. col. U.S. Army, 1968—71. Recipient Triton Rsch. award Triton Bioscis., Inc., 1985, Sadusk award Peralta Cancer Inst., 1986, others. Master: AAUP (exec. com. 1983—85); mem.: No. Calif. Pathology Soc. (pres. 1990—96), Sacramento Pathology Soc. (bd. dirs. 1985—96), Internat. Assn. Breast Cancer Rsch. (bd. dirs. 1984—96, pres. 2003—), Internat. Acad. Pathology, Pluto Soc., Sigma Xi. Avocations: basketball, skiing, jogging. Office: U Calif-Davis Ctr for Comparative Medicine 98 County Rd & Hutchison Dr Davis CA 95616 Business E-Mail: rdcardiff@ucdavis.edu.

CARDILE, PAUL JULIUS, fine arts dealer; b. N.Y.C., July 30, 1948; s. Julius Joseph and Mary Lola (Contrucci) C. BA, Queens Coll., N.Y.C., 1969, MA, 1971; MPhil, Yale U., 1974, PhD, 1976. Asst. prof. SUNY, Albany, 1975-76, Newcomb Coll., New Orleans, 1976-77, Cleve. State U., 1977-78; asst. prof., mus. dir. Denison U., Granville, Ohio, 1978-84; owner Cardile Galleries, N.Y.C., 1984—. Appraiser Assn. of Am., N.Y.C., 1985—, bd. dirs., 1995—. Author: Paintings in Churches and Sacred Places in Cortona, 1982; contbr. articles to profl. jours. Historian Orthodox Knights Hospitaller of St. John of Jerusalem. Humanities fellow NEH, 1982-83. Mem. Portuguese Heritage Found. (adv. coun. 1991—). Republican. Roman Catholic. Home: 880 5th Ave # 6H New York NY 10021-4951 Office: RF Stuart 444 Park Ave S New York NY 10016

CARDILLO, JOHN POLLARA, lawyer; b. Ft. Lee, N.J., July 1, 1942; s. John E. and Margaret (Pollara) Cardillo; m. Linda Bentey, Sept. 25, 1976; children: John Thomas, Joseph Pollara, Margaret Celia, Mark Luigi. BA, Furman U., 1964; postgrad., W.Va. U., 1965; JD, U. S.C., 1968. Bar: S.C. 1968, N.Y. 1970, Fla. 1972, U.S. Ct. Appeals (2d cir., 4th cir. 5th cir. 11th cir.) 1972, U.S. Dist. Ct. (ea. and so. dists.) N.Y. 1972, U.S. Dist. Ct. S.C. 1968, U.S. Dist. Ct. (so. and mid. dists.) Fla. 1974, U.S. Tax Ct. 1972, U.S. Supreme Ct. 1984. Assoc. Cardillo & Corbett, N.Y.C., 1968-71, Mays & McLellan, Columbia, S.C., 1971-72, Sorokoty, Monaco & Cervelli, Naples, Fla., 1972-75; ptnr. Monaco, Cardillo & Keith, P.A., Naples, 1975-96, Cardillo, Keith & Bonaquist, P.A., 1997—. Mem. Furman U. Alumni Bd. Dirs., 1984-89; active Environ. Adv. Coun., Collier County, Fla., 1983-87, past chmn.; past pres. Pine Ridge Civic Assn.; bd. dirs. YMCA Collier County, past pres., 1978-80, United Arts Coun. of Collier County, pres., 1991-92, bd. dirs. Big Bros., 1974-76; past pres. Naples Leadership Sch., 1987-88; mem. Leadership Collier, 1992; mem. Gov.'s Task Force on Drug Abuse, 1985; bd. advisors Gene and Mary Sarazen FDN, 1997—; trustee Edison C.C., 1998-99; founding bd. dirs. Neighborhood Health Clinic, 1998—; pres. Naples Area C. of C., 1990-95, past pres., 1995. Recipient Pioneer Preeminent award YMCA, 1984, Fla. Bar Humanitarian award, 2001, Naples Daily News Outstanding Citizen, 2005, Jefferson award for Pub. Svc. Mem. ATLA, ABA, Acad. Fla. Trial Lawyers, Fla. Bar (20th jud. cir., bd. govs. 1992-2002), Collier County Bar Assn. (past pres. 1975-76, Lifetime Achievement award, Lion of Law award for professionalism), S.C. Bar Assn., Assn. Bar City N.Y., Naples Area C. of C., Inns Of Ct. (founding bd. dirs. Thomas Biggs chpt. 2002). Home: 395 Ridge Dr Naples FL 34108-2933 Office: Cardillo Keith & Bonaquist PA 3550 Tamiami Trl E Naples FL 34112-4999 Business E-Mail: johnpcardiollo@ckblaw.com. E-mail: ckblaw@ckblaw.com.

CARDIN, BENJAMIN LOUIS, congressman, lawyer; b. Balt., Md, Oct. 5, 1943; s. Meyer M. and Dora (Green) C.; m. Myrna Edelman, Nov. 24, 1964; children: Michael, Deborah. BA cum laude, U. Pitts., 1964; JD (hon.), U. Md., 1967; LLD (hon.), U. Balt., 1990, U. Md., 1993, Balt. Hebrew U., 1994, Goucher Coll., 1996. Bar: Md. 1967. Pvt. practice law, Balt., 1967-87; mem. Md. Ho. of Del., 1967-86, chmn. ways and means com., 1974-79, spkr. of house, 1979-86; mem. US Congress from 3d Md. Dist., Washington, 1987—, asst. Dem. whip, ways and means com., human resources and social security subcoms., 1991—, steering com. Dem. caucus, 1991—, com. on stds. and ofcl. conduct, 1991-97, chair orgn., study and review com. of Dem. caucus, 1997—, mem. homeland security com. Chmn. MD Legal Svc. Corp., 1988-95; commr. Commn. on Security and Cooperation in Europe, 1993—. Contbr. Bd. visitors U. Md. Sch. Law, 1993—; trustee St. Mary's Coll., 1988-99, Goucher Coll., 1999—. Recipient Small Bus. Coun. of Am. Congrl. award, 1993, 99, Jacob K. Javits award Am Psychiat. Assn., 1999, Md. Psychiatric Soc. Friend of Psychiatry Award, 1988; Common Cause of Md. Ann Hogan Meml. Award, 1087; Rep. of Yr. award Nat. Assn. Police Orgn., 1998, Md. Bar Found. Vernon Eney award, 1996, Md. Save Our Streams' Living Stream award, 1996, Digestive Disease Nat. Coalition Publ. Policy Leadership award, 1996, The Coalition for a Lead Safe Environment, Alliance to End Childhood Lead Poisoning: the H. John Heinz III Nat. Leadership Award, 1994; ABA Pro Bono Publico Award, 1989; Hunting S. Williams award, 1995, H. John Heinz III Nat. Leadership award, 1994, Nat. Multiple Sclerosis Soc. Rep. of the Yr. award, 1993, Israel Freedom award, 1992, U. Md. Law Sch. Alumni Assn. Cardin Pro Bono award, 1990, Congl. Advocate of Yr. award Child Welfare League of Am., 2000; named to Concord Coalition's Deficit Hawk Honor Roll, 1998, 99, The Am. Med. Assoc. Dr. Nathan Davis Award for Publ. Svc., 1999; Congressional Advocate of the Yr. Award, Child Welfare League of Am, 2000; Nat. Leadership Award for Svc. to Children and Families, Casey Family Svc., 2000; Congressional Leadership Award, the Am. Coll. of Emerg. Physicians, 2001; Congressional Champion Award, The Nat. coalition for Cancer Rsch., 2002; Legislator of the Yr., Am. Assoc. of Health Plans, 2003. Mem.: Md. Bar Assn., ABA (Pro Bono Pub. award 1989), Balt. City Bar Assn. Democrat. Jewish. Office: US Ho Reps 2207 Rayburn Bldg Washington DC 20515-2003*

CARDINALE, GERALD, state legislator, dentist; b. Bklyn., Feb. 27, 1934; s. Gaspar and Mary (Modica) C.; m. Carole Nina Petrullo, 1959; children: Marisa, Christine, Kara, Gary, Nicole. BS, St. John's U., 1955; DDS, NYU, 1959. Dentist, Ft. Lee, N.J., 1959—; asst. prof. dentistry Columbia U., N.Y.C., 1971-80; mayor Town of Demarest, N.J., 1974-79; mem. N.J. Gen. Assembly, Trenton, 1980-81, N.J. Senate, Trenton, 1982—. Minority whip N.J. Senate, 1985, asst. minority leader, 1987, dep. majority leader, 1994-2001. Trustee Dumont Cmty. Ctr. for Mental Health, 1976; vol. Bergen-Passaic unit for Retarded Citizens; mem. Demarest Planning Bd. Mem. ADA, Ft. Lee Athletic Club, Elks. Republican. Office: 350 Madison Ave Cresskill NJ 07626-1342 Office Phone: 201-567-2324.

CARDINALE, KATHLEEN CARMEL, retired medical center administrator; b. Donegal, Ireland, July 13, 1933; came to U.S., 1958, naturalized, 1966; d. Denis and May (Cannon) O'Boyle; m. Anthony Cardinale, Aug. 28, 1965. BA, Jersey City State Coll., 1971, MA, 1973. RN, N.Y., U.K.; cert. nursing adminstr. advanced; nat. managed care cert., 1996. Nurse Walton Hosp., Liverpool, Eng., 1955; staff nurse, acting-in-charge Manhattan Gen. Hosp., N.Y.C., 1958-59; charge nurse, acting-in-charge Met. Hosp., N.Y.C., 1959-60; charge nurse, relief supr. Manhattan Gen. Hosp., N.Y.C., 1960-64, asst. dir. nursing, 1964-68, staffing coord., 1968-70; acting assoc. dir. nursing Bernstein Inst., N.Y.C., 1970; clin. supr., clin. specialist Beth Israel Med. Ctr., N.Y.C., 1971-73; asst. dir. nursing Cabrini Med. Ctr., N.Y.C., 1974-77, assoc. DON, 1977-78, v.p. nursing svcs., 1978-94, sr. v.p. nursing svcs., 1994-2000; ret., 2000. Mem. ANA, Greater N.Y. Hosp. Assn. (mental hygiene com.), Am. Hosp. Assn., Am. Orgn. Nurse Execs., Dean and Dirs., N.Y.C. Inc. (sec. 1993-94), Am. Coll. Health Care Execs. (assoc.). Home: 545 E 14th St New York NY 10009-3020 Personal E-mail: nungie0713@yahoo.com.

CARDINALI, ALBERT JOHN, lawyer; b. N.Y.C., Apr. 24, 1934; s. John and Ines (Clara) C.; m. June DuRose Seaman; children: Kathleen, John, Raymond, Kenneth, Scott, Jeffrey. BA, CCNY, 1955; LL.B., Columbia U., 1958; LL.M., NYU, 1965. Bar: N.Y. 1961. Asso. Thacher, Proffitt & Wood, N.Y.C., 1960-68, partner, 1969—. Served with AUS, 1958-60. Mem. ABA, N.Y. State Bar Assn., Assn. Bar City N.Y. Clubs: Shenorock Shore (Rye, N.Y.); University (N.Y.C.). Office Phone: 212-912-7633. E-mail: acardinali@tpw.com.

CARDMAN, LAWRENCE SANTO, physics professor, researcher; b. Mt. Vernon, N.Y., Oct. 7, 1944; s. Michael L. and Alice (Willis) C.; m. Helen-Andrea Fox; children: Andrew Lawrence, Michael Allan, Zena Maria. BA, Yale U., 1966, PhD in Physics, 1972. Instr. physics Yale U., New Haven, 1971—72, rsch. assoc., 1972; NAS/NRC postdoctoral fellow Nat. Bur. Stds., 1972—73; asst. prof. U. Ill., Urbana, 1973—78, assoc. prof., 1978—82, prof., 1982—95, adj. prof., 1995—, co-prin. investigator nuc. physics lab. Champaign, 1982—89, 1992; dep. assoc. dir. physics Continuous Electron Beam Accelerator Facility, Newport News, Va., 1993—96; assoc. dir. for physics Thomas Jefferson Nat. Accelerator Facility, Newport News, Va., 1996—; prof. U. Va., Charlottesville, 2002—. Vis. scientist Centre D'Etudes Nucleaire Saclay, France, 1980-81, Continuous Electron Beam Accelerator Facility, Newport News, Va., 1989-90; adj. prof. Coll. William and Mary, Williamsburg, Va., 1995—. Nat. Acad. Scis.-NRC Postdoctoral Rsch. fellow, 1972-73. Fellow Am. Phys. Soc.; mem. Sigma Xi. Avocations: woodworking, electronics, computers, cooking. Office: Jefferson Lab 12000 Jefferson Ave Newport News VA 23606 Office Phone: 757-269-7032. Business E-Mail: cardman@jlab.org.

CARDONA, MANUEL, physics professor; b. Barcelona, Catalonia, Spain, July 9, 1934; s. Juan and Angela (Castro) C.; m. Inge Hecht; children: Michael, Angela, Steven. Licenciado en Ciencias, U. Barcelona, 1955; DSc, U. Madrid, 1958; MSc, Harvard U., 1958, PhD, 1959; degree (hon.), Brown U.; Dr. (hon.), U. Autónoma de, Madrid, 1985, U. Autónom de Barcelona, 1985, U. Regensburg, Germany, 1994, Sherbrooke U., Can., 1994, U. La Sapienza, Roma, 1995, U. Toulouse, 1998, U. Thessaloniki, 2001, Masaryk U., Brno, 2002, Valencia U., 2004. Mem. tech. staff RCA Labs, Zurich, Switzerland, 1959-61, Princeton, N.J., 1961-64; assoc. prof. physics Brown U., Providence, 1964-66, prof. physics, 1966-71; dir. Max Planck Inst. for Solid State Rsch., Stuttgart, Germany, 1971-2000, emeritus, 2000—. Adj. prof. U. Stuttgart, 1973—, U. Konstanz, 1990—; lectr. Air New Zealand, 2001; mem. French Nat. Com. for Evaluation Sci. Rsch., 1999—2001. Editor-in-chief Solid State Comm., Oxford, Eng., 1992-2004; mem. bd. editors Physica Status Solidi, Berlin, 1971—; assoc. editor Phys. Rev. Letters, Upton, N.Y., 1989-92; editor Solid State Sci. Series Springer, 1975—; author: Modulation Spectroscopy, 1969, Fundamentals of Semiconductors, 1995, 3d edit., 2001; others; contbr. numerous articles to profl. jours. Recipient N. Monturiol medal, Govt. of Catalonia, 1984, Great Cross of Order of Alfonso X el Sabio, Spain, 1987, Principe de Asturias Found. award, 1988, J.M. Marci von Kronland medal, Czechoslovak Spectroscopic Soc., Prague, 1989, Sci. prize, Catalonian Sci. Found., 1990, Medaglia Teresiana, U. Pavia, Italy, 1992, Italgas prize, 1993, Max Planck Rsch. prize, 1994, Ernst Mach medal, Czech Phys. Soc., 1999, Sir Nevill Mott medal and prize, Inst. Physics, London, 2001, Medaglia Matteucci, Italian Acad. Scis., 2004, Blaise Pascal medal in Physics, European Acad. Scis., 2004; fellow, World Innovation Found., 2001. Fellow: Inst. of Physics (London), Am. Phys. Soc. (Frank Isakson prize 1984, John Wheatley award 1997); mem.: NAS of U.S. (ordinary mem.), Internat. Union Pure and Applied Physics (chmn. semicondrs. commn. 1996—2002), Royal Acad. Scis. of Spain (corr. mem.), Academia Europaea, Mex. Acad. Scis. (corr.), German Phys. Soc., European Phys. Soc., Acad. Scis. of Barcelona (corr. mem.), A.F. Ioffe Inst. (hon.). Lutheran. Office: Max Planck Inst Heisenbergstr 1 70569 Stuttgart Germany Office Phone: 49-711-6891710. Business E-Mail: m.cardona@fkf.mpg.de.

CARDONA, RODOLFO, Spanish language and literature educator; b. San Jose, Costa Rica, Jan. 17, 1924; came to U.S., 1943, naturalized, 1950; s. Jose Ismael and Julia (Cooper) C.; m. Electra Ducas, Aug. 1, 1954; children: Eleni Maria, Alexander Xavier, Michael Anthony, Christopher Pericles. BA, La. State U., 1946; PhD, U. Wash., Seattle, 1953. Consul of Costa Rica, San Diego, 1943-44; asst. instr. fine arts and Spanish La. State U., 1946-47; asst. prof. Am. Inst. Fgn. Trade, Phoenix, 1947-48; instr. U. Wash., 1948-53; hon.

consul Costa Rica, Seattle, 1948-53, asst. prof. Western Res. U., also hon. consul Cleve., 1953-56; asst. prof., then assoc. prof. Chatham Coll., Pitts., 1956-60; prof., then chmn. dept. Hispanic langs. U. Pitts., 1961-69; hon. consul Costa Rica, Pitts., 1956-69; prof. Spanish, chmn. dept. Spanish and Portuguese U. Tex., Austin, 1969-78; Univ. prof., dir. Univ. Profs. Program Boston U., 1978-88, prof. emeritus, 1991—. Resident dir. Internat. Inst., Madrid, 2000—. Author: Ramón: A Study of Gómez de la Serna and His Works, 1957, Del Geroismo ala Caquexia: Los Episodios Nacionales de Galdos, 2005; co-author: Visión del esperpento; editor: Novelistas españoles de hoy, 1959, La sombra de Benito Pérez Galdós, 1964, Doña Perfecta, 9th edit., 1984, Greguerias, 9th edit., 1997, La viuda blanca y negra by R. Gomez de la Serna, 1988; Novelistas españoles de postguerra, 1977; co-editor: Teatro selecto de Galdós, 1973; founder, editor: Anales galdosianos; contbr. articles to profl. jours. Andrew Mellon postdoctoral fellow, 1960-61; grantee Am. Council Learned Socs., 1967-68; grantee Univ. Research Inst., 1973-74; fellow Nat. Endowment Humanities, 1973-74 Mem. Phi Beta Kappa, Phi Kappa Phi, Pi Mu Epsilon, Phi Sigma Iota. Mem. Eastern Orthodox Ch. Home: 56 Bay State Rd Boston MA 02115-3108 Personal E-mail: rodolfo@localnet.com.

CARDONE, BONNIE JEAN, freelance/self-employed photojournalist; b. Chgo., Feb. 21, 1942; d. Frederick Paul and Beverly Jean Rittschof; m. David Frederick Cardone, June 9, 1963 (div. 1978); children: Pamela Susan, Michael David. BA, Mich. State U., 1963. Editorial asst. Mich. State Dental Assn. Jour., Lansing, 1963-64; asst. editor Nursing Home Adminstr. mag., Chgo., 1964-65, Skin Diver Mag., L.A., 1976-77, sr. editor, 1977-81, photographer, 1981—, exec. editor, 1981-97, editor, 1997-99; mystery novelist, 1999—. Author: Fireside Diver, 1993; co-author: Shipwrecks of Southern California, 1989. Named Woman Diver of Yr. Women's Scuba Assn., 1999; recipient Calif. Scuba Svc. award St. Brendan Corp., 1999; named to Women Diver's Hall of Fame, 2000, Women's Scuba Assn. Mem. Calif. Wreck Divers Club (Wreck Divers Hall of Fame, 2003), Hist. Diving Soc. (bd. dirs. 1997-2001). E-mail: bjcardone@hotmail.com.

CARDOSO, ANTHONY ANTONIO, artist, educator; b. Tampa, Fla., Sept. 13, 1930; s. Frank T. and Nancy (Mesina) C.; m. Martha Rodriguez, 1954; children: Michele Denise, Toni Lynn. BS in Art Edn., U. Tampa, 1954; BFA, Minn. Art Inst., 1965; MA, U. South Fla., 1975; PhD in Art, Elysion Coll. Calif., 1981. Art instr., head fine arts dept. Jefferson H.S., Tampa, 1952-67, Leto H.S., Tampa, 1967—; supr. art and humanities Hillsborough County Sch., Tampa, 1985—91. Bd. dirs., supr. art Hillsboro County Schs.; rep. Tampa Art Coun.; artist, 1952-87. One-man shows include Warren's Gallery, Tampa, 1974, 75, 76, Tampa Realist Gallery, Tampa, 1975; group shows include Rotunda Gallery, London, End., 1973, Raymon Duncan Galleries, Paris, France, 1973, Brussells (Belgium) Internat., 1973; represented in permanent collections Minn. Mus., St. Paul, Tampa Sports Authority Art Collection, Tampa Arts' Coun.; executed murals Tampa Sports Authority Stadium, 1972, Suncoast Credit Union Bldg., Tampa, 1975, Kotler Gallery Exhibit, Tampa, 2004, Centro Asturiano Ball Room Gallery, 2004. Recipient Prix de Paris Art award Raymon Duncan Galleries, 1970, Salon of 50 States award Ligoa Duncan Gallery, NYC, 1970, Latham Found. Internat. Art award, 1964, XXII Bienniel Traveling award Smithsonian Instn., 1968-69, Purchaase award Minn. Mus., 1971, 1st award Fla. State Fair, 1967, Gold medal Accademia Italia, 1981-82, Medallion Merit, Internat. Parliament, Italy, 1984, Statue of Vittoria award for centro studi and richerche, Italy, 1988, Accademia D'Europa, Premio Palma D'Oro D' Europa, Italy, 1989—, El Prado Gallery, 1990—, Merit award Festival Arts Hillsborough County Tampa, 1994-2002, El Prado Gallery, Tampa, 1999-2004. Democrat. Roman Catholic. Office: El Prado Art Gallery 3208 W Nassau St Tampa FL 33607-5145 Office Phone: 813-876-3629.

CARDOZA, DENNIS, congressman; b. Atwater, Calif., Mar. 31, 1959; m. Kathleen McLoughlin; children: Joey, Brittany, Elaina. BA, U. Md., 1983. Intern Rep. Martin Frost, Washington; mem. Calif. Assembly, 1996—2002; congressman 18th Dist. Calif. U.S. Ho. Reps., 2003—, mem. agr. com., mem. com. on resources, mem. com. on sci. Mem. Atwater City Coun., 1984, Merced City Coun., 1994. Named Legis. of Yr., Calif. Sheriff's Assn., 2001, Calif. Sherirf's Assn., 2002, U. Calif., 2001, Small Bus. Roundtable, 2001, Small Bus. Assn., 2001. Democrat. Office: 435 Cannon HOB Washington DC 20515-0518

CARDOZIER, VIRGUS RAY, higher education educator; b. Montgomery, La., Apr. 2, 1923; s. James C. and Lelia M. C.; m. Nancy Pattison Fyfe, Dec. 29, 1955. BS, La. State U., 1947, MS, 1950; PhD, Ohio State U., 1952; postgrad., U. Mich., 1967. Adult edn. tchr. and supr. La. schs., 1947-50; edn. specialist in industry, 1952-57; assoc. prof. U. Tenn. Coll. Edn., Knoxville, 1957-60; prof., chmn. rural edn. U. Md., College Park, 1960-70, prof. higher edn., 1968-70; v.p. for acad. affairs U. Tex. of Permian Basin, Odessa, 1970-74, prof. higher edn. and behavioral sci., 1970-82, pres., 1974-82; sr. acad. policy adviser U. Tex. System, 1982-83; prof. higher edn. U. Tex., Austin, 1983-97, prof. emeritus, 1997—. Vis. prof. Pa. State U., 1968; vis. scholar UCLA, 1983; cons. in field. Author: American Higher Education: An International Perspective, 1987, Colleges and Universities in World War II, 1993, The Mobilization of the United States in World War II, 1995; co-author, editor: Important Lessons from Innovative Colleges and Universities, 1993, University of Texas-Permian Basin: A History, 1998; contbr. articles to profl. jours. Bd. dirs. Am. Assn. State Colls. and Univs., 1981-82. With U.S. Army, 1943-45, PTO. Named Outstanding Grad. Ohio State U. Centennial Celebration, 1969. Mem. Am. Sociol. Assn., Am. Assn. for Higher Edn., Acad. Polit. and Social Scis., Assn. for Study of Higher Edn., Nat. Assn. of Scholars, Phi Delta Kappa, Omicron Delta Kappa. Office: U Tex Coll Edn Austin TX 78712

CARDOZO, BENJAMIN MORDECAI, lawyer; b. N.Y.C., May 15, 1915; s. Sidney Benjamin and Eva Cecile (Mordecai) C.; m. Barbara Ruth Schaffer, Sept. 21, 1941; children: Enid Cardozo Lamcn, Ellen Cardozo Sonsino. BA, Dartmouth Coll., 1937; postgrad., Columbia U., 1938; JD, NYU, 1941. Bar: N.Y. State bar 1942, U.S. Supreme Ct. bar 1947, Conn. bar 1954. Mem. staff Moreland Commn. Workmen's Compensation Investigation, N.Y. State, 1941, Office Alien Property, U.S. Dept. Justice, Washington, 1946-49; assoc. Cardozo & Nathan, N.Y.C., 1949-51, Cardozo & Cardozo, P.C., N.Y.C., 1952—; pvt. practice, N.Y.C. Mem. ABA, New York County Lawyers Assn., Assn. Bar City N.Y., Yale Club, Met. Club. Home: 325 E 79th St New York NY 10021-0954 Office: 488 Madison Ave Rm 1100 New York NY 10022-5702 Office Phone: 212-838-6120.

CARDOZO, MICHAEL A., lawyer; b. N.Y.C., June 28, 1941; s. Harmon and Lucile Cardozo; children: Hedy, Sheryl. AB, Brown U., 1963; JD, Columbia U., 1966. Bar: N.Y. 1966, U.S. Dist. Ct. (so. dist.) N.Y. 1967, U.S. Ct. Appeals (2d cir., 7th cit., 9th cir. and 3d cir.), U.S. Supreme Ct. Law clk. hon. Edward C. McClean U.S. Dist. Ct. (so. dist.) N.Y., N.Y.C., 1966-67; assoc. Proskauer Rose Goetz & Mendelsohn, N.Y.C., 1967-74, ptnr., 1974—2002; corp. counsel City of New York, 2002—. Chair Columbia U. Law Sch. Bd. Visitors, 1999. Fellow: Am. Coll. Trial Lawyers; mem.: Fund for Modern Courts (chair 1999—2002), Assn. Bar City N.Y. (pres. 1996—98). Democrat. Jewish. Office: 100 Church St New York NY 10007-2601

CARDOZO, RICHARD NUNEZ, marketing professional, educator, entrepreneur; b. Mpls., Feb. 13, 1936; s. William Nunez and Miriam (Honig) C.; m. Arlene Rossen, June 29, 1959; children: Miriam, Rachel (dec.), Rebecca. AB, Carleton Coll., 1956; MBA, Harvard U., 1959; PhD (Ford Found. fellow, Kaiser fellow), U. Minn., 1964. Asst. prof. bus. adminstrn. Harvard U., 1964-67; assoc. prof. mktg. U. Minn., 1967-71, prof., 1971—2000, Curtis L. Carlson chair in entrepreneurial studies, 1987-2000, prof. entrepreneurial studies, strategic mgmt., 2000—02, prof. emeritus, 2002—; dir. Ctr. for Exptl. Studies in Bus., 1969-73, chmn. dept. mktg., 1975-78; dir. Case Devel. Ctr., 1980-2000, Entrepreneurial Studies Ctr., 1987-2000. Dir. Nat. Presto Industries, Brownstone Distbg.; Fulbright lectr. Hebrew U., Jerusalem, 1980; vis. prof. bus. adminstrn. Harvard U., Grad. Sch. Bus., 1982-83; adj. prof. U. Miami, 2003—; cons. in field. Author: (with others) Problems in Marketing, 4th edit, 1968; Product Policy: Cases and Concepts, 1979; contbr. articles to profl. jours. Served with USAR, 1961. Fulbright fellow London Sch. Econ., 1956-57; Sr. scholar Fla. Internat. U., 2003—. Mem. Am. Mktg. Assn., AAAS, Product Devel. and Mgmt. Assn., Acad. Mgmt. Home: 202A Sunrise Dr Key Biscayne FL 33149 E-mail: dickcardozo@aol.com.

CARDUCCI, JUDITH WEEKS BARKER, artist, retired social worker; b. Norwood, Mass., Feb. 25, 1935; d. Harold O. and Catherine E. (Stone) Barker; m. Dewey J. Carducci, June 22, 1961; 1 child, David E.B. BA, U. Maine, 1956; MS, Columbia U., 1958. Coor. psychiatry and social work programs Cleve. VA Med. Ctr., Brecksville, Ohio, 1964-94; now artist, 1994—. Instr. art workshops, Cuyahoga Valley Art Ctr., Cuyahoga Falls, Ohio; mem. faculty Portrait Soc. Am. Mag., Am. Artists Mag., 1997, 2001, Artist's Mag., 1998, 2000, book, The Best of Portrait Painting, 1998, Internat. Artist, 1999, 2000, Pastel Artist Internat., 1999, 2001, mag., 2003, Pastel Jour., 1999, mag., 2003, book, Beautiful Things, 2000, Paint! Figure & Portrait, 2000, juried art shows include, State Tchrs. Retirement Sys., 1997, 1998 (Purchase award, 1997), Pastel Soc. Am., Nat. Arts Club, Am. Artists Profl. League, Salmagundi Club, Hilton Head Art League, Grand Exhbn., Akron, Portrait Soc. Am., Reston, Va., Degas Pastel Soc., New Orleans, Pastel Soc. of the West Coast, Calif., Butler Inst. Am. Art, Youngstown, Ohio, KLH Fine Art Competition, Bennington (Vt.) Ctr. Fine Art, Cahoon Mus. Am. Art, Mass., Lexington (Ky.) Art League (Best of Show), Cin. Art Club (3d prize, 2003), one-woman shows include Gallery 732, Akron Women's City Club, 1997, Hudson (Ohio) Galleries, 1997, Akron Jewish Cmty. Ctr., 1997, Moos Gallery, Western Res. Acad., Ohio, exhibited in group shows at Churski Gallery, Bath, Ohio, 1996—, Veerhoff Gallery, Georgetown, Va., exhibitions include Butler Inst. Am. Art, Youngstown, Ohio, Spaces Gallery, Cleve., Summit Art Space, Akron, Ohio, Represented in permanent collections Ohio Edn. Assn., State Tchrs. Retirement Sys., Rep. Sav. Bank, Hudson Libr. and Hist. Soc., Cuyahoga Valley Youth Ballet, Hudson C. of C., City of Hudson, Case-Barlow Hist. Farm, Cleve. State U., Hosp. for Spl. Surgery., N.Y.C., U. Maine Mus. Art; author: (represented in book) How Did You Paint That--100 Ways to Paint People, 2004 (Internat. Artist award); co-author: (book) The Caring Classroom-A Guide for Teachers Troubled by the Difficult Student & Classroom Discription, 1984; Exhibited in group shows at Cin. Art Club Nat. Show, 2003. Recipient Best of Show nat. pastel competition LaFond Galleries, Portrait Soc. Am. Internat. Competition, Best of Show, 2005. Mem.: Hudson Soc. Artists (pres. 1996—97), Am. Artists Profl. League, Portrait Soc. Am. (charter, bd., faculty), Akron Soc. Artists (Best of Show award), Degas Pastel Soc. (award of Excellence 1998, Patrons Purchase award 2001, Daler-Rowney award 2001, Award of Merit 2002), Pastel Soc. Am. (Art Times award, David B. Korostoff Purchase award), Cin. Art Club, Salmagundi Club, Phi Kappa Phi, Phi Beta Kappa. Home: 197 Sunset Dr Hudson OH 44236-3347 Office Phone: 330-650-4069. E-mail: djcarducci@aol.com.

CARDWELL, HAROLD DOUGLAS, SR., retired rehabilitation services professional; b. Varnell, Ga., July 17, 1926; s. Arlie Amber and Hettie Ellen (Eledge) C.; m. Priscilla Dean Rumley, July 3, 1954; children: Harold Douglas, Jr., Ruth Ellen Cardwell-Landau. AA, Daytona Beach C.C., 1972; student, U. Fla., 1970; BA, Fla. Tech. U., 1974; postgrad., Clemson U., 1975. Registered landscape architect Fla. Chem. operator Fercleve Chem. Corp., Oak Ridge, Tenn., 1945-46; draftsman C.M. Price Constrn. Co., Daytona Beach, Fla., 1947-48; bookkeeper, expediter W.A. Cardwell Constrn. Co., Gatlinburg, Tenn., 1948-49; office mgr., sales rep. J.H. Gordon Lumber Co., St. Augustine, Fla., 1949-51; asst. mgr. King Bros. Lumber Co., St. Augustine, 1951-56; pvt. practice landscape architect Port Orange, Fla., 1956-67; sr. rehab. specialist State of Fla. Divsn. of Blind Svcs., Daytona Beach, 1967-99, ret., 1999. Vice chmn. Daytona Beach Preservation Bd., 1987-98; adv. mem. task force Daytona Beach City Govt., 1987; vice chmn. Volusia County Hist. Commn., Deland, Fla., 1989-92; mem. adv. bd. Volusia County Hist. Preservation Bd., Deland, 1992-94; adv. mem. Flagler Centennial Com., Tallahassee, Fla., 1986; pres. Fla. Anthropol. Soc., Gainesville, 1988-89; chmn. Daytona Beach Preservation Bd., 1998—. Recipient Historian of Yr. award Volusia County Hist. Commn., 1988, Lazarus award for Preservation, Fla. Anthropol. Soc., 1988. Mem. Am. Hort. Therapy Assn. (registered hort. therapist, nat. treas. 1978-80), Fla. Nurserymen and Growers Assn. (bd. dirs. 1963-64, 68-69), Halifax Hist. Soc. (bd. dirs. 1974—), Fla. Hist. Soc., Lions (Pres.' award in leadership Port Orange/South Halifax club 1988). Democrat. Methodist. Avocations: history, anthropology, historical tools, pre-historic tools, writing, research. Home: 1343 Woodbine St Daytona Beach FL 32114-5740

CARDWELL, KENNETH HARVEY, architect, educator; b. Los Angeles, Feb. 15, 1920; s. Stephen William and Beatrice Viola (Duperrault) C.; m. Mary Elinor Sullivan, Dec. 30, 1946; children: Kenneth William, Mary Elizabeth, Ann Margaret, Catherine Buckley, Robert Stephen. AA, Occidental Coll.; AB, U. Calif.-Berkeley; postgrad., Stanford U. Lic. architect, Calif. Draftsman Thompsen & Wilson Architects, San Francisco, 1946-48, Michael Goodman, Architect, Berkeley, Calif., 1949; architect W.S. Wellington, Architect, Berkeley, 1950-59; prin. Kolbeck, Cardwell, Christopherson, Berkeley, 1960-66; prof. dept. arch. U. Calif.-Berkeley, 1950-82; prin. Kenneth H. Cardwell Architect, Berkeley, 1982—. Author: Bernard Maybeck, 1977. Pres. Civic Art Commn., Berkeley, 1963-65; mem. Bd. Adjustments, 1967-69, Alameda County Art Commn., 1969-72. Served to 1st lt. USAAF, 1941-45. Decorated D.F.C.; decorated Air medal with 3 oak leaf clusters; Rehman fellow, 1957; Graham fellow, 1961; recipient Berkeley citation U. Calif., 1982. Fellow: AIA; mem.: Berkeley Hist. Soc. (pres. 1997—2000), Alpha Rho Chi. Home and Office: 1210 Shattuck Ave Berkeley CA 94709-1413

CARDWELL, MICHAEL STEVEN, obstetrician, educator; b. Salem, Ind., Apr. 3, 1954; s. Carlie and Gladys Cardwell; m. Dannette Marie Littell, Oct. 8, 1983; children: R. Roxanne, Michael S. II. BS, Purdue U., 1974; MD, Ind. U., 1978; MPH, St. Louis U., 1991; JD, U. Toledo, 1992; MBA, Bowling Green State U., 1997. Diplomate Am. Bd. Ob-Gyn, Am. Bd. Maternal-Fetal Medicine, Am. Bd. Diagnostic Sonography. Intern, resident U. Ill. St. Francis Hosp. Med. Ctr., Peoria, Ill., 1979—82; fellow Baylor Coll Medicine, Houston, 1982—84; dir. maternal-fetal medicine Rockford (Ill.) Meml. Hosp., 1984—86, Bapt. Hosp., Nashville, 1986—88, U. Mo., Columbia, 1988—90; with The Toledo Hosp., 1990—92; dir. Maternal Fetal Medicine St. Vincent Med. Ctr., Toledo, 1991—96, dir. maternal fetal medicine, 2003—05, Riverside Hosp., 1996—2001. Advisor Mo. Low Birth Weight Program, Jefferson City, Mo., 1988—; physician advisor Planned Parenthood Ctrl. Mo., Columbia, 1988—90, Planned Parenthood, N.W. Ohio, 1990—; peer reviewer New Eng. Jour. Medicine, 1988—; mem. Perinatal Adv. Com., Jefferson City, 1989—90; asst. clin. prof. Meharry Med. Coll., Nashville, 1986—88; asst. prof. U. Mo., Columbia, 1988—90; mem. clin. faculty Med. Coll. Ohio, Toledo, 1990—; clin. instr. Ohio U. Sch. Osteopathy, 1993—. Contbr. articles to med. jours. Leader 4-H Club, Hardinsburg, Ind., 1968-72; asst. scoutmaster Boy Scouts Am., Livonia, Ind., 1970-72. Recipient teaching award Am. Acad. Family Practice, 1984. Fellow Am. Coll. Obstetricians and Gynecologists, Am. Coll. Preventive Medicine; mem. AMA, APHA, Soc. Perinatal Obstetricians, So. Med. Assn., Ohio Perinatal Assn., Alpha Omega Alpha. Republican. Mem. Christian Ch. (Disciples Of Christ). Avocations: travel, americana. Home: 7863 Brint Rd Sylvania OH 43560 Office: 3335 Meijer Dr Toledo OH 43617 Office Phone: 419-251-3704. E-mail: mdjbob@aol.com.

CARDWELL, NANCY LEE, editor, writer; b. Norfolk, Va., Apr. 2, 1947; d. Joseph Thomas Cardwell and Martha (Bailey) Underwood BA in Econs., Duke U., 1969; MS in Journalism, Columbia U., 1971. Copy editor Wall Street Jour., N.Y.C., 1971-73, reporter, 1973-76, editor fgn. dept. and Washington bur., 1977-80, night news editor, 1981-83, nat. news editor, 1983-87, asst. mng. editor, 1987-89; sr. editor Bus. Week mag., N.Y.C., 1989-91; editor Habitat World, Habitat for Humanity Internat., Americus, Ga., 1991-94; freelance editor/writer, 1994—. Episcopalian.

CARDWELL, THOMAS AUGUSTA, III, retired research scientist, retired personnel director; b. Oklahoma City, July 25, 1943; s. Thomas Augusta Jr. and Hilda Ogreta (Box) C.; m. T.J. Hopkins, 1992; children: Jill Suzanne, Mark Christopher, Robert M. Hopkins, Kevin D. Hopkins. BBA, Tex. A&M U., 1965; MS, U. So. Calif., 1976; PhD, Pacific Western U., L.A., 1988; DLitt (hon.), London Inst. for Applied Rsch., 1993. Commd. 2d lt. USAF, 1965, advanced through grades to col., 1982; ret., 1993; F-4 fighter pilot 390th Tactical Fighter Squadron USAF, Da Nang Air Base, Republic of Vietnam, 1967; F-106 pilot 11th Fighter Interceptor Squadron USAF, Duluth, Minn., 1968-72, ASTRA dep. chief staff for sys. and logistics Washington, 1973-74, dir. acad. tng. and pubs. Interceptor Weapons Sch. Tyndall AFB, Fla., 1974-77, program and planning officer Washington, 1977-81, dep. comdr. ops. 323d Flying Tng. Wing Mather AFB, Calif., 1982-84; chief strategy div. Orgn. of Joint Chiefs of Staff, Washington, 1984-85; comdr. 601st Tactical Control Wing USAF, Semach Air Base, Germany, 1985-87; asst. dep. chief staff for plans and prog. U.S. Air Forces in Europe, Ramstein Air Base, Germany, 1987-88; dep. asst. chief staff and vice comdr. Air Force Ctr. for Studies and Analyses, Washington, 1988-90; comdr. Air Force Studies and Analyses Agy., Washington, 1990-93; sr. program mgr. joint and comml. programs Sci. Applications Internat. Corp., McLean, Va., 1993-95, divsn. mgr. command and control ops.; v.p., ops. mgr. C2 Ops., McLean, Va., 1995-96; v.p. internat. and comml. bus. devel. ADSI Ops., 1996-97; v.p. info. tech., internat. sys. ops. McLean, 1997—2002; v.p., dep. ops. mgr., divsn. mgr. internat. sys. ops, 2002—. Lectr. in field. Author: Command Structure for Theater Warfare, 1984, 2d edit., 1991, Air Land Combat--An Organization for Joint Warfare, 1992; contbr. articles to profl. jours. Donor Washington Performing Arts Soc.; mem. Washington Opera Guild, Wolf Trap Assocs., Kennedy Ctr. Stars, Libr. Congress Assocs., Corcoran Gallery of Art, Air Mus. Britain (founder). Decorated Legion of Merit, DFC, Air Medal. Mem. Nat. Air and Space Soc. (founder), Studies and Analyses Assn., Air Force Assn., Red River Valley Fighter Pilot Assn., Air Force Mus., Mil. Ops. Rsch. Soc., Assn. Former Students Tex. A&M U., Air War Coll. Alumni Assn., Armed Forces Communication and Electronics Assn., Tex. State Soc. Washington, Tex. Breakfast Club of Washington, Old Crows, Am. Legion, VFW, Order of Daedalians (flight adj. 1978-80, vice flight capt. 1987-88), Mil. Order of World Wars. Republican. Episcopalian. Home: 3025 John Vaughan Rd Williamsburg VA 23185 Office: Sci Applications Internat Corp 1710 SAIC Dr Mc Lean VA 22102-3701 Business E-Mail: cardwellt@saic.com.

CAREK, DONALD J(OHN), child psychiatry educator; b. Sheboygan, Wis., Aug. 10, 1931; s. Peter and Rose (Gergisch) C.; m. Frances M. Schaefer, Jan. 28, 1956; children: Carla, Thomas, Therese, Peter, Mary Beth, Christopher MD, Marquette U., 1956. Diplomate Am. Bd. Psychiatry and Neurology (examiner in child psychiatry, psychiatry). Intern Walter Reed Army Hosp., 1956-57; resident U. Mich. Hosps., 1959-63; pediatrician Fort Meyer Dispensary, Arlington, Va., 1958-59; instr. psychiatry U. Mich., Ann Arbor, 1962-65, asst. prof., 1965-66; dir. day care Children's Psychiat. Hosp., Ann Arbor, 1965-66; assoc. prof. psychiatry and pediatrics Med. Coll. Wis., Milw., 1966-74, acting chmn. div. human behavior, 1970-73, prof. psychiatry, 1974-76; pres. med. staff Milw. Psychiat. Hosp., 1971-73; prof. psychiatry and pediatrics, chief youth divsn. Med. U. S.C., Charleston, 1976-96, emeritus prof. psychiatry, 1996—; staff psychiatrist Vols. in Medicine, Hilton Head, SC, 2004—. Co-author: Guide to Psychotherapy, 1966; author: Principles of Child Psychotherapy, 1972; mem. editorial bd. Am. Jour. Child & Adolscent Psychiatry, 1988-93; contbr. articles to profl. jours. Bd. dirs. Cedarcrest Girls Residential Treatment Ctr., 1969-71. Capt. USAR, 1956-59. Fellow Am. Acad. Child Psychiatry (com. on adolescent psychiatry 1979-85, com. on psythotherapy 1986-90), Am. Psychiat. Assn., Am. Coll. Psychiatrists (membership com. 1991-94, 95-98); mem. AMA, Am. Orthopsychiatry Assn., AAAS, Am. Psychosomatic Soc., Soc. Profs. Child Psychiatry, S.C. Med. Assn. (mental health com. 1992-93), S.C. Dist. Cr. Am. Psychiat. Assn., Charleston County Med. Soc., S.C. State Bd. Med. Examiners (med. disciplinary commn. 1992-95), Alpha Omega Alpha, Alpha Sigma Nu, Best Doctors in America Southeast Region, 1995. Fellow Am. Acad. Child Psychiatry (life, com. on adolscent psychiatry 1979-85, com. on psychotherapy 1986-90), Am. Psychiat. Assn., Am. Coll. Psychiatrists (membership com. 1991-98); mem. AMA, AAAS, Am. Orthopsychiatry Assn., Am. Psychosomatic Soc., Soc. Profs. Child Psychiatry, S.C. Med. Assn. (mental health com. 1992-93), S.C. Dist. Cr. Am. Psychiat. Assn., Charleston County Med. Soc., S.C. State Bd. Med. Examiners (med. disciplinary commn. 1992-95), Alpha Omega Alpha, Alpha Sigma Nu. Roman Catholic. Home: 97 Nightingale Ln Bluffton SC 29909 Office: Med Univ SC 171 Ashley Ave Charleston SC 29425-0001 Office Phone: 843-792-2436. Personal E-mail: djfmcarek@davtv.com.

CARELL, STEVE, comedian, actor; b. Concord, Mass., Aug. 16, 1963; m. Nancy Walls, 1996; children: Elizabeth Anne, John. Grad., Denison U. Performed with theater groups including Second City, Chgo., The Goodman, Wisdom Bridge. Actor: (films) Curley Sue, 1991, Over the Top, 1997, Tomorrow Night, 1998, Suits, 1999, Street of Pain, 2002, Bruce Almighty, 2003, Sleepover, 2004, Anchorman, 2004, Melinda and Melinda, 2004, Bewitched, 2005; (TV films) Life As We Know It!, 1991, H.U.D., 2000; (TV series) Saturday Night Live, 1996—2002, (and writer) The Dana Carvey Show, 1996, Over the Top, 1997, The Daily Show with Jon Stewart, 1999—2004, Watching Ellie, 2002—03, Come to Papa, 2004, The Office, 2005—; actor, writer, prodr.: (films) The 40 Year-Old Virgin, 2005. Office: The Daily Show 513 W 54th St New York NY 10019*

CAREN, ROBERT POSTON, aerospace transportation executive; b. Columbus, Ohio, Dec. 25, 1932; s. Robert James and Charlene (Poston) C.; m. Linda Ann Davis, Mar. 27, 1963; children: Christopher Davis, Michael Poston. BS, Ohio State U., 1953, MS, 1954, PhD, 1961. Sr. physicist N.Am. Aviation, Columbus, 1959-60; assoc. research scientist research and devel. div. Lockheed Missiles and Space Co., Inc., Palo Alto, Calif., 1962-63, research scientist, 1963-66, sr. mem. research lab., 1966-69, mgr. def. systems space systems div., 1969-70, mgr. infared tech. R & D div., 1970-71, research dir., 1972-76, chief engr., 1976-86, v.p. gen. mgr. R & D div., 1986—, corp. v.p. sci. and engring., 1987-98; chmn. LITEX Inc., 1998—2000. Bd. dirs. LITEX Corp., Superconducting Tech. Inc.; mem. U.S./Israel Sci. and Tech. Commn., 1997—. Contbr. articles to profl. jours.; patentee in field. Fellow AIAA, AAAS, AAS, Soc. Automotive Engrs.; mem. NAE, IEEE (sr.), Am. Def. Preparedness Assn. (past chmn. rsch. divsn.), Am. Phys. Soc., Aerospace Industries Assn. (past chmn. tech. and ops. coun.), Calif. Coun. on Sci. and Tech., Sigma Pi Sigma, Pi Mu Epsilon. Home: 6039 Gleneagles Cir San Jose CA 95138-2372 Office: 1220 Ventura Blvd Ste 2250 Sherman Oaks CA 91403-5338 Personal E-mail: rcaren@comcast.net.

CARENDI, JAN R., insurance company executive; b. Lomas de Zamora, Argentina, Mar. 12, 1945; Exec. trainee Skandia Ins. Co. Ltd.; dep. chief exec. Skandia Mexico (Reassurance Life and P/C), 1971—81; pres., CEO Skandia Colombia Group (Primary Life and P/C), 1982—86; exec. v.p., COO internat. life ops. Skandia Internat. Ins. Corp., 1986—88; sr. v.p., mem. corp. mgmt. group, COO assurance and fin. svcs. Skandia Ins. Co. Ltd., 1988—93, exec. v.p., mem. exec. mgmt. group, COO Skandia Assurance and Fin. Svcs., 1993—96, sr. exec. v.p., mem. exec. mgm.t group, CEO Skandia Assurance and Fin. Svcs., 1996—98, CEO Skandia Assurance and Fin. Svcs., 1998—2000, dep. CEO Skandia Group, 1998—2002, sr. advisor to exec. bd., 2002—03; CEO Skandia New Markets, Inc., 2001; mem. bd. mgmt. Allianz AG, Munich, 2003—. Chmn., CEO Am. Skandia, Inc., 1987—2000. Office: Firemans Fund Ins Co 777 San Marin Dr Novato CA 94998

CARESS, STANLEY MALCOLM, political science educator; b. Calif., 1951; BA, Calif. State U., San Jose, 1972, MA, 1974; PhD, U. Calif., Riverside, 1978. Lectr. Calif. State U., Long Beach, 1982-92; prof. State U. West Ga., Carrollton, 1992—. Vis. prof. U. Nev., Las Vegas, 1996-97; assoc. dir. Ctr. for Future Democracy, Fountain Valley, Calif., 1990—. Contbr. articles to profl. jours. Dem. nominee Calif. State Assembly, 1984, 92. Mem. Am. Soc. for Pub. Adminstrn. (exec. coun. Ga. chpt.), Am. Polit. Sci. Assn., Western Polit. Sci. Assn., Ga. Polit. Sci. Assn. E-mail: scaress@westga.edu.

CARET, ROBERT LAURENT, academic administrator; b. Biddeford, Maine, Oct. 7, 1947; s. Laurent J. and Anne (Santorsola) C.; m. Elizabeth Zoltan; children: Colin, Katherine, Katalyn Ford, Kellen Ford. BA in Chemistry & Math., Suffolk U., 1969; PhD in Organic Chemistry, U. NH, 1974; DSc (hon.), Suffolk U., 1996; DHL (hon.), Nat. Hispanic U., 1997, San Jose U., 2004. Dean Coll. Natural and Math. Scis. Towson (Md.) State U., 1981-87, prof. chemistry, 1994—, assoc. v.p., 1985-86, exec. asst. to pres., 1986-87, provost, exec. v.p., 1987-95, pres., 2003—, San Jose (Calif.) State U., 1995—2003. Bd. dirs. Coll. Bound Found., Md. Bus. Coun.; mem. workforce investment bd. Gov., 2005—. Author: (with A.S. Wingrove) Quimca Organica, 1984, Organic Chemistry, 1981, (with P. Plante) Myths and Realities in Higher Education Administration, 1990, (with K. Denniston and J.J. Topping) Principles and Applications of Organic and Biological Chemistry, 1995, 2d edit., 1997, Principles and Applications of Inorganic, Organic and Biological Chemistry, 1992, 4th edit. (General, Organic and Biochemistry), 2004, Foundations of Inorganic, Organic and Biological Chemistry, 1995; contrb. chpts. to monographs and articles to profl. jours. Chmn. Baltimore County Higher Edn. Adv. Bd., Towson, 1989-1994; co-chmn. Balt. Sci. Fair/Kiwanis, Towson, 1983-88; bd. dirs. San Jose Repertory Theater, 1995-2001, bd. dirs. San Jose Opera, Calif. State U. Inst., 1995-2003. Named one of Silicon Valley's 100 Power Brokers, San Jose Mag., 2003; recipient Employee Incentive award, State of Md., 1987, Outstanding Chemistry Tchr. award, Md. Inst. Chemists, 1971, Award for Excellence, Suffolk U. Gen. Alumni Assn., 1986, Tomas Rivera Leadership award, Nat. Hispanic U., 1999, Univ. Partnership award, 2002, Outstanding Pres. award, All Am. Football League, 2001, Achievement award, Italian-Am. Heritage Found., 2001; Albert W. Diniak fellow, U. N.H., 1972, Lester A. Pratt fellow, 1972. Mem. AAUP (Towson State U. chpt., exec. com. 1978-81, v.p. 1975-80, divsn. and dept. rep. 1975-80), NCAA (predidl. adv. com. 2004—, coun. pres. 2004—), Am. Assn. Higher Edn., Am. Assn. Univ. Adminstrs. (Md. membership rep. 1986-1989), EDUCOM (instl. rep. 1986-87), Am. Chem. Soc. (Chesapeake sect. alt. counselor 1979-87, exec. com. 1978-87, mem.-at-large 1978-79, com. mem. 1978-87), Am. Coun. Edn. (Leadership Commn., 2000, Internat. Commn., 1997), Am. Assn. State Colls. and Univs. (adv. bd. 1986—, Kellogg Leadership bd., state rep. 1989-1989, joint venture Silicon Valley bd. dirs. 1997-2003, co-chair econ. devel. team 1996-98, co-chair econ. prosperity coun. 1998-2000, bd. dirs. 2004—, rep. to ACE bd. dirs. 2005—), Coalition Met. Univs. (v.p. bd. dirs. 2004—, program and pub. policy com. 2005—), Silicon Valley Mfg. Group (bd. dirs. 1988-2003), San Jose C. of C. (bd. dirs. 1995-2001, Leadership in Excellence award 1999), Center Club Balt. (house com. 2004—, mem. Md. Gov.'s Workforce investment bd.), Sigma Xi (Towson State U. chpt. pres. 1975-76), Sigma Zeta, Phi Beta Chi, Omicron Delta Kappa. Avocations: jogging, tae kwan do, cross country skiing, golf. Office: Towson Univ 8000 York Rd Towson MD 21252-0001 Office Phone: 410-704-2356.

CARETTO, ANTONIA, psychologist; b. Garden City, Mich., Sept. 11, 1962; d. Antoni Charles Caretto and Harriet Pearl Moskovitz. BA in Psychology, U. Mich., 1984; MA in Clin. Psychology, Calif. Sch. Profl. Psychology, 1987, PhD in Clin. Psychology, 1991. Lic. clin. psychology Mich. Mental health worker First Hosp. Corp., Vallejo, Calif., 1987—91; asst. case mgr. US Behavioral Health, Emeryville, Calif., 1991—92; fellow Hawthorn Ctr., Northville, Mich., 1992—94; psychologist Adult-Youth Develop. Svcs., Farmington, Mich., 1994—96, Davis Counseling Ctr., Farmington Hills, Mich., 1996—2002, ptnr., 1999—2005; pvt. practice Antonia Coretto PhD P.L.L.C., Farmington Hills, Mich., 2002—. Med. adv. bd. OCD Found. Mich., Livonia, Mich., 1998—; mental health affiliate U. Mich. Comprehesive Gender Svcs. Program, Ann Arbor, Mich., 1998—. Mem.: Obsessive Compulsive Disorder Found., Harry Benjamin Internat Gender Dysphoria Assn. Avocations: travel, photography.

CAREW, THOMAS JAMES, neuroscientist, educator; b. Calif. m. Mary Jo Carew. BS in Psychology, Loyola U., Los Angeles; MS, Calif. State U., Los Angeles; PhD, U. Calif., Riverside, 1970. Prof. psychiatry Columbia U. Coll. of Physicians & Surgeons, 1970—76, NYU Sch. of Medicine, 1976—83; prof. Yale U., 1983—90, John M. Musser prof., chair dept. psychology, 1990—99; prof. neurobiology & behavior U. Calif., Irvine, Calif., 1999—2001, Donald Bren prof. & chair Ctr. for Neurobiology of Learning & Memory, 2001—. Author over 140 articles published in various journals; co-author: (books) Perspectives in Neural Systems and Behavior, 1989, Mechanistic Relationships Between Development and Learning, 1998; author: Behavioral Neorobiology, 2000. Recipient Merit award, NIH, 1990, Dylan Hixon prize, 1990. Fellow: AAAS, Am. Acad. Arts & Sciences; mem.: Soc. of Experimental Psychology. Achievements include research in neural basis of behavior and animal behavior. Office: U Calif 2205 Biological Sciences 2 301 Qureshey Rsch Lab Irvine CA 92697-4550

CAREY, ANTHONY MORRIS, lawyer; b. Balt., May 31, 1935; s. Anthony Morris and Louise (Waterman) C.; m. Eleanor MacKey, Oct. 7, 1967. AB, Princeton U., 1957; LLB, Harvard U., 1963; MLA, Johns Hopkins U., 1970. Bar: Md. 1963, U.S. Dist. Ct. (fed. dist.) Md. 1965, U.S. Supreme Ct. 1968. Assoc. Venable, Baetjer & Howard, Balt., 1963-67, ptnr., 1972—79, 1987—2003; former chmn. environ. dept., asst. atty. gen. State of Md., Balt., 1967-69; spl. asst. for energy affairs HUD, Washington, 1979-81; pres. Carey-Tidewater, Inc., Balt., 1981-86; regional dir., gen. counsel HEC Energy Corp., Balt., 1986-87. Former bd. dirs. Carey Machinery Supply Co., Inc., Balt.; former bd. dirs. Eberhard Faber, Inc; former exec. sec. Md. Bd. Ethics. Contbr. Former trustee Citizen's Planning and Housing Assn.; former dir. Nat. Civic League, Denver, 1979-90; chmn. bd. trustees Balt. Sch. for the Arts Found., current chmn. emeritus bd. overseers; vice chmn. Lillie Carroll Jackson Mus.; trustee, sec. Robert Garrett Fund for Surg. Treatment of Children; mem. Balt. City Commn. on Resource Conservation and Recycling. With USAF, 1957-60. Mem. ABA, Md. State Bar Assn., Balt.City Bar Assn., Ivy Club, Hamilton St. Club. Democrat. Episcopalian. Avocations: skiing, hiking, reading. Office: Venable LLP 1800 Merc Bank & Trust Bldg 2 Hopkins Plz Ste 2100 Baltimore MD 21201-2982 also: Venable LLP 575 7th St NW Washington DC 20004 Office Phone: 410-244-7620, 202-344-4804. Office Fax: 202-344-8300, 410-244-7742. Business E-Mail: amcarey@venable.com.*

CAREY, ARTHUR BERNARD, JR., editor, columnist; b. Phila., May 16, 1950; s. Arthur Bernard and Mary Louise (Lynch) C.; m. Katherine Ann White, Apr. 14, 1973 (div. Feb. 1980); m. Tanya Marie Walters, July 17, 1982; 1 child, Edward Lynch AB, Princeton U, 1972; MS, Columbia U., 1975. Editor Fedn. Telephone Workers of Pa., Phila., 1972-74; reporter Bucks County Courier Times, Levittown, Pa., 1975-77, Phila. Inquirer, 1977—. Author: In Defense of Marriage, 1984, The United States of Incompetence, 1991; editor: That's Livin', 1984 Term trustee The Episcopal Acad., Merion, Pa., 1982-88, alumni trustee, 1990-93; mem. com. to nominate alumni trustees Princeton U., 1989-92. Recipient Edward J. Meeman Conservation award Scripps-Howard Found., 1977, Best Story of the Yr. award Nat. Conf. Sunday Mags., 1983, George Washington Honor medal Freedoms Found., 1984, Disting. Journalism award Epilepsy Found. Am., 1997, Robert Joplin Sci. Writers award Am. Orthopedic Foot and Ankle Soc., 1998; Robert E. Sherwood Traveling fellow Columbia U., 1975; best feature story Pa. Soc. Newspaper Editors, 1986, 91. Mem. Soc. Profl. Journalists (best newsfeature N.J. chpt. 1979) Democrat. Episcopalian. Avocations: running, weightlifting, carpentry, antique jeeps. Home: 928 Clover Hill Rd Wynnewood PA 19096-1631 Office: Phila Inquirer 400 N Broad St Philadelphia PA 19130-4099 Office Phone: 215-854-4588. E-mail: acarey@phillynews.com.

CAREY, CATHERINE ELLEN, small business owner; b. Burlington, Mass., May 18, 1941; d. Clarence William and Mary Aglae (Dube) Ingalls; m. Edward Francis Carey, Sr., Oct. 7, 1973; 1 child, Edward F., Jr. At, Northeastern U., 1970-73, Essex Agricultures Tech., Rowley, Mass., 1977-78, Whittier Regional Vocat. Sch., Merrimac, Mass., 1980, Custom Decorating Inst., Santa Ana, Calif., 1980-84; student, Internat. Correspondence Schs., Scranton, Pa., 1990-92. Asst. bookkeeper High Carbon & Wire Corp., Millbury, Mass., 1965-68; pub. relations New Eng. Newspaper Supply Co., 1968—69; tech. aide Mitre Corp., Bedford, 1969—74; tailor, restorer of heirloom gowns Rowley, 1979—98, Bedford, NH, 1998—. Owner Edward F. Carey Jr. Disc Jockey. Contbg. author: New England Bride Mag., 1984-2000. Active Rowley Hist. Soc., Wenham Hist. Assn. and Mus., Inc. Mem. NAFE, Nat. Trust, Rowley C. of C. (bd. dirs., sec. 1983-1998). Roman Catholic. Office Phone: 603-647-2464.

CAREY, CHASE, broadcast executive; BA, Colgate U., 1976; MBA, Harvard U., 1981. Sr. v.p. Columbia Pictures, 1981—88; exec. v.p. & CFO Fox Inc., 1988—92, COO, 1992—94; chmn. & CEO Fox TV Group, 1994—2000; co-COO News Corp., 1997—2002; dir., pres. & CEO Sky Global Networks, Inc., 2001—02; pres., CEO DIRECTV Group, 2003—. Bd. dirs. News Corp., 1996—, Fox Entertainment Group, Inc., 1992—2002, News Am. Inc., 1998—2002, NDS Group, Inc., 1996—2002, Gemstar-TV Guide Internat., Inc., 2000—02, British Sky Broadcasting plc, 2003—, Gateway, Inc., Yell Finance B.V. Bd. trustees Colgate U. Office: DIRECTV Group 2230 E Imperial Hwy El Segundo CA 90245*

CAREY, DAVID, publishing executive; BA, UCLA. Pub. Smart Money Mag.; pub. House & Garden Conde Nast Pubs., NYC, 1996—98, pub. The New Yorker, 1998—2001; CEO bus. info. group Gruner & Jahr Pub., NYC, 2001; v.p. & pub. The New Yorker Conde Nast Pubs., NYC, 1998—2005, pres., bus. group, 2005—. Office: Conde Nast Pubs 4 Times Sq New York NY 10036*

CAREY, DAVID P., judge, career military officer; married; 1 child. Grad., Tulane U., Ohio No. U. Law Sch., Army Command Gen. Staff Coll., Army War Coll. Entered active duty U.S. Army, 1977, advanced through ranks to brigadier gen., legal assistance officer, chief mil. justice Fort Devons, Mass., def. counsel Republic of Korea, internat. law specialist we. command Fort Shafter, Hawaii, officer-in-charge br. VII Corps office staff judge advocate Ludwigsburg, Germany, 1985—88, with litigation divsn. Pentagon, exec. officer for judge advocate Europe, 1992—94, staff judge advocate 101st Airborne Divsn. (air assault) and Ft. Campbell, 1994—97, chief litigation divsn., 1997—2000, judge advocate Europe and Seventh Army Heidelberg, Germany, 2000, asst. JAG civil law and litigation Arlington, Va., comdr., chief judge legal svcs. agency. Decorated Legion of Merit with two oak leaf clusters, Meritorious Svc. Medal with three oak leaf clusters, Army Commendation Medal with oak leaf cluster, Army Achievement Medal. Office: JAGC US Army Pentagon Washington DC 20310-1500

CAREY, DAVID R., JR., history professor; b. Kwajelein, Marshall Islands; s. David and Margot Carey; m. Sarah Johnson. Spanish lang. and culture tng., IDEAL, Cuernavaca, Mex., 1990; Kaqchikel lang. and culture summer program, Tulane U., 1994—96; BA in Polit. sci., U. Notre Dame, 1990; MA in Latin Am. studies, Tulane U., 1995, PhD in Latin Am. studies, 1999. Instr. Tulane U., 1995—99; tchr. Caminos, Pathways Learning Ctr., San Francisco, 1999—2000; asst. prof. history U. So. Maine, 2000—. Mem. women's studies dept. U. So. Maine, 2001—; resident dir., program coord. Summer in Mex. Study Abroad Program Tulane U. and U. Iberoamericana of Mexico City, 1996—97; presenter, lectr. in field. Author: Our Elders Teach Us: Maya-Kaqchikel' Historical Perspectives: Xkib 'ij kan qate' qatata', 2001, A History of the Kaqchikel People, 2004; contbr. articles to profl. jours.; consulting editor: Mex. issue Faces: People, Places and Cultures, 2000; contbr. entries to encys.; author: Engendering Mayan History: Kagchilal Women As Conduits and Agents of the Past 1875-1970. Vol. Holy Cross Assocs., Los Andes, Chile, 1990—92. Recipient Albert J. Beveridge Rsch. grant, Am. Hist. Assn., 2003, John Anson Kittredge Ednl. Fund grant, 2003, Fulbright-Hays Dissertation Rsch. grant for Guatemala, 1997, Fulbright U.S. Student Program Rsch. grant for Guatemala, 1997, Fgn. Lang. and Area Studies fellowship, 1995, Tinker Found. grant, 1994, acad. fellowship, Tulane U., 1993—99, travel grant for rsch. presentation, Tulane Grad. Sch., 1998, S.W. Labor Studies Assn. scholarship, 2000, Alfred B. Thomas Book award, Southeastern Coun. Latin Am. Studies, 2002, Best Article award, Latin Am. and Caribbean sect. So. Hist. Assn., 2002. Office: U So Maine 37 College Ave Gorham ME 04038 Business E-Mail: dcarey@usm.maine.edu.

CAREY, DREW, actor; b. Cleve., May 23, 1958; Attended, Kent State U.; PhD (hon.), Cleve. State U., 2000. Acting debut on The Tonight Show, 1991; actor: (films) Coneheads, 1993; prodr.: The Big Tease, 1999; actor(voice): Robots, 2005,: (TV films) Freaky Friday, 1995, Sex, Drugs and Freedom of Choice, 1998; (TV series) The Drew Carey Show, 1995—2004; exec. prodr.: Drew Carey's Green Screen Show, 2004—; host, prodr. (TV series) Whose Line Is It Anyway?, 1998—2005, exec. prodr. (TV movie) Geppetto, 2000, TV guest appearances include The Torkelsons, 1991, Late Night with Rita Sever, 1998, Star Search, 1988, George Carlin Show, 1995, Lois & Clark: The New Adventures of Superman, 1993, Home Improvement, 1991, Ellen, 1994, Sabrina, the Teenage Witch, 1996, Weird Al Show, 1997, Dharma & Greg, 1997, Larry Sanders Show, 1992, star comedy spls. for Showtime: Full Frontal Comedy, Drew Carey, Human Cartoon; author: Dirty Jokes and Beer, 1997; host 25th Ann. Am. Music Awards, 1999. Formerly with USMC. Recipient Editor's Choice award, TV Guide, 1999, People's Choice award for best actor in a new series, CableACE award. Mem.: Delta Tau Delta.*

CAREY, EDWARD JOHN, utilities executive; b. N.Y.C., Jan. 16, 1944; s. Edward John and Mary Elizabeth (Hopkins) C.; m. Maureen A. McCullough, June 4, 1977; children: Christine, Caroline. BA, Fordham U., 1971. With N.Y. Central R.R., 1962-68; with Consol. Edison Co., N.Y.C., 1968-99; ret., 1999. Past bd. dirs. Salvation Army, Greater N.Y. Adv. Bd. Home: 17 Richmond Hills Irvington NY 10533-2301

CAREY, EDWARD MARSHEL, JR., accountant; b. Washington, Pa., June 12, 1942; s. Edward Marshel and Mildred Elizabeth (Bradley) Carey; m. Naomi Ruth Davis, June 1, 1964; children: Martha Ann, Mary Louise. BS in Bus. Adminstrn., Greenville (Ill.) Coll., 1964. Acct. GM Corp., Anderson, Ind., 1964—68, supr. acctg., 1968—70; staff acct. Carter, Kirlin & Merrill LLP, Indpls., 1970—74, ptnr., 1974—87, mng. ptnr., 1988—2000, tax ptnr., 2001—. Pres. CKM Mgmt., Inc., Indpls., 1985—. Mem.: AICPA (dir. Indpls. chpt. 1977—83, treas. 1978—79, pres. 1979—80), Inst. Internal Auditors (dir.), Am. Mgmt. Assn., Nat. Assn. Accts., Greenville Coll. Alumni Assn. (dir., treas. Ind. chpt. 1980—82), Indpls. Athletic Club. Republican. Methodist. Home: 215 Royal Oak Ct Zionsville IN 46077-1039 Office: Carter Kirlin & Merrill LLP CPAs 9102 N Meridian St Ste 555 Indianapolis IN 46260-1809 Office Phone: 317-844-8881. Personal E-mail: edcareyckm@aol.com.

CAREY, ERNESTINE GILBRETH (MRS. CHARLES E. CAREY), writer, educator; b. N.Y.C., Apr. 5, 1908; d. Frank Bunker and Lillian (Moller) Gilbreth; m. Charles Everett Carey, Sept. 13, 1930; children: Lillian Carey Barley, Charles Everett. BA, Smith Coll., 1929. Buyer R. H. Macy & Co., N.Y.C., 1930-44, James McCreery, N.Y.C., 1947-49. Carey writer and lectr. Book reviewer, 1949—, syndicated newspaper articles, 1951, (with Lillian Moller Gilbreth) (McElligott medallion Assn. Marquette U. Women 1966); author: Jumping Jupiter, 1952, Rings Around Us, 1956, Giddy Moment, 1958, Off and Away, 1998, Blubby, 1999, (with Frank B. Gilbreth, Jr.) Cheaper by the Dozen, 1948 (Prix Scarron French Internat. Humor award 1951, more than 53 translations), Belles on Their Toes, 1950; contbg. author: Smith Voices—Selected Works by Smith College Women, 1990, 99; lifetime papers represented in collections at Smith Coll.; also mag. articles and book revs. Bd. dirs. Right to Read, Inc., 1968—, co-chmn., 1967; lay adv. com. Manhasset (N.Y.) Bd. Edn.; trustee Manhasset Pub. Libr., 1953-59, v.p., 1956-59; trustee Smith Coll., 1967-72; active in care-preservation and current student use of Frank B. and Lillian M. Gilbreth lifetime papers at Purdue U., Smith Coll. and internationally. Montgomery award Friends of Phoenix Pub. Libr., 1981, honored guest Ariz. Lib. Friends, 1994; recipient Internat. Mgmt. award: the Gilbreth Medal, Soc. for Advancement of Mgmt., 1996. Mem. Authors Guild Am. (life mem., mem. guild council 1955-60), PEN, North Shore Club, Smith Coll. Club (asst. chmn. scholarship com. L.I. chpt. 1950-59), Smith Coll. Club (vice chmn. scholarship com. Phoenix chpt.). Home: 701 W Herbert Ave # 115 Reedley CA 93654-3941

CAREY, FRANCIS JAMES, investment banker; b. Balt., Mar. 24, 1926; s. Francis James and Marjorie (Armstrong) C.; m. Emily Norris Large, June 8, 1956 (dec. Apr. 1997); children: Francis James III, Elizabeth P. Carey Boden, Henry Augustus, Emily Norris, Frances Carey MacMaster. Student, Princeton, 1944; AB, U. Pa., 1945, JD, 1949. Bar: Pa. 1950. Law sec. to justice Supreme Ct. Pa., 1950-51; with firm Reed Smith Shaw & McClay, Phila., 1951-87, ptnr., 1956—87, counsel, 1987-92; pres. bd. dirs. W.P. Carey & Co., Inc., 1987—98; chmn., CEO, bd. dirs. Carey Diversified LLC, N.Y.C., 1998-2000; vice chmn., chmn. exec. com., bd. dirs. W.P. Carey & Co. LLC, 2000—; pres., bd. dirs. W.P. Carey Internat. LLC, 2000—. Mem. faculty U. Pa., 1946-47; bd. mgrs., mem. exec. com. Western Savs. Bank, 1970-82; pres., mem. bus. adv. com. Bus. Coun. for UN, 1994—2002; trustee Investment Program Assn., 1990-2000, chmn., 1998-2000; mem. Senatorial Trust, 1992—. Mem. Com. of Seventy, Phila., 1957-58; mem. Lower Gwynedd Twp. (Pa.) Planning Commn., 1962-75, sec., 1962-65; trustee Germantown Acad., Fort Washington, Pa., 1961—, pres., 1966-72; trustee Md. Hist. Soc., 2002—; overseer Sch. Arts and Scis., U. Pa., 1983-90; mgr. Law Alumni Soc., U. Pa., 1962-66; jr. warden St. Martin's-in-the-Field, Biddeford Poole, Maine, 2003-04, sr. warden, 2004-; trustee Md. Hist. Soc., 2002—. Served to lt. USNR, 1943-45, PTO. Mem. ABA, Pa. Bar Assn. (chmn. real property, probate and trust law sect. 1966-67, chmn. conf. group to cooperate with Pa. Land Title Assn. 1970-77), Phila. Bar Assn. (chmn. com. on civil legis. 1962), Soc. Mayflower Descs. in State of N.Y., Fourth Street Club, St. Anthony Club (Phila.), Sunnybrook Golf Club (Plymouth Meeting, Pa.), Racquet and Tennis Club, The Brook Club, St. Anthony Club (N.Y.), Abenakee Club (Biddeford Pool, Maine), Biddeford Pool Yacht Club, Md. Club (Balt.). Republican. Episcopalian. Home: 485 Lewis Ln Ambler PA 19002-5116 Office: WP Carey & Co LLC 50 Rockefeller Plz Fl 2 New York NY 10020-1607 E-mail: fcarey@wpcarey.com.

CAREY, JACK H., publishing executive; b. Phila., Dec. 25, 1950; s. Jack H. and Kathryn M. C.; m. Marsha C. Johnson, Dec. 15, 1973. BA, Allegheny Coll., 1973; MA, Syracuse U., 1975. Abstractor, indexer, editor Congl. Info. Svc., Bethesda, Md., 1975-81, staff writer, 1981-83, sr. copywriter, 1983-86, promotion mgr., 1986-89, dir. comms., 1989-97; advt. and promotions mgr. Bernan Assocs., 1997-2000; sr. copywriter Sallie Mae, Inc., 2000—. Mgr. direct mail, sales collaterals. Mem. Direct Mktg. Assn. Washington. Office: Sallie Mae Inc 12061 Bluemont Way Reston VA 20190

CAREY, JAMES HENRY, banker; b. Elizabeth, N.J., May 22, 1932; s. Charles C. and Adelyne (Bilyeu) C.; m. Nancy Mershon Ferrenz, Aug. 14, 1954; children: Jane Meredith, Christopher James, George Mershon, David James. BA cum laude, Brown U., 1953; postgrad., Sch. Bus. Adminstrn., N.Y. U., 1956-59. With Chase Manhattan Bank, N.Y.C., 1955-86, asst. v.p., 1961-63, v.p., 1963-68, exec. v.p., 1976-86, Hambro Am. Bank & Trust Co., N.Y.C., 1968-69, pres., 1969-72, also bd. dirs.; pres., chmn. bd. First Empire Bank N.Y. (formerly Hambro Am. Bank & Trust Co.), N.Y.C., 1972-75; exec. v.p. Chase Manhattan Corp., N.Y.C., 1976-86; pres., CEO The Berkshire Bank N.Y., N.Y.C., 1989-92; mng. dir. Briarcliff Fin. Assocs., N.Y.C., 1992—2002; chmn., dir. ABX Air, Inc., Wilmington, Ohio, 2002—. Bd. dirs. Midland Co., Asset Mgmt. Variable Series Funds, Inc. Bd. dirs. The Rayburn Found., Am. Mus. Flyfishing. Lt. (j.g.) USNR, 1953-55. Mem. The Dorset (Vt.) Field Club, Mid Ocean Club (Bermuda), The Sky Club, Phi Beta Kappa, Delta Tau Delta. Episcopalian. Office: PO Box 859 Manchester VT 05254-0859 E-mail: jhcarey@together.net.

CAREY, JANA HOWARD, lawyer; b. Huntsville, Ala., Apr. 20, 1945; d. Ernest Randall and Mary Regna (Baites) Howard; m. James Johnston Hale Carey, Jan. 15, 1983. BS in Home Econs., Auburn U., 1967; MS in Audiovisual Communications, Towson State U., 1973; JD, U. Balt., 1976. Bar: (U.S. Ct. Appeals (4th cir.)) 1977, (U.S. Dist. Ct. (Md. dist.)) 1978, (U.S. Ct. Appeals (3d cir.)) 1994, (U.S. Supreme Ct.) 1995, (U.S. Ct. Appeals (Md. cir.)) 1996. Tchr. Hampton High Sch., Melbourne, Australia, 1967; home economist U. Ga., Athens, 1967-70, devel. specialist state youth program, 1970-72, U. Md., College Park, 1972-73; clk. appellate div. Pub. Defender's Office, Balt., 1974; assoc. Venable, Baetjer & Howard, Balt., 1975, 76-84, ptnr., 1994—2003, past chair labor and employment group, 1995-97. Spkr in field. Co-author: (book) Legal Aspects of the Employment Relationship: An Introduction for the General Practitioner, 1978; mem ed bd: Employment Testing Law and Policy Reporter, Nat Employment Law Inst Adv Bd, Am Employment Law Coun Adv Bd; contbr. articles to profl jours. Chair dean's adv coun U. Balt. Law Sch.; pres. U. Balt. Edn. Found., U. Balt. Bd. Visitors; past mem pres adv coun St Mary's Col, Pension Oversight Comn Anne Arundel County. Named Top 100 Women for Outstanding Achievement, Daily Record, 1997, 2000, 2002; recipient Circle of Excellence, 2002, Univ. Baltimore Alumnae of Yr., 1999, Distinguished Alumnae Award, 2004. Mem.: ABA (past chair sect. coun. labor and employment law sect., past mgt. co-chair insts. and meetings com., EEOC liaison com. sects. com. equal employment opportunity law, mem. standing com. CLE, dep. chair labor & employment law com. sect. pub utility, comm, transp, health law forum, commn. on women in the profession), Univ. Baltimore Women's Bar Assn., Nat Asn Women Lawyers (past mem. gender bias com.), Am Col Labor and Employment Lawyers, Nat Labor Lawyers Adv Comt CUE. Personal E-mail: janahowardcarey@comcast.net.

CAREY, JOHN, judge; b. Phila., June 11, 1924; s. Henry Reginald and Margaret Howell (Bacon) Carey; m. Patricia F. Frank, Feb. 24, 1951; children: Henry Frank, John, Douglas, Jennifer Patricia. Grad., Milton Acad., 1942; BA, Yale U., 1947; LLB, Harvard U., 1949; LLM in Internat. Law, N.Y.U., 1965; LLD, U. W.I., 1985. Bar: Pa. 1950, N.Y. 1957. Practiced in, Phila., 1949-55; asst. dist. atty., 1952-54; cons. spl. com. fed. loyalty-security program Assn. Bar City N.Y., 1955-56; ptnr. Coudert Bros., 1961-87; justice N.Y. Supreme Ct., 1987; judge Westchester County Ct., White Plains, N.Y., 1988-94; mem. faculty NYU Law Sch., 1966-73; jud. hearing officer N.Y. State, 1995—. Author: UN Protection of Civil and Political Rights, 1970; editor: United Nations Law and Reports, 1966—. Alt. mem. subcommn. promotion and protection human rights UN, 1966—91, alt. rep. human rights commn., 1968; mem. Rye (N.Y.) City Coun., 1964—68, 1972—74, mayor, 1974—82; trustee Little Harbor Chapel, Portsmouth, NH. Mem.: ABA, Coun. Fgn. Rels., Am. Soc. Internat. Law (v.p. 1987—88), Assn. Bar City of N.Y., N.Y. State Bar Assn., Phi Beta Kappa. Home and Office: 860 Forest Ave Rye NY 10580-3145 Office: County Ct House White Plains NY 10601 Office Phone: 914-967-1290. Personal E-mail: jncarey@westnet.com.

CAREY, JOHN, language educator, critic; b. London, Apr. 5, 1934; s. Charles William and Winifred Ethel (Cook) C.; m. Gillian Mary Booth, Aug. 13, 1960; children: Leo, Thomas. BA, St. John's Coll., Oxford, Eng., 1957; PhD, Oxford U., 1960. Lectr. Christ Church Coll., Oxford, 1958-59; rsch. fellow Balliol Coll., Oxford, 1959-60; tutorial fellow Keble Coll., Oxford, 1960-64, St. John's Coll., 1964-75; Merton prof. English lit. Oxford U., 1976-2001. Prin. book reviewer Sunday Times, London, 1977—; hon. fellow St. John's Coll., Balliol Coll., Oxford, fellow British Acad., 1996. Author: Milton, 1969, The Violent Effigy, 1973, Thackeray: Prodigal Genius, 1977, John Donne: Life, Mind and Art, 1981, Original Copy: Selected Reviews and Journalism, 1987, The Faber Book of Reportage, 1987, The Intellectuals and the Masses, 1992, The Faber Book of Science, 1995, The Faber Book of Utopias, 1999, Pure Pleasure, 2000, What Good Are the Arts?, 2005. Served to lt. Brit. Army, 1953-54. Fellow Royal Soc. Lit. Avocations: bee-keeping, gardening, swimming. Home: 57 Stapleton Rd Headington Oxford England Office: Merton Coll Oxford England Personal E-mail: john.carey53@ntlworld.com.

CAREY, JOHN ANDREW, investment company executive; b. Glendale, Calif., May 27, 1949; s. John Nelson and Dorothea Ruth (Bordwell) C.; m. Harriet Ruth Stolmeier, June 19, 1982; children: Julia Scott, Elizabeth Bordwell. BA, Columbia U., 1971; AM, Harvard U., 1972, PhD, 1979. Chartered fin. analyst. Teaching fellow Harvard U., Cambridge, Mass., 1973-78; sr. council rep. Yankelovich, Skelly & White, Stamford, Conn., 1977-79; analyst Pioneer Investment Mgmt., Inc., Boston, 1979-81, sr. analyst, 1981-83, v.p., 1983-98, sr. v.p., 1998—2002, exec. v.p., 2002—. V.p.

Pioneer Scout, Inc., Boston, 1984-89, v.p. Pioneer Fund, 1987—, Pioneer Equity-Income Fund, 1992—, Pioneer Income Fund, 1994-96, Pioneer Variable Contract Trust, 1995—. Author: Judicial Reform in France before the Revolution of 1789, 1981. Treas. Newton Hist. Soc., Mass., 1983—87, Musicians of the Old Post Rd, 1998—; trustee Longy Sch. Music, 2001—. Mem.: CFA Inst., Boston Security Analysts Soc., Boston Athenaeum, Harvard Club of Boston. Republican. Episcopalian. Home: 14 Yarmouth Rd Wellesley Hills MA 02481-1249 Office: Pioneer Investment Mgmt Inc 60 State St Fl 18 Boston MA 02109-1800 Office Phone: 617-742-7825.

CAREY, JOHN CLAYTON, pediatrician, educator, medical geneticist; b. Balt., 1946; MD, Georgetown U., 1972. Diplomate Am. Bd. Med. Genetics, Am. Bd. Pediatrics. Prof pediatrics U. Utah Med. Ctr., Salt Lake City. Co-author: Medical Genetics, 1988, 3d edit., 2003, Care of the Child with Trisomy 18/13, 1996, rev. edit. 2000. Softly Written, Softly Spoken, 2002; editor-in-chief Am. Jour. Med. Genetics; contbr. over 200 articles to profl. jours. Med. advisor Support Orgn. Trisomy 18, 13 and Related Disorders, Utah Birth Defects Network, Pregnancy Risk Line. Office: U Utah Med Ctr Pediatrics 2C412 SOM 50 N Medical Dr Salt Lake City UT 84132-0001 Office Phone: 801-581-8943. Business E-Mail: john.carey@hsc.utah.edu.

CAREY, JOHN EDWARD, communications executive; b. Albany, N.Y., Sept. 21, 1949; s. John Edward and Lillian Rose (Murdock) C.; m. Nicolette Anne Yianilos, Oct. 26, 1974; children: Theodore, Anna. BA, Tulane U., 1971. Pres. FOI Svcs., Inc., Rockville, Md., 1976-95, Gaithersburg, Md., 1995—. Office: FOI Svcs Inc 704 Quince Orchard Rd Ste 275 Gaithersburg MD 20878-1751 Office Phone: 301-975-9400. E-mail: jcarey@foiservices.com.

CAREY, JOHN LEO, lawyer; b. Morris, Ill., Oct. 1, 1920; s. John Leo and Loretta (Conley) C.; m. Rhea M. White, July 15, 1950; children: John Leo III, Daniel Hobart, Deborah M. BS, St. Ambrose Coll., Davenport, Ia., 1941; JD, Georgetown U., 1947, LLM, 1949. Bar: Ind. 1954, DC 1947, Ill. 1947. Legis. asst. Senator Scott W. Lucas, 1945-47; spl. atty. IRS, Washington, 1947-54; since practiced in South Bend; ptnr. Barnes & Thornburg, 1954—, now of counsel; law prof. taxation Notre Dame Law Sch., 1968-90. Trustee LaLumire Prep. Sch., Laporte, Ind. Served with USAAF, WW II; to lt. col. USAF, Korean War. Decorated D.F.C., Air medal. Mem. ABA (bd. govs. 1986-89, treas. 1990-93), Ind. Bar Assn. (pres. 1976-77), St. Joseph County Bar Assn., Signal Point Country Club, Quail Valley City Club. Office: 600 1st Source Bank Ctr 100 N Michigan St South Bend IN 46601-1630 Home: 940 St Annes Ln Vero Beach FL 32967

CAREY, KAREN J., education educator; b. Tahlequah, Okla., May 12, 1962; d. Eugene and Bertie Carter; m. John David Carey, Aug. 6, 1983; children: Megan, Mallory, Madison. BS in Elem. Edn., Northeastern State U., 1983, MS in Ednl. Adminstrn., 1995; EdD in Adult Edn., U. Ark., 2001. Elem. tchr. Spring Brand Ind. Sch. Dist., Houston, 1984—86, Moore (Okla.) Pub. Sch., 1986—92; prof., dir. orientation Northeastern State U., Tahlequah, Okla., 2000—03, prof., dir. honors program, 2002—05, prof. edn., 2004—. Adv. bd. gifted and talented com. Tahlequah Pub. Sch., 2002—05. Faculty sponsor Honors Scholars Student Govt. Assn., 2002—; univ. rep. AAUW, Tahlequah, 1994—; sponsor Soroptimist Internat., Tahlequah, 2003—. Grantee, Nat. Collegiate Honors Coun., 2001—02. Mem.: Nat. Coll. Honors Coun., Am. Edn. Rsch. Assn., Tahlequah Pub. Sch. Tennis Booster Club (pres. 2001—05), Phi Delta Kapa. Baptist. Avocations: tennis, travel, cooking. Home: 808 W Downing Tahlequah OK 74464 Office: Northeastern State Univ 600 N Grand Ave Tahlequah OK 74464

CAREY, MARIAH, vocalist, songwriter; b. Huntington, NY, Mar. 27, 1970; d. Alfred Roy and Patricia Carey; m. Thomas Mottola, June 5, 1993 (div. March 5, 1998) Back up vocalist with Brenda K. Starr. Albums: Mariah Carey, 1990, Emotions, 1991, Mariah Carey MTV Unplugged, 1992, Music Box, 1993 (Grammy nomination, Best Pop Female Vocal for "Dreamlover"), Merry Christmas, 1994, Daydream, 1995, Butterfly, 1997, #1's, 1998, Rainbow, 1999, Charmbracelet, 2002, Through the Rain, 2003, Emancipation of Mimi, 2005; appeared in movies All That Glitters, 1998, The Bachelor, 1999, (mini series) Motown 40: The Music Is Forever. Recipient Grammy awards Best New Artist of 1990, Best Pop Vocal Performance by Female, 1990. Office: Columbia Records 550 Madison Ave New York NY 10022-3211

CAREY, PAUL RICHARD, biophysicist; b. Dartford, Kent, Eng., June 17, 1945; arrived in Can., 1969; s. Charles Richard and Winifred Margaret (Knight) C.; m. Julia Smith, Sept. 4, 1966 (div. May 1991); children: Emma, Sarah, Matthew; m. Marianne Pusztai, Mar. 7, 1992. BS in Chemistry with honors, U. Sussex, Eng., 1966, PhD, 1969. Postdoctoral fellow Nat. Rsch. Coun., Ottawa, Ont., Can., 1969-71, rsch. officer, 1971-94; mgr. Ctr. for Protein Structure Design, head protein lab. Inst. for Bio. Scis., Ottawa, Ont., Can., 1987-93; prof. dept. biochemistry Case Western Res. U., 1995—, dir. Cleve. Ctr. Structural Biology, 2000—. Mem. internat. adminstrv. com. Internat. Conf. on Lasers and Biol. Molecules, 1987—, adj. prof. Dept. Biochemistry, U. Ottawa, 1987-94, prof., 1994; prof. dept. biochemistry Case Western Reserve U. Author: Biochemical Applications of Raman and Resonance Raman Spectroscopies, 1982; contbr. over 200 articles to profl. jours.; patentee in field. Fellow Chem. Inst. Can.; mem. Am. Chem. Soc., Can. Protein Engring. Network (Adminstrv. body 1990-93), Internat. Network Protein Engring. Ctrs. Achievements include first demonstration of resonance Raman spectroscopy providing vibrational spectrum of a substrate or drug in active site of an enzyme; generation of first quantitative relationship between active site bond lengths and reactivity by combining resonance Raman spectroscopy, enzyme kinetics and x-ray crystallography; elucidation of mechanism of sunlight degradation of biological insecticide from B. thuringiensis; research on use of lasers in fingerprint detection. Office: Case Western Res U Dept Biochemistry Cleveland OH 44106-4935 Business E-Mail: paul.carey@case.edu.

CAREY, PETER KEVIN, reporter; b. San Francisco, Apr. 2, 1940; s. Paul Twohig and Stanleigh M. (White) C.; m. Joanne Dayl Barker, Jan. 7, 1978; children: Brendan Patrick, Nadia Marguerite. BS in Econs., U. Calif., Berkeley, 1964. Reporter San Francisco Examiner, 1964, Livermore (Calif.) Ind., 1965-67, editor, 1967; aerospace writer, spl. projects and investigative reporter San Jose (Calif.) Mercury, 1967—. Pulizer prize juror, 2002—03. Recipient Pulitzer prize for internat. reporting Columbia U., 1986, George Polk award L.I. U., 1986, Investigative Reporters and Editors award, 1986, staff Pulitzer prize for gen. reporting, Columbia U., 1990, Thomas L. Stokes award Washington Journalism Ctr., 1991, Malcolm Forbes award Overseas Press Club of Am., 1993, Gerald Loeb award UCLA Grad. Sch. Mgmt., 1993; NEH profl. journalism fellow, Stanford U., 1983-84. Mem. Internat. Consortium of Investigative Journalists, Soc. Profl. Journalists, Investigative Reporters and Editors. Avocation: classical piano. Office: San Jose Mercury-News 750 Ridder Park Dr San Jose CA 95190 Business E-Mail: pcarey@mercurynews.com.

CAREY, PETER PHILIP, novelist; b. Bacchus Marsh, Australia, May 7, 1943; m. Alison Summers, Mar. 16, 1985; 2 children. LittD, U. Queensland, Australia, 1989; LHD, The New Sch., 1998; DHC, Monash U., Australia, 2000. Tchr. creative writing NYU, Princeton (N.J.) U., Columbia U., NYC Author: The Fat Man in History, 1974, War Crimes, 1979, Bliss, 1981, Illywhacker, 1985, Oscar and Lucinda, 1989 (Booker prize), (with Wim Wenders) Until the End of the World, 1990, The Tax Inspector, 1991, The Unusual Life of Tristan Smith, 1994, The Big Bazoohley, 1995, Jack Maggs, 1997 (Commonwealth prize 1998), True History of the Kelly Gang, 2000 (Commonwealth prize 2001, Booker prize 2001), My Life as a Fake, 2003, Wrong About Japan, 2005. Recipient NSW Premier's Literary award, Miles Franklin award (3), Nat. Book Coun. award (2), Age Book of Yr. award (3), Victorian Premier's Literary award. Fellow Royal Soc. Lit. Office: c/o Binky Urban ICM 40 W 57th St New York NY 10019-4001

CAREY, ROBERT MUNSON, medical educator, physician; b. Lexington, Ky., Aug. 13, 1940; s. Henry Ames and Eleanor Day (Munson) C.; m. Theodora Vann Hereford, Aug. 24, 1963; children: Adonice Ames, Alicia Vann, Robert Josiah Hereford. BS, U. Ky., 1962; MD, Vanderbilt U., 1965; Doctor Honoris Causa, Fed. U. Ceara, Brazil, 1998. Diplomate Am. Bd. Internal Medicine, Am. Bd. Endocrinology and Metabolism, Nat. Bd. Med. Examiners. Intern in medicine U. Va. Hosp., Charlottesville, 1966; jr. asst. resident in medicine N.Y. Hosp.-Cornell Med. Ctr., N.Y.C., 1968-69, sr. asst. resident, 1969-70; instr. endocrinology, dept. medicine Vanderbilt U. Sch. Medicine, Nashville, 1970-72; postdoctoral fellow in medicine St. Mary's Hosp. Med. Sch., London, 1972-73; asst. prof. internal medicine, endocrinology and metabolism U. Va. Sch. Medicine, Charlottesville, 1973-76, assoc. prof., 1976-80, prof., 1980—, James Carroll Flippin prof. medical sci. and dean, 1986—2002, prof. u., 2002—, David A. Harrison III disting. prof. medicine, 2002—, assoc. dir. Clin. Rsch. Ctr., 1975-86, prof., dean emeritus, 2002—, head. div. endocrinology and metabolism, dept. internal medicine, 1978-86, chmn. gen. faculty, chmn. med. adv. com., chmn. exec. com., 1986—. Attending staff U. Va. Hosp., Charlottesville, 1973—, pres. clin. staff, 1977-79, vice chmn. med. policy com., 1986—, adv. bd. 1986—; mem. study sect. on exptl. cardiovascular scis. NIH, 1982-85; mem. cardiovascular and renal adv. com. USDA, 1988—; vis. prof. div. nephrology, U. Miami Med. Sch., Fla., 1979, 83, 84, Hosp. das Clinicas da Univ., Fed. do Ceara, Forteleza, Brazil, 1981, hypertension div. Mt. Sinai Sch. Medicine, N.Y.C., 1981, div. pediatric endocrinology N.Y. Hosp.-Cornell Med. Ctr., 1981, dept. endocrinology St. Vincent's Hosp., Univ. Coll., Dublin, Ireland, 1982, depts. physiology and endocrinology Mayo Grad. Sch. Medicine, Rochester, Minn., 1984, div. rsch. Cleve. Clinic Found., 1984, Genentech, Inc., San Francisco, 1984, divs. endocrinology and metabolism U. Mass., U. Pa. Sch. Medicine, Boston U. Med. Sch., 1984, U. N.C. Sch. Medicine, 1985, Harvard Med. Sch., Boston, 1987, Jefferson Med. Coll., 1988; Bley Stein vis. prof. endocrinology U. So. Calif., 1987; Pfizer vis. prof. in pharmacology U. Chgo., 1988; co-organizer 3d Internat. Meeting on Peripheral Actions of Dopamine, Charlottesville, 1989; v.p. Va. Ambulatory Surgery, Inc., 1986—; speaker, presenter numerous nat. and internat. profl. meetings and congresses. Author: (with E.D. Vaughn) Adrenal Disorders, 1988; co-editor: Hypertension: An Endocrine Disease, 1985; mem. editorial bd. Jour. Clin. Endocronlogy and Metabolism, 1981-84, Hypertension jour., 1983-84, Am. Jour. Physiology: Heart and Circulatory Physiology, 1987-89, Am. Jour. Hypertension, 1987—; author over 150 articles, revs., papers for profl. jours., contbr. 19 chpts. to books. Mem. exec. com. and fin. com. U. Va. Health Services Found., 1986—; bd. dirs. Va. Kidney Stone Found., Inc., 1986—, The Harrison Found., Inc. U. Va., 1986—, Dyslexia Ctr., Charlottesville, 1986—. Surgeon (lt. comdr.) USPHS, 1966-68, res., 1968—. Recipient Attending Physician of Yr. awrd dept. internal medicine U. Va. Med. Ctr., 1983-84, Disting. Alumnus award and Founder's medal Vanderbilt U.; USPHS fellow Vanderbilt U., 1970-72; recipient numerous NIH grants as co-prin. and prin. investigator, 1972—; named to Hall Disting. Alumni, U. Ky., 2000. Master ACP (program com. regional meeting 1987); fellow Coun. for High Blood Pressure Rsch. AHA (program com. 1984-86, exec. and long rang planning coms. 1992—; chair-elect 2002-); mem. Inst. Medicine of NAS, Am. Heart Assn. (established investigator 1975-80), Va. affiliate Am. Heart Assn. (bd. dirs. 1977-83, pres. 1979-80, Disting. Service award), The Endocrine Soc. (fin. com. 1988—, chair devel. com. 1991-92), Am. Fedn. Clin. Rsch. (so. sect. councilor 1978-81, nominating com. 1982), So. Soc. Clin. Investigation (nominating com. 1982, sec.-treas. 1985-86), Inter-Am. Soc. for Hypertension, Am. Soc. Clin. Investigation, Am. Clin. and Climatol. Assn., Am. Soc. Hypertension (intersocietal affairs com. 1986—), Internat. Soc. Hypertension, Assn. Am. Physicians, AMA, Albemarle County Med. Soc., Med. Soc. Va., Assn. Am. Med. Coll.s Coun. of Deans, Inst. of Medicine, Nat. Acad. of Scis., The Raven Soc., Alpha Omega Alpha (Disting. Med. Alumnus award Vanderbilt U. 1994). Home: Pavilion Vi East Lawn Charlottesville VA 22903 Office: U Va Sch Medicine PO Box 801414 Charlottesville VA 22908-1414

CAREY, SARAH COLLINS, lawyer; b. N.Y.C., Aug. 12, 1938; d. Jerome Joseph and Susan (Atlee) Collins; m. James J. Carey, Aug. 28, 1962 (div. 1977); 1 child, Sasha; m. John D. Reilly, Jan. 27, 1979; children: Sarah Reilly, Katherine Reilly. BA, Radcliffe Coll., 1960; LLB, Georgetown U., 1965. Bar: D.C. 1966, U.S. Supreme Ct. 1977. Soviet specialist USIA/U.S. Dept. State, 1961-65; assoc. Arnold & Porter, Washington, 1965-68; asst. dir. Lawyers Com. for Civil Rights, Washington, 1968-73; ptnr. Heron, Burchette, Ruckert & Rothwell/predecessor firms, Washington, 1973-90; chair CIS Practice Steptoe and Johnson, Washington, 1990-99; chair CIS Practice, sr. ptnr. internat. Squire, Sanders & Dempsey, Washington, 1999—. Cons. Ford Found., 1975—83; bd. dirs. Yukos Oil Co. Bd. dirs. Acad. for Ednl. Develop., 2004—; chair bd. dirs. Eurasia Found., 1994—; bd. dirs. Russia-Am. Enterprise Fund, 1993—95, Def. Enterprise Fund, 1994—2001, Georgetown U. Sch. Law Inst. Pub. Representation, 1971—85, Am. Arbitration Assn., 1975—82, Women's Fgn. Policy Group. Mem.: Atlantic Coun., Coun. Fgn. Rels. Democrat. Office: 1201 Pennsylvania Ave NW Washington DC 20004-2401 Business E-Mail: scarey@ssd.com.

CAREY, STEVENS ANTHONY, lawyer; b. Santa Monica, Calif., Mar. 30, 1951; s. Edward Macdonald and Elizabeth Crosby (Heckscher) Carey; m. Indy Shriner, Mar. 20, 1987; children: Lauren, Meagan. BA, U. Calif. Berkeley, 1973, MA, 1975, JD, 1978. Bar: Calif. 1978, N.Y. 1988. Assoc. Lawler, Felix & Hall, L.A., 1977; rsch. asst. Appellate Conf. IRS, San Francisco, 1977—78; assoc. Lawler, Felix & Hall, L.A., 1978—83; ptnr. Pircher, Nichols & Meeks (formerly Lawler, Felix & Hall), L.A., 1984—. Contbr. articles to profl. jours. Bd. mem. Calif. Trust Pub. Schs. Mem.: ABA, L.A. County Bar Assn. (real estate sect.), Calif. State Bar Assn. Avocations: swimming, music. Home: 1110 Benedict Canyon Dr Beverly Hills CA 90210 Office: Pircher Nichols Meeks 1925 Century Park E #1700 Los Angeles CA 90067 Office Phone: 310-201-8904. Business E-Mail: scarey@pircher.com.

CAREY, THOMAS CHARLES, elementary school educator, music educator; b. Syracuse, N.Y., Jan. 27, 1953; s. Charles Francis Carey and Janet Tillou; m. Janet Gay Wilson, Aug. 2, 1975; children: Kelly, Seth, John. BMus, Heidelberg Coll., 1975; student, U. No. Iowa, 1976, Bowling Green (Ohio) State U., 1978—85, U. Findlay, 1999—. Tchr. music Waterloo (Iowa) Pub. Schs., 1975—76, Findlay (Ohio) City Schs., 1976—85; tchr. elem. sch. Van Buren (Ohio) Local Sch., 1988—. Violinist Lima (Ohio) Symphony Orch., 1976—; instr. music U. Findlay, 1999—; co-concertmaster Lima (Ohio) Symphony Orch., 2002—. Chmn. St. Paul Luth. Ch., Jenera, Ohio, 1995—96. Mem.: Ohio Edn. Assn., Nat. Edn. Assn., Ohio Music Educators Assn., Music Educators Nat. Conf. Home: 454 Mountain Ash Arlington OH 45814 Office: Van Buren Local Schs 301 S Main St Van Buren OH 45889 Office Phone: 419-299-3416. Personal E-mail: tcarey@bright.net.

CAREY, TIMOTHY S, medical educator; b. Milton, Mass., Jan. 12, 1951; s. Edmund L. and Eleanor Carey; m. Kathleen Dalton, 1981; children: William H., Samuel L., Joseph M. BA, Colby Coll., 1972; MD, U. Vt., 1976; MPH, U. NC, Sch. Pub. Health, 1985. Lic. NC Bd., 1983, cert. Am. Bd. Internal Medicine, 1979. Physician Frontier Nursing Svc., Hyden, Ky., 1979—83; Robert Wood Johnson clin. scholar U. NC Chapel Hill, 1983—85, asst. to assoc. to prof., medicine and social medicine, 1985—. Dir. U. NC Chapel Hill, Cecil G. Sheps Ctr. Health Svcs. Rsch., 2000—. Mem., exec. coun. NC Coll. of Internal Medicine, NC, 1995; mem. Orange County Bd. of Health, NC, 2003. Comdr. US Pub. Health Svc., 1979—82. Recipient Cmty. Svc. award, Interfaith Coun. Social Svcs., 2003, Laureate, ACP, 2003, Cecil G. Sheps Disting. Investigator award, Sheps Ctr. Health Svcs. Rsch., Sara Graham Kenan Prof. of Medicine award, U. NC Chapel Hill, 2004, Northrop award, Am. Osteo. Assn., 2004; various grants, NIH, AHRQ, 1988 through the present. Fellow: ACP; mem.: Soc. of Gen. Internal Medicine. Achievements include research in health svcs. rsch. on the patterns of care for back pain, access to care, and evidence-based practice. Office: Sheps Ctr Health Svcs Rsch CB 7590 U NC Chapel Hill Chapel Hill NC 27599

CAREY, WILLIAM BACON, pediatrician, educator; b. Phila., Dec. 6, 1926; s. Henry Reginald and Margaret (Bacon) Carey; m. Ann Lord McDougal, July 21, 1956; children: Katharine Blayney, Laura Bacon, Elizabeth McDougal. BA, Yale U., 1950; MD, Harvard U., 1954. Diplomate Am. Bd. Pediatrics. Intern Phila. Gen. Hosp., 1954-55; resident in pediatrics Children's Hosp. of Phila., 1955-57, 59-60; dir. sect. on behavioral pediatrics Children's Hosp. Phila., 1989—; practice medicine specializing in pediatrics Media, Pa., 1960-89. Instr. pediat. U. Pa. Sch. Medicine, Children's Hosp. Phila., 1961—73, assoc. in pediat., 1973—79, clin. asst. prof., 1979—82, clin. assoc. prof., 1982—90, clin. prof., 1990—. Co-editor: (book) Developmental-Behavioral Pediatrics, 1983, 1992, 1999, Clinical and Educational Applications of Temperament Research, 1989, Prevention and Early Intervention: Individual Differences as Risk Factors for the Mental Health of Children, 1994; author (with S. C. McDevitt): Coping with Children's Temperament: A Guide for Professionals, 1995; author: (with M. Jablow) Understanding Your Child's Temperament, 1997, revised edit., 2005; contbr. articles to profl. jours.; developer Infant Temperament Questionnaire, 1970, co-developer Toddler Temperament Scale, 1978, Behavioral Style Questionnaire, 1976, Middle Childhood Temperament Questionnaire, 1980, Early Infancy Temperament Questionnaire, 1990, BASICS Behavioral Adjustment Scale, 2002. Pres. Friends of Wyck (House), Germantown, Phila., 1980—; bd. dirs. Benchmark Sch., Media, Pa., 1989—. Capt. M.C. U.S. Army, 1957—59. Recipient Wistar-Haines award, 2001. Fellow: Am. Acad. Pediat. (Rsch. grantee 1975, 1980, 1985, Aldrich award 1991, Practitioner Rsch. award 1992); mem.: Coll. Physicians Phila., Phila. Pediatric Soc. (bd. dirs. 1969—71), Soc. Devel. and Behavioral Pediat. (exec. coun. 1983—85, pres-elect 1989—90, pres. 1990—91), Ambulatory Pediatric Assn., Soc. Rsch. Child Devel., Am. Pediat. Soc., Inst. Medicine NAS, Penn Club, Franklin Inn Club, Phi Beta Kappa. Home: 511 Walnut Ln Swarthmore PA 19081-1140 Office Phone: 215-590-1467. Personal E-mail: wbcarey@worldnet.att.net. Business E-Mail: carey@email.chop.edu.

CAREY, WILLIAM POLK, investment banker; b. Balt., May 11, 1930; s. Francis J. and Marjorie A. (Armstrong) C. Grad., Pomfret Sch., 1948; student, Princeton, 1948—50; BS in Econs., Wharton Sch., U. Pa., 1953; ScD (hon.), Ariz. State U., 1998; DCS (hon.), CUNY, 2003. V.p., gen. mgr. A. J. Orbach Co., Plainfield, NJ, 1955—58; prin. W. P. Carey & Co., Bloomfield, NJ, 1958—63; pres., dir. Internat. Leasing Corp., N.Y.C., 1959—89; chmn. exec. com., dir. Hubbard, Westervelt & Mottelay, Inc. (now Merrill Lynch Hubbard, Inc.), N.Y.C., 1964—67; dept. head Loeb, Rhoades & Co. (now Lehman Bros.), N.Y.C., 1967—71; vice chmn. investment banking bd., dir. corporate finance duPont Glore Forgan Inc., 1971—73; pres., dir. W.P. Carey & Co., Inc. and affiliates, N.Y.C., 1973—83, chmn., 1983—; gen. ptnr. Corp. Property Assocs. (CPA), N.Y.C., 1978—97, chmn. CPA series of pub. ltd. partnerships and real estate investment trusts, 1979—. Chmn. Carey Instnl. Properties, N.Y.C., 1991—, W.P. Carey & Co. LLC, W.P. Carey Internat. LLC, 2000—; chmn. exec. com. Carey Diversified LLC, 1997-2000; adv. com. U.S. Treasury Dept., 1986-92; exec. in residence Harvard Bus. Sch., 1999; advisor W.P. Carey Sch. Bus., Ariz. State U. Trustee Johns Hopkins U., Newcomer Soc.; adv. bd. Johns Hopkins Sch. Advanced Internat. Studies; life trustee Gilman Sch. Balt., Pomfret Sch., Conn.; trustee, mem. exec. com. Rensselaerville (N.Y.) Inst., 1979—; chmn. bd. trustees Oxford Mgmt. Ctr. Assocs. Coun., 1984-94, hon. trustee 1994—; mem. coun. mgmt. Templeton Coll., Oxford U., 1970-95; chm. St. Elmo Found., W.P. Carey Found., Pa. Inst. for Econ. Rsch., 2001—; dir. (hon.) Edmund Niles Huyck Preserve; mem. leadership com. James A. Baker III Inst. for Pub. Policy Rice U.; gov. Nat. Assn. Real Estate Investment Trusts, 1993-97; chmn. bd. overseers Rensselaerville Inst. Conf. Ctr., 2000—. 1st lt. USAF, 1953-55. Estab. William Polk Carey prize in econs., Carey term chairs in econs. and fin. U. Pa., Carey chair in math. Pomfret Sch., Carey prize in math. Calif. Inst. Tech., Armstrong law prize Ariz. State U. Mem. Soc. Mayflower Descs. (gov. emeritus), White's (London), The Pilgrims, The Brook, Newcomen Soc., Racquet and Tennis Club, Univ. Club, Penn Club (N.Y.), St. Elmo Club (Phila. and N.Y.C.), Maryland Club (Balt.), Harvard Faculty Club (Cambridge), N.E. Harbor Fleet (N.E. Harbor, Maine), Johns Hopkins Club, Delta Phi. Episcopalian. Home: 525 Park Ave New York NY 10021-8141 also: Fullerlea Rensselaerville NY 12147 Office: 50 Rockefeller Plz New York NY 10020-1605

CAREY-SHULER, BARBARA, county commissioner; BA in Speech, Fla. A&M U., 1961; M in Comms. and Speech, Ohio State U., 1962; M in Guidance, U. Miami, 1969; EdD in Edn., U. Fla., 1978. County commr. dist. 3 Miami Dade County, Fla., 1979—; chair Miami Dade County Commn., Fla., 2002—04; exec. dir. office of multicultural programs Dade County Pub. Schs., 1990-92, asst. supt., 1992-96. Office: 111 NW 1st St Miami FL 33128-1902

CARFAGNA, VINCENT O., physician; b. Syracuse, NY, Feb. 15, 1931; s. Cosmo and Livia Irma (Franceschetti) Carfagna; m. Bernice Irene Czerwinski, July 2, 1960; children: Michael Dominick, Catherine Ann, Christopher Cosmo Casimir. BS, LeMoyne Coll., 1953; MD, Creighton U., 1959. Diplomate Am. Bd. Family Practice. Intern, gen. practice resident Mercy Hosp., Buffalo, 1959—61, attending physician, 1961—, chmn. pharmacy and therapeutics, 1981—91, chmn. dept. family practice, 1997—. Sch. physician East Aurora (NY) Pub. Schs., 1963—96, on-field football med. officer, 1963—95. With U.S. Army, 1953—58. Named Man of Hr., East Aurora Jaycees; recipient Outstanding Svc. Placque, East Aurora Football Boosters, Golden Stethoscope award, Erie County chpg. NY State Acad. Family Physicians. Fellow: Am. Acad. Family Physicians. Roman Catholic. Avocations: tennis, gardening, Nordic skiing. Office: 323 Main St East Aurora NY 14052

CARFORA, JOHN MICHAEL, economics professor, academic administrator; b. New Haven, Conn., July 24, 1950; s. John Michael and Rose Mary (Mitro) C.; m. Linda Louise Palmer, July 22, 1972; 1 child, Rachel Ellen. BS, U. New Haven, 1973, MPA, 1975; MS in Econs. and Polit. Sci., London Sch. Econs., 1978; AM, Dartmouth Coll., 1985; EdM, Harvard U., 1993. Rsch. asst. London Sch. Econs. and Polit. Sci., 1980-81; lectr. polit. sci. Albertus Magnus Coll., New Haven, 1982-83; lectr. econs. and quantitative analysis U. New Haven, 1982-83; program cons. Dartmouth Coll., 1984-85, assoc. prof. internat. econ. Sch. Internat. Tng., 1985-90; v.p. rsch. and acad. affairs, dir. Soviet-Am. projects Global-Genesis, Internat. Cons., 1989-91, dir. east and west projects, 1992-94; asst. dean for rsch. and sponsored programs Ind. State U., Terre Haute, 1994-95; dir. grants and sponsored programs Simmons Coll., Boston, 1995-97; assoc. dir. grants and contracts Dartmouth Coll., Hanover, NH, 1997—2002; dir. office rsch. & sponsored programs Boston Coll., 2002—. Ednl. cons. USSR Acad. Mgmt., Moscow, 1991-92; vis. asst. prof. U.S. Dept. Def., Europe, 1979-80; vis. sr. lectr. Poly. of Ctrl. London, 1980; vis. asst. prof. internat. rels. So. Conn. State U., New Haven, 1982; cons. Commonwealth Acad. Mgmt., Moscow, 1992-94. Mem. editl. bd. Rsch. Mgmt. Rev.; contbr. articles to profl. jours. With USAR, 1970-76. Recipient Roy E. Jenkins award, 1972; fellow Radio Free Europe-Radio Liberty, 1979, Internat. Rsch. and Exchs. Bd., 1981-84. Mem. ASTD, AAUP, Am. Assn. Advancement Slavic Studies, Nat. Assn. Fgn. Student Advisors (internat. educators), Am. Acad. Polit. Sci., Am. Econ. Assn., Am. Polit. Sci. Assn., Am. Assn. for Higher Edn., Am. Assn. for Adult and Continuing Edn., Nat. Coun. Univ. Rsch. Adminstrs. (bd. dirs., chmn. internat. commn. on rsch. adminstrn. 2004—), Acad. Polit. Sci., N.E. Slavic Assn., Soc. Rsch. Adminstrs., Royal Acad. Pub. Adminstrn. (Eng.), Atlantic Econ. Soc., Am. Friends of the London Sch. Econs. (Conn. program chmn. 1981-85, N.H.-Vt. program chmn. 1985-87, alumni bd. dirs. 1983-92). Office: Office Sponsored Programs Boston Coll Chestnut Hill Chestnut Hill MA 02467 Office Phone: 617-552-4950. Business E-Mail: john.carfora@bc.edu.

CARGILL, LANCE, lawyer, state representative; b. Oklahoma City, Okla., Sept. 13, 1971; s. Bill and Sharon Ann (Sieman) Cargill; m. Amber Smith. BS in Econs. and Polit. Scis., Okla. State U., 1993; JD, U. Vanderbilt, 1996. Bar: Okla. Lawyer Sole Practive, Harrah, Okla.; rep. Ho. Reps., State of Okla., Okla. City, 2001—. Adj. prof. econs., Okla. City; mem. subciom. on pub. safety and judiciary to appropriations and budget com. Okla. Ho. Reps., Okla. City, 2001—, mem. banking and fin., energy and utility regulation, wildlife coms., 2001—. Republican. Office: 2300 N Lincoln Blvd Rm 500-A Oklahoma City OK 73105 Home and Office: 4288 Deer Park Harrah OK 73045 E-mail: cargillla@lsb.state.ok.us.

CARGO, DAVID FRANCIS, lawyer, former governor; b. Dowagiac, Mich., Jan. 13, 1929; s. Francis Clair and Mary E. (Harton) C.; children: Veronica Ann, David Joseph, Patrick Michael, Maria Elena Christina, Eamon Francis. AB, U. Mich., 1951, M of Pub. Adminstrn., 1953, JD, 1957. Bar: Mich. 1957, N.Mex. 1957, Oreg. 1974. Pvt. practice, Albuquerque, 1957; asst. dist. atty., 1958-59; mem. N.Mex. Ho. of Reps., 1962; gov. N.Mex., 1967-71; practice law Santa Fe, 1970-73, Portland, Oreg., 1973-83. Bd. dirs. N.Mex. State Lottery Authority; mem. Interstate Compact. Chmn. Four Corners Regional Commn., 1967-71, Oil and Gas Conservation Commn.; chmn. N.Mex. Young Reps., 1959-61, Clackamas County Rep. Ctrl. Com.; mem. Israel Bond Com.; former mem. bd. govs. St. John Coll.; bd. dirs. Albuquerque Tech. Vocat. Sch.; chmn. governing bd. Albuquerque Tv.I. C.C.; mem. Albuquerque City Pers. Bd., N.Mex. State Lottery Authority; adv. bd. mem. N.Mex. State Fair; exec. bd. Found. for Open Govt.; bd. dirs. N.Mex. State Libr. Found.; elected state chair libr. bond chmn., 2002; pres. Calvin Coolidge Found. and Libr.; bd. dirs. N.Mex. State Lottery, Cumbres and Toltec R.R.; founder David F. Cargo Cmty. Libr., Mora, N.Mex. With U.S. Army, 1953-55. Named Man of Yr. Albuquerque Jr. C. of C., 1964, Congregation Albert Brotherhood Man of Yr., 2001, 2002; recipient Outstanding Conservationist award N.Mex. Wildlife Assn., 1969, 70; David F. Cargo Libr., Mora, N.Mex., named in his honor. Mem. Mich. Bar Assn., Oreg. Bar Assn., N.Mex. Bar Assn., Albuquerque Bar Assn., Isaac Walton League (past v.p. N.Mex.), World Affairs Coun. Oreg. (pres.), Interstate Oil and Gas Compact, Isaak Walton League Oreg., Hispano C. of C., Am. Leadership Conf. (bd. dirs.), Nat. Fedn. Blind, Oreg. State Film Commn., KC. Home: 6422 Concordia Rd NE Albuquerque NM 87111-1228

CARGO, WILLIAM IRA, retired ambassador; b. Detroit, Feb. 27, 1917; s. Ira Wiles and Nina (Lathrop) C.; m. Margaret Grace Ludwig, June 21, 1938; children: David Paul, Ruth. AB, Albion Coll., 1937, LLD, 1963; AM, U. Mich., 1938, PhD, 1941; student Russian lang., Naval Tng. Sch., Boulder, Colo., 1944-45; LLD, Waynesburg Coll., 1970. Instr. polit. sci. U. Mich., 1941-42, Colo. Coll., 1942-43; staff Dept. State, 1943-78, Bur. UN Affairs, 1946-53, dep. dir. office dependent area affairs, 1952; assigned Nat. War Coll., 1953-54; adviser U.S. delegations Gen. Assembly, Trusteeship Council Sessions, 1946-53; alternate U.S. rep. UN Com. on Non-self-governing Terrs., 1952; U.S. rep. UN vis. mission Trust Terrs. Tanganyika, Italian Somaliland, Ruanda-Urundi, 1951; assigned to U.S. Mission to NATO and European regional orgns. in connection with spl. internat. trade problems, Paris, 1954-57; dep. dir. Office of UN Polit. and Security Affairs, Dept. State, 1957-58, dir., 1958-61; dep. U.S. rep. Internat. Atomic Energy Agy., Vienna, 1961-63; dep. chief of mission, minister-counselor Am. embassy, Karachi and Rawalpindi, Pakistan, 1963-67; dep. U.S. rep. to NATO minister, Brussels, 1967-69; career minister U.S. Fgn. Service, 1969; dir. policy planning staff Dept. State, Washington, 1969-73; US amb. to Nepal, 1973—76; sr. insp. Fgn. Service Inspection Corps., Washington, 1976-78, cons., 1979-83; adviser U.S. delegation UN Gen. Assembly, 1957, Gen. Conf. of IAEA, Vienna, 1958, alt. U.S. rep., 1961, 62; adviser U.S. del. Conf. Discontinuance Nuclear Weapons Tests, Geneva, 1959; vice-chmn. U.S. del. Conf. to Amend Single Conv. Narcotic Drugs, Geneva, 1972. Co-author: (autobiography) Wherever the Road Leads, 1997. Served with USNR, 1944-46. Recipient Meritorious Svc. award, Dept. State. Mem. Am. Fgn. Svc. Assn., Diplomatic and Consular Officers Ret., Phi Beta Kappa, Delta Sigma Rho, Phi Mu Alpha. Methodist. Home: Vantage House # 313 5400 Vantage Point Rd Columbia MD 21044-2696

CARHART, HOMER WALTER, retired research scientist; b. Orange, Calif., May 21, 1914; s. Walter D. and Ethel (Shepherd) C.; m. Julia M. Holzapfel, June 15, 1940; children: Martha Jean, David Henry. BS, Dakota Wesleyan U., 1934; MA, U. S.D., 1935; PhD in Organic Chemistry, U. Md., 1939. Asst. prof. Gallaudet Coll., Washington, 1939-42; rsch. chemist Naval Rsch. Lab., Washington, 1942-52, head fuels br., 1952-70, head chem. dynamics br., 1970-86, dir. Navy Tech. Ctr. for Safety and Survivability, 1986-94, sr. scientist emeritus, 1994—. Mem. sec. of treas. Blue Ribbon Com. on Tanker Hazards, 1962-63; USN mem., del. Am., Brit., Can., and Australian Quadripartite Coms. on Fuels, 1964-94; mem. USN Working Group in Submarine Atmosphere Control, 1966-71; mem. Nat. Acad. Scis./NRC Com. on Hazardous Materials, 1966-75, chmn. Elec. Hazards Panel, 1966-75, chmn. Electrostatics Panel, 1969-75, chmn. indsl. hazards com., 1982-89; fire panel mem., spl. cons. NASA Apollo 204 (Fatal) Fire Rev. Bd., 1967; mem. exec. group, dir. Navy Labs. Planning Panel for Enhanced Aircraft Carrier Survivability, 1967-68; chmn. USN Panel on Hydrogen as a Potential Fuel, 1973, USN Inter-Labs. Com. on Pers. Adminstrn., 1973-75; chmn. dir. Navy Labs. Advanced Tech. Objectives Working Group for Fire Rsch., 1973-76; mem. Coordinating Rsch. Coun. Diesel Com., 1950-66; chmn. Ignition Quality Investigation Group, 1956-66, Compression Ignition Adv. Group, 1960-65; chmn. Aviation Fuel Safety Task Force (Adv. to FAA), 1974-76; chmn. NAS/NRC Com. on Indsl. Hazards, 1982-89; mem. Dept. of Labor Joint Soviet/Am. Task Force on Safety in the Chem. Industry, 1991. Contbr. articles to profl. publs.; patentee in field. Recipient USN Meritorious Civilian Svc. award, 1945, Dept. of Navy Recognition of Achievement award, 1975, USN Superior Civilian Svc. award, 1965, USN Disting. Civilian Svc. award, 1979, Winning Team, Federally Employed Women, Inc. award, 1989, Robert Dexter Conrad award for outstanding achievemnet in naval sci. and engring., 1991, Naval Rsch. Lab. Lifetime Achievement award, 1994, Harry C. Bigglestone award for excellence in written comm. of fire protection concepts, 1990, Jack Bono Engring. Comms. award, 1995, Ann. Homer W. Carhart award for excellence in damage control/fire protection established by Chief of Naval Ops; elevated to rank of Meritorious Sr. Exec. by Pres. Bush, 1989, Naval Rsch. Lab. Award for Innovation, 1998. Mem. Am. Chem. Soc. (alt. councilor 1954-56), Chem. Soc. Washington (mgr. 1953, mem. com. on rels. and status com. 1954, chmn. budget com. 1957, chmn. edn. com. 1965-66, chmn. long range planning com. 1967-70), Combustion Inst. (charter), U.S. Naval Inst., Naval Submarine League, Surface Navy Assn., Navy League U.S., Phi Kappa Phi, Sigma Xi. Avocations: musical composition, plant hybridization, photography. Office: Naval Rsch Lab Code 6108 Washington DC 20375-0001

CARICO, OPAL LEE, retired elementary school educator; b. New Tazewell, Tenn., May 9, 1929; d. Raleigh David and Myrtle Rose (Bunch) Lester; m. Joyce Darrell Carico, Nov. 25, 1956; 1 child, Thomas Darrell. BS cum laude, East Tenn. State U., 1977, MEd, 1982, postgrad., 1989—. Cert. elem. and spl. reading tchr. Sec. Tenn. Eastman co., Kingsport, Tenn., 1958-62; tchr. Sullivan County Bd. Edn., 1978—94; mth. tchr., coach math bowl team, 1989—94; ret., 1994. Participant Fantasy Lit. Workshop Nat. Inst. for the Humanities, Johnson City, Tenn., 1985, Mathcaps Workshop Nat. Sci. Found., Johnson City, 1987, 88. Vol. tchr. Spl. Class for Gifted Students, Blountville, Tenn., 1985, 86, Salvation Army, 1994-96, Meals on Wheels, 1994-2000. Recipient Who's Who Among America's Tchrs., 1992. Mem. Tenn. Edn. Assn., Nat. Edn. Assn., Sullivan County Edn. Assn., Phi Kappa Phi. Avocations: gardening, reading, decorating. Home: 412 Meadow Ln Kingsport TN 37663-2546

CARINO, AURORA LAO, psychiatrist, health facility administrator; b. Angeles, Philippines, Jan. 11, 1940; arrived in U.S., 1967; d. Pedro Samson and Hilaria Sanchez (Paras) Lao; m. Rosalito Aldecoa Carino, Dec. 2, 1967; children: Robert, Edwin, Antoinette. AA, U. of the East, Manila, 1961; degree in Medicine, U. of the East, Quezon City, Philippines, 1966. Lic. psychiatrist N.Y., Va., Conn., Fla.; cert. Am. Bd. Psychiatry and Neurology. Resident in pediat. U. of the East-R.M. Meml. Hosp., Quezon City, 1966-67; rotating intern Stamford (Conn.) Hosp., 1967-68; resident in psychiatry Norwich (Conn.) Hosp., 1968-71, staff psychiatrist, 1971-75; staff psychiatrist, unit chief, acting clin. dir. Harlem Valley Psychiat. Ctr., Wingdale, NY, 1975-80; svc. chief Fla. State Hosp., Chattahoochee, 1982-83; unit chief Hudson River Psychiat. Ctr., Poughkeepsie, NY, 1983-89, dep. med. dir., acting clin. dir., 1989-90, asst. to clin. dir., 1990-93, dep. med. dir.-admissions, 1993-97. Cons. Dept. Mental Hygiene, Dutchess County, Poughkeepsie, 1976—. Mem.: Am. Psychiat. Assn. Republican. Roman Catholic. Avocations: gardening, country music, recording/listening to spiritual enhancement. Home: 10 Millbank Rd Poughkeepsie NY 12603-5112

CARIOLA, ROBERT JOSEPH, artist; b. Bklyn., Mar. 24, 1927; Grad., Pratt Inst. Art Sch., 1954; student, Pratt Graphic Ctr., 1958-59. Instr. art La Salle Acad., Oakdale, N.Y., 1963-65. Instr. creative painting workshop Nat. Art League, Douglaston, Queens, N.Y.; condr. art workshops in mixed media painting Bd. Continuing Edn. One-man shows include Long Beach Mus., N.Y., 1985, East Meadow Libr. Gallery, 1990, Merrick Symphony Performance Lobby of Hall, 1990, Vatican Pavilion-N.Y. World's Fair, 1964; exhibited in group shows at Boston Mus. Printmakers Exhbn., 1962, Corcoran Gallery Art, Washington, 1963, Pa. Acad. Fine Arts, Phila., 1963, Nat. Acad. Design, N.Y.C., 1970, Signature Gallery, Va., 1986, Cath. Mus. Arts and Antiquities, Olympic Towers, N.Y.C., 1995-96; represented in permanent collections Landing Gallery, Woodbury, Soundview Gallery, Pt. Jefferson, N.Y.; contbr.: Illustrator Writer's Ann., 1958, Sign Mag., 1971, art mags.; executed murals in Sr. Citizen Ctr., Wantagh, N.Y., 1989, cmty. Rm. St. Johns Luth. Ch., Merrick, N.Y., 1992, also schs.; created, installed 4-sided Indian Monument dedicated to Meroke Tribe Indians-1643, Merrick, N.Y., 1993; painted murals and mosaics in 4 chapels; created metal, wood, and concrete sculptures, faceted stained glass windows St. Johns Cemetery Mausoleum, Queens, N.Y; created 3 large bronze and brass wall sculptures, 2 mosaics and 3 large etched glass windows and doors at St. Raymonds Cemetery Mausoleum, Bronx N.Y., painted life sized horse casting for Nassau County's Horses of a Different Color fund raising project, installed at Wheatley Plaza in Greenvale, L.I.,N.Y. 2003, created 4 foot bronze statue of Mother Theresa holding a baby, donated to Our Lady of Lourdes Ch., Massapequa, NY, dedicated June 2004. Recipient Ann. Painting prize Hofstra, 1957, Purchase award Hofstra, 1957, Operation Democracy prize Locust Valley, N.Y., 1958, 1st prize for painting John Kennedy Cultural Ctr. Bankers Trust, 1971, Grumbacher Cash award Silvermine Artists Guild, New Canaan, Conn., 1976, Best in Show award Bayshore C. of C. Art Festival, 1979, 1st prize Long Beach (N.Y.) Mus., 1984; grnatee Tiffany Grants, 1965, 66, N.Y. State Creative Arts Program, 1988, Nassau County, 1989, Wantagh Creative Arts Program, 1992; subject of feature article in Equine Images, fall, 1991. Address: 1844 Gormley Ave Merrick NY 11566-3009 Office Phone: 516-378-5379. E-mail: artist@robertcariola.com.

CARITHERS, DIANN YVONNE, nursing educator; b. Musgrave Harbour, Newfoundland, Canada, Dec. 27, 1956; arrived in U.S., 1957; d. John Ansley Crawford and Sara Harris; m. Gregory Van Crawford, Sept. 8, 1979; 1 child, Jennifer A. BSN, Vanderbilt U., 1979; MS, U. South Ala., 1984. Cert. clin. nurse specialist, Am. Nurse's Assn., 1993. Legal nurse cons. Carithers Medical-Legal Consulting, Mobile, Ala., 1992—2005; assoc. prof. U. Mobile, 1993—. Bd. dirs. Home of Grace, Mobile, 2000—04. Mem.: ANA, Gulf Coast Legal Nurse Assn., Nat. League for Nurses, Am. Assn. Legal Nurse Consultants, Ala. States Nurses Assn. (assoc.; fin. com. 2003—05), Sigma Theta Tau (Zeta Gamma chpt., Omicron Theta chpt.). Republican. Baptist. Avocations: reading, travel. Home: 6713 Chimney Top Dr South Mobile AL 36695 Office: University of Mobile College Parkway Mobile AL 36613 Office Phone: 251-442-2455. E-mail: dcarithers@comcast.net.

CARIUS, MICHAEL LEE, emergency medicine physician; b. Peoria, Ill., July 5, 1947; s. Marvin W. and Geraldine E. (Rapp) C.; m. Maura Ann Dugan (div. Apr. 1990); m. Kathleen Patricia Cilimberg, Feb. 24, 1996; children: Lauren, Jennifer, Brandon. BS in Biology, Trinity Coll., 1969; MD, U. Colo., 1973. Diplomate Am. Bd. Emergency Medicine, recert., Am. Bd. Family Practice, recert., Nat. Bd. Med. Examiners; lic. physician, Conn.; cert. ACLS instr. and provider, ATLS provider, APLS provider and instr. Rotating intern Naval Regional Med. Ctr., San Diego, 1973-74; resident in emergency medicine dept. emergency medicine U. So. Calif.-L.A. County Med. Ctr., 1981-83; staff emergency physician Middlesex (Conn.) Meml. Hosp., 1983-87, assoc. emergency dept. dir., 1985-87; chmn. dept. emergency medicine St. Vincent's Med. Ctr., Bridgeport, Conn., 1988-94; staff emergency physician Hosp. of St. Raphael, New Haven, Conn., 1994-95; chmn. dept. emergency medicine Norwalk (Conn.) Hosp., 1995—. Instr. dept. surgery divsn. emergency medicine U. Conn. Sch. Medicine, Farmington, 1994—. With USN, 1974-77, with USAF, 1977-81. Fellow Am. Coll. Emergency Physicians (bd. dirs. 1996—); mem. AMA, Conn. State Med. Soc., Conn. Coll. Emergency Physicians (sec., treas., pres.-elect, pres., bd. dirs. 1984—), Fairfield County Med. Assn. Office: Norwalk Hosp 5 Maple St Norwalk CT 06850 Address: American College of Emergency Physicians 1125 Executive Cir Irving TX 75038-2522

CARIUS, ROBERT WILHELM, mathematics professor, retired military officer; b. Peoria, Ill., Jan. 4, 1929; s. Henry Clarence and Mary Magdalen (Wilhelm) C.; m. Geraldine Mary Sullivan, Mar. 16, 1957; children: Patricia, Mary, Linda, Robert, Daniel, Sara. BS in Naval Sci, U.S. Naval Acad., 1951; BS in Aero. Engring, U.S. Naval Postgrad. Sch., 1958; MS in Nuclear Engring, Iowa State Coll., 1959. Commd. ensign USN, 1951, advanced through grades to rear adm., 1977, served with Fighter Squadron 74, 1953-56, served with U.S.S. Bennington, 1959-61, project mgr. U.S. AEC, 1964-65, served with Air Anti-Submarine Squadron 33, 1962-63, command officer Air Anti-Submarine Squadron 29, 1966-68, exec. officer U.S.S. Princeton, 1968-70, R & D br. head Dept. Navy, 1970-71, command officer U.S.S. New Orleans San Diego, 1971-73, mem. staff Anti-Submarine Wing Pacific, 1973-77, comdr. Anti-Submarine Wings Atlantic, Naval Air Sta. Jacksonville, Fla., 1977-79, with aviation programs Dept. Navy, from 1979; instr. physics Ark. Coll., Batesville, 1983-85, asst. prof. physics, 1986—. Bd. govs. USO, Jacksonville. Mem. exec. bd. United Way of Jacksonville, N.E. Fla. coun. Boy Scouts Am.; pres. Independence County United Way. Decorated Legion of Merit, Air medal, Meritorious Service medal; recipient Spl. award United Way of Jacksonville, 1979 Mem. U.S. Naval Acad. Alumni Assn., Assn. Naval Aviation, Ret. Officers Assn., Ark. Hist. Soc., Batesville Symphony Assn., Naval Helicopter Assn., U.S. Naval Inst., Jacksonville C. of C. (gov.) Clubs: Rotary. Roman Catholic. Home: 2630 Antioch Rd Cave City AR 72521-9249 Office: Lyon Coll Batesville AR 72501 *Personal integrity and honesty to oneself have been key elements in my life's philosophy. Attempting to understand the people you work with and treating them as you prefer to be treated were other essential principles. Lastly, always do your very best in all endeavors, and you never have to look over your shoulder with regret.*

CARL, ALLEN LAURENCE, surgery educator; b. Queens, N.Y., Apr. 14, 1953; s. O. Edward and Muriel (Lerner) C.; m. Susan A. Ross, Dec. 26, 1981; children: Alissa, Andrew, Scott, Danielle. BA with honors, SUNY, Binghamton, 1975; MD, SUNY, Buffalo, 1979. Diplomate Nat. Bd. Med. Examiners, Am. Bd. Orthopaedic Surgery; lic. surgeon, N.Y. Intern in gen. surgery Albert Einstein Hosp., Bronx, N.Y., 1979-80; resident in orthop. surgery, clin. instr. SUNY, Stony Brook, 1980-81; resident in orthop. surgery Bellevue Hosp., N.Y.C., 1981-85; fellow in spinal surgery Toronto (Ont., Can.) Gen. Hosp., 1985-86; asst. prof. orthop. surgery Albany Med. Coll., 1986-91, assoc. prof. orthop. surgery, 1991-97, prof. orthopedic surgery, 1997—, vice chmn. orthop. surgery, 1993—, assoc. prof. pediat., 1994—. Cons. and presenter in field; mem. N.Y. State Spinal Cord Injury Rev. Bd. Contbr. articles to Head and Neck Surgery, Contemporary Orthops., Foot and Ankle, Spine, Jour. of Bone Joint Surgery Am., Jour. Trauma, Med. Outlook for Orthop. Surgeons, Jour. Orthop. Trauma, Current Opinions in Orthops., Jour. Orthop. Techniques. Fellow ACS, Am. Acad. Orthop. Surgeons, Acad. Pain Mgmt., The Spine Jour., Am. Orthop. Assn.; mem. Am. Spine Injury Assn., Am. Spinal Injury Soc., N.Am. Spine Soc. (mem. profl. and tech. liaison com., mem. subcom. materials and devices), New Eng. Spine Study Group, Ea. Orthop. Assn., Internat. Soc. Minimal Intervention in Spinal Surgery, Scoliosis Rsch. Soc. (mem. instrumentation com., internat. traveling fellow), Acad. Orthop. Soc., Group Internat. Cotrel-Dubousset, Cervical Spine Rsch. Soc Achievements include patents for Dynamized Anterior Vertebral Body Fixation Device (concept and structure), Shape Memory Scoliosis and Limb Implant; patents pending for virtual reality 3-D spinal imaging and implant placement. Office: Albany Med Coll Divsn Orthopaedic Surgery A 61 OR Albany NY 12208 E-mail: alcsar@nycop.rr.com.

CARL, DAN R., lawyer; b. 1952; BA, Stanford U.; JD, U. Calif. Pvt. practice; assoc. Gray, Cary, Ames & Frye, San Diego, 1978—80; with Berg, Ziegler, Lichtman & Anderson, San Francisco, Horwich & Warner, San Francisco; corp. counsel Sybase, Inc., Dublin, Calif., 1989—92, assoc. gen. counsel, 1992—96, v.p., 1996, dir. European legal affairs England, 1997—99, v.p., gen. counsel, sec. Dublin, Calif., 1999—. Office: Sybase US Hdqs One Sybase Dr Dublin CA 94568

CARL, HERMAN E., computer scientist, educator, chemistry professor; s. Robert Charles and Anna Marie Carl; m. Judith Ann Cooper, July 10, 1983; children: Robert Calvin, Michelle Marie. BS in Chemistry, St. Francis Coll., Pa., 1976; MA in Chemistry, Ind. U. Pa., Pa., 1989. Pa. Tchg. Cert. Pa. Dept. of Edn., 1977, Prin. Cert. Pa. Dept. of Edn., 1994. Adjundt chemistry instr. Mt. Aloysius Jr. Coll., Cresson, Pa., 1976—77; chemistry & physics tchr. Columbia Borough Sch. Dist., Pa., 1977—81; computer sci., sci. tchr. Portage Area Sch. Dist., Pa., 1981—. Elec. newspaper web designer Pandya Computers, INC, Ebensburg, Pa., 1998—2000. Com. mem. Boy Scouts of Am., Ebensburg, Pa., 1996; musican No. Cambria Cmty. Band, Pa. NSF grant, 1989, Nat. Sci. Found. grant, NSF, 1998, H.S. Instrument grant, Spectroscopy Soc. of Pitts., 1988, 1992, 2004. Mem.: ASCD, Sci. Alliance (assoc.; treas. 1992—95), IUP Physics Alliance (assoc.), Pa. State Educator Assn. (assoc.), Pa. Jr. Acad. of Sci. Sponsor (assoc.; treas. region 6 2005). Roman Catholic. Avocations: photography, computers. Office: Portage Area Sch Dist 85 Mountain Ave Portage PA 15946 Office Phone: 814-736-9636.

CARL, JEFFERY, art educator; b. Arlington Heights, Ill., Jan. 5, 1976; s. Don and Judith Carl. MFA, No. Illinios U., 2001. Asst. prof. art Judson Coll., Elgin, Ill., 2001—. One-man shows include Gallery 214 No. Ill. U., DeKalb, Ill., 1999, Grace Luth. Ch., River Forest, Ill., 2001, Ferguson Gallery Concordia U., Iver Forest, Ill., 2001, DeKalb (Ill.) Gallery, 2004, exhibited in group shows at Quincy (Ill.) Art Ctr., 2000, LRC Gallery Nicolet Coll., Rhinelander, Wis., 2001. Jail min., DeKalb County, Ill., 2001—04; h.s. youth dir. Vineyard Christian Fellowship, DeKalb, 2005. Mem.: Coll. Art Assn., Christians in Visual Arts. Avocation: music. Office: Judson Coll 1151 N State St Elgin IL 60123 Office Phone: 847-628-1031. Business E-Mail: jcarl@judsoncollege.edu.

CARL, ROBERT E., retired marketing company executive; b. Sept. 1, 1927; s. Elmer T. Carl and Marion R. (Pack) C.; m. Linda Arlene Sutton, Aug. 30, 1967; children: Melanie Ruth, Robert Brady, Camber Carleen. BS, U. Kans., 1950; grad. in real estate, So. Meth. U., 1965; cert. in investment analysis, N.Y. Inst. Fin., 1967. V.p. sales promotion Wm. S. Henson, Inc., Dallas, 1951—54; pres., COO Jones-Carl, Inc., Dallas, 1954-62; v.p. mktg. comms. Modern Am. Corp., Dallas, 1962-70; v.p. sales Dunn Properties of Tex., Inc., Dallas, 1970-71; sr. v.p. mktg. svcs. Vantage Cos., Dallas, 1971-84; pres. Mktg. Mgmt. Sys., Dallas, 1984-90; v.p. The Premium Group, Inc., 1990-92; mem. Dallas Cable TV Bd., 1981-83; v.p. mktg. Availent Mortgage Co., 2000—02. Co-founder Liberty Christian H.S., Dallas, 1995. Contbr. articles to profl. jours. Dir. comms. Rep. Party Dallas County; precinct chmn. Dallas County Grand Jury, election judge. Recipient Chevalier and Legion of Honor Degrees Internat. Supreme Coun. of Order of De Molay, 1957, Silver Anvil award Pub. Rels. Soc. Am., 1958, Eagle Scout with four palm awards. Mem. Sales and Mktg. Execs. Dallas (pres. 1976-77, Disting. Salesman's award 1954), S.W. Found. Free Enterprise (pres. 1975-76), Tex. Indsl. Devel. Coun., Nat. Assn. Corp. Real Estate Execs., Sales and Mktg. Execs. Internat. (sr. v.p.), Tex. Econ. Coun., Nat. Assn. Indsl. and Office Parks, Internat. Platform Assn., Dallas Advt. League, U. Kans. Alumni Assn. (life), Big D Toastmasters Club (pres. 1966), Press Club Dallas, Greater Dallas Pachyderm Club (chmn.), Park City Club (bd. govs. 1989-92), Masons (32d degree), Shriners, Dervish Club, Dallas Jr. C. of C. (bd. dir.). Home: 6337B Diamondhead Cir Dallas TX 75225 E-mail: rec4209@aol.com.

CARLE, ERIC, artist, author; b. Syracuse, N.Y., June 25, 1929; s. Erich Wilhelm and Johanna (Oelschlager) C.; student Akadamie der Bildenden Kunste, Stuttgart, Germany, 1946-50; m. Dorothea Wohlenberg, June 5, 1954 (div. Mar. 1967); children: Cirsten, Rolf; m. Barbara A. Morrison, June, 1973. Poster designer U.S. Info. Center Germany, Stuttgart, 1950-52; designer promotion dept. N.Y. Times, N.Y.C., 1952-55; art dir. pharm. advt. L.W. Frohlich Co., N.Y.C., 1955-63; guest instr. Pratt Inst., N.Y.C., 1963; exhibited in group shows including Soc. Illustrators, Am. Inst. Graphic Arts, 1970; author, illustrator: 1, 2, 3 to the Zoo, 1968, The Very Hungry Caterpillar, 1970, Pancakes, 1970, The Tiny Seed, 1970, Do You Want To Be My Friend?, 1971, The Secret Birthday Message, 1972, Walter The Baker, 1972, The Rooster Who Set Out To See The World, 1972, Have You Seen My Cat?, 1973, I See A Song, 1973, All About Arthur, 1974, The Mixed Up Chameleon, 1975, Eric Carle's Storybook, 1976, The Grouchy Ladybug, 1977, Hans Christian Andersen by Eric Carle, 1978, Watch Out! A Giant!, 1978, Tales from Aesop, 1980, The Honeybee and the Robber, 1981, What's for Lunch?, 1982, Let's Paint a Rainbow, 1982, Catch the Ball, 1982, The Very Busy Spider, 1984. Papa, Please Get the Moon for Me, 1986, All Around Us, 1986, A House for Hermit Crab, 1987, Animals, Animals, 1989, Dragons, Dragons, 1989, The Very Quiet Cricket, 1991, Draw Me A Star, 1992, Today is Monday, 1993, 10 Little Rubber Ducks, 2005. With AUS, 1952-54. Recipient Silver medal City of Milan., 1989, 10 Best Book of Yr. N.Y. Times, 1969, 10 Best poster of Yr. 1952, 1st prize for children's books Internat. Childrens Book Fair, 1970, 72, Deutscher Jugendbuch preis, 1970, 72, selection du Grand Prix des Treize, 1972, 73, Readers prize, Japan, 1975, one of best children's books, Eng., 1971. *

CARLEN, PETER LOUIS, neuroscientist, educator, science administrator, researcher; b. Edmonton, Alta., July 22, 1943; m. 1970; 2 children. MD, U. Toronto, 1967. Intern Montreal (Que., Can.) Gen. Hosp., 1967-68, resident internal medicine, 1968-69; instr. neurophysiology, dept. zoology Hebrew U., Jerusalem, 1969-70; resident neurology U. Toronto, 1970-72; fellow neurophysiol. neurobiol. unit Hebrew U., Jerusalem, 1972-74; sr. physician, head neurol. program Addiction Rsch. Found. Clin. Inst., 1974-94; staff neurologist Toronto Western Hosp., U. Toronto, 1974; rsch. assoc. Playfair Neurosci. Unit U. Toronto, 1979-89, assoc. prof. dept. medicine and physiology, 1981-88, prof. dept. medicine & physiology, 1989—; dir. neurosci. unit Toronto Hosp., 1989-99. Fellow Can. Neurol. Soc., Am. Acad. Neurology, Am. Neurol. Assn.; mem. AAAS, Soc. Neurosci., Can. Physiol. Soc. Office: U Toronto -Toronto Western Hosp 399 Bathurst St Toronto ON Canada M5T 2S8

CARLESON, ROBERT BAZIL, public policy consultant; b. Long Beach, Calif., Feb. 21, 1931; s. Bazil Upton and Grace Reynolds (Wilhite) Carleson; m. Betty Jane Nichols, Jan. 31, 1954 (div.); children: Eric Robert, Mark Andrew, Susan Lynn; m. Susan A. Dower, Feb. 11, 1984. Student, U. Utah, 1949—51; BS, U. So. Calif., 1953, postgrad., 1956—58. Adminstrv. asst. City of Beverly Hills, Calif., 1956-57; asst. to city mgr. City of Claremont, Calif., 1957-58; sr. adminstrv. asst. to city mgr. City of Torrance, Calif., 1958-60; city mgr. City of San Dimas, Calif., 1960-64, Pico Rivera, Calif., 1964-68; chief dep. dir. Calif. Dept. Pub. Works, 1968-71; dir. Calif. Dept. Social Welfare, 1971-73; U.S. commr. welfare Washington, 1973-75; pres. Robert B. Carleson & Assocs., Sacramento and Washington, 1975-81, chmn. Washington, 1987—93, 2002—, San Diego, 1993—2001; pres. Innovative Environ. Svcs. Ltd., Vancouver, Canada, 1992; spl. asst. to U.S. pres. for policy devel. Washington, 1981-84; prin., dir. govt. rels. KMG Main Hurdman, Washington, 1984-87; dir. transition team Dept. HHS, Office of Pres.-Elect, 1980-81; spl. adviser Office of Policy Coordination; sr. policy advisor, chmn. welfare task force Reagan Campaign, 1980. Bd. dirs. Fed. Home Loan Bank of Atlanta, 1987-90, I.E.S., Ltd., Can., Transenviro Co., USA, Churchill Co., USA; adv. com. Fed. Home Loan Mortgage Corp., 1985-87; mem. strengthening family policy coun. Nat. Policy Forum, Washington, 1994. Eagle Scout q.m. sea scout, 1948; lt. gov. Calif. Boys' State, 1948; adv. coun. gen. govt. Rep. Nat. Com., Washington, 1980-81; sr. fellow Free Congress Found., 1994—; founder, chmn. Am. Civil Rights Union, 1998—. Officer USN, 1953-56, USNR, 1956-67. Mem.: Capitol Hill Club, Army and Navy Club (Washington), Rotary (pres. 1964), Masons. Home and Office: 175 Cameron Station Blvd Alexandria VA 22304 Personal E-mail: rcarleson@aol.com.

CARLETON, DON EDWARD, history center administrator, educator, writer; b. Dallas, Jan. 22, 1947; s. Edward Preston and Wilma Jo (Smith) C.; m. Suzanne Marie Young, Jan. 2, 1974; children: Ian Alexander, Aunna Fleur. BS, U. Houston, 1969, MA, 1974, PhD, 1978. Tchr. Friendswood Ind. Sch. Dist., Tex., 1969-71; teaching fellow U. Houston, 1971-75; research asst. Southwest Ctr. for Urban Research, Houston, 1974-75; dir. Houston Met. Research Ctr., 1975-79, Barker History Ctr., Austin, 1979-91, Ctr. for am. History, U. Tex., Austin, 1991—. Urban adv. editor Handbook of Tex., Austin, 1983—95; sr. lectr. dept. history U. Tex., Austin, 1985—, dept. journalism, 1997—; J.R. Parten chair in Archives Am. History, 1989—; cons. Amon Carter Mus., Ft. Worth, 1983, Birmingham (Ala.) Pub. Libr., 1978. Editorial bd. Southwestern Hist. Quar., 1980-90; author: Who Shot the Bear?, 1984, Red Scare!, 1985, (Coral Tullis best book award Tex. Hist. Assn. 1986), A Breed So Rare: The Life of J.R. Parten, Liberal Texas Oilman, 1896-1992, 1998 (Tex. Inst. Letters Book award 1998), Being Rapoport: Capitalist With a Conscience, 2002; editor: Focus on America Series, 1999-; oral hist., mem. bd. advs. Pioneers of Television Project, Acad. Television Arts and Scis., L.A., 1998-; contbr. articles to profl. jours. Recipient Presdl. Excellence award, U. Tex., Austin, 1982; grantee, Parten Found., 1982, O'Connor Found., 1982. Fellow: Tex. Inst. Letters, Tex. State Hist. Assn. (grantee 1983); mem.: Philos. Soc. Tex., Headliners Club Austin. Democrat. Avocations: reading, travel. Office: U Tex Ctr Am History ANB Austin TX 78713-7330 Business E-Mail: d.carleton@mail.utexas.edu.

CARLETON, JOSEPH GEORGE, JR., lawyer, state legislator; b. Bklyn., July 21, 1945; s. Joseph G. and Ellen (Gabriel) C. AB, Dartmouth Coll., 1969; JD, Boston U., 1972. Atty. Calderwood & Ouellette, Dover, N.H., 1972-79; pvt. practice Wells, Maine, 1979-83, 88—; atty., ptnr. Patterson Carleton & Mongue, Wells, 1983-88; mem. Maine Ho. of Reps., Augusta, 1990-98, asst. Rep. leader, 1994-96; commr. Gov.'s Blue Ribbon Commn. on Health, 2000, Maine Health Performance Coun., 2001—02. Chmn. Wells Site Rev. Bd., 1985-86; town meeting moderator Town of Wells, 1983—; mem. adv. bd. York County Tech. Coll., 1996-2003. Sgt. N.H. Air N.G., 1966-74. Mem. Wells C. of C. (pres. 1984), Elks, Masons. Republican. Avocations: golf, history, politics. Home and Office: PO Box 369 Wells ME 04090-0369 E-mail: atty@maine.rr.com.

CARLETON, MARY RUTH, development professional, consultant; b. Sacramento, Feb. 2, 1948; d. Warren Alfred and Mary Gertrude (Clark) Case; m. Bruce A. Hunt, Jan. 21, 1989. BA in Polit. Sci., U. Calif., Berkeley, 1970, MJ, 1974; postgrad., San Diego State U. TV news anchor, reporter Sta KXAS-TV, Ft. Worth, 1974-78, Sta. KING-TV, Seattle, 1978-80, Sta. KOCO-TV, Oklahoma City, 1980-84, Sta. KTTV-TV, L.A., 1984-87; news anchor Sta. KLAS-TV, Las Vegas, 1987-91, Sta. KNV-TV, 1991-93, Sta. UNLV-TV, 1993-94; broadcast instr. Okla. Christian Coll., 1981-84, UCLA, 1985-87; broadcast instr., dir. Women's Ctr. U. Nev., Las Vegas, 1991-94, news dir. univ. news Sta. UNLV-TV, 1992-94; asst. dean devel. San Diego State U., 1994-97; v.p., dir. devel. Scripps Found., 1997-99; v.p. instl. advancement Holy Names Coll., Oakland, Calif., 1999-2001; assoc. v.p. advancement U. San Francisco, 2001—. V.p. exec. com. West Coast Conf.; cons. in field. Bd. dirs. World Neighbors, Oklahoma City, 1984-89, Allied Arts Coun. So. Nev., Las Vegas, 1988-94, Nev. Inst. for Contemporary Art, 1988-94, Las Vegas Women's Coun., 1993-94, Friends of Channel 10, 1991-94, United Way, Las Vegas, 1991-94, secret witness bd., 1991-94; bd. dirs. Case Dist. VII, 1998—, conf. chair, 2003. Recipient Broadcasting award UPI, 1981, Nat. award for best documentary, 1990, Tri-State award for best newscast, 1990, Emmy award, L.A., 1986, L.A. Press Club award, 1986, 90, Nat. awaad for documentaries UPI, 1990, Woman of Achievement Media award Las Vegas C. of C., 1990; named Best Environ. Reporter, Okla. Wildlife Fedn., 1983, Disting. Woman of So. Nev., Woman of Achievement, Las Vegas Women's Coun., 1990. Mem. AARP (mem. nat. econ. issues team 1992-94, state legis. com.), Women in Comm. (Clarion award 1981, Best Newscaster 1990), Soc. Profl. Journalists, Press Women, Investigative Reporters, Calif. Alumni Assn. (bd. dir. 2002—), Sigma Delta Chi. Democrat. Roman Catholic. Avocations: tennis, gourmet cooking. Office: Univ San Francisco 2130 Fulton St San Francisco CA 94117-1080 Office Phone: 415-422-6606. E-mail: carleton@usfca.edu.

CARLETON, WILLARD TRACY, retired finance educator; b. Boston, May 3, 1934; s. Frank Nagle and Margaret Lally (Parker) C.; married; children: James, Sarah, Leslie, Julia. AB, Dartmouth Coll., 1956, MBA, 1957, MA (hon.), 1971; MA in Econs., U. Wis., 1961, PhD in Econs., 1962. Acct. C.F. Rittenhouse & Co., Boston, 1956; mem. labs. staff Bell Telephone Labs., Inc., N.Y.C., 1957-58; teaching asst. econs. dept. U. Wis., 1958-59, research asst., 1959-61; economist Fed. Res. Bank St. Louis, 1961-63; asst. prof. fin. Grad. Sch. Bus. Adminstrn., NYU, 1963-65, assoc. prof., 1965-66; assoc. prof. quantitative methods and managerial econs. Sch. Bus., Northwestern U., 1966-67; assoc. prof. fin. and econs. Amos Tuck Sch. Bus. Adminstrn., Dartmouth Coll., 1967-70, prof. fin. and econs., 1970-73, Leon E. Williams prof. banking and fin., 1973-74; William R. Kenan Jr. prof. bus. adminstrn. U. N.C., Chapel Hill, 1974-84; Karl Eller prof. fin. U. Ariz., Tucson, 1984—99, Donald R. Diamond prof. fin., 1999—2001, prof. fin emeritus, 2001. Author: A Theory of Financial Analysis, 1966, Corporate Finance, 1985; contbr. articles to profl. jours. Trustee Coll. Retirement Equities Fund, N.Y.C., 1980—84, Tchrs. Ins. and Annuity Assn., N.Y.C., 1984—2003, Coll. Retirement Equities Fund, 2003—. Mem. Fin. Mgmt. Assn. (pres. 1977-78), Western. Fin. Assn. (bd. dir. 1986-89), Am. Fin. Assn. (bd. dir. 1973-75), Am. Econ. Assn., Fin. Economist Roundtable. Episcopalian. Avocations: fishing, reading, music. Home: 4911 E Parade Ground Loop Tucson AZ 85712

CARLEY, GEORGE H., state supreme court justice; b. Jackson, Miss., Sept. 24, 1938; s. George L. Jr. and Dorothy (Holmes) C.; m. Sandra M. Lineberger, 1960; 1 child, George H. Jr. AB, U. Ga., 1960, LLB, 1962. Bar: Ga. 1961. Pvt. practice, Atlanta and Decatur, Ga., 1961-71; ptnr. McCurdy & Candler, Decatur, Ga., 1971-79; also spl. asst. atty. gen. Office. Atty. Gen.; judge Ct. Appeals Ga., 1979-89, chief judge, 1989-91, presiding judge, 1991-93; justice Ga. Supreme Ct., Atlanta, 1993—. Chmn. bd. visitors U. Ga. Law Sch., 1995-96. Bd. Visitors U. Ga. Law Sch.; past pres. U. Ga. Law Sch. Assn. Coun., 1989-90, active, 1986-91; trustee Ga. Legal History Found., Inc.; active Holy Trinity Episc. Ch., Decatur. Mem. ABA, State Bar Ga., Ga. Bar Found., Lawyers Club Atlanta, Old Warhorse Lawyers Club (pres. 1997-98), Joseph Henry Lumpkin Am. Inn of Ct. (pres. 1994-95), Pythagoras Lodge, Scottish Rite. Office: Ga Supreme Court State Office Annex Bldg 244 Washington St Atlanta GA 30334-9007*

CARLILE, JANET LOUISE, artist, educator; b. Denver, Apr. 26, 1942; d. Jessie Crawford and Alice Essie (Williams) Carlile. BFA, Cooper Union, 1966; MFA, Pratt Inst., 1971. Prof. Bklyn. Coll., CUNY, 1971—; prin., owner, dir. Red Mountain Gallery, Ouray, Colo., 2001—. Founder Incline Village (Nev.) Fine Arts Ctr., 1966—68; instr. Sch. Visual Arts, N.Y.C., 1968—70, Printmaking Workshop, N.Y.C., 1971, Scarsdale (N.Y.) Studio Workshop, 1971—73, SUNY-Stony Brook, L.I., 1976, Bard Winter Coll., Rhinebeck, NY, 1980; head printmaking, asst. dir. Bklyn. Mus. Art Sch., 1971—77; dir. Bklyn. Coll. Press, 1977—2003; cons. Woodstock (N.Y.) Sch. Art, 1980—84; judge Alpine Artists Show, Ouray, Colo., 1989; judge Landscape Painting Show Woodstock Art Assn., 1995; owner, dir. Red Mountain Gallery, Ouray, Colo. One-woman shows include Blue Mountain Gallery, N.Y.C., 1980, Stetson U., Deland, Fla., 1995, Fairleigh Dickinson Coll., Teaneck, N.J., 1995, exhibited in group shows at Associated Am. Artists Gallery, N.Y., 1971—81, Bklyn. Mus., 1976, Ulster County Artists Show, N.Y. State Coun. Show, 1984, Alpine Artists Show Ouray County, 1987, IRT Bklyn. Mus. Sta., work appears in, Libr. of Congress Collection, Washington. Sec. San Juan Vista Landowners Assn., Ridgway, Colo., 1980—86. Recipient Hirshorn Purchase prize, Soc. Am. Graphic Artists, 1969, Best of Show award, Alpine Artists Show Ouray County, 1987, Creative Incentive award, Rsch. Found., CUNY, 1992, 1996—, Pollack/Krasner Found. award, 2002—03; fellow, Pratt Inst., Bklyn., 1971; grantee NEA workshop, Colo. Coun. Arts; scholar full scholarship, Cooper Union, N.Y.C., 1962—66. Mem.: Am. Acad. Arts and Letters, Ouray County Arts Assn. (pres. 1991—93). Avocation: Avocations: hiking, backpacking, skiing, yoga, rock climbing. Office: Brooklyn Coll Art Dept Bedford at Ave H Brooklyn NY 11210 Office Phone: 970-325-4668.

CARLILE, ROBERT TOY, lawyer; b. Phila., July 27, 1926; s. Robert and Eva (MacQueen) C.; m. Gill S. Carlile; children: Robert A., Regan J. BBA, U. Miami, 1949; JD, U. Fla., 1958. Bar: Fla. 1958. Assoc. Grimditch & Smith, Deerfield Beach, Fla., 1958-60; sole practice Deerfield Beach, 1960-65, 73-91, Boca Raton, Fla., 1991-95, Palm City, Fla., 1994—; ptnr. Carlile & Pulskamp, Deerfield Beach, 1965-69, Carlile, Pulskamp & Fletcher, 1969-72, Carlile & Fletcher, 1972-73. City atty., Deerfield Beach, 1963-68, 88-91; mcpl. judge, 1971-77. With U.S. Army, 1944-46, USAF, 1951-53. Mem. Fla. Bar Assn., Broward County Mcpl. Judges Assn. (v.p. 1975), Deerfield Beach C. of C. (pres. 1966), Kiwanis (pres.), Billiken (pres.), Shriners, Jesters (dir. 1994), Phi Alpha Delta. Democrat. Office: 3945 SW Bimini Cir S Palm City FL 34990-1340 Office Phone: 561-220-2228. E-mail: rcarlile@bellsouth.net.

CARLIN, BETTY, education educator; b. N.Y.C. d. Samuel and Rose Sara (Bernstein) Grossberg; m. Arthur S. Carlin, July 18, 1953 (dec.); children: Lisa Anne Skinner, James Howard. BA, UCLA, 1952; MA, U. Calif., Berkeley, 1955. Educator L.A. Sch. Dist., 1952-55; owner Carlin's Shoes, L.A., 1952-68; educator Berkeley (Calif.) Sch. Dist., 1957-58; master tchr. spl. programs Calif. State Coll., Hayward, 1967-84; educator U. Calif., Berkeley, 1984-86; tchr. demonstrator C.V.U. Sch. Dist.; student tchr. supr. Calif. State U., Hayward. Co-owner Art-Car Corp., 1978-88. Creator ednl. videos for children Study in Characteristics of an Effective and Loving Mother, Children's Play as Related to Intelligence, An Eclectic Approach to Teaching Reading. Mem. Nat. Tchrs. Assn., Calif. Tchrs. Assn., Commonwealth Club, San Francisco Opera Guild. Avocations: swimming, opera, theater, gardening, vocal study.

CARLIN, DAVID H., lawyer; b. N.Y.C., Mar. 18, 1943; AB, Columbia U., 1964; JD, NYU, 1967. Bar: N.Y. 1967. With Hall, Dickler, Lawler, Kent & Friedman, NYC; joined Loeb and Loeb, NYC, 1985, mng. ptnr., NY office, 1992—96, mng. ptnr. LA, 1996—98, former co-chmn. NYC, 1998, ptnr. Frequent lecturer on advertising issues; adjunct prof., grad. program in direct mktg. Mercy Coll. Mem.: Am. Advertising Federation (legal affairs com.). Office: Loeb and Loeb 345 Park Ave New York NY 10154-0037 Office Phone: 212-407-4970. Office Fax: 212-407-4990. Business E-Mail: dcarlin@loeb.com.

CARLIN, DENNIS J., lawyer; b. Chgo., Aug. 23, 1941; s. Herbert E. and Lillian (Schneider) C.; m. Fern Carlin, Nov. 25, 1964; children: Gregory A., H. David, Stuart B. BBA, U. Wis., 1963; JD, DePaul U., 1967; LLM in Taxation, Georgetown U., 1971. Bar: Ill. 1967; CPA. Auditor Checkers, Simon & Rosner, Chgo., 1963-67; assoc. tax ct. litigation divsn. IRS, Washington, 1967-71; ptnr. Frankel, McKay, Orlikoff, Denten & Kostner, Chgo., 1971-77, Horwood & Carlin, Chgo., 1977-82, Gardner, Carton & Douglas, Chgo., 1982—, vice-chmn., 1998—2003. Contbr. articles to profl. jours. Mem. atty. divsn. Jewish United Fund; bd. dirs., exec. com., vice-chmn. Coun. for Jewish Elderly. Mem. ABA, Am. Coll. Tax Counsel, Chgo. Bar Assn. (former chmn. fed. tax com.), Nat. Strategy Forum, NYU Inst. Fed. Taxation, DePaul U. Alumni Coun., Am. Israeli C. of C., Twin Orchard Country Club. Avocations: golf, skiing, reading, music, theater. Office: Gardner Carton & Douglas LLC 191 N Wacker Dr Ste 3400 Chicago IL 60606-1698 Office Phone: 312-569-1264. Business E-Mail: dcarlin@gcd.com.

CARLIN, DONALD WALTER, retired food products executive, consultant; b. Gary, Ind., Aug. 27, 1934; s. Walter Joseph and Mabel (Ebert) C.; m. Kathleen Susan McCone, Jan. 21, 1961; children: Michael Scott, Karen Mary, Mark Steven. BS in Engring, U. Notre Dame, 1956; LLB, U. Mich., 1959; grad., Advanced Mgmt. Program, Harvard U., 1978. Bar: Ind. 1959, Ill. 1960. Assoc. to ptnr. Soans, Anderson Luedeka & Fitch, Chgo., 1960-72; sr. atty. Kraft Inc., Glenview, Ill., 1972-73, v.p., asst. gen. counsel, 1974-79, sr. v.p., gen. counsel, 1979-81, sr. v.p., gen. counsel, sec., 1981-86, v.p., assoc. gen. counsel, 1986-89; v.p., dep. gen. counsel Kraft Gen. Foods, Northfield, Ill., 1989-92. Mem. bd. visitors Sch. Medicine, U. Calif.-Davis, 1990—. Mem. ABA (hon.; com. corp. law depts. sect. bus. law), Assn. Gen. Counsel (emeritus), Westmoreland Country Club (bd. dirs. 1989-94, pres. 1993-94), Notre Dame Club (Chgo.), Ironwood Country Club (pres. 2000-03, bd. dirs. 2000-03). Home and Office: 333 Regentwood Rd Northfield IL 60093-2762 also: 73-106 Galleria Ct Palm Desert CA 92260

CARLIN, GEORGE DENIS, comedian, actor; b. N.Y.C., May 12, 1937; m. Brenda Hosbrook, 1961 (dec. 1997); 1 child, Kelly Radio announcer Sta. KJOE, Shreveport, La., Sta. WEZE, Boston, Sta. KXOL, Ft. Worth, Sta. KDAY, L.A. Numerous TV appearances on Merv Griffin Show, Mike Douglas Show, Tonight Show (over 130), numerous other TV variety shows; regular on TV programs, Away We Go, 1967, John Davidson Show, 1966, Shining Time Station, 1992, The George Carlin Show, sitcom on Fox TV, 1994-95; syndicated TV spl. The Real George Carlin, 1973; miniseries Streets of Laredo, 1995; movies include: With Six You Get Eggroll, 1968, Car Wash, 1976, Americathon, 1979, Outrageous Fortune, 1987, Justin Case, 1988, Bill & Ted's Excellent Adventure, 1989, Working Trash, 1990, Bill and Ted's Bogus Journey, 1990, Prince of Tides, 1991, Dogma, 1999, Jay and Silent Bob Strike Back, 2001, Scary Movie 3, Happily N'Ever After, 2003, Jersey Girl, 2004; TV specials include Drawing on My Mind, 1985, George Carlin: Playin' with Your Head, 1986, The Envelope, 1986, What Am I Doing In New Jersey?, 1988, Doin' It Again, 1990, Jammin' In New York, 1992, Back In Town, 1996, George's Best Stuff, 1996, George Carlin: 40 Years of Comedy, 1997, You Are All Diseased, 1999, Personal Favorites, 2001, Complaints and Grievances, 2001; albums include Burns & Carlin at the Playboy Club Tonight, 1960, Take-Offs and Put-Ons, 1967, FM & AM, 1972 (Grammy for best comedy recording), Occupation: Foole, 1973, Class Clown, Toledo Window Box, An Evening with Wally Londo Featuring Bill Slaszo, 1975, Indecent Exposure, On the Road, 1977, A Place for My Stuff, 1982, The Carlin Collection, Carlin on Campus, Playin' With Your Head, What Am I Doin' in New Jersey?, Parental Advisory: Explicit Lyrics, Jammin' in New York, 1993 (Grammy for spoken comedy album), The Little David Years: 1971-1977, 2000, Brain Dropping, 2000, (Grammy for spoken comedy album), Napalm & Sillyputty, 2001, (Grammy for spoken comedy album); author Sometimes A Little Brain Damage Can Help, 1983, Brain Droppings, 1997, Napalm and Silly Putty, 2001, When Will Jesus Bring the Pork Chops?, 2004. Office: Carlin Prodns 11911 San Vicente Blvd Los Angeles CA 90049-5086

CARLIN, HERBERT J., electrical engineering educator, researcher; b. N.Y.C., May 1, 1917; s. Louis Aaron and Shirley (Salzman) C.; children: Seth Andrew, Elliot Michael; m. Mariann J. Hartmann, June 29, 1975 B.E.E., Columbia Coll., 1938, M.E.E., 1950; PhD in Elec. Engring., Poly. Inst. N.Y., 1947. Engr. Westinghouse Corp., Newark, 1940-45; from asst. to assoc. prof. Poly. Inst. Bklyn., 1945-60, prof., head electrophysics, 1960-66; J. Preston Levis prof. engring. Cornell U., Ithaca, N.Y., 1966—, dir. elec. engring., 1966-75. Mem. adv. panel Nat. Bur. Standards, Boulder, Colo., 1967-70; mem. rev. com. Lehigh U., Bethlehem, Pa., 1966-74, U. Pa., Phila., 1979-82; vis. prof. Ecole Normale Superieure, Paris, 1964-67, MIT, Boston, 1973-74; vis. scientist Nat. Ctr. for Telecommunications, Issy Les Moulineaux, France, 1979-80; vis. lectr. U. Genoa, Italy, summer 1973, U. London, Dec. 1979, The Technion, Haifa, Israel, Mar. 1980, Tianjin U., China, summer 1982, Univ. Coll., Dublin, Ireland, summer 1983, Polytech. of Turin, Italy, summer 1985, 91, Fed. Polytech., Lausanne, Switzerland, summer 1992. Co-author: Wideband Circuit Design, 1997. Fellow NSF, 1964; recipient Outstanding Achievement award U.S. Air Force, 1965 Fellow IEEE (chmn. profl. group on circuit theory 1955-56, Centennial medal 1985) Home: 8 Highland Park Ln Ithaca NY 14850-1452 Business E-Mail: hjc2@cornell.edu.

CARLIN, JAMES BOYCE, elementary education educator, consultant, writer; b. Paducah, Ky., June 19, 1932; s. Lois Whitfield and Flora Lee (Newton) C.; m. Hellon Lillian Upchurch, June 22, 1968; 1 child, Rhonda Hope. AA, Paducah Jr. Coll., 1952; BA, Murray (Ky.) State U., 1954; MA, Vanderbilt U., 1957; EdD, U. Miss., 1969. Cert. standard elem. life tchr., Ky. Tchr. Hendron Elem. Sch., Paducah, 1954-63; asst. prof. Mid. Tenn. State U., Murfreesboro, 1964-67; supr. reading instrn. Meridian (Miss.) Schs., 1967-68; asst. prof. U. Miss., University, 1968-69; prof. elem. edn. Murray State U., 1969-91, West Ga. Coll. at Dalton, Ga., 1991-93; assoc. prof. Austin Peay State U., Clarksville, Tenn., 1993-97. Cons. to elem. schs. Contbr. articles to profl. jours. Mem. Internat. Reading Assn. (pres. Murray area 1974-75), Assn. for Childhood Edn. Internat. (internat. exec. bd. 1988-91, Outstanding Mem. award 1988), Ky. Assn. for Childhood Edn. (state pres. 1979-81), Rotary (pres. Murray 1987-88), Kappa Delta Pi. Democrat. Baptist. Office Phone: 386-668-5192.

CARLIN, JOHN WILLIAM, archivist; b. Salina, Kans., Aug. 3, 1940; s. Jack W. and Hazel L. (Johnson) C.; m. Ramona Hawkinson, 1962 (div. 1980); children: John David, Lisa Marie; m. Lynn Lady, 1997. BS in Agr., Kans. State U., 1962, PhD (hon.), 1987. Farmer, dairyman, Smolan, Kans., 1962-79; mem. Kans. Ho. of Reps., 1971-79, speaker of ho., 1977-79; gov. State of Kans., Topeka, 1979-87; pres. Econ. Devel. Assocs., Inc., 1987-92; partner Carlin & Associates, Topeka, 1989-95; vice-chmn. Midwest Superconductivity, Inc., Lawrence, KS, 1990-94; partner Clark Publishing, Inc., Topeka, 1991-95; archivist of the U.S. Nat. Archives & Records Admin., Washington, 1995—2005. Vis. prof. pub. adminstrn. and internat. trade Wichita State U., 1987-88; chmn. Nat. Govs. Assn., 1984-85, Midwestern Govs. Conf., 1982-83. Democrat. Lutheran.

CARLIN, MARIAN P., secondary school educator; b. NYC, N.Y., July 4, 1949; d. Gerard Richard and Wanda Priscilla (Duglin) Preville; m. Howard Sandy Carlin, Aug. 9, 1969; children: Jonathan, Jason, Jennifer, Jillian. BS History, Mercy Coll., 1985; MSED, LI U., 1993. Profl. diploma ednl. adminstrn. Long Island U., 2000. Tchr. Lakeland High Sch., Shrub Oak, NY, 1991—2001, CW Stanford Mid. Sch., Hillsborough, NC, 2002—. Tutor Lakeland Sch. Dist., Scrub Oak, 1991—99, pvt. practice, Mohegan Lake, 1991—97. Editor: Substitute Teacher's Handbook, 1997. Mem.: NCMSA, NCAE, NSTA, ASCD. Avocations: mentoring, travel, reading, music, exercise. Home: 3736 Hermine St Durham NC 27705-2134 E-mail: max.carlin@orange.k12.nc.us.

CARLIN, PAUL VICTOR, legal association executive; b. McKeesport, Pa., Nov. 11, 1945; BA, Grove City Coll., 1967; JD, Dickinson Law Sch., 1970. Bar: Pa. 1971, D.C. 1978, U.S. Dist. Ct. (we. dist.) Pa. 1971, U.S. Dist. Ct. D.C. 1978, U.S. Supreme Ct. 1979. Asst. atty. gen. Pa. Atty. Gen.'s Office, 1971; exec. dir. Balt. City Bar Assn., 1981-84, Conn. Bar Assn., Rocky Hill, 1984-85, Md. State Bar Assn., Balt., 1985—. Exec. v.p. Pro Bono Resource Ctr., 1990—; asst. sec. treas. Md. Bar Found.; founder Sr. Law Ctr., Phila., 1978, 59th St. Legal Clinic, Phila., 1977. Editor: CCH Government Contracts Reporter, 1972. Mem. Am. Soc. Assn. Execs. (mem. devel. com. 1995-97, legal sect. coun. 1997—), Legal Mut. Liability Soc. Md. (charter, bd. dirs. 1986—), Phila. Bar Assn. (dir. legal svcs. 1975-77), ABA (standing com. lawyer referral 1977-80, standing com. delivery of legal svcs. com. 1987-89, standing com. assn. com. 1992-96, standing com. on legal assts. 1996-99), DC Bar (dir. pub. svc. activities 1977-81), Nat. Assn. Bar Execs. (state del. 1987-89, treas. 1989-91, v.p. 1991, pres. elect 1992, pres. 1993, Bolton award for profl. excellence), Internat. Inst. Law Assn. Chief Execs., Mid.-Atlantic Bar Conf., So. Conf. Bar Pres.'s. Office: Md State Bar Assn Inc 520 W Fayette St Baltimore MD 21201-1781 Office Phone: 410-685-7878. Business E-Mail: pcarlin@msba.org.

CARLIN, SETH A., musician, educator; b. N.Y.C., Feb. 8, 1945; s. Herbert Jacob and Esther Beth Carlin; m. Maryse Christiane Rodé, June 3, 1947; children: Tova Juliette, Daniel Guillaume. Licence de Concert Premier Nommé, Ecole Normale de Musique, Paris, 1965; BA cum laude, Harvard U., 1969; MS in Piano, Juilliard Sch., 1970. Asst. prof. music Hiram (Ohio) Coll., 1970—73; piano instr. Phillips Exeter (NH) Acad., 1973—79; prof. music, head piano program Washington U., St. Louis, 1979—. Piano soloist Friedenhauer Kammerkonzerte, Berlin, 1999, St. Louis Symphony Orch., 2002; fortepiano soloist Philharmonia Baroque, San Francisco, 2000. Musician: (CD) Sonata and Bagatelles of Beethoven, 1990, Solo Fortepiano Music of Schubert, 1993, 2004, Four-hand Fortepiano Music of Schubert, 2001; performer: cycle of complete Schubert Fortepiano sonatas, Merkin Hall, NY, Marboro Music Festival, Newport Music Festival, Santa Fe Music Festival, Great Performers at Lincoln Ctr. Mozart Marathon. Bd. trustees Westfield Ctr. for Keyboard Studies, 2000—. Recipient prize, Internat. Busoni Piano Competition, 1973, CD Rec. of Mo. award, Alte Musik Actuelle mag., 2000; grantee, Nat. Endowment for Arts, 1989. Mem.: Coailtion for Environ., Sierra Club. Avocations: tennis, hiking, windsurfing. Office: Washington U Campus Box 1032 Saint Louis MO 63130

CARLIN, SYDNEY, state representative; b. Wichita, Kans., Nov. 20, 1944; m. John Carlin; 4 children. BS in Social Sci. City commr. City of Manhattan, Kans., 1993—96, mayor, 1996—97; state rep. Dist. 66, Kans., 2003—. Democrat. Roman Catholic. Office: 284-W State Capitol 300 SW 10th Ave Topeka KS 66612 Office Phone: 785-296-7665. Business E-Mail: carlin@house.state.ks.us.

CARLINER, DAVID, lawyer; b. Washington, Aug. 13, 1918; s. Louis and Cassie (Brooks) C.; m. Miriam Kalter, Jan. 24, 1944 (dec. Aug. 9, 1994); children: Geoffrey Owen, Deborah Joan (Mrs. Robert Remes). Student, Am. U., 1935-36, U. Va., 1936-38, student in law, 1938-40; LLB, Nat. U., 1941. Bar: Va. 1940, D.C. 1946. Atty. JAG Office Army Dept., Washington, 1946; Washington rep. New Coun. Am. Bus., Washington, 1946-48; pvt. practice, 1948-50; ptnr. Wasserman and Carliner, 1950-67; of counsel Chapman Duff and Lenzini, 1968-74; ptnr. Carliner and Gordon, 1974-84, Carliner and Remes, Washington, 1984—. Vis. lectr. Fgn. Svc. Inst., Dept. State, USIA, Harvard U., 1985. Author: Rights of Aliens, 1977; co-author The Rights of Aliens and Refugees, 1990. Nat. bd. dirs. ACLU, 1965-83, gen. counsel, 1976-79; chmn. Internat. Human Rights Law Group, 1978-86, Washington Home Rule Com., 1966-70; co-chmn. D.C. Com. for Re-Orgn. Plan, 1967-68; chmn. Washington chpt., mem. nat. exec. coun. Am. Jewish Com., 1969-71; mem. nat. adv. coun. Amnesty Internat., 1969—; Bd. dirs. Am. Coun. for Nationalities Svcs., 1977-89, Internat. League for Human Rights; trustee Washington Inst. Values in Pub. Policy, 1984-88. With AUS, 1941-45. Recipient Oliver Wendell Holmes award, 1966, Human Rights award Ctr. for Human Rights and Constl. Law, 1994, Isaiah award Am. Jewish Com., 1998. Mem. ABA (chmn. immigration and nationality com. adminstrv. law sect. 1979-83, mem. coun. administrv. law sect. 1983-87, Brookings Instn. coun., Washington 1995—), Fed. Bar Assn. (chmn. com. immigration and naturalization 1961-62), D.C. Bar (vice chmn. opinions com. ethics 1974-76, bd. dir. 1980-83), Va. State Bar, Am. Law Inst., Am. Immigration and Naturalization Lawyers Assn. (Jack Wasserman Meml. award 1994), Cosmos Club (Washington). Office: 1150 Connecticut Ave NW Ste 610 Washington DC 20036-3817 E-mail: dcarliner@remes.com.

CARLINER, GEOFFREY OWEN, economist, director; b. Washington, Sept. 21, 1944; s. David and Miriam (Kalter) C.; m. Astrid Synnove Skrikerud, July 31, 1971; children: Anders Benjamin, Hannah Emily Brooke. AB cum laude, Harvard U., 1966; MA, U. Calif., Berkeley, 1968, PhD, 1972. Rsch. assoc. U. Wis., Madison, 1971-73; asst. prof. U. Western Ont., London, Ont., Can., 1974-80; sr. staff economist Coun. of Econ. Advisors, Washington, 1980-83, staff dir., 1983-84; exec. dir. Nat. Bur. of Econ. Rsch., Cambridge, Mass., 1984-95; dep. dir. Inst. for Internat. Econs., Washington, 1995-97; prin. Charles River Assocs., Boston, 1997—2001. Vis. asst. prof. U. Calif., Berkeley, 1976-77, vis. assoc. prof. Babson Coll., Wellesley, 2001-03, vis. prof. Boston U., 2004-. Co-editor: Politics and Economics in the Eighties, 1991; contbr. articles to profl. jours. Recipient Joint Coun. of Econ. Edn. award, 1976. Mem. Am. Econ. Assn., Boston Com. Fgn. Rels. (exec. dir.

2001—), Boston Econ. Club (exec. com.), Conf. for Rsch. on Income and Wealth (exec. com. 1985-95), Internat. Seminar on Internat. Trade (steering com. 1988-95). Business E-Mail: carliner@bu.edu.

CARLINI, JAMES, management consultant; b. Berwyn, Ill., Aug. 27, 1954; s. Harvey Reno and Helen Dorothy (Stan) C.; m. Holly R. Haupin, Sept. 29, 1979. MusB, Roosevelt U., 1976, BS in Computer Sci., 1978; MBA in Mgmt. Info. Systems and Mktg., DePaul U., 1982. Info. systems designer Western Electric div. Bell Labs., Naperville, Ill., 1977-79; software engr. Motorola, Schaumburg, Ill., 1979-81; mgr. Ill. Bell, Chgo., 1981-83; dir. telecommunications and computer hardware cons. Arthur Young & Co., Chgo., 1983-86; pres. Carlini & Assocs., Inc., Hinsdale, Ill., 1986—. Adj. prof. Technol. Inst. Sch. Speech Northwestern U., Evanston, Ill., 1986—, grad. sch. bus. DePaul U., Chgo., 1986-89; dir. Teledata Hong Kong; mem. adv. bd. COMDEX. Editorial adv. bd. mem. Cabling Bus. Mag.; editl. columnist Eprairie.com; contbr. articles to profl. jours. Pres. Mental Health Bd., Berwyn, 1983; village trustee East Dundee, Ill., 2005—; apptd. mem. Fox Valley Cable Commn. Recipient Northwestern U. Alumni Prof.'s award, 1995, Disting. Tchg. award Northwestern U., 1996. Mem. Assn. Cabling Profls. (dir. End User Coun., infrastructure cons., cabling facilities integrator, network cabling and applications integrator), Internat. Trade Assn., Data Processing Mgmt. Assn. (bd. dirs. 1988-96, Chgo. chpt. pres. 1994-96, Spkrs. award, Outstand Instrs. award 1993), Intelligent Bldg. Inst. (chmn. definitions com.), DAV (citation 1979), East Dundee Econ. Devel. Commn., Federal Comms. Bar Assn. Roman Catholic. Avocations: yachting, golf. Office: Carlini & Assocs Inc 445 Greenwood Ave Dundee IL 60118-1011 Office Phone: 773-370-1888. Personal E-mail: carlini@carlinij.com.

CARLISLE, CASEY ALLEN, chemist, educator; b. Trenton, Fla., Sept. 20, 1949; s. Eddie Roy and Meveree Martha Carlisle; m. Marianne M. Bonnell, Aug. 6, 1970; children: Jonathan Edward, Allen Bryce, Kerry Brett, Kristofer Robin, John Paul, Sandra Rose, James M. AA, Fla. Coll., Temple Terrace, 1969; BA in Edn., U. Fla., 1974, MA in Edn., 1976; Ednl. Specialist in Sci. Bus. Edn. and Computers, Nova U., 1986. Cert. in chemistry, biology, mid. sch. sci., health edn., elem., ednl. supervision and leadership, Fla. Tchr. Trenton (Fla.) Elem. Sch., 1974-76; tchr. sci. Dixie County H.S., Cross City, Fla., 1976-90, chmn. dept. sci., 1984-90; tchr. chemistry/sci. Santa Fe High sch., Alachua, Fla., 1990—, chmn. dept. sci., 1994—. Instr. sci. Lake City C.C., 1984-90. Minister N.E. Ch. of Christ, 2004—; mem. sch. bd, Gilchrist County, Trenton, Fla., 1978—82. Avocations: farming, computers, home improvement. Home: 4022 SE 17th Trl Trenton FL 32693-4611 Office: Santa Fe High School 16331 US Highway 441 Alachua FL 32615-5281

CARLISLE, DALE L., lawyer; b. Walla Walla, Wash., Apr. 24, 1935; BA, U. Idaho, 1957; JD, George Washington U. School of Law, 1960. Judge advocate USAF, 1960—63; asst. U.S. atty. Wash. State (western dist.), 1964—66; with Gordon, Thomas, Honeywell, Malanca, Peterson & Daheim PLLC, Tacoma, 1966—; gen. counsel Levitt West, Inc., 1970—73; mng. ptnr. Gordon, Thomas, Honeywell, Malanca, Peterson & Daheim PLLC, Tacoma, 1990—2000, of counsel. Mem.: Wash. State Bar Assn. (pres.-elect 2000—01, pres. 2001—02, bd. govs. 1999—2002). Address: 1201 Pacific Ave Ste 2200 Tacoma WA 98402-4314 Mailing: PO Box 1157 Tacoma WA 98402 Office Phone: 253-620-6401. E-mail: dcarlisle@gth-law.com.

CARLISLE, DOUGLAS R., managed health care company executive; Former mgr. fin. Vt. Am. Corp.; former COO Belknap Hardward, Louisville; contr. health care divsn. Humana, Inc., 1986—91, v.p. Fla. region, 1991—97, regional v.p., 1997—99, sr. v.p. market ops., 1999—2002, sr. v.p. Sr. Products, 2002—. Office: Humana Inc 500 W Main St Louisville KY 40202

CARLISLE, ERVIN FREDERICK, university provost, educator; b. Delaware, Ohio, Mar. 20, 1935; s. Ervin Frederick C. and Winnifred (Lucas) Pope; children: Lindy, Rebecca, Ginna, Jana; m. Barbara, Sept. 28, 1973. BA, Ohio Wesleyan U., 1956; MA, Ohio State U., 1957; PhD, Ind. U., 1963. Mem. faculty Ohio U., Athens, 1962-63, DePauw U., Greencastle, Ind., 1963-66; asst. prof. dept. English Mich. State U., East Lansing, 1966-68, assoc. prof., assoc. chmn. dept. English, 1968-72, prof., 1972-79, chmn. dept. English, 1979-81, asst. to pres., 1981-85; provost, exec. v.p. for acad. affairs Miami U., Oxford, Ohio, 1985-89; sr. v.p., provost Va. Poly. Inst. and State U., Blacksburg, 1989-94, William E. Lavery prof., 1995-2000, William E. Lavery prof., sr. v.p. and provost emeritus, 2000—; spl. advisor to minister of higher edn. and the v.p, Zayed U., United Arab Emirates, 2001—. Editor: American Poetry and Prose, 1970; author: The Uncertain Self, 1973, Loren Eiseley, 1983. Served to 1st lt. USAF, 1957-60. NEH fellow, 1972-73; NEH grantee, 1978, 80 Mem. MLA (chmn. lit. and sci. divsn. 1983). Home: 1227 N Lakeside Dr Lake Worth FL 33460 E-mail: efredcarlisle@bellsouth.net.

CARLISLE, JAMES PATTON, entrepreneur; b. Miami Beach, Fla., May 7, 1946; s. William Olin and Evelyn Obie (Ogden) C.; m. Laima Kirstina Launags; children: Alexandra Ji-Anne, Erika Li, Wendy Laubach, Scott Reidenbach. BA, Auburn U., 1969; MDiv, Emory U., 1976. Ordained to ministry Meth. Ch., 1975. Adminstrv. asst. Radney for Lt. Gov. Ala. campaign, 1969-70; asst. adminstr. Lee County Head Start, Auburn, Ala., 1970-72; assoc. pastor 10th St United Meth. Ch., Atlanta, 1974-76; dir. continuing edn. No. Ga. Ann. Conf. United Meth. Ch., Atlanta, 1975-78; program dir. Ctr. Profl. Devel. in Ministry, Lancaster, Pa., 1978-80; pres. Carlisle Leadership Group, 1989-99, The de Bono Group, 2000—; program master trainer Edward de Bono Thinking Methods, 2000—. Dir. Ctr. for Profl. Devel. in Ministry, Lancaster Theol. Sem., 1980—90; exec. dir. Ctr. for Creative Ch. Leadership, 1990—2004; cons. on devel. of distributorships and trainers in S.Am. to debemo Thinking Sys. global distbr. for Edward de Bono Thinking Methods; distbr. Edward de Bono Thinking Methods, Mex., Argentina, Brazil, Colombia; dir. programs and continuing edn. events; pres. New Think Inst., 2004—. Contbr. articles to profl. jours. Leader career planning events for clergy Uniting Ch. of Australia, Australia and N.Z.; elder N.Y. Ann. Conf. United Meth. Ch.; bd. dirs. Phila. Human Resources Planning Group; clergy mem. N.Y. Ann. Conf. of United Meth. Ch. Mem. OD Network,Soc. Advancement Continuing Edn. for Ministry, Omicron Delta Kappa. Achievements include first to introduce debono methods to corporations in China. Home and Office: 1722 Niblick Ave Lancaster PA 17602-4826 Office Phone: 217-299-5811. Business E-Mail: jpc@debonogroup.com.

CARLISLE, JAY CHARLES, II, lawyer, educator; b. Washington, Apr. 8, 1942; s. Jay C. and Opal Fiske C.; m. Frances Bell, Nov. 22, 1970 (div.); 1 child, Marie Bell; m. Janessa C. Nisley, June 22, 1984. AB, UCLA, 1965; JD, U. Calif., Davis, 1969; postgrad., Columbia U., 1969-70. Bar: N.Y. 1970, N.Mex. 1972, U.S. Dist. Ct. (so., ea. and we. dists.) N.Y. 1971, U.S. Ct. Appeals (2d cir.) 1975, U.S. Supreme Ct. 1975. Asst. trial counsel ITT, Hartford, 1970-71; assoc. Bigbee, Bryd, Carpenter & Crout, Santa Fe, 1971-73; pvt. practice law, 1973-75; asst. dean faculty of law SUNY, 1975-78; from asst. prof. to prof. of law Pace Univ., White Plains, N.Y., 1978—. Spl. master N.Y. Supreme Ct., 1980—; commr. N.Y. Task Force on Women and Cts., 1984-86; adj. prof. Fordham U., 1987-88, 90-91, N.Y. Law Sch., 1993—, Quinnipiac U. Law Sch., 2001—; referee N.Y. State Commn. on Jud. Conduct, 1999—; bd. editors Weinstein, Korn & Miller, NY Civil Practice, 2002—; pres. Bklyn. chpt. N.Y. Civil Liberties Union, 1987-1988; apptd. chief judge NY. Author, editor: numerous articles, books in field. Apptd. chair pub. adv. coun. N.Y. Temp. Commn. on Local Govt. Ethics, 1992-94; mem. Yonkers Police Profl. Stds. Rev. Bd., 1993-95; commr. N.Y. Task Force on Cameras In the Cts., 1996-97; mem. vestry Christ Episcopal Ch., Hudson, N.Y, 2004—; elected to vestry, 2004—. Recipient Harrison Tweed award ABA/Am. Law Inst. Fellow: Am. Bar Found. (life); mem.: Assn. of Bar of City of N.Y., N.Y. State Bar Assn., Rotary (team leader to Mex. 2000, pres. Hudson chpt. 2002—03, dir. spl. needs 2003—, Paul Harris fellow). Republican. Episcopalian. Office: Pace U Sch Law 78 N Broadway White Plains NY 10603-3796 Office Phone: 914-422-4234. Business E-Mail: jcarlisle@law.pace.edu.

CARLISLE, LILIAN MATAROSE BAKER (MRS. E. GRAFTON CARLISLE JR.), writer, lecturer; b. Meridian, Miss., Jan. 1, 1912; d. Joseph and Lilian (Flournoy) Baker; m. E. Grafton Carlisle, Jr., Jan. 9, 1933; children: Diana, Penelope. Student, Dickinson Coll., 1929-30, Pierce Coll. Bus. Adminstrn., 1930-31; BA, U. Vt., 1981, MA, 1986, PhD (hon.), 2005. Adminstrv. sec. RAF Ferry Command, Montreal, Can., 1942; exec. staff. mem. in charge collections, research Shelburne (Vt.) Mus., 1951-61; exec. sec. Burlington Area Community Health Study, 1963, coord., 1964; asst. coord. Vt. Mental Retardation Planning Project, 1965; project dir. 4-county Champlain Valley Medicare Alert, 1966; dir. publ. rels. Champlain Valley Agrl. Fair, 1968-77; lectr. U. Vt. Elder Hostel program, 1976-77. Mem. faculty Vacation Coll., 1980-83. Co-author: The Story of the Shelburne Museum, 1955, Profile of the Community, 1964, Environmental and Personal Health of the Community, 1964, Vermont Clock and Watchmakers, Silversmiths and Jewelers, 1970; also numerous catalogs on collections at Shelburne Mus.; editl. cons. Burlington Social Survey, 1967; editor: Historic Guide to Burlington Neighborhoods, 1991, vol. II, 1997, vol. III, 2003; contbr. articles to profl. jours. Pres., Burlington Comty. Coun. for Social Welfare, 1959-61, 1971-73; chmn. bd. Champlain Sr. Citizens, 1977-79, justice of peace, 1979-81; pres. Chittenden County Extension Adv. Com., 1977-78; chmn. publs. com. Vt. Bicentennial Commn., 1974-77; mem. Vt. Ho. of Reps., 1968-70. Recipient Cmty. Coun. Disting. Citizen award, 1978, cert. of award for Excellence in Cmty. Svc. DAR, 1996, Lifetime Achievement award Preservation Burlington, 2004., Lifetime Achievement award Ctr. for Rsch. on Vt., 2005 Mem. Vt. (trustee, chmn. mus. com. 1967), N.Y. (faculty seminar) Chittenden (pres. 1969-72, editor Heritage Series of 10 books about Chittenden County towns 1972-76) hist. socs., Vt. Old Cemetary Assn., Vt. Folklore So., League Vt. Writers (dir. 1962, v.p., pres. 1967-69), Am. Pen Women (pres. Green Mountain br. 1980-82), Order Women Legislators (pres. Vt. br. 1972-74), Meml. Soc. Vt. (pres. 1989-94), Zonta Club (pres. 1964-65), Chi Omega, Conglist. Home: 117 Lakeview Ter Burlington VT 05401-2901 Office Phone: 802-862-0554.

CARLISLE, LINDA ELIZABETH, lawyer; b. San Antonio, Dec. 17, 1948; d. Charles and Elizabeth (Chalkley) Herrera; m. Charles Larry Carlisle, Aug. 22, 1969; 1 child, Zachary Charles. BA in Biology, U. Tex., 1970; JD, Cath. U., 1980; MLT, Georgetown U., 1984. Bar: D.C. 1980, U.S. Ct. Appeals (D.C. cir.) 1980, U.S. Tax Ct. 1981, N.Y. 1990. Assoc. Cadwalader, Wickersham & Taft, Washington, 1980-84, ptnr., 1987-91; atty., adv. office tax legislation Dept. Treas., Washington, 1984-85, spl. asst. to asst. sec. tax policy, 1985-87; shareholder McClure, Trotter & Mentz, Washington, 1991-95; ptnr. White & Case, Washington, 1995—. Mem. bd. contbrs. Jour. of Taxation of Investment. Mem. ABA (sect. taxation, fin. transactions com.), Fed. Bar Assn., Am. Law Inst., Bar Assn. Dist. Columbia (tax sect., chair fin. products com.), N.Y. State Bar Assn. (sec. taxation and fin. instruments com.), Internat. Fiscal Assn. Republican. Home: 3215 Newark St NW Washington DC 20008-3346 Office: White & Case LLP 701 13th St NW Washington DC 20005 Office Phone: 202-626-3666.

CARLISLE, RICK, professional basketball coach; b. Ogdensburg, NY; m. Donna Carlisle. Attended, U. Maine; BA in Psychology, U. Va., 1984. Player Boston Celtics, 1984—87; asst. coach NJ Nets, 1992—94, Portland Trail Blazers, 1994—97, Ind. Pacers, 1997—2000; head coach Detroit Pistons, 2001—03, Ind. Pacers, 2003—. Named winner NBA Championship, 1985—86. Achievements include teams that have ranked no lower than 16th in the league in scoring and have ranked in the top-10 during four of those seasons. Avocations: golf, piano. Office: Ind Pacers 125 S Pennsylvania St Indianapolis IN 46204*

CARLISLE-FRANK, PAMELA L., writer, researcher, consultant; d. James E. and Barbara Carlisle; m. Joshua M. Frank, Mar. 13, 1988. BA with honors, U. Chgo., 1985, MA, 1986; PhD, U. Calif., Irvine, 1991. Rschr. The Hardiness Inst., Chgo., 1983-86, U. Chgo., 1983-86, U. Calif., Irvine, 1987-91, Eastern N.Mex. U., Portales, 1991-92; rsch. cons. Rsch. Inst. on Addictions, Buffalo, 1992; co-founder, pres. Found. Interdisciplinary Rsch./Edn. Promoting Animal Welfare, (FIREPAW), 1992—; self employed rsch. cons. San Francisco, NY, 1992—98; prof. Ea. N.Mex. U. Cons. Crisis Ctr., Clovis, N.Mex., 1991-92, Mental Health Resources, Clovis, 1992-93; adj. instr. Coll. San Mateo, Calif., 1997-98, Russell Sage Coll., Troy, N.Y., 1999; prof. Green Mountain Environ. Coll., 2000-01. Co-author: Addictive Behaviors in Women, 1994, Silent Victims: Recognizing and Stopping Animal Abuse, 2005; contbr. articles to newspapers, mags., profl. jours. Vol. Homeless Teens, San Francisco, 1995—98. Regents fellow, 1998; U. Calif. Irvine rsch. fellow, 1990. Mem.: APA, Internat. Soc. Anthrozoology, Psychologists for Ethical Treatment of Animals, Am. Sociol. Assn. (sect. animals and soc.). Avocations: writing novels, hiking, painting. Office Phone: 518-462-5939. E-mail: drpfrank@firepaw.org.

CARLO, PAULA WHEELER, historian, history professor, researcher; d. Howard Earl and Marion Frieda Wheeler; m. Gerald Richard Carlo, Aug. 19, 1973; children: Jeremy Paul, Jennifer Lynn. PhD in History, CUNY, N.Y.C., 2001. Adj. lectr. Coll. of SI, NY, 1979—95; assoc. prof. Nassau CC, Garden City, NY, 1995—. Author: The Huguenots of Colonial New Paltz and New Rochelle (Nat. Huguenot Soc. book award, 2001), Huguenot Refugees in Colonial New York: Becoming American in the Hudson Valley, 2005; contbr. chapters to books, articles to encys., to profl. jours. Recipient Faculty Disting. Achievement award, Nassau CC, 2003, Chancellor's award Excellence in Tchg., 2004; grantee, Huguenot Soc. of Am., 2001, 2002, 2004; Lehman Grad. Fellowship, NY State Higher Edn. Services, 1978—82. Mem.: Am. Soc. of Ch. Historians, Omohundro Inst. of Early Am. History and Culture, Orgn. of Am. Historians, Am. Hist. Assn. Avocations: travel, research, writing, public speaking. Business E-Mail: carlop@ncc.edu.

CARLOCK, JOHN BRUCE, JR., language educator; b. Pitts., Sept. 21, 1925; s. John Bruce and Sydney Jane (Whiteside) C.; m. Ruth Olive McCardle, Oct. 19, 1948; children: Elizabeth Kehl, Rebecca Riley, John Bruce III, David Matthew (dec.). BA, Wesleyan U., 1951; PhD, U. S.C., 1973. Prof. English, Erskine Coll., Due West, SC, 1973—, chmn. dept. English. Dir. theatre studies Erskine Coll., Due West, 1973-91. Editor: (jour.) Voice of Sanity, 1988—. Bd. dirs. Upstate S.C. chpt. ACLU, Abbeville (S.C.) Opera House, pres., 1995-96. Served USAF, 1943—46, Maj. USAF, 1951—69, Vietnam. Decorated Bronze Star USAF, Air Force Commendation medal. Mem. MLA, Beta Theta Pi. Democrat. Avocations: reading, writing, speaking, orcharding. Home: Burning Tree Farm 247 Arborville Rd Donalds SC 29638 Office: Erskine Coll PO Box 458 Due West SC 29639

CARLOCK, MAHLON WALDO, II, (STEVE CARLOCK), lawyer; b. Indpls., June 3, 1955; s. Mahlon Waldo and Betty Lou (Dobbs) C.; m. Robin Elaine Wall Carlock, Dec. 1, 1984; children: Caleb Michael, Hannah Mary. AB, Ind. U., Bloomington, 1977; JD, Ind. U., Indpls., 1981. Bar: Ind. 1981. Dir. Student Asst. Commn., Indpls., 1977-81; atty. pvt. practice, Indpls., 1981-84; v.p., corp. counsel U.S.A. Group, Inc., Indpls., 1985-94; atty. pvt. practice, Indpls., 1994—. Mem., 1982-86, pres., 1986 Warren Twp Sch. Bd., Indpls. Author: The Reindeer Rule, 1997, Is Christianity Relevant?, 1998. Elder Trinity Luth. Ch., Indpls., 1997—. Named Hon. Father God and Wife, Indpls., 1987, 91. Mem. Ind. Bar Assn., Indpls. Bar Assn., Am. Corp. Counsel Assn. Republican. Avocations: family, golf, god.

CARLO-MELENDEZ, ARNALDO, mathematics educator; b. Mayaguez, P.R., Oct. 1, 1953; s. Asdrubal Ali and Herolida (Melendez) Carlo; divorced; 1 child, Arnaldo Ali. BA, U. S. Fla., 1975. Cert. math. tchr., grades 6-12, Fla. Math. tchr. U.S. Peace Corps., Washington, Montverde (Fla.) Acad. Mem. ASCD, Nat. Coun. Tchrs. Math., Phi Kappa Phi. Home: PO Box 560469 Montverde FL 34756-0469 E-mail: mva2math@hotmail.com.

CARLOTTI, RONALD JOHN, food scientist; b. Martins Ferry, Ohio, Sept. 20, 1942; s. John Peter and Mary Rose (Pilla) C.; m. Eileen Theresa Dorsey, May 17, 1969; children: Lori Ann, Christina Maria, Jennifer Ann, Theresa Maria. Student, Wheeling (W.Va.) Jesuit Coll., 1960—63; BS, Ohio State U., 1964; MS, W.Va. U., 1966, PhD, 1970; MM, Aquinas Coll., 1996. Postdoctoral fellow dept. biochemistry U. Iowa, Iowa City, 1971—72, asst. rsch. scientist dept. pediats., 1973—74; corp. nutritionist Kellogg Co., Battle Creek, Mich., 1974—77; mgr. nutrition/basic rsch. Frito Lay divsn. Pepsico, Dallas, 1977—82, prin. scientist new products Frito Lay divsn., 1982—85; sr. rsch. scientist Amway Corp., Ada, Mich., 1985—89; dir. food sci. and tech. Country Home Bakers, Grand Rapids, Mich., 1990—93; pres. Carlotti and Assocs., Grand Rapids, 1994; pres., CEO Natura Inc., Lansing, Mich., 1995—2001, corp. sec., 2002—, bd. dirs. Tech. rep. Snack Food Assn., Crystal City, Va., 1978-82, Grocery Mfrs. Am., Washington, 1975-77; nutritionist Am. Frozen Food Assn., Washington, 1990-93; vis. asst. prof. chemistry Grand Valley State U., Allendale, Mich., 2002; adj. faculty mem. Davenport U.; regulatory affairs and devel. specialist Ranir Corp., Grand Rapids, 2002—. Contbr. articles to profl. jours. Pres. Mary Immaculate Sch. Bd., Dallas, 1981-83. Recipient Lovable Spud award, Nat. Potato Promotion Bd., Denver, 1981. Mem. Am. Chem. Soc., Am. Assn. Cereal Chemists, Inst. Food Tech. Roman Catholic. Achievements include start-up of new biotechnology-based food and chemical ingredients company, development of patented taste-appealing shelf-stable blend of fruit juice and milk, development of patented antioxidant system protecting food, pharmaceuticals and plastics against air and/or photo-oxidation, development of first nutritionally improved (low fat/low calorie) prototype of Tostitos Baked tortilla chips, of new high potency dry dog food for Amway Corp., of a series of nutritionally improved fruit pies for diabetics, of a specially formulated pumpkin pie which will not allow for the growth of pathogenic bacteria innoculated after baking in testing required to verify that the product can be stored at ambient temperature for up to five days; initiation of tech. and regulatory functions for corporate products. Home: 6921 Maplecrest Dr SE Grand Rapids MI 49546-9208

CARLOTTI, STEPHEN JON, lawyer; b. Providence, Apr. 28, 1942; s. Albert Edward and Rose C.; m. Nancy Ann Arnold, Sept. 16, 1961; children: Stephen J., Cristina C. AB, Dartmouth Coll., 1963; LLB, Yale U., 1966. Bar: R.I. 1966, U.S. Ct. Mil. Appeals 1967, U.S. Ct. Appeals (9th cir.) 1969, U.S. Dist. Ct. R.I. 1970, U.S. Supreme Ct. 1972. Assoc. Hinckley, Allen, Salisbury & Parsons, Providence, 1966, 70-72; ptnr. Hinckley, Allen, & Snyder, Providence, 1972-89, 91, mng. ptnr., 1986-89, 92-96; with The Mut. Benefit Life Ins. Co., Newark, 1989-91. Chmn. Town Com., 1975-76; trustee Roger Williams U., 1978-93; chmn. Healthcare Provider Svcs.; dir. R.I. Pub. Expenditures Coun. Capt. JAGC, U.S. Army, 1967-70. Mem. ABA, R.I. Bar Assn., R.I. Country Club (1st v.p.), Univ. Club. Republican. Roman Catholic. Avocations: golf, sailing. Office: Hinckley Allen & Snyder 1500 Fleet Ctr Providence RI 02903-2319 Office Phone: 401-274-2000. Business E-Mail: scarlotti@haslaw.com.

CARLOZZI, CATHERINE L., corporate communications consultant, writer; b. Berea, Ohio, July 25, 1953; d. Charles Henry and Carol Louise (Jones) Bader; m. Nicholas Carlozzi, Jan. 4, 1975. BA in English summa cum laude, Denison U., 1975; MA in English with distinction, U. Wis., 1976. Tchg. asst. U. Wis., Madison, 1976-77; editor Visual Edn. Cons., Madison, 1977-78; copywriter advt. Walnut Equipment Leasing, Ardmore, Pa., 1978-79; assoc. nat. dir. publs. Laventhol & Horwath, Phila., 1979-84; sr. assoc., mgr. spl. projects, v.p. Brown Boxenbaum, N.Y.C., 1984-91; prin. Carlozzi Comm. Cons., Cedar Grove, N.J., 1991—. Trustee Montclair, N.J. Art Mus., 1993-2004. Recipient Dir.'s award Montclair Art Mus., 1994, 2000. Mem. N.Y. Women in Comm. (v.p. membership 1999-2002, co-v.p. programs 2002-, Liz Hoover award 1999), Phi Beta Kappa. Avocation: sailing. Home and Office: 334 Crestmont Rd Cedar Grove NJ 07009-1908

CARLQUIST, JOHN FREDERICK, microbiologist, immunologist; b. Salt Lake City, May 25, 1948; s. John Howard and Beatrice (Degenkolbe) C.; m. Pamela Woodbury, Aug. 22, 1975; children: John David, William Christopher. BS, U. Utah, 1971, PhD, 1977. Rsch. asst. dept. microbiology U. Utah Coll. of Medicine, Salt Lake City, 1967-69; microbiologist Utah State Dept. Health, Salt Lake City, 1970-71; microbiologist, curator Pure Culture Lab. U. Utah Coll. of Medicine, Salt Lake City, 1972-73, teaching asst. Dept. Microbiology, 1973-75, teaching fellow Dept. Microbiology, 1976-77; postdoctoral fellow Dept. Bioengring. U. Utah, Salt Lake City, 1977-78; rsch. asst. Dept. Pathology LDS Hosp., Salt Lake City, 1979-82, rsch. assoc. Dept. Medicine Divsn. Cardiology, 1982-86, rsch. scientist head cardiology rsch. lab., 1986—; rsch. instr., rsch. assoc. prof. Dept. Internal Medicine U. Utah Sch. of Medicine, Salt Lake City, 1988-91, 91—; dir. molecular pathology Internat. Health Care Lab., Salt Lake City, 1998—. Contbr. numerous articles to profl. jours. English instr. Guadalupe Cultural Ctr., Salt Lake City, 1971; youth councilor, chaperone St. Mary's Cath. Ch., Park City, Utah, 1979; dist. rep. Park City Cmty. Citizens Coun., 1980. Recipient Am. Soc. for Microbiology Student Rsch. award, 1976, 77, Frat. Order of Eagles award for Cardiovascular Rsch., 1990, Grad. fellowship U. Utah, 1973; grantee Deseret Found. Rsch., 1980, 85, 88, Am. Heart Assn., 1984, 87, 90, NIH, 1989, 90. Mem. AAAS, Am. Soc. for Microbiology, Transplantation Soc., Park City Ski Patrol (avalanche advisor 1990—, Outstanding Patroller award 1990, 91), Nat. Ski Patrol, Am. Assn. Immunologists, Fedn. of Am. Socs. for Exptl. Biology, Kappa Sigma. Avocations: running, skiing, guitar, amateur radio, rock climbing. Office: LDS Hosp Divsn Cardiology 8th Ave C St Salt Lake City UT 84143-0001

CARLSEN, JAMES CALDWELL, musicologist, educator; b. Pasco, Wash., Feb. 11, 1927; s. Theodore N. and Eunice (Caldwell) C.; m. Mary Louisa Baird, May 1, 1949; children: Philip C., Douglas A., Susan A., Kristine L. BA, Whitworth Coll., 1950; MA, U. Wash., 1958; PhD, Northwestern U., 1962. Pub. sch. tchr., Almira, Wash., 1950-53; pub. sch. tchr. Portland, Oreg., 1953-54; mem. faculty Whitworth Coll., 1954-63, U. Conn., 1963-67; prof. music U. Wash., Seattle, 1967-92, head div. systematic musicology, 1968-92, ret., 1992, emeritus prof. music, 1992—. Rsch. assoc. Stäatliches Institut für Musikforschung, West Berlin, Germany, 1973-74; adj. prof. psychology U. Wash., 1979-92; vis. lectr. Instituto Investigaciones Educativas, Buenos Aires, 1981, Ind. U., 1985, Centro de Investigacion en Educacion Musical del Collegium Musicum, Buenos Aires, 1994; vis. scholar U. Bergen, Norway, 1986; disting. vis. prof. music Aichi U. Edn., Japan, 1992; Housewright eminent scholar chair in music Fla. State U., 1998. Author: Melodic Perception, 1965; editor Jour. Research in Music Edn, 1978-81; assoc. editor Psychomusicology, 1980-01; cons. editor Jour. Music Perception and Cognition, Japan, 1998—. Condr. Spokane Symphonic Band, Wash., 1957-60; music dir. Walla Walla Choral Soc., 1997. Served with AUS, 1945-47. Danforth Tchr. Study grantee, 1960-61; grad. fellow Presbyn. Ch., 1961-62; Fulbright-Hays grantee, 1973-74; recipient Soc. Rsch. in Music Edn. Sr. Researcher award, 1994. Mem. AAUP, Music Educators Nat. Conf., Music Edn. rsch. Coun. (past chmn.), Coll. Music Soc., Soc. for Music Perception and Cognition, Internat. Soc. Music Edn. (chmn. rsch. commn. 1976-80), Internat. Soc. Music Edn. Rsch. Commn. Seminars (hon. life), Internat. Soc. Music Edn. (hon. life), Walla Walla Symphony Soc. (bd. dirs. 1997-2003). Home: 845 Fern Ct Walla Walla WA 99362-8857

CARLSEN, MARY BAIRD, clinical psychologist; b. Salt Lake City, Utah, Aug. 31, 1928; d. Jesse Hays and Susannah Amanda (Bragstad) Baird; m. James C. Carlsen, May 1, 1949; children: Philip, Douglas, Susan, Kristine. Student, St. Olaf Coll., 1946-47; BA, Whitworth Coll., 1950; MA, U. Conn., 1967; PhD, U. Wash., 1973. Profl. organist, piano tchr., Wash., Oreg., Ill., Conn., 1949-68; staff counselor Presbyn. Counseling Svc., Seattle, 1976-79; pvt. practice clin. psychologist, marriage therapist, cognitive, devel. psychology, career devel. Seattle, 1978-95; cons. creative aging Walla Walla, 1996—. Chmn. sr. adult adv. coun. Seattle Parks Dept., 1975-76; adv. bd. Northwest Ctr. for Creative Aging, 1995-98; mem. steering com. Quest Learning Inst., Walla Walla, Wash., 1997-2001, mem. faculty, 1997—; mem. nat. adv. bd. Ctr. for Creative Retirement, Asheville, N.C., 1998-2001. Author: Meaning-Making: Therapeutic Processes in Adult Development, 1988, Creative Aging: A Meaning-Making Perspective, 1991, 2d edit., 1996, Transformational

Meaning-Making and the Practices of Career Counseling, 1991; contbr. chpts. to books and articles to profl. jours. Grantee PEO Rsch., 1972, U. Wash. Women's Guidance Ctr., 1972. Mem. APA, Am. Soc. Aging, Nat. Coun. on Aging.

CARLSMITH, CHRISTOPHER, history professor; s. J. Merrill and Lyn K. Carlsmith. AB, Stanford U., 1986; MA, U. Va., 1995, PhD, 1999. History dept. chair, head residence The Am. Sch. Switzerland (TASIS), Lugano, 1989—92; instr. U. Va., Charlottesville, 1995—97; history faculty Noble & Greenough Sch., Dedham, Mass., 1999—2000; asst. prof. history dept. U. Mass., Mass., 2001—. Contbr. articles to profl. jours., chpts. to books. Steering com. Cmty. Teamwork, Inc., Lowell, 2004—; dir. Stanford Club New Eng., Boston, 2001—. Recipient History Dept. Tchg. award, U. Mass. Lowell History Dept., 2002—03, Exceeding Expectations Faculty award, U. Mass. Lowell Student Govt. Assoc., 2003—04; fellow, Stanford U., I-HUM Program, 2000—01; Joseph Healey Rsch. grantee, U. Mass., 2001. Mem.: Renaisssance Soc. Am., Am. Hist. Assoc. Avocation: outdoor leadership (amc). Office: U Mass History Dept 850 Broadway St Lowell MA 01854-3099 Office Phone: 978-934-4277. Office Fax: 978-934-3023.

CARLSMITH, ROGER SNEDDEN, chemistry and energy conservation researcher; b. N.Y.C., Oct. 2, 1925; s. Leonard Eldon and Hope (Snedden) C.; m. Thelma Kathleen Sutton, July 31, 1954; children: David, Nancy Lynn. AB in Chemistry cum laude, Harvard, 1948; MSCE, MIT, 1960. Rsch. engr. Oak Ridge Nat. Lab., Oak Ridge, Tenn., 1950—62, group leader, 1962—70, sect. mgr., 1970—78, prog. dir. conservation and renewable energy, 1978—94; ret., 1994. Mem. Gov.'s Energy Task Force, Tenn., 1972-74, adv. com. Fed. Power Commn., Washington, 1973; bd. dirs. Am. Coun. Energy Efficient Economy., Washington, Tenn. Citizens Wilderness Planning. Author: (book with others) World Energy Conference Survey of Energy Resourses, 1974. Sgt. USAF, 1943-46. Recipient Sadi Carnot medal for achievements in energy conservation rsch. Dept. Energy, 1996. Mem. AAAS, Sierra Club, The Wilderness Soc. Achievements include research and development of advanced technology for improved energy efficiency, alternative energy sources, environmental impacts of energy, energy and the economy. Home: 1052 W Outer Dr Oak Ridge TN 37830-8641

CARLSON, ALAN DOUGLAS, lawyer; b. Omaha, May 24, 1951; s. John Peter and Elizabeth Jean (Pflasterer) C.; m. Sarah Louise Ware, June 28, 1975 (div. Mar., 1995); children: Elizabeth, Anne, Sally. AB, Augustana Coll., Rock Island, Ill., 1973; postgrad., Luth. Sch. Theology, 1974-75; JD, Creighton U., 1978. Bar: Nebr. 1978, U.S. Dist. Ct. Nebr. 1978, Colo. 1981, U.S. Dist. Ct. Colo. 1981, U.S. Ct. Appeals (10th cir.) 1989. Staff asst. govt. rels. Luth. Coun. USA, Washington, 1973-74; assoc. Holtorf, Kovarik & Nuttleman, Gering, Nebr., 1978-80; ptnr. Hopp, Carlson & Beckmann, Longmont, Colo., 1981-89, Ozer, Kiel, Trueax, Pribila & Kullman, P.C., Denver, Colorado Springs, Colo., 1989-91, Ozer and Carlson, Ft. Collins, Colo., 1990-91, Carlson & Swanson PC, Ft. Collins, 1999—2004, Carlson, Swanson & Dumler PC, Ft. Collins, 2004—. Guest lectr. Trial Advocacy Program U. Colo. Sch. Law; adj. faculty Regis U., 1999—, Colo. Christian U., 2000—; mem. Cross Creek Ranch Enterprises LLC; chmn. bd. Cross Creek Ranch Horsemanship Camp. Del. County Rep. Conv., Nebr. Rep. Conv., 1976, Colo. Rep. Conv., 1988; mem. subcom. social ministry Rocky Mountain Synod, Denver, 1984-88, adv. bd. Luth. Office Govt. Ministry, Denver, 1984-92; intern for U.S. Sen. Mark Hatfield, 1971; long range planning bd. St. Vrain Sch. Dist. Mem. ATLA, Colo. Bar Assn., Colo. Trial Lawyers Assn. (speakers bur.), Alliance Def. Fund, Nat. Litigation Acad., Christian Legal Soc., Longmont C. of C. (vice chmn. govt. affairs com. 1988-89). Republican. Avocations: showing horses, tournament tennis. Office: Carlson Swanson & Dumler PC 125 S Howes Ste 800 Fort Collins CO 80521 Office Phone: 970-482-0808. E-mail: adc@csdlawoffice.com.

CARLSON, ARNE HELGE, former governor; b. N.Y.C., Sept. 24, 1934; s. Helge William and Kerstin (Magnusson) C.; children by previous marriage: Arne H. Jr., Anne Davis; m. Susan Shepard, July 12, 1985; 1 child, Jessica Shepard. BA, Williams Coll., 1957; postgrad., U. Minn., 1957-58. Mem. advt. staff Control Data, Bloomington, Minn., 1962-64; councilman Mpls. City Council, 1965-67; ind. businessman Mpls., 1968-69; legislator Minn. Ho. Reps., St. Paul, 1970-78; state auditor State of Minn., St. Paul, 1978-90, gov., 1991-99; chmn. bd. Am. Express Funds, Mpls., 1999—. Bd. dirs. Minn. Land Exch. Bd., St. Paul; trustee Minn. State Bd. Investment, St. Paul, 1979-99. Bd. dirs. Exec. Coun., St. Paul, KidsFirst Scholarship Fund Minn., 1999-2002, Fairview Lakes Regional Health Care, 2002-04; sec. Minn. Housing Fin. Agy., St. Paul, 1979-91; past pres. Pub. Employees Retirement Assn., St. Paul, 1985-88; adv. bd. mem. Nat. Heritage Acad., 2001—; mem. Nat. Gov.'s Assn., Midwest Gov.'s Assn., Great Lakes Govs.; mem. Nat. Ednl. Goals Panel of Nat. Gov.'s Assn. Bush Found. Leadership fellow, 1971; recipient Children's Champion award Minn. Children's Def. Fund, Nat. Audubon Soc. award, Small Bus. Guardian award Nat. Fedn. Ind. Businesses, 1994, Great Blue Heron award N.Am. Waterfront Mgmt. Plan/U.S. Fish & Wildlife Svc., 1995; named Rep. of Yr. Nat. Ripon Soc., 1993. Bd. dirs. Exec. Coun. St. Paul, sec. Minn. Housing Fin. Agy., St. Paul, 1979-91; past pres. Pub. Employees Retirement Assn., St. Paul, 1985-88; mem. Nat. Gov.'s Assn. (chmn. com. on human resources, mem. Nat. Ednl. Goals Panel), Rep. Gov.'s Assn., Midwest Gov.'s Assn., Great Lakes Govs. Republican. Avocations: reading, squash, U. Minn. basketball and football games. Office: Am Express Funds 901 Marquette Ave Ste 2810 Minneapolis MN 55402-3268 Home: 145 Holly Ln N Minneapolis MN 55447

CARLSON, ARTHUR EUGENE, accounting educator; b. Whitewater, Wis., May 10, 1923; s. Paul Adolph and Dorothy Adeline (Cooper) C.; m. Lorraine June Bronson, Aug. 19, 1944; 1 child, George Arthur. EdB, U. Wis., Whitewater, 1943; MBA, Harvard U., 1947; PhD, Northwestern U., 1954. Instr. Ohio U., 1947-50; lectr. Northwestern U., 1950-52; from asst. prof. to prof. acctg. Washington U., St. Louis, 1952-88, prof. emeritus, 1988—. Vis. prof. U. Hawaii, 1963-64. Author: College Accounting, 1967, 7th edit., 1993, Accounting Essentials, 1973, 5th edit., 1991. Chmn. Robert Meml. Endowment Fund, University City, Mo., 1972-2004, trustee Police and Fire Pension Bd., 1979-88. Mem. Inst. Mgmt. Accts. (past pres.), Assn. Sys. Mgmt. (past pres., Disting. Svc. award 1973), Soc. Profs. Emeriti Washington U. (pres. 1995, disting. bus. alumni awards com. 1998—), Kiwanis (pres. 1969). Republican. Episcopalian. Avocations: bowling, gardening. Home: 801 S Skinker Blvd # 9A Saint Louis MO 63105-3265 Business E-Mail: carlson@olin.wustl.edu.

CARLSON, BRUCE MARTIN, anatomist; b. Gary, Ind., July 11, 1938; s. Martin E. and Esther (Granquist) C.; m. Jean Ann Hyslop, Aug. 18, 1968; children: Martin, James. BA, Gustavus Adolphus Coll., 1959; MS, Cornell U., 1961; MD, PhD, U. Minn., 1986. Exchange scientist Inst. of Devel. Biology, Moscow, 1965-66; Fulbright fellow Hubrecht (Netherlands) Inst., 1973-74; Joshiah Macy scholar U. Helsinki, Finland, 1981-82; exchange scientist Inst. of Physiology, Prague, Czechoslovakia, 1971; asst. prof. of anatomy to prof. U. Mich., Ann Arbor, 1966—, prof. biology, 1979—, chmn. dept. anatomy and cell biology, 1988-2000, rsch. scientist Inst. Gerontology, 1989—, dir. Inst. Gerontology, 2000—04. Fellow Fetzer Inst., Kalamazoo, Mich., 1990-96, trustee, 1998—; mem. study sects. NIH, 1986-90, Nat. Bd. Med. Examiners, 1994-96; NIH Fogerty fellow, U. Otago, Dunedin, New Zealand, 1999-00. Author: The Regeneration of Minced Muscles, 1972, Patten's Foundations of Embryology, 1974, 4th edit., 1981, 5th edit., 1988, 6th edit., 1996, Regeneration (in Russian), 1986, Human Embryology and Developmental Biology, 1994, 3d edit., 2004; editor: From Message to Mind, 1988, Regeneration and Transplantation, 1990, numerous others. Recipient Disting. Alumni award Gustavus Adolphus Coll., 1979, Newcomb-Cleveland prize AAAS, 1972, 650th Anniversary medal, Charles U., Prague, silver medal Russian Acad. Nat. Scis., 2004, H. Gray award Am. Assn. Anatomists, 2004. Fellow: AAAS, Russian Acad. Natural Scis.; mem.: Gerontol. Soc. Am., Internat. Soc. Devel. Biology, Soc. Devel. Biologists, Assn. of Anatomy, Cell Biology and Neurobiology Chairpersons (pres. 1995), Am. Soc. Ichthyologists and Herpetologists, Am. Soc. Zoologists (divsn. chmn. 1987—89), Am. Assn. Clin. Anatomists, Am. Assn. Anatomists (nominating com. 1991, exec. com. 1994, pres. 1997—99). Lutheran. Achievements include invention of techniques of free muscle transplantation. Home: 3838 Curlew Ln Ann Arbor MI 48103-9404 Office: U Mich Inst of Gerontology Ann Arbor MI 48109

CARLSON, BRUCE WILLIAM, diversified holding company executive; BS in Acctg., U. Buffalo, 1969. CPA, N.Y. Mgr. Arthur Andersen & Co., Rochester, N.Y., 1969-77; v.p. fin. Andco Inc., Buffalo, 1977-86; v.p., corp. contr. Delaware North Cos., Inc., Buffalo, 1986—. Mem. AICPA, Beta Gamma Sigma. Office: Delaware North Cos Inc 40 Fountain Plz Buffalo NY 14202 Business E-Mail: bcarlson@dncinc.com.

CARLSON, CHRISTOPHER TAPLEY, lawyer; b. N.Y.C., Mar. 7, 1949; s. David Bret and Jane (Tapley) C.; m. Jane Fisher, Aug. 22, 1970; children: Caroline, Jonathan. Bar: Mass. 1973, U.S. Supreme Ct. 1980. Assoc. Hale and Dorr, Boston, 1973-79, jr. ptnr., 1979-83, sr. ptnr., 1983-89; ptnr. Gilmore Rees and Carlson, Franklin, Mass., 1989—. Mem. estate planning curr. com. Mass. Continuing Edn. New Eng. Law Inst., Inc., Boston, 1982-93; mem. exec. com. Boston Estate Planning Council, 1987-91; mem. Boston Estate Planning and Probate Forum, 1989—; lectr. Law Boston U. Sch. Law, 1982-84. Trustee William Lawrence Camp, Center Tuftonboro, N.H., 1975-90. Fellow Am. Coll. Trust and Estate Counsel; mem. Weston Golf Club. Office: Gilmore Rees & Carlson 20 Walnut St Wellesley MA 02481-2104

CARLSON, CURTIS EUGENE, orthodontist, periodontist; b. Mar. 30, 1942; m. Dona M. Seely; children: Jennifer Ann, Gina Christine, Erik Alan. BA in Divisional Scis., Augustana Coll., 1965; BDS, DDS, U. Ill., 1969; cert. in periodontics, U. Wash., 1974, cert. in orthodontics, 1976. Dental intern Oak Knoll Navy Hosp., Oakland, Calif., 1969-70; dental officer USN, 1970-72; part-time dentist VA Hosp., Seattle, 1972-73; part-time periodontist Group Health Dental Coop., Seattle, 1973-76, part-time orthodontist, 1976-78; clin. instr. U. Wash., 1976; prin. Bellevue (Wash.) Orthodontic and Periodontic Clinic, 1976—; clin. instr., trainer Luxar Laser Corp., Bothell, Wash., 1992—. Presenter in field. Master of ceremonies Auctioneer Friendship Fair, Augustana Coll., 1965, orientation group leader, 1965, mem. field svcs. com. for high sch.recruitment, 1965; orthodontic advisor Seattle Study Clubs, 2001-. Fellow Am. Coll. Dentists; mem. ADA, Am. Acad. Periodontology, Am. Assn. Orthodontics, Western Soc. Periodontology (bd. dirs. 1984-85, 86, program chmn. 1986, v.p. 1988, pres. elect 1989, pres. 1990), Seattle King County Dental Soc. (grievance, ethics and pub. info. coms.), Wash. State Dental Assn., Wash. State Soc. Periodontists (program chmn., pres. elect 1987, pres. 1988, 89), Wash. Assn. Dental Specialists (com. rep. 1987, 88, 89), Wash. State Orthodontic Soc., Wash. State Soc. Periodontists, Pacific Coast Soc. Orthodontics, Omicron Kappa Upsilon (dental hon. fraternity), Pi Upsilon Gamma (social chmn. 1964, pres. 1965). Home: 16730 Shore Dr NW Seattle WA 98155-5634 Office: Bellevue Orthodontic/ Periodontic Clinic 1248 112th Ave NE Bellevue WA 98004-3712 Office Phone: 425-453-1202. E-mail: orthoperio@aol.com.

CARLSON, CURTIS R., electronics research industry executive; BS in Physics, Worcester Polytechnic Inst.; MS, PhD, Rutgers U. Mem. tech. staff RCA Lab. (became Sarnoff Corp. and part of SRI, 1987), Princeton, NJ, 1973-1981; founder, leader high definition TV program Sarnoff Corp. subs. SRI Internat., Princton, NJ, 1981-84; dir. Info. Systems Lab, 1984-90; vp, info. systems Sarnoff Corp., 1990-95; exec. v.p. Sarnoff Corp. subs. SRI Internat., Princton, NJ, 1995-98, past head ventures and licensing; pres., CEO SRI Internat., Menlo Park, Calif., 1998—. Co-founder, exec. dir. Nat. Info. Display Lab., 1990; past mem. adv. bd. USAF; past mem. rsch. lab. tech. assessment bd. U.S. Army; active Joint. Civilian Ops. Conf., 1996; vis. distg. sci., U. of Wash., 1998; served on several govt. task forces; cons. and presenter in field. Author 15 U.S. patents in the fields of image quality, image coding and computer vision. Recipient Dr. Robert H. Goddard award for profl. achievements, Worcester Polytechnic Inst., 2002. Mem. IEEE, Soc. Motion Picture and TV Engrs., Highlands Group (charter mem.), Sigma Xi, Tau Beta Pi. Avocation: violin. Address: SRI Internat 333 Ravenswood Ave Menlo Park CA 94025-3493 E-mail: inquiry.line@sri.com.

CARLSON, CYNTHIA JOANNE, artist, educator; b. Chgo. d. Ivan Morris and Ruth (Holmes) Carlson. BFA, Sch. Art Inst., Chgo., 1965; MFA, Pratt Inst., Bklyn., 1967. Instr. Phila. Coll. Art., 1967-72, U. Colo., Boulder, 1972-73; asst. prof. painting Phila. Coll. Art., 1973; assoc. prof. Phila Coll. Art., 1979-82; prof. Phila. Coll. Art., 1982-87, Queens Coll., CUNY, 1987—. One-woman shows include Allen Meml. Art Mus., Oberlin, Ohio, 1980, Milw. Art Mus., 1982, Pam Adler Gallery, N.Y.C., 1983, Albright-Knox Art Gallery, Buffalo, 1985, Queens Mus., Flushing, N.Y., 1990, Charles More Gallery, Phila., 1990—96, AIR Gallery, N.Y.C., 1992, Neuberger Mus., Purchase, N.Y., 1999, exhibited in group shows at Contemporary Art Ctr., Cin., 1980, Whitney Mus. Art, N.Y.C., 1980, Hayden Art Gallery, MIT, Cambridge, 1981, Jacksonville (Fla.) Art Mus., 1982, Represented in permanent collections Guggenheim Mus., N.Y.C., Bklyn. Mus. Art, Phila. Mus. Art, Richmond (Va.) Mus. Fine Arts, Denver Art Mus., Allen Meml. Art Mus., commn., L.A. Metro Rail Sys., 1992—93, Criminal Justice Ctr., Phila., Dept. Arts and Culture, 1995. Grantee, NEA, 1975, 1978, 1981, 1987, Creative Artists Pub. Svc., 1978. Home: 139 W 19th St New York NY 10011-4105 Office: CUNY Queens Coll Art Dept Klapper # 172 Flushing NY 11367-0904 Personal E-mail: ccarlson607@yahoo.com. Business E-Mail: ccyncyn@earthlink.net.

CARLSON, DALE ARVID, retired university dean; b. Aberdeen, Wash., Jan. 10, 1925; s. Edwin C.G. and Anna A. (Anderson) C.; m. Jean M. Stanton, Nov. 11, 1948; children: Dale Ronald, Gail L. Carlson Manahan, Joan M. Carlson Lee, Gwen D. Carlson Lundgren. AA, Grays Harbor Coll., 1947; BSCE, U. Wash., 1950, MSCE, 1951; PhD, U. Wis., 1960. Registered profl. engr., Wash., 1955. Water engr. City of Aberdeen, 1951-55; asst. prof., assoc. prof., prof., chmn. dept. civil engring. U. Wash., Seattle, 1955-76, dean Coll Engring., 1976-80, dean emeritus, 1980—, dir. Valle Scandinavian Exch., 1980—2002; chmn. dept. civil engring. Seattle U., 1983-88, acting dean sci. and engring., 1990, dean sci. and engring., 1990-92. Vis. prof. Tech. U. Denmark, Copenhagen, 1970, Royal Coll. Agr., Uppsala, Sweden, 1976, 78; mem. adv. com. Scandinavian Studies Dept. U. Wash., 2003-. Contbr. articles to profl. jours. Exec. bd. Pacific N.W. Synod Luth. Ch. in Am., chmn. fin. com., 1980-84, treas., 1986-87, bd. edn., fin. com. Evang. Luth. Ch. in Am., 1987-91; v.p. Nat. Luth. Campus Ministry, 1988-91; treas. N.W. Washington synod Evang. Luth. Ch. in Am., 1996-2000, mem. synod candidacy com., 2001—; exec. bd. Nordic Heritage Mus., 1981-86; bd. dirs. Hearthstone Retirement Ctrs., 1984-93, Evergreen Safety Coun., 1980-86. With AUS, 1943-45. Named Outstanding Grad. Weatherwax H.S., Aberdeen, 1972, Outstanding Grad. Grays Harbor Coll., 1947; guest of honor Soppeldagene, Trondheim, 1978. Mem. ASCE, Internat. Water Acad., Am. Soc. Engring. Educators, Am. Acad. Environ. Engring., Am. Water Works Assn., Am. Scandinavian Found., Swedish Am. C. of C. (bd. dirs. 1994-99), Norwegian Am. C. of C., Rainier Club, Rotary, Phi Beta Kappa, Sigma Xi, Chi Epsilon. Home: 9235 41st Ave NE Seattle WA 98115-3801 Business E-Mail: dcarlson@engr.washington.edu.

CARLSON, DALE BICK, writer; b. N.Y.C., May 24, 1935; d. Edgar M. and Estelle (Cohen) Bick; children: Daniel, Hannah. BA, Wellesley Coll., 1957. Lic. wildlife rehabilitator. Founder, pres. Bick Pub. House, 1993—. Founder, pres. Bick Pub. House, 1993—. Author children's books, adult books, Perkins the Brain, 1964, The House of Perkins, 1965, Miss Maloo, 1966, The Brainstormers, 1966, Dracula, 1967, Frankenstein, 1968, The Electronic Teabowl, 1969, Warlord of the Genji, 1970, The Beggar King of China, 1971, The Mountain of Truth, 1972 (Spring Festival Honor book, named Am. Libr. Assn. Notable Book), Good Morning Danny, 1972, Hannah, 1972, The Human Apes, 1973 (named Am. Libr. Assn. Notable Book), Girls Are Equal Too, 1973;: 2d edit., 2000 (named Am. Library Assn. Notable Book), Baby Needs Shoes, 1974, Triple Boy, 1976, Where's Your Head?, 1971 (Christopher award), The Plant People, 1977, The Wild Heart, 1977, The Shinning Pool, 1979, Lovingsex for Both Sexes, 1979, Boys Have Feelings Too, 1980, Call Me Amanda, 1981, Manners That Matter, 1982, The Frog People, 1982, Charlie the Hero, 1983—85, The Jenny Dean Science Fiction Mysteries, The Mystery of the Shining Children, The Mystery of the Hidden Trap, The Secret of the Third Eye, The James Budd Mysteries, The Mystery of Galaxy Games, The Mystery of Operation Brain, 1985, Miss Mary's Husbands, 1988, Basic Manuals in Wildlife Rehabilitation, 6 vols., 1993—94, Basic Manuals for Friends of the Disabled Series, 1995—96, Living With Disabilities, 1997, Wildlife Care for Birds and Mammals, 1997, Stop the Pain: Mediations for Teenagers, 1998 (N.Y. Pub. Libr. Best Books, 2000), Confessions of a Brain-Impaired Writer: A Memoir, 1998; Stop the Pain: Adult Meditations, 2000; editor: What Are You Doing With Your Life, 2001, In and Out of Your Mind: Teen Science, Human Bites, 2002 (named Best Book, N.Y. Pub. Libr., 2003), Who Said What? Philosophy Quotes for Teens, 2003 (Voya Honor award, 2003), The Teen Brain Book, 2004 (Book of Yr. finalist Foreword Mag., 2004), The Teen Talk Book, 2005. Mem. Authors League Am., Authors Guild. Address: 307 Neck Rd Madison CT 06443-2755 Office: Agent Hagenbach-Bender 20 Gutenbergstrasse Bern Switzerland Business E-Mail: bickpubhse@aol.com.

CARLSON, DAVID BRET, retired lawyer; b. Jamestown, N.Y., Aug. 16, 1918; s. David Albert and Gertrude (Johnson) C.; m. Jane Tapley, Apr. 12, 1947; children: Christopher Tapley, David Kurt, Nancy Berners-Lee. AB, Brown U., 1940; LL.B., Harvard U., 1947. Bar: N.Y. 1947, U.S. Supreme Ct. 1972. Assoc. Debevoise & Plimpton, N.Y.C., 1947-53, ptnr., 1953-87. Contbr. articles to profl. publs. Mem. ABA, N.Y. State Bar Assn., Bar Assn. City of N.Y. Home: PO Box 32 275 W Falmouth Hwy West Falmouth MA 02574

CARLSON, DAVID EDWARD, journalism educator, journalist, consultant; b. Duluth, Minn., June 25, 1951; s. Carl Alfred Carlson and Frances Rita Gueroult; m. C. Jeanne Reynolds, May 27, 1984; children: Christopher Troy Reynolds, Laura Catherine Reynolds, Kelly Anne Reynolds. BJ, Drake U., 1973. Regional editor Chronicle-Tribune, Marion, Ind., 1973—81; editor The Kingman Daily Miner, Kingman, Ariz., 1984—87, The Albuquerque Tribune, 1987—93, dining critic, 1989—93, The Gainesville Sun, Gainesville, Fla., 1999—; new media columnist Am. Journalism Rev., College Park, Md., 1999—2000; dir., interactive media lab, Coll. Journalism and Comm. U. Fla., Gainesville, 1993—, prof. new media journalism, 2002—. Pres. The Albuquerque (N. Mex.) Press Club, 1991—92; lectr. in field. Contbr. columns to magazines, columns in newspapers. Scoutmaster Boy Scouts of Am., Thoreau, N.Mex., 1983—85; mem. Kirkwood Environ. Improvement Assn., Gainesville, Fla., 1996—98. Recipient Dozens of journalism awards, 1993-present; fellow, The Poynter Inst., 1994, 2004, Am. Press Inst., 1995, 1996; grantee, Russian Ctr. for Cyberjournalism, 1994, 1995, 1996, 1997, The NY Times Co., 1995, 1996, 1997, U.S. Dept. State, 1998, 2003. Mem.: Am. Soc. Newspaper Editors, Online News Assn., Investigative Reporters and Editors, Soc. Profl. Journalists (nat. pres. elect 2004—05, nat. sec.-treas. 2003—04, mem. exec. com. 1997—, pres. 2005—), The Albuquerque Press Club. Achievements include development of first journalism-related site on the World Wide Web; first interactive newspaper based on a personal computer. Avocations: cooking, piloting small aircraft, computing, woodworking, sports car racing. Office: U Fla 3219 Weimer Hall Gainesville FL 32611 Office Phone: 352-846-0171.

CARLSON, DAVID EMIL, physicist, researcher; b. Weymouth, Mass., Mar. 5, 1942; s. Emil Algot and Anne Alice (Salomaa) C.; m. Mary Ann Lewinski, June, 1966; children: Eric, Darcey. BS in Physics, Rensselaer Poly. Inst., 1963; PhD in Physics, Rutgers U., 1968. Research scientist U.S. Army Nuclear Effects Lab., Edgewood Arsenal, Md., 1968-69; head photovoltaic device research RCA Labs., Princeton, N.J., 1970-83; dep. gen. mgr., dir. research Solarex Thin Film Div., Newtown, Pa., 1983-86, gen. mgr., 1986-88, v.p., 1988-98; chief scientist BP Solar, 1999—. Contbr. articles to profl. jours.; patentee in field. Served to capt. Signal Corps U.S. Army, 1968-70, Vietnam. Decorated Bronze Star medal; recipient Ross Coffin Purdy award Am. Ceramic Soc., 1976, Outstanding Achievement award RCA Labs., 1973, 76, Walton Clark medal Franklin Inst., 1986, Karl W. Boer Solar Energy medal of merit U. Del. and Internat. Solar Energy Soc., 1995. Fellow IEEE (co-recipient Morris N. Liebmann award 1984, William R. Cherry award 1988); mem. Am. Phys. Soc., Am. Vacuum Soc., Sigma Xi. Achievements include inventor amorphous silicon solar cell, 1974. Home: 217 Yorkshire Dr Williamsburg VA 23185-3912 Office: BP Solar 630 Solarex Ct Frederick MD 21703 Office Phone: 301-698-4256. Business E-Mail: dave.carlson@bp.com. *My career in science has resulted from a curiosity about the workings of nature and a desire to use the phenomena and materials of nature to benefit society.*

CARLSON, DAVID RUSCO, lawyer; b. San Antonio, Apr. 17, 1961; s. Robert Dalner C. and Penelope Rusco; m. Kay Marie Lethlean, Apr. 28, 1983; children: Josiah, Erica, Lauren, Noah, Japheth. BA in English, Portland State U., 1986; JD, Ariz. State U., 1989. Bar: Idaho 1990, Oreg. 1990, U.S. Dist. Ct. Oreg. 1990, U.S. Dist. Ct. Idaho 1990, Ariz. 1994. Prosecutor Malheur County Dist. Atty., Vale, Oreg., 1990-93; county atty. Malheur County, Vale, Oreg., 1993-96; atty. pvt. practice, Vale, Oreg., 1993—. Instr. Treasure Valley C.C., Ontario, Oreg., 1990-94, mem. budget bd., 1991-97, vice chair, 1997-2000, chair, 2000—, bd. dirs.; mem. Malheur County Commn. Juvenile Drug Ct. Policies and Implementation; lectr. theory and practice of "domestic violence" cases. Scout leader Boy Scouts Am., 1983—. Mem. Nat. Assn. Criminal Defense Lawyers, Oreg. Criminal Defense Lawyers Assn. (bd. dirs. 1995—). Republican. Mem. Lds Ch. Avocations: travel, current events, family, reading. Office: 449 Washington St E Vale OR 97918-1254

CARLSON, DESIREE ANICE, pathologist; b. Clinton, Iowa, June 10, 1950; d. Donald Richard and Bernice Elfriede (Jacobs) C. MD, Duke U., 1975. Diplomate in anat. and clin. pathology, blood banking and cytopathology Am. Bd. Pathology. Resident in pathology U. Wash., Seattle, 1975-76, N.E. Deaconess Hosp., Boston, 1976-77, Peter Bent Brigham Hosp., Boston, 1977-79; pathologist W. Roxbury VA Med. Ctr., Boston, 1979-82; med. dir. blood bank Univ. Hosp., Boston, 1982-90; assoc. chief pathology N.E. Meml. Hosp., Stoneham, Mass., 1990-93; chief pathology Brockton (Mass.) Hosp., 1993—, sec., treas. med. staff, 2001—02, v.p. med. staff, 2003—04, pres. med. staff, 2005—. Asst. prof. pathology Boston U. Sch. Med., 1983—; cons. pathology Brigham and Women's Hosp., Boston, 1984-95; mem. adv. bd. ARC, Dedham, 1982-96. Contbr. chapters to books, articles to profl. jours. Recipient Outstanding Contbd. Article award Med. Lab. Observer, 1988. Mem. Coll. Am. Pathologists (N.E. regional commr. 1991—), Am. Med. Women's Assn., Am. Assn. Blood Banks, Mass. Med. Soc. (coms.), Mass. Pathology Soc., N.E. Pathology Soc. (sec. 1996-98, treas. 1998-2000, pres.-elect 2000-01, pres. 2001-02, joint sponsored activities coord. 2002-04). Republican. Presbyterian. Avocations: dance, aerobics. Office: Brockton Hosp 680 Centre St Brockton MA 02302-3395 Office Phone: 508-941-7321. Business E-Mail: dcarlson@brocktonhospital.org.

CARLSON, DEVON MCELVIN, architect, educator; b. Topeka, Dec. 1, 1917; s. Gustave Elvin and Gertrude M. (Swanson) C.; m. Mary E. Ackley, June 14, 1949; children: Mitchell Lans, Martha Sue, Judith Ann, Peter DeVon. BS in Architecture, U. Kans., 1941; BS in Archtl. Engring. with honors, U. Colo., 1947; MS in Architecture, Columbia U., 1949. Mem. faculty U. Colo., 1943-81, prof., chmn. dept. architecture and archtl. engring., 1959-62, dean Sch. Architecture, 1962-70, dean Coll. Environ. Design, 1970-71, dean emeritus, 1981—, mem. steering com. Creative Arts Program, 1959-80. Lectr. civic and profl. groups; past mem. Colo. Bd. Examiners Architects, pres., 1964-65. Co-author: An Approach to Architectural Design, 1950, Architecture/Colorado, 1966; contbr. articles to profl. jours. Past mem. Boulder Landmarks Bd.; advisor emeritus Nat. Trust for Hist. Preservation; mem. Colo. Hist. Preservation Rev. Bd., 1980-84, 85-93. Recipient Stearns award 1972, Disting. Alumnus award U. Kans., 1984; Columbia U. scholar, 1948. Fellow AIA (bd. dirs. Colo. chpt. 1966-67, pres. 1969, nat. scholarship com. chmn. 1977-78, mem. nat. com. on hist. resources 1978—, Silver medal Western Mountain region 1980, Carlson Lecture series established in his honor 1981); mem. Nat. Coun. Archtl. Registration Bds. (exam-devel. com. 1962-76, 87-93, chmn. 1975, editor Handbook 1976), Colo. Soc. Architects (pres. 1980), Assn. Coll. Schs. Architecture, Am. Soc. Engring. Edn. (past chmn. Colo. chpt.), Boulder C. of C., Rocky Mountain Liturg Art Assn., Hist. Boulder, Hist. Denver, Soc. Archtl. Historians, Scarab Club, Triangle Club, Rotary (bd. dirs.), Tau Beta Pi, Delta Phi Delta, Chi Epsilon. Address: 5472 White Pl Boulder CO 80303-1227

CARLSON, DONALD OTTO, magazine publisher, editor; b. Gary, Ind., Oct. 4, 1926; BA in Journalism, History, English, Ind. U., 1949. Spot news reporter Walla Walla (Wash.) Union Bulletin; mem. staff Inside Mich., Vance Pub. Corp., Chgo.; editor various, Chgo. and N.Y.C.; prin., owner CMN Assocs., Inc., Calif., 1964—. Editor (pub.): Automated Builder, 1974—; observed: Automated Builder mags. 40th Anniversary with edit. no. 392, Feb. 2004, —; author: Dictionary/Ency. of Industrialized Housing, 1995—, How to Start an Inner City Housing Plant, 1999—, Shelter All Victims of Emergencies and Disasters, 2000—, How and Why to Buy a Factory Built Home, 2001—. Founder Automated Builders Consortium, 1993, ABC Saved shelter, 1999. Recipient five nat. journalism awards; named Factory-Built Housing's Man of the 20th Century, Allen Newsletter, Indpls., 2000; charter mem. Hall of Fame, Modular Bldg. Inst., 2001. Mem. Soc. Profl. Journalists, Wood Truss Council Am. (hall of fame 1988), Wood Found. Inst. (co-founder 1980). Office Phone: 805-642-9735. E-mail: info@automatedbuilder.com.

CARLSON, DONNA, art association administrator, director; b. Grand Junction, Colo., Jan. 16, 1936; d. Vincent Grasso and Evalyn Eileen Holley; m. Leslie M. Carlson (div.). BA, U. Denver, 1956; MFA, U. S.D., 1957. Founder theater Thresholds, N.Y.C., 1962—69; dir. adminstrn. Art Dealers Assn. Am., N.Y.C. Mem.: Phi Beta Kappa. Office: Art Dealers Association America 575 Madison Ave New York NY 10022 Office Phone: 212-940-8590. Business E-Mail: adaa@artdealers.org.

CARLSON, EDWARD C., anatomy educator; b. Iron Mountain, Mich., Feb. 22, 1942; s. Clarence H. and Rachel O. (Olsen) C.; m. Pam R. Carlson, 1995; children: Scott Edward, Susan Rebecca. BA, Bethel Coll., 1964; PhD, U. N.D., 1970. Spl. instr. dept. biology Bethel Coll., St. Paul, 1964-66; instr. anatomy U. Ariz., Tucson, 1970-72, asst. prof., 1972-77; assoc. prof. human anatomy U. Calif., Davis, 1977-81, prof., 1981—; chmn. dept. anatomy and cell biology U. N.D., Grand Forks, 1981—. Rsch. anatomist Calif. Primate Rsch. Ctr., Davis, 1982-85, rsch. affiliate, 1985—; co-dir. N.D. Diabetes Ocular Rsch. Ctr., Grand Forks, 1988—. Contbr. articles to profl. jours. Rsch. grantee Juvenile Diabetes Found., Am. Heart Assn., NIH, EPSCOR, NSF. Mem. Am. Assn. Anatomists, Am. Soc. for Investigative Pathology, Am. Soc. Cell Biology, Microcirculatory Soc. Avocations: running, fishing, skiing. Office: U ND Dept Anatomy & Cell Biol Grand Forks ND 58202 Office Phone: 701-777-2101.

CARLSON, ERIK B., lawyer; b. 1947; BA, Dartmouth College; JD, George Washington U. Law Sch. Sr. atty. Western Crude Oil Inc.; asst. gen. counsel Davis Oil Co.; sr. v.p., gen. counsel, sec. Duke Energy Field Svcs. (formerly Associated Natural Gas Corp.), 1983—98, TransMontaigne Inc., Denver, 1998—. Office: TransMontaigne Inc 370 17th St Ste 2750 PO Box 5660 Denver CO 80217 Office Phone: 303-626-8265. Office Fax: 303-626-8228. Business E-Mail: ecarlson@transmontaigne.com.

CARLSON, FREDA ELLEN, secondary school educator, educational association administrator; b. Wilmington, Ohio, Jan. 4, 1914; d. Heber W. and Hazel (Reed) Custis; m. Raymond A. Carlson, June 15, 1940; children: Susan Ann Lapp, Philip Reed. MA in Adminstrn., Toledo U., 1967, MA in Teaching and Reading, EdS, 1972. Tchr. elem. Highland Sch., Sylvania, Ohio, 1963-68; from tchr. to supr. Lucas County Schs., Toledo, 1968-76, cons. to tchrs., 1969-76, ret., 1976. Tchr. adult continuing edn. Toledo U., 1961-76. Guardian ad litem Ohio Juvenile Ct., 1976-84: Sarasota County High Sch. Acad. Olympics, 1991—. Recipient Woman of Toledo award St. Vincent Hosp. Guild, 1984. Mem. Internat. Reading Assn. (pres. 1980-81), Nat. Middle Sch. Assn. (sec. 1978-79), AAUW (1st v.p. 1990—), Phi Delta Kappa, Pi Lambda Theta (pres. 1970-72), Delta Kappa Gamma (pres. 1974-76), Phi Kappa Phi. Republican. Lutheran.

CARLSON, GEORGE ARTHUR, artist; b. Elmhurst, Ill., July 3, 1940; s. William Emanuel and Mathilda Katherine (Jorgensen) C.; m. Pamela Gustavson Hatzenbiler, May 9, 1981; children: Solon Emil, Andra Sean, Erin Hatzenbiler Vaughan, Eric Hatzenbiler. Student, Am. Acad. Art, Chgo., Art Inst. Chgo., U. Ariz.; DFA (hon.), U. Idaho. Lectr. 1st U.S./Soviet Art Summit, Tretyakov Mus., Moscow, 1989. One man exhbns. include Indpls. Mus. Art, 1979, 85, Smithsonian Inst., Washington, 1982, Southwest Mus., L.A., 1988, Autry Western Heritage Mus., 1993, Gilcrease Mus., Tulsa, 1994, Ft. Worth Zoo Art Gallery, 1995-96; one man shows include Saks Gallery, Colorado Springs, Colo., 1972, Kennedy Galleries, N.Y.C., 1976, Bishop Galleries, Scottsdale, Ariz., 1977, Stremmel Galleries, Reno, 1978, 81, Grand Cen. Galleries, N.Y.C., 1980, O'Grady Galleries, Chgo., 1977, 83, Gerald Peters Gallery, Santa Fe, N.Mex., 1977, 85, 88, 92, Gerald Peters Gallery, Dallas, 1987, Farber Gallery Fine Arts, Indpls., 1989, Kneeland Gallery, Sun Valley, Idaho, 1990, 93, 94, Fenn Galleries, 1993, The Art Spirit Gallery, 2001, Nicholas Gallery, Billings, Mont., 2002, Matthew -Chase Gallery, Santa Fe, 2002; featured in group exhbns. including Phoenix Art Mus., Denver Art Mus., Denver Natural History Mus., Penrose Library at U. Denver, Gillette Pub. Library, Wyoming, Nat. Acad. Western Art, Oklahoma City, 1973-90, The Peking Exhibit, Beijing, Peoples Republic of China, 1981, Artists of Am. Show, Denver, 1981-2000, Nat. Sculpture Soc., N.Y.C., 1982-83, 86, 90, Mus. Western Art, Denver, 1985, Gilcrease Mus., Tulsa, 1985, Ft. Smith (Okla.) Art Ctr., 1986, Kyoto (Japan) World Expn. Hist. Cities, 1987, Sonoma County Mus., Santa Rosa, Calif., 1987, Western & Wildlife Mus., Jackson Hole, Wyo., 1988, Amerika Haus, Berlin, 1990, Nat. Acad. Design, N.Y.C., 1990, Hubbard Mus., Riudoso, N.Mex., 1990, Hakone Open-Air Mus.,Tokyo, 1991, Denver 7 Show Nat. Cowboy Hall of Fame, 1992, 93, others; represented in pub. and corp. collections including Indpls. Mus., Genesee Mus., Rochester, N.Y., Denver Pub. Library, Denver Natural History Mus., Los Angeles Athletic Club, Cherokee Nat. Hist. Soc., Chakota, Okla., Corning (N.Y.) Mus., Anshutz Collection, Denver, Outdoor Mus. Art, Denver, Rockwell Mus., Pitts., Bank of Am., Las Vegas, Boatmans Bankshare, Inc., St. Louis, Brownsville (Tex.) Nat. Bank, Mountain States Bank, Denver, Rocky Mountain Bank, Denver, Sierra Nev. Arts Mus., Reno, Nat. Cowboy Hall of Fame, Oklahoma City, Mobile Oil Corp.; represented in various pvt. corp. and mus. collections, including U.S. Embassy, Copenhagen, Tucson Mus. Art, Manville Corp., Denver, L.A. Athletic Club, Rockwell Internat., others; sculptures include Bill Cosby, 1979, Bill Harrah, 1981, Early Day Miner, Washington Park, Denver, 1980, Of One Heart, Genesee Country Mus., 1982, Of One Heart, Mus. of Outdoor Arts, Englewood, Colo., 1985, I'm the Drum, Bank Am., Las Vegas, 1987, The Greeting, Genesee Mus., 1988, Eiteljorg Mus., 1989, Paul Robeson Cen. State U., Wilberforce, Ohio, 1990, Phylicia Rashad, 1991, I'm the Drum, Colo. Springs Fine Arts Ctr., 1994, Old Blue, Amon Carter Mus., Ft. Worth, 1995, Ennis Cosby, 1997, Mane of Wind-Neck of Thunder, Kirkland, Wash., 1999, Conqueror, Leanim Free Mus., Boulder, Colo., 2005, Autry Mus. Western Heritage, 2005; featured in various bibliographies and films. Served with USAR, 1963-69. Recipient gold medal Nat. Acad. Western Art, 1974, 78, 80, 85, 89, Prix de West, 1975, Silver medal, 1976, 81, 88, Robert Lougheed award, 1989, Gold medal, 1989; Merit award Western Rendezvous Show, 1983, Kenneth T. and Eileen Morris Found. award Sculpture, Autry Nat. Mus., 2003, Gold medal Sculpture, Calif. Art Club, 2003, Mary Bell Grant award, Coors Invitational, 2003. Mem. Nat. Sculpture Soc., Nat. Acad. Western Art (Gold medal 1974, 78, 80, 85, (2) 1989, Best of Show 1975, Silver medal 1976, 81, 88). Address: PO Box 28 Harrison ID 83833-0028

CARLSON, GEORGE CLARENCE, JR., state supreme court justice; b. Greenwood, Miss., May 23, 1946; s. George Clarence and Gusta Christine (Wooley) C.; m. Jane Ivy Russel, July 25, 1970; children George Russel, Meredith Christine. BS in History, Miss. State U., 1969; JD, U. Miss., 1972; grad., Nat. Jud. Coll. U. Nev., Reno, 1982. Bar: Miss. 1972, U.S. Dist. Ct. (no. dist.) Miss. 1972. Practiced law, Panola County, Miss., 1972-82; cir. ct. judge 17th Jud. Dist. Miss., Batesville, 1982—2001; justice Miss. Supreme Ct., 2001—. Sch. bd. atty. S. Panola Sch. Dist., 1972-82; state chmn. Miss. Sch. Bds. Assn. Coun. of Sch. Bd. Attys., 1980-81; mcpl. judge pro tem City of Batesville, 1979-82; atty. 2d ct. dist. Indsl. Devel. Authority, Panola County, 1980-82; mem. Govs'. Criminal Justice Task Force, 1991, Commn. on the Cts. in the 21st Century, 1992-93; vice-chair Miss. Circuit Judges Conference, 1998-99, chair 1999-2000. Elected del. precinct, county, congl. dist. caucuses and to state Dem. conv., 1976. Named Boss of Yr. Panola County Legal Secs. Assn., 1981; elected King Batesville Jr. Aux. Charity Ball, 1985. Fellow Miss. Bar Found.; mem. ABA, Miss. Bar Assn. (bd. dirs. young lawyers divsn. 1975-78), Panola County Bar Assn. (pres. 1975-76), Am. Judges Assn., William C. Keady Am. Inns of Ct. (past pres.). Presbyterian. Avocations: golf, skiing. Office: Miss Supreme Ct PO Box 779 Batesville MS 38606-0779 Business E-Mail: jcarlson@mssc.state.ms.us.

CARLSON, JANE CARTWRIGHT, painter; b. Boston, Sept. 1, 1928; d. Richard Chase and Florence (Kinsley) Cartwright; m. Byron Leslie Carlson, 1948; children: Gary, Douglas, Wesley. Student, Mass. Coll. Art, 1946-47. Mem. Am. Watercolor Soc. (dir. 1980-85), Allied Artists of Am., Audubon Artists, Knickerbocker Artists, Am. Artists Profl. League. Address: PO Box 1288 Boca Grande FL 33921-1288

CARLSON, JANET FRANCES, psychologist, educator; b. Newport, R.I., Oct. 3, 1957; d. Robert Carl and Alice Marion (Orina) Carlson; m. Kurt Francis Geisinger, Sept. 22, 1984. BS summa cum laude, Union Coll., Schenectady, 1979; MA in Clin. Psychology, Fordham U., 1982, PhD in Clin. Psychology, 1987. Lic. psychologist NY, cert. sch psychologist NY. Clin. psychology intern Conn. Valley Hosp., Middletown, Conn., 1983-84; rsch. fellow Schering-Plough Found., Bronx, N.Y., 1984-85; psychologist I Creedmoor Psychiat. Ctr., Queens Village, N.Y., 1985-86; psychologist Hallen Sch., Mamaroneck, N.Y., 1986-88; asst. prof. psychology Fordham U., Bronx, N.Y., 1988-89; asst. prof. sch. and applied psychology Fairfield (Conn.) U., 1989-93, dir. sch. and applied psychology programs, 1989-90; from asst. prof. counseling and psychol. svcs. to prof. SUNY, Oswego, 1993—2002, assoc. dean Sch. Edn., 1998-2001; prof. psychology, head dept. gen. academics Tex. A&M U., Galveston, 2002—. Cons. N.Y.C. Bd. Edn. Office Rsch., Evaluation and Assessment, 1988—92; vis. asst. prof. psychol. LeMoyne Coll., Syracuse, NY, 1992—93; dir. Office Tchg. Resources in Psychol., 2001—. Recipient Sugarfree scholarship, 1984—85; grantee Sigma Xi, 1984—85. Fellow: APA; mem.: NASP, N.Y. Assn. Sch. Psychologists, Northeastern Ednl. Rsch. Assn. (ed newsletter 1988—91, bd dirs. 1990—93, pres. 1995—96), N.Y. State Psychol. Assn., Eastern Psychol. Assn., Am. Ednl. Rsch. Assn., Sigma Xi, Psi Chi, Phi Kappa Phi (pres. 1995—96). Avocations: wildlife preservation, conservation issues.

CARLSON, JANET LYNN, county commissioner, consultant; b. Grants Pass, Oreg., Nov. 1, 1953; d. Howard Wilkie and Ruby Brock; m. Dee Kevin Carlson; children: Erika Lynn McCauley, Justin Brock, Christian David. BA, Willamette U., 1971—75; MA, Brigham Young U., 1975—77; PhD, U. of Oreg., 1995—97. French tchr. & activities dir. Evergreen Jr. H.S., Hillsboro, Oreg., 1981—87; budget & policy analyst Oreg. Exec. Dept., 1989—91; budget dir. & regional coord. Oreg. Commn. on Children & Families, 1991—95; cons. - children & families programs Salem, 1996—; com. adminstr. Oreg. Ho. of Representatives, Oreg., 1997—99; county commr. Marion County, Oreg., 2003—. Mem. Oreg. Commn. on Black Affairs, 2001—03, Governor's Task Force on the Future of Seniors & Persons with Disabilities, Salem, 2002—03, Keizer RIVERR Task Force, Keizer, Oreg.; bd. dirs. & exec. com. mem. Mid-Valley Behavioral Care Network, Salem; treas. Marion County Fair Bd., Salem, 2003—; commn. and exec. com. mem. Marion County Children & Families Commn., Salem, 2003—; mem., human services & edn. com. Nat. Assn. of Counties, Washington, 2004—; bd. dirs. Marion County Housing Authority, Salem, 2003—; mem., past chair Salem-Keizer Sch. Dist. Cmty. Involvement Adv. Com., 2003—; legislative com., bd. of directors Assn. of Oreg. Counties, 2005—; mem. State Interagency Coordinating Coun. for Early Intervention & Early Childhood Spl. Edn., 2001—03, Oreg. Commn. on Children & Families, 2001—03. State rep. Oreg. Ho. of Representatives, 2001—03. Recipient Eagle award for Vision and Innovation in State Govt., Oreg. Exec. Dept., 1992, Disting. Svc. award, Vol. Recognition, City of Salem, Oreg., 2000, Presenter and Participant, Ensuring Student Success Through Collaboration, Coun. of Chief State Sch. Officers, 1994—95. Mem.: Soc. for Prevention Rsch., Family Support Am., Assn. for Supervision & Curriculum Devel. Church Of Jesus Christ Of Latter-Day Saints. Avocations: dance, weightlifting, music. Office: Marion County Bd of Commn PO Box 14500 Salem OR 97309 Office Phone: 503-588-5300. E-mail: jcarlson@co.marion.or.us.

CARLSON, JENNIE PEASLACK, bank executive; b. Ft. Thomas, Ky., June 11, 1960; d. Roland A. and Shirley (Willen) Peaslack; m. Charles I. Michaels, Aug. 13, 1983 (div. May 1989); m. Richard A. Carlson, May 2, 1992. BA in English, Centre Coll., 1982; JD, Vanderbilt U., 1985. Bar: Ohio 1985, Minn. 2002. Atty. Taft, Stettinius & Hollister, Cin., 1985-91; sr. v.p., dep. gen. counsel Star Banc Corp., Cin., 1991—95; gen. counsel Star Bank Corp., Firstar Corp, 1995—2001; dep. gen. counsel U.S. Bancorp, 2001, exec. v.p., human resources Mpls., 2002—. Office: US Bancorp US Bancorp Ctr 800 Nicollet Mall Minneapolis MN 55402 Office Phone: 612-303-7699. E-mail: jennie.carlson@usbank.com.

CARLSON, KAREN BETH, elementary school educator; b. Rochester, N.Y., July 4, 1967; d. Barton Kent and Lucinda Ellen (Wells) C. BS in Edn., Miami U., 1989; MS in Edn., Pace U., 1993. Cert. elem. educator Ohio, N.Y. Substitute tchr. Yorktown Ctrl. Sch., NY, 1989-90; tchr. Riverdale Country Sch., Bronx, 1990-93; tchr. 4th grade Siwanoy Sch., Pelham, 1993—96; tchr. 3d & 5th grades Hendrick Hudson Sch., 1996—98; tchr. grades 1 and 5 computers and math. Dows Ln. Elem. Sch., Irvington, NY, 1998—2001, math. specialist, 2001—03, tchr. 2d grade, 2003—. Author: Pound Ridge Remembers, 1990. Avocations: tennis, boating, water-skiing, cooking, travel. Home: 19 Meadow Ln Katonah NY 10536-1535

CARLSON, KATHLEEN, not-for-profit fundraiser, writer, journalist; b. San Nicholaas, Aruba, Netherlands Antilles, June 23, 1946; arrived in Milw., Wis., 1952; d. Arthur Hughborn Mendes and Wilhelmina Leanora (Hill) Bunyan; m. Vernon Marcus Carlson, Aug. 6, 1999; m. Roman Harry Januchowski, July 6, 1966 (dec. Sept. 1968); m. Timmons Wells, May 2, 1978 (div. Sept. 1996). BA in English, U. of Wis., 1972; MS in Journalism, Northwestern U., 1973; MA in English, U. of Wis., 1988. Cert. Resource Devel. Specialist Coun. for Resource Devel., DC, 1991, Cert. Fundraising Exec. Nat. Soc. of Fund Raising Executives, Alexandria, Va., 1996-1999. Compliance monitor, planner, grants, coord. Milw. County Exec., 1980—83; asst. admin. Sr. Citizens Svs. Inc., 1983—84; auditor Milw. County, 1984—87; prog. monitor Milw. Employment Training Inc., 1988; external programs spec. Waukesha County Tech. Coll., Pewaukee, 1989—91, devel. coord., 1991—. Wis. state coord. Coun. for Resource Devel., DC, 1992—96; mem. Wis. Mfg. Curriculum Consortium, Pewaukee, 1994—; region V dir. elect Coun. for Resource Devel., 1996—97, region V dir., 1998—99. Author: (poetry book) Deep Night, 1970; contbr. var. newsletters and jours., 1985—91, poetry book Journey of the Heart, 2002. Recipient Hon. Citation, Acad. Am. Poets, 1970—71; grantee Edit. Internship, Assn. for Edn. in Journalism, 1971, Reporting Internship, The Mil. Jour., 1970. Mem.: Coun. for Resource Devel. (2003 v.p. for Annual Nat. Conf. 2002—03), Minority Graphic Arts Orgn. Inc. (sec. 1983—), YWCA of Waukesha (sec. of bd. 1998—2000, chair, Diversity Task Force 1999—2004). Avocations: writing poetry and music, ballroom dancing, skiing. Office: Waukesha County Technical College 800 Main St Pewaukee WI 53072 Office Phone: 262-691-5523. Business E-Mail: kcarlson@wctc.edu.

CARLSON, KATHLEEN BUSSART, law librarian; b. Charlotte, NC, June 25, 1956; d. Dean Allyn and Joan (Parlette) Bussart; m. Gerald Mark Carlson, Aug. 15, 1987. BA in Polit. Sci., Ohio State U., 1977; JD, Capital U., 1980; MA in Libr. and Info. Sci., U. Iowa, 1986. Bar: Ohio 1980 (inactive). Editor Lawyers Coop. Pub. Co., Rochester, N.Y., 1980-83; asst. state law libr. State of Wyo., Cheyenne, 1987-88, state law libr., 1988—. Mem. Bd. Adjustment, City of Cheyenne, 2001—; 2d v.p., bd. dirs. Wyo. coun. Girl Scouts U.S., Casper, 1990—92, 1st v.p., bd. dirs., 1993—96. Mem. Am. Assn. Law Librs. (indexing legal periodical lit. adv. com. 1993-96, chair 1994-96, scholarship com. 1996-98, citation format com. 1998-2000, 2002-2003, fair bus. practices com. 2000-02, exec. bd. 2003—, edn. com. State Ct. and County Law Librs. sect. 1991-92, sec.-treas. 1992-95, chair grants com. 1997-98 nominating com. 1998-99, co-chair membership com., chair edn. com. 2000-01), Western Pacific Assn. Law Librs. (pres. 1996-97, 2003-04), Wyo. Libr. Assn. (sec. acad. and spl. librs. sect. 1990-92, pres. 1994-95), Bibliog. Ctr. for Rsch. (trustee 1991-95), Zonta (pres. local club 2002-03), Kappa Delta, Beta Phi Mu. Avocations: arts and crafts, baking, travel. Home: 911 E 18th St Cheyenne WY 82001-4722 Office: State Law Libr 2301 Capitol Ave Cheyenne WY 82002-0001 Office Phone: 307-777-7509. Business E-Mail: kcarls@state.wy.us.

CARLSON, KAY MARIE, artist, educator; b. Marshfield, Wis., Aug. 29, 1948; d. Delmer Roland and Florence (Biechler) C.; m. Robert Vigil, Jan. 1, 1982 (div. Aug. 1987). BA in English Lit., U. Wis., 1970; postgrad., San Francisco Art Inst., 1971-74. English tchr. Antioch West Coll., San Francisco, 1973; gallery asst. Source Gallery, San Francisco, 1978-79; art dir., sales mgr. Vorpal Gallery, San Francisco, 1979-81; artist in residece Tomales (Calif.) Bay Schs., 1986; art tchr. Talampais Cmty. Edn., Mill Valley, Calif., 1992—. Cons. to artists Amsterdam Art Sight and Insight Ctr., Marin County, Calif., 1985—, bd. dirs., 1997; founder, project dir. Marin Open Studios, Sausalito, Calif., 1993-96; art curator Concordia Argonaut Club, San Francisco, 1988—; artist trip leader Wilderness Tours, Bolinas, Calif., 1987-88; sec., mem. com. Indsl. Ctr. Bldg., Sausalito, Calif., 1994-97; represented by Mus. Modern Art Gallery, San Francisco, Interart Gallery, Walnut Creek, Calif., The Art Club, Oakland, Calif. One woman shows include BankAm World Hdqrs., San Francisco, 1979, Henry Gifford Hardy Gallery, San Francisco, 1987, Mill Valley Libr. Gallery, 1990, Jessup OrangeWorks Gallery, San Anselmo, Calif, 1991, U. Wis. Marshfield Wood County Ctr., 1991, Ames Corp., San Rafael, 1992, Pt. Reyes Seashore Lodge, Olema, Calif., 1992, CCC Gallery, Tiburon, 1993, Bank of Marin, 1994, U. San Francisco, 1994; exhibited in group shows at Escalle Winery, Bank of Marin, Coll. of Marin, 1991, Bolinas (Calif.) Mus., 1991, Artisans Gallery, Mill Valley, 1991, Marin County Fair, San Rafael, 1991, 93 (1st Pl.), San Francisco Artists Guild, 1991, Grants Pass (Oreg.) Mus. Art, 1991, 92, Indsl. Ctr. Bldg., 1992, Marin Agrl. Land Trust, Ross, Calif., 1992, Marin Open Studios, Sausalito, 1993, Mill Valley City Hall, 1993, Shorebirds Gallery, Tiburon, 1994, Artisans Gallery, 1995, numerous others; executed mural St. Francis Hosp.; represented in permanent collections at BankAm., Itel Corp., Boston, U.S. Dept. Labor, EPA, San Francisco, Fireman's Fund Ins. Co., Seattle, numerous others. Sec. bd. dirs. Marin Art Coun., San Rafael, Calif., 1991-96. Studio: # 33 Indsl Ctr Bldg 480 Gate 5 Rd Sausalito CA 94965-1461 Home: 135 W J St Benicia CA 94510-3165

CARLSON, KAYE LILIEN, retired music educator; b. Mpls., Minn., July 23, 1947; d. Herbert Richard and Hilma Emma Hermann; m. Jerry Dale Carlson; children: Richard Dale, Sharon Kristine. BA, Augsburg Coll., Mpls., 1969; MusM, Mankato State U., 1980. Band dir. Anoka-Hennepin Ind. #11, Anoka, Minn., 1969—70, Fridley Mid. Sch., Fridley, Minn., 1970—, ret., 2003. Supr. student tchrs. Fridley Mid. Sch., 1970—, music dept. chairperson, 1987—94; chair, nat. rsch. com. Band Lit. List. Facilitator of after care groups St. Mary's Rehab. Ctr., Mpls., 1989—92; facilitator of student support groups Fridley Mid. Sch., Fridley, Minn., 1985—90. Mem.: NEA, Fridley Edn. Assn., Edn. Minn., Minn. Band Dirs. Assn., Music Educator's Nat. Conf., Am. Sch. Band Dirs. Assn. (past sec. of Minn. chpt., past state chair, panel moderator 1985). Avocations: reading, travel, activities with my family. Home: 1690 Canyon Ln New Brighton MN 55112 Personal E-mail: jerrykaye@hotmail.com.

CARLSON, KENNETH GEORGE, data processing executive; b. Duluth, Minn., Dec. 14, 1949; s. George Bernard and Laura Anna (Larson) C.; m. Stephanie Venn Petersen, Sept. 20, 1969; children: Laura, Anna. BSEE, U. Minn., 1972. Cert. in data processing; cert. systems profl. Systems programmer U. Minn. Computer Ctr., Mpls., 1969-74; dept. mgr. United Computing System, Kansas City, Mo., 1974-80; computer scientist Computer Scis. Corp., Falls Church, Va., 1980-82; pres., chmn. bd. LSS Data Sys., Mpls., 1982—86, 1987—2001, chmn. bd., chief tech. officer, CEO, 2001—; v.p. Minn. Supercomputer Ctr., Mpls., 1986-87, asst. to exec. v.p., 1987-90. Data processing advisor Johnson Community Coll., Overland Park, Kans., 1975-78; bd. dirs., chief fin. officer Superior Resources, Duluth, 1985—. Republican. Mem. United Ch. of Christ. Avocations: travel, running, bicycling, astronomy.

CARLSON, LAWRENCE ARVID, retired English language educator, real estate agent; b. San Diego, Dec. 29, 1935; s. Arvid Fritiof and Ruth Mathilda (Hedman) C.; m. Patricia Catherine Barlow, Sept. 8, 1963; children: Lawrence Stephen, Janine Catherine. BA in History, Roanoke Coll., 1957; MS in Edn., S.D. State U., 1962; MA in English, Calif. State U., Fullerton, 1966; grad., Realtor Inst., 2002. Cert. e-PRO Internet Profl. Tchr. Edison Jr. H.S., L.A., 1962—63, Anaheim H.S., Calif., 1963—66; prof. English Orange Coast Coll., Costa Mesa, Calif., 1966—2001; ret., 2001; instr. karate Orange Coast Coll., Costa Mesa, 1984—95. Sales assoc. Real Estate Offices, San Juan Capistrano, Calif., 1994—. Host, writer (ednl. TV show) Creative Writers Viewpoint, 1975. Horseback riding tour leader Rock Creek Pack Sta., Bishop, Calif., 1990-95; leader 4-H, Orange County, Calif., 1983-93; vol. Liberty Walk, Dana Point, Calif., 1997. Maj. USMCR, 1957-67. Recipient Excellence award Nat. Inst. Staff Orgnl. Devel., 1993, President's Club award, Re/Max of Calif. and Hawaii, 2003. Mem. Nat. Assn. Realtors, Calif. Assn. Realtors, Orange County Assn. Realtors, Faculty Assn. Calif. C.C.'s, San Juan Capistrano C. of C. Democrat. Lutheran. Avocations: horseback riding, Karate, surfing. Office: Ste A-102 32241 Camino Capistrano San Juan Capistrano CA 92675 Office Phone: 949-487-6567. Personal E-mail: ranchcarlson@earthlink.net. Business E-Mail: carlsons@larandpat.com.

CARLSON, LEROY THEODORE, JR., telecommunications industry executive; b. 1946; AB, Harvard U., 1968, MBA, 1971. Fin. analyst, mgr. fin. analysis and planning, mgr. acctg. Singer Corp., 1971-74; v.p. Telephone and Data Systems, Inc., 1974-78, exec. v.p., 1978-81, pres., 1981-86, pres., CEO, 1981—; chmn. bd. Am. Paging Sys., Inc., 1998. Chmn. bd. Am. Paging, Inc., TDS Telecomm., U.S. Cellular Corp., Am. Portable Telecom. Mem. U.S. Telephone Assn. (bd. dirs.), Nat. Rural Telecom. Assn. (bd. dirs.). Office: Telephone & Data Sys Inc 30 N La Salle St Ste 4000 Chicago IL 60602-2587*

CARLSON, MARIAN BILLE, geneticist, researcher, educator; b. Princeton, N.J., Oct. 19, 1952; d. B.C. and L.W. Carlson; m. Stephen P. Goff, Oct. 15, 1977; children: Sarah Carlson, Thomas Carlson. BA summa cum laude, Harvard U., 1973; PhD with distinction, Stanford U., 1978. Asst. prof. genetics Columbia U., N.Y.C., 1981-87, assoc. prof., 1987-88, prof., 1988—, prof. microbiology, 1991—, sr. assoc. dean for rsch., 2005. Mem. genetic basis of disease rev. com. NIH, 1991-95; mem. sci. adv. com. Damon Runyan-Walter Winchell Cancer Rsch. Fund, 1992-96. Assoc. editor Genetics, 1988-95, 97-99; mem. editl. bd. Molecular and Cellular Biology, 1987-2004, Cell Metabolsim, 2005, Current Opinion in Genetics and Devel., 1991—, editor, 97-2003, Microbiol. and Molecular Biol. Rev.; contbr. chpts. to books, articles to profl. jours. Mem. basic sci. adv. com. March of Dimes, 1993-95, mem. sci. adv. coun., 1996—; coun. mem. Harvey Soc., 1998-2001. NSF fellow, 1973-76, Jane Coffin Childs fellow, 1976-81; recipient Irma T. Hirschl Career Sci. award, 1982-87, Lamport award for basic rsch. Columbia U., 1987, Faculty Rsch. award Am. Cancer Soc., 1988-92, NIH Merit award, 1996. Fellow AAAS, Am. Acad. Microbiology, Am. Acad. Arts & Sci.; mem. Genetics Soc. Am. (bd. dirs. 1994-96, v.p. 2000, pres. 2001), Am. Soc. Microbiology (lectr. ASM Found. for Microbiology 1990-91), Phi Beta Kappa, Sigma Xi. Office: Columbia U 701 W 168th St New York NY 10032-2704 Office Phone: 212-305-6314. Business E-Mail: mbc1@columbia.edu.

CARLSON, MARVIN ALBERT, theater educator; b. Wichita, Kans., Sept. 15, 1935; s. Roy Edward and Gladys (Nelson) C.; m. Patricia Alene McElroy, Aug. 20, 1960; children— Geoffrey, Richard. BS, U. Kans., 1957, MA, 1959; PhD, Cornell U., 1961. Instr. speech and drama Cornell U., Ithaca, N.Y., 1961-62, asst. prof., 1962-66, assoc. prof. theatre arts, 1966-73, prof., 1973-79, chmn. dept., 1966-68, 73-78; dir. Cornell U. (Univ. Theatre), 1963-64, 65-66; prof. theatre and drama Ind. U., Bloomington, 1979-86, prof. comparative lit., 1984-86, disting. prof., 1986—; exec. officer PhD program in theatre Grad. Ctr. CUNY, 1986-95; Sidney E. Cohn chair in theatre CUNY, 1988—. Walker-Ames lectr. U. Wash., 1994. Author: Andre Antoine's Memories of the Theatre-Libre, 1964, The Theatre of the French Revolution, 1966, The French Stage in the Nineteenth Century, 1972, The German Stage in the Nineteenth Century, 1972, Goethe and the Weimar Theatre, 1978, The Italian Stage from Goldoni to D'Annunzio, 1981, Theories of the Theatre, 1984, The Italian Shakespearians, 1985, Places of Performance, 1989, Theatre Semiotics, 1990, Deathtraps, 1993, Performance, 1996, Voltaire and the Theatre of the Eighteenth Century, 1998, The Haunted Stage, 2001. Recipient George Jean Nathan award, 1994, ATHE Career Achievement award, 1995, Calloway prize, 2001; Guggenheim fellow, 1968, Ind. U. Soc. for Humanities fellow, 1993. Fellow Am. Theatre Assn.; mem. Am. Soc. Theatre Rsch. (Outstanding Achievement award 2000), Internat. Assn. Theatre Critics, Am. Theatre in Higher Edn., Internat. Fedn. Theatre Rsch., Nat. Theatre Conf. Home: 20 E 35th St New York NY 10016 Office: CUNY Grad Grad Ctr Program in Theatre 365 Fifth Ave New York NY 10016-4334 Office Phone: 212-817-8877. Business E-Mail: mcarlson@gc.cuny.edu.

CARLSON, NORMAN A., retired federal agency administrator; b. Sioux City, Iowa, Aug. 10, 1933; s. Albert N. and Esther (Hollander) C.; m. Patricia Helen Musser, Sept. 8, 1956 (dec. Feb. 1994); children: Lucinda M., Gary N.; m. Phyllis J. Rohan, May 23, 1997. BA, Gustavus Adolphus Coll., 1955; MA, State U. Iowa, 1957, Princeton U., 1966. Parole officer Dept. Justice, U.S. Penitentiary, Leavenworth, Kan., 1957-58; casework supr. Fed. Correctional Inst., Ashland, Ky., 1958-60; asst. supr. instl. programs Fed. Bur. Prisons, Dept. Justice, Washington, 1960-62, project officer, 1962-65, exec. asst. to dir., 1966-70; dir. Fed. Bur. Prisons, 1970-87; sr. fellow Hubert Humphrey Inst. Pub. Affairs, U. Minn., Mpls., 1987-88; prof. dept. sociology U. Minn., Mpls., 1988-98. Nat. Inst. Pub. Affairs fellow Princeton U., 1965-66; recipient Arthur S. Flemming award, 1972, Roger W. Jones award for exec. leadership, 1978, Atty. Gen.'s award for exceptional service, 1981 Mem. Am. Correctional Assn. (past pres., mem. exec. com., E.R. Cass award 1981) Home: 15745 W Vale Dr Goodyear AZ 85338-8757 E-mail: ncarl123@aol.com.

CARLSON, P(ATRICIA) M(CELROY), writer; b. Guatemala City, Guatemala, Feb. 3, 1940; (parents Am. citizens); d. James Benjamin and Alene (Jones) McElroy; m. M.A. Carlson, Aug. 20, 1960; children: Geoffrey, Richard. BA, Cornell U., 1961; MA, Cornell, 1966, PhD, 1974. Instr., lectr. psychology and human development Cornell U., Ithaca, N.Y., 1973-78. Mem. bd. dirs. Bloomington Restorations, Inc., 1982-84. Author: (with M. Potts, R. Cocking and C. Copple), Structure and Development in Child Language, 1979, Audition for Murder, 1985, Murder is Academic, 1985, Murder is Pathological, 1986, (with Richard Darlington) Behavioral Statistics, 1987, Murder Unrenovated, 1988, Rehearsal for Murder, 1988, Murder in the Dog Days, 1991, Murder Misread, 1991, Bad Blood, 1991, Gravestone, 1993, Bloodstream, 1995, Renowned Be Thy Grave, 1998, Murder, They Wrote II, 1998, The First Lady Murders, 1999, Murder Most Celtic, 2001; fourteen short stories. Chair Ithaca Environ. Commn., 1975-78; bd. dirs. Historic Ithaca, 1976-77. Mem. Mystery Writers Am. (bd. dirs. 1990-92, editor Mystery Writers Ann. 1993-96, 98-2000), Sisters in Crime (internat. sec. 1990-91, v.p. 1991-92, pres. 1992-93). Address: Vicky Bijur Literary Agy 333 W End Ave New York NY 10023-8128

CARLSON, RICHARD A., interior designer; m. Helen Carlson (dec.). BA, Pratt Inst.; postgrad., Oxford (Eng.) U. Joined Swanke, Hayden, Connell Archs., N.Y.C., 1968, prin., 1979, prin.-in-charge interior design, 1979—, mem. exec. com. Bd. mem. Creative Ctr. for Women with Cancer Chips Soup Kitchen. Named to, Interior Design Mag. Hall of Fame; recipient Nat. Hist. Preservation award, 1992, Gold medal award, Nat. Arts Club, 2001. Fellow: Inst. Bus. Designers (pres. N.Y.C. chpt.), Internat. Interior Design Assn. (Ron Wallin Disting. Merit award). Roman Catholic. Office: SHCA 295 Lafayette St New York NY 10012

CARLSON, RICHARD GREGORY, accountant; b. Chgo., Aug. 24, 1949; s. Richard George and S. Diane (Russell) C.; m. Annette Claire Bonneville, Aug. 30, 1969 (div. May 1982); children: Scott Richard, Amy Kristin; m. Pamela Catherine Punzelt, Sept. 25, 1982. BBA, Western Mich. U., 1971. CPA, Ill. With Deloitte & Touche, Chgo., 1971—80, ptnr., 1980—, dir. Chgo. real estate svc. ctr., 1980-91, mng. dir. nat. real estate svcs., 1991—2003, global mng. dir., 2004—. Author: Real Estate Accounting and Reporting Handbook, 1995; editor Real Estate Accounting and Taxation Journal, 1991-93, Real Estate Strategies, 1991—; contbr. articles to profl. jours. Mem. MIT Real Estate Ctr., 1995—; adv. bd. Ctr. Real Estate Studies Ind. U.; mem. bd. advisors Real Estate Fin. Jour., 1993—; bd. dirs. Western Mich. U. Found., 1986, mem. investment com., 1986-88, 91-97, mem. exec. com., 1988-97, vice-chmn., 1992-93, chmn. 1994-97; bd. dirs. Pin Oak Homeowners Assn., treas. 1982-86. With USAR, 1971-77. Recipient Disting. Acctg. Alumni award Western Mich. U., 1987, Disting. Alumni award 1993. Mem. AICPA, Am. Acctg. Assn. (Midwest regional steering com. 1983-87), Ill. Soc. CPAs, Internat. Coun. Shopping Ctrs., Western Mich. U. Alumni Assn. (bd. dirs. 1984-91, treas. 1984-86, pres. 1986-88), Nat. Assn. Real Estate Cos., Real Estate Roundtable. (bd. dirs. 1992—2001, pres. coun. 2001—), Nat. Coun. Real Estate Investment Fiduciaries (acctg. com. 1985—, pres. elect 1997, bd. dirs. 1993-99, pres. 1998-99),Urban Land Inst. (bd. trustees, 2002—); Plaza Club (Chgo.), Westmoreland Country Club (Wilmette, Ill., bd. dirs. 1988-92, treas. 1988-92), Ironwood Country Club (Palm Desert, Calif.). Republican. Office: Deloitte & Touche 2 Prudential Plz Chicago IL 60601 Home: Apt 5201 540 N State St Chicago IL 60610-7244

CARLSON, RICHARD WARNER, journalist, broadcast executive, federal agency administrator, diplomat; b. Boston, Mass., Feb. 10, 1941; adopted s. W.E. and Ruth Miriam (Rafuse) C.; m. Patricia Caroline Swanson; children: Tucker McNear, Buckley Peck. Student, U. Miss., 1961-62; LLD (hon.), Calif. Western U., 1988. Editl. asst. L.A. Times, 1962-63; writer, columnist UPI, San Francisco, Sacramento, 1963-66; investigative reporter, anchorman ABC-TV, San Francisco, 1966-71, anchorman, polit. editor L.A., 1971-75; anchorman Sta. KFMB-TV (CBS), San Diego, 1975-77; prodr., writer, dir. documentary films NBC-TV, Burbank, Calif., 1974; anchorman, host Carlson & Co., CBS-TV, San Diego, 1975-76; sr. v.p. Gt. Am. First Bank, San Diego, 1977-84; dir. USIA/Voice of Am., Washington, 1985-91; U.S. amb. to Republic Seychelles, 1991-92; pres., CEO Corp. for Pub. Broadcasting, 1992-97; CEO Kingworld Pub. TV, Washington, 1997-99; vice chmn. Found. for the Def. of Democracies, Washington, 2003—; columnist The Hill Newspaper, Washington, 2003—. Vice chmn. Found. for the Def. of Democracies; bd. dirs. Exec. Info. Svc., Radio Voyager, Inc.; pres. Gately-Carlson Cons.; lectr., cons. in field. Chmn. San Diego Coalition, 1980-81; gov. Scripps Meml. Hosps., La Jolla, 1981-90, Banff (Can.) TV Festival, 1996—, Am. Ctr. Children's TV, 1996—; mem. Calif. State Rep. Ctrl. Com., 1982-85; appointed Pres.'s Coun. Peace Corps, 1982-84; mem. La Jolla Planned Dist. Bd., 1982-84; bd. dirs. Sharp Hosp. Found., 1983—, Scripps Inst. Medicine and Sci., 1995—; mem. La Jolla Town Coun., 1983-85; mem. San Diego Crime Commn., 1984-85; trustee Fund for Am. Studies, 1988-91; mem. Rosalind Russell Arthritis Found., 1985-91; dir. Georgetown Club, 1995—. Recipient investigative reporting awards AP, 1968, 76, 77, awards news analysis, 1968, 69, 75, Nat. Headliners award, 1968, Emmy award best investigative reporting, 1977, Golden Mike award best documentary, 1972, investigative reporting, 1975, best commentary, 1975, George Foster Peabody award, 1976, L.A. Press Club Grand award, 1976, San Diego Press Club award, 1976, 77, 79, Friend of Lithuania award Knights of Lithuania, 1988, Jose Marti award Cuban Am. Polit. Soc., Miami, Fla., 1988, Broadcast Pioneer award, 1997. Mem. Nat. Press Club, Thunderbird Country Club (Rancho Mirage, Calif.), Mid-Ocean Club (Tuckerstown, Bermuda), Georgetown Club, Met. Club, Diplomatic and Consular Officers Retired, The Pilgrims (N.Y.C.), Am. Ambs. Episcopalian. Office Phone: 202-207-0185. Business E-Mail: rwc@defenddemocracy.org.

CARLSON, ROBERT CHARLES, financial planner, writer; BS in Fin. Mgmt. with high honor, Clemson U., 1979; MS in Acctg., JD, U. Va., 1982. CPA Md.; bar: DC 1982. Law clk. US Dept. Justice, Washington, 1982, US Dept. Edn., Washington, 1982-83; editor Tax Savs. Report, Balt., 1983-85, Fin. Independence, Balt., 1983-85, Tax Wise Money (formerly Tax Avoidance Digest), Balt., 1985—97, Bob Carlson's Retirement Watch, 1991—; prin. R.C. Carlson Adv., Fairfax, Va., 1988-94; pres. Ctr. for Retirement Security, Inc., Fairfax, 1992—; mng. mem. Carlson Wealth Advisors, LLC. Mem. Va. Fiscal Alternative Commn., Richmond, 1989-91; trustee, vice chmn. Fairfax County, Va. Employees' Retirement System, 1992—, chmn. 1995—; trustee Va. Retirement Sys., 2000-05 Author: Tax Savings Through Short-Term Trusts, 1985, 199 Loopholes That Survived Tax Reform, 1987, How to Handle and Win a Federal Tax Appeal, 1988, Retirement Tax Guide, 1989, rev. 4th edit. 1994, How to Slash Your Mutual Fund Taxes, 1990, 2d rev. edit. 1991, Tax Wise Money Strategies, 1995, Estate Planning Strategies, 2d edit., 1998, New Rules of Estate Planning, 2003, New Rules of Retirement, 2005 Treas. 10th Dist. Rep. Com., Fairfax, 1988-92; treas. No. Va. Rep. Bus. Forum, Alexandria, 1990—, Atoka Country Supper Com., Springfield, Va., 1989-92; chmn. Fairfax Area Young Reps., Annandale, Va., 1989-91; treas. Wahlquist for Senate, 1988-94, Butler for Congress, 1992-94; chmn. Sully Dist. Rep. Com., Fairfax County, Va., 2004—. Named one of Outstanding Young Men of Am., U.S. Jaycees, 1983. Mem. D.C. Bar Assn., Conservative Club, Sully Dist. Rep. Com. (chmn., 2004-), Phi Kappa Phi, Phi Gamma Sigma. Home: PO Box 222070 Chantilly VA 20153-2070 Personal E-mail: bcarlson@retirementwatch.com.

CARLSON, ROBERT CODNER, industrial engineering educator; b. Granite Falls, Minn., Jan. 17, 1939; s. Robert Ledin and Ada Louise (Codner) C.; children: Brian William, Andrew Robert, Christina Louise. BSME, Cornell U., 1962; MS, Johns Hopkins U., 1963, PhD, 1976. Mem. tech. staff Bell Tel. Labs., Holmdel, N.J., 1962-70; asst. prof. Stanford (Calif.) U., Stanford, 1970-77, assoc. prof., 1977-82, prof. indsl. engring., 1982-2000, prof. mgmt. sci. & engring., 2000—. Program dir., lectr., cons. various spl. programs U.S., Japan, France, 1971—; cons. Japan Mgmt. Assn., Tokyo, 1990—, Boeing, L.A., 1998--, GKN Automotive, London, 1989—, Rockwell Internat., L.A., 1988—; vis. prof. U. Calif., Berkeley, 1987-88, Dartmouth Coll., Hanover, N.J., 1978-79; vis. faculty Internat. Mgmt. Inst., Geneva, 1984, 88. Contbr. articles to profl. jours. Recipient Maxwell Upson award in Mech. Engring. Cornell U., 1962; Bell Labs. Systems Engring. fellow, 1962-63, Bell Labs. Doctoral Support fellow, 1966-67. Mem. INFORMS (chmn. membership com. 1981-83), Inst. Indsl. Engrs., Am. Soc. Engring. Edn., Am. Prodn. and Inventory Control Soc. (bd. dirs. 1975-81), Confrerie des Chevaliers du Tastevin, Tau Beta Pi, Phi Kappa Phi, Pi Tau Sigma. Avocations: wine tasting, travel. Office Phone: 650-723-9110. Business E-Mail: r.c.carlson@stanford.edu.

CARLSON, ROBERT EDWIN, lawyer; b. Bklyn., Oct. 11, 1930; s. Harry Victor and Lenore Marie (Hanrahan) C.; m. Maureen Eleanor Donnelly, Aug. 24, 1963; children: John T., Katherine L., Elizabeth A., Robert E. Jr. BS, U. Oreg., 1953; JD, U. Calif., San Francisco, 1958; LLM, Harvard U., 1963. Bar: Calif. 1959, U.S. Dist. Ct. (ctrl. dist.) Calif. 1959, U.S. Ct. Appeals (9th cir.) 1959. Assoc. Kindel & Anderson, L.A., 1958-63, ptnr., 1963-67, Agnew, Miller & Carlson, L.A., 1967-80, Hufstedler, Miller, Carlson & Beardsley, L.A., 1980-88, Paul, Hastings, Janofsky & Walker LLP, L.A., 1988—, chmn. corp. practice group investment mgmt., 1988—2001. Pres. Constl. Rights Found., LA, 1978-80, LA County Bar Found., 1988-89; exec. com. bus. sect. LA Bar Assn., 1982-89; bd. dirs. Legal Aid Found., LA. Bd. dirs. Westridge Sch. for Girls, Pasadena, Calif., 1985-91, Trust for Pub. Land, San Francisco, 1987—; chair bd. Skid Row Housing Trust, LA, 1989-2000, Pasadena Cmty. Found.; bd. visitors Santa Clara Law Sch., 1986-92. With U.S. Army, 1953-55. Recipient Griffin Bell award Dispute Resolution Svcs., Inc., 1992, Katherine Krause award Inner City Law Ctr., 1996. Mem. ABA (securities com., co-chair com. devel. investment svcs., task force to prepare guidebook for dirs. mut. funds 1995, chair youth edn. for citizenship, Chgo. 1982-85), Calif. State Bar (corp. com. 1990-94), Valley Hunt Club, Chancery Club, Calif. Club. Democrat. Avocations: hiking, tennis, reading, skiing. Office: Paul Hastings Janofsky & Walker LLP 515 S Flower St Fl 23 Los Angeles CA 90071-2300 Office Phone: 213-683-6299. Office Fax: 213-627-0705. Business E-Mail: robertcarlson@paulhastings.com.

CARLSON, ROBERT JAMES, bishop; b. Mpls., June 30, 1944; s. Robert James and Jeanne Catherine (Dorgan) C. BA, St. Paul Sem., 1964, MDiv, 1976; JCL, Catholic U. Am., 1979. Ordained priest Roman Catholic Ch., 1970. Asst. St. Raphael Ch., Crystal, 1970—72; assoc. St. Margaret Mary Ch., Golden Valley, 1972—73, adminstr., 1973—76; vice chancellor Vocation Office, 1976—79, dir., 1977; chancellor Archdiocese, 1979—84; pastor St. Leonard of Port Maurice, Mpls., 1982—84; aux. bishop St. Paul and Mpls., Mpls., 1983—94, Archdiocese of St. Paul and Mpls., Mpls., 1984—94; apptd. coadjutor Bishop of Sioux Falls, SD, 1994—95, Sioux Falls, SD, 1995—; bishop of Sioux Falls, 1995—2005; bishop of Saginaw, 2005—. Author: Going All Out: An Invitation to Belong, 1985. Pres. Nat. Found. Cath. Youth Ministry, Washington, 1989—97; bd. govs. N.Am. Coll. Rome, 1997—2001; Sioux Falls Humane Soc., 2003—05; Episcopal moderator Nat. Cath. Com. on Scouting, 1993—97, USA/Can. coun. Serra Internat., 1996—2001; bd. dirs. St. Paul Sem., 1993—2000; hon. canon Ch. Holy Sepulchre, 2003; bd. dirs. Mt. Angel Sem., Portland, Oreg., 1995—2001, St. John V. Coll. Sem., U. St. Thomas, St. Paul, 1997—2001, Hennich-Glennon Sem., St. Louis, 1998—2001. Decorated Papal Knight, Knight Comdr. with star Holy Sepulchre of Jerusalem; recipient Friendship award, Knights and Ladies of St. Peter Claver, 1990, St. De LaSalle Meml. award, Cretin H.S. Alumni Assn., 1990, Humanitarian of Yr. award, S.D. Right to Life, 1998, Our Lady of Guadalupe medal, Inst. for Priestly Formation, 2003. Mem.: Canon Law Soc. Am., Serra Internat. (Dist. Svc. award 2002), Cosmopolitan Club of Sioux Falls (Disting. Svc. award 2002). Roman Catholic. Avocation: hunting. Office: The Chancery 5800 Weiss St Saginaw MI 48603 Office Phone: 989-797-6615. Business E-Mail: rcarlson@dioceseofsaginaw.org.

CARLSON, ROBERT MARSHALL, health facility administrator; b. Jamestown, N.Y., Oct. 6, 1950; s. Marshall Lawrence and Alice (Christine) C.; m. Robin Shankey, May 29, 1987; children: Todd Marshall, Scott Thomas. BS, Bowling Green (Ohio) State U., 1972; postgrad. in pub. health, U. Utah, 1972; ME in Health Edn., U. Toledo, 1977. Planning analyst, then found. dir. Riverside Hosp., Toledo, 1975-78; hosp. planning coord. Med. Coll. Ohio, Toledo, 1978-80, asst. hosp. dir. for ambulatory programs, 1980-81; cons. P.M.S. (Planning & Mgmt. Services) Inc., Bloomington, Minn., 1981-82; dir. health tech. mktg., sr. cons. Ellerbe Cons. Group, Bloomington, 1983-85; mktg. dir. Ellerbe Assocs. Inc., Mpls., 1986; v.p. Ellerbe Assocs., 1987-89, Export USA Publs., Mpls., 1989-91; dir. physician svcs. HealthEast, St. Paul, 1991-95; exec. adminstr. OSF Med. Group, OSF Healthcare Systems, Peoria, Ill., 1995-99; dir. clin. svcs. Phycor, Inc., Nashville, 1999-2000; sr. assoc. Progressive Healthcare, Inc., Nashville, 2000—02; adminstr. Medicine Patient Care Ctrs., Vanderbilt U. Med. Ctr., Nashville, 2003—. Served to commdr., Med. Svc. Corps., USNR, 1972-98. Mem. Med. Group Mgmt. Assn., Am. Coll. Med. Practice Execs., Assn. Mil. Surgeons of U.S., Profl. Ski Instrs. Am., Res. Officers Assn., Phi Kappa Phi, Kappa Sigma. Lutheran. Office: Vanderbilt Univ Med Ctr 2568 TVC Nashville TN 37232-5999

CARLSON, ROBERT MICHAEL, artist; b. Bklyn., Nov. 19, 1952; s. Sidney Carlson and Vickey (Mihaloff) Woodward; m. Linda Schneider; m. Mary Elizabeth Fontaine, Feb. 24, 1984; 1 child, Nora. Student, CCNY, 1970-73; studied with Flora Mace and Joey Kirkpatrick, Pilchuck Glass Sch., 1981, studied with Dan Dailey, 1982. Teaching asst. Pilchuck Sch., Stanwood, Wash., 1986, 88, mem. faculty, 1989-90, 92, 95, Pratt Fine Arts Ctr., Seattle, 1988-90, Penland (N.C.) Sch. Crafts, 1994, Bild-Werk Sch., Germany, 1996-2000. Mem. artists adv. com. Pilchuck Sch., 1989, 90; vis. artist Calif. Coll. Arts and Crafts, Oakland, 1989, Calif. State U., Fullerton, 1991, blossom summer program Kent State U., Ohio, 1991, U. Ill., Urbana-Champaign, 1993, Toledo Mus. of Art Sch., 1994; visual-artist-in-residence Centrum Found., Port Townsend, Wash., 1992; prof. artist-in-residence Pilchuck Sch., Wash. One-man shows include Foster White Gallery, Seattle, 1987, 90, 92, The Glass Gallery, Bethesda, Md., 1988, Heller Gallery, N.Y.C., 1989, 95, Betsy Rosenfield Gallery, Chgo., 1991, 92, MIA Gallery, Seattle, 1994, Habitat Gallery, Florida, 1998, 2001, William Traver Gallery, Seattle, 2000, 04, others; exhibited in group shows at Traver Gallery, Seattle, 1984, 89, Mindscape Gallery, Evanston, Ill., 1984, 86, Tucson Mus. Art., 1984 (Purchase award), 86 (Award of Merit), Hand and Spirit Gallery, Scottsdale, Ariz., 1985, 86, Craftsman Gallery, Scarsdale, N.Y., 1985, Robert Kidd Gallery, Birmingham, Mich., 1985, 88, Gazebo Gallery, Gatlinburg, Tenn., 1985, The Glass Gallery, Bethesda, Md., 1986 (Jurors award), 91, 92, 94, Artists Soc. Internat., San Francisco, 1987 (Critics Choice award), William Traver Gallery, Seattle, 1987, 90, 91, 92, Japan Glass Artcrafts Assn., Tokyo, 1987, Heller Gallery, 1988, 89, 90, 91, 93, 94, 95, 96, 97, Washington Sq. Ptnrs., 1988, Foster White Gallery, 1988, 90, Bellvue Art Mus., Wash., 1988, 91, 94, Am. Arts and Crafts Inc., San Francisco, 1989, Mus. Craft and Folk Art, San Francisco, 1989, Great Am. Gallery, Atlanta, 1989, Dorothy Weiss Gallery, San Francisco, 1989, Habitat Gallery, Farmington Hills, Mich., 1990, 93, Philabaum Gallery, Tucson, 1990, Greg Kucera Gallery, Seattle, 1990, Connell Gallery, Atlanta, 1990, Net Contents Gallery, Bainbridge Island, Wash., 1991, Seattle Tacoma Internat. Airport Installation, 1991, 95, Pratt Fine Arts Ctr., Seattle, 1991, Crystalex, Novy Bor, Czechoslovakia, 1991, Whatcom County Mus., Bellingham, Wash., 1992, Art Gallery West Australia, 1992, 1004 Gallery, Port Townsend, 1992, Bainbridge Island Arts Coun., 1992, MIA Gallery, 1993, Betsy Rosenfield Gallery, Chgo., 1993, Blue Spiral Gallery, Asheville, N.C., 1995, Huntington Mus., 1996, Salem Art Assn., 1996, Judy Yovens Gallery, Houston, 1997, Internat. Glass Art Exchange, Tucson, 1997, Habatat Gallery, Boca Raton, Fla., 1998, Habatat Gallery, Farmington Hills, Mich., 1998, Tampa (Fla.) Mus. Art, 1998, Traver Gall., 2001, Glass Gall., 2001, Habatat Gall., 2000, Glasmus., 2000, Kentucky Art & Luak Gall., 2000; represented in permanent collections Corning (N.Y.) Mus. Glass, Tucson Mus. Art, Toledo Mus. Art, Tampa Mus. Art, Glasmuseum Frauenau, Germany, Glasmuseum Ebeltoft, Denmark, Valley Nat. Bank, Phoenix, Fountain Assocs., Portland, Oreg., Iceland Air Co., Reykjavik, Iceland, Crocker Banks, L.A., Davis Wright Tremain, Seattle, Meiwa Trading Co., Tokyo, Safeco Ins. Corp., Seattle, Crystalex Corp., L.A. County Mus. Art, Indpls. Mus. Art. Bd. dirs. Am. Craft Coun., 1996-99. Fellow Tucson Pima Arts Coun., 1987, NEA, 1990; John Hauberg fellow, 2000. Mem. Glass Art Soc. (conf. lectr. 1991, bd. dirs. 1992-94, v.p. 1993-94, pres. 1995-96, Lifetime Mem. award 2004). Office: PO Box 11590 Bainbridge Island WA 98110 Office Phone: 206-842-3206. E-mail: bobway@qwest.net.

CARLSON, ROGER ALLAN, retired manufacturing executive, accountant; b. Mpls., Dec. 12, 1932; s. Carl Albert and Borghild Amanda (Anderson) Carlson; m. Lois Roberta Lehman, Aug. 20, 1955; children: Gene, Bradley. BBA, U. Minn., 1954. CPA Minn. Investment mgr. Mayo Found., Rochester, Minn., 1963-83; contr. Luth. Hosp. and Homes Soc., Fargo, ND, 1983-84; v.p., treas. Crenlo Inc., Rochester, 1984-94, also bd. dirs., part owner, 1984-99. Pres. Ability Bldg. Ctr., Rochester, 1974—75; bd. dirs. Samaritan Bethany, Inc., Rochester, 1991—95. Capt. U.S. Army, 1955—57. Mem.: AICPA, Minn. Soc. CPA's. Avocations: hunting, fishing, genealogy. Home: 14334 Harbour Landings Dr Fort Myers FL 33908-4906

CARLSON, ROGER DAVID, psychologist, educator, minister; b. Berkeley, Calif., Nov. 19, 1946; s. George Clarence and Elizabeth (Norris) C.; m. Ema T. Paviolo, June 11, 1977 (div. 1994); children: Erik Andreas Paviolo, Lucas Sven Paviolo, Justin Nikolaus Paviolo. AB, Calif. State U., Sacramento, 1968, MA, 1969; PhD, U. Oreg., 1972; cert. theol. studies, Pacific Sch. of Religion, 1994; MDiv, Pacific Sch. Religion, 1996. Ordained deacon, 1996, elder, 1998 United Meth. Ch.; lic. psychologist Pa., 1977, Calif., 2001, Oreg., 2002. Assoc. prof. psychology Lebanon Valley Coll., Annville, Pa., 1972-85; rsch. assoc. Eugene Pub. Schs., 1985-87; assoc. prof. edn. Williamette U., Salem, Oreg., 1987-88; assoc. prof. psychology Ea. Wash. U., 1991-92; adj. prof. Linfield Coll., 1993—; pastor Coburg (Oreg.) United Meth. Ch., 1992-94, Florence (Oreg.) United Meth. Ch., 1994—2001, Covenant United Meth. Ch., Reedsport, Oreg., 1995—99, 1st United Meth. Ch. of Stayton, Oreg., 2001—03, Bennett Chapel United Meth. Ch., Portland, Oreg., 2003—; assoc. prof. psychology Pacific U., 2005—. Vis. scholar dept. history and philosophy of sci. Cambridge (Eng.) U., 1979-80; life sr. mem. Wolfson Coll., Cambridge U.; vis. assoc. prof. psychology Whitman Coll., Walla Walla, Wash., 1988-89, 90-91, cons., 1989—; psychologist, pvt. practice, 1977-1985, 2001—. Author books, contbr. rsch. papers, jour. articles and book chpts. on numerous subjects in field. Mem. Friends Radio Sta. KPFA, v.p. 1969, pres. 1970; Wolfeboro Pioneer, Boy Scouts Am., 1959; co-founder, Pathways of Faith, Florence, Oreg., 1998; bd. dirs., Ecumenical Ministries Oreg., 2003-04; v.p. Oreg. Soc. of Clin. Hypnosis, 2005—. Recipient Presdl. Sports award. Fellow Am. Coll. Heraldry; mem. APA, Oreg. Psychol. Assn., Oreg. Soc. Clin. Hypnosis (v.p. 2005—), Am. Psychol. Soc., Am. Coll. Psychology, Soc. for Philosophy and Psychology (mem. exec. com. 1975-76), SAR, Airplane Owners and Pilots Assn., Sons Union Vets. Civil War, Am. Radio Relay League, Order of St. Luke, Psi Chi. Methodist. Office Phone: 503-245-2929. Business E-Mail: r.d.carlson.80@cantab.net.

CARLSON, RONALD LEE, law educator; b. Davenport, Iowa, Dec. 10, 1934; s. Arthur A. and Louise (Sehmann) C.; m. Mary Murphy, Apr. 10, 1965; children: Michael, Andrew. BA, Augustana Coll., 1956; JD (Clarion DeWitt Hardy law scholar), Northwestern U., 1959; LL.M. (E. Barrett Prettyman law scholar), Georgetown U., 1961. Bar: Ill. 1959, Iowa 1959, D.C. 1960, U.S. Supreme Ct. 1966. Mem. firm Betty, Neuman, McMahon, Hellstrom & Bittner, Davenport, Iowa, 1961-65; U.S. commr. So. Dist. Iowa, 1964-64; prof. law U. Iowa, Iowa City, 1965-73, Washington U., St. Louis, 1973-84; John Byrd Martin prof. law U. Ga., 1984-95, Fuller E. Callaway prof. law, 1995—. Vis. prof. Wayne State U., Detroit, 1974, Detroit, 1976—77, Detroit, 1979, U. Tex., 1978, St. Louis U., 1982—86, 1988, U. Iowa, 1986—87, 1996, Ohio State U., 2003; cons. Legis. Com. Criminal Code Revision Iowa, 1969—73; lectr. Nat. Coll. State Judiciary, Reno, 1974, Nat. Coll. Dist. Attys., West Palm Beach, Fla., 1980, Chgo., 83, Inst. Cont. Legal Edn., Atlanta, 1990, 2000—04, Amelia Island, 2001, Nat. Pract. Inst., Kansas City, 1991, 93, 98, Omaha, 91, 96, 2001, Davenport, 00, Des Moines, 1991, Chgo., 91, San Francisco, 91, San Francisco, 96, St. Louis, 1992—93, St. Louis, 1997—98, St. Louis, 2000, Honolulu, 1992, 94, 96, 2001, New Orleans, 1992, 2001, 03, Seattle, 1992, Minn., 1992—97, 2001, 03, Boston, 1992, Houston, 92, Houston, 97, Cleve., 92, 97, 2001, Tampa, 1992, Miami, 92, San Diego, 93, L.A., 93, Phoenix, 93, 96, Detroit, 93, Portland, 93, Denver, 93, 95, Washington, 93, 97, Little Rock, 93, 97, 98, Newark, 94, Richmond, 94, Atlanta, 1994—95, 1997, N.Y.C., 94, Birmingham, 95, Oklahoma City, 95, Nashville, 95, 2001, Salt Lake City, 1995, Charlotte, 98, Phila., 98, 2002, Las Vegas, 1998, Hartford, 2000, Columbus, 2000—02, Raleigh, 2001, Providence, 02; moderator Robert Vance Forum on The Bill of Rights, 1990—96, 2002—03; Founder's Day lectr. U. Ga., 2005. Author: Criminal Law Advocacy, 1982, Successful Techniques for Civil Trials, 1983, rev. edit., 1992, Adjudication of Criminal Justice, 1986, Pocket Proof of Facts, 1993, Trial Handbook for Georgia Lawyers, 2003, Student's Guide to Elements of Proof, 2004, Criminal Justice Procedure, 2005; author: (with M. Ladd) Cases on Evidence, 1972; author: (with J. Yeager) Criminal Law and Procedure, 1979; author: (with M. Bright) Maine Objections at Trial, 1991, New Hampshire Objections at Trial, 1992, Oregon Objections at Trial, 1992; author: (with A. Montgomery and M. Bright) Minnesota Objections at Trial, 1992; author: (with R. Aronson and M. Bright) Washington Objections at Trial, 1992; author: (with J. Young, K. Curtis, and M. Bright) Virginia Objections at Trial, 1998; author: (with E. Imwinkelried, E. Kionka and K. Strachan) Evidence Teaching Materials for an Age of Science and Statues, 2002; author: (with M. Bright and E. Imwinkelried) Objections at Trial: A Concise Guide, 2002; author: (with E. Imwinkelried) Dynamics of Trial Practice: Problems and Materials, 2002. V.p. alumni bd. Augustana Coll., Rock Island, Ill., 1968; com. mem. Ga. State Bar Assn. Recipient Roscoe Pound Found. Jacobson award, ATLA, 1987. Mem.: ABA (Harrison Tweed award 2000), Ga. Trial Lawyers Assn. (Lifetime Achievement award 2005),

Fed. Ins. and Corp. Counsel, Am. Inns. of Ct., Fed. Practice Inst. (dir. 1980—83), dean 1985—89), Iowa Bar Assn., Fed. Bar Assn. (chmn. law sch. divsn. 1978—79, nat. coun. 1994—95, Earl W. Kintner award 1992), Am. Assn. Law Schs. Republican. Office: U Ga School of Law Sch of Law Athens GA 30602 Office Phone: 706-542-5186. Business E-Mail: mlfield@uga.edu. *Proper application of law provides the key to resolution of disputes: local, national, and international. As a teacher of law to judges, lawyers and students, it is my goal to educate in a manner which contributes to this needed resolution of conflict in a positive way.*

CARLSON, SHAWN ERIC, physicist, educator; b. San Francisco, Mar. 11, 1960; s. Devere Milfred Carlson Jr. and Beverly Ann Bennett; m. Michelle Lynn Tetreault, 1994; children: Katherine Joanne, Erik Philip, Jennifer Elizabeth. BS in Physics, Applied Math., U. Calif., Berkeley, 1981; MS in Physics, UCLA, 1983, PhD in Physics, 1989. V.p. R & D Flowgram Software Assocs., San Francisco, 1989-91; rsch. physicist, astrophysicist Lawrence Berkeley Labs., 1982-94; founder, exec. dir. Soc. Amateur Scientists, 1994—; co-founder Tinkers Guild Pubs., 1999; chief tech. officer Personal Genetics, 2000—01; founder, CEO Bright Sci., LLC, 2003—; creator labrats.org, 2005, scifair.org, 2005; ind. cons. sci. and tech., 1995—. Adj. prof. physics, San Diego State U., 1995—; sci. and tech. cons. CSICOP 1985—; vis. scholar Brown U., 2002—; speaker in field. Author: Satanism in America, 1989, Core Concepts in Physics, 1997, The Amateur Scientist-The Complete 20th Century Collection (CD-Rom), 2000, The Amateur Astronomer, 2000, The Amateur Biologist, 2001; columnist Sci. Am. Mag., 1995-2001; Humanist Mag., Buffalo, 1991-93, MAKE Mag., 2005—; numerous radio and TV appearances. Investigator faith-healers, Satanism, religious miracles, astrology for Com. Scientific Examination of Religion, Buffalo, 1987, 89. Fellow MacArthur Found., 1999; named Headliner of Yr., San Diego Press Club, 2000; recipient San Diego State U. Svc. award, 2000. Mem. AAAS, Am. Astron. Soc., Nat. Assn. Sci. Writers, Sigma Xi, Labrats Sci. Club. Office: Soc Amateur Scientists 5600 Post Rd Ste 114-341 East Greenwich RI 02818 Office Phone: 401-398-7001. Business E-Mail: scarlson@sas.org.

CARLSON, STACY C., former motion picture association executive; b. Burbank, Calif., Sept. 6, 1960; BA in Econ., Calif. State U., 1982; MBA, Stanford U., 1988. Legis. asst. to Rep. Bill Thomas, 1982-84; chief of staff Kern County Bd. Suprs., 1984-86; various positions including sr. v.p. strategic planning and spl. projects Silicon Valley Bank, Santa Clara, Calif., 1989-93; minority staff dir. Com. House Adminstrn., 1993-94; staff dir. Com. House Oversight, 1995—97; mng. dir. emerging growth divsn. Imperial Bank (now Comerica), 1997—99; sr. advisor for pub. law & policy Akin, Gump, Strauss, Hauer & Feld, LLP, 1999—2004; dir. Washington DC office Office Gov. Calif., 2004; exec. v.p. govt. affairs Motion Picture Assn. Am., Encino, Calif., 2005.*

CARLSON, STEPHEN, publishing executive; b. Mpls., Minn. BA, U. Vt., 1963—67. News dir. WJOY Radio, Burlington, Vt., 1968—70; capitol bur. chief Burlington Free Press, Vt., 1970—75; chief legis. asst. U.S. Rep. James Jeffords, Wash., DC, 1975—87; publisher Upper Access Inc., 1990—. Cons. misc. polit. campaigns, Vt., 1990—2002; pres. Hinesburg Record, Inc., 1992—96. Contbg. editor: Journal of Light Construction, 1987—94; author: (book) Low Tax, 1989, Best Home for Less. Mem.: Pubs. Mktg. Assn. (bd. dirs. 2005—). Home: P O Box 457 Hinesburg VT 05461 Office Phone: 802-482-2988. Business E-Mail: steve@upperaccess.com.

CARLSON, SUZANNE OLIVE, architect; b. Worcester, Mass., Aug. 20, 1939; d. Sigfrid and Helga (Larson) C. BS, RI Sch. Design, 1963. Jr. ptnr. Dingnam-Fauteux & Ptnrs., Worcester, 1969-70; ptnr. Richard Lamoureux Assoc., Worcester, 1970-75, Herron & Carlson (AIA), Worcester, 1975-96; arch. Edgecomb, Maine, 1997—. Guest lectr. Holy Cross Coll., 1969-70. Chmn. Worcester Hist. Commn., 1976-88; trustee Worcester Heritage Soc., 1982-88, Park Spirit of Worcester Inc., 1987—, Friends of Ft. Edgecomb, 2005-; v.p. Lincoln County Hist. Assn., 2001—; trustee Worcester Girls Inc. of Worcester, pres. 1989-92, 95-2002, sec. 1994-95; trustee Performing Arts Sch. Worcester, 1977-86, v.p. 1980-85; trustee Cultural Assembly Greater Worcester, 1981-86, v.p., 1982-83; pres. Edgecomb Hist. Soc., 1997—. Recipient European Honors Program grant Rome, Italy, 1961-62; recipient AIA School medal for excellence, 1963. Mem. AIA (exec. bd. Ctrl. Mass. chpt. 1969-71, sec.-treas. 1970-71, v.p. 1971-72, pres. 1972-73), Mass. Soc. Archs. (exec. bd. 1972-74, v.p. 1975, pres. 1976), New Eng. Regional Coun. Archs. (pres. 1977), New Eng. Antiquities Rsch. Assn. (membership chair 1982-84, 90-94, resource devel. chair 1994—, graphics dir. jours. 1982—, publs. chair 1995—, trustee 1990—). Home and Office: Suzanne O Carlson Architect 94 Cross Point Rd Edgecomb ME 04556-3208 Office Phone: 207-882-8155. E-mail: krosspt@lincoln.midcoast.com.

CARLSON, TERRANCE L., lawyer, aerospace transportation executive; b. Superior, Wis., Jan. 21, 1953; s. Einar August and Carol (McAuley) C.; m. Jeanette Michele Leehr, Mar. 13, 1987; children: Aurora Brita Leehr, Henry Einar, Stephen Michael. BS in Bus. with high distinction, U. Minn., 1975; JD cum laude, U. Mich., 1978. Bar: Calif. 1978, U.S. Dist. Ct. (cen. dist.) Calif. 1978. With Gibson, Dunn & Crutcher, 1978-94, London, 1981-87, ptnr.-in-charge Hong Kong, 1987-89; v.p., gen counsel Allied Signal Aerospace, Torrance, CA, 1994; dep. gen. counsel AlliedSignal (now Honeywell Internat.); sr. v.p. bus. devel., gen. counsel, sec. PerkinElmer Inc., 1999—2001; sr. v.p., gen. counsel, corp. sec. Medtronic Inc., Mpls., 2001—. Adj. prof. London Law Ctr. U. Notre Dame, 1983-87, Pepperdine U., London, 1984; exec. dir. Annual Multi-Species Invitational (Since 1973). Contbr. articles to legal publs. Mem. Soc. English and Am. Lawyers (com. 1985-87), Royal Auto. Club, Am. Club. Avocations: fishing, guitar. Office: Allied Signal Aerospace 2525 W 190th St Torrance CA 90504-6002 also: Medtronic Inc 710 Medtronic Pky NE Minneapolis MN 55432-5604

CARLSON, THOMAS DAVID, lawyer; b. Mpls., Aug. 17, 1944; s. David W. and Grace M. (Laser) Carlson; m. Jane A. Gleeson; children: Amy A., Ryan T., Madeline Jane. BA, Colgate U., 1966; JD cum laude, U. Minn., 1969. Bar: Minn. 1969, U.S. Dist. Ct. Minn. 1969, U.S. Supreme Ct. 1973. Law clk. to Hon. Earl R. Larson U.S. Dist. Ct. (fed. dist.) Minn., Mpls., 1969-70; assoc. Best & Flanagan, Mpls., 1970-74, ptnr., 1974-91, Lindquist & Vennum, Mpls., 1991—. Trustee Groves Acad.; asst. varsity hockey coach Edina HS. Fellow: Am. Coll. Trust and Estate Counsel; mem.: ABA, Hennepin County Bar Assn., Minn. State Bar Assn., Colgate U. Alumni Assn. (trustee), Spring Hill Golf Club (bd. dirs.), Colgate Silver Puck Club (trustee), Minikahda Club, Mpls. Club. Office: Lindquist & Vennum 4200 IDS Ctr Minneapolis MN 55402

CARLSON, THOMAS JOSEPH, real estate developer, lawyer; b. St. Paul, Jan. 12, 1953; s. Delbert George and Shirley Lorraine (Willardson) C.; m. Chandler Elizabeth Campbell, July 15, 1973; 1 child, Thomas Chandler. BA, George Washington U., 1975; JD, U. Mo., Kansas City, 1979. Reporter Springfield (Mo.) News-Leader, 1975-76; editor Buffalo (Mo.) Reflex, 1976-77; assoc. Woolsey Fisher, Springfield, 1980-83; pvt. practice law Springfield, 1983-86; ptnr. Carlson & Clark, 1986-93, Carmichael, Carlson, Gardner & Clark, Springfield, 1993-94; mayor City of Springfield, 1987-93, 2001—; U.S. Bankruptcy trustee Springfield, 1982-98; pvt. practice, 1994-98. CEO, Resorts Mgmt., Inc., 1995—; bd. dirs. ITEC Attractions, Inc., Great So. Bancorp; lectr. in field. Contbr. articles to profl. jours. Mem. Springfield City Coun., 1983-87, 1997—2001, Airport Bd. Springfield, 1994-97; chmn. Springfield-Branson Leadership Com., 1993—; bd. dirs. Mo. Cmty. Devel. Corp. Iniative, Mo. Commn. on Intergovtl. Cooperation; mem. bd. govs. S.W. Mo. State U., 2003-; adv. coun. Fannie Mae Southwestern Regional Housing and Cmty. Devel.; mem. Ozark Trail coun. Boy Scouts Am. Mem. Mo. Bar Assn. (Disting. Young Lawyer award 1989). Presbyterian. Office: 205 W Walnut Ste 200 Springfield MO 65806-2115

CARLSON, TIMOTHY A., music educator; b. Ashtabula, Ohio, May 9, 1967; s. Barbara J. and David E. Carlson; m. Elizabeth A. Helwig; children: Katherine, Erica. B in Music Edn., Otterbein Coll., 1989; M in Music Edn., VanderCook Coll. Music, 1993; M in Instnl. Tech., Kent State U., 2001. Lic. music tchr., cert. tech. tchr. Dir. bands Elmwood Local Schs., Ohio, 1989—91, Grand Valley Local Sch., Orwell, Ohio, 1991—2002, computer tchr., 1998—. Mem.: Ohio Music Educators Assn. (tech. chair dist. 5 2000—), Music Educators Nat. Conf. Office: Grand Valley High Sch 44 N School St Orwell OH 44076 Office Phone: 440-437-6260. Personal E-mail: tcarlson@orwell.net.

CARLSON, TUCKER, political analyst, writer, television host; b. San Francisco, Calif., May 16, 1969; s. Richard and Patricia Buckley (Stepmother); m. Susie Andrews, 1991; children: Lillie, Buckley, Hopie. Attended, Trinity Coll., Conn. Writer Policy Review, Wash., DC; staff writer Arkansas Democrat-Gazette, Little Rock; co-host Spin Room CNN, 2000—01, co-host Crossfire, 2001—05, political analyst Wash. bureau; host & mng. editor Tucker Carlson: Unfiltered PBS, 2004—05; anchor MSNBC, 2005—, host The Situation With Tucker Carlson, 2005—. Regular contributor to The Weekly Standard & Esquire; articles in NY Times, NY Mag., Reader's Digest, Wall Street Journal, Forbes, GQ. Author: Politician, Partisans and Parasites: My Adventures in Cable News, 2003. Office: One MSNBC Plaza Secaucus NJ 07094

CARLSON, VICTORIA THILDA, merchant banker; b. Minn., Oct. 12, 1937; d. Herman Edwin and Nora Deming Carlson. BA, Ctr. Biblical Counselling, 2001; BA in acctg., Metro. State U., 1986. Cert. Am. Inst. Banking, 1972. Securities clk. to income collection clk. First Bank Mpls., Mpls., 1960—86; corp. action specialist First Trust Co., St. Paul, 1986—97; asst. acct. Inspiration Ministries, Walworth, Wis., 2002—04; owner Vicky's Sewing Parlor, 2005—. Author: (poetry) Miracles of Joy, 2000. Tchr. woman's bible study Inspiration Ministires. Nominee Alumni of Yr., Metro. State U., 2002; named to Nat. Author Registry, Iliard Press, 2001, Pres. award for Literary Excellence, 2001; recipient 1000 Hour award, Courage Ctr., Rose & Jay Phillips award, 1995, Oticon Focus on People award, Oticon Hearing Aid Co., 2003. Avocations: travel, sewing, bicycling, writing. Office: Inspiration Ministries Hwy 67 at County Rd F Walworth WI 53184 Office Phone: 262-275-6131. Personal E-mail: rejoiching@aol.com.

CARLSON, WALTER CARL, lawyer; b. Chgo., Sept. 14, 1953; s. LeRoy T. and Margaret (Deffenbaugh) C.; m. Debora M. DeHoyos, June 20, 1981; children: Amanda, Greta, Linnea. BA magna cum laude, Yale U., 1975; JD magna cum laude, Harvard U., 1978. Bar: Ill. 1978, US Dist. Ct. (no. dist.) Ill. 1980, (ea. dist.) Wis. 1992, US Supreme Ct. 1991. Law clk. to presiding justice U.S. Dist. Ct. No. Dist., Chgo., 1978-80; ptnr. securities litigation Sidley, Austin, Brown & Wood LLP, Chgo., 1986—, mem. exec. com., 2002—. Bd. dirs. Telephone and Data Sys., Inc., Chgo. (non-exec. chmn.), mem. and former chmn. audit com. 1989-2001, chmn., 2002-; bd. dirs. U.S. Cellular Corp., 1989—, chmn. audit com. 1989-2001; bd. dirs. Aerial Comm., Inc., 1996-2000. Mem. Dist. 65 Sch. Bd., Evanston, Ill., 1993-2001, pres., 1997-2001. Mem. ABA, U.S. Supreme Ct. Hist. Soc., Am. Judicature Soc., Seventh Cir. Bar Assn., Chgo. United. Office Phone: 312-853-7734. Business E-Mail: wcarlson@sidley.com.

CARLSON, WILLIAM CLIFFORD, manufacturing executive, director, retired military officer; b. Detroit, Feb. 7, 1937; s. William and Marion Lucille Carlson; m. Jane Elder, Jan. 28, 1960 (div. Jne 1987); children: David, Scott, Jennifer Carlson-Burns; m. Linda Darlene Reid, June 6, 1991. BS in Edn., U. N.Mex., 1959; MS in Physics, U.S. Naval Postgrad. Sch., Monterey, Calif., 1965; MS equivalent, U.S. Naval War Coll., Newport, R.I., 1975. Commd. U.S. Navy, 1959, advanced through ranks to rear admiral, officer, 1959-92, mgr. ASW combat sys. Naval Sea Sys. Command Washington, 1982-88, asst. dep. cmdr. Naval Sea Sys. Command, 1988-91, cmdr. Naval Undersea Warfare Ctr., 1991-92, ret., 1992; dir. advanced programs Scientific Atlanta Instrumentation Group, 1993-94; v.p. mktg. & sales Scientific Atlanta SPS Group, 1994-95; dir. surface ship ASW combat system programs Lockheed Martin, Syracuse, NY, 1995—2002. Mem. Acoustical Soc. Am., U.S. Naval Inst., U.S. Navy League, Surface Warfare Assn. Avocations: trout fishing, fly tying, skiing. Home: 3996 Pompey Hollow Rd Cazenovia NY 13035-9523 E-mail: wcarlso1@twcny.rr.com.

CARLSON ARONSON, MARILYN A., language educator; b. Gothenburg, Nebr., July 24, 1938; d. Harold N. and Verma Elnora (Granlund) C.; m. Paul E. Carlson, July 31, 1959 (dec. Sept. 1988); 1 child, Andrea Joy; m. David L. Aronson, July 8, 1995. BS in Edn., English and Psychology, Sioux Falls Coll., 1960; MA in History, U. S.D., 1973, MA in English, 1992, EdD in Ednl. Adminstrn., 1997. Tchr. English and social scis. curriculum coord. Beresford (S.D.) Pub. Sch., 1960-78; tchr. English and social scis. Sioux Empire Coll., Hawarden, Iowa, 1979-85; instr. English and ESL, Midwest Inst. for Internat. Studies, Sioux Falls, S.D., 1985-89; asst. prof. English Augustana Coll., Sioux Falls, 1989-97, asst. prof. English and edn., 1997-2000; acad. affairs coord. acad. evaluation U. S.D., Vermillion, 2000—02; assoc. acad. dean Nat. Am. U., Sioux Falls, 2002—03, acad. dean, 2003—. Part time instr. psychology Northwestern Coll., 1985; part time instr. English and lit. Nat. Coll., 1985-88; part time instr. English and history Augustana Coll., 1986-89; presenter in field. Author: Visions of Light: Flannery O'Connor's Themes and Narrative Method, 1992, A Higher Education Perspective: Themes and Narrative Methods of Flannery O'Connor and Eudora Welty, 1997; Plains Goddesses: Heroines in Willa Cather's Prairie Novels, 1995; contbr. articles and revs. to profl. publs. including The Social Sci. Jour., others. Humanities Scholar evaluator Rainbow Project and Increasing Cultural Understanding Seminar, 2000; evaluator Profl. Devel. Conf. Native Am. Curriculum, Rapid City, S.Dak., 2001; mem. S.D. Humanities Coun., 2003—. Recipient Internat. Prof.'s Exch. award Sor Trondelag Coll., Trondheim, Norway, Jan. 1999; named Tchr. of Yr. Beresford (S.D.) Pub. Schs., 1976; S.D. Humanities scholar, 1993—; Bush mini-grantee, 1993, Internat. Studies grantee, 1994, 98, 99, S.D. Humanities Spkr.'s Bur. grantee, 1996—, . Mem.: Delta Kappa Gamma. Home: 29615 469th Ave Beresford SD 57004-6457 Office: Nat Am U 2801 S Kiwanis Ave Sioux Falls SD 57105 Office Phone: 605-334-5430.

CARLSSON, BO AXEL VILHELM, economics professor; b. Ulricehamn, Sweden, July 22, 1942; s. Carl Axel Valentin and Dagmar Elisabet (Karlsson) C.; m. Glenda Joyce Bishop, Dec. 28, 1965; children: Eric, Mark, Amy. BA, Harvard U., 1968; MA, Stanford U., 1970, PhD, 1972; Docent, Uppsala U., Sweden, 1980. Sr. rsch. assoc. Indsl. Inst. Econ. and Social Rsch., Stockholm, 1972-84, dep. dir., 1977-81; Umstattd prof. indsl. econs. Case Western Res. U., Cleve., 1984-2000, de Windt prof. indsl. econs., 2000—, chmn. dept. econs., 1984-87, assoc. dean rsch. and grad. programs Weatherhead Sch. Mgmt., 1996—2001, dir. PhD programs and rsch., 2001—05, faculty dir. and exec. doctor mgmt. program, 2005—. Vis. scholar MIT, 1982; cons. World Bank, Washington, 1983-87, Swedish Fedn. Industries, Stockholm, 1984-89; min. of fin. Stockholm, 1993-94, Econ. Commn. for L.Am., 1996; project dir. Sweden's Tech. Sys., Stockholm, 1987—; mem. Indsl. and Sci. Coun., Nat. Bd. Tech. Devel., 1987-98; chair sci. adv. bd. Danish Rsch. Unit for Indsl. Dynamics, 1996—; mem. internat. evaluation panel Acad. of Finland, 2004. Author: Technology and Industrial Structure, 1979, Industrial Subsidies, 1980, Swedish Industry Facing the 80s, 1981; editor: Industrial Dynamics, 1989, Technological Systems and Economic Performance, 1995, Technological Systems and Industrial Dynamics, 1997, Technological Systems in the Bio Industries: An International Study, 2002. Mem. Swedish cultural orgns. Mem. Europe Assn. Rsch. Indsl. Econs. (pres. 1983-85, exec. com.), Am. Econ. Assn., Ea. Econ. Assn. (bd. dirs. 1989-92), Internat. J.A. Schumpeter Soc. (prize selection com. 1988-90, 94-96, 2002-04), Assn. Christian Economists. Methodist. Home: 2708 Rochester Rd Cleveland OH 44122-2167 Office: Case Western Res Univ Weatherhead Sch Mgmt Dept Econs Cleveland OH 44106-7235 Office Phone: 216-368-4112. Business E-Mail: Bo.Carlsson@case.edu.

CARLSTON, JOHN A., allergist; b. N.Y.C., Nov. 9, 1932; s. Ramon R. and Genevieve P. (Poss) C.; m. Jean L. Lawson, June 21, 1958; children: Ann, Kimberly, Susan. BS in Biology and Philosophy, Coll. of Holy Cross, 1954; MD, Yale U., 1958. Diplomate Am. Bd. Allergy and Immunology. Intern Akron (Ohio) Gen. Hosp., 1958-59, resident in internal medicine, 1959-61; fellow in allergy U. Pitts., 1961-62; instr. medicine in allergy U. Ill., Chgo., 1962-64; assoc. in medicine Northwestern U., Chgo., 1964-69; active staff in medicine Virginia Beach (Va.) Gen. Hosp., 1969—; assoc. prof. in medicine Eastern Va. Med. Sch., Norfolk, Va., 1974—. Bd. cert. Allergy, 1974, 77, 80, 83, 87, 93. Contbr. articles to profl. jours. Lt. col. U.S. Army Med. Corps, 1967-69. Fellow Am. Coll. Allergy and Immunology, Am. Acad. Allergy and Immunology; mem. Va. Allergy Assn., S.E. Allergy Assn., Va. Beach Med. Soc. (pres. 1976), Allergy Rehab. Found. (cons.). Republican. Episcopal. Avocations: Go, travel, skiing, golf, tennis. Office: Asthma and Allergy Specialists Ltd 1704 Sir William Osler Dr Virginia Beach VA 23454-3003

CARLTON, ALFRED PERSHING, JR., lawyer; b. Raleigh, N.C., Aug. 27, 1947; s. Alfred P. and Katherine (Singleton) C.; m. Blair Creech Carlton, Apr. 21, 2001; children: Mary Elizabeth, Troy Eugene. BSBA, U. N.C., 1969, JD, 1975; MPA, U. Dayton, 1973; LLD, Stetson U., 2002, U. Denver, 2003. Bar: N.C. 1975, U.S. Dist. Ct. (ea. dist.) N.C. 1975, U.S. Ct. Appeals (4th cir.) 1976, U.S. Supreme Ct. 1993. Pvt. practice, Raleigh, 1975-77; counsel N.C. Bankers Assn., Raleigh, 1977-79; sec., gen. counsel Bancshares N.C., Inc., Raleigh, 1979-82; adj. prof. law Campbell U., Buies Creek, N.C., 1979-82; ptnr. Sanford, Adams, McCullough & Beard, Raleigh, 1983-89; shareholder McNair & Sanford, Raleigh, 1990-95; ptnr. The Sanford Holshouser Law Firm, Raleigh, 1995—2001, Kilpatrick Stockton LLP, 2002—. Founding chmn. State Law Resources Inc., 1999—. Active City of Raleigh Hist. Properties and Hist. Dists. Commn., 1978-82; exec. bd. Occoneechee coun. Boy Scouts Am., 1983-94; trustee U. N.C. at Wilmington, 1997—; mem. Chief Justice's Commn. on Professionalism, 1998-2001. 1st lt. Med. Svc. Corps, USAF, 1970-73. Fellow Am. Bar Found.; mem. ABA (ho. of dels. 1982-84, 1987—, chmn. of the house 1996-98, bd. govs. 1996-98, chmn. standing com. on jud. independence 1998-2001, pres.-elect 2001-02, pres. 2002-2003), N.C. Bar Assn. (bd. govs. 1981-82, 92-95), Am. Law Inst., N.C. Legis. Rsch. Commn. (study com. on pub. financing 1985-88). Democrat. Episcopalian. Avocations: tennis, gardening. Office: Kilpatrick Stockton LLP 3737 Glenwood Ave Ste 400 Raleigh NC 27612 E-mail: apcarlton@kilpatrick.com.

CARLTON, BUZZ (CLYDE GORDON CARLTON JR.), singer, songwriter, entertainer, recording artist; b. Richmond, Va., Aug. 8, 1962; Owner Millhouse Records. Instr. music United Meth. Ch., Richmond, 1998—99. Performances include Nat. Anthem, Richmond Braves Baseball Game, 1989, 90, also TV, radio, and concerts; singer Freedom of Speech, 2001; albums include: Blame It On the Blues, 2002, Just This Side of the Blues, 2005; author (song) What a Lie Vol. Salvation Army, Richmond, 1996—99. Mem.: Songwriters Guild, ASCAP. Democrat. Avocations: nature, psychology, philosophy. Office: Buzz Carlton LLC PO Box 8382 Richmond VA 23226-0382 Office Phone: 804-840-6640. E-mail: buzz@singerbuzz.com.

CARLTON, CHARLES MERRITT, retired linguistics educator; b. Poultney, Vt., Dec. 12, 1928; s. Clarence Rann and Margaret Louise (Pennell) C.; m. Mary MacDonald, Aug. 31, 1957; children: David, John, Stephen. AB, U. Vt., 1950; MA, Middlebury Coll., 1951; PhD, U. Mich., 1963. Instr. Mich. State U., East Lansing, 1958—62; asst. prof. U. Mo., Columbia, 1962-66; prof. French and Romance linguistics U. Rochester, N.Y., 1966-99; ret.; asst. dir. NDEA French Inst., U. Vt., Burlington, summer 1964; lectr. U.S. State Dept Seminars, Brasov, Romania, summer 1972, U. Ky., Cluj, Romania, summer 1977; reader NEH, 1974—, dept edn. title VI programs, 1993. Fulbright lectr., 1971-72, Romania, 1986, Brazil. Author: Studies in Romance Lexicology, 1965, A Linguistic Analysis of a Collection of Late Latin Documents Composed in Ravenna Between A.D. 445-700: A Quantitative Approach, 1973, Romanian Poetry in English Translation: An Annotated Bibliography and Census (1740-1996), 1997; bibliographer: Romanian Language and Linguistics, 1973, 75-91, Comparative Romance Linguistics Newsletter; co-translator: (G. Doca) Acquisition Grammar of Romanian, 1995, (A. Marino) The Biography of the Idea of Literature, 1996; editor: Comparative Romance Linguistics newsletter, 1970-71. Fulbright fellow, Paris, 1950-51; fellow NSF, summer 1965, Nat. Def. Fgn. Lang., summer 1970; Fulbright grantee, 1974, 78, 82, 88, Romania, IREX grantee, 1982, 91. Mem.: UN Assn. Rochester, Soc. Romanian Studies, Romanian Studies Assn., Am. Romanian Acad., Am. Assn. Advancement Slavic Studies, Rennes-Rochester Sister City Com., Sigma Delta Pi. Home: 3 Thornfield Way Fairport NY 14450-3023 E-mail: charlesmcarlton6@cs.com.

CARLTON, DONALD MORRILL, retired research, development and engineering executive; b. Houston, July 20, 1937; s. Spencer William and Ruth (Morrill) C.; m. Elaine Yvonne Smith, Jan. 28, 1961; children: Donna Kay, Spencer Frank, Monica Elaine. BA, U. St. Thomas, Houston, 1958; PhD, U. Tex., Austin, 1962. Mem. staff, then group leader Sandia Corp., Albuquerque, 1962-65; with Tracor, Inc., Austin, 1965-69, asst. dir. research, 1968-69; pres., chmn. bd. Radian Corp., Austin, 1969-95; pres., CEO Radian Internat., LLC, Austin, 1996-98, ret., 1998. Bd. dirs. Am. Elec. Power Co., Smith Barney Investment Series Trust, Nat. Instruments Corp., Temple-Inland, Crystatech Corp.; mem. mgmt. com. Signature Sci.; chmn. Utex Austin. Past chmn. natural sci. adv. coun. U. Tex., Austin, mem. Engring. Found. adv. coun., mem. adv. coun. Electric Power Rsch. Inst. Mem. Am. Chem. Soc., Tex. Taxpayers and Rsch. Assn. (past chmn.), Austin C. of C. (past dir.), Tex. C. of C. (past chmn.). Home: 403 N Weston Ln Austin TX 78733 Office: URS/RADIAN PO Box 201088 Austin TX 78720-1088 Office Phone: 512-419-5750.

CARLTON, MICHAEL, magazine editor; B, Colgate Univ. With Phila. Inquirer; exec. editor So. Living, Birmingham, 1999; editor Coastal Living, 1999—2001, Yankee Mag., Dublin, NH, 2001—. Dir. pub. rels. Island of Bermuda; travel editor Dallas Times Herald, Denver Post. Syndicated columnist: Wash. Post-L.A. Times. Recipient seven Lowell Thomas awards for travel writing. Office: Yankee Mag PO Box 520 1121 Main St Dublin NH 03444*

CARLTON, PAUL KENDALL, JR., physician; b. Roswell, N.Mex., May 13, 1947; s. Paul Kendall and Helen C. (Sweat) C.; m. Dorothea Janice Prichard, July 5, 1969; children: Paul Kendall III, Christianne Joy, Stephanie Jill, Luke Jeffrey. BS, USAF Acad., 1969; MD, U. Colo., 1973, DSc (hon.), 2003. Diplomate Am. Bd. Surgery, 1980, 1990, 2000. Commd. 2d lt. USAF, 1969, advanced through grades to lt. gen., 1999; resident in surgery Wilford Hall Med. Ctr., San Antonio, 1973-78; comdr. USAF Hosp. Torrejon, Madrid, 1985-88, Scott Med. Ctr., Scott AFB, Ill., 1988-91; command surgeon Air Edn. and Tng. Command, San Antonio, 1991-94; comdr. Wilford Hall Med. Ctr., San Antonio, 1994-99, surgeon gen., 1999—2002; prof., dir. Homeland Security Health Sci. Ctr. Tex. A&M, 2002—. Decorated Air medal, Legion of Merit (2), Def. Disting. Svc. medal, Airman's medal; recipient Hoekton Silver award AMA, 1978, Nathan Davis award, AMA, 2001. Fellow ACS (gov. 1992-96). Avocations: hunting, flying. Office: Tex A&M U Health Sci Ctr Homeland Security Dir College Station TX 77845 also: 7th Fl 301 Farrow St College Station TX 77840-7896 Office Phone: 979-458-7246.

CARLTON, TERRY SCOTT, chemist, educator, retired chemist; b. Peoria, Ill., Jan. 29, 1939; s. Daniel Cushman and Mabel (Smith) C.; m. Claudine Fields, 1960; children: Brian, David. BS, Duke U., 1960; PhD (NSF grad. fellow 1960-63), U. Calif., Berkeley, 1963. Mem. faculty Oberlin (Ohio) Coll., 1963—, prof. chemistry, 1976-2001, prof. emeritus, 2001—, chmn. dept., 1980-83. Vis. prof. chemistry U. N.C., Chapel Hill, 1976 Co-author: Composition, Reaction and Equilibrium, 1970. Home: 143 Kendal Dr Oberlin OH 44074-1906 Office: Oberlin Coll Dept Chemistry and Biochemistry Oberlin OH 44074-1097 E-mail: terry.carlton@oberlin.edu.

CARLUCCI, DAVID R., information technology executive; BA in Polit. Sci., Univ. Rochester. With IBM, 1976—2002; v.p. mktg., channel mgmt IBM Personal Computer Co. NA, 1990—92; v.p. sys., industries, svcs. IBM Asia Pacific, 1993—95; gen. mgr. IBM Printing Sys. Co., 1995—97; chief info.

officer IBM, 1997—98, gen. mgr., S/390 divsn., 1998—2000; gen. mgr. IBM Americas, 2000—02; COO IMS Health, Fairfield, Conn., 2002—04, pres., 2002—, CEO, 2004—. Office: IMS Health 1499 Post Rd Fairfield CT 06824 Office Phone: 203-319-4700.*

CARLUCCI, FRANK CHARLES, III, former secretary of defense; b. Scranton, Pa., Oct. 18, 1930; s. Frank Charles, Jr. and Roxanne (Bacon) C.; m. Marcia Myers, Apr. 15, 1976; children: Karen, Frank, Kristin. AB, Princeton U., 1952; postgrad., Sch. Bus. Adminstrn., Harvard U., 1956; postgrad. hon. dr. degree, Wilkes Coll., Kings Coll., 1973; LLD (hon.), U. Scranton, 1989. With Jantzen Co., Portland, Oreg., 1955-56; fgn. svc. officer US Dept. State, 1956—69, vice consul, econ. officer Johannesburg, 1957-59, second sec., polit. officer Kinshasa, Democratic Republic of Congo, 1960-62, officer in charge Congolese polit. affairs, 1962-64, consul gen. Zanzibar, 1964-65, counselor for polit. affairs Rio de Janeiro, 1965-69; asst. dir. Office Econ. Opportunity, Washington, 1969, dir., 1971; assoc. dir. Office Mgmt. & Budget, 1971—72, dep. dir., 1971—72; undersec. US Dept. Health, Edn. & Welfare, 1972-74, 1977—78; US amb. to Portugal US Dept. State, Lisbon, 1974—77; dep. dir. CIA, Washington, 1978-81; dep. sec. US Dept. Def., Washington, 1981—83, sec., 1987-89; pres. Sears World Trade, Inc., Washington, 1983-84, chmn., CEO, 1984-86; asst. to the Pres. for national security affairs Nat. Security Coun., Washington, 1986-87; vice chmn. Carlyle Group, Washington, 1989-93, chmn., 1993—2003, chmn. emeritus, 2003—. Mem. Coun. on Fgn. Rels.; trustee RAND Corp.; co-chair RAND Ctr. for Middle East Pub. Policy; chmn. emeritus Acad. Diplomacy; bd. dir. Quaker Oats Co., SunResorts, Ltd., N.V., Encysive Pharms. Served as lt. (j.g.) USNR, 1952-54. Recipient Superior Honor award, 1969, Superior Svc. award Dept. State, 1971, HEW Disting. Civilian Svc. award, 1975, Def. Dept. Disting. Civilian award, 1977, Disting. Intelligence medal, 1981, Nat. Intelligence Disting. Svc. medal, 1981, Presdl. Citizens award, 1983, Woodrow Wilson award, 1988, James Forrestal Meml. award, 1988, Woodrow Wilson award, 1988, Herbert Roback Meml. award, 1989, George C. Marshall award, 1989. Business E-Mail: frank.carlucci@carlyle.com.

CARLUCCI, JOSEPH P., lawyer; b. Port Chester, NY, Aug. 21, 1942; m. Elizabeth Smith; children: Susan Elizabeth, Kathleen Ann. B.S, in Econs., Georgetown U., 1964; JD, Fordham U., 1967. Bar: NY 1969. Ptnr. Pierro & Carlucci, Port Chester, N.Y., 1969-76; pvt. practice, Rye, N.Y., 1977-78; mng. ptnr. Cuddy & Feder & Worby LLP, White Plains, N.Y., 1979-99. Chief legis. counsel to N.Y. senator from Westchester County, 1971-73; chief counsel N.Y. State Select Com. on State's Economy, 1973-74. Co-founder, v.p. Rye Town-Port Chester Rep. Club, 1972; trustee Village of Port Chester, 1974-77; chmn. Port Chester Indsl. Devel. Agy., 1974-76; mem. Westchester County Econ. Devel. Coun., 1976-80, Narcotics Guidance Coun. Port Chester, 1970-74; chmn. Met. N.Y. YMCA Key Leaders Conf., 1984; mem. Parent's Coun., Wheaton Coll., 1986-87; bd. dirs. Port Chester YMCA, 1970-79, sec., 1972-77, v.p., 1978; mem. Port Chester Govt. Study Commn., 1971-73; commr. appraisal White Plains and Greenburgh Urban Renewal; counsel to South Shore Hotline, 1973-74; mem. Port Chester Pub. Employees Rels. Bd., 1973-77; mem. adv. bd. bd. dirs. Salvation Army, 1973-77; mem. adv. bd. Security Title and Guaranty Co., 1986-90; bd. dirs. Rye YMCA, 1979-87, pres., 1982-85, trustee, 1989—; trustee Rye Hist. Soc., 1979-83, 90-96, sec., 1980-81, v.p., 1982-83, 92-94, pres., 1994-96; interviewer alumni admissions program Georgetown U., 1988-96; bd. visitors Pace U. Sch. Law, 1990—; bd. dirs. Vol. Ctr. United Way Westchester County, 1991-97; mem. Westchester divsn. Cardinal's Com. for Laity, 1991-2001, vice chmn., 1992, chmn., 1993-95; mem. paralegal curriculum adv. com. SUNY-Westchester C.C., 1994; bd. dirs. March of Dimes Birth Defects Found., 1994-96, Westchester Bus. Partnership, 1995-98, Westchester Partnership for Econ. Devel., 1996-97, Jacob Burns Film Ctr., Ind., 2000—; trustee Westchester Arts Coun., 2000-2004, Mercy Coll., 2002-. Recipient Golden R award Rennaissance Project, Inc., Gold Man award YMCA, 1985, Cmty. Svc. award Rotary Internat. Club, 1995. Mem. ABA (vice-chmn. econs. of law practice com. on lawyering skills 1984-85), N.Y. State Bar Assn., Westchester County Bar Assn. (real property com. 1978-82), Port Chester-Rye Bar Assn. (sec. 1970-75, pres. 1976-77, bd. dirs. student assistance svcs. alcohol and drug abuse prevention program 1989-95, adv. bd. 1995—), Westchester C.C. Found. (bd. dirs. 1997—), Real Estate Fin. Assn. (bd. dirs. 2000-03), Coveleigh Club (bd. govs. 1978-86, sec. 1979, v.p. 1980, pres. 1981-84), Georgetown U. Met. Club (bd. dirs. 1980-82), Hundred Club Westchester (bd. dirs.). Office: Cuddy & Feder LLP 90 Maple Ave White Plains NY 10601 Office Phone: 914-761-1300. Business E-Mail: jcarlucci@cuddyfeder.com.

CARLUCCI, WILLIAM PHILIP, lawyer; b. Scranton, Pa., Sept. 26, 1955; m. Christine Vanderlin; 3 children. AB, Lycoming Coll., 1976; JD, Temple U., 1979. Bar: Pa. 1979, Lycoming County 1979, U.S. Dist. Ct. Md. 1980, U.S. Dist. Ct. Pa. 1980, U.S. Supreme Ct. 1988. Ptnr. Elion, Wayne, Grieco, Carlucci, Shipman & Irwin, Williamsport, Pa. Mem.: Lycoming Law Assn. (treas. 1986—87, mem. exec. com. 1988—90, v.p., pres.-elect 1991, pres. 1992), Pa. Bar Assn. (v.p. 2003—04, pres.-elect 2004—, mem. bd. govs. 1993—96). Office: Elion Wayne Grieco Carlucci Shipman & Irwin 125 E Third St Williamsport PA 17701 Office Phone: 570-326-2443. Office Fax: 570-326-1585. E-mail: elionwayne@suscom.net, ewcarlucci@suscom.net.

CARLUZZO, LEWIS R., federal judge; b. NJ, 1949; Diploma, Villanova U., 1971, JD, 1974. Bar: NJ 1974. Law clk. NJ Superior Ct. Judge; assoc., city prosecutor Bridgeton, NJ, 1975; atty., office of chief counsel, dist. counsel's office IRS, Washington, 1977—83, spl. trial atty. litigation, 1983—92, spl. trial atty. large case, 1992—94; spl. trial judge US Tax Ct., 1994—. Office: US Tax Ct 400 Second St NW Washington DC 20217

CARMACK, MILDRED JEAN, retired lawyer; b. Folsom, Calif., Sept. 3, 1938; d. Kermit Leroy Brown and Elsie Imogene (Johnston) Walker; m. Allan W. Carmack, 1957 (div. 1979); 1 child, Kerry Jean Carmack Garrett. Student, Linfield Coll., 1955-58; BA, U. Oreg., 1967, JD, 1969. Bar: Oreg. 1969, U.S. Dist. Ct. Oreg. 1980, U.S. Ct. Appeals (9th and fed. cirs.) 1980, U. S. Claims Ct. 1987. Law clk. to Hon. William McAllister Oreg. Supreme Ct., Salem, 1969-73, asst. to ct., 1976-80; asst. prof. U. Oreg. Law Sch., Eugene, 1973-76; assoc. Schwabe, Williamson & Wyatt, Portland, Oreg., 1980-83, ptnr., 1984-96, ret., 1996. Writer, lectr., legal educator, Oreg., 1969—; mem. exec. bd. Appellate sect. Oreg. State Bar, 1993-95. Contbr. articles to Oreg. Law Rev., 1967-70. Mem. citizen adv. com. State Coastal Planning Commn., Oreg., 1974-76, State Senate Judiciary Com., Oreg., 1984; mem. bd. visitors Law Sch. U. Oreg., 1992-95; mem. Oreg. Law Commn. Working Group on Conflict of Laws, 2000. Mem. Oreg. State Bar Assn., Order of Coif.

CARMAN, GREGORY WRIGHT, federal judge; b. Farmingdale, N.Y., Jan. 31, 1937; s. Willis B. and Marjorie (Sosa) C. Exch. student, U. Paris, 1956-57; BA, St. Lawrence U., 1958; JD, St. John's U., 1961; Judge Adv. Gen. honors grad., U. Va. Law Sch., 1962. Bar: N.Y. 1961. Atty. Carman, Callahan & Sabino, Farmingdale, N.Y., 1964-83; councilman Town of Oyster Bay, N.Y., 1972-81; mem. 97th Congress from 3d Dist. N.Y., 1981-82; U.S. Congl. del. I.M.F. Cong., 1982; judge U.S. Ct. Internat. Trade, N.Y.C., 1983—96, 2003—, acting chief judge, 1991, chief judge, 1996—2003. Statutory mem. Jud. Conf. U.S., 1991. Capt. AUS, 1962-64. Fellow Am. Bar Found.; mem. ABA, N.Y. State Bar Assn. (cts. and cmty. com.), Nassau County Bar Assn., Nassau Lawyers Assn., St. John's Law Rev. Republican. Episcopalian. Office: US Ct Internat Trade 1 Federal Plz New York NY 10278-0001*

CARMAN, LAURA JUNGE, lawyer; b. New Orleans, Mar. 23, 1952; d. Lester Ernest and Bernice D. Junge; m. Allen Solari Carman Jr., Feb. 23, 1986; 1 child, Richard Junge Carman. BA magna cum laude, Vanderbilt U., 1974; JD, Tulane U., 1977. Bar: La. 1977, U.S. Dist. Ct. (ea. dist.) La. 1978. Pvt. practice, New Orleans, 1978—. Assoc. adj. prof. Tulane U., New Orleans, 1983-87, fellow, Amer. Coll. of Trust and Estate Couns. Author: Louisiana Succession Pleadings: A Systems Approach, 1986, Louisiana Successions (2d edit., 1998), 1991. Recipient Tchr. Recognition award Tulane U., 1986-87. Mem. New Orleans Bar Assn. (past chairperson com. on probate trusts and estate planning), La. Bar Assn. (past pres. sect. on immovable property, probate and estate trusts). Office: 228 Saint Charles Ave Ste 1100 New Orleans LA 70130-2611 E-mail: ljcaplc@aol.com.

CARMAN, MARY ANN, realtor, writer, retired medical/surgical nurse; b. Wichita, Kans., Jan. 5, 1953; d. Herbert William and Alberdine Esther Kumba; m. Randy Paul Carman, Apr. 8, 1972 (dif. Sept. 27, 1990); children: Chad William, Kenneth Franklin. AA, San Bernadino Valley Coll., 1980; AS in Nursing, SUNY, 1993. Lic. practical nurse, Calif., 1980; Realtor 2003. Disaster team mgr. ARC / BSA Explorer Post, Albuquerque, 1982—84; nurse Veterans Med. Ctr., Tucson, 1990—2001; fiction author self employed, 1998—; REALTOR Long Realty Co., 2003—04; realtor Real Estate Mktg. Profls., Tucson, 2004—. Author: Never To Love. Mem. Nat. Writers Union, Tucson, 2002—03. Mem.: Women's Coun. REALTORS Tech., Tucson Assn. REALTORS (fair & affordable housing com. 2003—04), Ariz. Assn. REALTORS, Nat. Assn. REALTORS, Ariz. Author's Assn., Soc. Southwestern Author's, Romance Writers Am. Avocations: writing, reading, travel. Home: Box 413 7739 East Broadway Blvd Tucson AZ 85710 Office: Real Estate Mktg Profls Tucson 2462-1 N Pantano Rd Tucson AZ 85715 Personal E-mail: maryann@maryanncarman.com. E-mail: maryann@mywordsworth.com.

CARMAN, RANDALL MILTON, SR., municipal official; b. Dallas, Feb. 13, 1958; s. Barbara O'Brien; 1 child, Randall M. Carman, Jr. AAS, Eastfield Coll., Mesquite, Tex., 1980; BA, U. Tex. Dallas, Richardson, 1983, MS, 1987. Sr. test validation specialist City of Dallas, 1990—2005. Mem.: APA (assoc.). Avocations: fishing, hunting, archery, reading, grandparenting. Home: 1307 Westridge Mansfield TX 76063 Office: City of Dallas Civil Svc Dept City Hall 1500 Marilla 1CS Dallas TX 75201 Office Phone: 214-670-5421.

CARMANY, GEORGE WALTER, III, finance company executive, consultant; b. NYC, Mar. 21, 1940; s. George Walter Carmany, Jr. and Merle (Harrold) Carmany; m. Judith Jermain Lawrence, Apr. 27, 1968; children: George W. W., Elizabeth C. Perreten. BA, Amherst Coll., 1962. V.p. Bankers Trust Co., N.Y.C., 1966—71; sr. v.p. Am. Express Co., N.Y.C., 1975—81; sr. exec. v.p. Am. Express Bank, Ltd., N.Y.C., 1981—90, The Boston Co., 1990—93; pres. G.W. Carmany & Co., Inc., Boston, 1994—. Vice chmn. Computerized Med. Systems, St. Louis, 2001—; sr. advisor EnGeneIC Pty. Ltd., Sydney, New South Wales, Australia, 2003—; dir. SunLife Fin., Inc., Toronto, Ontario, Canada, 2004—, Macquarie Infrastructure Co., N.Y.C., 2004—; chmn. Helicon Therapeutics, Farmingdale, N.Y. Mem. pres.'s cir. The Nat. Acads., Wash., 2002—; chmn. The New Eng. Med. Ctr. Hosps, Boston, 1996—97; vice chmn. Lifespan, Inc., Providence, 1997—2002; chmn. bd. assocs. The Whitehead Inst., Cambridge, Mass., 2001—03; trustee Bentley Coll., Waltham, Mass., 1990—. Lt. USNR, 1962—66. Recipient Disting. Svc. award, Amherst Coll., 2001. Mem.: Racquet and Tennis Club, Ft. Worth Boat Club, Shinnecock Yacht Club (commodore 1983—87), Royal Sydney Yacht Squadron, Somerset Club, N.Y. Yacht Club (trustee 1996—). Republican. Episcopalian. Avocations: ocean racing, game fishing, hunting. Home: 4 Lime St Boston MA 02108 Office: GW Carmany and Co Inc One Boston Pl Ste 1650 Boston MA 02108 Office Phone: 617-542-5918.

CARMEAN, C. WILLIAM, lawyer; b. 1952; BA, Yale U., 1975; JD, NYU, 1982. Bar: NY 1982. Assoc. Breed, Abbott & Morgan, NYC; assoc. gen. counsel Bristol-Myers Squibb Co., Princeton, NJ, 1988—90; corp. counsel Quantum Chem. Corp., 1990—93; assoc. gen. counsel Millennium Chemicals, Inc., Hunt Valley, Md., 1993—98, v.p. legal, 1998—2001, sr. v.p., gen. counsel, sec., 2002—. Office: Millennium Chemicals Inc 20 Wright Ave Ste 100 Hunt Valley MD 21030 Office Phone: 410-229-4400. Office Fax: 410-229-5003. E-mail: bill.carmean@millenniumchem.com.

CARMEAN, JERRY RICHARD, broadcast engineer; b. Greenfield, Ohio, Apr. 2, 1938; s. Clyode B. and Mary F. (Hedges) C.; m. Patricia H. Carmean; 1 child, Steven. BS in Edn., Ohio U., 1965, BS in Elec. Engring., 1984. Registered profl. engr., Ohio; lic. FCC gen. class radiotelephone operator. Tchr. New Philadelphia (Ohio) High Sch., 1965-66; broadcast engr. Ohio U. Telecommunications Ctr., Athens, 1966-81, dir. engring., 1981-92; pvt. broadcast engring. cons., 1992—. Cons. Sta. WLGN, Logan, Ohio, 1964-2000; tech. cons. Sta. 4VEH, Cap Hatien, Haiti. Served with U.S. Army, 1961-64. Mem. NSPE, Ohio Soc. Profl. Engrs., Antique Wireless Assn., Soc. Broadcast Engrs., Men for Missions Internat., Athens County (Ohio) Amateur Repeater Assn., The Planetary Soc., Rotary. Avocations: astronomy, photography, amateur radio, antiques. Home: 16341 Calico Ridge Rd Logan OH 43138-9416 Office: Sta WLGN Logan Broadcasting Co 1 Radio Ln Logan OH 43138-8762

CARMEL, PETER W., neurosurgeon; BA, U. Chgo., 1956; MD, NYU, 1960; D of Med. sci. in Neuroanatomy, Columbia U., 1970. Mem. faculty Columbia U., 1967—98; attending neurosurgeon Columbia-Presbyn. Med. Ctr., 1967—98; prof. neurol. surgery, dir. pediat. neurol. surgery Coll. Physicians and Surgeons of Columbia U., N.Y.C.; chair dept. neurol. surgery N.J. Med. Sch., 1994—; co-med. dir. Neurol. Inst. N.J., 1999—. Lectr. in field. Contbr. articles to profl. jours., chapters to books. Named one of Top Drs. 2003, N.J. Monthly Mag., Best Drs. in Am., Am. Health Mag., Woodward/White. Mem.: AMA (neurosurg. rep. ho. of dels., former chair coun. on long range planning, trustee), Nat. Found. Brain Rsch., Nat. Coalition Rsch. in Neurol. Diseases and Stroke, Am. Assn. Neurol. Surgeons, Congress Neurol. Surgeons. Office: Drs Office Ctr Neuro--90 Bergen St Newark NJ 07103-2425 Office Phone: 973-972-2905. Business E-Mail: carmel@umdnj.edu.

CARMEN, IRA HARRIS, political scientist, educator; b. Boston, Dec. 3, 1934; s. Jacob and Lida (Rosenman) Carmen; m. Sandra Vineberg, Sept. 6, 1958 (div. June 1999); children: Gail Deborah, Amy Rebecca; m. Lawrence Lowell Putnam, Mar. 16, 2000. BA, U. N.H., 1957; MA, U. Mich., 1959, PhD, 1964. Asst. prof. Ball State U., 1963-66; assoc. prof. Coe Coll., 1966-68; prof. polit. sci. U. Ill., 1968—. Mem. Inst. Genomic Biology U. Ill., 2004—; mem. recombinant DNA adv. com. NIH, 1990—94; vis. lectr. Tamkang U., Taiwan, 1991; participant numerous internat. meetings. Author: Movies, Censorship, and the Law, 1966, Power and Balance, 1978, Cloning and the Constitution, 1986, Politics in the Laboratory: The Constitution of Human Genomics, 2004; contbr. articles to profl. jours. Sr. advisor Bush-Quayle Nat. Jewish Campaign Com., 1988; mem. Pres. George Bush's Inaugural Educators Adv. Com., 1989; guest del. Rep. Nat. Conv., 1992; mem. Rep. Nat. Com., Rep. Jewish Coalition, Straight Talk Am. Vis. scholar, Yale Law Sch., 1981. Mem.: AAAS, Assn. Politics and Life Scis. (chmn. coun. 2000—03), Am. Soc. Gene Therapy, Human Genome Orgn., Phi Beta Kappa. Office: U Ill Dept Polit Sci Urbana IL 61801 Office Phone: 217-333-3880. Business E-Mail: icarmen@uiuc.edu.

CARMENT, THOMAS MAXWELL, accounting educator, consultant, researcher; b. Cleve., Mar. 13, 1945; s. Charles Albert and Helen Marie C.; m. Deborah Lee Grant, Sept. 7, 1968; children: Rebecca L. Carment Schiehing, John M., David T. BA in Econs., Okla. State U., 1967, MBA, 1971, PhD in Bus. Adminstrn., 1991. CPA, Okla. Fin. analyst Ford Motor Co., Detroit, 1969-71; mktg. rep. Burroughs Corp., Detroit, 1971-72; asst. divsn. treasury mgr. Conoco, Inc., Houston, 1972-77; v.p. Power Pak Co., Inc., Conroe, Tex., 1977-78; prof. acctg. Northeastern State U., Tahlequah, Okla., 1979—. Chmn. faculty adv. com. Okla. State Regents for Higher Edn., Oklahoma City, 1995-96; cons. Intelligent Media, Venice, Calif., 1995-99; cons. LSCI, Colorado Springs, Colo., 1992-99. Author various procs. Pres., mem. exec. com. Goodwill Industries, Muskogee, Okla., 1993-96; pres. faculty coun. Northeastern State U., 1993-95; scoutmaster Boy Scouts Am., 1987-99. Recipient Dist. award of merit and Scoutmaster Awd. of Merit, 1998, Boy Scouts Am., 1995; travel grantee, 1990, 96, 99, summer rsch. grantee, 1984. Mem. AAUP, Am. Acctg. Assn., Inst. Mgmt. Accts., Okla. Soc. CPAs, Acad. Internat. Bus., Optimist Club (exec. com. 1995-98, pres. 1999—). Democrat. Presbyterian. Avocations: bicycling, hiking, camping, travel. Office: Northeastern State U 600 N Grand Ave Tahlequah OK 74464-2301

CARMI, SOFIA, artist, educator; b. Jerusalem, Apr. 19, 1956; arrived in U.S., 1962; d. Joseph Carmi and Lusia Fogel Carmi. BA in Humanities, New Coll. Calif., 1988, MA in Psychology, 1989; BA, Ontario Coll. Art, 1978. Tchr. art pvt. practice, Amsterdam, 1993—95, Berlin, San Francisco, 1996, LEAP Art, 2000—02, Matrix Art Kids, Sacramento, 2002—03; art activity specialist Family Svc. San Francisco, 2003; tchr. Am. Acad. of English, San Francisco, 2005—. Tchr. art Santa Cruz Arts Coun., Calif., 1992—93, San Jose Mus. Art, 1989—91; tchg. asst. art history New Coll. Calif., San Francisco, 1987; libr. media and art San Francisco Art Inst., 1985. Illustrator: Parabola Mag., 2000; exhibitions include San Francisco Women's Art Gallery, 1986, 1989, 1995, Judah Magnes Mus., 1990, Campbell/Thiebaud Gallery, San Francisco, 1991, Jewish Hist. Mus., Amsterdam, 1995, Frederick Spratt Gallery, San Jose, Calif., 1996, Synagogue for the Arts Gallery, N.Y.C., 2000, 2000, Ctr. Contemporary Art, Sacramento, 2003, Calif. Breast Cancer Rsch. Program Symposium, San Diego, 2003, Graystone Gallery, San Francisco, 2004, Calif. Inst. Integral Studies, 2004, slide registry, Nat. Mus. of Women's Art, Washinggon, D.C., Israel Mus., Jerusalem. Grantee, Fred Ball, Sacramento, 2003, Change Inc., N.Y.C., 2001, Artist Space, N.Y.C., 1989. Mem.: Women's Caucus of Art (bd. dirs. 1990). Home: 3440 20th St #206 San Francisco CA 94110 Personal E-mail: bsquared@inreach.com.

CARMICHAEL, ALEXANDER DOUGLAS, engineering educator; b. Sliema, Malta, July 19, 1929; arrived in US, 1970, permanent resident; s. Adam and Jane (Hamilton) Carmichael; m. Rose Margaret Whittaker, Sept. 1, 1951; children: Gillian Ruth, Alison Rose, Peter Stewart. B.Sc., Plymouth Tech. Coll., London U., 1949; PhD, Cambridge U., 1958. Head aero. rsch. group Bristol-Siddely Engine Co., Bristol, England, 1958—60; chief engr. Dracone Developments Ltd., London, 1960-61; sr. project engr. No. Research and Engring. Corp., Cambridge, Mass, 1961-64; research fellow Imperial Coll. Sci. and Tech., London, 1964-68; tech. adv. English Electric Co. Ltd., Rugby, 1968-70; prof. power engring. MIT, 1970-96; prof. emeritus, 1996—. Fellow: Soc. Naval Archs. and Marine Engrs. (v.p. N.E. region 1991—94); mem.: Whitworth Soc. (London). Home: 319 Stearns St Unit 11 Carlisle MA 01741 Office: MIT Dept Ocean Engring Cambridge MA 02139 E-mail: adcarmic@mit.edu.

CARMICHAEL, DAVID BURTON, physician; b. Santa Ana, Calif., Sept. 12, 1923; s. David Burton and Phyllis (Adams) C.; m. Ava Louise Smith, Dec. 26, 1944; children: Catherine Ann, Heather Sue, Linda L., Ava L. Student, Graceland U., 1940-42; BA, MD, U. Iowa, 1946; postgrad., Harvard U., 1949-50; LL.D. (hon.), Graceland U., Iowa, 1985. Diplomate Am. Bd. Internal Medicine. Clin. and research fellow medicine Mass. Gen. Hosp., Boston, 1949-50; cons. cardiovascular diseases U.S. Naval Hosp., San Diego, Camp Pendleton, 1956-86, U.S. VA, 1960-82; chief dept. medicine Scripps Meml. Hosp., La Jolla, Calif., 1961-63, 65-67, chief staff, 1970-71. Clin. prof. medicine U. Calif. at San Diego, 1968—; pres. De Anza Lab. Corp., 1962-72, Carmichael-Carson Med.-Clin. Lab. Corp., 1962-75; sr. ptnr. Med. Clinic; founding med. dir. Cardiovascular Inst. Scripps Meml. Hosps., 1985-96; pres. Orange County Pioneer Coun., 1993-94; trustee GDE Systems, Inc., 1992-94. Contbr. articles to profl. jours. Trustee Millicent Rogers Mus., Taos, N.Mex., 1986—90, Graceland U., Iowa, 1987—, Rancho de las Golondrinas Mus., Santa Fe, 1989—. Rear adm. med. insp. gen. USNR. Decorated Legion of Merit; recipient Alumni Disting. Service award Graceland U., 1967. Master ACP (gov. So. Calif. region III 1972-76, Laureate award 1991); fellow Am. Coll. Cardiology (dir., sec. 1975, trustee 1979-85, Disting. Fellow award 1994, Mastership 2001), Am. Coll. Chest Physicians; mem. AMA (chmn. specialty soc. and service delegation 1985-87, 93-96, mem. grad. med. edn. adv. com. 1983—89, chmn., 1985-87, chmn. sect. council on clin. cardiology, Disting. Svc. award 1997), Am. Heart Assn., San Diego County Heart Assn. (pres. 1959-60), San Diego Biomed. Research Inst. (pres. 1958-59, 62-63, vice chmn. residency rev. com. internal medicine 1971-78), San Diego Soc. Internal Medicine (pres. 1959-61). Republican. Mem. Community Ch. of Christ. Home: 8333 Calle Del Cielo La Jolla CA 92037-3033 Personal E-mail: ASCDBC@aol.com. *This country, with its Christian heritage, gives to the vast majority the opportunity to serve and often, the chance to excel. The guidance of parents and instructors should never be forgotten, nor should the sacrifices of those who have allowed us to preserve our freedom.*

CARMICHAEL, DAVID RICHARD, lawyer; b. Sept. 4, 1942; BS, UCLA, 1964, JD, 1967. Bar: Calif. 1968. Assoc. Adams, Duque & Hazeltine, L.A., 1967-72; gen. counsel The Housing Group, Irvine, Calif., 1972-77; assoc. counsel Pacific Mut. Life Ins. Co., 1977-81, v.p., assoc. gen. counsel, 1981-89, corp. sec., 1981—83, 2nd v.p., assoc. gen. counsel, 1983—92, v.p., investment counsel, 1989-92, sr. v.p., gen. counsel, 1992—. Dir. & chmn. Ca. Life & Health Ins. Guarantee Assn.; dir. Assn. Ca. Life Ins. Companies, Assn. Life Ins. Counsel. Office: Pacific Life Ins Co 700 Newport Center Dr Newport Beach CA 92660-6307

CARMICHAEL, DONALD SCOTT, retired lawyer, retired corporate financial executive; b. Toledo, Feb. 19, 1912; s. Grey Thornton and Edna Earle (Jaite) C.; m. Mary Glenn Dickinson, May 28, 1940; children: Mary Brooke McMurray, Pamela Hastings Keenan. AB, Harvard U., 1935, student Sch. Law, 1935-37; LLB, U. Mich., 1942. Bar: Ohio 1942. Staff dept. law City of Cleve., 1938-40; chief renegotiation br. Cleve. Ordnance Dist., War Dept., 1942-46; practiced in Cleve., 1946; asst. sec. Diamond Alkali Co., 1946-48, sec., 1948-57, gen. counsel, 1957-58; v.p.-gen. counsel Stouffer Corp., 1959-60, exec. v.p., 1960-64; practiced in Cleve., 1964-71; pres. Schrafft's divsn. Pet, Inc., N.Y.C., 1971-75, Sportsvc. Corp., Buffalo, 1975-80, Del. North Cos., Inc., Buffalo, 1980-89, vice chmn., 1989; officer, dir. various corps.; dir., cons. Editor: F.D.R; Columnist, 1947; Contbr. to law revs. Mem. Cuyahoga County Charter Commn., 1959; chmn.; mem. Cleve. Met. Services Commn., 1957-59, President's Task Force on War Against Poverty, 1964; Del. Democratic Nat. Conv., 1960, 64; mem. Cuyahoga County Dem. Exec. Com.; Chmn. bd. trustees Cuyahoga County Hosps., 1958-64, Urban League, Karamu House. Mem. ABA, Ohio Bar Assn., Cleve. Bar Assn., Union Club Cleve., Chagrin Valley Hunt Club, Harvard Club N.Y.C., River Club N.Y.C., Buffalo Club, Phi Gamma Delta. Home: 21 Hardscrabble Ln Lyme NH 03768

CARMICHAEL, JAMES VINSON, JR., library and information science educator; b. Atlanta, Nov. 27, 1946; s. James Vinson and Frances Elizabeth (McDonald) C.; m. Karen Bryce Powers, June 18, 1969 (div. Sept. 1973). BA, Emory U., 1969, MLN, 1977; PhD, U. N.C., 1988. Inventory control clk. Lockheed Aircraft, Marietta, Ga., 1969, logistics asst., 1969-70; trust adminstrv. asst. Trust Co. Bank, Atlanta, 1970-76; ref., instrn. libr. Ga. Coll., Milledgeville, Ga., 1977-81; instr. U. N.C., Chapel Hill, 1988-89, Greensboro, 1988-89, asst. prof. libr., info. scis., 1989-95, assoc. prof. libr., info. sci., 1995-00, prof., 2000—. Editor: Daring To Find Our Names: The Search for Lesbigay Library History, 1998; contbr. articles to profl. jours. Recipient Louis Round Wilson award Southeastern Libr. Assn., 1988, Franklin M. Garrett award Atlanta Hist. Soc., 1990, Disting. Alumni award Univ. N.C., Chapel Hill, 1995, Edmund Pearson award 2001. Mem. ALA (chair libr. history round table 1995-96, mem. com. status of women 1993-96), N.C. Libr. Assn. (Ray Moore award 1992, 94, chair coll. and univ. sec., 2001-03), Assn. Libr. and Info. Sci. Edn. Home: 2403 Cottage Pl Greensboro NC 27455-2912 Office Phone: 336-334-3478. E-mail: Jim_Carmichael@uncg.edu.

CARMICHAEL, JUDY LEA, record industry executive, concert jazz pianist; b. Lynwood, Calif., Nov. 27, 1952; d. John Alvin and Jeanne Pauline (Boock) Hohenstein. Student, Calif. State U., Long Beach, 1970-73, Calif. State U., Fullerton. Owner C&D Prodns., N.Y.C., 1989—. Chmn. jazz fellowships com. NEA, Washington, 1990-91; featured on Nat. Pub. Radio, Marian McPartland's Piano Jazz, 1990, Morning Edition Nat. Pub. Radio, also TV programs Entertainment Tonight, CBS, Sunday Morning with Charles Kuralt, 1993. Performed as pianist at Breda Jazz Festival, The Netherlands, 1986, Carnegie Hall, N.Y.C., 1988, 89, Rio de Janeiro, 1989, Peggy Guggenheim Mus., Venice, Italy, 1990, Am. Acad., Rome, 1990, 91, USIA Tour, Portugal, 1991, Spain, 1991, India, 1988, China, 1992, Singapore, 1994, S. Am., 1996, major U.S. tours 1993-95, also L.A., Zurich, Switzerland,

Paris, Cannes, France; performer Stanford Symphony Pops with Skitch Henderson, 1997; author (music) Judy Carmichael's Complete Book of Stride Piano, 1987, You Can Play Stride Piano, 1996; prodr., artist (LP's) Jazz Piano, 1983, Two Handed Stride, 1980, (CD's) Trio, 1989, Old Friends, 1991, Pearls, 1985, ...And Basie Called Her Stride, 1993, Judy, 1994, Chops, 1995, PianoDisc, 1995, QRS piano rolls, 1996, (CD and player piano formats) High on Fats and Other Stuff, 1997; featured on CBS Sunday Morning with Charles Osgood, Entertainment Tonight, Prairie Home Companion, Nat. Pub. Radio's Morning Edit.; jazz editor Sheet Music mag., 1989-90; host, creator, prodr. Judy Carmichael's Jazz Inspired, Nat. Pub. Radio, 2000—, Pub. Radio Internat. on Sirius Satellite Network; stage show with Steve Ross 2000-2003 aboard QEII and throughout Europe and U.S., and QEII, Canary Islands, Lisbon, Atlantic crossing; tour of Australia and New Zealand, 2004; performer Robert Redford's Sundance Cantata, 2004, Sundance Film Festival, 2005, QMII concerts, 2005; prodr. (radio show) Dog Talk, 2005—; contbr. numerous articles to profl. jours NEA fellow, grantee; Grammy award nominee, 1980; chosen to be Steinway artist, 1986; nominated for Mac award Manhattan Assn. Cabarets and Clubs for Stage Show with Steve Ross, 1996. Avocations: golf, softball, tennis, skiing. Office Phone: 631-725-3603. Personal E-mail: judy@judycarmichael.com.

CARMICHAEL, ROBERTA KAY, writer; b. Daytona Beach, Fla., Dec. 11, 1956; d. James Lawton and Barbara Kent Coward; m. Del Carmichael, July 5, 1974; 1 child, Joseph. Grad. H.S., Crescent City, Fla.; Breaking into Print Diploma, Long Ridge Writers Group, West Redding, Conn., 2000. Tchr. Kiddie Korner Nursery Sch., Crescent City, 1972—77; freelance writer Homosassa, Fla., 2000—. Contbr. articles to publs. Phys. therapy vol. Citrus Meml. Hosp., Inverness, Fla., 1992—93. Mem.: Pisgah Camping Club. Avocations: writing, reading, woodcarving, hiking, horseback riding. Home: 3610 S Springbreeze Way Homosassa FL 34448

CARMICHAEL, WILLIAM DANIEL, management consultant, educator; b. Denver, Sept. 5, 1929; s. Fitzhugh Lee and Anna Devona (Sullivan) C.; m. Faith Young, June 21, 1958; children: Amy, Philip Fitzhugh, Daniel Owen. AB, Yale, 1950; MA, MPA, Princeton, 1952, PhD, 1959; BLitt (Rhodes scholar), U. Oxford (Eng.), 1955; LLD (hon.), U. W.I., 1989. Legislative analyst U.S. Bur. Budget, 1955-56, budget analyst, 1956-57; lectr. econs. and pub. affairs Princeton, 1957-60, asst. prof., 1960-62; dir. undergrad. program Woodrow Wilson Sch. Pub. and Internat. Affairs, 1958-62; prof. econ. policy, dean Grad. Sch. Bus. and Pub. Adminstrn., Cornell U., 1962-68; rep. Ford Found., Brazil, 1968-71, head Latin Am. and Caribbean, 1971-77, Middle East and Africa, 1977-81, v.p. for developing country programs, 1981-89; exec. dir. Ea. European programs Inst. Internat. Edn., N.Y.C., 1989-93. Cons. on edn. and econ. devel., 1993—. Bd. dirs. Human Rights Watch, So. African Legal Svcs. and Edn. Program, Film Aid Internat., Future Generations. Mem. Coun. on Fgn. Rels., Assn. Am. Rhodes Scholars, Phi Beta Kappa. Home and Office: 603 W Lyon Farm Dr Greenwich CT 06831-4363 Office Phone: 203-532-1461. E-mail: wdcarm@optonline.net.

CARMODY, ARTHUR RODERICK, JR., lawyer, director; b. Shreveport, La., Feb. 19, 1928; s. Arthur R. and Caroline (Gaughan) C.; m. Renee Aubry, Jan. 26, 1952 (div. 1980); children: Helen Bragg, Renee, Arthur Roderick, Patrick, Timothy, Mary, Virginia, Joseph; m. Mary Wells, Sept. 1, 1990. Grad. with honors, N.Mex. Mil. Inst.; BS, Fordham U., 1949; LLB, La. State U., 1952. Bar: La. 1952, U.S. Supreme Ct. 1971. Mem. firm Wilkinson, Carmody & Gilliam and its predecessors, Shreveport, 1952—. Bd. dirs. Kansas City So. Transport Co., Kansas City, Shreveport and Gulf Terminal Co., Shreveport Braves Baseball Club (Tex. League), Sta. KDAQ-FM Pub. Radio, pres., 1991, chmn., 1992, RED River Pub. Radio Network; mem. Shreveport Steamer (World Football League) Partnership; pres. Touchdown Club of Shreveport, 1960. Author: Legal Problems in the Development and Mining of Lignite, 1976; legal history columnist Shreveport Bar Review, 1995—; La. adv. editor The Insurance Bar, 1961—. Chmn. Met. Shreveport Zoning Bd. Appeals, 1959—72; mem. gov.'s ad hoc com. for preparation rules and regulations for mining and reclamation of lignite in State of La., Dept. Conservation, 1978—79; mem. select com. for rev. stds. juc. conduct Supreme Ct. La., 1994—; nat. bd. dirs. N.Mex. Mil. Inst., Roswell, 1967—68; pres. bd. trustees Jesuit H.S., 1976—82; chmn. bd. govs. Loyola Found., Shreveport, 1991—94; trustee Schumpert Med. Ctr., 1965—85; adv. bd. La. State U., Shreveport, 1982—86; bd. dirs. La. State U. Found., Baton Rouge, Agnew Day Sch., Shreveport, 1970—82, Ridgewood Montessori Sch., Christus Schumpert Health Sys. Found.; bd. trustees La. State Paul M. Hebert Law Ctr. 1st lt. USAR, 1948—50. Recipient Alumni Achievement award Fordham U., 1995; named Hon. Alumnus, elected to Ring of Honor Loyola Coll. Prep., 1993; named to N.Mex. Mil. Inst. Hall of Fame, 1994. Master: Am. Inns of Ct.; fellow: La. Bar Assn. (mem. com. on lawyer and judicial conduct 1996—), Am. Coll. of Trial Lawyers, La. Bar Found. (life); mem.: ABA, Mil. Order Stars and Bars, Crossed Saber Soc., Soc. for Civil War History, Soc. for Mil. History, U.S. Horse Cavalry Assn., North La. Civil War Round Table, Res. Officers Assn., La. Civil Svc. League, Soc. Hosp. Counsel, Rlwy. and Locomotive Hist. Soc., Kansas City So. Hist. Soc., Shreveport C. of C. (dir. 1968—70), Pub. Affairs Rsch. Coun., Nat. Legal Ctr. for the Pub. Interest, La. Assn. Bus. and Industry, Tarshar Soc., La. R.R. Assn. (exec. com. 1992—), Mid-Continent Oil and Gas Assn. (exec. com. 1984—), Am. Arbitration Assn. (panel arbitrators), Nat. Acad. Law and Medicine, La. Assn. Def. Counsel, Internat. Assn. Def. Counsel, Nat. Assn. R.R. Trial Counsel, Trial Attys. Am., Coll. Master Advocates and Barristers, La. Law Inst., Am. Judicature Soc., Univ. Assocs. of La. State U., Supreme Ct. of La. Hist. Soc., Scribes Soc., Nat. Soc. SAR (pres. Galvez chpt. 1997), Confederate Meml. Lit. Soc., La. Hist. Assn., North La. Hist. Soc., Federalist Soc., Fifth Fed. Cir. Bar Assn., U.S. Supreme Ct. Hist. Soc., Shreveport Bar Assn. (pres. 2003), Fed. Bar Assn., Kappa Alpha Order, Sovereign Mil. Order of Malta, Phi Delta Phi. Home: 255 Forest Ave Shreveport LA 71104-4506 Office: Wilkinson Carmody & Gilliam 1700 Beck Bldg 400 Travis St Shreveport LA 71101-3108 Office Phone: 318-221-4196. E-mail: Acarmody@wcglawfirm.com.

CARMODY, CAROL J., transportation executive; BA, U.of Oklahoma; M in Public Administration, American U. Aviation staff member Senate Commerce Comm., 1988—94; U.S. rep. to the Council Internat. Civil Aviation Org., Montreal, 1994—99; mem. Nat. Transportation Safety Bd., Washington, DC, 2000—05, vice chmn., 2001—02; dir. transp. initiatives Nat. Acad. Pub. Adminstrn., 2005—. Office: Nat Acad Pub Adminstrn Ste 1090 E 1100 New York Ave, NW Washington DC 20005-3934 Office Phone: 202-204-3666. E-mail: ccarmody@napwash.org.

CARMODY, JAMES ALBERT, lawyer; b. St. Louis, Nov. 21, 1945; m. Helen Tippy Valin, mar. 22, 1969; children: Paul Valin, Leigh Christin. BA, Vanderbilt U., 1967; JD, U. Ark., 1973. Bar: Tex. 1974, U.S. Dist. Ct. (so. dist.) Tex. 1974, U.S. Ct. Appeals (5th and 10th cirs.) 1975, U.S. Supreme Ct., 1996. Assoc. Mabry & Gunn, Texas City, Tex., 1974-75; mcpl. ct. judge Texas City, Tex., 1975; assoc. Chamberlain & Hrdlicka, Houston, 1975-78, ptnr., 1978-89, Keck Mahin & Cate, Houston, 1989-94, Carmody & Yokubaitis, L.L.P., Houston, 1995-2000. Assoc. editor U. Ark. Law Rev., 1973. Incorporator, Gulf Coast Big Bros. and Sisters, Inc., Galveston County, Tex., 1975; mem. St. Maximillian Cath. Community Bldg. Com., Houston, 1985-88; mem. CANN Uniform Dispute Resolution Policy Task Force, 2001-2003. Lt. USN, 1967-71. Mem.: Houston Bar Assn. (arbitrator fee dispute com. 1977—2003), Galveston County Jr. Bar Assn. (pres. 1975, Outstanding Young Lawyer award 1975), Nat. Arbitration Forum (mem. panel of arbitrators), Entrepreneurship Inst. Houston (chmn. 1991—94), Delta Theta Phi (master insp. 1983—85, dean Houston alumni senate 1988, found. bd. dir.). Republican. Roman Catholic. Avocations: amateur radio, international travel. Office: Ste 820 6363 Woodway Houston TX 77057 E-mail: carmody@lawyer.com.

CARMODY, RICHARD PATRICK, lawyer; b. Chgo., June 2, 1942; s. Thomas Francis and Margaret (Tully) C.; m. Alison Pierce Cutter, Dec. 27, 1968; children: Elizabeth Carmody Gonzalez, Emily Pierce Carmody. BA, U. Ill., 1964; JD, Vanderbilt U., 1975. Bar: Ala. 1975, U.S. Dist. Ct. (no., mid. and so. dists.) Ala. 1975, U.S. Ct. Appeals (11th cir.) 1985, U.S. Supreme Ct. 1988. Assoc. Lange, Simpson, Robinson & Somerville, Birmingham, Ala., 1975-81, ptnr., 1981—2002; chmn. exec. com. Lange, Simpson Robinson & Somerville, Birmingham, Ala., 1987-93; ptnr. Adams and Reese/Lange Simpson LLP, Birmingham, 2003—. Mem. Am. Bankruptcy Inst., Washington, 1985—, co-chair ethics com. 1999—; bd. dirs. Am. Bd. Cert., 2000—, mem. exec. com., 2001-03, mem. faculty com., 2004—. Bd. dirs. Birmingham coun. Campfire Boys and Girls Inc., 1978-90, pres., 1983-85; bd. dirs. Ala. region NCCJ, 1995—, state chair, 2000-02; bd. dirs. St. Vincent's Hosp. Foudn., 2002—; active Leadership Birmingham, 1998—. Fellow Am. Coll. Bankruptcy, 1999—. Mem. Ala. Bar Assn. (chmn. bankruptcy and comml. law sect. 1985, exec. com. 1986-93), Greystone Golf & Country Club, Kiwanis. Roman Catholic. Avocations: golf, sports. Office: Adams & Reese LLP 2100 3d Ave N Ste 1100 Birmingham AL 35203 Office Phone: 205-250-5033. Business E-Mail: richard.carmody@arlaw.com.

CARMON, HAGGAI, lawyer; b. Tel Aviv, Nov. 5, 1944; came to U.S., 1985; s. Yehiel and Ida Carmon; m. Rakeffet Avissara, Mar. 7, 1978; children: Ittai, Dria, Irin, Yahel. LLB cum laude, Tel Aviv U., 1981; MA, St. John's U., NYC, 1987. Bar: Israel 1983. Ptnr. Carmon & Co. Law Offices, Israel and NYC, 1983—, Carmon & Carmon, NYC. Rep. US Govt. in Israel legal matters. Author (novels) Triple Identity, 2005; Contbr. articles to profl. publs. Hon. chief del. to USA, Israeli Labor Party, 1985-87; v.p., bd. dirs. Israel Am. C. of C. and Industry, 1979-85. Mem. ABA (assoc.) NY State Bar Assn., Assn. Trial Lawyers Am. Avocation: scuba diving. Office: Law Office 767 3rd Ave New York NY 10017*

CARMONA, JOSÉ ANTONIO, Spanish language educator, English language educator; b. Remedios, Las Villas, Cuba, Mar. 9, 1960; came to U.S., 1971; s. Felix and Maria Gloria (Reyes) C.; 1 child, Alberto José. BA, Drew U., 1983; MA, Columbia U., 1984, EdM, 1986, postgrad in Hispanic culture & lit. U.S., 1986—. Cert. Spanish tchr. K-12, N.J., ESL. Spl. edn. tchr. grades 5, 6. P.S. 121 N.Y. Bd. Edn., N.Y.C., 1984; ESL instr. Hispanic Inst. Rsch. & Devel., Paramus, N.J., 1985-86; adj. prof. of Spanish Bergen C.C., Paramus, 1985-87; instr. Spanish Drew U., Madison, N.J., 1987-91; ESL instr. Emerson Adult Edn. Program, Union City, N.J., 1988-89; adj. assoc. prof. Spanish County Coll. of Morris, Randolph, N.J., 1988; adj. prof. Spanish Coll. St. Elizabeth, Convent Station, N.J., 1990; instr., coord. ESL and Spanish Hudson County C.C., West N.Y., N.J., 1990-94, asst. prof. ESOL, modern lang. coord., 1994-96; supr. student tchrs. of Spanish William Paterson Coll., Wayne, N.J., 1996; prof. modern langs./EOSL Daytona Beach (Fla.) C.C., 1996—, chair dept. modern langs./ESL, 1999—, chair ESOL, 2001—04. Case worker Angel Guardian Home, Bklyn., 1983; coord. Hispanic Leadership Program, St. Elizabeth Coll., Convent Station, 1989-90, Gov.'s Sch. on the Environ. Stockton State Coll., Pomona, N.J., 1989-93, co-dir. 1993; faculty adviser Hispanic House students, Drew U., Madison, 1987-91, acad. adviser and counselor to 1st and 2nd yr. students, other adminstrv. duties; freelance translator, 1985—; lectr. and or presenter at many nat. and internat. ednl. confs.; vis. prof. Flagler Coll., St. Augustine, Fla., 2003—; vis. adj. prof. edn. Bethune-Cookman Coll., Daytona Beach, 2005. Author: Adolescent Blues (poetry) 1992, Distinct Voices: A Multicultural Anthology for ESL Writers, 1996; co-author: Mixed Media: Authentic Reading for the Beginning ESL Student (text), 1993, Topics and Trends: First Authentic Readings for ESL Writers, 1994 (text), Exploremos: Spanish for the Community College Student, 2001; contbr. over 80 poems to Spanish and English mags, 1988—. Mem. Hispanic Affairs Adv. Com. Dept. Community Affairs, Trenton, N.J., 1989-91,community, Affirmative Action Com., Drew U., Madison, 1989-91; adv. bd. mem. Drew U. EOF program, Madison, 1990-95, Selective Svc. Bd., West N.Y., 1992-96; bd. dirs. Jose Marti Scholarship Fund, Union City, 1979—, Hudson County 4-Coll. Consortium, 1992, N.E. Fla. Tchrs. of English as 2d Lang., 2000—, pres., 2002-2004; bd. dirs. Magdalene, Inc., 2000-2001, pres. exec. bd., 2001—, Fla. Adult Edn. ESOL Task Force, 2002--. Recipient Hon. Literary Essay award Cuban Lions Club in Exile, Union City,1976, Outstanding Alumnus award N.J. Ednl. Opportunity Fund Profl. Assn., Newark, 1989, Golden Poet award World of Poetry, Calif., 1989, Frances B. Sellers award, Drew U. E.O.F. Alumni Assn., Madison, 1990. Mem. NEA (rev. panel bd. dirs. higher edn. jour. Thought and Action 1996-99, plaque for svc. to the jour. 1999), MLA, Fgn. Lang. Educators N.J., N.Y. Met. Assn. for Devl. Edn., TESOL (N.J. higher edn. rep. 1992-96, bd. dirs. N.E. Fla. 2002—, pres. 2005—), Hispanic Assn. for Higher Edn., Circulo Cultural Pan Am., Acad. Am. Poets, Trio (N.J. bd. dirs. 1991-92), Fla. Assn. Cmty. Colls., Sigma Delta Pi, Kappa Delta Pi., Epsilon Omega Psi., TESOL (pres., 2005—) Roman Catholic. Avocations: writing, reading, dance. Office: Daytona Beach CC 1200 Internat Speedway Blvd Daytona Beach FL 32120-2811 Office Phone: 386-506-4568. Business E-Mail: carmonj@dbcc.edu.

CARMONA, RICHARD HENRY, United States Surgeon General; b. N.Y.C., Nov. 22, 1949; m. Diana Sanchez; 4 children. BS, U. Calif., San Francisco, 1976, MD, 1979; MPH, U. Ariz., 1998. Prof. surgery U. Ariz., 1985—2002; dir., trauma services Tucson Med. Ctr., 1985—93; CEO Kino County Cmty. Hosp., 1995—96, Pima Health Care System, 1997—99; surgeon gen. US Dept. Health & Human Services, 2002—. Dep. sheriff, SWAT team mem. Pima Cty. Sheriff's Dept., 1986—2002; chmn. Ariz. So. Regional Emergency Med. System, 1990—2002. With U.S. Army, 1967—70. Office: Office of Surgeon Gen 5600 Fishers Ln Rm 18-66 Rockville MD 20857

CARMONY, MARVIN DALE, retired linguist, educator; b. nr. Richmond, Ind., Feb. 27, 1923; s. Harry Edgar and Ellen (Brown) C.; m. Mary Joan Nicholson, May 31, 1947; children— Ronald Dee, Kathryn Lynn. Student, Valparaiso Tech. Inst., 1941-42, Olivet Nazarene U., 1947-49; AB, Ind. State U., 1950, MA, 1951; PhD, Ind. U., 1965. Radio operator Am. Airlines, Chgo., 1942-44; tchr. high schs. Pendleton and Shelbyville, Ind., 1953-59; from instr. English to assoc. prof. English and linguistics Ind. State U., Terre Haute, 1959-69, prof., 1969-88, assoc. dean Coll. Arts and Scis., 1970-86. Cofounder Ind. Place-Names Survey, 1968, dir., 1968-70; co-founder Ind. Names (now Hoosier Folklore), 1970, gen. editor, 1970-88. Author: (with D.F. Carmony) Indiana Dialects in Their Historical Setting, 1972, rev. edit., 1979, (with Ronald Baker) Indiana Place Names, 1975; also articles. Trustee Olivet Nazarene U., 1967-70, mem. alumni bd. dirs., 1995-2000. With U.S. Mcht. Marine, 1944-46; vet. USCG. Am. Council Learned Socs. fellow, 1964-65 Mem. Am. Dialect Soc. (adv. bd. publs. 1972-77, 82-86, pres. 1981-82), Soc. Wireless Pioneers, Am. Names Soc. (editorial bd. Names 1977-84), Linguistic Soc. Am., Nat. Soc. XVII Century Colonial Dames (Disting. Svc. award 1975), Phi Delta Lambda, Phi Delta Kappa, Sigma Tau Delta. Methodist. Home: 227 Madison Blvd Terre Haute IN 47803-1911

CARNABUCI, FRANK J., III, headmaster; b. Nov. 23, 1951; BA, Drew U., 1973; MA in Edn., Columbia U., Harvard U. Asst. headmaster Dalton Sch., NYC; headmaster Birch Wathen Lenox Sch., 1992—. Contbr. (book) The Dalton School, 1992, Founding Mothers and Others, 2002. Office: Birch Wathen Lenox Sch 210 E 77th St New York NY 10021 Office Phone: 212-861-0404. Office Fax: 212-879-5309.*

CARNAHAN, BRICE, chemical engineer, educator; b. New Philadelphia, Ohio, Oct. 13, 1933; s. Paul Tracy and Amelia Christina (Gray) C. BS, Case Western Res. U., 1955, MS, 1957; PhD, U. Mich., 1965. Lectr. in engring. biostats. U. Mich., Ann Arbor, 1959-64, asst. prof. chem. engring. and biostatics, 1965-68, assoc. prof., 1968-70, prof. chem. engring., 1970—. Vis. lect. Imperial Coll., London, England, 1971-72; vis. prof. U. Pa., 1970, U. Calif.-San Diego, 1986-87; mem., chmn. Curriculum Aids for Chem. Engring. Edn. com. Nat. Acad. Engring., 1974-75 Author: (with H.A. Luther and J.O. Wilkes) Applied Numerical Methods, 1969, (with J.O. Wilkes) Digital Computing and Numerical Methods, 1973; Editorial bd.: Jour. Computers and Fluids, 1971—, Computers and Chemical Engineering, 1974—. Mem. communications com. Mich. Council for Arts, 1977—. Recipient Chem. Engr. of Yr. award Detroit Engring. Soc., 1987, 3M award Am. Soc. for Engring. Edn., 1990. Fellow AIChE (Computers in Chem. Engring. award 1980, chm. CAST div. 1981); mem. AAAS, Assn. for Computing Machinery, Soc. for Computer Simulation, Sigma Xi, Sigma Nu.

CARNAHAN, JEAN, former senator; m. Mel Carnahan (former governor) (dec. 2000); children: Randy(dec.), Russ, Robin, Tom. BA in Bus. and Pub. Admin., George Washington U. First lady of Mo., 1993—2000; U.S. senator, 2001—02. Mem. armed svcs. com, small bus. and entrepreneurship com., gov. affairs com., commerce, sci. and transportation com., special com. aging, State of Mo.; co-founder Children in the Workplace; spkr. for domestic violence, cancer, osteoporosis, mental health, drug problems. Author: If Walls Could Talk, 1998, Christmas at the Mansion: Its Memories and Menus, 1999, Don't Let the Fire Go Out, 2004; contbr.: Vital Speeches of the Day, 1999, Will You Say a Few Words, 2000. Recipient Robert C. Goshorn award for pub. svc., State of Mo. Martin Luther King, Jr. Special Achievement award, Child Adv. of Yr. award, Boys' and Girls' Town Mo., 1995, Citizen of Yr., March of Dimes, 1997, Woman of Yr., St. Louis Zonta Clubs Internat., 1999. Bd. mem. William Woods U. Democrat. Achievements include representing her husband's posthumously won seat in the U.S. Senate from 2001 to 2002 after he and their son, Randy, tragically died in a plane crash.

CARNAHAN, JOHN ANDERSON, retired lawyer; b. Cleve., May 8, 1930; s. Samuel Edwin and Penelope (Moulton) C.; m. Katherine A. Halter, June 14, 1958; children: Peter M., Allison E., Kristin A. BA, Duke U., 1953, JD, 1955. Bar: Ohio 1955. Pvt. practice, Columbus, Ohio, 1955-78; ptnr. Arter & Hadden, Columbus, 1978-99; in-house counsel The XLO Group, Cleve., 2000—04; ret. Lectr. Ohio Legal Ctr. Inst., 1969, 73-74. Editor Duke Law Jour., 1954-55; chmn. bd. editors Ohio Lawyer, 1986-91; contbr. articles to profl. jours. Chmn. UN Day, Columbus, 1960; pres. Capital City Young Republican Club, 1960; bd. dirs. Columbus Cancer Clinic, pres., 1978-81; bd. dirs. Columbus chpt. ARC, 1979-87; mem. governing bd. Hannah Neil Mission, Inc., 1974-78; chmn. Duke Alumni Admissions Adv. Com., 1965-79. Named one of Outstanding Young Men of Columbus, 1965. Fellow Am. Bar Found. (life, chmn. Ohio fellows 1988-95), Columbus Bar Found. (life); mem ABA (ho. of dels. 1984-95), Ohio State Bar Found. (trustee 1986-90), Nat. Conf. Bar Pres., Ohio State Bar Assn. (coun. of dels. 1965-67, exec. com. 1977-81, 82-85, pres.-elect 1982-83, pres. 1983-84, Ritter award for outstanding contbns. adminstrn. justice 1987), Columbus Bar Assn. (bd. govs. 1970-72, sec.-treas. 1974-75, pres. 1976-77, Professionalism award 1996), Kit Kat Club (past pres.). Presbyterian. Home and Office: 767 S 5th St Columbus OH 43206-2145 E-mail: jac583@aol.com.

CARNAHAN, ORVILLE DARRELL, retired state legislator, retired academic administrator; b. Elba, Idaho, Dec. 25, 1929; s. Marion Carlos and Leola Pearl (Putnam) C.; m. Colleen Arrott, Dec. 14, 1951; children: Karen, Jeanie, Orville Darrell, Carla. BS, Utah State U., 1958; MEd, U. Idaho, 1962, EdD, 1964. Vocat. dir., v.p. Yakima (Wash.) Valley Coll., 1964-69; chancellor Eastern Iowa C.C. Dist., Davenport, 1969-71; pres. Highline Coll., Midway, Wash., 1971-76; assoc. Utah Commn. for Higher Edn., Salt Lake City, 1976-78; pres. So. Utah U., Cedar City, 1978-81, Salt Lake C.C., Salt Lake City, 1981-90, pres. emeritus, 1990—; mem. Utah Ho. of Reps., 1993-99; ret., 1999. Cons. in field. Active Boy Scouts Am. Served with U.S. Army, 1952-54, Korea. Mem. Am. Vocat. Assn., NEA, Idaho Hist. Soc., Utah Hist. Soc., Alpha Tau Alpha, Phi Delta Kappa, Rotary Internat. Mem. LDS Ch. Home: 1653 Cornerstone Dr South Jordan UT 84095-5501 Office: Salt Lake CC 4600 S Redwood Rd Salt Lake City UT 84123-3197 E-mail: odcarn@comcast.net.

CARNAHAN, ROBERT PAUL, civil engineer, educator, researcher, consultant; b. Bradenton, Fla., July 22, 1936; s. Robert Dewey and Marion (Wilbur) C.; m. Geraldine Schott, July 30, 1938; children: Robert P. Jr., Christopher T., Sean P. BCE, U. Fla., 1959; MS in Sanitary Engring., U. N.C., 1964; PhD, Clemson U., 1973. Registered profl. engr., Fla., Va., Md. Commd. 2d lt. U.S. Army, 1959, advanced through grades to lt. col., 1975; co. comdr. 92d Engring. Battalion, Ft. Bragg, N.C., 1960-61; project officer U.S. Environ. Hygiene Agy., Edgewood Arsenal, Md., 1961-63; instr. Med. Field Service Sch., San Antonio, 1966-68; sr. environ. engr. 20th Pvt. Med. Unit, Vietnam, 1968-69; project officer U.S. Army Med. Research and Devel. Command, Washington, 1973-75; project devel. officer U.S. Army Material Devel. and Research Ctr., Ft. Belvior, Va., 1975-79; divsn. chief EPA br. U.S. Army Med. Bioengring. Rsch. and Devel. Lab, Frederick, Md., 1979-80. Adj. rsch. prof. dept. chemistry Am. U., 1976-77; adj. prof. dept. civil, mech. and environ. engring. George Washington U., 1979-80; asst. prof. dept. civil engring. and mechs. U. South Fla., 1980-84; assoc. prof. dept. civil engring. and mechs. U. South Fla., 1984-89, prof. dept. civil engring. & mechs., 1989-93, assoc. dean rsch. Coll. of Engring., 1993—. Contbr. numerous articles to profl. jours. Decorated Legion of Merit, Bronze Star with oak leaf cluster, Meritorious Service Medal with oak leaf cluster, Army Commendation medal with oak leaf cluster; recipient Silver medal for research and devel. Am. Def. Preparedness Assn., Rsch. award U.S. Dept. of Army Rsch., Comdr.'s award for tech. Meradcom. Mem. ASCE, Nat. Soc. Profl. Engrs., Am. Inst. Chem. Engrs., Am. Chem. Soc., Water Pollution Control Fedn., Am. Water Works Assn., N.A. Membrane Soc., Internat. Desalination Assn., Am. Desalting Assn. (Hall of Fame 1998), Fla. Engring. Soc., Internat. Assn. Water Pollution Research, Am. Acad. Environ. Engrs. (cert.), Sigma Xi, Chi Epsilon, Tau Beta Pi. Democrat. Roman Catholic. Home: 506 Terrace Hill Dr Tampa FL 33617-3850 Office: U South Fla Coll Engring Rsch Office 4202 E Fowler Ave Tampa FL 33620-8000 E-mail: carnahan@eng.usf.edu, gcarnahan@msn.com.

CARNAHAN, ROBIN, state official; b. Mo. d. Mel and Jean Carnahan. BA in Econ., with honors, William Jewell Coll., Liberty, Mo.; JD, U. Va. Sch. Law, 1986. Atty. Thompson & Mitchell, St. Louis; spl. asst. to chmn. Export-Import Bank of US; Sec. of State State of Mo., 2004—. Democrat. Office: Office of Sec of State 208 State Capitol Jefferson City MO 65101 Fax: 573-751-2490. Office Phone: 573-751-4936.

CARNAHAN, RUSS (JOHN RUSSELL CARNAHAN), congressman, lawyer; b. Rolla, Mo., July 10, 1958; m. Debra Carnahan; children: Austin, Andrew. Attended, U. Mo., Rolla, 1976—77, Richmond Coll., London, Eng., 1978; BS, U. Mo., Columbia, 1979; JD, U. Mo., Columbia Sch. Law, 1983. Atty. BJC Healthcare, 1995—; mem. Mo. Ho. Reps., 2000—04, US Ho. Reps., 109th Congress, 3d Dist. Mo., 2005—. Mem. Mo. joint com. Terrorism, Bio-terrorism and Homeland Security; dep. majority whip Mo. Dem. Orgn.; chmn. Mo. Ho. Dem. Caucus; mem. adv. com. citzenship edn., health care law com. Mo. Bar; mem. Civil and Adminstrv. Law com., State Courts Automation Com. Mem. Compton Heights Neighborhood Assn.; mem. Friends Tower Grove Park Mo. Botanical Gardens and DeMenil Mansion; mem. Landmarks Assn. St. Louis, State Hist. Soc. Mo., St. Louis Regional Commerce and Growth Assn., Pub. Policy Com.; mem. govt. rels. com. United Way Greater St. Louis; chmn. Miss. River Parkway Commn.; others. Recipient Lewis & Clark Statesman award, St. Louis Regional C. of C., 2002, Legis. award, St. Louis Bus. Jour., 2002. Mem.: Bar Assn. Mo. (Legis. award 2002), Bar Assn. Met. St. Louis. Democrat. Office: US Ho of Reps 1232 Longworth Ho Office Bldg Washington DC 20009 Office Phone: 202-225-2671.*

CARNALL, TIMOTHY W., music educator; b. Ft. Wayne, Ind., Mar. 12, 1967; s. Jerry Wayne and Donna Rae (Bercot) Carnall; m. Sandra Elizabeth Carnall, July 19, 1997; 1 child, Samuel William Wayne. BS in Music Edn., Ball State U., 1990. Tchr., band dir. N. Decatur Jr./Sr. H.S., Greensburg, Ind., 1990—91, Ft. Wayne, Ind., Elkhart (Ind.) Ctrl. H.S. Pvt. music tchr., 1990—; judge ISSMA, Ind., 1995—. Mem.: Ind. Music Educators, Ind. Band Masters. Home: 1302 Briarwood Dr Elkhart IN 46514 Office: Elkhart Ctrl High Sch 1 Blazer Blvd Elkhart IN 46516

CARNASE, THOMAS PAUL, graphics designer, consultant; b. Bronx, NY, Sept. 15, 1939; Assoc. B.F.A., N.Y.C. Community Coll., 1959. Assoc. designer Sudler & Hennessey, Inc., N.Y.C., 1959-64; pres., designer Bonder & Carnase Studio, Inc., N.Y.C., 1964-68; v.p., ptnr. Lubalin, Smith, Carnase, Inc., N.Y.C., 1969-79; pres. Carnase, Inc., N.Y.C., 1979—, Carnase Computer Typography, N.Y.C., 1979—, World Typeface Ctr., Inc., N.Y.C., 1981—. Mem. adv. com. N.Y.C. Community Coll., 1977—; guest lectr./juror art dirs. clubs, schs., univs. throughout world Exhibited in group show Whitney Mus.

Am. Art, N.Y.C.; editor Ligature jour., 1981—; designer numerous typefaces; represented in permanent collection at Cooper Hewitt Nat. Design Mus. Recipient award of Excellence, Communication Arts mag.; cert. of Distinction Creativity mag.; archived drawings and records gifted to The Cary Graphic Arts Collection at Rochester Inst. Tech., 2004. Mem. N.Y. Art Dirs. Club, N.Y. Type Dirs. Club, Soc. Publ. Designers, Am. Inst. Graphic Arts Office: Carnase Inc 21 Dorset Rd Scarsdale NY 10583

CARNEAL, GEORGE UPSHUR, lawyer; b. N.Y.C., May 31, 1935; AB, Princeton U., 1957; LLB, U. Va., 1961. Bar: Va. 1961, D.C. 1962. Law clk. to judge U.S. Ct. Appeals, D.C. Circuit, 1961-62; assoc. Hogan & Hartson, Washington, 1962-68, ptnr., 1973—, dir. aviation practice group. Spl. asst. to sec. Dept. Transp., Washington, 1969-70; gen. counsel FAA, Washington, 1970-73; lectr. Georgetown U. Law Ctr., 1965-68; chmn. bd. trustees D.C. Bar Clients Security Trust Fund, 1973-78; gen. counsel Nat. Aeronautic Assn., 1984—. Decisions editor: Va. Law Rev, 1960-61; contbr. articles to legal jours. Bd. govs. Flight Safety Found., 1982-95; mem. exec. com. Princeton U. Alumni Coun., 1984-87; bd. dirs. Nat. Aviation Rsch. Inst., 2001-03. Mem. ABA, Fed. Bar Assn., Raven Soc., Order of Coif. Clubs: Princeton (pres. 1984-86), Aero (pres. 1982) (Washington), Metropolitan, Chevy Chase. Office: Hogan & Hartson 555 13th St NW Washington DC 20004-1161 Office Phone: 202-637-6546. Office Fax: 202-637-5910. Business E-Mail: gucarneal@hhlaw.com.

CARNEIRO, ROBERT LEONARD, curator, anthropologist; b. N.Y.C., June 4, 1927; s. Anthony Mario and Serafina (Garrigo) Carneiro; m. Barbara Ora Bode, Aug. 7, 1980; 1 child, Brett Rodrigo. BA, U. Mich., 1949, MA, 1952, PhD, 1957. Instr. anthropology U. Wis., Madison, 1956-57; asst. curator anthropology Am. Mus. Natural History, N.Y.C., 1957-63, assoc. curator anthropology, 1963-69, curator anthropology, 1969—. Ethnographic field work Kuikuru Indians, Brazil, 1953—54, Brazil, 1975, Amahuaca Indians, Peru, 1960—61, Yanomamo Indians, Venezuela, 1975; vis. prof. UCLA, 1968, Pa. State U., University Park, 1973, U. Victoria, BC, Canada, 1977; adj. prof. anthropology Columbia U., 1992—. Co-editor: Essays in the Science Culture, 1960, Leslie A. White: Ethnological Essays, 1987; editor: Herbert Spencer: The Evolution of Society, 1967; author: The Chiefdom: Precursor of the State, 1981, The Muse of History and the Science of Culture, 2000, Evolutionism in Cultural Anthropology: A Critical History, 2003. Recipient Monks Meml. prize, Inst. Humane Studies, 1973;, Robert L. Carneiro Disting. Univ. professorship in anthropology established in his name U. Mich., 2005. Fellow: AAAS (chmn. nominating com. sect. H 1982—83), Am. Anthrop. Assn., N.Y. Acad. Scis. (vice chmn., chmn. anthropology sect. 1981—83, 1983—85), Linnean Soc. London; mem.: Nat. Acad. Scis. Achievements include research in one of the leading theories of the origin of the state. Office: Am Mus Natural History Central Pk W At 79th St W New York NY 10024 Office Phone: 212-769-5897. E-mail: carneiro@amnh.org.

CARNELL, RICHARD SCOTT, law educator; b. Bronxville, N.Y., June 20, 1953; s. Corbin Scott and Carol Beth (Young) C. BA in History magna cum laude, Yale U., 1975; JD, Harvard U., 1982. Bar: Calif. 1982, U.S. Dist. Ct. (no. dist.) Calif. 1982, U.S. Ct. Appeals (9th cir.) 1984, U.S. Supreme Ct. 1987. Assoc. Broad, Schulz, Larson & Wineberg, San Francisco, 1982-84; atty. Bd. Govs., FRS, Washington, 1984-87; counsel to com. on banking, housing, and urban affairs U.S. Senate, Washington, 1987-88, sr. counsel to com. on banking, housing, and urban affairs, 1989-93; asst. sec. fin. instns. Dept. Treasury, Washington, 1993-99; assoc. prof. law Fordham U., N.Y.C., 1999—. Anglican. Office: Fordham U Sch Law 140 W 62nd St New York NY 10023-7407

CARNELL, TERESA BURT, lawyer; b. Phila., Sept. 15, 1964; BA cum laude, U. Del., 1986; JD, U. Md., 1992. CPA; bar: Md. 1992, U.S. Ct. Appeals, Fourth Cir., U.S. Dist. Ct. (Dist. Md.). Legis. counsel Md. Gen. Assembly's Dept. Legis. Svcs.; assoc. Ballard Spahr Andrews & Ingersoll, LLP; of counsel Venable LLP, Baltimore, 2004—. Mem. Econ. Matters Com.; lectr. in field. Contbr. Named one of Baltimore's Top Lawyers: The Next Generation, Baltimore Mag., 2003; recipient Cunningham Award. Mem.: ABA, Md. State Bar Assn. (co-chair Com. Corp. Laws, formerly, Bus. Law Sect.), Omicron Delta Kappa, Pi Sigma Alpha. Office: Venable LLP 1800 Mercantile Bank & Trust Bldg 2 Hopkins Plaza Baltimore MD 21201 Office Phone: 410-244-7526. Office Fax: 410-244-7742. E-mail: tcarnell@venable.com.*

CARNER, CHARLES ROBERT, JR., screenwriter, director; b. Chgo., Apr. 30, 1957; s. Charles Robert Carner Sr. and Barbara (Shields) Traeger. BA, Columbia Coll., 1978. Asst. to dir. TV show Dummy, Chgo., 1978; casting asst. film My Bodyguard, Chgo., 1979; story editor Tony Bill Prodns., Venice, Calif., 1979-81; screenwriter Fred Weintraub Prodns., Beverly Hills, Calif., 1981-82, Catalina Prodn. Group, Sherman Oaks, Calif., 1983-84, Trian Prodns./CBS-TV, Los Angeles, 1984-85; screenwriter, dir. Tristar Prodns., Los Angeles, 1985-89. Author: (screenplays) Seduced, 1985, Gymkata, 1985, Let's Get Harry, 1986, Blind Fury, 1988, Eyes of a Witness, 1991; writer, dir. TV series Midnight Caller, 1990, Reasonable Doubts, 1992, The Untouchables, 1993, TV movie A Killer Among Friends, 1992, One Woman's Courage, 1994, Vanishing Point, 1997, The Fixer, 1997, Who Killed Atlanta's Children?, 1999, Crossfire Trail, 2000, Crhsitmas Rush, 2002, Judas, 2003. Active East African Wildlife Soc., Kenya, Los Angeles, 1984—. Recipient Best Student Film award Chgo. Internat. Film Festival, 1978. Mem. NRA (life), Writers Guild Am., Sierra Club (life). Roman Catholic. Home and Office: 26039 Mulholland Hwy Calabasas CA 91302-1946

CARNER, GEORGE, foreign service executive, economic strategist; b. N.Y.C., Sept. 2, 1945; s. Joseph Carner Ribalta and Esther Cadefau; m. Michele Colette Delamotte, Apr. 20, 1968; children: Shawn L., Deric A. BA in Internat. Affairs, U. N.C., 1965; postgrad., Inst. Polit. Sci. La Sorbonne, Paris, 1966; MA in Internat. Affairs, George Washington U., 1971; student, Fgn. Svc. Inst., 1975. Internat. trade specialist U.S. Dept. Commerce, Washington, 1967-71; asst. program officer Agy. for Internat. Devel., Rabat, Morocco, 1971-75, dep. program officer Kabul, Afghanistan, 1976-79, program planning officer Manila, 1979-82, officer-in-charge India Washington, 1982-84, chief policy plan/eval. DP/AFR, 1984-86, dep. mission dir. Dakar, Senegal, 1986-88, mission dir. Tunis, Tunisia, 1988-91, Antan, Madagascar, 1991-94, Managua, Nicaragua, 1994-98, Guatemala City, Guatemala, 1998—2002; U.S. rep to OECD/DAC Paris, 2003—. Speaker, panelist Nat. Assn. of Schs. Pub. Affairs and Adminstrn., Honolulu and N.Y.C., 1981, 83, Harvard U., Boston, 1984. Contbr. articles to profl. jours. and procs. Recipient Superior Honor award Agency for Internat. Devel., Washington, 1978, Presdl. Meritorious Svc. awards The White House, 1987, 2000. Mem. Am. Fgn. Svcs. Assn., East-West Ctr., Rotary. Avocations: listening to jazz, art, scuba diving, nature walks. Address: USOECD PSC116 OECD/AID APO 09777 France

CARNES, EDWARD E., federal judge; b. Albertville, Ala., June 3, 1950; BS, U. Ala., Tuscaloosa, 1972; JD cum laude, Harvard U., 1975. Asst. Ala. atty. gen. Office Atty. Gen., 1975—92; cir. judge U.S. Ct. Appeals (11th cir.), Montgomery, Ala., 1992—. Mem.: Jud. Conference Adv. Com on Criminal Rules, 1997- (chmn, 2001-), Fed. Judges Assn. Office: US Courthouse Frank M Johnson Jr Fed Bldg 15 Lee St Ste 408 Montgomery AL 36104-4096 also: Elbert P Tuttle US Ct Appeals Bldg 56 Forsyth St NW Atlanta GA 30303*

CARNES, JAMES EDWARD, retired electronics executive; b. Cumberland, Md., Sept. 27, 1939; s. Roy Clifton and Alta (Wigfield) C.; m. Nancy Louise Zolto, Nov. 27, 1977; 1 child, Gillian. BS in Engring. Sci., Pa. State U., 1961; MA in Elec. Engring., Princeton U., 1967, PhD in Elec. Engring., 1970; PhD (hon.), Thomas Edison State Coll., 1994, Kean U., 1998. Mem. tech. staff RCA Labs., Princeton, NJ, 1969-77; mgr. tech. application RCA Consumer Electronics, Indpls., 1977-80, dir. new products lab, 1980-82, div. v.p. engring., 1982-87; v.p. consumer electronics and info. scis. David Sarnoff Rsch. Ctr. (subs. SRI Internat.), Princeton, NJ, 1987-90, pres., COO, 1990-93, pres., CEO, 1993—2002, sr. advisor, 2002—03; sr. v.p. SRI Internat., 1990-95; chmn. bd. Sensar, Inc., Princeton, NJ, 1992-2000, Orchid Biocomputer Inc., 1995-97, Sarnoff Digital Comm., Inc., 1996-97. Dir. Sarnoff Real Time Inc., Sarif, Inc., Delsys Pharm. Corp., Orchid Biocomputer, Inc., Sarnoff Digital Comms., Nova Corp., SRI Internat., C-Cor Inc., Village at Pa. State, 2004—; short course lectr. UCLA, 1978-81, Am. U. Washington, 1976, Ctrl. Poly. Inst., London, 1974. Contbr. articles to profl. jours. Campaign chmn. Princeton Area United Way, 1992, bd. dirs., 1992-94, 1st v.p., 1993-94; chmn. bd. trustees United Way Greater Mercer County, 1994-96; chmn. sci. adv. bd. Rider Coll., 1990-92; trustee Rider U., 1993-2002, Ind. Coll. Fund. N.J., 1990-96, Thomas Edison State Coll. Found., 1992—, Am. Boychoir Sch., 1995-2002, Regional Planning Partnership, 1997-2002; mem. bd . overseers N.J. Inst. Tech., 1993-98; co-chair Prosperity N.J., 2000-02. Lt. USN, 1961-65. Recipient David Sarnoff Outstanding Achievement award RCA, 1981, Engr. of Yr. award Ctrl. N.J. Engring. Coun., 1991, Humanitarian award NCCJ, 1994, Citizen of Yr. award Mercer County C. of C., 1996, N.J. Tech. Coun. High Tech. Hero award, 1999, N.J. Network Chmn.'s award, 2000; named to Jr. Achievement Bus. Hall of Fame, 1998, Am. Electronics Assn. N.J. High Tech Hall of Fame, 1999, Acad. Digital TV Pioneers, 2002. Fellow IEEE (Centennial medal 1984, Region I award 1993); mem. Am. Electronics Assn., Nat. Acad. Engring., Pa. State U. Alumni Assn. (coun., exec. com., Outanding Engr. Alumnus award 1992, Pres. and Exec. dir. award 1995, Disting. Alumnus award 1996, v.p. 1997-99, pres. 1999-2001, alumni fellow 2003). Achievements include inventor in field. Avocations: flying, golf. Home: 7038 Kingsmill Ct Bradenton FL 34202 Personal E-mail: jim.carnes@psualum.com.

CARNES, JOSEPH SYDNEY, clergyman; b. Memphis, Dec. 2, 1929; s. Samuel Leslye and Marion Rachel (Weaver) C.; m. Annie Frank Rutledge, June 22, 1952; children: Jane Ann, Joseph Sydney Jr., James Rutledge, John David. BS, Memphis State U., 1956; MDiv, Tex. Christian U., 1962, D Ministry, 1979. Ordained to ministry Christian Ch. (Disciples of Christ), 1949; cert. pastoral counselor Parkland Hosp., Dallas. Min. of membership 1st Christian Ch, Eugene, Oreg., 1962-65, sr. min. Nampa, Idaho, 1965-72, Lakeview Christian Ch., Dallas, 1972-81, Oak Cliff Christian Ch., Dallas, 1981—. Pres. Christian Chs. in Idaho, Boise, 1971. Co-author: Communion Meditations, 1966. Founding dir. Nampa Christian Housing, 1967; bd. dirs. Mercy Hosp., Nampa, 1968-72, Idaho Mental Health Dept., 1969-72. Col. Tex. State Guard, chief chaplains, 1972-94. Recipient Disting. Min. of Yr. award, Tex. Christian U., 2003. Mem. Mil. Chaplains Assn. U.S.A. (local pres. 1972—), Masons (33d degree, chaplain 1988-95), Lions (local pres. 1981-82), Order Ea. Star. Republican. Avocations: fishing, hunting, world travel. Home: Wedgewood Twr Apt 615 2511 Wedglea Dr Dallas TX 75211-2041 Office: 1222 W Kiest Blvd Dallas TX 75224-3233 E-mail: jsydney1@aol.com.

CARNES, JULIE ELIZABETH, judge; m. Stephen S. Cowen. AB summa cum laude, U. Ga., 1972, JD magna cum laude, 1975. Bar: Ga. 1975. Law clk. to Hon. Lewis R. Morgan U.S. Ct. Appeals (5th cir.), 1975-77; spl. counsel U.S. Sentencing Commn., 1989, commr., 1990-96; asst. U.S. Atty. U.S. Dist. Ct. (no. dist.) Ga., Atlanta, 1978-90, judge, 1992—. Office: US Courthouse 75 Spring St SW Ste 2167 Atlanta GA 30303-3309

CARNESALE, ALBERT, academic administrator; b. Bronx, NY, July 2, 1936; m. Robin Gerber, Apr. 6, 2002; children: Keith, Kimberly. BME, Cooper Union, 1957; MS, Drexel U., 1961, LLD (hon.), 1993; PhD, NC State U., 1966, LLD (hon.), 1997; AM (hon.), Harvard U., 1979; ScD (hon.), NJ Inst. Tech., 1984. Prof. NC State U., Raleigh, 1962—69, 1972—74; chief Def. Weapons Systems U.S. Arms Control and Disarmament Agy., Washington, 1969—72; prof. John F. Kennedy Sch. of Govt., Harvard U., Cambridge, Mass., 1974—97, acad. dean, 1981—91, dean, 1991—95; provost, Lucius N. Littauer Prof. Pub. Policy and Adminstrn. Harvard U., 1994—97; chancellor UCLA, 1997—. Author: Nuclear Power Issues and Choices: Report of the Nuclear Energy Policy Study Group, 1977, Living with Nuclear Weapons, 1983, Hawks, Doves and Owls: An Agenda for Avoiding Nuclear War, 1985, Superpower Arms Control: Setting the Record Straight, 1987, Fateful Visions: Avoiding Nuclear Catastrophe, 1988; co-author: New Nuclear Nations: Consequences for US Policy, 1993. Recipient Gano Dunn award Outstanding Profl. Achievement, Cooper Union, NYC. Fellow: Am. Acad. Arts and Scis.; mem.: LA World Affairs Coun., Internat. Inst. for Strategic Studies, Coun. on Fgn. Rels. Office: UCLA Office of the Chancellor 405 Hilgard Ave Los Angeles CA 90095-1405*

CARNESI, KENNETH BRIAN, lawyer; b. N.Y.C., May 29, 1953; s. Frank and Angela (Dinardo) C.; m. Daria Mary Chmil, July 22, 1978; children: Kenneth Brian Jr., Katherine Elizabeth. BA, Bklyn. Coll., 1975; MPS, L.I. U., 1977; JD, N.Y. Law Sch., 1982. Bar: N.Y. 1983. Bank officer Chemical Bank, N.Y.C., 1978-82, counsel, 1982-84; ptnr. Carnesi & Assocs., Garden City, N.Y., 1984—; pres. Banfinanz Internat., Inc., N.Y.C., 1996—. Bd. dirs. The Prime Mint, Inc., N.Y.C., FAS Fragrances, Inc., N.Y.C., Granite State Mint, Inc., Amherst, N.H. Contbr. articles to profl. jours. Recipient Elsberg award, N.Y. Law Sch., N.Y.C., 1982, Human Rights Jour. award, 1982, Businessman of Yr. award, U.S. Presdl. Bus. Commn., 2003. Mem. Nassau County Bar Assn., ABA, Am. Mgmt. Assn. Republican. Roman Catholic. Office: 1225 Franklin Ave Garden City NY 11530 Office Phone: 516-227-0500. E-mail: kcarnesi@hotmail.com.

CARNESOLTAS, ANA-MARIA, lawyer; b. Havana, Cuba, Feb. 9, 1948; came to U.S., 1962; d. Manuel Ramon and Zenaida de las Mercedes C.; 1 child, Caroline. BA, U. Calif., Santa Barbara, 1970; JD, Loyola U., L.A., 1978. Bar: Calif. 1978, Fla. 1979. Dep probation officer Probation Dept., Santa Barbara, Calif., 1970-73; personnel analyst Dept. Personnel, L.A., 1973-77; dep. dist. atty. Dist. Atty.'s Office, L.A., 1978-80; asst. U.S. atty. U.S. Atty.'s Office, Miami, Fla., 1980-82; pvt. practice law, Miami, 1982-83, Coral Gables, Fla., 1985-89; asst. city atty. City Atty.'s Office, Miami, 1983-85; judge Dade (Fla.) County Ct., 1989-93; pvt. practice, 1993-2002; atty. Englander & Fischer, PA, 2004—; lectr. YMCA, Miami, 1983-89; adj. prof. Fla. Internat. U.; prof. Miami-Dade C.C., 1989-92; hearing officer Dade County Pub. Schs., Miami, 1985-89; legal commentator Sta. TeleMiami, Fla., 1997—; legal commenrator WCMQ, Miami, 1993-97. Bd. dirs. Am. Heart Assn., M iami, 1983-86, YWCA, 1985-89, Alzheimer's Disease and Related Disorders Assn., 1987. Named Disting. Advocate, Loyola Law Sch., 1978. Mem. ATLA, St. Petersburg Bar Assn., Nat. Assn. Women Judges (outreach com., task force on minority concerns, internat. cmty. outreach com.), Conf. County Ct. Judges (edn. com., small claims com., civic proc. rules com.), Calif. Probation Parole and Corrections Assn. (v.p. 1972-73), Cuban Am. Attys. Council (sec. 1979-80), Cuban Am. Bar Assn. (dir. 1983, 88, sec. 1984), Dade County Bar Assn., ABA, Fla. Assn. Women Lawyers, Fed. Bar Assn., Latin Bus. and Profl. Women's Club (pres. 1984-85, v.p.), Cuban Women's Club. Republican. Roman Catholic. Office: 1900 S Bayshore Dr Miami FL Office Phone: 727-898-7210. E-mail: amc4/aw@aol.com, acarnesoltas@efpalaw.com.

CARNEY, BRADFORD GEORGE YOST, lawyer, educator; b. Oct. 25, 1950; s. Blanchard Donald and Anne Carolyn (Yost) C.; m. Gail Elaine Hasson, Jan. 6, 1973: children: Jason Bradford, Brandon Burroughs. BA, Washington Coll., 1972; JD, U. Balt., 1976. Bar: Md. 1977, U.S. Dist. Ct. Md. 1978, U.S. Supreme Ct. 1982. Ptnr. Callahan, Calwell, Laudeman, Balt., 1982—87, Weinberg and Green, Balt., 1987—96; of counsel Royston, Mueller, McLean & Reid LLP, Towson, Md., 1996—. Asst. prof. law Villa Julie Coll., Stevenson, Md., 1983-97, assoc. prof., 1997-2000, adj. prof. law, 2000—. Bd. trustees Boys' Latin Sch., Md., 1988-93. Mem. ABA, Nat. Assn. Criminal Def. Lawyers, Md. State Bar Assn., Md. Criminal Def. Attys. Assn., Balt. County Bar Assn., Balt. City Bar Assn., U. Balt. Alumni Assn. (bd. govs. 1984-87), Boys' Latin Sch. Alumni Assn. (bd. dirs. 1983-, pres. 1986-88). Home: 474 Five Farms Ln Lutherville Timonium MD 21093-2954 Office: Royston Mueller McLean & Reid LLP 102 W Pennsylvania Ave Towson MD 21204-4526 Office Phone: 410-823-1800. Personal E-mail: bcarney@rmmr.com.

CARNEY, JOHN C., JR., lieutenant governor; b. Claymont, Del. m. Tracey Quillen; children: Sam, James. BA in English, Dartmouth Coll., 1978; MPA, U. Del. Assoc. dir. Cath. Youth Orgn., Wilmington; staff asst. U.S. Senator Joseph R. Biden, 1986-89; dep. chief adminstrv. officer New Castle County, 1989-94, acting dir. pub. works; dep. chief of staff Gov. Carper, 1994-97; sec. of fin. State of Del., 1997-2000, lt. gov. Dover, 2000—. Bd. dirs. Cath. Youth Orgn. Democrat. Office: Tatnall Bldg Dover DE 19901

CARNEY, JOHN F., III, academic administrator; BA in Civil Engring., Merrimack Coll., 1963; MA, Northwestern U., 1963, PhD, 1966. Rsch. scientist Northwestern U., 1966; asst. prof. U. Conn., 1966—69, assoc. prof., 1969—74, prof., 1974—81; prof., head Auburn U., 1981—83; prof. civil engring. Vanderbilt U., 1983—96, assoc. dean for grad. affairs, 1993—96, assoc. dean for rsch. and grad. affairs, 1993—96; provost, v.p. for acad. affairs Worcester Poly. Inst., Mass., 1996—2005; chancellor U. Mo., Rolla, 2005—. Editor: Effectiveness of Highway Safety Improvements, 1986. Mem.: ASCE, Soc. Automotive Engrs. Office: U Mo 1870 Miner Circle Rolla MO 65409 Office Phone: 573-341-4416. E-mail: jfc3@umr.edu.*

CARNEY, JOSEPH BUCKINGHAM, lawyer; b. Greensburg, Ind., July 8, 1928; s. Edward O. and Grace Rebecca (Buckingham) C.; m. Constance J. Caylor, July 8, 1950; children: Elizabeth, Joseph Buckingham Jr., Julia, Sarah. AB, DePauw U., 1950; LLB, Harvard U., 1953. Bar: D.C. 1953, Ind. 1953, U.S. Dist. Ct. (so. dist.) Ind. 1953, U.S. Supreme Ct. 1957, U.S. Ct. Appeals (7th cir.) 1961; ind. cert. mediator. Assoc. Hogg, Peters & Leonard, Ft. Wayne, Ind., 1953-54, Baker & Daniels, Indpls., 1957-62, ptnr., 1992—95, mem. mgmt. com., 1993-94, sec., 1994, of counsel, 1996—. Mem. lawyers com. Nat. Ctr. State Cts., Williamsburg, Va., 1985—; assoc. Environ. Law Inst., Washington. Chmn. bd. dirs. Parkinson Awareness Assn. Ctrl. Ind., Inc.; past pres. Interfaith Homes, Inc., Indpls.; past chmn., elder Northwood Christian Ch., Indpls. 1st lt. U.S. Army, 1954-57. Recipient Disting. Alumni award DePauw U., 1984. Mem. ABA, Ind. Bar Assn., Indpls. Bar Assn., Am. Judicature Soc., 7th Cir. Bar Assn. (pres. 1983-84), Univ. Club, Columbia Club, Contemporary, Lawyers Club Indpls. (past pres.), Phi Eta Sigma, Phi Gamma Delta (bd. dirs. 1974-78, sec. 1976-78, pres. 1980-82), Phi Gamma Delta Ednl. Found. (bd. dirs., pres. 1996-98). Avocations: scuba diving, travel, photography. Office: Baker & Daniels 300 N Meridian St Ste 2700 Indianapolis IN 46204-1782 Office Phone: 317-237-0300.

CARNEY, J.W., JR., lawyer; b. New Bedford, Mass., Apr. 28, 1952; s. James William and Lucille (Parent) C.; m. Joy B. Rosen; children: Julia, Nathaniel. BA, Holy Cross Coll., 1975; JD, Boston Coll., 1978. Bar: Mass. 1978, U.S. Dist. Ct. Mass. 1979, U. S. Ct. Appeals (1st cir.) 1982, U.S. Supreme Ct. 1991. Trial lawyer Mass. Pub. Defenders Com., Boston, 1978-83; asst. dist. atty. Middlesex Count Dist. Atty's. Office, Cambridge, Mass., 1983-88; ptnr. Carney & Bassil, Boston, 1989—. Chmn. adv. bd. Nat. Mock Trial Competition, Boston, 1987—. Contrbg. author: Massachusetts Courtroom Evidence, 1988, Massachusetts Criminal Defense, 1990. Fellow Am. Coll. Trial Lawyers; mem. Nat. Assn. Trial Lawyers, Mass. Assn. Criminal Defense Lawyers, Mass. Bar Assn., Boston Bar Assn., Boston Coll. Law Sch. Alumni Assn. (sec. 1987-89, treas. 1989—), Lawyers Assistance Strike Force (co-chmn. 1992-), Fed. Ct. Criminal Justice Act Bd (2001-), Mass. Judicial Nominating Com. (2002-, vice chmn. 2002-2003), Women's Lunch Place (Homeless Shelter) (bd. dirs. 1996-) . Avocations: new wave music, playing basketball, watching the Boston Celtics, Horace Rumpole. Office: Carney & Bassil 20 Park Plz Ste 800 Boston MA 02116-4308 Office Fax: 617-338-5587. Business E-Mail: jcarney@CarneyBassil.com.

CARNEY, MARGARET LOU, historian, curator; b. Iowa City, Apr. 30, 1949; d. Robert Gibson and Dorothy (Briscoe) Carney; m. William John Walker, Dec. 28, 2002. BA in Anthropology, U. Iowa, 1971, cert. in secondary tchg., 1972, MA in Art History, 1981; MPhil in Art History, U. Kans., 1986, PhD in Asian Art History, 1989. Collections mgr., asst. prof. U. Oreg. Mus. Art, Eugene, 1986—87; dir., chief curator Blanden Meml. Art Mus., Ft. Dodge, Iowa, 1987—90, Schein-Joseph Internat. Mus. Ceramic Art, Alfred, NY, 1991—2002, Ross C. Purdy Mus. Ceramics, Westerville, Ohio, 2002—04; curator Blair Mus. Lithophanes, Toledo, 2004—. Mus. cons. Herbert Hoover Presdl. Libr. and Mus., West Branch, Iowa, 1980—81; tchr. Taipei (Taiwan) Lang. Inst., 1981, Zhengzhou U., Henan, China, 1983—84; asst. prof. art history Alfred U., 1991—2002; cons. Baggs Meml. Libr., 1997, Ohio State U., 2002, Eva Ziesel, 1998, MacKenzie-Childs, Ltd., 2000, Axner Co., Inc., 2000, Corning, Inc., 2001, Virginia A. Groot Found., 2001—02; vis. faculty Ohio State U., Columbus, 2002, Columbus, 03; adj. faculty Bowling Green (Ohio) State U., 2004. Contbr. articles to profl. jours.; mem. editl. bd. Interpreting Ceramics, 2000—. Founding com. mem. Save Our Archtl. Resources, Ft. Dodge, 1989—90; mem. cmty. attitude com. Ft. Dodge C. of C., 1989—90; mem. design com. Ft. Dodge Main St. Program, 1988—90; bd. dirs., v.p. Sta. KTPR Pub. Radio Cmty. Adv. Bd., Ft. Dodge, 1988, pres., 1989—90; panel mem. Iowa Arts Coun., 1987—90; bd. dirs. Iowa Arts Coalition, 1990. Recipient Chancellor's award for Excellence in Profl. Svc., SUNY, 1999, Hon. Mention, Am. Assn. Mus. Publ. Design Competition, 1999; grantee, Bei Shan Tang Found., 1984—85; Nat. Resource fellow, U. Kans., 1982, 1986—87, Kress Found. fellow, 1982, Smithsonian Sr. fellow, Renwick Gallery, 1993—94, Smithsonian grantee, 1999, Study Abroad scholar, U. Kans., 1983—84, 1984—85, Fulbrate-Hays Rsch. grantee, 1986—87, Arthur and Lea Powell Found. grantee, 1992—98, Smithsonian Vis. Scholar Rsch. grantee, Nat. Mus. Am. Art, 1994, Doty Rsch. grantee, Tile Heritage Found., 1998—99, 2002—03. Fellow: Am. Ceramic Soc. (program co-chair design divsn. 1995—96, co-chair elect 1996—97, trustee, dir. 1996—2001, mem. ceramic mus. com. 1997—2000, co-chair com. outreach 2001—04, mem. W. David Kingery award com. 2003—); mem.: Societé Internationale de la Ceramique, Nat. Coun. Edn. Ceramic Arts, Coll. Art Assn., Assn. Asian Studies, Archeol. Inst. Am., Am. Ceramic Cir. (Rsch. grantee 1991—92), Am. Assn. Mus. Avocations: bassoon, gardening, ice skating. Home: 2364 Barrington Dr Toledo OH 43606 Office: Blair Mus Lithophanes 5403 Elmer Dr Toledo OH 43615 Office Phone: 419-245-1356. Office Fax: 419-535-5770. Personal E-mail: margaretcarney@sbcglobal.net. Business E-Mail: mcarney@lithophanemuseum.org.

CARNEY, MICHAEL, orchestra leader; b. N.Y.C., Nov. 27, 1937; s. Edward M. and Jacqueline (Soutar) C.; m. Lisa Marshall, May 9, 1997. BA, Northwestern U., 1959. Securities analyst Butcher & Sherrerd Co., Phila., 1964-66; investment mgr. Barnes & Tucker Co., Haverford, Pa., 1966; orchestra leader Michael Carney Music, N.Y.C., 1970—. Mem. vis. com. Northwestern U. Sch. Music., Evanston, Ill., 1983—. Trustee Boys Club N.Y., 1981—. Mem.: Bohemian Club, River Club. Republican. Office: 305 Madison Ave Ste 449 New York NY 10165 Office Phone: 212-353-5301.

CARNEY, RITA J., educational association administrator; b. Hoboken, N.J., July 17, 1941; BA, Beaver Coll., Glenside, Pa., 1962; MA, Seton Hall U., South Orange, N.J., 1965; EdD, Columbia U., 1977; MA, Princeton Theol. Sem., 1980. Tchr. Latin and English, Phillipsburg (N.J.) Pub. Schs., 1962-65; guidance counselor Jefferson Twp. Pub. Schs., Oak Ridge, NJ, 1965-67; admin. asst. Supt./H.S. prin. Madison Twp. Pub. Schs., Old Bridge, NJ, 1967—70; program devel. N.J. Dept. Edn., Trenton, 1970—75; county supt. schs. Middlesex County, NJ, 1975—80; N.J. asst. commr. for rsch., planning and evaluation; assoc. v.p. for acad. adminstrn. Temple U., Phila.; asst. to pres., v.p. for acad. and student affairs Georgian Ct. Coll., Lakewood, NJ, 1990—2001. Lectr. presenter profl and ch related orgns; consult planning and orgn analysis. Pres. Diocesan Pastoral Coun., Trenton, Blessed Sacrament Parish Coun., Trenton, NJ, Hiltonia Civic Assn., Trenton; chmn. exec. com. Mercy Higher Edn. Colloquium, 1994—2000. Mem.: Soc Col and Univ Planning (state rep 1996—2000). Home: 32 N Avon Dr Jackson NJ 08527-3975 E-mail: ritacarney@care2.com.

CARNEY, ROBERT THOMAS, lawyer; b. Youngstown, Ohio, Mar. 28, 1947; s. Thomas P. and Mildred B. (Keeling) C.; m. Victoria L. Schrecengost, May 21, 1977; children: Brian, Michael. BS in Physics, Northwestern U., 1969; JD, Georgetown U., 1972. Bar: Ohio 1972, D.C. 1974, U.S. Ct. Appeals (fed. cir.), U.S. Ct. Fed. Claims, U.S. Tax Court, U.S. Patent and Trademark

Office, U.S. Supreme Ct. Law clk. U.S. Dist. Ct., Cleve., 1972-73; trial atty. tax divsn U.S. Dept. Justice, Washington, 1973-79; ptnr. tax atty. Lee, Toomey & Kent, Washington, 1979-88, Dow, Lohnes & Albertson, Washington, 1988-90, Rogers & Wells, Washington, 1990-96; ptnr. Fulbright & Jaworski, Washington, 1996-98, Ernst & Young, Washington, 1998—. Adj. prof. Georgetown U. Law Sch., Washington, 1987—. Mem. Murdoch Inn of Ct. (master, sec.-treas.). Office: Ernst & Young 1225 Connecticut Ave NW Ste 700 Washington DC 20036-2621 Office Phone: 202-327-6420. Business E-Mail: robert.carney@ey.com.

CARNEY, ROGER FRANCIS XAVIER, retired military officer; b. Bklyn., Oct. 20, 1933; s. Frank Clement and Clara Helen (Muller) Carney; m. Linda Ann Bowlus, Aug. 11, 1963 (div. Mar. 1993); children: Kevin James, Stephen Jason, Brian Andrew. BS, Purdue U., 1960, MS in Indsl. Adminstrn., 1963; grad., U.S. Army Command and Gen. Staff Coll., 1975, U.S. Army War Coll., 1979; MA, U. Conn., 1992. Commd. 2d lt. U.S. Army, 1960, advanced through grades to lt. col., 1976; comdr. 583d Ordnance Co., Muenster, Germany, 1969-72; R&D coord. Army Material Comman Field Office, Kirtland AFB, N.Mex., 1972-74; logistic staff officer CENTAG Signal Support GP (NATO), Seckenheim, Germany, 1975-78; chief nuc. weapons logistic element G4 CENTAG (NATO), Seckenheim, 1978; comdr. 15th Ordnance Bn., Darmstadt, West Germany, 1978-80; prof. mil. sci. head dept. Worcester (Mass.) Poly. Inst., 1980-84; prof. mil. sci., head dept. Fitchburg (Mass.) State Coll., 1980-84, Nichols Coll., Dudley, Mass., 1982-84, dean student affairs, 1985-98, dir. Robert C. Fischer Inst., 1998—2004; ret., 2004. Mem. Worcester Com. Fgn. Rels., Worcester Econ. Club. Decorated Legion of Merit, Bronze Star. Mem.: DAV, Purdue Alumni Assn., Mil. Officers Assn. Am., U. Conn. Alumni Assn., Assn. Former Intelligence Officers, Assn. U.S. Army, Am. Legion, Pi Lambda Theta, Alpha Sigma Pi (pres. Purdue U. chpt. 1959—60). Democrat. Home: 7 Thayer Pond Dr Apt 11 North Oxford MA 01537-1134 Personal E-mail: carney33@earthlink.net.

CARNEY, STEPHEN PATRICK, insurance company executive; b. Morristown, NJ, Aug. 14, 1950; s. Stephen M. and June K. Carney; m. Patricia Ann Davis, Oct. 29, 1989. BS, Coll. William & Mary, 1972, JD, 1980. Bar: Md. 1981. Law clk. to Hon. J. Calvitt Clarke, Jr. U.S. Dist. Ct. (ea. dist.) Va., Norfolk, 1980-81; labor assoc. Venable, Baetjer & Howard, Balt., 1981-84, assoc. real estate, 1984-88; gen. counsel, sec. Med. Mut. Liability Ins. Soc. Md., Hunt Valley, 1988-89, v.p., gen. counsel, sec., 1989-99, sr. v.p., gen. counsel, sec., 1999—. Bd. dirs. Med-Lantic Mgmt. Svcs. Inc., Health Liability Alliance; mem. Gov.'s Adv. Com. on Practice Parameters, Balt., 1993—. Bd. dirs. Md. chpt. March of Dimes, Balt., 1990—, mem. exec. com., chair pub. affairs com., 1993—2003, chair bd. dirs., 2003—. Recipient Alumni Svc. award Coll. William & Mary, 1998; named Pub. Affairs Com. Mem. of Yr. March of Dimes, White Plains, N.Y., 1998. Mem. ABA, Am. Corp. Counsel Assn., Physician Insurers Assn. Am. (legal sect.), Md. State Bar Assn., William & Mary Law Sch. Found. (bd. dirs., pres. 2003-). Avocations: sailing, golf, travel, classic cars. Office: Med Mut Liability Ins Soc Md 225 Internat Cir Hunt Valley MD 21030

CARNEY, THOMAS DALY, lawyer; b. Detroit, Mar. 28, 1947; s. William C. and Mary L. (Daly) C.; m. Anne C. Filson; children: Thomas, David, Kristen. BA, U. Mich., 1969, JD, 1972. Bar: Mich. 1972. Assoc., Cross, Wrock, Miller & Vieson, Detroit, 1973-77, mem. firm, 1977-79; corp. counsel Hoover Universal, Inc., Ann Arbor, Mich., 1979-81, sec., gen. counsel, 1981-83, v.p., sec., gen. counsel, 1983-86; counsel Dickinson, Wright, Moon, Van Dusen & Freeman, Detroit, 1986-87, ptnr., 1988—94; named v.p., gen. counsel, sec. Borders Group Inc., Ann Arbor, Mich., 1994, now sr. v.p, gen. counsel, sec. Mem. ABA, Mich. Bar Assn.; Am. Soc. Corp. Secretaries, Assn. Corp. Counsel. Club: Barton Hills Country (Ann Arbor). Office: Borders Group Inc 100 Phoenix Dr Ann Arbor MI 48108

CARNEY, WILLIAM PATRICK, medical educator; b. Dillon, Mont., July 1, 1938; s. Thomas James and Helen Catherine (Ballard) C.; children: Christopher Patrick, Mark Daniel; m. Sharon Loreta Sonnek, Aug. 14, 1965. BA, St. Thomas U., Kenmore, Wash., 1960; BS, Western Mont. U., 1962; PhD, U. Mont., 1967; MPH, Johns Hopkins U., 1976. Cert. secondary tchr. in biol. scis. Rsch. assoc. Minot (N.D.) State U., 1967-69; commd. lt. USN, 1969, advanced through grades to capt., 1986; rsch. parasitologist Naval Med. Rsch. Inst., Bethesda, Md., 1969-70, 74-75; dir. parasitology dept. Naval Med. Rsch. Unit No. 2, Jakarta, Indonesia, 1970-74, dept. dir. Taipei, Taiwan, 1976-79, lab. and scientific dir. Jakarta, 1979-81; program mgr. Naval Med. Rsch. Devel. Command, Bethesda, 1981-84; lab. dir. Naval Bioscis. Lab., Oakland, Calif., 1984-87; prof., dir. grad. program Uniformed Svcs. U., Bethesda, 1987-91, ret., 1991; project mgr. schistosomasis rsch. project in Cairo Med. Svc. Corp. Internat., Arlington, Va., 1991-95; prof., dep. chair dept. preventive medicine Uniformed Svcs. U., Bethesda, Md., 1995—. Exec. com. bd. dirs. Gorgas Meml. Inst., Bethesda; cons. Vector Biology and Control Project, Arlington, 1989-94, Am. Inst. Biol. Scis., Washington, 1987—. Contbr. articles to profl. jours. Smokejumper USFS, 1962-64; adult leader Boy Scouts Am., Taipei, 1976-79. Decorated Legion of Merit. Mem. Am. Soc. Parasitologists, Am. Soc. Tropical Medicine and Hygiene, Helminthological Soc. Washington, Sigma Xi, Phi Sigma. Republican. Roman Catholic. Avocations: scuba diving, auto repair, carpentry, masonry, welding. Office: Uniformed Svcs U Dept Preventive Medicine 4301 Jones Bridge Rd Bethesda MD 20814-4712 E-mail: pcarney@usuhs.mil, pat-and-sharon@erols.com.

CARNICELLI, MATTHEW JOHN, literary agent, editor, writer; b. Lebanon, N.H., Aug. 8, 1964; s. Thomas Anthony Carnicelli and Anne Lindsay Calver, Pamela Stone (Stepmother); life ptnr. Brian Michael Lange. BA, Wash. U., St. Louis, 1986; MA, U. Toronto, 1990. Editor Penguin USA, N.Y.C., 1990—95, sr. editor, 1995—97, Contemporary Books, N.Y.C., 1997—2000; exec. editor McGraw-Hill, N.Y.C., 2000—04; pres. Carnicelli Lit. Mgmt., N.Y.C., 2004—. Home: 7 Kipp Rd Rhinebeck NY 12572 Office: Carnicelli Literary Mgmt 108 E 17th St New York NY 10003 Office Phone: 212-979-0101. E-mail: matthew@carnicellilit.com.

CARNICERO, JORGE EMILIO, aeronautical engineer, transportation executive; b. Buenos Aires, July 17, 1921; came to U.S., 1942, naturalized, 1950; s. Alberto and Ana (Sulimeau) C.; m. Jacqueline Joanne Damman, Feb. 22, 1946; children— Jacqueline Denise, Jorge Jay. Student, U. LaPlata, Argentina, 1939—41, Rensselaer Poly. Inst., 1945. Chief engr. Dodero Airlines, Argentina, 1945, Flota Aerea Mercante, Argentina, 1945-46; v.p. Air Carrier Svc. Corp., Washington, 1946, exec. v.p., 1947-55, chmn. bd. dirs., dir., 1955-88; ret., 1988. Past chmn., bd. Dyncorp (formerly Calif. Ea. Aviation, then Dynalectron Corp.); pres., bd. dirs. Blue Cove, Inc., N.Y., Inter-Properties, Inc., Del., Trans-Am. Aero. Corp., Del., Round Hill Devel. Ltd., Jamaica. Bd. visitors Sch. Fgn. Service, Georgetown U., Washington; mem. council Rensselaer Poly. Inst., Troy, N.Y., mem. adv. bd. mech., aero. and mechanics dept. Fellow Royal Aero. Soc.; mem. Argentine-Am. C. of C. (bd. dirs.), Univ. Club, Met. Club, Congl. Country Club, Georgetown Club. Home: 3949 52nd St NW Washington DC 20016-1925 Office: 1313 Dolley Madison Blvd Mc Lean VA 22101-3926 Office Phone: 703-556-4412. Personal E-mail: jccarjc@aol.com.

CARNIE, KAY C., artist, educator; b. NYC, June 8, 1942; d. James Ogden and Allegra MacCulloch Combes; m. Donald Ross Carnie, June 6, 1964; children: David, Michael. BA, Fla. So. Coll., 1964; MA, San Jose State U., 1988, MFA, 1993. Profl. artist, Cupertino, Calif., 1993—; instr. Palo Alto Art Ctr., Calif., 1996—99, San Mateo Cmty. Edn., Calif., 1999; tchr. Coll. of San Mateo, 2000—. Juror fine arts Santa Clara County Fair, San Jose, 1991, 97. Splash 4, 1996, Painting Great Pictures from Photographs, 1999, Capturing Texture, 2002, Splash 8, 2004. Mem. Nat. Watercolor Soc. (signature), Midwest Watercolor Soc. (signature), Calif. Watercolor Assn. (signature), Watercolor West (juried mem.). Avocations: piano, photography, travel. Home and Office: 10439 Heney Creek Pl Cupertino CA 95014 Personal E-mail: kccarnie@aol.com.

CARNIOL, PAUL J., plastic and reconstructive surgeon, otolaryngologist; b. NYC, Sept. 26, 1951; s. David A. and Diane (Hadler) C.; m. Renie Rich, Jan. 3, 1976; children: Michael P., Alan R., Eric T. BA, NYU, 1972; MD, U. Pa., 1976. Diplomate Am. Bd. Otolaryngology, Am Bd. Facial Plastic and Reconstructive Surgery, Am. Bd. Cosmetic Surgery, Am. Bd. Med. Examiners. Resident in surgery U. Pa., Phila., 1976-77, resident in plastic and reconstructive surgery, 1981-83; resident in surgery North Shore U. Hosp., Manhasset, NY, 1977-78; resident in surgery and otolaryngology, clin. tchg. fellow Harvard Med. Sch., Boston, 1978-81; attending plastic surgery, head and neck surgery Overlook Hosp., Summit, NJ, 1983—; clin. assoc. prof. U. Medicine and Dentistry of NJ, Newark. Cons. aesthetic, laser and reconstructive and plastic surgery; instr. courses on lasers in plastic surgery, facial rejuvenation; chief sect. otolaryngology Overlook Hosp., 1992-97; police surgeon, Summit and New Providence, NJ; mem. bd. health New Providence, 2002—, emergency response team, 2003—; lectr., presenter in field. Editor: Laser Skin Rejuvenation, 1998, Facial Rejuvenation, 2001; spl. editor: Am. Jour. Cosmetic Surgery, mem. editl. bd.: Jour. Cosmetic and Laser Therapy; contbr. articles to profl. jours. Interviewer for admissions com. U. Pa., Phila., 1987—. Recipient Cmty. Svc. award, Ciba-Geigy, Summit, 1978, Found. award, NYU, 1972, Alumni Gold Medal award, 1972, Silver Shield, PBA 55, 2003. Fellow: ACS (coun. mem. NJ chpt. 2004—), Am. Acad. Cosmetic Surgery, Am. Acad. Facial Plastic and Reconstructive Surgery (dir. courses lasers, facial plastic surgery and cosmetic surgery 1996—98, care com., chmn. new tech. and surg. devices com. 1998—2000, v.p. R & D 2001—03), Am. Acad. Otolaryngology, Nead and Neck Surgery; mem.: AMA, Med. Soc. N.J. (trustee 2005—), Union County Med. Soc. (planning com. 1986—89, pres. 2003—04, chmn. program com., exec. com., bd. dirs.), NJ Acad. Otolaryngology (pres. 1993—96, 1997—), NJ Med. Soc. (coun. on med. svcs.), Internat. Soc. Cosmetic Laser Surgery (v.p. 2001—03), Phi Beta Kappa. Achievements include included in Top Cosmetic Surgeons in N.J., N.J. Life Magazine and Castle Connelly Medical, Ltd., 2004. Avocations: golf, fishing, bicycling, Karate. Office: 33 Overlook Rd Ste 202 Summit NJ 07901-3562 Office Phone: 908-598-1400.

CARNOCHAN, WALTER BLISS, retired humanities educator; b. N.Y.C., Dec. 20, 1930; s. Gouverneur Morris and Sibyll Baldwin (Bliss) C.; m. Nancy Powers Carter, June 25, 1955 (div. 1978); children— Lisa Powers, Sarah Bliss, Gouverneur Morris, Sibyll Carter; m. Brigitte Hoy Fields, Sept. 16, 1979. AB, Harvard, 1953, A.M., 1957, PhD, 1960. Asst. dean freshmen Harvard U., 1954-56; successively instr., asst. prof., assoc. prof., prof. English, Stanford (Calif.) U., 1960-94, prof. emeritus, 1994—, chmn. dept. English, 1971-73, dean grad. studies, 1975-80, vice provost, 1976-80, dir. Stanford Humanities Ctr., 1985-91, Anthony P. Meier Family prof. humanities, 1988-91, Richard W. Lyman prof. humanities, 1993-94, Richard W. Lyman prof. emeritus, 1994—, acting dir. Stanford Humanities Ctr., 1999. Mem. overseers com. to visit Harvard Coll, 1979-85, mem. bd. advisors Ehrenpreis Ctr. for Swift Studies, 1984—. Author: Lemuel Gulliver's Mirror for Man, 1968, Confinement and Flight: An Essay on English Literature of the 18th Century, 1977, Gibbon's Solitude: The Inward World of the Historian, 1987, The Battleground of the Curriculum: Liberal Education and American Experience, 1993, Momentary Bliss: An American Memoir, 1999. Trustee Mills Coll., 1978-85, Athenian Sch., 1975-88, Berkeley (Calif.) Art Mus., 1983-96, 98-2001. Home: 138 Cervantes Rd Portola Valley CA 94028-7725 Business E-Mail: carnoch@stanford.edu.

CARO, IVOR, dermatologist; b. Johannesburg, June 2, 1946; came to U.S., 1975; s. Herbert and Rachel (Eisenstein) C.; m. Sheryl Helaine Marsden, Dec. 14, 1969; children: Howard Seth, Glen. MB, BCh, U. Witwatersrand, 1969. Diplomate, Am. Bd. Dermatology. Resident U. Witwatersrand, Johannesburg, 1971—74; fellow St. John's Hosp., London, 1974—76; asst. prof. U. N.C., Chapel Hill, 1975—78; pvt. practice Seattle, 1978—99; dir. internat. program dermatology Harvard Med. Sch., Boston, 1999—2003; dir. dermatol. clin. investigation unit Mass. Gen. Hosp./ Harvard Med. Sch., 2000—03; med. dir. dermatology Genentech, South San Francisco, 2003—. Clin. prof. U. Wash., Seattle, 1978-99; chief of dermatology, attending dermatologist Va. Mason Med. Ctr., Seattle, 1978-99. Contbr. to profl. publs. and textbooks. Fellow: Am. Acad. Dermatology; mem.: Pacific Dermatol. Soc., New Eng. Dermatol. Soc., Noah Worcester Dermatol. Soc. (sec., treas. 2000—04, pres. 2004—05), Seattle Dermatol. Soc. (pres. 1987—88). Office: Genentech 1 DNA Way MS 84 South San Francisco CA 94080 Office Phone: 650-225-6370. E-mail: icaro@gene.com.

CARO, ROBERT ALLAN, author; b. NYC; s. Benjamin and Cele (Mendelow) C.; m. Ina Joan Sloshberg, June 9, 1957; 1 child, Chase Arthur. AB cum laude, Princeton U., 1957; DLitt (hon.), Merrimack Coll., 1983, L.I. U., 2003; LHD (hon.), New Sch. for Social Rsch., 1997. Reporter New Brunswick Home News, NJ, 1957-59, Newsday, Garden City, NY, 1960-66; Nieman fellow Harvard U., Cambridge, Mass., 1965-66. Historian, biographer, 1967—. Author: The Power Broker: Robert Moses and the Fall of New York, 1974 (Pulitzer prize for biography 1975, Francis Parkman prize Soc. Am. Historians 1975, Selected by Modern Libr. as 1 of 100 Best Nonfiction Books Written in English during the 20th Century), The Years of Lyndon Johnson: The Path to Power, 1982 (Nat. Book Critics award for biography 1983, Tex. Inst. Arts and Letters award for non-fiction 1983), The Years of Lyndon Johnson: Means of Ascent, 1990 (Nat. Book Critics Cir. award for biography 1991), The Years of Lyndon Johnson: Master of the Senate, 2002 (Nat. Book award for non-fiction 2002, Pulitzer prize for biography 2003, L.A. Times Book prize for biography 2003, Carl Sandburg award in Lit. 2004, award Chgo. Pub. Libr. Found. 2003). Bd. dir. Fund for City NY, NY Soc. Libr., Theatre for New Audience. Recipient Soc. of Silurians award, 1964, Deadline Club, 1964, 65, spl. citation NY chpt. AIA, 1975, H.L. Mencken prize Free Press Assn., 1983, award in lit. Am. Acad. and Inst. Arts and Letters, 1986, Lifetime Achievement in Arts award Guild Hall Acad. Arts, 1992, Pulitzer Prize for biography, 1975, 2003; co-recipient ann. polit. book award Washington Monthly, 1975, 83, 91. Fellow Soc. Am. Historians (Francis Parkman prize); mem. Authors Guild Am. (bd. dir. 1976—, pres. 1980-82), PEN Am. Ctr. (mem. exec. bd. 1986-88, v.p. 1989-92), Century Club. Office: Robert A Caro Inc 250 W 57th St Ste 2215 New York NY 10107-2209 Office Phone: 212-582-4845. E-mail: Randeltracy@aol.com.

CARO, WILLIAM ALLAN, dermatologist, educator, pathologist; b. Chgo., Aug. 16, 1934; s. Marcus Rayner and Adeline Beatrice (Cohen) Caro; m. Ruth Fruchtlander, June 15, 1959 (dec.); children: Mark Stephen, David Edward; m. Joan Peters, Oct. 18, 1997. Student, U. Mich., 1952-55; BS in Medicine, U. Ill., 1957, MD, 1959. Intern Cook County Hosp., Chgo., 1959-60; resident in internal medicine U. Ill. Rsch. and Ednl. Hosps., 1960-61; resident in dermatology Hosp. U. Pa., 1961-62, 64-66; Earl D. Osborne fellow dermal pathology Armed Forces Inst. Pathology, Washington, 1966-67; asst. in medicine U. Ill. Coll. Medicine, 1960-61; asst. instr. U. Pa. Med. Sch., 1961-62, 64-66; from asst. prof. to assoc. prof. dermatology Northwestern U. Med. Sch., 1967—81, prof., 1981—; pvt. practice specializing in dermatology Chgo., 1967—. Chief dermatology sect. MacDonald Army Hosp., Ft. Eustis, Va., 1962—64; attending physician Chgo. Wesley Meml. Hosp., 1969—72, Northwestern Meml. Hosp., 1972—, mem. med. exec. com., 1977—79; cons. Rehab. Inst. Chgo., Mcpl. Tb Sanitarium Chgo., 1968—74. Mem. editl. bd. Curtis, 1975—; assoc. editor: Year Book Pathology and Clin. Pathology, 1977—80. Mem. medicine adv. bd. U. Ill. Coll. Medicine, 1988—; trustee Northwestern Meml. Hosp. Chgo., 1986—87, bd. dirs., 1988—91, Northwestern Meml. Corp., 1987—2000, mem. exec. com., 1988—91. Served as capt. M.C. USAR, 1962—64. Mem.: AMA, Am. Bd. Dermatology (diplomate 1966, bd. dirs. 1981—91, v.p. 1989—90, pres. 1990—91), Dermatology Found. (Clark W. Finnerud award 2002), Pacific Dermatol. Assn., Internat. Soc. Dermatology, Am. Soc. Dermatopathology (pres.-elect 1995—96, bd. dirs. 1995—2000, pres. 1996—97), Am. Dermatol. Assn. (bd. dirs. 1993—98, v.p. 2004—05), Chgo. Dermatol. Soc. (editor trans. 1971—73, pres. 1983—84, Founders award 1992), Am. Acad. Dermatology (Gold award sci. exhibit 1970), U. Ill. Med. Alumni Assn. (exec. bd. 1977—80), Phi Kappa Phi, Alpha Omega Alpha. Office: 676 N Saint Clair St Ste 1840 Chicago IL 60611-2927

CAROL, JOY HAUPT, writer, educator; b. Lincoln, Nebr., Apr. 28, 1938; d. Wilson J. and Alma J. (Weilage) Haupt. BA in Edn., Nebr. Wesleyan U., 1959; postgrad., Scarritt U., 1960-61; MA in Counseling Psychology, U. Md., 1968; postgrad., NYU, 1974-75; MA in Spirituality, Gen. Theol. Sem., 1998; LHD (hon.), Nebr. Wesleyan U., 1994. Tchr., dir. Project Head Start various pub. schs., 1959-60, 64-68; project dir. Meth. Ch. Edn. Sys., Karachi, Pakistan, 1961-63; psychol. counselor pub. and pvt. schs., 1969-73; founder, dir. Union Ctr. for Women, Bklyn., 1973-76; assoc. exec. dir. YWCA Bklyn., 1978; mem. staff UN Devel. Program, Suva, Fiji, 1979-80; program officer Ford Found., N.Y.C., 1980-82; program devel. officer Cultural Info. Svcs., N.Y.C., 1983-84; dir. Asia/Pacific region Save the Children, Westport, Conn., 1984-93; dir. internat. programs Christian Children's Fund, Richmond, Va., 1993-95; dir. devel. Internat. Women's Tribune Ctr., N.Y.C., 1996-97. Cons. UN/World Coun. Chs., N.Y. and Asia, 1976-77, 84, women's orgns., Oslo, 1974, Trauma Response Assistance for Children, 2002-03. Author: You Don't Have to be Rich to Own a Brownstone, 1971, (Women in Devel. publ.) But We're Not Afraid to Speak Anymore, 1976, (booklet) Already I Feel the Change, 1989, Towers of Hope, 2002, Finding Courage, 2002, Journeys of Courage, 2004; author ofcl. report on end of Internat. Women's Decade, UN Devel. Program, 1985; contbr. numerous articles to mags. Bd. dirs. Vietnamese Meml. Assn., Ctrl. Europe Inst., 1990—, United Meth. Ch.; mem. nat. adv. coun., bd. dirs. Nebr. Wesleyan U., 1992—; co-founder self-help cmty. ctr. CHIPS, Bklyn., 1972-75; nat. convernor U.S. Forum on Vietnam, Cambodia, Laos, N.Y., 1990-95; co-founder, vol. Project Reach Youth, N.Y.C., 1965-68; vol. support groups for brain tumor patients at area hosps., Richmond, 1992-94, vol. chaplain Bellevue Hosp., 1997-98, hospice vol., 1994-98, spiritual dir., 1997-2005; vol. chaplain Am. Red Cross, 2001-05; vol. Ctrl. Pk. Conservancy, 2002-05. Named one of Outstanding Women of Am., 1966; named Outstanding Educator in U.S., U.S. Jaycees, Colo., 1966, Outstanding Woman, Bklyn. City Coun., 1970. Mem. AAUW, NOW, Women's Internat. League for Peace and Freedom, Soc. for Internat. Devel. Avocations: writing, reading, hiking, music, gardening. Home: 549 W 123rd St Apt 13H New York NY 10027-5040

CAROLAND, WILLIAM BOURNE, structural engineer; b. Clarksville, Tenn., July 9, 1929; s. Enoch Arden and Jennie Wimberly (Bourne) C.; m. Eloise Joyce Crickard, June 3, 1957; children: Richard Bradley, Jennifer Dorothy. Student, U. Tenn., 1947-52. Registered surveyor, Ky., 1967-2000; profl. engr., Ky., 1967-, Tenn., 1972-2004, Fla., 1972-2001, W.Va., 1972-2004, Mich., 1972-2004, Ind., 1974-2004. Survey party chief King & Clark Engrs., Clarksville, 1955-56, Michael Baker Jr., Inc., Jackson, Miss., 1956-57, asst. designer Charleston, W.Va., 1957-62, project supr. Louisville, 1962-63, designer Charleston, 1963-64; bridge designer Vogt, Ivers & Assocs., Cin., 1964-65; sr. structural engr. Brighton Engring., Frankfort, Ky., 1965-73; chief bridge engr. Beam, Longest & Neff, Indpls., 1973-79; with Am. Cons. Engrs., Lexington, Ky., 1979—2001, chief bridge engr., 1988—; ret., 2001. Cons. in field; mem. Am. Cons. Engrs. Coun. Contbr. papers to profl. publs. With U.S. Army, 1952-55. Recipient Welded Steel Design award Lincoln Arc Welding Found., 1974, Welded Steel Design hon. mention, 1975, silver award 1999; Bridge Design award Prestressed Concrete Inst., 1977, 92, Grand Conceptor award Am. Consulting Engrs. Coun., 2001. Avocations: woodworking, photography. Home: 604 S Broadway St Georgetown KY 40324-1136 *When I was growing up my father always told me there is no such word as can't. Over the years I have come to agree with this. If we believe and work hard it can be done.*

CAROL ANN, artist, educator; Exhibited in group shows at World Fine Art's Gallery, N.Y.C., 2003, Agora Gallery, at Mali Villas Boas Galeria, Caribé Galeria de Arte, Centro Cultural de Suzano, Sao Paulo, Brazil, at Omma Center of Contemporary Art, Crete, Greece, Vera Simoes, Sao Paulo, Matiz Art Galeris, Escritorio de Arte Vera, exhibitions include Biennale Internazionale Dell'Arte Contemporanea, Florence, Italy, Ninth Fine Art's Gallery, V.I., international art competition Art Challenge, (award of merit, 2002). Home: 11736 Zenobia Loop Westminster CO 80031 Personal E-mail: artcarolann@aol.com.

CARONE, GABRIELA ROXANA, philosophy educator, dancer; Lic. in Philosophy, U. Buenos Aires, 1989; PhD in Philosophy, King's Coll., U. London, London, 1995. Asst. prof. U. Buenos Aires, 1989—95; prof. philosophy U. Colo., Boulder, 1996—. Exec. com. Argentine Soc. Ancient Philosophy, Buenos Aires, 1989—95; vis. fellow Harvard U. Ctr. for Hellenic Studies, 2004—; guest lectr. King's Coll., London, 1993—94. Author: The Notion of God in Plato's Timaeus, 1991, Plato's Cosmology and Its Ethical Dimensions, 2005; co-author: Platon: Timeo; mem. editl. bd.: Methexis, An Argentine Jour. Ancient Philosophy, 1989—96; contbr. chapters to books, articles to profl. jours. (leading article). Recipient Brit. Coun. award, 1992—95, Tchg. award, U. Colo., 2002; fellow, NEH, 2004; CONICET fellow, 1989—92, 1995—97, Laurance S. Rockefeller fellow, Ctr. for Human Values, Princeton U., 2003—04. Address: Harvard Univ Ctr for Hellenic Studies 3100 Whitehaven St NW Washington DC 20008

CARONE, NICOLAS, artist; b. New York City, New York, June 4, 1917; Stud., Nat. Acad. of Design. Founding mem. New York Studio School; teacher, painting Yale U., Columbia U., Brandeis U., Cornell U., Cooper Union, School of Visual Arts, Skowhegan School. Exhibitions include Solo Exhibitions, Frumkin Gallery, Stable Gallery, Staempfli Gallery, exhibitions include Group Exhibitions, Museum of Modern Art (Rome), Brussels World's Fair, The Venice Biennale, The Tate Gallery, The Geitain Group (Japan), Represented in permanent collections, The Whitney, Metropolitan Museum of Art, The Hirshhorn, The Baltimore Museum of Art. Named National Academician, 2001; recipient The Rome Prize; fellow Fullbright Fellowship; grantee William Copely Grant, Am. Acad. of Arts and Letters, Childe Hassam Grant.

CARONIS, GEORGE JOHN, insurance executive; b. Columbus, Ohio, Dec. 8, 1933; s. John George and Effie (Zarafonetis) C.; m. Shirley Ann Milburn, June 7, 1958; 1 child, Kevin M. BA, Ohio State U., 1955, MA, 1960. CLU; ChFC; chartered property and casualty underwriter; CFP. Asst. dean of men Ohio State U., Columbus, 1957-60; assoc. gen. agt. Tice Ins. Co., Columbus, 1960-74; v.p. pensions and estate planning Midland Mut. Life Ins. Co., Columbus, 1974-77; v.p. bus. devel. Bank One Trust Co., Columbus, 1977-79; v.p. fin. svcs. Kientz and Co., Columbus, 1979-82; dir. mktg. Nationwide Ins. Cos., Columbus, 1982-87; mktg. mgr. Aetna Life and Casualty Co., Columbus, 1987-89; v.p. advanced underwriting Western Res. Life Assurance Co., Clearwater, Fla., 1989-91, v.p. mktg., 1991—2001; sr. v.p. Asset Accumulation Group, Aegon U.S.A., 1994-98; exec. v.p. Aegon Equity Group, 1998—2001; registered prin. ProVise Mgmt. Group, LLC, 2002—. Bd. dirs. Mass. Fidelity Trust Co. 1st lt. U.S. Army, 1955-57. Recipient Thomas Arkle Clark award Alpha Tau Omega, 1955, Alumni Centennial award Ohio State U., 1970, Ralph D. Mershon award Ohio State U., 1990. Fellow Life Mgmt. Inst.; mem. Ohio State Alumni Assn. (nat. pres. 1983-85), Ohio State U. Found. (nominating com.), Nat. Assn. Life Underwriters, Am. Soc. CLUs and ChFCs. Home: 1371 River Oaks Ct Oldsmar FL 34677-4829 Office: Western Res Life Assurance 1371 River Oaks Ct Oldsmar FL 34677-4829

CAROOMPAS, CAROLE JEAN, artist, educator; b. Oregon City, Oreg., Nov. 14, 1946; d. John Thomas and Dorothy Lietta (Dirks) C. BA, Calif. State U., Fullerton, 1968; MFA in Painting, U. So. Calif., 1971. Instr. El Camino Coll., Torrance, Calif., 1971—72; vis. artist Calif. State U., Northridge, 1972—75; instr. Immaculate Heart Coll., L.A., 1973—76; vis. artist Calif. State U., Fullerton, 1976—78; instr. U. Calif., Irvine, 1976—80, Claremont (Calif.) Grad. Sch., 1976—79, Art Ctr. Coll. of Design, Pasadena, Calif., 1978—86, UCLA Ext., 1984—93; prof. fine arts Otis Coll. Art and Design, L.A., 1981—. Vis. artist Anderson Ranch Art Ctr., Aspen, Colo., 1996, 98, 2005. One-woman shows include Jan Baum Art Gallery, L.A., 1978-82, Karl Bornstein Gallery, L.A., 1985, L.A. Contemporary Exhbns., 1989, U. Calif., Irvine, 1990, Sue Spaid Fine Art, L.A., 1992, 94, P.P.O.W., N.Y.C., 1994, Otis Coll. of Art and Design Art Gallery, 1997-98, Mark Moore Gallery, Santa Monica, 1997, 99, 2000, Western Project, Culver City, Calif., 2004; exhibited in group shows at Pasadena Mus. Art, 1972, Whitney Mus. of Art, 1978, Mus. Modern Art, N.Y.C., 1976, L.A. County Mus., 1982, Corcoran Gallery of Art, 43rd Biennial Exhbn. of Contemporary Am. Painting, Washington, 1993, Under Contstrn. Armory Ctr. for Arts, Pasadena, 1995, UCLA Hammer Mus. of Art, L.A., 1996, L.A. County Mus. Art, 1996, Beaver Coll., 1996, L.A. Mcpl. Art Gallery, 1997, UCLA Hammer Mus. Art, 2000, Calif. State U., Fullerton, 2001, San Jose Mus., 2002, Rosamund Felson Gallery, Santa Monica, Calif., 2003, Lewis and Clark Coll., Portland, Oreg., 2003, San Luis Obispo Art Ctr., 2003, In-A-Gadda-Da-Vida, Baby, Western Project, Culver City, 2004; also a vocalist; recs. include 2 individual albums and inclusion in The Record: 13 Vocal Artists; contbr. articles to Paris Rev., Dreamworks, Whitewalls. Recipient Visual Arts Funding Initiative, Calif. Cmty. Found., 2005; NEA grantee, 1987, 1993, Faculty Devel. grantee, New Sch. Social Rsch., 1989, Support grantee, Esther and Adolph Gottlieb Found., 1993, Guggenheim Meml. fellow, 1995, Individual Artist's fellow, City of L.A. Cultural Affairs Dept., 2000. Office: Otis Coll Art and Design 9045 Lincoln Blvd Los Angeles CA 90045-3505 Office Phone: 310-838-0609.

CAROSELLI, WILLIAM R., lawyer; b. Braddock, Pa., Dec. 14, 1941; s. Rudolph G. and Josephine (Rodrequez) C.; m. Dusty Elias Kirk; children: Clay R., Alyssa; BA, Brown U., 1963; JD, Dickinson Sch. Law, 1966. Bar: U.S. Dist. Ct. (we. and mid. dists.) Pa. 1967, U.S. Ct. Appeals (3d cir.) 1968, U.S. Ct. Appeals (D.C. cir.) 1970. Assoc., McArdle, Harrington, Feeney & McLaughlin, Pitts., 1966-72; asst. solicitor Allegheny County Law Dept., Pitts., 1972-74; ptnr. Caroselli, Beachler, McTiernan & Conby, Pitts., 1972—; mem. disciplinary bd. Pa. Supreme Ct., 1996-2002, chmn., 2000. Co-author: Pennsylvania Workers' Compensation Practices and Procedure, 1982, 85. Trustee Pa. Trial Lawyers Polit. Action Trust, Harrisburg, C.C. Mellor Library, Pitts., 1971-75; Hearing Officer Disciplinary Bd. Supreme Ct. Pa., 1991-93; trustee St. Edmunds Acad., Pitts., 1982-88, Winchester Thurston Sch, 1989-94; bd. dirs. Greater Pitts. Coun. Boy Scouts of Am., 1989, 93; bd. dirs. Easter Seals Western Pa., 2002, pres., 2001-04; bd. dirs. Pitts. Opera, 2005—; mem. Pa. Supreme Ct. Civil Rules Commn., 1989-95, Gov.'s Med. Malpractice Task Force Com., 2002-03; permanent trustee Dickinson Sch. Law Pa. State U. Fellow Internat. Acad. Trial Lawyers (bd. dirs. 2002), Am. Coll. of Trial Lawyers; mem. ABA, Am. Bd. Trial Advocates, Pa. Bar Assn. (chmn. workers compensation sect. 1984), Pa. Trial Lawyers Assn. (pres. 1985-86), Western Pa. Trial Lawyers Assn. (pres. 1984), ATLA (bd. govs. 1986-88, state del. 1980-82, exec. bd. 2000-2001), The Rivers Club, Edgewood Club (pres. 1971-75), Pitts. Golf Club. Democrat. Office: Caroselli Beachler McTiernan & Conboy 312 Blvd Of The Allies Pittsburgh PA 15222-1925 Home: 108 Woodland Rd Pittsburgh PA 15233 Business E-Mail: wrc@cbmclaw.com.

CAROTHERS, A.J., scriptwriter; b. Houston, Oct. 22, 1931; s. A.J. and Vivian (Gibson) C.; m. Caryl Enid Volkman, Nov. 7, 1959; children: Cameron, Christopher, Andrew. BA, UCLA, 1954. Story editor Studio One, 1958; assoc. prodr. Playhouse 90 CBS TV, LA, 1959-60; contract writer Walt Disney Prodns., Burbank, Calif., 1961-68; writer-prodr. Lorimar, Culver City, Calif., 1986-87. Guest lectr. UCLA; writer Music Ctr. Spotlight Awards, 1989-2004. Author: (screenplays) Miracle of the White Stallions, 1962, Emil and the Detectives, 1964, The Happiest Millionaire, 1967, Never a Dull Moment, 1968, Hero At Large, 1980, The Secret of My Success, 1987; (TV movies) The Making of a Male Model, 1984, Summer Girl, 1983, Forever, 1977, The Thief of Bagdad, 1978; creator, author, cons. (TV series) Nanny and the Professor, 1970-72; creator, writer (TV mini-series) Friends, 1979; creator, writer, exec. producer (TV series) Goodnight, Beantown, 1982-83, (mus. play) Busker Alley, 1994; writer (TV series) Studio One, 1958, My Three Sons, 1960-61, The Dupont Show, 1960-61, The Investigators, 1961, (TV spl.) Goldilocks, 1971; writer (play) Two Can Play, 2004. V.p. Fraternity of Friends, LA, 1986—. With US Army, 1954-56. Recipient Disting. Artists award, Club 100 of LA Music Ctr., 1990; Gold Lone Star award, Houston Film Festival, 1982; named Disting. Alumnus, KinKaid Sch., 1997. Mem. Motion Picture Acad. (writer's br. exec. com.), UCLA Theater Arts Alumni Assn. (bd. dirs. 1984-88), Sons of the Rep. of Tex Home and Office: 1379 Midvale Ave Los Angeles CA 90024-6218 Office Phone: 310-476-6552.

CAROTHERS, DONNA J., biochemist, educator, writer; b. Hollywood, Calif., Apr. 9, 1954; d. Elzy Lee and Mauna June (Williams) C. m. Allen Eric Tracht, Sept. 14, 1986; children: Michael Edward, Diane Sarah, Daniel Carothers Tracht. BS with distinction, Centre Coll., Ky., 1976; MS, U. Louisville, 1979; PhD, Case Western Res. U., 1987. Rsch. asst. U. Louisville, Ky., 1979; rsch. assoc. Case Western Reserve U., Cleve., 1987-89; adj. instr. Cuyahoga C.C., Cleve., 1990; test item writer ACT, Iowa, 1990—; specialist reviewer Sci. Books and Films, Washington, 1990—; vol. scientist Sci. by Mail, Boston, 1990—. Contbr. articles and book revs. to profl. jours., chpts. to books. Nat. Merit scholar, 1972-76; NIH fellow, 1979-83. Mem. AAAS, Am. Chem. Soc., N.Y. Acad. Scis., Ohio Acad Sci., Ky. Acad. Sci., Internat. Soc. Twin Studies, Nat. Book Critics Circle, Phi Beta Kappa, Iota Sigma Pi, Phi Alpha Theta, Omicron Delta Kappa. Avocations: genealogy, creative writing, needlecrafts. Home: 3066 Scarborough Rd Cleveland Heights OH 44118-4065

CAROTHERS, ROBERT LEE, academic administrator; b. Sewickley, Pa., Sept. 3, 1942; s. Robert Fleming and Mary (Skinner) C.; children: Robert Kennedy, Shelley Rye, Matthew K. BA in English, Edinboro U., 1965; MA, Kent State U., 1966, PhD, 1969; JD, U. Akron, 1980. Bar: Pa. 1981. Prof. English, dean, v.p. Edinboro U., 1968-83; pres. S.W. State U., Marshall, Minn., 1983-86; chancellor Minn. State U. Sys., St. Paul, 1986-91; pres. U. R.I., Kingston, 1991—. Author: Freedom and Other Times, 1972; John Calvin's Favorite Son, 1980. Served with AUS, 1960-68. Recipient Humanitarian award, Urban League RI, 2000, Jean Hicks award, RI Nat. Conf. for Cmty. and Justice, 2000, History Makers Salute, RI Historical Soc., 2001, Silver Anniversary Honor Roll award, Am. Cancer Soc. Mem.: Nat. Inst. Alcohol Abuse and Alcoholism (com. campus drinking 1999—2002). Avocation: fishing. Home: 56 Upper College Rd Kingston RI 02881-2022 Office: URI Office of the Pres Green Hall 35 Campus Ave Kingston RI 02881-1303 Office Phone: 401-874-2444. Office Fax: 401-874-7149. E-mail: muskrat@uri.edu.

CAROVANO, JOHN MARTIN, not-for-profit developer; b. Tacoma, May 9, 1935; s. John and Elda C. (Martin) C.; m. Barbara Bevins, June 14, 1958; children: Kristen, Kathryn. BA, Pomona Coll., 1957, LL.D., 1979; MA, U. Calif. at Berkeley, 1961, PhD, 1965; LL.D., Hamilton Coll., 1974. Research asst., teaching fellow U. Calif. at Berkeley, 1959-63; instr. econs. Hamilton Coll., Clinton, N.Y., 1963-65, asst. prof., 1965-68, asso. prof., 1969-74, acting provost, 1971-72, provost, 1972-74, pres. coll., 1974-88; dir. N.Y. office The Nature Conservancy, 1988-94, planned giving officer, 1994—. Financial economist Office Tax Analysis, U.S. Dept. Treasury, Washington, 1968-69; chmn. N.Y. Com. of Selection, Rhodes Scholarship Trust, 1978-82; trustee Commn. on Ind. Colls. and Univs. N.Y., 1980-83 Mem. Democratic Com., Clinton, 1970-74. Served with AUS, 1957-58. Home: # 407 87 Railroad Pl Saratoga Springs NY 12866 Office: Nature Conservancy Ste 10 110 Spring St Saratoga Springs NY 12866 E-mail: carovano@nycap.rr.com.

CAROZZA, GERALD NICHOLAS, JR., lawyer; b. Bronx, N.Y., July 8, 1960; s. Gerald Nicholas and Juana B. (Luchessi) C.; m. Ruthellen Purdy, Dec. 14, 1985; children: Jacqueline P., Peter John, Julia F.B. BA, Boston U., 1982; JD, Villanova U., 1985. Bar: Pa. 1985, N.J. 1988. Assoc. Marshall, Dennehey, Warner, Coleman & Goggin, Phila., 1985, Jos. A. Marrazzo & Assocs., Pennsauken, N.J., 1988-93; sr. atty. Resolution Trust Corp., Valley Forge, Pa., 1993-96; v.p., gen. counsel The Mountbatten Surety Co., Inc., Bala Cynwyd, Pa., 1997-2000; bond counsel, claims mgr. Selective Ins. Co. Cm., Branchville, N.J., 2000—. Lectr. Hagerstown (Md.) Jr. Coll., 1986-87; asst. prof. mil. sci. Villanova U., 1999-2000. Capt. U.S. Army, 1986-88; with Res. Mem. Pa. Bar Assn. Office: Selective Ins Co Am 40 Wantage Ave Branchville NJ 07890 Office Phone: 973-948-1823. E-mail: gncarozza@hotmail.com.

CARP, DANIEL A., consumer products company executive; b. Wytheville, Va. BBA in Quantitative Methods, Ohio U.; MBA, Rochester Inst. Tech.; MS in Mgmt., MIT. Stats. analyst Eastman Kodak Co., Rochester, NY, various postions in market rsch. and mgmt., gen. mgr. sales Kodak Can., gen. mgr. consumer electronics divsn., asst. gen. mgr. Latin Am. region, 1986-88, v.p., gen. mgr., 1988-90, gen. mgr. European Mktg. Cos., 1990—95, exec. v.p., asst. COO, 1995-97, pres., COO, 1997-2000, pres., CEO, 2000, chmn., pres., CEO, 2000—01, chmn., CEO, 2001—05, chmn., 2005—. Bd. dirs. Tex. Instruments Inc.; mem. Bus. Council. Sloan fellow Sloan Sch. of Mgmt., MIT; recipient Leadership award, 2001, Person of the Yr. award, 2004, PhotoImaging Manufacturers & Distributors Assn. Office: Eastman Kodak 343 State St Rochester NY 14650-0001*

CARP, LARRY, lawyer; b. St. Louis, Jan. 26, 1926; s. Avery and Ruth C. Student, U. Mo., Columbia, 1944; cert., Sorbonne U., Paris, 1946; BA, Washington U., St. Louis, 1947; postgrad., Grad. Inst. Internat. Studies, Geneva, 1949; JD, Washington U., St. Louis, 1951. Bar: Mo. 1951, U.S. Dist. Ct. (ea. dist.) Mo. 1951. Mem. U.S. Dept. of State, Washington, 1951-53; mem. staff Senator Paul H. Douglas (Dem. Ill.), Washington, 1953-54; assoc. Fordyce, Mayne, Hartman, Renard, and Stribling, St. Louis, 1954-63; sole practice St. Louis, 1963-68; ptnr. Carp & Morris, St. Louis, 1968-90, Carp, Sexauer and Carr, St. Louis, 1990-94, Carp and Sexauer, St. Louis, 1994—. Assoc. counsel, acting chief counsel U.S. Senate Subcom. on Constitutional Rights, Washington, 1956; life mem. bd. trustees Acad. Sci., St. Louis, 1984—; mem. St. Louis Regional U.S. Export Expansion Coun., 1964-74; mem. Mo. Commn. on Human Rights, 1966-78, vice chmn., 1977-78; vice chmn., bd. dirs. Pastoral Counselling Inst. for Greater St. Louis, 1964-91; mem. adv. bd. George Engelmann Math. and Science Inst., 1992-96; bd. dirs. St. Louis Ctr. for Internat. Rels., 1998—; legal advisor Image, Inc., St. Louis, 1998-2003. Co-author: (musicals) Pocahontas, The Pied Piper, Androcles; author: (musicals) For the Love of Adam, The Red Ribbon, Famous Last Words, GOD KNOWS!; contbr. articles to newspapers and profl. jours. Mem. Common Cause, 1966-78, chmn. Mo. chpt., 1973-75; bd. dirs. Internat. Inst. of Metro St. Louis, 1980-86, English Speaking Union, St. Louis, 1985—, Mo. Prison Arts Program, 1999-2003; U.S. presdl. appointee as sr. adviser and U.S. pub. del. to UN 55th Gen. Assembly, 2000-2001. With U.S. Army, 1944-46, ETO. Decorated (2) Battle Stars; Rotary Internat. fellow Grad. Inst. Internat. Studies, Geneva, 1948-49; award for Outstanding Service in Recognition of Spl. Needs of Hispanic Community IMAGE, St. Louis, 1984. Fellow Am. Acad. Matrimonial Lawyers (cert.); mem. ABA (immigration law coord. com., 1989, chmn. immigration law com. gen. practice sect. 1981-86), Mo. Bar Assn., Bar Assn. Met. St. Louis (chmn. internat. law and trade com. 1973-79, chmn. immigration law com. 1989-92), Am. Immigration Lawyers Assn., UNA-USA Assn. (bd. dirs. St. Louis chpt. 1999-2003), Phi Delta Phi. Office: Carp and Sexauer 225 S Meramec Ave Ste 325 Saint Louis MO 63105-3511 Office Phone: 314-863-4300. Office Fax: 314-727-0308. Business E-Mail: carpandsexauer@msn.com.

CARPEL, EMMETT FRANKLIN, ophthalmologist, consultant; b. Phila. MD, Hahnemann U., 1968. Cert. Am. Acad. of Ophthalmology, 1976. Fellow U. Wash., Seattle, 1971—72, resident, 1972—75; staff Health Partners, Mpls., 1975—, Hennepin County Med. Ctr. HFA, Mpls., 1975—, Hennepin Faculty Assocs., Bloomington, Minn., 1975—. Cons. U. Minn., 1991. Contbr. articles various profl. jours., 1975—2002. Capt. U.S. Army, 1969—71. Recipient Edn. Tchg. award, Group Health, 1993. Fellow: Am. Acad. Ophthalmology; mem.: Minn. Acad. Ophthalmology (bd. mem. 2000—), Royal Coll. Ophthalmologists. Achievements include patents for medical devices. Office: Health Partners 8600 Nicollet Ave So Bloomington MN 55420

CARPENETI, WALTER L., state supreme court justice; b. San Francisco, Jan. 25, 1945; m. Anne Dose, 1969; children: Christian, Marianna, Lia, Bianca. AB in History with distinction, Stanford U., 1967; JD, U. Calif., Berkeley, 1970. Law clk. Justice John H. Dimond Alaska Supreme Ct., 1970-71; partner Carpeneti & Carpeneti, San Francisco, 1972-74; supervisor Alaska Public Defender Agency, Juneau, Alaska, 1974-78; partner Carpeneti & Council, Juneau, 1978-81; judge Alaska Superior Ct., Juneau, 1981-98; justice Alaska State Supreme Ct., Juneau, 1998—. Mem. Alaska Judicial Council, 1980—81, Alaska Commn. on Judicial Conduct, 1992—95. Mem. Nat. Council on Alcoholism, 1980—83, Gastineau Council on Alcoholism, 1975—78. Office: Alaska Supreme Ct PO Box 114100 Juneau AK 99811-4100 Office Phone: 907-463-4771.

CARPENTER, ANGIE M., small business owner, editor, state legislator; b. Bay Shore, N.Y., Sept. 30, 1943; d. Joseph and Ida (Gullo) Linarello; m. Joe David Carpenter, Apr. 13, 1964; children: Richard, Robert. Student, Nassau C.C., 1962-63. Office mgr., graphic designer, typographer Merrick (N.Y.) Typographers and Maverick Pubs., 1966-76; founder, v.p. AC Typesetters and Printing, Inc., West Islip, NY, 1976-93; dep. presiding officer Suffolk County Legislature. Editor, pub., co-founder West Islip Record, 1986-91; columnist The Graphic, The Beacon, 1985-87. Chmn. publicity com., trustee Babylon/West Islip Windmill Com., Inc., Babylon, N.Y., 1986—, ASK US, 1987-98; trustee West Islip After-Sch.-Care program, 1987-97, Our Lady of Consolation Geriatric Care Ctr.; chmn. West Islip Youth Enrichment Svcs., 1986-87; mem. govt. action coun. L.I. Assn., 1987; mem. recycling panel Town of Islip, 1987; chairperson TOI Blue Ribbon Com. on Recycling, 1987-88; trustee Suffolk County Vanderbilt Mus., 1990-93; vice chair Suffolk County Salvation Army Adv. Bd.; mem. Suffolk County Legislature, 1993—, dep. presiding officer, chmn. pub. safety com., vice chmn. budget and fin. Mem. West Islip C. of C. (v.p., mchts. dir. 1982-84, pres. 1985, 86, 87, 88), Govt. Fin. Officer's Assn. Republican. Roman Catholic. Office: Office County Legislature 4 Udall Rd West Islip NY 11795-2341 Office Phone: 631-854-4100. Personal E-mail: angiecarp930@aol.com. E-mail: angie.carpenter@co.suffolk.ny.us.

CARPENTER, ARTHUR LLOYD, education educator; s. Arthur Betz and Mildred Carpenter; m. Madeline Mae Daue, Aug. 1, 1953; children: Thomas Wayne, James Paul, Lee Arthur. BS, Ea. Mich. U., 1951; MS, Mich. State U., 1956; postgrad. studies, Wayne State U., 1957, U. Mic., 1958-66. Cert. elem., secondary tchr. (permanent), Mich. Tchr. Jefferson Consol. Schs., Monroe, Mich., 1951-53, Plymouth (Mich.) Comty. Schs., 1953-55; asst. prof. edn. U. No. Iowa, Cedar Falls, 1956-64; coord. instrnl. materials Wayne-Westland Comty. Sch., Wayne, Mich., 1964; asst. prof. edn. Ea. Mich. U., Ypsilanti, Mich., 1964-90. Cons. Iowa and Mich. schs., 1957-90, Fed. Correctional Prison, Milan, Mich., 1966; cons. with Nat. Coun. Accreditation of Tchr. Edn. Nebr. Wesleyan U., Lincoln, 1969. Film producer: 12 films for U. No. Iowa, 1957-64; Slide sets and F.S. 14 produced for U. No. Iowa, 1957-64; contbr. articles to 15 profl. publs.; photography reproduced in numerous mags.; book reviewer for several publishers. Recipient Red Balloon award Detroit Assn. Film Tchrs., 1970, 2d prize in Wayne Behling Meml. Photographic Contest, Ann Arbor, Mich., 1987. Mem. Wayne Hist. Soc. (bd. dirs., pres.), Mich. Bird Banders Assn. (pres.), Mich. Audubon Soc. (com. chmn.), Washtenaw Audubon Soc. (pres.), Mich. Natural Area Coun., Mich Photographic Hist. Soc. Home: 3646 S John Hix Rd Wayne MI 48184-1047

CARPENTER, BOGDANA MARIA MAGDALENA, language educator; b. Czestochowa, Poland, June 2, 1941; came to U.S., 1965; d. Jozef Konrad and Maria (Gordon) Chetkowska; m. John Randell Carpenter, Apr. 15, 1963; children: Michael, Magdalena. MA, Warsaw U., 1963; PhD, U. Calif., Berkeley, 1974. Asst. prof. U. Wash., Seattle, 1974-83, U. Mich., Ann Arbor, 1983-85, assoc. prof., 1985-91, prof., 1991—, chmn. dept. Slavic lit. and langs., 1991—. Adv. coun. Wilson Ctr. East European Program, Washington, 1985-90; selection com. Internat. Rsch. and Exch., Princeton, N.J., 1987-88; discipline adv. com. Coun. for Internat. Exch. Scholars, Washington, 1989-90. Author: Poetic Avantgarde in Poland, 1918-1939, 1983, Monumenta Polonica, 1989 (1st prize Am. Coun. of Polish Cultural Clubs 1991); translator: Selected Poems of Zbigniew Herbert, 1977 (Poetry Soc. Am. prize 1979), Z. Herbert's Report from the Besieged City, 1987, Still Life with a Bridle, 1991 (Columbia U. Translation Ctr. Merit award 1992), Mr. Cogito, 1993; assoc. editor: Cross Currents, 1987—; contbr. articles and revs. to profl. jours. Fulbright-Hays grantee, 1976, IREX grantee, 1976, NEH grantee, 1987-88, ACLS grantee, 1990-91. Mem. Am. Assn. for Advancement Slavic Studies (exec. bd. Midwest chpt. 1989—), Am. Assn. Tchrs. Slavic and East European Langs. Office: U Mich Dept Slavic Lit & Langs 3040 Mlb Ann Arbor MI 48109

CARPENTER, CAROLYN, elementary school educator; b. Passaic, N.J., Apr. 24, 1948; d. Roman and Mary Petrisin; m. John Burnett Carpenter, Jr.; 1 child, Sarah Mary. BA, Paterson State U., 1970. Tchr. Netcong (N.J.) Elem. Sch., 1970—. Title I coord. Netcong Elem. Sch., affirmative action officer, 1979, 2004—05. Leader, vol. Girl Scouts of Am., Netcong, 1973, 1991—93; vol. Booster Club Bangor (Pa.) H.S., 1996—98, mem. Band Parents, 1996—98. Named Tchr. of Yr., Netcong Elem. Faculty, 1991. Mem.: N.J. Edn. Assn., Netcong Tchr.'s Assn. (pres. 1973—74). Democrat. Lutheran. Avocations: cooking, crocheting, travel. Home: 208 Frutchey Ct Mount Bethel PA 18343

CARPENTER, CHARLES COLCOCK JONES, internist, educator; b. Savannah, Ga., Jan. 5, 1931; s. Charles Colcock Jones and Alexandra (Morrison) C.; m. Sally R. Fisher, Nov. 29, 1958; children— Charles Morrison, Murray Douglas, Andrew Fisher. AB, Princeton, 1952; MD, Johns Hopkins, 1956. Diplomate: Am. Bd. Internal Medicine (mem. bd. 1976—, exec. com. 1980—, chmn. 1983-84). Intern Johns Hopkins Hosp., Balt., 1956-57, resident, 1957—59, 1961—62; practice medicine, specializing in infectious disease, 1962-73; asst. prof. medicine Johns Hopkins, 1962-67, assoc. prof., 1967-69, prof., 1969-73; physician-in-chief Balt. City Hosps., 1969-73; prof., chmn. dept. medicine Case Western Res. Sch. Medicine, 1973-86; physician-in-chief Case Western Res. Univ. Hosp., 1973-85; prof. medicine Brown U., 1986—, dir. Internat. Health Inst., 1993—98. Dir. Cholera Research Program, Johns Hopkins Center Med. Research and Tng., Calcutta, India, 1962-64; chmn. cholera panel U.S.-Japan Coop. Med. Sci. Program, 1965-72; mem. U.S.-Japan Coop. Med. Sci. Program (U.S. del.), 1973—2000, chmn., 1990-2000; mem. adv. bd. Sch. Medicine Johns Hopkins U., 1982-97; mem. Nat. Adv. Coun. Allergy and Infectious Diseases, 1985-89; chmn. extramural cons. AIDS exec. com. NIH, 1986-87, nat. adv. com. for AIDS, NIH, 1992-93; chmn. adv. coun. AIDS Rsch., NIH, 1995-2000; dir. Lifespan/Tufts/Brown Ctr. for AIDS Rsch., 1998-. Trustee Internat. Ctr. for Infectious Disease Rsch., Bangladesh, 1979-83, Internat. Child Health Found., 1985-96, Miriam Hosp., 1992-97. Sr. asst. surgeon USPHS, 1959-61. Recipient John E. Fogarty Internat. Health Recognition Award, NIH, 2003, John H. Chafee Award for Leadership in Healthcare, Am. Heart Assn., 2004. Fellow ACP (master 1992, Distinguished Physician award, 2003), AAAS (chmn. med. scis. sect. 1994-96); mem. Inst. Medicine NAS, Am. Soc. Clin. Investigation, Assn. Am. Physicians (sec. 1975-81, councillor 1981-86, v.p. 1986-87, pres. 1987-88), Infectious Diseases Soc. Am. (Smadel medal 1991), Johns Hopkins Soc. Scholars, Johns Hopkins Med. and Surg. Assn. (pres. 1995-97), Order of the Sacred Treasure (Japan). Home: 12 Half Mile Rd Barrington RI 02806-4104 Office Phone: 401-793-4025.

CARPENTER, CHARLES CONGDEN, retired zoologist; b. Denison, Iowa, June 2, 1921; s. Harry Alonzo and Myrtle Ruth (Barber) C.; m. Mary F. Pitynski, Sept. 2, 1947; children— Janet Eleanor, Caryn Sue, Geoffrey Congden. BA, No. Mich. Coll. Edn., Marquette, 1943; postgrad., Tarleton State Coll., Stephenville, Tex., 1943-44, Stanford U., 1944, Wayne U., 1945; MS, U. Mich., 1947, PhD, 1951. Lab. asst. zoology No. Mich. Coll. Edn., 1941-43; teaching asst. zoology U. Mich., 1946; asst. herpetology and mammalogy Biol. Sta., summer 1948, teaching fellow zoology, 1947-51, instr. zoology, 1951-52; instr. U. Okla. Biol. Sta., Norman, summer 1952, U. Okla., 1953, asst. prof. zoology, 1953-59; assoc. prof. zoology, curator reptiles U. Okla. and, U. Okla. Biol. Sta., 1959-66, prof. zoology, curator reptiles, 1966-87, prof. emeritus zoology, curator emeritus reptiles and amphibians, 1988; rsch. assoc. in herpetology Dallas Zoo, 1980. Expdns. and field studies U. Mich. Paleontol. Expdn., Kans. and, Colo., 1947, Jackson Hole Research sta., Grand Teton Nat. Park, 1951, field trips throughout, Mexico and; S.W., U.S., 1979—88; Galapagos Islands Expdn., 1962; expdns. to islands of Gulf of Calif., 1964; invited scientist mem. Galapagos Internat. Sci. Project to Galapagos Islands, Ecuador and; Cocos Island, 1964—88; sec. Animal Research Council, Oklahoma City Zoo, 1972-74, 78—88, chmn., 1980 Contbr. articles to profl. jours. Served with AUS, 1943-46. Recipient Disting. Alumni award No. Mich. U., 1972; Regents award U. Okla., 1980; numerous grants NSF; numerous grants N.Y. Zool. Soc.; numerous grants U. Okla. Alumni Devel. Fund; numerous grants U. Okla. Research Inst. Fellow Animal Behavior Soc. (sec. 1966-68), Okla. Acad. Sci. (pres. 1970, Outstanding Scientist award 1991), Herpetologist League (v.p. 1972-73, pres. 1974-75); mem. Am. Ornithologists Union, Am. Soc. Zoologists, Am. Inst. Biol. Sci., Ecol. Soc. Am., Am. Soc. Ichthyologists and Herpetologists, Wilson Ornithol. Soc., Southwestern Assn. Naturalists (bd. govs. 1965-68, pres. 1968-69, permanent sec. 1971-76, W. Frank Blair award 1987), Am. Soc. Mammalogists, Brit. Ecol. Soc., Soc. Study Amphibians and Reptiles, Explorers Club, Wilderness Soc., Nature Conservancy, Sigma Xi, Phi Kappa Phi, Phi Sigma. Home: 1218 Cruce St Norman OK 73069-4440 Office: U Okla Dept Zoology 730 Van Vleet Oval Norman OK 73019-6120

CARPENTER, CHRIS, professional baseball player; b. Exeter, NH, Apr. 27, 1975; m. Alyson Carpenter; 1 child, Sam. Pitcher Toronto Blue Jays, 1997—2002, St. Louis Cardinals, 2002—. Named Nat. League All-Star Starting Pitcher, 2005. Office: St Louis Cardinals 250 Stadium Plz Saint Louis MO 63102-1722 Home: Bedford NH*

CARPENTER, DAVID ALLAN, lawyer; b. Cambridge, Mass., May 16, 1951; s. David Lawrence and Jane (Boucher) C.; m. Nancy Joan Surdyka, Apr. 29, 1973. BS in Bus. Adminstrn., Bucknell U., Lewisburg, Pa., 1972; MBA in Fin., Temple U., Phila., 1975; JD, Rutgers U., 1981. Banking officer Girard Bank, Phila., 1972-77, mng. ptnr., 1983-85, mng. ptnr. Mid Atlantic region, 1985-89, mng. ptnr. Atlantic region, 1989-92; nat. dir. litigation and claims svcs. Coopers & Lybrand, Phila., 1987-92, nat. dir. fin. adv. svcs. Boston, 1992-94; founding ptnr. Ptnrs. for Mkt. Leadership, Inc., Atlanta, 1995—; ptnr. Ptnrs. for Corp. Renewal, Phila., 1997—. Co-editor: Proving and Pricing Construction Claims, 1990, Environmental Dispute Handbook, 1991; contbr. articles to profl. jours., chpts. to books. Mem. Inst. Mgmt. Consultants, Turnaround Mgmt. Assn., Beta Gamma Sigma. Address: PO Box 903 Great Barrington MA 01230-0903 Office: Ptnrs for Mkt Leadership Inc 400 Galleria Pkwy SE Ste 1500 Atlanta GA 30339-3122 Office Phone: 800-984-1110.

CARPENTER, DAVID ERWIN, county official, land use planner; b. Appleton, Wis., Oct. 20, 1939; s. Erwin Carl and Othilia Mary (Killian) Carpenter; m. Linda Louise Simkins, June 22, 1961 (div. Apr. 15, 1983); children: Bradley John, Robert Anthony, Paige Elizabeth; m. Mary Starr Griffin, May 18, 1991. BS, U. Wis., 1962, MS, 1979. Planner Wis. Dept. Devel., Madison, 1963-66, Fond du Lac County, Wis., 1966-68; supr. county planning Wis. Dept. Devel., Madison, 1968-69; assoc. dir. Southeastern Wis. Health Systems Agy., Milw., 1969-77; dir. planning St. Mary's Hosp. Med. Ctr., Madison, 1977-84; dir. mktg. St. Mary's Svcs., Madison, 1984-86; pres. David Carpenter Assocs., Madison, 1986-89; dir. planning Dodge County Planning and Devel., Juneau, Wis., 1989-95, exec. dir., 1995—. Author: Solid Waste Recycling Plan, 1991, Outdoor Recreation Plan, 1995. Sec.-treas. Ice Age Pk. and Trail Found., Madison, 1990; mgr. Dodge County Heritage Preservation, Beaver Dam, 1991—97; vol. Columbus (Wis.) Downtown Devel. Corp., 1992, Columbus Main St. Program, 1992—95; mem. exec. com. Flyway Area Labor-Mgmt. Coun., Horicon, 1993—98; mem. Columbus Ad Hoc Econ. Devel. Com., 1994; pres. Rock River Coalition, Watertown, 1995—97, chmn. comm. com., 1997—98; docent Monona Terr. Cmty. and Conv. Ctr., Madison, 1999—; active City of Columbus Planning Commn., 2000—05; bd. dirs. Columbus Area Aquatic Ctr., 2000—03; mem. Skilaufers, Inc., 2001—, bd. dirs., 2002—05, pres., 2003—05; mem. Seth Peterson Cottage Conservancy, Inc., 2002—; vol. Wis. Pub. TV, 2002—; trustee Columbus United Meth. Ch., 1992—2003, pres., 1998—2003. Recipient Foward Wis. award, 1994, Elmer Kohlbeck Friend of Tourism award, 1995, Svc. award, Rock River Coalition, 1998. Mem.: Western Pa. Conservancy, Wis. Hist. Soc., League Am. Bicyclists, Olbrich Bot. Soc., Charles E. Brown

Archeol. Soc. (pres. 1992—95), Wis. Archeol. Soc. (Eileen Swiggum award for Contbn. 2001), Am. Planning Assn., Phi Sigma Kappa. Avocations: archaeology, art, history, gardening, bicycling. Office: Dodge County Planning & Devel 127 E Oak St Juneau WI 53039-1329 Business E-Mail: dcarpenter@co.dodge.wi.us.

CARPENTER, DAVID WILLIAM, lawyer; b. Chgo., Aug. 26, 1950; s. William Warren and Dorothy Susan (Jacobs) C.; m. Jane Ellen French, Aug. 18, 1973 (div. Jan. 2001); children: Johanna Lindsay, Julie Rachel; m. Orit Karni, Mar. 26, 2004. BA cum laude, Yale U., 1972; JD magna cum laude, Boston U., 1975. Bar: Mass. 1975, Ill. 1979, DC 1980, US Ct. Appeals (1st cir.) 1977, U.S. Dist. Ct. (no. dist.) Ill. 1979, DC 1995, U.S. Ct. Appeals 3rd. cir. 1981, DC cir. 1982, 7th cir. 1982, 10th cir. 1985, 8th cir. 1986, 9th cir. and 11th ciruits 1987, 2nd, 5th and 6th circuits, 1990, 4th cir. 2000, U.S. Supreme Ct. 1981. Law clk. to presiding justice US Ct. Appeals (1st cir.), Portland, Maine, 1975-77, US Supreme Ct., Washington, 1977-78; assoc. Sidley & Austin (now Sidley Austin Brown & Wood LLP), Chgo., 1978-82; ptnr. Sidley Austin Brown & Wood LLP, Chgo., 1982—, and mem. exec. com., 1994—. Lectr. Ill. Inst. Tech., Chgo., 1980-82. Bd. dirs., sec. Chgo. Coun. for Young Profls., 1985-90; bd. dirs., exec. com. Brennan Ctr. for Justice, NYC, 1995-2004; bd. dirs. Lyric Opera Chgo., 1999—. Democrat. Mem. United Ch. Christ. Office: Sidley Austin Brown & Wood LLP Bank One Plz 10 S Dearborn St Chicago IL 60603 Office Phone: 312-853-7237.

CARPENTER, DELBERT STANLEY, educational administration educator; b. Wichita Falls, Tex., May 18, 1950; s. Delbert Stanley Sr. and Nancy (Williams) S.; m. Noralyn Gray, July 13, 1973 (div. Mar. 1986); m. Janet Ann Stewart, July 15, 1989 (div. June 1993); m. Linda Jan Meerdink Evans, June 15, 1994; 1 child, Susanne Gray Carpenter; stepchildren: Robert Scott Evans, Peter Clark Evans. BS, Tarleton State U., 1972; MS, East Tex. State U., 1975; PhD, U. Ga., 1979. Actuarial technician A.S. Hansen, Inc., Dallas, 1972-74; grad. asst. ctrl. housing office East Tex. State U., Commerce, 1974-75; men's resident dir. Oglethorpe U., Atlanta, 1975-77; grad. asst. rsch., tchg., counseling and human devel. dept. U. Ga., Athens, 1977-79; dean students U. Ark., Monticello, 1979-81; asst. dir. devel. Tex. A&M U., College Station, 1982-84, from asst. prof. ednl. adminstrn. to assoc. prof., 1985-95, prof., 1995—2003; prof., chair ednl. adminstrn. and psychol. svcs. dept. Tex. State U., San Marcos, 2003—. Mem. editl. bds. various profl. jours.; contbr. articles to profl. jours. Named Outstanding Doctoral Alumnus, Students Affairs Adminstrn. U. Ga., 1995, Disting. Tchg. award Assn. Former Students Coll. of Edn., 1996. Mem. Assn. for the Study Higher Edn. (exec. dir. 1987-98, Disting. Svc. award 1996), Am. Coll. Pers. Assocs. (Annuit Coeptis award 1995, Sr. Scholar 2000, chair 2001-04, Esther Lloyd-Jones Profl. Svc. award 2004), Nat. Assn. Student Pers. Adminstrn. (mem.-at-large nat. bd. 2001-03), South Assn. for Coll. Student Affairs (Melvene Hardee award 1997), Alpha Phi Omega (pres., bd. dirs. 1986-90, Nat. Disting. Svc. award 1990, trustee endowment fund 1996—, chair 1997—), Alpha Chi. Avocations: golf, reading, travel. Home: 129 Mountain Laurel Way Bastrop TX 78602 Office Phone: 512-245-8851. Business E-Mail: stanc@txstate.edu.

CARPENTER, DERR ALVIN, retired landscape architect; b. Sunbury, Pa., Jan. 18, 1931; s. Alvin Witmer and Katharine (Rockefeller) C.; m. Helen Longden Hedge, Apr. 10, 1954; children: Mary Katharine Carpenter Denault, Melissa Sue Carpenter Sciumbata. BS, Pa. State U., 1953. Registered landscape architect. Chief landscape architect La. State Parks, Baton Rouge, 1955-58; asst. dir. City Parish Planning Com., Baton Rouge, 1958-62; chief planning and engring. Pa. State Parks, Harrisburg, 1962-67; pres. Derr A. Carpenter & Assocs., Camp Hill, Pa., 1967-73; v.p. Smith, Miller & Assocs. Inc., Camp Hill and Kingston, Pa., 1973-86, Rettew Assocs. Inc., Mechanicsburg and Lancaster, Pa., 1987-90; self employed landscape architect Mechanicsburg, 1990—2003. Lectr. Pa. State U., Harrisburg Area C.C., 1973-2003, Susquehanna U.; mem. legis. com. Pa. Recreation and Park Soc., University Park, 1982-90; bd. dirs. Pa. State Arts and Architecture Alumni Bd., University Park, 1985-95. Mem. Camp Hill Shade Tree Commn., 1968-87; councilman Tree of Life Luth. Ch., Linglestown, 1994-98, bldg. com., fellowship com., social ministry com.; bd. dirs. Park Adv. Bd., Cumberland County, Pa., 1978-84; bd. dirs. YMCA, Harrisburg, 1974-80, Capital Region Econ. Devel. Corp., 1988-93; chair Zoning Commn., 1989, Dauphin County Open Space Commn., 1989-92. With U.S. Army, 1953-55. Pa. State U. Alumni fellow, 1984 Fellow Am. Soc. Landscape Architects (trustee 1977-80, 1983, pres. chpt. 1973-77, nat. ethics com. chmn. 1984-87, dir. legislation 1968-90, Disting. Svc. award 1981, cert. appreciation 1984); mem. Susquehanna River Tri-State Assn. (pres. 1980-82, Leadership award 1982, bd. dirs.), Pa. Nursery Mktg. Adv. Coun. (chmn. 1976-77, bd. dirs. Outstanding Achievement award 1972), Pa. State Alumni Assn. of Harrisburg (pres. 1983-85, bd. dirs., Leadership award 1985). Lodges: Torch (bd. dirs. 1976-81), Rotary (bd. dirs. 1968-82), Masons. Republican. Lutheran. Avocations: gardening, hiking, reading, printing, massage. E-mail: laguy3@juno.com.

CARPENTER, EDMUND NELSON, II, retired lawyer; b. Phila., Jan. 27, 1921; s. Walter S. and Mary (Wootten) C.; m. Carroll Morgan, July 18, 1970; children: Mary W., Edmund Nelson III, Katherine R.R., Elizabeth Lea; stepchildren: John D. Gates, Ashley du Pont Gates. AB, Princeton U., 1943; LLB, Harvard U., 1948; LLD (hon.), Widener U., 1985, U. Del., 1999. Bar: Del. 1949, U.S. Supreme Ct. 1957. Assoc. Richards, Layton & Finger, Wilmington, Del., 1949-53, ptnr., 1953-78, dir., 1978-91, pres., 1982-85; ret., 1991. Dep. atty. gen. State of Del., 1953-54, spl. dep. atty., 1960-62; chmn. Del. Superior Ct. Jury Study Com., 1963-66, Del. Supreme Ct. Cts. Consol. Com., 1985-87; mem. Del. Gov.'s Commn. Law Enforcement and Adminstrn. Justice, 1969; chmn. Del. Supreme Ct. Adv. Com. on Profl. Fin. Accountability, 1974-75, Del. Jud. Nominating Commn., 1977-83, Del. Superior Ct. Study Com., 1991-92; mem. Long Range Cts. Planning Com., 1976-89, Del. Ct. Common Pleas Study Com., 1992, Del. Supreme Ct. Com. on Judicial Code of Conduct, 1991-93; co-chmn. Del. Justice Ctr. Com., 1994-97; mem. lawyers adv. com. U.S. Ct. Appeals (3d cir.) 1975-80, chmn., 1975-77; chmn. local rules com. U.S. Dist. Ct. Del., 1978-83, Del. Ct. on the Judiciary Rules Com., 1996-98; bd. dirs. Bank of Del., Barclay's Bank. Trustee Wilmington Med. Ctr., 1965—, U. Del., 1971-77, Princeton U., 1974-85, 86-91, Winterthur Mus., 1991-99, World Affairs Coun. Wilmington, 1968-80, Woodrow Wilson Found., 1985—, Lawrenceville Sch., 1953-74, trustee emeritus, 1974—; trustee Nat. Humanities Ctr., 1995-98, U.S. Supreme Ct. Hist. Soc., 2004—; bd. dirs. Good Samaritan Inc., 1973—, pres., 1998—; trustee U.S. Superior Ct. Hist. Soc., 2004—; mem. Del. Health Care Injury Ins. Study Commn., 1976-80. With U.S. Army, 1942-46, 50-52 Decorated Bronze Star, Soldier's medal, Chinese Order of the Flying Cloud with four battle stars; recipient 1st State Disting. Svc. award, Del. State Bar Assn., 1984, Josiah Marvel Cup award Del. State C. of C., 1990, Benjamin Franklin Disting. Pub. Svc. award Am. Philos. Soc., 1996, Am. Inns of Ct. Professionalism award U.S. Ct. Appeals, 3d cir., 2003, Sister Eva Fink award Ministry of Caring, 2003. Fellow Am. Coll. Trial Lawyers, Am. Bar Found.; mem. ABA (ho. of dels. 1979-86), Del. State Bar Assn. (pres. 1971-72, Presdl. citation 1987), ATLA, Am. Judicature Soc. (bd. dirs. 1974-83, exec. com. 1978-80, v.p. 1980-81, pres. 1981-83, Justice award 1991). Home and Office: 600 Center Mill Rd Wilmington DE 19807-1502 E-mail: Nedcarp@aol.com.

CARPENTER, GENE BLAKELY, crystallography and chemistry educator; b. Evansville, Ind., Dec. 15, 1922; s. Leland A. and Juanita (Blakely) C.; m. Elizabeth E. Corkum, Apr. 15, 1949; children— Jonathan R., Anne E. BA, U. Louisville, 1944; MA, Harvard U., 1945, PhD, 1947. NRC fellow Calif. Inst. Tech., 1947-48, research fellow, 1948-49; instr. Brown U., 1949-52, asst. prof., 1952-56, asso. prof., 1956-63, prof., 1963-88, prof. emeritus, 1988—. Guggenheim fellow U. Leeds, Eng., 1956-57; vis. prof. U. Groningen, The Netherlands, 1963-64; Fulbright-Hayes lectr. U. Zagreb, Yugoslavia, 1971-72; vis. scientist Oak Ridge Nat. Lab., 1980, U. Göttingen, Fed. Republic of Germany, 1987, U. Canterbury, Christchurch, New Zealand, 1989. Author: Principles of Crystal Structure Determination, 1969; Contbr. articles to sci. jours. Mem. Am. Crystallographic Assn., Am. Chem. Soc. Home: 229 Medway St Apt 309 Providence RI 02906-5300 Office: Brown U Dept Chemistry Providence RI 02912-0001 Office Phone: 401-863-3389. E-mail: gene_carpenter@brown.edu.

CARPENTER, GEORGE ROBERT, artist; b. Boston, Dec. 13, 1928; s. George Gillis and Daisy Winifred Carpenter; m. Virgina A. forsyth, Oct. 14, 1966. One-man shows include Wilkes Coll., Wilkes-Barre, Pa., Rockport (Mass.) Art Assn., Red Piano Gallery, Hilton Head Island, S.C., quadrangle Gallery, Dallas, Hallway Gallery, Washington, Down East Gallery, Washington, Continental Galleries, Ontreal, Que., others; group shows include Acad. Artists Assn., Springfield, Mass., Anchorage Fine Arts Mus., Black Hills State Coll., Spearfish, S.C., cheyenne (Wyo.) Western Galleries, Copley Soc., Boston, Charles and Emma Frye Mus., Seattle, Mainstreams, Marietta, Ohio, Nat. Acad. of Design, N.Y., Rockport Art Assn., Salmagundi Club, N.Y., Wouthwestern Watercolor Soc., Dallas, others; represented in pub. and pvt. collections includingMerck Pharma., Miami U., Ohio, Mills coll., Oakland, Calif., Nat. Steamship Lines, Can., No. Trust Offices, Chgo., others. Mem. adv. bd. Coastal Conservation Assn., Maine, 1997—. Mem. Rockport Art Assn., Watercolor USA Honor Soc., Masons, Shriners, Lions. Avocation: fishing. Office: George Carpenter Gallery Perkins Cove Ogunquit ME 03907

CARPENTER, GORDON RUSSELL, retired lawyer, banker; b. Denton, Tex., Feb. 6, 1920; s. Solomon Lafayette and Grace L. (Fowler) C.; m. Muriel E. James, Sept. 18, 1943 (dec.); m. Mary Alice Borah, Aug. 4, 1962. BS, North Tex. State U., 1940; postgrad., Georgetown U., 1941-42; LL.B., So. Meth. U., 1948. Bar: Tex. 1947, U.S. Supreme Ct. 1960. Announcer KDNT, Denton, Tex., 1940-41; spl. agent FBI, 1941-46; exec. sec. Southwestern Legal Found., Dallas, 1947-56; exec. dir., 1956-58; adminstrv. asst. to dean Law Sch. So. Meth. U., 1951-58, asst. prof. law, 1956-68, pres. Law Alumni, 1959-60; trust officer 1st Nat. Bank, Dallas, 1958-60, v.p., 1960-79; v.p., sr. fin. planning officer InterfFirst Bank, Dallas, 1979-84. Pres. Law Alumni Assn., 1959. Bd. regents Tex. Sch. Trust Banking, 1981-82; bd. trustees Hatton W. Sumners Found., 1959—, exec. dir., 1985-95; chmn. North Tex. State U. Ednl. Found.; chmn. Luth. Med. Sys. Tex. Found., 1980-83; vice chmn. Farmers Br. Hosp. Authority, 1976-77. Recipient Pres.'s award State Bar Tex., 1963, Bd. Dirs. award, 1971, Gene Cavin award for excellence in con. legal edn., 1998, Disting. Law Alumni award So. Meth. U., 2001, Disting. Pub. Svc. award Hatton W. Sumners Found., 2004. Fellow Tex. Bar Found.; mem. ABA (chmn. publs. com. mineral and natural resources law sect. 1958-64), State Bar Tex. (chmn. cont. legal edn. com. 1952-54, 58-66, chmn. real estate, probate and trust law sect. 1964-65), Dallas Bar Assn. (dir. 1960-61, 65-66, chmn. centennial com. 1972-73), Dallas Bar Found. (trustee, sec.-treas.), Tex. Bankers Assn. (chmn. trust divsn. 1980-81), Soc. Former Spl. Agts. FBI (pres. 1963), Brookhaven Country Club, Masons, Delta Theta Phi. Republican. Presbyterian. Office: 325 N Saint Paul St Ste 3920 Dallas TX 75201-3821

CARPENTER, JAMES, glass innovator; BFA in Sculpture, RI Sch. of Design, 1972. Cons. Corning Glass Works, Corning, NY, 1972—82; pres. James Carpenter Design Assoc., Inc., NYC, 1978—. Named a MacArthur Fellow, 2004; recipient Inst. Honor, Am. Inst. of Arch., 1991, DuPont Benedictus award (hon. mention), 2003. Office: James Carpenter Design Assoc 4th Fl 145 Hudson St New York NY 10013

CARPENTER, JANELLA ANN, retired librarian; b. Knoxville, Tenn., Sept. 20, 1936; d. J. Beecher Carpenter, M. Janella Hooper. BS, U. Tenn., 1958; MA, George Peabody Coll. Tchrs., 1963. Cert. tchg. cert. N.C., 1958. Libr. Elizabeth Elem. Sch., Charlotte, NC, 1958—63, Merry Oaks Elem. Sch., Charlotte, NC, 1963—64; libr., media specialist Rama Rd. Elem. Sch., Charlotte, NC, 1964—88; ret., 1988. Sch. area rep., tchrs. adv. coun. Charlotte-Mecklenburg Schs., Charlotte, NC, 1983—88. Bd. dirs. Newport/Cocke County Mus., Newport; mem. Newport Regional Planning Commn., Newport, 1995—, Newport/Cocke County Tourism Coun., Newport, 1995—2002; mem. coordinating com. for growth planning Newport/Cocke County, Newport, 1998—2002; newsletter editor Dead Pigeon River Coun., Newport, 1989—93. Named Carpenter Ctr., Rama Rd. Elem. Sch., 1988. Mem.: ALA, DAR, Classroom Tchrs. Assn. (pres. 1975—76), Profl. Educators N.C. (life; 1st pres. 1979—82), Newport Garden Club, Alpha Omicron Pi, Beta Sigma Phi, Delta Kappa Gamma. Republican. Baptist. Avocations: amateur desktop printing, painting, genealogy, gardening, football. Personal E-mail: janella@planetc.com.

CARPENTER, J.D., academic administrator; b. Logan, W.Va., June 9, 1967; s. Jean L. and Charles L. Carpenter; m. Lisa J. Barker, June 11, 1994. BS, W.Va. U., 1985—89, MS, 1989—91, EdD, 1998—2002; Edn. Specialist, Marshall U. Grad. Coll., 1998—2001. Resident dir. Concord Coll., Athens, W.Va., 1991—94; dir. of residence life Salem-Teikyo U., Salem, W.Va., 1995—95; dir. of campus life Bluefield State Coll., W.Va., 1995—2001; assoc. vp for ops./student devel. Mountain State U., Beckley, W.Va., 2001—. Membership coord. Region II - Nat. Assn. of Student Pers. Administrators, Washington, 1999—; naspa liaison W.Va. Assn. of Student Pers. Administrators, Beckley, W.Va., 2000—. Pres. Gamma Beta Phi Nat. Honor and Svc. Soc., Oak Ridge, Tenn., 1998—99; W. Va. state coord. Basset Hound Rescue of Old Dominion, Charlottesville, Va., 1998—2003; deacon Parkview Bapt. Ch., Bluefield, Va., 2002—03. Mem.: Nat. Assn. of Student Pers. Administrators (assoc.), W.Va. Assn. of Student Pers. Administrators (assoc.). Independent. Baptist. Avocations: camping, fishing, travel, photography. Office: Mountain State U PO Box 9003 Beckley WV 25802 E-mail: jd@mountainstate.edu.

CARPENTER, JEFFREY PALMER, vascular surgeon, researcher; b. Sunbury, Pa., Nov. 25, 1959; s. John Andrew and Jane (Curran) C.; m. Judith Trachtenberg, May 31, 1985; children: John, Katharine. BA, Amherst Coll., 1981; MD, MDiv, Yale U., 1986. Diplomate Am. Bd. Surgery. Prof. surgery U. Pa., Phila. Office Phone: 215-662-2029.

CARPENTER, JOANN DEAKIN, history professor; b. Bangor, Maine, Aug. 9, 1955; d. Donald Frederick and Sylvia Hanson Deakin; m. Bruce Michael Carpenter, June 15, 1984; 1 child, Michael Hanson. BA, Wofford Coll., 1977; MA, PhD, Emory U., 1987. Prof. history Fla. C.C., Jacksonville, Fla., 1988—. Author supplements Prentice-Hall, Upper Saddle, NJ, 1999—; faculty dir. NEH-Faces of America Fla. C.C., Jacksonville, 2001—02. Cons. Boys and Girls Club, Jacksonville, 2003—. Mem.: Orgn. American History, So. Hist. Assn. (recruiting officer 1988—), Am. Hist. Assn. Democrat. Luth. Avocations: reading, needlecrafts, cooking. Office: Florida Community Coll Jacksonville 11901 Beach Blvd Jacksonville FL 32246 Office Phone: 904-646-2415. Office Fax: 904-646-2315. Business E-Mail: jcarpent@fccj.edu.

CARPENTER, JOHN HOWARD, director, screenwriter; b. Carthage, N.Y., Jan. 16, 1948; s. Howard Ralph and Milton Jean (Carter) C; m. Sandra Ann King, Dec. 1, 1990; 1 child, John Cody. Student, U. So. Calif., 1972. Co-writer, editor, composer: (short film) The Resurrection of Bronco Billy, 1970 (Academy award best live action short subject 1970); writer, prodr., dir., composer: (films) Dark Star, 1974; writer, dir., composer: (films) Assault on Precinct 13, 1976, Halloween, 1978, The Fog, 1980, Escape from New York, 1981, Prince of Darkness, 1987, They Live, 1988; writer, prodr., composer: (films) Halloween II, 1981; prodr., composer: (films) Halloween III: Season of the Witch, 1982; dir.: (films) The Thing, 1982, Starman, 1984, Memoirs of an Invisible Man, 1992, In the Mouth of Madness, 1994, Escape from L.A., 1996, Vampires, 1998, Halloween H2O, 1998; (TV movies) Elvis, 1979; dir., composer: (films) Christine, 1983, Big Trouble in Little China, 1986; exec. prodr.: (films) The Philadelphia Experiment, 1984, (TV movies) John Carpenter Presents Body Bags, 1993; writer: (films) The Eyes of Laura Mars, 1978, Black Moon Rising, 1986, (TV movies) Zuma Beach, 1978, Better Late Than Never, 1979, El Diablo, 1990, Blood River, 1991; writer, dir.: (TV movies) Someone's Watching Me!, 1978; composer: (films) Halloween V: The Revenge of Michael Myers, 1989. Mem. ASCAP, Dirs. Guild Am. West, Writers Guild Am. West. Avocations: music, helicopter piloting. Office: ICM 8942 Wilshire Blvd Beverly Hills CA 90211-1934

CARPENTER, JOHN MARLAND, engineer, physicist; b. Williamsport, Pa., June 20, 1935; s. John Hiram and Ruth Edith (Johnson) Carpenter; m. Rhonda DeCardy, 1991; children: John Marland Jr., Kathryn Ann, Susan Marie, Janet Elaine. BS in Engring. Sci, Pa. State U., 1957; MS in Nuclear Engring, U. Mich., 1958, PhD, 1963. Fellow Oak Ridge Inst. Nuclear Studies, 1957-60; postdoctoral fellow Inst. Sci. and Tech., U. Mich., 1963-64, mem. faculty univ., 1964-75, prof. nuclear engring., 1973-75; vis. scientist nuclear tech. br. Phillips Petroleum Co., 1965; solid state sci. div. Argonne (Ill.) Nat. Lab., 1971-72, 73; physics div. Los Alamos Sci. Lab., 1973; sr. physicist solid state sci. div., mgr. intense pulsed neutron source project Argonne Nat. Lab., 1975-77, program dir., 1977-78, tech. dir., 1978—. Mem. U.S. del. to USSR on fundamental properties of matter, 1977; co-founder Internat. Collaboration on Advanced Neurton Sources, 1977; vis. scientist Japanese Lab. for High Energy Physics, 1982, 93; mem. indsl. and profl. adv. coun. Coll. Engring., Pa. State U., 1984—87; mem. nat. steering com. Advanced Neutron Source, 1986—95, mem. exec. com.; mem. grad. faculty Iowa State U., 1988—93; mem. internat. sci. coun. AUSTRON, Austria, 1993—; mem. external rev. com. Accelerator Prodn. Tritium Project Los Alamos Nat. Lab., N.Mex., 1995—98; mem. internat. adv. com.Scientific Coun. on Condensed Matter Investigations with Neutrons Russian Ministry of Sci. and Tech., 1996—; sr. tech. advisor exptl. facilities divsn. SNS Oak Ridge Nat. Lab., 1999—; vis. scientist Rutherford Appleton Lab., 1997—; mem. steering com. spallation neutron source Oak Ridge Nat. Lab., 1996—98, sci. adv. com. for spallation neutron source, 1996—2001. Author: (with Motoharu Kimura) Living with Nuclei, 1993, editor; patentee nuclear instrumentation, neutron scattering, time dependent neutron thermalization, pulsed spallation neutron sources, neutron scattering instrumentation, structure and dynamcs of amorphous solids. Presdl. appointee vis. com. dept. nuclear engring. MIT, 1989-95. Recipient Disting. Svc. award, U. Mich. Dept. Nuc. Engring., 1967, L.J. Hamilton Disting. Alumnus award, 1977, Disting. Performance award for work at Argonne Nat. Lab., U. Chgo., 1982, Ilja M. Frank prize, Joint Inst. Nuc. Rsch., 1998, merit award, Dept. Nuc. Engring. and Radiol. Scis., U. Mich. Alumni Soc., 2001. Fellow Condensed Matter Physics Divsn, Am. Phys. Soc.; mem. Am. Nuclear Soc. (sect. chmn. 1974-75), Neutron Scattering Soc. Am. (mem. subcom. on pulsed spallation sources 1993—, mem. pulsed source steering com.). Office: Argonne Nat Lab Intense Pulsed Neutron Source Argonne IL 60439 E-mail: jmcarpenter@anl.gov.

CARPENTER, JOHN R., finance educator; b. Phila., Pa., July 31, 1962; s. Frank Lewis and Hannelore Carpenter; m. Carol Sue Huguelet, June 22, 1985; children: J. David, Rosa Mae, Anna Deborah. BS in Forestry, Mich. Technol. U., 1984; MS in Bus. Adminstrn., Boston U., 1989; MDiv, Grand Rapids Theol. Sem., Mich., 2000; postgrad. in Applied Mgmt. and Decision Sci., Walden U., Mpls., 2003—05. Engring. officer US Army Corps of Engring., Washington, 1984—90; engr. mgmt. US Fish and Wildlife Svc., 1990—96; adj. prof. of bus. and mgmt Cornerstone U., 1997—; adj. prof. of sustainable bus. Aquanis U., Grand Rapids, 2004—; adj. faculty Taylor U. Ctr. for Lifelong Learning, Ind., 2005—. Chaplain Boy Scouts of Am., Grand Rapids, 1999—; health officer Gerber Boy Scout Reservation, Twin Lakes, Mich., 2005—. Mem. Cornerstone U. Alumni Assn., 2000—, Boston U. Alumni Assn., 2002—; charter mem. Citizen Flag Alliance, 1994—; mem. Mich. Technol. U. Alumni Assn., Houghton, Mich., 1984—, Nat. Arbor Day Found., 2003—, Am. Legion, Mich., 2004—; chaplain Boy Scouts of Am., Grand Rapids, 1998—; adult leader Venturing BSA Crew 2219, 2001—; trainer, tchr. Kent Dist. BSA, 2002—; com. mem. Venture BSA Crew 9099, Twin Lakes, Mich., 2004—; mem., fin. sec. Trinity Bapt. Ch., 2000—. Capt. U.S. Army, 1984—90, Fort Dix, NJ, Frankfurt Germany, Washington DC. Recipient God and Svc., PRAY, Boy Scouts of Am., and Trinity Bapt. Ch., 2003, Kent Dist. award of merit, Boy Scouts Am., 2005. Mem.: Christian Bus. Faculty Assn., Decision Sci. Inst., Math. Assn. of Am. Avocations: camping, hiking, fishing, reading. Home: 3049 Windover Dr NE Grand Rapids MI 49525

CARPENTER, KATHRYN HAMMELL, library director, educator; b. Beloit, Wis., Jan. 1, 1954; d. Jay Barnes Hammell and Josephine Anne Winter; m. John Charles Carpenter, Dec. 26, 1986; 1 child, Caleigh Sage. AB in Sociology, U. Ill., 1976, MSLS, 1977. Cert. Acad. Health Info. Profls. Med. Libr. Assn., 1991, Med. Libr. Assn. Asst. edn. and social sci. libr., vis. instr. U. Ill., Urbana, 1977—78; documents libr., instr. Libr. Health Scis., U. Ill. at the Med. Ctr., Chgo., 1979—80, interlibrary loan libr., asst. prof., 1980—83; acquisitions libr., assoc. prof. Libr. Health Sciences, U. Ill., Chgo., 1983—87; bibliographer for the health sciences, assoc. prof. U. Ill., Chgo., 1988—93; u. libr., assoc. prof. Valparaiso (Ind.) U., 1993—98; libr. dir., prof. of libr. sci. Purdue U. Calumet, Hammond, Ind., 1998—. Dir. at large Academic Librs. Ind., Indpls., 2004—05, dir., 2005—. Editor: (assn. jour.) Libr. Adminstrn. & Mgmt., 2005; author: (annual price index) Prices of U.S. and Foreign Published Materials, 1989—96, (collection mgmt.) Competition, Collaboration, and Cost in the New Knowledge Environment, 1996, (reference book) Sourcebook on Parenting and Child Care, 1995, (the acquisitions librarian) Forecasting Expenditures for Library Materials: Approaches and Techniques, 1989; co-author: (annual price index) U.S. Periodicals Price Index; assoc. editor: assn. jour. Libr. Adminstrn. & Mgmt., 2001—02. Dir. Hammond Reads, 2003—05; sec., dir. Montessori Children's Schoolhouse, Inc., Hammond, 2003—. Recipient Cert., HERS/Bryn Mawr Summer Inst. for Women in Higher Edn. Adminstrn., 1985; grantee Moellering Library's Self-Development Initiatives, Lilly Endowment Inc., 1995; Gov.'s Summer fellow, State of Ill., 1975. Mem.: Am. Assn. for Higher Edn., ALA (dir. at large Libr. Adminstrn. and Mgmt. Assn. 2003—05), Woodmar-Hammond Kiwanis. Avocations: resistance training, skiing, golf, fashion. Office: Purdue University Calumet 2200 169th St Hammond IN 46323 Office Phone: 219-989-2249. Business E-Mail: carpent@calumet.purdue.edu.

CARPENTER, KENNETH JOHN, nutrition educator; b. London, May 17, 1923; came to U.S., 1977; s. James Frederick and Dorothy (George) C.; m. Daphne Holmes, June 22, 1944 (dec. 1974); 1 child, Roger Hugh; m. Antonina Pecoraro, June 18, 1977. BA, U. Cambridge, Eng., 1944, PhD, 1948, ScD, 1974. Mem. sci. staff Rowett Inst., Aberdeen, Scotland, 1948-56; lectr., then reader in nutrition U. Cambridge, 1956-77; prof. nutrition U. Calif., Berkeley, 1977-91. Author: History of Scurvy and Vitamin C, 1986, Protein and Energy, 1994, Beriberi, White Rice and Vitamin B, 2000; editor: Pellagra, 1982. Kellogg fellow Harvard U., 1955-56, Commonwealth fellow Cen. Food Tech. Rsch. Inst., Mysore, India, 1961, fellow Sidney Sussex Coll., Cambridge, U.K., 1961-77. Fellow Am. Inst. Nutritional Sci.(Atwater medal 1993, Hatch medal 1993); mem. History of Sci. Soc. Avocations: art history, gardening. Home: 6201 Rockwell St Oakland CA 94618-1350 Office: U Calif Dept Nutritional Sci Berkeley CA 94720-3104 Office Phone: 510-642-1038. E-mail: kcarp@uclink.berkeley.edu.

CARPENTER, LINDA MEERDINK, nursing educator; d. Peter B. and Geneva H. Meerdink; m. Delbert Stanley Carpenter, June 25, 1994; children: Robert Scott Evans, Peter Clark Evans. BSN, U. N.Mex, Albuquerque, 1966—70; MSN, U. Ark. for Med. Scis., Little Rock, 1978—80; PhD, U. Ariz., Tucson, 1987—93. Cert. Nurse Practitioner in Family Practice, Ark. State Bd. Nursing, 1980, in Maternal and Child Health Nursing Practice, Am. Nurses' Assn., 1989. Nursing instr. U. N.Mex, Albuquerque; RN St. Joseph's Hosp., Albuquerque, 1971—72; clin. nurse specialist Ark. Children's Hosp., Little Rock, 1980—83; asst. prof. U. Ark. for Med. Scis., Little Rock, 1980—85; instr. U. Ariz., Tucson, 1985—93; project coord., accelerated pathways for second degree students U. Ariz. Coll. Nursing, Tucson, 1992—94, coord. for academic affairs, 1993—94; dir. Blinn Coll. Assoc. Degree Nursing Program, Bryan, Tex., 1994—97; divsn. chair, family health nursing U. Tex. of Austin Sch. Nursing, 1997—99; asst. dean, student and clin. affairs U. Tex. Sch. Nursing, Austin, 1998—2005, assoc. prof. clin. nursing. Cons. Am. Internat. Health Alliance, Almaty, Kazakhstan, 1994; immunization edn. project consulting Tex. A&M U. Kinesiology Dept., College Station, 1995—98, gestational diabetes tng. project, 1996—98.

Contbr. articles to profl. jours. Adminstrv. dir. Friends of Children's Wellness Ctr., Tex., 2000—05; cons. U. Tex. Elem. Sch., Austin, 2003—05, Austin CC Health Inst., Tex., 2002—05. Mem.: Assn. for the Study of Higher Edn. (curriculum com. 1992—94). Home: 129 Mountain Laurel Way Bastrop TX 78602 Office: Univ Texas 1700 Red River Austin TX 78701 Office Phone: 512-232-4799. Office Fax: 512-232-4777. E-mail: lcarpenter@mail.utexas.edu.

CARPENTER, MARGARET S. (MOLLY CARPENTER), artist; b. Wilmington, Del., Jan. 21, 1960; d. Richard Paulett and Margaret Marvel Sanger; m. Samuel Preston Carpenter, Oct. 4, 1981; children: Benjamin Sanger, Margaret Paulett. Student, Pa. Acad. Fine Arts, Phila., 1978—79, Frudakis Acad. Fine Arts, 1978—81. Apprentice Charles Cropper Parks, Wilmington, 1977-80; sculptor, Salem, 1981—. One-woman shows include Gallery 50, Bridgeton, N.J., 1983, 86, 92, Gloucester C.C., 1988, Vineland Pub. Libr., 1988; exhibited in group shows, including Wilmington Christmas Shop Artists' Gallery, 1981-2000, Glassboro State Coll., 1989, Longwood Gardens, Kennett Square, Pa., 1993, Rockfeller Ctr., 1996, Independence Seaport Mus., Phila., 1996, The Coliseum, N.Y.C., 1996, Ronald McDonald House, 1996-98, 2003, Nat. Sculpture Soc., 1997, Catherine Lorillard Wolfe Art Club, Nat. Arts Club, N.Y.C, 1999, Del. Art Mus., 1999, Olympic Regional Devel. Assn., Mus., 2000, Goodwill Games Mus., 2000; represented in permanent collections Independence Seaport Mus., Du Pont Children's Hosp., Wilmington, 1989; commns. include Constl. Compass Rose, Del. Heritage Commn. for U.S. Constn. Bicentennial, Legis. Hall, Dover, 1987, bas relief sculpture to honor Judge Samuel Desimone, Bar Assns. Cumberland, Salem and Gloucester Counties, N.J., 2000; portrait sculptures include Vince Gioaya, Robert Kasey, Dr. Martin Luther King Jr.; designer rooms class Phila. Flower Show, 1990-2001. Bd. dirs. Salem County Arts Alliance, 1997—, v.p., 2000—; mem. arts com. Salem County Cultural and Heritage Commn., 1998—; bd. dirs. Salem County Cultural and Heritage, 1998—. Recipient numerous best of show awards, award sculpture AIDS Del., 1998; creator of Achievement Award in Sculpture, Creative Grandparenting Del., 2000. Mem. Nat. Sculpture Soc. Home: 465 Kings Hwy Salem NJ 08079 E-mail: sculptor@mollycarpenter.com.

CARPENTER, MARK WARREN, social sciences educator; b. Long Beach, Calif., Nov. 11, 1949; s. Philip Benham and Nancy Anne (Banchor) C. BA in Comm., Calif. State U., Fullerton, 1974, MPA, 1977; MA in Behavioral Sci., Calif. State U., Dominguez Hills, 1982; MA in Edn., U. Calif., Riverside, 1994. Life cert. tchr. cmty. coll. sociology; life cert. FCC. Editor, rsch. analyst, project coord. Govt. edn. Ctr., L.A., 1975-76; rsch. fellow Calif. State U., Dominguez Hills, 1980-81, mem. staff registrar's office Fullerton, 1984-87; tchg. asst. U. Calif., Riverside, 1987-88; lectr., mem. faculty dept. sociology Riverside C.C., 1989—. Founder, World Citizens Institute, 1986. Author/compiler: (ednl. directory) After Work in Los Angeles, 1976; author, editor: (gen. plan element) Torrance Energy Awareness Monograph, 1978. Sgt. U.S. Army, 1969-71, Vietnam. Mem. Am. Ednl. Rsch. Assn., Am. Soc. Pub. Adminstrn. (mem. higher edn. and govt. rels. com.), Sociology of Edn. Assn., Assn. Environ. Profls., Calif. Coop. Edn. Assn., Internat. Assn. Cognitive Edn., Internat. Platform Assn., Com. for Expanded Ednl. Opportunity, So. Calif. Assn. Govts., Mensa. Avocations: surfing, writing. Home: PO Box 8116 Moreno Valley CA 92552-8116 Office: Riverside C C 4800 Magnolia Ave Riverside CA 92506-1242 E-mail: mark.carpenter@rcc.edu.

CARPENTER, MICHAEL A., financial services executive; b. London, Mar. 24, 1947; came to U.S., 1971; s. Walter and Kathleen Mary C.; m. Mary Aughton, Mar. 1, 1975; children: Nicholas James, Abigail Lee. BSc with joint honors, U. Nottingham, Eng., 1968; LLD (hon.), U. Nottingham; MBA, Harvard U., 1973. Bus. analyst Mond div. Imperial Chem. Industries, Runcorn, England, 1968-71; cons., mgr. Boston Cons. Group, 1973-78, v.p., 1978-83; v.p. bus. devel. and planning GE Capital Corp., Fairfield, Conn., 1983-86, exec. v.p. Stamford, Conn., 1986—89, GE Financial Services Inc., 1986—89; chmn., pres., CEO Kidder Peabody & Co. Inc., 1989—94; exec. v.p. Travelers Group, Hartford, 1994—98, chmn., CEO, pres. life and annuity, 1995—98, vice chmn., 1998; chmn., CEO Salomon Smith Barney, N.Y.C., 1998—2002, Citigroup Global Investments, N.Y.C., 1998—. Bd. dirs. NYC Investment Fund, Mikronite Techs., Inc. Baker scholar Harvard Bus. Sch., 1973 Office: Citigroup Global Investments 399 Park Ave, 3rd Fl New York NY 10022

CARPENTER, MICHAEL H., lawyer; b. Huntington, W.Va., Mar. 3, 1953; BA, Ohio State U., 1974, JD, 1977. Bar: Ohio 1977. Former ptnr. Jones, Day, Reavis & Pogue, Columbus, Ohio; ptnr. Carpenter & Lipps LLP, Columbus, 1994—. Mem. Order of Coif, Phi Beta Kappa. Office: Carpenter & Lipps LLP 280 Plaza Ste 1300 280 N High St Columbus OH 43215 Office Phone: 614-365-4100. Business E-Mail: carpenter@carpenterlipps.com.

CARPENTER, MYRON ARTHUR, manufacturing executive; b. Jacksonville, Ill., Nov. 12, 1938; s. Paul Floyd and Margaret Esther C.; m. JoAnn Fisher, June 22, 1963. BA in Acctg, U. Ill., 1960. C.P.A., Mo. Staff acct. Arthur Young & Co., St. Louis, 1960-67, audit mgr., 1967-71; controller Bank Bldg. & Equipment Corp., St. Louis, 1972-78; v.p., treas. Bank Bldg. & Equipment Corp. Am., St. Louis, 1978-82, v.p. fin., treas., 1982-83, sr. v.p., chief fin. officer, 1983-90; v.p. fin., adminstrn. Gemco, Inc., Collinsville, Ill., 1991—. Author: (with Neal W. Beckman) Purchasing for Profit, 1979. Served with U.S. Army, 1961. Mem. AICPA, Mo. Soc. CPAs, Delta Phi.

CARPENTER, NANCY J., health science association administrator; Assoc. dir. H.A. Chapman Inst. Med. Genetics, Tulsa, Okla.; pres. Am. Bd. Med. Genetics, 2001—. Adj. prof. biochemistry Okla. State U. Office: H A Chapman Inst Med Genetics 4502 E 41st St Tulsa OK 74135-2553 Business E-Mail: ncarpenter@hillcrest.com.

CARPENTER, NATHANIEL DENNARD, nursing administrator; b. Phila., Feb. 2, 1959; s. Marvin Dennard and Rose Ann (Heath) Carpenter; m. Jennifer Jones, Mar. 2001; children: Jeffrey Nathan, Eric Randolph; 1 child from previous marriage, Natalie Deneen. Lic. practical nurse, James Martin Sch., Phila., 1982. Staff nurse Med. Coll. Pa., Phila., 1982-85; nursing coord. Hosp. Home Care Greater Phila., 1985-86; staff nurse Kimberly Quality Care, Phila., 1986-90; staff nurse ICU St. Agnes Med. Ctr., Phila., 1987-90; asst. resident health coord. Logan Sq. East, Phila., 1989-92, resident health coord., 1991-94; staff nurse New Ralston House, Phila., 1994—97, asst. primary instr. P&A nursing, 2003—. Author: Vital Signs, 1990. Vol. speaker Planned Parenthood, Phila., 1982-85. With USAF, 1976-77. Avocations: reading, sports. Home: 5209 Harlan St Philadelphia PA 19131-4022 Office: Logan Sq East 2 Franklin Town Blvd Philadelphia PA 19103-1238 E-mail: nuheart1@netzero.net.

CARPENTER, PAULA JO, elementary school educator; b. New Martinsville, W. Va., June 1, 1963; d. James Marlin and Gwenola Jo (Norton) C. BS, David Lipscomb Coll., 1984. Tchr. middle sch. Ga. Christian Sch., Valdosta, tchr. first grade, 1987-89; kindergarten tchr. Palm Beach Christian Sch., W. Palm Beach, Fla., 1984-87; dir. Humpty Dumpty Playsch., Inc., Lake Park, Ga., 1989-90; kindergarten tchr., chorus dir. Ga. Christian Sch., Valdosta, Ga., 1990-91, 1st grade tchr., 1991-92, 95—, 1st and 2d grade tchr., 1992-94. Named Tchr. of Yr. 1986, Palm Beach Christian Sch. Mem. Women's Orgn. for Serving Youth (rec. sec.), Internat. Reading Assn. Mem. Ch. of Christ. Home: 5512 Danieli Pl Lake Park GA 31636-2128

CARPENTER, PEARL ELIZABETH, artist; b. Balt., May 7, 1939; d. James William and Lillian Elizabeth (Wyble) Truett; m. Harry F. Carpenter, Aug. 16, 1958; children: Harry F. III, Donald Alan, David James. Student, Washington Coll., Chestertown, Md., 1957—58. Owner Shades Mother Nature, Glen Burnie, Md., 1979—; instrnl. aide Anne Arundel County Bd. Edn., Md., 1973—79; instr. Anne Arundel CC, 1981—99; ret., 1999. Tchr. line dancing Anne Arundel Sr. Ctrs., 1999—; tchr. color pencil painting at sr. ctrs. Anne Arundel C.C.; also cake decorating, panoramic sugar eggs Anne Arundel Sr. Ctrs.; cons. Harundale Mall, Glen Burnie, 1985. Exhibitions include, Annapolis, Md., Chesapeake, Essex Wildfowl Expositions, Glen Burnie HS Artisans Exhibit, Officers Wives, Ft. Meade, Md., others, Represented in permanent collections Senator Mattingly, Ga.; author, pub.: poems Ponderings, 1982, book The Duck Book 1 and 2, 1984, rev. edit., 1988, Painting Textured Carvings, 1991, newsletter News, Views and Revs., 1985—90; grain paintings process, 1980. Chmn., founder PTA Block Parent Program, 1974—75; pres. Glen Burnie HS Band Parents, 1980—81, cons., 1982—, promoter, dir. artisan's showcase, 1987—89. Named Best in Show, AA Carvers, 1993; recipient awards for woodcarvings and decoy paintings, 1988—. Mem.: Nat. Carvers Assn., Arundel Carvers Club, Moose. Democrat. Avocations: reading, water sports, art, travel.

CARPENTER, RAY WARREN, engineering educator, materials engineer; b. Berkeley, Calif., 1934; s. Fritz Josh and Ethel Thordis (Davisson) C.; m. Ann Louise Leavitt, July 10, 1955; children: Shannon R., Sheila A., Matthew L. BS in Engring., U. Calif., Berkeley, 1958, MS in Metallurgy, 1959, PhD in Metallurgy, 1966. Registered profl. engr., Calif. Sr. engr. Aerojet-Gen. Nucleonics, San Ramon, Calif., 1959-64; sr. metallurgist Stanford Rsch Inst., Menlo Park, Calif., 1966-67; mem. sr. rsch. staff Oak Ridge (Tenn.) Nat. Lab., 1967-80; prof. Solid State Sci. & Engring. Ariz. State U., Tempe, 1980—, prof. chem. and materials engring., 2003—, dir. Facility for High Resolution Electron Microscopy, 1980-83, dir. Ctr. for Solid State Sci., 1985-91, also bd. dirs. Ctr. for Solid State Sci. Chmn. doctoral program on sci. and engring. of materials, 1987-90, 94-98; vis. prof. U. Tenn., 1976-78; adj. prof. Vanderbilt U., Nashville, 1979-81. Contbg. author books; contbr. articles to profl. rsch. jour. and symposia; editor Phys. and Material Scis., Jour. of the Microscopy Soc. of Am., 1994-97; editor Microscopy and Microanalysis, 1995-2000; dep. editor Acta Materialia, 2001--. Recipient awards, Internat. Metallographic Soc. and Am. Soc. for Metals competition, 1976, 77, 79; Faculty Disting. Achievement award Ariz. State U. Alumni Assn., 1990. Mem. Electron Microscopy Soc. Am. (pres. 1989, dir. phys. sci. 1980-83), Metall. Soc. of AIME, Materials Rsch. Soc., Am. Phys. Soc., Am. Ceramic Soc., Sigma Xi. Office: Ariz State U Ctr Solid State Sci Tempe AZ 85287-1704 Office Phone: 480-965-4549. Business E-Mail: carpenter@asu.edu.

CARPENTER, RICHARD NORRIS, retired lawyer, energy consultant; b. Cortland, NY, Feb. 14, 1937; s. Robert P. and Sylvia (Norris) C.; m. Elizabeth Bigbee, Aug. 1961 (div. June 1975); 1 child, Andrew Norris; m. Leslie Nordby, July, 1991. BA magna cum laude, Syracuse U., 1958; LLB, Yale U., 1962. Bar: N.Y. 1962, N.Mex. 1963, U.S. Dist. Ct. (no. dist.) N.Y., U.S. Dist. Ct. N.Mex., U.S. Ct. Appeals (D.C. and 10th cirs.), U.S. Supreme Ct. Assoc. Breed, Abbott & Morgan, N.Y.C., 1962, Bigbee & Byrd, 1963—67; ptnr. Bigbee Law Firm et al., 1967—78, Carpenter et al. Law Firm, 1978—97; ptnr., co-owner Carpenter & Nixon, 1997—2000; owner Carpenter Law Firm, 2000—02; ret., 2002. Spl. asst. atty. gen., State of N.Mex., 1963-74, 90-96; sec. Bokum Corp., Miami, Fla., 1969-70; bd. dirs. Bigbee Cattle Co., 1978-86, Sandia TV Corp., 1975. Adv. bd. Interstate Mining Compact, N.Mex., 1981-88; elder 1st Presbyn. Ch., Santa Fe, 1978-80, 86-89, bd. trustees, 1975-77, pres., 1977; bd. dirs. Santa Fe Cmty. Coun., 1965-67, Santa Fe Prep. Sch., 1981-84, pres., 1982-84; bd. trustees St. Vincent Hosp. Found., Santa Fe, 1980-82, v.p. 1983-84; bd. trustees St. Vincent Hosp., 1980-86, 1987-2001, chmn. 1985-86, 90-93, 1998-2000; bd. dirs. Santa Fe YMCA, 1964-69, pres., 1969; trustee Santa Fe Prep. Permanent Endowment Fund., 1987-90; bd. trustees, treas. Con Alma Health Found., 2002—; bd. regents N.Mex. Tech., 2003—, sec., treas., 2004—; bd. dirs. N.Mex. Edn. Assistance Found., 2003—; bd. trustees Archdiocese of Santa Fe Cath. Found., 2003—; mem. jt. city-county Santa Fe Energy Task Force, 2004—. Rotary Found. fellow, Panjab U., Pakistan, 1959-60. Mem. N.Mex. Bar Assn., N.Y. State Bar Assn., The Best Lawyers of Am., Phi Beta Kappa, Pi Sigma Alpha, Phi Beta Phi. Home and Office: 1048 Bishops Lodge Rd Santa Fe NM 87501-1009 E-mail: rncarpenter@aol.com.

CARPENTER, ROBERT C., state legislator, retired banker; b. Franklin, N.C., June 18, 1924; m. Helen Carpenter. Student, Ind. U., Kokomo, 1947, Purdue U., 1950, U. Va., 1964, Western Carolina U. V.p. bank, 32 yrs.; ret.; mem. N.C. Senate, Raleigh, 1988—. Ranking minority mem. appropriations com. on Dept. Transp., judiciary I com., mem. appropriations/base budget com., commerce com., pensions and retirement and aging com., vice chmn. transp. com. Mem. Am. Legis. Exch. Coun.; commr. Macon County, N.C., 1978-82. Pilot USN, 1943-45. Mem. Am. Legion, KC, Rotary. Republican. Roman Catholic. Office: NC Senate 300 N Salisbury St Raleigh NC 27603-5925 also: 29 Admiral Dr Franklin NC 28734-1981

CARPENTER, RON D., music educator; b. Lyons, Kans., Oct. 22, 1966; life ptnr. Tim M. Outland. MusB in Edn., No. Ariz. U., 1985—90, M of Ednl. Leadership, 1995—97. Dir. of choirs Hendrix Jr. H.S., Chandler, 1993—; artistic dir. Phoenix Children's Chorus, 1993—. Day camp dir. U. of Miami Choral Camp, Coral Gables, 1999—. State officer Ariz. Music Educators Assn., Phoenix, 1998—2000. Mem.: Am. Choral Directors Assn. (standards com. 1999—2001, Invitation to perform at conv. 1998). Achievements include Bronze and SilverCertificate at the World Choral Olympics 2000 and 2004. Avocations: travel, weight training. Office: Hendrix Junior High School 1550 W Summit Pl Chandler AZ 85224 Personal E-mail: azmisterc@aol.com.

CARPENTER, ROSALIE T., education educator, consultant; b. Braddock, Pa., Apr. 6, 1954; d. Frank William and Clara Zezzo Tigano; m. Stephen G. Carpenter, Jan. 7, 1978; children: Claire Elizabeth, George Wilson II. BA, Wesleyan U., 1976; MA, Marshall U., 1983; EdD, W.Va. U., 1994. Asst. prof. Fairmont (W.Va.) State Coll., 1995—96, Waynesburg (Pa.) Coll., 1996—2000; assoc. prof. Washington & Jefferson Coll., Washington, Pa., 2000—, dir. elem. edn. Cons. Ednl. Futures, Morgantown, W.Va., 1990—. Mem.: Coun. Exceptional Children, Nat. Assn. Edn. Young Children, Kappa Delta Epsilon (counselor). Avocations: walking, strength training, exercise. Business E-Mail: rcarpenter@washjeff.edu.

CARPENTER, RUSSELL H., JR., lawyer; b. Providence, May 17, 1941; AB, Princeton U., 1963; BPhil in Politics, Oxford U., Eng., 1965; LLB, Yale U., 1968. Bar: D.C. 1968. Law clk. to Hon. David Bazelon U.S. Ct. Appeals (D.C. cir.), 1968-69; mem. Covington & Burling, Washington. Contbr. articles to profl. jours. Rhodes scholar. Mem. Order Coif. Office: Covington & Burling PO Box 7566 1201 Pennsylvania Ave NW Washington DC 20004-2401 E-mail: rcarpenter@cov.com.

CARPENTER, SHEILA JANE, lawyer; b. Kyoto, Oct. 16, 1950; d. Chester Elwin and Betty (Boulger) C.; m. William Joseph McCarthy, May 26, 1973; 1 child, Diana Elizabeth. BA, Purdue U., 1972; JD, Yale U., 1975. Bar: Md. 1975, U.S. Dist. Ct. Md. 1976, D.C. 1977, U.S. Dist. Ct. D.C. 1978, U.S. Supreme Ct. 1980, U.S. Dist. Ct. (no. dist.) Ohio 1980, U.S. Claims Ct. 1982, U.S. Ct. Appeals (D.C. cir.) 1983, U.S. Ct. Appeals (4th and Fed. cirs.) 1984, U.S. Ct. Appeals (8th cir.) 2000, U.S. Ct. Appeals (5th cir.) 2004. Assoc. Weinberg & Green, Balt., 1975-77, Sutherland, Asbill & Brennan, Washington, 1977-82, ptnr., 1982-96, Jorden Burt LLP, Washington, 1996—. Pub. svc. com. Sutherland, Asbill & Brennan, 1990-94, chair, 1990-92, chair litigation group Washington office, 1991-93; web chair life, health and disability com. Def. Rsch. Inst., 2000-04. Contbr. articles to profl. jours. Fellow Am. Bar Found.; mem. ABA (mem. excess surplus lines and reins. com. TIPS sect., vice chmn. 1992-94, chair 1995-96, vice chair pub. regulation ins. commn. TIPS sect. 1995-2000, mem. life ins. com. TIPS sect., vice chair 2004-), Am. Arbitration Assn. (arbitrator large complex case panel), Md. Bar Assn., Phi Beta Kappa. Office: Jorden Burt LLP Ste 400E 1025 Thomas Jefferson St NW Washington DC 20007-5208 Office Phone: 202-965-8165. E-mail: sjc@jordenusa.com.

CARPENTER, STANLEY DEAN MACDONALD, military officer, educator; b. Raleigh, NC, Aug. 28, 1953; s. William Lester and Mattie Frances (Wallace) Carpenter; m. Jennifer Ann Wells, June 1, 1985 (div. Mar. 1998); children: Christopher Kenneth Wells, William Gerald Wells Wells, Samantha Theresa Wells. BA, U. of NC, 1975; MA in Lit., U. of St. Andrews, Scotland, 1978; PhD, Fla. State U., 1998; Diploma in Strategic Studies, US Naval War Coll., 2000. Real Estate Broker's Lic. NC State, 1987. Advanced through grades to capt. USN, 1979—; task leader Booz Allen & Hamilton, Inc., Arlington, Va., 1984—87; dep. program mgr. LSA, Inc., Arlington, 1988—90; grad. student/instr. Fla. State U., 1991—98; prof. of strategy/policy US Naval War Coll., 1998—, command historian, strategy/policy divsn. head, Coll. of Distance Edn. Adj. prof. of history Am. Mil. U., Manassas Pk., Va., 1996—, Salve Regina U., Newport, RI, 1999—. Author: (book) Mil. Leadership in the Br. Civil Wars: "The Genius of this Age", 2003; contbr. numerous articles in ency., conf. papers, and book reviews. Vol. Boy Scouts of Am., 1961, Portsmouth Cmty. Theater, RI, USS NC Hist. Detachment, Wilmington, NC, 1998—. Recipient Phi Alpha Theta, FSU Delta Chpt., 1992; grantee Clan Donald Ednl. and Charitable Trust scholarship, 1975—77, Richard C. Maguire scholarship, Rock Island Arsenal Hist. Soc., 1992—95, Henry J. Reilly Mem. Grad. scholarship, Res. Officers Assn. of the US, 1992—94. Fellow: Res. Officers Assn.; mem.: Navy League of the US, RI Employer Support to the Guard and Res., Naval Res. Assn., Royal United Services Inst., US Naval Inst., Triangle U. Security Inst., Fla. Conf. of Historians, Armed Forces Comm. and Electronics Assn., The Hist. Soc., Am. Hist. Assn. Avocations: cmty. theater, reenacting, scouts. Office: US Naval War Coll 686 Cushing Rd Newport RI 02841 Home: Apt 406 2121 W Main Rd Portsmouth RI 02871-1045

CARPENTER, STEPHEN WESLEY, director, screenwriter; b. Ft. Worth, Sept. 12, 1957; s. James and Ruth Carpenter. BA, UCLA, 1979, MFA, 1981. Writer, dir., cinematographer: (films) The Dorm That Dripped Blood, 1984, The Power, 1985, The Kindred, 1987; cinematographer Torment, 1985; writer: (films) The Servants of Twilight, 1991, Blue Streak, The Man, 2005; writer, dir.: (films) Soul Survivors, 2001.*

CARPENTER, SUSAN KAREN, defender; b. New Orleans, May 6, 1951; d. Donald Jack and Elise Ann (Diehl) C. BA magna cum laude with honors in English, Smith Coll., 1973; JD, Ind. U., 1976. Bar: Ind. 1976. Dep. pub. defender of Ind. State of Ind., Indpls., 1976-81, pub. defender of Ind., 1981—; chief pub. defender Wayne County, Richmond, Ind., 1981. Bd. dirs. Ind. Pub. Defender Coun., Indpls., 1981—; Ind. Lawyers Comm., Indpls., 1984-89; trustee Ind. Criminal Justice Inst., Indpls., 1983—. Mem. Criminal Code Study Commn., Indpls., 1981—, Supreme Ct. Records Mgmt. Com., Indpls., 1983—, Ind. Pub. Defender Commn., 1989—, Ind. Supreme Ct. Commn. on Race and Gender Fairness, 2000—. Mem. Ind. State Bar Assn. (criminal justice sect.), Nat. Legal Aid and Defender Assn., Nat. Assn. Defense Lawyers, Phi Beta Kappa. Office Phone: 317-232-2475. Business E-Mail: scarpenter@iquest.net.

CARPENTER, TED GALEN, political scientist; b. Ladysmith, Wis., Oct. 1, 1947; s. Jay Dee and Magdalene (Stuner) C.; m. Barbara Lynette Bethke, May 11, 1968; children: Lara, Amber, Brian. BA, U. Wis., Milw., 1970, MA in History, 1971; PhD in History, U. Tex., 1980. Rsch. assoc. ideas and action project U. Tex., Austin, 1980-83; fgn. policy analyst Cato Inst., Washington, 1985-87, dir. foreign policy studies, 1987-95, v.p. def. and fgn. policy studies, 1996—. Cons. Profl. Mgmt. Resources, Austin, Tex., 1983-84. Author: A Search for Enemies: America's Alliances After the Cold War, 1992, Beyond NATO: Staying Out of Europe's Wars, 1994, The Captive Press: Foreign Policy Crises and the First Amendment, 1995, Peace & Freedom: Foreign Policy for a Constitutional Republic, 2002, Bad Neighbor Policy: Washington's Futile War on Drugs in Latin America, 2003; co-author: The Korean Conundrum: America's Troubled Relations with North and South Korea, 2004; editor: Collective Defense or Strategic Independence: Alternative Strategies for the Future, 1989, NATO at 40: Confronting a Changing World, 1990, America Entangled: The Persian Gulf Crisis and Its Consequences, 1991, The Future of NATO, 1995, Delusions of Grandeur: The United Nations and Global Intervention, 1997, NATO's Empty Victory: A Postmortem on the Balkan War, 2000, NATO Enters the 21s Century, 2001; co-editor: The U.S.-South Korean Alliance; Time for a Change, 1992, NATO Enlargement: Illusions and Reality, 1998, China's Future: Constructive Partner or Emerging Threat?, 2000; contbg. editor National Interest, 2005—; meml. editl. bd.: Jour. Strategic Studies, meml. editl. adv. bd.: Mediterranean Quar.; contbr. articles to profl. jours. Mem.: Coun. on Fgn. Rels., Acad. Polit. Sci. Mem. Unitarian Ch. Office: Cato Institute 1000 Massachusetts Ave NW Washington DC 20001-5400 Business E-Mail: tcarpenter@cato.org.

CARPENTER, VICTORIA J., lawyer; b. Evanston, Ill., Mar. 08; d. Robert Duane and Jaqueline Joan Carpenter. BA, U. Ill., 1979; MA, U. Mo., 1983; JD, Ill. Inst. Tech., 1996. Bar: Ill. 2001, U.S. Ct. Appeals (4th cir.) 2001, U.S. Dist. (no. dist.) Ill. 2001. Ind. contractor, Chgo., 1996—2001; pvt. practice, 2001; bankruptcy assoc. Legal Rescues, Chgo., 2003—. Bd. dirs. Kindred Hearts Inc., Evanston, Ill., 1990—. Mem.: ABA, Chgo. Bar Assn., Ill. State Bar Assn., Pi Delta Phi. Office Phone: 312-307-2336. E-mail: vjcmajd@aol.com.

CARPENTER, VIRGIE MAE, retired librarian; b. Pine Bluff, Ark., Oct. 3, 1934; d. William Clyde Clemons and Martha Pearl (Murdock) Jones; m. Bruce McKinley Tipton, Dec. 16, 1960 (dec. May 1979); m. Thomas F. Carpenter, Feb. 15, 1980. BS, Henderson State U., 1959; MLS, Tex. Woman's U., 1960. Tchr. Social Hill Elem. Sch., Malvern, Ark., 1956-59; libr. Malvern Jr. HS, 1960—2000; ret., 2000. Student Coun., Malvern, 1961-84. Sponsor Libr. Club, 1960—2000. Mem. NEA, Ark. Edn. Assn., Ark. Libr. Assn., Malvern Edn. Assn. Baptist. Avocations: reading, handicrafts, flower arranging. Home: 925 Clardy St Malvern AR 72104-4448

CARPENTER, WILL DOCKERY, chemical company executive; b. Moorhead, Miss., July 13, 1930; s. Horace Aubrey and Celeste (Brian) C.; m. Hellen E. Dodd, Mar. 26, 1960; children: Celeste, Bill. BS in Agronomy, Miss. State U., 1952; MS in Plant Physiology, Purdue U., 1956, PhD in Plant Physiology, 1958, DSc (hon.), 1999; grad. exec. program in bus. adminstrn., Columbia U., 1980. Research biochemist Monsanto Co., St. Louis, 1958-60, agrl. research chemist, 1960-61, staff agrl. devel., 1961-65; mgr. market devel. Monsanto Agrl. Div., St. Louis, 1965-71; dir. product devel. Monsanto Agrl. Products Co., St. Louis, 1971-77, dir. environ. ops., 1977-80, dir. environ. mgmt./environ. policy staff, 1980-84, gen. mgr. tech., 1984-86; v.p. technology Monsanto Agrl. Co., St. Louis, 1986-90, v.p., gen. mgr. new products, 1990-92; chmn., bd. dirs. Agridyne Techs. Inc. Served to capt. U.S. Army, 1952-54, Korea. Fellow Weed Sci. Soc. Am. (treas. 1975, pres. 1980); mem. Indsl. Biotech. Assn. (bd. dirs. 1986—), Chem. Mfrs. Assn. (chmn. environ. mgmt. com. 1982-84, chmn. chem. warfare disarmament com. Washington 1985—), North Cen. Weed Control Conf. (pres. 1977, hon. mem. 1982). Office: 456 Conway Meadows Dr Chesterfield MO 63017-9625 E-mail: wdchdc@aol.com.

CARPENTER, WILLIAM MORTON, language educator, writer; b. Cambridge, Mass., Oct. 31, 1940; s. James M. and Dorothy N. (Sauer) C.; m. Joanne Laventis, 1962 (div. 1987); 1 child, Matthew; m. Donna Gold; 1 child, Daniel. BA, Dartmouth Coll., 1962; PhD, U. Minn., 1967. Instr. U. Minn., Mpls., 1963-67; asst. prof. U. Chgo., 1967-72; mem. faculty dept. lit. Coll. of Atlantic, Bar Harbor, Maine, 1972—, faculty dean, 1983-89. Bd. dirs. Maine Acad. Coalition, Augusta. Author: The Hours of Morning, 1981, Rain, 1986, Speaking Fire at Stones, 1992, A Keeper of Sheep, 1994, Wooden Nickel, 2002. Recipient Neruda prize U. Okla., 1979, Contemporary Poetry award Assoc. Writing Program, 1981, Black Warrior Rev. prize U. Ala., 1984, Morse prize Northeastern U., 1985; NEA fellow, Venice, Italy, 1985, Inst. for Human Ecology fellow 1989—, Yaddo Ctr., fellow 1984, MacDowell Colony fellow, 1985. Office: Coll of Atlantic 105 Eden St Bar Harbor ME 04609-1105 Office Phone: 207-288-5015. E-mail: carpenter@coa.dv.

CARPENTER, WOODROW WILSON, manufacturing executive, ceramics engineer; b. Snyder, Ill., Sept. 11, 1915; s. Marion Ernest and Margaretta (Fawver) Carpenter; m. Fay D. Turner, Nov. 24, 1939 (div. 1959); 1 child, Gay M. Caldwell; m. Irmgard K. Toberg, Sept. 3, 1960. BS in Ceramic Engring., U. Ill., 1939. Rsch. engr. Ingram Richardson Mfg. Co., Frankfort, Ind., 1939-54; dir. rsch. Barrows Porcelain Enamel Co., Cin., 1954-58; chmn.

bd. Ceramic Coating Co., Newport, Ky., 1958-97, Thompson Enamel, inc., Bellevue, Ky., 1997—. Founder mag. Glass On Metal, 1982, W.W. Carpenter Enamel Found., 2003. Lt. col. AUS, 1941-46, PTO Mem. Enamelist Soc. (founder). Avocations: magic, puzzles, golf. Home: PO Box 7 Cold Spring KY 41076 Office: 650 Colfax Ave Bellevue KY 41073-1621 Office Phone: 859-291-3800.

CARPENTER-MASON, BEVERLY NADINE, quality assurance professional, medical/surgical nurse, pediatric nurse practitioner, consultant, writer; d. Frank Carpenter and Thelma Deresa (Williams) Carpenter Smith; m. Sherman Robert Robinson Jr., Dec. 26, 1953 (div. Jan. 1959); 1 child, Keith Michael Robinson; m. David Solomon Mason Jr., Sept. 10, 1960; 1 child, Tamara Nadina Mason. Grad., Shadyside Hosp. Sch. Nursing, Pitts.; BS, St. Joseph Coll., North Windham, ME, 1979; MS, So. Ill. U., 1981; PhD, Columbia Pacific U., 1995. RN Pa., DC, Fla., cert. PNP; state ombusman long term care North Pinellas Pasco County Long Term Care Ombudsman Coun., parish nurse 2004, lay spkr. 1999, lay del. Fla. Conf. United Meth. Ch., 1998. Staff nurse med. surgery, ob-gyn neonatology and pediat. Pa., NY, Wyo., Colo. and Washington, 1954—68; mgr. clinician dermatol. svcs. Malcolm Grow Med. Ctr., Camp Spring, Md., 1968—71; PNP Dept. Human Resources, Washington, 1971—73; asst. DON Glenn Dale Hosp., Md., 1973—81; nursing coord. medicaid divsn. Forest Haven Ctr., Laurel, Md., 1981—83, spl. asst. to supr. for med. svcs., 1983—84; spl. asst. to supt. for quality assurance Bur. Habilitation Svcs., Laurel, 1984—89; exec. asst. quality assurance coord. Mental Retardation Devel. Disabilities Adminstrn., Washington, 1989—91, also bd. dirs.; owner, prin. BCM Assocs., 1992—; coord. quality assurance health svcs. divsn. UPARC, Clearwater, Fla., 1993—94. Mem. exec. com. Am. Found. Edn. Healthcare Quality, 1995—97; bd. dirs. Dist. V, Fla. Dept. HHS, 1997—2002; cons., lectr. in field. Author: (book) Quality Assurance: Toward a Paradigm of Universality, 1995; mem. editl. bd., case study editor: Am. Jour. Quality Assurance, 1985—; contbr. articles to profl. jours. Mem., star donor ARC Blood Dr., Washington, 1975—91; mem. health and human svcs. bd. Fla. Dept. Children and Families, 1997—2000, cons. Dist. XI, 1998; bd. dirs. Pinellas County (Fla.) Coun., Pinellas County WAGES Coalition, 1999; mem. Parish Nurse Assn., 2004—; vol. chief cons. Am. Bd. Med. Quality 2005 Cert. Examination Devel., 2005—; vol. curriculum specialist cons. Accreditation Coun. for Edn. and Tng., 2001—; lay del. United Meth. Ch. Fla. Conf., 1998—; bd. ordained ministry apptd. by the bishop of United Meth. Ch., 2004—; bd. dirs. North Pinellas divsn. Am. Cancer Soc., 2002—04; bd. trustees, dir. Upper Pinellas Assn. Retarded Citizens Bd./Found., 2002—; chair nominations com. Prince Georges Nat. Coun. Negro Women, Md., 1984—85; exec. sec. Pipers Meadow Home Owners Assn., 1993—2001; mem. Long Term Care Fla. State Ombudsman Coun., 2000—. Named Woman of the Yr., 1990—96; recipient awards, Dept. Air Force and DC Govt., 1966—92, Della Robbia Gold medallion, Am. Acad. Pediat., 1972, John P. Lamb Jr. Meml. Lectureship award, E. Tenn. State U., 1988, Outstanding Svc. award, U.S. Congress Adv. Bd. Svc., 1991. Fellow: Am. Coll. Med. Quality (Disting., case study editor, mem. jour. editl. bd. 1985—2004, chmn. publs. com. 1987—2003, asst. treas. 1988—93, Svc. award 1999); mem.: NAFE, Internat. Platform Assn., Healthcare Quality Inst., Assn. Retarded Citizens, Am. Bd. Quality Assurance and Utilization Rev. Physicians (asst. treas. 1988—94, chair exam. com. 1990—93, chief proctor exam. com. 1995—97, Chmn. of the Yr. award 1992, presdl. citation, Calvin R. Openshaw Svc. award 1993), Am. Assn. Mental Retardation (conf. lectr. 1988), Top Ladies Distinction (1st v.p. 1986—91), World Cir. Lang. Club (1st v.p. 2003—05), Soroptimists Internat. (sec. Pinellas chpt. 1999, Achievement in Healthcare award 1997), Order Ea. Star (Achievement award Deborah chpt. 1991). Democrat. Avocations: studying languages, travel, reading, writing, collecting antiques. Personal E-mail: drbevearpmason@aol.com.

CARPENTIERI, SARAH C., neuropsychologist, researcher, clinical psychologist; b. Naples, Italy, Aug. 30, 1967; m. James F. Asbury. BBA/BA, U. Notre Dame, 1989; MS, U. Memphis, 1991, PhD, 1994. Lic. psychologist, neuropsychologist. Rschr. St. Jude Children's Hosp., Memphis, 1990—94; psychology intern Harvard Med. Sch. /Children's Hosp., Boston, 1994—95; neuropsychology post-doctoral fellow Harvard Med. Sch., 1995—97; instr., asst. psychology and neuropsychologist Harvard Med. Sch., Boston, 1997—; assoc. rsch. and neuropsychologist Children's Hosp., Boston, 1997—. Lead investigator pediatric brain tumor rsch. program Children's Hosp., Boston, 1998—; cons. Dana Farber Cancer Inst., Boston, 2001—. Contbr. articles to profl. jours. Fellow VanVleet, U. Memphis, 1993—94; grantee Rsch., Pitino Found., 1999—2000, Murphy Child's Trust, 1999—2000, S&S Found., 1997—2003. Mem.: APA, Nat. Acad. Neuropsychology, Internat. Neuropsychology Soc. Personal E-mail: sarah.carpentieri@carpenburymed.com.

CARPER, FERN GAYLE, small business owner, writer; b. Pitts., Jan. 28, 1934; d. Phillip Jack and Jean Edith (Epstein) Whitman; m. Robert S. Carper, Aug. 3, 1958; children: Pamela Hope, Bruce Alan. Diploma, Taylor Alderdice HS, 1952. Exe. sec. J.J. Gumberg & Co., Pitts., 1952—58; author, owner Pete The Toad Enterprises, Potomac, Md., 2000—. Author: Pete The Toad and Friends, 2002. Democrat. Achievements include development of line of Pete The Toad stuffed animals and tee shirts. Avocations: oil and acrylic artist, still life painting, singing. Home: 9203 Gatewater Terr Potomac MD 20854 Office: Pete The Toad Enterprises 9203 Gatewater Terr Potomac MD 20854 Office Phone: 301-279-0926.

CARPER, GERTRUDE ESTHER, small business owner, real estate developer; b. Jamestown, N.Y., Apr. 13, 1921; d. Zenas Mills and Virgie (Lytton) Hanks; m. J. Dennis Carper, Apr. 5, 1942; children: David Hanks, John Michael Dennis, Michelle Kristen. Student violinist, Nat. Acad. Mus., 1931-41; diploma fine arts, Md. Inst. of Art, 1950; voice student, Frazier Gange, Peabody Inst. Music, 1952-55. Interior decorator O'Neill's (Importers), Balt., 1942-44; auditor Citizens Nat. Bank, Covington, Va., 1945-46; owner, developer Essex Yacht Harbour Marina, Balt., 1955—, owner, developer St. Michael's Sanctuary wildlife preserve, 1965—. Jewelry designer, 1987—; portrait artist, 1947—; exhibited one-woman shows Ferdinand Roten Gallery, Balt., 1963, Highfield Salon, Balt., 1967, Le Salon des Nations a Paris, 1985, Ducks and Geese of North Am., 1986, Series of Lighthouses, 1991; exhibited group shows Md. Inst. Alumni Show, 1964, Essex Libr., 1981, Hist. Preservation of Am., Hall of Fame, 1989, others; works included in collections including Prestige de la Peinture d'Aujourd'hus dans le Monde, 1990, Artists and Masters of the Twentieth Century, 1991; author: Expressions for Children, 1985, Fidere, 1993, Mentation, 1993; contbr. articles and poetry to ch. publs. and newspapers. Vol. tchr. of retarded persons, 1942—; leader Women's Circle at local Presbyn. chs., 1952-87, mem. 40 yrs. of choir svc. Mem. Md. Inst. Art Alumni Assn. (life), Grand Coun. World Parliament of Chivalry (Nobless of Humanity citation), Nat. Mus. Women in the Arts (charter, Washington). Avocations: raising orchids, reading, writing essays and poetry. Office: Essex Yacht Harbour Marina 500 Sandalwood Rd Baltimore MD 21221-5830

CARPER, KEITH ALAN, music educator, musician; b. West Hamlin, W.Va., Sept. 15, 1958; s. Bobby Shoat Carper and Jewel Marie Bell Charper; m. Julie Ann Johns, Dec. 27, 1994; 1 child, Nichole Lynn. BA, Marshall U., 1981, MA, 1986. Asst. band dir. Hamlin H.S., 1981—84, Duval H.S., Griffithsville, W.Va., 1984—86; band dir. Summes Valley H.S., Willowwood, Ohio, 1986—87, Fairland H.S., Proctorville, Ohio, 1987—. Musician (prin. trumpet): Lincoln Brass Quintet, 1971—, Huntington (W.Va.) Symphony Orch., 1985—. Mem.: Am. Fed. Musicians (v.p. 1989—90), Lawrence County Band Dir. Assn. (treas. 1997—), Ohio Music Edn. Assn. (pres. dist. 17 2005—). Home: 2226 Circle Dr Milton WV 25541 Office: Fairland High Sch 21630 SR 243 Proctorville OH 45669

CARPER, THOMAS RICHARD, senator, former governor; b. Beckley, W.Va., Jan. 23, 1947; s. Wallace Richard and Mary Jean (Patton) C.; m. Martha Stacy, Jan. 1, 1986; children: Christopher Thomas, Benjamin Michael. BA in Econs., Ohio State U., 1968; MBA, U. Del., 1975. Indsl. devel. specialist Del. div. Econ. Devel., Dover, 1975-76; state treas. State of Del., Dover, 1976-83; mem. 98th-102nd Congresses from Del., Washington, 1983-93; governor of Del., 1993-2001; U.S. senator from Del., 2001—; mem. banking, housing and urban affairs com., envt. and public works com., govtl. affairs com. Fund-raising chmn. Big Bros.-Big Sisters of Del., 1985, 93; hon. chair Del. Spl. Olympics, 1987—; bd. vice chair Jobs for America's Grads., 1996—. Lt. USN, 1968-73, capt. Res., 1973-91. Mem. Nat. Govs. Assn. (vice chmn. 1997-98, chmn. 1998-99). Democrat. Presbyterian. Office: US Senate 513 Hart Senate Office Bldg Washington DC 20510*

CARPLES, STEVEN ARTHUR, marketing professional; b. Hartford, Conn., Mar. 3, 1954; s. Charles E. and Florence Diana (Land) C.; m. Joan Rachel Malman, June 21, 1981; children: Jeremy, Matthew. BA, U. Rochester, 1972-76; M of Pub. and Pvt. Mgmt., Yale U., 1979-81. Mental health worker McLean Hosp., Belmont, Mass., 1976-78; sales rep. Leonard Silver Mfg., E. Boston, Mass., 1978-79; product mgr. Gen. Foods Corp., White Plains, N.Y., 1981-85; segment mgr. M & M/Mars, Hackettstown, N.J., 1985-92; dir. mktg. The Walt Disney Co., Orlando, Fla., 1992-95; sr. v.p. corp. mktg. Select Comfort Corp., Mpls., 1995-96; sr. v.p. mktg. and bus. devel. John Ryan Co., Mpls., 1997-98; v.p. mktg. and sales Schwan Food Co. (Back Home Foods), Mpls., 1998-99; mng. ptnr. Greer & Assocs., Mpls., 1999—2002; prin. Synergistics Cons., 2002—. Mem. Phi Beta Kappa. Avocations: hiking/backpacking, tennis, golf, skiing. Personal E-mail: carples@mn.rr.com.

CARPP, CAROLYN CLAIRE, retired elementary school educator; b. Litchfield, Ill., May 4, 1936; d. Joseph Victor and Stella Esther (Sammons) Emmons; m. Charles Walter Carpp, June 14, 1957 (div. 1970): children: Charles J., Curtis A. BA, Seattle Pacific U., 1958; MA, Ctrl. Wash. State U., 1974. Tchr. Highline Schs., Seattle, 1958-59, Shoreline Schs., Seattle, 1959-63, Lake Washington Sch. Dist., Kirkland, Wash., 1963—2001; ret., 2001. Mem.: NEA, Am. Guild Mus. Artists (N.W. rep. 1978—2002), Lake Washington Edn. Assn., Wash. Edn. Assn., Internat. Orgn. Women Pilots (gov. N.W. sect. 1991—93, internat. dir. 1993—96, internat. sec. 1996—98, v.p. 1998—2000), Airplane Owners and Pilots Assn., Seattle Opera Assn. (chorister 1964—89), Exptl. Aircraft Assn., Wash. Pilots Assn., The Ninety-Nines, Inc., Alpha Delta Kappa, Delta Kappa Gamma (pres. Alpha Nu chpt. 1990—91). Presbyterian. Avocations: flying, singing, travel. Home and Office: 14401 NE 30th Pl Apt 24B Bellevue WA 98007-3203 Personal E-mail: carpp99@hotmail.com.

CARR, ALBERT ANTHONY, retired organic chemist; b. Covington, Ky., Dec. 20, 1930; s. Albert Anthony and Virginia Charlotte (Wendel) C.; children: Virginia I., Michael P., Gregory J., Jerome R. BS, Xavier Univ., 1953, MS, 1955; PhD, Univ. Fla., 1958; LLD (hon.), Xavier U., 1994. Rsch. chemist Wm. S. Merrell Co., Cin., 1958-65; sect. head Merrell Nat. Labs., Cin., 1965-76; sr. sect. head Richardson-Merrell Inc., Cin., 1976-85; assoc. scientist Merrell Dow Rsch. Inst., Cin., 1985-88, sr. assoc. scientist, 1988-92; disting. scientist Marion Merrell Dow Rsch. Inst., Cin., 1992-95. Disting. rsch. fellow Hoechst Marion Roussel, Cin., 1995-97; lectr. Xavier U., 1962-68; ind. cons. to pharm. industry, 1997-99; cons. in field, 1997-99. Contbr. articles to profl. jours.; patentee in field. Named Chemist of Yr., Cin. Am. Chem. Soc., 1987; recipient Disting. Scientist award Tech. Soc. Coun. Engrs., 1988, Am. Chem. Soc. award Creative Invention, 1993, Perkin medal for applied chemistry Am. Sect. Soc. Chem. Industry, 1999. Mem. AAAS, Am. Chem. Soc. (Creative Invention award 1993), N.Y. Acad. Scis. Achievements include selection of 14 of the many compounds he discovered for devel.; survival of 7 two marketed, tested in humans.

CARR, ANNE ELIZABETH, theology studies educator; b. Chgo., Nov. 11, 1934; d. Frank James and Dorothy Margaret (Graber) C. AB, Mundelein Coll., 1956; AM, Marquette U., 1963, U. Chgo., 1968, PhD, 1971; DDiv (hon.), Jesuit Sch. Theology, 1983; LHD (hon.), Loyola U., 1995; ThD (hon.), Cath. Theol. Union, 2000. Instr. Mundelein Coll., Chgo., 1963-66, asst. prof., 1966-71, Ind. U., Bloomington, 1972-74; asst. prof., asst. dean U. Chgo. Divinity Sch., 1975-78, assoc. prof., assoc. dean, 1978-88, prof., 1988—. Donnelan vis. prof. Trinity Coll., Dublin, Ireland, 1983. Author: Theological Method of K. Rahner, 1977, Transforming Grace, 1988, Search for Wisdom and Spirit, 1988; editor: (with E.S. Florenza) Women, Work and Poverty, 1987, Motherhood: Experience, Institution, Theologu, 1989, Women's Special Nature?, 1991; bd. cons. Jour. of Religion, 1975-86, co-editor, 1987-94; assoc. editor Horizons, 1974—; editorial bd. Concilium, 1985-91. Trustee Mundelein Coll., Chgo., 1977-91. Postdoctoral fellow Harvard Divinity Sch., 1983-84, John Courtney Murry award, 1997. Mem. Am. Acad. Religion (program com. 1978-80), Cath. Theol. Soc. Am., Coll. Theology Soc. Roman Catholic. Office: U Chgo Divinity Sch 1025 E 58th St Chicago IL 60637-1509

CARR, ARTHUR CHARLES, psychologist, educator; b. Buffalo, Nov. 27, 1918; s. John E. and Katherine (Haas) C. BS, Buffalo State Tchrs. Coll., 1941; MA, Tchrs. Coll. Columbia U., 1946; PhD, U. Chgo., 1952; postgrad., William Alanson White Inst., 1953-54, Inst. Group Therapy, 1957-58, N.Y. Soc. Clin. Psychologists, 1954, 60. Diplomate: Am. Bd. Examiners in Profl. Psychology, N.Y. State Edn. Dept. Trainee clin. psychology VA, 1947-52; sr. clin. psychologist Creedmoor State Hosp., Queens Village, N.Y., 1952-56; prin. clin. psychologist N.Y. State Psychiat. Inst., N.Y.C., 1956—; ret.; asst. prof. psychology Adelphi Coll., Garden City, N.Y., 1952-56; asso. prof. med. psychology, dept. psychiatry Coll. Physicians and Surgeons, Columbia U., 1956-71, prof., 1971-78, prof. emeritus, 1978—; prof. psychology in psychiatry Cornell U. Med. Coll., 1978-89. Author: (with Shervert Frazier) Introduction to Psychopathology, 1964, (with Herbert Hendin, William Gaylin) Psychoanalysis and Social Research, 1965; author, editor: (with others) Loss and Grief, 1970, Psychosocial Aspects of Terminal Care, 1972, The Terminal Patient, 1973, Anticipatory Grief, 1974, Bereavement: Its Psychosocial Aspects, 1975, Grief, Selected Readings, 1975, The Mouth in Critical and Terminal Illness, 1980, Education of the Medical Student in Thanatology, 1981, Adolescent Marijuana Abusers and their Families, 1981, Bernard Schoenberg: Contributions to Psychiatry, Education of the Health Professional, Thanatology and Ethical Values, 1984, Principles of Thanatology, 1987, Psychodynamic Psychotherapy of Borderline Patients, 1989; editor-in-chief: Man and Medicine, 75-80; cons. editor, 1980—; editorial bd., cons. editor: Jour. Projective Techniques, 1967-73; asso. editor: Jour. Abnormal Psychology, 1966 70, Jour. Thanatology, 1971—; contbr. articles to profl. jours. Served to maj. AUS, 1941-46. Fellow Am. Psychol. Assn., Soc. Projective Techniques (dir. 1961-64, pres. 1971-72); mem. Eastern, N.Y. State psychol. assns., N.Y. Soc. Clin. Psychologists. Home: 560 Riverside Dr New York NY 10027-3202

CARR, BOB, congressman, lawyer; b. Janesville, Wis., Mar. 27, 1943; s. Milton Raymond and Edna (Blood) C.; m. Kathleen Smith; 1 child, Alexandra Anne; stepchildren: Jennifer McCloskey, Christopher McCloskey. BS, U. Wis., 1965, JD, 1968; postgrad., Mich. State U., 1968—69. Bar: Wis. 1968, Mich. 1969, U.S. Supreme Ct. 1973. Mem. staff of minority leader Mich. State Senate, 1968-69; adminstrv. asst. to atty. gen. State of Mich., Lansing, 1969-70, asst. atty. gen., 1970-72; counsel to spl. joint com. on legal edn. Mich. Legislature, Lansing, 1972; mem. 94th-96th, 98th-103rd Congresses from 6th (now 8th) Mich. Dist., Washington, 1975-80, 83; appropriations com., 1983-95; chmn. transp. subcom. appropriations, 1993-95; sr. v.p. The Jefferson Group, Inc., 1996-98, Henry J. Kaufman & Assocs., Washington, 1997-99, Carr Sherman Minjack, Washington, 1999—. Mgmt. cons., 1995-; sr. fellow UCLA Sch. Pub. Policy, 2000-01. Mem. U.S. Assn. Former Mems. Congress (bd. dirs. 2001—), Supporters Civil Soc. Russia (bd. dirs. 2003—) Democrat. Office: 2775 Unicorn Ln NW Washington DC 20015-2233 Office Phone: 202-244-3032.

CARR, CAROLYN KINDER, art gallery director; b. Providence, R(I; BA in Art History, Smith Coll.; MA in Art History, Oberlin Coll.; PhD in Art History, Case Western Reserve U. Instr. art history Kent (Ohio) State Univ., 1963-65, 67-68; art critic Akron (Ohio) Beacon Jour., 1968-73; chief curator Akron Art Mus., 1978—83; asst. dir. for collections Nat. Portrait Gallery, Washington, 1984-90, dep. dir., chief curator, 1991—. Vis. lectr. Akron U., Spring 1975, '76; organizer numerous art exhbns. Akron Art Mus., 1978—83, Nat. Portrait Gallery, 1984—. Contbr. articles to art publs. including Nat. Portrait Gallery, The Dictionary of Art, Am. Art, The Am. Art Jour., Dialogue, Currier Gallery of Art Bull.; author: art catalogs for exhibitions at Akron Art Mus., Chrysler Mus. of Art, Nat. Portrait Gallery and Smithsonian Instn. Office: Nat Portrait Gallery 750 9th St NW Box 37012 Washington DC 20013-7012 Office Phone: 202-275-1867. Business E-Mail: carrc@si.edu.

CARR, CASSANDRA COLVIN, communications company executive; b. Champaign, Ill., Nov. 14, 1944; d. A.B. and Irene Colvin; m. Edward M. Carr, Nov. 27, 1970. BA, Vanderbilt U., 1966; MA, U. Tex., 1973. Div. mgr. revenue requirements Southwestern Bell Telephone Co., Austin, Tex., 1985, div. mgr. congl. asst. program Washington, 1986; dir. govt. rels. Southwestern Bell Corp., St. Louis, 1986-87, mng. dir. govt. rels., 1987-88, v.p. fin., treas., 1988, sr. v.p. fin., treas., 1988-90, v.p. revenues and pub. affairs Austin, Tex., 1990—, sr. v.p. human resources San Antonio, Tex., sr. exec. v.p. external affairs. Commr. St. Louis Regional Conv. and Sports Complex Authority; bd. dirs. The Arch Funds, Inc., St. Louis, The Conf. Bd., N.Y.C., Found. Women's Resources, Austin. Recipient YWCA Leader award YWCA of St. Louis, 1988. Mem. Fin. Execs. Inst., Nat. Assn. Corp. Treasurers, St. Louis Club, Forest Hills Country Club. Office: SBC Communications Inc PO Box 2933 175 E Houston 6th Fl San Antonio TX 78299-2933 Home: 4400 River Garden Trl Austin TX 78746-2016

CARR, CHARLES LOUIS, retired religious organization administrator; b. Rockport, Ind., Sept. 9, 1930; s. Louis E. and Loris B. (Lindsey) C.; m. Shirley R. Cron, Nov. 15, 1950; children: Kathleen Carr Wright, Charles Stephen, Jeffrey Louis, David Wayne. Student, Ind. State U., 1949-50, So. Bapt. Theol. Sem., 1965-67; BS, Oakland City U., 1978, DD, 1994. Ordained to ministry Gen. Assn. Gen. Bapts., 1957. Pastor East Oolitic Gen. Bapt. Ch., Bedford, Ind., 1959-63, Mt. Zion Gen. Bapt. Ch., Indpls., 1963-65, Hunsinger Lane Gen. Bapt. Ch., Louisville, 1965-67; missionary to Saipan Mariana Islands, 1967-73; exec. dir. Gen. Bapt. Fgn. Mission Soc., Poplar Bluff, Mo., 1973-96; ret., 1996; pastor Wyatt United Meth Ch., 1997—, Dogwood United Meth Ch., 1997—. Author: Seed, Soil and Seasons, 1988; contbr. articles to various publs. Home: 706 S 9th St Poplar Bluff MO 63901-5639 E-mail: carrsson@ims-1.com.

CARR, COLLEEN KLONARIS, lawyer, special education educator; b. Montgomery, Ala., Aug. 07; d. James Dimond and Jessie (Miaoulis) Klonaris; m. Charles F. Carr, July 15, 1973 (div. Apr. 1985); children: Charles F. Jr., Conley James. BS, U. Ala., 1973, MS, 1976, AA, 1978; postgrad., U. Notre Dame, London, 1988; JD, Birmingham Sch. Law, 1989. Tchr., head tchr. U. Ala., Tuscaloosa, 1973-74; tchr. home econs. Partlow State Sch., Tuscaloosa, 1974-75; tchr. reading Tuscaloosa County Bd. Edn., 1975-76; tchr. learning disabilities Mountain Brook Bd. Edn., Birmingham, 1976-84, Homewood (Ala.) Bd. Edn., 1986—2001. Home economist So. Living Mag., Birmingham, 1985; pvt. practice law, Birmingham, 1994—; asst. atty. gen. Dept. of H.R. (DHR), 2002—. Mem. Svc. Guild, Birmingham, 1985-91, Music Club, Birmingham, 1985-92. Mem. Ala. State Bar, Birmingham Bar Assn., Am. Bar Assn., NEA, Ala. Edn. Assn., Homewood Edn. Assn. Avocations: exercising, running, reading, movies, cooking. Office: 1117 22d St South Birmingham AL 35205 Office Phone: 205-939-0000.

CARR, CYNTHIA, lawyer; b. San Antonio, Nov. 4, 1953; d. Robert Claude Carr and Alta Mae (Bletsch) Holmes; m. Marc Allan Wallman; children: Lydia Michael, Aidan Holmes. BA, Austin Coll., 1975; JD, Harvard U., 1984; LLM, NYU, 1990. Bar: N.Y. 1985, Conn. 1988. Coord. Cambodian sect. Internat. Rescue Com., Bangkok, Thailand, 1980-81; legal intern Mental Health Legal Advisers Com., Boston, 1982-83; assoc. White & Case, N.Y.C., 1984-87; assoc. gen. counsel, exec. dir. planned giving Yale U., New Haven, 1988-2000; gen. counsel Save the Children, Westport, Conn., 2000—. Vis. lectr. Yale U. Law Sch., New Haven, 1988-90. Vol. Peace Corps, West Africa, 1975-77, 79-80; bd. dirs. Yale Law Sch. Early Learning Ctr., 1990-95; trustee Yale U. Hong Kong Charitable Trust, 1997-2000, Oak Leaf Endowment Trust for Yale, 1997-2000. Mem. ABA (vice chair lifetime and charitable gift planning com. 2000—, probate and trust divsn. 2000-01), Conn. Bar Assn. (mem. charitable giving exempt orgns. subcom.), Trusts and Estates Mag. (charitable giving mini bd. mem. 1996-99), Jewish Found. New Haven (tax and legal com. 1999—), Conn. Planned Giving Group (bd. dirs. 2000-01). Home: 30 Hawley Rd Hamden CT 06517-2128 Office: Save the Children 54 Wilton Rd Westport CT 06880-3131 Office Phone: 203-221-4035. Business E-Mail: ccarr@savechildren.org.

CARR, DANIEL BARRY, anesthesiologist, endocrinologist, medical researcher; b. N.Y.C., Apr. 6, 1948; s. Andrew Joseph and Florence (Glassman) C.; m. Justine M. Meehan, Nov. 11, 1978; children: Nora, Rebecca, Andrew. BA, Columbia U., 1968, MA, 1970, MD, 1976. Diplomate Am. Bd. Internal Medicine (subsplty. bds. Endocrinology and Metabolism, Anesthesiology, Pain Mgmt.). Intern Columbia-Presbyn. Med. Ctr., N.Y.C., 1976-78; resident med. svc. Mass. Gen. Hosp., Boston, 1978-79, endocrine fellow, 1979-82, staff physician endocrine unit, 1982-94, clin. assoc. physician, clin. rsch. ctr., 1982-84, fellow in anesthesiology, 1984-86, dir. analgesic peptide rsch. unit, 1986-94, staff physician anesthesia svc., co-dir. anesthesia pain unit, 1986-91, dir. divsn. pain mgmt., 1991-94; anesthetist, 1992-94; instr. medicine Harvard U. Med. Sch., 1982-84, asst.prof., 1984-88, assoc. prof., 1988-94; rsch. staff Shriners Burn Inst., Boston, 1986-94; Saltonstall prof. Pain Rsch. in anesthesia and medicine Tufts-New England Med. Ctr., 1994—; dir. pain mgmt. rsch. Caritas St. Elizabeth's Med. Ctr., 1998—. Co-chair acute and cancer pain mgmt. guideline panels Agy. for Health Care Policy and Rsch., U.S. Dept. HHS, 1990—94; vice chair rsch. dept. anesthesia New Eng. Med. Ctr., 1994—; pain rev. editor Cochrane collaboration rev. group Pain, Palliative and Supportive Care, 1998—; mem. Gov. Mass. Spl. Commn. Pain Mgmt., 1993—98; tech. expert Agy. Healthcare Rsch. and Quality, 1999—2002; chair pain outcomes expert com. JCAHO-AMA-NCQA, 2002—03. Editor-in-chief IASP Pain: Clinical Updates, 1993—; mem. editl. bd. Clin. Jour. Pain, 1988—, Jour. Clin. Anesthesia, 1995—, Anesthesia and Analgesia, 1996-99, Acute Pain, 1998—, Jour. Pain, 1999—, Pain Medicine, 1999—, Pain, 2001--; contbr. articles, rsch. reports, essays, revs. to profl. librs. Daland fellow Am. Philos. Soc., 1980-83. Mem. Am. Pain Soc. (bd. dirs. 1994-97), Am. Acad. Pain medicine (bd. dirs. 1995-98, sec. 2003-), France-Am. Pain Soc. (pres. 1996-98), Am. Soc. Anesthesiologists, Internat. Assn. for Study Pain (coun. 1996-99), Endocrine Soc., Soc. for Neurosci., Internat. Anesthesia Rsch. Soc., Assn. Univ. Anesthetists, Alpha Omega Alpha. Achievements include research on pain, analgesic peptides and stress responses; relationship between analgesia and clinical outcome; systematic reviews and guidelines for improved pain treatment in hospital, hospice and home care settings. Office: New Eng Med Ctr-Dept Anesthesia 750 Washington St Boston MA 02111-1526 E-mail: daniel.carr@tufts.edu.

CARR, DAVID TURNER, physician; b. Richmond, Va., Mar. 12, 1914; s. John Ernest and Mary Lela (King) Carr; m. Rosemary Rudow, June 18, 1948 (div. 1953); 1 child, Jennifer Anne Carr Oderkirk; m. Christine Nadeau, Dec. 27, 1979. Student, U. Richmond, 1931-33; MD, Med. Coll. Va., 1937; MS in Medicine, Mayo Grad. Sch. Medicine, 1947. Intern, then asst. resident Grady Hosp., Atlanta, 1937-39; resident chest diseases Bellevue Hosp., N.Y.C., 1940-41; fellow medicine Mayo Clinic, 1943-47, cons. medicine, 1947-79, chmn. dept. oncology, 1975; dir. Mayo Comprehensive Cancer Ctr., 1975; assoc. dir. Ctr. Cancer Control, 1976-79; prof. medicine Mayo Med. Sch., 1964-79, M.D. Anderson Hosp. and Tumor Inst., Tex. Med. Ctr., Houston, 1979-92; med.-legal cons., 1992—. Mem.-at-large bd. dirs. Am. Lung Assn., 1959—74, v.p., 1971—72; bd. dirs. Rochester Civic Theatre, 1951—70, pres., 1965—67; bd. dirs. at large Am. Cancer Soc., 1967—74, pres. Minn. divsn., 1974—75, mem. am. joint com. cancer, 1971—79, chmn. am. joint com. cancer, 1979—82. Fellow: AAAS, ACP; mem.: Am. Thoracic Soc. (v.p. 1963—64), Internat. Assn. Study Lung Cancer (v.p. 1974—76, pres. 1976, treas. 1976—82), Ctrl. Soc. Clin. Rsch., Peruvian Atni-Tb Assn. (hon.), Rochester C. of C. (pres. 1959—60). Achievements include research in in pulmonary diseases. Home and Office: PO Box 9300 Rancho Santa Fe CA 92067 Office Phone: 858-759-1798.

CARR, EDWARD A., lawyer; b. Borger, Tex., July 31, 1962; AB with honors and distinction, Stanford U., 1984; JD, UCLA, 1987. Bar: Tex. 1988, D.C. 1989, U.S. Dist. Ct. (so. dist.) Tex. 1989, U.S. Ct. Appeals (5th cir.) 1989, U.S. Ct. Appeals (fed. cir.) 1989. Assoc. Vinson & Elkins, Houston, 1988-97, ptnr., 1997—. Lectr. in field; spkr. in field. Contbr. articles to profl. jours.; contbg. author Business and Commercial Litigation in Federal Courts, 1998, Texas Legal Ethics in the American Legal Ethics Library, Cornell Law School, 1998, mem. UCLA Law Rev., 1985—87, mem. editl. bd., 1986—87. Fellow Tex. Bar Found. (life), Coll. State Bar Tex.; mem. ABA (sects. antitrust law, litigation), Am. Judicature Soc. (life), D.C. Bar, Fed. Bar Assn., State Bar Tex. (chmn. dist. 4B5 grievance com., 2000-05, panel chmn.), Houston Bar Assn. Address: Vinson & Elkins LLP First City Tower 1001 Fannin St Ste 2300 Houston TX 77002-6760

CARR, EDWARD ALBERT, JR., pharmacologist, educator, physician; b. Cranston, RI, Mar. 3, 1922; s. Edward Albert and Florence (Hodge) C.; m. Nancy Albosta, Dec. 27, 1952; children: Sharon L., Cynthia F. AB summa cum laude, Brown U., 1942; MD cum laude, Harvard, 1945. Rsch. fellow, instr. pharmacology Harvard Med. Sch., 1948-51; exch. fellow St. Bartholomew's Hosp., London, 1952-53; mem. faculty U. Mich. Med. Sch., Ann Arbor, 1953-74, prof. pharmacology, 1962-74, prof. internal medicine, 1967-74, dir. program investigative clin. pharmacology, 1962-74; mem. sr. staff Univ. Hosp., 1957-74; dir. Upjohn Ctr. Clin. Pharmacology, 1966-74; prof. medicine, prof. and chmn. dept. pharmacology Med. Sch., U. Louisville, 1974-76; prof. medicine, pharmacology and therapeutics Med. and Dental Sch., SUNY, Buffalo, 1976-92, emeritus prof. medicine, pharmacology and therapeutics, 1992—, chmn. dept. pharmacology and therapeutics, 1976-88. Mem. sr. staff, chmn. therapeutics com. Louisville Gen. Hosp., 1974-76; lectr. U. Helsinki, 1972, Autonomous U. Barcelona, 1974, Japan Med. Assn., 1977, Swedish Acad. Pharm. Sci., Stockholm, 1977, Esteve Found. Symposium, Mallorca, 1988; cons. Ann Arbor VA Hosp., 1954-74, Louisville VA Hosp., 1974-76, Buffalo VA Hosp., 1976-2002, Erie County Med. Ctr., 1978-92; hon. vis. prof. Prince Henry and Prince of Wales Hosp., Sydney, Australia, 1973. Co-author: Radioisotopes in Biology and Medicine, 1964; also articles. Mem. Nat. Joint Commn. on Prescription Drug Use, 1976-80; mem. coop. studies evaluation com. US VA, 1980-83; chmn. pharmacology com. Am. Inst. Biol. Sci., Walter Reed Army Inst. Rsch., 1985-86; vol. Niagara Hospice, 1992-2002, bd. dir., 1992-95, 1996-2002. Fellow ACP (emeritus); mem. Am. Thyroid Assn. (emeritus), Am. Soc. Pharmacology and Exptl. Therapeutics (emeritus) (exec. com. clin. pharmacology div. 1984-86), Am. Soc. Clin. Pharmacology and Therapeutics (emeritus, pres., 1974-75, Henry W. Elliott award 1981), Soc. Nuclear Medicine (emeritus), Ctrl. Soc. Clin. Rsch. (emeritus), Endocrine Soc. (emeritus), Phi Beta Kappa, Sigma Xi, Alpha Omega Alpha. Home: 2 Gothic Ledge Lockport NY 14094-9702

CARR, EDWARD GARY, psychology professor; b. Toronto, Aug. 20, 1947; came to U.S., 1969; s. Saul Isaac and Anne (Goldsmith) C.; m. Ilene Wasserman, Aug. 2, 1987; 1 child, Aaron. BA, U. Toronto, 1969; PhD, U. Calif., San Diego, 1973. Lic. psychologist, N.Y. Asst. prof. psychology SUNY, Stony Brook, 1976—81, assoc. prof., 1981—85, prof., 1985—2000, leading prof., 2000—. Dir. rsch. and continuing edn. Devel. Disabilities Inst., Smithtown, N.Y., 1976—. Author: In Response to Aggression, 1981, How to Teach Sign Language, 1982, Communication-Based Intervention for Problem Behavior, 1994; author monograph. Recipient Disting. Rsch. award Assn. for Retarded Citizens; Woodrow Wilson fellow. Fellow: APA (Applied Rsch. award in Behavior Analysis); mem.: Assn. for Positive Behavior Support (pres. 2003—06). Office: SUNY Dept Psychology Stony Brook NY 11794-2500 Business E-Mail: edward.carr@sunysb.edu.

CARR, FIRPO WYCOFF, bible scholar, educator, writer; b. LA, Sept. 17, 1954; s. Oscar James and Ophelia Priscilla Carr; m. Mary Bethe Richards, June 17, 1979 (div. Nov. 22, 1989); 1 child, Danielle Corrin. B Info. Sys. Mgmt., U. San Francisco, 1984—86; M in Mgmt., U. Redlands, 1986—88; PhD, Pacific Western U., 1988—90. Adj. prof. U. Phoenix, Los Angeles, Calif., 1993—, UCLA, 1994—; prof. Mt. St. Mary's Coll., Brentwood, Calif., 2002—03. Author: (book) Germany's Black Holocaust: 1890-1945 (Nat. Best Seller, 2004), The Divine Name Controversy (Vol. I), Wicked Words: Poisoned Minds (Nat. Best Seller), Search for the Sacred Name, A History of Jehovah's Witnesses (Nat. Best Seller), Jehovah's Witnesses: African American, Are Gays Really Gay?. Min. Christian Congregation, 1975—2004; bd. dirs. Cri-Help Drug Rehab., North Hollywood, Calif., 1994—2004. Achievements include first to photograph, in color, and digitize pages from the oldest most complete Hebrew Bible located at the time in the Soviet Union; research in biblical manuscripts, written in Hebrew and other ancient languages, known as the Dead Sea Scrolls; discovery of the obscured divine name of God using an advanced IBM computer. Office: Scholar Tech Institute of Research Inc 4067 Hardwick St #330 Lakewood CA 90712 Office Phone: 800-501-2713. Personal E-mail: firpocarr@aol.com.

CARR, GAIL D., director; b. Plymouth, N.H., Apr. 10, 1952; d. Donald Guy and Muriel Barnard Kenneson; m. William Michael Carr, Oct. 8, 1977; children: Melanie Elizabeth Smith, Bethany Christine. BS in Elem. Edn., Plymouth State U., 1974, MEd in Counseling, 1988, cert. of Advanced grad. Study, 1998. Cert. career devel. facilitator Nat. Career Devel. Assn., 2001. Ast. dir. continuing edn./grad. studies Plymouth State U., 1986—90, dir. continuing edn., 1990—. Leader Girl Scouts Am., Rumney, NH, 1996—2001; co-founder Piano Monster Festival-Summer; ch. pianist Gateway Alliance Ch., Plymouth, 1991—2005. Recipient Alumni Achievement award, Plymouth State Alumni Orgn., 2000, Award for Pub. Svc., N.H. State Grange, 2001, Grafton County Pomona Grange, 2001, Distinuished PAT award, Plymouth State PAT Senate, 2002. Mem.: Phi Kappa Phi (pres., v.p., historian 1995—99). Home: PO Box 335 115 Stone Hill Rd Rumney NH 03266 Office: Plymouth State Univ 17 High St Plymouth NH 03264 Office Phone: 603-535-2228. Office Fax: 603-535-2823. Business E-Mail: gailc@plymouth.edu.

CARR, GARY THOMAS, lawyer; b. El Reno, Okla., July 25, 1946; s. Thomas Clay and Bobbye Jean (Page) C.; m. Ann Elizabeth Smith, Jan. 5, 1985. AB, Washington U., St. Louis, 1968, BSCE, 1972, JD, 1975. Bar: Mo. 1975, U.S. Dist. Ct. (ea. and we. dists.) Mo. 1975, U.S. Ct. Appeals (8th cir.) 1977, U.S. Ct. Appeals (fed. cir.) 1980, U.S. Ct. Appeals (5th cir.) 1991, U.S. Ct. Fed. Claims, 2004. Jr. ptnr. Bryan, Cave, McPheeters & McRoberts, St. Louis, 1975-83, ptnr., 1984-99. Lectr. law Washington U., 1978-82, adj. prof., 1982-85; sec., dir. Bruton-Stroube Studios, Inc., 1978—. Trustee Parkview Subdiv. Assn., St. Louis, 1982-90, 2003—. 1st lt. U.S. Army, 1968-71, Vietnam. Mem. ABA, Mo. Bar Assn., St. Louis Bar Assn., Order of Coif. Avocations: woodworking, hunting, fishing, automobiles. Office: PO Box 300129 Saint Louis MO 63130-0430 Office Phone: 314-725-6464. E-mail: gtc10485@aol.com.

CARR, GEORGE FRANCIS, JR., retired lawyer; b. Bklyn., Feb. 11, 1939; s. George Francis and Edith Frances (Schaible) C.; m. Patricia Louise Shiels, Jan. 30, 1965; children: Frances Virginia, Anne McKenzie, Margaret Edith. BA, Georgetown U., 1961; LLB, Harvard U., 1964. Bar: Ohio 1964, U.S. Dist. Ct. Ohio 1964. Assoc. Kyte, Conlan, Wulsin & Vogeler, Cin., 1964-70, ptnr., 1970-78, Frost & Jacobs, Cin., 1978-82; sec., counsel Baldwin-United Corp., Cin., 1982-84, v.p., spl. counsel, 1984-85; sole practice Cin., 1985-86; ptnr. Douglas, Carr and Pettit, Milford, Ohio, 1987-88; staff v.p., assoc. gen. counsel Penn Cen. Corp., Cin., 1988-92, Gen. Cable Corp., Highland Heights, Ky., 1992-95, ret., 1995. Treas. Cave Hill Farm Property Owners Assn., Cin., 1998—, Heritage Club Co., Cin., 2003—. Bd. dirs. Ctr. for Comprehensive Alcoholism Treatment, Cin., 1975-87, pres., 1980-83; bd. dirs. NCCJ, Cin., 1975-82. Served with U.S. Army, 1965—67. Avocations: real estate construction and development, geology, hiking, physical fitness. Home: 7150 Ragland Rd # 4 Cincinnati OH 45244-3148

CARR, GERALD FRANCIS, language educator; b. Pitts., Dec. 29, 1930; s. James Patrick and Hannah (Sweeney) C.; m. Irmengard Rauch, June 12, 1965; children: Christopher, Gregory. EdB, Duquesne U., 1958; MA, U. Wis., 1960, PhD, 1968. Instr. in German Duquesne U., Pitts., 1960-62, asst. prof. German, 1964-68; tchg. asst. U. Wis., Madison, 1962-64; asst. prof. German Ea. Ill. U., Charleston, 1968-70, assoc. prof. German, 1970-75, prof. German, 1975-87, Calif. State U., Sacramento, 1987—. Co-editor: Linguistic Method: Essays in Honor of Herbert Penzl, 1979, The Signifying Animal: The Grammar of Language and Experience, 1980, Language Change, 1983, The Semiotic Bridge, 1989, On Germanic Linguistics, 1992, Insights in Germanic Linguistics I, 1995, Insights in Germanic Linguistics II, 1996, Semiotics Around the World, 1996, Essays for Irmengard Rauch, 1998, New Insights in Germanic Linguistics I, 1999, New Insights in Germanic Linguistics II, 2000, New Insights in Germanic Linguistics III, 2002; series editor: Studies in Old Germanic Languages and Literatures, assoc. editor: Interdisciplinary Jour. for Germanic Linguistics and Semiotic Analysis. Cpl. USMC, 1951—54. Dist. tchg. fellow, U. Wis., 1966. Mem. MLA, Internat. Assn. for Semiotic Studies (co-dir. 5th congress 1994), Am. Coun. Tchrs. Fgn. Lang., Semiotic Soc. Am., Am. Assn. Tchrs. of German, Soc. German Philology, Calif. Fgn. Lang. Tchr. Assn., Semiotic Circle Calif., Kappa Phi Kappa, Delta Phi Alpha. Avocations: books, antiques. Office: Calif State U 6000 J St Sacramento CA 95819-2605 Office Phone: 916-278-6379.

CARR, GERALD PAUL, retired astronaut, retired engineer, retired marketing professional, retired military officer; b. Denver, Aug. 22, 1932; s. Thomas Ernest and Freda (Wright) C.; divorced; children: Jennifer, Jamee, Jeffrey, John, Jessica, Joshua; m. Patricia Musick, Sept. 14, 1979 BS in Mech. Engrng., U. So. Calif., 1954; BS in Aero. Engrng., U.S. Naval Postgrad. Sch., 1961; MS in Aero. Engrng., Princeton U., 1962; DSc (hon.), St. Louis U., 1976. Registered profl. engr., Tex. Commd. 2d lt. USMC, 1954, advanced through grades to col., 1974, ret., 1975; jet fighter pilot U.S., Mediterranean, Far East, 1956-65; astronaut NASA, Houston, 1966-77; comdr. 3d Skylab Manned Mission, 1973-74; sr. v.p. CAMUS, Inc., Huntsville, Ark.; ret. Adv. bd. Nat. Space Soc., Space Dermatology Found. Bd. trustees U. of the Ozarks. Recipient Group Achievement award NASA, 1971. Distinguished Service medal, 1974; Gold medal City of Chgo., 1974; Gold medal City of N.Y., 1974; Alumni Merit award U. So. Calif., 1974; Distinguished Eagle Scout award Boy Scouts Am., 1974; Robert J. Collier Trophy, 1974; Robert H. Goddard Meml. trophy, 1975; FAI Gold Space medal; others; inductee Astronaut Hall of Fame, 1997. Fellow Am. Astronautical Soc. (Flight Achievement award 1975); mem. NSPE, Marine Corps Assn., Marine Corps Aviation Assn., Soc. Exptl. Test Pilots, U. So. Calif. Alumni Assn., Tau Kappa Epsilon. Presbyterian. Home and Office: 1655 Madison 1200 Huntsville AR 72740-0919 Business E-Mail: camusinc@direcway.com.

CARR, GILBERT RANDLE, retired railroad executive; b. Rockford, Ill., Jan. 4, 1928; s. Audra Clifford and Marjorie (Lantz) C.; m. Marion Minnie Heinemann, Mar. 28, 1953; children: John W., James M. BS in Accounting and Mgmt, U. Ill., 1950. With Arthur Andersen & Co., Chgo., 1950—57; with C. & N. W. Transp. Co., 1957-88, comptroller, 1967-79, v.p., comptroller, 1979-88; ret., 1988. Served with AUS, 1946-47. Lutheran. Home: 1425 Linden Ave Park Ridge IL 60068-5545

CARR, GLADYS JUSTIN, publishing executive, consultant, editor, writer; b. N.Y.C. d. Jack and Mollie (Marmor) Carr. BA, MA, Smith Coll.; postgrad., Cornell U. Sr. editor Prentice-Hall, Inc., Englewood Cliffs, N.J., 1969; exec. editor Cowles Comm., Inc., N.Y.C., 1969-71; editl. dir., editor-in-chief Am. Heritage Press, N.Y.C., 1971-75; sr. editor McGraw-Hill, Inc., N.Y.C., 1975-81, editor in chief, editorial dir., chmn. editorial bd., 1981-89, v.p., pub., 1988-89, HarperCollins Pubs., Inc., N.Y.C., 1989-2000; mng. dir. GJ Carr Assocs., N.Y.C., 2000—. Contbr. articles, fiction and poetry to literary and profl. jours. Marjorie Hope Nicholson trustee fellow, Smith Coll., Ford Found., Walter Francis Wilcox fellow, Cornell U. Mem. PEN Am. Ctr., Women's Media Group, Acad. Am. Poets, Poetry Soc. Am., Nat. Arts Club, Exec. and Chemists Club, Smith Coll. Club (N.Y.C.), Phi Beta Kappa. Home and Office: 920 Park Ave New York NY 10028-0208 also: 1 Boulder Ln East Hampton NY 11937-1047

CARR, GREGG K., surgeon; b. Birmingham, Ala., Mar. 31, 1962; s. William N. and Sendra C.; m. Juli Carr; children: Evans, Jordan, Sara, Grace. BSCE, Auburn U., 1986; MD, U. Ala., 1994. Resident surgeon Greenville (S.C.) Hosp. Sys., 1994—99; fellow in orthopedic surgery Am. Sports Medicine Inst., Birmingham, 1999—2000; founder So. Orthopaedic Specialists, Birmingham, 2000—. Mem.: Am. Acad. Orthopaedic Surgeons, AMA, Am. Orthopaedic Surgery Sports Medicine Soc., Am. Sports Medicine Fellowship Soc.

CARR, HAROLD NOFLET, investment company executive; b. Kansas City, Kans., Mar. 14, 1921; s. Noflet B. and Mildred (Addison) C.; m. Mary Elizabeth Smith, Aug. 5, 1944; children: Steven Addison, Hal Douglas, James Taylor, Scott Noflet. BS, Tex. A&M U., 1943; postgrad., Am. U., 1944-46. Asst. dir. route devel. Trans World Airlines, Inc., 1943-47; exec. v.p. Wis. Central Airlines, Inc., 1947-52; mem. firm McKinsey & Co., 1952-54; pres. North Central Airlines, Inc., Mpls., 1954-69, chmn. bd., 1965-79; chmn. Republic Airlines, Inc., 1979-84, chmn. exec. com., 1984-86; chmn. Carr and Assocs., 1986—. Professorial lectr. mgmt. engrng. Am. U., 1952-62; mem. bd. nominations Nat. Aviation Hall of Fame; mem. exec. adv. com. Minn. Aviation Hall of Fame. Trustee Tex. A&M Rsch. Found.; mem. pres.'s coun. of advisors Tex. A&M U. Mem. Nat. Aero. Assn., World Bus. Coun., Am. Mgmt. Assn., Nat. Trust Historic Preservation, Pine Beach Peninsula Assn., Am. Econ. Assn., Tex. A&M Former Students Assn., Nat. Aviation Club, Aero Club (Washington),Mpls. Club, Twelfth Man Found. (dir., Coll. Sta., Tex.), Tex. A&M Century Club, Gull Lake Yacht Club (Brainerd, Minn.), Wings Club (N.Y.C.), Stearman Alumnus (Wichita, Kans.), Briarcrest Country Club, Beta Gamma Sigma. Episcopalian. Office Phone: 979-846-1765.

CARR, IRIS CONSTANTINE, artist, writer; b. Smyrna, Turkey, Aug. 4, 1922; d. John and Julia Kyrides Constantine (parents Greek citizens); m. Herman Edgar Carr Jr., 1947; 3 children. Diploma in dental nursing, Boston Sch. Dental Nursing, 1942; BA, Simmons Coll., 1970, postgrad., 1990-91, DeCordova Mus. Sch., 1986—. Anesthetist for oral surgeon, Boston, 1942-43; exec. med. sec. Boston Evening Clinic, 1943-44; lab. sec., dir. Boston Dispensary, 1944-45, Children's Hosp., Boston, 1944-47; editl. asst. Internat. Rsch. and Publs., 1947—; developed improved interlibr. loan svc. Wellesley Coll. Libr., 1964. Demonstrator watercolor technique Needham (Mass.) Arts Festival, 1996. One woman show at Needham Village Gallery, 1991, Needham Travel Svc. Bur., 1998-99; group shows include Mass. Med. Soc., 1999, Needham and Wellesley Art Assn., 1999, Needham Libr., 1999, Mass. Med. Soc. Alliance (Best in Show award); contbr. articles to profl. jours.; contbg. editor Mass. Med. Soc. Alliance. Recipient over 14 awards for pastel, watercolor and oil paintings. Mem. Mass. Med. Soc. Alliance (pub. rels. com. 1985-94, contbg. editor 1995—), Dedham Art Assn. (featured artist), Wellesley Soc. Artists (bd. dirs., registration com. 1994—), Needham Art Assn. (bd. dirs., publicity com., pres. 1989-90, co-inaugurated 1st art gallery 1990), Nat. Mus. Women in Arts, Mus. Fine Arts, Boston. Democrat. Home: 14 Ingleside Rd Needham MA 02492-4239

CARR, JACK LESLIE, economics professor, consultant; b. Toronto, Ont., Can., Aug. 9, 1944; s. Meyer and Marion (Pinkus) Carr; m. Honey Feldman, Dec. 27, 1965; children: Elana, Adam, David. B.Com., U. Toronto, 1965; M.A., U. Chgo., 1968, Ph.D., 1971. Asst. prof. econs. U. Toronto, 1968—73, assoc. prof., 1973—78, prof., 1978—; rsch. assoc. Inst. Policy Analysis, 1968—. also assoc. chmn., dir. grad. studies; vis. assoc. prof. UCLA, 1975—76. Econ. cons. Bell Can., Montreal, Que., 1968—70, Can. Bankers Assn., Toronto, 1980—84, Ont. Supreme Ct., Toronto, 1981, Can., Govt., Ottawa, Ont., 1977—79; econ. commentator on fed. budget CBC; econ. commentator TV and radio, Toronto, 1968—85. Author: Cents and Non Sense: The Economics of Canadian Policy Issues, 1972, Wage and Price Controls: Panacea for Inflation or Prescription for Disaster, 1976, Liability Rules and Insurance Markets, 1981, Tax-Based Income Policies: A Cure for Inflation, 1982. Woodrow Wilson Found. fellow, U. Chgo., 1965, Lily Honor fellow, Eli Lily Fund, U. Chgo., 1965—68, Can. Council leave fellow, UCLA, 1975—76, Social Sci. and Humanities Research Coun. leave fellow, U. Toronto, 1982—83. Mem.: Am. Econ. Assn., Can. Econ. Assn., Can. Profs. for Peace in Middle East. Home: 163 Banbury Rd Don Mills ON Canada M3B 2L7 Office: U Toronto 150 St George St Toronto ON Canada M5S 1A1 Office Phone: 416-978-5396. Business E-Mail: jcarr@chass.utoronto.ca.

CARR, JAMES GRAY, federal judge; b. Boston, Nov. 14, 1940; s. Edmund Albert and Anna Frances C.; m. Eileen Margaret Glynn, Dec. 17, 1966; children: Maureen M., Megan A., Darrah E., Caitlin E. AB, Kenyon Coll., 1962; LLB, Harvard U., 1966. Bar: Ill. 1966, Ohio 1972, U.S. Dist. Ct. (no. dist.) Ill. 1966, U.S. Dist. Ct. (no. dist.) Ohio 1970, U.S. Supreme Ct. 1980. Assoc. Gardner & Carton, et al., Chgo., 1966-68; staff atty. Cook County Legal Asst. Found., Evanston, Ill., 1968-70; prof. U. Toledo Law Sch., 1970-79; magistrate judge US Dist. Ct. (no. dist.) Ohio, Toledo, 1979-94, judge, 1994—, chief judge, 2005—. Adj. prof. law Chgo. Kent Law Sch., 1969, Loyola U., Chgo., 1970; reporter, juvenile rules com. Ohio Supreme Ct., Columbus, 1971-72; reporter, mem. nat. wiretap com. U.S. Congress, Washington, 1976-77. Contbr. articles to profl. law jours. Founder, bd. dirs. Child Abuse Ctr., Toledo, 1970-84; active Lucas County Mental Health Bd., Toledo, 1984-89, Lucas County Children Svcs. Bd., Toledo, 1989-94. Fulbright fellow, 1977-78. Mem. ABA (reporter, elec. survey stds. 1979-80, mem. task force on tech. and law enforcement 1995-99, mem. task force on jury initiatives 1995-98), Toledo Bar Assn. (bd. dirs.), Phi Beta Kappa. Roman Catholic. Office: US Dist Ct 203 US Courthouse 1716 Spielbusch Ave Toledo OH 43624-1363 Office Phone: 419-259-6420. E-mail: james_g_carr@ohnd.uscourts.gov.

CARR, JAMES PATRICK, lawyer; b. Cheverly, Md., Apr. 13, 1950; s. Lawrence Edward Jr. and agnes (Dyer) C.; m. Mona L. Kyle, May 28, 1986; children: James P. Jr., Kristin, Kevin, Sean. BA, U. Notre Dame, 1972, JD, 1976. Bar: Md. 1976, Calif. 1977, U.S. Dist. Ct. (cen. dist.) Calif. 1977, U.S. Dist. Ct. (so. dist.) Calif. 1986. Assoc. Carr, Jordan et al, Washington, 1976-77; ptnr. Breidenbach, Swainston et al, L.A., 1977-84, Harney, Wolfe, Shaller & Carr, L.A., 1984-88, Carr & Shaller, L.A., 1988-89; pvt. practice law L.A., 1989—. Mem. Am. Bd. Trial Advs., Assn. Trial Lawyers Am., Consumer Attys. Calif., Consumer Attys. Assn. L.A. Democrat. Roman Catholic. Office: 11755 Wilshire Blvd Ste 1170 Los Angeles CA 90025-1539 Office Phone: 310-444-7179. E-mail: jpc@jpcarrlaw.com.

CARR, JAMES REVELL, writer, curator, retired museum director; b. Bryn Mawr, Pa., Aug. 11, 1939; s. Clinton DeWitt and Asta Marie (Knudsen) C.; m. Mary Elizabeth Bump, June 25, 1963 (div. Oct. 1986); children: James Revell III, George McKelvy; m. Barbara Palmer, Apr. 15, 1989. BA, Rutgers U., 1962; MA, U. Pa., 1969. Teaching asst. U. Pa., Phila., 1968-69; archeologist N.J. State Mus., Trenton, 1968-69; rsch. assoc. Mystic Seaport Mus. Inc., Mystic, Conn., 1969-70, chief curator, 1970-78, dir., 1978—2001, pres., 1988—2001, dir. emeritus, 2001—. Pres. Internat. Congress Maritime Mus., Liverpool, Eng., 1984-87, Coun. Am. Maritime Mus., 1981-84; trustee Nat. Trust for Historic Preservation, Washington, 1983-92; accreditation commr. Am. Assn. Mus., Washington, 1988-94; chmn. Nat. Maritime Heritage Task Force, Washington, 1981-84. Author: Amerikanische Schiffsbuilder, 1976, All Brave Sailors, 2004; contbr. chpts. to books, articles to profl. jours.; TV commentator Operation Sail, WBZ-TV, Boston, 1976, with Peter Jennings on ABC-TV, 1986, Columbus Celebration, Pub. Broadcast Sta., 1992. Corporator Lawrence and Meml. Hosp., New London, Conn., 1979-86; mem. vestry Calvary Ch., Stonington, Conn., 1978-81; mem., sec. Navy Adv. Com. Naval History. Lt. USNR, 1962-67. Mem. Am. Antiquarian Soc., Century Assn., Newcomen Soc. Avocations: running, skiing, sailing. Mailing: 75 Seawood Park Rd New Harbor ME 04554

CARR, JEFFREY W., lawyer, manufacturing executive; BA in Govt. and Fgn. Affairs, U. Va.; JD with honors, Georgetown U. Law Ctr. Founder, mgr. Internat. Adv. Svcs. Group, Ltd.; law clk. Judge Schwartz, U.S. Dist. Ct., Del.; atty., internat. trade Willkie Farr & Gallagher, Washington; atty. Wald Harkrader & Ross, Washington; internat. counsel FMC Technologies, Phila., 1993—97, assoc. gen. counsel, energy & airport sys. bus. groups, 1997—2001, v.p., gen. counsel Chgo., 2001—. Office: FMC Technologies 200 E Randolph Dr Chicago IL 60601*

CARR, JESSE METTEAU, III, lawyer, engineering executive; b. Roanoke, Va., Sept. 3, 1952; s. Jesse Metteau Jr. and Martha Ann (Niday) C.; m. Amelia Kathryn Tynes, May 6, 1983 (div. Oct. 1985); m. Floy Simpson Holloman, Oct. 14, 2000. BSEE, La. State U., 1974, JD, 1977. Bar: La. 1978, Tex. 1979; registered profl. engr., Tex., Wash., Oreg., Pa., Ind., Ohio, Ga., La., Miss., Ill.; diplomate Am. Coll. Forensic Examiners, Am. Bd. Forensic Engring. and Tech. Elec. engr. Southeastern Chem., Reserve, La., 1974-77; control systems engr. J.E. Sirrine Co., Houston, 1977-83; pvt. practice cons. Houston, 1983-84; control systems engr. Jacobs Engring., Houston, 1985-86; mng. gen. ptnr. Carr/Sperry Design, Houston, 1985-87, Tech. Ventures Group, Houston, 1987-90; v.p. Intellex Corp., Houston, 1986-92, pres., chmn., 1992—, also bd. dirs.; mng. gen. ptnr. Tech. Ventures Group, Houston, 1987-90. V.p. East Tex. Co., Inc., 1994-2001, pres., chmn., 2001—; bd. dirs. Mimics Inc., Houston, East Tex. Co., Washington, Ga. Cub Scout leader Boy Scouts Am., Houston, 1987-90. Mem. IEEE, ABA, La. Bar Assn., Tex. Bar Assn., Am. Inst. Chem. Engrs., Internat. Soc. Pharm. Engrs., Am. Soc. Agrl. Engrs., S.W. Assn. Biotech. Cos., Instrument Soc. Am., Assn. Energy Engrs., Tau Beta Pi, Omicron Delta Kappa, Eta Kappa Nu. Republican. Methodist. Avocations: skiing, backpacking.

CARR, JOHN S., trade association administrator; Air traffic contr. Kansas City Internat. Airport, Chgo. Terminal Radar Approach Control, Cleve. Hopkins Airport; pres. Nat. Air Traffic Contrs. Assn., Washington, 2000—. With USN, 1976—80. Office: NATCA 1325 Massachusetts Ave NW Washington DC 20005

CARR, LARRY DEAN, not-for-profit executive; b. Mt. Vernon, Ill., Apr. 22, 1947; s. Jewell Dean and Mary Janet (Lawrence) C.; 1 child, Lisa Diane. BS in Fin., U. Ill., 1969. CPCU. Analyst Allstate Ins. Co., Northbrook, Ill., 1970-75, controller Svc. Rev. Arlington Heights, Ill., 1975-76, regional controller Rochester, N.Y. and Murray Hiil, N.J., 1976-80, exec. info. dir. Northbrook, 1980-82, dir. mktg., 1982-83; v.p. Crum and Forster Personal Ins. Co./U.S. Fire Ins. Co., Basking Ridge, N.J., 1983-84, sr. v.p., 1984-85, exec. v.p., 1985-86, chmn. bd. dirs., pres., CEO, 1986-90, also bd. dirs.; CEO Viking Inc. Co., 1986-90, Nat. Gen. Ins.Co., 1986-91; exec. v.p. Motors Ins. Corp., 1991; pres., CEO Presbyn. Ch. Found., 1993-99; pres., founding dir., chmn. bd. dirs. New Covenant Trust Co., N.A., 1997-99; pres. case mgmt. divsn. Concentra Managed Care, Inc., Waltham, Mass., 2000—02; COO Greater Boston Aid to the Blind, Inc., 2002—03, Jewish Guild for the Blind, 2003—. Treas., bd. dirs. Somerset Hills YMCA, Basking Ridge, 1984-85; trustee Kent Place Sch., 1989-90; mem. adv. bd. Resource Ctr. for Women and Their Families, 1989-90; dir. Jarvie Commonweal Svc., 1994-99, Ky. Shakespeare Festival, 1997, Presbyn. Outlook Found., 2000—. Served with USAR, 1969-74. Mem. Pres.' Assn., Am. Mgmt. Assn., Delta Sigma Pi. Republican. Presbyterian. Avocations: swimming, skiing. Office Phone: 212-712-9957. Business E-Mail: carrl@jgb.org.

CARR, LAWRENCE EDWARD, JR., lawyer; b. Colorado Springs, Colo., Aug. 10, 1923; s. Lawrence Edward and Lelah R. (Rubert) C.; m. Agnes Isabel Dyer, Dec. 26, 1946; children— Mary Lee, James Patrick, Lawrence Edward III, Eileen Louise, Thomas Vincent. BS, U. Notre Dame, 1948, LL.B., 1949; LL.M., George Washington U., 1954. Bar: Colo. 1949, D.C. 1952, Md. 1961. With Travelers Ins. Co., 1949-51; practiced in Washington, 1952—; sr. ptnr. Carr Goodson, PC, Washington, 1984—2001, Carr Maloney, PC, 2001—. Mem. adv. coun. U. Notre Dame Coll. Law, 1985—. With USMCR, 1943-46, 51-52; col. Res.; ret. Fellow Am. Bar Found.; mem. ABA (ho. of dels. 1973-75), Bar Assn. D.C. (dir. 1969-71, pres. 1974-75), D.C. Def. Lawyers Assn. (pres. 1978-79), Bar Assn. D.C. Rsch. Found. (pres. 1985-86). Home: 111 Storm Haven Ct Stevensville MD 21666-3707 Office: Carr Maloney PC 1615 L St NW Ste 500 Washington DC 20036-5652 Office Phone: 202-310-5501. Business E-Mail: lec@carmaloney.com.

CARR, LES, psychologist, educator; b. Bklyn., Mar. 7, 1935; s. Sam and Sara (Berman) Carr; children: Lincoln Damian, Sharon Rose, Lewis Wade, Faith Theresa. BA, NYU, 1957; MA, New Sch. for Social Rsch., N.Y.C., 1959; PhD, Vanderbilt U., 1963. Diplomate Am. Bd. Med. Psychotherapists (fellow), lic. psychologist Calif., cert. psychologist, R.I. Rsch. and clin. intern Rockland State Hosp., N.Y.C. Dept. Mental Hygiene, 1958-59; cons. clin. psychologist to sr. clin. psychologist Ctrl. State Hosp., Nashville, 1962-64; sr. coord. psychol. svcs. U. R.I., Providence, 1963-68; prof., chmn. psychology dept., dean Summer Sch., Salve Regina Coll., Newport, R.I., 1966-70, v.p. acad. affairs, 1969-71; project dir. Newport Hosp., 1967-71; pres. Lewis U., Lockport, Ill., 1971-76; dean of faculty Columbia Pacific U., San Rafael, Calif., 1977—2000; pres. Columbia Commonwealth U., 2000—. Pres., dir. Elder 100 Plus, Inc., Somerset, Calif.; staff psychologist San Quentin State Prison, 1989—2000; former ednl. cons. to sultan and min. of edn., Oman; staff psychologist No. Calif. Women's Facility, 2000—03. Past chmn. R.I. Gov.'s Task Force on Mental Health Rehab.; chmn. bd. dirs. Sr. U., Richmond, Can.; mem. nat. adv. coun. Profl. Children's Sch., N.Y.C.; past chmn. adv. bd. dirs. Comprehensive Mental Health Ctr., Newport; past bd. dirs. Regional Ballet Soc., Joliet, Ill., R.I. Rehab. Assn.; past chmn. bd. trustees St. Mary's Acad., Nauvoo, Ill.; past mem. exec. com. R.I. Gov.'s Commn. on Vocat. Rehab. With U.S. Army, 1958. Mem.: APA, Calif. Psychol. Assn. Home: 7900 Shenandoah Ln Somerset CA 95684-9597 Office Phone: 530-620-1112. Office Fax: 530-620-6427.

CARR, OSCAR CLARK, III, lawyer; b. Apr. 9, 1951; s. Oscar Clark Carr Jr. and Billie (Fisher) Carr Houghton; m. Mary Leatherman, Aug. 4, 1973; children: Camilla Fisher, Oscar Clark V. BA in English with distinction, U. Va., 1973; JD with distinction, Emory U., 1976. Bar: Tenn. 1976, U.S. Dist. Ct. (we. dist.) Tenn. 1977, (no. dist.) Miss. 1977, U.S. Ct. Appeals (6th cir.) 1985, (5th cir.) 1995, U.S. Dist. Ct. (so. dist.) Miss. 2000; cert. mediator Tenn. Assoc. Glankler Brown, PLLC (formerly Glankler, Brown, et al, Memphis, 1976-82, ptnr., 1982—, chief mgr., 1998-00. Mem. Emory Law Coun., 2004—. Treas., vestryman St. John's Episcopal Ch., Memphis, 1988—91, sr. warden, 1991; mem. Commn. on Ministry Diocese of West Tenn., 1987—90; King of Carnival Memphis, 1994; bd. dirs. West Tenn. chpt. Juvenile Diabetes Found., 1998—, dir., 1998—2002; bd. dirs. Memphis Ballet Soc., 1980, Memphis-Shelby County Unit Am. Cancer Soc., Memphis Oral Sch. Deaf, 1988—91, Carnival Memphis. Recipient Living and Giving award, West Tenn. chpt. Juvenile Diabetes Rsch. Found., 2002. Fellow Tenn. Bar Found.; mem. ABA, Tenn. Bar Assn. (we. dist. coun. environ. law 1992—), Memphis-Shelby County Bar Assn. (bd. dirs. 1985-87), Memphis Country Club (atty. 2004-). Office: Glankler Brown PLLC 1700 One Commerce Sq Memphis TN 38103 Office Phone: 901-525-1322. Business E-Mail: ocarr@glankler.com.

CARR, PAMELA M., elementary school educator; b. Manchester, N.H., Dec. 3, 1967; d. Edgar R. and Pauline L. Begin; m. Seth P. Carr, May 7, 1994; 1 child, Meaghan E. MS, So. N.H. U., 1992. Cert. bus. educator N.H., 1992, mktg. educator N.H., 1992, computer educator N.H., 2000. Tchr. Merrimack (N.H.) H.S., 1994—96, Newmarket (N.H.) Jr. Sr. H.S., 1996—99, Hampton (N.H.) Acad. Jr. H.S., 1999—. Adj. faculty Hesser Coll., Manchester, NH, 1994—96, N.H. Cmty. Tech. Coll., Stratham, NH, 1996—2000. Fellow, State of N.H. and So. N.H. U., 1991—92. Mem.: NEA, Seacoast Ednl. Assn., Internat. Soc. Tech. in Edn., Nat. Bus. Edn. Assn. Office: Hampton Academy Junior High School 29 Academy Avenue Hampton NH 03842 Office Phone: 603-926-2000.

CARR, PATRICIA ANN, community health nurse; b. Teaneck, N.J., Dec. 6, 1949; d. John O. and Elizabeth (Nestor) Olsen. Diploma, Mt. Sinai Hosp. Sch. Nursing, N.Y.C., 1970. RN, Ga., Fla.; AIDS cert. RN; cert. clin. rsch. coord. Asst. DON Taylor Meml. Hosp., Hawkinsville, Ga., 1979-81; staff nurse ICU Shands Teaching Hosp., Gainesville, Fla., 1981-82; staff nurse Venice Hosp., 1982-84; field nurse Fla. Home Health Svcs. Sarasota Inc., 1986-93; regulatory compliance coord. Fla. Home Health Svcs., Sarasota, 1993-96; program clin. coord. Cmty. AIDS Network, Inc., Sarasota, 1996-98; clin. studies coord. Infectious Diseases Assocs., Sarasota, 1998—. Contbr. articles to publs. Mem. APHA, Assn. Nurses in AIDS Care, Home Health Nurses Assn., Intravenous Nurses Soc., Assn. Practitioners in Infection Control, Assn. Clin. Rsch. Profls. Office: Infectious Diseases Assocs 1425 S Osprey Ave Ste 1 Sarasota FL 34239-2900 Office Phone: 941-366-0776. Personal E-mail: patcarr2@verizon.net.

CARR, PETER WILLIAM, chemistry professor; b. Bklyn., Aug. 16, 1944; s. Peter V. and Kathleen T. Carr; m. Leah Phillips, 1966; children: Sean, Erin, Kelly. BS in Chemistry, Polytech Inst. Bklyn., 1965; PhD in Analytical Chemistry, Pa. State U., 1969. Rsch. asst., assoc. Brookhaven Nat. Lab., 1965, 66; postdoctoral assoc. Stanford U. Med. Sch., 1968; faculty mem. U. Ga., 1969-77; prof. chemistry U. Minn., 1977—. Cons. Leeds and Northrup, Hewlett Packard, 3M Co., Cabot Inc.; pres. ZirChrom Separations, Inc., 1995-2002; pres. Symposium Analytical Chemistry in Environment, 1976. Mem. editl. adv. bd. Analytical Chemistry, Talanta, Jour. Chromatography, LC/GC, Chromatographia, Separation Sci. and Tech.; contbr. numerous articles to profl. jours. Recipient L.S. Palmer award Minn. Chromatography Forum, 1984, Benedetti-Pichler award Am. Microchem. Soc., 1990, award in Fields Analytical Chemistry Ea. Analytical Symposium, 1993, S. Nogare award Del. Valley Chromatography Forum, 1996, award in chromatography ISCO, 1997, award in separation sci. Ea. Analytical Symposium, 2000, Pitts. Conference award in analytical chemistry, 2004. Mem. Am. Chem. Soc. (chmn. subdivsn. chromatography and separation sci. of Analytical Chemistry divsn. 1988-89, Chromatography award 1997), Minn. Chromatography Forum. Office: U Minn Dept Chemistry 207 Pleasant St SE Minneapolis MN 55455-0431 Office Phone: 612-624-0253. Business E-Mail: carr@chem.umn.edu.

CARR, RICHARD RAYMOND, editor, public relations executive; b. Des Moines, Jan. 26, 1934; s. Raymond William and Myra Reuss (Stevens) C.; m. Kathryn S. Chapman, Jan. 9, 1954; children: Rochelle Carr Needham, Stephen Todd Carr. BJ, Kans. State U., 1956. News editor Headlight & Sun, Pittsburg, Kans., 1956-60; pub. rels. adminstr. Pittsburg State U., 1960-85; pub. rels. advisor Tri-Lakes Cmty. Theatre, Branson, Mo., 1985-87; mng. editor Alumni Today quar. jour. Ctrl. Mo. State U., Warrensburg, 1988-99, ret., 1999. Mem. Soc. Profl. Journalists, Kansas City Press Club, Alpha Tau Omega (trustee chpt.), Lions Club (past pres.), Kiwanis Club (past pres.). Methodist. Avocations: reading, collecting, history. Home: 99 Hawthorne Hill Dr Warrensburg MO 64093-2904 E-mail: rcarr@iland.net.

CARR, ROBERT WILSON, JR., retired chemistry educator; b. Montpelier, Vt., Sept. 7, 1934; s. Robert Wilson and Marie (Soucy) C.; m. Betty Lee Elmer, June 21, 1958; children: Kevin, Terrell, Kathryn. BS, Norwich U., 1956; MS, U. Vt., 1958; PhD, U. Rochester, 1962. NIH fellow Harvard U., 1963-65; asst. prof. U. Minn., 1965-69, asso. prof., 1969-75, prof. dept. chem. engring. and materials sci., 1975, prof. emeritus. Vis. prof. U. Cambridge, 1971-72, MIT, 1995; guest prof. U. Göttingen, Fed. Republic Germany, 1982. Asst. editor: Jour. Phys. Chemistry, 1970-80. Served to 1st lt. U.S. Army, 1963. NSF fellow, 1971-72; Fulbright fellow, 1982 Mem. Am. Chem. Soc., Am. Aviation Hist. Soc., Interam. Photochem. Soc., Am. Inst. Chem. Engrs., Sigma Xi. Mem. Congregational Ch. Office: U Minn Dept Chem Engring & Material Scis Minneapolis MN 55455

CARR, RONALD EDWARD, ophthalmologist, educator; b. Newark, Sept. 17, 1932; s. Frank Edward and Mildred (Sasso) C.; m. Nancy May Gould, June 8, 1957; children: Peter Richardson, Jacqueline Marie, Timothy Edward. AB, Princeton U., 1954; MD, Johns Hopkins U., 1958; M.Sc., NYU, 1963. Intern Bellevue Hosp., N.Y.C., 1958-59; resident NYU Med. Ctr., N.Y.C., 1959-63; clin. assoc. NIH, Bethesda, Md., 1963-64, assoc. ophthalmologist, 1964-65; asst. prof. ophthalmology NYU Med. Ctr., 1965-67, assoc. prof., 1967-71, prof., 1971—. Author: Visual Electrodiagnosis, 1981, Electrodiagnostic Testing of the Visual System, 1990. Served to lt. comdr. USPHS, 1963. Recipient Knapp award AMA, 1966 Fellow Am. Acad. Ophthalmology, ACS; mem. Am Ophthal. Soc., N.Y. Ophthal Soc., Assn. Research in Ophthalmology Clubs: Princeton, Stone Horse Yacht. Republican. Episcopalian. Home: 130 E End Ave New York NY 10028-7553 Office: NYU Med Ctr 530 1st Ave New York NY 10016-6402 Office Phone: 212-263-7360. E-mail: nancycarr2@aol.com.

CARR, RUTH MARGARET, plastic surgeon; b. Waco, Tex., July 2, 1951; MD, U. Okla., 1977. Intern U. Okla. Med. Sch., Oklahoma City, 1977-78; resident U. Okla. Health Sci. Ctr., Oklahoma City, 1978-81, UCLA, 1981-83; plastic surgeon St. John's Hosp., 1989—. Clin. asst. prof. UCLA, 1983—, U. So. Calif., 1984-. Mem.: Bay Surgical Soc. (pres. 2004), Calif. Soc. Plastic Surgeons (parlanentarian 2004—05), Am. Soc. Plastic Surgeons. Office: 1301 20th St Ste 470 Santa Monica CA 90404-2082 Office Phone: 310-315-0222. Business E-Mail: rcarr@ucla.edu.

CARR, STEPHEN HOWARD, materials engineer, educator; b. Dayton, Ohio, Sept. 29, 1942; s. William Howard and Mary Elizabeth (Clement) C.; m. Virginia W. McMillan, June 24, 1967; children: Rosamond Elizabeth, Louisa Ruth. BS, U. Cin., 1965; MS, Case Western Res. U., 1967, PhD, 1970. Coop. engr. Inland divsn. GM, Dayton, 1960-65; asst. prof. materials sci. and engring. and chem. engring. Northwestern U., Evanston, Ill., 1970-73, assoc. prof., 1973-78, prof., 1978—, dir. Materials Rsch. Ctr., 1984-90, asst. dean engring., 1991-93, assoc. dean engring., 1993—. Cons. in field. Contbr. articles to profl. jours. Recipient Outstanding Alumni Achievement award U. Cin. Coll. Engring., 1993. Fellow Am. Soc. for Metals Internat., Am. Phys. Soc.; mem. AIChE, Soc. Automotive Engrs. (Ralph R. Teetor award 1980), Plastics Inst. Am. (Ednl. Svc. award 1975), Am. Chem. Soc., Soc. Plastics Engrs., Materials Rsch. Soc. Achievements include patents in plastics and textiles fields. Home: 2704 Harrison St Evanston IL 60201-1216 Office: Northwestern U 2145 Sheridan Rd Evanston IL 60208-0834 Business E-Mail: s-carr@northwestern.edu.

CARR, THOMAS A., real estate company executive; s. Oliver T. Carr, Jr.; married; three sons. BA, Brown U.; MBA, Harvard U. With Cadillac Fairview; dir. Oliver Carr Co., 1991—2005; devel. project mgr. CarrAmerica Realty Corp., Washington, 1985—93, CFO, 1993-95, pres., dir., 1993—2002, COO, 1995-97, CEO, 1997—, chmn., 2000—. Mem. Nat. Assn. Real Estate Investment Trusts, Young Pres. Orgn., Fed. City Coun., Internat. Devel. Rsch. Coun. Avocation: sailing. Office: 1850 K St NW Washington DC 20006-2213

CARR, TRACY A., musician, educator; d. Raymond H. and Naomi B. Carr. MusB, U. R.I., 1987; MusM, Miami U., Oxford, Ohio, 1990; D of Musical Arts, U. So. Calif., 1994. Assoc. prof. music Ea. N.Mex U., Portales, 1999—. Oboist Trio Encantada, Portales, N.Mex., 1999—. Musician: (solo and chamber musician) various national and international performances. Mem.: Internat. Double Reed Soc. Office: Music Ea NMex Univ Station 16 Portales NM 88130 Office Phone: 505-562-2681. Personal E-mail: tracy.carr@enmu.edu.

CARR, WALTER JAMES, JR., research physicist, consultant; b. Knob Noster, Mo., May 6, 1918; s. Walter James and Alice Frances (Koch) C.; m. Winifred Walker Schultz, Mar. 21, 1953; children: James Lawrence, Robert David. BSEE, U. Mo., Rolla, 1940; MEE, Stanford U., 1942; DSc in Physics, Carnegie-Mellon U., 1951. Engr. Westinghouse Electric R&D, Pitts., 1942-51, section mgr., 1951-57, adv. physicist, 1957-65, mgr. solid state theory, 1965-70, cons., 1970-85; ind. cons. Pitts., 1985—. Physicist Atomic Energy Establishment, Harwell, Eng., 1962. Author: AC Loss and Macroscopic Theory of Superconductors, 1983, 2d edit., 2001. Named to Acad. Elec. Engring., U. Mo., Rolla, 1981. Fellow Am. Phys. Soc., IEEE; mem. Univ. Club. Avocation: tennis. Home: 1460 Jefferson Heights Rd Pittsburgh PA 15235-5220 Business E-Mail: wjamescarrjr@att.net.

CARR, WALTER STANLEY, lawyer; b. Chgo., May 5, 1945; s. Robert Adams and Margaret (Wiley) C.; m. Mary Baine, Sept. 20, 1969. BS, U. Pa., 1967; JD, U. Chgo., 1970. Bar: Ill. 1970. From assoc. to ptnr. McDermott, Will & Emery, Chgo., 1970-86; v.p. Miami Corp., Chgo., 1987—. Pres. Hull House Assn., Chgo., 1989; bd. dirs. Planned Parenthood Assn. Chgo. Area, 1980—. Mem. ABA, Ill. Bar Assn., Chgo. Bar Assn., Chgo. Estate Planning Council. Clubs: Univ. (Chgo.). Home: 507 W Briar Pl Chicago IL 60657-4633 Office: Miami Corp 410 N Michigan Ave Ste 590 Chicago IL 60611-4252

CARR, WILLARD ZELLER, JR., retired lawyer; b. Richmond, Ind., Dec. 18, 1927; s. Willard Zeller and Susan (Brownell) C.; m. Margaret Paterson, Feb. 15, 1952; children: Clayton Paterson, Jeffrey Westcott. BS, Purdue U., 1948; JD, Ind. U., 1951. Bar: Calif. 1951, U.S. Supreme Ct. 1963. Former ptnr. Gibson, Dunn & Crutcher, Los Angeles, 1952—. Mem. nat. panel arbitrators Am. Arbitration Assn.; former labor relations cons. State of Alaska; lectr. bd. visitors Southwestern U. Law Sch.; mem. adv. council Southwestern Legal Found., Internat. and Comparative Law Ctr. Trustee Calif. Adminstrv. Law Coll.; bd. dirs. Employers' Group, Calif. State Pks. Found., L.A. coun. Boy Scouts Am.; mem. Mayor's Econ. Devel. Policies Com.; past chmn. Pacific Legal Found.; past chmn. men's adv. com. Los Angeles County-U. So. Calif. Med. Ctr. Aux. for Recruitment, Edn. and Service; past chmn. bd. Wilshire Republican Club; past mem. Rep. State Ctrl. Com.; past mem. pres.'s coun. Calif. Mus. Sci. and Industry; mem. Nat. Def. Exec. Res., L.A. World Affairs Coun.; chmn. bd. councilors Andrus Sch. Gerontology, U. So. Calif.; bd. dirs., sec. L.A. Police Meml. Found.; past chmn. L.A. sect. United Way; mem. adv. com. Los Angeles County Human Rels. Commn., past commr., Calif. State World Trade Commn.; active L.A. chpt. ARC. Fellow Am. Bar Found.; mem. Internat. Bar. Assn. (past chmn. labor law com. of bus. law sect., past chmn. labor employment practice group), The Federalist Soc., Calif. Bar Assn., L.A. County Bar Assn., L.A. C. of C. (past chmn. 1991), Calif. C. of C. Office: Gibson Dunn & Crutcher 333 S Grand Ave Ste 4400 Los Angeles CA 90071-3197 Office Phone: 213-229-7238. Business E-Mail: wcarr@gibsondunn.com.

CARRAHER, CHARLES JACOB, JR., corporate communications specialist; b. Sept. 22, 1922; s. Charles Jacob and Marcella Marie (Hager) C.; m. Joyce Ann Root, June 13, 1947; children: Cynthia A., Craig J. Grad. pub. schs., Norwood, Ohio. With Cin. Enquirer, 1937-72, office mgr., circulation mgr., admin. asst. to exec. v.p., 1947-66, dir. employee cmty. rels., 1966-72, corp. sec., 1969-72; exec. v.p., ptnr. Sub Suburban Newspapers Inc., 1973-77; asst. dir. devel. Sta. WCET-TV, 1977-79; v.p. Garrett Computer Inc., 1979-81. Participant numerous symposia. Mem. bd., v.p. Cin. Conv. and Visitors Bur., 1966-72; mem. Cin. Manpower Planning Coun., 1972; bd. dirs. Cen. Psychiat. Clinic, 1970-80, Mental Health Assn., 1970-72, Great Rivers coun. Girl Scouts U.S.A., 1969-74; v.p. bd. dirs. Neediest Kids of All, 1969-72; bd. dirs. Greater Cin. Urban League, 1971-74, 75-78. Lt. USAF, WWII, ETO. Decorated Air medal with cluster. Mem. Greater Cin. C. of C. (chmn. human resources devel. com. 1972), Beta Gamma Sigma. Republican. Home and Office: 10848 Lake Thames Dr Cincinnati OH 45242-3105

CARRAHER, MARY LOU CARTER, art educator; b. Cin., Mar. 9, 1927; d. John Paul and Martha Leona (Williams) Carter; m. Emmett Carraher, Nov. 6, 1943 (div. July 1970); children: Candace Lou Holsenbeck-Smith, Michael Emmett, Cathleen C. Kruska. Student, U. Cin., 1946-48, Calif. State U., 1973-74. Lifetime credential in adult edn.: art, ceramics, crafts, Calif. Substitute tchr. Cobb County Schs., Smyrna, Ga., 1961-63; art tchr. pvt. lessons Canyon Country, Calif., 1968-72; adult edn. art tchr. Wm. S. Hart H.S. Dist., Santa Clarita, Calif., 1973-97; children's art and calligraphy cmty. svcs. Coll. of the Canyons, Santa Clarita, Calif., 1976-96. Fine arts coord. Santa Clarita Sr. Ctr., 1998—; founder, bd. dirs. Santa Clarita Art Guild, 1972-80; art dir. European tours Continental Club, Canyon Country, 1977-81; art tour guide and travel cons. Northridge (Calif.) Travel, 1981-91; vol. art tchr. stroke patients Henry Newhall Meml. Hosp., Valencia, Calif., 1993-96; craft tchr. for respite care program, Newhall, Calif., 1995-96, Respite Care Ctr., Santa Clarita Valley Sr. Ctr., 1995-96; art tour guide, Andulusia, Spain, 1997, 99. Artist, author History of Moreland School District, San Jose, California, 1965; prin. works include Paintings for each season of Church Year, 1970's, Baptismal painting, 1988, Sr. Ctr. Watercolors Ctr. Scenes, 1993, Watercolors of Christmas Charity Home Tour, 1993, Henry Mayo Newhall Meml. Hosp., 1997, 1999, 2001, 2002, 2003, 2004, murals painted for Christian Ch. and Sr. Ctr., 1997—99, mall st. painting for charity, 2000. Tchr., mem. Santa Clarita United Meth. Ch., 1966-96; judge for art contests and exhibits, Santa Clarita, 1973-96; mem. Santa Clarita Valley Hist. Soc., 1989-96; mem. Alumni Assn., Norwood (Ohio) City Schs., 1993-96; leader art tours to Spain, 1997, 99, 2002, Italy, 2001, Portugal, 2002, Australia, New Zealand and Fiji, 2003; designer certs, with scenes of Sr. Ctr., Cir. of Friends certs; leader art tour Rhine River Cruise, France, 2003-2004, Rhone River Tour, 2003, 04. Recipient Bravo award nomination for Outstanding Achievement in Art, 1995, Sr. of Yr. Santa Clarita Valley Sr. Ctr. and Svc. Newspaper "The Signal", 1995, Christian Svc. award Santa Clarita United Meth. Ch., 1988; invited by Citizen Amb. Program of People to People Internat. to join U.S. del. to assess bus. and trade opportunities of the craft industry in China. Mem. Santa Clarita Valley Arts Coun., Hosp. Home Tour League, Nat. Women in the Arts (charter, Washington). Republican. Methodist. Avocations: travel, art related crafts, reading.

CARRAHER, SHAWN MICHAEL, investment company executive, management educator; b. Kansas City, Kans., Nov. 9, 1966; s. Charles E. and Loyalea Velda (Zimmerman) C.; m. Sarah Carlene Laine, July 6, 2001; children: Shawn Michael, Charles. BBA with honors, Fla. Atlantic U., 1987; MBA, U. Cin., 1988; PhD, U. Okla., 1992. Delivery specialist Dayton Daily News, Beavercreek, Ohio, 1980-85; pres., owner Carraher & Sons, Beavercreek, 1982-87; tchr. U. Kans., Lawrence, 1988; rschr. Fla. Atlantic U., Boca Raton, 1989-90, U. Okla., Norman, 1990-92; vis. asst. prof. U. Wis., Milw., 1992-94; assoc. prof. Calif. State U., Chico, 1994-95, Ind. State U., Terre Haute, 1995-98, Ind. U., Bloomington, 1998-2000; prof. mgmt. and global entrepreneurship Tex. A&M U., Commerce, 2000—04; Virginia Brewczynski Endowed chair entrepreneurial studies, dir. Ctr. Emerging Tech. and Entrepreneurial Studies, Cameron U.; prof. mgmt. and global entrepreneurship Cameron U., Lawton, Okla., 2004—. Pres. Carraher & Carraher Cons. Group, 1997—; cons. City of Norman, 1990-91, USAF, 1990-92, Pratt & Whitney, West Palm Beach, Fla., 1990; spkr. at more than 600 profl. presentations on goal-setting and mgmt. devel., including U. Okla., Norman, 1992; dir. Internat. Family Bus. Ctr., Tex. A&M U., 2002— Author: (12 video tapes) Industrial Psychology, 1992; contbr. 80 articles to profl. jours. Pres. Christians In Action, Beavercreek, 1984-85; treas. Campus Crusade for Christ, Norman, 1991-92 Shuman fellow U. Okla., 1991; recipient Outstanding Reviewer award for Careers Divsn. of the Acad. of Mgmt., SW Acad. Mgmt. Disting. Reviewer award, 1997, 2000, Midwest Acad. Mgmt. Disting. Reviewer award, 2000, Southern Mgmt. Assn. Outstanding Reviewer award, 2000, Outstanding Educator award internat. divsn. US Assn. Small Bus. and Entrepreneurship, 2004. Mem. Acad. Mgmt. (chair elect 2000-01), Am. Ednl. Rsch. Assn., Am. Psychol. Soc., So. Mgmt. Assn.(bd. dir. 2000-03, program chmn., 2002-03, chmn. mgmt. history and future trends track), S.W. Acad. Mgmt (rep at large 1998-2001, program chair elect, 2001-02, pres. 2004-05), U.S. Assn. Small Bus. and Entrepreneurship (program chair, chair elect, sec. 2000-01, program chair internat. divsn., 2001-02, Fulbright sr. specialist 2002, 2004, Outstanding Educator award), Acad. Internat. Bus., Internat. Small Bus. Inst. Assn. (pres. elect), Acad. Internat. Bus. (chmn. international mgmt. and bus. track, asst. v.p. program chair, divns. chmn., 2002-03, competitive papers chmn., 2003—) Avocations: research, speaking on goal-setting, martial arts, weight-lifting, cooking. Home: 5012 Malcolm Rd Lawton OK 73505 Office: Ctr Emerging Tech and Entrepreneurship Studies Sch Bus Cameron U 2800 W Gore Blvd Lawton OK 73505 Business E-Mail: scarraher@cameron.edu.

CARRASCO, JOSÉ ANIBAL, recreational therapist; b. San Juan, PR, Sept. 11, 1964; s. Aníbal Carrasco and Rosa Margarita Ayala; m. Nora Liz O'Neill, Oct. 27, 1990; children: Jonathan Andrés, Mario Alejandro. *Spouse, Nora Liz Carrasco-O'Neill, received a BA (Magna Cum Laude) in 1987 from the University of Puerto Rico and has a Master in Music Therapy 1994 from Florida State University. Son, Jonathan Andres, a trombone player, was selected to the 2005 All-District Honor Band - the Florida Bandmasters Association, District III; he plays piano and currently attends the Magnet Program at the Cobb Middle School in Tallahassee, Florida. Son, Mario Alejandro, who plays violin, has been selected twice to attend the Gifted Program at Astoria Park Elementary School in Tallahassee, Florida.* BA, U. PR, 1988; M in music therapy, Fla. State U., 1994. Rehab. therapist, music therapist Alzheimer's Unit 16, Fla. State Hosp., Chattahoochee, Fla., 1993—95; rehab. therapist, music therapist Ctrl. Forensic Unit, Fla. State Hosp., Chattahoochee, Fla., 1995—; vis. asst. prof. Coll. of Music, Fla. State U., Tallahassee, 2002—. Grad. asst., music dir. Salsa Fla. Caribbean Ensemble, Ctr. for Music of The Americas, Fla. State U. Coll. of Music, Tallahassee, 1988—91; latin music ensemble dir. Colonial H.S., Orlando, Fla., 1990—91; dir. Latin Jazz Band Latin Attitude, Tallahassee, 1993—. *Mr. Carrasco has over 23 years of performing and teaching experience. As a graduate assistant, he taught college students the essential techniques and styles of salsa music and led the Salsa Ensemble to performances at popular Calle Ocho Festival, Miami, 1990, and Fiesta on Flagler, West Palm Beach, 1993, 1994. As visiting professor he increased enrollment in his ensemble attracting students who traditionally seek jazz ensembles. Some high profile performances with his group Latin Attitude include The Tallahassee Jazz & Blues Festival in 1999, 2000, 2003, 2005; The Florida Park Festival in 2002, 2004; and 2004 Reception at the Florida Governor's Mansion for Spanish Prime Minister, Jose Maria Aznar.* Musician (musical dir., co-producer): Feel The Rhythm; musician: Trompetas Con Trovadores by Elías Lopés & Co., Huellas by Tony Croatto, Tony Croatto. Student mem. Fla. State U. Equal Opportunity Com., Tallahassee, 1989—90. Recipient Dist. Performance as Dir. of Salsa Fla., Ctr. for Music of The Americas, Fla. State U. Sch. of Music, 1988-1990, Davis Productivity award, State of Fla., 1997, 5 Years Svc. award, Fla. Dept. of Children and Families, 1998. Avocations: music arranging, electronic music and keyboards, computers, outdoors, classical music. Home: 2198 Foster Dr Tallahassee FL 32303 Office: Fla State Hospital Ctrl Forensic US Hwy 90 PO Box 1000 Chattahoochee FL 32324 Office Phone: 850-663-7632. Home Fax: 850-386-3701. Personal E-mail: papo@latinattitude.com.

CARRASQUEL-BELANDRIA, JOSE RAMON, language educator; b. Caracas, Venezuela, June 2, 1965; s. Jose Carrasquel-Hurtado and Maria Belandria-Belandria. PhD in romance linguistics, U. Wash., 1995. Spanish lectr. Stanford U., Calif., 1997—98; prof. No. Ill. U., DeKalb, 1999—. Editl. reviewer U. of Michigan-Dearborn, Fgn. Lang. Annals, Mich., 2001—; editl. cons. Houghton Mifflin Co., Boston, 2000—; faculty assoc. No. Ill. U., Ctr. for Latino and L. Am. Studies, 1999—. Contbr. conference Adnominal and pronominal reflexes of Latin demonstratives in Early Ibero-Romance (XVth Internat. Conf. on Hist. Linguistics in Melbourne, Australia, 2001); author: (articles) various profl. jours. (Internat. Conf. on Lang. Variation in Europe, in Barcelona, Spain, 2001, Fourth Hispanic Linguistics Symposium, 2002). Lobbyist Chgo. Chpt. of LGIRTF at Heartland Alliance, 1999—2000. Fellow Tchg. fellowship, U. Wash., 1990-1995, U. Oreg., 1988-1990; grantee Rsch. and Artistry award, Grad. Sch. at No. Ill. U., Summer 2002; scholar Study Abroad scholarship, Fundacion Gran Mariscal de Ayacucho, 1983-1988. Master: Phi Sigma Iota, Internat. Honor Soc. for Fgn. Languages (hon.; faculty adv. 1999); mem.: Am. Assn. of Tchrs., Spanish and Portuguese (assoc.), Linguistic Assn. of the S.W. (assoc.; conf. presenter 1995). Avocations: human/equal rights, education, internat. affairs, multiculturalism and diversity of all kinds, scholarships.

CARR-DUGAS, ANN BRIDGET, elementary school educator; b. Boston, Oct. 12, 1964; d. Robert Denvir and Mary Elizabeth Carr; m. Alan Joseph Dugas, Sept. 19, 1996; children: Marc Alan Dugas, Brigitte Therese Dugas, Raymond Paul Dugas. BA, U. Mass., 1989. Cert. tchr. grades 5 - 12 geography and sci. Mass., 1990. Tchr. sci. Quincy H.S., Mass., 1990—2000; naturalist, tchr. (summer program) South Shore Natural Sci. Ctr., Norwell, 1990—94; tchr. 5th grade Epiphany Mid. Sch., Dorchester, 2000—. Evening study hall proctor Epiphany Mid. Sch., 2000—, supr. intern tchrs., 2000—02, grade 5 summer intensive program, 2005—; supr. student tchr. Quincy H.S.,

1994—95. Nursery coord. St. Michael's Episcopal Ch., Milton, Mass., 2002—05. Mem.: Nat. Audobon Soc. Independent. Avocations: skiing, camping. Home: 27 Rock View Rd Milton MA 02186 Office: Epiphany Mid Sch 154 Centre St Dorchester MA 02124 Office Phone: 617-326-0425 306. Office Fax: 617-326-0424. Personal E-mail: anncarr@hotmail.com. E-mail: adugas@epiphanyschool.com.

CARRELL, DANIEL ALLAN, lawyer; b. Louisville, Jan. 2, 1941; s. Elmer N. and Mary F. (Pfingst) C.; m. Janis M. Wilhelm, July 3, 1976; children: Mary Monroe, Courtney Adele. AB, Davidson Coll., 1963; BA, Oxford U., 1965, MA, 1969; JD, Stanford U., 1968. Bar: Va. 1972, U.S. Dist. Ct. (ea. dist.) Va. 1972, U.S. Ct. Appeals (4th cir.) 1975, U.S. Dist. Ct. (we. dist.) Va. 1985. Asst. prof. U.S. Mil. Acad., West Point, N.Y., 1968-71; assoc. Hunton & Williams, Richmond, Va., 1971-79, ptnr., 1979-95; prin. Carrell, Rice & Rigsby, Richmond, Va., 1996—. Hearing officer Commonwealth of Va., 2000—. Active Richmond Rep. Com., 1974—; co-counsel Dalton for Gov. campaign, Richmond, 1977; counsel Obenshain for Senate campaign, Richmond, 1978; treas. Va. Victory '92; state fin. chmn., fin. com., state ctrl. com. and budget com. Rep. Party Va., 1993-96; bd. dirs. Southampton Citizens Assn., 1985-2001; pres. Davidson Coll. Alumni Assn., 1987-88; trustee Davidson Coll., 1987-88; bd. dirs. Needle's Eye Ministries, 1986-90, adv. bd., 1990—, bd. dirs. U-Turn, Inc., 2001-; elder, trustee Stony Point Reformed Presbyn. Ch., 1993—; moderator James River Presbytery Presbyn. Ch. Am., 1998, 2001; chmn. com. constl. bus. Presbyn. Ch. Am., 2003—. Rhodes scholar, 1962; recipient Merit award Sports Illustrated Mag., 1963. Mem. ABA (chmn. exemption and Noerr Doctrine com. 1986-87, antitrust sect.), Va. Bar Assn. (chmn. young lawyers joint law-related edn. com. 1978-79, young lawyers fellow award 1980), Va. State Bar (chmn. com. on legal edn. and admission to bar 1984-91, bd. govs. sect. edn. lawyers 1992-99. dist. com. discipline 2001-03), Richmond Bar Assn., Christian Legal Soc., Westwood Club. Avocations: tennis, basketball, theater, concerts. Home: 3724 Custis Rd Richmond VA 23225-1102 Office: Carrell Rice & Rigsby 7275 Glen Forest Dr Richmond VA 23226-3772 Office Phone: 804-285-7900. Personal E-mail: lexrex3dac@aol.com.

CARRELL, HAMMEL LEE, jewelry designer; b. Lovington, N.Mex., Dec. 3, 1941; s. Hammel and Sudie Lee (Foust) C.; m. Linda Lee Koch; 1 child, Sativa Sunny Day January. BA, Ea. N.Mex. U., 1965; BFA, N.Mex. State U., 1973, MA, 1974; MFA, U. Kans., 1977. Owner, mgr. Fuego Del Sol, Cloudcroft, N.Mex., 1971-74, Platoro Del Fuego, Las Cruces, N.Mex., 1972-74; instr. design U. Kans., Lawrence, 1974-77; co-owner, mgr. The Oxbow Gallery, Lawrence, 1976-77; asst. prof. art No. Ariz. U., Flagstaff, 1977-80; designer, planner Carrell Carpet and Interiors, Austin, 1980-82; owner Creative Solutions, Austin, 1982-84; dir., founder The Austin Sch. of Jewelry and Design, Austin, 1984-97; owner New Horizon Studio, Austin, 1988—, Reflections of the West Gallery, Spicewood, 1998—2004. Juror N.Mex. Designer-Craftsmans show, 1978, Albuquerque Designer-Craftsman competition, 1981, N.Mex. State U. Art Undergrad. Shows, 1972-74, Grad. and Faculty Shows, 1973-74. Group shows include Contemporary Jewelry show N.Mex. State Fair, 1972, Tex. Christian U., 1973, N.Mex. Gallery, 1973, Gallery Plus, Los Alamos, N.Mex., 1974, Nat. Metal Invitational Traveling Exhibit, U.S., Australia and New Zealand, 1975, Grad. Thesis Exhibit, Lawrence, Kans., 1977, S.W. Metalsmithing Exhbn., 1979, The Westside Gallery, Phoenix, 1980-82, Columbine Gallery, Breckenridge, Colo., 1984, Magic Mountain Gallery, Taos, N.Mex., 1985, Applied Arts Gallery, Austin, Tex., 1986, Littlefield Gallery, Austin, 1987, Red Poppy Gallery, Georgetown, Tex., 1988-90, El Taller Gallery, Austin, 1994-95, Spirit Echos Gallery, Austin, 1995—, Western Design Conf., 1998 (selected 1 of 2000 Artists/Designers 20th Century). Elected v.p. Art Students League N.Mex. State U., elected student rep. to faculty meetings. With USAF, 1966-70. Assistantship N.Mex. State U., U. Kans.; grantee Matthey-Johnson Inc. Mem. Spicewood Arts Soc. (bd. dirs. 2000—), Delta Sigma Pi, Alpha Rho Gamma. Avocations: writing, painting, jewelry, sculpture, ceramics. Office: PO Box 196 Spicewood TX 78669-0196 E-mail: reflectwest@isp.com, leenlinda@texasreflections.com.

CARRELL, TERRY EUGENE, manufacturing executive; b. Monmouth, Ill., July 1, 1938; s. Roy Edwin and Caroline Hilma (Fillman) Carrell; m. Bonnie Lee Clements, July 11, 1964; children: Philip Edwin, Andrew David. AB, Monmouth Coll., 1961; MBA, Calif. State U., L.A., 1967; D in Bus. Adminstrn., U. So. Calif., 1970; AAS, Ivy Tech. State Coll., 1991. Engr. Argonne Nat. Lab., 1957—59, Mass. Inst. of Tech. Rsch. and Engring., 1959—62; from sr. engr. to prin. engr. reconnaissance and comm. N.Am. Aviation, 1962-67; mgr. avionics analysis and techs. B-1 divsn. Rockwell Internat., 1967-73; dir. engring. Morse Controls divsn., 1973-74; gen. mgr. Morse Controls divsn. Incom Internat. Inc., 1974-78; pres. Morse Controls, 1978—82, Heim Bearings, 1982—85; gen. mgr. Stewart-Warner Corp., 1985-88; pres. Stewart Warner South Wind Corp., 1988-95, Stewart Warner Electronics Corp., 1991-95; pres., COO Nartron Corp., 1995-97; pres. Image Moulding and Frame, Inc., Image Arts, Inc., 1997-99, TECorp, Inc., 1997—, Best Weld, Inc., 1998—. Cons. in field; lectr. U. So. Calif., 1967—70. Contbr. articles to profl. jours. Nat. coun. Boy Scouts Am., 1980—85; active Hudson (Ohio) Econ. Devel. Com., 1979—82; mem. svc. rev. panel United Way Summit County, 1980; bd. dirs., coun. commr. Boy Scouts Am., 1980—85. NDEA fellow, 1961—63. Mem.: Boating Industry Assn. (chmn. steering task force 1974—85), Am. Boat and Yacht Coun. (dir. 1980—88), Hudson C. of C. (trustee 1976—78). Achievements include patents in field. Office: 1315 W 18th St Anderson IN 46016-3800 Office Phone: 765-641-7720. E-mail: tcarrell@iquest.net.

CARREN, JEFFREY P., lawyer; b. Chgo., Oct. 8, 1946; AB with high honors, U. Ill., 1968; JD, Northwestern U., 1972. Bar: Ill. 1973, U.S. Dist. Ct. (no. dist.) Ill. 1973, U.S. Ct. Appeals (7th cir.) 1976, U.S. Supreme Ct. 1980. Formerly ptnr. Winston & Strawn, Chgo.; ptnr. Laner, Muchin, Dombrow, Becker, Levin & Tominberg Ltd., Chgo., 1994—. Editor notes and comments Northwestern U. Law Rev., 1971-72/ Edmund James scholar. Mem. ABA (tax and bus. sects.), Ill. State Bar Assn. (employee benefits sect.), Chgo. Bar Assn. (employee benefits com), Am. Arbitration Assn. (panel arbitrators), Phi Eta Sigma. Office: Laner Muchin et al 515 N State St Chicago IL 60610-4324 Office Phone: 312-467-9800. E-mail: jcarren@lanermuchin.com.

CARRERA, JAGANATH, acupuncturist, yoga educator; b. Elizabeth, N.J., Jan. 23, 1950; s. Peter Daniel and Maria Felicita Carrera; m. Mary Ellen Janaki Schmidt, June 28, 1980. B in Religious Studies, SUNY, N.Y.C., 1995; M in Acupuncture, Tri State Coll. Acupuncture, 1998. Diplomate Nat. Coun. for Cert. Acupuncture and Oriental Medicine, 1998, cert. acupuncturist N.J., Va., N.Y., 1998, Swedish Inst. of Massage and Allied Sci., 1978; Raja yoga instr. Integral Yoga Internat., 1987; instr. Integral Yoga Internat., 1975, tchr. trainer Integral Yoga Internat., 1980, registered tchr. Yoga Alliance, 2002. Exec. dir. Integral Yoga Inst., New Brunswick, NJ, 1975—87; vice pres., adminstr. Satchidananda Ashram-Yogaville, Buckingham, Va., 1987—94; dean studies Ea. Sch. Acupuncture and Traditional Medicine, Montclair, NJ, 1997—2002, v.p. Monclair, NJ, 2002—, clinic supr.; hatha yoga instr. Integral Yoga Internat., 1974—, raja yoga instr., 1975—, meditation instr., 1974—, yoga tchr. trainer, 1976—. Hatha yoga instr. Integral Yoga Ministry, 1974—, mediation instr., 1974—, raja yoga instr., 1975—, exec. dir., 1975—87, yoga tchr. trainer, 1976—, bd. mem., 1980—; adv. bd. New Sem., N.Y.C., NY, 1998—; spiritual advisor One Spirit Learning Alliance, N.Y.C., NY, 2000—; bd. govs. Ea. Sch. Acupuncture, Montclair, NJ. Contbr. articles to profl. jours. Recipient Guru Tattwa Ratnam award, Integral Yoga Internat., 1986. Achievements include originator and devloper of Integral Yoga Ministry; development of co-developer of Integral Yoga Raja Yoga and Integral Yoga meditation teacher trainings. Office: Integral Yoga Inst 2103 Maple Ave Fair Lawn NJ 07410 Office Phone: 201-796-7585. Personal E-mail: revjaganath@yahoo.com. E-mail: iyiyoga@aol.com.

CARRERAS, FRANCISCO JOSÉ, retired academic administrator, foundation administrator; b. San Juan, PR, May 13, 1932; s. Francisco and Antonia (Muriente) C.; m. Ana Elisa Carreras, Mar. 29, 1964; children: Inés María, María Soledad, Irene María, Marianne, Francisco José, María del Pilar. Student, Instituto Superior de Estudios Clásicos, Havana, Cuba, 1954-57; BA, Universidad Pontificia de Comillas, Santander, Spain, 1959; MA, Fordham U., 1960; PhD, Universidad Pontificia Gregoriana, Rome, 1966. Mem. faculty U. P.R., Rio Piedras Campus, 1962-69, acad. asst. to dir., 1967-69, dir. humanities dept., 1967-68; pres. Cath. U. P.R., Ponce, 1969-81; academician P.R. Acad. Arts and Scis., 1970; exec. dir. Angel Ramos Found., Inc., San Juan, P.R., 1984—; mem. P.R. State Commn. on Post-Secondary Edn., 1973. Dir. Banco Popular de P.R. Author: Filosofía de la Coordinación de José Vasconcelos, 1971, Incógnita y Revelación, 1981; also articles. Adv. Sociedad Puertorriqueña UNESCO, 1973; pres. P.R. Endowment for Humanities, 1977; bd. dirs. Angel Ramos Found., 1977; bd. dirs. Damas Hosp., 1978, P.R. Acad. Arts and Scis., 1980; adv. bd. dirs. Orgns. Universidades Católicas de América Latina, 1976. Recipient Pres.'s medal Ana G. Mendez Univ. Sys.-P.R., 2000. Mem. Fundación Puertorriqueña Humanidades (pres. 1977), Ponce Sales and Mktg. Execs. Assn., Alpha Phi Omega, Phi Delta Kappa. Clubs: Rotary, Lions. Roman Catholic. Home: 1 St C-16 Villas Del Pilar San Juan PR 00926 Office: Angel Ramos Found Inc PO Box 362408 San Juan PR 00936-2408 Office Phone: 787-763-3530. Business E-Mail: fcarreras@farpr.org.

CARRERE, CHARLES SCOTT, law educator, judge; b. Dublin, Ga., Sept. 26, 1937; 1 son, Daniel Austin. BA, U. Ga., 1959; LLB, Stetson U., 1961. Bar: Ga. 1960, Fla. 1961. Law clk. U.S. Dist. Judge, Orlando, Fla., 1962—63; asst. U.S. Atty. Mid. Dist. Fla., 1963—66, 1968—69, chief trial atty., 1965—66, 1968—69; ptnr. Harrison, Greene, Mann, Rowe & Stanton, 1970—80; judge Pinellas County, Fla., 1980—96; vis. prof. law Stetson Coll. Law, 1997—98, Cumberland Law Sch., 1998—99. Recipient Jud. Appreciation award St. Petersburg Bar Assn., 1996, Alumnus of Yr. award Stetson Student Bar Assn., 1998. Mem. State Bar Ga., Fla. Bar, Phi Beta Kappa. Presbyterian. Address: PO Box 22034 Gateway Mall Sta Saint Petersburg FL 33742 also: PO Box 7177 Seminole FL 33775-7177 Office Phone: 727-395-9444. Fax: 727-395-0444.

CARREY, JIM, actor; b. Newmarket, Ont., Can., Jan. 17, 1962; s. Percy and Kathleen Carrey; m. Melissa Womer, Mar. 28, 1987 (div. Dec. 11, 1995); 1 child, Jane; m. Lauren Holly Sept. 23, 1996 (div. July 29, 1997). Performances include (TV series) The Duck Factory, 1984, In Living Color, 1990-94 (also writer); (TV films) Mike Hammer: Murder Takes All, 1989, Doing Time on Maple Drive, 1992; (films) Finders Keepers, 1984, Once Bitten, 1985, Peggy Sue Got Married, 1986, The Dead Pool, 1988, Earth Girls Are Easy, 1989, Pink Cadillac, 1989, High Strung, 1991, Ace Ventura: Pet Detective, 1993 (also screenwriter), The Mask, 1994, Dumb and Dumber, 1994, Batman Forever, 1995, Ace Ventura: When Nature Calls, 1995, The Mask's Revenge, 1996, Liar, Liar, 1996, The Cable Guy, 1996, The Truman Show, 1997 (Golden Globe award for best performance by an actor in a motion picture 2000), Simon Birch, 1998, Man on the Moon, 1999 (Golden Globe for best performance by an actor in a motion picture 2000), Me, Myself and Irene, 2000, How the Grinch Stole Christmas, 2000, The Majestic, 2001, Bruce Almighty, 2003, Eternal Sunshine of the Spotless Mind, 2004, Lemony Snicket's A Series of Unfortunate Events, 2004. Star on the Hollywood Walk of Fame, 2000; named one of 50 Most Powerful People in Hollywood, 2004, 2005. Office: UTA 9560 Wilshire Blvd Fl 5 Beverly Hills CA 90212-2401*

CARRICK, BRUCE ROBERT, publishing company executive; b. N.Y.C., Feb. 5, 1937; s. Charles L. Jr. and Virginia S. (Brewster) C.; m. Ann Ewing; children: Charles L., Meredyth E., James B. BA in History, Princeton U., 1961. Various positions Western Pub. Co., N.Y.C., 1961-64, Doubleday & Co., N.Y.C., 1964-68, London, 1964—68; sr. editor Charles Scribner & Sons, N.Y.C., 1968-71, Macmillan Co., N.Y.C., 1971-74; dir., v.p. H.W. Wilson Co., N.Y.C., 1975-96; pub. cons., writer, 1996—. Served with U.S. Army, 1956-58. Mem. Princeton Club. Home and Office: 304C Heritage Hills Dr Somers NY 10589-1716

CARRICK, KATHLEEN MICHELE, law librarian; b. Cleve., June 11, 1950; d. Michael James and Genevieve (Wenger) C. BA, Duquesne U., Pitts., 1972; MLS, U. Pitts., 1973; JD, Cleve.-Marshall U., 1977. Bar: Ohio 1977, U.S. Ct. Internat. Trade 1983. Rsch. asst. The Plain Dealer, Cleve., 1973-75; head reference SUNY, Buffalo, 1977-78, assoc. dir., 1978-80, dir., asst. prof., 1980-83; dir., assoc. prof. law Case Western Res. U., Cleve., 1983—. Cons. Mead Data Central, Dayton, Ohio, 1987-91. Author: Lexis: A Research Manual, 1989, From Litchfield to Lexis: A Bibliography of American Legal Education, 2004; contbr. articles to profl. jours. Fellow Am. Bar Found.; mem. ABA, Am. Law Inst., Am. Assn. Law Librs., Assn. Am. Law Schs., Scribes. Home: 1317 Burlington Rd Cleveland OH 44118-1212 Office: Case Western Res U 11075 East Blvd Cleveland OH 44106-5409 Office Phone: 216-368-6357. Business E-Mail: kxc4@case.edu.

CARRICO, DONALD JEFFERSON, retired transportation executive; b. Dallas, June 15, 1944; s. Ivan and Helen Mae (Jefferson) C.; m. Prudence Louise Cornish, Aug. 17, 1968; children: Bryan Jefferson, Alan Jefferson. BSBA, Ohio State U., 1967; MA in Bus. Mgmt., Cen. Mich. U., 1977. Commd. 2d lt. USAF, 1967, advanced through grades to maj., 1979; various supervisory positions USAF Air Freight Terminals, 1967—72; mgr. passenger travel and cargo br. USAF Transp. Div., Rickenbacker AFB, Ohio, 1972—74; transp. and air terminal insp. USAF Insp. Gen. Team, 1974—76; liaison officer US Naval Supply Ctr., Pearl Harbor, Hawaii, 1976—78; transp. staff officer USAF Hdqrs. Tactical Air Command, Langley AFB, Va., 1978—83; chief transp. USAF Transp. Div., Incirlik AB, Turkey, 1983—85, Williams AFB, Ariz., 1986—88; vehicle fleet mgr. V&B Svcs., Phoenix, 1989—91; asst. mgr. dispatch svcs. Phoenix Transit Sys., 1991—92, ops. mgr., 1993—95, logistics mgr., 1996—98, ops. dir., 1998—2004, ret., 2004. Logistics chief Gilbert Food Bank Cmty. Food Dr., Gilbert, Ariz., 1987, chmn., 1988; asst. cubmaster Pack 282 Boy Scouts Am., Gilbert, 1987; mem. Town of Gilbert Gen. Plan Rev. Task Force, 1992-93, total quality mgmt. rsch. panel Transp. Rsch. Bd., Washington, 1992-95; transp. coord. Super Bowl XXX, Tempe, 1995-96, City of Phoenix Millennium Celebration, 1999-2000. Decorated Bronze Star; recipient excellence award City of Phoenix, 1998. Avocations: community planning, automotive restoration, travel. Home: Ste 804-B 425 Ena Rd Honolulu HI 96815 Personal E-mail: djc4410@verizon.net.

CARRICO, HARRY LEE, retired judge; b. Washington, Sept. 4, 1916; s. William Temple and Nellie Nadalia (Willett) C.; m. Betty Lou Peck, May 18, 1940 (dec. 1987); 1 child, Lucretia Ann; m. Lynn Brackenridge, July 1, 1994. Jr. cert., George Washington U., 1938, JD, 1942; LLD (hon.), U. Richmond, 1973, George Washington U., 1987; LLD, Coll. William & Mary, 1993; LLD (hon.), Shenandoah U., 2004. Bar: Va. 1941. With Rust & Rust, Fairfax, Va., 1941-43; trial justice Fairfax, Va., 1943-51; pvt. practice, 1951-56; judge 16th Jud. Cir., Va., 1956-61; justice Va. Supreme Ct., Richmond, 1961-81, chief justice, 1981—2003, sr. justice, 2003—. Chmn. bd dirs. Nat. Ctr. for State Cts., 1989-90; vis. prof. law and civic engagement Law Sch. U. Richmond, 2004. With USNR, 1945-46. Recipient Alumni Profl. Achievement award George Washington U., 1981. Mem. McNeill Law Soc., Conf. Chief Justices (bd. dirs. 1985-91, 1st v.p. 1987, pres.-elect. 1988, pres. 1989-90, co-chmn. nat. jud. coun. 1991-97), Order of Coif, Phi Delta Phi, Omicron Delta Kappa. Episcopalian. Office: Supreme Court of Va 100 N 9th St 4th Fl Richmond VA 23219 Office Phone: 804-786-2023. Business E-Mail: hcarrico@courts.state.va.us.

CARRICO, KIMBERLY ANNE, elementary school educator; b. Modest, Calif., Oct. 23, 1954; d. Jack R. and Aloha V. Carrico; 1 child, Chance Scott. BA, Calif. State Stanislaus, 1994. Tchr. Hidahl Elem. Sch., Ceres, Calif., Joel Hidahl Elem. Sch., Ceres. Leader citizenship and sci. 4-H; mem. Friends Ceres Libr., 1990—2005, Project Wild Calif., 1990—2005. Named Tchr. of the Yr., Order of Eastern Star, 2003. Avocations: skydiving, white-water rafting, waterfalls. Home: PO Box 1711 Ceres CA 95307 Office: Ceres Unified Sch Dist Ceres CA 95307

CARRICO, STEPHEN J., construction company executive; b. 1954; Grad., Ctrl. Mich. U., 1977. CPA. With Straka, Jarackas & Co., Detroit, 1977-84; various positions Hensel Phelps Constrn. Co., Greeley, Colo., 1984—, now v.p. fin. Office: Hensel Phelps Construction 420 Sixth Ave Greeley CO 80632*

CARRICO, VIRGIL NORMAN, physician; b. Cumberland, Md., Aug. 28, 1940; s. Virgil Norman and Lucille E. Carrico; m. Nina Lois Lemper, Aug. 17, 1963; children: Pamela Beth Carrico-Miller, Sandra Kelly (dec.). BA, Wabash Coll., 1962; MD, Ind. U., 1966. Diplomate Am. Bd. Family Practice. Intern Marion County Gen. Hosp., Indpls., 1966-67; resident in family practice Akron (Ohio) City Hosp., 1970-72, chief resident in family practice, 1972, assoc. dir. family practice residency, 1972; chief family practice Bryan Cmty. Hosp., chief of staff, 1977-78, preceptor Bryan Area Health Edn. Ctr.; past preceptor cmty. medicine Med. Coll. Ohio, Toledo, clin. asst. prof. family medicine, clin. prof. family medicine; past preceptor preventive medicine and family practice Ohio State U.; med. dir. Bryan Area Health Edn. Ctr. Past pres., bd. dirs. Bryan Med. Group, Inc. Contbr. articles to profl. jours. Trustee YWCA, Bryan, Ohio, v.p., 1990-92; bd. dirs. United Fund, pres., 1990-92; bd. dirs. Jr. Achievement, 1981-83, Bryan Area Found. Capt. USAF, 1967-70. Fellow Am. Acad. Family Physicians (bylaw coms. 1989, 90, 91, 92, nat. chmn. 1993, chmn. patient care svcs. commn. 1988-89, chmn. mem. svcs. commn. 1989-90); mem. Soc. Tchrs. Family Medicine, Ohio Acad. Family Medicine, Am. Acad. Family Medicine, Williams County Med. Soc. (pres. 1976-79, sec.-treas., v.p. 1980-83), Ohio Acad. Family Physicians (del. to ho. of dels. 1972-85; pres. Fulton County chpt. 1973-85, chmn. resident affairs subcom., nominating com., student awards, fin. com., ref. com. of the ho. of dels.; treas. 1985-87, v.p. 1987-89, bd. dirs. 1983-92, pres.-elect 1990-91), Rotary Internat. Avocations: golf, travel, reading. Office: Bryan Med Group 442 W High St Bryan OH 43506-1681 Office Phone: 419-636-4517. Personal E-mail: bmg@bright.net.

CARRIER, FRANCE, medical educator; b. Beauport, Que., June 9, 1961; d. Philippe Carrier and Therese Pare; m. Steven I. Hirschfeld; 1 child, Joshua Samuel. PhD, U. Montreal, 1988. Postdoctoral fellow Biotechnology Rsch. Inst., Montreal, 1988—89; vis. assoc. NIH, Bethesda, Md., 1989—91; vis. scientist Nat. Cancer Inst. NIH, Bethesda, 1991—98; prof. medicine U. Md., Balt., 1998—. Mem. Greenebaum Cancer Ctr., Balt. Contbr. articles to profl. jours., chapters to books. Internat. fellow, Human Frontier Sci. Program Orgn., 1990, Rsch. grantee, NIH, 1999—2003, 2001—02, Am. Cancer Soc., 2000—02, 2004—, A-T Children's Project, 2003—04, 2005—. Mem.: Am. Assn. for Cancer Rsch. (sponsor, Brigid Leventhal award 2002), N.Y. Acad. Scis., Cosmos Club (Elected mem. 1999). Achievements include patents for methods for determining the presence of functional p53 in mammalian cells research in genotoxic stress-response, cancer progression, chromatin remodeling. Office: U Md 108 N Greene St Baltimore MD 21201-1503 Office Phone: 410-706-5105. Business E-Mail: fcarr001@umaryland.edu.

CARRIER, RACHEL ESTHER, music educator, director; b. Dayton, Ohio, Dec. 22, 1949; d. Robert Richard Folkerth and Amber Mae Spitler; m. Harold Gene Carrier, Jan. 27, 1968; children: Bryan Patrick, Alan Brent. BA in Performing Arts, Wittenberg Univ., 1975; student, Sinclair Coll., 1986—87, Wright State U., 1987—90; studied with, Douglas MacCash, 1964—84, D. Maddafore, 1968—73, Joan Swank. Cert. dental asst. nat., 1980. Orthodontic asst. Drs. King, Mayerson, Pope, Dayton, 1968—73; dental forensic asst. Wm. Bernard Weaver, D.M.D, Dayton, 1978—93; vocal instr. Northmont H.S., Clayton, Ohio, 1994—. Music cons. Bel Canto Young Singers Music Club, Dayton, 1997—; dir. children's drama and show choir Miami-Montage Children's Theater, Vandalia, Ohio, 1996—98; dir. children's choir Concord United Meth. Ch., Englewood, Ohio, 1973—74, asst. dir. music, youth dir., 1977—92; youth choir dir. Englewood (Ohio) United Meth. Ch., 1989—91; dir. music Vandalia (Ohio) United Meth. Ch., 1993—98; dir. music ministries and drama and Christian edn. Shiloh Ch., Dayton, 1998—, dir. christian edn., 1998—2001; vocal judge Regional Star Search, Cincinnati-Dayton, Ohio, 2004; dir. Music Ministries and Drama. Singer: George Washington Episc. Ch., Dayton (Ohio) Opera. Dir. Dayton (Ohio) Performing Arts Programs, 1998—2003. Named Woman of the Yr., Am. Biog. Assoc., 2001. Mem.: Dayton Music Club (corr.; cons. to the jr. music club 1998—2003), The Fellowship/Music and Worship Arts (corr.), Ohio Fedn. of Music Clubs (state festival chmn. 1998—), Ohio Ea. Star (past matron 1979—80, State of Ohio Vocalist 1978, 1979, 1980, 1982, 1984). Republican. Protestant. Avocations: breeding english springer spaniels, swimming, acting, gardening, directing handbells. Home: 4339 Gorman Ave Englewood OH 45322 Office: Shiloh Church UCC 5300 Philadelphia Dr Dayton OH 45415 Office Phone: 937-277-8953. Personal E-mail: rachcar898@aol.com. E-mail: rachelcarrier@shiloh.org.

CARRIER, RONALD EDWIN, academic administrator, director; b. Bluff City, Tenn., Aug. 18, 1932; s. James Murphy and Melissa (Miller) C.; m. Edith Marie Johnson, Sept. 7, 1955; children: Michael Lavon, Linda Lois Carrier Frazee, Jennine Marie. BS, Ea. Tenn. State U., 1955; MS in Econs., U. Ill., 1957, PhD in Econs., 1960; Doctorate (hon.), William and Mary Coll., Bridgewater Coll., Jacksonville State U., Francis Marion U. Assoc. prof. econs. U. Miss., Oxford, 1960-63; dir., prof. Bur. Bus. and Econ. Rsch., Memphis U., 1963-66, provost, v.p. acad. affairs, 1966-71; pres., chancellor James Madison U., Harrisonburg, Va., 1971—2002, pres. emeritus, 2002—; pres. Ctr. Innovative Tech., Herndon, Va., 1986-87. Chancellor Romanian Am. U. Author: Plant Locations: A Theory and Explanations, 1968; contbr. articles and monographs to profl. publs. Mem. White House Conf. Balance Econ. Growth; mem. Va. Indsl. Facilities Study Commn., 1972-75; chmn. Va. Land Use Adv. Com., 1974-77, Va. Gov.'s Electricity Costs Commn., 1975—; mem. Va. Gov.'s Energy Resource Adv. Commn., 1975-76, Gov.'s Regulatory Reform Adv. Bd., 1983, Joint Subcom. to Study Coal Slurry Pipeline Feasibility, 1983, ethics com. Senate Va., 1999, Va. Higher Edn. Steering Commn., 2002. Earheart fellow 1958-60; recipient Ben Franklin award Memphis Printing Industry, 1966, faculty award East Tenn. State U., 1955, Disting. Svc. award Jr. C. of C., 1965, Virginian of Yr. award Va. Assn. Broadcasters, 1982; named Outstanding Virginian, FHA, 1990; cultural laureate Va.; named Outstanding Virginian FFA, 1991. Mem.: Sigma Phi Epsilon, Omicron Delta Gamma, Omicron Delta Kappa. Methodist. Office: James Madison U MSC 5730 Harrisonburg VA 22807 Home: 209 Divot Dr Harrisonburg VA 22802 Office Phone: 540-568-8181. Business E-Mail: carriere@jmu.edu.

CARRIER, WARREN PENDLETON, retired university chancellor, writer; b. Cheviot, Ohio, July 3, 1918; s. Burly Warren and Prudence (Alfrey) C.; m. Marjorie Jane Regan, Apr. 3, 1947 (dec.); 1 child, Gregory Paul; m. Judy Lynn Hall, June 14, 1973; 1 son, Ethan Alfrey. Student, Wabash Coll., 1938-40; AB, Miami U., Oxford, Ohio, 1942; MA, Harvard U., 1948; PhD, Occidental Coll., 1962. Asst. prof. English U. Iowa, 1949-52; assoc. prof. Bard Coll., 1953-57; lit. faculty Bennington, 1955-58; vis. prof. Sweet Briar (Va.) Coll., 1958-60; prof. Deep Springs (Calif.) Coll., 1960-62, Portland (Oreg.) State U., 1962-64; prof., chmn. English dept. U. Mont., Missoula, 1964-68; assoc. dean. prof. English and comparative lit., chmn. comparative lit. Livingston Coll., Rutgers U., 1968-69; dean Coll. Arts and Letters, San Diego State U., 1969-72; v.p. acad. affairs U. Bridgeport, Conn., 1972-75; chancellor U. Wis., Platteville, 1975-82. Author: The Hunt, 1952, Bay of the Damned, 1957, Toward Montebello, 1966, Leave Your Sugar for the Cold Morning, 1977, The Diver, 1986, Death of a Chancellor, 1986, An Honorable Spy, 1992, Murder at the Strawberry Festival, 1993, An Ordinary Man, 1997, Death of a Poet, 1999, Justice at Christmas, 1999, Risking the Wind, 1999, Coming to Terms, 2004; founder Quar. Rev. of Lit.; editor: Guide to World Literature, 1980; co-editor: Reading Modern Poetry, 1955, 68, Literature from the World, 1981; assoc. editor: Western Rev., 1949-51; contbr. articles, poems, revs. to lit. mags. Mem. Jud. Commn. Wis. Vol., Am. Field Service attached to Brit. Army, India-Burma, 1944-45. Recipient award for poetry Nat. Endowment for Arts, 1972; Colladay prize for poetry, 1986 Mem. Nat. Coun. Tchrs. English, Royal Soc. Arts, Wis. Acad. Arts and Scis., Phi Beta Kappa. Home: 69 Colony Park Cir Galveston TX 77551-1737

CARRIERE, MARGARET E., energy executive; BS, Georgetown U., 1973; JD, So. Meth. U., 1979. With legal dept. Halliburton, Houston, v.p. legal and assoc. gen. counsel, v.p. human resources, regional chief counsel for Europe and Africa England, 1986—88, 1994—98, v.p. and sec., legal Houston, 2002—. Mem.: Am. Soc. Corp. Secs., Am. Corp. Counsel Assn., Tex. State Bar Assn., La. State Bar Assn. Office: Halliburton Ste 2400 PO Box 42807 5 Houston Ctr 1401 McKinney Houston TX 77242-2807 Office Phone: 713-759-2617.

CARRIERI, ARTHUR HELMUT, physicist, researcher; b. Phila., June 15, 1953; s. Philip and Margot Carrieri. AB, Temple U., 1976; MS, Pa. State U., 1978. Sr. rsch. physicist U.S. Army Rsch., Devel. and Engring. Command, Edgewood Chem. Biol. Ctr., Aberdeen Proving Ground, Md., 1983—. Roman Catholic. Achievements include patents for neural network pattern recognition systems; infrared Mueller matrix detection and ranging system, thermal luminescence sensor, chemical imaging sensor and laser beacon, earth monitoring satellite system, others. Avocation: scuba diving. Home: 3105 K Cardinal Way Abingdon MD 21009 Office: US Army Edgewood Chem & Biol Ctr 5183 Blackhawk Rd Aberdeen Proving Ground MD 21010-5424 Office Phone: 410-436-5943. Personal E-mail: ahcarrie@hotmail.com. Business E-Mail: arthur.carrieri@us.army.mil.

CARRIG, KENNETH J., food products executive; m. Lisa Carrig; 3 children. BS in Labor Econs., Cornell U., 1981. With PepsiCo; head human resources Continental Airlines, 1995—97; global practice leader human capital practice Andersen Cons.; v.p., chief adminstrv. officer Sysco Corp., Houston, 1998—99, sr. .v.p. adminstrn., 1998—2004, exec. v.p., chief adminstrv. officer, 2004—. Fellow: Nat. Acad. of Human Resources. Office: Sysco Corp 1390 Enclave Pky Houston TX 77077-2099

CARRIGAN, CHARLES ROGER, geophysicist; b. Altadena, Calif., Sept. 7, 1949; s. Charles Francis and Alyce (Krosley) C.; m. Suzanne Lundin, Feb. 21, 1976; children: Alisa Lynn, Charles Jonathan. BA in Astronomy and Physics, UCLA, 1971, MS in Geophysics, 1973, PhD in Geophysics, 1977. Rsch. assoc. UCLA, 1979-80; tech. staff mem. Sandia Nat. Labs., Albuquerque, 1980-89; physicist Lawrence Livermore Nat. Lab., Livermore, Calif., 1989-97, group leader flow and transport group, 1997—, prin. investigator Vadose Zone Obs., 1997—. Patentee in field; contbr. articles to profl. jours. Deacon Grace Bapt. Ch., Tracy, Calif., 1993-94, chmn. bd. 1994-95, 97—. Fellow Cambridge (Eng.) U., 1977-79, NATO, 1977. Mem. Am. Geophys. Union, Sigma Xi, Sigma Pi Sigma. Avocations: music, reading, walking. Office: Lawrence Livermore Nat Lab PO Box 808 Livermore CA 94551-0808

CARRIGAN, DAVID OWEN, history educator; b. New Glasgow, N.S., Can., Nov. 30, 1933; s. Ronald and Marion Constance (Hoare) C.; m. Florence Catherine Nicholson, June 21, 1958; children: Nancy, Janet, David, Glen, Sharon, Douglas. BA, St. Francis Xavier U., 1954; MA, Boston U., 1955; PhD, U. Maine, 1966. Asst. prof. history St. Francis Xavier U., 1957-61, assoc. prof., 1961-67; assoc. prof. history Wilfred Laurier U., 1967-68; prin., dean arts Kings Coll., U. Western Ont., 1968-71; pres. St. Mary's U., Halifax, N.S., 1971-79, prof., 1979-99, prof. emeritus, 1999—. Author: Canadian Party Platforms, 1867-1968, 1968, Crime and Punishment in Canada: A History, 1991, Juvenile Delinquency in Canada a History, 1998; contbrs. articles to profl. jours. Former trustee Inst. Research on Public Policy; past mem. Can. Council; past bd. dirs. Can. Assn. for Treatment and Study of Families Mem.: Phi Kappa Phi. Office: St Mary's Univ Halifax NS Canada B3H 3C3

CARRIGAN, JIM R., arbitrator, mediator, retired judge; b. Mobridge, S.D., Aug. 24, 1929; s. Leo Michael and Mildred Ione (Jaycox) C.; m. Beverly Jean Halpin, June 2, 1956. Ph.B., JD, U. N.D., 1953; LL.M. in Taxation, NYU, 1956; LLD (hon.), U. Colo., 1989, Suffolk U., 1991, U. N.D., 1997. Bar: N.D. 1953, Colo. 1956. Asst. prof. law U. Denver, 1956-59; vis. assoc. prof. NYU Law Sch., 1958, U. Wash. Law Sch., 1959-60; Colo. jud. adminstr., 1960-61; prof. law U. Colo., 1961-67; partner firm Carrigan & Bragg (and predecessors), 1967-76; bd. regents U. Colo., 1975-76; justice Colo. Supreme Ct., 1976-79; judge U.S. Dist. Ct. Colo., 1979-95. Mem. Colo. Bd. Bar Examiners, 1969-71; lectr. Nat. Coll. State Judiciary, 1964-77, 95; bd. dirs. Nat. Inst. Trial Advocacy, 1971-73, 78—, chmn. bd. 1986-88, also mem. faculty, 1972—; adj. prof. law U. Colo, 1984, 1991—; bd. dirs. Denver Broncos Stadium Dist., 1996—. Editor-in-chief: N.D. Law Rev., 1952-53, Internat. Soc. Barristers Quar., 1972-79; editor: DICTA, 1957-59; contbr. articles to profl. jours. Bd. visitors U. N.D. Coll. Law, 1983-85. Recipient Disting. Svc. award Nat. Coll. State Judiciary, 1969, Outstanding Alumnus award U. N.D., 1973, Regent Emeritus award U. Colo., 1977, B'nai Brith Civil Rights award, 1986, Thomas More Outstanding Lawyer award Cath. Lawyers Guild, 1988, Oliphant Disting. Svc. award Nat. Inst. Trial Advocacy, 1993, Constl. Rights award Nat. Assn. Blacks in Criminal Justice (Colo. chpt.), 1992, Disting. Svc. award Colo. Bar Assn., 1994, Amicus Curiae award ATLA, 1994, Colo. Trial Lawyers Assn. Lifetime Achievement award, 2000. Fellow Colo. Bar Found., Boulder County Bar Found.; mem. ABA (action com. on tort system improvement 1985-87, TIPS sect. long range planning com., 1986-97; coun. 1987-91, task force on initiatives and referenda 1990-92, size of civil juries task force 1988-90, class actions task force 1995-97), Colo. Bar Assn., Boulder County Bar Assn., Denver Bar Assn., Cath. Lawyers Guild, Inns. of Ct., Internat. Soc. Barristers, Internat. Acad. Trial Lawyers (bd. dirs. 1995—), Fed. Judges Assn. (bd. dirs. 1985-89), Am. Judicature Soc. (bd. dirs. 1985-89), Tenth Circuit Dist. Judges Assn. (sec. 1991-92, v.p. 1992-93, pres. 1994-95), Order of Coif, Phi Beta Kappa. Roman Catholic. Office: Judicial Arbiter Group 1601 Blake St Ste 400 Denver CO 80202-1328 Personal E-mail: carrigan2350@earthlink.net. E-mail: info@jagine.com.

CARRIGAN, MARTIN DENNIS, lawyer, educator; b. Mansfield, Ohio, Nov. 22, 1959; s. Michael Robert and Marilyn Jane (Simpson) C.; m. Catherine Marie Goertemiller, Oct. 29, 1988. BA, U. Notre Dame, 1981; JD, U. Toledo, 1985; MBA, U. Findlay, 1995; PhD, LaSalle U., 1997. Ptnr. Fuller & Henry, Toledo, 1985-97; prin. Carrigan Law Offices, Toledo, 1997—. Asst. prof. Mgmt., U. Findlay, Ohio, 1997—; bus. cons. Katoy Enterprises, Maunee, 1990-92. Mem. Ohio State Bar Assn. Avocation: skiing. E-mail: carrigan@lawyer.com.

CARRIGAN, ROBERT, technology media company executive; BBA, Boston U. Intern Digital News, IDG Co., New Eng. regional mgr., ea. sales mgr.; various sr. sales mgmt. positions PC World, IDG, v.p., assoc. pub.; sr. v.p. Spinner.com; sr. v.p. Key Accounts Group Am. Online, Inc.; pub., pres., CEO Computerworld, IDG Co. Office: Computerworld One Speen St Framingham MA 01701 Business E-Mail: bob_carrigan@computerworld.net.

CARRIGAN, WILLIAM THOMAS, III, writer; b. Havana, Cuba, Nov. 8, 1921; arrived in U.S., 1923; s. William Thomas, Jr. and Ethel Harrison (Kilpatrick) Carrigan; m. Theodora Clarine Belland, Dec. 20, 1945; children: Bonnie Ann, Denise Elaine. BS, U. Md., College Park, 1943. Info. officer NIH, Bethesda, Md., 1944—85; sci. writer, editor Howard Hughes Med. Inst., Chevy Chase, Md., 1986—97; freelance fiction writer Potomac, Md., 1944—97, Sarasota, Fla., 1997—. Author: (novels) Manic, 2001, The Runaway Clock, 2001, Seldom Go By, 2002, The Parachute Plant, 2002, The Burden of Matter, 2005. Avocations: music, bridge.

CARRIKER, MELBOURNE ROMAINE, retired marine biologist; b. Santa Marta, Colombia, Feb. 25, 1915; s. Melbourne Armstrong Jr. Carriker and Carmela Myrtle Flye; m. Meriel Roosevelt McAllister, Oct. 17, 1943; children: Eric Berkeley, Bruce Leaycraft, Neal Armstrong, Robert Romaine. BA, Rutgers Univ., New Brunswick, N.J., 1939; PhD, U. Wis., 1943; degree of sci. (hon.), Beloit Coll., 1968. From instr. to asst. prof. zoology Rutgers U., New Brunswick, NJ, 1946—54; assoc. prof. zoology U. N.C., Chapel Hill, 1954—61; supervisory fishery rsch. biologist, chief shellfish mortality program Biol. Lab. U.S. Bur. Comml. Fisheries, Oxford, 1961—62; 1962dir. systematics-ecology program Marine Biol. Lab., Woods Hole, Mass., ind. investigator, 1972—73; prof. marine studies U. Del., Lewes, 1973—85, prof. emeritus, 1985—. Numerous adj. professorships, rsch. fellowships in field. Author: Vista Nieve, Adventures of an early 20th century naturalist and his family in Colombia, S. A., 2001, Taming of the Oyster, A History of Evoling Shellfisheries and the National Shellfisheries Association, 2004, The Bird Call of the Rio Beni, Adventures of Father and Son on an Ornithological Expedition in the Jungles of Western Bolivia, South America in 1994-1995, 2005; contbr. more than 100 articles to profl. publs. Pres. Partners of the Americas, Lewes-Newark, Del. Lt.(j.g.) USNR, 1943—45, PTO. Mem.: Am. Malacological Soc. (pres. 1985—87), Atlantic Estuarine Rsch. Soc. (pres. 1961—62), Nat. Shellfisheries Assn. (pres. 1955—57). Home: 23 Hoornkill Ave Lewes DE 19958 Office: U Del Grad Coll Marine Studies Pillottown Rd Lewes DE 19958 Office Phone: 302-645-4274. Personal E-mail: carriker@udel.edu.

CARRIKER, ROBERT CHARLES, history professor; b. St. Louis, Aug. 18, 1940; s. Thomas B. and Vivian Ida (Spaunhorst) C.; m. Eleanor R. Gualdoni, Aug. 24, 1963; children: Thomas A., Robert M., Andrew J. BS, St. Louis U., 1962, AM, 1963; PhD, U. Okla., 1967. Asst. prof. Gonzaga U., Spokane, Wash., 1967-71, assoc. prof., 1972-76, prof. history, 1976—2002, disting. prof. Coll. Arts and Scis., 2003—. Author: Fort Supply, Indian Territory, 1970, 90, The Kalispel People, 1973, Father Peter De Smet, 1995, 1998, (with Harry Fritz) America Looks West, 2002, Ocian in View!, 2005; editor: (with Eleanor R. Carriker) Army Wife on the Frontier, 1975, (with William L. Lang) Great River of the West, 1999; book rev. editor Columbia mag., 1987—. Mem. Wash. Lewis and Clark Trail Com., 1978-99; commr. Wash. Maritime Bicentennial, Olympia, 1989-92; bd. dirs. Wash. Commn. for Humanities, Seattle, 1988-94. Burlington No. Found. scholar, 1985, 96; recipient Disting. Svc. award Lewis and Clark Trail Heritage Found., 1989. Mem. Wash. State Hist. Soc. (trustee 1981-90, v.p. 1993-2000), Western Hist. Assn., Phi Alpha Theta (councilor 1985-87). Roman Catholic. Avocations: travel, photography, cartography. Office: Gonzaga U 502 E Boone Ave Spokane WA 99258-0001 Business E-Mail: carriker@gonzaga.edu.

CARRINGER, PAUL TIMOTHY, marketing executive; b. St. Paul, Apr. 8, 1958; s. Donald Fred and Violet Johanna (Wermter) C.; m. Patsy Sue Mullins, Sept. 12, 1986. AA, Columbus Tech. Inst., 1981; BSBA, Franklin U., 1982; MBA, Ohio U., 1986. V.p. Carringer Bus. Svc., Columbus, 1981—88; account exec. Jones, Anastasi & Lennon Advt., Columbus, 1987—89; dir. pub. affairs YMCA of Ctrl. Ohio, Columbus, 1989—; pres. OCC Comm. (formerly CaringDirect Corp.), Columbus, 1989—; account exec. Zook Advt. Inc., 1992, Mills/James Prodns., Columbus, 1992—97; pres. Caring Direct Mktg. Solutions, Columbus, 2000—. Grad. staff asst. Ohio U., Athens, 1985-86; mem. faculty Franklin U. Coll. Bus. Adminstrn., 1999—; vice-chmn. Clintonville Inc., 2000—. Commr. Clintonville Area Commn., Columbus, 1995—, chmn. 1997—. Served with USAR, 1977-83. Mem. Columbus Area C. of C. (mgr. 1984-85, cons. 1985), Columbus Advt. Fedn. Republican. Pentecostal. Avocations: running, reading, computers, model building. Office: Caring Direct Mktg Solutions Ste 100 254 S Grubb St Columbus OH 43215 E-mail: paul@occommunications.com, paul@rocketmail.com.

CARRINGER, ROBERT, language educator; b. Knoxville, Tenn., May 12, 1941; m. Sonia Raysor, Sept. 7, 1968. AB, U. Tenn., 1962; MA, Johns Hopkins, 1964; PhD, Ind. U., 1968. Asst. prof. English U. Ill., Urbana, 1970-76, assoc. prof. English, 1976-84, disting. prof., 1985, prof. English and film, 1985—2003, prof. emeritus. Author: Ernst Lubitsch, 1978 (Choice Outstanding Acad. Book award 1979), The Making of Citizen Kane, 1985, rev. edit., 1996, Magnificent Ambersons: A Reconstruction, 1993; editor: The Jazz Singer, 1979; contbr. articles to profl. jours.; prodr. laserdiscs; assoc. Ctr. for Advanced Study, 1983-84. Mem. editl. bd.: Am. Studies, Quar. Rev. Film and Video, Cinema Jour. Recipient Instrnl. Tech. awards Amoco Corp., 1980, Apple Computer, 1988; Rsch. grantee NEH, 1986-87; fellow in cognitive psychology U. Ill., 1990-91; Getty scholar Getty Rsch. Inst., 1996-97. Mem.: MLA (chmn.film divsn. exec. com. 1981), Phi Beta Kappa, Phi Kappa Phi. Home: 50 County Rd 1675N Seymour IL 61875 Business E-Mail: fergus@uiuc.edu.

CARRINGTON, GARY, psychologist; b. Cleveland, OH, Feb. 26, 1969; s. Marjorie Carrington; children: Gary, Imari, Inaya. BA, Morehouse Coll., Atlanta, GA, 1992; MA psychology, Kent State U, Kent, OH, 1995, PhD coun. psychology, 2003. Psychologist pvt. practice, Cleveland, Ohio; prof. Tri-C, Cleveland, Ohio. Cons. Diversified Consultants, Cleveland, Ohio. Mentor, 2000—03. Vol. Urban League, Cleveland, Ohio; tutor Project Learn, Cleveland, Ohio. Mem.: Am. Coun. Assoc. (assoc.), Am. Psychol. Assoc. (assoc.). Home: 3734 Silsby Rd University Heights OH 44118

CARRINGTON, MICHAEL DAVIS, criminal justice and security consultant; b. South Bend, Ind., Mar. 9, 1938; s. Herman Lakin and Margaret (Davis) C.; m. Lynn Ogden, Feb. 8, 1958; children: Michael O. (dec.), Jill A., Elizabeth A., Gretchen L. BA, Ind. U., 1970; MALS, Valparaiso U., 1971. Parole officer State of Ind., South Bend, 1970-71; chief probation officer St. Joseph County, South Bend, 1971-74; dir. pub. safety City of South Bend, 1974-76, mayor's asst., 1976-80; adj. assoc. prof., dir. safety, security, police Ind. U., South Bend, 1979-94; presdl. appointment as U.S. Marshal Northern Dist. of Ind., South Bend, Ind., 1994—2002; ret. U.S. Marshall's Svc., 2002—. Cons. in pvt. security Pan Am. Games, Indpls., 1987; cons. on Bur. Motor Vehicles security study Gov. of Ind., 2003-04; security advance agt. Olympic Torch Relay, Ind., 1984, Hands Across Am., Ind., 1986. Mem. Ind. Parole Bd., 2004—05. Named Ky. Col., 1984, Hon. Big Bro. of Yr., 1974; recipient Sagamore of the Wabash award, 1984, 2002, 2004, Disting. Alumnus award, Coll. Arts and Scis., Ind. U., South Bend, 2002. Mem.: Assn. of Threat Assessment Profls. Presbyterian. Avocations: travel, reading, walking, working. Office: Box 96 South Bend IN 46624 Office Phone: 574-210-8575.

CARRINGTON, PAUL DEWITT, lawyer, educator; b. Dallas, June 12, 1931; s. Paul and Frances Ellen (DeWitt) C.; m. Bessie Meek, Aug., 1952; children: Clark DeWitt, Mary Carrington Coults, William James, Emily Carrington. BA, U. Tex., 1952; LLB, Harvard U., 1955. Bar: Tex. 1955, Ohio 1962, Mich. 1967. Practice, Dallas, 1955; teaching fellow Harvard U., 1957-58; asst. prof. law U. Wyo., 1958-60, Ind. U., 1960-62; assoc. prof. Ohio State U., 1962-65; prof. U. Mich., 1965-78; dean Duke U. Sch. Law, Durham, N.C., 1978-88, prof., 1978—. Reporter civil rules adv. com. Jud. Conf. of U.S., 1985-92. Author: (with Meador and Rosenberg) Justice on Appeal, 1977, (with Meador and Rosenberg) Appeals, 1994, (with Babcock) Civil Procedure, 1977, 3d edit., 1983, Stewards of Democracy, 1999, Spreading America's Word, 2005. Active Ann Arbor (Mich.) Bd. Edn., 1970-73; pres. Pvt. Adjudication Ctr., Inc., 1988-94, chmn., 1995-2002. With U.S. Army, 1955-57. Guggenheim fellow, 1988-89. Fellow: Am. Acad. Appellate Lawyers, Am. Acad. Arts and Scis., Am. Bar Found.; mem.: ABA, Am. Law Inst. Office: Duke U Sch Law Durham NC 27708-0362 Office Phone: 919-613-7040. Business E-Mail: pdc@law.duke.edu.

CARRION, RICHARD L., bank executive; b. San Juan, P.R., 1952; BS, U. Penn.; MS in Mgmt. Info. Systems, MIT. Pres. Ban Ponce Corp.; chmn., CEO Banco Popular de P.R.; chmn., pres., CEO Popular Inc. Bd. dirs. Nynex Corp., 1995—97, Verizon Comm., 1997—, Wyeth, 1997—; mem. exec. bd. Internat. Olympic Com., 2004—. Office: Banco Popularde Puerto Rico 209 Munoz Rivera Avenue Hato Rey PR 00918

CARRITHERS, JOSEPH EDWARD, English composition and literature educator; b. Red Bay, Ala., July 28, 1963; s. Edward Walden and Dessie Lee McClure. BA in Comm./Journalism, Miss. State U., Starkville, 1985, BA in English/History, 1987, MA in English, 1990, U. So. Calif., 1992, PhD in English, 2003. Reporter Comml. Dispatch, Columbus, Miss., 1985-88; mng. editor Starkville Daily News, 1988-90; asst. lectr. U. So. Calif., L.A., 1990-94; ESL instr. Don Martin Coll., Monterey Park, Calif., 1991; part-time prof. Mt. San Antonio Coll., Walnut, Calif., 1991-94; lectr. Woodbury U., Burbank, Calif., 1993-94; prof. English Fullerton (Calif.) Coll., 1994—. Mem. faculty senate Fullerton Coll. 1996-2002, pres. 1998-2001, mem. Planning and Consultative Coun., Fullerton Coll., 1997-2005 Contbr. poetry to Forum; contbr. articles to Frontiers, Men's Fitness, Jour. Popular Film and TV Mem. MLA, United Faculty, Nat. Coun. Tchrs. English, Am. Studies Assn., Gay and Lesbian Assn. Dist. Employees, Lambda Soc. (advisor). Office: Fullerton Coll 321 E Chapman Ave Fullerton CA 92832-2011

CARRO, CECILIA, political economist, researcher; b. Buenos Aires, Apr. 11, 1978; d. Daniel Hector Carro and Dina Esther Milovan de Carro. BA, Furman U., Greenville, S.C., 2000; postgrad., Georgetown U., 2005. Program rsch. asst. Inter-Am. Dialogue, Washington, 2001—02, program assoc. Inter-American Dialogue, 2002—04. Mem. Argentina 2020, Washington, 2003; rep. Centro de Estudiantes Lenguas Vivas, Buenos Aires, 1990—95; mem., student rep. Internat. Minority Coun. Furman U., Greenville, SC, 1997—2000. Iverson Brookes Academic Scholarship, Furman U., 1996—98, Howle Academic Scholarship, 1996—2000, Howes Academic Scholarship, 1999—2000. Mem.: Pi Sigma Alpha Nat. Polit. Sci. Honor Soc. Bapt. Avocations: pianist, swimming, tennis.

CARRO, ERIC F., neurosurgeon; b. San Juan, P.R., Dec. 1, 1949; BS, U. P.R., 1970, MD, 1974. Diplomate Am. Bd. Neurol. Surgery. Assoc. prof. U. P.R., San Juan, 1982—; pvt. practice neurosurgery, 1981—. Mem.: Caribbean Assn. Neurol. Surgeons, Am. Assn. Neurol. Surgeons. Office: 73 Santa Cruz St Office 207 Bayamon PR 00961 Office Phone: 787-740-2166. Personal E-mail: ecarro@caribe.net.

CARROL, EDWARD NICHOLAS, psychologist; b. Newark, June 22, 1943; s. Wilfred and Ruth (Gluck) C.; m. Anne Marie McDonald, May 27, 1973 (div. May 1989); 1 child, Abbe Galen; m. Virginia Paisley Herbruck, Oct. 6, 1996. BA, Columbia U., 1965; MA, NYU, 1970, U. Del., 1975, PhD, 1979. Diplomate Am. Acad. Pain Mgmt. Dir. Pain Clinic, VA Med. Ctr., Cleve., 1979—2003, dir. pain psychology Pain Mgmt. Ctr., 2003—. Mem. Internat. Assn. Study of Pain, Midwest Pain Soc. Republican. Jewish. Avocations: dogs, classical and country music. Home: 21490 Claythorne Rd Shaker Heights OH 44122-1964 Office: VA Med Ctr Pain Mgmt Ctr 10701 East Blvd Cleveland OH 44106-1702 Office Phone: 216-791-3800 x 4480.

CARROLL, ADELINE F., special education educator; b. Chester, Pa., June 30, 1949; d. Relda Cirilli; children: Colleen Dinae, Kathleen Marie Hagan, Michael Thomas, Richard Wallace. BS, West Chester U., 1971; Masters Degree, Calif. State U., Fullerton, 1998. Elem. tchr. Pa. Delco Sch. Dist., Aston, 1971—77; 2d grade tchr. St. Edwards Sch., Dana Point, Calif., 1986—94; 4th grade tchr. Carl Hankey Elem. Sch., Mission Viejo, Calif., 1994—97; resource specialist Aliso Viejo (Calif.) Mid. Sch., Aliso Viejo, 1997—; univ. lectr. Calif. State U., Fullerton, 1998—. Support provider BTSA, Alsio Viejo, 2001—; conf. presenter Dist. Profl. Devel. Acad., Aliso Viejo, 1998—; resource specialist assessors panel mem. Orange County Dept. of Edn., Costa Mesa, Calif., 2000—; conf. facilitator Calif. League of Mid. Schs., Maui, Hawaii, 2001, San Francisco, 02. Religious edn. tchr. St. Timothy's Ch., Laguna Niguel, Calif., 1986—88. Recipient Edn. award, Nat. Down Syndrome Congress, 1997. Roman Catholic. Home: 11 Rollins Pl Laguna Niguel CA 92677 Office: Aliso Viejo Mid Sch 111 Park Ave Aliso Viejo CA 92656 Personal E-mail: addiecarroll@cox.net.

CARROLL, ANDREW PATRICK KEATING, writer; b. Washington, Sept. 27, 1969; s. Thomas Edmund and Mara Grace Carroll. BA, Columbia U., 1992. Exec. dir., co-founder The Am. Poetry and Literacy Project, Washington, 1993—. Bd. dirs. Literacy Vols. of Am., Washington, 1994—. Author: Volunteer USA, 1991, Golden Opportunities: A Volunteer Guide for Americans over 50, 1994, War Letters: Extraordinary Correspondence from American Wars, 2001, Behind the Lines: Powerful and Revealing American and Foreign War Letters--and One Man's Search to Find Them, 2005. Named Tomorrow's Leaders Today, Pub. Allies, 1993, Person of the Week, ABC World News Tonight, 1994; recipient Pres. award IONA Sr. Svcs., 1994. Office: The Am Poetry & Lit Project PO Box 53445 Washington DC 20009-9445*

CARROLL, BARRY JOSEPH, manufacturing and real estate executive; b. Highland Park, Ill., Jan. 22, 1944; s. Wallace Edward and Lelia (Holden) C.; m. Barbara Ann Pehrson, July 16, 1965; children: Megan, Sean, Deirdre, Colleen, Oona. Student, Boston Coll., 1961-63; AB, Shimer Coll., 1966; MBA, Harvard U., 1969. Lic. real estate broker, Ill. Account rep. Amerad Advt. Service, Chgo., summers 1966, 67; staff analyst Jamesbury Valve Co., Worcester, Mass., 1968; asst. to pres. Am. Gage & Machine Co., Elgin, Ill., 1969; pres. J.C. Deagan Co., Chgo., 1969-77; v.p. Internat. Metals & Machines, Des Plaines, 1977-92, also bd. dirs.; v.p. Katy Industries, Elgin, 1984-94, also bd. dirs.; pres. Katy Comm., Inc. (WIVS-AM, WXRD-FM, WAIT AM/FM), 1986-92, Sta. W45AJ-TV, Rockford, Ill., 1989-92. V.p., bd. dirs. Pehrson-Long Assocs., Real Estate Mgmt., Am. Machine & Sci. Inc., CRL Inc., Carroll Internat. Corp. (chmn. 1992), GFS Holdings Co.; bd. dirs. XPS Mktg. Inc. Author: (monograph) Talking with Business, 1986; author of appendix/editor: What I Do Best: The Biography of Wallace Edward Carroll, 1992; editor/author: Private Means/Public Ends, 1987; author: Lake Forest, A Very Special Place, 1996; producer, dir. indsl. films, including In There Punching, 1965, The Story of Mallet Instruments, 1975, Digging Lake County, 1999; dir./host (cable TV series) Area Arts, 2000—. Spl. asst. U.S. Sec. Edn., Washington, 1983-84; Presdl. Exch. exec., Washington, 1983-84; bd. govs. United Rep. Fund, Chgo., 1986-92; mem. Nat. Inst. Edn. Commn. Edn. and Tech., U.S. Dept. Edn., 1984-85; trustee Shimer Coll., 1970—, chmn. bd. trustees, 1975-78; trustee Barat Coll., Lake Forest, 1983—2001, life trustee, 1999—; trustee St. Xavier U., Chgo., 1988-94, Lake County Regional Sch. Bd., 1993—; bd. trustees Am. Ireland Fund, 1982-2001, sec., 1991-99; bd. dirs. Lake Forest Symphony, 1970—, Pageant of Peace/Nat. Christmas Tree, 1987-2000, Lake Forest Symphony Sch. of Music., 1991—, Roosevelt U., Chgo., 1996-2005, U. Ill. Eye Rsch. Inst., 1996—; bd. dirs. Chgo. Crime Commn., 1993—, treas., 1994-98; mem., chmn. Lake Forest Cultural Arts Commn., 1997—; chair adv. bd. Inst. Metro. Affairs Roosevelt U., 1998—; trustee Auditorium Theatre Roosevelt U., 2003—, chmn. fin. com., 2003—. Shimer fellow Shimer Coll., Mt. Carroll, Ill., 1972, Shimer Hero award Shimer Coll., Waukegan, Ill., 1980, Dr. Letters, 1995. Mem. Woods Hole Oceanographic Inst. Assn., Ill. Mfrs. Assn. (bd. dirs. 1989-2005, treas. 1991-95), Assn. for Mfg. Tech. (bd. dirs. chmn. pub. affairs com. 1988-93), dir. Elawa Farm Commn., Lake Forest, Onwentsia Club (Lake Forest), Chgo. Club, Met. Club (Washington), East Chop Beach Tennis and Yacht Clubs (Martha's Vineyard Island), Edgartown Yacht Club, Bath and Tennis Club (Palm Beach, Fla.), Soc. Colonial Wars in the State of Ill. (treas. 1988-94, gov. 1998-2000), Nat. Soc. Colonial Wars (dep. gov. gen. 2002—) Soc. of the Cin. Avocations: flying, sailing, skiing, scuba diving, photography. Office: Wildwood LLC 60 N Stonegate Lake Forest IL 60045 E-mail: bcarroll@carrollintl.com.

CARROLL, BILLY PRICE, artist; b. Memphis, Nov. 27, 1920; d. Robert Ray and Olive (Thomas) Price; m. Robert Ray Hosmer, May 3, 1941 (div. Aug. 1948); 1 child, Nadia Jan Woodall; m. David Donald Carroll, Dec. 25, 1964. Student, Memphis Acad. Arts, 1939-40, Farnsworth Sch. Painting, 1949, 50-51, Accademia Delle Belle Arte, Florence, Italy, 1959; also pvt. study, various museums, Uffizi, Florence, Italy. Lectr., Chinese, Western painting; lectr. Fine Arts Mus., Little Rock, Ark., 1954, Brooks Art Gallery, 1957, 62, 63, 69, 77, National TV interview, tape, Taiwan 1969, interview, Taipei, 1969, Lynchburg Fine Arts Ctr., 1971, 83, Memphis State U. Gallery, 1987, Memphis U., Lecture Memphis Racquet Club, Gallery Eng. Speaking Union, 1990, Memphis Brooks Mus. Art, 1984, 91, Shainberg Gallery, Memphis, state conv. Nat. League Am. Pen Women. One-man shows include Fine Arts Mus., Little Rock, 1953, McCaughen and Burr Gallery Fine Arts, St. Louis, 1954, 64, 88, Brooks Meml. Art Gallery, Memphis, 1956, Greenville (Miss.) Art Assn., 1963, Hong Kong, 1968, Taiwan Nat. Art Center, Teipei, 1969, Mpls. Aquatennial Festival, 1970, Lynchburg Fine Arts Ctr., Va., 1971, 83, Memphis Brooks Mus. Art, 1984, Christian Bros. U. Art Gallery, 1993, Memphis Botanical Gardens, 2002, others; exhibited in group shows at Fla. Artists Group, 1952-53, 57-58, Brooks Meml. Art Gallery, 1953, 61, 66-67, Painting of Year Exhbn., Atlanta, 1955, Mo. Athletic Club, St.

Louis Fine Arts Collection, 1954, 1st Hunter Ann., Chattanooga, 1960, Swanberg Gallery, 1987; represented in permanent collections Ga. Inst. Tech., Atlanta, Mo. Athletic Club, St. Louis, U. Tenn., Memphis, Memphis State U., United Chinese Bank, Hong Kong, Dr. Sun Yat Sen, 1st Pres. of China, City Hall Gallery of Memphis Mayor Wyeth Chandler, Portrait of Morrie Moss, major donor to Memphis Brooks Mus. Art, Christian Bros. U. Art Gallery, Judge Hu Anderson, Ct. Appeals, Jackson, Supreme Ct. Justice John Swepston, Memphis, Dean of Shelby County Jurists Judge Robert Hoffman, Memphis, Senator Howard Baker, Sr. Circuit Ct. Judge Harry Adams, Memphis, Circuit Ct. Judge Robert Hoffman, Memphis, two bishops of Tenn. Episcopal Diocese, Edmund P. Dandridge, Memphis, William E. Sanders, Knoxville, Mayor Elliott Shearer, Lynchburg, Va., Judge U.S. Bankruptcy Ct., Judge William Leffler U.S. Bankruptcy Ct., U.S. Circuit Judge Harry Wellford, Memphis, others, portrait Blanche Spain Christian Bros. U., 1993; permanent collections include garden sculpture Memphis Botan. Gardens. Recipient Oil-first and Hon. award Tenn. Nat. League Am. Pen. Women, 1969, others; Jay Hambridge Found. fellow, 1954, Huntington Hartford Found. fellow, 1958. Mem. Memphis Brooks Mus. Art League. Home: 3232 W Lakewood Dr Memphis TN 38128 E-mail: bpcarrollstudio@aristotle.net.

CARROLL, CHARLES MICHAEL, music educator; b. Otterbein, Ind., Mar. 5, 1921; s. James William and Catherine Doretta (Bohan) C.; m. Mary Lipford Rosenbush, Sept. 4, 1951; children: Charles Michael, Mary Catherine, Theresa Jane, William Rosenbush. BM, Ind. U., Bloomington, 1949; MM, Fla. State U., Tallahassee, 1951, PhD, 1960. Asst. coordinator music services Ind. U., 1949-50; instr. music Fla. State U., 1950-53; concert mgr. symphony orchs. Toledo, Washington, Savannah, Ga., 1953-58; prof. music Pensacola (Fla.) Jr. Coll., 1960-64; prof. St. Petersburg (Fla.) Jr. Coll., 1964-89, chmn. communications dept. Music critic Tallahassee Democrat, 1950-53, St. Petersburg Evening Independent, 1976-86. Author: The Great Chess Automaton, 1975; contbr. articles to profl. jours., and encyclopaedias. Served to capt., AUS, 1942-46, ETO. Mem. Am. Symphony Orch. League (v.p. 1955-56), Am. Musicol. Soc. (nat. council 1974-77, chmn. chpt. 1974-76), Am. Soc. Eighteenth-Century Studies (exec. bd. region 1974-82, regional pres. 1979-80), Coll. Music Soc. (editor 1979-83, nat. council 1978-81, chmn. chpt. 1979-80), Société d'Etudes Philidoriennes (conseiller bibliographique 1988—). Home: 1701 80th St N Saint Petersburg FL 33710-3703

CARROLL, DAVID M., communications professional; b. Apr. 12, 1957; BS in Bus. Admin., Univ. of North Carolina. With First Union Corp. (now Wachovia Corp.), Charlotte, 1981—; pres. First Union Ga. First Union Corp., Ga., 1994-97, pres. First Union Fla., 1997-99, exec. v.p., chief E-commerce officer Charlotte, 1999—2001; sr. exec. v.p., Head of Corp. Support Services Wachovia Corp., 2001—, sr. exec. v.p., Head of Merger Integration, 2001—. Office: Wachovia Corp 1 Wachovia Ctr Charlotte NC 28288

CARROLL, DAVID PAUL, social welfare administrator; b. N.Y.C., Nov. 22, 1935; s. Hugh Felix Carroll and Gertrude Jordan. BA in Physics, Cath. U. Am., Washington, 1958; M in Physics, Brown U., 1963; PhD in Sci. Edn., NYU, 1978. Data processing cons. Diocese Bklyn., 1965-68; founder, dir. Data Sys. Ctr. Archdiocese N.Y., N.Y.C., 1968-79, asst. to chancellor, 1979-82; dir. rsch. Pope John Paul II Ctr., N.Y.C., 1982-85; asst. to sec. gen. Cath. Near E. Welfare Assn., N.Y.C., 1985—. Adj. asst. prof. St. John's U., Jamaica, N.Y., 1978-86; adj. prof. NYU, 1981-97; mid. east advisor Holy See Permanent Mission to UN, N.Y.C., 1985—. Co-author: The Ethics of Nuclear Deterrence, 1991; contbr. over 70 articles to profl. publs. Co-chair Muslim/Roman Cath. Dialogue, N.Y.C., 1985—; treas. Bros. of Christian Schs. Found., Oak Brook, Ill., 1987—; bd. dirs. Future Millenium Found., Arlington, Va., 1996—, St. Thomas Aquinas Coll., Sparkill, N.Y., 1998—. Recipient Cross Pro Ecclescia Pro Pontifice Roman Cath. Pontiff, 1995. Mem. Cath. Acad. Scis. (founder, sec. 1987—), Equestrian Order Holy Sepulchre Jerusalem (knight comdr. with star 1987), Cath. Assn. Scientists & Engrs., Scholars Social Justice. Avocations: model railroading, canoeing, hiking, backpacking, classical music. Home: 367 Clermont Ave Brooklyn NY 11238 Office: Cath Near E Welfare Assn 1011 1st Ave Ste 1552 New York NY 10022 E-mail: bad@cnewa.org.

CARROLL, DEBRA ANN, science educator; b. Lafayette, La., Aug. 9, 1951; d. Frank Joseph (Stepfather) and Betty Jean Dias; children: Candace Michelle, Miranda Cay Usie, Anthony Charles. BS, Stephen F. Austin State U., Nacogdoches, Texas, 1973; MEd, U. La., Lafayette, 1997. Tchr. Lafayette Parish Sch. Sys., 1980—2002, lead sci. tchr. mid. schs., 2001—. Tchr. cons. Nat. Writing Project Acadian Divsn., Lafayette, 1989. Mem.: ASCD, Nat. Educators Assn., Nat. Sci. Tchrs. Assn. Home: 701 Idlewood Blvd Lafayette LA 70506 Office Phone: 337-962-2648. Personal E-mail: debracarroll@bellsouth.net. E-mail: dacarroll@lpssonline.com.

CARROLL, DEIRDRE HOLDEN, psychiatric nurse practitioner, educator, medical researcher; b. Lake Forest, Ill., Jan. 1, 1973; d. Barry Joseph and Barbara Pehrson Carroll. BSN, Boston Coll., Chestnut Hill, Mass., 1995; MSN, Yale U., 2000; student, Boston Coll., 2003—. Cert. psychiatric-mental health clinical nurse specialist, Conn., adult nurse practitioner, Conn., lic. advanced practice RN, Conn., RN Conn., Ill. Staff nurse Lake Forest Hosp., 1996, Rush North Shore Med. Ctr., Skokie, Ill., 1996—98, Ariaú (Brazil) Jungle Towers, 1998; clin. faculty Yale U. Sch. of Nursing, New Haven, 2002—04, clin. preceptor. Co-investigator/clin. rsch., clin. faculty Yale U. Sch. Medicine, Child Study Ctr., New Haven, 2000—; psychiat. nurse practitioner Yale U. Sch. of Medicine, Child Study Ctr., New Haven, 2000—04; co-investigator Rsch. Units in Pediatric Psychopharmacology, New Haven, 2000—; presenter in field. Contbr. articles to profl. jours. Mem. Am. Ireland Fund. Mem.: DAR, Nat. League for Nurses, Am. Pyschiatric Nurses Assn., Ea. Nursing Rsch. Soc., Coun. Fgn. Rels. Ill., Boston Coll. Nurses Assn., Ill. Nurses Assn., Conn. Nurses Assn., Am. Coll. of Nurse Practitioners, Internat. Soc. of Psychiatric-Mental Health Nurses, Irish-Georgian Soc., Yale Alumnae Assn., Landmarks Preservation Soc. Ill., Boston Coll. Alumni Assn., USTA, PA of Diving Instructors, Women's Athletic Club of Chgo., Yale Club of NYC, Boston Coll. Honor Soc., Sigma Theta Tau Internat. (named to Yale U. Honor Soc. 2001, named to Boston (Mass.) Coll. Honor Soc. 2004). Achievements include research in psychopharmacology and behavioral interventions for the treatment of children and adolecents with serious mental illness and developmental disorders. Avocations: international travel, classical piano, tennis/squash, photography, scuba diving. Home: 17B Harbour VLG Branford CT 06405-4436 E-mail: Carroldc@bc.edu.

CARROLL, DONNA M., academic administrator; MA, U. Cin., 1977, PhD in Edn., 1981. Program dir. U. Cin.; dean of students Fairleigh Dickenson U., Madison, NJ, Mt. Vernon Coll., Washington, v.p. devel.; sec. Fordham U., 1991—94, exec. sec. Bd. Trustees, 1991—94; pres. Dominican U., River Forest, Ill., 1994—. Recipient Chief Exec. Leadership award, Coun. Advancement and Support of Edn., 2004. Office: Dominican U 7900 W Division River Forest IL 60305

CARROLL, EARL HAMBLIN, federal judge; b. Tucson, Mar. 26, 1925; s. John Vernon and Ruby (Wood) C.; m. Louise Rowlands, Nov. 1, 1952; children— Katherine Carroll Pearson, Margaret Anne BSBA, U. Ariz., 1948, LLB, 1951. Bar: Ariz., U.S. Ct. Appeals (9th and 10th cirs.), U.S. Ct. of Claims, U.S. Supreme Ct. Law clk. Ariz. Supreme Ct., Phoenix, 1951-52; assoc. Evans, Kitchel & Jenckes, Phoenix, 1952-56, ptnr., 1956-80; judge U.S. Dist. Ct. Ariz., Phoenix, 1980—, sr. judge, 1994—. Spl. counsel City of Tombstone, Ariz., 1962-65, Maricopa County, Phoenix, 1968-75, City of Tucson, 1974, City of Phoenix, 1979; designated mem. U.S. Fgn. Intelligence Surveillance Court by Chief Justice U.S. Supreme Ct., 1993-99; chief judge Alien Terrorist Removal Ct., 1996-01, 2001—. Mem. City of Phoenix Bd. of Adjustment, 1955-58; trustee Phoenix Elem. Sch. Bd., 1961-72; mem. Gov.'s Council on Intergovtl. Relations, Phoenix, 1970-73; mem. Ariz. Bd. Regents, 1978-80. Served with USNR, 1943-46; PTO Recipient Nat. Service awards Campfire, 1973, 75, Alumni Service award U. Ariz., 1980, Disting. Citizen award No. Ariz. U., Flagstaff, 1983, Bicentenial award Georgetown U., 1988, Disting. Citizen award U. Ariz., 1990, Sidney S. Woods Alumni Svc. award, 2000. Fellow Am. Coll. Trial Lawyers, Am. Bar Found.; mem. ABA, Ariz. Bar Assn., U. Ariz. Law Coll. Assn. (pres. 1975), Sigma Chi (Significant Sig award 1991), Phi Delta Phi. Democrat. Office: US Dist Ct US Courthouse Ste 521 401 W Washington SPC 48 Phoenix AZ 85003-2151 Office Phone: 602-322-7530.

CARROLL, FRANCES LAVERNE, librarian, educator; b. Scammon, Kans., Dec. 6, 1925; d. Robert Allen and Truda Hilda (Flanagan) C. BS in Ed., Kans. State Tchrs. Coll., 1948; MA in Libr. Sci., U. Denver, 1956; postgrad., Western Res. U., 1957; PhD in Edn., U. Okla., 1970. Bookkeeper Baxter Springs Bank, Kans., 1944; tchr. English and journalism high sch. Caney, Kans., 1947-49; libr. Field Kindley Meml. HS, Coffeyville, Kans., 1949-54; librarian Coffeyville Jr. Coll., 1954-62; supr. elem. sch. libraries Coffeyville, 1957-62; asst. prof. library sci. U. Okla., Norman, 1962-67, assoc. prof., 1972-75, acting dir. sch. library sci., 1974-75, prof., 1975-86, emeritus, 1986—. Head library studies Nedlands Coll. Advanced Edn. (formerly Western Australian Secondary Tchrs. Coll.), Perth, 1977-81; guest lectr. Drexel Inst. Tech., Phila., 1964, U. London, 1972, Pahlavi U., Shiraz, Iran, 1976, Beijing Fgn. Studies U., 1992; dir. US Office Edn. Inst., 1966, 67, 69. Author: (with Mary Meacham) The Library at Mount Vernon, 1977, Exciting, Funny, Scary, Short, Different and Sad Books Kids Like, 1984, More Exciting, Funny, Scary, Short, Different and Sad Books Kids Like, 1992, (with Pat Beilke) Guidelines for the Planning and Organization of Sch. Libr. Media Ctr., 1979, Guidelines for Planning and Organization of Library Media Centers, 1990, Arabic translation, 1995, Recent Advances in Sch. Librarianship, 1981, (with John Harvey) Internationalizing Libr. Ed., 1987; nat. series editor: Reading for Young People, 1979-85; editor: (with Philip Schwartz) Biog. Directory of Nat. Librarians, 1989, Destination Discovery! Activities and Resources for Studying Columbus and Other Explorers, 1994, (with Susan Houck) Internat. Biog. Directory of Nat. Archivists, Documentalists and Librarians, 1996, (with John Harvey and Susan Houck) Internat. Librarianship, 2001; contbr. articles to profl. jour. US Office Edn. grantee, 1969 Mem. AAUW, AAUP, ALA, Okla. Student Libr. Assn. (state sponsor 1963-84), Okla. Libr. Assn., Internat. Rels. Round Table (chmn. membership 1970-74), Internat. Fedn. Libr. Assn. (chmn. sect. sch. libr. 1973-77), Delta Kappa Gamma, Phi Delta Kappa, Beta Phi Mu. Office: Sch Library & Info Studies 401 W Brooks St Norman OK 73019-6032

CARROLL, FRANK EDWARD, JR., radiologist, medical researcher; b. Phila., Oct. 25, 1941; s. Frank Edward Sr. and Marie Elizabeth (Mullin) C.; m. Saramae Dorothy Dever, Sept. 4, 1965; children: Frank Leonard, Mark Edward. BS in Biology, St. Joseph's Coll., 1963; MD, Hahnemann Med. Coll., 1967. Diplomate Am. Bd. Radiology. Rsch. asst. Hahnemann Med. Coll. and Hosp., Phila., 1965-66; rotating intern U.S. Naval Regional Med. Ctr., Oakland, Calif., 1967-68; submarine med. officer U.S. Submarine Med. Sch., U.S. Naval Submarine Base, Gorton, Conn., 1968, SSBN 659 Will Rogers Polaris Nuclear Submarine, 1968-69; staff physician Armed Forces Staff Coll., Norfolk, Va., 1969-70; diagnostic radiology resident St. Mary's Hosp. and Med. Ctr., San Francisco, 1970-72; resident, fellow, rschr. U. Calif. San Francisco Sch. Medicine, 1972-73; asst. prof. diagnostic radiology Yale U. Sch. Medicine, New Haven, 1973-74; staff radiologist Broadway Hosp., Vallejo, Calif., 1974-75, Franklin (Pa.) Regional Med. Ctr., 1975-83; asst. prof. diagnostic radiology Vanderbilt U. Med. Ctr., Nashville, 1983-87, chief sect. pulmonary imaging, 1983—2000, assoc. dir. divsn. diagnostic radiology, 1984, dir. lab. radiologic rsch., 1984-85, assoc. prof. diagnostic radiology, 1987-94, dir. diagnostic radiology, 1985-89, assoc. prof. physics and astronomy, 1993-99, prof. diagnostic radiology, 1994—2004, emeritus prof. diagnostic radiology, 2004—, prof. physics and astronomy, 1999—; founder Mxisystems, Inc., Nashville. Adj. asst. prof. diagnostic radiology Duke U. Med. Ctr., Durham, N.C., 1981-83; cons. in field; referee jours. in field, including Investigative Radiology, Acad. Radiology, Radiology, Chest, Jour. Applied Physiology, Archives of Internal Medicine, Am. Jour. Neuroradiology, others; grant reviewer NIH, Washington. Contbr. articles to profl. jours., chpts. to books. Bd. dirs. Nashville Opera, 1988-94, Franklin Emergency Ambulance Svc., 1975-83, St. Patrick's Sch. Bd., 1975-83; asst. scoutmaster Boy Scouts Am., Franklin, 1975-83, physician and merit badge counselor, Nashville, 1983—; pres. Am. Cancer Soc., Franklin, 1975-83; design prodn. vol. Cheekwood Fine Arts Mus., Nashville, 1995—. Lt. comdr. USNR, 1963—73, submarine med. officer USNR, 1968—71, base physician Armed Forces Staff Coll., 1970—71. Fellow Am. Coll. Radiology, Am. Coll. Chest Physicians; mem. Am. Soc. Laser Medicine and Surgery, Soc. Photo-Optical Instrumentation Engrs., Soc. for Magnetic Resonance Imaging, Assn. Univ. Radiologists, Radiol. Soc. N.Am., Soc. thoracic Radiology, Tenn. Radiologic Soc., Mid. Tenn. Radiologic Soc. Achievements include production of pulsed, tunable, monochromatic X-rays by the free electron laser; designed and commissioned dedicated tabletop laser tunable, synchrotron source for monochromatic 3-D mammography without breast compression, k-edge imaging, auger cascade radiotherapy, phase contrast imaging, time-of flight imaging and protein crystallography; evaluation of lung water by magnetic resonance imaging. Home: 1216 Vintage Pl Nashville TN 37215-4707 Office: Vanderbilt U Med Ctr Emeritus Office 211 Oxford House Nashville TN 37232-4245 Business E-Mail: frank.carroll@vanderbilt.edu.

CARROLL, FRANK JAMES, lawyer, educator; b. Albuquerque, Feb. 10, 1947; s. Francis J. and Dorothy (Bloom) C.; m. Marilyn Blume, Aug. 9, 1969; children: Christine, Kathleen, Emily. BS in Acctg., St. Louis U., 1969; JD, U. Ill., 1973. Bar: Iowa 1973, U.S. Dist. Ct. Iowa, U.S. Tax Ct., U.S. Ct. Appeals (8th cir.); CPA, Mo., Iowa. Acct. Arthur Young & Co., St. Louis, 1969-70; shareholder Davis, Brown, Koehn, Shors & Roberts, P.C., Des Moines, 1973—. Lectr. law Drake U. Law Sch., Des Moines, 1976-86, lectr. Sch. of Bus., 1988-92; bd. dirs. Iowa Agr. Devel. Authority, Iowa State Bar Assn. Mem. commr.'s adv. group IRS, Washington, 1989; mem. grad. tax adv. bd. U. Mo. Kansas City Sch. Law, 1995. Mem. ABA, Iowa Bar Assn. (chair bus. law sect. 1995-98, chair corp. counsel sect. 2001-2003, bd. govs. 2003-), Polk County Bar Assn. (bd. dirs. 2003-), Des Moines C. of C., Wakonda Club, Des Moines Variety Club (bd. dirs. 1998), Beta Gamma Sigma. Home: 5725 Harwood Dr Des Moines IA 50312-1203 Office: Davis Brown Koehn Shors Roberts PC 666 Walnut St Ste 2500 Des Moines IA 50309-3904 Office Phone: 515-288-2500. Business E-Mail: frankcarroll@lawiowa.com.

CARROLL, GEORGE JOSEPH, pathologist, educator; b. Gardner, Mass., Oct. 14, 1917; s. George Joseph and Kathryn (O'Hearn) C. BA, Clark U., Worcester, Mass., 1939; MD, George Washington U., 1944. Diplomate Am. Bd. Pathology. Intern Worchester City Hosp., 1944-45; resident in medicine Doctors Hosp., Washington, 1945-46; resident in pathology Sibley Hosp., Washington, 1948-49, VA Hosp., Washington, 1949-50; asst. pathologist D.C. Gen. Hosp., 1950-51, assoc. pathologist, 1951-52; pathologist Louise Obici Meml. Hosp., Suffolk, Va., 1952—, sec. med. staff, 1956-59, chief of staff, 1959-60, 67-69; pathologist Chowan Hosp., Edenton, N.C., 1952-71, Southampton Meml. Hosp., Franklin, Va., 1952—, Greensville Meml. Hosp., Emporia, Va., 1961—. Instr. pathology Georgetown U. Sch. Medicine, 1950-52; instr. bacteriology Am. U., Washington, 1950-51; assoc. clin. prof. pathology Med. Coll. Va., Richmond, 1968-70; clin. prof. pathology Va. Commonwealth U., 1970—; prof. dept. pathology Eastern Va. Med. Sch., Norfolk, 1974—; sec.-treas. Va. Bd. Medicine, 1967-86, treas., 1971-86. Contbr. articles to med. jours. Served with U.S. Army, 1946-48. Fellow ACP, Coll. Am. Pathologists, Am. Soc. Clin. Pathologists (bd. dirs. 1969—, pres. 1977—), Internat. Acad. Pathology; mem. AMA, So. Med. Assn. (Va. councilor 1965-70, pres. 1973-74), Med. Soc. Va., 4th dist. Med. Soc. (pres. 1968-70), Seaboard Med. Soc. (pres. 1957), George Washington Med. Soc., Tri-County Med. Soc. (pres. 1971-73), Am. Soc. Clin. Pharmacy Therapeutics, Va. Soc. Pathology (pres. 1973-74), Soc. Nuclear Medicine, Am. Assn. Blood Banks, Am. Cancer Soc. (bd. dirs. Va. div. 1955-62), Va. Med. Svc. Assn. (bd. dirs. 1960-71), Rotary. Home: 219 Northbrooke Ave Suffolk VA 23434-6647

CARROLL, HARVEY FRANKLIN, retired chemistry and nutrition educator; b. New Haven, Aug. 25, 1939; AB, Hunter Coll., CUNY, 1961; PhD, Cornell U., 1969. Sr. chemist Uniroyal Chem., Naugatuck, Conn., 1968-69; prof. phys. scis. Kingsborough C.C./CUNY, Bklyn., 1969—2003, prof. emeritus, 2003—. Vis. prof. Hebrew U., Jerusalem, 1979-80. Mem. Am. Chem. Soc., Sigma Xi.

CARROLL, HOWARD WILLIAM, state legislator; b. July 28, 1942; s. Barney M. and Lyla (Price) C.; m. Eda Stagman, Dec. 1, 1973; children: Jacqueline, Barbara. BBA, Roosevelt U., 1964; postgrad., Loyola U., 1964-65; JD, DePaul U., 1967. Bar: Ill. 1967. Staff atty. Chgo. Transit Authority, 1967-71; pvt. practice, 1971-74; ptnr. Carroll & Sain, Chgo., 1974—; mem. Ill. Senate, Springfield, 1973-99, asst. minority leader, 1993-99, chmn. appropriations com., 1977-93. Mem. Legis. Info. System Commn., Ill. Comprehensive Health Ins. Bd.; vice chmn. State Employees Suggestion Award Bd.; mem. fed. budget and taxation com. State-Fed. Assembly; mem. Assembly Com. on State's Legis. Fiscal Affairs and Oversight; prof. complemental faculty Rush U. Coll. Health Scis., Chgo.; lectr. in field. Mem. Ill. Ho. of Reps., 1971-72; chmn. fin. com. Chgo. and Cook County Dem. Crtl. Com., 1982-84, treas., 1984-2000; committeeman 50th Ward Dem. Orgn., 1980-2000; mem. platform com. Ill. Dem. Com., 1974—; former mem. youth adv. bd. Dem. Nat. Com.; del. nat. and Ill. Dem. convs.; v.p. Young Dem. Clubs Am., 1971-73, also former gen. counsel; mem. exec. bd. Atlantic Alliance Young Polit. Leaders, 1970-73; active numerous civic orgns.; mem. exec. com. Jewish Nat. Fund, 1977—; vice chmn. bd. trustees Weiss Meml. Hosp. Found.; officer Jewish Cmty. Rels. Coun.; former chair govt. affairs Jewish Fedn. Met. Chgo.; founder Howard W. Carroll Found.; vice chmn. Jewish Found. Met. Chgo., Jewish United Found, Northshore Ctr. Performing Arts Found. Recipient numerous awards, including cert. of appreciation Decalogue Soc. Lawyers, 1972, Hemophilia Found. Ill., 1988, City Colls. Chgo., 1992, Disting. Svc. award State of Israel Bonds, 1974, Self-Help Assn., 1986, citation for meritorious svc. DAV, 1986, Legislator of Yr. award Child Care Assn. Ill., 1988, Ill. Coun. on Long Term Care, 1988, Outstanding Legislator award Am. Acad. Ophtholmology, 1989, Legis. Advocacy award Ill. Coun. for Gifted, 1991, Founders medal Montay Coll., 1992, Peace Advocate award Ill. Coalition Against Domestic Violence, 1998, Spl. award Comprehensive Health Ins. Plan, Chgo., Ill., 1998, award Northshore Ctr. Performing Arts, 1999, Spl. Svc. award Anti Defamation League, 2001, Ytshak Rabin Visionary award State of Israel, 2003; named Ill. Health Care Outstanding Legislator of Yr., 1995. Mem. Chgo. Bar Assn. (Disting. Lawyer and Legislator award 1974), Zionist Orgn. Chgo., Masons (32d degree), B'nai B'rith (bd. dirs. West Rogers Park, chmn. Anti-Defamation League 1978-80, mem. exec. com. and chmn. spl. events Greater Chgo. coun., bd. dirs. Budlong Woods chpt.) Office: 7250 N Cicero Ave Lincolnwood IL 60712 Home: 31 Indian Hill Rd Winnetka IL 60093-3940 Office Phone: 847-568-7000. Business E-Mail: senhwc@carrollandsain.com.

CARROLL, J. SPEED, lawyer, consultant, corporate financial executive, writer; b. Sherman, Tex., Apr. 23, 1936; s. Horace Bailey and Mary Joe (Durning) C.; m. Martha Coleman Huff, Apr. 12, 1957; 1 child, Charles Durning. BA, U. Tex., 1957; LLB cum laude, Harvard U., 1962. Bar: N.Y. 1964, U.S. Supreme Ct. 1971, Japan (fgn. legal cons.) 1993-95. Assoc. Cleary, Gottlieb, Steen & Hamilton, N.Y.C. and Paris, 1963-70, ptnr. N.Y.C., London, Tokyo, 1971-97, counsel, 1997—2002; mng. dir., gen. coun. EMP Global, Washington, 1997—. Cons. fgn. law Nagashima & Ohno, Tokyo, 1964-65; instr. Internat. Law Inst., Washington, 1973-83; bd. dirs. Mitsubishi Trust and Banking Corp., U.S.A., N.Y.C., Standard Infrastructure Fund Mgrs. (Africa) Ltd., Mauritius. Contbr. chapters to books and articles to profl. jours. Mem. Coun. on Fgn. Rels., N.Y.C., 1973—; trustee Parker Sch. Internat. and Comparative Law Columbia U., 1992—, French Inst./Alliance Francaise, N.Y.C., 2004—. Lt. USNR, 1957-59. Knox fellow Harvard U., 1962-63. Mem. Phi Beta Kappa. Office: EMP Global 2001 Pennsylvania Ave NW Washington DC 20006-1850

CARROLL, JAMES EDWARD, lawyer; b. Milford, Mass., July 9, 1952; s. James William and Anna (Bertoni) Carroll; children: Jonathan Patrick, Benjamin James, Jeremy David. BS, Fairfield U., 1974; MA, U. R.I., 1977; JD cum laude, Suffolk U., 1983. Bar: Mass. 1983, N.Y. 1999, U.S. Dist. Ct. Mass. 1984, U.S. Ct. Appeals (1st cir.) 1984, U.S. Tax Ct. 1989, U.S. Supreme Ct. 1995, N.Y. (U.S. Dist. Ct.) 2002. Tchr. Prout Meml. High Sch., Wakefield, R.I., 1974-76, Walpole (Mass.) High Sch., 1976-83; assoc. Gaston Snow & Ely Bartlett, Boston, 1983-86; trial atty. U.S. Dept. Justice, Washington, 1986-88; assoc. Hale & Dorr, Boston, 1988; ptnr. Peabody & Arnold, Boston, 1988-95; founding ptnr. Cetrulo & Capone, LLP, Boston, 1995—. Mem. criminal justice panel, U.S. Dist. Ct. Mass., 1993—. Contbr. articles to law rev. Bd. dirs. Am. Cancer Soc. Mem.: ABA, Supreme Jud. Ct. Hist. Soc., Nat. Assn. Criminal Def. Attys., Assn. Bar City N.Y., N.Y. State Bar, Boston Bar Assn., Mass. Bar Assn. (spkr. 1991—92), Phi Delta Phi. Roman Catholic. Avocations: running, baseball, football, children's soccer. Home: 23 Forest Edge Rd Easton MA 02375 Office: 2 Seaport Ln Boston MA 02210-2001 Office Phone: 617-217-5500. Business E-Mail: jcarroll@cefcap.com.

CARROLL, JAMES EDWIN, child neurologist, researcher; b. Joplin, Mo., May 15, 1945; s. George Henry and Sarah Frances (Montee) C.; m. Shirley Ann Carol Rohlander, July 1, 1967; children: John, Peter, Ruth, Rebecca, Timothy, Matthew, Lydia, Elizabeth. BS, U. Louisville, 1966, MD, 1969. Diplomate Nat. Bd. Med. Examiners, Am. Bd. Pediat., Am. Bd. Psychiatry and Neurology. Resident in pediat. Louisville (Ky.) Children's Hosp., 1969-71; resident in child neurology U. Colo., Denver, 1973-76; fellowship, faculty Washington U., St. Louis, 1976-84; chief child neurology, prof. Med. Coll. Ga., Augusta, 1984-88; prof., dir. pediat. tng. program Kuwait U., 1988-90; prof., dir. child neurology, vice chmn. neurology Med. Coll. Ga., Augusta, 1990—. Co-dir. Jerry Lewis Neuromuscular Rsch. Ctr., Washington. U., 1982-84; dir. Muscular Dystrophy Clinic, Med. Coll. Ga., 1991—; mem. Ga. Myasthenia Gravis Med. Adv. Bd., 1985-88. Author book chpts.; contbr. over 60 articles to profl. jours. Mem. exec. bd. United Cerebral Palsy of Ctrl. Savannah River Area, Augusta, 1985-88. Served to lt. comdr. USN, 1971-73. Recipient Investigator award NIH, 1979-83, grant NIH, 1986-89, Meritorious Honor award for scv. in Embassy in Kuwait, U.S. Dept. State, 1990. Fellow Am. Acad. Pediat., Am. Acad. Neurology; mem. Soc. for Pediat. Rsch., Am. Neurol. Assn. Republican. Presbyterian. Achievements include characterization of biochemical findings in a number of neuromuscular diseases. Home: 2711 Hunters Xing Augusta GA 30907-4710 Office: Med Coll Ga Child Neurology CJ2103 Augusta GA 30912 Office Phone: 706-721-3371. Business E-Mail: jcarroll@mail.mcg.edu.

CARROLL, JAMES J., lawyer; b. Chgo., Jan. 10, 1948; BS magna cum laude, DePaul U., 1969, JD summa cum laude, 1972. Bar: Ill. 1972, U.S. Tax Ct. 1980, U.S. Supreme Ct. 1981. Of counsel Sidley & Austin, Chgo., 1995-99, ptnr., 1978-95; dir., pres. Wrigley Mgmt. Inc., Chgo., 1995-99; trust counsel Northern Trust Co., 1999—. Lectr. Ill. Inst. for Continuing Legal Edn. Editor-in-chief DePaul Law Rev., 1971-72. Sec. Lakewood Estates Homeowners Assn.; bd. dirs. David and Ruth Barnow Found., 1979, Wrigley Family Found., 1993-99; active Ill. Atty. Gen.'s Charitable Adv. Coun. With USAR, 1970-76. Mem. Ill. State Bar Assn. (chmn. children's rights subcom. 1972-73), Chgo. Bar Assn. (probate practice com. 1977-88, lectr.), Death and Tax Soc., Law Club Chgo., Legal Club Chgo., Phi Eta Sigma, Beta Alpha Psi. Office: Northern Trust Co 181 W Madison St M 9 Chicago IL 60675-0001 E-mail: jjc@notes.ntrs.com.

CARROLL, JAMES P., lawyer; b. Washington, D.C., Aug. 22, 1952; BA with honors, Georgetown Univ., 1974; JD with honors, Catholic Univ., Washington, 1977. Bar: Md. 1977, D.C. 1978, US Dist. Ct. D.C. 1978, US Ct. Appeals D.C. cir. 1978, N.C. 1996. Ptnr. real estate dept., mng. ptnr. Charlotte office & mem. mgmt. com. Cadwalader Wickersham & Taft, Charlotte, NC. Adj. prof. George Washington Univ., 1985—96. Mem.: ABA (chmn., Real Property Probate & Trust Law sect. Securitization com. 2002—04). Office: Cadwalader Wickersham & Taft LLP 227 W Trade St Charlotte NC 28202 Office Phone: 704-348-5116. Office Fax: 704-348-5200. Business E-Mail: james.carroll@cwt.com.

CARROLL, JANE HAMMOND, artist, writer, poet; b. Greenville, SC, May 15, 1946; d. Charles Kirby and Margaret (Cooper) Hammond; m. Robert Lindsay Carroll Jr., Feb. 3, 1968; children: Jane-Gower, Robert Lindsay III. BA, U. SC, 1968. Tchr. A.C. Flora High Sch., Columbia, S.C., 1968-70; exec. field dir. N.E. Ga. Girl Scout Coun., Athens, 1970-71; asst. dir. AID-Vol. Greenville, 1971-73; author, artist Winston Derek Pubs., Nashville, 1985—. Author: Grace, 1987 (Gov.'s Collection 1988), Intimate Moments, 1987 (Gov.'s Collection), Dayspring, 1989; one-woman shows include Williams Salon, Atlanta, 1989, 92-95, 99-2000, 05, Galerie Timothy Tew, Jenny Pruitt Realty, 1989, Ariel Gallery, Atlanta, 1996, Revis Lewis Gallery, Greenville, 2002; group shows include Fine Art Mus. of the South, Mobile, Beyond the Wall, 1990, Sumner Mus. Archives, Mus. Archives, Washington, 1992, Internat. Pastel Show, Ga., 1991, 95, Savannah Nat. (1st pl. award in drawing), Telfare Mus. Savannah, 1995, 2000, 02, 04, Telfare Art Fair, Ariel Gallery, 1995-99, Calloway Garden, 1998, Cathedral of St. Philips, Atlanta, 2000, Nat. Art Exhbn. South Cobb Alliance, 2000, 02-03, Ga. Nat. Fair, Perry, (Drawing prize, Merit award), Holly Mitchell Fine Art, Greenville, 2004; permanent collections represented Greenville Meml. Hosp., SC, Embassy Suites, Ill., Macan Motor Cars, Ga., Jenny Pruitt Reality, Ga., others; commns. include Landscape, Portraits, family, others; pub. and pvt. collections; author numerous poems. Bd. mgr. Greenville Jr. League, 1971-73; artist for fundraiser Rehab. Edn. for Handicapped Adults and Children, Atlanta, 1992-95; vol. artist Arts in the Atlanta Project, 1993, Symphony of Greenville Art Sale fundraiser, 2002. Mem. Nat. League Am. Pen Women (chair art's program 1984-2000, Achievement award 1987, 89, 93-98), Atlanta Artist Club (v.p. 1984-85, Merit mem.). Presbyterian. Avocations: travel, reading, outdoor activities, yoga. Home and Office: 2979 Majestic Cir Avondale Estates GA 30002-1611 Office Phone: 404-294-8167. E-mail: janescapeltd@cs.com.

CARROLL, JOHN, professional basketball coach; m. Beverley Carroll; 1 child, Austin. BA in Psychology, Dickinson Coll., 1977. Starter Dickinson Coll., Carlisle, Pa., 1973—77; grad. asst. basketball coach U. Del., 1977—79; head basketball coach Bloomfield (N.J.) Coll., 1979—82; asst. coach Seton Hall, 1982—89; head basketball coach Duquesne U., 1989—95; advance pro scout Portland (Oreg.) Trail Blazers, 1995—96, Orlando (Fla.) Magic, 1996—97; asst. coach Boston (Mass.) Celtics, 1997—2004, head coach, 2004.

CARROLL, JOHN DOUGLAS, mathematical and statistical psychologist, educator; b. Phila., Jan. 3, 1939; s. John Joseph and Nolie Fay (Godwin) C.; m. Sylvia Stevens Booma, Jan. 2, 1965; children: Gregory Alan, Steven Douglas. BS with honors, U. Fla., 1958; PhD, Princeton U., 1963. Research asst. dept. psychology Yale U., 1961-63; math.-statis. psychologist Bell Labs., Murray Hill, NJ, 1963-65, 66-89; Bd. of Govs. prof. mgmt. and psychology Rutgers Bus. Sch., Newark, 1990. Asst. prof. indsl. engring. and ops. rsch. NYU, 1965-66, adj. assoc. prof. stats., 1968-70; acting prof. psychology U. Calif.-San Diego, 1975-76; acting prof. social sci. U. Calif.-Irvine, 1975-76; adj. prof. stats. Baruch Coll., CUNY, 1971, adj. prof. mktg. U. Pa., 1978-79; Procter & Gamble adj. prof. of mktg. U. Pa., 1987-89; vis. rsch. prof. cognitive sci. U. Calif. Irvine, 1993. Contbr. numerous articles and chpts. to profl. publs.; author computer programs for multidimensional analysis of behavioral sci. data; assoc. editor: Psychometrika, 1973—, Jour. Exptl. Psychology, 1978-88; mem. editl. bd. Jour. Classification, 1984—, Jour. Mktg. Rsch., 1994—; editor Methodika, 1987-93. Ednl. Testing Service psychometric fellow, 1958-61; NIMH fellow, 1959-61 Fellow AAAS, APA (active Div. 5, pres.-elect 1990-91, pres. 1991-92, APA Disting. Sci. Contbn. award 1989), Am. Psychol. Soc. (William James fellow 1989), Am. Statis. Assn. (program chair stats. in mktg. sect. 1992, chair stats. in mktg. sect. 1993-94, mem. exec. com. 1991-95); mem. Psychometric Soc. (trustee 1971-77, 81-83, 84-87, 93-96, pres. 1975-76, mem. editl. coun. 1975-81), Classification Soc. N.Am. (governing coun. 1974-77, pres. 1980-83, bd. dirs. 1984-96), Internat. Fedn. Classification Socs. (rep. to coun. 1984—, v.p./pres.-elect 1995, pres. 1996—), Soc. Multivariate Exptl. Psychology (editl. adv. bd. 1980-81, pres. 1982-83), Ea. Psychol. assn., Psychonomic Soc., Soc. Math. Psychology, Am. Mktg. Assn., Assn. for Consumer Rsch., Soc. for Consumer Psychology, Inst. for Ops. Rsch. and Mgmt. Scis., Phi Beta Kappa, Sigma Xi, Beta Gamma Sigma. Home: 14 Forest Dr Warren NJ 07059-5802 Office: Rutgers Business School Management Rutgers U 111 Washington St Newark NJ 07102-3027 Office Phone: 973-353-5814. Business E-Mail: dcarroll@rci.rutgers.edu.

CARROLL, JOHN SAWYER, newspaper editor; b. NYC, Jan. 23, 1942; s. John Wallace and Margaret (Sawyer) C.; m. Kathleen Kirk, May 1, 1971 (div. Sept. 1982) children: Kathleen Louise, Margaret Adriane; m. Lee Huston Powell, Nov. 1985. BA in English lit., Haverford Coll., 1963. Reporter Providence Jour.-Bull., 1963-64, Balt. Sun, 1966-72, fgn. corr. Vietnam, 1967-69, fgn. corr. Mid. East, 1969, reporter Washington, 1969-72, editor, sr. v.p., 1991—2000; v.p. Times Mirror Co., 1998—2000; city editor, met. editor Phila. Inquirer, 1973-79; exec. v.p., editor Lexington Herald-Leader, Ky., 1979-91; editor LA Times, 2000—05, exec. v.p., 2000—05. Pulitzer Prize juror, 1987, 89, 94; mem. Pulitzer Prize Bd., 1994-2003, chmn., 2002. Served with U.S. Army, 1964-66 Recipient Leadership Award Am. Soc. Newspaper Editors, 2004, Burton Benjamin Meml. Award Com. to Protect Journalists, 2004; named Nat. Press Found. Editor of Yr., 1998; Nieman Fellow Harvard U., 1971-72; vis. journalist fellow Queen Elizbeth House, U. Oxford, 1988. Fellow: Am. Acad. Arts & Sciences.*

CARROLL, JOSEPH J(OHN), lawyer; b. N.Y.C., Sept. 18, 1936; s. James J. and M. Catherine (Molloy) C.; m. Barbara Ann Lediger, May 16, 1959; 1 child, Barbara Ann (dec.). BS, Manhattan Coll., 1958; LLB, St. John's U., 1963; LLM, NYU, 1968. Bar: N.Y. 1964, U.S. Supreme Ct. 1967. Ins. underwriter Atlantic Mut. Ins. Co., N.Y.C., 1959-63; pub. adminstrn. intern N.Y. State Housing Fin. Agy., N.Y.C., 1963-64, adminstrv. asst., 1964-67; assoc. Mudge, Rose, Guthrie, Alexander & Ferdon, N.Y.C., 1967-77, ptnr., 1977-95; of counsel Sullivan Donovan & Gentile, P.C., N.Y.C., 1995—2003, Centilman, Balem, Alder & Hyman LLP, 2003—. Mem. nat. coun. trustees Nat. Jewish Med. and Rsch. Ctr., Denver; trustee Manhattan Coll., N.Y.C., Queen of the Most Holy Rosary Parish, Roosevelt, N.Y. Mem.: ABA (health law sect.), Nat. Assn. Coll. and Univ. Attys., Am. Health Lawyers Assn., N.Y. State Bar Assn. (mcpl. health law sects.), Baldwin Public Library (bd. trustees). Office Phone: 516-546-8233.

CARROLL, JULIAN MORTON, lawyer, retired governor, state senator; b. Paducah, Ky., Apr. 16, 1931; s. Elvie B. and Eva (Heady) C.; m. Charlann Harting, July 22, 1951; children: Kenneth Morton, Iva Patrice, Bradley Harting, Ellyn Kriston. AA, Paducah Jr. Coll., 1952; AB, U. Ky., 1954, LLB, 1956. Bar: Ky. 1956. Ptnr. Emery & Carroll, Paducah, 1960—68; mem. Ky. Ho. of Reps., 1962-71, speaker, 1968-71; lt. gov. State of Ky., 1971-74, gov., 1974-79; of counsel Reed, Scent & Walton, Paducah, 1968-71; ptnr. Carroll & Assocs., Frankfort, Ky., 1980—; mem. Ky. State Senate, 2004—. Chmn. Nat. Conf. Lt. Govs., 1974, Nat. Govs. Assn., 1978-79. Trustee Paducah Jr. Coll., Regency U. Lt. USAF, 1956-59. Recipient Minerva award U. Louisville, 1977, Man of Yr. award Advt. Club Louisville, 1978. Mem. ABA, Ky. Bar Assn., Franklin County Bar Assn., Optimist Club, Phi Delta. Democrat. Avocation: golf. Office: Carroll & Assocs 25 Fountain Pl Frankfort KY 40601-1942 Office Phone: 502-223-8806. Personal E-mail: jmc75farm@aol.com. E-mail: julian.carroll@lrb.ky.gov.

CARROLL, KATHLEEN LINDA, literature and language educator; b. Buffalo; d. Morgan Emmanuel Davies and Kathryn Lorraine Sheffler; m. John Francis Carroll IV, July 11, 1970; children: Sheila Marie, Kathryn Leah. BA, SUNY, Potsdam, 1969; MEd, Millersville U., Pa., 1973; PhD, U. Md., College Park, 1990. English instr., asst. dir freshman writing U. Md., College Park, 1980—91, program dir., CAST, 1993—95; asst. prof., English Essex CC, Md., 1991—93; sr. instrnl. designer Arthur Andersen, St. Charles, Ill., 1999—2002; dir., gen. edn. Aurora U., Ill., 2002—. Cons. Full Circle Internat., Brussels, 1995—98, Chgo., 1998—99. Contbr. articles to profl. jours.; editor: A Century of Manufacturing, 2002. Mem.: Kiwanis Internat. (adv. 2003—). Avocations: golf, sewing, gardening. Office: Aurora Univ 347 S Gladstone Ave Aurora IL 60506

CARROLL, KENNETH G., lawyer; b. Winston-Salem, NC, Feb. 1, 1952; BA, Wake Forest Univ., NC, 1982, JD, 1985. Bar: NC 1985. Mem. mgmt. com. Womble Carlyle Sandridge & Rice, PLLC, mem. recruiting com., mem. professionalism com., mng. mem. Research Triangle, NC, chmn. assocs. com., chmn. salaried mem. com. Notes and comments editor Wake Forest Law Review, 1984—85. Mem. United Way-Triangle; Habitat for Humanity. Mem.: ABA, NC Bar Assn. (mem. curriculum com., bus. law sect.), Wake County Bar Assn. Mailing: Womble Carlyle Sandridge & Rice PLLC PO Box 13069 Research Triangle Park NC 27709 Office: Womble Carlyle Sandridge & Rice PLLC 2530 Meridian Pwky Ste 400 Durham NC 27713 Office Phone: 919-484-2318. Office Fax: 919-484-2368. Business E-Mail: kcarroll@wcsr.com.

CARROLL, KENT JEAN, retired naval officer; b. Newton, Iowa, Aug. 22, 1926; s. Lee A. and Mabel E. (McCormick) C.; m. Betty M. Harrington, Mar. 29, 1947; children: Craig, Debra Carroll Rollins, Lance S., Maureen Burt. BS in Naval Sci., U. Notre Dame, 1946; grad., U.S. Naval Postgrad. Sch., 1955, Naval War Coll., 1960, Army War Coll., 1965; BA in Internat. Affairs, George Washington U., 1965. Ensign USN, 1946, advanced through grades to vice adm., 1979; svc. in Korea and Vietnam; comdr. U.S.S. Sablefish, 1959-60, Submarine Divsn. 81, Divsn. 82, 1968-69, 69, U.S.S. Blue Ridge, 1970-72, Amphibious Squadron 10, 1972-73, Task Force 65, 1974-75, Naval Inshore Warfare Command, Atlantic Fleet, 1974-75, U.S. Naval Forces Marianas, 1975-77; dir. J-4 OJCS, Washington, 1977-81; comdr. Mil. Sealift Command, Washington, 1981-83. Decorated Navy D.S.M. with cluster, Def. D.S.M., Legion of Merit with 2 clusters; recipient John Paul Jones award Navy League, 1977; Presdl. citation for humanitarian svc., 1976, Rev. William Corby C.S.C. award U. Notre Dame, 1995. Mem. English Speaking Union (bd. dirs. 1999—). Home: Country Club NC 1600 Morganton Rd X 30 Pinehurst NC 28374-6862 E-mail: kcarroll@nc.rr.com.

CARROLL, LA SHUN LA RUE, endodontist; b. N.Y.C., N.Y., Mar. 1, 1977; s. Marggio Carroll. BA in Philosophy and Natural sci., CUNY, 2000; cert. in med. emergencies in dentistry, 2004; MS in Gen. Studies, Suffield Coll. and U., 2004; DDS, SUNY, 2005. Lic. info. sys. tech. h.s. level N.Y.C. Bd. of Edn.; BLS: CPR-AED for primary healthcare providers Am. Heart Assn., EMT-B Emergency Med. Svcs., N.J., cert. adv. cardiac life support healthcare Practitioners 2005. Retail salesperson Edison Bros., Inc., World Trade Ctr., NY, 1994—95; med. libr. NYU. Sch. of Medicine, 1994—95, info. sys. technologist, 1995—96; adminstr. Aux. of Tisch Hosp., NYU. Med. Ctr., 1996—97; staff rsch. pathology NYU Sch. of Medicine, 1997—2000. Student rschr. NYU Med. Ctr. Honors Program, N.Y.C., 1993—95; adminstr. symposia on hydrocephalus and spina-bifida Aux. at Tisch Hosp., N.Y.C., 1996—97; rschr. NASA Specialized Ctr. for Rsch. and Tng., Raleigh, NC, 1997; chemistry tchg. asst. for visually impaired students Bernard M. Baruch Coll., N.Y.C., 1998—99; asst. instr. nat. jour. of chem. edn. conf. workshop Jour. of Chem. Edn., Sacred Heart U., Conn., 1999; vol. NYU Med. Ctr., N.Y.C., 1996—97; vol. guest spkr. sr. oral health awareness at local nursing home U. at Buffalo Sch. of Dental Medicine, 2002, vol. guest spkr. local and inner-city pub. elem. schs. for ann. Children's Smile Day, 2002—; mem., vol. minority affairs com. U. Buffalo Sch. of Dental Medicine, Buffalo, 2003—; oral cancer screener SUNY Buffalo Sch. of Dental Medicine Oral Health Screening Program, 2003—; specialty endodontic residency program, N.Y., 2005—. Contbr. articles and reports to profl. jours. Vol. student dr. oral cancer screening of physically and/or developmentally disabled Spl. Olympics, Buffalo, 2002; vol. EMT Emergency Med. Svcs., Monroe County, Pa., 2004—05; vol. comm. outreach program Buffalo Zoo, NY, 2004. Recipient Spl. Recognition award for peer mediation, Murry Bergtraum H.S., NY, NY, 1993, Excellence Scholarship in Philosophy, CUNY, 2000, Arthur A. Schomburg fellowship, SUNY, Buffalo, 2001—05, Barrett scholarship, 2001—02, Class of 1964 scholarship for outstanding scholastic achievement, 2002, Tucker scholarship for top 25 students, SUNY Buffalo Sch. of Dental Medicine, 2002, SUNY, Buffalo, 2003, U. Buffalo Sch. of Dental Medicine Gen. scholarship, SUNY Buffalo Sch. of Dental Medicine, 2003, Outstanding Volunteerism award, Murry Bergtraum H.S., N.Y.C., 1994, Spl. Recognition award for peer mediation, 1995, CRC Press Chemistry Achievement award for outstanding scholastic achievement in chemistry, CRC Press, 1999, N.Y.C. Alliance for Minority Participation in Rsch. scholarship, NYC Alliance, CUNY, 1999; scholar Robert C. Weaver Incentive Scholarship, Bernard M. Baruch Coll. (CUNY), 1999. Mem.: Braille Sch./Blindness Related learning, Nat. Assn. Emergency Med. Techs., Nat. Registry Emergency Med. Techs., Am. Student Dental Assn., Acad. of Gen. Dentistry (assoc.), Internat. High IQ Soc. (life), Bernard M. Baruch Alumni Assn. (life), N.Y.C. Alliance for Minority Participation (scholarship 1999), Golden Key Nat. Hon. Soc. (life), Nat. Scholars Hon. Soc. (life), Student Hon. Soc. (life), Delta Epsilon Iota (life). Avocations: drawing, philosophy and logic, biblical hebrew and linguistics, science and medicine, writing. Personal E-mail: lcarroll@buffalo.edu. E-mail: lcarroll@lmcmc.com.

CARROLL, LUCY ELLEN, theater director, educator; b. NYC, Oct. 11; d. Edward Joseph and Lucy Sophie (Czapszys) C. B in Music Edn., Temple U., 1968; MA, Trenton State Coll., 1973; D in Musical Arts, Combs Coll. Music, Phila., 1982. Cert. tchr. music, N.J., Pa., Nat. Cert., 1991. Tchr. music Log Coll. Jr. High Sch., Pa., 1968-72, Ind. (Pa.) High Sch., 1972-73, William Tennent High Sch., Warminster, Pa., 1973-98, dir. mus. theater, 1973-98; choir dir. St. John Bosco Parish Choir, 1999—2001; organist, dir. Carmelite Monastery, Phila., 1996—. Music coord. Centennial Schs., 1991-98; founder, dir. Madrigal Singers, Warminster, Pa., 1971-98; choral dir. Cabrini Coll., Radnor, Pa., 1974-77, First Day Singers, Phila., 1979-83, Combs Coll. Music, Phila., 1981-84, 87-88; choral adjudicator various Music festivals, 1973-98; theatre dir., Villa Joseph Marie (Holland), 1998-99; del. Internat. Arts Conf., Cambridge, Eng., 1992; adj. assoc. prof. Westminster Choir Coll., Princeton, 2002—; lectr. in field. Singer (operas Ambler Festival) Street Scene, 1970, Death of Bishop of Brindisi (premiere); (Robin Hood Dell) La Boheme; dir. (jazz theater piece N.Y.C.) Murder of Agamemnon, 1980, (drama) Power of Love (1705), 1986, (outdoor music theater) Vorspiel (Pa. Historic Commn. 1989); editor The Monastery Hymnal, 2002, Music of the Ephrata Cloister, 2003; columnist Polyphony mag., Adoremus Bulletin, 2002—; creator Churchmouse Squeaks cartoons, Monastery Mice cartoons; author The Music of EPHRATA, 2003, The Bastet Worry-Stone and Other Tales, 2004; contbr. articles to profl. jours. and mags. Dir. Monastery Choir, Phila., 2001—. Recipient awards Writers of Future, 1985, 87, Andrew Ferraro award Combs Coll. Music, 1989, plaque for svc. to music Bucks County Commr., 1991, Disting. Citizen medal Southampton Twp., 1994, Harmony award Country Gentlemen Nat. Soc. for Preservation and Encouragement Barbershop Quartet Singing in Am., 1994; Scholar-In-Residence, Pa. Hist. and Museum Commn.; named Humanities Spkr. for 2000, Pa. Humanities Coun. Mem. Am. Choral Dirs. Assn., Sci. Fiction Fantasy Writers of Am., Am. Musicol. Soc., Am. Guild Organists, Organ Hist. Soc., Latin Liturgy Assn., Del. Valley Composers (choral cons. 1988-90), Hist. Soc. Pa., Smithsonian Assocs., Musical Fund Soc. of Phila., Soc. for Am. Music, Pa. Music Educators Assn. (adv. bd. 1986-87, contbg. writer Spotlight on Tchg. Chorus 2003), Nat. Assn. State Tchrs. of the Yr., Ephrata Cloister Assocs., Kelpius Soc. (editor newsletter 2004—, v.p., chair rsch. publs. 2005—), Sigma Alpha Iota. Republican. Roman Catholic. Avocation: travel. Home: 712 High Ave Hatboro PA 19040-2418 Personal E-mail: LucyCarroll@att.net.

CARROLL, MARGARET AILEEN, member of Canadian parliament; b. Halifax, N.S., Can., June 1, 1944; m. D. Kevin Carroll, Nov. 11, 1968; children: Joanna, Daniel. BA, St. Mary's U., Halifax, 1965; BEd, York U., Toronto, Ont., Can., 1989. Adminstr. Law Firm of Carroll, Heyd, 1990—; M.P. from Barrie-Simcoe-Bradford Ho. of Commons, Canada. Mem. justice and environ. coms.; vice chair Ctrl. Ont. Caucus; v.p., major shareholder Canadiana Curtains, Barrie, Ont., Inc., 1976-88; chair bd. referees, Unemployment Ins. appeals process, 1994-95; mem. Ont. Film Rev. Bd., 1990-91; formerly with Can. Internat. Devel. Agy., Toronto, and Province of Ont. Fed.-Provincial Affairs Secretariat, Toronto Elected alderman Ward 2, City of Barrie; past chair capital campaign New Barrie Pub. Libr.; past chair St. Joseph's H.S. Pvt. Bd.; past mem. bd. dirs. Barrie Food Found. Office: House of Commons 125 Confederation Bldg Ottawa ON Canada K1A 0A6 and: Constituency Office 7 Anne St S, Unit 4 Barrie Canada L4N 2C4 Office Phone: 7057265959. Fax: 613-996-7923.

CARROLL, M(ARGARET) LIZBETH CARR, art educator, graphics designer, photographer; b. Washington, Feb. 9, 1936; d. J. Franklin and Dorothy Mae (Colborn) Carr; m. Eugene R. Carroll, Jr., June 2, 1979 (div. May 2000); children: Kyung Soo Kim, Whan Kim. BFA in Studio Art, U. D.C., 1979; MFA in Visual Comm. & Photography, George Washington U., 1984; postgrad., Union Inst. and Univ., 2004—. Visual info. specialist U.S. Fed. Govt., Washington, 1966—84; graphics designer Office of the Comptr. of the Currency, Dept. of the Treasury, Washington, 1984—94, sr. graphics designer, 1994—99; adj. assoc. prof. fine arts U. D.C., Washington, 1989—; asst. prof. lectr. in art George Washington U., Washington, 2001—. Adv. for Native Am. artists/pvt. cons. ArtDirections, Washington, 1994—. Author, photographer: Native Peoples Mag., 1995, Piecework Mag., 1998, Am. Rivers, Pres.'s Coun. Environ. Quality, U.S. Congl. Record, Friends of the Earth, U.S. Nat. Pk. Svc., Nat. Pks. Conservation Assn., Sierra Club, Wilderness Soc. in support of conservation and wilderness legis.; Represented in permanent collections U.S. Dept. Interior, Grand Canyon Nat. Pk., exhibitions include Gallery 42, U. D.C., 2003, exhibited in group shows at Martin Luther King, Jr. Libr., Washington, 2003, U. D.C., 1976—79, Cath. U. Am., 1979; others. Home: 3313 Runnymede Pl NW Washington DC 20015-2415 Office: Univ DC Dept Mass Media Visual & Performing Arts 4200 Connecticut Ave NW Washington DC 20008

CARROLL, MARK THOMAS, lawyer; b. Queens, N.Y., May 12, 1956; s. Bernard James and Thalia (Antypas) C.; m. Joanne Mary Grinnell, Aug. 4, 1979; children: Stephen, Thomas. BA, Columbia U., 1977; JD, Harvard U., 1980. Bar: Pa. 1980, U.S. Ct. Appeals (3d cir.) 1980, U.S. Dist. Ct. (ea. dist.) Pa. 1980. Assoc. Duane, Morris & Heckscher, Phila., 1980-82; asst. dir. ALI-ABA, Phila., 1982-85, dir. office of publs., 1985—. Bd. dirs. Bradford Glen Homeowners Assn., 1988-90; founding mem. Joseph's People Com. Mem. ABA, Assn. for Continuing Legal Edn. (pres. 2003-04). Republican. Roman Catholic. Home: 1402 Ashcom Dr Downingtown PA 19335-3566 Office: ALI-ABA 4025 Chestnut St Ste 500 Philadelphia PA 19104-3099 Office Phone: 215-243-1656. Business E-Mail: mcarroll@ali-aba.org.

CARROLL, MARY COLVERT, corporate executive, honorary trade representative of Nepal; b. Milw., June 5, 1940; d. Frederick Rolfing and Helen (McCall) Colvert; m. Andrew David Carroll; children: Sherri L. Oberg, Andrew David Carroll III. BA mgna cum laude, U. Miami, Fla., 1966. Bd. dirs. Aqua Am. Inc., Bryn Mawr, 1979—; chmn. bd. Friends Independence Nat. Hist. Park, Phila., 1978-81; bd. dirs. Urban Affairs Coalition, Phila., 1979-90, advisor, 1990—; pres., founder Friends Conversation Hall, Phila., 1982-83; bd. dirs. Internat. House, Phila., 1982—98; chmn., founder Nat. Parks Mid-Atlantic Council, Phila., 1982—; vice chmn. bd. Nat. Parks and Conservation Assn., Washington, 1982-88; bd. dirs. Phila. First Econ. Devel. Coalition, 1983-90; chmn., founder, bd. dirs. Phila. Hospitality, Inc., 1998—2000; bd. dirs. World Affairs Council, Phila., 1984-88; bd. trustees Bryn Mawr (Pa.) Presbyn. Ch., 1984-90; mem. bd. advisors Independence Hall Assn., Phila., 1984-86; vice chair Phila. Hist. Preservation Corp., 1986-93; vice chmn. bd. Fort Mifflin on Del., Inc., Phila., 1986—2001; trustee William Penn Found., Phila., 1987-93. Hon. trade rep. of Nepal, 2002—. Bd. dirs. Met. YMCA, Preservation Action, 1993-97. Recipient Civic Environ. award Found for Architecture, 1983, Conservation Service award U.S. Dept. Interior, 1978, Friend of Nepal award Assn. Nepalis in the Americas, 2002, Woman of Distinction award Lake Forest Acad., 2005. Mem. Merion Cricket Club. Presbyterian. Home and Office: PO Box 654 Naalehu HI 96772

CARROLL, MARY PATRICIA, writer; b. Chgo., June 28, 1938; d. Anthony Bernard Carroll and Marie Cecilia Delaney. Student in writing, Columbia Coll., U. Fla.; BS in Humanities magna cum laude, Loyola U., Chgo., 1961, MSW, 1965; DSW, Smith Coll., 1970. Caseworker II Cook County Dept. Pub. Assistance, Chgo., 1961—64; sr. psychiat. social svc. worker Chgo. Bd. Health, Lower North Cmty. Mental Health Ctr., 1964—66; sch. social worker Sch. Dist. #81, Schiller Park, Ill., 1966—68; dist. dir. Family Svc. Assn. Greater Boston, 1970—73; program rep. United Cerebral Palsy Assns., N.Y.C., 1973—75; assoc. prof. George Williams Coll., 1975—77, Ind. U.-Purdue U., Indpls., 1977—81; assoc. prof., chmn. social work dept. U. Alaska, Anchorage, 1981—85; writer Mary P. Caroll Enterprises, 1985—. Contbr. articles, essays, short stories, poems to profl. and lit. publs. Recipient Hon. Mention award for fiction Writers Digest, 1987, for poetry, 1999, 2003; fellow VA Pub. Health, 1963-65, NIMH, 1968-70. Mem. Poetry Soc. of Va., Live Poets Soc., Amnesty Internat., Acad. Am. Poets, Nat. Com. to Preserve Social Security and Medicare, Friends of Libr of Alexandria Va. Duncan Br., Natural Resources Def. Coun., Humane Soc. of U.S., Sierra Club. Democrat. Roman Catholic. Avocation: outdoor activities. E-mail: wnm4444@aol.com.

CARROLL, MILTON, oil industry executive; BS, Tex. So. Univ., 1973. Founder, chmn., CEO Instrument Products Inc., Houston, 1977—; bd. dir. CenterPoint Energy Inc., Houston, 1992—, bd. chmn. Dir. Houston Endowment Inc., TEPPCO Partners, Ocean Energy, Health Care Svcs. Corp. Mailing: CenterPoint Energy PO Box 1700 Houston TX 77251-1700*

CARROLL, PETE, college football coach; b. San Francisco, Sept. 15, 1951; m. Glena Carroll; children: Brennan, Nathan, Jaime. BS in Bus. Adminstrn., Univ. Pacific, 1973, MS in Physical Edn., 1976. Grad. asst., wide receivers coach Univ. Pacific Tigers, 1974—75, grad. asst., secondary coach, 1975—77; grad. asst., secondary Univ. Ark. Razorbacks, 1977—78; secondary coach Iowa St. Univ. Cyclones, 1978, Ohio St. Univ. Buckeyes, 1979; def. coord., secondary coach North Carolina St. Wolfpack, 1980—82; asst. head coach, offensive coord. Univ. Pacific Tigers, 1983; def. backs coach Buffalo Bills, 1984—85, Minn. Vikings, 1985—90; def. coord. N.Y. Jets, 1990—94, head coach, 1994; defensive coord. San Francisco 49ers, 1995—97; head coach New England Patriots, 1997-99; head coach, defensive coord. U. So. Calif. Trojans, LA, 2001—. Achievements include head coach, co-nat. champions USC Trojan's, 2004, nat. champions, 2005. Office: Univ Southern Calif 203 Heritage Hall Los Angeles CA 90089

CARROLL, RAOUL LORD, lawyer, investment banker; b. Washington, Mar. 16, 1950; s. John Thomas and Gertrude Barbara (Jenkins) C.; m. Elizabeth Jane Coleman, Mar. 22, 1980; children: Alexandria Nicole, Christina Elizabeth. BS, Morgan State U., 1972; JD, St. Johns U., Jamaica, N.Y., 1975; postgrad., Georgetown U., 1980-81. Bar: N.Y. 1976, D.C. 1979, U.S. Dist. Ct. D.C. 1979, U.S. Supreme Ct. 1979, U.S. Dist. Ct. (so. and ea. dist.) N.Y. 1982. Asst. U.S. atty. Office U.S. Atty., Dept. Justice, Washington, 1979-80. Assoc. mem. U.S. Bd. Vets. Appeals, Washington, 1980-81; ptnr. Hart, Carroll & Chavers, Washington, 1981-86, Bishop, Cook, Purcell & Reynolds, Washington, 1986-89; gen. counsel U.S. Dept. Vets. Affairs, 1989-91; pres. Govt. Nat. Mortgage Assn., HUD, 1991-92; COO, M.R. Beal & Co., 1993-95; gen. ptnr. Christalex Ptnrs., Inc., 1995—, Am. Ctr. for Internat. Leadership, Balt.; chmn. Christian Bros. Investment Svcs., Inc., N.Y.C. Trustee The Enterprise Found., Columbia, Md. Capt. U.S. Army, 1975-79. Decorated Joint Service Commendation medal, Army Commendation medal; named Outstanding Young Man Am., U.S. Jaycees, 1979. Em. N.Y. State Bar Assn., D.C. Bar Assn., Washington Bar Assn., Asst. U.S. Attys. Assn., Omega Psi Phi. Republican. Baptist.

CARROLL, RAY DEAN, SR., veterinarian; b. Barry, Tex., Oct. 19, 1927; s. James William and Blanche Estelle (Jordan) C.; m. Lula Pearl Mayfield, June 6, 1957; children: James William, Ray Dean Jr. Assoc., Hillsboro Jr. Coll., 1948; BS in Animal Sci., Tex. A&M U., 1950, DVM, 1957. Vet. Carroll &

Harpe Animal Hosp., Corsicana, Tex., 1957—; instr. Navarro Coll., Corsicana, 1970-95. Author: Beef Cattle Science Handbook, vol. 16, 1979. Mem. found. bd. Navarro Coll., 1985—, vice-chmn., trustee, 1990. With USN, 1945-46, 51-52. Mem. AVMA, Tex. Polled Hereford Assn. (pres. 1992-96), Navarro County Ext. Beef Commn. (chmn. 1960—). Democrat. Methodist. Home: 2203 Highland Cir Corsicana TX 75110-1611 Office: Carroll & Harper Animal Hosp 2508 W 2nd Ave Corsicana TX 75110-2520 Office Phone: 903-872-4686.

CARROLL, RICHARD ELLIS (DICK CARROLL), minister, educator, writer, actor, artist; b. Tampa, Fla., Dec. 22, 1955; s. James Carlton Sr. and Shirley Mae (Bailey) C.; m. Sherry Lynn McGee, July 9, 1988. BA, Palm Beach Atlantic Coll., 1981; MDiv, Southwestern Bapt. Theological Seminary, 1984, MA in Communications, 1986. Asst. dir. continuity Sta. WFUZ-FM, Ocala, Fla., 1981-82; internship in master control Sammons Cable of Ft. Worth, 1985; media cons. Rehab., Edn., Advocacy for Citizens with Handicaps, Ft. Worth, 1987-88; personal and profl. workshop leader Carroll & Carroll Enterprises, Ft. Worth, 1989—; min. missions and discipleship Fairview Bapt. Ch., Austin, Tex., 1995-99; pastor Pond Springs Bapt. Ch., 2000—. Pub. access cable producer Sammons Cable, Ft. Worth, 1986-88. Author, dir., actor Memoirs of the Fisherman; author: Three One Man Shows, 1986, (TV movie) Fire and Rain, 1989, (movies) Problem Child, 1990, Ruby, 1991. Served with U.S. Army, 1974-80. Recipient Albert G. Wade Acting Award Palm Beach Atlantic Coll., 1981, Girl Scout Svc. award, 1990; named one of Outstanding Young Men in Am. Mem. Alpha Psi Omega, Fellowship of Christian Communicators. Democrat. Avocations: writing, martial arts, swimming, scuba diving, line art. Home: 1718 Greening Way Leander TX 78641-8620 Office: Pond Springs Bapt Ch 13461 Pond Springs Rd Austin TX 78729 Office Phone: 512-258-1447. *Learning to see the world through Jesus's eyes, to feel with Jesus' heart and to act with Jesus' tender touch is the only thing that will change our world.*

CARROLL, ROBERT LYNN, biology professor, paleontologist, curator, museum director; b. Kalamazoo, May 5, 1938; s. John Henry and Arvella Mae (Wickerham) Carroll; m. Helen Louise Swaim, June 22, 1961 (dec. Jan. 1972); 1 child, David Lynferd; m. Anna Di Turi, Sept. 26, 1987. BS, Mich. State U., 1959; MA, Harvard U., 1961, PhD, 1963. NRC postdoctoral fellow McGill U., Montreal, Que., Can., 1962-63, asst. prof. zoology, 1964-69, assoc. prof. biology, 1969-74, prof. biology, 1974—, Strathcona prof. zoology, 1987—; curator vertebrate paleontology Redpath Mus., McGill U., 1965—, dir., 1985-90, 98-99, chmn. dept. biology, 1990-95. Vis prof biol Sir George Williams Univ, Montreal, 1965—66. Author: (book) Vertebrate Paleontology and Evolution, 1987, Patterns and Processes of Vertebrate Evolution, 1997; co-author: Paleontology - The History of Life, 1989; editor: Leposondyli, 1998; co-editor: Paleontology, The Evolutionary History of Amphibians, 2000; editor (assoc ed): Can Jour Earth Scis, 1984—93, Jour Vertebrate Paleontology, 1989—92; editor: (consulting ed) Trans Royal Soc Edinburgh: Earth Scis, 1993—; editor: (technical ed) Jour Paleontology, 2000—. Mem educ bd Linn Soc London, 1999—. Recipient Billings Medal for contbns to paleontology, Geological Asn Can; fellow NSF Postdoctoral, Brit Mus, London, 1963—64. Fellow: Linnean Soc., Royal Soc. Can. (Miller medal 2001); mem.: World Congress Herpetology (treas. 1989—94), Am. Soc. Zoologists, Soc. Vertebrate Paleontology (hon.; pres. 1982—83, Romer-Simpson medal 2004), Paleontological Soc. (Schuchert award 1978), Soc. Study Evolution. Avocations: hiking, singing. Office: Redpath Mus/McGill Univ 859 Sherbrooke St W Montreal PQ Canada H3A 2K6 Office Phone: 514-398-4086 ext. 4090. E-mail: robert.carroll@mcgill.ca.

CARROLL, ROBERT W., retired management consultant; b. Ossining, N.Y., May 29, 1923; s. John Francis and Catherine Veronica (Coyne) C.; m. Mary Bernardine Dugan, June 1, 1946; children: Kevin, Dennis, Terrence, Maura, Monica. Student, Sch. Commerce, NYU, 1952-56, Mgmt. Inst., 1957. With N.Y. Cen. R.R., 1942-68, asst. to sec., 1953-54, asst. sec., 1954-59, sec., 1959-68; sr. asst. sec. Penn Cen. Transp. Co., 1968-70, sec., 1971-76, also former v.p., sec., dir. several railroad, real estate, trucking and fin.-oriented subsidiaries, 1971-76; exec. dir. adminstrn. Law Offices La Brum and Doak, Phila., 1976-88; prin. Robert W. Carroll & Assoc., Mgmt. Cons., Radnor, Pa., 1989-93. Corp. sec. Pitts. and Lake Erie R.R. Co., 1959-79; v.p., sec., dir. Montour R.R. Co., Montour Land Co., Youngstown and So. Ry. Co., 1959-79; rep. Kissel Blake Orgn., Inc., 1983-89. Served with USCGR, 1942-46. Recipient Legion of Honor Chapel of the Four Chaplains, 1984. Mem. ABA (law office adminstrv. assoc. 1985-89), Internat. Assn. Legal Adminstrs. (bd. dirs. 1987-88, v.p. 1987—, pres.-elect Phila. chapter 1988), VFW, Soc. Friendly Sons St. Patrick, Pa. Soc. K.C. (4), World Affairs Coun. Phila., Am. Soc. of Corp. Secs., Inc., Overbrook Golf Club (Bryn Mawr, Pa.). Home: 9 Ridgewood Rd Wayne PA 19087-3713

CARROLL, ROBERT WAYNE, mathematics professor; b. Chgo., May 10, 1930; s. Walter Scott and Dorothy (Le Monnier) C.; m. Berenice Jacobs, Sept. 7, 1957 (div. June 1974); children: David Leon, Malcolm Scott; m. Alice von Neumann, Sept. 1974 (div. Mar. 1977); m. Joan Miller, Jan. 1979 (dec. Apr. 2001), m. Denise Bredt, May 2003. BS, U. Wis., 1952; PhD, U. Md., 1959. Aero. research scientist NASA, Cleve., 1952-54; NSF postdoctoral fellow, 1959-60; asst. prof. Rutgers U., 1960-63, assoc. prof., 1963-64; assoc. prof. math. U. Ill., Urbana, 1964-67, prof., 1967-97, prof. emeritus, 1997—. Author: Abstract Methods in Partial Differential Equations, 1969, Transmutation and Operator Differential Equations, 1979, Transmutation, Scattering Theory and Special Functions, 1982, Transmutation Theory and Applications, 1985, Mathematical Physics, 1988, Topics in Soliton Theory, 1991, Quantum Theory, Deformation and Integrability, 2000, Calculus Revisited, 2002, Fluctuations, Information, Gravity, and the Quantam Potential, 2005; co-author: Singular and Degenerate Cachy Problems, 1976; assoc. editor Jour. Applicable Analysis, 1970—; contbr. over 190 articles to profl. jours. Served with U.S. Army, 1954-57. Mem. Am. Math. Soc., Am. Phys. Soc. Avocations: foreign languages, cello. Home: 1314 Brighton Dr Urbana IL 61801-6417 Office: Univ Ill Math Dept Urbana IL 61801 Business E-Mail: rcarroll@math.uiuc.edu.

CARROLL, ROSEMARY FRANCES, historian, educator, lawyer; b. Providence, Oct. 15, 1935; d. Francis Edward and Katherine Loretta (Graham) C. AB, Brown U., 1957; MA, Wesleyan U., 1962; PhD, Rutgers U., 1968; JD, U. Iowa, 1983. Bar: Iowa 1983. Asst. prof. history Notre Dame Coll., N.Y.C., 1968-70; vis. asst. prof. history Denison U., Granville, Ohio, 1970-71; asst. prof. history Coe Coll., Cedar Rapids, Iowa, 1971-75, assoc. prof. history, 1975-84, prof. history, 1984—2000, chair dept. history, 1988—2000, affirmative action officer, 1973-98, prelaw advisor, 1988-98, rep. Truman Found., 1988—98, faculty rep. Rhodes Scholarship Trust, 1993-98, faculty rep. Brit. Marshal Scholarship, 1996-98, Henry and Margaret Haegg disting. prof. history, 2000—01, Henry and Margaret Haegg disting. prof. history emerita, 2001—. Contbr. articles to profl. jours. Vol. lawyer Legal Services Corp. Iowa, Cedar Rapids, 1984—2003, mem. adv. coun., 1985—2003. Olmsted fellow Hoover Presdl. Libr. Assn., 1987-92, Hoover grantee, 1992-94, NEH grantee, 1992-93. Mem. ABA, AAUP, AAUW, Iowa Bar Assn. (legal heritage com. 1988-2002), Linn County Bar Assn. (continuing legal edn. com. 1990-2002), Linn County Women Atty. (treas. 1990-91), Orgn. Am. Historians (membership com. 1978), So. Hist. Assn. (membership com. 1986-87, 88-89, 96-98), So. Assn. Womens Historians (pres. 1975-76, membership com. 1987-88, 89-90, 96-98), Am. Hist. Assn., Phi Kappa Phi. Roman Catholic. Avocations: bicycling, swimming. Home (Summer): 33 Nicholson Middletown RI 02842-5409 Office Phone: 401-846-3908. E-mail: rfcarroll1@aol.com.

CARROLL, ROY, retired academic administrator; b. England, Ark., Dec. 8, 1929; m. Eleanor Kate Moorefield, 1953; children: Jane, Linda. BA cum laude, Ouachita Bapt. U., 1951; MA, Vanderbilt U., 1959, PhD, 1964. Math. tchr. Baker H.S., Columbus, Ga., 1955; asst. prof. history and polit. sci. Mercer U., Macon, Ga., 1959-65; prof. history, chmn. dept. history and polit. sci. Armstrong State Coll., Savannah, Ga., 1965-69; prof. history, chmn. dept. history Appalachian State U., Boone, NC, 1969-79; v.p. planning gen. adminstrn. U. NC Sys., 1979-90, 91-96, sr. v.p., v.p. acad. affairs, 1996-99, ret., 1999; interim chancellor U. NC, Asheville, 1990-91. Mem. NC Justice Edn. and Tng. Stds. Commn., 1979-90, chmn. planning com., 1981-88; mem. adv. bd. Inst. Transp. Rsch. and Edn., Rsch. Triangle Park, 1980—; bd. dirs. Western NC Devel. Assn., 1990-91, NC State Employees Credit Union, 1990-91, Rsch. Triangle Inst., 1996-2000; trustee Appalachian State U., 2000—. Contbr. articles to profl. jours. Inf. officer U.S. Army, 1951-53, Japan, Korea. Fulbright scholar, Eng., 1958-59. Home: 6811 Huntingridge Rd Chapel Hill NC 27517-8673 Office: U NC Gen Adminstrn PO Box 2688 Chapel Hill NC 27515-2688 E-mail: rcl@ga.unc.edu.

CARROLL, SEAN B., research scientist, geneticist, biologist, educator; b. Sept. 17, 1960; m. Jamie Carroll; 2 children; 2 stepchildren. BA, Wash. U.; PhD in Immunology, Tufts U., 1983. Prof. molecular biology, genetics, and med. genetics U. Wis., Madison, Howard Hughes Med. Inst. investigator, 1990—. Co-author: From DNA to Diversity: Molecular Genetics and the Evolution of Animal Design, 2004; author: Endless Forms Most Beautiful: The New Science of Evo Devo and the Making of the Animal Kingdom, 2005. Named one of 50 Future Leaders 40 and Under, Time mag., 1994; recipient Presdl. Young Investigator Award, NSF, Shaw Award, Milw. Found., Herbert W. Dickerman Award, Wadsworth Ctr., NY State Dept. Health. Mem.: AAAS. Office: U Wis 201a RM Bock Labs 1525 Linden Dr Madison WI 53706 Office Phone: 608-262-6199. Office Fax: 608-265-2004. E-mail: sbcarrol@wisc.edu.

CARROLL, WARREN HASTY, retired historian; s. Herbert Allen and Gladys Harry Carroll; m. Anne Westhoff, June 7, 1967. BA, Bates Coll., 1953; MA, Columbia U., 1954, PhD, 1957; LLD (hon.), Christendom Coll., 1999. Instr. history Ind. U., Bloomington, Ind., 1957—58; asst. command historian Second AF Strategic Air Command, Barksdale AFB, La., 1958—59; legis. asst. Congressman John G. Schmitz, Washington, 1960—62; founder, pres. Christendom Coll., Front Royal, Va., 1975—85, prof. history, 1985—2002, ret., 2002. Bd. dirs. Christendom Ednl. Corp., Front Royal, Seton Sch., Manassas, Va., Aid to Ch. in Russia, Leesburg, Va. Author: 1917-Red Banners, White Mantle, 1981, Our Lady of Guadalupe and the Conquest of Darkness, 1983, History of Christendom, 1985, 1987, The Guillotine and the Cross, 1986; contbr. The Tarrans Chronicles, 2002. With Signal Corps. U.S. Army, 1955—57, Japan. Mem.: Fellowship of Cath. Scholars. Republican. Roman Cath. Avocation: writing. Office: Christendom College 134 Christendom Drive Front Royal VA 22630 Personal E-mail: warren.h.carroll@trincomm.org.

CARROLL, WILLIAM, publishing company executive; Mgr., dir. Auto Book Press, Coda Publs.; dir., N.Mex. Books Coda Publs., Raton, N.Mex. Office: New Mex Books Coda Publs PO Box 71 Raton NM 87740-0071

CARROLL, WILLIAM J., municipal official; b. Aug. 24, 1944; BS in Acctg., Univ. Toledo, 1969; grad. Adv. Mgmt. Program, Harvard Bus. Sch., 1994. Gen. mgr., after market prodn. divsn. Hayes-Dana, 1987—89, v.p., after market prodn. divsn., 1989—93, pres., 1993—95, Dana Distribution Svc. Group, 1995—96, pres., diversified products and distribution, 1996—97, pres., automotive sys. group, 1997—2004, pres., COO, 2004; dir., econ., cmty. devel. City of Toledo, Ohio, 2004—. Office: City of Toledo Ste 1710 One Government Ctr Toledo OH 43604 Office Phone: 419-245-1286.

CARROLL, WILLIAM KENNETH, lawyer, educator, psychologist, theologian; b. Oak Park, Ill., May 8, 1927; s. Ralph Thomas and Edith (Fay) C.; m. Frances Louise Forgue; children: Michele, Brian. BS in Edn., BA in Philosophy, Quincy Coll., Ill., 1950; MA, Duquesne U., 1964; STL, Cath. U., 1965; PhD, U. Strasbourg, France, 1968; JD, Northwestern U., 1972. Bar: Ill. 1972, U.S. Dist. Ct. (no. dist.) Ill 1972, U.S. Ct. Appeals (7th cir.) 1973; lic. clin. psychologist, Ill. Asst. editor Franciscan Press, Chgo., 1955-60; asst. prof. psychology and religion Carlow Coll., Pitts., 1962-65, Loyola U., Chgo., 1968-70; staff atty. Fed. Defender Program, Chgo., 1972-75; prof. law John Marshall Law Sch., Chgo., 1975—. Bd. dirs. Am. Inst. Adlerian Studies; law reporter ABA Criminal Justice Mental Health Stds. Project, 1981-83; cons. legal issues Am. Psych. Assn.; standing com. on mental health law, Ill. Author: (with Kosnik et al.) Human Sexuality, 1977; Eyewitness Testimony, Strategies and Tactics, 1984, 2d edit., 2003; contbg. author: By Reason of Insanity, 1983, Law for Illinois Psychologists, 1985, Law and Mental Health Professionals, 2002. Bd. dirs. Chgo. Sch. Profl. Psychology, 1978-82; bd. adv. Ill. Sch. Profl. Psychology, 1985. Recipient Am. Juris award, 1970; U. Chgo. scholar, 1968-69. Fellow Inst. Social and Behavioral Pathology (chmn. 1987—); mem. ABA, AAUP, APA (Outstanding Contbn. to Psychology award 1998, com. on legal issues 1995—), Ill. Psychol. Assn., Cath. Theol. Soc. Am. Avocation: pvt. pilot. Office: John Marshall Law Sch 315 S Plymouth Ct Chicago IL 60604-3968 Office Phone: 312-987-1447. Business E-Mail: 7carroll@jmls.edu.

CARROTHERS, GERALD ARTHUR PATRICK, environmental and city planning educator; b. Saskatoon, Sask., Can., July 1, 1925; BArch, U. Man., Can., 1948, MArch, 1951; MCP, Harvard U., 1953; PhD, MIT, 1959. Lectr. architecture U. Man., Winnipeg, 1948-52; research asst. regional sci. Mass. Inst. Tech., Cambridge, 1953-56; asst. prof. town and regional planning U. Toronto, Ont., Can., 1956-60; assoc. prof. to prof. city planning U. Pa., Phila., 1960-67, chmn. dept. city planning, 1961-65; founding dir. Inst. Environ. Studies, 1965-67; prof. York U., Downsview, Ont., 1968—, founding dean faculty environ. studies, 1968-76. Chmn. U. Toronto-York U. Joint Program in Transp., 1971-78; adviser Central Mortgage and Housing Corp., Can., 1967-77; vis. prof. U. Nairobi, Kenya, 1978-80; mem. founding bd. dirs. Can. Urban Inst., 1988. Fellow World Acad. Art and Sci., Royal Archtl. Inst. Can., Can. Inst. Planners (founding editor Plan Can., 1959, councillor 1968-70); mem. Am. Inst. Cert. Planners (life), Am. Planning Assn. (charter), Regional Sci. Assn. (founding mem., founding editor Papers 1954, pres. 1970-71), Ont. Assn. Architects (life), Ont. Profl. Planners Inst. (founding registrar, founding bd. dirs. 1985). Home: 24 Bertmount Ave Toronto ON Canada M4M 2X9 Office: York U Fac Environ Studies 4700 Keele St Toronto ON Canada M3J 1P3

CARROW, JOHN C., computer company executive; b. Crystal City, Mo. BS, US Mil. Acad., 1966; MS in EE and Computer Sci., U. Ill., 1973. Commd. 2d lt. U.S. Army, advanced through grades, ret.; sys. engr., large scale info. sys. Gen. Electric; various sr. mgmt. positions GE Aerospace Info. Mgmt. Systems/Mgmt. Data Systems; chief info. officer, history City of Phila., 1993—96; chief info. officer Unisys Corp., 1996—, v.p., worldwide info. tech., 1996—. Chmn. bd. Red Cross (Southeastern Pa. Chpt.). Served to major U.S. Army. Named Pub. Ofcl. of Yr., Governing mag., 1996. Office: Unisys Corp Unisys Way Blue Bell PA 19424*

CARROW, LEON ALBERT, physician; b. Chgo., Jan. 18, 1924; s. Charles and Mollie (Sachs) C.; m. Joan Twaddell, June 21, 1974; children by previous marriage— Elizabeth, James. BS, U. Chgo., 1945, MD, 1947. Intern Cook County Hosp. and Chgo. Lying-in Hosp., 1947-48; resident Chgo. Wesley Meml. Hosp., Chgo. Maternity Center, 1949-51; sr. attending physician in obstetrics and gynecology Northwestern Meml. Hosp., 1954-91, sr. attending physician emeritus, 1991—, also past chief of staff. Asso. prof. obstetrics and gynecology Northwestern U. Med. Sch., 1967-73, prof. clin. obstetrics and gynecology, 1973-91, prof. emeritus, 1991—. Contbr. articles to profl. jours. Served with AUS, 1944-46; to capt. USAF, 1952-53. Fellow A.C.S.; mem. Ill., Chgo. med. socs., AMA, Chgo. Gynecology Soc., Am. Soc. Cytology, Central Assn. Obstetrics and Gynecology. Home: 566 Cedar St Winnetka IL 60093-2338

CARROW, MILTON MICHAEL, law educator; b. N.Y.C., Sept. 13, 1912; s. Samuel and Ethel (Berlin) Carrow; m. Betsey Wood Hall, Nov. 2, 1940 (div. 1968); children: David M, Thomas E, Deborah, James H, Emily W; m. Eve Wagner Cooper, Feb. 28, 1969 (div. 1986); m. Barbara M Barski, Nov. 2, 1996. AB, Syracuse U., 1933, postgrad., 1933-34; JD, Harvard U., 1937. Bar: NY 1938. Assoc. Legal Aid Soc., Rochester, N.Y., 1937-38, Lincoln Epworth & Nathan Sweedler, 1938-42, Emil Schlesinger, 1946-48; pvt. practice, 1948-53; ptnr. Lavine & Carrow, N.Y.C., 1953-59, Landis, Carrow, Benson & Tucker, N.Y.C., 1959-70, Carrow, Bernson, Hoeniger, Freitag & Abbey, 1970-73; dir. Ctr. for Adminstrv. Justice, ABA, 1973-77, Nat. Center for Adminstrv. Justice, Consortium of Univs. of Washington Met. Area, 1977-79; pres. Nat. Center for Adminstrv. Justice, 1979-82. Adj. asst. prof. Law Sch. NYU, 1964—68; cons. Nat. Adv. Com. Civil Disorders, 1967; mem. faculty appellate judges seminar Inst. Jud. Adminstrn., 1969—70; vis. prof. Nat. Law Ctr. George Washington U., 1973—80; adj. prof. Georgetown U., 1980—81, rsch. prof. pub. policy, 1983—; vice chmn. Weston Charter Comm., Conn., 1965—66; counsel UN We Believe, 1962—72; vis. intervenor XVIII Internat. Congress Adminstrv. Scis., Madrid, 1980; US rep. to standing com. law and sci. pub. adminstrn. Internat. Inst. Adminstrv. Scis., 1982; cons. Block Island Charter Commn., 1988—89. Author: (book) Background of Administrative Law, 1948, The Licensing Power in New York City, 1968; author (with J D Nyhart) Law and Science in Collaboration, 1983; editor (with Robert Paul Churchill and Joseph J Cordes): Democracy, Social Values and Public Policy, 1998; contbr. articles to profl jours; editor: Working Paper series, Grad Program in Pub Policy, 1985—. Dir. Washington Ctr. George Washington U., 1988—. With AUS, 1943—46. Mem.: ABA (chmn. sect. adminstrv. law 1971—72), Assn. Bar City NY (chmn. com. adminstrv. law 1964—67), Arts Club Washington (trustee, endowment com. 2001—). Home: 914 25th St NW Washington DC 20037-2191 Personal E-mail: mcarrow@earthlink.net.

CARROW, ROBERT DUANE, lawyer, barrister; b. Marshall, Minn., Feb. 5, 1934; s. Meddie Joseph and Estelle Marie (Kough) C.; m. Jacqueline Mary Givens, Sept. 3, 1960; children: Leslie, Tamara, Amelia, Vanessa, Creighton, Jessica, Ramsey. Student, U. Colo., 1952; BA, U. Minn., 1956; JD, Stanford U., 1958. Bar: Calif. 1959, U.S. Supreme Ct. 1978, Eng., 1981, N.Y. 1983. Pvt. practice, Calif., 1959—; barrister London, 1981—. Judge pro tem Superior Ct. of Calif., San Francisco, 1992—. Bd. editors Minn. Law Rev., 1956-57. Mayor City of Novato, Calif., 1964-66. Fellow Ctr. Internat. Legal Studies, Soc. Advanced Legal Studies (assoc.); mem. ABA (accredited mediator), N.Y. Bar Assn., L.A. Bar Assn., San Francisco Bar Assn., Internat. Bar Assn., Chartered Inst. Arbitrators, Assn. Conflict Resolution, Honourable Soc. Mid. Inn of Ct. Address: Chambers 33 Bedford Row London WC1 4JR England Office: Goldstein & Musto 1 Embarcadero Ctr Ste 500 San Francisco CA 94111-3607 also: 7 Mount Lassen Dr Ste C134 San Rafael CA 94903-1170

CARR-RUFFINO, NORMA, finance educator; b. Fort Worth, Dec. 15, 1932; d. Robert L. and Lorene Dickeson Carr; m. Randell H. Smith, July 20, 1951 (div. Jan. 1973); children: Randell H. Smith II, Brian F. Smith, Erica Carr; m. Alfred Ruffino, Jan. 6, 1979. BBA, Tex. Wesleyan U., 1968; MBA, U. N. Tex., 1969, PhD, 1973. V.p. Randy's, Inc., Ft. Worth, 1965—70; vocat. office edn. coord., tchr. Ft. Worth Pub. Schs., 1970—73; prof., mgmt. San Francisco State U., 1973—. Contbr. chapters to books, articles to profl. jours.; author: Diversity Success Strategies, 1999, The Innovative Woman: Hot Skills for the New Economy, 2001, Business Students Guide, 3d edit., 2004, The Creative Intelligence Model: Building Innovative Skills, 3d edit., 2004, Managing Diversity: People Skills for a Multicultural Workplace, 6th edit., 2004, The Promotable Woman, 4th edit., 2005, Making Diversity Work, 2005; mem. editl. bd. Women in Mgmt. Rev., 1991—. Ref. Calif. State Bar Ct., 1985—. Named Alumna of Yr., Tex. Wesleyan U., 1988; named one of Top 100 Women Alumna (100th anniversary), 1991. Mem.: 21st Century World, Internat. Assn. Bus. and Soc., World Future Soc., Women's Leadership Forum of Dem. Party, Acad. Mgmt. Home: 1414 Alameda San Mateo CA 94402 Office: San Francisco State U Coll of Bus 1600 Holloway Ave San Francisco CA 94132-1722 Office Phone: 650-345-8372. Business E-Mail: ncr@sfsu.edu.

CARRUTH, HAYDEN, poet; b. Waterbury, Conn., Aug. 3, 1921; s. Gorton Veeder and Margery Tracy Barrow (Dibb) C.; m. Sara Anderson, Mar. 14, 1943; 1 child, Martha Hamilton; m. Eleanore Ray, Nov. 29, 1952; m. Rose Marie Dorn, Oct. 28, 1961; 1 child, David Barrow II; m. Joe-Anne McLaughlin, Dec. 29, 1989. AB, U. N.C., 1943; MA, U. Chgo., 1948; LLD, New Eng. Coll., 1987, Syracuse U., 1993. Editor-in-chief Poetry mag., 1949-50; assoc. editor U. Chgo. Press, 1950-51; project adminstr. Intercultural Publs. Inc., N.Y.C., 1952-53; poetry editor Harper's mag., 1977—88. Poet-in-residence Johnson State Coll., 1972-74; adj. prof. U. Vt., 1975-78; prof. English Syracuse (N.Y.) U., 1979-91, prof. emeritus, 1991—. Author: The Crow and the Heart, 1959, Journey to a Known Place, 1961, Norfolk Poems, 1962, Appendix A, 1963, North Winter, 1964, Nothing for Tigers, 1965, Contra Mortem, 1967, After the Stranger, 1965, For You, 1970, The Clay Hill Anthology, 1970, The Voice That Is Great Within Us, 1970, The Bird-Poem Book, 1970, From Snow and Rock, from Chaos, 1973, Dark World, 1973, The Bloomingdale Papers, 1975, Loneliness, 1976, Aura, 1977, Brothers, I Loved You All, 1978, Almanach du Printemprs Vivarois, 1979, Working Papers, 1982, The Mythology of Dark and Light, 1982, The Sleeping Beauty, 1982, If You Call This Cry a Song, 1983, Effluences from the Sacred Caves, 1983, Asphalt Georgics, 1985, Lighter than Air Craft, 1985, The Oldest Killed Lake in North America, 1985, The Selected Poetry of Hayden Carruth, 1986, Mother, 1986, Sitting In: Selected Writings on Jazz, Blues & Related Topics, 1986, Sonnets, 1989, Tell Me Again How the White Heron Rises and Flies Across the Nacreous River at Twilight Toward the Distant Island, 1989, Collected Shorter Poems, 1946-91, 92, Suicides and Jazzers, 1992, Collected Longer Poems, 1994, Selected Essays and Reviews, 1995, Scrambled Eggs and Whiskey, 1996, Reluctantly, 1998, Beside the Shadblow Tree, 1999, Faxes to William, 2000, Doctor Jazz, 2001, Letters To Jane, 2004; mem. editl. bd. Hudson Rev., 1971—. Sr. fellow N.Y. Found. Arts, 1993. Recipient Vachel Lindsay prize, 1954, Bess Hokin prize, 1956, Levinson prize, 1958, Ann. Poetry award Brandeis U., 1959, Harriet Monroe Poetry prize U. Chgo., 1960, Helen Bullis prize U. Seattle, 1962, Carl Sandburg prize, 1963, Emily Clark Balch prize, 1964, Gov.'s medal State of Vt., 1974, Shelley award Poetry Soc. Am., 1978, Lenore Marshall prize, 1979, Morton Zabel prize, 1968, Whiting Writers award, 1986, Sarah Josepha Hale award, 1988, Ruth Lilly Poetry prize, 1990, Nat. Book Critics Circle award in poetry, 1993, Lannan award for poetry, 1995, Nat. Book award for Poetry, 1996; named Vt. poet laureate, 2002; fellow Bollingen Found., 1962, John Simon Meml. Guggenheim Found., 1965, 79, sr. fellow Nat. Endowment for Arts, 1988; grantee Nat. Found. on Arts and Humanities, 1967, 74. Home: RR 1 Box 128 Munnsville NY 13409-9549

CARRUTH, PATTI JO, nursing director; b. San Diego, Sept. 1, 1958; d. Robert William and Constance (Cooper) Berg; m. Christopher James Peterson, June 6, 1981 (div. Apr. 1988); m. Denis Grady Carruth, Oct. 7, 1989; 1 child, Savannah Rose. BSN, San Jose State U., 1980. Cert. oncology nurse, Oncology Nursing Soc. Staff RN ortho/neuro Washington Hosp., Fremont, Calif., 1981-89, asst. mgr. ortho/neuro, 1989-92; dir. in-patient and outpatient oncology Touro Infirmary, New Orleans, 1992-96, oncology clin. specialist, 1996; clin. rsch. assoc. Alton Ochsner Med. Found. Hosp., New Orleans, 1996-97; clin. edn. specialist vascular access HOC Corp., Atlanta, 1997—. Mem. Nat. Assn. Vascular Access Networks, New Orleans Oncology Nurses (dir.-at-large 1993-94, mem. program planning 1994, Metro Atlanta Oncology Nursing chpt. 1998—). Republican. Baptist. Avocations: arts and crafts, gardening, horseback riding. Office: HOC Corp 2109 Otoole Ave San Jose CA 95131-1338

CARRUTHERS, THOMAS NEELY, lawyer; b. Columbia, Tenn., Oct. 11, 1928; s. Thomas Neely and Ellen Douglas (Everett) C.; m. Dale Gilder Jones, Feb. 7, 1959; children: Thomas Neely III, Virginia Carruthers Smith, Catherine Everett. AB, Princeton U., 1950; LLB, Yale U., 1955. Assoc. Bradley, Arant, Rose & White, Birmingham, Ala., 1955-63, ptnr., 1963—, chair exec. com. and mng. ptnr., 1990-95. Mem. editl. bd. Yale Law Jour., 1953-55. Trustee Children's Hosp. Ala., pres. 1996-97; trustee Ala. Shakespeare Festival, Leadership Ala., pres. 1995-96, chmn., 1996-97; trustee Birmingham Mus. Art., chmn., 1995-2002; trustee Birmingham Legal Aid Soc., 2004—, chmn., 2005—; chmn. Gov.'s Tax Reform Task Force, 1991-92, exec. sec. devel. com., 1992-93; bd. dirs., dir. Comm. Found. Greater Birmingham, chmn., 1999-2002; bd. dirs. 2020 Birmingham Com., Ala. Dept. of Archives and History; bd. advisors Cumberland Law Sch., chmn., 1993-95;

chancellor, Episcopal Diocese of Ala., 2003—; chmn. Constl. Reform Task Force, 2005—; chmn. exec. com. Ala. Acad. Honor, 1999—; active Boy Scouts Am., Birmingham, exec. bd. Birmingham Coun.; chmn. fin. com. Lakeshore Found., 2005— Recipient Thurmond Arnold Appellate Competition prize Yale U., 1954, Birmingham-So. Coll. medal Honor, 1992, award for pub. svc. Birmingham Bar, 1998, Brotherhood and Sisterhood award NCCJ, 2000, commendations: State Ala., Ala. Commn. Higher Edn., Jacksonville State U., Silver Beaver award Boy Scouts Am.; named Humanitarian of Yr., 1997. Fellow: Am. Bar Found.; mem.: ABA, Birmingham Bar Assn. (Outstanding Lawyer of Yr. award 2001), Ala. Bar Assn., Am. Law Inst., Am. Tax Policy Inst. (past trustee), Am. Coll. Tax Counsel, So. Fed. Tax Inst. (pres. 1993—94, trustee, past chmn.), Internat. Bar Assn., Mountain Brook Club, Rotary (pres. 1992—93, Spain-Hickman award 2003). Episcopalian. Office: Bradley Arant Rose & White One Federal Pl 1819 5th Ave N Birmingham AL 35203 Office Phone: 205-521-8263. E-mail: tcarruthers@bradleyarant.com.

CARSCH, RUTH E., librarian, consultant; b. London, May 3, 1945; arrived in U.S., 1949; d. Harry and Ellen Margot (Adler) Carsch; 1 child, Zachariah Robert. BA, Hunter Coll. CUNY, 1967; MS, Columbia U., 1968; cert. in info. sys. mgmt., U. Calif., Santa Cruz, 1999, U. Calif. Berkeley Libr. Futures Inst., 1997. Cert. libr. N.Y., Calif. Reference libr. N.Y. Pub. Libr., 1968-70; tech. info. specialist Bechtel, Inc., San Francisco, 1972-75; rsch. assoc. Erick & Lavidge Mkt. Rsch. Assocs., San Francisco, 1980-86; instrnl. reference libr. San Mateo County CC Dist., 1987—; reference libr. San Francisco Pub. Libr., 2001—. Cons. Port Authority N.Y. and N.J., 1982—84, Camp, Dresser, McKee Engrs., Boston, 1988, Met. Mus. Art & Getty Trust, 1992, Calif. Conservation Corps., 1992, Miriam and Peter Haas Fund, 1995, Oreg. Shaekspeare Festival, 1995, Oak Grove Sch. Dist., San Jose, Calif., 1998, Skidmore Owings Merrill, San Francisco, 2000; Hong Kong bd. trade ICT Expo, 2004. Mem.: No. Calif. Architecture-Engrng. Librs. Roundtable, Art Librs. Soc. Office: 1453 Rhode Island St San Francisco CA 94107-3248 Business E-Mail: recarsch@mzinfo.com.

CARSON, BENJAMIN SOLOMON, neurosurgeon; b. Detroit, Sept. 18, 1951; s. Robert Solomon and Sonya (Copeland) C.; m. Lacena Rustin, July 6, 1975; children: Murray Nedlands, Benjamin Solomon Jr., Rhoeyce Harrington. BA, Yale U., 1973; MD, U. Mich., 1977; DSc (hon.), Gettysburg Coll., 1988, N.C. A&T, 1989, Andrews U., 1989, Sojourner-Douglas Coll., 1989, Shippenburg U., 1990, Jersey City State Coll., 1990, Southwestern Adventist Coll., 1992, U. Mass., Boston, 1992, Marygrove Coll., 1993, U. Detroit-Mercy, 1994, Spalding U., 1994, Western Md. Coll., 1994, Morgan State U., 1994, Long Island U., 1994, N.C. State U., 1994, Tuskegee U., 1995, Yale U., 1996, Del. State U., 1996, Med. U. South Africa, Medunsa, 1997, GMI Engrng. and Mgmt. Inst., 1997, U. Del., 1997, Coll. William and Mary, 1998. Diplomate Am. Bd. Neurol. Surgery. Surg. intern Johns Hopkins Hosp., Balt., 1977-78, neurosurg. resident, 1978-82, chief resident, 1982-83; sr. registrar Sir Charles Gairdner Hosp., Perth, W. Australia, 1983-84; dir. pediatric neurosurgery, prof. neurosurgery, plastic surgery, oncology & pediatrics Johns Hopkins Hosp., Balt., 1985—; co-dir. Johns Hopkins Craniofacial Ctr., Balt. Bd. dirs. Kellogg Co. Author: Pediatric Neurooncology, 1987, Achondroplasia, 1988, Gifted Hands, 1989, Think Big, 1996, The Big Picture, 1999; contbr. jour. articles. Mem. med. adv. bd. Children's Cancer Found., Balt., 1987—; hon. med. chmn. Md. Red Cross, Balt., 1987—. Recipient Am. Black Achievement award Ebony mag., Hollywood, Calif., 1988, Cum Laude award Am. Radiol. Soc., Chgo., 1982, Candle award Morehouse U., Atlanta, 1989; Paul Harris fellow Rotary Internat., 1988; Named one of Top 100 Black Physicians in Am. by Black Enterprise Mag., 2001. Mem. Am. Assn. Neurol. Surgeons, Congress Neurol. Surgeons, AAAS, Pediatric Oncology Group, Nat. Med. Assn. Seventh Day Adventist. Office: Johns Hopkins Hosp 600 N Wolfe St #811 Baltimore MD 21287-0005

CARSON, BRAD ROGERS, former congressman; b. Winslow, AZ., Mar. 11, 1967; m. Julie. BA with honors, Baylor U., 1967; MA in politics, philopsophy and econ., Oxford; JD, U. Okla. Coll. Law, 1994. Atty. pvt. practice; White House fellow, spl. asst. to Sec. Defense Spl. Projects, 1997-98; mem. US Ho. of Reps. (2nd dist.) Okla., 2001—05. Vice-chair Congl. Native Am. Caucus. Mem. Phi Beta Kappa. Mem. Blue Dog Coalition, New Democrat Coalition; mem. First Baptist Ch. Claremore.

CARSON, CHARLES HENRY, electrical engineer; b. Malden, Mass., July 18, 1930; s. Philip Stanley and Margaret (Mitchell) C.; m. Olivia Rose Marie Barto, Apr. 23, 1967; children: Cynthia, Craig, Marcia, Claudia. Student, Northeastern U., Boston, 1956, postgrad., 1966. Devel. engr. microwave Raytheon, Bedford, Mass., 1953-56; sr. engr., dept. mgr. Airtron Inc., Cambridge, Mass., 1956-58; co-founder, v.p., dir. ops. Ferrotec Inc., Newton, Mass., 1958-70; dir. corp. mkt. planning MA/COM, Burlington, Mass., 1970-75; chmn., founder, chief exec. officer Carson Assocs., Inc., Milford, Mass., 1975—. Bd. dirs. Carson Assocs., Inc., Milford; co-founder, bd. dirs. Colonial Cablevision, Revere, Mass., 1976-86; co-founder, v.p. mktg., bd. dirs. Ferrotec Inc., Newton, 1958-70. Inventor in field; contbr. articles to profl. jours. Commr. Indsl. devel. Commn., Milford, 1968-70; minuteman Mass. Ind. Devel. Commn., 1969-73; bd. dirs. Order of St. Mary the Virgin, 1993. With USN, 1948-53. Mem. U.S. Polo Assn. (del. 1986-96), R.I. Tuna Tournament (dep. dir. 1973-77), Galilee Tuna Club (pres. 1976-77), Newport Polo Club (del. 1989-90). Avocations: polo, giant tuna fishing, sailing, shooting. Office: Carson Assocs Inc 5 Kellett Dr Milford MA 01757-4013

CARSON, CHRISTOPHER LEONARD, lawyer; b. Washington, Dec. 28, 1940; s. Leonard O. and Evelyn (Watters) C.; m. Cynthia Caffey, Dec. 27, 1963; 1 dau., Melissa Ann. AB, Duke U., 1962; JD, U. Mich., 1965. Bar: N.Y. 1965, Fla. 1968, Ga. 1970. Assoc. Olwine, Chase, O'Donnell & Weyher, N.Y.C., 1965-66; ptnr. Hansell & Post, Atlanta, 1969-89, Jones Day, Atlanta, 1989—. Contbg. author: Modern Real Estate Transactions; contbr. articles to legal publs. and mags. Bd. dirs., adv. coun. Atlanta Area Boy Scouts Am., 1974-80; bd. dirs. Young Life Urban Atlanta, 1983—87. Lt. sr. grade USNR, 1966-69. Fellow Am. Coll. Coml. Fin. Lawyers; mem. ABA (Uniform Comml. Code Com., Subcoms. on Secured Transactions and Letter of Credit 1982-95), Southeastern Bankruptcy Law Inst. (dir. 1973—, pres. 1980-81, chmn. 1981-82), Atlanta Bar Bankruptcy Sect. (chmn. 1981-82), Ga. Bar Uniform Code Com. (chmn. 1984-87), Cherokee Club. Republican. Baptist. Avocations: running, reading, travel. Office: Jones Day 1420 Peachtree St NE Ste 800 Atlanta GA 30309-3053 Office Phone: 404-581-8035. Business E-Mail: clcarson@jonesday.com.

CARSON, CULLEY CLYDE, III, urologist, educator; b. Westerly, R.I., Feb. 25, 1945; s. Culley Clyde Jr. and Dorothy (Scarborough) C.; m. Mary Jo McDonald, Aug. 10, 1970; children: Culley Clyde IV, Hilary. BS, Trinity Coll., 1967; MD, George Washington U., 1971. Diplomate Am. Bd. Urology. Intern Dartmouth Med. Ctr., 1971-72, resident surgery, 1971-73; fellow urology Mayo Clinic, Rochester, Minn., 1975-78; instr. urology U. Minn. Mayo Med. Sch., Rochester, 1978; asst. prof. urology Duke U. Med. Ctr., Durham, N.C., 1978-84, assoc. prof., 1984-88, prof., 1988-93, Rhodes Disting. chair, 1993—; prof., chmn. urology U. N.C., Chapel Hill, 1993—, Rhoads disting. prof., 2000—. Chief urology Durham VA Hosp.; mem. new drug panel U.S. FDA; mem. exec. com. U.S. Pharmacopea. Author: Endourology, 1985, Atlas of Urologic Endoscopy, 1986, Impotence, 1992, 98, Complications of Invasive Procedures, 1995, Textbook of Erectile Dysfunction, 1999; editor-in-chief Mediguide to Urology, 1994—, Contemporary Urology, 1997—; contbr. chpts. to urol. texts. Maj. M.C., USAF, 1973-75. Recipient Calvin Klopp Rsch. award, 1971, Friedman rsch. prize, 1971, Cristol Mayo Alumni award, 1992, Jesse H. Neal award, 2001; named Command Flight Surgeon of Yr., USAF, 1974; Rsch. fellow Am. Heart Assn., 1969, O'Dea travel fellow, 1978. Fellow ACS, Am. Surg. Assn.; mem. AMA, AAAS, Am. Assn. Genitourinary Surgeons, Am. Urol. Assn. (pres. Southeast sect. 2004), Sexual Medicine Soc. (pres. 2003), Internat. Soc. Urology, Am. Fertility Soc., Univ. Urol. Forum, N.Y. Acad. Scis., Mayo Alumni Assn., Gov.'s Club, Carolina Club, Trinity Club (Hartford), Sigma Xi, Psi Chi, Alpha Omega Alpha. Home: 2719 Spencer St Durham NC 27705-5720 Office: U NC Hosps Chapel Hill NC 27599-7235 Office Phone: 919-966-2574. Personal E-mail: culleyccarson3@hotmail.com. Business E-Mail: carson@med.unc.edu.

CARSON, DENNIS A., immunologist, researcher, cancer biologist; married. BA, Haverford Coll.; MD, Columbia U., 1970; postgraduate rsch. tng., Salk Inst. Former divsn. head immunology Scripps Clinic and Rsch. Found.; resident U. Calif., San Diego, postdoctoral fellow, 1974—77, prof. medicine, 1995—, dir. Sam and Rose Stein Inst. Rsch. Aging; dir. Rebecca and John Moores U. Calif. Cancer Ctr., 2003—. Founder, bd. dirs. Dynavax Tech. Corp., San Diego, Salmedix Inc., San Diego; founder Vical Inc., San Diego, Triangle Pharm. Inc., San Diego. Recipient Bruce F. Cain Meml. award, Am. Assn. Cancer Rsch., 2004, Lee C. Howley Sr. prize for arthritis rsch., Arthritis Found. Mem.: NAS. Achievements include development of new agent called 2-chlorodeoxyadenosine (2-CdA), now marketed as the drug Leustatin, for the treatment of hairy cell leukemia, other lymphoid cancers, multiple sclerosis, and psoriasis. Avocations: reading, walking. Office: U Calif San Diego 9500 Gilman Dr La Jolla CA 92093 Office Phone: 858-822-1213.

CARSON, DORA A., secondary school educator; b. Dayton, Ohio, Nov. 3, 1945; d. Neely C. and Mary A. (Whitelow) Sampson; m. Alfred N. Carson, Mar. 18, 1967; 1 child, Tyra Lynne. BS, Wright State U., 1972, MS, 1978. Prin. Meadowdale High Sch., Dayton, Ohio, 1969—. NFL Teacher of the Year, 1992. Mem. Dayton Adminstrs. Assn. Home: 1233 Sunnyview Ave Dayton OH 45406-1927 Office: Meadowdale HS for Internat Studies 4417 Williamson Dr Dayton OH 45416 Office Phone: 937-542-7030. Business E-Mail: dcarson@dps.k12.oh.us.

CARSON, JAMES WOOD, psychologist; b. Greensboro, NC, Dec. 19, 1951; s. Nancy Wood and George Washington Mordecai (Stepfather); m. Kimberly Maynard Carson, May 16, 1998. PhD, U. NC, 2002. Lic. Psychologist NC, 2003. Postdoctoral fellow Duke U. Med. Ctr., 2002—05, asst. clin. prof., 2005—. Swami in Saraswati Order Gurudev Siddha Peeth, Ganeshpuri, Maharashtra, India, 1982—93. Pres. Heart of It Found., Durham, NC, 2005. Mem.: APA, Assn. for Behavioral and Cognitive Therapies, Soc. of Behavioral Medicine. Achievements include research in first study examining effect of mindfulness meditation on couples' relationships; first study examining effects of loving-kindness meditation. Avocation: Carolina basketball. Home: 4625 W Cornwallis Rd Durham NC 27705 Office: Duke Univ Medl Ctr 2200 W Main St Ste 340 Durham NC 27705 Office Phone: 919-416-3407. Office Fax: 919-416-3458. Personal E-mail: jim@yogaatthethreshold.com. E-mail: jim.carson@duke.edu.

CARSON, JAY WILMER, pathologist, educator; b. Ki-Jang, Korea, Oct. 6, 1933; came to U.S., 1960; s. Han Kyu and Jin Chan (Son) Cha; m. Jennifer C. White, June 28, 1968 (dec. Aug. 1990); m. Teresa M. Alberda, July 14, 1995. MD, Seoul Nat. U., 1958. Diplomate Am. Bd. Pathology. Intern Bellevue Hosp. Ctr., N.Y.C., 1961-62; resident in pathology Albert Einstein Coll. Medicine, N.Y.C., 1963-66; fellow U. Montreal, Que., Can., 1967-68; chief anatomic pathology VA Hosp., Martinez, Calif., 1969-91; dir. cytopathology VA Med. Ctr., San Francisco, 1992-96; assoc. clin. prof. U. Calif. Med. Sch., San Francisco, 1992—. Aviation med. examiner FAA, Oklahoma City, 1987-96; assoc. clin. prof. U. Calif., Davis, 1985—; hosp. comdr. 347th Gen. Hosp., Sunnyvale, Calif., 1992-1993, 6253d Army Hosp., Santa Rosa, Calif., 1994-96. Patentee needle aspiration device. Mem. chmn.'s adv. bd. Nat. Rep. Com., Washington, 1995-96. Col. USAR, 1971-96. Decorated Order of Military Med. Merit, Meritorious Svc. Medal with one oakleaf cluster, Sr. Flight Surgeon Badge. Fellow Coll. Am. Pathologists; mem. Internat. Acad. Pathology, Assn. Mil. Surgeons U.S. (life), Res. Officers Assn. (life), U.S. Army War Coll. Alumni Assn. (life), Soc. U.S. Army Flight Surgeons (life). Avocations: skiing, sailing, music. Home: 1550 Sorrel Ct Walnut Creek CA 94598-4800 Personal E-mail: jntcarson@astound.net.

CARSON, JEFFREY L., internist; b. Phila., Oct. 11, 1951; s. Albert Carson and Jackie Zeitz; m. Susan Carson, June 1977; children: Josh, Jennie, Rachael, Dylan. BA in Polit. Sci., U. R.I., 1973; MD, Hahnemann Med. Coll., 1977. Diplomate Am. Bd. Internal Medicine. Chief med. resident Hahnemann Med. Coll. and Hosp., Phila., 1979-80; Henry J. Kaiser fellow U. Pa./Hosp., Phila., 1981-82; asst. prof. medicine UMDNJ - Rutgers Med. Sch., Camden, N.J., 1982-87; assoc. prof. medicine UMDNJ - Robert Wood Johnson Med. Sch., New Brunswick, N.J., 1987-94, chief, Divsn. of GIM, 1987—, prof. of medicine, 1987—, Richard G. Reynolds chair, 1996—. Sr. internat. fellow U. Oxford, U.K., 1995-96; mem. epidemiology study sect. NIH, Bethesda, 1990-94, reviewers res., 1994-98; adhoc reviewer Agy. for Health Care Policy and Rsch., Bethesda, 1990—. Rsch. grantee Agy. for Health Care Policy and Rsch., 1993, NIH, 1990-95, Ortho-Biotech, Bridgewater, N.J., 1995. Fellow am. Coll. Physicians; mem. Soc. Gen. Internal Medicine (chair mid-atlantic sect. 1990-91, other offices)l. Avocations: sailing, coaching little league baseball. Office: UMDNJ-RWJ Med Sch 125 Paterson St New Brunswick NJ 08901-1962 Business E-Mail: carson@umdnj.edu.

CARSON, JOANNE, art educator, artist; BA, U. Ill.; MFA, U. Chgo. Prof. & chairperson art dept. U. at Albany, SUNY. One-woman shows include, Bklyn. Mus., 2002, Plus Ultra Gallery, Bklyn., 2001, Sylvia Schmidt Gallery, New Orleans, 1994, Ruth Siegel Gallery, N.Y.C., 1990, Options, Mus. Contemporary Art, Chgo., 1985, exhibited in group shows at Spring Exhibit, AAAL, 2002, New Works on Wood, Fleming Mus., Burlington Vt., 2001, Frederick Weisman Collection, New Orleans Mus., 1997, Whitney Biennial, Whitney Mus. Am. Art, N.Y.C., 1985. Recipient Purchase Prize Sculpture, AAAL, 2002; Rome Prize Fellowship Painting, Am. Acad. Rome, Artists Fellowship, Nat. Endowment Arts. Office: University at Albany, SUNY Art Dept 1400 Washington Ave FA 216 Albany NY 12222 Office Phone: 518-442-4020. Office Fax: 518-442-4807.*

CARSON, JOHNNIE, former ambassador, academic administrator; b. Chgo., Apr. 7, 1943; s. Dupree and Aretha (Rhodes) C.; m. Anne Diemer; Feb. 8, 1969; children: Elizabeth, Michael Dupree, Katherine Anne. BA, Drake U., 1965; MA in Internat. Rels., U. London, 1975. Tchr., vol. U.S. Peace Corps, Tanzania, 1965-68; fgn. svc. officer U.S. Dept. State, Washington, 1969—; polit. officer U.S. Embassy, Lagos, Nigeria, 1969-71; internat. rels. officer U.S. Dept. State, Washington, 1971-74; dep. chief of mission U.S. Embassy, Maputo, Mozambique, 1975-78; staff dir. fgn. affairs com. subcom. on Africa U.S. Ho. of Reps., Washington, 1979-82; dep. polit. counselor U.S. Embassy, Lisbon, Portugal, 1982-86, dep. chief of mission Gaborone, Botswana, 1986-90; Am. amb. Am. Embassy, Kampala, Uganda, 1991-94, Am. amb. to Zimbabwe Harare, 1995-97; prin. dep. asst. sec. for African Affairs Dept. of State, Washington, 1997-99, U.S. amb. to Kenya Nairobi, Kenya, 1999—2003; sr. v.p. Nat. Def. Univ., 2003—. Contbr. to numerous Congl. Studies on Africa, also to book; author articles on Africa and refugees. Mem. NAACP, African Studies Assn. Baptist. Avocations: tennis, reading, cross country skiing, hiking, fishing. Office: Nat Def Univ Fort Lesley J McNair Washington DC 20319-5066

CARSON, JULIA M., congresswoman; b. Louisville, July 8, 1938; 2 children. Ed., Ind. U., 1960-62, St. Mary of the Woods, 1976-78. Mem. Ind. Ho. of Reps., Indpls., 1972-76, Ind. Senate, 1976-90, U.S. Congress from 7th Ind. dist. (formerly 10th), 1997—. Mem. fin. svcs. com., 1997—, Vets. Affairs com., 1997—. V.p. Greater Indpls. Prog. Com.; nat. Dem. committeewoman; trustee YMCA; bd. didrs. Pub. Svc. Acad. Recipient Woman of Yr. Ind. award, 1974, Outstanding Leadership award AKA, Humanitarian award Christian Theol. Sem. Mem. NAACP, Urban League, Nat. Coun. Negro Women. Democrat. Baptist. Office: 1535 Longworth HOB Washington DC 20515-1410

CARSON, KIRK, music educator; b. Wewoka, Okla., July 23, 1954; s. Richard Lynn Van Bover and Joreene Carson; widowed; 1 child, Steven Kirk II. MusB, Okla. City U., 1980, M in Performing Arts, 1985. Dir. choral activities We. Okla. State Coll., Altus, 1999—. Bd. dirs. Shortgrass Arts Coun., Altus, 2001—; founder, dir. Altus Youth Choir, 2000—02, Western Jazz Ensemble, Altus, 2001—. Mem.: Nat. Assn. Tchrs. Singing, Am. Choral Dir. Assn., Internat. Assn. Jazz Educators. Office: We Okla State Coll 2801 N Main Altus OK 73521 Home: 5511 Fox Hill Rd Parkville MO 64152 Personal E-mail: kirkcarson@yahoo.com.

CARSON, LINDA MARIE, elementary school educator; b. La Salle, Ill., Aug. 3, 1947; d. Francis Harold and Dorothy Groleau; m. Randolph William Carson, Aug. 20, 1971; children: Sean, Kevin, Bethany. BS in Edn., No. Ill. U., 1969, MS in Edn., 1978. Cert. elem. tchr., Ill. Elem. tchr. Dist. 300, Dundee, Ill., 1969-85; instr. ESL, Elgin (Ill.) Community Coll., 1986; tchr. Dist. 15, McHenry, Ill., 1986—. Instr. ACT rev. McHenry County Coll., Crystal Lake, Ill., 1991. Co-pres. Eastview Sch. PTO, Algonquin, Ill., 1981-82; pres. Algonquin Women's Club, 1987-89. Communist. Home: 631 Webster St Algonquin IL 60102-2869 Office: Valley View Sch 6515 W State Route 120 Mchenry IL 60050-7450

CARSON, MARGARET, human services administrator; d. Chief and Lena Mae Carson. Cert. dietian cooking Vigo County Health Dept., Ind., nurses tng. Vigo County Health Dept., Ind., CPR Vigo County Health Dept., Ind., home health Vigo County Health Dept., Ind.; RN Vigo County Sch. of Nursing, 1965. Home health nurse numerous; organizer variuos cmty. svc. projects with the sole purpose of ending hunger and poverty. Mem. regional bd. Los Angeles County Food Bank, Calif., 1998—2003; music dir., mem. choir 54th St. Seventh Day Adventist Ch., L.A., 1999—2002, dir. cmty. svcs. program. Recipient Cmty. Services Dir. of the Yr., L.A. City Cmty. Svc. Dept., 2001, Excellence in Serving Your Cmty., L.A. City Mayor's Office, 2002. Democrat. Seventh-Day. Avocations: serving her community, singing, fundrasing, interior decorating, catering for the less fortunate. Office: SDA Ch Cmty Svcs 1973 W 54th Street Los Angeles CA 90062-2610 Office Phone: 323-292-2762. Business E-Mail: office@54thstreetsda.org.

CARSON, SAMUEL GOODMAN, retired bank executive; b. Glens Falls, NY, Oct. 6, 1913; s. Russell M.L. and Mary (Goodman) C.; m. Alice Williams, Oct. 14, 1939; children: Russell L., Frances Elizabeth (Mrs. Thomas E. Brady Jr.), Mary Goodman (Mrs. John A. Fedderke), Kathryn Williams (Mrs. Robert Richards), Samuel Goodman. BA magna cum laude, Dartmouth Coll., 1934. With Aetna Life Ins. Co., 1934-68; with Toledo Trust Co., 1967-84, exec. v.p., 1968, pres., 1969-84, chief exec. officer, 1970-84, chmn., 1976-84; chmn., dir. Toledo Trustcorp, Inc., 1976-84, ret., 1984. Dir. Kiemle-Hankins Co., Plastic Technologies, Inc., Carson Assocs., Inc. Mem. Ottawa Hills Bd. Edn., 1954-66; pres. United Appeal Greater Toledo Area, 1969, campaign chmn., 1964; Bd. dirs., trustee Toledo chpt. ARC, 1950—, chmn., 1959-61; trustee Toledo Hosp., 1960—, v.p., 1963-65, pres., 1966-69; bd. dirs. Community Chest Greater Toledo, 1962-65, pres., 1965; pres. Boys' Club Toledo, 1961-64, trustee, 1957—; trustee Toledo Mus. Art, 1967—, sec.-treas., 1969, v.p., 1973-78, pres., 1978-80. Recipient Service to Mankind award Sertoma Club Toledo, 1965, Man and Boy award Boys' Clubs Am., 1966, Pacemaker of Yr. award U. Toledo Coll. Bus. Adminstrn. Alumni Assn., 1969 Mem. Toledo Area C. of C. (trustee 1961-62, 73-76, pres. 1974-75), Phi Beta Kappa, Phi Gamma Delta. Clubs: Rotarian, Toledo Country, Toledo. Lodges: Rotary. Republican. Congregationalist. Office: 425 Madison Ave Toledo OH 43604-1229

CARSON, SHARON LYNN, education educator; b. San Antonio, Texas, Dec. 4, 1959; d. Robert L. and Carol A. (Ashbaugh) Buckley; m. James F. Carson Jr., Mar. 7, 1981. BBA, Our Lady of the Lake U., 1986; MBA, S.W. Tex. State U., 1991. Head cashier Sommers Drug Store, San Antonio, Texas, 1977-81; store mgr. San Antonio Area Coun. of Girl Scouts, 1981-83; dept. head Winns Store Inc., San Antonio, 1983-86; merchandiser Western Auto Supply Co., San Antonio, 1986-87; instr. Palo Alto Coll., San Antonio, 1987-89; substitute tchr. San Antonio Ind. Sch. Dist., 1989-91. Instr., faculty advisor Palo Alto Coll., San Antonio, 1991, adj. faculty, 1991—, coord. workforce edn., 2002-. Coord. workforcw edn., 2002—; co-leader San Antonio Girl Scouts, San Antonio, 1987-88; Presbyn. Women of Mission Presbytery. Mem. Nat. Notary Assn. (com. for Holistic Grading PAC), Am. Mktg. Assn., Texas Jr. Coll. Tchrs. Assn., Palo Alto Faculty Senate, Our lady of the Lake Alumni Assn., Incarnate Word Coll. (fashion adv. com.), Tex. Assn. Coll. Tech. Educators, Girl Scout Alumni. Presbyterian. Avocations: sewing, crocheting, bowling, gardening, reading. Office Phone: 210-921-5167. Business E-Mail: carsonclan@yahoo.com.

CARSON, SOL KENT, artist, educator; b. Phila., June 7, 1917; s. Philip Pasach and Sarah Carson; m. Thelma Clearfield-Carson; 1 child, Kent Steven. Student, Zeckwer-Hahn Acad., Phila., 1937; BFA with honors, Temple U., 1944, BS with honors in Edn., 1945, MEd in Fine Arts with distinction, 1946, postgrad., 1957, NYU, 1958; PhD, U. Italy, 1960. Asst. Temple U., Phila., 1940—45, dir. dept. visual art, 1944—47, dir. dept. art Eckels Coll., 1946—55, prof., 1946—55; cons. art Bristol Twp. Sch. Dist., Pa., 1956—66; prof. art dept. Wis. State U., Superior, 1965; assoc. prof. art dept. Millerville State U., Lancaster, Pa., 1966—79, assoc. prof. emeritus, 1979—. Mus. cons. U. Pa., 1945—46; art tchr. Phila. (Pa.) Bd. Edn., 1947—58; commn. Los Gatos (Calif.) Art Selection Panel. Represented in permanent collections Phila. Mus. Art Archives, Phila. Libr., Temple U., exhibitions include Mus. Modern Art, Acad. Fine Arts, Fed. Arts Galleries, Internat. League for Peace and Freedom, Tyler Galleries, Temple U., Millersville State Coll., Civic Ctr. Mus., Phila., Harrisburg State Bldg., Pa. Fellow, Temple U.; scholar, Barnes Found. Mem.: NEA, AAUP, Pa. State Ednl. Assn., Artist Equity, Assn. Higher Edn., Phi Delta Kappa. Achievements include development of Three new depts.: Visual Edu., Printmaking, Printmaking II, Temple U. Avocations: music, poetry. Home: 447 Alberto Way C128 Los Gatos CA 95032

CARSON, STEVEN DOUGLAS, science educator, biomedical researcher; b. Apr. 9, 1951; s. Harvey Arthur and Evelyn (Rule) C., Jr.; m. Sharon McLaren (div. 1985); 1 child, Shawn Kevin. BA, Rice U., 1973; PhD, U. Tex., Galveston, 1978. Asst. in chemistry EPA, Houston, 1972-73; rsch. asst. U. Tex. Med. Br., Galveston, Tex., 1973-78; rsch. assoc. Yale U., 1982, lectr., 1982-83; chemist pathology lab. VA, Denver, 1982-84; asst. prof. U. Colo. Sch. Medicine, Denver, 1982-88; assoc. prof. U. Nebr. Sch. Medicine, Omaha, 1988-93, prof., 1993—. Author rsch. papers, book chpt.; patentee in field. Recipient New Investigator award NIH, 1983, Rsch. Career Devel. award, 1988; fellow Robert Welch Found., 1970-72; grantee NSF, 1978-79, NIH, 1979-97, 2003, Am. Heart Assn., 1986, 97, 2001. Mem. AAAS, Am. Soc. Biochemistry and Molecular Biology, Am. Soc. Human Genetics, N.Y. Acad. Sci., Am. Heart Assn., Internat. Soc. Thrombosis and Haemostasis. Home: 12817 Chandler St Omaha NE 68138-6017 Office Phone: 402-559-4710. Personal E-mail: 73632.3623@compuserve.com. Business E-Mail: scarson@unmc.edu.

CARSON, STEVEN LEE, newspaper publisher; b. N.Y.C., Mar. 23, 1943; s. Harold and Mathilde (Seidel) C.; m. Yvonne DeDrozizhki, Aug. 8, 1971 (dec. Feb. 1980). BA, NYU, 1964, MA, 1965. Archivist, conf. dir. Nat. Archives, Washington, 1967—73; chmn. White House Conf. Pres. & Children, Washington, 1974; conf. dir. The Manuscript Soc., 1974—80; editor, writer Manuscript Soc. News, Washington, 1987—2003, The Lincoln Forum Bull., 2004—. Dir. history pavilion Hall of Fame Great Am., N.Y.C., 1964; editor Pres. Commn. Civil Disorders, Washington, 1968; mem. (charter) Hildene Robert Todd Lincoln estate; TV commentator; spkr. in field. Author: Maximilien Robespierre, 1988; (plays) The Last Lincoln, Princess Alice; contbr. articles to profl. jours. Speechwriter The White House, U.S. Congress, Md. Ho. Dels., 1974—; historian Rock Creek Cemetery, Washington, 1997—. Recipient NYU Heights Daily News Alumni award, 1964, medal, N.Y. Civil War Roundtable, 1969, Archival medal, Republic of Korea, 1972, Internat. Psychohistory Assn. award, 1983, Lincoln Group of N.Y. award, 1988, 1992, Man of the Month award, Washington Bus. Jour., 1989, Surratt Soc. award, 1993, delivered ofcl. Lincoln Day Address, Ford's Theatre, Washington, 1996, award, Rowfant Club, 1996, Smithsonian lectr., 1999—, delivered ofcl. Lincoln Day Address, Ford's Theatre, Washington, 2005; grantee, Md. Commn. Humanities, 1986, 1987, U.S. Dept. Interior, 1985; Ford Found. fellow, 1964, Johns Hopkins U. Chas Carroll Fulton fellow, 1965. Fellow:

The Manuscript Soc.; mem.: Washington Ind. Writers, Nat. Writers Union, Nat. Press Club, Walt Whitman Leaves of Grass Sesquicentennial Comn., U.S. Abraham Lincoln Bicentennial Com. (trustee 2003—), Abraham Lincoln Inst. (trustee 1997—), Lincoln Group D.C. (pres. 1985—88, Lincoln Recognition award 2003), Lincoln Forum (trustee 1997—), Lincoln Group III (trustee 1986—91), NYU Soc. of the Torch, NYU Perstare et Praestare, NYU Hon. Soc. Avocation: collecting historic manuscripts & letters. Office: 8811 Colesville Rd Ste 506 Silver Spring MD 20910-4332

CARSON, THOMAS BODE, bank executive, consultant; b. Washington, May 30, 1932; s. Thomas D. and Margaret (Bode) C.; m. Anne Conover; 1 child, Natalie Ambrose. BA, Princeton U., 1954; MA, Georgetown U., 1998. V.p. Chase Manhattan Bank, N.Y.C., 1960-68; sr. ops. officer Inter-Am. Devel. Bank, Washington, 1969-89; cons. Washington, 1990—. Author: Beyond the American Dream: Work and Wealth in the 21st Century, 1998. 1st lt. U.S. Army, 1955-57. Fellow Woodrow Wilson Found., 1955. Mem. World Future Soc. (lectr.), Met. Club Washington, Chevy Chase Club, Knickerbocker Club, Phi Beta Kappa. Democrat. Episcopalian. Avocations: futurism, classical music. Home: 3323 Nebraska Ave NW Washington DC 20016

CARSON, VAN, lawyer; BA, Mt. Union Coll., 1963; LLB, Duke U., 1966. Bar: Ohio 1966, registered: Supreme Ct. Ohio 1966, US Ct. Appeals (6th cir.) 1976, US Supreme Ct. 1981, US Ct. Appeals (7th cir.) 1993, US Ct. Appeals (DC cir.) 1993, US Dist. Ct., DC 1996. Ptnr. Squire, Sanders & Dempsey LLP, Cleve., chmn., Environ., Health & Safety Practice Group. Exec. com. mem. & vice chmn. of bd. dir. Ohio C. of C. Mem.: Ohio State Bar Assn. (environ. law com.), Cleve. Bar Assn. (environ. law com.), ABA (Litig. Sect.), Order of Coif. Office: Squire Sanders & Dempsey LLP 4900 Key Tower 127 Public Sq Cleveland OH 44114-1304 Office Phone: 216-479-8559. Office Fax: 216-479-8780. Business E-Mail: vcarson@ssd.com.

CARSON, VIRGINIA HILL, oil and gas executive; b. L.A., Dec. 4, 1928; d. Percy Albert McCord and Flora May (Newking) Schultz; m. John Carson, Dec. 30, 1950 (dec.). BA in Internat. Rels., U. Calif., Berkeley, 1949; postgrad., Stanford U., 1948, UCLA, 1951. Gen. office worker UN, San Francisco, 1949; ind. oil and gas profl. U.S., Can., Cuba, 1953-73; supr., specialist, Sun Exploration & Prodn. Co. (named changed to Oryx Energy Co.), Dallas, 1978-83, profl. analyst, 1983-92; lit. rschr. and freelance editor, 1992—. Mem. Dallas Coun. World Affairs, 1984-2003, Dallas Mus. Fine Arts, 1984—; vol. Reading and Radio Resources, 1992—. Nominated to pres.'s coun. Am. Inst. Mgmt., N.Y.C., 1974. Address: PO Box 12530 Dallas TX 75225-0530

CARSON, WALLACE PRESTON, JR., state supreme court justice; b. Salem, Oreg., June 10, 1934; s. Wallace Preston and Edith (Bragg) C.; m. Gloria Stolk, June 24, 1956; children: Scott, Carol, Steven (dec. 1981). BA in Politics, Stanford U., 1956; JD, Willamette U., 1962. Bar: Oreg. 1962, U.S. Dist. Ct. Oreg. 1963, U.S. Ct. Appeals (9th cir.) 1968, U.S. Supreme Ct. 1971, U.S. Ct. Mil. Appeals 1977; lic. comml. pilot FAA. Pvt. practice law, Salem, Oreg., 1962-77; mem. Oreg. House of Reps., 1967—71, majority leader, 1969—71; mem. Oreg. State Senate, 1971—77, minority floor leader, 1971—77; judge Marion County Cir. Ct., Salem, 1977-82; assoc. justice Oreg. Supreme Ct., Salem, 1982-92, chief justice, 1992—. Dir. Salem Area Community Council, 1967-70, pres., 1969-70; mem. Salem Planning Commn., 1966-72, pres., 1970-71; co-chmn. Marion County Mental Health Planning Com., 1965-69; mem. Salem Community Goals Com., 1965; Republican precinct commiteeman, 1963-66; mem. Marion County Rep. Central Exec. Com., 1963-66; com. predinct edn. Oreg. Rep. Central Com., 1965; vestryman, acolyte, Sunday Sch. tchr., youth coach St. Paul's Episcopal Ch., 1935—; task force on cts. Oreg. Council Crime and Delinquency, 1968-69; trustee Willamette U., 1970—; adv. bd. Cath. Ctr. Community Services, 1976-77; mem. comporehensive planning com. Mid-Willamette Valley Council of Govts., 1970-71; adv. com. Oreg. Coll. Edn. Tchr. Edn., 1971-75; pres. Willamette regional Oreg. Lung Assn., 1974-75, state dir., exec. com., 1975-77; pub. relations com. Williamette council Campfire Girls, 1976-77; criminal justice adv. bd. Chemeketa Community Coll., 1977-79; mem. Oreg. Mental Health Com., 1979-80; mem. subcom. Gov's Task Force Mental Health, 1980; You and Govt. Adv. Com. Oreg. YMCA, 1981—. Served to col. USAFR, 1956—59. Recipient Salem Disting. Svc. award, 1968; recipient Good Fellow award Marion County Fire Svc., 1974, Minuteman award Oreg. N.G. Assn., 1980; fellow Eagleton Inst. Politics, Rutgers U., 1971 Mem. Marion County Bar Assn. (sec.-treas. 1965-67, dir. 1968-70), Oreg. Bar Assn., ABA, Willamette U. Coll. Law Alumni Assn. (v.p. 1968-70), Salem Art Assn., Oreg. Hist. Soc., Marion County Hist. Soc., Stanford U. Club (pres. Salem chpt. 1963-64), Delta Theta Phi. Office: Oreg Supreme Ct Supreme Ct Bldg 1163 State St Salem OR 97310*

CARSON, WILLIAM MORRIS, manpower planning and development advisor; s. Edward Belmont and Frances Lucretia (Powell) C.; children: Lincoln Bruce Carson, Adrien Lee Allen, Anthony Lunt Carson, Karen Tracy Carson. BS, Columbia U., 1949; MA, Johns Hopkins U., 1951; postgrad., U. Chgo., 1955, London Sch. Econs., 1956; diploma in Arabic, Middle East Ctr. Arab Studies, 1969. Cairo corr. MBS, 1951-53; asst. prof. Mid. East Studies, SAIS, 1955-56; tng. officer U.S. AID, 1958-64; indsl. rels. staff analyst ARAMCO, Dhahran, Saudi Arabia, 1964-70; mgr. mgmt. deve. and tng. Saudi Arabian Airlines, Jeddah, 1970-72; chief tng. sect. UN Devel. Programme, N.Y.C., 1973-75; mgr. mgmt. devel. and tng. Sulvania Tng. Ops., Waltham, Mass., 1975-76; dir. tng. Ingersoll-Rand Constrn. Svcs., Winston-Salem, N.C., 1977-79; sr. advisor manpower planning and devel. Internat. Human Resources Devel. Corp., Boston, 1979-83; gen. mgr. ITECO divsn. Saudi Tng. Svcs., Riyadh, Saudi Arabia, 1983-84; mng. dir. Arab Resources Devel. Corp., Mass., 1984-87; mgr. Turkish tech. projects GE Internat. Svc. Corp., 1987-92; prin. Carson & Assocs., Balt., 1992-96, Nat. Manpower Strategies, 1997—. Cons. UN; Middle East Inst. fellow; Ford Found. area fellow. Co-author: International Manpower Planning: The Developing World, 1982; also articles. Recipient Outstanding Performance award AID. Fellow Royal Anthrop. Inst. Gt. Britain and No. Ireland, Inst. Comml. Mgmt.; mem. Ineamus Meloria Honor Soc. Address: 1908 C St Forest Grove OR 97116-2308 E-mail: wlmcrsn@prodigy.net.

CARSTAIRS, SHARON, legislator; b. Halifax, N.S., Can., Apr. 26, 1942; d. Vivian and Harold Connolly; m. John Esdale Carstairs, 1966; children: Catherine, Jennifer. BA in Polit. Sci. and History, Dalhousie U., 1962; MA in Tchg. of History, Smith Coll., 1963; postgrad., Georgetown U., 1964, U. Calgary, 1968; LLD (hon.), Brandon U., 2003. Tchr. Dana Hall Sch. for Girls, Wellesley, Mass., 1963-65, Calgary (Alta.) Separate Sch. Bd., 1965-71; chmn. bd. referees Unemployment Ins. Commn., 1973-77; tchr. St. John's Ravenscourt Sch., Winnipeg, Man., 1978-81, St. Norbert (Man.) Collegiate, 1982-84; elected leader Liberal Party in Man., 1984; elected mem. Man. Legis. Assembly, River Heights, 1986—; elected leader Ofcl. Opposition, 1988-90; apptd. to Senate, 1994—; apptd. dep. leader of the govt. in the Senate, 1997-99; leader of the govt. in the Senate, 2001—03; minister with spl. responsibility for palliative care, 2001—03. Scriptwriter, narrator Calgary and Region Ednl. TV, 1967-69. Brownie leader, Halifax and Winnipeg; mem. Parks and Recreation Bd., City of Calgary; fund-raiser Manitoba Heart Found.; canvasser Can. Cancer Soc., Alta., Man., Alta. Soc. for the Mentally Retarded; vol. Man. Mus. of Man and Nature; bd. mem. Women and the Arts, Nursing Coun. Man.; campaign worker provincial elections, Nova Scotia, 1948, 52, 56, 60; exec. positions Dalhousie U. Liberal Club, Nova Scotia, 1958-62; nat. exec. Univ. Liberals, Nova Scotia, 1960-62, others; poll capt. Fed. elections, Alta. 1965, 68, 72, 74; exec. Alta. Women's Liberal Assn., 1965-68; sec. Liberal Party, Alta., 1968-70, v.p., 1972-74, pres., 1975-77, nat. exec. 1975-77; Calgary Regional v.p., Liberal Party Alta., 1970-72; mem. Fed. Campaign com., Alta. 1972, 74, Man. 1983—; candidate Provincial Liberal, Alta. 1975; poll worker Ft. Rouge Provincial constituency, Man., 1977, Ft. Garry Fed. constituency, Man., 1979-80; office mgr, Tuxedo Provincial constituency, Man., 1981; exec., River Heights Provincial constituency, Man., 1983—; mem. Man. Legislative Assembly 1986—; elected leader Official Opposition, Man., 1988-90. Recipient Dalhousie U. Entrance scholarship, Dalhousie U. scholarship, Smith Coll. Grad. fellowship. Mem. Winnipeg C. of C. Liberal Party Can.

CARSTARPHEN, EDWARD MORGAN, III, lawyer; b. Ancon, Panama Canal Zone, Oct. 25, 1957; s. Edward Morgan and Norlavine (Carson) C.; m. Celia LaRae Rawlings Buchalski, June 3, 1979 (div. Apr. 1990); 1 child, Lucy Catherine; m. Darleen Colton, Aug. 29, 1991; 1 child, Desirae Dixon Peters. BA cum laude, Vanderbilt U., 1979; JD, U. Tex., 1982. Bar: Tex. 1982, U.S. Dist. Ct. (so. dist.) Tex. 1983, U.S. Ct. Appeals (5th cir.) 1984; cert. in civil trial law Tex. Bd. Legal Specialization. Assoc. Holtzman & Urquhart, Houston, 1982-84; briefing atty. to chief justice Tex. State Ct. Appeals for 6th Dist., Texarkana, 1984-85; ptnr. Brockway & Carstarphen, Houston, 1985-86, Powers & Carstarphen, Houston, 1987; of counsel Woodard, Hall & Primm, P.C., Houston, 1988-91, ptnr., 1991—2001. Contbr. articles to profl. publs., chpt. to book. Fellow Tex. Bar Found.; mem. State Bar Tex., Phi Delta Phi. Office: Ellis Carstarphen Dougherty & Goldenthal PC 720 N Post Oak Rd Ste 330 Houston TX 77024

CARSTEN, ARLAND LEON, radiobiologist, researcher, educator, consultant; b. Hastings, Minn., Apr. 17, 1930; s. John Peter Carsten and Alfreda Victoria Rydeen; m. Marcia Carsten; 1 child, Stephanie. BS, Minn. State U., 1953; MS, PhD, U. Rochester, 1957. Diplomate Am. Bd. Health Physics. Rsch. assoc. in neurology Columbia U., N.Y.C., 1964—74; from asst. scientist to sr. scientist Broohaven Nat. Lab., Upton, NY, 1957—. From adj. rsch. assoc. prof. to prof. of pathology SUNY, Stony Brook, 1971—. Contbr. articles to profl. jours. Mem. and bd. dirs. Bellport Beach Property Owners Assn., East Patchogue, NY, 1966—. Staff sgt. U.S. Army, 1950—51. Recipient Bausch & Lomb Sci. award, 1948; fellow in radiol. physics, Atomic Energy Commn. Mem.: L.I. (N.Y.) Am. Nuclear Soc. (exec. bd.), Internat. Soc. Exptl. Hematology (founding bd. mem.), Bioelectromagnetics Soc., Gentic Toxicology Assn., Environ. Mutagen Soc., Health Physics Soc., Radiation Rsch. Soc. (various coms.). Avocations: golf, tennis, skiing, sailing, music. Office: Brookhaven Nat Lab Bldg 703 Upton NY 11973

CARSTEN, JACK CRAIG, venture capitalist; b. Cin., Aug. 24, 1941; s. John A. and Edith L. C.; m. Mary Ellis Jones, June 22, 1963; children: Scott, Elizabeth, Amy. BS in Physics, Duke U., 1963. Mktg. mgr. Tex. Instruments, Dallas, Houston, 1965-71, integrated circuits gen. mgr. Houston, 1971-75; v.p. sales and mktg. Intel Corp., Santa Clara, Calif., 1975-79, v.p., microcomputer gen. mgr., 1979-82, sr. v.p., components gen. mgr., 1982-87; gen. ptnr. U.S. Venture Ptnrs., Menlo Park, Calif., 1988-90; venture capitalist Tech. Investments, Los Altos, Calif., 1990-99, Horizon Ventures LLC, Los Altos, 2000—. Bd. dirs. Comerica Bank-CA, and several privately held firms. Contbr. articles to profl.jours. Office: Horizon Ventures LLC 4 Main St Los Altos CA 94022-2998 E-mail: jack@carsten.com.

CARSTENS, JANE ELLEN, retired library science educator; b. New Iberia, La., Apr. 19, 1922; d. Charles John and Marie Claudia (Blanchet) C. BA in Elem. Edn., U. Southwestern La., 1942; BS in LS, La. State U., 1945; MS in LS, Columbia U., 1955, DLS, 1975. Asst. libr. Hamilton Lab. sch. and instr. libr. sci. U. Southwestern La., Lafayette, 1942-54, asst. prof., 1954-65, assoc. prof., 1965-75; children's librarian/storyteller N.Y. Pub. Libr., N.Y.C., 1947, 48-49; vis. lectr. U. Minn., Mpls., 1955-56, summer 59, La. State U., Baton Rouge, summer 1958, State Coll. Iowa, Cedar Falls, summer 1963; prof. libr. sci. U. Southwestern La., Lafayette, 1975-94. Vis. lectr. Syracuse U., summers 1962, 64, U. Tex., Austin, summers 1976-86, 89. Trustee Our Lady of Wisdom Cath. Ch., 1995-2005 Named Tchr. of Yr., Amoco, 1982, Outstanding Alumna, U. Southwestern La., 1986; recipient Essae Culver Disting. Svc. award La. Libr. Assn., 1987, Alumni Faculty Excellence award Blue Key, 1990, Faculty Advisor of Yr. award U. Southwestern La. Student Govt. Assn., 1992, Point of Excellence award Kappa Delta Pi, 1992, Outstanding Tchr. award USL Found., 1994; Blue Key Faculty/Student Staff Directory dedicated to her, 1994-95; Lifetime Achievement award, Coll. Edn.Chpt., ULI Alumni Assn., 2005. Mem. ALA, Assn. Libr. and Info. Sci. Edn., Assn. Libr. Svc. to Children (mem. Newbery award com. 1989-90), Am. Assn. Sch. Librs., La. Libr. Assn. (pres. 1959-60), Young Adult Libr. Svc. Assn., Lafayette Pub. Libr. Found., Univ. Women's Club, Phi Kappa Phi (pres. USL chpt. 1984-85), Delta Kappa Gamma (pres. Alpha chpt. 1988-90). Roman Catholic. Home: 214 Saint Joseph St Lafayette LA 70506-4535 also: ULL La Lafayette PO Box 40298 Lafayette LA 70504-0001

CARSTENS, MARILYN, freelance/self-employed music educator; b. Detroit, Feb. 24, 1930; d. Aldor John Carstens and Catherine Nettleton; m. Patrick Douglas Smiley, July 13, 1986; children: Joy Catherine, Carroll Lynn. BA, Holy Names U., 1987, MA in Culture and Creation Spirituality, 1988; cert. in Level 1 Orff Schlwerk, Ariz. State U., 1982; cert. in Level 2 Orff Schlwerk, U. Calif., Santa Cruz, Calif., 1983. Prin., owner Marilynn Carstens Music Studio, 1963—2005. Dir. choir sch. Christ Luth. Ch., Clarendon, Calif. Mem.: Nat. Guild The Am. Coll. Musicians, The Am. Coll. Musicians, Music Tchrs. Assn. Calif. (chmn. improvisation 1978—2004, transitional chmn. 2005). Office: Marily Carstens Music Studio 2449 Fairoak Ct San Jose CA 95125

CARSTENSEN, EDWIN LORENZ, retired biomedical engineer, retired biophysicist; b. Oakdale, Nebr., Dec. 8, 1919; s. August Hans and Opal Lois (Norwood) C.; m. Pam McDonald, Aug. 1, 1947; children: Richard Lorenz, Allen Brent, Laura Lee, Loretta Dee, Christina Marie. BS, Nebr. State Tchrs. Coll., 1941; MS, Case Inst. Tech., 1947; PhD, U. Pa., 1955. Mem. sci. staff div. war rsch. Columbia U., 1942-45; head lab. sect. U.S. Navy Underwater Sound Reference Lab., Orlando, Fla., 1945-48; rsch. assoc. Moore Sch. Elec. Engring., U. Pa., 1948-55, asst. prof. elec. engring., 1955-56; prin. investigator U.S. Army Biol. Lab., Fort Detrick, Frederick, Md., 1956-61; assoc. prof. elec. engring. U. Rochester, 1961-73, prof., 1973-88, Arthur Gould Yates prof. engring., 1988-90, Arthur Gould Yates prof. engring. emeritus, 1990—, dir. biomed. engring., 1971-83, prof. biophysics, 1981-90, univ. mentor, 1982—, sr. scientist in elec. engring., 1990—. Dir. Rochester Ctr. for Biomed. Ultrasound, 1986-90. Author: Biological Effects of Transmission Line Fields, 1987; contbr. numerous articles to profl. publs. Fellow Acoustical Soc. Am., IEEE, Am. Inst. Ultrasound in Medicine; mem. Biophys. Soc., Biomed. Engring. Soc., Nat. Acad. Engring. Democrat. Home: 103 Eastland Ave Rochester NY 14618-1027 Office: U Rochester Dept Elec/Computer Engring Rochester NY 14627 Personal E-mail: ecarsten@rochester.rr.com.

CARSTENSEN, FRED VERNON, economics educator; b. Seattle, Apr. 29, 1944; s. Vernon and Mary Buffum Carstensen; m. Mildred G. Eubanks, July 5, 1975; 1 child, Erin H. BA, U. Wis., 1966; MA, Yale U., 1969, PhD, 1976. Instr. U. Chgo., 1970—71, 1972—75; asst. prof. U. Va., Charlottesville, 1975—82; assoc. prof. U. Conn., Storrs, 1982—96, prof., 1996—, dir. Ctr. for Econ. Analysis, 1997—. Home: 3 Mallard Dr Bloomfield CT 06002-2227 Office: Dept Econ Rm 330 341 Mansfield Rd Storrs Mansfield CT 06269-1063 E-mail: fred.carstensen@uconn.edu.

CARSWELL, JANE TRIPLETT, retired family physician; b. Raeford, N.C., Feb. 26, 1932; d. Arthur Dula and Madeline Mapp (Warburton) C. Student, Flora Macdonald Coll., 1950-52; AB in Chemistry, U. N.C., 1954; MD, Med. Coll. Va., 1958. Diplomate Am. Bd. Family Practice. Resident Med. Coll. Va., Richmond, 1958-61; practice medicine specializing in family medicine Harlan, Ky., 1961-62, Lenoir, N.C., 1962—. Chmn. Lenoir Human Relations Com., N.C., 1962-64; vice-chmn. Caldwell County Council Status of Women, Lenoir, 1976-78 Mem. Caldwell County Med. Soc. (pres. 1965), N.C. Acad. Family Physicians (N.C. Family Physician of Yr. award 1983), N.C. Med. Soc., Am. Acad. Family Practice (Nat. Family Dr. of Yr. award 1984) Presbyterian. Avocations: hiking, backpacking, skiing, photography.

CARSWELL, LOIS MALAKOFF, agricultural products executive, consultant; b. N.Y.C., Mar. 2, 1932; d. Arthur and Dora (Krechevsky) Malakoff; m. Donald Carswell, Oct. 12, 1957; children: Anne Carswell Tang, Alexander, Robert Ian. AB magna cum laude, Radcliffe Coll., 1953; cert. in bus. adminstrn., Harvard U. and Radcliffe Coll., 1954. Editor Dell Pub. Co., N.Y.C., 1954-56; publicist Ruth E. Pepper Co., N.Y.C., 1957-58; vol. Bklyn. Botanic Garden, 1964—, co-chmn. plant sales, 1967—, co-chmn. capital campaign, 1984-88, chmn. bd. dirs., 1989-98, chmn. emeritus, 1998—. Chmn. Coalition Living Mus. N.Y. State, N.Y.C., 1980—; cons. N.Y. State Natural Heritage Trust, 1982—. Office: Bklyn Botanic Garden 1000 Washington Ave Brooklyn NY 11225-1008 Office Phone: 718-623-7225. E-mail: loiscarswell@bbg.org.

CART, JON ROBERT, music educator, musician; MusB, DePauw U.; MusM, Ind. U.; D of Musical Arts, U. Md., 2001. Chair dept. music and theater arts Shippensburg (Pa.) U., 2000—. Tchg. artist apprentice Domingo-Cafritz young artist program Washington Nat. Opera, 2004—. Mem. SHAPE, Shippensburg, 2000—02. Mem.: Coll. Music Soc. Avocations: swimming, bicycling, hiking. Office: Shippensburg U 1871 Old Main Dr Shippensburg PA 17257 Office Phone: 717-477-1638.

CARTAINO, CAROL ANN, editor; b. NYC, Dec. 7, 1944; d. Pietro Michael and Ann Wanda (Scotch) C.; 1 child, Clayton Collier-Cartaino. BA, Rutgers U., 1966; postgrad., NYU, 1967-68. Cert. English tchr., N.J. Prodn. editor trade book Prentice-Hall, Inc., Englewood Cliffs, N.J., 1966-68, from asst. to assoc. editor trade book, 1968-72, editor trade book, 1972-77; editor-in-chief Writer's Digest Books, Cin., 1978-86, freelance editor and collaborator, 1986—; editl. dir. Don Aslett, Inc., Pocatello, Idaho, 1987-93, Marsh Creek Press, Pocatello, Idaho, 1993—; assoc. Collier Assoc. Literary Agy., Seaman, Ohio, 1987-94; proprietor freelance editing and book cons. svc. White Oak Edits., 1987—; proprietor Carol Cartaino, Lit. Agt., 1994—. Speaker in field; instr. in writing So. State C.C., Hillsboro and Wilmington, Ohio, 1989—. Author: Keeping Work Simple, 1997, Get Organized, Get Published!, 2001. Vol. nurses aide Hackensack (N.J.) Hosp. State of N.J. scholar, 1962-66, Emerson (N.J.) PTA scholar, 1962. Roman Catholic. Avocations: hiking, photography, gardening, nature study. Home and Office: 2000 Flat Run Rd Seaman OH 45679-9412 Office Phone: 937-764-1303. E-mail: cartaino@aol.com.

CARTE, TRACI, information scientist, educator; PhD, U. Ga., 1999. Asst. prof. U. Okla., Norman, 1999—. Office: Univ Okla College of Business Norman OK 73019 Office Phone: 405-325-0741.

CARTER, ALICE T., journalist; b. Pitts., Dec. 18, 1946; d. Oliver Andrew and Mary Alice (Sample) Thompson; m. Roderick R. Carter, Oct. 31, 1970; children: Barker Thompson, Mary Alice BA in Liberal Arts, Western Coll. for Women, 1968. Prodr. Winter Theatre Co., Pitts., 1980-84; reporter, theater critic North Hills News Record, Cranberry, Pa., 1988-97; arts and entertainment writer Pitts. Tribune Rev., 1997-99, theatre critic, 1999—. Mem. Am. Theatre Critics Assn. Home: 119 Hawthorne Rd Millvale PA 15209-1915 Office: Pitts Tribune Review The DL Clark Bldg 503 Martindale St Pittsburgh PA 15212-5746 E-mail: acarter@tribweb.com.

CARTER, ASHLEY HALE, physicist, educator; m. Eva Horvath Carter; children: Deborah Anne, Sarah Judith, Ashley Hale, Jr. AB, Harvard Coll., 1946; PhD, Brown U., 1963. Rsch. assoc. Woods Hole Oceanographic Instn., Mass., 1946—47; dept. head AT&T Bell Labs., Whippany, NJ, 1953—90; adj. prof. physics Drew U., Madison, NJ, 1975—, dir. Charles A. Dana Rsch. Inst. for Scientists Emeriti, 1999—. Author: (book) Classical and Statistical Thermodynamics, 2001. Lt. (j.g.) USN, 1943—46. Mem.: Acoustical Soc. Am., Am. Assn. Physics Tchrs., Am. Phys. Soc. Democrat. Avocations: literature, art, music, essay writing. Office: Drew U Hall of Scis 322 Madison NJ 07940 Office Phone: 973-408-3687. Business E-Mail: acarter@drew.edu.

CARTER, BARRY EDWARD, law educator; b. LA, Oct. 14, 1942; s. Byron Edward and Ethel Catherine (Turner) C.; m. Kathleen Anne Ambrose, May 17, 1987; children: Gregory Ambrose, Meghan Elisabeth. AB with great distinction, Stanford U., 1964; MPA, Princeton U., 1966; JD, Yale U., 1969. Bar: Calif. 1970, DC 1972. Program analyst Office of Sec. Def., Washington, 1969—70; mem. staff NSC, Washington, 1970—72; rsch. fellow Kennedy Sch., Harvard U., Cambridge, Mass., 1972; internat. affairs fellow Coun. on Fgn. Rels., 1972; assoc. Wilmer, Cutler & Pickering, Washington, 1973—75; sr. counsel Select Com. on Intelligence Activities, U.S. Senate, Washington, 1975; assoc. Morrison & Foerster, San Francisco, 1976—79; assoc. prof. law Georgetown U. Law Ctr., Washington, 1979—89, prof., 1989-93, 96—, dir. internat. and transnational programs, 2005—; exec. dir. Am. Soc. Internat. Law, Washington, 1992—93; acting undersec. for export adminstrn. U.S. Dept. Commerce, Washington, 1993—94, dep. undersec., 1994—96; dir. Internat. and Transnational Programs, Georgetown U. Law Ctr., 2005—. Vis. prof. law Stanford U. Law Sch., 1990; bd. dirs. RWE Nukem, Inc., 1998—; chmn. adv. bd. Def. Budget Project, 1990—93; mem. UN Assn. Soviet-Am. Parallel Studies Project, 1976—87; adv. coun. Zurich Emerging Markets Solutions, 2001—. Author: International Economic Sanctions: Improving the Haphazard U.S. Legal Regime, 1988 (Am. Soc. Internat. Law Cert. of Merit, 1989); co-author: International Law, 4th edit., 2003; editor: Internat. Law: Selected Documents, 2005—; contbr. articles to profl. jours. With U.S. Army, 1969—71. Mem.: ABA, Am. Soc. Internat. Law (hon. v.p. 1993—99, counselor 1999—2000), Coun. on Fgn. Rels., DC Bar Assn., Calif. Bar Assn., Am. Law Inst., Am. Bar Found., Phi Beta Kappa. Democrat. Roman Catholic. Home: 2922 45th St NW Washington DC 20016-3559 Office: Georgetown U Law Ctr 600 New Jersey Ave NW Washington DC 20001-2075 Office Phone: 202-662-9322. Business E-Mail: carter@law.georgetown.edu.

CARTER, BETSY L., magazine editor; b. N.Y.C., June 9, 1945; d. Rudy and Gerda Cohn; m. Gary Hoenig. BA, U. Mich., 1967. Editorial asst. McGraw Hill, 1967—68; editor co. mag. Am. Security and Trust Co., 1968—69; editorial asst. Atlantic Monthly, 1969—70; researcher Newsweek, N.Y.C., 1971—73, asst. editor, 1973—75, assoc. editor, 1975—80; sr. editor Esquire Mag., N.Y.C., 1980—81, exec. editor, 1981—82, sr. exec. editor, 1982—83, editorial dir., 1983—85; creator, editor-in-chief New York Woman, N.Y.C., 1988; editor-in-chief New Woman mag., N.Y.C., 1994—97; founding editor-in-chief AARP's My Generation, 1999—2003. Author: (memoir) Nothing to Fall Back On, 2002, (novel) Orange Blossom Special, 2005; contbr. to Atlantic, Washington Post, Glamour, Oprah, New York mag. Mem.: Am. Soc. Mag. Editors (exec. com. 1988—91, v.p. 1997—). E-mail: bcarter@nyc.rr.com.

CARTER, BRUCE L.A., biotechnologist, director; BSc with honors in Botany, U. Nottingham, Eng.; PhD in Microbiology, Queen Elizabeth Coll., U. London. Lectr. Trinity Coll., U. Dublin, Ireland, 1975—82; head molecular genetics G.D. Searle & Co., Ltd., 1982—86; v.p. R&D ZymoGenetics, Seattle, 1986—88, pres., 1988—94, chmn. bd., 1994—98, pres., CEO, 1998—, chmn., 2005—, dir., 1987—; corp. exec. v.p., chief sci. officer Novo Nordisk A/S, 1994—2000. Office: ZymoGenetics Inc 201 Eastlake Ave E Seattle WA 98102-3702*

CARTER, C. MICHAEL, lawyer; b. Apr. 18, 1945; BS in Acctg., U. Calif., Berkeley, 1967; JD, George Washington U., 1973. Atty. Winthrop Stimson Putnam & Roberts; divsn. counsel Singer Co., 1981—83; sr. corp. counsel, asst. sec. R.J. Reynolds Inc., 1983—87; sr. v.p., opers., bd. mem. Concurrent Computer Corp., 1987—94; exec. v.p., gen. counsel, corp. sec. Pinkerton's, Inc., 1994—2000; sr. v.p., gen. counsel, corp. sec. Dole Food Co., Westlake Village, Calif., 2000—. Bd. dirs. Dole Food Co., Inc., Westlake Village, Calif. Bd. trustees George Washington U. Office: Dole Food Co One Dole Dr Westlake Village CA 91362 Business E-Mail: michael_carter@na.dole.com.

CARTER, CALVIN H., JR., materials engineer; married; 2 children. BS in Materials Engring., NC State U., 1977, MS in Materials Engring., 1980, PhD in Materials Engring., 1983. Co-founder Cree Inc. (formerly Cree Rsch. Inc.), Durham, NC, 1987—, exec. pres., dir., 1987—2000, dir. materials tech., 1987—. Recipient Nat. Medal of Tech. award, US Dept. Commerce, 2002. Office: Cree Inc 4600 Silicon Dr Durham NC 27703

CARTER, CHARLEATA A., cancer researcher, developmental biologist, cell biologist, toxicologist; b. Asheville, N.C., Dec. 6, 1960; d. Charles E. and Oleata J. Carter. BS in Biology, Mars Hill Coll., 1981; MA, Appalachian State U., Boone, N.C., 1983; PhD, Clemson U., 1988. Nat. Rsch. Svc. Award fellow U. N.C., Chapel Hill, 1988-91; Intramural Rsch. Tng. Award fellow Nat. Inst. Environ. Health Sci., Research Triangle Park, N.C., 1991-93; assoc. scientist Lovelace Biomed. & Environ. Rsch. Inst., Albuquerque, 1993-94, Nat. Ctr. for Toxicol. Rsch., Jefferson, Ark., 1994-95; asst. prof. dept. ob-gyn. U. Ark. for Med. Scis., Little Rock, 1995—. Dir. The Confocal Laser Scanning Microscope Facility, Ark. Cancer Rsch. Ctr., Little Rock, 1996—. Contbr. articles to profl. jours. Mem. Am. Soc. for Cell Biology, Am. Assn. Cancer Rsch., Metastasis Rsch. Soc., Sigma Xi (grantee 1986). Achievements include research in extracellular matrix and cytoskeletal structural alterations induced by oncogenes, chemicals and growth factor pathways and involvement of these protein alterations in tumorigenesis and metastasis, retinoid reversion of endometrial adenocarcinoma cells toward the normal, differentiated phenotype, developmental biology, toxicology and tumorigenesis in fish. Office: U Ark Med Sci Dept Ob-Gyn Slot 518 4301 W Markham St Little Rock AR 72205-7101

CARTER, CHARLES WILLIAMS, management consultant, management educator; b. Dobbs Ferry, N.Y., Jan. 24, 1922; s. Frederic Dewhurst and Betty Williams C.; m. Priscilla Gleason Carter, Nov. 11, 1944; children: Charles W. Jr., John Tower, Anne Timothy, Stuart Herrick, Mary Elizabeth. BE in Mech., Yale U., 1942. Profl. engr. Mass.; cert. mgmt. cons.; cert. quality and reliability engr. Engr. George S. Armstrong, Inc., N.Y.C., 1945-47; quality control engr. Bigelow-Sanford Cpt C., Thompsonville, Conn., 1947-52; staff cons. Rath & Strong, Inc., Boston, 1952-59; pres. Product Integrity Co., Enfield, Conn., 1959—. Adj. prof. mgmt. Rensselaer Polytech. Inst., Hartford, Conn., 1955-90; dir. Greenfield Components Corp., Mass., 1965-75, Kinematics Corp., Wareham, Mass., 1970-80, Allied Cmty. Svcs., Enfield, Conn., 1993—. Contbg. editor: Quality Control Handbook, 1962. With USNR, 1943-45, PTO. Fellow Am. Soc. Quality (Brumbaugh award 1952, Goldthwait award 1978, Scalise award 1995); mem. Rotary Internat. Avocations: music composing, arranging, conducting and singing, golf. Home: 49 The Laurels Enfield CT 06082-2355

CARTER, CRIS, retired professional football player, sportscaster; b. Middletown, Ohio, Nov. 25, 1965; Student, Ohio State U. With Phila. Eagles, 1987—89; wide receiver Minn. Vikings, 1990—2001; mem. Miami Dolphins, 2002; co-host Inside the NFL, 2002—. Named to Pro Bowl, 1993, The Sporting News NFL All-Pro team, 1994; recipient NFL Man of the Yr. award, 1999. Achievements include holding NFL single-season record for most pass receptions, 122, 1994.

CARTER, CURTIS LLOYD, museum director, aesthetics and philosophy educator, author; b. Moulton, Iowa, Oct. 1, 1935; s. Lloyd Joseph and Helen Edna (Wood) C.; m. Jean Elaine Watson, June 12, 1960; 1 child, Curtis Lloyd, Jr. BA, Taylor U., 1960; MDiv., Boston U., 1963, PhD., 1971. Instr. Marquette U., Milw., 1969-71, asst. prof., 1971-84, prof., 1984—, chmn. com. fine arts, 1975-84; dir. Haggerty Mus. Art, Marquette U., 1984—; chmn. Nat. Bicentennial Dance Conf., Cambridge, Mass., 1976; panelist, referee NEH Individual Research Project, Washington, 1983, Media Panel, Washington, 1984; chmn., speaker World Congress Aesthetics, Montreal, Can., 1984, Joyce and Vico Conf., Venice, Italy, 1985; advisor Bay View High Sch., Milw., 1982— . Gen. editor and essayist: (Art Mus. Catalogue) Selected Works, 1984. Contbr. articles and essays to profl. jours. and publs. Founding pres., bd. dirs. ARTREACH Milw., 1975—; v.p., bd. dirs. Charles Allis Art Mus., Milw., 1979—; bd. dirs. Music From Almost Yesterday, Milw., 1978—, Wis. Heritages, Inc., Milw., 1979—, Goals for Greater Milw. 2000, 1982—, Studio Watts Artist's Housing Project, Los Angeles, 1982—, Milw. Ctr. Photography, 1982— . Grantee Wis. Arts Bd., 1979, NEA, 1979, 80, 81, Inst. Mus. Services, 1982, 84, Mellon Found., 1982, Wis. Humanities, 1984, J. Paul Getty Trust, 1985. Mem. Am. Assn. Museums, Am. Philos. Assn., Am. Soc. for Aesthetics (nat. conf. chmn. 1980), Am. Dance Guild (chmn. nat. bicentennial dance conf. 1976, mem. nat. exec. com.), Hegel Soc. Am., Semiotics Soc. Am., Coll. Art Assn., Am. Assn. U. Adminstrs., Nat. Dance Critics Assn., Internat. Metaphysical Soc. (chmn.-speaker World Cong. Philosophy, Montreal, Can. 1983), Milw. Area Mus. Assocs. Avocation: travel. Home: 2609 E Menlo Blvd Milwaukee WI 53211-2649 Office: Haggerty Museum Art Marquette U 13th Clybourn Milwaukee WI 53233*

CARTER, CURTIS WILLIAM, communications executive; b. Cleve., Dec. 9, 1969; s. Vivian Marie Townsell; m. Janet Sue Schuesler, Oct. 14, 1999. BS in Bus. Mgmt., David N. Myers U., 1999. Pres. and owner Carter's Tax Svc., Bedford Heights, Ohio, 1993—97; prof. basketball player Can. Harlem Kings, Toronto, 1997—98; legal adminstr. Adv.'s Legal Ctr., Inc., Santa Ana, Calif., 1999—2002; profl. basketball player Sugar Land Sharks, Houston, 2002, KB Drita, Gjilan, 2003, Orange County Crush, Am. Basketball Assn., 2004—05; v.p. and bd. dirs. New Soul Records, Inc., Irvine, Calif., 2002—03; pres., CEO, chmn. of bd. Crossover Broadcast Network, Inc., Santa Ana, 2003—. Author: The Road to the NBA: The Other Side, vols. I and II, 2005. Mem.: Orange County Paralegal Assn., Songwriters Club of Am. (life). Avocations: writing, reading case law, sports, travel. Office: Crossover Broadcast Network Inc 2781 W MacArthur Blvd # B 608 Santa Ana CA 92704 Office Phone: 714-454-4424. Personal E-mail: ceocbn@aol.com.

CARTER, DANIEL PAUL, lawyer, educator; b. Massillon, Ohio, Mar. 22, 1948; s. Harry A. and Anna Jean (Steiner) C.; m. Regina Ranieri, July 9, 1983; children: Emily Hedges, Daniel Paul Jr., Anne Baldwin, Elizabeth Regina. BS, St. Joseph's Coll., Phila., 1971; JD, Villanova U., 1974. Bar: Pa. 1974, Ohio 2002, U.S. Dist. Ct. (ea. dist.) Pa. 1980, U.S. Ct. Appeals (3d cir.) 1981, U.S. Dist. Ct. (mid. dist.) Pa. 1985, U.S. Ct. Claims 1986, U.S. Dist. Ct. (we. dist.) Pa. 1989, U.S. Supreme Ct. 1991, U.S. Ct. Appeals (1st cir.) 1995, U.S. Dist. Ct. (no. dist.) Ohio 1996. Asst. prof. of law, dir. admissions Widener U., Wilmington, Del., 1974-79; ptnr. LaBrum & Doak, Phila., 1979-86, Shaffer, Palma, Dougherty & Carter, West Chester, Pa., 1986-87, Murphy & O'Connor, Phila., 1988-90; founding ptnr. Timby Brown & Timby, Phila., 1990-96; ptnr., head environ. dept. Buckley King LPA, Cleve., 1996—. Counsel jury study Delaware County, Media, Pa., 1976; adj. prof. law Widener U., 1984-89. Legal counsel Pa. Young Reps., 1977-78; regional legal counsel Young Rep. Nat. Fedn., 1978-79; chmn. Cuyahoga County Lawyers for Bush Cheyney, 2004; exec. com., fin. com. Cuyahoga County Rep. Party, 2004—. Named One of Outstanding Young Men of Am., Jaycees, 1979. Mem. NRA, Del. County Bar Assn., Phila. Bar Assn., Pa. Bar Assn. (vice-chmn. law sch. liaison 1981-82), Ohio Bar Assn., Ohio Assn. Civil Trial Attys., Cleve. Bar Assn., Def. Rsch. Inst. Republican. Episcopalian. Home: 30651 Brookwood Dr Pepper Pike OH 44124-5422 Office: Buckley King LPA 1400 Fifth Third Ctr 600 Superior Ave E Cleveland OH 44114-2652 Office Phone: 216-363-1400. Business E-Mail: carter@bucklaw.com.

CARTER, DAVID ALLEN, chemist, educator; b. Santa Fe, Aug. 30, 1958; s. Keith Delano and I. Darlene Carter; m. Gretchen Anne Carter, Feb. 27, 1988; children: Jonathan David, Rachel Anne, Autumn Belinda. BS, Wayland Bapt. Coll., 1980; PhD, U. Ariz., 1996. H.S. tchr. So. Bapt. Fgn. Mission Bd., Mombasa, Kenya, 1982—84; asst. prof. Okla. Bapt. U., Shawnee, 1994—2000, Angelo State U., San Angelo, Tex., 2000—. Grad. rsch. asst. Los Alamos (N.Mex.) Nat. Lab. Office: Angelo State Univ Dept Chemistry and Biochemistry San Angelo TX 76909 Office Phone: 325-942-2181. Personal E-mail: dacarter76-wwia@yahoo.com.

CARTER, DAVID GEORGE, SR., university administrator; b. Dayton, Ohio, Oct. 25, 1942; s. Richard Walter and Esther Mae (Dunn) C.; children: Ehrika Aileen, Jessica Faye, David George Jr. BS, Cen. State U., 1965; MEd, Miami U., 1968; PhD, Ohio State U., 1971. Cert. elem. tchr., Ohio. Prin. Dayton Pub. Schs., 1969-70, supr., 1970-71, unit facilitator, dist. supt., 1971-73; asst. and assoc. prof. Pa. State U., State College, 1972-77; assoc. dean and prof. edn. U. Conn., Storrs, 1977-82, assoc. v.p. acad. affairs, 1982-88; pres. East Conn. State U., Willimantic, 1988—. Corporator Liberty Bank, 1999—, dir., 2000—; chair bd. visitors Marine Corps Univ., 2003-04. Contbr. articles to profl. jours. Bd. dirs. New England Regional Exch., Framingham, Mass., 1981-86, Haitian Health Found.; mem. Gov.'s Task Force on Jail and Prison Overcrowding. Named Young Man of Yr. Dayton C. of C., 1973, Disting. Alumnus Ctrl. State U., Wilberforce, Ohio, 1988, Man of Yr., African Am. Affairs Commn., 2000—; inducted into Donald K. Anthony Achievement Hall of Fame Ctrl. State U., 1993; recipient Roy Wilkins Civil Rights award NAACP, 1994; 39th Americanism award Conn. Am. Legion, 1994; recipient Greater Hartford NAACP award of honor, 2001, Good Citizen award, Conn. Grand Lodge Order Sons of Italy in Am., 2001, Educator of Yr. award Greater Hartford Assn. of Negro Bus. and Profl. Woman's Club, 2003, Whitney M. Young Jr. Svc. award Urban Scouting Com. Conn. Rivers Coun. Boy Scouts Am., 2003. Mem. Nat. Orgn. Legal Problems of Edn. (bd. dirs. 1980-83), NCAA (chair pres.' commn. divsn. III 1995-97, pres.'s commn. 1991-97), Am. Ednl. Rsch. Orgn., Am. Coun. on Edn. (bd. mem. 1999-2005, exec. com. 2001-03, chair fin. and audit com. 2002-05), Am. Assn. State Colls. and Univs. (dir. 2001—, chair bd. dirs. 2002-03, chair elect 2002, past chair 2004), Internat. Assn. U. Pres. (chair N.Am. council 2004-05), Phi Delta Kappa, Pi Lambda Theta, Phi Kappa Phi, Sigma Pi Phi. Home: 9 Charles Ln Storrs Mansfield CT 06268-2308 Office: East Conn State U 83 Windham St Willimantic CT 06226-2211

CARTER, DAVID LAVERE, retired soil scientist, retired researcher, retired consultant; b. Tremonton, Utah, June 10, 1933; s. Gordon Ray and Mary Eldora (Hirschi) C.; m. Virginia Beutler, June 1, 1953; children: Allen David, Roger Gordon, Brent Ryan. BS, Utah State U., 1955, MS, 1957; PhD, Oreg. State U., 1961. Soil scientist USDA Agrl. Research Service, Corvallis, Oreg., 1956-60, research soil scientist, line project leader Weslaco, Tex., 1960-65; rsch. soil scientist USDA Agrl. Rsch. Svc., Kimberly, Idaho, 1965-68, supervisory soil scientist, rsch. leader, 1968-86, supervisory soil scientist, rsch. leader, dir., 1986-96; pvt. cons. Kimberly, 1992—2004; ret., 2002. Cons., adviser to many projects and orgns. Contbr. articles to profl. jours.; author, co-author books. Recipient Emmett J. Culligan award World Water Soc. Fellow Am. Soc. Agronomy (cert.), Soil Sci. Soc. Am. (cert.); mem. Soil Conservation Soc. Am. (Soil Conservation award 1985), Internat. Soc. Soil Sci., Western Soc. Soil Sci., Internat. Soc. Soil Sci., OPEDA. Mem. Lds Ch.

CARTER, DENNIS LEE, marketing professional; b. Louisville, Oct. 23, 1951; s. Bernard Lee and Opal Delores (Jaggers) C.; m. Janice Lea Herbert, Dec. 31, 1976; children: Serra Kimberly, Scott Winston. BSEE, BS in Physics, Rose Hulman Inst., Terre Haute, Ind., 1973; MSEE, Purdue U., 1974, DSc (hon.), 1996; MBA, Harvard U., 1981. Instr. elec. engring. tech. Purdue U., West Lafayette, Ind., 1975; collateral engr. Rockwell-Collins, Cedar Rapids, Iowa, 1975-76, design engr., 1976-79; product mktg. engr. Intel Corp., Santa Clara, Calif., 1981-83, software products mktg. mgr., 1983-85, tech. asst. to pres., 1985-89, end-user mktg. mgr., 1989-90, gen. mgr. end-user components divsn., 1990-91, dir. corp. mktg., 1991-92, v.p., dir. corp. mktg., 1992-98, v.p., dir. strategic mktg., 1998—. Inventor radio reception path monitor for a diversity sys., 1985. Episcopalian. Avocation: baseball.

CARTER, DENNIS R., music educator, band director, musician; b. Alton, Ill., Oct. 25, 1970; s. Sharrel L. and Shirley A. C. BM in Music Edn., Millikin U., Decatur, Ill., 1993; A in Fine Arts in Music, Lewis and Clark C.C., Godfrey, Ill., 1990. Band dir. Mt. Pulaski Cmty. Sch. Dist., Mt. Pulaski, Ill., 1993—95, Triad Cmty. Unit Sch. Dist. No. 2, Troy, Ill., 1995—. Mem.: Am. Fedn. of Musicians, Ill. Grade Sch. Music Assn. (pres. 2001—), Madison County Band Directors Assn. (pres. 2002—03), Ill. Music Educators Assn. (chmn. of jr. divsn. bands dist. VI 1999—2002). Home: 417 Washington East Alton IL 62024-1319 Office: Triad Mid Sch 9539 US Highway 40 Saint Jacob IL 62281 Personal E-mail: dcjazz1@charter.net. E-mail: dcarter@triad.madison.k12.il.us.

CARTER, DIXIE, actress; b. McLemoresville, Tenn. m. Hal Holbrook, May 27, 1984. Student, U. Tenn., Southwestern U., Memphis; B in English, Memphis State U. Actress: The Winter's Tale, Oklahoma!, Kiss Me Kate, Carousel, The King and I; broadway: Sextet, 1974, Pal Joey, 1976, The Master Class, 1997, Thoroughly Modern Millie, 2004; off broadway Fathers and Sons, (Drama Desk nomination), Jesse and the Bandit Queen (Theatre World award), A Coupla White Chicks Sitting Around Talking, Buried Inside Extra (TV series) One Life to Live, 1974, The Edge of Night, 1974-76, On Our Own, 1977-78, Out of the Blue, 1979, Filthy Rich, 1982-83, Diff'rent Strokes, 1984-85, Designing Women, 1986-93, Ladies Man, 1999, Family Law, 1999-2002; (films) The Killing of Randy Webster, (TV films) Gambler V: Playing for Keeps, 1994, Dazzle, 1994, Judith Krantz's Dazzle, 1995, Gone in the Night, 1996, Comfort and Joy, 2003; (instructional video) Dixie Carter's Unworkout, 1993; author: Trying to get to Heaven: Opinions of a Tennessee Talker, 1996. Avocations: family, singing.

CARTER, DONALD PATTON, retired advertising executive; b. Richmond, Mo., July 30, 1927; s. R. D. and Lillian (Patton) Carter; m. Susan Virginia Wurst, Apr. 22, 1950 (dec. Apr. 1980); children: Jeffrey, Stephen, Carol; m. Carol Holzrichter, Dec. 27, 1983. Student, U. Louisville, 1945-46; BS, U. Mo., 1948; MBA, U. Pa., 1950. With Continental Color Press, Inc., Kansas City, Mo., 1950-52; pres. Nasco, Inc., Kansas City, Kans., 1953-54; from v.p. to pres. Biddle Co., Bloomington, Ill., 1955-68; pres. Post Keyes Gardner Inc., Chgo., 1968-78, also bd. dirs.; chmn., pres. Cunningham & Walsh Inc., Chgo., 1978-83, exec. v.p. NY, 1978-83, also bd. dirs.; chmn. bd. dirs. Modu-line Industries, 1982-97; ret., 1997. Instr. econs. and bus. adminstrn. Kansas City (Mo.) Jr. Coll., 1950—52; trustee Thomson-McKinnon Mut. Funds, 1983—96, PIMCO Multi-Mgr. Mut. Funds, 1996—. With USNR, 1945—47. Named Young of the Yr., Jr. C. of C., 1961. Mem.: Bob O'Link Golf Club, Knollwood Country Club, Phi Kappa Psi. Home: 950 Gloucester Crossing Lake Forest IL 60045-4900

CARTER, EDWARD GRAYDON, editor; b. Canada, July 14, 1949; s. E.P. and Margaret Ellen Carter; 4 children; m. Anna Scott, May 21, 2005. Student, Carleton U., U. Ottawa. Editor The Can. Rev., 1973—77; writer Time, 1978—83, Life, NYC, 1983—86; founder, editor Spy, 1986—91; editor NY Observer, 1991—92; hon. editor Harvard Lampoon, 1989; editor in chief Vanity Fair, NYC, 1992—. Exec. prodr. (documentaries) 9/11, CBS, 2002; prodr.: (documentaries) The Kid Stays in the Picture, 2002; author: Vanity Fair's Hollywood, 2000, What We've Lost, 2004, Oscar Night: 75 Years of Hollywood Parties, 2004. Named Editor of Yr., Advertising Age, 1996, Adweek mag., 1997, 2003; recipient Nat. Mag. Award for General Excellence for magazines with circulation over 1,000,000, 1997, 1999, Nat. Mag. Award for Photography, 2000, 2002, Nat. Mag. Award for Reporting, 2000, Nat. Mag. Award for Reviews and Criticism, 2003. Mem.: Brook Club, Washington (Conn.) Club. Avocations: fly fishing, canoeing. Office: Conde Nast Media Group Vanity Fair Mag 4 Times Sq Fl 22 New York NY 10036-6522

CARTER, ELLIOTT COOK, JR., composer; b. N.Y.C., Dec. 11, 1908; s. Elliott Cook and Florence (Chambers) Carter; m. Helen Frost-Jones, July 6, 1939; 1 child, David. AB, Harvard U., 1930, AM, 1932, MusD (hon.), 1970, New Eng. Conservatory Music, 1961, Swarthmore Coll., 1956, Princeton U., 1967, Boston U., 1970, Yale U., 1970, Oberlin Coll., 1970, Cambridge (Eng.) U., 1983. Music dir. George Balanchine's Ballet Caravan, 1936—40; tchr. St. John's Coll., Annapolis, Md., 1940—42; cons. O.W.I., 1943—44; tchr. Greek and math.; tchr. music theory and composition Peabody Conservatory, Balt., 1946—48; dir., pres. Am. sect., Internat. Soc. Contemporary Music, 1946—52; assoc. prof. music Columbia U., N.Y.C., 1948—50, Queen's Coll., N.Y.C., 1955—56; tchr. Am. studies Salzburg (Austria) Seminars, 1958; lectr. music seminar Princeton (N.J.) U., 1959—60; prof. of composition Yale U., New Haven, 1960—62; Am. del. East-West Encounter, Tokyo, 1962; composer in residence Am. Acad. in Rome, 1963, 1967, Am. Sch., West Berlin, 1964; prof. of composition Julliard Sch. Music, N.Y.C., 1967—84; Andrew D. White Prof.-at-Large Cornell U., Ithaca, NY, 1967—68. Composer: (symphonies/orchestral) Symphony, Suite from Pocahontas, 1939 (Juilliard pub. award, 1940), Symphony No. 1, 1942, Holiday Overture, 1944 (1st prize Ind. Music Publishers Contest, 1945), Suite, From the Minotaur, 1947, Elegy, 1952, Variations for Orchestra, 1954—55, Double Concerto (Sibelius medal, 1961, Critics' Cir. award, 1961), Piano Concerto, 1964—65, Concerto for Orchestra, 1968—69, A Symphony of Three Orchestras, 1976, Penthode, 1984—85, A Celebration of Some 100 x 150 Notes, 1986, Oboe Concerto, 1988, Remembrance, 1988, Anniversary, 1989, Violin Concerto, 1990 (Grammy award Best Contemporary Composition, 1994), Allegro Scorrevole, 1996 (Prince Rainier Found. Music award, 1998), Clarinet Concerto, 1997, (symphony) Sum fluxae pretium spei, 1996, Asko Concerto, 2000, Cello Concerto, 2000 (commissioned by the Chgo. Symphony Orch.), Boston Concerto, 2002 (commissioned by Boston Symphony), Dialogues, 2003, Reflexions, 2004, (chamber/instrumental) Canonic Suite, 1939 (BMI pub. prize, 1945), Pastoral, 1940, Elegy, 1941, Piano Sonata No. 1, 1945—46, Woodwind Quintet, 1948, Cello Sonata, 1948, Eight Études and a Fantasy, 1949—50, Eight Pieces for Four Timpani/Recitative and Improvisation, 1950—66, String Quartet No. 1, 1950—51 (1st prize Internat. Quartet Competition, Liège, Belgium, 1953), Sonata, 1952, String Quartet No. 2, 1959 (Pulitzer prize for music, 1960, Critics'Cir. award, UNESCO award, Naumburg award, 1956), String Quartet No. 3, 1971 (Pulitzer prize for music, 1973), Canon for Three: In Memoriam Igor Stravinsky, 1971, Duo, 1973—74, Brass Quintet, 1974, A Fantasy About Purcell's Fantasia Upon One Note, 1974, Birthday Fanfare for Sir William Glock's 70th, 1978, Night Fantasies, 1980, Triple Duo, 1982—83, Changes, 1983, Canon for Four: Homage to William, 1984, Esprit rude/Esprit doux, 1984, Riconoscenza per Goffredo Petrassi, 1984, String Quartet No. 4, 1986, Enchanted Preludes, 1988, 1994, Con Leggerezza Pensosa (Omaggio a Italo Calvino), 1990, Scrivo in Vento, 1991, Quintet for Piano and Winds, 1991, Trilogy for Harp and Oboe, 1992, Gra for clarinet alone, 1993, Figment for cello alone, 1994, Fragment for string quartet, 1994, esprit rude/esprit doux II, 1995, String Quartet No. 5, 1995, more than 90 for piano, A Six-Letter Letter (for Paul Sacher's 90th Birthday) for English Horn alone, 1996, Luimen, 1997, Quintet for Piano and String Quartet, 1997, Tempo e tempi, 1999, Mosaic, 2004, (vocal, choral) My Love is in a Light Attire, 1928, Tarantella, 1936, Harvest Home, To Music, Let's Be Gay, Heart Not So Heavy As Mine, Tell Me Where is Fancy Bred?, The Defense of Corinth, 1941, Three Poems of Robert Frost, 1943, The Difference, The Harmony of Morning, 1944, Musicians Wrestle Everywhere, 1945, Emblems, 1947, A Mirror on which to Dwell, 1975, Syringa, 1978, In Sleep, In Thunder, 1981, Of Challenge and Of Love, 1995, Two Diversions for piano, 1999, (statement) Remembering Aaron, for violin alone, 1999, (fantasy) Remembering Roger for violin alone, 1999, Rhapsodic Musings for violin alone, 2000, (ballet) Pocahontas, 1936, The Minotaur, 1947, (opera) What Next?, 1998, (incidental music) Philocetes, 1931, Mostellaria, 1936. Trustee Am. Acad. in Rome. Named Commandeur dans l'Ordre des Arts et des Lettres, France, 1987, Commendatore in the Order of Merit of the Republic of Italy, 1991; recipient Am. Composers' Alliance prize, 1943, Acad.-Inst. award in Music, Am. Acad. and Inst. of Arts and Letters, 1950, Guggenheim fellowships, 1945, 1950, Prix de Rome, 1953, Harvard Glee Club medal, 1967, Gold medal, Am. Acad. and Inst. of Arts and Letters, 1971, Handel medallion, 1978, Ernst von Siemens Musik-Preis, Munich, 1985, MacDowell medal, 1983, George Peabody medal, 1984, Nat. Medal of Arts, Nat. Endowment for the Arts, 1985. Mem.: Acad. Santa Cecilia (Rome), Acad. der Kunste (Berlin), Am. Composers Alliance (bd. dirs. 1939—52, treas. 1949—50), Am. Acad. Arts and Scis., Nat. Inst. Arts and Letters, Internat. Soc. Contemporary Music (bd. dirs. 1946—52, pres. U.S. sect. 1952), League Composers (bd. dirs. 1939—52). Address: Boosey & Hawkes Inc 35 E 21st St New York NY 10010-6212

CARTER, EMILY ANN, physical chemist, researcher, educator; b. Los Gatos, Calif., Nov. 28, 1960; d. David and Rebecca (Blumberg) C.; m. Bruce E. Koel, 1994; 1 child, Adam. BS in Chemistry, U. Calif., Berkeley, 1982; PhD in Chemistry, Calif. Inst. Tech., 1987. Postdoctoral rsch. assoc. U. Colo., Boulder, 1987—88; asst. prof., physical chemistry UCLA, 1988—92, assoc. prof., 1992—94, prof., 1994—2002, prof. chemistry and materials sci. and engring., 2002—04; prof. mech. and aero. engring., applied and comp. math. Princeton U., 2004—. Mem. Def. Sci. Study Group, 1996-97; vis. scholar in physics Harvard U., 1999; cons. Inst. for Def. Analysis, 1998-, Los Alamos Nat. Lab., 2000-, mem. theoretical divsn. rev. com., 2000-05; vis. scholar in aeronautics Calif. Inst. Tech., 2001; UCLA dir. modeling and simulation Calif. Nano Systems Inst., 2000-04; McDowell lectr. U. B.C., 2002; Merck-Frosst lectr., Concordia U., 2005. Mem. editl. bd. Jour. Phys. Chemistry, 1995-00, Surface Sci., 1994-99, Ency. Chem. Physics and Phys. Chemistry 1996-01, Chem. Phys. Letters, 1998-, Phys. Chem. Comm., 1998-2002, Chem. Phys. Chem., 2000-, Jour. Chem. Phys., 2000-02, Modeling and Simulation in Materials Sci. and Engring., 2001-, SIAM Multiscale Modeling and Simulation Jour., 2001-; guest editor Jour. Phys. Chem., 1999-00; contbr. numerous articles to tech. jours; given over 260 invited lectures. Recipient rsch. innovation recognition awards Union Carbide Co., 1990, 91, New Faculty award Camille and Henry Dreyfus Found., 1988, Hanson-Dow award for excellence in tchg., 1998, others; NSF Presdl. Young Investigator award, 1988, Dreyfus Tchr. Scholar award, 1992, Alfred P. Sloan fellow, 1993, Internat. Acad. of Quantum Molecular Sci. medal, 1993, Exxon faculty fellow, 1993, Glen T. Seaborg Rsch. award, 1993, Herbert Newby McCoy Rsch. award, 1993, Peter Mark Meml. award Am Vacuum Soc., 1995, Dr. Lee vis. rsch. fellow Oxford U., 1996, UCLA Hanson-Dow award, 1998, UCLA Dean's Recognition award for rsch., 2002. Fellow AAAS, Am. Vacuum Soc., Am. Phys. Soc., Inst. of Physics; mem. Am. Chem. Soc., Material Rsch. Soc., Sigma Xi, Phi Beta Kappa. Democrat. Jewish. Avocations: theater, films, cooking, reading, tennis. Office: Princeton U Dept MAE E Quad Rm D404A Princeton NJ 08544-5263 Home: 34 Wellington Ct Belle Mead NJ 08502 Office Phone: 609-258-5391. Business E-Mail: eac@princeton.edu.

CARTER, FRANCES TUNNELL (FRAN CARTER), fraternal organization administrator; b. Springville, Miss. d. David Atmond and Mary Annie (McCutcheon) Tunnell; m. John T. Carter; children: Wayne, Nell Branum. BS, U. So. Miss., 1946; MS, U. Tenn., 1948; EdD, U. Ill., 1954. Elem. sch. tchr., Thaxton, Miss., 1942-43, Cumberland, Miss., 1943-44; tchr. high sch. home econs. Randolph, Miss., 1944-45, Maben, Miss., 1946-47; instr. Wood Coll., Mathiston, Miss., 1947—48, East Central Jr. Coll., Decatur, Miss., 1948-49; prof. home econs. Clarke Coll., Newton, Miss., 1950-56; prof. Samford U., Birmingham, Ala., 1956-84; editor, children and youth products and resources Woman's Missionary Union, Birmingham, 1983-85; pres. CarterCraft, Inc., Birmingham, 1985-89; nat. exec. dir. Kappa Delta Epsilon, Birmingham, 1987—2003. Vis. prof. Hong Kong Bapt. U., 1965-66, Anhui Normal U., People's Republic of China, 1987; medical/dental mission team mem. Honduras, Mex., 1983-; tchr. workshops in China, 1988, 90, 92, 95, 97, 2000; tchr. workshops in Indonesia, 1993; lectr. in symposium at invitation of Russian Edn. Ministry, Moscow, 1994, U. Nanjing, People's Republic of China, 1997; curriculum writer Bapt. Brotherhood Commn., 1986-90; writer N.Am. Mission Bd., 1995-98. Author: Sammy in the Country, 1960, Tween-Age Ambassador, 1970, Ching Fu and Jim, 1978; co-author: Sharing Times Seven, 1977, also short stories, articles; feature writer: Crusader Mag., 1986-95, The Current, 1987-2003; editor 103 Rosie Stories, 2001. Tchr. Sunday sch. Bapt. Ch., Birmingham, 1980—; mem., lt. col. CAP, 1968—, bd. dirs. Aerospace Edn. Ala. Wing, 1991-94, dir. pub. affairs regional S.E., 1994-95; v.p. Women's Civic Club of Birmingham, 1997-98, 2002-03; placement officer ESL Sch., 1995-98, pres., 1982-83, Test of English as a Fgn. Lang. tchr., 1998--. Recipient Career Achievement award Profl. Fraternity Assn., 1988, Outstanding Alumnae award Wood Coll., 1992, Outstanding award Kappa Delta Pi, 1992, Brewer award for Aerospace Edn. Southeast region CAP, 1994, Vol. of Yr. award Nat. Profl. Fraternity Assn., 1999, Lillian K. Keil award WWII Vets. Com., Washington, D.C., 2004; named Birmingham's Woman of Yr., 1977, Birmingham's Vol. of Yr., 1980, Silver rep. Dist. 6 Ala. Nat. Silver Haired Congress, 1991-96, Ala. Silver Haired Legislator Dist. 55 Jefferson County, 1996—, cert. Rosie the Riveter reunion, Little White House, Warm Springs, Ga., 1997; named to Sr. Citizen Hall of Fame, 2002. Mem. AARP (local pres. 1988-89, asst. state dir. 1989-93, Nat. Cmty. award 1992), Birmingham's Women C. of C. (pres. 1975-76, 2003-04), Nat. League Am. Pen Women (3rd v.p. 1988-90, nat. pres. 1994-96), Ala. League Pen Women (pres. 1970-72), Birmingham League Am. Pen Women (pres. 1968-70, 76-78), Ala. Writers Conclave (pres. 1978-79), Ala. State Poetry Soc. (pres. 1979-82), Ala. Federated Women's Clubs (dist. dir. 1988-90, Outstanding Woman of Ala. Club award 1988), Freedoms Found. Valley Forge (pres. Birmingham area chpt. 1990-91), Nat. Fellowship Bapt. Educators (sec. 1987-93), Birmingham Bus. and Profl. Club (pres. 1986-87), Am.

Rosie the Riveter Assn. Inc. (founder, pres. 1998-2003, nat. exec. dir. 2003—), Kappa Delta Epsilon (nat. pres. 1980-85, exec. dir. 1987-2003, co-dir. ESL Sch. 1994-98), Alpha Delta Kappa, Delta Kappa Gamma, Phi Delta Kappa (Nat. Profl. Fraternity Assn. award 1999, cert. emeritus 2000), Birmingham Civic Club (v.p. 2003-04), Birmingham Women's C. of C. (pres. 2003-04), Samford U. Retired Faculty Assn. (pres. 2004-) Home and Office: 3470 Loch Ridge Dr Birmingham AL 35216 Office Phone: 205-822-4106. Personal E-mail: fran.carter@juno.com.

CARTER, GENE, judge; b. Milbridge, Maine, Nov. 1, 1935; s. K.W. and S. Loreta (Beal) C.; m. Judith Ann Kittredge, June 24, 1961; children: Matthew G., Mark G. BA, U. Maine, 1958, LLD (hon.), 1985; LLB, NYU, 1961. Bar: Maine 1962. Ptnr. Rudman, Winchell, Carter & Buckley (and predecessors), Bangor, Maine, 1965-80; assoc. justice Maine Supreme Jud. Ct., 1980-83; from judge to sr. dist. judge U.S. Dist. Ct. Maine, 1983—2003, sr. dist. judge, 2003—. Chmn. adv. com. on rules of civil procedure Maine Supreme Jud. Ct., 1976-80. Chmn. Bangor Housing Authority, 1970-77. Mem. Am. Trial Lawyers Assn., Internat. Soc. Barristers, Am. Coll. Trial Lawyers. Office: US Dist Ct 156 Federal St Portland ME 04101-4152

CARTER, GENE RAYMOND, professional association executive; b. Staunton, Va. BA, Va. State U.; MA, Boston U.; EdD, Columbia U., 1973; LLD (hon.), Va. State U.; LittD, Old Dominion U. Various teaching and ednl. adminstrv. pos., 1960-92; exec. dir. ASCD, 1992—. Cons. various colls. and univs. Bd. dirs. Norfolk So. Corp.; mem. adv. bd. Edn. Commn. of the States. Recipient Brotherhood citation Nat. Conf. of Christians and Jews, 1985, Presdl. citation Nat. Assn. Equal Oppty. in Higher Edn., 1985, Outstanding Sch. Supt. in Va. in 1985 award John F. Kennedy Ctr. for the Performing Arts, 1985, Nat. Supt. of the Yr. award Am. Assn. Sch. Adminstrs., 1988, Annual Leadership for Learning award Am. Assn. Sch. Adminstrs., 1990, Disting. Alumni award Teacher's Coll. Columbia U., 1991. Office: ASCD 1703 N Beauregard St Alexandria VA 22311-1714 Home: 10910 Chatham Ridge Way Spotsylvania VA 22553 E-mail: gcarter@ascd.org.

CARTER, HARRY ROBERT, fire protection consultant; b. Neptune, N.J., July 29, 1947; s. Harry Barringer and Stella (Napiorkowski) C.; m. Jacalyn Roberta Miller, Apr. 29, 1972; children: Ellen, Kathleen, Todd. AA, Brookdale Coll., 1971; BA, Thomas Edison State Coll., 1975; BS magna cum laude, Jersey City State Coll., 1976; MA, Rutgers U., 1979; PhD, Western States U., 1984, Capella U., 2005. Fire fighter Rahway (N.J.) Fire Dept., 1972-73, Newark (N.J.) Fire Dept., 1972-77, fire capt., 1977-90, battalion fire chief, 1990-97, dep. to divsn., 1997-99, ret., 1999. Assoc. prof., Mercer County Coll., West Windsor, N.J., 1999—; adj. prof. Ocean County Coll., Toms River, N.J., 1977-81; pres. Carter Fire Protection, Inc., Adelphia, N.J., 1980—; fire marshal N.J. Army Nat. Guard, 1981-91. Author: Management in the Fire Service, 1989, Managing Fire Service Finances, 1989, Understanding Fire Behavior, 1995, Strategic Planning and Fire Protection, 1996, Tactics in Fire Department Management, 1997, Firefighting Strategy and Tactics, 1998, Management in the Fire Service, 3d edit., 1998, It's All About Me, 2002; contbr. articles to profl. jours. Vol. firefighter, officer Howell Twp. Fire Co. # 1, Adelphia, NJ, 1971—, tng. officer, 1978—91, fire chief, 1991; fire commr. fire dist. # 2 Howell Twp. Bd. Fire Commrs. Mem. ISFSI (bd. dirs. 1989-2001, pres. bd. dirs. 1999, chmn. bd. commrs.), N.J. Soc. Fire Instrs. (bd. dirs. 1978-80, pres. 1980-82), Nat. Fire Protection Assn. (adv. coun. 1975-90), Internat. Assn. Fire Chiefs (scholarship 1975-76), Internat. Assn. Fire Fighters, Wall-Spring Lake Lodge F & AM (past master), VFW, Am. Legion, Optimist Internat. Republican. Avocations: military music, playing the tuba, poetry, collecting military medals. Home: PO Box 100 Adelphia NJ 07710-0100

CARTER, HENRY MOORE, JR., retired foundation executive; b. Portsmouth, Va., Mar. 10, 1932; s. Henry and Debbie (McCoy) C.; m. Martha Rhea Greene, Aug. 21, 1954; 1 dau., Ann Clair. BA, Randolph-Macon Coll., 1953; MA, Vanderbilt U., 1954. Tchr. English, Norfolk County Public Schs., Portsmouth, 1954-59, head dept. English, 1957-59; headmaster Bollingbrook Sch., Petersburg, Va., 1959-66; dir. public relations Randolph-Macon Coll., Ashland, Va., 1966-68; dir. Randolph-Macon Fund, 1968-69, dir. devel., 1969-77; pres. Winston-Salem (N.C.) Found., 1977-97. Pastmem. adv. com. Kate B. Reynolds Trust for Poor and Needy; former chair bd. dirs. N.C. Ctr. for Nonprofits; former sec. Winston-Salem Campaign Coordinating Com. Past chmn., bd. dirs. coord. com. Winston-Salem Crime Stoppers; past chmn. Emergency Loan Fund, Southeastern Coun. Founds., N.C. Assn. Cmty. Founds., Forsyth Common Vision Coun., Old Salem Inc; past mem. adv. bd. Mary Baldwin Coll.; former sec.-treas. Twin City Devel. Corp; past chmn. bd.; past bd. dirs. Crosby Scholars Cmty. Partnership, Hospice Found., Forsyth Tech. Coll. Found.; ret. pres. Waccamaw Cmty. Found. Carnegie fellow, 1953-54. Mem. Litchfield Country Club, Rotary. Republican. Methodist. Personal E-mail: grants1sc@verizon.net.

CARTER, HERBERT EDMUND, retired university official; b. Mooresville, Ind., Sept. 25, 1910; s. George Benjamin and Edna (Pidgeon) C.; m. Elizabeth Winifred DeWees, Aug. 30, 1933; children— Anne Winsett, Jean Elizabeth. AB, DePauw U., 1930, ScD, 1952; AM, U. Ill., 1931, PhD, 1934, ScD, 1974, U. Ind., 1974, U. Ariz., 1984; LHD, Thomas Jefferson U., 1975. Instr. chemistry U. Ill., 1933-35, asso., 1935-37, asst. prof., 1937-43, asso. prof., 1943-45, prof., 1945-71, acting dean grad. coll., 1963-64, head dept. chemistry and chem. engring., 1954-67, vice chancellor for acad. affairs, 1967-71; coordinator interdisciplinary programs U. Ariz., Tucson, 1971-77, head dept. biochemistry, 1977-81; rsch. fellow Office Arid Lands Studies, 1981—, spl. asst. to v.p. rsch., 1984-90, coord. interdisciplinary programs, 1987-90. Mem. Pres.'s Com. on Nat. Medal of Sci., 1963-66; mem. nat. sci. bd. NSF, 1963-76, chmn., 1970-74; mem. Citizens Commn. Sci., Law and Food Supply.; Mem. exec. com. div. chemistry and chem. tech. NRC, 1949-55, 57-68 Mem. editorial bd. Bio Chem. Preparations; editor-in-chief, Vol. I.; contbr. to tech. pubIs. Trustee Assn. Univs. for Argonne, 1980-83, Nutrition Found., 1972-85. Awarded Rector Scholarship, Rector Fellowship DePauw U.; Eli Lilly & Co., Annual award ($1,000 and bronze medal to biochemist under 35 years of age showing promise in research), 1943; Am. Oil Chemists Soc. award in lipid chemistry, 1966 Mem. Am. Chem. Soc. (dir., asso. editor Bio-Chemistry 1961-67, William H. Nichols medal N.Y. sect., also Spencer award Kansas City sect. 1969), Am. Inst. Nutrition (sec. 1945-47), Am. Soc. Biol. Chemists (editorial bd. 1951-60, editorial com. 1963-66, pres. 1956-57), Nat. Acad. Scis. (chmn. section biochemistry 1963-66, mem. council 1966-69), Blue Key, Phi Beta Kappa, Sigma Xi, Phi Eta Sigma, Lambda Chi Alpha, Gamma Alpha, Alpha Chi Sigma. Democrat. Presbyterian. E-mail: hcarter@earthlink.net.

CARTER, HODDING, III, (WILLIAM HODDING CARTER), former foundation administrator, video specialist, commentator; b. New Orleans, Apr. 7, 1935; s. William Hodding and Betty Brunhilde (Werlein) C.; m. Margaret A. Wolfe, June 21, 1957 (div. 1978); children: Catherine Ainsworth, Elizebeth Fearn, William Hodding IV, Margaret Lorraine; m. Patricia M. Derian, 1978. BA, Princeton U., 1957; LLD (hon.), Stetson Coll., 1980, Kenyon Coll., 1984; LittD (hon.), Tusculum Coll., 1983; LLD (hon.), George Washington U., 1986, N.Y. Inst. Tech., 1987; LHD (hon.), U. Maine, 1985, U. San Diego, 1991, Millsaps Coll., 1998, U. SC, 2004. Reporter Delta Democrat-Times, Greenville, Miss., 1959-62, mng. editor, 1962-66, editor, pub., 1966-77; asst. sec. state for pub. affairs, dept. spokesman US Dept. State, Washington, 1977-80; vis. prof. Am. U., 1980; anchorman and chief corr. Inside Story, PBS, 1981-84; chief corr., exec. editor Capitol Jour., PBS, 1985-86; pres. MainStreet TV Prodn. Co., 1985-95; Knight chair in pub. affairs journalism U. Md., 1995-98; pres., CEO John S. and James L. Knight Found., Miami, 1998—2005. Vis. prof. Duke U., 1990; oper. editl. columnist Wall St. Jour., 1980-91. Author: The South Strikes Back, 1959, The Reagan Years, 1988; contbr. to books, newspapers and mags.; commentator on TV and radio; columnist Newspaper Enterprise Assn., 1992-95. Co-chmn. Young Dem. Clubs Miss., 1965-68; founding mem. Loyal Dems. of Miss., 1968; mem. Charter Commn. Dem. Party, 1973-74; del. Dem. Conv., 1968, 72, 76, Dem. Mini Conv., Kansas City, Mo., 1974; mem. campaign staff Johnson for Pres., 1964, Carter for Pres., 1976; mem. exec. com. So. Regional Coun., 1969-75, Miss. Dem. Party, 1976-79; trustee Princeton U., 1983-98; dir. Dreyfus Corp. Funds; bd. dirs. Century Found., Found. for the Mid South, Enterprise Corp. of the Delta, Ind. Sector; former chmn. Action Coun. for Peace in the Balkans, Am. Com. for U.S.-Soviet Rels. Recipient Editl. award, Soc. Profl. Journalists, 1961, Disting. Achievement award, U. So. Calif. Sch. Journalism, 1972, 4 Emmy awards for pub. affairs TV, 1984—85, Edward R. Murrow award for best fgn. documentary, 1984; Nieman fellow, Harvard U., 1965—66. Mem.: Pen/Am., Nat. Press Club, Coun. Fgn. Rels., Tarratine Club. Episcopalian.

CARTER, JAINE M(ARIE), human resources specialist, director; b. Chgo., Oct. 29, 1946; d. Bruno and Louise Kucinski; m. James Dudley Carter, Apr. 8, 1970; children: Paul, Todd. BS, Northwestern U., 1968; PhD, Walden U., 1988. Mgmt. cons. to bus., 1964—69; chmn. bd. Pers. Devel., Inc., Palatine, Ill., 1969—; dir. women's divsn. Lake Forest (Ill.) Coll. Advanced Mgmt. Inst., 1970—. Writer, lectr., tchr., cons. mgmt. devel. programs; faculty AMA; speaker weekly cable TV series Life Skills; pres. bd. dirs. Family Renewal Inst., 1991—96. Author: (book) How to Train for Supervisors, 1969, Career Planning Workshop for Women, 1975, Training Techniques That Bring About Positive Behavioral Change, 1976, Assertive Management Role Plays, 1976, Understanding the Female Employee, 1976, Rx for Women in Business, 1976, New Directions Needed in Management Training Programs, 1980, The Burnout of Retirement, 1983, Successfully Working with People, 1984, Assertiveness Training for Supervisors, 1985, Successfully Managing People, 1986, The New Success, 1986, Employee Assistance Program Handbook, 1988, Stay Out of Your Own Way-And Get the Job You Want, 1989, He Works/She Works-Successful Strategies for Working Couples, 1996; columnist: Scripps- Howard News Svc., Balancing Work and Family, 1996—2004; moderator, content expert (TV spl.) Commitment to Quality, Nat. Tech. U., 1989; author: (TV series) Executive Communications, 1988 prodr.: (TV series) Relationships, 1992; creator, prodr., host (TV series) Choices, 1992, 1993, host (radio talk show), 1992—96, columnist Scripps-Howard News Svc. He Works/She Works, 1996—, co-host (radio talk show) Your Own Business!, 1993—97. Mem.: Pres.'s Forum (exec.dir.), SAG, Am. Mgmt. Assn., AGVA, AFTRA. *People can only be free when they are able to take personal responsibility for their actions, turn their back on the expectations of others, and confidently pursue their own unlimited realitites.*

CARTER, JAMES C., apparel executive, lawyer; b. Pendleton, Oreg., Aug. 7, 1948; AB in economics, Stanford U., 1971; JD, U. Oreg., 1976. Bar: Oreg. 1976, US Fed. Ct. 1978. With Schulte Anderson Downes & Carter, Portland, Oreg.; gen. counsel US and Americas Nike, Inc., Beaverton, Oreg., 1998—2003, v.p., gen. counsel, 2003—, also chief legal officer. Mem.: Oreg. Assn. Def. Counsel. Office: Nike Inc 1 Bowerman Dr Beaverton OR 97005-6453

CARTER, JAMES CLARENCE, pastor, educator; b. N.Y.C., Aug. 1, 1927; s. James Clarence and Elizabeth (Dillon) C. BS in Physics, Spring Hill Coll., 1952; MS in Physics, Fordham U., 1953; STL in Theology, Woodstock Coll., 1959; PhD in Physics, Cath. U. Am., 1956. Ordained priest Roman Cath. Ch., 1958. Instr., asst. prof. Physics Loyola U., New Orleans, 1960-67, assoc. prof. of Physics, 1967—, v.p., 1970-74, pres., 1974-95, chancellor, 1995-2001; pastor Immaculate Conception Parish, New Orleans, 2001—04. Bd. dirs. Met. Area Com.; mem. higher edn. facilities com. State La., 1971-73, Am. Council's Commn. on Leadership in Higher Edn., 1975-78; bd. trustees Loyola U. Chgo., 1981-90; chmn. Mayor's Com. Ednl. Uses CATV, 1972. Contbr. articles to profl. jours. Mem. adv. com. New Orleans Pub. Library for the NEH Grant, 1975; bd. dirs. Greater New Orleans Area United Way, 1976-82, La. Ednl. TV Authority, 1977-83, 95-; bd. trustees Regis U., 1980-90, 94—, U. San Francisco, 1991-2000, St. Joseph's U., 1993—2004. Recipient Torch of Liberty award Anti-Defamation League of B'nai B'rith, 1983. Mem. Palmes Academiques, So. Assn. of Colls. and Schs. (exec. council of the commn. on colls.), Am. Phys. Soc., Am. Assn. Physics Tchrs., Assn. Jesuit Colls. and Univs. (chmn. acad. v.p. conf. 1971-74, chmn. 1991-94, exec. dir. 1996), Nat. Assn. Ind. Colls. and Univs. (bd. dirs. 1977-82), Am. Council Edn., Sigma Xi. Office: Loyola U New Orleans New Orleans LA 70118 Office Phone: 504-865-2168. E-mail: jcarter@loyno.edu.

CARTER, JAMES H., state supreme court justice; b. Waverly, Iowa, Jan. 18, 1935; s. Harvey J. and Althea (Dominick) C.; m. Jeanne E. Carter, Aug. 1965; children: Carol, James. BA, U. Iowa, 1956, JD, 1960. Law clk. to judge U.S. Dist. Ct., 1960-62; assoc. Shuttleworth & Ingersoll, Cedar Rapids, Iowa, 1962-73; judge 6th Jud. Dist., 1973-76, Iowa Ct. Appeals, 1976-82; justice Iowa Supreme Ct., Des Moines, 1982—. Office: Iowa Supreme Ct Judicial Branch Bldg 1111 E Ct Ave Des Moines IA 50319 Business E-Mail: james.carter@jb.state.ia.us.

CARTER, JAMES HAL, JR., lawyer; b. Ames, Iowa, Sept. 25, 1943; s. James H. Sr. and Louise (Benge) Carter; m. Theresa Carter; children: Janet, Faith, Katherine. BA, Yale U., 1965, LLB, 1969. Bar: N.Y. 1971, U.S. Ct. Appeals (2d cir.) 1971, U.S. Dist. Ct. (so. dist.) N.Y. 1972, U.S. Dist. Ct. (ea. dist.) N.Y. 1975, U.S. Supreme Ct. 1976, U.S. Ct. Internat. Trade 1980, U.S. Dist. Ct. Conn. 1981, U.S. Ct. Appeals (1st and 5th cirs.) 1984, U.S. Ct. Appeals (fed. cir.) 1988, U.S. Ct. Appeals (3d cir.) 1990, U.S. Dist. Ct. (no. dist.) N.Y. 1992, U.S. Dist. Ct. (we. dist.) Mich. 1992. Law clk., Hon. Robert Anderson U.S. Ct. Appeals (2d cir.), 1969-70; with Sullivan & Cromwell, LLP, N.Y.C., 1970—77, ptnr., 1977—. Lectr. internat. comml. arbitration Practicing Law Inst. Corr. editor: Internat. Legal Materials; contbr. articles to profl. jours. Mem. adv. bd. Ctr. for Am. and Internat. Law; bd. dirs. Am. Bar Found. Fulbright scholar, Cambridge (Eng.) U., 1965—66. Mem.: ABA (past chair internat. law and practice sect., former co-chmn. internat. comml. arbitration com.), Am. Arbitration Assn. (chmn. bd. dirs.), Coun. Fgn. Rels., Assn. Bar City of N.Y. (former chmn. internat. affairs coun.), N.Y. State Bar Assn. (former chmn. internat. dispute resolution com.), Am. Law Inst., Am. Soc. Internat. Law (pres. 2004—), U.S. Coun. Internat. Bus. (mem. com. arbitration). Office: Sullivan and Cromwell LLP 125 Broad St 32d Fl New York NY 10004-2498 Office Phone: 212-558-4000. Business E-Mail: carterj@sullcrom.com.

CARTER, JAMES HARVEY, psychiatrist, educator; b. Maysville, N.C., May 11, 1934; s. Thomas and Irene (Barber) C.; m. Jettie Lucille Strayhorn, Aug. 21, 1957 (dec. Sept. 1987); 1 child, James Harvey; m. Elsie Richardson, Aug. 26, 1988; 1 child, Saunia Carter-Wilson BS, N.C. Ctrl. U., Durham, 1956; MD, Howard U., 1966; MDiv, Shaw U., Raleigh, NC, 1999. Diplomate Am. Bd. Psychiatry and Neurology, Am. Bd. Forensic Examiners. Rotating intern Walter Reed Army Hosp., Washington, 1967; resident in gen. adult psychiatry Dorothea Dix/Duke Med. Ctr., Raleigh-Durham, N.C., 1969-70; assoc. dept. psychiatry Duke U., Durham, 1971-74, asst. prof., 1974-78, assoc. prof., 1978-83, prof., 1983—; sr. psychiatrist Dept. Correction, Raleigh, 1974—. Lectr. N.C. Found. for Alcohol and Drug Studies, U. N.C., Wilmington, 1989-95. Editor Epikrisis. Bd. dirs. Gov.'s Inst. on Alcohol and Substance Abuse, 1992-94; co-founder Drug Action of Wake County, Raleigh. Served to Col. M.C., U.S. Army, 1958-94. Decorated Order of Mil. Merit; recipient Profl. Designation A, U.S. Army Surg. Gen., 1985, Order of the Oak Leaf Pine Gov.'s award, 1999, Salomon Carter Fuller award, Am. Psychiatric Assn., 2003; E.Y. Williams clin. scholar, 1994; Josiah Macy Faculty fellow, 1970-74; Falk fellow, 1971-72. Fellow Am. Psychiat. Assn. (life; disting.; Solomon Carter Fuller award 2003); vice chair com. on chronic mental illness), Orthopsychiat. Assn.; mem. AMA, N.C. Med. Soc. (life), Alpha Kappa Mu, Alpha Omega Alpha. Achievements include founding of various drug awareness programs. Office: Duke U Med Ctr PO Box 3106 Durham NC 27715-3106 Office Phone: 919-684-6102. Office Fax: 919-681-7504. Personal E-mail: jcarter511@aol.com, jcarter511@bellsouth.net.com. Business E-Mail: carte049@mc.duke.edu.

CARTER, JANE FOSTER, agricultural industry executive; b. Stockton, Calif., Jan. 14, 1927; d. Chester William and Bertha Emily Foster; m. Robert Buffington Carter, Feb. 25, 1952 (dec. Dec. 1994); children: Ann Claire Carter Palmer, Benjamin Foster; m. Frank Anthony Bauman, Aug. 15, 1998 (div. Aug. 2003). BA, Stanford U., 1948; MS, NYU, 1949. Pres. Colusa (Calif.) Properties, Inc., 1953—; owner Carter Land and Livestock, Colusa, 1965—; pres. Sartain Mut. Water Co., Inc., 1992—2003, Carter Mut. Water Co. Inc., 2003—, J&B Rice Farms, Inc., Colusa, 1996—. Sec./treas. Carter Farms, Inc., Colusa, 1975—94, pres., 1994—2002; bd. dirs. Colusa Bean Growers, Inc., 1996—2002, sec., 1998—2002. Author: If the Walls Could Talk, Colusa's Architectural Heritage, 1988; author, editor: Colusa County Survey and Plan for the Arts, 1981—83, Implementing the Colusa County Arts Plan, 1984—86. Adv. mem. Calif. Gov.'s Commn. Agr., Sacramento, 1979—82; trustee Calif. Hist. Soc., 1979—89, regional v.p., 1984—89; mem. Calif. Reclamation Bd., 1982—96, sec., 1986—96; mem. Calif. Hist. Resources Commn., 1994—2001, vice chair, 1996—97, chair, 1997—99; mem. Colusa Heritage Preservation Com., 1976—2000, chmn., 1977—83, vice chmn., 1983—91, sec., 1997—2000; bd. dirs. Colusa Cmty. Theatre Found., 1980—99; trustee Calif. Preservation Found., 1989—95; del. Rep. Nat. Conv., Kans. City, Mo., 1976, Detroit, 1980, Dallas, 1984; mem. Calif. Rep. Ctrl. Com., 1976—94; bd. dirs. English-Spkg. Union U.S., N.Y.C., 1995—2001, English-Spkg. Union, San Francisco, 1992—, pres., 1993—95, v.p., 1995—; bd. dirs. Leland Stanford Mansion Found., Sacramento, 1992—; bd. dirs. Colusa County br. Am. Cancer Soc., 1960—86, chmn., 1964—86. Recipient award of Merit for Hist. Preservation, Calif. Hist. Soc., 1989, Design award, Calif. Preservation Found., 1990, Pres.'s award, 2001, Citizens award, English-Speaking Union U.S., 2002, Congl. Order Merit, Nat. Rep. Congl. Com., 2003. Mem.: Sacramento River Water Contractors Assn. (sec. 1992—2003, mem. exec. com. 1974—2003), Francisca Club (San Francisco), Kappa Alpha Theta. Episcopalian. Avocations: travel, the arts, historic preservation. Home and Office: 4746 River Rd Colusa CA 95932-4200

CARTER, JEAN GORDON, lawyer; b. Fort Belvoir, Va., July 30, 1955; d. Thomas Laney and Cleone (Hunter) Gordon; m. Michael L. Carter, Sept. 17, 1977; children: Christina Jean, William Gordon. BS magna cum laude with honors in Accountancy, Wake Forest U., 1977; JD with high honors, Duke U., 1983. Bar: N.C. 1983; CPA; bd. cert. specialist in estates. Acct. Arthur Andersen & Co., Charlotte, N.C., 1977-80; atty. Moore & Van Allen, Raleigh, N.C., 1983-90; ptnr. Hunton & Williams, Raleigh, N.C., 1990—. Mem. Am. Coll. Trusts and Estates Coun., N.C. Bar Assn., Wake County Estate Coun. (pres. 1991-92), Order of Coif, Phi Beta Kappa. Democrat. Presbyterian. Avocation: reading. Home: 3913 Stratford Ct Raleigh NC 27609-6351 Office: Hunton & Williams 1 Hannover Sq Ste 1400 Raleigh NC 27601-2947 Office Phone: 919-899-3088. E-mail: jcarter@hunton.com.

CARTER, JEANIE, performing company executive; b. Decatur, Ill., May 16, 1950; children: James L. Cook, Abigail G. Cook, Sarah E. Mason;. B in music, Millikin U., 1972. Cons. Hewitt Assoc., Lincolnshire, Ill., 1989—2000; vocal instr. Willow Creek Arts Ctr., South Barrington, Ill., 2002—03; pres., artistic dir. Bel Canto Studios, Barrington, Ill., 2001—. Voice lessons Clare Kittner, Northbrook, Ill., 1972—85, Willow Creek Arts Ctr., South Barrington, 2002—03; mem. Willow Creek, McHenry County vocal team, 2005. Composer: Footprints, 2002. Soprano soloist 1st Presbyn. Ch., Libertyville, Ill., 1972—92; vocal ministry Willow Creek Cmty. Ch., South Barrington, 2002—03. Mem.: Nat. Assn. Tchr.'s Singing, Music Tchr.'s Nat. Assn. Office: 217 Park Ave Barrington IL 60010 Office Phone: 847-382-2560, 847-682-9601. Business E-Mail: jeaniecarter@belcantostudios.com.

CARTER, JEANNE WILMOT, lawyer, publishing executive; b. Iowa City, Iowa, Oct. 25, 1950; d. John Robert and Adelaide Wilmot (Briggs) Carter; m. Daniel Halpern, Dec. 31, 1982; 1 child, Lily Wilmot. BA cum laude, Barnard Coll., N.Y.C., 1973; MFA, Columbia U., 1977; JD, Yeshiva U., N.Y.C., 1986. Bar: N.Y. 1987. Assoc. Raoul Lionel Felder, P.C., N.Y.C., 1986—; pres., co-owner, dir. Ecco Press, Hopewell, N.J., 1992—. Author: Dirt Angel, 1997, Tales from the Rain Forest, 1997; editor: On Music, 1994; contbr. articles to profl. jours. and books including Reading the Fights, N.Am. Rev., O'Henry Prize Stories 1986, Antaeus, Antioch Rev., Arts and Entertainment Law Jour., Ont. Rev., Denver Quar., Jour. Blacks in Higher Edn., others. Bd. dirs. Nat. Poetry Series, 1981—, AIDS Helping Hand, N.Y.C., 1987-95, Planned Parenthood of Mercer County, 1998—; vol. litigator Womanspace, Princeton, N.J., 1994; mem. Jr. League of N.Y.C., 1980-91; chmn. Princeton Alcohol and Drug Alliance, 2000—; pres. bd. Corner House Found., 2004—. N.Y. Found. of the Arts fellow, 1989. Mem. ABA, N.Y. State Bar Assn.

CARTER, JEFFREY RICHARD, music educator; b. New Orleans, La., July 17, 1961; s. Vincent Richard Carter and F. Marie Blocher. MA, Ctrl. Mo. State U., Warrensburg, 1996; D Musical Arts, U. Kans., Lawrence, 2000. Owner Carter Studios, Blue Springs, Mo., 1989—99; musical dir. The Jacomo Chorale, Blue Springs, Mo., 1990—99; asst. prof. music Ky. Wesleyan Coll., Owensboro, Ky., 1999—2000; asst. prof. music performance; dir. u. singers Ball State U., Muncie, Ind., 2000—, coord. undergraduate programs in music, 2004—. Youth and student activities chmn. Am. Choral Dirs. Assn. (Nat.), Okla. City, 2005—. Composer: (choral composition) Phos Hilaron (Opus Award (Mo. Choral Dirs. Assn.), 1999), The Oxen; contbr. articles pub. to profl. jour. Choirmaster Grace Episcopal Ch., Muncie, Ind., 2002—05; dir. music First Presbyn. Ch., Lawrence, Kans., 1997—99. Named Student Orgn. Outstanding Leader, Ball State U., 2005; grantee Enriching the Four-Year Choral Experience, Lilly Found./Ball State U., 2003-2005. Mem.: Elgar Soc., Music Educators Nat. Conf., Am. Choral Dir. Assn. (divisional bd. mem. 2004—05, Nat. Student Chpt. of Yr. 2005), Herbert Howells Soc., Pi Kappa Lambda, Phi Mu Alpha Sinfonia (hon.). Episcopal. E-mail: jrc@jeffreycarter.us.

CARTER, JEROME N., human resources specialist, paper company executive; With Union Camp Internat. Paper Co., Stamford, Conn., 1980—81, plant indsl. rels. mgr. to asst. divsn. mgr. indsl. and pub. rels., 1981—87, dir. indsl. rels., 1987—97, sr. v.p. human resources, 1999—. Spkr. in field. Office: Internat Paper Co 400 Atlantic St Stamford CT 06921 Office Phone: 203-541-8000.*

CARTER, JERRY WILLIAMS, digital artist, mosaicist, forensic art consultant; b. Wichita, Kans., Apr. 19, 1941; s. Jerry Williams and Dorrice (Snyder) C. Student, Sch. Chgo. Art Inst., 1968-69; BA, U. Md., 1968; student, L'Ecole Nat. Sup. Beaux Arts, Paris, 1970-71, Acad. di Belli Arti da Ravenna, Italy, 1971-72; student Dept. Interior Architecture, U. Helskinki, 1972-73; MFA, Antioch U., 1981. Art dir., designer ABC-TV, Washington, 1966-68; art tchr., lectr. various schs. U.S. and Finland, 1970-74; freelance artist, 1972—; pvt. practice as tech. forensic art adviser, 1984—. Artist-in-residence Iittala-Nuutajarui Glass Factory, Finland, 1989-91, Artistic Agy. of NSZZ Solidarnosc, Gdansk, Poland, 1990; dir. Human Rights Andri Sakharov Movement Project, Moscow. Prin. works include glass, mosaic and ceramic sculpture Vista Internat. Hotel, Wasington, glass collage Pinacotecca Comunale da Ravenna, metal sculpture Phillips Collection Washington, cast concrete and glass mosaic monument Second Genesis Am. Peace Monument Peace Park, Ravenna; exhbns. include Nat. Mus. Am. Art, Smithsonia, Washington, Assn. Moscow Artists, Georgian Cultural Ctr., Moscow; solo exhbn. Natcher Ctr., NIH, Bethesda, Md., 1997-98; represented in permanent collections Loggetta Lombardesca, Ravenna, Phillips Gallery, Washington, Kunstgewerbemus. der Stadt Köln, Germany, Nat. Finnish Glas Mus. Mem. scholarship rev. com. Finland and U.S. Senate Scholarship Youth for Understanding, Washignton, 1983. Recipient Ravenna medallion Mayor of Ravenna, 1984; Am. winner European Internat. Coun. on Monuments and Sites, Rome, 1984; grantee Art Barn Assn., 1984, Fulbright Italiana, 1984. Mem. Internat. Assn. Contemporary Mosaicists (U.S. rep., founding mem. bd. dirs.), Finlandia Found. (treas. 1981-82, cultural chmn. 1976-80, 82-83). Avocations: music, travel, reading, gardening, space probe collection. Office: 10602 Bucknell Dr Silver Spring MD 20902-4254

CARTER, JIMMY (JAMES EARL CARTER JR.), 39th President of the United States; b. Plains, Ga., Oct. 1, 1924; s. James Earl and Lillian (Gordy) C.; m. Rosalynn Smith, July 7, 1946; children: John William, James Earl III, Donnel Jeffrey, Amy Lynn. Student, Ga. Southwestern Coll., 1941-42, Ga. Inst. Tech., 1942-43; BS, U.S. Naval Acad., 1946 (class of 1947); postgrad., Union Coll., 1952-53; LLD (hon.), Morris Brown Coll., 1972, Morehouse

Coll., 1972, U. Notre Dame, 1977, Emory U., 1979, Kwansei Gakuin U., Japan, 1981, Ga. Southwestern Coll., 1981, N.Y. Law Sch., 1985, Bates Coll., 1985, Centre Coll., 1987, Creighton U., 1987; DEng (hon.), Ga. Inst. Tech., 1979; PhD (hon.), Weizmann Inst. Sci., 1980, Tel Aviv U., 1983, Haifa U., 1987; DHL (hon.), Cen. Conn. State U., 1985. Farmer, warehouseman, Plains, Ga., 1953-77; mem. Ga. Senate, 1963-67; gov. State of Ga., Atlanta, 1971-75; President of United States, 1977-81; disting. prof. Emory U., Atlanta, 1982—. Leader internat. observer teams Panama, 1989, Nicaragua, 1990, Dominican Republic, 1990, Haiti, 1990, Guyana, 1992, Venezuela, 1998, Nigeria, 1999, Indonesia and East Timor, 1999, Mexico, 2000, China, 2001, Jamaica, 2002, Guatemala, 2003; host peace negotiations Ethiopia, 1989; conflict mediator North Korea, Liberia, Haiti, Bosnia, Sudan, 1994, Sudan, Uganda, 1999, Venezuela, 2002-2003 Author: Why Not the Best?, 1975, A Government as Good as Its People, 1977, Keeping Faith/Memoirs of a President, 1982, Negotiation: The Alternative to Hostility, 1984, The Blood of Abraham, 1985, (with Rosalynn Carter) Everything to Gain: Making the Most of the Rest of Your Life, 1987, An Outdoor Journal, 1988, Turning Point: A Candidate, A State, and a Nation Come of Age, 1992, Talking Peace: A Vision for the Next Generation, 1993, Always a Reckoning, 1995, Living Faith, 1996, Sources of Strength: Meditations on Scripture for a Living Faith, 1997, The Virtues of Aging, 1998, An Hour Before Daylight: Memoirs of Rural Boyhood, 2001, Christmas in Plains: Memories, 2001, The Hornet's Nest: A Novel of the Revolutionary War, 2003, Sharing Good Times, 2004. Mem. Sumter County (Ga.) Sch. Bd., 1955-62, chmn., 1960-62; mem. Americus and Sumter County Hosp. Authority, 1956-70; mem. Sumter County (Ga.) Library Bd., 1961; chmn. congl. campaign com. Dem. Nat. Com., 1974; founder Carter Ctr. Emory U., 1982; bd. dirs. Habitat for Humanity, 1984-87; chmn. bd. trustees Carter Ctr., Inc., 1986—, Carter-Menil Human Rights Found., 1986—, Global 2000 Inc., 1986—; chmn. Coun. of Freely-Elected Heads of Govt., 1986—; chmn. Coun. Internat. Negotiation Network, 1991—. Served to lt. USN, 1946-53. Recipient Gold medal Internat. Inst. Human Rights, 1979, Internat. Mediation medal Am. Arbitration Assn., 1979, Martin Luther King Jr. Nonviolent Peace prize, 1979, Internat. Human Rights award Synagogue Coun. Am., 1979, Conservationist of Yr. award, 1979, Harry S. Truman Pub. Svc. award, 1981, Ansel Adams Conservation award Wilderness Soc., 1982, Disting. Svc. award So. Bapt. Conv., 1982, Human Rights award Internat. League for Human Rights, 1983, World Meth. Peace award, 1985, Albert Schweitzer prize for Humanitarianism, 1987, Edwin C. Whitehead award Nat. Ctr. for Health Edn., 1989, Jefferson award Am. Inst. Pub. Svc., 1990, Phila. Liberty medal, 1990, Spirit of Am. award Nat. Coun. for Social Studies, 1990, Physicians for Social Responsibility award, 1991, Aristotle prize Alexander S. Onassis Found., 1991, Félix Houphouet-Boigny Peace prize UNESCO, 1995, Nobel Peace prize, 2002. Democrat. Office: Carter Ctr 1 Copenhill 453 Freedom Pkwy NE Atlanta GA 30307-1406*

CARTER, JOHN BOYD, JR., retired oil industry executive, bank executive; b. Ft. Worth, Oct. 19, 1924; s. John Boyd and Enlie (Corder) C.; m. Susie Ann Browne, Feb. 9, 1946 (div. Dec. 1968); children: Catherine Browne Malone, John Mason; m. Winifred Trimble Runnells, Feb. 23, 1970 (div. Jan. 1987); m. Elizabeth Langston Bayless, Apr. 29, 1987. Student, Kemper Mil. Sch., 1941-43, U. Tex., 1943-46, Babson Coll., 1946-47. Mortgage loan supr. Am. Gen. Investment Corp., 1947; ind. oil operator, 1948-49; sec., treas. Tex. Fund, Inc., 1949-52, mem. investment adv. bd., 1951-58; pres. Tex. Fund Rsch. and Mgmt. Assocs., 1950-52; ind. oil operator and fin. cons., 1952-58; Southwestern rep. Lehman Bros., 1959-65, gen. ptnr., 1965-77, mng. dir., 1970-77; sr. v.p., dir. Pogo Producing Co., 1977-86; former chair bd. dirs. Houston Nat. Bank; dir. Sterling Bank. Chmn. bd. dirs. B.C.M. Tech., Inc.; pres., bd. dirs. High Prairie Ranch Co.; adv. bd. Technas Ventures, Austin, Tex. Trustee Baylor Coll. Medicine, Howard Florey Inst., Melbourne, Australia. Bd. dirs. Robert Kleberg Found., Pvt. Enterprise Rsch. Corp. Tex. A&M U., Tex. State Hist. Soc. Mem. Houston Country Club, U.S. Seniors Golf Assn., Bayou Club, Pilgrims Club (N.Y.C.), Brook Club (N.Y.C.), Sigma Alpha Epsilon. Home: 5422 John Dreaper Dr Houston TX 77056-4231 Office: 5757 Memorial Dr Houston TX 77007-8011 Office Phone: 713-868-5345.

CARTER, JOHN CHARLTON See HESTON, CHARLTON

CARTER, JOHN DALE, organizational development coordinator; b. Tuskegee, Ala., Apr. 9, 1944; s. Arthur L. and Ann (Bargyh) C.; m. Veronica Louise Helen Hopper, Oct. 12, 1986; children: Annelise Grace, Hopper Carter. AB, Ind. U., 1965, MS, 1967; PhD (NDEA fellow), Case Western Res. U., 1974. Dir. student affairs Dental Sch. Case Western Res. U., Cleve., 1974-75, asst. prof. applied behavioral sci., 1974-90, asst. dean orgn. devel. and student affairs, 1975-78; pres. John D. Carter and Assocs., Inc., Cleve., 1969—; ptnr. Portsmouth Cons. Group, 1984—. Chmn. bd. Gestalt Inst. Cleve., 1974-80, chmn. orgn. and systems devel. program, 1980—, program dir., fin. dir. 1981-86, dir. corp. svcs., 1989-95, dean of faculty, 1992-96; pres. Orgn. and Systems Devel. Ctr., 1996—; mem. exec. bd. Nat. Tng. Labs., 1975-78; faculty Am. U., 1980-90, 94-96; mem. Nat. Tng. Labs., 1976—; bd. dirs. Behavioral Sci. Found., Cleve., Orgn. Devel. Network, 1999—; exec. bd. Fielding Inst., 1987-89; preceptor Shri Ram Chandra Mission, Sahag Marg Meditation, 1993—; Gestalt Inst. Cleve., 1996—; bd. mem. ODN Orgn. Devel. Network, 1999—. Author: Counselling the Helping Relationship, 1975, Managing the Merger Integration Process, 1986, Institutionalizing Change, 1995. Hon. fellow Gestalt Inst. Cleve., 1999. Fellow Gestalt Inst. of Cleve. (hon.); mem. Internat. Assn. Applied Social Scientists (cert. cons. Internat.), Kappa Alpha Psi (pres. Alpha chpt. 1964-65), Alpha Phi Omega. Home and Office: 2232 Harcourt Dr Cleveland OH 44106-4622

CARTER, JOHN FRANCIS, II, lawyer; b. Washington, Dec. 21, 1939; s. John F. and Majorie (Thomas) C.; children: J. F. III, Marion; m. Catherine Dulany Turner, 2000. AB, Princeton U., 1963; JD, U. Tex., 1970. Bar: Tex. 1970, US Supreme Ct. 1977. Analyst Rotan Mosle, Houston, 1967-68; ptnr. Hutcheson & Grundy, Houston, 1970-90, mng. ptnr., 1990-94; sr. counsel Akin, Gump, Strauss, Hauer & Feld, Houston, 1996-98; atty. pvt. practice, Houston, 1998—. Mem. State Bar Grievance Commn., Houston, 1976-79; internat. sr. advisor to dep. sec. U.S. Dept. Energy, 1994-96. Co-author: Incorporation in Texas, 1980. Chmn. Tex. Arts Alliance, 1981-82, Mcpl. Art Commn., Houston, 1988-90; pres. Arts Coun., Houston, 1983-84; chmn., sec. Harris County Dem. Party, Tex., 1988-90; mem. host com. Econ. Summit, Houston, 1989-90; chair Planned Parenthood of Southeastern Va., 2005—; Capt. Spl. Forces, US Army, 1963-67, Panama, Vietnam. Named a Tex. Super Lawyer, 2003—; named one of Best Lawyers in Am., 1996—; recipient Cert. Outstanding Svc. award, US Dept. State, 1996. Mem. ABA (com. chair 1987-94), Houston Club, Tejas Breakfast Club, Univ. Cottage Club, Princeton Club N.Y., Phi Delta Phi. Avocations: music, ballet, history. Office: The Carter Law Office 3417 Milam St Houston TX 77002-9531 Office Phone: 713-724-5440. Personal E-mail: jackcarter@aol.com.

CARTER, JOHN LOYD, lawyer; b. Clayton, N.Mex., Oct. 2, 1948; s. John Allen and Ruth (Laughlin) C.; m. Dorel Susan Payne, Sept. 20, 1975; children: Matthew, Caroline, Susan. BA, So. Meth. U., 1970, JD cum laude, 1973. Bar: Tex. 1973, U.S. Ct. Appeals (5th and 11th cirs.) 1975, U.S. Ct. Appeals (D.C. cir.) 2004, U.S. Supreme Ct. 1976, U.S. Dist. Ct. (so. dist.) Tex. 1974, U.S. Dist. Ct. (no. dist.) Tex. 1978, U.S. Dist. Ct. (ea. dist.) Tex. 1985, U.S. Dist. Ct. (we. dist.) Tex. 1999. Assoc. Vinson & Elkins, Houston, 1973-80, ptnr., 1980—. Editor-in-chief: Southwestern Law Jour., 1972—73. Fellow Am. Coll. Trial Lawyers, Am. Bar Found., Tex. Bar Found., Houston Bar Found., Order of the Coif, Barristers. Office: Vinson & Elkins 2300 First City Tower Houston TX 77002-6760 Office Phone: 713-758-2124. E-mail: jcarter@velaw.com.

CARTER, JOHN RICE, congressman, lawyer; b. Houston, Nov. 6, 1941; s. John James and Elizabeth (Rice) Carter; m. Erika Theodora Van Bruegel, June 15, 1968; children: Gilianne, John, Theodore, Danielle. BA, Tex. Tech U., 1965; JD, U. Tex. Sch. of Law, 1969. Bar: Tex. 1969. Counsel Tex. Legis. Council, Austin, 1969—72; pvt. practice Round Rock, Tex., 1973—81; city judge, 1978—80; dist. judge Tex. Dist. 277, Georgetown, 1981—2002; mem. US Ho. of Reps. from 31st Tex. dist., 2003—, counsel, agr. com., 1973. Chmn. planning com., Round Rock, Tex., 1975—78. Mem.: Williamson County Bar Assn. (pres. 1976), Round Rock Jaycees (pres. 1975, Jaycee of Yr. 1975). Republican. Office: US Ho of Reps 408 Cannon Ho Office Bldg Washington DC 20515*

CARTER, JOHN ROBERT, retired physician; b. Buffalo, Apr. 21, 1917; s. John Harvey and Gertrude Ann (Buckpitt) C.; m. Adelaide Briggs, May 8, 1943; children— Marilyn Anne, Jeanne Catherine. BS, Hamilton Coll., 1939; MD, U. Rochester, 1943. Diplomate: Nat. Bd. Med. Examiners. Intern State U. Iowa, 1943-44, resident, 1944-48, asst. dept. pathology, 1944, from instr. to asso. prof., 1944-55, prof., 1955-59; prof., chmn. dept. pathology and oncology U. Kans. Med. Center, 1960-66; prof. pathology dept. orthopedics Case Western Res. U., Cleve., 1981—2001, dir. Inst. Pathology, chmn. dept. pathology, 1966-81; prof. emeritus, 1987—; ret., 1995. Cons. VA Hosp., U.S. Army Hosp., U.S. Penitentiary, Watkins Meml. Hosp.; Past chmn. pathology study sect. NIH; mem. pathology tng. grant com. Nat. Inst. Gen. Med. Scis.; mem. pathology adv. council Central VA Office; mem. sci. adv. bd. Armed Forces Inst. Pathology.; Bd. dirs. Univs. Asso. Research and Edn. Pathology; past pres. Mem. editorial bd.: Am. Jour. Pathology. Served to lt. USNR, 1946-48. Mem. AMA, AAAS, Cleve. Acad. Medicine, Path. Soc. Gt. Britain and Ireland, Am. Assn. Pathologists and Bacteriologists (past pres.), Internat. Acad. Pathology, Am. Soc. Clin. Pathology, Am. Soc. Exptl. Pathology, Am. Soc. Investigative Pathology, Coll. Am. Pathologists, Soc. Exptl. Biology, AAUP, Central Soc. Clin. Research, Phi Beta Kappa, Sigma Xi, Alpha Omega Alpha. Home: 36570 Ridge Rd Willoughby OH 44094-4106 Personal E-mail: jrcarter51@hotmail.com.

CARTER, JOHN SWAIN, museum director, consultant; b. Exeter, N.H., May 11, 1950; s. John F. C. and Ethel Mae Carter; m. Karin Carter, Aug. 8, 1978; 1 child, Elsbeth. BS in Psychology, U. Mass., 1973; MA in History of Tech., U. Del., 1979. Editor The Am. Neptune, Salem, Mass., 1979-82; curator Peabody Mus. Salem, 1979-82; dir. Maine Maritime Mus., Bath, 1982-89; pres. Phila. Maritime Mus., 1989-96, Independence Seaport Mus., 1996—. Vice chmn. Internat. Congress Maritime Mus., Oslo, 1987-93; bd. dirs. Phila. City Sail, Cushing Acad., 1999— Herreshoff Marine Mus., 1991-2003, Merchant's Fund, 1995-2003; bd. dirs. Springside Sch., v.p., 1996-98; bd. dirs. Pa. Fedn. Mus., 1997—, pres., 2002—. Author: Wood Book, 1980, (catalogs) Am. Traders, Maritime Arts, 1982. Mem. Am. Assn. Mus. (mem. coun. 1987-90), Coun. Am. Maritime Mus. (pres. 1986-90), Mus. Coun. Phila. (pres. 1991-93), Bostonian Soc., Union League, Corinthian Yacht Club, Phila. Cricket Club, Phila. Club, N.Y. Yacht Club, Cruising Club of Am., Edgartown Yacht Club, Royal Bermuda Yacht Club, Club Odd Volumes. Office: Independence Seaport 211 S Columbus Blvd Philadelphia PA 19106-3199

CARTER, JOHN TILTON, JR., lawyer; b. Bennettsville, S.C., Nov. 16, 1950; s. John Tilton Sr. and Jessie (Tucker) C.; m. Faye Keene, Sept. 2, 1977; children: John Tilton III, Karianne. AA, Wingate Coll., 1971; BA, U. N.C., Charlotte, 1973; JD, U. N.C., Chapel Hill, 1976. Bar: N.C. 1976, U.S. Dist. Ct. (ea. dist.) N.C. 1980; cert. family law specialist. Instr. paralegal law Fayetteville (N.C.) Tech. Inst., 1976-77; asst. dist. atty. State of N.C., Jacksonville, 1977-80; ptnr. Warlick, Milsted, Dotson & Carter, Jacksonville, 1980—. Sr. warden St. Anne's Episc. Ch., Jacksonville, 1986-87. Mem. N.C. Acad. Trial Lawyers, N.C. Bar Assn., Onslow County Bar Assn. (pres. 1991-92). Democrat. Avocation: crafting stained glass. Office: Warlick Milsted Dotson & Carter PO Drawer 766 320 New Bridge St Jacksonville NC 28540-4756

CARTER, JULIA MARIE, secondary school educator; b. Topeka, May 2, 1958; d. Jack Earnest and Bonita Aileen (Hatfield) Estes; m. Dan W. Carter; children: John-Thomas, Jessica Raye. BA, Ouachita Bapt. U., 1982; MBA, U. Phoenix, 2003; PhD candidate, Capella U. Cert. tchr. K-12, Ark., Fla., Md., Va., Pa., Mich., Ohio, Iowa. Tchr. French Dunbar Jr. High, Little Rock, 1989-91; tchr. Mt. Vernon (Ark.) Schs., 1991; tchr. French Cathedral Sch., Little Rock, 1991-92; tchr. St. Mark's Episcopal Sch., Oakland Park, Fla., 1992-93; tchr. French Miramar (Fla.) High Sch., 1993-96, Benjamin Franklin Sch., 1996—98, West Village Acad., 1999—2000, Detroit Public Sch., 2000—01, Bettendorf (Iowa) Pub. Schs., 2001—, Davenport (Iowa) Pub. Schs., 2003—. Owner Carter's Ednl. Svcs.; author, presenter in field. Vol. Chicot Elem., Little Rock, 1989-90, Silver Lake Mid. Sch., North Lauderdale, Fla., 1992-93, Miramar High Sch., 1993-95; mem. Ednl. Materials Equality Com., Little Rock, 1990-91. Fullbright scholar, 1989. Mem. Am. Assn. Tchrs. French (Prof. du Laureat 1989, 92), Am. Fedn. Tchrs. Democrat. Methodist. Avocations: travel, historic research, writing. Home: 3946 Madison St Dearborn Heights MI 48125-2156

CARTER, KENNETH CHARLES, geneticist; b. Flagstaff, Ariz., Nov. 28, 1959; s. James Frank and Norma (Barker) C. AA, AS, York Coll., 1980; BS in Biology, Abilene Christian U., 1983; PhD in Genetics, U. Tex. Med. Br., 1989. Grad. asst. U. Tex. Med. Br., Galveston, 1984-89; postdoctoral fellow U. Mass. Med. Sch., Worcester, 1989-93; scientist Human Genome Scis., Inc., Rockville, Md., 1993-98; pres. Internat. Genetics Assocs., Inc., Rockville, Md., 1998-99; CEO, pres. Avalon Pharms., Inc., Rockville, Md., 1999—. Contbr. articles to profl. jours. Recipient award for outstanding rsch. on aging Rose and Harry Walk Found., 1989, Muscular Dystrophy Assn., 1990, award for outstanding alumnus U. Tex. Med. Br., 1999; Kempner fellow J. B. Kempner Found., 1989, Human Genome fellow NIH, 1991. Mem. Am. Soc. for Cell Biology, AAAS, Microscopy Assn. Am., Thursday Group. Home: 10316 Cavanaugh Ct Rockville MD 20850-5401

CARTER, LA RAE DUNN, music educator; b. Salt Lake City, Oct. 17, 1932; d. Charles Oscar Dunn and Gretta Smith Haslam-Dunn; m. Ronald G. Carter, Aug. 7, 1956; children: Gary, Eric, Thomas, Jeffrey, John, Kristen, Karen, Shannon, Joseph. BA, Brigham Young U., 1954, MA, 1955; D in Musical Arts, Claremont U., 1996; cert. in tchr. edn., Boise State U., 1982. Music tchr. Boise Sch. Dist., 1954—56; vocal instr. Brigham Young U., Provo, Utah, 1956—57; music tchr. Nebo Sch. Dist., Springville, Utah, 1982—86; choral instr. Claremount (Calif.) Sch. Dist., 1987—99, chair fine arts depts., 1989—98; dir. choral activities Park City (Utah) H.S., 1999—, chair fine arts dept., 2001—. Dist. music team leader Park City Sch. Dist., 2001—03. Recipient Bravo award for the Arts, L.A. Music Ctr., 1996—97. Mem.: Utah Music Educators Assn., Music Educators Nat. Conf., Am. Choral Dirs. Assn., Utah Sch. Activities Assn. (region choral chmm. 1999—). Republican. Mem. Lds Church. Office: Park City High Sch 1750 Kearus Blvd Park City UT 84060 E-mail: rcarter@parkcityus.com.

CARTER, LINDA WHITEHEAD, oncological nurse, educator; b. Bluefield, W.Va., Dec. 20, 1941; d. Lee Joseph and Kathleen (Witherspoon) Whitehead; m. J. Stephen Carter, Mar. 11, 1961; children: Paul Scott, Kristin Hope. Student, Westmoreland Coll., Youngwood, Pa., 1980-83, St. Vincent Coll., Latrobe, Pa., 1984-85; BSN, Carlow Coll., Pitts., 1986; MSN, U. Pitts., 1992. RN Pa., cert. advanced oncology nurse, clin. nurse specialist. Oncology staff nurse Westmoreland Hosp., Greensburg, Pa., 1986-93, facilitator support group, 1988-93, oncology educator, 1990-93; clin. nurse specialist Magee Women's Hosp., Pitts., 1993-94; homecare nurse, 1996—; home care nurse U. Pitts. Med. Ctr. Home Care, Pitts., 1996-99; case mgr., 1996—. Faculty Carlow Coll. Divsn. Nursing, Pitts., 1993-97; grad. asst. Pitts. Cancer Inst., 1990; grad. clin. nurse specialist Allegheny Gen. Hosp., Pitts., 1991-92; nurse of hope Am. Cancer Soc., 1987, mem. pub. edn. com. Westmoreland Unit, 1987-88, mem. nursing edn. com., 1987-94, mem. profl. edn. com., 1990-93, bd. dirs., 1989-92. Mem. editl. rev. bd. Oncology Nursing Forum, 1994-98. Named Vol. of Yr., Am. Cancer Soc., 1988, Pa. Div. scholar, 1987, Nat. scholar, 1989-91. Mem. ANA, Pa. Nurses Assn., Nat. League for Nursing, Oncology Nursing Soc. (nominating com. Greater Pitts. chpt. 1990-91, newsletter com. 1992-93, chair awards com. 1997-2001, Found. liaison com. chair), Internat. Soc. Nurses in Cancer Care, Sigma Theta Tau. Home: 2922 Bryer Ridge Ct Export PA 15632-9393 E-mail: lcarter@prodigy.net.

CARTER, LUTHER FREDRICK, university president; b. Kenova, W.Va., May 30, 1950; s. Luther and Elaine (Jones) C.; m. Theresa Siskind, Dec. 18, 1975 (div. 1988); 1 child, Bryan; m. Florence Roach, Feb. 29, 1992; 1 child, Luke. BA, U. Ctrl. Fla., 1972; MPA, U. S.C., 1976, PhD in Polit. Sci., 1979; LHD (hon.), U. Charleston, 1992, Lander U., 1998, The Citadel, 2000. Assoc. prof. polit. sci. Coll. of Charleston, S.C., 1981-85, chmn. dept. polit. sci., 1985-87; sr. exec. asst. to gov. State of S.C., Columbia, 1987-91; exec. dir. S.C. Budget and Control Bd., Columbia, 1991-99; pres. Francis Marion U., Florence, S.C., 1999—. Rsch. fellow Nat. Def. U., 1983-84; mem. Pres. Com. on White House Fellowships, 2000-04; chief of staff to Gov. of S.C. sabbatical, 2003. Author: Personnel: Managing Human Resources, 1985; editor: Government in the Palmetto State, 1983, Mobilization and the National Defense, 1985, Government in the Palmetto State: Toward the 21st Century, 1993, The South Carolina Governor: The Emergence of an Institution, 2003. Active S.C. Humanities Coun., Columbia, 1988-94; trustee Winthrop U., Rock Hill, S.C., 1989-93, S.C. Ednl. TV Endowment, 2000—. 1st lt. USMC, col. USMCR. Recipient State Exec. award, Nat. Govs. Assn., 1999, Ralph Brown award, AAUP, 2002; fellow Rsch. fellow, Nat. Def. U., 1983—84. Mem. Am. Polit. Sci. Assn., So. Polit. Sci. Assn., Am. Soc. for Pub. Adminstrn., Southeastern Conf. on Pub. Adminstrn. (chmn. 1984, Pugliese award 1987), Am. Assn. U. Profs. (Ralph Brown award 2002), Fedn. German-Am. Club (Lvcius Clay medal 2004), S.C. C. of C.(Pub. Ofcl. of Yr. award 2003). Roman Catholic. Home and Office: Francis Marion U 4822 E Palmetto St Florence SC 29506-4530 Office Phone: 843-661-1210. E-mail: lcarter@fmarion.edu.

CARTER, LYNDA, actress, entertainer; b. Phoenix, July 24, 1951; m. Ron Samuels May 28, 1977 (div. 1982); m. Robert Altman Jan. 29, 1984; 2 children. Student, U. Ariz. Beauty and fashion dir. Maybelline Cosmetics; profl. motivational spkr. Actor: (TV series) Wonder Woman, 1976-79, Partners in Crime, 1984, Hawkeye, 1994, (TV films) The New Original Wonder Woman, 1975, A Matter of Wife...and Death, 1976, The Last Song, 1980, Born to Be Sold, 1981, Hotline, 1982, Rita Hayworth: The Love Goddess, 1983, Stillwatch (also exec. prodr.), 1987, Mike Hammer: Murder Takes All, 1989, Daddy, 1991, Posing: Inspired by Three Real Stories, 1991, When Friendship Kills, 1996, She Woke Up Pregnant, 1996, Family Blessings, 1996, A Prayer in the Dark, 1997, Someone to Love Me: A Moment of Truth Movie, 1998, Terror Peak, 2003, (films) Bobbie Jo and the Outlaw, 1976, Lightning in a Bottle, 1993, Super Troopers, 2001, The Creature of the Sunny Side Up Trailer Park, 2004, Sky High, 2005, The Dukes of Hazzard, 2005; singer: (album) Portrait, 1978. Hon. crusade chmn. Am. Cancer Soc., 1985-86; hon. chairperson Exceptional Children Found., 1987-88. Named Miss World-USA, 1972; recipient Hispanic Woman of Yr. award, 1983, Golden Eagle award, 1986. Office: William Morris Agy 151 S El Camino Dr Beverly Hills CA 90212-2775*

CARTER, MAE RIEDY, retired academic official, consultant; b. Berkeley, Calif., May 20, 1921; d. Carl Joseph and Avis Blanche (Rodehaver) Riedy; m. Robert C. Carter, Aug. 19, 1944; children: Catherine, Christin Ann. BS, U. Calif., Berkeley, 1943. Ednl. adviser, then program specialist div. continuing edn. U. Del., Newark, 1968-78; asst. provost women's affairs, exec. dir. status of women Office Women's Affairs, U. Del., 1978-86; mem. adv. bd. Rockefeller Family Grant Project, 1979-83. Regional v.p. Del. PTA, 1960-62; pres. Friends Newark Free Library, 1968-69; mem. fiscal planning com. Newark Spl. Sch. Dist., 1972. Author: Research on Seeing and Evaluating People, 1982, (with Geis and Butler) Seeing and Evaluating People, 1982, revised, 1986, (with Haslett and Geis) The Organizational Woman: Power and Paradox, 1992, also papers and reports in field. Recipient Outstanding Svc. award Women's Coordinating Coun., 1977, 79, Spl. Recognition award Nat. U. Extension Assn., 1977, award for credit programs, 1971, Creative Programming award, 1971, medal of distinction U. Del., 1998; AAUW grantee, 1968; Fulbright grantee, 1976; annual award named for returning Adult Students, 1988—, named to Del. Women Hall of Fame, 1995, professorship named for, in Women's Studies, 2003. Mem. AAUW (past br. pres.), LWV, NOW, Legal Momentum, Nat. Women's Polit. Caucus, Global Fund Women, Planned Parenthood, Freedom From Hunger, Population Comm. Internat. Democrat. Home: 604 Dallam Rd Newark DE 19711-3110

CARTER, MARJORIE JACKSON, special education educator, consultant; b. Moulton, Ala., Dec. 2, 1946; d. Johnnie Henry Stover and Marie Edith McDaniel; m. Youncy Pippin Carter, June 27; 1 child, Coreen Marie Diaz. BS in Edn., Slippery Rock (Pa.) U., 1968; MEd in Spl. Edn., U. Pitts., 1974. Cert. tchr. Pa., tchr. spl. edn., social studies, learning disabilities, mental retardation Fla. Spl. edn. tchr. Pitts. Bd. Edn., 1974—79; program specialist Fla. Atlantic U., Boca Raton, 1981—82; program dir. Ann Storck Ctr. for the Disabled, Ft. Lauderdale, Fla., 1982—83; tchr. spl. edn. Broward County Schs., Ft. Lauderdale, 1982—. Mem. com. Cmty. Action Plan, Ft. Lauderdale, 2000—; bd. dirs. Wiggins-Henry Found., Pembroke Pines, Fla., 2001—. Democrat. Baptist. Avocations: real estate investment, tutoring, aerobics. Office: Dillard HS 2501 NW 11th St Fort Lauderdale FL 33311

CARTER, MARSHALL NICHOLS, stock exchange executive; b. Newport News, Va., Apr. 23, 1940; s. Marshall Sylvester and Préot (Nichols) C.; m. Mary Meehan, June 20, 1964; children: Christina Ann, Marshall William. BSCE, U.S. Mil. Acad., 1962; MS in Ops. Rsch., Systems Analysis, USN Postgrad. Sch., 1970; MA in Internat. Affairs, George Washington U., 1976. Commd. 2d lt. USMC, 1962, advanced through grades to maj., 1975; served in Vietnam, 1966-67, 70-71; resigned, 1976; White House fellow US Dept. State, Washington, 1975-76; v.p. internat. dept. Chase Manhattan Bank, N.Y.C., 1976-78; dir. budgeting Chase Manhattan Corp., N.Y.C., 1978-81; product and prodn. risk mgmt. exec., div. exec. internat. trade procucts Chase Manhattan Bank, N.Y.C., 1981-84, sr. v.p. global securities svcs., 1988-91; exec. v.p. banking, sales and svcs. Chase Lincoln First Bank, Rochester, N.Y., 1985-88; pres., COO State St. Bank & Trust Co., Boston, 1991, CEO, 1992—2000, chmn., 1993—2001; fellow, Ctr. for Pub. Leadership Harvard U., 2001—05; chmn. N.Y. Stock Exch., NYC, 2005—. Chmn. bd. trustees, Boston Med. Ctr.; bd. dirs. NY Stock Exch., 2003-, Am. Bankers Assn., CEDEL, Euroclear & Nat. Securities Clearing Corp.; mem. exec. com. Livraison Valeurs Mobilieres, Luxembourg; co-chair, Working Group Group of Thirty, London, 1988-95; mem. Sinai peacekeeping surveillance del. Dept. State, 1975, mem. internat. relief efforts, Guatemala, Italy, Mali., 1975; chair, Mass. Gov.'s Spl. Advisory Task Force on Massport folowing the events of Sept. 11, 2001 Sr. coord. Tri-State United Way, N.Y.C., 1989. Col. USMCR, 1985. Decorated Navy Cross, Bronze Star, Purple Heart. Mem. Internat. Soc. Securities Adminstrs. Republican. Roman Catholic. Avocations: flying, tennis, skiing. Office: NY Stock Exch 11 Wall St New York NY 10005*

CARTER, MARY ANDREWS, paralegal; b. Greenville, S.C., Sept. 27, 1958; d. Harold M. Andrews and Mary Nancy Dollar; m. Donald P. Carter, Aug. 1, 1982 (div. Sept. 27, 1986); children: Christina Marie, Jason Paul. Diploma in paralegal, Greenville Tech., 1988. Paralegal Alan. O Campbell, P.E., Inc., Sullivan's Island, SC, 1995—99; pvt. practice, 1999—2001; paralegal Campbell, Schneider & Assocs., John's Island, SC, 2001—. Mem. adv. coun. Clark Acad., Charleston, 1998—2000; guardian, litem State of S.C., Charleston, 1999—2004. Office: Campbell Schneider and Assocs 3690 Bohicket Rd Ste 1D Johns Island SC 29455

CARTER, MICHAEL ALLEN, nursing educator; b. Springfield, Mo., Feb. 13, 1947; s. William Franklin and Mary Alyne Kelly; m. Sarah Ann Jennings, July 4, 1969; 1 child, Elizabeth Ruth. BS in Nursing, U. Ark., 1969, MS in Nursing, 1973; D of Nursing Sci., Boston U., 1979. Cert. family nurse practitioner. Instr. U. Ark., Little Rock, 1972-73; nurse practitioner VA Hosp., Bedford, Mass., 1974-75; asst. prof. Boston U., 1975-76, U. Colo., Denver, 1976-79, assoc. prof., 1979-82; prof., coll. dean U. Tenn., Memphis, 1982-2000, univ. disting. prof., 2000—. Chmn. Vis. Nurses Assn., Memphis. 1st lt. Nurse Corps, U.S. Army, 1969-71. Named Vol. of Yr. Salvation Army, Denver, 1978; recipient Better Life award Tenn. Health Care Assn., 1988.

Fellow Am. Acad. Nursing; mem. Nat. Acads. Practice (Disting. practitioner). Home: 369 Belmont Acres Cir Tumbling Shoals AR 72581 Office: U Tenn Coll Nursing 877 Madison Ave Memphis TN 38103-3408 Business E-Mail: mcarter@utmem.edu.

CARTER, NANETTE CAROLYN, artist; b. Columbus, Ohio, Jan. 30, 1954; d. Matthew Gameliel and Frances (Hill) C. BA, Oberlin Coll., 1976; MFA, Pratt Inst. of Art, 1978. Tchr. art Dwight Englewood Prep Sch., Englewood, NJ, 1978-87; profl. artist, 1987-92, CCNY, 1992-93; vis. lectr. Pratt Inst. of Art, Bklyn., 2001—. Artist-in-residence Triangle Workshop, Pine Plains, NYC, 1991. One-woman shows include Ericson Gallery, NYC, 1983, G.R. N'Namdi Gallery, Detroit, 1984, 86, 92-2002, Birmingham, Mich., 1989, 92, 96, 99, Chgo., 1999-2002, Cinque Gallery, NYC, 1985, Montclair (NJ) Art Mus., 1988, Jersey City (NJ) Mus., 1990, June Kelly Gallery, NYC, 1990, 94, 97, 2000, 04, Southampton (NY) Coll., 1991, Franklin Marshall Coll., Lancaster, Pa., 1992, Kebede Fine Arts, LA, 1992, Sande Webster Gallery, Phila., 1993, 95, 97, 99, 2001, 03, Alitash Kebete, LA, 1995, Hodges-Taylor Gallery, Charlotte, NC, 1997, Noel Gallery, Charlotte, N.C., 2004; exhibited in group shows at Bklyn. Mus., 1981, Newark Mus., 1985, Pa. Acad. Fine Arts, Phila., 1986, Clocktower Gallery, NYC, 1986, Associated Am. Artists Gallery, NYC, 1986, Wennigger Gallery Boston, 1987, Kenkelaba Gallery, NYC, 1987, Fashion Moda Gallery, Bronx, NY, 1988, Studio Mus. in Harlem, NY, 1988, Louisa McIntosh Gallery, Atlanta, 1990, Sande Webster Gallery, 1990, East Hampton Ctr. for Contemporary Art, NY, 1990, Space Gallery, Cleve., 1991, Mary Ryan Gallery, NYC, 1991, New Visions Gallery, Ithaca, NY, 1991, Bennington (Vt.) Coll., 1991, The Rifle Gallery, Columbus, Ohio, 1991, Bristol-Myers Squibb Co., Princeton, NJ, 1992, The Nat. Mus. of Woman in the Arts, Washington, 1992, The Paine Webber Art Gallery, NYC, 1993, Mus. Art, R.I. Sch. of Design, Providence, 1994, 98, Pratt's Inst.'s Manhattan Ctr., NYC, 1995, Skoto Gallery, NYC, 1995, Phila. Mus. Art, 1996, Wayne State U., Detroit, 1996, Pitts. Ctr. for Arts, 1996, W.Va. Wesleyan Coll., Buckhannon, 1996, Yale U. Art Gallery, New Haven, 1996, Spelman Coll. Mus. Fine Art, Atlanta, 1996, Rush Art, NYC, 1997, The Schomburg Ctr., NYC, 1998, Louis Ross Gallery, NYC, 1998, Nabisco, East Hanover, NJ, 1998, The Parish Art Mus., Southampton, NY, 1998, Elise Goodheart Gallery, Sea Harbor, NY, 1998, RI Sch. Design, Providence, 1998, Arlene Bujese Gallery, East Hampton, NY, 1999, Nat. Arts Club, NYC, 1999, Concordia Coll., Ann Arbor, Mich., 2000, Ark. Arts Ctr., Little Rock, 2000, Lambert Gallery, Atlanta, 2004, Rongio Gallery, Bklyn., 2004, and numerous others; represented in permanent collections Planned Parenthood, NYC, Jane Zimmerli Art Mus., Rutgers U., New Brunswick, NJ, Jersey City Mus., Libr. of Congress, Washington, ARCO, Phila., Reader's Digest, Pleasantville, NY, Schomburg Libr., NYC, Salomon Bros., NYC, Newark Mus., Herbert Johnson Mu., Art, Cornell U., Ithaca, NY, Studio Mus. Harlem, NY, MCI Telecomm., Chgo., Times Mirror, NYC, AT&T, NJ, IBM, Stamford, Conn., Lang Comm., Randolph, Vt., Merck Pharm. Co., Phila., Johnson & Johnson, Inc., New Brunswick, Pepsi-Cola, NYC, Motown Corp., L.P., LA, Am. Express, Mpls., Mus. Art RI Sch. Design, Providence, Yale Gallery of Art, New Haven, Conn., USA Assurance, San Antonio, Tex., Nextel Corp., LA, GE, Fairfield, Conn., Cochran Found., La Grange, Ga., Rutgers Grad. Sch. Mgmt., Newark, ARCO, Phila., Magic Johnson Enterprises, LA, Nissho Iwai Am. Corp., NYC, Pa. Acad. Fine Arts, Phila., Lucent Tech., Basking Ridge, NJ, Butler Inst. Am. Art, Youngstown, Ohio, Conkling Gallery, Minn. State Univ., Mankato, MN, 2002; Group shows: Jacktilton Gallery, NYC; Exhibit A Gallery, NYC; Pfizer Incorp., NYC, 2002; and numerous others. Grantee Nat. Endowment for Arts, 1981, The Jerome Found., 1981, NJ Coun. on Arts, 1985, NY Found. for Arts, 1990, The Pollock-Krasner Found., 1994, Wheeler Found., NYC, 1996, Fellowship, Lower East Side Printshop, NYC, 1997, Fellowship, Brandywine Workshop, Philadelphia, 1999

CARTER, NEVILLE LOUIS, geophysicist, educator; b. LA, Aug. 21, 1934; s. Herman Louis and Maribelle (Sheller) C.; m. Susan Ruth Orton, Aug. 1, 1987; children from previous marriage: James Neville, Lindsay Louis, Jenifer June. AB, Pomona Coll., 1956; MA, UCLA, 1958, PhD, 1963; postgrad. (Fulbright fellow), U. Oslo, Norway, 1958-59. Research assoc. Inst. Geophysics, UCLA, 1963; research geologist Shell Devel. Co., Houston, 1963-66; assoc. prof. geology and geophysics Yale U., New Haven, 1966-71; prof. geophysics SUNY-Stony Brook, 1971-78; prof., head dept. geophysics, faculty assoc. Ctr. for Tectonophysics, Tex. A&M U., College Station, 1978-83, dir., 1984-89; faculty assoc. Geodynamics Rsch. Inst., Tex. A&M U., 1984-96; prof. emeritus geology and geophysics Tex. A&M U., 1996—. Author, editor numerous publs. in field. Mem. Am. Geophys. Union (pres. tectonophysics sect. 1974-76), Sigma Xi. Home: PO Box 1442 Crescent City CA 95531-1442

CARTER, PEYTON FRANKLIN, III, accountant; b. NYC, Oct. 17, 1969; s. Peyton Franklin Carter, II and Elizabeth Ann Scott; m. Elizabeth Clayton Ketterson, Sept. 26, 1998; children: Parker Upshur, Peyton Franklin IV. BA in Polit. Sci., New Eng. Coll., 1994. Fund acct. State St. Bank & Trust, Boston, 1994—95, auditor, 1995—96, client svc. mgr., 1996—96, account mgr., 1997—99, corp. trainer, 1999—2001, acctg. officer, 2001—01; acctg. oversight mgr. Columbia Mgmt. Group - Fleet Bank, Boston, 2001—03; group mgr. Bisys Hedge Fund Svc., Boston, 2003—04; asst. contr. Anchorage Capital Group, NYC, 2005—. Author: Who Was Richard Brayne?, 2002, Hitherto Above Reproach, 2003, The Bartons' Quest For Liberty, 2003, The Carters of Amelia County, Virginia, 2003. Trustee New Eng. Coll., 2005; elected town meeting mem. Town Legislature, Brookline, Mass., 2000—02. Mem.: Soc. War of 1812 (v.p. 2002—03), Union Club Boston, SAR (asst. sec. 2000—03), Mason (jr. deacon 2004—). R-Liberal. Unitarian Universalist. Avocations: tennis, travel, musical composition. Home: 150 Southfield Ave #1136 Stamford CT 06902 Office: Anchorage Capital Group 650 Madison Ave 26th Fl New York NY 10022

CARTER, PHYLLIS LEIGH LIMBAUGH, secondary school educator; b. St. Louis, May 22, 1958; d. Leonard William and Wanda Louise (McGee) Limbaugh; m. Robert C. Carter, July 22, 1995; 1 child, Daniel Lee. BS in Secondary Edn., SE Mo. State U., 1980; MEd, U. Mo., St. Louis, 1982. Jr. high sch. tchr. math. Parkway Sch. Dist., Chesterfield, Mo., 1980-86, math. specialist, 1986-87, sr. high sch. tchr., 1987—, workshop presenter, 1986—, dept. chair, 1995—. Co-author: Pre-Algebra Mathematics, 1987. Chpt. 2 grantee, 1990-91. Mem. ASCD, Nat. Coun. Tchrs. Math., Mo. Coun. Tchrs. Math. (workshop presenter 1986, 89, 91), Math. Educators Greater St. Louis. Office: Parkway North High Sch 12860 Fee Fee Rd Saint Louis MO 63146-4498

CARTER, QUINCY, professional football player; b. Decatur, GA, Oct. 13, 1977; 2 children. Degree in edn., U. Ga. Quarterback Dallas Cowboys, 2001—04, N.Y. Jets, 2004—. Achievements include drafted by the Chicago Cubs (MLB) and spent 3 years in their farm system before turning to the NFL. Office: c/o New York Jets 1000 Fulton Ave Hempstead NY 11550

CARTER, RICHARD DUANE, finance educator; s. Herbert Duane and Edith Irene (Richardson) C.; m. Nancy Jean Cantrell, Sept. 3, 1955; 1 child, Erich Richardson. AB, Coll. William and Mary; MBA, Columbia U.; PhD, UCLA, 1968. Sr. advisor, dir. Taiwan Metal Industries Devel. Ctr. (under auspices of ILO), 1966-67; dir. UNDP, cons. svcs., Taiwan, 1966-67; chief exec. officer Human Resources Inst., Baton Rouge, 1968-70; liaison advisor Internat. Inst. Applied Systems Analysis, Vienna, 1975; U.S. rep., dir. indsl. mgmt. and cons. svcs. program UN Indsl. Devel. Orgn., Vienna, 1970-75; mem. East-West Trade and Mgmt. Commn., 1973-75; sr. advisor, dir. Korean Inst. Sci. and Tech. (under auspices of UN), Seoul, 1974-75; dean Sch. Bus. Quinnipiac Coll., Hamden, Conn., 1977-80; chmn. bd. TCG Industries, Inc., N.Y.C., 1980—; prof. mgmt., program coord. Fairfield (Conn.) U., 1980-84; founder, mng. dir. Internat. Mgmt. Consortium, Vienna, Westport and Millerton, N.Y., 1975—; assoc. mem. Seminar on Orgn. and Mgmt. Columbia U., 1975-89, vice-chmn. Seminar on Orgn. and Mgmt., 1976-89, chmn. rsch. and publ. com. Seminar on Orgn. and Mgmt., 1983-89; mng. dir. Wainwright & Ramsey Securities, Inc., N.Y.C., 1985—2005. Mem. editorial bd. Indian Adminstrv. and Mgmt. Rev., New Delhi, 1974-76; author: Management: In Perspective and Practice, 1970, The Future Challenges of Management Education, 1981; also numerous articles and revs. Trustee Dingletown Community Ch., Greenwich, Conn., 1978-87; mem. adv. coun. Calif. Coll. Tech., L.A., 1978—. Recipient Disting. Alumni medallion (Olde Guarde), Coll. William and Mary, 2001. Fellow Internat. Acad. Mgmt.; mem. Acad. Mgmt., Am. Mgmt. Assns. (pres.'s council, dir. 1976-77), N.Am. Soc. Corp. Planning, N.Am. Mgmt. Coun. (bd. dirs. 1983-87), Soc. Internat. Orgn. Devel., Mensa, Triple Nine Soc., Explorers Club, Sharon (Conn.) Country Club, Beta Gamma Sigma, Kappa Sigma (rotary internat. chair 2004-). Office Phone: 707-785-3504. *Success depends upon the art of optimizing the skills of confrontation, accommodation and cooperation.*

CARTER, RICKEY E, medical educator; PhD, Med. U. SC, 2002. Dir. info. sys. The Clin. Innovation Group, Charleston, SC, 1998—2003; asst. prof. Med. Univ. SC., Charleston, SC, 2003—. Office: Med U SC 135 Cannon St Charleston SC 29425 Office Phone: 843-876-1100.

CARTER, ROBERT B., delivery service executive; b. Taiwan, 1959; B, U. Fla.; MBA, U. South Fla. V.p. info. and telecomm. FedEx Corp., 1993—98, chief tech. officer, 1998—2000, exec. v.p., chief info. officer Memphis, 2000—. Bd. dir. Saks Inc. Named Chief Tech. Officer of Yr., Infoworld, 2000, one of top tech. innovators, Info. Week mag, 2004. Office: FedEx 942 S Shady Grove Rd Memphis TN 38120

CARTER, RONALD MARTIN, SR., pharmaceutical company executive; b. Chgo., Nov. 18, 1925; s. Jack Edward and Anna (Press) C.; m. Joy Wolf, Nov. 14, 1946; children: Ronald M. Jr., Craig Alan. Student, U. Ill., 1942-43, 45-46. Sales mgr. Preston Labs., Inc., Chgo., 1948-52; v.p. Myers-Carter Labs., Inc., Phoenix, 1952-69, pres., 1969-75, Carter-Glogau Labs., Inc., Glendale, Ariz., 1975-86, Steris Labs., Inc., Phoenix, 1987—, The Pharmikon Co., 1987—. Cons. Internat. Exec. Service Corp., Stamford, Conn., 1985—. Served as cpl. U.S. Army, 1943-45. Mem. Drug, Chem. Allied Trades, Generic Pharm. Industry Assn., Nat. Assn. Pharm. Mfrs., Nat. Pharm. Alliance (pres. 1983-84). Clubs: Arizona, Plaza (Phoenix). Democrat. Jewish. Avocations: hunting, fishing. Home: 5707 N 40th St Phoenix AZ 85018-1108 Personal E-mail: roncar@cox.net.

CARTER, ROSALYNN SMITH, former First Lady of the United States; b. Plains, Ga., Aug. 18, 1927; d. Edgar and Allie (Murray) Smith; m. James Earl Carter, Jr., July 7, 1946; children: John William, James Earl III, Donnel Jeffrey, Amy Lynn. Grad., Ga. Southwestern Coll.; DHL (hon.), Morehouse Coll., 1980; LLD (hon.), U. Notre Dame, 1987. First Lady of U.S., Washington, 1977—81; Disting. fellow dept. women's studies Emory U., Atlanta, 1990—. Vice chair, bd. trustees The Carter Ctr., chair Mental Health Task Force Carter Ctr.; pres., bd. dirs. Rosalynn Carter Inst. for Caregiving of Ga. Southwestern State U.; co-founder Every Child by Two Campaign for Early Immunization. Author: First Lady from Plains, 1984, (with Jimmy Carter) Everything to Gain: Making the Most of the Rest of Your Life, 1987, Helping Yourself Help Others: A Book for Caregivers, 1994, Helping Someone With Mental Illness: A Compassionate Guide for Family, Friends and Caregivers, 1998. Adv. bd. mem. Habitat for Humanity; mem. Ga. Gov.'s Commn. to Improve Svcs. for Mentally and Emotionally Handicapped, 1971; hon. chmn. Pres.'s Commn. on Mental Health, 1977-78. Recipient Vol. of Decade award Nat. Mental Health Assn., 1980, Presdl. Citation APA, 1982, Nathan S. Kline medal of merit Internat. Com. Against Mental Illness, 1984, Disting. Alumnus award Am. Assn. State Colls. and Univs., 1987, Dorothea Dix award Mental Illness Found., 1988, Dean's award Columbia U. Coll. Physicians and Surgeons, 1991, Notre Dame award for internat. humanitarian svc., 1992, Eleanor Roosevelt Living World award Peace Links, 1992, Nat. Caring award The Caring Inst., 1995, Kiwanis World Svc. medal Kiwanis Internat. Found., 1995, Jefferson award Am. Inst. for Pub. Svc., 1996, Presdl. Medal of Freedom, 1999; named to Nat. Women's Hall of Fame, 2001. Fellow: Am. Psychiat. Assn. (hon.). Democrat. Office Phone: 404-331-3900.

CARTER, ROY ERNEST, JR., retired journalist, educator; b. Ulysses, Kans., Apr. 7, 1922; s. Roy Ernest and Inez (Anderson) C.; m. Ruby Maxine Rice, Mar. 28, 1948; children: Phyllis Diane, Patricia Inez, Susan Dolores. BA, Ft. Hays State U., 1948; MA, U. Minn., 1951; PhD, Stanford U., 1954; Prof. h.c., U. Chile, 1982. Reporter, editor, editorial writer various newspapers, 1942-48, 51; high sch. tchr. Hutchinson, Kans., 1948-50; assoc. prof., chmn. dept. journalism Ohio Wesleyan U., 1951-52; acting assoc. prof. journalism Stanford U., 1952-54; research prof. journalism, mem. Inst. Research in Social Sci. of U. N.C., 1954-58; prof. journalism, sociology and internat. relations U. Minn., 1958-90, prof. emeritus, 1990—, prof. ind. and distance learning. Lectr., Quito, Ecuador, 1961, Chile, Argentina, Uruguay, 1991; vis. prof. U. Chile, 1962-63, 82, U. Concepción, Chile, 1964, 66-68, 91, U. Costa Rica, 1971, 84, U. Pernambuco, Brazil, 1972, U. P.R., 1978-79, 86, Cath. U. Uruguay, 1987, U. del Salvador, Buenos Aires, 1989, Fla. Internat. U., 1992-96, U. Md., 1996-98; cons. to mktg., pub. opinion rsch. firms, internat. orgns. Author: North Carolina Press-Medical Study, 1957, (with R.O. Nafziger, D.M. White et al.) Introduction to Mass Communication Research, 1963; Assoc. editor of: Journalism, Quarterly, 1958-63; Contbr. articles to sci. jours. Recipient Kellogg Found. grant Stanford, 1952-53, sr. Fulbright-Hays award Chile, 1962-63, sr. Fulbright-Hays award Costa Rica, 1971, sr. Fulbright award Argentina, 1989, Social Sci. Research Council grants, 1962, 68; Rotary fellow, Uruguay, 1987 Fellow Am. Sociol. Assn.; mem. Assn. Edn. Journalism, World Assn. Pub. Opinion Research, Sigma Delta Chi, Phi Kappa Phi. Episcopalian. Achievements include research in Costa Rica, 1975, 91, El Salvador and Chile, 1976, P.R., 1979, Uruguay, 1982-89, 93—, Colombia, 1993, Peru, 1994. Office: U of Minn Journalism Sch 206 Church St SE Minneapolis MN 55455-0488

CARTER, Corey SHAWN See JAY-Z

CARTER, STEPHEN LISLE, law educator; BA, Stanford U., 1976, JD, 1979. Bar: DC 1981. Law clk. to presiding justice U.S. Ct. Appeals (D.C. cir.), 1979-80, U.S. Supreme Ct., 1980-81; assoc. Shea & Gardner, Washington, 1981-82; asst. prof. Yale U., New Haven, 1982-84, assoc. prof., 1984-85, prof., 1986—91, William Nelson Cromwell prof. law, 1991—. Author: Reflections of an Affirmative Action Baby, 1991, The Culture of Disbelief, 1993, The Confirmation Mess, 1994, Integrity, 1986, The Dissent of the Governed, 1998, Civility, 1998, God's Name in Vain, 2000, The Emperor of Ocean Park, 2002. Office: Yale Law Sch PO Box 208215 New Haven CT 06520-8215*

CARTER, STEVE, state attorney general; b. Lafayette, Ind. m. Marilyn Carter; 3 children. BA in Econs. (hon.), Harvard U., 1976; JD, MBA, Ind. U. Chief city-county atty. Indpls.-Marion County; chief of staff Former Mayor Stephen Goldsmith Ind.; legis. counsel Ind. State Senate; chief of staff, agrl. asst. Ind. Lt. Gov. John Mutz; atty. gen. State of Ind., 2001—. Mem.: Nat. Assn. of Atty. Gen. (pres.-elect). Republican. Office: Ind Govt Ctr S 5th Fl 302 W Washington St Indianapolis IN 46204

CARTER, SYLVIA, journalist; b. Keokuk, Iowa; d. Charles Sylvester and Frances Elizabeth (Smith) C. B of Journalism, U. Mo., 1968. Intern Quincy (Ill.) Herald-Whig, 1966, Detroit Free Press, 1967; reporter The N.Y. Daily News, 1968-70; successively gen. assignment reporter, edn. reporter, food writer, restaurant critic, food columnist Newsday, Melville, NY, 1970—; food writer, restaurant critic N.Y. Newsday, N.Y.C., 1985-95; founder, editor Kidsday Newsday, Melville, columnist, 2005—. Author: Eats: The Best Little Restaurants in New York, 1988, Eats N.Y.C.: A Guide to the Best, Cheapest, Most Interesting Restaurants in Brooklyn, Queens and Manhattan, 1995; contbr. to Family Circle and other publs. Trustee Anne O'Hare McCormick Scholarship Fund, N.Y.C., 1988—; bd. dirs. Art Inst. N.Y., 2003-05. Recipient Feature Writing award U. Mo., 2000; nominee James Beard Journalism awards, 2001. Mem. Newswomen's Club N.Y. (pres. 1990-92, bd. dirs., Front Page award 1982). Democrat. Presbyterian. Avocations: reading, collectibles, hiking, music, cooking. Home: 111 Waverly Pl New York NY 10011-9142 also: 46 Crescent Bow Ridge NY 11961-2915 Office Phone: 631-775-9534. E-mail: sylviacarter@optonline.net.

CARTER, THOMAS, film director, television producer; b. Austin, Tex. s. Allen and La Fray Carter. Diploma, S.W. Tex. State U. Exec. producer TV series Equal Justice, 1989-90 (Emmy awards 1990, 91); dir. TV pilots including Miami Vice, Equal Justice, St. Elsewhere, Midnight Caller, A Year in the Life; dir. TV series including 8 episodes of Hill Street Blues (DGA award 1985); dir. TV movies Under the Influence, Divas, 1995, Bronx County, 1998, Partners in Crime, 2003; dir. feature films Swing Kids, 1993, Metro, 1997, Save the Last Dance, 2001; exec. prodr., dir., Coach Carter, 2005, (TV films) Divas, 1995, Hack, 2002, (TV Series) Hack, 2002-04; TV appearances include Good Times, 1976, M*A*S*H, 1977, What's Happening, 1977, Lou Grant, 1978, Hill Street Blues, 1982.

CARTER, T(HOMAS) BARTON, law educator; b. Dallas, Aug. 6, 1949; s. Sydney Hobart and Josephine (Wren) C.; m. Eleonore Dorothy Alexander, June 3, 1978 (div. 1988); 1 child, Richard Alexander. BA in Psychology, Yale U., 1971; JD, U. Pa., 1974; MS in Mass Communication, Boston U., 1978. Bar: Mass. 1974, U.S. Dist. Ct. Mass. 1975, U.S. Ct. Appeals (1st cir.) 1975. Asst. prof. law Boston U., 1979-85, assoc. prof., 1985-96, prof., 1996—; pvt. practice Boston, 1974—. Pres. Tanist Broadcasting Corp., Boston, 1981—2001. Co-author: The First Amendment and the Fourth Estate, 1985, 9th edit., 2004, The First Amendment and the Fifth Estate, 1986, 6th edit., 2003, Mass Communications Law in a Nutshell, 1988, 5th edit., 2000. Mem. ABA, Assn. for Edn. in Journalism and Mass Comm. (clk. 1981-82, asst. head 1982-83, head 1983-84), Broadcast Edn. Assn. (chair law and policy divsn. 1989-90), Fed. Comm. Bar Assn., Univ. Club. Avocation: bridge. Home: 109 Commonwealth Ave Apt 6 Boston MA 02116-2345 Office: Boston U 640 Commonwealth Ave Boston MA 02215-2422 Office Phone: 617-353-3482. E-mail: comlaw@bu.edu.

CARTER, THOMAS SMITH, JR., retired rail transportation executive; b. Dallas, June 6, 1921; s. Thomas S. and Mattie (Dowell) C.; m. Janet R. Hostetter, July 3, 1946 (dec. 1981); children: Diane Carter Petersen, Charles T., Carol Carter Koehler. BSCE, So. Meth. U., 1944; MS in Engring. Mgmt., Kans. U., 1991. Registered profl. engr., Mo., Kans., Okla., Tex., La., Ark. With Mo. Kans. Tex. R.R., 1946-54, chief engr., 1954-61, v.p. ops., 1961-66; v.p. Kansas City So. Rlwy. Co., La. and Ark. Rlwy. Co., 1966-74; pres. Kansas City So. Rlwy. Co., 1973-86, chmn. bd., 1981-91; pres. La. and Ark. Rlwy. Co., 1974-86, chmn. bd., 1981-91, CEO, 1981-91; ret., 1991. With U.S. Corps of Engrs., 1944-46. Fellow ASCE; mem. NSPE, Am. Rlwy. Engring. and Maintenance Assn. (life), Hide-A-Way Lake Club. Home: 131 Clubview Dr Lindale TX 75771-5054

CARTER, VINCE, professional basketball player; b. Jan. 26, 1977; Grad., U. N.C., 2001. Forward Toronto (Can.) Raptors, 1998—2004, New Jersey Nets, 2004—. Mem. NBA All Star Team, 2000, 01, 02, 03, 05; pres. Visions in Flight Inc. Established Embassy of Hope Found. Named mem., 1995 USA Basketball Jr. Tam, World Championships, Goodwill Amb., Big Bros./Big Sisters Am.; named to NCAA Tournament All-East Regional Team, 1997, 1998, Schick All-Rookie 1st Team; recipient Schick Rookie of Yr. award, 1998—99. Office: c/o NJ Nets 390 Murray Hill Parkway East Rutherford NJ 07073*

CARTER, WILFRED WILSON, retired finance company executive, retired controller; b. Providence, Feb. 22, 1923; s. Leo and Florence (Wilson) C.; m. Elsa Aulisio, June 17, 1950; children— Linda J., Donald J., Paul J., Gregory J. AA, Roger Williams Coll., 1951; student, Bryant Coll., 1958-62. Sec., tax mgr. Nicholson File Co., East Providence, 1940-73; controller Columbia Chase Corp. (name changed to Chase Corp.), Braintree, Mass., 1973-84, v.p. fin., controller, 1984-88, CEO, pres., treas., CFO, 1988-91, chmn. bd. dirs., CEO, treas., 1991-93, chmn. bd. dirs., 1993-94; ret., 1994. Vestryman All Saints Meml. Ch., Providence, R.I., 1968-76, 94-2000, treas., 1968-76. With USAAF, 1942-46. Mem. Tax Exec. Inst. Episcopalian (vestryman 1968-76, 94-2000, treas. 1968-76). Home: 720 Putnam Pike Unit 607 Greenville RI 02828-1448

CARTER, WILLIAM G., lawyer; b. Oct. 1940; BS, LLB, U. Oreg. Bar: Oreg. 1965. Pres.-elect Oreg. State Bar, 2003—04, pres., 2004—. Office: PO Box 70 Medford OR 97501 Office Phone: 541-773-8471.

CARTER, WILLIAM GERALD, non-profit corporation executive; b. Bethany, Mo., Jan. 12, 1929; s. William Young and Leah Genevieve (Cover) C.; m. Geralyn Gail Finlay, July 22, 1951; children: Kathryn Carter Gee, Karen Carter Winn, William Ralph. BSc, U. Mo., 1950. Assoc. editor Nat. Livestock Prodr., Chgo., 1950-51; comml. specialist Farmland Industries, Kansas City, Mo., 1953-54; advt. dir. MFA Oil Co., Columbia, Mo., 1954-58; ptnr. Neds & Wardlow Advt. Agy., Springfield, Mo., 1958-68; chmn., pres. Tri-State Pharm Co., Oklahoma City, 1968-81; real estate broker W.G. Carter Real Estate, Oklahoma City & Foster City, Calif., 1981-96; founder, chmn. Am. Acad. Vols. in Edn., Foster City, Calif., 1994-2000. Spl. agent intelligence U.S. Army, 1951-53. Named Young Man of Yr., C. of C., Springfield, 1964. Mem. Optimist Internat. (mem. various coms. 1981-89, v.p., bd. dirs. 1984, chair coms. 1985-87, v.p. Optimist Vols. for Youth, Inc. 1992-99). Republican. Methodist. Avocations: reading, writing. Home and Office: 1909 NW Quail Trl Lees Summit MO 64081-1614

CARTER, WILLIAM H., chemicals executive; CFO Borden Inc., Columbus, Ohio. Office: Borden Inc 180 E Broad StFl 30 Columbus OH 43215

CARTER, WILLIAM HAROLD, SR., physicist, researcher, electrical engineer; b. Houston, Nov. 17, 1938; s. William Henry and Fannie Augusta (Simpson) Carter; children: William Harold Jr., Elizabeth Lee. BSEE, U. Tex., 1962, MSEE, 1963, PhD, 1966. Rsch. asst. U. Tex., Austin, 1962-66; program dir. Office of R&D, CIA, Washington, 1966—69; rsch. assoc. U. Rochester, N.Y., 1969-70; rsch. physicist Naval Rsch. Lab., Washington, 1971-93; prof. U. Nebr., Lincoln, 1981-82; instr. Johns Hopkin's U., Balt., 1989-93; program dir. NSF, Arlington, Va., 1993—95. Vis. rsch. fellow U. Reading, Eng., 1976-77; vis. scientist applied physics lab. Johns Hopkin's U., Columbia, Md., 1991-92. Contbr. articles to profl. jours. Cellist Alexandria (Va.) Symphony, 1979-88, Georgetown Symphony, 1981-2003. Capt. U.S. Army, 1967-69. Fellow Optical Soc. Am. (topical editor jour. 2000-03), Internat. Soc. for Optical Engring. (chmn. tech. coun. 1980-82, chmn. pub. com. 1981-83, chmn. fellows com. 1986); mem. IEEE (sr., conf. chmn. 1988), Am. Phys. Soc., Cosmos Club, Sigma Xi, Tau Beta Pi, Eta Kappa Nu. Achievements include co-discovery of the quasi-homogeneous source model; research in optical coherence, in applications of speckle phenomena, and in processing images and data from optical sensors. Home: 8301 Cherry Valley Ln Alexandria VA 22309-2117

CARTER, WILLIAM JOSEPH, lawyer; b. Balt., Sept. 1, 1949; s. Henry Merle and Florence (Rogan) C.; m. Monica Anne Urlock, July 17, 1976. BS in Psychology, Va. Poly. Inst., 1971; JD, Coll. William and Mary, 1974. Bar: Va. 1974, Pa. 1974, Md. 1980, D.C. 1980, Colo. 2004, U.S. Dist. Ct. D.C. 1981, U.S. Dist. Ct. Md. 1983, U.S. Dist. Ct. (ea. dist.) Va. 1985, U.S. Ct. Claims 1977, U.S. Tax Ct. 1977, U.S. Ct. Mil. Appeals 1975, U.S. Ct. Appeals (D.C. and 4th cirs.) 1979, U.S. Ct. Appeals (fed. cir.) 1982, U.S. Ct. Appeals (6th cir.) 1988, U.S. Ct. Appeals (3d and 5th cirs.) 1992, U.S. Ct. Appeals (11th cir.) 2002, U.S. Supreme Ct. 1977. Commd. 2d lt. U.S. Army, 1971, advanced through grades to capt., 1974, served with JAGC, 1971-79, resigned, 1979; assoc. Carr, Jordan, Coyne & Savits, Washington, 1979-84; shareholder Carr, Goodson & Lee, P.C., 1984-95, Carr Goodson Lee & Warner Profl. Corp., Washington, 1996-98, Carr Goodson Warner Profl. Corp., Washington, 1999-2000, Carr Goodson, P.C., Washington, 2000—01, Carr Maloney, P.C., Washington, 2001—. Mem. Deans adv. roundtable Coll. Sci., Va. Poly. Inst. Author: Appellate Practice Handbook for Maryland,

Virginia and District of Columbia, 1996; editor: Appellate Practice Manual for the District of Columbia Court of Appeals, 1992. Mem.: ABA, D.C. Bar Assn. (cts. and adminstrn. of justice sect., ct. rules com., chair 1998—2001), Counsellors, Bar Assn. D.C., Rotary (pres. Olney, Md. chpt. 1999—2000). Episcopalian. Avocations: ice hockey, tennis, music, scuba diving, skiing. Office: Carr Maloney PC Ste 500 1615 L St NW Washington DC 20036 Office Phone: 202-310-5500. Business E-Mail: wjc@carrmaloney.com.

CARTER, WILLIAM WALTON, physicist, researcher; b. Pensacola, Fla., Nov. 7, 1921; s. Eugene Hudson and Nannie (Ledyard) C.; m. Elizabeth Jean Dedick, June 11, 1945; children— Carolyn A., Susan J., Judith J., Paul W. BS, Carnegie Inst. Tech., 1943; MS, Calif. Inst. Tech., 1948, PhD, 1949. Atomic and thermonuclear weapon R&D group leader weapons physics group, weapons div. Los Alamos Sci. Lab., 1949-59, mem. joint working com.; chief scientist Army Missile Command, Redstone Arsenal, 1959-67; asst. dir. nuclear programs, def. research and engring. Office Sec. Def., Washington, 1967-71; assoc. dir. Harry Diamond Labs. U.S. Army, 1971-74, tech. dir., 1975-84, also chmn. staff devel. council; sr. scientist Pacific-Sierra Rsch., Arlington, Va, 1984-94; scientific cons. nuclear treaty monitoring, 1994—. Designer, deployer instruments to verify nuclear treaties; chmn. steering com. Huntsville Rsch. Inst. Served to lt. USNR, 1944-46. Asso. fellow AIAA; mem. AAAS, Am. Phys. Soc., Am. Inst. Physics. Achievements include design of air samplers for worldwide network of sensors to monitor non-proliferation and nuclear test ban treaties; installation first unit in Turkmenistan; being project leader for first thermonuclear weapon to enter regular national stockpile. Home: 250 Pantops Mountain Rd Apt 5219 Charlottesville VA 22911 Office Phone: 434-972-2454, 434-972-2454. Personal E-mail: wwcarter@wcbr.us.

CARTER, YVONNE BREAUX, retired librarian; b. Crowley, La., Aug. 3, 1922; d. Valentin D. and Annie H. (Oertling) Breaux; m. Walter R. Carter, Apr. 23, 1943. BS in Edn. with high distinction, U. Southwestern La., 1943; BS in Libr. Sci., George Peabody Coll. Tchrs., 1950, MA, 1960, EdS, 1966. Cert. tchr. and libr. La. State Devel. of Edn. Tchr., libr. Vermillion Parish Sch. Bd., Abbeville, La.; prin. Sardis (Tenn.) HS, 1944—45; tchr. Calcasieu Parish, Lake Charles, La., 1942-43; libr. U.S. Office of Edn., 1967-76; adminstrv. libr. U.S. Dept. of Edn., Washington, 1976-93; ret., 1993. Asst. prof. Northwestern State U., Natchitoches, La., 1964—65, U. Southwestern La., 1966—67. Mem. Lafayette Pub. Libr. Found. Bd. Kappa Kappa Iota scholar, Delta Kappa Gamma Epsilon scholar. Mem.: DAR (regent Galvez chpt. 1998—2004, state libr. 2004—), AAUW, ALA, La. Libr. Assn., Am. Assn. Sch. Librs., Women in Arts, Attakapas Hist. Assn., Women's Club Lafayette, Nat. Soc. Daus. War 1812 (state historian 2002—03, chpt. pres. 2004—), Nat. Soc. DAR (state libr. 2004—), United Daus. Confederacy, Beta Phi Mu, Delta Kappa Gamma, Kappa Delta Pi. E-mail: ycarter@bellsouth.net.

CARTER, ZACHARY W., lawyer; BA, Cornell U., 1972; JD, NYU, 1975. Bar: N.Y., U.S. Dist Ct. (ea. dist.) N.Y., U.S. Dist. Ct. (so. dist.) N.Y., U.S. Ct. Appeals (2d cir.), U.S. Supreme Ct. Asst. U.S. atty. U.S. Dist. Ct. (ea. dist.) N.Y., 1975-80; mem. Patterson, Belknap, Webb & Tyler, 1980-81; exec. asst. dist. atty. King County Dist. Atty's. Office, Bklyn., 1982-87; exec. asst. to dep. chief adminstrv. judge N.Y. City Cts., 1987; judge criminal ct. City of N.Y., 1987-91; U.S. magistrate judge E.D.N.Y., 1991-93; U.S. atty. ea. dist. N.Y. U.S. Dept. Justice, Bklyn., 1993-99; ptnr., trial, regulatory & tech. group Dorsey & Whitney, N.Y.C., 1999—, and chair, white collar crime & civil fraud group. Chmn., bd. dir. Hale House. Mem. N.Y. Bar Assn. (chmn. Mayor's adv. com. on jud. selection). Office: Dorsey & Whitney LLP 250 Park Ave New York NY 10177-1500 Office Phone: 212-415-9345. Office Fax: 212-953-7201. E-mail: carter.zachary@dorseylaw.com.

CARTER-JOHNSON, JEAN EVELYN, management consultant; b. Front Royal, Va., Sept. 22, 1956; d. William Robert Carter and Hilda Mae Jett; m. Ronald Malcolm Johnson, Sept. 27, 1985; 1 child, Sherard Akeem Johnson. Dental Assistance Cert., Montgomery Jr. Coll., Takoma Park, Md., 1977, AA, 1978; BSBA, Southeastern U., Washington, 1990. Licensing info. asst. Nuc. Regulatory Commn., Silver Spring, Md., 1982—86; freedom info. act/privacy act specialist U.S. Info. Agy., Washington, 1986—88; paralegal Fed. Trade Commn., Washington, 1988—2001; mgmt. analyst Dept. Commerce, Silver Spring, Md., 2001—. Freedom info. act/privacy act program mgr. Nat. Oceanic and Atmospheric Adminstrn., Silver Spring, Md., 2001—. Mentor Young Adult Orgn., 2004. Fellow: Md. State Bd. Dental Examiners (lic. 1977). Avocations: reading, writing, cooking, piano, coin collecting/numismatics. Home: 7510 Somerset Terr Frederick MD 21702 Office: Dept Commerce 1315 Eastwest Hwy Silver Spring MD 20901 Personal E-mail: jeancj@adelphia.net.

CARTER-MILLER, JOCELYN, retail executive; BSc in Acctg., U. Ill., Urbana-Champaign; MBA in Mktg. and Fin., U. Chgo. CPA. Various sr. level positions Mattel, Inc., 1984—91; corp. v.p., chief mktg. officer Motorola, Inc., 1992—2002; exec. v.p. Office Depot, Inc., Delray Beach, Fla., 2002—, chief mktg. officer, 2002—. Bd. dir. Principal Fin. Group, Inc. Author (with Melissa Giovagnoli): Networlding: Building Relationships and Opportunities for Success, 1998. Office: Office Depot Inc 2200 Old Germantown Rd Delray Beach FL 33445

CARTHY, MARK PATRICK, financial executive; b. Dublin, Aug. 8, 1960; came to U.S., 1982; s. Francis Fenton and Mairead (Maguire) C.; m. Vera Maria Trojan, Aug. 26, 1989. BChemE, U. Coll. Dublin, 1982; MChemE, U. Mo., Rolla, 1983; MBA, Harvard U., 1987. Sr. engr. Intel Corp., Santa Clara, Calif., 1983-85; venture capital assoc. Alan Patricof Assocs., London, 1986; assoc. mergers and acquisitions Shearson Lehman Hutton, N.Y.C., 1987-88; product mgr. mktg. dept. Millipore Corp., Bedford, Mass., 1988-92; dir. bus. devel. Vertex Pharms., Inc., Cambridge, Mass.; sr. dir. bus. devel. Cubist Pharms. Inc., Cambridge, Mass., 1992—97, chief bus. officer, 1997—98; biotech. portfolio mgr. Morningside Ventures, 1998-2000; gen. ptnr. Oxford Biosci. Ptnrs., Boston, 2000—. Jefferson Smurfit fellow U. Mo., 1982. Mem. World Affairs Coun. Boston, Stephens Green Club, Dublin, Ireland. Avocations: golf, rugby, classical music. E-mail: mcarthy@oxbio.com.

CARTIER, BRIAN EVANS, consumer products company executive; b. Providence, Apr. 12, 1950; s. Clarence Joseph and Mary Anna (Evans) C. BA, R.I. Coll., 1972; MEd, Springfield (Mass.) Coll., 1973. Exec. dir. Arthritis Found. Conn., Hartford, 1976-78, dep. exec. dir. N.Y. chpt. N.Y.C., 1979; exec. dir. Found. for Chiropractic Edn. and Rsch., Arlington, Va., 1979-90, Nat. Ct. Reporters Assn., 1990-98; CEO Nat. Assn. Coll. Stores, Oberlin, Ohio, 1998—. Mem. Am. Mgmt. Assn. (cert. assn. exec.), Am. Soc. Assn. Execs., US C. of C. Republican. Roman Catholic. Office: NACS 500 E Lorain St Oberlin OH 44074-1238

CARTISANO, LINDA ANN, lawyer; b. Phila., Dec. 11, 1953; d. S. James and Anna M. (Morley) C. BA cum laude, Widener U., 1974; JD, Temple U., 1978. Bar: Pa. 1978, U.S. Dist. Ct. (ea. dist.) Pa. 1979. Pvt. practice law, Chester, Pa., 1978—; asst. city solicitor City of Chester, 1982-96; solicitor Chester Devel. Office, 1985-90, Darby Creek Joint Authority, Springfield, Pa., 1987—, Borough Of Upland, Upland, Pa., 1988—; counsel Chester Redevel. Authority, Chester, 1986-92, acting exec. dir., 1989. Custody conciliator Del. County Ct. Common Pleas, Media, Pa., 1996—; solicitor City of Chester, Pa., 1996—; asst. solicitor County of Delaware, 1999—. Mem. Widener-PMC Alumni Assn., Chester, 1978, v.p. 1996—; mem. Chester City Health Assn., 1981-91, Chester-Widener Community Commn. Mem. Pa. Bar Assn., Delaware County Bar Assn., Chester Coun. Republican Women. Roman Catholic.

CARTLEDGE, RAYMOND EUGENE, retired paper company executive; b. Pensacola, Fla., June 12, 1929; s. Raymond H. and Meddie (Brookins) C.; m. Gale Perry, June 30, 1962; children: John R., Perri Ann, Susan R. BS, U. Ala., 1952; postgrad., Harvard Bus. Sch., 1970. With Procter & Gamble Co., 1955-56, Union Camp Corp., Wayne, NJ, 1956-70, 80-94, pres., COO, 1983-86, chmn., pres., CEO, 1986-94; pres., CEO Clevepak Corp., White Plains, NY, 1971-79; chmn. Savannah Foods, 1996-97. Past chmn. Am. Paper Inst.; trustee Am. Enterprise Inst.; trustee, life councillor The Conf. Bd.; bd. dirs. Blount Internat., Graftec Internat.; past chmn. Inst. Paper Sci. and Tech. Served with U.S. Army Airborne Infantry, 1952-55. Office: #235 15 Lake St Savannah GA 31411-2913 Office Phone: 912-598-3214. E-mail: recart1929@aol.com.

CARTLIDGE, EDWARD SUTTERLEY, mechanical engineer; b. Trenton, N.J., Feb. 5, 1945; s. Leon James and Agnes Jean (Cinkay) C.; m. Marilyn Spinuzza, July 21, 1979. BS in Marine Engring., U.S. Mcht. Marine Acad., 1968; MSME, N.J. Inst. Tech., 1971; MBA, Temple U., 1982; MA, Biblical Theol. Sem., 2001. Registered profl. engr., Pa., Ill., Del., Md., N.J., Va., Wis., Calif., Fla. Marine engr. Seatrain Lines, 1968-69; performance engr. Foster Wheeler Corp., Livingston, N.J., 1969-71; cons. engr. Fluor, Sargent & Lundy, and Kuljian Corp., 1971-75; chief engr. Gimpel Corp., Langhorne, Pa., 1976-79; sr. R&D engr. Yarway Corp., Blue Bell, Pa., 1979-82; sr. project process engr. and power utilities supr. Merck & Co., Inc., West Point, Pa., 1982-91; sr. project mgr. Conmec, Inc., Bethlehem, Pa., 1992-93, Edward S. Cartlidge, PE and Assocs., Blue Bell, Pa., 1993—2000; mgr. facilities engring. Cardinal Health, Inc., Softgel Pharm. Mfg., St. Petersburg, Fla., 2000—04; mfgr. rep. Tom Evans Environ. Water/Waste Products Inc., Lakeland, Fla., 2005—. Cons. Pharm., Polymer, Utilities, Semiconductor, Steel Fab., Gideon; Christian fin. counselor, lectr., seminar leader. Bd. dirs. Grand Old Gospel Fellowship. Served to comdr. USNR, 1968-91. Mem. NSPE (chpt. pres.), ASME, ASHRAE, AWWA, Fla. Engring. Soc., Pa. Soc. Profl. Engrs. (Young Engr. of Yr. 1980), Naval Res. Assn., Nat. Fire Prevention Assn., Gideons Internat. (camp pres.). Home: 901 Stratford Manor Dr Brandon FL 33510-2810 Office Phone: 813-380-8608. E-mail: ec@tomevans.com.

CARTMELL, NATHANIEL MADISON, III, lawyer; b. N.Y.C., Oct. 22, 1951; s. Nathaniel Madison Jr. and Ruth Kincer (Davies) C.; m. Suzanne Cameron Pettus, Jan. 3, 1981; children: Nathaniel Madison IV, Edmund Winston, Samuel Chapman Davies. BA, Yale U., 1973; JD, Vanderbilt U., 1978. Bar: Calif. State 1983, D.C. 1980, Va. State 1978. Mem. faculty Williston Northampton Sch., Easthampton, Mass., 1973-75; assoc. Hunton & Williams, Richmond, Va., 1978-80, Washington, 1980-81; atty. U.S. Synthetic Fuels Corp., Washington, 1981; assoc. Pillsbury Madison & Sutro LLP, Washington, 1982-83, San Francisco, 1983-86; ptnr. Pillsbury Winthrop Shaw Pittman, LLP, San Francisco, 1987—2005, mgr. corp. and securities group, 1994-96, chair mergers and acquisitions specialty team, 1999—2004; ptnr., co-chair mergers & acquisitions practice group Pillsbury Winthrop Shaw Pittman LLP, San Francisco, 2005—. Alumni bd. dirs. Vanderbilt Law Sch., 1998-2001; alumni coun. Phillips Acad., 1997-2000; bd. govs. Phelps Assn., 2004—; bd. dirs. YMCA, San Francisco, 2004—. Mem. ABA (mem. fed. regulation of securities com., bus. law sect. 1990—), Calif. State Bar (mem. corps. com., bus. law sect. 1989-91). Episcopalian. Office: Pillsbury Winthrop Shaw Pittman LLP 50 Fremont St San Francisco CA 94105 Office Phone: 415-983-1570. Office Fax: 415-983-1200. Business E-Mail: nathaniel.cartmell@pillsburylaw.com.

CARTNER, DAVID STEVEN, claims representative, retired military officer; b. Boonville, Mo., Dec. 9, 1950; s. John Elmer Cartner and Helen Taylor; m. Donna Jane Dutton, June 30, 1973; children: Stephanie Ann, Jonathan Roy. Grad. Non-Commd. Officers Acad., 8th Army, 1974; BS, U. State NY, Albany, 1985. Cert. assoc. in claims Ins. Inst. Am., assoc. in ins. svcs. Ins. Inst. Am., assoc. in mgmt. Ins. Inst. Am. Platoon sgt. Torii Sta., Japan, 1971—75; shift supr. Kelly AFB, San Antonio, 1975; tng. NCO Vint Hill Farms Sta., Warrenton, 1975—77; attache technician Am. Embassy, Ankara, Turkey, 1977—79, ops. coord. Kabul, Afghanistan, 1979—80, asst. army attache Nicosia, Cyprus, 1985—88; spl. projects officer Def. Intelligence Agy., Washington, 1980—81; ops. coord. Am. Embassy, Paris, France (incl. Monaco), 1981—84, asst. army attache Belize City, Belize, 1988—91; sr. field claims rep. Mo. Farm Bur., Sikeston, 1991—. Mem., chmn. City of Sikeston Pk. Bd., Mo., 1997—2003; bd. govs. USO; nat. aide de camp VFW, Mo., 2002—03, nat. gen. resolutions com., 2003—05, nat. POW/MIA com., 2003—04, post comdr. Sikeston, Mo., 2001—02; vol. hunter edn. instr. Mo. Dept. Conservation, Mo., 1995—2005; asst. scoutmaster, dist. com., unit commr. Boy Scouts Am., Mo., 1995—2005; dist. comdr. VFW, Mo., 2003—05, dept. youth activities and patriot's pen chmn., 2004—05. Chief warrant officer U.S. Army, 1970—91. Decorated Armed Forces Expeditionary medal, NCO Profl. Devel. Ribbon w/3 devices, Army Svc. Ribbon, Overseas Svc. Ribbon w/5 device, Army Meritorious Unit Citation, Air Force Outstanding Unit award, Expert Marksman, Rifle, Pistol, Machine Gun, Grenade, Def. Meritorious Svc. Medal w/2 Oak Leaf Clusters Dept. of Def., Joint Svc. Commendation Medal w/1 Oak Leaf Cluster, Army Commendation medal, Joint Svc. Achievement medal, Army Good Conduct Medal, 2d award, Nat. Def. Svc. Medal w/Bronze Star, Vietnam Svc. medal; named Instr. of Yr., Mo. Hunter Edn. Instrs. Assn., Honor Grad., Def. Intelligence Coll., 1977, All-State Post Comdr., VFW, 2002, All-State Dist. Comdr., 2005; recipient Dist. Award of Merit, Cherokee Dist., Boy Scouts Am., Scoutmaster's Tng. Award, Greater St. Louis Area Coun., Boy Scouts of Am., God & Svc. Award, Vigil Honor, Anpetu-We Lodge, Order of the Arrow, Lodge Advisor's award, Anpetu-We Lodge, Order of Arrow, medal of the City of Paris, Silver Echelon, Mayor Jacques Chirac, City of Paris, 1984, Scouters Achievement award, VFW, 2005. Mem.: NRA (cert. range safety officer, rifle, shotgun, and muzzleloading instr.), VFW (life), Mil. Officers Assn. Am., PA Diving Instrs. (master scuba diver trainer), Mo. Hunter Edn. Instrs. Assn., Elks, Am. Legion. Conservative. Methodist. Avocations: hunting, fishing, scuba diving, shooting. Home: 109 Linda Dr Sikeston MO 63801 Office: Mo Farm Bur 1901 E Malone Ave Sikeston MO 63801 Personal E-mail: dscartner@charter.net. E-mail: dcartner@mofb.com.

CARTNER, JOHN A., III, marine company executive; b. Jacksonville, N.C., Nov. 6, 1947; s. John Alexander II and Anna Gertrude (Hardison) C.; m. Tanya Lynn Morris; children: Christian W.J., Natalie V.O. BS, U.S. Mcht. Marine Acad., 1969; MS, U. Ga., 1974, PhD, 1975; MBA, Ga. State U., 1978. Asst. prof. bus. adminstrn. U. Ga., 1979-80; dir. marine transp. Grumman Corp., Bethpage, N.Y., 1980-81; v.p. IMA Resources, Inc., Washington, 1981-82; pres. Phillips Cartner & Co., Inc., Alexandria, Va., 1982-84, chief exec. officer, 1984-88, chmn., 1989—. Bd. dirs. Alexandria Seaport Found., Inc., First Windsor Corp., Alexandria. Contbr. numerous articles to profl. jours. Vestryman Grace Episcopal Ch., Alexandria, 1986; bd. dirs. U.S. Mcht. Marine Acad. Found., Kings Point, N.Y., 1983-86. Lt. USNR, 1969-73; master U.S. Mcht. Marine, 1969-82. Mem. Soc. Naval Architects and Marine Engrs., Am. Soc. Naval Engrs., U.S. Mcht. Marine Acad. Alumni Assn. (Outstanding Profl. Achievement award 1984, Supt.'s Trophy 1982). Republican. Episcopalian. Office: Phillips Cartner & Co Inc 700 N Fairfax St Alexandria VA 22314-2040

CARTO, DAVID DRAFFAN, lawyer; b. St. Paul, Jan. 10, 1956; s. David Lawrence and Frances Eleanor (Draffan) Carto; m. Carolyn Elizabeth Maikis, Sept. 6, 1981; children: David Willis, Anne Donnelly. BA, Ohio Wesleyan U., 1978; JD, Case Western Res. U., 1981. Bar: Ohio 1981, U.S. Dist. Ct. (no. dist.) Ohio 1981, U.S. Ct. Appeals (6th cir.) 1992, U.S. Supreme Ct. 1991. Assoc. Weldon, Huston & Keyser, Mansfield, Ohio, 1981-86, ptnr., 1986—. Bd. govs. Discovery Sch., 1987-97; bd. dirs. Richland County Heart Assn., Mansfield, 1983-84, Mansfield Art Ctr., 1986-96, Kingwood Ctr., 1996—, Rehab. Svcs. of North Ctrl. Ohio, 2000—. Mem.: Richland County Bar Assn., Ohio State Bar Assn., Our Club (Mansfield), Univ. Club, Kiwanis (bd. dirs. Mansfield 1983—87, v.p. 1988—89, pres. 1989—90). Republican. Avocations: skiing, tennis, hunting, golf. Office: Weldon Huston & Keyser LLP 28 Park Ave W Mansfield OH 44902-1648 E-mail: dcarto@whkmansfield.com.

CARTON, JAMES ALFRED, oceanographer, educator; b. Highland Park, Ill., July 10, 1954; s. Robert Wells and Jean (Keating) C.; m. Allison Joan Mankin, Aug. 15, 1983; children: Samuel, Molly. BSE, Princeton U., 1976, MA, 1980, PhD, 1983; MS, U. Wash., Seattle, 1979. Rsch. fellow theoretical physics Harvard U., Cambridge, Mass., 1983-85; asst. prof. U. Md., College Park, 1985-90, assoc. prof., 1990-97, prof., 1997—. Co-chair adv. bd. Atlantic Climate Change Program, Silver Spring, Md., 1994—. Mem. adv. bd. Societ Jour. Phys. Oceanography, Moscow, 1990-94; contbr. articles to profl. jours. Mem. Am. Geophys. Union, Am. Meteorol. Soc., Sigma Xi (pres. College Park chpt. 1996—). Achievements include studying oceanic causes of low frequency climate variability.

CARTON, LONNIE CAMING, educational psychologist; b. Balt. d. Daniel and Shirley (Cooper) Caming; m. Edwin B. Carton; children: Evan, Deborah, Paula. BS, Johns Hopkins U.; MS, U. Md.; PhD, Pa. State U. Tchr. Laurel (Md.) H.S.; instr. Pa. State U., State College, Temple U., Phila.; newspaper columnist Delaware County Times, Chester, Pa.; instr., then asst. prof. Tufts U., Medford, Mass., 1964—80; learning sys. cons. Tufts New Eng. Med. Ctr., Boston, 1968—73. Broadcast journalist CBS Radio, N.Y.C., 1974—; family support sys. cons. Boston Ptnrs. in Edn., 1985—; ind. cons., lectr., workshop leader in field; guest appearances of various radio and TV shows; family lit. cons. Mass. Dept. Edn., 2001—; cons., dir. teen and family resources Warm 2 Kids, Inc., 2003—; adv. panel SeaWorld Entertainment. Author: Mommies, 1960, Daddies, 1963, Raise Your Kids Right, 1980, No is a Love Word, 1992, (cassette tapes) Parenting Preschoolers from the Park Bench, 1999; sr. editor Edn. Today, Boston, 1992-98; broadcast journalist Voice of Am., 1995-98; contbr. articles to profl. publs. Grantee Gannet Found., U.S. Dept. Edn., Mass. Dept. Edn., U.S. Dept. Hwy. Safety, Mass. Gov.'s Alliance Against Drugs; recipient Nat. Media award APA, 1978, 80, San Francisco State Broadcast Media award, 1983, Contbn. to Lives of Children award UNICEF, Margaret Sanger Soc. award Planned Parenthood, 1985, Don Bosco Friend of Youth award Salesian Soc., awards from Mass. Psychol. Assn., Nat. Comnn. Against Drunk Driving, Gabriel Broadcaster's and Allied Communicators, Mass. Soc. Against Cruelty to Children, 1988; named to One Hundred Most Remarkable Women in Mass., Boston Woman's Mag., 1989, Freedoms Found., George Washington medal for pub. comms., 1998. Avocations: tennis, spectator football, reading. Office: The Learning Ctr PO Box 204 New Town MA 02456-0204 E-mail: ebclcc@aol.com.

CARTWRIGHT, ABIGAIL CAROLINE, academic administrator; b. Knoxville, Tenn., June 26, 1979; d. John Maurice and Grace Martha Cartwright. BA in commn., Radford U., 1997—2001; MA in edn., Va. Poly. Inst. & State U., 2001—03. Grad. asst. Va. Poly. Inst. & State U., Blacksburg, Va., 2001—03; residence coord. Kutztown U. of Pa., Kutztown, Pa. Mem.: PA Coll. Pers. Assn.

CARTWRIGHT, BRENDA YVONNE, counselor, educator; d. Louise Ethel Haynie. Bachelors, Western Md. Coll., 1972; Masters, U. Mich., 1979; Doctorate, George Wash. U., 1996. Cert. rehab. counselor Commn. on Rehab. Counselor Cert., lic. profl. counselor D.C. Bd. Profl. Counseling, cert. counselor Nat. Bd. Cert. Counselors, mental health counselor Hawaii. Spl. edn. tchr. Mich. Sch. for Deaf, Flint, 1972—76; vocat. rehab. counselor Bur. Rehab., Flint, 1976—79; vocat. rehab. specialist Rehab. Svcs. Adminstrn., Washington, 1979—98; asst. prof. Coppin State U., Balt., 1998—2001, U. Hawaii, Honolulu, 2001—05, assoc. prof., 2005—. Cons. U.S. Dept. Edn., Washington, 1980—, U.S. Social Security Adminstrn., Balt., 1990—92, Children's Nat. Med. Ctr., Washington, 1996—2001, U.S. HUD, Washington, 2000—01, Social Security Adminstrn., Office Hearings and Appeals, Honolulu, 2002—; lectr. Gallaudet U., Washington, 1996, Bowie (Md.) State U., 2000, U. D.C., Washington, 2001. Contbr. tng. videotape, instrnl. manual (Bobbie Atkins Rsch. award, 2004), articles to refereed jours., chapters to books. Recipient Andrew Woods Adv. of Yr. Meml. award, D.C. Rehab. Assn., 1983, Sr. Communicator of Quarter award, USN, RAF Edzell, 1989, Thinking Out of the Box award, U. Hawaii Coll. Edn. Faculty Senate, 2004, Excellence in Tchg. award, Coll. Edn., U. Hawaii, 2005; scholar, George Wash. U., 1991—95; Minority fellow, U. Md., 1999. Mem.: NEA, Am. Counseling Assn. (Rsch. award 2005), APA, Am. Counseling Assn., Assn. Assessment Counseling and Edn. (award 2005), Hawaii Rehab. Counseling Assn., Hawaii Counseling Assn., Am. Rehab. Counseling Assn., Nat. Coun. Rehab. Educators, Rehab. Assn. Hawaii (sec., bd. dirs.), Nat. Assn. Multicultural Rehab. Concerns (membership chairperson, bd. dirs., Sylvia Walker Edn. award 2004), Nat. Hawaiian Edn. Assn., Nat. Rehab. Assn. (Mid-Atlantic Region Humanitarian award 1984), Delta Sigma Theta (chaplain, sec., scholarship com. chairperson). Office: U Hawaii WA2-221 1776 University Ave Honolulu HI 96822 Office Phone: 808-956-4386. Business E-Mail: bcartwri@hawaii.edu.

CARTWRIGHT, BRIAN GRANT, lawyer; b. Seattle, May 29, 1947; s. John Brydonne and Helen Ruth (Engman) C.; m. Jean Claudia Libby, Jan. 5, 1975; children: Grant, Eliot, Bryce. BS, Yale U., 1967; PhD, U. Chgo., 1971; JD, Harvard U., 1980. Bar: D.C. 1981, U.S. Dist. Ct. D.C. 1981, U.S. Ct. Appeals (D.C. cir.) 1981, Calif. 1984. Law clk. U.S. Ct. Appeals (D.C. cir.), Washington, 1980-81, U.S. Supreme Ct., Washington, 1981-82; assoc. Latham & Watkins, L.A., 1982-88, ptnr., 1988—, mem. exec. com., 1994-98; lectr. U. Calif., Los Angeles, 1999—. Mem. Los Angeles County Bar Assn. (mem. exec. com., bus. and corps. law sect. 1992-99), Inst. Corp. Counsel (bd. govs. 2004-). Office: Latham & Watkins 633 W 5th St Ste 3800 Los Angeles CA 90071-2007 Office Phone: 213-485-1234.

CARTWRIGHT, CAROL ANN, university president; b. Sioux City, Iowa, June 19, 1941; d. Carl Anton and Kathryn Marie (Weishapple) Becker; m. G. Phillip Cartwright, June 11, 1966; children: Catherine E., Stephen R., Susan D. BS in Early Childhood Edn., U. Wis., Whitewater, 1962; MEd in Spl. Edn., U. Pitts., 1965, PhD in Spl. Edn., Ednl. Rsch., 1968. From instr. to assoc. prof. Coll. Edn. Pa. State U., University Park, 1968-72, from assoc. prof. to prof., 1972-79, dean acad. affairs, 1981-84, dean undergrad. program, vice provost, 1984-88; vice chancellor acad. affairs U. Calif., Davis, 1988-91, prof. human devel., 1988-91; pres. Kent (Ohio) State U., 1991—. Bd. dirs. First Energy Corp. (formerly Ohio Edison), Akron, 1992—, KeyCorp., Cleve., PolyOne Corp., The Davey Tree Expert Co., Kent; exec. bd. Nat. Coun. for Accreditation Tchr. Edn., 2002—; chair NCAA Exec. Com.; mem. N.E. Ohio Coun. Higher Edn., Knight Commn. Intercollegiate Athletics, 2000. Editorial bd. Topics in Early Childhood Special Education, 1982-88, Exceptional Education Quarterly, 1982-88. Pres., bd. dirs. Child Devel. Coun. of Center County, Title XX Day Care Contractor, 1977-80; bd. dirs. Center County United Way, State College, Pa., 1984-88, Urban League of Greater Cleve., 1997—; bd. mem. Davis (Calif.) Art Ctr., 1988-91, Davis Sci. Ctr., 1989-91; bd. dirs. Ohio divsn. Am. Cancer Soc., 1993-2000, nat. bd. dirs., 1993—; mem. nat. bd. First Ladies Libr.; bd. trustees Woodrow Wilson Internat. Ctr. for Scholars, 1999—; bd. dirs. Ctr. for Rsch. Librs., 2002—. Named to Ohio Women's Hall of Fame; recipient Disting. Alumni award, U. Wis.-Whitewater, U. Pittsburgh Sch. Edn., Clairol Mentor award, Women of Achievement award, YWCA of Greater Cleve., Franklin Delano Roosevelt award for Excellence, March of Dimes. Mem. AAUW, Am. Coun. Edn. (Commn. on Women in Higher Edn., 2003-), Am. Ednl. Rsch. Assn., Am. Assn. for Higher Edn., Nat. Assn. State Univs. and Land-Grant Colls., Coun. for Exceptional Children, the Greater Akron Chamber, Cleve. Tomorrow. Roman Catholic. Avocations: walking, reading, travel. Home: 1703 Woodway Rd Kent OH 44240-5917 Office: Kent State U Office of the President PO Box 5190 Kent OH 44242-0001 E-mail: carol.cartwright@kent.edu.

CARTWRIGHT, DERRICK, museum director; BA, U. Calif., Berkeley; MA, UCLA, 1988; PhD in Art Hist., U. Mich., 1994. Prof. art hist. U. San Diego, 1993—98; dir. Musée d'Art Américain, Giverny, France, 1998—2000, Hood Mus. Art, Dartmouth Coll., 2000—04, San Diego Mus. Art, 2004—. Co-curator Lateral Thinking: Art of the 1990s, José Clemente Orozco in the United States, 1927-1934. Office: San Diego Mus Art PO Box 122107 San Diego CA 92112-2107*

CARTWRIGHT, JAMES E., career military officer; b. Rockford, Ill., Sept. 22, 1949; Grad., U. Iowa, 1971, Naval Flight Sch., 1973; grad. with distinction, Air Command and Staff Coll., 1986; MA in Nat. Security and Strategic Study, Naval War Coll., 1991. Commd. 2d lt. USMC, 1971, advanced through grades to gen., 2004; line divsn. officer VMFA-333 USS NIMITZ, 1975—77; aircraft maintenance officer VMFA-235, 1979—82; adminstrn. officer, officer-in-charge deployed carrier ops. VMFAT-101, 1983—85; asst. program mgr. for engring. F/A 18 Naval Air Systems

Command, 1986—89; comdr. Marine Aviation Logistics Squadron 12, Iwakuni, Japan, 1989-90, Marine Aircraft Group 24, Kanoehoe Bay, Hawaii, 1991-92; dep. aviation plans, policy, and budgets Marine Hdqrs., Washington, 1992-94; fellow MIT, 1994; comdr. Marine Aircraft Group 31, 1994-96; assigned to Dir. Force Structure, Resources, and Assessment, The Joint Staff, Washington, 1996-97, dep. dir., 1997-98; dep. comdr. USMC Forces Atlantic, 1999—2000; commdg. gen. 1st Marine Aircraft Wing, 2000—02; dir., force structure, resources & assessment (J-8) The Joint Staff, 2002—04; comdr. US Strategic Command, Offutt AFB, 2004—. Office: US Strategic Commd 901 SAC Blvd Ste 2A1 Offutt A F B NE 68113

CARTWRIGHT, KEROS, hydrogeologist, researcher; b. LA, July 25, 1934; s. Eugene Ewing and Charlotte Lucy (Searle) C.; m. Sharon Miller, July 5, 1955 (dec.); children: Sylvia, Jennifer; m. Jennifer Elizabeth Moberley, Mar. 9, 1962 (div. Sept. 1988); children: David, Bridget; m. Madalene Rose Tierney, Feb. 16, 1990. AB in Geology, U. Calif., 1959; MS in Geology, U. Nev., 1961; PhD in Geology, U. Ill., 1973. Cert. profl. geologist, profl. hydrologist. Hydrogeologist Humboldt River Rsch. Project, Winnemucca, Nev., 1959-61, Ill. State Geol. Survey, Champaign, 1961-2000, head hydrogeology and geophysics sect., 1975-84, prin. scientist and head gen. and environ. geology group, 1984-88, prin. rsch. scientist, 1988-99, chief scientist emeritus, 1999—; adj. prof. geology No. Ill. U., DeKalb, 1979—, U. Ill., Urbana, 1985—. Cons. pvt. practice in hydrogeology, N.Am. and Europe, 1968—, U.S. Environ. Protection Agy. Sci. Adv. Bd., Washington, 1983—, Savannah River Site Environ. Adv., Aiken, S.C., 1988—. Mem. editorial bd. Elsevier Sci. Publ. Jour. of Hydrology, 1982-85; contbr. articles to profl. jours. Named Disting. Lectr. Assn. Groundwater-Water Scientists and Engrs., 1987; recipient Cert. Appreciation U.S. Environ. Protection Agy., 1988. Fellow: Geol. Soc. Am. (officer hydrogeology sect. 1975—78, mem. editl. bd. Jour. Water Resources Rsch. 1975—81, chmn. 1978—79, Bull. 1981—83, mem. governing coun. 1993—97, chmn. publs. com., Birdsall disting. lectr. 1987—88, George B. Maxey Disting. Svc. award 1991), Explorers Club; mem.: ASTM (vice chmn. subcom. D-14 1984—88), Internat. Assn. Hydrogeologists (U.S. com. 1985—89), Am.Water Resources Assn., Am. Geophys. Union (assoc. editor 1975—81), Am. Inst. Hydrology (mem. editl. bd. Jour. Hydrol. Sci. and Tech. 1985—). Avocation: farming. Office: Ill Geol Survey 615 E Peabody Dr Champaign IL 61820-6918 Business E-Mail: redoaks@soltec.net.

CARTWRIGHT, NANCY, actress, television producer; b. Kettering, Ohio, Oct. 25, 1957; d. Frank and Miriam Cartwright; m. Warren Murphy, Dec. 24, 1988; children: Lucy Mae, Jackson. Student, Ohio U., 1976—77; BA in theatre, UCLA, 1981. Founder Cartwright Entertainment Inc. Author: (biography) My Life as a 10-Year-Old Boy, 2000; prodr.: (animated internet series) The Kellys, 2001—; actor(voice): (TV series) The Richie Rich/Scooby-Doo Hour, 1980, Richie Rich, 1981, Monchichis, 1983, Saturday Supercade, 1983, Alvin & the Chipmunks, 1983, The Shirt Tales, 1983—85, The Snorks, 1984, Galaxy High School, 1986, My Little Pony and Friends, 1986, Pound Puppies, 1986, Popeye and Son, 1987, (voice of Bart Simpson) The Tracy Ullman Show, 1987—89, (voice) Fantastic Max, 1988, (voice, Bart Simpson/Nelson/Todd Flanders/Ralph Wiggum/others) The Simpsons, 1989— (Emmy award outstanding voice-over performance, 1992), (voice) Dink, the Little Dinosaur, 1989, Goof Troop, 1992, Raw Toonage, 1992, Bonkers, 1993, Animaniacs, 1993 (Daytime Emmy awards honors for contbg., 1996), Problem Child, 1993, The Pink Panther, 1993, Aladdin, 1993, 2 Stupid Dogs, 1993, The Critic, 1994, Timon and Pumbaa, 1995, The Twisted Adventures of Felix the Cat, 1995, Toonsylvania, 1998, Pinky, Elmyra & the Brian, 1998 (Daytime Emmy awards honors for contbg., 1999), Mike, Lu & Og, 1999, Big Guy and Rusty the Boy Robot, 1999—, God, the Devil and Bob, 2000, (voice of Chuckie) Rugrats, 2001—04, (voice of Rufus) Kim Possible, 2002, (voice of Chuckie) All Grown Up, 2003, (voice): (videos) The Land Before Time VI: The Secret of Saurus Rock, 1998, Wakko's Wish, 1999, Timberwolf, 2002, Kim Possible: The Secret Files, 2003; (TV films) Kim Possible: A Stitch in Time, 2003; (films) The Chipmunk Adventure, 1987, The Little Mermaid, 1989, Petal to the Metal, 1992, Rugrats Go Wild!, 2003,; (TV films) Marian Rose White, 1982, The Rules of Marriage, 1982, Deadly Lessons, 1983, Not My Kid, 1985, Yellow Pages, 1988, On Hollywood Blvd., 1988, Precious Victims, 1993, Vows of Deception, 1996, Suddenly, 1996; (films) Twilight Zone: The Movie, 1983, Flesh & Blood, 1985, Godzilla, 1998; (plays) The Transgressor, 1980, Guys and Dolls, 1984, Coming Attractions, 1985, In Search of Fellini, 1995 (DramaLogue award best performance one-person show, 1996), Cat's Meow, 1998. Cofounder Neko Tech Learning Ctr., Ghana, W. Africa, 2000; mem., commr. Citizens Commn. on Human Rights, 1996—; active with Famous Fone Friends, The World Literacy Crusade, Make A Wish Foundation, The Way to Happiness Internat. Recipient Am. Libr. Assn. award, 1992, Elizabeth Andersch award, 1992, County of LA Pub. Libr. award, 1994, Annie award for outstanding individual achievement for voice acting field of animation, Internat. Animated Soc., 1995, PMA Star Power award, 2000. Mem.: Screen Actors Guild. Office: Cartwright Entertainment Inc 9420 Reseda Blvd #572 Northridge CA 91324

CARTWRIGHT, PAUL COLBY, library director; s. Billie Lee Cartwright and Mary Frances Sullivan; m. Wendy Claire Davis, Oct. 17, 1987; children: Cathryn C., Joseph Tyler Davis. B in History, Hendrix Coll., 1986; MLS, U. So. Miss., 1988. Asst. dir. Madison County Libr., Canton, Miss., 1988—93; dir. Copith-Jefferson Regional Libr., Hazlehurst, Miss., 1993—2003, Yazoo (Miss.) Libr. Assn., Yazoo, Miss., 2003—. Pres. Cartwright Estate Liquidation Inc., Yazoo, 1993—; appraiser of artwork and manscripts. Sec. Yazoo Main St. Assn., 2003—; pres. Yazoo Hist. Preservation Commn., 2003—. Fellow: Rotary; mem.: Yazoo County C. of C., Lions. Republican. Baptist. Avocation: antiques. Office: Yazoo Libr Assn 310 N Main St Yazoo City MS 39194-4253 E-mail: pcartw@yazoo.lib.ms.us.

CARTWRIGHT, PETER, electronics company executive; b. 1930; m. June Cartwright; 4 children. BS, Princeton U.; MS in engring., Columbia U. Lic. NY, Calif. With General Electric Co.; engr. Gibbs and Hill Archtl. Engring., 1979—84; pres., CEO, founder, chmn. Calpine, San Jose, Calif., 1984—. Officer civil engring. corps. USN. Recipient Business Leader of Yr. within the "Scientific American 50", Scientific American, 2004. Office: Calpine 50 W San Fernando St Ste 500 San Jose CA 95113-2433*

CARTY, AMOS W., lawyer; b. V.I., 1966; m. Verna Carty. Chief legal counsel Legis.; counsel to Gov., 1997; COO Roy Lester Schneider Hosp. Mem.: V.I. Bar Assn. (ABA del. 2003, pres. 2004—, pres.-elect 2003—04). Office: Roy Lester Schneider Hosp PO Box 307223 VDS Charlotte Amalie St Thomas VI 00802 Office Phone: 340-714-6331. Office Fax: 340-714-6316. E-mail: awcarty@rlhospital.org.

CARTY, ARTHUR JOHN, science policy advisor, research administrator; b. Hookergate, County Durham, Eng., Sept. 12, 1940; arrived in Can., 1965; naturalized, 1969; George M. and Evelyn Carty; m. Helene Cloutier, Sept. 3, 1967; children: Richard, Stephane, Roxanne. BSc, U. Nottingham, Eng., 1962, PhD, 1965; DSc honoris causa, U. Rennes, France, 1986, Carleton U., Ottawa, Can., 1997, U. Waterloo, Can., 1997; Prof. Honoris Causa, Nat. Chiao-Tung U., Taiwan, 1998; DSc honoris causa, Acadia U., N.S., Can., 1999, McMaster U., Hamilton, Can., 2000, Queen's U., Kingston, Can., 2001. Asst. prof. chemistry Meml. U. Nfld., St. John's, Can., 1965-67, U. Waterloo, Ont., Can., 1967-69, assoc. prof. chemistry, 1969-75, prof. chemistry, 1975-94, chmn. dept. chemistry, 1983-89, dean rsch., 1989-94; pres. Nat. Rsch. Coun. Can., Ottawa, Ont., 1994—; mem. Sch. Grad. Studies and Rsch. U. Ottawa, 1995—. Dir. Guelph-Waterloo Ctr. for Grad. Work in Chemistry, 1975-79; chmn. chem. grants selection com. Nat. Scis. and Engring. Rsch. Coun. Can., 1980-81, mem. targeted rsch. com., 1992-95, chair internat. peer rev. com. Can. Microelectronics Corp., 1994; mem. rsch. grants reallocations com. Natural sci. and engring rsch coun. of Canada. 1997; mem. adv. bd. Steacie Inst. Molecular Scis., NRC, 1990-94; bd. dirs. Waterloo Ctr. for Groundwater Rsch., 1992-94, Ont. Ctr. for Materials Rsch., 1991-94, Can. Indsl. Innovation Ctr., 1990-94, Fields Inst. for Rsch. in Math. Scis., 1991-97; mem. mgmt. bd. Inst. for Chem. Scis. and Tech., 1989-94; mem. R&D adv. coun. Dept. Nat. Def., 1996—, Environment Can., 1996—; mem. internat. adv. bd. Asia Pacific Eco. Cooperation Ctr. for Tech. Foresight, Thailand, 1997—, numerous others. Mem. Waterloo Econ. Devel. Com., 1990-93; mem. internat. intellectual property com. Intelligent Mfg. Sys., 1992-94; mem. rsch. adv. com. Royal Victoria Hosp., London, 1993-94; bd. dirs. Can. Inst. Tech. for Environ., 1992-94, Ont. Ctr. for Environ. Techs. Applications, 1993-94; mem. selection com. phase II of program Network Ctrs. Excellence, 1994—; bd. dirs. Intelligent Mfg. Systems Corp., 1994-2000, Comm. Rsch. Ctr., 1995—, Math. of Info. Tech. and Complex Systems, 1999—, Can. Stroke Network, 2000—, Genome Can., 2000—, Communitech Assn. Inc., 2000—; chmn. Can. Light Source Inc., 1999—; mem. Can. Space Agy. Adv. Coun., 2000; mem. exec. com. Soc. Chem. Industry, 1994-2000; mem. Can. Nuclear Safety Commn., 2000—. Recipient Royal Soc. award Nuffield Found., 1974, Purvis award Soc. Chem. Industry, 1997; Officer of the Ordre Nat. du Mérite (France), 1998, officer Order of Can., 2001. Fellow Royal Soc. Can. (chmn. pub. awareness of sci. com. 1990-94); mem. Am. Chem. Soc., Can. Soc. for Chemistry (v.p. 1989-90, pres. 1990-91, Alcan award 1984, E.W.R. Steacie award 1995), Chem. Inst. Can. (Montreal medal 1996), Royal Soc. Sci. (policy com. 1998—), Engring. Inst. Can. (hon.). Office: Nat Sci Adv to Prime Minister Privy Council Office 85 Sparks St Ottawa ON K1A 0A3 Canada

CARTY, DONALD J., former airline company executive; b. Toronto, July 23, 1946; m. Ana Carty; 3 children. Grad., Queen's U., Kingston, Ont., 1968, Harvard U., 1971. With Air Canada, 1971—73, Canadian Pacific Rwy.; gen. mgr. Montcel Distbrs. unit Celanese Can. Ltd., Montreal, 1973—78; sr. v.p. fin. Americana Hotels, 1978—79; v.p., ops. rsch. American Airlines, 1979—80, v.p. profit improvement, 1980—81, v.p., controller, 1981—83, sr. v.p., controller, 1983—85, sr. v.p. airline planning, 1987-89; pres., CEO CP Air, 1985—87; exec. v.p. fin. and planning AMR and Am. Airlines, DFW Airport, Tex., 1989-95; pres. AMR Airline Group and Am. Airlines, Inc., DFW Airport, Tex., 1995-98; chmn., pres., CEO AMR Corp., Ft. Worth, 1998—2002, chmn., CEO, 2002—03. Bd. dirs. Dell computer Corp., 1992-, Sears, Roebuck & Co. Bd. trustees Queen's U. Recipient The Order of Canada, 2003.

CARTY, HEIDI MARLENE, finance educator, researcher; b. Salt Lake City, July 19, 1967; d. Richard Eathel Coon and Sharon (Pitcher) Smith; m. Shawn Patrick Carty. BS in Psychology with honors cum laude, Loyola U., 1992, MA in Rsch. Methodology and Stats., 1994, PhD in Rsch. Methodology and Stats., 1998. Rsch. asst. Loyola U. Med. Ctr., Maywood, Ill., 1993, Loyola U., Chgo., 1993-94, grad. asst. statis. computing, 1992-94; statis. cons. Iota, Inc., Chgo., 1993-95; grad. asst. rsch. methodology Loyola U., Chgo., 1994-96; statis. cons. U. San Diego, 1996-98; asst. prof. rsch. Hofstra U., Hempstead, N.Y., 1998-99; prin. rsch. analyst and info. Univ. Calif. San Diego, San Diego, 1999—. Part-time lectr. Loyola U., Chgo., 1992-96; lectr. biology dept. U. San Diego, 1998—; lectr. Grad. Sch. Bus. and Mgmt., U. Phoenix, online; test reviewer Buros Inst. Mental Measures, 2002—; part-time lectr. U. Phoenix Online, 2002—. Contbr. articles to profl. jours. Recipient grad. assistantship Loyola U., 1992-94, 94-96; scholar Nat. AMBUCS, 1991. Fellow Am. Ednl. Rsch. Assn.; mem. APA, Am. Ednl. Rsch. Assn., Assn. for Instnl. Rsch., Calif. Assn. for Instnsl. Rsch., Psi Chi (pres.), Alpha Epsilon Delta, Sigma Xi. Avocations: sailing, reading, jogging, movies, theater. Office: UCSD 9500 Gilman Dr La Jolla CA 92093-5004 Office Phone: 858-534-4053. E-mail: hcarty@ucsd.edu.

CARTY, RITA MARY, dean, nurse; b. Pitts., Dec. 23, 1937; d. Ignatius and Frances (Brisini) Cardillo; m. Wayne Lee Carty, Aug. 20, 1966; 1 child, Gina Marie. Diploma in Nursing, Ohio Valley Gen. Hosp., McKees Rocks, Pa., 1958; BSN, Duquesne U., 1965, PhD (hon.), 1995; MSN, Cath. U., 1966, DNSc, 1977. Sch. nurse South Fayette Twp. Sch. Dist., McDonald, Pa., 1958-60; charge nurse Ohio Valley Gen. Hosp., McKees Rocks, Pa., 1960-62, instr., 1962-65; asst. prof. Cath. U., Washington, 1966-72, lectr., 1972-74; dir. nursing div. univ. affiliated program Georgetown U., Washington, 1978-81; assoc. prof., grad. program coordinator George Mason U., Fairfax, Va., 1981-85, chmn. dept. nursing, 1985-93, dean and prof. sch. nursing, 1993—, dean, prof. Coll. Nursing and Health Sci., 1993—; dir. Inst. of Post. Grad. Health Sci., 1991—. Dir. WHO Collaborating Ctr., 1991—. Contbr. articles to profl. jours. Mem. Luxmanor Citizens Assn., Rockville, Md., 1985—. Recipient Bice Lectureship award, sch. nursing U. Va., Charlottesville, 1984, Progress of Excellence award region III Nat. U. Continuing Edn., 1985, Chief Nurse Officer award, 1992. Fellow Am. Acad. Nursing; mem. ANA, Va. Soc. Profl. Nursing (bd. dirs. 1985-87), Am. Assn. Coll. Nursing (bd. dirs. 1987-90, pres. 1990-92), Nat. League Nursing (exec. com. 1987-89), Cath. U. Nurses Alumnae (pres. 1979-81), Golden Key Soc. (hon.), Sigma Theta Tau (1st v.p. 1970-73). Roman Catholic. Avocations: horse back riding, painting, drawing. Office: George Mason U Coll Nursing & Health Sci 4400 University Dr Fairfax VA 22030-4444

CARUCCI, JOHN A., physician; b. Lyndhurst, NJ, Dec. 17, 1963; s. John Joseph and Dorothy Ann Carucci; m. Ingrid Helena Olhoffer, Aug. 21, 1999; 1 child, Isabella Ann. BA, Columbia U., 1981—85; MS, New York U., 1985—87; MD, PhD, SUNY, 1994. Cert. dermatology Am. Bd. of Dermatology, 1998, Mohs Micrographic Surgery Am. Coll. of Mohs Micrographic Surgery and Cutaneous Oncology, 2000. Dir., mohs micrographic and dermatologic surgery Cornell-New York Presbyn. Hosp., New York, 2001—. Contbr. articles to profl. jours. including the Jour. Am. Acad. Dermatology, Archives of Dermatology, Dermatol. Surgery (Presdl. Citation from the Am. Acad. of Dermatology, 2001), chapters to books. Recipient career devel. award in dermatol. surgery, Dermatology Found., 2003; Dermatologist Investigator Rsch. fellows, 1998—99. Mem.: Internat. Transplant Skin Cancer Collaborative (bd. of dirs. 2001—, chmn. rsch. com.). Roman Catholic. Avocations: guitar, musical composition, running, weight training. Office: New York Presbyterian Hospital 525 East 68 th Street New York NY 10021 Office Phone: 212-746-7273. Business E-Mail: jac2015@med.cornell.edu.

CARUNCHIO, FLORENCE REGINA, financial planner; b. Jersey City, July 30, 1952; d. Alfred Peter and Florence Concetta (Pirozzi) Carunchio. BA summa cum laude, Montclair State U., 1975. CFP; lic. ins. provider N.J., N.Y., Va., Fla.; tchr. psychology and social studies K-12 N.J. Tchr. social studies St. Michael's Acad., Palisades Park, NJ, 1975—79; coord. film libr. and youth programs World Vision, Midland Park, 1981—82; owner Gifts of the Magi, Westwood, 1982—84; exec. asst. to CEO, Biomatrix, Inc., Ridgefield, 1985—94; assets mgr. Balden Assoc., Ridgefield, 1985—94; personal fin. advisor Am. Express Fin. Advisors, Paramus, 1995, advanced advisor, 1996—2002, sr. fin. advisor, 1999—2002. Advisor of record pension plan, I.U.O.E. Am. Express Fin. Advisors, Paramus, 2000—05; spkr. in field. Avocations: music, literature, Bible translation and distribution. Office: Am Express Fin Advisors Wash Town Ctr 285 Pascack Rd Ste 7 Township Of Washington NJ 07676

CARUS, MILTON BLOUKE, children's periodicals publisher; b. Chgo., June 15, 1927; s. Edward H. and Dorothy (Blouke) C.; m. Marianne Sondermann, Mar. 3, 1951; children: Andre, Christine, Inga. BS in Elec. Engring, Calif. Inst. Tech., 1949; postgrad. in Chemistry, U. Freiburg, Germany, 1949-51; postgrad., Sorbonne U., Paris, 1951. Devel. engr. Carus Chem. Co., Inc., LaSalle, Ill., 1951—55, asst. gen. mgr., 1955—61, exec. v.p., 1961—64, chmn., CEO, 1964—90, Carus Corp., Peru, 1990—; editor Open Ct. Pub. Co., 1962—67, pub., pres., 1967—88, pub., 1988—89, sr. cons., 1989—; pub. Cricket mag., 1973—89; sr. cons. Cricket mag. group, 1989—2000, chmn., 2000—. Treas. Bookbird Internat. Bd. Books Young People, 1994-1996. Chmn. Ill. Valley Cmty. Coll. Com., 1965-67; pres. Internat. Baccalaureat N.Am. Inc., 1977, chmn., 1980-89; mem. IBO Coun., Geneva, 1977-94; co-trustee Hegeler Inst., 1968-89, chmn., 1989-; mem. employment and tng. com. U.S. Chamber, 1981-85; mem. Nat. Coun. on Ednl. Rsch. Nat. Inst. Edn., Dept. Edn., 1982-85, vice chmn., 1983-85; trustee Parliament of World's Religious, 1988—; mem. Ill. Gov.'s Task Force on Sch.-to-Work, 1994-96. Mem. Ill. Valley Indsl. Assn. (pres. 1970—), Chem. Mfrs. Assn. (dir. 1977-80), Ill. Mfrs. Assn. (dir. 1972-77, 1988-99, chmn. edn. com. 1988—), LaSalle County Hist. Soc. (dir. 1979-85), Phila Soc., Ill. State C. of C. (edn. com. 1973-75). Avocations: reading, travel, music, gardening, languages. Office: Carus Corp Hdqrs 315 5th St Peru IL 61354-2859 Office Phone: 815-224-6674. Business E-Mail: mbcarus@caruschem.com.

CARUSO, ADRIENNE IORIO, retired language educator; b. Saratoga Springs, N.Y., May 30, 1926; d. Andrew and Josephine Pompay Iorio; m. Carl Thomas Caruso, June 27, 1953 (dec. Feb. 2, 2001). BA, N.Y. State Coll. Tchrs., Albany, 1948, MA, 1951. Cert. tchr. N.Y. Dept. Edn. Tchr. English, French, art and libr. Oppenheim Ephratah Ctrl. Sch., NY, 1948—50; tchr. English Corinth H.S., 1951—52, Saratoga Springs Secondary Sch. Complex, 1952—82. Practice tchr. supr. Saratoga Springs City Sch. Dist.; faculty advisor Nat. Honor Soc.; faculty advisor yearbook, book club, others Saratoga Springs Secondary Complex. Permanent mem. Saratoga Performing Arts Ctr.; donor U. at Albany Found., NY; v.p. Saratoga Springs Ret. Tchrs. Assn., 1985—97; pres. Ladies Aux. BPOE Lodge 161, 1985—86; past bd. mem. and treas. LWV. Mem.: AAUW (life; past pres. Sarasota Springs br. 1983—85, 1990—91), Catholic Daughters of Am., N.Y. State Retired Tchrs. Assn. (life; past pres. Ea. zone 1995—98, honoree 1990), Hist. Soc. Saratoga Springs, Friends Saratoga Springs Pub. Libr., SUNY Albany Alumni (life; bd. dir. 2000—). Republican. Roman Catholic. Avocations: art, dance, music, photography, travel. Home: 280 Lake Ave Saratoga Springs NY 12866-3735

CARUSO, DANIEL F., lawyer, judge, former state legislator; b. Greenwich, Conn., Dec. 12, 1957; s. Frederick A. Caruso and Ruth Collins. BA, U. Conn., 1980; JD, U. Vt., 1983. Bar: Conn. 1983, U.S. Dist. Ct. Conn. 1984. Atty. Paul M. Tymniak & Assocs., Fairfield, Conn., 1984-88; sole practice Fairfield, 1988-97; mem. Conn. Gen. Assembly, Hartford, 1989-94, asst. house minority leader, 1992-94, ranking mem. gen. law com., 1991; judge of probate Probate Dist. of Fairfield, 1995—; adminstrv. judge Probate Dist. of New Cannan, 2001, Probate Dist. of Greenwich, 2002; atty. Owen, Schine & Nicola, P.C., Fairfield, Conn., 1997—. Co-chmn. House Rep. Policy Group on Drug Control Strategy; mem. gen. law com. Conn. Gen. Assembly, 1991-94, mem. judiciary com., 1989-94, mem. regulation rev. com., 1989-94; 2d v.p. Conn. Probate Assembly, 2004—. Mem., advisor Nat. Heritage Trust Adv. Bd., 1990-91; treas. Town of Fairfield, 1993-95, mem. bd. fin., 1985-89; del. Rep. Nat. conv., Houston, 1992. Mem. Kiwanis, Eagle Scouts Am., Pi Sigma Alpha, Phi Alpha Theta, Alpha Phi Omega. Roman Catholic. Home: 160 Fairfield Woods Rd Apt 61 Fairfield CT 06825-3348 Office: 53 Sherman St Fairfield CT 06824-5821

CARUSO, DAVID, actor; b. Queens, N.Y., Jan. 17, 1956; s. Charles and Joan C.; m. Sherry Maugans (div.); m. Rachel Ticotin (div.); 1 child, Greta; m. Margaret Caruso (div.). Appearances include (film) An Officer and a Gentleman, 1982, First Blood, 1982, Thief of Hearts, 1984, Blue City, 1986, China Girl, 1987, Twins, 1988, King of New York, 1990, Hudson Hawk, 1991, Mad Dog and Glory, 1993, Kiss of Death, 1994, Jade, 1995, The Split, 1997, Cold Around the Heart, 1997, The Split, 1998; (TV movies) Crazy Times, 1981, The First Olympics-Athens 1896, 1984, Into the Homeland, 1987, Rainbow Drive, 1990, Mission of the Shark, 1991, Judgement Day: The John List Story, 1993, Gold Coast, 1997; (TV series) N.Y.P.D. Blue, 1993-94 (Best Actor - Drama Golden Globe award 1994, Best Actor in Drama series Emmy award nominee 1994), Michael Hayes, 1997, CSI: Miami, 2002-; (TV miniseries) Baseball, 1994, Gold Coast, 1997. Office: William Morris Agy c/o Scott Lambert 151 S El Camino Dr Beverly Hills CA 90212-2775*

CARUSO, NICK J., energy executive; BA in Acctg., La. State U. Various positions, including controller, gen. auditor to v.p. fin., CFO Shell Oil Co., Houston, 1969—2001; exec. v.p., CFO Dynegy, Inc., Houston, 2002—. Office: Dynegy Ste 5800 1000 Louisiana Houston TX 77002-5050 Office Phone: 713-507-6400.

CARVALHO, JOSEPH, III, museum director, library director; b. Kinston, N.C., Aug. 28, 1953; s. Jose Jr. and Janine M. (Gagnon) C.; m. Gayle Elizabeth Conklin, Oct. 16, 1976; children: Alyssa Gayle, Michael Armand. BA, Westfield State Coll., 1975; MA, Coll. William and Mary, 1977; M in Libr. and Info. Sci., U. R.I., 1984. Instr. Westfield (Mass.) State Coll., 1976; dir. History Mus. Conn. Valley Hist. Mus., Springfield, 1986-94; pres., exec. dir. Springfield Libr. and Mus. Assn., 1994—. Dir. Inst. for Mass. Studies, Westfield State Coll., 1990; bd. dirs. Mass. Found. for Humanities, 2004—. Author: Black Families of Hampden County, Mass.: 1650-1855, 1984; editor: Guide to the History of Massachusetts, 1988; assoc. editor: Labor in Massachusetts, 1990; assoc. editor Hist. Jour. Mass., 1978—; exec. prodr. (video documentary) The Making of the Dr. Seuss Nat. Meml., 2001. Bd. dirs. Urban League Greater Springfield, 1992—2003; v.p. Indian Motorcycle Mus., Springfield, 1996—; founder, bd. dirs. Springfield Bus. Improvement Dist., 1998—. Recipient Commendation, Am. Assn. for State and Local History, 1989, Excellence in Programming award Cable TV Endowment, Springfield, 1991, 92, 93, Video Hist. Documentary award New Eng. Hist. Assn., Providence, 1993. Mem. Nat. Geneal. Soc. (book rev. editor Nat. Geneal. Soc. Quarterly 1987-95, Nat. award for advancing geneal. rsch. publs. 1996), Am. Assn. Mus., Acad. Cert. Archivists (cert. archivist), Assn. Profl. Genealogists (regional trustee 1992-96), New Eng. Mus. Assn. Avocation: sculpting. Office: Springfield Libr & Mus Assn 220 State St Springfield MA 01103 Office Phone: 413-263-6800 259. E-mail: jcarvalho@springfieldmuseums.org.

CARVALHO, JULIE ANN, psychologist; b. Washington, Apr. 11, 1940; d. Daniel Henry and Elizabeth Cecilia (Gardiner) Schmidt; children: Alan R., Dennis M., Melanie D., Celeste A., Joshua E. BA with high honors, U. Md., 1962, postgrad., 1962-63, 68-73; MA, George Washington U., 1966; postgrad., Va. Poly. Inst., 1979-88; Dal studies in curriculum and instrn., Argosy U., 2003—. Social sci. rsch. analyst Mental Health Study Ctr., NIMH, Adelphi, Md., 1963-67; edn. and tng. analyst Computer Applications, Inc., Silver Spring, Md., 1967-68; edn. program specialist, program analyst Nat. Ctr. for Ednl. R&D, U.S. Office of Edn., Washington, 1969-73; equal opportunity specialist Office of Sec., HEW, Washington, 1973-77; legis. program, civil rights analyst Office for Civil Rights Dept. Health and Human Svcs., Washington, 1977-85; ind. cons. Adj. lectr. No. Va. C.C., George Mason U., Montgomery Coll., Strayer U., Park U., Shepherd Coll., Germanna Coll., U. Md. U. Coll., Va. Internat. U., Prince William Hosp., Fairfax County Pub. Schs., Fairfax County Dept. Social Svcs., all Washington area, 1986—; proposal evaluator HUD, HHS, 1989—; presenter in field. Contbr. articles to profl. jours. Bd. dirs. Child Care Ctrs., 1970—76, HEW Employees Assn., 1973—78; steering com. Alliance for Child Care, 1975—80. Mem.: ASPA (condr. panels 1975, 1991), APA (panel condr. 1969—75, editor Bull. of Peace Psychology 1991—97, divsn. 48), Unitarian Universalists for Social Justice (bd. dirs. Balt.-Washington region 2003—), Federally Employed Women (nat. editor 1975—79), Psychologists Soc. Responsibility (cons.), Capitol Area Social Psychologists Assn. (conf. chmn. 1985, 1993), Fairfax County Assn. for the Gifted (pres. 1980), Phi Alpha Theta, Psi Chi, Alpha Sigma Lambda (hon.). Home and Office: PO Box 11500 Alexandria VA 22312-0500 Office Phone: 703-453-9119. E-mail: visionaries@pocketmail.com.

CARVER, DAVID HAROLD, pediatrician, educator; b. Boston, Apr. 18, 1930; s. Elias and Lottie (Jaffe) C.; m. Patricia Jo Nair, Aug. 2, 1963; children: Randolph Nair, Rebecca Lynn, Leslie Allison. AB magna cum laude, Harvard U., 1951; MD, Duke U., 1955. Intern Johns Hopkins Hosp., 1955-56; rsch. fellow pediatrics Cleve. Met. Hosp., 1956-58; jr. asst. resident Children's Hosp. Med. Center, Boston, 1958-59, sr. asst. resident, 1959-60, chief resident, 1960-61, USPHS spl. rsch. fellow Harvard Med. Sch., 1961-63; asst. prof. pediatrics Albert Einstein Coll. Medicine, 1963-66; from assoc. prof. to prof. pediatrics Johns Hopkins U. Med. Sch., 1966-76; prof. pediatrics U. Toronto Med. Sch., 1976-88; physician-in-chief Hosp. Sick Children, Toronto, 1976-86; chmn. dept. pediatrics U. Toronto, 1976-86; prof., chmn. dept. pediatrics Robert Wood Johnson Med. Sch., New Brunswick, N.J., 1988-2001, prof. pediat., 2001—, assoc. dean faculty affairs, 2001—04, spl. advisor to the dean, 2004—. Mem. study sect. USPHS Ctr. Disease Control, 1971-73; mem. provincial research grants rev. com. Ont. Ministry Health, 1977-83, chmn., 1981-83 Assoc. editor: Textbook of Pediatrics, 14th edit, 1968, 15th edit., 1972, 16th edit., 1977; mem. editl. bd. Pediatrics, 1973-79. With USPHS, 1956-58. Recipient Schaffer award clin. teaching Johns Hopkins U. Med. Sch., 1973, Bain award for clin. teaching Hosp. Sick Children, 1978, Kennedy Sr. scholar, 1966-73 Mem. Am. Acad. Pediatrics (com. on infectious diseases 1973-79), Infectious Disease Soc. Am., Am. Soc. Virology, Internat. Soc. Interferon Research, Canadian Infectious Disease Soc., Am. Soc. Microbiology, Soc. Pediatric Research, Am. Pediatric Soc., Can. Pediatric Soc., Harvard Club Princeton. Home: 220 Sayre Dr Princeton NJ 08540-5852 Business E-Mail: carver@umdnj.edu.

CARVER, GEORGE ALLEN, JR., retired lawyer; b. Washington, Nov. 8, 1940; s. George Allen and Barbara Ellen (Bristol) C.; m. Joan Page, Dec. 13, 1964; children: George Allen III, Robert William. BS, U.S. Mil. Acad., 1964; JD, U. Va., 1972. Bar: Va. 1972, D.C. 1978, U.S. Ct. Appeals (D.C. cir.) 1979, U.S. Ct. Appeals (9th cir.) 1986, U.S. Ct. Appeals (4th cir.) 1988. Trial atty. gen. crimes sect. Criminal divsn. U.S. Dept. Justice, Washington, 1972-76, trial atty. pub. integrity sect., 1976-81, dir. conflicts of interest crimes br., pub. integrity sect., 1981-88, dep. chief fraud sect., 1988-92, prin. dep. chief fraud sect., 1992-95, sr. counsel to chief asset forfeiture/money laundering sect., 1995-96, dep. chief, sr. counsel to the chief, 1996-2000; ret., 2000. Capt. inf. U.S. Army, 1964-69. Decorated Silver Star, Bronze Star, Purple Heart. Avocations: photography, fishing, boating, walking, reading. Home: 6049 Makely Dr Fairfax Station VA 22039-1324

CARVER, GLORIA JEAN, documentation specialist; d. Floyd Albert Carver and Kathryn Elizabeth Onstead/Carver; 1 child, Jacklynne. BA, Concordia U., 1988; MS, Cardinal Stritch U., 1995. LPN, Pa. Documentation adminstr. ADC Telecomms., Bloomington, Minn., 1984—97; documentation analyst Ciprico, Plymouth, Minn., 1997—2003; documentation specialist Micro Dynamics, Eden Prairie, Minn., 2003—. Mem.: Am. Soc. of Quality, Amaranth, Ea. Star. Avocations: motorcycling, fishing, needlecrafts, camping. Home: 2400 W 140th St Burnsville MN 55337 Office: Micro Dynamics 6201 Bury Dr Eden Prairie MN 55346

CARVER, JEFFREY ALLAN, writer; b. Cleve., Aug. 25, 1949; s. Robert D. and Mildred Sherrick Carver; m. Allysen Evans Palmer, Sept. 7, 1986; children: Alexandra, Julia. BA, Brown U., 1971; M of Marine Affairs, U. R.I., 1974. Scuba diving instr. Nat. Assn. of Underwater Instrs., Mass., R.I; Quahog diver Narragansett, R.I., 1974. Word processing cons., Cambridge, 1984-85; webmaster The Star Rigger's Net, 1996—; tchr., lectr., developer, on-air host distance learning satellite broadcast series Sci. Fiction and Fantasy Writing, 1995. Author: 14 novels including Eternity's End, 2000, The Chaos Chronicles, vol. 1-3, Dragons in the Stars, 1992, Dragon Rigger 1993, From a Changeling Star, 1989, Down the Stream of Stars, 1990, The Infinity Link, 1984, (CD ROM and online) Writing Science Fiction & Fantasy, 2000; consulting instrl. designer, editor, 2000—. Mem. Sci. Fiction and Fantasy Writers of Am., The Authors Guild. Avocations: reading, scuba diving, hiking, camping with family. E-mail: jeff@starrigger.net.

CARVER, JOHN H., medical association administrator; b. Buffalo, Dec. 27, 1965; s. Robert L. Carver and Katherine E. Smith; stepfather, Gerald J. Smith; m. Paula D. Deinhart, Oct. 18, 1992; children: Madeline Haase, Charles John. BS in Bus./Mgmt. Econs., SUNY, Buffalo, 1988; C.M.R. in Sci. and Medicine, Bus. Healthcare, Cert. Med. Representative Inst., 1997; postgrad., St. Bonaventure U., 2001, MS in Exec. and Profl. Leadership, 2002; MBA in Internat. Bus .Adminstrn., Beijing Inst. Tech., 2001. Forms products broker Moore Bus. Products, Amherst, N.Y., 1990-92; med. liaison, ctrl. nervous sys. specialist Solvay Pharms., Inc., Marietta, Ga., 1992-97; founding mgr. Med. Sci. Liaison Programs, Forest Labs., Inc., N.Y.C., 1997—2001, sr. ctrl. area mgr., 2001—. Adj. instr. in pharmacology Lake Erie Coll. Osteo. Medicine, Erie, Pa., 1996-98; bd. dirs. Westfield Devel. Corp., N.Y., 2001-2002. Mem.: Classical Ballet of We. NY (bd. dirs.), Lockport City Ballet (bd. dirs.). Avocations: yacht racing, flying sail planes, downhill skiing, mountain biking, photography, archery. Office: Forest Labs Inc 909 Third Ave New York NY 10022-4731 E-mail: John.Carver@FRX.com.

CARVER, KIMBERLY, music educator; b. Battle Creek, Mich., Sept. 30, 1961; d. Michael and Janet Betanzos; m. Joseph Carver, Dec. 26, 1997; children: Alexander Blaise Tomann, Julia Frances Tomann. AS, Orange County CC, Middletown, NY, 1981; BFA, SUNY, Buffalo, 1981—84; MS, Western Conn. State U., Danbury Conn., 1989. Cert. Edn. Conn., 1989. Dir. of choirs Middletown H.S., NY, 1985—94; dir. of choirs and drama Valley Ctrl. H.S., Montgomery, NY, 1994—. Dept. chairperson Valley Ctrl. H.S., Montgomery, 1999—; wedding svc. vocalist Riverwood Studio, 1985—; advisor Tri-M Music Honor Soc. at Valley Ctrl. H.S., 2005—; auditorium mgr. Valley Ctrl. H.S., 1997—; pvt. vocal instr. The Riverwood Studio, Marlboro, NY, 1985—. Singer: (benefit performer) Back to Bacharach. Mem.: MENC, Am. Choral Dirs. Assn., NY State Sch. Music Assn. Roman Catholic. Achievements include development of Creator of The Riverwood Studio, Inc. This is a vocal performance company that provides educational practice cd's to individuals to prepare them for any solo performance. www.theriverwood-studio.com. Office: Valley Ctrll High Sch 1175 Rt 17K Montgomery NY 12549 Office Phone: 845-457-2400 (7169). Home Fax: 928-438-3105; Office Fax: 845-457-4056. Personal E-mail: kcarver@hvc.rr.com. E-mail: kcarver@vcmail.ouboces.org.

CARVER, NORMAN FRANCIS, JR., architect, photographer; b. Jan. 27, 1928; m. Joan Willson, Aug. 15, 1953; children: Norman F. III, Cristina. Grad., Yale. Practice architecture, Kalamazoo; prof. advanced photography Kalamazoo Inst. Arts, 1971-86. Vis. lectr., critic Carnegie Inst. Tech., Mich. State U., Yale U., MIT, So. Ill. U.; guest lectr. King Faisal U., Saudi Arabia, 1981. Exhibited photography U.S. and abroad; photographs published in Aperture, House Beautiful, Horizon, others; author: Form and Space of Japanese Architecture, 1955, 3d edit., 1993, Silent Cities of Mexico and the Maya, 1966, rev. edit., 1986, Italian Hilltowns, 1979, rev. edit., 1995, Iberian Villages - Spain and Portugal, 1981, Japanese Folkhouses, 1984, rev. edit., 2003, North African Villages, 1989, Greek Island Villages, 2001. Recipient Fulbright awards to Japan, 1953-54, 64, silver medal Archtl. League, 1962, award Archtl. Record, 1960, 61, 62, Robert Hastings award Mich. Soc. Architects, 1987. Home: 3201 Lorraine Ave Kalamazoo MI 49008-2003

CARVER, PETER JAMES, education educator, director; s. Richard James and Dorothy (Nikodem) Carver; m. Lisa Wiggins, Sept. 9, 2000. BA, Stetson U., 1992; MA, Tex. Woman's U., 1995; MFA, U. New Orleans, 2000. Mng. dir. Tulane Summer Lyric Theatre, 1998—2000; exec. dir. Asheville (NC) Cmty. Theatre, 2000—02; adj. instr. Asheville-Buncombe Tech. CC, 2002—; adj. prof. U. SC Upstate, 2002—04, U. NC, Asheville, 2002—. Founder Poetry at an Uncouth Hour Stetson U., De Land, Fla., 1991—; cons. in field; host Western NC Theatre League Unified Audition, 2004—05. Dir.: (plays) This is Our Youth, 2002, The Velveteen Rabbit, 2003—04, The Boys Next Door, 2004; columnist, reviewer Critical Rev., 2003. Grantee, Asheville Area Arts Coun., 2001, Cmty. Found. WNC, 2002. Mem.: Rotary. Home: 18 Moffitt Hill Dr Asheville NC 28805 Personal E-mail: thestagepicture@aol.com.

CARVER, RITA, fundraising consultant; b. Minden, Nebr. d. Jess Albert and Marguerite Florence Ford; children: David Christopher, Heather Michelle; m. Kris E. White, Apr. 30, 2004. BS in Comm., Dallas Bapt. U., 1976; MA in human scis., Our Lady of the Lake, 2000. Freelance writer, 1976—82; account exec. Walvoord, Killian, McCabe, Dallas, 1982—86; sr. v.p. Resource Devel., Inc., Plano, Tex., 1986—2001; pres. R-Designs Inc., Plano, 2001—. Instr. Resource Inst., Springfield, Mo., 1986-99. Creative dir.: Portraits of Hope, 1996; editor: He Leadeth Me, 1999. Vol. Collin County Children's Adv. Ctr., Plano, 1999—. Named Outstanding Young Women of Am., 1980, Most Stressed Out Bus. Traveler, Rosewood Hotel and Resorts, 1994. Mem. AAUW, NAFE, Sierra Club, Plano C. of C. Methodist. Avocations: scuba diving, writing, dance, travel. Office: R-Designs Inc 752 Nicklaus Dr Plano TX 75025 Office Phone: 972-527-2265. Personal E-mail: rmcrdi@aol.com.

CARVEY, DANA, actor, stand up comedian; b. Missoula, Mont., Apr. 2, 1955; m. Paula Zwaggerman. Student communication arts, San Francisco U. Appeared in TV films Alone at Last, 1980, Whacked Out, 1981, Hot Shots, 1986; TV series One of the Boys, 1982, Blue Thunder, 1984, Saturday Night Live, 1986— (Emmy award Outstanding Individual Performance in Variety or Musical Program 1989, 90, 91, 93); appeared in films including Halloween II, 1981, Racing with the Moon, 1984, This is Spinal Tap, 1984, Tough Guys, 1986, Moving, 1988, Opportunity Knocks, 1990, Wayne's World, 1992, Wayne's World II, 1993, Clean Slate, 1994, The Road to Wellville, 1994, Trapped in Paradise, 1994, The Shot, 1996, Little Nicky, 2000, The Master of Disguise, 2002; (TV series) The Dana Carvey Show, 1996; appeared on TV: Saturday Night Live, 25th Anniversary, 1999, Saturday Night Live: Best of Phil Hartman, 1998. Recipient Am. Comedy award, 1990.

CARVILLE, JAMES, JR., (CHESTER JAMES CARVILLE), political scientist, consultant; b. Fort Benning, Ga., Oct. 25, 1944; s. Lucille Carville; m. Mary Matalin, Nov. 25, 1993; 2 children. Grad., La. State Univ. Litigator, Baton Rouge, 1973—79; cons. Bob Casey's 1986 Penn. gubernatorial race, Sen. Harris Wofford's 1991 campaign; chief strategist, cons. Bill Clinton's 1992 presdl. campaign; cons. Gov. Jim Florio's 1993 re-election campaign, N.J., Ehud Barak's campaign for Prime Min. Israel, 1999. Co-host CNN's Crossfire; ptnr. Hawthorne Lane Restaurant, San Francisco; spkr. in field. Author: We're Right, They're Wrong: A Handbook for Spirited Progressives, 1996, ...And the Horse He Rode in on: The People vs. Kenneth Starr, 1998, Stickin': The Case for Loyalty, 2000; co-author (with Mary Matalin): All's Fair: Love, War and Running for President, 1994; (with Paul Begala) Buck Up, Suck Up... and Come Back When You Foul Up, 2003, (with Jeff Nussbaum) Had Enough?, 2003, (with Patricia C. McKissack) Lu and the Swamp Ghost, 2004; actor: (films) The People vs. Larry Flynt, 1996, Old School, 2003, Wedding Crashers, 2005; (TV series) Boston Common, 1996, Arli$$, 1997, (voice only) King of the Hill, 1997, Mad About You, 1998, Spin City, 1999, (voice only) Family Guy, 2000; appearance (documentaries) The War Room, 1993, The Hunting of the President, 2004, (TV-polit. series) K Street. Named Campaign Mgr. of the Year, Am. Assn. of Political Consultants, 1993. Avocation: watching reruns of the andy griffith show. Office: Gaslight Inc 424 S Washington St Lower Level Alexandria VA 22314 Office Phone: 703-739-7777. Business E-Mail: james@carville.info.

CARWELL, HATTIE VIRGINIA, health physicist; b. Bklyn., July 17, 1948; d. George and Fannie (Tunstall) C. BS in Chemistry/Biology, Bennett Coll., 1970; MS in Radiation Sci., Rutgers U., 1971; postgrad., U. Calif., Berkeley, 1973-75. Rsch. asst. Thomas Jefferson U. Hosp., Phila., 1970-72; health physicist AEC, Upton, N.Y., 1972-73, Energy Rsch. Adminstrn., Oakland, Calif., 1973-80; internat. nuclear safeguards insp. and group leader Internat. Atomic Energy Agy., Vienna, Austria, 1980-85; health physicist U.S. Dept. Energy, Oakland, Calif., 1985-90, program mgr. for high energy and nuclear programs, 1990-91, program mgr. Berkeley, Calif., 1991-93, ops. br. chief, 1993-94, ops. team head, 1994—. Asst. environ. survey team leader Dept. Energy, Washington, 1987; lectr. U. Calif.-Berkeley, Stanford U., Cabrillo Coll., Can. Coll., Tougaloo Coll; dir. Mus. African Am. Tech. Sci. Village. Author: Blacks In Science: Astrophysicist to Zoologist, 1977, In Pursuit of Excellence: Dr. Warren Henry - World Class Scientist, 1998, Solar Cooker Design Training Guide, 1996, African American Achievements in Air and Space, 2003; contbr. sci. articles to profl. jours. Co-founder, chmn. Devel. Fund for Black Students in Sci. and Tech., Washington, 1983—; dir., co-founder Mus. African Am. Tech. Sci. Village, 2000—; bd. dirs. Nat. Inventors Hall of Fame Found., 2001—05; treas. Nat. Coun. Black Scientists and Engrs., 2001—05. Named inductee, Black Coll. Hall of Fame, 1991, included in exhibit, The African Am. Presence in Physics, 1999; recipient Fed. Cmty. Svc. award, 1977, Elijah McCoy award, 1989, vol. recognition, Dept. Energy, 1990, Disting. Alumni award, 1992, Image award, Bennett Coll., 1997, Inspiring Scientist award, Jr. Ctr of Art and Science of Oakland, 2002, Outstanding Woman in Sci. award, Nat. Tech. Assn., 1998. Mem.: NAACP (life), No. Calif. Coun. Black Profl. Engrs. (pres. 1986, 1987, sec. 1988, pres. 1994, 1995, sec. 1996—99, pres. 2000—05), Inst. Materials Mgmt. (treas. Vienna chpt. 1985), Nat. Health Physics Soc., Nat. Tech. Assn. (James C. Jones Humanitarian award 2000, Outstanding Woman Scientist Award 1998). Avocations: writing, travel. Home: 4622 Meldon Ave Oakland CA 94619-2646

CARY, ALICE SHEPARD, retired physician; b. Gaziantep, Turkey, June 2, 1920; (parents Am. citizens); d. Lorrin Andrews and Virginia (Moffat) Shepard; m. Otis Cary, Dec. 9, 1944; children: Beth D., Ann B., Frank B., Ellen Cary Bearn. *Husband, Otis Cary, was born in Otaru, Japan on October 20, 1921. His degrees were BA from Amherst College, 1946, MA from Yale University, 1951, and LHD from Doshisha University, 1992. He attended the US Navy Language School in Berkeley, California, and Boulder, Colorado 1942-1943 and until 1945 interrogated Japanese prisoners of war in Hawaii, Attu and Saipan. From 1947 until 1992 he was on the facilities of both Amherst College and Doshisha University, Kyoto, Japan. He authored, edited, or translated numerous books and articles, many of them in Japanese. Kyoto Prefecture gave him their "Cultural Award" in 1984, Kyoto City in 1989, and in 1987 he received an Imperial Decoration: Order of the Sacred Treasure, third class.* BA, Wellesley Coll., 1942; MD, Yale U., 1945. Intern, resident New Haven Hosp., 1945-47; physician Doshisha U. Health Ctr., Kyoto, Japan, 1947-50, Japan Bapt. Hosp., Kyoto, 1955-95; dir. Aoibashi Family Clinic Counseling Ctr., Kyoto, 1981-91; ret., 1996. Assoc. missionary United Ch. Bd. World Ministries, N.Y.C., 1947-96. Mem. adv. com. on women's issues UN Women's Decade, Prime Min.'s Office, Tokyo, 1970—75; trustee Piedmont (Calif.) Cmty. Ch. Recipient 40th Anniversary award Coll. Women's Assn. Japan, 1989, internat. contbn. award City of Kyoto, 1992. Mem.: East Bay Chpt. UN Assn., U.S.A. Democrat. Mem. United Ch. of Christ. Home: 33 Linda Ave Apt 1601 Oakland CA 94611-4817

CARY, ANNE O., economist, retired diplomat; b. Washington, Sept. 8, 1952; d. Charles O. and Jean (Cochran) C.; m. John F. McNamara, June 26, 1982; children: John McNamara, Elizabeth McNamara, James McNamara. Student, Trinity Coll., Dublin, Ireland, 1972-73; BA, U. Wis., 1973; MA, Stanford U., 1984. Internat. economist Civil Aeronautic Bd., Washington, 1974; fgn. svc. officer Dept. of State, Washington, 1974-76, U.S. Mission to European Community, Brussels, Belgium, 1976-78, U.S. Emb., Port-au-Prince, Haiti, 1978-80, Paris, France, 1980-83, Addis Ababa, Ethiopia, 1985-87, New Delhi, India, 1987-89, European Community Affairs, Dept. of State, Washington, 1989-91; consul gen. U.S. Consulate, Casablanca, Morocco, 1992-95; macroeconomist U.S. Embassy, Pretoria, 2000—. Mem. Fgn. Svc. Res. Corps, 1995—. Dean Rusk fellow Georgetown U., Washington, 1991-92.

CARY, JAMES DONALD, journalist; b. Douglas, Ariz., Oct. 7, 1919; s. Leon Barker and Ruth F. (Dunlap) C.; m. Norma Frances Goben, Dec. 18, 1942; 1 son, James Christopher. BA, U. Ariz., 1941; MS in Journalism, Northwestern U., 1948. Reporter Miami Beach Evening Sun, Miami, Fla., 1945-46, Miami Daily News, 1946-47, Ariz. Times, Phoenix, 1947-48; reporter AP, Phoenix, 1949-54, Tokyo Bur., 1954-60, news editor, 1959-60; desk editor Washington Bur., 1960-65; White House/State Dept. corr. Copley New Service, Washington, 1965-73, bur. chief, 1973-78, sr. corr., 1978-81. Vis. prof. Brigham Young U., 1983-84 Author: Japan Today: Reluctant Ally, 1962, Tanks and Armor in Modern Warfare, 1965, (computer disk novel) The Fires of Mammon, 1994, (novel) Seeds: Search for the Descendants of Christ, 2004. Served from 2d lt. to capt. AUS, 1941-46, ETO. Decorated Silver Star, Purple Heart (2).; Recipient Copley Ring of Truth awards, 1966, 72, Ariz. Press Club award., Brigham Young U. Disting. Service cert. Mem. Nat. Press Club. Home: 2604 Aspen Way Boynton Beach FL 33436-6614 E-mail: caryonjim@aol.com.

CARY, NOEL DEMETRI, history educator; b. June 22, 1950; BS in Physics, U. Calif., Davis, 1971; MA in Astronomy, U. Va., 1973; PhD in History, U. Calif., Berkeley, 1988. Scientific programmer Computer Sci. Corp., Silver Spring, Md., 1974-76, Informatics Inc., 1978-79; adj. asst. prof. Montana State U., 1986-87; instr. Swarthmore Coll., 1987-88; asst. prof. Coll. Holy Cross, 1989-93, assoc. prof., 1993—. Vis. asst. prof. Oakland Univ., 1988-89. Author: The Path to Christian Democracy, 1996. Office: Coll Holy Cross Dept History Worcester MA 01610 Business E-Mail: ncary@holycross.edu.

CARY, WILLIAM STERLING, retired church executive; b. Plainfield, N.J., Aug. 10, 1927; s. Andrew and Sadie C.; m. Marie B. Phillips; children: Yvonne, Denise, Sterling, Patricia. BA, Morehouse Coll., 1949, also D.D.; MDiv, Union Theol. Sem., 1952; LL.D., Bishop Coll.; D.D., Elmhurst Coll.; L.H.D., Allen U., Ill. Coll.; MDiv, Union Theol. Sem. Ordained to ministry Baptist Ch., 1948; pastor Butler Meml. Presbyn. Ch., Youngstown, Ohio, 1953-55, Interdenominational Ch. of Open Door, Bklyn., 1955-58, Grace Congl. Ch., N.Y.C., 1958-68; area min. Met. and Suffolk assns. N.Y. Conf. United Ch. Christ, 1968-75; pres. Nat. Coun. Chs., N.Y.C., 1972-75; conf. min. Ill. Conf. United Ch. Christ, 1974—94, conf. min. emeritus, 2001. Chmn. United Ch. Christ Council Conf. Execs., Council Religious Leaders Met. Chgo., 1986-92; mem. governing bd. Nat. Council Chs.; mem. rep. consultation on ch. union United Ch. of Christ; mem. exec. council United Ch. of Christ; mem. Council on Ecumenism, Ch. World Service, Pres.'s Adv. Com. Vietnam Refugees; lectr. in field. Named One of 100 Most Influential Blacks in Am. for 1974-75 Ebony mag. Address: 206 Le Moyne Pkwy Oak Park IL 60302-1122

CARYL, WILLIAM R., JR., orthodontist; b. Syracuse, N.Y., Sept. 7, 1953; s. William R. and Joyce L. (Downs) C.; m. Deborah S. Auerbach, Apr. 25, 1975; children: Mark R., David M. BA in Biology, SUNY, Buffalo, 1975, DDS, 1979; MS in Oral Biology, Loyola U. of Chgo., Maywood, Ill., 1981. Assoc. orthodontist William B. Drake, DDS, MS, Liverpool, N.Y., 1981-84; orthodontist pvt. practice, Camillus, N.Y., 1983—. Mem. adv. bd. Fairmount Gardens, Syracuse, N.Y., 1994-2000; co-chair Ctrl. N.Y. Study Group for Dentofacial Abnormalities, 1993-95. Nat. ski patroler Nat. Ski Patrol System Camillus Ski Assn., 1969-71, 81-93. Mem. ADA, Am. Assn. Orthodontists, Am. Cleft Palate Craniofacial Assn., Syracuse Dental Seminar (program chair, sec. 1987-88, 88—, pres. 89, 89-90, 2000-01), Rotary Internat. (sec., pres. 1989-90). Avocations: sailing, skiing, bicycling, tennis, reading. Office: 5102 W Genesee St Camillus NY 13031-2327 E-mail: wcaryljr@aol.com.

CASAD, ROBERT CLAIR, legal educator; b. Council Grove, Kans., Dec. 8, 1929; s. Clair L. and Eula Imogene (Compton) C.; m. Sally Ann McKeighan, Aug. 20, 1955; children: Benjamin Nathan, Joseph Story, Robert Clair, Madeleine Imogene. AB, U. Kans., 1950, MA, 1952; JD with honors, U. Mich., 1957; S.JD, Harvard U., 1979. Bar: Kans. 1957, Minn. 1958, U.S. Dist. Ct. Kans. 1957; U.S. Ct. Appeals (10th cir.) 1985. Instr. law U. Mich., Ann Arbor, 1957-58; assoc. firm Streater & Murphy, Winona, Minn., 1958-59; asst. prof. law U. Kans., Lawrence, 1959-62, assoc. prof., 1962-64, prof., 1964-81, John H. and John M. Kane prof. law, 1981-97; John H. and John M. Kane prof. law emeritus, 1997. Vis. prof. UCLA, 1969—70, U. Ill., 1973—74, U. Calif., Hastings, 1979—80, U. Colo., 1982, U. Vienna, 1986, U. Mich., 1986, U. Valladolid, 1988, Chuo U., 1992, U. Salamanca, 1995, Emory U., 2001—02. Author: Jurisdiction and Forum Selection, 1988, 2nd edit., 1999, Jurisdiction in Civil Actions, 1983, 2d edit., 1991, (with Richman) 3d edit., 1998, Expropriation Procedures in Central America and Panama, 1975, (with others) Kansas Appellate Practice, 1978, Civil Judgment Recognition and the Integration of Multiple State Associations, 1982, Res Judicata in a Nutshell, 1976; (with Fink and Simon) Civil Procedure: Cases and Materials, 2d edit., 1989, (with Gard) Kansas Code of Civil Procedure Annotated, 4th edit., 2003, (with Clermont) Res Judicata: A Handbook on its Theory, Doctrine and Practice, 2001; contbr. numerous articles to legal jours. Mem. civil code adv. com. Kans. Jud. Coun. 1st lt. USAF, 1952-53. Recipient Coblentz prize Sch. Law, U. Mich., 1957, Rice prize U. Kans. Law Sch., 1976, 83, 84, 88, 89, medal Dana Fund for Internat. and Comparative Legal Studies, 1981, Balfour Jeffrey Rsch. prize U. Kans., 1984; Ford fellow, 1965-66, fellow in law Harvard U., 1965-66, OAS fellow, 1976, NEH fellow, summer 1978; grantee Dana Fund for Internat. and Comparative Legal Studies. Mem. Am. Law Inst., ABA, Kans. Bar Assn., Order of Coif. Democrat. Home: 1130 Emery Rd Lawrence KS 66044-2515 E-mail: casad@ku.edu, casad@sunflower.com.

CASADESUS, PENELOPE ANN, advertising executive, film producer; b. Calcutta, India, Sept. 20, 1940; came to U.S., 1980; d. Francis John and Betty (Walker) Copeland; m. Jean-Claude Casadesus, Jan. 20, 1960; children: Caroline, Sebastian. Gen. Cert. of Edn., Godolphin Sch., Eng. Head of prodn. S.S.C.B. Lintas, Paris, 1975—78, Grey-France, Paris, 1978—80, Grey Worldwide, N.Y.C., 1980, exec. producer Internat. Health and Beauty divsn., 1991—, sr. v.p., group prodr. Ind. film producer, 1984—. Author, producer (screenplays) Transvaal Episode, The Cuckoo.

CASALE, ALFRED STANLEY, thoracic and cardiovascular surgeon; b. Passaic, NJ, Nov. 28, 1955; s. Alfred Stanley and Regina Josephine (Cembor) C.; m. Mary Louise Cavell, Aug. 1, 1976; 1 child, Katherine. BA, Johns Hopkins U., 1976, MD, 1980. Diplomate Am. Bd. Surgery, Am. Bd. Thoracic Surgery; cert. Surg. Critical Care. Intern Johns Hopkins U., Balt., 1980-81, resident in surgery, 1981-85, resident in thoracic surgery, 1985-88, asst. prof., 1988-90; surgeon Mid Atlantic Surg. Assocs., Morristown, N.J., 1990-2000, ptnr., 1993—2000; chief cardiac surgery U. Hosp., UMD N.J., Newark, 2000—01; dir. cardiothoracic surgery Geisinger Wyoming Valley Med. Ctr., Wilkes-Barre, Pa., 2001—; surg. dir. Heart Inst., Geisinger Health Sys., Danville, PR, 2002—. Assoc. chief cardiac surgery Atlantic Health Sys., Florham Park, NJ; chief cardiac surgery Gen. Hosp. Ctr., Passaic, NJ, 2000; mem. cardiovasc. health adv. panel N.J. Dept. Health, Trenton; assoc. prof. N.J. Med. Sch., UMD N.J., 2000—01. Contbr. articles to profl. jours. Dir. Madison YMCA, N.J., 1990-96, Am. Heart Assn., Morristown, 1990-2001, Luzerne County, 2002—, Kirby Child Care Ctr., Madison, 1992-96. Fellow Am. Coll. Surgeons, Am. Coll. Cardiology, Am. Coll. Chest Physicians; mem. Assn. Acad. Surgery (Resident Rsch. award 1984), Internat. Soc. Heart Transplantation, Soc. Thoracic Surgery. Avocations: skiing, tennis, fishing, shooting. Office: Geisinger Wyo Valley Med Ctr 1000 E Mountain Blvd Wilkes Barre PA 18711 Office Phone: 570-820-6017. Business E-Mail: ascasale@geisinger.edu. E-mail: al@casale.org.

CASALE, THOMAS BRUCE, medical educator; b. Chgo., Apr. 21, 1951; m. Jean M. Casale; 1 son, Jeffrey G. BS cum laude, U. Ill., 1973; MD, Chgo. Med. Sch., 1977. Diplomate Am. Bd. Internal Medicine, Am. Bd. Allergy and Immunology. Resident in internal medicine Baylor Coll. Medicine, Houston, 1977-80; med. staff fellow lab. clin. investigation NIAID, NIH, Bethesda, Md., 1980-84; from asst. prof. to prof. internal medicine U. Iowa, Iowa City, 1984-94, prof. internal medicine, 1994-96; dir. Nebr. Med. Rsch. Inst., 1996-99; adj. prof. pediatrics Coll. Medicine U. Nebr., 1996—; clin. prof. medicine Creighton U., Omaha, 1997-99, prof., assoc. chair dept. medicine, dir. clin. rsch., 1999—, chief allergy/immunology, 2001—. Chief med. staff fellow lab. clin. investigation, NIAID, NIH, Bethesda, 1982-83; attending physician VA Med. Ctr., Iowa City, 1984-96, staff physician, 1986-96, clin. investigator, 1991-96; asst. dir. tchg. allergy/immunology divsn. dept. internal medicine U. Iowa, Iowa City, 1989-92, acting dir., 1992, dir., 1993-96, faculty inerdisciplinary immunology grad. degree program U. Iowa, 1993-96; bd. dirs. Am. Bd. Allergy and Immunology, Am. Acad. Allergy, Asthma and Immunology; reviewer over 15 profl. and sci. jours. Contbr. over 200 articles to profl. publs.; mem. editl. bd. Jour. Allergy Clin. Immunology, 1988-93, clin. asthma revs., 1996-99, Allergy & Clinical Immunology Internat., 1997-2002, Jour. World Allergy Org., 2003—; editor Respiratory Digest, 1999—, Ann. Allergy, Asthma & Immunology, 1999—. Mem. asthma technical adv. group Am. Lung Assn., 1989-96. Lt. commdr. USPHS, 1980-83, USPHS Res., 1983—. Recipient Dr. John J. Sheinin Rsch. award Chgo. Med. Sch., 1977, Clin. Investigator VA, 1991-96, Am. Soc. Clin. Investigation, 1992; grantee NIH, 1986-91, 87-90, 92-93, 93-94, VA Merit

Rev., 1986-89, 89-92, 92-96, Environ. Health Sci. Core Ctr., 1990-96, Novartis Pharms., 1997—, Sepracor, Inc., 1997, Immune Tolerance Network, 2003—, others. Fellow ACP, Am. Acad. Allergy Immunology (cutaneous allergy com. 1985-90, postgrad. edn. com. 1988-91, chmn. 1989-90, program com. dermatologic diseases sect. 1988-93, sec. 1989-90, vice chmn. 1990-91, chmn. 1991-92, prof. edn. coun. 1998—, chair 1998—, sec. 1993-95, vice chair 1995—, chmn. bronchoalveolar lavage com. 1991-95, 98—, others), Am. Coll. Allergy Immunology (profl. allergy/immunology edn. com. 1989-94); mem. Am. Acad. Allergy Asthma Immunology (bd. dirs. 2001—, sec., treas. 2004—), Am. Fedn. Clin. Rsch., Am. Thoracic Soc. (sec. allergy immunology and inflammation scientific assembly 1990-91, chair-elect 1991-93, chair program com. 1992-93, chair 1993-95, long-range planning and policy com. sci. assembly on allergy immunology and inflammation 1991-96, sci. conf. com. 1991-93, bd. dirs. 1993-95, chair asthma adv. com. 1995-99), Am. Bd. Allergy and Immunology (bd. dirs. 1999—, co-chmn. 2003-04), Iowa Soc. Allergy Immunology (pres. 1987-89), Am. Assn. Immunologists, Midwest Sect. Am. Fedn. Clin. Rsch., Ctrl. Soc. Clin. Rsch., Am. Soc. Clin. Invest., Am. Lung Assn. (mem. rsch. coordinating com. 1996-99), European Respiratory Soc. Office: Creighton U Dept Medicine 601 N 30th St Ste 5850 Omaha NE 68131-2137 Fax: 402-280-4115. E-mail: tbcasale@creighton.edu.

CASALS, ROSIE, retired professional tennis player; b. San Francisco, Sept. 16, 1948; Profl. tennis player, 1968—; nat. championships and major tournaments include U.S. Open singles (finalist), 1970, 71, U.S. Open doubles, 1967, 71, 74, 82, U.S. Open mixed doubles, 1975, Wimbledon doubles, 1967, 68, 70, 71, 73, Wimbledon mixed doubles, 1971, 73, finalist with Dick Stockton, 1976, Italian doubles, 1967, 70, Family Circle Cup (winner), 1973, Wightman Cup, 1967, 76-81, Bridgestone doubles championships (finalist), 1975, Spalding mixed doubles, 1976, 77, U.S. Tennis Assn. Atlanta doubles, 1976, Fedn. Cup, 1967, 76-81; winner 1st Virginia Slims tournament, 1970; 3d place Virginia Slims Championships, 1976, 4th place, 1977, 78; winner Murjani-WTA championship, 1980; Fla. Fed. Open doubles, 1980; pres. sports promotion co. Sportswoman, Inc., Sausalito, Calif., 1981—; Virginia Slims Legends Tour, 1995—. Mem. Los Angeles Strings team, World Team Tennis, 1975-77; founder Women's Sports Legends Inc. Virginia Slims Event tennis winner, 1986, doubles winner (with Martina Navratilova), 1988, 89; inducted in to Marin Women's Hall of Fame, 1995, Internat. Tennis Hall of Fame, Newport, R.I., 1996, Bay Area Sports Hall of Fame, 2000, African Am. and Ethnic Hall of Fame, 2005. Mem. Women's Internat. Tennis Assn. (bd. dirs.). Office: PO Box 537 Sausalito CA 94966-0537 Office Phone: 760-772-9411. E-mail: sportswomn@aol.com.

CASAMASSIMA, CHRISTOPHER T., lawyer; b. LA, Oct. 5, 1975; m. Lindsay Dinn Casamassima, Aug. 31, 2003. BA, U. Pa., Phila., 1997; JD, U. Calif., LA Sch. Law, 2000. Bar: Calif. 2000, U.S. Ct. Appeals (9th cir.) 2000, U.S. Dist. Ct. 2001. Atty. Kirkland & Ellis LLP, 2000—. Mentor Everybody Wins, 2002—. Named Rising Star, So. Calif. Super Lawyers, 2004, 2005. Mem.: ABA (mem. criminal procedure com. antitrust sect. 2002—), LA County Bar Assn., Italian Am. Lawyers Assn. Home: 2294 Ronda Vista Dr Los Angeles CA 90027 Office: Kirkland & Ellis LLP 777 S Figueroa St #3700 Los Angeles CA 90017 Office Phone: 213-680-8353.

CASANOVA, ALDO JOHN, sculptor; b. San Francisco, Feb. 8, 1929; s. Felice and Teresa (Papini) C.; children: Aviva, Liana, Anabelle. BA, San Francisco State U., 1950, MA, 1951; PhD, Ohio State U., 1957. Asst. prof. art San Francisco State U., 1951-53; asst. prof. Antioch (Ohio) Coll., 1956-58; asst. prof. art Tyler Sch. Art, Temple U., Phila., 1961-64, Tyler Sch. Art, Temple U. (Italy campus), Rome, 1968-70; prof. art Scripps Coll., Claremont, Calif., 1966—, chmn. art dept., 1971-73; vis. prof. SUNY, 1981; faculty mem. Skowhegan Sch. Painting and Sculpture, Maine, summers 1973-74. One-man shows include Esther Robles Gallery, L.A., 1967, Santa Barbara (Calif.) Mus., 1967, Calif. Inst. Tech., 1972, Carl Schlosberg Fine Arts, L.A., 1977, SUNY, 1981, Casanova Retrospective Williamson Galleries, Claremont Colls., Calif. 2002; represented in permanent collections Whitney Mus., San Francisco Mus. Art, San Diego Mus. Sculpture Garden, Hirshhorn Collection, Cornell U., Columbus (Ohio) Mus., UCLA Sculpture Garden, Calif. Inst. Tech., Pasadena, Univ. Judaism, L.A., Air and Space Mus., Washington, Collection of Nat. Acad. of Design, N.Y.C., 1993, Robert Feldmuth Meml. Commn., W.M. Keck Sci. Ctr., Claremont, Calif., 1995, Orange County Mus., Calif., 1996, Rancho Santa Ana Botanic Gardens, Claremont, Calif. Recipient Prix-de-Rome Am. Acad. in Rome, 1958-61; Louis Comfort Tiffany award, 1970 Fellow: Am. Acad. in Rome; mem.: NAD, Nat. Sculpture Soc. Democrat. Roman Catholic.

CASARELLA, WILLIAM JOSEPH, physician; b. Dunmore, Pa., Nov. 17, 1937; s. Rocco F. and Madeline M. Casarella; m. Carolyn A. Hughes, June 18, 1966; children: Jennifer, Gregory. BA, Yale U., 1959; MD, Harvard U., 1963. Intern U. Pa. Hosp., 1963—64; resident in medicine Boston City Hosp., 1966—67; resident in radiology Columbia U.-Presbyn. Med. Center, 1967—70, attending radiologist, 1970—81; prof. radiology Columbia U. Coll. Physicians and Surgeons, N.Y.C., 1977—81; chmn. dept. radiology Emory U., Atlanta, 1981—; exec. assoc. dean Emory U. Sch. Medicine, Atlanta, 1986—; pres. Am. Bd. Radiology, 1998—99. Contbr. articles to med. jours. Nat. bd. dirs. Am. Cancer Soc. Served to capt. Med. Corps U.S. Army, 1964—66. Fellow: Am. Coll. Radiology; mem.: Soc. Chmn. Acad. Radiology Depts. (sec.-treas. 1989—, pres.-elect 1991), Am. Roentgen Ray Soc. (exec. coun. 1988—), Soc. Cardiac Angiography, N.Y. Roentgen Soc., Ea. Radiol. Soc., Assn. Univ. Radiologists, N.Am. Soc. Cardiac Angiography, Radiol. Soc. N.Am., Am. Heart Assn., Soc. Cardiovasc. Radiology (pres. 1979). Office Phone: 404-712-4996. Business E-Mail: william_casarella@emoryhealthcare.org.

CASAREZ, RUEBEN CHARLES, lawyer; b. El Paso, Tex., Sept. 26, 1953; s. Ramon and Irene (Lucero) C.; m. Nicole J. Bremner, Nov. 13, 1982. AB in Psychology, Stanford U., 1975; JD, U. Tex., 1979. Bar: Tex. 1979. Assoc. Butler & Binion, Houston, 1979-87, ptnr., 1988-95; sr. counsel Wells Fargo Bank, Houston, 1995—. Pres. Houston Housing Fin. Corp., 1992-94. Mem. ABA, Hispanic Bar Assn. Houston (pres. 1991-92), Mexican Am. Bar Assn. Houston, Assn. for Advancement Mexican Ams. (gen. counsel 1992-98). Democrat. Roman Catholic. Office: Wells Fargo Bank PO Box 3326 MAC T5008-022 Houston TX 77253-3326 Office Phone: 713-284-5528.

CASAS, LAURIE ANN, plastic surgeon; b. May 26, 1956; married; 2 children. BS, BA, U. Ill., Champaign/Urbana, 1974—78; MD, Northwestern U. Med. Sch., Chgo., 1978—82. Diplomate Am. Bd. Plastic Surgery. Resident, gen. surgery Northwestern U. Med. Ctr., Chgo., 1982—85, resident, plastic surgery, 1985—88; microsurgery rsch. fellow So. Ill. U., Springfield, 1988; aesthetic plastic surgery fellow NYU, N.Y.C., 1989; breast reconstruction fellow St. Joseph Hosp., Atlanta, 1989; clin. instr., surgery Northwestern U. Med. Sch., Chgo., 1987—88, asst. prof., surgery, 1990—2001, assoc. prof., surgery, 2001—; adj. staff, asst. attending in plastic/reconstructive surgery Evanston Hosp., Ill., 1990, assoc. attending in plastic/reconstructive surgery, 1992, attending in plastic/reconstructive surgery, 1996; co-dir., ctr. for plastic and aesthetic surgery Glenbrook Hosp., Glenview, Ill., 1990—95, adj. staff, asst. attending in plastic/reconstructive surgery, 1990, assoc. attending in plastic/reconstructive surgery, 1992, attending in plastic/reconstructive surgery, 1996; acting head, divsn. plastic surgery Evanston Hosp. Corp., Ill., 1993—96; head, divsn. plastic surgery Evanston Northwestern Healthcare, Glenbrook Hosp., Glenview, Ill., 1996—. Mem. editl. bd. Plastic Surgery Today, 2000, Guide to Aesthetic Plastic Surgery, 2000, Your Image, 2002—03, editor-in-chief Aesthetic Soc. News, 2000—. Fellow: Am. Coll. Surgeons; mem.: AMA, Ill. Med. Soc., Plastic Surgery Rsch. Coun., Internat. Soc. Aesthetic Plastic Surgery, Midwestern Assn. Plastic Surgeons, The Rhinoplasty Soc., Chgo. Med. Soc., Chgo. Plastic Surgery Soc., Am. Soc. Plastic Surgery, Am. Soc. Aesthetic Plastic Surgery. Office: 2050 Pfingsten Ste 270 Glenview IL 60025

CASAS, MARTHA, education educator; b. Huntington Pk, Calif. d. Roberto Rubio and Enriqueta Garcia Casas. BS in Edn., U. Tex., El Paso, 1978; MA in edn., U. Tex. at El Paslo, 1991; EdD, Harvard Grad Sch. of Edn., 1997. Elem. sch. tchr. El Paso Ind. Sch. Dist., 1978—91; doctoral student Harvard Grad. Sch. Edn., 1991—95; curriculum specialist El Paso Ind. Sch. Dist., 1993—99; asst. prof. in tchr. edn. U. Tex. at Permian Basin, Odessa, 1999—2001, U. Tex., El Paso, 2001—. Author: (book) Grolier's Encyclopedia Latina, 2003. Grant, Hervey Found., 2003, Univ. Tex. at El Paso, 2004. Mem.: Assn. Edn. Rsch. Assoc., Assoc. for Supervision of Curriculum Develop., Phi Delta Kappa Internat. Avocations: dance, gardening, swimming, travel. Home: 1213 Cambria Cove El Paso TX 79912 Office: Univ Tex at El Paso 500 W University El Paso TX 79968 Personal E-mail: mcasas@utep.edu.

CASASENT, DAVID PAUL, electrical engineer, educator, data processing executive; b. Washington, Dec. 8, 1942; s. Harold Kane and Delta (Fletchall) C.; m. Paula Timko; children: Candace, Erin, Maureen, Tod, Jon. BSEE, U. Ill., Urbana, 1964, MS, 1965, PhD, 1969. Prof. elec. engring. Carnegie Mellon U., Pitts., 1969—; pres. Unicorn Sys., Inc., Pitts., 1983—. Dir. Ctr. for Optical Data Processing, Pitts. Editor: Optical Data Processing, 1978; contbr. more than 700 articles to tech. jours. Recipient Thomas K. Benedict award AIAA, 1979; named George Westinghouse prof. Carnegie-Mellon U., 1980. Fellow IEEE (local pres. 1971-72, Barry Carlton award 1976), Optical Soc. Am. (local pres. 1975-77), Soc. Photo-Optical Instrumentation Engrs. (gov. 1982-85, 87-90, pres. 1993, exec. bd.), Internat. Neural Network Soc. (gov. 1992-95, 1998-00, pres. 1999). Republican. Roman Catholic. Avocations: travel, basketball, volleyball. Home: 133 Woodland Farms Rd Pittsburgh PA 15238-2021 Office: Carnegie Mellon U Dept Elec & Computer Engring Pittsburgh PA 15213-3890

CASATI, FABIO, engineer; b. Como, Italy, Jan. 28, 1971; s. Giulio Casati and Antonia Zocca. PhD, Politecnico di Milano, Milan, Italy, 1998. Engineer, Italy, 1996, cert. engr. With Hewlett-Packard, Palo Alto, Calif., 1998, sr. rsch. scientist, 1999—. Author: (book) Web Services, 2003. Achievements include initiated research in bus. process intelligence and web services. Office: Hewlett-Packard 1501 Page Mill Rd MS 1142 Palo Alto CA 94304 Office Phone: 650-236-8437. Business E-Mail: fabio.casati@hp.com.

CASAZZA, JOHN ANDREW, electrical engineer, energy executive; b. Bklyn., Jan. 3, 1924; s. John Andrew and Jane (Granata) C.; m. Madeline Russo, Apr. 24, 1949; children: John Anthony, Joan Bernadette Casazza Fram. Student, Cooper Union, 1941-43; BEE, Cornell U., 1945. Registered profl. engr., N.J. Successively system planning and devel. engr., gen. mgr. planning and rsch., v.p. planning and rsch. Pub. Svc. Electric & Gas Co., Newark, 1946-77; v.p. Stone & Webster Mgmt. Cons., N.Y.C., 1977-79; pres. Casazza, Schultz & Assocs., Inc., Arlington, Va., 1979-90; chmn. bd. CSA Energy Cons., 1991-97; pres. Am. Edn. Inst., 1994—. Mem. energy engring. bd. NRC, 1988—94; mem. rsch. adv. com. Elec. Power Rsch. Inst., Palo Alto, Calif., 1976—77; mem. U.S. Energy Assn. World Energy Conf., 1983—92; bd. dirs. Ga. Sys. Ops. Co.; mem. Power Engineers Supporting Truth, 2003—. Contbr. numerous articles to profl. publs. Pub. trustee N.J. Marine Scis. Consortium, 1973-79; treas. N.J. Energy Rsch. Inst., 1977; mem. N.J. Gov.'s Panel on Solar Energy, 1975-77. Ensign USN, 1943-45. Fellow IEEE (life, chmn. energy policy com. 1981-82, chmn. environ. quality com. 1984-85, U.S. activities bd. citation of honor 1985, Herman Halperin award 1990, U.S. activities bd. dirs. VII profl. leadership award 1992); mem. Internat. Conf. on Large High Voltage Electric Sys. (Exec. com. U.S. nat. com. 1974-93, Atwood assoc. 1986—, spl. citation 1982, Philip Sporn award 1994), Springfield Golf and Country Club. Roman Catholic. Avocations: golf, writing. Office: Am Edn Inst 8208 Donset Dr Springfield VA 22152-1810 Office Phone: 703-569-3579. Personal E-mail: jackcasazza@aol.com.

CASAZZA, WILLIAM JAMES, insurance company executive, lawyer; b. Cambridge, Mass., 1955; BA, Tufts U., 1977; MBA, U. Notre Dame, 1979; JD, Cornell U., 1985. Bar: N.Y. 1985, Conn. 1993; CPA, Pa. 2001. With Ernst & Whinney, CPAs, 1979-83, Sullivan & Cromwell, 1985-92, Aetna Inc., Hartford, Conn., 1992—, v.p., dep. gen. counsel, 1997—, corp. sec., 1999—, sr. v.p., 2004—05, gen. counsel Hartford, 2005—. Mem. ABA. Office: Aetna Inc 151 Farmington Ave Hartford CT 06156-0002 Office Phone: 860-273-1773. Business E-Mail: casazzawj@aetna.com.

CASBERGUE, JOHN P., medical educator; b. Angleton, Tex., Jan. 14, 1932; s. Selim F. and Nona (Chase) C.; m. Eugenia Szpieg, Feb. 24, 1962 (div. 1979); children: Paul A., Maria A., Lisa A.; m. Helen E. Hagens, Dec. 21, 1985; children: Jennifer E., Frances A. Burigana. RN, Fla. State U., 1955; MA, Mich. State U., 1961, PhD, 1974. Assoc. prof. Ohio State U., Columbus, 1962-72, Mich. State U., East Lansing, 1973-78, prof., 1978-81, prof. emeritus, 1981—93; v.p. ednl. affairs Applied Med. Data Inc., Ann Arbor, Mich., 1981—; pres. Casbergue and Assocs. Inc., East Lansing, 1985—2005. Cons. WHO, Colombia, Guatemala, 1971, numerous med. schs. in Eng., Can., U.S., 1972-93, Nat. Libr. of Medicine, USPHS, Mich. Jud. Inst., Am. Dietetic Assn., Am. Hosp. Assn., Can. Coll. Family Physicians. Contbr. articles to profl. jours. Served to 1st lt. USAF, 1955-60. Fellow Soc. Advancement of Food Service Research (pres. 1972-73). Universalist-Unitarian. Home: 1301 Tomah Dr Mount Pleasant MI 48858-4144

CASBON, LINDA, artist, educator; b. El Paso, Tex., Jan. 10, 1959; d. Lewis and Marillyn Casbon; m. David Poses, Oct. 28, 2000. BENVD, U. of Colo., 1981; MFA, Kent State U., 1986. Vis. lectr. U. Mass., Dartmouth, 2000—01; vis. asst. prof. Ohio U., Athens, 2000—00; adj. assoc. prof. Hofstra U., Hempstead, NY, 2003—, NYU, 2005. Trustee Watershed Ctr. for Ceramic Arts, Newcastle, Maine, 1999—; guest lectr. Tyler Sch. of Art, Elkins Park, Pa., 2004—04; vis. artist U. of Tenn., Knoxville, Tenn., 2003—03; guest lectr. RISD, Providence, 2001—01; vis. artist Bennington Coll., Bennington, Vt., 2000—00. Exhibition, Generations.04 at AIR Gallery, Paintings and Forms, Materia Prima. Sec. Watershed Ctr. for Ceramic Arts, Newcastle, Maine, 2004—05. Fellow Kohler Arts in Industry Program, John Michael Kohler Art Ctr., 2002; Artist's Residency grantee, The Bemis Found., 1992—93, Artist fellow, NY Found. for the Arts, 1997. Mem.: Coll. Art Assn. (assoc.).

CASBON, MONICA LYNN, accountant; b. Michigan City, Ind., Aug. 10, 1955; d. Frank John and Mary Frances (Ray) K.; m. Robert D. Casbon, Sept. 30, 2000; 1 child, Katie Frances. BS in Bus., Ind. U. N.W., Gary, 1991, MBA, 1994. Cons. Hair Master, Chesterton, Ind., 1977-94; acct. SB Assocs., Valparaiso, Ind., 1994—; auditor State Bd. Accounts, 1998—2001; acct. McDonough Assocs., Chgo., 2000—03. Precinct com. person Porter County, Ind., 1989-91; fin. chmn. St. Patricks Festival, Chesterton, 1993, 94; vol. Spring Valley Homeless Shelter, Valparaiso, 1993—, Hilltop Neighborhood House, Valparaiso, 1997—. Mem. NAFE, Inst. Mgmt. Accts. Republican. Roman Catholic. Avocations: golf, reading, running, volunteer work. Home: 560 S 400 W Hebron IN 46341

CASCIANO, DANIEL ANTHONY, biologist, educator; b. Buffalo, Mar. 1, 1941; s. Frederick James and Rose Ann C.; m. Gertrude Ann Tara, Aug. 22, 1964; children: Anne, Jonathan. BS, Canisius Coll., 1962; PhD in Cell Biology, Purdue U., 1971. Rsch. asst. Roswell Park Meml. Inst., Buffalo, 1963-64; rsch. asst. dept. biol. scis. Purdue U., Lafayette, Ind., 1965-66, tchg. asst., 1969, rsch. trainee, 1966-71; trainee NIH, 1966-71; postdoctoral investigator U. Tenn., Oak Ridge Nat. Labs., 1971-73; assoc. prof. dept. biochemistry and molecular biology U. Ark. for Med. Scis., Little Rock, 1974-90, prof. dept. biochemistry and molecular biology, 1990—, prof. dept pharmacology and toxicology, 1990—; rsch. biologist Nat. Ctr. Toxicology Rsch., Jefferson, Ark., 1973, program dir. divsn. mutagenesis rsch., 1976-78, dir. divsn. genetic toxicology, 1979-97, dir. divsn. genetic and reproductive toxicology, 1997-99, dep. dir. for rsch., 1999-2000, acting dir., 1999-2000, dir., 2000—. Contbr. articles to profl. jours. Mem. Tissue Culture Assn., Environ. Mutagen Soc., AAAS, Beta Beta Beta. Home: 47 Marcella Dr Margeux Pl Little Rock AR 72223-9172 Office: FDA Nat Ctr Toxicological Rsch Jefferson AR 72079 Office Phone: 870-543-7517. Business E-Mail: dcasciano@nctr.fda.gov.

CASCINO, ANTHONY ELMO, JR., lawyer, insurance company executive; b. South Bend, Ind., Aug. 21, 1948; s. Anthony E. and Lorayne (Allegretti) C.; m. Mary Anne Dory, July 28, 1973; children: Anthony Elmo III, Christine Anne, Caroline Stephanie. BA, Loyola U., Chgo., 1970; JD, Ill. Inst. Tech., 1974; M of Mgmt., Northwestern U., 1987. Bar: Ill. 1974, U.S. Dist. Ct. (no. dist.) Ill. 1974, U.S. Supreme Ct. 1996. Div. counsel CF Industries, Inc., Long Grove, Ill., 1974-79; sec., gen. counsel Energy Coop., Inc., Rosemont, Ill., 1979-83; v.p., gen. counsel GHR Energy Corp., Good Hope, La., 1983; dep. gen. counsel AM Internat., Inc., Chgo., 1983-86; v.o, bus. devel. Multigraphics divsn. AM Internat., Mt. Prospect, Ill., 1986-88; exec. v.p., sec., gen. counsel, bd. dirs. United Fin. Group Inc. of Ill., Oak Brook, 1988-96; ptnr., exec. v.p. Tait Adv. Svcs., 1997-2000; v.p. Corp. Legal Warrior Ins. Group, 2000—02, Cascino & Assocs. PC, 2002—; sec., gen. counsel Echelon Property and Casulty Ins. Co., Chgo., 2004—. Bd. dirs. Oak Brook Property and Casualty Ins. Co., First Oak Brook Corp. Syndicate, United Comml. Affiliated, Inc., Combined Adjustment Co., Inc., Ctrl. State Ins. Co., Inc., Echelon Property and Casualty Ins. Co.; mem. inquiry bd. Atty. Registration and Disciplinary Commn., 1992-96; alt. trustee Ill. Ins. Exch., 1988-97; arbitrator Cook County Mandatory Arbitration Program, 1997—; lectr. Ill. Inst. Continuing Edn., 1986Corp. Goverance Conf., 2004. Contbg. author: Commercial Damage, 1984; contbr. articles to profl. jours. Bd. dirs. Chgo. Cmty. Loon Fund, 1999—; bd. advisors St. Joseph Sem. Coll., Archdiocese Chgo., 1999—; mem. adv. com. postgrad. programs Ill. Inst. Tech., 1987-88; hon. chmn. Tony C. and Carole Segal PAtient Assistance Fund; mem. bd. adv. Cath. Charities of Archdiocese Chgo., 2004. Mem. ABA, Fed. Energy Bar Assn., Ill. State Bar Assn., Chgo. Bar Assn. (vice chmn. ins. law com., 2004, chmn. ins. law com., 2004-2005, Dupage County Bar Assn., Art Inst. Chgo., Lyric Opera of Chgo. (Glencoe chpt.), Bar and Gavel Soc., DuPage Club, Union League Club (Chgo.), Club Internat. (Chgo.), Bob O'Link Golf Club. Democrat. Roman Catholic. Home: 385 Lincoln Ave Glencoe IL 60022-1521 Office: 875 N Michigan Ave Ste 1430 Chicago IL 60611 Office Phone: 312-654-6183. Business E-Mail: tcascino@eisgroup.net.

CASCIO, MICHAEL JOSEPH, television production and programming executive; b. Arlington, Va., July 5, 1950; s. Morris Frank and Blanche Rose (Borzomati) C.; m. Jane Kashlak, Apr. 7, 1979 (div. Jan. 1987); m. Cynthia Weber, Feb. 14, 1988. BA, U. Va., 1972; MA, Am. U., 1973. Reporter, news dir. Sta. WUVA, Charlottesville, Va., 1968—72; anchorman, writer, editor news interview program Jefferson Cable TV, Charlottesville, 1971—72; exec. prodr., reporter, announcer Sta. WAMU-FM, Washington, 1972—73; intern, prodn. asst. Sta. WTTG-TV, Washington, 1973; news dir., reporter, prodr. spls. Sta. WHYY-TV, Wilmington, Del. and Phila., 1973—78; prodr. N.J. Nightly News, reporter, prodr. Congress Watch Sta. WNET-TV, Newark and N.Y.C., 1978—79; dir. pub. affairs, news prodr., exec. prodr. Sta. WPVI-TV, Phila., 1979—90; sr. v.p. programming A&E Network, 1997—99; v.p. cable programming devel. NBC News, 1999—2001; exec. v.p., gen. mgr. Animal Planet Network, Discovery Comm., Inc., 2001—03; sr. v.p. Nat. Geog. Channel, 2004—. Tchr. comm. Wilmington Coll., 1974, tchr. journalism U. Del., Newark, 1977 Dir. pub. affairs, exec. prodr. numerous local programs for WPVI-TV including Prime Time, Visions; dir. documentary prodn. Arts and Entertainment Network, 1990, v.p. documentary programming, 1993; exec. in charge TV programs including A&E Investigative Reports with Bill Kurtis, A&E Biography Am. Justice, City Confidential, The Real West with Kenny Rogers, American Justice, Class of the 20th Century with Richard Dreyfuss, other network TV programs, Ancient Mysteries. Recipient Blue Ribbon Addy award Phila. Advt. Club, 1983, Coun. Spanish Speaking Orgns. award, Phila., 1984, Phila. Emmy award, 1984, 96, Scleroderma Rsch. Found. award, 1984, Sarah award Women in Comm., 1985, Top honors N.J. Broadcasters Assn., 1985, Pa. Assn. Broadcasters award, 1985, Best Documentary, 1988, Best Pub. Affairs Program Series, 1988, 2d Ann. Highway Safety award State of N.J., 1986, Del. award MADD, 1987, Commendation award Am. Women in Radio and TV, 1987, Nat. Assn. TV Program Execs. Iris award, 1988, Best Documentary Series award Ace, 1993, Best Consumer/Bus. Program award, 1993, Cable Ace award, 1995, Emmy award for outstanding investigative journalism, 1996, Emmy award for outstanding hist. programming, 1996, Cable Ace award for best ednl. instnl. program, 1996, Cable Ace award for best pub. affairs spl. or series, 1996, Emmy award for outstanding info. series, 1997.

CASE, BILL, management consultant, state representative; b. Akron, Ohio, Dec. 10, 1954; s. Harry and Julianne Case; m. Darlene Case; children: Bradley, Kimberly. BS in Parks and Recreation Adminstrn, Appalachin State U., N.C., 1977. Councilman Midwest City, Okla., 1990—94, mayor, 1993—94. Vice chmn. county and mcpl. govt. com. Okla. Ho. Reps., Okla. City, 1995—, mem. subcom. on natural resources and regulatory svcs to appropriatiions and budget com., 1995—, mem. human svcs., transp (subcom. on railways) coms., 1995—; mem. joint spl. com. on internat. devel. Okla. Ho. Reps.-Senate, Okla. City, 1995—. Grad. Midwest City Leadership Class, 1991; bd. dirs. Mid-Del-Tinker 100 Club. Socialist. Office: 2300 N Lincoln Blvd Rm 539 Oklahoma City OK 73105 Home and Office: 1319 Alviola Ave Oklahoma City OK 73110 E-mail: casebi@lsb.state.ok.us.

CASE, CHARLES DIXON, lawyer; b. Manning, S.C., Mar. 23, 1952; s. James E. and Jennie (Stout) C.; m. Margie Toy, Aug. 28, 1982; children: J. Everett II, Elliot T. BS in Physics, N.C. State U., 1973; JD, Harvard U., 1977. Bar: N.C. 1977, U.S. Dist. Ct. (ea., mid. and we. dists.) N.C., U.S. Supreme Ct. Environ. atty., ptnr. Moore & Van Allen, 1977-92; ptnr. Hunton & Williams, Raleigh, N.C., 1992—. Adj. prof. law Campbell U., Buies Creek, N.C., 1981-84; hearing officer N.C. OSHA Safety and Health Rev. Bd., Raleigh, 1981-84; chmn. Wake County Bd. Adjustment, Raleigh, 1979-83; mem. N.C. Hazardous Waste Study Commn., 1982. Co-author: Toxic Tort and Hazardous Substance Litigation, 1995; contbr. articles to profl. jours. Pres. Coll. Phys. and Math. Scis. Found., N.C. State U. 1994-95, bd. dirs., 1991-98, 2000—; bd. dirs. Jr. Achievement Ea. N.C., 1994-98, Camp Kanata, 1997—; mem. bd. visitors N.C. State U., 1995—, chmn., 1999-2000. Home: 1540 Carr St Raleigh NC 27608-2302 Office: Hunton & Williams PO Box 109 Raleigh NC 27602-0109 Office Phone: 919-899-3045. E-mail: ccase@hunton.com.

CASE, COLLEEN MAE, computer scientist, educator; b. Aurora, Ill., Nov. 3, 1952; d. Harry Sherman, Jr. and JoAnne Mae (Rife) Case; children: William Matt, Thomas Wesley, Corey Isaac. BS, U. Wis., LaCrosse, 1981; MLS, Ea. Mich. U., 1991. Cert. computer sci. tchr. Mich. Sys. analyst Midwest Regional Tech-Unisys Corp., Okemos, Mich., 1981-88; computer instr. UAW/Ford Computer Learning Ctr., Wixom, Mich., 1989-95; video prodr. Creative Media Cons., Livonia, Mich., 1990-95; assoc. prof. computer graphics tech. Schoolcraft Coll., Livonia, 1996—. Tech. editor: Course Techs. and other publ., 1996—. Mem.: Assn. for Computing Machinery (SIGGRAPH dir. for edn.). E-mail: ccase@schoolcraft.cc.mi.us, colleen_case@siggraph.org.

CASE, DAVID BARTLETT, internist, educator; b. Plainfield, NJ, Mar. 17, 1942; s. George and Caroline (Bartlett) C.; m. Jean Brookhart, Aug. 2, 1969; children; Thayer Stimson, Nelson Chipman. AB, Princeton U., 1964; MD, Columbia U., 1968. Intern, then asst. resident Johns Hopkins Hosp., Balt., 1968-70; fellow Columbia Presbyn. Hosp., N.Y.C., 1972-75; asst., then assoc. prof. Cornell U. Med. Coll., N.Y.C., 1975-84, clin. assoc. prof., 1984—. Mem. Council on High Blood Pressure Research, 1979—; vis. lectr. Columbia U. Coll. of Physicians and Surgeons, 1997—. Contbr. chapters to books, articles to profl. jours. Recipient Andrew Mellon Tchr. Scientist award Cornell U., 1978. Master ACP (gov. downstate I); fellow Am. Coll. Clin. Pharmacology, Am. Heart Assn. Achievements include research in hypertension. Office: 635 Madison Ave New York NY 10022-1009 Office Phone: 212-857-4660. Personal E-mail: dbmdny@aol.com.

CASE, DAVID KNOWLTON, management consultant; b. Worcester, Mass., Mar. 26, 1938; s. Frederic Howard and Frances Mary (Knowlton) C.; m. Caroline Porter Richards, Feb. 2, 1974; children— Elizabeth, Sarah BA, Yale U., 1961; grad. mktg. mgmt. program, Harvard U., 1973. Pub. rels. rep. U.S. Steel Corp., Pitts., 1962-66; comms. dir. John Hancock Ins. Co., Boston, 1966-70; asst. v.p. Shawmut Bank, Boston, 1970-76; devel. dir. Boston Ctr.

for the Arts, 1977; dir. Plimoth Plantation, Plymouth, Mass., 1977-90, pres., CEO, 1990-96; owner, CEO Case Consulting, Norwell, Mass., 1997—; ptnr. Case & Mann, Osterville, Mass., 2000—. Bd. assocs. ARTS/Boston, 1988—; pres. emeritus, hon. dir. English-Speaking Union, Boston; pres. emeritus, dir. Plymouth County Devel. Coun., 1988—; mem. adv. bd. S.E. Mass. Am. Automobile Assn., 1988—, Three Bays Preservation, Inc., Osterville; mem. external rels. com. Milton Acad. Recipient Golden Coin award Bank Mktg. Assn., 1973, Nat. award Bus. Com. Arts, N.Y., 1975, Leadership award Soc. Mayflower Descendants, 1994, Jackson Bowl award Milton Acad., 1995, Silver medal SAR, 1996, Lifetime Achievement award Mass. Office Travel and Tourism, 1997. Mem. Am. Assn. Mus., New Eng. Mus. Assn., Colonial Soc., Soc. Colonial Wars in Commonwealth of Mass., Yale Club (Boston and N.Y.), Harvard Club (Boston), The Beach Club (Centerville, Mass.). Republican. Episcopalian. Home and Office: 378 River St Norwell MA 02061-2205 also: PO Box 361 205 Seapuit Rd Osterville MA 02655-1819 Office Phone: 508-540-8169. Personal E-mail: dkcrcase@aol.com.

CASE, DONNI MARIE, investment company executive; b. Chgo., Feb. 20, 1948; d. Donald Milton and Felecia Virginia (Krantz) Schuette; m. Lawrence Lee Hewitt, Apr. 20, 1996. BA in Econs., U. Ill., 1970. Pres. FRB/Weber Shandwick, Chgo., 1972—. Bd. dirs. Inst. Bus. and Profl. Ethics Depaul U. Mem.: Chicago Network, TEC Internat. Home: 2417 N Geneva Ter Chicago IL 60614-5914 Office: FRB/Weber Shandwick 676 N St Clair 13th Fl Chicago IL 60611-1803

CASE, DOUGLAS MANNING, lawyer; b. Cleve., Jan. 3, 1947; s. Manning Eugene and Ernestine (Bryan) Case; m. Marilyn Cooper, Aug. 23, 1969. BA, U. Pa., 1969; JD, MBA, Columbia U., 1973. Bar: N.Y. 1974, N.J. 1975, Calif. 1980, Ohio 1991, Fla. 2000. Assoc. Brown & Wood, N.Y.C., 1973-77; corp. counsel PepsiCo Inc., Purchase, NY, Irvine, Calif., 1977—83, Nabisco Brands Inc., N.Y.C., East Hanover, N.J. and London, 1983-89; asst. gen. counsel Chiquita Brands Internat., Inc., Cin., 1989-92; prin. Douglas M. Case Law Offices, Cin., Vero Beach, Fla., 1993—. Lectr. numerous seminars. Contbr. articles to profl. jours. Chmn. Olde Colonial Dist.; active Morris-Sussex area coun. Boy Scouts Am., 1986—88; sec., trustee Marble Scholarship Com., N.Y.C., 1983—88; trustee Cin. Opera Guild, 1994—99, pres., 1997—98, chmn., 1998—99, hon. trustee, 1999—; bd. dirs., mem. exec. com. Cin. Opera Assn., 1997—98. Mem.: ABA, Quality in Law (chmn. 1996—98), Cin. Bar Assn. (continuing legal edn. chair internat. law com. 1994—96, chair solo and small firm practitioners com. 1995—97, sec. 1996—97, vice chair 1997—98, chair 1998—2000), Fla. Bar Assn., Internat. Bar Assn., Munich Sister City Assn. Greater Cin. (chmn. econ. devel. com. 1995—96), Vero Beach Yacht Club, Bent Pine Golf Club, Kenwood Country Club, Columbia Bus. Sch. Club (N.Y.C.) (pres., bd. dirs. 1974—79), Morris County Golf Club, Met. Club (N.Y.C.), Lawyers Club Cin. (mem. exec. com. 1995—2000, treas. 1996, sec. 1997, 2d v.p. 1998, 1st v.p. 1999, pres. 2000). Avocation: golf. Office: 501 Bay Dr Vero Beach FL 32963-2163 Personal E-mail: dcaselaw@bellsouth.net.

CASE, EDWARD E., congressman, lawyer; b. Hilo, Hawaii, Sept. 27, 1952; m. Audrey Case; children: David, Megan, James, David. BA, Williams Coll., 1975; JD, U. Calif., 1981. Aide to U.S. Rep. Spark Matsunaga from Hawaii, Washington, 1975—78; clk. to Hon. William Richardson Hawaii Supreme Ct., 1981—82; clk. Hawaii State. Dept. Labor; from assoc. to mng. ptnr. Carlsmith Ball, Honolulu, 1983—; mem. Hawaii Ho. of Reps., 1994—2002, majority leader, 1999—2000; mem. from 2d Hawaii dist. U.S. Ho. of Reps., Washington, 2002—, mem. edn. and workforce com., agr. com., small bus. com. Mem. Manoa Neighborhood Bd., Honolulu, 1985—89. Named Legislator of Yr., Honolulu Weekly, 1995, Small Bus. Hawaii, 2000, New Economy Legislator of Yr., Hawaii Tech. and Trade Assn., 2000. Democrat. Office: US Ho of Reps 115 Cannon Ho Office Bldg Washington DC 20515 also: 5104 Prince Kuhio Fed Bldg Honolulu HI 96850*

CASE, ELDON DARREL, materials science educator; b. Logan, Kans., Aug. 23, 1949; s. Eldon George and Ila Marie (Lewis) C.; m. Linda Lee Lubken, Aug. 29, 1975 (div. Mar. 1993); 1 child, Carl Allen; m. Rebecca J. Ervin, 1996. BA in Physics and Math., U. Colo., 1971; MA in Physics, U. No. Colo., 1975; PhD in Materials Sci., Iowa State U., 1980. Rsch. asst. dept. materials sci. Iowa State U., Ames, 1976—80; NRC postdoctoral assoc. Nat. Bur. Stds., Gaithersburg, Md., 1980—82; rsch. engr. materials sci. and mining engrng. U. Calif., Berkeley, 1982—85; asst. prof. metallurgy, mechanics and materials sci. Mich. State U., East Lansing, 1985—89, assoc. prof., 1988—99, prof., 1999—. Cons. Indsl. Tech. Inst., Ann Arbor, Mich., 1990, Westinghouse, West Mifflin, Pa., 1991-92; judge Nat. Am. Indian Sci. and Engrng. Fair, 1993-2001; grand awards judge Internat. Sci. and Engrng. Fair, 2000; mem. internat. sci. com. ACUN-3 Advanced Composites, Sydney, Australia, 2000-01; mem. external adv. bd. Dept. Materials Sci. and Engrng. Iowa State U., 2004-; mem. editl. bd. Jour. Materials Engrng. and Performance, 2005- Assoc. editor Internat. Jour.of Applied Ceramics Tech., 2003—; contbr. over 125 articles to profl. jours. and conf. proc. including Jour. Materials Sci., Materials Sci. Engrng., Applied Physics Letters. Spkr. sch. groups Okemos (Mich.) Pub. Schs., 1986-90; asst. with middle-sch. activities Episcopal Ch., East Lansing, 1988-92; judge Nat. Am. Indian Sci. and Engrng. Fair, 1993-2001. Recipient Tchr.-Scholar award Mich. State U., 1989, Withrow Excellence in Tchg. award Engrng. Coll. Mich. State U., 1993, 95, 98; Regents scholar U. Colo., 1967-71; grantee NASA, 1987, NSF, 1987-90, Mich. State U., 1989, AFOSR, 2001—. Fellow Am. Ceramic Soc.; mem. AAUP, ASM (chair advanced joining tech. com. 1999—, tech. programming bd. for joining critical tech. sector 1999—), Nat. Inst. Ceramic Engrs., The Metall. Soc. (sec. structural materials div. 1988-91, chair non-metall. com. 1988-91), Sigma xi; fellow Am. Ceramic Soc. (pres. Mich. sect. 1998-2004, officer nominating com. engrng. ceramics divsn., internat. sci. adv. com. for ACUN-3 advanced composites symposium Sydney, Australia, 2000-01). Democrat. Achievements include first neutron scattering study from microcracks in a polycrystalline ceramic; statistical analysis of water drop impact damage cracks in infrared windows; microwave sintering and joining of ceramics and ceramic composites; adhesion studies of diamond thin-films on brittle substrates; thermal-shock and thermal fatigue studies on ceramics and ceramic composites, microwave sintering and joining of ceramics. Home: 4469 Fairlane Dr Okemos MI 48864-2407 Office: Materials Sci and Mechanics Sci Dept East Lansing MI 48824 Office Phone: 517-353-6715. Business E-Mail: casee@egr.msu.edu.

CASE, ELIZABETH JOY, psychology research administrator; b. Phila., Oct. 12, 1948; d. Edward N. and Helene (LeBlanc) C. BS in Edn./Spl. Edn., Ashland Coll., 1970; MA in Spl. Edn., Fairfield U., 1975; PhD, U. N.Mex., 1985. Cert. tchr. spl. edn. K-12, regular edn. K-12, adminstr. Tchr. second grade Mansfield (Ohio) Pub. Schs., 1969-70; supr., tchr. spl. edn. Greenwich (Conn.) Pub. Schs., 1970-78; cons. Nat. Learning Disabilties Assistance Project, Washington, 1976-78; instr. Fairfield (Conn.) U., 1975-79; grad. asst., fellow U. N.Mex., Albuquerque, 1978-81, instr., 1980-85; cons. IBM, White Plains and Arwork, N.Y., 1976-81; asst. prin. Albuquerque Pub. Schs., 1981-82, coord. spl. edn., 1989—93; with Minn. Dept. Edn., 1993—97; dir. rsch. Harcourt/Psychol. Corp., 1997—. Cons. Office of Spl. Edn., U.S. Dept. Edn., Washington, 1980—; dir. regional large sch. testing programs, mid-continent Harcourt Edn. Measurement, 1999—, grants and devel. Minn. Dept. Children, Families, and Learning, Minn. Assessment Project, Rsch. on Spl. Populations Harcourt Assessment, Inc./The Psychol. Corp.; presenter in field. Contbr. articles to profl. jours./publs. Chmn. Gov.'s Com. on the Concerns of the Handicapped, Santa Fe, N.Mex., 1988—; pres. Civitan/Sierra Vista, Albuquerque, 1989, Albuquerque Wheelchair Tennis Assn., 1985; pres., CEO World Inst. on Disabilities, 1997-98; adv. bd. Protection and Advocacy, Albuquerque, 1988-90; vice-chmn. N.Mex. Vols. for the Outdoors, Albuquerque, 1988-91; bd. dirs. Very Spl. Arts, 1984—, Easter Seal Fundraiser, 1976—, Spl. Olympics, 1986—. Named Vol. of the Yr., N.Mex. Vols. for the Outdoors, 1988, Nat. Woman's Single Champion/Nat. Wheelchair Tennis Assn., Irvine, Calif., 1985, Most Inspirational Tennis Player, 1985, Outstanding Leader in Elem. Edn., Ashland, Ohio, 1976, Conn. Outstanding Young Woman, Hartford, 1976. Mem. N.Mex. Coun. Exceptional Children (treas. 1990-92), Am. Ednl. Rsch. Assn., Phi Delta Kappa (pres. local chpt. 1990-91). Office: Harcourt Assessment Inc 19500 Bulverde Rd San Antonio TX 78259 Office Phone: 210-339-5433.

CASE, GREGORY C., insurance company executive; BA summa cum laude, Kans. State Univ.; MBA, Harvard Univ. Ptnr., head fin. svc. & global ins. practices McKinsey & Co., 1988—2005; pres. & CEO Aon Corp., Chgo., 2005—. Office: Aon Corporation 200 E Randolph St Chicago IL 60601*

CASE, JAMES HEBARD, lawyer; b. Lihue, Hawaii, Apr. 10, 1920; s. Adrial Hebard and Elizabeth (McConnell) C.; m. Suzanne Catherine Espenett, Sept. 18, 1948; children: Edward E., John H. (dec.), Suzanne D., Russell L., Elisabeth C. Marguleas, Bradford Case. AB, Williams Coll., 1941; JD, Harvard U., 1949. Bar: Hawaii 1949, U.S. Supreme Ct. 1985. Assoc. Pratt, Tavares & Cassidy, Honolulu, 1949-51, Carlsmith & Carlsmith, Hilo, Hawaii, 1951-59; ptnr. Carlsmith Ball, Honolulu, 1959—2002, of counsel, 2002—. Bd. dirs. ML Resources, Honolulu. Trustee Hanahauoli Sch., Honolulu, 1970-82, Ctrl. Union Ch., Honolulu, 1984-88, Arcadia Retirement Residence, Honolulu, 1985-91. Lt. comdr. USNR, 1943-46, PTO. Mem. ABA, Hawaii Bar Assn., Hawaii Yacht Racing Assn. (bd. dirs. 1994-2000), Pacific Club (bd. dirs. 1978-82), Kaneohe Yacht Club (Honolulu). Republican. Congregationalist. Avocations: sailing, tennis. Home: 3757 Round Top Dr Honolulu HI 96822-5043 Office: Carlsmith Ball PO Box 656 Honolulu HI 96809-0656 Office Phone: 808-523-2501. Business E-Mail: jhc@carlsmith.com.

CASE, KAREN ANN, lawyer; b. Milw., Apr. 7, 1944; d. Alfred F. and Hilda M. (Tomich) Case. BS, Marquette U., 1963, JD, 1966; LLM, NYU, 1973. Bar: Wis. 1966, U.S. Ct. Claims 1973, U.S. Tax Ct. 1973. Ptnr. Meldman, Case & Weine, Milw., 1973-85, Meldman, Case & Weine divsn. Mulcahy & Wherry, S.C., 1985-87; Sec. of Revenue State of Wis., 1987-88; ptnr. Case & Drinka, S.C., Milw., 1989-91, Case, Drinka & Diel, S.C., Milw., 1991-97, CoVac, 1997—. Lectr. U. Wis., Milw., 1974-78; guest lectr. Marquette U. Law Sch., 1975-78; dir. WBBC, 1998—. Contbr. articles to legal jours. Mem. gov.'s Commn. on Taliesin, 1988, gov.'s Econ. Adv. Commn., 1989-91, pres.'s coun. Alverno Coll., 1988-94, nat. coun., 1998-2000; bd. dirs. WBCC, 1998—. Fellow Wis. Bar Found. (dir. 1977-90, treas. 1980-90); mem. ABA, Milw. Assn. Women Lawyers (founding mem., bd. dirs. 1975-78, 81-82), Milw. Bar Assn. (bd. dirs. 1985-87, law office mgmt. chair 1992-93), State Bar Wis. (bd. govs. 1981-85, 87-90, dir. taxation sect. 1981-87, vice chmn. 1986-87, 90-91, chmn. 1991-92), Am. Acad. Matrimonial Lawyers (bd. dirs. 1988-90), Nat. Assn. Women Lawyers (Wis. del. 1982-83), Milw. Rose Soc. (pres. 1981, dir. 1981-83), Friends of Boerner Bot. Gardens (founding mem., pres. 1984-90), Profl. Dimensions Club (dir. 1985-87), Tempo Club (sec. 1984-85). Office: CoVac 9803 W Meadow Park Dr Hales Corners WI 53130-2261 Office Phone: 414-425-5672. *Delegate tasks for responsibility and accountability. then spend the resulting freed time nourishing your soul. Resign yourself to the fact that the tasks will not be completed as you would have but they will be done, sometimes with more creativity. Give credit and praise always.*

CASE, KENNETH EUGENE, industrial engineering educator; b. Oak Ridge, Tenn., Aug. 12, 1944; s. Richard Thaddeus and Vera Lavone (Peyton) C.; m. Frances Lynn Curlee, Jan. 21, 1966; children: Kristin Lynn, David Rex. BSEE, Okla. State U., 1966, MS in Indsl. Engrng., 1967, PhD in Indsl. Engrng., 1969. Lic. profl. engr., cert. quality engr., Am. Soc. Quality, reliability engr., Am. Soc. Quality, quality auditor, Am. Soc. Quality, quality mgr., Am. Soc. Quality, prodn. and inventory mgmt., Am. Prodn. and Inventory Control Soc., 1990, six sigma black belt, Am. Soc. Quality. Asst. prof. indsl. engrng. Va. Poly. Inst., Blacksburg, 1969-73, assoc. prof. indsl. engrng., 1973-74; mgmt. scientist GTE Data Services, Tampa, Fla., 1974-75; assoc. prof. indsl. engrng. Okla. State U., Stillwater, 1975-78, prof., head indsl. engrng., 1980-82, prof. inden. engrng., 1978-87, regents prof. inden. engrng., 1987—, dir. MS in Engrng. and Tech. Mgmt. Program, 1997—2002. Dir. MS in Engrng. and Tech. Mgmt. Program Okla. State U., Stillwater, Okla., 1997—2002; sr. examiner Malcolm Baldridge Nat. Quality award Dept. of Commerce, 1988, 89, 90, panel of judges, 91, 92, 93. Co-author: Principles of Engineering Economic Analysis, 1977, 4th edit., 1998, Introduction to Industrial and Systems Engineering, 1977, 3d edit., 1993 (IIE Book of Yr. 1979), Profit Through Quality, 1978. Com. chmn. troop 828 Boy Scouts Am., Stillwater, 1985-88. Named Outstanding Engrng. Prof. Okla. State U., 1983, Disting. Eagle Scout Boy Scouts Am., 1986; recipient L.E. Tinker award Boy Scouts Am., Albert Holzman Disting. Edn. award, 1991, Regents Disting. Teaching award Okla. State U., 1992, Silver Beaver award Boy Scouts Am., 1994. Fellow: Am. Soc. Quality (editl. bd. Jour. Quality Tech. 1979—97, editl. bd. Quality Mgmt. Jour. 1993—, nat. dir. 1999—2001, treas. 2001—02, pres.-elect 2002—03, pres. 2003—04, chmn. of bd. 2004—, past sect. chmn., Berg award 1978, Eugene L. Grant medal 2003), Inst. Indsl. Engrs. (internat. pres. 1986—87, Award of Excellence 1980, Disting. Svc. award 1984, Frank and Lillian Gilbreth Indsl. Engrng. award 2002); mem.: NSPE, NAE (peer com. chair sect. 8, membership com., nominating com.), Am. Prodn. and Inventory Control Soc., Internat. Acad. Quality (academician 1990—, bd. dir., editor IAQ Contact), Am. Soc. Engrng. Edn. (George Westinghouse award 1989), Okla. Soc. Profl. Engrs. (Okla. Outstanding Engr. 1987), Am. Radio Relay League (Conn. chpt.), Order of Arrow, Sigma Chi. Home: 2416 Tanglewood Cir Stillwater OK 74074-1717 Office: Okla State U Sch Indsl Engrng and Mgmt Stillwater OK 74078-5018 Office Phone: 405-744-6952. E-mail: kcase@okstate.edu.

CASE, LARRY D., agricultural education specialist; b. Norborne, Mo., Aug. 8, 1943; s. Burr Jr. and Eva Marie (Harper); m. Joy Leona Vandivort, June 18, 1966; children: Jeffrey Dale, Rebecca Joy, Matthew Edward. BS in Agriculture, U. Mo., 1966, MEd, 1972, EdD, 1983; LHD (hon.), SUNY, Cobleskill, 1990. Life cert. agriculture tchr. Tchr. Northwestern High Sch., Mendon, Mo., 1966, Orrick (Mo.) Sch. Dist., 1966-69, Lexington (Mo.) R-V Sch. Dist., 1969-73, vocat. dir., 1973-74; dir. vocat. edn. Lexington La-Ray Area Vocat. Sch., 1974-77; supr. agrl. edn. Mo. Dept. Elem. & Sec. Edn., Jefferson City, 1977-78, state dir. agrl. edn., 1978-84; ednl. program specialist-agriculture U.S. Dept. Edn., Washington, 1984—. Chmn. bd. Future Farmers Am., Alexandria, 1984, Nat. Coun. for Vocat. Tech. Edn. in Agr., Alexandria, 1984-93, Nat. Postgrad. Agrl. Students Orgn., Alexandria, 1984; pres. Future Farmers Am. Found., Alexandria, 1984; adj. prof. Pa. State U., University Park. Contbr. articles on agrl. edn. and internat. travel related to agrl. edn. Active deacon Fredericksburg (Va.) Bapt. Ch., 1984—, Sunday sch. tchr., 1984—; pres. Motts Row Property Owners Assn., 1988-89. Recipient Hon. Am. Farmer degree Future Farmers Am., 1984, Citation of Merit, U. Mo. Coll. of Agr., 1990. Mem. Future Farmers Am. Alumni Assn. (life), Am. Vocat. Assn., Nat. Assn. State Suprs. Agrl. Edn. (sec. 1980-84), Nat. Vocat. Agr. Tchrs. Assn. (life), Nat. Planning Assn. (food and agr. com.), Phi Delta Kappa, Alpha Gamma Rho (nat. hon. mem.). Office: US Dept Edn OVAE 330 C St SW Washington DC 20202-0001*

CASE, MARY ANNE, law educator; b. 1957; BA magna cum laude, Yale U., 1979; grad. study, Ludwig Maximilians U., Munich, 1979—80; JD cum laude, Harvard U., 1985. Bar: NY 1986. Litig. assoc. Paul, Weiss, Rifkind, Wharton & Garrison, NYC, 1986—90; assoc. prof. law U. Va. Sch. Law, 1990—95, prof., 1995—96, Class of 1996 prof. law, 1996—99; prof. U. Chgo. Law Sch., 1999—2003, Arnold I. Shure prof. law, 2003—. Vis. prof. law NYU Sch. Law, 1996—97, 1999, U. Chgo. Law Sch., 1998; Bosch pub. policy fellow Am. Acad. Berlin, 2004. Office: U Chgo Law Sch 1111 E 60th St Chicago IL 60637 Office Phone: 773-834-3867. E-mail: macase@law.uchicago.edu.

CASE, PAUL WATSON, JR., communications executive; b. Elmira, N.Y., Dec. 4, 1949; s. Paul Watson and Josephine Pharr (Pollock) C.; m. Laura Lee Moseley, Dec. 12, 1972; 1 child, Brian M. BA, U. Colo., 1971. Cert. in computer programming, cert. in data processing, Inst. Cert. Computer Profls. Programmer analyst Boulder Daily Camera, Colo., 1968—73; v.p. Mr. Steak Inc., Denver, 1973—83, United Cable TV Corp., Denver, 1983—88, United Artists Entertainment Corp., Denver, 1988—90; pres. Caspen, Inc., Larkspur, Colo., 1990; CEO Interactive TV Network Inc., Denver, 1991—97; founding prin. Spectralliance LLC, Denver, 1998—; mng. dir. Case Ventures, 2001—; pres. Kolani Distillers, 2002—. Mem. Colo. Open Systems Consortium (founder., chmn. 1992-95), Cable Data User Com. (chmn. 1986-88). Home: 6561 N Pike Cir Larkspur CO 80118-9713 Office: Spectralliance LLC Ste 700 4600 S Ulster St Denver CO 80237 Office Phone: 303-681-3325. E-mail: pcase@spectralliance.com.

CASE, RICHARD PAUL, electronics executive; b. Akron, Ohio, May 13, 1935; s. Charles Robert and Barbara (Ebinger) C.; m. Virginia Carolyn Quallich, Sept 1, 1956; children: Duane, Ralph, Glenn, Ellen, Sarah, Eileen, Katherine, Melinda. BSEE, Case Inst. Tech., Cleve., 1956; MSEE, Syracuse U., 1985. Registered profl. engr., Conn. Tech. engr., then sr. programmer IBM, 1956-65, mgr. programming ctr. Kingston, N.Y., 1965-66, dir. systems architecture, 1966-71, dir. advanced systems, 1971-75, cons. to dir. rsch. Thomas J. Watson Rsch. Ctr. Yorktown Heights, N.Y., 1975-77, dir. advanced systems devel. Data Processing Product Group, 1977-78, dir. tech. ops. for System Products Div., 1979-81, v.p. devel. ops. Gen. Tech. Div. White Plains, N.Y., 1981-82, dir. product lab. Endicott, N.Y., 1983, v.p. for devel. Systems Tech. Div., 1983-84, dir. tech. pers. devel., 1984-86, dir. univ. rels. and tech. programs, 1986-87, dir. systems analysis, 1987-91, dir. tech. strategy devel. Armonk, N.Y., 1991-97; commr. Pres.'s Commn. on Critical Infrastructure Protection, Washington, 1997-98; ind. computer cons., 1998—. Panelist Nat. Computer Conf., Anaheim, Calif., 1975, Comp-Con, Washington, 1975, 4th IEEE Careers Conf., 1985, NRC Panel on Reliability, Integrity and Privacy in Telecommunications, 1985-86, TECHWORLD Symposium, Washington, 1987, Ann. Jud. Conf. 2d Jud. Cir. U.S., Bolton Landing, N.Y., 1989, 2d Nat. Conf. on Ct. Mgmt., Phoenix, 1990; participant in Air Force Studies Bd. Workshop on Software Devel. and Procurement, Woods Hole, Mass., 1976; mem. sponsors adv. com. Ctr. for Integrated Systems, Stanford U., 1980-84; mem. adv. com. Office of Tech. Assessment, Congress of U.S., 1983; keynote speaker Conf. on Automation and Robotics, Pa. State U., 1983, Symposium on Bus. and the Creative Process, AIESEC, R.I., 1985, Computer Integrated Mfg. and Communications, Anaheim, Calif., 1985; speaker numerous symposiums and confs.; ind. computer cons., 1998—. Chmn. editorial bd. Systems Programming Series, 1975—; contbr. articles to profl. jours. Chmn. evaluation PFG Com., Met. N.Y. Synod, Luth. Ch. in Am., 1973-77; bd. dirs., treas. Mid-Hudson Philharm. Orch., 1974-77; bd. dirs. Binghamton Symphony Orch., 1983-84, Greenwich Symphony Orch., 1989—; trustee Wagner Coll., S.I., N.Y., 1982-88, Nat. Tech. U., 1984-88; trustee, chmn. exec. com. Computer Mus., Boston, 1989—; bd. dirs. nat. judge Nat. Math. Counts Found., 1992—. Recipient Outstanding Invention award IBM, 1965, award for excellence in principles of mgmt. and quantative methods Inst. Certification of Computer Profls., 1976. Fellow IEEE (mem. com. engrng. accreditation activities 2004—); mem. Assn. for Computing Machinery, Sigma Xi (assoc.), Tau Kappa Alpha, Tau Beta Pi, Eta Kappa Nu. Office: 40 Bush Ave Greenwich CT 06830-7067 Office Phone: 203-869-5498. Personal E-mail: case004@attglobal.net.

CASE, RICHARD W., sports association executive; m. Barbara Case; two children. Sec. gen. USA Baseball (formerly U.S. Baseball Fedn.), 1980—. Bd. dirs. U.S. Olympic Com.; cons., advisor and dir. in field; producer instrnl. videotapes, books and brochures with a concentration in the areas of player and coach tng., vol. enlistment, accident prevention, juv. delinquency, and youth tournament operation in all sports. Recipient USA Baseball Pres.'s award, Am. Baseball Coaches Assn. award of honor, Centenary medal Juan Antonio Samaranch, Internat. Olympic Com. Pres., others; inducted into Nat. Jr. Coll. Athletic Assn. Hall of Fame, Nat. Assn. Intercollegiate Athletics Hall of Fame, Nat. Police Assn. Hall of Honor; recipient numerous hon. citizenship and commendation awards. Mem. Internat. Baseball Assn. (sec. gen.). Office: USA Baseball 4825 Creekstone Dr Ste 200 Durham NC 27703-6051

CASE, ROBERT BROWN, physician; b. Columbus, Ohio, July 19, 1920; s. William Lyman and Margaret (Brown) C.; m. Nan Barkin, Nov. 9, 1973; 1 child, Lisa Case. BA, Ohio Wesleyan, 1943; BS, MIT, 1943; MD, Columbia U., 1948. Diplomate Am. Bd. Internal Medicine. Intern and resident St. Luke's Hosp., N.Y.C., 1948-52, chief lab. of exptl. cardiology, 1956-95, sr. attending physician, 1971-95; rsch. fellow Harvard Sch. of Pub. Health, Boston, 1952-54; rsch. assoc. Nat. Heart Inst., Bethesda, Md., 1954-56; prof. emeritus medicine Columbia U., N.Y.C., 1991—. Chief cardiac consultation clinic N.Y.C. Dept. Health, 1962-70; mem. cardiovascular study sect. Nat. Heart Inst., 1970-74. Mem. editl. bd. Circulation Rsch., 1977-85; contbr. articles to profl. jours. With USPHS, 1954-56. Rsch. Career devel. grant NIH, 1962-72. Felow Am. Physiol. Soc., N.Y. County Med. Assn., N.Y. State Med. Assn., Am. Heart Assn., Am. Fedn. for Clin. Rsch. Home and Office: 130 E 75th St New York NY 10021-3277 Office Phone: 212-249-5613. E-mail: rcasemd@nyc.rr.com.

CASE, STEPHEN M., healthcare investment company executive, former media and entertainment company executive; b. Honolulu, Aug. 21, 1958; m. Joanne Case (div.); 3 children; m. Jean Case. BA in Polit. Sci., Williams Coll., 1980. With mktg. dept. Procter & Gamble, 1980—82; mng. new pizza devel. Pizza Hut divsn. PepsiCo, 1982—83; with Control Video, 1983—85, Quantum Computer Svcs., 1985—92; CEO America Online, 1992—2001, chmn., 1995—2001, AOL Time Warner, N.Y.C., 2001—03, Exclusive Resorts LLC, Denver, 2004—; chmn., CEO Revolution Health Group, 2005—. Named Named Entrepreneur of Yr., Inc. Mag., 1994. Avocation: reading political science and social history. Office: Exclusive Resorts LLC Ste 500 1530 16th St Denver CO 80202*

CASE, TAMMY, bank executive; BBA magna cum laude, Upsala Coll., 1995; grad. with honors, U. Del., 1998. Platform asst. to asst. br. mgr. Nat. Bank Sussex County, 1977—81, adminstrv. asst. to asst. cashier, 1981—86, asst. v.p., compliance officer, 1986—89, v.p., 1989—93; sr. loan officer Newton (NJ) Trust Co., 1993—, sr. v.p. bus. banking svcs., 2001—. Chair Sussex County C. of C., past chair govt. legis. com.; past chair ARC; trustee Patriots Path Boy Scout Coun., Ct. Appointed Spl. Advocates; past chair found. bd. SCARD; mem. interfaith hosp. network Sparta Presbyn. Ch.; bd. dirs. Sussex County Econ. Devel. Ptnrship. Named one of 25 Women to Watch, US Banker Mag., 2003; recipient Vol. of Yr. award, Sussex County C. of C., 2001, Women of Yr. award, Patriot's Path Boy Scout Coun., 2001. Office: Newton Trust Co 29 Trinity St Newton NJ 07860

CASE, TED JOSEPH, biologist, educator; b. Sioux City, Iowa, July 19, 1947; BS with honors, U. Redlands, Calif., 1969; PhD, U. Calif., Irvine, 1974. Postgrad. rsch. entomologist U. Calif., Davis, 1973-75; asst. prof. dept. biol. scis. Purdue U., West Lafayette, Ind., 1975-78; asst. prof. dept. biology U. Calif., San Diego, 1978-82, assoc. prof., 1982-86, prof., 1986—, chair dept. biology, 1992-94. Assoc. editor Oecologia, 1986-92, U. Calif. Publs. in Entomology, 1980-92, Evolution, 1984-88, Ecology, 1994—; contbr. numerous articles to profl. jours. Named Outstanding Alumnus, U. Redlands, 1979; Woodrow Wilson fellow, 1969; grantee NSF, 1984-87, 88-91, 90-91, 91-92, 93—, Apple Computer Co., 1987, Nat. Geog. Soc., 1988-91, 92-93, Calif. Dept. Fish and Game, 1995-96, Calif. Met. Water Dist., 1995—, others. Fellow Am. Acad. Arts & Sci.; mem. Am. Soc. Naturalists, Ecol. Soc. Am. Office: U Calif at San Diego Dept Biology La Jolla CA 92093*

CASE, THOMAS LOUIS, lawyer; b. Dallas, June 14, 1947; s. Donald L. and Ellen (Hanson) C.; m. Bonnie Nally, July 8, 1972. BA, Vanderbilt U., 1969, JD, 1972; cert. civil trial law, Tex. Bd. Legal Specialization. Bar: Tex. 1972, U.S. Dist. Ct. (no. dist.) Tex. 1973, U.S. Dist. Ct. (we. and ea. dists.) Tex. 1978, U.S. Dist. Ct. (so. dist.) Tex. 1979, U.S. Dist. Ct. (ea. dist.) Ark. 1981, U.S. Ct. Appeals (5th cir.) 1977, U.S. Supreme Ct. 1978, U.S. Ct. Appeals (8th cir.) 1984, U.S. Ct. Appeals (11th cir.) 1981. Assoc. Johnson, Bromberg, Leeds & Riggs, Dallas, 1972-77; ptnr. Bickel & Case, Dallas, 1977-84, St. Claire & Case, Dallas, 1984-93, Thomas L. Case & Assocs., P.C., Dallas, 1993-2000; shareholder Case Carter Salyers & Henry, Dallas, 2000—01; ptnr. Bell, Nunnally & Martin, Dallas, 2002—. Mem. ABA, Tex.

Bar Assn., Tex. Assn. Def. Coun., Dallas Assn. of Def. Counsel, Dallas Bar Assn. Office: Bell Nunnally & Martin 3232 McKinney Ave Ste 1400 Dallas TX 75204 Office Phone: 214-740-1422. Business E-Mail: tomc@bellnunnally.com.

CASEBEER, DOUGLAS KELLEY, artist, consultant; b. Joplin, Mo., Nov. 1, 1956; s. Charles William and Sue (Dalby) C.; nm. Susan Roscoe, Dec. 22, 1979; children: Emily Clara, Logan Oliver. Student, U. Okla., 1974-76, Mo. Western Stat Coll., 1977-78; BFA in Ceramics, Wichita State U., 1980; MFA in Ceramics, Alfred U., 1982. Dir. ceramics and sculpture program, instr., resident artist Anderson Ranch Arts Ctr., Snowmass Village, Colo., 1985—, program dir. artist-in-residency program, 1987—, dir. programs, 1995-97. Tchg. asst. advanced pottery and kilns N.Y. State Coll. Ceramics, Alfred U., 1980-82; instr. ceramics Jamaica Sch. Art, Kingston, 1984; ceramic cons. UN Indsl. Devel. Orgn., Vienna, Austria, 1982-85, German Agy. for Tech. Cooperation, Eschborn, 1985, Govt. of Nepal, Kathmandu, 1985, USIS, Washington, 1993, Hui Noeau Visual Arts Ctr., Makawao, Maui, Hawaii, 1998; prof. ceramics U. Ga., Cortona, Italy, 1993; mem. nat. adv. bd. Aspen Ednl. Rsch. Found., Woody Creek, Colo., 1998—; co-leader, instr. Gobardia project Potters to Nepal, ceramics study tour, Deohkuri, Dang Dist., Nepal, 1993-00; condr. workshops, lectr., vis. artist, 1983—; co-leader, instr. ceramics study tour Potters to Nepal Gobardiya Project Anderson Ranch Arts Ctr., Deohkuri, Dang Dist., Nepal, 1993-2001. Exhibited in numerous group shows, 1978—, latest being Foothills Art Ctr., Golden, Colo., 1995, 98, Auckland (New Zealand) Studio Potters, 1996, 2000, U. So. Colo., Pueblo, 1996, Taller Huara-Huara, Santiago, Chile, 1996, Daniel Arvizu Gallery, Santa Ana, Calif., 1996, Mus. Nebr., Kearney, 1996, S.E. Ind. U., New Albany, 1997, Grosvenor Gallery, Kingston, Jamaica, 1997, Coll. of Ozarks, Point Lookout, Mo., 1997, Roundtree Art Ctr., Denver, 1997, Contemporary Artifacts Gallery, Brea, Ky., 1997, Greenwich House Pottery, N.Y.C., 1997, 98, 99, Adelson Gallery, Aspen, Colo., 1998, Evelyn Siegel Gallery, Ft. Worth, 1998, 2000, Ching-Tao Fang Ceramics Gallery, Kaohsiung, Taiwan, 1998, Odyssey Gallery, Asheville, N.C., 1999, Islip Art Mus., New Islip, N.Y., 1999, Yoyokaku Gallery, Karatsu-Chi, Saga, Japan, 1999, Gallery Ichibankan, Fukuoka, Japan, 1999, Andrews U., Beriens Springs, Mich., 2000, Hibberd/McGrath Gallery, Breckenridge, Colo., 2000, Signature Gallery, Atlanta, 2000, Nassau County Mus. Art, Nassau, N.Y., 2000, Kreeger Pottery Gallery, Harwich, Mass., 2000, Pub. Libr. Charlotte (N.C.), 2001, Archie Bray Found., Helena, Mont., 2001, Indigo Gallery, Kathmandu, 2001, Blue Spiral Gallery, Asheville, N.C., numerous others; represented in permanent collections Islip Art Mus., Contemporary Ceramics Arts Inst., Taipei, Taiwan, Auckland Art Mus., Jamaica Nat. Gallery, Stetson U., Bemidji (Minn.) State U., Eccelson Harrison Mus. Art, Utah State U., Logan, N.Y. State Coll. Ceramics, Alfred U., Topeka Pub. Libr., also pvt. and corp. collections; work reviewed in newspapers and mags. Mem. Am. Craft Coun., Coll. Art Assn., Nat. Coun. on Edn. Ceramic Arts, Colo. Artist Craftsmen Assn. (bd. dirs. 1990-91). Achievements include development variety of kilns in U.S. and Caribbean; research on glazes and clay bodies in relation to demands of final project; discovered and developed 5 clays and variety of basic minerals for manufacture of ceramic products, 3 stoneware and 2 earthenware clays, 3 varieties of silica, dolomite, limestones, gypsum, haematite, steatite, and prophyry granites for feldspars. Office: Anderson Ranch Arts Ctr PO Box 5598 5263 Owl Creek Rd Snowmass Village CO 81615 E-mail: dcasebeer@andersonranch.org.

CASEBEER, LINDA LOUISE, medical educator; b. Boone, Iowa, Apr. 8, 1947; d. Paul Fredrick and Hazel Arlene (Wickstrom) Gallmeier; m. Norman Leslie Shillman, Dec. 22, 1968 (div. Oct. 1983); children: Holly, Lisa, Wendy, Rachael; m. Edwin Frank Casebeer Jr., July 23, 1988; 1 stepchild, John. BA in Polit. Sci., N.C. State U., 1969; MEd, The Citadel, Charleston, S.C., 1983; PhD in Instrnl. Systems Tech., Ind. U., 1991. Elem. tchr. Colleton County Sch., Roundo, S.C., 1970-73; tchr. Christ Luth. Presch., Hilton Head Island, S.C., 1979-82; instrnl. designer Meth. Hosp., Indpls., 1985-90, dir. acad. affairs dept., 1990-95; assoc. dir., asst. prof. U. Ala. Sch. Medicine, Birmingham, 1995—2003, assoc. prof., 2003—. Mem. Accreditation Coun. for Continuing Med. Edn. Contbr. poetry to profl. jours. Recipient Vol. award Accreditation Coun. for Continuing Med. Edn., 2000, Soc. Acad. Cm Rschr. of Yr. award, 2004. Mem. Alliance Continuing Med. Edn. (rsch. award 1995, provider/industry award 1997), Am. Med. Informatics Assn., Assn. Am. Med. Colls Group on Ednl. Affairs. Democrat. Lutheran. Home: 1500 21st Way S Birmingham AL 35205-5002 Office: U Ala Sch Medicine 1521 11th Ave S Birmingham AL 35205-3503 E-mail: casebeer@uab.edu.

CASEI, NEDDA, mezzo soprano; b. Balt. d. Howard Thomas and Lyda Marie (Graupman) Casey; m. John A. Wiles, Jr., 1971 (div. 1979); m. Samuel Strasbourger, 1983 (dec. 1987). Cert., Mozarteum, Salzburg, Austria, 1959; B in Performing Arts Adminstrn. magna cum laude, Fordham U., 1982; studied voice with, William P. Herman, N.Y.C., Vittorio Piccinini, Milan, Italy, Loretta Corelli, N.Y.C.; also student piano, langs., modern dance, ballet. Tchr. master classes, lectr. univs. and festivals. Judge vocal competitions for Met. Opera, Fulbright Scholarship, Rosa Ponselle Internat. Competition, Savannah Festival, George London Found. Competition, First Internat. Vocal Competition, Baku, Azerbaijan, and others; vis. prof. Aichi Prefectural U. Fine Arts and Music, Nagoya, Japan; guest prof. Flaine Festival/Paris Conservatory, Haut Savoie, France, Mannes Coll. Music, New Sch. Social Rsch., N.Y.C., Internat. Vocal Arts Inst., Tel Aviv; pvt. tchr. Operatic debut Theatre Royal de la Monnaie, Brussels, 1960, with La Scala, Milan, Met. Opera, N.Y.C., 1964; operatic performances at Met. Opera, 1964-86, Basel Stadttheater, Gran Liceo, Barcelona, Teatro Carlo Fenice, Genova, San Remo Festival, Trieste Opera, Opera du Rhin, Strasbourg, Salzburg Festspielhaus, Teatro San Carlo, Naples, Chgo. Lyric Opera, Bogota Opera, Caracas Opera, Pitts. Opera, Vancouver Opera, Cape Town Opera, Brno Opera, Bratislava Opera, Kosice Opera, Prague Opera, Miami Opera, Houston Opera, San Diego Opera, Hartford Opera, Phila. Opera, Toledo Opera, Dayton Opera, Memphis Opera, Mobile Opera, Los Angeles Opera, Boston Opera, N.J. Opera, Taipei Opera, Opera of Mexico City; performances in numerous mus. festivals, concerts, recitals and operatic guest appearances in Europe, South Africa, Cen. Am., S.Am., Can., U.S., Far East, Middle East and Australia, including Detroit Symphony, Cin. Orch., Toronto Symphony, Liepzig Gewandhaus Philharm., Phila. Orch., Brussels Philharm., NY Philharm.; performed on radio and TV in Holland, Belgium, Leipzig, Japan, U.S., German Dem. Republic, Fed. Republic of Germany, Hong Kong, Singapore; performed at White House, Washington; made various recs. Supraphon, Everest, Nonesuch, Concert Hall, Vanguard, CETRA, VAI, others; contbr. articles to profl. jours.; guest editor Opera Quar. Coord. mus. events and benefits for Internat. Ctr. for Disabled, Morningside Home, Aging in Am. Gerontol. Acad.; mem. adv. bd. Fordham U at Lincoln Ctr., 1984—; bd. dirs. Theatre for a New Audience, Am. Coun. for Arts, Nat. Cultural Alliance, Songs of Love; mem. Career Transition for Dancers Nat. Adv. Bd. Recipient Outstanding Young Singers award, 1959, Martha Baird Rockefeller Found. award, 1962, 1964, Woman of Achievement award, 1969, Cmty. Leaders and Noteworthy Americans, 1975—76, Outstanding Achievement award on behalf of Arts and Edn., Opera Music Theater Internat. and Children's Emergency Med. Fund, 2000, Outstanding Lifetime Achievement award, Licia Albanese/Puccini Found., 2001, Extraordinary Women award, 2000, honors at, 100 Year Verdi Celebration by Met. Opera. Mem. AFTRA, Actors Equity, Am. Guild Mus. Artists (nat. pres. 1983-93. chmn. Emergency Relief Fund 1983-94), Nat. Assn. Tchrs. Singing (bd. govs.), N.Y. Singing Tchrs. Assn., The Players, James Beard Found. E-mail: neddanewyork@nyc.rr.com, neddanagoya@guitar.ocn.ne.jp.

CASEIRAS, JO ANN STRIGA, artist, educator; b. Bklyn., Dec. 17, 1950; d. Michael Striga and Stella Mary Lango; m. Frank Caseiras, May 21, 1983; children: Michael Allen, Kevin Frank, Amanda Beth, Robert Anthony. BFA, St. John's U., Jamaica, N.Y., 1972; MFA, SUNY, New Paltz, 1975. Tchr. continuing edn. SUNY, New Paltz, 1974-75, prof. Buffalo, 1976-78; tchr. Marlboro (N.Y.) Elem. Continuing Edn., 1980-82; parent advocate Rondout Valley Ctrl. Sch. Dist., Accord, N.Y., 1992-97, tchr. program for the handicapped, 1999—. Exhibited in shows at Reavin Gallery, New Paltz, N.Y., 1976, Benjamin's Works of Art, Buffalo, 1977, Art Zone 208, New Paltz, 1979, Mamaroneck Artists Guild, White Plains, N.Y., 1979, Womanart Gallery, N.Y.C., Schenectady (N.Y.) Mus., 1980, New Rochelle (N.Y.) Art Assn., 1994, Heritage Art Gallery, Poughkeepsie, N.Y., 1995, St. John's U., Jamaica, N.Y., 1996, Heritage Gallery, Rhinebeck, N.Y., 1997, Highland (N.Y.) Cultural Art Ctr., 1996-98, Coffey Gallery, Kingston, N.Y., 1998, Woodstock (N.Y.) Art Assn., 1995—, First Union Bank, New Paltz, 2000, Marbletown Arts Assn., 2002, Marbletown Tricentennial Exhbn., 2003. Recipient Mortimer L. Medrich Meml. award, 1979. Mem.: Woodstock Art Assn., Art Soc. Kingston, Downs Syndrome Assn. Democrat. Roman Catholic. Avocations: sports, swimming, piano, photography. Personal E-mail: jstrigacaseiras@aol.com.

CASELLA, JIM, marketing professional; CEO Round1; 1st pres., CEO PennNet (now called PennEnergy); CEO Reed Bus. Info. U.S., 2002—. Sr. position pub. co. Harcourt; pres. ABC Mag.; COO IDG. Office: Reed Internat Bus US 360 Park Ave S 18th Fl New York NY 10010-1710 Business E-Mail: jcasella@reedbusiness.com.

CASELLA, RUSSELL CARL, physicist; b. Framingham, Nov. 6, 1929; s. Rosario and Lena Casella; m. Marilyn Smith, Jan. 27, 1952; children: Sheryl M., Cynthia L. Conturie. BS in Physics, MIT, 1951, MS in Physics, 1953; PhD in Physics, U. Ill., 1956. Physicist Cambridge (Mass.) AF Rsch. Ctr., 1951-52; teaching and rsch. asst. physics dept. U. Ill., Urbana, 1953-55, rsch. fellow physics dept., 1955-56, rsch. assoc. physics dept., 1956-58; theoretical physicist IBM T.J. Watson Rsch. Ctr., Yorktown Heights, N.Y., 1958-65, Nat. Inst. Standards and Tech., Gaithersburg, Md., 1965-95. Contbr. articles to profl. jours. Recipient Silver medal U.S. Dept. Commerce, 1973. Mem. Am. Phys. Soc., Sigma Xi. Achievements include development of theory of condensed-matter and of elementary-particle physics; research in (broken) symmetries; neutron scattering; Bose condensation of excitons; tests of time reversal and CPT symmetries in Kaon physics; neutrino scattering; topology in neutron interferometry; high-temperature superconductivity; hydrogen in metals; quark-parton-sea content of the nucleon in deep-inelastic electroweak scattering. Home: 1485 Dunster Ln Potomac MD 20854-6107

CASELLAS, JOACHIM, art gallery executive; b. Gerona, Spain, Aug. 1, 1927; came to U.S., 1954; s. Juan and Dolores Farres (Carrera) C.; m. Elizabeth Reed Brannon, Mar. 17, 1952 (dec. Dec. 1984); m. Janice Mary Bezverkov, May 29, 1990 (dec. Apr. 2002). BA, Gerona Coll., 1948; MA, Sacred Heart Coll., 1953. Curator Mus. Provincial, Gerona, Spain, 1952; art appraiser Feist Co., N.Y.C., 1952-68, Mahan Co., New Orleans, 1968-72; pres. Casell Gallery, New Orleans, 1972—. One-man shows include Ft. Walton (Fla.) Beach Mus. Art, 1987. Mem. Ocean Springs Yacht Club. Republican. Episcopalian. Avocations: photography, gardening, travel, antiques, boating. Home: 107 Shearwater Dr Ocean Springs MS 39564-4828 Office: Casell Gallery 818 Royal St New Orleans LA 70116-3115 Office Phone: 504-524-0671. Personal E-mail: joaquin_cas@msn.com. E-mail: casellartgallery@bellsouth.net.

CASELLAS, SALVADOR E., judge; b. 1935; BS in Fgn. Svc. cum laude, Georgetown U., 1957; LLB magna cum laude, U. P.R., 1960; LLM, Harvard U., 1961. Ptnr. Fiddler, Gonzalez & Rodriguez, 1962-72, 77-94; sr. judge U.S. Dist. Ct. P.R., San Juan, 1994—. Mem. P.R. Acad. Jurisprudence, P.R. Commn. on Bicentennial of U.S. Constn., 1987-89; aide to Sec. of U.S. Army, 1985-89, emeritus, 1990—. Dir. Alliance for Drug Free P.R., 1993-94. 1st lt. U.S. Army, 1961-62, Res., JAGC, 1963-67. Recipient Comdrs. medal Second U.S. Army, 1990, P.R. Nat. Guard medal, 1990. Mem. ABA, Am. Bar Found., P.R. Bar Assn., P.R. Bar Assn. Found., Caparra Country Club, Banker's Club. Office: US Courthouse Ste 342 Viejo San Juan PR 00901

CASERTA, JENNIFER, school psychologist; b. Mt. Vernon, NY, Aug. 8, 1977; d. Basilio and Margaret Caserta. A in Liberal Arts, Dutchess C.C., 1997; B in Psychology, Fairleigh Dickinson U., M in Psychology, 2000; EdS in Mental Health Counseling, Seton Hall U., 2005. Cert. sch. psychologist Marist Coll. Poughkeepsie, NY, 2002. Svc. coord. ARC Dutchess County, Pleasant Valley, NY, 2000—01; clinician, sch. psychologist Anderson Sch., Staatsburg, 2001—04; sch. psychologist Kearny H.S., NJ, 2004—. Mem.: NASP, Assn. Play Therapy, Order Sons Italy Am., Chi Sigma Iota, Kappa Delta Pi. Roman Catholic. Office Phone: 201-955-3015.

CASE-SCHMIDT, MARY E., pathologist, educator; b. Jefferson City, Mo., Feb. 27, 1943; BA, U. Mo., 1965; MD, St. Louis U. Sch. Medicine, 1969. Resident in pathology St. Louis U. Sch. Medicine, St. Louis, 1969—71, asst. in pathology, 1969—73; postdoctoral fellow Nat. Inst. Neurol. Disease and Stroke, St. Louis, 1971—72; resident in neuropathology St. Louis U. Sch. Medicine, 1972—73, instr. in pathology, 1973—75; vis. asst. prof. neuropathology U. Mo., Sch. Medicine, Columbia, Mo., 1975—77; asst. prof. pathology St. Louis U. Sch. Medicine, 1975—81; cons. neuropathology St. Luke's Hosp., East and West, 1973—77; asst. med. examiner St. Louis County, 1975—88, City of St. Louis, 1977—80; assoc. prof. pathology St. Louis U. Sch. Medicine, 1981—99; dep. chief med. examiner City of St. Louis, 1980—85; cons. neuropathology St. John's Mercy Hosp., St. Louis, 1973—88; spl. projects, divsn. forensic and environ. pathology St. Louis U. Sch. Medicine, 1985—; chief med. examiner St. Charles County, 1986—, St. Louis County, 1988—, Jefferson County, 1992—, Franklin County, 1993—; prof. pathology St. Louis U. Health Scis. Ctr., 1999—, co-dir., divsn. forensic pathology, 1996—. Dean's adv. bd. St. Louis U., 2000—; bd. dirs. Greater St. Louis Region Critical Incident Stress Mgmt. Team, 1995—; mem. Nat. Medicolegal Rev. Panel for Devel. Guidelines for Death Invest. for Nat. Inst. Justice, 1996—. Recipient Spl. Leadership award for Professions, Meto. St. Louis YWCA, 1990, Norman Westbrook "Hall of Fame" award, Mo. Police Juvenile Officers Assn., 1992, Recognition award "Teen Drinking and Driving", St. Louis Metro. Med. Soc., 2001, Spl. Recognition award, St. Charles Crime Stoppers, 2002. Fellow: Am. Acad. Forensic Sci. (ethics com. 2001—), Am. Soc. Clin. Pathology, Coll. Am. Pathologists; mem.: AMA, Nat. Assn. Med. Examiner (bd. dir. 2000—, exec. com. 2001—), Am. Assn. Neuropathologists, Internat. Acad. Pathology, St. Louis Path. Soc., St. Louis Metro. Med. Soc., Am. Profl. Soc. on Abuse of Children, Mo. State Med. Assn., Mo. Network of Cert. Pathologists for Child Death Autopsies (chmn. 1996—), Am. Journal Forensic Medicine and Pathology. Office: St Louis U Sch Medicine Dept Pathology 1402 S Grand Saint Louis MO 63104-1004

CASEY, BARBARA JEANNE, marketing professional; b. Glen Cove, N.Y., Mar. 6, 1970; d. William Royal DeMeo and Barbara Louise (Anderson) Terry; m. John Edward Casey, Sept. 12, 1998. BA, U. So. Calif., 1992; MBA, Columbia U., 1998. Client svcs. rep. Christie's Inc., N.Y.C., 1992-93, adminstr., 1993-94, overseas liaison, 1994-96; assoc. mktg. mgr. Time Inc., N.Y.C., 1998-99; dir. mktg. Onview.com, N.Y.C., 1999—2001; v.p. client rels. Chilton Investment Co., Inc., 2001—. Mem. jr. com. Search and Care, Inc., 1993—. Mem. N.Y.C. Alumni Club (v.p. 1996-98, co-pres. 1998-2002), Doubles Club (assocs. com. 1993—), Delta Gamma (v.p. programming alumni club 1994-95). Avocations: dogs, tennis, golf, skiing, arts and entertainment. Home: 945 Fifth Ave Apt 3D New York NY 10021-2655 Office: Onview dot com 300 Park Ave 19th Fl New York NY 10022

CASEY, BARBARA LOUISE, writer, consultant; b. Carrollton, Ill., July 11, 1944; d. George Dallas and Charlotte Louise (Barbour) Casey; m. Willis Robert Casey, Feb. 17, 1979 (dec. June 1992); children: Carlotta Brown-Harward, Rene Louise Mathews BA English and History summa cum laude, N.C. Wesleyan Coll., 1975; student, U. N.C., 1963-68, N.C. State U., 1968-70, Kings Bus. Coll., 1962-63. Dir. alumni and pub. rels. N.C. Wesleyan Coll., 1975-77; staff dept. athletics N.C. State U., 1977-79; freelance writer, editl. cons., lit. agt. Wellington, Fla., 1986—. Guest author Book Fest the Palm Beaches, 1993-94., panelist, 1994; judge pathfinder awards program, Palm Beach Post, 1994— Author: Leilani Zan, 1992, Grandma Jock and Christabelle, 1994, Shyla's Initiative, 2002, The Coach's Wife, 2004; author numerous poems; contbr. articles to local newspapers and popular mags Mem. Soc. Children's Book Writers and Illustrators (Fla. regional advisor), Fla. Freelance Writers, Poets of the Palm Beaches, Book Group of South Fla. Personal E-mail: bcasey@publishersupdate.com.

CASEY, BERNARD J., lawyer; b. June 4, 1942; s. Andrew J. and Theresa (Lennon) C.; m. Kathleen A. Wall; children: Brendan, B. John. AB, Providence Coll., 1964; JD, Catholic U., 1967. Bar: R.I. 1967, D.C. 1971, Calif. 2003, U.S. Supreme Ct. 1972, U.S. Cir. Ct. (D.C. cir., 4th cir., 6th cir.). Assoc. Gall, Lane & Powell, Washington, 1971-76, ptnr., 1976, Reed Smith LLP, Washington, 1976—. Bd. dirs. Cath. Charities, 1994-99, chmn., 1997-98. Served to capt. AUS, 1967-71. Decorated Bronze Star medal. Mem. ABA (litigation com.), Barristers, Lawyers Club, Univ. Club (bd. govs. 1989-97, pres. 1990-92), Chevy Chase Country Club. Roman Catholic. Home: 1920 Jones St San Francisco CA 94133 Office: Reed Smith LLP Two Embarcadero Ste 2000 San Francisco CA 94111 Office Phone: 415-659-5959.

CASEY, BEVERLY ANN, retired postmaster; b. Decaturville, Tenn., Aug. 6, 1949; d. Willie Hugh and Lillian Blanche (Ivy) Tillman; m. John Robert Casey, Jan. 19, 1969 (div. 1982); children: John Gary, Kimberly Jean. Student, Jackson State C.C., 1982-84. Sec. State of Tenn., Western Inst., Western Institute, 1969-76; clk. U.S. Postal Svc., Western Institute, 1977-82, postmaster, 82-84, Pickwick Dam, Tenn., 1984—2005, officer-in-charge Stantonville, Tenn., 1998, Michie, Tenn., 1984; ret., 2005. Dir.-at-large women's adv. coun. U.S. Postal Svc., 1983-88. Bd. dirs. Pickwick Med. Clinic, 1986; vol. Hardeman chpt. St. Jude, Bolivar, Tenn., 1983, Hospice, 1996; mem. parents advancement com. Wesleyan Coll., 1991-94; town chmn., activities chmn. Reelfoot coun. Girl Scouts U.S., 1980-84 Recipient Appreciation award Girl Scouts U.S., 1983, Vol. Svc. award Tenn. chpt. Cystic Fibrosis Found., 1982, Vol. Appreciation cert. Western Mental Health, 1984, cert. of appreciation Tenn. Partnership Missions, 1997. Mem. Nat. League Postmasters (v.p. Tenn. br. 1984-86, 200004, Postmaster of Yr. 2003), 380 Postmasters Assn. (pres. 1983-84). Baptist. Avocations: walking, gardening. Office: US Postal Service Pickwick Dam TN 38365 Home: 2025 Hamburg Loop Savannah TN 38372

CASEY, CAROLE LYNN, elementary school educator, music educator; b. Baytown, Tex., Dec. 27, 1969; d. Douglas Lawrence and Vicki Carolynn Haddon; m. Randy Lee Casey, Apr. 26, 1967; children: Abigail Vaugh, Megan Ann. BA in English, BA in Music, U. Houston, 1995, M in Curriculum and Instrn. and Elem. Edn., 1997. Cert. tchr. in elem. edn. and English Tex., 1997. Tchr. 2nd grade self contained Pumphrey Elem., Baytown, Tex., 1997—2000, 4th grade lang. arts tchr., 2000—01, 5th grade sci. and math. tchr., 2001—05, 3rd grade math. and sci. tchr., 2005—; inst. percussion Robert E. Lee H.S., 2001—; tchr. percussion pvt. lesson Baytown Jr. H.S., 2004—. Tutorial tchr. Pumphrey Elem., 1997—. Musician: Baytown Cmty. Band, Baytown Symphony Orch.; composer (musician): (percussion ensemble) Kodo Stomp (Walt Disney Superior Percussion Ensemble, 2002); composer: (conductor) America: Old Beat, New Drummer (All Sch. Dist. Performance, 2004). Mem. Civil War Preservation Trust, Baytown, 2001—, Friends Gettysburg, Pa., 2003—. Recipient Superior Drum Line, Sulpher Music Contest, 2001—05. Mem.: Trooper Drum Corps Alumni (life), Sigma Alpha Iota (life; pres. 1995—97), Tau Beta Sigma (life; v.p. 1992—95). Home: 1705 Woodlawn Dr Baytown TX 77520 Office: Pumphrey Elem Sch 4901 Fairway Dr Baytown TX 77521 Office Phone: 281-420-4655. Personal E-mail: clcasey@gccisd.net.

CASEY, DANIEL ARTHUR, lawyer; b. Pitts., May 8, 1956; s. Robert Louis and Rosemary (Doran) C.; m. Maria Cristina Pena, Aug. 1, 1981; children: Patricia, Robert, Andrew. BS, Wheeling Coll., 1978; JD, Georgetown U., 1981. Bar: Fla. 1981, U.S. Dist. Ct. (so. dist.) Fla. 1986, U.S. Ct. Appeals (11th cir.) 1986, U.S. Dist. Ct. (mid. dist.) Fla. 1989. Asst. State Atty. Dade County State Atty., Miami, Fla., 1981-86; assoc. Kirkpatrick and Lockhart, Miami, 1986-89, ptnr., 1990—2004; adminstrv. ptnr. & mem. exec. com. Kirkpatrick & Lockhart Nicholson Graham LLP, Miami, 2005—. Adj. prof. law Nova U. Law Sch., 1989-96. Contbr. articles to profl. publs. Nat. bd. dir. YMCA of the USA; past pres. YMCA So. Broward County; mem. Ins. Info. Council; past pres. Greater Hollywood C. of C. Mem.: Dade County Bar Assn. (bd. dir.), Alpha Sigma Nu. Office: Kirkpatrick & Lockhart Nicholson Graham LLP Ste 2000 201 S Biscayne Blvd Miami FL 33131-2399 Office Phone: 305-539-3324. Office Fax: 305-358-7095. Business E-Mail: dcasey@klng.com.

CASEY, EDWARD PAUL, manufacturing executive; b. Boston, Feb. 23, 1930; s. Edward J. and Virginia (Paul) C.; m. Patricia Pinkham, June 23, 1950 (dec. Nov. 1996); children: Patricia Estes Casey Shepherd, Tyler Casey White, Jennifer Paul Casey, Sheila Pinkham Casey McManus, Virginia Louise Casey Pettengill; m. Mary Ann Patton, Mar. 28, 1998. AB, Yale U., 1952; MBA, Harvard Coll., 1955. With Davidson Rubber Co., Dover, N.H., 1950-65; COO McCord Corp., Detroit, 1965-78, pres., 1965-78; COO Ex-Cell-O Corp., Troy, Mich., 1978-81, CEO, pres., 1981-86, chmn., 1983-86; vice chmn. Textron Inc., 1986-87; pres. E. Paul Casey Assocs., 1987-89; mng. gen. ptnr. Metapoint Ptnrs., Peabody, Mass., 1989-97, chmn., 1997—2004, chmn. emeritus, 2004—. Trustee Henry Ford Health Care Sys., Detroit; chair Hobe Sound Cmty. Chest, Fla. Mem. Chief Execs. Orgn., Harvard Bus. Sch. Club So. Fla., N.Y. Yacht Club (N.Y.C.), Yondotega Club (Detroit), Ea. Yacht Club (Marblehead, Mass.), Yale Club (N.Y.C.), Jupiter Island Club, Hobe Sound Yacht Club (Jupiter Island, Fla.). Home: 330 S Beach Rd Hobe Sound FL 33455-2606

CASEY, GEORGE WILLIAM, JR., career military officer; b. Japan, July 22, 1948; BS in Internat. Rels., Georgetown U., 1970; MA in Internat. Rels., U. Denver. Commd. 2nd lt. U.S. Army, 1970, advanced through grades to gen., 2003, various positions, 1970-82, exec. officer 1st Battalion, 10th Infantry, 4th Divsn. Ft. Carson, Colo., 1982-84, sec. gen. staff 4th Infantry Divsn., 1984-85, comdr. 1st Battalion, 10th Infantry, 4th Divsn., 1985-87; congl. program coord. Office of the Chief of Legis. Liaison, Washington, 1988-89; spl. ast. to Chief of Staff U.S. Army, Washington, 1989-91, chief of staff 1st Cavalry Divsn. Ft. Hood, Tex., 1991-93, comdr. 3rd Brigade, 1st Cavalry Divsn., 1993-95; asst. chief of staff G-3 (ops.), V Corps. U.S. Army Europe, 1995; chief of staff V Corps. U.S. Army Europe and Seventh Army, Germany, 1995-96, asst. divsn. comdr. 1st Armored Divsn., 1996-97; asst. dep. dir. politico-mil. affairs J-5 The Joint Staff, Washington, 1997-99; comdg. gen. U.S. Army Europe, 1st Armored Divsn., 1999—2001; dir. for strategic plans, policy Joint Staff, Washington, 2001—03, dir., 2003; vice chief of staff U.S. Army, Washington, 2003—04; comdr. Multi-Nat. Force-Iraq, 2004—. Decorated Legion of Merit with 2 oak leaf clusters, Def. Meritorious Svc. medal, Meritorious Svc. medal, Army Commendation medal with oak leaf cluster, Army Achievement medal with oak leaf cluster.

CASEY, GERARD WILLIAM, retired food products executive, lawyer; b. N.Y.C., Nov. 12, 1942; s. William Gerard and Bridget (Carmody) C.; m. Lani St. John; children: Jennifer, William, Thomas, Andrew, Patrick. BS in History, Fordham Coll., 1963; MA in History, NYU, 1966; JD, Fordham U., 1967. Bar: N.Y. 1969. Criminal investigator U.S. Army, U.S., Korea, 1967-69; v.p., gen. counsel Pepsi Cola Co., PepsiCo, Inc., Puchase, NY, 1969—2001. Mem. Friendly Sons of St. Patrick, White Plains, 1987—; dir., chmn. bd. mgrs. Lincoln Hall Sch., Lincolndale, N.Y., 1988-91. Mem. ABA, N.Y. State Bar Assn., Am. Corp. Counsel Assn., VFW. Roman Catholic. Home: 45 E 72nd St New York NY 10021

CASEY, H(ORACE) CRAIG, JR., electrical engineering educator; b. Houston, Dec. 4, 1934; s. H.c. and Mae (Walls) C.; m. Jean Anne Merritt, June 14, 1960 (div. 1983); children: Anne, Michael; m. Jacqueline Lucas, Jan. 22, 1983. BSEE, Okla. State U., 1957; MSEE, Stanford U., 1959, PhD, 1964. Devel. engr. Hewlett-Packard, Palo Alto, Calif., 1957-62; mem. tech. staff Bell Labs., Murray Hill, NJ, 1964-79; chmn. dept. elec. engring. Duke U., Durham, NC, 1979-94, prof. elec. engring., 1979—. Mem. Dept. of Def. Adv. Group Electron Devices, Washington, 1975-79; bd. dirs. Acme Elec., 1984-91. Author: Heterostructure Lasers, 1978, Devices for Integrated Circuits: Silicon and III-V Compounds, 1999. Fellow IEEE (pres. Electron Devices Soc. 1988-89, editor centennial issue Trans. on Electron Devices 1984); mem. Am. Phys. Soc. Office: Duke U Dept Elec Engring Durham NC 27706 Business E-Mail: hcc@ee.duke.edu.

CASEY, JAMES B., librarian; b. Syracuse, NY, June 29, 1950; s. John Joseph and Louise (Countryman) C.; m. Diane Dates, Nov. 16, 1984; children: Nathan, Jeremy. MLS, SUNY, Geneseo, 1973; MA, Cleve. State U., 1979; PhD, Case Western Res. U., 1985. Head librarian Ohio Hist. Soc., Columbus, 1983-84; dir. Pickaway County Pub. Libr., Circleville, Ohio, 1984-92, Oak Lawn (Ill.) Libr., 1992—. Editor: Libby Prison Autograph Book, 1984. Grant rev. com. Ill. State Libr. Constrn., 1999—. Recipient Heath Lit. award, Am. Numis. Assn., 1980, Heath Literary award, Am. Numismatic Assn., 1980. Mem. ALA (mem. coun. 1996—), Ill. Libr. Assn. (pub. policy com. 2001—). Avocation: coin collecting/numismatics. Home: 9717 Parkside Ave Oak Lawn IL 60453-3657 Office: Oak Lawn Libr 9427 Raymond Ave Oak Lawn IL 60453-2405 E-mail: drjbc92@lib.oak-lawn.il.us.

CASEY, JOHN ALEXANDER, lawyer; b. Wisconsin Rapids, Wis., Apr. 7, 1945; s. Samuel Alexander and Ardean A. AB, Stanford U., 1967; JD, U. Mich., 1970. Ptnr. Quarles & Brady, Milw., 1970—. Office: Quarles & Brady 411 E Wisconsin Ave Ste 2040 Milwaukee WI 53202-4497 Office Phone: 414-277-5383. Business E-Mail: jac@quarles.com.

CASEY, JOHN DUDLEY, writer, language educator; b. Worcester, Mass., Jan. 18, 1939; s. Joseph Edward and Constance (Dudley) C.; m. Jane Barnes, June 10, 1967 (div. 1980); children: Maud, Nell; m. Rosamond Pinchot Pittman, June 27, 1982; children: Clare, Julia. BA, Harvard U., 1962, LLB, 1965; MFA, U. Iowa, 1968. Prof. English U. Va., Charlottesville, 1972-92, U. Iowa, 1998, U. Va., 1999—. Lit. executor Estate of Breece D'J Pancake, 1979—; resident scholar Am. Acad. in Rome, 1990-91. Author: An American Romance, 1977 (runner up Ernest Hemingway award 1977), Testimony and Demeanor, 1979 (Friends Am. Lit. award 1980), Spartina, 1989 (Nat. Book award 1989), Supper at the Black Pearl, 1995, The Half-life of Happiness, 1998; co-translator: You're an Animal, Viskovitz (By A. Boffa), 2002; contbr. stories (O. Henry award 1989), essays maj. nat. mags. including New Yorker, Esquire. With USAR, 1959-60. Guggenheim fellow, 1979-80, Nat. Endowment for Arts fellow, 1983, resident Am. Acad. in Rome, 1990-91; grantee Strauss living AAAL, 1992-97. Mem. PEN. Avocation: rowing. Office: U Va Dept English Bryan Hall Charlottesville VA 22903-3289 also: Michael Carlisle Carlisle & Co 24 E 64th St New York NY 10021-7201

CASEY, JOHN PATRICK (JACK CASEY), public relations executive, political scientist; b. Syracuse, N.Y., July 19, 1928; s. Patrick Joseph and Ellen (Loftus) C.; m. Ursula Casey, Feb. 3, 1951 (div. 1975); children: Michael, Gretchen, John, Patrick; m. Mary Lou Butcher, May 2, 1982. BA, U. Toledo, 1958. Reporter Toledo Times, 1951-56; staff writer Detroit Free Press, 1956-61; spl. asst. to mayor City of Detroit, 1962-66; v.p. MG and Casey Communications Inc., Detroit, 1966-82; pres., chief exec. officer Casey Communications Mgmt. Inc., Southfield, Mich., 1982-90; chmn. Casey Butcher Ventures, Bloomfield Hills, Mich., 1990—. Polit. analyst Sta. WJR-Radio, Detroit, 1966—99, Sta. WDIV-TV, Detroit, 1978-87, WKBD-TV, Detroit, 1989—2000; speaker in field. Contbr. articles to various publs. Campaign mgr. Re-elect Mayor Cavanagh, Detroit, 1966; chmn. Commn. on Community Rels., City of Detroit, 1968-70. With U.S. Army, 1946-48. Recipient Page One awards Newspaper Guild, Detroit, 1957, 58; other awards for news coverage, pub. rels. Mem. Pub. Rels. Soc. Am. (pres. Detroit chpt. 1981-82, counselors acad., pub. affairs sect., inducted in Detroit chpt. Hall of Fame 1994), Plum Hollow Country Club, Mission Hills Country Club. Democrat. Avocations: classical music, reading, golf. Home: 3864 Vista Ln Orchard Lake MI 48323-1678 also: 12504 Prestwick Ct Rancho Mirage CA 92270-1481

CASEY, JOHN T., hospital administrator; b. 1945; Grad., U. Ala., 1972. With Shands Tchg. Hosp., U. Fla., Gainesville, 1972-73, Cathedral Rehab. Ctr., Jacksonville, Fla., 1973-76, Presbyn. St. Luke's Hosp., Denver, 1976-82; pres. Meth. Health Sys., Memphis, 1985-90; pres., CEO Samaritan Found., Phoenix, 1990-91; pres., COO Am. Med. Holdings, Inc., Dallas, 1991—95; vice chmn. Tenet Healthcare Corp., 1995—97; chmn., CEO Physician Reliance Network, Inc., 1997—99; bd. dirs. MedCath Inc., 2000—, pres., 2003—04, CEO, 2003—05, chmn., 2003—. Served USN, 1967-69. Office: MedCath Inc 10720 Sikes Pl Ste 300 Charlotte NC 28277*

CASEY, KAREN ANNE, banker; b. Bklyn., Oct. 5, 1955; d. Stanley Joseph and Helen Katherine (Kosowski) Mozeleski; m. Dennis Joseph Casey, May 14, 1977; children: Christopher Sean, Erin Michelle. BBA, Baruch Coll., CUNY, 1977. CPA, NY, CFP. Jr. acct. Coopers & Lybrand, NYC, 1977-78, sr. acct., 1978-79, supr., 1979-81; asst. fin. contr. Gulf Internat. Bank, NYC, 1981-82, fin. contr., 1982; v.p., fin. contr. Allied Irish Banks plc, NYC, 1982-87, sr. v.p., fin. contr., 1988-89, sr. v.p. mgmt. support svcs., 1989-92, sr. v.p., CFO, 1992-94, sr. v.p., head pvt. fin. svcs., 1994-2001, sr. v.p., head retail and bus. banking, 2001—04; sr. v.p. Greater Cmty. Svcs. Inc., Little Falls, NJ, 2004; exec. v.p. Greater Cmty. Bank/Bergen Comml. Bank, Little Falls, 2005—. Bank rep. to Inst. Cert. Fin. Planners, 1991—. Mem. AICPA. Roman Catholic. Avocations: gardening, golf, tennis, reading. Office: Greater Cmty Svcs Inc 7 Center Ave Little Falls NJ 07424 Personal E-mail: kcasey55@aol.com.

CASEY, KEITH ALLEN, accountant; b. Michigan City, Ind., Jan. 18, 1961; s. Russell Noal and Juanita Amy (Church) C. BS, Purdue U., 1983; MS in Adminstrn., U. Notre Dame, 1993. CPA, Ind; cert. mgmt. acct., govt. fin. mgr. Cost acct. Joy Mfg. Co., Michigan City, Ind., 1984-85; mfg. acct. Wheel Horse Products, South Bend, Ind., 1985-86; contr., treas. Michigan City (Ind.) Pub. Library, 1986—97; contr. No. Ind. Commuter Transp. Dist., Chesterton, Ind., 1997—; pres. DynaFuture, LLC, Michigan City, 2003—. Instr. Ivy Tech. Coll., 1988-89, Purdue U., 1989-97, Ind. U., South Bend, 1994-96 Mem. AICPA, Ind. CPA Soc. (assoc.), Inst. Mgmt. Accts. (sec. bd.), Assn. of Govt. Accts. Home and Office: 3756 N 700 W La Porte IN 46350-8551 Office Phone: 219-874-4221 ext 221. E-mail: caseyks@netnitco.net.

CASEY, KENNETH LYMAN, neurologist; b. Ogden, Utah, Apr. 16, 1935; s. Kenneth Lafayette and Lyzena (Payne) C.; m. Jean Louise Madsen, June 21, 1958; children— Tena Jeanette, Kenneth Lyman, Teresa Louise. BA, Whitman Coll., Walla Walla, Wash., 1957; MD with honors, U. Wash., Seattle, 1961. Diplomate Am. Bd. Neurology and Psychiatry. Intern in medicine Cornell U. Med. Center-N.Y. Hosp., 1961-62; USPHS officer lab. neurophysiology NIMH, 1962-64; fellow in psychology McGill U., Montreal, Que., Can., 1964-66; mem. faculty U. Mich. Med. Sch., Ann Arbor, 1966—, prof. neurology and physiology, 1978—; resident in neurology U. Mich Hosp., 1971-74; chief neurology svc. VA Med. Center, Ann Arbor, 1979—2002, cons. in neurology, 2002—. Sci. adv. com. Santa Fe Neurol. Inst., 1984—. Assoc. editor Clin. Jour. Pain, 1984—, Pain, 1991—; editor-in-chief Am. Pain Soc. Jour. Pain Forum, 1991-99; contbr. articles to profl. jours., chpts. to books. Grantee, NIH, 1966—; Spl. fellow, 1964—66, Bristol-Myers rsch. grantee, 1988—93. Fellow Am. Acad. Neurology; mem. Am. Physiol. Soc., Am. Acad. Neurology, Am. Neurol. Assn., Soc. Neurosci., Am. Pain Soc. (pres. 1984-85, F.W.L. Kerr Basic Sci. Rsch. award and lecture 1998), Wayne County Med. Soc. (Rhoades lectr. and medalist 2002), Internat. Assn. Study Pain, Phi Beta Kappa, Sigma Xi, Alpha Omega Alpha (J.J. Bonica disting. lectr. and awardee 1991). Unitarian Universalist. Achievements include named lectureship established in his honor by Pfizer Co. in 2002. Home: 2775 Heatherway St Ann Arbor MI 48104-2852 Office: VA Med Ctr Neurology Svc 2215 Fuller Rd Ann Arbor MI 48105-2300 Business E-Mail: kencasey@umich.edu.

CASEY, KIMBERLYN LORETTRE, artist, painter, educator; b. Dexster, Maine, Apr. 10, 1964; d. Terry F. and Jeanette (Turcotte) Casey; m. Mar. 18, 1958. Student, Chautauqua Sch. Art; BS in Art Edn., U. N.H., Plymouth, 1982; postgrad., U. N.H., Durham, 1983-84, Mass. Coll. Art, Boston, 1985-86; MFA in Painting and Printmaking, CUNY, N.Y.C., 1997. Cert. tchr. K-12, N.H., Mass. Owner Creative Corner Studio Sch., Dover, N.H., 1991-95; tchr. workshops U. N.H., Durham, 1992-94; prof. art Plymouth (N.H.) State Coll., 1998—. Mem. pilot program drawing early age Ipswich (Mass.) Pub. Schs., 1997; artist-in-residence N.H. Teen Program Workshop On Star Island; roster artist state coun. arts Barn Gallery, Ogunquit, Maine Exhibited drawings at U. Utah, Ogden, 2000, Currier Gallery of Art, Manchester, N.H., 2000, Newport (N.H.) Art Ctr., 2002; contbr. articles to profl. jours. Recipient Vt. Studio Ctr. Alumni award, 1994, award Charles Edison Fund, 1995, LLerman Trust Found. award, 2001; Ruth Farkau scholar Chautauqua Instn. N.Y., 1996; N.H. Coun. on the Arts painting grantee and fellow, 1999; grantee Ora Lerman Charitable Trust, 2002, N.H. State Coun. on Arts, 2002. Fellow Coll. Art Assn.; mem. CHADD, ADD, ADHD Children, Ogunquit (Maine) Art Assn., Kappa Delta Phi. Avocations: swimming masters, skiing, hiking, camping. Home: 244 Locust St Dover NH 03820-4034 E-mail: kimberlync@hotmail.com.

CASEY, M. MICHAEL, food products executive; BS in Econ., MBA, Harvard Coll. V.p. W.R. Grace & Co.; dir. Family Restaurants, 1986—88; pres., CEO El Torito Restaurants, Inc., 1988—93; exec. v.p., CFO Family Restaurants, Inc., 1993—95; sr. v.p., CFO Starbucks, Seattle, 1995—97, exec. v.p., CFO, chief adminstrv. officer, 1997—. Office: Starbucks PO Box 34067 Seattle WA 98124-1067

CASEY, MAUD L, writer, educator; b. Iowa City, Dec. 9, 1968; d. John D. Casey and Jane Barnes. BA, Wesleyan U., 1991; MFA in Creative Writing, U. Ariz., 1994. Tchr. fiction U. Ariz., Tucson, 1994—95; fiction tchr. New Sch. Social Rsch., N.Y.C., 1995; tchg. asst. Wesleyan U., Middletown, Conn., 2000; adj. asst. prof. Ill. Wesleyan U., Bloomington, 2000—02. Book reviewer NY Times Book Rev., 1997—, Elle mag., 1997—, Newsday, N.Y.C., 1997—, Salon, N.Y.C., 1997—; freelance writer Paper, Poets and Writers, N.Y.C., 1998—. Author: (novels) The Shape of Things to Come, 2001 (NY Times Notable Book of Yr., 2001), (short stories) Drastic, 2002. Recipient spl. mention, Pushcart prize, 1997; fellow, Vt. Studio Ctr., 2001, UCross Found., Clearmont, NY, 2002. Personal E-mail: maud.casey@verizon.net.

CASEY, MICHAEL D., biotechnology company executive; With Ortho Pharm. Corp., v.p. sales and mktg., 1985—89; pres. McNeil Pharm., 1989—93; pres., COO Genetic Therapy, Inc., 1993—95; exec. v.p. Schein Pharm., Inc., 1995—96, pres. retail and specialty products divsn., 1996—97; chmn., pres., CEO and dir. Matrix Pharm., Inc., Fremont, Calif., 1997—.

CASEY, MICHEAL WILLIAM, portfolio manager; b. Indpls., Oct. 4, 1955; s. Robert Ellsworth and Mildred Jane (Holland) C.; m. Christine McCarthy, Apr. 11, 1991 (div. Sept. 1997); children: Kathleen Maura, Thomas Robert, James Patrick. AB, Ind. U., 1978; MS, London Sch. Econs., 1985; PhD, New Sch. Social Rsch., 1996. Translator U. Graz, Austria, 1978-80; tchr. math. Peace Corps, Sierra Leone, 1981-83; economist McCarthy, Crisanti & Matthei, NYC, 1986—90; internat. economist Maria Ramierz, Inc., NYC, 1990—96; portfolio mgr. Federated Investors, NYC, 1996—2002; pres. Discretionary Global Mgmt., NYC, 2002—. Mem.: Ea. Econ. Assn., Am. Econ. Assn., Downtown Economists Club, Forecasters Club. Personal E-mail: mikecasey@rcn.com.

CASEY, MURRAY JOSEPH, physician, educator; b. Armour, S.D., May 1, 1936; s. Meryl Joseph and Gladice (Murray) C.; m. Virginia Anne Fletcher; children: Murray Joseph Jr., Theresa Marie, Anne Franklin, Francis Xavier, Peter Colum, Matthew Padraic. Student, Chanute Jr. Coll., 1954-55, Rockhurst Coll., 1955-56; AB, U. Kans., 1958; MD, Georgetown U., 1962; postgrad., Suffolk U. Law Sch., 1963-64, Howard U., 1965, U. Conn., 1977; MS in Mgmt., Cardinal Stritch Coll., 1984; MBA, Marquette U., 1988; cert. in Theology, Creighton U., 2003—. Diplomate Nat. Bd. Med. Examiners, Am. Bd. Ob-Gyn. Intern USPHS Hosp.-Univ. Hosp., Balt., 1962-63; staff physician USPHS Hosp., Boston, 1963-64; rsch. staff Lab Infectious Diseases, Nat. Inst. Allergy and Infectious Diseases, NIH, Bethesda, Md., 1964-66; virologist, resident physician Columbia-Presbyn. Med. Ctr. also Francis Delafield Hosp., N.Y.C., 1966-69, USPHS sr. clin. trainee, 1969-70; fellow gynecol. oncology, resident dept. surgery Meml. Hosp. Cancer and Allied Diseases, Meml. Sloan-Kettering Cancer Ctr., N.Y.C., 1969-71; Am. Cancer Soc. fellow, 1969-71; ofcl. observer in radiotherapy U. Tex. M.D. Anderson Hosp. and Tumor Inst., Houston, 1971; vis. scientist Radiumhemmet Karolinska Sjukhuset and Inst., Stockholm, 1971; asst. prof. ob-gyn U. Conn. Sch. Medicine, 1971-75, asso. prof., 1975-80, dir. gynecologic oncology, 1971-80, also mem. med. bd.; Linson fellow Am. Coll. Surgeons Commn. on Cancer, 1979—89, 1995—; prof., assoc. chmn. dept. ob-gyn U. Wis. Med. Sch., 1980-89; prof., chmn. dept. ob-gyn. Creighton U., Omaha, 1989-94; chief ob-gyn. and dir. gynecologic oncology St. Joseph Hosp., Creighton U. Med. Ctr., Omaha, 1989-94; dir. gynecologic oncology Creighton Cancer Ctr., 1996—. Faculty coun. Creighton U., 1992—93, 1995—, acad. coun., 1992—93, 1995—, mem. instl. rev. bd., 1994—, rank and tenure com., 1998—2001, cancer ctr. adv. bd., 1994—, prin. investigator Cancer Ctr., 2001—02; bd. dirs. Mo. Valley Consortium, Cmty. Coop. Oncology Program; chief ob-gyn Mt. Sinai Med. Ctr., Milw., 1980—82, dir. gynecologic oncology, 1980—89, also mem. med. exec. com.; chmn. research adv. com., mem. council Conn. Cancer Epidemiology Unit. Editor, contbr. articles in sports medicine to profl. jours., chpts. to books; rsch. in oncogenesis and tumor immunology. Bd. dirs., mem. exec. com., chmn. profl. edn. com. Hartford unit Am. Cancer Soc., dir. Milw. divsn., exec. com. 1985-87, v.p., 1985-86, pres.-elect, 1986-87, 1st v.p. exec. com. Wis. divsn. 1987-89, bd. dirs., chmn. profl. edn. com., 1987-89, bd. dirs., 1989-96, exec. com. Nebr. divsn., 1989-93, pub. edn. and communications com., profl. edn. com. vice chair, 2nd v.p., 1990-91, 1st v.p., pres.-elect, 1991-92, pres., 1992-93, bd. dirs. Douglas County unit, 1993—; mem. mayor's adv. com. Cancer Survivors Park, City of Omaha, 1991-92; mem. Parks and Recreation Bd., City of Omaha, 1993-94; mem. med. svcs. 1980 Winter Olympic Games, Lake Placid, N.Y.; mem. med. supervisory team U.S. Nordic Ski Team. Lt. (j.g.) USPHS, 1962-64, lt. comdr., 1964-66; col. USAR, 1988-93. Fellow: ACS, Am. Coll. Ob-Gyn; mem.: AAAS, Omaha Ob-Gyn. Soc., Milwaukee Gynecologic Soc., Assn. Mil. Surgeons, Am. Urogynecol. Soc., Lake Placid Sports Medicine Soc. (v.p. 1981—84, pres. 1984—86), Soc. Meml. Gynecol. Oncologists (exec. bd. 1979—84, pres. 1982—83), Internat. Assn. for Advancement of Humanistic Studies in Medicine, N.Am. Menopause Soc., Internat. Menopause Soc., Am. Soc. Clin. Oncology, Am. Radium Soc., Internat. Gynecol. Cancer Soc., New Eng. Assn. Gynecol. Oncologists (pres. 1980—81), European Soc. Gynecol. Oncologists, Soc. Gynecol. Oncologists, Am. Fertility Soc., Am. Assn. Gynecologic Laparoscopists, Am. Soc. Colposcopy, N.Y. Acad. Scis., Am. Coll. Sports Medicine, Cen. Assn. Ob-Gyns., Soc. of Gynecol. Surgeons, St. George Soc., Cedarburg C. of C. (dir. 1983—85, Ambassadors com. 1983—89, chmn. bus. indsl. program com. 1985, 1987—89, hon. life mem., amb. emeritus), Beta Gamma Sigma. Office: Creighton U Sch Medicine Dept Ob-Gyn 601 N 30th St # 4810 Omaha NE 68131-2137

CASEY, PAUL ARNOLD, writer, producer, photographer, composer, director; b. Inglewood, Calif., Dec. 10, 1934; s. Paul Franklyn and Orilee Corinne (Gray) C. AA, BA, UCLA. Pres., genetics cons. CSCA Internat., Sun Valley, Calif.; pres., tech. advisor Solenz Corp., Wilmington, Del. Dramaturg L.A. Playwrights Group, 1996; dir., CEO L.A. Playwrights Group. Author: Open the Coffin, 2005, (poetry) Songs of Youth, 1951; writer TV show Lassie, 1969; photographer wildlife: Girl Scouts Calendar, 1995; developer breed of cat: Calif. Spangled, 1971-86; inventor power lens, 1967; prodr. (theatrical) Original Sins; dir.: (film and theatrical prodn.) Smoke Screen; playwright: Anna & Ylenna; playwright Jewel Box Theatre Ctr. for Performing Arts, 1998-02. With USN, 1953-54. Recipient Nat. Humane Soc. award, 1965, Meritorious Achievement award Contbn. to Sci., 1998; scholar U.S. Govt. scholar, 1954. Mem. L.A. Playwrights Group (gen. sec. 1995-96, bd. dirs. 1998-99). Achievements include invention of wind driven desalination and water purification plant, 2001. Avocations: wildlife photography, astronomy, archaeology, natural power systems technology. Office: CSCA International PO Box 368 Sun Valley CA 91353-0368 E-mail: paulcase6@yahoo.com.

CASEY, RICHARD CONWAY, federal judge; b. 1933; BA, Holy Cross, 1955; JD, Georgetown U., 1958. Asst. US atty. criminal div. So. Dist. NY, Dept. Justice, 1959—63, chief internal security unit, 1960—63; counsel Special Commn. State of NY, 1963—64; assoc. Brown & Wood, 1964—69, ptnr., 1970—84, of counsel, 1984—97; judge U.S. Dist. Ct. (so. dist.) NY, 1997—. Served U.S. Army, 1958, served U.S. Army, 1961—62. Recipient Blessed Hyacinth Cormier O.P. Medal at the Angelicum in Rome, 1999. Mem.: Assn. Bar City NY, ABA. Office: 500 Pearl St Room 1350 New York NY 10007-1316*

CASEY, ROBERT REISCH, lawyer; b. New Orleans, May 19, 1946; s. Robert Taylor Casey and Merlyn Lucille (Reisch) Weilbaecher. BBA in Acctg. magna cum laude, U. Notre Dame, 1968; JD, Tulane U., 1971; LLM in Taxation, NYU, 1973. Bar: La. 1971. Ptnr. Jones, Walker, Waechter, Poitevent, Carrere and Denegre, Baton Rouge, 1971—. Mem. bd. editors Tulane Law Rev., 1970-71. Mem. ABA (chmn. partnership com. tax sect. 1982-84, mem. coun. 1985-88, sec. 1988-90, vice chmn. 1989-91), Order of Coif, Beta Gamma Sigma, Beta Alpha Psi. Avocations: golf, French horn. Office Phone: 225-248-2090. Business E-Mail: rcasey@joneswalker.com.

CASEY, THOMAS CLARK, retired trust company executive, investment advisor; b. Akron, Ohio, Dec. 17, 1929; s. Thomas W. and Portia (Clark) C.; m. Tanya Seely, July 2, 1958 (dec.); children: Tate, Doug, John, Gary, Brad, Nina, Mimi, Tom W.; m. Suzanne Rhodes, Apr. 5, 1997. BA, Bowdoin Coll.; MBA, Stanford U.; CFSC, Northwestern U. Registered investment advisor, SEC, 1995. Sales rep. Acushnet Co., New Bedford, Mass., 1953-55, Reeves Rubber Co., San Clemente, Calif., 1957-59; gen. mgr. Polymer Corp., Santa Ana, Calif., 1959-61; from trust officer to pres. 1st Am. Trust Co., Santa Ana, 1965-95; registered investment advisor pvt. practice, 1995—. Bd. dir. First Am. Trust F.S.B., 1999—. Trustee Bowdoin Coll., 1989—2001; bd. dirs. Hoag Meml. Hosp., 1982—95; chmn. Orange County com. So. Calif. Bldg. Fund, 1986—94; co-chmn. capital expenditure rev. com. United Way, 1982—; chair bd. dirs. Hoag Hosp. Found., 1995—99; bd. dirs. Newport Ctr. Assn., 1976—2002, pres., 1979; trustee Newport-Mesa Unified Sch. Dist., 1969—77, pres., 1975—77; bd. dirs. Orange County Bar Found., 1995—2001; bd. dirs., mem. exec. com. Alzheimers Assn. Orange County, 2000—. Named Outstanding Vol. of Yr., Orange County, Calif., 2003. Mem.: Orange County Soc. Investment Mgrs., Calif. Bankers Assn., L.A. Soc. Fin. Analysts, Soc. Preservation New Eng. Antiquities. Avocations: golf, skiing, snorkeling, travel. Office: Ste 1100 620 Newport Ctr Dr Newport Beach CA 92660-8011

CASEY, THOMAS JEFFERSON, energy executive, environmentalist, entrepreneur; Student, U.S. Naval Acad., 1964—65; MBA, Harvard U., 1970; postgrad., U. London/Am. U., 1997. Pres., COO New Eng. Furniture Group, Boston, 1968—71; chmn., CEO Commonwealth Industries, Inc., N.Y.C., 1971—75, Quantum Renewable Energy, N.Y.C., 1991—; pres., gen. mgr. Damson Oil Corp. AMEX, N.Y.C., Houston, 1975—80; founder, chmn., CEO Sovereign Group, Ltd., N.Y.C., 1980—90. Guest lectr. Wharton Grad. Sch. Bus. Adminstrn.; former mem. faculty internat. mgmt. Northeastern U. Sch. Mgmt. and Adminstrn., Boston; sr. fin., investment advisor several Fortun 500 cos., sovereign fgn. govts. and internat. fin. instns. Environ. activist. Avocations: golf, tennis, sailing, skiing, flying. Office: Quantum Renewable Energy Inc 730 5th Ave Ste 900 New York NY 10019-4105

CASEY, THOMAS W., finance company executive; BS in Acctg., Kings Coll., Wilkes-Barre, Pa. Audit supr. Coopers & Lybrand, 1984—90; with Citicorp, 1990—92; from advisor/contr., to analyst GE Capital Corp., 1992—99, sr. v.p., CFO GE Fin., 1999—2002; exec. v.p., CFO Washington Mut., Inc., Seattle, 2002—. Mem. Pres.'s Coun. Washington Mut., Inc. Office: Washington Mut Inc 1201 3d Ave Seattle WA 98101

CASH, ALAN SHERWIN, electronics engineer; b. Chgo., Oct. 28, 1938; s. Edward A. and Mildred M. Cash; m. Carole M. Hoffman, July 31, 1966; children: Susan, Jody. BS in Indsl. Engring., U. Ill., 1961; MBA, Northwestern U., 1969. Registered profl. engr., Calif.; cert. electrostatic discharge engr. and technician; cert. IRCA provisional auditor, Internat. Register Cert. Auditors. Sr. process engr. Cook Electric Co., Morton Grove, Ill., 1973-75; sr. indsl. engr. Motorola, Carol Stream, Ill., 1975-77; supr. indsl. engring. def. sys. divsn. Northrop Grumman, Rolling Meadows, Ill., 1977-80, mgr. tech. svcs. def. sys. divsn., 1980-84, mgr. advance mfg. tech. def. sys. divsn., 1984-86, mgr. tng. ctr. def. sys. divsn., 1986-95; ops. program engr., 1995—; category C instr., examiner, ISO 9000, ISO 1900, and AS 9100, ISO 14001 lead assessor Dept. Def., electrostatic discharge site coord., 1997—. Mem. Nat. Soldering Std. Working Coms., 1990-93, mem. IPC J-stds. coms.-001, 002, 003, 004, 005, 006, 1990—, mem. IPC Term and Definitions Com. Mem. Nat. Assn. Radio and Telecomm. Engrs. (cert. engr., technician), Inst. Indsl. Engring. (pres. North Suburban Ill. chpt. 1982-83, program chmn. Dist. 8, 1984—, spouses program chmn. 1992 internat. conv., Midwest chpt. ESD assoc. libr. chmn., pres. 1998, treas. 2000), Inst. Indsl. Engrs., Assn. Old Crows, U. Ill. Alumni Assn., Northwestern U. Alumni Assn., Northwestern Club Chgo., ESD Assn. (Midwest chpt.). Office: Northrop Grumman ES-DSD-RMS 600 Hicks Rd Rolling Meadows IL 60008-1098 Office Phone: 847-259-9600. Business E-Mail: alan.cash@ngc.com.

CASH, ARTHUR LEE, JR., lawyer, editor; b. Winston-Salem, N.C. AB, Wash. U., 1989, JD, 1994. Bar: Ill. 1994, D.C. 1995, N.C. 2003. Sr. atty. editor West Group, Deerfield, Ill., 1995-2000; editor ABA, Chgo., 2001—04. Mem. ABA, N.C. Bar Assn. Office: 3447 Robinhood Rd Ste 210 Winston Salem NC 27106 Office Phone: 336-768-6336. Business E-Mail: lee@leecashlaw.com.

CASH, CAMILLE GENEVA, physician; b. Balt., Oct. 8, 1969; d. William Henry, III and Cheryl (Griffin) Cash; m. Roderick Delano Lowe, June 3, 1995; children: Lauren Shelby Lowe, Kennedy Camille Lowe, Christopher Delano Lowe. BS, Howard U., 1991; MD, Baylor U., 1995. Diplomate Am. Bd. Surgery, 2002. Intern in gen. surgery Christus St. Joseph Hosp., 1995—96, resident in gen. surgery, 1996—2002, fellow in plastic surgery, 2002—. Mem.: ACS, Houston Soc. Plastic Surgery, Harris County Med. Soc., Tex. Soc. Plastic Surgery, Tex. Med. Assn. Roman Catholic. Office: 1315 St Joseph Pkway Ste 1305 Houston TX 77002 Home: 4218 Roseneath Dr Houston TX 77021-1550 Personal E-mail: cashmd@hotmail.com.

CASH, JAMES IRELAND, JR., retired business educator; b. 1948; s. Juanita Cash; m. Clemmie Cash; 2 children. BS in math., Tex. Christian U., 1969; MS in computer sci., PhD in mgmt. info. systems, Purdue U.; LLD (hon.), Babson Coll., 2003. Mem. faculty Harvard Bus. Sch., 1976—2003, prof., 1985—2003, James E. Robison Prof. Bus. Adminstrn., chmn. MBA Program, 1992—95, sr. assoc. dean., chmn. HBS Pub., 1998—2003. Bd. dirs. Phase Forward Inc., Chubb Corp., 1996—, GE, 1997—, Sci.-Atlanta Inc., 2001—, Microsoft Corp., 2001—; bd. advisors Egenera Inc.; dir. Cash Concours program The Concours Group; part-owner Boston Celtics, 2003—. Co-author: (books) Global Electronic Wholesale Banking, 1990, Corporate Information Systems Management: Issues Facing Senior Managers and Corporate Information Systems Management: Text and Cases, 1992, Building the Information-Age Organization: Structure, Control and Information Technology, 1994; author: Business Decision Making with Lotus 1-2-3, articles in acctg. and info. tech. journals; co-editor: The Information Systems Challenge: Survey Research Methods, 1991. Bd. trustees Harlem Children's Zone, Babson Coll., Mass. Gen. Hosp., Partners Healthcare, Newton-Wellesley Hosp.; overseer Boston Mus. Sci.; founding mem. coun. Nat. Mus. African Am. History and Culture, Smithsonian Instn., 2004—. Recipient Bert King Award for Svc. to the Cmty., Afro-Am. Student Union, Harvard Bus. Sch., 2002. Office: Harvard Bus Sch Soldiers Field Boston MA 02163*

CASH, MARY FRANCES, minister, retired civilian military employee; d. Hugh Lester and Myrtle Victoria (Byrd) Flucas; m. William Hadley Cash, May 7, 1966; children: Aleta Grace Pearson, William Anthony, Antonio Hadley. Diploma, Atlantic Bus. Coll., 1961; Assoc. in Religious Edn., Washington Saturday Coll., 1996; Masters Degree in religious edn., Bethel Bible Coll./Seminary, 2003. Ordained elder African Meth. Episcopal Ch., 1999. Sec., stenographer Dept. Human Resources, Washington, 1964—77; adminstr. Flu-Bea Enterprises, Landover, Md., 1977—80; substitute tchr.

Pineview Elem. Sch., Valdosta, Ga., 1980—81; sec. Moody AFB, Valdosta, 1981—82, Andrews AFB, Camp Spring, Md., 1982—92, Dept. Def., Va., 1992—94; pastor Cmty. African Meth. Episcopal Ch., Whitehall, Ark., 1998. Leader, trainer Girl Scout Coun. Am., Washington, 1971—79, Valdosta, Ga., 1980—82, Washington, 1982—96; mem. adv. bd. Duke Ellington Sch. Art, Washington, 1986; instr. Summer Tchg. Program for Children, Jonesboro, 1996—2000; dir. Saturday Sch. Brown Meml. African Meth. Episcopal Ch., Washington, 1990—96. Named Mother of the Yr., Brown Meml. African Meth. Episcopal Ch., 1988; recipient Spl. Svc. award, Girl Scout Coun. Nations Capitol, 1994, Superior award, Young and Adult Missionary Soc., 1996. Mem.: East No. Ark. Annual Conf. of the 12th Episcopal Dist. (Sec. 2002—). Office: Cmty AME Ch 12th Episcopal Dist 1998 Poff Ln Jonesboro AR 72401 Personal E-mail: revmfc3@aol.com.

CASH, RICHARD M., gifted and talented educator, director, educator, consultant; b. Antigo, Wis., Dec. 8, 1957; s. Cecil H. and Elizabeth Anne Cash. B in Theatre, U. Wis., 1981; postgrad. in elem. edn., U. Minn., 1988; M in Curriculum and Instrn.-Gifted Edn., U. St. Thomas, 1995, EdD, 2001. Tchr. 1-6 Minn., 1988. Curriculum specialist/program coord. Capitol Hill Magnet Sch., St. Paul Pub. Schs., St. Paul, 1989—99; coord., gifted edn. Rochester Pub. Schs., Rochester, Minn., 1999—2001; dir., gifted edn. Bloomington Pub. Schs., Minn., 2001—. Adj. prof., gifted edn. Minn. State U., Mankato, Minn., 2001—; ednl. cons. nRich Ednl. Consulting, Savage, Minn., 2001—. Dir.(co-author): (childrens theater) Tales of Five Continents, Little Red: Life in the Hood, The Birds, Comedia del Delight (Nat. Childrens Play Writing Contest award, 1998). Sec. Minn. Assn. Supervision and Curriculum Devel., Minn., 2002. Mem.: Minn. Coun. Gifted and Talented (exhibitors chair 1999—2001), Minn. Educators Gifted and Talented, Coun. Exceptional Children, Nat. Assn. Gifted Children (co-chair, nat. task force 2002). Avocations: weight training, running, travel, music, theater. Home: 14071 Alabama Ave S Savage MN 55378 Office: Bloomington MN Pub Schs 1350 W 106th St Bloomington MN 55431 Office Phone: 952-681-6438. Office Fax: 952-681-6533. Personal E-mail: rcash@integraonline.com. E-mail: rcash@bloomington.k12.mn.us.

CASH, ROY DON, retired gas and petroleum company executive; b. Shamrock, Tex., June 27, 1942; s. Bill R. and Billie Mae (Lisle) C.; m. Sondra Kay Burleson, Feb. 20, 1966; 1 child, Clay Collin. BS in Indsl. Engring., Tex. Tech U., 1966. Former engr. Amoco Prodn. Co.; v.p. Mountain Fuel Supply, Salt Lake City, 1976-79; pres. Wexpro Co., Salt Lake City, 1979-80; pres., CEO Mountain Fuel Supply Co., Salt Lake City, 1980-84, Questar Corp., Salt Lake City, 1984-85, pres., chmn., CEO, 1985—2003, now bd. dirs. Bd. dirs. Zions Bancorp., Aegis Ins. Svcs., Inc., Nat. Fuel Gas, TODCO. Trustee Holy Cross Hosp., 1987-90, Salt Lake Organizing Com. of 2002 Olympic Winter Games, 1991—2002, So. Utah U., 1992-97; bd. dirs. Utah Symphony Orch., Salt Lake City, 1983-86, 93—2004, Gas Rsch. Inst., 1991-93, Lubbock Symphony Orch., 2003—, Tex. Tech Found., 2002—. Mem. Soc. Petroleum Engrs., Rocky Mountain Oil and Gas Assn. (bd. dirs., pres. 1982-84), Utah Mfrs. Assn. (bd. dirs. 1983-89, chmn. 1986), Pacific Coast Gas Assn. (bd. dirs. 1981-85, 87-97, chmn. 1993-94), Am. Gas Assn. (bd. dirs. 1989-95), Am. Petroleum Inst. (bd. dirs. 1986-91), Nat. Petroleum Coun., Ind. Petroleum Assn. of Am., Salt Lake Area C. of C. (bd. dirs. 1981-84, 89-92, chmn. 1991-92), Alta Club, Jeremy Ranch Golf and Country Club. Avocations: boating, skiing, tennis, fishing, hunting. Office: Questar Corp PO Box 45433 Salt Lake City UT 84145-0433

CASH, SWIN (SWINTAYLA MARIE CASH), professional basketball player; b. McKeesport, Pa., Sept. 22, 1979; d. Kevin Menifee (Stepfather) and Cynthia Cash. Grad., U. Conn., 2002. Basketball player McKeesport High Sch., McKeesport, Pa., U. Conn., 1998—2002; basketball player, forward Detroit Shock, WNBA, 2002—; founder Swin Cash LLC. Mem. USA Basketball Women's Senior Nat. Team, 2004. Named Parade Magazine, USA Today and Street & Smith All-Am. first team, 1998, Gatorade Pa. Player of the Yr., 1998, Kodak/WBCA All-District I, 2002, Final Four Most Outstanding Player, 2002; named to All-Big East third team, 2000, All-Big East second team, 2001, All-Big East first team, 2002, AP All-American second team, 2001, Kodak/WBCA & US Basketball Writers Assn. All-Am. first team, 2002, WNBA All-Star Team, 2003, all-WNBA second team, 2003. Achievements include mem. NCAA Divsn. 1 Nat. Championship Team, U. Conn., 2000, 2002; mem. WNBA Championship Team, Detroit Shock, 2003; mem. US Women's Basketball Team, Athens Olympic Games, 2004. Office: USA Basketball 5465 Mark Dabling Blvd Colorado Springs CO 80918-3842

CASH, SWINTAYLA MARIE See CASH, SWIN

CASH, W. LARRY, health products executive; CPA AICPA. With Humana Inc., 1973—96; v.p., group CFO Columbia/HCA, 1996—97; exec. v.p. Cmty. Health Sys., Brentwood, Tenn., 1997—, CFO, 1997—. Bd. dir. Cmty. Health Sys., Cross Country, Inc. Mem.: Healthcare Fin. Mgmt. Assn., Am. Assn. Health Plans, Tenn. Soc. CPAs. Office: Community Health Systems 155 Franklin Rd Ste 400 Brentwood TN 37027-4600

CASH-CLARK, REGINA L., editor, writer; b. Bennettsville, S.C., Sept. 15, 1968; d. Ralph L. and Mae A. Cash; m. Charles E. Clark, II, Aug. 18, 2000. BA, Syracuse U., 1990; MFA, Sarah Lawrence Coll., Bronxville, N.Y., 2000. Editor Syracuse U. Hons. Program, 1988-90; mktg. asst. ABC Internat., Secaucus, N.J., 1991-93; prodn. asst. Kevin Wendle Prodns., N.Y.C., 1993; sales/mktg. rep. Harlem Spirituals Inc., N.Y.C., 1994; asst. editor Essence Mag., N.Y.C., 1994-98, freelance editor, 1999—. Adj. faculty Ramapo Coll. of N.J., Mahwah, N.J., 2001—. Author: When Autumn Cries, 2000. Mem. Eta Pi Upsilon (co-v.p. 1988-89). Avocations: fitness activities, singing, art. Home: 142 Main Ave 6A Passaic NJ 07055-5423 E-mail: reginaluv@aol.com, reginaclark@ecofaith.com.

CASHEN, HENRY CHRISTOPHER, II, lawyer, government agency administrator; b. June 25, 1939; s. Raymond and Catherine C.; m. Leslie Renchard, June 28, 1967 (div. 1982); children: Raymond II, Hayley Holloway, Henry Christopher III; m. Diana Knowles Pryor, June 4, 1988. AB, Brown U., 1961; grad., U. Mich. Law Sch., 1963. Bar: Mich. 1964, U.S. Supreme Ct. 1969. Mem. firm Dickinson, Wright, McKean & Cudlip, Detroit, 1964-69; dep. counsel to Pres. U.S., Washington, 1969-70, dep. asst. to, 1970-73; mem. firm Dickstein, Shapiro & Morin (and predecessor), Washington, 1973—. Mem. Barristers Soc., D.C. Mich. bar assns., Fed. Nat. Mortgage Assn. (bd. dirs. 1985-91), Country Club of Detroit, The Brook, Met. Club, Chevy Chase Club, Psi Upsilon Phi Delta Phi. Republican. Roman Catholic. Office: 2101 L St NW Washington DC 20037-1526 Office Phone: 202-828-2213. E-mail: cashenh@dsmo.com.

CASHEN, NORENE ANNETTE, writer; b. Detroit, Nov. 18, 1967; A in Gen. Edn., St. Clair County C.C., 1994; student, Oakland U., 1997—. Freelance writer The Rocket, Seattle, 1995, Times Herald, Port Huron, Mich., 1995-97, New Times, Kansas City, 1996-97, Met Times, Detroit, 1996—. Contbr. to: Musichound's Guide to R & B, 1997; contbr. articles to Alternative Press Mag., Cleve. With U.S. Army, 1988-91. Home: 22875 Lakeshore Dr Saint Clair Shores MI 48080-2580

CASHION, ANN, food service executive; b. Jackson, Miss. B, Harvard U., 1976; postgrad., Stanford U., 1976—78. With Oh-la-la!, San Francisco, 1982; chef Restaurant Nora, Washington, Dakota; head chef Austin Grill, Washington, 1988; exec. chef Jaleo, Washington, 1993—95; chef, owner Cashion's Eat Pl., Washington, 1995—; ptnr. Johnny's Half Shell, 1999—. Named Chef of Yr., Restaurant Assn. Met. Washington, 1997, Am. Express Best Chef Mid-Atlantic, James Beard Found., 2004. Mem.: So. Foodnays Alliance. Office: Cahions Eat Pl 1819 Columbia Rd NW Washington DC 20009-2005 Office Phone: 202-797-1819.

CASHION, DEENA DIANNE, social studies educator, pastor; b. Fort Worth, Tex., Apr. 6, 1945; d. Charles T. and Nadine Hazel Stamp; m. J. W. Cashion, June 27, 1964; children: Jace, Paige Michelle. PhD, Heath Missions Coll., 2001. Ordained Rhema Ministerial Assn. Internat., 1992. Prof. Greek and Hebrew studies Heath Missions Coll., Phila., 1998—; pastor Glorious Gathering Christian Fellowship, Bartonsville, Pa., 1995—. Pres. Walk Free Farm, Saylorsburg, Pa., 1980—. Author: The Master Potter & His Clay (Christian Svc. awards, Gov. Pa. and Mayor Phila., 2002), Digging For Gold in the Ancient Greek & Hebrew Manuscripts, Purim. Dir. Life Skills Trade Acad., Inc., Deleware Water Gap, Pa., 2003—04. Conservative. Avocations: quilting, art. Office: WOFM Inc PO Box 993 Saylorsburg PA 18353

CASHMAN, GIDEON, lawyer; b. N.Y.C., Sept. 10, 1929; s. Abba Morris and Rachel (Cashman) Cashman; m. Kathryn Batchelder, 1985; children: Adam Parker, Lindsey Avril, Emily Parker Hyle. AB, NYU, 1951; JD, Columbia U., 1954. Bar: D.C. 1954, N.Y. 1954. Asst. counsel Waterfront Commn. N.Y., 1954-55; asst. U.S. atty. criminal divsn. So. Dist. Ct. N.Y., 1958-61, chief criminal apls., 1959-61; assoc. Christy Perkins & Christy, N.Y.C., 1961-63; sr. ptnr. Pryor, Cashman, Sherman & Flynn LLP, N.Y.C., 1963—. Lectr. trial tactics Practicing Law Inst.; bd. dirs. Irvington Inst. for Med. Rsch. Trustee Friars Found., Heart Rsch. Found., Eugene O'Neill Teatre Ctr. 1st lt. U.S. Army, judge advocate Gen.'s Corps, 1955-58. Mem. ABA, N.Y. State Bar Assn., Assn. Bar City N.Y., N.Y. County Lawyers Assn., Friars Club (N.Y.C.). Jewish. Home: 812 Park Ave New York NY 10021-2759 Office: 410 Park Ave New York NY 10022-4441

CASHMAN, MICHAEL RICHARD, small business owner; b. Owatonna, Minn., Sept. 26, 1926; s. Michael Richard and Mary (Quinn) C.; m. Antje Katrin Paulus, Jan. 22, 1972 (div. 1983); children: Janice Katrin, Joshua Paulus, Nina Carolin. BS, U.S. Mcht. Marine Acad., 1947; BA, U. Minn., 1951; MBA, Harvard U., 1953. Regional mgr. Air Products & Chems., Inc., Allentown, Pa., 1959-64, then pres. so. div. Washington, 1964-68; mng. dir. Air Products & Chems., Inc. Europe, Brussels, 1968-72; internat. v.p. Airco Indsl. Gasses, Brussels, 1972-79; pres. Continental Elevator Co., Denver, 1979-81; assoc. Moore & Co., Denver, 1981-84; prin. Cashman & Co., Denver, 1984—. Committeeman Denver Rep. Com., 1986—, congl. candidate, 1988; chmn. "Two Forks or Dust" Ad Hoc Citizens Com. Lt. (j.g.) USN, 1953-55. Mem. Bldg. Owners and Mgrs. Assn., Colo. Harvard Bus. Sch. Club, Am. Rights Union, Royal Golf de Belgique, Belgian Shooting Club, Rotary, Soc. St. George, Phi Beta Kappa. Avocations: skiing, golf, sailing, guitar, opera. Home: 2512 S University Blvd Apt 802 Denver CO 80210-6152

CASHMAN, WAYNE, professional athletics coach; b. Kingston, Ont., Can. m. Lyn Cashmar; children: Scott, Becky. NHL vet. Bruins NHL, 18 seasons; scout to asst. coach N.Y. Rangers, 1986-92; assoc. coach Tampa Bay Lightning, 1995—. Mem. two Stanley Cup Championship teams/Bruins, Boston, 1970, 72, five Stanley Cup Finals appearances; currently ranks third on Bruins and 80th on the NHL all-time list in games played, with 1,027. Office: Philadelphia Flyers First Union Ctr 3601 S Broad St Ste 2 Philadelphia PA 19148-5297

CASI, PAUL ALDO, II, lawyer; b. Cin., Oct. 14, 1969; s. Paul A. and Joan Y. (Wright) C.; m. Karen A. Laclare, Jan. 2, 1990; children: Paul III, David J., Mark E. BA, Vanderbilt U., 1991; JD, U. Louisville, 1994. Bar: Ky. 1994, Ind. 1994, U.S. Dist. Ct. (ea. and we. dists.) Ky., 1994, U.S. Dist. Ct. (no. and so. dists.) Ind. 1994, U.S. Ct. Appeals (6th cir.) 1998. Law clk. Mulhall, Turner, Hoffman & Coombs, Louisville, 1992-94, atty., 1994-99, Hoffman & Casi PLLC, Louisville, 1999—. Sr. editor law rev. Jour. Family Law, 1993-94, mem. law rev., 1992-93; mem. law rev. Jour. Law and Edn., 1992-93. Mem. ATLA, ABA, Ky. Acad. Trial Attys. (bd. govs. 1998—), Ind. Trial Lawyers Assn. Roman Catholic. Avocations: politics, tennis, basketball, fishing. Home: 6719 Harrods View Cir Prospect KY 40059-9475 Office: Hoffman & Casi PLLC 440 S 7th St Ste 100 Louisville KY 40203-1967 Office Phone: 502-584-0404. E-mail: pac@hoffman-casi.com.

CASIANO, KIMBERLY, publishing executive; b. NY; m. Juan Woodroffe; children: Natalia, Juan Antonio. BA in politics and Latin Am. studies, Princeton U.; MBA, Harvard. Founded Caribbean Mktg. Overseas Corp., Wash., DC, 1981—88; v.p. Casiano Comm., 1988—94, pres., CEO, 1994—. Bd. mem. Ford Motor Co., 2003—, mem. fin. bd. com., mem. nom. com., mem. corp. governance com., mem. environ. and pub. policy com. Bd. trustees Hispanic Coll. Fund; mem. bd. dirs. Young Pres. Orgn. (YPO) PR chpt. Named one of Elite Women, Hispanic Bus. mag., 2004. Achievements include apptd. to US Savings Bond Nat. Com. by US Treas. Sec. Office: Casiano Comm 1700 Ave Fernandex Juncos San Juan PR 00909-2938 Office Phone: 787-728-3000. Office Fax: 787-268-1001.

CASIDA, JOHN EDWARD, toxicology and entomology professor; b. Phoenix, Dec. 22, 1929; s. Lester Earl and Ruth (Barnes) Casida; m. Katherine Faustine Monson, June 16, 1956; children: Mark Earl, Eric Gerhard. BS, U. Wis., 1951, MS, 1952, PhD, 1954; D (hon.), U. Buenos Aires, 1997. Research asst. U. Wis., 1951-53, mem. faculty, 1954-63, prof. toxicology & entomology, 1959-63, U. Calif.-Berkeley, 1964—; scholar-in-residence Bellagio Study and Conf. Center, Rockefeller Found., Lake Como, Italy, 1978. Messenger lectr. Cornell U., 1985; Sterling B. Hendricks lectr. USDA and Am. Chem. Soc., 1992; dir. Environ. Chemistry and Toxicology Lab., U. Calif., Berkeley, 1964—; William Muriece Hoskins chair in chem. and molecular entomology U. Calif., Berkeley, 1996—, faculty rsch. lectr., 1998; lectr. in sci. Third World Acad. Scis., Buenos Aires, 1997. Author: rsch. pubIs. With USAF, 1953. Named Jeffery lectr., U. New South Wales, Australia, 1983; recipient medal, 7th Internat. Congress Plant Protection, Paris, 1970, Disting. Svc. award, USDA, 1988, Wolf prize in Agrl., 1993, Koro-Sho prize, Pesticide Sci. Soc. Japan, 1995; fellow Haight traveling fellow, 1958—59, Guggenheim fellow, 1970—71. Fellow: Entomol. Soc. (Bussart Meml. award 1989); mem.: NAS, European Acad. Scis., Soc. Environ. Toxicology and Chemistry (Founder's award 1994), Pesticide Sci. Soc. Japan (hon.), Soc. Toxicology (hon.), Am. Chem. Soc. (Internat. award rsch. pesticide chemistry 1970, Spencer award in agrl. and food chemistry 1978), Royal Soc. UK (fgn.). Home: 1570 La Vereda Rd Berkeley CA 94708-2036

CASIDA, KATI, artist; b. Viroqua, Wis., Mar. 28, 1931; d. Gerhard Aniel and Eloise Margaret (Nedland) Monson; m. John Edward Casida, Jne 16, 1956; children: Mark Earl, Eric Gerhard. BS in Art Edn., U. Wis., 1953. Tchr. art Beaver Dam (Wis.) Schs., 1954-55, Upsala Coll., East Orange, N.J., 1955-56, Spring Harbor Sch., Madison, Wis., 1960, Adult Vocat. Sch., Madison, 1961; freelance artist, sculptor Berkeley, Calif., 1963—. Founder, coord., pub. rels. dir. Nordic 5 Arts, San Francisco Bay area, 1993—. Sculpture commns. include pub. art, Oakland, Calif., Viroqua, Wis., San Francisco, Palo Alto, Calif., Dallas, Brea, Calif., Santa Clara, Calif.; invitational solo sculpture exhbn. Gallery 555, Oakland Mus., 2002-2003, Steel Gallery, San Francisco, 2005, Walaker Gallery, Solvorn, Norway, 2005; contbr. articles to Hellenic Jour., 1974— Recipient Pub. Art Sculpture award Divsn. Cultural Arts, City of Oakland, Calif., 1992. Mem. Internat. Sculpture Ctr., Pacific Rim Sculpture Group, Calif. Soc. Printmakers, Headlands for Arts, Am.-Scandinavian Found., Nat. Mus. Women in Arts, Kala-Printmakers, Greek Cypriots No. Calif. Avocations: Greek folk dancing, travel, photography. Home: 1570 La Vereda Rd Berkeley CA 94708-2036 Office Phone: 510-845-4956. Personal E-mail: kefi328@sbcglobal.net.

CASILLAS, SHERRY LYNN, secondary school educator; b. Morenci, Ariz., Nov. 5, 1948; d. Murl H. and Lydia Marie (Spring) Sylvester; m. Nolbert G. Casillas, May 21, 1981; children: Caleb Quinn, Jena Marisa. MS in Edn., No. Ariz. U., 1971; EdS, U. Ariz., 1977. Cert. tchr. Ariz. Tchr. Hayden H.S., Winkelman, Ariz., 1971—81, Globe (Ariz.) H.S., 1994—. After sch. tutor, Globe; sponsor Nat. Honor Soc., 2002—05, The Papoose sch. newspaper, 1996—2005. Leader and tchr. vacation Bible sch. Globe Christian Ctr., 1994—. Mem.: Journalism Edn. Assn., Ariz. Interscholastic Press Assn. (bd. dirs. 2000, Forest Martin award: Journalism Tchr. of Yr. 2004). Republican. Avocations: swimming, reading, crafts. Office: Globe H S 501 E Ash Globe AZ 85501

CASINI, JANE SLOAN, wholesale distribution executive; b. Richmond, Va., Sept. 22, 1947; d. James Turner and Jane Patrick (Coleman) Sloan; m. Mauro Casini (div.). Student, Villa Mercede, Florence, Italy. Owner, Richmond and Washington; retailer; leather salesman Florence. Bd. dirs. Va. Home for Boys, Richmond, 1991. Office: Jane Casini 5407 Lakeside Ave Richmond VA 23228

CASKEY, CAROLINE T., lab administrator; b. 1967; m. Sam Goodner. BA, Duke U.; MBA, Rice U., Houston, 1993. V.p. Laboratories for Genetic Svcs.; founder, pres., CEO Identigene Corp., Houston, 1993—. Bd. dir. Tex. Lyceum. TV appearances Dateline NBC, NBC Nightly News, Today Show. Mem.: Young Entrepreneur's Orgn. Office: Identigene Corp 5615 Kirby Ste 800 Houston TX 77005

CASKEY, CHARLES THOMAS, biotechnology executive, biology and genetics educator; b. Lancaster, S.C., Sept. 22, 1938; m. Peggy Ann Pearce, 1960; children: Clifton, Caroline. Student, U. S.C., 1956-58; MD, Duke U., 1963; DSc (hon.), U. S.C., 1993. Diplomate Am. Bd. Internal Medicine. Intern, resident dept. medicine Duke Med. Sch., 1963-65; rsch. assoc. Nat. Heart & Lung Inst., Bethesda, Md., 1965-67, head sect. med. genetics, 1970-71; sr. investigator Lab. Biomed. Genetics NIH, Bethesda, 1967-70; chief sect. med. genetics, prof. medicine, prof. biochemistry Baylor Coll. Medicine, Houston, 1971—, investigator Howard Hughes Med. Inst., 1976—, dir. Robert J. Kleberg, Jr. Ctr. for Human Genetics, 1980-94, dir. med. scientist tng. program, 1982-93, prof. cell biology, 1982-94, dir. and prof. molecular genetics Inst. Molecular Genetics, 1985-92, prof. molecular genetics Inst. Molecular Genetics, 1985-94, Henry and Emma Meyer chmn. molecular genetics, 1987-94, dir. Human Genome Ctr., 1991-94, chmn. dept. molecular and human genetics, 1994-95; sr. v.p. rsch. Merck Rsch. Labs., 1995-99; adj. prof. Baylor Coll. Medicine, Houston, 1995—; pres., CEO Cogene BioTech Ventures, Houston, 2000—; disting. prof., inst. molecular medicine U. Tex. Health Sciences Ctr., Houston. Josiah Macy, Jr. faculty scholar Med. Rsch. Coun. Cambridge (Eng.) U., 1979-80; dir. NATO ASI on Somatic Cell Genetics, 1980-81, NATO/EMBO/FEBS Spetsai European Molecular Biology Course, 1983, 87; Bernard Sachs lectr. Child Neurology Soc., 1993; Roy E. Moon disting. lectr. sci. Angelo State U., 1994; Samuel Rudin disting. vis. prof. Columbia U., N.Y.C., 1994; mem. biochem. test com. Nat. Bd. Med. Examiners, 1977-81, chmn. biochem. test com., 1981-84, mem. coord. com. for FLEX, 1984-86, mem.-at-large, 1984-88; chmn. sci. adv. bd. Xytronyx Inc., 1984-90; acad. assoc. Nichols Inst., 1987-92; liason mem. program adv. com. on human genome NIH, 1989-92; chair adv. panel forensic uses DNA tests U.S. Congress Office Tech. Assessment, 1989-90; mem. mapping the human genome adv. com. U.S. Dept. Energy, 1986-89; mem. adv. panel mapping the human genome U.S. Congress Office Tech. Assessment, 1987-88; mem. human genome coord. com. Dept. Energy, 1989-94, gov.'s bd. Tex. Academy of Sci., Engring. and Medicine, 2004; trustee, pres. Merck Genome Rsch. Inst., Inc., 1996—; pres. Academy of Medicine, Engring. and Sci. of Texas; chmn. bd. Lexicon Genetics Inc., Odessey Thera Corp.; bd. dirs., Kodiak Technologies, EnVivo Pharmaceuticals, Athersys Corp. Author: Somatic Cell Genetics, 1982; author: (with others) Prebiotic and Biochemical Evolution, 1971, Frontiers of Biology: The Mechanism of Protein Synthesis and Its Regulation, 1972, The Enzymes, 1974, The Kidney in Systemic Disease, 1976, Protein Synthesis, 1976, Molecular Mechanisms of Protein Biosynthesis, 1977, Tay-Sachs Disease Screening and Prevention, 1977, Nonsense Mutations and tRNA Suppressors, 1979, Strauss and Welt Diseases of the Kidney, 3d edit., 1979, Gene Amplification, 1982, Internal Medicine, 1983, Advances in Gene Technology: Human Genetic Disorders, 1984, After Barney Clark: Reflections on the Utah Artificial Heart Program, 1984, Pediatric Neurology, 1986, Clinical Endocrinology, 1986, Gene Transfer, 1986, Molecular Biology of Homo Sapiens, 1986, Medical and Experimental Mammalian Genetics: A Perspective, 1987, Human Genetics, 1987, Molecular Neurobiology in Neurology and Psychiatry, 1987, Current Neurology, vol. 9, 1988, Textbook of Internal Medicine, 1988, Nucleic Acid Probes in Diagnosis of Human Genetic Diseases, 1988, Molecular Genetics of Brain, Nerve, and Muscle, 1989, Molecular Genetics of Diseases of Brain, Nerve, and Muscle, 1989, The Metabolic Basis of Inherited Disease, 6th edit., 1989, PCR Technology: Principles and Applications of DNA Amplification, 1989, The Polymerase Chain Reaction, 1989, PCR Protocols: A Guide to Methods and Applications, 1989, Genetic Engineering, Principles and Methods, vol. 11, 1989, The Science and Practice of Pediatric Cardiology, vol. 1, 1990, Ribosomes and Protein Synthesis: A Practical Approach, 1990, Etiology of Human Disease at the DNA Level, 1991, PCR: A Practical Approach, 1991, Neurodegenerative Disorders: Mechanisms and Prospects for Therapy, 1991, Reproductive Risks and Prenatal Diagnosis, 1991, Antisense RNA and DNA, 1991, Biomonitoring and Carcinogen Risk Assessment, 1991, Legal and Ethical Issues Raised by the Human Genome Project, 1991, Advances in Forensic Haemogenetics, 1992, Gene Mapping - Using Law and Ethics as Guides, 1992, The Code of Codes, 1992, Antisense Strategies, 1992, Molecular Basis of Neurology, 1993, Genetic Engineering, Principles and Methods, 1993, Genetics and Society, 1993, numerous other chpts. to books; mem. editorial bd. Archives Biochemistry and Biophysics, 1975-78, Jour. Biol. Chemistry, 1978-83, Annals Intenal Medicine, 1980-83, Molecular Biology and Medicine, 1982-90, Somatic Cell and Molecular Genetics, 1983-94, Trends in Genetics, 1985-90, Genomics, 1987-90, Molecular and Cell Biology, 1988-90, Human Gene Therapy, 1990—, Jour. AMA, 1991-94, Genetic Epidemiology, 1992-94, Human Mutation, 1992—, Circulation, 1993—; mem. bd. reviewing editors Sci., 1991—. Mem. Human Genome Orgn., 1988—, pres., 1993—; mem. task force on genetics Muscular Dystrophy Assn., 1989-94. With USPHS, 1965-67. Recipient Borden Rsch. award, Disting. Alumnus award Duke U. Med. Sch., 1991, Wadsworth award N.Y. State Dept. Health, 1992, Svc. Merchandise Leadership award Muscular Dystrophy Assn., 1992, Basic Biomed. Rsch. prize Giovanni Lorenzini Med. Found., 1993, Lucy Wortham James Basic Rsch. award Soc. Surg. Oncology, 1994, Norberto Montalbetti Milan award, 1994, The Coriell medal Coriell Inst., 1995, 5th Milano award in memory of Norberto Montalbetti, 1995. Fellow AMA (founding), AAAS (sci. innovation program com. 1991-93), Am. Coll. Physicians, Am. Acad. Microbiology, Royal Soc. Medicine Found.; mem. Nat. Acad. Scis., Am. Fedn. Clin. Rsch., Am. Soc. Biochemistry and Molecular Biology, Am. Soc. Clin. Investigation, Am. Soc. Human Genetics, Am. Soc. Cell Biology, Am. Coll. Med. Genetics, Assn. Am. Physicians, Fedn. Am. Socs. for Exptl. Biology, N.Y. Acad. Scis., So. Soc. Clin. Investigation, Soc. Inherited Metabolic Disorders, Inst. Medicine Nat. Acad. Scis., Royal Soc. Medicine, Baylor Med. Alumni Assn. (disting. faculty mem. 1993), Alpha Omega Alpha. Office: Cogene BioTech Ventures 5 Post Oak Park 4400 Post Oak Pkwy Ste 1400 Houston TX 77027

CASKEY, GRADY EDWARD, secondary school educator, artist; b. Jonesboro, La. s. James Thomas and Kathleen Parker Caskey; m. Deborah Joyce Clarkson, May 29, 1993; children: Ashley Diane, Jodi Leigh. BFA, U. Southwestern La., 1996; MS in Edn., U. Tenn., 1999. Cert. tchr. K-12 art Tenn. Dept. Edn. Owner ServiceMaster Bldg. Maintenance, Lafayette, La., 1976—86; roughneck Penrod Drilling Co., Dallas, 1987—91; tchr. Blount County Sch. Sys., Maryville, Tenn., 1999—. Illustrator: Southern Forests, 1995; Derelict I, 1996, Derelict II, 1997. Soccer coach Heritage H.S., 2002—; soccer referee U.S. Soccer Fedn., 1984—2000; Sunday sch. tchr. East Bayou Bapt. Ch., Lafayette, 1997. Mem.: Tenn. Artist Assn., Tenn. Art Educators Assn., Nat. Art Educators Assn. Republican. Baptist. Home: 4323 Thunderhead Mountain Vista Walland TN 37886 Office: Blount County Sch Sys 831 Grandview Maryville TN 37803

CASLINI, CORRADO, molecular biologist; b. Seriate, Italy, Feb. 23, 1966; m. Amparo Serna; children: Gabriel children: Sofia. BSc, U. Milan, Italy, 1990; PhD, M. Negri Inst. Pharmacol. Rsch., Milan, 1993, U. Milan, Italy, 1996. Postdoctoral fellow St. Jude Children's Rsch. Hosp., Memphis, 1994—97, M.Tettamont Rsch. Ctr., Pediatric Clinic, U. Milan, S. Gerarda Hosp., Manzi, Italy, 1997—99; rsch. assoc. U. Milan, Gerorda Hosp., Monza, Italy, 2000—01; postdoctoral assoc. Fox Chase Cancer Ctr., Phila., 2001—05; rsch. asst. prof. U. Mich. Med. Sch., Ann Arbor, 2005—. Contbr. articles to profl. publs. Fellow Associazione Italiana per la Ricerca sul Cancro and

Fondazione Italiana per la Ricerca sul Cancro, 1994—96, Associazione Italiana per la Ricerca sul Cancro, 1993—94. Mem.: Ordine Nazionale dei Biologi. Office: Univ Mich Med Sch M2246 Med Sci I 1301 Catherine St Ann Arbor MI 48109-0602 Office Phone: 734-615-1508.

CASNER, TRUMAN SNELL, lawyer; b. Balt., Oct. 9, 1933; s. A. James and Margaret (Snell) Casner; m. Elizabeth Lyons, June 12, 1954 (dec. Aug. 1997); children: Richard Dana, Elizabeth Anne, Abigail Lee; m. Cynthia Ferris Evans, May 29, 1999. BA cum laude, Princeton U., 1955; LLB cum laude, Harvard U., 1958. Bar: Mass. 1958. Law clk. to Chief Justice Raymond Wilkins, Mass. Supreme Judicial Ct., 1958-59; assoc. firm Ropes & Gray, Boston, 1959-68, partner, 1968—, mng. ptnr., 1994-99. Bd. dirs. State St. Corp., State St. Bank and Trust Co. Active Belmont Town Meeting, 1971—95; trustee, exec. com. Belmont Hill Sch., 1966—94, pres., 1985—89, chmn., 1989—2001; sec., trustee, mem. exec. com. Pine Manor Coll., 1973—79; overseer, trustee Boston Mus. Sci., 1981—; trustee Old Dartmouth Hist. Soc. (New Bedford Whaling Mus.), 2000—. Mem.: Am. Law Inst., Tavern Club, Cruising Club of Am., Kittansett Club, Comml. Club of Boston, New Bedford Yacht Club. Episcopalian. Home: 54 Fairgreen Pl Chestnut Hill MA 02467-2710 Office: Ropes & Gray One International Pl Boston MA 02110 E-mail: tcasner@ropesgray.com.

CASO, ANTHONY T., lawyer; b. 1955; BA in Polit. Sci., magna cum laude, La Verne Coll., 1976; MBA, Golden Gate U.; JD, U. Pacific, McGeorge Sch. Law. Bar: Calif. 1979. Joined Pacific Legal Found., Sacramento, sr. v.p. and gen. counsel. Adj. prof., McGeorge Sch. Law U. Pacific. Office: Pacific Legal Foundation 3900 Lennane Dr Sacramento CA 95834 Office Phone: 916-419-7111. Business E-Mail: atc@pacificlegal.org.

CASON, ALAN C., lawyer; b. Havre de Grace, Md., 1958; BS, U. Md., College Park, 1980; JD, U. Md., Balt., 1983. Bar: Md. 1984, DC 1985, US Dist. Ct. Dist. Md. Dep. county atty. Harford County, Md., 1988—90; assoc. Shapiro & Olander, 1990—93, McGuireWoods LLP, Balt., 1993—95, ptnr., 1995—, mng. ptnr. Balt. office, 2003—. Bd. mem. N.E. Md. Waste Disposal Authority, 1990—93. Adv. bd. U. Md. Cancer Ctr., 1996—2000. Named U. Md. Sch. Law Alumnus of Yr. Mem.: Monumental City Bar Assn., Balt. City Bar Assn. (chmn. minority clerkship program), Nat. Assn. Bond Lawyers, Nat. Bar Assn., Md. State Bar Assn. (mem. coun. bus. law sect.), U. Md. Alumni Assn. (mem. exec. com., fin. com.), Terrapin Club (bd. mem.), M Club. Office: McGuireWoods LLP Ste 1000 7 St Paul St Baltimore MD 21202-1671 Office Phone: 410-659-4433. Office Fax: 410-659-4481. Business E-Mail: acason@mcguirewoods.com.

CASPAR, JOHN M., manufacturing executive; BS, Drexel Inst. of Tech.; MBA, Okla. State U. Exec. v.p. internat., CFO Mitek, Inc., St. Louis, 1987-94; v.p., CFO Petrolite Corp., St. Louis; fin. cons.; sr. v.p. fin., CFO DT Industries, Inc., Springfield, Mo., 2001—. Office: DT Industries Inc 907 W 5th St Dayton OH 45407-3306

CASPARIUS, KATHY M., mathematician, department chairman; b. Augusta, Maine, Aug. 24, 1952; d. John Joseph and Charity Ellis Muslawski; m. Daniel Lowell Casparius, Feb. 14, 1974; children: Amanda Glazier, John. BS in Secondary Math., U. Maine, 1973; MBA, Thomas Coll., 1992, MS in Computer Tech. Edn., 1996. Cert. secondary sch. tchr. Maine, 2004. Math. tchr. Augusta (Maine) Sch. Dept., 1978—, tech. coord., 1996—. Bd. advisors Maine Math and Sci. Alliance, Augusta, 2002—; adj. assoc. prof. Thomas Coll., Waterville, Maine, 1990—; instr. in field. Recipient Tchr. Achievement award, Tandy Corp., 1992. Mem.: ASCD, NEA, Assn. Tchrs. Math. in Maine, Nat. Coun. Tchrs. Math., Augusta Edn. Assn. (pres. 1997—2000), Math. Educators Assn. (chair leadership com. 1999—99). Home: 33 Oak Hill Road Monmouth ME 04259 Office: Cony High School 120 Cony Street Augusta ME 04330 Office Phone: 207-626-2460. Home Fax: 207-626-2541. Business E-Mail: kcasparius@augustaschools.org.

CASPER, CHARLES B., lawyer; b. Boise, Idaho, June 9, 1952; s. John Blaine and Joyce Lucile (Mercer) C.; m. Brenda Cheryl Bowers, Aug. 28, 1976; children: Timothy L., Jonathan B. BA, Yale U., 1974; JD, U. Va., 1977; MDiv, Princeton Theol. Sem., 1985. Bar: Utah 1977, U.S. Dist. Ct. Utah 1977, U.S. Ct. Appeals (10th cir.) 1978, U.S. Supreme Ct. 1982, Pa. 1985, U.S. Dist. Ct. (ea. dist.) Pa. 1989, U.S. Ct. Appeals (3d cir.) 1989, U.S. Dist. Ct. N.J. 1990, N.J. 1990. Assoc. Fabian & Clendenin, Salt Lake City, 1977-82, shareholder, 1982; assoc. pastor Arch St. United Meth. Ch., Phila., 1985-89; assoc. Montgomery, McCracken, Walker & Rhoads, LLP, Phila., 1989-92, ptnr., 1992—, vice chmn. litigation dept., 1996-98, 2002—04. Bd. dirs. Ptnrs. Sacred Places, 1999-2003, chmn., 2003—. Evangelical Svcs. for the Aging Found., 1996-99, United Meth. Neighborhood Svcs., Phila., 1987-93, Parent-Infant Ctr., Phila., 1990-93; com. chair Utah Heritage Found., Salt Lake City, 1979-82; mem. local bd. Emergency Food and Shelter Program, 1988-98, chair, 1998—. Recipient Svc. award Utah Heritage Found., 1982, United Way Committed Cmty. Vol. award, Pa., 2005. Mem. ABA, Utah State Bar Assn., N.J. Bar Assn., Pa. Bar Assn., Phila. Bar Assn. Republican. Office: Montgomery McCracken Walker and Rhoads LLP 123 S Broad St Fl 24 Philadelphia PA 19109-1099 Office Phone: 215-772-1500.

CASPER, GERHARD, retired academic administrator, law educator; b. Hamburg, Germany, Dec. 25, 1937; s. Heinrich and Hertha Casper; m. Regina Koschel, Dec. 26, 1964; 1 child, Hanna. Legal state exam, U. Freiburg, U. Hamburg, 1961; Dr.iur.utr., U. Freiburg, Germany, 1964; LLM, Yale U., 1962, LLD (hon.), 2000, John Marshall Law Sch., 1982, Chgo.-Kent Coll. Law, 1987; PhD (hon.), Uppsala U., 2000. Asst. prof. polit. sci. U. Calif., Berkeley, 1964—66; assoc. prof. law and polit. sci. U. Chgo., 1966—69, prof., 1969—76, Max Pam prof. Am. and fgn. law, 1976—80, William B. Graham prof. law, 1980—87, William B. Graham disting. svc. prof. law, 1987—92, dean law sch., 1979—87, provost, 1989—92; prof. law Stanford U., 1992—, pres., 1992—2000, pres. emeritus, 2000—, Peter and Helen Bing prof. undergraduate edn., 2000—, sr. fellow Inst. Internat. Studies. Vis. prof. law Cath. U., Louvain, Belgium, 1970, U. Munich, 1988, 91. Author: Realism and Political Theory in American Legal Thought, 1967, Separating Power, 1997; co-author: (with Richard A. Posner) The Workload of the Supreme Court, 1976; co-editor: The Supreme Ct. Rev., 1977-91, Successor trustee Yale U., 2000—; bd. dirs. Am. Acad. in Berlin, 2000—; bd. trustees Ctrl. European U., Budapest. Fellow Am. Acad. Arts and Sciences; mem. Internat. Acad. Comparative Law, Am. Bar Found. (bd. dirs. 1979-87), Coun. Fgn. Rels., Am. Law Inst. (coun. 1980—), Am. Philos. Soc., The Trilateral Commn., 1996—, Order pour la mérite für Wissenschaften und Kunste. Office: Stanford U Stanford Inst for Internat Studies E114 Encina Hall Stanford CA 94305-6055 Office Phone: 650-723-2482. E-mail: gcasper@stanford.edu.

CASPER, JULIE ANN, geographer, writer; b. Salt Lake City, Feb. 18, 1958; d. Beverly Farr and Thomas Alden Kerr; m. Jerel Grant Casper, Dec. 20, 1997; children: Jaclyn Kerr Tygesen, Jennifer Ann Clifton, Kristina Danielle Romney, Jaida Nicole. BS, U. Utah, 1980, MS, 1984, PhD, 1996. Dental asst., Salt Lake City, 1974—82; cartographer US Bur. Land Mgmt., Salt Lake City, 1977—90, geographer, 1990—. Author: The Snow Eagle: Riddle of the Stone Tablet, The Snow Eagle: Escape Through the Kayawati, The Snow Eagle: Quest for the Shattered Orb; contbr. articles to popular mags. Educator, fund raiser Alzheimer's Assn., Chgo., 1999—2003; pres. Intermountain divsn. Am. Soc. Photogrammetry and Remote Sensing, 1993—94. With N.G. USAF, 1981—84. Mem.: Nat. Writers Assn., Pacific N.W. Writers Assn., S.W. Writers Assn., Mystery Writers of Am., Soc. Children's Book Writers and Illustrators (assoc.). Mem. Lds Ch. Avocations: hiking, kayaking, horseback riding, travel.

CASPER, LEONARD RALPH, American literature educator; b. Fond du Lac, Wis., July 6, 1923; s. Louis and Caroline (Eder) C.; m. Linda Velasquez-Ty, June 2, 1956; children: Gretchen Gabrielle, Kristina Elise. BA, U. Wis., 1948, MA, 1949, PhD, 1953. Grad. asst. U. Wis., 1949-51; instr. Cornell U., 1952-53; asst. prof. U. Philippines, 1953-56, Fulbright lectr., 1962-63, summer 1973; mem. faculty Boston Coll., 1956—, prof. contemporary Am. lit., 1963-93, prof. emeritus, 1993—99; lectr. RSVP, 2001—03. Dir. creative writing U. RI, 1958; lectr. in field. Author: Robert Penn Warren: The Dark and Bloody Ground, 1960, The Wayward Horizon: Essays on Modern Philippine Literature, 1961, The Wounded Diamond: Studies in Modern Philippine Literature, 1964, New Writing from The Philippines: A Critique and Anthology, 1966, A Lion Unannounced: 12 Stories and a Fable, 1971, Firewalkers: Concelebrations 1964-1984, 1987, In Burning Ambush: Essays, 1985-90, 1991, The Opposing Thumb: Decoding Literature of the Marcos Regime, 1995, Sunsurfers Seen from Afar: Critical Essays, 1991-96, 1996, The Blood Marriage of Earth and Sky: The Later Novels of Robert Penn Warren, 1997, The Circular Firing Squad, 1999, Green Circuits of the Sun: Studies in Philippine and American Literature, 2002; editor: Six Filipino Poets, 1955, Modern Philippine Short Stories, 1962; co-editor (with T.A. Gullason): The World of Short Fiction: An International Collection, 1962; contbg. editor Panorama, Manila, 1955—61, Drama Critique, 1956—62, Solidarity, Manila, 1966—78, Literature East and West, 1969—81, Aquila, 1975—79, Pilipinas, 1987—2002. Served with F.A., AUS, 1943-46. Recipient Ford Found. Pub. award, Nat. Coun. on Arts award, 1970, Rockefeller Found. Residency award, Bellagio, Italy, 1994; Stanford Creative Writing fellow, 1951-52; Bread Loaf Creative Writing scholar, 1961; rsch. grantee Am. Coun. Learned Socs.-Social Sci. Rsch. Coun., 1965, Asia Soc., 1965; Creative Writing grant Boston Coll.; rsch. travel grantee Am. Philos. Soc., 1968-69. Home: 54 Simpson Dr Framingham MA 01701-4076

CASPER, RICHARD HENRY, lawyer; b. Chgo., Nov. 4, 1950; s. Edson Lee and Dorothy Ellen (Klemp) C.; m. Betty Gene Ward, Aug. 26, 1972; children: Terrance, Laura, Russell, Jeremy. AB, Bowdoin Coll., 1972; JD, Northwestern U., 1975. Bar: Wis. 1975, U.S. Dist. Ct. (ea. dist.) Wis. 1975. Assoc. Foley & Lardner LLP, Milw., 1975-82, ptnr., 1982—, chmn. comml. transactions & bus. counseling practice group. James Bowdoin scholar Bowdoin Coll, 1972. Mem. Wis. Bar Assn., Milw. Bar Assn., Order of the Coif. Office: Foley & Lardner LLP Firstar 777 E Wisconsin Ave Milwaukee WI 53202-5367 Office Phone: 414-297-5612. Business E-Mail: rcasper@foley.com.

CASPERSEN, FINN MICHAEL WESTBY, diversified financial services company executive; b. N.Y.C., Oct. 27, 1941; s. Olaus Westby and Freda Caspersen; m. Barbara Caspersen, June 17, 1967. BA With honors in Econs., Brown U., 1963; LLB cum laude, Harvard U., 1966; DHL (hon.), Johns Hopkins U., 1999; various hon. degrees. Assoc. Dewey, Ballantine, Bushby, Palmer & Wood, N.Y.C., 1969-72; chmn. bd., chief exec. officer, mem. exec. com. Beneficial Corp., Wilmington, Del., 1976-98; chmn. bd. dirs., CEO Knickerbocker LLC. Past bd. dirs., mem. exec. com. Beneficial Nat. Bank; chmn. bd. dirs. Beneficial Bank, Plc; bd. advisors Inst. Law and Econs., U. Pa.; past chmn. Coalition for Better Transp.; past co-chair Prosperity N.J.; pres. emeritus U.S. Equestrian Team; chmn. internat. coun., dir. Hosp. for Spl. Surgery. Emeritus trustee Brown U.; former chmn. Save Ellis Island; moderator, bd. dirs. Shelter Harbor Fire Dist.; pres. O.W. Caspersen Found.; trustee BGCN Life Camp Inc.; chmn. bd. trustees Peddie Sch., Hightstown, N.J.; former chmn. bd. trust Gladstone Equestrian Assn. Inc.; past bd. dirs. Drumthwacket Found.; charter mem. Partnership for N.J., New Brunswick; mem. Martin County Econ Devel. Coun.; bd. dirs. Coalition of Svc. Industries, Inc., Washington, 1982-95, vice chair, 1995; chmn. World Pair Championship, 1993; chmn. Princeton World Cup Regatta, 2000; chmn., CEO Princeton Internat. Regatta Assn.; mem. corp. Cardigan Mountain Sch.; mem. exec. com. Harvard Resources Com.; trustee BGCN Life Camp Inc., John Carter Libr.; chmn. dean's adv. com. Harvard Law Sch.; past dir. Clay Math. Inst. Lt. USCG, 1966-69; tpwn commr. Jupiter Island. Recipient Pres.'s medal Johns Hopkins U., Ethics in Bus. award BBB, 1992, Gov.'s award Alexander Hamilton Econ. Devel., 1997, President's medal Brown U., 1997, Brightest Star award Boys and Girls Clubs Newark, Inc., 1997, Humanities Citizen of Yr. award N.J. Coun. for Humanities, 1999; named Civic Leader of Yr., YMCA, 1982, Citizen of Yr., Morristown Meml. Hosp., 1993. Mem. Am. Fin. Svcs. Assn. (bd. dirs., chmn. govt. affairs com., chmn. membership com., adminstrn. com., past chmn.), Fla. Bar Assn., N.Y. Bar Assn., Harvard Club, Knickerbocker Club, Univ. Club, Wilmington Club, Shelter Harbor Golf Club (founder, chmn.). Office: Knickerbocker LLC Hobe Sound Office Plz 11450 SE Dixie Hwy Hobe Sound FL 33455

CASPERSEN, SIDNEY J., state agency administrator; BS in Law Enforcement, Jacksonville State U., Jacksonville, Ala.; studied advanced criminal investigation, U. Ala.; studied undercover and pub. corruption in-svc. tng., FBI Acad., Quantico, Vir. Police officer, Anniston, Ala., 1969; sr. spl. agent Nat. Automobile Theft Bur., 1974—78; with FBI, NYC, spl. agt., organized crime unit Birmingham, Ala., program mgr., supervisory agt. NYC, supervisory spl. agt., violent fugitive task force and the pub. corruption unit, asst. chief, spl. ops.; supervisory spl. agt. Russian Counter-Intelligence; asst. dir. intelligence NY State Office Pub. Safety, 2002, dep. dir., 2002; dir. NJ Office Counter-Terrorism, Trenton, NJ, 2002—. Recipient Outstanding Contbn. to Law Enforcement award, Marine Corps Law Enforcement Found. Office: NJ Office Counter Terrorism 25 Market St PO Box 091 Trenton NJ 08625-0091 Office Phone: 609-341-3434. Office Fax: 609-341-2958.

CASS, DAVID, economist, educator; b. Honolulu, Jan. 19, 1937; s. Phil and Muriel (Dranga) C.; m. Janice Vernon, Sept. 14, 1959 (div. July 1983); children— Stephen, Lisa. BA, U. Oreg., 1958; PhD in Econs. and Stats., Stanford U., 1965; D (hon.), U. Geneva, 1994. From asst. to assoc. prof. Yale U., New Haven, 1964-70; prof. econs. Carnegie-Mellon U., Pitts., 1970—74, U. Pa., Phila., 1974-88, Paul F. and E. Warren Shafer Miller prof. econs., 1988—, dir. Ctr. for Analytic Rsch. in Econs. and the Social Scis. Prof. econs. European Union Inst., Italy, 1996—97. Contbr. articles to profl. jours.; co-editor: Selected Readings in Macroeconomics from Econometrica, 1974; The Hamiltonian Approach to Economics, 1976. 1st lt. USAR, 1959-65. Guggenheim fellow, 1970-71; recipient Morgan prize U. Chgo., 1976; Sherman Fairchild Disting. Scholar Calif. Inst. Tech., 1978-79; NSF grantee, 1971-91. Fellow Am. Econ. Assn. (disting.), Econometric Soc., Am. Acad. Arts and Scis.; mem. Phi Beta Kappa. Office: Univ Pa 435 McNeil/6297 3451 Walnut St Philadelphia PA 19104 E-mail: dcass@ssc.upenn.edu.

CASS, MARY LOUISE, librarian; b. Jersey City, May 27, 1956; d. Eugene Louis and Catherine (Reynolds) Cass; m. Edward John Skillin, Dec. 2, 2000. BA in History, Rutgers U., 1978, MLS, 1979. Cataloguer Fairleigh Dickinson U., Madison, NJ, 1979-81; mgr. Montclair Pub. Libr., 1982-96, br. dir., 1996—. Bibliographer (book) Suicide, 1991. Treas. Upper Mountain Gardens Bd., Montclair, 1998-2003. Mem. ALA (pres. cmty. info. sect. 1991-92). Democrat. Roman Cath. Home: 29 Upper Mountain Ave Montclair NJ 07042-1919 Office: Montclair Pub Libr 185 Bellevue Ave Upper Montclair NJ 07043 Office Phone: 973-744-0500. Business E-Mail: mlskillin@montlib.org.

CASS, RONALD ANDREW, lawyer, former dean; b. Washington, Aug. 12, 1949; s. Millard and Ruth Claire (Marx); m. Susan Nezamian; 1 child, Daniella Helena; children: Laura Rebecca, Alexander Stephen. BA with high distinction, U. Va., 1970; JD with honors, U. Chgo., 1973. Bar: Md. 1973, D.C. 1974, U.S. Dist. Ct. D.C. 1974, U.S. Ct. Appeals (D.C. cir.) 1974, U.S. Supreme Ct. 1977, Va. 1979. Law clk. to chief judge U.S. Ct. Appeals (3d cir.), Wilmington, Del., 1973-74; assoc. Arent, Fox, Kintner, Plotkin & Kahn, Washington, 1974-76; asst. prof. law U. Va. Sch. Law, Charlottesville, 1976-81; assoc. prof. law Boston U., 1981-83, prof., 1983-95, dean Law Sch., 1990—2004, dean emeritus, 2004—, Melville Madison Bigelow prof., 1995—2004; legal advisor Office Plans and Policy, FCC, Washington, 1987-88; mem. U.S. Internat. Trade Commn., Washington, 1988-90, vice chmn., 1989-90; pres. Cass & Assoc., PC, 2004—. Cons. comm. program Aspen (Colo.) Inst., 1977-78, Adminstrv. Conf. U.S. Washington, 1980-87, Helsell, Fetterman, Martin, Todd & Hokanson, Seattle, 1984-85, Assn. Trial Lawyers Am., Phila., 1985-87, UN Conf. Trade and Devel., Geneva, 1991, U.S. Dept. Justice, 1998, Microsoft Corp., 1998—, TransKaryotic Therapies, 2004-05; spl. cons. Nat. Econ. Rsch. Assn., Cambridge, Mass., 1990-94; arbitrator Biogen v. Schering-Plough, 1999-2000, Telesisa Sistemas v. Lucent Tech., 2000-2002, UPS v. Canada, 2001-; adj. scholar Am. Enterprise Inst., Washington, 1993-; sr. fellow Internat. Ctr. Econ. Rsch., Turin, 1996-97, 99-2002, 04—; sesquicentennial assoc. Ctr. Advanced Studies U. Va. Law Sch., 1980-81; mem. nat. adv. bd. Case Western Res. U. Sch. Law, 1996-97; disting. lectr. U. Francisco Marroquin, Guatemala City, 1996, IMADEC Internat. Bus. Sch., Vienna, 2000, U. Aix en Provence, 2002, Boston U. London Program, 2002; vis. prof. U. Lyon, 2004—. Author: Revolution in the Wasteland: Value and Diversity in Television, 1981, (with Colin S. Diver) Administrative Law: Cases and Materials, 1987, (with Colin S. Diver and Jack M. Beermann) Administrative Law: Cases and Materials, 2nd edit., 1994, 3d edit., 1998, 4th edit., 2002, (with John R. Haring) International Trade in Telecommunications, 1998, The Rule of Law in America, 2001, (with Michael Knoll) International Trade Law, 2003; contbr. articles and essays to profl. jours., also chpts. to books. Bd. dirs. Northwestern Va. Health Systems Agy., Culpeper, 1980; bd. govs. Sightsavers Internat., Washington, 1989-91; bd. dirs. Telecomm. Policy Rsch. Conf., Washington, 1989-91, sec.-treas. 1989-90, vice chmn., 1991-92; bd. dirs. New Eng. Legal Found., 1994-2002, New England Coun., 1995-2004, Ralph Papitto Sch. Law, Roger Williams U., 2005—, Mass. 9/11 Fund, 2002-05; bd. overseers Boston Bar Found., 1992-94, Supreme Jud. Ct. Hist. Soc., 1997-2000; sr. Europe Discussion Group, Ctr. for Strategic and Internat. Studies, 1989-96; bd. advisors George Mason U. Law Sch. Law & Econs. Ctr., 1996-99, Inst. Dem. Comm., Boston, 1991-92, Fundación de la Commn. Social, Madrid, 1995—, IMADEC Internat. Bus. Sch., Vienna, 1999-2001, Legal Issues in Econ. Integration, Amsterdam, 2000—, Competition Policy Internat., 2005—. Fellow Am. Bar Found.; mem. ABA (adminstrv. law and regulatory practice sect., coun. 1993-95, chair 1998-99, legal edn. and admission bar sect., review commn. 1994-95, ho. of dels. 2000-02), Am. Law Inst., Am. Law Deans Assn. (bd. dirs. 1995-2004, pres. 1995-97), Mont Pelerin Soc., Boston Bar Assn. (coun. 1992-95), Adminstrv. Conf. U.S. (pub. mem. 1990-95, govt. mem. 1988-90), Transatlantic Policy Network (U.S. Working Group), Order of Coif, Federalist Soc. (internat. law, exec. com. 2001—, chmn. 2004—), Phi Beta Kappa. Republican. Jewish. Home and Office: 10560 Fox Forest Dr Great Falls VA 22066 Business E-Mail: roncass@cassassociates.net.

CASSADY, DANIEL BENNET, music educator; b. Des Moines, Iowa, Mar. 14, 1951; s. James Neal and Inez Bardella Cassady; m. Lori Janine Becker, July 29, 1988; children: Nathan, Megan; m. Dixie Lee Miller, Aug. 2, 1975 (div. July 31, 1985); 1 child, Michael. MusB, The U. of Iowa, 1973, MA, 1984. Cert. Tchr. State of Iowa, 1973, lic. Iowa Bd. Ednl. Examiners, 73. Band dir. Graettinger Cmty. Sch., Graettinger, Iowa, 1973—76, Hawley Elem. Sch., Fort Dodge, Iowa, 1976—77, Ft. Dodge Sr. H.S., Fort Dodge, Iowa, 1976—95; dir. of bands Iowa Ctrl. C.C., Fort Dodge, Iowa, 1995—, instr. humanities, 1995—. Guest dir. Reggie Schive Summer Jazz Camps, Storm Lake and Okoboji, Iowa, 1982—, Southwestern C.C. Summer Jazz Camps, Creston, Iowa, 1985—97. Musician: (albums) Brass Transit, 1998. Orch. mgr., trombonist, arranger Ft. Dodge Civic Glee Club, Fort Dodge, 1976; active various capacities Karl L. King Mcpl. Band, 1977, bd. dir., 1977. Recipient Excellence award, Nat. Inst. for Staff and Orgnl. Devel. U. of Tex., Austin, 1999. Mem.: NEA, Iowa H.S. Music Assn. (adjudicator 1979—), Music Educators Nat. Conf. (north ctrl. rep. 1996—2000), Iowa Bandmasters Assn. (county chmn. jazz com. 1973, county chmn.coll. affairs com. 1973), Iowa Alliance for Arts Edn., Internat. Trombone Assn., Internat. Jazz Educators Assn., Am. Sch. Band Directors Assn. (sgt. at arms 1997). Methodist. Avocations: billiards, jazz, motorcycling. Home: 1801 Lainson Avenue Fort Dodge IA 50501-8531 Office: Iowa Central Community College 330 Avenue M Fort Dodge IA 50501 E-mail: cassady@triton.iccc.cc.ia.us.

CASSADY, HAROLD LEE, music educator; b. Pitts., Pa., Feb. 6, 1966; s. Harold Lee and Mary Vaux Cassady; children: Connor, McKenna. BS in Mktg., Lehigh U., 1988, MBA, 1998; BS in Music Edn., Moravian Coll., 1996. Cert. Tchr. Pa. Dept. Edn., 1996. Sales mgr. Macy's, Allentown, Pa., 1988—89; acct. exec. AT&T, Parsippanny, NJ, 1989—94; dir. of bands Stroudsburg H.S., Stroudsburg, Pa., 1996—. Mem.: NEA, Percussive Arts Soc., Pa. Music Educators Assn., Music Educators Nat. Conf. Republican. Office: Stroudsburg High School 1100 West Main Street Stroudsburg PA 18360 Home: 1319 Coolbaugh St Stroudsburg PA 18360-8917 Office Phone: 570-421-1991.

CASSADY, SHAWN LAWRENCE, psychiatrist; b. Balt., Dec. 16, 1958; s. John Howard Jr. and Mary Katharyn (Feeley) C.; m. Denise Eve Lally, Apr. 13, 1985; children: Maureen Kathryn, Sean Joseph, Colin Francis. BS in Chemistry, Loyola Coll., 1980; MD, U. Md., 1985. Diplomate Am. Bd. Psychiatry and Neurology. Rsch. asst. med. chemistry Loyola Coll, Balt., 1978; chemist quality control A.A.I. Corp., Cockeysvile, Md., 1980—81; toxicologist C.L.A.M.P., Timonium, Md., 1982—83; resident U. Md. Dept. Psychiatry, Balt., 1985—89; cons. psychiatry Loch Raven V.A. Med. Ctr., Balt., 1986—88; rsch. asst. prof. Md. Psychiat. Rsch. Ctr. U. Md. Sch. Medicine, Balt., 1992—; staff psychiatrist State of Md. Dept. Health and Mental Hygiene, Harford County, 1992—97; cons. psychiatry Balt. V.A. Med. Ctr., 1993—94. Med. dir. mobile treatment svcs. Harford County Mental Health and Addictions, Bel Air, Md., 1992-97; rsch. asst. prof. dept. psychiatry U. Md., 1991—; psychiat. cons. Key Point Health Svcs., Md., 1997—. Contbr. chpt. to book and articles to profl. jours. Rsch. fellow Md. Psychiat. Rsch. Ctr., Catonsville, 1989-92; recipient New Investigator award new clin. drug evaluation unit NIMH, 1992. Mem. Am. Psychiat. Assn., Md. Psychiat. Soc. Democrat. Roman Catholic. Avocations: bagpipes, mandolins, irish banjo, piano. Office: Key Point Health Svcs 135 N Parke St Aberdeen MD 21001 Office Phone: 443-625-1600. E-mail: SCassadyMD@aol.com.

CASSADY, ZOE ANNE, theater educator, director; d. Roy Alfred and Kari Lenora Scheidecker; m. Donald Joseph Cassady, Oct. 23, 1993; 1 child, Kieran Madison. BA, Concordia U., River Forest, Ill., 1992. Cert. tchg. type 9 with endorsements Ill., camp dir. Am. Camping Assn. Program dir. Luth. Camp Assn., Woodland Pk., Colo., 1980—81; exec. dir. Camp Lutherhaven, Albion, Ind., 1982—88; mgr. Somewhere in Time, Ottawa, Ill., 1987—92; program dir. Gov.'s State U., U. Pk., 1988—89; creativity asst. Steppenwolf Theatre, Chgo., 1989—90; tchr. and drama dir. Rock Falls (Ill.) H.S., 1992—94, Streator Twp. H.S., 1994—. Sec. Ind. section Am. Camping Assn., 1984—86; dir. Camp Fire of LaSalle County, Ottawa, 1990—93, Engle Ln. Theatre, Streator, Ill., 1991—. Contbr. articles to periodicals; actor: (plays) Bus Stop, 1991 (Best Actor, 1991); dir.: Little Shop of Horrors, 1990 (Best Dir., 1990); set designer: Arsenic and Old Lace, 1992 (Best Set Design, 1992). Reading tchr. Laubanch Literacy, Ft. Wayne, Ind., 1985—88; vol. tchr. Am. Red Cross; election judge LaSalle County, Ill., 1991. Recipient Cmty. Svc. award, Streator Area C. of C., 1996, 1999, 2003, Excellence in Tchg. award, LaSalle County Regional Office of Edn., 2001. Mem.: Am. Fedn. Tchrs. (Streator local) (Ill. corr. sec. 1995—2003), Nat. Forensic League, Nat. Coun. of Tchrs. of English. Lutheran. Avocations: swimming, hiking. Office: Streator Twp HS 600 N Jefferson Streator IL 61364 Office Phone: 815-672-0545. E-mail: thespus@verizon.net.

CASSANI, MARGARETA-ERMINIA, writer; b. Detroit, Dec. 4, 1952; d. Peter Henry and Elizabeth Jane (Vansyckle) C.; 1 child, Kristin Suzanne. BFA, Ea. Mich. U., 1978; MA, Wayne State U., 1985, postgrad., 1990-95. Media specialist Sinai Hosp., Detroit, 1988-94; owner Media rising, Livonia, Mich., 1994—. Author numerous articles, short stories to profl. jours. Mem. AAUW, NOW. Democrat. Avocations: exercise, travel, history, films, politics.

CASSARA, FRANK, artist, educator, printmaker; b. Partinico, Italy, Mar. 13, 1913; came to U.S., 1913, naturalized, 1936; s. Gaspare and Rosalia (Savarino) C.; m. Gretchen Jean Grathwohl, Dec. 28, 1946; children: Christina, Francesca. Student, U. Iowa, summer 1956, Atelier 17, Paris, summer 1958; MS in Design, U. Mich., 1954. Supr. easel painting sect. WPA, 1937; instr. Detroit Sch. Art, 1935-36, Soc. Arts and Crafts, Detroit, 1946-47; prof. U. Mich., Ann Arbor, after 1947, prof. emeritus. Instr. Nat. Music Camp, Interlochen, Mich., summers 1948-49 Illustrated manuscript published in Artists Proof, A Collectors Edition, 1963; one-man shows include: U. Man., Can., Winnipeg, Flint (Mich.) Inst. Arts, Toledo Mus., 1983, Kalamazoo Art Ctr., U. Maine, Orono, U. Ill., Urbana, U. Oreg., Corvallis, U. Nebr., Lincoln; group shows include: 7th Internat. Prints, Chgo. Art Inst., Mus. Palace Legion of Honor, San Francisco, Gallerie Nees Morphes, Athens, Greece, Bklyn. Mus., Achenbach Found. Graphic Arts, San Francisco, Okla. Art Ctr., Oklahoma City, Internat. Conf. Hand Papermakers, Boston, 1980, Internat. Papermakers, Birmingham Art Assn., Ella Sharp Mus. and Slusser Gallery; represented in permanent collections at Bibliotecque Nationale, Paris, Stadelijk Mus., The Netherlands, Libr. of Congress, USIA Agy., Nat. Mus. Am. Art, Smithsonian Instn., Washington; mural executed East Detroit Post Office, 1939, Sandusky (Mich.) Post Office, 1941, Lansing (Mich.) Water Conditioning Plant, 1941, renovated, 1989, Palio, Ann Arbor, 1996. Served with U.S. Army, 1942-46. Decorated 2 Bronze Stars.; Grantee Rackham Research Found., U. Mich., 1957-61, 68; Recipient over 50 awards in National and regional exhibitions. Mem. Ann Arbor Art Assn. (past pres., dir. 1954-62), Nat. Acad. Design. Achievements include being the innovator of two white grounds for etching.

CASSAVETES, NICK, film director, actor; b. NYC, May 21, 1959; s. John Cassavetes and Gena Rowlands. Dir.: (films) She's So Lovely, 1997, John Q, 2002, The Notebook, 2004; exec. prodr. (TV movies) The Incredible Mrs. Ritchie, 2003; writer (films) Blow, 2001; dir., writer: (films) Unhook the Stars/Décroche les étoiles, 1996; actor: A Woman Under the Influence, 1974, Mask, 1985, The Wraith, 1986, Quiet Cool, 1986, Black Moon Rising, 1986, Under the Gun, 1988, Assault of the Killer Bimbos, 1998, Blind Fury, 1989, Desperation Rising, 1989, Object of Desire, 1990, Backstreet Dreams, 1990, Delta Force 3: The Killing Game, 1991, Sins of the Night, 1993, Sins of Desire, 1993, Body of Influence, 1993, Broken Trust, 1993, Mrs. Parker and the Vicious Circle, 1994, Twogether, 1994, Class of 1999 II: The Substitute, 1994, Black Rose of Harlem, 1996, Me and the Gods, 1997, Face/Off, 1997, Conversations in Limbo, 1998, Life, 1999, The Astronaut's Wife, 1999, (TV movies) Reunion, 1980, Shooter, 1988, Just Like Dad, 1995. Office: c/o DGA 7920 W Sunset Blvd Los Angeles CA 90046-3300

CASSEL, CHRISTINE KAREN, physician; b. Mpls., Sept. 14, 1945; d. Charles Moore and Virginia Julia (Anderson) Cassel. AB, U. Chgo., 1967; MD, U. Mass., 1976. Diplomate Am. Bd. Internal Medicine (chmn. 1998-99). Intern, resident in internal medicine Children's Hosp., San Francisco, 1976—78; fellow in bioethics Inst. Health Policy Studies, U. Calif., San Francisco, 1978—79; fellow geriatrics Portland (Oreg.) VA Hosp., 1979—81; asst. prof. medicine and public health U. Oreg. Health Scis. U., 1981—83; asst. prof. geriatrics and medicine Mt. Sinai Med. Ctr., N.Y.C., 1983—85; prof. medicine, prof. pub. policy U. Chgo., 1989—95, chief gen. internal medicine, 1985—95; chmn. and prof. geriatrics and medicine Mt. Sinai, 1995—2002; dean sch. of medicine Oreg. Heatlh and Sci. U., 2002—03; pres., CEO Am. Bd. Internal Medicine and ABIM Found., 2003—. Author: Ethical Dimensions in the Health Professions, 1981, 1993, Geriatric Medicine: Principles and Practice, 1984, 2003, Nuclear Weapons and Nuclear War: A Sourcebook for Health Professionals, 1984. Bd. dirs., chmn. Greenwall Found. Henry J. Kaiser Family Found. faculty scholar, 1982—85, Hastings Ctr. fellow. Master: ACP (regent 1989—97, pres. 1997—98); fellow: Am. Geriatrics Soc.; mem.: Am. .Soc. Law and Medicine (bd. dirs.), Soc. Health and Human Values (pres. 1986), Physicians for Social Responsibility (dir. 1983—86, pres. 1988—89), Inst. of Medicine of NAS. Office: Am Bd Internat Medicine Found Ste 1700 510 Walnut St Philadelphia PA 19106-3699 E-mail: casselc@abim.org.

CASSEL, JOHN ELDEN, accountant; b. Apr. 24, 1934; s. Elbert Emry and Erma Ruth (McDowell) C.; m. Mary Lou Malcom, June 3, 1953; children: John Elden, James Edward, Jerald Eugene. Plant mgr., asst. gen. mgr. Baker and Taylor Co., Oklahoma City, 1966—71; paymaster, officer mgr. Robberson Steel Co., Oklahoma City, 1971—76; pvt. investor, 1976—. Methodist. Home: 2332 NW 118th St Oklahoma City OK 73120-7404 E-mail: cassel5@hotmail.com.

CASSEL, JOHN MICHAEL, plastic surgeon; b. Miami, Mar. 25, 1948; m. Robyn Cassel, July 12, 1987; children: (twins) Adrienne and Brandon. BS, U. Miami, 1972, MD, 1978. Diplomate Am. Bd. Plastic Surgery. Gen. surg. intern U. Va., Charlottesville, 1978-79, gen. surg. resident, 1979-80, Cedars-Sinai Med. Ctr., L.A., 1980-81; jr. resident in plastic surgery U. Miami Sch. Medicine, 1981-82, sr. resident in plastic surgery, 1982-83; microsurgery and hand surgery fellow Ralph K. Davies Med. Ctr., San Francisco, 1984; pvt. practice plastic surgery Miami, 1985—. Clin. assoc. prof. plastic surgery U. Miami Sch. Medicine, 1984—. Fellow Am. Coll. Surgeons; mem. Am. Soc. Plastic & Reconstructive Surgeons, Am. Soc. Aesthetic Plastic Surgeons. Avocations: sculpture, stained glass, gem cutting, jewely design & fabrication. Office: 8950 N Kendall Dr Ste 106 Miami FL 33176-2131

CASSELL, ERIC JONATHAN, physician; b. NYC, Aug. 29, 1928; s. Hyman William and Anne (Lake) Goldstein; m. Joan M. Fishman, Oct. 17, 1957 (div. 1987); children: Justine, Stephen; m. Patricia M. Owens, May 26, 1990. BA, Queens Coll., 1950; MA, Columbia U., 1950; MD, NYU, 1954; DHL (hon.), Med. Coll. Pa., 1985. Intern 3d med. divsn. Bellevue Hosp., N.Y.C., 1954—55, asst. resident 3d med. divsn., 1955—56, physician 3d, 4th med. divsn., 1965—66; USPHS trainee in infectious diseases Weill Med. Coll., Cornell U., N.Y.C., 1959—61; clin. prof. pub. health Cornell U., N.Y.C., 1971—; attending physician French Hosp., N.Y.C., 1961—74; assoc. attending physician Mt. Sinai (N.Y.) Hosp., 1966—71; assoc. dir. ambulatory care Community Med., Mt. Sinai, 1966—68; attending physician N.Y. Presbyn. Hosp., 1984—; asst. resident 3d med. divsn. Bellevue Hosp., N.Y.C., 1958—59. Clin. assoc. prof. medicine NYU, 1965—66, Mt. Sinai Hosp., 1966—71; bd. dirs. Hasting's Ctr., Garrison, NY; commr. Nat. Bioethics Adv. Commn., 1997—2001; vis. investigator Meml. Sloan Kettering Cancer Ctr., 1999—; adj. prof. medicine McGill U., Montreal, Canada, 2005—. Author: Healer's Art, 1976, Place of Humanities in Medicine, 1984, Talking with Patients (2 vols.), 1985, The Nature of Suffering, 1991, 2d edit., 2004, Doctoring: The Nature of Primary Care Medicine, 1997; editor: Changing Values in Medicine, 1979. Capt. M.C. U.S. Army, 1956—58. Master: ACP; fellow: N.Y. Acad. Medicine; mem.: Inst. of Medicine of NAS. Democrat. Jewish. Avocations: woodworking, metalworking. Personal E-mail: eric@ericcassell.com.

CASSELL, KAY ANN, librarian; b. Van Wert, Ohio, Sept. 24, 1941; d. Kenneth Miller and Pauline (Zimmerman) C. BA, Carnegie-Mellon U., 1963; M.L.S., Rutgers U., 1965; MA, Bklyn. Coll., 1969. Reference librarian Bklyn. Coll. Library, 1965-68; adult svcs. cons. NJ State Libr., Trenton, 1968-71; libr. cons.-vol. Peace Corps, Rabat, Morocco, 1971-73; adult svcs. cons. Westchester Libr. System, White Plains, NY, 1973-75; dir. Bethlehem Pub. Libr., Delmar, NY, 1975-81, Huntington (N.Y.) Pub. Libr., 1982-85; exec. dir. Coordinating Coun. Lit. Mags., NYC, 1985-87; univ. libr. New Sch. Social Rsch., 1987-88; assoc. dir. collections and svcs. br. librs. NY Pub. Libr., 1989—. Adj. faculty Grad. Sch. Libr. Sci., SUNY, Albany, 1976-78, Palmer Sch. Libr. and Info. Scis., L.I. U., 1986-90, Grad. Sch. Info. and Libr. Sci., Pratt Inst., 1994—; chmn. cmty. adv. com. Capital Dist. Humanities Program, Albany, 1980-81; bd. dirs. Literacy Vols. of Suffolk, Bellport, N.Y., 1981-85; chmn. N.Y.C. Sch. Libr. Sys. Coun., 1991-94; treas. Libr. Pub. Rels. Coun., 1993-98, pres., 1999-2000. Mem. ALA (pres. reference and adult svcs. divsn. 1983-84, chair membership com. 1991-95, coun. 1992—, chair pub. com. 1999-01, chair human resources com., 2003-04), Freedom to Read Found., NY Libr. Assn. (pres. reference and adult svcs. sect. 1975-76), Feminist Press (bd. dirs.), Beta Phi Mu. Office: NY Pub Libr Office Collections & Svcs 455 5th Ave New York NY 10016-0118 Business E-Mail: kcassell@nypl.org.

CASSELL, LUCILLE RICHARDSON, small business owner; b. Sikeston, Mo., Feb. 23, 1958; d. Glen and Cenia (McCaster) Richardson; m. Arthur Earl Cassell, Apr. 12, 1986; children: Christopher Glen, Bryan Mitchell, David Arthur, Aaron Lamar. AA in Edn., S.E. Mo. State U., 1980; deaconess lic., Green Meml. Bible Inst.-Coll., Sikeston, 1982. Shoe packer Wohl Shoe Co., Sikeston, 1980-84; sales clk. J.C. Penney, Sikeston, 1984-85; bookeeper, teller Bank of Sikeston, 1985-86; computer operator Sta. KBSI-TV, Cape Girardeau, Mo., 1986-89; data clk. Falcon Cable TV, Sikeston, 1989-90; owner, mgr. Wee=Care Daycare Ctr., Charleston, 1990-99; pres. CBD Enterprises, Inc., Charleston, 1999—; tchr. kindergarten Sikeston (Mo.) Pub. Schs., 2000, Charleston (Mo.) Pub. Schs., 2001. Author: (poem) The Best That I Can Be, 1995; patented disposable diapers, adult diapers; patentee in field. Participant walk-a-thons Cystic Fibrosis Found., Charleston, 1992; leader Kid's Beat Program, Opportunity COGIC Drill Team; youth drill team; presentation History of Fancy Bottom Diapers Sikeston Local Libr., Cape Girardeau Pub. Lib., Charleston Pub. Lib.; vol. Delta Med. Ctr., Sikeston, 1990; Sunday sch. tchr. Green Meml. Ch., Sikeston, Mo., 1985—86, Opportunity Ch., Charleston. Mem. Ch. of God in Christ. Avocations: reading, volleyball, music, bowling. Home: PO Box 284 Charleston MO 63834-0284 Personal E-mail: casscbd@aol.com.

CASSELL, WILLIAM COMYN, retired college president; b. Vallejo, Calif., Oct. 8, 1933; s. Comyn R. and Emily E. (Duckwith) C.; m. Jeanne Taylor, Dec. 27, 1955; children: Paul, Susan, David. BA, Pomona Coll., 1956; MA, Claremont Grad. Sch., 1969; LHD (hon.), Lakeland Coll., 1977; LLD, William Penn Coll.; D in Bus. Adminstn., Won Kwang U.; MBA, DLitt, Heidelberg Coll. Broker Hornblower and Weeks, Inc., Orange, Calif., 1958-64; asst. to treas. Claremont (Calif.) Coll., 1964-65; dir. income trusts and bequests Calif. Inst. Tech., Pasadena, 1965-69; dir. devel. and pub. relations Menninger Found., Topeka, 1969-70; dir. devel. U. Denver, 1970-74; pres. Coll. of Idaho, Caldwell, 1974-80, Heidelberg Coll., Tiffin, Ohio, 1980-96, pres. emeritus, 1996—. Cons. Ford Found., Phelps-Stokes Fund, Congress of No. Marianas Islands, numerous colls. and govt. agys., 1983—; hon. royal consul gen. Nepal; bd. dirs. Fifth-Third Bank No. Ohio. Author: The Case for Deferred Giving, 1966, Deferred Giving Programs: Administration and Promotion, 1972; editorial adv. bd.: Ednl. Record. Mem. Parks and Recreation Commn., Claremont, 1967-69, City Coun., Bow Mar, Colo., 1967-69; mem. adv. bd. Salvation Army, Caldwell, Western Electric Fund; trustee Caldwell Meml. Hosp., chmn., 1976; mem. Idaho newspaper carrier scholarship selection com.; mem. Missions on Am. Mgmt. and Ednl. Techniques to Indonesia and Jamaica; mission leader Thailand on Edn. and Mgmt.; mem. White House Adv. Com. on Libr. and Tech., White House Conf.; mem. Ohio Higher Edn. Facilities Commn., Depository Libr. Commn. of U.S.; adv. com. chmn. bd. Western Ind. Coll. Funds; bd. dirs. Tiffin YMCA, Wood River Cmty. YMCA, 2005-; chair Ketchum/Sun Valley Transit Authority; jr. warden St. Thomas Episcopal Ch.; chair adv. bd. Minn. Pub. Radio of Wood River Valley, 2000—; sec., bd. dirs. The Arts Found. for the Wood River Valley. Capt. USAR, 1957-58. Recipient Brakeley award for Outstanding Coll. Devel. Am. Alumni Coun., 1968, Nat. Fund Raising Coun. award, 1969; named Outstanding Young Man of Yr., Claremont, Calif., 1967, an Idaho Disting. Citizen, 1977, hon. VIP Sta. KIDO, Boise, Citizen of Yr. City of Tiffin, 1991. Mem. Coun. for Advancement of Support of Edn., Caldwell C. of C. (exec. bd. dir.), Tiffin C. of c. (bd. dirs., v.p.), Internat. Assn. Univ. Pres. (exec. com.), World Bus. Coun., North Cen. Accreditation Assn. (commr.), Am. Coun. on Edn. (commn. internat. edn.), Rotary (fellows selection com. dist., Citizen of Yr., Tiffin, Ohio 1991), Ketchum Sun Valley Rotary Club (mem. internat. projects com. Rotary dist.). Home: PO Box 1688 Sun Valley ID 83353-1688

CASSELL, WILLIAM WALTER, retired accounting operations consultant; b. Chgo., Apr. 10, 1917; s. Charles F. and E. Margaret (Jackson) C.; m. Rosamond Mary Fisher, May 13, 1944; children: Anne, Gerald, Douglas, Mary. Student, U. Wash., 1936-38, Syracuse U., 1943-44; grad., Am. Inst. Banking, 1957, Grad. Sch. Savs. Banking, 1965, Savs. Banks Mgmt. Devel. Program, U. Mass., 1970. Officer's asst. Syracuse (N.Y.) Savs. Bank, 1959-66, treas., 1966-71, v.p., 1971-75, sr. v.p., controller, 1975-77, exec. v.p., 1977-83, cons., 1983, also dir.; dir. State Bank of Chittenango, 1963—73, 1983—2005, Credit Bur. Syracuse, 1976-83, Consumer Credit Counseling Service, 1979-83. Chmn. bd. dirs. State Bank of Chittenango, 1993-2005, SBC Fin. Corp., 1993-2005 Bd. dirs. Syracuse Symphony Orch., 1979-81, Opera Theater of Syracuse, 1982-84; pres. Madison County Hist. Soc., 1982-84. Served with U.S. Army, 1941-45, ETO. Decorated Bronze Star Mem. Am. Inst. Banking, Fin. Execs. Inst. (pres. Syracuse chpt. 1971-72). Clubs: Men's Garden of Am, Monarch of Syracuse. Republican. Methodist. Home: 131 W Genesee St Chittenango NY 13037-1501 *To find happiness in little things each day; to be all I am capable of being, judged within the framework of my own real values and to make others glad I came this way—this is the measure of a life worthwhile: contentment, not complacency.*

CASSELLA, DENNIS GENE, retired county official; b. Pratt, Kans., Oct. 24, 1946; s. Barney Joseph and Norma Jeanne Cassella. AA, Sacramento C.C., 1970; BA in History/Polit. Sci., U. Calif., Davis, 1971; MPA, East Tex. State U., 1975. City pers. dir. City of Texarkana, Ark., 1971—75; dir. adminstrv. svcs. Ark. Dept. Local Svcs., Little Rock, 1975—76; dir. gen. svcs. County of Nevada, Calif., 1977—2002; ret., 2002. Dir. emergency svcs. County of Nevada, 1988-2003; sr. adj. prof. Golden Gate U., Sacramento, 1979—. Mem. Nevada City (Calif.) Police Cmty. Rels. Commn., 1991—93, Nevada City Bicentennial of the Constn. Commn., 1986—; commr. Grass Valley (Calif.) Pers. Com., 2003—. Mem. Nevada County Libr. Found. (pres. 1998-99), Gold Country Lions (pres. 1987, 2004), Hospice of the Foothills (bd. mem.). Home: 205 Cypress Hill Dr Grass Valley CA 95945 E-mail: henryv@nccn.net.

CASSELLA, WILLIAM NATHAN, JR., retired not-for-profit organization executive; b. Alton, Ill., July 14, 1920; s. William Nathan and Martha (Stanly) C.; m. Margaret Powers Crowley, June 22, 1946 (dec. Nov. 1987); children: John Woodson, Stephen Rowan, Mark Crowley, William Kent. AB, U. Ill., 1942; MS, Syracuse U., 1943; A.M., Harvard, 1951, PhD, 1953. Research asst. Pub. Adminstrn. Clearing House, Washington, 1946; instr., then asst. prof. polit. sci. U. Mo., 1948-54; with Nat. Mcpl. League, 1953-90, exec. dir., 1969-85, project coord., 1985-90; sr. assoc. Inst. Pub. Adminstrn., 1988—. Rsch. assoc. Govt. Affairs Found., 1954-57; vis. assoc. prof. pub. adminstrn. Columbia, 1957; sr. rsch. assoc. Columbia (Met. Region Program), 1957-61; mem. adv. com. state and local govt. stats. Bur. Census, 1962-65, chmn., 1963-65; mem. area devel. adv. bd. Com. Econ. Devel., 1964-66; cons. Adv. Commn. Intergovtl. Rels., 1967-89. Author: Constitutional Aspects of Metropolitan Government, 1961, also articles; contbg. editor Nat. Civic Rev., 1954-85, chmn. editorial bd., 1969-85. Mem. Greenburgh (N.Y.) Bd. Edn., 1961-64; mem. Westchester County Planning Bd., 1962-97, vice chmn., 1967-72, chmn., 1973-97, Hudson River Valley Greenway Compact Commn., 1997—, Conservation Adv. Bd., Dobbs Ferry, N.Y., 1997—; bd. dirs. Westchester County Indsl. Devel. Agy., 1976-83; trustee Pub. Adminstrn. Service, 1969-76; governing bd. Governmental Affairs Inst., 1969-76. Served to lt. USNR, 1943-46. Mem. Am. Polit. Sci. Assn., Am. Soc. Pub. Adminstrn., Govtl. Rsch. Assn., Internat. City/County Mgmt. Assn., Nat. Acad. Pub. Adminstrn., Regional Plan Assn. N.Y., Phi Beta Kappa, Alpha Kappa Lambda, Delta Sigma Pi, Omicron Delta Kappa, Pi Alpha Alpha. Episcopalian. Home: 100 Buena Vista Dr Dobbs Ferry NY 10522-3521 E-mail: wncassella@aol.com.

CASSELLI, HENRY CALVIN, JR., artist, painter; b. New Orleans, Oct. 25, 1946; m. Donna Madden, June 5, 1971; 1 child, Dana Nicole. Student, John McCrady Sch. Fine and Applied Arts, 1967. Solo shows include Smithsonian Inst., Washington, 1968, 71, Lauren Roberts Mus., 1972, Far Gallery, N.Y.C., 1974-77, Hunter Mus., Tenn., 1981, Am. Watercolor Soc., 1971-86, Greenville (S.C.) Mus., 1980, others; permanent collections include New Orleans Mus., Albany Mus., Ga., The White House, Lauren Rogers Mus., Grover M. Herman Fine Arts Ctr, Libr. Congress, N.Y. Pub. Libr., Nat. Portrait Gallery, Washington. Served with USMC, 1967-70. Decorated Bronze Star medal with combat V.; named official NASA artist for space shuttle. Mem. NAD, Am. Watercolor Soc. (v.p. 1979-80, nat. juror 1979, High Winds medal 1976, 77, 79, 88, Silver medal 1986, Gold medal 1987.) Office: 4015 N Labarre Rd Metairie LA 70002-1820*

CASSELMAN, WILLIAM E., II, lawyer; b. Washington, Pa., July 8, 1941; s. William E. and Lucy C.; m. Mia Kang, June 15, 1993; children: Katharine Carr, Lee Wilson. BA, Claremont-McKenna Coll., 1963; postgrad., U. Madrid, 1963-64; JD, George Washington U., 1968. Bar: Va. 1968, D.C. 1972, U.S. Supreme Ct. 1975. Legis. asst. to Robert McClory U.S. Ho. of Reps., 1965-68; staff asst. Office of Pres., 1969, dep. spl. asst. to Pres., 1969-71, counsel to Pres., 1974-75; gen. counsel Gen. Svcs. Adminstrn., 1971-73; legal counsel to Vice Pres. U.S., 1973-74; ptnr. Ambrose & Casselman, P.C., 1975-79; pvt. practice Washington, 1979-82; ptnr. Dorsey & Whitney, 1982-84, Popham, Haik, Schnobrich & Kaufman, Ltd., Washington, 1985-93; of counsel Stairs Dillenbeck Finley & Rendon, N.Y.C., 1993—; pvt. practice Washington, Va., 1993—. Mem. adminstrv. conf. U.S., 1971-73; adv. mem. Nat. Conf. Commrs. on Uniform State Laws, 1975; mem. Gerald R. Ford Commemorative Com., 1977-82; bd. dirs. gen. counsel, mem. fin. com., fellow Georgetown U. Ctr. for Internat. Bus. and Trade (formerly Nat. Ctr. Export-Import Studies), 1983-93. Recipient Disting. Alumni Achievement award George Washington U., 1975. Mem. ABA, Fed. Bar Assn. (chmn. gen. counsels com. 1973-74, nat. coun. 1974-79, Disting. Svc. commendation 1974), George Washington Law Assn. (bd. dirs. 1976-81), Nat. Trust for Hist. Preservation (mem. com. on legal svcs. 1978-80), Delta Theta Phi, Theta Chi. Republican. E-mail: weclawfirm@aol.com.

CASSELS, MARTHA BEASLEY, realtor, real estate developer; b. Greenwood, S.C., Oct. 22, 1932; d. Hugh Alton and Ora Faith (Mitchell) Beasley; m. Marion Carlyle Crenshaw, Jr., June 25, 1953 (div. 1979); children: Marion Carlyle III, William Frank, Hugh Charles, Faith Byrd; m. Samuel Jones Cassels, III, Oct. 6, 1979 (div. 1999). BA, Converse Coll., 1953. Cert. residential specialist Realtors Nat. Mktg. Inst., 1979. Tchr. Carr Jr. H.S., Durham, N.C., 1953-55, 1st Congl. Pre Sch., Branford, Conn., 1964-66; dir. Barfield Kindergarten, Durham, 1966-68, Duke Meml. Pre Sch., Durham, 1968-74; sec. corp. Bob Gunter Realty, Inc., Durham, 1972-77; owner Crenshaw Co., Inc., Durham, 1977-79, Cassels Real Estate, Montgomery, Ala., 1980—. Pres. Hampton Killingsworth, Inc. 1990—, Montgomery Area Bd. Realtors, Ala. Bd. Realtors, 1979—, Nat. Bd. Realtors, Chgo., 1974—. Mem. County Bd. Edn., Durham, 1972—79; patron theatre dept. Ala. State U., Montgomery, 1994—; active Montgomery Zoo; bd. dirs. Scott and Zelda Fitzgerald Mus., Montgomery, 1986—, sponsor statewide lit. contest for high schs. and colls. Named Top Prodr., Montgomery Area Bd. Realtors, 1981; recipient Top Residential award Montgomery Area Bd. Realtors, 1982, 10 Consecutive Yrs. of Multi Millions award Montgomery Area Bd. Realtors, 1990. Mem.: YMCA, AAUW, Greater Montgomery Home Builder Assn., Prattville C. of C., Montgomery Area C. of C., C.E.O. Roundtable, Jr. Twentieth Century Club, Mobile Yacht Club. Episcopalian. Avocations: reading, swimming, sailing. Office: Cassels Real Estate 623 S Perry St Montgomery AL 36104-5890

CASSENS, NICHOLAS, JR., ceramics engineer; b. Sigourney, Iowa, Sept. 8, 1948; s. Nicholas and Wanda Fern (Lancaster) C.; m. Linda Joyce Morrow, Aug. 30, 1969; 1 son, Randall Scott. BS in Ceramic Engring., BSChemE, Iowa State U., 1971; MS in Material Sci. and Engring., U. Calif., Berkeley, 1979. Jr. rsch. engr. Nat. Refractories and Minerals Corp., Livermore, Calif., 1971-72, rsch. engr., 1972-74, sr. rsch. engr., 1974—77, staff rsch. engr., 1977-84, sr. staff rsch. engr., 1984—2002; sr. mgr. product devel. Refractory and Advanced Specialties Inc., Stockton, Calif., 2003; quality assurance mgr. Cametoid Technologies. Inc., Alameda, Calif., 2004—. Mem. Am. Ceramic Soc. Democrat. Achievements include patentee in field U.S., Australia, S.Am., Japan, Europe. Home: 4082 Suffolk Way Pleasanton CA 94588-4117 Office: 818 McCloy Ave Rough and Ready Island Stockton CA 94550

CASSERLY, JAMES LUND, lawyer; b. Norfolk, Va., Dec. 26, 1951; s. James Robert and Patricia (Lund) C.; m. Kathleen Ann Flynn, Apr. 25, 1981; 1 child Laura Flynn. AB magna cum laude, Tufts Coll., 1973; JD, Columbia U., 1976. Bar: D.C. 1976, U.S. Dist. Ct. D.C. 1980, U.S. Ct. Appeals (D.C. cir.) 1981. Law clk. to trial judges U.S. Ct. Fed. Claims, Washington, 1976-77; law clk. to judge Marion Bennett U.S. Ct. Appeals Fed. Cir., Washington, 1977-78; assoc. Wilkinson, Cragun & Barker LLP, Washington, 1978-82, Squire Sanders & Dempsey, Washington, 1982-85, ptnr., 1985-94; sr. legal advisor to Commr. Susan Ness FCC, Washington, 1994-99; ptnr. Mintz Levin Cohn Ferris Glovsky & Popeo PC, Washington, 1999—2002, Willkie Farr & Gallagher LLP, Washington, 2003—. Home: 2839 Allendale Pl NW Washington DC 20008 Office: Willkie Farr & Gallagher LLP 1875 K St NW Washington DC 20006-1238 Office Phone: 202-303-1119. Personal E-mail: jlcasserly@aol.com. Business E-Mail: jcasserly@willkie.com.

CASSIDY, DONALD L., financial analyst; b. Cambridge, Mass., June 25, 1945; s. Francis Joseph and Ethel Dorothy (Lange) C. BS in Econs., U. Pa., 1967. Asst. to pres. Spear & Staff, Inc., Wellesley, Mass., 1973-74; sr. analyst Arthur D. Little Decision Resources, Cambridge, 1974-86; sr. research analyst Boettcher & Co., Inc., Denver, 1986, v.p., 1987-89; sr. analyst, mgr. closed-end funds svcs. Lipper Inc., Denver, 1990-95, mgr. money flows analysis, 1999—. Author: Plugging Into Utilities, 1993, It's When You Sell That Counts, 1996, 30 Strategies for High-Profit Investment Success, 1997, When the Dow Breaks, 1999, Trading on Volume, 2001. Umpire Little League Baseball, 1970-96; chmn. bd. dirs. Citizens for Ltd. Taxation, Boston, 1978-84, author, drafter tax-limitation initiative ballot question, 1980. Served with U.S. Army, 1968-70. Mem. Am. Assn. Individual Investors (nat. spkrs. bur.), Denver Soc. Securities Analysts, CFA Inst. (nat. spkrs. bur.). Libertarian.

CASSIDY, EUGENE PATRICK, pathologist; b. NYC, July 21, 1940; s. Eugene Zachary and Anita Hilda (Corsi) C.; m. Hollis Elizabeth Ward, Sept. 25, 1965; 1 child, Meredith. BA, Williams Coll., 1962; MD, Yale U., 1966. Diplomate Am. Bd. Pathology. Intern Yale-New Haven Hosp., Conn., 1966-67; resident then fellow in pathology and lab. medicine Yale U. Med. Ctr., 1967-70; dir. pathology Appalachian Lab. for Occupational Respitory Disease, Morgantown, Wis., 1970-72; pathologist Clarkson Hosp., Omaha, 1972-78, Scripps Hosp., Encinitas, Calif., 1978-84; dir. pathology Marshalltown (Iowa) Med. and Surgical Ctr., 1984—. Asst. prof. W.Va. U. Sch. Medicine, Morgantown, 1970-72, U. Nebr. Sch. Medicine, Omaha, 1974-78. Contbr. articles to profl. jours. Served with USPHS, 1970-72. Fellow Internat. Acad. Pathology, Coll. Am. Pathologists, Am. Soc. Clin. Pathologists; mem. AMA, Am. Assn. Blood Banks. Republican. Avocations: music, architecture. Home: 505 Craig Cir Marshalltown IA 50158-6303 Office: Marshalltown Med & Surg Ctr 3 S Fouth Ave Marshalltown IA 50158-2924 Business E-Mail: cassidy@marshmed.com.

CASSIDY, JACK, academic administrator, educator; b. Phila., Mar. 12, 1941; married; 2 children. BA in English, Gettysburg Coll., Phila., 1962; MEd in Secondary Edn., Temple U., Phila., 1965, PhD in Ednl. Psychology, 1975. Tchr. Hawaii Dept. Pub. Instrn., Island Kauai, Lihue, 1965-69; instr. Temple U., 1970-71; reading supr. Newark (Del.) Sch. Dist., 1972-78; prof. Millersville (Pa.) U., 1998; assoc. dean coll. Edn. Tex. A&M Univ., Corpus Christi, 1998—. Spl. cons. Ednl. Testing Svc., 1977-93. Sr. author: Basic Life Skills, Macmillan Lit. Series, Read-Reason-Write, Scribner Reading Series; contbr. articles to profl. jours. Coach Community Swim Teams, Kapaa, Hawaii, 1967-68. Mem. Internat. Reading Assn. (legis. com. 1975-76, dir. 1976-79, pres. 1982-83), Diamond State Reading Assn. (pres. 1974-75), Nat. Coun. Tchrs. English, Assn. for Supervision and Curriculum Devel., Nat. Coun. Accreditation Tchr. Edn. (exec. bd. 1986-88, chmn. 1988-89, 1997-2000), Coll. Reading Assn. (dir. 1994-97, pres. 1999-2000), Phi Delta Kappa. Home: 322 Santa Monica Pl Corpus Christi TX 78411-1612 Office: Early Childhood Devel Ctr Tex A&M Univ 6300 Ocean Dr Corpus Christi TX 78412-5503 Office Phone: 361-825-5611. Business E-Mail: jcassidy@falcon.tamucc.edu.

CASSIDY, JAMES MARK, construction company executive; b. Evanston, Ill., June 22, 1942; s. James Michael and Mary Ellen (Munroe) C.; m. Bonnie Marie Bercker, Aug. 1, 1964 (div. Dec. 1981); children: Micaela Marie, Elizabeth Ann, Daniel James; m. Patricia Margaret Mary Murphy, Sept. 15, 1984. BA, St. Mary's Coll., 1963. Estimator Cassidy Bros., Inc., Rosemont, Ill., 1963-65, project mgr., 1965-67, v.p., 1967-71, exec. v.p., 1971-77, pres., 1978—. Trustee Plasterer's Health & Welfare Trust, 1971-92; chmn. labor liaison com. Laborers Internat. Union N.Am. and Assn. Wall and Ceiling Industries, 1982-85, chmn. labor-mgmt. group, 1985-88; chmn. Chicagoland Assn. Wall and Ceiling Contractors' Carpenters Union Negotiating Team, 1983—; trustee, vice chmn. laborers dist. coun. Chgo. and Vicinity Laborers-Employers Cooperation and Edn. Trust Fund, 1999—. Area fund leader

Constrn. Industry Salute to Boy Scouts Am., 1975; mem. president's coun. St. Mary's Coll. With U.S. Army, 1963-64, N.G., 1964-69. Mem. Chgo. Plastering Inst., Builder Uppers Club (pres. 1973-74), Chicagoland Assn. Wall and Ceiling Contractors (pres. 1976-79), Great Lakes Coun., Internat. Assn. Wall and Ceiling Contractors (chmn. 1977), Constrn. Employers Assn. Chgo. (bd. dirs. 1976—, pres.-elect 1989-90, pres. 1991-93, chmn. com. labor-mgmt. rels. 1983-93), Chicagoland Safety Coun. (bd. dirs. 1988-92), Joint Conf. Bd. Cook County (chmn. 1996-97, 98-99, 2003-04), Assn. Wall and Ceiling Industries Internat. (bd. dirs. 1978-81, 88-89, fin. v.p. 1990, 2d v.p. 1991, pres.-elect 1992, pres. 1993), Park Ridge County Club (Ill.) (bd. dirs. 1994-97), Eagle Creek Country Club (Naples, Fla.).

CASSIDY, JOHN FRANCIS, JR., industrial technology executive; b. Troy, N.Y., Nov. 26, 1943; s. John F. Sr. and Beverly A. (Blowers) C.; m. Paulina C. DiBacco, July 24, 1965; children: Rachel, Sean. BEE, Rensselaer Poly. Inst., 1965, MEE, 1967, PhD, 1969. Various R & D mgmt. positions GM, 1969-81; with control systems R & D GE Corp. R & D Labs., 1981-89; corp. dir. tech. mgmt. United Techs. Corp., 1989-92; dir. United Techs. Rsch. Ctr., 1992-93, v.p., 1993-98; sr. v.p. sci. and tech. United Techs. Corp., Hartford, Conn., 1998—. Bd. mem. Conn. Tech. Council; corp. mem. Charles Stark Draper Lab., Inc, Cambridge; mem. adv. bd. Georgia Tech Research Inst. Mem.: Soc. of Automotive Engrs., IEEE, Conn. Acad. of Sci. and Engring. Office: United Techs Rsch Ctr MS 129-04 411 Silver Ln East Hartford CT 06118-1127 E-mail: cassidjf@utrc.utc.com.

CASSIDY, JOHN HAROLD, lawyer; b. St. Louis, June 18, 1925; s. John Harold and Jennie (Phillips) C.; m. Marjorie Blair, Nov. 26, 1947; children: Patricia, John, Brian. AB, Washington U., 1949, JD, 1951. Bar: Mo. 1951, U.S. Dist. Ct. (ea. dist.) Mo. 1951, U.S. Ct. Appeals (8th crct.) 1951, U.S. Supreme Ct. 1955. Atty. U.S. Govt., St. Louis, 1951-56; pvt. practice St. Louis, 1956-59; atty. Crown Zellerbach Corp., San Francisco, 1959-61, Ralston Purina Co., St. Louis, 1961-89, v.p., 1975-85, v.p., sec., sr. counsel, 1985-89. Served with U.S. Mcht. Marine, 1943-45. Mem.: ABA, Am. Soc. Corp. Secs., St. Louis Bar Assn., Mo. Bar Assn. Republican.

CASSIDY, MIKE, online game company executive; Student in piano, Berkelee Coll. Music, Boston; BS in Aerospace Engring., MIT, 1985, MS in Aerospace Engring., 1986; MBA, Harvard Bus. Sch., 1991. Co-founder, CEO Stylus Innovation (acquired by Artisoft in 1996), Direct Hit (acquired by Ask Jeeves in 2000), Ultimate Arena (now Xfire, Inc). Spkr. in fields of tech. and online gaming. Office: Xfire Inc 200 Middlefield Rd Ste 102 Menlo Park CA 94025

CASSIDY, RICHARD ARTHUR, environmental engineer, water resources specialist; b. Manchester, N.H., Nov. 15, 1944; s. Arthur Joseph and Alice Ethuliette (Gregoire) C.; m. Judith Diane Maine, Aug. 14, 1971; children: Matthew, Amanda, Michael. BA, St. Anselm Coll., 1966; MS, U. N.H., 1969, Tufts U., 1972. Field biologist Pub. Svc. Co. N.H., Manchester, 1968; jr. san. engr. Mass. Divsn. Water Pollution Control, Boston, 1968-69; aquatic biologist Normandeau Assocs., Bedford, N.H., 1969-70; hydraulic engr. New Eng. divsn. U.S. Army Civil Engrs., Waltham, Mass., 1972-77; engr. northwestern divsn. Portland (Oreg.) dist. U.S. Army Civil Engrs., 1977-81, supr., environ. engr., 1981-99, environ. engr. northwestern divsn. Portland, 2000—03; ptnr. Am. Voyageur Enterprises, Beaverton, Oreg., 2003—. Interpretive guide, 2003—; cons. water resources specialist, 2003—. Contbr. articles to books and profl. jours. Den leader Cascade Pacific coun. Cub Scouts Am., Beaverton, Oreg., 1982-83, Webelos leader, 1984-85, 90-91, troop committeeman, 1985-87, asst. scoutmaster, 1992, scoutmaster, 1993-94, 95-2001; mem. Planning Commn. Hudson, N.H., 1976-77. Recipient commendation for exemplary performance Mo.-Miss. flood, 1973, commendation for litigation defense, 1986, commendation for mgmt. activities, 1987, 1991, Comdr.'s award for civilian svc., 1997, Achievement medal for civilian svc., 2000, Silver Beaver award, Boy Scouts Am., 2003. Mem. Am. Inst. Hydrology (cert., profl. ethics com. 1986, v.p. Oreg. sect. 1987-89, pres. Oreg. sect. 1990-92, nat. treas. 1995-2000), Internat. Tng. in Comm. (pres. West Way Club 1989-90), Nat. Assn. for Interpretation (cert.). Home: 7655 SW Belmont Dr Beaverton OR 97008-6335 Office: Am Voyageur Enterprises 7655 SW Belmont Dr Beaverton OR 97008 Office Phone: 503-646-0958. E-mail: cassidy@historytoursnw.com, richardcassidy@comcast.net.

CASSIDY, ROBERT CHARLES, JR., lawyer; b. Beaumont, Tex., May 16, 1946; s. Robert Charles and Peggy (Timken) C.; m. Leslie Fleming Iben, Sept. 2, 1949; children: Robert Charles III, Thomas Reinhard, Leslie Anne Vallandingham. BA, Johns Hopkins U., 1968; JD, U. Pa., 1973; LLM, Georgetown U., 1977. Bar: Pa. 1973, U.S. Dist. Ct. D.C. 1975, U.S. Ct. Appeals (D.C. cir.) 1975, U.S. Ct. Internat. Trade 1982, U.S. Ct. Appeals (fed. cir.) 1982. Asst. counsel Office of Legis. Counsel U.S. Senate, 1973-75, internat. trade counsel Com. on Fin., 1975-79; gen. counsel Office of U.S. Trade Rep., Exec. Office of Pres., Washington, 1979-81; ptnr. Kaye, Scholer, Fierman, Hays & Handler, Washington, 1982-83, Wilmer Cutler Pickering Hale and Dorr, Washington, 1983—, trade group leader, 1985—2001, internat. practice group leader, 1995—2000. With U.S. Army, 1968—70. Mem.: ABA (chmn. internat. trade law com. 1986—89), Am. Soc. Internat. Law., D.C. Bar Assn. Office: Wilmer Cutler Pickering Hale and Dorr 2445 M St NW Washington DC 20037-1487 Office Phone: 202-663-6740. Business E-Mail: Robert.Cassidy@wilmerhale.com.

CASSIDY, SAMUEL H., lawyer, humanities educator; children: Rachael, Sarah, Samuel H. IV. BA, U. Okla., 1972; JD, U. Tulsa, 1975; postgrad., Harvard U., 1991. Bar: Okla., 1975, U.S. Supreme Ct. 1977, U.S. Ct. Appeals (10th cir.), 1977, Colo. 1982. Pvt. practice law, 1975—; mem. Colo. State Senate, 1991-94; lt. gov. State of Colo., 1994-95; pres. Jefferson Econ. Coun., 1995-97; pres., CEO Colo. Assn. Commerce and Industry, 1997-2000; chair dept. bus. ethics and legal studies U. Denver, 2001—. Bd. dirs. Capital Reporter; instr. U. Tulsa, 1978-81, Tulsa Jr. Coll., 1979; owner High Country Title Co.; developer of residential and commercial real estate, pres. Sam Cassidy, Inc. oil and gas exploration and production co., mem. agriculture and natural resources com., 1991-92, state, mil. and vet. affairs com., 1991-92, local govt. com. 1991, legal svcs. com. 1991-92, hwy. legis. review com. 1991-93, nat. hazards mitigation coun., 1992-93, appropriations com., 1993, judiciary com., 1993; pres. Econ. Devel. Coun. of Colo., 1997-98; exec. com. legis coun., 1993-94, senate svcs. com. 1993; elected Senate Minority Leader, 1993-94, exec. com. Colo. Gen. Assembly; sr. fellow U. Denver, 1997—. Bd. dirs. Colo. DLC, 1993-95, Leadership Jefferson County, Rocky Flats Local Impacts Initiative, dir.; chmn. bd. Arts Comm., Inc. Named Outstanding Legislator for 1991 Colo. Bankers Assn., ACLU Outstanding Legis. 1994; recipient Outsatnding Legis. Efforts award Colo. Counties, Guardian of Small Bus. award, NFIB, 1992, 94; fellow Gates Found., 1991, U. Denver sr. fellow. Mem. Colo. Bar Assn. (bd. gov. 1993-94), S.W. Colo. Bar Assn., Nat. Conf. State Legis. (Colo. rep., task force on state-tribe rels.), Rotary (hon. mem., sustaining Paul Harris fellow), Club 20 (bd. dirs.), San Juan Forum (chmn., bd. dirs.). Avocations: fine art photography, skiing, fishing. Home: # 128 2800 S University Blvd Denver CO 80210 E-mail: scassidy@du.edu. *Leaders must nurture the positive. They must identify and promote issues which concern the whole community and the future of their grandchildren. They cannot indulge themselves in the profits of the politics of division. This is a vision which is hard to sell next November but which clearly distinguishes leaders from politicians.*

CASSIDY, SUZANNE BLETTERMAN, medical educator; b. N.Y.C., Jan. 12, 1944; d. Maurice and Helene (Soldinger) Bletterman; m. Paul Stark Cassidy, June 25, 1969; 1 child, Joshua Kemp Cassidy; m. Dale Alan Kirshnitz, May 29, 1988. BA, Reed Coll., Portland, Oreg., 1965; MS, Vanderbilt U., Nashville, Tenn., 1973, MD, 1976. Diplomate Am. Bd. Med. Genetics, Am. Bd. Pediatrics. Resident in pediatrics U. Wash., Seattle, 1977-79, fellow in med. genetics, 1979-81; asst. prof. pediatrics U. Conn., Farmington, 1981-87, assoc. prof., 1987-88, asst. prof. ob-gyn., 1986-88, dir. div. med. genetics, dept. pediatrics, 1984-88; assoc. prof. pediatrics U. Ariz., Tucson, 1988—, dir. genetics fellowship tng. program, 1988—. Bd. dirs. Prader-Willi Syndrome Assn., St. Louis Park, Minn. Editor newsletter Mountain States Regional Genetics Network, 1988—; contbr. numerous articles to med. jours., chpts. to books. March of Dimes, Birth Defects Found. grantee, 1985, 86, 87. Mem. Am. Soc. Human Genetics, Am. Acad. Pediatrics, Teratology Soc., Western Soc. Human Genetics, Am. Bd. Med. Genetics, Am. Bd. Pediatrics. Democrat. Jewish. Avocations: fashion, interior design.

CASSIDY, VICTOR MONOD, editor, writer, curator, art critic; b. Madison, Wis., Nov. 30, 1940; s. Frederic Gomes and Helene Lucille (Monod) C.; m. Ingrid Louise Hammer, Mar. 1962 (dec. 1964); 1 child, Alexander; m. Naomi Neusues, Aug. 4, 1969 (div. 1977); 1 child, Mark; m. Donna Marie Hapac, Feb. 18, 1984. BA in English, Columbia U., 1962; MA in Econs., U. Wis., 1966. With Motorola, Inc., Chgo., 1966-69; editor Ency. Brit., Chgo., 1969-72; writer, rschr., Ithaca, N.Y., 1972-74; tech. editor Sargent & Lundy, Chgo., 1974-80; sr. editor Specifying Engr. Cahners Inc., Des Plaines, Ill., 1980-84; editor Modern Metals Mag. Delta Comms., Chgo., 1984-95; prin. Market Advantage, 1995-97; mng. editor Software Strategies mag. Putman Pub. Co., Chgo., 1997—. Panelist Ill. Arts Coun., Chgo., 1979-80. Contbr. articles to profl. jours.; appears in ArtNet.com, Art in America, Black & White, Sculpture. Bd. dirs. Chgo. Chamber Choir, 1977-80, Chgo. New Art Assn., 1982-85, Chgo. String Ensemble, 1981-83, N.A.M.E. Gallery, Chgo., 1981-84, Art Encounter, 1995-97. NEH rsch. grantee, 1972-73; recipient awards Ill. Arts Coun., 1988, 90, Graham Found., 1990. Mem.: Chgo. Art Critics Assn. Republican. Roman Catholic. Avocations: curating, organizing art exhibitions. Home: 4922 N Moody Ave Chicago IL 60630-2912 E-mail: 2717west@cocentric.net.*

CASSIDY, WILLIAM ARTHUR, geology and planetary science educator; b. NYC, Jan. 3, 1928; s. John and Nellie (Briel) C.; m. Beverly J. Griffith, Aug. 29, 1959; children: Shauna Lynne, Laura Dawn, Brian John. BS in Geology, U. N. Mex., 1952; PhD in Geochemistry, Pa. State U., 1961. Seismic computer Superior Oil Co. of Calif., Midland, Tex., 1952-53; research scientist Lamont Geol. Obs., Palisades, N.Y., 1961-67; assoc. prof. geology and planetary sci. U. Pitts., 1968-80, prof., 1981-98, prof. emeritus, 1998—. Trustee Univ. Space Research Assn., Columbia, Md., 1975-82, chmn., 1978-79; chmn. meteorite working group Lunar and Planetary Sci. Inst., Houston, 1977-83 Author: Meteorites, Ice and Antarctica, 2003; contbr. articles to profl. jours. Served with USNR, 1945-46. Recipient Antarctic Svc. medal NSF, 1978; Fulbright student, 1953-54; grantee NSF, NASA. Mem. Am. Geophys. Union, Meteoritical Soc. (Barringer award 1995), Antarctican Soc. (Washington). Office: U Pitts 200 Space Research Coordination Ctr Pittsburgh PA 15620-3332 Office Phone: 412-624-8886. Business E-Mail: ansmet@pitt.edu.

CASSILL, HERBERT CARROLL, artist; b. Percival, Iowa, Dec. 24, 1928; s. Howard Earl and Mary Elizabeth (Glosser) C.; m. Jean Kuniko Kubota, Aug. 23, 1951; children: Sarah Elizabeth, J. Aaron. Student, Purdue U., 1944-45; B.F.A., State U. Iowa, 1948, M.F.A., 1950. Instr. printmaking State U. Iowa, Iowa City, 1953-57; prof., head dept. printmaking Cleve. Inst. Art, 1957-91, prof. emeritus, 1991—. One man shows include Oakland (Calif.) Art Mus., Ohio State U., Columbus, Cleve. Inst. Art, U. Wis., William Busta Gallery, 1990, 93, 96, 2001; group shows include Library of Congress, Washington, Bklyn. Art Mus., Bradford Internat. Invitational, 1984; represented in permanent collections, Mus. Modern Art, N.Y.C., Cleve. Mus. Art, Oakland Art Mus., San Francisco Art Mus., and others. Tiffany fellow printmaking, 1953 Home: 3084 Coleridge Rd Cleveland OH 44118-3556 Office: 11141 East Blvd Cleveland OH 44106-1710 E-mail: hcprint@hotmail.com.

CASSIMATIS, PETER JOHN, economics professor; b. Greece, Jan. 30, 1928; came to U.S., 1946, naturalized, 1946; s. John G. and Coula N. (Lourantos) C.; m. Margaret Ann Nell, Nov. 30, 1958; 1 son, Gregory. BCE, CUNY, 1953, MBA, 1961; PhD, New Sch. Social Research, 1967. Registered profl. engr., N.Y.; cert. cost analyst. Project mgr. several mgmt. and engring. cons. firms, 1953-64; prof. econs. and finance Fairleigh Dickinson U., Teaneck, N.J., 1964-99, emeritus prof. econs. and finance, 1999—. Vis. prof. Center for Planning and Econ. Research, Athens, Greece, 1972-73 Author: Economics of the Construction Industry, 1970, Construction and Economic Development, 1975, The Construciton Industry in Greece, 1976, Engineering Economics, 1988, Managerial Economics, 1996; contbr. articles to profl. jours. Served with AUS, 1946-47. Research fellow Found. Econ. Edn., 1970 Mem. Am. Econ. Assn., Eastern Econ. Assn., Nat. Assn. Bus. Economists, Acad. Internat. Bus., World Future Soc., Fin. Mgmt. Assn. Home: 19 Lorraine Dr Eastchester NY 10709-2008 Office: Fairleigh Dickinson U Economics Dept Teaneck NJ 07666

CASSINELLI, JOSEPH PATRICK, astronomy educator; b. Cin., Aug. 23, 1940; s. Herbert John and Louise Margaret (Schlottman) C.; m. Mary LeFever; children: Joseph Michael, Carolyn Marie, Mary Kathleen. BS in Physics, Xavier U., 1962; MS in Physics, U. Ariz., 1965; PhD in Astronomy, U. Wash., 1970. Research asst. Kitt Peak Nat. Obs., Tucson, 1963-65; research engr. Boeing Co., Seattle, 1965-66; postdoctoral research assoc. Joint Inst. for Lab. Astrophysics, Boulder, Colo., 1970-72; postdoctoral fellow U. Wis., Madison, 1972-73, asst. prof., 1973-77, assoc. prof., 1977-81, prof., 1981—, chmn. astronomy dept., 1986-89. Vis. scientist Space Astronomy Lab., Utrecht, the Netherlands, 1975-76, Space Telescope Sci. Inst., 1991, High Altitude Obs., 1998; Donders chair U. Utrecht, 1985; sr. vis. fellow dept. physics and astronomy U. Glasgow, Scotland, 1998. Co-author: Introduction to Stellar Winds, 1999. Langley Abbot research fellow Harvard Smithsonian Ctr. for Astrophysics, 1981; Fulbright research fellow Sonnenborgh Obs., 1986. Mem. Am. Astron. Soc., Internat. Astron. Union. Roman Catholic. Home: 1520 Chandler St Madison WI 53711-2210 Office: U Wis Astronomy Dept 475 N Charter St Madison WI 53706-1582 Business E-Mail: cassinelli@astro.wisc.edu.

CASSITY, MICHAEL DAVID, music therapy educator; b. Alexandria, Va., Oct. 18, 1945; s. Dale Max and Lucile Bessie Cassity; m. Julia Ellen Cravey, July 1, 1989; children: Sharel, Christopher, Austin. BA in Psychology, S.W. Bapt. U., Bolivar, Mo., 1971; M in Music Therapy, Loyola U., New Orleans, 1975; PhD, U. Iowa, 1985. Cert. music therapist. Music therapy intern S.E. La. Hosp., Mandeville, 1974; supr. edn. Belle Chasse (La.) State Sch., 1975—77; grad. asst. music therapy U. Iowa, Iowa City, 1977—79; asst. prof. music therapy Slippery Rock (Pa.) State U., 1979—81; prof., dir. music therapy S.W. Okla. State U., Weatherford, 1981—2001; prof., dir. music therapy dept. Drury U., Springfield, Mo., 2001—. Pianist S.W. Playhouse Theater, Clinton, Okla., 1998—2001; prof. emeritus Bd. Regents of Okla. Colls., Oklahoma City, 2001. Author: Multimodal Psychiatric Music Therapy, 1998; contbr. articles to profl. jours. Grant writer Barry Count Bd. for Developmentally Disabled, 2004, Lawrence County Bd. for Developmentally Disabled, 2004. Served with N.G., 1966—71. Mem.: Am. Music Therapy Assn. (pres. S.W. Region 1985—87, editl. bd. Jour. Music Therapy 2001—, assembly of dels. 1996—2001, Hon. award for outstanding contbns. to rsch. 1998). Republican. Baptist. Avocations: piloting private plane, playing jazz piano. Home: 4598 S Quail Creek Ave Springfield MO 65810 Office: Drury U 900 N Benton Ave Springfield MO 65802 Office Phone: 417-873-7370. E-mail: mcassity@drury.edu.

CASSO, JAMES C., social worker, mental health services professional; b. Berlin, Conn., Apr. 1, 1978; s. Joseph P. and Hedwig Casso. MSW, U. of Conn., 2002—04. Psychology rsch. asst. So. Conn. State U., New Haven, 2000—01; vocat. counselor Cmty. Mental Health Affiliates, Bristol, Conn., 2002—. DeBlois Found. scholarship, Dairy Mart, 1998—2001. D-Liberal. Avocations: music, hiking, mountain biking, weightlifting.

CASSO, RAMIRO RAUL, retired physician, academic administrator; b. Laredo, Tex., Aug. 4, 1922; s. Francisco Margarito and Josefa (Villarreal) C.; m. Emma Laurel, July 18, 1949; children: Thelma Casso Morales, Lydia Casso Tummel, Sylvia Casso Filoteo, Daniel, David. *Biographee is tenth generation maternal descendant of Captain Diego de Villarreal, of Viscaya, Spain, the first Villarreal to settle in Northern Mexico, about 1590. Biographee is third generation maternal descendant of Anastacio Villarreal, who in 1767 settled in Spanish land-grant, Porcion 43, with Rio Grande River frontage, in what is today western Hidalgo County, Texas. Dr. and Mrs. Emma Laurel Casso have five married children: Thelma (Pete); Lydia (Ken); Sylvia (divorced); Daniel (Araceli); David (Vicki). Grandchildren: Marcus and Michelle Morales; Evan and Kurt Tummel; Christopher and Sabrina Filoteo; Andrew and Matthew Casso; Allie and Jake Casso.* BSME, Tex. A&M U., 1943; BA in Chemistry, Baylor U., 1952; MD, U. Tex., Dallas, 1956. Diplomate Am. Bd. Family Practice. Hydraulic engr. Internat. Boundary and Water Commn., Laredo, 1948-50; tchr. math. Martin H.S., Laredo, 1946-48; med. intern Robert B. Green Hosp., San Antonio, 1956-57; pvt. family med. practice McAllen, Tex., 1957—95; ret., 1995; v.p. instnl. advancement South Tex. C.C., Hidalgo-Starr County C.C. Dist., McAllen, 1995—2002. Adj. prof. Tex. A&M U. Health Sci. Ctr., 1999-2004; bd. dirs. McAllen Mcpl. Hosp./McAllen Med. Ctr. Hosp., 1975-85; founder, bd. dirs. Hidalgo County Health Care Corp., 1975-85; mem. nat. adv. bd. health rsch. facilities NIH, Washington, 1964-67; participant White House Confs. on Food and Food Nutrition and Health, Washington, 1965-69; spkr. on pub. health and primary care issues pertaining to South Tex. and U.S.-Mex. borderlands; presenter Hispanic health issues position Tex. Minority Health Conf., Houston, 1999. Mem. McAllen Ind. Sch. Dist. Sch. Bd., 1959-65; mem., v.p. Tex. Bd. Health, Austin, 1977-81, 91-97; mem. Texas Human (Employment) Rights Commn., Austin, 1983-87; established charity clinic for farm workers United Farmworkers, McAllen, 1970; bd. dirs. Area Health Edn. Ctr., 1997-98; pres., bd. dirs. El Milagro Clinic Bd., 1998—; founder El Milagro Primary Care Clinic, McAllen, Tex., 2000. Capt. anti-aircraft arty. U.S. Army, 1943-46. Named McAllen Man of Yr., McAllen C. of C., 1996, Notable Rio Grande Valley Hispanic, U. Tex.-PanAm., Edinburg, 1999, 100 Outstanding Hispanic-Ams. in Tex. in 20th Century Latino Monthly Mag., 2000; recipient Bishop Medeiros Golden Deeds award Tex. AFL-CIO and United Farmworkers, 1970, yearly award Hidalgo County Women's Polit. Caucus, 1991, Disting. Citizen award League United L.Am. Citizens, 1997, Living Legend award South Tex. C.C., 2002, Golden Trowel Masonic award City of Rio Grande and McAllen Tex. Lodges, 2003; Dr. Ramiro R. Casso S.T.C.C. Nursing and Allied Health Ctr. bldg. named in his honor, 2001. Fellow Am. Acad. Family Physicians; mem. AMA (life), Tex. Med. Assn. (life). Democrat. Baptist. Avocations: travel, reading, hunting, fishing. Home: 3400 W Pecan Mcallen TX 78501 Office: El Milagro Clinic 1001 E Vermont St Mcallen TX 78501

CASSON, ALAN GRAHAM, thoracic surgeon, researcher; b. Birmingham, Eng., Apr. 22, 1958; arrived in Can., 1981; m. Sharon Margaret Coffey; 1 child, Angela. MB ChB, Manchester (Eng.) U., 1981; MSc, Meml. U., St. John's, Nfld., Can., 1986. Asst. prof. surgery and oncology U. Western Ont., Canada, 1991-93; asst. prof. surgery, program dir. thoracic surgery U. Toronto, Canada, 1994-97; prof. thoracic surgery U. of Warwick, England, 1997-98; cons. thoracic surgery Heartlands Hosp., Birmingham, England, 1997-98; prof. surgery, head divsn. thoracic surgery Dalhousie U., Halifax, Canada, 1998—. Author: Oncogene Activation in Esophageal Cancer, 1992, Key Topics in Thoracic Surgery, 1999, Molecular Biology of Cancer, 2004; mem. editl. bd. Jour. Surg. Oncology, Diseases of the Esophagus; contbr. chpts. to surg. textbooks and articles to profl. jours. Fellow ACS, Royal Coll. Surgeons Can., Am. Coll. Chest Physicians (Young Investigator award 1993); mem. Internat. Soc. for Diseases of the Esophagus, Am. Assn. for Thoracic Surgery, Am. Assn. Cancer Rsch., Soc. Thoracic Surgeons. Avocations: fly fishing, squash, sailing. Office: Divsn Thoracic Surg 1278 Twr Rd Victoria Bldg 7-008 Halifax NS Canada B3H 2Y9 Office Phone: 902-473-2281. Business E-Mail: thoracic@dal.ca.

CASSON, RICHARD FREDERICK, lawyer, hotel executive; b. Boston, Apr. 11, 1939; s. Louis H. and Beatrix S. C. AB, Colby Coll., 1960; JD, U. Chgo., 1963. Bar: Ill. 1963, Mass. 1964. Ptnr. Casson & Casson, Boston, 1967-68; assoc. counsel, corp. sec. Bankers Leasing Corp., 1968-75; asst. gen. counsel, corp. sec. Commonwealth Planning Corp., 1975-76; assoc. gen. counsel, asst. sec. Prudential Capital Corp., 1976-92; pres. Autumn Crest Corp., 1991-98; v.p. Casseden Corp. Asst. innkeeper Jackson House Inn, Woodstock, Vt. Capt. JAGC U.S. Army, 1964-67. Decorated Bronze Star. Jewish. Home and Office: 6648 John Smith Ln Hayes VA 23072 E-mail: rfcasson@verizon.net.

CASSON MADDEN, CHRIS, entrepreneur, interior designer; m. J. Kevin Madden; children: Patrick, Nick. Student, Fashion Inst. Tech. Founder, CEO Chris Madden, Inc., Rye, NY, 1995—; photographer Sports Illustrated; with Random House, G.P. Putnam & Sons, Farrar, Straus & Giroux. Design expert Today Show, Good Morning Am., Oprah, CBS Sunday Morning, CNN; nat. spokesperson JC Penny Home Collection, 2003—. Author: The Complete Lemon, 1979, The Summer House Cookbook, 1979, Baby Hints Handbook, 1982, Baby's First Helpings: Super-Healthy Meals for Super-Healthy Kids, 1984, Kitchens: Information and Inspiration for Making the Kitchen the Heart of the Home, 1993, Bathrooms: Inspiring Ideas and Practical Solutions for Creating a Beautiful Bathroom, 1996, Chris Madden's Guide to Personalizing Your Home: Simple, Beautiful Ideas for Every Room, 1997, A Room of Her Own: Women's Personal Spaces, Clarkson Potter, 1997, Getaways: Carefree Retreats for All Seasons, 2000, Bedrooms: Creating the Stylish Comfortable Room of Your Dreams, 2001, Chris Casson Madden's New American Living Rooms, 2003; co-author: Interior Visions: Great American Designers and the Showcase House, 1988, Rooms With a View: Two Decades of Outstanding American Interior Design from the Kips Bay Decorator Show Houses, 1995, Interior Details: The Designers' Style, 1996; columnist: Interiors by Design; host (TV series) Interiors By Design, HGTV, 1995—.

CASSTEVENS, CHARLES FRANKLIN, JR., music educator, minister; b. Elkin, N.C., Jan. 25, 1964; s. Charles Franklin and Nonnie Etta Casstevens; m. Holly Anne Hykes, Sept. 26, 1998; 1 child, Trevor Jordan. BS in Music and Bus., Wingate (N.C.) U., 1986; MAT, Winthrop U., 1993. Min. to music/youth Mineral Springs Bapt. Ch., Jonesville, NC, 1982; min. to youth South Florence (S.C.) Bapt. Ch., 1985; ch. accompanist Union Bapt. Ch., Monroe, NC, 1985; min. to music/youth New Salem Bapt. Ch., Monroe, 1985—; music specialist Benton Heights Elem. Sch., Monroe, 1986—. Accompanist Charlotte (N.C.) Children's Choir, 1998; chmn. youth com. Union Bapt. Assn., Monroe, 2001—; chmn. site base Benton Heights Elem. Sch., Monroe, 2002—, chmn. splty. areas, 2003—. Named Tchr. of Yr., Benton Heights Elem. Sch., 1995. Mem.: Music Educators Nat. Conf. Republican. Baptist. Avocations: tennis, arts events, travel. Home: 1507 Buena Vista Dr Monroe NC 28112 Office: Benton Heights Elem Sch 1200 Concord Ave Monroe NC 28110 Office Phone: 704-296-3100. Office Fax: 704-296-3106. E-mail: music4cfcj@aol.com.

CASSULLO, JOANNE LEONHARDT, foundation administrator; b. Glen Cove, NY, Dec. 2, 1955; d. John Louis and Dorothea Louise (Leonhardt) C. BA in English, Elementary Ed., & Fine Arts, Roanoke Coll., Salem, Va., 1978; MFA, So. Meth. U., 1982. Cert. tchr. elem. edn., Va. Dir. counseling and edn. PCI, Inc., Ft. Worth, 1978-80; gallery asst. Washburn Gallery, Inc., NYC, 1983-86; pres. Dorothea L. Leonhardt Found., NYC, 1988—. Contbr. articles to profl. jours. Trustee Whitney Mus. Am. Art, NYC, 1985—, v.p.; bd. dirs. Phoenix House Found., Inc., NYC, 1982—, Bklyn. Acad. Music, 1989—, Children of Alcoholics Found., NYC, 1990—, RxART, Children's Advocacy Ctr. of Manhattan, Housing Enterprises for Less Privileged (HELP USA). Helena Rubinstein fellow in Mus. Studies, Whitney Mus. Am. Art, 1982-83. Mailing: c/o Whitney Mus Am Art 945 Madison Ave New York NY 10021*

CAST, ANITA HURSH, small business owner; b. Columbus, Ohio, July 11, 1939; d. Charles Walter and Hulda Marie (Ramsey) Hursh; m. William R. Cast, Apr. 1, 1961; children: Jennifer, Carter, Meghan. BA, DePauw U., 1961. Ptnr. Cast Hursh and Assocs., Ft. Wayne, Ind., 1982—; pianist Words and Music, Ft. Wayne, 1983—; owner Anita Cast's Wearable Art, Ft. Wayne, 1986—. Bd. dirs. Fort Wayne Philharm., Indpls. Internat. Violin Competition; past pres. Ind. U. Friends of Music, Ind. Endowment for the Arts; mem. adv. bd. Leadership Ft. Wayne. Author: (arts section) New History of Fort Wayne. Advisory bd., pres. Am. Symphony Orch. League, vol., v.p., 1985—86;

commr. Ind. Gov.'s Mansion Commn., 1987, Ind. Arts Commn., 1979—87; bd. dirs. Ft. Wayne Philharm., pres., 1977—79; mem. Mayor's Bicentennial Exec. Bd., 1989—94, Ind. Cultural Congress Hon. Com.; active Ft. Wayne's Celebrate 2000 Com.; bd. dirs. WBNI Nat. Pub. Radio, Ft. Wayne; chmn. bd. dirs. Fine Arts Found., Ft. Wayne, 1988; pres. bd. dirs. Ind. Endowment Arts; chmn. bd. dirs. Arts United Greater Ft. Wayne, 1988—90; bd. dirs. Arts United; pres., bd. dirs. Ind. U. Friends Music, 1995—97, past pres. exec. com.; v.p. adv. bd. Leadership Ft. Wayne; pres. Met. YMCA, Ft. Wayne, 1986—. Named Miss Ind.; recipient Sagamore of the Wabash awards (2); Lily Endowment Leadership fellow. Mem.: Quest Club (pres.), Duodecimo Club (hon.). Republican. Episcopalian. Avocations: music, cooking, golf, hiking, reading. Home and Office: Anita Cast Wearable Art 4401 Taylor St Fort Wayne IN 46804-1913

CASTAGNA, VANESSA J., retail executive; b. Muncie, Ind., 1949; m. Neil Castagna. BS in psychology and speech comm., Purdue U., 1971. With Lazarus most recently as sr. v.p. and gen. mgr., 1972—85; v.p. merchandising - women's Target Stores, 1985—92; sr. v.p., gen. merchandising mgr. - women's and jr.'s Marshall's Stores, Mass., 1992—94; sr. v.p., gen. mdse. mgr. - home decor, furniture, crafts, children's apparel Wal-Mart Stores, Bentonville, Ark., 1994—96, sr. v.p., gen. mdse. mgr. - women's and children's accessories and apparel, 1996—99; exec. v.p. J.C. Penney Co., Inc., Plano, Tex., 1999—2004; COO JC Penney Stores, Merchandising, & Catalog, 1999—2001; pres., COO J.C. Penney Stores, Catalog, & Internet, 2001—03; chmn., CEO JC Penney Stores, Catalog, & Internet, 2003—04; chmn. Mervyns, 2005—; with Cerberus Capital Management LP, 2005—. Chair Women's Leadership Coun. United Way of Met. Dallas; bd. dirs. JC Penney Afterschool Fund, Nat. Minority Supplier Devel. Coun., Cox Sch. Bus. So. Methodist U. Named one of most powerful women, Forbes mag., 2005. Office: Cerberus Capital Mgmt 299 Park Ave New York NY 10171*

CASTAGNA, WILLIAM JOHN, federal judge; Student, U. Pa., 1941-43; LLB, JD, U. Fla., 1949. Bar: Fla. 1949. Ptnr. MacKenzie, Castagna, Bennison & Gardner, 1970-79; judge U.S. Dist. Judge (mid. dist.) Fla., 1979—, now sr. judge. Democrat.

CASTALDI, DAVID LAWRENCE, health products executive; b. Logansport, Ind., Jan. 27, 1940; s. Lawrence J. and Ruth (Speitel) C.; m. Judith A. Pille, June 18, 1966; children: Valerie A., Maria C. BBA maxima cum laude, U. Notre Dame, 1962; MBA with high distinction, Harvard U., 1966. Sec., bd. dirs. Mid-West Spring Mfg. Co., Inc., Chgo., 1961-71; with Baxter-Travenol Labs., Inc., 1971-87, exec. v.p. Artificial Organs divsn. Deerfield, Ill., 1976-77, pres. hyland therapeutics divsn. Glendale, Calif., 1977-87; founder, pres., CEO, bd. dirs. BioSurface Tech., Inc., Cambridge, Mass., 1987-94. Bd. dirs. Biolink Corp., Middleboro, Mass., chmn. bd. dirs., 1995-98, CEO, 1996-98; founder, chmn., bd. dirs. Cadent Med. Corp., Bedford, Mass., 1996-2000, CEO, 1998-1999; chancellor Roman Cath. Archdiocese Boston, 2001; bd. dirs. Nabi Biopharms, Boca Raton, Fla., Embrex Inc., Durham, N.C., Biolex Inc., Pittsboro, N.C., Tissue Regeneration Inc., Medford, Mass., Harbus Investors, Inc., St. Petersburg, Fla.; bd. dir. Mass. Biotechnology Coun., 1989-93, treas., 1991-93. Mem. bd. of transplantation svcs. ARC, 1988-90, nat. skin adv. coun., 1990-92; mem. gov.'s biotech. subcom., 1991; trustee St. John's Sem., Brighton, Mass., Voice of the Faithful Inc., chmn. bd. trustees, 2005—. With U.S. Army, 1962-64. Republican. Roman Catholic.

CASTAÑEDA, CARMELITA PATRICE, ROSIE, education educator; d. Manuel Joseph Castaneda and Carmelita Woerner. BS in Phys. Edn., Calif. State U., Sacramento, Calif., 1985; MS in Phys. Edn., Va. Poly. and State U., Blacksburg, Va., 1992; D in Social Justice Edn., U. Mass., Amherst, Mass., 2002. Instr. U. Mass., Amherst, Mass., 1998—2001, Westfield State Coll., Westfield, Mass., 2001—02; asst. prof. U. Wyo., Laramie, Wyo., 2002—. Employee tnr. Office of Trg. and Devel. U. Mass., Amherst, Mass., 1998—2002; diversity cons. Romney Assoc., Inc., Amherst, Mass., 2001—02. Editor: (coll. textbook) Readings for Diversity and Social Justice; author: Teaching and Learning in Diverse Classrooms: Faculty Reflections on Their Experiences and Pedagogical Practices of Teaching Diverse Populations. Recipient Profl. Devel. Award, Ctr. for Tchg. U. Mass. Amherst, 1996; grantee Rsch. Study: Tchrs. of Color in Diasporic Contexts, Faculty Grant and Aid, 2002, Intergroup Dialogue Rsch. Study, Chancellors Commn. on Civility and Human Rels., 1997, Preservice Tchrs. Experiences to Wyo. Indian Schs., Presidents Adv. Coun. on Women and Minorities, Fall 2003 and Spring 2005. Mem.: Nat. Network Ednl. Renewal, Na. Assn. Chicana and Chicano Studies, Nat. Coun. of La Raza, Am. Ednl. Rsch. Assn., Nat. Assn. for Multicultural Edn. Achievements include Crystal Light Nat. Aerobic Champion; Fla. State Body Bldg. Championship. Avocations: travel, horseback riding. Office: Univ Wyoming Dept 3374 1000 E Univ Ave Laramie WY 82071 Office Phone: 307-766-3126. Office Fax: 307-766-2018. Personal E-mail: carmelit@uwyo.edu.

CASTAÑEDA, JAMES AGUSTIN, language educator, golf coach; b. Bklyn., Apr. 2, 1933; s. Ciro Castañeda and Edna May Sincock; m. Terrill Lynn McCauley, Sept. 14, 1957; 1 child, Christopher James; m. Clara Luz Gutiérrez, Dec. 9, 1991. BA summa cum laude, Drew U., 1954; MA, Yale U., 1955, PhD, 1958; Certificat d'Aptitude à l'Enseignement du Français à l'Etranger, Université Paris, 1957; postgrad., Universidad de Madrid, 1957—; student summer inst. tchrs. fgn. langs., Purdue U., 1959. Asst. to assoc. prof. Spanish and French Hanover (Ind.) Coll., 1958-61; asst. prof. Spanish Rice U., Houston, 1961-63, assoc. prof. Spanish, 1963-67, prof. Spanish, 1967—. Vis. prof. Spanish U. So. Calif., 1959, U. N.C., 1962, 68, Western N.Mex. U., 1970; Florence Purington vis. prof. Mt. Holyoke Coll., 1976-77; prof. summer program Hispanic studies in Spain Rice U., 1979, 82, 83-90, head freshman baseball coach, 1962-67, asst. varsity coach, 1962-83, chmn. dept. Classics, Italian, Portuguese, Russian and Spanish, 1964-72, moderator television series, 1964-67, 68-69, head golf coach, 1983-98; lectr., dir., adviser and sponsor numerous acad. and other coms. in field. Author: A Critical Edition of Lope de Vega's Las paces de los reyes, y Judía de Toledo, 1962, introducción, edición, 1971, Agustín Moreto, 1974, Mira de Amescua, 1977, El esclavo del demonio, 1980; contbr. numerous articles to profl. jours. Chmn. interview team in Europe Kent Fellowship Program, 1968; active Internat. Good Neighbor Coun. Rose Meml. scholar Drew U., 1950-54, Varsity Club scholar, Alumni Assn. Meml. scholar, Fulbright scholar Université de Paris, 1956-57, scholar Instituto de Cultura Hispánica, 1971; Danforth fellow Yale U., 1954-58, teaching fellow 1958—; named Miembro Titular, Instituto de Cultura Hispánica de Madrid, 1972, Hon. Master Will Rice Coll., 1976, Spanish Tchr. of Yr. and Fgn. Lang. Tchr. of Yr., Tex. Fgn. Lang. Tchrs.' Assn., 1982; recipient Drew U. Alumni Achievement award in Humanities, 1973, Will Rice Coll. James St. Fulton Svc. award 1973, Bklyn. Cadets Alumni Assn. Achievement award, 1976, Spanish Heritage award 1982, Disting. Svc. award Assn. Rice Alumni, 2000; named to Drew U. Athletics Hall of Fame, 1997. Mem. Am. Assn. Spanish and Portugese (numerous coms. and offices), Am. Assn. Tchrs. French, Am. Coun. Tchrs. Fgn. Langs. (del. affiliate assembly, 1970-75), S. Ctrl. Modern Lang. Assn. (various coms. and offices), Houston Area Tchrs. Fgn. Langs. (various coms. and offices), Modern Lang. Assn. (various coms. and offices), Inst. Hispanic Culture Houston (founding mem. 1966, numerous other coms. and offices), Hispanic Soc. Am. (hon.), Sigma Delta Pi (hon. pres. 1998). Office: Rice Univ 6100 Main St Houston TX 77005-1892 Office Phone: 713-348-3248. Business E-Mail: spangolf@rice.edu.

CASTEEL, CAMILLE, school system administrator; EdD, Nova Southeastern U. Fischler Grad. Sch. of Edn. and Human Svcs., 1991. 1st grade tchr. to supt. Chandler (Ariz.) Unified Sch. Dist., 1971—91, supt., 1991—. Named Ariz. Nat. Supt. of Yr., 2002; recipient Excellence award, Ariz. Sch. Pub. Rels. Assn., Achievement award, Ariz. Year Round Edn. Assn. Office: Chandler Unified Sch Dist 1525 W Frey Rd Chandler AZ 85224

CASTEEN, JOHN THOMAS, III, academic administrator; b. Portsmouth, Va., Dec. 11, 1943; s. John Thomas and Naomi Irene (Anderson) C.; children: John Thomas IV, Elizabeth, Lars. BA with high honors, U. Va., 1965, MA, 1966, PhD, 1970; LLD, Shenandoah Coll. and Conservatory Music, 1984; DHL, Bentley Coll., 1992; hon. degree, Piedmont (Va.) C.C., 1992; DPA, Bridgewater Coll., 1993; D honoris causa, U. Athens, Greece, 1996; DHL (hon.), Transylvania U., 1999. Asst. prof. English U. Calif., Berkeley, 1970—75; assoc. prof., dean admissions U. Va., Charlottesville, 1975—82; adj. prof. Va. Commonwealth U., Richmond, 1982—85; prof. English, pres. U. Conn., Storrs, 1985—90; pres. U. Va., 1990—, George M. Kaufman presdl. prof. of English, 1990—. Bd. dirs. NCAA, Wachovia, Inc., Sallie Mae, Ctrl. Va.'s Pub. Broadcasting; mem. Assn. Acad. Health Ctrs.' Coun. Health Scis. and Univ.; mem. com. Nat. Inst. on Alcohol Abuse and Alcoholism and Misuse on Coll. Campuses; chair Coun. for Higher Edn. Accreditation, 2000—. Author: 16 Stories, 1981; contbr. articles to various publs.; mem. editl. adv. bd. The Presidency. Sec. edn. Commonwealth of Va., Richmond, 1982-85; trustee Mariner's Mus., 1990—. Coll. Entrance Exam Bd., N.Y.C., 1980-90, chmn. 1986-88; mem. So. Regional Edn. Bd., 1982-85. New Eng. Bd. of Higher Edn., 1986-90; mem. nat. adv. com. Nat. Domestic Violence Media Campaign, 1992—; dir. Am. Coun. on Edn., 1993-96. Recipient Outstanding Virginian award, 1993, Gold medal award Nat. Inst. Social Scis., 1998. Mem. Assn. Am. Univs. (exec. com.), So. Assn. Colls. and Schs. (chair commn. on colls. 1995-97, pres.-elect 1997, pres. 1998), Assn. Governing Bds. Colls. and Schs. (coun. of pres. 1992—), Keswick Club, Farmington County Club, Commonwealth Club (Richmond), Phi Beta Kappa. Episcopalian. Office: P O Box 400224 Charlottesville VA 22904 E-mail: jtc@virginia.edu.*

CASTEL, JEAN GABRIEL, lawyer, educator; b. Nice, France, Sept. 17, 1928; s. Charles A. and Simone (Ricour de Quinsac) C. Lic., U. Paris, 1948; JD, U. Mich., 1953; SJD, Harvard U., 1957; LLD (hon.), Aix-Marseille, France, 1988. Created queen's counsel. From asst. prof. to assoc. prof. law McGill U., 1954-57; now prof. emeritus law Osgoode Hall Law Sch., York U., Toronto. Author: International Law as Interpreted and Applied in Canada, 1978, Canadian Criminal Law: International and Transnational Aspects, 1981, Extraterritoriality in International Trade, 1988, The Canadian Law and Practice of International Trade, 1991, 2d edit., 1997, Canadian Conflict of Laws, 5th edit., 2002; editor: Can. Bar Rev., 1957-83. Mem. spl. group for settlement of disputes under Can.-U.S. Free Trade Agreement, 1989-93. Served with French Resistance, 1943-45. Decorated officer Order of Can., officier Ordre Nat. du Merite, chevalier Légion d'Honneur, Order of Ont.; recipient medal Law Soc. Upper Can., John Read medal Internat. Law. Fellow Acad. Arts and Scis., Royal Soc. Can.; mem. Can. Bar Assn. (hon.), Internat. Acad. Comparative Law (assoc.). E-mail: jgcastel@sympatico.ca.

CASTEL, NICO, tenor, educator; b. Lisbon, Portugal, Aug. 1, 1935; s. Felix and Margalitt (Castel) Kalinhoff; 1 child, Alexandra. BA, Temple U., 1952. Artist in residence Mannes Coll. of Music, N.Y.C., 1980—. Instr. diction and langs. Mannes Coll. Music, Juilliard Sch. Music, Internat. Vocal Arts Inst., Tel Aviv, Finnish Nat. Opera, Helsinki, Aspen Festival, Colo.; diction coach Met. Opera; stage dir. opera; adj. faculty Boston U.; founder N.Y. Opera Studio, Vassar Coll Author: The Nico Castel Book of Ladino Songs, A Singers' Manual of Spanish Lyric Diction, The Complete Puccini, Verdi, Mozart Wagner Libretti with phonetics and translation; Debuts include, N.Y. City Opera, 1965, Metropolitan Opera, 1970; permanent artist, Metropolitan Opera; extensive concert tours, U.S., S.Am., Europe; tchr. master classes in multilingual diction and style; trans. over 70 operas With U.S. Army, 1952-54. Mem. Am. Guild Mus. Artists. Democrat. Jewish. Home: 214 W 92nd St Apt 77E New York NY 10025-7455 Office: c/o Met Opera Lincoln Ctr New York NY 10023 Office Phone: 212-799-3100. Personal E-mail: nccastel@aol.com.

CASTEL, P. KEVIN, federal judge; b. NYC, Aug. 5, 1950; 2 children. BS, St. John's U., Jamaica, N.Y., 1972, JD, 1975; LLD (hon.), St. John's U., 2004. Bar: N.Y. 1976, U.S. Dist. Ct. (so. and ea. dists.) N.Y. 1976, U.S. Ct. Appeals (2nd cir.) 1979, U.S. Supreme Ct. 1983, U.S. Ct. Appeals (fed. cir.), 1986, U.S. Ct. Appeals (10th cir.), 1988, U.S. Ct. Appeals (3rd cir.) 1989, U.S. Ct. Appeals (4th cir.) 1991, U.S. Ct. Appeals (7th cir.) 1995, U.S. Ct. Appeals (11th cir.) 1997. Law clk. to judge U.S. Dist. Ct. (so. dist.) N.Y., 1975-77; assoc. Cahill Gordon & Reindel, N.Y.C., 1977-83, ptnr., 1983—2003; judge U.S. Dist. Judge (so dist.) N.Y., 2003—. Mem. departmental disciplinary com. appellate divsn. 1st dept., 1987—93, hearing panel chair, 1991—93, mem. policy com., 1997—2002. Articles editor St. John's Law Rev., 1974-75. Mayor's panel Martin Luther King Jr. Inst. for Law and Social Justice, 1987—89; nat. chmn. ann. giving campaign St. John's U., 1994—95; bd. dirs. Legal Aid Soc., 2000—03. Recipient Pres.'s medal St. John's U., 2000. Fellow: N.Y. Bar Found., Am. Bar Found.; mem.: Fed. Bar Coun. (sec. 1983—85, chmn. publs. com. 1984—95, trustee 1985—93, v.p. 1988—90, chmn. program com. 1995—98, trustee 1997—2002, pres. 2000—02), Assn. Bar City of N.Y. (com. profl. and jud. ethics 1994—97, coun. on jud. adminstrn. 1997—2000), N.Y. State Bar Assn. (com. on cts. of appellate jurisdiction 1979—86, com. fed. cts. of appellate jurisdiction 1979—86, com. fed. cts. 1986—89, chmn. com. fed practice 1989—91, exec. vice chmn. comml. and fed. litig. sect. 1991—92, chmn. 1993—94, ho. of dels. 1994—95), St. John's U. Law Sch. Alumni Assn. (bd. dirs. 1991—, v.p. 1998—), Supreme Ct. Hist. Soc. Office: US Dist Ct So Dist NY 500 Pearl St New York NY 10007-1790

CASTELE, THEODORE JOHN, radiologist; b. New Castle, Pa., Feb. 1, 1928; s. Theodore Robert and Anne Mercedes (McNavish) C.; m. Jean Marie Willse, Oct. 20, 1951; children: Robert, Ann Marie, Richard, Mary Kathryn, Thomas, Daniel, John. BS, Case Western Res. U., 1951, MD, 1957. Diplomate Am. Bd. Radiology, 1962. Intern then resident U. Hosps. Cleve., 1957-61, fellow, 1961-62; dir. of radiology Luth. Med. Ctr., Cleve., 1968-75, 77-89, chief of staff, 1975-81; pres. Med. Ctr. Radiologists, Inc., Cleve., 1978-95; v.p. med. and copr. devel. Health Cleve. Inc., 1989-91; chmn. Lakeshore Radiology Inc., Cleve., 1991-96, emeritus chmn., 1996—. Med. editor sta. WEWS-TV-ABC, Cleve., 1975-99; chmn. bd. Med. Cons. Imaging Co., Cleve., 1981-97; asst. clin. prof. radiology Case Western Res. U., chmn. dean's tech. coun. Sch. Medicine, 1996—, chmn. vis. com. Cleve. Health Scis. Libr., chmn. campaign for future of acad. medicine, 1998—. Exec. editor Prime mag., 2000—. Chmn. Southwestern dist. Greater Cleve. coun. Boy Scouts Am., 1969, 73; mem. bd. med. cons. Cleve. Police Dept., pres., 1988-90; trustee Comty. Dialysis Ctr., chmn. 1997-99, chmn. emeritus, 2000—; active Luth. Med. Ctr. Found., chmn. bd. trustees, 1969-75, pres., 1988-90; trustee Case Western Res. U., Blue Cross/Blue Shield Ohio, Greater Cleve. Hosp. Assn., Fairview Health, Luth. Med. Ctr., 1975-80, Fairview Hosp. Found.; bd. trustees Fairview Luth. Hosp. Found., 1999—, No. Ohio Lung Assn.; chmn. Health Mus. Cleve., 1996—, Humility of Mary Healthcare Sys., 1995-98; dir. Coun. Pub. Reps. for NIH, 1999-2001. With USN, 1946-47. Recipient Order of Merit award Boy Scouts Am., 1971, Silver Beaver award, 1972, Nat. Disting. Eagle Scout award, 1984, Frances Payne Bolton Sch. of Nursing Disting. Svc. award, 1990, Outstanding Philanthropist award Nat. Soc. of Fundraising Execs., 1991, Alumnus of the Yr. award Dept. Radiology of Case Western Res. U., 1996, LMC Found. Women's Bd. award, 1996, Luth. Hosp. award Fairview Health Sys. Bd., 1996, Midwest Nursing Rsch. Soc. Media award, 1998, Lamplighter Humanitarian award 2001; named Knight of the Equestrian, Order of the Holy Sepulchre of Jerusalem, 1993—; recipient Magis award St. Ignatius H.S.; named to Med. Hall of Fame, Case Western Res. U., Cleve. Mag., 1999, No. Ohio Italian-Am. Found., 1999. Fellow Am. Coll. Radiology; mem. AMA (Physician Spkr. Gold award 1978, 80, Silver 1979, Bronze 1978, Benjamin Rush award 1989, Golden Achievement award Golden Age Ctrs., 1996, chmn. Ohio del. 1987-96), Ohio State Med. Assn. (5th dist. councilor 1977-79, Spl. award 1979, Disting. Svc. award 1997), Cleve. Radiol. Soc. (pres. 1969-70), Cleve. Med. Libr. Assn. (pres. 1996, 97-98), Case Western Res. U. Med. Alumni Assn. (pres. 1971-72, 91-92, Disting. Svc. award 1987, Spl. Trustees award 1997, Univ. medal 1998), Cleve. Acad. Medicine (pres. 1974-75, Disting. Mem. award 1990, Disting. Svc. award 1984, Spl. Honor award and portrait 1998), Ohio State Radiol. Soc. (Silver award 1990). Home: 18869 Canyon Rd Cleveland OH 44126-1703 Office: Case Western Reserve Univ Sch Medicine Cleveland OH 44106

CASTELL, SIR WILLIAM MARTIN, health products executive; b. London, Apr. 10, 1947; s. William Gummer and Gladys (Doe) C.; m. Renice Mendelson, 1971; children: Sarah, Claire, William. BA with honors, City of London Coll., England; D Soc. Sci. (hon.), Brunel Univ., 2004. FCA. With Wellcome Found., 1975—86; mng. dir. Wellcome Biotech., 1984—87; comml. dir. Wellcome plc, 1987—89; chief executive Amersham plc, England, 1990—2004; pres. & CEO GE Healthcare, England, 2004—; vice chmn., exec. officer General Electric Co., 2004—. Vis. fellow Green Coll., 1993—; companion Inst. Mgmt., 1995—; non-exec. dir. Marconi plc (formerly GEC); chmn. The Prince's Trust, 1998—. Trustee Natural Hist. Mus., London; bd. mem. Inst. Life Scis., Univ. Mich.; vis. fellow Green Coll., Oxford; chmn. The Prince's Trust, 1998. Named knight, 2000, Lt., Royal Victorian Order, 2004; fellow (hon.), Acad. Med. Sci. Mem.: Ins. Chartered Accountants (fellow 1980). Office: GE Healthcare Amersham Pl Little Chalfont Buckinghamshire HP7 9NA England*

CASTELLANETA, DAN (DANIEL LOUIS), actor; b. Chgo., Sept. 10, 1958; m. Deb Lacusta. Grad., No. Ill. U. Actor, writer, originator (TV series) Homer Simpson's voice, The Simpsons, 1987 (2 Emmys, 1992, 1993), voiceover Homer Simpson, Grampa Abe Simpson, Krusty the Klown, Barney Gumble, Groundskeeper Willie, Mayor Quimby, Hans Moleman, Sideshow Mel, The Simpsons, 1989— (Primetime Emmy for voice-over performance, 2004), Tiny Toon Adventures, 1990, Chula The Tarantula, Fievel's American Tails, 1991, Dr. Emmett Lathrop Doc Brown, Back to the Future, 1991, Mister Thickley, Taz-Mania, 1991, Megavolt, Darkwing Duck, 1991—95, Mittens, Bill, Eek! The Cat!, 1992, Genie, Icafrak, Aladdin, 1993, Grandpa Steely Phil, Willie the Golly Olly Man, Early, Dr. Murray Steiglitz, Nick Vermicelli, Hey Arnold!, 1996, Charles' father, The Tick, 1994, (TV films) Comet and Blitzen, The Online Adventures of Ozzie the Elf, 1997, Postman, Olive, the Other Reindeer, 1999 (Annie award, 1993), (films) All Dogs Go to Heaven, 1996, Grandpa Steely Phil, Nick Vermicelli, Hey Arnold! The Movie, 2002, Thing One and Thing Two, The Cat in the Hat, 2003; actor: (TV series) Tracy Ulman Show, (guest appearance) Alf, 1986, LA Law, 1986, Married...with Children, 1987, Murphy Brown, 1988, Wings, 1990, Dream On, 1990, Bagdad Café, 1990, Dinosaurs, 1991, Rugrats, 1991, Mad About You, 1992, Grace Under Fire, 1993, Bakersfield, P.D., 1993, NYPD Blue, 1993, Frasier, 1993, Animaniacs, 1993, Duckman, 1994, Friends, 1994, George Carlin Show, 1994, The Critic, 1994, Drew Carey Show, 1995, Cybill, 1995, Nash Bridges, 1996, Everybody Loves Raymond, 1996, Johnny Bravo, 1997, That '70s Show, 1998, Hercules, 1998, Batman Beyond, 1999, Futurama, 1999, Yes, Dear, 2000, Jackie Chan Adventures, 2000, Buzz Lightyear of Star Command, 2000, Reba, 2001, Adventures of Jimmy Neutron: Boy Genius, 2002, Lucky, 2003, The Pitts, 2003; actor (TV films) Lady Against the Odds, 1999, Tracey Takes on New York, 1993, Related by Birth, 1994, The Computer Wore Tennis Shoes, 1995, My Giant, 1998, Rhapsody in Bloom, 1998, Laughter on the 23rd Floor, 2001, Behind the Camera: The Unauthorized Story of Charlie's Angels, 2004, (films) Nothing in Common, 1986, War of the Roses, 1989, Love Affair, 1994, The Client, 1994, The Settlement, 1999, Return to Neverland, 2002, Adventures in Homeschooling, 2004. Mem. Chgo. Second City. Achievements include has a trademark phrase d'oh from the Simpsons added to the Oxford Dictionary. Office: The Simpsons c/o Twentieth TV Matt Groening's Office PO Box 900 Beverly Hills CA 90213

CASTELLANI, LAWRENCE P., automotive company executive; With Tops Friendly Markets, Buffalo, 1962—97, from stock boy to managerial positions, 1962—75, dir. ops., 1975—91, pres., CEO, 1991—97; exec. v.p. Ahold USA Royal Ahold NV, 1997—98, pres. support svc. for S.Am. stores, 1998—2000; CEO Advance Auto Parts Inc., Roanoke, Va., 2000—05, chmn., 2003—. Office: Advance Holding Corp 5673 Airport Rd NW Roanoke VA 24012

CASTELLANO, JOSEPH ANTHONY, retired chemist, management consulting firm executive; b. NYC, Oct. 28, 1937; s. Joseph and Marie Antoinette (Gallo) C.; m. Rosalie Ann Fantaci, Aug. 28, 1960; children: Joseph, Thomas, Laura. BS in Chemistry, CCNY, 1959; MS in Chemistry, Poly. Inst. N.Y., 1964, PhD in Chemistry, 1969. Cert. profl. chemist; cert. community coll. instr. Research chemist Witco Chem. Co., Paterson, N.J., 1959-62; sr. research chemist Thiokol Chem. Corp., Denville, N.J., 1962-65; mem. tech. staff, project mgr. RCA Labs., Princeton, N.J., 1965-73; chmn., CEO Princeton Materials Sci., 1973-75; ops. mgr. Fairchild Camera and Inst. Corp., Palo Alto, Calif., 1975-77; mgr. ops. Kylex, Mt. View, Calif., 1977-78; pres. Stanford Resources, San Jose, Calif., 1978—2002. Publisher: Electronic Display World, The Electronic Display Industry Svc.; cons. scientist Princeton U., 1970-72; lectr. Rutgers U., Kent State U., SUNY-Binghamton, NASA Rsch. Ctr., USAF Materials Lab., Office Naval Rsch., IBM Rsch. Ctrs., RCA Labs., Motorola, others. Author: Handbook of Display Technology, 1992, Liquid Gold, 2005; contbr. articles to profl. jours. Recipient RCA Doctoral Study award 1966, RCA Labs. Outstanding Achievement award, 1967, R&D Mag. IR-100 award, 1968, David Sarnoff Team award in sci., 1969, PATCA award for guidance and exceptional svc., 1983, Svc. cert. Soc. Motion Picture Scientists and Engrs., 1989, Spl. Recognition award Soc. Info. Display, 2000, 25 Yr. Svc. award iSuppli Corp., 2002. Fellow Am. Inst. Chemists; mem. AAAS, Am. Chem. Soc., Am. Assn. Advancement Sci., N.Y. Acad. Sci., Royal Chem. Soc., Soc. Info. Display, Profl. and Tech. Cons. Assn., Soc. Tech. Comm., N.Y. Acad. Sci., Sigma Xi. Roman Catholic. Achievements include patents in field. Home: 7017 Elmsdale Dr San Jose CA 95120-3225 Personal E-mail: drjcast@aol.com.

CASTELLANO, JOSEPHINE MASSARO, medical records specialist; d. Ignazio and Maria Massaro Castellano. BS in Med. Tech., Fla. State U., 1952; tchrs. cert., U. Tampa, 1955; MA, Columbia U., 1961. Med. technologist St. Joseph's Hosp., Tampa, Fla., 1952—55; tchr. Hillsborough County Sch. Bd., Tampa, 1955—85; med. records specialist Robert Martinez, M.D., Tampa, 1985—95, David L. Castellano, DDS, Tampa, 1996—, Domenic M. Castellano, DDS, Tampa, 1996—. Mem.: AAUW (mem. adv. bd. 1999—2002), Christian Med. Found. (mem. adv. bd. 1996—2003), Kappa Delta Pi (mem. adv. bd. 2000—02). Roman Catholic. Avocations: reading, horseback riding, tennis, gardening, bowling. Home: 305 N Hesperides St Tampa FL 33609-2020 Office: David L and Domenic M Castellano DDS 8365 W Hillsborough Ave Tampa FL 33615-3899

CASTELLANO, MARK JOSEPH, music educator; b. Oceanside, NY, Aug. 5, 1957; s. Salvatore Francis and Carmela Cecelia Castellano. MusB in edn., La. State U., 1975—79; MusM in edn., U. of Southwestern La., 1983—85. Profl. Educator's Certificate Fla. Dir. of bands Acadia Parish Pub. Schools, Rayne, La., 1980—82; asst. to the dir. of bands U. of Southwestern La., Lafayette, La., 1985—87; dir. of bands Mariner H.S., Cape Coral, Fla., 1987—93, Three Oaks Mid. Sch., Ft. Myers, Fla., 1993—; adj. instr. of music Barry U., Ft. Myers, Fla. Instr., summer music camps Music Found. of SW Fla., Ft. Myers, Fla., 1994—; v.p. Teachers Assn. of Lee County, Ft. Myers, Fla.; instr., summer staff devel. inst. Sch. Dist. of Lee County, Ft. Myers, Fla., lee county core curriculum writing team for music, Ft. Myers, Fla. Mem. Music Program Exploration Task Force, Fla. Gulf Coast U., Ft. Myers, Fla., 2000—01; chmn. and founding mem. Unified Arts Coun., Sch. Dist. of Lee County, Ft. Myers, 1995—98; mem. Bargaining Team, Teachers Assn. of Lee County, Ft. Myers, 1998—2004; chmn., crisis com. Teachers Assn. of Lee County, Ft. Myers, 1997—99; founding mem. Lee County Arts for a Complete Edn., Ft. Myers; mem. Polit. Action Com., Teachers Assn. of Lee County, Ft. Myers, Fla., 1999—2004. Named Tchr. of Distinction, Golden Apple Tchr. Recognition Program, Found. for Pub. Edn., Lee County, 1997, 1998, 2000, 2003; recipient Outstanding Grad. Student, Music Dept., Music Dept., U. of Soutwestern La., 1984, Finalist, Golden Apple Tchr. Recognition Program, Found. for Pub. Edn., Lee County, 1999 and 2001; Music scholarship, La. State U., 1975—79, Grad. Tchg. Assistantship, U. of Southwestern La., 1983—85. Mem.: NEA, Island Coast Educators (mem. polit. action com. 2000—), Internat. Horn Soc., Am. Sch. Band Directors Assn., Am. Fedn. of Teachers, Fla. Edn. Assn., Tchrs. Assn. Lee County (v.p.

2002—04, mem. membership devel. team 2003—), Music Educators Nat. Conf., Fla. Music Educators Assn., Fla. Bandmasters Assn., Pi Kappa Lambda, Phi Mu Alpha Sinfonia. Avocations: fishing, writing, reading. Office Phone: 239-267-9272.

CASTELLANOS, JOSEPHINE FALCON, insurance agent, composer; b. Havana, Cuba, 1933; arrived in U.S., 1962; d. Manuel Falcon and Rita Maria dela Portilla; m. Hector Manuel Castellanos, Apr. 9, 1955 (dec. 2002); 1 child, Josefina. Degree, Ins. Sch., Miami, Fla.; student, Normal Sch. Kindergarten Tchrs., Havana, Cuba. Tchr. kindergarten, Havana, Cuba; customer rep. First Federal and Fin. Fed. Savings and Loan Assn., Miami; ins. agent Fortis Ins., Miami; freelance songwriter, composer Miami. Songwriter: Come Back to Me, 2005, Hazme Vibrar, 2005. Mem.: Third Order Discaled Camelites. Republican. Roman Cath. Office Phone: 305-383-3174.

CASTELLANOS-BRANDON, ALBA G., secondary school educator; b. Vedado, Cuba, Oct. 12, 1957; d. Jesus René Castellanos Gomez and Ana Maria Brandon Merino. AA and AS, William Rainey Harper Coll., 1979; BA in Edn., U. Ill., Chgo., 1987; MA in Edn., Roosevelt U., 2001. Tchr. various dists. to River Trails Dist. #26, Mt. Prospect, Ill., 1988—2001; tchr. William R. Harper Coll., Palatine, Ill., 1985—, Schaumburg (Ill.) Twp. Dist. #54, 2001—. Mem. multicultural com., Schaumburg, Ill., 2001—. Author: (novels) Images of Winter, 1993, (manuscripts) various, including Resolving the Misconceptions of LD Labeling in the Reading Domain, 1999. Avocation: reading, writing, arts, crafts, outdoor sports.

CASTELLI, ALEXANDER GERARD, accountant; b. N.Y.C., May 3, 1929; s. Gerard and Carmela (Canzoneri) C.; m. Michelina Castelli, Jan. 8, 1961; children— Gerard, Alexander, JoAnn. BS, N.Y. U., 1958. C.P.A., N.Y., Md., 1970. Chief accountant Daitch Crystal Dairies, Inc., Bronx, N.Y., 1965-68; asst. controller Alexander's, Inc., N.Y.C., 1968-70; v.p., treas. Bond Stores, Inc., N.Y.C., 1970-73; v.p. fin. McBrides, Inc., Washington, 1973-77; mng. ptnr. Castelli & Catudal, P.A., 1977—. Bd. advisers Nat. Bank of Washington. Served with CIC AUS, 1951-53. Recipient Founder's Day award NYU, 1958 Mem. Am. Inst. CPA's, N.Y. State Soc. CPA's, Beta Gamma Sigma. Roman Catholic. Home: 10009 Gainsborough Rd Rockville MD 20854-4276 Office: 7925 Glenbrook Rd Bethesda MD 20814-2441 E-mail: agcast@aol.com.

CASTELLI, TIM, publishing executive; BA, Duke U. Various sales positions P.C. Mag., Boston, 1992—98, Chicago, 1992—98, San Francisco, 1992—98, West Coast assoc. pub., 1998—99, nat. assoc. pub., 1999—2000, pub. N.Y.C., 2000—; v.p. P.C. Mag. Group, 2003—05; assoc. pub. Maxim, 2005—.

CASTELLINI, MARY MERCER, author; b. Portland, Oreg., Apr. 4, 1923; d. Reuben Howard and Alma Evangeline (Holmes) Mercer; m. Edgar Aldo Castellini, Aug. 25, 1946 (dec. Febr. 1983); children: Edgar M., Anita M. BA in Am. Civilization, Dominican Coll., 1974. Bot. rschr. at Herbarium Calif. Acad. Scis., San Francisco, 1984-87. Author: A Victorian Heritage in Old Cow Hollow, 1977, Herbarium Messages from California Flora, 1978, Herbarium: A Noetic Herbal Expedition, 1979; contbr.: An Anthology of American Women Writers, 1979; exhibitor, lectr., artist San Francisco Pub. Libr., 1977, Marin (Calif.) Pub. Libr./Marin Civic Ctr., 1977, Tiburon Pub. Libr., 1991, Golden Gate Theol. Sem., Mill Valley, Calif., 1992—. Den leader Boy Scouts Am., Stuart Hall Sch. for Boys, San Francisco, 1955-57; leader Girl Scouts U.S., Convent of the Sacred Heart, San Francisco, 1957-59; mem. Mothers' March on Polio, Polio Soc., San Francisco, 1955; freshman YWCA pres. U. Wash., Seattle, 1943; mem. chorus Emeritus Coll. of Marin. Named Outstanding Californian, Rare Books and Calif. History, The Bancroft Libr., U. Calif. Berkeley, 1993—. Mem. Ina Coolbrith Cir. (life), AAUW (Washington, life, Individual grant Ednl. Found. 1977-78, 78-79), Calif. Bot. Soc., Alpha Chi Omega. Avocations: writing, studying, vol. work, swimming, hiking. Home and Office: 212 Mountain View Dr Healdsburg CA 95448-4315

CASTELLINO, RONALD AUGUSTUS DIETRICH, radiologist, educator; b. N.Y.C., Feb. 18, 1938; s. Leonard Vincent and Henrietta Wilhelmina (Geffken) C.; m. Joyce Cuneo, Jan. 26, 1963; children: Jeffrey Charles, Robin Leonard, Anthony James. Student, Creighton U., Omaha, 1955-58, MD, 1962. Diplomate: Am. Bd. Radiology. Rotating intern Highland Alameda County Hosp., Oakland, Calif., 1962-63; USPHS/Peace Corps physician Brazil, 1963-65; resident in diagnostic radiology Stanford U. Hosp., 1965-68, chief resident, 1967-68; asst. prof. radiology Stanford U. Med. Sch., 1968-74, assoc. prof., 1974-81, prof., 1981-93, chief diagnostic oncologic radiology, 1970-89, chief CT body scanning, 1979-89, dir. div. diagnostic radiology and assoc. chmn. dept. radiology, 1981-86, acting chmn. dept. diagnostic radiology and nuclear medicine, 1986-89, prof. emeritus N.Y.C., 1993—; chair dept. radiology, Carroll and Milton Petrie chair Meml. Sloan Kettering Cancer Ctr., N.Y.C., 1990-98; prof. radiology Cornell Med. Sch., 1994-98, chief med. officer R-2 tech., 1998—. Mem. U.S. Cancer del., People's Republic China, 1977 Co-editor: Pediatric Oncologic Radiology, 1977; assoc. editor; Lymphology, 1973-97, Investigative Radiology, 1985-94, Academic Radiology, 1994-97, Radiology, 1986-94, Postgrad. Radiology, 1986-98; contbr. numerous rsch. papers to profl. jours., chpts. to books. Recipient T.F. Eckstrom Fund award, 1978; Guggenheim fellow, 1974-75 Mem.: N.Y. Acad. Medicine, N.Y. Roentgen Soc., Calif. Acad. Medicine, N.Am. Soc. Lymphology (charter), Soc. Cancer Imaging (charter), Soc. Thoracic Radiology (charter), Calif. Radiol. Soc., Calif. Med. Assn. (adv. panel sect. radiology 1972—89), Western Angiography Soc. (charter), Internat. Cancer Imaging Soc. (charter), Am. Roentgen Ray Soc., Soc. Cardiovascular and Interventional Radiology (charter), Radiol. Soc. N.Am., Assn. Univ. Radiologists (exec. com. 1981—85), Am. Coll. Radiology, Internat. Soc. Lymphology (exec. com. 1975—85), Am. Soc. Therapeutic Radiation Oncologists (hon.), Alpha Omega Alpha. Office: R-2 Tech 1195 W Fremont Ave Sunnyvale CA 94087 Office Phone: 408-481-5600. Personal E-mail: rcastellino@sbcglobal.net. Business E-Mail: rcastellino@r2tech.com.

CASTELLO, JOE, JR., lawyer; b. Coronado, Calif., Feb. 1, 1943; s. Joseph William Sr. and Fern (Noel) C.; m. Kathie Means, Sept. 11, 1981; 1 child, Matthew Noel; 1 stepchild, Heather Jo Means. BA, U. Fla., 1965; JD, Stetson U., 1971. Bar: Fla. 1971, U.S. Dist. Ct. (mid. dist.) Fla. 1971. Assoc. mem. Trenam, Simmons, Kemker, Scharf, Frye & O'Neill, Tampa, Fla., 1969-79; assoc., ptnr. Holland & Knight, Lakeland, Tampa, Fla., 1979-81; pvt. practice Tampa, 1981—. Office: 4202 E Fowler Ave USF 30538 Tampa FL 33620-8001 Office Phone: 813-866-4842. E-mail: joe@honestlawyer.us.

CASTEN, RICHARD FRANCIS, physicist; b. N.Y.C., Nov. 1, 1941; s. Daniel F. and Constance Mary (Bell) C.; m. Jo Ann Daly, June 6, 1964. BS magna cum laude, Coll. of the Holy Cross, 1963; PhD, Yale U., 1967. Postdoctoral fellow Niels Bohr Inst., Copenhagen, 1967-69, Los Alamos (N.Mex.) Sci. Lab., 1969-71; asst. scientist Brookhaven Nat. Lab., Upton, N.Y., 1971-73, assoc. scientist, 1973-76, scientist, 1977-81, sr. scientist, 1981-96, group leader nuclear structure group, 1981-96; prof. physics, dir. A.W. Wright Nuclear Structure Lab. Yale U., New Haven, Conn., 1995—. Chmn. N.Am. steering com. for Isospin Lab. Radioactive Beam Facility, 1989-2002, co-chmn. RIA steering com., 2002-03, mem. Nuc. Sci. Adv. Com., 1998-2000, chmn. 2002—; guest prof. U. Cologne, Germany, 1985—; mem. panel on basic nuclear data NAS, 1990-92; mem. long-range plan working group Nuc. Sci. Adv. Com., 1989, 95, 2001; mem. subcom. on implementation of long-range plan, 1991; mem. spl. emphasis panel NSF, 1993; U.S. rep. Megasci. Forum for Nuc. Physics, Subpanel on Intense Beams and Target Sys., 1997, 98; co-chair writing panel for Columbus White Paper on sci. opportunities with an advanced ISOL facility, 1997; chair ISAC/TRIUMF rev. com., 1997; mem. Can. NSERC com. on subatomic physics, 1999-2001; mem. panels internat. rev. of standing and potential of physics rsch. in U.K., 2001, 05; co-convenor 1995 TUNL Town Meeting on Nuc. Structure and 2000 Rare Isotope Accelerator Workshop; chair Nustar Pac for new GSI Pair facility, 2004-2005; numerous other nat. and internat. coms.; co-organizer seven internat. confs. on nuc. physics; adv. coms. for many internat. confs.; spkr. in field. Author: Nuclear Structure from a Simple Perspective, 1990, rev. edit., 2000; co-author, co-editor: Algebraic Approaches to Nuclear Structure, 1993; mem. editl. bd. (Jours.) Nuclear Physics News Internat., Internat. Jour. Modern Physics, Modern Physics Letters, assoc. editor Phys. Rev. C, 2001—; contbr. over 400 articles to profl. jours. Pres. Jo Ann and Richard Casten, Ltd., 1973—. Danforth fellow, 1963-67; recipient Sr. Alexander von Humboldt prize, 1983; honoree Internat. Nuc. Structure Conf., Jackson, Wyo., 2002. Fellow AAAS, mem. Am. Phys. Soc. (exec. com. divsn. nuc. physics 1991-93, chmn. task force to rev. jour. Phys. Rev. C 1995, C-12 com. on internat. cooperation in nuclear physics 2004—), Sigma Xi. Achievements include discovery of O(6) symmetry of IBA model and other experimental verifications of the IBA including extensive study of 168-Er and 196-Pt; invention of symmetry triangle of the IBA known as the Casten Triangle; co-inventor of consistent Q formalism; evolution of nuclear structure with nucleon number, valence p-n interaction, NpNn scheme and P-factor, quenching of the N=20 and Z=64 shell gaps, fragility of magicity; research in generalization of the Federman-Pittel mechanism for the onset of deformation in nuclei; radioactive nuclear beams, Q-invariants, application of Landau theory to equilibrium structure of nuclei; development of signatures of nuclear structure, ARC method of complete spectroscopy; first to use the GRID technique for nuclear structure studies, evidence for large hexadecapole deformations in odd-A nuclei, extensive tests of Coriolis mixing in nuclei; discovery of empirical examples of E (5) and X (5) critical point symmetries for nuclear phase transition regions; co-discovery of new evidence for multi-phonon states in nuclei, global correlations of nuclear observables; co-discovery of anharmonic vibrator and tripartite correlations of nuclear observables; co-discovery of nuclei in the internal arc of regularity of symmetry triangle; new interpretation of EO transitions; first intermediate energy Coulomb excitation in inverse kinematics; mapping of structural evolution in nuclei. Office: Yale Univ Wright Nuc Structure PO Box 208124 New Haven CT 06520-8124 Office Phone: 203-432-6174. Business E-Mail: rick@riviera.physics.yale.edu.

CASTENELL, LOUIS ANTHONY, academic administrator; b. NYC, Oct. 2, 1947; s. Louis Anthony Sr. and Marguerite (Barzon) C.; m. Mae Beckett, May 3, 1975; children: Louis Calvin, Elizabeth M. BA, Xavier U., 1968; MS, U. Wis., Milw., 1973; PhD, U. Ill., 1980. Cert. counselor and tchr. Elem. tchr. Orleans Parish Schs., New Orleans, 1968; academic advisor U. Wis., Milw., 1970-74; alumni dir. Xavier U., New Orleans, 1974-77, dean Grad Sch., 1980-89; dean Coll. Edn. U. Cin., 1990-99, U. Ga., 1999—. Cons. in field. Contbr. chpts. to books and articles to profl. jours. Mem. edn. commn. Nativity Sch., Cin., 1990, NAACP, 1990; mem. steering com. Cin. Youth Collabarative, 1990; bd. dirs. Tri-State Edn. and Tech. Found., Cin., 1990. Sgt. U.S. Army, 1968-69, Korea. Recipient Presdl. Citation, Assn. Multicultural Counseling, Washington, 1983. HEW fellow, 1978-80, Pedro Zamora award Contbns. to Diversity, 2003, Am. Coun. Edn. Bd. Svc. award, 2003, U. Ga. Diversity Leadership award, 2003, Disting. Alumni in Higher Edn., U. Ill., 2002, Outstanding Faculty, Kappa Delta Epsilon, 2000. Mem. AACD, Am. Edn. Rsch. Assn., Am. Assn. Colls. Tchrs. Edn. (chmn. bd. dirs. 2001—), Nat. Bd. Profl. Tchg. Stds., Assn. Tchr. Educators, State U. Deans Edn., Kappa Delta Pi, Phi Delta Kappa. Democrat. Roman Catholic. Avocations: reading, travel, photography. Home: 1320 Beverly Dr Athens GA 30606-7610 Office: U Ga Coll Edn Aderhold Hall G-3 Athens GA 30602

CASTER, JACQUELINE JACOBS, not-for-profit executive; d. Walter Harvery Jacobs and Dorothy Jacobs Duncan; m. Andrew Ian Caster, Oct. 15, 1989; children: Bryce William, Jocelyn Lily. BA, Pomona Coll., 1979; M in City and Regional Planning, Harvard U., John Fitzgerald Kennedy Sch. Govt., 1983; JD, Boston U. Sch. Law, 1983. Bar: Calif. 1984. Atty. Loeb and Loeb, Los Angeles, Calif., 1983—86; mgr. market rsch. Disney Devel. Co., Burbank, 1987—90; pres. Jacqueline Caster Consulting, Pacific Palisades, 1990—2000; founder, pres. Everychild Found., Pacific Palisades, 2000—. Mem. adv. bd. Alternative Living for the Aging, Los Angeles, 2004—, Blue Heron Found., Los Angeles, 2004—. Named Woman of Yr., Santa Monica-Westside YWCA, 1985; recipient Humanitarian award, First Star Found., 1984. Mem.: Calif. State Bar (licentiate). Office: Everychild Found PO Box 1808 Pacific Palisades CA 90272 Office Phone: 310-573-2153.

CASTETTER, WILLIAM BENJAMIN, retired education educator, educational director; b. Shamokin, Pa., Aug. 31, 1914; s. Edward Franklin and Stella (Zimmerman) C.; m. Roberta Vera Breitmeyer, Aug. 6, 1947. BS, U. N.Mex., 1936. MA, 1937; PhD, U. Pa., 1948. Cert. tchr. sci. and fgn. langs., Pa. Tchr., prin. Melrose (N.Mex.) Sch. Dist., 1937-40; prof. Lebanon Valley Coll., Annville, Pa., 1947-49, U. Pa., Phila., 1949-81, dir. edn. svc. bur., 1970-81. Author: (textbook) The Human Resources Function in Educational Administration, 1950—; contbr. articles to profl. jours. Capt. U.S. Infantry, 1943-45. Recipient Tchg. and Svc. award Phi Delta Kappa, U. Pa. Chpt., Phila., 1980. Republican. Episcopalian. Avocations: wood working, gardening. Home and Office: Waverly Heights 1400 Waverly Rd Apt B323 Gladwyne PA 19035-1254 Office Phone: 610-645-8682.

CASTIGLIA, PATRICIA ANNE THORSON, dean, nursing educator; b. Johnson City, N.Y. d. Theodore William and Isabelle Alice (Lane) Thorson; children: Karen, Patricia, Joseph. Diploma in Nursing, St. Vincent's Hosp., N.Y.C., 1955; BSN, U. Buffalo, 1962; MSN, SUNY, Buffalo, 1965; PhD, SUNY, 1976. RN, N.Y.; cert. sch. nurse tchr., N.Y. Staff nurse Our Lady of Lourdes Hosp., Binghamton, NY, 1955-56; asst. head nurse Hosp. of the Good Shepherd, Syracuse, NY, 1956; sch. nurse tchr. North Collins Cen. Sch., North Collins, NY, 1956-62; clin. instr. SUNY, Buffalo, 1965-73; asst. prof. Niagara U., NY, 1976-77; from asst. prof. dir. ind. study to assoc. prof. SUNY, Buffalo, 1977-89, assoc. dean, 1983-89; acting dean, assoc. prof. SUNY at Buffalo Coll. Nursing, 1989; dean, prof. Coll. Nursing and Health Scis. U. Tex., El Paso, 1990—2002, asst. to pres. for health affairs, 2001—02, prof. emeritus, 2002—, SUNY, Buffalo, 1991—, cons. for higher edn. issues; interim assoc. dean U. Tex. Med. Br., San Antonio, 2004. Stockholder, treas. Profl. Nurse Consultants P.C., Buffalo; pediatric nurse practitioner Erie County Health Dept., Buffalo, 1982-89; vis. prof. SUNY Buffalo, 2003; dean emeritus Am. Assn. Colls. Nursing, 2003; interim assoc. dean acad. affairs SON, WTMB, 2004-. Author chpts. to books; chair book of yr. awards Pediatric Nursing, 1986-88; manuscript reviewer Pediatric Nursing, Clin. Nurse Specialist, 1985—; editor: Jour. of Pediatric Health Care; co-editor: Child Health Care: Process and Practice, 1992; contbr. articles to MCN, Pediatric Nursing, Jour. Pediatric Health Care. Recipient Reach award YWCA, 1995, Charles and Shirley Leavell Endowed chair; named Nurse of Yr., Tex. Nurse Assn. 1996, Woman of the Yr. in Edn., El Paso Commn. for Women, 1996; grantee P.I. Kellogg Cmty. Partnership; SUNY Faculty Exch. scholar, Albany, 1985. Fellow Am. Acad. Nursing; mem. NAPNAP, N.Y. State Nurses Assn., Coalition of Nurse Practitioners, U. Buffalo Alumni Assn., St. Vincent's Alumni Assn., Rotary Internat., Sigma Theta Tau. Roman Catholic. Avocations: travel, piano, theater, reading, knitting. E-mail: pcastiglia@adelphia.net.

CASTILE, RAND (JESSE RANDOLPH III), retired museum director; b. NC, 1938; s. Jesse Randolph II and Pauline Virginia (Simmons) C.; m. Sondra Meadow Myers, 1960; children: Leath Willow, Heather Rain. BA, Drew U., Madison, N.J., 1960; diploma, Urasenke Tea Ceremony, Kyoto, Japan, 1967; LHD (hon.), Drew U., 1992. With ARTnews, NYC, 1963-65; dir. edn. Japan Soc., NYC, 1967-71, dir. performing arts, 1981-86, dir. Japan House Gallery, 1971-86; dir. Asian Art Mus., San Francisco, 1986-94, dir. emeritus, 1994—. Vis. com. Met. Mus. Art, 1974-99; sec., mem. US-Japan Cultural and Ednl. Conf., 1972-86; mem. Maine Art Commn., 1997-2001, vis. com. Asian Art, Mus. Fine Arts, Boston, 2000-2004; sr. adv. Sherman E. Lee Inst. Japanese Art, 2000-2002; mem. North Atlantic Cultural Coun., 2002-; mem. Can.-Am. Cultural Bd., 2003-. Author: The Way of Tea, 1971, 79; (exhbn. catalogue) Japanese Art Now: Tadaaki Kuwayama & Rikuro Okamoto, 1980, other catalogues; editor: Japanese Art Exhibitions with Catalogue in US, 1980; contbr. articles to profl. jour. Panelist Calif. Arts Coun., 1986-91; bd. dir. West-East Coun. Cathedral Ch. of St. John the Devine, 1977-86, AAM/ICOM, 1982-85, Japan Soc. No. Calif., 1986-95, San Francisco Bay Area Dance Coalition, 1986-88, Rock and Roll Mus., San Francisco, 1988-89, U. San Francisco Ctr. for Pacific Rim, 1989-95, Seoul-San Francisco Sister City Com., 1987-93, Nat. Maritime Mus., San Francisco, 1989-93; mem. internat. adv. com. Ctr. for Internat. Contemporary Arts, 1989-95; chair co-chair gov. State Calif. awards for Art and Philanthropy, 1990-94, others; chmn. Eastport Area Millenium Festival, 1997-2000; mem. vis. com. Mus. Fine Arts, Boston. Fulbright-Hayes fellow, 1966-67; recipient Mayor's award of Honor for Arts and Culture, NYC, 1982, Plowshares Humanitarian award, 1990, Harry Mattin award Eastport Area C. of C., 2000, award Global Heritage Fund, 2004. Mem. Assn. Art Mus. Dirs. (emeritus), Am. Assn. Mus. (bd. dirs. Internat. coun. 1982-86), Mus. Trustee Assn. (adv. coun. of dirs. 1989-95), Am. Fedn. Arts (nat. exhbn. com. 1980-95), Acad. Lacquer Rsch. Tokyo (Am. sec. 1977-86), Japan Soc. No. Calif. (bd. dir. 1986-95, mem. collections com. Farnsworth Mus. 2000-), Century Assn., St. Croix Country Club (bd. dirs. 2001—), Herring Cove Golf Club.

CASTILLA, VINIVIO SORIA, professional baseball player; b. Oaxaca, Mexico, July 4, 1967; Grad. high sch., Mexico. Player Atlanta Braves, 1991-92, 2002—03, Tampa Bay Devil Rays, 1999—2001, Houston Astros, 2001, Colo. Rockies, 1993-99, 2004, Washington Nationals, 2005—. Named Nat. League All-Star Team, 1995, 1998 Achievements include led Nat. League in RBI's (131), 2004. Office: Wash Nationals 2400 East Capitol St SE Washington DC 20003

CASTILLE, RONALD D., state supreme court justice; b. Miami, Fla., Mar. 16, 1944; s. Henry and Marie Nash Castille. BS in Econs., Auburn U., 1966; JD, U. Va., 1971. Asst. dist. atty., 1971-81; chief asst. dist. atty. Career Criminal Unit, 1982-84; dep. dist. atty. Pre-Trial Unit, 1984-85; dist. atty. Phila., 1986-91; with litigation dept. Reed Smith Shaw & McClay, Phila., 1991-93; justice Pa. Supreme Ct., 1993—. Mem. Appellate Ct. Procedural Rules Com., 1994-96; liaison justice Ad Hoc Com. on Evidence, 1994-, Criminal Procedural Rules Com., 1994-, Minor Ct. Rules Com., 1994-. Co-chmn. Pa. Anti-Crime Coalition for George Bush for Pres., 1988, 92; commr. Presidents' Commn. on Model State Drug Laws, 1992; mem. Pa. Advisory Com. of U.S. Commn. on Civil Rights, 1992-; bd. dirs. mem. Nat. Alliance for Model State Drug Laws, 1993-, Pa. Ctr. for Adapted Sports, 1996-. Lieutenant USMC, 1966—68. Decorated Bronze Star with Combat V, Purple Heart (2); recipient Disting. Pub. Svc. award Pa. County and State Detectives Assn., 1987, Layman award Pa. Chiefs of Police Assn., 1987, Spirit of Am. award Inst. for Study of Am. Wars, 1988, Pres.'s award for Outstanding Svc., Nat. Dist. Attys. Assn., 1991; named Man of Yr., Fraternal Order of Police Lodge #5, 1988, Outstanding Disabled Vet. of Yr., Nat. Disabled Am. Vets., 1988. Mem. Nat. Dist. Attys. Assn. (v.p. 1986-91), Pa. Dist. Attys. Assn. (legis. chmn. 1986-91). Office: 1818 Market St Ste 3730 Philadelphia PA 19103-3639

CASTILLO, CARMEN, staffing company executive; b. Mallorca, Spain; Founder, pres., CEO Superior Design Internat., 1992—. Bd. mem. Fla. Regional Minority Bus. Coun. Named Minority Supplier Yr. (for Superior Design Internat.), Nat. Minority Supplier Devel. Coun. (NMSDC), 2002, 34th Largest Hispanic Bus. in US, Hispanic Fortune mag., 2002, Class III Supplier Yr., Ga. Minority Supplier Devel. Coun., 2002, NY/NJ Minority Purchasing Coun., 2002; named to Top 200 Fla. Pvt. Co., Fla. Trend, 2000; recipient Corporate Plus award, Nat. Minority Supplier Devel. Coun. (NMSDC), 1997. Achievements include featured in Women's Enterprise mag., 2003. Office: 6365 NW 6th Way Ste 360 Fort Lauderdale FL 33309 Office Phone: 954-938-5400. Office Fax: 953-772-5061.

CASTILLO, CRAIG Y., military officer, physician; b. Honolulu, Feb. 2, 1963; s. Albert and Masako Castillo; m. Yukari Koizumi Castillo, July 30, 1992; 1 child, Trisha Y.; 1 child, Memysha Y. BA, U. Calif., 85; MD, George Washington U., 1989; MPH, Harvard U., 1996. Lic. physician Hawaii, 1990, diplomate Am. Bd. Occuptl. Medicine, 1998, Am. Bd. Aerospace Medicine, 1997. Commd. lt. USAF, 1996, advanced through grades to lt. col., 2001—, resident Sch. Aerospace Medicine Brooks City Base, Tex., 1996—98, chief aerospace medicine Charleston AFB, SC, 1998—2000, flight commdr. Yokota AFB, Japan, 2000—02, specialist internat. health, 2002—03, commdr. Hollomen AFB, N.Mex., 2004—; student Nat. Inst. Def. Studies, Tokyo, 2003—04. Named Flight Surgeon of Yr., PACAF, 2003. Mem.: Aerospace Med. Assn. (Julian Ward award 1998). Home: 3479 Rosewood Ave Alamogordo NM 88310 Office: 49 ADOS 280 First St Holloman Afb NM 88330

CASTILLO, DAN A., health facility administrator; b. Lakewood, Calif., Feb. 28, 1972; s. Delfin Albert and Tobi Hein Castillo (Stepmother), Marlene Mendoza; m. Sayge Drotar, Oct. 3, 1998; 1 child, Emma Lauren. BS, U. So. Calif., 1994. Health adminstr. Alamitos Dermatol. Med. Group, Inc., Los Alamitos, Calif., 1998—2004, Newport Children's Med. Group, Newport Beach, Calif., 2004—. Recipient Book Dedication award, Rotary Club Lakewood, 1996. Mem.: Am. Coll. Med. Practice Execs. (assoc.), Med. Group Mgmt. Assn. (assoc.), Am. Bd. Quality Assurance and Utilization Rev. Physicians (assoc.). D-Conservative. Avocations: volleyball, surfing, guitar. Office: Newport Children's Med Group 1401 Avocado Ave #802 Newport Beach CA 92660 Office Phone: 949-644-0970.

CASTILLO, JOSEPHINE, small business owner, educator; b. Brownsville, Tex., Oct. 14, 1950; d. Douglas Ernest and Mary Castillo. Home econs. edn., Tex. Women's U., 1973. Tchr. CVAE Brownsville (Tex.) Independent Sch. Dist., 1973—74; tchr. Houston, 1974—79; home economist Microwave Oven Ctr., Houston, 1979—86, Club Party, Houston, 1986—87, Landlock Seafood, Houston, 1987—88; family consumer scis. tchr. Houston Independent Sch. Dist., 1988—. Mem.: FCST Houston, FCSTAT. Democrat. Roman Catholic. Avocations: crafts, sewing, cooking, reading mystery books. Home: 17515 Canton Forest Richmond TX 77469 Office: Southwest Dem Promotions PO Box 940755 Houston TX 77094-7755 Business E-Mail: jcastillo@teacher.esc4.com.

CASTILLO, LUIS ANTONIO DONATO, professional baseball player; b. San Pedro de Macoris, Dominican Republic, Sept. 12, 1975; Infielder Fla. Marlins, Miami, 1996—. Named to Nat. League All-Star Team, 2002—04; recipient Nat. League Gold Glove Award, 2003—04. Achievements include mem. World Series Champion Florida Marlins, 1997, 2003. Office: Fla Marlins Pro Player Stadium 2267 Dan Morino Blvd Opa Locka FL 33028 Fax: 305-626-7428.

CASTILLO, MARIO ENRIQUE, artist, educator; came to U.S., 1955, naturalized, 1965; s. Manuel Castillo and Maria Enriquez de Allen. Cert., Ill. Inst. Design, 1964; BFA, Sch. of Art Inst. Chgo., 1969; MFA, Calif. Inst. Arts, 1972; postgrad., U. So. Calif., 1969—70, Pasadena City Coll., 1977, Calif. State U. L.A., 1980—81, Calif. State U., Dominguez Hills, 1986—88, East L.A. City Coll., 1982, Nat. U., Inglewood, Calif., 1990, Columbia Coll., Chgo., 1996. Designer J.M. Pateros Studios, Inc., Chgo., 1965, Lukas & Assocs., Chgo., 1966; instr. Pilsen Settlement House, Chgo., 1967; comml. artist Chgo. Bd. Edn., 1968; instr. United Christian Cmty. Svc., Chgo., 1968—69; mural dir. Halsted Urban Progress Ctr., 1968, Dept. Human Resources, Chgo., 1969, McHenry Coll., Crystal Lake, Ill., 1992, No. Ill. U., DeKalb, 1993, Joliet Jr. Coll., Ill., 1994, Coll. of Lake County, Grayslake, Ill., 1994, U. Guadalajara, Ocotian, Mexico, 1995, SAIC & Lincoln Park Cultural Ctr., Chgo., 1996, Bemis Found., Omaha, 1996, Triton Coll., River Grove, Ill., 1997; tchg. asst. Calif. Inst. Arts, Valencia, 1970—72, instr., 1972—73, Santa Monica City Coll., Calif., 1973; mem. faculty dept. art U. Ill., Champaign, 1973—76; comml. artist L.A., 1977; instr. art Immaculate Heart Coll., Hollywood, Calif., 1979—80, Pacific Asian Consortium in Edn., 1980—81, E.C.F. Art Ctr., L.A., 1986—90, L.A. Unified Sch. Dist., 1986—90, Instituto Comercial Artistico, Maywood, Calif., 1987, Lexicon Sch. Langs., 1987—88, Plaza de la Raza, 1989—90; mem. faculty art dept. Columbia Coll., Chgo., 1990—. Panelist at Northeastern Ill. U., Chgo., 1974, Coll. Art Assn., Chgo., 1975, Columbia Coll., Chgo., 1992, 94, 96, Chgo. Artist Coalition, 1993, Nat. Assn. Chicano Studies, Chgo., 1994, 96, Suburban Fine Arts Ctr., Highland Park, Ill., 1995, U. Guadalajara, Jalisco, 1995; presenter workshop Human Rights Portfolio, Chgo., 1994, Chgo.,

1995; guest lectr. Galeria J.M. Velazco, Mexico City, 1975, Centro de la Causa, Chgo., 1975, Latino Cultural House, Champaign, 1975, U. Ill., Champaign, 1975, 76, Corpus Christi (Tex.) State U., 1978, McHenry County Coll., 1991, 92, Northwestern U., 1991, Columbia Coll., Montebello Sch. Dist., 1990, No. Ill. U., DeKalb, 1993, Triton Coll., River Grove, Ill., 1993, 94, Prospectus Gallery, Chgo., 1993, Joliet (Ill.) Jr. Coll., 1994, St. Cloud (Minn.) State U., 1994, MacMurry Coll., Jacksonville, Ill., 1994, Coll. of Lake County, 1994, Nat.-Louis U., Chgo., 1995, Melrose Park (Ill.) Pub. Libr., 1995, Mobil Art Gallery, Jacksonville, Ill., 1994, Northeastern U., Chgo., 1995, Harold Washington Libr., Chgo., 1995, Munster Ind. Cultural Ctr., 1995, U. Guadalajara, Ocotlan, Jalisco, 1995, 96, CCC Art Gallery, Chgo., 1995, Winnetka (Ill.) Cultural House, 1995, No. Ill. U., DeKalb, 1995, U. Guadalajara, La Barranca Campus, 1996, Lincoln Park Cultural Ctr., Chgo., 1996, Triton Coll., River Grove, 1996, 97; art juror Weisman Scholarship CCC, Chgo., 1993, Old Town Art Fair, Chgo., 1994, Hokin Gallery CCC, Chgo., 1995, Weisman Best of Show, Chgo., 1996; curator art exhibitions U. Ill., Champaign, 1975, Columbia Coll., Chgo., 1994, 95, Triton Coll., 1995, No. Ind. Arts Assn., Munster, 1995, 11th Street Art Gallery CCC, 1995, Hokin Ctr. Gallery, Columbia Coll., 1996; interior designer El Mercado Co., L.A. 1981-83; regular performer musical program Noches Rancheras, East L.A., Calif., 1981-83; cons. in field. One-man shows include Scholarship and Guidance Assn., Chgo., 1968, Calif. Inst. of the Arts, Burbank, 1971, Valencia, Calif., 1972, Latino Cultural House, U. Ill., Champaign, 1976, Inst. for Hispanic Cultural Studies, Santa Monica, Calif., 1989, Orlando Gallery, Sherman Oaks, Calif., 1989, Sangre De Cristo Arts and Conf. Ctr., Pueblo, Colo., 1991, Prospectus Gallery, Chgo., 1991, 93, McHenry County Art Gallery, 1991, No. Ill. U. Art Gallery, DeKalb, 1993, Atwood Art Ctr., St. Cloud U., 1994, MacMurry Coll., Jacksonville, Ill., 1994; numerous group shows including Fresno Art Mus., Calif., 1991, San Francisco Art Mus., 1991, San Francisco Mus. of Modern Art, 1991, Albuquerque Mus., 1991, Denver Art Mus., 1991, 93, Expo, 1993, San Antonio Mus. of Art, 1993, Nat. Mus. of Am. Art, 1993, Chgo., 1993, 94, Chgo. Latino Film Festival, 1994, Las Artes Galeria, Omaha, 1994, Open Windows Gallery, Chgo., 1994, S. Suburban Coll., South Holland, Ill., 1994, Columbia Coll., Chgo., 1994, 95, J.R. Shapiro Gallery, Oak Park, 1994, Cath. Theol. Union, Chgo., 1995, John Linsey Dallery, Oak Park, 1995, Hokin Gallery CCC, Chgo., 1995, Oak Park Art League, 1995, Pilsen Artist to Artist, Chgo., 1996, Prospecturs Gallery, Chgo., 1998, CCC Faculty Exhbn., Chgo., 1996, Richard Love Gallery, Chgo., 1996, La Llorona Gallery, Chgo., 1997, Prospectus Art Gallery, Chgo., 1997, Mexican Fine Arts Ctr. Mus., 1997, Chgo. Hist. Soc., 1996, 97, Mus. Contemporary Art, Chgo., 1996, 97, numerous others film screenings U.S., Europe, and Mexico; commd. muralist in public locations and pvt. residences; represented in permannet collections: Sara Lee Corp., Chgo., Mexican Mus. of Fine Arts, Chgo., San Francisco Mus. of Art, San Francisco Mus. of Contempory Art, Tucson Mus. of Art, Latino Inst., Chgo., Columbia Coll., Chgo., Bell Telephone Co., Chgo., Lake Meadows Assn., Chgo., Scholarship and Guidance Assn., Chgo., City of Chgo., San Antonio Art Mus., Guadalupe Cultural Arts Ctr., Denver, Evergreen State Coll., Olympia, Wash., Chgo. Humanities and Art Coun., Denver, Ariztlan, Inc., Phoenix, Mira, Chgo., Centro Cultural de La Raza, San Diego, San Diego Art Mus, Albuquerque Mus., San Francisco Art Mus., San Diego Mus. Contemporary Art, Denver Art Mus., Mex. Mus., San Francisco, Portland Art Mus., Nat. Mus. Am. Art, Washington, numerous group exhibitions include: Norris Gallery Cultural Arts Ctr., 1997, Instituto Cultural Puertoriqueno, 1998, Chgo. Athenaeum, Schaumburg, 1998, Ill. State Museum, 1999, Guadalupe Cultural Ctr., 2000; also numerous pvt. collections. Contbr. articles to numerous publications. Active contributor to cultural organizations. Recipient numerous awards including nat. gold medal, gold keys and certs. Scholastic Mag., 1963-65, cert. of merit N.Y. Times, 1965, 1st Prize award, Chgo. Police Dept., 1964, 1st Prize award Chgo. Assn. Commerce & Industry, 1965, 1st Pl. award U. Ill. Chgo. LASP design competition, 1st prize Maldef Art Competition, 1989, 1st pl. ESDC's Archtl. Relief Design Competition for New Homes in Chgo., 1992; artist to represent Midwest in nat. workshop, UCLA, 1988, artist to represent Latino culture in Spanish TV comml., 1989, 1st prize Homewood (Ill.) C. of C., 1967, 1st prize Fiesta del Quinto Sol, Chgo., 1974, 1st prize Mus. Sci. and Industry, Chgo., 1975, 1st prize for 18th St. banner design, Chgo., 1994; Am. Film Inst. grantee, 1972; Oakley fellow U. So. Calif., 1969-70; Scholarship and Guidance Assn. grantee, 1965-68, Ford Found. grantee, 1975; named Artist of Yr., Latino Inst., 1991. Achievements include rsch. in Perceptualism (the phenomena of after-images and optical illusions in paintings to create the feeling of the 4th dimension and alterations in color perception, visual investigations into discovering peculiar ways of presenting the human condition on this planet using superimposed layers of different states of realities and warping images and space so as to turn them "up-side-down"; composing numerous songs. Home: 10101 S Avenue M Chicago IL 60617-5925 Office: Columbia Coll Dept Art & Design 600 S Michigan Ave Chicago IL 60605-1900 Office Phone: 312-344-7590. Business E-Mail: mcastillo@colum.edu. E-mail: mario@mariocastillo.com.

CASTILLO, RUBEN, federal judge; b. Chgo., 1954; BA, Loyola U., 1976; JD, Northwestern U., 1979. Bar: Ill. 1979. Assoc. Jenner & Block, Chgo., 1979—84; asst. U.S. atty. (No. dist.) Ill. US Dept. Justice, 1984—88; regional counsel Mexican Am. Legal Def. & Edn. Fund, Chgo., 1988—91; ptnr. Kirkland & Ellis, Chgo., 1991-93; judge U.S. Dist. Ct. (no. dist.) Ill., 1994—. Adj. prof. Northwestern U., 1988—; vice chair, U.S. Sentencing Commn., 1999-. Mem. ABA, Latin Am. Bar Assn., Chgo. Bar Found., Chgo. Coun. of Lawyers (v.p. 1991-93). Office: U S Courthouse 2378 Dirksen Bldg 219 S Dearborn St Chicago IL 60604-1702

CASTILLO, SUSAN, school system administrator; b. LA, Aug. 14, 1951; m. Paul Machu. BA, Oreg. State U., 1981. Mem. staff Oreg. Pub. Broadcasting Radio, 1979-82; journalist, reporter legis. sessions Sta. KVAL-TV, Salem, 1991, 93, 95, journalist, reporter Eugene, 1982-97; mem. Oreg. State Senate, Salem, 1997—2002, vice chair edn. com., mem. health and human svcs. com., mem. transp. com., asst. Dem. leader legis. sessions, 1999, 2001; supt. pub. instrn. State of Oreg., Salem, 2003—. Leader Oreg. Women's Health & Wellness Alliance. Mem. Gov.'s Task Force on DUII, 1997, Gov.'s Task Force on Cmty. Right to Know; bd. dirs. Oreg. Commn. on Hispanic Affairs, 1997, Birth to Three, Oreg. Environ. Coun.; mem. adv. com. Oreg. Passenger Rail Adv. Coun.; mem. Labor Comm.'s Adv. Com. on Agrl. Labor; vice-chair Farm Worker Housing Task Force. Democrat. Achievements include being the first Hispanic woman to serve in Oregon legislature. Office: Oregon Dept Education 255 Capitol St NE Salem OR 97301-0203*

CASTLE, DIAN KIRSCHLING, staff development specialist, consultant; b. Wis. Rapids, Wis., May 24, 1942; d. Roman Anthony and Edna Sophie (Hostvedt) Kirschling. B.A., Mt. Mary Coll., 1969; M.S., Chgo. State U., 1978. Cert. tchr., Wis.; nat. cert. counselor, career counselor. Recreation leader City of Phila., 1969-70; tchr., Wis., Pa., 1970-74; social worker Dept. of Pub. Aid, Joliet, Ill., 1974-78; dir., coordinator Joliet Community Anti-Crime Orgn., 1978-79; counselor Joliet Jr. Coll., 1979; guidance dir. Assumption High Sch., Wis. Rapids, 1979-82; counselor Kansas City Sch. Dist., Mo., 1983-84; inservice specialist Kans. State Dept. of Edn., Topeka, 1984-86; cons. Global Industries Co., Wis. Rapids, 1980— . Contbr. articles to profl. jours. Mem. Wis. Council of Social Agencies, 1979-82, pres., 1982; mem. Adv. Council for Career Edn., Wis. Rapids, 1979-82, Shawnee Mission, Kans., 1983-84; mem. Mayor's Council on Edn., Kans. City, Mo., 1983-84. S.E. Wis. Sci. Fair scholar, 1965. Mem. Nat. Staff Devel. Council, Am. Assn. Counseling and Devel. (cert.), AAUW, Nat. Vocat. Guidance Assn., Am. Soc. Tng. and Devel., Nat. Soc. Performance and Instrn., U.S. Tennis Assn., Sigma Tau Delta, Alpha Kappa Delta, Phi Alpha, Phi Delta Kappa, Kappa Delta Pi. Roman Catholic. Club: Smithsonian (Washington). Avocations: tennis; skiing; ballet; camping; sports.

CASTLE, EMERY NEAL, agricultural and resource economist, educator; b. Eureka, Kans., Apr. 13, 1923; s. Sidney James and Josie May (Tucker) C.; m. Merab Eunice Weber (dec.), Jan. 20, 1946; 1 child, Cheryl Diana Delozier; m. Betty Thompson, Mar. 18, 2000. BS, Kans. State U., 1948, MS, 1950; PhD, Iowa State U., 1952, LHD (hon.), 1997. Agrl. economist Fed. Res. Bank of Kansas City, 1952-54; from asst. prof. to prof. dept. agrl. econs. Oreg. State U., Corvallis, 1954-65, dean faculty, 1965-66, prof., head dept. agrl. econs., 1966-72, dean Grad. Sch., 1972-76, Alumni disting. prof., 1970, prof. univ. grad. faculty econs., 1986—93, dir. rural studies program, 2001—03; v.p., sr. fellow Resources for the Future, Washington, 1976-79, pres., 1979-86. Vice-chmn. Environ. Quality Commn. Oreg., 1988-95; pres. Acad. for Lifelong Learning, Oreg. State U., 2002-03. Editor: The Changing American Countryside: Rural People and Places, 1995; mem. editl. bd. Land Econs., 1969—. Recipient Alumni Disting. Service award Kans. State U., 1976; Disting. Service award Oreg. State U., 1984 Fellow AAAS, Am. Assn. Agrl. Economists (pres. 1972-73), Am. Acad. Arts and Scis. Home: 4649 SW Hollyhock Cir Corvallis OR 97333 Office: Oreg State U 227 Ballard Corvallis OR 97331 Office Phone: 541-737-1428. E-mail: emerycastle@comcast.net.

CASTLE, HOWARD BLAINE, retired religious organization administrator; b. Toledo, July 15, 1935; s. Russell Wesley and Letha Belle (Hobbs) C.; m. Patricia Ann Haverty, Aug. 12, 1957; 1 child Kevin Blaine. AB, Marion Coll., 1958; postgrad., Valparaiso U., 1960. Pastor The Wesleyan Ch., Valparaiso, Ind., 1958-60, Toronto, Ohio, 1963-69; assoc. pastor Northridge Wesleyan Ch., Dayton, Ohio, 1960-63; exec. dir. gen. dept. youth Wesleyan Ch. Hdqrs., Marion, Ind., 1968-72, dir. field ministries gen. dept. Sunday schs., 1972-74, exec. dir. curriculum, 1980-81; mng. editor WIN Mag., Marion, Ind., 1969-72; asst. gen. sec. Gen. Dept. of Local Ch. Edn., Marion, Ind., 1974-80; gen. dir. estate planning Wesleyan Ch. Internat Ctr., Indpls., 1982—2002, ret., 2002. Editor Ohio dist. The Wesleyan Ch., Columbus, 1961-69; gen. conf. del. The Wesleyan Ch., Anderson, Ind., 1968, Greensboro, N.C., 2000. Writer: Curriculum-Religious Adult Student/Teacher, 1982—, Light from the Word, 1982—. Mem. Christian Holiness Partnership, Christian Stewardship Assn., Christian Mgmt. Assn. Mem. Wesleyan Ch. Avocations: music, reading. Personal E-mail: castlehb@aol.com. *Life's choices impact more than any other factor the measure of our success and achievements. Circumstances cannot defeat one who chooses to rise above them by acting in accord with his choice.*

CASTLE, JAMES CAMERON, information technology executive; b. Peoria, Ill., Nov. 4, 1936; s. Charles Cameron and Betty Evelyn (Shaw) C.; m. Dorothy Patricia Gorbandt, June 7, 1958; children: James Charles, Patricia Elizabeth. BS, U.S. Mil. Acad., 1958; MSEE, U. Pa., Phila., 1963, PhD, 1966. Pres., chief exec. officer Honeywell Bull Network Info. Svcs., S.A., Paris, 1975-78; gen. mgr. GE, Daytona Beach, Fla., 1978-80; v.p. ops. Honeywell, Inc., Billerica, Mass., 1980-82; exec. v.p. Memorex Corp., Santa Clara, Calif., 1982-84; pres. TGB Info. Systems, Inc., N.Y.C., 1984-87; chmn., pres., CEO Infotron Systems Corp., Cherry Hill, NJ, 1987—91; CEO Teradata Corp., El Segundo, Calif., 1991-92; chmn., CEO USCS Internat., Sacramento, 1992—2002; pres., CEO Castle Info. Techs., Manhattan Beach, 2000—. Bd. dirs. ADC Telecomms., Mpls., PMI Group, Inc., San Francisco, S.W. Water Co., LA, VeriFone, Inc., San Jose; pres. Chief Exec. Orgn., Bethesda, Md.; trustee West Point (N.Y.) Assn. Grads. 1st lt. U.S. Army, 1958-61. Mem. World Presidents Orgn.

CASTLE, JAY FRANK, lawyer; b. Sarasota, Fla., July 24, 1963; s. Frank Douglas and Nan Hunter Castle; m. Jennifer Annette Levi, Feb. 14, 1993; children: Jaager, Maddux, Lillian. BA with high honors, U. Fla., 1985; JD with distinction, Emory U., 1988. Bar: Ga. 1988, Fla. 2003, U.S. Dist. Ct. (no., mid. and so. dists.) Ga., U.S. Ct. Appeals (11th cir.). Assoc. King & Spalding, Atlanta, 1988—92, Lord Bissell & Brook, 1992—93; ptnr. Holt Ney Zatcoff & Wasserman, 1993—2003; group leader litigation Winn-Dixie Stores, Inc., 2003—. Mem.: ABA, Am. Trial Lawyers Assn. Office: 5050 Edgewood Ct Jacksonville FL 32203

CASTLE, JOHN KROB, merchant banker; b. Cedar Rapids, Iowa, Dec. 22, 1940; s. Clyo F. and Emma (Krob) C.; m. Marianne Sherman, Sept. 20, 1969; children: William Sherman, John Sherman, James Sherman, David Alexander. SB, MIT, 1963; MBA with high distinction, Harvard U., 1965; LHD (hon.), N.Y. Med. Coll., 1988. Assoc. Donaldson, Lufkin & Jenrette, Inc., N.Y.C., 1965-68, v.p., 1968-71, exec. v.p., 1971-73, mng. dir., 1973-80, chief operating officer, 1979-84, pres., 1980-86, chief exec. officer, 1985-86; pres., chief exec. officer Branford Castle, Inc., N.Y.C., 1986—; also founder, chmn., CEO Castle Harlan, Inc., N.Y.C., 1987—, also founder, chmn., chief exec. officer, 1987; chmn., gen. ptnr. Castle Harlan Ptnrs. II, III and IV. Bd. dirs. Morton's Restaurant Group, Inc., Marie Callender's, AdobeAir, Inc., Advanced Accessory Sys., LLC, Horizon Lines, Inc. Author: Financial Executives Handbook: Dividend Policy and Equity Financing, 1970, The Strategy of Corporate Financing: Packaging a Merger of Acquisition, 1971, Acquisition and Merger Negotiation Strategy, 1971; co-pub. Castle Connolly Guide, 1994, 1995, 1997—2004, Parent's Helper, 1996. With N.Y. Med. Coll., chmn. bd., 1979-90; mem. corp. MIT, 1987-2000; mem. vis. com. dept. econs; trustee The Whitehead Inst. for Biomed. Rsch., N.Y. Presbyn. Hosp.; chmn. Rhodes Scholar Selection Com., N.Y. State, 1986-90, Columbia-Presbyn. Health Sci. Adv. Coun.; endowed Castle Krob Fellowship for grad. study in econs. MIT, Castle Krob Fund for rsch. support at N.Y. Med. Coll., Castle Krob Devel. Chair in econs. MIT, John K. Castle Publs. Fund on Ethics, Politics and Econs., Yale U. Mem. Links Club, Met. Club, Harvard Club, N.Y. Yacht Club, Palm Beach Polo Club, Doubles Ltd., Club Collette. Home: 1095 N Ocean Blvd Palm Beach FL 33480-3230 Office: Castle Harlan Inc 150 E 58th St New York NY 10155-0002 Business E-Mail: jcastle@castleharlan.com.

CASTLE, JOYCE, mezzo soprano; b. Beaumont, Tex., Jan. 17, 1939; d. George Malicky and Ethel Lucille Reed; m. Wendell Castle (div.); m. Bruce Brewer (div.). BFA in voice/theatre, U Kans., 1961; MA, Eastman Sch. Music, 1966. Prin. artist N.Y.C. Opera, 1983—, Met. Opera, N.Y.C., 1985—, Chgo. Lyric Opera, Seattle Opera Co., Santa Fe Opera, opera cos. throughout U.S., Europe, Tel Aviv, Japan, Brazil. Artist in residence U. Kans., 2001—. Singer: (Operas) (world premiere) Dream of Valentino by D. Argento, Central Park by Michael Torke, (N.Am. premiere) The Handmaid's Tale, (albums) (by G. C. Menotti) The Medium, The Consul, (by L. Bernstein) Candide (Grammy Best Opera Recording, 1986). Mem.: AGMA, Actors Equity, Mu Phi Epsilon. Office: U Kans Dept of Music and Dance Murphy Hall Lawrence KS 66045

CASTLE, MICHAEL N., congressman, lawyer; b. Wilmington, Del., July 2, 1939; s. J. Manderson and Louisa B. Castle. BA, Hamilton Coll., 1961; JD, Georgetown U., 1964. Bar: Del. 1964, D.C. 1964. Assoc. Connolly Bove and Lodge, Wilmington, 1964-73, ptnr., 1973-75; dept. atty. gen. Del., 1965-66; mem. Del. Ho. of Reps., 1967-69, Del. State Senate, 1969-77; ptnr. Schnee and Castle (P.A.), 1975-80; lt. gov. State of Del., Wilmington, 1981-85, gov., 1985-93; prin. Michael N. Castle (P.A.), 1981—; mem. US Congress from Del., 1993—, mem. edn. and workforce com., intelligence com., chmn. subcom. edn. reform, chmn. tech. and tactical intelligence. Mem. Del. Ho. of Reps., 1966-67, Del. State Senate, 1968-76, minority leader, 1976 Bd. dirs. Boys Club of Wilmington. Mem. Del. State Bar Assn., ABA, Council State Govts., Nat. Gov.'s Assn., Rep. Gov.'s Assn., Southern Gov.'s Assn. Republican. Roman Catholic. Office: US Ho of Reps 1233 Longworth Bldg Washington DC 20515-0801*

CASTLE, WILLIAM EUGENE, retired academic administrator; b. Thomas, S.D., Sept. 5, 1929; s. Eugene Albert and Kathryn E. (Barkley) C.; m. Diane Lee Sklar, Aug. 8, 1963. BS, No. State Tchrs. Coll., 1951; MA, U. Iowa, 1958; PhD, Stanford U., 1963. Tchr. Faulkton (S.D) High Sch., 1951; instr. St. Cloud (Minn.) Tchrs. Coll., 1958-60, Central Wash. Tchrs. Coll., Ellensburg, 1961; asst. prof. U. Va., 1963-65; asso. sec. for research and sci. affairs Am. Speech, Lang. and Hearing Assn., Washington, 1965-68; dean Nat. Tech. Inst. for Deaf, Rochester Inst. Tech., N.Y., 1968-79, v.p., 1979-95, dir., 1977-95. Author: The Effect of Narrow Band Filtering on the Perception of Certain English Vowels, 1964. Served with USAF, 1952-56. Named Outstanding Alumnus, No. State Coll., 1984 Mem. Am. Speech Lang. and Hearing Assn., Alexander Graham Bell Assn. for Deaf (pres. 1982-84, 90-92). Home: Cypress Landing 104 Roanoke Ln Chocowinity NC 27817-8809 *Though it took more than one-third of the years I have thus far spent, a great sense of relief from skepticism and cynicism occurred for me when I reasoned within myself that life is the only absolute and that the greatest component of feeling and the finest advocacy are that of love, not just for fellow human beings but for all parts of life that reflect beauty. Without these two prime thoughts and without lifegiven talents, integrity, and flexibility for living cooperatively with others, I would have no sense of success.*

CASTLEBERRY, JAMES NEWTON, JR., retired law educator, dean; b. Chatom, Ala., Dec. 28, 1921; s. James Newton and Nellie (Robbins) C.; m. Mary Ann Blocker, Feb. 12, 1944 (dec.); children: Jean, Nancy, James III (dec.), Elizabeth, Cynthia, Robert, Mary Ann. JD magna cum laude, St. Mary's U., 1952; diploma in comparative law, Nat. U. Mex., 1960; diploma in tchg. of comparative law, Strasburg, 1963. Bar: Tex. 1952. Asst. atty. gen. State of Tex., 1953-55; prof. law St. Mary's U., San Antonio, 1955-92, dean, 1978-89, dean emeritus, 1989—, ret., 1992. Dir. St. Mary's U. Summer Program in Internat. and Comparative Law, Innsbruck, Austria, 1986-89; exec. dir. Tex. Ctr. for Legal Ethics and Professionalism, 1990-92; lectr. comparative law fgn. legal study tours Corp. for Profl. Confs., 1990—. Co-author: Water & Water Rights, 1970; contbr. articles to law jours. Bd. dirs. San Antonio Conservation Soc.; trustee Tex. Supreme Ct. Hist. Soc. Mem. ABA, Am. Bar Found., San Antonio Bar Assn., Tex. Bar Found., San Antonio Bar Found., Tex. State Bar, Phi Delta Phi (internat. pres. 1977-79). Home: 7727 Woodridge Dr San Antonio TX 78209-2223

CASTLE-HUGHES, KEISHA, actress; b. Donnybrook, WA, Australia, Mar. 24, 1990; d. Tim Castle and Desrae Hughes. Actor: (films) Whale Rider, 2002 (New Zealand Film and TV award for best actress, 2003, Acad. award nomination for best actress, 2004), Star Wars: Episode III-Revenge of the Sith, 2005. Mailing: Creative Artists Agy c/o Kim Hodgert 9830 Wilshire Blvd Beverly Hills CA 90212-1825

CASTLEMAN, ALBERT WELFORD, JR., physical chemist, educator; b. Richmond, Va., Jan. 7, 1936; s. Albert W. and Mildred L. Castleman; m. Heide Gisela Engel, Mar. 10, 1976; children: Sharon Beth, Robert Gill, Clifton Carl. BChemE, Rensselaer Poly. Inst., 1957; MS, Poly. Inst. Bklyn., 1963, PhD, 1969; PhD (hon.), U. Innsbruck, Austria, 1987. Leader chemistry rsch. group Brookhaven Nat. Lab., 1958-75; adj. prof. atmospheric chemistry depts. earth and space sci. and mechanics SUNY, Stony Brook, 1973-75; prof. chemistry, CIRES fellow U. Colo., Boulder, 1975-82; prof. chemistry Pa. State U., University Park, 1982—, Evan Pugh prof. chemistry, 1986—, adv. bd. Particulate Materials Ctr., 1987-94, mem. Ctr. for Materials Physics, 1993—, Eberly disting. chair in sci., 1999—, prof. physics, 1999; adv. bd. Ctr. for Nanoscale Sys. Materials Va. Commonwealth U., 1992—. Vis. prof. Physics Inst., Leopold-Franzens U., Innsbruck, Austria, 1981, 84, 99; mem. rev. com. chem. physics programs, Oak Ridge Nat. Lab., 1979, adv. com. to lab. dir. chem. physics programs, Health and Safety Divsn., 1987-90, chmn., 1990, mem. Dept. Energy rev. com. for chem. physics and radiol. physics program, 1985, Fulbright guest prof., 1990; adv. to Dept. Energy on chem. physics pertaining to energy related environ. programs, 1980; mem. ad hoc. panel on atmospheric chemistry Com. on Atmospheric Scis., NRC, NAD, 1980; mem. rev. com. for radiol. and environ. rsch. divsn. Argonne Univs. Assn. Argonne Nat. Lab., 1977-81, chemistry divsn., Argonne, 1988; mem. various rev. and adv. coms. Nat. Ctr. for Atmospheric Rsch., U.S. Dept. Energy U.S. Nuc. Regulatory Commn.; cons. Mfg. Chemists Assn., 1975-80, nuc. divsn. Oak Ridge Nat. Lab., 1976-86, E.I. Dupont de Nemours, 1989—2000; chmn. subcom. on ions, aerosols and radioactivity Internat. Commn. Atmospheric Electricity, 1976-80; sr. scientist von Humboldt awardee Tech. Hochschule Darmstadt, 1987, Philipps U., Marburg, Germany, 1988, U. Wuerzburg, 1998; bd. dirs. chem. sci. and tech. NRC-NAS, 2001—. Mem. editl. bd. Jour. Phys. Chemistry, 1985-88, 2000—, sr. editor, 1988-98; mem. editl. bd. Jour. Am. Chem. Soc., 2002—, Chem. Phys. Letters, 1995—, Jour. Cluster Sci., Internat. Jour. Mass Spectrometry and Ion Proc., 1987-90, Jour. Chem. Physics, 1985-87, Jour. Atmospheric Chemistry, 1982-94, Aerosol Sci. and Tech., 1982-86, Advances in Chem. Physics, 1995—, Nano Letters, 2000—, Springer Series in Chem. Physics, 2003—, Chem. Physics, 2003—; co-editor, mem. editl. bd. Zeitschrift fer Physick D., 1987-90; mem. chem. physics editl. adv. bd. Rsch. Trends; contbr. articles to profl. jours. Recipient Sr. Scientist Alexander von Humboldt award, 1986, Sr. Scientist Fulbright award, 1990, Wilhelm-Jost-Meml. Lecture award, 2000; Sherman Fairchild Disting. scholar, Calif. Inst. Tech., 1977; NSF Creativity Award grantee, 1985-87; Japanese Soc. for Promotion Sci. fellow, 1983, 97, Fellow AAAS, Am. Acad. Arts and Scis., Am. Phys. Soc., N.Y. Acad. Scis.; mem. Nat. Acad. Scis., Am. Chem. Soc. (Creative Advances in Environ. Sci. and Tech. award 1988), Am. Geophys. Union, Am. Assn. Aerosol Rsch., Materials Rsch. Soc., Sigma Xi, Phi Lambda Upsilon. Home: 425 Hillcrest Ave State College PA 16803-3419 Office: Pa State U Dept Chemistry 152 Davey Lab University Park PA 16802-6300

CASTLEMAN, BREAUX BALLARD, health management company executive; b. Louisville, Aug. 19, 1940; s. John Pryor and Mary Jane (Ballard) Castleman; m. Sue Ann Foreman (div. 1995); children: Matthew B., Shea B.; m. Patricia Templin, 2002. BA in Econs., Yale U., 1962; postgrad., NYU, 1963. Mgmt. trainee Bankers Trust Co., N.Y.C., 1963-65; mng. dir. Castleman and Co., Houston, 1965-71; dir. program planning, econ. U.S. Dept. HUD, Ft. Worth, Dallas, 1971-73; v.p., office mgr. Booz Allen and Hamilton, Dallas, Houston, 1973-85; mng. dir. Castleman Group, Houston, 1985-87; CEO Kelsey-Seybold Clinic, P.A., Houston, 1987-95; pres. physician resources divsn. Caremark Internat., Inc., 1994-96; pres. Scripps Clinic, La Jolla, Calif., 1996-99; CEO Physia Corp., Houston, 2000—; pres., CEO Syntiro Healthcare Svcs., Inc., Irvine, Calif., 2001—. Contbr. articles to profl. jours. Candidate state legislature, Houston, 1968. Mem. Am. Med. Group Assn. (bd. dirs. 1996-99), Planning Forum (chmn. 1985-86), Yale Club N.Y., Presidio Golf Club. Office Phone: 949-923-3212. Personal E-mail: xcastleman@aol.com.

CASTLEMAN, LOUIS SAMUEL, retired metallurgist, educator; b. St. Johnsbury, Vt., Nov. 24, 1918; s. Max and Fannie (Svetkey) C.; m. Mildred Blanche Rubin, Jan. 25, 1948; children— Michael Z., David A., Steven J., Daniel J. BS, Mass. Inst. Tech., 1939, D.Sc., 1950. Plant metallurgist Sunbeam Electric Mfg. Co., Evansville, Ind., 1939-41; sr. scientist, supr., acting sect. mgr. Westinghouse Atomic Power Div., Pitts., 1950-54; metall. specialist Gen. Telephone & Electronics Labs., Inc., Bayside, N.Y., 1954-64; prof. phys. metallurgy Poly. U., N.Y., 1964-89, prof. emeritus, 1989—. Cons. phys. metallurgy. With AUS, 1941-46; lt. col. Ret. Recipient Distinguished Tchr. award Poly. Inst. N.Y., 1975 Fellow AAAS; mem. Am. Soc. Metals (chpt. chmn. 1963-64), Am. Inst. Mining, Metall. and Petroleum Engrs., Am. Phys. Soc., Metal Sci. Club N.Y. (pres. 1973-74), Sigma Xi. Democrat. Jewish religion. Home: 120 Morris Ave Apt C5 Rockville Centre NY 11570-4240 Office: 6 Metrotech Ctr Brooklyn NY 11201-3840 E-mail: lcastlem@optonline.net.

CASTON, J(ESSE) DOUGLAS, medical educator; b. Ellenboro, N.C., June 16, 1932; s. Lemuel Joseph and Myrtice Elizabeth (Vassey) C.; m. Marry Ann Keeter, June 1, 1958; children: John Andrew, Elizabeth Anne, Mary Susan. AB, Lenoir Rhyne Coll., 1954; MA, U. N.C., 1958; PhD, Brown U., 1961. Fellow Carnegie Instn., Washington, Balt., 1961-62; asst. prof. anatomy Case Western Res. U., Cleve., 1962-71, assoc. prof., 1971-76, prof., 1976-98, co-dir. Devel. Biology Ctr., 1971-77, prof. emeritus, 1999—. Cons. Diamond Shamrock Corp., Cleve., 1975-77; coordinator Core Acad. Program, Sch. Medicine, 1985-94. Patentee folate assay, methotrexate assay; contbr. numerous articles to sci. jours., 1962— . Served with AUS, 1954—56. Fellow H.W. Wilson, 1956; grantee USPHS, 1963—, Cancer Soc., 1963— Mem. Am. Chem. Soc., AAAS, Am. Soc. Zoologists and Developmental Biologists, Biophys. Soc., Soc. Cell Biology, Am. Assn. Anatomists Episcopalian.

CASTOR, JON STUART, electronics executive; b. Lynchburg, Va., Dec. 15, 1951; s. William Stuart and Marilyn (Hughes) Castor; m. Stephanie Lum, Jan. 7, 1989; 1 child, David Jon. BA, Northwestern U., 1973; MBA, Stanford U., 1975. Mgmt. cons., Menlo Park, Calif., 1981-96; pres., CFO TeraLogic, Inc., 1996—2000, CEO, 2000—02; sr. v.p., gen. mgr. Oak Tech. Inc., Sunnyvale, 2002—03, Zoran Corp., Sunnyvale, 2003—04; bd. dirs. Genesis Microchip,

2004—. Bd. dirs. Genesis Microchip, Alviso, Calif., Artimi, Cambridge, England. Dir. midwest consumer adv. bd. FTC, 1971—73; v.p., bd. dirs. San Mateo coun. Boy Scouts Am., 1991—93, bd. dirs. Pacific Skyline coun., 1994—2003; trustee Coyote Point Mus. Environ. Edn., San Mateo, 1992—95. Achievements include patents in field.

CASTORINO, SUE, communications executive; b. Columbus, Ohio, May 5, 1953; m. Randy Minkoff, Oct. 23, 1983. BS in Speech, Northwestern U., Evanston, Ill., 1975. Grad. fellow Ohio Gov.'s Sch., Columbus, 1975; producer, community affairs Sta. WBBM-TV, Chgo., 1975; news anchor, reporter Sta. WBBM, Chgo., 1981—86; news reporter Sta. WHTH-AM/FM, Newark, Ohio, 1975; news anchor, reporter Sta. WERE, Cleve., 1975—78, Sta. WWWE, Cleve., 1978—81; founder, pres. Sue Castorino: The Speaking Specialists, Chgo., 1986—. Pvt. voice coach; active internat. exec. comm. tng. in media, crisis and issue mgmt.; presenter, lectr. in field. Author: North Shore Mag., 1987—92. Recipient Golden Gavel award, Chgo. Soc. Assn. Execs., 1991, various news reporting awards, AP. UPI, Chgo., 1981—86. Avocations: sports, film, accomplished pianist. Office: The Speaking Specialists Ste 2602 435 N Michigan Ave Fl 2602 Chicago IL 60611-4001 Office Phone: 312-527-2252.

CASTORO, ROSEMARIE, sculptor; b. Bklyn., Mar. 1, 1939; d. Michael Peter and Camille C. Student in painting, Mus. Modern Art, N.Y.C., 1955-56; BFA cum laude, Pratt Inst., Bklyn., 1963. Tchr. Sch. Visual Arts, N.Y.C., 1971, Hunter Coll., N.Y.C., 1972, Calif. State U., Fresno, 1973, Syracuse (N.Y.) U., 1975, U. Colo., Boulder, 1977, Stockton State U., N.J., 1983, Boston Mus. Sch., 1983, Am. U., Corciano, Italy, 2000. Lectr. art Boston Mus. Sch. Art, 1971, 80, New Sch. Social Rsch., N.Y.C., 1972, 73, Phila. Coll. Art, 1974, Atlanta Coll. Art, 1974, Rome Art Assn., N.Y. State, 1975, Syracuse (N.Y.) U., 1975, U. Calif., Berkeley, 1976, Suzuki-Walker, Sausalito, Calif., 1976, Art Inst. Sch., Chgo., 1980, Pratt Inst., N.Y.C., 1982, 95, C.W. Post, L.I., N.Y., 1984, San Jose (Calif.) U., 1984, 85, N.J. Ctr. for Visual Arts, Summit, 1989, Ecole Nat. Superieure des Beaux-Arts, Paris, 1995. One-woman shows include Tibor de Nagy Gallery, N.Y.C., 1971, 1972, 1973, 1975, 1976, 1978, 1981, 1983, 1985, 1989, Hal Bromm Gallery, 1976, 1978, 1979, 1980, 1983, 1987, 1991—92, 1997, 2002, Julian Pretto, 1978, 1979, Marion Deson, Chgo., 1981, Am. Ctr., Paris, 1983, Eaton/Shoen Gallery, San Francisco, 1984, 1986, Newark Mus., 1991, Arnaud Lefebvre Gallery, Paris, 1993, 1995, 1997, 1998, 1999, 2003, 2004, Stella R Graphics, Paris, 1993, Eaton Fine Arts, West Palm Beach, Fla., 2000, 2004, exhibited in group shows at Bklyn. Mus., 1963, Tibor de Nagy Gallery, 1966, Stable Gallery, 1966, Dwan Gallery, N.Y.C., 1968, 1969, Richard Feigen Gallery, 1968, Paula Cooper Gallery, 1969, 1971, Vancouver (B.C., Can.) Art Gallery, 1970, Stadtische Kunsthalle, Dusseldorf, Germany, 1970, Allen Art Mus., Oberlin, Ohio, 1970, Hundred Acres Gallery, N.Y.C., 1970, 112 Greene St Gallery, 1971, 1972, Richard Gray Gallery, Chgo., 1972, Storm King Art Gallery, Mountainville, N.Y., 1972, 1974, 1975, Grapestake Gallery, San Francisco, 1975—76, Moore Coll. Art, Phila., 1977, John Weber Gallery, N.Y.C., 1977, Hal Bromm Gallery, 1977, 1981—82, 1985—87, Indpls. Mus. Art, 1978, Whitney Mus. Am. Art, N.Y.C., 1978, Nancy Lurie Gallery, Chgo., 1978, Smithsonian Instn., Washington, 1980, Hunter Mus. Art, Chattanooga, Tenn., 1980, Banco Gallery, Brescia, Italy, 1980, Hirshhorn Mus. and Sculpture Garden, Washington, 1981, Pratt Inst. Art Gallery, Bklyn., 1981, Eaton/Shoen Gallery, 1982, 2003, Maier Mus. Art, Lynchburgh, Va., 1983, 1990, Laguna Gloria Art Mus., Austin, Tex., 1985, Mus. Modern Art, N.Y.C., 1985, Newark Mus., 1987, Marvin Seline Gallery, Houston, 1990, Jan Baum Gallery, LA, 1990, Stellar Graphics, Paris, 1992, Galerie Arnaud Lefebvre, 1993, 1995—96, 2001, 2003, 2004, Henry St. Settlement, N.Y.C., 1993, Athenaeum Music & Arts Libr., La Jolla, Calif., 1995, Beaumanoir, Le Leslay, France, 1995, 2004, PS #1, N.Y.C., 2004, many others, commns. include, Battery Park City, N.Y.C., 1978, GSA, Topeka, Kans., 1979, Am. Ctr., Paris, 1983, Athena Found., L.I., N.Y., 1986, Woodstock '94, Saurgerties, N.Y., 1994, others, Represented in permanent collections Allen Art Mus., Oberlin, Ohio, Boca Raton (Fla.) Mus., Bank of Am., Calif., Chase Manhattan Bank, N.A., GSA, Washington, Mus. Modern Art, N.Y.C., Newark Mus., Fonds Nat. d'Art Contemporain, Paris, Univ. Art Mus., U. Calif., Berkeley, U. Mass., Woodward Found., Washington, others. Treas. HIV-Arts, N.Y.C., 1994—2005. Guggenheim fellow, 1971; grantee Woodward Found., 1970, CAPS, 1972, 74, NEA, 1974-75, 84-85, Tiffany Found., 1977, Pollock-Krasner Found., 1989-90, 97-98. Home: 151 Spring St # 6 New York NY 10012-3850 Personal E-mail: rcastoro@earthlink.net.

CASTRIOTTA, RICHARD J., medical educator, physician; b. Winchester, Mass., Dec. 21, 1945; s. Louis and Mary Castriotta; m. Laura Gillespie, Feb. 19, 1983; 1 child, Gabrielle. AB, Holy Cross Coll., 1967; MD, U. Bologna, Italy, 1974. Diplomate internal medicine Am. Bd. Internal Medicine, 1978, pulmonary disease Am. Bd. Internal Medicine, 1980, sleep medicine Am. Bd. Sleep Medicine, 1989. Rsch. asst. Mass. Gen. Hosp., Boston, 1967—74; med. resident Hosp. St. Raphael, New Haven, 1974—78; pulmonary fellow U. Conn. Health Ctr., Farmington, 1978—80; asst. prof. of medicine and pathology U. Conn. Sch. Medicine, Farmington, 1981—92, assoc. prof. clin. medicine, 1992—95; dir. pulmonary medicine Mt. Sinai Hosp., Hartford, Conn., 1981—85, dir. Sleep Disorders Ctr., 1983—95, asst. chief medicine, 1991—95, interim chief medicine, 1992—93; med. dir. Meml. Hermann Hosp. Sleep Disorders Ctr., Houston, 1995—; assoc. prof. internal medicine U. Tex. Med. Sch., Houston, 1995—2002, prof. internal medicine, 2002—, dir. divsn. pulmonary, critical care and sleep medicine, 2004. Dir. Hartford Health Dept. Chest Clinic (for Tb), 1981—94; med. dir. Pulmonary Physiology Lab. Mt. Sinai Hosp., Hartford, 1981—95, med. dir. Blood Gas Lab., 1981—92, med. dir. respiratory therapy dept., 1981—95, chmn. ethics com., 1986—95, med. dir. ICU, 1991—92; mem. Sch. Medicine. coun. U. Conn. Health Ctr., Farmington, 1992—95; chmn. tb elimination adv. com. State Conn., Hartford, 1992—95; chmn. sleep medicine sect. Conn. Thoracic Soc., 1992—95; chmn. ethics meeting group Conn. Hosp. Assn., Wallingford, 1993—95; chmn. ethics com. St. Francis Hosp. and Med. Ctr., Hartford, 1995—95; med. adv. com. Blue Cross and Blue Shield Tex., Richardson, 1996—; faculty senate U. Tex. Med. Sch., Houston; sleep fellowship program dir. U. Tex. Health Sci. Ctr., Houston; chmn. futility rev. and ethics com. Meml. Hermann Hosp., Houston. Mem. Conn. Opera, Hartford, 1994—95. Fellow: Am. Coll. Chest Physicians (vice chair sleep network steering com. 2004—, steering com. sleep inst. 2005—), Am. Acad. Sleep Medicine (sleep inst. steering com. 2004—); mem.: So. Sleep Soc. (pres. 2003—05), Am. Thoracic Soc. Home: 2406 Reba Dr Houston TX 77019 Office: Univ Tex Med Sch Ste I-274 6431 Fannin Houston TX 77030 Office Phone: 713-500-6828. Personal E-mail: castriotta@sbcglobal.net. E-mail: richard.j.castriotta@uth.tmc.edu.

CASTRO, ALEXANDRO C., commonwealth supreme court justice; b. Tinian, Northern Marianas, Apr. 23, 1952; m. Carmen Moses; children: Patrick, Eric, Yvonne, Alex Jr., Rodney, Ariel. BL, U. Papua New Guinea, 1979. Bar: U.S. Ct. Appeals (9th cir.), U.S. Dist. Ct. No. Mariana Islands. Mem. Rota Mcpl. Coun., 1972; asst. prosecutor Atty. Gen.'s Office, 1979—86, atty. gen., 1986—89; assoc. judge Northern Mariana Islands Superior Ct., 1989—93, presiding judge, 1993—98; assoc. judge Northern Mariana Islands Supreme Ct., 1998—. Office: House of Justice Guma Hustisia, Imwaal Aweewe PO Box 502165 Saipan MP 96950 Business E-Mail: cnmilaw@itecnmi.com.

CASTRO, JAN GARDEN, writer, art educator, consultant; b. St. Louis, June 8, 1945; d. Harold and Estelle (Fischer) Garden; 1 child, Jomo Jemal. Student, Cornell U., 1963—65; BA, U. Wis., 1967; pub. cert., Radcliffe Coll., 1967; MA in Tchg., Washington U., St. Louis, 1974, MA, 1994. Life cert. tchr. secondary English, speech, drama and social studies, Mo. Tchr., writer, St. Louis, 1970—; dir. Big River Assn., St. Louis, 1975-85; adj. prof. humanities Lindenwood Coll., 1980—. Co-founder, dir. Duff's Poetry Series, St. Louis, 1975-81; founder, dir. River Styx P.M. Series, St. Louis, 1981-83; arts cons. Harris-Stowe State Coll., 1986-87; vis. scholar Am. Acad. in Rome, summer 2000. Contbg. author: rev. books San Francisco Rev. Books, 1982—85, Am. Book Rev., 1990—93, Mo. Rev., 1991, New Letters, 1993, 1996, Tampa Rev., 1994—2000, The Nation, Am. Poetry Rev., Sculpture Mag., 1997—; author: (poetry) Mandala of the Five Senses, 1975, The Art and Life of Georgia O'Keeffe, 1985, 1995, Memories and Memoirs...Contemporary Missouri Authors, 2000, (poetry) The Last Frontier, 2001—, Sonia DeLaunay: La Moderne, 2002—; editor: (jours.) River Styx mag., 1975—86; co-editor: (essays) Margaret Atwood: Vision and Forms, 1988; co-prodr.(TV host, co-prodr.): (shows) The Writers Cir., Double Helix, 1987—89; contbg. editor: (jours.) Sculpture Mag. Seeking St. Louis, Voices from a River City, 1670—2000. Mem. University City Arts and Letters Commn., Mo., 1983-84. NEH fellow UCLA, 1988, Johns Hopkins U., 1991, Camargo Found. fellow (Cassis, France), 1996; recipient Arts and Letters award St. Louis Mag., 1985, Editor's award and editor during G.E. Younger Writers award to River Styx Mag., Coord. Coun. for Lit. Mags., 1986, Arts award Mandrake Soc. Charity Ball, 1988, Leadership award YWCA St. Louis, 1988. Mem. MLA, CAA, PEN Am. Ctr., Nat. Coalition Ind. Scholars, Margaret Atwood Soc. (founder). Home: 7420 Cornell Ave Saint Louis MO 63130-2914 Office: LCIE Coll Lindenwood U Saint Charles MO 63301 E-mail: jan_g_castro@mail.com.

CASTRO, LEONARD EDWARD, lawyer; b. L.A., Mar. 18, 1934; s. Emil Galvez and Lily (Meyerholtz) C.; 1 son, Stephen Paul. A.B., UCLA, 1959, J.D., 1962. Bar: Calif. 1963, U.S. Supreme Ct. 1970. Assoc. Musick, Peeler & Garrett, Los Angeles, 1962-68, ptnr., 1968— . Mem. ABA, Los Angeles County Bar Assn.Bd. editors, note and comment editor: UCLA Law Review, 1961-62. Contbd. chpts. to books. Panelist, spkr., various legal edn. programs. Office: Musick Peeler & Garrett 1 Wilshire Blvd Ste 2000 Los Angeles CA 90017-3876

CASTRO, MARIA GRACIELA, medical educator, geneticist, researcher; b. Buenos Aires, Mar. 2, 1955; d. Nestor Antonio Castro and Maria Esther Rodriquez; m. Pedro Ricardo Lowenstein, Jan. 12, 1988; 1 child, Elijah David Lowenstein. BSc 1st class in Chemistry, Nat. U. La Plata, Argentina, 1979, MSc in Biochemistry, 1981, PhD in Biochemistry, 1986. Fogarty postdoctoral fellow Lab. Neurochemistry and Neuroimmunology NICHHD/NIH, Bethesda, Md., 1986-88; sr. rsch. fellow Lab. Molecular Endocrinology, dept. biuochemistry and physiology U. Reading, England, 1988-90; lectr. dept. molecular and life scis. U. Abertay, Dundee, Scotland, 1991-92; lectr. in neurosci., dept. physiology U. Wales Coll., Cardiff, 1991-95; sr. lectr. medicine Sch. Medicine U. Manchester, England, 1995-98, prof. molecular medicine, 1998—, dir. molecular medicine and gene therapy unit, 1996—. Expert Women in Sci. Tech., Sheffield, England, 1996—; neurosci. panel Wellcome Trust, England, 1999—; co-dir. dept. molecular medicine Cedar-Sinai Med. Ctr., 2001—; co-dir. bd. govs. Gene Therapeutics Rsch. Inst., Cedars Sinai Med. Ctr., 2001—; prof. medicine UCLA, 2002—, prof. molecular and med. pharmacology, 2004—. Mem. editl. bd.: Jour. Endocrinology, Jour. Molecular Endocrinology, Current Gene Therapy, Gene Therapy, Pituitary, 2000, Neuro Molecular Medicine, 2001—; contbr. articles to profl. jours. Rsch. grantee, Brit. Heart Found., 1997, Med. Rsch. Coun., 1998, Biotech. and Biol. Rsch. Coun., 1999—2000, Wellcome Trust, 1999, NIH, 2003—. Mem.: Nat. Inst. Neurol. Disorders and Stroke, Internat. Soc. Nerovirology (founding mem.), Soc. Neurosci., Endocrine Soc., Am. Gene Therapy Assn. Achievements include patents in field; research in program development of gene therapy for chronic neurological diseases and brain cancer. Business E-Mail: castromg@cshs.org.

CASTRO, MARY MCDERMOTT, language educator; b. East Liverpool, Ohio, Apr. 13, 1952; d. Robert James and Elizabeth Costello McDermott; 1 child, Sarah Elizabeth. BA, Seton Hill, 1974; MA, Ohio U., 1976. Tchr. Spanish, Mercyhurst Prep. Sch., Erie, Pa., 1976—78; lectr. in Spanish, U. Minn., Duluth, 1979; tchg. asst. in English, U. Pitts., 1979; tchg. asst. in Spanish, U. N.C., Chapel Hill, 1980—83; lectr. in Spanish, N.C. State U., Raleigh, 1984—90, U. N.C., Charlotte, 1990—. Dir. of Spanish lang. & culture in Costa Rica program U. N.C., Charlotte, 1993—, Sigma Delta Pi advisor, 1995—2005; instr. English, Inst. Anglo-Mexicano, Jalapa, Mexico, 1982. Named Outstanding Tchr., N.C. Gen. Assembly, 1994, 1996. Mem.: Fgn. Lang. Assn. N.C., Am. Coun. on Tchg. of Fgn. Langs., Am. Assn. Tchrs. of Spanish and Portuguese, N.C. State U. Acad. Outstanding Tchrs. (life). Avocation: dog breeding. Home: 2520 Savannah Hills Dr Matthews NC 28105 Office: University of North Carolina-Charlotte 9201 University City Blvd Charlotte NC 28223-0001 Office Phone: 704-841-9126. Personal E-mail: marysec88@aol.com.

CASTRO, PAULETTE, elementary school educator; b. Goodrich, Mich., Dec. 27, 1947; d. Paul and Betty Jane (Nelles) Bindig; m. Steve Allen Castro, May 4, 1974; children: Melanie, Christopher. BA, U. Mich., 1972; MS, U. So. Calif., 1980. Cert. tchr., Mich., Kans., Calif., Colo., Va. Tchr. kindergarten LaPetite Acad., Colorado Springs, Colo.; tchr. Fairfax County Pub. Schs., Springfield, Va. Capt. U.S. Army, 1972-77.

CASTRO, RAUL HECTOR, lawyer, retired governor, retired ambassador; b. Cananea, Mexico, June 12, 1916; arrived in US, 1926, naturalized, 1939; s. Francisco D. and Rosario (Acosta) C.; m. Patricia M. Norris, Nov. 13, 1954; children— Mary Pat, Beth. BA, Ariz. State Coll., 1939; JD, U. Ariz., 1949; LL.D. (hon.), No. Ariz. U., 1966, Ariz. State U., 1972, U. Autonoma de Guadalajara, Mex. Bar: Ariz. 1949. Fgn. service clk. Dept. State, Agua Prieta, Mexico, 1941-46; instr. Spanish U. Ariz., 1946-49; practiced in Tucson, 1949-51; dep. county atty. Pima County, Ariz., 1951-54; county atty., 1954-58; judge Superior Ct., Tucson, 1958-64, Juvenile Ct., Tucson, 1961-64; U.S. ambassador to El Salvador, San Salvador, 1964-68, to Bolivia, La Paz, 1968-69; practice internat. law Tucson, 1969-74, Phoenix, 1980—; gov. Ariz., 1975-77; U.S. ambassador to Argentina, 1977-80; operator Castro Pony Farm, 1954-64. Pres. Pima County Tb and Health Assn., Tucson Youth Bd., Ariz. Horseman's Assn.; Bd. dirs. Tucson chpt. A.R.C., Tucson council Boy Scouts Am., Tucson YMCA, Nat. Council Christians and Jews, YWCA Camp; Bd. Mem. Ariz. N.G., 1935-39. Recipient Outstanding Naturalized Citizen award Pima County Bar Assn., 1964, Outstanding Am. Citizen award D.A.R., 1964; Pub. Service award U. Ariz., 1966; John F. Kennedy medal Kennedy U., Buenos Aires. Mem. Am. Fgn. Service Assn., Am. Judicature Soc., Inter-Am. Bar Assn., Ariz. Bar Assn., Pima County Bar Assn., Nat. Council Crime and Deliquency (bd. dirs.), Assn. Trial Lawyers Am., Council Am. Ambassadors, Nat. Assn. Trial Judges, Nat. Council Juvenile Ct. Judges, Fed. Bar Assn., Nat. Lawyers Club, Phi Alpha Delta. Clubs: Rotarian. Democrat. Roman Catholic.

CASTRO, VALENTINO, psychologist, counseling administrator; b. Humacao, P.R., Oct. 6, 1950; s. Vale and Dolores (Mulero) Castro; m. Angelica Alba, Sept. 13, 2001; children: Daniel, Raoul, Jorge, Deborah, Ariana. M in Planning, U. PR, Rio Piedras, 1976; EdD, Interamerican U., PR, 1987; specialist in sch. psychology, Govs. State U., University Park, Ill., 1998; resp. clin. psychology, Ill. Sch. Profl. Psychology, Rolling Meadows, 2000. Lic. sch. psychologist Fla. Dept. Health, Fla. Bd. Edn., Fla. Dept. Edn., profl. planner PR Dept. of State, nat. cert. school psychologist Nat. Sch. Psychology Cert. Sys. Rehab. counselor Dept. Social Svcs., Humacao, PR, 1971—76; profl. planner V&C Planning Assocs., San Juan, Miami, 1976—83; prof. Interam. U., San Juan, 1983—87; dir. evaluation Met. U., San Juan, 1984—85; prof. Phoenix U., San Juan, 1984—89; dir. evaluation Regional Colls. Adminstrn. U. PR, Rio Piedras, 1986—87; h.s. advanced math and stats. tchr. Chgo. Pub. Schs., 1991—96; sch. psychologist Cicero (Ill.) Pub. Schs., 1998—99, Dist. 141, Elgin, Ill., 1999—2000, Manatee County Sch. Bd., Bradenton, Fla., 2000—, Spl. Edn. Coop., Woodstock, Ill., 2000—01, Duval County Pub. Schs., Jacksonville, Fla., 2001—02; sr. psychologist Fla. State Prison, Starke, Fla., 2002—03. Cons. McNeill Labs., Las Piedras, 1983—87, PR Med. Bd., San Juan, 1987—91; com. mem. Manatee County Sch. Evaluation Com., Bradenton, Fla., 2004—; crisis specialist Nat. Orgn. For Victims Assistance, Fla., 2000—, NASP, Bethesda, Md., 2001—; social security reform commn. Office of Gov., San Juan, 1976—77; cons. Office of Gov., San Juan, 1983—91, PR Legislature (Senate) Edn. Reform Commn., San Juan, 1987—89, Johnson & Johnson, PR, 1987—90; cons., trainer Ponce Mcpl. Govt., 1990—91; cons. Dept. Children and Families, Chgo., 1996—97; testing cons., examiner Harcourt Pub., Dallas, 2003—. Contbr. articles to profl. jours. Troop chmn. Boys Scouts, Humacao, PR, 1976—80; mem. Chatholic Charities, Chgo., Woodstock, 2000—01; chmn. bd. dirs. Comm. and Social Svcs. Org., Chgo., 1992—2001; mem. Govs. Commn. on Child Wefare, Springfield, Ill., 1998—2000. Recipient Scholastic Achievement award, Interam. U., 1987; fellow, Nat. Edn. Acad., 1998; scholar, Nat. Mental Health Inst., 1974. Mem.: NASP, APA, Am. Planning Assn. (assoc.). Office: Manatee County Sch Bd 215 Manatee Ave W Bradenton FL 34221 Office Phone: 941-708-8770. Personal E-mail: castrov@fc.manatee.k12.fl.us.

CASTRO-BLANCO, JAMES, law educator; b. Bronx, N.Y., 1959; Bachelor, SUNY, Albany, 1988; JD, Bklyn. Law Sch., 1991. Litigation assoc. Winthrop Stimson Putnam & Roberts; asst. U.S. atty. Ea. Dist. N.Y.; asst. dean, adj. prof. law St. John's U. Sch. Law; mgr. assoc. devel. Shearman & Sterling. Mem. faculty N.Y.C. Corp. Counsel Trial Program, 1999—; coach mock trial teams Bklyn. Law Sch. and St. Johns U. Sch. Law. Mem. Mayor's adv. com. on judiciary, N.Y.C.; exec. coun. Network of Bar Leaders. Mem.: N.Y. State Bar Assn. (com. on legal edn. and admission to bar), Assn. of Bar of City of N.Y. (com. on recruitment and retention of lawyers). Office: St Johns U 8000 Utopia Pkwy Jamaica NY 11439

CASTROGIOVANNI, GARY J., management educator, researcher; b. Chgo. s. Raymond R. and Evelyn Castrogiovanni. BBA, Loyola U., Chgo., 1979; MBA, DePaul U., Chgo., 1982; PhD, Tex. Tech. U., Lubbock, 1987. Vis. asst. prof. McGill U., Montreal, Canada, 1986—87; asst. prof. La. State U., Baton Rouge, 1987—94; vis. assoc. prof. U. Houston, 1994—98; assoc. prof. U. Tulsa, 1998—. Comms. coord. So. Mgmt. Assn., 2004—, newsletter editor, 2003—04. Mem. editl. rev. bd. Jour. Mgmt., 1999—; contbr. articles to profl. jours. Recipient Best Reviewer - Strategy, So. Mgmt. Assn., 2001. Mem.: U.S. Assn. for Small Bus. and Entrepreneurship, Acad. Mgmt., Strategic Mgmt. Soc. Democrat. Roman Catholic. Office: Coll Bus Univ Tulsa 600 S Coll Ave Tulsa OK 74104-3189 Business E-Mail: gary-castrogiovanni@utulsa.edu.

CASTRO-KLAREN, SARA, Latin American literature professor; b. Arequipa, Sabandia, Peru, June 9, 1942; d. José Andrés and Zoila Rosa (Rivas) Castro-Valdivia; m. Peter F. Klaren, Sept. 3, 1962; 1 child, Alexandra. BA, UCLA, 1962, MA, 1965, PhD, 1968. Asst. prof. Dartmouth Coll., No. Hampshire, N.H., 1970-84; chief Hispanic div. Lib. of Congress Fed. Govt., Washington, 1984-86; prof. Latin Am. lit. Johns Hopkins U., Balt., 1986—. Dir. program Latin Am. Studies, JHU. Author: El Mundo Magico de J.M. Arquedas, Lima, 1973, Mario Vargas Llosa, Analisis Introductorio, Lima, 1988, Escritura Sujeto y Transgresión, Mex., 1989, Understanding Mario Vargas Llosa, U.S.C., 1990; editor: Women's Writing in Latin America, 1991, Latin American Women's Narrative: Practices and Theoretical Perspectives, 2003, Beyond Imagined Communities: Reading and Writing the Nation in Nineteenth Century Latin America, 2003. Fellow Woodrow Wilson Ctr. for Scholars, Washington, 1977-78. Mem. MLA, AAUP, Latin Am. Studies Assn. Avocation: gardening. Home: 9438 Rabbit Hill Road Great Falls VA 22066

CASTRONOVO, THOMAS PAUL, architect, consultant; b. Chgo., Apr. 7, 1932; s. Paul Thomas and Nancy (Racina) C. Student, U. Akron, 1949-51; BArch, Ohio State U., 1955. Registered architect, Ohio, Calif., Colo., Fla. Intern architect E.J. Guran, Architect, Akron, Ohio, 1957-58, A.W. Petersen, Architect, Akron, 1958-60; pres., owner Thomas P. Castronovo, Architect, Akron, 1960—. Chmn. Akron Urban Design and Fine Arts Commn.; mem. Akron Civic Design Awards Com., 1972, Akron Regional Devel. Bd., 1983-87. 1st lt. USAF, 1955-57. Mem. AIA (bd. dirs. Akron chpt. 1987-90), Architects Soc. Ohio, Pi Kappa Epsilon (Akron U. chpt., pres. alumni 1982-84, mem. Hall of Fame 1982). Avocations: tennis, skiing, gardening, cooking, boating. Office: 1175 N Main St Akron OH 44310-1047

CASTRO-PONCE, CLARA ESTHER, Spanish language educator; b. San Juan, P.R. d. Alfredo and Gladys A. (Ponce-Castro) Castro-Mesa; m. Guray Tas, July 19, 1997. BA magna cum laude, U. P.R., 1988; MA, Brown U., Providence, 1990, PhD, 2000. Tchg. asst., fellow Brown U., Providence, 1989-94, instr. Brown Learning Cmty., 1992-94; vis. asst. prof. Spanish North Park Coll., Chgo., 1995-97; asst. prof. Spanish Allegheny Coll., Meadville, Pa., 2000—02. Contbr. articles to profl. jours. Recipient Bernard E. Bruce award Brown U., 2001, Jose Marti award U. P.R., 1988, Cert. of Recognition, Chancellor of U., 1988; Demmler Endowment grantee Allegheny Coll., 2001, Dorothy Danforth-Compton Found. Rsch. Travel grantee, 1993, fellow, 1988-93, dissertation fellow, 1994. Mem. AAUP, MLA, Asociación Hispánica Medieval, Medieval Acad. Am., Golden Key. Avocations: travel, reading, tennis, music. Home: 91 Crenshaw Dr Flanders NJ 07836-4721

CASTURO, DON JAMES, venture capitalist; b. McKeesport, Pa., Nov. 9, 1942; s. Charles and Elizabeth B. (Barno) C.; m. Judith K. Erkman, Aug. 22, 1964; children: Don J.E., Christian D.E. BA, Mich. State U., 1964; MBA, U. So. Calif., 1966. Participant mgmt. devel. program Mellon Bank, Pitts., 1966-67, investment rschr., 1967-69, asst. invesment officer, 1969-71, investment officer, 1971-73, asst. v.p., 1973-82; v.p. mgr. Venture Capital Investments, 1982-88; gen. ptnr. Point Mgmt. Group, Pitts. Bd. dirs. GALT Technologies, Inc., Tri Foods, Inc., Lloyd's Food Products, Inc., Network Data Corp., Creativators, Inc., Meretek Diagnostics, Southdown Trading, Inc., The Steak-umm Co., SpaElegance.com., Inc. Co-chmn. enrichment program Mich. State U.; bd. dirs. Upper St. Clair Athletic Assn. Mem. Pitts. Soc. Fin. Analysts (past pres., chmn. exec. com., dir.), Chartered Fin. Analyst Inst., Nat. Venture Capital Assn., Pitts. Venture Capital Assn. (founding mem., past pres., bd. dirs.), Sigma Nu. Republican. Orthodox Catholic. Home: 2339 Morton Rd Pittsburgh PA 15241-3301 Office: Point Mgmt Group 130 7th St 400 Century Bldg Pittsburgh PA 15222-3409

CASWELL, DOROTHY ANN COTTRELL, performing arts association administrator; b. N.Y.C., Dec. 18, 1938; d. Donald Peery and Eleanor Hildaborg (Westberg) Cottrell; m. Allen Edward Caswell, Oct. 24, 1959; children: David Alan, Bruce Leland. Student, Carleton Coll., Northfield, MN., 1956-59; AB in Psych., George Wash. U., 1960-61; postgrad. in vocal performance, SUNY, Oneonta, 1971-76. Sec. U.S. Fgn. Service, Tunis, Tunisia, 1959-61; mng. dir. Glimmerglass Opera, Inc., Cooperstown, N.Y., 1975-78; exec. dir. Upper Catskill Community Council on the Arts, Oneonta, N.Y., 1978-80; devel. officer Catskill Arts Consortium, Oneonta, 1981-83; devel. cons. Otsego Urban Rural Self-Devel. Assocs., Inc., Oneonta, 1982-83; co-founder, pres. Catskill Choral Soc., 1970-76, 81-84; assoc. producer Orpheus Theatre, Inc., Oneonta, 1984-91; voice tchr. Oneonta, 1984—; ptnr., co-owner OnStage Prodn. Svcs., 1991—. Cons., arts adminstrv. Dorothy Caswell Assocs., Oneonta, 1981—; past pres., mem. sub-area coun. Health Sys. Agy. NE, NY, mem. planning adv. group, rev. adv. Actor(film series Susquehanna Stories): WSKG-TV Pub. TV, 1990—. Mem. chorus Glimmerglass Opera, Cooperstown, 1974—; mem. mil. acad. selection com. Congressman Sherwood Boehlert, NY, 1993—; mem. Otsego County Health Planning Adv. Coun. Otsego Publ Health Partnership; bd. dirs. Otsego County Tourism Bur., 1987—90, Oneonta Downtown Coalition, 1982—84. Recipient Honored for Outstanding Performance and Svcs. to Cmty., SUNY, 1975. Democrat. Avocations: painting, performing arts, gardening, swimming.

CASWELL, FRANCES PRATT, retired English language educator; b. Brunswick, Maine, June 25, 1929; m. Forrest Wilbur Caswell, June 30, 1956; children: Lucy Caswell Hilburn, Helen Caswell Watts, Harold F. BA, U. Maine, 1951; MA, U. Mich., 1955. Tchr. English, Bridgton (Maine) High Sch., 1951-54, Grosse Point (Mich.) High Sch., 1955-56; instr. South Maine Tech. Coll., South Portland, 1968-84, chmn. dept., 1984-93. Bd. dirs. Maine Vocat. Region 10, 1993-2003. Author: Growing Through Faith, A History of the Brunswick United Methodist Church, 1821-1996, 1996; contbg. author: Brunswick, Maine, 250 Years A Town, 1989. Pres. United Pejepscot Housing Inc., Brunswick, 1987-93. Mem. AAUW, Casco Bay Art League. Methodist. Avocations: painting, gardening.

CASWELL, HELEN RAYBURN, artist; b. Long Beach, Calif., Mar. 16, 1923; d. Odis Claude and Helen (Kepner) Rayburn; m. Dwight Allan Caswell, Dec. 27, 1942; children: Dwight Allan Jr., Philip, Mary, Christopher, John. Student, U. Oreg., 1939—42. Author, illustrator (of 32 books represented in pvt.and corp. collections.). Episcopalian. Home: 13207 Dupont Rd Sebastopol CA 95472-9787

CASWELL, RANDALL SMITH, physicist; b. Eugene, Oreg., Feb. 7, 1924; s. Albert Edward and M. Constance (Edwards) C.; m. Jean M. Miller, June 14, 1945; children: William Edward (dec.), Virginia Lee, Anne Marden, Ellen Sue, Wendy Jean (dec.), Julia Constance. SB, MIT, 1947, PhD in Physics, 1951. Assoc. prof. physics U. Ky., 1950-52; rschr. particle solid state physics Oak Ridge Nat. Lab., 1952; physicist neutron physics Nat. Bur. Standards, 1952-69; dep. dir. Ctr. Radiation Rsch., 1969-78, chief nuclear radiation divsn., 1978-85; chief ionizing radiation divsn. Nat. Inst. Standards & Tech., Gaithersburg, Md., 1985-94, ret., 1994. Adj. prof. physics Am. U. 1957-71; mem. Nat. Coun. Radiation Protection & Measurements, 1967-91; chmn. neutron measurements sect. Adv. Com. Standards Ionizing Radiation Measurement, Bur. Internat. des Poids et Measures, 1969-89; mem. Internat. Commn. Radiation Units & Measurement, 1975-2002, sec., 1979-2002; chmn. sci. panel Com. Interagy. Radiation Rsch. and Policy Coord. Office Sci. and Tech. Policy, 1984-94. Assoc. editor Radiation Rsch., 1977-80. Recipient Silver medal, US Dept. Commerce, 1961, Gold medal, 1979, Rosa award, Nat. Inst. Stds. and Tech., 1991, Disting. Svc. award, Coun. Ionizing Radiation Measurements and Stds., 2000. Fellow Am. Physics Soc.; mem. Radiation Rsch. Soc. (Disting. Svc. award, 2000). Office: Nat Inst of Stds Tech Physics Rm C229 Radiation Physics Bldg 245 Gaithersburg MD 20899-0001 Office Phone: 301-975-5525.

CASWELL HARRIS, LUCKY JEAN, community health nurse; b. Montgomery, Ala., Oct. 21, 1950; d. Lizzie Mae and Luck Caswell; m. Mabry McCarley Harris Sr., Aug. 21, 1971; children: Mabry McCarley Harris Jr., Meka Monique Harris. A in Bus. Mgmt., Cuyahoga C.C., 1997. Problem gambling asst. Ohio Lottery Commn., Cleve., 1996—98, media specialist, 1998—2001, cmty. svc. coord., 2001—. Mem. pub. rels. com., steering com. State of Ohio Combined Charities, Columbus, 1992—; bus. cons. Jamocha Art Ctr., Cleve., 1999—; customer svc. cons. United Way, Cleve., 1999—; mentor Rotsky Found. for Mentors, Cleve., 1999—; customer svc. cons. United Way, Columbus, Ohio, 1999—; mem. State of Ohio Tng. Assn., Cleve., 2000—; founder Mothers Of Mil., Cleve., 2001—; mem. policy and procedures State of Ohio Combined Charities, Columbus, 2001—; fund raising cons. New Spirit Revival Ctr., Cleveland Heights, Ohio, 2003—. Editor: (women's newsletter) Wake Up Sisters; author (poetry): From the Womb to Wounded to Wonderful, 2004. Selection com. Cmty. Shares, Cleve., 2000—03; bd. dirs. Cmty. Health Charities, Columbus, Ohio, 2002—04; mem. steering com. First Lady of Ohio, Reach Out Now Awareness Program for Students; vol. Alzheimer's Assn., Cleve., 1998—2001. Recipient Outstanding Cmty. Svc. award, State of Ohio, 1985, Cert. of Recognition award, Gov. of Ohio, 1996 to 2002, Coll. Fund/UNCF, 1997, 1998, United Way of Ohio, 1998, 1999. Mem.: NAFE (assoc.), ARC (assoc.), Rotsky Found. for Mentors (assoc.), Nat. African Am. Spkrs. Assn. (assoc.), Womens Entrepreneurs of Am. Inc. (assoc.), So. Christian Leadership Conf. (assoc.). Avocations: poetry, mentoring, travel, gardening, family. Home: 2112 Hampstead Rd Cleveland Heights OH 44118-2509 Personal E-mail: lady1luck1@aol.com.

CATALANO, CARL PHILIP, small business owner; b. Chgo., May 13, 1953; s. Philip Thomas and Arlene Margret (Hora) C.; m. Maria Rosa Diaz, Feb. 14, 1983. AS, Miami (Fla.) Dade Community Coll., 1984, AA, 1985; student, Am. Inst. Med. Law, 1986; BS in Audio Engring., Kennedy-Western U., 1993, PhD in Mgmt. Info. Sys., 2002. Cert. TV and radio broadcaster FCC, Nat. Radio Inst. (NRI), 1993. Drummer Queens Kidds, Miami and Ft. Lauderdale, Fla., 1970-74; show drummer Kickin, Fla., 1974-76; producer I.J.E. Distbrs. Inc., Hollywood, Fla., 1976-79; coord. internet tech., v.p., case mgr., computer engr. Catalano Registry Inc., Hialeah, Fla., 1979—; owner, prodr. Soundtrack Rec., Hialeah, 1986-96, Studio-K Prodns., Miramar, Fla., 1996—; computer programmer, arranger Final Chpt. Inc., 1988-89. Stage and location gripper Channels 1 and 2, Miami, 1984-85; free-lance programmer drum computer, photographer, Miami and Hialeah, 1983—; musician various studios, Fla., 1983— Appeared in (TV show) Miami Vice, 1985; (film) Mean Season, 1985. Mem. NYU Navi Quest Group, Marsh Affinity Group, NOP World/CMP Profl. Developers Panel, Eweek Advisory Panel, Tech. Rsch. Advisory Bd., Rep. Nat. Com., Rep. Presdl. Task Force. Mem. IEEE Computer Soc., Computer Security Inst., Nat. Drum Assn., Am. Bd. Risk Mgmt. Profls. (diplomate), Assn. Computing Machinery (adv. bd.), South Fla. Musicians Assn. (adv. panel eweek), Microsoft Ptnrs., Microsoft Bus. Solutions, Network Solutions, Computer Security Inst. Home: 2522 SW 180th Ave Miramar FL 33029-5191 Office Phone: 954-292-3744. E-mail: ccatalano@acm.org.

CATALANO, GERALD, accountant; b. Chgo., Jan. 17, 1949; s. Frank and Virginia (Kreiman) C.; m. Mary L. Billings, July 4, 1970; children: James, Maria, Gina. BSBA, Roosevelt U., 1971. CPA, Ill. Jr. acct. Drebin, Lindquist and Gervasio, Chgo., 1971, Leaf, Dahl and Co., Ltd., Chgo., 1971-77, prin., 1978-80, ptnr., 1980-82; prin. Gerald Catalano, CPA, Chgo., 1982-83; ptnr. Barbakoff, Catalano & Assocs., Chgo., 1983-87; pres. Barbakoff, Catalano & Caboor Ltd., Chgo., 1993—. V.p. Tri-City Oil, Inc., Addison, Ill., 1983-93; treas. Uncle Andy's, Inc., 1991-94; corp. officer Bionic Auto Parts, Inc.; bd. dirs. EDT, Inc., treas., 1993—; ptnr. PetCatMusic Publ., 1996—; owner IEP Record Group, 1996—, dir. United Community Lisle, IL, 2001-. Pres. Young Dems., Roosevelt U., 1967-71; trustee U. Ill. Russo Scholarship Fund, 1989—; dir. Elmhurst Jaycees, 1976. Mem. AICPA, ASCAP (assoc.), NARAS (assoc.), Ill. CPA Soc., Theosophical Soc. Roman Catholic. Office: 1 S 376 Summit Ave Oakbrook Terrace IL 60181 E-mail: jerryc@catboor.com.

CATALANO, JANE DONNA, lawyer; b. Schenectady, N.Y., Feb. 21, 1957; d. Alfred and Joan (Futscher) Martini; m. Peter Catalano, June 18, 1988. BA, SUNY, Plattsburgh, 1979; JD, Albany Law Sch., 1982. Bar: N.Y. 1983, U.S. Dist. Ct. 1983. Atty. Pentak, Brown & Tobin, Albany, N.Y., 1982-87, Niagara Mohawk Power Corp., Albany, 1987—. Mem. N.Y. State Bar Assn., Albany County Bar Assn. Home: 7 Blackburn Way Latham NY 12110-1943 Office: National Grid 1125 Broadway Albany NY 12204 Office Phone: 518-433-5257. Business E-Mail: jane.catalano@us.ngrid.com.

CATALANO, LOUIS WILLIAM, JR., neurologist; b. Bklyn., Apr. 20, 1942; s. Louis William and Aileen (Bobb) C.; m. Diana Catalano; children: Louis William III, Jamea Elizabeth, Adriana Louise. BS cum laude, U. Pitts., 1963, MD, 1967. Diplomate Am. Bd. Psychiatry and Neurology, Am. Bd. Electroencephalography, Am. Bd. Pain Medicine, Am. Bd. Med. Examiners. Intern Presbyn.-St. Luke's Hosp., Chgo., 1967-68; rsch. assoc. NIH, Bethesda, Md., 1968-70; fellow neurology The Neurol. Inst., N.Y.C., 1970-73; clin. asst., prof. neurology U. Pitts. Sch. Med., 1973—; pvt. practice Greensburg, Pa., 1973—. Staff Latrobe (Pa.) Area Hosp., 1973—, Westmoreland Regional Hosp., Greensburg, 1973—, Indiana (Pa.) Hosp., 1983—; cons. Jeannette (Pa.) Mercy Hosp., 1984—, Frick Cmty. Health Ctr., Mt. Pleasant, Pa., 1991—, Torrance (Pa.) State Hosp., 2000—; lectr. in field. Contbr. articles to profl. jours. Pres. Neurol. Inst. We. Pa.; bd. dirs. Epilepsy Found. Western/Cen. Pa., 2000— Spl. fellow Columbia U., NIH, 1970-73, epilepsy minifellow, Bowman Gray Sch. Medicine, Winston-Salem, N.C., 1988. Fellow: Am. Acad. Neurology, Royal Soc. Medicine; mem.: AMA, European Fedn. Neurol. Socs., Pitts. Neurosci. Soc., Latrobe Acad. Medicine, Westmoreland County Med. Soc., World Fedn. Neurology, Pa. Med. Soc., Am. Sleep Disorders Assn., Am. Acad. Clin. Neurphysiology, Am. Soc. Neuroimaging, Am. Med. Electroencephalographic Assn., Am. Acad. Pain Mgmt., Alpha Omega Alpha, Sigma Xi. Avocations: sport fishing, scuba diving, skiing, travel. Office Phone: 724-537-0885.

CATALANOTTO, FRANK A., dentist, association executive; DMD, U. Medicine and Dentistry NJ, 1968. Fellow in pediat. dentistry Harvard U. and Children's Hosp. Med. Ctr., Boston, 1968—71; faculty mem. Harvard U., 1971—72; assoc. epidemiologist US Navy Great Lakes Dental Rsch. Inst., 1972—74; asst. prof. pediat. dentistry Dept. Pediat. Dentisty, U. Conn. Health Ctr., 1974—85, founding dir. sch. faculty practice, dir. predoctoral program and postdoctoral residency in pediat. dentistry; chair pediat. dentistry U. Tex. Health Sci. Ctr., San Antonio, 1985—88; assoc. dean acad. planning faculty devel. U. Medicine and Dentistry, NJ Dental Sch., 1988—89, assoc. dean rsch., indsl. rels. and profl. devel., 1989—95; dean U. Fla. Coll. Dentistry, 1995—2002; prof. pediat. dentistry U. Fla., 2002—. Co-founder, prin. investigator NIH-supported Conn. Chemosensory Clinical Rsch. Ctr., 1980—85, Northeastern Minority Oral Health Rsch. Ctr., NJ, 1992—95; cons. basic sci. curriculum Commn. Dental Accreditation, ADA, 1989—97; mem. adminstrv. bd. ADEA Coun. Deans, 1996—2000; pres.-elect Am. Dental Edn. Assn., 2003, pres., 2004—; edt. bd. Pediat. Dentistry jour., Am. Dental Acad.; mem. nat. affairs com. Am. Assn. Dental Rsch., 1989—95; mem. adv. com. on training in primary care medicine and dentistry US Dept. Health's Health Resources and Svc. Adminstrn. Co-author more than 60 sci. publ. Recipient Rsch. Career Devel. award, Nat. Inst. Health. Office: Univ Fla Coll Dentistry PO Box 100405 Gainesville FL 32610-0405 Office Phone: 352-392-2911. Office Fax: 352-392-8195. Business E-Mail: fcatalanotto@dental.ufl.edu.

CATALDO, JENNIFER, elementary school educator; d. Marlin Elwyn Whitney and Loretta Ligor; m. Zac A Cataldo, Sept. 1, 1991; children: Jesse, Maia, Jaramie. BA in psychology, Boston U., 1990; MA in tchg., Simmons Coll., 1991. Elementary School Teacher Mass. Tchr. Old Orchard Sch., Newhall, Calif., 1992—94, Winchester Pub. Sch., Mass., 1994—. Avocations: gardening, writing. Office: Winchester Pub Sch Ambrose Sch Winchester MA 01890

CATALFO, ALFRED, JR., (ALFIO CATALFO), lawyer; b. Lawrence, Mass., Jan. 31, 1920; s. Alfio and Vincenza (Amato) C.; m. Caroline Joanne Mosca (dec. Apr. 1968); children: Alfred Thomas, Carol Joanne, Gina Marie; m. Gail Varney, 1988. BA, U. N.H., 1945, MA in History, 1952; LLB, Boston U., 1947, JD (hon.), 1969; postgrad., Suffolk U. Sch. Law, 1955-56, Am. Law Inst., N.Y.C., 1959. Bar: N.H. 1947, U.S. Dist. Ct. 1948, U.S. Ct. Appeals 1978, U.S. Supreme Ct. 1979. Pvt. practice, Dover, N.H., 1948—; ptnr. Catalfo Law Firm, Dover, 1980—; county atty. Strafford County, Dover, N.H., 1949-50, 55-56; bd. immigration appeals U.S. Dept. Justice, 1953—; football coach Berwick Acad., South Berwick, Maine, 1944, Mission Catholic H.S., Roxbury, Mass., 1945-46. Author: Laws of Divorces, Marriages, and Separations in New Hampshire, 1962, History of the Town of Rollinsford, 1623-1973, 1973. Pres. Young Dems. of Dover, 1953-55; 1st vice-chmn. Young Dems., N.H., 1954-56; mem. Strafford County Dem. Com., 1948-75; vice-chmn. N.H. Dem. Com., 1954-56, 1st chmn., 1956-58, chmn. spl. activities, 1958-60; del. Dem. Nat. Conv., 1956-60, 76; chmn. N.H. Dem. Conv., 1958, conv. dir., 1960; mem. Dem. state exec. com., 1960-70; Dem. nominee for U.S. Senate, 1962; vice-chmn. Dover Cath. Sch. Com., 1969-71; mem. Dover Bd. Adjustment, 1960-65; apptd. lt. commdr. N.H. Govs. Mil. Staff. Pilot U.S. Naval Air Corp., lt. commdr. USNR, 1942-44. Recipient keys to cities of Dover, Somersworth, Concord, Berlin, Manchester and Rochester N.H., 6 nat. plaques DAV, 3 disting. svc. awards Am. Legion, Am. Legion Life Membership award, spl. recognition award Berwick Acad., 1985. Mem. ABA, N.H. Bar Assn., Strafford County Bar Assn. (v.p. 1966-67, pres. 1968-69), Assn. Trial Lawyers Am., N.Y. State Trial Lawyers Assn., Mass. Trial Lawyers Assn., N.H. Trial Lawyers Assn., Tex. Trial Lawyers Assn., Nat. Assn. Criminal Def. Lawyers, N.H. Assn. Criminal Def. Lawyers, Am. Judicature Soc., Phi Delta Phi, DAV (judge adv. N.H. dept. 1950-68, 72—; comdr. chpt. 1953-54, comdr. N.H. 1956-57), Am. Legion (life, chmn. state conv. 1967, 77, 84), Navy League, N.H. Hist. Soc., Dover Hist. Soc., Rollinsford Hist. Soc., Eagles Club, Sons of Italy, Lions, Elks, K.C. (grand knight 1975-77), Moose, Lebanese Club. Clubs: Eagles (Somersworth, N.H.), Sons of Italy (Portsmouth, N.H.). Lodges: Lions, Elks, K.C. (grand knight 1975-77), Moose, Lebanese (Dover). Home: 20 Arch St Dover NH 03820-3602 Office: 450 Central Ave Dover NH 03820-3451

CATALFO, BETTY MARIE, health service executive, nutritionist; b. N.Y.C., Nov. 2, 1942; d. Lawrence Santo and Gemma (Patrone) Lorefice; children— Anthony, Lawrence, Donna Marie. Grad. Newtown High Sch., Elmhurst, N.Y., 1958. Sec., clk. ABC-TV, N.Y.C., 1957-60; founder, lectr., nutritionist Weight Watchers, Manhasset, N.Y., 1964-75; founder, pres. Every-Bodys Diet, Inc. dba Stay Slim, Queens, N.Y., 1976—; dir. in-home program N.Y. State Dept. Health, N.Y.C., 1985—; founder, pres. Delitegul Diet Foods, Inc., 1988—; lectr. in field. Author: 101 Stay-Slim Recipes, 1983, Get Slim and Stay Slim Diet Cook Book, rev. ed., 1987, Diet Revolution, 1991, Holiday Cookbook, 1992, Fat Counts in Fast Food Spots, 1992, Choose to Loose!, 1993, You Are Not Alone, 1993, Eating Out, 1994, Change or Select, 1994, Calories Do Count!, 1994, Fat Free Receipes, 1994; author, dir., producer: (video) Dancersize for Overweight, 1986, Get Slim and Stay Slim Diet Cook Book, Eating Right for Your Life, Hello It's Me and I'm Slim, (videos) Stay Slim Line Dancing, 1989, Stay Slim Food Facts, 1989, Help Me Before I Give In, 1990, A New Year A New You!, 1991, Relax and Meditate, 1991, Come Shop with Me, 1991, Change or Accept, 1993, The Bag Lady, 1993, Sneak Eater, 1993, Sins That Every Dieter Makes, 1994, Stay Slim from Start to Finish, 1994, Here's Some Helpful Diet Tips, 1994, What Every Smart Dieter Knows, 1994, Mirror Mirror on the Wall, 1994, Weight Management Techniques, 1995; author, editor: (video) Eating Right For Life, 1985, Isometric Techniques for Weight Reduction, Dance Your Calories A-Weigh; author, producer: (video) Eating Habits, 1986—; (video) Isometric Techniques for Weight Reduction, 1986, Patience Is a Virtue When Weight Loss is the Goal, 1986, Slow Down You Eat to Fast, 1994, Always Giving Never Receiving, 1994, Relax and Don't You Worry, 1994; producer, dir.: (video) Positive and Negative Diet Forces, 1987, (video) Hello It's Me and I'm Thin, 1987, (video) Dance Your Calories A-Weigh, 1987, (video) Positive and Negative Diet Forces, 1987. Sponsor, lectr. St. Pauls Ctr., Bklyn., 1981—, Throgs Neck Assn. Retarded Children, Bronx, 1985—; active ARC, LWV, Am. Italian Assn., United Way Greenwich, Council Chs. and Synagogues, Heart Assn., N.Y. Meals on Wheels, 1985—, Health Assn. Fairfield County, Food Svcs. for Homeless People, 1993, 94, 95; chairperson, sponsor Battered Women, 1994—. Named Woman of Yr., Bayside Womens Club, N.Y., 1983, O, PK Woman of Yr., 1986—, Woman of Yr. Richmond Boys Club, 1987, Woman of Yr. Bronx Press Club Assn., 1987; recipient Merit award for Svc. Cath. Archdiocese of Bklyn., 1985, Merit award Svcs. Cath. Archdioces of Bklyn. and Queens, 1992, 93, 94, Community Service award Sr. Citizens Sacred Heart League Bklyn./Queens Archdiocese. N.Y. State Nutritional Guidance for Children Nat. Assn. Scis. Mem. Nat. C. of C. for Women (Woman of Yr. 1987, 90), Pres.'s Coun. on Nutrition, Roundtable for Women in Food Service, Bus. and Profl. Women's Club, Pres. Council for Phys. Fitness, Nat. Assn. Female Execs., Assn. for Fitness in Bus. Inc., Nat. Assn. Female Bus. Owners. Democrat. Roman Catholic. Club: Mothers Sacred Heart Sch. (chairperson 1979-82). Avocations: reading; travel, golf, family. Home: 21422 27th Ave Flushing NY 11360-2608 also: 58 Riverview Ct Greenwich CT 06831-4127 Office: 10005 101st Ave Ozone Park NY 11416-2601

CATALFOMO, PHILIP, retired university dean; b. Providence, Dec. 27, 1931; s. Antonio and Frances (Di Giuseppe) C.; m. Magdalena Wettstein, Jan. 8, 1962; children— Kristina, Anthony Werner. BS, Providence Coll., 1953, U. Conn., 1958; MS, U. Wash., Seattle, 1960, PhD, 1962. Mem. faculty Oreg. State U., 1963-75, prof. pharmacognosy, 1966-75, head dept., 1966-75; prof. pharmacognosy, dean Sch. Pharmacy, U. Mont., Missoula, 1975-86; dean coll. health scis. U. Wyo., Laramie, 1986-91; ret., 1991. Author research articles fungal metabolism. Served with AUS, 1953-55. Gustavus A. Pfeiffer Meml. research fellow, 1969-70 Home: 81800 Old Hwy # 93 Dayton MT 59914

CATALLO, HEATHER, newscaster; b. Mich. Graduate, S.I. Newhouse Sch. of Pub. Comm., Syracuse, N.Y. Reporter WTVH-TV, Syracuse, NY; police beat reporter KREM-TV, Spokane, Wash.; investigative reporter WXYZ-TV, Detroit, 1999—, anchor Sunday morning and noon shows, 1999—. Recipient Hearst Nat. TV award Excellence, 1998. Office: WXYZ-TV 20777 W Ten Mile Rd Southfield MI 48037

CATANESE, ANTHONY JAMES, academic administrator; b. New Brunswick, N.J., Oct. 18, 1942; s. Anthony James and Josephine Marlene (Barone) C.; m. Sara Jean Phillips, Oct. 23, 1968; children: Mark Anthony, Michael Scott, Mark Alexander. BA, Rutgers U., 1963; M in Urban Planning, NYU, 1965; PhD, U. Wis., 1968. Asst. prof. city planning Ga. Inst. Tech., Atlanta, 1967-78, assoc. prof., 1968-73, chmn. doctoral studies com., 1970-73; James A. Ryder prof. transp. and planning, dir. Ryder program in transp. U. Miami, Coral Gables, Fla., 1973-75; dean Sch. Architecture and Urban Planning U. Wis., Milw., 1975-82; prof. architecture and urban planning, provost Pratt Inst., N.Y.C., 1982-84; dean Coll. Architecture, U. Fla., Gainesville, 1984-89; pres. Fla. Atlantic U., Boca Raton, 1989—2002, pres., prof., 1990—2002; pres. Fla. Inst. Tech., Melbourne, 2002—. Sr. Fulbright prof., Colombia, 1971-72; sr. cons. State of Wis., 1965-67, sr. planner State of N.J., 1963-67; pres. A. J. Catanese & Assocs., Inc., 1967—; mem. pres. commn. NCAA, 1991-93. Author: Scientific Methods of Urban Analysis, 1972, New Perspectives on Urban Transportatio Research, 1972, Systematic Planning-Theory and Applications, 1970, Planners and Local Politics: Impossible Dreams, 1973, Urban Transportation in South Florida, 1974, Personality, Politics and Planning, 1978, Introduction to Urban Planning, 1979, Introduction to Architecture, 1979, The Politics of Planning and Development, 1984, Ubran Planning, 1988; contbr. articles to profl. jours. Chmn. Mid. DeKalb County Dem. Party, 1969-71, mem. 5th Congl. Dist. Dem. caucus, 1971; aide-de-camp Gov.'s Office, State of Ga., 1971-72; mem. Ga. Dunes Studies Commn., 1972-73; bd. dirs. Archtl. Rsch. Ctrs. Consortium, 1976—; mem. Urban Policy Task Force, Carter presdl. campaign, 1976, 80; pres. Park West Redevel. Corp., 1976-78; chmn. Milw. City Plan Commn., 1978-82; bd. dirs. Goals for Milw. 2000, 1978-82, Environ. Edn. Found. Fla.; chmn. Gainesville (Fla.) Planning Bd., 1986-89. With USAR, 1961-63. Recipient fellowships State of N.J. Act of 1927, 1962-63, Werner Hegemann Found., 1963-65, Wis. Alumni Rsch. Found., 1965-68, Richard King Mellon Trust, 1966-67, Ford Found., 1967, Nat. Endowment Arts, 1980. Mem. Am. Inst. Planners (bd. govs., v.p. 1971-74), Am. Inst. Cert. Planners (mem. exec. com. 1971-74), Am. Planning Assn., Transp. Rsch. Bd., Regional Sci. Assn., Am. Acad. Polit. and Social Scis., Assn. Coll. Schs. Planning, Heritage Club, Wycliff Club, Tower Club. Office: Fla Inst Tech 150 W University Blvd Melbourne FL 32901 Office Phone: 321-674-7232. Business E-Mail: catanese@fit.edu.

CATANGUI, MICHAEL AGUILAR, entomologist, researcher; b. Polangui, Albay, Philippines, Jan. 2, 1962; arrived in U.S., 1986; s. Felipe Portem and Myrna Aguilar Catangui; m. Concepcion Marco Vendiola, Nov. 30, 1991; children: Lauren Michelle, Sean Michael, Adam Mitchell. BS, U. Philippines, Los Banos, Laguna, 1981; MS, S.D. State, Brookings, 1987; PhD, U. Nebr., Lincoln, 1992. Diplomate applied parasitology and entomology Inst. for Med. Rsch. / Malaysia, 1984. Instr. U. Philippines, Los Banos, Philippines, 1982—86; grad. rsch. asst. S.D. State, Brookings, 1986—87, U. Nebr., Lincoln, 1987—92; postdoctoral rsch. assoc. S.D. State, 1992—95, ext. assoc., 1995—98, asst. prof., 1998—2002, assoc. prof., 2002—. Mem. arbovirus surveillance group S.D. Dept. of Health, Pierre, mem. Gypsy Moth com., 1998—; thesis advisor S.D. State, Brookings, 1999—. Contbr. articles to profl. jours. Panelist, Garden Line S.D. Pub. TV, Brookings, 1998; participant West Nile Virus roundtable U.S. Senator Tim Johnson, Sioux Falls, 2003. Recipient Disting. Grad. Student award, Widaman Trust, 1989, Dean's Team award, S.D. State U. Coll. of Agr., 2003. Mem.: Entomol. Soc. of Am. Roman Catholic. Achievements include research in economic and environmental impacts of transgenic Bt-corn crops. Avocations: reading, travel, listening to oldies music, web design, lawn and garden. Home: 2613 S Rutgers Ave Sioux Falls SD 57106 Office: SD State Univ Medary Ave Brookings SD 57007 Office Phone: 605-688-4603. Office Fax: 605-688-4602. E-mail: michael_catangui@sdstate.edu.

CATANIA, A(NTHONY) CHARLES, psychologist, educator; b. NYC, June 22, 1936; s. Charles John and Elizabeth (Lattarulo) C.; m. Constance J. Britt, Feb. 10, 1962; children: William John, Kenneth Charles. BA in Psychology with highest honors, Columbia U., 1957, MA, 1958. Postdoctoral research fellow Harvard U., 1961-62; sr. pharmacologist Smith, Kline & French Labs., Phila., 1962-64; asst. prof. NYU, 1964-66, asso. prof., 1966-69, prof., chmn. dept. psychology, 1969-73; prof. dept. psychology U. Md. Baltimore County, Catonsville, 1973—2004, program co-dir. master's track in applied behavior analysis, 2004—; mem. psychobiology com. NSF, 1982-85. Vis. prof. Keio U., Tokyo, 1992. Author: Learning, 1979, 4th edit., 1998; co-author: (with E. Shimoff and B.A. Matthews) Behavior on a Disk, 1989; editor: Contemporary Research in Operant Behavior, 1968; co-editor: (with T.A. Brigham) Handbook of Applied Behavior Analysis, 1978, (with S. Harnad) The Selection of Behavior: The Operant Behaviorism of B.F. Skinner, 1988, (with P.N. Hineline) Variations and Selections, 1996, (with V.G. Laties) B.F. Skinner's Cumulative Record, definitive edit., 1999; editor: Jour. Exptl. Analysis Behavior, 1966-69, rev. editor, 1969-76, 83-91; assoc. editor: Behavioral and Brain Scis., 1980—; mem. bd. editors various jours.; contbr. articles to profl. jours.; contbr. chpts. to textbooks. Recipient James McKeen Cattell Sabbatical award, 1986-87, Outstanding Sci. Contbns. to Psychology award Md. Psychol. Assn., 1993, Outstanding Contbr. Behavior Analysis award No. Calif. Assn. Behavior Analysis, 1990; NSF grantee, 1965-67, 74-79, 82-88, USPHS grantee, 1967-73, 79-83; Fulbright sr. rsch. fellow, Wales, Bangor, 1986-87. Fellow APA (pres. divsn. 25 1976-79, 96-98, Don Hake award divsn. 25); mem. Assn. Behavior Analysis (pres. 1982-83, chair publ. bd. 1992-95, pres. Md. chpt. 2001-02), Ea. Psychol. Assn. (dir. 1979-82), Soc. Exptl. Analysis of Behavior (pres. 1966-67, 81-83, v.p. 2003—), Lang. Origins Soc. (program chair 1996), Md. Assn. Behavior Analysis (pres. 2001-02), Icelandic Assn. Behavior Analysis (hon. founding mem. 2004). Home: 10545 Rivulet Row Columbia MD 21044-2420 Office: U Md Baltimore County Dept Psychology Baltimore MD 21250-0001 Office Phone: 410-455-3002. Business E-Mail: catania@umbc.edu.

CATANZARITE, DAVID M., theater educator, director; b. Dayton, July 15, 1957; s. Francis Joseph and Maya Spector Catanzarite; m. Karen T. Lin, Oct. 12, 2001; 1 child, Antonio. BA in English, Stanford U., 1978; MA in Theatre, San Francisco State U., 1987; MFA in Theatre, U. So. Calif., 1994. Cert. secondary tchg. credential Calif. State U., 1988. Theatre program coord. Dana Mid. Sch., LA, 1988—92; lectr. U. So. Calif., 1992—94; instr. Calif. Arts Project UCLA, 1993—97; asst. prof. theatre Pomona Coll., Claremont, Calif., 1995—98, Towson U., Balt., 1998—99; theatre coach itinerant LA Unified Sch. Dist., 2000—02, arts edn. adv., 2002—. Exec. bd. mem. Calif. Ednl. Theatre Assn., 1988—98; coord. new play devel. workshop Assn. for Theatre in Higher Edn., 1997—2000; edn. adv. bd. UCLA Fowler Mus., 2000—. Author: Deconstructing Brecht, Internat. Brecht Yearbook, 1996; artistic dir. Bertolt Brecht Centennial Festival, LA, 1998; dir.: Faustathon Goethe 250th Birthday, 1999. Mem.: Calif. Ednl. Theatre Assn., Soc. of Stage Dirs. and Choreographers, Black Theatre Network. Avocation: internat. travel. Office: Los Angeles Unified Sch Dist Arts Edn Br 333 Beaudry Ave 16th Fl Los Angeles CA 90017 Office Phone: 213-241-4527. Business E-Mail: david.catanzarite@lausd.net.

CATANZARO, DANIEL FRANK, molecular biologist, educator; b. Sydney, Australia, Apr. 4, 1957; came to U.S., 1990; m. Cathy L. Budman; 2 children. BA in Biol. Scis. with honors, Macquarie U., 1978; PhD in Physiology and Molecular Biology, U. Sydney, 1986; MBA, Columbia U., 2000. Vis. rsch. biochemist U. Calif., San Francisco, 1985; lectr. in eukaryotic molecular genetics U. Sydney, 1986-90; asst. prof. physiology in medicine Cornell U. Med. Coll., 1990-95; assoc. prof. Weill Med. Coll., Cornell U., N.Y.C., 1995-99, assoc. prof. physiology in cardiothoracic surgery, 1999—. Dep. editor basic sci. Am. Jour. Hypertension, 1999-2001; co-exec. editor Am. Jour. Hypertension, 2002-; contbr. articles and revs. to profl. jours. Postgrad. scholar U. Sydney Faculty of Medicine, 1979-81; recipient investigatorship award Am. Heart Assn., 1995. Fellow AHA High Blood Pressure Rsch. Coun.; mem. Endocrine Soc., Am. Soc. Hypertension (Young Scholars award 1993). Office: Cornell U Weill Med Coll Cardiovascular Ctr A-863 1300 York Ave New York NY 10021-4805

CATAPANO-FRIEDMAN, ROBERT STEPHEN, lawyer; b. Orange, N.J., Feb. 27, 1952; s. Carmen Sam Catapano and Carolyn (Marton) Scalo; m. Lisa K. Friedman, Dec. 22, 1974; children: Sarah Ann, Rebecca Koren. BS in Biology, Yale U., 1974; JD, Suffolk U., 1978; LLM in Taxation, NYU, 1983. Bar: Mass. 1978, U.S. Ct. Appeals (1st cir.) 1979, N.J. 1980, N.Y. 1988, U.S. Dist. Ct. (no. dist.) N.Y. 1992. Assoc. Gargill & Sassoon, Boston, 1978-79; house counsel Liberty Mutual Ins. Co., Boston, 1979-80; assoc. Fox & Fox, Newark, 1980-81; assoc. tax counsel Gulf & Western, Inc., N.Y.C., 1981-83, Allied-Signal, Inc., Morristown, N.J., 1983-88; assoc. Walter, Conston, Alexander & Green, P.C., N.Y.C., 1988-92; ptnr. Maynard, O'Connor & Smith, Albany, N.Y., 1992-93; pvt. practice Albany, N.Y., 1993—; of counsel Fox & Fox, Newark, 1993-96. Instr. bus. law Bay State Jr. Coll., Boston, 1979-80. Contbr. articles to profl. jours. Pres. Congregation Beth El, Bennington, Vt., 1993-94. Mem. N.Y. State Bar Assn. (tax sect., mem. com. Qualified Plans and Nonqualified Employee Benefits), Albany County Bar Assn. Avocations: golf, basketball, jogging, water sports, horseback riding. Office: 744 Broadway Albany NY 12207-2331 E-mail: catapan@worldnet.att.net.

CATCHINGS, TAMIKA DEVONNE, professional basketball player; b. Stratford, NJ, July 21, 1979; d. Harvey Catchings and Wanda Cathings. Grad., U. Tenn., 2001. Basketball player U. Tenn., 1997—2001; profl. basketball player Ind. Fever, WNBA, 2001—. Mem. USA Basketball Women's Sr. Nat. Team, 2004. Host Catch the Fever basketball camp, 2002, 2003, Catch the Fitness clinic, 2003. Named Naismith Player of Yr., 2000, AP Player of Yr., 2000, US Basketball Writers Assn. Player of Yr., 2000, Kodak/WBCA Player of Yr., 2000, Coll. Women's Basketball Player of Yr., ESPY Awards, 2001, WNBA Rookie of the Yr., 2002; named to WNBA All-Star Team, 2002, 2003, First Team All-WNBA, 2002, 2003; recipient Reynolds Soc. Achievement Award, Mass. Eye and Ear Infirmary, Off-Season WNBA Cmty. Assist Award, 2002, 2003. Achievements include mem. US Women's Basketball FIBA Jr. World Championship Gold Medal Team, 1997; mem. US Women's Basketball FIBA World Championship Gold Medal Team, 2002; mem. US Women's Basketball Team, Athens Olympics, 2004. Office: 125 S Pennsylvania St Indianapolis IN 46204

CATCHPOLE, JUDY, state official; m. Glenn Catchpole; children: Glenda, Fred, Katie. BA in Edn., U. Wyo. Former state supt. pub. instrn. State Dept. Edn., Cheyenne, Wyo.; mem. Wyo. Higher Edn. Assistance Authority, 2002—. Exec. dir. Wyoming Rep. Party; mem. Wyoming Land and Investment bd., CCSSO Bd. Dirs., U. Wyo. Bd. Trustees, Edn. Commn. of States Commr., STARBASE Bd. Dirs., pres. Mem. Wyo. Sch. Bds. Assn. (past vice chmn.), Wyo. Early Childhood Assn. (past pres.). Office: Wyo Dept Edn 2300 Capitol Ave Fl 2 Cheyenne WY 82002-0050

CATE, JAN HARRIS, lawyer; b. NYC, Jan. 9, 1964; BA with honors, Univ. Calif., San Diego, 1986; JD, Boston Univ., 1989. Bar: Calif. 1989. Ptnr., leader Bank Fin. practice Pillsbury Winthrop Shaw Pittman, LA. Contbr. articles to profl. jours. Mem.: LA County Bar Assn. Office: Pillsbury Winthrop Shaw Pittman Suite 2800 725 S Figueroa St Los Angeles CA 90017 Office Phone: 213-488-7539. Office Fax: 213-629-1033. Business E-Mail: jan.cate@pillsburylaw.com.

CATE, RICHARD H., school system administrator; BS, U. Vt.; MPA in Pub. Adminstrn., U. Albany. CFO NY State Dept. Edn., exec. dep. commr., COO, commr. of edn., 2003—. City mgr. Barre City, Vt.; past mem. Barre City Coun.; exec. dir. Vt. Supt. Assn. Office: Vt Dept Edn 120 State St Montpelier VT 05620-0002 Office Phone: 802-828-3135. Office Fax: 802-828-3140.*

CATELL, PADMA JOY, psychologist, marriage and family therapist; b. N.Y.C., Jan. 17, 1944; d. Joseph Cicatelli and Belle (Mishkind) Diamond. BA in Biology, CUNY-Hunter Coll., 1969; MA in Biology, CUNY, 1971; PhD in Psychology, Calif. Inst. Integral Studies, 1984. Lic. psychologist, lic. marriage & family therapist, Calif. Biomed. rsch. grad. fellow CUNY-Hunter Coll., 1971; counselor Cathedral Hill Hosp., San Francisco, 1971-75; co-founder, dir. Buena Vista Women's Svcs., San Francisco, 1975-81; dir. Buena Vista Counseling Ctr., San Francisco, 1979—; prof. psychology Calif. Inst. Integral Studies, San Francisco, 1984—, dean Sch. Healing Arts, 1993—96; ptnr./therapist Mariposa Counseling Ctr., San Rafael, Calif., 1992—. Pres. Coalition for Med. Rights of Women, San Francisco, 1974-76. Mem. APA, Calif. Assn. Marriage and Family Therapists. Avocations: photography, sculpting, travel. Office: Buena Vista Counseling Ctr 801 Portola Dr San Francisco CA 94127-1234 Office Phone: 415-435-7787.

CATELL, ROBERT BARRY, gas industry executive; b. Bklyn., Feb. 1, 1937; s. Joseph Daniel and Belle (Mishkind) Cicatelli; m. Joan Kathryn Weigand, June 25, 1971; children: Laura Anne, Erica Anne; children by previous marriage: Robert Edward, Carla Ann, Donna Theresa. BME, CCNY, 1958, MME, 1964. Registered profl. engr. Asst. v.p. Bklyn. Union Gas Co., 1974-78, v.p., 1978-82, sr. v.p., 1982-84, exec. v.p., 1984-86, exec. v.p., COO, 1986-90, pres., COO, 1990-91, pres., CEO, 1991-96; chmn., CEO Key Span Energy Corp. (formerly Bklyn. Union Gas Co.), 1996—. Trustee Independence Savs. Bank, Bklyn., 1984—, Gas. Rsch. Inst., 1992; mem. regional adv. com. Chase Bank; chmn. N.Y. State Energy Assn., L.I. Assn. Mem. N.Y. Serda Bd.; chmn. N.Y.C. Partnership; mem. N.Y. State Bus. Coun., vice chmn. Mem. Am. Gas Assn., Soc. Gas Lighting. Avocations: swimming, golf, tennis. Office: Key Span Corp One Metrotech Ctr Brooklyn NY 11201

CATES, ANNA L., language educator; b. Brunswick, Maine, 1971; d. Carleton Enos Cates and Saundra Mae McMeans. BA in English, Asbury Coll., 1995; MA in English, Ind. State U., 1997, PhD in Curriculum and Instrnl. English, 2002. With Ind. State U., Terre Haute, 1995—2002, Lodge Grass (Mont.) H.S., 2002—03, Great Basin Coll., Ely, Nev., 2003—04, Wilmington (Ohio) Coll., 2004; online prof. Corintrian Coll., 2003—, So. N.H. U., 2004—. Author: Lumenor of Dragon Mountain, 2003, (poetry) Paper Cuts: Poems for the Bruised, 2003, Gemeinschaft: Poems for the Common Good, 2003. Mem.: NCTE, MIA, Delta Kappa Gamma. Avocations: writing, piano. Home: 405 Nunn Ave Wilmington OH 45177 E-mail: catesanna@hotmail.com.

CATES, DENNIS LYNN, education educator; b. Dallas, Nov. 25, 1946; s. Robert N. and Wanda June (Boyd) C.; m. Sue Anne Sadler, Aug. 9, 1975. BA, Tex. Tech U., 1968, MEd, 1976, EdD, 1986; MA, Sul Ross State U., 1981. Cert. secondary edn. tchr., deficient vision, learning disabilities, mental retardation, supervision, mid-mgmt., orientation and mobility instr. Tchr. Eagle Pass (Tex.) Ind. Sch. Dist., Beeville (Tex.) Ind. Sch. Dist., Levelland (Tex.) Ind. Sch. Dist.; tchg. asst. Tex. Tech. U., Lubbock; asst. prof. West Tex. State U., Canyon, 1986-89, U. S.C., Columbia, 1989-95, dir. Ctr. for Excellence in Spl. Edn. Tech., 1992-93; assoc. prof. Cameron U., Lawton, Okla., 1995-2000, prof., 2000—04; cons., 2004—. Presenter numerous profl. confs.; field reviewer edn. jours. and pubs. Contbr. articles to profl. jours. Sgt. USAF, 1969-73. Grantee Consultation Tchrs. grant, 1981—82. Mem.: AAUP, ASCD, Assn. Tchr. Edn., Assn. Edn. and Rehab. for Blind and Visually Impaired (chmn. Divsn. 3 1998—2000, past chmn. 2000—02, newsletter editor Divsn. 3 1998—2004), Am. Coun. for Rural Spl. Edn. (bd. dirs. 1998—2004, chmn.-elect 2000—02, chmn. 2002—03, past chmn. 2003—04), Coun. for Exceptional Children (pres. Okla. chpt. 2001—02, treas. Okla. subdivsn. devel. disabilities divsn. 2001—04, past pres. Okla. chpt. 2002—03), Am. Ednl. Rsch. Assn., Internat. Assn. Spl. Edn., Am. Assn. Mental Retardation, Nat. Coun. Geog. Edn., Nat. Coun. for Social Studies, Phi Delta Kappa. E-mail: rebmevon@prodigy.net.

CATES, GILBERT, television producer, theater director, film producer; b. N.Y.C., June 6, 1934; s. Nathan and Nina (Peltzman) Katz; m. Jane Betty Dubin, Feb. 9, 1957 (div.); children: Melissa Beth, Jonathan Michael, David Sawyer, Gilbert Lewis; m. Judith Reichman, Jan. 25, 1987; stepchildren: Ronit Reichman, Anat Reichman. BS, Syracuse U., 1955, MA, 1965. Prof. theatre, film and TV UCLA, 1990—, dean, 1990-99; with Cates-Doty Prodns., Inc.; prodr. dir. Geffen Playhouse, L.A., 1995—. Com. mem. 1 drama dept. Syracuse U., 1969-73. TV prodr., dir. Haggis Baggis, 1959, Camouflage, 1961-62, Internat. Showtime, 1962-64, Hootenanny, 1962, To All My Friends on Shore, 1972, The Affair, 1974, After the Fall, 1974, Johnny, We Hardly Knew Ye, 1977, The Kid From Nowhere, 1982, Country Gold, 1982, Faerie Tale Theatre, 1982, Hobson's Choice, 1983, Consenting Adult, 1984, Child's Cry?, 1986, Fatal Judgement, 1988, One More Time, 1988, Muffin Man, 1989, Call Me Anna, 1990, Absolute Strangers, 1991, Overruled, 1992, Confessions-Two Faces of Evil, 1994, Innocent Victims, 1995, A Death in the Family - Masterpice Theatre, 2001, Collected Stories-PBS, 2002; film prodr., dir.: The Painting, 1962, Rings Aroung the World, 1967, I Never Sang for My Father, 1970, Summer Wishes, Winter Dreams, 1973, Dragonfly, 1976, The Promise, 1978, The Last Married Couple in America, 1979, O God, Book II, 1980, Backfire, 1986; theatrical prodr.: You Know I Can't Hear You When the Water's Running, 1967, I Never Sang for My Father, 1968, The Chinese and Doctor Fish, 1970, Solitaire-Double Solitaire, 1971; dir.: Voices, 1972, Tricks of the Trade, 1980, Collected Stories, 1999, Under the Blue Sky, 2002, Paint Your Wagon, 2004; prodr.: Ann. Acad. Awards, 1990-1995, 97-99, 2001, 03-05, To Life, America Celebrates Israel's 50th (CBS-TV), 1998, America Celebrates Ford's Theater (ABC-TV), 1999, 2000, 02, 03, 04, 05, CBS at 75, 2003. Bd. dirs. Israeli Cancer Rsch. Fund, 1992-94. Recipient Best Short Film award Internat. Film Importers and Distbrs., 1962, Chancellor'smedal Syracuse U., 1974, Emmy award, 1991, Star on Hollywood Walk of Fame, 1994, Jimmy Doolittle award L.A. Theater, 1998, Best Prodn. Ovation award, 1999, Lifetime Dirs. Achievement award Caucus of Prodrs., Writers and Dirs., 1998, Arents award Syracuse U., 2003. Mem. Dirs. Guild Am. (hon. life award 1990, v.p. Ea. region 1965, Western region 1980—, pres. 1983-87, Robert B. Aldrich award 1989, nat. sec.-tras. 1997—, Pres.'s award 2005), Acad. Motion Picture Arts and Scis. (bd. govs., chmn. bd. dirs. 1985-94, 2003—), Women in Film (bd. dirs. 1993-94. v.p. 2003), League N.Y. Theatres, Friars Club (gov. 1980—). Office: 10920 Wilshire Blvd Ste 820 Los Angeles CA 90024-6510 *Craft is freedom.*

CATES, JO ANN, librarian, consultant, writer; b. Ft. Worth, June 25, 1958; d. Charles Kimbrough and Lydia Joe (Sachse) C.; children: Jacob Abraham Frank, Mabel Rose Frank. BS in Journalism, Boston U., 1980; MLS, Simmons Coll., 1984. Advt. asst. Boston Phoenix, 1978-79; med. serials asst. Mass. Gen. Hosp., Boston, 1979-80; editorial asst. Exceptional Parent Mag., Boston, 1980-81; libr. reference asst. Lesley Coll., Cambridge, Mass., 1981-84; head reference libr. Lamont Libr., Harvard U., Cambridge, Mass., 1984-85; chief libr. Poynter Inst. for Media Studies, St. Petersburg, Fla., 1985-91; head transp. libr. Northwestern U., Evanston, Ill., 1991-94; regional rsch. mgr. Ctr. for Bus. Knowledge Ernst & Young, 1997—2001; libr. dir. Columbia Coll., Chgo., 2001—04, dean of the libr., 2004—. Tchr. News Libr. and Newsroom Seminars Poynter Inst., 1990-91; mem. Harvard Com. on Instrn. Libr. Use, 1984, mem. adv. com. on book and serial budgets, 1991-94; cons. journalism orgns. Calif., Fla., Mass., 1984—; mem. Acad. Affairs Commn., 2001—; book reviewer Libr. Jour., Choice, 1985-2000, Am. Reference Book Annual, 1993—; knowledge mgmt. column editor B&F Divsn. Bull., 1999-2000. Author: Journalism: A Guide to the Reference Literature, 1990, 3d edit., 2004; editor Transp. Divsn. Bull., 1992-94; mem. editorial bd. Footnotes, 1991-94; contbr. articles to profl. jours. Mem. Transp. Rsch. Bd. Info. Svcs. Com., 1991-94; media intern Dem. Nat. Com., Boston, 1979-80. Scholar Women in Comm., 1976-78; Trustee scholar Boston U., 1978-80; Simmons Coll. grantee, 1982-84. Mem. Spl. Librs. Assn., Assn. for Edn. in Journalism and Mass Comm., Suncoast Info. Specialists (pres. 1990-91). Am. Libr. Assoc. Home: 540 Hinman Ave Apt 4 Evanston IL 60202-3081

CATES, MARSHALL E., pharmacist, medical educator; b. Ripley, Tenn., Oct. 16, 1962; s. Franklin E. Cates and Geneva S Palmer; m. Deborah L. Bailey, Dec. 16, 1988; children: Dalton M., Bailey P. BS in Biology, Rhodes Coll., Memphis, 1984; PharmD, U. Tenn., Memphis, 1991. Registered pharmacist Tenn., 1991, Ala., 1996, cert. psychiat. pharmacist Bd. Pharm. Specialties, 1996. Psychiat. pharmacy practice resident U. Tenn., Memphis, 1991—92; clin. pharmacy specialist in psychiatry VA Med. Ctr., Salt Lake City, 1992—95; asst. prof. pharmacy practice Samford U. McWhorter Sch. of Pharmacy, Birmingham, Ala., 1995—2001, assoc. prof. pharmacy practice, 2001—. Program dir. psychiat. pharmacy practice residency VA Med. Ctr., Tuscaloosa, Ala., 1997—2003. Editl. bd. psychiatry panel (biomed. jour.) Annals of Pharmacotherapy, reviewer, Pharmacotherapy, American Journal of Health-System Pharmacy. Recipient Excellence in Pharmacy award, Mylan Pharms. Inc., 1991. Fellow: Am. Soc. Health-Sys. Pharmacists; mem.: Am. Assn. Coll. Pharmacy (faculty del. 2001—02), Coll. Psychiat. and Neurologic Pharmacists (chair membership com. 1999—2000), Ala. Soc. Health-Sys. Pharmacists (bd. dirs. 2002—03, pres.-elect 2004—), Rho Chi Pharm. Honor Soc., Phi Lambda Sigma Pharmacy Leadership Soc. Achievements include first to Established the first accredited Psychiatric Pharmacy Practice Residency in the state of Alabama; Was among the first group of pharmacists to become board certified in psychiatric pharmacy. Office: Samford Univ Sch Pharmacy 800 Lakeshore Dr Birmingham AL 35229 Office Phone: 205-726-2457. Business E-Mail: mecates@samford.edu.

CATES, SUE SADLER, educational diagnostician; b. Ft. Worth, Aug. 7, 1947; d. Randall and Mary Jo (Merkt) Sadler; m. Dennis Lynn Cates, Aug. 9, 1975. BA, Baylor U., 1970; MEd, Sul Ross State U., 1977. Cert. tchr., counselor, ednl. diagnostician, Tex. Tchr. spl. edn. Eagle Pass (Tex.) Ind. Sch. Dist., 1974-76, Beeville (Tex.) Ind. Sch. Dist., 1976-80; supr., ednl. diagnostician Sinton (Tex.) Ind. Sch. Dist., 1980-81; counselor, diagnostician Snyder (Tex.) Ind. Sch. Dist., 1981-86; ednl. diagnostician Pampa (Tex.) Ind. Sch. Dist., 1987-89; elem. counselor Richland County Sch. Dist., Columbia, S.C., 1989-95; ednl. diagnostician Wichita Falls (Tex.) Ind. Sch. Dist., 1995-97, Graham (Tex.) Ind. Sch. Dist., 1997-98, Carrollton-Farmers Branch (Tex.) Ind. Sch. Dist., 1998-2000, Cedar Hill Ind. Sch. Dist., 2000-01, Arlington (Tex.) Ind. Sch. Dist., 2001—02, Ft. Worth (Tex.) Can! Acad. Charter Sch., 2002—, Ft. Worth Can! Acad. Charter Sch., 2002, Van Zandt/Rains County SSA-Edgewood Ind. Sch. Dist., 2003—04, Rains Ind. Sch. Dist., Emory, 2004—. Bd. dir. Scurry County Sheltered Workshop, 1981-85, Tex. Assn. Children with Learning Disabilities, 1976-77, 81-83; coach Tex. Spl. Olympics, Beeville, amd Sinton, 1978-81; mem. sanctuary choir Floral Heights United Meth. Ch., Wichita Falls, 1995-98, Stephen Ministry, 1992-2005, Stephen Ministry L.T.C., 2005—, tchr. Sunday sch., youth coord. Mem. NEA, AAUW, Tex. Ednl. Diagnosticians' Assn., Coun. Exceptional Children, Coun. Ednl. Diagnosticians, Assn. Supervision and Devel., Nat. Assn. Workshop Dirs., Tex. State Tchrs. Assn., Tex. Classroom Tchrs. Assn., Am. Assn. Counseling and Devel., Tex. Assn. Counseling and Devel., Tex. Ednl. Diagnosticians Assn., Phi Delta Kappa, Zeta Phi Eta. Avocations: swimming, coin collecting/numismatics, travel, singing, jewelry. Home: 321 Harbor Landing Dr Rockwall TX 75032-2414 Office: Rains ISD Spl Svcs PO Box 247 Emory TX 75440 Office Phone: 903-473-2222 ext 4121. Personal E-mail: bu70@prodigy.net.

CATHELL, DALE ROBERTS, judge; b. Berlin, Md., July 30, 1937; s. Dale Parsons Cathell and Charlotte Robert (Hocker) Terrell; m. Charlotte M. Kerbin; children: Kelly Ann, Dale Kerbin, William Howard. Student, U. Md., 1962-64; LLB, U. Balt., 1967; cert., Nat. Jud. Coll., 1983. Bar: Md. 1967. Atty. City of Ocean City, Md., 1970-76; assoc. judge Md. Dist. Ct., Worcester County, 1980-81; judge Md. Cir. Ct., Worcester County, 1981-89, Ct. Spl. Appeals, 1st Appellate Cir., 1989-97, Md. Ct. Appeals, 1998—. Instr. WOR-WIC C.C., 1973, Salisbury State U., 1978; adj. prof. law U. Balt., 1997—; mem. family and domestic rels. law com. Md. Jud. Conf., 1995-97, past mem. exec. com. Author: From Lands Over, 2003, Scent of Lilacs, 2005. Mem. Pub. Service Commn. Adv. Panel, Md., 1970, charity revision com. Mayor City Council, Ocean City, 1970; mem. Worcester County Shoreline Com., Md., 1971; mem. charter revision com. City of Ocean City, 1973, mem. utility consumer adv. panel, 1978; creator Alt. Com. Service Program, Md., 1980—; organizer Legal Intern Program Pub. Schs., Worcester County, 1981—. Served in USAF, 1955—59. Mem. Md. Bar Assn. (jud. appointment com. 1970), Worcester County Bar Assn. (pres. 1970), Balt. City Bar Assn. Democrat. Episcopalian. Office: Md Ct Appeals PO Box 4306 Salisbury MD 21803-4306 Office Phone: 410-543-6014.

CATHEY, MARY ELLEN JACKSON, religious studies educator; b. Florence, S.C., Jan. 12, 1926; d. John William and Mary Ellen (Heinrich) Jackson; m. Henry Marcellus Cathey, May 31, 1958; children: Mary Emily Cathey Ewell, Henry Marcellus Jr. AB, Winthrop Coll., 1947; MRE, Presbyn. Sch. Christian Edn., Richmond, Va., 1953. Cert. Christian educator. Tchr. English, drama Jenkins Jr. High Sch., Spartanburg, S.C., 1947-51; dir. Christian edn. First Presbyn. Ch., Anderson, S.C., 1953-56, Bethesda (Md.) Presbyn. Ch., 1956-59; organizer, dir. Co-op Nursery Sch., Bethesda Presbyn. Ch., 1967-70; dir. Christian edn. Potomac Presbyn. Ch., Potomac, Md., 1977-83, Bethesda Presbyn. Ch., 1983-85, Nat. Presbyn. Ch., Washington, 1985-88; freelance cons. and educator Nat. Capital Presbytery, Washington, 1988—. Edn. cons. Covenant Presbyn. Ch., Arlington, Va., 1987, First Presbyn. Ch., Arlington, 1989-91, Lewinsville Presbyn. Ch., McLean, 1990; elder Nat. Presbyn. Ch., 1990—; elder commr. Gen. Assy., Presbyn. Ch., Milw., 1992. Author hymn text: God Almighty, God Eternal, 1956, others, numerous poems; co-author: Confirmation Guidebook, 1988, The Circle of Wholeness, 1991. Mem. Nat. Leadership Ctr., Washington, 1999—2000; mem. pres.;s adv. coun. Union Sem.-Presbyn. Sch. Christian Edn., Richmond, Va.; pub. trustee Washington Theol. Consortium; elder Presbyn. Ch. USA, copmmr. gen. assembly, 1992. Recipient Sparkler Award Presbyn. Sch. of Christian Edn. Alumni/ae Coun., 1991. Mem. Hymn Soc. U.S. and Can., Presbyn. Writers' Guild, Presbyn. Assn. Musicians, Assn. Presbyn. Ch. Educators, Nat. Capital Presbytery Educators. Avocations: travel, theater, music, dance, writing. Home and Office: 1817 Bart Dr Silver Spring MD 20905-4418

CATHEY, PATRICE ANTOINETTE, secondary school educator, director; b. Buffalo, Oct. 13, 1954; d. Eulis Merle and Ruth Houston Cathey; children: Jonathan Eulis Barr, Patrick Jason Barr, Stephan James Barr. BA, Canisius Coll., 1995—98, EdM, 2000—02; PhD, Walden U., 2002—. Cert. of Interior Design J.R. Powers Sch., 1982. Founder/dir. Poetically Speaking Poetry Workshops For Children, Buffalo, 1995—, Ethics and Etiquette, Buffalo, 1996—; writers in edn. instr. Just Buffalo Lit. Ctr., 1996—2000; tchr. St. John Christian Acad., Buffalo, 1997—2000; academic coord. Upward Bound of Buffalo State Coll., 2000—01; dir. Liberty Partnerships Program, Buffalo, 2001—. Comm. coord. B.E.A.M.-Buffalo-Area Engring. Awareness for Minorities, 1996—; founder/pub. Onya Pub., Buffalo, 1998—; dir. of mentoring/tutoring Liberty Partnerships Program, Buffalo, 2001—. Actor: (performance poetry) A Woman of Her Words; author: (cd) Perhaps Virginia, When Poems Take Wings...Life Poems, 2003, numerous poems. Mem. Cmty. Sch. #53, Buffalo, 2001—02; vol. Darwin Martin Ho., Buffalo, 2002, Albright Knox Art Gallery, Buffalo. Recipient Distinguished Alumni Award, The Buffalo Sem., 2002, Uncrowned Queens, African Am. Women Cmty. Builders of Western N.Y., 2001; scholar Academic Scholarship, Women's Bus. Soc. of Amherst, 1997. Mem.: Internat. Soc. of Poets (award 2000), Poetry Soc. of Am., The Acad. of Am. Poets, Women in Higher Edn., Nat. Assn. of U. Women, Nat. Assn. of Black Sch. Educators, AEEE, The Jr. League of Buffalo, Alpha Kappa Alpha Sorority. Office: Liberty Partnerships Program 1300 Elmwood Avenue-CLL-E103 Buffalo NY 14222 Personal E-mail: patricecathey@yahoo.com. E-mail: catheypc@buffalostate.edu.

CATHEY-GIBSON, SHARON SUE RINN, principal, academic administrator; b. Reed City, Mich., June 11, 1940; d. Sherwood and Ellen (Hutson) Rinn.; children: Joel A. Cathey, Julie A. Maez, Sharon Sue Rinn Cathey-Gibson, Aug. 27, 1996; m. Warren Gibson. BA in Edn., San Francisco State U., 1962; postgrad., U. Mich., 1972-74, U. Calif., 1975-77; MA in Edn., U. Nev., 1988, EdD in Curriculum and Instrn., 1991. Tchr. Laguna Salada Union Sch. Dist., Pacifica, Calif., 1962-64, Redwood City (Calif.) Sch. Dist., 1964-66, Lapeer (Mich.) Sch. Dist., 1970-74; tchr., choral dir. Pine Middle Sch., Reno, 1978-84; tchr. Washoe County Sch. Dist., Reno, 1985—, adminstrv. elem. edn. cons., 1991-92; adminstrv. cons. Nev. State Dept. Elem. Edn., Carson City, 1990—; prin. Anderson Elem. Sch., Reno, 1992—, Elizabeth Lenz Elem. Sch., 1994, Libby Booth Sch., Reno, 1994-97; prof., adminstr. Sierra Nev. Coll., 1994—2002, adminstr., 1997—2002, ret., 2002; asst. prof. U. Nev., Reno, 2002—, cons. for literacy, 2001—05; cons., ptnr., editl. staff Superior Edn. and Leadership Inc.; interim dir. Ctr. Learning & Literacy, U. Nev., Reno, 2004—05. Statewide exec. dir. tchr. edn. Thompson Learning Ctr., Reno, 1987—89, diagnostician, 1987—89; asst. U. Nev., Reno, 1988—90; adminstr., prof. and coord. sch. based programs, dir. tchr. edn. dept. Sierra Nev. Coll.; ct. apptd. spl. adv. worker; cons., editor Superior Learning & Leadership Corp.; ptnr. Superior Learning Co.; cons., presenter in field. Adminstr., founder, and pres. Sierra Advocates for Family Equity. Recipient Celebrate Literacy award, Internat. Reading Assn., 2003; grantee, Nev. ESSA, 1977. Mem.: AAUW (pres. 1976—2005), Nev. Assn. Coll. Tchrs. Edn., Nat. Coun. Tchrs. English, Nat. Reading Assn., Internat. Reading Assn. (state pres. 1992, local pres. 1993—94, Literacy award 1995, Celebrate Literacy award 2003), Washoe County Tchrs. Assn., Kiwanis (Reno Sunrisers chpt. sec. 1995—98, pres. 2001—02, Kiwanian of Yr. 2003, Disting. Club Pres. 2003), Kappa Delta Epsilon (adviser), Delta Kappa Gamma (state pres. 1989—91, chptr. pres. 2004—, chair nominating com.), Phi Kappa Phi, Golden Key (hon.; ct. appted spl. advocate 2002—05). Republican. Episcopalian. Avocations: music, art, swimming. Home: 2550 Comstock Dr Reno NV 89512-1347 E-mail: sharons@gbis.com.

CATHOU, RENATA EGONE, chemist, consultant; b. Milan, June 21, 1935; d. Egon and Stella Mary Egone; m. Pierre-Yves Cathou, June 21, 1959. BS, MIT, 1957, PhD, 1963. Fellow, rsch. assoc. in chemistry MIT, Cambridge, 1962-65; rsch. assoc. Harvard U. Med. Sch., Cambridge, 1965-69, instr., 1969-70; rsch. assoc. Mass. Gen. Hosp., 1965-69, instr., 1969-70; asst. prof. dept. biochemistry Sch. Medicine, Tufts U., 1970-73, assoc. prof., 1973-78, prof., 1978-81; pres. Tech. Evaluations, Lexington, Mass., 1983-2000; sr. cons. SRC Assocs., Park Ridge, N.J., 1984-93. Sr. investigator Arthritis Found., 1970-75; vis. prof. dept. chemistry UCLA, 1976-77; mem. adv. panel NSF, 1974-75; mem. bd. sci. counselors Nat. Cancer Inst., 1979-83; ind. cons. and writer. Mem. editl. bd. Immunochemistry, 1972-75; contbr. chpts. to books and articles to profl. jours. MIT Company Founders citation, 1989; NIH predoctoral fellow, 1958-62; grantee Am. Heart Assn., 1969-81, USPHS, 1970-81. Mem. AAAS, Am. Soc. for Biochemistry and Molecular Biology, Am. Assn. Immunologists, U.S. Power Squadron (past dist. lt. comdr.), Charles River Squadron (past comdr.), Circumnavigators Club. Avocations: photography, opera, fine arts. Personal E-mail: rcathou@aol.com.

CATLETT, ELIZABETH, sculptor, educator, printmaker; b. Washington, Apr. 15, 1919; d. John and Mary (Carson) C.; m. Francisco Mora, Oct. 31, 1946; children: Francisco Mora, Juan Mora, David Mora. BS Art cum laude, Howard U., 1936; MFA, State U. Iowa, 1940; studied with Ossip Zadkine, N.Y.C., 1943; HLD (hon.), Morgan State U., 1993, Tulane U., 1995; DFA (hon.), Spellman Coll., 1995, Parsons Sch. Design, 1995, New Sch. Social Rsch., N.Y.C., 1995. Art dept. head Dillard U., New Orleans, 1940-42; instr., promotions dir. G.W. Carver Sch., N.Y.C., 1944-45; head sculpture coll. Nat. Autonomous U. Mex., 1959-76. One-woman shows include Barnett Aden Gallery, Washington, 1947-48, Nat. Sch. Fine Arts, Mexico City, 1962, Modern Art Mus., Mexico City, 1970, Studio Mus. Harlem, 1971-72, New Orleans Mus. Art, 1983, Ark. Art Centennial, 1984, Miss. Mus. of Art, 1986, Montgomery (Ala.) Mus. of Art, 1991, Jane Kelly Gallery, N.Y.C., 1993. Recipient 1st prize sculpture Golden Jubilee Nat. Exposition, 1941, Tlatlico prize 1st Sculpture Biannual, 1962, Xipe Totec prize 2d Sculpture Biannual, 1964, 1st Prize sculpture Atlanta U. Annual, 1965, 1st Purchase prize Nat. Print Salon, 1969, Alumni award Howard U. Washington, 1979, Honor award Outstanding Achievement Visual Arts Nat. Women's Caucus Art Conf., San Francisco, 1981, James Van der Zee award Phila. Mus. Art, 1983, award Amistad Rsch. Ctr., New Orleans, 1990, Candace award Art Nat. Coalition

100 Black Women, N.Y.C., 1991, numerous commns., 1966-92; named honoree Nat. Sculpture Conf., Ohio, 1987; grants Julius Rosenwald Found., 1945-47, Brit. Coun. Great Britain, 1971.*

CATLETT, RICHARD H., JR., retired lawyer; b. Boston, May 1, 1921; s. Richard Henry and Martha Barton (Taylor) Catlett; m. Marion Frances Buckey, Apr. 3, 1948 (dec. Sept. 1967); children: Ross C. Rose, Richard H. III, Thomas Y., Maria C. Eldredge; m. Barbara Ann L'Orange, May 1, 1969. BSEE, Va. Mil. Inst., 1943; LLB, U. Richmond, 1952. Engr. C&P Tel. Co., Richmond, Va., 1946-47, Catlett-Johnson Corp., Richmond, Va., 1947-50; assoc., ptnr. Christian & Barton, Richmond, Va., 1952-76; ptnr. McGuire Woods LLP, Richmond, Va., 1976-91; ret., 1991. Bd. dirs. James River Corp., gen. counsel, sec., 1969—90; gen. counsel Signet Banking Corp., Richmond, 1985—89; adj. asst. prof. law U. Richmond, 1990—93. Chmn. City of Richmond Personnel Bd., 1971—80; dir. Westminster-Canterbury Corp., Richmond, 1985—89, chmn., 1987—89; mem. vestry St. James Episc. Ch., Richmond, 1954—75. 1st lt. U.S. Army, 1943—46, ETO. Mem.: ABA, Va. State Bar Assn. (chmn. bus. law sect. 1972—73), Va. State Bar (chmn. bus. law sect. 1971—72), Commonwealth Club (Richmond), Country Club Va. (dir. 1966—69, 1971—74). Home: 300 N Ridge Rd #26 Richmond VA 23229 Office Phone: 804-775-4308. E-mail: rcatlett@mcguirewoods.com.

CATLEY-CARLSON, MARGARET, not-for-profit executive; b. Nelson, B.C., Oct. 6, 1942; d. George Lorne and Helen Margaret Catley; m. Stanley F. Carlson, Oct. 30, 1970. BA with honors, U. B.C., 1966, LLD (hon.), 1994; postgrad., Inst. Internat. Rels., U. W.I., St. Augustine, Trinidad and Tobago, 1970; LLD (hon.), U. Regina, 1985; LittD (hon.), St. Mary's U., 1985; LLD (hon.), Concordia U., 1989, Mt. St. Vincent U., 1990, Carleton U., 1994, U. Calgary, 1994. Joined Dept. External Affairs, Canada, 1966, with, 1970-74, asst. under-sec., 1981-82; 2d sec. Can. High Commn., Colombo, Sri Lanka, 1968, econ. counsellor London, 1975-77; v.p. Can. Internat. Devel. Agy., 1978, sr. v.p., acting pres., 1979-80, pres., 1983-89; asst. sec. gen. UN; dep. exec. dir. ops. UNICEF, 1981—83; fellow Ryerson Poly. U., 1986; dep. min. Health and Welfare Country Can., 1989—92; pres. Population Coun., NYC, 1993—99. Chmn. Global Water Partnership; chmn. water resource adv. com. Group Suez, Paris; chmn. change devel. and mgmt. team CGIAR, Washington, 2001; vice-chair Internat. Devel. Rsch. Ctr., Ottawa; chmn. Ctr. Agr. Rsch. Dry Areas, Syria; mem. 2020 vision policy, global food policy Internat. Food Policy Rsch. Inst., Washington; with Libr. Alexandria, Egypt, Inter-Am. Dialogue, Washington; clin. prof. Tulane U., New Orleans. Home: 249 E 48th St Apt 8A New York NY 10017

CATLIN, DON H., molecular pharmacologist, educator; Pharmacologist, dir. Olympic Analytical Laboratory, UCLA. Prof. molecular and med. pharmacology UCLA. Contbr. articles to profl. jours. Led the effort to isolate and analyze tetrahydrogestrinone (THG). Office: UCLA Sch Medicine UCLA Olympic Analytical Lab 2122 Granville Ave Los Angeles CA 90025 Office Phone: 310-825-2635. Office Fax: 310-206-9077. Business E-Mail: dcatlin@ucla.edu.

CATLIN, FRANCIS IRVING, physician; b. Hartford, Conn., Dec. 6, 1925; s. Robert Irving and Frances Rose (Maleski) C.; m. Rebecca Vaughan Graham, June 11, 1948; children: Robert, Andrew, Martha. AA, Princeton U., 1949; MD, Johns Hopkins U., 1948, DSc, 1959. Diplomate: Am. Bd. Otolaryngology. Intern Union Meml. Hosp., Balt., 1948-49; resident in otolaryngology Johns Hopkins Hosp., Balt., 1950, 52-54; from instr. to assoc. prof. Johns Hopkins U. Med. Sch., Balt., 1956-72; prof. otorhinolaryngology and communicative scis. Baylor U. Med. Sch., Houston, 1972-91, prof. emeritus, 1991—. Chief otolaryngology svc. Tex. Children's Hosp., 1972-91, emeritus staff, 1991—, mem. credentials com., 1989—. Contbr. articles to med. jours. Capt. M.C. USAF, 1950-52. Fellow Am. Otol. Soc.; mem. AMA, ASTM (F29 com. on anesthesia and respiratory equipment 1989-2004), Tex. Med. Soc., Am. Acad. Otolaryngology, Am. Coun. Otolaryngology, Am. Laryngological, Rhinological and Otol. Soc., Am. Speech and Hearing Assn. (life). Republican. Episcopalian. Home: 13307 Queensbury Ln Houston TX 77079-6013

CATLIN, ROBERT A., academic administrator, consultant, urban planner; b. Chgo., June 14, 1940; s. Robert T. and Julia J. Catlin; m. Ethel C. Catlin, Dec. 16, 1977; children: Janell, Michelle. BS, Ill. Inst. Tech., 1961; MS in Urban Planning, Columbia U., 1972; PhD in Am. Govt., Claremont U., 1976. Chair dept. polit. sci. U. South Fla., Tampa, 1977-82; chair dept. minority studies Ind. U., Gary, 1982-87; dean Coll. Social Scis. Fla. Atlantic U., Boca Raton, 1987-89; prof. urban planning U. Fla., Gainesville, 1989-92; dean Coll. Arts and Scis. Rutgers U., Camden, 1992-99; provost, v.p. for acad. affairs Calif. State U., Bakersfield, 1999—. Urban planner Mpls., L.A., Balt., N.Y.C., Washington, 1961-72; asst. prof. urban planner Calif. State Polytechnic U., Pomona, 1972-76. Author: Land Use Planning, Growth Management and Environmental Protection, 1997, Racial Politics and Urban Planning, 1993. Planning commr. Hillsborough County Planning Com., Tampa, 1979-81; transit commr. Hillsborough County Transp. Bd., Tampa, 1981-83; chair airport bd. dirs. Gary Airport Authority, 1985-87. Mem. Am. Inst. Cert. Planners.

CATMULL, EDWIN E., computer graphics engineer; b. Parkersburg, W. Va., Mar. 31, 1945; married; 5 children. BS in Computer Sci. and Physics, U. Utah, PhD in Computer Sci., 1974. V.p. computer div. Lucasfilm, Ltd., 1979—86; co-founder, pres. Pixar Animation Studios, Emeryville, Calif., 1986—88, CTO, chmn., 1988—91, pres., 1991—. Named to High-Tech Hall of Fame, Utah Information Technol. Assn., 2001; recipient Coons award., 1993, Academy award of Merit, 2001. Mem. NAE, Acad. Motion Picture Arts and Scis. (Sci. and Tech. engring. award, sci. and tech. awards com.). Achievements include research in computer graphics, video editing, video games, digital video, digital computer graphics and animation. Office: Pixar Animation Studios 1200 Park Ave Emeryville CA 94608

CATO, GLORIA MAXINE, retired secondary education educator, school program administrator; b. Covington, La., Mar. 22, 1942; d. Dan and Roxieana (Washington) Smith; widowed; 1 child, Mark. BS, Southern U., 1965; MS, Pepperdine U., 1974. Tchr. Los Angeles Unified Sch. Dist., 1965-81, counselor, magnet program coordinator, 1981—, PUSH for Excellence program coordinator, 1978-80, student activities coordinator, 1982-84, coll. advisor, 1984-85, personnel specialist, tchr. advisor, 1986-87, asst. prin., 1992—99; ret., 1999. Edn./counselor cons. L.A. Unified Sch. Dist. Trustee L.A. Ednl. Allance Restructuring Now. Recipient Community-Sch. Service award City of Los Angeles, 1978; named to Top Ladies of Distinction, 1992. Charter mem. NEA, Nat. Assn. Biology Tchrs. (finalist Tchrs. award 1978), Magnet Coordinator Assn., Los Angeles Counselors Assn.; mem. United Tchrs. Los Angeles, Associated Adminstrs. L.A., Assn. Calif. Sch. Adminstrs., Asst. Prin. Secondary Counseling Svcs. Orgn., Phi Delta Kappa, Alpha Kappa Alpha (Mu Beta Omega chpt.). Democrat. Baptist. Home: 3661 Kensley Dr Inglewood CA 90305-2230

CATOE, BETTE LORRINA, pediatrician, educator; b. Apr. 7, 1926; d. John Booker and Laura Beola (Adams) C.; m. Warren J. Strudwick, Sept. 17, 1949; children: Laura Christina, Warren J., William J. BS cum laude, Howard U., 1948, MD, 1951. Intern Freedmen's Hosp., Washington, 1951-52; pediat. resident Howard U./Freedman's Hosp., 1952-55, practice medicine specializing in pediatrics Washington, 1956—2003; cons. Govt. of D.C. Income Maintenance Adminstrn., Washington, 2003—; instr. bacteriology Howard U., 1955-57; mem. staff Providence Hosp., Columbia Hosp., Howard U. Hosp., Wash., Hosp. Ctr.; sch. health officer Dept. Health, Washington, 1960-64; clin. instr. Howard U., 1956-58; health cons., 2003—; cons. income maint. admin. Govt. D.C., 2003—. Mem. D.C. Health Planning Adv. Coun., 1967-77, chmn. 1973-77; chmn. D.C. Devel. Disabilities Adv. Coun., 1970-74; mem. D.C. Mayor's Commn. on Food and Nutrition, 1971-72, Mayor's Commn. on Maternal and Child Health, 1978-84, appt. vice chmn. Pub. Benefit Corp., 1997-2001; mem. D.C. Commn. Jud. Tenure and Disabilities, 1977-2001, chmn. Bd. Public Benefit Corp. of D.C., 1998-2001; bd. govs. St. Alban's Sch., 1978-84; bd. dirs. D.C. Health and Welfare Coun., 1968-73, pres., 1973-74; del. Democratic Nat. Conv., 1976; bd. dirs. Met. Washington Health and Welfare Coun., 1970-72, Parent Coun. of Washington, 1974-75, Met. Med. Founds., Inc., Silver Spring YMCA, 1977-80, Kingsburg Ctr., 1997-99; mem., chair emergency med. com. Mayor's Health Policy Coun., 1998-2001; cons. income maintenance adminstrn. Govt. of D.C. Dept. Human Svcs., 2003—. Mem.: NAACP, AMA, Women's Aux. Medico-Chirurg. Soc., Assn. Comprehensive Health Planners (dir. 1975—77), Urban League, Am. Med. Women's Assn., Nat. Med. Assn. (chmn. pediat. sect. 1981—83), D.C. Chirurg. Soc. (trustee 1996—99, nominating com. 2000—03, jud. legis. com. 2001—03), Women's Nat. Dem., Jack and Jill Am., Carrousels Club (nat. v.p. 1986—88, nat. pres. 1988—90), Links Club, Century Club of Nat. Assn. Negro Bus. and Profl. Women's Clubs (pres. 1985—89), Alpha Kappa Alpha. Home and Office: 1748 Sycamore St NW Washington DC 20012-1031 Personal E-mail: bcatoemd@aol.com.

CATOLINE-ACKERMAN, PAULINE DESSIE, small business owner; b. Ft. Worth, Dec. 17, 1937; d. Byron Hillis and Dessie Elizabeth (Plumlee) Doggett; children: Sherry Lou, Brenda Lynn; m. Donald Ralph Ackerman, Feb. 19, 1993. BA in Bus. Mgmt. (labor rels. specialty), Hiram Coll., 1989. Sec. Gen. Am. Life Ins. Co., Ft. Worth, 1956-57, Kelly Girl Svcs., Youngstown, Ohio, 1965-69; legal sec. Burgstaller, Schwartz & Moore, Youngstown, 1962-65, Green, Schiavoni, Murphy & Haines, Youngstown, 1969-71, Flask & Policy, Youngstown, 1971-83; sec. Western Res. Care System, Youngstown, 1983-87, exec. sec., 1987-90; owner, mgr. Pauline's Place, Youngstown, 1993—; legal sec. Henderson, Covington, Stein, Donchess & Messenger Law Firm, 1993-94; exec. adminstrv. asst. to pres. CEO, sr. v.p. Internat. Renaissance Developers, Youngstown, 1994-96; adminstrv. asst. to v.p. and client svc. mgr. Bank One Investment Mgmt. & Trust Group, Youngstown, 1996—2000; admin. assoc. regional divsn. Am. Heart Assn., Youngstown, 2000—01; owner, mgr. Paulines Pl., 2001—; staff Kelly Svcs., Youngstown, Ohio, 2001—. Pres. PTA, Cottage Hills, Ill., 1968-69, brownie and scout leader, 1968-69. Mem. Mahoning County Legal Secs. Assn. (v.p. 1973-74, editor monthly booklet 1974-75), Exec. Link, Missionary Group Club. Democrat. Methodist. Avocations: painting, reading poetry, tennis, swimming, horseback riding. Home: 3961 Cannon Rd Youngstown OH 44515-4604

CATON, SCOTT BRENON, history professor; b. Brockport, N.Y., July 22, 1960; s. Brenon Phelps and Bonnie (Rohr) Caton; m. Bonnie Lee Marshall, Aug. 21, 1982; children: Emily, Elizabeth, Brooke, Catherine, Victoria, Alexander. BA in Religion and Philosophy, Roberts Wesleyan Coll., Rochester, N.Y., 1986; MAR, Westminster Theol. Seminary, Phila., 1988; PhD in History, U. Rochester, N.Y., 1998. History prof. Roberts Wesleyan Coll., Rochester, NY, 1990—; prof., founding faculty mem. Northeastern Seminary, Rochester, NY, 1998—. Cons. Adept Gifted and Talented Program, BOCES, Rochester, NY, 1998—; curriculum writer Barnes & Noble U., 2002—03. Author: The Compleat Minister: The De Profundis Sermons of Jonathan Mitchel, 1998. Mem.: Am. Chesterton Soc. (founding mem., Rochester, N.Y. chpt.), Am. Soc. Church History, Am. Hist. Assn. Roman Catholic. Avocations: camping, classical music, hiking, travel. Home: Branches 223 Lyell Ave Spencerport NY 14559 Office: Roberts Wesleyan Coll 2301 Westside Dr Rochester NY 14624 Office Phone: 585-594-6336. Business E-Mail: catons@roberts.edu.

CATRON, STEPHEN BARNARD, lawyer, real estate developer, director; b. Bowling Green, Ky., Feb. 4, 1949; s. Eugene and Gladys (Bell) C.; m. Deborah Faye Grigsby, Nov. 28, 1981. BA, Western Ky. U., Bowling Green, 1971; JD, U. Miss., 1974. Bar: Ky. 1974, Miss. 1974, Tenn. 1988, U.S. Dist. Ct. (we. dist.) Ky. 1974, U.S. Dist. Ct. (no. dist.) Miss. 1974, U.S. Supreme Ct. 1982, U.S. Ct. Appeals (6th cir.) 1983. Atty. Ky. Dept. Human Resources, Bowling Green, Ky., 1974-75; atty., ptnr. Reynolds, Catron, Johnson & Hinton, Bowling Green, Ky., 1975-95, Lewis, King, Krieg, Waldrop and Catron, P.C., Bowling Green, Ky., 1995-2001; ptnr. Wyatt, Tarrant & Combs, LLP, Bowling Green, Ky., 2001—04; dir. real estate devel. Bridgemont Devel. Group, LLC, 2004—05; cons. Pinnacle View Consulting, LLC, 2005—. Pres. Bowling Green-Warren County Bar, 1989-90; chair., bd. trustees Ky. IOLTA Fund, Frankfort, Ky., 1990-94; bd. dirs. Nat. Assn. IOLTA Programs, Chgo., 1991-92. Author: Kentucky Corporations Law, 1989. Bd. dirs. Bowling Green (Ky.) Human Rights Commn., 1976-78; vice chair Ky. Ednl. TV Auth., Lexington, Ky., 1988-92; bd. regents Western Ky. U., Bowling Green., 1991-92; chairperson Bowling Green-Warren County Indsl. Authority; trustee Western Ky. U. Found. Fellow Am. Bar Found.; mem. Ky. Bar Assn. (bd. govs. 1992-2000, v.p. 2000-01, pres.-elect 2001-02, pres. 2002-03). Democrat. Episcopalian. Avocations: reading, jogging, golf, computers. Home: 509 Saint Charles Ln Knoxville TN 37922 Office: Pinnacle View Consulting LLC 2732 Florence Dr Pigeon Forge TN 37863 Office Phone: 865-453-9983. Business E-Mail: scatron@pinnacleviewconsulting.com.

CATSIMATIDIS, JOHN ANDREAS, retail chain executive, airline executive; b. Nissiros, Greece, Sept. 7, 1948; came to U.S., 1949, naturalized, 1950; s. Andreas John and Despina (Emmanulides) C. BS in Engring., NYU, 1970. Chmn., CEO Gristedes Foods, 1969—, Red Apple Cos. (Gristedes, Red Apple stores), N.Y.C., 1970—, United Refining Inc., Warren, Pa., 1986—. Chmn., CEO Sloan's Supermarket, N.Y.C. Pres. Greek Orthodox Ch. of Am., 2001—02. Recipient Humanitarian award NCCJ, 1978, Am. Jewish Com., 1982, Nat. Kidney Assn., 1986; Entrepreneurship award NYU Bus. Sch., 1987. Mem.: Young Men Philanthrapic League, Westside C. of C., N.Y. Athletic Club, Wings, N.Y. U. Club. Office: Red Apple Group 823 11th Ave New York NY 10019-3557

CATTANACH, ROBERT EDWARD, JR., lawyer; b. Thorp, Wis., Jan. 14, 1949; s. Robert Edmund Sr. and Irene Louise (Papierniak) C.; m. Terry Theirl, June 9, 1972; children: Philip, Sarah, Katherine. BS, U.S. Naval Acad., 1972; JD, U. Wis., 1975. Bar: Wis. 1975, U.S. Supreme Ct. 1980, Minn. 1983, U.S. Dist. Ct. (8th cir.) 1989. Spl. counsel to Sec. of Navy, Washington, 1976-78; trial atty. U.S. Dept. of Justice, Washington, 1978-80; ptnr., chair litigation dept. Oppenheimer Wolff & Donnelly, St. Paul, 1983-94; ptnr., co-chmn., telecom. Dorsey & Whitney, Mpls., 1994—. Articles editor U. Wis. Law Rev., 1974-75. Mem. St. Paul Heritage Preservation Commn., 1993-98. Mem. ABA, Wis. Bar Assn. (pres. non-resident divsn. 1990-92), Minn. Bar Assn., Fellow, Am. Bar Found. Avocations: cross-country skiing, bicycling. Office: Dorsey & Whitney LLP 50 S 6th St Ste 1500 Minneapolis MN 55402-1553 Office Phone: 612-340-2873. Office Fax: 612-340-2868. Business E-Mail: cattanach.robert@dorsey.com.

CATTANEO, JACQUELYN ANNETTE KAMMERER, artist, educator; b. Gallup, N.Mex., June 1, 1944; d. Ralph John and Gladys Agnes (O'Sullivan) Kammer; m. John Leo Cattaneo, Apr. 25, 1964; children: John Auro, Paul Anthony. Student, Tex. Woman's U., 1962-64. Portrait artist, tchr., Gallup, N.Mex., 1972. Coord. Works Progress Adminstrn. art project renovation McKinley County, Gallup, Octavia Fellin Performing Arts wing dedication, Gallup Pub. Libr.; formation com. mem. Multi-Modal/Multi-Cultural Ctr. for Gallup; exch. with Soviet Women's Com. USSR Women Artists del., Moscow, Kiev, Leningrad, 1990; Women Artists del. and exch., Jerusalem, Tel Aviv, Cairo, Israel; mem. Artists Del. to Prague, Vienna and Budapest; mem. Women Artists Del. to Egypt, Israel and Italy, 1992, artist del., Brazil, 1994, Greece, Crete, Turkey, Spain, 1996, N.S. and Ont., N.B., PEI, Can., 2000. One-woman shows include Gallup Pub. Libr., 1963, 66, 77, 78, 81, 87, Gallup Lovelace Med. Clinic, Santa Fe St. Open House, 1981, Gallery 20, Farmington, N.Mex., 1985—, Red Mesa Art Gallery, 1989, Soviet Retrospect Carol's Art & Antiques Gallery, Liverpool, N.Y., 1992, 97, N.Mex. State Capitol Bldg., Santa Fe, 1992, Lt. Govt. Casey Luna-Office Complex, Women Artists N.Mex. Mus. Fine Arts, Carlsbad, 1992, Rio Rancho Country Club, N.Mex., 1995; exhibited in group shows including Navajo Nation Libr. Invitational, 1978, Santa Fe Festival of the Arts Invitational, 1979, N.Mex. State Fair, 1978, 79, 80, Catharine Lorrilard Wolfe, N.Y.C., 1980, 81, 84, 85, 86, 87, 88, 89, 90, 91, 92, 2004, 2005, 4th ann. exhbn. Salmagundi Club, 1984, 90, 98, 3d ann. Palm Beach Internat., New Orleans, 1984, Fine Arts Ctr., Taos, 1984, The Best and the Brightest O'Brien's Art Emporium, Scottsdale, Ariz., 1986, Gov.'s Gallery, 1989, N.Mex. State Capitol, Santa Fe, 1987, Pastel Soc. West Coast Ann. Exhbn., Sacramento Ctr. for Arts, Calif., 1986-90, gov.'s invitational Magnifico Fest. of the Arts, Albuquerque, 1991, Assn. pour la Promotion du Patrimone Artistique Française, Paris Nat. Mus. of the Arts for Women, Washington, 1991, Artists of N.Mex., Internat. Nexus '92 Fine Art Exhbn., Trammell Corw Pavillion, Dallas, Carlsbad (N.Mex.) Mus. Fine Art; represented in permanent collections Zuni Arts and Crafts Ednl. Bldg., U. N.Mex., C.J. Wiemar Collection, McKinley Manor, Gov.'s Office, State Capitol Bldg., Santa Fe, Hist. El Rancho Hotel, Gallup, Sunwest Bank, Fine Arts Ctr., Taos, Armand Hammer Pvt. Collection, Wilcox Canyon Collections, Sadona, Ariz., Galaria Impi, Netherlands, Woods Art and Antiques, Liverpool, N.Y., Stewarts Fine Art, Taos, N.Mex., Rehoboth McKinley Christian Hosp. & Sacred Heart Cathedral, Gallup, NM. Mem. Dora Cox del. to Soviet Union-U.S. Exch., 1990. Recipient Cert. of Recognition for Contbn. and Participation Assn. pour la Patrinome du Artistique Français, 1991, N.Mex. State Senate 14th Legislature Session Meml. # 101 for Artistic Achievements award, 1992, Award of Merit, Pastel Soc. West Coast Ann. Membership Exhbn., 1998, award N.Mex. State Ho. Reps. for Artistic Achievement, 2001, Holbein award for excellence in painting Pastel Soc. West Coast Internat. Juried Exhbn., 1st pl. pastel award Catherine Lorillard Wolfe Art Club Mems. Exhbn., N.Y.C., 2004; honored for preservation of WPA Dept. Edn. N.Mex. State Ho. of Reps., 2001. Mem. Internat. Fine Arts Guild, Am. Portrait Soc. (cert.), Oil Painters of Am., Pastel Soc. Am. (signature, Award of Merit 2004), Pastel Soc. of West Coast (cert., signature, Hobein award, award of excellence mem.'s show 1999), Mus. N.Mex. Found., N.Mex. Archtl. Found., Mus. Women in the Arts, Fechin Inst., Artists' Co-op (co-chair), Gallup C. of C., Gallup Area Arts and Crafts Coun. (nat. and internat. artist of distinction award 1997), Catharine Lorillard Wolfe Art Club of N.Y.C. (oil and pastel juried membership, 2nd Pl. Pastel award 2005), Oil Painters of Am., Pastel Soc. N.Mex., Soroptimists (Internat. Woman of Distinction 1990), almagundi Art Club. Address: 210 E Green St Gallup NM 87301-6130 Office Phone: 505-722-4090. E-mail: cattaneo@cnetco.com.

CATTELAN, MAURIZIO, artist; b. Padua, Italy, 1960; Projects 65, Mus. Modern Art, NY, 1998, 48th Venice Biennale, La Biennale di Venezia, Venice, 1999, Apr. 1999, Galleria Massimo De Carlo, Milano, 1999, Au-delà du spectacle, Centre Pompidou, Musée National d'Art Moderne, Paris, 2000, Over the Edges, Stedelijk Mus. voor Acutuele Kunst, 2000, 49th Venice Biennale, La Biennale Di Venezia, Venice, 2001, Irony, Fundación Joan Miró, Barcelona, 2001, Recaptured Nature, Marian Goodman Gallery, NY, 2002, Accrochage I: Photographs, Van de Weghe Fine Art, NY, 2002, Hollywood is a Verb, Gagosian Gallery, London, 2002, Felix, Mus. Contemporary Art, Chgo., 2002, Dreams & Conflicts: Dictatorship of the Viewer, La Biennale di Venezia, Venice, 2003, It happened tomorrow, La biennale d'art contemporain de Lyon, 2002, Whitney Biennial Exhbn., Whitney Mus. Am. Art, 2004, Bodily Space: New Obsessions in Figurative Sculpture, Albright-Knox Art Gallery, Buffalo, NY, 2004, The Big Nothing, Inst. Contemporary Art, Phila., 2004, None of the above, Swiss Inst., NY, 2004. Mailing: c/o Marian Goodman Gallery 24 West 57th St New York NY 10019*

CATTELL, HEATHER BIRKETT, psychologist; b. Carlisle, eng., Dec. 16, 1936; came to U.S., 1958; d. Wilfred B. and Anne Birkett; m. Russel B. Shields, June 10, 1958 (div. 1968); children: Vaughn, Gary, Heather Luanne; m. Raymond B. Cattell, May 9, 1981. BA, U. Hawaii, 1974, MA, 1977, PhD, 1979. Lic. clin. psychologist, Hawaii. Dir. rsch. Salvation Army, Honolulu, 1979-81; pvt. practice Honolulu, 1981—. Lectr., workshop leader, U.S., Australia, Can., and United Kingdom, 1989—. Author: The 16PF: Personality in Depth, 1989, The Cattell Comprehensive Personality Inventory, 1998. Mem. Phi Beta Kappa.

CATTERALL, MARLENE, Canadian legislator; b. Ottawa, Ont., Can., Mar. 1, 1939; d. Paul and Isobel Petzold; m. Ron Catterall, July 14, 1962; children: Karen, Chris, Cheryl. Ed., Carleton U. Alderman City of Ottawa, 1976-85; coun. mem. Regional Municipality Ottawa-Carleton, 1976-85; mem. from Ottawa West Ho. of Commons, 1988-97, apptd. parliamentary sec. to pres. of treasury bd., 1993, mem. from Ottawa W., Nepean, 1997—. Apptd. dep. govt. whip, 1994; apptd. chief govt. whip, 2001; mem. Justice Com., Bd. Internal Economy. Mem. coun. women Friends of Can. Mus. Civilization. Liberal. Roman Catholic. Office: House of Commons Rm 451-S Centre Block Ottawa ON Canada K1A 0A6 E-mail: cattem@parl.gc.ca.

CATTERALL, WILLIAM A., pharmacology, neurobiology educator; b. Providence, Oct. 12, 1946; s. William V. and Alice C.; children: W. Douglas, Elizabeth R.; m. Christine E. BA in Chemistry, Brown U., 1968; PhD in Physiol. Chemistry, Johns Hopkins U., 1972. Postdoctoral research fellow Lab. of Biochem. Genetics NIH, Bethesda, Md., 1972-76, staff scientist, 1976-77; assoc. prof. dept. pharmacology U. Wash., Seattle, 1977-82, prof., 1982—, chmn. dept. pharmacology, 1984—, chmn. interdisciplinary com. on neurobiology, 1986—. Editor: Molecular Pharmacology, 1986—90; contbr. chapters to books, articles to profl. jours. Recipient Young Scientist award Passano Found., 1981, Jacob Javits Neurosci award, NIH, 1984, 91, Basic Sci. prize Am. Heart Assn., 1992, Bristol Myers Squibb award, 2003; numerous grants. Mem. Nat. Acad. Sci., Inst. of Medicine, Am. Acad. Arts and Sci., Am. Soc. Pharmacology and Exptl. Therapeutics, Soc. for Neurosci., Am. Soc. Biol. Chemists. Avocations: sailing, skiing. Office: Univ Wash Dept Pharmacology PO Box 357280 Seattle WA 98195-7280

CATTO, HENRY EDWARD, former government official, retired ambassador; b. Dallas, Dec. 6, 1930; s. Henry Edward and Maurine (Halsell) C.; m. Jessica Oveta Hobby, Feb. 15, 1958; children: Heather, John, William, Elizabeth. BA, Williams Coll., 1952; JD (hon.), U. Aberdeen, 1990. Ptnr. Catto & Catto, San Antonio, 1955—2003, ret., 2003; dep. rep. Orgn. Am. States, Washington, 1969-71; ambassador to El Salvador, 1971-73; U.S. chief protocol White House, Washington, 1974-76; ambassador to UN, Geneva, 1976-77; asst. sec. def. Pentagon, Washington, 1981-83; vice chmn. H & C Communications, 1983-89; amb. to U.K., 1989-91; dir. U.S. Info. Agy., Washington, 1991-93; adj. prof. U. Tex., San Antonio, 1993—. Mem. Coun. on Fgn. Rels., N.Y.C., 1973; vice chmn. The Aspen Inst., 1993—; chmn. Atlantic Coun. U.S., 1999—. Mem. Metro Club (Washington). Republican. Office: 200 Navarro San Antonio TX 78205

CATTRALL, KIM, actress; b. Liverpool, Eng., Aug. 21, 1956; d. Dennis and Shane Cattrall; m. Larry Davis, 1975 (div.); m. Andre J. Lyson, 1982 (div. 1989); m. Mark Levinson, Sept. 4, 1998. Student, London Acad. Music and Dramatic Art, Banff Sch. Fine Arts, Alta., Can.; grad., Am. Acad. Dramatic Arts, N.Y.C. Actor: (films) Rosebud, 1975, Tribute, 1980, Ticket to Heaven, 1981, Porky's, 1982, Police Academy, 1984, Turk 182!, 1985, City Limits, 1985, Hold-Up, 1985, Big Trouble in Little China, 1986, Mannequin, 1987, Masquerade, 1988, Palais Royale, 1988, Midnight Crossing, 1988, The Return of the Musketeers, 1989, La Famiglia Buonanotte, 1989, Honeymoon Academy, 1990, Bonfire of the Vanities, 1990, Star Trek VI: The Undiscovered Country, 1991, Split Second, 1992, Breaking Point, 1993, Live Nude Girls, 1995, Above Suspicion, 1995, Where Truth Lies, 1996, Unforgettable, 1996, Exception to the Rule, 1997, Modern Vampires, 1998, Baby Geniuses, 1999, The Devil and Daniel Webster, 2001, 15 Minutes, 2001, Crossroads, 2002, Ice Princess, 2005, others; (TV films) Sins of the Past, 1984, Miracle in the Wilderness, 1992, Double Vision, 1992, Two Golden Balls, 1994, Running Delilah, 1994, OP Center, 1995, The Heidi Chronicles, 1995, Every Woman's Dream, 1996, Invasion, 1997, Creature, 1998, 36 Hours to Die, 1999, Sex and the Matrix, 2000; (TV series) Angel Falls, 1993, Sex and the City, 1998—2004 (SAG award, 2001, Golden Globe award, 2002, Women in Film Lucy award, 1999); (TV miniseries) Wild Palms, 1993, (various TV guest appearances); co-author (with Mark Levinson): Satisfaction, 2002; actor: (plays) Whose Life Is It Anyway?, 2005. Office: c/o Jeffrey Witjas William Morris Agy 151 El Camino Dr Beverly Hills CA 90212*

CATUZZI, JEROME PRIMO, JR., lawyer; b. NYC, Aug. 23, 1938; s. J.P. Sr. and Ida (Ghezzi) C.; m. Chantal Mauricette Marais, Nov. 10, 1979; children: Daniella Firenze, Vanessa Carmen, Lee. BA, Columbia U., 1958; JD, Georgetown U., 1961; LLM in Internat. Law, NYU, 1963; PhD in Internat. Bus., La Salle U., 1998. Bar: NY, DC, Asesor Legal, Spain 1973. Assoc. Baker & McKenzie, NYC and Chgo., 1963-65; gen. counsel, exec. v.p. Royal Bus. Fund Corp. (Amex), NYC, 1965-72; exec. v.p., gen. counsel Holmes Protection, Inc. (Amex); internat. counsel, mng. dir. Occidental S.A., Madrid and Geneva, 1972-84; counsel US Consulate, Costa del Sol, Spain, Sotogrande; U.S. gen. counsel Soparind S.A., NYC and Paris, 1984-86; resident US ptnr. Berlioz, Ferry, David, Lutz & Rochefort, NYC, 1986-88; resident prin. J.P. Catuzzi, Jr. & Assocs., NYC, 1989—; internat. counsel, 1987. Adj. prof. law and fin. C.W. Post campus LI U., NYC, 1985—; nat. lectr. Internat. Bus. Network, NYC and Santa Monica, Calif., 1980-84; internat. cons. Eums Pharma, S.A., Geneva, Switzerland, Magellan, GmbH, MNG Industries, GmbH, Fed. Republic Germany, GEFI Holdings, Ltd., Gibraltar, ChartHouse Holdings, Ltd., Ireland, Galia, Ltd., Lausanne, Switzerland, Centro Geotecnico, S.R.L., Rome, Geosaf, Inc., Montreal, Can., Hanover Trust House, Ltd., Ireland; internat. coun. Chropi, S.A., Greece, Igos Comm., S.A., Paris, Ireland; gen. internat. counsel Centrum European Securities, Ltd., Geneva, Switzerland; int. counsel golden Hat Resources, Inc., Vancouver, BC, Canada; gen. counsel Orbis Capital Investment, Ltd., Dublin, Ireland South Winds, LLC, Isle of Man; cons. Fond D'aide au Devel. NGO Econ. and Social Coun. UN, Geneva, NYC, 1999—; prin. KI-Int. Mgmt. Group, London; gen. counsel, prin. Seaforth Meridian Hedge Fund, London, 2004—. Legis. cons. to Gov. Rockefeller div. human rights State of NY, Albany, 1968-70; mem. legal com. NY County Rep. Party, 1967-72. Mem. Confrerie des Chevalier du Tastevin (NYC) (chevalier 1985—), Knights of Malta. Roman Catholic. Personal E-mail: ilmaestro7@hotmail.com. Business E-Mail: ilmaestro@mail2world.com.

CATZ, BORIS, endocrinologist, educator; b. Troyanov, Russia, Feb. 15, 1923; came to U.S., 1950, naturalized, 1955; s. Jacobo and Esther (Galbmillon) C.; m. Rebecca Schechter; children: Judith, Dinah, Sarah Lea, Robert. BS, Nat. U. Mex., 1941, MD, 1947; MS in Medicine, U. So. Calif., 1951. Intern Gen. Hosp., Mexico City, Mex., 1945-46; prof. sch. medicine U. Mex., 1947-48; instr. medicine U. So. Calif., 1952-54, asst. clin. prof., 1954-59, 1959-83, clin. prof., 1983—; pvt. practice L.A., 1951-55, Beverly Hills, Calif., 1957—. Chief Thyroid Clinic L.A. County Gen. Hosp., 1955-70; sr. cons. thyroid clin. U. So. Calif., L.A. Med. Ctr., 1970—; clin. chief endocrinology Cedars-Sinai Med. Ctr., 1983-87. Author: Thyroid Case Studies, 1975, 2d edit., 1981; contbr. numerous articles on thyroidology to med. jours. Capt. U.S. Army, 1955-57. Rsch. fellow medicine U. So. Calif., 1949-51; Boris Catz lectureship in his honor Thyroid Rsch. Endowment Fund, Cedars Sinai Med. Ctr., 1985. Fellow ACP, Am. Coll. Nuclear Medicine (pres. elect 1982), Royal Soc. Medicine, Am. Thyroid Assn. (Disting. Svc. award 2001); mem. AMA, AAAS, Cedars Sinai Med. Ctr. Soc. History of Medicine (chmn.), L.A. County Med. Assn., Calif. Med. Assn., Endocrine Soc., Am. Thyroid Assn., Soc. Exptl. Biology and Medicine, Western Soc. Clin. Rsch., Am. Fedn. Clin. Rsch., Soc. Nuclear Medicine, So. Calif. Soc. Nuclear Medicine, N.Y. Acad. Scis., L.A. Soc. Internal Medicine, Collegium Salerni, Cedar Sinai Soc. History Medicine, B'nai B'rith Club, The Profl. Man's Club (past pres.), Phi Lambda Kappa. Home: 300 S El Camino Dr Beverly Hills CA 90212-4212 Office: 435 N Roxbury Dr Beverly Hills CA 90210-5027 Office Phone: 310-273-1766.

CATZ, SAFRA, computer software company executive; Various investment banking positions Donaldson, Lufkin & Jenrette, 1986—94, sr. v.p., 1994—97, mng. dir., 1997—99; sr. v.p. Oracle Corp., Redwood City, Calif., 1999, exec. v.p., 1999—2004, co-pres., 2004—, also bd. dir., 2001—; co-pres. PeopleSoft Inc., Pleasanton, Calif., 2004—. Named one of Most Powerful Women, Forbes mag., 2005. Office: Oracle Corp 500 Oracle Pkwy Redwood City CA 94085 Address: PeopleSoft Inc 4460 Hacienda Dr Pleasanton CA 94588-8618*

CAUCHON, MARTIN, former Canadian government official; b. La Malbaie, Que., Can., Aug. 23, 1962; Lic. in Civil Law, U. Ottawa, 1984; ML in Internat. Law, U. Exeter, 1990. Practiced civil and comml. law, 1985-93; mem. Parliament. Govt. of Can., Ottawa, 1993—, pres. Liberal Party Can. Que., 1993-95, vice. chmn. standing com. pub. accts., 1994, chmn. Can.-France Inter-Parliamentary Assn., 1994-95, mem. standing com. human resources devel., 1994-96, sec. state responsible for Can. econ. devel. Montreal, 1996—2002, mgr. Can.-Quebec infrastructure works agreement, cmty. futures program, min. of nat. revenue, 1999—2002, min. of justice & attorney gen., 2002—03, min. with polit. responsibility for Que., 2002—03. Liberal Party Can.

CAUDILL, SAMUEL JEFFERSON, architect; b. Tulsa, June 5, 1922; s. Samuel Jefferson and Maymie Starling (Boulware) C.; m. Joy Maxwell, May 31, 1952; children: Jody Caudill Cardamone, Julie Hertzberg, Samuel Boone, Robert Maxwell, Anne Goertzen BArch, Cornell U., Ithaca, N.Y., 1946. Registered architect Colo., Calif., Idaho, Ariz. Prin. architect Samuel J. Caudill, Jr., Aspen, Colo., 1954-59, Caudill Assocs. Architects, Aspen, 1959-80; pres. Caudill Gustafson & Assocs. Architects, PC, Aspen, 1980-87; pres., CEO Caudill Gustafson & Assocs., Architects, PC, Aspen, 1992—; pres. Caudill Gustafson Ross & Assocs., Architects, P.C., Aspen, 1987-92. Mem. Pitkin County Planning and Zoning Commn., Colo., 1955-58; mem. outdoor edn. com. Colo. Dept. Edn., 1966-68; chmn. Pitkin County Bd. Appeals, 1970; mem. Colo. Water Quality Control Commn., 1977-80. Wildlife rep. adv. bd. Bur. Land Mgmt. Dept. Interior, Grand Junction, Colo., 1969-75, 80-85; chmn. citizens adv. com. Colo. Hwy. Dept. for I-70 through Glenwood Canyon, 1975-92; chmn. Colo. Wildlife Commn., 1978-79. Recipient Outstanding Pub. Service Bur. Land Mgmt., 1975; named to Aspen (Colo.) Hall of Fame, 1998. Fellow AIA (Community Svc. award 1976, Architect of Yr. award 1992, mem. emeritus 1995); mem. Colo. Soc. Architects (pres. 1983), Colo. Coun. on Arts and Humanities, Aspen C. of C. (pres. 1956-57), Masons, Shriners (Denver). Home: 1055 Stage Rd Aspen CO 81611-1096 Office: Caudill Gustafson & Assocs Architects PC 234 E Hopkins Ave Aspen CO 81611-1938

CAUDILL, TOM HOLDEN, military analyst; b. St. Augustine, Fla., June 21, 1945; s. Julian Terrill and Alta Jane (Holden) C.; 1 child, Mara Julia. BA in History, East Tenn. State U., 1967, MA in Internat. Rels., 1977; MA in Mgmt. Sci., Webster U., 1980. Instr. English as second lang., polit. sci., mgmt. sci. U.S. Peace Corps, Loei, Thailand, 1970-73; instr. English as second lang., polit. sci., mgmt. sci. Steed Coll., Johnson City, Tenn., 1973-76; instr. Internat. Ctr. U. Tex., Austin, 1976-77; tng. specialist Air Tng. Command USAF, Lackland AFB, Tex., 1977-80, tng. specialist Logistics Command Wright-Patterson AFB, Ohio, 1980-81, logistics mgmt. specialist, 1981-85, chief, policy and procedures Internat. Logistics Ctr., 1985-88, chief policy and analysis, 1986—, chief plans and devel., 1988; dir. Arabian programs Internat. Logistics Ctr., 1991-95; exec. fellow Woodrow Wilson Sch. Govt. Princeton U., 1995-96; dep. dir. internat. programs Air Force Security Assistance Ctr., 1996; chief prodn. policy Hdqtrs. Air Force Material Command, Wright Patterson AFB, Ohio, 1997-99; dir. ops. mgmt. Air Force Security Assistance Ctr., Wright Patterson AFB, Ohio, 1999-2000, dir. case mgmt., 2000—. Vis. instr. English as a second lang., polit. sci., mgmt. sci. Antioch Coll., Yellow Springs, Ohio, 1986—; asst. dep. plans policy mgmt. systems, 1988, dir. plans and policy, 1988, tech. lead integrated logistics support, acquisition logistics div., 1988—, instr. mgmt. sci. Author: Textbook in Logistics 1988, Policy Regulations/Procedural Instructions 1986—; contbr. articles to profl. jours., 1987—. Adminstr. Refugee Assistance Program, Greene County, Ohio, 1981-84, AFS chpt. v.p.; Scoutmaster Buckeye Trails coun. Girl Scout U.S., Yellow Springs, 1982-86; active Dayton (Ohio) Coun. on World Affairs, 1984—; pres. local chpt. Am. Field Svc., Greene County, 1988—. Mem LWV (fin. chm. Greene county chpt. 1987—). Democratic. Methodist. Avocations: travel, scouting, reading, writing. Office: Global Mgmt Air Force Security Assistance Ctr Wright Patterson Afb OH 45433 E-mail: Tom.Caudill@wpafb.af.mil.

CAUDILL, WILLIAM HOWARD, lawyer; b. Memphis, Mar. 18, 1951; s. John W. Caudill and Elizabeth (Rivers) Stayton; m. Chris Looney, Sept. 2, 1978; children: Lucy L., W. Christopher. BSBA, U. Ark., 1973; M in Pub. Acctg., U. Tex., 1977, JD, 1978. Bar: Tex. 1978, U.S. Dist. Ct. (so. dist.) Tex. 1978, U.S. Tax Ct. 1978, U.S. Claims Ct. 1978, U.S. Ct. Appeals (5th cir.) 1978; CPA. Ptnr. Fulbright & Jaworski, LLP, Houston, 1986—. Mem. Tex. Quarter Dollar Coin Design Com., 2002-04; mem. vestry St. John the Divine Episc. Ch., Houston, 1982-86, 89-93; coun. del. Episcopal Diocese of Tex., 2003-2005; res. Meml. Endowment Fund, 1995—. Mem.: ABA (chair CLE subcom. 1994—2000, chair spl. projects subcom., vice chair, chair partnership com. 1994—2005, tax sect.), Am. Coll. Tax Counsel, State Bar Tex. (dir. tax course 1986—87, bd. dirs. taxation sect. 1987—92, chair-elect 1990, chair 1991—92). Avocations: fishing, music, golf. Office: Fulbright & Jaworski LLP 1301 Mckinney St Ste 5100 Houston TX 77010-3031 Office Phone: 713-651-5292. E-mail: wcaudill@fulbright.com.

CAUGHLIN, STEPHENIE JANE, organic farmer; b. McAllen, Tex., July 23, 1948; d. James Daniel and Betty Jane (Warnock) C. BA in Family Econs., San Diego State U., 1972, MEd, 1973; M in Psychology, U.S. Internat. U., San Diego, 1979. Cert. secondary life tchr. Owner, mgr. Minute Maid Svc., San Diego, 1970-75; prin. Rainbow Fin. Svc., San Diego, 1975-78; tchr. San Diego Unified Sch. Dist., 1973-80; mortgage broker Santa Fe Mortgage Co., San Diego, 1984-88; owner, sec. Nationwide Metals Corp.; owner, gen. mgr. Seabreeze Organic Farm, 1984—. Sec. Arroyo Sorrento Assn., Del Mar, Calif., 1978—; co-founder Slow Food San Diego Co-founder, treas. Slow Foods San Diego Convivium. Mem. Greenpeace Nature Conservancy, DAR, Sierra Club, Jobs Daus. Republican. Avocations: horseback riding, swimming, skiing, gardening. Home and Office: 3909 Arroyo Sorrento Rd San Diego CA 92130-2610 Office Phone: 858-481-0209. E-mail: info@seabreezed.com, stephenie@seabreezed.com.

CAULEY, JAMES ROBERT, lawyer; b. Milw., Apr. 9, 1952; children: Anne, Thomas. AB with highest honors, U. Notre Dame, 1974; MA, Brown U., 1977; JD magna cum laude, U. Minn., 1980. Bar: Wis. 1980, U.S. Dist. Ct. (ea. dist.) Wis. 1980, U.S. Dist. Ct. (we. dist.) Wis. 1985, U.S. Ct. Appeals (7th cir.) 1986. Assoc. Foley & Lardner, Milw., 1980-86; div. counsel Johnson Controls, Inc., Milw., 1986-89, group counsel, 1989-93; corp. counsel Best Power Technology, Inc., 1993-95, gen. counsel, 1995; gen. counsel Best Power unit Gen. Signal Power Systems, Inc., Waukesha, Wis., 1995—98; asst. gen. counsel Gen. Signal Corp., Waukesha, Wis., 1997-98; group gen. counsel SPX Corp., Waukesha, Wis., 1998—2005, segment gen. counsel, 2005—. Editor U. Minn. Law Rev., 1979-80. Brown U. Fellow, 1976. Mem. ABA, Wis. Bar Assn., Milw. Bar Assn., St. Thomas More Lawyers Soc. (bd. govs. 1986-93, pres. 1988), Order of Coif, Phi Beta Kappa. Office: SPX Corp 400 S Prairie Ave Waukesha WI 53186-5969 Home: 5020 N Woodruff Ave Whitefish Bay WI 53217 Office Phone: 262-513-0600.

CAULEY, PATRICK C., lawyer; BS, JD, U. Mich. CPA. Ptnr. Bodman, Longley & Dahling, LLP, Detroit; asst. gen. counsel Hayes Lemmerz Internat., Inc., Northville, Mich., 1999—2004, v.p., gen. counsel, sec., 2004—. Office: Hayes Lemmerz Internat 15300 Centennial Dr Northville MI 48167 Office Phone: 734-737-5000.

CAULFIELD, JAMES BENJAMIN, pathologist, educator; b. Mpls., Jan. 1, 1927; s. Linus Joseph and Olive Bell (Curtis) C.; m. Virginia Walsh, Jan. 28, 1950; children: Ann, John, Clare. BA, Miami U., Oxford, Ohio, 1947; BS, U. Ill., 1948, MD, 1950. Intern Henrotin Hosp., Chgo., 1950-51; resident U. N.C., Chapel Hill, 1951-52, U. Kans. Med. Ctr., Kansas City, 1954-55; vis. investigator Rockefeller Inst., N.Y.C., 1955-56; instr. pathology Harvard U., 1959-64, asst. prof., 1964-70, assoc. prof., 1970-75; asst. pathologist Mass. Gen. Hosp., Boston, 1960-64, assoc. pathologist, 1964-75; prof., chmn. dept. pathology U. S.C., 1975-85; prof. pathology U. Ala., Birmingham, 1985—. Adj. prof. Med. U. S.C., Charleston, 1981-85; rsch. on collagen network of heart and changes associated with alterations in the network. Contbr. articles to profl. jours. Served with USN, 1944-46, 52-54. Mem. Am. Soc. Cell Biology, Am. Soc. Pathology, Internat. Acad. Pathology, Fedn. Exptl. Pathology, Electron Microscopy Soc., Internat. Study Group for Heart Research (treas. Am. sect. 1972-85), N.Y. Acad. Scis., Harvard Club, Boston Athenaeum Club, Sigma Xi, Phi Eta Sigma. Office: U Ala Dept Pathology 506 Kracke Bldg 619 19th St S Birmingham AL 35233-0001

CAULFIELD, JEROME JOSEPH, lawyer; b. Phila., Aug. 9, 1949; s. Charles Patrick and Pauline Gertrude (Riley) C.; m. Rosita Noyes Murray, Aug. 4, 1973; children: Andrew, Alexandra. BS in Fgn. Svc., Georgetown U., 1971; JD, Am. U., 1974; LLM, NYU, 1977. Bar: N.Y. 1976, U.S. Tax Ct. 1980, U.S. Dist. Ct. (so. dist.) N.Y. 1986. Assoc. Carter, Ledyard & Milburn, N.Y.C., 1978-83, ptnr., 1984-99, mng. ptnr., 1999—2003, mem. exec. com., 2003—. Contbr. articles to profl. jours. Bd. dirs. Impact on Hunger Inc., 1984-86. Mem. ABA, N.Y. State Bar Assn., Assn. of Bar of City of N.Y. Roman Catholic. Home: 35 Stanwich Rd Greenwich CT 06830-4842 Office: Carter Ledyard & Milburn LLP 2 Wall St Fl 13 New York NY 10005-2072 Office Phone: 212-732-3200. Business E-Mail: caulfield@clm.com.

CAULFIELD, JOAN, director, educator; b. St. Joseph, Mo., July 17, 1943; d. Joseph A. and Jane (Lisenby) Caulfield; m. Alan Warne, Sept. 7, 1996. BS in Edn. cum laude, U. Mo., 1963, MA in Spanish, 1965, PhD, 1978; postgrad. (Mexican Govt. scholar), Nat. U. Mexico, 1962-63. TV tchr. Spanish Kansas City (Mo.) pub. schs., 1963-68; tchr. Spanish, French Bingham Jr. High Schs., Kansas City, 1968-78; asst. prin. S.E. High Sch., Kansas City, 1984; prin. Nowlin Jr. High Sch., Independence, Mo., 1984-86, Lincoln Coll. Preparatory Acad., Kansas City, Mo., 1986-88; asst. supt. Kansas City, 1988-89; part-time instr. U. Mo.-Kansas City; dir. English Inst. Rockhurst Coll., summers 1972-75; coord. sch. coll. rels. Rockhurst U., 1989-2001, chmn. edn. dept.; adj. prof. St. Louis U.; pres., CEO The Brain Inc., 2001—. Mem. nat. steering com. Brain-Based Learning Network, facilitator; assessor dept. elem. and secondary edn. State Mo.; mem. women's coun. bd. U. Mo.-Kansas City, 1994-98, pres. 1998-; pres., CEO The Brain Inc.; vis. social scientist Midwest Rsch. Inst.; adj. prof. Baker U. Co-Author: Inciting Learning: a Guide to Brain Compatible Instr.; Bridging the Learning/Assessment Gap: Showcase Teaching; contbr articles to profl. jours. Active Sister City Commn., Kansas City, 1980—, Kans.' Quality Performance Assessment Team, Metro-Vision Task Force; ofcl. translator to mayor on trip to Seville, Spain, 1969; bd. dirs. Kansas City chpt. NCCJ, Expo '92 World's Fair, Seville, transl., 1992, St. Theresa's Acad., 1991-94, Kansas City Acad. of Learning; selected leadership training Greater Mo.; trainer Harmony in a World of Difference, 1989-93; task force C. of C. bd. dirs.; edn. alumni bd. U. Mo., Kansas City; del. leader Spain People to People Internat., 1997; trustee Kansas City Pub. Libr. mem. mayor's commn. on race, Kansas City; mem. adv. bd. NCCJ, 2002—. Named Outstanding Secondary Educator, 1973. Mem.: MLA (contbr. jour.), ASCD, Mo. Mid. Sch. Assn. (contbr. jour.), Am. Assn. Tchrs. Spanish and Portuguese, Nat. Assn. Secondary Sch. Prins., Magnet Schs. Am. (contbr. jour.), Friends of Art, Friends of Seville, Sigma Delta Pi, Phi Kappa Phi, Delta Kappa Gamma (state scholar 1977—78, contbr. jour. Bull.), Phi Delta Kappa, Phi Sigma Iota, Kappa Delta Pi. Presbyterian. Home: 431 W 70th St Kansas City MO 64113-2022 Personal E-mail: joancaulfield@prodigy.net.

CAULFIELD, SHARON ELIZABETH, lawyer; b. Santa Rosa, Calif., Jan. 16, 1956; d. Edward Nelson Caulfield and Alicelee (Freeman) Ewan; m. Edmund Daniel Andrews, Dec 28, 1976; children: Daniel Graham, Caroline Elizabeth. Student, U. Calif., Berkeley, 1974-76; BA in Anthropology, U. Colo., 1979, JD, 1982. Bar: Colo. 1982, U.S. Dist. Ct. Colo. 1982, U.S. Ct. Appeals (10th cir.) 1982. Legal writing instr. U. Colo. Sch. Law, Boulder, 1981-82; assoc. Davis Graham & Stubbs, Denver, 1982-88, ptnr., 1988-93, practice leader health care group, 1991-93; mem. Caplan & Earnest, L.L.C., Boulder, 1993—. Mem. Leadership Denver, 1989. Mem. ABA, Am. Health Lawyers Assn., Healthcare Fin. Mgmt. Assn., Colo. Bar Assn., Denver Bar Assn., Colo. U. Boulder Alumni Assn. (pres. 1991-92, bd. dirs. 1985-93). Democrat. Episcopalian. Avocations: mountain climbing, travel, cooking. Office: Caplan & Earnest 2595 Canyon Blvd Ste 400 Boulder CO 80302-6737

CAULLWINE, DAWN QUINT, quality engineer; b. Lewes, Del., Aug. 9, 1958; d. Donald Eugene and Juanita Johnson Quint; m. René O. Caullwine; children: Amber, Brandi. BSChemE, U. Del., Newark, 1979, MBA, 1988. Cert. quality engr., quality mgr., ASQ, Six Sigma Black Belt. 1st line supervisor DuPont, Richmond, Va., 1979—81, fibers system analyst Charlotte, NC, 1981—85, mgr. fibers data Wilmington, Del., 1985—86, corp. quality engr. Newark, Del., 1986—95, kevlar quality engr. Richmond, Va., 1995—2001, AFS black belt, 2001—03, kevlar quality mgr., 2003—. Office: DuPont AFS 5401 Jefferson Davis Hwy Richmond VA 23234 Office Phone: 804-383-2914.

CAUNA, NIKOLAJS, physician, medical educator, scientist; b. Riga, Latvia, Apr. 4, 1914; came to U.S., 1961; s. Nikolajs and Marija (Manika) C.; m. Dzidra Priede, June 23, 1942. MD, U. Latvia, 1942; M.Sc., U. Durham (Eng.), 1954, D.Sc., 1961. Lectr. anatomy U. Latvia, Riga, 1942-44; gen. practice medicine Sarsted and Eschershausen, West Germany, 1944-46; acting chmn. anatomy dept. Baltic U., Hamburg, Germany, 1946-48; lectr. anatomy Med. Sch. U. Durham (Eng.), 1948-57, reader, 1958-61; prof. anatomy Sch. Medicine U. Pitts., 1961-84, chmn., 1975-83, prof. emeritus, 1984—. Mem. editorial bd. Anat. Record, 1969-91, Histology and Histopathology, 1985-90; contbr. articles to profl. jours. Recipient Golden Apple award (tchr. of year) U. Pitts., 1964, 67, 73; research grantee Royal Soc. Eng., 1958-60; USPHS grantee, 1962-82; Am. Cancer Inst. grantee, 1961. Mem. AAAS, Anat. Soc. Gt. Britain and Ireland, Am. Assn. Anatomists, Royal Micros. Soc., Anatomische Gesellschaft, Histochem. Soc., Am. Soc. Cell Biology, Internat. Assn. for Study Pain. Achievements include research in normal and pathol. sensory receptor organs, in autonomic control mechanism, in devel. and evolution of sense organs and limbs. Home: 5850 Meridian Rd Apt 311C Gibsonia PA 15044-4811

CAUSEY, ROBERT LOUIS, philosopher, educator, consultant; b. Los Angeles, Apr. 13, 1941; s. Robert Vester and Gertrude (Bloom) C.; m. Sandra Lee Shliff, Jan. 25, 1964; children— Britt Ann, Diane Sue. BS, Calif. Inst. Tech., 1963; PhD, U. Calif., Berkeley, 1967. Asst. prof. dept. philosophy U. Tex., Austin, 1967-73, asso. prof., 1973-79, prof., 1979—, chmn. dept. philosophy, 1980-88; co-founder, assoc. dir. U. Tex. Artificial Intelligence Lab., 1984-97. Cons. NSF, 1979-81; spkr. numerous confs., univs., broadcasts; cons. to U.S. Army and various pvt. corps. and univs. Author: Supplement to Logic, Sets, and Recursion, 2002, Logic, Sets, and Recursion, 1994, rev. edit., 2001, Unity of Science, 1977; co-author: Introduction to Artificial Intelligence and Expert Systems, Video-Course, 1988; contbr. articles and revs. to philos. and sci. jours.; author various ednl. and exptl. computer programs. NSF fellow, NSF grantee, 1973-74, 79-81; U. Tex. Rsch. Inst. grantee, 1979; rsch. scientist, U.S. Army Rsch. Office grantee, 1984-89; U. Tex. Dean's fellow, 1997. Mem.: Assn. Computing Machinery, Am. Assn. Artificial Intelligence, Philosophy of Sci. Assn. (bd. govs. 1980—81), Am. Philos. Assn. (mem. com. on computer use in philosophy 1994—97, rev. editor electronic newsletter on philosophy and computers 1996—2001). Achievements include development of new system for automated defeasible reasoning. Office: Univ Tex Dept of Philosophy Waggener Hall # 316 Austin TX 78712 Business E-Mail: rlc@cs.utexas.edu.

CAUTHEN, CHARLES EDWARD, JR., retired retail executive, management consultant; b. Columbia, S.C., Oct. 26, 1931; s. Charles Edward and Rachel (Macaulay) C.; m. Hazel Electa Peery, June 13, 1959; children: Portia Cauthen White, Rachel Cauthen Rohrer, Sara Cauthen Landfear, Sidney Cauthen Bullard. BA, Wofford Coll., 1952; cert. Charlotte Meml. Hosp., Sch. Hosp. Adminstrn., 1956; MS in Bus. Adminstrn. and Labor Mgmt., PhD in Bus. Adminstrn., Kennedy-Western U., 1986; LLD, Montreat-Anderson Coll., 1991. Asst. adminstr. Union Meml. Hosp., Monroe, N.C., 1956-58; adminstr. Lowrance Hosp., Inc., Mooresville, N.C., 1958-61; v.p., mgr. Va. Acme Market, Bluefield, W.Va., 1961-68; v.p. Acme Markets and A-Mart Stores (now Acme Markets of Tazewell, Va., Inc.), North Tazewell, Va., 1965-87; adminstr. Lowrance Hosp., Inc., Mooresville, N.C., 1958-61; v.p., mgr. Va. Acme Market, Bluefield, W.Va., 1961-68; v.p. Acme Markets and A-Mart Stores (now Acme Markets of Tazewell, Va., Inc.), North Tazewell, Va., 1965-87, exec. v.p., 1968-71, pres., 1971-87; provost, pres. King Coll., Bristol, Tenn., 1987—92; pres. Doran Devel. Corp., 1971-87, Big A Market, Inc., 1981-87. Cons. in field, 1992—2000. Author: Evaluation of the Small Company for Strategic Planning, Merger or Acquisition, 1987. Deacon, elder, trustee Westminster Presbyn. Ch., Bluefield, W.Va.; mem. Internat. Adv. Coun. Han Nam U., Korea, 1991; mem. exec. bd., 1992-2001; bd. dirs. Internat. Inst. Christian Studies, 1993-97, Tenn. Inst. for Pub. Policy, 1994-2001. Served to 1st lt. AUS, 1952-54. Mem. W.Va. Assn. Retail Grocers (v.p., dir. 1968-82), Va. Food Dealers Assn. (dir. 1978), Bluefield Sales Exec. Club (dir. 1965-67), Rotary (bd. dirs. 1966). Republican. Home and Office: 100 Muirfield Williamsburg VA 23188

CAUTHORNE-BURNETTE, TAMERA DIANNE, family nurse practitioner, healthcare consultant; b. Richmond, Va., Apr. 13, 1961; d. Robert Francis Cauthorne and Lois Avery (Lloyd) Cumashot; m. William Nichols Burnette, Dec. 3, 1983. BSN, U. Va., 1983; postgrad., Med. U. S.C., 1988; MSN, Old Dominion U., 1993, grad. cert. in women's studies, 1994; postgrad., Univ. Coll., Oxford (Eng.) U., 1996. RN, Va.; family nurse practitioner. Staff nurse, charge nurse gynecology-oncology unit U. Va. Med. Ctr., Charlottesville, 1983, staff nurse, charge nurse high-risk labor and delivery, ICU, 1984-85; staff nurse, charge nurse, preceptor med. ICU Med. U. S.C., 1985-87, staff nurse ICU, 1988; staff nurse, charge nurse med.-surg. ICU, progressive care Stuart Cir. Hosp., Richmond, Va., 1988-90; staff nurse pediat. and neonatal ICU Childrens' Hosp. of the King's Dau., Norfolk, Va., 1990, staff nurse, team leader neonatal ICU, 1990-91; pvt. health care cons., 1993—; with Delmar Pub., 1994—; pres. The Foxmont Co., LLC, 1995—; with Sussex Ctrl. Health Ctr., 1995; men's responsibility clinic coord. Planned Parenthood, 1996; chief nurse practitioner med. svcs. Va. League Planned Parenthood, 1997-99; pvt. practice Air Park Med., Ashland, Va., 1999-2001; with James Jones and Assocs. Ob-gyn., 2001. Cons. Old Dominion U. Coll. Health Sci., Sch. Nursing, 1993—, undergrad. clin. facility, 1994—; condr. analysis of Russian and Ukrainian health care system; breast self-exam instr. Am. Cancer Soc., 1982—; presenter at profl. confs.; mng. mem. The Foxmont Co., L.L.C.; mem. adj. faculty Sch. Nursing U. Va., 1996; primary med. provider Va. League Planned Parenthood, 1997; mem. clin. faculty sch. of nursing Va. Commonwealth U., 1999, assoc. prof., 2001. Contbg. author A Quick Reference for Health Assessment, 1997, Clin. Companion to Health Assessment and Physical Examination, 1998; contbr. articles to profl. jours. Vol. Ronald McDonald House, 1980-83; docent Spoleto Festival USA, 1984-92, MacArthur Meml. Mus., 1991; vol. receptionist info. ctr. Gibbes Art Gallery, 1987-89; vol. ARC Blood Donation Ctr., 1986-92; mem. coun. U. Va. Coll. of Health Scis.; mem. adv. coun. U. Va. Sch. Nursing, 1997—; chmn. Va. Nurses PAC, 2002. Named Vol. of Yr., U. Va. Sch. Nursing. Fellow Internat. Pedagogical Acad./Moswoc. Order of Omega Nat. Honor Soc., Raven Honor Soc. U. Va., Sorenson Inst. Polit. Leadership U. Va.; mem. AACN, DAR, AAUW, Va. Coalition for Nurse Practitioners, U. Va. Sch. Nursing Alumnae Assn. (pres., CEO 1994—, adv. coun. 1997—), Jr. League Va. (chair state pub. affairs com.), Virginians Patient Choice Coalition, Jr. League Norfolk and Virginia Beach (state pub. affairs vice chmn./lobbyist 1995), Daus. of Confederacy, Carolina Art Assn., S.C. Hist. Soc., Confederate Meml. Lit. Soc., U. Va. Coll. Health Scis. Coun., Alpha Delta Pi (chmn. nat. panhellenic rels. com., nat. by-laws and resolutions com.), Sigma Theta Tau. Avocations: riding, raising and showing thoroughbred racing horses, collecting sporting art, foxhunting.

CAUTHRON, ROBIN J., federal judge; b. Edmond, Okla., July 14, 1950; d. Austin W. and Mary Louise (Adamson) Johnson. BA, U. Okla., 1970, JD, 1977; MEd, Cen. State U., Edmond, Okla., 1974. Bar: Okla. 1977. Law clk to Hon. Ralph G. Thompson US Dist. Ct. (We. Dist.) Okla., 1977-81; staff atty. Legal Svcs. Ea. Okla., 1981-82; pvt. practice law, 1982-83; spl. judge 17th Jud. Dist. State Okla., 1983-86; magistrate US Dist. Ct. (We. Dist.) Okla., Oklahoma City, 1986-91, judge, 1991—, chief judge. Editor Okla. Law Rev. Bd. dirs. Juvenile Diabetes Found. Internat., 1989-92; mem. nominating com. Frontier Coun. Boy Scouts Am., 1987, Edmond Ednl. Endowment;

trustee, sec. First United Meth. Ch., 1988-90. Mem. ABA, Okla. Bar Assn., Okla. County Bar Assn. (bd. dirs. 1990— bench and bar com.), McCurtain County Bar Assn. (pres. 1986), Am. Judicature Soc., Nat. Assn. Women Judges, Fed. Bar Assn., Nat. Coun. Women Magistrates (bd. dirs. 1990-91), Okla. Jud. Conf. (v.p. 1985), Am. Inns of Ct. (pres. 1991-92), Order of Coif, Phi Delta Phi. Office: US Courthouse 200 NW 4th St Ste 3108 Oklahoma City OK 73102-3029*

CAVA, MICHAEL PATRICK, chemist, educator; b. Bklyn., Feb. 13, 1926; s. Michael R. and Catherine (Lombardo) C.; m. Esther Laden, June 11, 1951; 1 son, John M.; m. Armelle Laden-Guinard, Dec. 21, 1998. BS, Harvard U., 1946; MS, U. Mich., 1948, PhD, 1951. Postdoctoral fellow Harvard U., 1951-53; from asst. prof. to prof. Ohio State U., 1953-65; prof. Wayne State U., Detroit, 1965-69; prof. chemistry U. Pa., Phila., 1969-85; prof. U. Ala., Tuscaloosa, 1985—. Mem. study sect. NIH, 1987-91. Author: (with M.J. Mitchell) Cyclobutadiene and Related Compounds, 1967; also numerous articles. Alfred P. Sloan Found. fellow. Mem. Am. Chem. Soc. Achievements include research on organic sulphur, selenium and tellurium compounds; organic condrs., benzocyclobutenes, natural products chemistry. Home: 440 Northshore Dr Tuscaloosa AL 35406-2012 Office: U Ala Dept Chemistry PO Box 870336 Tuscaloosa AL 35487-0001 Office Phone: 205-348-8454. E-mail: michael_cava@comcast.net.

CAVA, ROBERT J., chemistry educator; BS, MS in Materials Sci. and Engring., MIT, 1974, PhD in Ceramics, 1977. Temp. mem. tech. staff Lincoln Lab., 1977; NRC postdoctoral fellow Nat. Inst. Standards and Tech., 1978; mem. tech. staff Bell Labs., 1979-85, disting. mem. tech. staff., 1985-96; prof. chemistry Princeton U., 1996—, chair dept. chemistry, 2004—; prof. Princeton Materials Inst., 1996—, assoc. dir., 1999—2001, acting dir., 2001—02. Vis. scientist Brookhaven Nat. Lab., Nat. Inst. Standards and Tech., Riso Nat. Lab., Denmark, Lab. Crystallography CNRS, Grenoble, France, Inst. Chem. Rsch., Kyoto U., Japan; chair NSF workshop on Future of Solid State Chemistry, 2001. Contbr. articles to profl. publs. Recipient Honor Scroll Award, Am. Inst. Chemists, 1990, Bernd Matthias Prize for new superconducting materials, 1996, Prize in the Chemistry of Materials, Am. Chem. Soc., 1997, Wulff Award in Materials Sci., 2000, Excellence in Tchg. Award, Princeton Engring. Coun., 2003. Fellow Am. Phys. Soc., Am. Ceramic Soc.; mem. NAS (John J. Carty Award for the Advancement of Sci., 2005), Materials Rsch. Soc. Achievements include 30 patent applications; research on solid state chemistry, synthesis, crystallography and phase equilibria of new transition metal oxide, chalcogenide, intermetallic and pnictide compounds with interesting magnetic and electronic properties. Office: Princeton Materials Inst Bowen Hall 70 Prospect Ave Princeton NJ 08540 Fax: (609) 258-6878.*

CAVAGLIERI, GIORGIO, architect; b. Venice, Italy, Aug. 1, 1911; came to U.S., 1939, naturalized, 1943; s. Gino and Margherita (Maroni) C.; m. Norma Sanford, Jan. 31, 1942. D. Archtl. Engring, Sup. Sch. Engring., Milan, Italy, 1932; student spl. city planning, Sup. Sch. Architecture, Rome, 1934. Apprenticeship N.Y. office R. Candela, Balt. offices J.O. Chertkof, also Benjamin Franklin, arch., 1934—39; propr. own firm N.Y.C., 1946—; adj. prof. Sch. Architecture Pratt Inst., 1956-69. Trustee Nat. Inst. Archtl. Edn., chmn. trustees, 1957-60; academician NAD. Prin. works in Milan, prior to World War II; prin. works include in the U.S., Fenton Hall reconstrn. Fredonia (N.Y.) Coll., Astor Libr. restoration and conversion to N.Y. Pub. Theatre, N.Y. Shakespeare Festival, Jefferson Market Courthouse restoration and conversion to N.Y. Pub. Libr., Branch Libr., Riverdale, N.Y., N.Y. Pub. Libr. main bldg. Periodical Dept., Pub. Sch. 32, S.I., Kip's Bay br. libr.; assoc. arch. Pension Bldg./Nat. Mus. Bldg. Arts, Washington; arch.-in-charge Rosary Hall, U.S. Mil. Acad. Mus.; Eldridge St. Synagogue restoration, N.Y.C.; Chapel of the Good Shepherd reconstrn., Roosevelt Island, N.Y. Served with C.E. AUS, 1943-45. Decorated Bronze Star; recipient Honor award AIA, 1968, House Improvement award, 1961; Bard award, spl. citation City Club N.Y., 1968; Illuminated scroll Mcpl. Art Soc. N.Y., 1966; Clients award N.Y. State Assn. Archs., 1964; Gold medal honor architecture Archtl. League N.Y., 1956; winner 1st prize nat. competition auditorium Rome, 1935, 3d prize competition city hosp. Cuneo, Italy., 1938, hon. mention Armed Forces bldgs. Rome World's Fair, 1938, 3d prize N.Y.C. Bd. Edn. archtl. competition for modernization Bronx Jr. H.S., 1967; cert. of merit for excellence in design N.Y. State Assn. Archs., 1976; 1st honor award ALA/AIA, 1976; Sidney L. Strauss Meml. N.Y. Soc. Archs., 1977; recipient award Excellence in Design N.Y.C. Art Commn., 1992, Design award for Preservation Gen. Svcs. Adminstrn., 1992; Outstanding Cert. for Competition N.Y.C. Bd. Edn., 1997, Lucy Moses award NY Landmark Conservancy, 2002, Bronze medal Fine Art Fedn. N.Y., 2002. Fellow AIA (pres. N.Y. chpt. 1970-71, Disting. Architecture award 1985, Honor award 1986, Presdl. citation 1990, Medal of Honor N.Y. chpt. 1990); mem. Mcpl. Art Soc. N.Y. (pres. 1963-65, 4th Ann. Preservation award 1992), Archtl. League N.Y. (v.p. 1961-63), Am. Soc. Interior Designers (v.p. 1984-85, 87-88, medal 1985), Fine Arts Fedn. N.Y. (pres. 1970-72, 74-76, 2000-01, Centennial Yr. honoree 1995), N.Y. Coun. Arts and Govt., N.Y.C. Victorian Soc. (Outstanding in Preservation award 1986). Democrat. Home: 75 Central Park W New York NY 10023-6011 Office: 250 W 57th St Ste 2511 New York NY 10107 Office Phone: 212-245-4207.

CAVALIER, GINA M., lawyer; b. Long Beach, Calif., Jan. 19, 1971; BA in Internat. Rels., summa cum laude, Boston U., 1993; JD cum laude, Georgetown U., 1996. Bar: NY 1997, DC 2000. Atty. Atty. Gen.'s Honors Program, US Dept. Justice; law clk. to Hon. Mary Ellen Bittner Drug Enforcement Adminstrn.; assoc., health care group Reed Smith; assoc., health law group Shaw Pittman; assoc., health care practice group Sonnenschein Nath & Rosenthal LLP, Washington, 2003—04, ptnr., 2004—. Mem.: Health Care Compliance Assn., Healthcare Businesswomen's Assn., DC Bar Assn., Am. Health Lawyers Assn. Office: Sonnenschein Nath & Rosenthal LLP Ste 600, E Tower 1301 K St NW Washington DC 20005 Office Phone: 202-408-9156. Office Fax: 202-408-6399. Business E-Mail: gcavalier@sonnenschein.com.

CAVALIERE, FRANK JOSEPH, lawyer, educator; b. N.Y.C., Dec. 29, 1949; s. Alfred and Margaret Joan Cavaliere. BA in Econs., Bklyn. Coll., 1970; BBA in Acctg., Lamar U., 1976; JD, U. Tex., 1979. Bar: Tex. 1979. Atty. Coke & Coke, Dallas, 1979-81, Weller, Wheelus & Green, Beaumont, Tex., 1981-84; pvt. practice law Beaumont, 1985—; from asst. to full prof. bus. law Lamar U., Beaumont, 1985—. Mem. editl. adv. bd. CPA Tech. and Internet Advisor, 2000—; tech. advisor Am. Law Inst.-ABA, 1998—, also continuing legal edn. spkr. Author (column) Web-Wise Lawyer, The Practical Lawyer, 1996; contbr. articles to profl. jours. Advisor Pi Kappa Alpha Fraternity, Beaumont, 1987-90, Delta Sigma Pi Fraternity, Beaumont, 1994-97. Lt. USNR, 1970-75. Mem. ABA, Tex. Bar Assn., Coll. of the State Bar Tex., Jefferson County Bar Assn., Phi Beta Kappa. Office: 148 S Dowlen Rd PMB 683 Beaumont TX 77707-1755 E-mail: cavfj@prodigy.net, cavalierfj@hal.lamar.edu.

CAVALIERE, ROSSELLA, neurologist; b. Tuscany, Italy, Nov. 24, 1957; arrived in U.S., 1987; d. Pietro Bastianini and Dora Landi; m. Ludovico Frank Cavaliere, June 8, 1986. MD summa cum laude, U. Bologna, Italy, 1984. Diplomate Am. Bd. Neurology. Neurology resident St. Vincent's Hosp. and Med. Ctr., N.Y.C., 1991—94, neuroimaging fellow, 1994—95; neurology attending physician Health Ins. Plan, N.Y.C., 1996; neurorehabilitation fellow Burke Rehab. Hosp., White Plains, NY, 1996—97, neurology attending physician, 1997—98; movement disorder fellow Beth Israel Med. Ctr., N.Y.C., 1998—99; neurology attending physician Helen Hayes Hosp., West Haverstraw, NY, 1999—. Mem.: Am. Acad. Neurology. Office: Helen Hayes Hosp Rt 9 West Haverstraw NY 10993

CAVALLARO, JOSEPH JOHN, retired microbiologist; b. Lawrence, Mass., Mar. 18, 1932; s. John and Salvatrice (Zappala) C.; m. Margaret Hare, Aug. 24, 1964; children: Theresa Margaret, Sandra Marie; m. Kathleen Frances Kraus, Dec. 2, 1972; children: Elizabeth Camille, Danielle Kay, Gina Kathleen. BS, Tufts U., 1952; MS, U. Mass., 1954; PhD, U. Mich., 1966. Pub. health sanitarian Hartford (Conn.) Health Dept., 1954-55, 57-61; tchg. asssoc. dept. microbiology U. Mass., Amherst, 1961-62; rsch. virologist Med. Rsch. Labs. Charles Pfizer & Co., Groton, Conn., 1966-67; rsch. assoc. dept. epidemiology Sch. Pub. Health U. Mich., Ann Arbor, 1967-70; microbiology, diagnostic immunology tng. br. Ctrs. for Disease Control, Atlanta, 1971-86, rsch. microbiologist anaerobic bacteria br., 1986-2000; ret., 2000. Lectr. resident pathologists Grady Meml. Hosp., Atlanta, 1975; asst. prof. pathology Morehouse Sch. Medicine, 1982-85, clin. assoc. prof., 1986-97; adj. asst. prof. pathology and lab. medicine Emory U. Sch. of Medicine, 1985-2000; cons. Pan Am. Health Orgn., Colombia and Brazil, 1976-77, WHO, 2003. Prin. author/co-author over 12 lab manuals; contbr. over 30 articles to profl. jours., 3 chpts. to books. Served with M.C., AUS, 1955-57. Registered specialist microbiologist Nat. Registry Microbiologist, Am. Acad. Microbiologist. Fellow Am. Acad. Microbiology; mem. Am. Soc. Microbiology, Am. Assn. Immunologists, N.Y. Acad. Sci., KC, Sigma Xi. Democrat. Home: 1325 Balsam Dr Decatur GA 30033-2905 Personal E-mail: cavallaro@mindspring.com.

CAVALLARO, MARY CAROLINE, retired physics professor; b. Everett, Mass., Feb. 2, 1932; d. Joseph and Domenica Cavallaro. BS, Simmons Coll., 1954, MS, 1956; EdD, Ind. U., 1972; postgrad., Tufts U., 1980-81. Inst. math. and physics Sweet Briar (Va.) Coll., 1955-56; instr. physics Simmons Coll., Boston, 1956-58, Randolph-Macon Woman's Coll., Lynchburg, Va., 1958-59; lectr. Boston U., 1960-61; asst. prof. physics Framingham (Mass.) State Coll., 1961-63; prof. physics Salem (Mass.) State Coll., 1963-94; ret., 1994. Cons. Introductory Phys. Scis. group Edn. Devel. Ctr., Newton, 1966; asst. to dean grad. studies Salem State Coll., 1971-78, coord. pre-engring. program, 1980-89, coord. secondary edn. program, 1989-91; vis. scholar Harvard U. Grad. Sch. Edn., Cambridge, Mass., 1989-90. Grantee, NSF, 1962. Mem.: MTA, NEA, AAUW, Am. Inst. Physics, Am. Assn. Physics Tchrs., Am. Phys. Soc., Ind. U. Alumnae Assn., Simmons Coll. Alumnae Assn., Pi Lambda Theta. Avocations: travel, reading, swimming. Home: 14 Winford Way Medford MA 02155-1526 Personal E-mail: mary46@comcast.net.

CAVALLO, JO ANN, language educator; b. Summit, NJ, May 21, 1959; d. Joseph Anthony and Jacqueline Amelia (Toth) C.; children: Maria Cristina, Alberto Joseph. Student, U. Florence, Italy, 1979-80, U. Valencia, Spain, 1980; BA, Rutgers U., 1981; student, Inst. French Studies, Avignon, 1982; MA, Yale U., 1984, PhD, 1987. Instr. dept. Italian Yale U., New Haven, 1983-86, instr. dept. Spanish, 1986-87, instr. Sch. Music, 1986-87; asst. prof. U. Wash., Seattle, 1987-88; assoc. prof. of Italian Columbia U., N.Y.C., 1988—. Mem. sci. com. Boiardo Quincentennial Celebration, Italy, 1993-94; founder and program dir. Columbia U. Summer Program in Scandiano, Italy, 1995-2001. Author: Boiardo's Orlando Innamorato: An Ethics of Desire, 1993; co-editor: Fortune and Romance: Boiardo in America, 1998; adapter: Orlando Innamorato for young readers, 2001; author: Il Maggio Epico Emiliano: ricordi, riflessioni, brani, 2003, The Romance Epics of Boiardo, Aristo, and Tasso: From Public Duty to Private Pleasure, 2004. Recipient scholarship Nat. Italian Am. Found., Washington, 1986, fellowship grant Columbia U. Coun. for Rsch. in the Humanities, 1989, 90. Mem. Am. Assn. for Tchrs. of Italian, Am. Assn. of Italian Studies, Renaissance Soc. Am., Am Folklore Soc., Phi Beta Kappa. Roman Catholic. Home: 733 Buchanan St Toms River NJ 08753-7207 Office: Columbia Univ Italian Dept 1130 Amsterdam Ave Hamilton Hall Rm 514 New York NY 10027 Office Phone: 212-854-4982. Business E-Mail: jac3@columbia.edu.

CAVANAGH, DENIS, gynecologist, obstetrician, educator, gynecological oncologist; MB, ChB, U. Glasgow, Scotland, 1952. Diplomate: Am. Bd. Obstetrics and Gynecology. Former prof. gynecology and obstetrics, chmn. dept. St. Louis U. Sch. Medicine, 1966-77; prof. obstetrics, gynecology, dir. gynecologic oncology U. South Fla. Coll. Medicine, 1977—. Fellow ACS, ACOG, Am. Gyn-Ob Soc., Royal Coll. Obstetricians and Gynecologists; mem. South Atlantic Assn. Obstetricians and Gynecologists, Soc. Gynecol. Oncologists, Soc. Pelvic Surgeons. Home and Office: 8701 Midnight Pass Rd #206A Sarasota FL 34242

CAVANAGH, HARRISON DWIGHT, ophthalmologist, educator; s. William Edwards and Marie Corrine (Logue) C.; m. Lynn Ayres Gantt, Dec. 27, 1964; 1 dau., Catherine DuVal. AB, Johns Hopkins U., 1962, MD (Joseph Collins scholar 1963-65), 1965; PhD in Biology, Harvard U., 1972. Life diplomate Am. Bd. Ophthalmology. Intern Johns Hopkins Hosp., 1965-66, resident in ophthalmology, 1969-73; fellow corneal surgery Mass. Eye and Ear Infirmary, Boston, 1973-75; instr. ophthalmology Johns Hopkins Med. Sch., 1969-73; asst. prof. Harvard U. Med. Sch., 1975-76; mem. faculty Emory U., 1976-87, F. Phinizy Calhoun prof. ophthalmology, chmn. dept., 1978-87; prof. Georgetown U., Washington, 1987-91; Disting. Univ. prof., vice chmn. dept. ophthalmology U. Tex. Southwestern Med. Ctr., Dallas, 1991-95, W. Maxwell Thomas chair prof., 1995—; med. dir., assoc. dean clin. svcs. Zale Lipsky U. Hosp./U. Tex. Southwestern Med. Ctr. Vis. prof. Georgetown U., 1986-87; cons., chmn. visual scis. study sect A NIH, 1980-84; Heed Found. scholar, 1973-74; sci. adv. panel Nat. Soc. Prevention Blindness, Knights Templar Found.; civilian cons. USAF, 1983-86, USN, Bethesda Naval Hosp., 1989-91; mem. neuroscis. behavior study sect. NIH, 1989-93; organizing com. 3rd-4th Internat. Conf. on Confocal Microscopy and 4th-5th Internat. Conf. on 3D Image Processing in Microscopy, 1991—. Editor-in-chief Jour. Cornea, 1989-96, Eye and Contact Lens Jour., 2002-2007; mem. editorial bd. Jour. Scanning, Bioimaging Jour.; contbr. articles to profl. jours. Recipient Heed Found. award, 1981, 2d Joseph Koplowitz lectr. Georgetown U., 1983, 14th Waldert lectr. U. Rochester, 1987, 5th Morton B. Sarver lectr. U. Calif., Berkeley, 1991, George Nissel lectr. Brit. Contact Lens Assn., 1997; 21st James McDonald lectr., Loyola U. Chicago, 1998, 3d Maxwell Boschner lectr., U. Toronto; recipient Sr. Scientific Investigators award Rsch. to Prevent Blindness, Inc., 1996. Fellow ACS, Internat. Coll. Surgeons, Am. Acad. Ophthalmology (hon., assoc. sect. govt. rels. and rsch. 1979-83, Honor Recognition award 1982, Whitney Sampson lectr. 1997, Sr. Achievement award 1999), Am. Acad. Optometry (hon., Max Shapiro award 2001, lectr. 2005), Royal Microscopy Soc., Royal Soc. Medicine; mem. Contact Lens Assn. Ophthalmologists Am. (pres. 1987, 20th Conrad Behrens medal lectr. 1989, Honor Recognition award 1988), Castroviejo Soc. Corneal Surgeons (pres. 1988-90, Honor Recognition award 1987, 96), Keratorefractive Soc. (bd. dirs.), Internat. Eye Found. Eye Surgeons, Internat. Soc. Contact Lens Rsch. (Montague Ruben medal 2005), New Eng. Ophthal. Soc., Assn. Rsch. in Vision and Ophthalmology (exec. sec.-treas. 1981-86, Honor Recognition award 1987), South-Ctrl. Eyebank Assn. (pres. 1997), Eye Bank Assn. Am. (bd. dirs. 1997-99, R. Townley Paton, M.D. award 2000, Bausch and Lomb Visionaries award 2005), Johns Hopkins Club, Park Cities Club, Harvard Club (Dallas, N.Y.), Order of St. John (U.S., U.K.), Phi Beta Kappa. Republican. Episcopalian. Home: 27 Lakeside Park Dallas TX 75225-8110 Office: U Tex Southwestern Med Ctr Dept Ophthalmology 5323 Harry Hines Blvd Dallas TX 75390-9057 Office Phone: 214-648-8074. Business E-Mail: dwight.cavanagh@utsouthwestern.edu.

CAVANAGH, JOHN HENRY, political economist; b. Boston, Aug. 20, 1955; s. James Ellsworth and Elizabeth (Brady) C.; m. Robin Broad, Apr. 26, 1982. BA, Dartmouth Coll., 1977; MPA, Princeton U., 1980. Asst officer econ. affairs UN Conf. on Trade and Devel., Geneva, 1977-78, 80-81; tech. officer World Health Orgn., Geneva, 1981-82; fellow Inst. for Policy Studies, Washington, 1983-95; co-dir. Inst. Policy Studies, Washington, 1996-97, dir., 1998—. Co-author: The World in Their Web, 1983, Alcoholic Beverages, 1985, From Debt to Development, 1986, Trade's Hidden Costs, 1988, Merchants of Drink, 1988, Trading Freedom, 1992, Plundering Paradise, 1993, Global Dreams: Imperial Corporations and the New World Order, 1994, Beyond Bretton Woods, 1994, Alternatives to Economic Globalization, 2004, Field Guide to the Global Economy, 2005. Co-coord. Debt Crisis Network, Washington, 1984-89; advisor World Coun. Chs., Geneva, 1984-85; bd. dirs. Internat. Labor Rights Fund, Washington, 1987—, Philippine Devel. Forum, 1989-95, Inter-Hemispheric Resource Ctr., 1993—; mem. Civil Soc. Com., UN Devel. Program, 2001—. Harbison fellow Princeton U., 1979. Democrat. Home: 214 Tulip Ave Silver Spring MD 20912-4202 Office: Inst for Policy Studies 733 15th St NW Ste 1020 Washington DC 20005

CAVANAGH, MICHAEL FRANCIS, state supreme court justice; b. Detroit, Oct. 21, 1940; s. Sylvester J. and Mary Irene (Timmins) C.; m. Patricia E. Ferriss, Apr. 30, 1966; children: Jane Elizabeth, Michael F., Megan Kathleen BA, U. Detroit, 1962, JD, 1966. Bar: Mich. 1966. Law clk. to judge Ct. Appeals, Detroit, 1966-67; atty. City of Lansing, Mich., 1967-69; ptnr. Farhat, Story, et al., Lansing, Mich., 1969-73; judge 54-A Dist. Ct., Lansing, 1973-75, Mich. Ct. Appeals, Lansing, 1975-82; justice Mich. Supreme Ct., Lansing, 1983—, chief justice, 1991—95. Supervising justice Sentencing Guidelines Com., Lansing, 1983-94, Mich. Jud. Inst., Lansing, 1986-94, 2001—; bd. dirs. Thomas M. Cooley Law Sch., 1979-88; chair Mich. Justice Project, 1994-95, Nat. Interbranch Conf., Mpls., 1994-95; supreme ct. liaison Mich. Indian Tribal Cts., Mich. State Cts. Bd. dirs. Am. Heart Assn. Mich., 1982—, chmn. bd. Am. Heart Assn. Mich., Lathrup Village, 1984-85; bd. dirs. YMCA, Lansing, 1978. Mem. ABA, Fed. Bar Assn., Ingham County Bar Assn., Inst. Jud. Adminstrn., Soc. of Irish/Am. Lawyers (pres. 1987-88). Democrat. Roman Catholic. Avocations: jogging, racquetball, fishing. Office: Mich Supreme Ct PO Box 30052 925 W Ottawa St Lansing MI 48933-1067 Office Phone: 517-373-8683.

CAVANAGH, PETER ROBERT, academic administrator, science educator, researcher; b. Wolverhampton, Staffordshire, Eng., July 31, 1947; came to U.S., 1972; s. John Joseph and Dorothy Ann (Stokes) C.; m. Magda Margalova, Dec. 21, 1968 (div. 1979); 1 child, Sasha; m. Ann Elizabeth Vandervelde, Apr. 18, 1981; children: Drew, Chris, Jennifer. BEd, U. Nottingham, Loughborough Coll., 1969; PhD, U. London, Royal Free Hosp. Sch. Med., 1972; DSc in Medicine, U. London, 2004. Rsch. asst. Royal Free Hosp. Sch. Med., London, 1969—72; asst. prof. Pa. State U., University Park, 1972-75, assoc. prof., 1975-81, prof. biomechanics, 1981—86, prof. locomotion studies, 1986—2002, dir. Ctr. Locomotion Studies, 1986—2002, prof. biobehavioral health, 1989—2002, rsch. dir. Diabetic Foot Clinic, 1989—2002; prof. medicine Pa. State U. Coll. Med., Hershey, 1993—2002; prof. orthop. surgery and rehab. Pa. State U., University Park, 1994—2002, disting. prof. kinesiology, medicine, orthopedics and rehab. and biobehavioral health, 1993—2002; v.p. rsch. DIApedia LLC, State College, Pa., 1999—; rsch. dir. Diabetic Foot Clinic, Milton S. Hershey Med. Ctr., Hershey, 1993—2002; Virginia Lois Kennedy chmn. dept. biomed. engring., acad. dir. Diabetic Foot Care Program, mem. Cleve. Clinic Found., 2002—; prof. molecular medicine Cleve. Clinic Lerner Coll. Medicine of Case Western Res. U., 2004—; co-dir. Cleve. Clinic Ctr. for Space Medicine, 2004—. Vis. prof. univ. dept. medicine Manchester Royal Infirmary, U. Manchester, Eng., 1990-91; cons. U.S. Olympic Com., Colorado Springs, Colo., 1984-90, NASA, Houston, 1986—, leader bone loss team Nat. Space Biomed. Rsch. Inst., 2004-; various athletic shoe and biomed. cos., U.S., Japan, Germany, 1978—; expert witness for patent and trademark, diabetic foot, foot injury, footwear and footprints and personal injury during gait. Author: The Running Shoe Book, 1980; co-author: The Physiology and Biomechanics of Cycling, 1978, The Biomechanics of Distance Running, 1990, The Foot in Diabetes: A Bibliography, various edits. 1992, 2000, The Foot in Diabetes, 2d and 3d edit., 1994, 2000; mem. editl. bd. Foot and Ankle Internat., 1994—, Internat. Jour. Lower Extremity Wounds, 2001-. Trustee Mus. Contemporary Art, Cleve., 2003—05. Mem. Internat. Soc. Biomechanics (pres. 1995-97, Muybridge medal 1987), Am. Coll. Sports Medicine (fellow 1983, trustee 1987-90, Wolffe lectr. 1987, Citation award 1997, Dill lectr. 2001), Am. Soc. Biomechanics (pres. 1986-87, Borelli award 1994), Am. Diabetes Assn. (chmn. foot coun. 1997-99, Pecoraro lectr. 2002), Aerospace Med. Assn., Orthop. Rsch. Soc., European Assn. Study Diabetes, Am. Soc. Bone and Mineral Rsch., Am. Orthop. Foot and Ankle Soc. (hon.), Melpomene Inst. Adv. Bd., IOC Olympic Acad. Sport Sci. Avocations: running, music, flying. Office: Cleveland Clinic Found 9500 Euclid Ave ND20 Cleveland OH 44195

CAVANAGH, RICHARD EDWARD, not-for-profit developer; b. Buffalo, June 15, 1946; s. Joseph John and Mary Celeste (Stack) C.; m. Patricia Sypher, 1995; 1 child. BA, Wesleyan U., Middletown, Conn., 1968; MBA, Harvard U., 1970. Assoc. McKinsey & Co. Inc., Washington, 1970-77, ptnr., 1980-88; exec. dir. fed. cash mgmt. U.S. Office Mgmt. and Budget, Washington, 1977-79; exec. dean Kennedy Sch. Govt. Harvard U., Cambridge, Mass., 1988-95; pres., CEO The Conf. Bd., Inc., NYC, 1995—. Domestic coord. Pres.' Reorgn. Project, The White House, Washington, 1978-79; mem. exec. com. Pres.' Pvt. Sector Survey on Cost Control, Grace Commn., 1982-83. Co-author: (with Donald K. Clifford Jr.) The Winning Performance: How America's High-Growth Midsize Companies Succeed, 1985, 2d edit., 1988 (pub. in 11 fgn. langs.). Trustee Ctr. for Excellence in Govt., 1985, 96—, Ednl. Testing Svc., 1997—, vice chmn., 2002-05; chmn. 2005—; trustee, dir. Black Rock Mut. Funds, 1994—; dir. Fremont Group, 1997—, The Guardian Ins., 1998—, Arch Chems., Inc., 1996—, Aircraft Fin. Trust, 1999—. Recipient Presdl. commendation, 1979, 80, 83. Mem. Coun. on Fgn. Rels., Wesleyan U. (trustee emeritus), Met. Club (DC), Harvard Club (NYC, Boston), Siwanoy Country Club (Bronxville, NY), The Links (NYC), Beta Theta Pi. Democrat. Roman Catholic. Office: The Conf Bd Inc 845 3rd Ave New York NY 10022-6600 Business E-Mail: richard.cavanagh@conference_board.org.

CAVANAGH, SHIRLEY BICKOFF, librarian; b. New Haven, Aug. 5, 1952; d. Sidney and Sylvia (Weinstein) Bickoff; m. Thomas E. Cavanagh, Aug. 16, 1991. BS, So. Conn. State U., 1974, MLS, 1982. Pub. svcs. asst. Yale U. Libr., New Haven, 1975-82; staff libr. So. Conn. State U., New Haven, 1982-85, assoc. libr., head access svcs. divsn., 1985—, ednl. tech. academic com. Author: LC Marvel: A Guide to the Virtual Electronic Library, 1995. Rsch. grantee Conn. State U., 1995, faculty devel. grantee, 1997. Mem. ALA, Assn. Coll. and Rsch. Librs., Conn. Libr. Assn. (exec. bd.), Gov. Documents Orgn. of Conn. (chair, sec.). Democrat. Jewish. Home: 8 Charlton Hill Rd Hamden CT 06518-2550 Office: So Conn State U 501 Crescent St New Haven CT 06515-1330 Office Phone: 203-392-5768. Business E-Mail: cavanaghs1@southernct.edu.

CAVANAGH, WILLIAM G., lawyer; b. Ctrl. Valley, NY, Apr. 22, 1950; BA, Syracuse U., 1972; JD, George Washington U., 1975; LLM, NYU, 1979. Bar: DC 1975, NY 1980, US Tax Ct. Law clk. to Judge Arthur L. Nims III US Tax Ct., 1979—80; ptnr., tax dept. Chadbourne & Parke LLP, NYC. Adj. asst. prof. Fordham U. Sch. Law, 1985; bd. adv. NYU Inst. Fed. Taxation. Contbr. articles to profl. jour. Mem.: Internat. Bar Assn., DC Bar, ABA, NY Bar Assn. Office: Chadbourne & Parke LLP 30 Rockefeller Plz New York NY 10112 Office Phone: 212-408-5388. Office Fax: 212-541-5369. Business E-Mail: wcavanagh@chadbourne.com.

CAVANAUGH, CHARLES DAVIS, computer scientist, educator; b. Tyler, Tex., Aug. 9, 1973; s. C.J. and Bonita Cavanaugh. AA, Tyler Jr. Coll., 1993; BS, U. Tex., Tyler, 1995, MS, 1997; PhD, U. Tex., Arlington, 2000. Cert. tchr. secondary edn. Tex. Rsch. asst. U. Tex., Tyler, 1996—97, asst. instr. computer sci. Arlington, 1998, grad. rsch. asst., 1997—2000; intern Naval Surface Warfare Ctr., Dahlgren, Va., 1998; asst. prof. computer sci. U. Mo., Rolla, 2000—01; asst. prof. Ctr. Advanced Computer Studies U. La., Lafayette, 2002—. Presenter confs. in field. Contbr. articles to profl. jours. Mem.: Assn. Computing Machinery (v.p. U. Tex. Tyler student chpt. 1996—97, sec. 1996), IEEE Computer Soc., Epsilon Delta Pi, Alpha Chi, Kappa Delta Pi, Phi Theta Kappa, Tau Beta Pi (life). Home: 13020 CR 2220 Whitehouse TX 75791 Personal E-mail: c.d.cavanaugh@att.net.

CAVANAUGH, JAMES HENRY, health products executive, retired federal official; b. Orange, N.J., Mar. 3, 1937; s. James H. and Madeline Rachel (McFerren) C.; m. Esther Sally Musselman, Jan. 20, 1962; children: Elizabeth Anne, Michael Patrick. BS, Fairleigh Dickinson U., 1959; MA, U. Iowa, 1961, PhD, 1964. Asst. adminstr. Princeton (N.J.) Hosp., 1961-62; asst. prof. hosp. and health care adminstrn. U. Iowa, 1964-66; spl. asst. to surgeon gen. USPHS, 1966-67, dir. office comprehensive health planning, 1967-68; dep. asst. sec. health and sci. affairs HEW, 1969-71; staff asst. for health affairs Pres. Nixon, The White House, 1971-73, asst. dir. domestic council, 1973-74, dep. dir., 1974-75; dep. chief White House staff for Pres. Ford, 1975-76; v.p. corp. devel. Allergan Pharms., Irvine, Calif., 1977-78, sr. v.p. sci. and planning, 1978-81; spl. cons. to Pres. Reagan, 1981; pres. Allergan Internat.,

1981-82, SmithKline BioSci. Labs., 1983-85, Smith Kline & French Labs. US, Phila., 1985-01, HealthCare Ventures, LLC. Founding bd. dirs. Marine Nat. Bank, Santa Ana Calif., Nat. Venture Capital Assn.; bd. dirs. MedImmune, Inc., Shire Pharms. Group, PLC, Diversa Corp., Vicuron, Advancis-Pharma. Mem. Pres.'s Export Council, 1981-85; bd. dirs. Proprietary Assn., 1980-82; trustee Nat. Com. for Quality Health Care, nat. chmn. 1988; trustee emeritus Calif. Coll. Medicine; mem. nat. adv. com. Am. Refugee Com. Recipient Disting. Alumnus award U. Iowa Coll. Medicine, Disting. Alumni Achievement award U. Iowa. Mem. Am. Hosp. Assn. (hon.), Pharm. Mfrs. Assn. (bd. dirs. 1986-88), Union League Club (Phila.), Nassau Club. Episcopalian (vestryman). Home: 554 Dorset Rd Devon PA 19333-1845 Office: HealthCare Ventures LLC 44 Nassau St Princeton NJ 08542-4506 Office Phone: 609-430-3930.

CAVANAUGH, JAMES MICHAEL, lawyer; b. Columbus, Ohio, Mar. 19, 1949; s. James Francis and Virginia (Allen) C.; m. Susan Boulineaux, Sept. 4, 1977; children: James, Thomas, Matthew, Daniel. BS, Ohio State U., 1971; JD, Stanford U., 1974. Bar: Ohio 1974, D.C. 1977, U.S. Dist. Ct. D.C. 1978, U.S. Claims Ct. 1981, U.S. Ct. Appeals (D.C. cir.) 1978, U.S. Ct. Appeals (fed. cir.) 1984. Atty.-advisor, Office of Gen. Counsel U.S. Dept. Commerce/Maritime Adminstrn., Washington, 1974-77, counsel Great Lakes region, 1976-77; assoc. Graham & James, Washington, 1977-80, ptnr., 1980—, mng. ptnr., chmn., 1987-92; ptnr. Holland & Knight LLP, Washington, mem. dir. com. Chmn. water transp. law com. Fed. Bar Assn., Washington, 1979-80; adj. prof. George Mason U. Sch. Law 1997-. Contbr. articles to profl. jours. Trustee Ctr. for Law and Social Policy, Washington, 1973-74. Mem. Maritime Law Assn. (assoc.), Maritime Adminstrv. Bar Assn., ABA, Phi Beta Kappa. Office: Holland & Knight LLP 2099 Pennsylvania Ave NW Ste 100 Washington DC 20006 Office Phone: 202-828-5084.*

CAVANAUGH, JANIS LYNN, protective services official, educator; b. Montebello, Calif., Feb. 15, 1952; d. William Franklin Cavanaugh and Anne Mildred Dederick; life ptnr. Jeanne Lynn Renner, Aug. 14, 1992. AS in Police Sci., Rio Hondo Coll., Whittier, Calif., 1973; BS in Criminal Justice, Calif. State U., L.A., 1995; MPA, U. of La Verne, Calif., 2000. Police officer El Monte Police Dept., Calif., 1972—77, Amtrak R.R. Police, L.A., 1977—84; asst. rangemaster Rio Hondo Police Acad., Whittier, 1977—96; prof. adminstrn. of justice and forensic sci. Rio Hondo C.C., Whittier, 1996—; coord. forensic sci. program & acad. La Puente Valley Regional Occupl. Program, City of Industry, Calif., 2003—, pub. safety coord., 1992—2000, instr., 2002—, supr., coord., 2000—02, supr., 2002—. Cons. Tri-Cities Regional Occupl. Program, Whittier, 2000—, East San Gabriel Valley Regional Occupl. Program, West Covina, Calif., 2002—, SE Regional Occupl. Program, Cerritos, Calif., 1995. Mem. Whittier Conservancy, 1984—; vol. ARC, Whittier, 1984—. Recipient Women of Yr. award, Soroptomist Orgn., 1996; Vocat. Ednl. Equipment grantee, State of Calif., 2001, Vocat. Ednl. grantee, 2003. Mem.: Am. Acad. Forensic Sci., Crim. Justice Educators, Forensic Sci. Club (advisor 2000—), Nat. Assn. Pub. Adminstrn. (assoc.), Rio Hondo Faculty Assn. (assoc.; sec. 1996—98), Calif. Assn. Criminal Justice Educators (assoc.; sec. 1994—96), Internat. Assn. Identification (assoc.), So. Calif. Assn. Fingerprint Officers (assoc.), Kiwanis Greater Whittier, NRA (life), Calif. Police Pistol Assn. (life), Alpha Gamma Sigma (assoc.; advisor 1996—2003, v.p. 2002—03). Presbyterian. Achievements include patents pending for forensic identification logo; forensic science curriculum. Avocations: combat shooting, hiking, photography. Home: 11743 North Circle Dr Whittier CA 90601 Office: La Puente Valley ROP 18501 E Gale Ave City Of Industry CA 91748 Office Phone: 562-699-6704. Personal E-mail: cavarenn@aol.com. E-mail: msforensics@janiscavanaugh.com.

CAVANAUGH, JOSEPH P., gas industry executive; CEO Star Gas Partners. Office: Star Gas Partners Clearwater House 2187 Atlantic St Stamford CT 06902

CAVANAUGH, KENNETH CLINTON, retired housing consultant; b. Fremont, Mich., Apr. 30, 1916; s. Frank Michael and Buryll Marie (Preston) C.; m. Barbara Blythe Boling, Feb. 24, 1979; children from previous marriage: Patricia Ann, James Lee, John Thomas. BS in Forestry, Mich. State U., 1939. County supr. Farm Security Adminstrn., USDA, Kalamazoo, 1939-43; community mgr. PHA, Willow Run, Mich., 1946-49, dir. fiscal mgmt. Washington, 1949-55, dir. elderly housing Housing & Home Fin. Agy., 1955-57, reg. dir. San Juan, P.R., 1957-58; dir. housing programs HUD, Washington, 1958-73; controller/dep. dir. San Francisco Housing Authority, 1973-78; pres. Ken C. Cavanaugh & Assocs., pvt. internat. housing and community devel. cons., Vista, Calif., 1978—; fin. finder Merrill Lynch-Huntoon Paige Co., San Francisco, 1979-81, Western Pacific Fin. Co., Newport Beach, Calif., 1981-83; gen. ptnr. The Knolls, Rogers, Ark., 1980-89. Exec. dir. Arlington (Va.) Youth Found., 1950-58; advisor Salvation Army adv. bd., Honolulu, 1985-88. Served to capt. USN, 1943-46, USNR, 1946-73. Recipient Superior Svc. award, Pub. Housing Adminstrn., 1956. Mem. Nat. Assn. Housing & Redevel. Ofcls., Ret. Officers Assn., Res. Officers Assn., Naval Res. Assn., Shadowridge Golf Club (Vista), Elks, Masons. Avocations: golf, travel. Home and Office: PO Box 749 Vista CA 92085-0749 E-mail: BlytheCav@aol.com.

CAVANAUGH, LUCILLE J., oil industry executive; b. Phila. Bachelor's, Immaculata Coll. With Exxon Mobil Corp., 1977—, gen. mgr. supply and engring., pres. credit corp., gen. mgr. west coast refining and mktg., v.p. global supply and distbn., v.p. human resources, 2002—. Bd. dirs. United Way Met. Dallas. Office: Exxon Mobil Corp 5959 Las Colinas Blvd Irving TX 75039-2298 Office Phone: 972-444-1000. Office Fax: 972-444-1198.*

CAVANAUGH, MICHAEL EVERETT, lawyer, arbitrator, mediator; b. Seattle, Dec. 23, 1946; s. Wilbur R. Cavanaugh and Gladys E. (Herring) Barber; m. Susan P. Heckman, Sept. 7, 1968. AB, U. Calif., Berkeley, 1973; JD, U. Wash., 1976. Bar: Wash. 1976, U.S. Dist. Ct. (we. dist.) Wash. 1977, U.S. Ct. Appeals (9th cir.) 1977, U.S. Dist. Ct. (ea. dist.) Wash. 1978. Staff atty. U.S. Ct. of Appeals (9th crct.) Calif., San Francisco, 1976-77; from assoc. to ptnr. Preston & Thorgrimson, Seattle, 1981-85; ptnr. Bogle & Gates, Seattle, 1985-97, assoc., 1977-81, ptnr., 1985-97; propr. Michael E. Cavanaugh, J.D., Arbitration and Mediation, Seattle, 1997—. Contbg. author: Employment Discrimination Law, 3d edit., 1995. Avocations: sailing, creative writing, music. Office: 1420 5th Ave # 2200 Seattle WA 98101-1346 Office Phone: 206-200-1935. E-mail: mec@cavanaugh-adr.com.

CAVANAUGH, ROBERT B., department store executive; BA in Econ., Providence Coll., 1973; MBA in Corp. Fin., U. Pa. Wharton Bus. Sch. Treas. J.C. Penney, mgr. of planning; v.p., treas. J.C. Penney Holding Co., 1996—99, exec. v.p., CFO, 2001—; CFO Eckerd (former J.C. Penney subs.), 1999—2001. Bd. dir. J.C. Penney Holding Co., 2002—. Office: J C Penny Co 6501 Legacy Dr Plano TX 75024

CAVANAUGH, STEPHANIE VON AMMON, psychiatrist, educator; b. Washington, May 26, 1942; m. James L. Cavanaugh, Jr.; children: Brendan James, Margaret Welch. BA, Sarah Lawrence Coll., 1963; BS, Northwestern U., 1964, MD, 1967. Diplomate Am. Bd. Psychiatry and Neurology (examiner 1976—). Intern Cook County Hosp., Chgo., 1967-68; fellow in psychiatry Hosp. U. Pa., 1969-72; clin. asst. psychiatry Maudsley Hosp., London, 1970; vis. resident in psychiatry adolescent inpatient unit Inst. Pa. Hosp., Phila., 1971; instr. psychiatry U. Pa., 1971-73, rsch. assoc. divsn. psychopharmacology, 1972-73; fellow in psychiatry Phila. Child Guidance Ctr., Phila., 1972-73; staff psychiatrist Phila. Gen. Hosp., U. Pa., 1972-73; asst., assoc. then prof. Rush Med. Coll., 1973—; asst., assoc. then sr. attending dept. psychiatry Rush Presbyn.-St. Luke's Med. Ctr., 1973—, chief psychiat. svcs., emergency and acute care program, 1973-98, chief consultation liaison svc., psychosomatic medicine, 1973—, dir. sect. psychosomatic ob-gyn., postpartum well-being, 1979—, dir. internal medicine psychiatry residency program, 1995—, dir. sect. internal medicine/psychiatry, 1996—. Asst. dir. methadone maintenance program West Phila. mental Health Consortium, 1968-69; co-dir. Woodlawn Counseling Ctr., 1968-69; cons. Phila. Gen. Hosp., 1971-73, Nat. Inst. Mental Health, 1979-85; spl. study sect. divsn. rsch. grants NIH, 1984—; coord. mental health team Commn. Experts UN Security Coun., 1994; presenter, lectr. in field. Author: (chpt.) Depression in the Practice of Primary Care Physicians, 1977, Postgraduate Medicine, 1979, Manual of Psychiatric Consultation and Emergency Care, 1984, Handbook of Studies in General Hospital Psychiatry, 1991, Principles and Practice of Emergency Medicine, 3d edit., 1992, 4th edit., 1998 (videotapes) Jacqueline, 1977, Mr. Domino, 1977, Common Problems in Family Practice, 1980; co-author: (chpt.) Psychiatric Update, The American Psychiatric Association Annual Review, Vol. III, 1984, Principles and Practice of Emergency Medicine, 3d edit., 1992, 4th edit., 1998, Psychiatry for Primary Care Physicians, 1998; mem. editl. bd. Psychosomatics, 1985—, Gen. Hosp. Psychiatry, 1985—, Psychosomatic Medicine, 1986—, Internat. Jour. Psychiatry Medicine, 1986—, Psychotherapy Psychosomatics, 1991—, Am. Jour. Cardiology, 1994—, Jour. Nervous Mental Diseases, 1994—; contbr. articles to profl. jours. Recipient Dorfman Jour. Paper award, 1995, 96; grantee Nat. Inst. Mental Health, 1976-79, 79-82, 83-86, Pfizer Pharm., 1981-83, Am. Cancer Soc., 1985-87, 87-88, MacArthur Found., 1994-95. Fellow Am. Psychiat. Assn. (com. med. student edn. 1983-86, task force cost effectiveness 1986-89), Acad. Psychosomatic Medicine (coun. 1991-94, task force outcome studies 1992—); mem. Internat. Coll. Psychosomatic Medicine, Am. Coll. Psychiatrists, Consortium Consultation-Liaison Psychiatrists (exec. coun.), Assn. Am. Med. Colls. (women's liaison officer 1995—), Am. Psychosomatic Soc. (coun. 1988-92, publs. com. 1992—, liaison com. 1992—), Assn. Acad. Psychiatrists (assoc. dir. consultation liaison sect. 1990—), Ill. Psychiat. Soc. (consultation Liaison com. 1983—, ethics com. 1990—), Psychosomatic Consortium Ill. (co-founder). Office: Rush-Presbyn St Luke's Med Ctr Dept Psychiatry 1653 W Congress Pkwy Chicago IL 60612-3833

CAVANAUGH, TOM RICHARD, artist, small business owner, retired art educator; b. Danville, Ill., July 19, 1923; s. Harry William and Hazel (Brown) Cavanaugh. BFA, U. Ill., 1947, MFA (McLellan fellow), 1950. Art and ednl. dir. Springfield (Ill.) Art Assn., 1947-49; mem. faculty Kansas City Art Inst., 1952-55, Washington U. Sch. Art, St. Louis, 1955-56; emeritus prof. painting and drawing La. State U., Baton Rouge, 1957—83; ret., 1983. Owner, dir. Bay St. Studio, Boothbay Harbor, Maine, 1950—, gallery g Art & Antiques. One-man shows include Chapellier Gallery, N.Y.C., 1963, La. State U., 1963, 1978, Griffith-Menard Gallery, Baton Rouge, 1986, Gallery of Art, 2003, exhibited in group shows at Met. Mus. Art, 1950, Whitney Mus., 1951—58, Nelson Gallery Art, 1952, Joslyn Mus. Art, 1954, Mulvane Art Mus., 1955, Kans. State Coll., 1956, Corcoran biennials, 1959, 1961, New Orleans Mus., 1959, Ark. Art Ctr., 1961, Represented in permanent collections Mead Corp., N.Y.C., Joslyn Mus. Art, New Orleans Mus., mural, Govt. Bldg., Baton Rouge. With U.S. Army, 1943—45. Fulbright fellow, Italy, 1956—57, McDowell Colony fellow, 1973. Mem.: Assn. Antique Dealers Am. (exec. bd. dirs.). Home: 8155 Gulf Blvd Navarre FL 32566-7115 Office Phone: 850-499-3139.

CAVANNA, DINO FRANCESCO, chemicals executive; b. Arona, Novara, Italy, Oct. 5, 1939; came to U.S., 1967; s. Carlo and Carla (Gelada) C.; m. Barbara Dziewulska, Nov. 30, 1946; children: Robert, Danielle. Degree in polit. and social scis., U. Milan, 1964; degree in internat. policy and indsl. diplomacy, Inst. Study Internat. Policy, Milan, 1965; degree in law, economy of European cmtys, Internat. Ctr. Studies and Documentation European Cmtys., Milan, 1966; postgrad., NYU, 1974. Exec. v.p. Indesit, Inc., N.Y.C., 1967-69, pres., 1969-82, Indesit Mfg., Harrison, N.Y., 1982-89, Domestic Appliances Trading of Am., Inc., N.Y.C., 1989-91; exec. v.p. The Tartaric Chems. Co., N.Y.C., 1991—2001, GC Chems. Corp., Larchmont, NY, 2001—. Mem. Italy-Am. C. of C. (N.Y.C. chpt., bd. dirs. 1996—, mem. adv. com. 1997—), Larchmont (N.Y.) Shore Club (bd. dirs. 1994—), Famija Piemonteisa Cultural Found. (bd. dirs. 1991, mem. exec. com. 1996—), European-am. C. of C. U.S., Inc. (N.Y.C. chpt. bd. dirs. 1998—). Avocations: tennis, historical social studies. Home: 38 Howell Ave Larchmont NY 10538-3249 Office: GC Chems Co 1890 Palmer Ave Larchmont NY 10538 E-mail: info@gcchemicals.com.

CAVARNOS, CONSTANTINE PETER, philosopher, writer; b. Boston, Oct. 19, 1918; s. Peter (Panagiotes) John and Irene (Maistrou) C. AB magna cum laude, Harvard U., 1942, AM, 1947, PhD, 1948. Tchg. asst. in philosophy Harvard U., Radcliffe Coll., 1945-46; teaching fellow in philosophy Harvard U., Cambridge, Mass., 1946-47; teaching asst. in philosophy Tufts U., Wellesley (Mass.) Coll., 1948-49; asst. prof. philosophy U. N.C., Chapel Hill, 1949-54; assoc. prof., prof. philosophy and Byzantine art Greek Orthodox Sch. Theology, Brookline, Mass., 1954-56; vis. assoc. prof. philosophy Wheaton Coll., Norton, Mass., 1965-67, Clark U., Worcester, Mass., 1967-68; pres. Inst. for Byzantine and Modern Greek Studies, Belmont, Mass., 1969—. Adj. prof. philosophy and Byzantine art Hellenic Coll., Brookline, 1978-82. Author: A Dialogue Between Bergson, Aristotle and Philologos, 1949, Byzantine Sacred Art, 1957, Anchored in God, 1959, Romanian edit., 2005, Man and the Universe in American Philosophy, 1959, Symbols and Proofs of Immortality, 1964, Modern Greek Philosophers on the Human Soul, 1967, 2d edit., 1987, Byzantine Thought and Art, 1968, Modern Greek Thought, 1969, The Holy Mountain, 1973, Plato's Theory of Fine Art, 1973, 2d edit., 1998, The Classical Theory of Relations, 1975, Plato's View of Man, 1975, Orthodox Iconography, 1977, Japanese edit., 1999, A Dialogue on G.E. Moore's Ethical Philosophy, 1979, Paths and Means to Holiness, 1980, Finnish edit., 1988, Romanian edit., 2002, Modern Orthodox Saints, Vols. I-XIV, 1971-2000, vol. 10 Romanian edit., 2003, St. Nectarios of Aegina, 1981, 2d edit., 1988, 95, The Future Life According to Orthodox Teaching, 1984, The Educational Theory of Benjamin Lesvos, 1984, Meetings with Kontoglou, 1985, Bysanttilainen Taide, 1987, The Goodness of God and the Self-Willed Wickedness of Man, 1987, St. Methodia of Kimolos, 1987, Smoking and the Orthodox Christian, 1988, Fasting and Science, 1988, The Hellenic-Christian Philosophical Tradition, 1989, New Library, Vol. 1, 1989, Vol. 2, 1992, Vol. 3, 1995, Vol. 4, 2002, Immortality of the Soul, 1993, Guide to Byzantine Iconography, Vol. I, 1993, Vol. II, 2001, Romanian edit. vols. I and II, 2005, Pythagoras on the Fine Arts as Therapy, 1994, Biological Evolutionism, 1994, 2d edit., 1997, Orthodox Christian Terminology, 1994, Cultural and Educational Continuity of Greece, 1995, To Haigion Oros (Greek version of The Holy Mountain 1973), 2000; editor: Greek Language and Culture: Their Vitality and Importance Today, 1995, Byzantine Churches of Thessaloniki, 1995, He Hiera Byzantine Techne, 1995, Spiritual Beauty, 1996, The Concept of Christian Love, 1996, The Seven Sages of Ancient Greece, 1996, Ecumenism Examined, 1996, Victories of Orthodoxy, 1997, Nikai tes Orthodoxias (Greek version of Victories of Orthodoxy), 2005, St. Nectarios' Study on Holy Icons, 1997, Byzantine Chant, 1998, Fine Arts as Therapy, 1998, St. Photios The Great: Philosopher and Theologian, 1998, Dostoievsky's Philosophy of Man, 1998, Koncepti i Dashurise Kristiane, 1998, The Hellenic Heritage, 1999, St. Gregory of Nyssa on the Human Soul, 2000, Plutarch's Advice on Keeping Well, 2001, Photios Kontoglou peri Byzantines Eikonographias kai Mousikes, 2001, Aristotle's Theory of the Fine Arts, 2001, Holiness: Man's Supreme Destiny, 2001, The Priest as Spiritual Father, 2002, Psychopheleis Didachai tou Photiou Kontoglou, 2003, Orthodoxy and Philosophy, 2003, Sacred Catechism of the Orthodox Church, 2003, Greek Letters and Orthodoxy, 2004, Fine Arts and Tradition, 2004. Sheldon Traveling fellow in philosophy, Harvard/Athens-Paris-Cambridge (Eng.)-Oxford, 1947-48, Fulbright Rsch. scholar U. Athens, 1957-59; recipient Archon of the Oecumenical Patriarchate, Constantinople, 1979, Ann. Faculty award Hellenic Coll., 1986, The Florovsky Theol. prize Ctr. for Traditionalist Orthodox Studies, 1992, Lifetime Achiev. award, Societe Internat. De Psychopathologie et D'Art-Therapie, Am. Soc. Psychopathology of Expression, 2004. Mem. Am. Philos. Assn., Metaphysical Soc. Am. (past treas. 1949), Am. Soc. Aesthetics, Internat. Inst. Arts & Letters, Revista Soc. Argentina Philosophy, Plomaritan Soc. Boston (past pres.), Ctr. Estudios Bizantinos Neohelénicos Fotios Malleros U. Chile (hon.). Greek Orthodox. Avocations: music, restoration of icons, walking. Office: Inst Byzantine & Greek Studies 115 Gilbert Rd Belmont MA 02478-2200 Office Phone: 617-485-6595.

CAVE, ELLIS, information technology executive; V.p. engring. Teknekron Infoswitch, Telephone Broadcasting Sys., 1979—89; dir. R&D Intervoice, Inc., 1989—2005, chief scientist, 2005—. Address: Intervoice Inc 17811 Waterview Pkwy Dallas TX 75252-8016

CAVE, KENT R., parks director; b. Elkin, NC, Oct. 6, 1952; s. John Marvin and Bessie Irene (Dezern) C.; m. Annette Gail Pruitt, May 28, 1983; children: John Carlton, Jacob Reuben, Benjamin Pruitt. BA, Appalachian State U., 1974, student, 1974—76, U. Tenn., 1976—80. Editl. asst. Papers of Andrew Johnson, Knoxville, 1976-80; Pk. ranger Blue Ridge Pky., Asheville, NC, 1975-77, Gt. Smoky Mountains Nat. Pk., Gatlinburg, Tenn., 1980-83, Andrew Johnson Nat. Hist. Site, Greeneville, Tenn., 1984-87, chief Pk. ranger, 1987-88, Ft. Pulaski Nat. Monument, Savannah, Ga., 1988-97; info. officer NPS E. Region Incident Mgmt. Team, 1994—; interpretive media br. chief, resource edn. Gt. Smoky Mountains Nat. Pk., Gatlinburg, 1997—. Active Bull St. Bapt. Ch., Savannah, 1992-97, dir. Royal Amb. youth group, 1993-97; active 1st Bapt. Ch., Gatlinburg, 1997—, mem. missions com., 1998-2000, bd. mem. Smoky Mountain Heritage Ctr., 2002-. Hilton Smith fellow U. Tenn., 1980. Mem. Nat. Park Svc. Employees and Alumni Assn. (life), Savannah Fed. Exec. Assn. (pres. 1991), Appalachian Studies Assn., Great Smoky Mountains Assn. (life). Avocations: woodworking, hiking, photography, history. Office: Gt Smoky Mountains Nat Park Resource Edn 107 Park Headquarters Rd Gatlinburg TN 37738-4102 Office Phone: 865-436-1262. E-mail: kent_cave@nps.gov.

CAVENDISH, KIM L. MAHER, museum administrator; b. Washington, Feb. 25, 1946; d. Joseph Wilson and Helen Elizabeth (Bell) Leverton; m. William Fredrick Maher, June 12, 1965 (div. 1980); 1 child, Lauren Robinson; m. Daryl Kent Cavendish, Feb. 26, 2000. Student, Duke U., 1963-65, George Washington U., 1966; BA in English, U. Fla., 1969. Social worker Fla. Health and Rehab. Svc., Gainesville, 1969-71, Delray Beach, 1972-74, fraud unit supr. West Palm Beach, 1974-76, direct svc. supr., 1977-78; ctr. dir. Palm Beach County Employment and Tng. Adminstrn., West Palm Beach, 1979-81; exec. dir. Discovery Ctyr., Inc., Ft. Lauderdale, Fla., 1981-92, Mus. Discovery & Sci., Ft. Lauderdale, 1992-94; CEO Va. Air and Space Ctr., Hampton, 1995-99; pres. Orlando Sci. Ctr., 2000—02, Mus. Discovery & Sci., Ft. Lauderdale, 2002—. Bd. dirs. Singing Pines Mus., Boca Raton, Fla., 1984-88, Broward Art Guild, Ft. Lauderdale, 1985-91, Va. Space Grant Consortium, Va. Aerospace Bus. Roundtable, Hampton, 1995—2000, Assn. Sci./Tech. Ctrs., 2002—, Giant Screen Theater Assn., 2005—; mem. Leaderhip Broward II, Ft. Lauderdale, 1983-84; mem. faculty Inst. New Sci. Ctrs., 1992; mem. Cultural Execs. Coun. Broward County. Recipient Cultural Arts award Broward Cultural Arts Found., 1985, Woman of Yr. award Women in Comm., 1990, Woman of Distinction award So. Fla. Mag., 1993; namedOutstanding Fundraiser, Fla. Assn. Nonprofit Orgns., 1994. Mem. Am. Assn. Mus., Assn. Sci. and Tech. Ctrs., Southeastern Mus. Conf., Va. Assn. Mus. (bd. dirs. 1999—), Fla. Sci. Tchrs. Assn. (bd. dirs.), Fla. Assn. Mus. (bd. dirs. 1989—, pres. 1993-95), Leadership Broward Alumnae (curriculum com. 1984—), Ft. Lauderdale Downtown Coun. (bd. dirs. 1992—), Women's Exec. Club, Phi Kappa Phi. Democrat. Methodist. Avocations: scuba diving, piano, creative writing, collecting art and antiques, painting. Office: Mus Discovery & Sci 401 SW 2nd St Fort Lauderdale FL 33311

CAVENEE, WEBSTER K., director; b. Sept. 12, 1951; BS in Biology, Kansas State U., 1973. Vis. rsch. scientist Ctr. Cancer Rsch. MIT, 1979—81; assoc. Howard Hughes Med. Inst., U. Utah, 1981—83; assist. then assoc. prof. microbiology & molecular genetics U. Cincinnati, 1983—86; vis. prof. Karolinska Inst., Stockholm, 1985; dir. Ludwig Inst. Cancer Rsch., prof. medicine, neurology, pathology, & human genetics McGill U., 1986—91; sokolow vis. prof. U. Calif., San Francisco, 1988, dir., prof. Ludwig Inst. for Cancer Rsch. LaJolla, 1991—. Mem. GM Adv. Council, Cancer Rsch. Found.; chair exec. com. World Alliance Cancer Rsch. Organizations, 2002; fellow Nat. Found. Cancer Rsch., 2003. Fellow: Am. Acad. Microbiology, Internat. Union Against Cancer, Am. Assn. Cancer Rsch.; mem.: NAS, Am. Soc. Clinical Investigation (hon.), Am. Soc. Microbiology, Am. Assn. for Advancement of Sci., Am. Soc. Human Genetics. Office: Ludwig Inst 9500 Gilman Dr La Jolla CA 92093-0660 E-mail: wcavenee@ucsd.edu.

CAVENY, LEONARD HUGH, mechanical engineer, aerospace scientist, consultant; b. Atlanta, Oct. 30, 1934; s. Elmer Leonard and Dorothy (Franklin) C.; m. Joyce Rodal, Apr. 10, 1957; children: Polly J., Rebecca R., Teresa L., Leslie Y., Susan C. BME, Ga. Inst. Tech., 1956, MSME, 1960; PhD in Mech. Engring., U. Ala., 1969. Registered profl. engr. Ala., 1965. Supr. aerothermodynamics Thiokol Chem. Corp., Huntsville, Ala., 1960-67; sr. tech. staff Princeton (N.J.) U., 1969-80; program mgr. Air Force Office Sci. Rsch., Washington, 1980-85; dep. dir. sci. and tech. Strategic Defense Initiative Orgn., Washington, 1985-93; dir. sci. & tech. Ballistic Missile Defense Orgn., Washington, 1993-97. Mem. Com. on Thermionic Rsch. and Tech. NRC, 2000—01, mem. com. to review NASA's pioneering revolutionary tech., 2002—, chair Air Force propulsiton proposal rev. panel, 2004—; cons. in field; nat. rsch. coun. Air Force Propulsion Proposal Review Panel, 2003—. Editor: Orbit-Raising and Maneuvering Propulsion, 1984; inventor in field. Lt. (j.g.) USN, 1956-59. Recipient Yuri Gagarin medal, Moscow, 1993. Fellow AIAA (chair elec. propulsion tech. com. 1984-86, chair Princeton sect. 1974-75, tech. chair internat. elec. propulsion conf. 1985, editorial adv. bd. 1988—, Wyld Propulsion medal 1997); mem. The Combustion Inst. Avocations: photography, construction, tennis. Home: 13715 Piscataway Dr Fort Washington MD 20744-6635 E-mail: lhcaveny@cs.com.

CAVERT, HENRY MEAD, physician, retired medical educator; b. Mpls, Mar. 30, 1922; s. William Lane and Mary (Mead) C.; m. June Lorraine Sederstrom, Jan. 27, 1946; children: John Mead (dec.), Harlan McCrea, Winston Peter. BS in Agrl. Biochemistry, U. Minn., 1942, MD, 1951, PhD in Physiology, 1952. Postdoctoral research fellow Am. Heart Assn., 1951-54; faculty U. Minn. Med. Sch., 1953-92, assoc. dean, 1964-92, prof. physiology, 1967-92, prin. investigator Gen. Clin. Rsch. Ctr., 1978-92, prof. emeritus, 1992—. Nat. Heart Inst. spl. rsch. fellow, vis. prof. biochemistry U. Edinburgh, Scotland, 1961-62; established investigator Am. Heart Assn., 1954-57; mem. program project com. B, Nat. Heart Inst., 1966-69; cons. Nat. Heart and Lung Inst., 1969-92. Author (with A.J. Carlson and V. Johnson): Machinery of the Body, 5th edit., 1961; author: also numerous articles. Mem. met. bd. dir. YMCA, Mpls., 1968-70, endowment com., 1988—, bd. mgmt. U. Minn. br., 1955-57, 77-83, 84-90, chmn., 1968-70, chmn. capital campaign endowment, 1992-95, chmn. capital bldg. campaign, 1998-99, capital campaign steering com., 2004—; mem. bd. parish edn. Am. Luth. Ch., 1958-72, Luth. Health Care Bangladesh, 1994—; trustee Minn. Med. Found., 1958-92, chmn. scholarship and loan com., 1960-68, chmn. honors and awards com., 1970-76, mem. spl. grants com., 1981—, chmn. student fin. aid com., 1984-92, active 1992-95, mem. planned giving com., 1991-2001, heritage soc. com., 2001— Recipient Harold S. Diehl award, 2001. Mem. AMA, Assn. Am. Med. Coll. (chmn. com. student aspects internat. med. edn. 1966-68, steering com. group on student affairs 1967-68, com. internat. rels. med. edn. 1968-75), Am. Physiol. Soc., Minn. Acad. Medicine (pres.-elect 1989-90, pres. 1990-91), Minn. Med. Alumni Soc. (bd. dir. 1992-98), Minn. Med. Assn. (pres. award 1988, mem. various coms.), Sigma Xi, Phi Lambda Upsilon, Alpha Omega Alpha, Gamma Sigma Delta, Alpha Zeta. Home: 2250 Luther Pl Condo #106 Saint Paul MN 55108

CAVETT, L JEAN, librarian; b. Ada, Okla., Oct. 20, 1946; d. Leon J. and Lenna M. Myers; m. Danny L. Cavett, July 12, 1968; children: Mark, Tonya Groves. Master in Libr. Sci. (MLS), U. of Okla., Norman, OK, 1980—83. Libr. dir. Midwest Christian Coll., Oklahoma City, Okla., 1975—85, Children's Hosp. of Okla., Oklahoma City, Okla., 1985—97. Coord. of reference services Rose State Coll., Midwest City, Okla., 1997—. Mem.: GOAL (Greater Okla. Area Health Sciences Libraries) (chair 2000—00). Christian Church. Avocation: camping, singing. Office: Rose State College 6420 SE 15th Midwest City OK 73110-2799

CAVIEZEL, JAMES PATRICK, actor; b. Mt. Vernon, Wash., Sept. 26, 1968; s. James and Maggie; m. Kerri Browitt, 1997. Student, Bellevue (Wash.) C.C., U. Wash.; student in Acting, U. So. Calif.; degree (hon.), King's Coll., 2003. Actor: (films) My Own Private Idaho, 1991, Diggstown, 1992, Wyatt Earp, 1994, Ed, 1996, The Rock, 1996, G.I. Jane, 1997, The Thin Red Line, 1998, Ride with the Devil, 1999, Frequency, 2000, Pay It Forward, 2000, Madison, 2001, Angel Eyes, 2001, The Count of Monte Cristo, 2002, High Crimes, 2002, I Am David, 2003, Highwaymen, 2003, The Final Cut, 2004, The Passion of the Christ, 2004, Bobby Jones, Stroke of Genius, 2004; (TV films) Children of the Dust, 1995; (TV series) The Wonder Years, 1992, Murder She Wrote, 1995. Office: c/o Pamela Cole United Talent Agency 9560 Wilshire Blvd Beverly Hills CA 90212-2400

CAVILEER, DENISE MARIE, poet; b. Point Pleasant, N.J., Nov. 21, 1973; d. Joseph G. and MaryLou Cooley; m. Matthew Patrick Cavileer; children: Kristina, Sarah, A.J. Cert. child devel. presch. tchr. Va., 1992. Tchr. in home day care, Chesapeake, Va., 1993—98. Contbr. anthology The Incandescent Jungle, 2001, anthology European edit. of poets by Nobel Press, 2003, other anthologies. Nominee Poet of the Year, 2002; recipient Achievement award, Poetry.com, 2001. Avocations: being with my children, writing, singing, music. Personal E-mail: Lyricalgirlpoet@aol.com.

CAVILEER, SHARON E., writer, public relations executive, consultant; b. Washington, Apr. 27, 1949; d. Douglas Richards and Grace Elizabeth Cavileer; m. Peter L. D'Alessandro; children: Jessica Flaherty, Rachel Pullen. BA in English, Kent State U., 1970, postgrad., George Mason U. Account exec. E.G. White & Assocs., Vienna, Va., 1983—85, Stackig, McLean, Va., 1985—88; pres. Cavileer & Co., Clifton, Va., 1987—; pub. rels. mgr. Prince William County Park Authority, Manassas, Va., 1992—99. Press officer The Freedom Mus., Manassas, 1999—2004; media relations staff Spotlight on the Arts, Fairfax, 1992; dir. Fairfax City Auto Dealers Assn., 1992—; lectr. in field. Author: Virginia Curiosities, 2002; contbr. stories to mags. and newspapers including Destinations, Home & Away, So. Living, Mid-Atlantic Travel, Washington Flyer, The Boston Herald, Cleveland Mag., others, articles to profl. jours. Mem.: Greater Manassas C. of C., Ctrl. Fairfax C. of C., Soc. Am. Travel Writers (Phoenix com. 2001—). Republican. Presbyterian. Office: Cavileer & Co 12950 Clifton Creek Dr Clifton VA 20124 Personal E-mail: cavileer2@aol.com.

CAVIN, KRISTINE SMITH, lawyer; b. Decatur, Ga., Mar. 26, 1969; d. Richard Theodore and Sherri (Nash) Smith; m. James Michael Cavin, May 13, 1995. BA, Furman U., 1991; JD, Calif. Western Sch. Law, 1995. Bar: Ga. 1995. Legal asst. Smith & Jenkins, P.C., Atlanta, 1991-92; intern child abuse and domestic violence unit San Diego City Atty.'s Office, 1995; assoc. Smith, Ronick & Corbin, L.L.C., Atlanta, 1995—. Mem. ABA, Nat. Assn. Women Lawyers, Nat. Assn. Profl. Mortgage Women, Mortgage Bankers Assn. (assoc.), Ga. Bar Assn., Ga. Assn. for Women Lawyers, Ga. Real Estate Closing Attys. Assn. (sec. 1997-2004, v.p. 2004—), Atlanta Bar Assn. Avocations: gourmet cooking, wine, gardening. Office: Smith Ronick & Corbin LLC 750 Hammond Dr NE Bldg 11 Atlanta GA 30328-5532 Office Phone: 404-256-9000. Business E-Mail: kristinecavin@closingattorney.com.

CAVIN, RUTH, editor; b. Pitts., Oct. 15, 1918; d. Abraham Jacob and Jennie Brodie; m. Bram Cavin, Nov. 25, 1946; children: Anthony, Emily, Nora. BS in Gen. studies, Carnegie Inst. Tech., Pitts., 1941. Editor various publ. hos., N.Y.C., 1946—. Mem.: Mystery Writers Am. (Lifetime Achievement 1990, Ellery Queen award 1988), Internat. Crime Writers, Women's Media Group. Avocation: acting. Office: St Martins Press 175 Fifth Ave New York NY 10010

CAVIOR, WARREN JOSEPH, communications executive; b. Boston, Sept. 18, 1929; s. Joel H. and Shirley (Miller) C.; m. Mariko Sanjo, Oct. 12, 1969; children— Mayu, Samuel. AB cum laude, Harvard, 1951; MA, Columbia, 1952; postgrad., Oxford U., 1952-53. Assoc. editor Forbes Mag., 1956-59; pres. Wall Street Consultants, Inc., N.Y.C., 1959-62, Warren J. Cavior & Co., N.Y.C., 1962-67; chmn. bd. Universal Communications Inc., N.Y.C., 1967-74; exec. v.p. Rogers, Cowan & Taplinger, Inc., N.Y.C., 1974-76; sr. v.p. Rogers & Cowan, Inc., N.Y.C., 1976-81; pres. Cavior Orgn., Inc., 1981—; chmn. The Am. Depositary Receipt Assn., 1993—; treas., dir. Wako Internat. Corp., 1962-67. Adv. bd.: Present Tense Mag. Chmn. Cavior Found., 1968—. Mem. Am. C. of C. in Japan. Office: 2 Fifth Ave New York NY 10011 Office Phone: 212-674-0408. E-mail: caviorg@aol.com.

CAVISH, JACQUELYN ANN, artist, educator; b. Riverside, Calif., Mar. 28, 1944; d. John Angus and Hope Florence (Franson) Ross; m. John David Richards, Apr. 1969 (div. 1973); 1 child, Clayton Andrew; m. Carl Walter Cavish, Nov. 10, 1979 (div. Aug. 1992). Student, U. Ariz., 1962-66; BA in Spanish, UCLA, 1968; MFA, U. Calif., Santa Barbara, 1988. Instr. art Wright Cultural Ctr., Port Hueneme, Calif., 1990—, Oxnard (Calif.) Coll., 1991—; curator of art Ventura County Mus. of Art, Channel Islands Harbor, Calif., 2002, Ventura County Maritime Mus. One-woman shows Ojai (Calif.) Valley Arts Ctr., 1989, Ventura (Calif.) Arts Commn., 1990, Wheeler Hot Springs Gallery, Ojai, 1991, Danica House, Ventura, 1992, Calif. Gold Coast Watercolor Soc., Ventura, 1993, Moorpark (Calif.) Coll., 1993, Alley Gallery, Carpinteria, Calif., 1994, State of the Arts Gallery, Olympia, Wash., 1994, Studio Gallery, Channel Islands Harbor, Calif., 1995, others; group shows include Ventura County Mus. History and Art, 1992, Conejo Valley Art Mus., Thousand Oaks, Calif., 1989-93, Santa Barbara (Calif.) Mus. Natural History, 1992, Midwest Watercolor Soc., Green Bay, Wis., 1993, N.E. Watercolor Soc., Goshen, N.Y., 1993, East Wash. Watercolor Soc., Richland, 1993, Clymer Mus. & Gallery, Ellensburg, Wash., 1993, Fremont Arts & Crafts Fair, Seattle, 1994, Yosemite Nat. Park, Calif., 1995, Pacific N.W. Arts & Crafts Festival, 1995. Chmn. Arts and Crafts Harbor Days, Port Hueneme, 1991-93. Recipient 2d place award Art Walk, Thousand Oaks, 1991, hon. mention Yosemite (Calif.) Renaissance Exhibit, 1991, Best of Show award Allied Artists Santa Monica Mountains, 1991, visual arts award Oxnard Cultural and Fine Arts Commn., 1992, 2003 Collection of City of Ventura, Calif. Mem.: Oxnard Art Assn. (pres. 1989), Calif. Gold Coast Watercolor Soc. (founding). Democrat.

CAVUTO, NEIL, newscaster, business journalist, television host; s. Pat and Kathleen Cavuto; m. Mary Cavuto. BA in Journalism, St. Bonaventure U., 1980. Journalist Investment Age mag., Wash., DC; weekend anchor WCAX, Burlington, Vt., 1982—85; reporter Nightly Bus. Report, PBS, 1985—89; host, Market Wrap, Power Lunch, Business Insiders CNBC, 1989—96; contributor Today Show, NBC, 1989—96; anchor, mng. ed. of bus. news FOX News Channel, 1996—2000, v.p. bus. news, 2000—, host, Your World With Neil Cavuto, 1996—, host, Cavuto on Business, 1999—. Author: More Than Money: True Stories of People Who Learned Life's Ultimate Lesson, 2004. Named one of most influential bus. journalists in Am., The Journalist and Financial Reporter; recipient 5 Cable ACE award nom. Office: FOX News Channel 1211 Ave Of Am New York NY 10036 Office Phone: 212-301-3000.

CAWLEY, CHARLES M., retired bank executive; Grad., Georgetown U. With Md. Nat. Bank, 1972; founder, exec. v.p. Md. Bank N.A. (now MBNA), 1982, pres., 1985—2002; CEO MBNA Am. Bank, N.A., 1990—2002; pres., dir. MBNA Corp., Del., 1991—2003, chmn., CEO Wilmington, Del., 2002—03; ret., 2003. Bd. dirs. MasterCard Internat. Exec. com. bd. dirs. Am. Quality Found.; bd. regents Georgetown U.

CAWLEY, JOSEPH DOUGLAS, retired reading professor; b. Savannah, Ga., Dec. 12, 1929; s. Henry Hughes and Bertha (Platt) C.; m. Grace Ashliman, June 21, 1951; children: Lorraine Cawley Gaufin, Carolyn Nielsen; m. Jacqueline Boss, May 22, 1987. BS, Brigham Young U., 1954; MS, U. Utah, 1961, PhD, 1970. Cert. elem. tchr., Utah, Ga. Tchr. Dekalb County Sch. Dist., Atlanta, Salt Lake City Sch. Dist.; asst. prof. edn. Adams State Coll., Alamosa, Colo.; prof., chmn. reading dept. Met. State Coll., Denver, prof. emeritus, 2001—. Author: Handbook for Experiential Education, 1988, From Alsace to South Carolina Jonas Beard, 1730-1796, Patriot, Statesman, 2002, From Lampertheim to South Carolina Reverend John Nicholas Martin, 2003, From Lampertheim to South Carolina Captain Daniel Strobel, 1775-1806, Patriot and Civic Leader, 2004. Mem. CCIRA (past pres., Pres. award), Kappa Delta Pi (Outstanding Counselor award), Phi Delta Kappa.

CAWLEY, LEO PATRICK, pathologist, immunologist; b. Oklahoma City, Aug. 11, 1922; s. Pat Bernard and Mary Elizabeth (Forbes) C.; m. Joan Mae Wood, June 20, 1948; children: Kevin Patrick, Karin Patricia, Kary Forbes. BS in Chemistry, Okla. State U., 1948; MD, Okla. Sch. Medicine, 1952. Diplomate Am. Bd. Pathology, Am. Bd. Nuc. Medicine, Am. Bd. Allergy and Immunology, Am. Bd. Med. Lab. Immunology, Am. Bd. Pathology in immunopathology. Intern Wesley Med. Ctr., Wichita, Kans., 1952-53, resident in pathology, 1953-54, Wayne County Gen. Hosp., Eloise, Mich., 1954-56, chief resident in pathology, 1956-57; clin. pathologist, asst. dir. lab. Wesley Med. Ctr., Wichita, 1957-69, dir. sci., 1965-86, dir. labs., 1969-77, dir. clin. immunology, 1979-86; med. dir. Roche Biomed. Lab., Wichita, 1979-86; dir. clin. labs. Vetazyme Corp., Tempe, Ariz., 1988—. Pres. Kilcawley Enterprises, 1986—. Author: Electrophoresis/Immunoelectric Phoresis, 1969; editor series Lab Med Little Brown, 1965-81; contbr. 210 articles to profl. jours. Pfc. USM, 1942-45. Fellow Am. Soc. Clin. Pathologist (bd. dirs. 1968, Disting. Svc. award 1980, Dist. Pathology edn. award 1998), Coll. Am. Pathologist; mem. AAAS, ACS, Am. Assn. Clin. Chemists, Alpha Pi Mu, Phi Lambda Upsilon, Alpha Omega Alpha. Avocations: reading, history. Office: KilCawley Enterprises 7135 E Main St Scottsdale AZ 85251-4315

CAWLEY, MICHAEL J., medical educator, pharmacist; s. Margaret and Paul A. Cawley; m. Angela Delnevo, June 2, 1996; 1 child, Ashley J. AAS, cert. in respiratory therapy, Luzerne County CC, 1987; BS in Pharmacy, Phila. Coll. Pharmacy and Sci., 1994, PharmD, 1996. Cert. pulmonary function technologist Nat. Bd. Respiratory Care, 1988, registered respiratory therapist Nat. Bd. Respiratory Care, 1992, pharmacist Pa., 1995. Cert. respiratory therapy technician Moses Taylor Hosp., Scranton, Pa., 1986—90; registered respiratory therapist Presbyn. Med. Ctr., Phila., 1990—97; residency in surgical critical care pharmacotherapy Phila. Coll. Pharmacy and Sci., 1996—97, clin. instr. in clin. pharmacy, 1996—97; asst. prof. clin. pharmacy Phila. Coll. Pharmacy/U. Scis., 1997—2003, assoc. prof. clin. pharmacy, 2003—; critical care clin. pharmacist Crozer-Chester Med. Ctr., Upland, Pa., 1997—. Cons. pharmacist Horizon Healthcare, Inc, Phila., 1997—99; jour. reviewer Annals of Pharmacotherapy, Cincinnati, 1997—, editl. bd. (critical care), 2003—; jour. reviewer Pharmacotherapy, Boston, 1997—, Critical Care Medicine, Balt., 2001—; editl. bd. RT Jour. Respiratory Care Practitioners, Marina del Rey, Calif., 1997—; cons. in field. Author: Pharmacotherapy, Burns, Journal of Neuroscience Nursing, RT Journal for Respiratory Care Practitioners, Annals of Pharmacotherapy, Journal of Pharmacy Practice. Mem.: Pa. Soc. Critical Care Medicine, Am. Coll. Clin. Pharmacy, Am. Soc. Health Sys. Pharmacist, Soc. Critical Care Medicine. Achievements include research in potential risk factors associated with thrombocytopenia in a surgical intensive care unit; open study of synercid (quinupristin/dalfopristin RP 59500) for emergency Use, infections due to resistant bacteria, treatment failure or in treatment intolerant patients; linezolid anaphylaxis and successful oral desensitization in a patient with myasthenia gravis; surveillance of resistant gram-positive bacteremia in the US. Office: Phila Coll Pharmacy 600 S 43rd St Philadelphia PA 19104-4495 Office Phone: 215-895-3136. Business E-Mail: m.cawley@usip.edu.

CAWLEY, PATRICIA BLONTS, secondary school educator; d. Edward Conrad and Donna Branch Blonts; m. Daniel Joseph Cawley, Mar. 12, 1994; 1 child, Seamus Patrick. BA, Old Dominion U., Norfolk, Va., 1993, MS, 2003. English tchr. Chesapeake (Va.) Pub. Sch. Communication dir. Women's Polit. Caucus, Norfolk, Va., 1992—99. Mem.: NEA (assoc.), Chesapeake Edn. Assn. (assoc.; comm. dir. 1997—99), Va. Edn. Assn. (assoc.), Va. Reading Coun. (assoc.), Southeastern Va. Assn. of Tchr. of English (assoc.), Va. Assn. of Tchr. of English (assoc.), Nat. Coun. of Tchr. of English (assoc.), Phi Kappa Phi. Democrat-Npl. Episc. Avocations: family, travel, literature.

CAWLEY, THOMAS J., lawyer; b. Carbondale, Pa., Oct. 7, 1943; BS, U. Scranton, 1966; LLB, U. Va., 1969. Bar: Va. 1969. Mem. Hunton & Williams LLP, Fairfax, Va., mng. ptnr., litig., intellectual property, antitrust McLean, Va. Mem. Am. Coll. Trial Lawyers. Office: Hunton & Williams PO Box 1147 1751 Pinnacle Dr Ste 1700 Mc Lean VA 22102-3836 Office Fax: 703-714-7410. Business E-Mail: tcawley@hunton.com.

CAWLEY, THOMAS M., lawyer; b. Cleve., June 1956; s. Edward Patrick and Francis Eileen (Holleran) C.; m. Barbara A.; children: Michael Christopher, Anne Caitlin. BS in Bus. and Econs., Grove City Coll., 1978; JD, Case Western Res. U., 1982. Bar: Ohio 1982, Fla. 1983. Ptnr. Cavitch, Familo, Durkin & Frutkin, Cleve., 1982—. Mem. Cleve. Bar Assn. Office: Cavitch Familo Durkin & Fru The E Ohio Bldg 14th Flr Cleveland OH 44114

CAWOOD, ALBERT MCLAURIN (HAP CAWOOD), retired newspaper editor; b. Harlan, Ky., Nov. 10, 1939; s. Frank Finley and C. Eugene (Barwick) C.; m. Sonia Barreiro, July 3, 1965; children: Romy Lanier, Shuly Xochitl. BA in English, Union Coll., 1962; MA in Journalism, Ohio State U., 1966. Asst. city editor Dayton (Ohio) Daily News, 1966, editorial writer, 1966-82, editorial page editor, 1982-99; ret., 1999. Author: The Miler, 2003. Vol. Peace Corps., Sierra Leone, 1962-64; chmn. Ohio Com. on Crime and Delinquency, 1969-70; bd. dirs. Engring. Sci. Found., Dayton, Ohio, 2003—04. Recipient Disting. Svc. award Nat. Soc. Profl. Journalists, 1968, Walker Stone award Scripps-Howard Found., 1984; named to Union Coll. Bus. and Profl. Hall of Fame. Mem. Am. Soc. Newspaper Editors, Nat. Conf. Editl. Writers, Engrs. Club Dayton (pres. 2003-04). Democrat. Home: 211 S Winter St Yellow Springs OH 45387-1730

CAWOOD, ELIZABETH JEAN, public relations executive; b. Santa Maria, Calif., Jan. 6, 1947; d. John Stephen and Gertrude Margaret (Shelton) Dille; m. Neil F. Cawood, Jan. 4, 1975; 1 child, Nathan Patrick. BA, Whitworth Coll., 1964-68. Dir. pub. info. Inland Empire Goodwill, Spokane, Wash., 1967-72; adminstrv. asst. N.W. Assn. Rehab. Industries, Seattle, 1973-74; pres., counselor Cawood, Eugene, Oreg., 1974—. Pres. Women in Comm., Inc., 1981-83; advisor U. Oreg. chpt. Pub. Rels. Soc. Am., 1987-91; active Benton Lane Lincoln Linn Region Stragegy Bd., 1993-99, chair, 1993-94; bd. dirs. AAA Oreg./Idaho, 1996—, SOLV, 1998-2003. Editor: Dictionary of Rehabilitation Acronyms, (newsletters) INTERCOM, Family Communicator, Oreg. Focus, (dictionary) Work-Oriented Rehabilitation Dictionary and Synonyms, 1st and 2nd edits. Bd. dirs. Laurel Hill Ctr., 1993—, v.p., 2001, pres. 2002-2004; bd. dirs. Lane County Boy Scouts Am., 1986-2001, Eugene Action Forum, 1981-86, Birth-to-Three, 1982-85, Lane County chpt. ARC, 1982-83, 84-89, Lane County chpt. Am. Cancer Soc., 1984-87, Eugene Opera, 1985-88, Joint Com. Econ. Diversification, 1985-89, 91-93, Lane County United Way, 1987-93, campaign cabinet, 2002-04, chair leadership, 2001-2003, Lane Econ. Com., vice chmn., 1990-95, chair, 1996-2001; bd. dirs. So. Willamette Pvt. Industry Coun., 1985-88, pres., 1988; chmn. Eugene Pvt. Industries Coun., 1981-83, vice chmn., 1983-84; chmn. Bus. Owners Network, Eugene, 1980-81; advisor Eugene Jr. League; trustee The Nature Conservancy, 1999—, exec. com., 2005—. Mem. LWV (bd. dirs. 1979), Pub Rels. Soc. Am. (bd. dirs. Columbia River chpt. 1987-88, pres. Greater Oreg. chpt. 1991-92, bd. dirs. 1991-93), Nat. Rehab. Assn. (pres. 1980-81), Profl. Women's Network (bd. dirs. Oreg. chpt. 1982), Eugene C. of C. (bd. dirs. 1980-87, 92-97, local govt. affairs coun. 1999-2002, mem. econs. devel. coun. 2002-2004, chmn. econ. devel. 1982-83, bd. dirs. exec. com. 1984-87, v.p. 1987, 93, chmn. edn. com., pres.-elect 1994, pres. 1995), Mid-Oreg. Advt. Club (bd. dirs. 1985-87), Oreg. Sales and Mktg. Execs. (bd. dirs. 1985-87), Eugene/Springfield Assn. Quality and Performance (chmn. 1991-93, bd. dirs. 1991-94), Internat. Assn. Sports and Human Performance (bd. dirs. 1993), Rotary (Eugene pub. rels. chair 2000-2004), Eugene City Club (bd. dirs. 1992-98, pres.-elect 1995, pres. 1996). Office: Cawood 1200 High St Ste 200 Eugene OR 97401-3266 Office Phone: 541-484-7052. Business E-Mail: liz@cawood.com.

CAWOOD, JENNY LIND, social worker, poet; b. Harlan, Ky., Aug. 15, 1940; d. James Abram and Lillian Greer Cawood; m. Hartwell Lynn Chenault, Mar. 1966 (div. 1986); children: James Cawood Chenault, Henry Brian Chenault. BA in Speech, Abilene Christian U., 1962; MSW, U. Louisville, 1966. LCSW Va. Dir. social work Battey State Hosp., Rome, Ga., 1967—68; clin. social worker Child and Family Svcs., Monroe, Mich., 1974—78; oncology social worker The Toledo Hosp., 1978—79; clin. social worker Ide Cmty. Mental Health, Toledo, 1979—80, Cmty. Mental Health Ctr. West, Toledo, 1980—84; unit social worker St. Albans Hosp., Radford, Va., 1984—85; clin. social worker Human Affairs Internat., Raleigh, NC, 1988. Mgr. rental properties. Avocations: poetry, doing poetry readings. Home: 11 Lavanda Lane Hot Springs Village AR 71909 Office Phone: 501-922-3436.

CAWS, MARY ANN, literature and language professor; b. Wilmington, NC, Sept. 10, 1933; d. Harmon Chadbourn and Margaret Devereux (Lippitt) Rorison; m. Peter Caws, June 2, 1956 (div. 1987); children: Hilary, Matthew. BA, Bryn Mawr Coll., 1954; MA, Yale U., 1956; PhD, U. Kans., 1962; DHL (hon.), Union Coll., 1983. Asst. instr. Romance langs. U. Kans., Lawrence, 1957-62, asst. editor Univ. press, 1957-58, vis. asst. prof., spring 1963; lectr. Barnard Coll. Columbia U., NYC, 1962-63; mem. faculty Sarah Lawrence Coll., Bronxville, NY, 1963-64, Hunter Coll. CUNY, NYC, 1966-88; prof. Grad. Sch. CUNY, NYC, 1969-88, exec. officer comparative lit. program Grad. Sch., 1977-79, exec. officer French program Grad. Sch., 1979-86, Disting. prof. French and comparative lit. Grad. Sch., 1983—, prof. English, 1985—, Disting. prof. French, comparative lit., English Grad. Sch., 1987—. Phi Beta Kappa vis. scholar, 1982-83; dir. NIH summer seminars for coll. tchrs., 1978, 85; mem. faculty Sch. of Criticism and Theory, Dartmouth U., 1988, Sch. Visual Arts, 1993; professeur associé Université de Paris VII, 1993-94; co-chair Henri Peyre Inst. for the Humanities, 1980-1996, French Inst., 1997-2002; lectr. NY Coun. for Humanities, 1992-96. Author: Surrealism and the Literary Imagination, 1966, The Poetry of Dada and Surrealism, 1970, The Inner Theatre of Recent French Poetry, 1972, The Presence of René Char, 1976, René Char, 1977, The Surrealist Voice of Robert Desnos, 1977, La Main de Pierre Reverdy, 1979, The Eye in the Text, Essays on Perception, Mannerist to Modern, 1981, André Breton, 1982, 96, The Metapoetics of the Passage, Architextures in Surrealism and After, 1982, Yves Bonnefoy, 1984, Reading Frames in Modern Fiction, 1988, Edmond Jabès, 1988, The Art of Interference: Stressed Readings in Visual and Verbal Texts, 1989, Women of Bloomsbury, 1991, Robert Motherwell: What Art Holds, 1996, Carrington and Lytton: Alone Together, 1996, The Surrealist Look: An Erotics of Encounter, 1997, Picasso's Weeping Women: The Life and Art of Dora Maar, 2000, Virginia Woolf: Illustrated Life, 2002, Robert Motherwell with Pen and Brush, 2003, Marcel Proust: Illustrated Life, 2003, To the Boathouse: A Memoir, 2004, Pablo Picolo, 2005; co-author: Bloomsbury and France: Art and Friends, 1999; editor: Dada-Surrealism, 1972, co-editor, 1980-2002, Le Siècle éclaté, 1974-78, About French Poetry from Dada to Tel Quel, 1974, Selected Poetry Prose of Stéphane Mallarmé, 1982, Selected Poems of St.-John Perse, 1983, Writing in a Modern Temper, 1984, Textual Analysis, 1986, Perspectives on Perception: Philosophy, Art, and Literature, 1989, City Images, 1992, Joseph Cornell's Theater of the Mind: Selected Diaries, Letters and Files, 1994, Manifesto: A Century of Isms, 2001, Mallarme in Prose, 2001, Surrealist Painters and Poets, 2001, Surrealist Love Poems, 2002, Vita Sackville-West: Selected Writings, 2002, Surrealism, 2004, Yale Anthology of Twentieth-Century French Poetry, 2004, Maria Jolas: Woman of Action, 2004; co-editor: Selected Poems of René Char, 1992, Contre-Courants: Les femmes s'écrivent à travers les siècles, 1994, Écritures de femmes: Nouvelles Cartographies, 1996; translator: Poems of René Char, 1976, Approximate Man and other Writings of Tristan Tzara, 1975, Mad Love, 1987, The Secret Art of Antonin Artaud, 1998, Ostinato, 2002; co-translator: Poems of André Breton, 1984, Communicating Vessels, 1990, Break of Day, 1999; chief editor Harper Collins World Reader, 1994, Manifesto: A Century of isms, 2001, Surrealist Painters and Poets, 2001, Mallarmé in Prose, 2001, Yale Anthology of Twentieth-Century French Poetry, 2004; contbr. articles to profl. jours. Decorated officier Palmes Académiques, France; fellow Guggenheim Found., 1972-73 NEH, 1979-80, Fulbright traveling fellow, 1972-73, Rockefeller Found. fellow, 1994, 2005; Getty scholar, 1990. Mem. MLA (exec. coun. 1973-77, v.p. 1982-83, pres. 1983-84), Am. Assn. Tchrs. French, Assn. for Study Dada and Surrealism (pres. 1982-86), Internat. Assn. Philosophy and Lit. (exec. bd. 1982—, chmn. 1984), Acad. Lit. Studies (pres. 1985), Am. Comparative Lit. Assn. (exec. com. 1981, v.p. 1986—, pres. 1989-91). Home: 140 E 81st St New York NY 10028-1805 Office: CUNY Grad Ctr 365 Fifth Ave New York NY 10016 Office Phone: 212-817-8371. E-mail: cawsma@aol.com.

CAWS, PETER JAMES, philosopher, educator; b. Southall, Eng., May 25, 1931; came to U.S., 1953; naturalized, 1995; s. Geoffrey Tulloh and Olive (Budden) C.; m. Mary Ann Rorison (div.); children: Hilary, Matthew; m. Nancy Breslin, Nov. 28, 1987; 1 child, Elisabeth. BS, U. London, 1952; MA, Yale U., 1954, PhD, 1956. Instr. natural sci. Mich. State U., 1956-57; asst. prof. philosophy U. Kans., 1957-60, assoc. prof., 1960-62, chmn. dept., 1961-62, Rose Morgan vis. prof., 1963; vis. prof. U. Costa Rica, 1961; exec. assoc. Carnegie Corp. N.Y., 1962-65, cons., 1965-67; prof. philosophy Hunter Coll., N.Y.C., 1965-82, chmn. dept., 1965-67; exec. officer Ph.D. program in philosophy CUNY, 1967-70, 81-82; Univ. prof. philosophy George Washington U., 1982—, dir. PhD Program in Human Scis., 1991-93; vis. prof. NYU, spring 1982, U.Md., spring 1985; tchr. New Sch. Social Research, 1965-67; mem. adv. bd. Learning Corp. of Am., 1968-74. Vis. scholar U. Kent, Canterbury, Eng., 1993-94; lectr. Smithsonian Resident Assocs. Program, 1988-95; mem. Coun. Philos. Studies, 1965-71; bd. dirs. Coordinating Coun. Lit. Mags., 1969-70; mem. Scientists Inst. for Pub. Info., 1967-94, treas., 1969-72, fellow, 1972-94, dir., 1975-80, vice chmn., 1975-79; mem. editl. bd. Environment, 1972-78; mem. bd. advisers, history of physics program Am. Inst. Physics, 1966-75; mem. NRC, 1967-70, Assembly Behavioral and Social Scis., 1973-77; nat. lectr. Sigma Xi, 1975-77; dir. Bicentennial Symposium of Philosophy; cons. in humanities LWV, 1978; vis. scholar Phi Beta Kappa, 1983-84; 1st Philip Morris Disting. lectr. in bus. and soc. Baruch Coll., N.Y.C., 1986; sr. fellow Christina River Inst., 2001—. Author: The Philosophy of Science, Systematic Account, 1965, Science and the Theory of Value, 1967, Sartre, 1979, Structuralism: A Philosophy for the Human Sciences, 1997, Yorick's World: Science and the Knowing Subject, 1993, The Capital Connection, 1993, Ethics from Experience, 1996; editor: Two Centuries of Philosophy in America, 1980, The Causes of Quarrel: Essays on Peace, War and Thomas Hobbes, 1989; mem. editl. bd. Jour. Enterprise Mgmt., 1976-81, Philosophy Documentation Ctr., mem. cmty. adv. bd. The News Jour., Wilmington, Del., 1998—2001. Bd. dirs. Newark (Del.) Symphony Orch., 2005—. Recipient Pres.'s medal Grad. Sch., CUNY, 1978; Am. Council Learned Socs. fellow Paris, 1972-73; Rockefeller Found. humanities fellow, 1979-80 Fellow AAAS (v.p. 1967); mem. Am. Philos. Assn. (dir., chmn. com. on internat. coop. 1974-84), Fedn. Internat. des Socs. de Philosophie (commn. on policy 1979-88, comité dir. 1978-88), Philosophy of Sci. Assn. (del.), Soc. Gen. Systems Rsch. (pres. 1966-67), Soc. Am. de Philosophie de Langue Française (v.p. 1989-92, pres. 1992-94), Elizabethan Club, Washington Philosophy Club (pres. 1988-89), Phi Beta Kappa (hon. Alpha chpt. D.C.). Home: 237 Cheltenham Rd Newark DE 19711-3617 Office: George Washington U Dept Philosophy Washington DC 20052-0001 Office Phone: 202-994-8685. E-mail: pcaws@gwu.edu.

CAWTHON, FRANK H., retired construction company executive; b. Kissimmee, Fla., Apr. 3, 1930; s. Benjamin Hill and Eva Elizabeth (Mullins) C.; m. Mary Elizabeth Dickert, July 10, 1959; 1 child, Frank H. Grad. high sch. Asst. sec.-treas. Orange Belt Truck & Tractor, Orlando, Fla., 1948-52, Murdock Constrn. Co., Inc., Orlando, 1954-59; sec.-treas. Amick Constrn. Co., Inc., Orlando, 1959-90; ret., 1990. Bd. dirs. Amick Constrn. Co., Inc. Bd. dirs. Conway Little League, Orlando, 1977. With U.S. Army, 1952-54. Mem. Cen. Fla. Rd. Bldrs. Assn. Democrat. Lutheran. Avocations: painting, gardening, fishing. Home: 391 Brushwood Ln Casselberry FL 32708-4955 Office: Amick Constrn Co 401 Ferguson Dr Orlando FL 32805-1009

CAWVEY, CLARENCE EUGENE, retired physician; b. Du Quoin, Ill., May 16, 1929; s. Clarence Eli and Lois Jane (Matheny) C.; m. Paulina Isabel Hincke, Sept. 12, 1953 (dec. Apr. 1973); children: Janet Edna, William Clarence, Paulina Ann, Jean Hincke; 1 stepchild, Douglas Lance Hester; m. Linda Mae Rice, Jan. 26, 1974. BA, Yale U., 1951; MD, U. Chgo., 1955. Diplomate Am. Bd. Family Practice. Intern Cook County Hosp., 1955-56; resident in psychiatry Brook Army Hosp., 1956-57; ptnr. Pinckneyville (Ill.) Med. Group, 1958—98; ret., 1998. Clin. asst. prof. Med. Sch. So. Ill. U., Springfield, 1976-2000, adv. com. continuing med. edn., 1977-2000; exec. com. Ctrl. Ill. Profl. Rev. Orgn., Champaign, 1988-2002; bd. dirs., chmn. First Nat. Bank, Pinckneyville. Founding mem., pres. Perry County Health Dept., Pinckneyville, 1970. Capt. U.S. Army, 1956-58. Fellow Am. Acad. Family Physicians; mem. AMA, Ill. State Med. Soc. (del. 1960-70), Perry County Med. Soc. Republican. Methodist. Avocations: skiing, photography, travel, gardening. Home: 204 W Laurel St Pinckneyville IL 62274-1019 Office Phone: 618-357-9393.

CAYETANO, BENJAMIN JEROME, former governor, former state senator and representative; b. Honolulu, Nov. 14, 1939; s. Bonifacio Marcos and Eleanor (Infante) C.; m. Vicky Tiu, 1997; children: Brandon, Janeen, Samantha, Cayetano, Marissa, William Liu. BA, UCLA, 1968; JD, Loyola U., 1971; LLD (hon.), U. Philippines, 1995; D in Pub. Svc. (hon.), Loyola Marymount U., 1998. Bar: Hawaii 1971. Practiced in, Honolulu, 1971-86; mem. Hawaii Ho. of Reps., 1975-78, Hawaii Senate, 1979-86; lt. gov. State of Hawaii, 1986-94, gov., 1994—2002. Adv. U. Hawaii Law Rev., 1982-84 Mem. bd. regents Chaminade U., 1980-83; chmn. Western Gov.'s Assn., 1999. Recipient UCLA Alumni award for excellence in pub. svc., 1993, UCLA Medal, 1995, Disting. Leadership award, UCLA John E. Anderson Sch. of Mgmt., 1995, Leadership award Harvard Found., 1996, Edward A. Dickson Alumnus of Yr. award UCLA, 1998, Disting. Alumnus of Yr., Loyola Law Sch., 2002. Democrat.*

CAYNE, BERNARD STANLEY, editor; b. NYC, Nov. 8, 1924; m. Helen M. Burgard, Apr. 11, 1953; children— Claudia Elizabeth, Douglas Andrew. Student, Cornell U., 1940-42; BS, Moravian Coll., 1945; postgrad., U. Pa., 1945-46; research fellow, Harvard U., 1953-55; MA, Columbia U., 1947. Head sci. dept. Adelphi Acad., 1946-47; instr. Bklyn. Coll., 1947-49; tchr. N.Y.C. Pub. Schs., 1948-49; head sci. sect., test devel. dept. Ednl. Testing Service, Princeton, N.J., 1949-53; dir. research Boston U. Coll. Basic Studies, 1953-54; sr. sci. editor Ginn & Co., Boston, 1955-61; v.p. Crowell-Collier Ednl. Corp., N.Y.C., 1961-68; exec. editor Collier's Ency., 1963-68, Collier's Ency. Yearbook, 1963-68; editor-in-chief Merit Students Ency., 1961-69, asst. editorial dir. corp., 1963-68; mng. editor, sch. div. Macmillan Co., 1968-69; editor-in-chief Ency. Americana, Danbury, Conn., 1969-90; v.p., editorial dir. Grolier, Inc., Danbury, 1980-90; creative dir. Readfern Group, Durham, NC, 1990—. Chmn. bd. editors: Harvard Edn. Rev, 1954. Fellow AAAS, Am. Psychol. Soc.; mem. N.Y. Acad. Scis., Am. Ednl. Rsch. Assn., Phi Delta Kappa. Home and Office: 2701 Pickett Rd #2044 Durham NC 27705

CAYNE, JAMES E. (JIMMY CAYNE), securities trader, diversified financial services company executive; b. Evanston, Ill., 1934; m. Patricia Cayne. Student, Purdue U. With Bonn Bush Mach, 1954-66, Lebenthal and Co., 1966-69; joined as retail salesman Bear Stearns and Co. Inc., 1969, gen. ptnr. retail dept., 1973, mem. office of the pres., 1985—88, sr. mng. dir., 1985, pres., 1988—2001, CEO, 1993—2001, chmn., 2001—, also bd. dirs. Served U.S. Army, Japan. Achievements include world-ranked bridge player, represented the US in multiple internat. competitions, including the 1990 championship. Avocation: bridge. Office: Bear Stearns & Co Inc 383 Madison Ave New York NY 10179*

CAYTAS, IVO GEORGE, lawyer; b. Plovdiv, Bulgaria, Feb. 3, 1958; s. George I. and Hilda (Plankl) Kaitasow. MA in Diplomacy, U. St Gallen, Switzerland, 1982, PhD in Law, 1984, PhD in Fin., 1986; LLM, Yale U., 1986. Bar: D.C. 1997, U.S. Ct. Internat. Trade, U.S. Claims Ct., U.S. Tax Ct., U.S. Dist. Ct. (so. and ea. dists.) N.Y. 1992, (no. and ctrl. dists.) Calif. 1992, U.S. Ct. Appeals (1st-11th cirs., fed. and D.C. cir.), U.S. Supreme Ct. 1996. Asst. to chmn. IMAG Corp., Vienna, Austria, 1979-80; ptnr. Caytas & Cie, St. Gallen, 1984-89, CCCC, St. Gallen, 1989-91; mng. dir. Swissconsult Corp., N.Y.C., 1990-91; pres., gen. counsel Swiss Am. Group Inc., N.Y.C., 1991-95; ptnr. Caytas & Assocs., 1996—. Bd. dirs. The London Ct. of Internat. Abritration. Author: Investment Banking, 1988, Global Political Risk, Modern Financial Instruments, 1992, Transnational Legal Practice, 1992; contbr. articles to profl. publs. Fellow Swiss Nat. Sci. Found., 1985, 88, Max Planck Inst., 1987; recipient Walther-Hug Found. award, 1984. Mem. ABA (sect. of internat. law and practice, internat. investment com., internat. taxation com.), Assn. of Bar of City of N.Y. (com. on govt. ethics), Calif. Bar Assn. (internat. law com., task force on internat. legal svcs.), Yale Club. Roman Catholic. Office: 146 W 57th St New York NY 10019-3301

CAYTON, DARRELL BROWNING, JR., lawyer; b. Washington, N.C., Oct. 7, 1962; s. Darrell Browning, Sr. and Peggy (Walker) C.; m. Paula Ann Hollowell, Aug. 6, 1994; 1 child, Douglas Browning. BSBA, U. N.C., 1984; JD, Campbell U., 1987. Bar: N.C. 1987; U.S. Dist. Ct. (ea. dist.) N.C. 1987. Assoc. Gaskins and Gaskins, Pa., Washington, N.C., 1987-90; pvt. practice Washington, 1990—. Mem. Walker Rd. Hunting Club, E. Carolina Hunting Club. Avocation: hunting. Office: 407 N Market St Washington NC 27889-4935 Office Phone: 919-975-3762.

CAYUSO, EMILY ANN, instructional coordinator; b. San Antonio, Oct. 23, 1954; d. Armando Octavio Cayuso and Anna Maria Barrera. BS in Elem. Edn., U. Tex., 1976; MEd, U. Incarnate Word, San Antonio, 1998. Cert. master reading tchr. Region 20, spl. edn. educator, deficient vision educator, elem. edn. educator, mental retardation educator, reading specialist. Tchr. spl. edn. Austin (Tex.) Ind. Sch. Dist., 1976—78, San Antonio (Tex.) Ind. Sch. Dist., 1978—84, tchr. elem. edn., 1984—98, reading recovery tchr., 1998—2002, campus instrnl. coord., 2002—. Ednl. cons. Ednl. Svc. Ctr. Region 20, San Antonio, 1998—. Author: Designing Teacher Study Groups, 2004, Flip for Comprehension, 2005. Mem.: Alamo Reacing Coun., Tex. Reading Assn., Internat. Reading Assn. Avocations: needlepoint, reading, antiques, gardening. Office: Will Rogers Elem 620 McIlvaine San Antonio TX 78212 E-mail: ecayuso@saisd.net.

CAYWOOD, CLARKE LAWRENCE, marketing educator, public relations executive; b. Madison, Wis., Mar. 13, 1947; s. Fred Lawrence and Marjorie Caroline (Clarke) C.; m. Mary Margaret Westing, Dec. 15, 1973; children: Matthew Shields, Emily Margaret, Graham Clarke. BBA, U. Wis., 1969, PhD, 1985; MPA, U. Tex., 1972. Asst. to gov. Exec. Office, Madison, 1969-70; research assoc. Lyndon Baines Johnson Sch. Pub. Affairs, U. Tex., Austin, 1971-72; legis. officer Office of Atty. Gen., Madison, 1972-74; exec. dir. Friends of Channel 21, Sta. WHA-TV, Madison, 1975-76; lectr. U. Wis., Whitewater, 1976-78; asst. prof. Marquette U., Milw., 1978-87; vis. asst. prof. U. Wis., Madison, 1987-89; assoc. prof. and dir. Medill Sch. Journalism, Pub. Rels., Integrated Mktg. Comm. Northwestern U., Evanston, 1989—. Bd. dirs. Biz360, DevLab, Direct Selling Edn. Found., Washington, Nat. Telemedia Coun., Madison; cons. Sony, Emerson Electric, Nat. Pub. Radio, IBM Corp., Scania, Kreab, Dairy Mgmt., Inc., Budgetel Corp., Wis., IBM-Europe, State of Wis. Author: The Handbook of Strategic Public Relations and Integrated Communication, 1997; pub. Jour. Integrated Comm.; contbr. articles to profl. jours. Adv. council Office of Lt. Gov., Madison, 1988; del. Wis. Rep. Party Conv., 1974-88; campaign dir. Scott McCallum, Wis., 1986; trustee Mus. Contemporary Art, Chgo.; bd. dirs. Chgo. Symphony. Mem.: Am. Acad. Advt., Am. Mktg. Assn., Assn. Edn. on Jour. and Mass Comm., Arthur W. Page Soc. (trustee), Pub. Rels. Soc. Am. (Silver Anvil co-chair, Educator of the Yr.), Beta Gamma Sigma. Republican. Presbyterian. Home: 100 Old Green Bay Rd Winnetka IL 60093-1512 Office: Northwestern U Medill Sch Evanston IL 60208-0001 Office Phone: 847-491-5665. E-mail: c-caywood@northwestern.edu.

CAZALAS, MARY REBECCA WILLIAMS, lawyer, nurse; b. Atlanta, Nov. 11, 1927; d. George Edgar and Mary Annie (Slappey) Williams; m. Albert Joseph Cazalas (dec.). *Her great-great-grandfather, General John Coffee, fought in the Battle of New Orleans. His son, Peter Coffee married Mary Donelson, who was niece of Mrs. Andrew Jackson. Their son, Major John A. Coffee, served in the Civil War. His daughter, Mary Stevens Coffee, married Dr. John George Slappey, prominent physician at Jeffersonville, Georgia. His grandfather was Hans (John) George Slappey, who fought in the Revolution, and his father was Robert Rutherford Slappey. His daughter, Mary Annie Slappey, married George Edgar Wiliams. His mother was Sarah Cobb of Kosiesco, Mississippi. He graduated from Mercer University and was Chief Dispatcher of Central of Georgia Railroad.* BS in Pre-medicine, Oglethorpe U., Atlanta, 1954; MS in Anatomy, Emory U., 1960; JD, Loyola U., 1967, Loyola U., New Orleans, 1967. RN, Ga.; Bar: La. 1967, U.S. Dist. Ct. (ea. dist.) La. 1967, U.S. Ct. Appeals (5th cir.) 1972, U.S. Supreme Ct. 1975, U.S. Ct. Appeals (fed. cir.) 1999. Gen. duty nurse, 1948-68; instr. maternity nursing St. Josephs Infirmary Sch. Nursing, Atlanta, 1954-59; med. rschr. in urology Tulane U. Sch. Medicine, New Orleans, 1961-65; legal rschr. for presiding judge La. Ct. Appeals (4th cir.), New Orleans, 1965-71; pvt. practice New Orleans, 1967-71; asst. U.S. atty., 1971-79; sr. trial atty. Equal Employment Opportunity Commn., New Orleans, 1979-84; owner Cazalas Apts., New Orleans, 1962—. Lectr. in field. Contbr. articles to profl. jours. Bd. advisors Loyola U. Sch. Law, New Orleans, 1974, v.p. adv. bd., 1975; active New Orleans Drug Abuse Adv. Com., 1976-80; task force Area Agy. on Aging, 1976-80, pres. coun. Loyola U., 1978—; adv. bd. Odyssey House, Inc., New Orleans, 1973; chmn. womens com. Fed. Exec. Bd., 1974; bd. dirs. Bethlehem House of Bread, 1975-79. Named Hon. La. State Senator, 1974; recipient Superior Performance award U.S. Dept. Justice, 1974, Cert. Appreciation Fed. Exec. Bd., 1975-78, Rev. E.A. Doyle award, 1976, Commendation for tchg. Guam Legislature, 1977, Career Achievement award Mt. de Sales Acad., 1995. Mem. Am. Judicature Soc., La. Sate Bar Assn., Fed. Bus. Assn. (v.p. 1976—, pres. 1976-78, bd. dirs. 1972-75), Fed. Bar Assn. (1st v.p. 1973, pres. New Orleans chpt. 1974-75, nat. coun. 1974-79), Assn. Women Lawyers, Nat. Health Lawyers Assn., DAR, Bus. and Profl. Womens Club, Am. Heart Assn., Emory Alumni Assn., Oglethorpe U. Alumni Assn., Loyola U. Alumni Assn. (bd. dirs. 1974-75, 77, v.p. 1976), Jefferson Parish Hist. Soc., Sierra Club, Zonta, Leconte Hon. Sci. Soc., Phi Delta Delta (merged with Phi Alpha Delta pres. 1970-72, bd. dirs., vice justice 1974-75), Alpha Epsilon Delta, Phi Sigma. Democrat.

CAZALOT, CLARENCE P., JR., oil industry executive; BS in Geology, La. State. U. Various positions with Texaco, 1972—2000, v.p., 1999—2000; pres., CEO Marathon Oil, 2000—. Mem. bd. advisors Maguire Energy Inst.; bd. dirs. Baker Hughes, US-Saudi Arabian Bus. Coun.; mem bd. mgrs. Marathon Ashland Petroleum LLC. Trustee Spindletop Charities; bd. dirs. Sam Houston Area Coun. Boy Scouts Am. Mem.: NAM (bd. dirs.), Am. Petroleum Inst. (bd. dirs.), All-American Wildcatters, Nat. Petroleum Coun., Am. Assn. Petroleum Geologists. Achievements include Member 25 Yr. Club, Petroleum Industry. Office: Marathon Oil 5555 San Felipe Rd Houston TX 77056

CAZDEN, COURTNEY B(ORDEN), education educator; b. Chgo., Nov. 30, 1925; d. John and Courtney (Letts) Borden; m. Norman Cazden (div. 1971); children: Elizabeth, Joanna. BA, Radcliffe Coll., 1946; MEd, U. Ill., 1953; EdD, Harvard U., 1965. Elem. tchr. pub. schs., N.Y., Conn., Calif., 1947-49, 54-61, 74-75; asst. prof. edn. Harvard U., Cambridge, Mass., 1965-68, assoc. prof., 1968-71, prof., 1971-95, Charles William Eliot prof. emerita, 1996—. Vis. prof. U. N.Mex. summer 1980, U. Alaska, Fairbanks, summer 1982, U. Auckland, N.Z., spring 1983, Bread Loaf Sch. of English, Vt., 1986—; chairperson bd. trustees Ctr. Applied Linguistics, Washington, 1981-85. Author: Child Language and Education, 1972, Classroom Discourse: The Language of Teaching and Learning, 2d edit., 2001, Whole Language plus Essays on Literacy in the US and New Zealand, 1992; co-editor: Functions of Language in the Classroom, 1972, English Plus: Issues in Bilingual Education, 1990; editor: Language in Early Childhood Education, rev. edit., 1981. Trustee Highland Ednl. and Rsch. Ctr., New Market, Tenn., 1982-84; bd. dirs. Feminist Press, Old Westbury, N.Y., 1982-84; clk. New Eng. regional office Am. Friends Svc. Com., Cambridge, 1989-92. Recipient Alumna Recognition award Radcliffe Coll., 1988; fellow Ctr. Advanced Study in Behavioral Scis., Stanford, Calif., 1978-79; Fulbright research fellow, New Zealand, 1987. Mem. Nat. Acad. Edn., Coun. on Anthropology and Edn. (pres. 1981, George & Louise Spindler award 1994), Am. Assn. Applied Linguistics (pres. 1985), Nat. Conf. on Rsch. in English (pres. 1993-94), Am. Ednl. Rsch. Assn. (exec. com. 1981-84, award for disting. contbns. to ednl. rsch. 1986). Mem. Soc. Of Friends. Office: Harvard U Grad Sch Edn Appian Way Cambridge MA 02138

CAZEAUX, ISABELLE ANNE MARIE, retired music educator; b. N.Y.C., Feb. 24, 1926; d. François and Marie-Anne (Fort) C. BA magna cum laude, Hunter Coll., 1945; MA in Musicology, Smith Coll., 1946; MS in Libr. Sci., Columbia U., 1959, PhD in Musicology, 1961. Licence d'Enseignement, Ecole Normale de Musique, Paris, 1950; Première Médaille, Conservatoire Nat. de Musique, Paris, 1950. Sr. music cataloguer, head sect. music and phonorecords cataloguing N.Y. Pub. Libr., N.Y.C., 1957-63; mem. faculty Manhattan Sch. Music, N.Y.C., 1969-82, Bryn Mawr Coll., Pa., 1963-92, chmn. dept., 1978-92, prof., 1972-92, Alice Carter Dickerman prof. emeritus music, 1992—. Vis. prof. Douglass Coll. Rutgers U., New Brunswick, N.J., 1978. Author: French Music in the 15th and 16th Centuries, 1975; editor: The Chansons of Claudin de Sermisy, 1974; translator: The Memoirs of Philippe de Commynes, 1969, 2d vol., 1973; contbr. articles to profl. jours. Recipient Libby van Arsdale prize Hunter Coll., 1945; fellow Smith Coll., 1945-46, Inst. Internat. Edn., 1948-50; Martha Baird Rockefeller Fund grantee, 1971-72, Herman Goldman Found. grantee, 1980. Mem. Am. Musicol. Soc. (coun. 1968-70, com. on status of women 1974-76), Music Libr. Assn., Soc. Française de Musicologie, Internat. Musicol. Soc. Roman Catholic. Avocations: opera, concerts. Home: 415 E 72nd St Apt 5FE New York NY 10021-4412

CAZEL, FRED A., JR., history professor; b. Asheville, N.C., Feb. 25, 1921; s. Fred Augustus Cazel and Agnes Miller Petrie; m. Ann Arie Jane Peters, 1946 (dec. 1983). AB, U. N.C., 1941; MA, Johns Hopkins U., 1943, PhD, 1948. Instr. Johns Hopkins U., Balt., 1947—48; asst. prof. U. Conn., Storrs, 1948—54, assoc. prof., 1954—62, prof., 1962—88, prof. emeritus, 1988—. Vis. asst. prof. U. Minn., Mpls., 1950; vis. prof. U. Calif., Berkeley, 1965—66; presenter in field. Editor: Feudalism and Liberty: Articles and Addresses of Sidney Painter, 1961, Foreign Accounts, 1982; co-editor (with Annarie P. Cazel): Early Subsidy Rolls, 1983; contbr. articles to profl. jours. Mayor Town of Mansfield, Conn., 1991—97, justice of peace, 1968—. John Martin Vincent fellow, Johns Hopkins U., 1941—43, 1946—47, Gastav Bissing fellow, 1951—52, Fulbright fellow, King's Coll., London, 1955—56. Fellow: Royal Hist. Soc.; mem.: AAUP, Conn. Acad. Arts and Scis., Conn. Hist. Soc., New Eng. History Tchrs. Assn., New England Medieval Conf. (exec. sec.), New Eng. Hist. Assn. (past pres.), Ecclesiastical Hist. Soc., Pipe Roll Soc., Conf. Brit. Studies, Medieval Acad. Am., Am. Hist. Assn., Phi Beta Kappa. Democrat. Avocations: gardening, travel, reading, local history. Home: 309 Gurleyville Rd Storrs Mansfield CT 06268-1439

CEBULKO, KAREN LEE, nursing consultant; b. Red Bank, NJ, Nov. 19, 1960; d. Edward Charles Apy and Helen Lee; m. Michael Richard Cebulko, Oct. 28, 1994; children: Courtney, Ryan, Nicole. BSN, U. SC, 1984. RN NJ, 1984, cert. legal nursing consultant, Med.-Legal Cons. Inst., Houston, 2001, nursing life care planner, NJ, 2004. RN Riverview Med. Ctr., Red Bank, NJ, 1984—90; nurse mgr., dir. admissions and mktg. Garden State Rehab. Hosp., Toms River, NJ, 1990—92; nurse adminstr., dir. admissions and bus. devel. New Beginnings at Lakehurst, NJ, 1992—94; pres., nurse cons. Healthcare 2000, Oceanport, NJ, 1994—99; regional nurse mgr., dir. case mgmt. and bus. devel. Ctrl. Jersey Rehab., Toms River, 1997—99; legal nurse cons., life care planner/analyst Oceanport, NJ, 1999—. Spkr. in field. Author: (tng. manual) Assessing Head Injury and Spinal Cord Injury Patients for Admission, 1991, Seven Systems of Success, 1999; contbr. (columns) NJ Am. Assn. Legal Nurse Consultants publ., 2002—. Mem. lifeline adv. bd. Ctrl. Jersey Red Cross, 1994—96; mem. corp. adv. com. Nat. Coun. Alcohol and Drug Abuse, 1994—95. Mem.: Nat. Alliance Cert. Legal Nurse Consultants, Am. Assn. Legal Nurse Consultants (pres. NJ chpt. 2005—, dir. at lg. 2002—03, edn. chair 2001—03), Am. Assn. Nurse Life Care Planners. Methodist. Avocation: running. Office Phone: 732-616-0400. Office Fax: 732-542-0801. E-mail: kcebulko@yahoo.com.

CECERE, DOMENICO, homebuilding company executive; b. June 10, 1949; BA in Fin. and Acctg., U. Okla. V.p. fin. indsl. controls Honeywell, Inc., v.p. fin. home and bldg. controlling bus., v.p. fin. European bus. Brussels; v.p., contr. Owens Corning, Toledo, 1993-95, pres. roofing sys. bus., 1995-98, sr. v.p., CFO, 1998-2000, exec. v.p., COO, 2000-01; cons. Gryphon Investors; sr. v.p., CFO KB Home, L.A., 2002—. Office: 7th Fl 10990 Wilshire Blvd Los Angeles CA 90024

CECH, THOMAS ROBERT, chemistry and biochemistry educator; b. Chgo., Dec. 8, 1947; m. Carol Lynn Martinson; children: Allison E., Jennifer N. BA in Chemistry, Grinnell Coll., 1970; PhD in Chem., U. Calif., Berkeley, 1975; DSc (hon.), Grinnell Coll., 1987, U. Chgo., 1991, Drury Coll., 1994, Colo. Coll., 1999, U. Md., Baltimore County, 2000, Williams Coll., 2000, Charles U., Prague, 2002, Ohio State U., 2003, Moscow State U., 2004. Postdoctoral fellow dept. biology MIT, Cambridge, Mass., 1975—77; from asst. prof. to assoc. prof. chemistry U. Colo., Boulder, 1978—83, prof. chemistry and biochemistry also molecular cellular and devel. biology, 1983—, disting. prof., 1990—; rsch. prof. Am. Cancer Soc., 1987—; investigator Howard Hughes Med. Inst., 1988—99, pres., 2000—. Co-chmn. Nucleic Acids Gordon Conf., 1984; Phillips disting. visitor Haverford Coll., 1984; Vivian Ernst meml. lectr. Brandeis U., 1984; Cynthia Chan meml. lectr. U. Calif., Berkeley; mem. Welch Found. Symposium, 1985; Danforth lectr. Grinnell Coll., 1986; Pfizer lectr. Harvard U., 1986; Hastings lectr., 92; Verna and Marrs McLean lectr. Baylor Coll. Medicine, 1987; Harvey lectr., 87; Mayer lectr. MIT, 1987; HHMI lectr., 89; T.Y. Shen lectr., 94; Martin D. Kamen disting. lectureship U. Calif., San Diego, 1988; Alfred Burger lectr. U. Va., 1988; Berzelius lectr. Karolinska Inst., 1988; Osamu Hayaishi lectr. Internat. Union Biochemistry, Prague, 1988; Beckman lectr. U. Utah, 1989; Max Tishler lectr. Merck, 1989; Abbott vis. scholar U. Chgo., 1989; Herriott lectr. Johns Hopkins U., 1990; J.T. Baker lectr., 90; G.N. Lewis lectr. U. Calif., Berkeley, 1990; Sonneborn lectr. Ind. U., 1991; Sternbach lectr. Yale U., 1991; W. Pauli lectr., Zurich, 92; Carter-Wallace lectr. Princeton U., 1992; Stetten lectr. NIH, 1992; Dauben lectr. U. Wash., 1992; Marker lectr. U. Md., 1993; Hirschmann lectr. Oberlin Coll., 1993; Beach lectr. Purdue U., 1993; Abe White lectr. Syntex, 1993; Robbins lectr. Pomona Coll., 1994; Bren lectr. U. Calif., Irvine, 1994; Wawzonek lectr. U. Iowa, 1994; Sumner lectr. Cornell U., 1994; Steenbock lectr. U. Wis., 1995; Murachi lectr. FAOB Congress, Sydney, 1995; Streck award lectr. U. Nebr., 1996; Gardner-Davern lectr. U. Utah, 1996; Priestley lectr. Pa. State U., 1996; Beckman lectr. Calif. Inst. Tech., 1996; Lemieux lectr. U. Alta., Canada, 1997; Hogg Award lectr. M.D. Anderson Cancer Ctr., 1997; DeCoursey Nobel lectr. Trinity U., 1998; Tschirgi lectr. U. Calif., San Diego, 1998; Boxer Meml. lectr. Robert Wood Johnson Med. Sch., 1998; Thomas lectr. U. Mo., 1999; Bachmann Meml. lectr. U. Mich., 1999; DuPont-Marshall lectr. U. Pa., 1999; Feodor Lynen lectr. Mosbach Germany, 2001; The Morgenthaler lectureship Case Wetern Res. U., 2001; Tercentenary Silliman lectr. Yale U., 2001; Nathans lectr. Johns Hopkins U., 2002; Tishler Prize lectr. Harvard U., 2002; Furlaud Disting. lectr. The Rockefeller U., 2002; non-resident fellow Salk Inst., 1999. Assoc. editor Cell, 1986—87, RNA Jour., mem. editl. bd. Genes and Devel.; contbg. editor: Sci. mag., 1999. Trustee Grinnell Coll. Named Westerner of Yr., Denver Post, 1986; named to Esquire Mag. Register, 1985; recipient medal, Am. Inst. Chemists, 1970, Rsch. Career Devel. award, Nat. Cancer Inst., 1980—85, Young Sci. award, Passano Found., 1984, Harrison Howe award, 1984, Pfizer award, 1985, U.S Steel award, NAS, 1987, V.D. Mattia award, 1987, Louisa Gross Horowitz prize, Columbia U., 1988, Newcombe-Cleveland award, AAAS, 1988, Heineken prize, Royal Netherlands Acad. Arts and Scis., 1988, Gairdner Found. Internat. award, 1988, Lasker Basic Med. Rsch. award, 1988, Rosenstiel award, Brandeis U., 1989, Warren Triennial prize, 1989, Nobel Prize in chemistry, 1989, Hopkins medal, Brit. Biochem. Soc., 1992, Feodor Lynen medal, 1995, Nat. Sci. medal, 1995, Mike Hogg award, M.D. Anderson, 1997, Wright prize, Harvey Mudd Coll., 1998, Gregor Mendel medal, Acad. Sci. Czech Republic, 2002; fellow, NSF, 1970—75, Pub. Health Svc.; rsch. fellow, Nat. Cancer Inst., 1975—77, Guggenheim fellow, 1985—86. Mem.: NAS, AAAS, RNA Soc. (v.p. 1993—96), European Molecular Biology Orgn., Am. Philos. Soc., Am. Acad. Arts and Scis., Am. Soc. Biochem. Molecular Biology, Inst. Medicine. Office: Howard Hughes Med Inst 4000 Jones Bridge Rd Chevy Chase MD 20815-6789 Office Phone: 301-215-8550. Office Fax: 301-215-8558. Business E-Mail: president@hhmi.org.*

CECHMANEK, ROMAN, professional hockey player; b. Gottwaldov, Czech Republic, Mar. 2, 1971; Goalie Phila. Flyers, 2000—03, Los Angeles Kings, 2003—. Named to All-Star World team as a rookie, 2000—01; recipient Olympic Gold medal, Czech Republic team, 1988. Office: LA Kings Staples Ctr 1111 S Figueroa St Los Angeles CA 90015

CECI, JESSE ARTHUR, violinist; b. Phila., Feb. 2, 1924; s. Luigi Concezio and Catherine Marie (Marotta) C.; m. Catherine Annette Stevens, Aug. 5, 1979. BS, Juilliard Sch. Music, 1951; license de concert, L'Ecole Normale de Musique, Paris, 1954; MusM, Manhattan Sch. Music, 1971. Assoc. concertmaster New Orleans Philharm. Orch., 1953-54; violinist Boston Symphony Orch., 1954-59, N.Y. Philharm. Orch., N.Y., 1959-62, Esterhazy Orch., N.Y.C., 1962-68; concertmaster Denver Symphony Orch., 1974-89, Colo. Symphony Orch., 1989-95. Over 50 performances of 22 major works; mem. Zimbler Sinfonietta, Boston, 1957-59; participant Marlboro Festival Chamber Orch. Vt., summmers 1960-62, 65, Marlboro Festival Chamber Orch. European-Israeli tour, 1965, Grand Teton Festival, Wyo., 1972, with Denver Duo, 1975—, N.Mex. Festival, Taos, 1980, Carmel (Calif.) Bach Festival, 1987—, Whistler (B.C., Can.) Mozart Festival, 1989-90, Bear Valley (Calif.) Festival, 1995—, Mendocino (Calif.) Festival, 1996—; mem. faculty Congress of Strings, Dallas, 1985, N.Y. Coll. Music, 1961-71, NYU, 1971-74, U. Colo., 1975-79; guest mem. faculty Univ. Denver, 1986; mem., assoc. concertmaster Casals Festival Orch., San Juan, P.R., 1963-77; violinist Cleve. Orch. fgn. tours, 1967, 73, 78, Cin. Symphony Orch. world tour, 1966; 1st violinist N.Y. String Quartet in-residence at U. Maine, Orono, summer 1969; guest violinist Fla. West Coast Symphony, Sarasota, 1993-98; concertmaster Minn. Orch., summers 1970-71, Denver Chamber Orch., 1985-90; guest concertmaster Pitts. Symphony Orch., Pitts., L.A., 1988, mem. N.Y. Philharmonia Chamber Ensemble in-residence at Hopkins Ctr., Dartmouth U., summer 1973; recitalist, Paris, 1963, Amsterdam, 1963, recitalist Carnegie Recital Hall, N.Y.C., 1963, Town Hall, N.Y.C., 1968, 70, Alice Tully Hall, N.Y.C., 1972; fgn. tour Pitts. Symphony Orch., 1989; soloist Royal Chamber Orch. Japan, 1997-98, appointment to concert master position of the Royal Chamber Orchestra and the Royal Metropolitan Orchestra of Japan, 1999—. Cpl. U.S. Army, 1943-46, PTO. Fulbright fellow Paris, 1951-52 Democrat. Roman Catholic. Office: Colo Symphony Orch 1031 13th St Denver CO 80204-2156

CECIL, ALEX THOMSON, travel executive; b. Birmingham, Ala., May 5, 1930; s. Alex Thomson and Martha (Lamar) C.; m. Jennifer Brown, Dec. 2, 1962 (div. 1976); children: Thurston, Lila; m. Jacqueline Bottger, May 10, 1980 (div. 1997); children: Julia, Caroline; m. E. Ritter, May 5, 1997; 1 child, Henry. Student, Ohio State U., 1950-52. Chmn., CEO, owner Auto-Europe, Inc., N.Y.C., 1953—97; chmn. Cognoscenti Health Inst., Orlando, Fla., 1999—. Office Phone: 617-492-4710. E-mail: acecil@europe.com.

CECIL, ALLAN, corporate communications executive; V.p. corp. comm., investor rels. National Gypsum, Mesa Petroleum Co.; v.p. investor rels. & corp. comm. Sonoco Products, Hartsville, SC, 1996—98, v.p. investor rels. & corp. affairs, mem. exec. com. Office: Sonoco Products One N 2d St Hartsville SC 29550

CECIL, BONNIE SUSAN, elementary school educator; b. Louisville, Sept. 29, 1951; d. Robert Lawrence and Mary Hedwig (Kluesner) C. BA in Edn., U. Ky., 1973; MS in Edn., Ind. U., 1978; postgrad., U. Louisville, 1988—. Tchr. grades 1-4 Roosevelt Cmty. Sch., Jefferson County, Ky., 1972-80; tchr. ages 6 and 7 Wandle Primary Sch., London, 1980-81; tchr. 1st grade Foster Elem. Sch., Jefferson County, 1981-82; tchr. ages 5-8 Brown Sch. Primary, Jefferson County, 1982—. Co-dir., instr. writing process for tchrs. Ky. Writing Insts. I and II, Boone County, 1986-88; instr. writing process insvc. Jefferson County Pub. Schs., 1988-89, workshop presenter on environ. edn., 1990, 92, supr. student tchrs., 1989-90, 92, 94, 95, 97; instr. lang. arts U. Louisville, 1990-91; participant Fulbright Tchr. Exch. Program, London, 1980-81, Brown Sch. Dream Team, 1992; presenter ann. conf. Ky. Assn. Edn. Young Children-Louisville Assn. for Children Under Seven, 1990; presenter Cmty. Learning Resource Conf., 1992; participant Louisville Writing Project, 1984-85, premier class Leadership Edn., 1986-87. Tchr. rep. J. Graham Brown Sch. PTSA, 1983-90, 92-97; tchr. rep. site-based decision making coun., 1996—; bd. dirs. Roosevelt Cmty. Sch., Inc., 1973-76; creator, dir. summer reading and writing program Portland Mus., Louisville, 1985; treas. Louisville Homefront Performances, Inc., 1986-87, sec., 1988-90, bd. dirs. 1984-96; state bd. dirs. Cmty. Farm Alliance, 2001-2002, v.p. Henry County chpt., 2001-. Recipient Golden Apple Achievement award Ashland Oil Co., 1989, Individual Tchr. Achievement award, 1992, Nat. Educator award Milken Family Found., 1994, ExCel award WHAS-TV and PNC Bank, 1995; named Jefferson County Elem. Tchr. of Yr., 1992, Ky. Elem. Tchr. of Yr., 1993, Ky. Tchr. of Yr., 1993, Milken Family Nat. Educator Project Mentor, 1998; grantee Ky. Arts Coun., 1986-87, Jefferson County Pub. Schs.-U. Louisville, 1989-91, U. Louisville, 1991, Rosenbaum Found., 1998; named Milken Virtual Workspace Mentor, 1998; inducted into The Commonwealth Inst. for Tchrs., 1998. Mem. ASCD, NEA, Assn. Childhood Edn. Internat., Nat. Coun. Tchrs. English (conf. presenter 1988, chmn., presenter nat. conf. 1992), Ky. Edn. Assn., Jefferson County Tchrs. Assn., Leadership Edn. Alumni Assn. Avocations: music, gardening, pets. Office: J Graham Brown Sch 546 S 1st St Louisville KY 40202-1816 E-mail: bcecil2@jefferson.K12.ky.us.

CECIL, CHARLES HARKLESS, artist, educator; b. Kansas City, Mo., May 12, 1945; s. Charles F. and Alice (Harkless) C.; m. Isabelle Claude Jeanne Touren, Dec. 30, 1982; 1 dau., Charlotte Alice Marcelle. BA, Haverford Coll., 1967; postgrad., Yale U., 1967-69. Co-dir. Studio Cecil-Graves, Florence, Italy, 1983-91; dir. Charles H. Cecil Studios, Florence, 1991—; instr. Villa Schifanoia, Grad. Studio Fine Arts, Florence, 1983-87. Exhibited in group shows at N.A.D., N.Y.C., 1979, 80, Dallas, 1983; represented in permanent collections at: Portrait Gallery, Haverford Coll., Pa., West Bend Gallery Fine Arts, Wis; executed: portrait Dr. Jonathon Rhodes for Am. Philos. Soc.; 10th Anniversary Exhibit of Charles H. Cecil Studios, London, 2001. NDEA grantee, 1967-69; Elizabeth Greenshields Found. grantee, 1970-73; John F. Stacey Found. grantee, 1980; R.H. Ives Gammell Studios Trust grantee, 1986-2001; recipient Julius T. Hallgarten First prize for oil painting, 1979, Benjamin Altman Second prize for landscape 155 Ann. Exhbn. Nat. Acad. Design, 1980 Home: Via Pandolfini 21 50122 Florence Italy Office: Charles H Cecil Studios Borgo San Frediano 68 50124 Florence Italy Office Phone: 0039-055285102. E-mail: cecilstudios@dada.it.

CECIL, DAVID ROLF, mathematician, educator; b. Tulsa, July 12, 1935; s. Neil McKinley and Ola Ethel (Turner) C.; m. Betty Lou Poe, June 14, 1958; 1 child, Eric Alan. Student (Pitts. Plate Glass Co. scholar), Carnegie Inst. Tech., 1954-55; BA, U. Tulsa, 1958; postgrad (fellow), Tulane U., 1958-59; MS, Okla. State U., 1960, PhD, 1962. Grad. teaching asst. Okla. State U., 1959-62; sr. research mathematician Atlantic Refining Co., 1962; asst. prof., then assoc. prof. math. North Tex. State U., Denton, 1962-69; prof. math. Butler U., Indpls., 1969-70, Tex. A&M U., Kingsville, 1970—, chmn. dept., 1980-85, asst. dean coll. arts and scis., 2000—04. Cons. Edn. Service Ctr. Region II, 1979-80, Air Force Office Sci. Rsch., Wilford Hall Med. Ctr., Tex., 1988-90; organizer Kingsville Computer Club, 1980; mem. credit com. Kingsville Area Educators Fed. Credit Union, 1979— Contbr. articles to math. jours. Faculty fellow North Tex. State U., 1968-69; Faculty fellow Tex. A&I U., 1971-73 Fellow Tex. Acad. Scis. (v.p. 1999, pres. 2001-2002); mem. Assn. for Computing Machinery, Am. Statistical Assn., Sigma Xi. Clubs: Kingsville Radio (pres. 1974). Methodist. Office: Tex A&M U Dept Math Kingsville TX 78363 Office Phone: 361-593-3198. Business E-Mail: d-cecil@tamuk.edu.

CECIL, DONALD, retired investment company executive; b. N.Y.C., Jan. 3, 1927; s. Leopold and Viola C.; m. Jane Grossman, Mar. 5, 1953; children: Alec, Leslie (twins). BS in Applied Econ., Yale U., 1947. V.p. Cecil Mfg. Co., 1947—58; securities analyst Ira Haupt & Co., 1958—61; sr. instl. rsch. analyst Eastman Dillon Union Securities, N.Y.C., 1961—63; from dir. instl. rsch. to sr. v.p. Shearson Hamill, Inc., N.Y.C., 1963—70; pres. Shearson Hamill Mgmt. Co., 1966—70; founding ptnr. Cumberland Assocs., N.Y.C., 1970—82; ret., 1982. Trustee 45 Merrill Lynch domestic, global and offshore mutual funds and trusts, 1977-99; bd. dirs. Rycote Adv. Panel, Geneva, Switzerland, Grey Global Group, 1978-87; chmn. valuation bd. Biotech. Investments, Ltd., London, 1986-99; dep. chmn. Internat. Biotech. Trust Ltd., London, 1994-2001; chmn. dirs. svc. com., Investment Com. Inst., Washington, 1996-2000. Chmn. Bd. Transp., Westchester County, White Plains, N.Y., 1978—; vice-chmn. bd. trustees SUNY Purchase Coll. Found., 1987—; sponsor I Have a Dream Found., Mt. Vernon, N.Y., 1987—; chmn. bd. Friends of Neuberger Mus., Purchase, 1989-91; sponsor, writing thru The Arts Program, Neuberger Mus., 1993-, sponsor Jandon Scholars Program Westchester County, 1999—; dir., treas. Ctr. for Ednl. Innovation/Pub. Edn. Assn. Mem. Chartered Fin. Analysts (cert.), N.Y. Econ. Club, N.Y. Soc. Security Analysts. Avocations: theater, travel, tennis. Office: Cumberland Assocs Rm 3803 1114 Avenue Of The Americas New York NY 10036-7703 Office Phone: 212-536-9727.

CECIL, ELIZABETH JEAN, writer; b. Biloxi, Miss., Apr. 13, 1938; d. Dudley Charles and Margaret Jean (Gilchrist) Andrews; m. Anthony Francis Cieslewicz (Cecil), Nov. 22, 1962; children: Stephen Charles, Sarah Jean. BA, Colo. State Coll., 1959; MA, Stanford U., 1963. Cert. speech and lang. pathologist, Wis. Speech-lang. pathologist Racine Unified Sch. Dist., Wis., 1963—95, ret., 1995. Author: (booklet essays) Jean's Stuff, 1993; author series of pictorial geneal. books. Office Vocat. Rehab. fellow Stanford U. Mem.: ASCD. Presbyterian. E-mail: writeshop@wi-net.com.

CECIL, J. ROBB, lawyer; b. 1960; BS, Mount St. Mary's Coll., Emmitsburg, Md.; JD, Univ. Balt. asst. state atty. Anne Arundel County, Md.; ptnr. McGowan, Cecil & Smathers, Laurel, Md. Named one of The Top Lawyers: The Next Generation, Baltimore Mag., 2003. Mem.: Assn. Trial Lawyers Am., Md. Trial Lawyers Assn. Office: McGowan Cecil & Smathers 317 Main St Laurel MD 20707

CEDAR, PAUL ARNOLD, church executive, minister; b. Mpls., Nov. 4, 1938; s. Carl Benjamin and Bernice M. (Peterson) C.; m. Jean Helen Lier, Aug. 25, 1959; children: Daniel Paul, Mark John, Deborah Jean. BS, No. State Coll., Aberdeen, S.D., 1960; MDiv, No. Bap. Theol. Sem., 1968, Calif. State U., Fullerton, 1971; DMin, Am. Baptist Sem. of the West, 1973. Ordained to ministry Evang. Free Ch. of Am., 1966. Youth for Christ, crusade dir. Billy Graham Evang. Assn., Leighton Ford Team, 1960-65; pastor Evang. Free Ch., Naperville, Ill., 1965-67, Yorba Linda, Calif., 1969-73; exec. pastor 1st Presbyn. Ch. Hollywood, Calif., 1975-81; sr. pastor Lake Ave. Congl. Ch., Pasadena, Calif., 1981-90; pres. Evang. Free Ch. Am., Mpls., 1990-96; chmn., CEO Mission Am., 1995—. Guest dean Billy Graham Sch. Evangelism, Mpls., 1983-2002; vis. prof. Fuller Theol. Sem., Pasadena, Talbot Theol. Sem., La Habra, Calif., Trinity Div. Sch., Deerfield, Ill. Author: How to Make Love Your Motive, 1977, Becoming a Lover, 1978, Seven Keys to Maximum Communication, 1980, Sharing the Good Life, 1980, Communicators Commentary, 1983, Strength in Servant Leadership, 1987, Mastering the Pastoral Role, 1991, Where Is Hope?, 1992, A Life of Prayer, 1998. Mem. Nat. Prayer Com. Mem. Christian TV and Film Commn., Internat. Students, Worldwide Leadership Coun., Caleb Ministries, Leadership Renewal Ctr., John M. Perkins Found., Revival Prayer Fellowship, Barnabas Internat., Pioneer Clubs. Mem. Evangelist Free Ch. Of Am. Avocations: athletics, music, writing, carpentry. *I am convinced that when all of life is over, only one thing will matter ultimately-fulfilling the will of God.*

CEDARBAUM, MIRIAM GOLDMAN, federal judge; b. N.Y.C., 1929; d. Louis Albert and Sarah (Shapiro) Goldman; married; 2 children. BA, Barnard Coll., 1950; LLB, Columbia U., 1953. Bar: N.Y. 1954, U.S. Dist. Ct. (so. dist.) N.Y. 1956, U.S. Ct. Appeals (2d cir.) 1956, U.S. Ct. Claims 1958, U.S. Supreme Ct. 1958, U.S. Dist. Ct. (ea. dist.) N.Y. 1980, U.S. Ct. Appeals (5th and 11th cirs.) 1981. Law clk. to judge Edward Jordan Dimock U.S. Dist. Ct. (so. dist.) N.Y., 1953-54, asst. U.S. atty., 1954-57; atty. Dept. Justice, Washington, 1958-59; part-time cons. to law firms in litig. matters, 1959-62; 1st asst. counsel N.Y. State Moreland Act Commn., 1963-64; assoc. counsel Mus. Modern Art, N.Y.C., 1965-79; assoc. litig. dept. Davis Polk & Wardwell, N.Y.C., 1979-83, sr. atty., 1983-86; acting village justice Village of Scarsdale, NY, 1978—82, village justice, 1982-86; judge U.S. Dist. Ct. (so. dist.) N.Y., 1986-98, sr. judge, 1998—. Trustee emerita Barnard Coll.; mem. com. defender svcs. Jud. Conf. U.S., 1993—99; mem. emerita bd. visitors Columbia Law Sch.; chmn. N.Y. State Selection Com. for Rhodes Scholarship. Contbr. articles to profl. jours. Recipient Medal of Distinction Barnard Coll., 1991; James Kent scholar. Mem. ABA (chmn. com. on pictorial graphic sculptural and choreographic works 1979-81, copyright com. fed. practice and procedure 1983-84), Am. Law Inst., Fed. Bar Coun., Copyright Soc. U.S.A. (trustee, exec. com. 1979-82), Supreme Ct. Hist. Soc., Am. Judicature Soc Jewish. Office: US Dist Ct US Courthouse 500 Pearl St Rm 1330 New York NY 10007-1312

CEDDIA, ANTHONY FRANCIS, university administrator; b. Boston, Mar. 4, 1944; s. Antonio John and Marie (Loungo) C.; m. Valerie Ann Mulkern, Apr. 15, 1966; children: Ann-Marie, Michael. BS in Edn., Northeastern U., 1965, MEd, 1968; EdD, U. Mass., 1980; postgrad. John F. Kennedy Sch. Govt., Harvard U., 1990; LLD (hon.), North Adams State Coll., 1990; cert. sr. exec. program in local govt., Harvard U., 1990; LLD (hon.), North Adams State Coll., 1990. Cert. counselor, secondary sch. tchr., Mass. Tchr. social studies, counselor Melrose High Sch., Mass., 1965-70; fin. aid and admissions ofcl. North Adams State Coll., Mass., 1970-73, dean of adminstrn, 1973-78, exec. v.p., 1978-81; acting pres. North Adams State Coll., Mass., 1979; pres. Shippensburg U., Pa., 1981—. Chmn. bd. Univ. Ctr., State System Higher Edn., Harrisburg, 1987-90; chmn. Commn. Univs. of Pa., 1986-88; mem. Sico Found., Sico Oil Corp., 1983—; mem. adv. bd. Orrstown Bank, Shippensburg, 1984-87. Mem. Cumberland County Transp. Bd., 1990; trustee Chambersburg Hosp. Bd., 1989—; mem. exec. com. South Ctrl. Pa. coun. Boy Scouts Am., 1982—, adv. panel Nat. Army ROTC, 1984—, chair, 1990-92; bd. dirs. Ams. for the Competitive System, 1981-87; chair divsn. II steering com. NCAA, 1990-92. Recipient Disting. Alumni Northeastern U., 1979 Mem. Am. Assn. State Colls. and Univs. (editor 1982-86, chmn. com. rsch. and liaison, com. on policy and purpose 1987-90), Am. Assn. Higher Edn., Mid. States Assn. Colls. and Schs. (commn. on higher edn. 1986-92), Nat. Intercollegiate Athletic Assn. (coun.). Home: PO Box 606 Shippensburg PA 17257-0606 Office: Shippensburg U Office of Pres 1871 Old Main Dr Shippensburg PA 17257-2299

CEDERBERG, JAMES, physics professor; b. Oberlin, Kans., Mar. 16, 1939; s. J. Walter and Edith E. (Glad) C.; m. Judith Ness, June 10, 1967; children: Anna Sook, Rachel Eun. BA, U. Kans., 1959; MA, Harvard U., 1960, PhD, 1963. Lectr., rsch. assoc. Harvard U., Cambridge, Mass., 1963-64; from asst. prof. to prof. St. Olaf Coll., Northfield, Minn., 1964—80, prof., 1980—92, Grace A. Whittier prof. sci., 1992—. Councilor Coun. on Undergrad. Rsch., 1985-91, 92-95, pres. physics coun., 1985-88; summer rsch. assoc. U. Mich., 1967, Harvard U., 1980; fellow Duke U., 1969-70, Harvard U., 1976-77; vis. prof. U. Washington, 1991-92, U. Canterbury, Christchurch, New Zealand, 1998-99. Recipient Distinguished Service Citation awd., Am. Assn. of Physics Teachers, 1993; fellow NSF, Woodrow Wilson fellowship; grantee various corps., NSF, RUI. Fellow: Am. Phys. Soc. (Undergraduate Rsch. prize 2002); mem.: Am. Assn. Physics Tchrs., Sigma Xi, Pi Mu Epsilon, Sigma Pi Sigma, Phi Beta Kappa. Lutheran. Office: St Olaf Coll 1520 Saint Olaf Ave Northfield MN 55057-1098 Office Fax: 507-646-3968. Business E-Mail: ceder@stolaf.edu.

CEDERING, SIV, poet, writer; b. Overkalix, Sweden, Feb. 5, 1939; came to U.S., 1953, naturalized, 1958; d. Hilding and Elvy (Wikstrom) C.; children: Lisa, Lora, David. Artist Elaine Benson Gallery, Bridgehampton, NY, 1991—98, Loveland Mus., Loveland, Colo., 1992, East End Arts Coun. Gallery, Riverhead, NY, 1992, Clayton-Liberatori Gallery, Bridgehampton, NY, 1991, Guild Hall Mus., East Hampton, NY, 2001, Hutchin Gallery, Green Vale, NY, 1993, Peconic Gallery, Riverheard, NY, 1993, East. New Mex. Univ., Portales, N.Mex., 1992, Nordic History Mus., 1998. Lectr. U. Mass., Amherst, 1973; cons. Coordinating Council Lit. Mags., 1972-75 Author: (poems and photographs) Cup of Cold Water, 1973, Letters from the Island, 1973; (poems) Letters from Helge, 1974, Two Swedish Poets, Gost Friberg and Goran Palm (transl. from Swedish), 1974, Mother Is, 1975, The Juggler, 1977, How to Eat a Fortune Cookie, 1977, Color Poems, 1978, Letters From the Floating World: New and Selected Poems, 1984, The Blue Horse, 1979; (children's poems) Leken i Grishuset, 1980 (books transl. into Japanese, Swedish); Oxen, 1981, Letters From an Observatory, 1998, Poetry Paintings, 2003, Adirondack Notebook, 2004; editor, translator: Det Blommande Trädet (The Flowering Tree, collection Am. Indian and Eskimo lyrics), 1973, You and I and the World, Poems by Werner Aspenström, 1980, Letters From The Observatory New and Selected Poem 1973-1998, 1998, Painting Poems, 2003, Adirondack Notebook, 2004; poems and prose published in several periodicals, including, Harper's, New Republic, Partisan Rev., Paris Rev., Quar. Rev. Lit., others, exhibited photography, Modernage Galleries, NYC, 1973. Recipient William Marion Reedy award Poetry Soc. Am., 1970, John Masefield Narrative Poetry award, 1969; Annapolis Fine Arts Festival poetry prize Md. Fine Arts Council, 1968; Photography prize Sat. Rev., 1970; Borestone Mountain Poetry award, 1974; Pushcart prize, 1977; Emily Dickinson award, 1978; NY State Council on Arts fellow, 1974; Swedish Writers Union stipend, 1979; grantee Swedish Writers Found., 1995-2000. Mem. Poetry Soc. Am. Home: PO Box 89 Sagaponack NY 11962-0089 Personal E-mail: siv@hamptons.com.

CEDOLINI, ANTHONY JOHN, psychologist; b. Rochester, N.Y., Sept. 19, 1942; s. Peter Ross and Mary J. (Anthony) C.; m. Clare Marie De Rose, Aug. 16, 1964; children: Maria A., Antonia C., Peter E. Student, U. San Francisco, 1960-62; BA, San Jose State U., 1965, MS, 1968; PhD in Ednl. Pscyhology, Columbia Pacific U., 1983. Lic. ednl. psychologist, sch. adminstr., marriage, family, child counselor, sch psychologist, sch. counselor, social worker, real estate broker, Calif. Ptnr. Cienega Valley Vineyards and DeRose Winery (formerly Almaden Vineyards) and Comml. Shopping Ctrs., 1968—; coord. psychol. svcs. Oak Grove Sch. Dist., San Jose, Calif., 1968-81, asst. dir. pupil svcs., 1977-81, dir. pupil svcs., 1981-83; pvt. practice, ednl. psychologist Ednl. Assocs., San Jose, 1983—. Co-dir. Biofeedback Inst. of Santa Clara County, San Jose, 1976-83; ptnr. in Cypress Ctr.-Ednl. Psychologists and Consultancy, 1978-84; cons., program auditor for Calif. State Dept. Edn.; instr. U. Calif., Santa Cruz and LaVerne Coll. Ext. courses; guest spkr. San Jose State U.; lectr., workshop presenter in field. Author: Occupational Stress and Job Burnout, 1982, A Parents Guide to School Readiness, 1971, The Effect of Affect, 1975; contbr. articles to profl. jours. and newspapers. Founder, bd. dirs. Lyceum of Santa Clara County, 1971—, Graham Owners Club of Calif. Avocations: collecting antique furniture and coins, stained glass, wine making, classic cars, wood carvings. Home and Office: 1183 Nikulina Ct San Jose CA 95120-5441 Office Phone: 408-997-2700. Personal E-mail: tonyced@pacbell.net.

CEDRASCHI, TULLIO, investment company executive; b. Zurich, Switzerland, Oct. 4, 1938; s. Guido and Ida (Colombara) C. Degree in Civil Engring., Coll. Tech., Zurich, 1960; MBA, McGill U., 1968. Civil engr., project mgr. Conrad Zschokke, Zurich, 1960-61, Bur. D'Etudes Quoniam, Paris, 1961-63, BBR Switzerland and Can., 1963-65, R. R. Nicolet and Assocs., Montreal, 1968—, gen. mgr. CN investment divsn., 1973-77, pres., CEO, 1977—. Bd. dirs. Toronto Stock Exch., Western Oil Sands Inc., Freehold Resources Ltd., Helix Investments. Bd. govs. emeritus McGill U.; bd. govs. Nat. Theatre Sch. Mem. Montreal Soc. Fin. Analysts, Hillside Tennis Club. Avocations: tennis, skiing. Home: # 605 2600 ave Pierre-Dupuy Habitat 67 Cite du Havre Montreal PQ Canada H3C 3R6 Office: CN Investment Divsn Fl 11 PO Box 11002 5 Pl Ville Marie Montreal PQ Canada H3C 4T2 also: CN 935 de la Gauchetiere St W Montreal PQ Canada H3C 3N4

CEDRONE, LOUIS ROBERT, JR., retired critic; b. Balt., June 25, 1923; s. Louis and Lucia (Mazzola) C.; m. Nancy Nelson, Sept. 11, 1954; children— Linda, David. BS, U. Md., 1951. With Balt. Evening Sun, 1951-92, drama-film critic, 1963-92, ret., 1992; corr. Variety, 1957-77, 82-85; TV show cablevision Critics Corner, 1982-85. Swimming instr. ARC, 1961-68. Served with inf. AUS, 1943-45. Decorated Purple Heart with oak leaf cluster, Bronze Star. Mem. Sigma Nu, Omicron Delta Kappa, Pi Delta Epsilon. Home: 9 Muirfield Ct Lutherville Timonium MD 21093-3905

CEFALO, ROBERT CHARLES, obstetrician, gynecologist; b. Boston, 1933; MD, Tufts U., 1959. Diplomate Am. Bd. Ob-Gyn. Intern Chelsea Naval Hosp., Boston, 1959—60; resident in ob.-gyn. U.S. Naval Hosp., Oakland, Calif., 1961—64; now prof. dept. ob-gyn. Med. Sch. U. N.C., Chapel Hill, and asst. dean, head of office grad. med. edn. Mem.: SGI, AMA, ACOG. Office: U NC Med Sch 214 Macnider Chapel Hill NC 27599-0001

CEFARATTI, ANTHONY JOSEPH, retired diplomat; b. Ossining, NY, Mar. 20, 1918; s. Andrew Joseph Cefaratti and Louise Agnes Fraino; m. Isabelle Anne-Marie Halgan d'Orbigny Cefaratti, Oct. 2, 1945; 1 child, Alessandra Isabelle. Mil., Leland Stanford U., 1938—41; BA, U. of Calif. at Los Angeles, 1941—42. Inf. officer U.S. Army, European theater, 1943—45; asst. comml. attache Dept. of State, West Germany, 1947; sec. U.S. del. Org. for European Econ. Coop., Paris, 1949—50; asst. pub. affairs officer Dept. of State, Washington, 1950—51; comml. counselor U.S. Embassy, Madrid, 1951—55; mng. dir. Patents Internat. Affiliates, London, 1958—61; pres. Dynamics Internat., Madrid, 1962—64; ret., 2000. Cons. for various org., Spain, 1988—92. Author: (screenplays) Rocio, The Spanish Mustang, 2003. Maj. infantry, 1945—46, France. Decorated Bronze Star U.S. Army, Gold medal Spanish Soc. Econ. and Sci., Res. Officers Assn. Spain; recipient Croix de Guerre, French Govt., 1944. Cath. Avocation: writing. Home: 19801 SW 110th Ct Apt 702 Miami FL 33157

CEHELSKA, OLGA M., music educator, flight instructor; b. Austria, Apr. 6, 1946; d. George Michael and Veronica Bronislava (Drozdowska) C. BMus magna cum laude, Temple U., 1968; MusM, U. Miami, 1978; MSc, Am. Coll. Holistic Health, 1995; PhD holistic nutrition, Clayton Coll. Natural Health, 1999. Cert. music educator, N.J.; cert. flight instr., FAA; cert. music therapist Nat. Assn. Music Therapy. Tchr. music Phila. Pub. Sch. System, 1967-71; flight instr. Tamiami Airport, Homestead Airport, Homestead, Fla., 1973-74, Fulton County Airport, Atlanta, 1974-75; intern activity therapy Ga. Mental Health Inst., Atlanta, 1974; dir. activity therapy Met. Psychiat. Ctr., Atlanta, 1974-75; coord. adult psychiat. day treatment North Dekalb Cmty. Mental Health Ctr., 1975-80; piano instr., 1962—; CEO Cehelska Piano Studio, 1991—; flight instr. Norfolk Airport, Va., 2000—. Musician Young Audiences of Va., Norfolk, 1990-95, cons. Dekalb County Day Program, 1975-80, Nutritional Wellness, Vairginia Beach, 2000—. Contbr. articles to profl. jours. Mem. Ukrainian Women's League of Am., Ukrainian Scouting, Ukrainian Dancers of Miami, Ukrainian Am. Club of Miami, Nat. Assn. Music Therapy, Aircraft Owners and Pilots Assn., Nat. Assn. Flight Instr., Sigma Alpha Iota Alumni, Tidewater Music Tchrs. Forum, Music Tchrs. Nat. Assn., Va. Music Tchrs. Assn. Ukrainian Catholic. Avocation: traditional Ukrainian music on bandura. Office: Cehelska Piano Studio/Nutr Wellness 2313 Beach Haven Dr Unit 103 Virginia Beach VA 23451-1263 Personal E-mail: OMCstudio@msn.com.

CEHELSKY, MARTA, scientific organization executive; BA, Barnard Coll., 1964; MA in Polit. Sci., Columbia U., 1968, PhD in Polit. Sci., 1974. News editor Latin Am. Rsch. Rev., 1970-71; vis. sr. rsch. assoc. U. Houston Inst. Urban Studies, 1974; asst. prof. dept. polit. sci. Bklyn. Coll., CUNY, 1971-76; pub. policy cons., 1967-68, 77-79; policy analyst Lyndon B. Johnson Space Ctr., 1977-79, NASA Hdqrs., 1979-80; spl. asst. Senator Ernest F. Hollings, Washington, 1983-84; from polit. analyst to exec. officer Nat. Sci. Bd. NSF, Washington, 1980—2002; sr. adv. sci. and tech., dept. Sustainable Devel. InterAm. Devel. Bank, 2002—. Author: Land Reform in Brazil: The Management of Social Change, 1979, Guatamala Election Factbook, 1966; contbr. chpts. to books, articles to profl. jours.; presenter in field. Charter mem. The Washington Gp. (bd. dirs.). Recipient Fulbright fellowship 1964, Fulbright Hays fellowship 1965, Ford For. Area fellowship, LEGIS Exec. fellowship, Nat. Def. Foreign Lang. fellowship, Barnard Soc. Proctors. Mem. AAAS, Am. Inst. Aeronautics and Astronautics, Exec. Women in Govt., Sr. Execs. Assn., Ukranian Physical Soc., Am. Astronautical Soc., Am. Pol. Sci. Assn. Office: InterAmerican Devel Bank 1300 New York Ave NW Washington DC 20577 Office Phone: 202-623-2176. E-mail: martace@secondee.iadb.org.

CEJAS, PAUL L., diplomat, executive; b. Havana, Cuba, Jan. 4, 1943; BBA in Acctg., U. Miami, 1969; PhD (hon.), Fla. Internat. U., 1988. CPA. Amb. to Belgium U.S. Dept. of State, 1998—; chmn., CEO PLC Investments, Inc. Founder, chmn., CEO CareFlorida Health Systems, Inc. Former chmn. Dade County Sch. Bd.; apptd. by Gov. Chiles to bd. regents State of Fla. U., 1994; chmn. Post-Summit Com. for the 1994 Hemispheric Summit of the Americas; chmn. Fla. Partnership of the Americas, 1994-97; rep. to U.S. Delegation to the Gen. Assembly of the Orgn. of Am. States, 1996, others. Office: 27 Blvd de Regent Box 002 Psc 82 APO AE 09710-0082

ČEJKA, JIŘÍ, retired chemist, researcher; b. Roudnice, N.L., Czech Republic, Sept. 2, 1929; s. Josef and Božena (Roudnická) C.; m. Marie Sedláčková, July 26, 1958; children: Jiří, Jan. MSc, Inst. Chem. Tech., Prague, Czechoslovakia, 1961, PhD, 1970; DSc, Acad. of Scis. of Czech Republic, 1994. Rsch. chemist Reagencia, Kralupy, Czechoslovakia, 1954-59, Glazura, Roudnice, 1959-72; head rsch. chem. divsn. Nat. Mus.-Natural History Mus., Prague, 1972-93, scientist, 1972-88, sr. rsch. scientist, 1988—, dir., 1991-2001, dir. emeritus, 2001—. Author: Secondary Uranium Minerals, 1990; editor Acta Mus. Nat. Prague, Hist. Natur., 1974-93; regional editor Czech Republic Art and Archaeology Tech. Abstracts, The Getty Conservation Inst., Marina del Rey, Calif., 1988-94; contbr. articles to profl. jours. Fellow: Scout History Assn.; mem.: Nat. Geog. Soc., Internat. Mineral. Assn., Commn. on New Minerals and Mineral Names (a new mineral named cejkaite to honor contributions to uranium mineralogy 1999), European Crystallographic Assn., Junák Assn. of Scouts and Guides of Czech Republic (award 1947, 1987, 1990, 1992, 1999, 2002, award A 2003, award B 2003—04), Crystallographic Soc., Slovak Chem. Soc., Czech Chem. Soc., Confederation Polit. Prisoners Czech Republic (award 1998), Scouts' Velen Fanderlik Troop (troop leader 1999—2001, award 1999). Achievements include patents in field. Avocations: classical music, jazz, fine arts, philosophy of the world scout movement. Home: Michálkova 1672 413 01 Roudnice N.L. Czech Republic Office: Nat Scis Mus of Nat Mus Václavské náměstí 68 115 79 Prague 1 Czech Republic Business E-Mail: jiri_.cejka@tiscali.cz.

CEKALA, CHESTER, lawyer; b. Attleboro, Mass., May 18, 1959; s. Chester and Eileen (Polefka) C.; m. Suzanne Collette Cloutier, June 21, 1981 (div. May 1989); 1 child, Allison Rene; m. Carol Lee Raleigh, Oct. 7, 1990; children: Samuel Chester, Andrew Robin. BS, Worcester Poly. Inst., 1982; JD, Suffolk U., 1987, MBA, 2001. Bar: Ohio 1987, Mass. 1996, U.S. Ct. Appeals (fed. cir.) 1989, U.S. Patent and Trademark Office 1988, U.S. Supreme Ct. 1996. Chem. engr. Moleculon Biotech, Cambridge, Mass., 1981-87; patent atty. Procter & Gamble, Cin., 1987-90, W.R. Grace & Co., Lexington, Mass., 1990-91, The Gillette Co., Boston, 1991-2000, sr group patent counsel, 2000—01, asst. patent counsel, 2001—. Mem. ABA, Am. Intellectual

Property Assn., Boston Bar Assn. (IP steering com. 2004—), Boston Patent Law Assn., Cin. Intellectual Property Assn. (sec. 1987-88). Avocations: sailing, bicycling, skiing. Office: The Gillette Co Prudential Tower Bldg Boston MA 02199 Office Phone: 617-421-7851. E-mail: chet_cekala@gillette.com.

CEKAUSKAS, CYNTHIA DANUTE, social worker; b. Detroit, Mar. 24, 1954; d. Vladas Algimantas and Isabel Gana (Stasiulis) Cekauskas; m. Randall Dean Voelker, Mar. 20, 2000. BA in Sociology, Madonna Coll., Livonia, Mich., 1976; MSW, U. Mich., 1979. Lic. clin. social worker La., Fla., LCSW. Psychiat. social worker Charity Hosp. New Orleans, 1982-84; social worker child and adolescent svc. DePaul Hosp., New Orleans, 1986-87; social worker, family adv. program mgr. Army Cmty. Svcs., Friedberg, Germany, 1988-89; social worker, family adv. program mgr., chmn. family adv. case mgmt. team Cmty. Counseling Ctr., Camp Zama, Japan, 1989-90; social worker, exceptional family mem. program mgr. Army Cmty. Svcs., Bamberg, Germany, 1990-91, alt. family adv., on-call crisis counselor Desert Storm, 1990-91; social worker, family advocacy rep., head dept. family adv. Naval Med. Clinic, New Orleans, 1991-96; social worker, family advocacy program mgr. Army Cmty. Svcs., Augsburg, Germany, 1997-98, Wiesbaden, Germany, 1998-2000; social worker, case mgr. Navy Family Advocacy Ctr., Norfolk, Va., 2000-01; social worker, family advocacy program mgr., exceptional family program mgr. U.S. Army Garrison Family Support Ctr., Miami, Fla., 2002—05. Presenter Child Abuse Prevention Bad Nauheim Elem. Sch., 1988—89. Contbr. articles to newspapers. Hosp. corpsman USN, 1979—82. Recipient Cmty. Support Svc. award, Giessen Mil. Cmty., 1988—89, Friend Bad Nauheim Elem. Sch. award, 1989, Commendation for Exceptional Svc., Cam Zama, 1991, Scroll of Appreciation for Desert Storm/Desert Shield, Bamberg, Germany, 1990—91, Outstanding Performance award, 1993—94, Presdl. Sports award for racewalking, 1996, Presdl. Sports award for aerobic dance, 1996, Presdl. Sports award for weight tng., 1996, Presdl. Sports award for endurance walking, 1996, 15 Yrs. Fed. Svc. cert. of recognition, U.S. Govt., 2002, Cold War cert. of recognition, 1999, Cert. of Appreciation for Vol. Svc. on behalf of U.S., Southern Comd., 2003—05, Cert. of Appreciation in Recognition of Outstanding Support to Miami, Knights Recruiting Battalion, 2003, 2005, Cert. of Appreciation for Special Solicitation Event in Support Victims of Asian Earthquake and Tsunami Disaster, 2005. Mem.: NOW, NASW, Acad. Cert. Social Workers, Sierra Club, Nat. Orgn. Victim Assistance, German Am. Social Club Hollywood, Florida. Democrat. Roman Catholic. Office: US Army Garrison Miami Family Support Ctr 3511 NW 91st Ave Miami FL 33172-1217 Office Phone: 305-437-2734. Business E-Mail: cekauskc@hq.southcom.mil.

CEKO, THERESA C., law educator, lawyer; BA, Univ. Chgo., 1981; JD, DePaul Univ., 1984. Clin. prof. Loyola Univ., Chgo., 1987—, dir. Cmty. Law Ctr., 1999—. Contbr. articles to Ill. Ct. publ. Office: Loyola University Chicago School of Law 1 E Pearson St Chicago IL 60611

CELEDONIO, FRANCISCO E., lawyer; s. Francisco and Mireya Celedonio; m. Monica Lopez, July 11, 2003. BA, Columbia U., 1982; JD, NYU, 1985. Bar: N.Y. 1987, U.S. Dist. Ct. (so. dist.) N.Y. 1987, U.S. Dist. Ct. (ea. dist.) N.Y. 1988, U.S. Ct. Appeals (2nd cir.) 2001. Jud. clk. U.S. Dist. Ct. (ea. dist.) Wis., Madison, 1985—86; atty. Paul, Weiss, Rifkind, Wharton & Garrison, N.Y.C., 1986—89; assoc. Dewey, Ballantine, Bushby, Palmer & Wood, N.Y.C., NY, 1989—90; atty. Aranda & Guttlein, N.Y.C., 1994; pvt. practice N.Y.C., 1994—. Mem. Criminal Justice Act Panel (so. and ea. dists.) N.Y. Mem.: N.Y. State Bar Assn., Nat. Assn. Criminal Def. Lawyers, Fed. Bar Coun., Assn. of the Bar of the City of NY. Office: Law Office of Francisco E Celedonio Ste 2510 401 Broadway New York NY 10013 Office Phone: 212-219-7533. Office Fax: 212-219-4094. Business E-Mail: fecdrq@yahoo.com.

CELENTANO, FRANCIS MICHAEL, artist, art educator; b. N.Y.C., May 25, 1928; s. Michael Anthony and Rafaela (Valentino) C. BA, NYU, 1951, MA in Art History, 1957. Lectr. C.W. Post Coll., L.I., N.Y., 1961-63, N.Y. Inst. Tech., Old Westbury, N.Y., 1965-66; from assoc. prof. to prof. Sch. Art, U. Wash., Seattle, 1966-93. One-man shows include Howard Wise Gallery, N.Y.C., 1963, Foster/White Gallery, Seattle, 1971, 73, 75, 78, Diane Gilson Gallery, Seattle, 1981, 82, Fountain Gallery, Portland, Oreg., 1983, Greg Kucera Gallery, Seattle, 1986, 89, 91, Safeco Plaza, Seattle, 1990, 95, Laura Russo Gallery, Portland, 1990, 2004, Woodside/Braseth Gallery, 1993, 95, 97, Bryan Ohno Gallery, Seattle, 2005; retrospective exhbn. Portland Ctr. for the Visual Arts, 1986, Whatcom County Mus., Bellingham, Washington, 1992; represented in permanent collections at Mus. of Modern Art, N.Y.C., Albright-Knox Mus., Buffalo, Seattle Art mus., Fed. Res. Bank of San Francisco, Wash. State Arts Commn., King County Arts Commn., U. Wash. Hosp., Seattle. Fulbright scholar Rome, 1958; fed. regional fellow in painting Western States Arts Fedn. Nat. Endowment for the Arts, 1990. E-mail: fcelent@u.washington.edu.

CELENTANO, SUZANNE, theater educator; b. Pitts., Nov. 4, 1967; d. Patrick Earl and Dixie Lea Carmack; m. Ronald Joseph Celentano, June 19, 1993; children: Christopher, Brandon, Sophia. BA in Comm. Arts and Theater, Allegheny Coll., 1989; MFA in Theater, U. Ala. and Ala. Shakespeare Festival, 1991. Cert. in group fitness, in pilates and yoga. Actor, dir., choreographer, 1992—; professorial lectr. dept. performing arts Am. U., Washington, 2003. Adj. instr. theater Coll. Charleston, Charleston, SC, 1992—95, St. Louis U., 1996—99; arts mgmt. cons., 1992—; spkr., presenter in field, 1992—. Dancer Am. Coll. Dance Festival Nat. Gala and Southeastern Gala, 1990; co-author: (book) Theatre Management: A Successful Guide to Producing Plays on Commercial and Nonprofit Stages, 1998; performer (actor, dancer): (films, TV and theater) April Is My Religion, 2001 (award); co. mem., dancer: Kathy Harty Gray Dance Theatre, 2003—; author: (plays) Phoenix Theatre; actor: Wilma Theatre, Ala. Shakespeare Festival, Walt Disney World. Theater coord. Piccolo Spoleto Festival, Charleston, 1994; bd. dirs. Lortan (Va.) Arts Found., 2002—05; 1st v.p. Lorton Sta. Elem. Sch. PTA, 2003—04. Recipient Nat. scholarship, Internat. Thespian Soc., 1985. Mem.: Southeastern Theatre Conf., Pilates Method Alliance (cert. instr. and master trainer of mat and apparatus), Officers Wives Clubs (scholarship coord. 1994—95, 2000—01), Officers Spouses Club (pres. 2001—02). Democrat. Roman Catholic. Avocations: director and choreographer, personal trainer, distance running, community activist, yoga. Home: 8710 Bitterroot Ct Lorton VA 22079 Personal E-mail: scelentano@aol.com.

CELENTINO, CHRISTOPHER, lawyer; b. Tarrytown, NY, July 2, 1962; BS, Northwestern U., 1984; JD cum laude, Georgetown U., 1987. Bar: Calif. 1987, US Dist. Ct. So., No., Ctrl. & Ea. Districts Calif. Assoc. Luce, Forward, Hamilton & Scripps LLP, San Diego, 1987—94, ptnr., 1994—2003, Duane Morris LLP, San Diego, 2003—, mng. ptnr. San Diego office, 2004—. Bd. dirs., mem. exec. com. Calif. Bankruptcy Forum; bd. dirs. San Diego Bankruptcy Forum, pres., 2002. Head coach & team mgr. Presidio Little League. Recipient Wiley M. Manual Award for Pro Bono Legal Svc., State Bar Calif., 1992, Frank Curran Humanitarian Award, San Diego Downtown Partnership, 1993. Mem.: Louis M. Welch Inn of Am. Inns Ct., San Diego Fin. Lawyers Group, San Diego County Bar Assn. (Annual Award for Outstanding Svc. to the Cmty. 1994), Northwestern U. Alumni Club San Diego, Georgetown U. Alumni Club San Diego. Office: Duane Morris LLP Ste 900 101 W Broadway San Diego CA 92101-8285 Office Phone: 619-744-2246. Office Fax: 619-744-2201. Business E-Mail: ccelentino@duanemorris.com.

CELESIA, GASTONE GUGLIELMO, neurologist; b. Genoa, Italy, Nov. 22, 1933; came to U.S., 1959, naturalized, 1970; s. Raffaele Amadeo and Ottavia (Tortrino) C.; m. Linda Irene Pike, Aug. 1, 1964; children: Gloria, Laura. MD, U. Genoa, 1959; MS, McGill U., Montreal, 1965. Diplomate Am. Bd. Psychiatry and Neurology in Neurology, Am. Bd. Psychiatry and Neurology in Clin. Neurophysiology. Intern Madison Gen. Hosp., Wis., 1960; fellow neurophysiology U. Wis., Madison, 1960-62, asst. prof. neurology, 1966-69, assoc. prof., 1970-73, prof., 1974-79, 1979-83; resident in neurology Montreal Neurol. Inst./McGill U., Montreal, Que., Can., 1962-66; chief neurology svc. VA Hosp., Madison, 1979-83; prof. neurology Loyola U., Chgo., 1983—99, chmn. dept. neurology, 1983-99, prof. neurology, 2000—03; cons. Exec. Svc. Chgo., 2003—. Cons. Exec. Svc. Core of Chgo. Editor in chief: Electroenceph. Clin. Neurophysiol., 1988-99; contbr. articles to profl. jours. Fellow Am. Acad. Neurology; mem. AMA, Am. EEG Soc., Am. Acad. Clin. Neurophysiology (pres. 1993-95), Am. Neurol. Assn., Ctrl. Assn. EEG, Wis. Neurol. Soc. Wis. Med. Alumni Assn., Wis. Neurol. Soc. (pres. 1975-76), Soc. Neurosci., Am. Epilepsy Soc., N.Y. Acad. Scis. AAAS, Am. Soc. Exptl. Med. Therapeutics. Office: 25 E Washington St Ste 1500 Chicago IL 60602-1804 Personal E-mail: g.celesia@comcast.net.

CELESTE, RICHARD F., academic administrator, former ambassador, former governor; b. Cleve., Nov. 11, 1937; s. Frank C.; m. Dagmar Braun, 1962; children: Eric, Christopher, Gabriella, Noelle, Natalie, Stephen; m. Jacqueline Lundquist; 1 child; 6 stepchildren. BA in History magna cum laude, Yale U., 1959; Ph.B. in Politics, Oxford U., 1962. Staff liaison officer Peace Corps, 1963, dir. Washington, 1979-81; spl. asst. to U.S. amb. to India, 1963-67; mem. Ohio Ho. of Reps., Columbus, 1970-74, majority whip, 1972-74; lt. gov. State of Ohio, Columbus, 1974-79, gov., 1983-91; mng. ptnr. Celeste & Sabety, Ltd., Columbus, Ohio, 1991—97; US amb. to India US Dept. State, New Delhi, 1997—2001; co-chair, Homeland Security Proj. The Century Found., 2002—; pres. Colorado Coll., 2002—. Mem. Ohio Dem. Exec. Com. Rhodes scholar Oxford U., Eng. Mem. Am. Soc. Pub. Adminstrn., Italian Sons and Daus. Am. Methodist. Office: Office Pres Colorado Coll 14 E Cache La Poudre St Colorado Springs CO 80903

CELIA, GEORGE, composer, writer; b. Ragusa, Italy, Mar. 17, 1921; came to U.S., 1923; s. Giorgio Giuseppe and Lucia Giovanna (Sola) C.; m. Rosemary Fern Walker, Apr. 26, 1958; 1 child, Georgene Fern. Student, Northwestern U., 1944-48, U. Chgo., 1968. Personnel mgr., asst. contr. Consolidated Radio Products Co., Chgo., 1949-55; office mgr., chief acct., contr., treas. Gulbransen Piano & Organ Co., Melrose Park, Ill., 1955-70; owner George Celia U. & Libr., 1971, Life Mgr. Co., Richardson, Tex., 1971-73, Get Organized Co., Richardson, 1973-97, Ultimate You, George Celia Creative Enterprises, Richardson, 1986-97, Midland, Tex., 1998—, Celia Ingram Comm. Spl. feature writer Chgo. (Ill.) Tribune, 1954. Composer (processional): The Triumph of Ideals, 1945; composer: March of the Nations-UN song, 1945, Fight Boys Fight Sport Song, 1945, Song of the Returning Soldier, 1945, Rispetto, 1989, Student's Procession on the Shoulder's of Giants, 2000, The Gladness, 2001, AnniMETsary Song, 2003, New Day Symphony, 2005; author: Focus Books, 1971, Ultimate You, 1989, Personal Magna Carta, 1989, The Triumph of Ideals, 1997, Love Affair with Every Day, 1997, Musikgarten & Art, 2000, Incredible Galleries, 2000, The Unstilled Quills, 2001, Keyboard Extravaganza, 2002, Historic Letter to Louisa, 2003, 6 Generations, 2004; author: (travel and autobiog. drama scenes) Roman Britain, 1992, Columbus 500th, Genoa Maternal Relatives Reunion, 1992, Rome, Paternal Relatives Reunion, 1992, Scafati (bordering Pompeii) Maternal Roots, 1992, Awed by Ragusa, Beautiful Sicilian City Scene, 1992, Ode to the Statue of Liberty and to the Marseillaise, 1992. Treas. City Coun. Campaign, Richardson, 1987. Mem.: Alpha Kappa Psi. Republican. Methodist. Avocations: composer, author, photographer, sports. Home: 3208 Whitney Dr Midland TX 79705-6246

CELL, GILLIAN TOWNSEND, retired historian, educator; b. Birkenhead, Cheshire, Eng., June 5, 1937; came to U.S., 1962; d. Thomas Edmund and Doris Abigail (Clark) Townsend; m. John Whitson Cell, Oct. 19, 1962 (dec.); children: Thomas K., Katherine A., John D. BA, U. Liverpool, Eng., 1959, PhD, 1964. Instr. U. N.C., Chapel Hill, 1965-66, asst. prof., 1966-70, assoc. prof., 1970-78, prof., 1978-91, affirmative action officer, 1981-83, chmn. dept. history, 1983-85, dean Coll. Arts and Scis., 1985-91; provost Lafayette Coll., 1991-93, Coll. of William and Mary, 1993—2003; ret., 2003. Author: English Enterprise in Newfoundland; 1577-1660, 1969; editor: Newfoundland Discovered, 1982. Home: 1152 Fearrington Post Fearrington Village NC 27312-5014 E-mail: gtcell@wm.edu.

CELLERY MCCALL, PATTI, librarian; d. Vivian L. and Leon Cellery; m. John R. Furr. MA, SUNY, Albany, 1998, MLS, 1999. Cert. libr. N.Y. State Dept. of Edn., 1999. Adult/youth svcs. libr. East Greenbush Cmty. Libr., NY, 2000—; corp. libr. Albany Molecular Rsch., Inc., NY, 2002—. Contbr. articles to profl. jours. Mem. Friends of U. Librs., Albany, NY, 2005. Mem.: Spl. Librs. Assn. (program planning com.), Hudson Mohawk Libr. Assn. (corr. sec./newsletter editor 2002), N.Y. Libr. Assn. (2005 conf. planner-ref. and adult svcs. sect. 2004). Avocations: hiking/fitness, military history, jazz, travel. Office: Albany Molecular Rsch Inc 26 Corporate Cir Albany NY 12203 Office Phone: 518-464-0279 2374. Business E-Mail: patti.mccall@albmolecular.com.

CELLI, ANDREW GEORGE, JR., lawyer; b. Rochester, N.Y., Nov. 7, 1965; s. Andrew George and Dolores R. (Licata) C.; m. Ellen Rose Unterberg, Mar. 10, 1990; children: Rebecca Rose, Hannah Andrea. BA, Hobart Coll., Geneva, N.Y., 1987; JD, NYU, 1990. Bar: N.Y. 1991, U.S. Dist. Ct. (so. dist.) N.Y. 1991, U.S. Dist. Ct. (ea. dist.) N.Y. 1991. Law clk. to Hon. Charles P. Sifton U.S. Dist. Ct. (ea. dist.) N.Y., Bklyn., 1990-91; assoc. Cravath, Swaine & Moore, N.Y.C., 1991-93, Richard D. Emery, P.C., N.Y.C., 1993-96; ptnr. Emery, Celli, Cuti & Brinckerhoff, L.L.P., N.Y.C., 1997—. Contbr. articles to profl. jours. Trustee NYU Law Pub. Svc. Fellowship Fund, 1992-94, Grand St. Settlement, N.Y.C., 1995—, Hobart and William Smith Colls., 1986-88; rschr. Abrams '92 Senate campaign, N.Y.C., 1991-92. Recipient Libel Def. fellowship Libel Def. Resource Ctr., N.Y.C., 1989-90. Mem. Police Abuse Lawyers Coalition (founding), Assn. of the Bar of the City of N.Y., Order of the Coif, Phi Beta Kappa. Democrat. Roman Catholic. Home: 993 Park Ave # 55 New York NY 10028-0809 Office: Emery Celli Cuti & Brinckerhoff LLP 1740 Broadway Fl 25 New York NY 10019-4315

CELLUCCI, PAUL (ARGEO PAUL CELLUCCI), former ambassador, former governor; b. Marlboro, Mass., Apr. 24, 1948; s. Argeo R. and Prisicilla Rose C.; m. Janet Garnett, 1971; children: Kate, Anne. BS, Boston Coll., 1970, JD, 1973. Atty. Kittredge, Cellucci and Moreira, Hudson, Mass., 1973-90; mem. Hudson charter commn. Hudson, 1970-71; selectman, 1971-77; state rep. Third Middlesex Dist., Mass., 1977-84; state senator Middlesex and Worcester Dists., Mass., 1985-90; lt. gov. State of Mass., 1991-97, gov., 1997—2001; U.S. amb. to Canada U.S. Dept. State, Ottawa, 2001—05; exec. v.p. corp. devel. Magna Entertainment Corp, 2005—. Capt. USAR, served in USAR 1970-1978. Recipient Haskins and Fells Found. award, 1969. Mem. ABA, Mass. Bar Assn., Elks, Sons of Italy. Republican. Roman Catholic. Office: Magna Entertainment Corp 337 Magna Dr L4G 7K1 Aurora ON Canada

CELLURA, A(NGELE) RAYMOND, psychologist; b. Rochester, N.Y., Dec. 22, 1932; s. Raymond Anthony and Helen (Balistrere) Cellura; children: Jon, Jane, Todd. BA, St. Francis Coll., 1957; MS, L.I. U., 1960, SUNY, New Paltz, 1960; EdD, U. Rochester, 1965. Lic. psychologist Mass., Ga. Psychologist City Sch. Dist., Rochester, 1961-63; sr. clin. psychologist N.Y. State Dept. Mental Hygeine, 1964-65; asst. dir. cmty. mental health rsch. tng. program Washington U., St. Louis, 1964-65, asst. prof. Grad. Inst. Edn., 1964-65; head dept. human devel. U. Mass., Amherst, 1965-68; assoc. prof. psychology R.I. Coll., Providence, 1968-70; pres. EDPSI, Inc., Sharon, Mass., 1970-89; psychologist IV, S.C. Dept. Mental Health, Columbia, 1989-91; med. cons. disability determination S.C. Divsn. Voc. Rehab., 1991-93; prin. Behavior Consults, Hartwell Ga., 1993—, Abbeville, S.C., 1993—. Mental health cons. Head Start program Ctrl. Savannah River Area-Econ. Opportunity Authority, Augusta, Ga., 1998—2000; trainee post-doctoral program in psychopharmacology U. Ga.-Ga. State U., 1999—2000; chief psychology svcs. Ga. Regional Hosp. Augusta, 2002—; bd. dirs. Psychosocial Treatment Svcs. E. Ctr. Regional Hosp., Augusta, 2003—. Author: Cellura's Cento, The Genomic Environment and Niche-Experience; contbr. articles to profl. jours. Mem.: AAAS, N.Y. Acad. Scis., Am. Psychol. Assn. Office: Behavior Consults 2418 Cedar Springs Rd Abbeville SC 29620-9803 E-mail: arcellura@wctel.net.

CELMER, VIRGINIA, psychologist; b. Detroit, June 26, 1945; d. Charles and Stella (Kopicko) C. BA in English, Marygrove Coll., 1968; MA in Theol. Studies, St. Louis U., 1977; PhD in Counseling Psychology, Tex. Tech. U., 1986. Lic. psychologist; lic. chem. dependency counselor; cert. diplomate in managed mental health care; bd. cert. alcohol and drug counselor level III diplomate; internat. cert. alcoholism and drug abuse counselor; cert. group psychotherapist; cert. sex addicion therapist level II. Chaplain Mercy Ctr. for Health Care Svcs., Aurora, Ill., 1977-81; grad. asst. counselor U. Counseling Ctr., Tex. Tech. U., Lubbock, 1982-86, pre-doctoral intern in counseling psychology, 1985-86; post-doctoral intern Consultation Ctr., San Antonio, 1986-89, staff psychologist, 1989-90; pvt. practice psychologist San Antonio, 1989—. Instr. dept. psychology Tex. Tech. U., Lubbock, 1981-85, Oblate Sch. Theology, San Antonio, 1989-90. Contbr. articles to profl. jours. Mem. APA, Tex. Psychol. Assn., Bexar County Psychol. Assn., Am. Group Psychotherapy Assn., San Antonio Group Psychotherapy Assn., Nat. Assn. Alcoholism and Drug Abuse Counselors, Tex. Assn. Alcoholism and Drug Abuse Counselors. Office: 5440 Babcock Rd Ste 110 San Antonio TX 78240-3946 Office Phone: 210-641-7400.

CELOTTA, ROBERT JAMES, physicist; s. Bart and Agnes Margaret (Comerford) C.; m. Beverly Kay Lauter, Nov. 20, 1966; children: Jennifer Ann, Daniel Wayne. BS in Physics, CCNY, 1964; PhD in Physics, NYU, 1969. Rsch. asst. IBM Watson Lab., N.Y.C., 1963-64; rsch. asst. dept. physics NYU, N.Y.C., 1964-69, instr., 1966-69; postdoctoral rsch. assoc. Joint Inst. Lab. Astrophysics, Boulder, Colo., 1969-71; physicist Nat. Inst. Standards and Tech., Gaithersburg, Md., 1971-86, fellow, 1987—. Mem. gen. com. Internat. Conf. on Physics of Electron and Atom Collisions, 1985—89; participant NSF-Nat. Coun. for Sci. and Tech. U.S.-L.Am. Coop. Sci. Program, 1984—86, U.S.-Spain Sci. Program, 1985—88, U.S.-Yugoslav Coop. Rsch. Program, 1978—87; vice chair Gordon Conf. on Magnetic Nanostructures, 1997—99, chair, 2000—02; mem. com. on emerging micro and nano technologies NRC, 2002—03. Series editor Methods of Exptl. Physics, 1981-95, Exptl. Methods in Phys. Scis., 1995—; mem. editl. bd. Rev. Sci. Instruments, 1982-85, vice chair Davisson-Germer Prize Com., 1990-91, chair, 1992-93, adv. com. Conf. on Magnetism and Magnetic Materials, 1996-97; contbr. articles to Phys. Rev. Letters, Science, Phys. Rev., Jour. Vaccum Sci. Tech., Jour. Applied Physics, Applied Physics Letters, Revs. Sci. Instruments, Sci., Jour. Physics, Jour. Magnetism and Magnetic Materials, Jour. Chem. Physics, numerous others; contbr. to conf. procs. Recipient Disting. Young Scientist award Md. Acad. Scis., 1978, Edward V. Condon award U.S. Dept. Commerce, 1980, IR-100 award R & D Mag., 1980, 85, Fed. Lab. Consortium award Excellence in Tech. Transfer, 1988, William P. Slichter award Nat. Inst. Stds. and Tech., 1992, Alumni Achievement award NYU, 1997. Fellow: AAAS (Centennial spkr. 1998—99), Washington Acad. Sci. (Outstanding and Disting. Career in Sci. award 1994), Am. Vacuum Soc. (Gaede-Langmuir prize 1994), Am. Phys. Soc. (exec. com. topical group on instrumentation and measurement scis. 2000—, mem. McGrody prize com. 2000—02). Achievements include patents for Absorbed Current Electron Polarization Detectors; Apparatus and Methods for Electron Spin Polarization Detection; Laser Controlled Nanolithography; developed photodetachment spectroscopy method for electron affinity measurement; pioneering measurements in polarized electron scattering from atoms and surfaces, scanning tunneling microscopy, surface magnetism and laser controlled atom deposition; developed the GaAs polarized electron source, the diffuse low energy polarization detector, the technique of scanning electron microscopy with polarization analysis (SEMPA), and autonomous atom assembly. Office: NIST 100 Bureau Dr Gaithersburg MD 20899-8412 Office Phone: 301-975-3710. Business E-Mail: Robert.Celotta@nist.gov.

CEMBALEST, ROBIN, arts editor, critic; B in Art Hist., Yale Univ. Editorial asst. Art Forum; staff Forward Newspaper; exec. editor ARTnews Mag., NYC, 1988—94, 1999—. Contbg. writer NY Times, Wall St. Jour. Lectr. in field. Mem. Nat. Found. for Jewish Culture. Recipient Nat. Headliner award, Silurians award for arts/cultural reporting. Office: ARTnews Magazine 48 W 38th St New York NY 10018-0042 Office Phone: 212-398-1690 112. Office Fax: 212-819-0394.

CENDALI, DALE MARGARET, lawyer; b. N.Y.C., Feb. 11, 1959; d. John Amos and Eleanor M. (Avocato) C.; m. John Francis Fitzpatrick, Sept. 12, 1987. BA summa cum laude, Yale U., 1981; JD, Harvard U., 1984. Bar: N.Y. 1985, U.S. Dist. Ct. (so. and ea. dists.) N.Y. 1985, U.S. Dist. Ct. (ea. dist.) Mich. 1988, U.S. Dist. Ct. (no. dist.) Calif. 2001, U.S. Ct. Appeals (2d cir.) 1989, U.S. Ct. Appeals (Fed. cir.) 1990, U.S. Ct. Appeals (9th cir.) 2001, U.S. Supreme Ct. 2002. Assoc. Fried, Frank, Harris Shriver & Jacobson, N.Y.C., 1984-91, O'Melveny & Myers, N.Y.C., 1991—. Editor-in-chief Harvard Jour. Legis. 1983-84; contbr. numerous articles to profl. jours. Named one of Am. Top 50 Women Litigators, Nat. Law Jour., The Magnificent 7 - IP's Best Young Trial Lawyers, IP Worldwide Mag., Nifty 50 - Harvard Law Sch. Women Alumnae, Harvard Law Bulletin. Mem. ABA (chair intellectual property com. litig. sect., programming co-chair 1993 litig. sect. ann. meeting), N.Y. State Bar Assn. (chair work for hire subcom. intellectual properties com. fed. and comml. sects.), Assn. of Bar of City of N.Y. (copyright and literary property com., media law com., chair trademark com.); Phi Beta Kappa. Avocations: theater, comic strips and books collector, sailing. Office: O'Melveny & Myers LLP Times Sq Tower 7 Times Sq New York NY 10036 Business E-Mail: dcendali@omm.com.

CENTAFONT, LUCY ANN ALEXANDER, occupational therapist, consultant; b. Anchorage, Alaska, Apr. 6, 1953; d. Robert C. and Lucy Ann (Morgan) Alexander; m. Richard A. Centafont, May 13, 1978; children: Ryan Alan, Jeffrey Richard, Lauren Ann. BS in Occupational Therapy, Temple U., 1977, MS, 1987; BS in Health Edn., Slippery Rock U., 1975. Occupational therapy cons. Bucks County Assn. for Retarded Citizens, Doylestown, Pa.; dir. occupational therapy Community Found. for Human Devel., Sellersville, Pa.; chief occupational therapy Rolling Hill Hosp., Elkins Park, Pa.; pvt. practice occupational therapy cons. Southampton, Pa. Mem. Am. Occupational Therapy Assn., Pa. Occupational Therapy Assn. (developmental disabilities spl. interest group, adminstrv. spl. interest group).

CENTANNI, ROSS J., engineering executive; b. 1946; With B.F. Goodrich Co., Hooker Chem. divsn. Occidental Petroleum; mgr. corp. planning Cooper Industries, Quincy, Ill., 1981, dir. mktg. Gardner-Denver Indsl. Machinery divsn., 1985-90, v.p., gen. mgr. Gardner-Denver Indsl. Machinery divsn., 1990-93; pres., CEO Gardner Denver, Inc., Quincy, 1993—, chmn. bd., 1998—. Office: 1800 Gardner Expy Quincy IL 62305-9364 Office Fax: 217-228-8247.

CENTNER, CHARLES WILLIAM, lawyer, educator; b. Battle Creek, Mich., July 4, 1915; s. Charles William and Lucy Irene (Patterson) C.; m. Evi Rohr, Dec. 22, 1956; children: Charles Patterson, David William, Geoffrey Christopher. AB, U. Chgo., 1936, AM, 1939, PhD, 1941; LLB, LaSalle Extension U., 1965; JD, Mich. State U., 1970. Bar: Mich. 1970. Asst. prof. U. N.D., 1940-41, Tulane U., New Orleans, 1941-42; liaison officer for Latin Am., Dept. State at Lend-Lease Adminstrn., 1942; assoc. dir. Western Hemisphere divsn. Nat. Fgn. Trade Coun., N.Y., 1946-52; exec. Ford Motor Co., Detroit, 1952-57, Chrysler Corp. and Chrysler Internat. S.A., Detroit and Geneva, Switzerland, 1957-70. Adj. prof. Pace U., N.Y.C., 1950-52, Wayne State U., Detroit, 1971-78, U. Detroit, 1970-72, Wayne County C.C., 1970-2001. Author: Great Britian and Chile, 1810-1914, 1941. Lt. comdr. USNR, 1942-45, Res., 1945-75. Mem. ABA, State Bar Mich., Oakland County Bar Assn., Masons. Republican. Episcopalian. Home: 936 Harcourt Rd Grosse Pointe Park MI 48230-1874

CENTO, WILLIAM FRANCIS, retired newspaper editor; b. St. Louis, Mar. 20, 1932; s. Frank and Augusta (Albietz) C.; m. Vera Ann Shaide, May 16, 1964. BS, St. Louis U., 1954. Gen. assignment reporter East St. Louis (Ill.) Jour., 1954-56; suburban editor Globe-Democrat, St. Louis, 1956-61; copy-editor Post-Dispatch, St. Louis, 1961-62; make-up editor Pioneer Press, St. Paul, 1962-65, wire editor, 1965-67, Sunday editor, 1967-73; graphics editor Pioneer Press & Dispatch, St. Paul, 1974-77; mng. editor St. Paul Dispatch,

1977-84; assoc. editor Pioneer Press, St. Paul, 1984-90. Owner Give Me Rewrite, West St. Paul, 1990—; editor, pub. Letter from Minn., West St. Paul, 1995—. Editor: Fifty and Feisty APME: 1933 to 1983, 1983. Recipient numerous awards including Twin Cities Newspaper Guild Page 1 award Makeup 1st pl. award, 1969, 71, 74, 2d pl., 1971, 72, Award of Appreciation, AP Mng. Editors Assn., 1983. Mem. Soc. Profl. Journalists, AP Mng. Editors Assn. (bd. dirs. 1982-88). Roman Catholic. Avocations: painting, graphic design. Home and Office: 111 Imperial Dr W Apt 103 West Saint Paul MN 55118-2249 Office Phone: 651-451-8565. E-mail: mnletter@aol.com.

CENTRELLO, GINA, publishing executive; Joined as copy editor Pocket Books, Simon & Schuster, 1981, exec. v.p. pub., 1993—94, pres. pub., 1994—99, Ballantine Books, 1999—2003, Random House Pub. Group, 2003—. Office: Random House Pub Group 1745 Broadway New York NY 10019

CENTRO, JUAN N., air transportation executive; b. Cuba; m. Ana Centro; 2 children. Attended, Miami Dade Cmty. Coll., Fla. Internat. U. Bus. Sch. With Flying Tiger Line, Inc., 1977—89, Fed. Express, 1989—, current pres. Latin Am. and Caribbean divsn. Dir. Beacons Coun. and World Trade Ctr., Miami; trustee Free Trade Area Ams. Bd. chmn. Internat. Kids Fund. Office: FedEx LAC HQ 701 Waterford Way Ste 1000 Miami FL 33126

CEPEDA, ORLANDO, retired professional baseball player; b. Ponce, P.R., Sept. 17, 1937; m. Miriam Cepeda; children: Orlando Jr., Hector, Malcolm, Ali Manuel. 1st baseman San Francisco Giants, 1958—66, St. Louis Cardinals, 1966—69, Atlanta Braves, 1969—72, Oakland Athletics, Calif., 1972, Boston Red Sox, 1973, Kansas City Royals, 1974; cmty. rep. San Francisco Giants, 1990—. Named Rookie of Yr. San Francisco Giants, 1958, Comeback Player of Yr., St. Louis Cardinals, 1966, Nat. League Most Valuable Player, 1967; named to Sports Hall of Fame, P.R., 1993, Baseball Hall of Fame, 1999; recipient Designated Hitter of Yr. award, 1973. Achievements include being lifetime .297 hitter with 379 home runs; making 1,364 RBIs; appearing in 3 World Series games; being an 11-time All-Star; hitting over .300 9 times in career. Office: c/o San Francisco Giants 3 Com Park San Francisco CA 94124-3904*

CEPHAS, DERRICK, lawyer; b. Cambridge, Md., Jan. 22, 1952; AB, Harvard Univ., 1975, JD, 1979. Counsel & dep. supt. of banks N.Y. State Banking Dept., 1983—85; gen. counsel Urban Develop. Corp., NY, 1985—86; adj. prof. Bklyn. Coll., 1986—89; chmn. N.Y. State Legislature Spec. Com. on Interstate Banking, 1987; Supt. of Banks N.Y. State Banking Dept., 1991—94; ptnr. Banking & Fin. dept. & mem. mgmt. com. Cadwalader Wickersham & Taft, N.Y.C. Bd. dir. Dime Savings Bank, NY, D.E. Shaw & Co. Office: Cadwalader Wickersham & Taft LLP 1 World Fin Ctr New York NY 10281 Office Phone: 212-504-6588. Office Fax: 212-504-6666. Business E-Mail: derrick.cephas@cwt.com.

CEPPOS, JEROME MERLE (JERRY CEPPOS), newspaper editor; b. Washington, Oct. 14, 1946; s. Harry and Florence (Epstein) C.; m. Karen E. Feingold, Mar. 7, 1982; children: Matthew, Robin. BS in Journalism, U. Md., 1969; postgrad., Knight-Ridder Exec. Leadership Program, 1989-90. Reporter, asst. city editor, night city editor Rochester (N.Y.) Democrat & Chronicle, 1969-72; from asst. city editor, to nat. editor, to asst. mng. editor The Miami (Fla.) Herald, 1972-81; various editl. positions, including assoc. editor San Jose (Calif.) Mercury News, 1981—83, mng. editor, 1983—85, exec. editor, sr. v.p., 1995-99; v.p. news Knight Ridder, 1999—. Bd. visitors Coll. Journalism, U. Md., 1999-; pres. Accrediting Coun. on Edn. in Journalism and Mass Comm. 2003-04. Recipient Journalism award, Soc. Profl. Journalists' Nat Ethics, 1997, Disting. Journalism Alumnus award, U. Md., 2001. Mem. AP Mng. Editors (immediate past pres.), Am. Soc. Newspaper Editors, Calif. Soc. Newspaper Editors (former mem. bd. dirs., past pres.), Soc. Profl. Journalists, Assn. for Edn. in Journalism and Mass Comm., No. Calif. Cancer Ctr. (bd. trustees), Silicon Valley Capital Club Office: Knight Ridder 50 W San Fernando St San Jose CA 95113-2429 E-mail: jceppos@knightridder.com.

CERCIELLO, ANN MARIE T., mathematics educator, church music director; b. Morristown, NJ, May 11, 1951; d. Lawrence and Theresa (DeCaro) Cerciello. BA, Coll. St. Elizabeth, Morristown, 1974. Cert. elem. sch. tchr. NJ, 1974, math tchr. NJ, 1976. Math. tchr., theater dir. Morristown Sch. Dist., Assumption Sch., 1975—76, Williamsport, Pa., 1985—87; math. tchr., theater dir., chorus accompanist Acad. St. Aloysius, Jersey City, 1975—78; math. tchr., chorus accompanist Jersey City Sch. Dist., Lincoln HS, 1987—88; math. tchr. Essex County Vo-Tech. Sch. Dist., Newark, 1989—91; math., chorus, theater tchr., dir. Montclair HS, NJ, 1995—, Mt. Hebron Mid. Sch., Montclair, 1995—. Piano tchr., 1970—96; ch. musician, 1970—; owner, prodr., dir. Touring Theater Co., NJ, 1982—87, Pa., 1982—87; math subject matter leader Montclair Sch. Dist., Mt. Hebron Mid. Sch., 1997—; com. mem. for curriculum evaluation, test materials Montclair Sch. Dist., 1996—. Donor, supporter So. Poverty Law Ctr.-tchg. tolerance, 1997—, Habitat for Humanity, 1997—, The Carter Ctr., 1997—, Emily's List, 2005—; various cmty. theater bds. NJ, 1975—2000. Named an honoree, Montclair Fund for Ednl. Excellence, 1995—; recipient Weston award, and nominee, pvt. donors Montclair Sch. Dist., 1995—. Mem.: Assn. Math. Tchrs. of NJ, Nat. Coun. Tchrs. of Math., Assn. Supervision and Curriculum Devel. Democrat. Avocations: reading, crossword puzzles, travel, dance. Home: 163 Williamson Ave Bloomfield NJ 07003 Office: Mt Hebron Middle Sch 173 Bellevue Ave Upper Montclair NJ 07043 E-mail: amtcmath@aol.com.

CERE, RONALD CARL, languages educator, consultant, researcher; b. N.Y.C., Oct. 22, 1947; s. Mindie Anthony and Edvige Clelia (Ruggero) C. BA, CUNY, 1968; MA, Queens Coll., 1969; PhD, NYU, 1974. Asst. prof. SUNY, Old Westbury, 1974-77, U. Ill., Urbana, 1977-80, U. Nebr., Lincoln, 1980-83, Gettysburg (Pa.) Coll., 1983-85; prof. Ea. Mich. U., Ypsilanti, 1985-90, 1990—. Cons. Trinity Dynamics, N.J., Harcourt Brace Jovanovich, Harper & Collins, D.C. Heath, Prentice-Hall, Random House, Scott Foresman Pub. Cos., 1985—; speaker, presenter in field. Author: Los Fabulistas, 1969, Exito Comercial, 3d edit., 2001; contbr. articles to profl. jours. Recipient James C. Healy award NYU, 1974. Mem. MLA, ASTD, Am. Assn. Tchrs. Spanish and Portuguese (dir. career svcs.), Am.Coun. Teaching Fgn. Langs., Soc. for Intercultural Edn., Tng. and Rsch., Southern Conf. Lang. Teaching (bd. advisors). Home: 2120 Glencoe Hills Dr Apt 8 Ann Arbor MI 48108-3017 Office: Ea Mich U Dept Fgn Langs 219 Alexander Hall Ypsilanti MI 48197-2255 Office Phone: 734-487-0433. Business E-Mail: rcere@emich.edu.

CEREZO, CARMEN CONSUELO, judge; b. 1940; BA, U. P.R., 1963, LLB, 1966. Pvt. practice, 1966-67; law clk. U.S. Dist. Ct., San Juan, 1967-72; judge Superior Ct., P.R., 1972-76, Ct. Intermediate Appeals, 1976-80, U.S. Dist. Ct., P.R., 1980-93, chief judge, 1993—; dist. judge. Office: Federico Degetau Fed Bldg Rm CH-131 150 Carlos Chardon Ave Hato Rey PR 00918-1761

CERF, VINTON GRAY, telecommunications company executive; b. New Haven, June 23, 1943; s. Vinton Thruston and Muriel (Gray) C.; m. Sigrid L. Thorstenberg, Sept. 10, 1966; children: David, Bennett. BS, Stanford U., 1965; MS in Computer Sci., UCLA, 1970, PhD in Computer Sci., 1972; PhD (hon.), Capitol Coll., Gettysburg Coll., U. Balearic Islands, U. Lulea, Swiss Fed. Inst. Tech.; PhD (hon.), George Mason U., U. Twente, U. Rovira and Virgili. Sys. engr. IBM Corp., 1965-67; prin. programmer UCLA, 1967-72; asst. prof. elec. engring. and computer sci. Stanford (Calif.) U., 1972-76; sr. programmer Jacobi Sys. Corp., Santa Monica, Calif., 1968-70; program mgr. info. processing techniques office Def. Advanced Rsch. Projects Agy., U.S. Dept. Def., Arlington, Va., 1976-81, prin. scientist, 1981-82; dir. sys. devel. MCI Comm. Corp., 1982-83; v.p. engring. MCI Digital Info. Svcs. Co., Washington, 1983-86; v.p. Corp. for Nat. Rsch. Initiatives, Reston, Va., 1986-94; sr. v.p. technology strategy MCI, Ashburn, Va., 1994—. Author: A Practical View of Communication Protocols, 1979. Named to Datamation Hall of Fame, 1989; recipient Kilby award, 1995, Silver medal Internat. Telecomms. Union, 1995, Industry Legend award Computer and Comms. Industries Assn., 1996, NEC Computer and Comm. prize, 1996, Computer Networks and Smithsonian Leadership award, 1996, Nat. Medal of Tech., 1997, Charles Stark Draper award, 2001, Prince of Asturias award, 2002; Marconi fellow, 1998. Fellow IEEE (Kobayashi award 1992, Alexander Graham Bell award 1997), AAAS, Assn. Computing Machinery (chmn. SIG Comm. 1987-91, coun. 1990-92, Software award), Internat. Fedn. Info. Processing, Internet Activities Bd. (chmn. 1979-82, 89-91), Internet Soc. (pioneer mem., trustee 1992-2002, pres. 1992-95, v.p. chpts. 1996-97, chmn. 1998-99); mem. Nat. Acad. Engrs., Sigma Xi. Office: MCI Data Svcs Divsn 2100 Reston Pkwy Rm 6002 Reston VA 20191-1244 E-mail: vinton.g.cerf@mci.com. *My entire working career has been focused on science and technology, in many forms—teaching, research, engineering management. The trait I have come to admire most among technical colleagues is absolute honesty in reporting or assessing results—blemishes and failures as well as successes.**

CERMAK, JACK EDWARD, engineer, educator; b. Hastings, Colo., Sept. 8, 1922; s. Joseph and Helen (Herman) C.; m. Helen Jane Carlson, Dec. 17, 1949; children: Douglas Karl, Jonathan Joel. BS, Colo. State U., 1947, MS, 1948; PhD, Cornell U., 1959; NATO postdoctoral fellow, Cambridge U., Eng., 1961-62. Mem. faculty Colo. State U., Ft. Collins, 1947—, prof. charge fluid mechanics and wind engring. program, also dir. Fluid Dynamics and Diffusion Lab., 1960-85, univ. disting. prof., 1986—, chmn. engring. sci. maj. program, 1963-72; pres., dir. Colo. State U. (Research Found.), 1965-72; pres. Cermak Peterka Petersen Inc., 1982—. Cons. in field; bd. mems. Univ. Corp. Atmospheric Research, 1966-67; pres., chmn. 10th Midwestern Mechanics Conf., 1966-67; dir. summer inst. fluid mechanics NSF, 1963, 65, 68, 72; chmn. 2d U.S. Nat. Conf. Wind Engring. Rsch., 1975, 5th Internat. Conf. Wind Engring., 1979; founding mem., pres. Wind Engring. Rsch. Council, Inc., 1979-85; co-chmn. U.S.-Japan Seminar Lab. Simulation of Stratified Shear Flows; co-dir. NATO Advanced Study Inst., 1993; mem. Colo. Gov.'s Sci. and Tech. Adv. Coun.; com. on army basic rsch. NRC, 1979-83. Mem. editl. bd. Indsl. Aerodynamics Abstracts, Mechanics Rsch. Comms., Internat. Jour. Wind Engring., Wind and Structures; contbr. articles to profl. jours. Fellow AAAS, AIAA (assoc.), ASCE (hon.; chmn. engring. mechanics divsn. 1965, chmn. wind effects com. structural divsn. 1991, chmn. aerodynamics com. aerospace divsn. 2004, Ernest E. Howard award, 2002, Jack E. Cermak medal established 2002, Robert H. Scanlan medal 2004), Am. Acad. Mechanics; mem. ASME (Freeman scholar 1974, disting. lectr. 1987-89), ASHRAE (mem. com. flow around bldgs.), NSPE (Outstanding Profl. Achievement award), Air and Waste Mgmt. Assn., Am. Soc. Engring. Edn. (chmn. mechanics divsn., Sr. Rsch. award 1987), Nat. Acad. Engring. (chmn. com. natural disasters, chmn. panel on wind engring. rsch.), Internat. Assn. Wind Engring. (chmn. bd. 1975-79, regional sec. N.Am. and S.Am. 1983—), Am. Meteorol. soc., Am. Geophys. Union, Instn. Civil engrs. (Scruton lectr. 1995), N.Y. Acad. Scis., Rotary, Sigma Xi (nat. lectr. 1976-77), Chi Epsilon. Home: 407 E Prospect Rd Fort Collins CO 80525-1058 Office Phone: 970-221-3371. Business E-Mail: jecermak@lamar.colostate.edu. *My thoughts and actions have been influenced always by a belief and an awareness that man, the near environment, and the far reaches of the universe are influenced by common natural laws. I believe that the order found in natural events, as revealed by scientific investigation, can someday become manifest in the behavior of man. Ultimately, through persistent and directed effort, I am confident that man will integrate religion, science, and technology to achieve harmony of man with man, and man with the environment. For the most part, my achievements and contributions to society can be attributed to the motivation and direction stemming from these convictions.*

CERMAK, JOHN FRANK, JR., lawyer; b. New Bedford, Mass., Nov. 27, 1956; s. John Frank Cermak Sr. and Barbara Jane (Cardoza) Savage. BA summa cum laude, Boston U., 1979; JD magna cum laude, Am. U., 1982. Bar: DC 1982, US Ct. Appeals DC Cir. 1982, US Ct. Appeals 9th Cir.& 4th Cir. 1984, US Ct. Appeals 5th Cir., 10th Cir. & 6th Cir. 1985, US Ct. Appeals 7th Cir. 1987, US Supreme Ct. 1988, Pa. 1989, Calif. 1990. Law clk. US Dist. Ct. Conn., New Haven, 1982-83, US Ct. Appeals 9th Cir., Phoenix, Seattle, 1983-84; trial atty. US Dept. Justice, Land Natural Resources Div., Washington, 1984-87; sr. assoc. Jones, Day, Reavis & Pogue, LA; atty. Rodi Pollock Pettker Galbraith & Cahill, LA; now shareholder, environ. & adminstrv. advocacy practice group Jenkens & Gilchrist, P.C., LA, mng. shareholder LA & Pasadena offices, firm v.p. bd. dirs. Settlement officer US Dist. Ct. Ctrl. Dist. Calif., 1998—. Mem.: ABA, Environ. Law Inst., Assn. Trial Lawyers of Am., Fed. Bar Assn., LA County Bar Assn., Valley Industry & Commerce Assn., LA Hdqs. Assn., Swiss Am. C. of C., German Am. C. of C., LA County C. of C. Avocations: travel, scuba diving, racquetball, photography. Office: Jenkens & Gilchrist PC 15th Fl 12100 Wilshire Blvd Los Angeles CA 90025-7120 Office Phone: 310-442-8885. Office Fax: 310-820-8859. Business E-Mail: jcermak@jenkens.com.

CERMINARA, FRANK, food products executive; Studied, W.Va. U.; BS, Wharton Sch. Business, U. Pa., 1972. Budget analyst Hershey Foods Corp., Pa., 1972—94, v.p., procurement, 1994—2001, v.p., CFO, treas., 2000—01, sr. v.p., CFO, 2001—. Office: Hershey Foods Corp PO Box 810 100 Crystal A Dr Hershey PA 17033-0810

CERNICA, JOHN N., engineering educator, civil engineer, consultant; b. Calvaser, Romania, May 14, 1932; arrived in U.S., 1945; s. John and Mary Cernica; m. Mary Patricia Marinelli, June 25, 1959; children: Kathy, Jude, Alice, Johanna, Patricia, Sarah. BE, Youngstown (Ohio) State U., 1954; MS in engring., Carnegie Mellon U., Pitts., 1955, PhD in engring., 1957. Registered Ohio, Tex., Fla., Ga., Ind., Iowa, DC, Ky., Md., Mich., NY, NJ, Miss., Pa., SC, Tenn., Va., W. Va., Nat. Cert. Prof. civil engring. Youngstown State U., 1958—, dept. head civil engring.; owner J.N. Cernica & Assoc., Cons. Engrs., Youngstown, Ohio, 1962. Panelist Nat. Sci. Found.; examiner Ohio Bd. Registration Profl. Engrs. and Surveyors. Author: (textbooks) Fundamentals of Reinforced Concrete, 1964, Strength of Materials, 1 edit., 1966, (Textbooks) Strength of Materials, Spanish edit., 1968, (textbooks) Strength of Materials, 2 edit., 1977, Strength of Materials, Chinese edit., 1982, Geotech. Engring., 1982, Soil Mechanics, 1994, Found. Design, 1994; contbr. scientific papers, articles to profl. jours. Recipient Ohio's Outstanding Engr., 1964, Man of the Yr. award, 1970, Outstanding Civil Engr., 1981, Disting. Prof. award, Youngstown State U. Mem.: Mahoning County Soc. of Profl. Engrs., Nat. Soc. of Profl. Engrs., Am. Soc. of Engring. Edn., Am. Concrete Inst., Am. Soc. of Civil Engrs., Sigma Tau, Sigma Xi, Phi Kappa Phi, Tau Beta Pi. Mailing: 611 Plymouth Dr Youngstown OH 44512

CERNUGEL, WILLIAM JOHN, consumer products company executive, distributor; b. Joliet, Ill., Nov. 19, 1942; m. Laurie M. Kusnik, Apr. 22, 1967; children: Debra, James, David. BS, No. Ill. U., 1964. CPA, Ill. Sr. supr. KPMG LLP, Chgo., 1964-70; asst. corp. contr. Alberto-Culver Co., Melrose Park, Ill., 1970-71, corp. contr., 1972—74, v.p., contr., 1974-82, v.p. fin., 1982-93, sr. v.p. fin., 1993-2000, sr. v.p., CFO, 2000—. Mem. bd. govs., treas. Gottlieb Meml. Hosp., Melrose Park; assoc. mem. bd. advisors Coll. Bus., No. Ill. U. Mem. AICPA, Am. Mgmt. Assn. (fin. coun.), Inst. Mgmt. Accts., Ill. Soc. CPAs, Fin. Exec. Internat., Lions. Home: 8111 Lake Ridge Dr Burr Ridge IL 60527-5977 Office: Alberto-Culver Co 2525 Armitage Ave Melrose Park IL 60160-1163

CERNY, ALLEN TERRY, art educator; s. Archie and Mary Cerny; m. Janice Cerny, Dec. 30, 1973; children: Jason, Brandon, Dillon. BS, Chadron State Coll., 1974; MEd, U. Nebr., 2002. Tchr. Ogallala (Nebr.) Pub. Schs., 1974—. Office: Ogallala HS 602 E G St Ogallala NE 69153-2249

CERNY, CHARLENE ANN, director; b. Jamaica, N.Y., Jan. 12, 1947; d. Albert Joseph and Charlotte Ann (Novy) Cerny; children: Elizabeth Brett Cerny-Chipman, Kathryn Rose Cerny-Chipman. BA, SUNY, Binghamton, 1969. Cert. Fundraising Exec. Curator Latin-Am. folk art Mus. Internat. Folk Art, Santa Fe, 1972-84, mus. dir., 1984-99; dir. instnl. advancement Santa Fe Prep. Sch., 1999—; founder Santa Fe Internat. Folk Art Market. Adv. bd. C.G. Jung Inst., Santa Fe, 1990-98. Mem. Mayor's Commn. on Children and Youth, Santa Fe, 1990-93, adv. bd. Recipient Exemplary Performance award State of N.Mex., 1982, Internat. Ptnr. Among Mus. award, Mayor's Recognition award, 1999, Mus. N.Mex. Regents award, 1999; Smithsonian Instn. travel grantee, 1976; Florence Dibell Bartlett Meml. scholar, 1979, 91; Kellogg fellow, 1983. Mem. Am. Assn. Mus. Internat. Coun. Mus. (bd. dirs. 1991—, exec. bd. 1991-95), Am. Folklore Soc., Mountain-Plains Mus. Assn., N.Mex. Assn. Mus. (chair membership com. 1975-77). Office: 1101 Camino De Cruz Blanca Santa Fe NM 87505-0349*

CERNY, JOSEPH, III, chemistry professor, retired dean, retired director; b. Montgomery, Ala., Apr. 24, 1936; s. Joseph and Olaette Genette (Jury) C.; m. Barbara Ann Nedelka, June 13, 1959 (div. Nov. 1982); children: Keith Joseph, Mark Evan; m. 2d Susan Dinkelspiel Stern, Nov. 12, 1983. BS in Chem. Engring., U. Miss.-Oxford, 1957; postgrad. Fulbright scholar, U. Manchester, Eng., 1957-58; PhD in Nuclear Chemistry, U. Calif.-Berkeley, 1961; PhD in Physics (hon.), U. Jyväskylä, Finland, 1990. Asst. prof. chemistry U. Calif., Berkeley, 1961-67, assoc. prof., 1967-71, prof., 1971—, chmn. dept. chemistry, 1975-79, head nuclear sci. div., 1979-84, assoc. dir. Lawrence Berkeley Lab., 1979-84, dean grad. div., 1985-2000, provost for research, 1986-94, vice chancellor for rsch., 1994-2000. Mem. Nat. Acad. Scis. Physics Commn., chair nuclear physics panel, 1983-86; mem. NASA Adv. Coun., Univ. Rels. Task Force, 1991-93, NRC Study of Rsch. Doctorates, 1992-95, chmn. nuc. sci. adv. subcom. edn., 2003-04. Editor: Nuclear Reactions and Spectroscopy, 4 vols., 1974; contbr. numerous articles to field to profl. jours. Served with U.S. Army, 1962-63. Recipient E.O. Lawrence award AEC, 1974, A. von Humboldt sr. scientist award, 1985; named to U. Miss. Alumni Hall of Fame, 1988. Fellow AAAS, Am. Phys. Soc.; mem. Am. Chem. Soc. (Nuclear Chemistry award 1984), Assn. Grad. Schs. (v.p., pres. 1992-94). Democrat. Home: 860 Keeler Ave Berkeley CA 94708-1324 Office: Lawrence Berkeley Nat Lab Univ Calif Bldg 88 Berkeley CA 94720 Office Phone: 510-486-7852. E-mail: jcerny@berkeley.edu.

CERNY, JOSEPH CHARLES, urologist, educator; b. Apr. 20, 1930; s. Joseph James and Mary (Turek) Cerny; m. Patti Bobette Pickens, Nov. 10, 1962; children: Joseph Charles, Rebecca Anne. BA, Knox Coll., 1952; MD, Yale U., 1956. Diplomate Am. Bd. Urology. Intern U. Mich. Hosp., Ann Arbor, 1956-57, resident, 1957-62; pvt. practice Ann Arbor, Detroit, 1962—. Pres. Resistors, Inc., Chgo., 1960—; from instr. to assoc. prof. urology U. Mich., Ann Arbor, 1962—77, clin. prof., 1971—, mem. instl. rev. bd. rsch. Med. Sch., 2001; chmn. dept. urology Henry Ford Hosp., Detroit, 1971—98, chmn. emeritus urology, 1998; cons. St. Joseph Hosp., Ann Arbor, 1973—; chief urology sect. dept. surgery Ann Arbor VA Hosp., 1999—. Mem. editl. bd. Am. Jour. Kidney Diseases, 1988—; contbr. articles to profl. jours., chapters to books. Bd. dirs. Ann Arbor Amateur Hockey Assn., 1980—83; pres. PTO Ann Arbor Pub. Schs., 1980; chmn. urology coun., mem. exec. com. Nat. Kidney Found. Mich., Ann Arbor, 1987—, bd. dirs., trustee, pres., 1988—, emeritus trustee, 1997, chmn. capital campaign, 2002. Lt. USNR, 1956—76. Recipient Disting. Svc. award, Nat. Kidney Found. Mich., 1993, Champion of Hope award, 1997, Disting. Career award, Henry Ford Hosp. Alumni, 2000. Fellow: ACS (pres-elect Mich. br. 1984—85, pres. 1985—); mem.: S.W. Oncology Group, Am. Fertility Soc., Am. Assn. Urologic Oncology, Soc. Univ. Urologists, Endocrine Surgeons, Am. Assn. Transplant Surgeons, Transplantation Soc. Mich. (pres. Mich. 1983—85, Disting. Svc. award 1982), Am. Urol. Assn. (pres. Mich. br. 1980—81, pres. N. Ctrl. sect. 1985—86, mem. fiscal affairs rev. commn. 1985—89, mem. manpower com. 1987—88, mem. tech. exhibits 1987—88, mem. jud. rev. com. 1987—91, mem. manpower com. 1990—92, mem. audit commn. 1992—96, mem. exec. commn. 1993—, bd. dirs., mem. audio-visual com., mem. program rev. com. 1994—, chmn., mem. work force com., mem. publs. com. 1995, chmn. publs. com. 1999, mem. jud. and ethics com. 1997—, Best Sci. Exhibit award 1978, Best Sci. Films award 1980, 1982), Internat. Soc. Urology, Am. Coll. Physician Execs., Am. Acad. Med. Dirs., Ann Arbor Racquet Club, Barton Hills Country Club. Avocations: tennis, fishing, civil war. Home: 2800 Fairlane St Ann Arbor MI 48104-4110 Office: U Mich Health Sys Sect Urology Dept Surgery 1500 E Medical Center Dr Ann Arbor MI 48109-0005 Office Phone: 734-615-3039. Business E-Mail: jocerny@umich.edu.

CERNY, LOUIS THOMAS, civil engineer, transportation engineer, consultant; b. Berwyn, Ill., Mar. 7, 1942; s. Thomas Alois and Rosalia Patricia (Havranek) C.; m. Lana Sally Taylor, June 6, 1964; children— Leonard, David BSCE, U. Ill., 1964, MS, 1965. Registered profl. engr., Ill., Miss. Rsch. asst. U. Ill., Urbana, 1964-65; various engring. positions Elgin, Joliet & Eastern Ry., Joliet, Ill., 1965-75; v.p., chief engr. Columbus & Greenville Ry., Miss., 1975-78; v.p. ops. Erie Western Ry., Huntington, Ind., 1978-79; exec. dir. Am. Ry Engring. Assn., Washington, 1979-94. Exec. dir. engring. divsn. Assn. Am. Railroads, 1979-97, cons., 1997—; leader engring. dels. to China, 1983, 84. Contbr. articles to profl. jours.; patentee in field Mem. Am. Railway Engring. and Maint.-of-Way Assn. Unitarian Universalist. Avocations: travel, photography, hiking, astronomy.

CERNY, WILLIAM, retired education educator, musician; b. N.Y.C., Dec. 27, 1928; s. Karl Otto Cerny and Martha Rossler; m. Mary Ann Cunningham, June 26, 1954; children: Elaine, Jean, Mary, Carol. BA magna cum laude, Yale Univ., New Haven, Conn., 1951; MusB, Yale Sch. of Music, New Haven, Conn., 1952, MusM, 1954. Profl. accompanist freelance, N.Y., 1954—59; assoc. prof. Eastman Sch. of Music, Rochester, NY, 1959—72; prof. Univ. Notre Dame, South Bend, Ind., 1972—2000. Chmn., music dept. Notre Dame Univ., South Bend, Ind., 1972—81; evaluator Nat Assoc. of Sch. of Music, Washington, 1980—95; classical piano concerts of music, throughout U.S.A. Musician (concert pianist and chamber musician): (concerts in scores) coll. and univ., 1965—96; musician: (explorations into piano lit.) weekly 1/2 hr. NPR Program, 1981—. Seaman USNR, 1948—57. Mem.: Phi Beta Kappa. Independent. Roman Catholic. Achievements include formed Wilmarc Rec., Inc., classical CD's 114, Cd's made available to Col. and Univ. throughout USA and abroad; a contbn. to ednl. cmty. Avocations: carpentry, sailing, fishing. Home: 2918 Caroline St South Bend IN 46614 Office Phone: 574-288-8741. E-mail: cerny.1@nd.edu.

CERONE, DAVID, academic administrator; m. Linda Sharon Cerone. Dir. and mem. summer faculty Meadowmount Sch. Music; prof. violin Oberlin Conservatory, 1962—71; chmn. string dept. and Kulas prof. Cleve. Inst. Music, 1971—81, pres., 1985—, Mary Elizabeth Callahan pres. chair; mem. violin faculty Curtis Inst. Music, 1975—85, head violin dept., 1981—85. Founder Cleve. Chamber Music Seminar, 1974; co-founder and dir. ENCORE Sch. Strings; bd. advisors Astral Artistic Svcs.; juror various violin competitions; bd. dirs. Univ. Cir., Inc., Avery Fisher Artist Program. Cleve. Orch. debut, 1987, former mem. Cleve. Chamber Players; musician: (violin and chamber ensemble) Donald Erb's View of Space and Time, 1987, Canterbury Trio, 1984—89. Mem. Leadership Cleve. Class of 1989. Named Person of Yr., Am. Italian Heritage, 1994; recipient No. Ohio Live Award of Achievement, 1986. Mem.: Suzuki Assn. (aux. dir. internat. bd.). Office: Cleve Inst Music 11021 East Blvd Cleveland OH 44106-1705 E-mail: ceroned@cs.com.*

CERRANO, ROBERT EDWARD, accountant; b. N.Y.C., Nov. 29, 1947; s. Edward F. and Mary M. (Audano) C.; m. Sherry L. Kibler, Jan. 31, 1970; children: Jason A., Anne M. BS in Acctg., Quincy Coll., 1969; MBA, Quincy U., 1995. State cert. FFII hazmat ops. Staff acct. Dancer, Fitzgerald, Sample, Inc., N.Y.C., 1969-70, Gray, Hunter, Stenn & Co., Quincy, Ill., 1970-72; pvt. practicw Quincy, 1972-78; mgr. fin. analysis Quincy Compressor div. Colt Industries, Inc., Quincy, 1978-85, mgr. gen. acctg., 1985-92, asst. contr., 1992-97, contr., 1998—. Coord. Lean Mfg., 2003—04, divsn. contr., 2004—; mem. review com. Quincy Pub. Schs., 2002—05. Treas. Pamel Bedford Dance Theatre, Inc., Quincy, 1979; advisor Jr. Achievement, Quincy, 1980; mem. Adams County Bd., 1982084; allocations com. United Way of Adams County, Quincy, 1984-88; St. Francis Solanus Parish Sch. Bd., 1986-88; vol.

firefighter, 2002—. Mem. Inst. Mgmt. Accts., Am. Legion (fin. officer Quincy chpt. 1971-76), Breakfast Optimists. Republican. Roman Catholic. Office: Enpro Industries Quincy Compressor Div 3501 Wisman Ln Quincy IL 62305-3116

CERRI, ROBERT NOEL, photographer; b. Boston, Dec. 25, 1947; s. Lawrence Alfred and Angelina (Arena) C. BA, Georgetown Coll., 1972. Dir., head counselor The Open Door, Boca Raton, Fla., 1972-77; actor, model Miami, 1977-79; photojournalist Newsweek/Nat. Geographic, Miami, 1979-85; comml. advt. photographer Miami, 1985-98; pres. RC Photo and Video Prodns., Miami, NY, LA, Orlando, The Caribbean, 1985—, Dream Light Prodns., 1994—, Robert Cerri Group, 2000—. Mem. USGA, Acad. Model Aeronautics, Tasters Guild, U.S. Golf Assn., Meeting Profl. Internat., Nat. Trust for Historic Preservation, Williamsburg Preservation Soc., PGA Ptnrs. Club. Republican. Avocations: golf, inline skating, horseback riding, travel, bicycling. Fax: 561-447-8684. Office Phone: 561-447-4245. Business E-Mail: rcerri@robertcerrigroup.com.

CERTAIN, VICKI LYNN, elementary school educator; b. Terre Haute, Ind., Nov. 27, 1945; d. Gene D. Rogers and Marjorie Ruth Sherwood; divorced; children: Angela Hayes, Marcus Dunn, Clay. BSc, Ind. State U., 1973, MSc, 1979. Substitute teacher, Fort Walters, Tex., 1966—67, Vigo County Sch. Corp., Terre Haute, 1974—77; elem. tchr. Pioneer Regional Sch. Corp., Royal Center, Ind., 1973, Deming Elem. Sch., Terre Haute, 1978—. Mem.: Internat. Reading Assn., Wabash Coun. Internat. Reading Assn. (sec., v.p., pres.-elect, pres., Outstanding Svc. award 1990, Pres. award 1999—2000), Phi Delta Kappa. Home: 2348 McKeen St Terre Haute IN 47802 Office: Deming Elem Sch 1750 8th Ave Terre Haute IN 47805

CERULO, MICHAEL LOUIS SUKE, music educator; b. Marlborough, Mass., Apr. 2, 1972; s. Louis John and Margret Ann Cerulo. BA, Berklee Coll. of Music, Boston, 1994. Shipping mgr. Mark Of the Unicorn, Cambridge, Mass., 1994—95; touring musician/co-owner Schleigho, Croton-On-Hudson, NY, 1994—; guitar tchr. N.Y.C. Guitar Sch., 2003—; asst. mgr. Cafe St. Barts, N.Y.C., 2003—04; touring musician Lynch, Catskill, NY, 2002—. Musician (composer, prodr., engr.): (solo cd) Michael Suke Cerulo, Jazz Guitar and Flute; musician: (composer, prodr.) (cd (by the band schleigho) Schleigho, (cd (schleigho) Farewell to the Sun, In The Interest of Time, Continent, Live at Hodown 2000. Scholar Wang scholar, Wang Computer, 1990, Sudbury Ednl. scholar, Sudbury Sch. Com., 1990. Mem.: Film Music Network. Home: 269 Devoe St Apt #1 Brooklyn NY 11211 Personal E-mail: suke@sukecerulo.com.

CERUTI-STACY, JAIME A., music educator, technologist, educator; b. Walpole, Mass., Jan. 12, 1976; d. VIrginia R. and Richard A. Ceruti; m. Richard A. Stacy, Aug. 7, 1999. BM in Edn., Va. Commonwealth U., 1998. Postgrad. Profl. Tchg. Lic. Va., 2003. Music tchr., lead tech. tchr. Salem Ch. Elem., Richmond, Va., 1998—. Dist. rep. Va. Music Educators Assn., Va., 2001—. Mem.: Assn. of Supervision and Curriculum Devel. Office Phone: 804-768-6215. Personal E-mail: jaime_stacy@ccpsnet.net.

CERUTTI, JOSEPH J., JR., conductor, music educator; b. Middletown, NY, Apr. 24, 1981; s. Joseph and Janet Cerutti. B in Music Edn., Five Towns Coll., Dix Hills, NY, 2004; postgrad., Boston U., 2004—. Founder/condr. David Johnson Singers, LI, NY, 2003—04; condr. LI Sound, Long Island, NY, 2002—04, Women of Note, Hudson, Mass., 2005—. Mem. faculty dir.'s coll. Harmony Coll., Ohio, 2005—. Asst. dir. (performance) Sounds of Concord (2nd Pl. North East Dist. of the Barbershop Harmony Soc., 2004); singer (choral participant): Carnegie Hall/Robert Shaw choral wkshp. Music dir. St. Lawrence of Canterbury Episc. Ch., Dix Hills, 2000—04. Mem.: Music Educators Nat. Confrence, Am. Choral Directors Assn., Barbershop Harmony Soc., Phi Sigma Eta. Presbyterian. Personal E-mail: jcerutti@coolgoose.com.

CERUTTI, PATRICK BERNARD, lawyer; b. Chgo., Jan. 31, 1945; s. Bernard C. and Kathleen A. (O'Connell) C.; m. Dee A. Leoni, June 15, 1968; children: Susan M., Gina M. BA, Gonzaga U., 1967, JD, 1971. Asst. corp. counsel City of Spokane, Wash., 1968-72; ptnr. Underwood, Campbell, Brock & Cerutti, P.S., Spokane, 1972-95, Lukins & Annis, P.S., Spokane, 1995—. Home: 5225 S Madelia St Spokane WA 99223-8134 Office: Lukis and Annis PS 1600 Washington Trust Fin Ctr 701 W Sprague Ave Spokane WA 99201-0466 Office Phone: 509-455-9555. E-mail: pcerutti@lukins.com.

CERVANTES, ANGEL RENTERIA, elementary school educator; b. Lake View Terrace, Calif., Oct. 24, 1972; s. Pedro M. and Alicia R. Cervantes. BA in History, Occidental Coll., 1994; MA in History, Claremont Grad. U., 1996. Cert. tchr. Calif. Substitute tchr. La Puente (Calif.) Unified Sch. Dist., 1996; tchr. L.A. Unified Sch. Dist., San Fernando, Calif., 1997—. Adj. prof. Glendale (Calif.) C.C., 2000—, La Mission Coll., Sylmar, Calif., 2002—03; ptnr., founder CRS Assocs., L.A., 2002—; exec. dir. Cervantes Fund for Social Justice, San Fernando, 2004—. Author: (children's activity books) San Fernando: A Short History, 2004, Cesar Chavez, 2004; exec. prodr., writer: (TV program) The Adventures of Dr. Cervantes and Captain Oiram, 2002—. Cultural arts commr. City of San Fernando, 1999—2003; bd. govs. Occidental Coll., Eagle Rock, Calif., 2001—; mem. Friends of Cesar Chavez Commemoration Com., San Fernando; chpt. chmn. United Tchrs. L.A., San Fernando, 1998—99; celebrity judge San Fernando City Coun., 2000—02. Recipient Svc. award, San Fernando City Coun., 2003. Mem.: Occidental Coll. Latino Alumni Assn. (treas. 2004—).

CERVANTES, LUIS AUGUSTO, neurosurgeon; b. Torreon, Mex., Mar. 5, 1953; came to U.S., 1976; s. Luis Augusto and Gloria (Galindo) C.; m. Joann Frances Emanuele, Feb. 10, 1979; children: Luis III, Sara, Francis, Nicolas, Juan Carlos, Mary Teresa. MD, Nat. U. Mex., 1976. Intern Suburban Hosp., Bethesda, Md., 1977-78; resident in surgery Washington Hosp. Ctr., 1978-79; resident in neurology George Washington U., Washington, 1979-80, resident in neurosurgery, 1980-84; chief neurosurgery sect. dept. surgery Meml. Hosp. Burlington County, Mount Holly, N.J., 1992—. Cons. in neurosurgery Deborah Heart and Lung Ctr., Browns Mills, N.J., 1999—. Fellow ACS, Internat. Coll. Surgeons; mem. Am. Assn. Neurol. Surgeons, Congress Neurol. Surgeons. Roman Catholic. Avocation: golf. Office: 110 Marter Ave Ste 309 Moorestown NJ 08057-3124 Office Phone: 856-727-1000. Personal E-mail: lacabron@aol.com.

CERVIA, JOSEPH STEVEN, medical educator; b. N.Y.C., Apr. 10, 1959; s. Joseph T. and Margaret (Bleier) C.; m. Denise Laura Blumberg, Aug. 10, 1986; children: David Michael, Lisa Danielle, Michael Jason. BS in Biology summa cum laude, St. John's U., 1980; MD, N.Y. Med. Coll., 1984. Diplomate Nat. Bd. Med. Examiners, Am. Bd. Internal Medicine, Am. Bd. Pediatrics, Subspeciality Bd. Infectious Diseases Internal Medicine and Pediatric; cert. HIV specialist. Intern in medicine, pediatrics Brookdale Hosp. Med. Ctr., Bklyn., 1984-85, resident in medicine, pediatrics, 1985-88; fellow in infectious diseases N.Y. Hosp. Cornell Med. Ctr., N.Y.C., 1988-90; asst. prof. medicine, pediatrics SUNY Health Sci. Ctr., Stony Brook, 1990-92; attending physician Nassau County Med. Ctr., East Meadow, N.Y., 1990-92; dir. pediatric-maternal HIV svc., 1990-92; asst. prof. pediatrics and medicine Cornell U. Med. Coll., 1992—96, assoc. prof. pediatrics and medicine, 1996—99. Mem. pediatric AIDS grant adv. bd. Nassau-Suffolk Health Sys. Agy., Plainview, N.Y., 1991-92; dir. Program for Children with AIDS, The N.Y. Hosp. Cornell Med. Ctr., 1992-1999, Comprehensive HIV Care and Rsch. Ctr., L.I. Jewish Med. Ctr., 1999-2004. Contbr. articles to profl. jours. Asst. scoutmaster Boy Scouts Am., Forest Hills, N.Y., 1977-80. Recipient Bausch and Lomb Hon. Sci. award, 1977, competitive and scholastic excellence scholarships, St. John's U., 1977-80, Harrison Scholarship award N.Y. Med. Coll., 1984, Henry Christian Meml. award Am. Fedn. Clin. Rsch., 1990. Fellow ACP, Am. Acad. Pediatrics, Pediatric Infectious Disease Soc., Infectious Disease Soc. Am., Am. Acad. HIV Medicine (bd. dirs.); mem. AAAS, AMA (physician's recognition award 1993—), Am. Soc. Microbiology, Am. Fedn. Clinic Rsch., AIDS Clin. Trials Group. Roman Catholic. Achievements include findings in the importance of the monocyte in leishmania donovani infection; immuno modulatory effects of granulocyte macrophage colony-stimulating factor and their T-cell dependence, characterizing long-term survival in children with AIDS; protection against serious bacterial infection in children with AIDS; factors influencing quality of life in children with AIDS and other infectious diseases issues. Home: 9 Pine Dr N Roslyn NY 11576-2015 Office: 2200 Northern Blvd Greenvale NY 11548 Office Phone: 516-801-9056. E-mail: joe_cervia@pall.com, jcervia@hotmail.com.

CERVILLA, CONSTANCE MARLENE, marketing consultant; b. Lafayette, Ind., Dec. 28, 1951; d. Norman Cimmino and Marilyn Jane (Stonebraker) C. AB, Harvard U., 1974, postgrad., 1974-75. Mktg. asst. Gen. Mills, Inc., Mpls., 1975-76; product dir. Pillsbury Co., Mpls., 1976-78; asst. v.p. Citicorp, N.A., Rochester, N.Y., 1978-80; cons. Bain & Co., Boston, 1980-81; owner, pres., CEO Core Group Mktg., Inc., Mpls., 1981—; co-founder, v.p. Mil. Communications Ctr., Inc., Mpls., 1983-89; co-founder Gift Certificate Ctrs., Inc., 1990—. Founder core group advancement spkr. Edn. Ministries Regarding Devel. Practices. Patentee in field. Mem. Bank Mktg. Assn., Harvard/Radcliffe Club Minn., Mpls. Harvard Club (N.Y.C.). Avocations: rowing, swimming, business development. Office: Core Group Mktg Inc 7171 Shady Oak Rd Eden Prairie MN 55344-3516

CERVONKA, DANIEL STEPHEN, medical educator; b. Phila., Sept. 1, 1963; s. Barbara Ann Cervonka. BS in Social and Health Svc., Roger Williams U., 1987; degree in Physician Assoc. Studies, Yale U., 1989; postgrad., Nova Southeastern U., 1998; M in Physician Assoc. Studies, U. Nebr., 2003; postgrad., Bond U. Lectr. surgery Yale U. Sch. Medicine, New Haven, 1990—93; chief physician assoc. Griffin Hosp., Derby, Conn., 1997—; pres., cofounder U. Physician Assocs., Fairifield, Conn., 1999—2003; v.p. mission devel. One World Medicine, Hamden, Conn., 2000—; asst. clin. prof. Quinnipiac U., Hamden, Conn., 2002—. Lectr. in surgery(emergency medicine) Yale U. Sch. of Medicine, New Haven, 1990—; assoc. dir. physician asst. dept. Cornell U. Med. Coll., NYC, 1992—95. Home: 39 AP Gates East Haddam CT 06423 Office: Griffin Hosp Emergency Medicine 130 Division St Derby CT 06418 E-mail: daniel.cervonka@yale.edu.

CESAR, KAMALA, dancer, educator; b. Bklyn., Dec. 9, 1948; d. Bruno Gonzales Cesar and Mary Kariwahawe Papnieau; m. Thomas Watson Buckner, Mar. 16, 1992; children: Robin, Paul, Tuy, Rana, Meera, Kiran. BA in Conservation of Natural Resources, U. Calif., Berkeley, 1976. Exec. dir., bd. dirs. The Balasaraswati Sch. of Music and Dance, N.Y.C., 1985—89; founder, artistic and exec. dir. Lotus Fine Arts Prodns. Inc., N.Y.C., 1989—, also bd. dirs. Artistic dir., performer (videotape) Bharata Natyam, The Sacred Dance of India, 1991. Named Am. Indian of Yr., Thunderbird Am. Indian Dancers, N.Y.C., 2002; recipient Ethnic Dance award, Dance Giant Steps, Inc., Bklyn., 1996; Folk Arts Apprentice, Nat. Endowment for the Arts, 1986. Democrat. Buddhist. Avocation: carnatic vocals. Office: Lotus Music and Dance Studios 109 W 27th St 8th Fl New York NY 10001 Business E-Mail: info@lotusarts.com.

CESARE, ALISON MARIA, art educator; b. Bethlehem, Pa., June 18, 1966; d. William Rolf Jackson and Jean Ernestine Cali; m. Thomas A. Cesare, Oct. 21, 1999; children: Reed J., Maria A. BS, Ind. U. of Pa., 1988. Cert. art edn. Kutztown U., 1993. Art tchr. Neshaminy HS, Langhorne, Pa., 1993—95, Nortre Dame Jr. Sr. HS, East Stroudsburg, Pa., 1996—97; art dept. coord. Pen Argyl Area HS, Pen Argyl, Pa., 1997—. Set design Pen Argyl HS, Pen Argyl, Pa., 1997—, freshman class co-adv., 2000—, ski club adv., 2004—05. Mem.: Monroe County Arts Coun., Pa. Edn. Ass. (bldg. rep. 2004—05). Office: Pen Argyl Area HS 501 W Laurel Ave Pen Argyl PA 18072 Office Phone: 610-863-1293. E-mail: cesarea@paprolog.net.

CESARE, CHRISTINE B., lawyer; BA magna cum laude, Conn. Coll., 1981; JD, Fordham U., 1984. Bar: NY 1985, Conn. 1986. Ptnr. comml. litig., mem. oper. group Bryan Cave LLP, NYC. Office: Bryan Cave LLP 1290 Ave of the Americas New York NY 10104 Office Phone: 212-541-1228. E-mail: cbcesare@bryancave.com.

CESARIO, ROBERT CHARLES, retail executive, consultant; b. Chgo., Apr. 6, 1941; s. Valentino A. and Mary Ethel (Kenny) C.; m. Susan Kay DePoutee; children: Jeffrey, Bradley. BS in Gen. Edn., Northwestern U., 1975; postgrad., DePaul U., 1975. Mgr. fin. ops. Midas Internat. Corp., Chgo., 1968-73; dir. staff ops. Am. Hosp. Supply Corp., McGaw Park, Ill., 1973-76; v.p. Car X Svc. Sys. Inc., Chgo., 1976-78, v.p. oil svcs., 1983-84; v.p. Chicken Unltd. Enterprises Inc., Chgo., 1978-83; pres. Growth Strategies, Inc., 1984-87; pres., CEO Lube Pro's Internat., Inc., 1987—2004. With USMC, 1960-62. Office: Franchise Strategies Inc 360 East Randolph St Ste 2103 Chicago IL 60601

CESNIK, JAMES MICHAEL, labor union administrator, publishing executive; b. Marshfield, Wis., Oct. 6, 1935; s. Ignatius Anthony and Mary Catherine (Bayuk) C.; m. Elizabeth Louise Havlik, Aug. 1, 1959 (div. 1987); children: Margaret Mary, Sarah Elizabeth, Michael Ignatius; m. Barbara E. Nelson, Jan. 1, 1990. BA, St. John's U., Collegeville, Minn., 1958. Reporter, Rice Lake (Wis.) Chronotype, 1958; reporter, copy, makeup and layout editor Mpls. Star & Tribune, 1958-64; internat. rep., asso. dir. rsch. and info., dir. rsch. and info. Newspaper Guild, CWA,AFL-CIO/CLC, Washington, 1965-75; editor Guild Reporter, 1973-93; v.p. Internat. Labor Press Assn., Washington, 1973-79, pres., 1980-82; sec.-treas. Internat. Labor Comm. Assn., Washington, 1984-87; editor Internat. Labor Comm. Assn. Reporter, Washington, 1983-84; sec.-treas. JBTM Enterprises Inc., Winchester, Va., 1989-91, 2002—, pres., 1991—2001, Signet Screen Printing and Embroidery, Winchester, Va., 1993—2001; ptnr. TJC LLC, Winchester, Va., 1999—. Elijah P. Lovejoy lectr. So. Ill. U., Carbondale, 1970; cons., 1993—; publs. cons., Falls Church, Va., 1993—. Mem. Falls Church (Va.) Democratic Com., 1970-84; founding mem. Falls Church Com. on Status of Women, 1975-76; pres. Montessori Sch. No. Va., 1970. Mem. Slovenian Heritage Com. Washington, Slovenian Choral Soc. Washington, Am. Slovenian Cath. Union, Soc. for Slovene Studies. Roman Catholic. Business E-Mail: jim@cesnik.com.

CESSNA, JANICE LYNN, systems administrator, information technology manager; d. Alexander Carl and Camilla Dorothy Wagenfohr; 1 child, Christopher Alexander. AS data processing, Pasco-Hernando C.C., New Port Richey, Fla., 1982—84, AA, 1995—97; BS in Computer Info. Systems, St. Leo U., St. Leo, Fla., 1998—2000; MS computer info. tech., Regis U., Denver, Colo., 2001—05. Info. processing mgr. Pasco-Hernando C.C., New Port Richey, Fla., 1985—90, programmer/analyst, 1990—96, systems mgr., 1996—98, dir. mgmt. info. services, 1998—. Chair/mem., tech. adv. Fla. Cmty. Coll. Computer Consortium, Pensacola, Fla., 1994—; mem., MISAT-FOR Fla. Cmty .Coll. Sys., Tallahassee, 1998—; mem. - CIO com. Fla. Cmty. Coll. Sys., Tallahassee, 1998—. Mem.: N.Am. UNISYS User Assn. (assoc.), The Fla. Assn. Ednl. Data Systems (assoc.), The Rotary Club (v.p.). Independent Thinkers. Luth. Avocations: exercise, travel, gardening, cooking, reading. Office: Pasco-Hernando Cmity Coll 10230 Ridge Road New Port Richey FL 34654 Business E-Mail: cessnaj@phcc.edu.

CETIN, ANTON, artist; b. Bojana, Croatia, Sept. 18, 1936; arrived in Can., 1968, naturalized, 1973; s. Tomo and Terezija (Grcic) C.; m. Milka Katalenic, Dec. 16, 1962; 1 child, Dawn Antonia. Diploma, Sch. Applied Arts, Zagreb, 1959; masters diploma, Acad. Fine Arts, Zagreb, 1964. One-man shows include Art Gallery Hamilton, 1978, Galeria Juan Martin, Mexico City, 1979, Gilman Galleries, Chgo., 1983, Mus. Arts and Crafts, Zagreb, 1986, Beverly Gordon Gallery, Dallas, 1987, Nat. and Univ. Libr., Zagreb, 1988, Oberhausmuseum, Passau, Germany, 1990, Sony Plaza Art Gallery, Tokyo, 1991, Gallery 7, Hong Kong, 1993, Museo del Chopo, Mexico City, 1993, Salas Nacionales de Cultura-Palais de Glace, Buenos Aires, Argentina, 1994, Museo Mcpl. de Arte J.C. Castagnino, Mar del Plata, Argentina, 1995, Mus. and Gallery Ctr., Zagreb, 1996, City Mus. Varazdin, Croatia, 1998, Art Gallery, Split, Croatia, 1998, Gallery Fine Arts & Waldinger Gallery, Osijek, Croatia, 2000, Herman Hesse Mus., Calw, Germany, 2000, Mercedes Zentrum, Stuttgart, Germany, 2000-01, Gallery Anton Cetín, Cazma, Croatia, 2001, State Archives and Gallery Kortil, Rijeka, Croatia, 2002, Gallery HKZ-Hrvatsko slovo, Zagreb, Croatia, 2003, Multicultural Gallery, Halifax, Can., 2003, Gallery Ministry of Fin., Zagreb, Croatia, 2003, Mus. Mimara, Zagreb, 2004, City Mus. Vukovar, Croatia, 2005, Gallery Kula, Split, Croatia, 2005, Mus. Mimara, Zagreg, 2005; group exhbns. include Mus. Modern Art, Crakow, Poland, 1972, Brockton Art Ctr., 1974, Nat. Libr. France, 1978, 2d Cabo Frio Internat. Print Biennial, Brazil, 1985, Del Bello Gallery, Toronto, 1986, 87, 89, 90, Crespano del Grappa, Italy, 1988, Nat. Libr. Can., 1990, Art Asia, 1993, Olympic Games, Atlanta, 1996, Shenzhen Fine Art Inst., Shenzhen Mus. Modern Art, Shanghai, 2000, Point K Galerie, Nice, France, 2001, Círculo del Arte, Barcelona, Spain, 2002, Six Stories, Multicultural Gallery, Halifax, Can., 2003, Centro Hist., Mexico City, 2004, CODA Mus., Apeldoorn, Holland, 2005, others; represented in permanent collections at nat. librs. France, Croatia, Can., U.N., Japan and Salas Nacionales-Palais de Glace, Buenos Aires, Museo del Chopo, Mexico City, Vatican, Italy, Mus. Arts and Crafts, Gallery Klovicevi dvori, Zagreb, Croatia, Can. Cultural Ctr., France, Circulo del Arte, Barcelona, Spain, Gallery Anton Cetin, Cazma, Croatia, others; author: Eve and the Moon, 1975; co-author: Amerika Croatan America, 1988. Named Artist of Yr., Can. Croatian Artists Soc., 1986; honored for outstanding merits in the field of culture, govt. of Croatia, 1995 Home: PH3 5 Greystone Walk Dr Scarborough ON Canada M1K 5J5 Office Phone: 1-416-264-8909. Personal E-mail: acetineve@sympatico.ca.

CETIN, MUJDAT, electrical engineer, researcher; PhD, Boston U., 2001. Post-doctoral assoc. MIT, Cambridge, Mass., 2001—02, rsch. scientist, 2002—. Panelist The Internat. Soc. for Optical Engring., Def. and Security Symposium, 2002—04; mem. tech. program com. The Internat. Soc. for Optical Engring., 2002—, IEEE Internat. Conf. on Image Processing, 2002—, IEEE Internat. Conf. on Acoustics, Speech, and Signal Processing, 2003—; spl. session organizer Internat. Conf. on Acoustics, Speech, and Signal Processing, 2005—; tech. reviewer sci. journals IEEE. Exec. bd. mem. The Turkish Am. Cultural Soc. of New Eng., Boston, 1997—98. Recipient Grad. of Yr., Bogazici U. Alumni Assn., 1993, Best Grad. Student award, Inst. of Measurement and Control, Manchester Sect., Eng., 1994, Best Engring. Rsch. award, Boston U. Science Day, 1998, Outstanding Paper award, Am. Geophysical Union, Fall Meeting, 2003; Fgn. and Commonwealth Office scholarship, The Brit. Coun., 1993-1994, Grad. Study scholarship, Turkish Edn. Found., 1993-1994, Doctoral Study Support scholarship, Turkish Sci. and Tech. Rsch. Coun. and NATO, 1995. Mem.: IEEE.

CETINKAYA, SILA, engineering educator; b. Izmir, Turkey, May 23, 1969; BS, Istanbul Tech. U., Turkey, 1985—89; MS, Bilkent U., Ankara, Turkey, 1989—91; PhD, McMaster U., Hamilton, Can., 1992—96. Asst. prof., indsl. engring. Tex. A&M U., College Station, 1997—2003, assoc. prof., indsl. engring., 2003—. Recipient Career award, NSF, 2001, Outstanding Young Industrial Engr. award, Inst. of Industrial Engrs., 2003; grantee, NSF, 2001—. Mem.: Inst. Indsl. Engrs., Inst. for Ops. Rsch. and Mgmt. Sci. Office: Texas A&M Univ Indsl Engring Dept College Station TX 77843-3131 Office Phone: 979-845-5597. Office Fax: 979-847-9005. Business E-Mail: sila@tamu.edu.

CETKOVIC-CVRLJE, MARINA, endocrinologist; b. Bjelovar, Croatia, Sept. 16, 1961; d. Ivo and Bozica (Pavlic) Cetkovic; m. Bogdan Cvrlje, Oct. 15, 1987; 1 child, Martina. MD, Med. Sch. Zagreb, 1986, MSc, 1991, PhD, 1997. Gen. practitioner Med. Ctr., Bjelovar, Croatia, 1986-88; rsch. asst. Inst. Ruder Boskovic, Zagreb, Croatia, 1988-92; vis. scientist dept. med. cell biology Med. Sch. Uppsala, Sweden, 1992-93; staff scientist Inst. Ruder Boskovic, 1993-94; postdoctoral fellow The Jackson Lab., Bar Harbor, Maine, 1994-97; dir. diabetes rsch. program Wayne Hughes Inst., St. Paul, 1997—. Mem. Am. Diabetes Assn. Roman Catholic. Avocations: walking, hiking, swimming. Office: Wayne Hughes Inst 2665 Long Lake Rd Ste 200 Saint Paul MN 55113-2535

CETRULO, JERRY, artist, sculptor; b. Jersey City, N.J., Sept. 10, 1941; s. Gerardo Cetrulo and Eva Augustine; m. Renate Cetrulo, 1961 (div.); children: Michael, Mark, Heidi; m. Barbara Cetrulo, Aug. 2, 1998. Customer engr. IBM, Cranford, N.J., 1967-99; ret., 1999; instr. Am. Woodcarving Sch., Wayne, N.J., 1992—. With U.S. Army, 1959-62. Avocations: woodcarving, painting. Home: 18 Cayuga Ave Rockaway NJ 07866-1012 Office: Am Woodcarving Sch 21 Pompton Plains Xrd Wayne NJ 07470-6326 Office Phone: 973-835-8555. E-mail: njcarver@optonline.net.

CETTO, LORRAINE MARY, music educator; b. Athol, Mass., Jan. 12, 1956; d. Edward Francis and Eleanor (Ryder) C. B in Music Edn., Anna Maria Coll., 1978; cert., U. Hartford, 1982; M in Performance, U. Conn., 1983. Cert. pub. educator. Vocal music tchr. Quaboag H.S., Warren, Mass., 1978-80, West Brookfield (Mass.) Elem. Sch., 1979-80; grad. asst. U. Conn., Storrs, 1981-83, part time prof., 1982-84; music dir. Our Lady Rosary Parish, Spencer, Mass., 1980-86, West Avon (Conn.) Congregation, 1987-90; dir. choral activities Hall H.S., West Hartford, Conn., 1983—. Guest conductor various Conn., Maine, Va., 1985—, RI Mid. Sch. All-State, 2005. Named Outstanding Sch. Educator, Neag Sch. Edn., U. Conn., 2003. Mem. Am. Choral Dirs. Assn. (exec. bd. 1988-2001, pres.-elect Conn. chpt. 1995-2001, Choral Dir. of Yr. Conn. chpt. 2004), Conn. Music Educators Assn., Music Educators Nat. Conf., Kodaly Educators. Democrat. Avocations: reading, hiking, cross country skiing. Office Phone: 860-232-4561.

CETTO, TERESA, precious metal jewelry designer; b. Athol, Mass. d. Robert and Pauline C. BS minor in Fine Arts, Fla. State U., 1976. Biol. illustrator Fla. State U., Tallahassee, 1975-77; exhibit designer, illustrator Cape Cod Mus. Natural History, Brewster, Mass., 1977-86; smithing instr. Creative Arts Ctr., Brewster, Mass. Illustrator: Mollusks of Cape Cod (Donald Zinn), 1984, Crabs of Cape Cod, 1986, Dragonflies of Cape Cod; exhibited in group show Smithsonian Natural History Mus., 1978-81. Mem. Artisans Guild Cape Cod, Soc. Cape Cod Craftsman, Soc. North Am. Goldsmith, Big Brothers, Big Sisters. Avocations: dance, music. Studio: Creative Arts Ctr 2623 Main St Brewster MA 02631

CEYANES, JASON WARREN, school system administrator; b. Texas City, Tex., Oct. 31, 1972; s. Robert Warren and Linda Marie Ceyanes; m. Kimberly Kay Harris, Dec. 15, 1972; children: Jason (Jace) Warren II, Sharayah Elizabeth, Chloe Kay, Joshuah Warren, Judson Harris, J. R. BA in Biol. Sci., U. Houston, Clear Lake, Tex., 1995, MS in Ednl. Mid-Mgmt., 1998; PhD in Ednl. Adminstrn., Tex. A&M U., College Station, 2004. Cert. provisional tchr. secondary Biology Tex. State Bd. Educator Cert., 1997, profl. mid-mgmt. adminstr. Tex. State Bd. Educator Cert., 1998, supt. Tex. State Bd. Educator Cert., 2003. Biology tchr. Dickinson (Tex.) Ind. Sch. Dist., 1995—97; phys. sci. tchr. Klein (Tex.) Ind. Sch. Dist., 1997—98; asst. prin. Magnolia (Tex.) Ind. Sch. Dist., 1998—2000; h.s. prin. Burton (Tex.) Ind. Sch. Dist., 2000—01; mid. sch. prin. Humble (Tex.) Ind. Sch. Dist., 2001—02; dir. spl. projects Montgomery (Tex.) Ind. Sch. Dist., 2002—. Presenter at profl. confs. Mem. West Conroe Bapt. Ch., Tex., 2004—. Mem.: Region VI Coun. Adminstrs. Spl. Edn. (treas. 2004—), Tex. Coun. Adminstrs. Spl. Edn., Tex. Assn. Secondary Sch. Prins., Tex. Assn. Sch. Adminstrs., Phi Delta Kappa. Avocations: reading, writing, singing. Home: 17337 Sunset Ranch Dr Montgomery TX 77316 Office Phone: 936-597-3015. Personal E-mail: jason@ceyanes.com.

CEYDELI, ADIL, surgeon; b. Gaziantep, Turkey, Nov. 22, 1974; s. Gungor and Canan Ceydeli; m. Lucia Buckman, Apr. 3, 2000; 1 child, Isabe. MD, Hacettepe Med. Sch., Ankara, Turkey, 1998; MS, N.J. Med. Sch., 2001. Lic. physician Ga. Surg. resident N.Y. Meth. Hosp., Bklyn., 2000—05; plastic surgery fellow Med. Coll. Ga., Augusta, 2005—. Recipient Best Resident Paper award, ACS, 2001, 2002, 2003, 2004. Mem.: ACS Resident Assn. (assoc.). Home: 2608 Berkshire at Townclub Augusta GA 30909 Personal E-mail: adilc@excite.com.

CEYER, SYLVIA T., chemistry professor; Grad. summa cum laude, Hope Coll., Holland, Mich.; PhD, U. Calif., Berkeley. Postdoctoral fellow Nat. Bur. Standards; faculty mem. dept. chemistry MIT, Cambridge, Mass., 1981—, J.C. Sheehan prof. chemistry. Recipient Recognition award for young scholars AAUW Ednl. Found., 1988, Nobel Laureate Signature award for Grad. Edn. in Chemistry, Am. Chem. Soc., 1993. Fellow AAAS, NAS (chmn. chemistry sect.), Am. Phys. Soc., Am. Acad. Arts and Scis. Office: MIT 6-217 Dept Chemistry 77 Mass Ave Dept Cambridge MA 02139-4307 Business E-Mail: stceyer@mit.edu.

CHA, CHARLES, surgical oncologist; b. Chgo. children: Alexia, Jacob. BA, MD, Northwestern U. Diplomate Am. Bd. Surgery. Resident in surgery U. Wis. Hosp. and Clinics, Madison, 1995—2000, chief resident in surgery, 2000—01; fellow in surg. oncology Meml. Sloan-Kettering Cancer Ctr., N.Y.C.; asst. prof. surgery Yale Sch. Medicine, New Haven. Recipient Benjamin Layton award for outstanding tchg., U. Wis. Dept. Surgery, 2001, Dennis Jahnigen Career Devel. award, Am. Geriat. Soc., 2004—, Ohse Surg. Rsch. award, Yale Dept. Surgery, 2005; NIH/NCI Rsch. fellow, 1993, David and Monica Gorin Sarcoma fellow, 2002—03. Mem.: Assn. VA Surgeons (awards com. 2005—), Assn. Acad. Surgery (membership com. 2005—), Pancreas Club, Soc. Am. Gastrointestinal Endoscopic Surgeons, Am. Soc. Clin. Oncology, Soc. Surg. Oncology, Soc. Surgery of Alimentary Tract, Am. Cancer Soc. (Faculty Fellowship Rsch. award 2004—), Am. Assn. Cancer Rsch. (assoc.). Achievements include research in SiRNA inhibition of angiogenesis in GI malignancy. Office: Yale Sch Medicine 330 Cedar St LH 118 New Haven CT 06520 Office Phone: 203-785-2380. E-mail: charles.cha@yale.edu.

CHA, SE DO, internist; b. Seoul, Korea, Dec. 17, 1942; came to U.S., 1966, naturalized, 1977; s. Young Sun and Hee Joo (Chang) C.; m. Elsa Jane Greene, Dec. 21, 1974; 1 child, Elizabeth. MD, Yon Sei U., 1966. Diplomate Am. Bd. Internal Medicine. Intern Presbyn.-U. Pa. Med. Ctr., Phila., 1966-67; resident in medicine Harrisburg (Pa.) Hosp., 1967-70; chief resident in medicine Roger Williams Gen. Hosp., Providence, 1970-71, cardiologist, 1973-75; fellow in cardiology Deborah Heart and Lung Center, Browns Mills, N.J., 1971-73, cardiologist, 1975—; from asst. dir. adult cardiac catheterization lab. to dir. Deborah Heart and Lung Ctr., Browns Mills, NJ, 1975—2003. Instr. Brown U., Providence, 1973-75. Contbr. articles to profl. jours. Fellow ACP, Soc. for Cardiac Angiography; mem. AMA, Fedn. Clin. Rsch., Am. Heart Assn. Office: Deborah Heart and Lung Ctr Trenton Rd Browns Mills NJ 08015 Office Phone: 609-893-6611. Business E-Mail: sdcha@msn.com.

CHA, SOYOUNG STEPHEN, mechanical engineer, educator; b. Inchon, Republic of Korea, June 25, 1944; arrived in U.S., 1974; s. Sang O. and Sook S. (Lee) C.; m. Young W. Park, Sept. 4, 1974. BS, Seoul (Republic of Korea) Nat. U., 1969; MS, Mich. State U., 1976; PhD, U. Mich., 1980. Project rsch. engr. Northrop Corp., Research Triangle Park, NC, 1979-84; prof., dir. opto-mech. lab. U. Ill., Chgo., 1984—. Co-chair Beijing Optical Diagnostics Symposium, 2002; spkr. in field. Editor: Optics Lasers in Engineering, numerous procs. vols.; contbr. more than 135 articles to profl. jours. Dept. of Energy fellow, 1987, NASA fellow, 1994, USAF fellow, 1996. Fellow Internat. Soc. Optical Engring. (conf. chair, co-chair 1991—), ASME (tech. com. 1983-87), Am. Soc. Aeronautics and Astronautics (tech. com. 1994-97, 1998—), Visualization Soc. Japan (conf. co-chair 1998, 2002). Methodist. Achievements include patent for holographic velocimetry. Office Phone: 312-996-9612. Business E-Mail: sscha@uic.edu.

CHABLANI, LACHMAN V., pathologist; b. Sind, Pakistan, Oct. 21, 1937; arrived in U.S., 1963; s. Vishindas M. and Sita V. Chablani; m. Nancy Elizabeth Blake, May 6, 1967; children: Malini Gillen, Aneel, Raj, Anisha. MD, U. Bombay, 1962. Diplomate in anatomic and clin. pathology Am. Bd. Pathology. Pathologist Mercy Hosp. Toledo, 1971—96; chief pathology, med. dir. lab. St. Charles Mercy Hosp., Oregon, Ohio, 1992—, chief of staff, 2002—03. Chief of staff Mercy Hosp., Toledo, 1987—89; pres. Acad. Medicine Toledo and Lucas County, 1995. Chmn. physician sect. United Way, Toledo, 1983, 1995; bd. mem. Mercy Health Ptnrs., Toledo, 2002—03. Fellow: Coll. Am. Pathologists; mem.: AMA. Home: 3153 Deep Water Ln Maumee OH 43537 Office: St Charles Mercy Hosp 2600 Navarre Ave Oregon OH 43616 Office Phone: 419-696-7216. E-mail: lachmanchablani@sbcglobal.net.

CHABOT, ELLIOT CHARLES, lawyer; b. Anniston, Ala., Mar. 29, 1955; s. Herbert L. and Aleen (Kerwin) C.; m. Christine H. Swan, July 3, 1998. BA with honors, U. Md., 1977; JD, George Washington U., 1980. Bar: D.C. 1980, U.S. Dist. Ct. D.C. 1981, U.S. Ct. Fed. Claims 1981, U.S. Ct. Internat. Trade 1981, U.S. Tax Ct. 1981, U.S. Ct. Appeals Armed Forces 1981, U.S. Temporary Emergency Ct. Appeals 1981, U.S. Ct. Appeals (D.C. cir.) 1981, U.S. Ct. Appeals (4th, 5th, 8th, 9th, 10th, 11th, fed. cirs.) 1982, U.S. Ct. Appeals (7th cir.) 1983. Applications analyst, atty., House Info. Systems U.S. Ho. of Reps., Washington, 1980-81, project leader integrated law revision and retrieval project, 1981-89, legal support project leader House Info. Sys., 1989-95, webmaster internet law libr., 1994-99, sr. sys. analyst, 1995—. Bd. dirs. Am. Revenue Assn., Rockford, Iowa, 1983—87, Threshold Services, Inc., Silver Spring, Md., 1984—89; v.p. Banor Housing Inc., Kensington, Md., 1987—88, dir., 1987—, v.p., 1990—2001. Columnist Aspen Hill Gazette, 1987-96. Pres. Aspen Hill (Md.) Civic Assn., 1985—95, dir., 1995—2000; adv. com. Aspen Hill Libr., 1972, 1986—2001; sec. Friends Aspen Hill Libr., 1994—96, dir., 1996—; chmn. Political Forum Com., 2005—; mem. exec. com. Allied Civic Group, Silver Spring, 1987—89, corr. sec., 1992—94; mem. Sta. 21 com. Kensington Vol. Fire Dept., 1989; mem. Greater Layhill Community Night Com., 1989, Aspen Hill Master Plan Citizens Adv. com., 1990—94, Wheaton Action Group, 1990—95; chmn. Wheaton Woods Recreation Ctr. Adv. Com., 1990; mem. Bauer Drive Community Ctr. Adv. Com., 1992—2002; bd. dirs. Strathmore-Bel Pre Civic Assn., 2003—; rec. sec. Dist. 19 Dem. Club, Montgomery County, 1983—86, 2d v.p., 1986—89, 1st v.p., 1989—92; sec. Montgomery County Dem. Party, 1994—, chmn. rules com., 1994—, chmn. Internet Svcs. com., 1995—2002, mem. ballot questions adv. com., 1988—90, 1998—2004; vice chmn. precint orgn. com. of the party opers. task force, 1991—92; area coord. Dist. 19, 1992—94, chmn. Precinct 13-43, 1987—92, treas. Precinct 13-45, 1978—85; campaign chmn. Dist. 19 Democratic Team, 1989—90; dir. dist. 3 Montgomery Citizens Polit. Action Com., 1991—92; sec. Montgomery County United Democrats, 1997—2002; mem. Md. State Dem. Ctrl. Com., 1994—, alt. mem. exec. com., 2002—04, mem. rules com., 2003—, mem. exec. com., 2004—; vice chmn. homeless com. Temple Shalom, Chevy Chase, Md., 1992—93; pres. Parkland Community Sch. Coun., Aspen Hill, 1983—87, 1994—96, v.p., 1971—73, mem. coun., 1970—74, 1982—96; chmn. community svcs. com. Greater Wheaton (Md.) Citizens Adv. Bd., 1986—92; chmn. Ga. Ave. Men's Shelter Adv. Bd., Aspen Hill, 1989—96, Community Edn. Devel. subcom. of Citizens Adv. com. to the Interagency Coordinating Bd. for Community Use of Ednl. Facilities and Svcs., 1985—88; dist. 3 v.p. Montgomery County Civic Fedn., 1990—91; exec. com. Robert E. Peary High Sch. PTA, Aspen Hill, 1972—73, Montgomery County Coun. com. on re-use of Peary High Sch., 1986, task force to examine the regional dist. act, 1991; corr. sec. Area 2 adv. coun. Montgomery County Pub. Schs., 1972—74, adv. com. spl. edn. programs, 1974; commr. Gov.'s Commn. on Student Affairs, Md., 1976—77; legal and acctg. div. steering com. Washington Israel Bonds, 1984—86; chmn. Kensington/Wheaton Human Svcs. Area Plan Adv. Group, 1988; sec. Robert E. Peary H.S. Alumni Assn., Aspen Hill, Md., 2001—. Recipient George Washington award, George Washington U., 1980, Donald R. Spivak award Montgomery County Interagency Coordinating Bd. Community Use of Edn. Facilities and Services, 1987, Total Quality Team award Chief Adminstrv. Officer of U.S. Ho. of Reps., 1996; named One of Outstanding Young Men, U.S. C. of C., 1982, Ky. Col. Hon. Order Ky. Cols., 1967, Citizen of Yr. Greater Wheaton Citizen's Adv. Bd., 1990, One of the Federal 100 Federal Computer Week, 1994. Mem. ABA, FBA, Internat. Law Inst. (mem. faculty legis. drafting 2000—), George Washington U. Law Alumni Assn. (pres. Capitol Hill chpt. 1987-89, sec. 1985-87), Phi Alpha Delta (clk. Jay chpt. 1979-80), Omicron Delta Kappa. Home: 3501 Beret Ln Aspen Hill MD 20906-3029 Office: US Congress House Info Resources H2-646 Ford Ho Office Bldg Washington DC 20515-6165 Office Phone: 202-226-6456.

CHABOT, HERBERT L., federal judge; b. N.Y.C., July 17, 1931; s. Meyer and Esther (Mogilansky) C.; m. Aleen Carol Kerwin, June 16, 1951; children: Elliot C., Donald J., Lewis A., Nancy Jo. BA, CCNY, 1952; LLB, Columbia U., 1957; LLM, Georgetown U., 1964. Bar: NY 1958. Staff counsel Am. Jewish Congress, 1957-60; law clk. U.S. Tax Ct., Washington, 1961-65, judge, 1978—2001, sr. judge, 2001—. Atty. Joint Congl. Com. Taxation, 1965—78. Del. Md. Constl. Conv., 1967-68. With U.S. Army, 1953—55. Mem. ABA, Fed. Bar Assn. Office: US Tax Ct 400 2nd St NW Washington DC 20217-0002 Office Phone: 202-606-8930.

CHABOT, JOYCE JENKINS, librarian; b. Roberts, Idaho, Mar. 6, 1924; d. Gordon Lorenzo Jenkins and Eva Parkinson (Packer) Cordon; m. Ambrose Billy Chabot, Apr. 18, 1945; children— David Stephen, Terry Lynne, Jeane Annette, Robert Neal, Peggy Sue, Donna Joyce, Barbara Elaine, Debra Eve, Ambrose Brent. Sc.B., U. Idaho, 1944; B.A. in French, U. Wash., 1968, 5th yr. teaching credential, 1969, M.A. in Librarianship, 1971. Sec. St. Nicholas Sch., Seattle, 1968-69, Monson Real Estate, Provo, Utah, 1972-73; librarian Provo Pub. Library, 1973—; library dir., prof. Stevens Henager Coll. Bus., Provo, 1983-86; book reviewer. Mem. Utah Library Assn., ALA, Utah Bus. Educators' Assn., Phi Kappa Phi, Beta Phi Mu, Lambda Delta Sigma. Mormon. Clubs: Etienne Literary, Squaw Peak Sam's (Provo); Sunburst Good Sam's (Orem, Utah), St. George's Color Country Good Sams., Ramblers, Daus. Utah Pioneers.

CHABOT, STEVEN J., congressman, lawyer; b. Cin., Jan. 22, 1953; s. Gerard Joseph and Doris Leona (Tilly) C.; m. Donna Daly, June 22; children: Erica, Randy. BA, Coll. William & Mary, 1975; JD, Salmon P. Chase Coll. of Law, 1978. Bar: Ohio; cert. tchr., Ohio. Tchr. St. Joseph Sch., Cin., 1975-76; atty. Cin., 1978-95; mem. city coun. City of Cin., 1985-90; commr. Hamilton County, Ohio, 1990-94; mem. U.S. Congress from 1st Ohio Dist., Washington, 1995—; internat. rels., judiciary, sm. bus. coms. Mem. internat. rels. with Africa, internat. econ. policy & trade, comml. & adminstrv. law, crime, procurement, exports & bus. opportunities coms. Republican. Roman Catholic. Avocations: reading, spending time with family. Office: US Ho of Reps 129 Cannon Ho Office Bldg Washington DC 20515-3501*

CHABRAJA, NICHOLAS D., equipment manufacturing executive, lawyer; b. Gary, Ind., Nov. 6, 1942; BA, Northwestern U., 1964, JD, 1967. Bar: Ind. 1967, Ill. 1968. Ptnr. Jenner & Block, Chgo., 1968-97; sr. v.p., gen. counsel Gen. Dynamics Corp., 1993-94, exec. v.p., bd. dirs., 1994-97, vice chair, 1996—97, chmn., CEO, 1997—. Spl. counsel to Ho. of Reps. re-Impeachment Trial of Judge Harry E. Claiborne before U.S. Senate, 1986. Fellow Am. Coll. Trial Lawyers; mem. ABA, Ill. Bar Assn., Chgo. Bar Assn. Office: General Dynamics Corp 3190 Fairview Park Dr Ste 1 Falls Church VA 22042-4523 Office Phone: 703-876-3000.*

CHACE, WILLIAM MURDOUGH, former university administrator, literature educator; b. Newport News, Va., Sept. 3, 1938; s. William Emerson and Grace Elizabeth (Murdough) Chace; m. JoAn Elizabeth Johnstone, Sept. 5, 1964; children: William Johnstone, Katherine Elizabeth. BA in English, Haverford Coll., 1961; MA in English, U. Calif., Berkeley, 1963; PhD in English, U. Calif., 1968; LLD (hon.), Amherst Coll., 1990, William Coll., 1992. Instr. Stillman Coll., Tuscaloosa, Ala., 1963—64; teaching asst. U. Calif., Berkeley, 1964—66, acting instr., 1967—68; asst. prof. English Stanford U., 1968—74, assoc. prof., 1974—80, prof., 1980, assoc. dean Sch. Humanities and Scis., 1981—85, vice provost for acad. planning and devel., 1985—88; pres. Wesleyan U., Middletown, Conn., 1988—94, Emory U., Atlanta, 1994—2003. Dir. Sun Trust Banks; cons. Hewlett-Packard, Hallmark Cards, Inc., Hawaiian Ednl. Fund, Midwestern Mgmt. Assn.; vis. prof. The Coll. Aboard the Delta Queen, 1979, 80, 82, The Coll. in Western Europe and Brit. Isles, 1985; lectr. to libr. assocs. Stanford U., 1976; lectr. 6th Internat. James Joyce Symposium, Dublin, 1977, MLAL Ann. Conv., 1977, 78, Tufts Symposium, 1978, English Conf. U. Calif., Berkeley, 1979, Eighth Internat. James Joyce Symposium, Dublin, 1982, IBM Internat. Bus. and Acad. Conf., Monte Carlo, 1984, Ezra Pound Centennial Colloquium, San Jose State U., 1985, Ann. Meeting of Assn. of Grad. Liberal Studies Programs, St. Louis, 1986, Chico State U., La. State U., 1987, U. Utah Sch. Medicine Pub. Lecture series, 1987, No. Calif. Sci. Meeting Am. Coll. Physicians, Monterey, Calif., 1987, 13th Internat. James Joyce Symposium, 1992; presenter Joyce and History conf. Yale U., 1990; spkr. Fleur Cowles Flair Symposium, U. Tex., Austin, 2000. Author: James Joyce: A Collection of Critical Essays, 1973, The Political Identities of Ezra Pound and T.S. Eliot, 1973, Lionel Trilling: Criticism and Politics, 1980; co-author: Graham Greene: A Revaluation, 1990; co-editor: Justice Denied: The Black Man in White America, 1970, An Introduction to Literature, 1985; co-editor: (with JoAn E. Chace) Making It New, 1972; contbr. articles to profl. jours. Home: 1325 Cowper St Palo Alto CA 94301 Office Phone: 404-727-6422. Personal E-mail: billchace@yahoo.com.

CHACHAVA, MAYA, art educator; arrived in U.S., 1992; d. Zurab Chachava and Dinara Georgeoliani; 1 child from previous marriage, Nini Gabunia. BFA in English, Tbilisi Pedagogical Inst., 1984; BFA in Spanish, Ctrl. Wash. U., 1997; MFA in Painting, U. Wash., 2000. Asst. prof. English Tbilisi Pedagogical Inst., 1985—90; asst. prof. art U. Utah, Salt Lake City, 2001—05, Ctrl. Wash. U., Ellensburg, 2005—. Grantee, Utah Arts Coun., 2002; Dee grantee, U. Utah, 2005. Mem.: Coll. Art Assn. Home: 506 N Anderson Ellensburg WA 98926 Office: Ctrl Wash U 400 E University Way Ellensburg WA 98926

CHACKES, KENNETH MICHAEL, lawyer, educator, mediator; b. St. Louis, Sept. 12, 1949; s. Alex and Shirlee (Radloff) C.; m. Carole Gail Breen, June 14, 1970; children: Laura Michelle, Andrew Scott, Brian Carl. BA in Psychology, Tulane U., 1971; JD cum laude, St. Louis U., 1976. Bar: Mo. 1976, U.S. Dist. Ct. (ea. and we. dists.) Mo. 1976, U.S. Ct. Appeals (8th cir.) 1976, U.S. Ct. Appeals (D.C. cir.) 1979, U.S. Ct. Appeals (7th cir.) 1981. Ptnr. Chackes & Hoare, St. Louis, 1976-84; vis. asst. prof. law Washington U., St. Louis, 1984-87; atty. Mo. Protection & Advocacy Svcs., St. Louis and Jefferson City, 1988-90, mng. atty., 1990-92; pvt. practice, of counsel Vines, Frankel, Rubin, Bond & Dubin, P.C., St. Louis, 1992-96; ptnr. Van Amburg, Chackes, Carlson & Spritzer, LLP, St. Louis, 1996—2003, Chackes, Carlson & Spritzer, LLP, St. Louis, 2003—. Adminstrv. hearing officer Mo. Dept. Elem. & Secondary Edn. Divsn. Spl. Edn., 1999—; adj. prof. law Washington U., 1982-83, 88, supr. clin. students, 1981-84, 88-89, 91—; appearances on TV shows Law Talk, 1985-86, Special People, Special Needs, 1989-90; judge Fed. Practice Tng. Inst., St. Louis, 1983, judge trial tng. program, 1986, 89, instr., 1984-85, 92; mem. fed. practice com. U.S. Dist. Ct. for Ea. Dist. Mo., chmn. subcom. on appointment of counsel in civil rights cases; mem. discovery abuse and civil jury instrns. subcom.; lectr. in field. Mem. editl. bd. St. Louis U. Law Jour. Exec. com. Access Resources of Mo., 1991-2002; mem. adv. com. on disabilities issues, HUD, 1990-91; mem. Coalition of Citizens with Disabilities of Greater St. Louis, 1989-2000, Mo. Coalition for Homeless, 1989-2000; steering com. St. Louis Lawyers' Project on Homelessness and Inadequate Housing, 1987-92; bd. dirs. Ctrl. Reform Congregation, 2001-2005, chair Israel Cir., 2002-2004. Recipient Legal Advocate award Mo. Assn. for Social Welfare, 1992, Equal Justice award Legal Svcs. of Ea. Mo., 1993. Mem. ABA (individual rights and responsibilities, labor and employment law and litigation sects.), Mo. Bar Assn., Nat. Employment Lawyers Assn. (pres. St. Louis chpt. 1995-98). Home: 8100 Gannon Ave Saint Louis MO 63130-3731 Office: 8390 Delmar Blvd Ste 218 Saint Louis MO 63124-2179 Office Phone: 314-872-8420. E-mail: kchackes@vccs-law.com.

CHACKO, GEORGE KUTTICKAL, information scientist, educator; b. Trivandrum, India, July 1, 1930; came to U.S., 1953. s. Geevarghese Kuttickal and Thankamma (Mathew) C.; m. Yo Yee, Aug. 10, 1957; children: Rajah Yee, Ashia Yo Chacko Lance. MA in Econs. and Polit. Philosophy, Madras U., India, 1950; postgrad., St. Xavier's Coll., Calcutta, India, 1950-52; B in Commerce, Calcutta U., 1952; cert. postgrad. tng., Indian Stat. Inst., Calcutta, 1951; postgrad., Princeton U., 1953-54; PhD in Econometrics, New Sch. for Social Rsch./New School U., N.Y.C., 1959; postdoctoral, UCLA, 1961. Asst. editor Indian Fin., Calcutta, 1951-53; comml. corr. Times of India, 1953; dir. mktg. and mgmt. rsch. Royal Metal Mfg. Co., N.Y.C., 1958-60; mgr. dept. ops. rsch. Hughes Semicondr. div., Newport Beach, Calif., 1960-61; cons., 1961-62; ops. research staff cons. Union Carbide Corp., N.Y.C., 1962-63; mem. tech. staff Research Analysis Corp., McLean, Va., 1963-65, MITRE Corp., Arlington, Va., 1965-67; sr. staff scientist TRW Systems Group, Washington, 1967-70; asst. in rsch. Princeton U., 1953—54; cons. def. systems, computer, space, tech. systems and internat. devel. systems, assoc. in math. test devel. Ednl. Testing Service, Princeton, N.J., 1955-57; asst. prof. bus. adminstrn. UCLA, 1961-62; lectr. Dept. Agr. Grad. Sch., 1965-67; asst. professorial lectr. George Washington U., 1965-68; professorial lectr. Am. U., 1967-70, adj. prof., 1970; vis. prof. def. systems Mgmt. Coll., Ft. Belvoir, Va., 1972-73; vis. prof. U. So. Calif., 1970-71, prof. systems mgmt., 1971-83, prof. systems sci., 1983-94, prof. emeritus, 1994; prof. mgmt. U. Pertanian/U. Putra, Malaysia, 1996—2000; prin. investigator IRPA project U. Pertanian, Malaysia, 1996-97; prof. U. Putra, Malaysia, 1997—2000; prof. tech. mgmt. Malaysian Grad. Sch. Mgmt., 1997—2000; founder chmn. Joint MIT-MGSM Pan-Asian Program in Mgmt. of Tech., 1997—2000; prof. mgmt. tech. Multimedia U., Cyberjaya, Selangor, 2001—; chmn. Centre of Excellence of Mgmt. Tech., 2001—02, sr. advisor, 2002—; sr. consultant to Profitera Corp. Malaysian Govt. Multimedia Development Corp. R&D Project: Electronic Enhancement of Receivables Realization, 2002—; consultant ptnr. Natl. Info. Tech. Coun., Govt. of Malaysia, 2003—; chmn., CEO George Chacko Mgmt. Sdn. Bhd., Kuala Lumpur, Washington D.C., 2003—; first vis. disting. prof. Indian Inst. of Mgmt., Ahmedabad, 2004; prof. mgmt. of tech. Multimedia U., Cyberjaya, 2001—. Sr. Fulbright prof. Nat. Chengchi U., Taipei, 1983-84, sr. Fulbright rsch. prof., 1984-85; prin. investigator and program dir. Tech. Transfer Project, Taiwan Nat. Sci. Coun., 1984-85; disting. fgn. expert lectr. Taiwan Ministry Econ. Affairs, 1986; sr. vis. rsch. prof. Taiwan Nat. Sci. Coun. Nat. Chengchi U., Taipei, 1988-89; sr. vis. rsch. prof. Dah-Yeh Inst. Tech., Dah-Tsuen, Chang-Hwa, Taiwan, 1993-94; vis. prof. Nat. Chengchi U., Taipei, 1993-94; v.p. program devel. Systems and Telecom. Corp., Potomac, Md., 1987-90; chief sci. cons. RJO Enterprises, Lanham, Md., 1988-89; cons. Med. Svcs. Corp. Internat., vector biology and control project U.S. Agy. for Internat. Devel., 1991; guest lectr. Tech. Univs. Tokyo, Taipei, Singapore, Dubai, Cairo, Warsaw, Budapest, Prague, Bergen, Stockholm, Helsinki, Berlin, Madras, Bombay, London, 1992, Yokohoma, Taipei, Hong Kong, Kuala Lampur, Madras, Bombay, Alexandria, Jerusalem, Cairo, Paris, London, 1993-94, Madrid, Bologna, Milan, Monte Carlo, Amsterdam, Vienna, Austria, Kuala Lampur, Bangkok, 1994; Bogta, Quito, Lima, Santiago, Buenos Aires, Rio De Janeiro, Johannesburg, Kuala Lumpur, 1996; USIA sponsored U.S. sci. emissary to Egypt, Burma, India, Singapore, 1987; USIA sponsored U.S. expert on tech. transfer and military conversion 1st Internat. Conf. on Reconstrn. of Soviet Republics, Hanover, Germany, 1992; keynote speaker 2d annual conf. on mgmt. edn. in China, Taipei, Taiwan, 1989, world conf. on transition to advanced market economies, Warsaw, Poland, 1992, annual conv. Indian Inst. Indsl. Engring., Hyderabad, India, 1993, First Sino-South Africa Bilateral Symposium on Tech. Devel., Taipei, 1994, First Asia-Pacific Convention on Bus. mgmt. Edn., Kuala Lumpur, 1996, Annual Conf. of Malaysian Soc. of Ops. Rsch. and Mgmt. Scis, 1997, Annual Conf. of Malaysian Inst. of Accts., 2001; Biannual Regional Conf. of CPA, Australia, 2001, Portland Intl. Conf. on Mgmt. of Engring. and Tech., 2003; mem. internat. adv. com. on restructuring strategies for electronics info. industry Asian Inst. Tech. Workshop, 1994, Technological Forecasting and Social Change, 1996—; mem. First Convention on Bus. and Mgmt. Edn., Kuala Lumpur, 1996, mem. Asian-Pacific Conf. on Mgmt. Sci., Malaysia, 1997; spkr. in field. Applying High Technology to Enhance Survival Chances, 2002, Chief 'Ntrepreneur Author: 37 books in field including Applied Statistics in Decision Making, 1971, Computer Aided Decision Making, 1972, Systems Approach to Public and Private Sector Problems, 1976, Operations Research Approach to Problem Formation and Solution, 1976, Management Information systems, 1979, Trade Drain Imperatives of Technology Transfer: U.S. Taiwan Concomitant Coalitions, 1985, Robotics/Artificial Intelligence/Productivity U.S.-Japan Concomitant Coalitions, 1986, Technology Management: Applications to Corporate Markets and Military Missions, 1988, The Systems Approach to Problem-Solving: From Corporate Markets to National Missions, 1989, Toward Expanding Exports Through Technology Transfer: IBM Taiwan Concomitant Coalitions, 1989, Dynamic Program Management: From Defense Experience to Commercial Application, 1989, Decision-Making Under Uncertainty: An Applied Statistics Approach, 1991, Operations Research/Management Science: Case Studies in Decision Making Under Structured Uncertainty, 1993, Invoking Intercessory Prayer Power: Mediating Modern-day Miracles, 1997, Targeting Strategies for Continuous Competitiveness: 33 Corporate, Country, and Cross-Country Applications for Information Technology (IT) Industry, 1988, Half-Indian, Half-Chinese, and All American, 1998, Synergizing Invention and Innovation for Missions and Markets: 31 Corporate, Country and Cross Country Applications in Integrating Technology and Territory within and Between Corporations and Countries, 2000, Survival Strategies of Hitech Corporations: 71 Case Studies of 285 years of Executive Experience in 20th Century Autobiographical Narratives, 2000, Comprehensive Strategy + TQM=Continuous Competitiveness: 64 Case Studies Integrating Operational Concepts of Quintet of Quality with Survival Strategies, 2001, Chief Technology Officer (CTO) Decisions to Dare for Coporate/Country Survival: 51 Case Studies in Anticipating, Acquiring, Adapting and Officer (CNO) Decision to Dare for Corporate/Country Survival: 44 Case Studies of Forming, Dissolving, and Re-forming Coalitions to Compete and Cooperate Simultaneously on the next "New, New" Thing, 2004, Pre-PhD Proposal Preparation: Problem Formation & Formulation: 39 Real-Life Applications (14 in Physical and Bilogical Sciences and 25 in Social and Behavioral Sciences), 2004, Pre-PhD Proposal Preparation: Problem Formation & Formulation Study Guide, 2004, Managing Unproven Technology Study Guide, 2004, Disequilibria Entrepreneurship: Concepts & Applications: 52 Case Studies in Investing in Opportunities of Disequilibria, 2004, Disequilibria Entrepreneurship Study Guide, 2004, Managing Unproven Technology: Concepts & Applications: 52 Cast Studies in Anticipating, Acquiring, Adapting and Applying High Technology to Enhance Survival Chances, 2005, Risking Resources in the Internet Economy: 41 Case Studies in Investing in Opportunities of Disequilibria, 2005; columnist: The Sunday Star, Kuala Lumpur, 1998-2003, Bus. Times, Kuala Lumpur, 2003, Asian Beacon, 2003; contbr. over 330 articles to profl. pubs.; editor, contbr. 25 books including The Recognition of Systems in Health Services, 1969, Reducing the Cost of Space Transportation, 1969, Systems Approach to Environmental Pollution, 1972, National Organization of Health Services-U.S., USSR, China, Europe, 1979, Educational Innovation in Health Services-U.S., Europe, Middle East, Africa, 1979, Management Education in the Republic of China: Second Annual Conference, 1989, Expert Systems: 1st World Congress Proceedings, 1991, Transition to Advanced Market Economies: Internat. Conf. Proceedings, 1992, Industrial Engineering Interfaces: Inndian Nat. Conf. Proceedings, 1993, Technological Development: 1st Sino-South Africa Bilateral Symposium Proceedings, 1994, Lenten Daily Devotions, 1996, Asia Pacific Convention on Dynamism and Invention in Management Education Procs., 1996, Foundations of Game Theory, 1997; mng. editor Jour. Astronautical Scis., 1969-75; guest editor Jour. Rsch. Comm. Studies, 1978-79; assoc. editor Internat. Jour. Forecasting, 1982-85; mem. internat. editl. bd. MalaysianJour.Mgmt. Scis., 1996-98. Active Nat. Presbyn. Ch., Washington, 1967-84, mem. ch. coun., 1969-71, mem. chancel choir, 1967-84, co-dean, ch. family camp, 1977, coord. life abundant discovery groups, 1979, chmn. worship com. Taipei Internat. Ch., 1984, founder, dir. Intercessory Prayer Power, 1984, mem. adult choir, 1983-85, 88-89, 93-96, chmn. membership com., 1985, chmn. stewardship and fin. com., 1985, chmn. com. Christian edn., 1988, Sunday Sch. supt., 1989, adult Sunday sch. leader, 1993; adult Sunday Sch. leader 4th Presbyn. Ch., Bethesda, Md., 1986-87, mem. sanctuary choir, 1985—96; participant 9th Internat. Ch. Mus. Festival, Coventry Cathedral, 1992; mem. Men's Ensemble, 1986-93; mem. Ministry Com. Men of 4th Rep. to Session, 1990—96; founder, dir. Prayer Power Partnership, 1990—; adult Sunday sch.

leader Kuala Lumpur Internat. Ch., 1996—98; mem. internat. adv. bd. Technol. Forecasting & Social Change, 1996—; sr. advisor Acacia Home Fellowship, Full Gospel Assembly, Kuala Lumpur, 1998-; charter mem. IndUS Entrepreneurs, Malaysian chpt. 2002—; mem. internat. adv. coun. Portland Internat. Conf. on Mgmt. & Engring. & Tech., 2003-. Recipient Gold medal Inter-collegiate Extempore Debate in Malayalam U. Travacore, Trivandrum, India, 1945, Yogic Exercises Competition U Travancore, 1946, Jr. Lectureship prize Physics Soc. U Coll., 1946, 1st prize Inter-Varsity Debating Team Madras, 1949, NSF internat. sci. lectures award, 1982, USIA citation for invaluable contbr. to America's pub. diplomacy, 1992, Commendation for 2 books on U.S. - Taiwan Technology Transfer by Presidential Palace, Taipei, 1993; Coll. scholar St. Xavier's Coll., 1950-52; S.E. Asia Club fellow Princeton U., 1953-54, Univ. fellow UCLA, 1961. Fellow AAAS (nat. coun. 1968-73, chmn. or co-chmn. symposia 1971, 72, 74, 76, 77, 78), Am. Astronautical Soc. (v.p. publs. 1969-71, editor Tech. Newsletter 1968-72, mng. editor Jour. Astronautical Scis. 1969-75), Ops. Rsch. Soc. Am. (vice-chmn. com. of representation on AAAS 1972-78, nat. coun. tech. sect. on health 1966-68, editor Tech. Newsletter on Health 1966-73); mem. Washington Ops. Rsch. Coun. (trustee 1967-69, chmn. tech. colloquia 1967-68, editor Tech. Newsletter 1967-68, Banquet chmn. 1992-93), Inst. Mgmt. Scis. (rep. to Internat. Inst. for Applied Systems Analysis in Vienna, Austria 1976-77, session chmn. Athens, Greece 1977, Atlanta 1977), World Future Soc. (editl. bd. publs. 1970-71), N.Y. Acad. Scis., Soc. Scientific Mgmt. and Ops. Rsch. (Egypt, 1st hon. fgn. mem.), Inst. for Ops. Rsch. and the Mgmt. Scis. (founding, INFORMS 1994); Kiwanis (charter 1st v.p., Life-time Hickson fellow 1995), Costa Mesa North Club (charter 1st v.p., dir.), Friendship Heights Club (charter pres., dir., Outstanding Svc. award 1972-73, Life award), Bethesda Club (disting. divsn. one svc. award, 1968, 70, capital dist. chmn. 1967, 69-70, 71-72, inter divsn. chmn. Green Candle of Hope Dinner, 1965-82), Capital dist. Found. 1982, Taipei-Keystone Club (disting. dir., spl. rep. of internat. pres. and counselor to dist. of Republic of China 1983-86, Pioneer Premier Project award Asia-Pacific conf. 1986, Legion of Honor 1985), Bethesda Club (dir. 1967-69, 95, chmn. internat. rels. 1991-2003, chmn. hon. com. 1992-2003, numerous coms. 1966—2003), Leisure World Kiwanis Club (chmn. internat. liaision on sibling rels. with Kiwanis Club of Kuala Lumpur, 2003-). Republican. Office: George Chacko Mgmt Bhd 14515 Fiske Dr Silver Spring MD 20906 E-mail: gkchacko2003@yahoo.com. *As one who was privileged to be born into a Christian family tracing itself to the founding in the year 52 of the Mar Thoma Syrian Church in Southwest India by Thomas the Doubting Disciple of Jesus Christ, I look upon the exciting encounters I have had with new ideas (such as Theory of Games) and new professions (such as Operations Research) as precious talents over which I exercise stewardship by enjoying excellence of effort and exposition toward a better tomorrow at home and abroad, as an Indian-American blest with a most supportive family.*

CHACKO, SAMUEL, association official; came to U.S., 1970; s. Chanda Pillai and Sosamma (Cheriyan) C.; m. Omana Chellimalayil George, May 21, 1979; children: Roshen Samuel, Renee Susan. BA in Econs., U. Kerala, 1963, MA in History, 1966, MA in Polit. Sci., 1968; BA in Social Sci., Olivet Nazarene U., Kankakee, Ill., 1971; MA in Comm., Govs. State U., 1974; postgrad., U. Ill., Chgo., 1981—86. Cert. in gerontology, cmty. nutrition. Dir. dept. aging Kankakee Land Community Action Agy., 1972—76; head sr. citizens dept. Oakland-Livingston Human Svcs. Agy., Pontiac, Mich., 1976—78; dir. Benton Harbor (Mich.) Area Parks and Recreation Bd., 1978—79; program analyst Ill. Migrant Coun., Chgo., 1980—84; dir. energy svcs. Community and Econ. Devel. Assn. Cook County, Inc., Chgo., 1985—2001; v.p. Cmty. and Econ. Devel. Assn. Cook County, Inc., Chgo., 2001—. Mem. Ill. State Commerce Commn. Task Force on Rewriting Utility Svc. Rules, 1995—, Ill. State Energy Assistance Program Working Group, 1991-93. Bd. dirs. NAACP, 1973-76; bd. dirs., Ea. Ill. U. Parents Club, 2000-. Mem.: Lions Club Internat. Office: Cmty and Econ Devel Assn Cook Cty Inc 208 S Lasalle St Ste 850 Chicago IL 60604-1000

CHADBURN, AMY, pathologist; b. Springfield, Oreg., Apr. 17, 1957; BS, Oreg. State U., 1979; MD, Stanford Med. Sch., 1983. Asst. prof. Columbia U., N.Y.C., 1989—94, Cornell U., N.Y.C., 1994—97; assoc. prof. Cornell U. Weill Med. Sch., 1997—2004; asst. attending pathologist Presbyn. Hosp. Columbia campus, N.Y.C., 1989—94, N.Y. Presbyn. Hosp., 1994—97, assoc. dir. immunopathology lab., 1994—2004, dir. immunopathology lab., 2004—. Pathologist AMC, Washington, 2001—; prof. pathology Weill Cornell Med. Coll., 2005—; attending pathologist N.Y. Presbyn. Hosp., 2005—. Named Best Dr. N.Y.C., Castle Connelly, 2000; recipient Arthur Purdy Stout award, Arthur Purdy Stout Soc., 1992. Mem.: Am. Soc. Clinical Pathologists, Soc. Hematopathology, U.S. and Canadian Acad. Pathology. Avocation: running. Office: NY Presbyn Hosp Cornell Campus Starr 715 525 E 68th St New York NY 10021

CHADEN, LEE A., food products executive; BS in Indsl. Engring., Purdue U.; MBA, U. Calif., Berkeley. Brand mgr. Procter & Gamble, 1966—70; sr. product mgr. Playtex Apparel, Inc., 1970—74, pres., Playtex Can., 1974—76, area v.p., internat. divsn., 1976—77, v.p., gen. mgr., family products divsn., 1977—79; ptnr. Mktg. Corp. of Am., 1979—81; prin. Gen. Consumer Elecs., 1981—83; CEO Interac Corp., 1983—85; gen. ptnr. Marketcorp Ventures, 1985—91; pres., U.S. and Westfar divsns. of Playtex Sara Lee Corp., 1991—94, pres., CEO, Sara Lee Intimates, 1994—95, v.p., 1995—98, sr. v.p., 1998—99, CEO, Sara Lee Branded Apparel, 1999—2001, sr. v.p., human resources, 2001—03, exec. v.p., 2003—, CEO, branded apparel unit, 2004—. Office: Sara Lee Corp Three First Nat Plaza Chicago IL 60602-4260

CHADICK, GARY ROBERT, lawyer; b. Manhasset, N.Y., June 19, 1961; s. Howard and Norma (Cohen) C.; m. Lori J. Branson, Sept. 22, 1990. BA cum laude, Union Coll., Schenectady, 1983; JD, George Washington U., 1986. Bar: Calif. 1987, U.S. Dist. Ct. (cen. dist.) Calif. 1987, D.C. 1988, U.S. Ct. Appeals (fed. cir.) 1988, Iowa, 2002. Research and writing asst. George Washington U., Washington, 1984-85; summer assoc. Epstein, Becker, Borsody and Green, Washington, 1985; assoc. McKenna & Cuneo, L.A., 1986-92; asst. gen. counsel, group counsel and div. counsel Litton Industries, Woodland Hills, 1992—2001; sr. v.p., gen. counsel, sec. Rockwell Collins, Inc., Cedar Rapids, 2002—. Lectr. SBA, Washington, 1985, Nat. Contracts Mgmt. Assn., Orange County chpt., L.A., 1987, Pepperdine Law Sch., 1988; in-house lectr. Terminations and Claims, 1990-91. Fed. Publs. Truth in Negotiation Act, San Jose, Calif., 1990; co-author: Cost Acctg. Standards: New Developments, 1989. Active Big Bros.-Big Sisters Program, Schenectady, 1982, United Way contbr. Mem. ABA (bus.law sec.), Nat. Contracts Mgmt. Assn., Am. Soc. Corp. Sec., Am. Corp. Counsel Assn., Nat. Assn.Stockplan Profls., Aerospace Industries Assn. (chmn. legal com. 1999-2000) Avocations: soccer referee, golf. Office: Rockwell Collins Inc 400 Collins Rd NE Cedar Rapids IA 52498

CHADSEY, HAROLD A., astronomer, physicist; s. Harold E. and Delores G. Chadsey; m. Carol Ellen Cooper, Nov. 9, 1991. BS, Centenary Coll., 1982; MS, Am. U., 1995; PhD, Kennedy-Western U., 2001. Astronomer U.S. Naval Obs., Miami, Fla., 1985—89, Washington, 1989—2004; physicist U.S. Dept. Navy, 2004—. GPS timing Precise Time & Time Interval, 1993—2004; timing and clock adviser USCG, Alexandria, Va., 1989—2004; atomic frequency stds., 1995—2004. Author: An Automated Quality Control System for Cesium Frequency Standards, 2001. Judge H.S. Sci. Fairs D.C. Pub. Schs., Washington, 1991—2002, Fairfax County Pub. Schs., 1998—; mentor H.S. students Dept. of the Navy, U.S. Naval Obs., 2002; chair HSSCI Fair Grand Prize Judges, 2004—05. Named Safety Rep., Naval Dist. Washington, 2002. Mem.: No. Va. Radio Control (pres. 1997), Quantico Flying Club, El Karubah Shrine. Avocations: building and flying remote control airplanes, private pilot.

CHADWICK, DEREK JAMES, foundation administrator; b. Carshalton, Surrey, Eng., Feb. 9, 1948; s. Dennis Edmund and Ida (Kay) Chadwick; m. Susan Reid, Dec. 20, 1980 (dec. May 15, 2002); children: Andrew John, Frederick Mark. BA in Chemistry, Oxford U., 1969, BSc, 1970, MA, D Philosophy, Oxford U., 1972. ICI fellow Cambridge U., 1972-73; Prize fellow Magdalen Coll., Oxford U., 1973-77; Royal Soc. European exch. fellow Eidgenössische Technische Hochschule, Zurich, Switzerland, 1975-77; lectr., sr. lectr., reader Liverpool U., 1977-88; vis. prof. U. Alsace, Mulhouse, France, 1988; dir. The Ciba Found. (now named The Novartis Found.), London, 1988—. Coun. mem. Louis Jeantet Found., Geneva, 1988-98, Assn. Med. Rsch. Charities, London, 1991-2000; vice-chmn., 1994-2000; coun. mem. Cou. Ctrl. Lab. of Rsch. Couns., 2002--; mem. steering com. Scientists Inst. for Pub. Info., N.Y.C., 1989-96; vis. prof. U. Trondheim, Norway, 1996-2003. Editor 55 books; author 100 papers and chpts. in sci. jours. and books. Fellow Royal Soc. Chemistry; mem. Am. Chem. Soc., Worshipful Soc. Apothecaries London, Hague Club Dirs. European Founds. (sec. 1993-97). Avocations: music, gardening, skiing. Office: The Novartis Found 41 Portland Pl London W1B 1BN England Office Phone: 44207-636-9456. E-mail: dchadwick@novartisfound.org.uk.

CHAE, HAN, medical researcher; s. Soo-Young Chae and Myoung-Geun Oh; m. Soo-Jin Lee, Jan. 12, 1999; 1 child, William J. PhD, Kyung Hee U., Seoul, Republic of Korea, 2000—03. Medical Doctor Republic of Korea, 1995. Chief of oriental medicine sect. Republic of Korean Army, Republic of Korea, 1995—98; rschr. Korean Inst. of Oriental Medicine, Seoul, Republic of Korea, 2000—03, Harvard Med. Sch., Boston, 2001—03, The Cleve. Clinic Found., Cleve., 2003—. Adv. com. mem. Assn. of Korean Oriental Medicine, Seoul, Republic of Korea, 1996—2001. Author: (book) Traditional Oriental Medicine for Mil. Med. Care; contbr. article in weekly newspaper. Exec. mgr. The Assn. for Neo Medicine, Seoul, Republic of Korea, 2000—01. First lt. Spl. Force Republic of Korean Army, 1995—98. Recipient Yellow Emperor Med. Prize, Kyung Hee U., 1991. Mem.: Korean Oriental Med. Soc., Korean Psychol. Assn., Soc. for Neuroscience. Achievements include research in first sci. publ. about Sasang typology; a traditional Korean med. typology widely used in Korea clinically for hundreds of years. Office: The Cleve Clinic Found 9500 Euclid Ave Cleveland OH 44195 Personal E-mail: han@chaelab.org.

CHAET, BERNARD ROBERT, artist, educator; b. Boston, Mar. 7, 1924; s. David and Golda (Benjamin) C.; m. Ninon Lacey, Dec. 14, 1951; 1 child, Leah. Student, Sch. Fine Arts, Boston, 1942-44, 48; BS, Tufts U., 1950; D.F.A. (hon.), Md. Inst. Coll. Art, 1985. Tchr. Boston Pub. Schs., Inst. Contemporary Art, Boston, 1951—; instr. painting Yale U., 1951-56, asst. prof., 1956-59, assoc. prof. painting, chmn. dept. art, 1959-62, prof. painting, 1969-90, William Leffingwell prof. painting, 1979-90, prof. emeritus, 1990—, dir. art. div. Summer Sch. Music and Art, 1960-66. Contbg. editor: Arts mag, 1956-59; org. exhbn. 20th Century Drawing, Yale U. Art Gallery, 1955; Represented in permanent colls., Worcester (Mass.) Art. Mus., Bklyn. Mus., DeCordova Mus., Lincoln, Mass., Brandeis U., Addison Gallery Am. Art, Andover, Mass., U. Calif. at Los Angeles, Fogg Mus., Harvard, Mus. Fine Arts Boston, Mus. Art R.I. Sch. Design, Yale Art Gallery, U. Mass., U. Conn., N.Y. U., State U. N.Y. at Cortland, Brown U.; Author: Artists at Work, 1960, The Art of Drawing, 1970, 3d edit., 1983, An Artist's Notebook: Materials and Techniques of Drawing and Painting, 1979; one-man shows, Boston, N.Y.C., White Museum of Cornell U., Boston Pub. Libr., 1989; group exhbns., Corcoran Gallery of Art, Modern Mus., Bklyn., Los Angeles County, Detroit museums, Art Inst. Chgo., Inst. Contemporary Art, Boston, Am. Drawings traveling show of French Museums, others, group shows, Mass. Inst. Tech., U. Ill., U. Nebr., Brandeis U. Recipient grant Nat. Found. Arts and Humanities, 1966-67 Home: 141 Cold Spring St New Haven CT 06511-2205*

CHAET, VICKY ISABEL, visual artist; b. Chgo., Dec. 27, 1941; d. Louis and Rose Chaet; m. John R. Manning. BFA in Ceramics, U. Chgo., 1963; MFA in Sculpture, Ceramics, U. Mass., 1971; MFA in Computer Graphics, Sculpture, Stanford U., 1973. Pvt. cons., art critiques for artists, 1979—2003; field instr. Antioch U. West, 1981; faculty visual thinking Coll. Engring., Boston U., 1978-79; guest lectr. Mass. Coll. of Art, 1978; instr. pottery Mudflat Sch., Cambridge, Mass., 1976-77; tchg. assoc. dept. art Stanford U., 1972-73; master painter Apprentice Alliance, 1992-96. One-person shows include Bergman Gallery, Chgo., 1968, Herter Gallery, Amherst, Mass., 1971, Sumner Gallery, Palo Alto, Calif., 1974, 75, 86, Live Art Gallery, San Francisco, 1992, 93, St. Paul Towers, Oakland, Calif., 1995, King Galleries, San Francisco, 1996, Post 814 Gallery, Milw., 2001-2002, Artspan Open Studio, San Francisco, 2002, 04; group exhbns. include Allen Art Mus., Oberlin, Ohio, 1973, Allyne Gallery, 1977, Riskin-Sinow Gallery, 1989-90, Nelson Morales Gallery, 1990 (all San Francisco), Dow and Frosini Art Gallery, Berkeley, 1991, Artreach, San Francisco, 1995, Jewish Cmty. Libr., San Francisco, 2003, 04, 05; works in pvt. collections at William Bonifas Fine Arts Ctr., Escanaba, Mich., Sundown Design Ltd., San Francisco, DeAnza Coll., Cupertino, Calif.; interview featured on TV program JobNET, San Francisco Viacomsix, 1995. Calif. State U. rsch. grantee, 1969, Women Artists History through Mudflat Sch. teaching grantee, 1977; Stanford U. fellow, 1971-73, vis. scholar, 1973-75; The Ragdale Found. artist residency, Lake Forest, Ill., 1988, 89; contbr. articles to profl. jours.; illustrator: Unravelling Smoke, 1975. Office: 339 Frederick St San Francisco CA 94117-3913 Office Phone: 415-665-5946.

CHAFE, WALLACE LESEUR, linguist, educator; b. Cambridge, Mass., Sept. 3, 1927; s. Albert J. and Nathalie (Amback) C.; m. Mary Elizabeth Butterworth, June 23, 1951 (div. 1980); children— Christopher, Douglas, Stephen; m. Marianne Mithun, Jan. 25, 1985 BA, Yale U., 1950, MA, 1956, PhD, 1958. Asst. prof. U. Buffalo, 1958-59; linguist Bur. Am. Ethnology, Smithsonian Instn., 1959-62; mem. faculty U. Calif.-Berkeley, 1962-86, prof. linguistics, 1967-86, U. Calif., Santa Barbara, 1986-91, prof. emeritus, 1991—, rsch. prof., 2003—. Author: Seneca Thanksgiving Rituals, 1961, Seneca Morphology and Dictionary, 1967, Meaning and the Structure of Language, 1970, The Pear Stories, 1980, Evidentiality, 1986, Discourse, Consciousness, and Time, 1994. Served with USNR, 1945-46. Mem. Linguistic Soc. Am., Am. Psychol. Assn., Am. Anthrop. Assn., Am. Psychol. Soc. Office: Univ Calif Dept Linguistics Santa Barbara CA 93106 Business E-Mail: chafe@linguistics.ucsb.edu.

CHAFE, WILLIAM HENRY, history professor; b. Boston, Jan. 28, 1942; s. William Robinson and Elsie (Crabtree) C.; m. Lorna Jane Waterhouse, July 12, 1964; children: Christopher Robert, Jennifer Elizabeth. AB, Harvard U., 1962; AM, Columbia U., 1966, PhD, 1971. Instr. Columbia Grammar Sch., N.Y.C., 1963-65, Vassar Coll., Poughkeepsie, N.Y., 1970-71; from asst. prof. to prof. Duke U., Durham, NC, 1971—79, prof., 1979—, Alice Mary Baldwin Disting. prof., 1988—, dean Faculty Arts and Scis., 1995—2004, vice provost undergrad. edn., 1999—2004. Author: The American Woman, 1972, Women and Equality, 1977, Civilities and Civil Rights, 1980 (R.F. Kennedy book award 1981), The Unfinished Journey, 1986, A History of Our Time, 1986, The Paradox of Change, 1991, Never Stop Running, 1993 (Sidney Hillman Found. book award 1994), The Road to Equality, 1994, Remembering Jim Crow, 2002 (Lillian Smith award, 2003). NEH fellow, 1974-75, 84-85, Rockefeller Found. fellow, 1978, Guggenheim fellow, 1989-90; grantee Nat. Humanities Ctr., Rsch. Triangle Pk., N.C., 1981-82, Ctr. for Advanced Study, Palo Alto, Calif., 1989-90. Fellow Soc. Am. Historians; mem. Am. Hist. Assn. (chmn. nominating com., 1987-88), Orgn. Am. Historians (co-chmn. program com. 1981-82, chair nominating com. 1991, exec. bd. 1993-96, pres. 1998-99), Am. Studies Assn., So. Hist. Assn. Avocations: sailing, tennis. Office: Duke U 224 Carr Building Box 90719 Durham NC 27706 Business E-Mail: william.chafe@duke.edu.

CHAFEE, INGRID ROBERTA HOOVER COLEMAN, retired language educator; b. Evanston, Ill., Dec. 12, 1934; d. Richard Thomas and Ingrid (Krogvig) Hoover; m. Samuel Henry Coleman III, Sept. 10, 1958 (wid. Oct. 1974); children: Robert D., Charles E.; m. Nathaniel Chafee, July 8, 1989. AB, Western Coll. of Miami, Oxford, 1956; MA, U. Va., 1959; PhD, Emory U., 1980. Part-time instr. Ga. State U., Atlanta, 1976—81; asst. prof. Morehouse Coll., Atlanta, 1981—83, 1990—95, assoc. prof., 1995—2004, acting chair dept. modern fgn. langs., 2000; ret., 2004. Tech. writer, trainer Am. Software, Inc., Atlanta, 1984-90; coord. European Program, Morehouse Ctr. for Internat. Studies, Atlanta, 1994-96; jour. referee Jour. of Assn. for W. Ga. Coll., 1996—. Contbr. articles to profl. jours. Coord. prisoner of conscience coms., Amnesty Internat., Atlanta, 1983-87. Mem. MLA, South Atlantic Modern Lang. Assn., Am. Assn. Tchrs. of French, Phi Beta Kappa. Democrat. Avocations: writing, listening to music, history, film, theater, swimming. Home: 476 Princeton Way NE Atlanta GA 30307-1131 E-mail: ingridcc@aol.com.

CHAFEE, LINCOLN, senator; b. Warwick, RI, Mar. 26, 1953; m. Stephanie Chafee; three children. BA in Classics, Brown U., 1975; postgrad., Mont. State U. Farrier various harness racktracks; planner Gen. Dynamics, Quonset Point, R.I., 1983; exec. dir. N.E. Corridor Initiative; del. R.I. Constnl. Conv., 1985; mem. Warwick City Coun., 1986—93; mayor City of Warwick, 1993—99; R.I. senator U.S. Senate, 1999—, mem. com. on environment and pub. works, chmn. subcom. on superfund, com. fgn. rels., chmn. subcom. near ea. and south Asian affairs, banking, housing and urban affairs com. Republican. Office: US Senate 141A Russell Senate Office Washington DC 20510-0001 also: Unit 1100 170 Westminster St Providence RI 02903-2104*

CHAFEL, JUDITH ANN, education educator; b. Rochester, N.Y., Apr. 8, 1945; d. James Arthur and Florence Joan (Santangelo) Chafel. AB, Vassar Coll., 1967; MSEd, Wheelock Coll, 1971; PhD, U. Ill., 1979. Cert. elem. tchr., Mass., N.J., N.Y. Tchr. Spruce St. Sch., Lakewood, N.J., 1972-74, Sodus (N.Y.) Primary Sch., 1974-76; grad. research and teaching asst. U. Ill., Urbana, 1976-79; vis. asst. prof. U. Tex., Austin, 1979-80; asst. prof. dept. curriculum and instrn. Ind. U., Bloomington, 1980-86, assoc. prof., 1986—2001, prof., 2001—; mem. profl. staff U.S. Ho. Reps., Washington, 1989-90. Adj. assoc. prof. philanthropic studies Ctr. on Philanthropy, 1991-2001; reviewer Hist. Publs. and Records Commn., Nat. Archives, Washington, 1979, Little, Brown and Co., Boston, 1982-84, Office for Ednl. Rsch. and Improvement, U.S. Dept. Edn., 1991, 93. Mem. editl. adv. bd. Early Child Devel. and Care, 1985—, Youth and Soc., 1995-2005, Jour. of Poverty: Innovations on Social, Political and Economic Inequalities, 1998—; cons. editor Early Childhood Rsch. Quar., 1988-91, 92-95; contbr. editor Am. Jour. of Orthopsychiatry, 2000—; reviewer, book editor; contbr. articles to profl. jours.; contbr. chapts. to books. Proffitt Endowment grantee, Ind. U., 1982, 88, 1998, Ctr. on Philanthropy grantee, 1991, Spencer Found. grantee, 1985, 98; Congl. Sci. fellow Soc. Rsch. in Child Devel., 1989. Mem. Soc. Rsch. in Child Devel. (program com. 1986, 92), Am. Ednl. Rsch. Assn. (program com. 1984, 86, 87, 91, 92, 94, 96-99, 2001, 03, 04, nominations com. 1986, 88, chair 1993-95, mem.-at-large spl. interest group on early edn. and child devel. 1991-93), Nat. Assn. Edn. Young Children (reviewer 1980—), Assn. Childhood Edn. Internat. (pub. com. 1982-84, bull. and pamphlets rev. editor jour. 1982-84, rsch. com. 1984-88), Nat. Soc. for the Study of Edn. Office: Ind U Sch Edn 3214 Education Bldg Bloomington IN 47405 E-mail: chafel@indiana.edu.

CHAFETZ, BARRY RICHARD, lawyer; b. Chgo., Dec. 16, 1946; s. David and Mildred (Dick) C.; m. Frances Therese Gawel, Apr. 2, 1968; children: Rochelle, Robyn, Ronald. BS, U. Ill., 1969, JD, 1972. Bar: Ill. 1972, U.S. Dist. Ct. (no. and cen. dists.) Ill. Asst. state atty., Mt. Vernon, Ill., 1972-74; assoc. Delano Law Offices, Springfield, Ill., 1975-80, Heller & Morris, Chgo., 1980, Leonard M. Ring & Assocs., Chgo., 1981-94; ptnr. Corboy & Demetrio, Chgo., 1994—. Mem. ABA, Ill. Bar Assn., Assn. Trial Lawyers Am., Ill. Trial Lawyers Assn. Office: 21st Fl 33 N Dearborn St Fl 21 Chicago IL 60602-3102 Home: 6338 Clarendon Hills Rd Willowbrook IL 60527-2133 Office Phone: 312-346-3191. E-mail: brc@corboydemetrio.com.

CHAFETZ, SIDNEY, art educator; b. Providence, Mar. 27, 1922; s. Isaac and Dora Chafetz; m. Adrienne Block Chafetz, June 11, 1982; children: Jonathan, Dan, Adam, Seth. BFA, RI Sch. of Design, 1947. Instr. Ohio State U., Columbus, Ohio, 1948—52, asst. prof., 1952—54, assoc. prof., 1954—56, prof. of art, 1956—88, prof. emeritus, 1988—2005. Vis. artist U. Ariz., Tucson, 1966, U. Wis., Madison, Wis., 1972, Portland Sch. of Art, Portland, Maine, 1971, Utah State U., Logan, Utah, 1972, Trinity U., San Antonio, 1994. Exhibitions include Holocaust Theme, 1992. Mem. Cultural Arts Comm., Upper Arlington, Ohio, 1973—77. T/5 U.S. Army, 1942—45. Recipient Ohio's Gov. award, Ohio Arts Coun., 1991, Outstanding Printmaker, Mid-Am. Print Coun., 1998, Major Cash award, Internat. Woodcut Exhibit, 1970; Fulbright grant, Paris, 1950—51, Fulbright Artist Residency, U. Belgrade, 1980, Ford Found. grant, Ohio State U., 1981. Mem.: Fulbright Assn., Nat. Acad. Design. Jewish. Avocations: reading, travel. Home: 1620 E Broad St 1002 Columbus OH 43203 E-mail: chafetz.1@osu.edu.

CHAFFEE, MARK ANTHONY, engineer; b. Rutland, Vt., Nov. 12, 1955; s. George Keen and Steria Korzun Chaffee; m. Monie Elizabeth Watson, July 21, 1984; children: J. Macklin, Quinn A., Griffith G., Aurora J., Cathal R. BA, Williams U., 1977; MS, Thayer Sch. Engring., 1983. From devel. engr. to prin. engr. Rockwell Automation (formerly Creonics), Lebanan, NH, 1983—2004, Mayfield Heights, Ohio, 2004—. Coach Upper Valley Lightning Soccer, Hanover, NH, 1993—2004; Sunday sch. tchr., deacon Grace Outreach, Lebanon, NH, 1991—98; elder Living Faith Fellowship, Claremont, NH, 1999—2002. Achievements include patents for in area of motion control. Avocations: running, ice hockey, tennis, golf, windsurfing. Office: Rockwell Automation 1 Allen-Bradley Dr Mayfield Heights OH 44124

CHAFFEE, PAUL CHARLES, newspaper editor; b. Racine, Wis., Aug. 10, 1947; s. Raymond Russell and Ellen Mary (Tiles) C.; m. Bonnie Louise Burmeister, Aug. 9, 1969. BA in Journalism, U. Minn., 1969. Reporter Grand Rapids (Mich.) Press, 1969-79, asst. met. editor, 1979-81; met. editor Saginaw (Mich.) News, 1981-88, editor, 1988—. Founding mem. adv. bd. dept. journalism Ctrl. Mich. U., Mt. Pleasant, 1987—, pres. bd. publs., 2004; past mem. Hispanic adv. bd. dept. journalism Mich. State U.; past pres. bd. dirs. Mich. AP Editl. Assn.; past bd. dirs. Mid Am. Press Inst. Bd. dirs. Salvation Army, Saginaw, 1986—, St. Charles (Mich.) Cmty. Schs. Found., 1994—, Westlund Child Guidance Clinic, 1995-99, Saginaw Bay Symphony, 1996—; steering bd. Leadership Saginaw; adv. bd. Saginaw County Jr. League; steering com. Bridge Ctr. Racial Harmony. Mem.: Nat. Assn. Hispanic Journalists, Soc. Profl. Journalists, Am. Soc. Newspaper Editors, Saginaw Country Club. Avocation: gardening. Office: Saginaw News 203 S Washington Ave Saginaw MI 48607-1283

CHAFFIN, CEAN, producer; Prodr.: (films, with Steve Golia) The Game, 1997, Fight Club, 1999; (films) Panic Room, 2002; actor: Lords of Dogtown, 2005. Recipient Grammy award Best Music Video-Short Form, 1995, 1996. Office: Anonymous Content 8522 National Blvd Ste 101 Culver City CA 90232-2454*

CHAFFIN, DON BRIAN, industrial engineering educator, research director; b. Sandusky, Ohio, Apr. 17, 1939; m. 1966; 3 children. B of Indsl. Engring., Gen. Motors Inst., 1962; MS in Indsl. Engring., U. Toledo, 1964; PhD in Engring., U. Mich., 1967. Registered profl. engr., Ohio; cert. prof. ergonomist. Quality ctrl. engr. New Departure Divsn. GM Corp., Ohio, 1960-62, inspection foreman, 1962-63; project engr. Micrometrical Divsn. Bendix Corp., Mich., 1963-64; asst. prof. phys. medicine U. Kans., 1967-68, asst. prof. indsl. engring., 1968-70, assoc. prof. indsl. engring., 1970-77; prof. indsl. and ops. engring. U. Mich., Ann Arbor, 1977-93, dir. Ctr. for Ergonomics, 1980-97, Disting. Univ. prof. and Johnson prof. indsl. engring. and biomed. engring., 1993—. Fellow AAAS, Human Factors Soc. (Paul Fitts award 1992), Am. Indsl. Hygiene Assn. (Edward Baier award 1994), Ergonomics Soc., Am. Inst. Med. and Biol. Engring.; mem. NSPE, NAE, Am. Inst. Indsl. Engrs. (Baker Disting. Rschr. award 1991), Am. Soc. Biomechanics (Borrelli award), Sigma Xi. Achievements include research on effects and applications of electromyography for measuring human performance, concepts of biomechanics for injury prevention in skeletal-muscle system; expanding the teaching of physiological, neurological and anatomical concepts related to the simulation of human motions and exertions in the design of operated systems in manufacturing and service organizations, and in vehicle operation and maintenance. Office: U Mich Ctr Ergonomies 1656 IOE Bldg Ann Arbor MI 48109-2117

CHAFFIN, JEFFREY G., dentist; s. Jere L. and Martha Chaffin; m. Sherry D. Nance, Oct. 15, 1993; children: Sawyer, Maison. BS, U. Tampa, 1988; DDS, U. Nebr., 1992; MPH, U. Mich., 2000. Diplomate Am. Bd. Dental Pub. Health, Am. Coll. of Healthcare Exec. Commd. lt. col. U.S. Army, 1992, resident Ft. Sill, Okla., 1992—93, officer in charge, Camp Carrol Dental Clinic Waegon, Republic of Korea, 1993—94, dental officer, Vizenza Dental Clinic Italy, 1994—97, dental officer, Ft. Drum Dental Clinic NY, 1997—98; resident Mich. Sch. Pub. Health, Ann Arbor, 1998—2000; dental pub. health officer U.S. Army Dental Command, San Antonio, 2000—. Lectr. European Dental Tng. Conf., Garmisch, Germany, 2002, Boston Coll. Sch. Pub. Health, 2003. Mem.: Am. Coll. of Healthcare Exec., Internat. Coll. Dentistry, Am. Dental Assn., Assn. Pub. Health Dentistry, Assn. Mil. Surgeons U.S. Avocations: skiing, travel.

CHAFFIN, JOHN B., minister, music educator; b. Cookeville, Tenn., Sept. 25, 1947; s. Marion and JoNell Chaffin; m. Kathy L. Wolfe, Apr. 9, 1977; children: Michael, Melody. MusB Edn., Murray (Ky.) State U., 1969; MusM in Choral Conducting, U.Ill., Champaign, 1973. Cert. Tchr. Ill. Choral tchr. Reidland H.S., Paducah, Ky., 1969—72, Hinsdale South H.S., Darien, Ill., 1973—74, Charleston (Ill.) H.S., 1974—76, Prospect H.S., Mt. Prospect, Ill., 1976—77, Russellville (Ky.) H.S., 1977—87; assoc. min. Columbia Ave. Ch. of Christ, Glasgow, Ky., 1987—91; min. Beedeville (Ark.) Ch. of Christ, 1991—92; choral & bible instr. Greater Atlanta Christian Sch., Norcross, Ga., 1992—. Composer: (choral arrangements) Various titles, 2000—. Mem.: Ga. Music Educators Assn., Music Educators Nat. Conf., Am. Choral Dirs. Assn. Office: Greater Atlanta Christian Sch 1575 Indian Trail-Lilburn Rd Norcross GA 30093 E-mail: johnch@gacs.pvt.k12.ga.us.

CHAFFIN, VERNER FRANKLIN, lawyer, educator; b. Martin, Ga., Sept. 26, 1918; s. Emory Franklin and Mabel (Verner) C.; m. Corinne Ethel Tison, July 17, 1943; children— Ethel, Verner Franklin, Mary Davis, John Edwards. AB, U. Ga., LL.B., 1942; J.S.D., Yale, 1961. Bar: Ga. bar 1942, Ala. bar 1953, U.S. Supreme Ct. bar 1965. Atty. Dept. Justice, 1946-47; mem. faculty U. Ala., 1947—57, U. Ga., Athens, 1957—, prof. law, 1954-69, Fuller E. Callaway prof., 1969—89, Fuller E. Callaway prof. emeritus, 1989—; mem. nat. labor panel Am. Arbitration Assn., 1957—89, mem. pub. employment disputes settlement panel, 1969—89; mem. panel arbitrators Fed. Mediation and Conciliation Service, 1973—89. Trustee Inst. Continuing Legal Edn. Ga., 1969-76 Author: Georgia Annotations to the Restatement (Second) Trusts, 1970, Studies in the Georgia Law of Decedents' Estates and Future Interests, 1979, The Rule Against Perpetuities in Georgia, 1984; Contbr. numerous articles to legal jours. Mem. permanent jud. commn. Gen. Assembly, Presbyn. Ch. U.S.A., 1972-75; elder 1st Presbyn. Ch., Athens, 1966-71, 74-79, 96-98; pres. Athens chpt. Am. Cancer Soc., 1968-69, Athens Community Concert Assn., 1966-67; with USN; Lt. Cmdr. USNR. Sterling fellow Yale, 1950-51 Fellow Am. Coll. Trust & Estate Council (life), Lawyers Found. GA (life), ABA; mem. Am. Law Inst., Pres. Athens Historical Soc., Western Circuit, Ga., Am. bar assns., Ga. Hist. Soc., Athens-Clarke Heritage Found., Blue Key, Sphinx, Order of Coif, Phi Beta Kappa, Phi Kappa Phi, Phi Delta Phi, Omicron Delta Kappa, Sigma Nu. Clubs: Athens City, Yale Club Ga. Home: 510 Riverview Rd Athens GA 30606-4830 Office: University of Georgia Law School Athens GA 30602

CHAFKIN, RITA M., retired dermatologist; b. N.Y.C., Apr. 11, 1929; d. Joseph and Dora (Winslow) Melnick; m. Samuel Chafkin, June 29, 1952; children: Elise Ceil Perkins, Marc David Chafkin (dec.). BA, NYU, 1949; MD, NYU Med. Sch., 1953; cert. in dermatology, NYU Postgrad. Med. Sch., 1957. Diplomate Am. Acad. Dermatology, 1959. Intern in internal medicine Kings County Hosp., Bklyn., 1953-54; dermatology resident Bellevue Hosp., N.Y.C., 1954-55; postgrad. trainee NYU Postgrad. Med. Sch., 1955-56, fellow in dermatology, 1956-57; precepteeship with Dr. Marion Sulzberger; pvt. practice dermatology Modesto, Calif., 1958-94; ret., 1994; assoc. clin. prof. dermatology U. Calif., Davis, 1975-97. Clinic dir. dermatology Stanislavs County Med. Ctr., Modesto, 1958-97. Artist in mixed media. Bd. dirs. Stanislaus County Med. Ctr. Found., 1982-97, pres. 1984-85. Recipient Tchr. of the Yr. award Stanislaus County Med. Ctr., Modesto, 1988, Founder's Dinner honoree, 1992. Fellow Am. Acad. Dermatology; mem. AMA, Calif. Med. Soc., San Francisco Dermatology Soc., Stanislaus County Med. Soc. (pres. 1983-84), Pacific Dermatology Assn. (fin. com. 1959—). Jewish.

CHAFUEN, ALEJANDRO ANTONIO, think-tank executive; b. Buenos Aires, 1954; m. Melanie Bailey; children: John, Gregory. Ins. Sch. Degree, Assn. Argentina de Companies de Seguros, Buenos Aires; BA in Econs., Grove City Coll.; M in Econ., Argentine Cath. U., Buenos Aires, 1978; diploma (hon.), Centro Internat. San Juan de la Penitencia, 1982; PhD in Econs. with distinction, Internat. Coll., 1984. Tchg. asst. econ. devel. Argentine Cath. U., 1977—78; prof. econs. Buenos Aires Stock Exch., 1979, 1980; assoc. prof. contemporary econ. policy ESEADE (Grad. Sch. Econs. and Bus. Adminstrn.), 1979—80, assoc. prof. critical history of econ. thought, 1979—85; prof. intro. to social scis. U. del Salvador, Buenos Aires, 1981; asst. prof. polit. economy and econ. policy U. Buenos Aires, 1981—85; assoc. prof. history of econ. thought Argentine Cath. U., Buenos Aires, 1983—85; prof. econs. Nat. Hispanic U., Oakland, Calif., 1987, 1988; dir. L.Am. affairs Atlas Econ. Rsch. Found., Va., 1985, dir. advisory programs, 1988—91, pres., CEO, 1991—. Rsch. fellow ESEADE (Grad. Sch. Econs. and Bus. Adminstrn.), 1979—85; rschr. Pérez Companc-U. Catolica Argentina Project, 1979—80; co-owner Milton Friedman's Free to Choose TV series rights, Argentina, 1981—83; vis. prof. U. Francisco Marroquin, Guatemala, 1984; external cons. McMaster Investments; former trustee Argentine Fin., Investment and Ins. Cos. Author: The Effect of Income Taxes on Capital Investments, 1983, Christians for Freedom: Late-Scholastic Economics, 1986, Economía y Etica: Raices Cristianas de la Economía Libre de Mercado, 1991, Cristiani per la liberta: Radici cattoliche dell'economia di mercato, 1999; co-author: Cristianismo y Libertad, 1984; editor: Apertura mag., 1982—83; contbr. chapters to books, articles to profl. jours. Mem. founding com. Donors Trust; trustee The Chase Found. Va., State Policy Network; active Govs. Commn. on Environ. Stewardship Commonwealth Va., 1996—; trustee The CEDICE Found.; v.p. bd. dirs. Friends of IEA Found.; active social affairs unit Internat. Adv. Coun., London; mem. adv. bd. Am. Means Bus., 1996—98; founding trustee The Acton Inst. for the Study of Religion and Liberty, Buckey Inst. (formerly Urban Policy Rsch. Inst.). Scholar, Centro de Estudios sobre la Libertad, Buenos Aires, 1978, Fundacion Pérez-Companc, Buenos Aires, 1979—80, Fundacion Ortega y Gasset, Spain, 1982, Inst. Torcuato Di Tella, Buenos Aires, 1982, Grove City (Pa.) Coll., 1984. Mem.: The Phila. Soc., Mont Pelèrin Soc., European Acad. Environ. Affairs (corr.). Office: Atlas Econ Rsch Found Ste 103 4084 University Dr Fairfax VA 22030

CHAGANTI, RAJU S., geneticist, educator, researcher; b. Samalkot, Andhra, India, Mar. 12, 1933; came to U.S., 1960. s. Sanyasi Raju and Seetasiromani (Vallury) C.; m. Seeta Ramam Kurada, Aug. 20, 1966; children: Seeta, Sara. BS with honors, Andhra U., 1954, MS, 1955; PhD, Harvard U., 1964. Diplomate Am. Bd. Med. Genetics. Mem. Med. Rsch. Coun. Radiobiology Unit, Harwell, England, 1967—71; rsch. assoc. N.Y. Blood Ctr., N.Y.C., 1971—73, assoc. investigator, 1973—76; asst. prof. Meml. Sloan-Kettering Cancer Ctr., N.Y.C., 1976—83, assoc. prof., 1983—87, prof., 1987—, William E. Snee chair N.Y.C., 1995—. Profl. assoc. N.Y. Hosp., N.Y.C., 1979—; founder, bd. dirs. Cancer Genetics, Inc., Hackensack, N.J., Karkigen, Inc., Hackensack, N.J. Editor: Genetics in Clinical Oncology, 1985; contbr. articles to profl. jours. Recipient research awards NIH, Nat. Cancer Inst., 1979—. Fellow AAAS, Am. Coll. Med. Genetics; mem. Am. Soc. Human Genetics, Harvey Soc. Achievements include research in the genetic basis of cancer development. Home: 235 Pascack Rd Hillsdale NJ 07642 Office: Meml Sloan-Kettering Cancer Ctr 1275 York Ave New York NY 10021-6094 Office Phone: 212-639-8121.

CHAGNONI, KATHLEEN, energy executive; BA with honors, Stanford U., 1981; JD, Columbia U., 1985. Assoc. O'Melveny & Myers, Washington, 1985—89, Hogan & Harlson, Balt., 1989—94; asst. v.p., assoc. group counsel USF&G Corp., 1996—98; v.p., corp. group gen. counsel St. Paul Cos., Inc., 1999—2003; v.p., gen. counsel, corp. sec. Constellation Energy, Balt., 2002—. Office: Constellation Energy Group 750 E Pratt St Baltimore MD 21202

CHAGULA, PAUL MACHIYA, information technology executive, consultant; b. Dar es Salaam, Tanzania, July 16, 1969; s. Wilbert Kumalija and Jane (Ubwe) C.; m. Aug. 1, 1993; 1 child, James M. Student, Westchester Bus. Inst., White Plains, N.Y., 1988-90. Troubleshooting asst., operational mgr. Bloomingdale's Inc., White Plains, 1990-91; pres. PC Courier Svc., Mt. Vernon, N.Y., 1991—; co-founder, v.p. J&P Cleaning Svc., Mt. Vernon, 1994—; founder, chmn., CEO, Tangible Techs. Internat. Inc., Bronx, N.Y., 1997—. Cons. Tanzania C. of C., Dar es Salaam, 1994-96; copy cons. Kinko's Inc., Mt. Kisco, N.Y. Advisor Tanzania Am. Assocs., N.Y.C., 1992-93, Chama Cha Mapinduzi, revolutionary party, Dar es Salaam, 1994, Govt. of Tanzania, N.Y.C., 1996. Avocations: consulting, advising, writing. Home: 56 Sheridan Ave Apt 4C Mount Vernon NY 10552-2525 Personal E-mail: chagula@hotmail.com.

CHAHINE, MOUSTAFA TOUFIC, atmospheric scientist; b. Beirut, Jan. 1, 1935; s. Toufic M. and Hind S. (Tabbara) C.; m. Marina Bandak, Dec. 9, 1960; children: Tony T., Steve S. BS, U. Wash., 1956, MS, 1957; PhD, U. Calif., Berkeley, 1960. With Jet Propulsion Lab., Calif. Inst. Tech., Pasadena, 1960—, mgr. planetary atmospheres sect., 1975—, sr. research scientist, mgr. earth and space scis. div., 1978-84, chief scientist, 1984—2001. Vis. scientist MIT, 1969-70; vis. prof. Am. U., Beirut, 1971-72; regent's lectr. UCLA, 1989-90; mem. NASA Space and Earth Sci. Adv. Com., 1982-85; mem. climate rsch. com. Nat. Acad. Scis., 1985-88, bd. dirs. atmospheric scis. and climate, 1988—; chmn. sci. steering group Global Energy and Water Cycle Experiment World Meteorol. Orgn., 1988-99; cons. U.S. Navy, 1972-76 Contbr. articles to profl. jours. Recipient medal for exceptional sci. achievements NASA, 1969, NASA Outstanding Leadership medal, 1984, William T. Pecora award, 1989, Jule G. Charney award, 1991, Losey Atmospheric Scis. award AIAA, 1993, NASA Exceptional Achievement medal, 2000, William Nordberg medal Com. on Space Rsch., 2002. Fellow AAAS, Am. Geophys. Union, Am. Phys. Soc., Royal Soc., Am. Meteorol. Soc.; mem. Internat. Acad. Astronautics, Sigma Xi. Office: 4800 Oak Grove Dr Pasadena CA 91109-8001 Office Phone: 818-354-6057. Business E-Mail: chahine@jpl.nasa.gov.

CHAHINIAN, A(RAM) PHILIPPE, oncologist; b. Paris, June 21, 1942; came to U.S., 1974; m. Marjorie Ellen; 1 child, Michael J. B., Buffon Coll., Paris, 1960; MD, Paris U., 1969. Diplomate Am. Bd. Internal Medicine, Am. Bd. Med. Oncology. Intern, resident Paris Univ. Hosps., France, 1968-74; fellow noeplastic diseases Mt. Sinai Sch. Medicine, N.Y.C., 1974-76, asst. prof., 1976-79, assoc. prof., 1980-88; prof. clin. medicine Coll. Physicians and Surgeons Columbia U., N.Y.C., 1990-92; prof. dept. medicine Mt. Sinai Sch. Medicine, N.Y.C., 1995—, prof., 1995—. Adj. prof. dept. neoplastic diseases Mt. Sinai Sch. Medicine, N.Y.C., 1992-95. Author: Lung Cancer, 1976; author (with others) of books; contbr. articles to profl. jours. Lt. Med. Corps, French Army, 1970. Rsch. grantee Nat. Cancer Inst., 1984. Fellow Am. Coll. Physicians; mem. Am. Soc. Clin. Oncology, Am. Assn. Cancer Rsch., Am. Fedn. Clin. Rsch., N.Y. Acad. Scis. Achievements include research in treatment of various cancers including lung cancer, asbestos related cancers, and mesothelioma by transplantation of human cancers into mice. Office: Mt Sinai Sch Medicine Dept NeoPlastic 1 Gustave L Levy Pl New York NY 10029-6500 Office Phone: 212-241-0484.

CHAI, LIANG, engineer; b. Hulin, Heilongjiang, China, Sept. 8, 1961; s. Peiquan Chai and Shuqin Guo; m. Sharon Lynn Johnson, June 24, 2004. BS, Beijing U., 1984, MS, 1987; MA, Princeton U., 1991, PhD, 1995. Rschr. U. Pa., Phila., 1995—97; sr. rsch. scientist Ferro Corp., Vista, 1997—2003; r&d dir. engr. powders divsn. Technic, Inc., Woonsocket, 2003—. Contbg editor ACerS/NIST Phase Diagram Program, Md., 2004—. Contbr. articles to profl. jours. Mem.: Am. Ceramic Soc., Internat. Microelectronics and Packaging Soc. (Best Paper of Session 2002). Achievements include research in microwave characterization of ceramic substrate systems for consumer and millitary applications; development of low cost material system for ceramic packaging; publicized technologies for low cost miniature consumer wireless devices. Home: 23 Calvin French Rd Sterling CT 06377 Office: Technic Inc 300 Park E Dr Woonsocket RI 02895 Office Phone: 401-769-7000. Office Fax: 401-769-2472. E-mail: lc@technic-epd.com.

CHAI, WINBERG, political science professor; b. Shanghai, Oct. 16, 1932; came to U.S., 1951, naturalized, 1973; s. Ch'u and Mei-en (Tsao) C.; m. Carolyn Everett, Mar. 17, 1966 (dec. 1996); children: Maria May-lee, Jeffrey Tien-yu. Student, Hartwick Coll., 1951-53, LittD, 2002; BA, Wittenberg U., 1955; MA, New Sch. Social Rsch., 1958; PhD, NYU, 1968; DHL, Wittenberg U., 1997; DL, Hartwick Coll., 2002. Lectr. New Sch. Social Rsch., 1957-61; vis. asst. prof. Drew U., 1961-62; asst. prof. Fairleigh Dickinson U., 1962-65, U. Redlands, 1965-68, assoc. prof., 1969-73, chmn. dept., 1970-73; prof., chmn. Asian studies CCNY, 1973-79; disting. prof. polit. sci., v.p. acad. affairs, spl. asst. to pres. U. S.D., Vermillion, 1979-82; prof. polit. sci., dir. internat. programs U. Wyo., Laramie, 1988—. Chmn. Third World Conf. Found., Inc., Chgo., 1982—; pres. Wang Yu-fa Found., Taiwan, 1989—; exec. editor Asian Affairs, 1997-. Author: (with Ch'u Chai) The Story of Chinese Philosophy, 1961, The Changing Society of China, 1962, rev. edit., 1969, The New Politics of Communist China, 1972, The Search for a New China, 1975; editor: Essential Works of Chinese Communism, 1969, (with James C. Hsiung) Asia in the U.S. Foreign Policy, 1981, (with James C. Hsiung) U.S. Asian Relations: The National Security Paradox, 1983, (with Carolyn Chai) Beyond China's Crisis, 1989, In Search of Peace in the Middle East, 1991, (with Cal Clark) Political Stability and Economic Growth, 1994, China Mainland and Taiwan, 1994, revised edit. 1996, Hong Kong Under China, 1998; editor: Saudi Arabia: A Modern Reader, 2005; co-translator: (with Ch'u Chai) A Treasury of Chinese Literature, 1965; co-author (with May-Lee-Chai) The Girl from Purple Mountain, 2001; contbg. editor: Encyclopedia of Modern Asia, 2003, Saudi Arabia: A Modern Reader, 2005. Haynes Found. fellow, 1967, 68; Ford Found. humanities grantee, 1968, 69, Pacific Cultural Found. grantee, 1978, 86, NSF grantee, 1970, Hubert Eaton Meml. Fund grantee, 1972-73, Field Found. grantee, 1973, 75, Henry Luce Found. grantee, 1978, 80, S.D. Humanities Com. grantee, 1980, Pacific Culture Fund grantee, 1987, 90-91. Mem. AAAS, AAUP, NAACP, Am. Polit. Sci. Assn., Am. Assn. Chinese Studies (pres.1978-80), N.Y. Acad. Scis., Internat. Studies Assn. Democrat. Home: 1071 Granito Dr Laramie WY 82072-5045 Office: Univ Wyoming Dept 3197 1000 E University Ave Laramie WY 82071-4098 Office Phone: 307-766-6484. E-mail: WinbergChai@aol.com. *Born in China and educated in the United States, I feel privileged to have experienced two rich cultures. My goals include promoting better understanding of all cultures and peoples.*

CHAIDARUN, SUSHELA SONGTANIN, endocrinologist, researcher; b. Sawankaloke, Sukhothai, Thailand, Apr. 13, 1963; arrived in U.S., 1994; d. Kittisak and Kanitha Songtanin; m. Sumet Chaidarun; children: Arthur Nachapon, Leo Pirapon, Tricia Tanyawan. MD, Chulalongkorn U., 1988; PhD, U. Birmingham, Eng., 1994; postgrad., Harvard U., 1994—98. Bd. certified internal medicine Am. Bd. Internat. Medicine, bd. certified endocrinology & metabolism. Postdoctoral rsch. fellow Mass. Gen. Hosp./ Harvard Med. Sch., Boston, 1994—98; med. resident internal medicine St. Vincent Hosp./Worcester Med. Ctr., U Mass. Med. Sch., Worcester, 1998—2001; endocrine clin. fellow U. Va. Health Sys., Charlottesville, 2001—03. Rsch. fellow /assoc. Harvard Med. Sch., Boston, 1994—98. Contbr. articles to profl. jours. Grantee Travel grant, Am. Endocrine Soc./Women in Endocrinology, 1996. Mem.: AMA, ACP (Med. Jeopardy Championship award Mass. chpt. 2000), Am. Assn. Clin. Endocrinologists, Am. Assn. Clinical Endocrinologists, Am. Endocrine Soc. Avocations: travel, swimming, cooking, piano, music. Office: Walla Walla Clin 55 W Tietan St Walla Walla WA 99362 Office Phone: 509-525-3720. Personal E-mail: schaidarun@hotmail.com. Business E-Mail: sushelac@wallawallaclinic.com.

CHAIFETZ, DAVID HARVEY, lawyer; b. Worcester, Mass., Nov. 6, 1942; s. Harry and Gertrude (Katz) C.; m. Edith Jakubs; children: Rosalyn, Pamela, Matthew. BS in Bus. Adminstrn., Clark U., 1965; JD, Boston Coll., 1968. Bar: Mich. 1968, U.S. Dist. Ct. (ea. dist.) Mich. 1968, U.S. Supreme Ct., 1995. Staff atty. Chrysler Corp., Highland Park, Mich., 1968-75; div. atty. Union Carbide Corp., N.Y.C., 1975-77, sr. div. atty., 1978-81, group counsel Danbury, Conn., 1981-85, asst. gen. counsel, 1985-92; gen. counsel Union Carbide Indsl. Gases Inc., Danbury, 1988-92; v.p., gen. counsel, sec. Praxair, Inc., Danbury, 1992—2004; mem. Town of Fairfield (Conn.) Police and Fire Retirement Bd., 2000—. Bd. dirs. Conn. Legal Svcs., Middlebury, 1991-92, 97—, Bridgeport Jewish Com. Found., 2001-, Conn. Yankee Coun; mem. Am. Israel Pub. Affairs Com., 2002—. Trustee U.S. China Legal Coop. Fund, 1998—2002. Mem. ABA, Conn. Bus. and Industry Assn. (bd. dirs. 1999-2003), Corporate Bar Assn. (chmn. pro bono com. 1990-93), Westchester-Fairfield Corp. Counsel Assn. (pres. 1988-89, bd. dirs. 1984-90), Coun. of Chief Legal Officers (conf. bd. 1997-2004). Avocations: golf, travel. Office: 35 Watergate Dr Apt 1405 Sarasota FL 34236

CHAIFETZ, MARSHAL LAWRENCE, educational consultant, educator; b. Stamford, Conn., Jan. 29, 1973; s. Alan Marvin Chaifetz, Rose Janet and Kenneth Blitz (Stepfather). BA, Ind. U., 1994, JD, 1997. Regional rep. Law Sch. Admission Coun., Newtown, Pa., 1997—99; dir. upward bound project Ind. U., Bloomington, 1999—, lectr., 2001—. Freelance computer cons., Bloomington, 1991—; grant reader US Dept. Edn., 2000—; ednl. cons., Bloomington, 2004—. Reviewer, editor: business book Grant Writing: Strategies for Developing Winning Proposals, 2d edit., Test Development: Guidelines, Practical Suggestions and Examples, education book Nonverbal Communication in the Classroom. Panel mem. consumer adv. panel Delta Airlines, Atlanta, 2003. Louis Stokes Alliance Minority Participation Program grant, US Dept. Edn., 2002—, Upward Bound Expansion Initiative grant, 2003—, Upward Bound grant, 2004—. Independent. Jewish. Home: 3209 E 10th St Apt I 2 Bloomington IN 47408 Office: Indiana Univ Upward Bound Project Smith Rsch Ctr Ste 100 Bloomington IN 47408 Personal E-mail: marshalchaifetz@gmail.com. Business E-Mail: mchaifet@indiana.edu.

CHAIKEN, BERNARD HENRY, internist, gastroenterologist; b. Bklyn., Oct. 14, 1927; s. Max and Esther (Golland) C.; m. Mildred Gilbert, Dec. 5, 1950; children: Barry Glenn, Caryl Joy Gordon. Student, NYU, 1944-45; MD, U. Tex., Dallas, 1949. Diplomate Am. Bd. Internal Medicine, subspecialty Bd. Gastroenterology. Intern Boston City Hosp., 1949-50; resident physician Cushing VA Hosp., Framingham, Mass., 1950-51, Phila. VA Hosp., 1953-54; staff physician VA Hosp. Dallas, 1954-55, VA Hosp., East Orange, N.J., 1955-56; attending physician Overlook Hosp., Summit, N.J., 1956—, St. Barnabas Med. Ctr., Livingston, N.J., 1956—. Vis. fellow Hosp. of U. Pa., Phila., 1954; clin. instr. Southwestern Med. Sch., U. Tex., Dallas, 1954-55; clin. asst. prof. medicine Seton Hall Coll. Medicine, Jersey City, 1956-58. Contbr. articles to med. jours. Capt. U.S. Army M.C., 1951-53. Fellow ACP, Am. Coll. Gastroenterology (Best Clin. Vignette Paper and Poster Presentation 1995); mem. Am. Soc. Internal Medicine, Am. Gastroenterol. Assn., Med. Soc. N.J., N.J. Gastroenterol. Soc. (pres. 1964-65). Avocation: collecting early american folk art. Home: 12 Taylor Rd Short Hills NJ 07078-2226 Office: 58 Chatham Rd Short Hills NJ 07078-2321 Office Phone: 973-376-5750.

CHAIKIN, MARY CARRIE, psychology librarian; b. Balt., Oct. 8, 1947; d. John Jr. and Mary (Fratta) Moscato; m. Philip Chaikin, Dec. 29, 1974; 1 child, Carrie Marie. BA, U. Balt., 1969; MLS, Rutgers U., 1981. Libr. Balt. City Hosp. Med. Libr., 1966-74; interlibr. loan tech. U. Ky. Med. Libr., Lexington, 1974-75; catalog libr. Ortho Pharms., Raritan, N.J., 1980-81; asst. psychiat. libr. Carrier Found., Belle Meade, N.J., 1981-83; asst. plasma physics libr. Princeton U., 1983-84, psychology libr., 1984—. Mem. Spl. Librs. Assn. (career guidance chair Princeton Trenton chpt. 1990-91, 92-93), Assn. Mental Health Librs. Home: 121 Wilshire Dr Belle Mead NJ 08502-5539 Office: Princeton U Psychology Libr Green Hall Princeton NJ 08540 Office Phone: 609-258-6084. Business E-Mail: mchaikin@princeton.edu.

CHAIKIN, PAUL M., physicist; PhD in physics, U. Pa. Henry DeWolf Smyth prof. physics Princeton U. Mem. sci. advisory bd. Arryx, Inc. Co-author: Principles of Condensed Matter Physics, 1995. Fellow, A.P. Sloan Found., Guggenheim. Fellow: Am. Physical Soc.; mem.: Am. Acad. Arts and Scis., Nat. Acad. Sci. Office: Princeton U Dept Physics PO Box 708 Princeton NJ 08544 Business E-Mail: chaikin@pupgg-princeton.edu.

CHAIM, DAVID ABEL, language educator; b. Queens, NY, May 22, 1968; arrived in US, 2002; s. Sigmar Chaim and Martha Ester Muniz de Chaim; m. Bernardita Ortega-Caez de Chaim, June 27, 1997. BA, U. Interamericana de PR, San Juan, 1992; MA in edn., U. Phoenix, 1994. Lic. lang. tchg. State of Ariz. ESL tchr., lang coord. IC PR Jr. Coll., San Juan, PR, 1994—99; ESL tchr. Escuela Dr. Jose Calso Bardosa, San Juan, PR, 1999—2002; Spanish tchr. Willcox HS, Willcox, Ariz., 2002—; Spanish assoc. prof. Cochise Coll., Willcox, Ariz., 2002—. Vol. firefighter Willcox Rural Fire Dept., Willcox, Ariz., 2002—. Mem.: Ariz. Tchrs. of Speakers of English as a Second Lang, Assn. for Symposium and Curriculum Devel. Cath. Avocations: golf, music, chess, basketball coaching. Office: Willcox HS 240 N Bisbee Ave Willcox AZ 85643 E-mail: cowboy@ssvecnet.com.

CHAIN, BOBBY LEE, electrical contractor, former mayor; b. Hattiesburg, Miss., Sept. 19, 1929; s. Zollie Lee and Grace (Sellers) C.; m. Betty Sue Green, June 30, 1967; children: Robin Ann, Laura Grace, Bobby Lee, John Webster. BS, U. So. Miss., Hattiesburg, 1957; DBA (hon.), William Carey Coll., Hattiesburg, 1983. Chief electrician Miss. Power & Light Co., Natchez, 1950—53; asst. to gen. supt. atomic energy plant Allegany Electric Co., Oak Ridge, 1954—55; owner, chmn. bd. Chain Electric Co., Hattiesburg, 1955, Chain Lighting & Appliance Co., Hattiesburg, 1960; owner, pres. Chainco, Inc., oil properties, Hattiesburg, 1974—2003; dir. Deposit Guaranty Nat. Bank, Jackson, Miss., 1965—2000; adv. dir. Am. South Bank, 2000—01; ret., 2003. Mem. Interstate Oil Compact Commn., 1972—; mem. nat. adv. coun. SBA, 1966-67; bd. dirs. Miss. Econ. Coun., 1991-93; mayor city of Hattiesburg, 1980-85; dir. Fed. Home Loan Bank of Dallas. Past mem., past pres. Miss. Trustees Instns. Higher Learning; past mem. and pres. So. Regional Edn. Bd., Mississippians for Quality Edn.; past chmn. Commn. on Efficiency in Govt., Miss. Econ. Coun.; mem. Miss. State Workforce Devel. Coun.; chmn. Pearl River County Dist. Workforce Coun.; past bd. dirs. Pub. Edn. Forum of Miss., chmn. Advanced Tech. Ctr., Pearl River Coll.; mem. commissioning com. USS John C. Stennis CVN-74 Aircraft Carrier, 1995; bd. dirs. Armed Forces Mus., Camp Shelby, Miss.; nat. coord. Trent Lott Nat. Ctr. Excellence Econ. Devel. and Entrepreneurship. With U.S. Army, 1950—51, Korea. Recipient Disting. Svc. award U. So. Miss., 1976, Hub award, 1979, Continuous Outstanding Svc. award, 1980, Liberty Bell award Forrest County Bar Assn., 1980, Svc. to Edn. award Phi Delta Kappa, 1980, Disting. Citizen award Pine Burr Area Coun. Boy Scouts Am., 1995; named to U. So. Miss., Miss. Bus. Hall of Fame, 1994, Noble Patron of Hon. Order St. George 155th Separate Armored Brigade; Bobby L. Chain Tech. Ctr. named in his honor; Bobby L. Chain Hattiesburg Mcpl. Airport named in his honor; Paul Harris fellow Rotary Internat., 1990; designated Friend of West Point, Assn. West Point Grads. Mem. Newcomen Soc. N.Am., U. So. Miss. Alumni Assn. (Outstanding Svc. award 1972, Sales and Mktg. Man of Yr. award 1981), Hattiesburg C. of C. (past dir.), Miss. Bus. Roundtable, Kiwanis, Hattiesburg Country Club (past pres.), U. So. Miss. Century Club, Shriners, Omicron Delta Kappa, Beta Gamma Sigma. Presbyn. Home: 312 6th Ave Hattiesburg MS 39401-4294 Office: PO Box 2058 Hattiesburg MS 39403-2058 E-mail: blc@bchain.com.

CHAIRES, JONATHAN BRADFORD, research scientist, educator; s. Clarence Bradford Chaires and Lydia Beld Hendricks; m. Deborah A. Levine, Sept. 18, 1981; 1 child, Laura Frances. BA, U. Calif., Santa Cruz, 1972; PhD, U. Conn., Storrs, 1978. NIH post doctoral fellow Yale U., New Haven, 1979—81; prof. U. Miss. Med. Ctr., Jackson, 1982—2004; Alexander Von Humboldt fellow Max Planck Inst. for Biophysics, Goettingen, Germany, 1989—90; James Graham Brown chair in biophysics U. Louisville, 2004—.

Chartered reviewer NIH, Bethesda, Md., 1997—2001. Editor: (books) Methods in Enzymology, vol. 340, 2001, Advances in DNA Sequence Specific Agents, vol. 2, 1996, DNA Binders and Related Subjects, 2005; mem. editl. bd. Biophys. Jour., Bethesda, Md., 2003—. Mem.: Am. Chem. Soc. (named Outstanding Chemist Miss. sect. 2000), Biophysical Soc., Sigma Xi. Achievements include patents for bis-anthracyclines with high activity against doxorubicin resistant tumors. Office: James Graham Brown Cancer Ctr 529 S Jackson St Louisville KY 40202 Office Phone: 502-852-1172. Office Fax: 502-852-1153. E-mail: j.chaires@louisville.edu.

CHAIT, ANDREA MELINDA, psychologist, behavior analyst; b. Buffalo, May 7, 1970; d. Marvin and Rochelle (Benatovich) C. BS in Health Edn., Ithaca (N.Y.) Coll., 1992; MEd in Spl. Edn., U. Fla., 1995, MA in Edn., 2001, PhD in Sch. Psychology, 2002. Lic. psychologist, bd. cert. behavior analyst. Substitute tchr. Cortland (N.Y.) H.S., 1992; tchrs. aid, substitute Stanley G. Falk, Cheektowaga, N.Y., 1993; pvt. spl. edn. tutor Buffalo and Gainesville, 1992—99; behavioral disorders tchr. Paul D. West Middle Sch., East Point, Ga., 1995-96; chair discipline com. spl. edn. dept. Paul P. West Middle Sch., East Point, Ga., 1995—; grad. tchg. asst. U. Fla., 1998-99; sch. psychologist internal sub. Browar Co. Pub. Schs., 2001—02; chief behavior analyst Clover Bottom Devel. Ctr., Nashville, 2004—. Adj. mem. faculty Santa Fe C.C., 2000-01; clin. coord. LEAP program Kennedy Krieger Inst., 2002-04.; chief behavior analyst Clover Bottom Devel. Ctr., 2004-. Vol. Task Force for Battered Women, Ithaca, 1991, Human Rights Orgn., Gainesville, 1993-94. Mem. APA, Nat. Assn. Sch. Psychologists, Pi Lambda Theta, Kappa Delta Pi, Phi Kappa Phi. Jewish. Avocations: reading, game devel., computers. Home: 113 Ryan Ct Nashville TN 37221

CHAIT, ARNOLD, retired radiologist; b. N.Y.C., Jan. 20, 1930; s. Irving and Tillie (Newman) C.; m. Joan Lois Oppenheim, Mar. 14, 1965; children: Andrea, Elizabeth, Caroline. BA, NYU, 1951; MD, U. Utrecht, Netherlands, 1957; MA (hon.), U. Pa., 1971. Diplomate Am. Bd. Radiology. Intern Kings County Hosp., Bklyn., 1958, resident in radiology, 1959-62; resident in pathology Manhattan Vets. Hosp., N.Y.C., 1959; instr. radiology SUNY, Bklyn., 1962-64, asst. prof. radiology, 1964-67, assoc. prof., 1967; asst. prof. radiology U. Pa., Phila., 1967-70, assoc. prof., 1970-74, prof., 1974-76, clin. prof., 1976-98; chief vascular radiology Hosp. U. Pa., 1969-76, dir. dept. radiology Grad. Hosp., 1976-88, pres. med. staff, 1981-83; prof. radiology Allegheny U. of the Health Scis., 1997—99; ret., 1999. Cons. radiology Bklyn. VA Hosp., 1962-67, Phila. VA Hosp., 1969-76, Phila. Naval Hosp., 1975-76 Contbr. articles to profl. jours. Fellow Coll. Physicians Phila., Am. Coll. Radiology; mem. Pa., Phila. County Med. Socs., Am. Roentgen Ray Soc., Phila. Roentgen Ray Soc. (pres. 1983-84), Radiol. Soc. N. Am., N.Y. Roentgen Soc., AAAS, Assn. U. Radiologists, Soc. Cardiovasc. Radiology Am. Heart Assn. (coun. on cardiovasc. radiology), Soc. Uroradiology, Soc. Cardiovasc. and Interventional Radiology. Home: 835 Chauncey Rd Narberth PA 19072-1303 E-mail: achait2000@yahoo.com.

CHAIT, FAY KLEIN, health administrator; b. Chgo., Jan. 12, 1929; d. Victor and Rose (Begun) Magid; m. Jerome G. Klein, June 27, 1948 (div. 1970); children: Leslie Susan Janik, Debra Lynne Maslov; m. Manuel Chait, Aug. 28, 1994. BA in English, UCLA, 1961; MA in Pub. Adminstrn., U. So. Calif., 1971. Cert. health adminstrn. Supr. social workers L.A. County, 1961-65; program specialist Econ. and Youth Opportunity Agy., L.A., 1965-69; sr. health planner Model Cities, L.A., 1971-72; dir. prepaid health plan Westland Health Svcs., L.A., 1972-74; exec. dir. Coastal Region Health Consortium, L.A., 1974-76; grants and legis. cons. Jewish Fed. Council of L.A., 1976-79; planning coun. Jewish Fed. Coun. of So. Fla., Palm Beach to Miami, 1979-82; adminstrv. dir. program in kidney diseases Dept. Medicine UCLA, 1982-84; exec. dir. west coast Israel Cancer Rsch. Fund, L.A., 1984-94; cons. to non-profit orgns. Santa Monica, 1994—. Cons. Arthritis Found., L.A., 1984, Bus. Action Ctr., L.A., 1982, Vis. Nurses Assn., L.A., 1982. Charter mem. L.A. County Mus. of Art, Mus. of Contemporary Art; cons. L.A. Mcpl. Art Gallery, 1979; mem. UCLA/Armand Hammer Mus. Fellow U.S. Pub. Health, U. So. Calif., 1970-71. Mem. APHA, UCLA Alumni Assn. (life), U. So. Calif. Alumni Assn. (life). Office Phone: 310-393-1644.

CHAIT, MAXWELL MANI, physician; b. Linz, Austria, Nov. 7, 1947; came to the U.S., 1953; s. Morris and Eva (Lederman) C.; m. Lynne Robin Milstein C.; children: Alanna Rose, Daniel Lawrence, Michael Paul. BA magna cum laude, U. Utah, Salt Lake City, 1969; BS cum laude, U. Calif., San Francisco, 1969, MD, 1972. Diplomate Am. Bd. Internal Medicine, 1975, Am. Bd. Gastroenterology, 1977; lic. N.Y., Utah. Intern st. medicine U. So. Calif. Med. Ctr., L.A. County, 1972-73; resident in medicine Cornell Coop. Hosps., North Shore U. Hosp., Manhasset, NY, 1973-75; fellow GI Cornell Coop. Hosps., Meml. Sloan-Kettering Cancer Ctr., NYC, 1975-77; attending physician White Plains (NY) Hosp., 1977—; asst. attending physician Columbia Presbyn. Med. Ctr., NYC, 1993—; asst. clin. prof. medicine Coll. Physicians & Surgeons of Columbia U., 1993—. Bd. dirs. Bd. Jewish Edn. Greater N.Y.; bd. trustees Crohn's & Colitis Found., 2000—02; lectr. in field. Pres. Westchester Assn. of Hebrew Schs., 1992-94; former mem. bd. trustees Temple Israel of White Plains; former coach baseball, softball, basketball Scarsdale Recreation Dept. Fellow Am. Coll. Gastroenterology, Am. Coll. Physicians; mem. Am. Gastroenterological Assn., Am. Soc. Gastrointestinal Endoscopy, N.Y. Acad. Gastroenterology, N.Y. Soc. Gastrointestinal Endoscopy, Westchester Acad. Medicine, Crohn and Colitis Found. of Am. (CMAC com.). Office: Hartsdale Med Group 180 E Hartsdale Ave Hartsdale NY 10530-3544 Office Phone: 914-725-2010. Personal E-mail: mdgi77@aol.com.

CHAITMAN, BERNARD RAYMOND, internist; b. Detroit, Dec. 23, 1943; MD, McGill U., 1969. Diplomate in internal medicine and cardiovasc. disease Am. Bd. Internal Medicine. Intern Jewish Gen. Hosp., Montreal, Can., 1969-70; resident internal medicine Royal Victoria Hosp., Montreal, Can., 1970-72; fellow cardiology U. Oreg. Hosps., Portland, 1972-74; dir. divsn. cardiology St. Louis U. Health Ctr., 1989—2001; prof. medicine St. Louis U. Med. Sch., 1983—. Fellow Am. Coll. Cardiology. Office: Saint Louis U Sch Medicine PO Box 15250 3635 Vista Ave at Grand Blvd Saint Louis MO 63110-0250 E-mail: chaitman@swbell.net.

CHAITMAN, HELEN DAVIS, lawyer; b. NYC, July 5, 1941; d. Philip and Miriam (Pfeffer) D.; m. Edmund Chaitman, Feb. 29, 1964 (div. 1978); children: Jennifer, Alison; m. George B. Gelman, Oct. 21, 1979. AB cum laude, Bryn Mawr Coll., 1963; JD, Rutgers U., 1976. Bar: N.J., 1976, N.Y. 1978, U.S. Dist. Ct. N.J. 1976, U.S. Dist. Ct. (so. and ea. dists.) 1978, U.S. Supreme Ct. 1981, Ct. Fed. Claims 2001, U.S. Ct. Appeals (8th cir.) 2002. Assoc. Paul, Weiss, Rifkind, Wharton & Garrison, N.Y.C., 1977-82; ptnr. Wilentz, Goldman & Spitzer, Woodbridge, NJ, 1983-87, Ross & Hardies, Somerset, NJ, 1987-99, Wolf Haldenstein Adler Freeman & Herz LLP, N.Y.C., 1999—2002, Phillips Nizer LLP, NYC, 2002—. Author: The Law of Lender Liability, 1990; contbg. author: Commercial Damages, 1985; editor Emerging Theories of Lender Liability, 1985-87. Mem.: ABA (chmn. comml. fin. svcs. com. 1994—97, sect. bus. law), Pub. Law Inst., Am. Law Inst. (sustaining mem. 1992—2005). Home: The Farm 115 Fairview Rd Frenchtown NJ 08825-3013 Office: Phillips Nizer LLP 666 Fifth Ave New York NY 10103-0084 also: 45 Essex St Hackensack NJ 07601 Office Phone: 212-841-1320. Business E-Mail: hchaitman@phillipsnizer.com.

CHAJET, CLIVE, brand and corporate image consultant; b. London, Feb. 27, 1937; came to U.S., 1950, naturalized, 1964; s. Henry W. and Anne (Kravis) C.; m. Bonnie Sue Loeb, Mar. 20, 1966; children: Lisa Ellen, Lori Menschell. BA, Columbia U., 1959. Acct. exec. Fuller, Smith & Rose, N.Y.C., 1960-63; designer Milprint, N.Y.C., 1963-65; exec. Gould Assocs., N.Y.C., 1965-72; founder Chajet Design Group, N.Y.C., 1972-83; chmn. Lippincott & Margulies, Inc., N.Y.C., 1983-96, Chajet Consultancy, 1997—. Bd. dirs. Triac Cos., Inc., Sr. Bridge Family Co., Inc. Author: Image by Design, 1991, From Corporate Vision to Corporate Reality, 1991, 2d edit., 1997. Trustee Town Sch., N.Y.C., 1980—83; bd. dirs. 92d St. YMHA, 1997—, Jewish Communal Fund, Am. Jewish Congress. Mem. Package Designers Coun. (pres. 1980-82), University Club. Jewish. Home: 1035 Fifth Ave New York NY 10028-0135 Office: Chajet Consultancy LLC 575 Madison Ave Fl 10 New York NY 10022-2511 Personal E-mail: thechaj@aol.com.

CHAK, AMITABH, gastroenterologist, researcher; b. Lucknow, India, June 11, 1959; arrived in U.S., 1966; s. Anand Mohan and Kusum Chak; m. Anjani Kaul, Dec. 18, 1988; children: Avinash, Ashwin. BS, Yale U., 1978, MS, 1979; MD, Columbia U., 1984. Asst. prof. CAse Sch. Medicine, Cleve., 1991—99, assoc. prof., 1999—2005. Fellow: Am. Soc. Gastrointestinal Endoscopy, Am. Gastroenterological Assn., Am. Coll. Gastroent., Am. Coll. Physicians. Office: U Hosps Cleve 1100 Euclid Ave Cleveland OH 44115 Office Phone: 216-844-5386.

CHAKRABARTI, DHRUVA RANJAN, computer engineer, researcher; s. Rajendra Mohan and Bithika Chakrabarti; m. Arundhati Chatterjee. BE, Jadavpur U., 1994; MS in Tech., Indian Inst. Tech., 1996; PhD, Northwestern U., 2000. Intern Regional Computer Ctr., Calcutta, India; software engr. Cadence Design Sys., Noida, India, 1996; rsch. asst. Northwestern U., Evanston, Ill., 1996—2000, tchg. asst., 1997; intern Sun Microsystems Rsch. Labs, Mountain View, Calif., 1998; software design engr. Hewlett-Packard Co., Cupertino, Calif., 2000—. Contbr. scientific papers to confs. and jours. in areas of parallelization and optimizing compilers. Recipient Silver medal, Sch. Engring., Jadavpur U., Calcutta, 1990—94; scholar, West Bengal Coun. Higher Secondary Edn., India, 1990; Cadence fellowship, Indian Inst. Tech., Kanpur, 1994—96, Henderson fellowship, Robert R. McCormick Sch. of Engring. and Applied Sci., Northwestern U., 1999—2000. Mem.: Assn. Computing Machinery. Achievements include patents pending for Improving run-time performance with call-site inline specialization; Cross-file inlining by using summaries and global worklist; Scalable cross-file inlining through locality-based transformation ordering; Cross-module inlining; Partitioning modules for cross-module optimization. Avocations: travel, photography. Office: Hewlett-Packard Company 19111 Pruneridge Avenue MS 4023 Cupertino CA 95014 Business E-Mail: dhruva_chak@yahoo.com.

CHAKRABARTI, SUBRATA KUMAR, marine research engineer; b. Calcutta, India, Feb. 3, 1941; came to U.S., 1964, naturalized, 1981; s. Asutosh and Shefali C.; m. Prakriti Bhaduri, July 23, 1967; children: Sumita, Prabal. BSME, Jadavpur U., Calcutta, India, 1963; MSME, U. Colo., 1965, PhD, 1968. Registered profl. engr., Ill. Asst. engr. Kuljian Corp., Calcutta, 1963-64, Simon Carves Ltd., Calcutta, 1964; instr. engring. U. Colo., Boulder, 1965-66; hydrodynamicist CB&I Tech. Svcs. Co. (formerly Chgo. Bridge and Iron Co.), Plainfield, Ill., 1968-70, head analytical group, 1970-79, dir. marine rsch., 1979-95, dir. structural devel., 1995-96; pres. Offshore Structure Analysis, Inc., Plainfield, 1996—. Vis. prof. U.S. Naval Acad., Annapolis, Md., 1986, 88, Indian Inst. Tech., Madras, 1996; prof. civil and mech. engring. dept. U. Ill., Chgo.; presenter in field. Author: Hydrodynamics of Offshore Structures, 1987, Nonlinear Methods in Offshore Engineering, 1990, Offshore Structure Modeling, 1994, Theory and Practice of Hydrodynamics and Vibration, 2002; editor: Fluid Structure Interaction in Offshore Engineering, 1994, Fluid Structure Interaction, 2001, Fluid Structure Interaction II, 2003; tech. editor Applied Ocean Rsch., 1998—, Numerical Modelling in Fluid-Structure Interactions, 2005; tech. editor: Handbook of Offshore Engineering, 2005—; mem. editl. bd. Applied Ocean Rsch., Marine Structures, Topics in Engring., Advances in Fluid Mechanics series, assoc. editor Energy Resources Tech., 1983—86; contbr. articles to profl. jours., chapters to books. Recipient Jadavpur U. Gold medal, 1963; U. Colo. fellow, 1968; named Outstanding New Citizen, 1981. Fellow AAAS, ASCE (publ. com. waterway divsn., James R. Croes Gold medal 1974, Freeman scholar 1979), ASME (exec. com., editor jour. offshore mechanics and arctic engring. divsn. 1986-96, chmn. divsn., 1987-88, awards com. 1983-2004, tech. session devloper, chmn. 1983—, chmn. tech. program com. 1988-89, tech. program chair, 2004, Ralph James award 1984, co-editor proc. internat. symposium, Offshore Mechanics and Arctic Engring. achievement award 1990, Ten Paper award 1991, Disting. Svcs. award 1998, Lifetime Achievement award 2005), NAS (com., design group, marine structures group 1989-91, chmn. 1992-95), Nat. Acad. Engring., Sigma Xi. Achievements include patents in field. Office: Offshore Structure Analysis Inc 13613 Capista Dr Plainfield IL 60544-7966 Office Phone: 815-436-4863. Personal E-mail: chakrab@aol.com. Business E-Mail: chakrab@uic.edu.

CHAKRABARTI, SUPRIYA, space astrophysicist; b. Howrah, India, June 22, 1953; came to U.S., 1975; s. Chiraranjan and Ranu Chakrabarti; m. Joanne Soljack, Dec. 17, 1983; children: Misha, Robin. BE, U. Calcutta, India, 1975; MS, U. Calif., Berkeley, 1980, PhD, 1982. Sr. fellow U. Calif., Berkeley, 1983-92; assoc. prof. astron. dept. Boston U., 1992-96, prof., 1996—, dir. Ctr. for Space Physics, 1997—, prof. dept. elec. and computer engring., 2001—. Mem. Ultraviolet/Visible and Gravitational Astrophysics Mgmt. Ops. Working Group, NASA, 1992-95, Universe Working Group, 2005-. Author: (ency.) Remote Sensing of the Upper Atmosphere, 1991; guest editor Optical Engring., 1993; editor conf. procs. in field. Mem. Am. Geophys. Union (life), Am. Inst. Physics, Am. Astron. Soc. Achievements include research in space instrumentation, planetary atmosphere and ionosphere, astrophysical plasma. Office: Boston U Ctr for Space Physics 725 Commonwealth Ave Boston MA 02215-1401 Office Phone: 617-359-5990. Business E-Mail: supc@bu.edu.

CHAKRABARTY, ANANDA MOHAN, microbiologist; b. Sainthia, India, Apr. 4, 1938; arrived in U.S., 1965; s. Satya Dos and Sasthi Bala (Mukherjee) Chakrabarty; m. Krishna Chakraverty, May 26, 1965; children: Kaberi, Asit. BSc, St. Xavier's Coll., 1958; MSc, U. Calcutta, India, 1960, PhD, 1965. Sr. rsch. officer U. Calcutta, 1964-65; rsch. assoc. biochemistry U. Ill., Urbana, 1965-71, prof. dept. microbiology Med. Ctr., 1979-89, disting. prof., 1989—; mem. staff GE R&D Ctr., Schenectady, NY, 1971-79. Editor: (book) Genetic Engineering, 1977, Biodegradation and Detoxification of Environmental Pollutants, 1982. Named Scientist of Yr., Indsl. Rsch. Mag., 1975; recipient Inventor of the Yr. award, Patent Lawyers' Assn., 1982, Pub. Affairs award, Am. Chem. Soc., 1984, Disting. Scientist award, EPA, 1985, Merit award, NIH, 1986, Pasteur award, 1991, Proctor & Gamble award, 1995; scholar, U. Ill., 1989. Mem.: Am. Soc. Biol. Chemists, Am. Soc. Microbiology. Home: 206 E Julia Dr Villa Park IL 60181-3340 Office: U Ill Med Ctr Dept Microbiology M/C 790 835 S Wolcott Ave Chicago IL 60612-7340 Office Phone: 312-996-4586. Business E-Mail: pseudomo@uic.edu.

CHAKRABARTY, DIPESH, history professor; PhD, Australian Nat. U., 1984. Prof. history dept. U. Chgo., prof. S. Asian languages & civilizations. Author: Habitations of Modernity: Essays in Wake of Subaltern Studies, 2002, Provincializing Europe: Postcolonial Thought & Historical Difference, 2000, Rethinking Working-Class History: Bengal, 1890-1940, 1989. Fellow: Am. Acad. Arts & Sci., 2004—; mem.: Am. Historical Rev. (editl. com.), Public Culture (editl. com.), Postcolonial Studies Jour. (founding editor), Critical Inquiry, Subaltern Studies Series (founding mem., co-editor). Office: University of Chicago 1130 E 59th St Chicago IL 60637 Office Fax: 773-834-3254, 773-702-8642.

CHAKRABORTY, HIMADRI S., physicist, researcher; s. Bhubaneswar and Sachi Chakraborty; m. Ruma De, Jan. 1, 1965; 1 child, Anzumaan Raumeyo. PhD, Phys. Rsch. Lab., Ahmedabad, India, 1995. Sr. project officer Indian Inst. Tech., Chennai, India, 1995—99; guest scientist Max-Planck-Insti. Physics of Complex Sys., Dresden, Germany, 1999—2001; rsch. assoc., instr. J R Macdonald Lab. Kans. State U., Manhattan, Kans., 2001—04; rsch. scientist physics and astronomy La. State U., Baton Rouge, 2004—. Contbr. over 75 articles to profl. jours. Mem.: Indian Soc. Atomic and Molecular Physics (life). Achievements include discovery of a number of new effects in the interactions of atoms/molecules/nano-particles/surfaces with light or charged-particle-beams. Office: Physics & Astronomy Louisiana State U 202 Nicholson Hall Baton Rouge LA 70803 Office Phone: 225-578-0554. E-mail: himadri@lsu.edu.

CHAKRABORTY, JOANA, physiologist, educator, science administrator; b. Calcutta, West Bengal, India, June 1, 1934; arrived in U.S., 1962; d. Mohadev and Nilima Mukherjee; m. Ajit Chakraborty; 1 child, Mellary. BS, Sci. Coll., Calcutta, 1954, MS, 1956; PhD, Inst. of Nuclear Physics, Calcutta, 1962. Rsch. asst. Inst. Nuc. Physics, Calcutta, 1960-62, lectr., 1964-69; postdoctoral asst. Iowa State U., Ames, 1962-63; Ford found. fellow Harbor Gen. UCLA Med. Ctr., 1969-70; dir. Electron Microscopy Lab. Med. Coll., Toledo, 1970-89; from asst. prof. to assoc. prof. Med. Coll. Ohio, Toledo, 1972—82, prof., 1982—, interim chmn., 1991-94. Spkr. in field. Author: Chemical Exposure and Toxic Responses, 1997; contbr. chapters to books, articles to profl. jours. Recipient World AIDS Found. award; Rsch. grantee, NIH, others. Mem.: AAAS, Internat. AIDS Soc., N.Y. Acad. Scis., Soc. Study Reproduction, Am. Soc. Andrology, Am. Soc. Cell Biology. Office: Med Coll Ohio 3035 Arlington Ave Toledo OH 43614-2570 Office Phone: 419-383-4149. Business E-Mail: jchakraborty@med.u.ohio.edu.

CHAKRAVARTI, ARNAB, oncologist, researcher; b. Bethlehem, Pa., Oct. 3, 1968; s. Kalidas and Anita Chakravarti; m. Kimberly Denise Chakravarti, Oct. 24, 1998. BA, Duke U., 1990; MD, U. Va., 1995. Resident in medicine Mass. Gen. Hosp., Harvard Med. Sch., Boston, 1996-99, chief resident in radiation oncology, 1999-2000, asst. radiation oncologist, 2000—. Mem. prostate cancer rsch. com. Radiation Therapy Oncology Group, 1999—; voting mem. neurooncology spore com. Dana-Farber Harvard Cancer Ctr., Boston, 2000—; voting mem. instnl. review bd. Dana-Farber/Ptnrs. Cancer Ctr., Harvard Med. Sch., 2000—. Contbr. articles to profl. jours. Pres. Linc of Duke U., Durham, N.C., 1989-90. Mem. AMA, AAAS, Am. Assn. Cancer Rsch. (Glaxo-Wellcome Rsch. award 2000, Novartis Rsch. award 2001), Am. Soc. Therapeutic Radiology Oncology (Nat. Resident Rsch. award 1999), Mass. Med. Soc. Avocations: meteorology, music, tennis, baseball, travel. Office: Mass Gen Hosp Dept Radiation Oncology Cox Basement Boston MA 02114 E-mail: achakravarti@partners.org.

CHAKRAVARTY, SUGATO, education educator, researcher; s. Ardhendu Sekhar Chakravarty and Chua Charkavarty. BSChE, Jadavpur U., Calcutta, India, 1984; MSME, U. Ky., 1988; PhD, Ind. U., Bloomington, Ind., 1994. Assoc. prof. Purdue U., West Lafayette, 1999—2003, prof., 2003—. Assoc. editor: Jour. Fin. Markets, 2005—. Achievements include research in Barclay's Global Investors Rsch. Award for best paper on capital markets/funds mgmt. on Australiasian markets for "Stealth trading in volatile markets," 2005 (with P. Kalev and L. Pham); Best Paper Award in the Eastern Finance Assn. Ann. Conf. for "The Effect of Decimalization on Trade Size and Adverse selection Costs" (co-authored with R. Van Ness and B. Van Ness), 2004; Winner of Q-Group Rsch. Award, 2001-2002. Office: Purdue Univ Matthews Hall West Lafayette IN 47906 Office Phone: 765-494-6427. Office Fax: 765-494-0869. Business E-Mail: sugato@purdue.edu.

CHAKRIN, LEWIS M., consumer products company executive; Degree in engring., NYU, 1969; M in Ops. Rsch., Columbia U., 1971; MBA in Fin., NYU, 1976, PhD in Fin., 1978. V.p. product mgmt. and consumer svcs. AT&T, 1998—2000; sr. v.p., chief strategy officer AT&T Wireless Svc., Inc., Redmond, Wash., 2000—01, exec. v.p. corp. strategy and bus. devel., 2001—. Office: AT&T Wireless Svcs Inc NE Bldg 1 7277 164th Ave Redmond WA 98052

CHALCRAFT, ELENA MARIE, actress, singer; b. Bklyn., Oct. 14, 1959; d. James Abdou and Vivian (Trovato) Edwards; m. Rory Charles Chalcraft, Aug. 1, 1992; 1 child, Christopher Aston. BA in Speech, English and Theater Arts, Shippensburg State Coll., 1981; MFA in Acting, Va. Commonwealth U., 1984. Human resources analyst APA, Washington, 1985-98; music dir. Our Lady Queen of Peace Ch., Arlington, Va., 1992-98; soprano Philomusica Chamber Choir, 1999—; ind. kitchen cons. The Pampered Chef, 1999—; soprano St. Bartholomew Choir, 2000—01; substitute tchr. South River Elem. Sch. and Corpus Christi Sch., 2005—. Substute tchr. South River Elem. Sch., 2005—, Corpus Christi Sch., 2005—. Actor, singer (plays): Man of La Mancha, 1988, Ben, 1989-90, Maryland Renaissance Festival, 1987-91, Ziggy, 1992, The Snow Queen, 1994; actor: (play) Broadway Bound, 1993, (tng. film) GAO, 1990; dramaturg (play) Ballets Russes and Drood, 1993. Mem. liturgy com. Our Lady Queen of Peace Ch., 1995-98. Roman Catholic. Avocations: reading, writing children's books, piano, cross-stitch, crosswords. E-mail: emcrcc@worldnet.att.net.

CHALEFF, CARL THOMAS, investment company executive; b. Inpls., Nov. 21, 1945; s. Boris Carl and Betty J. (Miller) C.; m. Carolyn F. Heath, Apr. 26, 1970 (div. Apr. 1985); children: Fritz. Eric; m. Darlene Finkel, Dec. 13, 1987. BS in Econs., Purdue U., 1969; MBA in Fin., Xavier U., 1976. Asst. v.p. Am. Can Corp., N.Y.C., 1969-70, sales mgr. Cin., 1970-73; account exec. Merrill Lynch, Cin., 1973-76; v.p. Oppenheimer, Chgo., 1976-81; assoc. dir. Bear Stearns & Co., Chgo., 1981-88; ptnr., mng. dir. CIBC Oppenheimer, 1988—; pres. Plaris Capital Ptnrs. Pres. bd. dirs. Nat. Kidney Found. of Ill.; exec. coun. U. Chgo. Childrens Hosp., Boy Scouts Am., 1992-94; former bd. dirs. AIDS Care, bd. dir. Adler Planetarium & Mus., Chgo., bd. dir., Jobs for Youth. Mem. Chgo. Bond Club, Am. Arbitration Assn., Nat. Bd. Arbitrators, East Bank Club, Rainbows (bd. dirs. 1984-96), Met. Club, Chgo. Mercantile Exch. Club, Chgo. Yacht Club, Ctr. for Excellence in Edn. (bd. dirs. 1990-92), Chgo. Filmmakers (bd. dirs. 1986-98). Avocations: sailing, skiing, tennis. Home: 55 W Goethe St Chicago IL 60610-7406 Office Phone: 312-327-5280. Personal E-mail: chaleff@rcn.com. Business E-Mail: chaleff@polarischicago.com.

CHALEFF, GERALD LAWRENCE, lawyer; b. Detroit, Nov. 24, 1941; s. Jules and Anne (Melick) C. BS, UCLA, 1963; LLB, Harvard U., 1966. Bar: Calif. 1966. Assoc. Lemaire & Mohi, L.A., 1966-68; dist. atty. L.A. County, 1967-68, pub. defender, 1968-77; ptnr. Lafaille, Chaleff & English, L.A., 1978-83; ptnr. Chaleff & English, L.A., 1982-98, former ptnr., Orrick, Herrington & Sutcliffe, LLP; pres., LA Bd. Police Commnrs., 1999-2000, guest lectr. in field. Mem. L.A. County Bar Assn. (trustee jud. appts. com., former pres.).

CHALFIE, MARTIN, biology professor; William R. Kenan, Jr. prof. bio. scis. Columbia U. Mem.: Nat. Acad. Scis. Achievements include being credited (with others) with popularization of green fluorescent protein in gene study. Office: Columbia U Dept Bio Sci 1012 Fairchild Ctr MC 2446 New York NY 10027 Office Phone: 212-854-8870. Business E-Mail: mc21@columbia.edu.

CHALFIN, SUSAN ROSE, psychologist, educator; b. Phila., Apr. 26, 1956; d. Harry Herbert and Arlene Sybil (Abrams) C.; m. Thomas Arthur Dughi, May 22, 1983. BA, Columbia U., 1978; postgrad., Wayne State U., 1978-79; MA, Clark U., 1982, PhD, 1990. Lic. psychologist, Fla. Rsch. asst. dept. psychology Barnard Coll., Columbia U., N.Y.C., 1976-78; grad. asst. Wayne State U., Detroit, 1978-79; psychometrican Spl. Edn. Program, Balt., 1984; family therapist, psychometrician Frederick County Spl. Edn. and Treatment Program, Frederick, Md., 1984-87; psychology assoc. Psychol. Counseling & Consultation Ctr., Glen Burnie, Md., 1987-88; behavioral specialist div. psychology Jackson Meml. Hosp., Miami, Fla., 1989-90; asst. prof. U. Miami, 1994—2002; clin. psychologist Jackson Meml. Hosp., 2002—. Cons. Hughes-Gaeda Ctr., Miami, 1989-90, Alliance for Psychol. Svcs., Miami, 1990-94; vol. faculty U. Miami, 2002—. Contbr. articles to profl. jours. Univ. scholar Clark U., 1979-80, Univ. fellow, 1980-81, rsch. fellow, 1981-82; fellow NIMH, 1982-83. Avocations: swimming, jogging, photography, bicycling. Office: 1695 NW 9th Ave Rm 1425 Miami FL 33136-1005

CHALIL, JOSEPH MATHEW, sales executive, consultant; b. Pala, Kerala State, India, June 30, 1973; arrived in US, 1999; s. Joseph Mathew Chalil and Claramma A. Scaria; m. Sumy T. Chalil, June 15, 1998; children: Mathew Joseph, Thomas Mathew. B in medicine and surgery, J.J.M. Med. Coll., Davangere, India, 1999; MBA, Davenport U., Warren, Mich., 2004. Lic. Dr. of medicine India. Adminstrv. fellow Henry Ford Health Sys., Detroit, 2002—03; profl. sales exec. TAP Pharm. Products, Inc., Lake Forest, Ill.,

2003—. Founder and dir. KTC Healthcare Inc., Union, NJ, 2002—. Named to Excalibur Guild, TAP Pharm. Products, Inc, 2004; recipient Will Hall Sayishu, TAP Pharm. Products, Inc., 2003, 2004. Achievements include research in multiple myeloma. Home: 7285 Millrock Ave Shelby Township MI 48317 Office Phone: 586-872-7370. Personal E-mail: drchalil@aol.com.

CHALK, DAVID, lawyer; b. Baltimore, May 18, 1967; BS summa cum laude, Univ. Baltimore, 1989; JD with honors, Univ. Md., 1992. Bar: Md. 1992, DC 1993. Atty. div. corp. fin., SEC; ptnr., co-chmn. Capital Markets practice group DLA Piper Rudnick Gray Cary, Balt. Adj. prof. Univ. Md. Sch. Law. Editor (assoc.): The Bus. Lawyer, 1991—92. Mem.: ABA, Md. State Bar Assn., Order of the Coif. Office: DLA Piper Rudnick Gray Cary 6225 Smith Ave Baltimore MD 21209-3600 Office Phone: 410-580-4120. Office Fax: 410-580-3120. Business E-Mail: david.chalk@dlapiper.com.

CHALK, JOHN ALLEN, SR., lawyer; b. Lexington, Tenn., Jan. 16, 1937; AA, Freed-Hardeman Coll., 1956; BS, Tenn. Tech. U., 1962, MA, 1967; JD, U. Tex., 1973. Bar: Tex. 1973, D.C. 1977; ordained to ministry Ch. of Christ, 1956. Pastor chs., Dayton, Ohio, 1956-60, Cookeville, Tenn., 1960-66, Abilene, Tex., 1966-71; assoc. Rhodes and Seamster, Abilene, 1973-74, Rhodes and Doscher, Abilene, 1974; ptnr. Rhodes, Doscher, Chalk and Heatherly, Abilene, 1975-78; gen. counsel La Jet, Inc., Abilene, 1978-84, also v.p., sec; exec. v.p. Dabney Corp., Dallas, 1984-86; pres. Dabney Capital, Dallas, 1984-86; assoc. Gandy, Michener, Swindle, Whitaker & Pratt, Ft. Worth, 1986, ptnr., 1987-93, Michener Larimore Swindle Whitaker Flowers Sawyer Reynolds & Chalk, Ft. Worth, 1993-2000, Whitaker Chalk Swindle & Sawyer LLP, Ft. Worth, 2000—. Pres. Equity, Inc., 1982-90; mem. strategic alliances com. for edn. Nat. Ct. Reporters Assn., 1994-95; dir. Tarrant County Bar Assn., 2004—; cert. master mediator Dispute Resolution Svcs. Tarrant County, Tex.; Tex. court-approved mediator; mem. panel of neutrals Am. Arbitration Assn., 1992—; contract mediator EEOC, Dallas, 1999-2001; mem. neutrals panel Internat. Ctr. Dispute Resolution, Dublin, 2003—; mem London Ct of Internat. Arbitration, 2003—. Author: The Praying Christ, 1964, Three American Revolutions, 1970, Jesus' Church, 1970, The Christian Family, 1973, Great Biblical Doctrines, 1973, The Devil, You Say!, 1974; author numerous articles on U.S. Dept. Edn. fed. student fin. assistance, domestic and internat. arbitration and mediation, also articles on religion; presenter in fields. Trustee Abilene Regional Mental Health Retardation Ctr., 1978—80, Christian Scholarship Found., Inc., Atlanta, 1980, chmn. bd., 1992—93; chmn. Abilene Bicentennial Com., 1975—76; mem. nat. adv. coun. Am. United for Separation of Ch. and State, 1979—82, pres. bd. trustees, 1981—82; featured spkr. radio and TV programs Herald of Truth, 1966—69; trustee Osteo. Health Care Found., Inc., Ft. Worth, 1987—96, sec.-treas., 1990—91, sr. v.p., pres.-elect, 1991—92, pres., 1992—93; mem. Strategy for 2000, City of Ft. Worth, 1995—2000; co-chair capital gifts campaign All Church Home for Children, Inc., 2003—05; bd. dirs. Health Care of Tex., Inc., 1987—2003, Ft. Worth Symphony Orgn., Inc., 2005—; dir. Ft. Worth Symphony Orch. Assn., 2005—. Named Top Atty., Ft. Worth Mag., 2003—04, Atty. of Excellence, Ft. Worth Bus. Press, 2003—04, Super Lawyer, Tex. Monthly, 2003, 2004; recipient, 2005. Fellow Tex. Bar Found. (life), Chartered Inst. Arbitrators London (chartered arbitrator), Tarrant County Bar Found. (founding, life); mem. ABA (acting assoc. editor, mem. editl. bd. Family Adv. 1977-78), Fed. Bar Assn., Coll. State Bar Tex. (maintaining fellow), Am. Health Lawyers Assn. (dispute resolution svc. panel of neutrals), Am. Arbitration Assn. (panel arbitrators and mediators), Internat. Ctrs. for Arbitration (panel arbitrators and mediators), Tex. Assn. Mediators, Tarrant County Assn. Mediators, State Bar Tex., Tarrant County Bar Assn. (dir.), Nat. Arbitration Forum (panel of neutrals). Home: 3601 Verde Vista Ct W Aledo TX 76008-3679 Office: Whitaker Chalk Swindle & Sawyer 3500 City Ctr II Fort Worth TX 76102-4186 Office Phone: 817-878-0575. Office Fax: 817-878-0501. Business E-Mail: jchalk@whitakerchalk.com.

CHALK, ROSEMARY ANNE, health science association administrator; b. Cin., May 25, 1948; d. John Henry and Virginia R. (Kamphaus) Chalk; m. Michael Anthony Stoto, June 28, 1986; children: Anna Murilius, Benjamin John. BA, U. Cin., 1970; postgrad., George Washington U., 1970-72. Policy analyst Libr. of Congress, Washington, 1972-75; rsch. fellow MIT, Cambridge, Mass., 1982-83; program dir. AAAS, Washington, 1976-86; cons. Harvard Sch. Pub. Health, Boston, 1986-87; study dir. Inst. of Med., Washington, 1987-89, Nat. Acad. Sci., Washington, 1989—; dir. Bd. on Children, Youth, and Families, Inst. of Med., Washington, 2000—. Cons. The Field Found., N.Y.C., 1986-87, The Acadia Inst., Bar Harbor, Maine, 1988-91; adv. com. on ethics and values studies NSF, 1984-87. Editor: Science, Technology and Society: Emerging Relationships, 1988; contbr. articles to profl. jours. Fellow AAAS (coun. and section officer 1987—), Fedn. Am. Scientists (coun. mem. 1982-90), Student Pugwash USA (bd. dirs. 1988—). Roman Catholic. Office: Inst Medicine NAS 500 Fifth Street NW Washington DC 20001

CHALKLEY, JACQUELINE ANN, retail company executive; b. Benson, Minn., Jan. 3, 1946; d. Vincent Otto and Dorothy Mildred (Alsaker) Kaehler; m. C. Wayne Callaway. BA in Art History cum laude, Brown U., 1967; MA, Columbia U., 1968; postgrad. in Contemporary Art, New Sch. for Social Rsch., NYC, 1968—70; postgrad. in Ceramics, U. Md., 1970—72. Art tchr. Summit (NJ) HS, 1968-70, Rockville (Md.) HS, 1970-74; adj. prof. ceramics Montgomery Coll., Rockville, 1974-78; owner Jackie Chalkley at Foxhall Sq., Washington, 1978-99, Jackie Chalkley at Willard Collection, Washington, 1986-99, Jackie Chalkley at Chevy Chase Plz., Washington, 1989-99; retail and product devel. cons., 1999—. Juror Rhinebeck Craft Fair, 1981, New Eng. Buyers Market, Boston, 1982, Craft Art 1982, Richmond, Va. Craft Show, 1983, Smithsonian Crafts Exhbn. 1983, Smithsonian Instn. Women's Com. Craft Show, 1984, Annie Albers fashion show at Renwick Gallery, 1984, Morristown Craft Fair, 1984, Washington Craft Show, 1986, Potomac Craftsmen's Guild Show, 1987, Harrisburg Arts Festival, 1987, Ceramic Guild Washington, 1987, Washington Guild Goldsmiths, 1987, 18th Bienniel Exhbn. Creative Crafts Coun., 1988, Art Balt., 2003-04, others; appointee screening com. Piedmont Craftsman's Guild, Winston-Salem, NC, 1983-86, DC Commn. Arts, 1983-85; hon. com. Brandeis Art Exhbn., 1984, Textile Mus., 1984-86. Featured in Ceramics Monthly, 1994, Women's Wear Daily, 1995. Hon. com. 34th St. Art Fair, John Eaton Sch., 1985; benefit com. Washington Charitable Fund, 1989; hon. bd. trustees DC chpt. Design Industries Found. for AIDS, 1989-90; auction benefit com. Washington Project for Arts, 1989, 90; benefit com. Source Theater, 1993, Corcoran Mus. Jazz Evening, 1993, Living Stage & Arena Theatre, 1997-99; hon. com. Lab Sch. Wash., 1992, Aid to Artisans DC, Cambodian Embassy, 2003; hon. benefit com. Arena Stage Living Theater, 1997-98; sponsor Wearable Art Fashion Show, Renwick Mus., 1993; juried Smithsonian Craft Show, 1994; hon. chair Friends of the Corcoran Mus. Benefit, 1999-2000, exec. com., 2001-02; chair Craft Leaders Caucus Day 2000; nat. resource bd. James Renwick Alliance of Renwick Mus., 2000-03, gala exec. com. Rincones Dance Theater, 2001—; fundraising chair Aid to Artisans Benefit, DC, 2005 Appeared on cover of Forecast Mag., 1978; recipient Best Taste in Washington award Washingtonian Mag., 1982, 1st Ann. Outstanding Accessories Merchandising award Accessories Mag., 1985; named one of 23 People to Watch in 1983, Washingtonian Mag., 1982; her apt. chosen as Residential Interior of Yr., Am. Soc. Interior Designers, 1985, 92; her store named 1986 Comml. Interior of Yr., Am. Soc. Interior Designers; nat. award for logo Am. Corp. Identity, 1988, 91 Mem. Am. Craft Coun., Washington Fashion Group, James Renwick Craft Leaders Caucus, Friends of the Corcoran Gallery of Art, Washington Performing Arts Soc. (impresario coun. 2001-), Nat. Gallery Art and Hishorn Mus. (cir. mem.). Avocations: travel, food, modern dance, visual arts, swimming. Office: Jackie Chalkley 2130 Cathedral Ave NW Washington DC 20008-1502

CHALLINOR, DAVID, retired scientist; b. N.Y.C., July 11, 1920; s. David and Mercedes (Crimmins) C.; m. Joan Ridder, Nov. 22, 1952; children: Julia M., Mary E., Sarah L., D. Thompson. BA, Harvard U., 1943; MF, Yale U., 1959, PhD, 1966. With Offerman-Anderson, Clayton & Co., Houston, 1947-51; cotton farmer Culberson County, Tex., 1951-53; asst. sec. First Mortgage Co., Houston, 1953-57; research asst. Conn. Agr. Expt. Sta., New Haven, 1959-60; dep. dir. Yale Peabody Mus., New Haven, 1960-65, acting dir., 1965-66; spl. asst. in tropical biology Smithsonian Instn., Washington, 1966-67, dep. dir. office internat. activities, 1967-68, dir. office internat. activities, 1968-70, asst. sec. sci., 1971-87, sci. advisor, 1988-95, scientist emeritus, 1996—; v.p. for No. Am. Charles Darwin Found., 1971-92. Contbr. articles to sci. jours. Trustee Manhattanville Coll., 1964-70, Environ. Law Inst., 1975-84, 86-92; bd. dirs. Environ. Def. Fund, 1982-94, African Wildlife Found., 1980-2004, chmn. bd. N Fixing Tree Assn., 1988-94, Ctr. for Marine Conservation, 1992-99. With USNR, 1943-46. Fellow AAAS; mem. Sigma Xi. Home: 3117 Hawthorne St NW Washington DC 20008-3540 Office: Smithsonian Inst Nat Zoo 3000 Connecticut Ave NW Washington DC 20008-2509 Office Phone: 202-633-4185.

CHALLONER, DAVID REYNOLDS, academic administrator, endocrinologist; b. Appleton, Wis., Jan. 31, 1935; s. Reynolds Ray and Marion (Below) C.; m. Jacklyn Davnes Anderson, Aug. 30, 1958; children: David Harvey, Laura Reynolds, Britt-Davnes. BS cum laude, Lawrence Coll., Appleton, 1956; postgrad., Cambridge (Eng.) U., 1958; MD cum laude, Harvard, 1961. Resident in internal medicine Columbia Presbyn. Hosp., N.Y.C., 1961—63; research assoc. Nat. Heart Inst., Bethesda, Md., 1963—65; chief med. resident and endocrinology research fellow U. Wash., Seattle, 1965—67; prof. medicine, asst. chmn. dept. Ind. U. Sch. Medicine, Indpls., 1967—75; vis. scholar Inst. Medicine, Nat. Acad. Sci., 1974; dean St. Louis U. Sch. Medicine, 1975—82; v.p. health affairs U. Fla., Gainesville, 1982—98; dir. Inst. for Sci. and Health Policy U. Fla., Gainesville, Fla., 1998—2002. Chmn. pres.'s com. on nat. med. sci. NIH, 1988-91, mem. dirs. adv. com., 1990-96; mem. com. sci., engring. pub. policy NAS, 1993-97; cons. Eli Lilly & co., NIH; mem. NAS Nat. Rsch. Coun. governing bd., 1997—; foreign sec. NAS, Inst. Med., 1998—. Served to lt. codr. USPHS, 1963—65. Recipient Harvard Med. Alumni award, 1961, Dr. William Beaumont award AMA, 1982, Disting. Alumnus award Lawrence U., 1987. Fellow AAAS; mem. Inst. of Medicine (fgn. sec. 1998—), Am. Fedn. Clin. Rsch.pres. 1975), Inst. Medicine, Nat. Acad. Sci., Am. Soc. Clin. Investigation, Endocrine Soc., Am. Diabetes Assn., Assn. Am. Physicians, Boylston Soc., Am. Clin. and Climatol. Assn., Phi Beta Kappa, Alpha Omega Alpha, Beta Theta Pi. Clubs: Racquet (St. Louis); Cosmos (Washington). Home: 2715 NW 22nd Dr Gainesville FL 32605-2975 Office: U Fla PO Box 103204 Gainesville FL 32610-3204

CHALMERS, DAVID B., petroleum executive; b. Denver, Nov. 17, 1924; s. David Twiggs and Dorrit (Bay) C.; 1 child, David B. BA, Dartmouth Coll., 1947; A.M.P., Harvard U., 1966. Various positions Bay Petroleum Co., Denver, 1951-55; various positions Tenneco Oil Co., Houston, 1955-67; v.p. Occidental Petroleum Corp., Houston, 1967-68; pres. Can. Occidental Petroleum Ltd., 1968-73; pres., chief exec. officer Petrogas Processing Ltd., 1968-73; officer Cansulex Ltd., 1968-73; chmn., chief exec. officer, dir. Coral Petroleum, Inc. and subs., Houston, 1973—. Served to lt. USMC, 1943-45, 49-50, Korea Mem. Am. Petroleum Inst., Petroleum Club of Houston, Lochinvar Golf Club, Houston Racquet Club, Denver Country Club, Houston Club. Republican. Episcopalian. Home: 5600 San Felipe St Unit 4 Houston TX 77056-2617 Office: Coral Oil and Gas Inc 909 Texas St Unit 202 Houston TX 77002-3197 Office Phone: 713-222-7304. Personal E-mail: coraloil@aol.com.

CHALMERS, NEIL R., secondary school educator; b. Willmar, Minn., Dec. 24, 1970; s. Gordon G. and Mary Margaret Chalmers; m. Aimee Marie Reis, July 6, 1996; children: Grace Elizabeth, Abigail Therese. AA, Willmar C.C., Willmar, Minn., 1991; BS Secondary Edn., No. State U., Aberdeen, S.D., 1995; M of Ednl. Leadership and Instrn., SW State U., Marshall, Minn., 2003. Lic. Minn. Tchg. Minn., 1995. Asst. women's basketball coach No. State U., Aberdeen, SD, 1993—95; 9-12 social studies tchr. Blue Earth Area H.S., Blue Earth, Minn., 1995—96; 7-12 social studies tchr. Albert Lea Area Sch., Albert Lea, Minn., 1996—. Mock trial coach Albert Lea H.S., Albert Lea, Minn., 2001—, head coach - girls basketball, 1996—2000, asst. coach - girls tennis, 1998—99, head coach - girls tennis, 1996—97, Blue Earth Area Schs., Blue Earth, Minn., 1995—96. Nominee Albert Lea Area Schs. Tchr. of the Yr., Tchr. of the Yr. Com., 1999-2005. Mem.: Am. Assn. of Educators. R-Consevative. Roman Cath. Avocations: student activities, politics, reading, writing, family. Office Phone: 507-379-5796.

CHALSTY, JOHN STEELE, investment banker; b. Port Elizabeth, Republic of South Africa, Nov. 7, 1933; came to U.S., 1955, naturalized, 1964; s. Frederick H. and Sarah S. (Lamprecht) C.; m. Jennifer Blomefield, Feb. 16, 1957; children: Susan Chalsty Neely, Deborah Ann. B.Sc. in Chemistry and Physics, U. Witwatersrand, 1952, B.Sc. with honors in Chemistry, 1953, M.Sc., 1954; MBA (Baker scholar), Harvard U., 1957. With Exxon Corp. (formerly Standard Oil Co.), N.Y.C., 1957-69; dir. Donaldson, Lufkin & Jenrette, Inc., N.Y.C., 1969-2000, pres., CEO, 1986—98, chmn., 1996—2000; prin., chmn. Muirfield Capital Mgmt. LLC, 2003—. Bd. dirs. NY Stock Exch. 1988-94, Occidental Petroleum Corp., 1996-, SoundView Technology Group, Inc., 2003-, AXA Financial, Inc., Sappi Ltd., Metromedia Internat. Group Inc., Metromedia Fiber Network, Inc., Creditex; vice chmn., NY Stock Exch., 1990-94, chmn. advisory bd. Silvercrest Asset Mgmt. LLC, 2003-, N.Y. Econ. Devel. Corp. Bd. dirs. Teagle Found. Inc., 1974—, chmn., 1997—; trustee Columbia U., St. Barnabas Med. Ctr.; pres. Lincoln Ctr. Theater; bd. dirs. Am. Ballet Theater, N.Y. Philharm. Mem. Short Hills (N.J.) Club, Harvard Club, Univ. Club (N.Y.C.).*

CHAM, DANIEL K., nuclear medicine physician, radiologist, medical researcher; s. James F. Cham and Wai Mui Kwan; m. Yenty Tioanda, June 9, 1999. MD, Chgo. Med. Sch., 1993—99, MS. Diplomate Am. Bd. Nuc. Medicine, 2003. Clin. rsch. instr. U. So. Calif., Dept. Radiology, Los Angeles, 2002—. Rschr. Human Genome Ctr., Lawrence Berkeley Lab., Calif., Harvard Med. Sch., Dept. Geriatric, Boston. Contbr. articles, scientific papers. Recipient Melvin Leichtling Oncology. Mem.: AMA, LA Radiol. Soc., Advance Molecular Imaging, Soc. Nuc. Medicine. Achievements include research in the Impact of PET/CT in oncological imaging. Office: Univ So Calif 1510 San Pablo St Ste 350 Los Angeles CA 90033 E-mail: cham@usc.edu.

CHAMBERLAIN, ADRIAN RAMOND, transportation engineer; b. Detroit, Nov. 11, 1929; s. Adrian and Leila (Swisher) C.; m. Melanie F. Stevens, May 19, 1979; children: Curtis (dec.), Tracy, Thomas (dec.). BS, Mich. State U., 1951, D Engring., 1971; MS, Wash. State U., 1952; PhD, Colo. State U., 1955; LittD, Denver U., 1974. Registered profl. engr., Colo. lic. real estate broker, Colo., 1981-91. Rsch. engr. Phillips Petroleum Co., 1955; rsch. coord., civil engr. Colo. State U., 1956-57, chief civil engr. sect., 1957-61, acting dean engring., 1959-61, v.p., 1960-66, exec. v.p., treas., governing bd., 1966-69, pres., 1969-80; chmn. bd. dirs. Univ. Nat. Bank, 1964-69, dir., 1964-74; pres., dir. Mitchell & Co., Inc., 1981-85; exec. v.p. Simons, Li & Assocs., Inc., 1985-87; pres., CEO, Chemagnetics, Inc., Ft. Collins, Colo., 1987-89; exec. dir. Colo. Dept. Hwys., Denver, 1987-91, Colo. Dept. Transp., 1991-94; v.p. engring. cons. firm Parsons Brinckerhoff, Denver, 1998—. Chmn. NSF Commn. Weather Modification, 1964-66; mem. Nat. Air Quality Criteria Adv. Com., 1967-70; vice chmn. rsch. and tech. coord. com. Fed. Hwy Admiinstrn. of Transp. Rsch. Bd., NRC, 1991-94. Colo. commr. Western Interstate Commn. on Higher Edn., 1974-78; pres. State Bd. Agr. Sys., 1978-80; trustee Cystic Fibrosis Found., 1971-84; bd. trustees Univ. Corp. for Atmospheric Rsch., 1967-72, 74-81, chmn. bd. trustees, 1977-79; pres. Black Mountain Ranch, Inc., 1969-85; bd. dirs. Nat. Ctr. for Higher Edn. Mgmt. Sys., 1975-80, chmn. bd. dirs., 1977-78; bd. visitors Air U., USAF, 1973-76, chmn., 1975-76; exec. com. Nat. Assn. State Univs. and Land Grant Colls., 1976-80, pres.-elect, 1978-79, chmn., 1979-80; mem. adv. coun. to dir. NSF, 1978-81; chmn. Ft. Collins-Loveland Airport Authority, 1983-86; bd. dirs. Synergetics Internat. Inc., 1987-90; mem. exec. com. strategic hwy. rsch. commn. Transp. Rsch. Bd. NRC, 1989-93, chmn. strategic transp. rsch. study hwy. safety, 1989-90, exec. com., 1991-96, vice-chmn., 1992, chmn., 1993; mem. Gov.'s Cabinet, State of Colo., 1987-94; mem. Info. Mgmt. Commn., 1988-93. Fulbright student U. Grenoble, 1955-56 Mem. ASCE, Am. Assn. State Hwy. and Transp. Ofcls. (policy com. 1987-92, v.p. 1990-91, pres. 1991-92, bd. dirs. 1992-94, chmn. standing com. on adminstrn. 1993-94), Am. Trucking Assn. (v.p. for freight policy 1994-98, mng. dir. found. 1998), Order of Aztec Eagle, Mex., Nat. Assn. Nat. Acads., Sigma Xi, Tau Beta Pi, Phi Kappa Phi, Chi Epsilon. Office: Parsons Brinckerhoff 1660 Lincoln St Ste 2100 Denver CO 80264-2001 Office Phone: 303-832-9091. Business E-Mail: chamberlain@pbworld.com.

CHAMBERLAIN, BARBARA KAYE, small business owner, communications executive; b. Lewiston, Idaho, Nov. 6, 1962; d. William Arthur and Gladys Marie (Humphrey) Greene; m. Dean Andrew Chamberlain, Sept. 13, 1986 (div.); children: Kathleen Marie, Laura Kaye; m. Daniel Eric Pocklington, Apr. 11, 1998. BA in English cum laude, BA in Linguistics cum laude, Wash. State U., 1984; MPA, Ea. Wash. U., 2002. Temp. sec. various svcs., Spokane, Wash., 1984-86; office mgr. Futurepast, Spokane, 1986-87; dir. mktg. and prodn. Futurepast: The History Co., Melior Publs., Spokane, 1987-88, v.p., 1988-89; founder, owner PageWorksInk, 1989—; mem. dist. 2 Idaho State Ho. of Reps., 1990-92; mem. Idaho State Senate, 1992-94; dir. comm. and pub. affairs Wash. State U., Spokane, 1998—. Adj. faculty North Idaho Coll., 1995, trustee, 1996-2001, bd. chair, 1999-2001. Author North Idaho's Centennial, 1990; editor Washington Songs and Lore, 1988. Bd. dirs. Mus. North Idaho Coeur d'Alene, 1990-91, Ct. Apptd. Spl. advocates, 1993-96; bd. dirs. Spokane Pub. Rels. Coun., 1999-2004, pres., 2002-03. Named Child Advocate Legislator of Yr., Idaho Alliance for Children, Youth and Families, 1993. Democrat. Office: 534 E Trent Ave Spokane WA 99210-1495

CHAMBERLAIN, BRIAN TODD, music educator; b. Henderson, Ky., 1973; s. Louis Earl and Pamela B. Chamberlain; m. Cindy Marie Chamberlain, 2001. B in Music Edn., U. Ky., 1995; MS, U. So. Oreg., 2002. Band dir. Harrodsburg (Ky.) H.S., 1995—99; music tchr. Northside Elem., Midway, Ky., 1999—2000; band dir. So. H.S., Louisville, 2000—. Prin. horn Ctrl. Ky. Concert Band, Lexington, 1999—. Mem.: Music Educators Nat. Conf., Ky. Music Educators Assn. Home: 222 Pinnacle Ct Frankfort KY 40601 Personal E-mail: btchamberlain@aol.com.

CHAMBERLAIN, CHARLES JAMES, railroad labor union executive; b. Ashton, Ill., Aug. 7, 1921; s. Charles Hubert and Katherine (Reitz) C.; m. Joyce Lois Swanson, June 27, 1942; children— Richard B., Charles M. Student pub. schs. With signal dept. C. & N.-W. Ry., 1938-57; grand lodge rep. Brotherhood of R.R. Signalmen, 1957-61, sec.-treas., 1961-67, pres., 1967—. Appointed Labor mem. by Pres. Carter to U.S. R.R. Retirement Bd., Chgo., 1977, reappointed, 1979-84, reappointed by Pres. Reagan, 1986-89, reappointed by Pres. Bush, 1989-92, ret. 1992; arbitrator Nat. Mediation Bd., 1996. Alderman DeKalb (Ill.) City Coun., 1949-57; pres. 4 Colonies Condo Assn., Crystal Lake, Ill., 1987—; chmn. St. John's Luth. Ch., Algonquin, Ill., 1990-91, 94—. Mem. Ry. Labor Execs. Assn. (chmn. 1970—) Home and Office: 740 St Andrews Ln Apt 33 Crystal Lake IL 60014-7043 Personal E-mail: brsrrb@aol.com.

CHAMBERLAIN, DANIEL ROBERT, college president; b. Mexico, Mo., Aug. 22, 1932; s. Ray Willis and Marianne Elizabeth (Horine) C.; m. Joyce F. Books, June 22, 1952; children: Rodney, Mark, Anthony, Priscilla, Aletha, Cynthia, Marianne. BA, Upland Coll., 1953; MA, Calif. State U., Los Angeles, 1957; postgrad., UCLA, 1958-59; D.Ed., U. So. Calif., 1967; DHL (hon.), Huntington Coll., 2000, Houghton Coll., 2001. Tchr., adminstr. Western Pilgrim Schs., El Monte, Calif., 1953-59; tchr. English and history Pasadena (Calif.) City Schs., 1959-63; chmn. div. profl. studies, acting pres. Upland Coll., 1963-65; asst. univ. dean for univ. wide activities SUNY, Albany, 1965-68; dean of coll. Messiah Coll., Grantham, Pa., 1968-76; pres. Houghton (N.Y.) Coll., 1976—. Lectr. on higher edn. and social scis. in People's Republic of China, 1984, 87, 88, 89. Pres. Calif. youth Wesleyan Ch., 1954-64; chmn. bd. dirs. Mile High Camp, Barton Flats, Calif., 1959-65; pres. men's commn. Christian Holiness Assn., 1975-80; bd. dirs. Commn. Ind. Colls. and Univs.; chmn. Ind. Coll. Fund, N.Y., Western N.Y. Consortium Higher Edn., 1976—; mem. gen. bd. adminstrn. Wesleyan Ch., 1988-92, 2000—; chmn. Western N.Y. Consortium Higher Edn., 1991-93; bd. dirs. N.Y. State Commn. on Ind. Colls. and Univs., 1994-97. Named One of 50 Most Outstanding Alumni, Calif. State U., L.A., 1997. Mem. Christian Coll. Consortium (chmn.), Council of Mennonite Coll. Deans (chmn.), Am. Assn. Higher Edn., Middle States Assn. Schs. and Colls. (evaluator, team chmn.), Wesleyan Edn. Council (chmn.), Lions, Phi Delta Kappa. Republican. Office: Houghton Coll Office of Pres Houghton NY 14744 Office Phone: 585-567-9310. Business E-Mail: daniel.chamberlain@houghton.edu.

CHAMBERLAIN, DIANE, psychotherapist, writer, social worker; b. Plainfield, N.J., Mar. 18, 1950; d. John and Anna Delores (Chamberlain) Lopresti; m. Richard David Chmielewski, Apr. 14, 1973 (div. 1993); m. David Earl Heagy, June 8, 1996. BSW, San Diego State U., 1975, MSW, 1978. Clin. social worker Social Advocates for Youth, San Diego, 1978-80; clin. social worker Sharp Meml. Hosp., San Diego, 1980-83, Children's Hosp. and Nat. Health Ctr., Washington, 1983-85; pvt. practice psychotherapy Alexandria, Va., 1985-92. Author: (novels) Private Relations, 1989, Lovers and Strangers, 1990, Secret Lives, 1991, Keeper of the Light, 1992, Fire and Rain, 1993, Brass Ring, 1994, Reflection, 1996, The Escape Artist, 1997, Breaking the Silence, 1999, Summer's Child 2000, The Courage Tree, 2001, Kiss River, 2003, In Her Mother's Shadow, 2004, Bay at Midnight, 2005; contbr. nonfiction articles to profl. jours. Mem. Novelists Inc. Democrat. Avocation: dog obedience training. Office: PO Box 1331 Vienna VA 22183-1331

CHAMBERLAIN, GEORGE ARTHUR, III, manufacturing company executive, venture capitalist; b. Boston, Sept. 14, 1935; s. George Arthur, Jr. and Mabel G. (Greene) C.; m. Judith Fehr, June 20, 1959; children— G. Randall, Cynthia L. AB, Wheaton (Ill.) Coll., 1957; MBA, Harvard U., 1961. Loan officer Worcester County Nat. Bank, Mass., 1961-65; v.p. fin., treas. Anderson Corp., Worcester, 1966-69; with Digital Equipment Corp., Maynard, Mass., 1969-92, treas., 1976-83, v.p. mfg., engring., mktg. fin., 1983-92; exec. v.p. Capitol Techs. Inc., 1993-94; CFO Marcam Corp., Boston, 1994-97, Radnet, Inc., Wakefield, 1997-2001, Media Map, Inc., Watertown, Mass., 2001, Neartek, Inc., Lakeville, Mass., 2001—. Trustee Consumers Savs. Bank, Worcester, 1970-85; adv. dir. ABN-AMRO Bank, Boston; bd. dirs. Mapics, Inc. Trustee Lawrence Acad., Groton, Mass.; past trustee Met. Ctr., Boston; bd. dirs. ARC Mass. Bay, 1986-94; overseer Sta. WGBH, Boston, 1988-94, Mus. Fine Arts, Boston, gov. sch., 1992—. With AUS, 1957-59. Mem. Fin. Execs. Inst.

CHAMBERLAIN, JEAN NASH, consultant, former county government department director; b. Chgo., Oct. 14, 1934; d. William Edmund and Virginia Jean (La Fon) Nash; m. James Staffeld Chamberlain, Dec. 29, 1953; children: James W., William S., Caren T., Martha J. Student, U. S.C., 1951-53. Dept. dir. Oakland County, Mich., 1982—2003; polit. dir. Tribune/United Cablevision, Huntington Woods, Mich., 1982; orgn. dir. polit. campaign, Oakland, Mich., 1983-84; dir. fin. Dan Murphy for Gov., Mich., 1985-86; exec. mgr. Greater Royal Oak (Mich.)/Oak Park C. of C., 1986-93; bus. and polit. cons. Royal Oak, Mich.; pres. JNC Consulting LLC. Bd. dir. Mich. Trust Bank. Chair Oak Park Bus. and Edn. Alliance; sec.-treas. Woodward Ave. Action Assn.; vice chair Rep. com., Oakland County, Mich., 1971—73; chair Rep. 18th congl. dist., 1973—77; del. Rep. Nat. Conv., Kansas City, Mo., 1976; bd. dir. Oakland County Mental Health Bd., Mich., 1976—93, chair, 1983—86; bd. dir. Nat. Heritage Route, Give A Christmas Yr. Around, Grand Nat., 8 Mile Blvd. Assn. Named among top thirty Outstanding Women State Mich., Mich.'s Womens Commn., 1998. Mem. Mich. State C. of C., Harnack Firefighters Scholarship Fund (bd. dirs.), Woodward Dream Cruise (bd. chair). Roman Catholic. Avocations: tennis, bridge, sports, cooking. Office Phone: 248-821-0665. E-mail: jean@jncconsulting.com.

CHAMBERLAIN, JOSEPH MILES, retired astronomer, educator; b. Peoria, Ill., July 26, 1923; s. Maurice Silloway and Roberta (Miles) C.; m. Paula Bruninga, Dec. 12, 1945; children: Janet Ann, Susan Louise, Barbara

Jean. BS, U.S. Mcht. Marine Acad., 1944; BA, Bradley U., 1947; AM, Tchrs. Coll. Columbia, 1950, EdD, 1962. Instr. Columbia Jr. High Sch., Peoria, 1943; instr. nav. War Shipping Adminstrn., 1944-45; boys sec. YMCA, Peoria, 1946-47; instr. U.S. Mcht. Marine Acad., Kings Point, N.Y., 1947-50, asst. prof., 1950-52; asst. curator Am. Museum-Hayden Planetarium, N.Y.C., 1952-53, gen. mgr., chief astronomer, 1953-56, chmn., 1956-64; asst. dir. Am. Mus. Natural History, 1964-68; dir. Adler Planetarium, Chgo., 1968-91, pres., 1977-91, ret., 1991. Prof. astronomy Northwestern U., 1968-78; professorial lectr. U. Chgo., 1968-71; led eclipse expdns. to Atlantic Ocean, 1972, 73, 94, Mexico, 1970, Can., 1954, 79, Ceylon, 1955, Pacific Ocean, 1977, 91, astro-geodetic expdns. to Can., 1956, 57, Greenland, 1958; dean coun. of sci. staff Am. Mus. Nat. History, 1960-62. Co-author: Planets, Stars and Space, 1957; author: Time and the Stars, 1964, also articles on popular astronomy. Active Boy Scouts Am., Met. Chgo. YMCA; trustee Lakeview Mus. Arts and Scis., Peoria, 1993—2003; bd. dirs. Heartland Water Resources Coun., 1995-98. Lt. USNR, 1945-46; staff Naval Res. Officers Sch. 1953-54, N.Y.C. Mem. Am. Astron. Soc., Internat. Astron. Union, Internat. Planetarium Dirs. Conf. (vice chmn. 1968-77, chmn. 1977-87), Am. Polar Soc., Am. Assn. Museums (mem. council 1965-77, v.p. 1971-74, pres. 1974-75), Mus. Trustee Assn. (bd. dirs. 1996-98), Peoria Hist. Soc. (trustee 1993-96), Ill. Valley Yacht Club, Univ. Club (Chgo.). Republican. Presbyn. (elder). Home: 5424 W Flagstone Dr Peoria IL 61615-9466

CHAMBERLAIN, KATHLEEN PATRICIA, humanities educator, writer; b. Cleve., Jan. 13, 1947; d. James Frederick and Ada Mae (Crowl) Egan; m. David John Chamberlain, Dec. 27, 1969 (div. May 1974); 1 child, David John Chamberlain Jr. BS in Edn., Ohio State U., 1969; MA in History, U. Colo., 1992; PhD in History, U. N.Mex., 1998. Freelance writer, 1969—74; mng. editor jour. Denver, 1974—84; tng. mgr. Am. Water Worker Assn., Denver, 1984—92; asst. prof. Castleton (Vt.) State Coll., 1998—2001, Ea. Mich. U., Ypsilanti, 2001—. Author: Under Sacred Ground, A History of Navajo Oil, 1922-1982, 2000. Susan Topham grant, Charles Redd Ctr., Brigham Young U., 1999—2000. Mem.: Orgn. Am. Historians, Am. Hist. Assn., Mich. Inst. Arts and Letters, Western History Assn., Phi Alpha Theta. Democrat. Mem. Christian Ch. Office: Ea Mich Univ Dept History 701 Pray Harrold Hall Ypsilanti MI 48197

CHAMBERLAIN, KATHRYN BURNS BROWNING, retired career naval officer; b. Rapid City, S.D., Jan. 17, 1951; d. George Alfred III and Mildred Doty Browning; m. Thomas Richard Masker, Apr. 19, 1975 (widowed Sept. 1978); m. Guy Caldwell Chamberlain III, Mar. 25, 1980 (div. Oct. 1988); children: Burns Doty, Anne Caldwell. BA, La. Tech. U., 1973; postgrad., Naval Postgrad. Sch., Monteray, Calif., 1978-79; MA, Auburn U., 1984; postgrad., U. Ill., 1994-96, Govs. State U., 1995-96. Ensign USN, 1974, lt. jg., 1976, lt., 1978, advanced through grades to comdr., 1983, surface warfare designation, 1980, joint staff officer, 1986, comdg. officer Mil. Sealift Command Office, 1986-88; comdr., exec. officer USNAVFAC, 1991-94; planner City of Montgomery, 1998—. Mem. Am. Inst. Cert. Planners, Am. Planning Assn., Urban and Regional Info. Sys. Assn. Home and Office: 364 Felder Ave Montgomery AL 36104-5616 Office Phone: 334-241-2699. Business E-Mail: kchamberlain@ci.montgomery.al.us. E-mail: kchamberlai1@earthlink.net.

CHAMBERLAIN, MARY, retired academic administrator, translator; b. Media, Pa., Mar. 26, 1928; d. Lloyd William Chamberlain, Sr. and Marie Gertrude Meloney. BA in Chemistry, Rosemont Coll., 1949; MS in French, Georgetown U., 1957, PhD in Linguistics and Spanish, 1965. Bus. office asst. Dunbarton Coll., Washington, 1950—58; prof. Spanish U. Md. Overseas, Torrejon Airbase, Spain, 1959—61; asst. edn. adviser USAF, Torrejon Airbase, Spain, 1959—61; asst. rschr. Bantu lang. Georgetown U., Washington, 1961—62; prof. Spanish and French Howard U., Washington, 1961—62; chief trainee selection Orgn. Am. States, Washington, 1962—89; ret. Translator: (chronicles) New Norcia Studies No. 9, 2001, New Norcia Studies No. 10, 2002. Roman Catholic. Avocations: music, opera, translations. Home: Apt 1013 2601 Woodley Pl Washington DC 20008

CHAMBERLAIN, NEIL CORNELIUS WOLVERTON, economist, emeritus educator; b. Charlotte, N.C., May 18, 1915; s. Henry Bryan and Elizabeth (Wolverton) C.; m. Mariam Kenosian, June 27, 1942 (div. June 1967); m. Harriet Feigenbaum, Aug. 9, 1968. AB, Western Res. U., 1937, MA, 1939; PhD, Ohio State U., 1942. Rsch. fellow Brookings Instn., 1941—42; rsch. dir. Labor and Mgmt. Ctr., Yale, 1946—49, asst. dir., 1949—54; asst. prof. econs. Yale, 1947—49, assoc. prof., 1949—54, prof. econs., 1959—67, Columbia, 1954—59, 1967—80, Armand G. Erpf prof. of modern corp., 1969—80, prof. emeritus, 1981—. Dir. program in Econ. Devel. and Adminstrn. Ford Found., 1957-60 Author: Collective Bargaining Procedures, 1944, The Union Challenge to Management Control, 1948, Management in Motion, 1950, Collective Bargaining, 1951, rev., 1965, 3d edit., 1986, Social Responsibility and Strikes, 1953, The Impact of Strikes, 1954, A General Theory of Economic Process, 1955, Labor, 1958, Sourcebook on Labor, 1958, The Firm: Micro- Economic Planning and Action, 1962, The West in a World Without War, 1963, The Labor Sector, 1965, rev., 1971, 80, Private and Public Planning, 1965, Enterprise and Environment, 1968, Beyond Malthus, 1970, The Place of Business in America's Future: A Study in Social Values, 1973, The Limits of Corporate Responsibility, 1973, Remaking American Values: Challenge to a Business Society, 1977, Forces of Change in Western Europe, 1980, Social Strategy and Corporate Structure, 1982, Intellectual Odyssey: An Economist's Ideological Journey, 1996; editor: Contemporary Economic Issues, 1969, rev., 1978, Business and the Cities, 1970; co-editor: Cases on Labor Relations, 1949, A Decade of Industrial Relations Research, 1958, Frontiers of Collective Bargaining, 1968; mem. editorial bd., editorial cons.: Mgmt. Internat, 1960-70; bd. editors: Am. Econ. Rev, 1957-59. Bd. dirs. Salzburg Seminar in Am. Studies, 1957-78; trustee Columbia Jour. World Bus., 1969-72, 75-80. Served from ensign to lt. USNR, 1942-46. Mem.: Indsl. Rels. Rsch. Assn. (exec. bd. 1955—58, pres. 1967, Lifetime Achievement award 2003), Am. Econ. Assn., Phi Beta Kappa. Home: 49 W 24th St New York NY 10010-3206

CHAMBERLAIN, OWEN, nuclear physicist; b. San Francisco, July 10, 1920; m. Babette Copper, 1943 (div. 1978); 4 children; m. June Steingart, 1980 (dec.); m. Senta Pugh, 1998. AB (Cramer fellow), Dartmouth Coll., 1941; PhD, U. Chgo., 1949. Instr. physics U. Calif., Berkeley, 1948—50, asst. prof., 1950—54, assoc. prof., 1954—58, prof., 1958—89, prof. emeritus, 1989—; civilian physicist Manhattan Dist., Berkeley, Los Alamos, 1942—46. Recipient Nobel prize (with Emilio Segre) in Physics, for discovery of anti-proton, 1959, The Berkeley citation, U. Calif., 1989, Loeb lectr., Harvard U., 1959; fellow Guggenheim, 1957—58. Fellow: Am. Acad. Arts and Scis., Am. Phys. Soc.; mem.: NAS, Berkeley Fellows. Office: U Calif Phys Dept Berkeley CA 94720-0001

CHAMBERLAIN, PAUL EDWARD, investment banker; s. William and Bernadette Chamberlain; m. Martha Elliott Witbeck, Aug. 15, 1992. Grad. magna cum laude, Princeton U.; MBA, Harvard U. Joined Morgan Stanley, 1990—, sr. assoc. equity capital markets NYC, principal, co-head West Coast Technol. Group Menlo Park, Calif., 1997—98, mng. dir., co-head of West Coast Techol. Group, 1998—. Named to Forbes Midas List, 2001, 2002, 2004. Office: Morgan Stanley 3000 Sand Hill Rd Bldg 4 Ste 250 Menlo Park CA 94025

CHAMBERLAIN, ROBERT GLENN, retired tool manfacturing executive; b. Cedar Rapids, Iowa, Feb. 17, 1926; s. Glenn Arlie and Ora Margarite (Castle) C.; m. Jane Helen Newlin, June 13, 1946; children: Carole, James, Sue, Patricia, Tracey. BSM.E., Iowa State U., 1949; postgrad., U. Wis.Milw. With Link-Belt Speeder, Cedar Rapids, 1949-54, Giddings & Lewis, Fond du Lac, Wis., 1954-83, group v.p. indsl. products, 1980-82, exec. v.p. machine tools, 1982-83, ret., 1983. Pioneer numerical control programmer, 1954-59. Mem. PTO; v.p. Bay Lakes coun. Boy Scouts Am., Menasha, Wis., 1982-89, exploring chmn. in sch., Dallas, 1981, exploring chmn. Area 1 NC region, Oak Brook, Ill., 1977; bd. dirs. Evergreen Retirement Cmty., 1989-94. With USNR, 1944-46. Recipient Silver Beaver award Boy Scouts Am., 1974, Silver Antelope award, 1983. Mem. Masons. Home: W2728 Oakwood Beach Rd Markesan WI 53946-8904 E-mail: rchamberlain1@juno.com.

CHAMBERLAIN, STEVEN PAUL, special education educator; b. Ft. Worth, May 12, 1963; s. D. Gilford and Anna Belle (Flynn) Chamberlain; m. Sylvia Lucia Montoya, May 26, 2001. BA in English, U. Tex., Austin, 1985, MEd in Spl. Edn., 1989; PhD, U. Tex., 1999. Cert. Spl Edn. Tchr. Tex. Edn. Agy., 1989, English as a Second Lang.Tchr. Tex. Edn. Agy., 1989, Secondary English Tchr. Tex. Edn. Agy., 1989, Secondary Econs.Tchr. Tex. Edn. Agy., 1989. Spl. edn. tchr. Manor (Tex.) Ind. Sch. Dist., 1989—94; rsch. asst. S.W. Ednl. Devel. Lab., Austin, Tex., 1997—99; asst. prof. spl. edn. U. Tex., Brownsville, 1999—. Contbr. articles to profl. jours., chapters to books. Bd. mem. Tex. Coun. for Exceptional Children, Tex., 2000—04. Mem.: Am. Ednl. Rsch. Assn., Nat. Assn. of Bilingual Edn., Coun. for Exceptional Children, Tex. Coun. for Exceptional Children (publications chair 2000—04). Office: U Tex 80 Ft Brown Brownsville TX 78520 Business E-Mail: steve.chamberlain@utb.edu.

CHAMBERLAIN, WILLARD THOMAS, retired metal products executive; b. New Haven, Nov. 22, 1928; s. Thomas Huntington and Alice Irene (Daley) C.; m. Harriet Halbert Keck, Nov. 20, 1965; children: Huntington Wilson, Amy Thatcher. B.E., Yale U., 1950; postgrad., Ill. Inst. Tech., 1951-53. With Armour Research Found., Chgo., 1951-53; asst. to tech. mgr. Anaconda Brass div. Anaconda Corp., Waterbury, Conn., 1953-56, tech. supr., 1956-60, metall. mgr. Torrington, Conn., 1960-61, mgr. devel. Waterbury, 1961-62, lab. mgr., 1962-64, mgr. research-tech. ctr., 1964-67, mgr. Valley Mills, 1967, Ansonia, 1967-70, mgr. prodn. planning, 1970-71, v.p. mfg., 1971-72, exec. v.p. Brass div., 1972-74, pres., 1974-80, Anaconda Industries, 1980; sr. v.p. Atlantic Richfield Co., 1980-82; pres. Arco Metals Co., 1982-85; sr. v.p. corp. affairs Atlantic Richfield Co., 1985-87; sr. v.p. govt. and pub. affairs ARCO, 1987-89. Mem. So. Calif. bus. com. Econ. Literacy Council Adv. of Calif. Mem. exec. bd. Waterbury Republican Town Com., 1964-70; commr. Waterbury Bd. Fin., 1966-67, chmn. charter revision com., 1966-67; mem. exec. bd. Mattatuck council Boy Scouts Am., 1965-72, Waterbury Assn. for Retarded Children, 1965-66; co-chmn. Clergy-Industry Conf., 1965-66; campaign chmn. Valley United Fund, 1970-71; bd. dirs. United Way, Central Naugatuck Valley, 1974, The Banking Ctr., 1974-81, Western Conn. Indsl. Council, 1974-81, Calif. State U. Found., Found. for Am. Communications, Los Angeles Arts Council; trustee Calif. Mus. Found., Harvey Mudd Coll.; bd. trustees Greater Los Angeles Partnership for the Homeless; bd. dirs. L.A. Habitat for Humanity. Recipient Outstanding Civic Leader award, 1967. Mem. Copper Devel. Assn., Aluminum Assn. (dir.), Am. Soc. Metals, Yale Engring. Assn., Greater Waterbury C. of C. (bd. dirs. 1974), Alliance Aging Rsch. (bd. dirs.), Am. Petroleum Inst. (emerging issues task force), Brookings Instn. (coun. mem.), Calif. State U. Found. (bd. dirs., compensation planning com., chmn. investment com.), Calif. State U. Bus. Assocs., Constl. Rights Found. (bus. adv. coun.), Econ. Literacy Coun. Adv. Calif. (so. Calif. bus. com.), Found. Am. Communications (dir.), Hugh O'Brian Youth Found., Math. Engring. and Sci. Achievement (industry adv. bd.), Nat. Action Coun. for Minorities in Engring., Nat. Minority Supplier Devel. Coun. (bd. dirs.), Nat. Wetlands Policy Forum, Nat. Wildlife Fedn. (vice chmn. corp. conservation coun.), Vols. of Am., L.A., Town Hall, U.S. C. of C., World Affairs Coun., Univ. Club L.A., Yale Club, So. Calif. Presbyterian. Home: 7115 Hawarden Dr Riverside CA 92506 E-mail: wtc91107@yahoo.com.

CHAMBERLAIN, WILLIAM EDWIN, JR., management consultant; b. St. Louis, June 8, 1951; s. William Edwin Sr. and Grace (Salisbury) C. AA in Bus. Mgmt., Mesa (Ariz.) C.C., 1983; BBA, U. Phoenix, 1988. Tng. and human resources devel. specialist Motorola, Inc., Phoenix, 1979-87; pres., seminar spkr. Chamberlain Cons. Svcs., Reno, 1987—. Curator, dir. ops. U.S. Wolf Refuge. Mem. Network for Profl. Devel. Avocations: wildlife preservation and management, hiking, backpacking, tennis, basketball, racquetball. Office Phone: 775-475-0510. Business E-Mail: bill@uswolfrefuge.org. *Personal philosophy: Better people make better workers and better workers make better people. A company's workforce is often its biggest investment, therefore efforts to develop its workers will often bring the biggest returns.*

CHAMBERLAND, KATHY LYNN, special education educator; b. Honolulu, Nov. 24, 1952; d. William Ernest Brooks Sr. and Vivian Jean Brooks; m. Michael John Chamberland, June 9, 1973; children: Ryan Patrick, Regan Elizabeth Hargrave, Kyle Barret. MusB in Edn., Southwestern Coll., 1974; MS, Emporia State U., 1982. Cert. tchr. Kans. State Dept. Edn., 1974, reading specialist Kans. State Dept. Edn., 1982. Tchr. music Unified Sch. Dist. 286, Sedan, Kans., 1974—82, tchr., 1982—90, tchr., reading specialist, 1990—. Chmn. lang. arts Unified Sch. Dist. 286, 1991—, coord. fed. programs, 1996—; adj. instr. Independence C.C., 1998—. Mem., past pres. Howard County Players, Sedan, 1991—2005; elder, music dir., worship com. chmn. First Christian Ch., 1979—2005. Mem.: Ea. Hills Reading Coun., Kans. Reading Assn. (Bill Martin Jr. award 2005—), Internat. Reading Assn., Beta Sigma Phi, Delta Kappa Gamma (past pres.). R-Liberal. Avocations: reading, music, travel. Home: 2067 Lariat Rd Sedan KS 67361-8827 Office Phone: 620-725-5611. Personal E-mail: chamberk@usd286-sedan-ks.org.

CHAMBERLIN, JOHN STEPHEN, investor, consumer products company executive; b. Boston, July 29, 1928; s. Stephen Henry and Olive Helen (McGrath) C.; m. Mary Katherine Leahy, Oct. 9, 1954; children— Mary Katherine, Patricia Ann, Carol Lynn, John Stephen Jr., Liane Helen, Mark Joseph. AB cum laude, Harvard U., 1950, MBA, 1953. Lamp salesman Gen. Electric Co., N.Y.C., 1954-57, mgmt. cons., 1957-60, mgr. product planning TV receiver dept. Syracuse, N.Y., 1960-63, mgr. mktg., gen. mgr. radio receiver dept. Utica, N.Y., 1963-70; exec. v.p., dir. Lenox Inc., Trenton, N.J., 1970-71; v.p., gen. mgr. housewares div. Gen. Electric Co., Bridgeport, Conn., 1971-74, v.p., gen. mgr. housewares and audio div., 1974-76; pres., chief exec. officer, dir. Lenox Inc., Lawrenceville, N.J., 1976-81, chmn., chief exec. officer, 1981-85; pres., chief operating officer Avon Products, Inc., N.Y.C., 1985-88; pvt. investor Princeton, N.J., 1988—. Sr. advisor Mancuso & Co., 1992—98. Trustee Univ. Med. Ctr. at Princeton, vice chmn. 1995, chmn., 2002; chmn. Princeton Health Care Sys., 2003. Mem. Bedens Brook Club, Harvard Club N.Y.C., Nassau Club. Home: 182 Fairway Dr Princeton NJ 08540-2410

CHAMBERLIN, MICHAEL JOHN, biochemistry professor; b. Chgo., June 7, 1937; s. John Windsor and Marian (McMichael) C.; m. Caroline Marie Kane, Jan. 31, 1981. AB, Harvard U., 1959; PhD, Stanford U., 1963. Asst. prof. virology U. Calif., Berkeley, 1963—67, assoc. prof. molecular biology, 1967—71, assoc. prof. biochemistry, 1971—73; prof., 1973—99, U. Calif., Berkeley, 1973, vice chmn. dept. biochemistry, 1983—88, prof. biochemistry and molecular biology, 1989; emeritus prof., 1999. Mem. physiol. chemistry study sect. NIH, 1970-74, molecular biology study sect., 1980-84; mem. study sect. Am. Heart Assn., 1983-86. Mem. editorial bd. Jour. Biol. Chemistry, 1975-78, Biochemistry, 1993—; contbr. articles to profl. jours. Recipient Charles Pfizer award Am. Chem. Soc., 1974. Mem. NAS, AAAS, Am. Acad. Arts and Scis., Am. Soc. Biochemistry and Molecular Biology, Am. Soc. Microbiology, Am. Acad. Microbiology, Phi Beta Kappa, Sigma Xi. Office: U Calif Dept Molecular/Cell Biology 401 Barker Hall Berkeley CA 94720-3208 E-mail: profmjc@berkeley.edu.

CHAMBERLIN, MICHAEL MEADE, lawyer; b. Omaha; s. Cecil Meade and Helen Gail (Russell) C. AB in Econs., Princeton U., 1972; JD, George Washington U., 1975. Bar: N.Y. 1976. Assoc. Shearman & Sterling, N.Y.C., 1975-83, ptnr., 1984-93; CEO, exec. dir. EMTA, 1994—. Avocations: conservation, running, choral music, skiing, flying. Business E-Mail: mchamb@emta.org.

CHAMBERLIN-DAVIS, ANN ELIZABETH, artist, writer; b. Plainfield, N.J., May 10, 1955; d. Earl Martin and Mary Helen Chamberlin; m. Steven Joseph Davis, Aug. 7, 1993. Student, Whitney Mus. Ind. Study, N.Y.C., 1975; BA, Rutgers U., 1977. Artist, author, linguist, Highland Park, N.J., 1986—. Author: (novels) The Writer, 1993, May Nancy, 1995, Her Other Life, 1997, The Conscience of Love, The Mistaken Identity of Gene Christopher Davison, My Stories are Ghosts; (short story) Slum City Memoirs, 1972. Pub. spkr. The Club, New Brunswick, N.J., 1986-93. Grantee N.J. State Coun. Arts, 1981, 93. Avocations: painting, writing, russian language, poetry, music. Home: 29 S Adelaide Ave Apt 1 Highland Park NJ 08904

CHAMBERS, ANNE COX, publishing executive, former diplomat; b. Dayton, Ohio; Student, Finch Coll., N.Y.C.; D in Pub. Svc. (hon.), Wesleyan Coll., 1982; DHL (hon.), Spelman Coll., 1983; LLD (hon.), Oglethorpe U., 1983; DHL (hon.), Brenau Coll., 1989; LLD (hon.), Clark Atlanta U., 1989. Chmn. bd. Atlanta Jour.-Constn.; Am. amb. to Belgium, 1977-81. Bd. dirs. Cox Enterprises, Inc. Bd. dirs. Atlanta Arts Alliance, High Mus. Art, Cmtys. in Schs., MacDowell Colony, Forward Arts Found., Emory Mus. Art and Archaeology, N.Y. Bot. Garden, Coun. Am. Ambs., Chmn.'s Coun., Met. Mus. Art, Fr.-Am. Found.; trustee Mus. Modern Art, Carter Ctr.; mem. internat. coun. Mus. Modern Art; mem. nat. com. Whitney Mus. Am. Art. Decorated Legion of Hon. (France). Mem. Coun. Fgn. Rels. Office: 6205 Peachtree Dunwoody Rd Atlanta GA 30328

CHAMBERS, AUDLEY C., music historian, educator, researcher; s. H. Chambers. Diploma in structural engring., South London Coll. Structural Engring., 1973—80; BSc in music edn., Oakwood Coll., 1981—86; MA in music history, Ohio State U., 1986—88; PhD, Northwestern U., 1989—99. Vocal/choral K-12 (music edn.) Dept. Edn., 1986, vocal/choral (music edn.) North Am. Divsn. Office Edn., 1986. Grad. tchg. assoc. Ohio State U., Columbus, Ohio, 1986—88; asst. prof. (music and black studies) Coll. Wooster, Wooster, Ohio, 1988—89; grad. tchg. assoc. Northwestern U., Evanston, Ill., 1989—94; vis. instr. music Columbia Coll., Chicago, 1990—90; asst. prof. music history and lit. Oakwood Coll., Huntsville, Ala., 1994—2003, assoc. prof. music history and lit., 2000—, chairperson dept. music, 2004—. Freelance music critiic Huntsville Times, Ala., 1999—2000; freelance music critic Decature Concert Assn./ Dectur Daily, Ala., 2000—04. Contbr. audio cassette The Aeolians, Live: A Centennial Celebration; musician: (Oakwood Coll. video cassette) Oakwood College: A Centennial of Service. Bd. mem. Huntsville Youth Symphony Orch., 1995—98. Grantee Faculty Retraining Grant, UNCF, 1999. Mem.: Hymn Soc., Soc. Am. Music, Internat. Adventist Music Soc., Ctr. Black Music Rsch., Am. Musicological Soc., Coll. Music Soc. Achievements include research in Frederic H. Cowen (1852-1935): Reception History of His songs for voice and Piano. Avocations: fell walking, hiking, camping, badminton, gourmet vegan cuisine.

CHAMBERS, CHARLES MACKAY, academic administrator, lawyer, consultant; b. Hampton, Va., June 22, 1941; s. Charles McKay and Ruth Ellanora (Wallach) C.; m. Barbara Mae Fromm, June 9, 1962; children: Charles M., Catherine M., Christina M., Carleton M. BS, U. Ala., 1962, MS, 1963, PhD, 1964; JD, George Washington U., 1976. Bar: Va. 1977, D.C. 1978, U.S. Patent and Trademark Office, 1978, U.S. Supreme Ct. 1980, U.S. Dist. Ct. D.C. 1985, U.S. Ct. Appeals (D.C. cir.) 1987, U.S. Dist. Ct. (ea. dist.) Va. 1988, U.S. Ct. Appeals D.C., 1987, U.S. Ct. Appeals (4th cir.) 1990, Mich. 1994; cert. comml. pilot, multiengine, land and instrument. Aerospace engr. NASA, Huntsville, Ala., 1962-63; rsch., teaching asst. U. Ala. Rsch. Inst., Huntsville, Ala., 1963-64; research fellow NASA, Cambridge, Mass., 1964-65; assoc. prof. U. Ala., Tuscaloosa, 1965-69; mng. dir. Univ. Assocs., Washington, 1969-72; prof., assoc. dean George Washington U., Washington, 1972-77; v.p., gen. counsel Council on Postsecondary Accreditation, Washington, 1977-83; exec. dir. Am. Inst. Biol. Sci., Washington, 1983-87; pres. Am. Found. Biol. Scis., Washington, 1987-93, Lawrence Tech. U., Southfield, Mich., 1993—. Cons., evaluator, accreditation rev. coun. commn. on instns. of higher edn. Noth Ctrl. Assn. Colls. and Schs., Chgo.; bd. dirs. Automation Alley, Mich. Sci. and Math. Alliance, Mich. Small Aircraft Transp. Sys. Author: (with others) Understanding Accreditation, 1983; pub. BioScience; contbr. chpts. to books. Mem. Diocesan Adv. Coun., Arlington, Va., 1978-84, Fairfax County (Va.) Dem. Com., 1979-95; judge No. Va. Sci. Fair, 1976—; trustee, sec. Southeastern U., Washington, 1983-87; trustee BIOSIS, Inc., Phila. and London, 1991-93; mem. Oakland County (Mich.) Workforce Devel. Bd., 1996—; bd. dirs. Automation Alley, 1999—, Detroit area coun. Boy Scouts Am. Recipient Citizenship award Am. Legion, 1959, Olive Branch award Editors and Writers Com., N.Y.C., 1986, Horace H. Rackham award Engring. Soc. Detroit, 2004; fellow NSF, 1964. Fellow AAAS; mem. ABA, AAUP, Am. Assn. Univ. Adminstrs. (pres. 1984-85), Engring. and Sci. Devel. Found. (bd. dirs., pres. 1996-2000, fellow Engring. Soc. 1997), Am. Coun. Edn. (bus. and higher edn. forum), Soc. Automotive Engrs., Nat. Soc. Black Engrs. (hon.), ESD-The Engring. Soc. (bd. dirs. 1999—), Assn. Ind. Colls. and Univs. Mich., Mich. Small Aircraft Transp. Program, Detroit Regional C. of C. (bd. dirs.), Circumnavigators Club, Detroit Econ. Club (bd. dirs.), Detroit Athletic Club, Cosmos Club, Capitol Hill Club, Phi Beta Kappa, Sigma Xi, Tau Beta Pi. Roman Catholic. Avocation: flying. Office: Lawrence Tech U 21000 W 10 Mile Rd Ste M351 Southfield MI 48075-1058 Personal E-mail: mail@charleschambers.com.

CHAMBERS, CLYTIA MONTLLOR, retired public relations consultant; b. Rochester, NY, Oct. 23, 1922; d. Anthony and Marie (Bambace) Capraro; m. Joseph John Montllor, July 2, 1941 (div. 1958); children: Michele, Thomas, Clytia; m. Robert Chambers, May 28, 1965. BA, Barnard Coll., N.Y.C., 1942; Licence en droit, Faculte de Droit, U. Lyon, France, 1948; MA, Howard U., Washington, 1958. Assoc. dir. dept. rsch. Coun. for Fin. Aid to Edn., N.Y.C., 1958-60; asst. to v.p. indsl. rels. Sinclair Oil Corp., N.Y.C., 1961-65; writer pub. rels. dept. Am. Oil Co., Chgo., 1965-67; dir. editorial svcs., v.p. Hill & Knowlton Inc., N.Y.C., 1967-77, sr. v.p., dir. spl. svcs. L.A., 1977-90, sr. cons., 1990—. Cons. and trustee Children's Inst. Internat., L.A., 1988-93. Co-author: The News Twisters, 1971; editor: Critical Issues in Public Relations, 1975. Mem.: Calif. Rare Fruit Growers (editor Fruit Gardener 1979—2000, editor emerita 2000—). Home: 11439 Laurelcrest Dr Studio City CA 91604-3872 Personal E-mail: clytia@sbcglobal.net.

CHAMBERS, CURTIS ALLEN, clergyman, church communications executive; b. Damascus, Ohio, Sept. 24, 1924; s. Binford Vincent and Margaret Esther (Patterson) C.; m. Anna June Winn, Aug. 26, 1946; children: David Lloyd, Curtis Allen II, Deborah Ann, Charles Cloyde. Th.B., Malone Coll., 1946; AB, Ind. Wesleyan U., 1947; B.D., Asbury Theol. Sem., 1950; postgrad., Oberlin Grad. Sch. Theology, 1951-53; S.T.M., Temple U., 1955, S.T.D., 1960; D.D. (hon.), Lebanon Valley Coll., 1967. Ordained to ministry Evang. United Brethren Ch., 1954. Pastor 1st Ch., Cleve., 1951-53, Rockville Ch., Harrisburg, Pa., 1953-59; editor adult pubs. Evang. United Brethren Ch., 1959-65; assoc. editor Ch. and Home mag., Dayton, Ohio, 1963-66, editor, 1967-69; asst. editorial dir. Together and Christian Advocate, Meth. Pub. House, Park Ridge, Ill., 1969; editor Together mag., 1969-73; acting editorial dir. gen. periodicals United Meth. Ch., 1971-72, editorial dir., 1972-73; gen. sec. United Meth. Communications, 1973-84; gen. mgr. Alternate View Network, 1984-85; minister edn. and communication First United Meth. Ch., Shreveport, La., 1985-87, minister pastoral care and communication, 1987-88; minister program and communication St. Paul's United Meth. Ch., Monroe, La., 1988-90; religious communication cons. Nashville, 1990—; assoc. pastor Andrew Price United Meth. Ch., Nashville, 1991-94. Book editor Evang. United Brethren Ch., 1965-68; co-editor Plan of Union, United Meth. Ch., 1965-68, Plan of Union, United Meth. Ch. (Book of Discipline), 1968, chmn. staff com. long range planning, 1969-72, mem. commn. on ch. union, 1965-68; dir. radio-TV relations gen. confs. Evang. United Brethren Ch., 1958, 62, 66, United Meth. Ch., 1966, 68; Chmn. commn. on ednl. media Nat. Council Chs., 1965-66, chmn. com. on audio visual and broadcast edn., 1962-65, exec. com. broadcasting and film commn., chmn. communications commn., 1975-78, v.p., 1975-78; chmn. Religious Communications Congress, 1980; named 1 of 12 editors sent to Middle East on fact-finding trip, 1969 Contbr. articles to religious lit. Served as capt. (chaplain) CAP, 1960-65. Recipient Distinguished Alumni award Malone Coll., 1967, 92, Alumni of Year, 1978, Distinguished Alumni award Goshen High Sch. Alumni Assn., 1992; named to Communicators Hall of Fame United Meth. Assn. Communicators, 1992. Mem. Aircraft Owners and Pilots Assn., United Meth. Assn. Communicators (v.p. 1968-72, Communicators' Hall of Fame 1992), World

Assn. Christian Communications (central com., chmn. Jour. editorial bd. 1975-82, chmn. periodical devel. com., exec. com., sec. 1978-82), Asso. Ch. Press (hon. life), Religious Pub. Relations Council. Clubs: Chgo. Press (Dayton), Torch (Dayton). Home: Westminster Village 1120 E Davis Dr Apt 423 Terre Haute IN 47802-4067 Office Phone: 812-238-8516. Personal E-mail: curtisa@joimail.com. *When I was young I thought that anything was possible for me and that I had a long, long time to achieve it. With maturity I have come to a recognition of mortality, finitude, a limitation of time and opportunity. Thus my life has taught me three things: 1) Choose the best. Life is too precious to squander it on the second rate. 2) Live for others. The quality of one's life is enhanced rather than diminished as one shares himself/herself with others. 3) Fulfill your dreams. Tomorrow may never come; act now so that life's opportunities may not be lost forever.*

CHAMBERS, CYNTHIA ANN, retired educator; d. Gloria Blanche and William David Powell; m. James Dennis Chambers, Oct. 14, 1982; stepchildren: Glenda June Evans, James Dennis Chambers Jr. children: Jennifer Lynn, Heather Lee. BS in Bus. Mgmt., U. Md., 1980; MS in Nat. Security Affairs, Georgetown U., 1991. Maj., asst .prof., exec. officer U.S. Mil. Acad., West Point, NY, 1994—97; tchr. El Paso Ind. Sch. Dist., Tex., 1997—99; asst. dist. mgr. H&R Block, Fort Worth, 1999—2000; grad. tchg. asst. U. Tex., Arlington, 2001—04. Co-chairwomen U. Tex. Webb Lectures, Arlington, 2002—03. Vol. Goodfellows Fund, Ft. Worth, 2002—04. Maj. U.S. Army, 1974—97. Decorated Legion of Merit U.S. Army; recipient Va. Garrett Cartographic Hist award, 2002, Univ. scholar Pres. Convocation for Acad. Excellence, U. Tex., Arlington, 2005; fellow, 2005. Avocations: travel, reading, walking tours, needlecrafts.

CHAMBERS, DONALD ARTHUR, biochemistry and molecular medicine educator; b. N.Y.C., Sept. 24, 1936; AB, Columbia U., 1959, PhD, 1972. Rsch. biochemist dept. surgery Harvard Med. Sch./Mass. Gen. Hosp., Boston, 1961-66; rsch. fellow in hematology dept. surgery Harvard Med. Sch./Beth Israel Hosp., Boston, 1967-68; faculty fellow in chem. biology Columbia U., N.Y.C., 1969-71; asst. rsch. biochemist Ctr. for Med. Genetics dept. medicine U. Calif. Med. Ctr., San Francisco, 1972-74, lectr. in biochemistry and biophysics, 1972-74, asst. prof. molecular biology and biochemistry, 1974-75; asst. prof. biol. chemistry and dermatology U. Mich., Ann Arbor, 1975-79, assoc. prof. biol. chemistry, 1979; prof. molecular biology U. Ill., Chgo., 1979—, prof. biol. chemistry, 1980—, rsch. prof. dermatology, 1981—, prof. biol. psychiatry, 1996. Assoc. mem. Dental Rsch. Inst. U. Mich., 1978-79, adj. rsch. investigator Dept. Biol. Chemistry, 1979—; dir. Ctr. for Molecular Biology of Oral Disease, U. Ill., Chgo., 1979—, interim head dept. biochemistry, 1985, head dept. biochemistry, 1986—; vis. scholar Green Coll., Oxford U., 1989-93, hon. vis. fellow, 1993—; sr. rsch. assoc. Wellcome Unit History of Medicine, Oxford. 2000--; fellow Honors Coll., 1985—, Phi Kappa Phi lectr., 1991, Sigma Xi lectr., 2001; nat. action com. Am. Assn. Dental Rsch., 1981—; study sect. rev. NIH, 1983-86, 92, 98—. Mem. editl. bd.: Perspectives in Biology and Medicine. Recipient James Howard McGregor prize Columbia U., 1971; named Inventor of Yr., U. Ill., 1990; fellow in hematology NIH, 1967-68, fellow in chem. biology, 1969-71; Rsch. grantee NIH, Am. Cancer Soc., Office of Naval Rsch.,1986—, Helene Curtis, Inc., 1988—, Tng. grantee NIH-NIGMS, 1975-79, NIH-NIAMDD, 1976-79, 77-80, NIH-NIDR-NIAMDD, 1980—, NIH-NCI, 1982-88, NIH-NIDCR, 2003-, NIH-NIAID, 2003-. Mem. AAAS, Am. Assn. Med. Colls., Am. Assn. Immunology, Am. Chem. Soc., Am. Fedn. Clin. Rsch., Am. Soc. Biol. Chemistry, Am. Soc. Cell Biology, Am. Soc. Microbiology, Internat. Assn. Dental Rsch. (com. on rsch. progress 1982-85, chmn. 1984-85, chmn. grad. tng. forum com. exptl. pathology sect. 1983), Assn. Dept. Chmn. Biol. Chemistry, Chgo. Assn. Immunologists, N.Y. Acad. Scis. (organizer meeting The Double Helix, 40 Yrs. 1993), Royal Soc. Medicine, Soc. Investigative Dermatology, Oxford Med. Alumni Assn. (N.Am. rep. 2000—), Green Coll. Oxford Soc. (N.Am. rep. 2000—), Athenaeum Club London, Phi Kappa Phi, Sigma Xi (NIDCR 1998, spl. emphisii panel), Sigma Xi (pres.-elect 2000, pres. 2001), Oxford Med. Alumni (N.Am Sec. 2001-). Achievements include patents (U.S., Can.) for method of determining periodontal disease, (with other) method of quantifying aspartate amino transferase in periodontal disease; research in role of cyclic nucleotides, prostaglandins, hormones and other regulatory factors in the regulation of cell function, proliferation and differentiation, in molecular medicine in neural-immune interactions, the regulatory mechanisms of host-microbial interactions, in the history and devel. of concepts in the bio-med. scis. Office: U Ill Coll Med Dept Biochemistry 1819 W Polk St # C 536 Chicago IL 60612-7331 also: Ctr Molecular Biol Oral Diseases 801 S Paulina St # C 860 Chicago IL 60612-7210 Office Phone: 312-996-1294. E-mail: donc@uic.edu.

CHAMBERS, EDWARD LACEY, JR., lawyer; b. High Point, N.C., July 28, 1946; s. Edward Lacey and Vera Elizabeth (Bailey) C.; m. Mary Ellen Atkins, Sept. 21, 1969 (div. July 1989); 1 child, Angela Marie (dec.); m. Jo Ann Wilson, July 24, 1993. BS, N.C. State U., 1968; JD, Coll. William and Mary, 1974. Bar: Va. 1974. Process engr. Allied Chem. Corp., Balt., 1968, 71; atty. Michalos & Overman, Newport News, Va., 1974-78, Schultz & Chambers, Yorktown, Va., 1978-80, Smiley & Chambers, Yorktown, Va., 1980-95; pvt. practice Yorktown, Va., 1995—. Bd. dirs., pres. March of Dimes, Virginia Beach, Va., 1981-95; mem. numerous bds. and coms. With U.S. Army, 1968-70. Named to Hall of Fame, March of Dimes, 1996. Mem. Va. State Bar (coun. 1989-96, numerous coms.). Avocation: golf. Home: 114 Pebble Beach Ln Williamsburg VA 23185 Office: 6021 George Washington Mem Hwy Yorktown VA 23692-2108

CHAMBERS, ELENORA STRASEL, artist; b. Strassel, Oreg. d. Augustine George and Frieda Rose (Westermann) Strasel; m. Edward Lucas Chambers, Oct. 9, 1954; children: Robert, Margaret L. BA, Marylhurst (Oreg.) Univ., 1942; student, Portland Art Mus. Sch., U. Miami, Fla., Fla. Internat. U. One person shows include Mirell Gallery, Coconut grove, Fla., 1961, Miami Mus. Modern Art, 1965, 80 Washington Sq. E., N.Y.C., 1983; Kendall Campus Art Gall., Miami, 1992, group exhbns. include Ringling Mus. Sarasota, Fla., 1956, Norton Gallery, West Palm Beach, 1956, Lowe Art Mus., Miami (award winner), 1957, 1976, Soc. of Four Arts, Palm Beach, 1958, 61, 62, 65, 67, 72, 74, 77, 81, Ft. Lauderdale Mus. Arts (award winner), 1964, 65, Profl. Women Artists, Lowe Art Mus., Miami, 1976, Mus. of Arts and Scis., Daytona Beach, Fla., 1979, Met. Dade County Coun. of Arts and scis., Miami, 1979, Lowe Levinson Gallery, Miami Beach, 1981, North Miami Mus. and Art Ctr., 1987, Metro-Dade Cultural Ctr., Miami, 1990, Mus. Contemporary Art, 1995, House Art Gallery, N.Y., 1996, Ambrosino Gallery, Miami, 1997, Ambrosino Gallery, Miami, 1998, Robert Hittel, Ft. Lauderdale, 1998, Dorsch Gallery, Miami, 1999, Kendall Campus Art Gallery, Miami, 2000, Snitzer Gallery, Miami, 2002; works in permanent collections Miami Mus. Modern Art, Hopkins-Easton Assocs., Omni Internat., many pvt. collections. Recipient Beaux Art award Lowe Art Mus., 1957, Hortt Meml. award Ft. Lauderdale Mus. Arts, 1964, Atwater Kent award 29th Ann. Exhbn. Contemporary Am. Paintings, Soc. Four Arts, 1967, 39th Ann. exhbn., 1977. Home: 5790 SW 51st Ter Miami FL 33155-6324

CHAMBERS, GLENN DARRELL, film company executive, art director; b. Butler, Mo., June 14, 1936; s. E. Glenn and Fern M. (Woods) C.; m. Marilyn Janell Henry, Aug. 29, 1959 (div. Jan. 1980); children: James D. (dec.), Russell G., Lindell C.; m. Jeannie Bay Erwin, Feb. 27, 1980; stepchildren: Robert Roemer, Matthew Roemer. BS, Ctrl. Mo. State U., 1958; MA, U. Mo.-Columbia, 1961; DSc (hon.) (hon.), Ctrl. Mo. State U., 2001. Area mgr. Mo. Dept. Conservation, Jefferson City, 1961-62, research biologist, 1962-69, biologist, photographer, 1969-79; regional dir. Ducks Unltd., Columbia, Mo., 1979-83, wildlife photographer, 1984-88; pres. Niska Art, Inc., Columbia, Mo., 1984—, Paddlefoot Prodns., Inc., 1994—. Motion picture specialist Mo. Dept. Conservation, 1988-95; exec. v.p. Mo. Bird Obs., 1988; freelance cinematographer, 1995—. Films include: (with Charles and Elizabeth Schwartz) Return of the Wild Turkey (2d place award Outdoor Writers Assn. Am.), 1971, The Show-Me Hunter (2d place award Outdoor Writers Assn. Am.), 1972, Wild Chorus: The Story of the Canada Goose (1st place award Outdoor Writers Assn. Am.), 1974, (Best Motion Picture award Wildlife Soc.), 1974; More Than Trees: Ecology of the Forest (2d place award Forestry Film Festival, 1st place award Outdoor Writers Assn. Am.), 1977, It's Your Choice, 1990 (Teddy Roosevelt award Mich. Outdoor Writers Assn.), Forests for the Future, 1991 (Teddy Roosevelt award Mich. Outdoor Writers Assn.), Back to the Wild, 1998 (3 TV Emmy awards); prodr. Otter Chaos, Nat. Geog. TV, 2000; tech. articles to Jour. Wildlife Mgmt., 1961-77; winner 1984-85 Mo. Waterfowl Stamp Design Contest; recipient TV Emmy award for Best Non-News Feature Glenn and the Geese, 1990, Where Eagles Soar, 1995 (2d Place award Assn. for Conservation Info.), Furbearers of Mo., 1997. Dist. chmn. Boonslick dist. Boy Scouts Am., 2001—04, exec. bd. Boonslick dist., 2004—. Recipient Outstanding Alumni award, U. Mo., 2004. Mem.: Mo. Conservation Heritage Found. (bd. dirs. 1990—), Conservation Fedn. Mo. (bd. dirs. 1998—, Conservationist of Yr. award 2001, Lifetime Achievement award 2002), Wildlife Soc. (E. Sidney Stephens award 1990). Democrat. Baptist. Home: 807 Cornell Columbia MO 65203-1828

CHAMBERS, HENRY GEORGE, orthopedic surgeon; b. Portsmouth, Va., June 22, 1956; s. Walter Charles and Teresa Frances (Fernandez) C.; m. Jill Annette Swanson, June 10, 1978; children: Sean Michael, Reid Christopher. BA summa cum laude in Biochemistry, U. Colo., 1978; MD, Tulane U. Sch. Medicine, 1982. Diplomate Am. Bd. Orthop. Surgery. Commd. 2d lt. U.S. Army, 1978, advanced through grades to maj., 1988; intern Fitzsimmons Army Med. Ctr., Aurora, Colo., 1982-83; orthopaedic surgery resident Brooke Army Med. Ctr., Ft. Sam Houston, Tex., 1983-87, chief resident, 1986-87, staff orthopaedic surgeon to asst. residency program dir., 1987-89, asst. chief surgeon orthopaedic surgery svc., 1990-92; staff orthopaedic surgeon DeWitt Army Hosp., Ft. Belvoir, Va., 1987; pediatric orthopaedic fellow San Diego Children's Hosp., 1989-90; asst. prof. surgery Uniformed Svcs. U. Health Scis., Bethesda, Md., 1987—; asst. program dir. Brooke Army Med. Ctr. Orthopaedic Surgery, 1987-92; assoc. prof. U. Calif.-San Diego Med. Ctr., 1989—; pvt. practice San Diego, 1992—; chmn. dept. orthopedic surgery San Diego Children's Hosp., 1997—2001, chief of staff, 2004—; med. dir. Motion Analysis Lab. Co-author: Long Distance Runner's Guide to Training, 1983, The Pediatric Spine—Principles and Practice, 2000, Fractures in Children, 2001; contbr. various articles to profl. jours. Physician, St. Vincent de Paul Clinic for Homeless, San Diego, 1989—; v.p. United Cerebral Palsy. Recipient Comdrs. award for outstanding rsch., Brooke Army Med. Ctr., 1987. Fellow: Am. Orthop. Assn., We. Orthop. Assn., Am. Acad. Orthop. Surgeons, Orthop. Rsch. Soc., Am. Acad. Pediats., Acad. Cerebral Palsy Devel. Medicine (treas.), Pediat. Orthop. Soc. N.Am., Acad. Orthop. Soc.; mem.: Union Concerned Scientist, Physicians for Social Responsibility, Handgun Control, Phi Beta Kappa. Democrat. Unitarian Universalist. Avocations: weightlifting, golf, bicycling. Home: 5458 Sandburg Ave San Diego CA 92122-4128 Office Phone: 858-966-6798. Business E-Mail: hchambers@chsd.org.

CHAMBERS, IMA LOUISE, secretarial skills educator, secretary; b. Ft. Worth, July 30, 1932; d. Thurman and Pearl (Linehan) Tyson; m. Billy Joe Chambers, Aug. 22, 1954; children: Joseph, Marc, Carol. BS, Tex. Wesleyan Coll., 1953; MEd, U. Mich., 1980. Cert. secondary and vocat. tchr., Mich., Tex., Wis., Ariz., Ohio. Travel counselor Am. Automobile Assn., Ft. Worth, 1949-55; stenographer Calif. Dept. Health, Berkeley, 1955-56; elem. tchr. Decoto (Calif.) Pub. Schs., 1956-58; shorthand tchr. Genoa Sch. Dist., Clay Ctr., Ohio, 1964-65; bus. tchr. New Miami H.S., Hamilton, Ohio, 1966-73, Genesee Area Vocat. Sch., Flint, Mich., 1974-81, Cisco H.S., Tex., 1985-88; sec. Pan Am. Oil Corp., Ft. Worth, 1958-60, Kelly Temp. Svcs., Inc., Milw., 1988-90; tchr. Bisbee H.S., Ariz., 1991—96; acctg. clk. Aegan Ins. Co., Fort Worth, 2000—03. Ch. tchr. So. Bapt. Ch., Tex., Calif., Ohio, Mich., Minn., Wis., 1956—, home missionary, S.E. Ariz., 1991-96. Mem. NEA, AAUW (pres. 1988-89), Delta Kappa Gamma (treas. 1994-96), Alpha Chi. Home: 3621 Scranton Dr Fort Worth TX 76118-5535

CHAMBERS, JACK ALLEN, application developer, educator; b. Hamilton, Ohio; s. Glen S. and H. Edna C.; m. Ruth Coe; children: Melissa Ann, Wendy Colleen AB, U. Miami, 1954; MA, U. Cin., 1955; PhD, Mich. State U. Dir. computer ctr. Mansfield (Pa.) U., 1972-74; dir. computing and comms. Calif. State U., Fresno, 1974-86, Duquesne U., Pitts., 1986-89; exec. dir. computing and comms. Loyola Coll., Balt., 1989-90; planning and info. rsch. ctr. mgr. Fla. C.C., Jacksonville, 1990-99, inter. dir. Assessment and Cert. Ctrs., 1999—2004, dir. program devel. for instrnl. tech., 2004—05, dir. learning technologies and profl. devel., 2005—; exec. dir. Organ. Learning Svcs., 2005—. Co-author: (with others) (book) Computer Assisted Instruction: Its Use in the Classroom, 1983; (chpt.) Motivating Students for Lifetime Learning in New Directions in Education and Training Technology, 1985; author: chpt. in Facilitating Academic Software Development, 1988; editor: (books) Selected Papers Fifth InternatConference on College Teaching and Learning, 1994, Sixth Conference, 1995, Seventh Conference, 1996, Eighth Conference, 1997, Ninth Conference, 1998, Tenth Conference, 1999, Eleventh Conference, 2000, Twelfth Conference, 2001, Thirteenth Conference, 2002, Fourteenth Conference, 2003, Fifteenth Conference, 2004, Sixteenth Conf., 2005. Grantee: James McKeen Cattell Fund, Calif. State Dept. Edn., Calif. State Univ. System, NSF, FIPSE. Office: Fla CC at Jacksonville 501 W State St Jacksonville FL 32202-4086 Office Phone: 904-632-3231. E-mail: jchamber@fccj.edu.

CHAMBERS, JAY LEE, clinical psychologist; b. Providence, Ky., Apr. 7, 1923; s. Jay Lea and Anna Royston (Griggs) C.; m. Willa Marie Browning, June 1, 1952 (dec. Aug. 1994); children: Ann Marie, Carol Louise; m. Elizabeth T. Burnette, Dec. 29, 1995. BA, George Washington U., 1948; MA, U. Ky., 1952, PhD, 1954. Chmn. psychology dept. Muskingum Coll., New Concord, Ohio, 1954-56; dir. psychol. svcs. Eastern State Hosp., Williamsburg, Va., 1956-58; dir. Charles L. Mix Meml. Fund, Inc., Americus, Ga., 1958-64; dir. psychol. svcs. Ky. State Hosp., Danville, 1964-66; clin. psychologist Student Health Svcs. Fla. State U., Tallahassee, 1966-70; dir. Ctr. for Psychol. Svcs. Coll. William and Mary, Williamsburg, 1970-90; pres. Motivation Analysis, Lexington, Va., 1991—. Contbr. articles to profl. jours. Served with USMCR, 1942-46. Mem. Am. Psychol. Assn., Southeastern Psychol. Assn., So. Soc. for Philosophy and Psychology. Democrat. Home and Office: 160 Kendal Dr # 205 Lexington VA 24450-1786 Office Phone: 540-462-3874. E-mail: ibis@kalexres.kendal.org.

CHAMBERS, JOAN LOUISE, retired librarian, retired dean; b. Denver, Mar. 22, 1937; d. Joseph Harvey and Clara Elizabeth (Carleton) Baker; m. Donald Ray Chambers, Aug. 17, 1958 BA in English Lit., U. No. Colo., Greeley, 1958; MS in L.S., U. Calif.-Berkeley, 1970; MS in Systems Mgmt., U. So. Calif., 1985; cert., Coll. for Fin. Planning, 1989. Libr. U. Nev., Reno, 1970-79; asst. univ. libr. U. Calif., San Diego, 1979-81, univ. libr. Riverside, 1981—85; dean librs., prof. Colo. State U., Ft. Collins, 1985-97, emeritus dean and prof., 1997—. Mgmt. intern Duke U. Libr., Durham, N.C., 1978-79; sr. fellow UCLA Summer, 1982; cons. tng. program Assn. of Rsch. Libraries, Washington, 1981; libr. cons. Calif. State U., Sacramento, 1982-83, U. Wyo., 1985-86, 94-95, U. Nebr., 1991-92, Calif. State U. System, 1993-94, Univ. No. Ariz., 1994-95. Contbr. articles to profl. jours., chpts. to books. Bd. dirs. Consumers Union, 1996—. U. Calif. instl. improvement grantee, 1980-81; State of Nev. grantee, 1976, ARL grantee, 1983-84. Mem.: PEO, Colo. Mountain Club, Phi Kappa Phi, Kappa Delta Phi, Phi Lambda Theta, Beta Phi Mu. Avocations: hiking, snow shoeing, skiing, bicycling, tennis. Home and Office: PO Box 1477 Edwards CO 81632-1477 E-mail: chambers@vail.net.

CHAMBERS, JOHN THOMAS, computer systems network executive; b. Cleve., Aug. 23, 1949; s. June and John Chambers; m. Elaine Prater, 1974; 2 children. BS, BA, W.Va. U., 1971, JD, 1974; MBA, Ind. U., 1975. Mktg. mgr. IBM, 1976—82; v.p. central U.S. ops. Wang Laboratories, 1983—87, sr. v.p., Americas/Asia/Pacific ops., 1987—89, sr. v.p., U.S. ops., 1989—90; sr. v.p. worldwide ops. Cisco Sys., Inc., San Jose, Calif., 1991-94, exec. v.p., 1994-95, pres., CEO, 1995—. Vice chmn. Nat. Infrastructure adv. coun., 2002—; Served on Bill Clinton Trade Policy com.; bd. dirs. Cisco Sys. Inc., 1993—, Clarify, Inc., San Jose, 1995—96, Arbor Software, Sunnyvale, Calif., 1995—96. Recipient Woodrow Wilson Award for corp. Citizenship, Woodrow Wilson Center for internat. ctr. for Scholars of the Smithsonian inst., Smithsonian Lifetime Achievement Award, Smithsonian, Presidential Award, Ron Brown Award for corp. Leadership, The bus coun., Frederick D. Patterson Award, United Negro coll. Fund. Office: Cisco Sys Inc 170 W Tasman Dr Bldg 10 San Jose CA 95134-1706 E-mail: jochambe@cisco.com.

CHAMBERS, JOHNNIE LOIS (TUCKER CHAMBERS), elementary school educator, rancher; b. Crocket County, Tex., Sept. 28, 1929; d. Robert Leo and Lois K. (Slaughter) Tucker; m. R. Boyd Chambers; children: Theresa A., Glyn Robert, Boyd James, John Trox. EdB, Sul Ross State U., Alpine, Tex., 1971. Tchr. 1st and 2d grades Candelaria (Tex.) Elem. Sch., 1971-73; head tchr. K-8 Ruidosa (Tex.) Elem. Sch., 1973-77, Presidio Ind. Sch. Dist. at Candelaria Elem. Sch., 1977-91, tchr. 2d and 3d grades, 1991-93, tchr. pre-kindergarten, kindergarten and 1st grade, 1993-98; acting prin. Candelaria Elem. and Jr. High, 1995-98, head tchr. pre-K to 8th grades, 1996-98, tchr. pre-K, kindergarten, 1st and 2d grades, 1996—99; tchr. pre-K-6 Redford (Tex.) Elem. Sch., 2001, tchr., 2001—. Mem. sight-base decision making, Presidio, 1991-94; mem. Chihuahuan Desert Rsch. Inst., Alpine, 1982-94. Leader Boy Scouts Am., Ruidosa and Candelaria, 1973-91, Cub Scout leader, 1973-91; chpt. mem. Sheriffs Assn. Tex., Austin, 1980; bd. dirs. Big Bend Regional Hosp. Dist., 2001—; mem. Ctr. for Big Bend Studies. Recipient awards Boy Scouts Am., 1969, 83, Litter Gitter award, 1994-95. Mem. Tex. State Tchrs. Assn., Tex. Fedn. Rep. Women, The Archaeol. Conservancy, Phi Alpha Theta. Avocations: hiking, camping, anthropologic digs, cave exploring, cooking. Home: 99 Retirement Cir Marfa TX 79843 Personal E-mail: johnnieltc@yahoo.com. Business E-Mail: johnnieltc@brooksdata.net.

CHAMBERS, JULIUS LEVONNE, lawyer; b. Montgomery County, N.C., Oct. 6, 1936; BA, N.C. Cen. U., 1958; MA, U. Mich., 1959; LLB, U. N.C., 1962; LLM, Columbia U., 1963. Bar: N.C. 1962, N.Y. 1986. Ptnr. Chambers, Ferguson, Stein, Chambers, Adkins, Gresham & Sumter, Charlotte, NC, 1964-84; dir., counsel NAACP Legal Def. and Ednl. Fund, N.Y.C., 1984-92; chancellor N.C. Ctrl. U., Durham, 1993-2000; with Ferguson, Stein, Wallas, Adkins, Gresham & Sumter, Charlotte, 2000—. Former trustee N.J. State Bd. Higher Edn.; former bd. visitors Harvard U., Columbia U. Law Sch.; former trustee U. Pa., mem. bd. overseers Law Sch.; former bd. dirs. Children's Def. Fund, Legal Aid Soc. N.Y. Mem. ABA (bd. editors ABA jour.), N.C. Bar Assn., Mecklenburg County Bar Assn., N.Y. State Bar Assn., Assn. of Bar of City of N.Y., Nat. Bar Assn., Assn. Black Lawyers N.C., Order of Coif, Order of Golden Fleece, Phi Alpha Theta. Office: Ferguson Stein Wallas Adkins Gresham & Sumter 741 Kenilworth Ave Ste 300 Charlotte NC 28204 Office Phone: 704-375-8461. E-mail: jchamb1230@aol.com.

CHAMBERS, KENTON LEE, botany educator; b. L.A., Sept. 27, 1929; s. Maynard Macy and Edna Georgia (Miller) C.; m. Henrietta Laing, June 21, 1958; children: Elaine Patricia, David Macy. AB with highest honors, Whittier Coll., 1950; PhD (NSF fellow), Stanford U., 1955. Instr. biol. scis. Stanford (Calif.) U., 1954-55; instr. botany, asst. prof. Yale U., New Haven, Conn., 1956-60; assoc. prof., prof. botany Oreg. State U., Corvallis, 1960-90, prof. emeritus, 1991—. Curator Herbarium, 1960-90; program dir. systematic biology NSF, Washington, 1967-68. Contbr. articles in field to profl. jours. Fellow AAAS; mem. Bot. Soc. Am. (Merit award 1990), Am. Soc. Plant Taxonomists, Am. Inst. Biol. Scis., Calif. Bot. Soc. Home: 4761 SW Hollyhock Cir Corvallis OR 97333-1385 Office: Oreg State U Herbarium Botany Dept Corvallis OR 97331-2902 E-mail: chamberk@science.oregonstate.edu.

CHAMBERS, LETITIA PEARL CAROLINE, consulting firm executive; b. Alva, Okla., Feb. 1, 1943; d. E. Wade and Anita (Sims) Chambers; m. Stephen Morelock, Mar. 1964 (div. 1970); 1 child, Melissa. BA, U. Okla., 1965; MS, Okla. State U., 1971, EdD, 1973. Tchr. Oklahoma City Pub. Schs., 1965-70, adminstr., 1973-74; dir. fed. programs N.Mex. State Edn. Agy., Santa Fe, 1974-75; sr. analyst US Senate Budget Com., Washington, 1976-77; minority staff dir. US Senate Spl. Com. on Aging, Washington, 1978; staff dir. US Senate Com. on Labor & Human Resources, Washington, 1979-81; pres. Chambers Assocs., Inc., Washington, 1982—2001; U.S. rep. to the UN gen. assembly 51st Session, N.Y.C., 1996; exec. dir. N.Mex. Commn. on Higher Edn., Santa Fe, 2004—05; mng. dir. Navigant Cons., Washington, 2005—. Pres. Coalition of Publicly Traded Partnerships, Washington, 1987-2004; dir. Adams Nat. Bank, Washington, 1989-94; dir. Stratego Investments, Prague, Cech Republic, 1997-2000; commr. Western Interstate Commn. on Higher Edn., 2004-05. Author various senate reports, policy studies. Chief budget adv. Clinton/Gore Transition, 1992—93; trustee Inst. Am. Indian Arts and Culture, Santa Fe, 1997—; elder Chevy Chase (Md.) Presbyn. Ch., 1986—89; bd. visitors U. Okla., 1995—2002; bd. dirs., chair IAIA Found.; bd. dirs. Internat. Shakespeare Guild, 1998—, Ctr. for Nat. Policy, 1993—2002. Recipient Disting. Alumni award U. Okla., 1998. Mem. Coun. for Excellence in Govt. (bd. dirs. 1990-2003), Cosmos Club. Avocation: landscape gardening. Office: Navigant Consulting 1801 K St NW Washington DC 20006 Home: 2022 Foothills Rd Santa Fe NM 87505 Office Phone: 202-679-2661.

CHAMBERS, MARJORIE BELL, historian; b. N.Y.C., Mar. 11, 1923; d. Kenneth Carter and Katherine (Totman) Bell; m. William Hyland Chambers, Aug. 8, 1945; children: Lee Chambers-Schiller, William Bell, Leslie Chambers Trujillo, Kenneth Carter. AB cum laude, Mt. Holyoke Coll., South Hadley, Mass., 1943; MA, Cornell U., 1948; PhD, U. N.Mex., 1974; LLD honoris causa, Ctrl. Mich. U., 1977; LHD (hon.), Wilson Coll., 1980, Northern Michigan U., 1982. Staff asst. Am. Assn. UN, League of Nations Assn., N.Y.C., 1944-45; program specialist dept. rural sociology Cornell U., Ithaca, N.Y., 1945-46, rsch. asst. dept. speech and drama, 1946-48; substitute tchr. Los Alamos (N.Mex.) Pub. Schs., 1962-65; project historian U.S. AEC, Los Alamos, 1965-69; adj. prof. U. N.Mex., Los Alamos, 1970-76, 84-85; pres. Colo. Women's Coll., Denver, 1976-78; dean Union Inst. and U. Grad. Sch. Interdisciplinary Arts and Scis., Cin., 1979—82, mem. core faculty Grad. Sch., 1979—; interim pres. Colby-Sawyer Coll., New London, N.H., 1985-86. Vis. prof. Cameron U., Lawton, Okla., 1974; commr., vice-chair N.Mex. Commn. on Higher Edn., Santa Fe, 1987-91; dir. N.Mex. Endowment for Humanities, 1995-2002, sec.-treas. 2001-2002; mem. bd. dirs. Coun. Ind. Colls. and Univs., Santa Fe, 1991-2001; rep. Los Alamos County Labor Mgmt. Bd.; lectr. U. N.Mex., Albuquerque, 1986. Contbr. articles to profl. jours. Coun. treas. Sangre de Cristo Girl Scouts Am., 2002; chair Los Alamos County Coun., 1976, councilor, 1975-76, 79; Rep.candidate N.Mex. 3d Congl. Dist., 1982, lt. gov. N.Mex., 1986; chair Sec. of Navy's Advisor Bd. on Edn. and Tng., Washington and Pensacola, Fla., 1981-89; chair Citizen Bd. of U.S. Army Command and Gen. Staff Coll., Fort Leavenworth, Kans., 1989-1992; acting chair, vice-chair adminstrn. Pres. Carter's Com. for Women, Washington, 1977-80; chair Pres. Ford's Nat. Adv. Bd. on Women's Ednl. Programs, Washington, Los Alamos County Pers. Bd., 1985-90, mem. bd., 1983-90; mem. nat. adv. coun . U.S. SBA, 1990-92; mem. Los Alamos and N.Mex. Rep. Ctrl. com., 1982—; trustee Colby-Sawyer Coll., New London, N.H., 1980-89; pub. mem. U.S. Dept. State Fgn. Svc. selection bd., 1978; mem. U.S. del. UN Conf. Women, Copenhagen, 1980; bd. dirs. N.Mex. Endowment for the Humanities, 1997—. Recipient Teresa d'Avila award Coll. St. Teresa, Winona, Minn., 1978, Disting. Woman award U. N.Mex. Alumni Assn., Albuquerque, 1990, N.Mex. Disting. Pub. Svc. award Gov. and Awards Coun., Albuquerque, 1991, Zia award U. N.Mex. Alumni Assn., 2001; named Outstanding N.Mex. Woman Gov. and Com. on Status of Women, Albuquerque, 1988, 89, Lifetime Achievement award, 2003. Mem. AAUW (life, U.S. rep. coun. 1973-75, nat. pres. 1975-79, pres. Edn. Found.), DAR, Bus. and Profl. Women (Los Alamos parliamentarian and dist. parliamentarian 1991-93), Nat. Women's Polit. Caucus (gov. bd. conv., keynoter, vice-chair Rep. caucus 1971-89), Internat. Women's Forum (founding mem. Colo. forum), N.Mex. Hist. Soc. (pres.), Los Alamos Hist. Soc. (pres., Sangre de Cristo Girl Scouts "Woman of Distinction" 1996). Presbyterian. Avocations: figure skating, skiing, swimming, painting, public speaking.

CHAMBERS, MILTON WARREN, retired architect; b. L.A., Aug. 5, 1928; s. Joe S. and Barbara N. (Harris) C.; m. Elizabeth M. Smith, Nov. 27, 1949; children: Mark, Michael, Daniel, Matthew. Student, Coll. of Sequoias, 1948-49, Harvard U., 1990. Lic. architect, Calif., Nev., Colo., Hawaii, Mont.; cert. Nat. Coun. Archtl. Registration Bds. Apprentice architect Kastner &

Kastner Architects, Visalia, Calif., 1950-57; project architect Wurster, Bernardi & Emmons, Architects, San Francisco, 1958-63, Claude Oakland, Architect, 1964-65; chief architect Bank of Am., 1965-68; pres., owner Milton W. Chambers, Architect, San Rafael, 1969-82, The Chambers Group, Architects, Rancho Mirage, 1983—99. Architect, designer St. Margaret's Episcopal Church, 1988. Foreman Marin County Grand Jury, San Rafael, 1976; mem. Archtl. Design Rev. Bd., Rancho Mirage, 1986-99; trustee Marywood Sch., Rancho Mirage, 1990-99, Rep. Pub. Devel. Authority (pres. 2003-2005), Friends of Stonerose Eocene Era Fossil Site, Rep. (pres. 2004-). Cpl. U.S. Army, 1946-48, PTO, 50-51. Mem. AIA (pres. Calif. Desert chpt. 1986-87, 96&, dir. Calif. coun. 1989-90, 96—), Rotary Internat., Terra Linda Rotary Club (pres. 1975-76, dist. gov. 1993-94), Rancho Mirage Rotary Club (pres. 1986-87). Republican. Episcopalian. Avocation: playing the banjo and guitar. Mailing: PO Box 1235 Republic WA 99166

CHAMBERS, ROBERT ANDREW, neuroscientist, psychopharmacologist; b. Campbellsville, Ky., Apr. 18, 1969; s. Henry Forrest and Peggy Atkinson Chambers; m. Joanna Elizabeth Zell, Dec. 21, 2001; 1 child, Gabriel Forrest. BS, Ctr. Coll., Ky, 1991; MD, Duke U. Sch. of Medicine, NC, 1996. Bd.Cert., Am.Bd. Psychiatry and Neurology Am. Bd. of Psychiatry and Neurology, 2001. Residency, fellow in psychiatry and translational neuroscience Yale U. Sch. of Medicine, New Haven, 1996—2002, asst. prof. of psychiatry, 2002—03, Ind. U. Sch. of Medicine, Indpls., 2003—. Dir., lab. for translational neuroscience of dual diagnosis disorders Ind. U. Dept. of Psychiatry, Indpls., 2003—. Recipient Phi Beta Kappa, Ctr. Coll., 1990, Lustman award, Yale U. Dept. of Psychiatry, 1999, Health Emotions Rsch. Inst. Scholar, U. of Wis. Dept. of Psychiatry, 2001, Raymond E. Houk scholar in Schizophrenia Rsch., Ind. U., 2003, Future Leaders in Psychiatry, Emory U. Dept. of Psychiatry, 2004, Career Devel. award, Nat. Inst. on Drub Abuse, 2005; grantee NARSAD Young Investigator award, Nat. Alliance for Rsch. on Schizophrenia and Depression, 2001. Mem.: Soc. for Biol. Psychiatry, Soc. for Neuroscience, Am. Psychiat. Assn. Achievements include discovery of Discovered and characterized addiction vulnerability in an animal model of schizophrenia, leading to a new area of basic science research focused on animal modeling of addictions in mental illness; research in Introduced first distributed neurocircuit-based theory for understanding addictions comorbidity in schizophrenia (Biological Psychiatry, 2001); Introduced first comprehensive neurobiodevelopmental theory on addictions and adolescent vulnerability to substance use disorders (American Journal of Psychiatry, 2003); First to describe the learning and memory effects of adult apoptosis/neurogenesis in artifical neural networks capable of synaptic plasticity-mediated learning (Neuropsychopharmacology, 2004); First discription of the distributed neural substrates involved in impulsivity and adolescent neurodevelopment leading to pathological gambling (Journal of Gambling Studies, 2003). Office: Indiana Univ Sch Medicine 791 Union Dr Indianapolis IN 46220

CHAMBERS, ROBERT HUNTER, III, academic administrator, historian, educator; b. Winston-Salem, N.C., Oct. 24, 1939; s. Robert Hunter and Hildred (MacDonald) C.; m. Alice Louise Grant, Aug. 18, 1962 (div. 1995); children: Lisa, Grant. AB, Duke U., 1962; B.D., Yale U., 1965; PhD, Brown U., 1969. Asst. prof., dean Davenport Coll. Yale U., New Haven, 1969-74; vis. fellow Clare Coll., Cambridge U., Eng., 1972-73; prof., dean Coll. Arts and Scis. Bucknell U., Lewisburg, Pa., 1975-84; vis. scholar Doshisha U., Kyoto, 1982; pres., prof. English Western Md. Coll., Westminster, 1984—2000; sr. cons. Marts & Lundy, Inc., Gainesville, Fla., 2001—; provost, dean Trinity Coll., U. Melbourne, Australia, 2004—. Founding dir. Wellway Ctrs., Inc., Ft. Worth, 1984—88, WMC Devel. Corp., 1985—88; presdl. chmn. Centennial Conf., Md. and Pa., 1986, 1998—99; mem. segmental adv. com. State Bd. Higher Edn., Annapolis, Md., 1985—88; mem. internat. adv. coun. U. Buckingham, England; mem. cmty. bd. Carroll Co. Health Svcs., Inc., 1988—2000; assoc. fellow Davenport Coll., Yale U. Author, editor: Twentieth Century Interpretations of All the King's Men, 1977. Contbr. articles to profl. jours. Bd. dirs. Ind. Coll. Fund of Md., Balt.,1984—; mem. coun. on grad. edn. Brown U., 1989; mem. City of Westminster Mayoral Task Force, 1990; co-chair spl. gifts Am. Heart Assn.; mem. task force on assessment Nat. Assn. Ind. Colls. and Univs., 1991-92, mem. commn. on state rels., 1992-95; mem. Gov.'s Edn. Policy Transition Team, 1994-95; mem. Md. Citizens for Arts; bd. dir. Coun. of Ind. Colls., 1997-2000. Rockefeller Brothers fellow, 1962-63; Nat. Endowment for the Humanities grantee, 1978, U.S.-Japan Friendship Commn. grantee, 1982; recipient Balt. Regional Coun. Govts. award, 1989. Mem.: NCAA (pres. coun. 1999—2000)), MLA, Internat. Assn. Univ. Presidents, Coun. on Econ. Edn. in Md. (trustee 1), Am. Studies Assn., Md. Ind. Coll. and Univ. Assn. (bd. dirs. 1984—2000, exec. com. 1985—88, 1991—2000, budget com. 1985—89, 1991, chair 1994—98), Mid. States Assn. Colls. and Schs. (commr. 1985—91, exec. com. 1986—91, vice chair 1987—89, chair 1990), Higher Edn. Commn., The Japan Soc., Nat. Assn. Ind. Colls. and Univs. (policy com. 1998—2000), Center Club, Yale Club, Rotary (hon. 1990), Phi Beta Kappa Assocs., Phi Beta Kappa. Avocations: running, reading, travel. Office: Trinity Coll U Melbourne Royal Parade Parkville Victoria 3052 Australia Business E-Mail: bchambers@trinity.unimelb.edu.au.

CHAMBERS, ROBERT WILLIAM, business broker; b. Atlanta, Apr. 4, 1943; s. Robert William Chambers and Mary Emily (Martin) Nalley; m. Wendy Ann Treneer, Dec. 28, 1967 (div. 1979); 1 child, Robert William III. AB, Princeton U., 1965; MA, Indiana U., 1970, PhD, 1974. Assoc. instr. Ind. U., Bloomington, 1970-73; instr. Kans. State U., Manhattan, 1973-74; gen. mgr. Standard Cellulose Products Inc., Atlanta, 1974-75; mgr. sales, ops. Disposable Plastic Systems Inc., Marietta, Ga., 1975-77; asst. v.p., account exec. instl. sales Robinson-Humphrey Co. Inc., Atlanta, 1977-80; columnist, fin. reporter Atlanta Journal, 1980-81; account exec. Hill and Knowlton (J. Walter Thompson Group), Atlanta, 1981-83; sr. v.p., sales mgr. ea. divsn. Colonial Investment Svcs. Inc., Boston, 1983-90; sr. fin. cons. The Gwent Group, Atlanta, 1990-92; v.p., treas. Rabun Gap Film Corp., Atlanta, 1993—; dir. Bus. Svcs. Div. Porraro and Assocs., Atlanta, 1993-95; mgr. accts. divsn. Atlanta Rsch. and Trading, 1994-95; regional mktg. dir. Stephens, Inc., Atlanta, 1996-97; fin. reporter Atlanta-Jour.-Constn., 1997—99; COO The Resource Ctr., Atlanta, 2000; CEO Chambers Capital Adv., 2002—. Ga. correspondent The Economist, London, 1978-83, 99-2000; Am. Bankers Assn. fellowship, 1998; asst. prof. Kennesaw State U., 2005. Chair bd. Oglethorpe U. Art Mus., 1998-2004. Mem.: The Authors Guild, Soc. Colonial Wars, Nine O'Clocks Club (Atlanta), Piedmont Driving Club, Rotary. Episcopalian. Home: 335 Franklin Rd NE Atlanta GA 30342-2711 Personal E-mail: robcha@bellsouth.net.

CHAMBERS, THOMAS EDWARD, academic administrator, psychologist; b. Cleve., Aug. 1, 1934; s. James Clyde and Mary Celestine (Malone) C. BA, U. Notre Dame, 1956, MA, 1962, PhD, 1976; MA, Holy Cross Coll., 1961; DHL (hon.), U. Portland, 2003, King's Coll., 2004. Lic. counselor, Ohio, La. Dir. student residences U. Notre Dame, Ind., 1969-73, dir. student activities, 1973-74, asst. v.p. student affairs, 1974-76; v.p. acad. affairs Ursuline Coll., Cleve., 1976-87; pres. Our Lady of Holy Cross Coll., New Orleans, 1987—2003; provincial adminstrn.-provincial counselor Congregation of Holy Cross Ind. Province, 2003—. Founder Internat. Student Leadership Inst., 1968; mem. exec. com. Sta. WLAE-TV, New Orleans, 1987—; pres. Willwoods Cmty., 2003—. Editor: For Leaders Only, 1975. Mem. exec. com. Met. Area Com., New Orleans, 1987—; trustee Gilmour Acad., Cleve., 1978—, United Way; chmn. Boy Scouts Am.; bd. dirs. King's Coll., Wilkes-Barre, Pa., 1989—, St. Joseph Sem. Coll., Will Woods Cmty., New Orleans, 1998—. Recipient Nat. League Nursing award of Ohio Nat. League Nursing, 1986, Trustee award Cathedral High Sch., 1987. Mem. Am. Psychol. Assn., Am. Cath. Colls. and Univs., Plimsoll Club, Internat. House Club. Roman Catholic. Office: Willwoods Comty Ste 345 3330 N Causeway Blvd Metairie LA 70002 Office Phone: 504-830-3701. Business E-Mail: tchambers@willwood.org.

CHAMBERS, THOMAS JEFFERSON, state supreme court justice; b. Yakima, Wash., Oct. 11, 1943; s. Thomas J. and Doris May (Ellyson) C.; m. Judy Larene Cable, June 11, 1967; children: Jolie, Jana, Tommy. BA in Polit. Sci., Wash. State U., 1966; JD, U. Wash., 1969. Bar: Wash., U.S. Dist. Ct. (we. and ea. dists.) Wash. 1969. Assoc. Lycette, Diamond & Sylvester, Seattle, 1969-71, Barokas & Martin, Seattle, 1972; sole practice Seattle, 1972—2001; justice Wash. Supreme Ct., 2001—. Mem. congestion com. Wash. State Cts., 1984, King County Mandatory Arbitration Council, 1981-86, Damages Atty. Roundtable, 1983-86. Editorial adv. bd. Everday Law mag.; contbr. articles to profl. jours. Mem. jud. evaluation com. Mcpl. League, 1982; volunteer Internat. Smile Power Found.; hon. bd. mem. Rise n' Shine Found. Mem. Wash. State Trial Lawyers Assn. (pres. 1985-86, pres.-elect 1984-85, bd. govs. 1976—, various coms.), Am. Bd. Trial Advs. (past. pres. Wash. chpt.), Am. Trial Lawyers Assn. (past mem. bd. govs.), Wash. State Bar Assn. (pres. 1996-97). Avocation: flying airplanes. Office: PO Box 40929 Olympia WA 98504-0929

CHAMBERS, VIRGINIA ANNE, music educator; b. Middlesboro, Ky., Jan. 28, 1931; d. Jason C. and Virginia Claire (Dobyns) C. MusB, U. Louisville, 1952; MusM, Eastman Sch. Music, 1964; PhD, U. Mich., 1970. Gen. elem. music tchr. Oak Ridge Pub. Schs., 1952-63, Rochester (N.Y.) Sch. Dist., 1963-64; prof. music SUNY-Geneso, 1964-66, Ea. Mich. U., Ypsilanti, 1966-68, U. Wis., Madison, 1968-75, U. Toledo, 1975—; ret., 1997. V.p., cons. Tometic Assocs., Ltd., Buffalo, 1980—. Author: Words and Music: An Introduction to Music Literacy, 1976; Tometics: Reading Rhythm Patterns, 1979; Piano Accompaniments for A Nichol's Worth, Vols. 3 and 4, 1982; editor: A Nichol's Worth, Vols. 3 and 4, Reading Tonal Patterns, 1984, Basic Keyboard Accompaniments, 1986, Tometics: Music for the Classroom Teacher, 1988, Tometics: Source Book for Music Theory and Aural Perception, 1988. Mem. Music Educators Nat. Conf., Ohio Music Educators Assn., Sonneck Soc., University Club. Avocations: needlepoint, travel. Home: 2129 Brookdale Rd Toledo OH 43606-3323 Office: U Toledo Ctr for Performing Arts Toledo OH 43606 E-mail: veecee@prodigy.net.

CHAMBERS, WILLIAM EDMOND, telephone techician, writer; b. Brooklyn, NY, Oct. 9, 1943; s. William Robert and Julia Mary (Lynch) Chambers; m. Marie Antoinette Kaczanowska, Aug. 29, 1964. Attended HS, Haaren, NYC, 1957—61; diploma HS equivalency, Stevens Inst. of Tech., Hoboken, NJ, 1961. Cert. merit United Way of Tri-State, 1980. Truck drivers helper M&M Transp., Queens, NY, 1961—62; constn. laborer Roman Stone Construction Co., Brooklyn, NY, 1962—65; tel. tech. NY Tel/Verizon, Manhattan, NYC, NY, 1965—91. Dir. MWA, NY, NY, 1970—74. Author: (novels) Death Toll, 1976, The Redemption Factor, 1980, The Tormentress, 2005, (short stories) Don't Kill a Karate Fighter; If I Quench Thee; A Better Way; One Up; Daddy's Little Girl; Night Service; Above Reproach; The Rationalist; Another Night to Remember, 1976—2005, (poem) An Ode to Freedom, 2000; author: (editor) (columns) Vital Signs; Bloodlines. Nominee Brooke Russell Astor Award, 2002; recipient leadership CWA, City of Hope, 1986, Couple of the Yr., Seneca Club/ Dem. Party, 1998, Seneca Club/ Dem., 2001, 2002, 2003, 2004, Seneca Club/Dem. Party, 2005. Mem.: Internat. Thriller Writers, Inc., Sisters in Crime, Pvt. Eye Writers of Am., Mystery Writers of America (hon.; N.Y. chpt. pres. 1995—97, exec. v.p. 2000—02). Democrat. Roman Catholic. Achievements include Novels, stories, and articles; influenced political reps. to acquire funds for new library. Avocations: history, reading, weightlifting, collecting books, politics. Home: 65 Meserole Ave Brooklyn NY 11222

CHAMBERS-BELIDA, CANDACE R., radio personality, writer, television producer, educator; b. Dayton, Ohio, May 25, 1958; d. James A and Sondra B Elmore; m. David P Belida, Aug. 26, 1995 (dec. Aug. 5, 1999); m. Freeman Chambers -First Husband 1979; 1 child, Elisha Anne Verity Chambers. Studied Acting/Pschology, U. of Cin., 1976—79; Assoc. Degree, Rancho Santiago Coll., Santa Ana, Calif., 1986—89. Lifestyles writer Pacific News and Rev., Anaheim, 1986—98; motivational spkr. Spkr. Platform, San Francisco, 2001—03; radio talk show host KHPY-Radio, Moreno Valley, Calif., 2002, KTYM-Radio, Los Angeles. Exec. prodr. KYOU-TV, Santa Ana, 1986—98; tv prodn. ABC-Network, 1991—92, CBS-Network. Author: Dare To Stand, The Secret Codes of Conduct for Marriage; prodr.: (TV series) Puttin' On the Ritz (Video Award, 1986); author: (screenplays) Hosea, Counterfeit Alliance, True Covenant. Founder, CEO Holy Hwy. Ministries, Internat.; spkr. Spkr. Platform, San Francisco, 2001—03. Recipient Leadership Awards, Video Awards. Achievements include appearing as guest on television shows, KCBS, KNBC, OCN, KOCE-TV, and at numerous book signings. Avocations: travel, reading, volunteer work. Office: Ewe Babe Productions Inc PO Box 10852 Costa Mesa CA 92627 Personal E-mail: cchamb7545@aol.com.

CHAMBERS-STEINBERG, WANDA, researcher; d. Abraham, Sr. and Lessie Dickey; m. George, III Steinberg. BS in Chemistry, Howard U., Washington, DC; MS in Chemistry, Am. U., Washington, DC; post grad., Touro U., Calif. Program and mgmt. analyst Office of Rsch.; mgmt. analyst Nat. Inst. of Edn.; mgmt. assoc. Toys R Us; grad. asst. U. of Md.; rsch. assoc. Bell Labs., 1982; rsch. asst. Howard U., 1983; program officer, rsch. analyst Office of Rsch. and Ednl. Improvement, 2003; program mgr. U.S. Energy Dept., Washington, 2003—. Nat. sci. fair judge local schs., Washington, 1987—2001; vol. Cancer.org, 2001, Vol. Match, 2001—03; tutor local schs. Washington; co-coord. GED program local orgn., Md., 1990—93. Recipient Performance awards, U.S. Dept. of Edn., 1990—2002, Sec. Innovation Team award, 1997; fellow MARC Scholar, NSF, 1981—83; scholar Nat. Competitive Scholar, Howard U., 1979—83. Mem.: Am. Chem. Soc. (corr.), APHA (corr.), Am. Math. Soc. (corr.), Am. Assn. for the Advancnement of Sci. (corr.), N.Y. Acad. of Scis. (corr.).

CHAMBLISS, LINDA R., obstetrician, consultant; b. Summit, NJ, Feb. 13, 1951; d. Robert E. and Alice (Dunne) C. BSN, Duke U., 1973; MD, Mich. State U., 1980; MPH, Johns Hopkins U., 2004. Diplomate with spl. certification in maternal-fetal medicine Am. Bd. Ob-Gyn. Pediat. intern U. Chgo., 1980—81; resident in ob-gyn. Cook County Hosp., Chgo., 1981—85; fellow in maternal-fetal medicine U. So. Calif.-LA County Hosp., LA, 1988—90; chief obstetrics Indian Health Svcs., Tuba City, Ariz., 1985-88; dir. obstetrics Maricopa Med. Ctr., Phoenix, 1990—; clin. prof. ob-gyn. U. Ariz., 2001—, clin. prof. family and cmty. medicine. Comdr. USPHS, 1985—. Recipient Alumna Excellence award Mich. State U., 1996, Nat. Faculty Excellence award Coun. on Resident Edn. in Ob-Gyn., 1995. Fellow ACOG; mem. AMA (cons.), AAUW, Soc. for Maternal Fetal Medicine, Am. Women's Med. Assn. Democrat. Office: Maricopa Med Ctr Dept Obstetrics 2601 E Roosevelt St Phoenix AZ 85008-4973 Office Phone: 602-344-5576, 602-344-5444. E-mail: olddoctor@excite.com.

CHAMBLISS, SAXBY, senator; b. Warrenton, NC, Nov. 10, 1943; m. Julianne Chambliss; 2 children. BA in Bus. Adminstrn., U. Ga., 1966; JD, U. Tenn., 1968. Atty., 1968—95; mem. U.S. Congress from 8th Ga. dist., 1995—2002, mem. agriculture com., armed svcs. com., 1996—2002; U.S. senator Georgia, 2003—. Mem. forestry, resource conservation & rsch. com., chmn. gen. farm commodities and risk mgmt. subcom., sen. select com. intelligence, sen. armed services com., sen. rules com. Republican. Office: Off of Senator Chambliss 416 Russell Senate Office Building Washington DC 20510*

CHAMILLARD, GEORGE W., electronics company executive; BS, Northeastern U., 1966, MBA. Various positions Terydyne Inc., Boston, 1969-96, pres., COO, 1996-97, pres., 1997—2003, CEO, 1997—2004, chmn., 2000—. Office: Teradyne Inc 321 Harrison Ave Boston MA 02118-2238*

CHAMIS, CHRISTOS CONSTANTINOS, aerospace scientist, educator; b. Sotira, Greece, May 16, 1930; arrived in U.S., 1948; s. Constantinos and Anastasia (Kyriakos) C.; m. Alice Yanosko, Aug. 20, 1966; children: Chrysanthe, Anna-Lisa, Constantinos. BS in Civil Engring., Cleve. State U., 1960; MS, Case Western Res. U., 1962, PhD, 1967. Draftsman, designer Cons. Engring., Cleve., 1955-60; rsch. asst. Case Western Res. U., Cleve., 1960-62, rsch. assoc., 1964-68; rsch. mathematician B.F. Goodrich, Brecksville, Ohio, 1962-64; aerospace engr. Glenn Rsch. Ctr. NASA, Cleve., 1968-78, sr. rsch. engr., 1978-86, sr. aerospace scientist, 1986—. Cons. Lawrence Livermore Labs., Calif., 1974-79; adj. prof. Cleve. State U., 1968—, Akron U., 1980—, Case Western Res. U., 1984—. Editor: Composites Analysis/Design, 1975, Test Methods and Design Allowables for Composites, 1979, 89; mem. editl. bd. Jour. Composites Rsch. and Tech., Reinforced Plastics and Composites, Internat. Jour. Damage Mechanics, Theoretical and Applied Fracture Mechanics; contbr. numerous articles to sci. jours.; patentee in field for Intraply Hybrid Composites and Exoskeletal Engine Concepts; rschr. in hygrothermal composite micromechanics, computational composite mechanics-computer codes, high-temperature composite structures, structural tailoring of engine structures, computational simulation of progressive fracture, engine structures computational simulations, computational simulation/tailoring of coupled multi-discipline problems, and probabilistic structural analysis. Served with USMC, 1952-53. Fellow ASME, AIAA (assoc. editor 1986-88), ASCE, ASTM, Soc. Advancement Materials and Process Engring., Soc. Automotive Engrs.; mem. Soc. Exptl. Mechanics, Am. Soc. Metals, Am. Soc. Composites, Soc. Engring. Sci., Am. Ceramic Soc., Sigma Xi. Home: 24534 Framingham Dr Cleveland OH 44145-4902 Office Phone: 216-433-3252. Business E-Mail: Christos.C.Chamis@nasa.gov.

CHAMOT, DENNIS, science policy executive; b. Bklyn., June 5, 1943; s. Joe and Sarah C.; m. Judith Ornstein, May 19, 1974; children: Jonathan, Joshua. BS in Chemistry, MS in Chemistry, Poly. Inst. Bklyn., 1964; PhD in Chemistry, U. Ill., 1969; MBA, U. Pa., 1974. Rsch. chemist E.I. duPont de Nemours and Co., Wilmington, Del., 1969-73; asst. to exec. sec. coun. unions for profl. employees AFL-CIO, Washington, 1974-77, asst. dir. dept. for profl. employees, 1977-84, assoc. dir. dept., 1984-90, exec. asst. to pres. dept., 1990-94; assoc. exec. dir. Commn. on Engring. and Tech. Sys., NRC, Washington, 1994—2000, Divsn. on Engring. and Phys. Sciences, NRC, 2001—. Mem. numerous coms. NRC, acting dir. bd. on infrastructure and constructed environment, 1994-95, acting dir. bd. on engring. edn., 1995; mem. adv. coun. NSF, 1984-89; mem. adj. faculty George Mason U., Fairfax, Va., 1983, 84; adj. asst. prof. Univ. Coll. U. Md., College Park, 1993—; mem. external rev. com. Nat. Inst. Occupl. Safety and Health; mem. adv. panel on info. tech., automation and the workplace Office Tech. Assessment, U.S. Congress, 1982-84; mem. nat. adv. com. for tng. in new tech. Work in Am. Inst., 1985-87; mem. rev. panel Ctr. on Edn. Quality of Workforce, U.S. Dept. Edn., 1990; provider testimony various congl. hearings; participant, presenter numerous profl. confs. and symposia. Contbr. numerous articles to profl. publs. Recipient Charles Gordon award Chem. Soc. Washington, 1986; travel grantee Swedish Inst., 1984; Mary E. Switzer meml. scholar Nat. Rehab. Assn., 1989. Fellow AAAS; mem. Am. Chem. Soc. (presenter, councilor 1975—, com. on profl. rels. 1988-89, chmn. subcom. on career support and mem. assistance 1990-91, chmn. subcom. on career support 1989, cons. 1992-93, chmn. com. on Project Seed 1992-94, chmn. divsn. profl. rels. 1982, chmn. mem. adv. bd. 1973, mem. com. on econ. status 1978-86, mem. task force on occupl. health and safety 1987-94, Henry Hill award 1992, chmn. coun. com. on econ. and profl. affairs, 2001-02, mem. coun. policy com., 2001-02; bd. dirs., 2002—, trustee group ins. plans, 2004—, exec. com. 2004—05), Soc. for Occupl. and Environ. Health (sec.-treas. 1978-82, plaque 1982), Sigma Xi, Phi Kappa Phi, Phi Lambda Upsilon. Office: NRC 500 Fifth St, NW Washington DC 20001

CHAMPAGNE, DUANE WILLARD, sociology educator; b. Belcourt, N.D., May 18, 1951; m. Carole Goldberg; children: Talya, Gabe, Demelza. BA in Math., N.D. State U., 1973, MA in Sociology, 1975; PhD in Sociology, Harvard U., 1982. Teaching fellow Harvard U., Cambridge, Mass., 1981-82, rsch. fellow, 1982-83; asst. prof. U. Wis., Milw., 1983-84, UCLA, 1984-91, assoc. prof., 1991-97, prof., 1997—. Publs. dir. Am. Indian Studies Ctr., UCLA, 1986-87, assoc. dir., 1990, acting dir., 1991, dir., 1991-02, affiliate faculty UCLA Native Nations Law and Policy Ctr., 2003-, acting dir. Tribal Learning Cmty. and Edn. Exch., 2004-05; adminstrv. co-head interdepartmental program for Am. Indian studies UCLA, 1992-93; mem. grad. rsch. fellowship panel NSF, 1990-92, minority fellowship com. ASA; cons. Energy Resources Co., 1982, No. Cheyenne Tribe, 1983, Realis Pictures, Inc., 1989-90, Sta. KCET-TV, L.A., 1990, 92, Salem Press, 1992, Book Prodns. Systems, 1993, Readers Digest, 1993, Rattlesnake Prodns., 1993. Author: American Indian Societies, 1989, Social Order and Political Change, 1992, Service Delivery for Native American Children in Los Angeles County, 1996, The ACCIP Community Service Report: A Second Century of Dishonor-Federal Inequities and California Indians, 2002; editor: Native Am. Studies Assn. Newsletter, 1991—92, Native North American Almanac, 1994, 2d edit., 2001, Chronology of Native North American, 1994, Native America: Potrait of the Peoples, 1994, Native American Activism: Alcatraz to the Longest Walk, 1997, Contemporary Native American Issues, 1999, Contemporary Native American Cultural Issues, 1999, Special Issue on Indigenous Issues: Hagar, International Social Science Review, 2001, Native American Studies in Higher Education: Models for Collaboration Between Indigenous Nations, 2002, The Future of Indigenous Peoples' Strategies for Survival and Development, 2003, Education, Social Development and Empowerment Among Indigenous Peoples and Minorities: The Case of the Palestinians, 2005, Education Social Development and Empowerment Among Indigenous Peoples and Minorities: International Perspectives, 2005, Indigenous Peoples and the Modern State, 2005; book rev. editor: Am. Indian Culture and Rsch. Jour., 1984—86; editor, 1986—2002; series editor: Contemporary American Indian Issues, 1998—; contbr. numerous articles to profl. jours. Mem. City of L.A. Cmty. Action Bd., 1993, L.A. County/City Am. Indian Commn., 1992—2005, chair, 1993, 1995—97, 2000—02, 2004, 2005, sec., 2002, vice chair, 1997—2000; mem. subcom. for cultural and econ. devel. L.A. City/County Native Am. Commn., 1992—93, 2004; bd. dirs. Ctr. for Improvement of Child Caring, 1993—, Greater L.A. Am. Indian Culture Ctr., Inc., 1993, incorporator, 1993; trustee Southwest Mus., 1994—97, Nat. Mus. Am. Indian, 1998—2003; master Coll. Humanities and Social Sci., N.D. State U., 1996. Recipient LA Sr. Health Peer Counseling Cmty. Vol. Cert. of Recognition, 1996; Writer of Yr. award Cir. Native Writers and Storytellers, 1999; honoree Nat. Ctr. Am. Indian Enterprise, 1999; grantee Rockefeller Found., 1982-83, U. Wis. Grad Sch. Rsch. Com., 1984-85, Wis. Dept. Edn., 1984-85, 87-88, 88-89, NSF, 1985-88, 88-89, Nat. Endowment for Arts, 1987-88, 91-92, NRC, 1988-89, Nat. Sci. Coun., 1989-90, John D. and Catherine T. MacArthur Found., 1990-91, Hayes Found., 1990-91, 92-93, Calif. Coun. for Humanities, 1991-92, Ford Found., 1990-92, Gale Rsch. Inc., 1991-93, 93-95, Rockwell Corp., 1991-93, GTE, 1992-93, Kellog Found., 1997-2000, Pequot Mus. and Rsch. Ctr., 1997-2002, So. Calif. Indian Ctr., 1998; Fund for the Improvement of Post Secondary Edn., 1998-2003, NEH, 2002—, Dept. Justice, 2001-05, NEH, 2003-05, San Manuel Band of Serrons Indians Endowment, 2004—; Am. Indian scholar, 1973-75, 80-82, Minority fellow Am. Sociol. Assn., 1975-78, RIAS Seminar fellow, 1976-77; Rockefeller Postdoctoral fellow, 1982-83, NSF fellow, 1985-88, Postdoctoral fellow Ford Found., 1988-89. Avocations: chess, jogging. Home: 2152 Balsam Ave Los Angeles CA 90025 Office: UCLA Native Nations Law and Policy Ctr Dept Sociology 264 Haines Hall Los Angeles CA 90095-1551 Office Phone: 310-852-2606. E-mail: champagn@ucla.edu.

CHAMPAGNE, RONALD OSCAR, medical association administrator; b. Woonsocket, R.I., Jan. 2, 1942; s. George Albert and Simone (Brodeur) C.; m. Ruth Inez DesRuisseux, Nov. 25, 1970 BA, Duquesne U., 1964; MA, Cath. U. Am., 1966, Fordham U., 1970, PhD, 1973. Instr. math. Sacred Heart U., Bridgeport, Conn., 1966-69; asst. prof. math. Manhattanville Coll., Purchase, N.Y., 1969-75, dir. advanced studies program, 1973-75; prof. math., v.p., dean of faculty Salem Coll., W.Va., 1975-82; prof. math., pres., trustee St. Xavier U., Chgo., 1982-94, pres. emeritus, 1994—; prof. philosophy, v.p. for devel. Roosevelt U., Chgo., 1996—2001; sr. v.p. devel. Alzheimer's Assn., 2001—. Author: LP Spaces of Complex Valued Functions, 1966; A Formalization of the Dialectical Development of Intelligence, 1974 Mem. Mat. Assn. Am., Philosophy of Sci. Assn., Carlton Club, Econs. Club Chgo., Exec. Club Chgo. Roman Catholic. Office: Alzheimers Assn 225 N Mich Ave Fl 17 Chicago IL 60601-7633

CHAMPINE, GEORGE A., computer scientist; b. Fairmont, Minn., May 16, 1934; s. A. Floyd and C. Genevieve (Northway) C.; m. Barbara Joan Nelson, Mar. 17, 1956; children: Renee, Mark, Lisa. BS in Physics, U. Minn., 1956, MS in Physics, 1959, PhD, 1975. Dir. rsch. Sperry Univac, St. Paul, 1979; v.p. engring. Exxon Enterprises, Florham Pk., N.J., 1980-81; dir. tech. Digital Equipment Corp. (acquired by Hewlett Packard), Maynard, Mass., 1981—. Adj. prof. U. Tex., Austin, 1984-86, MIT, Cambridge, Mass., 1986-88, U. Mass., Lowell, 1987-92. Author: Computer Technology, 1978, Distributed Computing, 1980, MIT Project Athena, 1991. Mem. IEEE Computer Soc., I.T. Alumni Soc. U. Minn. (past pres.). Methodist. Avocations: photography, music, genealogy, jogging. Business E-Mail: george.champine@computer.org.

CHAMPION, HALE (CHARLES HALE CHAMPION), political science professor, public information officer; b. Coldwater, Mich., Aug. 27, 1922; s. Paul Upham and Ruth Emma (Hungerford) C.; m. Marie Ozine Tifft, Aug. 21, 1952; children: Thomas Paul, Katherine Marie. BA, Stanford U., 1952. Journalist UPI, Milw. Jour., Sacramento Bee, San Francisco Chronicle, Reporter mag., 1946-49, 52-58; legis. asst. to Congressman Andrew J. Biemiller of Wis., 1950; press and exec. sec. to Gov. Edmund G. Brown of Calif., 1958-60; dir. fin. State of Calif., 1961-66; dir. Boston Redevel. Authority, 1968-69; v.p. fin., planning and ops. U. Minn., Mpls., 1969-71; v.p. fin. Harvard U., Cambridge, Mass., 1971-76, exec. dean John F. Kennedy Sch. Govt., 1980-87; undersec. HEW, Washington, 1977-79; chief of staff to Gov. Michael S. Dukakis of Mass., Boston, 1987-88; lectr. John F. Kennedy Sch. Govt. Harvard U., 1989-91; chmn. Champion-Murphy Assocs., 2004—. Mem. Presdl. Task Force Reorgn. Fed. Govt., 1966-67, Presdl. Task Force Role of Univ. in Urban Affairs, 1967-68; chmn. Mass. Joint Legis.-Exec. Com. Fed. Base Conversion, 1973-74; chmn. Presdl. Commn. on Nat. Health Ins., 1977-78. Bd. dirs. Kaiser Family Found., 1984-92, chmn., 1989-92; bd. dirs. Ctr. for Study of Social Policy, 1986—, chmn., 1998—. Served with AUS, 1942-46. Nieman fellow Harvard U., 1956-57; fellow John F. Kennedy Inst. Politics, 1967 Mem. Nat. Acad. Pub. Adminstrn. (trustee 1980-86). Democrat. Office: Harvard Univ John F Kennedy Sch Govt 79 Jfk St Cambridge MA 02138-5801 Office Phone: 617-499-0033. E-mail: hale@champtionmurphy.com.

CHAMPION, KENNETH STANLEY WARNER, physicist; b. Sydney, NSW, Australia, Dec. 7, 1923; s. Cecil Alexander Buckingham and Ellen Catherine (Moxham) C.; m. Mavis Audrey Hinckley, Nov. 27, 1948; children: Annette, Gwendalyn, Geoffrey, Sandra. BS, U. Sydney, 1945; PhD, U. Birmingham, Eng., 1951. Asst. lectr. physics U. Queensland, Australia, 1946-49; rsch. fellow Australian Nat. U., 1949-52; rsch. assoc. MIT, Cambridge, Mass., 1952-54; asst. prof. physics Tufts U., Medford, Mass., 1954-59; rsch. scientist, sr. scientist Atmospheric Physics/Br. Chief, 1959-64; sr. exec. AF Cambridge Rsch. Labs./Phillips Lab., 1964-94. Brit. Coun. Rsch. scholar, 1947-49; vis. prof. U. Adelaide, Australia, 1964; presenter in field in 21 countries. Contbr. articles to 6 internat. profl. jours. Co-pres. PTA, Lexington, Mass., 1965-75. Fellow Phys. Soc. of London; mem. AIAA (assoc. fellow), N.Y. Acad. Scis., Am. Phys. Soc., Am. Geophys. Union, Am. Meteorol. Soc., Sigma Xi. Episcopalian. Achievements include being a pioneer in early plasma fusion oriented rsch.; pioneer in space rsch. with rocket and satellite measurements and development of internationally accepted atmospheric models. Home: 6 Rolfe Rd Lexington MA 02420-2308

CHAMPION, MICHAEL EDWARD, physician assistant, clinical perfusionist; b. Oroville, Calif., Jan. 30, 1954; s. Robert Joseph and Shirley Anne (Rowland) C.; m. Marie S. Sittner, Oct. 8. 1990. AS, Cuyahoga C.C., 1980; BS, USNY, Albany, 1983; MEd, Boston U., 1986; M of Med. Sci., St. Francis Coll., 1996; postgrad., U. London, 1999, Nova Southeastern U. clin. perfusionist ABCVP. Enlisted U.S. Army, 1972, advanced through grades to maj., 1994; ret., 1994; aviation medicine physician asst., 1980-87; chief physician asst./perfusionist Letterman Army Med. Ctr., 1989-91; founding physician asst./perfusionist Madigan Army Med. Ctr., 1991-94; cardiac surgery mgr., chief physician asst/perfusionist Mercy Med. Ctr., Janesville, Wis., 1994-96; dir. cardiac svcs. Hutchinson (Kans.) Hosp., 1996-98; v.p. projects Champion Constrn., Inc., Wichita, Kans., 1997—; sr. physician asst./perfusionist Hays (Kans.) Med. Ctr., 1998—2002; chief perfusionist Wilford Hall Med. Ctr., San Antonio, 2001—. Clin. instr. U.S. Army Physician Asst. Program, 1981-84, U.S. Army Adult Nurse Practitioner Program, 1982; EMS instr. Fayetteville Tech. Inst., 1983; instr. MEDEX program U. Washington, 1992-95, MMS programs St. Francis Coll., Loretto, Pa., 1996—; CEO Champion and Assocs., LLC; organizer Surg. Physician Asst. course, Jamaica, 1995; CEO Operational Med. Solutions, LLC, 2002—. Contbr. articles to profl. jours. Treas. Rock County Rep. Party, Janesville, 1994; mem. Red Cross, Am. Cancer Soc., EAA Young Eagles Program. Mem. Am. Acad. Physician Assts. (rsch. rev. com. 1984, profl. and continuing edn. com. 1988, vets. caucus bd. dirs. 1989-91, vets. caucus pres. 1991-92, chmn. pilots assn. 1995, chmn. vets. caucus awards 1992-95, jud. affairs com. 1994, vice chmn. surg. congress 1994-96, chmn. 1996-97, Outstanding Svc. award 1989), Wis. Acad. Physician Assts. (chair legis. com., sec. 1995, pres.-elect 1996), Soc. Army Physician Assts. (life, chief del. 1983-84, v.p. 1984-85, pres. 1985-86, 98-99), Assn. Physician Assts. in Cardiovasc. Surgery, Assn. Mil. Surgeons of U.S. (life, Physician Asst. ot Yr. 1992), Am. Soc. Extracorporeal Tech., Am. Heart Assn., Am. Acad. Med. Adminstrs., Am. Coll. Cardiovasc. Adminstrs., Assn. Physician Assts. i Anesthesia (founder 2003). Republican. Roman Catholic. Avocation: private pilot. Home: 1322 Walkers Way San Antonio TX 78216-7709

CHAMPION, NORMA JEAN, communications educator, state legislator; b. Oklahoma City, Jan. 21, 1933; d. Aubra Dell (dec.) and Beuleah Beatrice (Flanagan) Black; m. Richard Gordon Champion, Oct. 3, 1953 (dec.); children: Jeffrey Bruce, Ashley Brooke. BA in Religious Edn., Cen. Bible Coll., Springfield, Mo., 1971; MA in Comm., S.W. Mo. State U., 1978; PhD in Tech., U. Okla., 1986. Producer, hostess The Children's Hour, Sta. KYTV-TV, NBC, Springfield, 1957-86; asst. prof. Cen. Bible Coll., 1968-84; prof. broadcasting Evangel U., Springfield, 1978—; mem. Springfield City Coun., 1987-92, Mo. Ho. of Reps., Jefferson City, 1993—2002, Mo. Senate, 2003—. Adj. faculty Assemblies of God Theol. Sem., Springfield, 1987—, pres. coun.; bd. dirs. Global U.; mem. Commn. on Higher Edn., Assemblies of God, 1998—, Mo. Film Commn., Mo. Pain Mgmt. Bd.; Mo. Film Commn., 2003-; spkr. Internat. Pentecostal Press Assn. World Conf., Singapore, 1989. Mem. bd Mo. Access to Higher Edn. Trust, 2003-, pain mgmt. bd., 2004-, Boys & Girls Town of Mo.; adv. coun. pain mgmt. Mo. Film Commn.; judge Springfield (Mo.) City Schs. Recipient commendation resolution Mo. Ho. of Reps., 1988; numerous award for The Children's Hour; Aunt Norma Day named in her honor City of Springfield, 1976. Mem. Nat. Broadcast Edn. Assn., Mo. Broadcast Edn. Assn., Nat. League Cities, Mo. Mcpl. League (human resource com. 1989, intergovtl. rels. com. 1990), Nat. Assn. Telecom. Officers and Advisors, PTA (life). Republican. Mem. Assemblies of God Ch. Avocations: gardening, reading, interior decoration. Home: 3609 S Broadway Ave Springfield MO 65807-4505 Office: Evangel Univ 1111 N Glenstone Ave Springfield MO 65802-2125 Business E-Mail: normachampion@senate.mo.gov.

CHAMPION, SARA STEWART, lawyer; b. Boston, Apr. 1, 1942; d. William Julius Champion and Mary Stewart Cunningham; m. Wayne L. Kinsey, Dec. 12, 1964 (div. Feb. 1971); m. John Q. Adams, Apr. 25, 1998 (div. Oct. 2000). BA, Duke U., 1963; MA, U. Calif., Davis, 1974; JD cum laude, N.Y. Law Sch., 1992. Bar: N.Y. 1992, Conn. 1992. Rsch. analyst Nat. Security Agy., Ft. Meade, Md., 1963-65; instr. Russian Def. Lang. Inst., Monterey, Calif., 1970-72; claims rep. Social Security Adminstrn., San Francisco, 1974-78, claims rep., ops. supr. N.Y.C., 1978-87; office adminstr. Bachelder Law Offices, N.Y.C., 1987-97, assoc., 1992-97, ptnr., 1997—2002; ptnr., shareholder, head NY exec. compensation practice Vedder, Price, Kaufman and Kammholz, N.Y.C., 2002—. Mem.: DAR, New Eng. Soc. (steward), Soc. Mayflower Descs. (bd. assts., steward), Colonial Dames Am., Silver Spring Country Club (Ridgefield, Conn.), Univ. Club, Wianno Yacht Club (Osterville, Mass.). Avocation: genealogy. Office: Vedder Price Kaufman & Kammholz 805 3d Ave New York NY 10022 Office Phone: 212-407-7785. E-mail: schampion@vedderprice.com.

CHAMPION, WILL, musician; b. Hampshire, England, July 31, 1978; Student in Anthropology, U. Coll. London. Drummer Coldplay, 1998—. Musician: (albums) Parachutes, 2000 (Grammy award: Best Alternative Music Album, 2001), A Rush of Blood to the Head, 2002 (Grammy awards: Best Alternative Music Album, 2002, Best Rock Performance By A Duo Or Group With Vocal for song "In My Place", 2002, Record Of The Yr. for song "Clocks", 2003), Live 2003, 2003. Office: Capital Records 1750 North Vine Street 10th Floor Hollywood CA 90028

CHAMPION-PREDMORE, CATHY M., music educator; b. Great Fallas, Mont., Mar. 21, 1959; d. Robert Edward Champion and Ruth Isabell Malmgren; m. Dan Roy Predmore, July 26, 1985. B in Music Edn., U. Mont., 1985. Presenter, founder Annual Jean Crockett Meml. Scholarship Recitals, 1995—. Mem. Music Tchrs. Nat. Assn. (cert.), Mont. State Music Tchrs. Assn. (cert., student affiliate advisor 1998-2001), Capital City Music Tchrs. Assn. (spring festival com. 1997-98, treas. 1998-2002), Helena Music Tchrs. Assn. (scholarship com. 1996—, tchrs. recital com. 1997—). Democrat. Methodist. Avocations: hiking, cross country skiing, crocheting, reading. Home: 2022 Grizzly Gulch Dr Helena MT 59601-9657

CHAMPLIN, CHARLES DAVENPORT, television personality, critic, writer; b. Hammondsport, N.Y., Mar. 23, 1926; s. Francis Malburn and Katherine Marietta (Masson) C.; m. Margaret Frances Derby, Sept. 11, 1948; children: Charles Jr., Katherine, John, Judith, Susan, Nancy. AB cum laude, Harvard U., 1947. Reporter Life mag., N.Y.C., 1948-49, corr. Chgo., 1949-52, Denver, 1952-54; asst. editor Life mag., N.Y.C., 1954—59; corr. Time mag., L.A., 1959-62, London, 1962-65; arts editor, columnist L.A. Times, 1965-91, prin. film critic, 1967-80, book critic, 1981-82. Host-commentator Ste. KCET-TV, L.A., ETV Network, Z Channel Cable TV, Bravo Channel, 1969-96; adj. prof. Loyola-Marymount U., L.A., 1969-86; adj. prof. U. So. Calif., 1986-96. Author: (with C. Sava) How to Swim Well, 1960, The Flicks, 1977, The Movies Grow Up, 1981, Back There Where the Past Was, 1989, George Lucas: The Creative Impulse, 1992, enlarged, 1997, John Frankenheimer: A Conversation, 1995, Woody Allen at Work, 1995, Hollywood's Revolutionary Decade, 1998, Tony's World, 1999, My Friend, You Are Legally Blind, 2001; contbr. numerous articles to mags. and publs. Bd. dirs. Am. Cinemateque; trustee L.A. Film Tchrs. Assn. With U.S. Army, 1944-46, ETO. Decorated Purple Heart; recipient Order Arts and Letters, France, 1977 Mem. PEN, L.A. Film Critics Assn., Authors Guild. Democrat. Home: 2169 Linda Flora Dr Los Angeles CA 90077-1408 E-mail: champc@aol.com.

CHAMPLIN, STEVEN KIRK, lawyer; b. Omaha, July 6, 1944; m. Marjorie Eckenberg, Mar. 15, 1969; children: Anne, Paul, Jane. BA, Vanderbilt U., 1966; JD cum laude, U. Minn., 1969. Bar: Minn. 1969, U.S. Dist. Ct. Minn., U.S. Ct. Appeals (8th cir.). Pub. defender Hennepin County, Mpls., 1972-73; assoc. Dorsey & Whitney, Mpls., 1969-70, 71-72, 73-75, ptnr., comml. litig., 1976—, and co- chmn., construction & design law. Capt. U.S. Army, 1970-71. Mem. USTA. Office: Dorsey & Whitney LLP 50 S 6th St Ste 1500 Minneapolis MN 55402-1553 Office Phone: 612-340-2913. Office Fax: 612-340-2868. Business E-Mail: champlin.steve@dorsey.com.

CHAMPNEY, RAYMOND JOSEPH, advertising and marketing executive, consultant; b. NYC, Aug. 6, 1940; s. Raymond Joseph and Florence (McConnell) C.; m. Anne Kelly, Jan. 10, 1976. Student, CCNY, 1961-63, NYU, 1965. With BBDO Advt., N.Y.C., 1964-66, McCann Erickson Advt., 1966-68, Clinton E. Frank Advt., 1968-71, Norman Craig & Kummel Advt., 1971-73, Doyle Dane Bernbach Advt., 1973-74, Guest Pub. Co., 1974-77, Bozell & Jacobs Advt., 1977-79; sr. v.p. Weekley & Assocs., 1980-84, pres. Weekley & Champney Advt. Dallas, 1984-86; pres., chief exec. officer Champney and Assoc. Advt., Dallas, 1986-92; pres. Champney Publicidad S.A. de C.V., Mexico City, 1987-92, Champney Fulfillment, 1987-92, RJC Internat., Bedford, Tex., 1992—. Dir. gen. Osama Al Madany/RJC Internat., Saudi Arabia, 1994—97; tab facilitator RJC Enterprises LLC-Cons., 2001. Served with U.S. Army, 1959-61. Mem. Sales Mktg. Execs., Dallas Ad League, Am. Mgmt. Assn., Presidents Assn.,. Am. Soc. Travel Agts., Hotel Sales and Mktg. Assn., Better Bus. Bur., Dallas C. of C., HEB C. of C. Home: 2300 Marshfield Dr Bedford TX 76021-7300 Office: PO Box 1072 Bedford TX 76095-1072 Office Phone: 817-318-1233. E-mail: raymond@rjcenter.com.

CHAN, CARLYLE HUNG-LUN, psychiatrist, educator; b. Clarksdale, Miss., July 4, 1949; s. Henry Howe and Jennie (Wong) C.; m. Patricia Meyer, June 18, 1977; children: Christopher, Diana. BS, U. Wis., 1971; MD, Med. Coll. Wis., 1975. Diplomate Am. Bd. Psychiatry and Neurology. Resident in psychiatry U. Chgo., 1975-78; postdoctoral fellow R.W. Johnson clin. scholar Yale U. Sch. Medicine, 1978-80; asst. prof. Med. Coll. Wis., Milw., 1980-86, assoc. prof., 1986-98; prof. Med. Coll. of Wis., Milw., 1998—; dir. residency edn. Med. Coll. Wis., Milw., 1987—, prof., 1998—, vice chair edn. and informatics, 1997—, dir. continuing med. edn., 1990—; dir. catchment area Milw. County Mental Health Complex, 1981-82; chief psychiatrist Psychiatrist Ctr., Columbia Hosp., Milw., 1982-87; dir. continuing med. edn. Soc. Tchg. Scholars, 1994. Dir. course annual psychiat. conf., 1982—; dir. Door County (Wis.) Summer Inst., 1987—. Asst. editor Asian-Am. Psychiatry Newsletter, Washington, 1983-84; assoc. editor Acad. Psychiatry Newsletter, 1991-94; contbr. articles to profl. jours. Bd. dirs. Planning Council for Mental Health and Social Service, 1983—. Jr. Faculty Devel. award NIMH, 1983-85; Community Devel. award Apple Computer Co., Milw., 1984, Parker Palmer award, 2004. Fellow Am. Psychiat. Assn (Disting.); mem. Am. Coll. Psychiatrists (pres.-elect 2005—), Wis. Psychiat. Assn. (pres. Milw. chpt. 1990-91, chair edn. com. 1995-), Assn. Acad. Psychiatry (regional coord. 1987-, regional coord. dir. 1993-96, treas. 1996-), Am. Assn. Dirs. Psychiat. Residency Tng. (sec. 1994-95, pres.-elect 1995, pres. 1996, treas. 1990-92, program com. chair 1993-94), Orgn. Program Dirs. Assns. (sec.-treas., chair 2004-), Wis. State Med. Soc., Milw. County Med. Soc. Med. Coll. of Wis., Soc. Teaching Scholars. Avocations: tennis, golf, running. Office: Med Coll Wis Dept Psychiatry 8701 W Watertown Plank Rd Milwaukee WI 53226-3548 Office Phone: 414-456-7250. Business E-Mail: cchan@mcw.edu.

CHAN, DAVID RONALD, tax specialist, lawyer; b. LA, Aug. 3, 1948; s. David Yew and Anna May (Wong) Chan; m. Mary Anne Chan, June 21, 1980; children: Eric, Christina. AB in Econs., UCLA, 1969, MS in Bus. Adminstrn., 1970, JD, 1973. Bar: Calif. 1973, U.S. Tax Ct. 1974, U.S. Ct. Appeals (9th cir.) 1974, U.S. Dist. Ct. (ctrl. dist.) Calif. 1980. Acct. Oxnard Celery Distbrs., L.A., 1968-73, Touche Ross & Co., L.A., 1970; tax prin. Kenneth Leventhal & Co. (name now E&Y Kenneth Leventhal Real Estate Group of Ernst & Young LLP), L.A., 1973—. Contbr. chpts. to books and articles to profl. jours. Founder, dir. Chinese Hist. Soc. So. Calif., L.A., 1975—; mem. spkrs. bur. L.A. 200 Bicentennial, L.A., 1981; spkr. Project Follow Through, L.A., 1981, EY Tax Forum, UCLA Real Estate Forecast, Merril Lynch Symposium, Calif. CPA Soc. Recipient Forbes Gold medal Calif. Soc. CPAs, L.A., 1970, Elijah Watt Sells cert. AICPA, L.A., 1970, cert. recognition Chinese Hist. Soc. So. Calif., L.A., 1985. Mem. So. Calif. Chinese Lawyers Assn., L.A. County Bar Assn., Chinese Am. CPAs So. Calif., Asian Bus. League, Chinese For Affirmative Action. Republican. Avocations: chinese cuisine, sports memorabilia, stamp collecting/philately. Office: E&Y Kenneth Leventhal Real Estate Group 725 S Figueroa St 5th Fl Los Angeles CA 90017-5418 Office Phone: 213-977-3310. E-mail: david.chan02@ey.com.

CHAN, HENRY ALBERT, minister; b. Golden Grove, East Bank, Guyana, Jan. 7, 1946; came to U.S., 1967, naturalized, 1977; s. Clarence Kenneth and Ruby Verna (Milner) C.; m. Jean Flora Langdon, Apr. 26, 1969; children: H. Anthony, Arin Dwayne, Natasha Laura. BS, SUNY, Saratoga Springs, 1978; MBA, Dowling Coll., Oakdale, N.Y., 1980; D.Pub. Adminstrn., Nova Southeastern U., Ft. Lauderdale, Fla., 1981; DMin, U. of the South, Sewanee, Tenn., 1987; M.Sacred Theology, Gen. Theol. Sem., N.Y.C., 1990; PhD in Pastoral Psychology, Grad. Theol. Found., Donaldson, Ind., 1994; Cert. of Grad., Mercer Sch. Theology, Garden City, N.Y., 1982. Ordained to ministry, Episcopal Ch., 1983. Long-range planning analyst Blue Cross/Blue Shield, N.Y.C., 1980-83; curate and rector Ch. of the Transfiguration, Freeport, N.Y., 1983-87; interim priest Christ Ch., Brentwood, N.Y., 1987; rector St. Peter's Episcopal Ch., Rosedale, N.Y., 1988—. Archdeacon of Demerara, Guyana, 1999; vicar Ch. of Transfiguration, Georgetown, Guyana, 1999. Bd. dirs. Liberty Park Non-Profit Housing Corp., Freeport, 1984-87; mem. Freeport Village Human rights Commn., 1986-87; mem. Peale Ctr. for Christian Living, 1996—. Mem. Christian Clergy, Queens Fedn. Chs., C.G. Jung Found. for Analytic Psychology, Inc. Avocations: fishing, reading, travel within caribbean region. Office: St Peters Episcopal Church 137-28 244th St Rosedale NY 11422-1828 E-mail: stpetersepisch@cs.com.

CHAN, JACKIE, actor, film director; b. Hong Kong, Apr. 7, 1954; s. Chi-Ping and Lee-Lee Chan; m. Lin Fong Chiao; 1 child: J.C. Trained, Peking Opera Sch. Films include: Little Tiger of Guangdong, Little Tiger from Canton, Hand of Death, 1975, New Fist of Fury, 1976, Shaolin Wooden Men, 1976, To Kill with Intrigue, 1977, Snake in the Eagle's Shadow, Snake and Crane Arts of Shaolin, Magnificent Bodyguards, 1978, Drunken Master, 1978, Spiritual Kung Fu, 1978, The Fearless Hyena, Dragon Fist, 1979, The Young Master, 1980, Half a Loaf of King Fu, Battle Creek Brawl, 1980, The Cannonball Run, 1981, The Dragon Lord, 1982, Marvelous Fists, 1982, Winners and Sinners, 1983, The Fearless Hyena Part 2, Project A, 1983, Cannonball Run II, 1984, Wheels on Meals, 1984, My Lucky Stars, 1985, The Protector, 1985, Twinkle Twinkle Lucky Stars, 1985, Heart of the Dragon, 1985, Police Story, 1986, Armour of God, 1987, Project A Part 2, 1987, Dragons Forever, 1987, Police Story II, 1987, Mr. Canton and Lady Rose, 1989, Amour of God II: Operation Condor, 1991, Island of Fire, 1991, Twin Dragons, 1992, Police Story III: Super Cop, 1992, City Hunter, 1993, Crime Story, 1993, Drunken Master II, 1994, Rumble in the Bronx, 1994, Thunderbolt, 1994, Police Story IV: First Strike, 1996, Mr. Nice Guy, 1997, Rush Hour, 1998, Who Am I?, 1998, Gorgeous, 1999, The King of Comedy, 1999, Gen-X Cops, 1999, Shanghai Noon, 2000, The Accidental Spy, 2001, Rush Hour 2, 2001, The Tuxedo, 2002, Shanghai Knights, 2003, The Medallion, 2003, Around the World in 80 Days, 2004. Recipient Lifetime Achievement award MTV, 1995, Best Picture award Hong Kong Film, 1989, Best Action Choreography Hong Kong Film, 1996, 99, 2002, Maverick Tribute award Cinequest San Jose Film Festival, 1998, PETA Humanitarian award, 1999, Internat. Lifetime Achievement award, Internat. Leadership Found., 2000, Taurus Hon. award, Outstanding Achievement for Acting in Actions Film, World Stunt awards, 2002. Named Goodwill Amb., 2004.

CHAN, JANET, editor-in-chief; children: Jack, Laura. Sr. editor Glamour Mag.; exec. dir. Good Housekeeping, Redbook; v.p., editor-in-chief Parenting Mag., 1996—. Editl. dir. Time Inc.'s Parenting Group including Healthy Pregnancy, Baby Talk, and Parenting mags. Office: The Parenting Group Inc 530 Fifth Ave 4th Fl New York NY 10036 Office Phone: 212-522-9808. Office Fax: 212-522-8750.*

CHAN, KIN FOONG, engineer; s. Weng Fai and Bee Keat; m. Indriani Chan. BS cum laude in elec. engring., U. of Tex. at Austin, 1992—96, MS in engring., 1996—97, PhD in elec. engring., 1997—2000. Co-op engr. Nat. Instruments Corp., Austin, Tex., 1994; optical rsch. engr. Ball Semiconductor, Inc., Allen, Tex., 2000—03; advanced devel. biomedical engr. Reliant Technologies, Inc., Palo Alto, Calif., 2003—04, sr. devel. engr., 2004—05; mgr. Biomedical Engring. Group, 2005—. Contbr. articles various profl. jours. Recipient Best Posters in Basic Sci., World Congress on Endourology, 1998—99, Tex. Excellence Tchg. Award, Tex. Exes Assn., 1999, Gordon Rsch. Conf. Grad. Student award, Gordon Rsch. Conferences, 2000; Whitaker Found. Conf. fellowship, Whitaker Found., 1997, Ray Fisher Meml.sScholarship, Tex. Exes Assn., 1998, Continuing U. fellowship, U. of Tex. at Austin, 1998—99, SPIE Ednl. Scholarship in Optical Sci. & Engring., Internat. Soc. for Optical Engring. (SPIE), 1999. Mem.: Am. Soc. for Laser Medicine and Surgery, Internat. Soc. for Optical Engring., Eta Kappa Nu, Tau Beta Pi. Achievements include patents for light modulation device and system; non-synchronous control of laser diode; patents pending for apparatus and method to treat heart disease using lasers to form microchannels; method and apparatus for monitoring and controlling laser-induced tissue treatment; research in dynamics of laser-tissue interaction; design of maskless microlithography; optical tracking and laser delivery sys. for dermatological application.

CHAN, LAWRENCE SIU-YUNG, dermatologist, educator; b. Hong Kong, Dec. 10, 1949; came to U.S., 1975; s. Cheong-Yin Chan and Chun-Fun Wu. AA, Montgomery Coll., Takoma Park, Md., 1978; student, Messiah Coll., Grantham, Pa., 1978-79; BS, BS, MIT, 1981; MD, U. Pa., 1985. Diplomate Am. Bd. Dermatology, Nat. Bd. Med. Examiners. Intern Rutgers Med. Sch., Camden, N.J., 1986-87; resident U. Mich., Ann Arbor, 1987-91; asst. prof. Wayne State U., Detroit, 1991-93, Northwestern U., Chgo., 1993—2002, dir. immunodermatology divsn., 1993—2002; assoc. prof. U. Ill., 2002—05, dir. immunology rsch., 2002—, prof., 2005—, head Dept. Immunology, 2005—. Adj. lectr. U. Mich., 1991-93. Editor: (sci. textbook) Animal Models of Human Inflammatory Skin Disease, 2003. Recipient Clin. Investigator award, NIH, Bethesda, 1996; grantee Merit Rev., VA Rsch. Com., 1996; Small Project, High-risk Project and Rsch. Project grantee, NIH, 2001. Fellow Am. Acad. Dermatology; mem. Soc. Investigative Dermatology, Ctrl. Soc. Investigative Dermatology (chmn. 1995), Dermatology Found. (Career Devel. award 1993), Am. Assn. Immunologists, Am. Soc. Investigative Pathology, Microcirculatory Soc., Alpha Omega Alpha. Achievements include identification of a novel skin basement membrane component, generation of an animal model of atopic dermatitis, generation of an animal model of an autoimmune hairloss disorder alopecia areata. Office: U Ill Dept Dermatology 808 S Wood Chicago IL 60612-3010 E-mail: larrycha@uic.edu.

CHAN, LOIS MAI, library and information science educator; arrived in U.S., 1956; d. Kar K. and Sau N. Mark; m. Shung Kai Chan, June 22, 1963; children: Jennifer M., Stephen Y. AB, Nat. Taiwan U., Taipei, 1956; MA, Fla. State U., 1958, MS, 1960; PhD, U. Ky., 1970. Asst. order libr. Purdue U., Lafayette, Ind., 1960-61, asst. cataloger, 1961-63; serials acquisition libr. Northwestern U., Evanston, Ill., 1963-64; asst. libr. Lake Forest Coll., Ill., 1964—66; serials cataloger U. Ky., Lexington, 1966-67, asst. prof. libr. sci., 1970-74, assoc. prof., 1974-80, prof., 1980—. Vis. lectr. U. Minn., Mpls., summer 1979, U. Hawaii, Honolulu, summer 1982; project cons. Online Computer Library Ctr., Dublin, Ohio, 1983-86, 2000—; chmn. Decimal Classification Editorial Policy Com., Washington, 1986-91. Author: Cataloging and Classification: An Introduction, 1981, 2d edit., 1994, Library of Congress Subject Headings, 1981, 4th edit., 2005, A Guide to the Library of Congress Classification 5th edit., 1999; co-author: Thesauri Used in Online Databases, 1988, Dewey Decimal Classification: A Practical Guide, 1994, 2d edit., 1996, Dewey Decimal Classification: Principals and Application, 2003. Recipient Gt. Tchr. award U. Ky. Alumni Assn., 1990, Disting. Svc. award Chinese-Am. Librs. Assn., 1992, Disting. Alumni award Fla. State U. Sch. Libr. and Info. Studies, 1996, Excellence in Tchg. award U. Ky. Coll. Comm. and Info. Studies, 2001. Mem.: MLA (Margaret Mann citation 1989). Mem. Christian Ch. (Disciples Of Christ). Office: U Ky Sch Libr And Info Sci Lexington KY 40506-0039 Office Phone: 859-257-5942. E-mail: loischan@uky.edu.

CHAN, LO-YI CHEUNG YUEN, architect; b. Canton, China, Dec. 1, 1932; came to U.S., 1942, naturalized, 1954; s. Wing tsit and Wai hing (Lei) C.; m. Mildred Wu, Sept. 1, 1957; children: Christopher, Leighton, Leicia. BA, Dartmouth Coll., 1954, DArts (hon.), 2004; MArch, Harvard U., 1959, postgrad. (Appleton fellow), 1959-60. Asso. firm I. M. Pei & Partners, N.Y.C., 1960-65; practiced architecture N.Y.C., 1965—2002. Adj. asst. prof. architecture Columbia, 1963-67; vis. critic Coll. Architecture, Cornell U., 1965-68, Harvard U., 1976, 78, 80, Mass. Inst. Tech., 1977; panelist Am. Arbitration Assn., 1972-80. Exhibitions include, The Museum of Modern Art, The Whitney Museum, Columbia U., Nat. Academy of Design, Boston Architectural Center. Bd. dirs. Parks Coun., N.Y.C., 1971-85, pres., 1974; trustee Cmty. Svc. Soc., N.Y.C., 1977-86, Henry St. Settlement, 1980-99, Lingnan Found., 1986—, chmn., 1990—, mem. N.Y.C. Art Commn., 1992-97, Berkshire Sch., 1992— trusteeColby-Sawyer Coll., 2003; active N.Y. State Coun. Arts, 1993-96; bd. dirs. Berkshire Taconic Cmty. Found., 2000—. With AUS, 1955-57. Nat. Endowment for Arts Design fellow, 1975-76 Fellow AIA (corp.); mem. Phi Beta Kappa. Home and Office: 270 Riverside Dr New York NY 10025

CHAN, MOSES HUNG WAI, physics educator, researcher; b. Xi-an, Shensi, China, Nov. 23, 1946; came to U.S., 1964, naturalized, 1984. BA magna cum laude, Bridgwater Coll., Va., 1967; MS, Cornell U., 1970, PhD, 1974. Asst. lectr. U. Hong Kong, 1969-70; asst. prof. U. Toledo, Ohio, 1976-79; asst. prof. Pa. State U., University Park, 1979-84, assoc. prof., 1984-86, prof. 1986-90, disting. prof., 1990—. Contbr. articles to profl. jours. Sr. rsch. fellow Inst. for Solid State Physics, U. Tokyo, summer 1982; NSF grantee; Fellow Am. Phys. Soc., Am. Acad. Arts & Sci.; mem. NAS; recipient Senior Rsch. Fellowship Japan Soc. for Promotion Sci., 1982, John Simon Guggenheim Fellowship, 1986, Fritz London Memorial prize in low temperature physics, 1996. Office: Pa State U Dept of Physics 104 Davey Lab University Park PA 16802*

CHAN, PETER WING KWONG, pharmacist; b. L.A., Feb. 3, 1949; s. Sherwin T.S. and Shirley W. (Lee) C.; children: Kristina Dionne, Kelly Alison, David Shoichi. BS, U. So. Calif., 1970, D in Pharmacy, 1974. Lic. pharmacist, Calif. Clin. instr. U. So. Calif., 1974-76; staff clin. pharmacist Cedars-Sinai Med. Ctr., L.A., 1974-76; 1st clin. pharmacist in ophthalmology Alcon Labs., Inc., Ft. Worth, 1977—. Formerly in Phila. monitoring patient drug therapy, teaching residents, nurses, pharmacy students, then assigned to Tumu Tumu hosp., Karatina, Kenya, also lectr. clin. ocular pharmacology tng. course, Nairobi, Cairo, Athens, formerly dist. sales mgr. Alcon/BP, ophthal. products div. Alcon Labs., Inc., Denver, v.p., gen. mgr. Optikem Internat., Sereine Products, Dvi., Optacryl, Inc., Denver, 1980-81, product mgr. hosp. pharmacy prodcuts Am. McGaw div. Am. Hosp. Supply Corp., 1981-83; internat. market mgr. IOLAB subs. Johnson & Johnson, 1983-86, dir. new bus. devel. Iolab Pharms., 1986-87. dir. Internat. Mktg., 1987-89, dir. new products mktg., 1989; bus. and mktg. strategies cons. to pharm. and med. device cos. Chan & Assocs., Northridge, Calif., 1989-98; regional mng. dir. Pacific Rim, Leiner Health Products, Inc., Carson, Calif., 1998-2000; clin. mktg. mgr. Cameron and Co., Inc., Torrance, Calif.; ptnr., chmn., CEO PreFree Techs. Inc., 1992-96; med. dir., Clin. Profl. Affairs, Nexstar Pharms., Inc., Boulder, 1996-97; ptnr. Vitamin Specialties Corp., 1993-95, JSP Ptnrs., Ltd., 1992—; med. dir., clin. and profl. affairs, Nexstar Pharm., Inc., Boulder, Colo.; regional mng. dir. Pacific Rim Leiner Health Products, 1998—; bd. dirs., mem. adv. bd. USA Health Alert; mem. adv. bd. All That's Natural II, Aptus Med. Group. Del. Calif. Youth Theatre at Paramount Studios, Hollyood, 1986-2002; bd. councillors U. So. Calif. Sch. Pharmacy, 1995—. Recipient Hollywood-Wilshire Pharm. assn. spl. award for outstanding svc., 1974. Mem. Chinese Am. Pharm. Assn., Am. Pharm. Assn. (ho. of dels. 1976-78), Calif. Pharm. Assn., Hollywood-Wilshire Pharm. Assn. (bd. dirs. 1972-76), Am. Soc. Hosp. Pharmacists, Am. Pharm. Assn. Acad. Pharmacy Practice, U. So. Calif. Assocs. (life), U. So. Calif. Gen. Alumni Assn., U. So. Calif. (steering com. lifescies info. networking coun.), Granada Hills H.S. Highlanders Booster Club (bd. dirs. 1991, 92, 93, chmn.-Project 2000), QSAD Centurions, U. So. Calif. Lifetime Assocs., Gamma Epsilon Omega Alumni Assn. (bd. dirs.), Phi Delta Chi, NRA (life), Golden Eagle, Calif. Rifle & Pistol Assn. (life). Republican. Home: 744 S Sierra Vista Ave Alhambra CA 91801-4520 Office: Chan and Assocs PO Box 90547 Pasadena CA 91109 also: Cameron and Co Inc 10606 Trademark Dr Ste 202 Rancho Cucamonga CA 91730 Fax: (310) 891-6899. E-mail: PChan388@Hotmail.com.

CHAN, PHILIP, retired dermatologist, retired military officer; b. Oceanside, N.Y., Oct. 14, 1946; s. Walter O. and Ann (Yee) C. BA, Harvard U., 1968; MD, Columbia U., 1972. Diplomate Am. Bd. Dermatology. Commd. capt. U.S. Army, 1973, advanced through grades to col., 1987; dermatologist Martin Army Cmty. Hosp., Ft. Benning, Ga., 1995-98; ret. U.S. Army, 1998; tchr. Tai Chi, Reiki, blues harmonica Columbus, Ga., 1999—. Adj. asst. prof. Uniformed Svcs. U. Health Scis., 1995—97; part-time instr. Rankin Arts Ctr., Columbus State U. Editor (govt. pub.) Procs. of Vesicant Workshop, 1987; conbtr. articles to profl. jours. Fellow Am. Acad. Dermatology; mem. AMA, Mensa, Assn. of Mil. Dermatologists, Internat. Assn. Reiki Profls., Tai Chi for Arthritis Assn. Home: 6300 Milgen Rd #1285 Columbus GA 31907-0962

CHAN, PHILIP J., medical educator; married; 3 children. BA cum laude in biology, Kalamazoo Coll., 1979; MS in Physiology, Mich. State U., 1981, PhD in Physiology, 1983. Diplomate Am. Bd. Bioanalysis. Dir. sperm processing & IVF and embryo transfer lab. Kennedy Meml. Hosps./U. Med. Ctr., Cherry Hill, NJ, 1983-87; dir. labs. Hillcrest Fertility Ctr., Tulsa, 1987-89; dir. andrology/male reproduction and molecular biology labs. Loma Linda (Calif.) U. Obstetrics Med. Group, 1989—. Mgr. info. sys. lab. computers and network Loma Linda U. Ob-Gyn. Med. Group, Inc., 1991—; from instr. to asst. prof. U. Medicine and Dentistry of N.J. Sch. Osteopathic Medicine, 1983-87; assoc. prof. Oral Roberts U. Sch. Medicine, 1987-89; from assoc. prof. to prof. Loma Linda U. Sch. Medicine, 1989—; mem. comparative medicine study sect. NIH, 1994-98, chmn. site visit Nat. Ctr. for Rsch. Resources, 1999; insp. Coll. Am. Pathologists, 1993—. Contbr. articles to profl. jours. Recipient Walter-MacPherson First Pl. Rsch. award The Walter E. Macpherson Soc., 1997, Outstanding Attending Staff Physician award WYETH, 2003. Mem. Am. Soc. Reproductive Medicine, Internat. Soc. Andrology, Internat. Primatological Soc., Am. Assn. Bioanalysts. Office: Loma Linda U Fac Med Office Dept Ob-Gyn Ste 3950 11370 Anderson St Loma Linda CA 92354-3450 Personal E-mail: pchann@yahoo.com.

CHAN, SHU-PARK, electrical engineering educator; b. Canton, China, Oct. 10, 1929; came to U.S., 1951, naturalized, 1965; s. Chi-Tong and Shui-Ying (Mok) C.; m. Stella Yok-Sing Lam, Dec. 28, 1956; children: Charlene Li-Hsiang, Yau-Gene. BEE, Va. Mil. Inst., 1955; MEE, U. Ill., 1957, PhD, 1963. Instr. elec. engring. and math. Va. Mil. Inst., 1957-59; instr. elec. engring. U. Ill., 1960-61, rsch. assoc., 1961-62, asst. prof. math., 1962-63; assoc. prof. elec. engring. U. Santa Clara, 1963-68, prof., 1968-92, chmn. elec. engring. and computer sci. dept., 1969-84; Nicholson Family Chair prof. Santa Clara U., 1987-92, prof. emeritus, 1992—, acting dean Sch. Engring., 1987-88; founder, pres. Internat. Technol. U., Santa Clara, 1994—; pres. Chu Hai Coll., Hong Kong, 1995-96. Prin. investigator NSF, NASA; Univ. fellow U. Ill., 1959-60; vis. spl. chair prof. elec. engring. dept. Nat. Taiwan U., 1973-74; spl. lectr. Acad. Sci., Peking, China, summer 1980; hon. prof. elec. engring. dept. U. Hong Kong, 1980-81; hon. prof. Anhuei U., China, 1982; spl. chair Tamkang U., Taipei, Taiwan, 1981; apptd. mem. J. William Fulbright Fgn. Scholarship Bd., 1991-93; founder, pres. Internat. Tech. U. Found., 1994—. Author: introductory Topological Analysis of Electrical Networks, 1969, (with others) Analysis of Linear Networks and Systems—A Matrix-Oriented Approach with Computer Applications, 1972, (with E. Moustakas) Introduction to the Applications of the Operational Amplifier, 1974; editor: Network Topology and Its Engineering Applications, 1975, Graph Theory and Applications, 1982. Chmn. bd., pres. Acad. Cultural Co., Santa Clara; founder, pres. China Exptl. U. Found., 1985—; chmn. Santa Clara County Bicentennial Chinese Festival Com.; pres. Chinese Arts and Culture Inst., 1976—; trustee Inst. Sino-Am. Studies, San Jose, Calif., 1971-76, West Valley-Mission C.C. Dist., Calif., 1988. Recipient Disting. Elec. Engring. Alumnus award U. Ill., 1983, 1991 Rschr. of Yr. award Sch. Engring., Santa Clara U., 1992, Courvoisier Leadership award in Edn., 1994; named Engr. of Yr. in Engring. Edn. San Francisco session AIAA, 1994, Chinese Am. Pioneer award Orgn. Chinese Ams., San Francisco, 1996; Hon. Prof. award S. China Normal U., Guangzhou, China, 1997—, Educator of Yr. award Chinese Consol. Benevolent Assn. and Chinese Consol. Women's Assn., 1999, Mayor's awrd City of San Francisco, 1999. Fellow IEEE (past chmn. circuit theory group San Francisco sect., chmn. asilomar conf. circuits and sys. 1970); mem. Am. Soc. Engring. Edn., Chineses Alumni Assn. U. Santa Clara (pres.), U. Santa Clara Faculty Club (pres. 1971-72), Sigma Xi, Tau Beta Pi, Eta Kappa Nu, Pi Mu Epsilon, Phi Kappa Phi. Home: 2085 Denise Dr Santa Clara CA 95050-4557 Office Phone: 408-556-9010. Business E-Mail: spchan@itu.edu. *I would like to attribute my personal success to the teaching of my father, the late General of the Army Chi-Tong Chan, who taught me the Four Principles of Goodness: Set a good goal in mind; acquire a good wealth of knowledge; exercise good self-discipline; and perform only good deeds.*

CHAN, SIU-WAI, materials science educator; m. Kung Yip Cheung; children: L.Y., K.Y. BS, Columbia U., 1980; ScD, MIT, 1985. Mem. tech. staff Bellcore, Murray Hill, N.J., 1985-86, Red Bank, N.J., 1986-90; assoc. prof. materials sci. Columbia U., N.Y.C., 1990—2002, prof., 2003—. Edn. coord. Chinese Sch. of CCC N.J., 1991-93. Presdl. Faculty fellow NSF, 1993; Guggenheim fellow, 2003-04. Office: Columbia U Sch Engring & Applied Sci 200 Mudd Bldg MC 4701 500 W 120th St New York NY 10027-8031 Business E-Mail: sc174@columbia.edu.

CHAN, SUCHENG, retired history educator, academic administrator; b. Peoples Republic of China, Apr. 16, 1941; came to U.S., 1957; d. Kock K. and Dora K.W. (Chen) C.; m. Mark K. Juergensmeyer, Sept. 21, 1969. BA, Swarthmore Coll., 1963; MA, U. Hawaii, 1965; PhD, U. Calif., Berkeley, 1973. Asst. prof. Sonoma State U., Cotati, Calif., 1971-72; from asst. to assoc. prof. U. Calif., Berkeley, 1974-84, prof., chair Asian Am. studies Santa Barbara, 1988—97, prof. Asian Am. studies and global studies, 1997—2001; prof. history, provost U. Calif. Oakes Coll., Santa Cruz, 1984—88, ret., 2001. Author: This Bittersweet Soil, 1986, Asian Americans: An Interpretive History, 1990, Asian Californians, 1991, Survivors: Cambodian Refugees in the United States, 2004, In Defense of Asian America Studies: The Politics of Teaching and Program Building, 2005; editor: Ethnic and Gender Boundaries in the U.S., 1989, Quiet Odyssey: A Pioneer Korean Woman in America, 1990, Income and Status Differences between White and Minority Americans, 1990, Entry Denied: Exclusion and the Chinese Community in America, 1991, Hmong Means Free: Life in Laos and America, 1994, Peoples of Color in the American West, 1994, Major Problems in California History, 1997, Claiming America: Constructing Chinese American Identitites in the Exclusion Era, 1998, Not Just Victims: Conversations with Cambodian Community Leaders in the United States, 2003, Remapping Asian American History, 2003, Chinese American Transnationalism the Flow of People, Resources and Ideas between China and America during the Exclusion Era, 2005; contbr. articles to profl. jours. Mem. Assn. Asian Am. Studies (pres. 1980-83, history and social sci. prize 1988, 91, 98), Am. Hist. Assn. (Louis Knott Koontz prize 1985, Pacific Coast Br. prize 1987), Orgn. Am. Historians, Immigration History Soc., Calif. History Soc., Agrl. Hist. Soc. (Theodore Saloutos prize 1986). Democrat.

CHAN, SUNNEY IGNATIUS, chemist, educator; b. San Francisco, Oct. 5, 1936; s. Sun and Hip-For (Lai) C.; m. Irene Yuk-Hing Tam, July 11, 1964; 1 son, Michael Kenneth. BSChemE, U. Calif., Berkeley, 1957, PhD in Chemistry, 1960; DSc honoris causa, Hong Kong Bapt. U., 2003. Asst. prof. chemistry U. Calif., Riverside, 1961—63; mem. faculty Calif. Inst. Tech., 1963—, prof. chem. physics, 1968—92, prof. biophys. chemistry, 1976—92, George Grant Hoag prof. biophys. chemistry, 1992—2001, exec. officer for chemistry, 1977—80, 1989—94, master student houses, 1980—83, chmn. faculty, 1987—89, George Grant Hoag prof. biophys. chemistry emeritus, 2002—; dir. Inst. of Chemistry, Academia Sinica, Taipei, Taiwan, 1997—99; disting. rsch. fellow Inst. Chemistry Academia Sinica, Taipei, 1997—, v.p., 1999—2003. R.T. Major lectr. U. Conn., 1998; Wilson T.S. Wang Disting. Internat. prof. Chinese U. Hong Kong, 1993; Reilly lectr. U. Notre Dame, 1973-74; Chan Meml. lectr. U. Calif., Berkeley, 1984; cons. in field. Author numerous articles in field. Recipient CB Net award in biophysics, 2005; Guggenheim fellow, 1968-69; Sloan fellow, 1965-67; NSF Postdoctoral fellow, 1960-61; Fogarty fellow NIH, 1986. Fellow AAAS, Biophys. Soc., Am. Phys. Soc.; mem. Academia Sinica, Am. Chem. Soc., Chinese Am. Chem. Soc. (chmn. bd. 1988-97), Am. Soc. Biochemistry and Molecular Biology (William C. Rose award 2004), Biophys. Soc. Taiwan (pres. 1998-2001), So. Calif. Chinese Engrs. and Scientists Assn. (Progress award 1971), Chinese Collegiate Colleagues So. Calif. (v.p. 1970-71, pres. 1971-72), Chinese Am. Faculty Assn. (pres. 1988, Achievement award 1991, Disting. Svc. award 2000), Third World Acad. Scis., Phi Beta Kappa, Sigma Xi, Tau Beta Pi, Alpha Chi Sigma, Phi Tau Phi (pres. 1981-83, nat. pres. 2004-) Home: 327 Camino Del Sol South Pasadena CA 91030-4107 Office: Calif Inst Tech Chem Dept Pasadena CA 91125-0001 Office Phone: 626-395-6508. Personal E-mail: sunneychan@yahoo.com. Business E-Mail: chans@its.caltech.edu.

CHAN, WAI-YEE, geneticist, educator; b. Canton, China, Apr. 28, 1950; arrived in U.S., 1974; s. Kui and Fung-Hing (Wong) Chan; m. May-Fong Sheung, Sept. 3, 1976; children: Connie Hai-Yee, Joanne Hai-Wei, Victor Hai-Yue, Amanda Hai-Pui, Bessie Hai-Lui. BSc with first class honors, Chinese U. of Hong Kong, 1974; PhD, U. Fla., 1977. Tchg. asst. dept. biochemistry and molecular biology U. Fla., Gainesville, 1974—77; rsch. assoc. U. Okla., Oklahoma City, 1978—79, asst. prof. dept. pediats., 1979—82, assoc. prof., 1982—89, asst. prof. dept. biochemistry and molecular biology, 1979—82, assoc. prof., 1982—89; prof. dept. pediats., biochemistry, molecular biology and cell biology Georgetown U., Washington, 1989—. Staff affiliate pediat. endocrine metabolism and genetic svc. Okla. Children's Meml. Hosp., Oklahoma City, 1979—89, dir. Clin. Trace Metal Diagnostic Lab., 1979—85, asst. sci. dir. Biochem. Genetics and Metabolic Screening Lab., 1980—87; co-dir. State of Okla. Tchg. Hosp., 1982—87. Editor: 2 books and monograph, Jour. Endocrine Genetics, Jour. Am. Coll. Nutrition, Jour. Current Molecular Medicine; contbr. articles to profl. jours. Assoc. mem. Okla. Med. Rsch. Found., Oklahoma City, 1987—89. Recipient Okla. Med. Rsch. Found. Merrick award, 1988; fellow NATO, 1979; scholar, Chinese U. Hong Kong, 1972—74, 1973—74. Mem.: Am. Coll. Nutrition, Endocrine Soc., Am. Assn. Immunology, Soc. Pediat. Rsch., Am. Soc. Cell Biology, Am. Soc. Human Genetics, Am. Soc. Biochem. Molecular Biology, Am. Inst. Nutrition. Achievements include patents for for application of pregnancy-specific glycoproteins; development of of in-vitro diagnostic method for Wilson's Disease. Home: 10708 Butterfly Ct North Potomac MD 20878-4209 Office: LCG NICHD NIH Bldg 49 Rm 2A08 49 Convent Dr MSC 4429 Bethesda MD 20892-4429 Office Phone: 301-451-8821. Personal E-mail: chanw@georgetown.edu. Business E-Mail: chanwy@mail.nih.gov.

CHAN, WILMA, state legislator; b. Boston; 2 children. BA, Wellesley Coll.; M. in Edn. Policy, Stanford U. Mem. Oakland (Calif.) Bd. Edn., 1990—94, Alameda County Bd. Suprs., Oakland, 1994—2000, Calif. State Assembly, Dist. 16, 2000—, majority leader, 2002—04, chair JALAC, 2004, chair edn. budget com., 2004, chair assembly health com., 2005, mem. transp., budget/edn., labor/employment coms., 2005. Mem. com. on health, aging & long term care, com. on jobs, economic develop. and economy, com. on govt. organization, com. on banking and fin. Calif. State Assembly, chair, select com. on Calif. children's sch. readiness and health, co-chair, select com. on language access to state svcs., vice chair, Asian-Pacific Islander legislative caucus, mem. legislative women's caucus, mem. environmental caucus, mem. internet caucus, mem. smart growth caucus. Office Phone: 510-286-1670. Business E-Mail: assemblymember.chan@assembly.ca.gov.

CHAN, WING-CHI, cultural organization administrator, musicologist; b. Hong Kong, Aug. 10, 1952; came to U.S., 1979; s. Hing and Mui-Fung (Leung) C.; m. Mina Chan, Jan. 1, 1979; children: Tidings, Leona, Dexter. BA, Chinese U., Hong Kong, 1978; MMus, No. Ill. U., 1981; postgrad., U. Amsterdam, 1991. Pres. Chinese U. Student Union, Hong Kong, 1977; rsch. asst. U. S.W. La., Lafayette, 1979; mgr. Charm's Trading Co., Houston, 1982; asst. to dir. coll. honors program U. Md., Catonsville, 1974—85; dir. devel. Washington Youth Orch., 1985—96; broadcaster Voice of Am. Radio, 1989—90, Fairchild Radio, Canada, 2001; exec. dir. Nat. Chamber Orch., Washington, 1992; D.C. commr. Nat. & Cmty. Svcs., 1994—97; v.p. Washington Symphony Orch., 1997—99; pres. Washington Cultural Internat. Inc., 1996—. Lectr., spkr. U. Md., College Park, 1983, 84, Tenri (Japan) U., 1986, Kingston Poly., London, 1988, Hong Kong U., 1990, 2003; Macao U. Sci. Tech., 2003; tour coord. Washington Youth Orch. to China, Hong Kong, Taiwan, Korea, Spain, France, Netherlands, and Russia, 1986-94; cons. NEA, Washington, 1989—, N.J. State Arts Coun., 1995, 97, S.C. Arts Commn., 1993; vis. assoc. prof. ShenYang Conservatory, China, 1992—; adj. prof. Green Mountain Coll., Vt. 2002—; artistic adv. China Nat. Symphony Orch., Bejing, 2001—; organizer conf. Asia 4th Pacific Life Underwriters Assns. Conf., Hong Kong, 1997; organizer seminar Aetna Sales Congr., Hong Kong, 1998; organizer Hong Kong New Youth Forum's 2004 U.S. Election observation tour. Recipient Supr. Svc. award Mayor of Washington, 1987. Mem. Assn. for Asian Studies, Am. Symphony Orch. League, Cultural Alliance Greater Washington. Office: Ste 201 419 7th St NW Washington DC 20004 Personal E-mail: wcichan@aol.com.

CHAN, YIUMO, biochemist; b. Hong Kong, June 25, 1967; s. Man and Kwok-ying Chan; m. Mei-hua Chen, Dec. 19, 2001. BS in Chemistry, U. Chgo., 1989, PhD of Devel. Biology, 1995. Postdoctoral fellow Harvard Med. Sch., Boston, 1995—2001; staff scientist Geisinger Hosp., Danville, Pa., 2001—. Adv. Coun. Healthcare Gerson Lehrman Group, NYC, 2001—; mem. Sci. Adv. Bd., Arlington, Va., 2002—. Co-author: Principles of Molecular Medicine, 1998; contbr. articles to profl. jours. Mem.: ACLU, AAAS, NY Acad. Scis., Am. Soc. Human Genetics (mentorship program), Amnesty Internat. Democrat. Achievements include discovery of genetic basis of an inherited skin blistering disease, Weber-Cockayne Epidermolysis Bullose Simplex; research in understanding muscular dystrophies and development of therapy for neuromuscular diseases. Avocations: reading, travel, art, coin collecting/numismatics, stamp collecting/philately. Office: Geisinger Hosp Weis Ctr for Rsch 100 N Academy Ave MC 26-11 Danville PA 17822 Office Phone: 570-271-6851. E-mail: ymchan@geisinger.edu.

CHANCE, F. EARLAYNE, artist; b. Austin, Tex., Oct. 29, 1942; d. (stepfather) Alford B. and Ermer Grace Hess; father: Earl J. Lee Summerrow; m. Kenneth D. Chance; children: Michael, Gregory A. Student, S.W. Tex. State U., 1961—63, U. Tex., Austin, 1963—64. Greenberg Pub. Co., Chester, NY, 1994-, Salmagundi Art Club, 1994, Irving (Tex.) Art Ctr., 1994—, Hill Country Art Found., Ingram, Tex., 2000-03, Contemporary Masters INvitational, Fredericksburg, Tex., 2005. Mem. Hays County Women's Polit. Caucus, San Marcos, Tex., 1989-96. Recipient Best of Show award PBS Sta. KLRU-TV, 1996. Mem. DAR, Daus. Republic of Tex., Kerrville C. of C., Oil Painters Am Methodist. Avocations: travel, photography, genealogy. Office: Chance Studio 220 Oak Hills Dr Kerrville TX 78028 Office Phone: 830-257-1529.

CHANCE, JANE, English literature educator; b. Neosho, Mo., Oct. 26, 1945; d. Donald William and Julia (Mile) C.; m. Dennis Carl Nitzsche, June, 1966 (div. Mar. 1969); 1 child, Therese; m. Paolo Passaro, Apr. 30, 1981,(div. May 2002); children: Antony Damian, Joseph Sebastian. BA in English with honors and highest distinction, Purdue U., 1967; AM in English, U. Ill., 1968, PhD of English, 1971. Lectr. U. Sask., Canada, 1971—72, asst. prof., 1972—73; asst. prof. English, Rice U., Houston, 1973—77, assoc. prof., 1977—80, prof., 1980—, dir. medieval studies program, 2005—; hon. rsch. fellow U. Coll. U. London, 1977—78. Sec., Scientia, Rice U., 1982-83, acting dir., 1983-84; dir. NEH Summer Seminar for Coll. Tchrs. on Chaucer and Mythography, 1985, NEH Inst. for Coll. Tchrs. on Medieval Women, 1997; pres., founder TEAMS, 1986-89; founder, dir. medieval studies program Rice U., 1986-92, 2005—; founding mem. Rice U. Commn. on Women, 1986-88; resident Rockefeller Found., Bellagio, Italy, 1988; mem. Sch. Hist. Studies, Inst. for Advanced Study, Princeton, 1988-89; vis. rsch. fellow Inst. for Advanced Studies in Humanities, U. Edinburgh, summer, 1994; Eccles fellow Humanities Ctr., U. Utah, 1994-95; spkr. in field; lectr. in field. Author: The Genius Figure in Antiquity and the Mid. Ages, 1975, Tolkien's Art: A Mythology for Eng., 1979, Woman as Hero in Old English Lit., 1986, The Lord of the Rings: The Mythology of Power, 1992;: rev. edit., 2001, Japanese trans., 2003, Medieval Mythography: From Roman North Africa to the Sch. of Chártres, AD 433-1177 (South Ctrl. MLA book prize, 1994), The Mythographic Chaucer: The Fabulation of Sexual Politics, 1995, Medieval Mythography, vol. 2: From the Sch. of Chartres to the Ct. at Avignon, 1177-1350, 2000; translator: Christine de Pizan's Letter of Othea to Hector, 1990; editor: The Mythographic Art: Classical Fable and the Rise of the Vernacular in Early France and Eng., 1990, Medievalism in the Twentieth Century, Studies in Medievalism, vol. 2:2, 1983, The Inklings and Others, vol. 3:3, 1990, Gender and Text in the Later Mid. Ages, 1996, rpt. pb., 2003, The Assembly of Gods, 1999, Tolkien the Medievalist, 2002 (finalist Mythopoeic award, 2005, 2005), Tolkien and the Invention of Myth: A Reader, 2004, Women Medievalists and the Academy, 2005 (Best Essay prize Soc. for Medieval Feminist Scholarship, 2005); co-editor: Approaches to Tchg. Sir Gawain, 1986, Mapping the Cosmos, 1985; gen. editor: Focus Libr. of Medieval Women, 1988—, Boydell & Brewer Libr. of Medieval Women, 1997—, series editor: Greenwood Guides to Hist. Events in the Medieval World, 2001—, Praeger Series on the Mid. Ages, 2003—, mem. editl. bd.: Coll. Lit., 2002—. Bd. dirs. Rice U. Press, 1981-88, Internat. Chaucer Studio, 2003—. NEH fellow, 1977-78, Guggenheim fellow, 1980-81, ACLS Travel grantee, 1982, Mellon leave Rice U., 1988, Disting. Faculty Tchg. fellow, 1995, Ctr. for Study Cultures fellow, 1998, NEH Fellow, St. Louis Univ. Ctr. for Med. Studies, 2003, Mellon Fellow, Pope Pius Vatican Film Libr., 2003; named in her honor Julia Mile Chance prize for tchng. Excellence 1997, Women's Ctr. IMPACT award Rice U., 1998; recipient Best Essay prize Soc. Medieval Femininist Scholarship, 2005. Mem. AAUP (Rice U. chpt. sec., treas. 1975-76), MLA, S.C. MLA, Scientia (acting dir. 1983-84, sec. 1982-83), Internat. Soc. Classical Tradition, Internat. Neo-Latin Soc., Tex. Faculty Assn. (exec. com., 1995-99, v.p., 1998-2000, Achievement award 1998), Tolkien Soc., Medieval Acad. Am., Internat. Arthurion Soc Avocations: book collecting, photography, travel. Office: Rice U Dept English MS 30 PO Box 1892 Houston TX 77251-1892 Office Phone: 713-348-2625. Business E-Mail: jchance@rice.edu.

CHANCE, KENNETH BERNARD, SR., endodontist educator, academic administrator; b. N.Y.C., Dec. 8, 1953; s. George E. and Janie L. (Bolles).; m. Sharon Lee Lewis, July 11, 1981; children: Kenneth Bernard, Dana Marie, Christopher, Jacquelyn. BS, Fordham U., 1975; DDS, Case Western Res. U., 1979; Cert. in Endodontics, U. Medicine and Dentistry N.J., 1982. Asst. attending Jamaica Hosp., Queens, N.Y., 1981-87; chief endodontics Kings County Med. Ctr., Bklyn., 1982-91; assoc. prof. endodontics U. Medicine and Dentistry N.J., 1987; also dir. external affairs N.J. Dental Sch.; asst. attending North Ctrl. Bronx (N.Y.) Hosp., 1983-91, Kingsbrook Jewish Med. Ctr., 1986-92; asst. dean external affairs and urban resource devel. N.J. Dental Sch., 1989-97; cons. Harlem Hosp., N.Y.C., 1982-90; health policy advisor to U.S. Senator Frank Lautenberg of N.J., 1991—99; dir. health policy program The Joint Ctr. Polit. and Econ. Studies, 1993-94; acting chmn. dept. endodontics N.J. Dental Sch., 1994-97; fed. rels. adv. com. U. Medicine and Dentistry N.J., 1994-97; dean, prof. endodontics Meharry Med. Coll. Sch. Dentistry, 1997-2000; prof., dir. divsn. endodontics U. Ky., Lexington, 2000—. Delivered commencement address Case Western Res. U., Sch. Dental Medicine, 2005. Min. of music, sr. organist Sharon Bapt. Ch., Bronx, 1983-91; mem. healthcare task force Congl. Black Caucus, 1994-2001; trustee Case Western Res. U., 2005—. Recipient Dr. Paul F. Sherwood award for excellence in endodontics Case Western Res. U. Dental Sch., 1979, Cmty. Svc. award U. Medicine and Dentistry N.J., 1997, Tenn. Outstanding Achievement award, 1998, Outstanding Academician award U. Medicine and Dentistry N.J., 1999, Disting. Alumnus of Yr. award, Case Western Res. U., 2004; Found. grant award U. Medicine and Dentistry N.J., 1984, Exceptional Merit award, 1985, Excellence award, 1990, Disting. Practioner award Nat. Acad. Practice Dentistry, 2001, Faculty award U. Ky., Sch. Dentistry, 2005; fellow Nat. Dental Leadership Devel. PEW, 1991, Robert Wood Johnson Health Policy, 1991, Pierre Fauchard Acad., 1996. Fellow Am. Coll. Dentists, Internat. Coll. Dentists; mem. ADA, Internat. Assn. Dental Rsch., Am. Dental Edn. Assn. (chair minority affairs sect. 2003), Am. Assn. Dental Schs., Nat. Dental Assn., Am. Assn. Endodontists, Greater Met. Dental Soc. N.Y. (pres.-elect 1986-87, v.p. 1984-86), Ky. Assn. Endodontists, Omicron Kappa Upsilon. Home: 2140 Mangrove Dr Lexington KY 40513 Office Phone: 859-323-7891. Business E-Mail: kbchan2@uky.edu.

CHANCE, STEVEN KENT, lawyer; b. Bryn Mawr, Pa., July 9, 1945; s. Henry Martyn and Elisabeth (Reese) C.; m. Colleen Benson Meyle; 1 child, Anna Benson. BA, Wesleyan U., 1967; MS, London Sch. Econs., 1968; JD, U. Pa., 1973. Assoc. Dechert Price & Rhoads, Phila., 1973-82, ptnr., 1982-84; dir. legal services Teleflex Inc., Limerick, Pa., 1984-86, v.p., dir. legal services, 1986—92, v.p., gen. counsel, sec., 1992—. Mem. ABA. Clubs: Corinthian Yacht (Phila.) (trustee 1986—); Cruising Am. Episcopalian. Home: 1212 Weybridge Ln Radnor PA 19087-4635 Office: Teleflex Inc 155 S Limerick Rd Royersford PA 19468-1603*

CHANCELLOR, BETTY ANN, elementary school educator; b. Shawnee, Okla., Oct. 15, 1940; d. Leon D. and Marie J. (Sontag) Shepherd; m. O. Duane Chancellor, Apr. 3, 1959 (dec. Mar. 1992); children: Terry Duahe, Delaina, Anita. BA cum laude, Okla. Bapt. U., 1973; MEd, Cen. State U., 1985. Tchr. 1st grade North Rock Creek Sch., Shawnee, Okla., 1973-78; tchr. 5th-6th grade sci. and social studies, primary gifted, talented North Rock Creek Schs., Shawnee, Okla., 1978-79, tchr. 4th grade, 1979-82, tchr. remedial reading and fed. programs, 1982-87, kindergarten tchr., 1987-89, 1st grade tchr., examiner kindergarten screening, 1989—. Mem. tchr. edn. com. Okla. Bapt. U., 1996—99. Edn. grant, Shawnee Edn. Found., 2003, 2005. Mem.: ASCD, NEA, Shawnee Assn. Children with Learning Disabilities (resource chmn.), Pottawatomie County Assn. Classroom Tchrs. (pres., v.p.), Pottawatomie County Reading Coun. (pres., bd. dirs.), Okla. Edn. Assn., North Rock Creek Edn. Assn. (treas.), Okla. Assn. Gifted, Creative and Talented, Okla. Reading Coun., Internat. Reading Assn., Okla. ASCD, Delta Kappa Gamma (pres. Alpha Beta chpt. Gamma State 1990—92), Kappa Delta Pi. Home: 37 River Bend Dr Shawnee OK 74804-9424 Office: North Rock Creek Sch 42400 Garretts Lake Rd Shawnee OK 74804-9301

CHANCELLOR, VAN, professional basketball coach; b. Louisville, Miss. m. Betty Chancellor; children: John, renee. Student, East Ctrl. Jr. Coll., Decatur, Miss.; B.Math. and Phys. Edn., Miss. State U., 1965, MEd, 1974. Head coach boys' basketball Noxapater (Miss.) H.S.; head coach women's basketball U. Miss., Oxford; head coach, gen. mgr. Houston Comets, 1997-99. Three time WNBA champions; USA Basketball Nat. Coach of Year, 2002. Achievements include head coach, USA Basketball Women's World Championship Team, 2002; head coach, gold medal US Women's basketball team, 2004 Olympics, Athens. Office: Houston Comets 1510 Polk St Houston TX 77002

CHANCELLOR, WILLIAM JOSEPH, agricultural engineering educator; b. Alexandria, Va., Aug. 25, 1931; s. John Miller and Caroline (Sedlacek) C.; m. Nongkarn Bodhiprasart, Dec. 13, 1960; 1 child, Marisa Kuakul BS in Agr., BSME, U. Wis., 1954; MS in Agrl. Engring., Cornell U., 1956, PhD, 1957. Registered profl. agrl. engr., Calif. Prof. agrl. engring. U. California.-Davis, 1957-94; prof. emeritus. Vis. prof. agrl. engring. U. Malaya, Kuala Lumpur, Malaysia, 1962-63; UNESCO cons. Punjab Agrl. U., 1976 Contbr. articles to profl. jours.; patentee transmission, planters, dryer, 1961-73 East/West Ctr. sr. Fellow, Honolulu, 1976 Fellow Am. Soc. Agrl. Engrs. (Kishida Internat. award 1984, John Deere Gold Medal award 2004); mem. Soc. Automotive Engrs., Sigma Xi: found. mem. Asian Assoc. for Agrl. Engring. Office: Univ of California Dept Biol & Agrl Engineering Davis CA 95616 Business E-Mail: wjchancellor@ucdavis.edu.

CHANDAN, JIT S., management consultant, educator; b. Jahania Mandi, India, Mar. 29, 1937; arrived in U.S., 1963; s. Gurdit Singh and Bhanwan Bai; m. Sundesh K. Chandan, July 21, 1968; children: Sunjit S. Chawla, Upjeet K. MS, Sheffield U., U.K., 1963, Columbia U., 1965, PE, 1966; MBA, Baruch Coll., 1972; PhD, Delhi U., India, 1977. Cert. 1st class colliery mgr. cert. Ministry of Fuel and Power, U.K. Asst. prof. N.Y. Inst. Tech., 1966—72; prof. Medgar Evers Coll. CUNY, 1977—. Author: Management Concepts and Strategies, 1998, Statistics for Business and Economics, 1997, Organizational Behavior, 1994, Strategic Management, 2004. Chair edn. and rsch. coms. Soc. Indian Academics of Am., N.Y.C., 1990—; gen. sec. Internat. Punjabi Soc., N.Y.C., 1972—92. Fellow King George VI Meml. fellowship, English Speaking Union, 1963—64. Mem.: Acad. Mgmt. Avocations: photography, travel, spiritual understanding. Home: 137-74 75 Rd Flushing NY 11367 Office: Medgar Evers Coll CUNY 1650 Bedford Ave Brooklyn NY 11225

CHANDLER, ALBERT BENJAMIN, III, congressman, former state attorney general; b. Lexington, Ky., Sept. 12, 1959; m. Jennifer Chandler; children: Lucie Brasher, Albert Benjamin IV, Russell Branham. BA in History with distinction, U. Ky., 1983, JD, 1986. Bar: Ky. 1986. Assoc. Brown, Todd & Heyburn, Lexington, Ky., Reeves & Graddy, Versailles, Ky.; auditor State of Ky., 1992—95, atty. gen., 1996—2003; mem. 108th Congress from 6th Ky dist., 2004—. Recipient Achievement of Yr. award, Assn. Govt. Accts., 1993—94. Mem.: ABA, Woodford County Bar Assn., Ky. Bar Assn. (named Outstanding Young Lawyer 1993). Democrat. Presbyterian. Office: 1117 Longworth House Office Bldg Washington DC 20515-1706*

CHANDLER, ALFRED DUPONT, JR., historian, educator; b. Guyencourt, Del., Sept. 15, 1918; s. Alfred Dupont and Carol (Ramsay) C.; m. Fay Martin, Jan. 8, 1944; children: Alpine Douglass Chandler Bird, Mary Morris Chandler Watt, Alfred Dupont III, Howard Martin. AB, Harvard U., 1940, AM, 1947, PhD, 1952, LLD (hon.), 1995; PhD (hon.), U. Leuven, Belgium, 1976, U. Antwerp, 1979; LHD (hon.), Babson Coll., 1982, Ohio State U., 1987; LLD (hon.), York U., Can., 1988, New England Coll., 1992; LLD (hon.), U. Del., 2002; DBA (hon.), Northeastern U., 2002. Research assoc. MIT, 1950-51, from instr. to prof., 1951-63; prof. history Johns Hopkins U., 1963-71, chmn. dept., 1966-70, dir. Center for Study Recent Am. History, 1964-71; Straus prof. bus. history Harvard U. Bus. Sch., 1971-89, prof. emeritus, 1989—. Vis. fellow All Souls Coll., Oxford U., 1975; vis. prof. European Inst. Advanced Studies in Mgmt., Brussels, 1979; Walker-Ames vis. prof. U. Wash., 1981; cons. U.S. Naval War Coll., 1954; mem. Nat. Adv. Council on Edn. Professions Devel., 1970-71; chmn. adv. hist. com. U.S. AEC (renamed ERDA 1974), 1969-77. Author: Henry Varnum Poor, 1956, Strategy and Structure (Newcomen award 1964), 1962, Giant Enterprise, 1964, The Railroads, 1965; co-author (with Stephen Salsbury): Pierre S. duPont, 1971; author: The Visible Hand (Pulitzer and Bancroft prizes for 1978); co-author (with Herman Daems): Managerial Hierarchies, 1980; co-author: (with Richard Tedlow) The Coming of Managerial Capitalism, 1985; author: Scale and Scope, 1990, Inventing the Electronic Century, 2001; editor: Papers of Dwight D. Eisenhower, 5 vols., 1970; co-editor: Big Business and The Wealth of Nations, 1997, The Dynamic Firm, 1998, A Nation Transformed by Information, 2000; editor (asst.): The Letters of Theodore Roosevelt, 4 vols., 1952—54; subject of The Essential Alfred Chandler, 1988; author: Shaping the Industrial Century, 2005; co-editor: Multinationals and the New Global History, 2005. Trustee Park Sch., Brookline, Mass., 1957-63, chmn. bd. 1961-63; trustee Brookline Pub. Libr., 1959-63, Roland Park Sch., Balt., 1964-70, Johns Hopkins U., 1971-81, Eleutherian Mills-Hagley Found., 1981-95, hon. trustee, 1995—. Lt. comdr. USNR, 1940-45. Recipient Pulitzer prize for history, 1978, Bancroft prize, 1978, award, Assn. Am. Pubs., 1991, Melamed prize, 1992, Eminent Scholar award, Acad. Internat. Bus., 2000; rsch. fellow, Harvard U., 1955, Guggenheim fellow, 1958—59. Mem. Am. Acad. Arts and Scis., Econ. History Assn. (trustee 1966-70, pres. 1971-72), Orgn. Am. Historians (exec. bd. 1969-72), Soc. for History Tech. (exec. coun. 1972-75), Am. Hist. Assn. (Scholarly Distinction award 1997), Soc. Am. Historians, Mass. Hist. Soc. (coun. 1977-83, John F. Kennedy award 2003), Bus. History Conf. (pres. 1977-78, Life Time Achievement award 2002), Am. Antiquarian Soc., Am. Philos. Soc., Brit. Acad., Japan Acad., Acad. Mgmt. (Scholarly Contbn. to Mgmt. award 1985), St. Botolph Club (Boston), Nantucket Yacht Club (Mass.). Episcopalian.

CHANDLER, ALICE, retired academic administrator, educational consultant; b. Bklyn., May 29, 1931; d. Samuel and Jenny (Meller) Kogan; m. Horace Chandler, June 10, 1954; children: Seth, Donald, Barnard C. AB, Columbia U., 1951, MA, 1953, PhD, 1960; LHD, Kean U., 1997, Ramapo Coll., 2001. Instr. Skidmore Coll., 1953-54; lectr. Columbia U. Barnard Coll., 1954-55, Hunter Coll., CUNY, 1956-57; from instr. to prof. CCNY, 1961-76, v.p. instl. advancement, 1974-76, v.p. acad. affairs, 1974-76, provost, 1976-79, acting pres., 1979-80; pres. SUNY Coll., New Paltz, 1980-96; interim pres. Ramapo Coll., 2000-2001. Cons. in higher edn., 1996—; bd. dirs. Mohonk Mountain House, N.J. Coun. Humanities. Author: The Prose Spectrum: A Rhetoric and Reader, 1968, The Theme of War, 1969, A Dream of Order, 1970, The Rationale of Rhetoric, 1970, The Rationale of the Essay, 1971, From Smollett to James, 1980, Foreign Student Policy: England, France, and West Germany, 1985, Obligation or Opportunity: Foreign Student Policy in Six Major Receiving Countries, 1989, Access, Inclusion and Equity: Imperatives for America's Campuses, 1997, Public Higher Education and the Public Good: Public Policy at the Crossroads, 1998, Paying the Bill for International Education: Programs, Purposes, and Possibilities at the Millenium, 1999. Lizette Fisher fellow. Mem. Lotos, Phi Beta Kappa. E-mail: hchand5066@aol.com.

CHANDLER, ARTHUR BLEAKLEY, pathologist, educator; b. Augusta, Ga., Sept. 11, 1926; s. Clemmons Quillian and Mary Isabella (Bleakley) Chandler; m. Jane Stoughton Downing, Sept. 2, 1953; children: Arthur Bleakley, John Downing. Student, U. Ga., 1943-44; MD, Med. Coll. Ga., 1948. Diplomate Am. Bd. Pathology. Intern Baylor U. Hosp., Dallas, 1948-49; resident in pathology, NIH trainee in cancer dept. pathology Med. Coll. Ga., 1950-51, asst. in pathology, 1949-50, mem. faculty, 1949—, prof. pathology, 1962-2000, chmn. dept., 1975-2000, emeritus prof., emeritus chmn., 2001—. Com. mem. Nat. Heart, Lung and Blood Inst., 1969—93. Mem. editl. bd. Haemostasis, 1975—83, Pathology Rsch. and Practice, 1987—2001;, author papers in field; contbr. chapters to books. Trustee Young Mens Libr. Assn. Fund, 1962—72, Historic Augusta, Inc., 1966—69, Augusta-Richmond County Mus., 1965—87, Dan Printup Meml. Trust, 1985—2000, Acad. Richmond County, 1984—. Officer AUS Med. Corps, 1951—53. Fellow Commonwealth Fund, Norway, 1963—64. Fellow: Thrombosis Rsch. Inst., Oslo; mem.: AMA, Sch. Medicine Alumni Assn. Med. Coll. Ga. (pres. 1996—97), Richmond County Med. Soc. (trustee 1984—2002, sec. 1987, v.p. 1988), Med. Assn. Ga., Ga. Heart Assn., Ga. Assn. Pathologists (pres. 1984—85), Am. Heart Assn. (chmn. coun. on thrombosis 1978—80, chmn. com. on coronary lesions and myocardial infarctions 1980—82, fellow coun. arteriosclerosis), Am. Soc. Hematology, Am. Assn. Pathologists, Coll. Am. Pathologists, Am. Assn. History Medicine, Internat. Soc. for History of Medicine, Internat. Soc. Thrombosis and Haemostasis, Internat. Acad. Pathology, Alpha Omega Alpha. Episcopalian. Home: 803 Milledge Rd Augusta GA 30904-4351 Office: Med Coll Ga Dept Pathology Augusta GA 30912

CHANDLER, AUSTIN GRACE, psychologist; BA in Psychology with honors, Columbia U., 1970, MA, 1972; PhD, Fordham U., 1982; postgrad. in Bus., U. N.C., Greensboro, 1990. Lic., clin. psychologist. Corp. cons. Farr Assocs., 1983-85; mem. adj. faculty, founder, dir. coll. counseling ctr. Greensboro Coll., 1985-92; founder, pres. Allied Counseling and Consulting Enterprises, 1992—; chief psychologist Evergreens Sr. Health Care Facilities, NC, 1997—2001; psychology cons. Therapeutic Alternatives, Inc., NC, 2002—03; dir. psychology Guilford Child Health, Inc., NC, 2003—. Mem. adj. faculty U. N.C., Greensboro; bd. dirs. Ashley Industries. Author: (with Jack Bornstein) Food is Killing You, 1997; contbr. articles to profl. jours. Bd. dirs. N.C. Aging and Mental Health Coalition. Recipient Psychologist of Yr. award N.C. Chiropractic Assn. Mem. APA, N.C. Psychol. Assn., Prescription Privileges for Psychologists Register (charter), Sigma Xi. Avocations: painting, writing, following the stock market, skiing. Office: Allied Counseling & Consulting Enterprises 8200 Crows Nest Ln Greensboro NC 27455-9294 Office Phone: 336-272-1050. Office Fax: 336-643-6850. Business E-Mail: austin_chandler@bellsouth.net.

CHANDLER, BRUE STANHOPE, III, hospital administrator; b. El Paso, Tex., Jan. 9, 1949; s. Brue Stanhope Jr. and Maxine (Mabry) C.; m. Susan Henderson, June 20, 1970; children: Hope Bennett, Mabry Susan. BIE, Ga. Inst. Tech., 1970; MHA, Ga. State U., 1975. Rsch. assoc. Ga. Med. Care Found., Atlanta, 1972-74; assoc. adminstr. Kennestone Hosp., Marietta, Ga., 1974-87; exec. v.p., COO Our Lady of Lake Regional Med. Ctr., Baton Rouge, 1987—. Instr. Ga. State U., Atlanta, 1979-86; preceptor Ga. Inst. Tech., Atlanta, 1982-87; adj. faculty U. Ala., Birmingham, 1991—. Bd. dirs. La. Health Ins. Assn., Baton Rouge, 1990—, bd. dirs. Hospice Found. Greater Baton Rouge, 1988, treas., 1992; mem. exec. bd. Instouma Area coun. Boy Scouts Am., Baton Rouge, 1988; com. mem. Capital Area United Way, Baton Rouge, 1991—, treas., 1993—. Fellow Am. Coll. Health Care Execs. (regent 1994—); mem. La. Hosp. Assn. (southeastern dist. pres. 1990), Ga. Hosp. Assn. (bd. dirs. north ctrl. dist., sec.-treas.), Southeastern Hosp. Conf. (bd. dirs. 1986), Rotary. Methodist. Office: Our Lady of the Lake Regional Med Ctr 5000 Hennessy Blvd Baton Rouge LA 70808-4367

CHANDLER, CHARLES Q., IV, energy executive; BA bus. adm., Kansas State Univ., 1975; MBA, Northwestern Univ., 1976. Pres., dir. INTRUST Fin. Corp.; chmn., CEO INTRUST Bank; chmn. bd. dir. Westar Energy. Bd. dir. Slavation Army, Wesley Medical Ctr., Kansas Soc. Crippled Children. Office: Westar Energy PO Box 889 Topeka KS 66601-0889 Office Phone: 785-575-6300.*

CHANDLER, CHRISTOPHER MARK (CHRIS CHANDLER), professional football player; b. Everett, Wash., Oct. 12, 1965; Degree in econ., Wash. State U., 1988. Quarterback Indpls. Colts, 1988—89, Tampa Bay Buccaneers, 1990—91, Phoenix Cardinals, 1991—93, L.A. Rams, 1994, Houston Oilers, 1995—96, Atlanta Falcons, 1997—2001, Chicago Bears, 2002—04, St. Louis Rams, 2004—; named Pro Bowl team, 1997. Office: c/o St Louis Rams 1 Rams Way Earth City MO 63045

CHANDLER, CYNTHIA LANYON, systems administrator; b. Madison, Wis., Nov. 11, 1954; d. Wesley E. and Vernia E. Lanyon; m. Richard S. Chandler, Aug. 9, 1986; children: Jeffrey Fremont, Jonathan Wesley. BA in Zoology, SUNY, Geneseo, 1975. Mgr. U.S. Joint Global Ocean Flux Study Data Mgmt. Office, Woods Hole, Mass., 1999—2005, Ocean Carbon and Biogeochemistry Data Mgmt. Office, Woods Hole, Mass., 2005—. Vol. Volunteers in Pub. Schools, Falmouth, Mass., 1991—2005. Mem.: Am. Soc. Info. Sci. and Tech. Independent. Avocations: hiking, kayaking, tennis, bicycling. Office: Woods Hole Oceanographic Inst MS 43 Woods Hole MA 02543 Office Phone: 508-289-2765.

CHANDLER, DAVID WOOD, music educator; b. Daytona Beach, Fla., Aug. 22, 1947; s. Daniel Frank and Louise McClung Chandler; m. Cheryle Ann Cain Chandler; children: DAvid Alan, Susan Elaine, Jereny Nicholas. B in Music Edn., Fla. State U., 1969. Cert. educator Fla. Music educator Glades County Sch. Bd., Moore Haven, Fla., 1969—74; v.p. Live Oak (Fla.) Gas Co., Inc., 1974—81, pres., 1981—99; music educator Lafayette County Sch. Bd., Mayo, Fla., 2001—. Choir dir. 1st Presbyn. Ch., Live Oak, 1974—94. Mem.: NEA, Fla. Educators Assn., Fla. Music Educators Assn., Rotary (pres. 1979, bd. dirs. 1978—88). Republican. Presbyterian. Avocations: gardening, fishing. Office: Lafayette High Sch 160 NE Hornet Dr Mayo FL 32066

CHANDLER, EDWARD WILLIAM, communication systems engineer, electrical engineer, electrical engineering educator; b. Milw., Oct. 10, 1953; s. Donald Harold and Helen Aleidia (Wonders) C.; m. Christine Anne Wohl, June 13, 1987; children: Rebecca Marie, Marcella Anne, Mary Elizabeth, Andrew Donald. BS, U. Wis., Milw., 1975; MSEE, Ill. Inst. Tech., 1978; PhD, Purdue U., 1985. Registered profl. engr., Wis. Electronics engr. Comms. and Electronics divsn. Motorola Inc., Schaumburg, Ill., 1976-77; instr. elec. engring. Milw. Sch. Engring., 1977-79, asst. prof., 1979-80, assoc. prof., 1982-84, prof., 1992—, acting head electronic comms. engring. tech. program, 1978-79, head, 1979-80, dir. elec. engring. program, 1982-84, dir. MS in Engring. program, 1992-2001, dir. elec. engring. tech. program, 2003—; asst. prof. elec. engring. Marquette U., Milw., 1984-86; sr. engr. Titan Corp. (formerly Govt Sys. divsn. M/A-COM, Inc.), San Diego, 1986-88, mem. tech. staff, 1988-92, engring. cons. Comms. and Electronic Warfare Divsn., 1992—. Lectr. U. Wis., Milw., 1979-83; invited lectr. Czech Tech. U., 1997-98, Tech. U. Budapest, 1998, Fachhoschchule, Lübeck, Germany, 2000; grad. instr. rsch. Purdue U., West Lafayette, Ind., 1980-82; rsch. cons. Naval Ocean Systems Ctr., San Diego, 1986. Contbr. articles to profl. jours. David Ross summer grantee, 1981; Faculty Rsch. grantee Milw. Sch. Engring., 1983; resipient Karl O. Werwath Engring. Rsch. award Sch. Engring., 2004. Mem. IEEE (sr., newsletter editor Milw. sect. 1985-86), Am. Soc. Engring. Edn., Armed Forces Comms. and Electronics Assn., Air Force Assn., Triangle, Sigma Xi, Tau Beta Pi, Eta Kappa Nu. Home: 7030 N Range Line Rd Glendale WI 53209-2621 Office: Milw Sch Engring 1025 N Broadway Milwaukee WI 53202-3109 Office Phone: 414-277-7337. Business E-Mail: chandler@msoe.edu.

CHANDLER, EDWIN RUSSELL, clergyman, writer; b. L.A., Sept. 9, 1932; s. Edwin Russell Sr. and Mary Elizabeth (Smith) C.; m. Sandra Lynn Swisher, Aug. 24, 1957 (div. 1977); children— Heather, Holly, Timothy John; m. Marjorie Lee Moore, Dec. 21, 1978; 3 stepchildren Student, Stanford U., 1950-52; BS in Bus. Adminstrn., UCLA, 1952-55; postgrad., U. So. Calif. Grad. Sch. Religion, 1955, New Coll., Edinburgh, Scotland, 1955-56; M.Div., Princeton Theol. Sem., 1958; grad., Washington Journalism Ctr., 1967. Ordained to ministry Presbyterian Ch., 1958. Asst. pastor 1st Presbyn. Ch., Concord, Calif., 1958-61; pastor Escalon Presbyn. Ch., Calif., 1961-66; reporter Modesto Bee, Calif., 1966-67; religion editor Washington Star, 1968-69; news editor Christianity Today, Washington, 1969-72; reporter Sonora Daily Union Dem., Calif., 1972-73; religion writer L.A. Times, 1974-92; interim pastor 1st Presbyn. Ch., Columbia, Calif., 1995-96. Author: The Kennedy Explosion, 1972, Budgets, Bedrooms and Boredom, 1976; co-author: Your Family--Frenzy or Fun?, 1977, The Overcomers, 1978, Understanding the New Age, 1988 (Silver Angel award 1989, Wilbur award 1989), Racing Toward 2001, 1992, Doomsday, 1993, Feeding the Flock, 1998; contbr. articles to profl. jours. Recipient Arthur West award United Methodist Communications Council, 1978, Faith and Freedom award Religious Heritage of Am., 1993; co-recipient Silver Angel award, Religion in Media, 1985 Mem. Religion Newswriters Assn. (pres. 1982-84, co-founder ann. Chandler award 2003, James O. Supple Meml. award, 1976, 1984, 86, John M. Templeton Reporter of Yr. award 1984, 87, 89), Phi Delta Theta Republican. Avocations: travel, beekeeping, birdwatching, theater. Home and Office: 14493 Kebra Ln Sonora CA 95370-9692 Personal E-mail: erchandler@aol.com.

CHANDLER, ELISABETH GORDON (MRS. LACI DE GERENDAY), sculptor, musician; b. St. Louis, June 10, 1913; d. Henry Brace and Sara Ellen (Sallee) Gordon; m. Robert Kirkland Chandler, May 27, 1946 (dec.); m. Laci de Gerenday, May 12, 1979 (dec.). Grad., Lenox Sch., 1931; pvt. study sculpture and harp; LHD (hon.), St. Joseph Coll., 2001. Mem. Mildred Dilling Harp Ensemble, 1934-45; prof. sculpture Lyme Acad. Fine Arts, 1976—, chair sculpture dept. Exhibited sculpture NAD, Nat. Sculpture Soc., Allied Artists Am., Nat. Arts Club, Pen and Brush, Lyme Art Assn., Mattatuck Mus., Catherine Lorillard Wolfe Art Club, Am. Artists Profl. League, Hudson Valley Art Assn., USIA, 1976-78, Lyme Art Ctr., 1979, retrospective exhbn. Lyme Acad. Fine Arts, 1987, Madison Gallery, 1987, Old State House, Hartford, Conn., 1989, Mellon Art Ctr., Wallingford, Conn., 1989, Fairfield U. Walsh Gallery, 1991, Brit. Mus., London, Am. Medallic Sculptors Assn. Traveling Exhbn., 1994, Slater Mus. Cropsey Found., 1995, Nat. Sculpture Exhbn. Lyme Acad. Fine Arts, 1995-96, Lever House, N.Y.C., 1996, America's Tower, 1996-98, Hillsdale (Mich.) Coll., 1997, Nat. Acad. Mus., N.Y.C., 1998; represented in permanent collections Aircraft Carrier USS Forrestal, Gov. Dummer Acad., James Forrestal Rsch. Ctr. of Princeton U., Lenox Sch., James L. Collins Parochial Sch., Tex., Storm King Art Ctr., Columbia U., Pace U., White Plains, N.Y., St. Patrick's Cathedral, N.Y.C., McAuley Ctr., St. Joseph's Coll., West Hartford, Conn., Nat. Acad. Mus.; designed and executed Brookgreen Gardens medal, Forrestal Meml. Medal, Timoschenko Medal for Applied Mechanics, Benjamin Franklin Medal, Albert A. Michelson Medal, Jonathan Edwards Medal, Shafto Broadcasting Award Medal, Enrichment of Life medal Soc. Medallists, Adlai Stevenson bronze bust for Woodrow Wilson Sch. of Princeton U., 250 Ann. George Washington medal,Owen R. Cheatham bronze bust for Ga. Pacific Bldg., Atlanta, Messiah Coll., Grantham, Pa., Adlai E. Stevenson High Sch., Ill., Queen Anne's County Courthouse Square, Md., Our Lady Mercy Hosp., N.Y.C., Albert A. Michelson bust in Hall of Fame for Great Americans, pvt. collections. Active mus. therapy divsn. Am. Theatre Wing, 1942-45; trustee The Lenox Sch., 1953-55; chmn. Associated Taxpayers Old Lyme, 1969-72; trustee Brookgreen Gardens, S.C., 1989-97; founder, life trustee Lyme Acad., Coll. Fine Arts, 1976, prof. sculpture, 1976—. Recipient 1st prize Bklyn. War Meml. competition, 1945, 1st prize sculpture Catherine Lorillard Wolfe Art Club, 1951, 58, 63, Gold medal, 1969, Founders prize Pen & Brush, 1954, 76, 78, Gold medal, 1957, 61, 63, 69, 74, 76, Am. Heritage award, 1968, Solo Show award, 1961, 69, 75, Thomas R. Proctor prize NAD, 1956, Dessie Greer prize, 1960, 79, 85, Sculpture prize Nat. Arts Club, 1959, 60, 62, Gold medal, 1971, Gold medal Am. Artists Profl. League, 1960, 69, 73, 75, prize, 1981, Anna Hyatt Huntington prize, 1970, 76, Harriet Mayer Meml. prize, 1961, Gold medal Hudson Valley Art Assn., 1956, 69, 74, Mrs. John Newington award, 1976, 78, Lindsey Morris Meml. prize Allied Artists Am., 1973, Gold medal, 1982, Sculpture prize Acad. Artists, 1974, Sydney Taylor Meml. prize Knickerbocker Artists, 1975, New Netherlands DAR Bicentennial medal, 1976, Pietro Montana Meml. prize Hudson Valley Art Assn., 1995, Citation, State of Conn., 1995, Govs. Arts award Conn. Commn. on the Arts, 2000, Gari Melchers award Artist's Fellowship, 2002; named Citizen of Yr., Town of Old Lyme, Conn., 1985. Fellow: Internat. Inst. Arts and Letters, Am. Artists Profl. League, Nat. Sculpture Soc. (coun. 1976—85, Tallix Foundry award 1979, John Spring Founders award 1986, John Cavanaugh Meml. prize 1991, Silver medal, citation 1992, Herbert Adams Meml. medal for svc. to Am. sculpture); mem.: NAD (academician), Conn. Comm. for the Arts (Govs. medal 2000), Am. Profl. Artists League, Coun. Am. Artists Socs., Lyme Art Assn. (pres. 1973—75), Catherine Lorillard Wolf Art Club, Pen and Brush, Am. Medallic Art Soc., Allied Artists Am., Nat. Arts Club, Fedn. Internat. de la Medaille. Home: 2 Mill Pond Ln Old Lyme CT 06371-1118*

CHANDLER, EVERETT ALFRED, lawyer; b. Columbus, Ohio, Sept. 21, 1926; s. Everett P. and Mary C. (Turner) C.; children: Wayne B., Brian E., V. Rhette; m. Mittie Rene Olion, Mar. 20, 1987 (div. Sept. 1991); 1 child, Mae Evette. BEd, Ohio State U., 1955; JD, Howard U., 1958. Bar: Ohio 1958, U.S. Dist. Ct. (no. dist.) Ohio 1962, U.S. Ct. Appeals (6th cir.) 1991, U.S. Tax Ct. 1967. Asst. county pros., Cuyahoga County, 1968-71; chief pros. City of Cleve., 1971-75; prin. Everett A. Chandler, Atty., Cleve. Author book rev. Cleve. State Law Jour., 1974. Chair bd. dirs. Cmty. Action Against Addiction, Cleve., 1975—, Crisis Intervention Team, Cleve., 1976-91; trustee Legal Aid Soc., Cleve., 1982-84, Boys Club Cleve., 1969-72; Dem. candidate for judge, Cuyahoga County, 1994. With USN, 1945-53. Mem. Norman S. Minor Bar Assn., Kappa Alpha Psi (past pres. 1980-83, 76-80, chmn. bd.). Democrat. Baptist. Avocations: golf, travel. Office: PO Box 28459 Cleveland OH 44128-0459 Home: 12450 Shaker Blvd Apt 306 Cleveland OH 44120-2044

CHANDLER, FAY MARTIN, artist; b. Norfolk, Va., Sept. 15, 1922; d. Howard Gresham and Alpine Douglas (Gatling) Martin; m. Alfred Dupont Chandler Jr., Jan. 8, 1944; children: Alpine C. Bird, Mary C. Watt, Alfred D. III, Howard Martin. BA, Sweetbriar Coll., 1943; MFA, Md. Inst. Coll. Art, Balt., 1967. Coord., dir. Fell's Point Gallery Md. Inst. Coll. Art, 1968-73; fellow Va. Ctr. Creative Arts, Sweetbriar, 1993. Bd. dirs. Md. Inst. Alumni Coun.; hon. bd. dirs. Mass. Vol. Lawyers for the Arts; founder, bd. dirs. The Art Connection, Boston; arts in edn. adv. coun. Harvard Grad. Sch. Edn.; mem. Coun. for the Arts at MIT. One-woman shows include Kenneth Taylor Little Gallery, Nantucket, 1973, 76, Fells Point Gallery, Balt., 1974, 76, Mills Gallery, Boston, 1974-88, Main St. Gallery, Nantucket, 1977, Ensign-Sibley Gallery, Nantucket, 1978, Sibley Gallery, Nantucket, 1980-85, Billiard Room Gallery, Cambridge, Mass., 1980, Helen Shlien Gallery, Boston, 1980, Bodley Gallery, NYC, 1980, St. Botolph Club, Boston, 1982, Stebbins Gallery, Cambridge, Mass., 1987, Bentley Coll., Waltham, Mass., 1987, Columbia (Md.) Ctr. for the Arts, 1987, Babcock Gallery Sweet Briar Coll., Va., 1993, Wenham (Mass.) Mus., 1993, Nantucket Island Sch. Design Gallery, 1994, Boston Ctr. For the Arts, 1995, Children's Mus., Boston, 1996, Decker Gallery/Md. Inst. Art, 1997, Steinbaum Krauss Gallery, NYC, 1997, Sacramento St. Gallery, Cambridge, Mass., 2002, Revolving Mus., Lowell,

Mass., 2003, Boston Ctr. for the Arts, 2005; exhibited in group shows. Bd. dirs. Friends of Art-Sweetbriar Coll., 2001—. Papers and slides chosen to be preserved Schlesinger Libr., Radcliffe Coll., Cambridge, Mass. Mem. Cambridge Art Assn Avocations: train trips, mystery books, philosophy. Home: 1010 Memorial Dr Apt 17E Cambridge MA 02138-4857 Studio: Engine House Studios 444 Western Ave Boston MA 02135-1016 Business E-Mail: fay@dougwatt.com.

CHANDLER, HUBERT THOMAS, former army officer; b. Charleston, W.Va., Dec. 8, 1933; s. Hubert Paris and Eleanor Lee (Gay) C.; m. Mary Frances Ritter, June 4, 1955; 1 son, Thomas Ritter. Student, Morris Harvey Coll., Charleston, 1951-52, U. Louisville, 1952-53; D.D.S., Balt. Coll. Dental Surgery, 1957; grad., Army War Coll., 1974. Diplomate: Am. Bd. Prosthodontics. Commd. Dental Corps U.S. Army, 1957, advanced through grades to maj. gen., dep. to chief Dental Corps, 1975-78, dep. comdr. Med. Command, dental surgeon, 1979-82, asst. surgeon gen., chief Dental Corps, 1982-86, dir. personnel Med. Dept., 1983-85; assoc. dean for profl. devel. Dental Sch., U. Md., Balt., 1988-92. Exec. com. Transatlantic council Boy Scouts Am., 1980-82; chmn. trust fund Girl Scouts Europe, 1981-82; pres. European Assn. Rod and Gun Clubs, 1981-82, Am. German Friendship Club, Heidelberg, W. Ger., 1981-82. Decorated D.S.M., Bronze Star, Meritorious Service medal, Army Commendation medal Fellow Am. Coll. Prosthodontists; mem. ADA. Office: 1714 Besley Rd Vienna VA 22182-2004 Personal E-mail: htchandler@earthlink.net.

CHANDLER, JAMES BARTON, international education consultant; b. Conway Springs, Kans., May 27, 1922; s. James Perry and Bessie May (Stone) C.; m. Madeleine Racoux, July 27, 1946; children: Paul A., Peter R., Michele A. Chandler Dore. AB, U. Kans., 1947, MA, 1949; postgrad., U. Mich., 1950—54. Asst. prof., fgn. student advisor Ea. Mich. U., 1953-55, 57-58; lang. edn. advisor Okla. A&M/Ethiopia, 1955-57, U. Mich./Laos, 1958-60; tchr. edn., advisor U.S. AID-Laos, Vientiane, Laos, 1960-61, edn. div. chief, 1961-63, asst. dir. manpower, industry, pub. administrn., 1965-69, deputy mission dir., 1969-73; higher edn. advisor U.S. AID-Tunisia, Tunis, Tunisia, 1963-65; dir. Office of Edn. AID, Washington, 1973-76, assoc. asst. adminstr., 1976-77; dir. Internat. Bur. Edn. UNESCO, Geneva, 1977-83; cons. Ann Arbor, 1983-88; St. Louis, 1989—. With Rotary, Vientiane, Laos, 1966-73, sec. 1968-69. Capt. U.S. Army, 1943-47, ETO. Decorated Bronze Star, Mo. WWII Air medal; recipient Meritorious Honor award AID, 1973, Disting. Career Svc. award, 1977, Cert. Appreciation Pres. Gerald Ford, 1975, Letter Appreciation Dir. Gen. UNESCO, Geneva, 1983, Cold War Recognition cert. Sec. Def., 1998; S.L. Whitcomb fellow U. Kansas, 1948-49, Ford Found. fellow, 1951-52, WWII medal, State of Mo. Mem. AAUP, Am. Acad. Social and Polit. Sci., Am. Fgn. Svc. Assn., NRA, Nat. Icarian Soc., Nat. Assn. Scholars, Nat. Parks and Conservation Assn., Am. Assn. Retired Persons, Nat. Wildlife Fedn., Archaeol. Inst. Am., Ind. Rights Found., Comparative and Internat. Edn. Soc., Diplomatic and Consular Officers Ret. (regional corr.), Nat. Assn. Ret. Fed. Employees (pres. Ann Arbor chpt. 1986-89, v.p. St. Louis chpt. 1989-90, pres. 1991-93, bd. dirs. 1992-93), Mo. Hist. Soc., Richmond Heights Srs. (v.p., pres.), Smithsonian Assocs., World Affairs Coun., Wilson Ctr. Assn., Nature Conservancy, Assn. Former Internat. Civil Servants, VFW, Am. Legion, 4th Cavalry Assn., Austrian Soc. of St. Louis, Soc. Francaise St. Louis (bd. dirs., v.p., pres., sec., sgt.-at.-arms), Ctr. for Internat. Understanding., Alliance Francaise, St. Louis-Lyon Sister Cities Com., Rotary (bd. dirs., officer 1992-2001, mid-county chpt. 2001—, sec. 2004—), St. Louis Discussion Club, Great Decisions Discussion Group, UN Assn. USA, Phi Beta Kappa, Pi Delta Phi, Phi Kappa Phi. Roman Catholic. Avocations: bowling, bridge, billiards, painting, writing memoirs, stamps and coins. Home and Office: 7449 Rupert Ave Richmond Heights MO 63117 Office Phone: 314-781-7727.

CHANDLER, JAMES E., publishing executive; m. Kathy Chandler; 2 children. V.p., dir. sales HarperCollins, Bantam Doubleday Dell, Barnes & Noble; joined Ingram Book Group, La Vergne, Tenn., 1997—; pres. Ingram Internat. Inc., La Vergne, Tenn.; chief comml. officer Ingram Book Group, pres., CEO, 2002—. Exec. coun. The Quills. Office: Ingram Book Group 1 Ingram Blvd La Vergne TN 37086 Office Phone: 804-643-5210.*

CHANDLER, JAMES JOHN, surgeon, educator; b. Dayton, Ohio, Nov. 13, 1932; s. James Kapp and Margaret Bertha (Paulson) Chandler; m. Fleur Elizabeth Varney, July 23, 1955; 1 child, Jennifer Hauge. AB, Dartmouth Coll., 1954, diploma in medicine, 1955; MD cum laude, U. Mich., 1957. Diplomate Am. Bd. Surgery. Intern Harvard Surg. Svc., Boston City Hosp., 1957-58, jr. asst. resident, 1958; resident, chief resident in surgery, clin. fellow Am. Cancer Soc. U. Oreg. Hosps., Portland, 1961-64, instr. surgery, 1964; courtesy staff, chmn. surgery Med. Ctr. at Princeton, NJ, 1972—92, pres. med. and dental staff, 1993-94; clin. prof. surgery U. Medicine and Dentistry N.J.-Robert Wood Johnson Med. Sch., Piscataway, 1976—; active staff Robert Wood Johnson U. Hosp., New Brunswick, NJ, 2000—. Cons. in surgery Princeton U.; trustee Med. Ctr. Princeton, 1993—94. Contbr. chapters to books, articles to profl. jours. Bd. dirs. Trinity Counseling Svc., 1968—, chmn., 1968—72; pres. Princeton Day Sch. PTA, 1976—78, trustee, 1976—81; mem. alumni coun. Dartmouth Med. Sch., 1981—86, Dartmouth Coll., 1983—86; active All Sts. Episcopal Ch., Princeton, 1965—. Lt. USN, 1958—60, served to lt. comdr. USNR, 1960—61. Fellow: ACS (pres. N.J. chpt. 1976—77, gov. 1981—87), Soc. Surg. Oncology, Am. Coll. Chest Physicians; mem.: AMA, Soc. Internat. Surgery, Soc. Surg. Alimentary Tract, Collegium Internationale Chirurgiae Digestivae, Med. Soc. N.J. (sec., chmn. surgery sect. 1967—69), Soc. Surgeons N.J., Am. Soc. Clin. Oncology, Gatineau Fish and Game Club, Bedens Brook Club, Nassau Gun Club (pres. 2001—02), Alpha Omega Alpha. Home: 95 Russell Rd Princeton NJ 08540-6729 Office: 1 Robert Wood Johnson Pl New Brunswick NJ 08903-0019 Office Phone: 732-235-7920. E-mail: chandljj@umdnj.edu.

CHANDLER, JAMES PHILLIP, law educator; b. Bakersfield, Calif., Aug. 15, 1938; s. Isaac and Lillie Mae Chandler; m. Elizabeth Thompson (div.); children: James P. IV, Elizabeth Lynne, Dennis Augustine, Ruth Rebekah, Isaac II, Aaron Daniel Pushkin, David Martin Thompson. BA, U. Calif., Berkeley, 1962; JD, U. Calif., Davis, 1970; LLM, Harvard U., 1971; LLD (hon.), La Academia Mexicana de Derecho Internacional, 1988. Bar: DC 1979, Pa. 1978, U.S. Dist. Ct. D.C., U.S. Dist. Ct. Md., U.S. Dist. Ct. (ea. dist.) Pa., U.S. Ct. Appeals (1st, 3d, 4th and 7th cirs.), U.S. Supreme Ct. Grad. fellow Harvard U., Cambridge, Mass., 1970—71; fellow Acad. Engring. of the NAS, Washington, 1971; faculty fellow engring. dept. Stanford U., Calif., 1972; disting. vis. prof. law U. Miss., Oxford, 1975; prof. law and dir. Computers in Law Inst. George Washington U. Nat. Law Ctr., Washington, 1977—93; mng. prin. The Chandler Law Firm, Chartered, Washington, 1979—; pres., bd. dirs. Nat. Intellectual Property Law Inst., Washington, 1993—. Vis. scholar Harvard U., Cambridge, 1984; cons. U.S. Gen. Acctg. Office, Washington, 1973—82, Computer Application in the Cts., Md. Ct. of Appeals, Adminstrv. Office of the Cts., Annapolis, 1974—76; mem. White House Nat. Infrastructure Assurance Coun., Washington, 1999. Contbr. articles to profl. jours. Mem.: Army-Navy Club DC. Avocation: racquetball. Home: 10621 River Rd Potomac MD 20854 Office: 2020 Pennsylvania Ave NW Washington DC 20006 Office Phone: 202-842-4800. Business E-Mail: chandler@nipli.org, professorchandler@chandlerlawfirm.com.

CHANDLER, JOHN WESLEY, educational consultant; b. Mars Hill, N.C., Sept. 5, 1923; s. Baxter Harrison and Mamie (McIntosh) C.; m. Florence Gordon, Aug. 25, 1948; children: Alison, John, Jennifer, Patricia. Student, Mars Hill Coll., 1941-43; AB, Wake Forest Coll., 1945, L.H.D. (hon.); B.D., Duke U., 1952, PhD, 1954; LL.D., Hamilton Coll., 1968, Colgate U., 1968, Williams Coll., 1973, Amherst Coll., 1974, Wesleyan U., 1978, North Adams State Coll., 1983; L.H.D., Wake Forest U., 1968, Trinity Coll., 1982, Middlebury Coll., 1983, Bates Coll., 1983, Beaver Coll., Duke U., 2002. Instr. philosophy Wake Forest Coll., 1948-51, asst. prof., 1954-55; asst. prof. religion Williams Coll., 1955-60, assoc. prof., chmn. dept., 1960-65, Cluett prof. religion, 1965-68, acting provost, 1965-66, dean faculty, 1966-68; pres. Hamilton Coll., Clinton, N.Y., 1968-73, Williams Coll., Williamstown, Mass., 1973-85, Assn. Am. Colls., Washington, 1985-90; ednl. cons. Korn/Ferry Internat., Washington, 1990-91, Acad. Search Cons. Svc., Washington, 1992—. Contbg. author: Miscellany of American Religion, 1963, Masterpieces of Religious Literature, 1963, also jour. articles and revs. Trustee Williams Coll., 1969-73; bd. visitors Wake Forest Coll., 1971-77, 79-91; bd. dirs. Williamstown Theatre Festival, 1973-85, Sterling and Francine Clark Art Inst., 1973-85; pres. New Eng. Assn. Schs. and Colls., 1977-78, Assn. Ind. Colls. and Univs. Mass., 1977-79; chmn. New Eng. Colls. Fund, 1978; trustee Duke U., 1985-94, chmn., 1993-94; trustee Randolph-Macon Woman's Coll., 1985-88, Phillips Collection, 1997-2001; dir. Value Line Funds, 1991—. Fulbright fellow India, 1963; Kent fellow. Mem. Phi Beta Kappa. Mem. United Ch. of Christ. Clubs: Williams; Cosmos (Washington). Office: Williams Coll Oakley Ctr Williamstown MA 01267 E-mail: John.W.Chandler@williams.edu.

CHANDLER, KENT, JR., lawyer; b. Chgo., Jan. 10, 1920; s. Kent and Grace Emeret (Tuttle) C.; m. Frances Robertson, June 19, 1948; children: Gail, Robertson Kent. BA, Yale U., 1942; JD, U. Mich., 1949. Bar: Ill. 1949, U.S. Dist. Ct. (no. dist.) Ill. 1949, U.S. Ct. Appeals (7th cir.) 1955, U.S. Ct. Claims 1958. Assoc. Wilson & McIlvaine, Chgo., 1949-56, ptnr., 1957-94, spl. counsel to firm, 1994-98; of counsel Bell Jones & Quinlisk, Chgo., 1998—. Bd. dirs. Internat. Crane Found. Mem. zoning bd. appeals City of Lake Forest, Ill., 1953-63, chmn., 1963-67, mem. plan commn., 1955-69, chmn., 1969-70, pres. bd. local improvements, 1970-73, mayor, 1970-73, mem. bd. fire and police commn., 1975-82, chmn., 1982-84. Served to maj. USMCR, 1941-46. Mem. ABA, Ill. State Bar Assn., Chgo. Bar Assn., Lake County Bar Assn., Lawyers Club Chgo. (pres. 1985-86), Univ. Club, Onwentsia Club (Lake Forest), Old Elm Club (Highland Park, Ill.). Republican. Presbyterian. Office: 200 W Adams St Ste 2600 Chicago IL 60606-5233 Office Phone: 312-606-8797.

CHANDLER, KIMBERLEY LYNN, educational administrator; b. Waynesboro, Va., Sept. 28, 1961; d. Alden Hugh and Cecille Frances (Brooks) C. BA in Elem. Edn., Coll. William and Mary, 1984, MA in Gifted Edn., 1992, PhD in Ednl. Policy, Planning and Leadership, 2004. Lic. educator, Va. Tchr. Fredericksburg (Va.) Pub. Schs., 1984-87, Henrico County Pub. Schs., Richmond, Va., 1987-98; gifted edn. resource specialist Hanover County Pub. Schs., Richmond, Va., 1998-2000; supr. enrichment programs, coord. of sci. K-12 Amherst County Pub. Schs., Va., 2000—03; cert. curriculum cons. Ctr. for Gifted Edn., 2002—; panel reviewer Jacob K. Javits Grant Program, U.S. Dept. Edn., 2002; postdoctoral fellow Ctr. for Gifted Edn. Coll. of William and Mary, Williamsburg, Va., 2003, curriculum coord., 2003—; acad. rev. team leader Va. Dept. Edn., 2004—. Summer sch. coord. Henrico County Pub. Schs., 1996, 97, staff devel. presenter, 1996, 97; curriculum cons. Coll. of William and Mary, Williamsburg, Va., 1996; presenter in field.; mem. gifted edn. staff devel. talent bank, mem. tchr. stds. com. Va. Dept. Edn.; mem. peer coaching program, Prin.'s Acad.; sch. renewal planning team facilitator Hanover County Pub. Schs.; mem. adj. faculty U. Va. Sch. Continuing and Profl. Studies, 2001—; instr. Casenex, Inc.; participant David L. Clark Grad. Student Seminar, 2003. Author: (curriculum unit) Literary Reflections, 1992; author: (with others) Aiming for Excellence-Gifted Program Standards: Annotations to the NAGC Pre-K-Grade 12 Gifted Program Standards, ERIC Research Report, 2002, (book review) Gifted and Talented International; editor (newsletter): Va. Assn. for the Gifted, 1999—. Vol. Hanover Humane Soc., 1994—, Habitat for Humanity Global Village Program, Nicaragua Disaster Relief Mission Team, 1999, Brazil VBS Mission Team, 2000; mem. Habitat for Humanity Global Village Team to South Africa, 2001. Recipient Doctoral Student award Nat. Assn. for Gifted Children, 2002, Hollingworth Rsch. award, 2003; grantee Henrico Edn. Found., 1997, Henrico Gifted Adv. Coun., 1997, Pntrs. in Arts grantee Richmond Arts Coun., 1996, Hanover Edn. Found., 1999, Coll. William and Mary, 2003; postdoctoral fellow Ctr. Gifted Edn., Coll. William and Mary, 2003—. Mem.: Va. Assn. for the Gifted (ex officio bd. dirs.), Va. Soc. for Tech. in Edn., Hanover County Prins. Acad., Nat. Assn. for Gifted Children (sec./treas. technol. divsn. 1997—99, sec./treas. profl. devel. divsn. 1997—99, chair profl. devel. divsn. 2003—, Harry Passow Classroom Tchr. scholarship 1997, Outstanding Curriculum award 2000, Doctoral Student award 2002, Hollingworth award 2003), Delta Kappa Gamma, Kappa Delta Pi (chpt. sec.). Home: 11444 New Farrington Ct Glen Allen VA 23059-1629 Office: Coll William and Mary Ctr for Gifted Edn PO Box 8795 Williamsburg VA 23187-8795 Personal E-mail: kchan11444@aol.com. Business E-Mail: klchan@wm.edu.

CHANDLER, LAWRENCE BRADFORD, JR., lawyer; b. New Bedford, Mass., June 20, 1942; s. Lawrence Bradford and Anne (Crane) C.; m. Madeleine Bibeau, Sept. 7, 1963 (div. June 1984); children: Dawn, Colleen, Brad. BS in Bus. Adminstrn., Boston Coll., 1963; LLB, U. Va., 1966, JD, 1970. Bar: Mass. 1966, U.S. Supreme Ct. 1967, Va. 1970, W.Va. 1993; diplomate Nat. Bd. Trial Advocacy; advocate Am. Bd. Trial Advocates. Ptnr. Chandler, Franklin & O'Bryan, Charlottesville, Va., 1971—. Pres. Western Va. Chpt., 1992-93. Capt. U.S. Army, 1967-71. Mem.: ATLA (chair state dels. 1993—94, exec. com. 1993—94, bd. govs. 1995—2001), ABA, Am. Assn. Profl. Liability Attys., Am. Soc. on Law, Medicine and Ethics, Am. Coll. Legal Medicine, Charlottesville Bar Assn., Nat. Bd. Trial Advocacy (bd. examiners), Am. Bd. Trial Advs. (pres. Va. chpt.), Va. Trial Lawyers Assn. (pres. 1985—86), Assn. U.S. Army (pres. 1971—73). Roman Catholic. Home: 1445 Old Ballard Rd Charlottesville VA 22901-9469 Office: Chandler Law Group PO Box 6747 Charlottesville VA 22906-6747 Office Phone: 434-971-7273. Personal E-mail: goofyc@mindspring.com.

CHANDLER, MARCIA SHAW BARNARD, farmer; b. Arlington, Mass., Aug. 22, 1934; d. John Alden and Grace Winifred (Copeland) Barnard; m. Samuel Butler Chandler, Aug. 31, 1952 (dec. 1986); children: Shawn Chandler Seddinger, Mark Thurmond, Matthew Butler. BA, Francis Marion Univ., Florence, S.C., 1976; MEd, U. S.C., 1985. Resource person United Cerebral Palsy of S.C., Dillon, 1976-79; instr. English Horry-Georgetown Tech. Coll., Conway, S.C., 1980-81; farm owner, mgr. Dillon; drama critic Dillon (S.C.) Herald, 1986—. Author: (with others) Best of Old Farmer's Almanac, First 200 Years, 1991, A Primer for the New Millennium, 1999; cover artist So. Bell Telephone Directory, 1988; artist Dillon County Lib., 1998. Bd. dirs., publicist, artist Dillon County Theatre, Inc., 1985—; publicist, bd. dirs., artist MacArthur Ave. Players, Dillon, 1990—; bd. dirs. Friends of Francis Marion U., 1985-95; pres. Dillon Area Arts Coun., 1980-85, Jr. Charity League of Dillon, 1960-75; nat. poetry judge DAR, 1982; Dunbar libr. com., Dillon County, 1998—; mem. SCDNR Scenic River Com., 2005. Recipient Honorable Commendation for civic involvement S.C. Ho. Reps., Mar. 22, 1990. Mem. Ctr. Environ. Edn., Internat. Fund Animal Welfare, Nature Conservancy, Sea Shepherd Conservation Soc., Humane Soc. U.S., Ocean Conservancy, Nat. Wildlife Fund, Animal Protection Inst., Nat. Humane Edn. Soc Avocations: snorkeling, animal welfare activities, theater, travel. Home: 309 E Reaves Ave Dillon SC 29536-1919 E-mail: marciacani@aol.com.

CHANDLER, MARGUERITE NELLA, real estate company executive; b. New Brunswick, N.J., May 16, 1943; d. Edward A. and Marguerite (Moore) Chandler; m. Ronald Wilson, May 30, 1964 (div. Nov. 1973); children: Mark Wilson, Adam Wilson; m. Richmond Shreve, Nov. 22, 1979; 1 child, Laura Shreve. BS in Acctg., Syracuse U., 1964; MS in Polit. Mgmt., George Washington U., 1968. Tax acct. Peat Marwick Mitchell, Providence, 1964; grant adminstr., psychology dept. Brown U., Providence, 1965; intern in devel. cons. Washington, 1973-75; prin., tng. cons. M. Chandler Assocs., 1975-76; mgmt. cons. Edmar Corp., Bound Brook, N.J., 1976-78, pres., chief exec. officer, 1978-90, pres., 1991—. Vol. Peace Corps, 1966—68, Somerset Cmty. Action Program, 1969—71; treas. Somerset County Day Care Assn., 1969—71; established Food Bank Network Somerset County, 1982, pres., 1982—85; established Worldworks Found., Inc., 1983; founder PeopleCare Ctr., 1984, pres., 1984—86; bd. dirs. United Way Somerset Valley, 1984—91, gen. campaign mgr., 1985—86; recorder Blue Ribbon Com. Ending Hunger in N.J., 1984—86; bd. dirs. N.J. Coun. Arts, 1986—87; mem. N.J. Gov.'s Task Force Pub./Pvt. Sector Initiatives, NJ, 1986—91; mem. adv. bd. US-USSR Youth Exch., Ptnrs. in Peacemaking, Giraffe Project; chmn. bd. dirs. Friends Retirement Inc., 1996—2002; Dem. candidate U.S. Congress Dist. 12, 1990; vol. Missionaries Charity, Calcutta, India, 1981; pres. bd. trustees N.J. Coun. Chs., 1985—90. Named Woman of the Yr., Women's Resource Ctr. Somerset County, 1983, Citizen of the Yr., N.J. chpt. Nat. Assn. Soc. Workers, 1986, Bus. and Profl. Women's Club, 1987, Person of the Decade, Courier-News, 1989, Bus. Person of the Yr., Bus. Ctrl. N.J. mag., 1993; recipient People's Champaion award, Somerset Family Planning Svc., 1985, Disting. Svc. award, N.J. Speech-Lang.-Hearing Assn., 1986, N.J. Women of Achievement award, Douglass Coll. and N.J. Fedn. Women's Clubs, 1986, Brotherhood award, Ctrl. Jersey chpt. Nat. Conf. Christians and Jews, 1986, Presdl. End Hunger award, Presdl. End Hunger award, 1987, Somerset Alliance for the Future Quality of Life award, 1996. Mem.: World Bus. Acad. (bd. dirs. 1988—89), Assn. N.J. Recyclers (pres. 1991—93), Regional Plan Assn. (bd. dirs. 1994—96), Somerset C. of C. (chmn. bd. dirs. 1989—90, chmn. strategic planning cultural and heritage com., tourism coun., Citizen of the Yr. 1985), Heritage Trail Assn. Somerset County (founder, pres. 1994—99), Crossroads Am. Revolution Assn. (pres. 2001—), Rotary (pres. Bound Brook-Middlesex 1993—94). Quaker. Avocation: quilting. Home: PO Box 250 Cape May Point NJ 08212 Office: PO Box 710 Bound Brook NJ 08805-0710 Office Phone: 732-469-9950.

CHANDLER, MARSHA, academic administrator, educator; BA, CCNY, 1965; PhD, UNC Chapel Hill, 1972; grad. in advanced Mgmt. Program, Harvard Bus. Sch., 2004. Prof. political econ. Univ. Toronto, 1977-96, dean arts and sci., 1990-97; sr. vice chancellor U. Calif., San Diego, 1996—. Vis. scholar Harvard U., 1995-96, 2004-05. Co-author: Trade and Transmissions, 1990, The Political Economy of Business Bailouts, 2 vols., 1986, The Politics of Canadian Public Policy, 1983, Public Policy and Provincial Politics, 1979, Adjusting to Trade: A Comparative Perspective, 1988; contbr. articles to profl. jours. Fellow, Royal Soc. of Canada, mem.dirs. San Diego Opera, Mingei Mus. Internatl. Folk Art (bd. dir.), UCSD Found. Bd. and the Charter 100, adv. com. on Fed. Judicial Appts., Canadian Inst. for Adv. Rsch.; trustee (bd. mem.), Art Gall. of Ontario, Mt. SInai Hosp., Huntsman Marine Sci. Ctr., Ontario Lightwave, Laser Rsch. Ctr. Office: U Calif 9500 Gilman Dr La Jolla CA 92093-5004

CHANDLER, MICHAEL JONATHAN, allergist, physician; b. Detroit, May 9, 1955; BS, U. Mich., 1977; MD, Wayne State U., 1981. Diplomate Am. Bd. Allergy & Immunology, Am. Bd. Internal Medicine. Resident in medicine Northwestern U., Chgo., 1981-84, fellow allergy & immunology, 1984-86; allergist Mt. Sinai Hosp., N.Y.C., 1986—, clin. instr. medicine, 1986—. Fellow Am. Assn. Allergy, Asthma & Immunology; mem. Am. Coll. Physicians. Office: 115 E 61st St New York NY 10021-8183

CHANDLER, ROBERT CHARLES, healthcare consultant; b. Birmingham, Ala., Apr. 15, 1945; s. Coleman Duke and Myrtle (Cleveland) C.; children: Jason Charles, Jonathan Robert. BS in Pharmacy, Samford U., 1968; MS in Hosp. and Health Adminstrn., U. Ala.-Birmingham, 1972. Registered pharmacist. Pharmacy intern Carraway Meth. Hosp., Birmingham, 1968-69; chief pharmacist Holy Family Hosp., Birmingham, 1969-70; v.p. Ft. Sanders Med. Ctr., Knoxville, Tenn., 1971-78; sr. v.p. Bapt. Med. Ctrs., Birmingham, 1978-79; exec. v.p. Princeton, 1979-85; pres. E. Tenn. Bapt. Hosp., Knoxville, 1985-90, The Bapt. Health Sys. East Tenn., Knoxville, 1986-90; ptnr. Ward Howell Internat., Atlanta, 1991-98, TMP Worldwide, Atlanta, 1998-99; sr. v.p., global practice leader Healthcare and Pharms., Stratford Group, Atlanta, 2000—01; exec. v.p., nat. practice leader for healthcare and life scis. DHR Internat., Atlanta, 2002—. Bd. dirs. Am. Healthcare Sys. San Diego, 1988-90; chmn. bd. dirs. SunHealth Care Plans Tenn., 1986-88; bd. dirs. Ala. Quality Assurance Found., Birmingham, 1984-85, Ala. Med. Rev., Birmingham, 1980-84; mem. adv. bd. Blue Cross/Blue Shield, Birmingham, 1983-85; mem. liaison com. Jefferson County Med. Soc., Birmingham, 1984-85; various faculty appts. U. Ala., Birmingham, Emory U. Sch. Medicine, Atlanta; divsn. chmn. United Way, Birmingham, 1984; bd. dirs. United Way Greater Knoxville, 1987-88, Knoxville Opera Co., 1988; Sunday sch. tchr. Dawson Bapt. Ch., Birmingham; deacon chmn. 1st Bapt. Ch., Knoxville, 1988-90. Recipient Cert. Appreciation, Tenn. Gov. Ray Blanton, 1978, Disting. Svc. award Tenn. Com. on Employment of Handicapped, 1978, Award of Excellence Ala. Pub. Rels. Coun., 1979. Fellow Am. Coll. Hosp. Adminstrs.; mem. Birmingham Regional Hosp. Coun. (pres.-elect 1985), Hosp. Alliance Tenn. (pres. 1987-88), Ala. Hosp. Assn. (trustee 1984-85), Birmingham C. of C. (chmn. health svcs. com. 1980), The Club (Birmingham), Rotary (mem. group study exch. 1977). Office: DHR International 100 Galleria Pkwy Ste 1150 Atlanta GA 30339

CHANDLER, ROBERT LESLIE, public relations executive; b. Phila., Mar. 3, 1948; s. Joel Leslie and Evelyn Laney (DeLaney) C.; m. Pamela Lin Gemmel, Sept. 22, 2002. AS, Atlantic C.C., 1969; BS, Bowling Green State U., 1971; MS, Ohio U., 1972; MBA in Hosp. Adminstrn., Wagner Coll., 1980. Dir. pub. rels. Athens (Ohio) Mental Health Ctr., 1972; internal comms. editor, pub. affairs dept. Owens-Corning Fiberglas Corp., Toledo, 1972-74; dir. cmty. rels. Wyandotte (Mich.) Gen. Hosp., 1974-76; v.p. asst. adminstr. mktg., pub. affairs Meth. Hosp., Bklyn., 1976-82; exec. v.p. Burson-Marsteller Pub. Rels., NYC, 1982-95; pres. Chandler Chicco Agy., 1995. Spl. cons. Am. Soc. Hosp. Mktg. and Pub. Rels./Am. Hosp. Assn., 1989—90; spkr. at numerous comms. confs. Contbr. articles to profl. jours. Mem. budget com. United Way Mich., 1975—76; bd. dirs. NY chpt. Am. Heart Assn. Recipient Healthcare Agy. of Yr. award Holmes Report, 2002-04, numerous other awards; named 7th in PR Week's Agy. rankings Top Pub. Rels. firms, 2004; Am. Heart Assn. NJ/NY State scholar, 1969. Mem. Pub. Rels. Soc. Am. (Silver Anvil awards), Am. Soc. Health Care Mktg. and Planning, Am. Coll. Healthcare Execs. (assoc.), Sigma Delta Chi, Kappa Tau Alpha. Office: Chandler Chicco Agy 450 W 15th St Ste 700 New York NY 10011-7014 Office Phone: 212-229-8400.

CHANDLER, SHERRY, writer, editor; b. Owenton, Ky., Feb. 15, 1945; d. Howard Kenneth and Katherine Botts (Keith) C.; m. Thomas Robert Williams, Aug. 9, 1972; children: Morgan Steele, Thomas Chandler. BA, Georgetown (Ky.) Coll., 1970; MA, U. Ky., 1972. Consumer affairs specialist William Wrigley Jr. Co., Chgo., 1973-77, consumer affairs supr., 1977-79; freelance writer Paris, Ky., 1979—; staff asst. U. Ky. Hosp., Lexington, 1988-90; data coord. U. Ky. Coll. Medicine, Lexington, 1990-92, editl. assoc., 1992-96; staff assoc. Sanders-Brown Ctr. on Aging, U. Ky., Lexington, 1996-99, sr. staff assoc., 1999—. Workshop leader Am. Med. Writers Assn., Rockville, Md., 1993-95. Author/performer: (radio commentary) Early World on WRVG Radio, 1999; peer reviewer (book) Biomedical Communications, 1997; author of poetry and short fiction. Mem. fourth Friday com. Lexington Art League, 1999—, site based com. Paris H.S., 1995-97; mem. strategic planning com. Paris Ind. schs., 1995-97; bd. dirs. Paris H.S. Band Boosters, 1994-96; mem. Ky. Coalition Against the Death Penalty, 1999—. Profl. Devel. grantee Ky. Arts Coun., 1989. Mem. Am. Med. Writers Assn. (subchpt. pres. 1993—), Bd. of Editors in the Life Scis., Ky. Writers Coalition, Ky. State Poetry Soc. Office: Sanders-Brown Ctr on Aging Univ of Ky 101 Sanders Brown Bldg Ky Lexington KY 40536-0001

CHANDLER, THEODORE LINDY, JR., lawyer, real estate company executive; b. South Boston, Va., May 13, 1952; s. Theodore Lindy and Jacqueline Anne (Hodnett) C.; m. Laura Lee Hankins, June 22, 1974; children: Katherine Anne, Rebecca Lee. BS in Commerce, U. Va., 1974; JD, U. Richmond, 1977. Bar: Va. 1977. With Williams, Mullen, Christian & Dobbins, Richmond, Va., 1977—; CEO & pres. LandAmerica Fin., Richmond, Va. Bd. dirs. Hilb, Rogal & Hamilton Co., Richmond, Lawyers Title Corp. Bd. dirs. Reeds Landing Community Assn., Richmond, 1988—, Theatre IV, Richmond, 1988—. Mem. Richmond Estate Planning Coun., Country Club Va., Capital Club, Commonwealth Club. Republican. Baptist. Avocations: golf, skiing, sailing, squash. Office: Williams Mullen Christian D 1021 E Cary St 17th Fl Richmond VA 23219

CHANDLER, VANESSA RENITA, education educator; d. Richard Lewis and Mary Elizabeth Chandler. BS, Ala. A&M U., 1981—85, MS, 1997—99. Program ops. dir. Girls Inc. of Huntsville, Huntsville, Ala., 1991—99; family and consumer sciences educator Huntsville City Schools, Huntsville, Ala., 2000—. Tng. cons. Girls Inc. of Am., Indianapolis, 1997—. Recipient Toyota Internat. Tchr. Program, Internat. Inst. of Edn., 2003. Mem.: Assn. for Career and Tech. Edn. (assoc.), Delta Sigma Theta (assoc.). Office: Lee HS 606 Forrest Circle Huntsville AL 35811 Office Phone: 256-428-8150 122. Office Fax: 256-428-8151. E-mail: vchandler@hsv.k12.al.us.

CHANDLER, WILLIAM HENRY, lawyer; b. Heminway, SC, May 5, 1948; s. William Jackson and Margaret Eloise (Nelson) C.; m. Ann Rodgers Tomlinson, July 31, 1982; children: Jared Witherspoon Nelson, Martha Elizabeth Hartman, Ann Paisley Snowden. AB, U. S.C., 1970, JD, 1973. Bar: S.C. 1973, U.S. Dist. Ct. (we. dist.) La. 1975, U.S. Dist. Ct. S.C. 1973, U.S. Ct. Mil. Appeals 1974. Ptnr. Chandler & Ruffin, Hemingway, S.C., 1978-84, Askins, Chandler, Ruffin & Askins, Hemingway, S.C., 1984—. Instr. bus. law Williamsburg Tech. Coll., Kingstree, SC, 1978—79, instr. state and local govt., 2002. Vice chmn. Williamsburg County Bd. Trustees, 1979—84, Williamsburg County Devel. Bd.; chmn. The Continuum of Care for Emotionally Disturbed Children, Williamsburg County Planning Commn., 2001—; mem. State Hist. Records Adv. Bd.; pres. Williamsburg Co. Forest Landowners Assn.; chmn. Williamsburg Co. Planning Commn.; supt. ch. sch. First Presbyn. Ch., Bossier City, La., 1975—77; lay spkr. Presbytery of the Pines Presbyn. Ch. U.S., Bossier City, 1976—77; ruling elder Indiantown Presbyn. Ch., Hemingway, 1980—; moderator, counsel, mem. judiciary com. The Presbytery of New Harmony; bd. dirs. Francis Marion Coll. Found., Williamsburg County Farm Bur.; vice chmn. Pee Dee Heritage Found.; bd. dirs. Williamsburg Regional Hosp. Found., Lake City Mus., Pee Dee Land Trust; atty. Town of Stuckey, SC, 1979—. Lt. col. USAF. Mem. ABA, SAR, Am. Legion, SC Geneal. Soc., SC Libr. Soc., French Higuenot Soc., SC Hist. Soc., Williamsburg County Bar Assn. (pres. 2005—), Francis Marian Trail Commn., Williamsburg County Hist. Soc. (pres.), Three Rivers Hist. Soc. (pres.), St. Andrews Soc. City of Columbia, Charleston Preservation Soc., Lions, Masons (Hemingway), Williamsburg Hometown C.C. (bd. dirs.), Hog Crawl Hunting Club, Wilson Lake Fishing Club, Phi Eta Sigma, Omicron Delta Kappa, Phi Delta Phi Home: 1949 Henry Rd Hemingway SC 29554 Office: PO Box 10 Hemingway SC 29554 Office Phone: 843-558-2588. E-mail: billchandler@ftc-i.net.

CHANDLER, WILLIAM KNOX, physiologist; b. Chgo., Oct. 13, 1933; s. William Knox and Margaret Belle (Colston) C.; m. Caroline Hardee Teague, June 6, 1957; children— William Knox, Janet Colston, Caroline Louise, Margaret Teague. AB, U. Louisville, 1955, MD, 1959. Postdoctoral fellow Physiol. Lab., Cambridge, Eng., 1962-65; staff asso. Lab. Biophysics, Nat. Inst. Neurol. Diseases and Blindness, Bethesda, Md., 1965-66; asso. prof. physiology Yale U. Sch. Medicine, 1966-72, prof., 1973—. Editor Physiol. Revs, 1968-74, Jour. Physiology, 1974-81, Jour. Gen. Physiology, 1990—. Served with USPHS, 1959-61, 65-66. Mem. NAS, Biophys. Soc., Physiol. Soc., Soc. Gen. Physiologists. Democrat. Home: 594 County Rd Guilford CT 06437-1035 Office: 333 Cedar St New Haven CT 06510-3206 Office Phone: 203-785-4066. E-mail: knox.chandler@yale.edu.

CHANDOR, STEBBINS BRYANT, pathologist; b. Boston, Dec. 18, 1933; s. Kendall Stebbins Bryant and Dorothy (Burrage) C.; m. Mary Carolyn White, May 30, 1959; children: Stebbins Bryant Jr., Charlotte White. BA, Princeton U., 1955; MD, Cornell U., 1960. Diplomate Am. Bd. Pathology. Intern Bellevue Hosp., N.Y.C., 1960-61, resident, 1965-66, Stanford U. Med. Ctr., Palo Alto, Calif., 1962-65; instr. Cornell U., Ithaca, NY, 1966; asst. prof. U. So. Calif. Med. Ctr., L.A., 1969-73, assoc. prof., 1974-76; prof., vice chmn. Sch. Medicine U. So. Calif., 1991—2004, prof. emeritus, 2004—, dir. immunopathology Med. Ctr., 1969-76, dir. labs. U. Hosp., 1991—2004; assoc. prof. SUNY, Stony Brook, 1976-80; prof., chmn. dept. pathology Marshall U. Sch. Medicine, Huntington, W.Va., 1981-91, assoc. dean for clin. affairs, 1990-91; pathologist Tripler Army Med Ctr, Honolulu, 1966-69; dir. clin. lab. Univ. Hosp., Stony Brook, 1978-80; dir. JMMS Labs., Huntington, 1981-91. Contbr. articles to profl. jours. Pres. San Marino Tennis Found., 1975; governing bd. U. Path. Consortium, 1999-2004. Served to maj. USAR, 1966-69. Decorated Army Commendation medal; recipient Physicians Recognition award AMA, 1983, 86, 89, 93, 99. Fellow Am. Assn. Med. Colls., Am. Soc. Clin. Pathologists (dep. commn. 1993-98, continuing edn. bd. dirs. 1990-96, chair by-law com., 1993-96, chmn. pathology group, 1993-98, v.p. 1997-98, pres. 1999-2000, mem. awards com. 2001-), Coll. Am. Pathologists (state commr. I&A program 1987-91, dist. commr. 1991-99); mem. Calif. Soc. Pathologists (sec.-treas. 1974-75, pres.-elect 1975-76), Assn. Am. Pathologists, W.Va. Assn. Pathologists (pres. 1985-86), Assoc. Path. Chmn. Acad. Clin. Lab. Physicians and Scientists (rep. CAS 1991-2003, adminstrv. bd. 1997-2003), Am. Assn. Med. Colls. (exec. coun. 1998-2000), L.A. Acad. Medicine, Princeton Club, Valley Club (v.p. 1975, bd. dirs. 1993), City Club (v.p. 1988-89, pres. 1989-90), San Gabriel Country Club, Valley Hunt Club, The Valley Club of Montecito. Republican. Episcopalian. Home: 2170 East Valley Dr Santa Barbara CA 93108 Office: 2011 Zonal Ave Los Angeles CA 90033-1034 Office Phone: 323-442-8591. Personal E-mail: sbcmcc@aol.com. Business E-Mail: chandor@usc.edu. *Have fun and make life enjoyable for those around you.*

CHANDRA, ABHIJIT, engineering educator; b. Kolkata, West Bengal, India, Jan. 4, 1957; arrived in US, 1980, naturalized, 1990; s. Ramesh Kumar and Sandhya (Dey) C.; m. Dolly Day, June 4, 1984; children: Koushik, Shoma. B of Tech. with honors, Indian Inst. Tech., 1978; MS, U. N.B., 1980; PhD, Cornell U., 1983. Sr. rsch. engr. GM Rsch. Labs., Warren, Mich., 1983—85; asst. prof. U. Ariz., Tucson, 1985—89, assoc. prof. engring., 1989—95; prof. Mich. Tech. U., Houghton, 1995—99; Engel prof., dir. Engel lab. Iowa State U., Ames, 1999—2004, prof., 1999—. Cons. Goodyear Tire and Rubber Co., Akron, Ohio, 1988-89, Advanced Ceramic Rsch., Tucson, 1990-95, ALCOA, Pitts., 1990-95, Thermoanalytics Inc., 1999-2001; chief tech. officer, bd. dirs. Actus Potentia, Inc. Author: Boundary Element Methods in Manufacturing, 1997; guest editor Internat. Jour. Solid Structures, 1994; contbr. over 90 articles to profl. jours. Alexander von Humboldt fellow, 1991; recipient Presdl. Young Investigator award NSF, 1987, Arc Welding Achievement award J. F. Lincoln Arc Welding Found., 1989. Fellow ASME (sec. So. Ariz. sect. 1988-89); mem. SME (Outstanding Paper award 1999), IEEE, Sigma Xi. Avocations: swimming, skiing, tennis, gardening, fiction writing. Business E-Mail: achandra@iastate.edu.

CHANDRA, ARUN, composer, educator; b. Allahbad, Uttar Pradesh, India, Aug. 2, 1954; s. Satish and Shimmi Chandra; m. Lori Blewett, June 20, 1994; children: Rian Naveen, Nuria Alina. MusD, U. Ill., Urbana, Illinois, 1989. Asst. prof. Nat. Chiao Tung U., Hsinchu, Taiwan, 1993—94; mem. faculty The Evergreen State Coll., Olympia, Wash., 1998—. Music dir., condr. The Olympia (Wash.) Chamber Orch., Olympia, 2000—04; founder The Performers' Workshop Ensemble, 1980—92, The School for Designing a Soc., 1992. Editor: When Music Resists Meaning: The Major Articles of Herbert Brun; composer: (songs) If Then What Now?, So Follows for guitar solo, Crocker for voice, digitally manipulated voice, and three percussionists, Lament for voice and computer, JDAM for four voices and computer, Three Times Four, The Gift Of Gab For Computer, Smear Pulse No Sneer, To Get To The Other Side for seven voices and computer, EarSong for solo speaker. Founder The Olympia (Wash.) Theatre Project, 2004. Mem.: Am. Soc. Cybernetics, Internat. Soc. Contemporary Music, Soc. Electro-Acoustic Music in U.S. Office: The Evergreen State College 2700 Evergreen Parkway Olympia WA 98505 Office Phone: 360-867-6077. E-mail: arunc@evergreen.edu.

CHANDRA, ASHISH, marketing professional, educator; b. Allahabad, India, Feb. 5, 1964; s. Suresh and Usha Chandra; m. Lea N. Chandra, June 1993; 1 child, Amitabh. M of Mgmt. Studies, Banaras Hindu U., Varanasi, India, 1989; MBA, U. La., Monroe, 1993, PhD, 1996. Mgmt. trainee Jaypee Rewa Cement Co., New Delhi, 1988; sales exec. Ravi Fans Pvt. Ltd., Varanasi, 1989; mktg. exec. Tara Consulting Svcs., Varanasi, 1990; mgmt. and mktg. cons. Mobile Express Lube, Monroe, 1992; asst. prof. Xavier U. of La., New Orleans, 1996-2000; mktg. cons. Memphis, W.Va., 1997; asst. prof. grad. coll. Marshall U., South Charleston, W.Va., 2000—02; assoc. prof. Marshall U. Grand Coll., 2002—. Editor: Hospital Topics, Internat. Conf. on Health Care Sys. Proceedings, 2000; contbr. articles to profl. jours. Rsch. grantee N. La. Area Health Edn. Ctr., 1995, Rsch. grantee CibaVision Ophthalmics, 1998. Mem.: Bus. and Health Adminstrn. Assn. (program chair 2000—01, pres. 2001—02, proceedings co-editor 2001), Assn. U. Programs Health Adminstrn., Acad. Mgmt., Assoc. of Collegiate Mktg. Educators (program chair 2004—05, pres. 2005—). Avocations: travel, outdoor sports. Office: Marshall U Grad Coll 100 Angus E Peyton Dr South Charleston WV 25303 E-mail: chandra2@marshall.edu.

CHANDRA, SATISH, psychologist; b. Dankaur, India, Dec. 22, 1944; arrived in U.S.A., 1966, permanent resident; s. Murari Lal and Yashoda Devi. BSc, U. Allahabad, 1961; BSEE with hons., Indian Inst. Tech., 1966; MA in Psychology, SUNY, 1975; postgrad., U. Rochester, 1969—71; postgrad. in Clin. Psychology, SUNY, 1971—77. Rsch. Dept. Psychology Harvard U., Cambridge, Mass., 1977—78; pvt. practice psychotherapy Cambridge, 1978—. Contbr. articles to profl. jours. Fellow, U. Rochester, 1969—70. Mem.: APS, Soc. Philosophy and Psychology, N.Y. Acad. Scis. Achievements include research in psychology led to end of B.F. Skinner's school of psychology. Office: PO Box 381629 Cambridge MA 02238 Office Phone: 617-407-0071.

CHANDRASEKARAN, BALAKRISHNAN, computer scientist, educator; b. Lalgudi, Tamil Nadu, India, June 20, 1942; came to U.S., 1963; s. Srinivasan and Nagamani Balakrishnan; m. Sandra Mamrak, Oct. 21, 1978; 1 child, Mallika. B in Engring., Madras U., Karaikudi, India, 1963; PhD, U. Pa., 1967. Devel. engr. Smith Kline Instruments, Phila., 1964-65; rsch. specialist Philco-Ford Corp., Blue Bell, Pa., 1967-69; asst. prof. computer and info. sci. Ohio State U., Columbus, 1969-71, assoc. prof., 1971-77, prof., 1977-95; sr. rsch. scientist, 1995—; dir. Lab. for Artificial Intelligence Rsch., Columbus, 1983—. Co-chmn. Symposium on Potentials and Limitations of Mech. Intelligence, Anaheim, Calif., 1971; chmn. Norbert Wiener Symposium, Boston, 1974; sci. dir. Summer Sch. on Computer Program Testing, SOGESTA, Urbino, Italy, 1981; vis. scientist Lawrence Livermore Nat. Lab., Livermore, Calif., summer 1981, cons. fall 1981; vis. scientist MIT Computer Sci. Lab., 1983; dir. NIH Artificial Intelligence in Medicine Workshop, 1984; organizer panel discussion on artificial intelligence and engring. ASME, 1985; vis. scholar Stanford U., 1990-91; keynote spkr. World Congress on Expert Sys., Mexico City, 1998, Internat. Conf. on Diagrammic Reasoning, Callaway Gardens, Ga., 2002; tech. Arca leader US Army Rsch. Labs. Tech. Alliance on Decision Architectures, 2001—. Editor: Diagrammatic Reasoning, 1995; co-editor Computer Program Testing, 1981; editor ACM Sigart Spl. Issue on Structure, Function, and Behavior, 1985; assoc. editor Artificial Intelligence in Engring., 1986—; mem. bd. editors Internat. Jour. Pattern Recognition & Artificial Intelligence, Med. Expert Systems, Artificial Intelligence in Engring.; assoc. editor Internat. Jour. Human-Computer Interactions, 1996—. Recipient Outstanding Paper award Pattern Recognition Soc., 1976; Moore fellow U. Pa., 1964-67. Fellow IEEE (editor-in-chief Expert Jour. 1990-94), Am. Assn. for Artificial Intelligence (chmn. workshops on diagrammatic reasoning 1992), Assn. for Computing Machinery; mem. Sys. Man and Cybernetics Soc. IEEE (v.p. 1974-75, pattern recognition com. 1969-72, assoc. editor Trans. 1973—, guest editor spl. issue on distributed program solving 1981). Democrat. Avocation: travel. Home: 2053 Iuka Ave Columbus OH 43201-1415 Office: Ohio State U Dept Computer and Info Sci 2015 Neil Ave Columbus OH 43210-1210 Office Phone: 614-292-0923. Business E-Mail: chandra@cse.ohio-state.edu, chandra+whoswho@cis.ohio-state.edu.

CHANDRASEKHAR, SUJANA S., otologist, educator, neurotologist; 4 children. BS cum laude, City Coll. N.Y., 1984; MD, Mt. Sinai Sch. Medicine, N.Y.C., 1986. Intern, residency otolaryngology NYU Med. Ctr., 1986—92; fellow in otology/neurology House Ear Inst., L.A., 1993; from asst. to assoc. prof. UMDNJ-N.J. Med. Sch., Newark, 1994—2001, dir. otology/neurotology, 1996—2001; assoc. prof. otolaryngology Mt. Sinai Sch. Medicine, N.Y.C., 2001—04, clin. assoc. prof. otolaryngology, 2004—. Dir. otology/neurotology Mt. Sinai Med. Ctr., N.Y.C., 2001—04, dir. cochlear implant program, 2001—. Recipient Honor award, AMA, 2000, Am. Acad. Otolaryngology-Head and Neck Surgery, 2002. Office: 1430 Second Ave Ste 110 New York NY 10021 Office Phone: 212-396-4327. E-mail: ssc@verizon.net.

CHANDRASOMA, PARAKRAMA TISSA, physician; b. Colombo, Sri Lanka, Mar. 4, 1948; U.S. s. Tissa and Gertrude Clara Chandrasoma; m. Nirmala Cherine Chandrasoma, Jan. 11, 1973; children: Shahin, Janak, Pradip. MBBS, U. Ceylon Med. Sch., 1971, MD, 1977. Chief surg. pathology L.A. Med. Ctr., 1982—, chief anatomic pathology, 1990—; prof. path0ology Keck Sch. Medicine, U. So. Calif., 1996—. Bd. dirs. UPA, L.A.; cons. in field. Author: Stereotactic Brain Biopsy, 1989, Concise Pathology, 1994, Gastrointestinal Pathology, 2000. Mem.: L.A. Pathological Soc., Am. Soc. Clin. Pathologists, Coll. Am. Pathologists. Avocations: photography, writing. Office: LAC & USC Med Ctr 1200 N State St Rm 16-905 Los Angeles CA 90033

CHANDROSS, EDWIN ARTHUR, chemist; b. NYC, Oct. 13, 1934; BS, MIT, 1955; MA, Harvard U., 1957, PhD, 1960. Mem. tech. staff Bell Labs., Murray Hill, NJ, 1959—2001; head dept. organic chemistry R&D Bell Labs./Lucent Techs., Murray Hill, 1980-94, dir. materials rsch. dept., 1994—2001; prin. materials rsch. dept. Materials Chemistry LLC, 2001—. Mem. editl. bd. Chem. Revs., 1978-, Jour. Am. Chem. Soc., 1995-2000, Jour. Organic Chemistry, 2002-04, Chemistry of Materials, 2004-, Nanoletters, 2005— Recipient Life Achievement award North Jersey sect. ACS, 1997, Bloch medal U. Chgo., 2001, Award Indsl. Innovation Am. Chem. Soc., 2001, Award Indsl. Chemistry Am. Chem. Soc., 2005. Fellow AAAS Achievements include over 60 U.S. patents in optical properties of polymers, and photosensitive materials; development of a process to remove impurities in materials used to make optical fibers; discovery of the chemiluminescent system that is the basis of the lightstick. Office: Materials Chemistry LLC 14 Hunterdon Blvd New Providence NJ 07974

CHANDY, DIPAK, internist, pulmonologist, medical educator; b. Coimbatore, India, Aug. 5, 1966; s. Chandy John and Mary Chandy; m. Nandini Mariam Matthan, Jan. 1, 1994; children: Rohan John, Anisha Mary. MBBS, U. Calcutta, 1984—89. Diplomate Am. Bd. Internal Medicine, 1995, Pulmonary Diseases Am. Bd. Internal Medicine, 1998, Critical Care Medicine Am. Bd. Internal Medicine, 1999. Asst. prof. clin. medicine NY Med. Coll., Valhalla, NY, 1995—96, asst. prof. medicine, 1999—; dir., pulmonary clinic Westchester Med. Ctr., Valhalla, 2000—, tb control officer, 2000—; program dir. Pulmonary Critical Care Fellowship Program N.Y. Med. Coll., Valhalla, 2004—. Office: New York Med Coll Pulmonary Lab Westchester Medical Ctr Valhalla NY 10595 Office Phone: 914-493-7518. Personal E-mail: nandipak@hotmail.com. Business E-Mail: chandyd@wcmc.com.

CHANEN, STEVEN ROBERT, lawyer; b. Phoenix, May 15, 1953; s. Herman and Lois Marion (Boshes) C. Student, UCLA, 1971-73; BS in Mass Communications, Ariz. State U., 1975, JD, 1979. Bar: Ariz. 1980, U.S. Dist. Ct. Ariz. 1980, U.S. Ct. Appeals (9th cir.) 1980, Calif. 1981, U.S. Dist. Ct. (no. dist.) Calif. 1982. Ptnr. Wentworth & Lundin, Phoenix, 1980-86, of counsel, 1986-87; pres. Chanen Constrn. Co., Inc., 1991—. Appointed bd. dirs. Ariz. Gov.'s Commn. on Motion Pictures and TV, 1986, chmn., 1990; fin. intermediary, chmn. bd. dirs. S.R. Chanen and Co, Inc.; pres. Media Tech. Capital Corp., 1987-91; bd. dirs. ILX, Inc.; pres., bd. dirs. Electronic Mail Sys. Inc. Bd. dirs. Anytown, Am., Phoenix, 1986—, COMPAS, Inc., Phoenix, 1986-92, Ariz. Sci. Ctr., Phoenix, 1987—, Mus. Theater Ariz., Phoenix, 1988-89, Ariz. Politically Interested Citizens; pres. bd. dirs. Cmty. Forum, Phoenix; bd. dirs. Phoenix Children's Hosp., Nat. Conf., Maricopa County C.C. Dist. Found. (pres.). Recipient J. Leonard Amdur Man of the Year award, Herberger Humanitarian of Yr. award, Ariz. Humane Soc., 2000, Leader of Distinction award, Anti-Defamation League. Mem. ABA (forum com. entertainment and sports industries 1981—), Ariz. Bar Assn., Calif. Bar Assn., Maricopa County Bar Assn., Assn. Trial Lawyers Am. Republican. Jewish. Office: 3300 N 3rd Ave Phoenix AZ 85013-4304

CHANES, LUIS ALBERTO, surgeon; b. Santiago, Chile, Dec. 11, 1958; came to U.S., 1960; s. Anthony and Rebeca (Llaneza) C. BS in Biomed. Engring., U. So. Calif., 1982; MS in Biomed. Sci., Barry U., 1984; MD, Ponce Sch. of Medicine, 1987. Diplomate Am. Bd. Ophthalmology. Pvt. practice, Santa Ana & Mission Viejo, Calif., 1992—. Fellow Am. Acad. Ophthalmology; mem. Calif. Assn. Ophthalmology, Orange County Soc. Ophthalmology, Am. Soc. of Cataract and Refractive Surgery. Avocations: skiing, classic cars, golf. Office: 27871 Medical Center Rd Ste 120 Mission Viejo CA 92691-6407 also: 2621 S Bristol St Ste 205 Santa Ana CA 92704 Office Phone: 949-364-6688.

CHANEY, CAROL A., music artist, educator; b. Flint, Mich., Mar. 23, 1952; d. Harold R. Chaney and Eleanor B. Murphy-Chaney. BA in Comm. (Video), U. Mich., 1988, MFA, 2003. Cryptanalyst US Army Security Agy., 1972—78; comedienne, joke writer N.Y.C. and Washington, 1976—79; entertainer Carson & Barnes Circus, Hugo, Okla., 1978; journalist, photographer Flint Jour., Mich., 1984—94; prodr., dir., animator WFUM-TV28 Pub. TV, Flint, Mich., 1984—2001; prodr., dir. WSMH-Fox66, Flint, Mich., 1986—95; instr., 3d and 2d animation Mott Coll., Flint, Mich., 1998—2001; lectr. 2d and 3d animation video prodn. U. Mich., Flint, 1994—2003, music technologist, 2001—. Media cons. depts. music and theatre U. Mich., Flint, 2001—; panelist Ottawa Animation Festival, Canada, 2003; adj. asst. prof. Sch. Art and Design U. Mich., Ann Arbor, 2003—; vis. prof. Sch. Comm., Dept. Film and Video Grand Valley State U., 2005—. Exhibitions include Louvre, Paris, 2003, one-woman shows include Mott Gallery, 2003, Media Union Gallery U. Mich., 2001, 2003, Kerrytown Playhouse, 2005, Max Fisher Symphony Hall, Detroit, 2005; artist, prodr., dir. (video and print media campaign) Little Bird and the Environment (distinction award Pub. Rels. Assn., 1991), artist, prodr., editor (video) Virtual Conductor. Dir. PRIDE, Flint, 1994—97; judge Kalamazoo Animation Festival, 2005; advisor spl. population Genesee County Dem. Party, Flint, 1997—99; bd. dirs. Greater Flint Arts Coun., 2001—02. Sgt. U.S. Army, 1972—78. Recipient medal, Freedom Found., 1973, Spl. Sect. award, Mich. Press Assn., 1979, spl. citation from gov.'s rep., Pub. Rels. Assn., 1987, Spl. Recognition award, Mich. Assn. Broadcasters, 2001, award of distinction, Pub. Rels. Assn., 2001. Mem.: Assn. Internat. du Film D'Animation, Am. MENSA, Women In Animation. Avocation: sailing. Office: U Mich 2000 Bonisteel Blvd Ann Arbor MI 48109-2069 Office Phone: 810-762-3037. Home Fax: 810-762-3326; Office Fax: 734-936-0469. E-mail: chaney@umich.edu.

CHANEY, DON, professional basketball coach; b. Baton Rouge, Mar. 22, 1946;, U. Houston, Houston, TX. Player Boston Celtics, Boston, 1968-75, Los Angeles Clippers, Los Angeles, CA, 1976-77, Boston Celtics, Boston, 1978-80; asst. coach Detroit Pistons, Detroit, 1980-83, San Diego, Los Angeles Clippers, 1983-85; head coach Los Angeles Clippers, Los Angeles, CA, 1985-87; asst. coach Atlanta Hawks, Atlanta, 1987-88; head coach Houston Rockets, Houston, 1988-92, Detroit Pistons, Auburn Hills, Mich., 1993-95; asst. coach N.Y. Knicks, 1996—2001, head coach, 2001—04. Named Coach of Year NBA, 1991.

CHANEY, GERALD M., retail executive; V.p. fin. and control fashion group Gen. Mills, Inc., 1983—85; exec. v.p. ops., CFO Crystal Brands, Inc., 1985—95; former COO Canadians Corp.; former exec. v.p., chief adminstrv. officer, CFO Petrie Retail, Inc.; former v.p. fin, CFO Kellwood Co., St. Louis; sr. v.p., CFO Polo Ralph Lauren Corp., N.Y.C., 2000—. Office: Polo Ralph Lauren Corp 650 Madison Ave New York NY 10022

CHANEY, NORMAN RICHARD, English studies educator; b. Brazil, Ind., Feb. 19, 1935; s. Hareld Ebon and Mildred Calista (Love) C.; m. Freda Mae Morris; children: Elizabeth, Paul, Heather; stepchildren: Adrian, Jacqueline, Vicki. BA in English, U. Indpls., 1960; MA in Comparative Lit., Ind. U., 1963; MDiv in Religion and Lit., Yale U., 1964; MA in Religion and Lit., U. Chgo., 1969, PhD in Religion and Lit., 1975. Tchr. Quinnipiac Coll., Hamden, Conn., 1961-63, Otterbein Coll., Westerville, Ohio, 1964-66, 70—, Elgin (Ill.) C.C., 1966-67; assoc. pastor Grace Meth. Ch., Naperville, Ill., 1967-68; tutor U. Chgo., 1969. Author: Theodore Roethke: The Poetics of Wonder, 1981, Six Images of Human Nature, 1990; contbr. articles to profl. jours. Elder United Meth. Ch., 1964—; pastor Hillsdale (Ind.) Meth. Ch.; singer Columbus (Ohio) Symphony Chorus, 1980-90. With Army Med. Corps, 1954-56. Grantee NEH, 1978, 87, 90, Otterbein Coll., 1970—. Mem. Am. Philos. Assn., MLA, Am. Acad. Religion. Avocations: music, woodworking, art, birdwatching, travel. Home: 7864 Newark Rd Mount Vernon OH 43050-9569 Office: Otterbein Coll Dept English Westerville OH 43081

CHANEY, VERNE EDWARD, JR., surgeon, foundation administrator, educator; b. Kansas City, Mo., July 16, 1923; s. Verne Edward and Adelaide (Hafner) C.; divorced; children: Christopher Edward, Steven Wood. BS, Va. Mil. Inst., 1951; MD, Johns Hopkins U., 1948, M.P.H., 1972; DSc (hon.), U. N.C., 2002. Diplomate: Am. Bd. Surgery, Am. Bd. Thoracic and Cardiac Surgery. Intern surgery Johns Hopkins U. Hosp., 1948-49, asst. resident, 1949-50, instr. anatomy, 1950-53; surg. resident N.C. Meml. Hosp., Chapel Hill, 1953-56; chief of surgery Albert Schweitzer Hosp., Deschappeles, Haiti, 1956-58; practice medicine specializing in thoracic surgery Monterey, Calif., 1958-61; pres. and founder Intermed Internat. Inc. (formerly Thomas A. Dooley Found.-INTERMED, Inc.), N.Y.C., 1961—; clin. prof. surgery U. Miami, 1976—; founder, pres. INTERMED, Geneva, 1976—. Patentee in field. Served from pvt. to capt. M.C. U.S. Army, 1944, 50-52. Decorated Silver Star medal; decorated Bronze Star medal with V, Purple Heart U.S., Croix de Guerre France, Order of Million Elephants Laos; recipient Disting. Svc. award Sch. Medicine U. North Carolina, 1991. Fellow ACS, Am. Coll. Chest Physicians; mem. N.Y. State Med. Soc., N.Y. Acad. Medicine, Am. Pub. Health Assn., Internat. Health Soc. (pres. 1987-88), Nathan A. Womack Surg. Soc., Internat. Soc. Surgeons, Nat. Soc. Fund Raising Execs., Explorers Club. Clubs: N.Y. Athletic, Sky, West Side Tennis. Republican. Episcopalian. Home: 530 E 72nd St Apt 16E New York NY 10021-4863 Office: Dooley Found Intermed 420 Lexington Ave Rm 2331 New York NY 10170-2332 Office Phone: 212-687-3620.

CHANEY, WILLIAM ALBERT, retired history professor; b. Arcadia, Calif., Dec. 23, 1922; s. Horace Pierce and Esther (Bowen) Chaney. AB, U. Calif., Berkeley, 1943, PhD, 1961. Mem. faculty Lawrence U., Appleton, Wis., 1952-99, George McKendree Steele prof. western culture, 1966-99, Steele prof. emeritus, 1999—, chmn. dept. history, 1968-71, 95-96. Vis. prof. Mich. State U., 1958. Author: The Cult of Kingship in Anglo-Saxon England: The Transformation from Paganism to Christianity, 1970, reprinted, 1999; contbr. articles to profl. jours. and encys. Grantee, Am. Coun. Learned Socs., 1966—67; Jr. fellow, Harvard Soc. Fellows, 1949—52. Fellow: Royal Soc. Arts; mem.: AAUP, MLA, Archeol. Inst. Am., Conf. Brit. Studies, Am. Soc. Ch. History, Medieval Acad. Am., Am. Hist. Assn. Episcopalian. Home: 215 E Kimball St Appleton WI 54911-5720 Office: Lawrence Univ Dept History Appleton WI 54912 Office Phone: 920-832-6676.

CHANG, BARBARA KAREN, medical educator; b. Milltown, Ind., Jan. 6, 1946; m. M.F. Joseph Chang-Wai-Ling, Oct. 6, 1967; children: Carla Marie Yvonnette, Nolanne Arlette. BA, Ind. U., 1968; MA, Brandeis U., 1970; MD, Albert Einstein Coll. Medicine, 1973. Diplomate Am. Bd. Internal Medicine, Am. Bd. Med. Oncology, Am. Bd. Hematology. Resident in internal medicine Montefiore Med. Ctr., Bronx, N.Y., 1973-75; fellow in hematology/oncology Duke U. Med. Ctr., Durham, N.C., 1975-78; staff physician VA Med. Ctr., Augusta, Ga., 1978-95, chief hematology/oncology, 1980-89, assoc. chief of staff edn., 1990-95; prof. medicine Med. Coll. Ga., Augusta, 1978-95; chief of staff, chief med. officer VA Med. Ctr., Albuquerque, 1995—2002; assoc. dean U. N.Mex. Sch. Medicine, Albuquerque, 1995—2002; cons. Capital Assets Realignment for Enhanced Svcs. Program VA Ctrl. Office, Washington, 2002—03, dir. program evaluation Office Academic Affiliations, 2003—. Mem. Sci. Adv. Bd., Washington, 1983-88; mem. expert panels computer applications Dept. Vets. Affairs, Washington, 1988-95. Contbr. numerous articles on cancer rsch. to profl. jours. Youth coord. Am. Hemerocallis Soc., Augusta, 1993-95, pres. local chpt. 1997, Albuquerque, garden judge 1997-2003, region 6 youth liaison, 2000-01, exhbn. judge, 2001—, nat. youth liaison com., 2003-05. Grantee Nat. Cancer Inst., Am. Cancer Soc., 1978-93; David M. Worthen award Acad. Excellence Dept. Vet. Affairs, 2000. Fellow ACP, Am. Soc. Clin. Oncology, Bioelectromagnetic Soc. (bd. dirs. 1983-86). Office: Dept Vets Affairs Med Ctr 1501 San Pedro Dr SE Albuquerque NM 87108-5153 Business E-Mail: barbara.chang@med.va.gov.

CHANG, CARMEN, lawyer; b. Nanjing, China, 1948; BA, Sarah Lawrence Coll., 1970; MA, Stanford U., 1973, JD with distinction, 1993. Bar: Calif. 1994, U.S. Ct. Appeals (9th cir.) 1994. With Wilson Sonisi Goodrich Rosati; ptnr. Shearman & Sterling, LLP, Menlo Park, Calif., 2003—. Spkr. in field; mem. adv. bd. Stanford Project Regions of Innovation and Entrepreneurship Asia-Pacific Rsch. Ctr. Stanford U., Stanford, Calif. Contbr. articles to profl. jours. Office: Wilson Sonsini Goodrich & Rosati 650 Page Mill Rd Palo Alto CA 94304 Office Phone: 650-838-3612. Office Fax: 650-838-3699. Business E-Mail: cchang@wsgr.com. E-mail: carmen.chang@shearman.com.

CHANG, CHAWNSHANG, science educator, lab administrator; b. Taichung, Taiwan, Nov. 26, 1955; came to U.S., 1980; s. Su-In Chang and Tsu-Hon Chang-Ko; m. Amly Liu, June 12, 1980; children: Eugene, Philip. BS, Nat. Taiwan U., Taipei, 1974-78; PhD, U. Chgo., 1985. Asst. prof. prostate cancer/male hormone action U. Chgo., 1988-90; asst. prof. U. Wis., Madison, 1990—93, assoc. prof., 1993-96, prof., 1996—97; George Whipple prof. U. Rochester, N.Y., 1997—. Patentee androgen receptor gene; contbr. articles to profl. publs. Chairperson Taiwanese Student Assn., U. Chgo., 1984-85. Lt. Taiwanese Army, 1978-80. Andrew Mellon Found. fellow, 1989-90; recipient Jr. Faculty award Am. Cancer Soc., Atlanta, 1990—, Pres. award Taiwan Urology Assn., 1999, Pres. award Taiwan Osteoporesis Assn., 1999. Fellow Japan Archology Soc. (hon.); mem. Am. Assn. for Cancer Rsch., The Endocrine Soc. (Ayerst Travel award 1988). Avocations: ping pong/table tennis, volleyball, music, swimming. Home: 19 Sandy Ln Pittsford NY 14534-1078 Office: U Rochester Dept Urology 601 Elmwood Ave Rochester NY 14642 Business E-Mail: chang@urmc.rochester.edu.

CHANG, CHING MING (CARL CHANG), engineering executive, mechanical engineer, educator, writer; b. Nanking, China; came to U.S., 1967; m. Birdie S.C. Chang, Dec. 18, 1964; children: Andrew L.P., Nelson L.A., Michele Chang. Dipl. Ing., Technol. U. Aachen, Germany, 1962; PhD, Technol. U. Aachen, 1967; MBA, SUNY, Buffalo, 1985. Registered profl. engr., N.Y., Va. Asst. prof. N.C. State U., Raleigh, 1968-73; sr. engr. to sr. devel. assoc. Praxair, Inc. (formerly Union Carbide Indsl. Gases), Tonawanda, N.Y., 1973-95, bus. devel. mgr., 1995-98; pres. CarlChang LLC Bus. Cons., Amherst, N.Y., 1998—; dir. analytical engring. O'Mara Cons. Engrs., Buffalo, 2001—02. Adj. prof. engring. SUNY, Buffalo, 1979-, cons. Great Am. Ins., Dresser-Rand, AccMed Tech. and Harper Internat. Author: Engineering Management: Challenges in the New Millennium, 2005; contbr. articles to profl. jour. Named Person of Yr. Tech. Soc. Coun., Buffalo, 1986. Mem. NSPE (pres. Erie-Niagara chpt. 1980-81, Disting. Svc. award 1981, Basinsky award 1984, Engring. Educator of Yr. award 1990, Praxair Special Recognition award for Technol. Leadership, 1992, Basinski-Wohler award 1994). Achievements include invention of holder of five U.S. patents, in the fields of electrostatic precipitation, turbomachinery, and artificial intelligence. Avocations: tennis, travel, computer games, writing, reading. also: SUNY Buffalo Dept Indsl Engring 323 Bell Hall Buffalo NY 14260 E-mail: CChangLLC@aol.com.

CHANG, CHING-JER, medicinal chemistry educator; b. Hsinchu, Taiwan, China, Oct. 17, 1942; came to the U.S., 1968; s. Tin-lian and Awei (Lai) C.; m. Shu-fang Kuo, Dec. 25, 1978; children: Philip, Sylvia. BS, Nat. Taiwan Cheng Kung U., 1965; PhD, Ind. U., 1972. Asst. prof. Purdue U., West Lafayette, Ind., 1973-78, assoc. prof., 1978-84, prof., 1984—. Mem. bioorganic and natural products chemistry study sect., NIH, Bethesda, Md., 1986-90, spl. study sect.,1985, 1991—; editl. adv. bd. Jour. Natural Products, 1989-99; reviewer Human Frontier Sci. Program, Strassbourg, France, 1992—, Hong Kong Govt. Rsch. Grant Coun., 1997—; mem. breast cancer rsch. study sect. Dept. Def., 1997-2002; N.Am. regional editor Jour. Asian Natural Products Rsch., 2002—. Contbr. articles to profl. jours. Mem. Am. Soc. Pharmacognosy (exec. com. 1993-97, 2004—), Am. Chem. Soc., Am. Assn. for Cancer Rsch., Phytochem. Soc. N.Am., Argentinian Soc. Organic Chemistry (hon. mem.). Achievements include patents in field. Office: Dept Medicinal Chemistry Purdue Univ West Lafayette IN 47907-2091 E-mail: cjchang@pharmacy.purdue.edu.

CHANG, CHRIS C.N., pediatric surgeon; b. Taiwan, China, June 20, 1943; s. Shu-Ming and Yu-Bow (Chow) C.; m. Rose Lee Chang, Mar. 4, 1972; children: Lynda, Steven. MD, Nat. Taiwan U., 1969. Intern Nat. Taiwan Univ. Hosp., 1968-69, resident in surgery, 1970-72, Albert Einstein Med. Ctr., Phila., 1972-76; resident in pediat. surgery St. Christopher's Hosp. for Children, Phila., 1976-78; dir. pediat. surgery Lehigh Valley Hosp., Allentown, Pa., 1993—. Fellow ACS, Internat. Coll. Surgeons, Am. Acad. Pediats.; mem. Am. Pediat. Surg. Assn. Office: Chop Specialty Care Ctr LV 2545 Schoenersville Rd Bethlehem PA 18017-7300 Office Phone: 484-884-3333. Office Fax: 484-884-3300. Business E-Mail: chris.chang@lvh.com.

CHANG, CHRISTOPHER Y., otolaryngologist, surgeon; s. Jin Y. and Sook H. Chang. BS magna cum laude, Yale U., 1996, MD, 2000. Gen. surgery intern Duke U. Med. Ctr., Durham, NC, 2000—01, otolaryngology-head & neck surgery resident, 2001—04, otolaryngology-head & neck surgery chief resident, 2004—05. Mem. exec. bd. iCORD, LLC, Durham, 2003—05. Creator and webmaster (website) Zenker's Diverticulum Website, webmaster Duke Otolaryngology-Head & Neck Surgery Website, creator and webmaster Y-Axis Yale School of Medicine Student Website; contbr. articles to profl. jours., chpts. to books. Recipient Social Enterprise Track 1st prize, Duke Bus. Sch. Start-Up Challenge, 2003; fellow, Yale U. Sch. Medicine, 1997. Achievements include patents pending for Methods and Systems for Searching, Displaying, and Managing Medical Teaching Cases in a Medical Teaching Case Database. Office Phone: 540-347-0505. E-mail: changcy@mac.com.

CHANG, CHUNG-CHE, hematopatholgist, medical researcher, medical educator; b. Tainan, Taiwan, July 25, 1958; s. Chu-Chang and Yeh-Ing Chang; m. Horng-Wen Hsieh, Aug. 18, 1970; children: Edwin, Ellen, Ayei Elizabeth. MD, Nat. Yang-Ming U., Taipei, Taiwan, 1983; PhD, Case Western Res. U., Cleve., 1990. Diplomate Am. Bd. Pathology, 1997. Asst. prof., dir. hematopathology fellowship Med. Coll. Wis., Milw., 1999—2003; assoc. prof. Baylor Coll. Medicine, Houston, 2003—, Weil Med. Coll. of Cornell Univ., 2003—. Dir. Chenn-Kung Town Group Med. Ctr., Taiwan, 1991—93; dir. hematopathology and flow cytometry lab The Meth. Hosp., Houston, 2003—. Pricipical investigator (novel research) Clonotypic B-cell In Myeloma; author: (manuscript) MUM1 In CLL; pricipal investigator (research) MDR1 In Childhood Leukemia. Grantee, NIH, 2003. Fellow: ASCP, Coll. Am. Pathologists (com. 1998—2003, scholar 1998, Tng. in Tech. award 1997). Achievements include development of computer software to diagnose Anemia; Quality Control System For Hematologic Analyzers. Office: The Meth Hosp 6565 Fannin Ms205 Houston TX 77030 Business E-Mail: jeffchang2@pol.net.

CHANG, CHUN-SHU, historian, educator, writer; b. Shandong, China, Apr. 25, 1934; arrived in U.S.A, 1957; s. Yun-an Chang and Ming-fang Kuo; m. Shelley Hsueh-lun Chang, Sept. 26, 1959; children: Chien-ju Jean, I-ju Deborah, Wei-chung Victor. BA in History, Nat. Taiwan U., Taipei, China, 1956; PhD., Harvard U., 1964. Richard Hudon prof. history U. Mich., Ann Arbor, 1966—83; from chair history to dept. head and dir. grad. studies The Chinese U. of Hong Kong, China, 1983—85; hon. prof. Chinese history The Peoples Republic of China, 1985—; vis. prof. Chinese history, dept. history Lanzhou U., Gansu, China, 1983, 1985, 1990; disting. vis. prof. Chinese History Taiwan, 1992; 29th Carl Becker lectr., 2002. Chair Internat. Conf. on Sung China, 1994; dir. Archeol. Expeditions, Gansu, China, 1982, 83, 85, 90, Summer Inst. of Han Studies, 1985. Author: The God of Soil in Ancient China, 1956, 1957, The Han Colonists and Their Settlements on the Chu-yen Frontier, 1966, Pre Modern China: A Bibliographical Introduction, 1971, revised edition, 1977, Han-tai pien-chiang shih lun-chi, 1975, War and Peace with the Hsiungnu in Early Han China: The Hsiungnu Challenge and the Origins of Han Wu-ti's Military Expansion, 200-133 B.C., 1979, South China in the Twelfth Century, 1982, Essays on the History of Northwest China, 1982, A New Critical Biography of the First Emperor, 260-210 B.C., 1985, (collection of Chinese poetry) Wei-ch'ing shih-chi, 1985—2003, Redefining History, 1998, State and Theatre in Seventeenth-Century China: Drama and Politics during the Ming-Ch'ing Transition, 2003, Nation, State, and Imperialism in Early China, ca. 1600 B.C. - 8 A.D., 2004, Frontier, Immigration and Empire in Han China, 129 B.C. -A.D.107, 2004; co-author (with Shelley Hsueh-lun Chang): Crisis and Transformation in Seventeenth-Century China: Society, Culture, and Modernity, 1998; editor: Two Studies in Chinese Literature, 1968, The Making of China, 1975, 2d edit., 2000, Sung-Yuan Studies, The Continent Magazine; contbr. articles to profl. jours and magazines; exhibitions include An Exhibition of Chinese Calligraphy The Language of Art, Ann Arbor, Mich, 2003. Nominee Pulitzer Prize, 1991; recipient The Warner G. Rice award for Outstanding Acheivements in Humanities, 1977, Sino-Am. Culture award, 1956; grantee The Am. Council of Learned Soc., Social Sci. Rsch. Coun., Ford Found., Harvard U., The Chinese U. of Hong Kong; Cultural Reconstruction Foundation. Mem.: The Am. Acad. of the Polit. and Social Sci. (delegate 1960s-2000), Assn. for Asian Studies (panel chair), Soc. of Xu Xiake Studies (Council mem.), Soc. of Sung-Yuan Studies (exec. editl. bd.), Am. Historical Assn. (chair). Avocations: basketball, Peking Opera. Office: U Mich Dept History 1029 Tisch Hall Ann Arbor MI 48109

CHANG, CLARENCE DAYTON, retired chemist; b. Tianjin, China, Mar. 8, 1933; came to U.S., 1939; s. Hsueh Tseng and Lucy Chang; m. Cheryl Schucker, June 28, 1958 (div. 1987); 1 child, Christopher E.; m. Elizabeth C. O'Donoghue, June 28, 1987; 1 child, Stephen D. AB, Harvard U., 1954. Project chemist Weyerhaeuser Co., Longview, Wash., 1954-55, Sugar Rsch. Found., N.Y.C., 1955-61; supr. M.W. Kellogg Co., Piscataway, N.J., 1961-70; sr. rsch. chemist Mobil R & D Corp., Princeton, N.J., 1970-74, rsch. assoc., 1974-81, rsch. scientist, 1981-84, sr. scientist, 1984-95, Mobil Tech. Co., Paulsboro, N.J., 1995-2000. Author: Hydrocarbons from Methanol, 1983; editor: Methane Conversion, 1988; also articles; over 200 U.S. patents in field. Recipient Hall of Fame, NJ Inventor's, 2005. Pem. Catalysis Soc. (excellence in catalysis award 1984), Am. Chem. Soc. (E.V. Murphree award 1992), Chinese-Am. Chem. Soc. (bd. dirs. 1993), N.Am. Catalysis Soc. (E.J. Houdry award 1999). Personal E-mail: cdchang@nji.com.

CHANG, DARWIN RAY, civil engineer; b. Jukao, Kiangsu, China, Aug. 1, 1917; came to U.S., 1945, naturalized, 1962; s. Wey and Susan (Hsiong) C.; m. Yen Ma, Dec. 23, 1961; children: Gordon, Susan, Martha, Leslie. BS, Chiao Tung U., Shanghai, China, 1940; MCE, Cornell U., 1946. Structural engr. Borsari Tank Corp., N.Y.C., 1951; project engr. Ebasco Internat. Corp., N.Y.C. 1956-60; prin. engr. Pub. Svc. Electric and Gas Co., Newark, 1960-80; mktg. mgr. Lehigh Utility Assos., Inc., South Plainfield, N.J., 1981-83; pres. D and Y Chang Enterprises Inc.; 1980—. Bd. visitors Drew U. Mem. N.J. Soc. Profl. Engrs., Chinese Inst. Engrs., Cornell Club of N.Y., Rotary. Presbyterian. Contbr. articles on esthetic transmission structures to trade mags. Home: 108 Green Ave Madison NJ 07940-2534 Office: 24 Main St Madison NJ 07940-1818

CHANG, DEBBIE I-JU, health programs and research executive, director; BS in Chem. Engring., MIT, 1984; MPH, U. Mich., 1987. Presdl. mgmt. intern Health Care Fin. Adminstrn. Office Legislation and Policy, 1987-89; sr. health policy advisor Senator Donald W. Riegle Jr., 1989-94; dir. office legis. and intergovt. affairs Health Care Fin. Adminstrn., Washington, 1994-98; dir. State Children's Health Ins. Program Health Care Fin. Adminstrn., Dept. HHS, 1997-99; dir. Medicaid coverage benefits and payments Health Care Fin. Adminstrn., Balt., 1998; dep. sec. health care financing Medicaid Md. Dept. Health and Mental Hygiene, Balt., 1999—2003; sr. v.p., exec. dir. Nemours Divsn. Health and Prevention Svcs., Del., 2004—. Contbr. articles to profl. jours. Office Phone: 302-444-9127. E-mail: dchang@nemours.org.

CHANG, DENNIS, lawyer; b. Carmel, Calif., Jan. 27, 1956; s. Kenneth Byung Cho Chang and Cynthia Mantell; m. Mina Lee, July 23, 1988; children: Eugene, Ethan, Luke, Kristie. Degree in sociology, Calif. State U., 1981; JD, U. Calif., San Francisco, 1986. Bar: Calif. 1988, U.S. Dist. Ct. (cen. and so. dists.) 1988. Assoc. in litig. Kim, Chung & Lim, L.A., 1986-88; ptnr. Chang & Lim, L.A., 1988-97, Park, Smith, Chang & Lim, L.A., 1997—. Trustee Korean Am. Mus., L.A., 1995—. Mem. L.A. County Bar (trustee 1991-93). Office: Ste 2800 1055 W 7th St Los Angeles CA 90017-2554

CHANG, EDWARD H., computer company executive; b. Taipei, Taiwan, Jan. 10, 1958; came to U.S., 1975; s. James T. and Yu-Chin Chang. BA, U. Hawaii, 1981; JD, Abraham Lincoln U., 2004. Cert. bus. counselor. Mktg. dir. Prometheus World Enterprise, Santa Ana, Calif., 1983-88; gen. mgr. Trans PC, Inc., Norwalk, Calif., 1989-91; v.p. consumer products Microtome, Inc., St. Louis, 1992-95; exec. dir. Lotus Profl., L.A., Calif., 1996—. Exec. dir. EKM Computer, Inc., Buena Park, Calif., 1997-99, LPS Telemgmt., L.A., 1995-2004 Bd. dirs. Vairotsana Found., pres., 1996-98, chair, 2004— Buddhist. Achievements include co-patent for system and apparatus for electronic communication. Office: Lotus Profl Media Tower II Rm 411 1600 Taft Ave Los Angeles CA 90028-3706 Business E-Mail: ehchang88@netscape.net.

CHANG, FRED H., music educator; s. S. I. and Y. S. Chang; m. E. Christina Chang, Apr. 22, 1989; children: Ross, Lauren. BA in Music Edn., Virginia Tech., 1986; M in Music Edn., U. Ala., 1999. With Rustburg (Va.) Secondary Sch., 1986—87; band dir. West Meckienburg H.S., Charlotte, NC, 1987—88, Bassett (Va.) Mid. Sch., 1988—93, Christiansburg (Va.) H.S., 1993—96, Bibb County H.S., Centreville, Ala., 1997—99, J.H. Rose H.S., Greenville, NC, 1999—2001, Chattahoochee H.S., Alpharetta, Ga., 2001—. Mem.: Music Educators Nat. Conf. Office: Chattahoochee High Sch 5320 Taylor Rd Alpharetta GA 30022

CHANG, HELEN T., municipal official; BA, Nat. Chung Hsing U.; MBA, Auburn U., Ala. Former instructor Inst. of Bus. Administration, Taiwan; former rsch. statistician U. Washington, Seattle; former admin. assoc. Baylor Coll. of Med., Houston; news anchor So. Chinese TV, 1988—91; former mem. advisory council on ed. statistics US Dept. of Ed., Washington; former mem. Tex. Statewide Hlth. Coord. Council, 1990—93; exec. asst. Off. of Mayor, Houston, 1992—, and dir. Internat. Affairs & Econ. Develop. Mem. Internat. Trade Com. of Greater Houston Partnership, Org. of Women in Internat. Trade-Houston, E.B. Cape Ctr. Sr. Professional Develop. Com., Houston Com. on Foreign Relations; founder & chair US Asian Bus. Partnership; chair Asian-Am. Heritage Assn. of Houston; pres. Chinese Women's Bus. Assn., Asian-Am. Voters' Coalition. Named Honorary Citizen, City of Dalian, China, 1997. Office: City of Houston 901 Bagby 4th Fl Houston TX 77002*

CHANG, HEMMIE, lawyer; b. Mar. 19, 1960; AB, Princeton Univ., 1981; JD, Harvard Univ., 1984. Bar: Mass. 1985. Law clk. Judge David S. Nelson, US Dist Ct. (Mass.); assoc. Ropes & Gray, Boston, 1985—93, ptnr. corp. dept., 1993—, head energy & utilities practice group. Bd. mem. South Cove Nursing Home; bd. mem. Cambridge Ctr for Adult Edn.; bd. mem. Commonwealth Sch. Mem.: Women's Corp. Counsel Network, Boston Law Firm Group. Office: Ropes & Gray 1 International Pl Boston MA 02110-2624 Office Phone: 617-951-7317. Office Fax: 617-951-7050. Business E-Mail: h.chang@ropesgray.com.

CHANG, HENRY C., library administrator; b. Canton, China, Sept. 15, 1941; came to U.S., 1964, naturalized, 1973; s. Ih-ming and Lily (Lin) C.; m. Marjorie Li, Oct. 29, 1966; 1 dau., Michelle. LLB, Nat. Chengchi U., 1962; MA, U. Mo., 1966; MA in Libr. Sci., U. Minn., 1968, PhD, 1974. Reader advisor Braille Inst. Am., L.A., 1965-67, dir. libr. svcs., 1990—; reference libr. U. Minn., Mpls., 1968-70, instr., libr., 1970-72, asst. head govt. document divsn., 1972-74; libr. dir., lectr. in social scis. U. of the V.I., St. Croix, 1974-75, dir. divsn. librs., museums and archeol. svcs., 1975-88; dir. V.I. Libr. Tng. Inst., 1975-76; coord., chmn. V.I. State Hist. Records Adv. Bd., 1976-88, pres., libr. cons., 1988-89; project dir. Calif. Telephone Reader Program, 2000—. Chmn. microfilm com. ACURIL, 1977-88; mem. V.I. Bicentennial Commn., 1975-77, Ft. Frederik Commn., 1975-76; adv. com. on rsch. tng. Caribbean Rsch. Inst., 1974-75; coord. Libr. Conf., 1977-87; project dir. cultural heritage project NEH, 1979-83; chmn. nat. collection devel. com. nat. libr. svcs. Libr. of Congress, 1998, chmn. western conf. group, 2001-04; commr. Accreditation Commn. for Acupuncture and Oriental Medicine, 2004—. Author: A Bibliography of Presidential Commissions, Committees, Councils, Panels and Task Forces, 1961-72, 1973, Taiwan Demography, 1964-71: A Selected Annotated Bibliography of Government Documents, 1973, A Selected Annotated Bibliography of Caribbean Bibliographies in English, 1975, A Survey of the Use of Microfilms in the Caribbean, 1978, Long-Range Program for Library Development, 1978, Institute for Training in Library Management and Communications Skill, 1979; contbr. numerous articles and book revs. on libr. sci. to profl. jours. Chmn. bd. dirs. Eden Found. for People with Disabilities, 1995—96; mem. adv. com. Nat. Std. and Guideline Svcs., Libr. Congress Network Librs., 2002—05. 2d lt. Taiwan Army, 1962—63. Named Mem. Staff of Yr., Coll. V.I., 1974—75; recipient Libr. Adminstrs. Devel. Program fellowship award, 1972, Cert. of Appreciation, Govt. V.I., 1985, Eden Found., 1999, L.A. Internat. Lions Club award, 1992, 1995, Driver Safety award, 1993, Cert. of Achievement, Braille Inst., 2001, Network Libr. of Yr. award, 2005;, Libr. of Congress, 2004—05; grantee, Nat. Commn. on Librs. and Info. Sci. Mem. ALA (counselor 1980-84), AAUP, Asian Pacific ALA (chmn. fin. com. 1993-96), Population Assn. Am., Am. Sociol. Assn., Chinese Am. Profl. Soc. Home: 3713 Lowry Rd Los Angeles CA 90027-1437 Office: Braille Inst Am 741 N Vermont Ave Los Angeles CA 90029-3594 Office Phone: 323-906-3185, 323-660-3880. Business E-Mail: dls@braillelibrary.org.

CHANG, HERNAN ROBERT, infectious disease consultant; s. Hector Chang and Julia Pinares. MD, San Marcos U., Lima, Peru, 1982, U. Geneva, Switzerland, 1988. Diplomate Am. Bd. Internal Medicine, 2000, Infectious Diseases Am. Bd. Infectious Diseases, 2002. Rsch. fellow Dept. Microbiology Inst. Tropical Medicine, Antwerp, Belgium, 1984—85; rsch. fellow Dept. Genetics and Microbiology U. Geneva Med. Sch., 1986—92; sr. lectr. Dept. Microbiology, Nat. U. Singapore, 1992—95; rsch. fellow Deaconess Hosp., Harvard Med. Sch., Boston, 1996—97; resident Salem Hosp., Mass., 1997—2000; fellow New Eng. Med. Ctr., Boston, 2000—01, Boston U. Med. Ctr., 2001—02; cons. Salem Hosp., Mass., 2002—04, Infectious Disease Cons., Jacksonville, Fla., 2004—. Chief resident Salem Hosp., Mass., 1999—2000. Contbr. articles to profl. jours. Recipient Maxwell Finland Award, Mass. Infectious Diseases Soc., 2002; grantee Rsch., Swiss NSF, 1993—95, Finanz-Pool 3R Found., Switzerland, 1988—91. Mem.: AMA, ACP, Mass. Med. Soc., Swiss Soc. for Cell Biology, Molecular Biology and Genetics, Swiss Soc. for Microbiology, European Soc. Clin. Microbiology and Infectious Diseases, Infectious Diseases Soc. Am., Am. Soc. for Microbiology, Mass. Med. Soc. (com. pubs. 2001—02), Am. Acad. HIV Medicine, Internat. Soc. Travel Medicine (cert. travel health 2003), Boston Med. Libr. (life; bd. trustees 2003—04), Intertel, Cerebrals, Top-One-Percent Soc., One-in-a-Thousand Soc., Glia Soc., Internat. Soc. for Philos. Enquiry, Triple Nine Soc., Mensa, Shriners, Scottish Rite, Grand Lodge of Mass. Office: Infectious Disease Consultants 11555 Central Pky #200 Jacksonville FL 32224

CHANG, HOWARD FENGHAU, law educator, consultant; b. Lafayette, Ind., June 30, 1960; s. Joseph Juifu and Mary Hsueh-mei C. AB in Govt. cum laude, Harvard Coll., 1982; M in Pub. Affairs, Princeton (N.J.) U., 1985; JD magna cum laude, Harvard U., 1987; SM in Econs., MIT, 1988, PhD in Econs., 1992. Bar: N.Y. 1989, D.C. 1989. Law clk. to hon. Ruth Bader Ginsburg U.S. Ct. of Appeals, Washington, 1988-89; asst. prof. law U. So. Calif. Law Sch., L.A., 1992-94, assoc. prof. law, 1994-97, prof. law, 1997-99, U. Pa., Phila., 1999—. Vis. assoc. prof. law Georgetown U. Law Ctr., Washington, 1996-97; prof. law Stanford Law Sch., 1998. Supervising editor Harvard Law Rev., 1986—87; contbr. articles to law jours. John M. Olin fellowship Dept. Econs. MIT, 1987, 90, 91; nat. merit scholar IBM, 1978. Mem. Am. Econ. Assn., Am. Law and Econs. Assn. Office: U Pa Law Sch 3400 Chestnut St Philadelphia PA 19104-6204 Office Fax: 215-573-2025. E-mail: hchang@law.upenn.edu.*

CHANG, HSUEH-LUN SHELLEY, historian, researcher, writer; b. Nanning, China, Sept. 18, 1934; d. Chun-su Loh and Chien-Yun Huang; m. Chun-shu Chang, Sept. 26, 1959; children: Chien-ju Jean, I-Ju Deborah, Wei-chung Victor. BA in History, Nat. Taiwan U., 1956; MA in History, Boston U., 1961. Rsch. assoc. Ctr. Chinese Study, Ann Arbor, Mich., 1984—. Vis. lectr. Chinese U. Hong Kong, 1983—85, U. Lan-chou China, 1984; vis. assoc. prof. U. Mich., Ann Arbor, 1987, 94, v.p. women's rsch. club, 91. Author: Windmills: A Collection of Essays, 1970, History and Legend, 1990; co-author: Crisis and Transformation in 17th-Century China, 1992, Redefining History, 1998. Mem.: Assn. Asian Studies, Am. Hist. Assn. Home: 3236 Bluett Dr Ann Arbor MI 48105

CHANG, ISABELLE C., librarian, educator, writer; b. Boston, Feb. 20, 1924; d. Que Wah Chin and June Hall; m. Min Chueh Chang, May 28, 1948; children: Francis Hugh, Claudia, Pamela. MA in English, Clark U., 1967; MA in Psychology, Anna Maria Coll., 1982. Lib. trustee Shrewsbury (Mass.) Pub. Lib., 1958-59, 65-68, lib. dir., 1959-64; tchr. English, audio visual and media coord., librarian Shrewsbury (Mass.) Schs., 1964-91, guidance counselor, 1980-91. Author: What's Cooking at Changs, 1959, Chinese Fairy Tales, 1965, Tales from Old China, 1969, Gourmet on the Go, 1970, The Magic Pole, 1977, Spag: The American Dream, 1992, Artemas Ward, 2002; (play) The Birth of the Pill, 2004 Shrewsbury Town Rep., 1997—. Recipient Disting. Writing Chandler Greene award, 1966. Mem. ALA (life), NEA (life), AAAS (life), AARP (dir. 1995—), Nat. Acad. Scis. (life), Mass. Tchrs. Assn. (life), Shrewsbury Hist. Soc. (life), Worcester Art Mus. (life). Home: 15 Fiske St Shrewsbury MA 01545-2721 Personal E-mail: isabellechang@aol.com.

CHANG, JAE CHAN, hematologist, oncologist, educator; b. Aug. 29, 1941; arrived in U.S., 1965; s. Tae Whan and Kap Hee (Lee) Chang; m. Sue Young Chung, Dec. 4, 1965; children: Sung-Jin, Sung-Ju, Sung-Hoon. MD, Seoul (Korea) Nat. U., 1965. Diplomate Am. Bd. Internal Medicine, Hematology, Med. Oncology, Am. Bd. Pathology (Hematology). Intern Ellis Hosp., Schenectady, NY, 1965—66; resident Harrisburg (Pa.) Hosp., 1966—69, fellow in nuclear medicine, 1969—70; fellow in hematology and oncology, instr. U. Rochester, 1970—72; chief hematology sect. VA Hosp., Dayton, Ohio, 1972—75; hematopathologist, co-dir. hematology lab. Good Samaritan Hosp., Dayton, 1975—2002, dir. oncology unit, 1976—2001, chief hematology and oncology sect., 1976—2003; clin. prof. medicine U. Calif., Irvine, Calif., 2003—, dir. hematology and oncology fellowship program, 2003—05; mem. Chao Family Comprehensive Cancer Ctr., U. Calif., Irvine, 2003—. Asst. clin. prof. Ohio State U., Columbus, 1972—75; assoc. clin. prof. Wright State U., Dayton, 1975—80, clin. prof., 1980—99, prof., 1999—2003, co-dir. hematology and med. oncology fellowship program, 1993—98; cons. hematology VA Hosp.; adv. com. Greater Dayton Area chpt. Leukemia Soc. Am., 1977; trustee Montgomery County Soc. Cancer Control, Dayton, 1976—85, Dayton Area Cancer Assn., 1985—88, Cmty. Blood Ctr., 1982—86, Hipple Cancer Rsch. Crt., 1999—2002. Contbr. articles to profl. jours., columns in newspapers. Recipient Med. Econ. Essay Competition award, 1990, Wright State U. Acad. of Medicine award, 1985, Laureate award, APC-ASIM Ohio Chpt., 2001, Spl. Commendation, Ohio Senate, 2002. Fellow: ACP; mem.: Montgomery Med. Soc. (dir. 1990—93), Dayton Soc. Internal Medicine (pres. 1989), Am. Soc. Clin. Oncologists, Am. Soc. Hematology. Office: UCI Med Ctr Div Hematology/ Oncology Chao Family Comp Cancer Ctr 101 The City Dr Orange CA 92868 Office Phone: 714-456-5153, 714-456-6578. Business E-Mail: jaec@uci.edu.

CHANG, JANE P., chemical engineering educator; BS, Nat. Taiwan U., 1993; MS, MIT, 1995, PhD, 1998. Engring. intern Merck and Co., Inc., Lansdale, Pa., 1994, Dow Chem. Co., Midland, Mich., 1994; postdoctoral mem. tech. staff Bell Labs, Lucent Technologies, Murray Hill, NJ, 1998—99; asst. prof. chem. engring. UCLA, 1999—2003, assoc. prof. chem. engring., 2003—. Vice chair com. undergrad. admission and rels. with schools UCLA, 2004—05. Contbr. articles to profl. jours. Named Prof. of Yr., UCLA, 2003—04; recipient Chancellor's Career Devel. award, 2000—02, Career award, Nat. Sci. Found., 2002, TRW Excellence in Tchg. award, TRW, 2002, Young Investigator award, Office of Naval Rsch., 2003, Hugo Schuck Best Paper award, Am. Automatic Control Coun., 2004; Rumbel Practice School Fellowship, MIT, 1993. Mem.: Material Rsch. Soc., Am. Vacuum Soc. (Coburn and Winters award 1996), Am. Inst. Chem. Engrs., Am. Physics Soc., Electrochem. Soc., Am. Chem. Soc., Phi Tau Phi. Office: UCLA Chem Engring Dept BH 5532-D 420 Westwood Plz Los Angeles CA 90095

CHANG, JEANNETTE, publishing executive; BS, CCNY. Advt. sales rep. Cosmopolitan mag. Hearst Mags., N.Y.C., 1973-77, fashion advt. mgr., 1977-79; dir. fashion mktg. Bazaar mag. Hearst Mags., N.Y.C., 1979-84; assoc. pub. Harper's Bazaar mag. Hearst Mags., N.Y.C., 1984-94, v.p., 1992-94, v.p., pub., 1994—2000; sr. v.p., internat. pub. dir. Hearst Mags., Intl., 2000—. Spkr. in field. Active City Meals on Wheels, Meml. Sloan Kettering Found., Susan G. Komen Breast Cancer Found. Named to YWCA Acad. of Women Achievers, 1992. Mem. Fashion Group Internat. (bd. dirs., chair cosmetic exec. women's com.). Office: Hearst Mags Intl 959 8th Ave Rm 306 New York NY 10019-3737

CHANG, JEFFREY CHAI, dentist, educator, researcher; b. Canton, China, Dec. 19, 1946; came to U.S., 1967; s. Po Wing and Wai Ming (Chan) C.; m. Frances Fuhman Liang; children: Sheila Sai, Kenneth Kiu. BA with honors, Northeastern U., 1971; DDS, Georgetown U., 1976; MS in Dentistry, U. Tex. Dental Br., Houston, 1996. Commd. 2d lt. U.S. Army, 1976, advanced through grades to maj., gen. dental officer Dental Corps Ft. Bliss, Tex., 1976-79, officer-in-charge Dental Clinic Pusan, Korea, 1979-80, asst. chief clinician dental activity Ft. Momouth, N.J., 1980-83, chief dental emergency svc. dental activity Ft. Hood, Tex., 1983—85, resigned, 1985; clin. asst. prof. Dental Sch. U. Calif., San Francisco, 1985-88; clin. asst. prof. NYU Coll. Dentistry, N.Y.C., 1988-90; asst. prof. U. Tex. Dental Br., 1990-92, assoc. prof., 1992—. Cons. VA Med. Ctr., San Francisco, 1987-88, St. Barnabas Hosp., Bronx, N.Y., 1988-90, VA Med. Ctr., Houston, 1993—, ADA Coun. on Sci. Affairs, 1996—; scientist Houston Biomaterials Rsch. Ctr., 1996—. Contbr. 40 articles, 20 abstracts to profl. jours. Col. USAR, 1996—. Master Acad. Gen. Dentistry; fellow Am. Coll. Dentists, Acad. Dentistry Internat., Internat. Coll. Dentists; mem. ADA, Am. Assn. Dental Rsch., Internat. Assn. Dental Rsch., Chinese Am. Drs. Assn. (bd. dirs. 1994-2001), Tzu-Chi Internat. Med. Assn., Am. Legion, Omicron Kappa Upsilon, Delta Sigma Delta. Avocations: soccer, stamps, contemporary music, photography, hi-fi systems. Home: 4123 Custer Creek Dr Missouri City TX 77459-1545 Business E-Mail: jeffrey.c.chang@uth.tmc.edu. E-mail: drjeffchang@gmail.com.

CHANG, JIM C. I., air force executive; b. Kiangsu, China, July 14, 1939; came to U.S., 1964; s. Jin-Chih and Shien-Wei (Hsiung) C.; m. Sue-Ying Hsu, May 1, 1987; 1 child, Dean C. BS, Taiwan Cheng Kung U., 1963; MS, Mich. Tech. U., 1966; PhD, Cornell U., 1971. Sr. scientist McDonald Douglas Co., Huntington Beach, Calif., 1973-74; group leader Westinghouse Co., Madison, Pa., 1974-78; br. chief materials div. Naval Rsch. Lab., Washington, 1978-88; mgr. materials, structures and space vehicles NASA, Washington, 1988-89; chief scientist Naval Air Systems Command, Arlington, Va., 1989-90; dir. aerospace and engring. Air Force Office of Sci. Rsch., Washington, 1990—. Chmn. sci. engring. coms. on materials, structures, fluid mechanics, propulsion and U.S. sci. and tech. policy Dept. Def., Washington; referee AIAA, ASME, ASTM Jour.; invited keynote and guest speaker in field. Assoc. editor Jour. Theoretical and Applied Fracture Mechanics; contbr. numerous articles to profl. jours. Chairman Asian-Am. EEO com. Naval Air Systems Command, 1990. Named Profl. Engr. of 1972, Memphis Engrs. Coun., 1972; recipient Invention award Ingersoll-Rand Co., 1967, Performance award, 1978-91, Naval Air Systems Command Performance award, NRL Alan Berman Publs. award, U.S. Air Force Sr. Exec. award. Mem. AIAA, ASME. Avocations: group singing, golf. Home: 7205 Greentree Rd Bethesda MD 20817-1507 Office: US Army Rsch Lab 2800 Powder Mill Rd Hyattsville MD 20783-1197

CHANG, KATHY KUHL, computer programmer, analyst; b. Olney, Ill., Oct. 26, 1956; d. John Joseph and Jeanette Catherine (Ochs) Kuhl; m. Michael Anthony DiSalvo, Aug. 31, 1985 (div. Dec. 1988). BS in Bus., Ea. Ill. U., 1977. Systems programmer, systems analyst, programmer/analyst Western Ill. U., Macomb, 1980-85; cons. Mattoon, Ill., 1985-86; programmer analyst St. Lucie County Sch. Bd., Ft. Pierce, Fla., 1986-88; sr. rsch. programmer U. Ill., Urbana, 1989—. Mem.: IEEE, NAFE. Home: 1619 Sangamon Dr Champaign IL 61821-4936 Business E-Mail: disalvo@uillinois.edu.

CHANG, KUK WON, theology educator, researcher, pastor; b. Yesan, Chungnam, Korea, Apr. 15, 1938; arrived in U.S., 1999; parents Hyun Tae Chang and Dae Jae Lee; m. Yeon Sook Lee, May 15, 1982; children: Sang Eun, Sang Young. BA, Seoul Nat. U., 1961, MA, 1967; AM, Duke U., 1971; PhD, Dr. Habil, Muenster U., 1980. Dir. Aram Inst. for Ancient Studies, Anyang, Republic of Korea, 1981—2001; pres. Korean Soc. for Ancient Near Ea. Studies, Seoul, 1983—2001; prof. Hansei U., Kunpo, 1990—2001. Vis. scholar Cornell U., Ithaca, NY, 1985—87; rsch. scholar Duke U., Durham, NC, 1999—2002; sec. gen. United Cultural Conv., Raleigh, NC, 2001—; sr. fellow Inst. for Interdisciplinary Studies, Pasadena, Calif., 1997—; advisor to dir. gen. Internat. Biog. Ctr., Cambridge, England, 2001—; dir. Inst. for Rschs. on Metatheology, Chapel Hill, NC, 2003—. Contbr. articles to profl. jours. 1st lt. Korean Army, 1963—67. Office: 223 Forbush Mountain Dr Chapel Hill NC 27514-1909 Office Phone: 919-960-2565. E-mail: kwpchang@hotmail.com.

CHANG, LING WEI, sales executive; b. Taiwan, China, July 27, 1960; arrived in U.S., 1976; d. Thomas T.P. and Hou Hsin (Wang) C. BEE, Cooper Union, 1982; MS, Syracuse U., 1989. Engr. Data Systems div. IBM Corp., Poughkeepsie, N.Y., 1982-85, sys. engr. U.S. mktg. and svcs. N.Y.C., 1985-90; adv. mktg. rep. N.Y. gov. br. IBM U.S., N.Y.C., 1991-92; acct. mgr. N.Y. Pub. Svcs. IBM N.Am., N.Y.C., 1993-94; br. mgr. LEXIS-NEXIS, N.Y.C., 1994-95; nat. account mgr. Computer Assocs. Internat. Inc., N.Y.C., 1996-99; acct. prin. Compaq Profl. Svcs., N.Y.C., 1999-2000, dir. N.Y./N.J. area, 2000—01; client prin. Hewlett-Packard Svcs., 2002—. Vol. City Hosp. Ctr. at Elmhurst, NY, 1978; jr. judge Nat. Energy Found., 1979—82; bd. mgrs. Queens Ctr. Pla. Condominium, 1990—92, v.p., 2004—. Mem.: Exec. Women's Golf Assn. (asst. sectional dir. Metro N.E., immediate past pres. Big Apple chpt.), Eta Kappa Nu, Tau Beta Pi. Avocations: piano, golf, skiing. Home: 87-08 Justice Ave Apt 10D Elmhurst NY 11373-4580 Office: Hewlett-Packard Co Tower 49 22d Fl 12 E 49th St New York NY 10017 Office Phone: 212-856-2364. Business E-Mail: ling.chang@hp.com.

CHANG, LYDIA LIANG-HWA, social worker, educator; b. Wuhan, Hubei, China, Sept. 25, 1929; came to U.S., 1960; d. Shu-Tze Yu-Rou and Jian-Bung (Young) C.; m. Norman Stock, Aug. 20, 1998; children: Elizabeth Shu-Mei L. Ip, George Shu-Ang Lee. Diploma in Spanish and Lit., U. Sorbonne, Paris, 1959; MSW, NYU, 1963; cert. in advanced social work, Columbia U., N.Y.C., 1977, PhD in Social Work, 1980. Cert. social worker, cert. sch. bilingual social worker, N.Y. Supr. Cath. Charities, N.Y.C., 1969-71; dir. mental health cons. ctr. Univ. Settlement, N.Y.C., 1971-73; psychotherapist Luth. Med. Ctr., Bklyn., 1974-78; assoc. prof. U. Cin., 1978-80; asst. prof. Borough of Manhattan C.C., N.Y.C., 1983-86; bilingual sch. social worker N.Y.C. Bd. Edn., 1987-98, instr. for staff devel. program, 1991-98; psychotherapist Western Queens (N.Y.) Consultation Ctr., 1998—2004; pvt. practice psychotherapy, 2005—. Govt. ofcl.; cmem. mty. sch. bd. Dist. 30 N.Y.C. Bd. Edn., 1999-2004; cons. Cath. Social Svc. Bur., Cin., 1978-80; faculty advisor Borough of Manhattan C.C., 1983-86. Author: numerous poems; contbr. articles to profl. jours. Adv. bd. Pub. Sys. of Schs., Cin., 1978-80, Orange County Asian Am. orgn., Goshen, NY, 1980-82; founder of the Shu-Tze Chang and Jian-Bung Young Chang Ednl. scholarship fund, China, 1996. Mem. NASW, Nat. Assn. Sch. Social Workers, Columbia Alumni Assn., Nankai Alumni Assn. (v.p. 1991-94), Am. Voters Assn., Asian-Am. Dem. Assn. Episcopalian. Avocations: flute, tai-chi-chuang, swimming, reading. Home: 77-11 35th Ave Apt 2P Jackson Heights NY 11372 E-mail: stockchang@msn.com.

CHANG, MARIAN S., filmmaker, composer; b. Atlanta, Aug. 19, 1958; d. C. H. Joseph and C. S. (Chun) Chang. MusB, Harvard U., 1981; MFA in Filmmaking, Columbia U., 1994. Composer, dir., choreographer Exptl. Theatre, Dance, Boston, 1981-88; composer for modern dance co. Performing Arts Ensemble, Boston, 1986-88; co-dir., choreographer, performer Theatre S., Boston, 1987-88; prodr., dir., writer, sound designer, composer N.Y.C., 1991—. Founder, prodr. Shy Artists Prodns., Boston, N.Y.C., 1988—94. Recipient 1st prize, Kansas City Music Scholarship Competition, 1976, Nino Cerruti Film award, 1995; fellow, Mass. Artists' Fellowship Program in Choreography, 1987, Mass. Artists' Fellowship Program in Music Composition, 1988; grantee, N.Y. Coun. Humanities, 1998. Achievements include first artist in Mass. Artists' Fellowship Program to receive awards in both music and choreography. Home: 220 E 27th St Apt 7 New York NY 10016-9234

CHANG, MICHAEL, professional tennis player; b. Hoboken, N.J., Feb. 22, 1972; s. Joe and Betty Chang. Round of 16 U.S. Open, NYC, 1988, 89, 91, 94, Wimbledon, London, 1989, 90, quarterfinalist, 1994; champion French Open, Paris, 1989, quarterfinalist, 1990, 91, finalist, 1995; semifinalist Australian Open, Melbourne, 1995, finalist, 1996, U.S. Open, NYC, 1996. Other tournaments include: semifinalist WCT Scottsdale (Ariz.) Open, 1987; champion Transamerica Open, San Francisco, 1988; semifinalist Volvo Tennis Indoor, Memphis, 1989, semifinalist, 1991; finalist Volvo Tennis L.A., 1989, 90, 93; champion Silk Cuts Championships, Wembley, Eng., 1989; semifinalist Sovran Bank Classic, Washington, 1990; champion Player's Ltd. Internat. Can. Open, Toronto, 1990; semifinalist Suntory Japan Open, Tokyo, 1991, 92; semifinalist Open de la Ville de Paris, 1991, 94; finalist Compaq Grand Slam Cup, Munich, 1991, 92; champion Diet Pepsi Indoor Challenge, Birmingham, Eng., 1991; semifinalist Thriftway ATP Championships, Cin., 1992, champion, 1993, 94, finalist, 1995; semifinalist Waldbaum's Hamlet Cup, L.I., N.Y., 1992; semifinalist Seiko Super Tennis, Tokyo, 1992, finalist, 1994, champion, 1995; semifinalist European Cmty. Championships, Antwerp, Belgium, 1992; finalist Salem Open, Hong Kong, 1992, champion, 1994, 95, champion, Osaka, 1993, champion, Kuala Lumpur, 1993, champion, Beijing, 1993, 94, 95; champion Volvo Tennis/San Francisco, 1992; champion Newsweek Champions Cup, Indian Wells, Calif., 1992, semifinalist, 1993; champion Lipton Internat. Players Championships, Key Biscayne, Fla., 1992; semifinalist Kroger St. Jude Internat., Memphis, 1993, finalist, 1998; Ford Australian Open, Melbourne, 1997, U.S. Open, N.Y.C., 1997; champion Indonesian Open, Jakarta, 1993; finalist Japan Open, Tokyo, 1994, semifinalist, 1995; champion Indonesian Men's Open, Jakarta, 1994; champion Comcast U.S. Indoor, Phila., 1994, finalist, 1995; champion AT&T Challenge, Atlanta, 1994, 95, Infiniti Open, L.A., 1996, U.S. Men's Clay Ct. Championships, 1997, Salem Open, Hong Kong, 1997, Legg Mason Tennis Classic, Washington, 1996, 97, Kroger St. Jude, 1997, Newsweek Champions Cup, Indian Wells, Calif., 1996, 97; finalist Sybase Open, San Jose, Calif., 1995, semifinalist, 1996, 1998; finalist ATP World Tour Championships, Frankfurt, Germany, 1995; mem. U.S. Davis Cup Squad, 1989-91; semifinalist du Maurier Open, Montreal, Canada, 1997; semifinalist Great Amer. Insurance ATP Championship, Cincinnati, Oh., 1997; semifinalist Heineken Open, Rosmalen, The Netherlands, 1997. Achievements include being the youngest player to win USTA Boys' Nat. Championships, 1987; youngest male to advance to semifinals of Super Series tournament, 1987; youngest male to win match at U.S. Open, 1987; youngest male to win match at Wimbledon, 1988; youngest player to win Super Series tournament, 1988; youngest player to be named to U.S. Davis Cup Squad, 1989; youngest male Grand Slam Champion in Open Era, 1989; youngest ever French Open Champion, 1989; first Am. since Tony Trabert to win French Open, 1989. Address: Advantage Internat 1751 Pinnacle Dr Ste 1500 Mc Lean VA 22102-3833

CHANG, PARRIS HSU-CHENG, government agency administrator, lawmaker, political science educator, writer; b. Chikou, Chiayi, Taiwan, Dec. 30, 1936; came to U.S., 1961; s. Chao and Liu (Chen) C.; m. Shirley Hsiu-chu Lin, Aug. 3, 1963; children: Yvette, Elaine, Bohdan. BA, Nat. Taiwan U., 1959; MA, U. Wash., 1963; postgrad., Pa. State U., 1963-64; PhD, Columbia U., 1969, cert. Asian studies, 1966. Research polit. scientist U. Mich., Ann Arbor, 1969-70; asst. prof. polit. sci. Pa. State U., University Park, 1970-72; vis. fellow Australian Nat. U., Canberra, 1978; vis. scholar Inst. Sino-Soviet Studies, George Washington U., Washington, 1979; assoc. prof. polit. sci. Pa. State U., University Park, 1972-76, prof., 1976-97, dir. Ctr. for East Asian Studies, 1989-93; mem. Legis. Yuan Parliament, Taiwan, China, 1993—2004; prof. emeritus polit. sci., 1997—; mem. bd. Taiwan Found. Democracy, 2003—; dep. sec.-gen. NSC, 2004—. Cons. The Rand Corp., Santa Monica, Calif., 1975-82, BDM, Vienna, Va., 1975—. Voice of Am., Washington, 1982—. Dept. State, 1983-84, Titan Sys., Vienna, 1985—; assoc. China cooun. Asia Soc., N.Y.C., 1976—; vis. prof. Columbia U., summer 1985, Sch. Internat. Studies, JFK Spl. Warfare Ctr., Ft. Bragg, N.C., 1985-86, Tokyo U. Fgn. Studies, 1986-87; pres. steering com. unrepresented Nations and Peoples Orgn., The Hague, 1993—; pres. Taiwan Inst. for Polit. Econ. and Strategic Studies, 1994—. Author: Radicals and Radical Ideology in China's Cultural Revolution, 1973, Power and Policy in China, 1975, 3d edit. 1990, Elite Conflict in the Post-Mao China, 1981, 2d edit. 1983; co-author, co-editor: If China Crosses the Taiwan Strait, 1993, Chinese View of Future Warfare: Taiwan's Response, 1998; columnist Newsweek, 1985-87. Fellow Fulbright Council Internat. Exchange of Scholars, 1977; research grantee Social Sci. Research Council, 1972; travel grantee Internat. Research Exchange Council, 1982, 85 Fellow Japan Soc. for Promotion of Sci.; mem. Assn. Asian Studies (pres. Mid-Atlantic region 1976-77), Inter-Univ. Seminar on Armed Forces and Soc., Am. Polit. Sci. Assn. Office: 3-2 Chingtao E Rd Taipei Taiwan Office Phone: 886 2 2311 5801, 8862 23913766. Office Fax: 886 2 2391 3760, 886 2 2331-2609. Personal E-mail: tipess@ms14.hinet.net. Business E-Mail: pchang@nscnet.gov.tw.

CHANG, PATTI, foundation administrator; b. Hawaii; BA in Internat. Rels., JD, Stanford U. Pres., CEO Women's Found., San Francisco, 1993—2003, Women's Found. Calif., San Francisco, 2003—. Past commr. San Francisco Commn. on the Environment. Mem.: Women's Inst. for Leadership Devel. for Human Rights (mem. adv. bd.), San Francisco Commn. on the Status of Women (past pres.), Nat. Com. for Responsible Philanthropy (nat. adv. bd.), GenderPAC (nat. adv. bd.), Women's Leadership Alliance, Asian Pacific Am. Women's Leadership Inst. (bd. mem.), Women's Funding network (chair bd. dirs., bd. mem.). Office: Womens Found Calif Ste 302 340 Pine St San Francisco CA 94014

CHANG, R. P. H., materials science educator; b. Chung King, Peoples Republic China, Dec. 22, 1941; s. Joseph K. Cho; m. Bennie Chang; children: Vivian, Samuel. BS in Physics, MIT, 1965; PhD in Plasma Physics, Princeton U., 1970. Postdoctoral fellowship Princeton Plasma Physics Lab., 1970-71; mem. tech. staff AT&T Bell Labs., Murray Hill, N.J., 1971-86; prof. Material Sci. & Engring. Northwestern U., 1986—. Dir. Materials Rsch. Ctr., 1989—. 7 original inventions 1977—; author over 170 sci. publs.; co-author chpts. in Plasma Diagnostics and Material Sci. & Engring.; co-editor: Plasma Synthesis & Etching of Electronic Materials, 1985. Fellow Am. Vacuum Soc.; mem. Am. Physics Soc., Materials Rsch. Soc. (pres. 1989), Internat. Union of Materials Rsch. Socs. (pres. 1991-92). Office: Northwestern U Dept Materials Sci Engring 2225 N Campus Dr Evanston IL 60208-0876

CHANG, REN FANG, physicist, researcher; b. Nanking, China, Jan. 14, 1938; came to U.S., 1962; s. C.F. and T.S. (Wong) Ch.; m. Elizabeth Anne Brabson, Apr. 27, 1968. BS, Taiwan U., 1960; PhD, U. Md., 1968. Rsch. assoc. U. Md., College Park, 1968-70, asst. prof., 1970-77, sr. rsch. assoc., 1977-78; physicist Nat. Inst. Standards and Tech., Gaithersburg, Md., 1978—. Recipient Apollo Achievement award NASA, 1969. Office: Nat Inst Standards And Tech Gaithersburg MD 20899-8364 E-mail: renchang@nist.gov.

CHANG, SAMUEL HENRY, computer scientist, educator; s. Zonba Chang and Suying Wang; m. Xiaoyuan Yu, Jan. 1, 1979; 1 child, Yu. Diploma, Xiamen U., Fujiang, China, 1978; MSEE, Cath. U. Am., 1991; PhD, George Mason U., 1997. Asst. rschr. Chinese Acad. Scis., Beijing, 1978—82; vice dir. Traffic Control Rsch. Inst., Guangzhou, China, 1983—87; rsch. asst. Cath. U. Am., Washington, 1990—91; rsch./tchg. asst. George Mason U., Va., 1992—94; cons. NIH, Md., 1995—97, U.S. Naval Rsch. Lab, Washington, 1998—99; program tech. leader Crown Comm., Md., 1999—2000; sr. software engr. Cambridge Rsch. Assocs., Va., 2000—01; sr. computer scientist Spatial Integrated Systems, Rockville, Md., 2002—. Part-time prof. Southea. U., Washington, 1998—; guest prof. Xiamen U., 2005—. Contbr. articles to profl. jours. ib computer vision imaging. Mem.: IEEE. Office: Spatial Integrated Systems 7524 Standish Pl Ste 100 Rockville MD 20855 Office Phone: 301-610-7965 ext. 108. Personal E-mail: changsamue@hotmail.com. Business E-Mail: sam.chang@sisinc.org.

CHANG, SIDNEY H., history professor; b. Wuchang, China, Jan. 1, 1934; PhD, U. Wis., 1967. Postdoctoral fellow Harvard U., Boston, 1969—70; prof. history Calif. State U., Fresno, 1996—2002, prof. emeritus history, 2002—. Office: Calif State U Dept History Fresno CA 93710 Office Phone: 559-278-4079. Business E-Mail: schang@csufresno.edu.

CHANG, STEVE, internet security company executive; BS in Applied Math., Fu-Zen Cath. Univ., Taiwan; MS in Computer Sci., Lehigh U. Engr. Hewlett Packard; founder Asia Tek, Inc., Taiwan; founder, chmn. Trend Micro, Calif., 1988—, CEO, 1988—2004. Named in FORTUNE Mag., 1996, Innovator of the Yr., Asia Bus. Leader awards, 2004; named one of 25 Movers and Shakers, ZDNet Asia, 2001; recipient Innovator of Yr. award, EDN Asia Mag., 1996, Stars of Asia award, Bus. Week Mag., 1997, 1998. Office: Trend Micro Inc Odakyy So Tower 10th Fl 2-2-1 Yoyogi Shibuya-ku Tokyo 1S1-8583 Japan also: Trend Micro Inc 10101 N De Anza Blvd Cupertino CA 95014

CHANG, SUN-YUNG ALICE, mathematics professor; b. Ci-an, China, Mar. 24, 1948; came to U.S., 1970; d. Fann Chang and Li-Ching Chen; m. Paul Chien-Ping Yang, Mar. 24, 1973; children: Ray Yang, Lusann Yang. BS, Nat. Taiwan U., 1970; PhD, U. Calif., Berkeley, 1974. Asst. prof. math. U. Md., College Park, 1977-79; prof. UCLA, 1981—, Princeton U., 1998—. Speaker Internat. Congress of Math., 1986, 2002. Sloan Found. fellow, 1977, 78; Guggenheim fellow, 1999. Mem. Am. Math. Soc. (v.p. 1989, 90, Ruth Lyttle Satter prize 1995), Am. Women in Math. Office: Princeton Univ/Dept Math Fine Hall Washington Rd Princeton NJ 08544-1000 Business E-Mail: chang@math.princeton.edu.

CHANG, SYLVIA TAN, health facility administrator, educator; b. Bandung, Indonesia, Dec. 18, 1940; came to U.S., 1963. d. Philip Harry and Lydia Shui-Yu (Ou) Tan; m. Belden Shiu-Wah Chang, Aug. 30, 1964 (dec. Aug. 1997); children: Donald Steven, Janice May. Diploma in nursing, Rumah Sakit Advent Indonesia, 1960; BS, Philippine Union Coll., 1962; MS, Loma Linda U., 1967; PhD, Columbia Pacific U., 1987. Cert. RN, PHN, ACLS, BLS instr., cmty. first aid instr., IV, TPN, blood withdrawal. Head nurse Rumah Sakit Advent, Bandung, Indonesia, 1960—61; critical care, spl. duty and medicine nurse, team leader White Meml. Med. Ctr., L.A., 1963—64; nursing coord. Loma Linda U. Med. Ctr., 1964—68; team leader, critical care nurse, relief head nurse Pomona Valley Hosp. Med. Ctr., Calif., 1966—67; evening supr. Loma Linda U. Med. Ctr., 1967—69, night supr., 1969—79, adminstrv. supr., 1979—94; sr. faculty Columbia Pacific U., San Rafael, Calif., 1986—94; dir. health svc. La Sierra U., Riverside, Calif., 1988—. Site coord. Health Fair Expo La Sierra U., 1988-89; adv. coun. Family Planning Clinic, Riverside, 1988-94; blood and bone marrow drive coord. La Sierra U., 1988—. Counselor Pathfinder Club Campus Hill Ch., Loma Linda, 1979-85, crafts instr., 1979-85, music dir., 1979-85; asst. organist U. Ch., 1982-88. Named one of Women of Achievement YWCA, Greater Riverside C. of C., The Press Enterprise, 1991, 2000, Safety Coord. of Yr. La Sierra U., 1995. Mem. Am. Coll. Health Assn., Pacific Coast Coll. Health Assn., Adventist Student Pers. Assn., Sigma Theta Tau. Republican. Seventh-day Adventist. Avocations: music, travel, collecting coins, shells and jade carvings. Home: 1025 Crestbrook Dr Riverside CA 92506-5662 Office: 4500 Riverwalk Pkwy Riverside CA 92515-8247 Office Phone: 951-785-2200. Business E-Mail: schang@lasierra.edu.

CHANG, TED T., chemist; b. Tainan, Taiwan, Oct. 6, 1935; arrived in U.S., 1961; s. Shei-huei and Ou-chiu Chang; m. Kay H. Hsu, Jan. 10, 1960; children: Grace, Susan, Diana. BS, Nat. Taiwan U., Taipei, 1957; MS, U. Va., 1963, PhD, 1965; postgrad., Calif. Inst. Tech., 1965—66. Lectr. Nat. Cheng-Kung U., Tainan, 1959—61; rsch. chemist Am. Cyanamid, Stamford, Conn., 1966—71, prin. rsch. scientist, 1979—86; group leader Wyeth Labs., Radnor, Pa., 1971—79; assoc. rsch. fellow Am. Cyanamid/Cytec, Stamford, 1986—92; rsch. fellow Cytec Industries, Stamford, 1992—. Tech. expert to China UN, 1984. Contbr. more than 50 articles to profl. publs. Mem.: Chinese Am. Soc. Mass Spectrometry (pres. 1981—98, hon. permanent pres. 1998), Am. Soc. Mass Spectrometry, Am. Chem. Soc. (mem. U.S. delegation to Sino-Japan conf. 1987). Achievements include research in mass spectrometry, polymer analysis, ionic liquids analysis, electrochemistry, ionic liquids analysis, colorimetry and atomic absorption spectroscopy; introduced tandem analytical techniques of TGA-GC-MS and TLC-FAB-MS. Home: 157 Dogwood Ln Stamford CT 06903 Office: Cytec Industries 1937 W Main St Stamford CT 06904 Office Phone: 203-321-2341. E-mail: ted.chang@cytec.com.

CHANG, THOMAS MING SWI, research scientist, biotechnologist, educator; b. Swatow, Kwantang, China, Apr. 8, 1933; arrived in Can., 1952; m. Lancy Yuk Lan Jin, June 21, 1958; children: Harvey, Victor, Christine, Sandra. BSc, McGill U., Montreal, Que., Can., 1957, MD, CM, 1961, PhD, 1965. Intern Montreal Gen. Hosp., 1961-62; rsch. fellow depts. physiology and chemistry McGill U., 1962-65, asst. prof. physiology, 1966-69, assoc. prof., 1969-72, prof. physiology, 1972—, dir. artificial organs rsch. unit, 1975-79, prof. medicine, 1975—, dir. artificial cells and organs rsch. ctr., 1979—, assoc. dept. chem. engring., 1985—2002, assoc. dept. chemistry, 1986—2001, prof. biomed. engring., 1990—, dir. MSSS-FRSQ rsch. group (d'equipe) on blood substitute in transfusion medicine, 2002—; lab. and clin. rschr. med. scis., biotech., biomed. engring. Montreal, 1962—. Mem. staff Royal Victoria Hosp.; hon. mem. staff Montreal Chinese Hosp., 1970—; cons. Montreal Children's Hosp., 1979—, Med. Rsch. Coun. fellow, 1962-65, scholar, 1965-68, career investigator, 1968-99; hon. prof. Nankai U., 1983—. Inventor artificial cells and blood substitutes; author: Artificial Cells, 1972, Biomedical Application of Immobilized Enzymes and Proteins, Vols. I and II, 1977, Artificial Kidney, Artificial Liver and Artificial Cells, 1978, Hemoperfusion-Kidney and Liver Supports and Detoxification, 1980, Hemoperfusion, 1981, Past, Present and Future of Artificial Organs, 1983, Microencapsulation and Artificial Cells, 1984, Hemoperfusion and Artificial Organs, 1985, Blood Substitutes, 1988, Blood Substitutes and Oxygen Carriers, 1993, Blood Substitutes: Principles, Methods, Products & Clinical Trials, Vol. I, 1997, II, 1998; editor-in-chief Artificial Cells, Blood Substitutes and Biotechnology; sect. editor Internat. Jour. Artificial Organs, 1977—, Trans. Am. Soc. Artificial Organs, 1977-2001; assoc. editor Biotechnology Ann. Rev., 1995—; mem. editl. bd. Jour. Biomaterial Med. Devel. and Orgn., 1972-87, Jour. Membrane Sci., 1975-92, Jour. Bioengring., 1975-79, Jour. Enzyme and Microbial Tech., 1978-86. Recipient Decorated officer, Order of Can., 1992—, Can. 125th Confereration medal, 1993, Queen Elizabeth Jubilee medal, 2002. Fellow Royal Coll. Physicians Can., Royal Soc. Can.; mem. Internat. Soc. Artificial Organs (trustee 1982-87, 89-92, congress pres. 1991, pres. 1994-96, immediate past pres. 1996-98), Can. Soc. Artificial Organs (pres. 1980-82), Internat. Soc. Artificial Cells, Blood Substitutes and Biotech. (hon. pres. 1990—, hon. congress pres. 1994, 97, 2001), Internat. Symposium Blood Substitutes (hon. pres. 2003—), Internat. Soc. Microencapsulations (hon.). Office: McGill U Artificial Organs Rsch Ctr 3655 Drummond St Rm 1006 Montreal PQ Canada H3G 1Y6 Office Phone: 514-398-3512. Business E-Mail: artcell.med@mcgill.ca.

CHANG, THOMAS S., radiologist; SB, MIT, 1981; MD, Washington U., St. Louis, 1985. Diplomate Am. Bd. Radiology, 1990, cert. clin. densitometrist Internat. Soc. Clin. Densitometry, 2000. Med. intern Pa. Hosp., Phila., 1985—86; diagnostic radiology resident Thomas Jefferson U. Hosp., Phila., 1986—90; imaging fellow Western Pa. Hosp., Pitts., 1990—91; asst. prof. of radiology U. Pitts. Sch. Medicine, Pitts., 1991—2000; staff radiologist U. Pitts. Med. Ctr., Pitts., 1991—2000; radiologist Weinstein Imaging Assocs., Pitts., 2000—. Manuscript reviewer Am. Jour. Roentgenology, 1998—; clin. image reviewer Mammography Accreditation Program, Am. Coll. Radiology, 1998—. Mem.: Am. Roentgen Ray Soc., Radiol. Soc. N.Am., Soc. Breast Imaging, Soc. Radiologists in Ultrasound, Mammographers' Soc. Pitts. (pres. 1999—2001), Pitts. Roentgen Soc. (pres. 2001—03), Pa. Radiol. Soc. (bd. dirs. 2001—04, editor, alt. councilor 2003—), Am. Coll. Radiology. Office: Weinstein Imaging Assocs 5850 Centre Ave 1st Fl Pittsburgh PA 15206

CHANG, VICTOR TSU-SHIH, oncologist, researcher, educator; b. Queens, N.Y., Nov. 28, 1956; s. Meng Hsiu and Chia Hwa (Chu) C. SB/SM in Chem. Engring., MIT, 1979; MD in Physiology with honors, NYU, 1983. Diplomate Nat. Bd. Med. Examiners, Am. Bd. Internal Medicine, Am. Bd. Hospice Palliative Medicine. PDIA faculty scholar; intern Johns Hopkins Hosp., Balt., 1983—84; rsch. assoc. Howard Hughes Med. Inst., Balt., 1984—85; intern, resident Good Samaritan Hosp., Balt., 1985—87, chief resident, 1987—88; fellow hematology-oncology Cornell U. Med. Coll., N.Y.C., 1988—91, fellow clin. pharmacology, 1991—92; fellow cancer pain Meml. Sloan Kettering Cancer Ctr., N.Y.C., 1992—93; asst. profl. clin. medicine U. Medicine and Dentistry N.J., N.J. Med. Sch., Newark, 1993—2001, assoc. prof., 2001—; staff physician East Orange (N.J.) VA Med. Ctr., 1993—; PDIA faculty scholar, 2000. Mem. Am. Soc. Clin. Oncology, Am. Pain Soc., Am. Soc. Hematology, Eastern Coop. Oncology Group (pain and symptom subcom. 1994—), Chinese Am. Med. Soc. (bd. dirs. 1992-96), Radiation Therapy Oncology Group, Chinese Alumni MIT (bd. dirs. 1989-91, newsletter contbr. 1990-92). Avocations: music, history.

CHANG, WALTER TUCK, SR., draftsman, real estate agent, religious studies educator; b. Honolulu, Feb. 16, 1920; s. Awai Abner and Clara Pa'a auao (Fairman) C.; m. Rita AnaMarie Yee Chang, Aug. 16, 1950 (div. June 1959); children: Walter Tuck Jr., Nani; m. Mercedes Arroyo Chang, June 15, 1961 (div. June 1973); m. Evelyn Show Chiao Huang, Aug. 25, 1973. BA in Indsl. Arts with honors, Tchr.'s credential, San Jose State U., 1945; postgrad. in trade and industry edn. and adminstrn., U. Calif., Berkeley, 1949—55; MA in Edn. and Adminstrn., San Francisco State U., 1959; postgrad. in elem. sch. adminstrn. and supv. of practice tchrs., U. Hawaii, 1959-64; postgrad. in indsl. arts and vocat. edn., U. Md., 1967-68. Gen. secondary credential, Calif., spl. subject supervision vocat. class A, spl. subject supervision vocat. class C1, spl. secondary life diploma in indsl. arts, secondary sch. adminstrn., supervision secondary sch. tchrs., Calif., spl. secondary life diploma in trade industry; profl. secondary cert. in indsl. arts, Hawaii. Drafting apprenticeship engring. and estimation dept. Hawaiian Elec. Co., Honolulu, 1937-39; journeyman machinist, leadman, nat. war manpower job instr. Joshua Hendy Iron Works, Sunnyvale, Calif., 1942-45; vocat. instr. San Jose State U., 1942-45; automotive machinist Garden City Sales and Svc. Co., San Jose, Calif., 1945-46; journeyman machinist Oliver M. Johnson Machine Shop, San Jose, Calif., 1946; machinist Food Machine Corp., San Jose, Calif., 1946; machinist, tool maker Ames Aero. Lab., NASA, Moffet Field, Calif., 1946-51; adult evening vocat. instr. Leland Evening H.S., San Jose, 1951; vocat. inst., supr., driver edn., tng. John Swett Union H.S., Crockett, Calif., 1951-59; journeyman machinist Oliver United Filters Inc., Oakland, Calif., 1952-53; vocat. dir., night prin. John Swett Union H.S., Crockett, Calif., 1952-59; indsl. arts, English, World Hist. instr. McKinley H.S., Honolulu, 1959-62; indsl. arts metal works instr. Kailua H.S., Oahu, 1962; indsl. arts tchr. edn. instr., supr. indsl. arts student tchrs. U. Hawaii Coll. Edn. Manoa Campus, Honolulu, 1962-64; drafting instr. archtl. engring., electronics and metals tech., autocad, supr. driver edn. tng. Kamehameha Schs., Honolulu, 1964-90. Built over 1,000 engines for liberty, cargo steam ships, minesweepers during WWII, 1942-45. Author: Getting Started With the Calipro, 1965, The Kidjel Ratio Concept in Designing and Drafting. Hawaiian musician entertainer ARC, Vet. Hosps. San Francisco Bay Area, 1942-49; Sunday Sch. tchr. Hayward (Calif.) Missionary Bapt. Ch., 1958-59, Missionary Bapt. Chs. on Oahu, Hawaii, 1960—; v.p. PTA of New Keolu Elem. Sch., 1961-62, v.p. monthly meetings; designed and built 3 chs. and 2 parsonages, Calif. and Hawaii; support Missionary Bapt. Chs. and Missions, U.S., Can., South Am., The Philippines, Japan, China, India, Africa, Russia, Jerusalem, 1958—. Recipient Nat. Merit Honor Soc. award, 1938, Best Auto-CAD Architecture in Hawaii award Sausilito Software, 1985, Nat. Hon. Edn. Fraternity Pin award Phi Delta Kappa, 1962, award Solid Wood Poi Pounder, Best Designed 4 Million Dollar Indsl. Arts Complex in Hawaii award Kamehameha Schs.; named Most Outstanding Alumni in field of edn., Kamehameha Alumni Assn., Honolulu, 1984. Mem. Oahu Indsl. Arts Tchrs. Assn. (exec. bd. 1959, v.p. in charge of monthly workshops 1960, pres. 1961), Epsilon Pi Tau, Kappa Delta Pi. Achievements include aiding in perfection of first working guided missile; implemented Unified Phonics into Keola Pub. Elem. Sch. curriculum. Avocations: photography, raising gold fish, travel, reading books, sports. Home: 94-1015 Uke'e Pl Waipahu HI 96797-4272

CHANG, WEI TSUN, music educator; b. Taipei, Taiwan, June 22, 1962; s. Joel Yuyu and Suzana Chang; m. Seanad Dunigan, June 11, 1988. MusB in Violin Performance, Ind. U. Bloomington, 1988; MusM in Chamber Music, NC Sch. of the Arts, 1991; D of Music Arts in Violin Performance, Mich. State U., 2005. Artist-in-residence Alma Coll., Mich., 1995—2002; asst. prof. violin Tenn. Technol. U., Cookeville, 2002—. Concertmaster Bryan Symphony Orch., Cookeville, Tenn., 2002—, Midland Symphony Orch., Midland, Mich., 1998—2002, West Shore Symphony, Muskegon, 1997—99, Alma Symphony, Alma, 1995—2002; soloist L'Orchestre de Chambre Antonio Vivaldi, Paris, 1997—2002. Author: (textbook) Music Appreciation: A Shared Experience; musician: (performance) Performance at Lincoln Center with the French Chamber Orchestra, Mozart Bicentennial at Lincoln Center. Recipient Tchg. Innovation award, Bd. Regents Distance Edn. Tenn., 2005. Mem.: Am. Fedn. Musicians. Achievements include first to Premier an American Composition at Fondation Danoise in Paris, France; Development of a Hybrid Course in Music using Multiple Intelligence; research in Developing a Humanities Course using Multiple Intelligence; Soloist with L'Orchestre de Chambre Francais Alberic Magnard in Spain; first to First to teach Music Appreciation course using Tablet PC; Fluent in five languages: Chinese, Portuguese, Spanish, French, and English. Avocations: painting, chess, travel, language, philosophy. Office: Tenn Tech U Box 5045 Cookeville TN 38505 Office Phone: 931-372-3714. Home Fax: 931-528-7482; Office Fax: 931-372-6279. Personal E-mail: chang1wt@gmail.com. E-mail: wtchang@tntech.edu.

CHANG, WILLIAM SHEN CHIE, electrical engineering educator; b. Nantung, Jiangsu, China, Apr. 4, 1931; s. Tung Wu and Phoebe Y.S. (Chow) C.; m. Margaret Huachen Kwei, Nov. 26, 1955; children: Helen Nai-yee, Hugh Nai-hun, Hedy Nai-lin. BSE, U. Mich., 1952, MSE, 1953; PhD, Brown U., 1957. Lectr., rsch. assoc. in elec. engring. Stanford (Calif.) U., 1957-59; asst. prof. elec. engring. Ohio State U., 1959-62, assoc. prof., 1962-65; prof. dept. elec. engring. Washington U., St. Louis, 1965—79, chmn. dept., 1965-71, dir. Applied Electronic Scis. Lab., 1971-79, Samuel Sachs prof. elec. engring., 1976-79; prof. dept. elec. and computer engring. U. Calif., San Diego, 1979—, chmn. dept., 1993-96. Author: Principles of Quantum Electronics, 1969, RF Photonic Technology in Optical Fiber Links, 2002, Principles of Lasers and Optics, 2005; Contbr. articles to profl. jours. Fellow: IEEE, Am. Optical Soc.; mem.: Am. Phys. Soc. Achievements include research in quantum electronics and guided wave optics. Home: 12676 Caminito Radiante San Diego CA 92130 Office: U Calif San Diego MS-0407 Dept Elec/Computer Engring La Jolla CA 92093-0407 Office Phone: 858-534-2737. Business E-Mail: wchang@ucsd.edu.

CHANG, WILLIAM ZHI-MING, research scientist; b. Shanghai, June 6, 1955; s. Yinfang Chang and Shanlin Chen; m. Sandra Schlachter, Aug., 1987; 1 child, Caroline Dagmar. BS, U. So. Calif., 1984, MS, 1985, PhD, 1992. Rsch. assoc. U. So. Calif., L.A., 1992-93; rsch. scientist Max Planck Soc. x-ray optics group Friedrich-Schiller U., Jena, Germany, 1993-96; sr. scientist advanced rsch. and applications corp. Aracor, Sunnyvale, Calif., 1996—. Contbr. articles to profl. jours. and books. Disting. scholar Microbeam Analysis Soc., San Jose, Calif., 1991, Boston, 1992. Mem. Optical Soc. Am. Achievements include patents in field. Avocations: opera, calligraphy. Home: 8592 Peachtree Ave Newark CA 94560-3342 Office: Rapiscan Systems 352 E Java Dr Sunnyvale CA 94089-1328 Office Phone: 408-733-7780. E-mail: wchang@rapiscansystems.com.

CHANG, WON, economist; b. Seoul, Republic of Korea, Jan. 7, 1969; s. Charlie H.J. Chang and Moon Sook Uhm. BA, NYU, 1992; PhD, Columbia U., 1999. Cons. The World Bank, Washington, 1997—2000; internat. economist U.S. Dept. Treasury, Washington. Contbr. articles to profl. jours. Achievements include research in Regional Integration Impact and Analysis. Office: US Dept Treasury 1500 Pennsylvania Ave NW Washington DC 20220 Personal E-mail: wchang_264@msn.com. E-mail: won.chang@do.treas.gov.

CHANG, WUNG, investment advisor, educator; b. Kangke Pyongbuk, Republic of Korea, Apr. 24, 1942; came to U.S., 1973; s. Jae Sun and Key Bok (Yoo) C.; m. Han Jin Yang, Nov. 14, 1970; children: Min, Won. *Wife, Han Jin Chang, is an RN and nurse manager at Temple Community Hospital, Los Angeles. Son, Min Chang, is an attorney at law, with an LLM and JD from Duke Law School. Min's wife, June (Kim) Chang, is a pharmacist with a PharmD from University of the Pacific, School of Pharmacy. Son, Won Chang, is an attorney at law, with a JD from Cornell Law School. Won's wife, Jenny (Ko) Chang, is also an attorney at law, with a JD from University of California Berkeley Law School.* MPA, Yon-Sei U., 1971; PhD in Bus. Mgmt., Union U., 1983. Editor-in-chief Korea Photo Times, Seoul, 1970—73; sec.-gen. Wum Found., L.A., 1986—87; sr. analyst Pacific Rsch. Inst., L.A., 1988—92; advisor Korea Travel News, Seoul, 1988—93; contr. U.S. Top Capital Corp., L.A., 1991—2000; sr. adv. Hypnosis Career Coll., 2002—; chancellor Lordland Univ., 2005—. Vice chmn. Mid-Wilshire Tng. Ctr. divsn. Adult and Career Edn., L.A. Unified Sch. Dist. Adv. Coun., 1994—96; vol. lectr. The Korean Sr. Citizens Assn. of San Fernando Valley Coll., 1995—96; co-chmn. Internat. Rsch. Inst. Govt. and Pub. Adminstrn., L.A., 1995—99; commentator Radio Korea, USA, 1997—2000; sr. advisor So. Calif.-Korean Fedn. Coun. of No. Korea, 1998—2001; adv. mem. So. Calif.-Korean Assn. of Pyung-An-Book-Do Province, 1999—. Mem. Rep. Presdl. Adv. Commn., Washington, 1991; active Rep. Senatorial Com., Washington, 1991; nat. campaign advisor Rep. Senatorial Inner Circle, Washington, 1995—; chmn. bd. dirs. Kang I. Lee Found., Inc., 2002—. Capt. Korean Army, 1966-70. Recipient Presdl. Order of Merit, 1991, Rep. Presdl. Task Force Wall of Honor, 1992, Rep. Senatorial medal of freedom, 2002. Avocations: fishing, swimming, music, baseball. Home: 7625 Radford Ave North Hollywood CA 91605-2858 Office Phone: 213-413-1155. E-mail: ushanchang@yahoo.com.

CHANG, YI-CHENG, insurance agent; b. Guang Dong, China, June 24, 1943; came to U.S., 1974; s. Jin-Xin and Man-Hua (Ling) C.; m. Rufina Hoi Tong Chung, Sept. 6, 1975; 1 child, Wen Zhong. BS, Hong Kong Bapt. Coll., 1968; MS, Mich. State U., 1976. Owner Self-Strength Air Conditioning, Hong Kong, 1962-68; asst. lab. mgr. Micro Electronics, Hong Kong, 1968-70; purchasing mgr. Gen. Electronics, Hong Kong, 1970-73; material controller Coltronics Ltd., Hong Kong, 1973-74; purchasing agt. Reese Finer Foods, Elk Grove Village, Ill., 1976-79; import clk. Charlotte Charles, Inc., Chgo., 1979-80; purchasing agt. Commodity Communication Corp., Lombard, Ill., 1980-82; agt. N.Y. Life, Chgo., Ill., 1982—. Spkr. at minority workship and Chinese market conf. N.Y. Life, 1988-89; commentator Chinese radio and TV, Chgo.; speaker nat. Chinese Market conf., 1993-98, 2d Worldwide Chinese Life Ins. Congress, Malaysia, 1998, Internat. Ins. Conf., Guangzhou, China, 1996, Inst. Internat. Rsch., Washington, 1996, others. Author: Easy & Practical Ways of Learning Swimming, 1971; columnist Chinese newspapers; contbr. articles to profl. jours. Mem. Orgn. of Chinese-Ams., Chgo., 1983—; founder, bd. dirs. Chgo. Chinese TV, 1990—; bd. dir. Light-a-Lamp Edn. Found., 1988, 89. Mem. Nat. Assn. Life Underwriters (strategic planning com. 1995-96), Life Underwriters Assn., Chgo. Life Underwriters Assn. (bd. dirs. 1992-94), Chinese Alliance No. Ill., Chgo.-Chinese C. of C. (bd. dirs. 1998-99), Chinese Am. C. of C. and Professions, Million Dollar Roundtable (life). Avocations: cooking, gardening, writing. Office: 211 W 22nd Pl # 3 F Chicago IL 60616-1901

CHANG, YING CHIH, engineering educator, researcher; d. Chau-Ting and Li-Yen Chang. PhD, Stanford U., 1998. Sr. engr. Maxmedia Calif. (Maxtor) Corp., San Jose, Calif., 1998; postdoctor Stanford (Calif.) U./ Affymetric Corp., 1998—99; prof. U. Calif., Irvine, 1999—2003; scientist Palo Alto Rsch. Ctr., Calif.; rsch. fellow Genomics Rsch. Ctr., Academia Sinica, Taipei, Taiwan, 2004—. Contbr. articles to profl. jours. (Engr. award, 1998). Fellow, Max Planck Inst., 1997; grantee, U. Calif., 2000—02, 2002—03. Mem.: AIChE, Materials Rsch. Soc., No. Am. Taiwanese Engineers Assn. (corr.; biotech. group leader 2002—03), Stanford Alumni Assn. (life). Achievements include patents for biochip and materials design.

CHANG, YOON IL, nuclear engineer; b. Seoul, Korea, Apr. 12, 1942; came to U.S., 1965; s. Paul Kun and In Sil (Hahn) C.; m. Ok Ja Kim, Dec. 19, 1966; children: Alice, Dennis, Eugene. BS in Nuclear Engring., Seoul Nat. U., 1964; ME, Tex. A & M U., 1967; PhD, U. Mich., 1971; MBA, U. Chgo., 1983. Mgr. spl. projects Nuclear Assurance Corp., Atlanta, 1971-74; asst. nuclear engr. Argonne (Ill.) Nat. Lab., 1974-76, group leader, 1976-77, sect. head, 1977-78, assoc. divsn. dir., 1978-84, gen. mgr. IFR program, 1984-94, dep. assoc. lab. dir. for engring. rsch., 1994—98, assoc. lab. dir. for engring. rsch., 1998—2002, interim lab. dir., 1999—2001, assoc. lab. dir. at large, 2002—. Recipient E. O. Lawrence award U.S. Dept. Energy, 1994. Fellow Am. Nuclear Soc. (Walker Cisler award 1997—). Home: 2020 Palmer Dr Naperville IL 60564-5664 Office: Argonne Nat Lab 9700 Cass Ave Argonne IL 60439-4803 Office Phone: 630-252-4856. E-mail: ychang@anl.gov.

CHANG, YUAN, neuropathologist, researcher, educator; m. Patrick S. Moore, 1989. MD, U. Utah. Neuropathologist, rschr. Columbia U., NY, 1992, prof. pathology, 1992; prof. dept. pathology U. Pitts. Sch. Medicine, 2002—. Mem. editl. bd.: Am. Jour. Pathology, Jour. Human Virology; contbr. articles and reviews in medical literature with Patrick S. Moore. Recipient Meyenburg Found. award Cancer Rsch., Robert Koch Prize, NYC Mayor's award for Excellence in Sci. and Tech., Paul A. Marks Prize, Meml. Sloan-Kettering Cancer Ctr., 2003, Charles S. Mott prize, GM Cancer Rsch. Found., 2003. Achievements include (with Patrick S. Moore, MD) discovery and characterization of the causative agent of Kaposi's Sarcoma-associated Herpes virus (KSHV) or human herpes virus 8 (HHV8); linked to other disorders that involve a compromised immune system. Office: U Pa Physicans Faculty and UPMC Pathology HCCLB 1 8 Pitts Pittsburgh PA 15122

CHANG-MOTA, ROBERTO, electrical engineer; b. Caracas, Venezuela, Dec. 28, 1935; came to US, 1948; s. Roberto W. and Mary C. (Mota) Chang; m. Alicia Santamaria-Gonzales, May 4, 1968; children: Roberto Ignacio, Roxana Ivette, Ricardo Ignacio. D of Elec. Engring., U. Ctrl. Venezuela, 1960; MS, U. Ill., 1962; AR, Harvard U., 1970; PhD, UCLA, 1983. Dir. sch. engring., prof. Ctrl. U., Caracas, 1964-69; prof., dean Simon Bolivar U., Caracas, 1971-77; pres. Colegio de Ingenieros de Venezuela, Caracas, 1974-79; dir. Venezuelan Power Co., Caracas, 1974-79; pres. L.Am. Orgn. Engring., Quito, Ecuador, 1977-79, Corporoil, Caracas, 1981-85, Audio Interface Corp., Caracas, 1983-96; v.p. ESCA Corp., Caracas, 1991-95; pres. 3R Corp., Caracas, 1995—; CEO, pres. Cositel Corp., 2002—, SSS Corp., 2002—; pres. 35 Corp., 2002, Inti Corp., Caracas. Spl. cons. Venezuelan Navy and Army, 1971-75, Venezuelan Congress, 1989-96; mem. tech. com. Venezuelan Supreme Election Coun., 1971-81, exec. dir., 1981-82, gen. dir., 1982-97; gen. dir. Consejo Nacional Electoral, 1991-98; cons. Ministry of Interior, 1990; v.p. Electronic Cir. Corp., 1991-2000; trustee Simon Bolivar U., 1985-98; bd. dirs. Sistemas y Procesos Automatizados, SEPAI Corp. Gen. dir. Nat. Election Coun., 1985-99; pres. Sistemas Electorales y Procesos Automatizados, 2001. Mem. IEEE, Am. Soc. Engring. Edn., Venezuelan Soc. Elec. and Mech. Engring. (pres. 1972-73), Instn. Elec. Engrs., Puerto Azul Club, Playa Pintada Club, Caracas Racquet Club. Roman Catholic. Home: 7861 SW 180th St Miami FL 33157-6216 also: Prados del Este Calle Colon Quinta Cumana Caracas 1080 Venezuela Personal E-mail: yasifu@gmail.com.

CHANIN, BERNARD, lawyer; b. Phila., Oct. 12, 1942; s. Benjamin and Irene (Holutin) C. BA, U. Pa., 1962, LLB cum laude, 1965. Bar: Pa. 1965, U.S. Supreme Ct. 1976. Law clk. to Samuel J. Roberts, Assoc. Justice Supreme Ct. Pa., Phila., 1965-66; ptnr. Wolf, Block, Schorr & Solis-Cohen, Phila., 1966—. Judge pro tem Phila. Ct. Common Pleas; mem. comml., constrn. and complex case panels Am. Arbitration Assn. Mem. ABA, Pa. Bar Assn., Phila. Bar Assn., Order of the Coif. Office: Wolf Block Schorr & Solis-Cohen 1650 Arch St Fl 22 Philadelphia PA 19103-2097 Office Phone: 215-977-2396. Business E-Mail: bchanin@wolfblock.com.

CHANIN, MICHAEL HENRY, lawyer; b. Atlanta, Nov. 11, 1943; s. Henry and Herma Irene (Blumenthal) C.; m. Margaret L. Jennings, June 15, 1968; children: Herma Louise, Richard Henry, Patrick Jennings. AB, U. N.C., 1965; JD, Emory U., 1968. Bar: Ga. 1968, D.C. 1981. Dir. So. Ctr. for Studies in Pub. Policy, Atlanta, 1968-69; asst. and acting legal officer 1st Coast Guard Dist., Boston, 1969-72; atty. Powell, Goldstein Frazer & Murphy, Atlanta, 1972-77; spl. asst. to sec. U.S. Dept. Commerce, Washington, 1977-78; dep. asst. to pres. The White House, Washington, 1978-81; ptnr. Powell, Gold stein LLP, Washington, 1981—. Served to lt. USCGR, 1969-72. Mem. ABA, D.C. Bar Assn., State Bar Ga. Democrat. Office: Powell Goldstein LLP 901 New York Ave NW Fl 3 Washington DC 20001-4432 Business E-Mail: mchanin@pogolaw.com.

CHANIN, ROBERT HOWARD, lawyer; b. Bklyn., Dec. 24, 1934; s. Frank and Irene (Goldfein) C.; m. Rhoda Paley, June 9, 1957; children: Jeffrey, Stacy, Lisa. BA, Bklyn. Coll., 1956; LLB, Yale U., 1959; MA, Columbia U., 1961. Bar: N.Y. 1959, D.C. 1969. Instr. in psychology New Haven Coll., 1956-59; staff atty. Law Sch. Columbia U., N.Y.C., 1959-62; assoc. Kaye, Scholer, Fierman, Hays & Handler, N.Y.C., 1962-68; gen. counsel NEA, Washington, 1968—, gen. counsel, dep. exec. dir., 1973-80. Profl. lectr. George Washington U. Law Sch., Washington, 1973-80; mem. Bredhoff & Kaiser, P.L.L.C., Washington, 1980—; trustee NEA Ins. Trust, Washington, 1975—. Author: The Law and Practice of Teacher Negotiations, 1970, The Law and Practice of Teacher Negotiations, 1974; contbr. articles to profl. jours. Mem. Nat. Orgn. Lawyers for Edn. Assn. (pres. 1969—). Office: Bredhoff & Kaiser PLLC 805 15th St NW Ste 1000 Washington DC 20005-2286

CHANNING, STOCKARD (SUSAN ANTONIA WILLIAMS STOCKARD), actress; b. N.Y.C., Feb. 13, 1944; d. Lester Napier and Mary Alice Stockard; m. Walter Channing, Jr., 1963 (div. 1967); m. Paul Schmidt, 1970 (div. 1976); m. David Debin, 1976 (div. 1980); m. David Rawle, 1982 (div. 1988). Attended, Radcliffe Coll.; BA in History and Lit., Harvard U. Actress movies include Up the Sandbox, 1972, The Fortune, 1975, The Big Bus, 1976, Sweet Revenge, 1977, The Cheap Detective, 1978, Grease, 1978, A Different Approach, 1978, The Fish That Saved Pittsburgh, 1979, Safari 3000, 1982, Without a Trace, 1983, The Men's Club, 1986, Heartburn, 1986, A Time of Destiny, 1988, Staying Together, 1989, Meet the Applegates, 1991, Married To It, 1991, Lunes de Fiel, 1992, Six Degrees of Separation (Acad. award nomination Best Actress), 1993, To Wong Foo, Thanks for Everything! Julie Newmar, 1995, Smoke, 1995, The First Wives Club, 1996, Up Close and Personal, 1996, Moll Flanders, 1996, Edie and Pen, 1997, Twilight, 1998, Lulu on the Bridge (voice), 1998, Practical Magic, 1998, The Venice Project, 1999, Other Voices, 2000, Isn't She Great, 2000, Where the Heart Is, 2000, The Business of Strangers, 2001, Life or Something Like It, 2002, Behind the Red Door, 2002, Bright Young Things, 2003, Le Divorce, 2003, Anything Else, 2003, Must Love Dogs, 2005; TV movies include Girl Most Likely to..., 1973, Lucan, 1977, Silent Victory: The Kitty O'Neill Story, 1979, Table Settings, 1984, Not My Kid, 1985, The Room Upstairs, 1987, Echoes in the Darkness, 1987, Tidy Endings, 1988, Perfect Witness, 1989, Lincoln, 1992, David's Mother, 1994, Mr. Willowby's Christmas Tree, 1995, An Unexpected Family, 1996, Lily Dale, 1996, The Prosecutors, 1996, An Unexpected Family, 1996, An Unexpected Life, 1998, The Baby Dance, 1998, The Truth About Jane, 2000, Confessions of an Ugly Stepsister, 2002, The Matthew Shepard Story, 2002 (Emmy Outstanding Supporting Actress in a Miniseries or a Movie, SAG award), Hitler: The Rise of Evil, 2003, The Piano Man's Daughter, 2003, Jack, 2004 (Outstadning Performer in a Children's Spl., Daytime Emmy award, Acad. TV Arts & Scis., 2005); TV series include Sesame Street, 1969, The Stockard Channing Show, 1980, Road to Avonlea, King of the Hill (voice), Batman Beyond (voice), 1999, The West Wing, 2001- (Emmy Outstanding Supporting Actress in a Drama Series 2002); actress (plays) A Day in the Death of Joe Egg, 1985 (Tony Actress in a Play, 1985), House of Blue Leaves, Four Baboons Adoring the Sun, The Little Foxes, Hapgood, Women In Mind, The Rink, The Golden Age, The Lion in Winter, They're Playing Our Song; TV mini series A Girl Thing, 2001. Office: ICM c/o Andrea Eastman 40 W 57th St Fl 16 New York NY 10019-4098*

CHANOCK, ROBERT MERRITT, pediatrician; b. Chgo., July 8, 1924; married; two children. BS, U. Chgo., 1945, MD, 1947, DSc (hon.), 1977. NRC fellow Children's Hosp., Cin., 1950—52; asst. prof. rsch. pediat. Coll. Medicine, U. Cin., 1954—56; asst. prof. epidemiology Sch. Hygiene and Pub. Health, Johns Hopkins U., 1956—57; surgeon USPHS, 1957—59, head respiratory viruses sect., 1959—61; chief lab. infectious diseases Nat. Inst. Allergy and Infectious Diseases, NIH, Bethesda, Md., 1968—. Nat. Found. Infantile Paralysis fellow, 1951—52; sr. rsch. fellow USPHS, 1956—57; virologist Children's Hosp. D.C., 1957—; mem. Internat. Nomenclature Com. Myxoviruses, 7th and 8th Internat. Microbiol. Congress, Armed Forces Epidemiology Bd., Com. Acute Respiratory Disease, 1960—62; assoc. mem. Com. Influenza, 1963—74; dir. Internat. Ref. Ctr. Lab. Mycroplasms, WHO, 1962; mem. Internat. Com. Nomenclature Bacteria, 1966; clin. prof. Georgetown U., 1970—71; mem. nominating com. NAS, 1979—80; mem. sci. rev. com. Scripps Clin. and Rsch. Found., 1986—89. Recipient E. Mead Johnson award pediatric rsch., 1964, Squibb Gorgas medal, Assn. Mil. Surgeons, 1972, Robert Koch medal, Fed. Republic of Germany, 1981, Virol prize, ICT Internat., 1990, Bristol-Myers Squibb award, Albert B. Sabin Gold medal. Mem. NAS, Soc. Pediat. Rsch., Am. Soc. Microbiology, Am. Epidemiol. Soc., Am. Epidemiology, Am. Pediat. Soc., Am. Soc. Clin. Investigation, Soc. Exptl. Biology and Medicine, Assn. Am. Physicians, Royal Danish Acad. Scis. (fgn. mem.). Office: NIH Inst Allergy Infectious Diseases Lab Infectious Diseases 7 Center Dr Rm 100 Bethesda MD 20817*

CHAO, ALLEN Y., pharmaceutical executive; m. Lee Hwa-Chao. PhD in Indsl., Physical Pharmacy, Purdue Univ., 1973, DSc (hon.), 2000. Founder Watson Pharm., Inc., Corona, Calif., 1984, CEO, 1985—, chmn., 1996—. Office: Watson Pharm, Inc 311 Bonnie Cir Corona CA 92880 also: Watson Pharm, Inc 360 Mt Kemble Ave PO Box 1953 Morristown NJ 07962*

CHAO, BEI TSE, mechanical engineering educator; b. Soochow, China, Dec. 18, 1918; arrived in U.S., 1948, naturalized, 1962; s. Tse Yu and Yin T. (Yao) C.; m. May Kiang, Feb. 7, 1948; children: Clara, Fred Roberto. BS in Elec. Engring. with highest honor, Nat. Chiao-Tung U., China, 1939; PhD (Boxer Indemnity scholar), Victoria U., Manchester, Eng., 1947. Asst. engr. tool and gage div. Central Machine Works, Kunming, China, 1939-41, asso. engr., 1941-43, mgr. tool and gage div., 1943-45; research asst. U. Ill., Urbana, 1948-50, asst. prof. dept. mech. engring., 1951-53, assoc. prof., 1953-55, prof., 1955-87, prof. emeritus, 1987—, head thermal sci. div., 1971-75, head dept. mech. and indsl. engring., 1975-87; assoc. mem. U. Ill. (Center for Advanced Study), 1963-64. Cons. to industry and govtl. agys., 1950-94; vis. Russell S. Springer prof. mech. engring. U. Calif., Berkeley, 1973; mem. reviewing staff Zentralblatt für Mathematik, Berlin, 1970-82; mem. U.S. Engring. Edn. Del. to Visit People's Republic of China, 1978;

mem. adv. screening com. in engring. Fulbright-Hays Awards Program, 1979-81, chmn., 1980, 81; mem. com. U.S. Army basic sci. rsch. NRC, 1980-83; Prince disting. lectr. Ariz. State U., 1984; bd. dirs. Aircraft Gear Corp., 1989-94. Author: Advanced Heat Transfer, 1969; tech. editor Jour. Heat Transfer, 1975-81; mem. adv. editl. bd. Numerical Heat Transfer, 1977-95; mem. hon. edit. bd. Internat. Jour. Heat and Mass Transfer, 1987-97, Internat. Comm. in Heat and Mass Transfer, 1987-97; contbr. numerous articles on mech. engring. to profl. jours. Recipient Outstanding Tchr. award, Ill. Mech. Engring. Alumni, 1978, Max Jakob Meml. award, ASME/Am. Inst. Chem. Engrs., 1983, Tau Beta Pi Daniel C. Drucker eminent faculty award, 1985; Univ. scholar, 1985. Fellow AAAS, ASME (hon.; Blackall award 1957, Heat Transfer award 1971, William T. Ennor Mfg. Tech. award 1992), Am. Soc. Engring. Edn. (Outstanding Tchr. award 1975, Western Electric Fund award 1973, Ralph Coats Roe award 1975, Benjamin Garver Lamme award 1984, Centennial Medallion 1993); mem. Nat. Acad. Engring., Academia Sinica, Chiao-Tung U. Alumni Assn. (pres. Midwest sect. 1975-76), Tau Beta Pi, Pi Tau Sigma (hon.). Home: 101 W Windsor Rd Apt 6103 Urbana IL 61802-6663 Office: Univ Ill 264 Mech Engring Bldg 1206 W Green St Urbana IL 61801-2906 Office Phone: 217-333-8880. Personal E-mail: btmchao@hotmail.com.

CHAO, CEDRIC C., lawyer; b. Cambridge, Mass., Apr. 9, 1950; BA, Stanford U., 1972; JD, Harvard U., 1977. Bar: Calif. 1977, U.S. Dist. Ct. (no. dist.) Calif. 1977, U.S. Ct. Appeals (9th cir.) 1979, U.S. Supreme Ct. 1988. Law clk.to Hon. William H. Orrick U.S. Dist. Ct. (no. dist.) Calif., San Francisco, 1977-78; asst. U.S. atty. U.S. Atty.'s Office, San Francisco, 1978-81; assoc. Morrison & Foerster, San Francisco, 1981-83, ptnr., 1983—. Lawyer del. 9th cir. judicial conf., 1990-92; chair magistrate judge selection com. No. Dist. Calif., 1996. Author: Creating Your Discovery Plan, 1999. Named One of Calif.'s Top 25 Lawyers Under Age 45, Calif. Law Bus., 1994. Fellow Am. Bar Found.; mem. ABA (standing com. fed. judiciary, 1991-94), State Bar Calif. (com. profl. responsibility and conduct 1980-84, exec. com. litigation sect. 1986-91, vice chair 1989-90, chair 1990-91), San Francisco Bar Assn. (bd. dirs. 1988-90), Am. Law Inst., Asian Am. Bar Assn. Greater Bay Area (bd. dirs. 1977-82, pres. 1982), 9th Judicial Cir. Hist. Soc. (trustee 2000—), San Francisco C. of C. (bd. dirs. 1996-99), Singapore Am. Bus. Assn. (bd. dirs. 1999—, pres. 2001), World Affairs Coun. No. Calif. (trustee 1994-99), Commonwealth Club Calif. (quar. chair 1989). Office: Morrison & Foerster 425 Market St San Francisco CA 94105-2482 E-mail: cchao@mofo.com.

CHAO, CHIA-CHUN, aerospace engineer; b. Kwei-yang, China, Nov. 17, 1939; came to U.S., 1963; s. Hsueh Yen and Wen Ru (Lu) C.; m. Jean Mei-Jen Kung, Aug. 3, 1968; children: Frank S., Sophia S. BS, Cheng-Kung U., Tainan, Taiwan, 1962; MS, Calif. Inst. Tech., 1964; Aero. Engring. Deg., Caltech U., 1968; PhD, UCLA, 1976. Project engr. ARA, Inc., West Covina, Calif., 1966-68; sr. engr. Jet Propulsion Lab., Pasadena, Calif., 1968-78; mem. tech. staff Aerospace Corp., El Segundo, Calif., 1978-80, engring. specialist, 1980-85, sect. mgr., 1985-95, sr. engring. specialist, 1995—. Instr. edn. program Aerospace Corp., 1980—; guest lectr. UCLA Extension, Westwood, 1985—. Contbr. articles to Jour. Astron. Scis. Pres. South Bay Chinese Sch., Rancho Palos Verdes, Calif., 1986-87, South Bay Chinese Choral Club, Rancho Palos Verdes, 1987-91. Recipient Def. Satellite Communications System Mission award Air Force Space Div., 1990, Best Paper of Conf. award AZAA, 1993. Fellow AIAA (assoc.); mem. Chinese Engrs. and Scientists So. Calif. Achievements include discovery of a method to avoid earth eclipses for high altitude earth satellite constellation; design of Chao tropospheric calibration model for JPL deep space tracking data calibration. Office: Aerospace Corp 2350 E El Segundo Blvd El Segundo CA 90245-4691

CHAO, ELAINE LAN (HSIAO LAN CHAO), secretary of labor; b. Taipei, Taiwan, Mar. 26, 1953; d. James S.C. and Ruth M.L. (Chu) C.; m. Mitch McConnell, 1993. AB, Mt. Holyoke Coll., 1975; MBA, Harvard U., 1979; LLD (hon.), Villanova U., 1989, St. John's U., 1991, Sacred Heart U., 1991, U. Notre Dame, 1998, St. Marys Coll., 2002, Fu-Jen Cath. U., 2003, Cath. U. Am., 2004; DHL (hon.), Niagara U., 1992, Bellarmine Coll., 1995, U. Toledo, 1995, Goucher Coll., 1996, U. Louisville, 1996, U. S.C., 2001, No. Ala. U., 2003, Centre Coll., 2003, Wingate U., 2004; DHum (hon.), Drexel U., 1992, Thomas More Coll., 1994, Ky. Wesleyan Coll., 1998; D Arts and Letters (hon.), Miami-Dade C.C., 2001; DPA (hon.), Campbellsville U., 2002, No. Ky. U., 2004; D Pub. Svcs. (hon.), DePauw U., 2002; D in Orgnl. Leadership (hon.), Regent U., 2003. Assoc. Gulf Oil Corp., Pitts., summer 1978; sr. lending officer Citicorp, NA, N.Y.C., 1979-83; v.p. capital markets group BankAmerica, San Francisco, 1984-86; dep. maritime adminstr. U.S. Dept. Transp., Washington, 1986-88; chmn. Fed. Maritime Commn., Washington, 1988; dep. sec. U.S. Dept. Transp., Washington, 1989-91; pres. United Way Am., Alexandria, Va., 1992-96; sr. editor, disting. fellow The Heritage Found., Washington; sec. U.S. Dept. Labor, Washington, 2001—. White House fellow, 1983-84; adj. asst. prof. Grad. Sch. Bus. Adminstrn., St. John's U., 1984; dir. Peace Corps., 1991-92. Recipient Young Achiever award Nat. Coun. Women U.S., Inc., 1986; Eisenhower Fellow Assn. fellow, 1984; named. one of 10 Outstanding Women of Am., 1988. Mem. Coun. on Fgn. Rels., Inc., Am. Coun. Young Polit. Leaders (bd. dirs. 1989), Harvard Bus. Sch. (vis. com. 1989, Outstanding Alumni award 1993), Harvard Club. Republican. Office: US Dept Labor Office of Sec 200 Constitution Ave NW Washington DC 20210*

CHAO, HOWARD H., lawyer; b. Taipei, Republic of China, June 13, 1954; came to U.S., 1958; s. Kuang-Chu and Jun-Jing (Su) C. BS in Math. with highest distinction, Purdue U., 1976; JD, U. Calif. Boalt Hall Sch. Law, Berkeley, 1980. Bar: Calif. 1980, U.S. Dist. Ct. (No. Dist. Calif.) 1980, Hong Kong, 1997. Assoc. O'Melveny & Myers LLP, Los Angeles, 1980—, ptnr. Menlo Park, Calif., partner-in-charge, Shanghai, chair, internat. practice group. Exec. sec. Los Angeles Com. Fgn. Relations, 1984-85; vis. prof. Fudan U., Shanghai, Republic of China, 1985, Beijing (Republic of China) U. of Internat. Bus., 1985. Assoc. editor Calif. Law Review, 1977—80. Rotary Internat. fellow, Geneva, 1979-80. Mem. Law Soc. Hong Kong, Phi Beta Kappa, Order of Coif. Office: O'Melveny & Myers LLP 2765 Sand Hill Rd Menlo Park CA 94025-7019 Address: O'Melveny & Myers LLP Kerry Centre 20F 1515 Nanjing Rd West Shanghai 200040 China also: O'Melveny & Myers LLP Suite 1905 Tower Two Lippo Ctr 89 Queensway Central Hong Kong Office Phone: 650-473-2628. Fax: 8621 5298 5500, 852 2522 1760; Office Fax: 650-473-2601. Business E-Mail: hchao@omm.com.

CHAO, JAMES MIN-TZU, architect; b. Dairen, China, Feb. 27, 1940; came to U.S., 1949; naturalized, 1962; m. Kirsti Helena Lehtonen, May 15, 1968. BArch, U. Calif., Berkeley, 1965. Registered arch., Calif., Ariz., Colo., Ill., N.Mex.; cert. instr. real estate, Calif. Intermediate draftsman Spencer, Lee & Busse, Archs., San Francisco, 1966-67; asst. to pres. Import Plus Inc., Santa Clara, Calif., 1967-69; job capt. Hammaberg and Herman, Archs., Oakland, Calif., 1969-71; project mgr. B A Premises Corp., San Francisco, 1971-79; constrn. mgr. The Straw Hat Restaurant Corp., San Francisco, 1979-81, mem. sr. mgmt., dir. real estate and constrn., 1981-87; mem. mktg. com. Straw Hat Coop. Corp., San Francisco, 1988-91; pvt. practice Berkeley, 1987—; dir. real estate Papillon Devel. Inc., 1998—. Pres. Food Svc. Cons. Inc., 1987-89; pres., CEO Stratsac, Inc., 1987-92; prin. arch. Alpha Cons. Group Inc., 1991-98; v.p. Intersyn Industries Calif., 1993-99; nat. tng. dir. Excel Telecom., Inc., 1995-99; CEO Nuts and Bolts Books, 1997—; lectr. comml. real estate site analysis and selection for profl. real estate seminars; coord. minority vending program, solar application program Bank of Am.; guest faculty mem. N.W. Ctr. for Profl. Edn.; mem. Nat. Coun. Archtl. Registration Bds., 1998—. Author: The Street-Smart Restaurant Development Handbook, 1996; patentee tidal electric generating system; author 1st comprehensive consumer orientated performance specification for remote banking transaction. Patron charter mem. Asian Art Mus., San Francisco, 2002—. Mem. Encinal Yacht Club (bd. dirs. 1977-78). Republican.

CHAO, JAMES SI-CHENG, maritime executive; b. Shanghai, Dec. 29, 1927; came to the U.S., 1959; s. Yi Jen and Yu Chin (Hsu) C.; m. Ruth Mu-Lan Chu, Nov. 12, 1951. BS, Nat. Maritime Coll., China, 1949; MBA, St. John's U., N.Y., 1964, DCS, 1979; LLD, Niagara U., N.Y., 1992. Cert. marine master certificate license. Marine officer, master port capt. Chinese Maritime Trust, Taiwan, 1949-59; asst. to dir. China Merchant Nav. Corp, N.Y.C., 1960-64; gen. mgr. exec. v.p. Foremost Maritime Corp., N.Y.C., 1964-69, pres., dir., 1969—; chmn. Foremost Group, N.Y.C., 1986—. Adj. prof. St. John's U., N.Y.C., 1977-83, trustee; hon. prof. Dalian Maritime U., Dalian, China, 1987—; hon. prof., pres. Shanghai Maritime Coll., China. Author: (monograph) International Shipping: Prospects and Opportunities, 1982; co-author: (monograph) Rise and Decline of the U.S. Shipping and Shipbuilding Industries, 1993. Bd. advisors St. John's U. Coll. of Bus. Adminstrn., N.Y., 1971—; hon. trustee Shanghai Jiao Tong U., China.; trustee St. John's U., 1995-2005, trustee emeritus, 2005—. Recipient medal of honor St. John's U., 1981, Ellis Island medal of honor, 2005; named Bus. Cmty. Leader Fed. Res. Bank of N.Y., 1976, 1981; named to Internat. Maritime Hall of Fame at UN, 2004. Mem. Chinese Maritime Assn. (pres. 1974—), Soc. Maritime Arbitrators, Chinese Opera (hon. mem., bd. dir. 1969—), Chiao Tung U. Alumni Assn. in Am. (chmn. 1989-99), Beta Gamma Sigma, Omicron Delta Epsilon (hon. mem.). Office: Foremost Maritime Group 60 E 42nd St 2212 New York NY 10165 E-mail: jscchao@aol.com.

CHAO, KWANG-CHU, chemical engineer, educator; b. Chongqing, China, June 7, 1925; came to U.S., 1954, naturalized, 1969; s. Chung-Pu and Jui-Pu (Chou) C.; m. Jiun-Ying Su, May 2, 1953; children: Howard Honshuen, Albert Honchi, Bernard Honwei. BS, Zhejiang (China) U., 1948; MS, U. Wis., 1952, PhD, 1956. Chem. engr. Taiwan Alkali Co., 1948-51, 52-54; research engr. Chevron Research Co., Richmond, Calif., 1957-63; asso. prof. Ill. Inst. Tech., Chgo., 1963-64, Okla. State U., 1964-68; prof. Purdue U., West Lafayette, Ind., 1968-93, Harry C. Peffer Disting. prof. chem. engring., 1989-93, Harry C. Peffer disting. prof. emeritus chem. engring., 1994—. Cons. to industry, 1964—; lectr., internat. scientist Nat. Sci. Coun., Taiwan, 1989; hon. prof. Beijing U. Chem. Tech., 1984—, Zhejiang U., 1988—. Author: (with R.A. Greenkorn) Thermodynamics of Fluids, 1975; Editor: Applied Thermodynamics, 1968, Equations of State in Engineering and Research, 1979; Equations of State-Theories and Applications, 1986. Co-founder, chmn./sec. bd.dirs. Am. Zhu Kezhen Edn. Found., 1995—. Recipient Donald Katz award Gas Processors Assn., 1994. Fellow Am. Inst. Chem. Engrs. (editorial bd. jour., also Ind. Engring. Chem. Ann. Revs.); mem. Am. Chem. Soc., AAUP, Sigma Xi, Omega Chi Epsilon. Home: 500 Lakemead Way Emerald Hills CA 94062-3919 Personal E-mail: chuchao@aol.com.

CHAO, MARSHALL, chemist; b. Changsha, Hunan, China, Nov. 20, 1924; came to U.S., 1955; s. Heng-ti and Hwei-yng C.; m. Patricia Hu, July 20, 1968; 1 dau., Anita A. BS, Nat. Central U., Nanking, China, 1947; MS, U. Ill., 1958, PhD, 1961. Tech. asst. Taiwan Fertilizer Co., Taipei, 1949-55; research chemist Dow Chem. Co., Midland, Mich., 1960-72, research specialist, 1973-80; research leader Dow chem. Co., Midland, Mich., 1980-86; sr. assoc. Omni Tech Internat., Ltd., Midland, 1986—. Author: Taiwan Fertilizers, 1951; editor newsletter Midland Chinese Christian Fellowship, 1987-94; contbr. articles to profl. jours.; patentee in field. Mem. Ch. Council Grace Bapt. Ch., Taipei, 1951-55; deacon 1st Baptist Ch., Midland, 1974-76. Univ. fellow U. Ill., 1957-60 Fellow Am. Inst. Chemists; mem. Am. Chem. Soc., Electrochem. Soc. (sect. chmn. 1973-74, 83-84, councilor 1974-76, 85—, vice chmn. 1964-65), Soc. Electronanalytical chemistry (charter), N.Y. Acad. Scis., Mensa, Sigma Xi, Phi Lambda Upsilon Clubs: Midland Chinese (chmn. 1975-76), Tittabawassee Toastmasters (sec.-treas. 1976-77). Home: 1206 Evamar Dr Midland MI 48640-7213 Office: Omni Tech Internat Ltd 2715 Ashman St Midland MI 48640-4449 E-mail: mschao@aol.com. *A man's intrinsic worth is measured by the good he has done his fellow men. As for outward signs of success, such as recognition or rewards, he should much rather have people wondering why he didn't get them than have people wondering why he got them at all.*

CHAO, RUTH, psychologist, researcher; b. Keelung, Taiwan, Apr. 1, 1967; arrived in U.S., 1996; d. Shi-yi Chao and Chin Chang. BS, Nat. Taiwan U., 1989; postgrad., U. Mo., 2000—. Clin. psychologist Samaritan Psychology Clinic, Chia-yi, Taiwan, 1994—96; rschr. U. Mo., Columbia, 2002—03, clin. supr., 2001—03; doctoral counselor Mich. State U., East Lansing, 2003—04. Cons. Mich. State U., East Lansing, 2003—04, coord., 2003—04. Author: (exhbn.) Listening to Clients' Voices (Winter Roundtable Scholarship, 2004), (vistas) Non-traditional Students on Counseling Needs, 2004, Clients' Perceptions of Mental Health Services, 2005, (book chpt.) Going through Cultural Barriers in Counseling, 2004, Integrating Taoism and Western Therapeutic Approaches in the Treatment of Anxiety, 2005, Integrating Holland's Theory with Tao-te Ching for Career Counseling, 2005; translator: (book) Abnormal Psychology, 1995, Social Psychology, 1995, Teaching and Learning, 1997; author: Historical Review of Multiculturalism, How Ethical is Contemporary Multicultural Training?, 2003, (exhbn.) Adult Students' Perspectives on Counseling and Education (ACCA Grant Award, 2004), Re-thinking Non-traditional College Students' Counseling Needs, 2004, Toward a Successful Experience at Graduate School, 2003, Gender and Smoking: A Qualitative Study, 2004, Minority Clients' Perspectives on Multicultural Competence, 2004, Counselors' Multicultural Self-awareness: A Way to Client Advocacy, 2004, A Qualitative Analysis of College Students' Smoking, 2003, (exhbn.) Creating a Hoslitic Environment for Clients (Rsch. and Profl. Devel. Award, 2003), College Smokers' Perspectives on Smoking (Rsch. Award, Sch. of Medicine, U. of Kans., 2003), Racial Identity Development in Minority Counselors (Winter Roundtable Scholoarship, Columbia U., 2002); contbr. articles to profl. jours. Christian student leader, Taipei, 1988—89. Recipient Multicultural Rsch. award, 2002, Outstanding Acad. Achievements award, 2002, Walter Scott Monroe Rsch. fellowship, 2002—03, Superior Rsch. award, 2004, Rsch. scholarship, Profl. R&D Support award, 2004. Mem.: APA, Am. Counseling Assn., Psi Chi (life). Office Phone: 573-462-0318. E-mail: ruth_chao2000@yahoo.com.

CHAO, TSAI CHUNG, physician, medical association administrator; b. Hangzhou, Zhejiang, China, Oct. 13, 1944; came to U.S., 1981; s. Chi Chang and Chi Hsiao (Sun) C.; m. Hsian Fang Hsiang; children: Charlene, James. Diploma, Zhejiang U. Sch. Medicine, 1969; MD, SUNY, N.Y.C., 1993. Diplomate Am. Bd. Phys. Medicine and Rehab. Ind. Med. Examiners, Am. Acad. Pain Mgmt. Surg. intern Xiaoshan County Hosp., Xiaoshan City, China, 1969-70; gen. practitioner Xiaoshan Coal & Iron Mining, 1970-72; surg. ho. physician Linpu People's Hosp., Xiaoshan City, 1972-74; surg. resident Zhejiang Med. U., Hangzhou City, 1974-80; surg. oncology fellow Hangzhou Cancer Inst., 1980; asst. prof., staff surgeon Zhejiang Med. U., Hangzhou City, 1980-81; instr. S. Baylo U., Garden Grove, Calif., 1984-86, SAMRA U. Oriental Medicine, L.A., 1985-86; surg. resident Interfaith Med. Ctr., Bklyn., 1986-88; rehab. medicine resident SUNY Downstate Med. Ctr., Bklyn., 1988-91, clinic asst. prof., attending physician, 1991-97, assoc. dir. rehab. med. residency program, 1997—. Course dir. continuing med. edn. program in med. acupuncture SUNY Downstate Med. Ctr., also dir. Low Back Pain Ctr. Contbr. articles to profl. jours. Fellow Am. Acad. Phys. Med. and Rehab.; mem. AMA, Am. Congress Rehab. Medicine, Am. Acad. Med. Acupunture, Am. Coll. Occupl. and Environ. Medicine, N.Y. Acad. Scis. Home: 330 E 38th St Apt 37N New York NY 10016-2782 Office: SUNY Health Sci Ctr PO Box 30 Brooklyn NY 11203-0030

CHAOVALITWONGSE, WANPRACHA, mathematician, researcher; b. Bangkok, Thailand, Apr. 22, 1979; s. Boonya and Vinij Chaovalitwongse. BS Engring., King Mongkut Inst. of Tech., Ladkrabang, Bangkok, Thailand, 1999; MS, U.Fla., Gainesville, 2000, PhD, 2003. Engr. internship Asia Multimedia Co. Ltd., Bangkok, 1998; grad. rsch. asst. U. Fla., Gainesville, 2000—03; post doctoral rsch. assoc. U. Fla., Gainesville, 2003—05, asst. prof. of indsl. and sys. engring., 2005—. Contbr. articles to profl. jours, chapters to books. Recipient Grad. Student Ann. Rsch. Excellence award, Dept. of Indsl. and Systems Engring., U. of Fla., 2003. Mem.: Inst. for Ops. Rsch. and the Mgmt. Sciences, Math. Programming Soc., Am. Epilepsy Soc., Soc. for Indsl. and Applied Math. Achievements include patents pending for Optimization of Multi-Dimensional Time Series Processing for Seizure Warning and Prediction; Efficient Transformation of Quadratic and Multi-Quadratic 0-1 Optimization Problems to Mixed Linear 0-1 Problems. Office: Dept Industrial and Systems Engring Rutgers Univ 96 Frelinghuysen Rd Rm 201 CORE Bldg Piscataway NJ 08854 Office Phone: 732-445-3469. E-mail: wchaoval@rci.rutgers.edu.

CHAPDELAINE, PERRY ANTHONY, JR., public health service officer, preventive medicine physician, educator; b. Mason City, Iowa, Feb. 23, 1950; s. Perry Anthony Sr. and Ruby Elizabeth (McCurley) C.; m. Catherine Joan Tidwell, May 22, 1981; 1 child, Rachel Maria. BA in Sociology, St. Ambrose U., 1972; MD, Meharry Med. Coll., 1989, MSPH, 1992. Diplomate Am. Bd. Preventive Medicine. CEO, pres. AC Projects Inc., Franklin, Tenn., 1974-86; epidemiologist Meharry Med. Coll., Nashville, 1992-95, asst. prof., 1993-95, 2001—03, dir. preventive medicine residency program, 1995; chief med. physician City of Nashville, Metro Health Dept., 1995-2000; pvt. cons. practice, 2000—. Cons. St. Thomas Hosp. Clin. Ethics Ctr., Nashville, 1993-98, Nashville Prevention Mktg. Initiative, 1994-96; med. dir. Samaritan Recovery Cmty., Nashville, 1993-95; mem. Access Med Plus Peer Rev. Com., Nashville, 1996-2000. Co-editor: The John W. Campbell Letters, 1985 (Hugo award nominee 1986). Mem. Alpha Chi, Alpha Omega Alpha. Avocations: writing, photography, dulcimer, hiking. Home: 5384 Village Way Nashville TN 37211 Office: Gen and Alternative Medicine 229 Ward Cir Ste B-12 Brentwood TN 37027 Office Phone: 615-377-6767. E-mail: docanthony1@yahoo.com.

CHAPEL, ROBERT CLYDE, theater director, educator; b. June 25, 1945; married. BA in TV, U. Mich., 1967, MA in Theatre, 1968, PhD in Theatre, 1974. Asst. prof. dept. theatre U. Ala., Ala., 1974-75; profl. actor LA, 1975-77; dir. devel. Force Ten Prod., LA, 1977-78; v.p. prodn. Trans-Atlantic Enterprises, LA, 1978-81; actor, dir. LA, 1981-83; dir. BFA mus. theatre program U. Mich., Mich., 1983-84; coordinating dir. MFA mus. theatre program Tisch Sch. of Arts NYU, NYC, 1984—86; co-prodr. Shubert Archives Series Lyceum Theatre, NYC, 1984-86; artistic dir. Music Theatre North, Potsdam, NY, 1986; freelance dir. NYC, 1986—88; dir. mus. theatre program San Diego State U., San Diego, 1988-90; prof., chair dept. drama U. Va., Va., 1990—2005; mng. dir. Heritage Repertory Theatre, Charlottesville, Va., 1990-94, prodr., artistic dir., 1995—; exec. dir. Va. Film Festival, Va., 1996—2000; prof. drama U. Va., 2005—. Chmn. pres. commn. on fine arts and performing arts U. Va., 1998-2001. Mem. SAG, AFTRA, Assn. for Theatre in Higher Edn., Nat. Assn. Schs. of Theatre, Actors Equity Assn., Soc. Stage Dirs. and Choreographers. Home: 1029 Hazel St Charlottesville VA 22902-4904 Office Phone: 434-924-8961. E-mail: rcc2u@virginia.edu.

CHAPELA, IGNACIO H., biologist, researcher; b. Mex. City, Mex., Sept. 12, 1959; s. Gonzalo Chapela Montañéz and Maria De La Luz Mendoza; m. Laura Garcia-Moreno, July 23, 1987; 1 child: Inés. Biologo, Nat. U. Mex., Mex. City, 1984; PhD, U. Wales, Cardiff, 1987. Scientist Sandoz, Ltd, Basel, Switzerland, 1989-91. Vis. prof. Cornell U., Ithaca, N.Y., 1987-88, 92-93; founder, scientific dir. Mycological Facility: Oaxaca (Mex.), 1994—; cons. World Bank Group, Washington, 1994, Pan-Am. Health Orgn., Washington, 1994; adv. bd. Andes Pharmaceuticals, Washington, 1995—; asst. prof. U. Calif., Berkeley. Contbr. articles to profl. jours. Fellow Instituto Nacional de Cardiologia, Mex. City, Mex., 1981-84; grantee Am. Philos. Soc., Phila., 1988, MacArthur Fdn., 1993, Vice Chancellors & Prins. of Brit. U., Wales, 1985-87. Mem. Brit. Mycological Soc. Ecology Com., 1985—, Mycological Soc. of Am., 1995—. Achievements include elucidation of symbiotic relationships of fungi and other organisms conservation through revaluation of biodiversity in Latin Am. Home: 3144 O St NW Washington DC 20007-3116 Office: U Calif Environ Sci Policy & Mgmt Berkeley CA 94720-0001

CHAPELLE, SUZANNE ELLERY GREENE, history professor; b. Phila., Sept. 21, 1942; d. John Channing and Jessie Horn (Myers) Ellery; m. Michael Thomas Greene, Sept. 15, 1972 (dec. 1973); 1 child, Jennifer; m. Francis Oberlin Chapelle, Apr. 14, 1984 (dec. 1999). BA, Harvard U., 1964; MA, Johns Hopkins U., 1966, PhD, 1970. Asst. prof. Am. history Towson State U., Balt., 1969-71; assoc. prof. Am. history Morgan State U., Balt., 1971-75, prof., 1975—, coord., environ. studies program. Author: Books for Pleasure, 1976, Baltimore: An Illustrated History, 1980, 2d rev. edit., 2000; sr. author: Maryland: A History of its People, 1986; revisions author: A Child's History of the World, 1994, African American Leaders of Maryland, 2000, The Maryland Adventure, 2001; mem. publs. bd. Md. Hist. Soc. Bd. dirs. Md. Interfaith Coalition for the Environment, 1997-2001, v.p., 1999-2001; bd. dirs. Md. Conservation Coun., 1999-2000; bd. trustees Irvine Nature Ctr., 2001—; mem. water quality adv. coun. Md., 2004—; mem. Md. State Dept. Edn. Social Studies Task Force, 2004—. Mem. Am. Hist. Assn., Am. Studies Assn. (mem. exec. bd. Chesapeake chpt. 1988-90), Popular Culture Assn. (bd. dirs. 1980-82), Orgn. Am. Historians, Md. Hist. Soc. (publs. com. 1998—), Mid-Atlantic Popular Culture Assn. (pres. 1977-80), Balt. County League Environ. Voters (exec. bd. 1992-96), Episcopal Diocese of Md. Com. on the Environ. (sec. 1994-2003), Ruxton-Riderwood Assn. (bd. govs. 1987-91), The Johns Hopkins Club, The Harvard-Radcliffe Club Md. Episcopalian. Home: 6021 Lakeview Rd Baltimore MD 21210-1033 Office: Morgan State U Hist Dept Baltimore MD 21251-0001 Office Phone: 443-885-3190. Personal E-mail: suechapelle@yahoo.com.

CHAPIN, DWIGHT ALLAN, columnist, writer; b. Lewiston, Idaho, June 16, 1938; s. Don Merle and Lucille Verna (Walker) C.; m. Susan Enid Fisk, Feb. 14, 1963 (div. 1973); children— Carla, Adam; m. Ellen Gonzalez, Aug. 10, 1983 BA, U. Idaho, 1960; MS in Journalism, Columbia U., 1961. Reporter Lewiston Morning Tribune, Idaho, 1956-62; reporter, editor Vancouver Columbian, Wash., 1962-65; sportswriter Seattle Post-Intelligencer, 1965-67, Los Angeles Times, 1967-77; columnist San Francisco Examiner, 1977-2000, San Francisco Chronicle, 2000—. Co-author: Wizard of Westwood, 1973; contbr. numerous articles to popular mags. Served with USNG, 1962-68 Recipient Sports Writing award AP, Calif./Nev., 1968-69; Baseball Writing award Am. Assn. Coll. Baseball Coaches Mem. Sigma Delta Chi (sports writing award Wash. state 1964, 65, 66) Democrat. Avocation: trading card and sports memorabilia collecting. Office: San Francisco Chronicle 901 Mission St San Francisco CA 94103-2988 Office Phone: 415-777-7201. E-mail: dchapin@sfchronicle.com.

CHAPIN, F. STUART, III, ecologist; BA in biology, Swarthmore Coll., 1966; PhD in bio. scis., Stanford U., 1973. Asst. and assoc. prof. U. Alaska, Fairbanks, 1973—84, prof. ecology, 1984—86, 1996—; asst. dir. Inst. Arctic Biology, 1981—83; prof. biology U. Calif., Berkeley, 1989—98. Vis. instr. biology Peace Corps U. Javeriana, Colombia, 1966—68. Co-author: Principles of Terrestrial Ecosystem Ecology, 2002; editl. bd. mem. Physiological Ecology Series, Ecology and Soc. Recipient Kempe award, 1996; fellow, Guggenheim, 1979. Mem.: Ecol. Soc. Am., Ecology Inst., Swedish Royal Acad. Agriculture and Forestry, Am. Acad. Arts and Scis., Nat. Acad. Scis. Office: U Alaska Inst Arctic Biology Dept Biology and Wildlife Fairbanks AK 99775 Business E-Mail: terry.chapin@uaf.edu.

CHAPIN, MARY Q., arbitrator, director, mediator, writer, performance artist; b. Shepherdstown, W.VA., May 5, 1933; d. Guy Estil and Anne Mildred (Jones) Quisenberry; m. Edward John Chapin Jr.; children: John Edward, Susan Q. (dec.). SUNY Regent's Degree, 1985; AAS, SUNY, Binghamton, BS, 1991. Pers. adminstr. Mohawk Valley Psychiatric Ctr., Utica, N.Y., 1976-89; arbitrator Am. Arbitration Assn., N.Y.C., 1989-99; pres. Dispute Resolution Internat., New Hartford, N.Y., 1993—; neutral chair NYSDOL Office of Labor Mgmt., Albany, N.Y., 1993—. Mem. adv. coun. on safety and security in N.Y. State schs. N.Y. State Dept. Edn., Albany, 1995-97; founder, mem., bd. dirs. Forum on Conflict and Concensus, 1993-941 chair Mohawk Valley Women's History Project, 1998—; host weekly TV show, Mohawk Valley Srs., Sta. WUTR, 2002—. Author: Woman's Suffrage: A Dream of Full Citizenship; author, performer An Afternoon with Susan B. Anthony. Pres. Utica/Rome Metro League of Women Voters, 1992-97; coord. Com. on Met. Orgn., 1995-97; coord. of multicultural commn. League of Women Voters Edn. Fund, 1997; trustee amerita Mohawk Valley Cmty. Coll., 1996-2002; Utica C. of C., 1995-98. Recipient Found. award The Found. of SUNY at Binghamton, 1992, Recognition award NYS League of Women Voters, 1995,

97, Recognition award U.S. LWV Edn. Fund, 1998, Labor Mgmt. award Office of Mental Health, 1988, Conservator of Women's History award NOW, 2002. Mem. AAUW, Central N.Y. Futurist, Bd. Neighborhood Ctr., Wentworth Golf Club. Home and Office: 56 Woodbrooke Rd New Hartford NY 13413-4805

CHAPIN, MARYAN FOX, civic worker; b. Easton, Pa., Apr. 26, 1933; d. Louis Rodman and Mary Catherine (Cannon) Fox; m. Richard Chapin, Nov. 3, 1956; children: Aldus Higgins II, Margery Rodman, Marya Marsh, Richard Dickinson. AB, Vassar Coll., 1954. Contr. Chapin's Market, Cambridge, 1986-88. Trustee Longy Sch. Music, 1974-75; pres. founding bd. trustees New Sch. Music, 1976-77; bd. dirs. Young Audiences of Mass., 1976-83, chairman, 1980-82; adv. bd. Wheelock Coll. Family Theatre, 1985-92; treas. Richards Libr., Georgetown, Maine; trustee Bowdoin Internat. Music Festival, 1994—, chmn., 1997-99. Bd. dir. Lark Soc. for Chamber Music, 1997-2004; Maine Arts Commr., 2001-2003. Mem.: New Eng. Conservatory (bd. overseers 1987—92). Home: 13 Knubble Rd Georgetown ME 04548

CHAPIN, MILES WHITWORTH, writer, actor; b. N.Y.C., Dec. 6, 1954; s. Schuyler Garrison and Elizabeth (Steinway) Chapin; m. Jennifer Iselin, Nov. 3, 1992; children: Elizabeth Steinway, Moses Iselin. H.S. Grad., Profl. Children's Sch., N.Y.C., 1972. Author: (book) 88 Keys, The Making Of A Steinway Piano; editor: (anthology) Tales From The Jungle: A Rainforest Reader; actor: (feature film) Man on the Moon, The People vs Larry Flynt, Buddy, Buddy, French Postcards, The Funhouse, Hair, Bless The Beasts And Children, Ladybug, Ladybug, Pandemonium, The Funny Farm, The Associate, Get Crazy, Young Goodman Brown, Howard the Duck, Hudson River Blues, To Find a Man. Bd. dirs. RARE Ctr. for Tropical Conservation, Arlington, Va., 1997—2003, Earth Comm. Office, LA, 1988—91, The Rene Dubos Ctr. for Human Environments, N.Y.C., NY, 1992—99; bd. trustees All Souls Ch., N.Y.C.; bd. dirs. Musica Viva, N.Y.C., 2002—04. Recipient James Beard award, 2005. Independent. Unitarian. Avocations: fly fishing, cooking, wood craft, travel.

CHAPIN, RICHARD, arbitrator, director; b. Boston, Dec. 25, 1923; s. Vinton and Elizabeth (Higgins) C.; m. Maryan Gainor Fox, Nov. 3, 1956; children: Aldus Higgins II, Margery Rodman Carr, Marya Chapin Lundgren, Richard Dickinson. SB, Harvard U., 1944, MBA, 1949; LLD (hon.), Emerson Coll., 1972. Asst. to treas. Anderson, Davis & Platt, Inc., 1946; journeyman machinist Yale & Towne Co., 1947; various adminstrn. and instnl. positions Harvard Grad. Sch. Bus. Adminstrn., 1949-67; pres. Emerson Coll., Boston, 1967-75. Exec. dir. Cheswick Ctr., 1976-84; bd. dirs. Advanced Mech. Tech., Inc., Alden Yachts, Inc.; hon. dir. Nickerson Lumber Co. Trustee Bigelow Found.; chmn. Riggs Cove Found.; vice chmn. Bigelow Lab. Ocean Sci. Served with USNR, 1942-46. Mem.: St. Botolph Club, NY Yacht Club. Home and Office: 13 Knubble Rd Georgetown ME 04548-9410 Personal E-mail: rchapin440@aol.com.

CHAPIN, RICHARD EARL, retired librarian; b. Danville, Ill., Apr. 29, 1925; s. Harry W. and Lula May (Briggs) C.; m. Eleanor Jane Lang, Aug. 15, 1949; children: Robert Lang, David Brian, Rebecca Anne. AB, Wabash Coll., 1948; MS, U. Ill., 1949, PhD, 1954; LHD (hon.), Wabash Coll., 1991. Reference asst. Fla. State U., 1949-50; libr. asst. U. Ill., 1950-53, vis. prof., 1957; asst. dir., asst. prof. Sch. Libr. Sci., U. Okla., 1953-55; assoc. libr., assoc. prof. Mich. State U., East Lansing, 1955-59, dir. librs., prof. journalism, 1959-89, dir. librs. emeritus, prof. emeritus, 1989—; libr. advisor United Arab Emirates U., 1989-92. Dir. Mich. State U. Press, 1986-90; cons. to govts., founds., colls., and univs.; bd. dirs. Ctr. for Rsch. Librs., 1978-83; bd. dirs. OCLC Users' Coun., 1980-83, pres., 1983. Contbr. articles to libr. periodicals and encys. Mem. East Lansing Human Relations Commn., 1966-69, chmn., 1969; mem. East Lansing Bd. Edn., 1970-74, 75, pres., 1973-74; bd. dirs. W.B. and Candace Thoman Found., 1991—. Served to lt. (j.g.) USNR, 1943-46. Mem. ALA, Mich. Library Assn. (pres. 1967), Assn. Research Libraries (bd. dirs. 1984-87), Blue Key, Sigma Chi, Phi Kappa Phi Home: 2539 Koala Dr East Lansing MI 48823-7211 E-mail: chapinR@msu.edu.

CHAPIN, SCHUYLER GARRISON, cultural organization administrator, dean; b. NYC, Feb. 13, 1923; s. L.H. Paul and Leila H. (Burden) C.; m. Elizabeth Steinway, Mar. 15, 1947 (dec. 1993); children: Henry Burden, Theodore Steinway, Samuel Garrison, Miles Whitworth; m. Catia Zoullas Mortimer, Sept. 15, 1995. Student, Longy Sch. Music, 1940-41; LHD (hon.), NYU, 1974, Hobart/William Smith Coll., 1974, Hofstra Coll., 1999; DLitt (hon.), Emerson Coll., 1976; MusD (hon.), Mannes Coll., New Sch., 1990, Curtis Inst. Music, 2000. Spot salesman NBC-TV, N.Y.C., 1947-51; gen. mgr. Tex and Jinx McCary Enterprises, N.Y.C., 1951-53; booking dir. Judson, O'Neill & Judd divsn. Columbia Artists Mgmt., 1953-59; dir. masterworks to v.p. creative svcs. Columbia Records divsn. CBS, 1959-63; v.p. programming Lincoln Center for the Performing Arts, 1964-69; exec. producer Amberson Enterprises, N.Y.C., 1969-71; acting gen. mgr. Met. Opera, N.Y.C., 1972-73, gen. mgr., 1973-75; dean faculty arts Columbia U., 1976-87, dean emeritus, 1987—; v.p. worldwide concert and artist activities Steinway & Sons, N.Y.C., 1990-92; commr. of cultural affairs City of N.Y., 1994—2002. Cons. Carnegie Hall Corp., 1979-87. Author: (autobiography) Musical Chairs, 1977, Leonard Bernstein: Notes from a Friend, 1992, Sopranos, Mezzos, Tenors, Bassos and Other Friends, 1995. Past chmn. Bagby Music Lovers Found.; past chmn., trustee Am. Symphony Orch. League, 1985-92; trustee Naumburg Found., 1949, Richard Tucker Found., 1975-92, Am. Inst. for Verdi Studies, 1975, Bklyn. Philharm., 1978-92, Lenox Music Theatre Group, 1984, Lincoln Ctr. Theatre, 1985-94, 2001—, Carnegie Hall Soc., 1987-94, 2001—, Curtis Inst. Music, 1986-92, Pres.'s Com. on Arts and Humanities, 1982-90, Redwood Libr. and Athenaeum, 1990-96; chmn., exec. com. Franklin and Eleanor Roosevelt Inst., 1982-2004, co-chair bd. govs., 2004—. 1st lt. Air Corps U.S. Army, 1942—46, China, Burma, India. Decorated chevalier Legion of Honor (France); recipient N.Y. State Conspicuous service cross, 1951, Christopher award, 1971, Emmy awards 1972, 76, 80, Gold Medal Nat. Arts Club, 1983. Fellow Am. Acad. Arts & Scis. Clubs: Century Assn. (N.Y.C.), Knickerbocker. Home: 655 Park Ave New York NY 10021-5937 Personal E-mail: SGC655@aol.com. *Throughout my career, and indeed my life, I have been fortunate to make my avocation my vocation. I've worked in, around, about and for the arts in a variety of ways. That, I hope, has brought as much happiness to others as it has to me. I have been privileged to be part of what a poet once called the Arts: the Signature of Man.*

CHAPKLIN GRIFFIN, PAMELA SUSAN, graphics designer, educator; b. Carle Place, N.Y., Aug. 10, 1951; d. Stephen and Lena Chapklin; m. Daryl Sharrock (dec.); 1 child, Kimani S. Griffin. BFA, Syracuse U., 1973; MFA (fellow 1975-76), Temple U., 1976; cert. in residential constrn., Forsyth Tech. Coll., 1985. Drawing/design faculty Cazenovia (N.Y.) Coll., 1978—82; design faculty N.C. Sch. Arts, Winston-Salem, 1982—. Master printer's asst. Fox Lithographic Studios, Mass., 1972; color correction specialist Transamerica Color Labs, NY, 1973; tech. illustrator, elec. draftsman, 1973—78; graphic designer Etcetera Graphics, Pa., 1977; graphic design, promotion Awareness Art Ensemble, Va., 1983—87; framing carpenter Dancy Constrn., N.Y.C., 1986; freelance graphic designer, 1990—; interior designer, painter Coconuts Comedy Club, N.Y.C., 1993. One-woman shows include Lowe Gallery, Syracuse (N.Y.) U., 1971, Tyler Sch. Art, Phila., 1976, Westbury (N.Y.) Libr., 1977, exhibited in group shows at Goods Gallery, Port Washington, N.Y., 1978, 1979, Long Beach (N.Y.) Mus., 1980, Porch Gallery, Winston-Salem, 1984, prin. works include Chapman Cultural Ctr., Cazenovia Coll., N.Y., 1981; scenic designer: (plays) Actor's Ensemble, 1987; scenic advisor, designer Yellow Sound, 1988; art dir.: (films) Music Lessons, 1994. Coord. AIDS Quilt Project Visual Arts Dept. N.C. Sch. Arts, 1992. Rockefeller grantee, 1994, Faculty Devel. grantee, Cazenovia Coll., 1980, N.C. Sch. Arts, 1983, 1985, 1991, Found. grantee, 1986. Home: 535 Banner Ave Winston Salem NC 27127 Office: NC Sch Arts Sch Design and Prodn 1533 S Main St Winston Salem NC 27127 Office Phone: 336-770-1219. E-mail: pgriffin6@triad.rr.com.

CHAPLIN, DAVID DUNBAR, medical research specialist, educator; b. London, Aug. 28, 1952; came to U.S., 1952; s. Hugh Jr. and Alice Elizabeth (Dougherty) C.; m. Jane Ellen Bryant; children: Vernon H., Rosalind K., Daniel B. AB, Harvard U., 1973; MD, PhD, Washington U., St. Louis, 1980. Intern, then resident Parkland Meml. Hosp., Dallas, 1980-82; post-doctoral fellow dept. genetics Harvard U. Med. Sch., Boston, 1982-84; asst. prof. medicine Washington U. Sch. Medicine, St. Louis, 1984-91, prof. medicine, 1995—; assoc. investigator Howard Hughes Med. Inst., St. Louis, 1984—. Assoc. editor: The New Biologist, 1990-92, Diabetes, 1992-96; contbr. articles to profl. jours. Mem. grants com. Arthritis Found., Atlanta, 1989-92, NIAID AITR, 1998—. Scholar Harvard U., 1972, 73; Jane Coffin Childs Fund for Med. Rsch. fellow, 1982-84. Mem. Am. Soc. Clin. Investigation, Am. Fedn. Clin. Rsch., Am. Assn. Immunologists, Am. Soc. Human Genetics, Assn., Assn. Am. Physicians, Alpha Omega Alpha. Democrat. Roman Catholic. Office: Howard Hughes Med Inst 10050 Clin Scis Res Bldg 660 S Euclid Ave # 8022 Saint Louis MO 63110-1010 E-mail: cahplin@im.wustl.edu.

CHAPLIN, HUGH, JR., preventive medicine physician, educator; b. N.Y.C., Feb. 4, 1923; m. Alice Dougherty, June 16, 1945; 4 children; m. Lee Nelken Robins, Aug. 5, 1998. AB, Princeton U., 1943; MD, Columbia U., 1947. Diplomate Am. Bd. Internal Medicine, Nat. Bd. Med. Examiners. Intern Mass. Gen. Hosp., Boston, 1947-48, resident, 1948-50; fellow in hematology Brit. Postgrad. Med. Sch., London, 1951-53; physician in charge Clin. Center Blood Bank, NIH, Bethesda, Md., 1953-55; Commonwealth Fund fellow Wright Fleming Inst. Microbiology, London, 1962-63, Josiah Macy Faculty scholar, 1975-76. Instr. in medicine Washington U. Sch. Medicine, St. Louis, 1955-56, asst. prof. medicine and preventive medicine, 1956-62, asso. dean, chmn. admissions com., 1957-62, asso. prof., 1963-65, prof., 1965, William B. Kountz prof. preventive medicine, 1965-83; dir. IWJ Inst. of Rehab., St. Louis, 1964-72; prof. pathology, dir. Barnes Hosp. Blood Bank, St. Louis, 1983-91; emeritus prof. pathology and medicine, 1991—; mem. Am. Standards Com. for Blood Transfusion Equipment; mem. subcom. on transfusion problems NRC, 1959-62, mem. com. on blood and transfusion problems, 1963-67; chmn. ad hoc blood program research com. ARC, 1967-73, bd. govs., 1978-84 Assoc. editor Transfusion, 1960-98; contbg. editor Vox Sanguinis, 1960-79. Served with USNR, 1942-45. Mem. Am. Fedn. Clin. Research, Central Soc. Clin. Research, Am. Soc. Clin. Investigation, Assn. Am. Physicians, Am., Internat. socs. hematology, Brit. Med. Research Soc., Brit. Royal Soc. Medicine, Am. Assn. Blood Banks (sci. program com. 1959-60, Emily Cooley award 1968, Morton Grove-Rasmussen award 1985), Phi Beta Kappa, Alpha Omega Alpha, Sigma Xi. Office: Washington U Sch Medicine Box 8118 4949 Barnes Hospital Plz Saint Louis MO 63110-1003 E-mail: hughchapln@yahoo.com.

CHAPLIN, PEGGY LOUIE, lawyer; b. Guantanamo Bay Naval Base, Cuba, Nov. 22, 1940; d. Raymond Gerard Fannon and Joan Marie (Carguil) Boyce. BS, Johns Hopkins U., 1971; JD, U. Md., 1973; LLM in Internat. Comml. Law, Georgetown U., 1983. Bar: Md. 1973, U.S. Dist. Ct. Md. 1973, U.S. Ct. Internat. Trade 1975, U.S. Ct. Appeals (fed. cir.) 1986, (D.C. cir.) 1988, U.S. Supreme Ct. 2003. V.p. Vanguard Shipping & Import, Balt., 1972-77, F.W. Myers & Co., Inc., Balt., 1977-84; assoc. Ober, Kaler, Grimes & Shriver, Balt., 1984-91, ptnr., 1992-97, Sandler, Travis & Rosenberg, P.A., Balt., 1997—. Chair Johns Hopkins U. Inst. of Policy Studies com. Logistics and the Economy, 1996-99. Contbr. articles to bar jours. Mem. Gov.'s Commn. World Trade Efforts, 1984, Balt. City Wage Commn., 1986-90, Md. Trade Policy Com., 1986; chair 2d Ann. Md. Internat. Trade Conf.; chair air cargo devel. com. BWI Econ. Devel. Coun., 1993-96. Mem.: NAFTA (chpt. 19 roster), Assn. Transp. Law, Logistics and Policy (newsletter editor Import/Export Regulation), Am. Assn. Exporters and Importers, Am. Arbitration Assn. (panelist), Md. Internat. Trade Assn. (pres. 1984—86), Women's Bar Assn. Md. (pres. 1977—78), Md. State Bar Assn. (chair internat. comml. law sect. 1991—92), Md. C. of C. (chmn. internat. trade com. 1984—97). Office: Sandler Travis & Rosenberg PA 111 S Calvert St Ste 2700 Baltimore MD 21202-6143 Office Phone: 410-385-5208. E-mail: pchaplin@strtrade.com.

CHAPMAN, ALAN JESSE, mechanical engineering educator; b. LA, June 22, 1925; s. Wallace Webster and Isabel (Smith) C.; m. Marjorie Bray, June 8, 1950; children: Alan Jesse, Katherine Lynn. BS in Mech. Engring, Rice U., 1945; MS, U. Colo., 1949; PhD, U. Ill., 1953. Registered profl. engr., Tex. Faculty Rice U., Houston, 1946—, prof. mech. engring., 1954-69, chmn. dept. mech. and aerospace engring. and materials sci., 1954-69, v.p., 1968—70, prof. emeritus, 1996—; dean G.R. Brown Sch. Engring., 1975-80, Harry S. Cameron prof. mech. engring., 1980—95. Cons. to Manned Spacecraft Ctr., NASA, Houston, 1961—95. Author: Introductory Gas Dynamics, 1970. Heat Transfer, 4th edit, 1984, Fundamentals of Heath Transfer, 1987. Pres. S.W. Athletic Conf., 1965-67; mem. coun. NCAA, 1968-73, pres., 1973-74. Served with USNR, 1942-45. Fellow AIAA (assoc.) ASME (hon.); mem. ASHRAE, Am. Soc. Engring. Edn., Sigma Xi, Tau Beta Pi. Home: 10031 Doliver Dr Houston TX 77042-2015 Office: Rice Univ PO Box 1892 6100 South Main Houston TX 77251 Office Phone: 713-348-4708. Business E-Mail: chapman@rice.edu.

CHAPMAN, ALGER BALDWIN, finance company executive, lawyer; b. Portland, Maine, Sept. 28, 1931; s. Alger Baldwin, Sr. and Elizabeth (Ives) Chapman; m. Beatrice Bishop, Oct. 30, 1983; children: Alger III, Samuel P., Andrew I., Henry H. BA, Williams Coll., 1953; JD, Columbia U., 1956. Bar: N.Y. 1957. Pres. Shearson, Hammill & Co., 1970-74; co-chmn. Shearson & Co., 1974-81; vice chmn. Am. Express Bank, 1982—86; chmn., CEO Chgo. Bd. Options Exch., 1986-97; vice chmn. ABN Amro, Inc., 1997—2001; chmn. ABN Amro Fin. Svcs, 1998—2004; dir. The Cambridge Group, Chgo., 2005—. Bd. dirs. HDO, Cantilever Tech., Arlington Capital; chmn. Prime Ins. Mem.: Econ. Club, Commercial Club, Met. Club (N.Y.C.), Racquet Club Chgo., Chgo. Club. Avocations: golf, reading. Home: 33 Hickory Hills Cir Little Rock AR 72212 Office: 227 W Monroe St Ste 3200 Chicago IL 60606 Office Phone: 312-961-9914.

CHAPMAN, ALVAH HERMAN, JR., retired newspaper executive; b. Columbus, Ga., Mar. 21, 1921; s. Alvah Herman and Wyline (Page) Chapman; m. Betty Bateman, Mar. 22, 1943; children: Dale Page Chapman Webb, Chris Ann Chapman Hilton. BS, The Citadel, 1942, hon. degree, 1971, Barry U., 1985, Fla. Internat. U., 1988, U. Miami, Coral Gables, Fla., 1989, U. Notre Dame, 1991. Bus. mgr. Columbus Ledger, 1945-53; exec. v.p., gen. mgr. St. Petersburg (Fla.) Times, 1953-57; pres., pub. Morning News and Evening Press, Savannah, Ga., 1957-60; exec. Knight-Ridder Newspapers, Inc., Miami, Fla., 1960-89, exec. com., 1960-2000; dir. Knight Ridder, 1962-2000; exec. v.p. Knight-Ridder Newspapers, Inc., 1967-73, pres., 1973-82, CEO, 1976-88, chmn., 1982-89, dir., chmn. exec. com., 1984-95; v.p., gen. mgr. Miami Herald, 1962-70, pres., 1970-82. Lectr. Am. Press Insts., Columbia; vice chmn., exec. com. Miami Coalition for Safe & Drug-Free Cmty.; mem. Pres.'s Drug Adv. Coun., 1989-92; chmn. emeritus Fla. Internat. U. Found.; bd. trustees Fla. Internat. U., 2001-2002; trustee John S. and James L. Knight Found., 1971-2002. Founder, chmn. emeritus Cmty. Anti-Drug Coalitions Am.; chmn. We Will Rebuild, 1992—93, Gov.'s Commn. on Homeless, 1992—94; founding chmn. Cmty. Partnership for Homeless, Inc., 1993—; mem. State's Commn. on the Homeless, 2000; bd. dirs. ARC Greater Miami and the Keys, 2001—04. Maj. USAAF, World War II. Decorated D.F.C. with 2 oak leaf clusters, Air medal with 5 clusters U.S., Croix de Guerre; named Outstanding Young Man, Columbus Jr. C. of C., 1952, Dade County's Outstanding Citizen of 1968-69, Brigham Young U. Internat. Businessman of Yr., 1984, Hon. Dir., Fla. C. of C., 1997; named one of 5 Outstanding Young Men in Ga., 1951, Legends of South Fla., South Fla. CEO Mag., 2004, 22 who Make a City Magic, Jr. Leagues, 2003; named to South Fla. Bus. Hall of Fame, 2000; recipient Citadel Palmetto award, 1985, Isaiah Thomas award, Rochester Inst. Tech., 1986, Joseph Wharton Statesman award, 1988, United Negro Coll. Fund's Disting. Svc. award, 1988, The Miami Herald Spirit of Excellence Lifetime Achievement award, 1989, Anne Ackerman Disting. Floridian award, 1991, LeRoy Collins Lifetime Achievement award, Leadership Fla., 1992, United Way Dorothy Shula award for Volunteerism, 1994, Salvation Army Red Shield award, 1994, ARC Humanitarian of Yr. award, 1994, Health Found. of South Fla. Concern award, 1995, Drum Maj. of Justice award, Miami-Dade C. C., 1996, Spirit of Martin Luther King Jr. Parade & Festivities Dinner Com. award, 1996, Citizen of Yr. award, Gray Panthers North Dade, 1996, Resolution State Fla., 1996, Lifetime Achievement award, Cmty. Anti-Drug Coalitions Am., 1999, Ellis Island medals of honor, 2000, Pontifical medal Benemerenti, 2000, Fla. Meml. Coll. Cmty. Leadership award, 2001, Pillar award, Fla. Internat. U., 2001, 1st recipient Cmty. Partnership for Homeless's Alvah H. Chapman, Jr. Humanitarian award, 2002, Corp. Citizenship award, Nat. Coalition for Homeless, 2002, Disting. Svc. award, Cmty. Anti-Drug Coalitions Am., 2004, Mayor's Lifetime Achievement award, 2004, Advocacy award, Homeless/Formerly Homeless Forum Inc., 2004, Peace and Unity award, St. Martin de Porres Assn., 2005, Disting. Svc. award, Cmty. Anti-Drug Coalitions Am., 2004, Mayor's Lifetime Achievement award, 2004, Advocacy award, Homeless Forum Inc., 2004, Peace and Unity award, St. Martin de Porres Assn., 2005; Alvan H. Chapman, Jr. Grad. Sch. Bus., Fla. Internat. U., named, 2001, Cmty. . Partnership for Homeless's Betty and Alvah Chapman, Jr. Ctr. named, 2002, inducted into, Arland D. Williams Soc. at The Citadel, 2002, Builders Assn. South Fla. Housing Hall of Fame, 2003, Fla. Newspaper Hall of Fame, 2004. Mem. Newspaper Assn. Am., Am. Newspaper Pub. Assn. (chmn., pres. 1986-87), So. Newspapers Pubs. Assn. (pres. 1976). Methodist. Home: Grove Harbour 1690 S Bayshore Ln # 10ab Miami FL 33133-4073 Office: Knight Ridder Inc One Herald Plz Miami FL 33132-1693 Office Phone: 305-376-3870.

CHAPMAN, BERT, government documents librarian; b. Marion, Ind., Feb. 19, 1962; s. Albert Thurman and Mildred Norris Chapman; m. Rebecca Ann Gick, Nov. 11, 2000. BA, Taylor U., 1984; MA, U. Toledo, 1986; MSLS, U. Ky., 1989. Reference/documents libr. Lamar U., Beaumont, Tex., 1989-94; govt. publs. coord., assoc. prof. libr. sci. Purdue U. Librs., West Lafayette, Ind., 1995—. Mem. com. on rare and endangered govt. publs. Govt. Documents Roundtable, 2002—03. Author: (book) Researching National Security and Intelligence Policy, 2004; contbr. articles to profl. jours. Mem. ALA (legis. com. mem. govt. documents roundtable 2000-2001, edn. com. mem. govt. documents roundtable 1998-99), Ind. Hist. Soc., Ind. Networking for Documents and Info. of Govt. Orgns. (chair 1998-99), Tex. State Hist. Assn. Republican. Presbyterian. Avocations: reading, music, travel, hiking. Office: 504 W State St West Lafayette IN 47907-2058 Office Fax: 765) 494-9007. E-mail: chapmanb@purdue.edu.

CHAPMAN, BRUCE DOUGLAS, remote sensing scientist, consultant; b. San Francisco, Mar. 3, 1959; s. Lynn Otis and Frances Louise (Barnes) C.; m. Scarlette Elizabeth Castillo, Feb. 9, 1996; children: Claire Louise, Eleanor Rose. AB in Physics and Astronomy, U. Calif., Berkeley, 1981; PhD in Planetary sci., MIT, 1986. Sr. mem. tech. staff Jet Propulsion Lab., Pasadena, Calif., 1986—. Bd. dirs. Webmetro, Pasadena, 1997-99. Author website and CD-roms. Hike leader Sierra Club, 1988—. Recipient Group Achievement award NASA, 1992, 94, 95. Office: Jet Propulsion Lab 4800 Oak Grove Dr Pasadena CA 91109-8001 E-mail: bruce.chapman@jpl.nasa.gov.

CHAPMAN, CAROLYN, broadcasting director; b. Portsmouth, Ohio, Feb. 4, 1933; d. Roger Donald and Flowery Alice (Callaway) Carr; diploma Portsmouth Interstate Bus. Coll., 1954, S. Ohio Manpower Tng. Ctr., 1965; m. Edward J. Chapman, May 13, 1966; children— Cheryl, Roger, Lisa, Mark, Edmond, Sean. Dep. probation officer Scioto County Juvenile Ct., Portsmouth, 1960-63: coder II, Aid for Aged, Ohio Dept. Pub. Welfare, Columbus, 1964; clk. typist II, Bur. Vital Stats., Dept. Health, Columbus, 1964, clk.-stenographer II, CD Div., 1966; clk.-stenographer ABC, Los Angeles, 1967, ops. coordinator, 1968-72, assoc. dir., on-air dir., 1972—; cons. in video tape and TV prodn.; mem. negotiating com. Teamsters Union, Los Angeles, 1970. Ch. sec. Findlay St. Meth. Ch., Portsmouth, 1959-63, chmn. women's day program, 1962, chmn. commn. on missions, 1959-62, del. ann. conf., Cleve., 1963, sec. ofcl. bd., 1959-62; pres. local chpt. Ohio Republican Council, 1959-62, mem. state bd., 1962, del. from Scioto County to State Rep. Conv., Ohio, 1962; mem. film editing com. Social Health and Hygiene Assn., 1961-62; tribute com. for Tribute to Dorothy Arzner, 1975; Los Angeles Jr. C. of C., 1977. Mem. ABC Employees Assn. (pres. Hollywood branch, 1971-73), Dirs. Guild Am. (council 1981-83). Address: PO Box 43025 Los Angeles CA 90043-0025

CHAPMAN, CONRAD DANIEL, lawyer; b. Detroit, July 31, 1933; s. Conrad F. and Alexandrine C. (Baranski) C.; m. Carol Lynn DeBash, Sept. 1, 1956; children: Stephen Daniel, Richard Thomas, Suzanne Marie. BA, U. Detroit, 1954, JD summa cum laude, 1957; LLM in Taxation, Wayne State U., 1964. Bar: Mich. 1957, U.S. Dist. Ct. (so. dist.) Mich. 1957. Former pres. chmn. of bd. Powers, Chapman, DeAgostino, Meyers & Milia, 1990—2003, of counsel Troy, Mich., 2004—. Mem. ABA, Detroit Bar Assn., Oakland Bar Assn., Met. Detroit Estate Planning Coun., Nat. Assn. Estate Planning Coun., Detroit Athletic Club, Detroit Golf Club. Office: Powers Chapman DeAgostino Meyers & Milia 3001 W Big Beaver Rd Ste 704 Troy MI 48084-3108

CHAPMAN, CRAIG E., lawyer; b. 1954; BA, Conn. Coll, 1977; JD, Case Western Reserve Univ., 1980. Bar: NY 1981. Atty. corp. fin., Sydney, Australia, 1981—83; assoc. Sidley Austin Brown & Wood LLP, NYC, 1983—92, ptnr., 1992—, resident ptnr. Tokyo, 1992—95, also now co-chmn. internat operations and practice devel. com. NYC. Mem.: ABA. Office: Sidley Austin Brown & Wood LLP 787 Seventh Ave New York NY 10019 Office Phone: 212-839-5564. Office Fax: 212-839-5599. Business E-Mail: cchapman@sidley.com.

CHAPMAN, CRAIG J., finance company executive; B in Econs. and Polit. sci., SUNY, Albany. Various exec. positions Household Fin. Corp.; pres. AMRESCO Residential Mortgage Corp., Irvine, Calif., 1997—98; pres., CEO Washington Mutual Fin. Corp., 1998—2004, head, mortgage banking bus., 2004—05; now pres., comml. group Washington Mut., Inc., mem. Pres.'s Coun., 2001. Bd. trustees Seattle Univ. Office: Washington Mut Inc 1201 3d Ave Seattle WA 98101

CHAPMAN, CYNTHIA B., lawyer; b. Bronxville, New York, July 7, 1965; BA in Art History, U. of Calif., San Diego, 1988; JD, U. of San Diego Law School, 1992. Bar: Texas, California. Assoc. English & Gloven, LLP, Seltzer, Caplan, Wilkens, and McMahon; partner Caddell & Chapman. Named one of top 50 Litigators, Nat. Law Journal, 2001, top 40 under 40 most successful litigators, 2002. Mem.: Houston Bar Assoc., Assoc. of Trial Lawyers of Am., Trial Lawyers for Public Justice. Office: Caddell & Chapman The Park in Houston Center 1331 Lamar Houston TX 77010

CHAPMAN, DALAINE, music educator; b. Syracuse, N.Y., Nov. 15, 1960; d. Harold Lewis and Ann Naum Chapman. AA, Brevard C.C., Cocoa, Fla., 1980; B of Music Edn., Fla. State U., 1983, MusM, 2002—. Cert. tchr. Fla. Dir. bands Bartow (Fla.) H.S., 1984—88, Southwest Jr. High, Palm Bay, Fla., 1988—98, Bayside H.S., Palm Bay, Fla., 1998—2001, Titusville HS, 2002—. Resource tchr, music k-12 Brevewal Pub. Schs., 2003—. French horn player Brass Quintet, Melbourne, Fla., 1991—. Mem.: Fla. Music Supr. Assn. (sec.), Fla. Music Educators Assn., Nat. Band Assn., Fla. Bandmasters Assn. (7th & 8th grade chair 1994—96, mid. sch/jr. high rep. 1996—98, all state band conductor, clinician 1999, Benevolence com. chair 2000—, adjudicator intern 2002—, 5 Yr. Superior award 1993, 1998). Home: 246 Van Loon Ave Palm Bay FL 32907

CHAPMAN, DAVID WILFRED, education educator; b. Bklyn., Nov. 5, 1947; s. Joseph Irvine and Shirley Elaine Chapman; m. Sigrid Margaret Hutcheson, Oct. 29, 1978. BA, Syracuse U., NY, 1969; MA, Colgate U., Hamilton, NY, 1970; PhD, Kalamazoo Coll., Mich., 1975. Prof. SUNY, Albany, NY, 1980—97; prof. Coll. Edn., U. Minn., Mpls., 1997—. Dir. Acad. Ednl. Devel., Washington, 1994—97; cons. UNICEF, NYC, 2002—03, Ministry Higher Edn., Oman, 2003—04. Co-editor: (book) The Evaluation of

Educational Efficiency, 1990, Adapting Technology for School Improvement, 2004; contbr. over 100 jour. articles and seven books in field. Mem.: Am. Ednl. Rsch. Assn., Comparative Edn. Soc. (bd. mem. 2002—). Home: 3357 St Louis Ave Minneapolis MN 55416

CHAPMAN, DIANA, academic administrator, social and behavioral sciences educator; BA, Wellesley Coll., 1966; MS, Boston U., 1971, PhD, 1983, LHD (hon.), 1994, Am. Coll. Greece, Athens, 1995, U. Mass., Amherst, 1999. Assoc. dir. Health Policy Inst. Boston U., 1985-90, prof. Sch. Pub. Health, Sch. Medicine, 1987-90, adj. prof., 1990—; chair dept. health and social behavior Harvard Sch. Pub. Health, Cambridge, Mass., 1990-93, adj. prof., 1990—; pres. Wellesley (Mass.) Coll., 1993—. Trustee WGBH Edn. Found., Boston, 1993-2000, Amherst (Mass.) Coll., 1998—; dir. State St. Corp., Boston, 1997—; chair internat. commn. Am. Coun. on Edn., 1998; consortium on financing higher edn. Asian U. for Women. Author: Corporate Physicians, 1987; co-author: Payer, Provide, Consumer, 1977; editor: Women, Work and Health: Challenges to Corporate Policy, 1980; contbr. chpt. to book. Recipient Book of the Yr. award Am. Jour. Nursing, 1980; Kellogg Nat. fellow, 1987-90. Mem. APHA, Am. Sociol. Assn., Soc. for the Study of Social Problems, Mass. Pub. Health Assn. Office: Wellesley Coll Office of the Pres Wellesley MA 02481-8268

CHAPMAN, DICK, retired journalist; b. Kansas City, Mo., Mar. 28, 1930; s. Rudolph Stanley and Clara Mae Chapman; m. Jean Hamilton (div.); children: Connie, Candice, Timothy, Michael; m. Barbara Susan Beerhalter, May 23, 1973. B Journalism, AB in Creative Writing, U. Mo., 1952. Reporter, announcer KCBD Radio, Lubbock, Tex., 1952—53; news dir. KWOS Radio, Jefferson City, Mo., 1953—57, KDWBTV, Jefferson City, 1956—57; reporter, asst. news dir. WCCO Radio, Mpls., 1957—93, outdoor reporter, 1959—60; ret., 1960. Author: When 'CCO Was Cookin' Book, 1995, The Bunjee Cord Bible, 1997. Pres. Twin City local chpt. AFTRA, Mpls., 1970—74; pres., founding mem. Minn. Press Club, Mpls., 1960—85; bd. dirs. Minn. chpt. Multiple Sclerosis Soc., Mpls., 1975; co-founder Muskies, Inc., Mpls., 1960. Recipient award for radio reporting and pub. svc., Soc. Profl. Journalists, 1955, 1965, Radio Pub. Svc. award, DuPont Corp., 1965, George Foster Peabody, 1965, Page One aard, Twin Cities Newspaper Guild, 1983, Good Youth News award, Lowell Thomas, 1987. Mem.: Moose, Elks. Avocations: fishing, hunting, bowling, bicycling. Home: 5400 Three Points Blvd # 315 Mound MN 55364

CHAPMAN, FAY L., lawyer; b. San Jose, Calif., Dec. 17, 1946; BA, UCLA, 1968; JD, NYU, 1972. Bar: N.Y. 1973, Wash. 1975. Atty. Foster Pepper & Shefelman, Seattle, 1979—97; exec. v.p., gen. counsel Washington Mutual, Inc., Seattle, 1997—99; sr. exec. v.p., gen. counsel Washington Mutual Inc, Seattle, 1999—. Mem. Amer Bar Assn., Wash. Bankers Assn., Wash. Savs. League. Office: Washington Mutual Inc 1201 3rd Ave Ste 1601 Seattle WA 98101-3033

CHAPMAN, GARY HOWARD, artist, educator; b. Xenia, Ohio, July 25, 1961; s. Gary Clarke Chapman and Kathleen Ann Cook; m. Bernadette Marie Chapman, Aug. 22, 1992; 1 child, Sadie Louise. BS, BA, Berea Coll., 1984; MFA, Cranbrook Acad. of Art, 1986. Prof. art U. Ala.-Birmingham, 1990—. Instr. Arrowmont Sch. of Arts and Crafts, Gatlinburg, Tenn., summers 1998, 2000, 2002, 2004; vis. artist SUNY, Plattsburgh, 2000, Ariz. State U., Tempe, 2001. One-person shows Wireglass Mus. of Art, 2001, Indpls. Art Ctr., 2003, U. Ark.-Little Rock, 2003, Jule Collins Smith Mus., 2004. Fellow Ala. State Coun. on Arts, 1995, 2001, Nat. Endowment for Arts, 1996; commd. artist Hoar Constrn. Co., Birmingham, 1999. Home: 1425 16th Ave S Birmingham AL 35205 Office: U Ala-Birmingham Dept Art and Art History Birmingham AL 35294 Office Phone: 205-934-4941. E-mail: painter@uab.edu, painter@aol.com.

CHAPMAN, GERALD FREDERICK, lawyer, banker; b. Jackson, Mich., Apr. 27, 1948; s. C. Joseph and Vera Ann Chapman; m. Mary Daugherty; children: Anne, Erin, John, Lindsay, Caroline. BA, Mich. State U., 1972; JD, U. Balt., 1978. Bar: Md., D.C., U.S. Dist. Ct. D.C., U.S. Dist. Ct. Md. Dep. dir. enforcement Fed. Home Loan Bank Bd., Washington, 1978-85; pres. Vista Fed. Savs. Bank, Reston, Va., 1985-92, City Nat. Bank, Washington, 1992-93; ptnr. Cooter, Mangold, Tompert & Chapman, Washington, 1993-97; prin. Gerald F. Chapman, LLC, Bethesda, Md., 1997—. Treas. Young Pres. Orgn., 1989-92. With U.S. Army, 1967-70. Mem. ABA. Democrat. Roman Catholic. Office: 6917 Arlington Rd Ste 214 Bethesda MD 20814-5289

CHAPMAN, GILBERT BRYANT, physicist; b. Uniontown, Ala., July 8, 1935; s. Gilbert Bryant and Annie Lillie (Stallworth) Chapman; m. Loretta Woodward, June 5, 1960 (dec. Sept. 1994); children: Annie L., Bernice M., Cedric N., David O., Ernest P., Frances Q. H., Gilbert Bryant III; m. Betty J. Ellis, June 27, 1999. BS in Math. and Chemistry, Baldwin Wallace Coll., Berea, Ohio, 1968; MS in Physics, Cleve. State U., 1973; MBA, Mich. State U., 1990; postgrad., Kent State U., Ohio, 1974-76, U. Windsor, Ont., Can., 2001—. Phys. sci. technician NASA-Lewis Rsch. Ctr., Cleve., 1953—68, emission spectroscopist, 1968—75, materials engr., 1975—77; sr. rsch. engr. Ford Motor Co., Redford Twp., Mich., 1977—83, project engr., 1983—86; adv. materials testing specialist Chrysler Corp., Highland Park, Mich., 1986—89, adv. materials specialist Madison Heights, Mich., 1989—91, advanced materials and product exec., 1991—95, advanced materials cons., 1995—98; sr. mgr. advanced materials and product devel. DaimlerChrylser Corp., Rochester Hills, Mich., 1998—2003, dir. advanced transp. tech., 2003—. Chmn. auto com. '87 Soc. Mfg. Engrs. Composites Group, Dearborn, Mich., 1987, chair bd. dirs., 96; chmn. ind. adv. bd. NDE/Ctr., Iowa State U., Ames, 1989, Ames, 90; mem. indsl. adv. bd. Inst. Mfg. Rsch., Wayne State U., Ctrl. State U., U. Tex.-Pan Am., U. Mich., Dearborn, Oakland U., Rochester, Mich.; chair Internat. Symposium Automotive Tech. and Automation Materials Conf., 1996, 98, Automotive Composites Consortium, 1996. Contbr. articles to profl. jours., chapters to books. Trustee Mt. Vernon Acad. Ohio, Ohio, 1972—76; lay adv. coun. Ohio Conf. SDA, 1974—77; lay leader, elder SDA Ch., Southfield, Mich., 1983—95, elder Farmington Hills, Mich., 2000—. With USAF, 1959—61. Named Black Engr. of the Yr., U.S. Black Engr. and Info. Tech. Mag., 1999; named one of Best and Brightest Profls., Dollars and Sense Mag., 1993; recipient Apollo Achievement award, NASA Lewis Rsch. Ctr., 1968, Group Achievement award, 1970, Mayor Archer's proclamation, Motor City Youth Fedn., 1994, Spirit of Detroit award, Detroit City Coun., 1994, Career Achievement award, U.S. Black Engr. and Info. Tech. Mag., 1999. Fellow: Am. Soc. Nondestructive Testing (cert. level III 6 NDT methods); mem.: SAE (award for excellence in oral presentation), ASTM, IEEE, ASM (mem. polymer composites program com. 1986), Soc. Mfg. Engrs. (chaired CMA adv. bd.), Soc. Applied Spectroscopy (Cleve. vice chair, sec.), Nat. Tech. Assn. (mem. Cleve. program com.), Fedn. Analytical Chemists, Engring. Soc. Detroit (mem. sci. com., ASM/ESD Best Paper award 1993), Can. Assn. Physicists, Am. Soc. Composites, Am. Phys. Soc., Am. Chem. Soc., Soc. Physics Students. Achievements include patents for infrared inspection method for friction welds in thermoplastics and advanced vehicle concepts; development of low-frequency ultrasonic inspection methods for polymer composites and adhesive bond joints; co-development of D.C. arc method of determining work functions of refractory alloys, spectrochemical analysis of microgram-size samples. Home and Office: Advanced Transp Techs 38671 Greenbrook Ct Farmington Hills MI 48331-2979 Office Phone: 248-324-5037. Personal E-mail: gbchapman2@aol.com. *The persistant pursuit of moral and ethical values, faith and the concomitant virtues while seeking to serve more effectively, can lead to a successful and satisfying life.*

CHAPMAN, GILBERT WHIPPLE, JR., publishing company executive; b. N.Y.C., July 1, 1933; s. Gilbert W. and Katherin (Bright) C.; m. Judith Coste, June 14, 1956; 1 child, Gilbert W. III BA, Yale U., 1956. Pub. McGraw-Hill, Inc., N.Y.C., 1958-72; exec. v.p., dir. Morgan Grampain, Inc., N.Y.C., 1971-75; pres. Pub. Group Esquire Inc., N.Y.C., 1975-78; pres., dir. Diversion Communications, Inc., N.Y.C., 1978-85, Kalo Communications, Inc., N.Y.C., 1985-91; chmn., CEO Cemark, Inc., 1991—. Trustee Village of Mill Neck, 1993—2000, Choate Sch., Wallingford, Conn., 1986—91, Pomfret Sch., 1980—86; bd. dirs. Planned Parenthood of Nassau County, 1985—2002, Planned Parenthood of Nassau County Found., 2000—, Cmty. Hosp. of Glen Cove, 1986—90, North Shore U. Hosp., 1990—94. Mem.: Piping Rock Club (pres. 2000—), Racquet and Tennis Club. Republican. Episcopalian. Home: Factory Pond Rd Locust Valley NY 11560-1405 Office: 13531 E Boundary Rd Midlothian VA 23112-3953

CHAPMAN, H. PERRY, art educator; BA, Swathmore Coll.; PhD, Princeton U. Assoc. chair, prof., Dept. Art Hist. U. Del. Co-curator (exhibiton) Jan Steen: Painter and Storyteller, Nat. Gallery Art & Rijksmuseum, Amsterdam, 1996—97; author: Rembrandt's Self-Portraits: A Study in Seventeenth-Century Identity, 1990; editor: U. Del. Art Bulletin, 2000—04. Fellow Woodrow Wilson Ctr., 1990—91, Nat. Endowment for Humanities, 1993—94, Guggenheim Meml. Found., 2004. Office: U Del Dept Art Hist Office 323 OCL 318 Old College Newark DE 19716-2516 Office Phone: 302-831-2242. E-mail: pchapman@udel.edu.*

CHAPMAN, HUGH MCMASTER, banker; b. Spartanburg, S.C., Sept. 11, 1932; s. James Alfred and Martha (Marshall) Chapman; m. Anne Allston Morrson, Dec. 27, 1958 (dec. Mar. 1993); children: Anne Allston, Rachel Buchanan, Mary Morrison; m. Janis Guzzle, Aug. 17, 2001. BSBA, U. N.C., 1955. With Citizens & So. Nat. Bank S.C., 1958-91, pres., 1971-74, chmn. bd., 1974-91; pres. Citizens & So. Corp., Atlanta, 1986-91; vice chmn. C&S/Sovran Corp., 1990-91; chmn. Nations Bank S., 1992-97; ret., 1997. Bd. dirs. Inman Mills., West Point Stevens, Williams Cos. Trustee East Lake Cmty. Fedn., Duke Endowment. 1st lt. USAF, 1955-57. Office: Bank of Am Plz 600 Peachtree St Fl 16 Atlanta GA 30308-2265

CHAPMAN, JACQUELYN SULLIVAN, retired elementary school educator; b. Chgo., June 6, 1928; d. Harold Patrick and Alyce Cecilia (Hagan) Sullivan; m. James H. Chapman, June 23, 1951; children: Kevin, Brian, Mark. BA, Clark Coll., Dubuque, Iowa, 1949; MusM, DePaul U., 1951; student, U. Galney, 1980, Coll. New Rochelle. Tchr. music various jr. high and high schs., spl. edn. educator, cons. Chgo. Bd. Edn., 1950-93; ret., 1993. Vol. Park Ridge (Ill.) Garden Club, 1972—, 20th Century Club, Park Ridge, 1993—, Park Ridge Women's Club, 1993—; active Found. Internat. Rels., Chgo., 1993—. Mem.: Clarke Coll. Alumnae Assn. (pres. 1960—65), Delta Kappa Gamma (pres. Kappa chpt. 1990—92, chmn. sect. music 1974—90). Roman Catholic. Avocations: travel, piano, literature, European antiques, opera. Home: 1604 S Western Ave Park Ridge IL 60068-5066

CHAPMAN, JOHN ANDREW, retired chamber of commerce executive; b. Evanston, Ill., Oct. 12, 1928; s. Roger Edington and Margaret Holloway (Morgan) Chapman; m. Betsy Miller, June 23, 1951; children: Andrew K., Jean M., Margaret(dec.), Peter S. BS, Northwestern U., 1950. Cert. Nat. Inst. Orgn. Mgmt., C. of C. exec. Asst. dir. pub. rels. Northwestern U., Evanston, 1950-54; asst. mgr. Joliet (Ill.) Assn. Commerce, 1954-57; mgr. Twin Cities Area C. of C., Benton Harbor/St. Joseph, Mich., 1957-67; pres. Muskegon Area Devel. Coun. and C. of C., Mich., 1967-74, Charleston (W.Va.) C. of C., 1974-94; mng. dir. Kanawha Pastoral Counseling Ctr., 1994-98; ret., 1998. Former chmn. Berrien County (Mich.) Planning Commn.; past treas. Tri-Cap, Inc.; mem. emeritus Salvation Army, Charleston; dir., past pres. Kanawha County Pub. Safety Coun.; bd. dirs. Good News Mountaineer Garage; former mem. Cmty. Coun. Charleston Job Corps; past chmn. Charleston Police Civilian Rev. Bd.; mem. U.S. Atty. Heavy Metal Task Force; co-chair Coun. Historic Orgns.; past vestryman St. John's, St. Edward's and St. Gregory's Episcopal Ch.; past warden St. Augustine's Episcopal Ch.; former bd. dirs. Charleston Symphony; bd. dirs. Charleston Renaissance Corp.; past v.p. Southwestern br. Mich. Children's Aid Soc.; past sec. Bishop Whittemore Found.; past treas. W.Va. Taxpayers Assn.; past pres. Charleston Leadership Coun. Pub. Safety; past vice-chair W.Va. Regional Cmty. Policing Inst.; vice-chair Eisenhower Math.-Sci. Consortium; dir., past v.p. Craik-Patton House, Inc.; treas. Craik-Patton House Found. Mem.: So. Assn. C. of C. Execs. (past pres., sec.), Am. C. of C. Execs. (bd. dirs.), Mich. C. of C. Execs. (past pres.), W.Va. C. of C. Execs. (past pres.), Anvil Club, Rotary. Republican. Home: 209 Ashby Ave Charleston WV 25314-1009 E-mail: johnandbetsy51@yahoo.com.

CHAPMAN, LEWIS DUANE, economist; b. Sept. 3, 1940; s. Lewis Ray and Alice Louise (Fullerton) Chapman; m. Mary Jane Angelacos, Aug. 16, 1961 (div. 1986); children: Erin Marie, Amy Nicole; m. Josephine Carol Crossley, Feb. 22, 1991 (div. 1998). BA, Mich. State U., 1961; PhD, U. Calif., Berkeley, 1969. Economist Oak Ridge (Tenn.) Nat. Lab., 1969—71; asst. prof. dept. applied econs. and mgmt. Cornell U., Ithaca, NY, 1971—76, assoc. prof., 1976—82, prof., 1982—, coord. Climate Change Rsch. Program, 1993—97. Leader, industry and the urban environ. U.S. AID, 1991—95. Author: Energy Resources and Energy Corporations, 1983, Environmental Economics, Theory, Application and Policy, 2000; mem. editl. bd.: Contemporary Econ. Policy, Internat. Jour. Environ. Sci. and Tech.; contbr. articles to 180 profl. jours. Task force on regional transmission Nat. Gov.'s Assn., 2001—02. Scholar, Fulbright Found., U. Natal, South Africa and U. Zimbabwe, 1991. Mem.: NAS (mem. nuc. power panel 1976—80, mem. electric power panel 1986, mem. U.S.-Czechoslovakia agr. and environ. panel 1986—87), Internat. Soc. Ecol. Econs., Western Econ. Assn. Internat., Assn. Environ. and Resource Economists, Internat. Assn. Energy Economists, Am. Econ. Assn. Avocations: hiking, tennis, travel, snow shoeing. Office: Cornell U 246 Warren Hall Ithaca NY 14853-7801 Office Phone: 607-255-4516.

CHAPMAN, LINDA LEE, computer company executive, consultant; b. Omaha, Apr. 27, 1965; d. Olin Parks Chapman and Phyllis May Chapman-Wakefield; m. Chris Barkley; children: Lea Lee Noell, Phillip Wayne Noell, Cameron David Barkley, Jasmine Lauren Barkley. Grad., Centennial H.S., Utica, Nebr., 1983. MCSE, MCP Microsoft, cert. product specialist NT 4.0 Enterprise Microsoft, product Ssecialist NT 4.0 Workstation Microsoft, product specialist NT 4.0 Server Microsoft, product specialist IIS 3.0 and Index Server Microsoft. LAN mgr. and programmer Wiig-Codr Underwriters, Omaha, 1986—93; sr. IT engr. MCI Consumer Markets, Austin, Tex., 1993—94; sr. migration cons. Levi-Strauss & Co., San Fransisco, 1994—95, Advanced Micro Devices (AMD), Austin, 1995—96; sr. migration cons., tech. project mgr. Continental Airlines, Houston, 1996—97; sr. migration cons., global arch. Dell Computer Corp., Round Rock, Tex., 1997—99, sr. product mgr., 1999—2000; pres., CEO, founder Migration Specialists Inc., Round Rock, 2001—. Recipient Outstanding Tech. Article award, 2000. E-mail: linda.chapman@migrationspecialistsinc.com.

CHAPMAN, LOREN J., psychology professor; b. Muncie, Ind., Jan. 5, 1927; s. Herbert L. and Lurana Gertrude (Treff) C.; m. Jean Marilyn Paulsen, June 6, 1953; children: Nancy, Laurence. AB cum laude, Harvard U., 1948; MS, Northwestern U., 1952, PhD, 1954. USPHS postdoctorate research fellow U. Chgo., 1954-56, instr., asst. prof., 1956-59; assoc. prof. U. Ky., Lexington, 1959-62; from assoc. prof. to prof. Southern Ill. U., Carbondale, 1962-67; prof. U. Wis., Madison, 1966-93, NIMH rsch. scientist, 1988-93; prof. emeritus, 1994—. Author: Disordered Thought in Schizophrenia, 1973; contbr. articles to profl. jours. Recipient Disting. Scientist award Soc. for Sci. Clin. Psychology, 1992; NIMH research grantee, 1952-97. Fellow AAAS, APA (Disting. Sci. award for application of psychology 1999); mem. Am. Psychopathol. Assn., Soc. Rsch. Psychopathology (pres. 1989, Joseph Zubin award 1992), Am. Psychol. Soc. (William James fellow 1995). Home: 129 Richland Ln Madison WI 53705-4834 Office: Univ Wis Dept Psychology 1202 W Johnson St Madison WI 53706-1611

CHAPMAN, MARY KATHRYN, elementary school educator; b. Birmingham, Ala., May 31, 1958; d. Vincent and Mary Helen (Treadwell) York; m. Jere Clark Chapman, Dec. 18, 1982; children: Lacy Dawn, John Luke. BS in Edn., Auburn U., 1980, MS, 1982. Cert. tchr., Ala., Tex. Tchr. elem. Fews Elem Sch., Montgomery, 1980—83; tchr. elem., computer rep. Morningview Elem. Sch., Montgomery, 1988—91; tchr. phys. edn. Jackson Elem. Sch., Abilene, Tex., 1983—85, Austin Elem. Sch., Abilene, 1986—87; tchr. W.L. Radney Elem. Sch., Alexander City, Ala., 1991—98, tchr. drama, 1991—94, mem. bldg. leadership team, 1994—95; tchr. Alexander City Mid. Sch., 1998—. Workshop presenter Montgomery Schs., 1990. Sunday sch. and Bible sch. tchr. Alexander City Ch. of Christ, 1991—; adult leader Girl Scouts U.S.A., Alexander City, 1992—; sponsor Alexander City Cheerleaders, 1992. Named Tchr. of Yr., Alexander City Sch., 1993, Alexander City C. of C., 1993; recipient Class Act award Sta. WSFA-TV, Montgomery, 1994. Mem. NEA, Ala. Edn. Assn. Avocations: gymnastics, swimming, reading, sewing, jogging. Home: 1953 Morningside Dr Alexander City AL 35010-3154 Office: Alexander City Mid Sch 359 State St Alexander City AL 35010

CHAPMAN, MATTHEW JOHN, music educator; s. David N. and Chapman, David N. and Christine Y. Chapman; m. Julie C. Anderson, Nov. 5, 1995; 1 child, Mackenzie Rose. MusB in Edn., Ill. State U., 1993. Ill. State Tchrs. Cert. Ill. Sch. Bd., 1993, Ill. Tchg. Cert. Ill. Music educator Flanagan Dist. #4, Ill., 1993—94, Illinios Valley Ctrl. Dist. #321, Chillicothe, Ill., 1994—. Dir.: (jazz band) Dist. #2 Jh Jazz Dir. (dir. of dist. #2 jh honors jazz band, 2000). Mem.: Ill. Music Educators Assn. Office: Mossville JH and Grade Sch 12207 N Old Galena Rd Mossville IL 61552 Office Phone: 309-579-2328. Home Fax: 309-579-2168; Office Fax: 309-579-2168. Personal E-mail: chapman_matthew@hotmail.com.

CHAPMAN, MAX C., JR., investment company executive; b. June 1943; MBA, Columbia Bus. Sch., 1969. Pres., COO Kidder, Peabody & Co; former co-chmn. of bd., CEO Nomura Securities Internat., NYC; former chmn. bd. Nomura Holding Am. Inc., 1996; former chmn. Gardner Capital Management Corp., NYC. Chmn. bd. Nat. Fish & Wildlife Found.; bd. overseers Columbia Bus. Sch., NYC; bd. trustees Intrepid Sea, Air, Space Mus. Mailing: Ste 2200 400 Park Ave New York NY 10022

CHAPMAN, MICHAEL SANDERS, music educator; b. Atlanta, Ga., Dec. 14, 1949; s. Harvey Holcomb Chapman Jr. and Marjorie Worsham Chapman. BME, Troy State U., 1972, MS, 1991. Band dir. Valdosta City Sch., Valdosta, Ga., 1972—81, Escambia County Sch., Pensacola, Fla., 1981—88, Decatur County Sch., Bainbridge, Ga., 1988—. Home: 1405 Pineland Dr Bainbridge GA 39819 Office Phone: 229-248-0233.

CHAPMAN, MICHAEL WILLIAM, orthopedist, educator; b. Newberry, Mich., Nov. 29, 1937; m. Elizabeth Casady; adopted sons: Mark, Craig. AA, Am. River Coll., Sacramento, Calif., 1957; BA, U. Calif., Davis, 1958; BS, U. Calif., San Francisco, 1959, MD, 1962. Diplomate Am. Bd. Orthopaedic Surgery (ad hoc appeal com. 1986, site visitor 1986, certification renewal com. 1985-88, certification renewal com. chmn. 1986-88). Intern San Francisco Gen. Hosp., 1962-63, asst. chief orthopaedic surgery svc., 1971-79, acting chief orthopaedic surgery svc., 1972-73; resident in orthopaedic surgery U. Calif., San Francisco, 1963-67, asst. prof. dept. orthopaedic surgery, Sch. Medicine, 1971-76, assoc. prof. dept. orthopaedic surgery, Sch. Medicine, 1976-79; resident in orthopaedic surgery U. Calif. Hosps., San Francisco, 1963-64, Samuel Merritt Hosp., Oakland, Calif., 1964, Highland-Alameda County Hosp., Oakland, 1965, Children's Hosp. of the East Bay, Oakland, 1966, Shriners Hosp., Honolulu, 1966-67; fellow Nat. Orthopaedic Hosp., London, 1967-68; chmn. dept. orthopaedic surgery U. Calif., Davis, Sacramento, 1979-99, prof. dept. orthopaedic surgery, 1981-2000, David Linn chair orthopaedic surgery, 1998-2001, prof. emeritus, 2000—. Panelist Calif. Crippled Children Svcs. Panel in Orthopaedic Surgery; cons. VA Hospital, Martinez, Calif.; co-chmn. Zimmer Trauma Panel, 1983-84; vis. prof. Fresno Valley Med. Ctr., 1975, Dept. Orthopaedics, U. Calif., Davis, 1976, U. Hawaii, Honolulu, 1977; vis. prof., cons. to Surgeon Gen. U.S. Army, Europe, 1978; vis. prof. U. Basel, Switzerland, 1979, Phoenix Orthopaedic Residency Program, 1979, Stanford U., 1981, U. Hawaii, 1982, U. So. Calif., L.A., 1984, SUNY, Buffalo, 1985, U. Utah, 1985, U. Iowa Coll. Medicine, 1987, Duke U. Sch. Medicine, 1988, U. Calif. Irvine, Div. Orthopaedics, 1990, U. S.C., 1990, Mass. Gen. Hosp., Harvard U., 1990, Boston U., 1994, Stanford U., 1995, Med. Coll. Pa., 1996, numerous others; also guest lectr. numerous instns.; insp. for residency rev. com. ad hoc appeal com. Accreditation coun. for Grad. Med. Specialist Site, 1983-86. Editor: (with M. Madison) Operative Orthopaedics, 1988 (Best New Book in Clin. Medicine Assn. Am. Pubs.); contbr. numerous articles and numerous abstracts to profl. jours.; presenter exhibits, audiovisual programs, some 500 other presentations; cons. editor Skiing Mag., 1973-77; mem. bd. assoc. editors Clin. Orthopaedics and Related Rsch., 1982-85, Internat. Med. Soc. Paraplegia, 1972-80; reviewer Jour. Bone and Joint Surgery, 1980-85, trustee, 1995-03, sec. to bd. trustees, 1999, chmn. bd. trustees, 2000; past reviewer New Eng. Jour. Medicine; patentee in field. With U.S. Army, 1968-70. Decorated Army Commendation medal; recipient Outstanding Tchg. award U. Calif., San Francisco, 1972, Outstanding Tchr. award U. Calif., Davis, 1984, 93; named One of Best 100 Doctors Am., Good Housekeeping Mag.; Fogarty Sr. Internat. fellow NIH, 1978-79, 80-81; grantee Johnson & Johnson, 1983-84, Zimmer Inc., 1983-85, 85-86, 87-90, Interpore Internat., 1985-86, 89-90, Collagen Inc., 1985-86, 88-89, Upjohn Inc., 1985-86, Orthopaedic Rsch. and Edn. Found., 1988-89. Mem. AMA (Physicians Recognition award 1989-96), ACS, Am. Acad. Orthopaedic Surgeons (bd. dirs. 1982-83, numerous coms., Zimmer award for Disting. Contbn. to Orthop. Surgery, 2002), Am. Orthopaedic Assn. (bd. dirs. 1985-86, pres. 1990-91, various coms.), Internat. Orthopaedic Assn., Assn. for Study of Internal Fixation (N.Am. chpt.), Internat. Soc. Orthopaedic Surgery and Traumatology, Internat. Soc. for Fracture Repair, Brit. Orthopaedic Assn., South African Orthopaedic Assn. (hon.), Am. Acad. Orthopaedic Surgeons, Am. Assn. for Surgery of Trauma, Am. Bd. Med. Spltys., Assn. Am. Med. Colls., Leroy C. Abbott Orthopaedic Soc., Austrian Trauma Assn., Paul R. Lipscomb Soc., Northwestern Med. Assn., Orthopaedic Rsch. Soc., Orthopaedic Trauma Assn., Sierra Club, U. Calif. San Francisco Alumni Assn., Western Orthopaedic Assn., Houston Orthopaedic Assn. (hon.), Calif. Med. Assn., Calif. Orthopaedic Assn., Sacramento-El Dorado Med. Soc., Wilson Interurban Orthopaedic Soc., Alpha Omega Alpha. Avocations: skiing, mountain climbing, backpacking, tennis, bicycling. Office: U Calif-Davis Sch Med Dept Orthopedics 4860 Y St Ste 3800 Sacramento CA 95817-2307

CHAPMAN, MORRIS HINES, denominational executive; b. Kosciusko, Miss. m. Jodi Francis; 2 children. Grad., Miss. Coll.; MDiv, D of Ministry, Southwestern Bapt. Theol. Sem.; hon. doctorates, S.W. Bapt. U., Miss. Coll. Pastor 1st Bapt. Ch., Albuquerque, 1974-79, Wichita Falls, Tex., 1979-92; pres. So. Bapt. Conv., 1990-92, pres., CEO, exec. com., 1992—. Pres. pastor's conf. So. Bapt. Conv., 1986, preacher Conv. Sermon, Las Vegas, 1989. Author: Faith: Taking God at His Word, The Wedding Collection. Office: Executive Committee Southern Baptist Convention 901 Commerce St Nashville TN 37203-3620

CHAPMAN, NATALIE PRICHARD, publishing executive; b. Palo Alto, Calif., Sept. 13, 1949; d. J. Warren and Virginia Carr Chapman; m. Galen Douglas Kirkland, May 31, 1986. BA, Smith Coll., 1971. Editor Holt, Rinehart & Winston, N.Y., 1972—85; sr. editor Consumer Reports Books, N.Y., 1987—89, Macmillan Publishing, N.Y., 1989—94, pub. Macmillan Books, 1994—98; v.p., pub. dir. Discovery Comms., N.Y., 1998—2000; pub. Creative Homeowner Press, Upper Saddle River, NJ, 2000—01; v.p., pub. culinary John Wiley & Sons Pubs., Hoboken, NJ, 2002—. Pres. Park River Ind. Dems., N.Y.C., 1989—91. Mem.: Women's Media Group, Internat. Assn. Culinary Profls. Home: 329 W 88th St New York NY 10024 Office: Wiley Publishing Inc 111 River St Hoboken NJ 07030-5773

CHAPMAN, ORVILLE LAMAR, chemist, educator; b. New London, Conn., June 26, 1932; s. Orville Carmen and Mabel Elnora (Tyree) C.; m. Faye Newton Morrow, Aug. 20, 1955 (div. 1980); children: Kenneth, Kevin; m. Susan Elizabeth Parker, June 15, 1981. BS, Va. Poly. Inst., 1954; PhD, Cornell U., 1957. Instr. chemistry Iowa State U., 1957-59, asst. prof., 1959-62, assoc. prof., 1962-65, Prof. chemistry, 1965-74; prof. chemistry UCLA, 1974—. Cons. Mobil Chem. Co., 1964—98. Recipient NYAS award, 1974, Founders prize, Tex. Instruments, George and Freda Halpern award in phothchemstry, N.Y. Acad. Scis., 1978, Outstanding Patent of Yr. award, Mobil Corp., 1992, Best Use of Info. Tech. in Edn. and Academia award, Computer World/Smithsonian Instn. Mem. Am. Chem. Soc. (award in pure chemistry 1968, Arthur C. Cope award 1978, Midwest award 1978, Havinga medal 1982, McCoy award UCLA, 1985). Home: 1213 Roscomare Rd Los Angeles CA 90077-2202 Office: UCLA Dept Chemistry 405 Hilgard Ave Los Angeles CA 90095-9000 E-mail: chapman@chem.ucla.edu.

CHAPMAN, PAUL B., oncologist; b. Chgo., 1955; MD, Cornell U., Ithaca, N.Y., 1981. Diplomate Am. Bd. Internal Medicine, Am. Bd. Med. Oncology. Intern U. Chgo. Hosp., 1981—82, resident, 1982—84; fellow Meml. Sloan-Kettering Cancer Ctr., N.Y.C., 1984; pvt. practice med. oncology N.Y.C., 1984—. Assoc. attending physician Meml. Sloan-Kettering Cancer Ctr., N.Y.C., 1992—; assoc. prof. medicine Cornell U. Med. Coll. Office: 1275 York Ave New York NY 10021-6007

CHAPMAN, PAUL H., pediatric neurosurgeon; BS in Biophysics, Yale U., 1960; MD, Harvard U., 1964. Diplomate Am. Bd. Pediatric Neurosurgery, Am. Bd. Neurosurgery. Resident in neurosurgery Mass. Gen. Hosp., 1972, unit chief pediatric neurosurgery, dir. cyclotron proton beam/neurosurg. radiosurgery unit; Nicholas T. Zervas prof. neurosurgery Harvard Med. Sch. Vis. neurosurgeon, neurosurg. radiation oncologist Mass. Gen. Hosp. Office: Mass Gen Hosp 55 Fruit St GRB502 Boston MA 02114

CHAPMAN, PETER HERBERT, investment company executive; b. Stockton, Calif., Mar. 6, 1953; s. Duff Gordon and Emalee (Sala) C.; m. Diane Chapman Clark; children: Charlotte Moseley, Alexander Clark. BA, Columbia U., 1977. V.p. Salomon Bros., Inc., N.Y.C., 1977-86, The First Boston Corp., N.Y.C., 1986—90; sr. vp. Bessemer Group, Inc., N.Y.C., 1991-92; exec. dir. CIBC Oppenheimer Corp., N.Y.C., 1993-99; chmn. PH Chapman Advisors, LLC, N.Y.C., 1999—; mng. dir. CDK Group LLC, N.Y.C, 2002—. Bd. dirs. C.D. Stimson Co., Seattle, 1988-92. Bd. dirs. Am. Internat. Sch., Florence, Italy, 1982-94, Mulsanne Capital Ltd Mem. Soc. Calif. Pioneers, The Links Club, Racquet and Tennis Club, Piping Rock Club, Knickerbocker Club, The Pilgrims, Tamasack Preserve, Mashomack Preserve Republican. Home: 923 Fifth Ave New York NY 10021-2649 Office Phone: 212-871-8500. E-mail: chapmail@ad.com.

CHAPMAN, RICHARD LEROY, public information officer, researcher; b. Yankton, SD, Feb. 4, 1932; s. Raymond Young and Vera Everette (Trimble) C.; m. Marilyn Jean Nicholson, Aug. 14, 1955; children: Catherine Ruth Hoff, Robert Matthew, Michael David, Stephen Raymond, Amy Jean Johnson. BS, S.D. State U., 1954; postgrad., Cambridge (Eng.) U., 1954-55; MPA, Syracuse U., 1958, PhD, 1967. With Office of Sec. of Def., 1958-59, 61-63; dep. dir. rsch. S.D. Legis. Rsch. Coun., 1959-60; mem. staff Bur. of the Budget, Exec. Office of Pres., Washington, 1960-61; profl. staff mem. com. govt. ops. U.S. Ho. of Reps., Washington, 1966; program dir. NIH, Bethesda, Md., 1967-68; sr. rsch. assoc. Nat. Acad. Pub. Adminstrn., Washington, 1968-72, dep. exec. dir., 1973-76, v.p., dir. rsch., 1976-82; sr. rsch. scientist Denver Rsch. Inst., 1982-86; mem. adv. com. Denver Rsch. Inst. U. Denver, 1984-86; ptnr. Milliken Chapman Rsch. Group Inc., Denver, 1986-88; v.p. Chapman Rsch. Group, Inc., Centennial, Colo., 1988—98, ret., 1998. Cons. U.S. Office Pers. Mgmt., Washington, 1977-81, Denver, 1986-98; cons. CIA, Washington, 1979, 80, 81, Arthur S. Fleming Awards, Washington, 1977-81; exec. staff dir., cons. U.S. Congressman Frank Denholm; lectr. on sci., tech., govt. and pub. mgmt. Author: (with Fred Grissom) Mining the Nation's Braintrust, 1992; contbr. over 70 articles and revs. to profl. jours. and congl. staff reports. Mem. aerospace com. Colo. Commn. Higher Edn., Denver, 1982-83; chmn. rules com. U. Denver Senate, 1984-85; bd. dirs. S.E. Englewood Water Dist., Littleton, 1984-88, pres. 1986-88; mem. strategic planning com. Mission Hills Bapt. Ch., 1986; bd. dirs. Lay Action Ministry Program, 1988-96, chmn. 1992-96; established Vera and Raymond Chapman Scholarship Fund, S.D. State U.; mem. Fairfax County Rep. Ctrl. Com., Va., 1969-71, Fairfax County Com. of 100, 1979-82. With U.S. Army, 1955-57, Korea, capt. Res. Syracuse U. Maxwell Sch. fellow, 1957-58, 63-64, Brookings Inst. fellow, 1964-65. Mem. Tech. Transfer Soc. (bd. dirs. 1987-95, Pres.'s award 1991, founder Colo. chpt., Thomas Jefferson award 1996), Fed. Lab. Consortium (nat. adv. com. 1989-98), S.D. State U. Found. (bd. dirs. 1992-98, vice chmn. 1994-96, chmn. bd. 1996-98), Southglen Country Club, Masons, KT, Order of DeMolay (Cross of Honor 1982), Rotary (fellow Internat. Found. 1954-55, Paul Harris fellow 1989). Republican. Avocations: hunting, fishing, golf, reading, gardening. *Treat all of life as an opportunity to learn and to contribute. As one enriches the lives of others, you receive great satisfaction and returns that cannot be imagined.*

CHAPMAN, ROBERT FOSTER, federal judge; b. Inman, S.C., Apr. 24, 1926; s. James Alfred and Martha (Marshall) Chapman; m. Mary Winston Gwathmey, Dec. 21, 1951 (dec. Sept. 1998); children: Edward, Foster, Winston; m. Mary Vail St. Georges, Sept. 30, 2000. BS, U. S.C., 1945, LLB, 1949, LLD (hon.), 1986, Coll. Charleston, 1999. Bar: S.C. 1949. Assoc. firm Butler & Moore, Spartanburg, 1949—51; partner firm Butler, Chapman & Morgan, Spartanburg, 1953—71; U.S. dist. judge for S.C., 1971—81; U.S. cir. judge, 1981—. Chmn. S.C. Rep. Party, 1961—63. Lt. USNR, 1943—46, lt. USNR, 1951—53. Recipient Nat. Patriot's award, Congl. Medal of Honor Soc., 1985. Fellow: Am. Coll. Trial Lawyers. Presbyterian. Home: PO Box 1043 Camden SC 29020-1043

CHAPMAN, ROBERT GALBRAITH, retired hematologist, administrator; b. Colorado Springs, Colo., Sept. 29, 1926; s. Edward Northrop and Janet Galbraith (Johnson) Chapman; m. Virginia Irene Potts, July 6, 1956; children: Lucia Tully, Sarah Northrop Bohrer, Robert Bostwick. Student, Westminster Coll., 1944-45; BA, Yale U., 1947; MD, Harvard U., 1951; MS, U. Colo., 1958. Diplomate Am. Bd. Internal Medicine and Pathology; lic. physician, Colo., Calif. Intern Hartford (Conn.) Hosp., 1951-52; resident in medicine U. Colo. Med. Ctr., Denver, 1955-58; fellow in hematology U. Wash., Seattle, 1958-60; chief resident in medicine U. Colo., Denver, 1957-58, instr. medicine, 1960-62, asst. prof. medicine, 1962-68, assoc. prof., 1968-91; chief staff VA Hosp., Denver, 1968-70; dir. Belle Bonfils Meml. Blood Ctr., Denver, 1977-91, retired, 1991. Regionalization com. Am. Blood Commn., Washington, 1985-87, Colo.sickle cell com., Denver, 1978-91, gov.'s AIDS Coun., 1987-88; trustee Coun. Community Blood Ctrs., v.p., 1979-81, pres., 1989-91, rsch. inst. bd. Palo Alto Med. Found., 1991-97. Contbr. articles to profl. jours. Treas. Carmel Valley Village Improvement Com., 1995—. Capt. USAF, 1953-55. USPHS fellow, 1958-60. Fellow ACP; mem. Am. Assn. Blood Banks, Mayflower Soc., Denver Med. Soc., Colo. Med. Soc., Western Soc. Clin. Rsch., Am. Radio Relay League, Alpha Omega Alpha. Mem. United Ch. Christ. Avocations: amateur radio, computers, investments, genealogy. Home: 47 La Rancheria Carmel Valley CA 93924-9424 E-mail: drrob@redshift.com.

CHAPMAN, ROBERT JAMES, psychiatrist, educator; b. Delaware, Ohio, July 10, 1936; s. Edward Samuel and Frances Mae (Stephenson) Chapman; m. Janice Holmes, June 18, 1960; children: Steven Holmes, Scott Edward, Erik Wellington. AB, Oberlin Coll., 1958; MD, Ohio State U., 1963. Diplomate Am. Bd. Psychiatry and Neurology. Instr., fellow, USPHS U. Rochester (N.Y.) Sch. Med., 1968-69; asst. prof. clin. psychiatry Dartmouth Med. Sch., Hanover, NH, 1969-79, asst. prof. cmty. and family med., 1976-79, assoc. prof. clin. psychiatry, 1980-94, adj. assoc. prof. psychiatry, 1994—2002, adj. assoc. prof. psychiatry emeritus, 2003—. Dir. comprehensive alcoholism svcs. program Dartmouth Med. Sch., Hanover, 1973—75, dir. Robert Wood Johnson Primary Care/Physician Mgr. residency program, 1977—79, dir. fellowship program rural cmty. psychiatry, 1979—81; dir. Mt. Ascutney Psychiat. Assocs., Windsor, Vt., 1984—94, Choate Psychiat. Assocs., New London, NH, 1995—99. Contbr. chapters to books, articles to profl. jours. With Peace Corps, Nigeria; mem. steering com. Upper Valley Health Care Coalition, White River Junction, Vt., Lebanon, NH, 1984—86; mem. Area Planning Coun., NH, 1977—80; bd. dirs. Planned Parenthood Assn. Upper Valley, Lebanon, 1970—78; chmn. profl. adv. com. Hanover Vis. Nurse Svc., 1979—80; bd. dirs. Hanover Conservation Coun., 2003—. Sr. asst. surgeon USPHS, 1964—66. Fellow: Am. Psychiat. Assn. (disting. life); mem.: AAAS, AMA, Global Health Coun., Physicians for Social Responsibility, N.H. Psychiat. Soc. (pres. 1983—84, chmn. ethics com. 1985—86), Union Concerned Scientists, Amnesty Internat., Human Rights Watch, Internat. Physicians for Prevention Nuc. War, Physicians for Human Rights. Avocations: camping, canoeing, photography, wilderness travel. Home: 33 Rip Rd Hanover NH 03755-1616

CHAPMAN, ROBERT LEE, III, real estate developer; b. Jacksonville, Fla., Dec. 14, 1946; s. Robert Lee Jr. and Elisabeth (Trotter) C.; m. Vicky Lee Patton, July 19, 1945; children: Margaret Patton, Robert Lee IV, Anna Elisabeth, Charlotte Elisabeth. BA, Duke U., 1971. Gen. mgr. Sta. WDBS-FM, Durham, N.C., 1971; dir. media ctr. Duke U., Durham, 1972-73; pres. Chapman Patton & Assocs., Durham, 1974-75, Learning Resources Network, Durham, 1975-90, Southlake Devel. Group, Clermont, Fla., 1990—2002, Southlake Utilities, Inc., Clermont, 1990—2002; mng. dir. The TND Fund, LLC, Durham, N.C., 1999—. Bd. dirs. Broadcasting Found. Am., N.Y.C., 1980-82, Coun. Entrepreneurial Devel., Research Triangle Park, N.C., 1982-86; cons. interactive tech., Burroughs Wellcome Co. and Glaxo, Inc., Research Triangle Park, 1982-86; coord. USA-USSR Summer Arts Festival; juror, Kammerer Meml. Filmmaking prize, Duke U., 1984-89. Editor: Arts Festival Planning Guide, 1974; exec. producer over 100 films and videos. Coord., Durham Bicentennial Commn., 1975-76; bd. dirs. Ctrl. Park Sch. for Children, 2001—, Historic Preservation Soc. of Durham, 2002—, Carolina Cinema Corp., Durham, 1978-82, Friends of Duke U. Arts Mus., Durham, 1986-89, Nat. Town Builders Assn.; chmn. N.C. Smart Growth Alliance, Chapel Hill; trustee, Duke Sch. for Children, Durham, 1986-90, Ctrl. Pk. Sch. for Children, Durham, 2002—; mng. dir. Traditional Neighborhood Devel. Ptnrs., LLC, 1999—. Mem. Samuel Cook Soc. (Duke U.), Order of Red Friars, Sigma Nu. Avocations: travel, jogging, backpacking, skin diving. Home: 2525 Lanier Pl Durham NC 27705-5005 Office Phone: 919-929-0336.

CHAPMAN, ROBYN LEMON, music educator; b. Ogden, Utah, Jan. 17, 1974; d. Kent Lowell Lemon and Joanette Avonne Emery, Steven George Piccoli (Stepfather) and Cathy S. Lemon (Stepmother), Rick Alden Emery (Stepfather); m. Christopher Carl Chapman, Apr. 8, 2001. MusB, U. of Nev., Las Vegas, 1992—98. License for Educational Personnel Nev., 1998, Residential Education Certificate Wash. Supt. of Pub. Instrn., 2002. Long term substitute Mike O'Callaghan Mid. Sch., Las Vegas, 1998, band dir., 1998—2001, Theron Swainston Mid. Sch., North Las Vegas, 2001—02; music specialist Totem Falls Elem. Sch., Snohomish, Wash., 2002—. Camp adminstr. U. of Nev., Las Vegas Bands, 1993—2002; mid. sch. honor band chair Clark County Sch. Dist., Las Vegas, 2000—02. Recipient New Tchr. of the Yr., Clark County Sch. Dist., 1998—99. Mem.: Women Band Dirs. Internat., Wash. Music Educators Assn., Nat. Band Assn., Music Educators Nat. Conf. D-Conservative. Church Of Jesus Christ Of Latter-Day Saints. Avocations: reading, bicycling, bowling. E-mail: roby_chapman@msn.com.

CHAPMAN, RONALD THOMAS, musician, educator; b. Bklyn., Dec. 16, 1933; s. William Leon and Rosamond (Walker) C.; m. Joyce Elaine Chase, Dec. 1966 (dec. May 1973); adopted child, Debra Anne (dec. July 1992); m. Virginia Marie Knochenhauer, Feb. 14, 1975 (dec. July 1989); stepchildren: Suzanne, Michael. BS cum laude, CUNY, 1982; MAT, Lehman Coll., 1983; PhD in Music in Higher Edn., NYU, 1989. Cert. tchr. music, N.Y., tchr. Spanish, N.Y. Toured with Leonard dePaur Infantry Chorus, 1953—55; mem. trio The Versatones, U.S. and Cam., 1955—59; vocalist, 1978—; asst. dir. men's choir Kingsborough C.C., 1980—82; asst. to dir. mixed chorus Lehman Coll. CUNY, 1982—83; instr. voice NYU, 1986—; instr. computer music for music tchrs. N.Y. Inst. Tech., 1987; tchr. music Hempstead Sch. Dist., 2002—. Pvt. instr. voice, piano, guitar, computerized music, music theory, sight singing and music lit., 1980—; substitute tchr. Hempstead (N.Y.) Sch. Dist., 1983-85, mem. faculty, 1988-89, tchr. adult edn., ESL, 1993—, tchr. group piano, group voice in continuing adult edn. program, 1993—, substitute music tchr., 2002-03; bd. dirs. Cultural Environ, Queens, N.Y.; adjudicator N.Y. Singing Tchrs. Assn., 1995. Performed in Spain, Japan, Thailand, The Philippines, Eng., Jamaica, Can., Vietnam, P.R., Fed. Republic of Germany, Laos, Portugal and U.S. including N.Y.C., Atlanta and Miami; TV appearances on Johnny Carson Show, Arthur Godfrey Talent Scouts, Gary Moore Show, Tex and Jinx Falkenburg Show, many others; rec. artist for Columbia Records, RCA Records, Island in the Sun soundtrack; appeared in Broadway play Kwamina; appearing nightly Fox Hollow, 1978-93, Caterer/Restaurant, Woodbury, N.Y., 1978—; starred in Playboy Club and Hotel Chain, 1960-67, (movies) Rueda de Sospechosos, 1963, (revue) The Ronnie Chapman Show, 1968-69; debuted by singing and accompanying himself on piano a medley of Broadway Show Tunes and Internat. Art Songs in various langs. Carnegie Hall, 1991, 92, 93, 94, 95, 96; Cafe Trilussa, 1996-97, J. DeCarlos Restaurant, Huntington, N.Y., 1998—. Bd. dirs. Cultural Environment, Queens, N.Y., 1978—; apptd. dep. gov. Am. Biog. Inst. Rsch. Assn., 1992. Mem. Internat. Assn. for Rsch. in Singing (rsch. assoc. Found. for Rsch. Singing), Nat. Assn. Tchrs. of Singing, N.Y. Singing Tchrs. Assn., N.Y. State Sch. Music Assn. (cert. to adjucate "Voice"), Internat. Assn. Jazz Educators, Chopin Found. N.Y., Am. Assn. Choral Dirs., Music Educators Nat. Conf., Music Tchrs. Nat. Assn., Assoc. Music Tchrs. League N.Y., Internat. Platform Assn., Am. Choral Dirs. Assn., Phi Delta Kappa (v.p. programs NYU chpt. 1988-89), Pi Kappa Lambda, Kappa Delta Pi (chpt. 3d v.p. 1994—) Achievements include being awarded a design patent for invention of a portable back rest/supporter, 1993. Home: 7 Taft Ave Hempstead NY 11550-4816 Office: Roncha Inc Nassau Plz Ste 26 1 Fulton Ave Hempstead NY 11550 Office Phone: 516-485-0795. E-mail: ronchamusic@aol.com.

CHAPMAN, RUSSELL LEONARD, botany educator; b. Bklyn., May 30, 1946; s. Russell Hood and Helen C.; m. Melanie Anne Chapman, June 28, 1969; children: Christopher John, Timothy Sean. BA, Dartmouth Coll., 1968; MS, U. Calif., Davis, 1970, PhD, 1973. NSF grad. fellow dept. botany U. Calif., Davis, 1971-73; asst. prof. dept. botany and plant biology La. State U., Baton Rouge, 1973-77, assoc. prof. dept. botany, 1977-83, prof. dept. botany, 1983—95, prof. dept. biol. sci., 1995—, assoc. dean Coll. of Arts and Scis., 1979-83, assoc. dean Coll. of Basic Scis., 1983-84, chmn. dept. botany, 1988-94, assoc. vice chancellor Office of Rsch. and Econ. Devel., 1994-96, interim exec. dir. Ctr. for Coastal, Energy and Environ. Res, 1995-96, exec. dir. Ctr. for Coastal, Energy and Environ. Resources, 1996-2001, dean Sch. of the Coast and Environment, 2001—, adj. prof. dept. oceanography and coastal scis. Mem. editl. bd.: Jour. of Phycology, Algologia, Molecular Phylogenetics and Evolution; assoc. editor Am. Jour. of Botany, 1995—; author book chpts. in field; contbr. articles to profl. jours. Bd. dirs. Baton Rouge (La.) Earth Day, Inc., 1990-92, Baton Rouge (La.) Symphony Orch., 2004—; mem. Found. for Hist. La., Baton Rouge, 1973—; trustee Johnston Sci. Found., 2000—, bd. dirs., 2001—; pres. bd. patrons La. State U. Opera, 2002—. Recipient Outstanding Undergrad. Teaching award Amoco Found., Inc., 1978, Disting. Faculty award La. State U. Alumni Fedn., Baton Rouge, 1981; Paul Harris fellow, 2000. Fellow Linnean Soc. London; mem. Phycol. Soc. Am. (sec., v.p., pres. 1985-90, bd. trustees 1994—), Botanical Soc. Am. (chmn. phycol. sect. 1983-85, fin. adv. com. 2000—), British Phycol. Soc., Internat. Phycol. Soc. (exec. coun. 2001—), Internat. Soc. for Evolutionary Protistology, Willie Hennig Soc., La. Soc. Electron Microscopy (treas., pres. 1976-80), Environ. Rsch. Consortium La. (bd. trustees 1998—, pres. 1999-2000, sec.-treas. 2000-01), Phi Kappa Phi, Sigma Xi, Omicron Delta Kappa. Episcopalian. Office: La State U Sch Coast & Environ 1002 R Energy Coast and Environ Bldg Baton Rouge LA 70803-4110 E-mail: chapman@lsu.edu.

CHAPMAN, SAMUEL GREELEY, political science professor, criminologist; b. Atlanta, Sept. 29, 1929; s. Calvin C. and Jane (Greeley) C.; m. Patricia Hepfer, June 19, 1949 (dec. Dec. 1978); children: Lynn Randall, Deborah Jane; m. Carolyn Hughes, June 1, 1991. AB, U. Calif.-Berkeley, 1951, MA, 1959. Officer Police Dept., Berkeley, 1951-56; police cons. Pub. Adminstrn. Service, Chgo., 1956-59; asst. prof. Sch. Police Adminstrn., Mich. State U., East Lansing, 1959-63; police chief Multnomah County, Portland, Oreg., 1963-66; asst. dir. Pres.'s Commn. on Law Enforcement and Adminstrn. of Justice, Nat. Crime Commn., Washington, 1966-67; prof. dept. polit. sci. U. Okla., Norman, 1967-91; prof. emeritus, 1991—; chmn. athletic council U. Okla., 1971-72, 79-80. Adj. prof. criminal justice U. Nev., Reno, 1995—; assoc.'s disting. lectr., 1985-86. Author: Dogs in Police Work, 1960, The Police Heritage in England and America, 1962, Police Patrol Readings, 1964, rev. edit., 1970, Perspectives on Police Assaults in the South Central United States, 1974, Short of Merger, 1976, Police Murders and Effective Countermeasures, 1976, Police Dogs in North America, 1979, 2d. edit., 1990, Cops, Killers and Staying Alive: The Murder of Police Officers in America, 1986; Murdered On Duty: The Killing of Police Officers in America, 1998; contbr. chpts. to books, articles to profl. jours. Mem. Norman City Council, 1972-83, mayor pro-tem, 1975-76, 79-80, 81-83. Recipient Amoco Found. award, 1986. Mem. Nev. Hist. Soc. (docent), Alpha Delta Phi. Republican. Home and Office: 680 Kane Ct Reno NV 89512-1354 Office Phone: 775-786-9011. Personal E-mail: sgchapman@charter.net.

CHAPMAN, STEPHEN JAMES, columnist; b. Brady, Tex., Feb. 25, 1954; s. Thurman James and Betty Dee (Sell) C.; m. Fern Brenda Schumer, Sept. 10, 1983, (div.); 3 children AB cum laude, Harvard Coll., 1976; student, U. Chgo. Sch. Bus., 1982-84. Assoc. editor The New Republic, Washington, 1978-81; editorial writer, columnist The Chicago Tribune, 1981—. Office: Chgo Tribune 435 N Michigan Ave Chicago IL 60611-4041

CHAPMAN, TERRY GLEN, lawyer; b. Chgo., Jan. 8, 1952; s. Bernard and Wilma J. Chapman; m. Susan Spier, Dec. 3, 1995. BS in Econs., MS in Acctg., U. Pa., 1973; JD, Northwestern U., Chgo., 1976. Bar: Ill. 1976, U.S. Dist. Ct. (no. dist.) Ill. 1976, U.S. Tax Ct. 1982; CPA, Ill. Assoc. Solomon, Rosenfeld, Elliott, Stiefel & Abrams, Chgo., 1976-82; ptnr. Abrams & Chapman, Chgo., 1983—. Vice chmn., bd. dirs. 1st Bus. Banccorp, Chgo., South Ctrl. Bank and Trust Co., Chgo. Office: Abrams & Chapman 321 S Plymouth Ct Ste 1200 Chicago IL 60604-3990

CHAPMAN, THOMAS WILLIAM, hospital executive; b. May 17, 1945; s. Alice Chapman; m. Cheryl Edmonds. BA, St. Anselm's Coll., 1968; postgrad., Boston Coll., 1968-69; MPH, Yale U., 1971. Adminstrv. resident Children's Hosp. Med. Ctr., Boston, 1970-71; sr. staff cons. Arthur D. Little, Inc., Cambridge, Mass., 1971-76, sr. cons. Washington, 1982-84; asst. exec. dir. Group Health Assn., Washington, 1976-78; pres. Provident Hosp., Balt., 1978-82, Greater Southeast Community Hosp., Washington, 1984-91, Greater Southeast Healthcare System, Washington, 1991-94; sr assoc. v.p. network dev., ceo The Univ. Hosp., Geo Wash. Univ. Med Ctr, Washington, 1994—. Lectr., Johns Hopkins U., Balt., Howard U., Washington, 1986—; guest lectr., Harvard U. Contbr. articles to profl. publs. Fellow Am. Coll. Healthcare Execs.; mem. AHA (mem. nominating com., governing coun. Met. Hosp. sect., mem. conv. adv. panel), D.C. Hosp. Assn. (chmn. bd. dirs. 1988-90), Am. Pub. Health Assn., Assn. Yale Alumni, Nat. Assn. Health Svc. Execs.

CHAPMAN, WILLIAM, baritone; b. LA; s. William Cloud and Augusta Jane (Kiel) C.; m. Irene Veronica Meyer, Sept. 15, 1957; children— Alexa Maria, Teren Cloud. BA in Drama, U. So. Calif. Propr. vocal studio, Los Angeles, 1967—. Mem. faculty U.S. Internat. U. Performing Arts Sch., San Diego, 1971-86; mem. extension faculty UCLA. Leading baritone N.Y.C. Opera, 1956—, also other opera houses, U.S. and Europe; opened Spoleto Festival as Macbeth in Macbeth, 1957; leading performer: Menotti's Maria Golovin as produced by David Merrick, Broadway, Frank Loesser's Greenwillow, Alvin Theater, (original prodn.) Candide, Martin Beck Theater; Broadway appearances as Charlie in Shenandoah, 1978-79, also in N.Y.C. Center revival of South Pacific; appeared as Frank Maurrant for N.Y.C. Opera, also PBS-TV; TV appearances on Wonderful World of Disney; Columnist: Notes for the Singing Actor, Voice Mag.; appearing as Cecil B. DeMille in 1996-97 Nat. Touring Co. of Sunset Blvd. Rockefeller grantee; recipient DramaLogue award for performance, 1992, various certs. of appreciation. Mem. Screen Actors Guild, Actors Equity, Am. Guild Variety Artists, AFTRA. E-mail: icy1@adelphia.net.

CHAPMAN COLLINS, JANICE, school system administrator; b. L.A. d. William and Milrene Hooks; m. Michael Dean Collins; children: Arshaun, Ashley. BA in Liberal Arts, Pepperdine U., 1979, EdM, 1985, MS in Sch. Mgmt. & Adminstrn., 1989, MA in Edn., 1985. Ryan Multiple Subject Credential Calif. Commn. Tchr. Credentialing, 1979, Sylvan Program Instr. Sylan Learning Ctr., 1998, Adminstrv. Svcs. Credential Calif Commn. Tchr. Credentialing, 2000, Cert. Profl. Devel. Trainer L.A. Unified Sch. Dist.-Calif., 2002. Elem. tchr. L.A. Unified Sch. Dist., 1979—92, instrnl. coord., 1992—94, advisor, 1994—96, mid. sch. tchr., 1996—99, adminstr., mentor tchr. program, 1999—2000, adminstr., mid. sch. programs, 2000—. Mentor tchr. L.A. Unified Sch. Dist., 1986—92, drop out prevention coord., Seventy-Fifth St. Sch., 1986—88, adult sch. tchr., 1987—89, program quality rev. team mem., 1990, ldpass/aemp facilitator, 1996—99, sylvan program instr., 1998—99, adminstrv. facilitator, phys. edn. focus group, 2000—, social studies adv. bd. mem., 2001—, mem.- secondary redesign com., 2003—, mem. Calif. phys. edn. content standards devel. com., 2004; cons. USC: Calif. writing project Calif. Subject Matter Projects, L.A., 1987—; mem. social studies adv. bd. Pearson Prentice Hall Pub., L.A., 2003—; mem. phys. content standards devel. com. Calif. Dept. Edn., mem. com. phys. edn. model content standards. Contbr. ednl. handbook, Successful Strategies Handbook, curriculum guide, History-Social Sci. Guidelines for Instrn.; co-author: America History For Our Nation, 2005. Founding mem. Nat. Campaign for Tolerance, Montgomery, Ala., 2005—; adminstrv. liasion L.A. Unified Sch. Dist. Nat. Campaign To Stop Violence, Washington, 2000—. Recipient Do the Write Thing Challenge 2003, Nat. Campaign to Stop Violence, 2003, 2004. Mem.: ASCD, Associated Adminstrs. L.A., Calif. Assn. Health Phys. Edn., Recreation and Dance, Orgn. Mgmt. Adminstrs., Calif. League Mid. Schools, Coun. Black Adminstrs. (profl. devel. com. 1998), Nat. Women's History Mus. (charter mem.), Pepperdine Alumni Assn., Phi Delta Kappa. Baptist. Avocations: travel, art collector, creative writing, theater. Office: LA Unified Sch Dist 333 S Beaudry Ave 25th Floor Los Angeles CA 90017 Office Phone: 213-241-4134. Business E-Mail: janice.collins@lausd.net.

CHAPMAN HOLLEY, SHAWN SNIDER, lawyer; b. L.A., Apr. 11, 1962; d. Henry Stewart and Freddi (Snider) King; m. Michael J. Chapman, Sept. 12, 1992. BA in English, UCLA, 1984; JD, Southwestern U., 1988. Bar: Calif. 1988, U.S. Dist. Ct. (ctrl. dist.) Calif. 1989. Deputy pub. defender L.A. County Pub. Defenders Office, 1988-94; mng. ptnr. The Cochran Firm (formerly Law Offices of Johnnie L. Cochran Jr.), L.A., 1994—. Commr. of community affairs Southwestern U. Sch. of Law, L.A., 1987. Mem. Black Pub. Defenders Assn., Black Women Lawyers, Langston Bar Assn. Democrat. Office: The Cochran Firm 4929 Wilshire Blvd Ste 1010 Los Angeles CA 90010-3825 E-mail: sholley@cochranfirm.com.

CHAPNICK, DAVID B., lawyer; b. N.Y.C., Apr. 24, 1939; s. H.M. and G. (Kraft) C.; m. Elaine Schlozman, Dec. 25, 1966; children: David Adam Lawrence, Melissa Rachel. AB with honors, Union Coll., 1959; LLB, NYU, 1962. Bar: N.Y. 1963. Law clk. to Hon. Warren E. Burger U.S. Ct. Appeals (D.C. cir.), Washington, 1962-63; pvt. practice N.Y.C., 1963-67; assoc. Simpson Thacher & Bartlett, N.Y.C., 1967-69, ptnr., 1970—2000, of counsel, 2001—. Trustee Union Coll., Schenectady, N.Y., 1991—, vice chmn., 1995-96, chmn., 1998-02; bd. govs. Wurzweiler Sch. Social Work, 2004—. Mem. N.Y. State Bar Assn., Assn. Bar City N.Y. Office: Simpson Thacher & Bartlett 425 Lexington Ave New York NY 10017-3954

CHAPOTON, JOHN EDGAR, lawyer, retired federal official; b. Galveston, Tex., May 18, 1936; s. Otis Byron and Grace Donaldson (Wayman) C.; m. Sarah Eastham, Jan. 5, 1963; children: John Edgar Jr., Clare Eastham. Student, Washington and Lee U., 1954-55; BBA with honors, U. Tex., 1958, LLB with honors, 1960. Bar: Tex. 1960, D.C. 1985. Assoc. Andrews, Kurth, Campbell & Jones, Houston, 1961-69; with Dept. Treasury, Washington, 1969-72, 81-84, tax legis. counsel, 1970-72, asst. sec. for tax policy, 1981-84; ptnr. Vinson & Elkins, Houston, 1972-81, mng. ptnr. Washington, 1984—2000; ptnr. Brown Investment Adv. & Trust Co., 2001—. Chmn. law firms div. United Way Capital Area, Washington, 1988-90; bd. dirs. Boys and Girls Clubs Greater Washington, 1990—, Meridian Internat. Ctr., 2001—. Recipient Achievement award Tax Soc. NYU, 1984. Fellow Am. Coll. Tax Counsel; mem. ABA (sect. taxation, vice chair govt. rels.), Tex. State Bar

Assn., D.C. Bar Assn., Am. Law Inst. Republican. Episcopalian. Avocation: golf. Office: Brown Investment Advisory Inc 1737 H St NW Washington DC 20006 Home: 18 W Kirke St Chevy Chase MD 20815 Office Phone: 202-496-2999. Business E-Mail: jchapoton@brownadvisory.com.

CHAPPARS, TIMOTHY STEPHEN, lawyer; b. Cin., July 23, 1952; s. Gregory S. and Helen (Maragos) C.; m. Laurie A. Kress, Dec. 24, 1986 (div. Sept. 1987); m. Laurie A. Kress, Apr. 18, 1990; children: Alexander T., Jake A., Madeline Claire. BS, Duke U., 1974; JD, U. Cin., 1978. Propr. Chappars Law Office. Mem. ATLA, Ohio Bar Assn., Ohio Acad. Trial Lawyers. Methodist. Avocations: tennis, piano, hiking, bicycling, skiing. Home: 2025 Winding Brook Way Xenia OH 45385-9382 Office: PO Box 280 Xenia OH 45385-0280 Office Phone: 937-374-0077.

CHAPPEL, DONALD R., petroleum pipeline company executive; b. Oct. 19, 1951; m. Erin Chappel. Grad., U. Ill. CPA, Ill. With Arthur Andersen & Co., Chgo., 1973—82, Beatrice Cos., Inc./Esmark, Inc., 1982—87, dir. N.Am. ops. analysis, dir. fin./ops. analysis and audit; joined Waste Mgmt., Inc., 1987, v.p., contr. chem. waste mgmt. divsn., v.p., contr. West and Mountain groups, v.p., contr. N.Am. solid waste ops., 1995-97, v.p., acting CFO, 1997-2000; sr. v.p., CFO The Williams Cos., Inc., Tulsa, 2003—. Office: One Williams Ctr Tulsa OK 74172

CHAPPELL, ANNETTE M., educational consultant, minister; b. Washington, Oct. 31, 1939; d. Joseph John and Annette B. (Harley) C.; m. Brian Thomas Flower, Sept. 3, 1960 (div. Mar. 1983); m. Frank Joseph Sanders, Apr. 8, 1985 (dec. Dec. 1995). BA in English, U. Md., 1962, MA, 1964, PhD, 1970; MDiv, Gen. Theol. Sem., 2003. Lectr. English Edn. div. U. Md., Eng., 1965-66, instr. English College Park, 1966-69; asst. prof. English Towson (Md.) U., 1969-72, assoc. prof., 1972-79, prof., 1979—99, spl. asst. to pres., affirmative action officer, 1974-77; dean humanistic, social and managerial studies Towson (Md.) State U., 1977-82, dean Coll. Liberal Arts, 1982-95, assoc. v.p. acad. affairs, 1995-99; ind. cons., 1999—; rector Ch. of the Redemption, Balt., 2003—. Contbr. articles to profl. jours. and book revs. to Ms Mag., Balt. Sun. Lay reader, chalicist All Saints Episcopal Ch., Reisterstown, Md., 1973-2003; pres. Baltimore County Commn. for Women, 1977-79; bd. dirs. Baltimore County Sexual Assault and Domestic Violence Center, 1978-83, pres., 1980-82. Mem. AAUP, MLA, Am. Assn. Higher Edn., Council Colls. Arts and Scis. (bd. dirs. 1984-86), Exec. Women's Council Md. (1st v.p. 1980, pres. 1981) Business E-Mail: achappell@towson.edu.

CHAPPELL, ASHLEY, music educator, musician; b. Mesquite, Tex., July 2, 1980; d. Rayburn Wayne and Marilyn Chappell. MusB summa cum laude, U. North Tex., 2002, M in Music Edn. summa cum laude, 2005. Choral dir. Plano ISD, Tex., 2002—04; music dir. St. Michael and All Angels Episcopal Ch., Dallas, 2004—; grad. asst. U. North Tex., Denton, 2004—. Musician (percussionist): (recording) Journey: Circles of Our Lives (Turtle Creek Chorale); musician: (music director) (musical) Live from Plano. Mem.: Percussive Arts Soc., Coll. Music Soc., Tex. Choral Dirs. Assn., Am. Choral Dir. Assn., Music Educators Nat. Conf., Tex. Music Educators Assn. Home: 4615 Vineyard Trail Mesquite TX 75150 Personal E-mail: musicalash@aol.com.

CHAPPELL, CHARLES FRANKLIN, meteorologist, consultant; b. St. Louis, Dec. 7, 1927; s. Hubert Guy and Wilma Halle (Lindsey) C.; m. Doris Mae Kennedy, Aug. 4, 1951; children— Christa Ann, Susan Lynne, Deborah Louise BS, Washington U., St. Louis, 1949; postgrad., St. Louis U., 1952-54; MS, Colo. State U., 1967, PhD, 1971. Flight data engr. McDonnell Aircraft Co., St. Louis, 1950-55; weather forecaster U.S. Weather Bur., Kansas City, Mo., 1956-67; research assoc. Colo. State U., Ft. Collins, 1967-70; assoc. prof. Utah State U., Logan, 1970-72; research meteorologist NOAA, Boulder, Colo., 1972-79, research dir., 1979-87; head applied sci. group Nat. Ctr. for Atmospheric Research, Boulder, 1988-89, sr. scientist coop. program for operational meteorology edn. and tng., 1989-94; meteolologist cons., Boulder, 1995—. Cons. meteorologist Midwest Weather Service, Kansas City, Mo., 1958-60 Assoc. editor Jour. Atmospheric Sci., 1984-87; contbr. articles to prof. jours. (Best Sci. Paper award in NOAA-Environ. Research Labs. 1981). Served as seaman 1st class USN, 1945-46 Recipient silver medal Dept. Commerce, 1957 Fellow Am. Meteorol. Soc.; mem. Nat. Weather Assn., Weather Modification Assn., Am. Geophys. Union, Phi Kappa Phi. Avocations: hiking, painting, gardening, piano. Home and Office: 3110 Heidelberg Dr Boulder CO 80305-7010 E-mail: chapmo@msn.com. *You can always accomplish more than you think, so do it.*

CHAPPELL, CHARLES RICHARD, space scientist; b. Greenville, S.C., June 2, 1943; s. Gordon Thomas and Mabel Winn (Ownbey) Chappell; m. Brenda Kay Taylor; 1 child, Christopher Richard. BA magna cum laude, Vanderbilt U., 1965; PhD in Space Sci., Rice U., 1968. Assoc. research scientist Lockheed Palo Alto (Calif.) Research Lab., 1968-70, research scientist, 1970-72, staff scientist, 1972-74; chief magnetospheric physics br. NASA-Marshall Space Flight Ctr., Huntsville, Ala., 1974-80, chief solar terrestrial physics div., 1980-87, assoc. dir. for sci., 1987-97; rsch. prof. physics, dir. sci. and rsch. comm. Vanderbilt U., Nashville, 1997—2002; rsch. prof. physics, dir. Vanderbilt Dyer Obs., Nashville, 2002—. Trainee NASA, 1966—68; selected as alternate payload specialist for the ATLAS-1 mission of the Space Shuttle, 1985; spl. asst. for environ. outreach to NASA adminstr., 1994—95; dep. dir. Global Learning and Observations to Benefit the Environment (GLOBE), 1994—95; vis. prof. scholar Freedom Forum First Amendment Ctr. Vanderbilt U., 1996—97; dir. Dyer Obs., 2003—. Author: (ency.) Plasmasphere, 1970, Spacelab Mission, 1985; contbr. articles to profl. jours. Recipient medal for Exceptional Sci. Achievement, NASA, 1981, 1984, Exceptional Svc. medal, 1998. Mem.: Congress of Space Rsch., Am. Geophys. Union, Internat. Acad. Astronautics, Phi Eta Sigma, Phi Beta Kappa. Methodist. Avocations: distance running, sailing. Home: 569 Midway Cir Brentwood TN 37027-5178 Office: Vanderbilt U Dyer Obs 1000 Oman Dr Brentwood TN 37027 Office Phone: 615-373-4897.

CHAPPELL, FRED DAVIS, language educator, poet; b. Canton, NC, May 28, 1936; s. James Taylor and Anne Mae (Davis) C.; m. Susan Nicholls, Aug. 2, 1959; 1 son, Christopher Heath. BA, Duke U., 1961, MA, 1964; LittD, U. N.C., Asheville, 1989, Spring Hill Coll., 1991. Prof. English U. N.C., Greensboro, 1964—. Adv. editor Skyhook, 1958-59, Red Clay Reader, 1964-65, Greensboro Rev., 1964—, Ga. Rev., 1990—. Author: It Is Time, Lord, 1963, The Inkling, 1965, Dagon, 1968, The World Between the Eyes, 1971, The Gaudy Place, 1972, Midquest, 1981, Moments of Light, 1982, Castle Tzingal, 1984, I Am One of You Forever, 1985, Source, 1985, The Fred Chappell Reader, 1988, First and Last Words, 1989, Brighten the Corner Where You Are, 1989, More Shapes Than One, 1992, C, 1993, Plow Naked, 1993, Spring Garden: New and Selected Poems, 1995, Farewell, I'm Bound To Leave You, 1996, A Way of Happening, 1998, Look Back All the Green Valley, 1999, Family Gathering, 2000, Backsass, 2004. Recipient Roanoke-Chowan Poetry prize N.C. Lit. Assn., 1979, Prix de Meilleur des Lettres Etrangers, 1973, N.C. award in lit. State of N.C., 1987, Bollingen prize for poetry, 1985, World Fantasy award World Fantasy Assn., 1992, 94, T.S. Eliot prize Ingersoll Found., 1993, Aiken Taylor Poetry award, 1996, Irene Lenore Heasley prize, 1999, SEBA Novel award, 2000, Eminescu medal for poetry, 2001, Appalachian Heritage Writers award, 2004, Thomas Wolfe award, 2005; N.C. Poet Laureate, 1997-2002; NDEA fellow, 1961-63; Rockefeller grantee, 1967-68, grantee Nat. Acad. Arts and Letters, 1968. Mem.: Order of the Longleaf Pine. Democrat. Avocations: books, wine, mischief. Office: U NC English Dept Greensboro NC 27412-0001 Office Phone: 336-275-8851.

CHAPPELL, JOHN CHARLES, lawyer; b. Minden, Nebr., Jan. 28, 1935; s. Charles Arthur and Eletta Hope (Pattison) C.; m. Joyce Joan Dawson, Sept. 1, 1957; children: Laura, Pamela, James, Allegra. BS in Edn., U. Nebr., 1956; JD, NYU, 1960. Bar: N.Y. 1960. Summer assoc. firm Dewey Ballantine, N.Y.C., 1959, assoc., 1960-68; ptnr. Dewey Ballantine LLP, N.Y.C., 1968-00, of counsel, 2000—. Served to 1st lt. U.S. Army, 1957. Root-Tilden scholar NYU, 1956 Mem.: Assn. Bar City N.Y. Home: 2 Galloping Hill Cir Holmdel NJ 07733-1848 Office: Dewey Ballantine LLP 1301 Ave Of The Americas New York NY 10019-6022

CHAPPELL, MILES LINWOOD, JR., art historian, educator; b. Norfolk, Va., June 6, 1939; s. Miles Linwood Sr. and Melrose Clarice (Debnam) C.; m. Marcial Cassada, July 23, 1966; children: Ashley, Oliver, Picot. BS in Chemistry, Coll. William and Mary, 1960; PhD in Art History, U. N.C., 1971. Prof. art history Coll. William and Mary, Williamsburg, Va., 1971—2005, chair dept., Chancellor prof. art history, 1987, prof. emeritus, 2005—. Artistic adv. bd. Interlochen Ctr. for Arts. Author: Cristofano Allori, 1984, Lodovico Cigoli, Disegni, 1992, The Fine Art of Drawing, 1993; co-author: Disegni dei Toscani, 1979, Lodovico Cigoli, tra manierismo e barocco, 1992, Renascence of the Florentine Baroque in "Dialoghi di storia dell'arte", 1998, The Artistic Education of Maria de'Medici, 2003, Cigoli's Treatise on Perspective in The Perspective Treatise, 2002; contbg. author: The Medici. Michelangelo and Late Renaissance Art, 2002; formulator and co-author: Form, Function and Finesse: Drawings from the Herman Found., 1983; co-editor L'Arte, Collezionismo, Conservazione: scritti in onore di Marco Chiarini, 2004; asst. editor: Studies in Iconography, 1978-80; mem. adv. bd. Eighteenth-Century Life, 1980-84, 85—; contbr. numerous articles on Renaissance and Baroque art to profl. jours. Mem. internat. survey of Jewish monuments, U. Ill., 1978. Harvard U. Ctr. for Italian Renaissance Studies fellow, Florence, 1980; Cité Internat. des Arts, 1995; recipient numerous rsch. grants. Mem. Kunsthistorisches Institut Florence, Phi Beta Kappa (Alpha chpt. award for scholarship 1987, v.p. 1992-93, 2003-05, Thomas Ashley Graves, Jr. award for excellence in tchg. 2005). Avocations: drawing, painting, music. Home: 139 Ridings Cv Williamsburg VA 23185-3903 Office: Coll William & Mary Dept Art History Williamsburg VA 23187 Office Phone: 757-220-1433. E-mail: mlchap@wm.edu.

CHAPPELL, MILTON LEROY, lawyer; b. Accra, Ghana, Mar. 25, 1951; (parents Am. citizens); s. Derwood Lee and Helen Jean (Freeman) C.; m. Margot Cecelia Shields, Dec. 18, 1972; children: Marton Gerald, Monet Louise. BA summa cum laude, Columbia Union Coll., 1973; JD, Cath. U., 1976; diploma, Nat. Inst. Trial Advocacy, Boulder, Colo., 1978; cert., U. Miami, 1982. Bar: Md. 1976, D.C. 1977, U.S. Ct. Appeals (4th, 5th, 9th and D.C. cirs.) 1977, U.S. Dist. Ct. D.C. 1978, U.S. Ct. Appeals (6th cir.) 1979, U.S. Supreme Ct. 1980, U.S. Ct. Appeals (11th cir.) 1981, U.S. Dist. Ct. Md. 1982, U.S. Ct. Appeals (7th cir.) 1988, U.S. Dist. Ct. (no. dist.) Calif., 1990, U.S. Ct. Appeals (3rd cir.) 2000. Sole practice, Silver Spring, Md., 1976—; staff atty. Nat. Right to Work Legal Def. Found., Springfield, Va., 1976—. Lectr. Columbia Union Coll., Takoma Park, Md., 1976-77; legal cons. JNA Elem. Sch., Takoma Park, 1980-83; gen. counsel Playgrounds Unltd., Inc., 1988-2000, Internat. Play Equipment Mfrs. Assn., Inc., 1995—, Park Dreams Internat., Ltd., 2000—; participant play settings subcom. recreation access adv. com. U.S. Archtl. and Transp. Barriers Compliance Bd., 1993-94. Contbr. to Ohio No. U. Law Rev., Govt. Union Rev., Calif. Pub. Employee Rels. Mem. Hillandale Civic Assn., Silver Spring, 1980—; legal cons., bd. dirs. Silver Spring Seventh-day Adventist Ch., 1976-84, Takoma Park.; participant U.S. Arch. and Trans. Barriers Compliance Bd., Recreation Access Adv. Com., Play Settings subcom., 1993-94. Mem. ABA, Md. Bar Assn. D.C. Bar Assn. Home: 10321 Royal Rd Silver Spring MD 20903-1616 Office: Nat Right to Work Legal Def Found 8001 Braddock Rd # 600 Springfield VA 22151-2110 Office Phone: 703-770-3329. Business E-Mail: mlc@nrtw.org.

CHAPPELL, TORRI P., elementary school educator; b. Okinawa, Japan, June 18, 1959; d. Kenneth M. and Carolyn (Mitchell) Pruitt; m. Gary Chappell, July 2, 1988. BA in Internat. Studies, Emory U., Atlanta, 1981; MBA, Thunderbird U., Glendale, Ariz., 1985; Cert., San Francisco State U., 1988. 5th grade tchr. Mill Valley (Calif.) Sch. Dist.; coord. training Marin County Sch. Vols., San Rafael, Calif. Home: 150 Morningside Dr San Anselmo CA 94960-1535

CHAPPELL, VIRGINIA, literature and language professor; b. Santa Ana, Calif., June 12, 1944; d. John George and Amy Elizabeth (Heilman) Chappell. AB, Brown U., 1966; MSJ, Columbia U., 1967; MAT in English, U. Wash., 1976, PhD in English, 1988. Reporter, copy editor Providence Jour., 1967—69; instr. English Air Am. Schs., Udorn, Thailand, 1973—74, U. Md. Far East Divsn., Udorn, 1975—76, U. Wash. Writing Ctr., Seattle, 1976—88; asst. prof. English Marquette U., Milw., 1988—95, assoc. prof. English, 1995—. Co-author: Reading Rhetorically, 2002, 2d edit.; co-editor: Balancing Acts, 1991. Mem.: MLA, Conf. on Coll. Composition, Coun. Writing Program Adminstrs. Episcopalian. Office: Marquette U English Dept Box 1881 Milwaukee WI 53201-1881 Office Phone: 414-288-6859. Office Fax: 414-288-5433. Business E-Mail: virginia.chappell@marquette.edu.

CHAPPELL, WALLACE, performing company executive; b. Dallas, Aug. 8, 1941; BA, Dartmouth Coll., 1963; MFA, U. Hawaii, 1965; postgrad., U. Minn. Staff dir. L.A. Music Ctr. Mark Taper Forum, 1969—75; assoc. artistic dir. Alliance Theatre, Atlanta, 1975—78; artistic dir. Repertory Theatre of St. Louis, 1980—83; dir. Hancher Auditorium, U. Iowa, 1986—2001; exec. dir. Am. Ballet Theatre, N.Y.C., 2001—04, Paul Taylor Dance Co., N.Y.C., 2004—. Cons., spkr., panelist, advisor, site visitor various orgns., including Nat. Endowment for Arts, Wallace Found., Assn. Performing Arts Presenters; bd. dirs. Iowa State Bank and Trust, Inc. Bd. dirs. Dance/USA, Iowa City C. of C. Mem.: Stage Soc. Dirs. and Choreographers, Internat. Soc. Performing Arts (pres. 1993—95). Office: 552 Broadway New York NY 10052 Office Phone: 212-431-5562. E-mail: wc@ptdc.org.

CHAPPELL, WILLARD RAY, physics educator, environmental scientist; b. Boulder, Colo., Feb. 27, 1938; s. Willard Bruce and Mildred Mary (Weaver) C.; m. Juanita June Benetin, Mar. 5, 1981; children: Ginger Ferguson, Robert Ferguson. BA in Math., U. Colo., 1962, PhD in Physics, 1965; A.M. in Physics, Harvard U., 1963. Postdoctoral research assoc. Smithsonian Astrophys. Obs., Cambridge, Mass., 1965-66; postdoctoral research assoc. Lawrence Livermore Lab., Calif., 1966-67; asst. prof. physics U. Colo., Boulder, 1967-70, assoc. prof., 1970-73, prof., 1973-76, prof. physics, dir. Ctr. for Environ. Scis. Denver, 1976—. Chmn. Dept. Energy Oil Shale Task Force, 1978-83; mem. adv. com. to dir. on health scis. Los Alamos Nat. Lab.; mem. Colo. Gov.'s Sci. Adv. Com., 1974-76, chmn., 1975-76 Author: Transport and Biological Effects of Molybdenum in the Environment, 1975 Served with U.S. Army, 1956-58 NSF fellow, 1962-65; grantee Fleishman Found., 1969-71, NSF, 1971-76, EPA, 1975-79, Dept. Energy, 1976-83, U.S. Bur. Mines, 1979-81 Mem. Am. Phys. Soc., AAAS, Soc. Environ. Geochemistry and Health (exec. com. 1981-83, 86-88, sec./treas. 1988—), Phi Beta Kappa Democrat. Office: U Colo Environ Scis PO Box 173364 Denver CO 80217-3364

CHAPPELLE, DAVID (DAVE CHAPPELLE, DAVE CHAPELLE), actor, comedian; b. Washington, Aug. 24, 1973; m. Elaine Chappelle; 2 children. Actor: (films) Robin Hood: Men in Tights, 1993, Undercover Blues, 1993, Getting In, 1994, The Nutty Professor, 1996, Joe's Apartment, 1996, Con Air, 1997, The Real Blonde, 1997, Bowl of Pork, 1997, Woo, 1998, You've Got Mail, 1998, 200 Cigarettes, 1999, Blue Streak, 1999, Screwed, 2000, Undercover Brother, 2002; (TV series) Buddies, 1996, Comedy: Coast to Coast, 1994, (voice) Crank Yankers, 2002; actor, writer, exec. prodr. (TV series) Chappelle's Show, 2003—05, actor, co-writer, and prodr. (films) Half Baked, 1998, writer and exec. prodr. (TV special) The Dave Chappelle Project, 1997, Dave Chappelle: Killin' Them Softly, 2000. Mailing: Gersh Agy 232 N Canon Dr Beverly Hills CA 90210*

CHAPPELLE, LOU JO, physical therapist assistant; b. Watertown, N.Y., Mar. 7, 1952; d. Harold Joseph and Alice Jean (Marcellus) Getman; m. Richard George Tobey, Aug. 14, 1982 (div.); m. Gerald E. Chappelle, Sept. 14, 1996; stepson, Scott C. AA, Hudson Valley Community Coll., 1972; BSE, State U. Coll., Cortland, N.Y., 1974; AAS, St. Philips Coll., 1981. Cert. elem. and secondary tchr., N.Y. Educator phys. edn., coach Gilbertsville (N.Y.) Central Sch., 1974-79, 1000 Islands Jr.-Sr. High Sch., Sand Bay-Clayton, N.Y., 1980-82; phys. therapist asst. II N.Y. State Veteran's Home, Oxford, 1982-91; phys. therapy asst. F.F. Thompson Health Sys., Inc., Canandaigua, N.Y., 1992-98, SunDance Rehab Corp, Ontario County Health Facility, 1998, Finger Lakes Vis. Nurse Svc., 1999—. EMT Gilbertsville (N.Y.) Emergency Squad, 1983-89. Capt. USAR, 1977-96. Decorated Army Achievement medal. Home: 4313 Deep Run Cv Canandaigua NY 14424-9777

CHAPPLE, JOHN H., telecommunications industry executive, former professional sports team executive; b. Syracuse, N.Y., Apr. 8, 1953; Grad., Syracuse U.; postgrad., Harvard U. Sr. mgmt. positions Rogers Cablesystems, 1978—83; sr. v.p. ops. Am Cablesystems, 1983—88; exec. v.p. ops. McCaw Cellular Comms., Inc. (became AT&T Wireless Svcs.), 1988—95; former exec. v.p. AT&T Wireless Svcs. (acquired McCaw); past chmn. Cellular One Group; pres., COO Orca Bay Sports and Entertainment parent co. of Vancouver Grizzlies (NBA), Vancouver Canucks (NHL), 1995—97; pres., CEO, chmn. of bd. Nextel Ptnrs., Kirkland, Wash., 1998—. Former chmn. Personal Comm. Industry Assn.; former vice chmn. Cellular Telecomm. Industry Assn.; former bd. of governors NHL and NBA; bd. of governors Fred Hutchinson Cancer Rsch. Bus. Alliance Bd. of Governors; adv. bd., Maxwell Sch. Syracuse U.; bd. dir. Cbeyond Comm., Atlanta, 2004—. Office: Chmn & CEO Nextel Partners 4500 Carillon Pt Kirkland WA 98033

CHAPPLE, THOMAS LESLIE, lawyer; b. Canandaigua, NY, Nov. 28, 1947; s. Howard Leslie and Elizabeth Chapple; m. Shelly Smith, July 17, 1982; children: Adam Roger, Hannah Elizabeth. BA, Cornell U., 1970; JD, Albany Law Sch., 1973. Bar: N.Y. 1974, U.S. Supreme Ct. 1981, Va. 1992. Atty. assoc. Nixon, Hargrave, Devans & Doyle, Rochester, NY, 1973-76; sec., asst. gen. counsel Gannett Co., Inc., Rochester, NY, 1977-79, assoc. gen. counsel., sec., 1979-81, v.p., assoc. gen. counsel, sec., 1981-91, gen. counsel, sec. McLean, Va., 1991-95, sr. v.p., gen. counsel, sec., 1995—2003, sr. v.p., chief adminstrv. officer, gen. counsel, 2003—. Sec. The Gannett Found., 1983-89. Mem. ABA, Assn. Corp. Counsel, N.Y. State Bar Assn., Sigma Pi Republican. Methodist. Office: Gannett Co Inc 7950 Jones Branch Dr Mc Lean VA 22107

CHAPUT, CHARLES J., archbishop; b. Concordia, Kans., Sept. 26, 1944; Student, St. Fidelis Coll., Capuchin Coll., Cath. U., U. San Francisco. Ordained priest Roman Cath. Ch., 1970, consecrated bishop 1988. Bishop, Rapid City, SD, 1988—97; archbishop Denver, 1997—. Office: Cath Pastoral Ctr 1300 S Steele St Denver CO 80210-2526*

CHAR, PATRICIA HELEN, lawyer; b. Honolulu, Mar. 23, 1952; d. Lincoln S. and Daisy Char; m. Thomas W. Bingham, Mar. 20, 1982; children: Matthew Thomas Bingham, James Nathan Bingham. BA, Northwestern U., 1974; JD, Georgetown U., 1977. Bar: Wash. 1977, U.S. Dist. Ct. (we. dist.) Wash. 1977, U.S. Dist. Ct. (ea. dist.) Wash. 1982, U.S. Ct. Appeals (9th cir.) 1981, U.S. Supreme Ct. 1984. Assoc. Bogle & Gates, Seattle, 1977-84; ptnr., mem. Bogle & Gates PLLC, Seattle, 1984-99; of counsel Garvey, Schubert & Barer, Seattle, 1999-2000; ptnr. Preston Gates & Ellis LLP, Seattle, 2000—. Author: Ownership By a Fiduciary, 1997. Trustee YWCA, Seattle-King County-Snohomish County, 1997-2005, United Way King County; vol. King County Big Sisters, United Way of King County, Seattle, 1987-90, Guardian Ad Litem Program, Seattle, 1987-93 Fellow Am. Coll. Trust and Estate Counsel; mem. ABA, Wash. State Bar Assn. (co-author chpts. 3 and 4 Wash. Civil Procedure Deskbook 1992). Office: Preston Gates & Ellis LLP 925 4th Ave #2900 Seattle WA 98104-1158 Office Phone: 206-623-7580. Business E-Mail: pchar@prestongates.com.

CHAR, VERNON FOOK LEONG, lawyer; b. Honolulu, Dec. 15, 1934; s. Charles A. and Annie (Ching) C.; m. Evelyn Lau, June 14, 1958; children: Richard, Daniel, Douglas, Charles, Elizabeth. BA, U. Hawaii, 1956; LLB, Harvard U., 1959. Bar: Hawaii 1959. Dep. atty. gen. Office of Atty. Gen., Honolulu, 1959-60, 62-65; ptnr. Damon Key Char & Bocken, Honolulu, 1965-89, Char, Sakamoto, Ishii, Lum & Ching, Honolulu, 1989—. Chmn. Hawaii Ethics Commn., Honolulu, 1968-75, Hawaii Bicentennial Com., 1986-91; mem. Hawaii Tourism Authority, 2003—. Mem. ABA (bd. govs. 1991-94), Hawaii Bar Assn. (pres. 1985), U. Hawaii Alumni Assn. (pres. 1989-90). Home: 351 Anonia St Honolulu HI 96821-2052 Office: Char Sakamoto Ishii Lum & Ching Davies Pacific Ctr 841 Bishop St Ste 850 Honolulu HI 96813-3957 Office Phone: 808-522-5133. Business E-Mail: vflchar@lawcsilc.com.

CHARANIA, BARKAT, real estate consultant; b. Ahmedabad, Gujrat, India, June 27, 1941; came to U.S., 1961; s. Ismail and Zenabai Charania; m. Jerilyn Lee Scott, Apr. 10, 1962 (div. May 1970); children: Sultana, Ramzan, Kalvin, Kevin, Stephen; m. Maher Kurani, Oct. 11, 1970; children: Munira, Rahim, Munira Moon. Student, Alpena (Mich.) Community Coll., 1961-62, U. Calif., L.A., 1962-63, U. Pa., 1965-68, Lincoln Tech. Sch., 1983. Cert. comml. investment mem.; cert. hotel adminstr. Pres. Eurindus, Inc., Cherry Hill, N.J., 1965-83, Airline Inn, Inc., Atlanta, 1980-83; owner B.C. Investments & Realty Co., Atlanta, 1985—; pres. Southern Inn, Inc., Chattanooga, 1987—; owner B.C. Hospitality Mgmt. Co., Atlanta, 1987—; pres. Trident Devel. Corp., Charleston, S.C., 1989—, BJM Hospitality, Inc., 1993—, ICI Long Distance Inc., 1995—, Universal Connect Corp., 1995—; CEO, CRM Ventures, LLC, 1997—, RBM Properties, LLC, 2000—; sr. assocs. Marcus & Millichap, Atlanta, 1996-97; CEO Charania Bros., LLC, 1999—, 786 Investments, LLC, 2003—, Small Axe, Inc., 2003—. Cons. Pattni Holdings, Atlanta, 1984—, Esmail Internat., Inc., Atlanta, 1986—, Harbour Enterprise, Chattanooga, 1987—, Shin Inc., Chattanooga, 1987—, ABC Inc., Chattanooga, 1988—. Ga. coord. Agakhan Found. U.S.A., Atlanta, 1988; chmn. Southeastern Enterprising People's Assn., 1990, 91. Mem. Atlanta Bd. Realtors, Nat. Assn. Realtors, Realtor Nat. Mktg. Inst., Comml. Investment Real Estate Coun., Edn. Inst., Internat. Real Estate Inst., Ismaili Commerce Club (v.p. Atlanta chpt. 1982), S.E. Region (chmn. Agakhan econ. planning bd. for U.S.A.), Internat. Real Estate Fedn. Republican. Avocations: reading, travel, swimming, tennis. Home and Office: 3000 Edmonton Green Ct Alpharetta GA 30022 Office Phone: 770-667-0460. Business E-Mail: bc@bcirealty.com. *People don't care how much you know until they know how much you care...about them. How far you go in life depends on your being tender with the young, compassionate with the aged, sympathetic with the striving, and tolerant of the weak and the strong. Because someday in life you will have all of these.*

CHARAP, STANLEY HARVEY, electrical engineering educator; b. NYC, Apr. 21, 1932; s. William and Esther Charap; m. Marilyn Novick, Aug. 7, 1955; children: Joshua David, Lawrence Gordon. BS in Physics, Bklyn. Coll., 1953; PhD in Physics, Rutgers U., 1959. Mem. rsch. staff IBM T.J. Watson Rsch. Ctr., Yorktown Heights, NY, 1958-64; rsch. scientist Rsch. div. Am.-Standard Inc., Piscataway, NJ, 1964, supr. solid state physics, 1965-66, mgr. physics and electronics, 1966-68; assoc. prof. elec. and computer engring. Carnegie Mellon U., Pitts., 1968-71, prof., 1971-96; prof. emeritus, 1997—; assoc. head dept. Carnegie Mellon U., Pitts., 1980-85, acting head dept., 1981-82, vice chmn. faculty senate, 1972-73, chmn. faculty senate, 1986-87, assoc. dir. Data Storage Systems Ctr., 1990-96. Cons. Westinghouse Rsch. Ctr., Pitts., 1969-84; mem. tech. staff Bell Labs., Whippany, NJ, summer 1973; sr. vis. fellow U. Wales, Cardiff, spring 1976; vis. scientist Control Data Corp., Mpls., summer 1987. Editor: Physics of Magnetism, 1964; contbr. to Magnetism & Metallurgy, 1969; contbr. over 60 tech. articles to profl. jours. V.p. Sch. Advanced Jewish Studies, Pitts., 1989—91. Recipient Tech. Achievement award, Nat. Storage Industry Consortium, 1998. Fellow IEEE (fellow com. 1997-99, Millennium medal 2000); mem. IEEE Magnetics Soc. (sec.-treas. 1987-88, v.p. 1989-90, pres. 1991-92, editor-in-chief IEEE Trans. on Magnetics 1982-86, editl. bd. IEEE Press 1989-91, IEEE Tech. activities bd., liaison coun. 1993, gen. chmn. Joint INTERMAG-MMM conf. 1994, Disting. Lectr. 1996, Achievement award 1998, chair Disting. Lectr. Program 2003-04), Am. Inst. Physics, Conf. on Magnetism and Magnetic Materials (treas. 1981-83, gen. chmn. 1986). Office: Carnegie Mellon Univ Dept Electrical Computer Engineering 5000 Forbes Ave Pittsburgh PA 15213-3890 E-mail: s.charap@ieee.org.

CHARASH, BRUCE D., cardiologist, educator; b. NYC, Apr. 8, 1956; BA in Chemistry, Cornell U., 1977; MD, Cornell U. Med. Coll., 1981. Lic. NY State, 1982, cert. Am. Bd. Internal Medicine, 1984, Cardiovascular Disease subspecialty 1987. Intern, internal medicine Mt. Sinai Med. Ctr., dept. of medicine, 1982, resident, internal medicine, 1982—84; instr. Cornell Med. Sch., 1986—87, asst. prof. medicine, 1987—93; fellow, divsn. cardiology NY Hosp.-Cornell Med. Ctr., 1984—86, asst. attending physician, 1986—91; sr. attending physician Lenox Hill Hosp., 1991—2005, chief cardiac care unit, 1991—2005; clin. assoc. prof. medicine NYU Med. Sch., 1993—2005; vis. assoc. prof. medicine SUNY Health Ctr., Bklyn., 1998—2005; assoc. prof. clinical medicine Columbia U., 2005—; attending physician New York-Presbyterian Hospital. Investigator in field. Contbr. to profl. publs., jours., abstracts, and chap. in books; author: Heart Myths, 1991. Daniel and Elaine Sargent Cardiology Fellow, 1985. Fellow: Am. Coll. of Cardiology; mem.: AMA, ACP, Am. Red. Cross-NY Chap. (med. dir. AED program), Alpha Omega Alpha, Phi Kappa Phi, Phi Beta Kappa. Office: 16 E 60th St Ste 330 New York NY 10022 Office Phone: 212-326-5746. Business E-Mail: bdc2104@columbia.edu.

CHARBONNEAU, REBECCA JEAN, music educator; b. Plymouth, Wis., Nov. 21, 1976; d. Dennis Edward and Shirley Malitta Roehrborn; m. Brian Jay Charbonneau, May 26, 2000; children: Faith, Abigail. BA in Music Edn., Lakeland Coll., Sheboygan, Wis., 2000. Gen. music, choral music tchr. Sheboygan Falls Mid. Sch., 2000—. Mem. chorus Sheboygan Symphony, 1995—, mem. symphony singers, 1995—, soloist; conductor apprentices. Honors chair Nat. Cmty. Finalist concert competition, Sheboygan Symphony; named Outstanding Sr., Lakeland Coll., Sheboygan, 2000. Mem.: NEA, Am. Choral Dirs. Assn., Wis. Edn. Assn. Mem. United Ch. Of Christ. Avocations: walking, exercise. Home: 717 Chicago St Sheboygan Falls WI 53085 Office Phone: 920-467-7880. Office Fax: 920-467-7885. Business E-Mail: rjcharb@sheboyganfalls.k12.wi.us.

CHAREN, MONA, columnist; b. N.Y.C., Feb. 25, 1957; d. George and Claire (Rosenfeld) C.; m. Robert P. Parker. BA, Columbia U., 1979; JD, George Wash. U., 1984. Editorial assoc. Nat. Review Mag., N.Y.C., 1979-81; speechwriter White House, Washington, 1984, assoc. dir., office of pub. liaison, 1985-86; speechwriter Jack Kemp for Pres., Washington, 1986; syndicated columnist Creators Syndicate, L.A., 1987—. Panelist The Capital Gang CNN, Washington. Contbr. articles profl. mags. and publs.; author: Useful Idiots, 2003, Do-Gooders, 2005. Republican. Jewish. Office: Creators Syndicate 5777 W Century Blvd Ste 700 Los Angeles CA 90045-5675 Personal E-mail: mcharen@cox.net.

CHARETTE, CECILE M., music educator; b. Lowell, Mass., Oct. 15, 1920; d. Arthur Joseph and Eva Marie (Croteau) C. MusB, U. Montreal, 1956, MusM, 1962; postgrad., Boston U., 1965-67. Joined Order of Holy Cross, 1939. Prof. music Basile Moreau Coll., St. Laurent, Canada, 1946—62, Notre Dame Coll., Manchester, NH, 1962—2002; pvt. music instr. Goffstown, NH. Choir dir., dir. operas, 1974-78. Mem. Nat. Assn. Tchrs. Singing (N.H. gov. 1978-84), Metro. Opera Guild. Roman Catholic. E-mail: cecilecha@aol.com.

CHARETTE, SHARON JULIETTE, library administrator; b. Woonsocket, RI, Apr. 24, 1956; d. Roland Alfred Lionel and Juliette Cecile (Lavoie) C. BA in French and English, R.I. Coll., 1978; MLS, U. R.I., 1981; cert. in computer info. systems, Bryant Coll., 1989; student, RISD, 1989—91. Asst. serials Wheaton Coll., Norton, Mass., 1978—79, catalog asst., 1979—82, libr. acquisitions, 1982—86; dir. libr. and instnl. rsch. New Eng. Inst. Tech., Warwick, RI, 1986—. Seamstress, designer, craftsman, 1976—; webmaster, publicist for Greg Bonin, 2002—; webmaster Charlie Hall's Ocean State Follies, 2005— Chair Franco Am. com. R.I. Heritage Commn., Providence, 1987-90, treas., 1982-87; costume designer Kaleidoscope Theatre, 2003—. Mem. ALA, New England Libr. Assn., R.I. Libr. Assn., No. R.I. Coun. of Arts, Theatre Works (costume designer 2001-05, web mgr. 2002-05), Mensa, TechACCESS of .I. (bd. dirs., sec. 1992-98, 2003—, chair 1998-2003, web mgr. 2002—04). Avocations: music, theater, costume design, website design, jewelry design. Home: 147 Greenville Rd North Smithfield RI 02896-7422 Office: New Eng Inst Tech 2500 Post Rd Warwick RI 02886-2244 E-mail: scharette3@cox.net.

CHARFOOS, LAWRENCE SELIG, lawyer; b. Detroit, Dec. 7, 1935; s. Samuel and Charlotte (Salkin) C.; m. Jane Emerson. Student, U. Mich., 1953-56; LLB, Wayne State U., 1959. Bar: Mich. 1959, Ill. 1965. Pvt. practice, Detroit, 1960-63; pres., ptnr. Charfoos & Christensen PC, Detroit, 1967—; theatrical producer, legitimate theater mgr. Chgo., 1963-67. Cons. med.-legal problems Mich. Med. Soc., Mich. Hosp. Coun., ATLA; US cts. com. State Bar Mich. Author: The Medical Malpractice Case: A Complete Handbook, 1974, Daughters at Risk, 1981, Personal Injury Practice, Technique and Technology, 1986; contbr. articles to profl. jours. Trustee Lawrence S. Charfoos Found. Elected to Inner Circle of Advocates, 1973 Mem. ABA, Mich. Bar Assn. (com. U.S. cts. 1999-2003), Detroit Bar Assn. (past dir.), Am. Bd. Profl. Liability Attys. (founder, past pres.), Internat. Acad. Trial Lawyers. Office: 5510 Woodward Ave Detroit MI 48202-3804 Office Phone: 313-875-8080. Business E-Mail: lcharfoos@c2law.com.

CHARLA, LEONARD FRANCIS, lawyer, publisher; b. New Rochelle, NY, May 4, 1940; s. Leonard A. and Mary L. Charla; m. Kathleen Gerace, Feb. 3, 1968 (div. Dec. 1988); children: Larisa, Christopher; m. Elizabeth A. Du Mouchelle, Aug. 27, 1993. BA, Iona Coll., 1962; JD, Cath. U., 1965; LLM, George Washington U., 1971. Bar: D.C. 1967, N.J. 1970, Mich. 1971. Tech. writer IRS, Washington, 1966-67; atty. adv. ICC, 1967, atty., 1968-69; mgmt. intern HEW, 1967-68; atty. Bowes & Millner, Transp. Cons., Newark, 1969-71; atty. legal staff GM, Detroit, 1971-85, sr. counsel, 1985-87, asst. gen. counsel, 1987-89; sr. v.p. Clean Sites Inc., Alexandria, Va., 1989-90; atty. Butzel Long, Detroit, 1990—2005; pres. Countinghouse Press, Inc., Bloomfield, Mich., 1997—. Mem. faculty Coll. Creative Studies, Detroit, 1978-89, adj. asst. prof., 1982-89; faculty art U. Mich., 1980, 84-89, adj. asst. prof. 1988-89; disting. vis. prof. U. Detroit Mercy Law Sch., 2004. Author: Never Cooked Before/Gotta Cook Now!, 1999; pub. A Letter from Marty (Mary O'Herron), 2004, The Freya Project (Phil Rosette), 2004. Bd. dirs. Gt. Lakes Performing Artists Assocs., 1983-85; bd. dirs. Mich. Assn. Cmty. Arts Agys., 1983-89, 92-93, vice-chair, 1986-88, chair, 1988-89; bd. govs. Cath. U. Am. Alumni, 1982-02, v.p., 1993-99; active Info. Network Superfund Settlements, 1988-2004; bd. regents Cath. U. Am., 1992-02, Birmingham Bloomfield Art Assn., 1987-88, 94-95; bd. dirs. Friends Modern Art, Detroit Inst. Arts, 1996-2003, v.p., 1998-03; bd. dirs. Art Ctr. Mt. Clemens, Mich., 1997-05, chair facilities com., 2001-04, v.p. 2001-04; bd. dir. Nat. Spkrs. Assn. of Mich., 2004-05. Fellow N.Y. State Regents, 1962; scholar Cath. U. Law Sch., 1962-65. Mem. ABA, Nat. Spkrs. Assn.,(Mem. of Yr., 2004, bd. mem. Mich. chpt., 2004-05) State Bar Assn. (arts com. entertainment and sports sect. 1979-, chmn., 1980-81, mem. coun. 92-). Office: Countinghouse Press 6632 Telegraph Rd #311 Bloomfield Hills MI 48301 Office Fax: 248-642-7192. E-mail: lcharla@comcast.net.

CHARLAND, WILLIAM A., JR., writer, educator, consultant; b. Mpls., July 25, 1937; s. William Alfred and Mildred Alice Charland; m. Margaret Ann Daniels (div.); children: Susan Ann Charland Burke, James William; m. Phoebe Lawson Lawrence, Apr. 17, 1984. BA, Yankton (S.D.) Coll., 1959; MDiv, Yale U., 1962; D of Religion, Chgo. Theol. Sem., 1968. Cert. tchr. English as fgn. lang. Woodrow Wilson Found. tchg. fellow Clark Coll., Atlanta, 1964—67; chaplain, asst. prof. religion Lake Forest Coll., 1968—71; dir. Univ. Without Walls Chgo. State U., 1971—76; cons. Union for Experimenting Colls. and Univs., 1971—76; dir. Project Transition Loretto Heights Coll., 1977—80; dir. profl. career devel. program, The Foresight Program U. Denver, 1980—87; adj. prof. Western N.Mex. U., Silver City, 1999—. Sr. fellow for employment and tng. Ctr. for the New West, 1988—2002. Author: Decide to Live: Adult Approaches to Values, 1979, Life-Work: Meaningful Employment in an Age of Limits, 1986, The Heart of the Global Village: Technology and the New Millennium, 1990, Career Shifting: Starting Over in a Changing Economy, 1993, The Complete Idiot's Guide to Changing Careers, 1998, Life-Work: A Career Guide for Idealists, 1999; contbr. articles to newspapers, mags., jours. Vol. Main St. Project, Silver City; mem. Right Sharing of World Resources Com., Phila., 1984—89; mem. oversight com. Mountain View Friends Meeting, Denver, 1985—2000; rep. Friends World Com., Phila., 1984—89. Finalist Rhodes Scholarship, 1958; grantee, U.S. Office of Edn. Fund for Improvement of Post-Secondary Edn., 1985—87. Mem.: BorderLinks. Mem. Soc. Friends. Avocations: music, sports, studying Spanish. Home: 622 N California St Silver City NM 88061 Personal E-mail: billandphoebe@yahoo.com.

CHARLES, ALLAN G., obstetrician, educator; b. N.Y.C., Nov. 15, 1928; s. Harry G. and Alice (Grotzky) C.; m. Phyllis V. J. Vail, June 28, 1957; children: Della Marie, Aaron Joseph, David Jonathan. AB cum laude, NYU, 1948, MD, 1952. Diplomate: Am. Bd. Ob-gyn. Intern Phila. Gen. Hosp., 1952-53; resident in ob-gyn. Mt. Sinai Hosp., N.Y.C., 1955-57, Michael Reese Hosp., Chgo., 1957-60, clin. asst., 1960-61, assoc. attending physician, 1961-69, attending physician, 1969—; co-dir. Michael Reese Hosp. (Rh-Investigative Clinic), 1963—, vice-chmn. dept. ob-gyn., 1971, pres. staff, 1978, bd. dirs., 1981-84; chief ob-gyn. Michael Reese Hosp., 1990-99; chmn. rsch. and edn. found. Michael Reese Hosp. Med. Staff, 1996-2000; pvt. practice specializing in office gynecology Chgo., 1960—. Courtesy staff Chgo. Lying-In-Hosp.; clin. asst. prof. ob-gyn. U. Ill. Coll. Medicine, Chgo., 1960-64, Chgo. Med. Sch., 1964-72; clin. prof. Pritzker Sch. Medicine, U. Chgo., 1972-84; attending physician Northwestern Meml. Hosp., 1984-90; prof. clin. ob-gyn. Northwestern U., 1983; clin. prof. ob-gyn. U. Ill. Coll. Medicine, 1991. Author: Rh Iso Immunization and Erythroblastosis Fetalis, 1969; Contbr. articles to profl. jours. Fellow Am. Coll. Obstetricians and Gynecologists, Internat. Coll. Surgeons (chmn. Am. sect. ob-gyn. 1979-83, sec., asst. treas. Am. sect.), Ctrl. Assn. Obstetricians and Gynecologists; mem. AMA, Ill., Chgo. med. socs., Chgo. Gynecol. Soc. (v.p. 1980—, sec. 1988-90, pres.-elect, 1992, pres. 1993-94). Achievements include developing substitute for uterine tube, Rh-sensitization. Home: 1150 N Lake Shore Dr Apt 22GH Chicago IL 60611 Office: 55 E Washington St Fl 37 Chicago IL 60602-2103 Office Phone: 312-263-5517. Personal E-mail: charles0920@sbcglobal.net.

CHARLES, CORY ANNE, television director, television producer; b. Bklyn., Oct. 3, 1965; d. John Thomas and Anne Jane Azumbrado; m. Nick Charles, Oct. 4, 1997; stepchildren: Katie, Jason. BA in Comms. cum laude, L.I. U., 1987; MA in Polit. Sci., U. Calif., Santa Barbara, 1988. Asst. dir. rsch. McLaughlin Group, Washington, 1989-90; rschr., editl. prodr. CNN, Atlanta, 1990-98; dir. internat. guest booking CNNI, Atlanta, 1998—2004, sr. dir., exec. prodr. internat. guest booking, 2004—; copy person N.Y. Daily News, 1986. Participant transatlantic forum BMW-Quandt Found. Fellow German Marshall Fund, 2001, 03, 04. Mem. Coun. on Fgn. Rels. Avocations: travel, reading, photography, animals, cooking. Office: CNN 1 CNN Center Atlanta GA 30303 E-mail: Cory.Charles@turner.com.

CHARLES, GEORGE P., religious studies educator; b. Pengugtali, Nelson Island, Alaska, Feb. 13, 1941; s. Nicholas Ayaginar and Elena Charles; m. Nancy Jean Furlow, Aug. 6, 1999. AA in Electronics Tech., U. Alaska, 1971; BA, Alaska Pacific U., 1991; MA, PhD, U. Calif., Santa Barbara, 2000. Asst. prof. dept. Alaska native and rural devel. Coll. Rural Alaska, Anchorage, 2002—; asst. prof. Alaska native studies U. Alaska, Fairbanks, 1999—2002. Carving yupiaq transformation masks & yupiaq graphic art; actor: (films) Legend of Spirit Dog; voice actor: On Deadly Ground; 13th Warrior. With U.S. Navy, 1965—69, Vietnam. Recipient Dennis Demmert Appreciatioin and Recognition award, Native Am. Bus. Leaders and Rural Student Svcs., 2002; fellow Grad. Opportunties fellow, U. Calif. Santa Barbara, 1994—98, Rowney fellow, 1995—96, Dissertation fellow, Ctr. Advanced Study, Oslo, Norway, 1998—99, Allaway fellow, U. Calif. Santa Barbara, 1998—99, Affirmative Action Dissertation fellow, 1998—99, Michaelson fellow, 1998—99. Mem.: SAG (assoc.). Achievements include research in Yupiaq Narrative from Family Stories. Avocation: yupiaq graphic art and carving. Office: Danrd/Cra 2221 E No Lights Blvd # 213 Anchorage AK 99508 E-mail: ffgpc@uaf.edu.

CHARLES, GERARD, performing company executive, choreographer; b. Folkstone, Eng. m. Catherine Yoshimura; 1 child, Max. Student, Royal Ballet Sch. Ballet master BalletMet, Les Grands Ballets Canadiens; profl. dancer Milw. Ballet, Ballet Internat., London; assoc. artistic dir. BalletMet Columbus, artistic dir., 2001—. Choreographer, tchr., restager of works internationally in field. Choreographer The Sleeping Beauty, Coppelia; artistic dir.: Cinderella. Choreographic fellow, Nat. Endowment for Arts. Office: BalletMet Columbus 322 Mount Vernon Ave Columbus OH 43215 E-mail: gcharles@balletmet.org.*

CHARLES, ISABEL, university administrator; b. Bklyn., Mar. 10, 1926; d. James Patrick and Isabel (Roney) C. BA, Manhattan Coll., 1954; MA, U. Notre Dame, 1960, PhD, 1965; postgrad., U. Mich., 1968-69. Chmn. dept. English Bishop Watterson High Sch., Columbus, Ohio, 1954-59, St. Mary of the Springs Acad., Columbus, 1959-62; asst. prof. English Ohio Dominican Coll., Columbus, 1965-68, acad. dean, exec. v.p., 1969-73; asst. dean Coll. Arts and Letters, U. Notre Dame, 1973-75, acting dean, 1975, dean, 1976-82, asst. provost, 1982-87, assoc. provost, 1987-95; assoc. provost emerita U. Notre Dame, 1995—. Contbr. articles to profl. jours. Mem. MLA, Assn. Am. Colls. Home: 1802 Stonehedge Ln South Bend IN 46614-6341

CHARLES, JONATHAN STEPHEN, application developer; b. Framingham, Mass., Nov. 18, 1975; s. Ronald Douglas and Joanne Barbara (Lenox) Charles. BA in Computer Sci., U. Maine, 1999; postgrad., U. Mass., 2003, Suffolk U., 2004—. Programmer U. Maine, Orono, Maine, 1997; tchr., resident counselor Musiker Discovery Programs, Inc., Roslyn, NY, 1998; embedded sys. software engr. Sync Rsch., Norton, Mass., 1999—2000, Mapletree Networks, Norwood, Mass., 2000—02. Author: (poetry) Lost Love, 2004. Vol. math tchr. ABCD Learning, Boston, 2002. Avocations: reading, tennis, skiing, writing, art. Business E-Mail: jonathan_charles@hotmail.com.

CHARLES, MICHAEL HARRISON, architectural interior designer; b. Feb. 8, 1952; s. Melvin Mowrer and Sylvia Ann (Cookus) C. BA, U. Fla., 1976; AS, Fla. Jr. Coll., 1982. Lic. interior designer, Fla. Ptnr., v.p. St. Johns Lighting Design, St. Augustine, Fla., 1978-81; archtl. interior designer KBJ Architects, Inc., Jacksonville, Fla., 1982-86; owner Michael H. Charles Assocs.-Comml./Resdl. Interior Design, N.Y., Fla., 1988—; dir. interior design DeWolff Ptnrship. Architects, Rochester, N.Y., 1986-88. Cons. in field, St. Augustine, Fla., 1984—. Featured in: Interior Designers of the U.S.A., 1991. Mem.: ASID (bd. dirs. upstate N.Y., Can. East chpt. 1996—99), Soc. of the Cin., English Speaking Union, Coun. Qualification Resdl. Interior Designers (nat. bd. dirs.), Internat. Interior Deisgn Assn., Interior Design Soc. (nat. bd. dirs. 1995), Order of St. Maurice and St. Lazarus, Pa. Soc. Sons of Revolution, St. George's Soc. N.Y. (bd. dirs.), Nat. Soc. Sons of Am. Colonists (v.p. gen. 2001, gov. Fla. chpt.), Pilgrims of the U.S., Soc. Sons St. George Phila., Order Stars and Bars (N.Y. comdr.), Nat. Soc. Descendants of Colonial Govs., Nat. Soc. CAR (chpt. organizing pres. 1963, sr. Fla. officer 1985—86), St. David's Soc. N.Y., St. Andrew's Soc. N.Y., St. Nicholas Soc., Huguenot Soc. Am. (life; coun. mem.), Order Ams. Armorial Ancestery (life), Flagon and Trencher (life), Descs. of Early Quakers (life), Soc. Colonial Wars (coun. mem.), Colonial Soc. of the Acorn, SAR (v.p. Fla. chpt. 1982—86, N.Y. chpt. bd.), Colonial Soc. Pa., Gen. Soc. War 1812 (Fla. State pres. 1993—98), Nat. Soc. Sons and Daus. of Pilgrims, Descendants of Colonial Clergy, Am. Priory Venerable Order St. John Jerusalem, Lansdowne Club (London), Knights Templar, The Ch. Club N.Y., Ponte Vedra (Fla.) Club, Sovereign Mil. Order of Temple of Jerusalem (grand officier), Masons (32 degree). Republican. Episcopalian. Avocations: boating, genealogy. Also: 18 Carrera St Saint Augustine FL 32084-3622 Office: 420E 58th St Apt 5B New York NY 10022-2346 E-mail: design@mhcharles.com.

CHARLES, ROBERT BRUCE, federal agency administrator, lawyer; b. Portsmouth, Va., Aug. 23, 1960; s. Roland Wilbur Charles Jr. and Doris Anne (Hassell) Babineau; m. Marina Timasheff, Oct. 16, 1988; children: Nicholas Westcote, Sophia Anne. AB, Dartmouth Coll., 1982; MA, Oxford U., 1984; JD, Columbia U., 1987. Bar: N.Y. 1989, Conn. 1989, Maine 1990. Law clk. to judge U.S. Ct. Appeals (9th cir.), Seattle, 1987-88; assoc. Kramer, Levin et al, N.Y.C., 1988-91, Weil, Gotshal & Manges, N.Y.C., 1991-92, Washington, 1993-95; dep. assoc. dir. office of policy devel The White House, Washington, 1992-93; chief staff, chief counsel nat. security, internat. affairs and criminal justice subcommittee U.S. Ho. of Reps., Washington, 1995-99; chief staffer Speaker's Task Force on Drug Free Am., 1997-99; prof. govt. and cyberlaw Harvard U. Extension Sch., 1998—2001; pres. The Charles Group, 1999—2003, 2005—; asst. sec. of state, internat. narcotics and law enforcement U.S. Dept. State, Washington, 2003—05. Summer assoc. The White House, Washington, 1982-84, Supreme Ct. India, 1985. Author: Narcots and Terrorism: Logic, Links, and Looking Forward, 2003; contbr. articles to profl. jours., chpts. to books. Active Coun. on Fgn. Rels. Theodore Roosevelt Assn. Officer USNR, 1998—. Keasbey scholar, Phila. 1982, Tony Patino fellow Columbia U., 1984; recipient Petra T. Shattuck Disting. Tchg. award Harvard U., 2000. Republican. Avocations: running, hiking, writing. E-mail: RCharlesZZ@aol.com.

CHARLES, SHAWN THOMAS, finance company executive; b. Los Angeles, Calif., Sept. 28, 1971; s. David Jon and David Jon Charles; m. Melissa Connie Johnson, Aug. 10, 2002. BA in polit. sci., Lenoir-Rhyne Coll., 1992—95. Housing specialist Western Piedmont Coun. of Governments, Hickory, NC, 1995—96; dir. of orgn. Com. to Re-elect Congressman Cass Ballenger, Hickory, NC, 1996—96; mktg. rep. Klingspor Abrasives, Hickory, NC, 1996—98; regional fin. services mgr. Henredon Furniture, Morganton, NC, 1998—. Chmn. Catawba County Rep. Party, Catawba County, NC, 2001—; parish coun. mem. St. Aloysius Cath. Ch., Hickory, NC, 2000—04. Specialist U.S. Army, 1989—92, Germany, with USAR. R-Consevative. Roman Catholic. Avocations: Tae Kwon Do, running, reading, hiking, chess. Home: 2402 27th Ave Cir NE Hickory NC 28601 Office: Henredon Furniture 400 Henredon Rd Morganton NC 28655 Office Phone: 828-432-5100 5127. Personal E-mail: shawncharles@catgop.com.

CHARLES, WALTER, actor; b. East Stroudsburg, Pa., Apr. 4, 1945; s. Theodore Edmund and Catherine Alexandra (Carstensen) Jacobsen. MusB, Boston U., 1968. Appeared in Broadway shows La Cage Aux Folles, Aspects of Love, Me & My Girl, Cats, Sweeney Todd, Grease, Knickerbocker Holiday, Call Me Madam, A Christmas Carol, Sunset Boulevard (Can. co.), Kiss Me Kate, Boys from Syracuse, Big River, The Woman in White, 2005, and others; off Broadway, Wit, The Immigrant; films: A Fine Mess, Weeds, Fletch Lives, Prancer, TV programs Cagney & Lacey, Kate & Allie, Law & Order: Criminal Intent, The Street, 1981 Tony Awards, PBS Great Performances, 1983 Grammy awards, All My Children, others, also various nat. tours, regional and stock theatrical prodns., commls. and voice-overs. Recipient Best Actor in Musical award Bay Area Drama Critics, 1984.

CHARLESWORTH, ARTHUR THOMAS, mathematics professor; b. Gainesville, Fla., Nov. 8, 1944; s. Arthur Riggs and Martha Jean (Hamilton) C.; m. Josephine Ann Owenby, Sept. 10, 1966; 1 child, Jonathan David. BS in Math., Stetson U., 1966; AM in Math., Duke U., 1968, PhD in Math., 1974; MS in Computer Sci., U. Va., 1983. Trajectory analysis engr. Apollo support dept. GE, Daytona Bch., Fla., 1966-67; instr. Jacksonville (Fla.) U., 1968-69, Randolph-Macon Coll., Ashland, Va., 1969-71; asst. prof. Queens Coll., Charlotte, N.C., 1974-76, U. Richmond, Va., 1976-82, assoc. prof., 1982-89, prof., 1989—. Sec. astronomy, math., physics sect. Va. Acad. Sci., 1977-78, chmn., 1978-79; treas. Md., D.C., Va. sect. Math. Assn. Am., 1980-82. Contbr. articles to profl. jours. Chmn. Trinity Meth. Comsn. on Missions, Richmond, 1981. Research grantee NASA Langley Rsch. Ctr., Hampton, Va., 1987, 88, 89, 90, 91, 92. Mem. IEEE, Assn. Computing Machinery, Omicron Delta Kappa, Sigma Xi. Avocations: hiking, rock collecting. Office: U Richmond Dept Math/Computer Sci Richmond VA 23173 Business E-Mail: charlesworth@richmond.edu.

CHARLESWORTH, DONNA, assistant principal; d. Harry and Agnes Phyllis Hurey; m. Norman Lewis Charlesworth, Apr. 21, 2000. BA, Glassboro (N.J.) State Coll., 1982; MEd, Rowan U., 1994. Tchr. Cherokee H.S., Marlton, NJ, 1984—, asst. prin., 1995—. Mem.: N.J. Prin. Suprs. Assn., Assn. Suprs. Curriculum Devel., Nat. Assn. Secondary Sch. Prins. Office: Cherokee High School 120 Tomlinson Mill Rd Marlton NJ 08053

CHARLESWORTH, ERNEST NEAL, allergist, immunologist, dermatologist, educator; b. Denver, June 11, 1945; s. Albert Ernest and Wilma Nadine (Wright) C.; m. Margaret Louise Gay, July 12, 1969; children: Richard Neil, Mark Edward. BS, U. Houston, 1967; MD, U. Tex., 1971. Diplomate Am. Bd. Allergy and Immunology, Am. Bd. Dermatology, Am. Bd. Internal Medicine, Diagnostic Lab. Immunology Bd. Commd. capt. USAF, 1971, advanced through grades to col., 1987;, ret. 1996; intern in medicine Wilford Hall USAF Med. Ctr., Lackland AFB, Tex., 1971-72, resident in dermatology, 1973-76, resident in internal medicine, 1984-86; staff dermatologist USAF Med. Ctr., Keesler AFB, Miss., 1976-78; pvt. practice in dermatology Jackson, Miss., 1978-81; clin. faculty dept. medicine U. Miss. Med. Sch., Jackson, 1979-81; chief dermatology svc. USAF Regional Med. Ctr., Clark Air Base, The Philippines, 1981-84; fellow in allergy and immunology Johns Hopkins U. Sch. Medicine, Balt., 1986-89, clin. faculty divsn. allergy and clin. immunology, 1988-89; asst. chief allergy-immunology svc. Wilford Hall USAF Med. Ctr., Lackland AFB, 1989-95; assoc. prof. medicine Uniformed Svcs. Univ. of The Health Scis., Bethesda, Md., 1990-92; clin. assoc. prof. U. Tex. Health Sci. Ctr., San Antonio, 1990-92; allergist/dermatologist Brenham (Tex.) Clinic Assn., 1995—. Cons. to surgeon gen. for dermatology PACAF Med. Command, Hickam AFB, Hawaii, 1981-84; presenter Harold S. Nelson Allergy-Immunology Symposium, Fitsimons Army Med. Ctr., Aurora, Colo., Johns Hopkins Asthma and Allergy Ctr., Balt., 16th Hawaii Dermatology Seminar, Maui. Contbr. articles to Arch. Dermatology, Jour. Mil. Assn. Dermatology, Jour. Clin. Investigation, Internat. Arch. Allergy Immunology, Insights in Allergy, Jour. Pediatrics, Jour. Investigative Dermatology. Recipient Clemens Von Pirquet Rsch. award Am. Coll. Allergy and Immunology, 1987. Fellow ACP (presenter), Am. Acad. Dermatology, Am. Coll. Allergy (presenter); mem. Am. Acad. Allergy and Immunology (dermatologic disease interest sect., presenter, Young Investigator award 1989), Assn. Air Force Allergists, Soc. Air Force Physicians, Soc. Investigative Dermatology, San Antonio Allergy Soc. (sec.). Episcopalian. Achievements include rsch. in late-phase allergic reaction sites, intractable sneezing, cutaneous late-phase response to allergen, decline in pulmonary function tests in extrinsic asthmatics immediately following immunotherapy. Home: 1207 Live Oak St San Angelo TX 76901-4144 Office: Shannon Clinic 215 E College San Angelo TX 76903

CHARLESWORTH, JEANNE ARLENE, secondary school educator; b. Paterson, NJ, Mar. 30, 1947; d. William A. and Elizabeth J. Grossmann; m. Jeffrey M. Charlesworth, Mar. 31, 1945; children: Andrew, Alan. BS, Douglass Coll., 1968; MEd, Arcadia Coll., 1981. Tchr. Hatboro-Horsham (Pa.) Sch. Dist., 1970—; pres. Mont-Bucks (Pa.) FCS Assn., 1993—95. Reviewer McGraw Hill, 2000, 03; presenter in field. Grantee, Hatboro-Horsham (Pa.) Edn. Found., 1989, 1991, 1992, 2003. Mem.: NEA, Am. Assn. Family and Consumer Scis. (chmn. membership Pa. chpt. 1998—2000, planning com. annual mtg. Pa. chpt. 1997, 2000, 2005), Nat. Assn. Edn. Young Children. Avocation: travel. Office: Hatboro Horsham High Sch 899 Horsham Rd Horsham PA 19044

CHARLIP, RALPH BLAIR, military officer, health facility administrator; b. Detroit, July 16, 1952; s. Jack Edward and Dorothea (Steinman) Charlip; m. Cynthia Lanell Sallas, May 23, 1987. BA, U. Ariz., 1976, MPA, 1977. Commd. 2nd lt. USAF, 1978, advanced through grades to lt. col., 1994; squadron comdr. USAF Regional Hosp., Langley AFB, Va., 1978-79, dir. patient adminstrn., 1979-80, plant mgr., 1980-81; dir. med. resource mgmt. USAF Clinic Andersen, Andersen AFB, 1981-82; dir. patient adminstrn. Malcolm Grow USAF Med. Ctr., Andrews AFB, Md., 1983-84; intern Data Systems Design Ctr., Gunter AFB, Ala., 1984-85; health policy devel. officer USAF Hdqs., Bolling AFB, DC, 1985-89; dir. patient adminstrn. USAF Med. Ctr., Wright-Patterson AFB, Ohio, 1989-92; assoc. dir. med. svcs. Air Nat. Guard Hqrs., Andrews AFB, 1992-94; dir. plans integration and mktg. Dept.

Def. Health Svcs. Region VII, Ft. Bliss, Tex., 1994-96; comdr. 423 Clinic, Upwood, England, 1996-97; adminstr. aerospace med. Armstrong Lab., Brooks AFB, Tex., 1997; dep. comdr. 59 Med. Support Group, Lackland AFB, Tex., 1997-99; assoc. adminstr. 59 Med. Wing, Lackland AFB, 1999-2000; dir. health adminstrn. ctr. VA, Denver, 2000—. Author: (book) Your Health Benefits, 1989. Recipient Ray Brown award, AMSUS, 2004. Fellow: Am. Acad. Med. Adminstrs., Am. Coll. Healthcare Execs. Office: VA HAC 300 S Jackson St Ste 444 Denver CO 80209-3134

CHARLOT, JOSEPH LEONCE, JR., preventive medicine physician; b. Bklyn., Oct. 19, 1967; s. Joseph Leonce and Marie Andree Charlot; m. Denise Michelle Johnson, July 11, 1967. BA, Rutgers U., 1986—90; MD, UMDNJ-Robert Wood Johnson Med. Sch., 1990—95; MPH, UMDNJ-Rutgers Sch. of Pub. Health, 1991—93. Med. Rev. Officer Med. Rev. Officer Certification Coun., Ill. State, 2001, Advanced Cardiac Life Support Am. Heart Assn., Ill. State, 2004, Basic Life Support Am. Heart Assn., Ill. State, 2004, Preventive Medicine Am. Bd. of Preventive Medicine, Ill. State, 2003, Am. Bd. of Preventive Medicine, Ill. State, 2004; Prison Religious Vol. Prison Fellowship, Va. State, 1999. Resident physician U. of Md. Med. Sys., Balt., 1995—97, Trover Clinic, Madisonville, Ky., 1997—98; locum tenens occupl. medicine physician Concentra Med. Centers, Richmond, Va., 1999—2000; resident physician Ft. Wayne Med. Found., Ft. Wayne, Ind., 2000—00; med. dir. Cmty. Occupl. Medicine, Elkhart, Ind., 2001—02; 2004plant occupl. medicine physician Daimler Chrysler Kokomo Transmission Plant, Kokomo, Ind., 2002; med. dir. US Health Works, Branford, Conn., 2004—. Prison religious vol. Prison Fellowship, Richmond, Va., 1999—2000; religious vol. Kokomo Rescue Mission, Kokomo, Ind., 2003—03; physician vol. Kokomo Cmty. Health Initative, 2002—03. Fellow Rsch. Fellowship, Robert Wood Johnson Med. Sch., 1991. Mem.: APHA (assoc.), AMA (assoc.), Am. Coll. of Preventive Medicine (assoc.), Christian Med. and Dental Associations (assoc.). Avocations: basketball, reading, computer programming, bicycling, weightlifting. Office: US Health Works 144 N Main St Branford CT 06405 Personal E-mail: jcharlot@earthlink.net.

CHARLSON, ALAN EDWARD, lawyer, retail executive; b. Indiana, Pa., 1948; m. Nancy Leavitt; 1 child. BS, U. Mich.; JD, U. Pitts. Bar: Pa. 1973, Mo. 1996. Assoc. gen. counsel The May Dept. Stores Co., St. Louis, 1977—79, asst. gen. counsel, 1979—81, counsel, 1981—82; exec. v.p., chief legal counsel May Centers Inc. subsid, 1982—88; sr. counsel The May Dept. Stores Co., St. Louis, 1988—98, sr. v.p., chief counsel, 1998—2001, sr. v.p., gen. counsel, 2001—. Mem.: ABA. Office: May Dept Stores Co 611 Olive St Ste 1750 Saint Louis MO 63101-1721

CHARLSON, MICHAEL LLOYD, lawyer; b. Pitts., Sept. 1, 1958; s. Benjamin Charlson and Sheila (Ostrow) Flodberg; m. Elizabeth Stone, Aug. 31, 1986. BS, MS in Biol. Sci., Stanford U., 1981; JD, U. Calif., Berkeley, 1985. Bar: Calif. 1985, D.C. 2002, U.S. Dist. Ct. (no. and ea. dists.) Calif. 1987, U.S. Ct. Appeals (9th cir.) 1990, U.S. Dist Ct. (cen. dist.) Calif., U.S. Dist. Ct. (so. dist.) Calif. 1992, U.S. Supreme Ct. 1994. Law clk. to Judge William C. Canby U.S. Ct. Appeals (9th cir.), Phoenix, 1985-86; ptnr. Heller, Ehrman, White & McAuliffe, Menlo Park, Calif., 1986—. Dir. Legal Aid Soc., San Mateo, Calif., 2000—, ODC/San Francisco, Calif., 2000—. Mem. atty. div. Jewish Fedn. San Francisco, 1987—. Mem. ABA (editorial bd. Litigation mag. 1989—92), Bar Assn. of San Francisco, Santa Clara (Calif.) Bar Assn., Order of Coif. Democrat. Home: 1412 Ashwood Dr San Mateo CA 94402-3434 Office: Heller Ehrman White & McAuliffe LLP 275 Middlefield Rd Menlo Park CA 94025-3506 Office Phone: 650-324-7000. Fax: 650-324-6020. E-mail: mcharlson@lewm.com.

CHARLSON, ROBERT JAY, atmospheric sciences educator; b. San Jose, Calif., Sept. 30, 1936; s. Rolland Walter and Harriet Adele (Stucky) C.; m. Patricia Elaine Allison, Mar. 16, 1964; children: Daniel Owen, Amanda Marcella. BS in Chemistry, Stanford U., 1958, MS in Chemistry, 1959; PhD in Atmospheric Scis., U. Wash., 1964; postgrad. (Fulbright scholar), London U., 1964-65; PhD (hon.), Stockholm U., 1993. Rsch. engr. Boeing Co., Seattle, 1959-62; rsch. asst. prof. dept. civil engring. U. Wash., Seattle, 1965-69, assoc. prof. atmospheric chemistry, 1969-71, assoc. prof. civil engring. and geophysics, 1971-74, prof. atmospheric chemistry in civil engring. geophysics and environ. studies, 1974-94, prof. atmospheric scis., 1985-98, adj. prof. chemistry, 1985-96, prof., 1996-98, prof. emeritus, 1998—; King Carl XVI Gustaf prof. environ. sci. Sweden, 1999-2000. Author: (with S.S. Butcher) An Introduction to Air Chemistry, 1972; assoc. editor: Jour. Applied Meteorology, 1971-73; co-editor: Global Biogeochemical Cycles, 1992; Earth System Science: From Biogeochemical Cycles to Global Change, 2000; mem. editorial bd. Jour. Boundary Layer Meteorology, 1971-86, Water, Air and Soil Pollution, 1971-85; contbr. articles on atmosphere chemistry to profl. jours.; patentee in field. Co-recipient Gerbier/Mumm award World Meteorol. Orgn., 1988; grantee USPHS, EPA, NSF, NASA, NOAA. Fellow Am. Meteorol. Soc., Am. Geophys. Union; mem. AAAS, Am. Chem. Soc., Sigma Xi, Phi Lambda Upson (hon.). Office: U Wash Dept Atmospheric Scis PO Box 351640 Seattle WA 98195-0001

CHARLTON, JENNIFER J., music educator; b. Great Falls, Mont., Jan. 3, 1968; d. Paul Leroy Carlson and Nadine Phylis Schoemer; m. Vince Dale Charlton, July 14, 1990. BE, Mont. State U., 1990. Tchr. music pvt. instr., 1992—. Ch. musician Valley Bapt. Ch., Huntley, Mont., 1990—; accompaniment for local music festival Billings, Mont., 1996—2002.

CHARLTON, JESSE MELVIN, JR., retired management educator, lawyer; b. Livonia, La., May 12, 1916; s. Jesse Melvin and Anna Lela (Medlin) C.; m. Mary Camp, Oct. 4, 1941; children: Jesse Melvin, Frances Anne. BS, La. State U., 1937, MBA, 1938; JD, Harvard U., 1951. Bar: U.S. Ct. Mil. Appeals 1952, U.S. Supreme Ct 1963, D.C. 1951. Instr. U. Ala., 1938-40; commd. 2d lt., inf. U.S. Army, 1940; advanced through grades to col. U.S. Army (Judge Adv. Gen.'s Corps), 1962; dep. comdr. Judge Adv. Gen. Sch., Charlottesville, Va., 1962-64; ret., 1964; mem. faculty U. New Orleans Coll. Bus., 1964-81, prof. mgmt., 1971-81, prof. emeritus, 1981—; asst. dean coll. bus. U. New Orleans, 1967-71, dean grad. sch., 1978-80. Author handbook; co-editor: Statistical Abstract of Louisiana, 5th edit, 1974. Decorated Bronze Star. Mem. D.C. Bar Assn. Republican.

CHARLTON, JOHN KIPP, pediatrician; b. Omaha, Jan. 26, 1937; s. George Paul and Mildred (Kipp) C.; m. Susan S. Young, Aug. 15, 1959; children: Paul, Cynthia, Daphne, Gregory. AB, Amherst Coll., 1958; MD, Cornell U., 1962. Intern Ohio State U. Hosp., Columbus, 1962-63; resident in pediatrics Children's Hosp., Dallas, 1966-68, chief resident in pediatrics, 1968-69; fellow in nephrology U. Tex. Southwestern Med. Sch., Dallas, 1969-70; pvt. practice medicine specializing in pediatrics, Phoenix, from 1970; chmn. dept. pediatrics Maricopa Med. Ctr., Phoenix, 1971-78, 84-93, pres. med. staff, 1991; med. dir., bd. dirs. Crisis Nursery, Inc., 1977—. Clin. assoc. prof. pediat. U. Ariz. Coll Medicine, asst. dean for student affairs, 2000—. Author articles and book revs. in field. Pres. Maricopa County Child Abuse Coun., 1977-81; bd. dirs. Florence Crittenton Svcs., 1980-83, Ariz. Children's Found., 1987-91; mem. Gov.'s Coun. on Children, Youth and Families, 1984-86. Officer M.C., USAF, 1963-65. Recipient Hon. Kachina award for volunteerism, 1980, Jefferson award for volunteerism, 1980, Horace Steel Child Advocacy award, 1993; named Clin. Sci. Educator of Yr., U. Ariz., 1997, 99, 2000, 2001. Mem. Am. Acad. Pediatrics, Ariz. Pediatric Soc., Maricopa County Pediatric Soc. (past pres.). Home: 6230 E Exeter Blvd Scottsdale AZ 85251-3060 Office: Maricopa Med Ctr 2601 E Roosevelt St Phoenix AZ 85008-4973 Office Phone: 602-344-5404. E-mail: kipp_charlton@medprodoctors.com.

CHARLTON, PAUL K., prosecutor, lawyer; b. 1960; m. Susan Charlton; 2 children. BA in Spanish, U. Ariz., 1983; JD, Ariz. State U., 1988. Law clk. to Atty. Gen. Bob Corbin; asst. atty. gen. Ariz. Atty. Gen. Office; asst. U.S. atty. US Dept. Justice, 1991—2001, U.S. atty. dist. Ariz., 2001—. Recipient Prosecutor of Yr., Fed. law Enforcement Officer's Assn., 1997. Office: Dist Ariz 2 Renaissance Sq Ste 1200 40 N Central Ave Phoenix AZ 85004-4408

CHARLTON, SHIRLEY MARIE, educational consultant; b. Nashville, Nov. 20, 1934; d. Ottis Ruby and Irene Lenoir (Cabler) C.; children: David Matthew Christian Sironen, Charlton Gwynn Cabler Sironen. BS, George Peabody Coll. Tchrs., 1954; MA in Ednl. Adminstrn. and Supervision, U. Tenn., Chattanooga, 1970. Cert. supr., Tenn. Classroom tchr. Albany (Ga.) Pub. Schs., 1954-55, 56-57, Orlando (Fla.) Pub. Schs., 1960-61, Grand Forks (N.D.) Pub. Schs., 1962-65; TV and resource tchr. Chattanooga Publ Schs., 1965-67, supr., 1967-97; cons., 1997-99. Mem. NEA, Tenn. Edn. Assn., Chattanooga Edn. Assn. (charter mem. negotiating team 1979-81), Alpha Delta Kappa (v.p. 1981-83). Episcopalian. Avocations: history, genealogy, acting, art, music.

CHARNAS, MICHAEL (MANNIE CHARNAS), investment company executive; b. Cleve., Sept. 24, 1947; s. Max and Eleanor (Gross) C.; m. Mimi F. Stein, June 10, 1990; 1 child from previous marriage, Matthew; 1 child, Max. BBA, Ohio State U., 1969, MBA in Fin., 1971. Page Ohio Ho. of Reps., 1969; mem. Ohio Staters, Inc., 1969; fin. analyst Addressograph-Multigraph, Inc., Cleve., 1971-73; asst. to pres., dir. planning and budget 1st Nat. Supermarkets, Inc (Pick-N-Pay), Cleve., 1975-78, asst. to pres., v.p. planning and budgets, 1978-79, sr. v.p. fin., adminstr., 1979-81, sr. v.p., CFO, adminstrv. officer Hartford Conn., 1981-86; founder Charnas Mktg. and Investment Co., 1986—; pres., owner Indsl. Pallet and Packaging Co., Beachwood, Ohio, 1986-94; regional v.p. Pallet Pallet, Inc. (formerly Indsl. Pallet and Packaging Co.), Toronto, 1995-97; co-owner Samm Properties and Samm Mgmt. Svcs., Ltd., 1998—; owner, operator Self Storage Facilities, Ohio and Fla.; co-owner Fat Burrito, Inc., a Qdoba Mexican Grill Restaurants franchise, Iowa, 2004—; owner/CEO Pallet Distbrs., Inc., 1999—2001; v.p., owner PMC Investment Group, 2003; franchisee of Qdoba Mexican Grill Restaurants, Cen. Ill, 1990—2005. Bd. dirs. Gorman-Lavelle Corp. Jewish. Avocations: tennis, reading, collecting modern classic cars. Office: 3659 Green Rd Ste 105 Cleveland OH 44122 Office Phone: 216-378-3306. E-mail: bizwiz924@cs.com.

CHARNESS, WAYNE SAMUEL, public relations executive; b. Montreal, Que., Can., June 3, 1954; came to U.S., 1972; s. Gerald Steven and Phyllis Selma (Rosenblatt) C.; m. Jeanie Stephan, Oct. 18, 1986. BA in Psychology, Nasson Coll., 1976; MS in Communications, Boston U., 1978. Account exec. Newsome & Co., N.Y.C., 1978-80, Fleishmin-Hillard, N.Y.C., 1980-82, account supr., 1982-84; mgr. client svc. Cohn & Wolfe, N.Y.C., 1984-85, v.p. client svc., 1985, v.p., group mgr., 1985-87; assoc. v.p., dir. pub. rels. and promotions Hasbro, Inc., Pawtucket, R.I., 1987-90, v.p. corp. communictions, 1990-97, sr. v.p. corp. comms., 1997—. Cons. Blackstone Valley C. of C., Pawtucket, 1987-88; bd. dirs. Kids Face, Nashville, 1991-95. Active Big Brothers, Springvale, Maine, 1974-75; pres. bd. dirs. Adoption R.I., 1997—; co-chair Gov. Task Force on Adoption, 1996—; bd. dirs. Providence Children Mus., 1993-97, Jewish Fedn. of R.I., 1990-96. Recipient Silver Anvil award Pub. Rels. Soc. Am., 1982. Mem. Psi Chi. Office: Hasbro Inc 1027 Newport Ave Pawtucket RI 02861-2500

CHARNEY, MELVIN, artist, architect, educator; b. Montreal, Que., Can., Aug. 28, 1935; s. H. and F. (Cassack) C.; m. Ann Korsower, May 29, 1960; 1 child, Dara Alexandra. BArch, McGill U., Montreal, 1958; MArch, Yale U., 1959. Prin. Melvin Charney, Architect, Montreal, 1964—; prof. U. Montreal, 1964-95. Mem. architects com. Am. Acad. Arts and Scis., Boston, 1968-69; co-dir. task force on housing Govt. of Can., Ottawa, 1970-71; mem. adv. com. Can. Centre for Architecture, Montreal, 1983-89; founding bd. dirs. Conseil des Arts et des Lettres, Quebec, 1994-97; invited prof. to numerous univs. One-man shows include Harvard U., 1977, Art Gallery of Ont., Toronto, 1978, Musee d'Art Contemporain, Montreal, 1979, P.S.1, N.Y.C., 1979, Can. Cultural Ctrs., Paris and Brussels, 1980, Mus. Contemporary Art, Chgo., 1982, Richard Gray Gallery, Chgo., 1982, 49th Parallel, Centre for Can. Contemporary Art, N.Y.C., 1982, 87, Agnes Etherington Art Centre, Kingston, Ont., 1983, represented Can. at the 42nd Venice Biennale, 1986, Renè Blouin Gallery, Montreal, 1987, 88, Ctr. for Can. Art, N.Y., 1987, Sable-Castelli Gallery, Toronto, 1988, 91, 92, 93, 95, 97, 99, 2001, 03, maj. retrospective Can. Centre for Architecture, Montreal, 1991-92, de Beyrie Gallery, Paris, 1994, Israel Mus., Jerusalem, 1996, Power Plant Gallery Contemporary Art, Toronto, 1995, Franc Basse-Normandie, Caen, France, 1997, Fondation pour l'architecture, Brussels, 1997; Can. Pavilion, 7th Venice Biennale of Architecture, 2000, major retrospective Musée d'art Contemporain de Montréal, 2002, Can. Mus. Contemporary Photography, Nat. Gallery, Ottawa, 2003-04; exhibited in group shows at Montreal Mus. Fine Arts, 1972, 83, Musee d'Art Moderne de la Ville de Paris, 1973, Institut d'Art Contemporain, Montreal, 1975, 76, XXI Olympic Games, Montreal, 1976, John Weber Gallery, N.Y., 1979, Max Protetch Gallery, N.Y.C., 1979, L.A. Inst. Contemporary Art, 1980, Vancouver Art Gallery, 1980, Centre George Pompidou, 1980, Musee du Que., 1981, 83, 85, 89, 91, 98, Akademie der Kunst, Berlin, 1983, Kunstverein, Stuttgart, 1983, Mus. Contemporary Art, Chgo., 1984, Internationalen Bauasstellung, Berlin, 1984, 17th Trianale di Milano, 1985, Centre internat. d'art contemporain, Montreal, 1985, 96, Musee d'art Contemporain de Montreal, 1987, 92, 99, 2000, Power Plant, Contemporary Art at Harbourfront, Toronto, 1988, The Canadian Ctr. Architecture, Montreal, 1989, 99, 00, Musee du Quebec, 1989, 91, Nat. Mus. Contemporary Art, Seoul, South Korea, 1990, Canadian Pavilion, V Biennale di Architettura, Venice, 1991, Passages, Ctr. d'art contemporain, Troyes, France, 1992, Musèe nat. d'art moderne, Paris, 1994, Ctr. Cultura Contemporania, Barcelona, 1994, Royal Festival Hall Galleries, London, 1995, Manchester City Art Gallery, 1995, Marlborough-Chelsea Gallery, N.Y., 1998, Espaid'art Contemporani de Castello, Spain, 2000, Bibliotheque Nat. de France, Paris, 2000, Concordia U. Art Gallery, 2001, Centre nationale de la photographie, Paris, 2002, others; sculpture commns. The Can. Tribute to Human Rights, Ottawa, 1986, Urban Sculpture Garden for Can. Ctr. Architecture, Montreal, 1987, Place Berri, Montreal, 1991, Esplanade Frontenac, Sherbrooke, Que., 2003-04; represented in permanent collections Nat. Gallery Can., Ottawa, Can. Coun. Art Bank, Ottawa, Art Gallery Ont., Toronto, Musee d'art contemporain, Montreal, Can. Ctr. Architecture, Montreal, Mus. Contemporary Art, Chgo., IBM Collection, Chgo., Fonds Nat. d'Art Contemporain, Paris, Musee du Quebec, Montreal Mus. Fine Arts, Frac Basse Normandie, France, Art Gallery Hamilton, Israel Mus., Jerusalem; contbr. articles to profl. jours. Decorated Order of Que., 2003; recipient Arts award Minister des Affaires Culturelles, 1967, research award Humanities and Social Scis. Coun., 1971, Berlin Arts award Deutcher Akademischer Austanschdienst, 1982, Sr. Arts award Can. Coun., 1983, 87, 96, Prix du Que. in visual arts, 1996, Lynch-Stanton award to disting. artists Can. Coun., 1997, Arts award Couseil Arts et Letters du Que., 2000. Mem. Royal Can. Acad., Ras. des Artists du Que, Royal Architectural Inst. of Can. Home: 3620 Marlowe Ave Montreal PQ Canada H4A 3L7 E-mail: mcharney@aol.com.

CHARNEY, NATALIE J., mental health services professional, educator, researcher; d. Frances E. and Leon A. Seidman; m. David Charney (dec.); 1 child, Melissa D Jonassen. BA cum laude, U. Pa., 1988, MA, MSEd, U. Pa., 1991; PhD in Health Care Adminstrn., Suffield U., 2005. Bd. cert. med. psychotherapist/psychodiagnostician, cert. cognitive behavioral therapist; co-occurring disorders profl. diplomate. Rsch. and adminstrv. assoc./acting dir. psychoendocrinology in psychiatry Hosp. U. Pa., Phila., 1972—82; pvt. practice Phila., 1991—; asst. adminstr. Phila. Mental Health Clinic, Phila., 1983—85; adminstr. sect. geriatric psychiatry Hosp. U. Pa., Phila., 1985—93; dir. family-based mental health svcs. Dr. Warren E. Smith CMH/MR/SA Ctrs., Phila., 1993—95, dir. mental health svcs. divsn., 1995—96; mgr. mental health svcs. divsn., vocat. rehab. programs Phila. OIC, 1998, 2004; dir. admissions, adult outpatient behavioral health svcs. and rsch. Cmty. Coun. for MH/MR, Inc., Phila., 1998—2004; clin. assoc. in psychiatry U. Pa. Med. Sch., Phila., 1992—, staff therapist Ctr. for Cognitive Therapy, 1992—. Project dir. Sobriety Through Out Patient Inc., Phila., 2004—; mem. Am. Bd. Psychotherapists and Psychodiagnosticians; presenter in field. Mem. editl. bd. The Med. Psychotherapist; contbr. articles to profl. jours. Recipient Cert. of Gratitude, Sled Toys for Tots, 1994. Mem.: APA (assoc.), Nat. Assn. Cognitive-Behavioral Therapists, Gerontol. Soc. Am. (rsch. edn. and practice com., pvt. sector task force 1989—92), Phila. Coalition of Cmty. Care Providers (mental health dirs. com., children's mental health com.), Pa. Cmty. Providers Assn. (family-home based subcom., mental health com. 1993—96). Office: Med Tower 255 S 17th St Ste 1907 Philadelphia PA 19103 Office Phone: 215-725-6080. Personal E-mail: ncharney@bellatlantic.net.

CHARNIN, JADE HOBSON, magazine executive; b. NYC, Mar. 12, 1945; d. John Louis Campo and Elizabeth (Anne) Stanton); m. David Alan Hobson,Dec. 30 (div. 1972); m. Martin Charnin, Dec. 18, 1984. BA, NYU, 1967. Asst. editor Glamour mag., N.Y.C., 1970; accessory editor Vogue mag., N.Y.C., 1970-78, fashion editor, 1978-81, fashion dir., 1981-86, creative dir. fashion, 1987-88; v.p., dir. creative svcs for fashion and design group Revlon Inc., 1988; exec. creative dir. Mirabella Mag., 1988-94; fashion dir. N.Y. Mag., 1994-98; freelance journalist, 1999—. Pres. Growing Things, Inc., 2002—; cons. editor Self mag., N.Y.C., 1979—81. Costume coord. for off-Broadways shows Upstairs at Oneals, 1981, Laughing Matters, 1989, Martin Charnin, the Hits and the M.S.'s, 1990. Mem.: ASPCA, Hort. Soc. N.Y., Am. Hort. Soc., Assn. Profl. Landscape Designers, Humane Soc. N.Y. (bd. dirs.), Wilton Garden Club (bd. dirs.). Avocations: opera, ballet, theater, skiing. Personal E-mail: jadehobson@aol.com.

CHARNS, MARTIN PAUL, management research administrator, educator; b. Cleve., Mar. 24, 1946; s. David Orland and Edna Miriam Charns; m. Judy Levin, Aug. 17, 1980; 1 child, David Matthew. BS, Case Inst. of Tech., 1967; MBA, Harvard U., 1969, DBA, 1973. Pres. Cambridge Interactive Sys., Inc, Newton, Mass., 1973—; dir. Mgmt. Decision and Rsch. Ctr., Boston, 1992—2004; prof. health svcs. Boston U. Sch. of Pub. Health, Boston, 1998—; dir. Ctr. for Orgn., Leadership and Mgmt. Rsch., Boston, 2004—. Spkr. in field. Author: (book) Collaboration in Health Care: The Hartford Hospital Experience, Collaborative Management in Health Care: Implementing the Integrative Organization, Health Care Organizations: A Model for Management (named one best mgmt. books, Hosps. Mag., 1984, selected for Ray E. Brown Collection, Am. Coll. Healthcare Execs.), (conf. presentation) Patterns of Coordination and Clinical Outcomes: A Study of Surgical Services. Recipient Best Paper award, Health Care Adminstrn. Divsn., Acad. of Mgmt., 1997; grantee, Robert Wood Johnson Found., 2002—05, VA Health Svcs. R&D, 2004—, 2004—; Baker scholar, Harvard U., 1969, John E. Thayer fellow, 1969. Mem.: Acad. of Mgmt. (chair health care adminstrn. divsn. 1987—88), Academy Health, Am. Coll. of Health Care Execs. (mem. com. on higher edn. 1980—82), Aircraft Owners and Pilots Assn., Tau Beta Pi, Sigma Xi. Avocation: aviation. Office: Boston U Sch Pub Health 715 Albany St Boston MA 02118-2526 Office Phone: 617-414-1431. Personal E-mail: mcharns@bu.edu.

CHARNVEJA, PAT S., civic leader, former oil and gas industry executive; b. Bangkok; came to US, 1961; m. Kitipot Charnveja; 3 children. Attended, W. Tex. A&M, Canyon, Tex., U. Houston. Various positions in oil and gas industry, 1976—98; mng. dir. PSKC Internat. LLC. Liaison Royal Thai Embassy & Royal Thai Consulate Gen. Founder & pres. Thai Am. Chamber of Commerce; pres. Thai Arts and Culture of Houston; former pres. Thai Assn. of Greater Houston; mem. bd. dirs. & former pres. Asian/Pacific Am. Heritage Assn.; mem. Focus Group for Leadership Ed. for Asian Pacifics, Inc.; mem. cultural diversity com. Holocaust Museum Houston; treasurer Asian Am. Voters' Coalition; adv. bd. mem. Asia Soc. Tex. Ctr.; mem. Chinese Cmty. Ctr., VN Teamwork. Office: Thai Am Chamber Commerce PO Box 681277 Houston TX 77268-1277 Office Phone: 281-477-8803. E-mail: prapatip@sbcglobal.net.

CHARON, RITA, medical educator; b. Providence, 1949; BA in Biology and Child Edn., Fordham U., 1970; MD, Harvard U., 1978; MA in English, Columbia U., 1990, MPhil in English, 1992, PhD in English, 1999. Resident Montefiore Hosp. and Med. Ctr., Bronx, NY; instr. in medicine Coll. of Physicians and Surgeons, Columbia U., 1983—88, asst. prof. medicine, 1983—88, asst. prof. clinical medicine, 1988—93, assoc. prof. clinical medicine, 1993—2001; asst. attending physician Presbyn. Hosp., N.Y.C., NY, 1982—93, assoc. attending physician, 1993—; prof. clinical medicine Coll. Physicians and Surgeons Columbia U., 2001—, dir. program in narrative medicine and clinical skills assessment program, 1996—. Editor-in-chief: Lit. and Medicine jour.; co-editor: (anthology) Stories Matter: The Role of Narrative in Medical Ethics, 2002. Named Outstanding Woman Physician of Yr., 1996; recipient Nat. award for innovation in med. edn., Soc. Gen. Internal Medicine, 1997; grantee Guggenheim fellowship, 2002; 1st recipient of Virginia Kneeland Frantz award for Outstanding Woman Dr. of Yr., 1987. Achievements include development of innovative new teaching method called the parallel chart systems which brings together literature and medicine. Office: Presbyn Hosp 9 E 105 Gen Medicine 622 W 168th St New York NY 10032

CHARPAK, GEORGES, physicist, nuclear scientist; b. Dabrovica, Poland, Aug. 1, 1924; naturalized, France, 1946; s. Maurice and Anna (Szapiro) C.; m. Dominique Vidal, 1953; children: Yves, Nathalie, Serge. BSc in Engring., Ecole des Mines de Paris, 1948; PhD in Physics, Collège de France, 1954; doctorate (hon.), U. Geneva, 1977, U. Thessalonica, Greece, 1993, Vrije Univ. Brussels, 1994, U. Coimbra, Portugal, 1994, U. Ottawa, Can., 1995, U. Rio de Janeiro, 1996. Lic. civil mining engr. Prof. Centre Nation de la Recherche Scientifique, 1948-59, Centre Européen pour la Recherche Nucléaire, Geneva, 1959—; rschr. Cern Lab. for Particle Physics, Geneva. Joliot-Curie prof. Ecole Supérieure de Physique et Chimie de la Ville de Paris, 1984—. Contbr. articles to profl. jours. With French Army, prisoner of war, Dachau. Decorated chevalier Legion of Honor, Mil. Cross 39-45, Croix de Guerre (France), Officer Nat. Order of Merit; recipient Paul Ricard prize French Soc. Physics, 1980, High Energy and Particle Physics prize, 1989, Nobel prize for physics, 1992. Mem. NAS (fgn. assoc.), French Acad. Scis. (Commissariat prize of Atomic Energy 1984), Austrian Acad. Scis. (hon.), Russian Acad. Scis. (fgn.), Lisboa Acad. Scis. (corr.), French Acad. Medicine (nat. corr. mem.). Achievements include invention of multiwire proportional chambers, drift chambers, diverse types of flash chambers without photography; development of particle detectors in high energy physics, installations for biological research using Beta-ray imagery; new fast gaseous detector adapted to accelerators to be constructed; research in in nuclear structure by reactions. Home: 22 rue Pierre et Marie Curie 75005 Paris France Office: CERN Lab for Particle Physics CH-1211 Geneva Switzerland Office Phone: +41-227672144.

CHARPENTIER, MARTI RAY, accountant, financial executive; b. Oakes, N.D., Feb. 28, 1955; s. Donald Alexander and Marcia Deloris (Remillard) C. BBA cum laude, U. N.D., 1977. CPA, Minn., N.D. Staff acct. Touche Ross & Co., Mpls., 1978-82, supr., 1982-83; mgr. fin. systems Dyco Petroleum Corp., Mpls., 1983-85; asst. controller Best Products Co., Inc., Mpls., 1985-87; contr. The King Cos. Inc., St. Paul, 1987-89; contr., asst. treas. Analysts Internat. Corp., Mpls., 1989—99, v.p. fin., treas., 1999—. Mem. Am. Inst. CPA's, N.D. Soc. CPA's, Minn. Soc. CPA's. Roman Catholic. Avocations: sports, fishing, hunting, camping. Home: 18934 Radford St Minnetonka MN 55345-6036 Office: Analysts Internat Corp 3601 W 76th St Minneapolis MN 55435

CHARPIE, ROBERT ALAN, physicist, researcher; b. Cleve., Sept. 9, 1925; s. Leonard Asbury and Dorothy (McLean) C.; m. Elizabeth Downs, July 12, 1947; children: Richard Alan, Carol Elizabeth, David Wayne, John Robert. BS with honors, Carnegie Inst. Tech., 1948, MS, 1949, D.Sc. in Theoretical Physics, 1950; D.H.L., Denison U., 1965; D.Sc., Alderson-Broaddus Coll., 1967; LL.D., Marietta Coll., 1975; D.Sc., Boston Coll., 1982. With Westinghouse Electric Corp., 1947-50; with Oak Ridge Nat. Lab., 1950-51, tech. asst. to research dir., 1952-54, asst. research dir., 1954-58, dir. reactor divsn., 1958-61; mgr. adv. devel. Union Carbide Corp., 1961-63, gen. mgr. devel. dept., 1963-64, dir. tech., 1964-66, pres. electronics divsn., 1966-68; pres. Bell & Howell Co., Chgo., 1968-69, Cabot Corp., Boston, 1969-86, also. bd. dirs., chmn. Waltham, Mass., 1986-88, Ampersand Ventures, Wellesley, Mass., 1988—. Trustee Mitre Corp., Boston, 1966-82, chmn., 1972-82; sec. gen. adv. com. AEC, 1959-63; mem. Nat. Sci. Bd., 1969-76; sci. sec., editor-in-chief proc., also asst. U.S. mem. 7 nation adv. com. 1st Internat. Conf. Peaceful Uses Atomic Energy, 1955; coordinator U.S. fusion research exhibit, 2d Conf., 1958; chmn. invention and innovation panel U.S. Dept. Commerce, 1965-67. Gen. editor: Internat. Monograph Series on Nuclear Energy, 1955-60; editor: Progress Series in Nuclear Energy, 1955-60, Jour. Nuclear Energy, 1955-60. Mem. Oak Ridge Bd. Edn., 1957-61; pres. Byram Hills Central Sch. Dist., 1966-68; trustee Carnegie Inst. Tech., 1962—. Recipient Alumni Merit award Carnegie Inst. Tech., 1957 Fellow Am. Phys. Soc., Am. Nuclear Soc. (dir.); mem. N.Y. Acad. Sci., Nat. Acad. Engring., Sigma Xi, Tau Beta Pi, Phi Mu Epsilon. Office: Ampersand Ventures 55 William St Ste 240 Wellesley MA 02481-4003

CHARRIERE, SUZANNE, architectural firm executive; Mng. ptnr. Corgan Assocs., Dallas. Rep. for firm Dallas (Tex.) Citizen's Coun. Pres. Friends of Dallas (Tex.) Police Assn.; adv. bd. Women's Mus., Dallas; bd. dir. Goodwill Industries, Dallas, Dallas (Tex.) Pks. and Trees Found. Mem.: Nat. Assn. Women Bus. Owners (Louise Razzio Pathfinder award 2004), Internat. Women's Forum (v.p.), Greater Dallas (Tex.) C. of C. (bd. dir.). Office: Corgan Associates Inc 501 Elm St Dallas TX 75202

CHARRON, JOSEPH L., bishop; b. Redfield, SD, Dec. 30, 1939; Ordained priest Roman Cath. Ch. 1967. Asst. theology prof. St. John's U., Collegeville, Minn., 1970—76; asst. gen. sec. U.S. Catholic Conf., 1976—79; assoc. gen. sec. Nat. Conf. Cath. Bishops, 1976—79; Kansas City Provincial dir. CPPS, 1979—87; aux. bishop Diocese of St. Paul/Mpls., 1990—93; bishop Diocese of Des Moines, 1994—. Admin. comm. Nat. Conf. Cath. Bishops/U.S. Cath. Conf. Mem.: Cath. Theol. Soc. Am., Soc. Precious Blood. Roman Catholic. Office: Chancery 601 Grand Ave Des Moines IA 50309*

CHARRON, PAUL RICHARD, apparel company executive; b. Schenectady, N.Y., Aug. 24, 1942; s. Richard Armand and Helen Marie (Barringer) C.; m. Kathy Lyn Herdt, June 29, 1974; children: Bradley, Ashley. BA, U. Notre Dame, 1964; MBA, Harvard U., 1971. Brand mgr. Procter & Gamble Corp., Cin., 1971-78; category mgr. Gen. Foods Corp., White Plains, N.Y., 1978-81; sr. v.p. sales, mktg. Cannon Mills Co., N.Y. and N.C., 1981-83; pres., chief operating officer Atwater Group, Inc., St. Paul, 1983-87; pres., chief oper. officer Brown & Bigelow, St. Paul, 1983-87; exec. v.p. VF Corp., Wyomissing, Pa., 1988-94; chmn., CEO Liz Claiborne Inc., N.Y.C., 1994—. Lt. USN, 1964-69, Vietnam. Decorated Meritorious Service medal. Office: Liz Claiborne Inc 1441 Broadway Fl 22 New York NY 10018-2088

CHARROW, JOEL, pediatrician, educator, geneticist, director; b. NYC, May 24, 1951; s. Saul David and Doris Elaine (Yates) C.; m. Martha K. McClintock, Oct. 23, 1982; children: Benjamin Whitmore, Julia Rachel. BS in Chemistry and Psychology, Antioch Coll., 1972; MD, Mt. Sinai Sch. Medicine, 1976. Diplomate Nat. Bd. Med. Examiners, Am. Bd. Pediatrics; diplomate in clin. genetics and biocehem. genetics. Am. Bd. Med. Genetics. Pediatric intern Children's Meml. Hosp./Northwestern U. Med. Sch., Chgo., 1976-77, resident in pediatrics, 1977-79, fellow in clin. and biochem. genetics, 1979-81; attending physician Children's Meml. Hosp., Chgo., 1981; from asst. prof. to assoc. prof. pediatrics Northwestern U. Med. Ctr., Chgo., 1981-94, prof. pediatrics, 2002—; dir. Genetics Lab., head sect. clin. genetics Children's Meml. Hosp., Chgo., 1991—. Mem. adv. bd. Fabry Disease Registry, 2001—. Contbr. chpts. to books, more than 50 articles to profl. jours. Regional coord. Internat. Collaborative Gaucher Group, 1994—; mem. health profl. adv. com. March of Dimes, Chgo., 1986-2004; mem. sci. adv. com. Nat. Tay-Sachs and Allied Diseases Assn., 1984—; mem. State of Ill. Genetic and Metabolic Diseases Adv. Com., 1989-97; mem. Genetics Task Force of Ill., 1982—, v.p., 1990-91, pres., 1991-93. Recipient Bela Schick Pediatric Soc. award Mt. Sinai Sch. Medicine, 1976. Fellow Am. Coll. Med. Genetics (founding), Am. Acad. Pediatrics; mem. Midwest Soc. for Pediatric Rsch., Soc. for Inherited Metabolic Disorders, Bone Dysplasia Soc., Internat. Neurofibromatosis Assn., Alpha Omega Alpha. Office: Children's Meml Hosp Sect Clin Genetics 2300 N Childrens Plz Chicago IL 60614-3394 Office Phone: 773-880-4462.

CHARTERS, ALEXANDER NATHANIEL, retired adult education educator; b. Verdant Valley, Alta., Can., Aug. 22, 1916; came to U.S., 1948, naturalized, 1957. s. Alexander Allen and Louisa Magdalena (Kern) C.; m. Margaret Anne MacNaughton, Mar. 29, 1952; children: A. William, David W., John C., Louisa A. Vike. BA, U. B.C., 1938; PhD, U. Chgo., 1948. Tchr. pub. schs., Fernie, B.C., 1939-41, Vancouver, 1941-42; asst. to dean Univ. Coll., Syracuse U., 1948-50, asst. dean, 1950-52, dean, 1952-64, asst. prof. Sch. Edn., 1950-54, assoc. prof., 1954-59, prof., 1959-83, prof. emeritus, 1983—, area chmn. for adult edn., 1950-80, univ. v.p. for continuing edn., 1964-73. Vis. faculty U. Chgo., 1958; UNESCO del. Internat. Conf. on Adult Edn., UNESCO, 1972; observer, del., Tokyo, 1972, Paris, 1985; coord. US participation pvt. sector CONFINTEA V, Hamburg, also observer and U.S. del., 1997, mem. U.S. del. team, 1997; cons. UNESCO Inst. for Edn., 1998; mem. standing com. 5th World Conf. on History of Adult Edn., 1991; mem. steering com. Internat. Assocs., 1991—; chmn. program com. Internat. Conf. Rethinking Adult Edn. for Devel., Ljubljana, Slovenia, 1993; adv. S. Rodriguez U., Caracas, Venezuela, 1994; external examiner adult edn. U. Madras, 1996; presenter edn. conf., Jena, Germany, 1996; cons. in adult edn. Inst. Pedagogida Rural, Venezuela, 1998; founding cons. Academic Inst. Educators of Adults, 1998; cons. to field. Author numerous books and publs. Mem. bd. Ctr. Study Liberal Edn. Adults, 1957-67, chmn., 1964-65; mem. Internat. Coun. for Adult Edn. (hon. 1998); founding mem., treas. Internat. Congress U. Adult Edn., 1962-67; mem. N.Y. State Adv. Bd. on Continuing Higher Edn.; chmn. Galaxy Conf. Adult Edn. Orgns., 1969; chmn. priorities com. Cmty. Chest and Coun.; trustee Chautauqua Inst., 1960-69; bd. mem. Laubach Literacy Internat., 1965-70, sec., 1967-70; trustee Ctrl. N.Y. UN Assn., Syracuse World Affairs Edn. Orgns.; mem. U.S. Nat. Com. UNESCO, presenter 5th world assembly, Cairo, 1994; bd. visitors U. Pitts., Washington U., St. Louis; founding mem., bd. dirs. Coalition Adult Edn. Orgn., 1964-82; exec. bd. dirs. Westminster Manor Ctr.; bd. dirs., treas. Vandercamp Conf. and Recreation Ctr., 1991-95, Ctrl. N.Y. Presbytery Conf. Ctr., 1991; clk. of session, elder Park Ctrl. Presbyn. Ch. With Royal Can. Naval Vol. Res., 1942-45. Recipient William Pearson Tolley medal for disting. leadership in adult edn. Syracuse U., 1986, Lifetime Achievement award Ctrl. N.Y. Coalition on Adult and Cont. Edn.; Alexander Charters Libr. Resources for Educators of Adults named for him Syracuse U., 1998. Mem. Assn. Continuing Higher Edn. (pres. 1947-48, Leadership citation 1973), Am. Assn. Adult Continuing Edn. (Pioneer award 1980), Nat. U. Continuing Edn. Assn. (pres. 1965-66, Bitner award 1973, Alexander N. Charters award 1999), Internat. Coun. Adult Edn. (founder 1972, chair documentation 1974, coord. confs., mem. Internat. Adult and Continuing Edn. Hall of Fame 1996, Scroll of Appreciation 1990), Internat. Soc. Comparative Adult Edn. (founding pres. 1992), Acad. Inst. Educators of Adults (founding cons. 1998), Ctrl. N.Y. Coalition on Adult and Continuing Edn. (lifetime achievement award 1998), Rotary (internat. Paul Harris fellow 1992), Beta Theta Pi. Home: 216 Lockwood Rd Syracuse NY 13214-2035 E-mail: ancharte@mailbox.syr.edu.

CHARTERS, ANN, literature educator; b. Bridgeport, Conn., Nov. 10, 1936; d. Nathan and Kate Danberg; m. Samuel B. Charters, Mar. 14, 1959; children: Mallay, Nora Lili. AB, U. Calif.-Berkeley, 1957; MA, Columbia U., 1960, PhD, 1965. Mem. faculty Colby Jr. Coll., New London, NH, 1961—63; lectr. Columbia U., 1965—66; asst. prof. Am. lit. N.Y.C. Community Coll., 1967-70; assoc. dean of the coll. Brown U., 1989-90; prof. Am. lit. U. Conn., Storrs, 1974—. Author: Nobody—Life and Times of Bert Williams, 1967, Kerouac, 1973, 2d edit., 1986, I Love—Story of Vladimir Mayakovsky and Lili Brik, 1979, The Story and Its Writer, 6th edit., 2002, The Beats: Literary Bohemians in Post-War America, 1983, Beats and Company: A Portrait of a Literary Generation, 1986, The Viking Portable Beat Reader, 1992, Major Writers of Short Fiction, 1993, The Viking Portable Jack Kerouac Reader, 1995, Selected Letters of Jack Kerouac, 1995, (with Samuel Charters) Literature and Its Writers, 1997; author intro. Penguin Classic edit. Three Lives and Q.E.D. (Gertrude Stein), On the Road (Jack Kerouac), Selected Letters of Jack Kerouac, vol. 2, 1999, The American Short Story and Its Writer, 1999, (with Samuel Charters) Blues Faces, 2000, Beat Down to Your Soul, 2000, The Portable Sixties Reader, 2003. Office: U Conn Dept English PO Box U-25 Storrs Mansfield CT 06269-0001 Office Phone: 860-486-2141. E-mail: acharters@uconn.edu.

CHARTERS, KAREN ANN ELLIOTT, critical care nurse, health facility administrator; b. Chelsea, Mass., Apr. 3, 1946; d. Albert Charles and Hazelle Marie (Kraus) Elliott; m. Byron James Charters, Feb. 4, 1972. Diploma, Grace New Haven Sch. Nursing, New Haven, Conn., 1967; student, So. Conn. State Coll., 1968, U. New Haven, 1974; BS in Healthcare Adminstrn., St. Leo Coll., 1999. CCRN. Asst. head nurse Yale New Haven (Conn.) Hosp., 1972-76; staff nurse critical care unit Hosp. Corp. Am., 1982—; relief clin. coord. Cmty. Hosp. of New Port Richey, Fla., 1987—, nursing supr., 1997—. Mem. AACN (bd. dirs. Gulf Coast chpt. 1990-91, 96-97, treas. 1991-93), Am. Heart Assn. (past bd. dirs.). Home: 7519 Clanton Trail Hudson FL 34667 Office: Cmty Hosp New Port Richey 5637 Marine Pkwy New Port Richey FL 34652

CHARTIER, KELLY ANN, music educator; b. Providence, Oct. 31, 1975; d. Paul and Patricia Lange; m. Matthew N. Chartier, Oct. 11, 2003. BS in Music Edn., R.I. Coll., 1998, MEd (hon.), 2002. Tchr. music Smithfield (R.I.) Sch. Dept., 1998—. Adj. prof. music R.I. Coll., Providence, 2001—; coach jr. varsity softball Moses Brown Sch., Providence, 2005—; coach women's tennis R.I. Coll., Providence, 2002—; pvt. instr. flute Axel Rod Music, Johnston, RI, 2004—. Vol. EMT-B Rehoboth (Mass.) Ambulance, 2003—. Recipient Sr. Female Athlete Helen Murphy award, R.I. Coll., 1998, Young Alumni award, 2005. Avocations: tennis, soccer, church choir, animals, swimming.

CHARTIER, KIRK LEE FREUND, business services executive; b. Chgo., July 27, 1963; s. George William Freund, Imogene Rasmussen; m. Michele Renee Chartier; children: Max children: Kate. BSCE with highest distinction, Worcester Poly. Inst., Mass., 1986; BA in Econs., Coll. of the Holy Cross, Worcester, 1986; MBA, Syracuse Un., 1996. Cert. mgmt. acct. 2001, instrument flight rating 1988, lic. comml. airline pilot 1988. Auditor GE Co., Fairfield, Conn., 1996—97; strategy dir. RCA, Inc., Irvine, Calif., 1997—98; sr. dir. Answerthink, Inc., Atlanta, 1998—2002; SVP cons. Commerce Quest, Tampa, Fla., 2002—. Examiner Malcolm Baldrige Nat. Quality Award, Washington, 1996—99. Lt. col. USMC, 1981—. Decorated Air Medal, Navy Commendation Medal (3); recipient Silver Medal---Leadership, Naval Assn., 1994. Mem.: Marine Corps Rse. Officer's Assn. (life). Republican. Episcopalian. Home: 2879 Normandy Dr NW Atlanta GA 30305 Personal E-mail: kirk_chartier@hotmail.com.

CHARTIER, MARY EILEEN, music educator; b. Alpena, Mich., Sept. 19, 1935; d. John Chester Brunette and Eileen Rosemond Woods; m. Duane Edward Chartier, Apr. 15, 1983; children: Joseph John Bonk, Julie Anne Bonk. AA, Delta Coll. Cert. Music Tchr. Mich. Music Tchrs. Assn., 1965. Sec. to mgr. Social Security Adminstrn., Bay City, Mich., 1954—57; pvt. music tchr. Mich., 1965—. Various positions Saginaw Tuesday Musicale, 1970—. Mem.: Music Tchrs. Bay County (cmty. outreach chmn. 1996—), Music Tchrs. Assn. (scholarship chmn. 1996—), Mich. Music Tchrs. Assn. (state bd. 2000—, Tchr. of Yr. award Saginaw chpt. 1991, Emeritus cert. 1990). Home and Studio: 3252 Pinehurst Dr Gladwin MI 48624-9738

CHARTIER, VERNON LEE, electrical engineer; b. Feb. 14, 1939; s. Raymond Earl and Margaret Clara (Winegar) C.; m. Lois Marie Schwartz, May 20, 1967; 1 child, Neal Raymond. BSEE, BS in Bus., U. Colo., 1963. Registered profl. engr., Pa.; cert. electromagnetic compatibility engr. Rsch. engr., cons. Westinghouse Electric Co., East Pitts., Pa., 1963-75; prin. engr. high voltage phenomena Bonneville Power Adminstrn., Vancouver, Wash., 1975-95; power sys. EMC cons. Portland, 1995—. Contbr. articles to profl. jours. Fellow IEEE (fellow com. 1993-96, 2004—, Herman Halperin Transmission and Distbn. award 1995, 3d Millennium medal 2000, chmn. Herman Halperin Transmission & Distbn. Award com. 2002-04); mem. Power Engring. Soc. of IEEE (chmn. transmission and distbn. com. 1987-88, chmn. fellows com. 1990-92), Internat. Conf. Large High Voltage Electric Sys. (Attwood Assoc. award 1999), Nat. Acad. Engring., Chartier Family Assn. Baptist. Home and Office: 13095 SW Glenn Ct Beaverton OR 97008-5664 Business E-Mail: vlchartier@ieee.org.

CHARTOFF, ROBERT IRWIN, film producer; b. N.Y.C. s. William and Bessie Chartoff; children: Jenifer, William, Julie, Charley, Miranda. AB, Union Coll., 1955; LLB, Columbia U., 1958. Producer: numerous films including Double Trouble, 1967, Point Blank, 1967, The Split, 1968, Leo the Last, 1969, They Shoot Horses Don't They, 1969, The Strawberry Statement, 1970, The Gang That Couldn't Shoot Straight, 1971, The New Centurions, 1972, The Mechanic, 1972, Up the Sandbox, 1972, Busting, 1974, Peeper, 1975, The Gambler, 1975, Rocky, 1976 (Acad. award for best picture), Nickelodeon, 1976, New York, New York, 1977, Valentino, 1977, Comes A Horseman, 1978, Uncle Joe Shannon, 1978, Rocky II, 1979, Raging Bull, 1980, True Confessions, 1981, Rocky III, 1982, The Right Stuff, 1983, Rocky IV, 1985, Beer, 1986, Rocky V, 1990, Straight Talk, 1992, In My Country, 2005. Office: Chartoff Prodns Inc 1250 6th St Ste 101 Santa Monica CA 90401-1612 E-mail: chartoffprod@cs.com.

CHARTON, MARVIN, chemist, educator; b. Bklyn., May 1, 1931; s. William and Elsie (Halpern) C.; m. Barbara Israel, Aug. 28, 1955; children—Michael, Sarah, Deborah. BS, CCNY, 1953; MA, Bklyn. Coll., 1956; PhD, Stevens Inst. Tech., 1962. Instr. chemistry Pratt Inst., Bklyn., 1956-61, asst. prof., 1961-64, assoc. prof., 1964-67, prof., 1967—, chmn. dept., 1969—. Vis. prof. Polymer Rsch. Inst., Poly. U., Bklyn., 1985—. Editor: Advances in Quantitative Structure Property Relationships Vol. 1, 1996, Vol. 2, 1999, Vol. 3, 2002; co-editor: Topics in Current Chemistry, vol. 114, 1983; contbr. articles to profl. jours.; mem. editl. bd.: Quantitative Structure Activity Relationships, Activity Relationships, Arkivoc, Drug Design Reviews, Current Computer-Aided Molecular Design. Fellow AAAS, Intrasci. Rsch. Found.; mem. Am. Chem. Soc., Internat. Group for Correlation Analysis in Chemistry, Internat. QSAR Soc., Royal Chem. Soc. London, N.Y. Acad. Scis., Sigma Xi. Avocation: collecting antiquarian chemistry books. Home: 1 Grace Ct Brooklyn NY 11201-4195 Office Phone: 718-636-3763. Business E-Mail: mcharton@pratt.edu.

CHARTRAND, DANNY LEWIS, secondary school educator, coach; b. Clarksville, Tenn., Dec. 12, 1957; s. David Edward Chartrand and Florence Neal; m. Mercedes Ellis Chartrand, Mar. 9, 1965; children: Cliff Ellis, Jacklyn Michelle. MA in Edn., Austin Peay State U., 1985. Cert. profl. educator Tenn., 1995. Musician: (music composition) Agnus Dei. Home: 1024 Hillshire Dr Clarksville TN 37043 Office: Rossview High School 1237 Rossview Rd Clarksville TN 37043 Personal E-mail: danny.chartrand@cmcss.net.

CHARTRAND, ROBERT LEE, information scientist; b. Kansas City, Mo., Mar. 6, 1928; s. Joseph Sterling, Jr. and Isabel Christine (Doherty) C.; m. Eleanor Salmon, Oct. 9, 1967; children: Leslie, Kevin; stepchildren: James, Jennifer. BA, U. Mo., Kansas City, 1948, MA, 1949; postgrad., La. State U., 1949-50, U. Mo., 1956. Staff Whatsoever Circle Community House, 1950; supr. phys. recreation welfare dept. City of Kansas City, Mo., 1951, chief rec. supr., 1956; mem. tech. staff Nat. Photo Intelligence Ctr., 1959; Mem. tech. staff Thompson-Ramo-Wooldridge (TRW), Denver and Canoga Park, Calif., 1959-61; with fed. system div. IBM Corp., Bethesda, Md., 1961-64, mgr. advanced systems mktg., 1964; mgr. applications devel. Planning Research Corp., Washington, 1964-66; specialist in info. sci. Congressional Research Service, Library of Congress, Washington, 1966-77, sr. specialist in info. policy and tech., 1977-88, sr. fellow in info. policy and tech., 1988-90. Fulbright-Hays lectr., 1968, UN lectr., 1979; cons. Pres.'s Commn. on Population Growth and Am. Future, 1970-71, U.S. Commn. Civil Rights, 1972-78, George Washington U., 1975-77, UNESCO, 1977, Exec. Office of Pres., 1977-82, Office of Tech. Assessment, 1979-89, NAS, 1981-83, Nat. Acad. Pub. Adminstrn. Sr. Res. Assoc., 1995—, sr. cons. Global Disaster Info. Network, 1997-2001, IRS, 1985-86, Dept. Energy, 1986, Fed. Election Com., 1976-77, U.S. Dept. Commerce, 1985-88, GSA, 1983, 86, 92-96, OMB, 1995-97, Fed. Emergency Mgmt. Agy., 1986-88, NASA, 1993, Carnegie Commn. on Sci., Tech. and Govt., 1993-94, NLM, 1994-95, Turner Edn. Svcs., 1994-96, inSite Learning, Inc., 2001-02, World Future Soc., 1997—, Nat. Reconnaisance Office, 2002; adj. fellow Ctr. for Strategic and Internat. Studies, 1990-95, sr. assoc., 2003—, Disaster Mgmt. Ptnrs., 2002; mem. STI bd. NAS/NRC, 1990-91, mapping sci. com., 1990-93; mem. adv. coun. Nat. Inst. Urban Search and Rescue, 1991—; mem. Extreme Info. Infrastructure (XII) Technical Working Group, 1999—; adj. prof. Am. U., 1974-78; lectr. U.S. Info. Agy., 1977; sr. lectr. UN Devel. Program, 1979; vis. prof. UCLA, 1982, U. Pitts., 1989, 1991-2001 mem. adv. bd. coll. info. studies U. Md., 1999—; lectr. Internat. Coll., 2000-04, Fla. Gulf Coast U., 2000-04; spl. advisor Open Systems Conf. Bd., 1990-94, Internat. Green Cross, 1993-94; mem. program adv. bd. Govt. Tech. Leadership Inst., 1998-2000; mem. adv. com. U.S. CSC, 1973-80, White House Conf. on Libr. and Info. Svcs., 1979-80; adv. NSF, 1977-79; mem. planning panel for toxicology and environment NLM, 1991-92; mem. adv. panel Dept. State, 1978-84; NLM, 1985-86, 91-92; mem. adv. bd. Chem. Abstracts Svc., 1979-84, Info. Inst., 1983-86, Econ. Devel. Found., 1985-90, Ency. Libr. and Info. Sci., 1986—, Internat. Design for Extreme Environments Assembly, 1991-95, Partnership for Intergovtl. Innovation (Pi2), 2000—, Internat. Energy Mgmt. & Engr. Soc., 1993, 94-96, S.W. Fla. Emergency Adv. Bd., 1993-99, Collier County Disaster Recovery Coalition Com., 1995-99, Collier County Pub. Safety Com., 1999-2000, Greater Naples Leadership Alumni Coun., 1999-2001; mem. bd. visitors FEMA Emergency Mgmt. Inst., 1987-89; proj. devel. cons. U. Mo., Kansas City, 1985-89, White House Conf. Libr. and Info. Svc., 1990-91; spl. cons. U. Mo. Sys., 1991, 93; nat. bd. dirs. Alliance of Info. and Referral Sys, 1994-98; bd. govs. Naples Inst., 1994-97, Internat. Coun. for Computer Commns., 1994—, sr. adv. Stennis Ctr. Pub. Svc., 1998-2000. Author: Systems Technology Applied to Social and Community Problems, 1971, Computers and Political Campaigning, 1972, (with others) State Legislature Use of Information Technology, 1978, Opportunities for the Use of Information Resources and Advanced Technologies in Congress, 1993; also congl. studies; editor, contbg. author: Information Support, Program Budgeting and the Congress, 1968; editor, contbg. author: Computers in the Service of Society, 1972, Critical Issues in the Information Age, 1991; editor: Hope for the Cities: A Systems Approach to Human Needs, 1971; co-editr, contbg. author: Information Technology Serving Society, 1979, Strategies and Systems for Disaster Survival, 1989; editorial bd.: Law and Computer Tech, 1968-82, The Information Society, 1979—, Hazard, 1979-95, Futures Res. Quar., 1987—, Am. Fedn. Info. Processing Socs. Washington Report, 1989-90; editorial adviser: Rutgers Jour. Computers and the Law, 1970-72, ASK, 1982-86, ASIS Bull., 1979-91; cons. editor: Info. Storage and Retrieval, 1969-74, SIAM News, 1976-79; contbr. articles to profl. jours. Trustee Windham Coll., 1974-76, Engring. Info., 1980-83, Capital Children's Mus., 1982-86; vice chmn. Friends of Montgomery County Libr., 1984-87; cons. advisor Smithsonian Inst., 1986-90; bd. dirs. Friends of Libr. Collier County, Fla., 1991—, v.p., 1993-95, pres.-elect, 1994, pres., 1995-96, exec. com., 1997-2000; mem. Leadership Collier Masters, 1996-97, class chmn., 1997-98, mem. adv. com., 1997-99; mem. MPA adv. com. Fla. Gulf Coast U., 1997-98, mem. external rels. coun., 1999—; active Greater Naples Leadership, 2000—. With U.S. Naval Intelligence, 1952-59. Decorated Cavaliere Ufficiale Italy; named to Govt. Computer News Hall of Fame, 1988; recipient Interagy. Com. on ADP award, 1976, Test of Time award, 1979, Alumni Achievement award, U. Mo., Kansas City, 1984, Internat. Emergency Mgmt. and Engring Soc. Life Achievement award, 1993, Libr. of Congress award for Superior Svc., 1988, Cert. of Appreciation, Congl. Rsch. Svc., 1988, Outstanding Svc. award, 1994. Fellow AAAS (sect. chmn. 1983-84); mem. Am. Soc. Info. Sci. and Tech. (cons. editor bull. 1974-90), cert. appreciation 1976, award of merit 1985, Pioneer award 1988, 99), Nat. Coun. on World Affairs, Nat. Acad. Pub. Adminstrn. (assoc.), Naval Intelligence Profls., Cosmos Club, Kenwood Golf and Country Club, Naples Bath and Tennis Club. Unitarian Universalist. *If there is to be a future, every effort must be expended by technologists and humanitarians alike to meld their philosophies and pragmatic undertakings. The global dimensions and impacts of mankind's major initiatives are inextricably related, and the ancients were prescient in their avowal that "where there is no vision, the people perish.".*

CHARWAT, ANDREW FRANCISZEK, engineering educator; b. Poland, Feb. 10, 1925; came to U.S., 1945; s. Franciszek and Wanda (Niec) C.; m. Halina M. Stieglitz, Aug. 18, 1948 (dec.); 1 child, Danuta K. Charwat McCall. M Engring., Stevens Inst. Tech., 1948; PhD, U. Calif., Berkeley, 1952. Aerodynamicist Propulsion Research Corp., Los Angeles, 1952-53; designer Northrup Aircraft Corp., Los Angeles, 1953-55; prof., dept. mech. and aerospace engring. UCLA, 1955-92, prof. emeritus, 1992—. Cons. to numerous industry and govt. agys., 1955—; expert witness various legal cases; dir. Univ. Study Ctr., Lyon and Grenoble, France, 1986-88. Contbr. over 80 articles and research papers. Guggenheim fellow, 1962. E-mail: acharwat@ucla.edu.

CHARYK, JOSEPH VINCENT, retired satellite telecommunications executive; b. Canmore, Alta., Can., Sept. 9, 1920; came to U.S., 1942, naturalized, 1948; s. John and Anna (Dorosh) C.; m. Edwina Elizabeth Rhodes, Aug. 18, 1945; children: William R., J. John, Christopher E., Diane E. B.Sc., U. Alta., 1942, LL.D., 1964; MS, Calif. Inst. Tech., 1943, PhD, 1946; D.Engring. (hon.), U. Bologna, 1974. Sect. chief Jet Propulsion Lab., Calif. Inst. Tech., 1945-46, instr. aeros., 1945-46; asst. prof. aeros. Princeton (N.J.) U., 1946-49, assoc. prof., 1949-55; dir. aerophysics and chemistry lab., missile systems div. Lockheed Aircraft Corp., 1955-56; dir. aero. lab. Aeronutronic Systems, Inc. subs. Ford Motor Co., 1956-58, gen. mgr. space tech. div., 1958-59; asst. sec. for research and devel. USAF, 1959, under sec., 1960-63, dir. nat. reconnaissance office, 1961—63; pres. Communications Satellite Corp., 1963-79, chief exec. officer, 1979-85, chmn., 1983-85, Draper Labs., 1987-90. Recipient Lloyd V. Berkner Space Utilization award, 1967, Disting. Aviation Aerospace Svc. award, 1973, Gugliemo Marconi Internat. award, 1974, TV Arts and Scis. Directorate award, 1974, Theodore Von Karman award, 1977, Goddard Astronautics award, 1978, award Computer and Comm. Found., 1985, Nat. Medal of Tech., 1987, Arthur C. Clarke award, 1992, Disting. Alumni award U. Alta., 1993. Fellow AIAA, IEEE; mem. Nat. Acad. Engring., Internat. Acad. Astronautics, Nat. Space Club, Chevy Chase Country Club, Gulf Stream Golf Club, Gulf Stream Bath and Tennis Club, Sigma Xi. Home: 790 Andrews Ave Apt A302 Delray Beach FL 33483-7257 Personal E-mail: chjv@msn.com.

CHARYTAN, LYNN R., lawyer; b. Oct. 29, 1965; BA summa cum laude, Columbia Univ.; JD magna cum laude, Harvard Univ., 1990. Bar: DC 1991, NY 1991. Law clk. Judge Stanley Sporkin, US Dist Ct. (DC dist.), 1990—91; in-house counsel Washington Post, 1991—93; ptnr., vice chmn. Comm. & E-Commerce dept. Wilmer Cutler Pickering Hale & Dorr, Washington. Mem.: ABA, Fed. Comm. Bar Assn., Phi Beta Kappa. Office: Wilmer Cutler Pickering Hale & Dorr 1801 Pennsylvania Ave NW Washington DC 20006 Mailing: Wilmer Cutler Pickering Hale & Dorr 2445 M St NW Washington DC 20037 Office Phone: 202-663-6455. Office Fax: 202-663-6363. Business E-Mail: lynn.charytan@wilmerhale.com.

CHASANOW, HOWARD STUART, retired judge, mediator; b. Washington, Apr. 3, 1937; 1 child from previous marriage, Andrea; m. Deborah Hovis Koss, May 15, 1l983. BA, U. Md., 1959, JD, 1961; LLM, Harvard U., 1962. Bar: Md. 1961, U.S. Supreme Ct. 1965. Asst. states atty. Prince George County, Upper Marlboro, Md., 1963-64, dep. states atty., 1964-67; judge Dist. Ct., Upper Marlboro, 1971-77, 7th Jud. Cir., 1977-90, Ct. Appeals of Md., 1990-99, ret., 1999. Lectr. Sch. Law U. Md., Balt., 1973—, Nat. Jud. Coll., Reno, 1980—, Am. Acad. Jud. Edn., 1984—; chmn. adv. bd. Sentencing Guidelines, Md., 1982-90, chmn. jud. adminstrn. sect., 1982-84; mem. Md. Commn. on Criminal Sentencing Policy, 1996—; mem. standing com. on rules of practice and procedure Ct. Appeals, 1985-90; mem. govs. task force to Revise Criminal Code, 1992—. Contbr. law rev. articles. Served with USAF, 1968-69. Address: 7849 Belle Point Dr Greenbelt MD 20770 Office Phone: 301-441-3366.

CHASE, BARBARA LANDIS, headmaster; b. Hershey, Pa., May 6, 1945; d. Floyd and Ruth Landis; m. David William Chase; children: Ashley Lawrence, Katherine Landis Chase. AB in History, Brown U., 1967; MLA, Johns Hopkins U., 1990. Tchr. 3rd grade Moses Brown Sch., Providence, R.I., 1967-68; tchr./dir. admissions Wheeler Sch., Providence, 1973-80; headmistress Bryn Mawr, Baltimore, Md., 1980-94; head of sch. Phillips Acad., Andover, Mass., 1994—. Contbr. articles to profl. jours.; presentations in field. Trustee Pike Sch., 1996-99, Sch. Yr. Abroad, 1994—, Tower Hill Sch., 1990-94, Brown U. 1995-2000; mem. Baltimore Ednl. Scholarship Trust, 1987-94, Baltimore Consortium Tchg. Am. History, 1987-90. Mem. Nat. Assn. Independent Schs. (bd. dirs. 1989-93, cons. 1988-89, chair sch. heads adv. com. 1986-88), Assn. Independent Md. Schs. (pres. bd. trustees 1986-88), The Headmasters Assn., Nat. Assn. Principals Schs. Girls, Headmistresses Assn. East.

CHASE, CHEVY (CORNELIUS CRANE CHASE), comedian, actor, writer; b. Woodstock, NY, Oct. 8, 1943; s. Edward Tinsley and Cathalene Crane (Widdoes) C.; m. Jayni Chase, 1982; children: Cydney Cathalene, Caley Leigh, Emily Evelyn. BA in English, Bard Coll., 1967; CCS, Inst. Audio Rsch., 1970. Artist MGM Records, 1968; writer for Mad mag., 1969; actor in his first film The Groove Tube, 1967-71; writer, actor Gt. Am. Dream Machine, 1971; dir., writer, actor, Nat. Lampoon Theatre Co., 1972-74, performing in Nat. Lampoon's Lemmings, off Broadway and on nat. tour; launched his career as a writer, actor in Sat. Night Live TV show, 1975-76; appeared on TV in Paul Simon Spl., host of The Chevy Chase Show, 1993; appeared in films Foul Play, 1978, Oh Heavenly Dog, 1980, Caddyshack in 1980, Caddyshack II in 1988, Seems Like Old Times, 1981, Under the Rainbow, 1981, Modern Problems, 1981, Vacation, 1983, Deal of the Century, 1983, Fletch, 1984 and Fletch Lives 1989, European Vacation, 1985, Spies Like Us, 1985, Follow That Bird, 1985, The Three Amigos, 1986, Funny Farm, 1988, The Couch Trip, 1988, Christmas Vacation, 1989, Nothing But Trouble, 1991, LA Story, 1991, Memoirs of an Invisible Man, 1992, Hero, 1992, Last Action Hero, 1993, Cops and Robbersons, 1994, Man of the House, 1995, National Lampoon's Vegas Vacation, 1997, Snow Day, 1999; he made appearances in Last Action Hero and Orange County. Recipient award for best script in comedy variety spl. Writers Guild, award best supporting actor in comedy variety series Nat. Acad. TV Arts and Sci.; won two Emmy Awards for Saturday Night Live and a third Emmy for co-writing The Paul Simon Special; hon. by Harvard Univ. Hasty Pudding Theatrical Group, 1992. Mem. Am. Fedn. Musicians, Stage Actors Guild, Actors Equity, AFTRA. Democrat. Office: Cornelius Prods PO Box 257 Bedford NY 10506-0257

CHASE, CLINTON IRVIN, psychologist, educator; b. Aug. 14, 1927; m. Patricia Cronenberger; 1 child. BS in Psychology with honors, U. Idaho, 1950, MS in Adminstrn., 1951; PhD in Ednl. Psychology, U. Calif.-Berkeley, 1958. Asst. to dean students Wash. State U., 1951-52; sch. psychologist Piedmont Pub. Schs., Calif., 1957-58; asst. prof. ednl. psychology Idaho State U., 1958-61, Miami U., Oxford, 1961-62, Ind. U., Bloomington, 1962-64, assoc. prof., 1964-68, prof., 1968-95; prof. emeritus Indiana U., Bloomington, 1995—; assoc. dir. Bur. Evaluative Studies and Testing Ind. U., Bloomington, 1962-70, dir., 1970-89, chmn. dept. ednl. psychology, 1970-74; dir. Ind. Testing and Evaluation Svc., Bloomington, 1976-87, Ind. Ctr. for Evaluation, 1988-94; owner, mgr. Ind. Testing and Evaluation Svc., 1990—. Author: (with H. Glenn Ludlow) Readings in Educational and Psychological Measurement, 1966, Elementary Statistical Procedures, 1967, 3d edit., 1984, Measurement for Educational Evaluation, 1974, 2d edit., 1978; (with L.C. Jacobs) Developing and Using Tests Effectively, 1992, Contemporary Assessment for Educators, 1999; mem. editl. bd. Jour. Edn. Measurement, 1985-97; contbr. more than 120 articles to profl. jours. Served with USN, 1945-46; to capt. USAF, 1952-55. Named Ky. Col., 1998. Fellow Am. Psychol. Assn. (divsn. 15), Am. Ednl. Rsch. Assn., Nat. Coun. on Measurement in Edn., Phi Beta Kappa, Kappa Delta Pi E-mail: chase@indiana.edu. *The careful establishment of objectives, and the persistant pursuit of objectives, are the primary ingredients of achievement.*

CHASE, COCHRANE, advertising agency executive; b. Berwyn, Ill., Feb. 6, 1932; s. Henry Cochrane and Roselyn (Scott) C.; m. Janis Valeria Kueber, June 19, 1954; children— Katherine Ann, Anthony Scott, Lisa Marie. BA, Wesleyan U., 1954. With steel warehousing div. Jessop Steel Co., Broadview, Ill., 1956-62, mgr. sales, 1961-62; with Jessop Steel Calif., Santa Fe Springs, 1963-64; asst. mgr. market rsch. Ducommun Metals & Supply Co., LA, 1964—65; v.p. Newport Advt. Inc., Newport Beach, Calif., 1965; pres. Cochrane Chase, Livingston & Co., Inc., Irvine, Calif., 1966, chmn. bd., CEO, 1966—88; chmn. emeritus AC&R/CCL, Irvine, Calif., 1988-89. Co-author: Marketing Problem Solver, 1973, Newport Financial Planner, 1985. Served with USNR, 1954-56. Home: 2162 Papaya Dr La Habra CA 90631-7917

CHASE, DANIEL EDWARD, lawyer; b. Trenton, N.J., Dec. 2, 1953; s. Daniel Anthony and Doris Marie (Keller) C.; m. Maryann DeAntonio, Oct. 2, 1982; children: Andrew, Nathaniel, Brian. AA, Mercer County Community Coll., Trenton, 1974; BA, Drew U., 1976; JD, Union U., Albany, N.J., 1979. Bar: N.J. 1979, U.S. Dist. Ct. N.J. 1979, U.S. Ct. Appeals 1989. Assoc. McKaughlin & Cooper, Trenton, 1980-88; ptnr. Teich, Groh & Frost, Trenton, 1988-95, Hartrough, Kenny & Chase, Trenton, 1995—. Mem. ABA, ATLA, N.J. State Bar Assn., Mercer County Bar Asssn. (bench bar com. 1990—). Office: Hartrough Kenny & Chase 3812 Quakerbridge Rd Hamilton NJ 08619-1003

CHASE, DAVID (DAVID DECAESARE), scriptwriter, television producer, television director; b. Mt. Vernon, N.Y., Aug. 22, 1945; Student in Filmmaking, Sch. Visual Arts, N.Y.; degree, NYU; MA in Film, Stanford (Calif.) U. Dir.: (TV series) Alfred Hitchcock Presents, 1985; writer, dir. (TV series) Almost Grown, 1988, writer Kolchak: The Night Stalker, 1974, (TV films) Grave of the Vampire, 1972, Moonlight, 1982, writer, prodr. (TV series) The Rockford Files, 1976—80 (Emmy award, 1977), writer, exec. prodr. I'll Fly Away, 1991 (Norman Felton award Prodrs. Guild Am., 1993), Northern Exposure, 1990, writer, prodr. (TV films) Off the Minnesota Strip, 1980 (Writers Guild Am. award, 1980, Emmy award, 1979), writer, prodr., dir. (TV series) The Soprano's, 1999— (Emmy award for College episode, 1998, Golden Globe award, 1999, Norman Felton award Prodrs. Guild Am., 2000, Outstanding Directorial Achievement award Dirs. Guild Am., 1999, Peabody award, 2000, Drama Series of Yr. award Am. Film Inst., 2001), prodr. (TV films) The Rockford Files: A Blessing in Disguise, 1995, writer, prodr., dir. The Rockford Files: The Punishment and Crime, 1996. Office: David Harbert United Talent Agency 9560 Wilshire Blvd Ste 500 Beverly Hills CA 90212*

CHASE, DAWN EILEEN, English language educator; b. Oak Park, Ill., Apr. 30, 1941; d. Ralph A. and Alice M. (Nischwitz) Eggert; m. Rowland K. Chase. BA, Knox Coll., 1966; MA, San Jose State U., 1975. Cert. secondary tchr., Calif. Tchr. English Campbell (Calif.) Union H.S. Dist., 1967-96, chair English dept., 1975-95; adj. English instr. San Jose (Calif.) State U., 1997-2000; univ. supr. tchr. edn. program Stanford (Calif.) U., 2001—. Tchr./cons. San Jose Area Writing Project, 1978—, mem. adv. bd., 1979-81, 95-97; presenter workshops on English edn., No. Calif., 1979—. Author, editor: (anthology) Looking Back, Moving Forward, 1992. Del. UN Conf. on Women, Beijing, 1995. Mem. Nat. Coun. Tchrs. of English, Calif. Assn. Tchrs. of English. Democrat. Avocations: reading, writing, travel. E-mail: dchase3@aol.com.

CHASE, ERIC LEWIS, lawyer; b. Princeton, N.J., Sept. 21, 1946; s. Harold William and Bernice Mae (Fadden) C.; m. Jamie Campbell, Dec. 29, 1979; children: Eric Campbell, Kathryn Dianne, John Harold. BA, Princeton U., 1968; JD cum laude, U. Minn., 1974. Bar: N.J. 1974, D.C. 1975, U.S. Ct. Appeals (3d cir.) 1979, U.S. Supreme Ct. 1981, U.S. Claims Ct. 1982, U.S. Tax Ct. 1982, N.Y. 1983, U.S. Ct. Appeals (2d cir.) 1988, U.S. Ct. Appeals (6th cir.) 2003. Trial atty. FCC, 1974-78; asst. U.S. atty. Dist. N.J., Newark, 1978-80; ptnr. Margolis Chase, Verona, N.J., 1980-90, Hannoch Weisman, Roseland, N.J., 1990-93, Bressler, Amery & Ross, Florham Park, N.J., 1993—. Prof. law of war Marine Corps Command and Staff Coll., Quantico, Va., 1990—99. Author: Automobile Dealers and the Law, 1994, 7th edit., 2000; contbr. articles on law and mil. to profl. publs., including N.Y. Times, Washington Post, Newsweek mag. With USMC, 1968-71; col. Res., ret. Mem. ABA (mem. task force on internat. criminal ct.), N.J. State Bar Assn. (franchise com 1997—, co-chair franchise com. 1999-2001). Office: Bressler Amery & Ross 325 Columbia Tpke Ste 8 Florham Park NJ 07932-1212 Office Phone: 973-514-1200. Business E-Mail: echase@bressler.com.

CHASE, EUGENE THOMAS, secondary school educator; b. Clark AFB, Philippines, May 25, 1968; s. Paul Edward and Marsha Ann (Skinner) Jakola. BA in Polit. Sci., U. Okla., 1990; MA in Polit. Sci., U. Ctrl. Okla., 1994. Cert. tchr. social studies, govt., history, Okla.; nat. bd. cert. tchr., 2001. Substitute tchr. Mid-Del Schs., Midwest City, Okla., 1991-92; tchr. govt. Edmond (Okla.) North H.S., 1992—. Acad. team coach Meml. H.S., Edmond, 1993-94. Mem. steering com. Okla. Closeup Found., Oklahoma City, 1993-94; parliamentarian Parkview Neighbor Assn., Oklahoma City, 1992; voter registrar Okla. County Election Bd., 1994. Named Tchr. of Yr., Edmond North H.S., 2002—03. Mem. Nat. Coun. for Social Studies, Phi Theta Kappa. Democrat. Mem. Christian Ch. (Disciples Of Christ). Avocations: politics, music, computers, reading, hockey. Office: Edmond North High Sch 215 W Danforth Rd Edmond OK 73003-5206

CHASE, J. SCOTT, lawyer; b. Houston, Tex, Mar. 14, 1946; s. Donald Lloyd and Jean Lou (Gamache) Chase; m. Jance Dahrling Chase, Nov. 22, 1968 (div.); 1 child, Jeffrey. BA Polit. Sci., U. Houston, 1968, JD, 1971. Bar: Tex. 1973, US Dist. Ct. Tex. 1978, US Dist. Ct. Mil. Appeals 1978. Assoc. counsel Campbell Taggart, Inc., Dallas, 1973—76; staff atty. Dr. Pepper Co., Dallas, 1976—, asst. sec., 1977—. Served USAR, 1971—73. Mem.: Dallas Assn. Young Lawyers (pres. 1982), Dallas Bar Assn. (dir. 1982, chmn. corp. counsel sect. 1981—82). Office: PO Box 225086 Dallas TX 75222-5086

CHASE, J. VINCENT, property manager; b. N.Y.C., Nov. 5, 1949; m. Addie Lee Pickus, Sept. 3, 1983. BS, U. Bridgeport, 1972. Pers. adminstr. Ins. Svcs. Office, N.Y.C., 1972-77; gen. mgr. pers. John Wiley & Sons, N.Y.C., 1977-79; pers. dir. CitiCorp, N.Y.C., 1979-83; pres., owner Colonial Square Shopping Ctr., Stratford, Conn., 1983—; mem. Conn. Ho. of Reps., Hartford, 1980-96, dep. minority leader, 1990-96; asst. treas. Conn. Office of the State Treasurer, Hartford, 1997-98, justice of the peace, 1996—2004; chief investigator U.S. Ho. of Reps., Washington, 1998—. Bd. dirs. Union Cemetery Assn; bd. trustees Stratford Libr. Assn.; candidate for U.S. Ho. or Reps. from 3d Dist. Conn., 1990; bd. mem. Stratford Red Cross, Stratford Vis. Nurse Assn., U. Bridgeport Alumni Assn., Kennedy Ctr., Sacred Heart U. Adv. Bd. Recipient Outstanding Svc. award Stratford Tenants' Coun., 1982, Man of Yr. award Stratford Civitan Club, 1983, Alumnus of Yr. award U. Bridgeport, 1990, Legislator of Yr. award Conn. Profl. Ins. Agts. Assn., 1991, Legislator of Yr. award Conn. Assn. Optometrists, 1993, Legislator of Yr. award Conn. Chiropractic Assn., 1994, Legislator of Yr. award Conn. Adoption Coun., 1996, Legislator of Yr. award U.S. Humane Soc., 1997. Mem. U. Bridgeport Alumni Assn. (bd. dirs.), Washington D.C.-Conn. Soc., Masons, Scottish Rite. Congregationalist.

CHASE, JAMES RICHARD, retired college president; b. Oxnard, Calif., Oct. 7, 1930; s. James Warren and Nina Marie (Fiscus) C.; m. Mary Corinne Sutherland, Dec. 16, 1950; children: Kenneth Richard, Jennifer Corinne. B. Theology, Biola Coll., 1951; BA, Pepperdine U., 1953, MA, 1954; PhD, Cornell U., 1961. Instr. Biola Coll., La Mirada, Calif., 1953-57, prof., chmn. dept. humanities, 1959-65, v.p. acad. affairs, 1965-70, pres., 1970-82, Wheaton (Ill.) Coll., 1982-93, pres. emeritus, 1993—. Teaching asst. Cornell Univ., Ithaca, N.Y., 1957-59; bd. dirs. World Christian Tng. Ctr., 1970-82; bd. dirs. Christian Coll. Coalition, 1977-79, chmn. bd., 1977-79; bd. dirs. Mission Aviation Fellowship, 1975-81, chmn. bd., 1978-81; bd. dirs. Western Coll. Assn., 1980-82 Mem. Nat. Assn. Ind. Colls. and Univs. (dir. 1980), Assn. Ind. Calif. Colls. and Univs. (mem. exec. com. 1978-82), Am. Assn. Bible Colls. (dir. 1974-80), Nat. Assn. Intercollegiate Athletics (pres. adv. com. 1976-82), Nat. Assn. Evangelicals (exec. com. 1984-92), We. Assn. Schs. and Colls. (sr. commn. 1981-82), Am. Assn. Pres. Ind. Colls. and Univs. (dir. 1980-85, v.p. 1982-85), Speech Communication Assn., Christian Coll. Consortium (chmn. 1986), Coalition (chmn. 1976), Fedn. Ind. Ill. Colls. and Univs. (exec. com., chmn. bd. 1989-91). Baptist.

CHASE, JEANNE NORMAN, artist, educator; b. Spokane, Wash., Feb. 15, 1929; d. John Henry and Violet Inez (Crosby) Norman; m. David Carl Chase, July 4, 1964. BFA in Painting, Calif. State U., Northridge, 1959. Instr. painting and drawing Ringling Sch. Art and Design, Sarasota, Fla., 1978-94, chmn. fine arts dept., 1983-85. Condr. workshops Ringling Workshop Series, Wildacres Retreat, N.C., 1984, 85; lectr. in field. Group and one-woman shows include Rauchbach Gallery, Bal Harbour, Fla., 1981, 83, Boca Grande (Fla.) Gallery, 1982, Tatem Gallery, Ft. Lauderdale, 1986, 87, St. Boniface Conservatory of Arts, Sarasota, 1988, Helios Gallery, Naples, Fla., 1989, Manatee C.C. Fine Arts Gallery, 1988, Phillips Gallery, Sanibel, Fla., 1991, Mickelson Gallery, Washington, 1989-94, Venice Art Gallery, Fla., 2003, others; nat. and internat. juried competitions Ridge Crest Art Assn., Winter Haven, Fla., 1980, Mason Keane Gallery, N.Y.C., 1981 (Best of Show), Tampa (Fla.) Mus. of Arts, 1982, El Paso Mus. Art, 1982, Columbia-Greene C.C., Hudson, N.Y., 1982, Edison C.C., Ft. Myers, Fla., 1982, 85, The Soc. of the Four Arts, Palm Beach, Fla., 1982, 87, The Capitol Gallery, Tallahassee, Fla., 1986, Tampa Mus., 1988, Binnewater Arts Ctr., N.Y.C., 1988, others.; represented in permanent collections former Pres. Jimmy and Roslyn Carter, Grace Lemon (collector), Indonesia, Bendix Avionies, Dr. and Mrs. Victor Maitland, Fla., Ringling Sch. Art and Design, Mr. and Mrs. E. Howland Swift III, Va., Chatahoochie Mus. Art, Ga., Dr. Artine Artinian, Fla., George Whitman, Shakespeare and Co., Paris, Veroingue Rabin Le Gall E'cole des Beaux-Arts, Paris, Donahoe Swift Assn., N.Y.C., Chonquing Mus., China, Spencer Mus. of Art, Kanas City; works published in book American Artists, an Illustrated Survey of Leading Contemporary Americans, 1986; subject in books: Female Artists in the United States: a Research and Resource File, 1986, 88, Artists and Their Cats, 1990, Drawings, Hylton-Leech Gallery, Sarasota, Fla., 1996; subject numerous newspaper articles; TV and video interviews: Focus on the Arts, Channel 4, 1980, A Fabric of Our Own Making, Ga. State U., 1981, Introduction to Jeanne Norman Chase, local sta., St. Augustine, Fla., 1991. Mem. Fla. Artists Group. Recipient Merit award Foster Harmon Gallery, Sarasota, 1991. Mem. Fla. Artists Group. Avocations: writing, piano, travel. Studio: 1817 Ingram Ave Sarasota FL 34232 Office Phone: 941-364-9132. E-mail: studiojnc@prodigy.net.

CHASE, JOHN DAVID, retired dean, retired internist; b. Detroit, Sept. 24, 1920; s. Clyde Harrison and Bonnie Lucille (Fogas) Chase; 1 child, Robert Winslow. AB, Wabash (Ind.) Coll., 1942; MD, Western Res. U., 1945. Diplomate Am. Bd. Internal Medicine. Intern Detroit Receiving Hosp., 1945—46; resident in internal medicine Wayne State U. Hosp., 1948—52; teaching fellow Nat. Heart Inst., 1952; with VA, 1952—78, dep. asso. chief med. dir. academic affairs Washington, 1970—73; chief med. service VA Hosp., Tacoma, 1973—74; chief med. dir. VA Central Office, Washington, 1974—78; assoc. dean clin. affairs U. Wash. Sch. Med., Seattle, 1978—81, dean Sch. Medicine, 1981—82, dean emeritus, 1983—. Mem. nat. adv. coun. Heart and Lung Inst., 1968—70, Regional Med. Programs, 1970—73, Nat. Libr. Medicine, 1972—73; mem. Nat. Adv. Coun. VA Edn., 1973, Nat. Adv. Coun. Health Svcs. Planning and Resources, 1976, Fed. Coordinating Coun. Sci., Engring. and Tech., 1976—78, Nat. Adv. Coun. Health Planning and Devel., 1976—; bd. govs. Armed Forces Inst. Pathology, 1976—78. With M.C. USNR, 1946—48. Recipient Disting. Svc. award, Wayne State U. Med. Sch., 1976. Fellow: ACP, Am. Coll. Chest Physicians; mem.: AMA (ho. dels.), Nat. Inst. Med., Am. Hosp. Assn. (trustee 1976—78), Assn. Mil. Surgeons U.S., Inst. Medicine. Home: 112 Frederick Rd Fredericksburg TX 78624 E-mail: jchase2@earthlink.net.

CHASE, KAREN HUMPHREY, elementary school educator; b. New Bedford, Mass., Nov. 17, 1948; d. Clifton Humphrey and Alice (Duffy) C. BA in Sociology, Stonehill Coll., 1970; MA in Edn., Lesley U., 2003. Cert. tchr. K-8, Mass. Elem. tchr. Minot (Maine) Consol. Sch., 1970-72; tchr. social studies George R. Austin Mid. Sch., Lakeville, Mass., 1972—2002, co-coord. students as mediators program, 1996—98; tchr. social studies Freetown-Lakeville Mid. Sch., 2002—. Dept. leader social studies, Austin Mid. Sch., Lakeville, 1976-80; supt. search team Freetown-Lakeville Sch. Dist., 1995. Actor/dir.: Your Theatre, Inc. New Bedford, Mass., 1985—; mem. Marion Arts Ctr., 1973—; 2nd v.p. Educators Assn. Freetown-Lakeville, 1991-93, 1st v.p., 1993-2003. Named Young Careerist of Yr., Bus. and Profl. Women, Wareham, Mass., 1979. Mem. Plymouth County Educators Assn. (Significant Svc. Honor award 1995), Mass. Tchrs. Assn., NEA, Nat. Coun. for Social Studies. Avocations: travel, reading, hiking, gardening, yoga. Home: 196 Clapp Rd Rochester MA 02770-4000 Office: Freetown-Lakeville Mid Sch 96 Howland Rd Lakeville MA 02347

CHASE, KAREN SUSAN, English literature educator; b. St. Louis, Oct. 16, 1952; d. Stanley Martin and Judith C.; m. Michael H. Levenson, Dec. 30, 1984; children: Alexander Nathan, Sarah Sophie. BA, UCLA, 1974; MA, Stanford U., 1977, PhD, 1980. Asst. prof. U. Va., Charlottesville, 1979-85, assoc. prof., 1985-91, prof., 1992—. Author: Eros and Psyche, 1984, George Eliot's Middlemarch, 1990; co-author: The Spectacle of Intimacy: A Public Life For The Victorian Family, 2000, Middlemarch in the Twenty-First Century, 2005. Office: Univ Va English Dept 219 Bryan Hall Charlottesville VA 22903

CHASE, OSCAR GOTTFRIED, law educator; b. 1940; s. Sidney and Helen G. Chase; m. Jane Monell, June 12, 1969; children: Arlo M., Oliver G. BA, NYU, 1960; JD, Yale U., 1963. Bar: NY 1963, US Dist. Ct. So. and Ea. Dists. NY 1968, US Ct. Appeals 2nd Cir. 1970, US Supreme Ct. 1972, US Ct. Appeals DC Cir. 1975. Staff mem voter edn. project Student Non-Violent Coordinating Com., Jackson, Miss., 1963-64; counsel Lower West Side Cmty. Corp., NYC, 1966-67; lawyer M.F.Y. Legal Services, Inc., 1967-68; asst. gen. counsel, dir. law reform Cmty. Action for Legal Services, Inc., 1968-72; prof. law Bklyn. Law Sch., 1972-78; vis. prof. law NYU Sch. Law, 1978-79, prof. law, 1980—, assoc. dean, 1990—94, vice dean, 1994—99, co-dir. Inst. Jud. Adminstrn., 2000—. Author: New York Civil Practice Law and Rules Manual, rev. edit., 1997; co-author: (with R. Barker) Civil Litigation in New York, 4th edit., 2002. Bd. dirs. Untapped Resources, Inc., 1970—81; mem. adv. com. ACLU Reproductive Freedom Project, 1977—82; mem. joint AALS/ABA Law Sch. Admission Coun. on Fin. Aid, 1991—94. Office: NYU Sch Law 40 Washington Sq S New York NY 10012-1099*

CHASE, ROBERT ARTHUR, surgeon, educator; b. Keene, N.H., Jan. 6, 1923; s. Albert Henry and Georgia Beulah (Bump) Chase; m. Ann Crosby Parker, Feb. 3, 1946; children: Deborah Lee, Nancy Jo, Robert N. BS cum laude, U. N.H., 1945, DSc (hon.), 1993; MD, Yale, 1947. Diplomate Am. Bd. Surgery, Am. Bd. Plastic Surgery. Intern New Haven Hosp., 1947—48, asst. resident, 1949—50, sr. resident surgery, 1952—53, chief resident surgeon, 1953—54; mem. faculty Yale Sch. Medicine, 1948—54, 1959—62, asst. prof. surgery, 1959—62; mem. faculty U. Pitts., 1957—59, resident plastic surgeon, also teaching fellow, 1957—59; attending surgeon VA Hosp., W. Haven, Conn., 1959—62, Grace New Haven Community Hosp., 1959—63; prof., chmn. dept. surgery Stanford Sch. Medicine, 1963—74, Emile Holman prof. surgery, 1972—; prof. surgery U. Pa., 1974—77; attending surgeon Pa. Hosp., Hosp. U. Pa., Grad. Hosp., Phila., 1974—77; pres., dir. Nat. Bd. Med. Examiners, Phila., 1974—77; prof. anatomy Stanford (Calif.) U., 1977—. Cons. plastic surgery Christian Med. Coll. and Hosp., Vellore, India, 1962; cons. to surgeon gen. USAF, 1970—; Benjamin K. Rank prof. Australasian Coll. Surgeons, 1974. Author: Atlas of Hand Surgery; editor: Videosurgery, 1974—; mem. editl. bd.: Med. Alert Communication, —; contbr. articles to profl. jours. Mem. bd. overseers Dartmouth Med. Sch., 1998-; mem. found. bd. U. N.H., 1998-. Maj. M.C. AUS, 1949—57. Recipient Francis Gilman Blake award, Yale Sch. Medicine, 1962, Henry J. Kaiser award, Stanford U. Sch. Medicine, 1978, 1979, 1984, 1986, 1990, 1993, Calif. Golden Apple award, 1991, Albion William Hewlett award, 1992, Pettee award, U. N.H., 1998; Robert A. Chase Ctr. for Upper Limb Surgery established at Stanford U., 2003. Fellow: ACS, Australasian Coll. Surgeons (hon.); mem.: AMA, NAS, Halsted Soc., Am. Soc. Most Venerable Order Hosp., St. John of Jerusalem, Inst. Medicine (exec. com. 1976, coun. 1986—), Soc. Univ. Surgeons, Found. Am. Soc. Plastic and Reconstructive Surgery (dir.), Am. Cancer Soc. (clin. fellowship com.), James IV Assn. Surgeons, Pacific Coast Surg. Soc., Western Surg. Assn., Soc. Clin. Surgery, Plastic Surgery Rsch. Coun., Am. Assn. Surgery Trauma, Am. Soc. Cleft Palate Rehab., Am. Soc. Surgery Hand (pres.), Conn. Med. Soc., Santa Clara County Med. Soc., Am. Surg. Assn., San Francisco Surg. Soc., Calif. Acad. Medicine (pres.), Am. Soc. Clin. Anatomists (hon.; pres.), South African Soc. Plastic and Reconstructive Surgery (hon.), South African Soc. Surgery Hand (hon.), Am. Assn. Plastic Surgery (hon.), Am. Assn. Clin. Anatomists (hon.; pres.), Am. Assn. Plastic Surgeons (hon.), Sigma Xi, Phi Beta Kappa. Home: 69 Pearce Mitchell Pl Stanford CA 94305 Office: Stanford U Div Anatomy 269 Campus Dr Stanford CA 94305-5102 Office Phone: 650-725-6618. E-mail: rchase6880@aol.com.

CHASE, SANDRA LEE, clinical pharmacist, consultant; b. Oak Park, Ill., July 31, 1959; d. William Warren and Charlene Lois (Johnson) Chase; m. Christopher Paul Bloch, Sept. 8, 1984; children: Kyle Thaddeus Bloch, Matthew William Bloch. Student, Mich. State U., 1977-80; BS in Pharmacy, U. Mich., 1983, PharmD, 1984. Lic. pharmacist Del., Mich., Pa.; cert. leader arthritis found. YMCA Aquatic Program. Rsch. asst. U. Mich., Ann Arbor, 1980-81; pharmacy intern Three Rivers (Mich.) Hosp., 1981, Cmty. Pharmacy, Ann Arbor, 1980-83; pharmacy intern, grad. intern St. Francis Hosp., Wilmington, Del., 1982-83; resident in hosp. pharmacy Thomas Jefferson U. Hosp., Phila., 1984-85, clin. pharmacist in cardiopulmonary medicine, 1985-89; sr. med. info. coord. ICI Pharms. Group, Wilmington, Del., 1989-92; clin. pharmacist Thomas Jefferson U. Hosp., Phila., 1989-93, clin. pharmacist drug use policy and clin. svcs., 1993-98; clin. pharmacy specialist Spectrum Health, Grand Rapids, Mich., 1999—. Adj. asst. prof. clin. pharmacy Temple U. Coll. Pharmacy, 1990—98, Ferris State U. Coll. Pharmacy, 1999—; clin. instr. in pharmacy practice Phila. Coll. Pharmacy and Sci., 1985—87, clin. asst. prof., 1987—88, clin. assoc. prof., 1988—98; instr. clin. care cardiopulmonary medicine in nursing Episcopal Hosp., Phila., 1986—88, Thomas Jefferson U. Hosp., Phila., 1985—91, Our Lady of Lourdes Med. Ctr., Camden, NJ, 1988—91; coord., prof. pharmacology and drug therapeutic for advanced nursing practice course Sch. Nursing Ctr. Profl. Devel., U. Pa., Phila., 1994—2001; mem. Pa. Osteporosis Soc. Bd., 1996—98; presenter in field. Mem. editl. bd.: RN, referee:; contbg. editor; mem. editl. bd.: Med. Econs., referee: AHFS Drug Info., Am. Druggist, Am. Jour. Hosp. Pharmacy, Nursing 96 Drug Handbook, Nursing 97 Drug Handbook, Pharmacotherapy, Annals of Pharmacotherapy, U. Hosp. Consortium Monographs; contbr. articles to profl. jours. Mem. adv. bd. Nursing Mothers Network; cert. leader aquatic program Arthritis Found. YMCA, 2000—; chmn. Coll. Pharmacy Alumni Soc., 2000—; mem. women's heart advantage steering com. Spectrum Health, 2003—; mem. alumni bd. govs. U. Mich. Coll. Pharmacy, 1991—97, 1998—2004, chair bd. govs., 2000—03; mem. Heartbeat Gala com. Am. Heart Assn., 2004—; mem. State of Mich. Task Force for Cardiovasc. Health, 2002—03; bd. dirs. U. Mich Alumni Soc., 2004—; chair edn. com. Mich. Soc. Health Sys. Pharmacists, 2001—; bd. dirs. Corey Lake Assn., 2003—. Fellow, Mich. Pharmacists Assn., 2001. Mem.: Am. Heart Assn., Aerobics and Fitness Assn. Am., Western Mich. Soc. Health-Sys. Pharmacists (bd. dirs. 1998—2000), Pediat. and Adult Asthma Network West Mich., Mich. Soc. Health Sys. Pharmacists (chair edn. com. 2000—), Mich. Pharm. Assn. (mem. exec. bd. 2002—, pres.elect 2005), Del. Pharm. Soc. (conv. com. 1990—94, ACPE com. 1990—94), Nat. Headache Found., Am. Diabetes Assn., Am. Pharm. Assn., Am. Soc. Health Sys. Pharmacists, Am. Coll. Clin. Pharmacy, U. Mich. Alumni Assn. (bd. dirs. 2004—), Rho Chi Pharm. Soc. Republican. Lutheran. Avocations: aerobics, waterskiing, cross country skiing, gardening. Office: Spectrum Health Dept Pharmacy 100 Michigan St NE Grand Rapids MI 49503-2560 Office Phone: 616-774-5264. E-mail: Sandra.Chase@spectrum-health.org.

CHASE, THOMAS NEWELL, neurologist, researcher, educator; b. Westfield, NJ, May 23, 1932; s. Newell Adams and Gudrun Margarethe (Eskesen) C.; 1 child, Thomas Newell. BS, MIT, 1954; postgrad., Columbia U., 1957-58; MD, Yale U., 1962; postgrad., Harvard U., 1963-66. Engr. Singer Mfg. Co., Bridgeport, Conn., 1954-55; technician Columbia U. Coll. Phys. and Surgs., 1957-58; intern in internal medicine Yale-New Haven Med. Center, 1962-63; asst. resident in neurology Mass. Gen. Hosp., Boston, 1963-64, resident, 1965-66; fellow in neuropathology Harvard U. Med. Sch., 1964-65; guest worker NIMH, Bethesda, Md., 1966-68, chief unit on neurology, 1968-70, chief sect. exptl. therapeutics, 1970-74; chief lab. of neuropharmacology Nat. Inst. Neurol. and Communicative Disorders and Stroke, Bethesda, 1974-76, dir. intramural research, 1974-83, chief pharmacology sect., 1976—2005; chief exptl. therapeutics br., 1983—2005; CFO Hamilton Pharrms., Inc., 2005—. Mem. sci. adv. bd. Nat. Parkinson Found.; mem. adv. bd. Nat. Ataxia Found., Astra-Zenica. Assoc. editor Jour. Psychiatry and Neurosci.; mem. editl. bd. Progress in Neuro-Psychopharmacology, Movement Disorders, Drug Devel. Rsch., Parkinsonian and Related Disorders, Contemporary Neurology, Current Treatment Options in Neurology, Jour. Neural Transmission, Neurotoxicology Rsch., Neurodegenerative Diseases; contbr. articles to med. jours. Served with Signal Corps U.S. Army, 1955-57. Recipient Winternitz prize in pathology, 1960, Ramsay prize for clin. medicine, 1961, diploma of recognition of merit for humanitarian svcs. Govt. of Bolivia, 1974, USPHS Meritorious Svc. medal, 1978, 96, USPHS Outstanding Svc. medal, 1991, Springer prize for Parkinson's disease rsch., 1994; summer fellow, 1960; USPHS summer fellow, 1961; Nat. Inst. Neurol. Diseases and Blindness spl. fellow, 1966-68. Fellow Am. Coll. Neuro-Psychopharmacology; mem. Am. Neurol. Assn., Am. Acad. Neurology, Am. Soc. Exptl. Neurotherapeutics (pres. 1997-2001), Soc. Neurosci., Internat. Soc. Neurochemistry, Am. Soc. Neurochemistry, Assn. for Rsch. in Nervous and Mental Disease, Internat. Brain Rsch. Orgn., Internat. Basal Ganglia Soc., World Fedn. Neurology, Movement Disorder Soc. Office: Hamilton Pharms Inc Ste 520 1825 K St NW Washington DC 20006

CHASE, WILLIAM ROBERT, television executive; b. Mt. Vernon, N.Y., Mar. 8, 1951; s. Irving Warren and Muriel Ada Chase. BA, Queens Coll., 1974; MS, Bklyn. Coll., 1976. Scenic and lighting dir. Bklyn. Coll. of CUNY, 1974-76; freelance lighting dir. N.Y.C., 1974—; unit prodn. mgr. various TV prodn. cos., 1983-87; prodn. mgr. Sta. WNET-TV/PBS, N.Y., 1979-87; dir. prodn. mgmt. Sta. WNET-TV, N.Y., 1987-88; dir. east coast prodn. HBO, Inc., N.Y.C., 1988-90, v.p. prodn., east coast, 1990—. Instr. Bklyn. Coll., 1976-85, N.Y. Inst. Tech., 1982-85. Assoc. producer Roanoak, 1985; unit prodn. mgr: (TV shows, mini-series, spls.) Kennedy, 1983, Finnegan Begin Again, 1984, Murder of Mary Phagan, 1987; line producer (TV series) Pee-Wee's Playhouse, 1986. Mem. Dirs. Guild Am., Nat. Acad. TV Arts and Scis. Avocations: photography, computers.

CHASEK, ARLENE SHATSKY, academic director; b. Newark, N.J., June 1, 1934; d. Herman and Rose (Sporn) Shatsky; m. Marvin B. Chasek, Apr. 10, 1960; children: Pamela S., Laura N., Daniel J. BA, Cornell U., 1956; MA, Columbia U., 1957; postgrad., U. N.D., 1972-74, Rutgers U., 1981-91. Tchr. English and journalism Elizabeth (N.J.) Pub. Schs., 1978-80, Summit (N.J.) Pub. Schs., 1978-80; coord. MA program Fairleigh Dickinson U., Teaneck, N.J., 1979-81; editor AT&T, Murray Hill, N.J., 1980-81; project coord. Consortium for Ednl. Equity, Rutgers U., New Brunswick, N.J., 1981-85, project dir., 1985-88, dir. spl. projects, 1988-93, dir. family involvement programs in math., sci. and tech., 1993-95, dir. Ctr. for Family Involvement in Schs., 1995—. Mem. steering com., N.J. coord. Am. Goes Back to Sch. initiative U.S. Dept. Edn., 1997. Author, editor: Rutgers Family Tools and Technology, 1994, Rutgers Family Science, 1993, Mathematics in Art/Art in Mathematics, 1986 (U.S. Dept. Edn. award 1987), From Jumping Genes to Red Giants: A Guide to High School Science Research; author: The Recruitment and Retention Challenge, 1982, Futures Unlimited, 1985 (Curriculum award am. Ednl. Rsch. Assn. 1986). Recipient Golden Apple award for Family Involvement Programs, Working Mother mag., U.S. Dept. Edn., and Tchrs. Coll. Columbia U., 1996. Mem. AAUW, LWV, NSTA, Nat. Assn. Equity Educators, Coop. Learning Assn., Internat. Tech. Edn. Assn., Assn. Math. Tchrs. N.J. Home: 9 Schindler Pl New Providence NJ 07974-1738 Office: Rutgers Univ Center for Math, Science, and Computer Busch Campus, SERC New Brunswick NJ 08903 E-mail: aschasek@aol.com.

CHASEMAN, JOEL, communications consultant; b. Feb. 18, 1926; m. Marlene Meyerson, Sept. 11, 1955; children: Martha Hope, Joanne Amy. BA, Cornell U., 1948. CEO Post-Newsweek Stas., Washington, 1973-90; chmn. NATAS, 1980-82; dir. Advt. Coun., 1986-90; prin. Chaseman Enterprises Internat., 1990—. Chmn. Advanced TV Test Ctr., 1987—93; CEO NevadaVision, Inc., 1990—2001, Hobby Craft Interactive Network, 1999—2002; chmn. adv. bd. Nearware Networks, 2001—; advisor Ctr. for Pub. Integrity, 2003—. Trustee Mus. Broadcasting, 1988. Mem. Assn. Maximum Svc. Telecasters (chmn. 1988-91), Nat. Assn. Broadcasters (bd. dirs. 1988-90). E-mail: joechase@wdn.com.

CHASEN, SYLVAN HERBERT, data processing executive, financial planner; b. Richmond, Va., May 19, 1926; s. Nathan and Hanna (Pass) C.; m. Catherine Hudlow, Mar. 25, 1946; children: Deborah Wyatt, Dianne Lipsey, Jane Morrison, Susan Mazur. Student, Va. Poly. Inst., 1943-44; BS in Engring, B. Chem. Engring., Ga. Inst. Tech., 1946; MS, Emory U., 1951. Registered investment advisor 1993. Math. instr. Ga. Inst. Tech., Atlanta, 1946-50; head computer facility Naval Air Test Ctr., Patuxent, Md., 1951-58; dir. advanced computing CAD and interactive graphics Lockheed-Ga. Co., Marietta, 1958-87; pres. Center CAD/CAM Tech., Inc. Adj. instr. Emory U., 1993-2005; cons. in field. Author: Geometric Principles and Procedures for Computer Graphics Applications, 1978, The Guide for the Evaluation and Implementation of CAD/CAM Systems, 1980, 2d edit., 1983. Served as ensign USN, 1944-46. Recipient Outstanding Contbns. award Gov. Md., 1957; recipient Disting. Contbns. award Soc. Mfg. Engrs., 1982 Mem. ASME, Soc. Mfg. Engrs., SIGGRAPH, NCGA Home: 760 Starlight Ct NE Atlanta GA 30342-2826

CHASIN, KEITH A., lawyer; b. N.Y.C., Dec. 11, 1957; s. Edwin Seymour and Lila Natalie C.; m. Diane Chasin, Aug. 31, 1980; children: Jessica, Nicole, Danielle. JD, U. Miami, Fla., 1982. Bar: Fla., U.S. Dist. Ct. Fla. Pvt. practice, 1982-85. Bd. dirs. YMCA, 1998-2000. Democrat. Jewish. Office: 9100 S Dadeland Blvd Ste 1704 Miami FL 33156-7817

CHASIN, MARTIN, art gallery director, consultant, educator; b. Bklyn., July 17, 1938; s. Saul and Frances M. (Rosenfeld) C.; m. Jessica Wolf, Nov. 12, 1989; 1 stepchild, Jonah Gelbach. Student, Bklyn. Coll., 1956-60, U. Pa., 1960-66, Oxford U., Eng, 1962, Free U. Berlin, 1962-63. Mem. faculty history Howard U., Washington, 1966-69; Am. Coun. Learned Socs. fellow Princeton U., 1969-73; mgr. Hannoch, Weisman, Stern & Besser, Newark, 1973-77; gen. mgr. Western Union Internat./Airsignal, N.Y.C., 1977-82; dir. mktg. Center Art Galleries, Honolulu, Hawaii, 1982-85; dir. ops. Greenwich Workshop, Trumbull, Conn., 1985. Author: (with others) History of the Crusades Vol. VI, 1990. Named Harrison fellow, Univ. fellow, U. Pa., 1963-66; recipient Fulbright Grant, Fulbright Commn., Washington, 1962. Fellow Royal Soc. Arts (London); mem. Am. Hist. Soc., Princeton Club of N.Y. Avocations: collector: books, 18th century english silver.

CHASKELSON, MARSHA INA, neuropsychologist; b. Brookline, Mass., Jan. 6, 1950; d. Hyman and Doris (Sacks) C.; m. Allen Noah Elgart, July 8, 1973; children: Jonah Elgart, Benjamin Elgart, Sarah Elgart. BA in Psychology, U. Mass., 1971; MEd in Spl. Edn., Boston Coll., 1972, PhD Counseling Psychology, 1985. Lic. psychologist; cert. sch. psychologist; cert. provider. Resource room specialist for emotionally disturbed Acton-Boxborough Regional Jr. High Sch., Acton, Mass., 1972-76; faculty mem., on-site facilitator Boston Coll., Chestnut Hill, Mass., 1976-77; in-patient coord., out-patient staff psychologist Kennedy Meml. Hosp., Brighton, Mass., 1977-80; contracted sch. psychologist Beverly (Mass.) Pub. Schs., 1981; contracted staff psychologist Human Resource Inst., Franklin, Mass., 1980-82, mental retardation coord., 1982-83; clin. specialist Alternatives, Unltd., Whitinsville, Mass., 1981-87; dir. Lexington Psychol. & Ednl. Resources, Lexington, Mass., 1987—. Psychology intern psychology dept. Kennedy Meml. Hosp., Brighton, 1976-77, post-doctoral psychologist Children's Hosp. Med. Ctr., Boston, 1984-85; post-doctoral neuropsychologist New Eng. Rehab. Hosp., Woburn, Mass., 1985-86; co-chairperson Lexington A.D.D. Parent Group, 1987-88. Mem. Am. Psychol. Assn., Assn. Higher Edn. and Disability., Coun. for Exceptional Children, Mass. Psychol. Assn., Worldwide Assn. for Children with Learning Disabilities. Democrat. Jewish. Office: Lexington Psychol & Ednl Resources 76 Bedford St Ste 26 Lexington MA 02420-4641 Office Phone: 781-863-5599. Business E-Mail: lexper@rcn.com.

CHASNOFF, BARRY A., lawyer; b. Houston, July 22, 1949; BA, Trinity U., 1971; JD with honors, U. Tex., 1974. Bar: Tex. 1974, US Dist. Ct. (we., no.and so. dists.) Tex. 1981, US Ct. Appeals (5th cir.) 1982, US Supreme Ct. 1983. Trial atty. office gen. counsel Dept. Transp., 1974-77; ptnr., head litig. practice and mem. mgmt. com. Akin, Gump, Strauss, Hauer & Feld LLP, San Antonio. Teaching quizmaster U. Tex. Sch. Law, 1973-74. Mem. ABA, State Bar of Tex. San Antonio Bar Assn., Tex. Bar Found., San Antonio Bar Found., Internat. Assn. Def. Counsel, Order of Coif. Office: Akin Gump Strauss Hauer & Feld LLP Ste 1500 300 Convent St San Antonio TX 78205-3732 Office Phone: 210-281-7001. Office Fax: 210-281-2035. Business E-Mail: bchasnoff@akingump.com.

CHASON, ROBERT, health facility administrator; Grad., Wilmington Coll.; MA, Miami U. Asst. exec. v.p., asst. v.p. bus. adminstrn., bus. mgr. State U. NY at Stony Brook, 1965—79; assoc. vice chancellor student affairs U. Calif. Davis Health Sys. U. Calif. Med. Ctr., 1979—94, dir. hosps. and clinics, chief operating officer, 2002—. Office: U Calif Davis Med Ctr 2315 Stockton Blvd Sacramento CA 95817

CHASSE, JOHN DENNIS, economics educator; b. Kalispell, Mont., July 30, 1934; s. Clarence Harry and Aurice Rose (Weller) C.; m. Linda Marie Negus, Jan. 2, 1977; children: Matthew, Paul. BA, Gonzaga U., 1961; MA, Regis Coll., 1968; PhD, Syracuse U., 1974. Rsch. asst. Syracuse (N.Y.) U., 1968-70; intern UN Devel. Programme, New Delhi, 1971; from asst. to assoc. prof. Savannah (Ga.) State Coll., 1973-79; pub. health advisor U.S. Office Internat. Health, Rockville, Md., 1976; assoc. prof. SUNY, Brockport, 1979—2001, prof. econs., 2001—. Vis. prof. U.S. Bur. Labor Stats., Washington, 1974. Contbr. articles to profl. jours. Home: 234 S Main St Brockport NY 14420-2247 Office: SUNY Dept Bus and Econs Brockport NY 14420

CHASSMAN, KAREN MOSS, educational administrator; b. Bklyn., Aug. 18, 1946; d. Bernard and Esther (Steier) Kahn; m. Robert Moss (div. 1973); 1 child, Jeff; m. Richard Chassman, Oct. 31, 1992 (dec. Feb. 1994). BA, Hunter Coll., 1967; MS in Edn., Bklyn. Coll., 1969, advanced cert. in lang. arts, 1978. Tchr. nursery, kindergarten and grades 1-6 Common Branches, 1967-78; sales rep., real estate broker various cos., 1978-91; dir., owner The Reading Improvement Ctr., East Islip, N.Y., 1991—. Mem. Islip C. of C., Islip Rotary (ednl. scholar 1992—). Avocations: aerobic exercise, antiques, travel. Office: Reading Improvement Ctr 2545 Middle Country Rd Centereach NY 11720 also: Reading Improvement Ctr 268 East Main St East Islip NY 11730 Office Phone: 631-581-0500. E-mail: readingcenter@aol.com, prinitch@aol.com.

CHASSMAN, LEONARD FREDRIC, retired labor union administrator; b. Detroit, Sept. 30, 1935; s. Joachim and Lillian (Abrams) C.; m. Phyllis Perlman, Aug. 25, 1957; children: Mark, Cheryl, Gregory. BA, UCLA, 1957. Rep. AFTRA, LA, 1959-63, SAG, LA, 1963-65; staff exec. Writers Guild Am., West, Inc., LA, 1965-77, exec. dir., 1978-82; nat. exec. sec. Screen Extras Guild Inc., 1982-84; Hollywood exec. dir. SAG Inc., 1984—2001, trustee SAG prodrs. pension and health funds; bd. dirs. Entertainment Industry Found. Pres. Hollywood Entertainment Labor Coun. Bd. dirs. L.A. Pvt. Industry Coun. E-mail: Lchassman930@aol.com.

CHAST, ROZ, cartoonist; b. Bklyn., Nov. 26, 1954; d. George and Elizabeth (Buchman) C.; m. William Franzen, Sept. 22, 1984; children: Ian, Nina. BFA, RISD, 1977. Contract artist The New Yorker Mag., N.Y.C., 1979—; cartoonist The Scis. Mag. Author: (cartoon collections) Unscientific Americans, 1982, Parallel Universes, 1984, Mondo Boxo: Cartoon Stories, 1987, The Four Elements, 1988, Proof of Life on Earth, 1991, The Party, After You Left: Collected Cartoons 1995-2003, 2004; illustrator of various books including The Joy of Being Single, 1992, Meet My Staff, 1998, Now I Will Never Leave the Dinner Table, 1999, Rationalizations to Live By, 2000, The New Yorker Book of Kids Cartoons, 2001, Weird and Wonderful Words, 2002, You're an Animal, Viskovitz!, 2003; work has been featured in Scientific American, N.Y. Times Mag., Rolling Stone, Nat. Lampoon.

CHASTAIN, BRANDI DENISE, professional soccer player; b. San Jose, Calif., July 21, 1968; m. Jerry Smith; 1 stepchild. Student, U. Calif., Berkeley, 1986—88; BA in TV Comm., Santa Clara U., 1991. Mem. U.S. Women's Soccer Team, 1996—; asst. coach women's soccer team Santa Clara U.; profl. soccer player San Jose CyberRays, 2001—03. Mem. Shiroke Serena, Japan, 1993, U.S. Olympic Soccer Team, Athens, 2004. Named World Cup Champion, 1999; recipient Gold medal, Atlanta Olympic Games, 1996, Gold Medal, Athens Olympic Games, 2004, Silver medal, Sydney Olympic Games, 2000. Achievements include mem. championship team U.S. Olympic Festival; CONCACAF Championship, N.Y., 1993. Office: c/o Santa Clara U Athletics Dept 500 El Camino Real Santa Clara CA 95050-4345 also: US Soccer Fedn 1801 S Prairie Ave # 1811 Chicago IL 60616-1319

CHASTAIN, DIANNA, elementary school educator; b. Bklyn., Dec. 21, 1943; d. Michael Angelo and Concetta (DeMondo) Bonacci; m. Edwin Gilbert Chastain, Feb. 25, 1967 (div. Oct. 1970); 1 child, Michele. BS in Elem. Edn., Fordham U., 1965; MS in Edn., Bklyn. Coll., 1991. Cert. elem. sch. tchr., N.Y. Tchr. N.Y.C. Dept. Edn., Bklyn., 1965—. Sci. fair judge N.Y. Acad. Sci., N.Y.C., 1990-2002, 04-05 Poll worker N.Y.C. Bd. Elections, 1986—. Republican. Avocations: swimming, walking. Home: 1123 Elm Ave Apt 2 Brooklyn NY 11230-5813 Office: NYC Dept Edn 65 Court St Brooklyn NY 11201-4916

CHASTAIN, KENNETH DUANE, retired foreign language educator, writer; b. Salem, Ind., July 20, 1934; s. Lloyd Lionel and Cristal Louise (Hoke) C.; m. Mary Janice McFadden, June 14, 1959; children: Kevin Duane, Brian Duane, Michael Allen. BS, Ind. U., 1956; MA, Ball State U., 1962; PhD, Purdue U., 1968. Tchr. Seymour HS, Ind., 1956-62, Columbus HS, Ind., 1962-64; grad. instr., prof. Purdue U., Lafayette, Ind., 1964-72; prof. Asbury Coll., Wilmore, Ky., 1972-73, U. Va., Charlottesville, Va., 1973-95, prof. emeritus, 1995—. Author: Developing S-L Skills, 1988, Spanish Grammar in Review, 1993, Exploraciones en la Literatura Hispanica, 1993, The Money Chase: Counting the Cost, 2000, Social Security and More: Comments on Government, 2001, English as a Communication System, 2001, Omri and the Boy, 2001, Imaginate, 2004. With U.S. Army, 1957-58. Recipient Florence Steiner Leadership in Fgn. Lang. Edn. award Am. Coun. Teaching Fgn. Langs., 1989. Avocations: exercise, gardening, nature, travel. Home: 2674 Bakers Chapel Church Rd Big Sandy TN 38221-5318 Personal E-mail: jkc373@compu.net.

CHASTAIN, MERRITT BANNING, JR., lawyer; b. Jan. 28, 1940; s. Merritt Banning and Lydia (Spock) Chastain; m. Virginia Anne Ferguson, July 21, 1962; children: Merritt Banning III, Grayson Anne Clarke. BS, U. Okla., 1962; JD, La. State U., 1967. Bar: La. 1967, U.S. Dist. Ct. (we. dist.) La. 1968, U.S. Dist. Ct. (ea. dist.) La. 1972, U.S. Ct. Appeals (5th cir.) 1972, U.S. Supreme Ct. 1979. Law clk. La. Ct. Appeals (2d cir.), Shreveport, La., 1967—68; assoc. Smitherman, Lunn, Chastain & Hill, Shreveport, 1968—72, ptnr., 1972—. Mng. dir. Nat. Assn. Pipe Coating Applicators, 1979—; spl. counsel La. Pub. Facilities Authority, 1985—87. Chmn. United Way of Shreveport/Bossier City, 1975, Ark.-La.-Tex. Ambs., Inc., 1989; pres. Vols. Am., 1976, Norwela Coun. Boy Scouts Am., 1977—78, Demoiselle Club, 1992, Cotillion Gov. Bd., 1989, Shreveport Opera, 1981—95, sec., 1981; trustee Loyola Coll. Prep. Sch., 1984—89, exec. com., 1985—89, pres. bd. trustees, 1986—87; chmn. bd. Loyola Found., Shreveport, La., 1987—88; corp. sponsor chmn. Arthritis Found. Telethon, 1990. Named Outstanding Young Man of La., La. Jaycees, 1975, Outstanding Young Man of Shreveport, Shreveport Jaycees, 1975; named to Hall of Fame, Nat. Assn. Pipe Coating Applicators, 2003. Mem.: ABA (La. mem. chmn. 1976—82), La. Law Inst., Shreveport Bar Assn. (exec. coun. 1971—75, sec.-treas. 1972, bd. govs. young lawyer's sect. 1967—74, pres. young lawyer's sect. 1974), La. State Bar Assn. (spl. com. 1974—75), So. Trace Country Club (Shreveport), Rotary, Shreveport Club. Republican. Episcopalian. Home: 330 Corinne Cir Shreveport LA 71106-6004 Office: Smitherman Lunn Chastain & Hill 333 Texas St Ste 717 Shreveport LA 71101-3673 Office Phone: 318-227-1990.

CHATARD, PETER RALPH NOEL, JR., aesthetic plastic surgeon; b. New Orleans, June 25, 1936; s. Peter Ralph Sr. and Alberta Chatard; m. Patricia Myrl White, Jan. 31, 1963; children: Andrea Michelle, Faedra Noelle, Tahra Deonne. BS in Biology, Morehouse Coll., 1956; MD, U. Rochester, 1960. Diplomate Am. Bd. Plastic Surgery, Am. Bd. Otolaryngology. Intern Colo. Gen. Hosp., 1960-61; asst. resident in gen. surgery Highland Gen. Hosp., Rochester, N.Y., 1963-64; resident in otolaryngology Strong Meml. Hosp., Rochester, 1964-67; resident in plastic and reconstructive surgery U. Fla., 1980-82; staff otolaryngologist Group Health Corp. of Puget Sound, Seattle, 1967-68; practice medicine specializing in otolaryngology Seattle, 1968-80; practice medicine specializing in plastic surgery, 1982—; clin. asst. prof. otolaryngology, head and neck surgery U. Wash., Seattle, 1975—. Plastic surgery cons. western sec. Maxillofacial Rev. Bd. State of Wash., 1982-90, cons. Conservation of Hearing Program, 1968-80; trustee Physicians and Dentist Credit Bur., 1974-80, 84-87, pres. 1976-77, 84-85; active staff mem. Northwest Hosp., Seattle; courtesy staff Swedish Hosp., Overlake Hosp., Bellevue, Stevens Meml. Hosp., Edmond, Wash., Seattle, others. Capt. USAF, 1961-63. Fellow ACS, Am. Rhinologic Soc., Seattle Surg. Soc., Am. Acad. Facial Plastic and Reconstructive Surgery, Am. Acad. Otolaryngology-Head and Neck Surgery, Northwest Acad. Otolaryngology and Head and Neck Surgery, Soc. for Ear, Nose and Throat Advances in Children, Pacific Oto-Ophthalmological Soc.; mem. Am. Soc. Plastic Surgery, Am. Soc. for Aesthetic Plastic Surgery, Inc., Lipoplasty Soc. N. Am., Wash. Soc. Plastic Surgeons, Nat. Med. Assn., King County Med. Soc., Wash. State Med. Assn., N.W. Soc. of Plastic Surgeons. Avocations: photography, cynology, microcomputing, architecture and design. Home: 13211 Frazier Pl NW Seattle WA 98177-4132 Office: AEsteem Aesthetic Plastic Surgery Inc 1200 N Northgate Way Seattle WA 98133-8916 Office Phone: 206-522-0200. Business E-Mail: aesteempsc@aol.com. E-mail: chatard@aol.com.

CHATEAUNEUF, JOHN EDWARD, chemistry educator, researcher; b. Lynn, Mass., Apr. 19, 1957; s. Edward Andre Chateauneuf and Blanche Louise Foley-Chateauneuf. BS in Chemistry, Salem (Mass.) State Coll., 1981; PhD in Chemistry, Tufts U., 1986. Rsch. assoc. Nat. Rsch. Coun. of Can., Ottawa, Ont., 1986-88; rsch. assoc. radiation lab. U. Notre Dame, Ind., 1988-90, mem. faculty, staff scientist, 1990-96; asst. prof. Western Mich. U., Kalamazoo, 1996-2000, assoc. prof., 2000—. Contbr. articles to profl. jours. Mem. AIChE, Am. Chem. Soc., Inter-Am. Photochem. Soc. Office: Western Mich U Dept Chemistry Kalamazoo MI 49008 Office Phone: 269-387-2879. E-mail: chateauneuf@wmich.edu.

CHATELAIN, DALIA DE LA PAZ, elementary school educator, educational consultant; b. Manzanillo, Oriente, Cuba, Oct. 13, 1954; arrived in U.S., 1967; d. Ciro V. and Dalia de la Paz; divorced; children: Katie, Kerri. BS, U. New Orleans, 1977; MA in Counseling, Our Lady of Holy Cross Coll., 1997. Lic. profl. counselor, nat. cert. sch. counselor, lic. marriage and family therapist. Tchr. Health and Phys. Edn. Archdiocese of New Orleans, Gretna, La., 1977-82; tchr. pre-kindegarten, kindergarten, resource bilingual tchr. Jefferson Parish Schs., Gretna., 1986-97, counselor, 1997—, bilingual counselor, 1998—. Co-chair Safe and Drug Free program, Gretna, 1996—. Vol. ARC, Gretna, 1994—; vol. Cath. ch., Gretna. Mem. Am. Counseling Assn., Am. Sch. Counselor Assn., La. Sch. Counselor Assn., Chi Sigma Iota (Alpha Zeta chpt. rep.-at-large 1997-98, pres. 1999-2000, Outstanding Mem. award 1998, pres. 1999—). E-mail: dalichat@cs.com.

CHATELAINE, KENNETH LEO, education educator, psychoanalyst; b. Mpls., Minn., Oct. 16, 1931; s. Frank Arthur Chatelaine and Rose L. Ney. BA, St. Thomas Universtiy, 1954—57; MLA, The Johns Hopkins U., 1967—69; PhD, The U. of Md., 1970—78; NcPsyA, The Wash. Sch. of Psychiatry, 1982—86. DABPS-Specialties, Child Psychology and Psychoanalysis Springfield, MO., 1992, lic. cert. profl. counselor State of Md., 1995, cert. instr. Nat. Air and Space Mus., Wash., DC, 1996, aerospace tech. specialist Nat. Air and Space Mus., Wash., DC, 1999. Prof. of psychology Anne Arundel C.C., Arnold, Md., 1970—; lectr. Shephard Pratt Sch. of Mental Health Studies, Towson, Md., 1981—82, Wash. Sch. of Psychiatry, 1982—83; psychoanalyst Pvt. Practice, Severna Park, Md., 1991—2002. Cons. Margaret Mahler Found., Philadelphia, 1995—; founder Anne Arundel County Mental Health Edn. Coalition, Annapolis, Md., 1982—90. Author: (book) Harry Stack Sullivan, The Formative Years, 1981, Good Me, Bad Me, Not Me, 1992, Harry Stack Sullivan, Founder of Interpersonal Psychiatry, (monogram) Harry Stack Sullivan, The Man and Clinican, 1991. Vice chmn. Md. State Mental Health Adv. Coun., 1980—85; mem. Anne Arundel Mental Health Adv. Com., Annapolis, Md., 1982—88. Recipient Centennial Spkr., APA, 1991. Mem.: Internat. Soc. for the Psychol. Treatment of Schizophrenia and Other Psychoses, Wash. Sch. of Psychiatry, APA (life). Achievements include rsch. scholar on the interpersonal theory of psychiatry. Avocations: skiing, tennis, sailing, flying. Home: 359 Gatewater Ct #402 Glen Burnie MD 21060 Office: Dr Kenneth L Chatelaine 124 Riggs Ave Severna Park MD 21146

CHATELIER, PAUL RICHARD, aviation psychologist; s. Paul and Mary Chatelier; m. Mary Lu Moss; children: Michael, Suzanne. BS in Biology, Chemistry, Psychology, U. Fla., 1960; MA in Psychology, U. Miss., 1962; postgrad., U. N.Mex., 1967-69. Commd. ensign USN, 1962, advanced through grades to capt., 1986; sr. v.p. strategic planning Perceptronics, Inc., Washington, 1986—93; with Office Sci. and Tech. Policy Exec. Office of Pres. U.S., Washington, 1993—96; dir. for edn. tech. edn. activity Dept. Def., Washington, 1996—. U.S. rep. on human factors NATO, Brussels, 1978—86; mem. task force tng. and wargaming Def. Sci. Bd., 1986—88, task force edn. and tng., 1999; U.S. rep. on tng. Tech. Coop. Panel, Washington, 1986—87; mem. indsl. adv. com. U. Ctrl. Fla. Inst. for Simulation and Tng.; edn. and tng. cons. Office Sci. and Tech. White Ho., 1993—96; workshop dir. internat. tng. and human factors; del. at large human factors and medicine panel NATO, 1999; dep. dir. Advanced Distributed Learning Co-Lab., Alexandria, Va., 1999—2001; cons. Potomac Inst. for Policy Studies, 2002—. Co-author: (book) Psychology of Reality, 1985; editor: Manprint & System Integ, 1988, International Human Factors, 1991, Advanced Technology for Training Design, NATO, 1993, Opening the Classroom Doors...Distance Learning, 1995, Virtual Reality Trainings Future?, 1997. Career advisor Fairfax County Pub. Sch., 1982—88. Mem.: Nat. Security Indsl. Assn. (chmn. manpower pers. tng. 1986—89), Va. Human Factors Soc. (pres. 1982—83), Nat. Human Factors Soc. (mem. exec. coun. 1982—85). Avocations: tennis, community activities. Home: 8021 W Point Dr Springfield VA 22153-3023 E-mail: pchat@mindspring.com.

CHATFIELD, MARY VAN ABSHOVEN, librarian; b. Bay Shore, NY; d. Cornelius and Elma Elizabeth (Sumner) van Abshoven; m. Robert W. Chatfield, June 22, 1963 (div. 1981); 1 child, Robert Warner Jr.; m. Alexander Watts, Jan. 6, 1996 (div. 2000). AB, Radcliffe Coll., 1958; SM, Columbia U., 1961; MBA, Harvard U., 1972. With library system Harvard U., Cambridge, Mass., 1961-92, librarian Bus. Sch., 1963-78, head libr., 1978-92; acting head libr. Countway Libr. Harvard Med. Sch., 1988-89; head libr. Angelo State U., San Angelo, Tex., 1992-95; collections care mgr. Fosterfields, Morristown, N.J., 1996-97; mgr. libr. svcs. Montclair (N.J.) Art Mus., 1997; exec. dir. Mendham (N.J.) Free Pub. Libr., 1997-99; coord. pub. svcs. Tom Green County Libr., San Angelo, Tex., 1999—2004; Concho Valley master gardener, docent, rschr. San Angelo (Tex.) Mus. Fine Arts, 2004—. Bd. dirs. Adult

Literacy Coun. San Angelo, Historic San Angelo, Inc. Episcopalian. Avocations: reading, embroidery, collecting, museum studies, public art. Home: 115 N Jackson St San Angelo TX 76901-3215 E-mail: marychat@wcc.net.

CHATHAM, LLOYD REEVE, lawyer; b. Jackson, Miss., Aug. 16, 1958; s. Archie Reeves Chatham and Anna C. Smith; m. Louise Lucas, July 2, 1983; 1 child, Christopher Lloyd. Student, Hinds Jr. Coll., Raymond, Miss., 1977-78; BS, Miss. State U., 1981; JD, Miss. Coll. Sch. Law, 1996. Bar: Miss. Supreme Ct. 1996, U.S. Dist. Ct. (no. and so. dist.) Miss. 1996, U.S. Ct. Appeals (5th cir.) 1996, Tex. 2003. Mgr. Miss. State U. Food Svcs., Starkville, 1981-83; gen. mgr. Dobbs Houses, Inc., Jackson, 1983-92; lawyer Waller & Waller, Jackson, 1996-99; pvt. practice Chatham Law Office, Brandon, Miss., 1999; corp. counsel Financial Technologies, Inc., Jackson, 1999—. Dir. Miss. Restaurant Assn., Jackson, 1989-92; v.p. Jackson Restaurant Assn., 1990, pres., 1991. Choir mem. St. Peters By-The-Lake, Brandon, Miss., 1997, Miss. Chorus, Brandon, 1998. Named Miss. Restaurant Mgr. of Yr., Miss. Restaurant Assn., Jackson, 1992. Mem. ABA, Miss. Bar Assn., Hinds County Bar Assn., Rankin County Bar Assn., Jackson Young Lawyers, Christian Legal Soc., Federalist Soc., Phi Delta Phi, Alpha Phi Omega (v.p., pres.). Avocations: antique collecting, travel, antique collecting, travel, music. Home: 1201 Martin Dr Brandon MS 39047-6448 Office: 200 Briarwood West Drive Jackson MS 39206 Office Phone: 601-863-2157. E-mail: chathaml@bellsouth.net.

CHATHAM, ROSEMARY GAIL MOOG, entrepreneur, musician, volunteer, composer; b. Perth Amboy, NJ, Jan. 30, 1956; d. Theodore and Harriet Sadie (White) Yuhasz; children: Mary Ellen Connell, Lisa Louise Clayore, Joseph Claude Clayore. Pres., tchr., spiritual advisor Blessing Club, Birmingham, Ala., 2000—; pres., owner Music For Meditation, Birmingham, Ala., 2003—, Head Stock-Transcending the Ordinary-Creating Body Atmospheres, Birmingham, Ala., 2004—. Founder Vietnam Veterans of Collier County, Inc., Naples, Fla., 1985—90; writer, tchr., keyboard cons. Music For Meditation, Birmingham, Ala., 2003—. Roarie Studios; composer, musician, engineer, producer, artist: CD No Grey Area, 2002, composer, musician, engineer, producer: CD Angel Prayers, 2003, Into The Light, 2003; author: (poetry) Eternal Portrait Series, 2003 (award winning digital photography artist), Endless Journeys, 2004. Mem. com. St. Matthews House shelter, Naples; dir., chmn. Collier County July 4th Parade, 1985—90; mem. rep. precinct com. Collier County Rep. Exec. Com., 1980—90; mem. St. Paul's Episcopal Ch., 1972—84, St. John's Episcopal Ch., 1985—, Ebenezer Missionary Baptist Ch., Birmingham, Ala., 1998—, Kenneth Copeland Ministries, 1998—, Joyce Meyer Ministries, 1998—. Nominee Poet of Yr. award, Internat. Soc. Poets, 2002, 2003, 2004; recipient Outstanding Citizen award, Youth Haven, Naples, 1988, Am. Legion, 1989, Outstanding Achievement award for God and Country, DAV, 1987, Outstanding Achievement award, VFW, 1988; subject of cover story in Vets. Day issue, Army Times, 1989. Mem.: Birmingham Art Assn., Ala. Designer/Craftsmen Assn. E-mail: rosemarychatham@yahoo.com.

CHATI, MANDAR KALIDAS, operations research specialist; arrived in U.S., 1993; s. Kalidas Madhav and Pratibha Kalidas Chati; m. Prachi Mandar Chati, Dec. 27, 1997; children: Prathamesh, Pranav. B in Tech., Indian Inst. Tech., Mumbai, 1993; MS, Iowa State U., 1995; PhD, Cornell U., 1999. Rschr. Gen. Electric, Niskayuna, NY, 1999—. Recipient Whitney award, Gen. Electric, 2000. Mem.: Am. Soc. Quality (cert.). Avocations: keyboards, languages, formula one cars.

CHATIGNY, ROBERT NEIL, federal judge; b. 1951; AB, Brown U., 1973; JD, Georgetown U., 1978. Atty. Williams & Connolly, Washington, 1981-83; ptnr. Chatigny and Palmer, Hartford, Conn., 1984-86, Chatigny & Cowdery, Hartford, 1991-94; pvt. practice Hartford, 1986-90; dist. judge U.S. Dist. Ct. Conn., Hartford, 1994—, chief judge. Office: US Dist Court 450 Main St Hartford CT 06103-3022

CHATILOVICZ, PETER, lawyer; b. Kenosha, Wis., Dec. 11, 1946; BA, Beloit Coll., 1969; JD magna cum laude, U. Miami, 1974. Bar: Fla. 1974, DC 1975. Mem. Seyfarth, Shaw, Fairweather & Geraldson, Washington; ptnr. Seyfarth Shaw LLP, Washington, mem. exec. com., mng. ptnr. Washington DC Office. Adj. prof. Georgetown U. Sch. Law, Washington, 1988—94. Editor-in-chief U. Miami Law Rev., 1973—74. Mem.: Hotel Assn. of Washington, DC, DC Bar Assn., Fla. Bar Assn. Office: Seyfarth Shaw LLP 815 Connecticut Ave NW Washington DC 20006-4004 Office Phone: 202-828-5330. Office Fax: 202-828-5393.

CHATLEN, STANLEY LEE, transportation executive; b. Washington, Nov. 6, 1937; s. Louis and Hannah (Fisher) C.; m. Patricia Adams, May 9, 1965 (dec. Nov. 1988); m. Martha Cahill, June 9, 1990; children: Sarah and Emily (twins), John Louis. BS, U Md., 1964; MBA, Wayne State U., 1968. Supr. Ford Motor Co., Detroit, 1964-66; divsn. traffic mgr. Chrysler Corp., Centerline, Mich., 1966-70; regional mgr. Airborne Freight Corp., Detroit, 1970-75; v.p., regional mgr. Shulman Air Freight, Chgo., 1975-78; v.p. svc. Associated Air Freight, New Hyde Park, N.Y., 1978-81; dir. mktg. and sales Pilot Air Freight, Newark, 1981-83; v.p. Central Air Freight, Inc., Valley Stream, N.Y., 1983-87; exec. v.p. Apollo Express Inc., Norwich, NY, 1987-88; pres. Chatlen Transp. Enterprises, Inc., Huntington, N.Y., 1988-97, New Media, Inc., 1996-98; v.p. sales Americold Logistics, Atlanta, 1998—2002; sr. ptnr. Stanley L. Chatlen, LLC, 2002—03; sales and mktg. mgr. Atlas Cold Storage, McDonough, Ga., 2003—. Instr. Henry Ford C.C., Dearborn, Mich., 1973-75, adv. bd., 1975; adj. prof. sales and mktg. SUNY, Westbury, 1997. Served with U.S. Army, 1958-60. Recipient Alcoa Found. award, 1964. Mem. Am. Mgmt. Assn., Coun. Logistics Mgmt. (dir. Atlanta Roundtable), Assn. Transp. Practitioners, Am. Soc. Transp. and Logistics, Delta Nu Alpha (past local dir.). Home: 3300 Sundew Ct Alpharetta GA 30005-4200 Office Phone: 404-514-9249. E-mail: schatlen@hotmail.com.

CHATLOS, WILLIAM EDWARD, management consultant; b. Turtle Creek, Pa., Aug. 28, 1927; s. Rudolph and Elizabeth (Mraz) C.; m. Margaret Eileen Jackson. Student, U. Pitts., 1946-47, Ursinus Coll., 1948-49; BS magna cum laude, Boston U., 1951; postgrad., N.Y. Inst. Fin., 1955-56. With Georgeson & Co., N.Y.C., 1952-81, prin. in charge mgmt. cons. for investor rels., 1957-81; prin. Chatlos & Co. Inc., North Caldwell, N.J., 1981—. Bd. dirs. Kelso Inst.; cons. state govts.; lectr. in field. Editor Trends in Mgmt.-Investor Rels., 1957-81; contbr. articles to profl. publs. Mem. Soc. Profl. Mgmt. Cons., Pub. Rels. Soc. Am., Am. Mgmt. Assn., Assn. Corp. Growth, Investor Rels. Assn. (pres. 1966-67), Nat. Investor Rels. Inst. (co-founder, pres. 1974-75). Office: Chatlos & Co Inc 302 Milanville Rd Beach Lake PA 18405

CHATMAS, JOHN THOMAS, art educator, artist; b. Marlin, Tex., Nov. 1, 1945; s. John and Frances Elizabeth (Wiggins) Chatmas; m. Karen Elizabeth Albrecht, Jan. 1, 1995; m. Mary Jo Lippard Albright (div.); 1 child, John Thomas Jr. BFA, U. Tex., 1964—68; MFA, Pratt Inst., 1968—70. Instr. McLennan Cmty. Coll., Waco, Tex., 1970—. Art edn. cons. McLennan Cmty. Coll., 1970—, art exhbn. curator, 1970—2000, art exhbn. coord., 1970—2000; art exhbn. judge Brazos River Festival, 1981—85. Exhibitions include Contemporary Art Ctr. of Ft. Worth, Tex., 1997, The Art Ctr., Waco, Tex., 1975, U. Art Gallery, Baylor U., Waco, 1972, Divadlo Arena, Czech Republic, 1996, Austin Mus. Art, 1995, NY U, 1980, U. Tex., 1979, Tex. Christian U., 1978. Visual Arts fellowship, Art Matters, Inc., 1990, Profl. Develop. grant, McLennan Cmty. Coll., 1985. Mem.: Tex. Cmty. Coll. Teachers Assn., Art Ctr. of Waco, Tex. Avocations: bicycling, reading, travel. Office: McLennan Cmty coll 1400 Coll Dr Waco TX 76708

CHATO, JOHN CLARK, mechanical and bioengineering educator; b. Budapest, Hungary, Dec. 28, 1929; s. Joseph Alexander and Elsie (Wasserman) C.; m. Elizabeth Janet Owens, Aug. 1954; children: Christine B., David J., Susan E. ME, U. Cin., 1954; MS, U. Ill., 1955; PhD, MIT, 1960. Co-op student, trainee Frigidaire div. GMC, Dayton, Ohio, 1950—54; grad. fellow U. Ill., Urbana, 1954—55; grad. fellow, inst. MIT, Cambridge, 1955—58, asst. prof., 1958—64; assoc. prof. U. Ill., Urbana, 1964—69, prof., 1969—96, prof. emeritus, 1996—, chmn. exec. com. bioengrig. faculty, 1972—78, 1982—83, 1984—85, asst. dean of engring., 1997—98. Cons. Industry and Govt., 1958—; dir., founder Biomed. Engring. Systems Team, Urbana, Ill, 1974-78; assoc. editor Jour. Biomech. Engring., 1976-82. Patentee in field; contbr. articles to profl. jours., chpts. to books on heat transfer, bio-heat transfer, refrigeration, air conditioning, cryogenics, and thermal systems. Com. mem. troop 6 Boy Scouts Am., Urbana, 1984—86; com. mem. Urbana Plan Commn., 1973—78; mem. adv. com. Urbana Park Dist., 1981—84; 2nd v.p. Champaign County Izaak Walton League, 1986, 1st v.p., 1987, pres., 1988—92, bd. dirs., state dir., 1992—; mem. Urbana Postal Customer Adv. Coun., 2002—; trustee 1st Presbyn. Ch., Urbana, 1976—78, 1999—2001, elder, 1982—85, 2004—; bd. dirs. Univ. YMCA, Champaign, Ill., 1976—78, 1987—90. Recipient Tobin award Champaign County Izaak Walton League, 1992, Cmty. Svc. award Urbana Park Dist., 1996, Russell Scott Meml. award, Cryogenic Engring. Conf., 1979; named Disting. Engring. Alumnus, U. Cin., 1972, U. Ill., 2005; NSF fellow 1961, Fogarty Sr. Internat. fellow 1978-79; Japan Soc. Promotion of Sci. fellow, 1997. Fellow: ASHRAE (treas. East Ctrl. Ill. chpt. 1984, sec. 1985, 1987, 1st v.p. 1988, pres. 1989), ASME (exec. com. bioengring. divsn. 1992—96, sec. 1993—94, chmn. 1994—95, Charles Russ Richards Meml. award 1978, N.R. Lissner award 1992, Dedicated Svc. award 2000), Am. Inst. Med. and Biol. Engrs.; mem.: IEEE (sr.), Am. Soc. Engring. Edn., Internat. Inst. Refrigeration (assoc.), Audubon Soc. Champaign County (bd. dirs. 1988—89, v.p. 1990, treas. 1991—93, v.p. 1995—96, treas. 1998—99, pres. 2000—02, bd. dirs. 2002, pres. 2005), Exch. Club Urbana (bd. dirs. 1989—91, 1995—96, pres.-elect 1996—97, pres. 1997—98, dist. dir. 2001—05). Achievements include research in fields of heat transfer, bio-heat transfer, refrigeration, air conditioning, cryogenics, and thermal systems. Avocations: tennis, photography, bird watching, hiking, kayaking. Office: U Ill Dept Mech Indsl Engring 1206 W Green St Urbana IL 61801-2906

CHATOFF, MICHAEL ALAN, lawyer; b. N.Y.C., Aug. 18, 1946; s. Alexander Zelig and Leona Rhoda (Weiss) C. BA, CUNY, 1967; JD, Bklyn. Law Sch., 1971; LLM, NYU, 1978. Bar: N.Y. 1971, U.S. Dist. Ct. (so. and ea. dists.) N.Y. 1978, U.S. Ct. Appeals (2d cir.) 1980, U.S. Supreme Ct. 1980. Reader Chgo. Title Ins. Co., N.Y.C., 1972; chief U.S. Code Congl. and Adminstrv. News West Pub. Co., Westbury, N.Y., 1972-97. Cons. N.Y. Sch. for Deaf, N.Y.C. Mayor's Office for Disabled, Westchester County Legis.; lectr. N.Y. State Dept. of Edn. Vocat. Ednl. Svcs. for Individuals with Disabilities, N.Y. Sch. Deaf, Lexington Sch. for Deaf, Parents for Deaf Awareness, Am. Profl. Soc. for Deaf, N.Y. Ctr. for Law and the Deaf, Coun. on Jewish Deaf Edn. and Rehab., Nat. Coun. on Deaf People and Deafness, NYU. Assoc. law editor Ency. on Deaf People and Deafness; contbr. articles to Nat. Law Jour., N.Y. Law Jour., Able Adv., Communication Outlook, Deaf Spectrum. Bd. dirs. Westchester Cmty. Svcs. for Hearing Impaired; counsel Conn. African-Am. Deaf Advocate; mem. Supreme Ct. Hist. Soc.; del. nominee Dem. Nat. Conv., 1992. Mem. ABA, Queens County Bar Assn., Assn. of Bar of City of N.Y., Nat. Assn. Deaf, Am. Contract Bridge League, Nassau Bar Assn. Avocations: bridge, jogging, weight-lifting. Home: 26909T Grand Central Pkwy Floral Park NY 11005-1010 Personal E-mail: mchatoff@aol.com.

CHATROO, ARTHUR JAY, lawyer; b. N.Y.C., July 1, 1946; s. George and Lillian (Leibowitz) C.; m. Christina Daly, Aug. 6, 1994; 1 child, Alexander. BChemE, CCNY, 1968; JD cum laude, New York Law Sch., 1979; MBA with distinction, NYU, 1982. Bar: N.Y. 1980, Ohio 1992, Calif. 1993, U.S. Patent Office 1998. Process engr. Std. Oil Co. of Ohio, various locations, 1968-73; process specialist BP Oil, Inc., Marcus Hook, Pa., 1974-75; sr. process engr. Sci. Design Co., Inc., N.Y.C., 1975-78; mgr. spl. projects The Halcon SD Group, N.Y.C., 1978-82; corp. counsel, tax and fin. The Lubrizol Corp., Wickliffe, Ohio, 1982-85, sr. counsel spl. investment projects, 1989-90; gen. counsel Lubrizol Enterprises, Inc., Wickliffe, 1985-89; chmn. Correlation Genetics Corp., San Jose, Calif., 1990-91; gen. counsel Agrigenetics Co., Eastlake, Ohio, 1990-92; gen. counsel, dir. comml. contracting Agrigenetics, L.P., San Diego, 1992-93; counsel Agrigenetics, Inc. dba Mycogen Seeds, Mycogen Corp., San Diego, 1994-97; dir. legal affairs Mycogen Corp., San Diego, 1997-98; exec. v.p. bus. devel., legal and regulatory affairs Global Agro, Inc., Encinitas, Calif., 1998-99; exec. v.p., gen. counsel Akkadix Corp., San Diego, 1999—2001; legal and bus. cons. San Diego, 2001—. Mem. Met. Parks Adv. com., Allen County, Ohio, 1973. Mem. ABA, AIChE, Am. Chem. Soc., N.Y. State Bar Assn., San Diego County Bar Assn., Am. Corp. Counsel Assn., Jaycees (pers. dir. Lima, Ohio chpt. 1972-73), Licensing Execs. Soc., Toastmasters, Omega Chi Epsilon, Beta Gamma Sigma. Clubs: Toastmasters. Avocations: sailing, photography, skiing. Home and Office: 3525 Del Mar Hts Rd # 285 San Diego CA 92130-2122 Office Phone: 858-775-0098. E-mail: achatroo@earthlink.net.

CHATT, ALLEN BARRETT, psychologist, neuroscientist; b. Phoenix, July 17, 1949; s. Arthur Beecher Ellis and Helen (Scheidt) Chatt; m. Gail Nancy Anguish, Aug. 21, 1971. BS in Psychology with honors, SUNY, Buffalo, 1971; MS in Psychology, Fla. State U., 1974, PhD in Psychology and Neuroscience, 1978. Rsch. asst. Fla. State U., Tallahassee, 1971-76; predoctoral fellow in neuroanatomy U. Tex. Med. Br., Galveston, 1977; postdoctoral fellow in neurology sch. medicine Yale U., New Haven, 1978-80, rsch. asst. prof. neurology Sch. Medicine, 1981-87, rsch. assoc. prof., 1988—91, retirement scholars chair, 1991; rsch. psychologist VA Med. Ctr., West Haven, Conn., 1978-84, sr. rsch. psychologist, 1985-90, sr. rsch. psychologist disability retirement pension, 1991—; founder, exec. dir., consulting psychologist Phoenix Fund for Neurologically Challenged, New Haven, Tallahassee, 1991—. Grant reviewer NSF, 1982—, NIH, 1982—, VA, 1982—; vis. prof. neuroscience Beijing Normal U., 1987, U. Glasgow, 1994—95; neuroscience reviewer Am. Psychol. Soc. Convs., 1991—; psychol. cons., case mgr. neurologically impaired; pvt. funding neurol. rsch.; courtesy prof. movement scis. Fla. State U., 1999—. Contbr. chapters to books, articles articles to profl. jours.; mem. editl. rev. bd. Brain Rsch., 1983—86, Exptl. Neurology, 1982—86, mem. editl. bd. Exptl. Brain Rsch., 1984—88, Quar. Jour. Exptl. Physiology, 1986. Sponsor Bobby Bowden Classic Fellowship Christian Athletes, 1992—, Bill Campbell Challenge Children's Miracle Network, 1996—99; mem. devel. bd. Sandels Fund Excellence Coll. Human Scis., Fla. State U., 1998, sponsor, 1999—; bd. dirs. Wal-Mart/Children's Miracle Network, No. Fla., 1996—99, Jennifer Harrison Fund, 1995—; judge Sam Walton Cmty. Leadership Scholarship Program, 1998—99, Phoenix Fund Collegiate Scholarship Human Scis., 2003; sponsor Jennifer Harrison Meml. Golf Tournament, 1991—2000, Freedom Scholarship Batavia HS Class 1965, 1992—, Camp Sunshine, 1992—, Goodspeed Opera Ho., 1995—, Fla. State U. Seminole Classic, 1998—2000, Boy's Town Invitational N. Fla., 1998—2000, Fla. State U., 1998—, Phoenix Fund Scholarship Applied Biomedical Undergraduate Study, 1999—; mem. Rep. Senatorial Inner Cir., Washington, 1985, Eisenhower Commn., 1995; life mem. Rep. Nat. Com., 1993—; mem. adv. bd. Ellingsworth Press, 1998—. Recipient Most Sr. Benefactor award, Children's Miracle Network, 1996—99, Gold Miracle Maker award, 1998, Platinum Miracle Maker award, 1999; Regents scholar, N.Y. State, 1965—69, VoHab scholar, 1965—71, Rsch. grantee, VA, 1978—91, NIH, 1982—87. Mem.: AAAS, Soc. Pain Practice Mgmt., Am. Epilepsy Soc., Soc. Neuroscience, Epilepsy Found. Am., Am. Psychol. Soc., Yale Neurology Alumni Assn. (charter), Fla. State U.'s Pres.'s Club. Republican. Methodist. Achievements include development of neurosurgical procedure increasing the effectiveness of stellate ganglion blocks for the treatment of relfex sympathetic dystrophy in humans; discovery of differential neuronal circuits involved in focal and secondarily generalized seizure activity in neocortical model of epilepsy; brain cells that become abnormal initially in focal and secondarily generalized seizure activity; mid brain neuronal circuits modulating pain; thermal evoked potential in humans and the localization of cortical cells responsive to pain. Home: 699 Goose Ln PO Box 1449 Guilford CT 06437-0549 also: 2949 Golden Eagle Dr E Tallahassee FL 32312-4008

CHATTEJEE, KANU, cardiologist, educator; b. Calcutta, India, Mar. 1, 1934; s. Gopal Lal and Basanti Chatterjee; m. Docey Edwards, May 9, 1975. MD, R.G. Kar Med. Coll., 1956. Cert. Internal Medicine Am. Bd. Internal Medicine, 1973, diplomate Cardiovascular Disease Am. Bd. Cardiology, 1975. Lucie Stern Prof. Medicine U. Calif., San Francisco, 1989—2002, Ernest Gallo Disting. Prof. Medicine, 2002—. Fellow: Royal Coll. Physicians London, Royal Coll. Physicians Edinburgh. Achievements include discovery of First to discover: post pacing t-wave changes; First to discover vasodilators in mitral regurgitation; First to discover relationship between endocardial potentials and ventricular volume. Office: Univ Calif San Francisco 505 Parnassus Ave Ste M-1182 San Francisco CA 94143-0124 Office Phone: 415-476-6079. Office Fax: 415-502-8627.

CHATTERJEE, ANJAN, automotive executive; BSEE, Indian Inst. Tech., Delhi; MS in Computer sci., George Washington U.; MBA, Stanford U. Former computer scientist space and tech. program NASA; former ptnr. A.T. Kearney; former dir., automotive sector leader McKinsey and Co.; sr. v.p. strategy and bus. planning Visteon Corp., Dearborn, Mich., 2003—, acting CFO, 2004—. Office: Visteon Corp 1700 Rotunda Dr Dearborn MI 48120

CHATTERJEE, JAYANTA, architecture and planning educator; b. Calcutta, India, Mar. 19, 1936; came to U.S., 1959; s. Hari Charan and Asha (Mukherjee) C.; m. Janet Ley Smith, Aug. 31, 1968; children: Eric, Brinda. BArch, Indian Inst. Tech., 1958; AA, Sch. Trop. Arch., 1959; M in Regional Planning, U. N.C., 1962; MArch in Urban Design, Harvard U., 1965. Asst. prof. U. of Cin., 1967-72, assoc. prof., 1972-77, assoc. dean, 1975-77, prof., 1977—, dir. sch. planning, 1977-82, acting dean, 1982-83, dean, 1982-2001, prof. arch. and planning, 2001—. Regional designer Met. Area Planning Commn., Boston, 1965-67; urban scholar Cities Recovery Program, Cleve., 1981-82. Co-author: The Partnership Planning, 1982, Rebuilding American Cities, 1983, Breaking the Boundaries, 1989; co-editor/founder: Jour. Planning, Education and Research, 1981-84. Mem. Ohio Eminent Scholar Rev. Panel, 1985, Urban Design Rev. Bd., Cin., 1988—; design review bd. U. Cin.; mem. historic conservation bd. City of Cin.; bd. dirs. Arts Consortium, Cin., 1983—87, Contemporary Arts Ctr., Cin., 1983—, Hillside Trust, Cin., 1983—84, Bethesda Hosp., Inc., Cin., 1982—95, Total Living Concept, Inc., Cin., 1976—88, Ctr. Mediation of Disputes, Cin., 1989—92, The Emery Ctr., Cin., 1988—90, Better Housing League, Cin., 1989—92, Archtl. Found., Cin., 1990—, pres., 2004—; bd. dirs. Season Found. for Good Govt., 2003—, pres., 1997—. Recipient Apple award Archtl. Fedn. Cin., 1996, Disting. Alumnus award U. N.C., 1996, Disting. Svc. award Assn. Coll. Schs. of Planning, 1991. Fellow Am. Inst. Cert. Planners (editl. bd. AICP Casebook 1991-93, tech. adv. bd. 1993-96); mem. AIA (assoc.; Thomas Jefferson award pub. arch. 2000), Am. Planning Assn. (pres. Ohio chpt. 1970-72, editorial adv. bd. Jour. APA), Ptnrs. of Ams. (Ohio-Parana), Assn. Collegiate Schs. of Planning (pres. 1983-85, Svc. award Instn. Jay Chatterjee 1998), Internat. Coun. Fine Arts Deans, Cin. Post/Corbett Found. (Lifetime achievement award in Arts 1999). Office: U Cin Coll of Design Architecture Art and Planning PO Box 210016 Cincinnati OH 45221-0016 Office Phone: 513-556-1204. Office Fax: 513-556-3288. Business E-Mail: Jay.Chatterjee@uc.edu.

CHATTERJEE, KAUSIK, education educator; s. Kamalesh and Madhabi Chatterjee; m. Juliana Kay Derksen; 1 child, Leena Brooklyn. BEE, Jadavpur U., 1992; M in nuc. engring., Indian Inst. of Tech., 1995; PhD of elec. engring., Rensselaer Poly. Inst., 2002. Adj. instr. Rensselaer Poly. Inst., Troy, NY, 2001—02; asst. prof. Calif. State U., Fresno, 2002—; vis. scientist MIT, Cambridge, 2004—. Govt. of india fellowship Indian Inst. of Tech., Kanpur, 1993—95; u. fellowship Ohio State U., 1995—96; intel doctoral fellow Rensselaer Poly. Inst., Troy, NY, 2001—02; nrc summer faculty fellow Air Force Rsch. Lab./Wright-Patterson AFB, Dayton, Ohio, 2004; nrc rsch. assoc. NASA, Langley, Hampton, Va., 2005—. Recipient Charles M. Close Doctoral prize, Rensselaer Poly. Inst., 2002; grant, Nat. Collegiate Inventors and Innovators Alliance, 2004—. Mem.: IEEE, APS, ACES. D-Liberal. Achievements include first to develop a floating random-walk algorithm for Maxwell-Helmholtz equations in heterogeneous problem domains, necessary for IC interconnect analysis; patents pending in field of develop a floating random-walk algorithm for Maxwell-Helmholtz equations at multiple wavelength length scales, necessary for IC interconnect analysis; first to develop a floating random-walk algorithm for a nonlinear PDE, namely the nonlinear Poisson-Boltzmann equation, with applications to plasma flow problems; develop a stochastic methodology for partial inductance extraction and the stochastic solution of the resultant RLC matrices. Avocations: running, cricket. Office: Mass Inst of Tech Room 10-171 Cambridge MA 02139 Office Phone: 617-253-2592. Personal E-mail: kausik@mit.edu.

CHATTERJEE, MAINAK, adult education educator; PhD, U. Tex., Arlington, Tex. Asst. prof. U. Ctrl. Fla., Orlando, Fla., 2002—.

CHATTERJEE, SANKAR, geology educator; b. Calcutta, India, May 28, 1943; arrived in U.S., 1976; s. Prafulla and Biva (Banerjee) C.; m. Sibani Mitra, Feb. 4, 1971; children: Soumya, Shuvu. BS, Jadaupur U., Calcutta, 1962, MS, 1964; PhD, Calcutta U., 1970; postdoctoral, Smithsonian Inst., 1978. Lectr., asst. prof. Indian Statis. Inst., Calcutta, 1968-75; asst. prof. George Washington U., Washington, 1976-78; asst. prof., curator Tex. Tech. U., Lubbock, 1976-78, assoc. prof., curator, 1984-87, prof., curator, 1987-94, Paul Whitfield Horn prof., 1994—. Vis. prof. U. Calif., Berkeley, 1976, U. Tubingen, Germany, 1991-92; curator of paleontology Mus. Tex. Tech. U., Lubbock, 1979—; rsch. assoc. Smithsonian Inst., 1979—. Author: Antarctica, 1985, New Concepts in Global Tectonics, 1992, The Rise of Birds: 225 Million Years of Evolution, 1997; contbr. numerous articles to profl. jours. Recipient Antarctic Svc. medal Dept. State, 1982, Sci. Achievement award Tex. Senate, 1991, Headliner award Women in Comm., 1992; grantee NSF, Nat. Geog. Soc., Am. Mus. Natural History, Field Mus. Natural History. Fellow: AAAS, Geol. Soc. Am. (Scientist of Yr.); mem.: Soc. Vertebrate Paleontology, Paleontological Soc., Golden Key. Avocation: music. Office: Mus of Tex Tech Univ 4th and Indiana Lubbock TX 79409 Office Phone: 806-742-1986. Business E-Mail: sankar.chattenga@ttu.edu.

CHATTERJEE, SHARMILA, marketing educator; b. Cuttack, Orissa, India, Dec. 4, 1961; arrived in U.S., 1986; d. Sunil N. and Pronoti Chatterjee; m. Arup K. Chakraborty, July 8, 1992; 1 child, Meenakshi. PhD in Mktg., U. Pa., 1994. Asst. prof. Fairfield (Conn.) U., 1995—98, Golden Gate U., San Francisco, 1998—2000, assoc. prof., chair dept. mktg., 2000—, Nagel T. Miner prof. bus., 2004—, prof., 2005—. Contbr. articles to profl. jours. Mem.: Informs, Am. Mktg. Assn. (mgr. collegiate activities San Francisco chpt. 1998—). Avocations: reading, music. Office: Golden Gate U 536 Mission St San Francisco CA 94105 Office Phone: 415-442-6519. Business E-Mail: schatterjee@ggu.edu.

CHATTERJEE, SOUMYA, rheumatologist; s. Phani Bhusan and Mira Chatterjee; m. Tamali Bhattacharyya, Nov. 20, 1989. MBBS, Calcutta Med. Coll., 1980—84; MD, U. of Calcutta, 1987—89; MRCP, Royal Coll. of Physicians of the UK, 1993; MS, U. of Mich. Sch. of Pub. Health, 2001—03. Asst. prof., divisin of rheumatology, dept of internal medicine Wayne State U., Detroit, 2001—03; staff rheumatologist Cleve. Clinic Found., 2004—. Patient care / tchg. / rsch. Cleve. Clinic Found. Fellow: Am. Coll. of Rheumatology; mem.: ACP, Scleroderma Clin. Trials Consortium. Office: Cleve Clinic Found /Desk A50 9500 Euclid Ave Cleveland OH 44195 Office Phone: 216-444-9945. Office Fax: 216-445-7569. Personal E-mail: chattes@ccf.org.

CHATTERJI, DEBAJYOTI, retired manufacturing executive; b. Puri, India, Aug. 4, 1944; came to U.S., 1967, naturalized, 1980; s. Kumud Chandra and Mrinmoyee (Mukherji) C.; m. Smee Banerjee, July 11, 1968; children: Ananya, Kooheli, Miabi. BS with honors, Utkal U., India, 1963; B in Metall. Engring., Indian Inst. Tech., Kharagpur, India, 1966; MS, Purdue U., 1968, PhD, 1971. Vis. scientist Wright-Patterson AFB, Ohio, 1971-73; with R & D Ctr., Gen. Electric Co., Schenectady, 1973-83, mgr. electrochemistry br., 1975-79; mgr. Chem. Systems and Tech. Lab., 1979-80, Inorganic

Materials and Structures Lab., 1980-83; v.p. tech. affairs The BOC Group, Inc., Murray Hill, NJ, 1983-89, chef exec. tech. activities, 1990, mng. dir. tech., 1990-99. Bd. dirs. The BOC Group, plc., Indsl. Rsch. Inst.; vis. prof. Lehigh U., 1999-2000; pres. Far Hills Group Inc. Chmn. editl. bd. Rsch. and Tech. Mgmt.; mem. editl. bd. R & D Mgmt.; contbr. articles to profl. jours.; patentee in field. Bd. dirs. BOC Found. for Environment, Imperial Coll., London; trustee Ananda Mandir, Inc. Recipient Disting. Engring. Alumnus award Purdue U., 1987, Maurice Holland award Ind. Rsch. Inst.; Disting. fellow Indian Inst. Mgmt., Calcutta; indsl. fellow Ctr. for Innovation Mgmt. Studies, NC State U. Mem. Internat. Assn. Mgmt. of Tech. (adv. bd.). Office: The BOC Group 100 Mountain Ave New Providence NJ 07974-2069

CHATTERTON, ROBERT TREAT, JR., reproductive endocrinology educator; b. Catskill, N.Y., Aug. 9, 1935; s. Robert Treat and Irene (Spoor) Chatterton; m. Patricia A. Holland, June 24, 1956 (div. 1965); children: Ruth Ellen, William Matthew, James Daniel; m. Astrida J. Vanags, June 4, 1966 (div. 1977); 1 child, Derek Scott; m. Carol J. Lewis, May 24, 1985. BS, Cornell U., 1958, PhD, 1963; MS, U. Conn., 1959. Postdoctoral fellow Med. Sch. Harvard U., 1963-65; rsch. assoc. div. oncology Inst. Steroid Rsch. Montefiore Hosp. and Med. Ctr., N.Y.C., 1965-70; asst. prof. Coll. Medicine U. Ill., 1970-72, assoc. prof. Coll. Medicine, 1972-79; prof. Med. Sch. Northwestern U., Chgo., 1979—. Mem. sci. adv. com. AID, chairperson Instnl. Rev. Bd. Northwestern U., 1982—83, mem. intellectual properties com., 1987—95, chairperson radiation safety com., 2000—02; dir. Immunoassay Facility, R. H. Lurie Cancer Ctr. Northwestern U. Med. Sch., 1997—; dir. clin. labs., dept. ob-gyn. Northwestern Med. Facutly Found., 1996—99, dir. shared clin. labs., 1999—. Contbr. articles to profl. jours. Grantee, NIH, 1972—90, 1995—, NSF, 1975, 1995—98, AID, 1971—86, Army Office Rsch., 1987—94. Mem.: AAAS, Chgo. Assn. Reproductive Endocrinologists (pres. 1987—88), Soc. Study Reproduction, Soc. Gynecologic Investigation, Endocrine Soc., Am. Chem. Soc., N.Y. Acad. Scis., Phi Kappa Phi, Sigma Xi. Presbyterian. Achievements include patents for method of totally suppressing ovarian follicular devel. and method of ovulation detection. Home: 6001 N Knox Ave Chicago IL 60646-5821 Office: Northwestern U Olson 8408 710 N Fairbanks Ct Chicago IL 606I1-3015 Office Phone: 312-503-5272. Business E-Mail: chat@northwestern.edu.

CHATTMAN, RAYMOND CHRISTOPHER, association executive; b. San Rafael, Calif., Apr. 11, 1956; s. Raymond Rene Chattman and Virginia Mae (Kirkland) Robinson; m. Patti Lyn Barnard Garbers, Feb. 14, 1975 (div. 1977); m. Dawn Irene Russell Kilpatrick, Aug. 21, 1993 (div. 1998); children: Christian Paige, Bradley Charles Kilpatrick. BS, SUNY, Albany, 1988; MBA, Averett Coll., 1995. Cert. assoc. exec. 2005. Dir. planning, ops. Comms. Media Group Inc., Alexandria, Va., 1981; comms. mgr. ANPA Found., Reston, Va., 1982-84; graphics editor Times-Herald Record, Middletown, N.Y., 1984-85; editor employee comms. Washington Gas Light Co., 1985-86; exec. dir., CEO Soc. Newspaper Design, Reston, 1986-96; dir. comm. and outreach AIAA, Reston, 1996—2005; v.p. Am. Chiropractic Assn., Arlington, Va., 2005—. Asst. coach Herndon (Va.) Optimist Youth Football, 1994, Herndon Youth Soccer, 1992. Served in U.S. Army, 1974-81, Korea, Germany, Res., 1981-90. Recipient Thomas Jefferson award Dept. Def., 1979, Keith L. Ware award Dept. Army, 1978, 83, 86, 87. Mem. Am. Soc. Assn. Execs., Nat. Assn. Govt. Communicators (blue pencil award 1978), Am. Mgmt. Assn., Greater Washington Soc. Assn. Execs. Avocations: travel, reading, golf. Office: Am Chiropractic Assn 1701 Clarendon Blvd Arlington VA 22209 Office Phone: 703-276-8800.

CHATTOPADHYAY, NAIBEDYA, physiologist, educator, researcher; b. Kharagpur, India, May 25, 1965; s. Nirmal Chandra and Minati Chattopadhyay. BSc with honors, Presidency Coll., Calcutta, 1985, MSc in Physiology, 1988; PhD in Endocrinology, S.G. PGIMS, Lucknow, India, 1994. Rsch. fellow Brigham & Women's Hosp., Boston, 1994-98, Harvard U. Sch. Medicine, Boston, 1994-98, instr. medicine, 1998—. Reviewer Am. Jour. Physiology, Endocrinology, European Jour. Neurosci; editor: Calcium-Sensing Receptor, 2001; contbr. numerous articles to sci. an dprofl. jours. Mem. Am. Physiol. Soc., Am. Soc. for Neurochemistry, N.Y. Acad. Scis., Endocrine Soc., Physiol. Soc. U.K., London Diplomatic Assn. (life). Office: Brigham and Women's Hosp 221 Longwood Ave Boston MA 02115 E-mail: nchattopadhyay@partners.org.

CHATURVEDI, PRAVIN R., pharmaceutical executive; B in Pharmacy, U. Bombay; PhD in Pharm. Scis., W.Va. U. With Alkermes Inc.; in charge of lead evaluation Vertex Pharmaceuticals Inc.; pres., CEO Scion Pharms., Inc., Medford, Mass., 2001—. Office: Scion Pharms Inc 200 Boston Ave Ste 3600 Medford MA 02155

CHATZINOFF, HOWARD, lawyer; b. Bklyn., Feb. 25, 1952; m. Leslie Chatzinoff. BSE with honors, Princeton U., 1974; JD, U. Va., 1977. Bar: NY 1978. Mem. Weil, Gotshal & Manges, NYC, ptnr. Lawyers com. NYC2012. Planning com. Ray Garrett Jr. Corp. and Securities Law Inst. Northwestern U. Sch. Law; exec. com. bd. dirs. Pub. Edn. Needs Civic Involvement in Learning (PENCIL); exec. com. NYC Adv. Bd. Enterprise Found. Mem. ABA (corp., banking and bus. law sect., comm. law com. 1985—). Office: Weil Gotshal & Manges 767 5th Ave 10th Fl New York NY 10153-0119

CHATZKY, HERBERT, music educator; b. Balt., Apr. 8, 1935; s. Samuel and Sonia (Greenspun) C.; m. Sally Anne Rush, Feb. 13, 1973; children: Christine, Lisa, David. BS, Juilliard Sch. of Music, 1957; MS, 1958, postgrad., 1959. Cert. tchr. music, Conn. Accompanying staff Juilliard Sch. Music, N.Y.C., 1952-57, tchr. class piano, 1958-60; instr. in piano Bowling Green (Ohio) State U., 1960-61; asst. prof. piano and accompanying Hart Coll. Music, Hartford, Conn., 1961-72; music staff South Windsor (Conn.) Sch., 1972-97; choirmaster Hartford (Conn.) Symphony Chorale, 1972-73, ofcl. pianist, 1962-73; dir. 2nd Congregational Ch., Manchester, Conn., 1967-86, North United Meth. Ch., Manchester, 1986—. Dir. Manchester Young Artist Competition, Conn., 1974—; music dir., sr. organist, Temple Beth Israel, Conn., 1986-98, dir. Jewish music competition Lake Placid Synagogue, 2004—; dir. Newcomb Friends for Music Concerts, Newcomb Young Composer Contest. Composer: (symphonic) Night Music for Orchestra, 1952, Variations, 1952, Music for Orchestra and Chorus: 29th Psalm, 1973; arranger for organ; Lincoln Portrait, 1978; performed concert series Lake Placid Synagogue. Performer holocaust music, Conn. Pub. Radio, Hartford, 1970, 2nd Congregational Ch., Manchester, 1978; dir. concert series Second Congregational Ch., 1975-86, Lake Placid Synagogue, 2003—; lectr. on sight-reading, New Eng. Piano Tchrs. Assn., 1967; trustee Newcomb United Meth. Ch.; v.p. Newcomb C. of C. Sgt. USANG, 1960-70. Recipient full piano scholarship Juilliard Sch. Music, 1952-57, french-horn scholarship, 1952-57; award of Philo-Music Soc., N.Y.C., 1955; winner of concerto competition, Juilliard Sch. of Music, 1958; concerto soloist under Arthur Fiedler, Hartford Symphony Orchestra, 1972. Jewish. Avocations: mountain climbing, hiking, reading, travel in motorhome. Home: PO Box 214 Newcomb NY 12852-0214 also: 5461 Rte 28N Newcomb NY 12852 Office Phone: 518-582-2206. Personal E-mail: hchatzky@frontierarto.net.

CHAU, PIN PIN, bank executive; b. Hong Kong; d. Waihing Wong; m. Raymond Chau; 1 child, Christine. BA, Coe Coll., 1965; MA in Asian hist., Yale U., 1967; grad., Stonier Grad. Sch. of Banking, Rutgers U. With Nat. Westminster Bank (now Fleet), 1970—87; chief lending officer United Orient Bank, N.Y.C., 1987—88, COO, 1988—89, pres., CEO, 1989—93. The Summit Nat. Bank, Atlanta, 1993—; CEO Summit Bank Corp., Atlanta, 1999—. Bd. dirs. Consumer Credit Counseling Service; exec. com. Ga. Dept. Industry, Trade and Tourism, 1999—. Bd. dirs. Atlanta Coll. Arts; bd. councilors Carter Ctr. Mem.: Internat. Women's Forum, Soc. Internat. Bus. Fellows (assoc.). Avocation: painting. Office: Summit Bank Corp 4360 Chamblee-Dunwoody Rd Atlanta GA 30341

CHAUDHARI, PRAVEEN, science administrator, materials physicist; b. Ludhiana, Punjab, India, Nov. 30, 1937; came to U.S., 1961; s. Hans Raj and Ved (Kumari) C.; m. Karin Romhild, June 13, 1964; children: Ashok, Pia. BS with honors, Indian Inst. Tech., Kharagpur, 1961; MS in Phys. Metallurgy, MIT, 1963, ScD in Phys. Metallurgy, 1966. Rsch. assoc. MIT, Cambridge, Mass., 1966; rsch. staff mem. IBM T.J. Watson Rsch. Ctr., Yorktown Heights, N.Y., 1966-70, mgr., 1970-80, dir. phys. scis., 1981-82, v.p. sci., dir. phys. scis., 1982-91, v.p. sci., tech. com., 1988-91, rsch. staff, 1991—2003; dir. Brookhaven Nat. Lab., Upton, NY, 2003—. Exec. sec. Presdl. Com. on Super Conductivity, 1988; mem. Presdl. Commn. on Super Conductivity, 1989; chmn. U.S. Liaison Commn. to Internat. Union of Pure and Applied Physics; mem. com. on Physics for the Next Decade, sponsored by NRC/NAS, Nat. Critical Tech. panel; chmn. sci. coun. Internat. Ctr. for Theoretical Physics, Trieste, Italy; chmn. adv. coun. math. and phys. scis. NSF; mem. governing bd. NY State Inst. Superconductivity. Author of papers on mechanical properties and defects in crystalline solids, amorphous solids, quantum transport, superconductivity and magnetic monopoles and neutrino mass experiments. Recipient Harry C. Gatos prize MIT, 1994, Nat. Medal Tech., 1995, Excellence award US Pan Asian Amer. C. of C., Liebmann prize IEEE, 1992, George Pake award Am. Phys. Soc., 1987. Mem.: NAS (mem. governing bd. physics and astronomy), Am. Acad. Arts and Sci., Nat. Acad. Engring., Am. Inst. Physics (mem.-at-large governing bd.), NY Acad. Scis. (mem. governing bd.). Office: Brookhaven Nat Lab PO Box 5000 Upton NY 11973

CHAUDHARY, RAVI I., pilot, aerospace engineer; b. Mpls., July 15, 1970; s. Surendra Pal Singh and Raj Mohini Chaudhary; m. Uma Raju, Nov. 29, 1996; children: Krishan Raju, Nina Angali. BS in Aero. Engring., U.S. Air Force Acad., 1993; MS in Indsl. Engring., St Mary's U., 1999. Cert. non-destructive test engr., Level III, USAF, Heller Corp., 1995, DOD Level III Acquistion, Test and Evaluation, USAF, 1999; lic. comml. pilot FAA, 1998, cert. AF Pilot Rating USAF, 2001, diver Padi, Tex., 1996. Delta II propulsion engr. USAF, L.A., 1993—97, flight test engr. Warner Robins, Ga., 1996—2001, C-17 aircraft comdr. Charleston, S.C., 2001—. Author: (flight test) Performance Reliability for Aircraft, 1998. Vol. diver S.C. Aquarium, Charleston, 2001—04. Maj. USAF, 1989—2005, Charleston AFB, S.C. Decorated Air Medal (3rd Cluster) USAF, Outstanding Unit with Valor, Co. Grade Officer of Yr. Kelly AFB; recipient NASA Stellar award, NASA Johnson Space Ctr., 2000; fellow NASA Grad. Student Rsch. Fellowship, NASA Marshall Space Flight Ctr., 1998. Master: AIAA (air transp., flight test tech rep. 1998—2004). Achievements include completion of the first-ever GPS Constellation. Home: 129 High Bridge Rd Summerville SC 29485 Personal E-mail: ravichaud@aol.com.

CHAUDHARY, SATVEER, state senator; b. June 12, 1969; BA, St. Olaf Coll., 1991; JD, U. Minn., 1995. Mem. Minn. Ho. Reps., 1996-2000, Minn. State Senate, 2000—, vice chair transp. com., mem. crime prevention com., edn. com., E-12 edn. budget divsn. com., fin. com., transp. and pub. safety budget divsn. com.; owner Chaudhary Cons. Law clk., intern Hennepin County Atty.'s Office, Minn.; aide Minn. Atty. Gen. Hubert H. Humphrey III. Co-chair Anoka County Legis. Delegation; hon. adv. coun. Asian-Pacific Endowment for Cmty. Devel.; mem. Coalition of Labor Union Women, Minn. Outdoor Heritage Alliance; hon. chair Minn. Cricket Assn.; mem. Minn. Welcome Com. for The Dalai Lama, U. Minn. Indsl. Rels. Adv. Coun., Twin Cities Internat. Citizen Award Com.; Fridley Human Resources Commn.; vol. Mounds View Festival in the Park; mem. New Brighton Hist. Soc., New Brighton Sportsmen's Club, Minn. Pheasants Forever Soc.; state affirmative action officer Minn. DFL Party; co-founder, chair Minn. Asian-Indian Dem. Assn.; bd. dirs. World Trade Ctr., St. Paul, A Blanket of Hope. Named Legislator of the Yr., Coll. Dems. of Minn., 1999; recipient Cert. of Commendation, Legal Aid Soc. of Minn., Cert. of Appreciation, DFL Party, 1995, Achievement award, Indian Assn. Minn. Mem.: New Brighton Eagles, Bass Anglers Soc. Am., Columbia Hts. Lions. Dfl. First Asian Indian sen. in Am. history and first Asian-Am. mem. of Minn. legis. Office: Minn Senate 75 Rev Dr Martin Luther King Jr Blvd Saint Paul MN 55155 E-mail: sen.satveer.chaudhary@senate.mn.*

CHAUDHARY, SHAUKAT ALI, ecologist, plant taxonomist; b. Sialkot, Punjab, Pakistan, Mar. 1, 1931; s. Allah-Rakha and Raisham Bibi (Din) C.; m. Zahida Sarwar, Oct. 22, 1967; children: Naveed, Naila, Ayesha, Samir. MSc, U. Punjab, Lahore, 1953; PhD, Wash. State U., 1965. Lectr. Gordon Coll., Rawalpindi, Punjab, 1953-54; asst. prof. Agrl. U., Faisalbad, Punjab, 1954-62, reader, head dept., 1965-70; sr. lectr. Am. U. Beirut (Lebanon), 1970-76; assoc. prof. Sana'a (Yemen) U., 1976-78; prof. and sr. scientist Am. U. Beirut on secondment to USDA Team in Saudi Arabia, Riyadh, 1978-89; sr. scientist UN FAO Team in Saudi Arabia, Riyadh, 1989—. Dean students Agr. U., Faisalabad, 1966-70; curator Nat. Herbarium Saudi Arabia, Riyadh, 1979—. Author: Weeds of Yemen, 1983, Weeds of Saudi Arabia and Arabian Peninsula, 1987, Weed Control Handbook for Saudi Arabia, 1985, Grasses of Saudi Arabia, 1989, Natural History of Saudi Arabia, 1992, Vegetation of Saudi Arabia, 1999, Flora of the Kingdom of Saudi Arabia I, 1999. Mem. Aril Soc. Internat. (dir. at large 1974-78), Pakistan Bot. Soc. (founding sec.-treas. 1968-69), Sigma Xi. Avocations: study of deserts, photography. Home: 3730 W Lake Dr Martinez GA 30907-9595

CHAUDHRI, JAVADE, lawyer; b. Nairobi, Kenya, Apr. 30, 1952; BS, Yale U., 1975, MS, 1977; JD, Georgetown U., 1980. Bar: DC 1980, Calif. 2000. Atty. Surrey & Morse, Washington, 1980—86; ptnr. Jones Day Reavis & Pogue (merger with Surrey & Morse), Washington, 1986—93; sr. ptnr. Winston & Strawn, Washington, 1993—99; v.p. law, dep. gen. counsel Gateway, Poway, Calif., 1999—2001, sr. v.p., gen. counsel, 2001—03; exec. v.p., gen. counsel Sempra Energy, San Diego, 2003—. Vis. faculty mem. Internat. Devel. Law Inst., Rome, Internat. Law Inst., Washington. Mem.: ABA, Internat. Bar Assn., DC Bar. Office: Sempra Energy 101 Ash St San Diego CA 92101-3017

CHAUDHURI, ALOKE, telecommunications industry executive; b. India; BS in Elec. Engring., Condordia U., Montreal, Can., 1990; MS in Elec. Engring., Concordia U., Montreal, Can., 1994. Sys. engr. TATA Inc., Jamshedpur, India, 1990—92; software developer IRIS, Montreal, Canada, 1992—94; sr. network engr. broadband netowrks Nortel Networks, Ottawa, Canada, 1994—97, network analyst, 1994—95, sys. arch. broadband networks, 1995—96; mgr. network mgmt. sys. integration Motorola, Inc., Horsham, Pa., 1997—99, sr. mgr., sys. integration, 1997—2001; v.p. tech. Xenon, Inc., Edison, NJ, 2001—02; chief tech. officer Netlink, Victor, NY, 2002—04; v.p. product mgmt. Soleo Comm., Fairport, NY, 2004—. Contbr. articles to profl. jours. Recipient Motorola Tech. Excellence award, 1998; Grad. fellowship, Concordia U., 1992. Achievements include patents for Route Optimization and Traffic Management in ATM Networks using Neural Computing. (U.S. Patent # 6, 411, 946). Office Phone: 585-641-4300. Business E-Mail: achaudhuri@soleocommunications.com.

CHAUHAN, NEELIMA B., neuroscientist, researcher; d. Vinayak S. and Sarala V. Athavale; m. Balwantsinh C. Chauhan, Dec. 5, 1977; children: Mihirsinh B., Nisha B. B in edn., MS U. Baroda, Baroda, Gujarat, India, 1982; MSc, PhD, MS U. Baroda, 1975—82. Rsch. physiologist R&D, Edward Hines, Jr. VA Med. Ctr., Hines, Ill., 1996—2000; asst. prof. Dept. Neuroscience, Finch U. Health Sciences, The Chgo. Med. Sch., 2000—02, NeuroAnesthesia, U. Ill., Chgo., 2002—; health scientist R&D, VA Chgo. Health Care Sys., 2002—. Contbr. articles, chapters to books. Cultural sec. Rajput Assn. N.Am., Chgo., 1997—98; mem. Swadhyaya, Chgo., 1998—2004. Grantee Rsch. project, NIH, 2004-2006, Rsch., Falk Found., 1999-2001. Mem.: Internat. Soc. Neurochemistry (life), Am. Soc. Neurochemistry (life), Soc. Neuroscience (life). Achievements include research in Design and development of ICV passive immunization in Alzheimer's disease; Use of statins in ameliorating Alzheimer's pathogenesis; Use of Propentofylline for concurrent management of plaques and tangles in Alzheimer's disease; Use of Acetyl-L-Carnitine for improving memory deficits in Alzheimer's disease; Use of herbal alternatives to ameliorate Alzheimer's pathogenesis. Office: R&D VACHCS Neuro Anesthesia UIC 820 S Damen Ave Chicago IL 60612 Office Phone: 312-569-7747. Business E-Mail: nchauhan@uic.edu.

CHAURASIA, VISHAL, physician, writer; b. Agra, India, Jan. 3, 1971; s. Raj and Renu Chaurasia; m. Shruti Chaurasia, Apr. 13, 1995. MBBS, All India Inst. Med. Scis., New Delhi, 1994. Diplomate Am. Bd. Internal Medicine. Intern Albert Einstein Coll. Medicine and Affiliated Hosps., Bronx, N.Y., 1994-95, resident, 1995-97; fellow SUNY, Buffalo, 1997-98; physician Med. Ctr. Eastern Ariz., Pima, 1998—2000; freelance emergency rm. physician Ariz., 1998—2003; hospitalist, 2003—; pvt. practice Safford, Ariz., 1999—2000. Chmn. ICU, respiratory, cardiology Mt. Graham Cmty. Hosp., Safford, Ariz., 1998-2000. Served with Naval Nat. Cadet Corps, 1986. Nat. Talent scholar Govt. of India, 1986. Mem.: MENSA, AMA, AOPA. Home: 9808 E Becker W Scottsdale AZ 85260 E-mail: chaurasia@email.com.

CHAUVEL, MARJORIE ANN, musician, music educator; b. Washington, Oct. 30, 1922; d. Allan Wells and Mary Isabel (Drummond) Gibson; m. Arthur L. Chauvel, Apr. 14, 1946; children: Ronald Cary, Nanette NaMarie Chauvel Bajka. Student, Curtis Inst. Music, 1941—46. Instr. harp New Sch. Music, Phila., 1944—45, Granott Sch. Music, 1943—45, Coll. Notre Dame, Belmont, Calif., 1955—81; prof. music, harp San Francisco State U., 1960—80, Conservatory Music, U. Pacific, Stockton, 1972—75; lectr. music, harp Stanford U., Palo Alto, 1979—. Harpist Nat. Orch. Assn., N.Y.C., 1940; harp soloist Curtis Syphpony, Phila., 1944, Scranton Philharmonic, Scranton, 1944, Norfolk Symphony, Va., 1943—44. Author: A Harp at the Wedding, 1980, Tunes I love to Play, 1982; musician: (arranger) numerous harp collections. Mem.: Santa Clara chpt. Am. Harp Assn., Am. Harp Assn. Avocation: golf. Home: 4100 Old Adobe Rd Palo Alto CA 94306 Office: Stanford U Braum Music Bldg Stanford CA 94305

CHAUVETTE, CLAUDE R., executive secretary; b. Montreal, Que., Can., Mar. 19, 1939; s. Bruno and Germaine (Handfield) C. BA, U. Montreal, 1959; postgrad., Ecole Polytechnique, Montreal, 1959-60; LSc Comm., LSc Compt., Hautes Etudes Comm., Montreal, 1963; CA, Can. Inst. Chartered Accts., Montreal, 1964. Pub. acct. Riddell Stead & Co., Montreal, 1963-67; asst. to v.p. Marine Industries, Montreal, 1967-71; contr. Forano Ltd., Plessisville, Can., 1971-73; sec.-treas. Demix Ltd., Demix (Laval) Ltd., Montreal, 1973-76; mgr. adminstrn. Montreal area St. Lawrence Cement Inc., Montreal, 1977-79, mgr. adminstrn. Que. div., 1979-81, treas., asst. sec., 1981-87, sec.-treas., 1987-2000, corp. sec., 2000—05. Mem. Can. Inst. Chartered Accts., Risk and Ins. Mgmt. Soc. Office: St Lawrence Cement Inc 1945 Graham Blvd Mount Royal PQ Canada H3R 1H1 E-mail: cchauvette@stlawrencecement.com.

CHAVARRIA, ANNA, artist, educator; arrived in U.S., 1976; d. Honorio Chavarria and Rosemary Kintler; 1 child, Ian Christopher. BFA, Sch. Visual Arts, N.Y., N.Y., 1983; cert. in Tchg., U. Tex., Edinburg, Tex., 1999. Tchr. English Berlitz Lang. Inst., Monterrey; tchr. sci. Pub. Sch. 149, N.Y.; tchr. elem. sch. Pub. Sch. 122, N.Y.; tchr. art McAllen (Tex.) Ind. Sch. Dist. Vol. artist Internat. Mus. Arts and Scis., McAllen. Named Tchr. of Yr., Lamar Acad., 2003; grantee, McAllen Edn. Found. Mem.: Tex. Art Edn. Assn. Avocations: reading, yoga. Office: McAllen ISD Lamar Acad 1009 N 10th St Mcallen TX 78501

CHAVE, CAROL, arbitrator, retired lawyer; b. Chgo., Jan. 30, 1948; d. Grant Carruthers and Priscilla Morrison (Shaw) C.; m. Robert Edmund Hand; children: Joshua, Chloe, Robert, Grant. BA, U. Chgo., 1970; MAT, Oakland U., 1971; JD, Loyola U., Chgo., 1976. Bar: Ill. 1976, N.Y. 1980. Tchr. corps intern Pontiac (Mich.) Pub. Schs., 1970-71; sec., receptionist Grad. Sch. Bus., U. Chgo., 1971; counselor Sonia Shankman Orthogenic Sch., Chgo., 1972; pvt. practice Chgo., 1976-78; asst. v.p., assoc. counsel Bank of Tokyo, N.Y.C., 1978-85; substitute tchr. N.Y.C. Pub. Schs., 1986-88; with Breckenridge Law Offices, 1986-88; sr. v.p., counsel, mgr. human resources Tokai Bank, N.Y.C., 1988-97; dir., counsel Deutsche Bank, N.Y.C., 1997-99; arbitrator Internat. Ctr. for Dispute Resolution, N.Y.C., 2001—. Arbitrator Am. Arbitration Assn., N.Y.C., 1986—. Vol. lawyer Chgo. Vol. Legal Svcs., 1977-78; designer playground PS 41 Parent Assn., Greenwich Village, N.Y., 1987. Avocations: weaving, dance. Personal E-mail: cchave@earthlink.net.

CHAVERS, BLANCHE MARIE, pediatrician, educator, researcher; b. Clarksdale, Miss., Aug. 2, 1949; d. Andrew and Mildred Louise C.; m. Gubare Mpambara, May 21, 1982; 1 child, Kaita. BS in Zoology, U. Wash., 1971, MD, 1975. Diplomate Am. Bd. Pediats. Intern U. Wash., Seattle, 1975-76, resident in pediatrics, 1976-78; instr. U. Minn., Mpls., 1982, asst. prof. pediatrics, 1983-90, assoc. prof. pediatrics, 1990-99, prof. pediatrics, 1999—. Attending physician dept. pediatrics, U. Minn. Sch. Medicine, Mpls., 1982. Co-editor: Am. Jour. Kidney Diseases, 2001—; contbr. articles to profl. jours. Recipient Clin. Investigator award NIH, 1982; Pediatric Nephrology fellow U. Minn., 1978-81. Mem. Am. Soc. Nephrology, Am. Soc. Pediatric Nephrology, Internat. Soc. Nephrology, Internat. Soc. Pediatric Nephrology, Am. Soc. Transplantation. Democrat. Methodist. Avocations: tennis, reading, collecting african artifacts, art. Office: Univ Minn MMC 491 420 Delaware St SE Minneapolis MN 55455-0348

CHAVES, JOSE MARIA, diplomat, lawyer, foundation administrator, educator; b. Bogotá, Colombia, Aug. 19, 1922; s. Carlos Chaves and María García de C.; m. Elena Gómez y Samperio; children: Cristina María, Tomás José. Bachiller, Bogotá, 1939, cert. in anthropology, 1942, JD, 1945; DSc (hon.), U. Antióquia, 1948; MA, Columbia U., 1951, PhD, 1953; LLD, U. Popayán, Colombia, 1957, Mercy Coll., 1991. Bar: Columbia 1944, Inter-American 1953. Editor in chief Revista Colegio del Rosario (arts and letters mag.), Colombia, 1944; gen. legal duties specializing in public adminstrn. Bogotá, 1942-45; instr. Romance langs. Columbia U., N.Y.C., 1945-48, 50-51; founder, 1st dean faculty U. Andes, Bogotá, 1948-49; head area studies Queens Coll. NYU, 1951-53; counselor Colombian Embassy, Washington, 1953-55; prof. internat. law U. Colombia, 1955-58, U. Paris, 1957; guest prof. internat. law and relations Brit. Council, various univs. Eng., Scotland, 1957; dir., chief exec. Am. Found. for Cultural Popular Action, Inc. (pvt. internat. orgn. for mass edn. by radio), N.Y.C., 1958—; amb. of Kyrgyzstan to UN, 1992—. Dir. Center Latin Am. Studies, CUNY; chmn. Hispanic Am. editorial bd. Grolier, Inc., 1971—; ambassador extraordinary, permanent del. Iberoam. Bur. Edn. to UN; A.E. and P., permanent rep. Grenada to OAS; permanent rep. orgn. Iberoam. Countries to UN and OAS, 1986—; alt. gov. World Bank and Internat. Monetary Fund, 1974-77, 94; chmn. C.I.P., 1972—; organizer, dir. tech. assistance mission Unitarian Service Com. in Latin Am.; dir. gen. Nat. Univ. Fund, Colombia, 1955-58; amb. extraordinary Spl. Mission to Brazil, 1995. Editor-in-chief: Grolier Spanish Universal Ency; author: Chaves Plan for settlement religious conflict between Caths. and Protestants in Latin Am; Author: Francisco de Vitoria. Founder International Law, 1945, Intergroup relations in the Spain of Cervantes, 1953, University Reform in Colombia, 1957. Pres. Assn. Latin Am. Unity, 1984; chmn. Summit Coun. World Peace, 1985-92; ambassador extraordinary and plenipotentiary of Kyrgyzstan to the UN, 1992-93. Decorated Legion of Honor (France); gran cruz Order of St. Constantine the Great; comdr., knight comdr. Grand Order Isabel La Católica (Spain); knight comdr. Alfonso El Sabio; grand cross Vasco N'nez de Balboa Panama, 1970; grand cross Juan P. Duarte Sanchez y Mella Dominican Republic, 1970, Medal of Jerusalem Israel, 1972; grand cross Order of Malta, 1976; grand cross Order Justice Law and Peace of Mex., 1977, grand cross Order Latin Am. Unity 1986, grand cross Order of St. Michael (Portugal), 1990; grand cross Order of Holy Cross of Jerusalem, 1991, grand cross of Saint Dennis of Zanthe, 1991; recipient medaglia universitaria U. Po Deo, Rome, 1957, medalla de los Andes U., 1958, medaille de Versailles, France, 1990, medalla Universidad, Lima, 1990, Lord Perry World prize for Edn., 1993, Order of Manas of Kyrgyzstan 1995. Mem. Internat. Law Assn., Inter-Am. Bar. Assn., Acad. Polit. Sci., MLA, Academia Hispano Americana, Assn. for Latin Am. Unity (founder, pres. 1984), Summit Coun. for World Peace (dir. 1987), Met. Club, Columbia U. Club (N.Y.C.), Quill Club USA (pres.), Brook Club, Phi Delta Kappa (v.p. Univ. World). Clubs: Metropolitan, Brook, Columbia U. (N.Y.C.), Quill of U.S.A. (pres.). Home: 118 E 60th St New York NY 10022-1103 Office: 401 5th Ave New York NY 10016-3317 *Faith in God is also faith in man. Service of man is also service of God. As we enter a new period of peace in the world, our faith can sustain our peace building efforts and help create a better life for all mankind.*

CHAVES-CARBALLO, ENRIQUE, neuropediatrician; b. San Jose, Costa Rica, Dec. 2, 1936; arrived in U.S., 1955, arrived in Saudi Arabia, 1996; s. Enrique Chaves and Celina Carballo; m. Vilma Irene Peralta, Aug. 26, 1961; children: Antonio, Maria, Miguel, Karen. MD, U. Okla., 1963. Diplomate Am. Bd. Psychiatry and Neurology, Am. Bd. Pediatrics. Prof. pediatrics and neurology Ea. Va. Med. Sch., Norfolk, 1979-89, U. Kans., Kansas City, 1990-94; chief pediatric neurology King Faisal Specialist Hosp. and Rsch. Ctr., Riyadh, Saudi Arabia, 1996—2002; fellow pediatrics Mayo Clinic, 1964—67, fellow neurology, 1972—75; clin. prof. pediatrics U. of Kans., Kans. City, 2003; clin. prof. hist. medicine U. Kans., Kans. City, Kans., 2004. Contbr. articles to profl. jours, chpts. to books; reviewer numerous jours. Recipient award Am. Neurol. Assn.; fgn. scholar Wesleyan U., 1955; grantee Rockefeller Archives, 1979. Fellow Am. Acad. Neurology; mem. Am. Assn. Hist. Medicine, Costa Rica Assn. Neuroscis. (hon.), Child Neurology Soc., Internat. Child Neurology Soc., Iberoam. Acad. Pediat. Neurology, Profs. Child Neurology, Soc. for Study of Inborn Errors of Metabolism, Soc. for Inherited Metabolic Disorders. Achievements include research in Reye syndrome and inborn errors of metabolism. E-mail: echaves17@hotmail.com.

CHAVEZ, ALBERT BLAS, financial executive; b. L.A., Jan. 1, 1952; s. Albert Blas and Yolanda (Garcia) Chavez; m. Irma Laura Cavazos, Dec. 21, 1996. BA, U. Tex., El Paso, 1979; MBA, Stanford U., 1985. CPA Calif. Mem. profl. staff Deloitte Haskins and Sells, L.A., 1980-83; planning analyst corp. fin. planning Boise (Idaho) Cascade Co., 1984; treasury analyst corp. treasury RCA Corp., N.Y.C., 1985; asst. contr. RCA/Ariola Records, Mexico City, 1986; fin. analyst corp. exec. office GE Co., Fairfield, Conn., 1987-90; corp. fin. cons. Entertainment Industry and Litigation Support Svcs., L.A., 1990-91; co-founder, sr. v.p., CFO El Dorado Comm., Inc., L.A., 1991-98; fin. cons. entertainment and tech. industries, 1999—2003; sr. v.p., CFO SiTV, Inc., L.A., 2003—. Bd. dirs., v.p., treas. L.A. Conservation Corp., 1990—; bd. dirs. Wave Cmty. Newspapers, 1999—2000. Mem.: AICPA, Calif. Soc. CPAs. Democrat. Home: 4820 Carmel Rd La Canada Flintridge CA 91011 Office Phone: 323-256-8900. E-mail: achavez@sitv.com.

CHAVEZ, BRENDA G., construction executive, real estate agent; d. Walter Samuel and Edythe Carleen (Campbell) Chavez; children: Regena Bean, Tamara Keeton, Lacey. BS in Bus. Mgmt. cum laude, Northwood U., 1992; MBA, U. Tex., 1994. Lic. real estate agt. Pres. Lone Star Model and Talent Agy., Inc., Houston, 1979—81, Total Rep Inc., Houston, 1982—85; sales mgr. MCN Constrn., Houston, 1982—96; pres., CEO Chavez Constrn. Co., Houston, 1991—. Owner, founder, dir. NBA Houston Rockets Cheerleaders, 1980—82, Second Bapt. H.S. Drill Team, Houston, 1984—86; bd. dirs. Houston Minority Bus. Coun., Hispanic Contractor's Assn., Houston Texans Hispanic Adv. Coun. Named Ms. Tex., 2004. Mem.: Mexican Am. Contractors Assn. (founder, exec. dir. 2002—), Profl. Cheerleaders Alumni Assn. (founder, exec. dir. 1995—). Avocations: weight training, ballroom dancing, jogging, decorating. Home: 11215 Marseilles Ln Houston TX 77082 Office: Chavez Service Cos Ste 300 5555 W Loop South Bellaire TX 77401 Office Phone: 713-680-0005. E-mail: xprocheerldr@yahoo.com.

CHAVEZ, EDWARD L., state supreme court justice; b. Santa Fe, Oct. 15, 1957; BA in Pers. Mgmt. with honors, Eastern New Mexico U., 1978; JD, New Mexico Sch. of Law, 1981. Bar: N.Mex 1981. Ptnr. Carpenter & Chavez, Ltd.; assoc. justice N. Mex. Supreme Ct., Santa Fe, 2003—. Spl. counsel N.Mex Disciplinary Bd., 1987—95; lectr. Nat. Inst. Trial Advocacy, 1998—99; adj. prof. U. N.Mex; chmn. disciplinary bd. Supreme Ct. N.Mex. Mem. Ctr. Civic Values; trustee U. N.Mex Mental Health Ctr., 1989; mem. Task Force Regulation Lawyer Advt., 1990. Fellow: Internat. Acad. Trial Lawyers, Am. Coll. Trial Lawyers; mem.: ATLA (minority del.), Hispanic Nat. Bar Assn., N.Mex. Hispanic Bar Assn., Am. Inns Ct., Trial Lawyers Pub. Justice, State Bar N.Mex, N.Mex Trial Lawyers Assn. (feature editor newsletter 1987—90, bd. dirs. 1990—, pres. 1997—98), Nat. Spinal Cord Injury Assn. Office: NMex Supreme Ct Box 848 Santa Fe NM 87504

CHAVEZ, JEANETTE, editor; BS in Journalism, U. Colo., 1973. Mem. staff Office of U.S. Rep. Spark Matsunaga, Washington, 1973—74; reporter Colorado Springs (Colo.) Sun, 1974—81; reporter, copy desk chief, city editor, news editor Ft. Collins (Colo.) Coloradoan; copy editor Daily Herald, Arlington Heights, Ill., 1981—82; copy editor, then news editor bus. sect. Chgo. Sun Times, 1982—84; dep. news editor Denver Post, 1984—86, news editor, 1987—88, asst. mng. editor, 1988—91, assoc. editor features, 1991—97, mng. editor, 1997—, mng. editor ops., 2000—. Office: Denver Post 1560 Broadway Denver CO 80202-1577

CHAVEZ, JOHN ANTHONY, lawyer; b. Auburn, Calif., Oct. 5, 1955; s. Marco Antonio and Barbara Ann (Lawrence) Chavez-Rivas. BA, U. Calif., Santa Barbara, 1977; JD, Stanford U., 1981. Bar: Calif. 1981, Tex. 1982, U.S. Dist. Ct. (so. and no. dists.) Calif. 1982, (cen. dist.) Calif. 1983, U.S. Dist. Ct. (so. dist.) Tex. 1982, (we. dist.) Tex. 1983, (no. dist.) Tex. 1991, N.Y. 1986, U.S. Dist. Ct. (ea. and so. dists.) N.Y. 1986, U.S. Supreme Ct. 1986. With legal dept. Exxon Co. U.S.A., Houston, 1981-85, N.Y.C., 1985-86; assoc. gen. counsel Sybron Corp., Saddlebrook, N.J., 1986-88, Crown Equipment Corp., New Bremen, Ohio, 1989-90; trial atty. Exxon Co. U.S.A., Houston, 1990-92; counsel complex litigation Exxon Chem. Co., Houston, 1992-95; counsel internat. oil and gas exploration Exxon Exploration Co., Houston, 1995-96; counsel antitrust, mergers and acquisitions Exxon Chem. Co., Houston, 1996-2000; counsel intellectual property licensing ExxonMobil Chem. Co., Baytown, Tex., 2000—04; counsel Intellectual Property Lic. Univation Techs., 2004—. Presenter numerous legal edn. seminars and programs. Contbr. articles to profl. jours. Mentor Ft. Bend Ind. Sch. Dist., 1998, Houston Bar Assn., 1998. Chancellor's scholar U. Calif., 1976; Univ. Svc. award for dist. svc. to campus cmty. U. Calif., Santa Barbara, 1977. Fellow Houston Bar Found.; mem. ABA (antitrust sect., vice chair corp. counseling com. 1998-2000, vice chair intellectual property com. 2000-03, vice chair Sherman Act sect. 2003—), Houston Bar Assn. (chair antitrust and trade regulation sect., 1997-98, vice-chair 1996-97, sec.-treas. 1995-96, coun. 1993-95), Wong Sun Soc. Republican. Avocations: hiking, theater, travel. Home: 4908 Cedar St Bellaire TX 77401 Office: Univation Techs 5555 San Felipe Rd Houston TX 77056 Office Phone: 713-892-3779. Business E-Mail: achaves@univation.com.

CHAVEZ, JOHN RICHARD, historian, educator; b. Pasadena, Calif., Jan. 12, 1949; s. Manuel and Andrea (Quiroz) Chavez; m. Lorena Jeanne Poirier, Aug. 11, 1984; children: Monica Antonia, David Mario. BA in English, Calif. State. U., L.A., 1971, MA in English, 1972, BA in Spanish, 1975; MA in Am. Culture, U. Mich., 1978, PhD in Am. Culture, 1980. Lectr. Calif. State U., L.A., 1980-81, Long Beach, 1981-84; vis. asst. prof. program in Am. culture U. Mich., Ann Arbor, 1984-86; asst. prof. dept. history Tex. A&M U., College Station, 1986-89; assoc. prof. history So. Meth. U., Dallas, 1989-97, prof., 1997—. Fulbright lectr., Spain, 2001. Author: (book) The Lost Land: The Chicano Image of the Southwest, 1984 (nominated Pulitzer prize, 1984), Eastside Landmark: A History fo the East LA Community Union, 1998; contbr. articles to profl. jours. Mem.: Western History Assn., Nat. Assn. Chicano Studies, Am. Studies Assn. Democrat. Roman Catholic. Office: So Meth U Dept History Dallas TX 75275-0176 E-mail: jchavez@smu.edu.

CHAVEZ, LINDA, civil rights organization executive; b. Albuquerque, June 17, 1947; m. Christopher Gersten Chavez; 3 children. BA, U. Colo., 1970; postgrad., UCLA, 1970-72, U. Md., 1974-75. Mem. staff House Judiciary Subcom. on Civil and Constl. Rights, Washington, 1972-74; asst. dir. legis. Am. Fedn. Tchrs., 1975—77; cons. civil rights sect. Office Mgmt. and Budget, Washington, 1977; editor Am. Educator mag., 1977-83; asst. to pres. Am. Fedn. Teachers, 1982—83; staff dir. U.S. Commn. on Civil Rights, 1983-85; dep. asst. to pres. and dir. Office Pub. Liaison Exec. Office of Pres., 1985-86; US Senate candidate Md., 1986; chmn. Nat. Commn. Migrant Edn., 1988—92; mem. UN Subcommission on prevention of discrimination and protection of minorities, 1992—96; founder, pres. Ctr. for Equal Opportunity, Washington, 1995—, Stop Union Polit. Abuse, 2001—; founder, chmn. Rep. Issues Campaign, 2003—. Bd. dirs. ABM Industries, Inc.; polit. analyst FOX News Channel; Pres. George Bush's nominee for Sec. Labor until she withdrew her name from consideration, 2001. Author: Out of the Barrio: Toward a New Politics of Hispanic Assimilation, 1991, An Unlikely Conservative: The Transformation of an Ex-Liberal, 2002; syndicated weekly columnist Chgo. Tribune; freelance columnist Wall St. Jour., Washington Post, The New Republic, Commentary, Crisis; appeared on To the Contrary, CNN & Co., Equal Time, The McNeil-Lehrer News Hour; host (radio show) Linda Chavez Show. Bd. dirs. Campaign to Prevent Teen Pregnancy. Recipient Living Legend award, Libr. of Congress, 2000. Mem.: Coun. Fgn. Rels. (co-chair com. on diversity 1998—2000). Office: Ctr for Equal Opportunity 14 Pidgeon Hill Dr Ste 500 Sterling VA 20165-6151*

CHAVEZ, MARTIN JOSEPH, lawyer, mayor; b. Albuquerque, Mar. 2, 1952; s. Lorenzo Armijo and Sara (Baca) C.; m. Margaret Aragon de Chavez, July 29, 1988; children: Martinique, Ezequiel Lorenzo. BS, U. N.Mex., 1975; JD, Georgetown U., 1978. Staff asst. U.S. Senate, Washington, 1976-77; dep. dir. LULAC Nat. Scholarship Fund, Washington, 1977-78; law clk. N.Mex. Atty. Gen., 1978-79; pvt. practice, 1979-86, 87-93, 98—; first and founding dir. N.Mex. Workers Compensation Adminstrn., 1986-87; mem. N.Mex. Senate, 1988-93; mayor City of Albuquerque, 1993-97, 2001—. Mem. Med. Rev. Commn., 1990—; bd. dirs. Senior Arts Project, 1987—, Tree New Mex., 1991-92. Mem. Citizens Rev. Bd., 1988—; bd. dirs. N.Mex. First, Sr. Arts; founding mem., bd. dirs. Tree N.Mex.; mem. Citizens Adv. Bd., N.Mex. Med. Rev. Commn., U.S. Conf. Mayors (adv. coun., urban water coun., homeland security comm.), Nat. Conf. Dem. Mayors (vice chair fin., 2003), Albuquerque/Bernalillo Water Utility Authority (chmn. 2003); Dem. candidate for Gov., 1998. Recipient Outstanding Young Men of Am. award, 1984, Appreciation award Friends of Albuquerque Petroglyphs, 1989, Cert. Appreciation, Am. Merchant Marines, 1989, Disting. Svc. award N.Mex. Dietetic Assn., 1989, Appreciation award West Mesa Little League, 1989, Excellence in Edn. award Friend of Edn., 1990, Appreciation award FHP N.Mex., Inc., 1990, Devoted and Invaluable Svc. award Indian Pueblo Cultural Ctr., 1990, Recognition award Ind. Ins. Agts. N.Mex., 1991, Accomplishment, Dedication and Performance award West Mesa High Sch., 1991, N.Mex. State Meml. award, 1991, Exemplary Dedication and Svc. award Sec. of State, 1991, Cert. Spl. Appreciation, MADD, 1991, Disting. Svc. award Hispanic Bar Assn., 1992, Legis. Recognition award Dem. Party N.Mex., 1992, Commitment to Edn. award Alamosa Elem. Sch., 1992, Recognition and Appreciation award N.Mex. First, 1992, Dedication award Albuquerque Hispano C. of C., 1993, Pride of N.Mex. award Hispanic Round Table, 1993; named Outstanding Youth Advocate, Youth Devel., Inc., 1993. Mem. N.Mex. State Bar Assn. (Pub. Svc. Recognition award 1989). Avocation: fly fishing. Office: Office of the Mayor PO Box 1293 Albuquerque NM 87103*

CHAVEZ, MARY ANN, osteopathic family physician; b. York, Pa., Dec. 6, 1942; d. Henry David Gross and Mary Ellen (Ness) Rhoads; m. Richard L. Ziegler, Dec. 24, 1965 (div. Jan. 1983); children: Richard L. Ziegler Jr., Mara L. Tammaro, Brian L. Ziegler. BS, Alvernia Coll., 1983; DO, Coll. Osteo. Medicine, Phila., 1992. Legal sec. Louis Sager, Esquire, Pottstown, Pa., 1962-67; homemaker, tailor in pvt. practice Pottstown, 1967-85; intern Riverside Hosp., Wilmington, Del., 1992-93, resident in family practice, 1993-95; pvt. practice Spring Grove, Pa., 1995-97, Lancaster, Pa., 1997-999, Chillicothe, Ohio, 1999-2000, Sullivan, Ind., 2001—. Pell grantee, Beog grantee Alvernia Coll., 1979-83. Mem. AMA, Am. Osteo. Assn., Am. Coll. Osteo. Family Physicians, Am. Acad. Osteopathy, Pa. Osteo. Med. Assn., York County Osteo. Med. Assn, Nat. Osteo. Women's Physicians Assn., Ohio Osteo. Medicine, Ohio State Med. Soc., Ind. State Med. Assn., Sullivan Rotary Club, Sullivan Bus. and Profl. Women's Club. Avocations: painting, piano, tailoring, gardening. Home: 204 W Giles St PO Box 450 Sullivan IN 47882-0450 Office: Sullivan Med Clinic 222 W Beech St Sullivan IN 47882 E-mail: maryann.chavez@verizon.net.

CHAVEZ, NELBA R., state agency administrator, former federal agency administrator; b. Mar. 9, 1940; BA in Sociology and Psychology, U. Ariz.; MSW, UCLA; PhD in Philosophy, U. Denver; student sr. exec. program in state and local govt., Harvard U. From therapist to exec. dir., CEO, COO La Frontera Ctr., Tuscon, 1971-89; prin. Chavez and Assocs., 1989-91; dir. juvenile probation svcs. City and County of San Francisco, 1991-94; adminstr. Substance Abuse and Mental Health Svcs. Adminstrn., U.S. Dept. Health and Human Svcs., Washington, 1994-2000; dep. dir. Ariz Dept. Econ. Security, 2003—. Bd. dirs. nat. coalition of Hispanic Health and Human Svc. Organs,; mem. U.S. Senate Hispanic Adv. Com., Pres. Nat. Coun. on Handicapped, White House Prevention Com. on Drug-Free Am. Mem. Tuscon Mayor's Task Force on Children. Recipient Outstanding Leadership award Ariz. State U., 1985, Dedication and Commitment award Tenth Ann. Chicano Conf., 1989, Disting. Svc. award Nat. Assn. Profl. Asian Am. Women, 1995, Mujer 95 award League United L.Am. Citizens, 1995, Rafael Tavares, MD, Meml. award Assn. Hispanic Mental Health Profls., 1995, Nat. Health Leadership award Nat. Coalition Hispanic Health and Human Svcs., 1997, Leadership award Fedn. Families for Children's Mental Health, 1997, Nat. Coun. on Aging award for Leadership in Health Promotion, 2000; named to Honor Roll Latino Behavioral Health Inst., 1998. Office: Ariz Dept Econ Security PO Box 6123 Phoenix AZ 85005

CHAVEZ, VICTOR EDWIN, judge; b. LA, Aug. 28, 1930; s. Raymond C. and Sarah (Baca) C.; children: Victoria, Catherine, Stephanie, Christopher, Robert, Elizabeth. BS, Loyola U., L.A., 1953, JD, 1959. Bar: Calif. 1960. Mem. firm Early, Maslach, Foran and Williams, L.A., 1960-69, Pomerantz and Chavez, L.A., 1969-90; judge L.A. Superior Ct., 1990—, asst. presiding judge, 1997, 98, presiding judge, 1999—2000. Mem. exec. com. L.A. Superior Ct., 1996, 2003—04. Mem. com. State Bar Examiners, 1972-76; del. to State Bar, 1971-75; bd. regents Loyola Marymount U., 1973-78. 1st lt. USAF, 1953-55. Mem. ABA (standing com. on fed. judiciary 1979-86), L.A. County Bar Assn., Mex.-Am. Bar Assn. of L.A.(pres. 1971), Am. Bd. Trial Advocates (pres. L.A. chpt. 1979), Law Soc., Internat. Acad. Trial Judges, Nat. Conf. Met. Cts. (bd. dirs. 2000—, exec. com. 2000—). Office: Dept 96 111 N Hill St Los Angeles CA 90012-3117 Office Phone: 213-893-1021.

CHAVEZ-THOMPSON, LINDA, labor union administrator; b. Lubbock, Tex., Aug. 3, 1944; m. Robert Thompson (dec.); 2 children. Union sec. Am. Fedn. State, County & Mcpl. Employees, 1967-71, internat. rep., 1971-73, asst. bus. mgr., bus. mgr., exec. dir. local 2399, 1973-95, exec. dir. coun. 42, 1977-95, nat. v.p. labor coun. L.Am. Advancement, 1986-96, internat. v.p., 1988-96, exec. dir. Tex. Coun. 42, 1977-95; v.p. AFL-CIO, Washington, 1993-95, exec. v.p., 1995—. Office: AFL-CIO 815 16th St NW Washington DC 20006-4145

CHAVIN, WALTER, biological sciences educator, researcher; b. N.Y.C., Dec. 6, 1925; s. Isidor and Fanny (Kesch) C. BS, CCNY, 1946; MS, NYU, 1949, PhD, 1954. Rsch. asst. N.Y. Aquarium, N.Y.C., 1947-48; instr. dept. zoology U. Ariz., Tucson, 1949-51; rsch. specialist dept. fishes Am. Mus. Natural History, N.Y.C., 1951-53; prof. biol. scis. Wayne State U., Detroit, 1953-90, prof. emeritus, 1990—; prof. radiology Wayne State U. Med. Sch., Detroit, 1975-80; dir. Radiation Biology Inst. Wayne State U., Detroit, 1959-71. Research assoc. Argonne (Ill.) Nat. Lab., 1955-58. Contbr. 225 articles to profl. jours. NSF Sr. Postdoctoral fellow, 1960-61; Rsch. grantee NSF, AEC, NIH. Fellow AAAS (sec. 1978-85), N.Y. Acad. Scis.; mem. Nat. Assn. Photoshop Profls., Am. Physiol. Soc., Am. Soc. Zoologists (treas., sec.), Soc. Exptl. Biology and Medicine (com. 1986-90), Endocrine Soc., Am. Orchid Soc., South Fla. Orchid Soc., Pan Am Orchid Soc., Am. Bonsai Soc., Gold Coast Bonsai Soc., Lighthouse Bonsai Soc., Palm Beach Bonsai Soc., Sigma Xi (chpt. pres. 1974), Palm Beach Digital Imaging Group, Boca Raton Mus. Art, Art League. Independent. Home: 16484 Bridlewood Cir Delray Beach FL 33445-6678 E-mail: raja25@bellsouth.net.

CHAVKIN, JEFFREY S., lawyer; BA, Tufts U., 1972; JD, Boston U., 1975; LLM, NYU, 1981. Bar: NY 1976. Ptnr., group leader Banking, Bus. and Pub. Fin. Bryan Cave LLP, NYC. Office: Bryan Cave LLP 1290 Ave of the Americas New York NY 10104 Office Fax: 212-541-1261. E-mail: jschavkin@bryancave.com.

CHAVKIN, NANCY FEYL, social worker, educator; d. Sampson Benjamin and Olive Marie Feyl; m. Allan Richard Chavkin, Aug. 27, 1979; 1 child, Laura Michelle. BA, Dickinson Coll., 1972; MSW, U. Ill., 1974; PhD, U. Tex., 1984. LCSW Tex. Social worker U. Ill., Champaign, Ill., 1973—75; social work Champaign (Ill.) Pub. Schs., 1975—79; prof. Tex. State U., San Marcos, Tex., 1987—; rsch. assoc. S.W. Ednl. Devel. Lab., Austin, Tex., 1984—87. Co-dir. Ctr. Children & Families, San Marcos, Tex., 1998—2004, Title IV-E Project, San Marcos, 1995—; bd. dir. Richter Inst. Social Work Rsch., San Marcos; dir. masters social work Tex. State U., San Marcos, 1998—2000. Author: Families and Schools in a Pluralistic Society, 1993, The Use of Research in Social Work Practice: A Case Study in School Social Work, 1993; co-author: Conversations with Louise Erdrich and Michael Dorris, 1994. Recipient Outstanding Coll. Tchg. award, Minnie Stevens Piper Found., 2002; grantee, U.S. Dept. Edn., 1989—92, 1991—93, Tex. Dept. Health and Human Svcs., 1995—2000. Mem.: NASW, Am. Edn. Rsch. Assn., Coun. Social Work Edn., Phi Alpha, Phi Beta Kappa. Achievements include research in family involvement in education, school social work, child welfare, and partnerships. Office: Texas State University-Social Work 601 University Drive San Marcos TX 78666 Office Phone: 512-245-2593. Home Fax: 512-245-8097; Office Fax: 512-245-8097. E-mail: nancychavkin@txstate.edu.

CHAVOUS, KEVIN P., lawyer; b. Indpls., May 17, 1956; s. Harold and Betty Chavous; m. Beverly Bass; children: Kevin, Eric. BA in Polit. Sci., Wabash Coll., 1978; JD, Howard U., 1981. Bar: Colo. 1983, DC 1983, Md. 1990, Va. 1990, US Dist. Ct. Dist Colo. 1983, US Dist. Ct. DC 1984, US Dist. Ct. Ea. Dist Va. 1990, US Dist. Ct. Dist. Md. 1990, US Ct. Appeals 10th Cir. 1983, US Ct. Appeals DC Cir. 1985. Atty. DC Pub. Defender Svc., Cadeaux & Taglieri, Washington; city councilman Ward 7 Washington City Coun., 1993—2004, past chair Com. on Edn., Libraries and Recreation; of counsel Arent Fox Kinter Plotkin & Kahn, Washington, 1998—99, 2001—02; v.p. legis. affairs Covad Comm., 1999—2001; of counsel Sonnenschein Nath & Rosenthal LLP, Washington, 2002—. Adj. prof. law Am. U., 2001—. Mem.: ABA, Trial Lawyers Assn. of Met. Washington (bd. governors 1991—93), Assn. Trial Lawyers of Am., Md. State Bar Assn., Colo. Bar Assn., Washington Bar Assn. (bd. dirs. 1990—96), Denver Bar Assn. Democrat. Episcopalian. Office: Sonnenschein Nath & Rosenthal LLP Ste 600, E Tower 1301 K St NW Washington DC 20005 Office Phone: 202-408-6381. Office Fax: 202-408-6399. Business E-Mail: kchavous@sonnenschein.com.

CHAWLA, NIKHILESH, engineering educator; b. Rio de Janeiro, Jan. 8, 1972; arrived in US, 1984, naturalized; s. Krishan Kumar and Nivedita Chawla; m. Anita Chawla. BS, N.Mex. Tech., 1993; MS, U. Tenn., 1994; PhD, U. Mich., 1997. Rsch. fellow U. Mich./Ford Motor Co., Ann Arbor, 1997-98; sr. devel. engr. Hoeganaes Corp., Cinnaminson, NJ, 1999; asst. prof. materials engring., grad. chair Ariz. State U., Tempe, 2000—, assoc. prof. materials engring., 2003—. Contbr. articles to profl. jours.; patentee in field. Recipient R.L. Thakur Meml. award, Indian Ceramic Soc., 1998, Office Naval Rsch. Young Investigator award, 2001, Early Career award, NSF, 2001; grantee, U.S. Automotive Materials Partnership, 2000. Mem. ASM (Bradley Stoughton award for Young Tchrs., 2004), Minerals, Metals and Materials Soc. (former chair young leaders com., chair composite materials com.). Hindu. Avocation: violin. Office: Ariz State U, Fulton Sch Engring Dept Chem/Materials Engrg Tempe AZ 85287-6006 Office Phone: 480-965-2402.

CHAWLA, TEJPAL SINGH, lawyer; BA in Polit. Sci. magna cum laude, Boston U.; JD with honors, George Washington U. Sch. of Law. Bar: Calif. Supreme Ct., DC Ct. of Appeals, US Dist. Ct., DC. Atty. Office of US Trade Repr.; law clerk to Judge Deborah K. Chasanow Fed. Dist. Ct.; law clerk to Judge Ann O'Regan Keary DC Superior Ct.; atty. Office of Congressman Joseph P. Kennedy II; assoc. Crowell & Moring LLP, 1998—; now legal counsel Sikh Mediawatch and Resource Task Force. Comr. DC Commn. on Asian Pacific Islander Affairs, 2002—05. Mem.: Assn. of Sikh Professionals, S. Asian Bar Assn., Asian Pacific Am. Bar Assn., DC Bar Assn. Office: Sikh Mediawatch and Resource Task Force PO Box 1761 Germantown MD 20875-1761 also: Crowell & Moring LLP 1001 Penn Ave NW Washington DC 20004*

CHAWNER, LUCIA MARTHA, language educator; b. Ithaca, N.Y., Dec. 2, 1933; d. Lowell Jenkins and Lucia Mary (Soule) Chawner; m. Movses Guichen Andreassian, Mar. 18, 1967 (div. June 1971). Student, Earlham Coll., 1951-53; BA, U. Colo., 1956; MA, So. Meth. U., 1975. Provisional cert. elem., secondary and talented and gifted Tex., profl. cert. reading specialist Tex. Tchr. grade 7 lang. arts and social studies Stonewall Jackson, Dallas Ind. Sch. Dist., 1959-63; reading clinician Reinhardt, Dallas Ind. Sch. Dist., 1963-66; Reading Resource Pilot Project Lakewood, Dallas Ind. Sch. Dist., 1972-74; devel. curriculum specialist El Centro Coll., Dallas County C.C. Dist., Dallas, 1977-78; English tchr. Health Magnet, Dallas Ind. Sch. Dist., 1979-95; univ. supervising tchr. U. Tex. Dallas, Richardson, 1996—. Part-time instr. El Centro & Richland Colls., Dallas, 1978—88, Brookhaven Coll., Farmers Branch, Tex., 1996—98; mem. English lit. textbook adoption com. Dallas Ind. Sch. Dist., 1988—89, chmn. English dept. Health Magnet, 1989—94, mgr. innovative grant, 1994—95. Region 7 chmn., nat. bd. dirs. English-Speaking Union, 1996—2000; co-leader child and youth study U. Md., Dallas, 1967—69; pres. English-Speaking Union, Dallas, 1992—96, mem. nat. edn. com., 1996—; mem. Leadership Arts Dallas Bus. Com. Arts, 1994—95; mem. World Affairs Coun. Greater Dallas. Named Tchr. of the Yr., Health Magnet, 1991, Rotary Tchr. of the Yr., 1993; recipient Nat. Merit award, English-Speaking Union, 2000; Advanced Study grantee, Dallas Ind. Sch. Dist., 1973, Instrnl. grantee, Richland Coll., 1980. Mem.: Brit. Am. Bus. Coun., Assemblage (pres. 1987—88), Friends SMU Librs. (bd. dirs. 1995—98), Dallas Mus. Art League (bd. dirs. 1997—2004), New Conservatory Dallas (bd. dirs. 1999—, sec. 2002—), Dallas Knife and Fork Club (bd. dirs. 2003—), Soc. Mayflower Descs., Dau. Brit. Empire (sec. 2003—), Pi Lambda Theta (chpt. pres. 2002—), Phi Delta Kappa, Delta Delta Delta. Avocations: sculpture, needlepoint, fitness exercise, travel. Office: PO Box 141179 Dallas TX 75214-1179 Office Phone: 972-883-2730.

CHAYES, JENNIFER TOUR, mathematical physicist, educator; b. N.Y.C., Sept. 20, 1956; d. Eli and Hedy Tour; m. Christian Borgs. BA summa cum laude, Wesleyan U., 1979; PhD, Princeton U., 1983. Postdoctoral fellow Harvard U., Cambridge, Mass., 1983-85, Cornell U., Ithaca, N.Y., 1985-87; prof. math. UCLA, 1987—; prof. math. and physics U. Wash., Seattle, 1997—; mgr. theory group Microsoft Rsch., Redmond, Wash., 1997—. Mem. bd. math. scis. NRC, Washington, 1997—; bd. govs. Inst. for Math. and its Applications, Mpls., 1998-2000; bd. mem. external adv. bd. Ctr. for Discrete Math. and Computer Sci., New Brunswick, N.J., 1997—; mem. adv. com. Office on the Pub. Understanding Sci., NAS, Washington, 2000—. Contbr. articles to profl. jours. Sloan Found. Rsch. fellow Alfred P. Sloan Found., 1989, NSF postdoctoral fellow, 1984. Mem. AAAS, Am. Math. Soc. (v.p. 1998-2001), Am. Phys. Soc., Internat. Assn. Math. Physics. Office: Microsoft Rsch 1 Microsoft Way Redmond WA 98052 Office Fax: 425-936-7429. E-mail: jchayes@microsoft.com.

CHAZELLE, BERNARD, computer science educator; b. Clamart, France, Nov. 5, 1955; s. Jean and Marie-Claire (Blanc) C.; m. Celia Martin, June 26, 1982; children: Damien, Anna. Engring. diploma, Ecole Nat. Supérieure des Mines de Paris, 1977; PhD, Yale U., 1980. Rsch. assoc. Carnegie-Mellon U., Pitts., 1980-82; from. asst. prof. to assoc. prof. Brown U., Providence, R.I., 1982-86; assoc. prof. Ecole Normale Superieure, Paris, 1985-86, Princeton (N.J.) U., 1986-89, prof., 1989—. Cons. Xerox Parc, Palo Alto, Calif., 1984, DEC SRC, 1984-93. Editor Algorithmica, Siam Jour. Computing, Jour. Algorithms, Computer Geometry: Theory & Applications, Internat. Jour. Computations Geometry and Applications, Discrete and Computational Geometry, Jour. Assn. for Computing Machinery; contbr. articles to profl. jours. Fellow French Ministry Fgn. Affairs, 1977, J.S. Guggenheim Meml. Found., 1994, NEC, 1998—. Fellow: Am. Acad. Arts & Sci., Assn. for Computing Machinery; mem.: European Acad. Sci. Avocation: blues guitar. Office: Princeton U Dept Computer Sci Princeton NJ 08544-0001 Office Phone: 609-258-5380. Business E-Mail: chazelle@cs.princeton.edu.

CHAZEN, HARTLEY JAMES, lawyer; b. N.Y.C., Feb. 14, 1932; s. Joseph and Helen (Jacobson) C.; m. Lois Audrey, Dec. 12, 1967; 1 child, Nicole Joanna. AB, CCNY, 1953; LLB, Harvard U., 1958; LLM, NYU, 1959. Bar: N.Y. 1959. Assoc. Hays, St. John, Abramson & Heilbron, N.Y.C., 1959-65, Shea & Gould, N.Y.C., 1965-68, Rosenman & Colin, N.Y.C., 1968-70; ptnr. Monasch Chazen & Stream, N.Y.C., 1970-82; pvt. practice N.Y.C., 1982-88; ptnr. Chazen & Fox, N.Y.C., 1988—; of counsel McLaughlin & Stern, N.Y.C., 1992-2000. Lectr. in field. Capt. USAR, 1958-68. Mem. Assn. Bar City N.Y., ABA (subcom. corp. taxation 1987—), Harvard Club. Home: 75 Perkins Rd Greenwich CT 06830-3510 Office: Chazen & Fox 767 Third Ave Fl 35 New York NY 10017 Office Phone: 212-588-1818. E-mail: hchazen@chazenfox.com.

CHAZEN, LEONARD, lawyer; b. Feb. 26, 1942; BA magna cum laude, Yale U., 1963, LLB, 1967. Bar: NY 1971. Gen. counsel, asst. corp. counsel, Bur. of Budget City of NY, 1972—73; ptnr. Covington & Burling, NYC, mem. mgmt. com. Visiting lectr. securities law Yale U. Author: Fairness from a Fin. Point of View in Acquisitions of Pub. Companies: Is 'Third Party Sale Value' the Appropriate Standard?, 1981, The Shareholder Rights Bylaw: Giving Shareholders a Decisive Voice, 1997, What Investment Mgrs. Need to Know About Charters & Bylaws, 1999. Mem.: Legal Aid Soc. (dir. 1990—94), Assn. Bar City NY (securities regulation com. 1977—79). Office: Covington & Burling 1330 Avenue of the Americas New York NY 10019-1010 Office Fax: 212-841-1096, 212-841-1010. Business E-Mail: lchazen@cov.com.

CHAZEN, STEPHEN I., oil industry executive; b. Buffalo, N.Y., Aug. 26, 1946; s. Michael M. and Marcia Chazen; m. Patricia L. Orr, Dec. 18, 1971. AB, Rutgers Coll., 1968; PhD, Mich. State U., 1973; MS, U. Houston, 1977. Lab. mgr. Northrop Svcs., Inc., Houston, 1973-77; dir. project evaluation Columbia Gas Devel. Corp., Houston, 1977-81; v.p. Merrill Lynch, Houston, 1982-86, mng. dir. N.Y.C., 1987-93; exec. v.p. Occidental Petroleum Corp., L.A., 1994—2004, sr. exec. v.p, 2004—, CFO, 1999—. Dir. Lyondell Chem. Corp., Houston, Premcor Inc., Old Greenwich, Conn. Mem. L.A. C. of C. (dir. 1996—). Home: PO Box 427 Pacific Palisades CA 90272-0427 Office: Occidental Petroleum Corp 10889 Wilshire Blvd Los Angeles CA 90024-4201

CHE, YEON-KOO, economics professor; b. Daejon, Republic of Korea, Sept. 15, 1961; s. Yunshik Che and Wolhang Yoo; m. Jinsook Cho, June 23, 1992; children: Woojin Constatine, Eric Joonho. PhD, Stanford U., Stanford, Calif., 1991. Asst. prof. U. Wis., Madison, Wis., 1991—97, assoc. prof., 1997—2000, prof., 2000—05, Columbia U., N.Y.C., 2005—. Editor Jour. of Indsl. Economics, United Kingdom, 2003—. Recipient NSF, 2003, Romnes Prize, U. Wis. Found., 1999; fellow Jon Olin Faculty Fellowship, Jon Olin Found., 1996, Shoemaker Fellowship, U. Wis. Found., 2005, Mary Claire Phipps Fellowship, 2005; grantee NSF, 1996, 1998, 2000, 2002. Mem.: Econometric Soc. Office: Columbia U Dept Econs 420 W 118th St 1016L New York NY 10027 Office Phone: 212-854-8276. Business E-Mail: yc2271@columbia.edu.

CHEADLE, DON, actor; b. Kansas City, Mo., Nov. 29, 1964; Actor: (TV series) Fame, 1982, L.A. Law, 1986, Hill Street Blues, 1981, The Bronx Zoo, 1987, Hooperman, 1988, Night Court, 1984, Booker, 1989, China Beach, 1988, The Fresh Prince of Bel-Air, 1990, Picket Fences, 1992, The Golden Palace, 1992, Hangin' with Mr. Cooper, 1992, The Simpsons, 1989, The Bernie Mac Show, 2001, ER, 2002; (TV films) Lush Life, 1993, Rebound: The Legend of Earl The Goat Manigault, 1996, The Rat Pack, 1998 (Golden Globe award for Best Performance in a Supporting Role, 1999), A Lesson Before Dying, 1999, Fail Safe, 2000; (films) Moving Violations, 1985, Punk, 1986, Hamburger Hill, 1987, Colors, 1988, Roadside Prophets, 1992, The Meteor Man, 1993, Things to Do in Denver When You're Dead, 1995, Devil in a Blue Dress, 1995, Rosewood, 1997, Volcano, 1997, Boogie Nights, 1997, Bulworth, 1998, Out of Sight, 1998, Mission to Mars, 2000, The Family Man, 2000, Traffic, 2000, Things Behind the Sun, 2000, Manic, 2001, Swordfish, 2001, Rush Hour 2, 2001, Ocean's Eleven, 2001, The Hire: Ticker, 2002, The United States of Leland, 2003, The Assassination of Richard Nixon, 2004, (also prodr.) Crash, 2004, Hotel Rwanda, 2004, Ocean's Twelve, 2004. Office: William Morris Agy Attn Arnold Rifkin 151 El Camino Dr Beverly Hills CA 90212*

CHEADLE, LOUISE, music educator, musician; b. Donora, Pa., July 4, 1935; d. Max Raphael and Helen Louise Busto; m. William George Cheadle, Feb. 12, 1959 (dec. Dec. 1993); children: William Robert, Amy Louise Fleming. BMusic, The Juilliard Sch., 1959. Founder, dir. Westminster Conservatory of Music/Rider U., Princeton, NJ, 1972—82; head piano dept. Amherst Summer Music Ctr., Raymond, Maine, 1971—72; adj. instr. music Bucks County C.C., Newtown, Pa., 1982-85; nationwide concert tours and workshops, various mgmts. and agys., throughout U.S., 1980s; nat. adjudicator Nat. Guild Piano Tchrs., Austin, Tex., 1999—; freelance recitals, workshops and pvt. tchg. includes Lincoln Ctr., Carnegie Hall, N.Y.C., 1980—. Debut recital with Pitts. Concert Soc., 1954; contbg. author: Teaching Piano, 1981; CD release Virtuoso Piano Music by Cecile Chaminate and Fanny Mendelssohn-Hensel, 2002. Bd. dirs., chair Cmty. Outreach. Juilliard Sch. scholar, 1956-59. Mem. Music Tchrs. Nat. Assn., N.J. Music Educators Assn. (bd. dirs., v.p.), N.J. Music Tchrs. Assn. (chair Young Artist Competition 1999, 2000, chair Master Class Competition 1999, 2000), Rossmoor (N.J.) Music Assn. (bd. dirs.), Piano Tchrs. Congress N.Y., Music Club of Princeton. Avocations: writing, reading, cooking, cultural events. E-mail: chealou@aol.com.

CHEAH, KEONG-CHYE, psychiatrist, educator; b. Georgetown, Penang, West Malaysia, Mar. 15, 1939; came to U.S., 1959; s. Thean Hoe and Hun Kin (Keong) C.; m. Sandra Massey, June 10, 1968; children: Chylynn, Maylynn. BA in Psychology, U. Ark., 1962; MD, U. Ark., Little Rock, 1967, MS in Microbiology, 1968. Diplomate Am. Bd. Psychiatry and Neurology (examiner 1982, 85); cert. Ark. State Sci. Bd., Ark. State Med. Bd. Intern U. Ark. Med. Ctr., 1967-68; resident VA Med. Ctr. and U. Ark. Med. Ctr., Little Rock, 1968-72; chief addiction sect. Little Rock VA Med. Ctr., 1972-73, staff psychiatrist, 1975-80; chief psychiatry American Lake VA Med. Ctr., Tacoma, 1981-86; chief consultation, liason Am. Lake divsn. Puget Sound Health Care Sys., Tacoma, 1986-94; asst. prof. medicine, psychiatry U. Ark., Little Rock, 1975-81; asst. prof. psychiatry and behavioral scis. U. Wash., Seattle, 1981-86, clin. assoc. prof., 1987—2002, clin. assoc. prof. emeritus, 2002—. Mem. dist. br. com. The CHAMPUS, 1977-91; surveyor Jt. Commn. for Accreditation of Healthcare Orgns., 1990-93; site visitor AMA Continuing Med. Edn., 1979-83; book reviewer Jour. Am. Geriatrics Soc., 1984-85; mem. task force alcohol abuse VA Med. Dist. 27, 1984, survey mem. Sytematic External Rev. Process, 1985; mem. mental health plan adv. com. State of Ark., 1976-81, chmn. 1979-81, chmn. steering com., 1979; mem. Vietnamese Resettlement Program, 1979; many coms. Am. Lake VA Med. Ctr. including chmn. mental health coun. 1981-84, utilization rev. com., 1981-86. Contbr. articles and abstracts to profl. jours.; presenter to confs. and meetings of profl. socs. Mem. Parents Adv. Com., Lakes H.S., Wash., 1987-91; mem. Mayor's Budget and Fin. Foresight Com., 1992—, chmn. 1990-92; sch. cons. Child Study Ctr. U. Ark., 1972-74; bd. dirs. Crisis Ctr. Ark., 1974-79, chmn. pub. rels. com., 1975-79, mem. pers. com. 1974, vice chmn. bd. 1977; pres. Chinese Assn. Ctrl. Ark., 1977; mem. gifted edn. adv. coun. Clover Park Sch. Dist. 400, Wash., 1983-85, Parent Tchr. Student Orgn. Recipient U.S. Govt. scholarship 1959, cert. merit State of Ark., 1973, Leadership award, Mental Health Svcs. Divsn., State of Ark., 1980. Fellow Am. Psychiat. Assn. (sec. treas. Asian Am. caucus 1985-87, pres. 1987-94); mem. Assn. Mil. Surgeons U.S., Wash. State Psychiat. Assn. (mem. peer rev. com. 1982-92, chmn. pub. psychiatry com. 1985-93, exec. coun. 1985-93), N. Pacific Soc. Neurology and Psychiatry Assn. (sec.-treas. 1986-99, pres. 1993), S. Puget Sound Psychiat. Assn., Assn. Chinese-Am. Psychiatrists, Chapel of Four Chaplains, Ark. Caduceus Club, Alpha Epsilon Delta, Psi Chi, Phi Beta Kappa, Alpha Omega Alpha. Avocations: reading, target shooting. Personal E-mail: kccheah@comcast.net.

CHEATHAM, BELZORA, writer; b. Lodi, Tex., Mar. 13, 1932; d. Calvin and Hattie Geneva Brown; m. Andy Cheatham, Sept. 9, 1950 (dec. Jan. 1979); children: Jacqueline, Russell E., David R. Divsn. head Sears Roebuck & Co., Chgo., 1970-93. Author: Whittaker Cemetery Index, 1995, The History of Whittaker Memorial Cemetery, 1996 (Tex. Hist. Marker award 1996), Slaves and Slave Owners of Bowie County, Tex., 1850, 1996. Mem. Afro-Am. Geneal. and Hist. Soc. Chgo. (treas. 1992-97, pres. 1999-2001). Methodist. Avocation: genealogy. E-mail: mscheats@aol.com.

CHEATHAM, JOHN BANE, JR., retired mechanical engineering educator; b. Houston, June 29, 1924; s. John Bane and Winnie (Carr) C.; m. Juanita Faye Burns, July 19, 1947; children— Preston, Curtis. BME, So. Methodist U., 1948, MS, 1953; ME, M.I.T., 1954; PhD, Rice U., 1960. Registered profl. engr. Design engr. Linkbelt Co., Dallas and Houston, 1949-50; rsch. engr. Atlantic Refining Co., Dallas, 1950-53; rsch. assoc., head drilling rschr. Shell Devel. Co., Houston, 1954-63; prof. mech. engring. Rice U., 1963-96; chmn. dept. mech. engring. and materials sci., 1994-96; pres. Cheatham Engring. Inc., Houston, 1977-94, Techaid Corp., Houston, 1978-88. Cons. in field. Contbr. to profl. jours.; tech. editor: Jour. Energy Resources Tech, 1979-81. Served to 2d lt. USAAF, 1943-45. Fellow ASME; mem. Am. Inst. Mining and Petroleum Engrs., Sigma Xi. Address: 5671 Longmont Dr Houston TX 77056-2344 Personal E-mail: john_cheatham@hotmail.com.

CHEATHAM, ROBERT WILLIAM, retired lawyer; b. St. Paul, June 4, 1938; s. Robert William and Hildegard Frances Cheatham; m. Kay C. Sarnecki, Mar. 20, 1964; children: Ann Marie, Lynn Marie, Paul William. BCE, U. Minn., 1961, JD, 1966. Bar: Calif. 1967, U.S. Dist. Ct. (no. dist.) Calif. 1967. Assoc. Brobeck, Phleger & Harrison, San Francisco, 1967-74, ptnr., 1974-88, Cheatham & Skovronski, San Francisco, 1988-96, Cheatham & Tomlinson, San Francisco, 1996-97, Cassidy, Cheatham, Shimko & Dawson, San Francisco, 1997-2000, Foley & Lardner, San Francisco, 2000—04; ret., 2004. Speaker on continuing legal edn., San Francisco. Co-author: Calif. Attorneys Guide to Real Estate Syndicates, 1970, Cheatham and Merritt California Real Estate Forms and Commentaries, 1984-90. Mem. ABA, Calif. Bar Assn. Business E-Mail: rwcheatham@aol.com.

CHEATHAM, WALLACE MCCLAIN, music educator; b. Cleveland, Tenn., Oct. 3, 1945; s. Martin Luther and Ollie Frances (Simpson) Cheatham; m. Willie Faye Watson, May 22, 1971; children: Tosca Carmé, Kimberly Ann. BS, Knoxville Coll., 1967; MS, U. Wis., Milw., 1972, DFA, 2002; PhD, Columbia Pacific U., 1982. Music tchr. Knoxville (Tenn.) City Sch. Sys., 1967—68, Unified Sch. Dist., Racine, Wis., 1968—71, Milw. Pub. Schs., 1971—2003. Presenter, cons. in field; composer in residence Menasha (Wis.) H.S., 2004; dir. music Brookfield (Wis.) Presbyn. Ch. Contbg. author: Challenges in Music Education, 1976; editor: Dialogues on Opera and the African American Experience, 1997; recordings include: U. Maine Singers, Spiritual Fantasy, Beginnings, Let God Arise; contbr. articles to profl. jours.; composer: My Soul is a Witness, Dese Bones Gonna Rise Again, I Belong To That Band, You Must Come In Through The Door, Sinner, Please Don't Let This Harvest Pass, When the Roll is Called Up Yonder, Glory Hallelujah, My Hope Is Built, On Our Knees, Kwanzaa Songs, Anthology of Art Songs, I Am A Soldier, Praise, Thanksgiving, Missa, Portraits, O Holy Yahweh, Hymn Suite, Ode To An Organism, Children Go Where I Send Thee, For Unto Us A Child is Born, Symphony No. 1, String Quartet No. 1, Over My Head, Passacaglia and Fugue, Drinking Of The Wine, Dies Irae, Theme and Variations on Austria, Charge From A Pauline Epistle, Statements From The Light, Do Not Press Me To Leave You, Yonder Comes Mary, He Shall Purify The Sons of Levi, The Glory of The Lord, Fanfare and Tocatta, Tone Poem, Three Preludes, Ode to a Destiny, Done Made My Vow, Stone in the Road, Pied Piper of Hamelin, Walk About Elders, Umukoro Songs, The inaugural anthem for the investiture of Coppin State Coll. Pres. Stanley Battle, 2003, Fanfare, Cannon and Postlude, others. Participant Operation Crossroads Africa, 1966. Named Milw. Pub. Schs. Disting. Music Tchr., 2002; recipient Sullivan-Spaights Prof. Leadership award, U. Wis., Milw., 1999, Lifetime Achievement award, Civic Music Assn. Milw., 2000, Morris D. Hayes award, Wis. Choral Dirs. Assn., 2003, Achievement award, Unity Grand chpt. Order of Ea. Star State of Wis., Prince Hall Affiliation, 2003, Knoxville Coll. Outstanding Alumni of Nat. Prominence award, 2004; profiled on Milw. Pub. TV, 2005. Mem.: Nat. Assn. Negro Musicians (Ctrl. Region scholarship chair), Internat. Consortium for the Music of Africa and its Diaspora (bd. mem.), Wis. Alliance Composers, Am. Choral Dirs. Assn., Music Educators Nat. Conf., Am. Guild Organists (svc. playing cert.), Phi Beta Sigma. African Methodist Episcopal. Home: 2961 N Fifth St Milwaukee WI 53212 Office Phone: 414-374-4215. Personal E-mail: FChea44172@aol.com.

CHEATHAM, WANDA M., music educator; b. Memphis, June 29, 1952; d. Roy Bennett Cheatham, Billie Jewel Cheatham. BS in Music Edn., U. Memphis, 1974, MEd in Music, 1983; student fgn. study program, Univ. of So. Miss., Vienna, Austria, 1991, Glasgow (Scotland) U., 1995; student, Univ. of Miss., 1997. Elem. music tchr. Memphis City Schs., 1975—81; h.s. choral dir. Evangelical Christian Sch., Cordova, Tenn., 1981—. Audition and rehearsal pianist Theatre Memphis, 1998, 2001. Organist Ctrl. Ch., Memphis, 1972—83, First Evangelical Ch., Memphis, 1984—2001; organist/music dir. St. Andrews Presbyn. Ch., Cordova, 2001—. Named a Outstanding Young Woman of Am., 1983; recipient, 1985, Outstanding Tchr. award, Tenn. Gov.'s Sch. for Arts, 1993, 1997, 1999. Mem.: Tenn. Music Educators Assn., Music Educators Nat. Conf., Am. Choral Dir. Assn. Presbyterian. Avocations: antiques, travel, reading, walking, gardening. Office: Evangelical Christian PO Box 1030 7600 Macon Rd Cordova TN 38088 Office Phone: 901-754-7217. Office Fax: 901-754-8123. E-mail: wcheatham@ecseagles.net.

CHEATWOOD, ROY CLIFTON, lawyer; b. Rome, Ga., Aug. 27, 1946; s. Herman Arthur and Dorothy Mary (Griffin) C.; m. Cynthia Morrison, June 27, 1969; children: Clifton, Scott, Dancy. BA, U. South Fla., 1968; JD, Tulane U., 1974. Bar: La. 1974, U.S. Dist. Ct. (ea. dist.) La. 1974, U.S. Dist. Ct. (mid. dist.) La. 1975, U.S. Ct. Appeals (5th cir.) 1975, U.S. Dist. Ct. (we. dist.) La. 1977, U.S. Supreme Ct. 1977, U.S. Ct. Appeals (11th cir.) 1981, U.S. Dist. Ct. (no. dist.) Tex. 1990. Assoc. Jones, Walker, Waechter, Poitevent, Carrere & Denegre, New Orleans, 1974-78, ptnr., 1978-91, Phelps Dunbar, New Orleans, 1991—2003, practice coord., comml. litigation practice group, 1992—2003, mem. mgmt. com., 1995—2002; shareholder Baker, Donelson, Bearman, Caldwell & Berkowitz, New Orleans, 2004—, office mgn. ptnr., 2004—. Adj. prof. La. State U., Baton Rouge, 1980, Loyola U., New Orleans, 1981, 84-86; faculty mem. Nat. Inst. Trial Advocacy, 1986-2003; master barrister Tulane Inn of Ct. Co-author: Louisiana Courtroom Evidence, 1993. Firm campaign rep. United Way, New Orleans, 1982, 98, recruiter, 1983-86, 88, acct. exec. area laywers, 1989; bd. dirs. Children's Bur., New Orleans, 1988, 1st v.p., 1991, pres., 1993-95; mem. session St. Charles Presbyn. Ch., 1988-91, session New Covenant Presbyn. Ch., 2000—03, clk. of session, chair pastor-nominating com., 2000—02. 1st lt. U.S. Army, 1968-71, Vietnam. Mem. ABA (litigation sect./vice chmn. 5th cir. trial practice com. 1975-76, co-chmn. 1976-78, judge regional nat. appellate adv. com. 1978, co-chmn. ann. litigation meeting 1981, judge nat. appellate adv. competition 1978, membership chmn. litigation sect. 1983-86), La. State Bar Assn. (bd. legal specialization 1998-2004, chmn. 2000-02). Office: 201 St Charles Ave Ste 3600 New Orleans LA 70170 Office Phone: 504-566-5200. Business E-Mail: rcheatwood@bakerdonelson.com.

CHEAVENS, JOSEPH D., lawyer; b. Dallas, Aug. 27, 1940; s. David A. and Alice (Dawson) C.; m. Georgine Roberts, Aug. 15, 1964; children: Mark, Joseph, Elizabeth, Sarah. BA magna cum laude, Baylor U., 1962; JD cum laude, Harvard U., 1965. Bar: Tex. 1965, US Dist. Ct. No. So. Ea. dist. Tex., US Ct. Appeals Fifth Sixth Eleventh Cir., US Supreme Ct. Assoc. Baker Botts LLP, Houston, 1965-72, ptnr., chmn. trial dept. & mem. exec. com., 1973—. Adj. prof. So. Tex. Coll. Law, 1967-68. Gen. counsel Concert Chorale Houston, bd. dirs.; pres. Houston Internat. Seaman's Ctr., bd. dirs. Named a Texas Super Lawyer, Texas Monthly mag. & Law & Politics Mag., 2003—04; named one of Top 100 Houston Region Super Lawyers, Texas Monthly mag. Law & Politics mag., 2003—04. Fellow Am. Coll. Trial Lawyers; mem. ABA, Tex. Bar Assn., Houston Bar Assn., Maritime Law Assn. (chmn. com. on maritime legislation, bd. dirs. 1992-95). Office: Baker Botts LLP One Shell Plz 910 Louisiana St Houston TX 77002-4995 Office Phone: 713-229-1250. Office Fax: 713-229-2850. Business E-Mail: joseph.cheavens@bakerbotts.com.

CHEBAANE, MOHAMED, water management specialist, consultant; s. Mohamed Ben Ahmed and Nessria Chebaane; m. Sallouha Ayari, Sept. 29, 1961; children: Ahmed Karim, Mohamed Amine, Wafa, Maher. Diploma of Advanced Studies, Faculte des Sciences de Tuins, Tunisia, 1977; BSc in Agr. Engring., Institut Nat. Agronomique de Tuins, Tunisia, 1979; MSc in Water sci., U. Paris VI, France, 1980; MSc in Hydrology, O.R.S.T.O.M, France, 1981; PhD, Colo. State U., 1987. Sefl-employed internat. cons., Falls Ch., Va., 2002—; prin. devel. specialist Devel. Alternatives Inc., Bethesda, Md., 2003—. Lectr. Institut Nat. Agronomique de Tunis, Tunisia, 1981—; sr. water mgmt. specialist Ministry of Water Resources, Muscat, Oman, 1988—; self-employed internat. cons., Fairfax, Va., 1997—; team leader Assoc. for Rural Devel., Burlington, Vt., 1999—; chief tech. advisor FAO, UN, Entebbe, Uganda, 2001—; lead cons. World Bank, Wash., 2002—. Author: (article) Jour. of Hydrology, 2004, (book) Springs in the Sultanate of Oman (Ministerial award, 1995), (articles) water resources publs. Regional pres. Tunisian Sci. Soc., Ft. Collins, Colo., 1986—88. Mem.: Internat. Water Resources Assn. Achievements include development of a new concept of horizontal precipitation for measurement of fog precipitation; developed a new gauge that measures both rain (vertical component) and mist (horizontal component); a new stochastic model for intermittent processes such as seasonal rainfall and flows in intermittent rivers; invited by ASCE as one of four world panelists on water utilities and environmental management, special international session on Water Management, ASCE Annual Meeting, Salt Lake City, 2004; played a key role, when he served in FAO and the World Bank, in promoting the Nile Basin Initiative and building capacity in Transboundary Water Resources Management in the 10 Nile Basin countries; development of a participatory approach for groundwater management. Office: Development Alternatives Inc (DAI) 7250 Woodmont Ave Ste 200 Bethesda MD 20814 Office Fax: 301-718-7968. E-mail: mohamed_chebaane@dai.com.

CHECCHI, ALFRED A., air transportation executive, financial consultant; b. 1948; BA, Amherst Coll., 1970; MBA, Harvard Univ., 1974. V.p. Marriott Corp., 1975-82; with Bass Bros., 1982-86; pres. Alfred Checchi Assocs., Inc., 1986—; co-chmn., bd. dirs. Wings Holdings Inc., 1997—; bd. dirs. Northwest Airlines, Inc., St. Paul, 1997—, co-chmn., 1991—97; pres. Washington Strategic Ptnrs., 2002—. Exec. and adv. bd. mem. J.E. Robert Cos., 2002—; exec. adv. bd. mem. Elizabeth Glaser Pediat. AIDS Founds. Office: Washington Strategic Ptnrs c/o JE Robert Cos 1650 Tysons Blvd Ste 1600 Mc Lean VA 22102

CHECCHI, VINCENT VICTOR, retired economist; b. Calais, Maine, Nov. 25, 1918; s. Arthur R. and Dina I. (Pisani) C.; m. Mary E. Pate, Aug. 2, 1941; children: Dina Ann, Mary Jane, Vincent Arthur. AB, U. Maine, 1940; postgrad., Harvard U., 1941; MA, George Washington U., 1942. Various posts in U.S. Government, Allied Military Government, UNRRA, The World Bank, 1941-50; founder, CEO, chmn. bd. dirs. Checchi and Co., Washington, 1951—, ret., 2004, chmn. of bd., 2004—. Co-author: Honduras, A Problem in Economic Development; contbr. articles to profl. jours. Home: 9206 Watson Rd Silver Spring MD 20910-4136 Office: Checchi and Co 1899 L St NW Ste 800 Washington DC 20036-3804 E-mail: checchi@checchiconsulting.com.

CHECKETTS, DAVID WAYNE, sports executive; b. Salt Lake City, Sept. 16, 1955; s. Clyde Alvin and Edith (Jones) C.; m. Deb Leishman, June 2, 1977; children: Spencer, Katie, Nathaniel, Andrew, Benjamin, Elizabeth. BS, U. Utah, 1979; MBA, Brigham Young U., 1981. Mgmt. cons. Bain and Co., Boston, 1980-83; exec. v.p. Utah Jazz, NBA, Salt Lake City, 1983-84, pres., 1984-87, pres., gen. mgr., 1987-88, gen. mgr., 1988-89; v.p. devel. NBA, NYC, 1990—91; pres. NY Knickerbockers, NBA, 1991—94; pres., CEO Madison Sq. Gardens, 1994—2001; founder, chmn. Sports Capital Partners, 2001—; chmn. SportsWest Comm., 2002—; prin. owner, operator MLS franchise, Salt Lake City, 2004—. Bd. dirs. JetBlue Airways Corp., 2000—, Citadel Broadcasting Corp., 2002—, McLeodUSA Inc., 2004—. Trustee Salt Lake Visitor and Conv. Bur., 1986. Mem. LDS Ch. Lodge: Rotary. Avocations: basketball, golf, water sports, photography.

CHEDID, ANTONIO, pathologist, educator, researcher; b. Barranquilla, Colombia, May 5, 1939; came to U.S., 1966; s. Aziz Antonio and Maria (Turbay) C.; m. Hoda Abi-Rached; children: Anthony John, Marie-Claude, Erica Houda. BS, Coll. of Barranquilla, 1954; MD, U. Madrid, 1962. Diplomate Am. Bd. Pathology. Intern Columbus Hosp., Chgo., 1967-68; resident in pathology Michael Reese Hosp., Chgo., 1968-72; instr. pathology Pritzker Sch. Medicine U. Chgo., 1972-73; asst. prof. pathology U. Cin. Coll. Medicine, 1973-76; assoc. prof. pathology Chgo. Med. Sch., North Chicago, Ill., 1976-84, prof. pathology, 1985—, prof. microbiology and immunology, 1995—, prof. medicine, 1997—. Author: (pen name Anthony Strong) The Phoenicians in History and Legend, 2002; current work: immunology of alcoholic liver disease and hepatitis C; specialties include pathology, medicine, hepatology and immunology. Mem. Am. Assn. Pathology, Internat. Assn. for Study of the Liver, Am. Assn. for Study Liver Diseases, Am. Soc. for Cell Biology, Fedn. Am. Socs. Exptl. Biology, Internat. Acad. Pathology. Home: 650 Rockefeller Rd Lake Forest IL 60045-3142 Office: Rosalind Franklin U Chgo Med Sch 3333 Green Bay Rd North Chicago IL 60064-3037 Office Phone: 847-578-3409. E-mail: antonio.chedid@rosalindfranklin.edu.

CHEE, CHENG-KHEE, artist, educator; b. Xienyou, Fujian, China, Jan. 14, 1934; arrived in came to U.S., 1962, naturalized, 1980; s. Ya-Jie and Xien-chun (Zheng) C.; m. Sing-Bee Ong, Aug. 28, 1965; children: Yi-Hung, Yi-Min, Wan-Ying, Yen-Ying. BA, Nanyang U., Singapore, 1960; MA, U. Minn., 1964. Asst. libr. Nanyang U., 1961-62; tchg. asst. U. Minn., Mpls., 1963-64, libr. Duluth, 1965-68, instr., 1968-80, asst. prof., 1981-88, assoc. prof., 1988—. One-man shows include Zhejiang Acad. Fine Arts, 1984, 87, Tweed Mus. Art, U. Minn., 1982-83, 91-92, Shanghai U. Acad. Fine Arts, China, 1987, Tianjin Acad. Fine Arts, China, 1988, Phipps Ctr. for Arts, Wis., 1991, Cannon Rotunda U.S. Ho. Office Bldg., Washington, 1993, Singapore Nat. Art Mus., 1997, Minn. Mus. Am. Art, 1997, Bloomington Ctr. for Arts, Minn., 2003; exhibited in group shows Am. Watercolor Soc. Ann., Nat. Acad. and Salmagundi Club, N.Y.C., 1975, 78, 79, 81, 91, 94-95, 98, 2001, 03, Foothills Art Ctr., Golden, Colo., 1976, 78, 80, 84, 90, 92-93, Allied Artists Am., Nat. Arts Club, N.Y.C., 1980, 82, 91-97, 99-2001, 03, Cmty. Arts Ctr., Old Forge, N.Y., 1982-83, 86, 89, 91-92, 95-98, 2000, 02-04, Nat. Watercolor Soc. Ann. Exhbn., 1983-85, 92, 96, 2002-03, Knickerbocker Artists USA Ann. Exhbn., 1980-81, 89-93, Sumi-e Soc. Am. Ann. Exhbn., 1979-84, 86, Mitchell Mus., Ill., 1983, Mpls. Inst. Arts, 1978, Nat. Taiwan Art Edn. Inst. Watercolor Exhbn. Artist of Taiwan, U.S. and Australia, 1994; author portfolio Cheng-Khee Chee Watercolors, 1984, 87, 91, 94, 96, (book) The Watercolor World of Cheng-Khee Chee, 1997; author exhbn. catalog, 1973-82, Retrospective Exhbn., 1982, China Exhbn. Tour, 1987, Singapore Nat. Art Mus. Exhbn., 1997, Bloomington Art Ctr., Minn., 2003; contbr. to books: Watercolor Energies, 1983, Learn Watercolor, The Edgar Whitney Way, 1994, Splash 3: Ideas and Inspirations, 1994, The Best of Watercolor, 1995, Splash 4: The Splendor of Light, 1996; illustrator: (children's books) Old Turtle, 1992 (AABBY award, Internat. Reading Assn. award 1993), Splash 5: The Glory of Color, 1998, The Best of Watercolor, Vol. 3, 1999, Swing Around the Sun, 2003, Noel, 2005. Recipient Gold medal of honor Allied Artists of Am. exhibit, 1980, Knickerbocker Artists Exhbn., 1989, Silver medal of honor Am. Watercolor Soc. Exhbn., 1991, High Winds medal Am. Watercolor Soc. Exhbn., 1994, Grand award Akron Soc. Artists Grant Nat. Exhbn., 1994, Colo. Centennial award Rocky Mountain Nat. Watermedia Exhbn., 1976, Grumbacher Gold medal Midwest Watercolor Soc. Exhbn., 1984, 85, 98, Gold award Ga. Watercolor Soc. Exhbn., 1985, 98, Gold medal and Purchase prize Knickerbocker Artists 43rd Ann. Grand Nat. Open Juried Exhbn., 1993, Chancellor's Disting. Svc. award U. Minn., 1994, Silver award Calif. Watercolor Assn., 1998; named Best in Show Sumi-e Soc. Am., 1984, 86, New Orleans Art Assn. 11th Nat. Art Exhbn., 1986, Western Colo. Watercolor Soc. Ann. Nat. Exhbn., 1993, Red River Watercolor Soc. 1st Nat.

Art Exhbn., 1994, La. Watercolor Soc. 26th Ann. Internat. Exhbn., 1996, Duluth Arts and Cultural Cmty. Enrichment award, 2004; Duluth's Cultural Amb. to the World, Mayor Doty, 1994, Arts and Culture Cmty. Enrichment award Duluth Depot Found., 2004. Mem. Am. Watercolor Soc. (Dolphin fellow), Nat. Watercolor Soc., Rocky Mountain Nat. Watermedia Soc., Allied Artists Am., Knickerbocker Artists USA, Transparent Watercolor Soc. Am. (Master Watercolorist), Watercolor USA Honor Soc., Sumi-e Soc. Am., others. Home: 1508 Vermilion Rd Duluth MN 55812-1526 Office Phone: 218-724-2554. Home Fax: 218-724-6153.

CHEEK, JAMES H., III, lawyer, educator; b. Nashville, Nov. 28, 1942; s. James H. and Anne H. C.; m. Sigourney Woods, June 1, 1968; children—James Howe, IV, Daniel W., Matthew H. AB, Duke U., 1964; JD, Vanderbilt U., 1967; LL.M., Harvard U., 1968. Bar: Tenn. 1967. Assoc. firm Shearman & Sterling, N.Y.C., 1967; asst. dean, asst. prof. law Vanderbilt U. Law Sch., 1968-70, adj. prof. law, 1970—; ptnr. Bass, Berry & Sims, PLC, Nashville, 1970—; chmn. legal adv. com. N.Y. Stock Exch., 1989-92. Vis. fellow Jesus Coll., Cambridge U., 1985—86; cons. Securities and Investments Bd. U.K., 1985—86; cons. comml. crime unit Commonwealth Secretariat, 1985—86; trustee Elliott E. Cheatham Fund; pres. dean's coun. Vanderbilt U. Law Sch., 1986—89, pres. law alumni bd., 1997—99; chair San Diego Securities Regulation Inst., 2000—04; chmn. legal adv. bd. NASD Inc., 1996—98; lectr. CLE at seminars and insts.; chair Nat. ABA Task Force on corp. responsibility, 2002—03. Contbr. articles to law jours. Trustee SEC Hist. Soc., 2000—02, Montgomery Bell Acad., Nashville, 2000—; chmn. Met. Nashville Airport Authority, 2000—. Recipient Disting. Alumnus award Vanderbilt Univ., 1994. Fellow Tenn. Bar Found. (trustee 1993-97); mem. ABA (chmn. subcom. on 1933 Act 1978-85, sec. com. on corp. law 1980-85, chmn. fed. regulation of securities com. 1987-91, chmn. sect. bus. law 1998-99, chmn. nat. task force on corp. responsibility 2002-03), Nashville Bar Assn., Am. law Inst., Order of Coif, Belle Meade Country Club, Queen's Club. Home: 4404 Honeywood Ave Nashville TN 37205-3404 Office: Bass Berry & Sims PLC Ste 2700 AmSouth Ctr 315 Deaderick St Nashville TN 37238-3001 Business E-Mail: jcheek@bassberry.com.

CHEEK, JAMES RICHARD, ambassador; b. Decatur, Ga., Apr. 27, 1936; s. Woodrow Wilson and Dorothy (Webb) C.; m. Carol Ruth Rozzell, Sept. 1, 1957; children— Leesa Lynn, Forrest Craig, Surya Tamang BA, Ark. State Tchrs. Coll., 1959; M. Internat. Service, Am. U., 1961. Dep. chief mission Am. Embassy, Montevideo, Uruguay, 1977—79; dep. asst. sec. state U.S. Dept. State, Washington, 1979—81; dep. chief mission Am. Embassy, Kathmandu, Nepal, 1982—85, charge d'affaires, chief mission Addis Ababa, Ethiopia, 1985—88; diplomat-in-residence Howard U., Washington, 1988—89; U.S. amb. to Sudan Am. Embassy, Khartoum, 1989—92, U.S. amb. to Argentina Buenos Aires, 1993—96; global cons., amb. in residence U. Ark., Little Rock, 1997—; pres. Am. Internat. Airports, LLC, 2002—. Served to capt. U.S. Army, 1954-56 Recipient spl. commendation Women's Orgn., Dept. State, 1979, Disting. Alumnus award U. Ark., 1992, U. Ctrl. Ark., 1997. Mem. Am. Fgn. Service Assn. (William R. Rivkin award 1974) Avocations: antique clocks, fishing, trekking, playing squash. Home: 31 Saint Andrews Dr Little Rock AR 72212-2908 Office: U Ark 2801 S University Ave Little Rock AR 72204-1099 Office Phone: 501-225-8452. E-mail: arkiecheek@aol.com.

CHEEK, JIMMY GEARY, academic administrator, agricultural studies educator; b. Gorman, Tex., Sept. 7, 1946; s. Geary B. and Mayme (Wright) C.; m. Ileen Griffin, Aug. 23, 1969; children: Jennifer Leigh, Jeffrey Stewart. BS with high honors, Tex. A&M U., 1969, PhD, 1975; MEd, Lamar U., 1972. Agrl. edn. instr. Beaumont (Tex.) High Sch., 1969-73; supr. manpower tng. Beaumont Ind. Sch. Dist., 1971-73; grad. fellow Tex. A&M U., College Station, 1973-74, instr., 1974-75; asst. prof. U. Fla., Gainesville, 1975-80, assoc. prof., 1980-85, prof., 1985—, asst. dean for acad. programs Coll. Agr., 1992-99, dean Coll. Agrl. and Life Scis., 1999—2004, sr. v.p. for agr. and natural resources, 2005—. Cons., seminar leader Pa. Coop. Extension Svc., 1985, Dept. Agrl. and Extension Edn., Pa. State U., 1985; cons. Gainesville (Fla.) Bd. Realty, Inc., 1988, 89, 90, 91, 92; review team mem. So. Assn. Colls. and Schs., 1977, 78; reviewer various books. Sr. author: (with others) Effective Oral Communication, 2d edit., 2000. Chair Rawlings Elem. Sch. Adv. Com., 1982-83, 85-86; pres. Rawlings Elem. Sch. PTA, 1985, v.p., 1984; mem. Ft. Clarke Sch. Adv. Com., 1987—; mem. Hidden Oak Elem. Sch. Adv. Com., 1988-90. Recipient Hon. Tex. State Future Farmers Am. degree, 1972, Hon. Fla. State Future Farmers Am. degree, 1978, Hon. Am. Future Farmers Am. degree, 1984, Outstanding Rsch. Paper award So. Agrl. Edn. Rsch. Conf., 1984, 88, 92; Merit award scholar Tex. A&M U., 1967-69; named of the 30 Notable Grads. Coll. Edn., Tex A&M U., 1999. Fellow Nat. Assn. Colls. and Tchrs. Agr. (Ensminger-Interstate Disting. Teaching award 1990); mem. Am. Vocat. Ednl. Rsch. Assn. (pres. 1986), Fla. Vocat. Assn. (pres. 1992), Am. Assn. Agrl. Edn. (v.p. 1991-92, Disting. Svc. award 1998), Am. Vocat. Assn., Nat. Vocat. Agr. Tchrs. Assn. (Outstanding Svc. award so. region 1987), Fla. Vocat. Agr. Tchrs. Assn., Fla. Assn. Vocat. and Adult Tchr. Educators, Nat. Future Farmers Am. Alumni Assn., Assn. Internat. Agrl. Edn., U. Fla. Agrl. Alumni and Friends, Sigma Xi, Phi Kappa Phi (pres. 2003—), Gamma Sigma Delta, Alpha Zeta, Phi Delta Kappa, Iota Lambda Sigma, Alpha Gamma Rho (hon.). Office: Sr Vice Pres Agriculture Natural Resources U Fla PO Box 110180 Gainesville FL 32611-0180 E-mail: jgcheek@ufl.edu.

CHEEK, MICHAEL CARROLL, lawyer; b. Fostoria, Ohio, Aug. 28, 1948; s. Carroll Wright and Mabel A. (Smith) C. BA, Hanover Coll., 1970; JD, U. Cin., 1974. Bar: Ohio 1974, Fla. 1974, U.S. Dist. Ct. (mid. dist.) Fla. 1975. Pub. defender, Clearwater, Fla., 1974-77; lawyer sole practice, 1977—. Vice chmn. bar grievance Clearwater, 1990—94; trustee Pinellas County Law Libr., Clearwater, 1977—92; chmn. Ct. Law Libr., 1982—89. Pres. 1st Step Corp., Clearwater, 1986-93; vice chmn. Long Ctr. Found., Clearwater, 1994-95; founder Head Start Learn-to-Swim Program, 1994. With Ohio NG, 1970—74, with Fla. NG, 1974—76. Mem. Nat. Assn. Criminal Def. Lawyers, Pinellas Criminal Def. Assn. (v.p. 1987).

CHEEK, TODD DAVID, music educator; b. Peoria, Ill., Sept. 13, 1975; s. David Franklin and Helen Mae Cheek; m. Kimberly Rae Blunt, June 8, 2002; 1 child, Peyton Daniel. BA in Music Edn., Eureka Coll., 1997. Choral dir. Cissna Park (Ill.) Sch., 1997—2000, Pontiac (Ill.) H.S., 2000—. Mem.: NEA, Am. Choral Dir. Assn., Music Educators Nat. Conf. Office: Pontiac Twp High Sch 1100 Indians Ave Pontiac IL 61764

CHEEKS, MAURICE EDWARD, professional basketball coach, retired professional basketball player; b. Chgo., Sept. 8, 1956; Grad., West Tex. State U., 1978. Guard Phila. 76ers, 1978-89, San Antonio Spurs, 1989-90, N.Y. Knicks, 1990—93; asst. coach Phila. 76ers, 1994—2001, head coach, 2005—, Portland Trialblazers, 2001—05. Mem. Nat. Basketball Assn. All-Star Team, 1983, 86-88; NBA Champion Phila. 76ers, 1983. Office: Phila 76ers 3601 S Broad St Philadelphia PA 19148

CHEELY, DANIEL JOSEPH, lawyer; b. Melrose Park, Ill., Oct. 24, 1949; s. Walter Hubbard and Edith Arlene (Orlandino) C.; m. Patricia Elizabeth Dorsey, May 14, 1977; children: Mary Elizabeth, Daniel, Katherine, Laura, Anne-Marie, Thomas, Susan, Michael, William. AB, Princeton U., 1971; JD, Harvard U., 1974. Bar: Ill. 1974, U.S. Dist. Ct (no. dist.) Ill. 1975, U.S. Ct. Appeals (7th cir.) 1975. Ptnr. Baker & McKenzie, Chgo., 1974-81, ptnr. litigation, 1981-85, capital ptnr. litigation, 1985-94; ptnr. Mauck, Bellande & Cheely, Chgo., 1994-2000, Bellande, Cheely & O'Flaherty, Chgo., 2000—05, Cheely, O'Flaherty & Ayres, Chgo., 2005—. Liaison counsel Asbestos Claims Facility, Chgo., 1985-88, bus. devel. com., 1987-90, Chgo. assoc. train com., 1988-91, chmn. Chgo. assoc. evaluation; liaison coun. Com. for Claims Resolution, 1988-89; cons. Midwest Theol. Forum, 2003—. Advisor Midtown Sports and Cultural Ctr., Chgo., 1974—; mem. River Forest Regular Reps., Ill., 1980-88, Ill. Rep. Assembly, Chgo., 1984—; pres. Cath. Evidence Forum, 1984—; pres. Ch. History Forum, 1994—; dir. Cath. Citizens of Ill., 1997—; bd. dirs. Cath. Lawyers Guild, 2000—; cons. Midwest Theological Forum, 2003-. Mem. ABA (vice chmn. environ. law sect. 1989-97), Ill. Bar Assn., Appellate Lawyers Soc. Ill., Chgo. Bar Assn., Trial Lawyers Club. Chgo., Serra Club (v.p. Chgo. chpt. 1988-89, 92-94, 96—, treas. 1989-92), United Rep. Fund, Phi Beta Kappa. Roman Catholic. Avocations: history, parent effectiveness training, education, christian apologetics, historical travel consulting. Office: Cheely O'Flaherty & Ayres 19 S La Salle St Ste 1203 Chicago IL 60603-1406 Office Phone: 312-853-8714. Business E-Mail: dcheely@lawchicago.net.

CHEEMA, ZAFARULLAH K., management consultant; b. Gakkhar, Pakistan, Apr. 21, 1934; arrived in U.S., 1957; s. Nasrulla Khan Cheema and Aisha Bibi Varraich; m. Bilquees Cheema, Aug. 12; children: Yusufullah, Shahjehan. BS in Pharmacy, U. Punjab, 1954; PhD, U. Tübingen, 1957; MBA, U. Chgo., 1983. Prof., chmn., chemistry dept. Knoxville (Tenn.) Coll., 1960—64; tech. supr. Allied Chem. (Honeywell), Morristown, NJ, 1964—71; prof., chmn., chemistry dept. Fairleigh Dickinson U., Madison, NJ, 1967—68; rsch. mgr. Keuffel and Essex Co., Morristown, NJ, 1971—78; v.p. Richarson Co. (WITCO), Melrose Pk., Ill., 1978—84, Polaroid Graphic Imaging, Waltham, Mass., 1985—2001. Cons. Oak Ridge (Tenn.) Nat. Lab., 1961—64, AMOCO Ctrl. Rsch., Napervill, Ill., 1984. Author: (publs.) Jour. Am. Chem. Soc., 1963—64. Achievements include patents for commercially successful products. Avocations: tennis, golf, hiking, reading, travel. Home: 5 Joan Ave Sudbury MA 01776 Business E-Mail: zcheema@gsb.uchicago.edu.

CHEESEBORO, MARGRIT, economics educator; b. Zurich, Switzerland; BA of Bus. Mgmt., U. Redlands, 1980; MSEd, U. So. Calif., 1981; MA in Ednl. Adminstrn., Calif. State U., L.A., 1982; postgrad, UCLA, 1990. Cert. tchr. and adminstr. Sch. office adminstr. Mid-City Alternative Sch., L.A., 1973-80; tchr. econ., govt., U.S. and world history Crenshaw H.S., L.A., 1982—; LEARN lead tchr., mentor tchr., chpt. chmn., co-chmn. governing bd., 1991-98. Bd. dirs. Baldwin Village Cmty. in Action, 1998—. Mem. United Tchrs. L.A. (chpt. chmn. 1991-98), Kappa Delta Pi. Home: 3525 S Bronson Ave Los Angeles CA 90018-3636

CHEESMAN, JOHN MICHAEL, corporate financial executive; b. Wichita, Kans., Feb. 4, 1943; s. Norman Carlyle and Anne Lucille (Norris) C.; m. Sharon Lindsey, Feb. 8, 1964 (div. 1968); children: Mary Kathleen, Deborah Kristine; m. Oksun Elledge, Aug. 29, 2000; children: James Richard, Anthony Wayne Elledge. AA in Math., Social Scis., Wichita State U., BBA, 1986, MA in Social Scis., 1987; MBA, W. Frank Barton Sch. Bus., Wichita, 1997; diploma, Inst. Lit., West Redding, Conn., 1993, grad. diploma, 1996; MS, Newman U., 2000. Cert. quality engr., Kans. Mgr. Guardian Industries, Wichita, 1966-72; supr. Cessna Aircraft Corp., Wichita, 1972-78; stats. analyst Boeing Airplane Co., Wichita, 1978-85; lead engr. Boeing Mil. Airplanes, Wichita, 1985-89; coord. prodn. conformance Boeing Comml. A/P Group, Wichita, 1994—2002; pres., CEO Portfolio Fin. Group, Inc., Wichita, Kans., 2004—. Founder, funder Mike Cheesman Endowed Bus. Scholar, Wichita State U. Found. Ebndowment Fund, 1997. Vol. United Meth. Urban Ministries Wichita, 1984—; numerous positions local and regional chpts. Boy Scouts Am., including commr. of scouting Quivira coun., Wichita; nat. staff mem. Boy Scouts Am., Fort A.P. Hill, Va., phys. arrangements group 1985, 89, 93, 97; leader United Meth. Men and Boys Retreat Youth Ministries, 1984—; chmn. United Meth. Neighborhood Outreach, 1988—; institutional rep. United Meth. Coun. on Ministries, Wichita; active Wichita-Sedgwick County Hist. Mus. Assn., 1985—, Rep. Nat. Com., 1981—, Nat. Rep. Congl. Com., 1986—, Wichita Children's Home, 1989—, Big Bros./Big Sisters, Wichita/Sedgwick County, 1989—; vol. leader Wichita Spl. Olympics, 1985—, chmn.; chmn. adv. bd. Rep. Nat. Com., 1994—; bd. dirs. Dept. Human Svcs., City of Wichita, 1991—, Citizens Participation Orgn., City of Wichita, 1998—; mem. state bd. examiners Kans. Award for Excellence Found., 2002—; commd. col. Conf. Air Force, 1985, Commemorative Air Force, 2000. Recipient Campaign Victory cert., 1983, Presdl. Achievement award Rep. Nat. Com., 1986, cert. of merit, 1990, Congl. cert. of appreciation, 1991; Presdl. cert. of recognition, 1991; Presdl. cert. of appreciation, 1992; Vice presdl. cert. of commendation, 1992; Congl. cert. of merit, 1992, Eisenhower Commn., 1995; George Meany award Nat. Fedn. Unions, 1986, God and Svc. award United Meth. Ch., 1986, Torch award Kans. West conf. United Meth. Ch., 1986, 88, Community Vol. of Yr. awards Boeing Co., 1987-89, Cross and Flame award United Meth. Ch., 1988, 91, Award of Merit Boy Scouts Am., 1988, God and Svc. award Presbyn. Ch. U.S.A., 1991, William M. Allen award Boeing Corp., 1989, Cert. of Appreciation Nat. Rep. congl. Com., 1990, 91, Wichita's First Citizen award First Nat. Bank, 1992, Disting. Commr. award Boy Scouts Am., 1993, Silver Beaver award Boy Scouts Am., 1993, Eagle Scout award Boy Scouts Am.; James E. West fellow, 1994; inducted as air and space leader NASA Exploration Wall of Honor/Smithsonian Air and Space Mus.; named Ky. col. Hon. Order of Ky. Cols., 1994. Mem. AIAA (sr.), Am. Computer Scientists Assn., Am. Mgmt. Assn., Adminstrv. Mgmt. Soc., Am. Soc. for Quality Control, Am. Assn. Family Counselors (cert. profl. counselor, nat. adv. bd. 1995—), Wichita State U. Alumni Assn. (life), Wichita State U. Soc. of 1895 (life), Wichita State U. Endowment Assn. (life), The Royal Aero. Soc., The Am. Air Mus. in Britain, Wichita Aero. Hist. Assn./Kans. Aviation Mus., U.S. Hist. Soc., United Meth. Men (past pres.), Nat. Assn. United Meth. Scouters (charter life, coord./chartered orgnl. rep.), Nat. Assn. Presbyn. Scouters (life), Nat. United Ch. of Christ Assn. Scouters (charter life Nat. Adv. Coun. 1984—), Orders and Medals Soc. Am., Medal of Honor Hist. Soc., Token and Medal Soc. Am., New Life Club (charter), The Augustan Soc. (charter), Masons (32 degree), Ky. Cols., Scottish Rite, York Rite, Shriners. Achievements include founded Mike Cheesman Endowed Bus. Scholarship Fund, Wichita State U. Found. Endowment Fund, 1997. Avocations: collecting, travel, reading.

CHEESMAN, KERRY LEE, biology educator, researcher; b. Santa Barbara, Calif., Sept. 28, 1954; s. Theodore Richard and Barbara Jean (Wyckoff) C.; m. Sara Day Cheesman, June 17, 1978; children: Ian Walling, Nathan Elisha. BA, U. Calif., Santa Barbara, 1976; PhD, U. Ill., 1981; MS, Ind. U., 1987. Rsch. asst. U. Ill. Med. Ctr., Chgo., 1977-80; rsch. assoc. Med. Sch. Northwestern U., Chgo., 1981-82, asst. prof., 1983-86, St. Francis Coll., Ft. Wayne, Ind., 1987-90, assoc. prof., 1991-92, Capital U., Columbus, Ohio, 1993—96, prof., 1996—, chair biology dept., 1994—2001. Assoc. dir. endocrine labs. Northwestern U. Med. Sch., Chgo., 1983-86; dir. med. tech. program St. Francis Coll., 1989-92; health prof. dir. Capital U., 1993-. Editor: Ohio Jour. Sci., 2004—. Bd. dirs. Habitat for Humanity, Ft. Wayne, 1985-92, Boy Scouts Am., Ft. Wayne, 1985-92, Columbus, Ohio, 1994—, Boy Scouts Am. Nat. Coun., 1999-, Native Am. Indian Ctr., Columbus, 1996-, Ohio Sci. & Ednl. Rsch. Assn., 1997-, Central Assn. Adv. in the Health Professions, 2002-. U. Calif. scholar, 1972. Mem. AAAS, Endocrine Soc., Soc. for Study Reprodn., Soc. for Health and Human Values, Soc. for Coll. Sci. Tchrs., N.Am. Assn. Environ. Edn., N.Y. Acad. Scis., Ohio Acad. Scis. (bd. dirs. 2004—), Nat. Sci. Tchrs. Assn., Nat. Assn. Biology Tchrs. Avocations: camping, backpacking, working with youth. Office: Capital U Biol Scis Dept 1 College and Main Columbus OH 43209-2394 Office Phone: 614-236-6951. E-mail: kcheesma@capital.edu.

CHEETHAM, ALAN HERBERT, paleontologist; b. El Paso, Tex., Jan. 30, 1928; s. Herbert and Hildegard Marguerite (Moreton) C.; m. Marjorie Rogers, Apr. 20, 1951; children: Alan Christopher, Jan Alison, Susan Hilarie, Hilary Taber. BS, N.Mex. Inst. Mining & Tech., 1950; MS, La. State U., 1952; PhD, Columbia U., 1959. Instr. paleontology La. State U., Baton Rouge, 1954-60, asst. prof., 1960-63, assoc. prof., 1963-66, cons. prof., 1966-72; assoc. curator Smithsonian Instn., Washington, 1966-69, curator, 1969-87, sr. invertebrate paleontologist, 1987-2001, sr. scientist emeritus, 2001—. Guest prof. U. Stockholm, 1964—65; adj. prof. U. N.Mex., 1994—97. Author: Geological Society of America, Memoir 91, 1963; editor: Animal Colonies, 1973, Fossil Invertebrates, 1987; contbr. articles to profl. jours. Recipient Raymond C. Moore medal for paleontol., 1997, Disting. Achievement Alumni award, N.Mex. Inst. Mining and Tech., 1990; fellow Humble Oil Co., 1951, NSF, 1952, 1961. Fellow: AAAS; mem.: Paleontol. Rsch. Instn., Soc. Sedimentary Geology, Paleontol. Soc. (medal 2001), Internat. Bryozoology Assn. Home and Office: 3101 Old Pecos Trail 647 Santa Fe NM 87505 Office Phone: 505-955-1840. Business E-Mail: cheetham@si.edu.

CHEEVER, GEORGE MARTIN, lawyer; b. Boston, Jan. 13, 1947; s. Francis Sargent and Julia Whitney (Martin) C.; m. Mary Margaret Duplain, Feb. 10, 1979; children: Charles Duplain, Frances Sargent, Mary Conner. AB, Harvard U., 1969; JD, U. Pa., 1973. Bar: Pa. 1973, U.S. Dist. Ct. (we. dist.) Pa. 1973, U.S. Ct. Appeals (3d cir.) 1978, U.S. Ct. Appeals (4th cir.) 1985, U.S. Ct. Appeals (7th cir.) 2004, U.S. Supreme Ct. 1992. Law clk. to assoc. justice Pa. Supreme Ct., Pitts., 1973—74; assoc. Kirkpatrick & Lockhart, LLP, Pitts., 1974—82; ptnr. Kirkpatrick & Lockhart Nicholson Graham, LLP, Pitts., 1982—. Mem. ABA, Am. Bankruptcy Inst., Pa. Bar Assn., Allegheny County Bar Assn., Turnaround Mgmt. Assn., Comml. Law League. Office: Kirkpatrick Lockhart Nicholson Graham LLP Henry W Oliver Bldg 535 Smithfield St Pittsburgh PA 15222-2312 Office Phone: 412-355-6544. E-mail: gcheever@klng.com.

CHEEVER, SUSAN, writer; b. N.Y.C., July 31, 1943; d. John and Mary Watson (Winternitz) C.; m. Robert Cowley, May, 1967 (div. 1975); m. Calvin Tomkins, II, Oct. 1, 1982; m. Warren James Hinckle III, June 10, 1989; children: Sarah Liley Cheever Tomkins, Warren James Hinckle IV. BA, Brown U., 1965. Tchr., Colo. Rocky Mountain Sch., Colo., 1965-67, Scarborough Sch., N.Y., 1968-69; writer Westchester-Rockland Newspapers, N.Y., 1970-72; editor, writer Newsweek Mag., N.Y., 1974-78; free lance writer, N.Y., 1978—; council mem. Authors Guild. Author: Looking for Work, 1980, A Handsome Man, 1981, The Cage, 1982, Home Before Dark, 1984, Doctors and Women, 1987, Elizabeth Cole, 1989, Treetops: A Famiy Memoir, 1991, A Woman's Life, 1994, Note Found In A Bottle, 1999, As Good As I Could Be, 2001, My Name is Bill, Bill Wilson's Life, 2004. Recipient Associated Press award, 1970; Guggenheim Found. fellow, 1984, nominee Nat. Book Critics Circle, 1984. Mem. Pen/Am. Ctr., Authors League. Democrat. Episcopalian E-mail: susancheever@aol.com.

CHEEVES, AMATINE CONNELLY, realtor; b. Sherman, Tex., Mar. 19, 1916; d. Ernest F. and Sallie Isabel Mercer; m. Tom Sylvester Connelly (dec. 1961); children: Mary Louise Connelly, Jack Joseph Connelly, Sylvia Ann Connelly; m. Ray Cheeves (dec.). Degree, Abilene Christian Coll., 1934. Cert. realtor. Realtor Connelly Realty, Dallas, 1952—. Named Tex. Woman Realtor of the Yr., 1972. Mem.: Tex. Women Coun. of Realtors (pres. 1972). Home: 1911 Newport Dallas TX 75224 Office: Connelly Realty 2743 S Hampton Rd Dallas TX 75224

CHEFITZ, JOEL GERALD, lawyer; b. Boston, Aug. 27, 1951; s. Melvin L and Bernice L (Kahn) Chefitz; m. Sharon P Garfinkel, 1972; children: Sandra Beth, Meira Sarah, Michael Hanan. AB cum laude, Boston U., 1972, JD magna cum laude, 1976. Bar: Ill 1976, US Dist Ct (no Dist) Ill 1977, US Ct Appeals (3d cir) 1981, US Supreme Ct 1983, US Ct Appeals (7th cir) 1984, US Ct Appeals (9th cir) 1993, US Ct Appeals (2d cir) 1994, US Ct Appeals (5th cir) 1996, US Ct Appeals (4th cir) 1998, US Ct Appeals (fed cir) 2000, US Ct Appeals (DC cir) 2001. Law clk. to presiding justice U.S. Dist. Ct. Mass., Boston, 1976-77; assoc. Kirkland & Ellis, Chgo., 1977-82, ptnr., 1982-86, Katten Muchin & Zavis, Chgo., 1986—2002, Howrey Simon Arnold & White, Chgo., 2002—. Editor: (jour) Boston Univ Law Rev, 1975—76; contbr. articles to profl jours. Bd. dirs. Legal Assistance Found. Met. Chgo., Gastrointestinal Rsch. Found. Scholar Am Jurisprudence, Boston Univ, 1973—76, CJS, 1975, Bigelow, 1976. Mem.: ABA, 7th Cir Asn, Chicago Bar Asn, East Bank Club. Office Phone: 312-595-1522. E-mail: chefitzj@howrey.com.

CHEH, HUK YUK, electrochemist, battery company executive; b. Shanghai, Oct. 27, 1939; s. Tze Sang and Sue Lan (Che) C.; m. An-li, July 26, 1969; children: Emily, Evelyn. BASc in Chem. Engring., U. Ottawa, Can., 1962; PhD in Chem. Engring., U. Calif., Berkeley, 1967. Mem. tech. staff AT&T Bell Labs., N.J., 1967-70; asst. prof. chem. engring. Columbia U., N.Y.C., 1970-73, assoc. prof., 1973-79, prof., 1979-82, Ruben-Viele prof., 1982—2001, Ruben-Viele prof. emeritus, 2001—, chmn. dept., 1980-86; v.p. tech. Duracell, Inc., 1999—. Program dir. NSF, 1978-79; vis. rsch. prof. Nat. Tsinghua U., Taiwan, 1977 Vice editor Chinese Battery Industry Jour.; contbr. articles to sci. jours.; patentee in biomaterials and in electrophoresis. Recipient Harold C. Urey award, 1980, sci. achievement award Am. Electroplaters and Surface Finishers Soc., 1989. Fellow Electrochem. Soc. (Electrodeposition Rsch. award 1988, Battery Tech. award 2000); mem. AIChE, Am. Electroplaters Soc., N.Y. Acad. Scis., Sigma Xi. Office: Duracell Berkshire Corp Park Bethel CT 06801 Office Phone: 203-796-4169. Business E-Mail: Huk_Cheh@Gillette.com.

CHEIT, EARL FRANK, economist, educator; b. Mpls., Aug. 5, 1926; s. Morris and Etta (Warshausky) C.; m. June Doris Andrews, Aug. 28, 1950; children: Wendy, David, Ross, Julie. BS, U. Minn., 1947, LLB, 1949, PhD, 1954. Rsch. economist, prof. Sch. Bus. Adminstrn. U. Calif., Berkeley, 1960—, exec. vice chancellor, 1965-69, dean Sch. Bus. Adminstrn., 1976-82, 90-91, dean emeritus Sch. Bus. Adminstrn., 1991—; dir. Inst. Indsl. Rels. Program officer in charge higher edn. and rsch. Ford Found., 1972-73; assoc. dir., sr. rsch. fellow Carnegie Coun. on Policy Studies in Higher Edn., 1973-75; sr. adv. con. Asian-Pacific econ. affairs Asia Found.; dir. CNF Transp., Inc., Shaklee Corp., 1976-2001, Simpson Mfg. Corp. Author: The Useful Arts and the Liberal Tradition, 1975, The New Depression in Higher Education, 1971, Foundations and Higher Education, 1979; editor: The Business Establishment, 1964. Trustee Richmond (Calif.) Unified Sch. Dist., 1961-65, Russell Sage Found., NYC, 1979-89, Mills Coll., 1991-; chmn. State of Calif. Wage Bd. for Agrl. Occupations, 1980-81. Office: U Calif Haas Sch Bus Berkeley CA 94720-1900 Office Phone: 510-642-2448. Business E-Mail: cheit@haas.berkeley.edu.

CHEITEN, MARVIN HAROLD, playwright, manufacturing executive; b. New Brunswick, N.J., Apr. 24, 1943; s. Samuel and Sarah (Peretzman) Cheiten. AB, Princeton U., 1965, MA, 1967, PhD, 1971. Ptnr. The Water Master Co., Highland Park, N.J., 1971-76, v.p., 1976-86, pres., 1986—. Author: (plays) Trial by Fire, 1972, Queen Jane, 1976, The Vault, 1978, The Golden Spy, 1996, Chowder, She Wrote, 1996, Le Coq d'Or, 2000, Zenobia, 2004, Miss Connections, 2005, (novella) The Long Hello, 1995, (essays) The fate of Princeton Graduate School, 1991, Touching a Goddess, 1996, Two Voices in the Darkness, 1997, To the Millstone, 1997, Escape from Raritan Prep, 1998, Songs for My Love, 2000, Return of the Plymouth, 2004, (lyrics) The Inn Cabaret, 1978—80, Deborah, 1996, A Princess in Death, 1998, Dorothea, 2000, Terry Catherine, 2001, Ballade to 911, 2002, The Hunting of the Deer, 2002, Go On, 2004, A Little English Girl, 2005; contbr. short stories; mem. editl. bd.: Princeton Alumni Weekly, 1983—87. Trustee Princeton Symphony Orch., 1993—, Friends of Theatre Intime, 1996—; mem. coun. Princeton U. Libr., 2002—; bd. dirs. Princeton Rep. Assn., 1972—74. Mem.: Alliance L.A. Playwrights, Dramatists Guild, Assn. Princeton Grad. Alumni (gov. bd. 1973—88), Campus Club, Nassau Club. Jewish. Office: The Water Master Co Highland Park NJ 08904

CHEKOL, TESEMA, research scientist; PhD, U. Md., 2000. Prin. rsch. scientist Battelle Meml. Inst., Aberdeen, Md., 2001—. Adj. prof. U. Md., Adelphi. Mem. Environment Com., Columbia, Md., 2004. Recipient Young Scholars award, Cosmos Club Found., Washington, 2000. Mem.: AAAS.

CHELAPATI, CHUNDURI VENKATA, civil engineering educator; b. Eluru, India, Mar. 11, 1933; came to U.S., 1957, naturalized, 1971; s. Lakshminarayana and Anjamma (Kanumuri) Chunduri. B.E. with honors, Andhra U., India, 1954; MS, U. Ill., 1959, PhD, 1962. Jr. engr. Office of Chief Engr., State of Andhra, India, 1954-55; asst. prof. structural engring. Birla Coll. Engring., Pilani, India, 1956-57; research asst. dept. civil engring. U. Ill., 1957-62; asst. prof. engring. Calif. State U., Los Angeles, 1962-65, assoc. prof. Long Beach, 1965-70, prof. civil engring., 1970—96, vice chmn. dept., 1971-73, chmn. dept., 1973-79, coordinator profl. engring. rev. programs, 1972-81, dir. continuing engring. edn., 1982—96, dir. CADDS Research Ctr., 1986—96; pres. C.V. Chelapati & Assos., Inc., Huntington Beach, Calif., 1979—2001. Cons. USN Civil Engring. Lab., 1962—68, 1975—94, Holmes & Narver, Inc., Anaheim, Calif., 1968—73; pres. Profl. Engring. Devel.

Publs., 1988—, Continuing Profl. Edn. Inst., 2000—, Irvine Inst. Tech., 2002—. Contbr. articles to profl. jours. Mem. ASCE, Am. Soc. Engring. Edn., Structural Engrs. Assn. So. Calif., Earthquake Engring. Research Inst., Seismol. Soc. Am., Am. Concrete Inst., Am. Inst. Steel Constrn., Sigma Xi, Chi Epsilon, Tau Beta Pi, Phi Kappa Phi. Home: 16292 Mandalay Cir Huntington Beach CA 92649-2107 Office: 8659 Research Dr Ste 201 Irvine CA 92618 Office Phone: 949-585-9137. *When a person is indeed fortunate enough to reach a position of responsibility, that person should even more zealously follow the path of truth and justice, keeping in mind the good of humanity. One should look for long range objectives and not be deterred by minor setbacks.*

CHELARIU, ANA RADU, library director; b. Bucharest, Romania, Nov. 19, 1946; m. Serban H. Chelariu; 1 child, Andrea. MA, U. Bucharest, 1972; MLS, Rutgers U., 1981. Indexer H. W. Wilson Co., N.Y.C., 1981-85; dir. Palisades Pk. (N.J.) Pub. Libr., 1981—99, Cliffside Park (N.J.) Pub. Libr., 1999—. Mem. Soc. Romanian Studies, N.J. Libr. Assn. Christian Orthodox. Office: Cliffside Park Pub Libr 505 Palisade Ave Cliffside Park NJ 07010 Office Phone: 201-945-2867. E-mail: chelariu@bccls.org.

CHELBERG, ROBERT DOUGLAS, army officer; b. Ironwood, Mich., Sept. 1, 1938; s. Raymond Rodahl and Marion Dora (Watson) C.; children: Robert, Kathryn. BS, U.S. Mil. Acad., West Point, N.Y., 1961; MBA, N.Mex. State U., 1973. Commd. 2d lt. U.S. Army, 1961, advanced through grades to lt. gen., 1991, ret., 1993; various assignments in U.S., Europe, Vietnam, 1961-78; student Nat. War Coll., Ft. McNair, Washington, 1978-79; asst. dir. pers. adminstrn. and svcs. Office Asst. Sec. Def. for Mil. Pers. Policy, Washington, 1979-80, staff dir., dep. to dep. asst. sec. def., 1980-81; comdr. 528th Arty. Group, U.S. Army So. Europe Task Force, 1981-83; chief of staff, dep. comdg. gen. Ft. Jackson, SC, 1983-86; asst. chief of staff, plans and policy Allied Forces So. Europe, 1986; exec. to supreme allied comdr. Europe, 1986-87; chief policy and programs br., policy div. Supreme Hdqrs., 1987-90; spl. asst. to supreme allied comdr. Europe for harmonization and verification Supreme Hdqrs., 1990; spl. advisor to sec.-gen. NATO, 1990-91; chief of staff U.S. European Command, Stuttgart, Germany, 1991-93; dep. dir. George C. Marshall European Ctr. for Security Studies, Garmisch, Germany, 1994-95; mng. dir. European region CUBIC Applications Inc., Stuttgart, Germany, 1995-98; sr. cons. European region Cubic Applications, Inc., 1998—2003; sr. advisor European affairs Econ. Devel. Partnership, Aiken, SC, 1999—; sr. fellow Joint Forces Staff Coll., 2001—; program mgr. Def. Threat Reduction Agy., European Field Office, 2003—. Dist. commr. Transatlantic coun. Boy Scouts Am., Brussels, Belgium, 1987-90, v.p. membership, 2004—. Decorated DSM, Def. Superior Svc. medal with oak leaf cluster, Army DSM. Legion of Merit, Bronze Star with four oak leaf clusters, 10 Air medals, Meritorious Svc. medal with oak leaf cluster; recipient Vet. of Yr. award VFW Post 3676, 1985, Outstanding Alumnus Svc. award Lake Superior State U., 1986, Army Exceptional Civilian Svc. award, 1995, Disting. Eagle Scout award, 1990; named to N.Mex. State U. Bus. Sch. Hall of Fame, 2001. Mem. Fedn. German-Am. Clubs (pres. 1994-96), S.C. Coun. Ret. Officers Assn. (v.p. 1999-2003), Rotary, Phi Eta Sigma, Phi Kappa Phi. Avocations: swimming, trap shooting.

CHELIOS, CHRISTOS K., professional hockey player; b. Chgo., Ill., Jan. 25, 1962; Student, U. Wis. With Montreal Canadiens, 1981—90; defenseman Chgo. Blackhawks, 1990—99, Detroit Red Wings, 1999—. Mem. NHL All-Rookie Team, 1984—85, NHL All-Star 1st Team, 1988—89, 1992—93, NHL All-Star 2d Team, 1990—91, WCHA All-Star 2d Team, 1982—83, Stanley Cup Champions Detroit Red Wings, 2002, U.S. World Cup Team, 1996, 2004, U.S. Olympic Hockey Team, Nagano, 1998, Salt Lake City, 2002. Named All Star Tournament Team, NCAA, 1982—83, All-Star First Team, The Sporting News, 1988—89, All-Star 2d Team, 1990—91, 1991—92; recipient James Norris Meml. Trophy, 1988—89, 1992—93. Achievements include won Silver medal, mem. U.S. Olympic Hockey Team, Salt Lake City Olympic Games, 2002; served as Captain to Team U.S.A, Salt Lake City Olympic Games, 2002, World Cup of Hockey, 2004. Office: Detroit Red Wings 600 Civic Center Dr Detroit MI 48226-4419

CHELL, BEVERLY C., lawyer; b. Phila., Aug. 12, 1942; d. Max M. and Cecelia (Portney) C.; m. Robert M. Chell, June 21, 1964. BA, U. Pa., 1964; JD, N.Y. Law Sch., 1967; LLM, NYU, 1973. Bar: N.Y. 1967. Assoc. Polur & Polur, N.Y.C., 1967-68, Thomas V. Kingham Esq., N.Y.C., 1968-69; v.p., sec., asst. gen. counsel, dir. Athlone Industries Inc., Parsippany, N.J., 1969-81; asst. v.p., asst. sec., assoc. gen. counsel Macmillan Inc., N.Y.C., 1981-85, v.p., sec., gen. counsel, 1985-90; vice chmn., gen. counsel K-III Holdings, N.Y.C., 1990-92; vice chmn., gen. counsel, sec. Primedia Inc. (formerly K-III Comm. Corp.), N.Y.C., 1992—. Adv. bd. U. Pa. Athletic Dept. Mem. Assn. of Bar of City of N.Y., Am. Soc. Corp. Secs. Home: 1050 5th Ave New York NY 10028-0110 Office: Primedia Inc 745 5th Ave Fl 23 New York NY 10151-0099

CHELLE, ROBERT FREDERICK, electric power industry executive, educator; b. New Brunswick, N.J., July 18, 1948; s. Robert and Frances (Brown) C.; m. Karen Ann Cederburg, Aug. 7, 1971; children: Robert, Pamela. BA, Bethany Coll., 1970; MBA, U. Dayton, 1972. Asst. contr. Tait Mfg. Co., Dayton, Ohio, 1972-73; pres. High Voltage Maintenance Corp., Dayton, 1973-99; dir. Crotty Ctr. for Entrepreneurial Leadership, U. Dayton, 1999—. Bd. dirs. The Siebenthaler Co., Dayton; adv. bd. U. Dayton Sch. Bus., 1994—. Contbr. articles to profl. jours. Chmn. Dayton C. of C., 1993, County Corp., Dayton, 1995. Recipient Cert. Appreciation Montgomery County Commn., Dayton, 1984-85, Up and Comer award for engring. City of Dayton, 1988. Mem. Nat. Elect. Testing Assn., Ohio Bar Assn. (mem. profl. ethics com. 2001—), Rotary (pres. 1984-85). Presbyterian. Avocations: yachting, fishing.

CHELLGREN, PAUL WILBUR, energy industry executive; b. Tullahoma, Tenn., Jan. 18, 1943; s. Wilbur E. Chellgren and Kathryn L. (Berquist) Chellgen; children: Sarah, Matthew, Jane. BS, U. Ky., 1964; MBA, Harvard U., 1966; diploma in devel. econ., Univ. Coll., Oxford, Eng., 1967. Assoc. McKinsey & Co., Washington and London, 1967—68; ops. analyst Office Sec. Def., Washington, 1968—70; adminstrv. asst. Boise Cascade Corp., Idaho, 1970—71, divsn. gen. mgr. L.A., 1971—72; gen. mgr. Universal Capital Corp., Kansas City, Mo., 1972—74; exec. asst. to chmn. Ashland (Ky.) Inc., 1974—77; adminstrv. v.p. Ashland Chem. Co., Columbus, Ohio, 1977—78, group v.p., 1978—80; sr. v.p., group oper. officer Ashland Inc., Covington, Ky., 1980—88, sr. v.p., CFO, 1988—92, pres., COO, 1992—96, pres., CEO, 1996—97, chmn., CEO, 1997—2002, ret. Bd. dirs. PNC Bank Corp., Centre Coll., The Conf. Bd.; adj. prof. No. Ky. U. Dir. Am. Friends of Univ. Coll. Oxford, Inc.; bd. dirs. Greater Cin. Found.; dir., trustee Taft Mus., Cin.; chmn. Cin. Mus. Art; trustee No. Ky. U. Found., Ea. Ky. U. Found. 1st lt. U.S. Army, 1968—70. Fellow: Univ. Coll. (Oxford, Eng.) (hon.); mem.: U. Ky. Fellows, Queen City Club (Cin.), Comml. Club, Met. Club. Home: 817 Squire Lake Dr Villa Hills KY 41017-1337 Office: 541 Buttermilk Pike # 207 Crescent Springs KY 41017 Office Phone: 859-341-1280.

CHELLINE, WARREN HERMAN, language educator, minister; b. Jonesport, Maine, Sept. 26, 1923; s. Herman Albert and Olive Viola (Yarwood) Chelline; m. Bonnibelle Nelson, Jan. 1, 1950 (dec. June 1991); 1 child, Eric Warren; m. Francis Nadine Woodside, Aug. 7, 1993. Student, Brown U., 1941-43; DD, Am. Div. Sch., 1956; BA, U. Mo., 1969, MA, 1970; MPhil, U. Kans., 1979, PhD, 1982. Cert. secondary edn. tchr. Mo., Kans. Clergy member Remnant LDS Ch., Independence, Mo., 1942—; prof. English lang. and lit. Mo. We. State U., St. Joseph, 1971-97, prof. emeritus, 1997—. Insp. U.S. Lighthouse Soc., 1997—. Author: (book) John Milton and Roger Williams, 1982; contbg. editor: Herald House Pubs., 1940—69; contbr. articles to profl. jours. Bd. dirs. Boy Scouts Am., Canada, 1946—, St. Joseph (Mo.) Pub. Libr., 1975—, St. Joseph Symphony, 1994—, Allied Arts Coun., 1995—; chmn. adv. bd. Salvation Army, 1989—. James E. West fellow, 1998. Mem.: Milton Soc. Internat., Soc. Profl. Journalists, Masons (chaplain 1988—, 32d degree), Kiwanis (disting. lt. gov. 1982—), Moila Shrine, Am. Legion. Avocations: clowning, lighthouses, circus lore, scottish bagpipe band. Home: Apt 1 421 N 25th St Saint Joseph MO 64501 Office: 620 Francis St Saint Joseph MO 64501 E-mail: wchelline@tdccapital.com.

CHELLIS, CONVERSE A., III, state representative, accountant; b. Stockton, Calif., Aug. 10, 1943; s. Converse A. Chellis Jr. and Adurline T. Chellis; m. Sharon Lee Hayes, Dec. 30, 1966; children: Tiffany, Converse IV. BS, The Citadel, 1965. CPA; diplomate Am. Bd. Forensic Acctg. Prin. Gamble, Givens & Moody, LLC; state rep. dist. 94 S.C. Legis., 1997—, chmn. rules com., mem. labor, commerce and industry com. Chmn. bus., commerce sub com. State Bd. Accountancy, 1990—93; mem. Acctg. Firms Assoc. Inc., 1982—99. Life mem. Hospice of Charleston, Inc./Bethany United Meth. Ch.; past treas. Alzheimer's Diseasn and Related Disorders Assn. Inc-Lowcountry chpt.; legis. mem. Info. Resource Coun.; chmn. Dochester County Legis. Del. Capt. USAF. Mem.: Summerville C. of C., Am. Coll. Forensic Examiners, S.C. Assn. CPAs (pres. 1985), Citadel Brigadier Club, Sertoma Club, Rotary. Republican. Office: State Capitol 519C Blatt Bldg Columbia SC 29211 Home: 119 Parkwood Dr Summerville SC 29483 E-mail: CAC@scstatehouse.net.

CHELSTROM, MARILYN ANN, political science educator, consultant; b. Mpls., Dec. 05; d. Arthur Rudolph and Signe (Johnson) Chelstrom. BA, U. Minn., 1950; LHD, Oklahoma City U., 1981. Staff asst. Mpls. Citizens Com. Pub. Edn., 1950—57; coord. policies and procedures Lithium Corp. Am., Inc., Mpls. and N.Y.C., 1957—62; dir. The Robert A. Taft Inst. Govt., N.Y.C., 1962—77, exec. v.p., 1977—78, pres., 1978—89, pres. emeritus, 1990—; polit. edn. cons., 1990—; pres. Chelstrom Connection, 1992—. Compiler (book) Tribute to Outstanding Minnesota Women, 2001. Home: 9600 Portland Ave Minneapolis MN 55420-4564 Office: 155 E 38th St New York NY 10016-2660

CHEMA, THOMAS V., government official, lawyer, academic administrator; b. East Liverpool, Ohio, Oct. 31, 1946; s. Stephen T. and Dorothy Grace (McCormack) C.; m. Barbara Burke Orr, Aug. 15, 1970; children: Christine, Stephen. AB, U. Notre Dame, 1968; JD, Harvard U., 1971. Bar: Ohio 1971, U.S. Supreme Ct. 1977. Assoc. Arter and Hadden, Cleve., 1971-79, ptnr. 1979-85, 1989-2003; of counsel Tucker, Ellis and West, 2003--; co-founder, pres. Gateway Cons. Group, Inc., 1994-; pres.Hiram Coll., Ohio, 2003--; exec. dir. Ohio Lottery Commn., Cleve., 1983-85, Gateway Econ. Devel. Corp. Greater Cleveland, 1990-95; chmn. Pub. Utilities Commn. Ohio, Columbus, 1985-89; chmn. Ohio Bldg. Authority, 1990-96. Candidate for Ohio Senate, 1980; campaign mgr., Senator Howard M. Metzenbaum, 1976; co-chmn. task force on violent crime, Cleve., 1981-83; trustee Hiram Coll., 1994—2003, Cleve. Works, Inc., 1995-98, Cleve. City Club, 1993-96, Sisters of Charity of St. Augustine Health Sys., 1994—, Hist. Gateway Neighborhood, Inc., 1995—; dir. Transtechnology, Inc., Fairport Funds. Mem. ABA (adv. coun.), Nat. Assn. Regulatory Utility Commrs., Nat. Assn. State Lotteries (bd. dirs.), Greater Cleve. Bar Assn., Ohio State Bar Assn., Cleve. Legal Aid Soc., Ohio Legal Assistance Found. (chmn. 1996-99), Electric Power Rsch. Inst., Sr. Citizens Resources Inc. (trustee), Hospice Coun. No. Ohio (sec., trustee, legal counsel), Citizens League, NAACP, League Women Voters, Am. Soc. Pub. Adminstrs. Trustee, St. Ignatius High Sch., Prospect Vision, Inc., Downtown Devel. Coords. Cleve. Found. Arch. Democrat. Roman Catholic. Club: City (Cleve., trustee 1993—). Avocation: skiing. Home: 18580 Parkland Dr Cleveland OH 44122-3469 Office: Office of President Hiram College Hiram OH 44234 Office Phone: 330-569-6112. Business E-Mail: chematv@hiram.edu.

CHEMBERLIN, PEG, minister, religious organization administrator; b. York, Nebr., Sept. 27, 1949; d. Charles Norman and Donna May (Chemberlin) Bean. BA cum laude, U. Wis., Parkside; grad., United Theol. Sem. Twin Cities, 1982. Ordained deacon Moravian Ch. Am., 1982, consecrated presbyter Moravian Ch. Am., 1986. Formerly dir. campus ministries, tchr., youth min.; also outreach min., parish intern pastor; exec. dir. Minn. Coun. Chs., 1995—. Former pres., former program chmn. Nat. Assn. Ecumenical and Interfaith Staff, 1992, 97; hon. campaign chair Minn. Ford Shane, 2003. Recipient Women of Excellence award Minn. Gov., 1994, NOVA Peace and Justice award, 1985; Angel of Reconciliation award, 2003. Mem.: Nat. Coun. of Ch. (exec. bd. 2003). Office: Minn Coun Chs 122 W Franklin Ave Minneapolis MN 55404-2447 Office Phone: 612-870-3600.

CHEMERINSKY, ERWIN, law educator; b. 1953; BS, Northwestern U., 1975; JD cum laude, Harvard U., 1978. Bar: Ill. 1978, D.C. 1979. Atty. civil divsn. US Dept. Justice, Washington, 1978—79; assoc. Dobrovir, Oates & Gebhardt, Washington, 1979—80; asst.prof.law De Paul U., Chgo., 1980—83, assoc. prof., 1983—84, U. So. Calif., LA, 1984—87, prof., 1987—2004; Alston & Bird prof. law Duke U., Durham, NC, 2004—. Vis. assoc. prof. U. So. Calif., 1983—84; mem. task force Diversity State Govt. Gov., 1999—2000; lectr. in field. Author: Interpreting the Constitution, 1987, 1990 Supplement to Federal Jurisdiction, 1990, 1992 Supplement to Federal Jurisdiction, 1992, Federal Jurisdiction, 1989, 4th edit., 2003, Constitutional Law: Principles and Policies, 1997, Constitutional Law, 2001, Supreme Ct. Rev.: October 2000 Term, 2001, 17th Annual Section 1983 Civil Rights Litigation, 2001, Fourth Annual Supreme Court Review: October 2001 Term, 2003; mem. editl. adv. bd.: Calif. Lawyer, 1994, Aspen (Colo.) Law & Bus., 2001—. Bd. dirs. Progressive Jewish Alliance, 2000—; bd. dirs., regional coun. Am. Jewish Congress, 1993—98; chmn. LA (Calif.) Charter Reform Commn., 1997—99. Mem.: AAUP (litigation com. 1991—95), ABA (tech. asst. constn. drafting), ACLU (bd. dirs. 1987—98, exec. com. 1991—98), Am. Assn. Law Schs. (planning com. mini workshop 1989, steering com. profl. responsibility 1987—90, task force profl. responsibility 1987). Office: Duke Law Box 90360 Durham NC 27708-0360

CHEMERS, MARTIN M., academic administrator, psychologist, educator; m. Barbara Goza Chemers; children: Michael, Holden. BS, U. Ill., 1964, MS, 1966, PhD, 1968. Asst. prof. psychology U. Del., 1968—70; prof., chmn. dept. psychology U. Utah, Salt Lake City, 1970—87; Henry R. Kravis prof. leadership and orgnl. psychology Claremont (Calif.) McKenna Coll., dir. Kravis Leadership Inst.; dean social scis. U. Calif., Santa Cruz, 1995—2003, interim provost, exec. vice chancellor, 2003—04, acting chancellor, 2004—, prof. psychology. Cons. in field. Author: An Integrative Theory of Leadership, 1997, 1999; co-author (with Fred Fiedler): Improving Leadership Effectiveness; contbr. articles to profl. jours. Recipient Sears-Roebuck Found. Tchg. Excellence and Campus Leadership award, 1991. Fellow: APA, Am. Psychol. Soc.; mem.: Soc. Exptl. Social Psychology (pres.-elect). Office: Univ Calif 1156 High St Santa Cruz CA 95064-1077

CHEMERS, ROBERT MARC, lawyer; b. Chgo., July 24, 1951; s. Donald and Florence (Weinberg) C.; m. Lenore Ziemann, Aug. 16, 1975; children: Brandon J., Derek M. BA, U. So. Calif., 1973; JD, Ind. U.-Indpls., 1976. Bar: Ind. 1976, Ill. 1976, U.S. Dist. Ct. (so. dist.) Ind. 1976, U.S. Dist. Ct. (no. and so. dists.) Ill. 1977, U.S. Ct. Appeals 7th cir.) 1977, U.S. Ct. Appeals (5th cir.) 1985. Assoc. Pretzel & Stouffer, Chgo., 1976-79, officer, 1979-81, dir., 1981—. Author: IICLE - Civil Practice, 1978, rev. edit. 1982, 87; IICLE Settlements, 1984. Mem. ABA, Ill. State Bar Assn., Chgo. Bar Assn., Def. Rsch. Inst., Ill. Def. Counsel, Appellate Lawyers Assn. Office: Pretzel & Stouffer One S Wacker Dr Chicago IL 60606

CHEN, ALLAN Y., oncologist, educator; s. Pao-Huei and Yin-O Chen. MD, Taipei Med. Coll., Taiwan, 1985; PhD, Johns Hopkins U., 1993. Cert. Am. Bd. Radiology (lic. radiation oncology). Adj. asst. prof. dept. pharmacology U. Medicine and Dentistry N.J.-Robert Wood Johnson Med. Sch., Piscataway, 1994—96; asst. prof. dept. radiation oncology Vanderbilt U. Med. Ctr., Nashville, 1998—2001, U. Calif.-Davis Med. Ctr., Sacramento, 2001—. Dir. stereotactic radiosurgery program U. Calif.-Davis, Sacramento, 2001—. Mem. rain exec. com. SWOG, 2004. Lt. comdr. active duty commn. corps. USPHS, 1996—98. Recipient Leukemia Soc. Spl. Fellowship award, 1993—94. Mem.: ASTRO, AACR. Office: U Calif-Davis Med Ctr 4501 X St Sacramento CA 95817 Office Phone: 916-734-8252.

CHEN, BINTONG, finance educator; s. Jinsong Chen and Meiling Ni; m. Yubei Zhang, Mar. 6, 1964; 1 child, Helen. BS, Shanghai Jiatong U., China, 1985; MS, U. Pa., 1987; PhD, Wharton Sch., 1990. From asst. to full prof. Wash. State U., Pullman, 1990—. Sr. editor Prodn. and Ops. Mgmt. Jour. Recipient Rsch. and Scholarship award, Wash. State Univ. Coll. of Bus., 1998, Tchg. award, 2004. Achievements include pioneering the non-interior point algorithm for complementarity related problems; the name is associated with the commonly used Chen-Harker-Kanzow-Smale function. Office: Wash State U Dept of Mgmt and Operations Pullman WA 99164 Office Phone: 509-335-4458. Office Fax: 509-335-7736. E-mail: chenbi@wsu.edu.

CHEN, CHARLES, music educator, musician; s. Bingran Chen and Yan Xu; m. Xiao Wang, July 2, 1998. BA, Ctrl. Conservatory of Music, Beijing, 1982; MA, Boston U., 1990; MusM, Kent (Ohio) State U., 1992; ArtsD, Ball State U., 1994. Prin. clarinetist Ctrl. Opera Ho. Orch., Beijing, 1982—87; asst. condr. Muncie (Ind.) Symphony Orch., 1992—94; music dir./condr. East Ctrl. Ind. Youth Symphony Orch., Muncie, 1992—94; condr./gen. mgr. Am. Youth Symphony, L.A., 1995—98; music dir./condr. All Chinese Musician Symphony Orch., L.A., 1996—99; music prof. Lock Haven U. of Pa., 1999—. Chief cons. Global Cultural Exch. Ctr., Lock Haven, 2001—; vis. prof. Shanghai Tongji U., 2002—. Chmn. Chinese Student Assn., Muncie, 1992—94. Mem.: Coll. Music Soc. (assoc.). Home: 214 W Waterb St #2A Lock Haven PA 17745 Office: Lock Haven U of Pa 139 Sloan Fine Arts Ctr Lock Haven PA 17745 E-mail: cchen@lhup.edu.

CHEN, CHENGCI, science educator, research scientist; arrived in U.S., 1992; s. Changtong Chen and Qingjie He; m. Wenxin Wang; children: David, Jonathan. BS, Beijing Agrl. U., 1984, MS, 1987, Oreg. State U., 1995, PhD, 1998. Rsch. asst./instr. Beijing Agrl. U., 1987—91; grad. rsch. asst. Oreg. State U., Corvallis, 1992—98; postdoctoral rsch. assoc. Oreg. State U./Columbia Basin Agrl. Rsch. Ctr., Pendleton, 1998—2001, asst. prof., sr. rschr., 2001—02; asst. prof. Mont. State U./Ctrl. Agrl. Rsch. Ctr., Moccasin. Affiliate asst. prof. Mont. State U./Land Resources and Environ. Scis., Bozeman, 2003—. Contbr. articles to profl. publs. Recipient Sci. and Tech. Advancement award, Edn. Commn. of China, 1991; grantee, USDA, 2003. Mem.: Western Soc. Crop Sci. (pres.-elect 2004), Assn. for Advancement of Indsl. Crops, Am. Soc. Soil Sci., Am. Soc. Agronomy. Achievements include development of microsprinkler irrigation technology for pear orchard grown on cracking clay soil in southern Oregon; research in seeding date effects on grain yield and water use efficiency of winter and spring wheat cultivars. Office: Mont State U/CARC HC90 Box20 Moccasin MT 59462 Office Phone: 406-423-5421. Business E-Mail: cchen@montana.edu.

CHEN, CHIN-CHIN, music educator; b. Taipei, Taiwan, Jan. 29, 1964; came to the U.S., 1991. MMus in Piano Performance, U. Ill., 1993, MMus in Music Theory, 1995, DMA in Composition/Theory, 2000. Tchg. asst. U. Ill., Urbana, 1995-99; asst. prof. Grand Valley State U., Allendale, Mich., 1999—2005. Adj. asst. prof. Millikin U., Decatur, Ill., 1998-99. Author: (music for vibraphone and tape) Points of Departure, 1996, (music for 2-channel tape) Points of No Return, 1997 (1st prize, Internat. Luigi Russolo, 1997), (music for violin and tape) Points of Arrival, 1998, (music for orch.) The Marks of Life, 1999, (music for two mezzo-sopranos, baritone, horn and percussion) Next Door, 2000, (music for carillon) Prior to Landing, 2001, (music for wind ensemble) Like a Chinese Waterfall, 2002, (music for 2-channel electroacoustic sounds) Snow of Ages, 2003, (music for soprano, vibraphone and cello) Autumn Heart, 2003, (music for 8-channel electroacoustic sounds) So Lonely Blooming, 2004, (music for vocal quartet and piano) Reminiscense, 2005. Recipient electroacoustic music commn. U. Ill., Urbana-Champaign, 1995, 98, percussion commn. Kalamazoo Symphony. Mem. Can. Electroacoustic Cmty., Soc. Composers, Inc., Soc. for the Electro-Acoustic Music in the U.S., Broadcast Music, Inc., Coll. Music Soc. Office: 11568 Brookland Dr Allendale MI 49401 E-mail: composee@yahoo.com.

CHEN, CHING JEN, mechanical engineering educator, research scientist; b. Taipei, Taiwan, July 6, 1936; came to U.S., 1960; s. I Sung Chen and T. Yen Chen; m. Ruei-Man, Aug. 14, 1965; children— Sandra, Anthony Diploma, Taipei Inst. Tech., 1957; MS in Mech. Engring., Kans. State U., 1962; PhD, Case Western Res. U., 1967. Design engr. Ta-Tung Grinding Co., Taipei, 1959-61; asst. prof. mech. engring. U. Iowa, Iowa City, 1967-70, assoc. prof., 1970-77, prof., 1977-82, chmn., prof. energy div., 1982-84, chmn., prof. dept. mech. engring., 1982-92; sr. rsch. scientist Iowa Inst. Hydraulic Research, 1970-92; mem. exec. com. Iowa Space Grant Coll. Consortium, 1990-92; dean Coll. Engring. Fla. A&M U.-Fla. State U., Tallahassee, 1992—. Cons. govtl. agys., mil. and industry Mem. editorial bd. Altas of Visualization, 1991-96, Atlas of Visualization 1991-95; evaluator Accreditation Bd. for Engring. and Tech., 1991-96; assoc. editor Jour. Engring. Mechanics, 1990-93; U.S. regional editor Internat. Jour. Visualization, 1997—; mem. editl. bd. Jour. Hybrid Methods in Engring.; contbr. articles to profl. publs. Old Gold fellow Iowa Found., 1968; U.S. sr. Scientist awardee Alexander von Humboldt Fund, Fed. Republic Germany, 1974; hon. prof. Wuhan Inst. of Hydraulic and Elec. Engring, Peoples Republic of China. Fellow ASME, ASCE; mem. AIAA, Am. Soc. Engring. Edn., Internat. Hydraulic Research, Am. Phys. Soc., Soc. Theoretical and Applied Mechanics (hon.) (Taiwan), Japan Soc. Visualization, Sigma Xi. Home: 4643 High Grove Rd Tallahassee FL 32309-2974 Office: FAMU-FSU Coll Engring 2525 Pottsdamer St Tallahassee FL 32310-6046 Office Phone: 850-410-6437.

CHEN, CHING-CHIH, information science educator, consultant; b. Foochow, Fukien, China, Sept. 3, 1937; came to U.S, 1959; d. Han-chia and May-ying (Liu) Liu; m. Sow-Hsin Chen, Aug. 19, 1961; children: Anne, Catherine, John. BA, Nat. Taiwan U., Taipei, 1959; MLS, U. Mich., 1961; PhD, Case Western Res. U., 1974. Asst. Sch. Libr. Sci. U. Mich., Ann Arbor, 1960-61, svc. libr., 1961-62; sci. reference libr. McMaster U., Hamilton, Ont., Can., 1962-63, head sci. libr., 1963-64; sr. sci. libr. U. Waterloo, Ont., Can., 1964-65, head engring., math. and sci. libr., 1965-68; assoc. sci. libr. MIT, Cambridge, Mass., 1968-71; asst. prof. Grad. Sch. Libr. and Info. Sci. Simmons Coll., Boston, 1971-76, asst. dean for acad. affairs, 1977-79, assoc. dean, prof., 1979-96, prof., 1979—. Cons. Am. Soc. Info. Sci./Cath. U. Am., 1976-77, Chung-Shan Inst. Sci. Rsch., Taiwan, 1977-87, Abt Assocs., Inc., 1980-82, Sci. and Tech. Info. Ctr. Nat. Sci. Coun., Taiwan, 1973-77, S.E. Asia Region WHO, 1980, 81, Engring. Info. Inc., 1982, UNESCO, Paris, 1984, Nat. Geog. Soc., 1985, Norman Bethuen U. Med. Scis. Libr., 1986, Getty Trust, 1988, USIA, 1988, Ont. Coun. Gradual Studies, 1989, FID, 1989, World Bank, 1990, UNESCO, 1991, DataConsult, Mex., 1991, Soros Found., 1992-93, USIA, 1993-95, UN Devel. Program, 1997, Tsinghua U., Taiwan, 1997, Nat. Sci. Coun., Taiwan, 1998—2001; mem. US President's Info. Tech. Adv. Com., 1997-2002; guest prof. Tsinghua U., Beijing, 1999-2002. Author, editor 36 books including Biomedical, Scientific and Technical Book Reviewing, 1976, Sourcebook on Health Sciences Librarianship, 1977, Quantitative Measurement and Dynamic Library Service, 1978, Scientific & Technical Information Sources, 2nd edit., 1987, (with others) Numeric Databases, 1984, HyperSource on Hypermdia/Multimedia Technologies, 1989, HyperSource on Optical Technologies, 1989, Optical Technologies in Libraries; Use & Trends, 1991, Planning Global Information Infrastructure, 1995, Consortium of Electronic Resources, 1999, IT and Global Digital Library Development, 1999, Global Digital Library Development in the New Millennium, 2001; editor-in-chief: Microcomputers for Information Management, 1983-96; mem. editl. bd.: Electronic Library, 1990-; also editor numerous conf. procs.; contbr. over 150 articles to profl. jours. Barbour scholar U. Mich., 1959-61, Case Western Res. U. fellow, 1973-74, NATO fellow, 1975, AAAS fellow, 1985; Emily Hollowell Rsch. grantee, 1972—, Simmons Coll. Fund Rsch. grantee, 1972-81, co-principal investigator NSF US-China Million Book Digital Libr. Grant Project, 2001-; recipient Disting. Svc. award Chinese-Am. Librs. Assn., 1982, Cert. of Appreciation, Asian-Pacific-Am. Librs. Assn., 1983, Disting. Alumni award U. Mich., 1983, Outstanding Svc. award Nat. Cen. Libr., 1986, Disting. Svc. award Asian-Am. Libr. Assn, 1992, Cindy award Assn. Visual Comm., 1992, Grazella Shepherd Meml. award for Excellence in Edn., Case Western Reserve U. Educator's Forum, 1999, NSF Internat. Digital Libr. Program award Chinese Memory

Net: U.S.-Sino Collaborative Rsch., 1999-2003, Ernest A. Lynton award Am. Assn. Higher Edn., 2001, NSF IDLP Project, Global Memory Net, 2002-05, NSF Internat. Digital Libr. Program award, 2004-. Fellow AAAS; mem. ALA (disting. svc. award 1989, Humphrey award 1996), AAUP, Am. Soc. Info. Sci. (best Info. Sci. Tchr. award 1983), Assn. Am. Libr. Schs., Assn. Coll. and Rsch. Librs., Libr. Info. Tech. Assn. (Gaylord Libr. and Info. Tech. Achievement award 1990, Outstanding Achievement Libr. Hi Tech. award 1994), New Eng. Libr. Assn. (Emerson Greenaway award 1994), Assn. Libr. and Info. Sci. Edn. (1st ALISE Pratt-Severn Nat. Faculty award 1997). Avocations: travel, stamp collecting/philately. Home: 1400 Commonwealth Ave Newton MA 02465-2830 Office: Simmons Coll 300 Fenway Boston MA 02115-5820 Office Phone: 617-521-2804. Business E-Mail: chen@simmons.edu.

CHEN, CHUN-HUNG, engineering educator; b. Kaohsiung, Taiwan, Oct. 27, 1964; came to U.S., 1991; s. Ping-Ho and Pao-Yu Chen; m. Mei-Mei Liu, June 15, 1991; 1 child, Valerie. PhD, Harvard U., 1994. Asst. prof. U. Pa., Phila., 1994-2000, acting grad. group chair, 1999-2000; assoc. prof. George Mason U., Fairfax, Va., 2000—. Cons. Computer Command and Control Co., Phila., 1997—. Recipient Grad. Assistance in Areas of Nat. Need award U.S. Dept. Edn., 1998; recipient Motion Planning and Simulation award U.S. Army Rsch. Office, 1997, Engring. Design award NSF, 1998, Robust Design Optimization award Sandia Nat. Labs., N.Mex., 1998, Small Aircraft Sys. Transportation Devel. award NASA, 2002, Info. Tech. Rsch. award NSF, 2003. Mem. IEEE (sr.; Best Paper in Automation award 2003), Inst. Ops. Rsch. and Mgmt. Scis. Achievements include development of simulation tool, 1992 (MasPar award); patents for optimal computing allocation, 1999 (Eliahu Jury award 1994). Avocations: trains, aircraft, weather forecasting. Office: George Mason U Dept Sys Engring & Ops Rsch 4400 University Dr MS 4A6 Fairfax VA 22030 Office Phone: 703-993-3572. Business E-Mail: cchen9@gmu.edu.

CHEN, CHUN-JEN, immunologist, researcher; b. Touliu City, Taiwan, Aug. 11, 1969; s. Yuan-Hong Chen and Shu-O Chang. PhD, U. Tex., 2002. Postdoctoral rsch. assoc. U. Mass. Med. Sch., Worcester, 2003—. 2d lt. Taiwan mil., 1993—95, Taiwan. Recipient Pres.' award, Nat. Taiwan U., 1989—90; fellow, U. Tex. Med. Br., Galveston, 2002—03. Mem.: Sigma Xi. Achievements include discovery of programmed cell death and cell cycle dysregulation induced by murine coronavirus. Home: 67 Frank St Apt164 Worcester MA 01604 Office: U Mass Med Sch 55 Lake Ave N Worcester MA 01655 Office Phone: 508-856-7571.

CHEN, COIN LIN, statistician; PhD, Purdue U., West Lafayette, Ind., 1998. Sr. rsch. statistician SAS Inst. Inc., Cary, NC, 1998—.

CHEN, CONCORDIA CHAO, mathematician; b. Peiping, China; came to U.S., 1955, naturalized, 1969; d. Chun-fu and Kwie Hwa (Wong) Chao; BA in Bus. Adminstrn., Nat. Taiwan U., 1954; MS in Math., Marquette U., 1958; postgrad. Purdue U., 1958-60, M.I.T., 1961-62; m. Chin Chen, July 2, 1960; children: Marie Hui-mei, Albert Chao. Teaching asst. Purdue U., Lafayette, Ind., 1958-60; system analysis engr. electronic data processing div. Mpls.-Honeywell, Newton Highlands, Mass., 1960-63; mgmt. planning asst. Lederle Labs., Am. Cyanamid Co., Pearl River, N.Y., 1964, computer applications specialist, 1967, ops. analyst, 1967; staff programmer IBM, Sterling Forest, N.Y., 1968-73, adv. programmer Data Processing Mktg. Group, Poughkeepsie, 1973-80, mgr. systems programming and systems architecture, Princeton, N.J., 1980-82, sr. systems analyst, 1982-83, data processing mktg. cons., Beijing, 1983-88; sr. planner IBM DSD, Poughkeepsie, 1988-92; program mgr. Chiang Indsl. Charity Found Ltd., 1993-94; mgr. software engring. China Weal Bus. Machinery Co., Ltd., Hong Kong, 1995-99, exec. gen. mgr., 1999-2001; prof. South China U. Tech., 2003—. Chmn. ednl. council Hudson region MIT. Mem. Am. Math. Soc., Soc. Indsl. and Applied Maths., MIT Club Hudson Valley (pres.). Home: 12 Mountain Pass Rd Hopewell Junction NY 12533-5331 Office: Flat E 32/F Tower 5 South Horizons Hong Kong E-mail: concordia@alum.mit.edu.

CHEN, DEANFORD FREDERICK, software engineer; b. Taiwan, Jan. 2, 1965; came to U.S. 1975; BS in Computer Sci., San Jose State (Calif.) U., 1991. Software devel. Computer Sci. Corp., Sunnyvale, Calif., 1993-94; software specialist Litton, San Jose, 1995—. Mem. IEEE Computer Soc., ACM, Toastmasters (awards, 1997, 98, 99), San Jose State Alumni Assn., U.S. Jaycees. Avocations: chess, sport, reading, travel, computers. Home: 5312 Ayrshire Dr San Jose CA 95118-3001

CHEN, DI, electronics executive, consultant, optical engineer; b. Chekiang, China, Mar. 15, 1929; came to U.S., 1954, naturalized, 1972; s. Hsun Yu and chien (Wang) C.; m. Lynn C. Wang, June 14, 1958; children: Andrew A.J., Daniel T.Y. BS, Nat. Taiwan U., 1953; MS, U. Minn., 1956; PhD, Stanford U., 1959. Asst. prof. U. Minn., Mpls., 1959-62; rsch. fellow Honeywell Co., Bloomington, Minn., 1962-80; tech. dir. Optical Peripherals Lab., Colorado Springs, Colo., 1980-84; co-founder, exec. v.p. tech. Optotech, Inc., 1984-89; pres. Chen and Assocs. Cons., 1989—. V.p. tech. and engring. Literal Corp., Colorado Springs, 1990-91; chmn., then co-chmn., advisor, sr. advisor Optical Data Storage, 1983-98. Topical editor Applied Optics Jour., 1991-97; contbr. articles to profl. jours, chpts. to ref. books; patentee in field. Founder, chair bd. dirs. Chinese Am. Assn. Minn., 1967—79. Recipient Honeywell Sweatt Scientists and Engrs. award, 1972. Fellow IEEE (life, chmn. IEEE-MAG Twin Cities chpt. 1974); mem. SPIE, Optical Soc. Am., Sigma Xi, Eta Kappa Nu. Office Phone: 952-472-1036. E-mail: dichen2127@frontier.net.

CHEN, FEN, mathematician, educator, researcher; b. Lutsao Village, Chia-Yi Shien, Taiwan, Nov. 28, 1939; arrived in U.S., 1979; s. Shin-Ting Chen and Susan Liaw; m. Ann-Hua Shieh, Aug. 10, 1966; children: Chu-Yi, Chu-Win. *Wife, Ann-Hua, is a musician. She grew up in a traditional Christian family. Her father, Re-Born Shieh, served as a pastor in an original church named Tainan Ti Pen Ching Presbyteria Church in Taiwan for 40 years. For her entire career she contributes her educational love and music to a blind student in the field of special education. Eldest daughter, Chu-Yi, is majoring in ministry of church. She is pursuing her career in as a pastor, to follow her mother and grandfather's steps. Second daughter, Chu-Wen, is a science teacher. She was majoring in biology with her curious mind including the beauty of nature and humans.* BS, Nat. Taiwan Normal U, Taipei, Taiwan, R.O.C., 1968; MEd, Tokyo U, 1977; postgrad., U. Mich., 1978—79, U. Wis., 1979—80; AGS, U Md., 1984. Math. tchr. Tailin Jr. H.S., Tailin, Chia-Yi, Taiwan, 1961—63, Pekung Sr. H.S., Pekung, Iling Shien, Taiwan, 1963—66, Taichung 1st Sr. H.S., Taichung City, Taiwan, 1966—70; math. instr. Tainan Pharmacy U, Tainan Shien, Taiwan, 1970—74; tchg. asst. U Md., College Park, 1981—83, vol. instr., 1982—86; substitute math. tchr. Prince George's and Montgomery County Pub. Schs., 1984—90; pvt. instr. Montgomery Coll., Md., 1985; substitute math. tchr. Fairfax County (Md.) Pub. Schs., 1990—98, Arlington (Va.) Pub. Sch. Sys., 1999—2002. *Career is an educator in mathematics, which is to educate a learner for growing intellectual powers including abilities of knowing, doing, reasoning and thinking. Thus, a mathematics curriculum must be well designed in terms of a learner's cognitive domain for expanding his or her mind in a lifetime. During his graduate study at Tokyo University of Education, his thinking mind was deeply influenced by Professor Yoshi-Nobu Wada (1913-1997) who was an outstanding educator in Japan. While he was a visiting student at the University of Wisconsin-Madison, his pedagory of designing and evaluating a mathematics curriculum was fruitfully enriched by Dr. Tom A. Romberg who is a well-known mathematics educator.* Author: Elem. Calculus, 1972, New Theory of Trisection, 1999, Regular Polygons Vol. I, 2001, Regular Polygons Vol. II. Fellow Kyo-Dai-Ken Math. Study Group, 1975—78. Mem.: Math. Edn. Rsch. Group (Tokyo), Nat. Coun. Tchrs. of Math., Am. Math. Soc., Math. Assn. Am. (assoc.). Achievements include new developments in the New Theory of Trisection to solve the most controversial trisection-problem in over 2500 years in the history of mathematics; first scholar to accomplish this; construction of a regular P-gon (P-3, P is a natural number); application of the new theory of trisection from a regular triangle, tetragon, pentagon, hexagon, heptagon, octagon, nonagon, decagon, undecagon, dodecagon, trisecagon, tetradecagon, pentadecagon. Home: 4520 King St No 902 Alexandria VA 22302 Office: Internat Sch Math & Scis Inst PO Box 16707 Alexandria VA 22302 Office Phone: 703-671-6176.

CHEN, FRANCIS F., physics and engineering educator; b. Canton, Kwangtung, Republic of China, Nov. 18, 1929; came to U.S., 1936; s. M. Conrad and Evelyn (Chu) C.; m. Edna Lau Chen, Mar. 31, 1956; children: Sheryl F., Patricia A., Robert F. AB, Harvard U., 1950, MA, 1951, PhD, 1954. Research staff mem. Princeton (N.J.) Plasma Physics Lab., 1954-69; prof. elec. engring. UCLA, 1969-94, prof. emeritus, 1994—. Chmn. plasma physics div. Am. Phys. Soc., N.Y.C., 1983. Author: Introduction to Plasma Physics and Controlled Fusion, 1974, 2d edit., 1984; contbr. over 200 articles to sci. jours. Fellow IEEE (Plasma Sci. and Application award 1994), Am. Phys. Soc. (James Clerk Maxwell Prize, 1995); mem. IEEE, Fusion Power Assocs., Am. Vacuum Soc. Avocations: tennis, marathons, photography, backpacking, woodworking. Office: Univ Calif 56-125B Engr IV Los Angeles CA 90095-1594 E-mail: ffchen@ee.ucla.edu.

CHEN, FRANCIS YONG, psychologist; b. Seoul, Republic of Korea, Feb. 16, 1963; arrived in U.S., 1970; s. Henry Yaoming and Yong Ja Park Chen. BA, Tex. State U., 1996, MA, 2000. Sch. psychologist Seguin (Tex.) Ind. Sch. Dist., 1999—2003, Grand Prairie (Tex.) Ind. Sch. Dist., 2003—04, Denton (Tex.) Ind. Sch. Dist., 2004—. Instr. U. Tex., San Antonio, 2001—03; presenter in field. Vol. Austin State Hosp., 1995—97, Outyouth, Austin, Tex., 1999—2001; co-sponsor Amnesty Internat., Denton, 2004—. Mem.: Nat. Assn. Sch. Psychologists, Tex. Assn. Sch. Psychologists (area IV rep. 1999—2003, webmaster 1999—).

CHEN, GANG, research scientist, educator; b. HanZhong, Shaanxi, China, Oct. 28, 1977; s. Xuwen Chen; m. Shu Zhang, May 10, 2002. B in Indsl. Engring., BE in Mech. Engring., Xi'an Jiaotong U., China, 1999; MS in Ops. Rsch. and Indsl. Engring., U. Fla., 2002, PhD in Ops. Rsch. and Indsl. Engring., 2003. Tchg. asst. U. Fla., Gainesville, 1999—2002, rsch. asst. Gaineville, 1999—2003, course instr. Gainesville, 2002—03; asst. v.p. Bank of Am., Dallas, 2003—. Chair, session on scheduling, informs ann. meeting Inst. for Ops. Rsch. and Mgmt. Scis., Atlanta, 2003; referee of jour. IIE Transactions, 2003, Naval Rsch. Logistics, 2004, Computational Mgmt. Scis., 2004. Invited presenter: numerous confs.; contbr. articles to profl. jours. Nominee Combined Doctoral Colloquium, INFORMS, 2003; recipient Achievement awards, U. Fla., 2000, 2001; scholarship, Xi'an Jiaotong U., 1995, 1996, 1997, 1999. Mem.: Material Handling and Mgmt. Soc., Inst. of Indsl. Engrs., Inst. for Ops. Rsch. and Mgmt. Scis., Tau Beta Pi. Achievements include development of Developed the first mathematical predictor and web-bade calculator of risk of Cesarean Section. Home: 8817 Southwestern Blvd #1222 Dallas TX 75206 Office: Bank of America 1401 Elm St 4th FL TX1-099-04-08 Dallas TX 75202 Personal E-mail: cgcn2003@fastmail.fm.

CHEN, GEORGE CHI-MING, energy company executive; b. Shanghai, Sept. 21, 1923; s. Harvey Kun-Fan and Margaret Wen-Yao (Sang) C.; m. Nora Tzu-Ling Pan, Oct. 15, 1953; children: Priscilla Hsu-Lu, Peter Hsu-Ling. BS, Harvard U., 1946. Mgr. Kian Gwan Co., Shanghai, 1947-49, Hong Kong, 1949-50, mng. dir. Taipei, 1950-51; chmn. George Chen & Co., Taipei, 1951-87, Lien Chen Ltd., Taipei, 1951-87; mng. dir. Shing Nung Group, Tai Chung, 1961-87; chmn. Shell Pacific Devel., Singapore, 1970-87. Trustee Northfield Mt. Hermon Sch., Mass., 1988-98, Libr. Found. of San Francisco, 1996—; mem. bd. overseers Harvard U., 1998—. Lt. Col. Chinese Army. Mem. China Petroleum Soc. (life). Republican. Roman Catholic.

CHEN, GUANG X., research company director; b. Feng Hua, Zhejiang, China, Sept. 2, 1962; s. Yizhao Chen and Ainu Chuang; m. Min Jiang, Feb. 4, 1963; children: Hanna Jamie, Henry James. PhD, U. Alta., Edmonton, Can., 1993. Sect. head New Sun Med. Works, Shengzhou, China, 1982—87; tech. dir., co. tech. dir. Fractionation Rsch., Inc., Stillwater, Okla., 1993—. Contbr. articles to profl. jours. Mem.: AIChE. Achievements include patents in field. Home: 5521 W 8 th Ave Stillwater OK 74074 Office: Fractionation Rsch Inc PO Box 2108 Stillwater OK 74076 Office Phone: 405-385-0354. Home Fax: 405-377-8043; Office Fax: 405-385-0357. Personal E-mail: gxchen1@cox.net. E-mail: gxchen@fri.org.

CHEN, HO-HONG H. H., industrial engineering executive, educator; b. Taiwan, Apr. 11, 1933; s. Shui-Cheng and Mei (Lin) C.; m. Yuki-Lihua Jenny, Mar. 10, 1959; children: Benjamin Kuen-Tsai, Carl Joseph Chao-Kuang, Charles Chao-Yu, Eric Chao-Ying, Charmine Tsuey-Ling, Dolly Hsiao-Ying, Edith Yi-Wen, Yvonne Yi-Fang, Grace Yi-Sing, Julia Yi-Jiun. Owner Tai Chang Indsl. Supplies Co., Ltd., 1967—; pres. Pan Pacific Indsl. Supplies, Inc., Ont., Canada, 1975—, Maker Group Inc., Md., 1986—, Wako Internat. Co., Ltd., Md., 1986—; CEO, pres. Nitor Co., Ltd., Taipei, Taiwan, 2000—. Prof. First Econ. U., Japan; commr. Overseas Chinese Affairs Commn., Taiwan; chmn. supervisory bd. Global Alliance for Democracy and Peace, Taiwan. Author: 500 Creative Designs for Future Business, 1961; A Summary of Suggestions for the Economic Development in Central America Countries, 1979; Access and Utilize the Potential Fund in Asia, 1980. Mem. Univ. Club (Washington), Kenwood Golf & Country Club (Bethesda, Md.). Office: PO Box 5674 Washington DC 20016-1274

CHEN, JAKE YUE, computer scientist, bioinformatician; s. Xianghua Chen and Guirong Zhao; m. Yang Liu. BS in BioChemistry and Molecular Biology, Peking U., Beijing, 1995; MS in Computer sci. and Engring., U. Minn., 1997, PhD, 2001. Bioinformatics computer scientist Affymetrix, Inc., Santa Clara, Calif., 1998—2002; head computational proteomics Myriad Proteomics, Inc., Salt Lake City, 2002—03; asst. prof. informatics and computer sci. Ind. U. - Purdue U., Indpls., 2004—. Chair, founder Bay Area Young Scientists Forum, Palo Alto, Calif., 2001—03; mem. steering com., co-founder Ind. Biomedical Entrepreneur Network, Indpls., 2004—; bd. dirs. Assn. of Chinese Bioinformaticians. Recipient Project Achievement awards, Affymetrix, Inc., 1999, 2000. Mem.: IEEE (sr.), Internat. Soc. of Computational Biology. Achievements include research in Large-Scale Genome/Proteome Data Management And Knowledge Discovery. Office: Ind Univ Sch of Informatics 535 W Michigan Ave #493 Indianapolis IN 46202 Office Phone: 317-278-7604. Home Fax: 775-659-0376. Personal E-mail: jakechen@iupui.edu.

CHEN, JIANHUA, computer science educator, researcher; BS in Computer Sci., Jilin U., China, 1982, MS in Computer Sci., 1985, PhD in Computer Sci., 1988. Tchr. discrete maths. jr. undergrads. computer sci. Jinan U., Canton, China, 1983; rsch. assoc. dept. computer scis. Jilin U., Changchun, China, 1985-87; sr. researcher, engr. China Software Technique Corp., Beijing, 1988; vis. asst. prof. dept. computer sci. La. State U., Baton Rouge, 1988-89, asst. prof. dept. computer sci., 1989-95, assoc. prof. dept. computer sci., 1995—. Prin. investigator NSF, 1994, LEQSF, 1995-97, LTRC, 1999-2000; panelist CISE/IRIS program NSF, 1993, 96, 98, 99, 2001; chair tech. session Fla. Artificial Intelligence Rsch. Symposium, Pensacola, 1994, 8th Internat. Symposium on Methodologies for Intelligent Sys., Charlotte, N.C., 1994, 9th Internat. Symposium on Methodologies for Intelligent Sys., Zakopane, Poland, 1996, program com. mem. 13th Internat. Symposium Methodologies Intelligent Sys., 2002; publ. chair N.Am. Fuzzy Info. Processing Soc. Internat. Conf., 2002. Reviewer jours.; contbr. numerous articles to profl. jours. Rsch. grantee U. Coun. Rsch., 1990. Mem. IEEE (chair tech. session Internat. Conf. Fuzzy Logic 1996), Am. Assn. Artificial Intelligence, Assn. Computing Machinery, Spl. Interested Groups SIGART, SIGMOD. Achievements include research in artificial intelligence, knowledge presentation and non-monotonic reasoning, logic programming, manchine learning, fuzzy logic and fuzzy systems, intelligent multimedia interface and intelligent tutoring. Office: La State U Dept Computer Science Baton Rouge LA 70803-0001 E-mail: jianhua@bit.csc.lsu.edu.

CHEN, JINGGUANG G., chemical engineer, educator; b. Tonghua, Jilin, China, Mar. 22, 1961; s. Mingzhe Chen; m. Wen Tao; children: Benjamin Z, Andrew Z. PhD, U. Pitts., 1988. Staff scientist Exxon Rsch. and Engring., Annandale, NJ, 1989—98; prof. chem. engring. U. Del., Newark, 2000—. Dir. Ctr. for Catalytic Sci. and Tech., Newark, 2000—. Contbr. more than 140 articles to sci. jours. Recipient Phila. Catalysis award, 2004; Varian Russell fellow, Am. Vacuum Soc., 1986, Humboldt rellow, Germany, 1989. Achievements include 16 patents. Office: U Del Dept Chem Engring Newark DE 19716 Office Phone: 302-831-0642. Office Fax: 302-831-2085.

CHEN, JIUHUA, physicist, geophysicist, educator; b. Shenyang, Liaoning, China, Dec. 2, 1962; arrived in U.S., 1994; s. Xixue Chen and Yukun Li; m. Hongyu Lu, Dec. 28, 1986; 1 child, Jeddy Chang. PhD, Nat. Lab. High Energy Physics, Tsukuba, Japan, 1994. Postdoctoral rsch. assoc. Ctr. High Pressure Rsch., Stony Brook, NY, 1994-96; rsch. asst. prof. geophysics SUNY, Stony Brook, 1996-2001, rsch. assoc. prof., 2001—, assoc. dir. Mineral Physics Inst., 2002—, acting dir. Mineral Physics Inst., 2004—. Mem. dissertation com. SUNY, Stony Brook, 1996—97, asst. dean admissions, 2005—; organizer workshop high pressure tech., ann. user's meeting Nat. Synchrotoron Light Source, Upton, NY, 1998. Author: (book) A Combined CCD/IP Detection System: Science and Technology of High Pressure, 2000. Fellow Rsch., Japan Soc. Promotion Sci., 1998; grantee, NSF, 1999—. Mem.: Japan Soc. High Pressure Sci. Tech., Am. Geophys. Union, Internat. Union Crystallography. Achievements include inventor in field. Office: SUNY Stony Brook ESS Bldg Stony Brook NY 11794-2100 Office Phone: 631-632-8058. Office Fax: 631-632-8140. E-mail: jiuhua.chen@sunysb.edu.

CHEN, JOHN CALVIN, psychiatrist, educator; b. Augusta, Ga., Apr. 30, 1949; s. Calvin H. Chen and Lora L. Liu. BA in History, Pacific Union Coll., 1971; MD, Loma Linda U., 1974; PhD in Philosophy, Claremont Grad. U., 1984; JD, UCLA, 1987. Bar: Calif. 1987, U.S. Dist. Ct. (ctrl. dist.) Calif. 1988; diplomate Am. Bd. Psychiatry and Neurology, Child and Adolescent Psychiatry. Resident in psychiatry Loma Linda U. Med. Ctr., 1975-77; fellow in child and family psychiatry Cedars-Sinai Med. Ctr., L.A., 1977-78; psychiat. cons. San Bernardino (Calif.) County Mental Health Dept., 1979-83; pvt. practice Claremont, Calif., 1980-84; fellow in child and adolescent psychiatry U. So. Calif., L.A., 1983-84; law clk. to Hon. William P. Gray U.S. Dist. Ct., L.A., 1987-88; mental health psychiatrist LA County Dept. Mental Health, LA, 1988-94, Alameda County Health Care Svcs. Agy., Fremont, Calif., 1994-97; physician specialist L.A. County Dept. Health Svcs., 1997—99; sr. physician, 1999—2003; attending physician Martin Luther King Jr. Hosp., L.A., 1997—; child and adolescent psychiatrist Augustus F. Hawkins Mental Health Ctr., L.A., 1997—2004, chief child/adolescent svc., 1998—2003; supr. psychiatrist L.A. County Dept Mental Health, L.A., 2003—04; staff Behavioral Neuroscience Rsch. Ctr., Charles Drew Univ., 2003—. Adj. instr. social scis., philosophy, Fullerton (Calif.) Coll., 1989-90; adj. asst. prof. psychiatry Charles Drew U., 1998—; asst. clin. prof. psychiatry UCLA Sch. Medicine, 1998-2004, assoc. clin. prof., 2004—; faculty Trinity Coll. Grad. Studies, 2004- Contbr. chapters to books Calif. hist., articles pub. to profl. jour. Univ. fellow, Claremont Grad. Sch., 1980—81. Office: 745 E Valley Blvd PMB 120 San Gabriel CA 91776-3549

CHEN, JOHN S., computer company executive; b. Hong Kong, July 1, 1955; came to U.S., 1974; s. Peter and Harmie (Lee) C.; m. Sherry Hai, Nov. 5, 1980; children: Jacqueline, Stephanie. BSEE, Brown U., 1978; MSEE, Calif. Inst. Tech., 1979. V.p. pres., gen. mgr. Unisys, Blue Bell, Pa., 1979-91; exec. v.p. Pyramid Tech., San Jose, Calif., 1991—92, COO, 1992—95, pres., 1993—95, CEO, 1995—97; pres. Sybase, Inc., Dublin, Calif., 1997—, chmn., CEO, 1998—. Mem., bd. dirs., Sybase, Inc., 1997-, Walt Disney Co., 2003-Republican. Roman Catholic. Office: Sybase Inc One Sybase Dr Dublin CA 94568*

CHEN, JOIE, news correspondent; b. Chgo., Aug. 28, 1961; married; 1 child. B in Journalism, M in Journalism, Northwestern U. Reporter Sta. WCIV-TV, Charleston, SC, 1983—85; from reporter to anchor Sta. WXIA-TV, Atlanta, 1985—91; host CNNI World News, Atlanta, 1991—94; news anchor CNN, 1994—2001; former co-host CNN Saturday Morning News and CNN Sunday Morning News, Atlanta, 1994-96; former co-anchor The World Today, CNN; news corr. CBS News, Washington, 2002—. Office: CBS News 2020 M St NW Washington DC 20036

CHEN, JULIE, newscaster; b. N.Y.C., Jan. 6, 1970; B in Broadcast Journalism and English, U. of So. Calif., 1991. Prodn. asst. ABC News, LA, 1990—91; prodr. ABC News One, Dayton, 1991—95; reporter WDTN-TV, Dayton, 1995—97; reporter, anchor WCBS-TV, N.Y.C., 1997—99; news anchor, substitute anchor The Early Show, 1999—2002; anchor CBS Morning News, 2002—. Substitute anchor CBS Morning News, 1999, This Morning, 1999; host Big Brother, 2000—. Office: CBS News 524 W 57th St New York NY 10019

CHEN, JUNJIE, anthropologist; b. Yuyao, Zhejiang Province, China, Oct. 8, 1968; s. Jiankang Chen and Huazhen Lu; m. Zhen Chen. PhD in Sociology, Peking U., Beijing, 1996. Asst. rsch. fellow Chinese Acad. Social Scis., Beijing, 1996—99. Grantee, Wenner-Gren Found. for Anthrop. Rsch., 2004; Rita and Arnold Goodman fellow, U. Ill., Urbana-Champaign. Mem.: Am. Anthrop. Assn. Avocations: swimming, hiking. Office: U Ill 607 S Mathews Ave Urbana IL 61801 Office Phone: 217-333-3616.

CHEN, KEVIN S., management executive, consultant, educator; b. Dover, N.J., Aug. 17, 1960; s. Irving S. and Judy Chen. BS, Stevens Inst. Tech., Hoboken, N.J., 1984, MS, 1988. Purchase parts planning mgr. Rowe Internat. Inc., Whippany, N.J., 1984-86; materials mgr. KDI/Triangle Electronics, Whippany, 1986-90; prodn. control supr. Micron Powder Systems, Summit, N.J., 1990-93; pres., CEO, Bus. Methods Corp., Randolph, NJ, 1995—. Dir. Bus. Methods Cons., Cedar Knolls, NJ, 1989—; registered and cert. profl. cons. to mgmt. Nat. Bur. Cert. Cons., 1993—2005, adv. coun., 1993—97, regional dir. (N.J.), 2001—05, nat. com. for continuing edn. in consultancy, 1999—2001; edn. dir. Vols. Morris County, Morristown, NJ, 2000; Dovia focus group chmn., coord., adv. coun. chair Project Blueprint, 2000; pres., CEO Logo In Motion, Randolph, NJ, 1999—; supr. Ctr. Assessment and Learning, County Coll. of Morris, 2000—. Mem. coll. coun. County Coll. of Morris, 2002—04, mem. acad. std. com., 2002—; hon. chair State of N.J. bus. adv. coun. Nat. Rep. Com., 2002—04; walk chair ADA, 1993—96, bd. dirs., 1995—97, mem. N.W. regional coun., 1993—97; mem. steering com. United Way's Mentoring Tng. and Cons. Ctr., 2001—02; vice chmn., chmn. spl. events., chmn. survey subcom. Randolph Township Environ. Com., 1985—89; dir. Custom Scholarship Search Program, 1991—94; instr. bus. County Coll. of Morris, 1996—98, instr., 2001—; racquetball events coord. Stevens Alumni Assn., 1994—2000; racquetball coord. Madison Area YMCA, 1999—2001; N.J. state dir. Cons. Inst., 1999—2001; bd. dirs. The Better Bus. Bur., NJ, 2001—02, Better Bus. Bur. N.J., 2005—. Recipient Nat. Leadership award, Nat. Rep. Congl. Com., Businessman of Yr., 2003—04, Ronald Reagan Gold medal, 2004. Mem.: NJ Bus. Tech. Edn. Assn. (bd. dirs.), Nat. Bus. Edn. Assn., NJ Regional Cons. Assn. (founder, regional dir., bd. dirs.), Delta Pi Epsilon. Avocations: racquetball, coaching, team sports. Home: PO Box 520 Mount Freedom NJ 07970-0520 Office: Business Methods Corp 503 State Route 10 E Randolph NJ 07869-2152 Personal E-mail: njconsultants99@aol.com.

CHEN, KUN-MU, electrical engineering educator; b. Taiwan, China, Feb. 3, 1933; came to U.S., 1957, naturalized, 1969; s. Tsa-Mao and Che (Wu) C.; m. Shun-Shun Chen, Feb. 22, 1962; children: Margaret, Katherine, Kenneth, George. BS, Nat. Taiwan U., 1955; MS, Harvard, 1958, PhD, 1960. Research assoc. U. Mich., 1960-64; vis. prof. Chao-Tung U., Taiwan, 1962; asso. prof. elec. engring. Mich. State U., 1964-67, prof., 1967-95, Richard M. Hong Endowed prof. elec. engring. Lansing, 1995—99, dir. elec. engring. grad. program, 1967-70, Richard M. Hong prof. emeritus, 1999—. Vis. prof. Tohoku U., Japan, 1989, Nat. Taiwan U., 1989. Author articles on electromagnetic radiation, plasma physics, electromagnetic bioeffects. Recipient Disting. Faculty award Mich. State U., 1976, Outstanding Achievement award in sci. and engring. Taiwanese Am. Found., 1984; Withrow Disting. scholar Coll. Engring., Mich. State U., 1993; C.T. Loo fellow, 1957; Gordon

McKay fellow, 1958-60. Fellow IEEE, AAAS; mem. Internat. Union Radio Sci. (commn. A, B and C), AAUP, Sigma Xi, Phi Kappa Phi, Tau Beta Pi. Home: 7585 Mona Ln San Diego CA 92130 Office: Mich State U Dept Elec Engring East Lansing MI 48824 E-mail: chen@msu.edu.

CHEN, LAN X., physician, educator; arrived in U.S., 1989; d. B. K. Xuan and R. L. Young; m. Tao Chen, Mar. 12, 1990; children: Sophia, Gavin. MD, Temple U., Phila., PhD, 1996. Intern Drexel U., 1996—97; resident Hahnemann/Drexel, 1997—99; attending physician Presbyn. Med. Ctr., UPHS, Phila., 2002—; asst. clin. prof. U. Pa., Phila., 2003—. Co-leader del. to China People to People, Pa. Grantee, Temple U. Med. Sch., 1995. Mem.: ACP, Am. Coll. Rheumatology. Office: U Pa PHI Bldg 2B 39th and Market St Philadelphia PA 19104 Office Phone: 215-662-8233. Office Fax: 215-823-6032.

CHEN, LIHTORNG ROBERT, lawyer, educator; b. Taiwan, Sept. 6, 1952; came to U.S., 1983; s. Su-Kuo and Su-Lien (Wu) C.; m. Ruei-Chu Catherine Li; children: Lida, Eileen. LLB, Soochow U., Taipei, 1977; MS, Mo. U., 1984; LLM, U. Miami, Fla., 1985; PhD, U. Wales, U.K., 1990. Researcher Republic of China Ministry of Econ. Affairs, Taipei, 1980-82; pvt. practice, 1985-90; assoc. prof. law Soochow U., 1991-92, Tunghai U. and Nat. Taiwan Ocean U., 1992—. Arbitrator Comml. Arbitration Assn. Republic of China, 1993—; sec.-gen. Marine Affairs Assn. Rep. China, 1997—; bd. dirs. Taiwan Water Co.; bd. dirs. Nat. Taiwan Ocean U., Law of the Sea Inst., 2004—. Internat. law editor Cambrian Law Rev., 1996—. Commr. adminstrv. appeal com. Ministry of Transp. and Comm. of Republic of China, 1995—; com. mem. adminstrv. appeal com. Ministry of Def. of Republic of China, 1998—; com. mem. adminstrv. appeal com. Coun. of Agrl. Exec. Yuan of Republic of China, 1997—, Commr. Comm. of administrv. appeal for Ministry of Foreign Affairs of Republic of China, 2002-; city counselor for Tainan gov. of Republic of China, 2002-.

CH'EN, LI-LI, literature and language educator, writer; b. Beijing, Apr. 6, 1934; came to U.S., 1951, naturalized, 1963; d. Shujen and Yu-wu (Kuan) C. BA magna cum laude, Wilson Coll., 1957, Litt.D., 1980; MA, Radcliffe Coll., 1958; PhD (Harvard-Yenching Inst. fellow, Ford Found. fellow), Harvard U., 1969. Prof. Chinese lang., lit. and comparative lit., dir. Chinese program Tufts U., Medford, Mass., 1972—94, prof. emerita, 1994—. Translator: Master Tung's Western Chamber Romance, 1977 (Nat. Book Award for Transl.); Contbr. articles to profl. jours. Am. Council Learned Socs. grantee, 1976-77; MacDowell Colony fellow, 1980; Michael Karolyi Found. fellow, 1980; Recipient Nat. Mag. Award for Fiction, Criticism, and Belles Lettres for short story Peking! Peking!, 1977 Mem. Phi Beta Kappa. Home: 186 Upland Rd Cambridge MA 02140-3624 Office: Tufts U Olin Hall Medford MA 02155

CHEN, LINCOLN CHIN-HO, former medical educator; b. Peoples Republic China, Feb. 12, 1942; came to U.S., 1949; s. Samuel S.T. and Winifred (Wan) C.; m. Martha Alter, July 1, 1967; children: Gregory, Alexis. BA magna cum laude, Princeton U., 1964; MD cum laude, Harvard U., 1968; MPH, Johns Hopkins U., 1973. Lic. doctor, Mass. Intern in internal medicine Mass Gen. Hosp., Boston, 1968-69, asst. resident in internal medicine, 1969-70; clin. fellow Harvard Med. Sch. Harvard U., Boston, 1969-70; chmn. population svcs. dept. Harvard Sch. Pub. Health Harvard U., Boston, 1987, Takemi prof. internat. health, 1987—97, study dir. Commn. on Health Rsch., 1987—97; clin. rsch. assoc. Nat. Inst. Allergy and Infectious Diseases NIH, D.C., Bangladesh, England, 1970-72; staff assoc. Population Coun., Washington, 1972-77; officer program for population Ford Found., Bangladesh, 1973-75, acting rep., 1976, project specialist devel. Internat. Ctr. for Health Rsch., 1977, rep., 1981-86; mem. White House Task Force on Internat. Health, 1977; sci. dir. IC Diarrhoeal Disease Rsch., B, Bangladesh, 1977-80; exec. v.p. strategy Rockefeller Found., 1997—2002; dir., global equity initiative, JFK Sch. Govt. Harvard U., 2002—. Vis. prof. nutrition U. Dhaka, Bangladesh, 1970-80; vis. assoc. prof. population sci. and internat. health Harvard U., Boston, 1980-81; vis. lectr. MIT, Cambridge, 1976-81; vis. scholar Bangladesh Inst. Devel. Studies, 1977-78; mem. U.S. panel U.S.-Japan Malnutrition Panel NIH, 1979-80; mem. global adv. com. UN Univ., 1980-83; mem. adv. com. on child survival revolution UNICEF, 1984—, chmn. CARE, 2001-. Editor, author (with others): Disaster in Bangladesh: Health Crisis in a Developing Nation, 1973; contbr. articles to profl. jours., chpts. to books. Recipient award NSF, 1964. Mem. Am. Pub. Health Assn., Population Assn. Am., AAAS, Internat. Union Nutritional Scis., Internat. Epidemiol. Assn., Nat. Coun. Internat. Health (bd. dirs. 1982-83), NAS (com. internat nutrition programs 1982-84, 86, subcom. on vitamin A), Internat. Ctr. Rsch. Women (bd. dirs. 1987), Phi Beta Kappa, Alpha Omega Alpha, Inst. Medicine, 2004. Office: JFK Sch Govt 79 John F Kennedy St Cambridge MA 02138

CHEN, LIPING, molecular biologist, researcher, biochemist; b. Fuzhou, Fujian, China, Jan. 14, 1955; came to U.S., 1989; d. Yueming and Yihua (Ye) C. MD, Fujian Med. Coll., Fuzhou, 1983; PhD in Biomed. Scis., Kent State U., 1993. Asst. lectr. in pharmacology Fujian Med. Coll., 1983-88; rsh. assoc. in molecular biology NEOUCOM, Rootstown, Ohio, 1991-93; rsch. scientist Gentest Corp., Woburn, Mass., 1993-94; rsch. fellow, immunology, molecular biology NIH, Nat. Inst. Allergy and Infectious Diseases, Bethesda, Md., 1994-97; rsch. fellow biochemistry, molecular biology HIH, Nat. Inst. Diabetes & Digestive & Kidney Diseases, 1997—. Cons. NIH Grant, Rootstown, Ohio, 1996—. Contbr. articles to profl. jours. Mem. AAAS, Am. Assn. Cancer Rsch., Am. Chem. Soc. Achievements include: co-developed procedures that identified first P450 with increased expression level in rat hepatic tumors; started new P450 subfamily; patent in process. Developed coexpression of P450 and oxidoreductase in baculovirus sys. by noticing that as a cofacor of P450s, oxidoreductase also degrades P450s; first study of interactions between purine receptor and ligands using surface plasmmon resonance. Office: NIH NIDDK Rm B1A 23 Bldg 8 Bethesda MD 20892-0001

CHEN, PENG-HSIN, composer, music educator; b. Tokyo, Dec. 2, 1964; d. Tsung-Tsing Chen and Mitsuko Ota; m. Christopher B Durrenberger, Dec. 29, 1965; children: Isabelle Ai Durrenberger, Leon Xin Durrenberger. Advanced studies in Composition for Motion Picture & TV, U. of So. Calif., 1993—94, MusM, 1990—93. Comml. & film music composer PH Music Prodn., Taipei, Taiwan, 1993—98; adj. instr. Wittenberg U., Springfield, Ohio, 2003—; comml. & Film music composer PH Music Prodn., LA, 1993—98. Composer: The Second Dream, Qing Xou Village, Dance Suite, Spring for Women Freshness. Office: Wittenberg University Ward St at North Wittenberg Avenue Springfield OH 45501-0720

CHEN, PETER PIN-SHAN, engineering educator, computer science and internet/web educator, data processing executive; b. Taishan, Kwangtung, China, Jan. 3, 1947; came to U.S., 1969; s. Man-See and T.T. Chen; m. Li-Chuang Ho; children: Victoria, Angela, Gloria Lily. BSEE, Nat. Taiwan U., Republic of China, 1968; MS, Harvard U., 1970, PhD, 1973. Student assoc. IBM, Yorktown Heights, N.Y., 1970; teaching fellow Harvard U., Cambridge, Mass., 1970-71; prin. engr. Honeywell, Waltham, Mass., 1973-74; vis. researcher Digital Equipment Corp., Maynard, Mass., 1974; asst. prof. MIT, Cambridge, Mass., 1974-78; assoc. prof. UCLA, 1978-82; Sinclair vis. prof. MIT, 1986-87; Foster Disting. Chair prof. La. State U., Baton Rouge, 1983—. Vis. prof. Harvard U., Cambridge, 1990, MIT, Cambridge, 1990-92; chmn. Chen & Assocs. Inc., Baton Rouge, 1978—; pres. ER Inst., Baton Rouge, 1980—. Author: Entity-Relationship Approach to Logical DB Design, 1978, ER to Systems Analysis, 1980, ER to Information Modeling, 1983; patentee in field. Tech. officer with Republic of China mil. svcs., 1968-69. Named to Data Mgmt. Hall of Fame, 2000; recipient Faculty Career award, UCLA, 1979, Info. Tech. award, Data Adminstrn. Mgmt. Assn., 1990, Gt. Paper in Computer Sci. Achievement award, Data Adminstrn. Mgmt. Assn. Internat., 2000, Stevens award, 2001, Allen Newell award, ACM/AAAI, 2002, Pan Wen-Yuan Outstanding Rsch. award, 2004, Disting. Faculty award, La. State U., 2005; Rsch. grantee, NSF, NIST, NIH, Dept. Def., Air Force, Air Force Office Sci. Rsch., Navy, others, 1978—. Fellow: AAAS, IEEE (Harry Goode award 2003), Assn. Computing Machines; mem.: European Acad. Scis. Office: La State Univ Computer Sci Dept Baton Rouge LA 70803-0001 E-mail: pchen@lsu.edu.

CHEN, PHILIP MINKANG, brokerage house executive; b. Chungking, Szechuan, China, Oct. 20, 1944; s. Yin Ching and Wansu (Wu) C.; m. Deborah Lynn Carlson, May 7, 1971; children: Martin, Emily. BME with distinction, U. Va., 1968; MS, Stanford U., 1969; JD, U. Minn., 1979. Bar: Minn. 1979, U.S. Dist. Ct. Minn. 1979, N.Y. 1982; registered profl. engr. Va., 1972, N.Y.; diplomate Am. Acad. Environ. Engrs., 1994. Copy boy Washington Star Newspaper, 1962-65; mech. engr. Pope, Evans & Robbins, Alex, Va., 1967-68; engr. Westinghouse Orec, Annapolis, Md., 1969-71; sr. environ. engr. Stone & Webster Engring. Corp., Boston, Denver, 1971-78; sr. engr. Dames & Moore, Denver, 1978; assoc. Dorsey & Whitney, Mpls., 1979-82, Mudge, Rose, Guthrie & Alexander, N.Y.C., 1982; mng. dir. Lehman Bros., N.Y.C., 1982-92; pres. Weston Internat., 1992-94; exec. v.p. Roy F. Weston, Inc., West Chester, Pa., 1992-94; investment banker The Chase Manhattan Bank, N.A., N.Y.C., 1995-96; mng. dir. South Africa Infrastructure Fund, Johannesburg, 1996-2000, PNC Capital Markets, Inc., Phila., 2003—05, ABN AMRO Bank NV, NY, 2005—, Vancouver, Canada, 2005—. Editl. adv. bd. American City and County Mag., 1986-87, Project Finance Monthly, 1989-92; mem. environ. technologies trade adv. com., Dept. Commerce, 1995-96, co-chmn. fin. subcom. Patentee for mooring system. Mem. Town Mtg. Winchester, Mass., 1973; past bd. dirs. U.S. Environ. Tech. Export Coun., Greater Phila. Internat. Network, Greater Phila. First Ptnrship. for Econ. Devel.; mem. The Union League of Phila., 1994-2001; participant Presdl. Bus. Devel. mission to Brazil, Argentina, and Chile, 1994. Mem. ABA (vice chmn. elec. power com. natural resources law sect. 1982-85, chmn. spl. com. on energy fin. 1988-89), ASME, Nat. Resource Recovery Assn. (adv. bd. U.S. conf. of mayors 1989), U. Va. Alumni Assn., Phi Sigma Kappa. Avocations: art, writing, fishing. Office: PNC Capital Markets Inc 1600 Market St Philadelphia PA 19103 Office Phone: 604-484-6058. E-mail: chenpm@aol.com, philip.chen@pnc.com.

CHEN, RAY GOW HWEI, art educator, department chairman, artist; b. Taipei, Taiwan, Jan. 9, 1962; s. Chi Wen Chen and Chang Wuo Kuo; m. Ann Mei Hui Huang, June 28, 2003. *Mother, Chang Hwa Gau, a well respected Ikebana teacher, was a founder of the Hwa Fu Flower Design Art Center in Keelung and his father, Chi Wen Chen, was the governor in Keelung, Taiwan. His sister Gow Yu is a musician and other sister, Gow Lin, former Miss Taiwan R.O.C. 1987, was an Ikebana and flower arrangement teacher and designer, and both are married.* BFA in Music, Nat. Taiwan Ednl. U., 1986; BFA in Ceramics, Ohio U., 1995; MFA in Ceramics & Ceramics Sculpture, Rochester Inst. Tech., 1997. Prof., ceramics dept. chair U. So. Maine, Gorham, Maine, 2001—; exhbn. dir. The Internat. Ceramics Group, Portland, Maine, 2005—. Symposium chmn. U. So. Maine, 2002, faculty senate, 2003—, symposium chmn., Maine, 2004—; juror Stretch Gallery, Charlotte, NC, 2004; vis. artist U. Mass., Dartmouth, Mass., 2004; presenter, spkr. Jingdezhen Ceramics Art Inst., Jingdezhen, China, 2004. *He was named Emerging Talent Artist for Ceramic Arts by the National Council on Education at the 2001 annual conference in Charlotte, NC. NCECA is a professional association of individuals and organizations whose interests, talents, and careers are focused on the ceramic arts. The annual NCECA conference is the world's largest event held in the field of ceramic arts. His career goal is to reach for the synthesis of contemporary communication and to contribute in the field of arts and higher education. He wants to connect boundaries of cultures, develop each individual artistic vocabulary through exhibitions, and increase his personal knowledge and philosophical world view.* Ceramic sculpture, Mother and Child (Emerging Talant Artist award, Nat. Coun. Edn. Ceramics Arts, 2001), Life (The 3rd Cheongju Internat. Biennale, Korea, 2003), Relationship (Sidney Myer Internat. award, Australia, 1999), Mother and Child (Altech Ceramics Triennial, South Africa, 2003), In Between (54 Concorso Internat. Della Mus. award, France, 2004). Deacon Portland Chinese Gospel Ch., Portland, 2004—. Soldier Mil. Police, 1982—86, Taiwan. Recipient Silver award, Forte Cup 20th Century Asian Pacific Art Internat., 1999, First Place, Internat. Art Vision 2.0, 2002, Elizabeth R. Raphael Founder's prize, Soc. Contemporary Craft Mus., 2003, Hon. Mention award, St. Petersburg Clay Nat., 2003, Gallery Internat., 2005; fellow Lormina Salter Fellowship, Balt. Clayworks, 1997; grantee Sculpture Excellence award, The Va. A. Groot Found., 2001, Faculty Profl. Devel. grant, U. So. Maine, 2001-2005, Internat. Exch. & Rsch. Found, 2004, Jingdezhen 1000 Yrs. Porcelain Internat. Rsch. grant, Jingdezhen Mcpl. People's Govt., Chian, 2004, Coll. Arts & Scis. Rsch. Creative award, U. So. Maine, 2004, 2005; scholar Nat. Coun. Edn. for Ceramic Arts, SHIMPO Co., Japan, 1993, Alfred L. & Ruby C. Davis Internat., Rochester Inst. Tech., 1997. Baptist. Avocations: travel, music, art collection, reading, exercise. Office: U So Maine 37 College Ave Gorham ME 04038-1032 Office Fax: 207-780-5759. Personal E-mail: raychenclay@msn.com. Business E-Mail: gowhwei.chen@maine.edu.

CHEN, SANDRA YI-TING, political organization worker; BA in Polit. Sci. & Chinese Lit., U. Calif., Riverside; attending, UCLA. Exec. dir. Ctr. for Asian Am. United for Self Empowerment, Pasadena. Dir. of mentorship Asian Professional Exchange. Adv. bd. mem. San Gabriel Valley YMCA, Make A Wish Found. of San Gabriel Valley; mem. League of Women Voters-Greater Pasadena. Office: Ctr for Asian Am United for Self Empowerment 260 S Los Robles Ave 118 Pasadena CA 91101*

CHEN, SHENGZAO, seismologist, consultant; s. Qiyan Chen and Zonglan Cheng; married, Dec. 26, 1982; children: Quinn, Christine. BS in Geophys., Peking U., 1977; MS in Geophys., Nanjing U., 1981, PhD in Geophys., 1986; PhD in Earthquake Seismology, Carleton U., 2000. Jr. lectr. Nanjing U., 1977—78; asst. prof., rschr. Nanjing Inst. Geology Mineral Resources, 1982—83; rsch. scientist Canmet Elliot Lake Lab., 1988—91, Laurenham U., 1991—95; seismologist Geomatrix Cons., Oakland, Calif., 2001—. Chief geophysicist China Chipper Gold Mines, Ltd., Ottawa, Canada, 1997—98; guest prof. Chengsha Inst., China, 1993—98; assoc. prof. Inst. Geophys.,State Seismoological Bur., 1989. Author: Coal Forming Tectonics & Evolution of China, 1994. Fellow, Inst. Geophys., State Seismological Bur., 1986—88. Mem.: Soc. Exploration Geophysicists, Seismological Soc. AM., Am. Geophys. Union. Office: Geomatrix Cons Inc 2101 Webster St 12th Fl Oakland CA 94612

CHEN, SHI-JIE (GARY), industrial engineer, educator; b. Taipei, Taiwan, June 10, 1967; arrived in U.S.A., 2001; s. Shie Chen and Jun Shao; m. Shu-Hwa (Dale) Ong, May 15, 1993. BS in engring., Feng-Chia U., Taiwan, 1989; MS in mech. engring., SUNY, Buffalo, 1996, PhD in indsl. engring., 1999. Asst. prof. Huafan U., Taipei, 1999—2000, Nat. Taipei U. of Tech., 2000—01, Mont. State U., Bozeman, 2001—. Primary investigator Nat. Sci. Coun., Taipei, 1999—2001. Contbr. articles to profl. jours. Sgt. Taiwan armed forces, 1989—91. Recipient Rsch. award, Nat. Sci. Coun., Taiwan, 1999, 2000; Rsch. grantee, 1999—2001. Mem.: IIE (faculty advisor 2001—), Alpha Pi Mu. Achievements include research in concurrent and management, project management, team management, and computer simulation of manufacturing systems. Office: Mont State U Dept Mech and Indsl Engring Bozeman MT 59717 Office Phone: 406-994-5942. Business E-Mail: gchen@ie.montana.edu.

CHEN, SHI-JIE, biophysicist; b. Hangzhou, Zhejiang, China, Dec. 18, 1965; s. Longxi Chen and Qunxian Zheng; m. Xiaoqin Zou, Aug. 23, 1993; children: Kyle Yu children: Hannah Shu. PhD, U.Calif.-San Diego, Calif., 1994. Asst. rsch. chemist U. Calif.-San Francisco, 1997—99; asst. prof. physics and biochemistry U. Mo.-Columbia, 1999—. Grantee Scientist Devel. Grant award, Am. Heart Assn. (Nat. Ctr.), 2001—04, NIH, 2003—. Achievements include research in devel. theories for biomolecular folding. Office: Univ Mo-Columbia Dept Physics and Biochemistry Columbia MO 65211 Business E-Mail: chenshi@missouri.edu.

CHEN, SHOEI-SHENG, retired mechanical engineer; b. Taiwan, Jan. 26, 1940; s. Yung-cheng and A-shu Chen; m. Ruth C. Lee, June 28, 1969; children: Lyrice, Lisa, Steve. BS, Nat. Taiwan U., 1963; MS, Princeton U., 1966, MA, 1967, PhD, 1968. Rsch. asst. Princeton U., 1965-68; asst. mech. engr. Argonne (Ill.) Nat. Lab., 1968-71, mech. engr., 1971-80, sr. mech. engr., 1980—2001; ret., 2001. Cons. to Internat. Atomic Energy Agy. to assist developing countries in R & D of nuclear reator systems components, 1977, 79, 80, 94; cons. NASA, NRC, Rockwell Internat., others. Author: Flow-Induced Vibration of Circular Cylinderical Structures, 1987; mem. internat. adv. editorial bd. Acta Mechanica Solida; adv. bd. JSME Internat. Jour.; assoc. editor Applied Mechs. Rev., Jour. of Pressure Vessels Tech.; contbr. articles to profl. jours. Recipient Disting. Performance award U. Chgo., 1986, ASME pressure vessel and piping medal, 2001. Fellow ASME (chmn. tech. subcom. on fluid and structure interactions pressure vessels and piping divsn. 1987-90, honors chmn. 1990-94, mem. exec. com. 1990-96, organizer symposia, tech. program chmn. 1994, conf. chair ASME/JSME pressure vessels and piping conf. 1995, pressure vessels and piping divsn., chmn. 1995-96, senate pres. 1997-98, honors and awards chair of materials and structures tech. group 1996-99), Instn. Diagnostic Engrs.; mem. Am. Acad. Mechanics, Acoustical Soc. Am., Sigma Xi. E-mail: sschen88@gnnil.com.

CHEN, SHUANG, computer science professional; b. China, Jan. 29, 1958; m. Hongwen Yan, Aug. 3, 1987; children: Jessica Y., Julia Y. BSEE, Nanjing Aeronautical U., 1982; MSEE, South China U. Tech., Guangzhou, China, 1985; MPH in Computer Engring., Rutgers U., 1990, PhD in Computer Engring., 1991. Mem. faculty South China U. Tech., Guangzhou, 1985-86; rsch. asst. Rutgers U., New Brunswick, 1986-91; sr. rsch. engr. Comm. Intelligence Corp., Redwood Shores, Calif., 1991-95; rsch. staff mem. IBM Thomas J. Watson Rsch. Ctr., Yorktown Heights, N.Y., 1995-98; pres., CEO, chmn. bd. Internat. Interactive Commerce, Ltd., Armonk, NY, 1999—2001; chmn. bd. Op40, Inc., White Plains, NY, 2002—. Author: (with others) Studies in Pattern Recognition, 1997; reviewer profl. jours. Mem. IEEE, Sigma Xi.

CHEN, SHU-CHING, computer science educator; b. Taoyan, Taiwan, Oct. 16, 1963; m. Mei-Ling Shyu; children: Winnie, Tiffany, Jonathan. MS in Computer Sci., Purdue U., 1992, MSEE, 1995, MSCE, 1996, PhD, 1998. Sys. engr. United World Chinese Comml. Bank, Taipei, Taiwan, 1988—90; rsch. asst. Ctr. Environ. and Regulatory Info., West Lafayette, Ind., 1996—98; assoc. prof. Fla. Internat. U., Sch. Computer Sci., Miami, 2004. Author: Semantic Models for Multimedia Database Searching and Browsing, 2000. Grantee, Fla. Dept. Ins., 2000—, NSF, 2000—02. Mem.: ACM, IEEE. Office: Fla Internat Univ 11200 SW 8th St ECS 354 Miami FL 33199 Office Phone: 305-348-3480. Business E-Mail: chens@cs.fiu.edu.

CHEN, SOW-HSIN, nuclear engineering educator, researcher; b. Chia-Yi, Taiwan, Mar. 5, 1935; came to U.S., 1958, naturalized, 1974; s. Pi-Yu Chen and Liang Hsu; m. Ching-Chih Liu, Aug. 19, 1961; children: Anne, Catherine, John. BS in Physics, Nat. Taiwan U., 1956; MS in Physics, Nat. Tsinghua U., 1958; MS in Nuclear Engring., U. Mich., 1962; PhD in Physics, McMaster U., 1964. Postdoctoral fellow AERE Harwell, Berkshire, U.K., 1965; asst. prof. physics U. Waterloo, Ont., Can., 1964-67; rsch. fellow Harvard U., Cambridge, Mass., 1967; asst. prof., then assoc. prof. nuclear engring. MIT, Cambridge, 1968-74, prof. nuclear engring., 1974—. Vis. prof. Tsinghua U., Peking, China, 1982, Ecole Superieure de Physique et Chemie, Paris, 1981, Univ. Konstanz, Germany, 1988, Univ. Bayreuth, Germany, 1988, Univ. Brodeaux I, France, 1991, 93; chmn. Gordon Conf., 1986; co-organizer ACS Conf., Conf. Colloid and Interface Sci.: Trends and Applications, 1985; dir. NATO ASI on Scattering Techniques Applied to Supramolecular and Non-Equilibrium Systems, 1980, Structure and Dynamics of Supramolecular Aggregates and Strongly Interacting Colloids, 1991. Author: Spectroscopy in Biology, Chemistry and Physics-Neutron, X-Ray and Laser, 1975, Scattering Techniques Applied to Supramolecular and Non-Equilibrium Systems, 1981, Micellar Solutions and Microemulsions: Structure: Dynamics and Statistical Thermodynamics, 1990, Structure and Dynamics on Strongly Interacting Colliods and Supramolecular Aggregates in Solution, 1992, Interaction of Photons and Neutrons with Matter-An Introduction, 1997; contbr. 350 articles to sci. jours. Alexander von Humboldt U.S. sr. scientist award Govt. of Germany, 1987-88, 95. Fellow AAAS, Am. Phys. Soc., Japan Soc. for the Promotion of Sci. (Rsch. fellow 1995); mem. Sigma Xi. Home: 1400 Commonwealth Ave Newton MA 02465-2830 Office: MIT 24-209 77 Mass Ave Cambridge MA 02139-4307 Office Phone: 617-253-3810. E-mail: sowhsin@mit.edu.

CHEN, STEPHEN S. F., retired diplomat; b. Nanking, China, Feb. 11, 1934; m. Rosa Te Chen; three children. BA, U. Santo Tomas, Philippines, 1957, MA, 1959; postgrad., U. Santo Tomas, 1959-60; DBA (hon.), Kensington U. Various positions in field to dir. gen. Coord. Coun. for N.Am. Affairs, L.A., 1988-89, dep. rep. Washington, 1989-93; vice-min. fgn. affairs Ministry Fgn. Affairs, China, 1993-96; dep. sec.-gen. Office of Pres., China, 1996-97; rep. TECRO, Washington, 1997-2000; ret., 2000. Avocation: languages.

CHEN, STEPHEN SHI-HUA, pathologist, biochemist; b. Taipei, Taiwan, Republic of China, Dec. 25, 1939; came to U.S., 1965; s. Ah-wen and Shun (Pan) C.; m. Hsin-Hsin Yii, July 5, 1969; children: Peter T., Margaret T. MD, Nat. Taiwan U., 1964; PhD, U. Pitts, 1972. Diplomate Am. Bd. of Pathology. Asst. prof. pathology U. Pitts., 1972-76; staff pathologist Presbyn. Hosp., Pitts., 1973-76; asst. prof. pathology dept. Stanford U., Palo Alto, Calif., 1976-80, clin. assoc. prof. pathology dept., 1980-96, clin. prof., 1996—; staff pathologist Veterans Affairs Med. Ctr., Palo Alto, 1976—. Contbr. articles to Jour. Cellular Physiology, Jour. Chromatography, Clinica Chimca Acta. Fellow Coll. Am. Pathologists; mem. Am. Soc. Investigative Pathology, U.S. and Can. Acad. Pathology Inc., Am. Soc. Clin. Pathologists, Am. Soc. Cytopathology. Achievements include chromatography of phospholipids. Office: Vets Affairs Med Ctr 113 3801 Miranda Ave Palo Alto CA 94304-1207

CHEN, TAK-MING, civil engineer, consultant; b. Changning, Hunan, China, July 29, 1936; came to U.S., 1970; s. Jenn-Chiu and Yin (Peng) C.; m. Taining Chou, July 1, 1973; children: Merry, Terry. BS in River/Harbor Engring., Taiwan Provincial Coll. of Marine Sci. and Tech., 1966; MSCE, U. Mo., 1971. Registered profl. engr., N.Y., Md., D.C. Project engr. Chinese Petroleum Corp., Taipei, Taiwan, 1973; structural designer Bellante, Clauss, Miller & Nolan, inc., Scranton, Pa., 1974-76; structural engr. Wayman C. Wings, Cons. Engrs., N.Y.C., 1978-80, Gibbs & Hills, Inc., N.Y.C., 1980-81; civil/structural engr. Bechtel Power Corp., Gaithersburg, Md., 1981-84; structural engr. Hazen & Sawyer, P.C., N.Y.C., 1984-85; civil/structural engr. N.Y.C. Dept. Sanitation, 1985-87; civil engr. N.Y.C. Dept. Bldgs., 1987-94, N.Y.C. Comptroller's Office, 1994—; pres. Chen's Cons. Engrs., Queens, N.Y., 1985-87. Bd. dirs. RFK Dem. Assn., Inc., Forest Hills, N.Y., 1994—. Recipient Cert. of Honor for leadership Dem. Nat. Com. Mem. NSPE, N.Y. State Soc. Profl. Engrs., Chinese Am. Assn. City of N.Y., MSM-UMR Alumni Assn., Comptr. Engrs. Assn. Home: 82-28 255th St Floral Park NY 11004 Office: New York City Comptrollers Office Bur of Engring 1 Centre St Rm 650 New York NY 10007 Office Phone: 212-669-2221. Personal E-mail: takchen@aol.com. Business E-Mail: tchen@comptroller.nyc.gov.

CHEN, TAR TIMOTHY, biostatistician, minister; b. Fuching, China, June 23, 1945; came to U.S., 1967, naturalized, 1979; s. Lin-Tsang and Ai-Ging (Chang) C.; m. Meei-Ming Li, Aug. 9, 1969; children: Stephen, Daniel. BS, Nat. Taiwan U., 1966; MS, U. Chgo., 1969, PhD, 1972; MDiv, Southwestern Bapt. Theol. Sem., 1989. Statistician Ill. Bell Tel., Chgo., 1971—73; asst. prof. Calif. State U., Hayward, 1973—74; vis. assoc. prof. Chung-Hsing U., Taichung, Taiwan, 1974—75; biostatistician Upjohn Co., Kalamazoo, 1975—79; asst. prof. biometrics M.D. Anderson Cancer Ctr. U. Tex., Houston, 1979—84; sr. biostatistician Alcon Labs., Fort Worth, 1984—89; math. statistician Nat. Cancer Inst., Bethesda, Md., 1989—98; prof., head biostats. sect. Greenebaum Cancer Ctr. U. Md., 1998—2001; pres. Timothy Statis. Cons., 2001—04; pastor St. Louis Chinese Gospel Ch., Chesterfield, Mo., 2004—. Contbr. articles to profl. jours. Deacon, Houston Chinese Ch., 1981-83, McKinney Meml. Bible Ch., Ft. Worth, 1988-89. 2d lt. Republic of

China Army, 1966-67. Fellow Am. Statis. Assn., Am. Scientific Affiliation; mem. Am. Assn. Chinese Studies, Internat. Chinese Statis. Assn., Evangelical Theol. Soc. Home: 79 Glen Cove Dr Chesterfield MO 63017-2755 Office Phone: 636-391-2112. E-mail: tar_timothy_chen@yahoo.com.

CHEN, WAI-FAH, civil engineering educator; b. Chekiang, China, Dec. 23, 1936; m. Lily Chen; children: Eric, Arnold, Brian. BS, Cheng-Kung U., 1959; MS, Lehigh U., 1963; PhD, Brown U., 1966. From asst. prof. to prof. civil engrng. Lehigh U., 1966-76; prof. civil engrng. Purdue U., Lafayette, Ind., 1976-92, head structural engrng., 1980-99, George E. Goodwin disting. prof., 1992-99; dean Coll. Engrng. U. Hawaii, Honolulu, 1999—. Cons. Exxon Products, 1979, Karagozian & Case Structural Engrs., 1985, Ga. Tech., 1987, Skidmore, Owings & Merrill, 1987, World Bank, 1988—. Editor-in-chief The Handbook of Structural Engineering, 1997, Bridge Engineering Handbook, 1999, Earthquake Engineering Handbook, 2002, The Civil Engrng. Handbook, 2d edit., 2002. Mem.: ASCE (hon.), Academia Sinica, Nat. Acad. Engrng., Am. Inst. Steel Constrn., Am. Concrete Inst., Am. Acad. Mech., Structural Stability Rsch. Coun., Internat. Assn. Bridge & Structural Engrng. Office: U Hawaii Coll Engrng 2540 Dole St Honolulu HI 96822-2303 Office Phone: 808-956-7727.

CHEN, WAI-KAI, electrical engineering and computer science educator, consultant; b. Nanking, China, Dec. 23, 1936; came to U.S., 1959; s. You-Chao and Shui-Tan (Shen) C.; m. Shirley Shiao-Ling, Jan. 13, 1939; children— Jerome, Melissa BS in Elec. Engrng., Ohio U., 1960, MS in Elec. Engrng., 1961; PhD in Elec. Engrng., U. Ill., Urbana, 1964. Asst. prof. Ohio U., 1964-67, assoc. prof., 1967-71, prof., 1971-78, disting. prof., 1978-81; prof., head dept. elec. engrng. and computer sci. U. Ill., Chgo., 1981-2001; vis. assoc. prof. Purdue U., 1970-71; v.p. acad. affairs Internat. Technol. U., 2000—04. Hon. prof. Tianjing U., Peoples Republic of China, 1990, Beijing U. of Posts and Telecomms., Beijing U. of Aeronautics and Astronautics, 1992. Author: Applied Graph Theory, 1970, Theory and Design of Broadband Matching Networks, 1976, Applied Graph Theory: Graphs and Electrical Networks, 1976, Active Network and Feedback Amplifier Theory, 1980, Linear Networks and Systems, 1983, Passive and Active Filters: Theory and Implementations, 1986, The Collected Papers of Professor Wai-Kai Chen, 1987, Broadband Matching: Theory and Implementations, 1988, Theory of Nets, 1990, Linear Networks and Systems: Computer-Aided Solutions and Implementations, 1990, Active Network Analysis, 1991, Modern Network Analysis, 1992, Computer-Aided Design of Comm. Networks World Scientific, 2000, Circuit Analysis and Feedback Amplifier Theory, 2005, Nonlinear and Distribution Circuits, 2005, Passive, Active and Digital Filters, 2005; editor: Brooks/Cole Series in Electrical Engineering, 1982-84; editor in chief Advanced Series in Elec. and Computer Engrng., World Sci. Pub. Co., Singapore, 1986—, Jour. Circuits, Systems and Computers, 1989—, The Circuits and Filters Handbook, 1995, 2d edit., 2002, The VLSI Handbook, 2000, Design Automation, Languages and Simulations, 2003, VLSI Technology, 2003, Memory, Microprocessor and ASIC, 2003, Analog Circuits and Devices, 2003, Logic Design, 2003; editor-in-chief The Elec. Engrng. Handbook, 2004—, Imperial Coll. Press, 1998—, others; editor The VLSI Series, 2000—; assoc. editor Jour. Circuits, Systems and Signal Processing, 1981-2004; editor in charge Advanced Series in Circuits and Systems, World Scientific Publ. Co., 1991—; sect. editor Encyclopedia of Physical Science & Technology, 1998-2001; editor-in chief Design Automation, Languages and Simulation, Memory, Microprocessor and ASIC, Analog Circuits and Devices, Logic Design, VLSI Tschmology, CRC Press, 2003, The Electrical Engineering Handbook, Academic Press, 2004. Recipient Lester R. Ford award Math. Assn. Am., 1967, Baker Fund award Ohio U., 1974, 78, Disting. Accomplishment award Chinese Acad. & Profl. Assn. in Mid-Am., 1985, Disting. Guest Prof. award Chuo U., Tokyo, 1987, Outstanding Svc. award Chinese Acad. & Profl. Assn. in Mid-Am., 1988, Outstanding Achievement award Mid-Am. Chinese Sci. & Tech. Assn, 1988, Disting. Alumnus award Elec. and Computer Engrng. Dept. Alumni Assn. U. Ill. Urbana-Champaign, 1988, Alexander von Humboldt award Alexander von Humboldt Stiftung, Fed. Republic of Germany, 1985, Rsch. award U. Ill. Chgo. Coll. Engrng., 2000, hon. prof. award Nanjing Inst. of Technology and Zhejing U., Peoples Republic of China, 1985, The Northeast U. Tech., East. China Inst. Tech., Nanjing Inst. of Posts & Telecommunications, AnHui U., Chengdu Inst. Radio Engrng., Wuhan Univ.; Rsch. Inst. fellow Ohio U., 1972, Japan Soc. for Promotion of Sci., 1986, Sr. U. Scholar award U. Ill., 1986, Ohio U. Alumni Medal Merit for Disting. Achievement in Engrng. Edn., 1987, Hon. Prof. award Hangzhan U. of Electronic Tech., China, 1990, Disting. Prof. award Internat. Technol. U., 1995, Hon. Prof. award Taichung U. Healthcare and Mgmt., Taiwan, 2002, Disting. Alumnus award Taipei U. Sci. and Tech., Taiwan, 2002, Certificate of Spl. Congl. Recognition, 2004. Fellow IEEE (Circuits and Sys. Soc. Meritorious Svc. award 1997, Edn. award 1998, Golden Jubilee medal 2000, Third Millennium medal 2000), AAAS; mem. NSPE, IEEE Cirs. and Sys. Soc. (adminstrv. com. 1985-87, exec. v.p. 1987, assoc. editor Trans. on Cirs. and Sys. 1977-79, editor 1991-93, pres.-elect 1993, pres. 1994), Md.-Am. Chinese Sci. and Tech. Assn. (bd. dirs. 1984-86, 89-93, pres. 1991-92), Chinese Acad. and Profl. Assn. Mid-Am. (advisor to bd. dirs. 1984-89, pres. 1986-87), Soc. Indsl. and Applied Math., Assn. Computing Machinery, Tensor Soc. Gt. Britain, Sigma Xi (sec.-treas. Ohio U. chpt. 1981), Phi Kappa Phi, Eta Kappa Nu. Office: Internat Technol U 3802 Belmont Ter Fremont CA 94539-8358 Office Phone: 408-556-9031. Business E-Mail: wkchen@ece.uic.edu.

CHEN, WENLIN, soil scientist, chemist; s. Angui and Laxiang Chen; m. June Q Li; children: Kevin S, LeeAnn. BS, Huazhong Agrl. U., Wuhan, China, 1982; MS, China Agrl. U., Beijing, China, 1988; PhD, Cornell U., Ithaca, New York, USA, 1994. Asst. scientist Chinese Acad. of Sciences, Beijing, 1988—90; post-doctoral rschr. U. of Minn., St. Paul, 1994—95; sr. chemist AgrEvo USA Co., Pikeville, NC, 1995—97; sr. scientist Syngenta Crop Protection, Inc., Greensboro, NC, 1997—. Contbr. book, scientific papers. Mem.: Soc. of Environ. Toxicology and Chemistry, Am. Geophys. Union, Soil Sci. Soc. of Am., Am. Chem. Soc. Achievements include research in Experimental Design, Mathematical Model Development, & Evaluation of Sorption Site Heterogeneity & Its Effects On Organic Chemical Transport In the environment; development of watershed scale exposure assessment methods; Model Development & Experimental Design To Reveal The Rate-Limiting Effect Of Time-Dependent Sorption On Bio-Degradation Of Organic Compounds In Soil. Office: Syngenta Crop Protection Inc 410 Swing Rd Greensboro NC 27409-2012 Office Phone: 336-632-2015.

CHEN, WESLEY, lawyer; b. NYC, Nov. 29, 1954; s. Tom Y.M. and Mary (Don) C.; m. Vivien Wong, Dec. 10, 1983; 2 children: Marissa, Jocelyn. BA, N.Y. U., 1976, JD, 1980. Bar: N.Y. 1981, U.S. Dist. Ct. (so. and ea. dists.) N.Y. 1981. Lawyer Meissner, Tisch & Kleinberg, N.Y.C., 1980-81; pvt. practice N.Y.C., 1982—85, 2003—, 1989—90; of counsel Serchuk, Wolfe & Zelermyer, White Plains, N.Y., 1985-88, ptnr. N.Y.C., 1995—2003, Cantwell & Chen, N.Y.C., 1988, Kimmelman, Sexter, Warmflash & Leitner, N.Y.C., 1990-91, Krasner & Chen, N.Y.C., 1992-94; pvt. practice, 2003—. Bd. dirs. United Orient Bank, N.Y.C., 1982-92, MFY Legal Svcs., Inc., 1993-96; mem. N.Y. State Banking Bd., 1992—. Mem. ABA, N.Y. State Bar Assn. (banking law com.), NY County Lawyers Assn. (banking law com.), Asian-Am. Bar Assn. NY, Chinese C. of C. (legal adviser 1982—). Office: 641 Lexington Ave Fl 20 New York NY 10022-4503 Office Phone: 212-751-7100.

CHEN, XIAO, process engineer; s. Mengcheng Chen and Huimei Xiao. PhD, U. Tex., Austin, 1996—2003. Key account technologist Applied Materials, Inc., Sunnyvale, Calif., 2003—. Contbr. articles to profl. jours. Mem.: IEEE. Achievements include research in the manufacturing of MOS capacitors on epitaxial Ge/Si1-xGex with high-k dielectrics using remote plasma chemical vapor deposition; high-resolution transmission electron microscopy of silicide formation and stability of Ni/Si and Ni/SiGe. Home: 5230 Birkdale Way San Jose CA 95138 Office: Applied Materials Inc 974 E Arques Ave Sunnyvale CA 94086 Office Phone: 408-584-7802.

CHEN, XIAO LUN, music educator, musician; s. Yu Xin Chen and Yu Jin Liu; m. Zhi Hui Li, Aug. 21, 1984; children: Xi En Owen, Katherine Lorris. MusM in Conducting and Voice, Eastman Sch. Music, NY, 1990. Choir dir. Perdido Bay United Meth. Ch., Pensacola, Fla., 2000—; dir. of choral activities Pensacola Jr. Coll., 1998—. Artistic dir. Choral Soc. Of Pensacola, Pensacola, 1998—. Dir.(singer): (choral conducting, solo singing) Choral Dir., Voice Tchr., Singer (Muriel Shugart Music award, 2000). Recipient Muriel Shugart Music award, NW Fla. Arts Coun., 2000. Mem.: Am. Choral Dir. Assn., Nat. Assn. of Tchrs. of Singing. Office: Pensacola Jr Coll 1000 College Blvd Pensacola FL 32504 Office Phone: 850-484-1810. Office Fax: 850-484-1835. E-mail: xchen@pjc.edu.

CHEN, XUMING, chemist, researcher; s. Caitao Chen and Xiuzhi Yi; m. Hua Zhong, Apr. 14, 1998; 1 child, Amy. Postgrad., SUNY, Stony Brook, 2002—. Chemical Engineer, BRICI, China, 1999. Group leader BRICI, Beijing, China, 1997—2000. Recipient Excellent In Grad. Polymer Rsch. award, Am. Chem. Soc., 2004. Mem.: Material Rsch. Soc. (licentiate), Am. Chem. Soc. (licentiate), Sigma Xi. Achievements include research in polymer nanocomposites. Home: B1016A Chapin Apts Stony Brook NY 11790 Office: Stony Brook Univ Dept of Chemistry Stony Brook NY 11974 Office Phone: 631-632-5779. Personal E-mail: xuchen@ic.sunysb.edu.

CHEN, YAN-HUA, medical educator; d. YueFu Chen; m. Qun Lu; children: Hope Lu, Wendy Lu. PhD, Emory U., Atlanta, 1993. Rsch. fellow Harvard Med. Sch., Boston, 1994—2000; asst. prof. East Carolina U. Sch. Medicine, Greenville, NC, 2000—. Grass Found. scholarship, Hopkins Marine Sta. of Stanford U., 1989. Mem.: Am. Soc. for Cell Biology. Achievements include research in Publish papers, presentations at national and international meetings. Office: Dept Anatomy and Cell Biology East Carolina Univ Sch Med Greenville NC 27858

CHEN, YEN-CHING KAREN, genetic epidemiologist; d. Tao Cheng and Chin-Cho ChengHo; m. Jen-Hau Howard Chen, June 25, 1973. DSc, Harvard U., 2001. Cert. environ. engr., Taiwan. Rsch. fellow Harvard Med. Sch., Boston, 2004—. Co-investigator Nat. Health Rsch. Insts., Taipei, 2001—; vis. scientist Harvard Sch. Pub. Health, Boston, 2001—; chair oral sect. annual meeting Internat. Soc. for Environ. Epidemiology, 2002. Contbr. articles to sci. publs. Grantee, NIH, 1998—. Mem.: Am. Assn. for Cancer Rsch. (assoc.). Achievements include research in insoluble arsenic in human urine; association between human papillomavirus and the risk of lung adenocarcinoma; arsenic methylation ability and the risk of bladder and skin cancer; genetic polymorphisms and the risk of hypertension. Avocations: swimming, instrument playing, travel, reading, art design. Office: Harvard Med Sch 181 Longwood Ave Boston MA 02115 Office Phone: 617-525-2105. Personal E-mail: chenkaren@yahoo.com. E-mail: karen.chen@channing.harvard.edu.

CHEN, YEN-CHU, physicist; arrived in US, 1990; s. Fai-Fan Chen and Ging-Ling Liao; m. Jennifer C. Chung, Mar. 21, 1962; 1 child, Rachel. B in Physics, Nat. Cheng Kung U., 1981, M in Physics, 1984; PhD, Nat. Cheng Kung U., Tainan, Taiwan, 1994. Postdoctoral staff Inst. Physics, Academia Sinica, Taipei, Taiwan, 1994—2001; vis. expert Nat. Sci. Coun., Taipei, 2001—; tching. asst. Nat. Cheng Kung U., 1987—88; rsch. asst. Inst. of Physics, Acad. Sinica, 1989—94. Co-leader CDF prodn. farm group The CDF Expt. at the Fermi Nat. Accelerator Lab., Batavia, Ill., 1998—. Vol., co-leader vol. tng. group Tzuchi Found., Midwest Region, USA, Chgo., 1998—2003. Buddhist. Achievements include development of The Data Acquisition System of the HyperCP experiment at the Fermilab; The CDF production farm computing system at the Fermilab. Office Phone: 630-840-5403.

CHEN, YU, acupuncturist, Chinese herbologist; b. Beijing, Sept. 10, 1942; arrived in U.S., 1985; d. Hai Chen and Xiu (Wang) C.; m. Paul L. Munson, Feb. 27, 1987; 1 child by previous marriage: Ming An. MD, Capital Med. Coll., Beijing, 1965; D Traditional Chinese Medicine, Chinese Traditional Med. Sch., Beijing, 1977; MS, Chinese Acad. Med. Sci., Beijing, 1981. Diplomate in acupuncture Nat. Comm. Cert. Acupuncture; cert. Chinese herbologist; lic. acupuncturist, Md. Physician Govt. China, Ching Yang, Gan Su, 1968-73; resident physician dept. ob-gyn. Worker's Hosp., Yen Shan Oil Factory, Beijing, 1974-78; attending physician dept. genetics Nat. Rsch. Inst. Family Planning, Beijing, 1982-83; WHO postdoctoral fellow Karolinska Inst., Stockholm, 1983-85; postdoctoral fellow dept. physiology U. Tex., Houston, 1985-87; postdoctoral fellow dept. pharmacology U. N.C., Chapel Hill, 1987-90; pvt. practice acupuncture and herbology Cmty. Wholistic Health Ctr., Carrboro, N.C., 1989-93; pvt. practice acupuncture, Chinese herbology, magnet therapy Pikesville and Parkville, Md., 1993—. Contbr. articles to profl. jours.; patentee in field; inventor of simple and effective way to treat panic attack by acupuncture and tiny hammer, ear magnet therapy to treat diabetes mellitus and control appetite, scalp magnet therapy to treat attention deficit disorder, herbal suppository for treatment of vaginal yeast infection, herbal treatment of AIDS meningitis. Recipient Best Essay award 1st Internat. Conf. Micro-Acupuncture Therapy, San Francisco, 1995. Democrat. Lutheran. Avocations: painting, photography, travel, classical music, gardening. Office: Beijing Acupuncture Chinese Herb & Magnetic Ctr 1401 Reisterstown Rd Baltimore MD 21208-6502 Office Phone: 410-484-4892. Personal E-mail: dryuchen@hotmail.com.

CHEN, YUANLIN, composer; s. Shifan Chen and Zongwen Zeng; m. Xilian Mo, Jan. 18, 2001. B.A., Ctrl. Conservatory of Music in Beijing, Beijing, China, 1978—83; MA, Ctrl. Conservatory of Music in Beijing, 1983—86; PhD in music, SUNY at Stony Brook, 1992—96. Composer Free Lance, NYC, 1996—; guest-prof. Ctrl. Conservatory of Music in Beijing, China, 2002—. Panelist of the cemc first electronic composition competition Contemporary Electronic Music Ctr., Beijing, China, 2004. Composer: (orchestra music) Away from Xuan, (classical) Chasing the Sun, (for percussion & wind instruments) Blowing Across the Sky, Striking Throughout the Earth. Red Cliff, Am. Composers Forum, 2003, Shijing Ste., 1999, 1998, Chasing the Sun, Mpls. Guitar Quartet, 2001, Thundering Across The Sky, Melody of China, 2002, Silk Rd. Ste., Silk Rd. Found., 1996. Mem.: Am. Music Ctr., Am. Composers Forum, Am. Soc. of Composers Authors and Publishers. Fax: 212-560-9368. Office Phone: 212-560-9368. Personal E-mail: yuanlinchen@hotmail.com.

CHEN, YUE, research scientist; s. Jioukuang Chen and Shuhui Zhang; m. Kelly Liu, Aug. 30, 1988; children: Langston, Katarina. PhD, U. Houston, 1990—95. Postdoctoral fellow Harvard U., Cambridge, Mass., 1995—97; rsch. fellow Harvard Med. Sch., Belmont, Mass., 1997—98, instr., 1998—2000, asst. prof., 2000—, dir. Visual Pschophysiology Lab., 2005—. Grantee, Nat. Alliance for Rsch. on Schizophrenia and Depression, 1998, 2000. Mem.: Am. Psychol. Soc., Soc. for Rsch. on Psychopathology, Soc. for Neuroscience, Am. Coll. Neuropsychopharmocology (assoc.). Office: McLean Hosp Harvard Med Sch 115 Mill St Belmont MA 02478 Office Phone: 617-855-3615. Office Fax: 617-855-3611. Business E-Mail: ychen@wjh.harvard.edu.

CHEN, ZHI, electrical engineering educator; b. Dazu, Chongqing, China; s. Jianguo Chen and Guoshu Huang; m. Chaoyuan Liu, Sept. 27, 1988; 1 child, Annie. BSEE, U. Electronic Sci. and Tech., Chengdu, Sichuan, China, 1984, MSEE, 1987; PhD in Elec. Engrng., U. Ill., 1999. Lectr., asst. prof. U. Electronic Sci. and Tech., 1987-92; asst. prof. U. Ky., Lexington, 1999—. Mem. tech. staff Lucent Techs., Orlando, Fla., summer 1998. Contbr. numerous articles to profl. jours.; patentee in field. Recipient Nat. award for invention Ministry of Sci. and Tech., China, 1995, Career award NSF, 2001; NSF grantee, 2000—. Mem. IEEE (sr. mem., Com. Prize Paper award 1992). Home: 4604 Hobbs Way Lexington KY 40515 Office: U Ky 453 Anderson Hall Lexington KY 40506 Fax: (859) 257-3092. E-mail: zhichen@engr.uky.edu.

CHEN, ZHIXIONG, engineering educator, researcher; b. Shanghai, Jan. 17, 1965; BA, MA, Shanghai Jiao Tong U., 1989; PhD, U. Pitts., 1997. Asst. prof. Shanghai Jiao Tong U., 1990—92; adv. software engr. IBM Rsch. Lab, Yorktown Heights, NY, 1997—2003; assoc. prof. Mercy Coll., Dobbs Ferry, NY, 2003—. Contbr. articles to profl. publs. Mem.: IEEE, Math. Assn. Am. Home: 46 Sandrock Ave Dobbs Ferry NY 10522 Office: Mercy Coll 555 Broadway Dobbs Fery NY 10522 Office Phone: 914-674-7532. Personal E-mail: zdragonet@gmail.com. E-mail: zchen@mercy.edu.

CHEN, ZONG, computer scientist, educator; b. Nanjing, Jiangsu, China, Apr. 17, 1971; s. Xin Chen and Manli Dong; m. Li Zhang, June 22, 1973. B, Nanjing U. Sci. and Tech., 1992; M, SE U., 1997; D, N.J. Inst. Tech., 2002. Rschr. N.J. Inst. Tech., Newark, 2003—04; asst. prof. Fairleigh Dickinson U., Teaneck, 2004—. Mem.: Upsilon Pi Epsilon (fairleigh dickinson u.), Sigma Xi (nj. inst. of tech.). Achievements include research in Pioneering research on dynamic handgrip recognition for biometric authentication. Home: 27 Jernee Dr East Brunswick NJ 08816 Office: Fairleigh Dickinson U 1000 River Rd T-BE2-01 Teaneck NJ 07666 Office Phone: 201-692-2721. Office Fax: 201-692-2773. Personal E-mail: zong71@yahoo.com. E-mail: zchen@fdu.edu.

CHENAULT, JAMES STOUFFER, judge; b. Richmond, Ky., May 1, 1923; s. Joe Prewitt and Russell (Stouffer) C.; m. Dorothy Neff, Apr. 21, 1960; children: Jean Russell. AB, Ea. Ky. U., 1949, LLD (hon.), 1975; LLB, U. Ky., 1949. Bar: Ky. 1949, U.S. Ct. Mil. Appeals 1956, U.S. Supreme Ct. 1960. Prosecuting atty. City of Richmond, Ky., 1950-57; commonwealth's atty. 25th Jud. Ct. of Ky., Clark, Jessamine and Madison Counties, 1964-66, cir. judge, 1966-80, chief cir. judge Clark and Madison Counties, 1980-93; chief regional judge Bluegrass Region of Ky., 1978-93; spl. judge Ky. Ct. of Appeals, 1973, Ky. Supreme Ct., 1984. Ky. rep. Nat. Ctr. State Cts., 1972-78; mem. Ky. Commn. on Corrections and Community Svc., 1973-77, Ky. Crime Commn. Cts. Sect., 1972-80, chmn., 1976-80, Task Force on Office for Pub. Advocacy, 1981-82, Gov.'s Jud. Adv. Coun., 1972-75, Ky. Jud. Coun., 1977-81, State and Fed. Jud. Coun., 1979-84; vol. faculty intensive trial seminar U. Ky., 1983, 85, 87, 90; lectr. So. Police Inst., 1970-80, Nat. Conf. Appellate Ctr. Clks., 1985, Nat. Conf. U.S. Dist. Ct. Clks., 1988, Nat. Conf. on Tech. and the Cts., Chgo., 1984, Denver, 1988, 3rd Fed. Jud. Cone, 1987, Ala. Appellate Judges Conf., 1990; adj. faculty Sch. Law Enforcement Ea. Ky. U., 1967-73; lectr. numerous state jud. confs.; presenter 1st Nat. Jud. State of the Art Conf., Phoenix, 1987. Councilman City of Richmond, 1949-50. Lt. (j.g.) USN, 1943-46, PTO. Recipient Outstanding Contbn. award Ky. Coun. Crime and Delinquency, 1974, Outstanding Contbn. award City of Richmond, 1977, Disting. Svc. award Dept. Mass Comm. Ea. Ky. U., 1993, Outstanding Trial Judge award Ky. Acad. Trial Attys., 1993, Ky. Chief Justice Spl. award, 1994; named Outstanding Alumnus Ea. Ky. U., Richmond, 1982; inducted into U. Ky. Law Sch. Hall of Fame, 2000. Mem. ABA (lectr., presenter ann. meeting San Francisco chpt. 1987), Am. Judicature Soc., Internat. Acad. Trial Judges, Ky. Bar Assn. (pres. younger lawyers conf. 1956-57), Ky. Assn. Cir. Judges (pres. 1970-75, editor newsletter 1976-93, Outstanding Contbn. award 1978), Ky. Commonwealth's Attys. Assn. (pres. 1965-66), Richmond C. of C. (Outstanding Svc. award 1983, Outstanding Achievement award 1989), Exch. Club (pres. Richmond chpt. 1955, Outstanding Lifetime Achievement award 2003), Elks. Avocations: Kentucky history, gardening. Home and Office: 302 High St Richmond KY 40475-1344

CHENAULT, KENNETH IRVINE, finance company executive; b. NYC, June 2, 1951; s. Hortenius and Anne N. (Quick) C.; m. Kathryn Cassell, Aug. 20, 1977; children: Kenneth I. Jr., Kevin A. BA, Bowdoin Coll., 1973; JD, Harvard U., 1977; PhD (hon.), Morgan State U., 1990, Stony Brook U., 1996, Adelphi U., 1995, Bowdoin Coll., 1996, Xavier U., 1997, S.C. State U., 1997, Howard U., 1998, U. Notre Dame, 1998; LLD, Iona Coll., 1996. Bar: Mass. 1981. Assoc. Rogers & Wells, NYC, 1977-79; cons. Bain & Co., Boston, 1979-81; dir. strategic planning Am. Express Co., NYC, 1981-83; from v.p. to sr. v.p. Am. Express Travel Related Svcs. Co., Inc., NYC, 1983-96, exec. v.p. platinum card/gold, 1986-88, exec. v.p. personal card divsn., 1988-89, pres. consumer card and fin. svcs. group, 1990-93, pres. U.S.A., 1993-95; vice-chmn. Am. Express Co., NYC, 1995-97, pres., COO, 1997-2000, chmn., CEO, 2001—. Bd. dirs. IBM, Am. Express Co., NYU Hosp.'s Ctr./NYU Sch. Medicine. Dean's adv. bd. Harvard Law Sch.; mem. Coun. Fgn. Rels., N.Y.C., 1988. Mem. ABA. Congregationalist. Office: Am Express Co Am Express Tower World Fin Ctr 200 Vesey St New York NY 10285-5104*

CHENEY, BRIGHAM VERNON, physical chemist, consultant; b. Salt Lake City, June 11, 1936; s. Silas Lavell and Klara (Young) C.; m. Marsali McAllister, Aug. 20, 1964; children: Jill, Mark Vernon, Heather, Karin, Brigham McAllister, John David. BA, U. Utah, 1961, PhD, 1966. Rsch. asst. U. Utah, 1964-66; rsch. scientist Upjohn Co., Kalamazoo, 1966-71, scientist, 1971-75, sr. rsch. scientist, 1975-98; cons. Vis. scientist Oxford (Eng.) U., 1986-87. Contbr. articles to profl. jours. Missionary LDS Ch., Germany, 1956-59, high councilor, Lansing, Mich., 1969-75, Grand Rapids, Mich., 1975-78, bishop, Kalamazoo, 1978-84; leader Boy Scouts Am., 1972-98. With U.S. Army NG, 1959-67. Mem. Am. Chem. Soc., Sigma Xi, Phi Eta Sigma, Sigma Pi Sigma. Home: 1765 N 2000 W Provo UT 84604-1128 Personal E-mail: bvcheney@iprovo.net.

CHENEY, DICK (RICHARD BRUCE CHENEY), Vice President of the United States; b. Lincoln, Nebr., Jan. 30, 1941; s. Richard Hebert and Marjorie Lauraine (Dickey) C.; m. Lynne Anne Vincent, Aug. 29, 1964; children: Elizabeth, Mary Claire. BA, U. Wyo., 1965, MA, 1966. Congl. fellow, staff of Rep . William Steiger US Ho. Reps., Washington, 1968—69; spl. asst. to dir. Office of Econ. Opportunity The White House, Washington, 1969—70, dep. to presdl. counselor, 1970—71, asst. dir. ops. Cost of Living Coun., 1971—73; ptnr. Bradley, Woods & Co., 1973—74; dep. asst. to Pres. The White House, Washington, 1974—75, asst. to Pres., 1975-77; mem. 96th-100th Congresses from Wyo., Washington, 1977—89, chmn. Republican Ho. Policy Comm., 1981—88, Ho. minority whip, 1988—89; sec. U.S Dept. Def., Washington, 1989-93; sr. fellow Am. Enterprise Inst., Washington, 1993-95; chmn., CEO, Halliburton Co., Dallas, 1995-2000; v.p. U.S., Washington, 2001—. Recipient Presdl. Medal of Freedom, The White House, 1991. Republican. Office: The White House 1600 Pennsylvania Ave NW Washington DC 20501*

CHENEY, JAMES ADDISON, civil engineering educator; b. Los Angeles, Feb. 2, 1927; s. Burton Howard and Esther Jesse (Dumaresq) C.; m. Frankyee Jane Jackson, June, 23, 1951 (dec. Oct. 1966); children: John Addison, Linanne Dando, Matthew Jackson, Sarah Allan, Sharla Ryan, Jennifer Dumaresq; m. Barbara Louise Chadwick, June 1967 (div. Feb. 1987); children: Michael Chadwick, David Grant; m. Elaine Disbrow Barratt, Apr. 1988. BS, UCLA, 1951, MS, 1953; PhD, Stanford U., 1963. Registered profl. civil engr., Calif. Assoc. engr. L.T. Evans, Foundation Engrs., Los Angeles, 1953-55; staff engr. Lockheed Missile and Space Co., Sunnyvale, Calif., 1955-65; prof. civil engrng. U. Calif., Davis, 1962-91, prof. emeritus civil engrng., 1991—. Contbr. over 50 articles to scientific jours. Served with USN, 1944-45. Recipient Silver Beaver award, Golden Empire coun. Boy Scouts Am., 2002. Fellow ASCE; mem. Alpha Sigma Phi. Republican. Episcopalian. Home: 418 Anza Ave Davis CA 95616-0404 Office: U Calif Dept Civil Engrng Davis CA 95616 E-mail: jacheney@ucdavis.edu.

CHENEY, LYNNE VINCENT, humanities educator, writer; b. Casper, Wyo., Aug. 14, 1941; d. Wayne and Edna (Lybyer) Vincent; m. Richard Bruce Cheney, Aug. 29, 1964; children: Elizabeth, Mary. BA, Colo. Coll., 1963; MA, U. Colo., 1964; PhD in 19th century Brit. lit., U. Wis., 1970. Freelance writer, 1970-83; lectr. No. Va. CC, 1968—71, George Washington U., Washington, 1972-77, U. Wyo., Casper, 1977-78; researcher, writer Md. Pub. Broadcasting, Owings Mills, 1982-83; sr. editor Washingtonian mag., Washington, 1983-86; chmn. NEH, Washington, 1986-93; W.J. Brady Jr. fellow Am. Enterprise Inst., Washington, 1993-95, sr. fellow, 1996—. Commr. U.S. Constitution Bicentennial Commn., Washington, 1985-87. Author: Executive Privilege, 1978, Sisters, 1981, Telling the Truth, 1995; (with others) Kings of the Hill, 1983, 96, (with Victor Gold) The Body Politic, 1988, (report) American Memory: A Report on the Humanities in the Nation's Public Schools, 1988, (essay) Academic Freedom, 1992, America: A Patriotic Primer, 2002, A is for Abigail, 2003; contbr. articles to profl. jours. Mem.

Women's Forum Washington. Mem. Congl. Club, Phi Beta Kappa, Kappa Alpha Theta. Republican. Methodist. Office: Am Enterprise Inst 1150 17th St NW Ste 1100 Washington DC 20036-4603

CHENEY, RICHARD EUGENE, public relations executive, psychoanalyst; b. Pana, Ill., Aug. 30, 1921; s. Royal F. and Nelle E. (Henke) C.; m. Betty L. McCray, Oct. 17, 1943; children: R. Christopher, Elyn G. Cheney MacInnis; m. 2d, Virginia B. Burns, Jan. 23, 1966; children: Benjamin, Anne. AB, Knox Coll., Galesburg, Ill., 1943; MA, Columbia U., 1960; postgrad., Ctr. Modern Psychoa. Studies, 1995. Assoc. editor Tide Mag., 1953; dir. pub. relations Tri Continental Corp., 1953-55; asst. mgr. pub. relations dept. Mobil Corp., 1955-60; chmn. bd., emeritus chmn. Hill & Knowlton, Inc., N.Y.C., 1987-91, 91—, chmn. bd., 1987-91, chmn. emeritus, 1991-93. Bd. dirs. Chattem Inc., Chattanooga, Stoneridge, Inc., Warren, Ohio, Rowe Furniture, Salem, Va. Served to lt. (j.g.) USNR, 1943-47, PTO. Mem. Soc. for Modern Psychoanalysis (trustee), Edgewood Club (Tivoli, N.Y.), Century Assn. Home: 108 E 86th St New York NY 10028-1024 Office: 108 E 86th St, 14 N New York NY 10028 Personal E-mail: dcheney212@earthlink.net.

CHENG, ALEXANDER HUNG-DARH, engineering educator, consultant; b. Taipei, Taiwan, May 25, 1952; came to U.S., 1976; s. Chia-hua and Yu-Chuen (Chwang) C.; m. Daisy T. Cheng, Nov. 23, 1979; children: Jacqueline, Julia. BS, Nat. Taiwan U., Taipei, 1974; MS, U. Mo., 1978; PhD, Cornell U., 1981. Asst. prof. Cornell U., Ithaca, 1981-82, Columbia U., N.Y.C., 1982-85; assoc. prof. U. Del., Newark, 1985-93, prof., 1993—2001; dept. chair, prof. U. Miss., Oxford, 2001—. Author: Multilayered Aquifer Systems, 2000; editor: Engineering Analysis with Boundary Elements, 1996; editor 9 books; editor-in-chief Progress in Water Resources Series, 1998—; assoc. editor Jour. Engrng. Mech., 1998—; contbr. over 100 articles to profl. jours. Recipient Basic Rsch. award U.S. Nat. Com. Rock Mechanics NRC, 1994, 99, Eminent Scientist award WIT. Mem. ASCE (chair, exec. com. engrng. mech. divsn., W.L. Huber Civil Engrng. prize 1994), Am. Geophys. Union, Am. Inst. Hydrology (v.p. acad. affairs). Office: U Miss Dept Civil Engrng University MS 38677 Office Phone: 662-915-5362. E-mail: acheng@olemiss.edu.

CHENG, CHU YUAN, economics professor; b. Kwangtung Province, China, Apr. 8, 1927; arrived in U.S., 1959, naturalized, 1964; s. Hung Shan and Shu Cheng (Yang) C.; m. Alice Hua Liang, Aug. 15, 1964; children: Anita tung I, Andrew Y.S. BA in Econs., Nat. Chengchi U., Nanking, China, 1947; MA, Georgetown U., 1962, PhD, 1964. Rsch. prof. Seton Hall U., 1960-64; sr. rsch. economist U. Mich., Ann Arbor, 1964-69; assoc. prof. Lawrence U., Appleton, Wis., 1970-71; assoc. prof. econs., chmn. Asian studies com. Ball State U., Muncie, Ind., 1971-73, prof. econs., 1974—. Vis. prof. George Washington U., Washington, 1963; cons. NSF, Washington, 1964—; rsch. mem. presdl. Coun. for Nat. Unification, China, 1992-98. Author: Scientific and Engineering Manpower in Communist China, 1966, The Machine-Building Industry in Communist China, 1971, China's Petroleum Industry: Output Growth and Export Potential, 1976, China's Economic Development: Growth and Structural Change, 1981, The Demand and Supply of Primary Energy in Mainland China, 1984, Taiwan as a Model for China's Modernization, 1986, Sun Yat-sen's Doctrine in Modern World, 1988, Taiwan Experience and China's Reconstruction, 1989, Behind the Tiananmen Massacre, Social, Political and Economic Ferment in China, 1990, Economic Development and Interaction between Two Sides of the Taiwan Straits, 1993, The Transformation of Social, Political and Economic Structure in China, 1994, China's Transition From A Planned to A Market Economy, 1994, Township-Village Enterprises: China's New Route to Industrialization, 1995, China's Economic Reform: Programs, Effects and Prospects, 1997, China's Economic Reform and Cross-Strait Economic Relations, 2000, Economies on the Two Sides of the Taiwan Straits: Reforms and Development, 1950-2000, 2002, Development of Contemporary Economic Thought in East and West, 2004. Bd. dirs., pres. Dr. Sun Yat-sen Inst., Chgo., 1978—. Grantee NSF, 1960-64, Social Sci. Rsch. Coun., 1965-67, 74, Chiang ching-Kuo Found., 1996. Mem. Am. Econ. Assn., Assn. Asian Studies, Assn. Comparative Econ. Studies, Am. Acad. Polit. and Social Sci., Assn. Chinese Social Scientists in N.Am. (bd. dirs., pres. 1994-96), Am. Assn. Chinese Studies (bd. dirs., pres. 1996-98), Chinese-Am. Soc. (pres. Washington 1989-92), Chinese Acad. and Profl. Assn. Mid-Am. (pres. 1983-84), Ind. Acad. Social Sci., Omicron Delta Epsilon. Home: 1211 N Greenbriar Rd Muncie IN 47304-2934 Office: Ball State U Coll Bus Rm 123 Muncie IN 47306-0340 Office Phone: 765-285-5366. Business E-Mail: ccheng@bsu.edu.

CHENG, CHUEN YAN, biochemist, educator; b. Hong Kong, June 18, 1954; came to the U.S., 1981, naturalized, 1993; s. C. Yin and Tak Ying (Ho) C.; m. Po Lee, Mar. 17, 1978; children; Yan Ho, Chin Ho. BS with honors, Chinese U., Hong Kong, 1978; PhD, U. Newcastle, Australia, 1982. Fellow Population Coun., N.Y.C., 1981-82, rsch. investigator, 1983-84, staff scientist, 1985-87, scientist, 1988-90, sr. scientist, 1991—; assoc. dir. Internat. Consortium on Male Contraception, N.Y.C., 1994-95, dir., 1996—. Asst. prof. Rockefeller U., N.Y.C., 1986-90; prof. U. Rome, 1990—; cons. Angelini Pharms., Inc., River Edge, N.J., 1985-91, Angelini Rsch. Inst., Rome, 1992-93, Fidia Pharms., Inc., Italy, 1997, Bioprogress Pharms., Rome, 2001—. Contbr. over 180 articles to profl. jours. Recipient Sea Horse award, Newcastle U., Australia, 1982. Mem. Am. Soc. Andrology (Best Sci. Paper award 1996), Endocrine Soc. (Richard E. Weitzman Meml. award 1988). Achievements include patents for abnormally glycosylated variants of alpha-2-macroglobulin and serum proteins used to detect autoimmune disease, monoclonal antibody specifically detects abnormal glycosylation site on alpha-1-antitrypsin used to detect autoimmune conditions, testicular protein that regulates androgen production for male fertility control; 3-substituted 1-benzyl-1H indazole derivatives as antifertility agents. Office: Population Coun 1230 York Ave New York NY 10021-6307 E-mail: ycheng@popcbr.rockefeller.edu. *Do what is right, not what is popular.*

CHENG, DAVID KEUN, engineering educator; b. Kiangsu, China, Jan. 10, 1918; came to U.S., 1943, naturalized, 1955; s. Han J. and Ying H.C.; m. Enid Kwok, Mar. 27, 1948; 1 child, Eugene. BS in Elec. Engring., Nat. Chiao Tung U., 1938; S.M., Harvard U., 1944, Sc.D., 1946; D.Engr. (hon.), Nat. Chiao Tung U., Taiwan, 1985; PhD (hon.), Xidian U., China, 1998. Electronics and project engr., rsch. labs. U.S. Air Force, Cambridge, Mass., 1946-48; asst. prof. elec. and computer engrng. Syracuse U., N.Y., 1948-51, assoc. prof., 1951-55, prof., 1955—, Centennial prof., 1970—. Hon. prof. Beijing Univ. Posts and Telecomm., 1982—, N.W. Inst. Telecomm. Engring., 1982—, Shanghai Jiao Tong U., 1985—, China; exch. scientist NAS, Hungary, 1972, Yugoslavia, 1974, Poland and Romania, 1978; liaison scientist Office of Naval Rsch., London, 1975-76; disting. European lectr. IEEE, 1975-76; pres., chmn., bd. trustees Li Instn. Sci. & Tech., 1992-98; cons. IBM, GE, TRW. Author: Analysis of Linear Systems, 1959, Field and Wave Electromagnetics, 1983, 2d edit., 1989, Fundamentals of Engineering Electromagnetics, 1993; cons. editor elec. sci. Addison-Wesley, 1961-78, elec. engrng. monographs Intext Edn. Pubs., 1969-72; mem. editorial bd. Jour. Electromagnetic Waves and Applications, 1987—; mem. internat. adv. bd. book series on Progress in Electromagnetic Rsch., 1989—; contbr. numerous articles to profl. jours. Recipient Disting. Achievement award Chinese Inst. Engrs., 1962, Disting. Engr. award Li Inst. Sci. and Tech., 1979; Guggenheim fellow, 1960-61; Chancellor's citation, 1981. Fellow IEEE, AAAS, Inst. Elec. Engrs. (U.K.); mem. AAUP, Am. Soc. Engring. Edn., N.Y. Acad. Scis., Sigma Xi (7 Best Paper prizes), Eta Kappa Nu, Phi Tau Phi (Disting. Svc. award 1975). Home: 4620 N Park Ave Apt 104E Chevy Chase MD 20815-4550 E-mail: chengkeun@aol.com.

CHENG, HENG-JIE, physician scientist; b. Harbin, China, June 27, 1958; came to U.S., 1984; s. Ji Cheng and Yu-Zhi Pan; m. Tina Sun; 1 child, Daniel. MD, Harbin Med. U., 1983; PhD, Wayne State U., 1991. Rsch. assoc. Wayne State U. Sch. Medicine, Detroit, 1991-93, Wake Forest U. Sch. Medicine, Winston-Salem, N.C., 1997—. Recipient Nat. Rsch. award NIH, 1999-2000. Mem. Am. Heart Assn., Am. Physiol. Soc. Home: 101 Bradford Lake Count Lewisville NC 27023 Office: Wake Forest U Sch Medicine Medical Center Blvd Winston Salem NC 27157 E-mail: hcheng@wfubmc.edu.

CHENG, HWEI H(SIEN), soil scientist, agronomic and environmental science educator; b. Shanghai, Aug. 13, 1932; arrived in U.S., 1951, naturalized, 1961; s. Chi-Pao and Anna (Lan) Cheng; m. Jo Yuan, Dec. 15, 1962; children: Edwin, Antony. BA, Berea Coll., 1956; MS, U. Ill., 1958, PhD, 1961; LLD (hon.), U. Minn., 2004. Lic. profl. soil scientist Minn. Rsch. assoc. Iowa State U., Ames, 1962-64, asst. prof. agronomy, 1964-65; asst. prof. dept. agronomy and soils Wash. State U., Pullman, 1965-71, assoc. prof., 1971-77, prof., 1977-89, interim chmn., 1986-87, chmn. program environ. sci. and regional planning, 1977-79, 88-89, assoc. dean Grad. Sch., 1982-86; prof., head dept. soil, water, and climate U. Minn., St. Paul, 1989—2002, prof. emeritus, 2002—. Vis. scientist Juelich Nuc. Rsch. Ctr., Germany, 1971-73, 79-80, Academia Sinica, Taipei, China, 1978, Fed. Agrl. Rsch. Ctr., Braunschweig, Germany, 1980; mem. acad. adv. coun. Inst. Soil Sci., Academia Sinica, Nanjing, China, 1987-2000; mem. adv. bd. Inst. Botany, Academia Sinica, Taipei, 1991-2000; mem. first sci. adv. bd. Dept. Ecology State of Wash., 1988-89; chief tech. advisor project on water-saving agr. for N.W. China, UNDP, 2001—04; mem. Nat. Acad. Bd. Agr. and Natural Resources, 2003—. Editor: Pesticides in the Soil Environment: Processes, Impacts, and Modeling, 1990; assoc. editor Jour. Environ. Quality, 1983-89; mem. editorial bd. Bot. bull. Academia Sinica, 1988—, Jour. Environ. Sci. and Health, Part B-Pesticides, Food Contaminants, and Agrl. Wastes, 2000—03; cons. editor: Pedosphere, 1991—; contbr. articles to profl. jours. Tech. adv. Mekong-Miss. River Partnership, 2003—. Recipient U. Minn. Coll. Agrl., Food and Environ. Scis. Internat. Achievement award, 2004; Fulbright rsch. scholar State Agrl. U., Ghent, Belgium, 1963-64. Fellow AAAS, Am. Soc. Agronomy (bd. dirs. 1990-2000, exec. com. 1994-2000, pres. 1998-99), Soil Sci. Soc. Am. (divsn. chair 1985-86, bd. dirs. 1990-93, exec. com. 1994-97, pres. 1995-96, chmn. Smithsonian soils exhibit com. 2002—); mem. Am. Chem. Soc., Soc. Environ. Toxicology and Chemistry, Internat. Soc. Chem. Ecology, Internat. Humic Substances Soc., Coun. for Agrl. Sci. and Tech., Soil and Water Conservation Soc., Minn. Assn. Profl. Soil Scientists (Soil Scientist of Yr. 2003), Inst. Internat. Devel. in Edn. and Agrl. and Life Scis. (chair bd. dirs. 2000—), Sigma Xi (pres. U. Minn. chpt. 1995-96), Miss. River Basin Inst. Internat. Coop. (chair, bd. dirs. 2004—), Phi Kappa Phi, Gamma Sigma Delta (pres. Wash. State chpt. 1988-89, Award of Merit U. Minn. chpt. 2000). Methodist. Office: U Minn Dept Soil Water and Climate 1991 Upper Buford Cir Saint Paul MN 55108-0010 Office Phone: 612-625-1244. Business E-Mail: hcheng@umn.edu.

CHENG, JIAN-YU, mechanical engineer, researcher, application developer; b. Shanghai, Aug. 2, 1960; arrived in U.S., 1996; s. Dewu Cheng and Fan Shen; m. Xiaolin Lu; children: Jinliu, Bridget. BS, U. Sci. and Tech. of China, 1982; PhD, U. of Sci. and Tech. of China, 1989. Asst. prof. U. of Sci. and Tech. of China, Hefei, China, 1988—91; postdoctoral fellow Inst. de Mecanique de Grenoble, Grenoble, France, 1991; Alexander von Humboldt fellow U. of Saarlandes, Saarbruecken, Germany, 1991—93; rsch. staff U. of Leeds, Leeds, England, 1993; fellow St. Francis Xavier U., Antigonish, Canada, 1994—96; sr. mech. project engr. Smith Internat., Inc, Houston, 1996—97; fellow U. of Del., Newark, Del., 1997—99; sr. rsch. scientist Dynaflow, Inc, Jessup, Md., 1999—2002; sr. software engr. Westover Cons., Inc., Silver Spring, Md., 2002—05; sr. computer scientist Computer Sci. Corp., 2005—. Contbr. articles to profl. jours. (Natural Sci. prize of Academia Sinica, China, 1993). Fellow, Alexander von Humboldt Found., Germany, 1991—93, Natural Sci. & Engring. Rsch. Coun. of Can., 1994—96; grantee, NOAA, 2001. Mem.: ASME. Avocation: travel. Home: 8538 Eastern Morning Rd Laurel MD 20723 Office: NOAA/NESDIS/CLASS 5627 Allentown Rd Suitland MD 20746 Personal E-mail: cheng_jj@hotmail.com. Business E-Mail: jianyu.cheng@noaa.gov.

CHENG, KUANG LU, chemist, educator; b. Yangchow, China, Sept. 14, 1915; came to U.S., 1947, naturalized, 1955; s. Fong Wu and Yi Ming (Chiang) C.; children: Meiling, Chiling, Hans Christian. PhD, U. Ill., 1951. Microchemist Comml. Solvents Corp., Terre Haute, Ind., 1952-53; instr. U. Conn., Storrs, 1953-55; engr. Westinghouse Electric Corp., Pitts., 1955-57; assoc. dir. research metals div. Kelsey Hayes Co., Utica, NY, 1957-59; mem. tech. staff RCA Labs., Princeton, N.J., 1959-66; prof. chemistry U. Mo., Kansas City, 1966-90, prof. emeritus, 1990—. Recipient Achievement award RCA, 1963, Benedetti-Pichler award Am. Microchem. Soc., 1989; N.T. Veatch award for Disting. rsch. and creative activity U. Mo., 1979; cert. of recognition U.S. Office of Naval Rsch., 1979, cert. of recognition Coll. Engring., Tex. A&M U., 1981; bd. trustees fellow U. Kansas City, 1984. Fellow AAAS, Chem. Soc. London; mem. Am. Chem. Soc. (Longtime Achievement award 2004), Electrochem. Soc., Soc. Applied Spectroscopy, Am. Inst. Physics. Achievements include discovery of intergacial triple layer, 2001; counterion triple layer in the interface structure. Office: U Mo Dept Physics Kansas City MO 64110 E-mail: chengk@umkc.edu. *Part of the art of research is to simplify complex phenomena and to elaborate the simple observations. Scientific research resembles gold prospecting — staying away from the spots crowded by people, exploring new territories.*

CHENG, LEO LING, biophysicist, researcher; b. Shanghai, Aug. 22, 1959; came to U.S., 1986; s. Jizhou Cheng and Yanzhuang Li; m. Emma Y. Wu, Dec. 15, 1985; children: Andrew Y., Amelia Y. MS in Chemistry, Nanjing (China) U., 1986; MA in Chemistry, Brandeis U., 1989, PhD in Chemistry, 1993. Postdoctoral fellow Harvard Med. Sch./Beth Israel Hosp., Boston, 1993-94, Harvard Med. Sch./Mass. Gen. Hosp., Boston, 1994-96, instr. pathology, 1997—2002, asst. prof. radiology and pathology, 2002—. Vis. scientist MIT, Cambridge, 1993-95; mem study sect. NIH, 2003—. Recipient 1st Ind. Rsch. Support and Transition award USPHS-NIH, 1999. Mem. Internat. Soc. Magnetic Resonance in Medicine. Home: 7 Village Way North Andover MA 01845 Office: Mass Gen Hosp/Harvard Med Sch Path Res CNY-7 149 13th St Charlestown MA 02129 Office Phone: 617-724-6593. E-mail: cheng@nmr.mgh.harvard.edu.

CHENG, LIANG, pathologist; b. Zhejiang, China, Nov. 9, 1965; came to U.S., 1988; MD, Beijing Med. U., 1987; MS, U. Ill., 1990. Diplomate Am. Bd. Pathology. Resident Case We. Res. U., Cleve., 1993—97, instr. pathology, 1994—97; fellow Mayo Clinic, Rochester, Minn., 1997—98; asst. prof. pathology Ind. U. Sch. Medicine, Indpls., 1998—, asst. prof. urology, 1999—. Spkr., cons. in field. Co-author: (chpts.) Therapeutics: Methods and Applications of Direct Gene Transfer, 1994, Immunotherapeutics Approaches for the Treatment of Cancer, 1995; editor: Essentials of Anatomic Pathology 2d edit., 2005; contbr. articles to profl. jours. Recipient Resident Competition award Cleve. Soc. Pathologists, 1997, Young Investigator Travel award, 1998, Eminent Scientist of Yr. Gold award, Internat. Rsch. Promotino Coun., 2000; Am. Cancer Inst. grantee, Clarian Value Fund grantee, Biomed. Rsch. Fund grantee, Dept. Def. grantee; Molecular Biology Lab. fellow U. Ill., 1990. Mem. AAAS, Am. Assn. Cancer Rsch., Am. Urologic Assn., U.S. and Can. Acad. Pathology (Stowell-Orbison award 1996), Coll. Am. Pathologists (cert. recognition), Am. Soc. Clin. Pathologists (cert. recognition), Internat. Soc. Urologic Pathology, Assn. Molecular Pathology. Office: Ind U Sch Medicine UH3465 550 University Blvd Indianapolis IN 46202-5149 Office Phone: 317-274-1756. Personal E-mail: liang_cheng@yahoo.com.

CHENG, LIANG, application developer, researcher; s. Deqing Cheng and Jiatong Yan; m. Chen Zhang. BSEE, Beijing U. Posts and Telecom., 1997, MSEE, 2000; MS, U. Calif., 2004, PhD, 2005. Rsch. asst. U. Calif., Irvine, 2000—05; software sys. designer Santa Clara, Calif., 2005—. Contbg. author Adaptation Techniques in Wireless Multimedia Networks. Fellow Calif. Inst. Telecomm. and Info. Tech.; scholar U. Calif. Sch. Info. and Computer Sci., 2002, U. Calif. Ctr. Pervasive Comm. and Computing, 2002, 2004. Mem.: ACM, IEEE. Achievements include patents pending for Systems And Methods For Video Compression For Low Bit Rate And Low Latency Video Communications. Personal E-mail: liang.cheng@gmail.com.

CHENG, MEI-FANG, psychobiology educator, neuroscientist; b. Kee Lung, Taiwan, Republic of China, Nov. 24, 1938; came to U.S., 1959; d. Chao-Chin Hsieh and Ai Tsu; m. Wen-Kwei Cheng; m. June 7, 1963; children: Suzanne, Po-Yuan, Julie. BS summa cum laude, Nat. Taiwan U., Taipei, 1958; PhD, Bryn Mawr Coll., 1965. Postdoctoral fellow U. Pa., Phila., 1965-68; asst. rsch. prof. Inst. Animal Behavior Rutgers U., Newark, 1969-73, assoc. prof., 1973-79, prof., 1979, acting dir. Inst. Animal Behavior, 1989—91, dir., 1991-95. Cons. NIMH, mem. neurosci. study sect., 1991-95; cons., mem. behavioral neurobiology br. NSF; mem. NIH Reviewers Res., 1995—; cons. numerous granting agys. Author: Advance in the Study of Behavior, 1979; co-editor: Reproduction: A Behavorial and Neuroscientific Perspective, 1986; assoc. editor Hormones and Behavior, 1986-96; cons. Brain Rsch., Sci., others; contbr. articles to profl. jours. Fulbright scholar, 1959; recipient Rsch. Scientist Devel. award NIMH, 1974-79, 79-84, Johnson & Johnson Discovery award, 1989, Hoechst-Celanese Innovative award, 1993, award of excellence in rsch. Rutgers Bd. Trustees, 1998. Mem. Internat. Conf. Neuroethology, Neurosci. Achievements include discovery that a bird's own songs stimulate the endocrine changes; demonstration of the vocal-auditory-endocrine pathways involved in voice and sound mediation of endocrine change, and provide anatomical basis for emotion-sharing theory of vocal communication; discovery of cell loss can trigger neurogenesis in the adult brain and may be harnessed for brain repair and functional recovery. Office: Rutgers U Dept Psychology 101 Warren St Newark NJ 07102-1811 Office Phone: 973-353-5440 226. Business E-Mail: mcheng@axon.rutgers.edu.

CHENG, SHIDE, engineer, researcher; s. Cheng Mindun and Gao Guiyin; m. Xiufeng Huang, Apr. 3, 1996; 1 child, Cheng Wanli. BS, Lanzhou U., China, 1989; MS, Nanjing U., China, 1992; PhD, Nanyang Technol. U., Singapore, 2001. Cert. electronic engr., Shenzhen, 1994. Sr. R&D engr. Tianma Microelectronics Co, Shenzhen, Guangdong, China, 1992—97; mem. tech. staff Phosistor Technologies Inc., Pleasanton, Calif., 2001—. Contbr. articles to profl. jours. Mem.: IEEE (sr.), Optical Soc. Am. Achievements include invention of deposition of c-axis oriented sol-gel $LiNbO_3$ on silicon; optical beam transformer module for light coupling between a fiber array and a photonic chip and the method of making the same; amorphous HTN-LCD with wide and uniform viewing angles; chirped acoustics supperlattice and ultra-high-frequency wideband acoustic/optic device; two-dimensional propagation in a surface acoustic wave device. Office: 21138 Commerce Pointe Dr Walnut CA 91789 Home: Apt D 18607 Colima Rd Rowland Heights CA 91748-2840 Business E-Mail: shide_cheng@hotmail.com.

CHENG, SUSAN, medical researcher; d. Tze-Chiang and Monica Cheng. BA magna cum laude, Harvard U., 1998; MD, McMaster U., 2003. Policy analyst NYC Dept. of Health, 1998—99; co-founder Idiom, Inc., Waltham, Mass., 1998—99; rsch. scholar Johns Hopkins U., Balt., 2004—05. Cons. Idiom, Inc., 1999—2000; freelance web designer, founder Silkview, Toronto, 2000—03. Contbr. book; author: (book chapter) Delirium, The Osler Medical Handbook, 2nd edition, Bleeding Disorders, The Osler Medical Handbook, 2nd edition, Hypercoagulable Disorders, The Osler Medical Handbook, 2nd edition, Globalizing an e-Commerce Web Site; contbr. articles to profl. jours., mags. Co-founder and dir. Health Advocacy Program, Project Health, Boston Med. Ctr., Boston, 1996—97; program dir., tchr. Partners Empowering Neighborhoods, 1994—96. Recipient 21st Action for Boston Cmty. Devel. award, Action Boston Cmty. Devel., Boston City Coun., 1995, Deans Summer Rsch. award, Harvard U., 1997, Burroughs Wellcome award Med. Student Rsch., Can. Insts. Health Rsch., 2001; scholar, Heart and Stroke Found., 2001, Yale U., New Haven, Conn., 2001—03, Harvard U., 1995—98; Frank and Doris Sercombe scholar, Heart and Stroke Found., 2001. Mem.: ACP (assoc.), Ont. Med. Assn. (assoc.), Can. Med. Assn. (assoc.), Am. Geriat. Soc. (assoc.), Soc. Geriatric Cardiology (assoc.). Achievements include design of Silkview Web Design projects.

CHENG, THERESA, neurosurgeon; d. Wayne and Florence Cheng. Degree in Biomed. Engring., Marquette U., 1982; MD, PhD, Med. Coll. Wis., Milw., 1989. Diplomate Am. Bd. Neurol. Surgeons, cert. Advanced Trauma Life Support ACS, 1996, Advanced Cardiac Life Support Am. Heart Assn., 1989; Eucharistic Ministry Cath. Ch., 1980. Tchg. asst. engring. level math. and physics Marquette U., Milw., 1979—82; tchg. asst. med. gross anatomy dept. anatomy and cellular biology Med. Coll. Wis., Milw., 1983—84, rsch. asst. dept. medicine, endocrinology, 1984, rsch. asst. dept. neurology, 1984, tchg. asst. med. neuroanatomy dept. anatomy and cellular biology, 1984—87, adj. instr. med. neuroanatomy dept. anatomy and cellular biology, 1987—89; neurosurgery resident Mayo Clinic, Rochester, Minn., 1989—95, postdoctoral fellow molecular genetics, 1992—93, spl. fellow neurosurgery, 1998—99; cons. neurosurgery Luther Midelfort, Mayo Health Sys., Eau Claire, Wis., 1995—2002, chmn. dept. neurosurgery, 2000—02; chief neurosurgery Affinity Health Systems, Oshkosh, Wis., 2002—. Contbr. articles to profl. jours. Med. dir. Think First Found., Eau Claire, Wis., 2000—02; co-director of neuro-peds-trauma icu Luther Midelfort, Mayo Health Sys., Eau Claire, Wis., 2001—02; eucharistic min. Cath. Ch., 1980—2003; bd. of directors Gold Cross Ambulance Svc., Fox Valley area, Wis., 2002—; elected to the med. exec. committe Luther Midelfort, Mayo Health Sys., Eau Claire, Wis., 2001—; pres. elect, bd. of directors, profl. adv. bd. Epilepsy Found. of Western Wis., Eau Claire, Wis., 1999—2002; bd. dirs. Dunn-Eau Claire-Pepin County Med. Soc., 1999—2002. Recipient 2nd Pl. award, Wis. State Fair, 1985; grantee, Mayo Clinic, 1992; scholar, Nicolet Clinic, 1979, 1980; Coll. scholar, AAUW, 1979, Med. Coll. of Wis. Summer Rsch. fellow, Med. Coll. Wis., 1983. Master: Epilepsy Found. Western Wis. (hon.); mem.: AAAS, Am. Assn. for Cancer RSch., Wis. State Med. Soc., Am. Assn. Neurol. Surgeons, Caduceus Soc., Samaritan Club, Alpha Epsilon Delta, Tau Beta Pi (life). Avocations: outdoor activities, sports and recreation, music, writing, community volunteering. Office: Affinity Health Systems Ste 203 2700 W Ninth Ave Oshkosh WI 54904 E-mail: tcheng@affinityhealth.org.

CHENG, TSEN-CHUNG, electrical engineering educator; b. Shanghai, Peoples Republic of China, Dec. 24, 1944; s. Yik Yu and Shun Lan (Tsui) C.; m. Doris Tin Gen Lee, Aug. 25, 1974; 1 child, Jason. BS, MIT, 1969, MSEE, 1970, ScD, 1974. Asst. prof. U. So. Calif., Los Angeles, 1974-80, assoc. prof., 1980-84, Lloyd F. Hunt prof., dir. electric power program, 1984—. Pres. T.C. Cheng ScD Inc., San Marino, Calif., 1981—; cons. Los Angeles Dept. Water and Power, 1984—, So. Calif. Edison Co., 1982—, Pacific Gas & Electric Co., San Francisco, 1982—, and numerous other pub. utilities and elec. and electronic mfrs. worldwide. Patentee in field; author over 120 publs. Recipient Outstanding Elec. Engrng. faculty award U. So. Calif., 1976, Engrng. Service award U. So. Calif., 1981. Fellow IEEE (relay com. award 1986, Best Paper award 1988), Sigma Xi, Eta Kappa Nu, Tau Beta Pi. Office: Univ of So Calif Phe 634 Dept Ee Ep # 634 Los Angeles CA 90089-0001 Office Phone: 213-740-4712. Personal E-mail: tccheng@socal.rr.com. Business E-Mail: tcheng@usc.edu.

CHENG, TSUNG O., cardiologist, educator; b. Shanghai, Mar. 30, 1925; came to U.S., 1950, naturalized, 1960; s. Keith S. and Fanny (Wang) C.; m. Marie Ellen Roe, June 18, 1955; children: Mark Dudley, Yvonne Joyce. BS, St. John's U., China, 1945; MD, U. Pa., 1950, MS in Medicine, 1956. Diplomate Am. Bd. Internal Medicine (subsplty. cardiovasc. disease), Nat. Bd. Med. Examiners. Intern St. Barnabas Hosp., Newark, 1950-51; resident in medicine Cook County Hosp., Chgo., 1952-55; fellow in cardiovasc. disease George Washington U., D.C. Gen. Hosp., Washington, 1955-56; instr. cardiology Harvard Med. Sch. Mass. Gen. Hosp., Boston, 1956-57; fellow in cardiorespiratory physiology Johns Hopkins U. Sch. Medicine and Hosp., 1957-59, staff cardiac cath. lab., 1957—59; practice medicine specializing in cardiology Washington, 1970—; asst. prof. medicine SUNY Downstate, 1959-70; assoc. prof. medicine George Washington U., 1970-72; chief cardiology D.C. Gen. Hosp., 1971-72; prof. George Washington U., 1972—. Dir. cardiac catheterization lab. George Washington U. Med. Ctr., 1972—78, assoc. dir. cardiology, 1972—75; asst. physician Cardiac Clinic Johns Hopkins Hosp., 1957—59; dir. cardiopulmonary lab. Bklyn. Hosp., 1959—66, co-chief Pediat. Cardiac Clinic, 1959—66, chief Adolescent Cardiac Clinic, 1961—66, attending physician Adult Cardiac Clinic, 1959—66; chief Pediat. Cardiac Clinic Cumberland Hosp., Bklyn., 1963—66; asst. chief cardiology VA Hosp., Bklyn., 1966—69, chief cardiovasc. lab., 1966—70, chief cardiology, 1969—70; asst. vis. physician Kings County Hosp. Med. Ctr., Bklyn., 1964—70; attending physician Univ. Hosp., SUNY, Bklyn., 1967—70; cons. Beth Israel Med. Ctr., N.Y.C., 1970—82; guest lectr. Chinese Med. Assn., 1972, 73, 75, 77, 79, 83, 86, 89, 92, Chinese

Ministry Health, 1990; prof. (hon.) Shanghai 2nd Med. Univ., 1986—, Qingdao Med. Coll., 1989—, Binzhou Med. Coll., 1992—, Taishan Med. Coll., 1992—, Tongji Med. U., Wuhan, China, 1994—, U. Cape Town (South Africa), 1995—, U. Natal, Durban, South Africa, 1995—; dir. (hon.) Quingdao Cardiovascular Rsch. Inst., 1990—; pres. (hon.) Dandong (China) 1st Hosp., Liaoning Province, 1988—, Shanghai St. Luke's Hosp., 1990—, Binzhou Med. Coll. Affil. Hosp., 1992—, Taishan Med. Coll. Affil. Hosp., 1992—, Jujiang (China) Med. Coll. Affil. Hosp., Jiangxi, 1994—, 2nd People's Hosp., Jin De Zhen, Jiangxi, 1994—; vis. prof. Peking Union Med. Coll., 1986—; cons. (hon.) Beijing Hosp., 1989—; vis. prof. Sun Yatsen Med. U., Canton, 1992—, Cairo U., Egypt, 1994—, U. Oxford, 1995—, U. Witwatersrand Med. Sch., Johannesburg, 1995—, U. Paris Hosp., Tenon, France, 1995—, Cath. U. Inst. Cardiology, Rome, 1996—; vis. prof. Inst. Clin. Physiology, Nat. Rsch. Coun. U. Pisa (Italy), 1996—, U. Milan; vis. prof. Inst. Pathol. Anatomy Med. Sch. U. Milan, 1996—; vis. prof. U. Dusseldorf (Germany), 1997—, U. Hamburg (Germany), 1997—, U. Hannover (Germany), 1997—, U. Melbourne (Australia), 1997—, U. NSW, Sydney, 1997—, U. Istanbul (Turkey), 1999—, U. Athens (Greece), 1999—, U. Córdoba (Spain), 2000—, U. Las Palmas (Spain), 2000—, U. Complutense, Madrid, 2000—; vis. prof. Med. Faculty Charite Humboldt U. Berlin, 2001—; vis. prof. Chinese U. Hong Kong, 2002—, Capital U. Med. Scis., Beijing, 2002—, U. Geneva, 2003—, U. Zurich, 2003—, U. Bern (Switzerland), 2003—, U. Tex., Houston, 2003—; hon. prof. U. Morón, Buenos Aires, 2003—; vis. prof. McMaster U., Hamilton, Ont., Canada, 2004—; v.p. Am. Ctr. Chinese Med. Sci., 1982—91; pres. Friends of St. Luke's Hosp., Shanghai, 1991—, chmn. bd., 1992—; dir. (hon.) Inst. Invasive Therapy PLA 150th Ctrl. Hosp., Luoyang, China, 1994—; disting. sr. visitor Royal Brompton Hosp./Nat. Heart and Lung Inst. London, 1995—; advisor (hon.) Guangdong Soc. Interventional Cardiology, Guangzhou, China, 1996—; pres. (hon.) China Heart Failure Assn., 2001—. Sr. editor: Vascular Medicine, 1983—88, Angiology, 1986—97; editor: The International Textbook of Cardiology, 1986, 1987, Percutaneous Balloon Valvuloplasty, 1992; mem. editl. bd.: Catheterization and Cardiovasc. Diagnosis, 1991—99, Catheterization and Cardiovasc. Interventions, 1999—2003, Jour. Noninvasive Cardiology, 1997—, Chinese Jour. Misdiagnostics, 1999—; co-editor: Congestive Heart Failure, 1991, Modern Cardiology, 1994, 2nd edit., 2002, Genetics of Cardiovasc. Diseases, 1995, Congestive Heart Failure, 2d edit., 1997, Textbook of Congestive Heart Failure, 2003; contbg. med. editor: Cortlandt Forum, 1997—98; contbr. articles to profl. jours. and textbooks. Fellow ACP, Am. Coll. Chest Physicians, Am. Coll. Cardiology (ofcl. rep. to stds. com. on catheters Assn. Advancement Med. Instrumentation 1971—), Am. Heart Assn., Coun. Clin. Cardiology, Soc. Cardiac Angiography and Interventions, Internat. Coll. Angiology, Am. Coll. Angiology, Soc. Geriat. Cardiology (founding), Royal Soc. Medicine; mem. AAAS, Am. Fedn. Clin. Rsch., Am. Heart Assn., Washington Heart Assn. Home: 7508 Cayuga Ave Bethesda MD 20817-4822 Office: George Washington U Med Ctr 2150 Pennsylvania Ave NW Washington DC 20037-3201 Office Phone: 202-741-2426. E-mail: tcheng@mfa.gwu.edu. *My goal in life is to serve the people the best way that I know, that is, through medicine which knows no international boundary. Perseverance, patience, hard work and selflessness will always be rewarded by the satisfaction of a job well done.*

CHENG, WAN-LEE, mechanical engineer, educator; b. Yi-Hsin, Chiang-Su, China, Dec. 28, 1945; arrived in U.S., 1971; s. Teh-Chih and Mei-Nung (Shih) Cheng; m. Viki Shu-Whei Lu, Dec. 16, 1972; children: Julie Wheichung, Paul Yichung, Lisa Yenchung. BS, Chung Yuan U., Taiwan, 1969; MEd, Sul Ross State U., 1972; PhD, Iowa State U., 1976. Mech. engr. Taiwan Power Co., Taipei, 1970-71; instr. Iowa State U., Ames, 1974-76; asst. prof., then prof. U. N.D., Grand Forks, 1976-85; prof., chmn. dept. design and industry San Francisco State U., 1985-2000, assoc. dean Coll. Creative Arts, 2000—. Cons. High-Tech Mobile Lab., N.D. Vocat. Edn. Dept., Bismarck, 1984—85; vis. prof. Nat. Sci. Coun. and Chung Yuan U., Taiwan, 1990—91; dean Coll. Design Chung Yuan Christian U., Taiwan, 1994—95. Author: computer software; contbr. articles to profl. jours.; mem. rev. bd. Jour. Indsl. Tech., 1986—. Session elder 1st Presbyn. Ch., Grand Forks, 1984—85, Lakeside Presbyn. Ch., 1989—91. Recipient Indsl. Arts Profl. Devel. award, N.D. Indsl. Arts Assn., 1985, Outstanding Tchg. and Faculty Devel. award, Burlington No. Found., 1985, Outstanding Profl. Indsl Tech. award, Nat. Assn. Indsl. Tech., 1992; 10 grants, U. N.D., 1979—85. Mem.: Chinese Am. Econ. and Tech. Devel. Assn. (pres. 1997—99), Chinese Inst. Engrs. (v.p. 1993), Soc. Mfg. Engrs. (sr.), Joint Alumni Assn. Chinese Univs. and Colls. No. Calif. (pres. San Francisco 1988—89), Chung Yuan Alumni Assn. No. Calif. (pres. San Francisco 1987—88), Epsilon Pi Tau (trustee Gamma Gamma chpt. Grand Forks 1984—85, Laureate award Beta Beta chpt. San Francisco 1991, Disting. Svc. award 2000), Phi Kappa Phi. Office: San Francisco State Univ Coll Creative Arts 1600 Holloway Ave San Francisco CA 94132-1722 Business E-Mail: wlcheng@sfsu.edu.

CHENG, WEI-TIH, insurance company executive; married; 2 children. Mgr. info. sys. IBM; v.p., info. sys. Meml. Sloan-Kettering Cancer Ctr., NYC; sr. v.p., chief info. officer Aetna Inc., Hartford, Conn., 2001—. Mem. editorial bd. several IT ind. pub. incl. ADVANCE for Health Info. Exec. and Topics in Healthcare Info. Mgmt. Recipient Info. Systems award, Healthcare Info. and Mgmt. Systems Soc., 1999, IS&CG Mgmt. Excellence award, IBM. Mem.: Coll. of Healthcare Info. Mgmt. Executives (charter mem., chmn., bd. trustees 1996, chmn. 1997). Achievements include voted chief info. officer of the year by peers in the healthcare industry; named John Gall Jr., chief info. officer of the year by the College of Healthcare Information Management Executives. Office: Aetna Inc 151 Farmington Ave Hartford CT 06156

CHENG, WILLIAM Y. Y., meteorologist, educator; s. Hang Sum Cheng and Fung Ting Chow. MSc in Atmospheric and Oceanic Scis., McGill U., Can., 1998; PhD in atmospheric sci., Colo. State U., 2002. Rsch. asst. McGill U., Dept. of Atmospheric and Oceanic Scis., Montreal, Canada, 1996—98, Colo. State U., Dept. of Atmospheric Sci., Fort Collins, Colo., 1998—2002; rsch. assoc. U. Utah, Dept. of Meteorology, 2002—04; rsch. asst. prof. U. of Utah, Dept. of Meteorology, Salt Lake City, 2004—. Contbr. articles to profl. jours. Mem.: Can. Meteorol. and Oceanog. Soc., Am. Geophys. Union, Am. Meteorol. Soc. Office: Univ Utah Dept of Meteorology 135 S 1460 E Room 819 Salt Lake City UT 84112-0110 Office Phone: 801-585-1416. Office Fax: 801-581-4362. E-mail: wcheng@met.utah.edu.

CHENG, WU C., retired patent examiner; b. Shanghai, Aug. 11, 1922; came to U.S., 1948; s. Ting-yih and Wei-chi (Kiang) C.; married 1963; 1 child, Robert C. BS, St. John's U., Shanghai, 1944; MS, Kans. State Coll., 1949; PhD, Ga. Inst. Tech., Atlanta, 1954. Asst. prof. to prof., head chemistry dept. Union U., Jackson, Tenn., 1955-66; assoc. prof. chemistry George Peabody Coll., Nashville, 1966-72; tchr. with rank I Lyman H.S., Longwood, Fla., 1972-75; asst. prof. chemistry to assoc. prof. physics Paine Coll., Augusta, Ga., 1975-89; patent examiner U.S. Dept. Commerce, Washington, 1990-99. Vis. instr. chemistry Ga. Inst. Tech., Atlanta, summer 1956; chemist No. Regional Rsch. Ctr., Peoria, Ill., summer 1976, 88; faculty rsch. participant Savannah River Lab., Aiken, S.C., summer 1977, Argonne Nat. Lab., Chgo., summer 1982, Oak Ridge (Tenn.) Nat. Lab., summer 1984; mem. faculty Rockwell Hanford (Wash.) Ops., summer 1979; faculty rsch. fellow USAF Acad., Colorado Springs, Colo., summer 1986. Contbr. articles to profl. jours. Mem.: N.Y. Acad. Scis., Ga. Acad. Sci., Am. Chem. Soc., Sigma Xi. Achievements include patents in field. Address: PO Box 211336 Augusta GA 30917-1336 E-mail: mayplay@aol.com.

CHENG, YU, anthropologist, consultant; b. HongAn, Hubei, China, June 10, 1973; s. Boyan Zhou and Xuewu Cheng; 1 child, Yi. PhD, Sun Yat-sen U., Guangzhou, China, 2004. Asst. prof. dept. anthropology Sun Yat-sen U., Guangzhou, 1999—; post doctoral fellow Ctr. for Interdisciplinary Rsch. on Aids, Yale U., New Haven, 2004—. Sr. cons. China Cross-Culture Cons. Ctr., Guangzhou, 2000—. Author: (book) Economics of Anthropology. Grantee, Urban China Rsch. Ctr., Albany U., 2000, Advanced Acad. Ctr. Hong Kong, 2002, Chinese Nat. Social Sci. Found., 2003, Guangzhou Social Sci. Found., 2003, Ctr. for Interdisciplinary Rsch. on Aids, Yale U., 2004. Mem.: Ethnicity Rsch. Assn. (assoc.). Achievements include ethnographic research on injection drug users in Guangzhou city. Home: 135 Xingang West Ro Guangdong Guangzhou 510275 China Office: Dept Anthropology Zhongshan Univ 135 Xingang West Rd Guangdong Guangzhou 510275 China Fax: 0086-20-84114286. Office Phone: 0086-20-84113160. Personal E-mail: yumoore@yahoo.com.cn.

CHENOK, PHILIP BARRY, accountant, educator; b. N.Y.C., Oct. 21, 1935; s. Irving and Anna C.; children from previous marriage: David, Daniel; m. Linda Stack, June 12, 1999. Student, NYU, 1957; postgrad., Grad. Sch. Bus., 1962. CPA, N.Y. Staff acct. Pogson, Peloubet & Co., 1957-61; mgr. spl. projects AICPA, N.Y.C., 1961-63; ptnr. Main Hurdman, N.Y.C., 1963-80; pres. AICPA, 1980-95; prof. acctg. NYU, 1995—2002. Mem. AICPA, N.Y. State Soc. CPAs, Am. Acctg. Assn.

CHENOWETH, KRISTIN, actress; b. Tulsa, Okla., July 24, 1968; MA in Opera, Oklahoma City U. Actor: (Broadway plays) Steel Pier, 1999 (Theatre World award), You're a Good Man, Charlie Brown, 1999 (Tony award Best Featured Actress, 1999, Drama Desk award, 1999, Clarence Derwent award, 1999, Outer Critics Circle award, 1999), Epic Proportions, 1999—2000, Funny Girl, 2002, Wicked, 2003—04 (Tony award nominee, Best Actress in a Musical, 2004); (plays) A New Brain, Scapin, The Fantasticks, Dames at Sea, Strike Up the Band, 1998, The Apple Tree, 2005; (TV series) LateLine, 1998, Frasier, 1993, Kristin, 2001, Baby Bob, 2002, Sesame Street, 2003—; (TV miniseries) Paramour, 1999; (TV films) Annie, 1999, The Music Man, 2003; (films) Topa Topa Bluffs, 2002, Bewitched, 2005; guest soloist: West Side Story Suite of Dances; singer: (albums) Let Yourself Go, 2001, As I Am, 2005. Metropolitan Opera award. Performed leading roles at Goodspeed Opera House, Guthrie Theatre, Paper Mill Playhouse, North Shore Music Theatre; guest soloist with National Symphony Orchestra, New York Philharmonic, London's Divas at Donmar series, Carnegie Hall, Lincoln Center and the Kennedy Center, and has performed with Placido Domingo, Paul Newman, Joshua Bell and Harvey Fierstein. Office: c/o SAG 360 Madison Ave #12 New York NY 10017-7111*

CHENOWETH-HAGE, HELEN P., former congresswoman; b. Topeka, Kans., Jan. 27, 1938; 2 children. Attended, Whitworth Coll., 1975-79; cert. in law office mgmt., U. Minn., 1974; student, Rep. Nat. Com. Mgmt. Coll., 1977. Bus. mgr. Northside Med. Ctr., 1964-75; state exec. dir. Idaho Rep. Party, 1975-77; chief of staff Congressman Steve Symms, 1977-78; campaign mgr. Symms for Congress Campaign, 1978, Leroy for Gov., 1985-86; v.p. Consulting Assocs., Inc., 1978—; mem. U.S. Congress from Idaho, Washington, 1995-2001; chairwoman Nev. Live Stock Assn., Hawthorne, Nev., 2003—; property rights activist. Mem. agriculture, resources, vets. affairs coms., chmn. forest subcom.; bd. dirs. Ctr. Study of Market Alternatives, Mountain States Legal Found.; chmn. bd. America 21. Deacon Capitol Christian Ctr., Boise. Republican. Office: Nev Live Stock Assn PO Box 639 Hawthorne NV 89415

CHENWORTH, JOSEPH ADAMS, secondary school educator; b. Seattle, July 8, 1940; s. Charles Francis and Mabel Alice (Adams) C.; m. Linda Ann Harrison, Aug. 2, 1965; children: Alan Joseph, David Alex, Eric Charles, Janica Lynn, Dallin Audy. AA in Civil Engring., U. N.C., Wilmington, 1960; BA in Math. and Physics, Greenville, 1963; grad. Air Force meteorology program, U. Utah, 1964-65; MSEd, U. So. Calif., 1970. Tchr. math., physics, chemistry, phys. sci. Tchr. math., physics, chemistry, meteorology Skyline H.S., Salt Lake City, 1970-80; dir. computer dept. JJ Johnson & Assoc. - Engring., Park City, Utah, 1980-85; indsl. engr., dir. ops. AngiPak corp., North Salt Lake City, Utah, 1985-88; tchr. physics, chemistry, math. Highland H.S. Salt Lake City Sch. Dist., 1988—. Adj. prof. edn. U. Utah, Salt Lake City, 1990—, adj. prof. math, physics Brigham Young U., Salt Lake City, 1993—; adj. prof. astronomy, meteorology, geology, math. Utah Valley State Coll., Heber City, 1999—. Contbr. article to 10-X mag. Mem. Utah Profl. Practices Adv. Commn., Salt Lake City, 1997-2003; mem. sch. bd., vp. Wasatch Sch. Dist., Heber City, Utah, 1983-91. Capt. USAF, 1963-70. Mem. Am. Phys. Soc., Am. Assn. Phys. Tchrs., Utah Amateur Radio Club, Salt Lake Astronomical Soc. Mem. Lds Ch. Home: 980 N Willow Way Heber City UT 84032-1043 Office: Highland HS 2166 S 1700 E Salt Lake City UT 84106-4123 E-mail: joseph.chenworth@slc.k12.ut.us, a87jc@arrl.net.

CHEO, LI-HSIANG S., education educator; b. Tainan, Taiwan, June 21, 1932; d. Chan Shen and Pu-Chan Shang; m. Bernard R Cheo, June 29, 1957; children: Lin-hsien Louise, Lin-Wen Wayne. BS, Cheng Kung U., 1955; MS, U. Calif., 1969; PhD, NYU, 1970. Asst. prof. math. NY Inst. Tech., 1970—72, William Paterson U. of NJ, 1972—74, program coord., assoc. prof. computer sci., 1974—79, prof. comp. sci., 1979—, chair computer sci., 1985—93. Program evaluator for computer sci. Accreditation Bd. for Engineers and Tech., 1993—; mem. Computer Sci. Com. Grant, NJ State Tech. and Engring. Mem.: Assn. for Computers of Machinery, Upsilon P Epsilon. Office: William Paterson U of NJ 300 Pompton Rd Wayne NJ 07470 Office Phone: 973-720-2517. Business E-Mail: cheol@wpunj.edu.

CHEPIGA, MICHAEL JOSEPH, lawyer; b. NYC, Jan. 14, 1948; s. Michael Andrew and Frances (Karasek) C.; m. Pamela Rogers, Nov. 21, 1970; children: Geoffrey Rogers, Emily Rogers. BA in English Lit., cum laude, Fordham U., 1970; PhD in English Lang. and Lit., NYU, 1975; JD, Yale U., 1979. Bar: N.Y. 1980, U.S. Ct. Appeals (2d cir.) 1986, U.S. Ct. Appeals (11th cir.) 1988, U.S. Dist. Ct. (so. dist.) N.Y. 1981, U.S. Dist. Ct. (ea. dist.) N.Y. 1983, U.S. Ct. Claims 1988. Tchr. English Washington Irving High Sch., N.Y.C., 1970-76; law clk. Hon. Milton Pollack, N.Y.C., 1979-80, Hon. Amalya Kearse, N.Y.C., 1980-81; assoc. Simpson, Thacher & Bartlett, N.Y.C., 1981-86, ptnr., mem. exec. com., 1986—. Bd. dirs. Legal Aid Soc. N.Y., exec. com., 1992—, v.p., 1994-96, pres., 1996—; adj. instr. English, writing skills LaGuardia C.C., L.I., N.Y., 1973-76; mem. bd. advisors Bank and Corp. Governance Law Reporter, 1988—. Mem. ABA (fellow), N.Y. State Bar Assn. (fed. cts. com. 1987-89), Assn. of Bar of City of N.Y. (fed. cts. com. 1992-95). Office: Simpson Thacher & Bartlett 425 Lexington Ave Fl 8 New York NY 10017-3954 Office Phone: 212-455-2598. Office Fax: 212-455-2502. Business E-Mail: mchepiga@stblaw.com.

CHEPOLIS, PAUL, musician; s. Stanley Paul and Margaret L. Chepolis; m. Meredith Allen, Apr. 17, 1979. MusB in Music Edn. and Jazz Studies, Temple U., Phila., 1993—98; MS in Instrnl. Design and Devel., Lehigh U., Bethlehem, Pa., 1999—2003. Dir., instrumental music Holland Twp. Sch., Milford, NJ, 1998—2004, instrnl. technologist, 2005—. Office: Holland Township Sch 710 Milford Warren Glenn Rd Milford NJ 08848 Office Phone: 908-995-2401. Personal E-mail: chepolisp1@rcn.com. E-mail: paul.chepolis@hts.k12.nj.us.

CHER, (CHERILYN SARKISIAN), singer, actress; b. El Centro, Calif., May 20, 1946; d. Gilbert and Georgia LaPiere; m. Sonny Bono, Oct. 27, 1964 (div. June 26, 1975); 1 child, Chastity; m. Gregg Allman, June 30, 1975 (div. Jan. 16, 1979); 1 child, Elijah Blue. Student drama coach, Jeff Corey. Singer with husband as team, Sonny and Cher, 1964-74; star TV shows: Cher, 1975-76, The Sonny and Cher Show, 1976-77; concert appearances with husband, 1977, numerous recs., TV, concert and benefit appearances with Sonny Bono; TV appearances, ABC-TV, 1978, appearance with Sonny Bono in motion pictures, Good Times, 1966, Chastity, 1969; film appearances include Come Back to the Five and Dime, Jimmy Dean, Jimmy Dean, 1982, Silkwood, 1983, Mask, 1985 (Best Actress, Cannes Internat. Film Festival), The Witches of Eastwick, 1987, Suspect, 1987, Moonstruck (Golden Globe award 1988, Acad. award for best actress 1988), 1987, Mermaids, 1990, The Player, 1992, Pret-a-Porter, 1994, Faithful, 1996, Tea With Mussolini, 1999; TV movies Club Rhino, 1990, If These Walls Could Talk, 1996, Happy Birthday Elizabeth: A Celebration of Life, 1997, AFI's 100 Years...100 Movies, 1998; helped form rock band, Black Rose, 1979; recorded albums include Black Rose, 1980, Cher, 1988, Heart of Stone, 1989 (Double Platinum and 3 Gold Singles), Love Hurts, 1991, It's A Man's World, 1996, The Casablanca Years, 1996, Believe, 1998 (Grammy award best dance recording 1999), Not Commercial, 2000, Living Proof, 2002; exec. prodr. Sonny & Me: Cher Remembers, 1998. also: Reprise Records 3000 Warner Blvd Burbank CA 19010-4694

CHERCOVER, MURRAY, television executive; b. Montreal, Que., Can., Aug. 18, 1929; s. Max M. and Betty (Pomerance) (dec.) C.; m. Barbara Ann Holleran, Aug. 8, 1953; children: Hollis Denny, Sean Peter. Grad., Acad. Radio TV Arts, Toronto, Ont., Can., Neighborhood Playhouse Sch. Theatre, N.Y.C. With Radio Sta. CFPA, Port Arthur, Ont., 1944-46, New Play Soc. Jupiter Theater, Toronto, 1946-48; exec. dir. Equity Library Theatre, N.Y.C., 1948-52; producer, dir. network TV drama Louis G. Cowan Agy., N.Y.C., 1948-52; with Canadian Broadcasting Co., 1952-60; exec. producer all prodn. Sta. CFTO-TV, Toronto, 1960, dir. programming, 1961; exec. v.p., gen. mgr. CTV TV Network Ltd., Toronto, 1966, pres., chief operating officer, 1968, pres., mng. dir., 1969—, pres., chief exec. officer, 1987-90, 1990—; pres. Chercover Communications, 1990—. Pres., dir. Avanti Mgmt. Ltd.; founding dir., fellow Internat. Coun. Nat. Acat. TV Arts and Scis.; past mem. adv. com. theatre arts George Brown Coll. Applied Arts and Tech.; past mem. adv. coun. film/TV prodn. program Humber Coll. Bd. dirs. Found. for Ocean Rsch. (founding), Can. Satellite Learning Svcs., Inc.; founding, past trustee Ruth Hancock Scholarship Found. Recipient Gold medal Can. Film and TV Assn., 1988, Rockie award for Lifetime Achievement Banff TV Festival, 1990, Excellence in Broadcasting Lifetime Achievement award Conestoga Coll., 1990, Achievement award for outstanding contbn. to broadcasting Broadcast Exec. Soc., 1991; named to Can. Broadcasting Hall of Fame, 1994. Fellow NATAS (founding dir. internat. coun., spl. citation 1989); mem. Acad. Can. Cinema and TV, Internat. Press Inst., Can. Assn. Broadcasters (Disting. Svc. gold ribbon medal 1986), Ctrl. Can. Broadcasters Assn. (past bd. dirs., Broadcaster of Yr. award 1990), Toronto Radio Control Club, Model Aeros. Assn. Can., Giant Scale Club (Oshawa), 403 RC Club, Seaton Valley R/C Flying Club. E-mail: chercover@sympatico.ca.

CHEREM, BARBARA BROWN, education educator; b. Detroit, May 4, 1946; d. Max Frederick and Dorothy Catherine (Bender) Brown; m. Gabriel Jerome Cherem, May 26, 1973; children: Mariah, Max. BA in English and Secondary Tchg., U. Mich., 1968; MA Ed. in Spl. Edn., Mich. State U., 1975; postgrad., Ea. Mich. U., 1984-86; PhD in Edn., Mich. State U., 1991, postgrad. Tchr. Romulus (Mich.) H.S., 1970-71; tchr. spl. edn. Hawthorn Children's Psychiat. Sch., Northville, Mich., 1971-73; program dir. Homme Home for Boys, Wittenberg, Wis., 1973-74; tchr. Wittenberg (Wis.)-Birnamwood H.S., 1973—74; pres., owner Learning Shop, Columbus, Ohio, 1974-77; tchr. cons. Jackson (Mich.) Pub. Schs., 1977-79; rsch. project dir. Ea. Mich. U., Mich. Evaluation Resource Ctr., 1979-81; rsch. and curriculum devel. grantee Ea. Mich. U., Ypsilanti, 1979-83; cmty. resource specialist Interpretation Ctr., Ann Arbor, Mich., 1981-83; acad. coord. adult mgmt. program Spring Arbor (Mich.) Coll., 1983-87, cons., with affiliate colls., 1984-90, dir. R&D, 1987-89, dir. R&D adult and continuing edn., 1989-91, assoc. prof. edn., 1991-93, prof., 1993—, prof., dir. instnl. assessment, 1994—. V.p. Interp Ctrl., Chelsea, Mich., 1979-89; presenter to 14 nat. confs., 1986-90; mem. bd. advs. Adult Faith Resources pls., 1988-91; cons. Mich. Dept. Social Svcs., Lansing and Detroit, 1989. Contbg. author, editor: Securing Occupational Achievement Through Readiness Sls, 1981, Parents in Parenting, 1993; contbr. articles to profl. jours. Trustee Chelsea (Mich.) Pub. Sch. Bd., 1986-90; mem. adminstrv. bd. First United Meth. Ch., Chelsea, 1983-85. Mich. State U. Scholars' fellow, 1988-89. Mem. AAUW, Am. Assn. Adult Continuing Edn. (trustee 1993—), Am. Assn. Sch. Adminstrs., Mich. Assn. Sch. Bds., Mich. Assn. Cmty. Adult Edn., Mich. Assn. Adult and Continuing Edn. (editl. bd. Options 1991-92, bd. dirs. 1993—), U. Mich Alumni club, Phi Delta Kappa, Alpha Delta Pi (philanthropy chair 1967). Avocations: reading, travel, internet, exercise, cooking. Office: Assessment Farmington PS 33000 Thomas St Farmington MI 48336-2347

CHERENZIA, BRADLEY JAMES, retired radiologist, consultant; b. Niagara Falls, N.Y., Aug. 22, 1931; s. Peter and Myrna (Bradley) C.; m. Paula Joyce, Mar. 9, 1978; children: Kevin, Lori, David, Robert, Lisa. BS in Pharmacy cum laude, U. Buffalo, 1953; MD, SUNY Upstate Med. Ctr., Syracuse, 1957. Cert. Am. Bd. Radiology, Am. Bd. Nuclear Medicine. Intern SUNY Upstate Med. Ctr. Hosps., Syracuse, 1957-58; resident in radiology Wayne State U. Sch. Medicine Hosps., Detroit, 1960-63; practice medicine specializing in radiology Diagnostic Radiology Cons., P.C., Warren, Mich., 1965-2000, also chmn. bd. dirs., ret., cons. Sr. attending radiologist St. John Macomb Hosp., med. dir. dept. diagnostic radiology. Served to capt. M.C., U.S. Army, 1958-60. Mem. AMA, Am. Soc. Nuc. Cardiology, Wayne County Med. Soc., Mich. State Med. Soc., Radiol. Soc. N.Am., Mich. Radiol. Soc., Am. Coll. Radiology, Soc. Nuclear Medicine, Am. Coll. Nuclear Medicine, Am. Coll. Physician Execs., Soc. Radiologists in Ultrasound, Am. Heart Assn., Am. Med. Tennis Assn. Republican. Roman Catholic. Avocations: photography, art, music, golf, tennis. E-mail: drbradrad@aol.com.

CHERIN, STEPHEN J., application developer, management consultant; b. N.Y.C., Apr. 12, 1962; Student, Baruch Coll., 1982-84; AA, L.A. City Coll., 2001; postgrad., Calif State U., L.A., 2001—. Mgr. data processing Salesman's Guide, N.Y.C., 1982-84; v.p. N.Y. Jour., N.Y.C., 1984-86; pres. Genesis Software, L.A., 1986—. V.p. pub. rels. Road Angels, L.A., 1986-88; programmer acctg. program EOMIDS, 1983, Datalink, 1985, E.Z. Acctg., 1989. Sgt. U.S. Army, 1979-81. Avocations: reading, philosophy, psychology, history.

CHERKASKY, MICHAEL G., insurance company executive; b. White Plains, NY, Mar. 2, 1950; m. Betsy Cherkasky; 4 children. BA, Case Western Reserve U., JD, 1975. Law clk. US Dist. Ct. (no. dist) Ohio; asst. dist. atty. NY County Dist. Atty. Office, 1978—85; mgr. Robert Morgenthau re-election campaign, 1985; asst. dist. atty. NY County Dist. Atty. Office, 1985—93, dep. bureau chief, trial bureau 40, 1983—84, bureau chief, trial bureau 40, 1984—85, head, Rackets Bureau, 1985—90, head, investigations divsn., 1990—94; chief NY office Kroll Associates, 1995—96, chief, N. Am. region, 1996—97, pres., COO, 1997—2001; pres., CEO Kroll Inc. (formerly The Kroll-O'Gara Co.), NYC, 2001—04; CEO Marsh Kroll, 2004; pres., CEO Marsh & McLellan Inc., NYC, 2004—. Supr. to the state prosecutors assigned to the Joint Terrorist Task Force investigating the World Trade Ctr. bombing NYC, 1993; compliance officer LI carting industry, 1994; election officer Internat. Brotherhood of Teamsters, 1997; ind. monitor LA Police Dept., 2001. Author: Forewarned: Why the Government is Failing to Protect Us and What We Must Do to Protect Ourselves, 2002. Office: Marsh & McLellan Inc 1166 Ave Americas New York NY 10036-2774*

CHERKASOVA, LUCY LUDMILA, computer scientist; b. Barnaul, Russia, Aug. 5, 1957; arrived in U.S., 1991; d. Alexander and Anfisa Orekhovsky; m. Vadim Kotov, Apr. 30, 1995; children: Helen, Andrew. MS in Math. and Computer Sci., Novosibirsk (Russia) State U., 1978, PhD in Computer Sci., 1984. Rschr. Computing Ctr. Russian Acad. Sci., Novosibirsk, 1984—88, sr. rschr. Inst. Info. Sys., 1988—91; rschr. Hewlett Packard Labs., Palo Alto, Calif., 1991—97, sr. scientist, 1997—. Mem. program coms. over 35 internat. confs. Contbr. over 100 articles to profl. jours. Mem.: IEEE (Appreciation cert. 2002). Achievements include patents in field. Office: Hewlett Packard Labs 1501 Page Mill Rd Palo Alto CA 94304 Office Phone: 650-857-3753.

CHERKEN, HARRY SARKIS, JR., lawyer; b. Phila., Dec. 8, 1949; s. Harry Sarkis and Lorna G. (Demurjian) Cherken. BA, Lafayette Coll., 1971; JD, Villanova U., 1976. Bar: Pa. 1976, U.S. Dist. Ct. (ea. dist.) Pa. 1976, U.S. Supreme Ct. 1983. Assoc. counsel Albert M. Greenfield & Co., Inc., Phila., 1976-79; assoc. Drinker, Biddle & Reath, Phila., 1979-84, ptnr., 1984—, co-chmn. real estate group, 1991—, mng. ptnr., 1996-2000. Assoc. Wharton Real Estate Rsch. Ctr., U. Pa., 1996—; adv. bd. Advanced Comml. Leasing Inst., Georgetown U. Law Ctr.; bd. dirs. Urban Outfitters, Inc., Mikronite Techs. Group, Inc., Law Dept. Am. U. Armenia. Trustee Kulicke Fund, Phila., 1985—, Balch Inst., 1992—2000, Woodmere Art Mus., 2002—; fellow trustee Armenian Assembly Am., 1986—, bd. dirs., 1988—2000, vice-chmn. bd. dirs., 1988—91, 1994—95; bd. dirs. Howard Karagheusian Commemorative Corp., 2003—; sec., bd. dirs. Reading Terminal Market Preservation Fund, 1991—. Mem.: ABA, Am. Coll. Real Estate Lawyers, Pa. Land Title Assn. (affiliate), Phila. Bar Assn., Pa. Bar Assn., Internat. Coun. Shopping Ctrs. (assoc.). Armenian Apostolic. Office: Drinker Biddle & Reath LLP One Logan Sq 18th & Cherry Sts Philadelphia PA 19103-6996 Office Phone: 215-988-2721. Office Fax: 215-988-2757. Business E-Mail: harry.cherken@dbr.com.

CHER KILLIGAN, BEATRIZ M., art educator; b. Buenos Aires, May 6, 1947; arrived in US, 1963; d. Sebuh Alfred and Katalina Cherkezian; m. Albert Richard Killigan, Dec. 21, 1963. AA in art edn., Miami Dade Coll., 1993; BFA magna cum laude, Fla. Internat. U., 1995; MFA cum laude, U. Miami, 1997. Prof., head admin. Am. Intercontinental U., Ill. Dept., Plantation, Fla., 2000—. Vice chair City of Coral Gables, Cultural Bd., Coral Gables, Fla., 1993—2001. Avocations: painting, sculpting, book art. Office: Am Intercontinental U 8151 W Peters Rd Plantation FL 33324 Office Phone: 954-446-6127. E-mail: bkilligan@aiufl.edu.

CHERLA, GAUTAM V., physician, nephrologist, researcher; s. Sastri B.N. and Kamala Sastri Cherla; m. Aparna Vadlamani, Nov. 24, 1999. MD, Andhra Med. Coll., Visakhapatnam, India, 1997. Diplomate Am. Bd. Internal Medicine. Ho. staff internal medicine Mt. Vernon Hosp./ NY Med. Coll., 1999—2002, chief ho. staff, 2001—02; postdoctoral rsch. fellow NY Med. Coll., Valhalla, 2002—03; clin. fellow in nephrology and hypertension U. Miami/ Jackson Meml. Hosp., Fla., 2003—, clin. fellow in interventional nephrology, 2004—. Contbr. articles to profl. jours. Mem.: Am. Soc. Diagnostic and Interventional Nephrology, Nat. Kidney found., Renal Physicians Assn., Am. Soc. Nephrology, AMA. Home: 13189 Sw 23rd St Miramar FL 33027 Office: U Miami 1600 NW 10th Ave Rm 7168 Miami FL 33027 Office Phone: 305-243-3583.

CHERMAK, GAIL D., audiologist, educator; BA in Comm. Disorders, SUNY, Buffalo; PhD, Ohio State U., 1975. Asst. prof. So. Ill. U., Edwardsville, Ill., 1975—77; prof. Wash. State U., Pullman, Wash., 1977—, chair dept. speech and hearing scis., 1990—, interim dean Coll. Liberal Arts, 1997—98, Edard Meyer disting. prof. Coll. Liberal Arts, 1999—2002. Author: (book) Central Auditory Processing Disorders: New perspectives, Handbook of Audiological Rehabilitation; contbr. articles to profl. jours. Named Disting. Faculty Mem., Wash. State U., 2002; fellow, Kellogg Found., 1986—89; grantee, U.S. Fulbright Program, 1990. Fellow: Am. Speech-Lang.-Hearing Assn. (cert. 1976), Am. Acad. Audiology; mem.: Intenat. Soc. of Audiology, Pan Am. Audiology Assn., Acoustical Soc. Am., Am. Auditory Soc. Avocations: gardening, boating. Office: Wash State Univ Dept Speech & Hearing Sci Pullman WA 99164-2420 Office Phone: 509-335-4526.

CHERMAYEFF, IVAN, graphic designer; b. London, Eng., June 6, 1932; s. Serge Ivan and Barbara Maitland (May) C.; m. Sara Anne Duffy, July 15, 1956; children: Catherine, Alexandra, Maro; m. Jane Clark, Sept. 24, 1978; 1 son, Sam. Grad., Phillips Acad., Andover, Mass., 1950; student, Harvard, 1950-52, Ill. Inst. Tech., 1952-54; BFA, Yale, 1955; LLD (hon.), Maine Sch. Art, 1981; BFA (hon.), Corcoran Sch. Art, 1991, U. of Arts, Phila., 1991. Asst. to Alvin Lustig (designer), 1955; asst. art dir. Columbia Records, 1956; ptnr. Brownjohn, Chermayeff & Geismar Assoc., 1956-59, Chermayeff & Geismar Inc., NYC, 1959—, Cambridge Seven Assoc., 1965-96. Bd. dir. Internat. Design Conf., Aspen, Colo., 1968-99; bd. dir. Mcpl. Art Soc. NY, 1972-76, Smithsonian Instn., 1988-96; trustee Mus. Modern Art, NYC, 1966-86, Archives of Am. Art, 1987-90, New Sch. Univ., 1988-2002; bd. overseers Parson's Sch. Design, 1988-2002; disting. vis. prof. UCLA, 1998; vis. prof. Kansas City Art Inst., Cooper Union; co-chmn. First Fed. Design Assembly, Nat. Endowment for the Arts and Humanities, 1973. Author: Observations on American Architecture, 1972, Ellis Island, 1987. Mem. com. on art and arch. Yale U.; mem. bd. overseers com. on visual and environ. studies Harvard U. Recipient Awards Art Dir. Club, NY, awards Am. Inst. Graphic Arts, awards Type Dirs. Club, Indsl. Arts, medal AIA, 1967, Gold medal Phila. Coll. Art, 1971, Claude M. Fuess medal Phillips Acad., 1980, Pres.'s award RISD, 1981, Yale Arts medal 1985, Grand Prix Biennale Brno, 1992; named to NY Art Dir. Club Hall of Fame, 1981, Soc. of Illustrators, gold medal, 2002. Mem. SPEE, Am. Inst. Graphic Arts (pres. 1963-66, Gold medal 1979), Nat. Soc. Indsl. Designers, Alliance Graphique Internat., Royal Soc. Arts and Commerce (Benjamin Franklin fellow), Royal Designer for Industry (RDI hon.), Century Assn., Yale Arts Assn. (past v.p.). Home: 140 E 81st St New York NY 10028-1805 also: Sheep's Hill North Salem NY 10560 Office: 15 E 26th St New York NY 10010-1505 E-mail: ic@cgnyc.com, ic@cgstudionyc.com.

CHERNESKY, RICHARD JOHN, lawyer; b. Scranton, Pa., July 27, 1939; s. Frank Peter and Mary C.; m. Alice Faye Nyfenger, Aug. 1, 1959; children: Christopher John, Joshua James. BA, Ohio St. U., 1963, JD, 1966. Bar: Ohio 1966. Ptnr. Smith & Schnacke, Dayton, Ohio, 1966-88; mng. ptnr. Chernesky, Heyman & Kress P.L.L., Dayton, 1988—. Bd. dirs. Am. Indoor Soccer Assn., Inc., 1992-96; pres. Ohio Sports Ctr., Miamisburg, Ohio, 1991—; trustee Hipple Cancer Rsch. Ctr., Kettering, Ohio, 1994-96, Dayton Internat. Aviation Corp., Inc., 1990-92; sec. Iams Co., 1997—. Bd. dirs. Miami Valley Hosp. Found., Dayton, 1987-88, Chapel of the Air, Wheaton, Ill., 1985-91, 94-95, Mike-sell's, Inc., 1994—, Dolly Inc., Tipp City, Ohio, 1989-93; trustee The Luth. Sch. of Dayton, 1988-91, The Waynesville Area Friends of the Parks, 1992—; mem. Luth. Social Svcs. Devel. Com., Dayton, 1987-93; chmn. Wayne Twp. Zoning Bd., Waynesville, 1987-95; bd. dirs. U.S. Soccer Fedn. Found., Inc., 1996—. Mem. Ohio State Bar Assn., Dayton Bar Assn., Dayton Better Bus. Bur. (bd. dirs. 1989-94). Home: 8027 New Burlington Rd Waynesville OH 45068-9705 Office: Chernesky Heyman & Kress PLL PO Box 3808 Ste 1100 10 Courthouse Plz SW Dayton OH 45401-3808

CHERNEV, MELVIN, retired beverage company executive; b. Bklyn., Nov. 29, 1928; s. Irving and Selma (Kulik) C.; m. Noemi Dohnert, May 29, 1955 (dec. July 1, 1985); 1 child, Celia Ann; m. Marlene G. Tonkin, Sept. 4, 1988. AB, Cornell U., 1950. Chief statistician Eversharp, Inc., N.Y.C., 1951-52, sales adminstr., 1952-55, asst. gen. sales mgr., 1955-58; sales promotion mgr. Internat. Latex Corp. (Playtex), N.Y.C., 1959-64, product mgr., 1964-66; pres. Snow White Corp., San Jose, Calif., 1966-67; dir. planning and research Fromm and Sichel, Inc., distbrs. Christian Bros. wines and brandy, San Francisco, 1967-70, dir. mktg. services, 1970-73, v.p. mktg. services, 1973-76, sr. v.p. mktg., 1976-77, exec. v.p., 1977-78, pres., chief operating officer, 1978-83, bd. dirs. Mem. Sacramento County Grand Jury, 2000—01; bd. dirs., trustee Cogswell Coll., San Francisco, 1976—86, chmn., 1983—85; bd. govs. City U., Seattle, 1985—99; bd. dirs., treas. The Lakes at Northridge Homeowners Assn.; pres. bd. dirs. Albert Einstein Residence Ctr., 1997—2000. Mem. Cornell Club No. Calif., Cornell Club (N.Y.C.), North Ridge Country Club (Fair Oaks, Calif.). Home: 7529 Pineridge Ln Fair Oaks CA 95628-4858 E-mail: mchernev@aol.com.

CHERNIACK, EVAN PAUL, geriatrician; s. Neil Stanley and Sandra Helene Cherniack; m. Maggie Velez, Aug. 13, 1992; children: Yitzchok Zev, Ariella Rochel. AB, Harvard U., Cambridge, Mass., 1978—82; MD, U. Cin., 1986. Resident SUNY Health Sci. Ctr., Bklyn., 1986—89; fellow Cornell U. Med. Coll., N.Y.C., 1989—92; asst. prof. Mt. Sinai Sch. Med., N.Y.C., 1992—2003; geriatrician Bronx VA Med. Ctr., NY, 1992—2001; geriatric rsch. coord. Jewish Home and Hosp., Bronx, NY, 2001—03; asst prof. U. Miami Sch. Medicine, Fla., 2003—; dir., geriat. clinic Miami VA Med. Ctr., Miami, Fla., 2003—. Reviewer Am. Geriat. Soc. Jour., L.A., 1992—. Editor: (medical textbook) Alternative Medicine for the Elderly. Office: Univ Miami Sch Med 1201 NW 16 St Miami FL 33125

CHERNIACK, NEIL STANLEY, pulmonologist, educator; b. Bklyn., May 28, 1931; s. Max and Rebecca (Roulnick) C.; m. Sandra Lebowitz, Dec. 31, 1954; children: Evan, Andrew, Emily. AB with honors, Columbia U., 1952; MD, SUNY, 1956; MA, U. Pa., 1972; hon. degree, Karolinska U., 1991. Cert. Am. Bd. Internal Medicine, 1962. Intern U. Ill., Chgo., 1956-57, resident, 1957-58, 60-62; resident, fellow Columbia Presbyn. Hosp., N.Y.C., 1962-64; practice medicine specializing in pulmonary disease Chgo., 1964-69, Phila., 1969-77, Cleve., 1977—95; asst. prof. medicine U. Ill., Chgo., 1964-68, assoc. prof., 1968-69, U. Pa., Phila., 1969-73, prof., 1973-77, Case Western Res. U., 1977—, chief pulmonary svc., 1977-89, prof. physiology, 1982—, assoc. dean, 1983-90, dean sch. medicine, v.p. med. affairs, 1990-95, vice chmn. div. gen. med. sci., 1986-90, vice chmn. dept. medicine, 1987-90; chief pulmonary svc., sr. attending physician Phila. Gen. Hosp., 1969-77; assoc. dir. pulmonary svc., attending physician U. Pa. Hosp., 1973-77, U. Hosps. of Cleve., Cleve. VA Med. Ctr.; vis. prof. Karolinska U., Stockholm, 1976-77, dir. clin. svc., 1995—2000; dir. of clin. svcs., acting chmn. dept. physiology & pharmacology U. Medicine & Dentistry N.J., Newark, 1995—97. External vis. com. Aga Khan U., Karachi, 1980—85; chmn. vis. com. neurosci. program Howard U., 1998—. Mem. editl. bd.: Circulation Rsch., Am. Rev. Respiratory Disease, Chest; editor: Jour. Applied Physiology, Handbook of Physiology; assoc. editor: Jour. Lab. Clin. Medicine, Respiration Handbooks of Physiology, Respiration and Respiratory Medicine Revs. Capt. USAF, 1958—60, with USAF, 1960—62. Mem.: N.Y. Clin. Soc., Neurosci. Soc., Ctrl. Soc. Clin. Rsch., Biomed. Engring. Soc. (bd. dirs. 1984—87, councilor 1986), Biogengring. Soc., Am. Physiol. Soc., Am. Lung Assn., Am. Thoracic Soc. (councilor 1982), Am. Soc. Clin. Investigation, Am. Assn. Physicians, Soc. Columbia Grads., Beta Sigma Rho, Alpha Omega Alpha, Phi Beta Kappa. Jewish. Avocation: digital art. Home: 11 Wood Dr Morris Plains NJ 07950-1509 Office: Univ Med Dental NJ Newark NJ 07103-2714 Office Phone: 973-972-7937. Business E-Mail: cherniac@umdnj.edu.

CHERNICHAW, MARK, broadcast executive, television producer, advertising executive, media consultant; b. Newark, Mar. 31, 1946; s. Nathan H. and Irma (Walker) C.; m. Pauline Papernik, Nov. 22, 1967; children: Adam, Ian. BA, U. Miami, Fla., 1969; MS, Bklyn. Coll., 1972. Assoc. prof. NYU, 1972-82; ind. TV prodr., dir., 1973-82; exec. prodr. TV commls., video, film prodns., exec.-in-charge of prodn. Avon Products, Inc., NYC, 1982-92; pres. Entertainment Enterprises Inc., 1991-96; exec. v.p. creative svcs. and prodn. SLP & Co., N.Y.C. and L.A., 1995—97; v.p. advt., promotion, prodn. The Home Shopping Network, USA Network, 1997—99; v.p. global comms. Prudential Fin., 1999—. Writer, prodr., dir. commls. ABC-TV Sweeps; exec. prodr., prodr., dir. shows featuring celebrities including John Glenn, George Burns, Henry Fonda, Bob Hope, Frank Sinatra, Ricki Lake, Martin Sheen, Cindy Crawford, Mary Hart, Whoopie Goldberg, Colin Powell; cons. NJ Coalition for Fair Broadcasting, Trenton; guest spkr. Directing TV seminars Video Comms. Congress; lectr. Video Expo, NY; judge Emmy, Clio awards. Dir. One Person Too Late, ABC-TV (Internat. Film and TV award), syndicated TV series The Road to the White House (represented in permanent collection Smithsonian Instn. and The Peabody Award Archives), CBS Sports segment, Cable TV series The Home Shopping Show, various nat. and regional TV commls. (Clio award); mem. editl. adv. bd. Video Mgr. mag.; contbr. articles to profl. jours. Polit. media cons. Recipient 1 Grand, 2 Gold, 4 Silver and 3 Bronze awards Internat. Film and TV, Grand award, Gold award Internat. Assn. Bus. Communicators. Mem. NIMA Internat., NATAS, Am. Film Inst., Internat. TV Assn. Avocations: music, sports, travel.

CHERNIGA, MICHAEL J., lawyer; b. Hartford, Conn., Dec. 23, 1955; BS in Fin., Fla. State Univ., 1978, JD with honors, 1981. Bar: Fla. 1981, US Dist. Ct. (mid. dist.) Fla. Shareholder, co-chair nat. health bus. group Greenberg Traurig LLP, Tallahassee. Adj. prof. health care law Fla. State Univ., 1999. Named one of the Legal Elite, Fla. Trend Mag., 2004. Mem.: ABA, Fla. Bar Assn., Am. Health Lawyers Assn., Fla. Health Care Assn., Fla. Hosp. Assn. Office: Greenberg Traurig LLP 101 E College Ave Tallahassee FL 32301-7742 Office Phone: 850-222-6891. Office Fax: 850-681-0207. Business E-Mail: chernigam@gtlaw.com.

CHERNIN, PETER, motion picture company executive; b. May 29, 1951; Pres. Lorimar Film Entertainment, 1988—89; pres. entertainment group Fox Broadcasting Co., L.A., 1989—92; chmn. Twentieth Century Fox Film Corp., now Fox Filmed Entertainment, Beverly Hills, Calif., 1992—; chmn., CEO The Fox Group, Beverly Hills, Calif., 1992—; pres., COO News Corp., 1996—. Bd. dirs. News Corp., E Trade. Office: Fox Inc Rm 5080 10201 W Pico Blvd Bldg 100 Los Angeles CA 90064-2606

CHERNIN, RUSSELL SCOTT, lawyer; b. Bklyn., Feb. 5, 1957; s. Julius and Sara Sidne (Fuchsman) C.; m. Diane M. Clay, Sept. 27, 1986. AB, Clark U., 1978; JD, George Washington U., 1981. Bar: Mass. 1981, U.S. Dist. Ct. Mass. 1983, U.S. Ct. Appeals (1st cir.) 1985. Law clk. FERC, Washington, 1979-81; assoc. Labovitz & Assocs., Worcester, Mass., 1982-83; pvt. practice Worcester, 1983—. Instr. bus. law Becker Jr. Coll., Leicester, Mass., 1985-89. Co-author handbook: Sex and the Law, 1979; contbr. to profl. publs. Mem. Legal panel Civil Liberties Union Mass., 1988. Mem. Mass. Bar Assn., Worcester County Bar Assn., Am. Arbitration Assn., Clark U. Alumni Assn. Avocations: scuba diving, skiing. Office: 390 Main St Worcester MA 01608-2583 Office Phone: 508-753-8118. Personal E-mail: loopehole26@verizon.net.

CHERNO, MELVIN, humanities educator; b. El Paso, Feb. 24, 1929; s. Sol and Deborah (Andes) C.; m. Dolores Ellen Himelstein, Dec. 25, 1950; children— Steven Philip, Paige Elise, Julie Rosanne AB, Stanford U., 1950; AM, U. Chgo., 1952; PhD, Stanford U., 1955. Instr. Bakersfield Coll., Calif., 1955-60; successively asst. prof., assoc. prof., prof. Oakland U., Rochester, Mich., 1960-80; Vaughan prof. tech., culture and comm. U. Va., Charlottesville, 1980-2000, Vaughan prof. emeritus humanities, 2001—, prin. second residential coll., 1991-95, 2000-01, co-prin., 1995-96. Co-editor: (4-vol. anthology) Western Society ..., 1967; editor, translator: (essay) Feuerbach on Luther, 1968; contbr. articles on historical topics to profl. jours. Former mem. Am. Hist. Assn., Am. Soc. Engring. Edn., So. Hist. Assn., Soc. for History of Tech., Soc. for Lit. & /Sci., Soc. for 19th Century Studies. Fellow Ford Found., 1953-55, Deutscher Akademische Austauschdienst, 1966, Inst. für Europäische Geschichte, 1966 Mem. Phi Beta Kappa. Home: 360 Forest Ave Apt 103 Palo Alto CA 94301 E-mail: melanddee@sbcglobal.net.

CHERNOFF, ALLAN, correspondent; BA in Am. Civilization, Brown U., 1981. Reporter, anchor, prodr. Sta. WBRU-FM, Providence, 1978-81; stringer Sta. WEAN-AM, Providence, 1981; newswriter Sta. KCBS-TV, L.A., 1981-82; reporter Fin. News Network, N.Y.C., 1983-86, corr., anchor This Morning's Bus., 1987-91; sr. corr. CNBC, N.Y.C., 1991—, anchor, reporter Mng. Your Money, 1991-94, corr., until 2000; sr. corr. pres. CNN, N.Y.C., 2000—. Interviewer Survivors of the Shoah Found.; freelance print journalist; contbr. Marketplace pub. radio; reporter NBC Nightly News, Today Show, NBC News at Sunrise, MCNBC; writer MSNBC.com. Mem. N.Y. Cares, In-Touch Radio Network. Mem. Soc. Profl. Journalists (two time winner best bus. reporting), Nat. Acad. TV Arts & Scis., N.Y. Fin. Writers' Assn. (interviewer survivor of Shoa Project), Deadline Club. Office: CNN One Time Warner Ctr New York NY 10019

CHERNOW, ANN LEVY, artist, art educator; b. NYC, Feb. 1, 1936; d. Edward P. and Mollie (Citrin) Levy; m. Philip Chenok, Aug. 11, 1957 (div. Jan. 1969); children: David Charles Chenok, Daniel Joshua Chenok; m. Burt Chernow, Dec. 11, 1970. MA, NYU, 1969. Instr. Mus. Modern Art, N.Y.C., 1966-71; prof., head art dept. Norwalk (Conn.) Cmty. Tech. Coll., 1974-96. Guest lectr., instr. studio and art history Silvermine Sch. Arts Silvermine Coll., 1968—80; vis. artist, lectr. Housatonic C.C., Conn., 1975—80; guest lectr. Am. Coll. in Paris, 1985, Salem State Coll., 1993, 94, Yale U., 1995, Westport Hist. Soc., 1994, Fairfield U., 1993; vis. artist CAP program Wesleyan U., 1979; coord. Bicentennial Exhbn. Norwalk C.C., 1976, Yale U. Art Gallery, 1996; master drawing class The Nat. Acad., N.Y.C., 2000—, N.Y.C., 2001; vis. artist and lectr. Bryn Mawr U., 2003, Ind. U., 2003; vis. artist Pa. Acad. Fine Arts, 2004, U. Ind., 2002. One-woman shows include Queens Coll., N.Y.C., 2000, Erlich Gallery, Marblehead, Mass., 2002, Uptown Gallery, N.Y.C., 2002, 2004, Raclin Gallery Ind. U., 2003, Print Ctr., Phila., 2003, Dorothy Rogers Fine Art, Santa Fe, N.Mex., 2003, Silvermine Guild, Conn., 2005, numerous others, exhibited in group shows at Millennium Portfolio of Time and Place, 1999—2001, Americas, 2000, Bklyn. Mus., 2001, Nat. Acad., 2001, NY Soc. Etchers, 2002, Nat Arts Club, NYC, 2002, Mus. City of NY, 2002, Salle des Fetes, Paris, 2003, Trois Rivieres, Can., 2003, Lessedra Gallery, Sophia, Bulgaria, 2004, Black Ch. Gallery, Dublin, 2004, Westport Arts Ctr., Conn., 2004, Housatonic Mus. Art, 2005, NAD, N.Y.C., 2005, numerous others, Represented in permanent collections Met. Mus. Art, Rose Art Mus., Brandeis U., Nat. Mus. Women in Arts, Washington, William Benton Mus. Art, Storrs, Conn., Mus. of City of N.Y., UN, Westport, Achenbach Found., San Francisco, New Britain Mus. Am. Art, Conn., Neuberger Mus., Purchase, N.Y., Housatonic Mus. Art Yale U., Mattatauk Mus., Lehigh U. Art Collection, Pa., Utah Mus. Fine Arts, U. Ariz. Art Collection, Lyman Allyn Mus., Conn., Bruce Mus., Butler Inst. Am. Art, Ohio, Rutgers U., Hofstra U., Elvejhem Mus., Wis., N.Y. Pub. Libr., Duxbury Mus. Mass., USO of Met. N.Y., Amity Art Found., Conn., Reading (Pa.) Pub. Mus., Portland (Oreg.) Art Mus., De Cordova Mus., Lincoln, Mass., Yale U. Art Gallery, Utah Mus. Fine Arts, Ohio Wesleyan U., Worcester Mus. Art, Mass., Oakland Mus., Calif., U.S.O. Greater Met. N.Y., Reading Pub. Mus., Pa., Transit Mus., N.Y.C., Bklyn. Mus., Libr. Congress, Nat. U. Coalition Taiwan, San Diego Mus. Art, Nat. Acad. N.Y.C., San Diego (Calif.) Mus.;, author numerous poems; contbr. articles to profl. jours.; artistic dir.: (documentaries) A Gathering of Glory. Active Westport Arts Adv. Com., Westport Schs. Permanent Art Collection Com. Named Conn. Woman of Decade in Arts, UN Assn., 1987, U.S.A. rep., Agart World Print Festival, Ljubljana, Slovenia, 1999, UN Artist of Yr., 2002; recipient Purchase award, Delta Internat. Prints, 1996, Etching award, L.A. Printmaking Soc., 1997, Painting award, Manhattan Arts Internat., 1997, Etching award, Audubon artists, 1997, Print Biennial Silvermine Guild of Art, Conn., 1998, Four winners award, Stamford Mus. & Nature Ctr., Conn., 1998, Eisner Found. award, 1998, Richard Florsheim award, 1998, Exhbn. award/Boston Printmakers and Delta Internat. awards, Print Club, 2001, Purchase award, Delta Internat. Prints, 2001, Trustees Merit award, Housatonic C.C., 2003, Legion of Honor award, Achenbach Found., San Francisco, Catalog Raisonée Graphics award, Amity Art Found., 2003, Lifetime Honors award, Silvermine Guild, Conn., 2004; fellow Yale Mellon, 1993—94; grantee Yale/Mellon, 1995; scholar Conn. Humanities Coun., 1980—. Mem.: N.Y. Etchers Soc., Print Club Albany, Print Club Phila., L.A. Print Soc., Boston Printmakers, Calif. Soc. Printmakers, Nat. Acad. Art, Nat. Acad. Art (elected Academician Graphics), Soc. Am. Graphic Artists (past coun.). Studio: 2 Gorham Ave Westport CT 06880-2531 Office Phone: 203-227-8016. Personal E-mail: ctfinearts@sbcglobal.net.

CHERNOW, BART, critical care physician; b. N.Y.C., June 26, 1947; BA, Queens Coll., 1968; MD, SUNY, N.Y.C., 1976. Internal medicine intern Nat. Naval Med. Ctr., Bethesda, Md., 1976-77, internal medicine resident, 1977-79, endocrine fellow, 1979-81; dir. rsch. dept. critical care medicine Bethesda Naval Hosp., 1981-85, head acad. affairs, 1985-86; assoc. prof. anesthesia Harvard Med. Sch., Boston, 1986-90; assoc. dir. surg. ICU Mass. Gen. Hosp., 1986-90; prof. medicine, anesthesia and critical care Johns Hopkins U. Sch. Medicine, Balt., 1990-99; physician-in-chief Sinai Hosp., 1990-97; program dir. John Hopkins U./Sinai Hosp. Program in Internal Medicine, 1990-97; vice dean for rsch. and tech. Sch. Medicine Johns Hopkins U. Sch. Medicine, 1997-99; pres., CEO GMP Cos., Inc., Ft. Lauderdale, Fla., 1999—2004, chief tech. officer, 2004—. Adj. prof. medicine Johns Hopkins U. Sch. Medicine, 1999—2005. Editor: Pharmacologic Approach to the Critically Ill Patient, 1983, 88, 94; editor-in-chief: Critical Care Medicine, 1990-97. Comdr. med. corps USNR, 1969-86. Recipient Achievement award Am. Coll. Nutrition, 1995. Fellow ACP (master), Am. Coll. Critical Care Medicine; mem. Soc. Critical Care Medicine (Presdl. citation 1997), Am. Coll. Chest Physicians (regent 1990-98, pres. 1996-97, master fellow, chair CHEST found.1996-2002). Home: 2100 N Ocean Blvd Ph 30 Fort Lauderdale FL 33305-1940 Office: GMP Cos Inc Ste 1701 One E Broward Blvd Fort Lauderdale FL 33301 Fax: 954-745-3511. Office Phone: 954-745-3503.

CHERNOW, RON, writer, journalist; b. Bklyn., Mar. 3, 1949; s. Israel and Ruth (Goldspinner) C.; m. Valerie Stearn, Oct. 22, 1979. BA in English summa cum laude, Yale U., 1970; MA in English, Cambridge (Eng.) U., 1972; LHD, Marymount Manhattan Coll., 2005, Hamilton Coll., 2005. Free-lance writer, N.Y.C., 1973-82; program officer for fin. policy studies The Twentieth Century Fund, N.Y.C., 1983-86; writer, essayist, lectr., book reviewer N.Y.C., 1988—; occasional columnist The Wall St. Jour., 1990-91; commentator Nat. Pub. Radio, 1994-97. Frum Meml. lectr., 1997; guest curator Mus. Am. Fin. History, 1998-99; hist. cons. WGBH Boston. Author: The House of Morgan, 1990, The Warburgs, 1993, The Death of the Banker, 1997, Titan, 1998, Alexander Hamilton, 2004; also 13 cover stories; contbr. articles to N.Y. Times, N.Y. Mag., Time mag., Bus. Week, Saturday Rev., Vanity Fair, Am. Heritage, Smithsonian and 30 other publs. Vice chmn. Cambridge U. Assn. of N.Y., 1986-87. Recipient Jack London award United Steelworkers, 1980, Nat. Book award Nat. Book Found., 1990, Books to Remember award N.Y. Pub. Libr., 1990, Ambassador Book award English Speaking Union, 1991, George S. Eccles prize Columbia Bus. Sch., 1993, Notable Book citation ALA, 1993, Annual Book award Colonial Dames Am., 1998, 2005, Scholar of Yr. award N.Y. Coun. Humanities, 1999, Ohiana Book award Ohiana Libr., 1999, Abraham Lincoln Literary award The Union League Club, 2000, Notable Book citation ALA, 2004, George Washington Book prize, 2005, Book award Yale Club of Boston, 2005, Washington Irving medal St. Nicholas Soc., 2005, Alexander Hamilton award Manhattan Inst., 2005, Annual Book award Colonial Dames Am., 2005 Mem. PEN (chmn. readers and writers com. 1994-98, trustee 1997-2003, sec. 1999, v.p. 2000-03, co-chmn. planning com. 2004), Authors Guild, Leo Baeck Inst., Wildlife Conservation Soc., The Nature Conservancy, Alexander Hamilton Hist. Soc. (mem. adv. bd. 2003—), N.Y. Hist. Soc., Century Assn., Orgn. Am. Historians, Internat. Vocal Arts Inst., Phi Beta Kappa (Couper lectr. 2004). Democrat. Jewish. Address: 63 Joralemon St Brooklyn NY 11201-4003

CHERNY, ROBERT WALLACE, historian, educator; b. Marysville, Kans., Apr. 4, 1943; s. Clarence L. and Lena M. (Hobbs) C.; m. Rebecca Ellen Marshall, June 11, 1967; 1 child, Sarah Catherine. BA with distinction, U. Nebr., 1965; MA, Columbia U., 1967, PhD, 1972. From instr. history to prof. San Francisco (Calif.) State U., 1971—81, prof., 1981—, assoc. dean behavioral and social scis., 1984, acting dean behavioral and social scis., 1985, chmn. history dept., 1987-92; interim dean undergrad. studies San Francisco State U., 2005—. Disting. Fulbright lectr. Moscow State U., 1996; vis. rsch. scholar U. Melbourne, 1997; mem. academic senate San Francisco (Calif.) State U., 1981-84, 95-2005, chmn. academic senate, 2002-04; cons. in field. Author: A Righteous Cause: The Life of William Jennings Bryan, 1985, rev. edit., 1994, Populism, Progressivism and the Transformation of Nebraska Politics, 1981, American Politics in the Gilded Age, 1869-1868, 1997; co-author (with William Issel): San Francisco, 1865-1932, 1986; co-author: San Francisco: Presidio, Port and Pacific Metropolis, 1981; co-author: (with Carol Berkin, Christopher L. Miller, James L. Gormly) Making America: A History of the United States, 1995, 3d edit., 2003; co-author: (with R. Griswold del Castillo and G. Lemke-Santangelo) Competing Visions: A History of California, 2005; co-editor (with William Issel and Keiran Taylor): American Labor and the Cold War: Unions, Politics and Postware Political Culture, 2004. Woodrow Wilson fellow, 1965-66, Woodrow Wilson dissertation fellow, 1969, NEH fellow, 1992-93. Mem. Am. Hist. Assn., Orgn. Am. Historians (treas. 2003-), S.W. Labor Studies Assn. (pres. 1982-86), Calif. Hist. Soc., Soc. Historians of Gilded Age and Progressive Era (pres. 1995), Nebr. State Hist. Soc., HNet--Humanities and Social Studies Online (pres. 2003, v.p. tchg. 2005—). Democrat. Office: San Francisco State U Dept of History 1600 Holloway Ave San Francisco CA 94132-4155

CHEROUTES, MICHAEL LOUIS, lawyer; b. Chgo., Apr. 27, 1940; s. Louis Samuel Cheroutes and Maria Jane (Zimmerman) Dodd; m. Trisha Flynn, Oct. 30, 1965; children: Michael Louis Jr., Trisha Francesca, Matthew Dodd. BA, Harvard U., 1962; LLB, Stanford U., 1965. Bar: Colo. 1965. Assoc., then ptnr. Sherman & Howard, Denver, 1965-85; chief of staff to Rep. Patricia A. Shroeder U.S. Ho. of Reps., Washington, 1972-74; ptnr. Davis, Graham & Stubbs, Denver, 1985-93, Hogan & Hartson LLP, various, Colo., 1993—, dir. pub. fin. practice group. Contbr. articles to profl. jours. Mem. Colo. Commn. on Higher Edn., 1988-91, chmn., 1989-91; mem. state bd. Gt. Outdoors Colo. Trust Fund, 1996-97. Mem. ABA, Colo. Bar Assn., Nat. Assn.

Bond Lawyers. Avocation: sailing. Office: Hogan & Hartson LLP One Tabor Ctr 1200 17th St Ste 1500 Denver CO 80202-5840 Office Phone: 303-899-7310. Business E-Mail: mlcheroutes@hhlaw.com.

CHEROVSKY, ERWIN LOUIS, lawyer, writer; b. Dover, NJ, Dec. 31, 1933; s. Sam and Ida (Bluestein) C.; m. Edith Mayer, June 26, 1966; children: Kim, Karen; children by previous marriage: Debra, Jill. AB, U. Rochester, 1955; LLB, Harvard U., 1958. Bar: N.Y. 1958, U.S. Dist. Ct. (so. dist.) N.Y. 1964, U.S. Ct. Appeals (2d cir.) 1964. Assoc. Stamer & Haft, N.Y.C., 1958-63, Summit Rovins & Feldesman, N.Y.C., 1963-68, ptnr., 1968-88, Proskauer Rose LLC, 1988-89; chmn., legal cost containment cons. WIK Cons. Inc., N.Y.C., 1992-97; pres. Old Quarry Devel., Englewood, N.J., 1996—. Sec. Space & Leisure Time, Ltd., N.Y.C., 1972-80, Ghiordian Knot, Ltd., N.Y.C., 1978-88, ORS Automation, Inc., Princeton, N.J., 1983-86, Cook United, Inc., Cleve., 1986; lit. agt. for Random House Russian-English Dictionary of Idioms, Sophia Lubensky, 1995, From Central Park to Sinai, Roy S. Neuberger, 2000. Author: The Guide to New York Law Firms, 1991, Competent Counsel: The Business Guide to Selecting, Hiring Lawyers and Monitoring Their Work, 1992; contbr. articles to profl. jours. Fellow Phi Beta Kappa Soc.; mem. N.Y.State Bar Assn., Assn. Bar City of N.Y., Fed. Bar Coun. (chmn. winter meeting 1980, mem. alternative dispute resolution com. 1984), Can. Club (N.Y.C.) (bd. govs. 1988-89, editor Maple Leaf 1984-89), Met. Club (N.Y.C.). Office Phone: 201-567-4505. Personal E-mail: cherovsky@aol.com.

CHERRINGTON, DAVID JACK, finance educator; b. Grace, Idaho, Oct. 28, 1942; s. Jack A. and Virginia Freebairn Cherrington; m. Marilyn Hope Daines, Feb. 12, 1944; children: David Richard, Nathan John, Jennifer Cherrington Throckmorton, Jill Cherrington Christensen. BS, Brigham Young U., 1966; MBA, DBA, Ind. U., 1970. Asst. prof. U. Ill., Urbana, 1970—73; prof. Brigham Young U., Provo, Utah, 1973—. Cons. Continental N.Am. Corp., Chgo., 1973—73; pres. Human Resource Assn. of Ctrl. Utah, Provo, Utah, 1986—88; vis. prof. U. Wis., Madison, 1977, U. So. Calif., Great Falls, Mont., 1978, Brigham Young U., Laie, Hawaii, 1980, U. Utah, Salt Lake City, 1993. Author: (reference book) The Work Ethic: Working Values and Values that Work, 1980, (on-line university course) Organizational Effectiveness, 2003 (3rd Pl. in Distance Learning Courses competition, 2004), (textbook) The Management of Human Resources, 1983, Organizational Behavior, 1987, (reference book) Rearing Responsible Children, 1989, Moral Leadership and Ethical Decision Making, 2000, (textbook) Organizational Effectiveness, 2002, (certification handbook) Human Resource Certification Preparation Program, volumes 1-6, (internet training course) Ethical Decision Making, Developing Moral Character. Dist. chmn. Neighborhoods in Action, Orem, Utah, 1998—2005; bishop Ch. of Jesus Christ of Latter-day Saints, Orem, 1995—2003, Provo, Utah, 1985—88. Recipient Outstanding Citizen award, Orem City Coun., 1993. Mem.: Acad. Mgmt., Soc. Human Resource Mgmt. (sr. profl. in human resources 1988). Mem. Lds Ch. Avocations: jogging, gardening, teaching. Home: 1123 East 120 South Orem UT 84097 Office: Brigham Young University 780 Tanner Building Provo UT 84602 Office Phone: 801-422-6828. Personal E-mail: david_cherrington@byu.edu.

CHERRY, ANDREW LAWRENCE, JR., social work educator, researcher; b. Dothan, Ala., Nov. 11, 1943; s. Andrew L. Cherry and Wyalene Cain; m. Mary Elizabeth Dillon, July 16, 1988. MSW, U. Ala., Tuscaloosa, 1974; D Social Work, Columbia U., 1986. Child welfare worker Escambia County Dept. Pensions and Securities, Brewton, Ala., 1968-72; psychiat. social worker Bryce State Hosp., Tuscaloosa, 1974-79; instr. Salisbury (Md.) State Coll., 1981-85; asst. prof. Marywood Coll. Sch. Social Work, Scranton, Pa., 1986-87; prof. Barry U. Sch. Social Work, Miami, Fla., 1987—2003; prof. mental health Sch. Social Work U. Okla., Tulsa, 2003—, endowed prof. mental health sch. social work, 2003—. Cons. Informed Families Dade County, Miami, 1990—98, Miami Coalition for Care to Homeless, 1991—93, NAACP Minority Media and Telecomm. Coun., 1992—2000; with drug abuse prevention program Cath. Charities, Miami, 1991—2000, Broward Children's Svc., Ft. Lauderdale, 1992—94, The Biscayne Inst., 1994—2004, St. Luke's Addiction Recovery Ctr., 1995—2000; interim dir. child welfare divsn. Cath. Charities, 1998—2000; evaluator project SAMHSA, Okla., 2004—. Author: The Socializing Instinct: Individual, Family and Social Bonds, 1994, A Research Primer for the Helping Professions: Methods, Statistics, and Writing, 2000, Examining Global Social Welfare Issues Using MicroCase, 2002, 2d edit., 2004; co-author: Social Bonds and Teen Pregnancy, 1992; co-editor: Teenage Pregnancy: A Global View, 2001, Substance Abuse: A Global View, 2002; contbr. articles to profl. jours. Scholar, NIMH, 1979. Fellow: Am. Orthopsychiat. Assn.; mem.: NASW, N.Y. Acad. Scis., Conf. Social Work Edn. Achievements include research in and devel. of the social bond theory; extensive work and rsch. among the mentally disabled, homeless, at-risk children and the addicted. Office: U Okla Tulsa Campus 4502 E 41st St Ste 2J02 Tulsa OK 74135-2512 Office Phone: 918-660-3633. Business E-Mail: alcherry@ou.edu.

CHERRY, CHAINEY KJELLIN, orchestra director, vocal aranger; b. Atlanta, Ga., Apr. 20, 1978; d. Kate White and George Alfred Jones; m. Forrest Leo Cherry II, July 23, 2004. MusB, Ga. So. U., 2001; MEd, U. West Ga., Ga., 2005. Music Educator Ga., 2001. Check retreival analyst Bank South, College Park, Ga., 1995—96; sales / promotional asst. Radio One of Atlanta, College Park, Ga., 1996—97; orch. dir. Clayton County Pub. Schools, College Park, Ga., 2001—. Orch. condr. Clayton County Honor Orch., Jonesboro, Ga., 2002—03; music tutor, Jonesboro, Ga., 2003—. Exec. coord. All Grown Up Inc., Atlanta, 2003—. Scholar, Dr. Dorothy Moore, 1996—98; HOPE grant, State of Ga., 1996—2000, Ga. So. U. Symphony Guild scholar, Ga. So. U. Music Dept., 1996—2001, Ga. So. Music scholar, Ga. So. U., 1996—2001. Mem.: Ga. Music Educators Assn. (assoc.).

CHERRY, DANIEL RONALD, lawyer; b. Mpls., Dec. 31, 1948; s. Clifford D. and Ruby E. (Norman) C.; m. Dianne Brown, Jan. 24, 1971 (dec.); children: Matthew A., Kathryn E.; m. Q. Rhea Walker, Oct. 25, 1998. SB, MIT, 1970; JD cum laude, Harvard U., 1976. Bar: Ohio 1976, U.S. Dist. Ct. (no. dist.) Ohio 1976, U.S. Patent and Trademark Office 1978, U.S. Ct. Appeals (6th and Fed. cirs.) 1982, Ill. 1987, U.S. Dist. Ct. (no. dist.) Ill. 1987. Assoc. Squire, Sanders & Dempsey, Cleve., 1976-85, ptnr., 1985-87; ptnr., prin. Welsh & Katz, Ltd., Chgo., 1987—. Co-author: Patent Practice, 1997. With USCG, 1970-73. Mem. ABA, Ohio State Bar Assn., Ill. State Bar Assn., Chgo. Bar Assn., Am. Intellectual Property Law Assn., Intellectual Property Law Assn. Chgo., Licensing Execs. Soc. Home: 1046 Vine St Winnetka IL 60093-1834 Office: Welsh & Katz Ltd 120 S Riverside Plz # 22 Chicago IL 60606-3913 Office Phone: 312-526-1526. E-mail: drcherry@welshkatz.com.

CHERRY, HAROLD, insurance company executive; b. Bronx, N.Y., June 20, 1931; s. Isidor and Esther C.; m. Maida Welt, Aug. 12, 1961; children—Gina, Joshua. BS cum laude, CCNY, 1953. With N.Y. Life Ins. Co., N.Y.C., 1956-89, 2d v.p., actuary, 1972-78, v .p., actuary, 1978-89; pres. Actuarial Study Materials, Merrick, N.Y., 1983—. Cons. in field. Served with U.S. Army, 1954-56. Fellow Soc. Actuaries; mem. Am. Acad. Actuaries, Nat. Assn. Watch and Clock Collectors (past pres. L.I. chpt.) Jewish. Office: Actuarial Study Materials 3217 Wynsum Ave Merrick NY 11566-5549

CHERRY, JAMES DONALD, pediatrician; b. Summit, N.J., June 10, 1930; s. Robert Newton and Beatrice (Wheeler) C.; m. Jeanne M. Fischer, June 19, 1954; children: James S., Jeffrey D., Susan J., Kenneth C. BS, Springfield (Mass.) Coll., 1953; MD, U. Vt., 1957; MSc in Epidemiology, London Sch. Hygiene and Tropical Medicine, 1983. Diplomate Am. Bd. Pediat., Am. Bd. Pediat. Infectious Diseases. Intern, then resident in pediat. Boston City Hosp., 1957-59; resident in pediat. Kings County Hosp., Bklyn., 1959-60; rsch. fellow in medicine Harvard U. Med. Sch.-Thorndike Meml. Lab., Boston City Hosp., 1961-62; instr. pediatrics U. Vt. Coll. Medicine, also asst. attending physician Mary Fletcher DeGoesbriand Meml. hosps., Burlington, Vt., 1960-61; asst. prof., then assoc. prof. pediat. U. Wis. Med. Sch., Madison, 1963-66; assoc. attending physician Madison Gen., U. Wis. hosps., 1963-66; dir. John A. Hartford Rsch. Lab., Madison Gen. Hosp., 1963-66. Mem. faculty St. Louis U. Med. Sch., 1966-73, prof. pediatrics, 1969-73, vice chmn. dept., 1970-73; mem. staff Cardinal Glennon Meml. Hosp. Children, St. Louis U. Hosp., 1966-73; chief divsn. infectious diseases UCLA Med. Ctr. UCLA Sch. Medicine, 1973-2000, prof. pediat., 1973–; acting chmn. dept. pediatrics UCLA Med. Ctr., 1977-79; attending physician, chmn. infection control com. UCLA Med. Ctr., 1975-93; cons. Project Head Start; vis. worker dept. cmty. medicine Middlesex Hosp. and Med. Sch., London, 1982-83; vis. worker Common Cold Rsch. Unit, 1969-70; acad. visitor U. Cambridge, Eng., 2000-01. Co-editor Textbook of: Pediatric Infectious Diseases, 1981, 5th edit., 2003; assoc. editor: Clin. Infectious Diseases, 1990-99; Am. regional editor: Vaccine, 1991-2000; author numerous papers in field; editl. reviewer profl. jours. Bd. govs. Alexander Graham Bell Internat. Parents Orgn., 1967-69. With USAR, 1958-64. John and Mary R. Markle scholar acad. medicine, 1964 Mem. AAAS, APHA, Am. Acad. Pediat. (mem. exec. com. Calif. chpt. 2 1975-77, mem. com. infectious diseases 1977-83, assoc. editor 19th Red Book 1982), Am. Soc. Microbiology, Am. Fedn. Clin. Rsch., Soc. Pediat. Rsch., Infectious Diseases Soc. Am., Am. Epidemiol. Soc., Am. Pediat. Soc., L.A. Pediat. Soc., Internat. Orgn. Mycoplasmologists, Am. Soc. Virology, Soc. Hosp. Epidemiologists Am., Pediat. Infectious Diseases Soc. (pres. 1989-91, Disting. Physician award 2003), Alpha Omega Alpha. Office: UCLA David Geffen Sch Medicine Dept Pediatrics Rm 22-442 10833 Le Conte Ave Los Angeles CA 90095-1752 Office Phone: 310-825-5226. Business E-Mail: jcherry@mednet.ucla.edu.

CHERRY, JOHN D., JR., lieutenant governor; b. Sulphur Springs, Tex., May 5, 1951; s. John D. Sr. and Margaret L. (Roark) C.; m. Pamela M. Faris, 1979; children: Meghan M., John D. BA, U. Mich., 1973, MA, 1984. Chmn. 7th Cong. Dist. Dem. Com., Mich., 1973-75; adminstrv. asst. Mich. State Sen. Gary Corbin, 1975-81; Mich. polit. dir. Am. Fedn. State, County & Munic Employees AFL-CIO, 1981-82; mem. Mich. Ho. Reps. from 79th dist., Lansing, 1983-86, Mich. Senate from 29th dist., 1987-95, Mich. Senate from 28th dist., lansing, 1995—2002; senate minority leader, mem. legis. coun.; lt. gov., 2003—. Mem. Genesee County Dem. Exec. Bd., 1983-2002; mem. Mich. Jobs Commn. Bd., 1996-2000; del. Dem. Nat. Conv., 1996, 2000, 04; treas. Nat. Lt. Govs. Assn., 2004-05; vice chair Great Lakes Commn., 2005-. Democrat. Mailing: PO Box 30013 Lansing MI 48909 Office Phone: 517-373-6800.*

CHERRY, KEVIN M., career planning administrator; b. Glen Cove, N.Y., Oct. 2, 1976; s. Peter Kevin and Brenda More Cherry. BA, Cath. U. Am., 1998, MA, 1999. Policy analyst Empower Am., Washington, 1996—. Editor: Index of Leading Cultural Indicators, 2001. Roman Catholic. Personal E-mail: kmcherry@hotmail.com. Business E-Mail: kmcherry@empower.org.

CHERRY, MARK JOSEPH, philosopher; b. San Diego, 1969; m. Mollie Cherry; children: Jacob, Thaddeus. BA, U. Houston, 1991; MA, Rice U., 1996, PhD, 1999. Instr. dept. philosophy St. Edward's U., Austin, Tex., 1999—. Editor: Persons and Their Bodies: Rights, Responsibilities, Relationships; author: (chpt.) Philosophy and Medicine: Framing the Field, Allocating Scarce Medical Resoures: Roman Catholic Perspectives, Bioethics and Moral Content, Natural Law and the Possibility of a Global Ethics, Japanese and Western Bioethics: Studies in Moral Diversity, Persons and Their Bodies: Rights Responsibilities, Relationships; editor: Allocating Scare Medical Resources: Roman Catholic Perspectives, Regional Perspectives in Bioethics, Religious Perspectives in Bioethics, Natural Law and the Possibility of a Global Ethics; sr. assoc. editor: Jour. Medicine Philosophy, 2002—, Christian Bioethics, 2002—, editor-in-chief: HealthCare Ethics Com. Forum, 2003—; editor: (book series) Annals of Bioethics, 2003—; author: Kidney for Sole by Owner: Human Organs, Transplantation and the Market. Office: Saint Edward's U 3001 S Congress Ave Austin TX 78704 E-mail: markc@admin.stedwards.edu.

CHERRY, PETER BALLARD, electrical products corporation executive; b. Evanston, Ill., May 25, 1947; s. Walter Lorain and Virginia Ames (Ballard) C.; m. Crissy Hazard, Sept. 6, 1969; children: Serena Ames, Spencer Ballard. BA, Yale U., 1969; MBA, Stanford U., 1972. Analyst Cherry Elec. Products Corp., Waukegan, Ill., 1972-74, data processing and systems mgr., 1974, treas., 1974-77; v.p. fin. and bus. devel. Cherry Elec. Products Corps., Waukegan, Ill., 1977-80; exec. v.p. Cherry Elec. Products Corp., Waukegan, Ill., 1980-82, pres., chief oper. officer, 1982-86; pres., chief exec. officer Cherry Corp., Waukegan, Ill., 1986-92, chmn., pres., 1992—. Trustee Lake Forest Coll., Ill., 1982-90; trustee Lake Forest Hosp., 1982—, chmn., 1989-92. Mem.Onwentsia Club. Office: Cherry Corp 10411 Corporate Dr Pleasent Prairie WI 53157

CHERRY, ROBERT STEVEN, III, municipal official; b. Chgo., Aug. 13, 1951; s. Robert Lee and Jean Louise (Curry) C. BA, Kensington U., 1988. With Chgo. Pk. Dist., 1968—2004, supr. beaches and swimming pool lifeguards south side, 2003, aquatic supr., 1983—2004; ret., 2004. Asst. capt. 37th precinct, 7th ward, City of Chgo., 1979-80, precinct capt., 1980-83, asst. precinct capt. 2d precinct, 42d ward, 1984-92, capt., 1992-2002. 1st lt. U.S. Army/Ill. Nat. Guard, 1970-82. Named one of Outstanding Young Men of Am., 1985. Mem. Am. Legion (Post 1976), Young Dems. Am. (Ill. del. 1985), Young Dems. Ill., Young Dems. Cook County, U.S. Water Polo, U.S. Lifesaving Assn., Res. Officers Assn. U.S., Pub. Svc. Employees Union, Lambda Alpha Epsilon. Roman Catholic. Avocations: reading, backgammon, ping pong/table tennis, swimming. Office Phone: 773-343-1282. E-mail: r.cherryiii@comcast.net.

CHERRY, SABRINA, psychiatrist; b. N.Y.C., Mar. 20, 1959; d. Sheldon H. and Gloria B. Cherry; m. Marc N. Gourevitch, Sept. 10, 1988; children: Rebecca, Ruth. BA, Brown U., 1981; MD, Harvard U, 1987. Diplomate in psychiatry Am. Bd. Psychiatry and Neurology. Attending psychiatrist N.Y. Presbyn. Hosp., N.Y.C, 1991; asst. clin. prof. psychiatry Columbia U., N.Y.C, 1993; pvt. practice psychiatry, N.Y.C, 1991. Faculty Columbia Ctr. for Psychoanalytic Tng., 1998. Office: 585 W End Ave # 1E New York NY 10024-1715

CHERRY, SANDRA WILSON, lawyer; b. Dec. 31, 1941; d. Berlin Alexander and Renna Glen (Barnes) Wilson; m. John Sandefur Cherry, Sept. 24, 1976; 1 child, Jane Wilson. BA, U. Ark., 1962, JD, 1975. Bar: Ark. 75, U.S. Dist. Ct. (ea. dist.) Ark. 79, U.S. Supreme Ct. 79, U.S. Ct. Appeals (8th cir.) 79. Tchr. social studies Little Rock Sch. Dist., 1966—70; chmn. social studies dept. Horace Mann Jr. H.S., Little Rock, 1970—72; asst. U.S. atty. Dept. Justice, Little Rock, 1975—81, 1983—, 1st asst. U.S. atty., 2002—; commr. Ark. Pub. Svc. Commn., Little Rock, 1981—83. Adj. instr. U. Ark. Sch. Law, Little Rock, 1980; mem. 8th cir. gender fairness task force, Ark. dist. ct. magistrate selection panel, 2001. Contbr. case note to Ark. Law Rev., 1975. Pres. bd. dirs. Gaines House, Inc.; pres. U. Ark. at Little Rock Law Sch. Assn., 1980—81, bd. dirs., 1982, Jr. League Little Rock, 1974, Ark. Cmty. Found., 1997—, Gov.'s Mansion Assn., 1998—2004, Good Shepherd Ecumenical Ctr., 2004—. Recipient Gayle Pettus Pontz award, U. Ark. Law Sch. Women Lawyers Assn., 1990. Mem.: Ark. Women's Forum, Little Rock C. of C., Ark. Bar Assn. (com. on the status of women and minorities), Ark. Women Lawyers Assn., Pulaski County Bar Assn. (bd. dirs. 1989—90, 1991—92, pres.-elect 1993—94, pres. 1994—), Ark. Bar Assn. (Ho. of Dels. 1984—86, sec.-treas. 1986—89, 8th cir. Gender Fairness Task Force 1989—94, Ho. of Dels. 1989—, tenured del. 1994, exec. coun. chair 1995—96, pres. 2001—02, Golden Gavel award 1992), Met. Coun., Phi Beta Phi. Republican. Presbyterian. Home: 1 River Bend Little Rock AR 72202 Office: US Atty's Office PO Box 1229 Little Rock AR 72203-1229 Business E-Mail: sandra.cherry@usdoj.gov.

CHERRY, SCHROEDER, federal agency administrator; BFA summa cum laude, U. Mich., 1976; M in Tchg. in Mus. Edn., George Washington U., 1978; EdD in Mus. Edn., Columbia U., 1988. Mus. educator Anacostia Mus., Smithsonian Inst., Washington; dir. edn. The Studio Mus. in Harlem; chief edn. N.Y.C. Transit Exhibit; mus. educator J. Paul Getty Mus., 1988—90; dir. edn. and cmty. Balt. Mus. Art, 1990—96; program officer Wallace-Reader's Digest Funds, 1996—2000; dep. dir. for edn. and pub. programs Md. Hist. Soc., 2000—02; dep. dir. mus. svcs. Inst. Mus. and Libr. Svcs., Washington, 2002—. V.p. African Am. Mus. Assn., 1984; commr. Balt. Coun. for Historic and Archtl. Preservation, 1992—95; ea. regional dir. mus. edn. divsn. Nat. Art Edn. Assn., 1993—95; tchr. trainer Nat. Gallery Art, 1994, Balt. County Pub. Schs., 1998; cons. proposals for humanities project Nat. Endowment for the Humanities, 1999; presenter, project dir., scriptwriter ednl. media prodns. Contbr. articles to profl. jours. Achievements include coordinated the Joshua Johnson Council, the oldest African-American support group established by a major museum. Office: Inst Mus and Libr Svcs Office Mus Svcs 1100 Pennsylvania Ave NW Room 609 Washington DC 20506

CHERRY, WILLIAM ASHLEY, surgeon, state health official, educator; b. Halls, Tenn., Oct. 25, 1924; s. and Bessie R. C.; m. Jacqueline Guidry, June 2, 1989; children by previous marriage: Neal, Darrell, Philip, Susan. BS, Tulane U., 1946, MD, 1949. Diplomate Am. Bd. Surgery. Rotating intern Phila. Gen. Hosp., 1949-51; resident gen. surgery La. State U. div. Charity Hosp., New Orleans, 1953-56, resident thoracic surgery, 1956-57, asst. chief fracture service, 1963-65; practice medicine specializing in gen. and thoracic surgery New Iberia, La., 1957-63; commd. med. officer USPHS, 1963; mem. surg. staff USPHS Hosp., New Orleans, 1963-66, dir., 1966-71, asst. chief surgery dept., 1963-65, dep. chief, 1965-66, dir., 1966-71; regional health dir. Health Services and Mental Health Adminstrn., HEW, USPHS, Region VI, Dallas, 1971-74; sec., state health officer La. Dept. Health and Human Resources, Baton Rouge, 1977-80; commd. ensign USN, 1946, advanced through grades to comdr., 1963; sr. surgeon, comdr. USPHS, 1963; advanced through grades to asst. surgeon gen., admiral; comdg. officer Naval Res. Med. Co. 8-32, 1953-55; ret., 1963; chief med. officer USCG, Washington, 1974-77; pres., CEO, S. La. Health Svcs. Inc., 1987; med. dir. Lallie Kemp Regional Med. Ctr., Independence, La., Div. Mental Retardation and Developmental Disabilities, State of La., Baton Rouge, 1992-93, La. Dept. Health and Hosps., 1992-93; CEO, La. Health Care Authority, 1993-96; staff Met. Health Group, 1996—. Asst. clin. dir. surgery Charity Hosp., 1956-57, vis. surgeon, 1963—; chief of surgery Iberia Parish Hosp., 1959-61; chief of staff Dauterive Hosp., New Iberia, 1962-63; clin. asso. instr., surgery dept. La. State U. Sch. Medicine, 1953-57, clin. instr., 1963-66, clin. asst. prof. surgery, 1966-67; clin. asso. prof. surgery Tulane U. Sch. Medicine, 1967-70; adj. asso. prof. health services adminstrn. Tulane U. Sch. Medicine (Sch. Pub. Health and Tropical Medicine), 1969-70, adj. prof., 1970-73, clin. prof. surgery, 1970— Contbr. articles to med. jours. Chmn. ofcl. bd. First Methodist Ch., New Iberia, 1960-62; mem. ofcl. bd. Carrollton Meth. Ch., New Orleans, 1964-66; chmn. La. Inter-Agy. Council for Tb, 1966-70; mem. exec. com. New Orleans Poison Control Center, 1966-71; mem. Health Goals Task Force, State of La., 1969-70; mem. Fed. Exec. Bd., New Orleans, 1970-71, Dallas, 1972-73; med. adv. to sec. Dept. Transp., 1974-77; pres. So. Inst. Human Resources, Atlanta, 1979-80; mem. La. Gov.'s Adv. Com. on Edn. of Handicapped Children, 1977-80. Recipient Querens-Rives-Shore award Tulane U. Sch. Medicine, 1949; USPHS Commendation medal, 1969; USPHS Meritorious Service medal, 1974; USPHS Disting. Service award, 1980; USCG Meritorious Service award, 1977; cert. of merit State of La., 1980; Grace A. Goldsmith Disting. Alumnus lectr. Tulane U. Med. Alumni Assn., 1974 Fellow ACS; mem. USPHS Clin. Soc., Nat. Tb Assn., James D. Rives Surg. Soc., Commd. Officers Assn., Mil. Order World Wars, La. Heart Assn., La. Tb and Respiratory Disease Assn. (dir. 1964—), La. Thoracic Soc., La. Pub. Health Assn., Assn. Mil. Surgeons of U.S., Phi Beta Kappa, Alpha Omega Alpha, Delta Omega. Home: 12674 S Highmeadow Ct Baton Rouge LA 70816-2528 Office: 4550 North Blvd Ste 100 Baton Rouge LA 70806-4013 Office Phone: 225-926-3343. Office Fax: 225-926-3346. Personal E-mail: quack_70817@yahoo.com.

CHERRYH, C. J., writer; b. St. Louis, Sept. 1, 1942; d. Basil L. and Lois Ruth (Van Deventer) C. BA in Latin, U. Okla., 1964; MA in Classics, Johns Hopkins U., 1965. Cert. tchr., Okla. Tchr. Oklahoma City Pub. Schs., 1965-77. Lectr. in field Author: (novels) Gate of Ivrel, 1976, Well of Shiuan, 1978, Brothers of Earth, 1976, Hunter of Worlds, 1976, The Faded Sun: Kesrith, 1977, The Faded Sun: Shon'Jir, 1978, Fires of Azeroth, 1979, The Faded Sun: Kutath, 1979, Hestia, 1979, Sunfall, 1981, Downbelow Station, 1981 (Hugo award for best novel 1982), Wave Without a Shore, 1981, The Pride of Chanur, 1982, Merchanter's Luck, 1982, Port Eternity, 1982, Forty Thousand in Gehenna, 1983, The Dreamstone, 1983, The Tree of Swords and Jewels, 1983, Chanur's Venture, 1984, Cuckoo's Egg, 1985, Visible Light, 1985, The Kif Strike Back, 1985, Angel with the Sword, 1985, Chanur's Homecoming, 1986, Exile's Gate, 1988, Cyteen, 1988 (Hugo award 1988, 89), Smuggler's Gold, 1988, Rimrunners, 1989, Rusalka, 1989, Chernevog, 1990, Yvgenie, 1991, Heavy Time, 1991, Rumrunners, 1991, Hellburner, 1992, Chanur's Legacy, 1992, Goblin Mirror, 1993, Faery in Shadow, 1993, Tripoint, 1994, Foreigner, 1994, Rider at the Gate, 1995, Invader, 1995, Fortress in the Eye of Time, 1995, Inheritor, 1996, Cloud's Rider, 1996, Lois & Clark, 1996, Finity's End, 1997, Fortress of Eagles, 1998, Precursor, 1999, Hammerfall, 2001, Forge of Heaven, 2004, Collected Short Fiction of C.J. Cherryh, 2004, Destroyer, 2005; editor: Flood Tide, 1990; translator: Stellar Crusade by Pierre Barbet, 1980, The Green Gods by Nathalie & Charles Henneberg, 1980, The Book of Shai by Daniel Walther, 1982; contbr. short stories to numerous mags. Woodrow Wilson fellow, 1965; recipient John W. Campbell award for best new writer, 1977, Hugo award for short story, 1979, for novel, 1982, 89, Locus award for best sci. fiction novel, 1988. Mem. Sci. Fiction Writers Assn., Alpha Lambda Delta, Phi beta Kappa. Avocations: galactic mapping, guitar and music composition, travel. Office: c/o Matt Bialer Sanford J Greenburger Assoc 55 Fifth Ave New York NY 10003*

CHERTOFF, MICHAEL, secretary of homeland security, former federal judge; b. Elizabeth, NJ, Nov. 28, 1953; m. Meryl Justin; 2 children. AB magna cum laude, Harvard U., 1975, JD magna cum laude, 1978. Bar: D.C. 1980, N.Y. 1987, N.J. 1990. Editor Harvard Law Review, 1978; summer assoc. Miller, Cassidy, Larroca & Lewin, 1978; law clk. to Hon. Murray I. Gurfein U.S. Ct. Appeals (2nd cir.), N.Y.C., 1978-79; law clk. to Justice William J. Brennan Jr. U.S. Supreme Ct., Washington, 1979-80; assoc. Latham & Watkins LLP, Washington, 1980-83, ptnr., 1994—2001; asst. U.S. atty. (So. dist.) NY US Dept. Justice, N.Y.C., 1983-87, 1st asst. U.S. atty. dist. NJ Newark, 1987-90, U.S. atty. dist. NJ, 1990—94, asst. atty. gen. criminal div. Washington, 2001—03; spl. counsel for Whitewater com. U.S. Senate, Washington, 1994—96; fed. judge U.S. Ct. Appeals, (3rd cir.), Newark, 2003—05; sec. US Dept. Homeland Security, Washington, 2005—. Mem. lawyer's adv. com. U.S. Dist. Ct. N.J., Newark, 1990-94, U.S. Atty. Gen.'s Adv. com. of U.S. Atty.'s, Washington, 1991-94. Recipient John Marshall award U.S. Dept. Justice, Washington, 1987. Office: US Dept Homeland Security 3801 Nebraska Ave NW Washington DC 20528

CHERUNDOLO, JOHN CHARLES, lawyer; b. Pitts., Nov. 24, 1948; s. Charles James and Margaret E. (Whitehead) C.; m. Elizabeth Flack, July 26, 1980; children: Allison Belle, Leane Elizabeth, James Charles. BA in Polit. Sci., Syracuse U., 1970, M Pub Adminstrn., 1972, JD, 1973. Bar: Ill. 1974, N.Y. 1974, U.S. Dist. Ct. (ea. dist.) Ill. 1974. Asst. gen. atty. Roper Corp., Kankakee, Ill., 1974-75; assoc. Hancock Law Firm, Syracuse, NY, 1975-80, Banbaum & Manaker, Syracuse, 1980-83; sr. ptnr. Cherundolo, Bottar & Leone, P.C., Syracuse, 1983—. Named All-Am. UPI, AP, Syracuse, 1970, Acad. All-Am., U.S. Coaches, Syracuse, 1970. Mem. Am. Coll. Trial Lawyers Assn. Trial Lawyers Am. (former state del., pres.'s coun.), Internat. Acad. Trial Lawyers, N.Y. State Trial Lawyers (past pres., bd. dirs.), Upstate Trial Lawyers Assn. (past pres.), Trial Lawyers for Pub. Justice (past state coord.), Onondaga County Bar Assn., Syracuse U. Varsity Club (bd. dirs. 1976—), Order of Coif. Roman Catholic. Avocation: sports. Home: 4443 Dolomite Dr Syracuse NY 13215-1500 Office: Cherundolo Bottar & Leone PC 407 S Warren St Syracuse NY 13202 Office Phone: 315-422-3466. E-mail: lumpyc@aol.com.

CHERY, LUDZEN A., mathematics educator; b. Hinche, Haiti, Nov. 4, 1947; arrived in US, 1986; s. Elius Chery and Adeleine Andou; m. Marie R. Paul, Dec. 8, 2004; children: Lissa G., Barbara, Amos, Rodney, Jessica. B of Laws, State U. Haiti, 1978; BA in Math., Jersey City U., 1993; MS, LI U., Bklyn., 1996; PhD, Lacrosse U., Miss., 1998. Cert. math. tchr. NJ, 1995, bilingual edn. NJ, 1995. Prof. history and Haitian lit. C.C. Maissoide, Haiti, 1978—86; tchr. math. Cicely Tyson H.S., East Orange, NJ, 1995—; adj. prof. Rutgers U., Newark, 2001—03. Mem.: Nat. Coun. of Teachers of Math. Office: Cicely Tyson School 161 Elmwood Avenue East Orange NJ 07017 Office Phone: 973-266-5970. Home Fax: 908-859-6651. Personal E-mail: ludzen2003@hotmail.com. E-mail: l.chery@eastorange.k12.nj.us.

CHERY, REGINALD, minister; b. Bklyn., July 12, 1968; s. Pierre Charlot and Viviane Chery; m. Bernadette L. Armstrong, Sept. 16, 2001. BBA in Computer Info. Sys., Baruch Coll., 1993; MDiv, Andrews U., 1997. Ordained elder, lic. min. Seventh-day Adventist Ch. Sales person Superior Computer Svcs., NYC, 1988; sys. analyst Rsch. Found. Mental Hygiene, NYC, 1992—93; bible worker assoc. evangelist Grand Concourse Seventh Day Adventist Ch., Bronx, NY, 1998; min. Gen. Conf. Seventh Day Adventist Chs., Silver Springs, Md., 1999—. Computer cons. Northeastern Conf. Seventh Day Adventists, Queens, NY, 1997; sch. chaplain Oakview Prep. Sch., Yonkers, NY, 1999—2002. Author: (manual) Straight Talk Youth Ministry. Recipient Police Athletic Leagues award, 1984. Mem.: Black Ministers Assn. Greater NY (assoc.). Seventh-Day Adventist. Achievements include design of Hotel Software. Avocations: basketball, reading, football, travel, weightlifting. Office: Gen Conf Seventh-day Adventists 12501 Old Columbia Pike Silver Spring MD 20904 Personal E-mail: ministerchery@aol.com.

CHESEBRO, JAMES WILLIAM, communications educator; b. Mpls., June 24, 1944; s. Floyd Jerome and Jeanette Mary (Campbell) C. BA, U. Minn., 1966, PhD, 1972; MS, Ill. State U., 1967. Instr. Concordia Coll., Moorhead, Minn., 1967-69; tchg. assoc. U. Minn., Mpls., 1969-72; assoc. prof. Temple U., Phila., 1972-81; prof. Queens Coll. CUNY, Flushing, 1981-89; dir. ednl. svcs. Nat. Comm. Assn., Annandale, Va., 1989-92; prof. Ind. State U., Terre Haute, 1992—2002, 2004—05; disting. prof. telecomm. Ball State U., Muncie, Ind., 2005—. Vis. prof. U. P.R., PR, 1980; adj. prof. George Mason U., Fairfax, Va., 1989—92; vis. prof. Ctr. for Media Design, Ball State U., 2002—04. Author: Analyzing Media, 1996; Computer-Mediated Communication, 1989; contbr. over 100 articles to profl. jours. Recipient Disting. Svc. award Nat. Kenneth Burke Soc., 1993. Mem. Nat. Commn. Assn. (pres. 1995-96, Golden Ann. Monograph award 1985, Disting. Svc. award 1997), Ea. Comm. Assn. (pres. 1982-83, Disting. Svc. award 1989, Hunt Scholarship award 1989, 97). Avocations: antiques, geneology. Office: Ball State Univ Dept Telecomm Muncie IN 47306 Office Phone: 765-285-1491. E-mail: jchesebro@ma.rr.com.

CHESER, RAYMOND NORRIS, III, healthcare company executive; b. Louisville, Oct. 17, 1947; s. Raymond N. II and Martha June C.; m. Elena Tymoshkina; 1 child, Stephanie Cheser. BS, Tex. A&M U., 1970, MS, 1976; MBA, U. Conn., 1983; DBA, Nova Southeastern U., 1996. Rsch. chemist The Dow Chem. Co., Freeport, Tex., 1970-76; engring., mfg. mgr. Johnson and Johnson, Skillman, N.J., 1977-80, Southington, Conn., 1980-92, dir. quality assurance, 1995-96; engring. mgr. C.R. Bard, Billerica, Mass., 1992-95; dir. continous improvement U.S. Surg. Corp., North Haven, Conn., 1997—2000; dir. quality United Health Group, Uniprise, Hartford, Conn., 2001—. Adj. faculty Boston U., 1994-95; adj. assoc. prof. Albertus Magnus Coll., New Haven, 1996—, U. New Haven, 2000—; spkr. in field. Contbr. articles to profl. jours. Bd. dir. New Britain Symphony, 1989-90. Recipient Shingo prize for mfg. rsch., 1999. Mem. Acad. Mgmt., Assn. Mfg. Excellence (Six Sigma Black Belt), Internat. Assn. Facilitators. Avocations: music composition, clay sculpture, art collector. E-mail: raymond.chester@snet.net.

CHESHIER, STEPHEN ROBERT, retired academic administrator, electrical engineer; b. Logan, Ohio, Feb. 21, 1940; s. George Robert Cheshier and Pauline Frazier (Magle) Mason; m. Katherine Joyce Hadley, June 5, 1960; children— David Mark, John Michael. BS in Physics, Memphis State U., 1970; MS in Elec. Engring., Purdue U., 1972; PhD in Engring. Edn., U. Ill., 1975. Cert. engring. technologist. Prof., head dept. elec. engring. tech. Purdue U., Lafayette, Ind., 1972-80; pres. So. Poly. State U., Marietta, Ga., 1980-97, pres. emeritus, 1997—. Cons. Sandia Labs., Albuquerque, 1976— Contbr. articles to profl. jours. Bd. dirs. Community Symposium Marietta, 1982-97, Cobb Edn. Consortium, 1997—; chmn. U. Ctr. in Ga.; founder Consortium for Polytech. Edn. Recipient James McGraw award McGraw-Hill Pubs., 1984; James G. Dwyer award Purdue U., 1975 Fellow IEEE (sr.), Accreditation Bd. for Engring. and Tech., Am. Soc. Engring. Edn. (chmn. 1981, 92, officer 1985-96), Ga. Soc. Profl. Engrs. (assoc.), Order of the Engr.; mem. Eta Kappa Nu, Tau Alpha Pi, Sigma Pi Sigma, Mensa, Kiwanis (bd. dirs. 1984-88). Mem. Ch. of Christ (elder). Avocations: travel, collecting, music, church work. Office: So Poly State U Pres Office 1100 S Marietta Pky Marietta GA 30060-2855

CHESLER, DORIS ADELLE, real estate professional; b. Lincoln, Ill., Sept. 23, 1924; d. Harry and Esther Pearl (Campbell) Schoth; m. Eugene Albert Aughenbaugh, May 23, 1943 (div. Sept. 1970); children: Judith C., Rodney E., Paula Sue; m. Arthur Bernard Chesler, Oct. 16, 1972 (dec. Oct. 1998). Lic. real estate broker Fla. Realtor, assoc. Kilgore Real Estate, Brandon, Fla., 1969—76; broker Doris A. Chesler, Brandon, 1976—. Den mother Cub Scouts Am., Tampa, 1961-62; leader 4-H Club, Decatur, Ill., 1956. Republican. Presbyterian. Avocations: interior decorating, sewing, gardening, music, painting. Office Phone: 813-681-4663.

CHESLER, EVAN ROBERT, lawyer; b. N.Y.C., July 17, 1949; s. Philip and Doris (Sims) C.; m. Diane Lynn Ackerman, May 30, 1970 (div. 1983); children: David Andrew, Matthew Lawrence, Rebecca Faye; m. Barbara Jean Gloven, Sept. 10, 1983. BA, NYU, 1970, JD, 1975; MA, Hunter Coll., 1973. Bar: N.Y. 1976, U.S. Dist. Ct. (so. dist.) N.Y. 1976, U.S. Supreme Ct. 1982, U.S. Ct. Appeals (2d cir.) 1982, U.S. Dist. Ct. (no. dist.) Calif. 1982. Tchr. N.Y.C. Bd. Edn., 1970-72; law clk. U.S. Dist. Ct. (so. dist.) N.Y., N.Y.C., 1975-76; assoc. Cravath, Swaine & Moore, N.Y.C., 1976-82, ptnr., 1982—, head of litig. Pres., Inst. Judicial Adminstrn., N.Y.U. Sch. Law. Mem. bd. overseers Faculty Arts & Scis, N.Y.U.; trustee NYS League Women Voteres Edn. Found.; mem. exec. com. Ctr. Pub. Resources. Author: The Russian Jewry Reader, 1973. Topics editor NYU Law Rev., 1974-75. Contbr. articles to legal jours. and chpts. to books. N.Y. Regents scholar, 1966-70, 72-75; Ctr. for Internat. Studies jr. fellow, 1974-75. Fellow Am. Coll. Trial Lawyers; mem. Assn. of Bar of City of N.Y., N.Y. State Bar Assn., ABA, Order of Coif. Democrat. Jewish. Office: Cravath Swaine & Moore Worldwide Plz Fl 38 825 8th Ave New York NY 10019-7475

CHESLER, GAIL, arts organization development executive; b. Phila., May 22; d. Leon William and Sylvia (Spiegel) C.; m. Richard Allen Lippe (div. May 1989); children; Wendy Ann, David Allen. BA in History, Beaver Coll.; MA in Performing Arts Adminstrn., NYU, 1988. Outreach coord. North Shore Cmty. Arts Ctr., Gt. Neck, N.Y., 1976-79; pub. rels. cons. Gt. Neck, 1979-85; dir. of devel. and mktg. ART/New York, N.Y.C., 1987-88; exec. dir. Jennifer Muller/The Works, N.Y.C., 1989; dir. of devel. Temple Beth-El, Gt. Neck, 1989-92; nat. dir. planned giving and endowments Women's Am. ORT, N.Y.C., 1993-96; planned giving officer N.Y. Presbyn. Hosp./Weill Med. Coll. of Cornell U., N.Y.C., 1996-2000; dir. planned and spl. gifts The Met. Opera, N.Y.C., 2000—. Co-founder, bd. dirs. Teen to Teen, Carle Place, N.Y., 1985-88. Mem. Planned Giving Group of Greater N.Y. (past pres. 1999—, pres. 1998-99, v.p. 1997-98, treas. 1996-97). Avocations: opera, travel, theater. Home: 128 Central Park S # 3B New York NY 10019-1565 Office: The Metropolitan Opera Lincoln Ctr New York NY 10023

CHESLEY, ANN MARIE, project administrator; b. Fitchburg, Mass., Nov. 9, 1972; d. Paul Weston and Florence Araxie Chesley. A of Applied Bus., Raymond Walters Coll., 1997; BA, Xavier U., 1998. From sales specialist to purchasing specialist Cin. Sub-Zero, 1991—99; health care regulatory affairs specialist Procter & Gamble Co., Cin., 1999—2000, project controls specialist, 2000—01; project planning specialist Belcan Engring. Group, Cin., 2001—03; ERP project adminstr., schedule and controls analyst Clopay Bldg. Products, Cin., 2003—05; project adminstr. Internat. Paper, Loveland, Ohio, 2005—. Vol. profl. devel. com. Project Mgmt. Inst., Cin., 2002—03; vol. perinatal cuddler Good Samaritan Hosp., Cin., 2000—03. Mem.: Project Mgmt. Inst. (cert.). Office: Internat Paper 6275 Tri-Ridge Blvd Loveland OH 45140 Office Phone: 513-965-3016. Business E-Mail: ann.chesley@ipaper.com. E-mail: achesley@xu.alumlink.com.

CHESLEY, STANLEY MORRIS, lawyer; b. Cin., Mar. 26, 1936; s. Frank and Rachel (Kinsburg) C.; children: Richard A., Lauren B. BA, U. Cin., 1958, LLB, 1960. Bar: Ohio 1960, Ky. 1978, W.Va. 1981, Tex. 1981, Nev. 1981. Ptnr. Waite, Schneider, Bayless & Chesley Co., Cin., 1960—. Contbr. articles to profl. jours. Past chmn. bd. commrs. on grievances and discipline Supreme Ct. Ohio; past pres. Jewish Fedn. Cin.; nat. vice chair, bd. govs., United Jewish Coms.; exec. bd., nat. bd. govs. Am. Jewish Com.; nat. bd. govs. Hebrew Uninon Coll.; exec. com. U.S. Holocaust Meml. Mus. Mem. bd. of dirs. Am. Jewish Joint Distbn ABA, ATLA, FBA, Am. Judicature Soc., Melvin M. Belli Soc., Ohio Bar Assn., Ky. Bar Assn., W.Va. Bar Assn., Tex. Bar Assn., Nev. Bar Assn., Cin. Bar Assn. Office: Waite Schneider Bayless & Chesley 1513 4th and Vine Tower Cincinnati OH 45202 Office Phone: 513-521-0267. Personal E-mail: wsbclaw@aol.com.

CHESNE, EDWARD LEONARD, physician; b. Chgo., June 11, 1931; m. Carol Chesne; children: Lauren, Christopher, Greig. BA, U. Chgo., 1950; MD, Northwestern U. Med. Sch., Chgo., 1955. Lic. phys., Ill., Calif., Hawaii, Guam, Saipan. Capt. U.S. Army, 1957. Fellow Am. Coll. Physicians, Am. Coll. Cardiology, Coun. Clin. Cardiology, Am. Heart Assn. Office: 1380 Lusitana St Ste 1002 Honolulu HI 96813-2461

CHESNEY, KENNY, country singer, songwriter; b. Knoxville, Tenn., Mar. 26, 1968; m. Renee Zellweger, May 9, 2005. Degree in advt., E. Tenn. State U., 1991. Performer Chuckie's Trading Post and Quarterback's Barbecue, Johnson City, Tenn.; resident performer The Turf, Nashville; publ. deal with Acuff-Rose, 1992; record contract with Capricorn, Tenn., 1993; with RCA, Subsidiary BNA, Tenn. Translator: (albums) In My Wildest Dreams, 1993; singer All I Need To Know, 1995, Me & You, 1996, I Will Stand, 1997, Everywhere We Go, 1999, Greatest Hits, 2000, No Shirt, No Shoes, No Problem, 2002, All I Want For Christmas is a Real Good Tan, 2003, When the Sun Goes Down, 2004 (Album of Yr. Country Music. Assn., 2004), (singles) Whatever It Takes, 1993, Tin Man, 1994, Somebody's Callin', 1994, Fall In Love, 1995, All I Need To Know, 1995, Granpa Told Me, 1995, Back In My Arms Again, 1996, Me & You, 1998, She's Got It All, 1997, That's Why I'm Here (#1), 1998, That's Why I'm Here (#2), 1998, I Will Stand, 1998, How Forever Feels, 1999, Team of Destiny, 1999, You Had Me From Hello, 1999, I Lost It, 2000, Don't Happen Twice, 2000, Young, 2002; singer: (guest appearance with Willie Nelson and Leon Russell) "Last Thing I Needed First Thing This Morning", Willie Nelson and Friends, Live and Kickin', 2003. Named Top New Male Vocalist, Acad. Country Music Awards, 1997, Top Male Vocalist, 2002, Entertainer of Yr., 2005, Country Music Assn., 2004; recipient Single Yr. for "The Good Stuff", Acad. Country Music Awards, 2003, Male Video of Yr. for song "I Go Back", Country Music Television Music award, 2005. Office: BNA Records Label c/o Cheryl Bevis PO Box 128558 Nashville TN 37212

CHESNEY, LEE ROY, JR., artist; b. Washington, June 1, 1920; s. Lee Roy and Rena Ruth (Beach) C.; m. Betty J. Lamb, Jan. 28, 1943; children: Lee Roy III, Terril Ann Bauer. B.F.A., U. Colo., 1946; M.F.A., U. Iowa, 1948; postgrad., U. Michoacan, Mex., 1950-51. Instr. drawing U. Iowa, 1947-50; prof. art, dir. printmaking, head grad. printmaking and painting U. Ill., Urbana, 1950-67; assoc. dean fine arts U. So. Calif., Los Angeles, 1967-72; prof. art, chmn. grad. art programs U. Hawaii, Honolulu, 1972-84, prof. emeritus, 1984—; Louis D. Beaumont vis. disting. prof. Washington U. Vis. artist Otis Art Inst., L.A., U. Colo., U. Wash., Mich. State U., Honolulu Acad. Arts Sch., Visual Arts Center, Anchorage, Portland (Oreg.,) State U., 1988, U. Fla., 1989, Lacoste Sch. Arts, France, 1989, UCLA, 1989-90; mem. com., nat. juror Sr. Fulbright Research Awards, 1968-71, com. chmn., 1969-71; mem. visual arts selection com., Calif. Arts Coun., 1990; juror Hawaii Print Exhbn., 1991, 10th Internat. Pacific Rim Exhbn. Hilo, Hawaii; mem. Pacific Rim Lectrs. and Workshops, 1992; artist-in-residence U. Tex., 1993, Pacific Rim Series, 1994. Symposium Amon Carter Mus., Ft. Worth, 1990, Archer M. Huntington Art Gallery, 1993; one-man shows include Newman Brown Gallery, Chgo., U. Fla., U. Louisville, U. Mich., U. Wis., Madison, Ohio State U., Ill. State U., Yoseido Gallery, Tokyo, Atrium Gallery, Seattle, Visual Arts Center, Anchorage, Washington U., St. Louis, U. Utah, U. Alaska, Am. Cultural Ctr., Paris, 1964, Fisher Galleries, U. So. Calif., 1968, State Fedn. Culture and Art, 1967—87, Honolulu Acad. Arts, 1973, Comsky Gallery, Beverly Hills, Calif., 1970—76, Downtown Gallery, Honolulu, 1975, BIMC Galerie, Paris, 1979, 1981, 1983, Galerie Sandoz, 1979, Cité Internat. des Arts, 1979, Honolulu Acad. of Arts, Focus Gallery, 1985, Contemporary Arts Center, Honolulu, 1980, 25-yr. retrospective exhbn. of prints circulated by U. Fla., 1977—80, retrospective exhbn. Portland State U., 1988, U. Fla., 1989, Printmaking 1985, Tallahassee, So. Graphics Coun. Emeritus Printmaker Exhbn. Knoxville Mus. Art, 1992, Williams Lamb Gallery, Long Beach, Calif., 1990, 1992, West Tex. A&M U., 1993, Oracle (Ariz.) Art Ctr., 1995, State Founds. and Arts, Hawaii, 1997, Parsons Sch. Design, Paris, 1998, solo exhbn. of paintings, Davis Dominguez Gall., Tucson, Ariz., 1999—2000, Hawaii State Mus. Art Inaugural Exhbn., 2003, exhibited in group shows at Am. Fedn. Arts traveling exhbn., Mus. Modern Art traveling exhbn., USIS traveling exhbn., Soc. Am. Graphic artists traveling exhbns., 1973—77, Nihon Sosaku Hanga Kyokai, 1957—84, Contemporary Am. Painting, Bucharest, 1977, Hawaii Nat. Biennial Print Exhbn., Honolulu Acad. Arts, 1971, 1973, 1975, 1977, 1978, 1980, 1983, BIMC Galerie, 1978, 1979, 1980, 1981, 1982, 1983, 70th Nat. Invitational Drawing Exhbn., Emporia, Kans., 1986, U. West Fla., 1986, Neville-Sargent Gallery, 1986, Northwest Printmakers, 1986, U. Calif., Davis, 1985, Calif. Artists exhbn. at Thomas Ctr. Gallery, Gainesville, Fla., 1987, 25th Anniversary Exhbn. State Found. for Culture and the Arts (reproduction), Honolulu, 1988, 50th Anniversary Exhbn. of Commd. Prints, Honolulu Printmakers, Honolulu Acad. of Arts, 1988, N.W. Print Coun. Exhbn., Australia, 1988, Overreact Gallery, Long Beach, 1989, U. Hawaii, Hilo, 1989, Williams Lamb Gallery, 1990, 1991, 1992, Worcester (Mass.) Art Mus., 1991, Amon Carter Mus., 1990, Ft. Worth, 1990, Artists Who Teach Exhbn., Champaign, Ill., 1990, Nelson Atkins Mus., Kansas City, 1990, Mona Bismark Found., Paris, 1991, Soc. Am. Graphic Artists (prize) Nat. Exhbn., N.Y.C., Internat. Exhbn. Artists of Lacoste, France, Paris, 1991, San Diego Art Inst. Invitational, 1991, Williams Lamb Gallery, Long Beach, Calif., 1991, 1992, 12th U. Dallas Nat. Print Exhbn., 1991, 1992, Nat. Exhbn. Copper Engraving, Portand, Oreg., 1992, Pacific States Biennial Exhbn., Hilo, 1992—94, Northwest Print Coun., Eugene, Oreg., 1993, Indpls. Mus. Art, 1993, Pacific Rim Internat., 1993, 1997 (award), Works on Paper, L.A., 1995, 1996, 1997, 1998, Southern Graphics Exhib. of Disting. Print Makers, Tampa, Fla., 1997, L.A. Print Soc. Exhbn., 1997, Portland Art Mus. Intern. Pr. Exhib., 1997, Davis Dominguez Gallery, Tucson, 1997, "Exclusively Etchings" Lankersheim Arts, Pacific Rim Internat. Monoprint Exhibition, Hilo, Hawaii, 1998, State Fedn. 30 yr. anniv. exhbn., Hofstra Univ. Mus. N.Y. Exhbn. "Abstract Expressionism: Then and Now", 2001, Tradition of Excellence, U. Hawaii Art Gallery, 2002, Hawaii State Art Mus. Grand Opening, Honolulu, 2002—03, 2005, Davis Domingus Gallery, Tucson, 2005, Cleve. Mus. Art, 2003, Represented in permanent collections Nat. Gallery Art, Washington, Biblioteque Nationale, Paris, Victoria and Albert Mus., London, Tokyo U. Fine Art, Tokyo Mus. Modern Art, Nat. Gallery Art, Stockholm, Tate Gallery, London, USIS, State Dept., Washington, Library of Congress, Bklyn. Mus., Mus. Modern Art, N.Y.C., Phila. Mus., Denver Mus., Dallas Mus., Pasadena Mus., Honolulu Acad. Arts, Hawaii Council for Arts, Art Inst. Chgo., Oakland Mus., L.A. County Mus., Seattle Mus., Worcester Art Mus., Am. Embassy, Bonn, Bank of Am., United Calif. Bank, U. Hawaii, IBM, Litton Industries Corp., Hartford Ins. Co., Fuji Bank Calif., Northrop Corp., 1st Hawaii Trust Bank, Mus. Contemporary Art, Honolulu, Portland (Oreg.) Mus. Art, 1993, Univ. Hawaii, Hilo, 1992, Indpls. Mus. Art, 1991-92, Elvehjem Mus. Art, Wis., West Tex. A&M U., 1993, Wycross Press, Auburn, Ala., 1994; contbr. Mem. Commn. for Founders' Portfolio for N.W. Printmakers, Portland, 1977. Served to capt. AUS, 1942-45. Recipient Francis G. Logan medal Art Inst. Chgo., 1962, Pauline Palmer award, 1966; Concora Found. prize, 1963; Vera List award Soc. Am. Graphic Artists, Am. Acad., Rome, 1964; appointee Cité Internat. des Arts, Paris, 1970, 78-83; Fondation Gardilanne-Moffat Studio award, 1978-80; purchase award Epinal (France) Biennial Invitational Exhbn., Pacific Rim Internat., 1993, 97; awards Hawaii State Found. for Culture and Arts, 1972, 74, 75, 78, 80; awards Honolulu Acad. Arts, 1973, 78; award San Diego Art Inst., 1991, Fulbright sr. rsch. award, 1956-57; U. Ill. rsch. grantee, 1963-64; Ford Found. faculty enrichment award, 1978, 82, Printmaker Emeritus award So. Graphics Coun., 1992. Mem. Coll. Art Assn. Am., Calif. Soc. Printmakers, N.W. Print Coun. (bd. dirs.), Japan Print Assn., Soc. Am. Graphic Artists, Color Print Soc., World Print Coun., L.A. Printmaking Soc. (hon. dir.), Honolulu Printmakers (past v.p., pres.), Painters and Sculptors League Hawaii, Hawaii Artists League, So. Graphics Coun., Fulbright Assn. Address: 14601 Whitfield Ave Pacific Palisades CA 90272-2645

CHESNEY, RUSSELL WALLACE, pediatrician; b. Knoxville, Tenn., Aug. 25, 1941; s. Jack and Helen Wallace (McColl) C.; m. Patricia Joan Cook, June 8, 1968; children: Karen, Christopher, Gillian. AB, Harvard U., 1963; MD, U. Rochester, 1968. Diplomate Am. Bd. Pediatrics. Intern then resident Johns Hopkins U. Hosp., Balt., 1968-70, 72-73; renal fellow NIH, Balt., 1970-72, Montreal Childrens Hosp., Montreal, Que., Can., 1973-75; asst. then prof. U. Wis., Madison, 1975-85; prof., vice chmn. U. Calif., Davis, 1985-88; prof., chmn. pediatrics U. Tenn., Memphis, 1988—. Mem. Rsch. Study Sect. NIH, Washington, 1983—88, mem. Nat. Kidney and Urology Diseases Adv. Bd., 1988—91; sec.-treas., pediat. dept. chmn. Am. Med. Schs., 1993—99, pres., 2001—03; mem. coun. Am. Pediat. Soc., 1995—2004, v.p., 2001—02, pres., 2002—03; chmn. Fed. Pediat. Orgn., 1995—96; Birdsong lectr. U. Va., 1995; vice chair Task Force on Pediat. Edn., 1996—99; chair Am. Bd. Pediats., 2000—02; bd. trustees Assn. Children's Hosps., 2002—. Contbr. articles to profl. jours., chpts. to text and med. books. Lt. comdr. USPHS, 1970-72, Balt. Recipient Founders award in Pediatric Rsch., So. Soc. Pediatric Rsch., 1993; Jour. Pediatrics lectr. U. Rochester, 1985, Paul Gaffney lectr. U. Pitts., 1988. Mem. Am. Pediat. Soc. (mem. coun. 1995-, v.p. 2001-02, pres. 2002-03), Am. Acad. Pediats. (pres. Tenn. state chpt. 1995-98, E. Meade Johnson award 1985, Nutrition award 1996, St. Geme award 2001, Henry Barnett award 2004, Founders award 2005), Soc. for Pediat. Rsch. (pres. 1986-87), Midwest Soc. for Pediat. Rsch. (pres. 1984-85), Am. Soc. for Pediat. Nephrology (pres. 1986-87), VA Merit Rev. Bd. (chmn. 1988-90). Office: U Tenn Dept Pediats 50 S Dunlap St Memphis TN 38103-4909 Office Phone: 901-572-3106.

CHESNOKOV, IGOR, biochemist, educator; arrived in U.S., 1992; m. Olga N. Shaburova, Oct. 18, 1986; children: Olga I. Chesnokova, Elena Chesnokova. MS, St. Petersburg (Russia) U., 1986, PhD in Biochemistry, 1990. Rsch. asst. prof. U. Calif., Berkeley, Calif., 1997—2001; asst. prof. U. Ala., Birmingham, Ala., 2002—. Contbr. articles to profl. jours. Grantee, NIH, 2005. Mem.: Genetics Soc., Biochemistry and Molecular Biology Soc. Achievements include research in DNA replication in eukaryotes. Office: University Of Alabama 720 20th Street South Birmingham AL 35294 Office Phone: 205-934-6975. E-mail: igor23@yahoo.com.

CHESNUT, DONALD BLAIR, retired chemistry professor; b. Richmond, Ind., Dec. 27, 1932; s. James Lyons and Naomi Irene (Wright) C.; m. Deborah Berry, Dec. 21, 1954; children— Lauren, Blair, Lynn. BS, Duke U., 1954; PhD, Calif. Inst. Tech., 1958. Postdoctoral fellow, instr. physics Duke U., Durham, N.C., 1957-58, assoc. prof. chemistry, 1965-71, prof. chemistry, 1971-98; prof. emeritus, 1999—; research chemist E.I. duPont de Nemours, Inc., Wilmington, Del., 1958-65. Mem. Am. Chem. Soc., Am. Phys. Soc., Sigma Xi. Home: 4404 Malvern Rd Durham NC 27707-5646 Office: Duke U Dept Chemistry Durham NC 27708 E-mail: donald.chesnut@duke.edu.

CHESNUT, NONDIS LORINE (ANGEL LOVE), education educator, writer; b. South Daytona, Fla., June 29, 1941; d. Anthony Valentine and Myrtle Marie (Allen) Campbell; m. Raymond Otho Chesnut, Aug. 25, 1962; 1 child, Starlina Mintina Chesnut Kladler. BS in English and Speech, Concord Coll., 1962; postgrad., Frostburg U., 1967; MEd, Shippensburg U., 1972; postgrad., W.Va. U., 1973; Advanced Grad. Specialist Degree, U. Md., 1974; postgrad., Md. State Dept. Edn., 1976-95, Inst. Children's Lit., 1995-97, Screenwriters Unlimited, 1997; writing coursework, Charter Oak State Coll., 2000. Cert. adminstr., secondary prin., elem. prin., reading splist., tchr. English and speech, drama. Tchr. English and speech Harpers Ferry (W.Va.) H.S., 1962-64; with Sears Roebuck, summer 1965; libr. Great Mills (Md.) H.S., 1968-69; tchr. English and reading North Hagerstown H.S., Hagerstown, Md., 1964-73; tchr. South Hagerstown H.S., Hagerstown, 1974-77; reading resource tchr. Woodland Way Elem. Sch., Hagerstown, 1977-83; adj. instr. grad. sch. Hood Coll., Frederick, Md., 1982-83; reading specialist Fountain Rock Elem. Sch., Hagerstown, 1983-85; tchr. Williamsport (Md.) H.S., 1985-95. Reading and lang. arts cons., Md., 1973-95, Fla., 1996-2000; adj. reading instr. Daytona Comm. Coll., 1996-97, Galaxy Middle Sch., 1997-98, drama, lang. arts, reading tchr., 1997-98, key source, 1999; instr. English and writing Bethune-Cookman Coll., fall 2000, adj. instr. reading, writing and English, learning specialist Daytona Beach C.C., 2001—, Learning Ctr. specialist, 2004-; spkr., presenter local, nat. and internat. workshops, 1973-2005; speech and debate coach. Writer for radio programs and advertisements for reading, 1986—, TV programs, 1974-78, 90-91; appeared on TV programs, 1974-78; co-editor column Beckley Post Herald, 1957-59; contbr. articles to newspapers and mags., 1964—; appeared in film Guarding Tess, 1993; screenwriter Heaven on Planet Earth, 2000; author (nonfiction) A Touch of Love From God, 2003, A Touch of Love From Heaven, 2005. Mem. debating team Concord Coll., 1961-62, mem. newspaper staff, 1959-61; mem. Washington County Network of Orgns., 1984-88; co-dir. Billy Bud, 1962; v.p. Women's Ind. Club, 1962, treas., 1961; sec.-treas. Fgn. lang. Club, 1961, Debate Club, 1961-62; treas. Meth. Youth Fellowship, 1961; pres. Tri-Hi-Y, 1959; legis. chairperson State of Md. Reading Coun., 1977-78; active Emmanuel Meth. Ch., White Sul, 1953-84, Life in Spirit Group, 1994-95, St. Ann's Roman Cath. Ch., 1994-95, Grace United Meth. Ch., 1984-95, Lady of Hope Cath. Ch., 1996—; mem. Fla. State Reading Coun., 1996-99. Recipient Pres.'s award State of Md. Reading Coun., 1981, Pres.'s award Washington County Reading Coun., 1981, Guidance Helping award, 1987, Voice of Democracy award VFW/Ladies Aux., 1992, Am. Heritage Writing award Williamsport Lions Club, 1995, numerous others; W.Va. Legislature scholar, 1959-62. Mem. AAUW (ednl. chairperson 1983-85, legis. v.p. 1986-87, cmty. chairperson 1987-89), NEA (publicity and scholarship coms., bldg. rep. 1989-95, del.), ASCD, VFW (chairperson Voice of Democracy 1989-95, VFW award 1989-95), Md. Dist. Am. Heritage Lions (Region II Lions award, Williamsport Am. Heritage Lions award 1995), State of Md. Internat. Reading Assn. Coun. (sec. 1975-79, v.p. elect 1979-80, v.p. 1980-81, pres. 1981-82, nominating chairperson 1982-83), Washington County Tchrs. Assn. (rep., scholarship chair, publicity), Internat. Reading Assn. (sec.-treas. sex differences in reading group 1976-77, 83-85, mem. gender differences in reading group 1985-86, mem. readability interest group, mastery learning interest group, del. convs., internat. rsch. com. 1976-77, 84-85, disabled learners interest group 1975-82), Washington County Reading Assn. (pres. 1981-82), Am. Legion (chairperson oratorial contest 1989-95, speech coach), Fla. Devel. Edn. Assn. (mem. com. registration 1996), Assn. Rsch. and Enlightenment. Democrat. Avocations: writing, swimming, dance, travel, psychology. Home: 107 Old Sunbeam Dr Daytona Beach FL 32119 E-mail: AngelLoveUs@aol.com.

CHESNUTT, JANE, publishing executive; b. Kenedy, Tex., Oct. 10, 1950; m. W. Mallory Rintoul. BJ, U. Tex., 1973. With Environment Information Ctr., NY, 1973; editorial asst. Am. Jour. Nursing, NYC, 1975-78; asst. editor Woman's Day mag., NYC, 1978—83, health editor, 1983—89, beauty, health, fashion editor, 1989-91, editor-in-chief, 1991—, sr. v.p., group editl. dir., 2002—. Sr. v.p. & group editl. dir. Transplant Am. Nat. Kidney Found. Mem. bus. adv. coun. Washington Irving H.S., N.Y.C. Named one of Editor of Yrl, Adweek, 1992, Top Players, Min Mag., 2000; recipient Editor of Yr., Adweek, 1992. Mem. Am. Soc. Mag. Editors, Women in Comms., Inc.

(Clarion award 1985, Headliner award 1996), YWCA Acad. of Achievers. Office: Woman's Day Mag Hachette Filipacchi Mags Inc 1633 Broadway New York NY 10019-6708 Office Phone: 212-767-6250. Office Fax: 212-767-5610.*

CHESNUTT, ROD MARTIN, music educator; s. Clarence and Natalie Brown Chesnutt; m. Jennifer Kathleene Wright, Oct. 22, 1970. BS in Music Edn., Tenn. Technol. U., 1981; MusM in Trombone Performance, Ark. State U., 1983; PhD in Music Edn., Fla. State U., 1995. Grad. tchg. asst. Ark. State U., Jonesboro, 1981—83; h.s. band dir. Trumann Pub. Schs., Trumann, 1983—87; dir. bands, supr. instrumental music Blytheville Pub. Schs.; tchg. asst. Fla. State U., Tallahassee, 1992—95; assoc. dir. bands U. Nebr., Lincoln, 1995—98; dir. bands State U. West Ga., Carrollton, 1998—99, Miss. State U., Starkville, 1999—2002; dir. symphonic, marching bands U. No. Iowa, Cedar Falls, 2002—. Condr, music dir. Starkville Symphony, 2001—03; adjudicator Parade of Bands, Moanalua, Hawaii, 2004—04, Ky. State Marching Championships, Bowling Green, 2000—03, SW Mo. Classic, Springfield, 2002—02, La. Showcase, Lafayette, 2000—00, Windfest, Syracuse, NY, 1997—2000; vis. prof. Charleston So. U. Grad. Symposium, SC, 1998—98, U. Mont. Grad. Music Edn. Program, Missoula, 1997—97; guest condr. Oahu All-District Band, Honolulu, 2004—04, SW Iowa All-District Band, Gilbertville, 2004—04, NE Iowa All-District Band, Oelwein, 2003—03, NE Miss. All-District Band, Fulton, 2001—01, Western Ky. Honor Band, Bowling Green, 2001—01, Mont. AA All-State Band, Kalispell, 2000—00; dir. U. No. Iowa Jr. Band Camp, Cedar Falls, 2003—; adjudicator Ill. State Concert Contest, Bloomington. Conductor (premiere) Bandancing; contbr. performance analyses; arranger (musical arrangement) American Quadrille, La Prima Donna, (musical arrangment) Trombone concerto; prodr.: (compact disc) Hear the Roar, Out of the Storm; conductor (premier) Danzante. Named Outstanding Young Men Am., 1988; recipient award of Merit, Nat. Music Clubs, 1991, Sudler trophy, Outstanding Collegiate Marching Band, John Phillip Sousa Found., 1996. Mem.: World Assn. Bands and Ensembles, Nat. Band Assn., Music Educators Nat. Conf., Iowa Music Educators Assn., Coll. Music Soc., Coll. Band Dirs. Nat. Assn. (state chair 2000—02), Iowa Alliance Arts, Phi Beta Mu, Pi Kappa Lambda (chpt. sec. 2003—05), Phi Mu Alpha, Kappa Kappa Psi (life; nat. vice pres., pres.-elect 2003—05). Achievements include research in International Conference of the World Association for Symphonic Bands and Ensembles, Schladming, Austria, July 5 - 12 1997; poster session, Biennial National Conference, College Band Director's National Association, Athens, GA, February-March 1997; Southern Division meeting of the College Band Director's National Association, Williamsburg, VA, February 1994. Avocations: gardening, cooking, fishing. Home: 1402 Cottage Row Cedar Falls IA 50613 Office: UNI Bands 48 GBPAC Cedar Falls IA 50614 Office Phone: 319-273-2025. Office Fax: 319-273-7306. E-mail: chesnutt@uni.edu.

CHESS, WILLIAM, public relations executive; BS in Mgmt. and Acctg., MBA in Fin., Fordham U. Air traffic controller USAF; with Lever Bros. Co., contr.; fin. v.p. Lever Foods; exec. v.p., CFO Ogilvy & Mather Pub. Rels.; sr. v.p. fin. Ogilvy & Mather; CFO Ogilvy & Mather Worldwide, 1993-95, CFO and COO, 1995, Ogilvy Pub. Rels. Worldwide, N.Y.C. Office: Ogilvy Worldwide 909 3rd Ave New York NY 10022-4731

CHESSELET, MARIE-FRANCOISE, neurologist, educator; MD, U. Paris VI, 1974, PhD in Neurosci., 1978. Attachee de recherches CNRS, Paris, 1978—80, head of rsch., 1981—84; prof. neurology UCLA/Reed Neurol. Rsch. Ctr., Calif. Contbr. articles to profl. jours. Recipient Merit award, NIMH, 1992—. Achievements include research in includes molecular mechanisms associated with movement disorders due to dysfunction of the basal ganglia such as those of Parkinson disease, Huntington disease and dystonia; on molecular mechanisms of cell death and neuroprotection in the basal ganglia; molecular mechanisms of neural repair in the striatum in the adult and during development. Office: UCLA Dept Neurology Reed Neurol Rsch Ctr 710 Westwood Plz Rm B-114 Los Angeles CA 90095

CHESSER, LEICLE E., corporate financial executive; Grad., Okla. State Univ. CPA. Accountant Arthur Young & Co.; v.p. fin., sec.-treas. HC Price Constrn. Co.; exec. v.p., CFO Spie Group, Inc., 1986—94, Comstock Group, Inc., 1990—94, EMCOR Group, Inc., Norwalk, Conn., 1994—. Office: EMCOR Group Inc 101 Merritt Seven Norwalk CT 06851

CHESSER, MICHAEL J., gas and electric power industry executive; BS, Ga. Tech. Univ.; MBA, Loyola Coll., Balt. With Balt. Gas & Electric; pres., COO Atlantic Energy Inc., 1994—98; pres., CEO Itron Inc., Spokane, Wash., 1999—2000, GPU Energy, Morristown, NJ, 2000—02; chmn., CEO United Water Resources, Harrington Park, NJ, 2002—03, Great Plains Energy, Kansas City, Mo., 2003—. Bd. mem. Edison Elec. Inst., Elec. Power Rsch. Inst. Trustee Univ. Mo., Kansas City, Midwest Rsch. Inst.; bd. mem. Heart of Am. United Way, Partnership for Children; mem. leadership bd. Mid-Am. Regional Council; mem. Civic Council Greater Kansas City, Kans. Bus. Edn. Partnership. Office: Great Plains Energy 1201 Walnut St Kansas City MO 64106 Mailing: Great Plains Energy PO Box 418679 Kansas City MO 64141-9679*

CHESSHIRE, MARY CLAIRE, lawyer; b. Balt., 1962; BS, Johns Hopkins U., 1989; JD, U. Balt., 1993. Bar: Md. 1993. Ptnr. Whiteford, Taylor & Preston LLP. Lectr. Villa Julie Coll. Paralegal Prog.; trainer Md. Assn. Non Profit Orgns. Mem. exec. com. Villa Julie Coll. Bd. Trustees. Mem.: ABA, Baltimore City Bar Assn., Nat. Assn. Pub. Pension Attys., Md. State Bar Assn. Office: Whiteford, Taylor & Preston LLP 7 Saint Paul St Baltimore MD 21202-1626 Office Fax: 410-347-9465. E-mail: mchesshire@wtplaw.com.

CHESSLER, RICHARD KENNETH, gastroenterologist, endocrinologist; b. N.Y.C., Apr. 6, 1944; BS, Fairleigh Dickinson U., Rutherford, N.J., 1965; MD, Chgo. Med. Sch., 1969. Diplomate Am. Bd. Internal Medicine and Gastroenterology. Asst. chief gastroenterology Englewood Hosp., N.J., 1982—, chief endoscopy, 1992-99; asst. prof. medicine Mt. Sinai Hosp., N.Y.C., 1994-97. Author: Chemical Technicians Ready Reference Book, 1996; mem. editl. bd. Practical Gastroenterology, 1977—. Fellow ACP, Am. Coll. Gastroenterology (bd. govs. 1989). Avocations: ski, racquetball, golf. Office: 1555 Center Ave Fort Lee NJ 07024-4612 Office Phone: 201-945-6564.

CHESSON, EUGENE, retired civil engineering educator, consultant, volunteer; b. São Paulo, Brazil, Dec. 1, 1928; s. Eugene and Mary Josie (Foy) C.; m. Marilyn Ryder Hershey, Aug. 21, 1954; children: Christopher Eugene, David Anson. BSC.E., Duke U., 1950; MS, U. Ill.-Urbana, 1956, PhD, 1959. Registered profl. engr., Ill., Del., Ariz. Refinery engr. Standard Oil Ind., Whiting, 1953; research asst., research assoc. civil engring. dept. U. Ill.-Urbana, 1953-59, asst. prof., 1959-62, assoc. prof., 1962-66; prof. civil engring. U. Del., Newark, 1966-86, dept. chmn., 1966-75, prof. emeritus, 1986—; pres. Chesson Engring., Inc., Newark, 1981-85; treas., project mgr. HPR Investors, L.C., Prescott, Ariz., 1992—2004, Sedona Pinon Woods Partnership, Prescott, 1992—2000; treas. Hershey Partnership, Prescott, 1993—. Contbr. articles in field to profl. jours. Mem. Nat. Def. Exec. Res., U.S. Dept. Transp., 1973-84; vol. Sharlot Hall Mus., Prescott, 2001—. Lt. (j.g.) Civil Engr. Corps, USN, 1950-53. Named Outstanding Young Faculty Mem., Dept. Civil Engring., U. Ill., 1962; Del. Outstanding Engr. Del. Soc. Profl. Engrs., 1981; recipient Teaching award AT&T Found., 1986 Fellow ASCE (pres. local sect. 1982-83); mem. Am. Soc. Engring. Edn. (W.E. Wickenden award 1981), No. Ariz. Geneal. Soc. (v.p., pres. 1989-91). Republican. Presbyterian. Home: 640 Cosmos Way Prescott AZ 86303-5049

CHESSON, MICHAEL BEDOUT, history professor, writer; b. Richmond, Va., Sept. 5, 1947; s. Wesley Earle and Virginia Winborne (Ramsey) Chesson; m. Jane B. Sherwin, July 2, 1988; children: Mark Allyn, Virginia Woodward. AB with high honors in History, Coll. William and Mary, 1969; postgrad. (Gilman fellow), Johns Hopkins U., 1972-73; PhD in History (Grad. fellow), Harvard U., 1978. Clk. R.F. & P. R.R., Richmond, 1966-69; park ranger-historian Colonial Nat. Hist. Park, Nat. Park Svc., Yorktown and Jamestown, Va., 1969-70, 72, 73; tchg. fellow Harvard U., 1975-78; asst. prof. history U. Mass., Boston, 1978-82, assoc. prof. history, 1982-96, prof. history, 1996—. Author: Richmond After the War, 1865-1890, 1981, Exile in Richmond: The Confederate Journal of Henri Garidel, 2001, The Journal of a Civil War Surgeon, 2003; co-author: Effective State Standards for U.S. History, 2003. Served to capt. USNR, 1969-2005, ret. Fellow Mass. Hist. Soc.; mem. Am. Hist. Assn., So. Hist. Assn., Va. Hist. Assn., Orgn. Am. Historians, Peabody Essex Mus., Cape Ann Hist. Assn., Mil. Hist. Soc. Mass., Naval Res. Assn., Res. Officer Assn., Fleet Res. Assn., Navy League. Clubs: Wardroom Club (Boston). Democrat. Office Phone: 617-287-6887. E-mail: michael.chesson@umb.edu.

CHESTER, ALEXANDER CAMPBELL, III, physician; b. N.Y.C., Dec. 21, 1947; s. Alexander C. II and Gladys (Edelhauser) C.; m. Kimberly Robinson Chester, Dec. 20, 1970; children: Kristin Elizabeth, Alexander C. IV. BS cum laude, Georgetown U., 1969; MD, Columbia U., 1973. Diplomate Am. Bd. Internal Medicine, Nat. Bd. Med. Examiners; advanced achievement in internal medicine; voluntary recert., 1998. Intern Georgetown U., Washington, 1973-74, resident in medicine, 1974-76, clin. fellow in nephrology, 1976-77, rsch. fellow in nephrology, 1977-78, clin. instr. medicine, 1978-80, clin. asst. prof. medicine, 1980-84, clin. assoc. prof. medicine, 1985-89, clin. prof. medicine, 1990—. Govs. com. for coll. affairs ACP, 1980-90; clin. prof. medicine Georgetown U. Med. Ctr.; reviewer Annals of Internal Medicine. Contbr. articles to profl. jours. and publs. Named one of Top Doctors, Washingtonian Mag., 1999, 2002, Area Outstanding Specialists, Checkbook mag., 1998, Area Outstanding Specialists Checkbook mag., 2002; featured in Consumers' Guide to Top Doctors, editors of Checkbook Mag., 2002, 03. Mem. AAAS, AMA, ACP (gov.'s nominating com.), Am. Soc. Internal Medicine (alt. del. Nat. Meeting 1980), Am. Fedn. Clin. Rsch., Hippocrates-Galen Med. Soc. (sec., treas. 1991-92, pres. 1993-94), Osler Soc. (sec., treas. 1986-88, pres. 1989-90), Nat. Kidney Found. (coun. clin. nephrology, dialysis and tranplantation, profl. adv. bd. 1983-86, program com. ann. kidney symposium 1983-86), N.Y. Acad. Scis., Am. Heart Assn. (coun. kidney 1988-90), Clinico-Pathol. Soc. (pres. 2003—), Am. Rhinologic Soc., Soc. for Study Human Behavior and Evolution, Pavlovian Soc. N.Am., Assn. Medicine and Psychiary, Am. Assn. Chronic Fatigue Syndrome, European Rhinologic Soc., Myalgic Encephalomyelitis Assn. (U.K.), Cosmos Club, Phi Beta Kappa. Achievements include research in nasal reflexes, sick building syndrome and chronic fatigue syndrome. Home: 4618 Laverock Pl NW Washington DC 20007-2544 Office: 3301 New Mexico Ave NW Ste 348 Washington DC 20016-3622 Office Phone: 202-362-4467. E-mail: achester@foxhallinternists.com.

CHESTER, JAMES A., music educator; b. Bay, Ark. s. Harvey Ray and Anna Florence (Brown) Chester; m. Julia Ellen Williams, May 31, 1963; children: Autumn Elizabeth Chester Marshall, Tiffany Paige Chester Parkhurst. BA, Harding Coll., 1965; M in Music Edn., Memphis State U., 1968. Cert. music tchr. grades K-12 Tenn. Tchr., choral dir. Crowley's Ridge Acad., Paragould, Ark., 1965—66, Memphis City Schs.-Treadwell, 1967—69, Harding Acad. Memphis, 1969—. Guest clinician Harding U. Christian H.S. Choral Festival, Searcy, Ark., 1984, guest clinician Lipscomb U., Nashville, 2001. Music min., worship leader Highland St. Ch. Christ, Memphis, 1968—. With U.S. Army, 1959—67. Named Outstanding Alumnus, Crowley's Ridge Acad., Paragould, Ark., 1984, Outstanding Tchr., Tenn. Govs. Sch. for the Arts, Nashville, 1990, Harding Acad. Secondary Tchr. of Yr., 1992; recipient Outstanding Tchr., Tenn. Govs. Sch. for the Arts, Nashville, 2004. Mem.: Tenn. Music Educator's Assn. (bd. mem. 1996—98, long-range planning com. 1999—2001), West Tenn. Vocal Music Educators Assn. (treas. 1990—94, pres. 1996—98, host jr. and sr. high honor choruses 1996—2002, past pres. 1998—2002), Am. Choral Dirs. Assn. (life). Mem. Ch. Of Christ. Avocations: carpentry, woodworking. Office: Harding Acad Memphis 1100 Cherry Rd Memphis TN 38117

CHESTER, JOHN JONAS, lawyer, educator; b. Columbus, Ohio, July 13, 1920; s. John J. and Harriet Bonnadine (Rice) C.; m. Cynthia Johnson, Apr. 18, 1959; children: John, James, Joel, Cecily. AB cum laude, Amherst Coll., 1942; JD, Yale U., 1948. Bar: Ohio 1948. Ptnr. Chester & Chester, Columbus, 1948-57, Chester & Rose, Columbus, 1958-70, Chester Willcox and Saxbe and predecessor firm, Columbus, 1971—. Spl. counsel Pres. of U.S., 1974. adj. prof. Ohio State U. Coll. Law. Past bd. dirs. Grant Riverside Meth. Hosps.; past chmn. Doctor's Hosp.; past chmn., bd. dirs. Ohio Health, 2001—; past trustee Doctor's Hosp., Columbus Sch. for Girls, Columbus Acad., Shepherd Hill Hosp., Ohio Hist. Found., Ohio Hist. Soc.; active Ohio Gen. Assembly, 1953-58. Lt. USNR, 1942-46. Mem. ABA, Ohio State Bar Assn., Columbus Bar Assn., Am. Coll. Trial Lawyers, Columbus Club, Columbus Athletic Club, Rocky Fork Hunt and Country Club. Republican. Episcopalian. Home: 4906 Riverside Dr Columbus OH 43220-2876 Office: Chester Willcox & Saxbe 65 E State St Ste 1000 Columbus OH 43215-3442 Office Phone: 614-221-4000. Business E-Mail: jackchester@cwslaw.com.

CHESTER, LINNES LEE, JR., healthcare association administrator; b. Hopkinsville, Ky., Dec. 15, 1958; s. Linnes Lee Chester, Sr. and Cozy Mae Chester. BS in health care admin., magna cum laude, SW Tex. State U., 1986; MS in logistics mgmt., Air Force Inst. of Tech., Wright-Patterson Air Force Base, OH, 1992; MS in sys. mgmt., U. Southen Calif., 1994. Cert. Health Care Management Am. Coll. of Healthcare Execs., 2001. Dir., patient affairs & med. readiness Peterson AFB Clinic, Peterson Air Force Base, Colo., 1986—89, dir., med. resource mgmt. & info. sys., 1989—90; dir., med. readiness 39rd Tactical Group Hosp., Incirlik, Turkey, 1990—91; grad. student Air Force Inst. of Tech., Wright-Patterson Air Force Base, Ohio, 1991—92; dir., med. logistics & pers. 42nd Med. Group, Loring Air Force Base, Maine, 1992—94; adminstr. Divsn. Medicine and Reid Health Clinic 59th Med. Wing, Lackland Air Force Base, Tex., 1994—97; exec. officer to the comdr. Air Force Inspection Agy., Kirtland Air Force Base, N.Mex., 1999—2000; fellow, managed care, resource mgmt. Long Beach Meml. Med. Ctr., Long Beach, Calif., 2000—01; dir. Dept. Def. Uniform Bus. Office Office of Asst. Sec. of Def. for Health Affairs, Falls Ch., Va., 2001—. Western regents adv. coun. Am. Coll. of Healthcare Execs., 2001—; adv. Presdl. Task Force Vets. Affairs-Dept. Def. Fin. Subcom. Mem. Pikes Peak Jaycees, Colo. Springs, Colo., 1988—90; instr. San Antonio Literacy Coun., San Antonio, 1996—97; co-chairman 59th Med. Wing Combined Fed. Campaign, Lackland Air Force Base, Tex., 1996—96. Lt. col. USAF. Decorated Meritorious Svc. medal Air Force, Mil. Outstanding Vol. Svc. medal; recipient Disting. Grad., Sch. of Healthcare Scis., Sheppard AFB, Tex., 1987, Air Force Med. Insp. of the Yr., Air Force Inspection Agy., 1998, Mil. Excellence in Healthcare Mgmt., Am. Coll. of Healthcare Execs., 2002. Fellow: Am. Coll. of Healthcare Execs.; mem.: Air Force Med. Svc. Corps Assn., Assn. of Mil. Surgeons of US, Air Force Assn. (life), Soc. of Logistics Engrs., Alpha Chi. Achievements include development of itemized medical billing at 127 military treatment facilites that aligned processes with industry standards; first automated appointment system in the continental United States; Persian Gulf medical evacuation operation ranked number one in 12 regions. Home: 3242 Chimney Rock Rd Abilene TX 79606-3356 Office: 7th Medical Support Squadron Dyess Afb TX 79607 Personal E-mail: linnes@sbcglobal.net. Business E-Mail: linnes.chester@dyess.af.mil.

CHESTER, LYNNE, foundation administrator, artist; b. Fargo, N.D., May 29, 1942; BA in Music, Hillsdale Coll., 1964; MA in Guidance Counseling, Mich. State U., 1965; PhD in Psychology, U. Mich., 1971. Tchr. Warren (Mich.) Consol. Schs., 1965-70; curriculum advisor Royal Oak (Mich.) Pub. Schs., 1974-75; co-founder, exec. dir. Peace Rsch. Found., Carmel, Calif., 1993-98. Assoc. Hillsdale Coll., 1989—; guest lectr. ceramics James Milliken U., Decatur, Ill., 1991; guest lectr. creative covergence Carl Cherry Ctr. for Art, Carmel, 1991, Compton lectr., Monterey, Calif., 1996—; mem. Nat. Assn. Fund Raising Execs., 1991-96; co-founder, bd. dirs. Monterey Peninsula Coll. Art Gallery, 1991—; guest juror Monterey County Essay Contest, 1997; cons. Monterey Mus. of Art; guest lectr. Hillsdale (Mich.) Coll., 1997; juror Monterey County Poetry Contest, 1993—; juror photographic show Beauty at the Heart of Things, Carl Cherry Ctr. for Arts, Carmel, 1999. Artist of multiple commd. sculptures for pvt. collections; also ceramics, sculpture and photographs in pvt. and corp. collections; represented in permanent collection at Krammert Art Mus., Champaign, Ill., Fresno (Calif.) Mus. Art; juried show Ctr. for Photographic Art, Carmel, Calif., 1996; art represented at Who's Who in Art, Monterey, 1989-96, Christmas Miniatures/Invitational Ctr. for Photographic Art, Carmel, 1996, Holiday Print Show Ctr. for Photographic Art, Carmel, 1996 (Dir.'s Choice 1996); author of poetry; juror essay contest Personal Heroes Monterey County K-12, 1997; juror poetry contest Monterey County 9-12 grades, Carl Cherry Ctr. for the Arts, 1993-2001; exhibited in photography show at Asilomer Conf. Ctr., Monterey Peninsula Airport, Pacific Grove Art Ctr., Carl Chevry Ctr., Seaside City Hall, Pacific Grove Mus. Natural History, 1995-98, Hillsdale Coll., 1997, Monterey Peninsula Airport, 1998, Calif. State U., Monterey Bay, 1998, Pacific Grove (Calif.) Art Ctr., 1998, Carl Cherry Ctr. for Arts, Carmel, Calif., 1998, Pacific Grove Mus. Nat. History, 1998, Salinas (Calif.) Courthouse, 1998, Asilomar Conf. Ctr., Pacific Grove, 1998, Prints Charming Gallery, Carmel, 1998, Triton Mus. Art, 1998, Pre-auction show KTEH, 1998, 2000, Triton Mus., 1998; one-woman show Prints Charming Gallery, Carmel, Calif., 2000; represented by Prints Charming Gallery and Carmel Express Internat. Co-founder Southfield (Mich.) Symphony, 1972, World Rhythms Festival, Carmel, 1994; mem. citizens adv. bd. City of Royal Oak, 1978-83; co-founder, bd. dirs. Monterey Bay Artists Day, Sta. KAZU-FM, 1987-89; pres., bd. dirs. Carl Cherry Ctr. for Arts, Carmel, 1988-94, 95, 97; bd. dirs. Monterey Peninsula Mus. Art, 1991-94, Carmel Pub. Libr. Found., 1991-94, Monterey Inst. for Rsch. in Astronomy, 1985-95, Cultural Coun. for Monterey County, 1993-98; fundraiser Student Art Gallery, Monterey Peninsula Coll., 1990-97, mem. mentors program Women Helping Women, 1998—. Recipient Citizens Adv. Coun. award City of Royal Oak, 1983, Best of Show award for monoprint Monterey Peninsula Coll., 1990, Poetry prizes Carl Cherry Ctr. for Arts, 1990-94, Benefactor of Arts award Monterey County Cultural Coun., 1992, 93, 94, Soccer Mgr./Coach of Yr. 1976-81, 1st pl. award photography contest Monterey Regional Park Dist. Celebration of Open Space, 1998; artist-in-residence Naubinway, Mich., 1997. Mem. AAUW, Internat. Platform Assn., Internat. Sculpture Ctr., Nat. Soc. Fund Raising Execs., Nat. Mus. Women in Art (charter mem.), Am. Crafts Coun., Sigma Alpha Iota (Ruby Sword of Honor 1963). Avocations: reading, playing piano, composing, hiking, photography. Home: 9645 Sandbur Pl Salinas CA 93907-1031

CHESTER, ROBERT SIMON GEORGE, lawyer; b. Chelmsford, Essex, England, Feb. 11, 1949; arrived in Can., 1971. s. Robert John and Elizabeth Poyitt (Forteath) C.; m. Anna Tharyan, Sept. 18, 1975; 1 child, Rahael Elizabeth Anna. BA, Oxford U., England, 1971, MA, 1979; LLM, Osgoode Hall Law Sch., Toronto, 2003. Bar: Ontario 1982, England and Wales 1988. Vis. lectr. Osgoode Hall Law Sch., Toronto, 1972-74; rsch. staff Ontario Law Reform Commn., Toronto, 1974-77; exec. counsel Dep. Atty. Gen. Ontario, Toronto, 1977-82; counsel policy devel. Ministry Atty. Gen., Ontario, 1982-85; dir. rsch. McMillan Binch, Toronto, 1985—2004; ptnr. KNOWlaw Group, Toronto, 1988—2004, Heenan Blaikie LLP, 2004—. Counsel Study on Access to Legal Svcs. by Disabled, Ontario, 1982-83; cons. Royal Commn. on Employment Equity, 1983-84, Royal Commn. on Electoral Reform, 1990-91, Royal Commn. on Aboriginal Peoples, 1992. Author: (with others) Environmental Rights in Canada, 1981, The Quality Pursuit, 1988, ABA Guide to Legal Marketing, 1995, Barristers and Solicitors in Practice, 1998; co-editor: Winning with Computers, 1991, 2d vol., 1993; contbr. articles to profl. jours. Trustee Coll. Law Practice Mgmt.; bd. dirs. Can. Rhodes Scholars Found. Can. Rhodes Found. scholar, 1972; fellow Coll. Law Practice Mgmt. Mem. ABA (chmn. New Media and Internet bd., chmn. edn. bd. law practice mgmt. sect. 1994-96, chmn. Techshow 1992-93), Can. Bar Assn. (com. legal opinions 1992—, Pres. tech. impact adv. group). Anglican. Home: 41 Walmsley Blvd Toronto ON Canada M4V 1X7 Office: Heenan Blaikie LLP Ste 2600 Royal Bank Plz S Tower 200 Bay St Toronto ON Canada M5J 2J4 Office Phone: 416-643-6905. Office Fax: 866-252-6067. Business E-Mail: simon.chester@mcmillanbinch.com, schester@heenan.ca.

CHESTER, RUSSELL GILBERT, JR., accountant, auditor; b. Lorain, Ohio, Aug. 6, 1947; s. Russell Gilbert and Elizabeth Jane (Eucker) C.; m. Martha Ann Mamula, Jan. 24, 1970 (div.); children: Sally Ann, Russell Theodore; m. Pamela Jean Huggins, Sept. 26, 1992. BS in Indsl. Mgmt., Purdue U., 1970; grad. with honors, USAF Comm. Analyst Sch., 1971; M Accountancy, Bowling Green State U., 1975; Exec. Mgmt. Program, U. Mich., 1985. CPA, Ohio; cert. systems profl. Staff and sr. acct. Arthur Andersen & Co., Cleve., 1975-77; chief internal auditor lighting fixture divsn. ITT, Vermilion, Ohio, 1977, comptr. Can. Lighting divsn. London, Ont., 1977-78, comptr. lighting fixture div. Vermillion, 1978-80; comptr., dir. pers., lighting fixtures div. Lithonia Lighting, Vermillion, 1980; supr. internal audit indsl. tech. group ITT, Chgo., 1980-81, mgr. internal audit engr. products group, 1981-83, dir. internal audit natural resources group Stamford, Conn., 1983-84; dir. audit svcs. Parker Hannifin Corp., Cleve., 1984-2001, v.p. audit, 2001—05; v.p. Enterprise Compliance, 2005—. Cons. Component Repair Tech. Mentor, Ohio, 1984-86, bd. dirs., 1986—; mem. acctg. student adv. bd. Cleve. State U., 1990-2000, Case Western Res. U., 1994-95. Asst. scoutleader Boy Scouts Am., Cleve., 1985; instr. Jr. Achievement, Cleve., 1986. Sgt. USAF, 1970-73. Mem. AICPA, Inst. Mgmt. Accts., Ohio Soc. CPAs, Inst. Internal Auditors (bd. dirs. Cleve.-Akron chpt. 1991-97, 99—, internat. conf. com. 1994-96, chmn. acad. rels. 1991-94, 1st v.p. 1994-95, pres. 1995-96, chmn. attendance and mem. 1996-98, dist. rep. 1997-2000), Assn. for Sys. Mgmt., Mfrs. Alliance for Productivity and Innovation (gen. auditors coun.), Am. Legion, VFW, Beta Alpha Psi. Republican. Avocations: stamp collecting/philately, coin collecting/numismatics, books, yachting, computers. Office: Parker Hannifin Corp 6035 Parkland Blvd Cleveland OH 44124-4141 E-mail: rchester@parker.com.

CHESTER, THOMAS JAY, physician; b. Bklyn., Apr. 20, 1947; s. Benjamin J. and Helen (Weltman) C.; m. Dawn C. Bryden, June 2, 1969; children: Janet A., Joyce E. BS in Life Science, MIT, Cambridge, 1968; MD, Stanford U., Palo Alto, Calif., 1973; MPH in Epidemiology, U. Wash., Seattle, 1978. Diplomate Am. Bd. Preventive Medicine. Lt. comdr. USPHS, 1972-78; med. epidemiologist Ctrs. for Disease Control and Prevention, Atlanta, 1975-78; chief state epidemiologist Ala. Dept. Pub. Health, Montgomery, 1978-81; dir. health svcs. Conoco, Inc., Houston, 1981-88; v.p. health systems ENSR Health Scis., Alameda, Calif., 1988-90; med. dir. superconducting Super Collider Lab., Waxahatchie, Tex., 1990-95; assoc. prof., acting chmn. Pub. Health & Preventive Medicine U. North Tex. Health Science Ctr., Fort Worth, 1993-95; v.p., med. dir. preventive health Mutual of Omaha, Nebr., 1996; med. dir. occupational health Fairview Clinics, Mpls., 1997-2000, med. dir. urgent care and splty. clinics, 1999-2000; med. dir. Fairview Employee Health, Mpls., 1999—2001; dist. health dir. North Ga. Health Dist., 2001—. Chmn. editl. com. (CD-ROM) ACOEM Physician's Silver Platter-Occupational Medicine, 1994-2000. Fellow ACP, Am. Coll. Preventive Medicine, Am. Coll. Occupl. and Environ. Medicine, Am. Coll. Epidemiology; mem. Okla. Occupl. Medicine Assn. (pres. 1986-87). Office: North Ga Health Dist 100 W Walnut Ave Ste 92 Dalton GA 30720

CHESTER, THOMAS LEE, chemist; b. Jacksonville, Fla., Sept. 28, 1949; s. Thomas Julian and Ruth (Poston) C.; m. Ellen Watts Quigley Dec. 28, 1970; children: Carolyn, Stephen. BS, Fla. State U., 1971; PhD, U. Florida, 1976. Chemist Verona divsn. Baychem Corp., Charleston, SC, 1971-72, Procter & Gamble Co., Cin., 1976—, sect. head, rsch., devel., 1980-00, prin. scientist, 2000-01, rsch. fellow, 2001—. Contbr. articles to profl. jours. Formerly mem. Citizens Com. of Commun. Devel., Forest Park, Ohio; pres. Supercritical Confs., 1991—. Mem. Am. Chem. Soc. (analytical fellowship com. 1983--). Episcopalian. Avocations: soccer, boy scouts america. Office: Procter and Gamble Co PO Box 538707 Cincinnati OH 45253-8707

CHESTNOV, RICHARD FRANKLIN, private investor; b. N.Y.C., Mar. 7, 1945; s. Alex and Hannah Chestnov; m. Stephanie Aizer, Aug. 29, 1981; 1 child, Alexis Kyle. BS, Pa. State U., 1966. Jr. sportswear buyer Bloomingdale's, N.Y.C., 1966-72; v.p. Huk-A-Poo Sportswear, N.Y.C., 1972-74; pres. Chego Internat., N.Y.C., 1974-89; chmn. Richarvey Ltd., Hong Kong,

1974-89. Bd. dirs. Jaclyn Inc., West New York, N.J. Fellow St. Andrews Country Club. Avocations: tennis, weight training, jogging. Home: 17142 White Haven Dr Boca Raton FL 33496-5921

CHESTNUT, JOHN WILLIAM, lawyer; b. Berwyn, Ill., July 3, 1940; s. James Edward and Alice Mary (Cotter) C.; m. Margaret Barbara Angland, Aug. 8, 1964; children: Edward, Nancy. BS cum laude, U. Notre Dame, 1962; JD cum laude, Northwestern U., 1965. Bar: Ill. 1965, U.S. Dist. Ct. (no. dist.) Ill. 1965, U.S. Supreme Ct. 1978, U.S. Ct. Appeals (fed. cir.) 1982. Assoc. Dawson, Tilton, Fallon & Lumgmus, Chgo., 1965-68; ptnr. Tilton, Fallon, Lumgmus & Chestnut, Chgo., 1968-94. Mem. editorial bd. The Trademark Reporter, N.Y.C., 1975—. Mem. ABA, Am. Intellectual Property Law Assn., Ill. State Bar Assn., Intellectual Property Law Assn. Chgo., Patent Law Assn. Chgo. (bd. govs. 1979-81). Office: Tilton Fallon Lungum & Chestnut 100 S Wacker Dr Ste 960 Chicago IL 60606-4002

CHESTON, SHEILA CAROL, lawyer; b. Washington, Nov. 5, 1958; d. Theodore C. and Gabrielle Joan (Hellings) C. BA, Dartmouth Coll., 1980; JD, Columbia U., 1984. Bar: N.Y. 1986, D.C. 1986, U.S. Dist. Ct. D.C. 1987, U.S. Ct. Appeals (D.C. cir.) 1987, U.S. Dist. Ct. (so. and ea. dists.) N.Y. 1989, U.S. Ct. Appeals (2d cir.), U.S. Supreme Ct. 1989. Law clk. to judge U.S. Ct. Appeals for 9th Cir., L.A., 1984-85; assoc. Wilmer, Cutler & Pickering, Washington, 1985-92, ptnr., 1992-93; gen. counsel Def. Base Closure and Realignment Commn., 1993; spl. assoc. counsel to Pres. of U.S., 1994; dep. gen. counsel Dept. Air Force, 1993-95, gen. counsel, 1995-98; ptnr. Wilmer, Cutler & Pickering, Washington, 1998—2002; sr. v.p., gen. counsel, sec. BAE Systems N.A., Rockville, Md., 2002—. Adj. prof. in internat. litig. Georgetown Law Sch., 1991—2003. Mem. ABA, D.C. Bar Assn., Women's Bar Assn., Am. Bar Found., Am. Soc. Internat. Law, Coun. on Fgn. Rels. Democrat. Episcopalian. Office: BAE Systems NA 1601 Research Blvd Rockville MD 20850-3173 E-mail: sheila.cheston@baesystems.com.

CHETTA, HOLLY ANN, transportation executive; b. New Orleans, Aug. 18, 1945; d. Henry John and Ernestine Rose (Blaise) C. BS, Tulane U., 1967, MS, 1970, MPH, 1977. Assoc. realtor Latter & Blum, New Orleans, 1978-83; adminstr. loan svc. First Fin. Bank, New Orleans, 1981-83; adminstr. USDA, New Orleans, 1982-84; pers. evaluator U.S. Dept. Transp., USCG, New Orleans, 1984-91, regional maritime pers. examiner, 1991—. Author: (poems) Toward the Twenty-First Century, 1985, New Year's Eve, 1984. Mem. Internat. Platform Assn. Republican. Roman Catholic. Avocations: pet training, poetry. Office: US Dept Transp US Coast Guard Exam Ctr 1615 Poydras St New Orleans LA 70112-1254 Home: 118 Wood Ave Metairie LA 70005-4206

CHEVALIER, DENISE ANN, director; b. Houston, May 4, 1978; d. James Donald and Adline Ann Chevalier. BA in Acctg., U. Miss., University, 2000; BBA in Mgmt., U. Houston Downtown, 2003; MS in Edn., Capella U., Mpls., 2004, post grad. in Edn., 2005—. Fin. aid advisor, Houston, 2001—03, C.C., Kingwood, 2003—04; dir. of fin. aid Proprietary Sch., Houston, 2003—. Mem.: NAACP, Am. Women In Univs., Tex. Assn. Fin. Aid Adminstrs., So. Poverty Law Ctr., Delta Sigma Theta. Roman Catholic. Home: 19515 Shinwood Humble TX 77346 Personal E-mail: denise1913@hotmail.com.

CHEVALIER, PAUL EDWARD, retired retail executive, lawyer; b. N.Y.C., Jan. 30, 1939; s. Arthur and Grace (Eaton) C.; 1 child, Marc. BA, Columbia U., 1960, LLB, MBA, Columbia U., 1966; AMP, Harvard U., 1979. Bar: Ill. 1968, U.S. Supreme Ct. 1974. Dir. labor rels. Carter Hawley Hale Stores, Inc., L.A., 1972-74, v.p. employee rels., 1974-86, sr. v.p. employee rels., 1986-93; pres. Chevalier Cons. Group, 1993-98. Vice chmn. Western Fed. Credit Union, 1989-93; bd. dirs., exec. com. Sedona Cultural Park, 2000—04; chmn. emeritus Jonathan Art Found. Past pres., bd. dirs. Calif. Employment Law Coun.; chmn. Art and Culture Commn., City of Sedona, 1999-2003; bd. dirs. Ariz. Humanities Coun., 2002-04. Lt. USN, 1960-66; mem. Harvard Bus. Sch. Alumni Coun., 1989-92, Mem. Nat. Retail Fedn. (chmn. employee rels. com. 1979-82), Calif. Retail Assn., Harvard Bus. Sch. Assn. (bd. dirs. 1980-90, pres. 1984-85). Personal E-mail: westwinds3@aol.com.

CHEVALIER, ROBERT, chemistry educator; s. Clyde and Joan Chevalier; m. Sally Chevalier, Aug. 1, 1998; children: Bryce, Owen. BA, BS in biology, Ohio State U., 1992—97; M in edn., Ashland U., 2000—03. Comprehensive Science Licensure Ohio Dept. of Edn., 2001. Interrogator U.S. Army, 1985—2000; chemistry and physics tchr. Bucyrus City Schools, Bucyrus, Ohio, 2000—05. Sgt. e-5 U.S. Army, 1985—2000, World. Decorated AR-COM, SWA medal U.S. Army. Conservative-R. Catholic. Avocations: hiking, fishing, camping. Office Phone: 419-562-7721. Personal E-mail: rlchevy@hotmail.com.

CHEVALIER, ROGER ALAN, astronomy educator, consultant; b. Rome, Sept. 26, 1949; came to U.S., 1962; s. Frank Charles and Marion Helen (Janhke) C.; m. Margaret Mary With, July 27, 1974.; children: Chase Arthur, Max Toussaint. BS in Astronomy, Calif. Inst. Tech., 1970; PhD in Astronomy (Woodrow Wilson and NSF fellow), Princeton U., 1973. Asst. astronomer Kitt Peak Nat. Obs., Tucson, 1973-76, assoc. astronomer, 1976-79; assoc. prof. astronomy U. Va., Charlottesville, 1979-85, prof. astronomy, chmn. dept., 1985-92, W.H. Vanderbilt prof. astronomy, 1990—; dir. Leander McCormick Obs., 1985-92. Cons. Lawrence Livermore Nat. Lab., Livermore, Calif., 1981-90; bd. trustees U. Space Rsch. Assn., 2000—. Contbr. numerous rsch. articles to Astrophys. Jour., other astronomy and physics jours. Recipient Heineman prize for astrophysics Am. Astron. Soc./Am. Inst. Physics, 1996; named Va. Outstanding Scientist, Sci. Mus. Va., 1991; Woodrow Wilson Found. fellow Princeton U., 1970-71, NSF fellow, 1970-73; elected to Nat. Acad. Scis., 1996. Mem. NAS, Am. Astron. Soc. (councilor 1988-91), Internat. Astron. Union, Ill. Sci. Lectr. Assn. (v.p. 1975-85), Univ. Space Rsch. Assn. (bd. trustees 2000—). Home: 1891 Westview Rd Charlottesville VA 22903-1632 Office: U Va Dept Astronomy PO Box 3818 Charlottesville VA 22903-0818

CHEVALIER, TRACY ROSE, writer; b. Washington, Oct. 1962; BA, Oberlin Coll., 1984; MA, U. East Anglia, 1994. Reference book editor, London, 1988—93; freelance editor, 1994—97. Author: The Virgin Blue, 1997, Girl with a Pearl Earring, 1999, Falling Angels, 2001, The Lady and the Unicorn, 2003; editor: Twentieth-Century Children's Writers, 1989, Contemporary Poets, 5th edit., 1991, Contemporary World Writers, 1993, Encyclopedia ofthe Essay, 1997. Office: c/o Jonny Geller Curtis Brown Haymarket House 28/29 Haymarket London SW1Y 4SP England

CHEVES, VERA LOUISA, retired librarian; b. Rockport, Mass., Nov. 13, 1908; d. Andrew Gustaf and Olga Amanda (Silen) Cederstrom; m. Robert Cheves, dec.; children: Robert (dec.), Constance. BS in Edn., Boston U., 1930; MLS, Simmons Coll., 1963. Libr. asst. Sawyer Free Libr., Gloucester, Mass., 1932-33; libr. Boston Pub. Libr., 1950-73; med. libr. Addison Gilbert Hosp., Gloucester, Mass., 1984-92. Organist Lanesville Congl. Ch., Gloucester, 1972—93. Home: 6 Hickory St Gloucester MA 01930-1112

CHEVIGNY, PAUL GRAVES, law educator; b. Seattle, July 12, 1935; s. Hector and Claire (Graves) C.; m. Bell Gale, July 24, 1964; children: Katy, Blue. BA magna cum laude, Yale U., 1957; LLB, Harvard U., 1960. Bar: NY 1961, US Dist. Ct. So. Dist. NY 1963, US Ct. Appeals 5th Cir. 1964, US Ct. Appeals 2nd Cir. 1969, US Supreme Ct. 1972. Assoc. Hughes Hubbard & Reed, NYC, 1961—64; dir. Harlem Neighborhood Legal Assistance, 1965-66; mem. legal staff NY Civil Liberties Union, 1966-77; assoc. prof. NYU Sch. Law, 1977—81, prof., 1981—, Joel S. and Anne B. Ehrenkranz prof. law. Author: Police Power: Police Abuses in New York City, 1969, Cops & Rebels, 1972, Criminal Mischief, 1977, More Speech: Dialogue Rights & Modern Liberty, 1988, Gigs: Jazz and the Cabaret Laws in New York City, 1991, Edge of the Knife: Police Violence in the Americas, 1995. Served U.S. Army, 1960—61. Mem. ABA, Assn. Am. Law Schools. Avocation: jazz music. Office: NYU Sch Law Vanderbilt Hall Rm 419 40 Washington Sq S New York NY 10012-1099 Office Phone: 212-998-6249. E-mail: chevigny@turing.law.nyu.edu.*

CHEVINS, ANTHONY CHARLES, retired advertising agency executive; b. Frackville, Pa., Apr. 1, 1921; s. Charles A. and Mary (Swade) C.; m. Margaret Macy, Sept. 18, 1948; children: Cheryl L., Christopher M., Cynthia M. AB in Eng. and Advt. magna cum laude, Syracuse U., 1947; postgrad., Columbia U., 1948-49. Writer Batten, Barton, Durstine & Osborn (advt.), 1948-51; with Cunningham & Walsh, 1951-87, sr. v.p., 1959-61, creative dir., 1958-61, exec. v.p., 1961-68, pres., chief operating officer, 1968-84, chmn., chief exec. officer, 1984-87, The C&W Group Inc., 1985-87; vice chmn. N.W Ayer Inc., 1987-90, also bd. dirs. Contbr. articles to mags. Mem. Nat. Advt. Rev. Bd.; mem. dean's adv. coun. Newhouse Sch.; bd. dirs. Medic Alert Found. Internat. Served to lt. USNR, 1941-45. Mem. Phi Beta Kappa, Alpha Delta Sigma. Clubs: Sky, Union League (N.Y.C.); Woodway Country (Darien, Conn.); Nat. Golf Links Am. (Southampton, L.I.); Ocean Reef, Card Sound (Key Largo, Fla.). Home: 10 South Rd Key Largo FL 33037-3729

CHEVIS, CHERYL ANN, lawyer; b. Ann Arbor, Mich., Nov. 9, 1947; d. Peter Paul and Antoinette (Slapinski) C.; m. Edwin Mahaffey Gerow, Nov. 18, 1976. BA, U. Wash., 1969, MA, 1974; postgrad. in Sanskrit, U. Chgo., 1974-77, JD, 1980. Bar: Ill. 1980, U.S. Dist. Ct. (no. dist.) Ill. 1980, U.S. Ct. Appeals (7th cir.) 1982, U.S. Tax Ct. 1982, Oreg. 1986. Tax assoc. Sidley and Austin, Chgo., 1979-80, Mayer Brown and Platt, Chgo., 1981-85; sr. tax atty. Perkins Coie, Portland, 1985-87, tax ptnr., 1987-99; assoc. gen. counsel Portland Gen. Electric, 1999—. Mem. faculty Ill. Continuing Legal Edn., Chgo., 1982; vis. lectr. U. B.C., Vancouver, Can., 1983; lectr. Chgo. Tax Club, 1983, Oreg. Securities Lawyers Bar, Bend, 1986, Internat. Employers Seminar, Portland, 1991. Contbr. articles to Jour. Taxation. Vol. atty. Com. Civil Rights Under Law, Chgo., 1982-85; exec. com., chair devel. com. Portland State U. Found.; exec. com., treas. Friends of Chamber Music; coun. mem. Oreg. Coun. for the Humanities. Grantee, Smithsonian Inst., 1981. Mem. ABA (tax sect., com. capital recovery and leasing), Oreg. State Bar (sister-bar com. with Lithuanian Lawyers Assn. 1997—). Avocations: music, theater, outdoor sports. Office: Portland Gen Electric 121 SW Salmon St Portland OR 97204-3713 Home: Apt 2504 1414 SW 3rd Ave Portland OR 97201-6625 Office Phone: 503-464-7193.

CHEVLI, RENATE NAREN, gynecologist, obstetrician; b. Hannover, Germany, 1937; d. Johann and Martha (Bruns) Schmidt; m. Naren A. Chevli, Sept. 18, 1965. MD, SUNY, Syracuse, 1971. Diplomate Am. Bd. Ob-Gyn. Intern St. Joseph's Hosp., Syracuse, 1971-72; resident in ob-gyn. SUNY Upstate Med. Ctr., Syracuse, 1972-76; pvt. practice Syracuse, 1976—. Fellow: ACOG; mem.: AMA, Onondaga County Med. Soc., N.Am. Menopause Soc., Med. Soc. NY State. Office: The Womens Place 4117 Medical Center Drive Fayetteville NY 13066 Office Phone: 315-329-4968.

CHEVRAY, PIERRE M., medical educator; s. René and Keiko Chevray; m. Keiko Yamaguchi, 1992; children: Kenji, Yukiko. BS, Mass. Inst. Tech., 1987; MD, PhD, Johns Hopkins U. Sch. Medicine, 1994. Cert. Am. Bd. Plastic Surgery, MD Tex., Md. Resident gen. surgery John Hopkins Hosp., 1994—98, resident plastic surgery, 1998—2000; asst. to assoc. prof. U. Tex. M.D. Anderson Cancer Ctr., Houston, 2000—; clin. asst. prof. Baylor Coll. Medicine, Houston, 2000—. Mem.: AMA, AAAS, Am. Soc. Reconstructive Microsurgery, Am. Soc. Plastic Surgeons. Office: U Tex MD Anderson Cancer Ctr 1515 Holcombe Blvd Unit 443 Houston TX 77030 Office Phone: 713-794-1247. Office Fax: 713-794-5492. E-mail: pchevray@mdanderson.org.

CHEVRAY, RENE, engineering educator; b. Paris, Feb. 6, 1937; came to the U.S., 1962; naturalized U.S. citizen, 1989; s. Robert and Marie-Louise (Fracher) C.; m. Keiko Uesawa, Aug. 9, 1964; children: Pierre-Yves Masaki, Veronique Mie. BS, U. Toulouse, France, 1962; Dipl. Ing. (French Govt. Highest scholar), Ecole Nationale Supérieure d'Electronique, d'Electrotechnique et d'Hydraulique de Toulouse, 1962; MS (Alliance Française of N.Y. fellow), U. Iowa, 1963, PhD, 1967; D.Sc., U. Claude Bernard, Lyon, France, 1978. Product and mfg. engr. Centrifugal Pumps Worthington, Paris, 1963-64; research assoc. Iowa Inst. Hydraulic Research, Iowa City, 1964-67; postdoctoral fellow, lectr. aeronautics Johns Hopkins U., 1967-69; asst. prof. SUNY, Stony Brook, 1969-72, assoc. prof., 1972-79, prof., 1979-82; prof. dept. mech. engring. Columbia U., N.Y.C., 1982-87, chmn. dept. mech. engring., 1987-90. Cons. physics of fluids and instrumentation; vis. prof. Japan Soc. for Promotion Sci., 1975; vis. prof., von. Humboldt fellow U. Karlsruhe, 1975-76 Author: Topics in Fluid Mechanics, 1993; contbr. articles to profl. jours.; rschr. in transport processes in fluids. Recipient Great Tchr. award Soc. Columbia Grads., 1993; Fulbright scholar, 1962-63; grantee NSF, 1970-73, 73-91, Dept. Energy, 1979-89, Office Naval Rsch., 1985-90, Whitaker Found., 1995—; Rsch. Found. SUNY Faculty Rsch. fellow, 1970-71. Mem. Internat. Assn. Hydraulic Rsch., Am. Phys. Soc., N.Y. Acad. Scis., Sigma Xi Home: 300 Riverside Dr Apt 10A New York NY 10025-5239 Office: Columbia U Mech Enging New York NY 10027

CHEW, E. BYRON, management consultant, educator; B.S. in Chem. Engring., Carnegie-Mellon U., 1966; PhD in Bus. Adminstrn., U. Ala., Tuscaloosa, 1971. Monaghan prof. mgmt. Birmingham So. Coll., Birmingham, Ala., 1981—; cons. Dr. E. Byron Chew and Associates, Birmingham, Ala., 1981—. Dean prof. divsn. of bus. Birmingham So. Coll., Ala., 1996—2002. Mem.: Acad. of Bus. Edn., Acad. of Mgmt. Office: Birmingham Southern Coll 900 Arkadelphia Rd Birmingham AL 35254 Office Phone: 205-226-4844.

CHEW, GEOFFREY FOUCAR, physicist; b. Washington, June 5, 1924; s. Arthur Percy and Pauline Lisette (Foucar) C.; m. Ruth Wright, June 10, 1945 (dec. Apr. 1971); children— Berkeley, Beverly; m. Denyse Odette Mettel, Dec. 30, 1971; children— Pierre-Yves, Jean-Francois, Pauline BS in Physics, George Washington U., 1944; PhD in Physics, U. Chgo., 1948. Research physicist Los Alamos Sci. Lab., N.Mex., 1944-46; research physicist Lawrence Berkeley Lab., Calif., 1948-49; asst. prof. physics U. Calif., Berkeley, 1949-50; asst. prof., assoc. prof. physics U. Ill., Urbana, 1950-56; prof. physics U. Calif., Berkeley, 1957—, chmn. dept. physics, 1974-78, Miller prof., 1981-82, dean physical scis., 1986-92. Group leader theoretical physics Lawrence Berkeley Lab., Calif., 1964-83; vis. prof. Princeton U., N.J., 1970-71; sci. assoc. CERN, Geneva, 1978-79; vis. prof. U. Paris, 1983. Author: S-Matrix Theory of Strong Interactions, 1961; Analytic S Matrix, 1966; contbr. articles to profl. jours. Chmn. passport com. Fedn. Am. Scientists, Washington, 1951-56 Recipient E.O. Lawrence award AEC, 1969, Disting. Alumni award George Washington U., 1974, Berkeley citation U. Calif., 1991; Churchill Coll. overseas fellow, 1962 Fellow Am. Phys. Soc. (Hughes prize 1962); mem. Nat. Acad. Scis., Am. Acad. Arts and Scis. Home: 10 Maybeck Twin Dr Berkeley CA 94708-2037 Business E-Mail: gfchew@lbl.gov.

CHEW, KEITH ELVIN, health facility administrator; b. Webb City, Mo., Jan. 1, 1957; s. David Elvin and Melinda Lou (Barker) C. BS in Physiology with distinction, U. Ill., 1979, MS in Biol. Sci., 1981, postgrad., 1981-83; MA in Health Svc. Adminstrn., Sangamon State U., Springfield, Ill., 1986. Instr. Sangamon State U., 1985-86; program dir. So. Ill. U. Sch. Medicine, Springfield, 1984-86; dir. bus. and clin. affairs Tex. Tech Health Sci. Ctr., Lubbock, 1986-88; cons. Profl. Cons. Svcs., Long Grove, Ill., 1988-90; adminstr. Primary Care Family Ctr., Libertyville, Ill., 1988-90; instr. Coll. St. Francis, Joliet, Ill., 1991; adminstr. North Suburban Clinic, Skokie, Ill., 1990-91; cons. KEC Healthcare Mgmt. Cons., Forest Lake, Ill., 1991-92; dir. practice mgmt. Contemporary Mgmt. Assocs., Inc., Portsmouth, N.H., 1992-95; exec. dir. Network, Health Mgmt. Ltd. Partnership-Drs. Hosp., Springfield, 1995-96, v.p., 1996-97; CEO Imaging Radiologists, MSO, Inc., Springfield and Chgo, 1998-99, Imaging Radiologists, LLC, Springfield and Chgo., 2000—02; prin. Vinculum Cons., LLC, 1998—. Author: reports and articles. Mem. Am. Coll. Med. Group Adminstrs. (cert. med. practice exec. 1994), Med. Group Mgmt. Assn., Healthcare Fin. Mgmt. Assn., Chgo. Health Exec. Forum. Avocations: music (aural and vocal), golf, fishing, aviation, gardening. Home: 18 Hawks Nest Chatham IL 62629-2016 Office Phone: 217-483-6467. E-mail: kechew@springnet1.com, kchew@vinculumconsulting.com.

CHEWNING, THOMAS N., energy executive; B in History, U. N.C., 1967; MBA, U. Pa., 1969. With Dominion Resources, Inc., Richmond, Va., 1987—, exec. v.p., 1996—, pres., CEO Dominion Energy subs. Address: PO Box 26532 Richmond VA 23261-6532 Office: 120 Tredegar St Richmond VA 23219-4306

CHEY, WILLIAM YOON, physician; b. Ki Jang, Korea, Jan. 21, 1930; s. Kee Bok and Myungkwon (Lee) C.; m. Fan K. Tang, May 21, 1959; children: William D., Donna C., Richard D., Laura C. MD, Seoul (Korea) Nat. U., 1953; MSc, U. Pa., 1962, DSc, 1966. Intern N.Y.C. Hosp., 1954-55, resident, 1955-56; resident in pathology Mount Sinai Hosp., N.Y.C., 1956-57; fellow in hepatology Seton Hall Med Coll., Jersey City, 1957-58; practice medicine specializing in gastroenterology Phila., 1967-71; attending physician Temple U. Med Center, Phila., 1963—; rsch. fellow in gastroenterology Samuel S. Fels Rsch. Inst., 1959-60; rsch. assoc. Samuel S. Fells Rsch. Inst., 1961, instr. medicine, 1961, assoc., 1963, asst. prof., 1965-68, assoc. prof., 1968-71; prof. medicine U. Rochester, N.Y., 1971-77, clin. prof., 1977-88, prof. medicine, 1988—; sr. attending physician, founding dir. Isaac Gordon Ctr. for Digestive Diseases and Nutrition, The Genesee Hosp., 1971-91; dir. divsn. gastroenterology and hepatology U. Rochester Sch. Medicine and Dentistry, 1992-2000; physician Strong Meml. Hosp., Rochester, 1992-2000; founding dir. William B. and Sheila Konar Ctr. for Digestive Liver Disease, Rochester, 1995—. Dir. Rochester Inst. Digestive Diseases and Scis., NY, 2000—; cons. gastroenterologist Canadaigua VA Hosp., Canadagiua, 1977—; hon. prof. Cath. U. Med. Coll., Seoul, Republic of Korea, 1983—; clin. prof. medicine Yunsei U. Sch. Medicine, 1984—; vis. prof. Peking Union Med. Coll., Chinese Acad. Med. Scis., Beijing, 1985—, Hallym U. Coll. Medicine, Choonchun, Republic of Korea, 1986—, Shanghai Med. U., 1987, Korea U. Coll. Medicine, Seoul, 1991—; mem. surgery and bioengring. study sect. Nat. Inst. Diaetes, Digestive and Kidney Diseases, NIH, Bethesda, Md., 1982—86. Contbr. articles to profl. and sci. jours and textbooks; mem. editorial bd. The Pancreas, Am. Jour. Physiology. Fellow Am. Coll. Gastroent.; mem. AAAS, Am. Fedn. Clin. Rsch., Am. Gastroent. Assn., Am. Physiol. Soc., Am. Assn. Study Liver Disease, Am. Pancreatic Assn. (pres. 1999-2000), Internat. Assn. Pancreatology, Am. Motility Soc., Am. Soc. Gastrointestinal Endoscopy, Am. Soc. Acupuncture, Am. Coll. Acupuncture, Sigma Xi. Home: 133 Crescent Hill Rd Pittsford NY 14534-2406 Office: 222 Alexander St Ste 3100 Rochester NY 14607

CHI, DENNIS S., oncologist, researcher; b. N.Y.C., May 4, 1964; s. Chul Young and Kyu Soo (Kim) C.; m. Hae-Young Lee, Mar. 14, 1992; children: Jessica, Stephanie, Andrew. BA magna cum laude, Columbia Coll., N.Y.C., 1986; MD, NYU, 1990. Diplomate Am. Bd. Ob-Gyn., Am. Bd. Gynecol. Oncology. Resident in ob-gyn. NYU Sch. Med., N.Y.C., 1990-94; fellow in gynecol. oncology Meml. Sloan Kettering Cancer Ctr., N.Y.C., 1994-97, clin. asst. surgeon gynecol. svc., 1997—, dir. med. student and resident edn., 1997—2002, dir. fellowship tng., 2002—. Lectr., presenter in field. Co-author: (with R.M. Lanciano and A. Kudelka) Cancer Management: A Multidisciplinary Approach, 3rd edit., 1999, 4th edit., 2000; (with W.J. Hoskins) Methods in Molecular Medicine: Ovarian Cancer, 2000; (with M. Hensley and K. Alektiar) The MD Anderson/Memorial Sloan-Kettering Handbook of Gynecologic Oncology, 2000; (with D.G. Gallup) Principles and Practice of Gynecologic Oncology, 3rd edit., 2000; contbr. articles to profl. jours. Recipient Trainee Investigator award Am. Fedn. for Clin. Rsch., 1994, Berlex Oncology Found. award, 1997, Stanley Zinberg Tchg. award NYU Downtown Med. Ctr., 2000. Fellow ACOG, Am. Cancer Soc.; mem. AMA, Soc. Surg. Oncology, Korean Am. Med. Assn., Soc. Gynecol. Oncologists, Am. Soc. Clin. Oncology, Assn. Profs. Gynecology and Obstet., Phi Beta Kappa. Office: Meml Sloan Kettering Cancer Ctr 1275 York Ave New York NY 10021 Home: 79 Wainwright Ave Closter NJ 07624-2919

CHI, JACOB, music educator; b. Qingdao, China, Dec. 9, 1952; arrived in U.S., 1981; s. Frank Chi and Linda Li; m. Lin Chang, July 11, 1987; children: Julius, Juliet. BA in Violin, Siena Heights U., 1985; MusM in Violin, U. Mich., 1987; DMA in Conducting, Mich. State U., 1996. Concert master Qingdao (China) Beijing Opera, 1970—74, condr., 1974—81; artist-in-residence U. So. Colo., Pueblo, 1991—93, assoc. prof. music, 1997—; asst. prof. music Miami U., Oxford, Ohio, 1993—97. Music dir. Pueblo Symphony, 1991—93, 1997—, Miami U. Symphony, Oxford, 1993—97. Composer: (Operas) Apricots Field, 1975. Home: 811 W Golfwood Dr Pueblo CO 81007 Office: Univ So Colo 2200 Bonforte Blvd Pueblo CO 81001

CHI, KEON SOO, editor, educator, researcher; b. Taegu, Korea, Nov. 26, 1936; came to U.S., 1965; s. Chong-Yun Chi and Pun-Sun Kim; m. Insoon Chi; children: Ronald, John. BA, Yonsei U., 1959; MA, Claremont (Calif.) U., 1968, PhD, 1970. Prof. polit. sci. Georgetown (Ky.) Coll., 1970—; sr. fellow Coun. of State Govts., Lexington, 1981—, academic dean, 1999—2001, editor jour. of state govt., 2000—; editor-in-chief The book of the State, 2001—. Contbr. chpts. to books and articles to profl. jours. Recipient Ky. Prof. of Yr. Carnegie Found., 1999; recipient James E. Webb award Am. Soc. for Pub. Adminstrn., 1996. Democrat. Presbyterian. Avocations: reading, travel, painting. Home: 3641 Gloucester Dr Lexington KY 40510 Office: Coun State Govts PO Box 11910 Lexington KY 40578

CHI, LOIS WANG, retired biology educator, research scientist; b. Fuchow, China, May 12, 1921; came to U.S., 1941; d. Leland and Ada (Pang) Wang; m. Henry Chi; children: Lanie, David, Joycelyn. BS, Wheaton Coll., 1945; MS, U. So. Calif., 1947, PhD, 1954. Rsch. fellow Loma Linda (Calif.) U., 1954-57; instr. to assoc. prof. biology Immaculate Heart Coll., L.A., 1957-66; assoc. prof. to prof. biology Calif. State U., Dominguez Hills, 1966-91, rsch. dir., 1979-86, prof. emeritus. Mem. NIH Nat. Adv. Allergy and Infectious Disease Coun., 1973-74; dir. Minority Biomed. Rsch. Program Calif. State U., Dominguez Hills, 1979-86, Minority Honor Program, 1982-86. Contbr. more than 30 articles to profl. jours. Co-founder, pres. and v.p. Chinese Am. Faculty Assocs. So. Calif., Chinese Am. Engrs. and Scientists Assocs. So. Calif. Home: 2839 El Oeste Hermosa Beach CA 90254-2234

CHIA, DAVID THIEN-SHING, internist, gastroenterologist; b. Sandakan, Malaysia, Mar. 24, 1942; came to U.S., 1966; s. Kiam Vun Chia and Su Lan Lo; m. Gloria Chia; children: Timothy Than-Han, Catherine Loo Ling. MD, Nat. Def. Med. Ctr., Taipei, Taiwan, 1996. Diplomate Am. Bd. Internal Medicine, Am. Bd. Gastroenterology. Rotating intern Resurrection Hosp., Chgo., 1966-67; resident in internal medicine and gastroenterology Bklyn. VA Hosp. and Downstate Med. Ctr., 1967-71; chief divsn. gastroenterology Phelps Meml. Hosp., Sleepy Hollow, N.Y., 1989-99; pvt. practice Sleepy Hollow, N.Y. Asst. prof. medicine N.Y. Med. Coll., N.Y.C., 1975. Fellow ACP, Am. Coll. Gastroenterology. Lutheran. Avocations: asian antiques, mountain bicycling. Office: 777 N Broadway Ste 305 Sleepy Hollow NY 10591-1040

CHIA, NING, history educator; b. Beijing, Dec. 14, 1955; d. Guangshi Jia and Fangying Sheng; m. Ko-Hsing Huang, June 18, 1983; children: Shenstone Chia Huang, Bellara Ann Sakda Huang. BA in World History, Beijing Normal U., 1981; grad. study, Ctrl. U. Nationalities, 1982—83; MA in U.S History, Ill. State U., 1985; PhD in Chinese History, Johns Hopkins U., 1991. From asst. prof. to assoc. prof. Ctrl. Coll., Pella, Iowa, 1991—2004, prof., 2004—. Bd. dirs. Chinese Hist., Inc., 1997—98; adminstrv. dir. Fulbright-Hays Pearl River Delta Faculty Devel. Summer Program in China, ASIAN-etwork and Hong Kong Am. Ctr., 2005—. Contbr. articles to journ., chapters to books. Bd. dirs. Pella Pub. Libr., 2002—06; apptd. mem. Commn. on Status of Iowans of Asian and Pacific Islander Heritage, Dept. Human Rights, 2004—. Fellow For Adv. Study in Chiina, Com. Scholarly Comm. with China, 1994—95. Mem.: Assn. Asian Studies, Am. Hist. Soc., Asianetwork (bd. dirs. 2003—06, Freeman Student-Faculty Fellowship Grant 2002). Avocations: fishing, photography, history book collecting, Chinese and Manchu calligraphy, classical music. Home: 209 Hemlock Dr Pella IA 50219 Office: Ctrl Coll 812 Univ St Pella IA 50219 Office Phone: 641-628-5323. Business E-Mail: chian@central.edu.

CHIAMES, CHRISTOPHER L., air transportation executive; BA in Journalism, Calif. State U., Fresno; MA in Journalism, U. Md.; MPA, Harvard U. Press sec. Former House Majority Whip Tony Coelho; mng. dir. pub. rels. Am. Airlines, 1996—2001; mng. dir. transp. and tousim pub. affairs practice Burson-Marsteller, 2001—02; sr. v.p. corp. affairs US Airways, Inc., Arlington, Va., 2002—. Office: US Airways 2345 Crystal Dr Arlington VA 22227

CHIANG, ALBERT CHINFA, polymer chemist; b. Pai-ho, Tainan, Taiwan, Jan. 3, 1946; came to U.S., 1973; s. Long and Ping (Su) C.; m. Geraldine Chin, June 4, 1978; 1 child, Scott Jinlong. BS, Nat. Chung-Hsing U., Taichung, Taiwan, 1970; MS, Georgetown U., 1977; PhD, Am. U., 1980. Teaching asst. Georgetown U., Washington, 1974-77, Am. U., Washington, 1977-80; assoc. chemist Pitney Bowes, Stamford, Conn., 1980-81, chemist, 1982-83, staff chemist, 1984-86, sr. chemist, 1987-89, tech. advisor, 1989-92; v.p. R&D Mearthane Products, Cranston, RI, 1992—. Mem. Chinese Oversea Scholar, Taipei, Taiwan, 1980—. Mem. adv. bd. Am. Security Coun., Washington, 1984. Dissertation fellow Am. U., 1979. Mem. Am. Chem. Soc. (rubber divsn. 1987—), Soc. Plastics Engring. (sr.), Photography of Sci. and Engring. Achievements include 23 patents; development of processes for preparation of polypheynlacetylene and desulfurization of coal; invention of materials for electrophotographic toners, high solid content emulsion formation, flourescent thermal transfer ribbon formation, new dual-step thermal transfer printing; research in rubber, photopolymers, thermal printing, silicone casting, polyurethane manufacturing; conducting polymers including conductive urethane, conductive silicone, acrylate, highly conjugated rubber and plastics, and high temperature superconducting material formation; non-impact printing technology and printing materials for postage meter and other mailing system machines; development and production of laser printer rollers including charge roller, developer roller, toner pick-up roller, paper transport roller; development of in-line skate and hockey wheel and live action skate wheel having a breaking mechanism, multiple-layer skate wheel and various track hockey wheel; toner for office machine application and medical grade urethane and silicone for medical applications; thermostat urethanes for pneumatic nail bumper application. Home: 10 Fox Hollow Ledyard CT 06339 Office Phone: 401-946-4400 3038. Business E-Mail: achiang@mearthane.com. E-mail: agschiang@aol.com.

CHIANG, CHIA-CHU, computer scientist, educator; b. Nan-Tou, Taiwan, Apr. 11, 1959; s. Yi-Ting Chiang and Chin-Nun Liao; m. Jung-Yung Wang; children: Robert, Michael, Jennifer. BBA, Soochow U., Taipei, Taiwan, 1981; MS, Ea. Mich. U., 1988; PhD, Ariz. State U., 1995. Software engr. ASG Co. (formerly Viasoft), Phoenix, 1996—2001; asst. prof. U. Ark., Little Rock, 2001—. Spkr. in field. Contbr. articles to profl. jours. 2d lt. Taiwanese Army, 1981—83, Taiwan. Recipient Outrageous Contbr., Viasoft Co., 1998. Mem.: ACM, IEEE, Upsilon Pi Epsilon, Tau Beta Pi, Phi Kappa Phi. Avocations: jogging, swimming, reading, travel. Office: University of Arkansas at Little Rock 2801 South University Ave Little Rock AR 72204-1099 Office Phone: 501-569-8142. Business E-Mail: cxchiang@ualr.edu.

CHIANG, JOHN YOUNG LING, biochemistry educator, researcher; b. Hangchew, CheKiang, China, July 29, 1947; came to U.S., 1970, naturalized, 1980; s. Ming-ming and Ya-Jung (Huang) C.; m. Lisa H. Kang, Aug. 3, 1973; children— Eric, David. B.S., Chung-Hsing U., Taichung, Taiwan, 1969; M.S., SUNY-Albany, 1973, Ph.D., 1976. Postdoctoral scholar U. Mich. Med. Sch., Ann Arbor, 1976-78; asst. prof. biochemistry and molecular pathology Northeastern Ohio U. Coll. Medicine, Rootstown, 1978-83, assoc. prof., 1983-88, prof., 1988—. Contbr. articles to profl. jours. NIH fellow, 1977-78; Pharm. Mfrs. Assn. Found. grantee, 1982-83; Am. Heart Assn. grantee, 1980-82; NIH grantee, 1983— . Mem. AAAS, Am. Soc. Biol. Chemists. Subspecialty: Biochemistry (medicine), Molecular biology. Current work: Biochemical research in studying the induction and regulation of enzymes involved in cholesterol and bile acid metabolism and liver detoxication enzymes. Home: 3020 Fox Burrow Dr Cuyahoga Falls OH 44224-4778 Office: Northeastern Ohio University College of Medicine 4209 State Route 44 Rootstown OH 44272

CHIANG, MICHAEL FRED, physician; b. Pitts., Aug. 6, 1970; BS, Stanford U., 1991; MD, Harvard U., 1996. Resident in ophthalmology Johns Hopkins Hosp., 1997—2000, fellow pediat. ophthalmology, 2000—01; asst. prof., ophthalmology and biomedical informatics Columbia U., N.Y.C., 2003—. Office Phone: 212-305-9535.

CHIANG, ROGER J., political organization worker; BA in Polit. Sci., U. Calif., Santa Barbara; student, Johns Hopkins U. With office of fed. govt. relations U. Calif.; staff mem. Office of Congressman Anthony C. Beilenson; rsch. asst. Wharton Sch., U. Pa.; various positions including dir. scheduling and advance & dir., ops. US Dept. of Housing and Urban Develop., repr. to White House Initiative on Asian Am. and Pacific Islanders, adv. to sec., 2000—01; dir., Asian Pacific Islander Am. outreach office Dem. Nat. Com., 2001—. Staff mem. Clinton/Gore 1996 campaign, Gore/Lieberman 2000 campaign. Adv. mem. Nat. Ctr. for Missing and Exploited Children; bd. mem. Indian Am. Leadership Incubator; steering com. mem. Asian Pacific Am. Inst., DC Cares. Named a Rising Asian Am. in Govt., Asian Am. Govt. Exec. Network; recipient President's Citation for Meritorious Svc. award, Secretary's award for excellence, US Dept. of Housing and Urban Develop., Outstanding Performance award. Office: Dem Nat Com Asian Pacific Islander Am Outreach 430 S Capitol St SE Washington DC 20003*

CHIANG, TZE I., economist, researcher, economist, consultant; b. Fuzhou, Fujian, China, Feb. 4, 1922; arrived in U.S., 1953; s. Swe-hwa and Wan-lun Chiang; m. Wei-chih Chou Chiang, Feb. 4, 1952 (dec. 1999); children: Chi, Ling, Ding. BA in Agrl. Econs., Fujian Christin U., Fuzhou, 1946; MS in Agrl. Econs., Okla. State U., 1955; PhD in Agrl. Econs., U. Fla., 1958. Tchr. Sin-Ding H.S., Fuzhou, 1946—47; asst. to gen. mgr. China Textile Industries, Inc., Shanghai, 1947—53; grad. asst. Okla. State U., Stillwater, 1954—55; rsch. asst. U. Fla., Gainesville, 1955—58; prin. rsch. scientist Ga. Inst. Tech., Atlanta, 1958—86. Advisor Qingdao (China) Spl. Econ. Zone, China, 1986; vis. scholar to scholar Ga. Inst. Tech., Atlanta, 1986; cons. tech. transfer China Tech., Atlanta, 1986—87. Contbr. articles to profl. jours. Mem.: Gamma Sigma Delta. Achievements include research in economic feasibility; market analysis; economic and industrial development; international trade. Avocations: reading, music, gardening. Home: 3165 Frontenac Ct NE Atlanta GA 30319

CHIANG, WEN, biophysicist, researcher; d. Lung and Cheng-Ping (Kuo) Chiang. BS, Tamkang U., 1989; MS, U. Del., 1992; PhD, U. Wis., Madison, 1999. Post doctoral rsch. assoc. Mich. State U., East Lansing, 1999—2003, rsch. asst. prof., 2003—. Ad hoc reviewer nat. rsch. initiative competitive grants program USDA, Washington, 2002. Grantee, Animal Initiative Industry Coalition, Mich. State U., 2002, USDA-NRICGP, 2005. Mem.: Am. Soc. Animal Sci., IFT, Biophysical Soc. Avocations: jogging, dance. Office Phone: 517-355-8474 198.

CHIANG, WEN-LI, hydrologist; b. Choulan, Republic of China, Apr. 14, 1946; came to U.S., 1972; naturalized, 1985; s. Pen-Hsiu and Yanagi (Shizuko) C.; m. Hsiu-lan Wang, Dec. 26, 1974; children: Dean Tsung, Charles. BS, Nat. Taiwan U., Taipei, Republic of China, 1969; MS, Nat. Cen. U., Chungli, Republic of China, 1972, U. Kans., Lawrence, 1977; PhD, U. So. Calif., 1980. Registered civil engr., Calif. Prin. engr. Tetra Tech Inc., Pasadena, Calif., 1979-87; prin. systems engr. undersea systems div. Honeywell Inc., Pasadena, 1987-88; prin. engr. Engring. Methods & Applications, Arcadia, Calif., 1988-90; sr. engr. Flow Sci., Inc., Pasadena, Calif., 1991—. Cons. Environment and Ocean Tech., Arcadia, Calif., 1990-91. Contbr. numerous articles to profl. jours. Recipient Sea grant NOAAt, 1976-79; NSF grantee, 1982-83. Mem. ASCE, Nat. Cen. Univ. Alumni Assn. So. Calif. (pres. 1986, chmn. bd. dirs. 1990), Sigma Xi, Tau Beta Pi. Avocations: reading, dance. Home: 1139 Calle Malaga Duarte CA 91010-2250 Office: Flow Sci Inc 723 E Green St Pasadena CA 91101-2111 Office Phone: 626-304-1134. Personal E-mail: chiangwenli@yahoo.com. Business E-Mail: wchiang@flowscience.com.

CHIANG, YUNG FRANK, law educator; b. Taichung, Taiwan, Jan. 2, 1936; came to U.S., 1961; s. Ruey-ting and Yueh-yin (Ho) C.; m. Quay-yin Lin, Nov. 1, 1969; children: Amy P., David H. LLB, Nat. Taiwan U., 1958; LLM, Northwestern U., 1962; JD, U. Chgo., 1965. Bar: Taiwan 1960, N.Y. 1974. Assoc. Yen & Lai Law Office, Taipei, Taiwan, 1960-61; editor The Lawyers Co-op Pub. Co., Rochester, N.Y., 1965; rsch. assoc. Harvard Law Sch., Cambridge, Mass., 1965-67; asst. prof. U. Ga. Sch. Law, Athens, 1967-72; assoc. prof. Fordham U. Sch. Law, N.Y.C., 1972-76, prof., 1976—. Vis. prof. Chuo U., Tokyo, 2005; bd. dirs. Taiwan Ctr., N.Y.C.; legal cons., vice-chmn. Asia Bank, N.A., Flushing, N.Y., 1983-88, also bd. dirs.; leader N.Y. judge and lawyers del. to China and Hong Kong, People to People Internat., 1994; organizer, moderator 5 Russian delegations to U.S., People to People Amb. Program, 1994-95; pres. Fordham U. Law Faculty Union, 2000—. Contbr. articles to profl. jours. Organizer, bd. dirs. The Taiwan Mcht. Assn. N.Y., Flushing, 1976-96, pres., 1980-84; pres. N.Y. chpt. Formosan Assn. for Pub. Affairs, Washington, 1991-92. Mem. N.Y. State Bar Assn., N.Am. Taiwanese Profs. Assn. (bd. dirs. 1994-2000, v.p. 1997-98, pres. 1998-99), Nat. Assn. of Securities Dealers (arbitrator 1976-98), Order of Coif. Avocations: reading, skiing, archery, swimming. Office: Fordham U Sch Law 140 W 62nd St New York NY 10023-7407 Office Phone: 212-636-6835. Business E-Mail: fchiang@law.fordham.edu.

CHIAO, LEROY, astronaut; b. Milw., Wis., Aug. 28, 1960; s. Tsu Tao and Cherry (Chu) Chiao; m. Karen Chiao, 2003. BS in Chemical Engring., U. Calif., Berkeley, 1983; MS, U. Calif., Santa Barbara, 1985, PhD in Chemical Engring., 1987. Postdoctoral researcher U. Calif., Santa Barbara, 1987; materials engr. Hexcel Corp., Dublin, Calif., 1987-89, Lawrence Livermore (Calif.) Nat. Lab., 1989-90; astronaut NASA, Houston, 1990—. Keynote commencement spkr. Dept. Engring., U. Calif., Berkeley, 1996, Santa Barbara, 96; lectr. Beijing Inst. Aeronautical Materials, 1988, Changsha Inst. Tech., 5th Dept., Peoples Republic of China, 1988; mission specialist STS-65, 1994, STS-72, 1996, STS-92, 2000. Contbr. Internat. Encyclopedia Composite Materials, 1989. Recipient NASA Space Flight medal, 1994, 1996, 2000, NASA Exceptional Svc. award, 1996, 2000, NASA Individual Achievement award, 2001, 2002, 2003, 2004, NASA Group Achievement award, 1995, 1997, NASA Going the Extra Mile award, 2004, Komarov Diploma, Fedn. Aeronautique Internationale, 1996, De La Vaulx medal, 1994, Korolev Diploma, 2002, Excellence award in Sci. and Tech., US Pan Asian Am. C. of C., 2003, 100 Most Influential Asian Americans in the 1990's award, A-Magazine, 2000. Mem. ASTM, AIAA, Soc. Advancement Material and Process Engring. Broke a nearly 30 year tradition of having at least one crewman with previous experience in piloting the capsule. Comdr. and NASA Sci. Officer of Expedition-10 headed for the International Space Station with Russian-US crew (with Salizhan Sharipov and Yuri Shargin) in the Soyuz TMA-5 on October, 2004, landed in April, 2005 (with Salizhan Sharipov and Roberto Vittori). First Asian-Am. to perform a spacewalk. First Am. to vote in presidential election while in space, 2004. Office: NASA-JSC 2101 NASA Rd 1 Houston TX 77058-3691*

CHIAPPETTA, CARRIE LYNN, elementary school educator, consultant; b. Greenwich, Conn., Apr. 9, 1968; d. Donald Dennis Chiappetta Sr. and Linda Haas Chiappetta. BA Internat. Studies, U. Dayton, 1990; MA in Slavic and East European Studies, U. Conn., 1994; MS in Edn., U. Bridgeport, Conn., 1996. Edn., Tchg. Conn., 1996. Mid. sch. math tchr. Scofield Magnet Mid. Sch., Stamford, Conn., 1996—; tchr. Stamford Bd. Edn., Conn., 1996—. Presenter U. Vt., Vt., 1997; dist. rep. Learn the Connected Math Program, Mich., 2000; dist. facilitator Stamford Bd. of Edn., 2000; math dept. liasion Scofield Magnet Mid. Sch., 2003—; presenter New Eng. League of Mid. Schs., Providence, 2003, Assn. of Tchrs. of Math. in Conn., Cromwell, Conn., 2003; participant 4th US-Russia Joint Conf. of Math. Edn., St. Petersburg, Russia, 2003; on-line mentor Mighty Mentor, 2004—; participant 10th Internat. Congress on Math. Edn. (ICME-10), Copenhagen, 2004, Nat. Coun. Tchrs. Math Nat. Conf., 2004—05, 4th Mediterranean Conf. on Math. Edn., Palmermo, Italy, 2005. Assoc. mem. Nat. Acads. Tchr. Adv. Com., 2004—05; primary leader People to People Student Amb., Greenwich/Stamford/New Haven, Conn., 2001—03; tchr. rep. Mid. Sch. Conn. Mastery Test Com., Conn., 2003—05, Stamford Dist. Mid. Sch. Math Action Com., 2003—05; state scorer for presdl. awardees PAEMST State Scoring Com., Conn., 2002; dist. tchr. rep. Stamford Dist. Mid. Sch. Math Action Com., 2003—05; sch. rep. Mid. Sch. Conn. Mastery Test Com., Stamford, Conn., 2003—05; state scorer for presdl. awardees PAEMST State Scoring Com., Conn., 2002—02. Recipient Presdl. award for Secondary Math., Washington, DC, 2001, Celebration of Excellence Award Recipient, CT State Dept of Edn., 2002, Conn. Edn. Assn. "Salutes" award, Conn. Edn. Assn., 2002, Stamford Edn. Assn. award, Stamford Edn. Assn., 2002; grantee Toyota TIME award, Toyota Motor Corp., 2004—06; People's Bank Mini grant, People's Bank, Stamford, Conn., 1998, 2000, 2001, 2002, 2003, 2004, Conn. Acad. Math, Sci. Tech. fellow. Fellow: Coun. of Presdl. Awardees in Math.; mem.: NEA, ASCD, Conn. Edn. Assn., Triangle Coalition, Assn. Tchrs. Math. in New Eng., Assn. Tchrs. Math. in Conn., Nat. Coun. Tchrs. Math., Stamford Edn. Assn. Independent. Avocation: travel. Home: 84 Midland Ave Stamford CT 06906 Office: Scofield Magnet Mid Sch 641 Scofieldtown Rd Stamford CT 06903 Office Phone: 203-977-2750. Office Fax: 203-977-2766. Personal E-mail: carrichip@aol.com.

CHIAPPONE, MARK, mathematics professor, researcher, financial planner; b. Norristown, Pa., May 3, 1970; s. Donald Albert Chiappone and Phylis Francis; m. Lina Ivette Lopez, Jan. 14, 1995; 1 child, Dominic Conrad. BS in Biology and Marine sci., U. Miami, 1991; MS in Marine Biology, Nova Southwestern U., 2000. Lic. life and health ins. agt. Fla.; mortgage broker Fla. Rsch. asst. U. Miami, Coral Gables, Fla., 1992—93; marine biologist Nature Conservancy, Coral Gables, 1993—99; rsch. scientist U. NC, Key Largo, Fla., 1999—; adj. faculty mem. in math. Miami Dade Coll., Homestead, Fla., 2000—; fin. planner Primerica Fin. Svcs., Cooper City, Fla., 2001—. Editor: Florida Key Site Characterization, 1996, Parque Nacional dal Este, 2000; contbr. articles to sci. jours. Vol. Rec. for Blind and Dislexic, Miami, 1997—99, Cmty. Blood Ctr., Miami, 2001—. Mem.: Fin. Planning Assn., Internat. Soc. Reef Studies. Democrat. Home: 10245 SW 154th Cir Ct # 108 Miami FL 33196 Office: U NC-Wilmington 515 Caribbean Dr Key Largo FL 33037 Office Phone: 305-453-9719. Office Fax: 305-453-9719. E-mail: mchiappone@adelphia.net.

CHIARA, MARGARET M., prosecutor, lawyer; BA, Fordham U.; MA Pace U.; JD, Rutgers U. Assoc. French and Lawrence, Cassopolis, Mich., 1979—82; prosecuting atty. Cass County Prosecutor's Office, 1982—96; adminstr. Trial Ct. Assessment Commn., 1997—98; policy and planning dir. Office of Chief Justice of Mich. Supreme Ct., 1999—2001; U.S. atty. (we. dist.) Mich. U.S. Dept. Justice, 2001—. Office: PO Box 208 Grand Rapids MI 49501 Office Phone: 616-456-2404.

CHIARAMIDA, SALVATORE, cardiologist, educator, health facility administrator; b. N.Y.C., Sept. 15, 1948; s. Joseph and Dina (DiBlasi) C.; m. Susan Postula, June 14, 1970; children: Todd, Tory. BS in Chemistry, Fordham Coll., 1970; MD, N.Y. Med. Coll., 1974. Diplomate Am. Bd. Internal Medicine, Am. Bd. Cardiovasc. Diseases. Intern North Shore U. Meml. Hosp., 1974-75, asst. resident in internal medicine, 1975-76, sr. resident in internal medicine, 1976-77, fellow in cardiology, 1977-79; fellow in medicine Cornell U. Med. Coll., 1975-77; chief cardiology Raritan Bay Med. Ctr., 1979-89, Our Lady of Mercy Med. Ctr., Bronx, NY, 1989—2000, assoc. dir. medicine, 1999—2000, COO, 1999, exec. v.p. clin. ops., 1999; dir. coronary care unit Med. Univ. S.C., Charleston, 2000—, prof. medicine, 2000—. Instr. cardiology North Shore U. Hosp., 1977-79; clin. instr. medicine U. Medicine and Dentistry N.J., 1981-83, clin. asst. prof., 1983; clin. assoc. prof. N.Y. Med. Coll., 1990—99, prof. clin. medicine, 1999-2002; cons. Woodbridge (N.J.) Devel. Ctr., 1989; v.p., trustee Mercy Care PHO, 1994-2000; bd. dirs. Cath. Health Care Network, Cath. Health Care Network Physicians Orgn., Servitas IPA, Cath. Healthcare Resources LLC, Benefice Health LLC, Cath. Health Care Sys.; prof. medicine Med. U. S.C., 2000—, dir. CCU, 2001—. Contbr. articles to profl. jours. Fellow: ACP, Am. Coll. Cardiology. Office: Med Univ SC Heart Ctr Divsn Cardiology 135 Rutledge Ave Ste 1201 PO Box 250592 Charleston SC 29464 Office Phone: 843-792-4457. Business E-Mail: chiara@musc.edu.

CHIARCHIARO, FRANK JOHN, lawyer; b. Sept. 11, 1945; s. Joseph Russell and Mary Catherine (Salmieri) C.; m. Judith Ann Penna, July 5, 1970; 1 child, Peter. BEE, Manhattan Coll., 1967; MSEE, NYU, 1970; JD, Bklyn. Law Sch., 1976. Bar: N.Y. 1977, U.S. Dist. Ct. (ea. and so. dists.) N.Y. 1977, U.S. Ct. Appeals (11th cir.) 1985, U.S. Ct. Appeals (4th cir.) 1989, U.S. Ct. Appeals (5th cir.) 1991, U.S. Supreme Ct. 1987. Engr. USN, Bklyn., 1968-72, USCG, N.Y.C., 1972-77; ptnr. Mendes & Mount, LLP., N.Y.C., 1977—. Contbr. articles to profl. jours. Decorated knight comdr. with star Order of Holy Sepulchre of Jerusalem. Mem. N.Y. State Bar Assn., Def. Rsch. Inst. Roman Catholic. Office: Mendes & Mount 750 7th Ave New York NY 10019-6834 Office Phone: 212-261-8278. Personal E-mail: frank.chiarchiaro@mendes.com.

CHIARELLA, DONALD JOSEPH GRAY, information systems specialist, educator; b. Kilmarnock, Scotland, June 21, 1956; s. Donald Joseph and Margaret Gray Chiarella; m. Misae Fox, Dec. 24, 1979; children: Donald H., Mia M., David A., Michaela F. BA in Urban Planning/Info. Sys. Mgmt., U. Md., 1979; MS in Tech. Mgmt., Am. U., 1988; PhD in MIS, Kennedy-Western, 2001. Cert. pub. adminstr. George Wash. U., 1996; urban planner 2004, data resources mgr. 2004. Computer specialist Navy Med., Bethesda, Md., 1977-86; prof. in computer mgmt. info. sys. U. Md. U. Coll., College Park, 1986—99; project leader Orkand Corp., Silver Spring, Md., 1988-89, R.S. Carsons, Bethesda, Md., 1989-90, Mneumonic Sys., 1990; govt. wide computer regulations analyst Gen. Svcs. Adminstrn., Washington, 1990-97; proj. leader Smartech, 1997; supervisory database adminstr. Md. State Govt., Hanover, 1997—; prof. CSI Anne Arundel CC, 2003—. V.p. Data Processing Mgmt. Assn., Am. U., Washington, 1987-88. Author: Programming in Natural, 1991, Life in God's Management Corps, 2002, One Plus One Equals Three: The Virtues and Value of Teamwork and Leadership, 2003, The Database Leader's Bible, 2003, others; author of 20 software applications. Pres. United Meth. Men, Cheltenham, 1987-88, Savage, Md., 1990-91; arch. bd. Spring Breeze Assn., Columbia, Md., 1994; vol. McCain for Pres. 2000, Alexandria, Va., 1999; Dem. chief judge Howard County, 2004. With USAF, 1974-75. Mem. IEEE Computer Soc., Inst. Transp. Engrs. (assoc.), Assn. Computing Machinery, Profl. Mgrs. (treas. 1992-93), Math. Assn. Am., Naval Inst. (life), Scottish Am. Found., Am. U. Alumni (life). Democrat. Avocations: home projects, writing, art, church. Home: 6335 Hanover Crossing Way Hanover MD 21076 Office: Md DOT 7491 Connelley Dr Hanover MD 21076 E-mail: dchiarella56@hotmail.com.

CHIARELLA, PETER RALPH, vintner; b. Bklyn., Dec. 6, 1932; s. C. Ralph and Catherine (Zinzi) C.; m. Frances M. Crane, Oct. 10, 1953; children: Ralph, Thomas, John, Karen. BBA, St. John's U., 1957. C.P.A., N.Y. Sr. accountant Peat, Marwick, Mitchell & Co., N.Y.C., 1957—61; asst. controller Bonwit Teller, N.Y.C., 1961—62; accounting mgr. plastics div. Celanese Corp., Newark, 1963—67; v.p., controller Clairol, Inc., N.Y.C., 1967—72; pres., dir. Kleinert's, Inc., Kutztown, Pa., 1972—77; v.p., corp. controller United Brands Co., N.Y.C., 1977—79; sr. v.p., chief fin. officer Max Factor & Co., Hollywood, Calif., 1979—83; sr. v.p. fin. and adminstrn. Syncor Internat., Sylmar, Calif., 1983—85; exec. v.p. Doctors' Co., Napa, Calif., 1985—92; pres. Cakebread Cellars, Inc., Rutherford, Calif., 1992—97; pres., CEO Crane Family Vineyards, Napa, 1999—. Mem. budget com. United Fund, Stamford, Conn., 1970; bd. dirs. Vis. Nurse Assn., L.A., 1983-90, Napa Valley Opera House, 1991-96, Napa Valley Coll. Found., 1991-99, Cakebread Cellars, Inc., Rutherford, 1992-2004; Napa Valley Fair Bd., 1994-2000, Napa Physicians IPA Bd., 1999-01, Pacific Vision Found., 2001—. With USN, 1952-54. Mem. AICPA, Fin. Execs. Inst., Delta Mu Delta. Home: 1051 Borrette Ln Napa CA 94558-9702 Office Phone: 707-259-0175. E-mail: peter@cranefamilyvineyards.com.

CHIARENZA, CARL, art historian, critic, artist, educator; b. Rochester, NY, Sept. 5, 1935; s. Charles and Mary Rose (Russo) C.; m. Heidi Faith Katz, Aug. 13, 1978; children: Suzanne Mari, Jonah Katz, Gabriella Christine. B.F.A., Rochester Inst. Tech., 1957; MS, Boston U., 1959; MA, 1964; PhD, Harvard U., 1972. Lectr. Boston U., 1963-64, instr. dept. fine arts, 1964-68, asst. prof., 1968-72, univ. prof., 1972-73, assoc. prof., 1973-80, prof. dept. art history, 1980-86, acting chmn. dept. art history, 1973-74, chmn. dept. art history, 1976-81; Fanny Knapp Allen prof. U. Rochester, N.Y., 1986-98, acting chmn. dept. art history, 1986-87, prof. emeritus, artist-in-residence, 1998—. Adj. vis. prof. Visual Studies Workshop, SUNY, 1972-73; vis. prof. Cornell U., 1991; Harnish vis. artist Smith Coll., 1983-84; vis. artist/scholar, U. Ga., Athens, 2002; artists adv. panel Artists Found., Boston, 1977-81; guest curator Inst. Contemporary Art, Boston, 1980-81; cons. Nat. Endowment for Arts, 1978-80, mem. Artists' Fellowships panel, 1982; bd. dirs. Photographic Resource Ctr.; trustee Visual Studies Workshop; lectr. in field. One-man shows include George Eastman House, 1995, Southeast Mus. of Photography, 1995, Rochester (NY) Inst. Tech., 1996, The Witkin Gallery, NYC, 1996, Kennedy Ctr. Gallery, Hiram Coll., 1997, High Mus. Art, Atlanta, 1997, U. Iowa Mus. Art, 1997, Stephen Cohen Gallery, LA, 1999, Robert Klein Gallery, Boston, 1999, Spectrum Gallery, Rochester, 1999, 2002, Troyer Gallery, Washington, 1999, Alan Klotz/Photocollect, NYC, 2000, U. RI, 2003, U. Rochester, 2003, Carl Solway Gallery, Cin., Ohio, 2004—05, Ctr. Photographic Arts, Carmel, Calif., 2005, others, numerous group shows including most recently, exhibited in group shows at Fitchburg Art Mus., 2001, DeCordova Mus. and Sculpture Pk., Lincoln, Mass., 2001, Boise (Idaho) Art Mus., 2001, Kiyosato (Japan) Mus. Photographic Arts, 2001, Adirondack C.C., 2001, Amon Carter Mus., Ft. Worth, Tex., 2002, Visual Studies Workshop Gallery, 2002, others, Represented in permanent collections LA County Mus. Art, Nat. Mus. Am. Art, Washington, Phila. Mus. Art, Mus. Modern Art, NYC, J. Paul Getty Mus., LA, Art Inst. Chgo., Cleve. Mus. Art, Mpls. Inst. Arts, Mus. Fine Arts, Boston, Houston, San Francisco Mus. Modern Art, Amon Carter Mus., Ft. Worth, others; author: Aaron Siskind: Pleasures and Terrors, 1982, Landscapes of the Mind, 1988, Evocations, 2002, The Peace Warriors of 2003, 2005, Solitudes, 2005; contbr. articles to over 180 profl. jours. Served with U.S. Army, 1960-62. Mass. Art and Humanities Found. fellow, 1975-76; Nat. Endowment for Arts fellow, 1977-78, 90-91; recipient Artist award Arts and Cultural Coun. for Greater Rochester, 1996, Artist-in-Residence award Hiram Coll., 1997, Spl. Opportunity Stipend award N.Y. Found. for the Arts, 1997, Disting. Alumnus of Yr., Rochester Inst. Tech., 1997, Honored Educator award Soc. for Photographic Edn., 1999, Lillian Fairchild Artist award, 1999, Best of Show award Nazareth Coll., 2000, 02, 04 Mem. Soc. Photographic Edn., Assn. Historians Am. Art. Office: U Rochester Morey # 424 Rochester NY 14627 Office Phone: 585-275-9249. Business E-Mail: ccrz@mail.rochester.edu. *I am a switch-hitter. I have always made, written about, or lectured about pictures. Because I seem to do each best when working in a concentrated spurt, I am often torn between these modes of communication. I work intuitively and in a state of agitation until things find their rightful place on a page or in a picture. It is as if I am reaching for a place of equilibrium or understanding as I move through the world from a position of essential ignorance about the meaning of life.*

CHIARENZA, FRANK JOHN, language educator; b. New Britain, Conn., Dec. 10, 1926; s. Sebastian X. and Josephine C. AB, Yale, 1949, PhD in Medieval Lit, 1956; MA in English, Rutgers U., 1950; certificate, Inst. for Ednl. Mgmt.; Sloan Found. grantee, Harvard, 1970. Lectr. English U. Conn., 1954-55; instr. English Hillyer Coll., Hartford, Conn., 1955-57; from asst. prof. to prof. Coll. Arts and Scis., U. Hartford, 1958-67, prof. English, 1978-89, emeritus, 1989, chmn. dept., 1958-67, acad. dean Coll. Arts and

Scis., 1967-78. Cons., reader English Coll. Entrance Exam. Bd., 1959—; reader advanced placement tests Ednl. Testing Service, Princeton, N.J., 1961—; chmn. for Conn., Nat. Council Coll. Publs. Advisers, 1966-67; adv. council Career Opportunity Program, 1970—; resource cons. Conn. Commn. for Higher Edn., 1972-73; chief reader Coll. Level Exam. Program, Ednl. Testing Service, N.J., 1978— Author: The Milk Glass Book, 1998; contbr. articles to profl. jours. Corporator Watkinson Sch., West Hartford, Conn.; bd. dirs. Nat. Milk Glass Collectors Soc., 1991—, pres., 1997-99; founder Frank Chiarenza Mus. of Glass, Meriden, Conn., Bd. Dirs., Rosa Ponselle Mus., Conn, Served with USNR, 1944-46. Fulbright grantee U. Rome, 1953-54. AAUP (pres. Hartford 1962-64), NEA, Am. Assn. Higher Edn., Am. Conf. Acad. Deans, Am. Coun. Edn., Conn. Acad. Arts and Scis., Nat. Milk Glass Collectors Soc. (bd. dirs. 1991—, v.p. 1994—, v.p., chmn. publs. com. 1994—, pres. 1997—), Yale Club. Home: 80 Crestview Dr Newington CT 06111-2405 Office: Dequaine Found 39 W Main Meriden CT 06451 E-mail: chiarenzaglassmuseum@snet.net, mgmfrank@aol.com.

CHIATE, KENNETH REED, lawyer; b. Phoenix, June 24, 1941; s. Mac Arthur and Lillian (Lavin) C.; m. Jeannette Jensen, Aug. 21, 1965; children: Gregory Jensen, Carley MaKay. BA with honors, Claremont Men's Coll., 1963; JD, Columbia U., 1966; postgrad., U. So. Calif. Law Sch., 1967. Bar: Calif. 1967, U.S. Dist. Ct. (cen. dist.) Calif. 1967, Ariz. 1971, U.S. Dist. Ct. Ariz. 1971, U.S. Dist. Ct. (no. Dist.) Calif. 1982. Law clk. presiding justice U.S. Dist. Ariz., 1971; ptnr. Lillick McHose & Charles, L.A., 1971-91, Pillsbury Winthrop, LLP (formerly Pillsbury Madison), L.A., 1991—. Arbitrator Los Angeles Superior Ct. Arbitration Panel, 1979-82; mcpl. ct. judge protem Los Angeles, 1979-81; vice chmn. Los Angeles Open Com., 1969-71. Named among Calif. Lawyers of Yr. 2000, Calif. Mag.; named one of So. Calif. Superlawyers, L.A. Mag., 2004. Mem. ABA, L.A. County Bar Assn., Calif. State Bar Assn., Ariz. State Bar Assn., Maricopa County Bar Assn., Am. Trial Lawyers Assn., L.A. Bus. Trial Lawyers Assn. Office: Quinn Emanuel Urquhart Oliver & Hedges LLP 865 Figueroa St 10th Fl Los Angeles CA 90017 E-mail: kenchiate@quinnemanuel.com.

CHIAVERINI, JOHN EDWARD, construction company executive; b. Providence, Feb. 6, 1924; s. John and Sadie (Ginsberg) C.; m. Cecile Corey, Mar. 31, 1951; children: Caryl Marie, John Michael. Cert. in advanced san. engring., U. Ill., 1945; BS in Civil Engring., U. R.I., 1947. Registered profl. engr., Mass., R.I. Project engr. Perini Corp., Hartford, Conn., 1950-51, project mgr., 1951-55, asst. project mgr. Pitts. and Que., 1955-61, v.p. Framingham, Mass., 1965-84, sr. v.p. San Francisco, 1984—; pres., dir. Compania Perini S.A., Colombia, 1961—; v.p., exec. mgr. Perini Yuba Assocs., Marysville, Calif., 1966-70, v.p. Western ops., 1970-78, 79-84, group v.p., 1978-79; sr. v.p. spl. projects Perini Corp., 1984-90, dir., asst. to chmn., 1991—. Mem. U.S. com. Internat. Commn. on Large Dams; bd. dirs. Bldg. Futures Coun., 1990—, vice chmn., 1993, chmn., 1994—; active Civil Engring. Rsch. Found., 1990—, mem. corp. adv. bd., 1992—. Served to 2d lt. USAAF, 1944-46. Recipient Golden Beaver award Supervision San Francisco Bay Area Coun. Boy Scouts Am., 1989, Good Scout award, 1989; named to R.I. Engring. Hall of Fame, 1997. Fellow ASCE (mem. exec. com. constrn. divsn., vice chmn. 1994-95, chmn. 1995—), Soc. Am. Mil. Engrs. (Acad. of Fellows 1997, pres. San Francisco post 1991-92, bd. dirs.); mem. NSPE (life), Am. Arbitration Assn., Calif. Soc. Profl. Engrs., Dispute Resolution Bd. Found., Beavers (bd. dirs.), Moles, Commonwealth Club of Calif., KC, Rotary (mem. dispute resolution bd. found.). Republican. Roman Catholic. Home and Office: Perini Corp 37 Dutch Valley Ln San Anselmo CA 94960-1045 Office Phone: 415-454-8251. Personal E-mail: ceejayIII@aol.com.

CHIAZZE, LEONARD, JR., biostatistician, epidemiologist, educator; b. Falconer, N.Y., June 19, 1934; s. Leonard and Jennie (Bondi) C.; m. Ellen Anne Bergman, June 12, 1954; children: Kathleen, Caroline, Michael, Ellen. AA, SUNY, Jamestown, 1953; BS, U. Buffalo, 1955, MBA, 1957; ScD, U. Pitts., 1964. Instr. stats. U. Buffalo, 1955—57; biostatistician Nat. Cancer Inst., Bethesda, Md., 1957—66, acting chief biometry br., 1975—76; asst. prof. Georgetown U. Sch. Medicine, Washington, 1966—69, assoc. prof., 1969—77, prof., 1977—, founder, dir. grad. program in biostats., 1970—94, dir. biostats. and epidemiology divsn., 1966—94, dir. occupl. health studies divsn., 1994—. Mem. com. toxicology NAS/NRC, 2000—04; vice chair Georgetown U. Instl. Rev. Bd., Washington; mem. data and safety monitoring bd. Nat. Inst. on Drug Abuse. Contbr. articles to profl. jours. Served with USPHS, 1957-66. Fellow: APHA, Am. Coll. Epidemiology; mem.: Soc. Occupl. and Environ. Health (past pres. governing coun.), Soc. Epidemiologic Rsch., Am. Statis. Assn., Sigma Xi, Beta Gamma Sigma. Home: 11237 Waycross Way Kensington MD 20895-1034 Office: Georgetown U 3750 Reservoir Rd NW Washington DC 20007-2111 E-mail: chiazzel@georgetown.edu.

CHICAGO, JUDY, artist; b. Chgo., July 20, 1939; d. Arthur M. and May (Levenson) Cohen. BA, UCLA, 1962, MA, 1964; doctorate (hon.), Russell Sage Coll., 1992, Lehigh U., 2000, Smith Coll., 2000, Duke U., 2003. Co-founder Feminist Studio Workshop, L.A., 1973, Through the Flower Corp., 1977; prof.-inresidence We. Ky. U., 2001; vis. artist Ind. U., 1999, Duke U., 2000, U. N.C., 2000, Calif. Poly. Inst., Pomona, 2003. Author: Through the Flower: My Struggle as a Woman Artist, 1975, The Dinner Party: A Symbol of Our Heritage, 1979, Embroidering Our Heritage: The Dinner Party Needlework, 1980, The Birth Project, 1985, Holocaust Project: From Darkness Into Light, 1993, Beyond the Flower: The Autobiography of a Feminist Artist, 1996, The Dinner Party, 1996, Women and Art: Contested Territory, 1999, Fragments from the Delta of Venus, 2004, Kitty City: A Feline Book of Hours, 2005; one-woman shows include, Pasadena (Calif.) Mus. Art, 1969, Jack Glenn Gallery, Corona del Mar, Calif., 1972, JPL Fine Arts, London, 1975, Quay Ceramics, San Francisco, 1976, San Francisco Mus. Modern Art, 1979, Bklyn. Mus., 1980, 2002, Parco Galleries, Japan, 1980, Fine Arts Gallery, Irvine, Calif., 1981, Musee d'Art Contemporain, Montreal, 1982, ACA Galleries, N.Y.C., 1984, 85, 86, 2004, 05, Nat. Mus. of Women in the Arts, 2002; group exhbns. include Jewish Mus., N.Y.C., 1966, 67, Whitney Mus., 1972, Winnipeg Art Gallery, 1975; represented in permanent collections Bklyn. Mus., San Francisco Mus. Modern Art, Oakland Mus. Art, Pa. Acad. Fine Arts, L.A. County Mus. Art, also numerous pvt. collections. Office: Through the Flower 107 Becker Ave Belen NM 87002 E-mail: throughtheflower@judychicago.com. *I am an artist, writer and committed to an enlarged role for art and a more humanized world.*

CHICCO, GIANFRANCO, healthcare communications executive; b. Maracay, Venezuela, Apr. 9, 1958; came to U.S., 1979; s. Giuseppe and Maria C.; 1 child, Marco Alesandro. BA in Health Scis., Kalamazoo Coll., 1980; MS in Comm., Boston U., 1982. Med. rschr. Biomechanics Lab. of Brigham and Women's Hosp. Harvard Med. Sch., Boston, 1980-82; sr. account supr. Edelman Pub. Rels. Worldwide, N.Y.C., 1982-86; v.p. Ruder-Finn, N.Y.C., 1986-88; sr. v.p., founder health and sci. comm. div. Rowland Worldwide, N.Y.C., 1988-90; exec. v.p., co-dir. healthcare group Burston-Marsteller, N.Y.C., 1990—95; prin., owner Chandler Chicco Agy., N.Y.C., 1995—. Recipient Big Apple award Pub. Rels. Soc. Am., 1988, Creativity in Pub. Rels. award, 1991. Office: 450 W 15th St New York NY 10011-7097 Fax: 212-229-8496.

CHICHETTO, JAMES WILLIAM, editor, educator; b. Boston, June 5, 1941; s. Francis Anthony and Christina McInnis C. B of Philosophy, Stonehill Coll., 1964; M of Theology, Holy Cross Coll., 1968; MA, Wesleyan U., 1978. Ordained to ministry, Cath. Ch. the Congregation of Holy Cross, 1968. Assoc. editor Gargoyle Mag., Cambridge, Mass., 1975-81, Conn. Poetry Rev., Stonington, 1981-84, 1984-88, asoc. editor, art editor, 1988-89, editor, 1989-91; prof. writing Stonehill Coll., North Easton, Mass., 1991—; art editor East & West Lit. Quar., San Francisco, 1995—. Author of poems, essays, revs. and plays. Mem. Easton Arts Coun., 1994-98. Recipient Sri Chinmoy award, 1986; NEA grantee, 1980, 83; NEH grantee, 1992. Fellow World Lit. Assn.; mem. Assn. Lit. Scholars. Democrat. Avocations: painting, sketching. Office: Stonehill Coll 430 Washington St Easton MA 02357 E-mail: JChichetto@stonehill.edu.

CHICHILNISKY, GRACIELA, mathematician, educator, economist, writer; b. Buenos Aires, Mar. 27, 1946; arrived in U.S., 1968, naturalized, 1992; d. Salomon Chichilnisky and Raquel Gavensky; children: Eduardo Jose, Natasha Sable. Student, MIT, 1967—68; MA, U. Calif., Berkeley, 1970, PhD in Math., 1971, PhD in Econs., 1976. Postdoctoral fellow Harvard U., 1974, lectr. dept. econs., 1975-77, fellow Harvard Inst. Internat. Devel., 1978; assoc. prof. Columbia U., N.Y.C., 1977—79, prof., 1980—, dir. Program on Info. and Resources, 1994—, prof. stats., 1996—, dir. Columbia Ctr. for Risk Mgmt., 1998—, UNESCO prof. math. and econs., 1995—99. CEO Cross Border Exch. Corp., 1999-2003, chmn. 2003-05; sr. adviser to pres., U. Ariz., 2004—; architect The Kyoto Protocol of the UN, 1995-2003; mem. presdl. cabinet Banco Ctrl. Republica Argentina, 1971-74; co-prin. investigator Urban Inst., Washington, 1975-77; vis. scholar Internat. Inst. Applied Sys. Analysis Laxenburg, Austria, 1975-77; prin. investigator U.S. Dept. Labor, 1977-78, Rockefeller Found. Project Internat. Rels., 1981-83; project dir. UN Inst. Tng. and Rsch., N.Y., 1979-83; chaired prof. econs. U. Essex, 1980-81; vis. prof. inst. math and its applications U. Minn., 1983-84, U. Siena, Italy, summers, 1991-93, 2002; vis. prof. Stanford Inst. Theoretical Econs., Stanford U., summers, 1991-93, dept. econs., Inst. Internat. Studies, 1993—, vis. prof. depts., econ. and ops. rsch. Stanford U., 1993-94; prof. missionaire U. des Antilles et de la Guyane, spring 1984-85; NSF prof. dept. math. U. Calif., Berkeley, 1985-86; CEO, chmn. FITEL Ltd., 1985-89; exec. dir. Sci. Internat. Ltd., 1989-90; vis. prof. U. Cath. Buenos Aires, Aug. 1993; cons. in field; UNESCO chair in math. and econs., Columbia U., 1995—; Salinbemi chair U. Siena, Italy, 1994-95; econ. architect The Kyoto Protocol, UN, 1994-2005 Co-author: Catastrophe or New Society? A Latin American World Model, 1976; author: (with G. Heal) The Evolving International Economy, 1986, Oil in the International Economy, 1991, Sustainability: Dynamics and Uncertainty, 1998, Mathematical Economics, 1998, Topology and Markets, 1998, Markets, Information and Uncertainty, 1998, Environmental Markets: Equity and Efficiency, 1999; assoc. editor Jour. Devel. Econs., 1976-86, Advances in Mathematics, 1985, Risk Decision and Policy; mem. various editl. bds.; contbr. articles to profl. jours. Mem. coun. Social Health and Welfare Soc.; bd. trustees Nat. Resources Def. Coun., 1994—. Recipient Internat. Rels. award Rockefeller Found., 1983-84; named Most Disting. Woman Economist, Newcombe Found. and Omega Delta Epsilon, 1991, Leif Johansen award U. Oslo, Norway, 1995; grantee NSF, 1974—; fellow Ford Found., 1967-69, Banco Ctrl. Republica Argentina, 1972-74, spl. fellow UN Inst. Tng. and Rsch., 1977-76. Office: Columbia U Stats Dept 1255 Amsterdam Ave 10th Fl New York NY 10027 Mailing: 335 Riverside Dr New York NY 10025 Office Phone: 212-678-1148. Business E-Mail: gcichilnisky@columbia.edu.

CHICKADONZ, GRACE HARLOW, dean; BSN, U. Kans., 1958; MS, U. Md., 1968, PhD, 1974; attended, Inst. Edn. Mgmt., Harvard U., 1985. Staff nurse U. Kans. Med. Ctr., Kansas City, 1958-59; instr. Enid (Okla.) Gen. Hosp. Sch. Nursing, 1959-61; staff nurse grants N.Mex. State Health Dept., 1961-63; staff nurse Arlington (Va.) County Health Dept., 1963-64; asst. prof. nursing Georgetown U., Washington, 1967-78; Robert Wood Johnson nurse faculty fellow in primary care U. Md., Balt., 1978-79, dir. nursing practice, psychophysiology clinic, dept. psychiatry, 1979-80; dean, prof. nursing Med. Coll. Ohio, Toledo, 1979-87, Syracuse (N.Y.) U., 1987—. Designer plan Ohio Commn. on Nursing Implementation Project, 1981-82; vice chancellor for health affairs' com. Deans and Dirs. of Baccalaureate Programs Rev. Com., 1981-86; pres. Ohio Coun. of Deans and Dirs. of Baccalaureate Programs and Grad. Programs, 1986-87; mem. N.Y. State Health Task Force, 1988; mem. statewide planning com. N.Y. State Legis. Nurse of Distinction Program, 1988-93; accreditation site visitor Calif. State U., Dominguez Hills, 1989; presenter in field. Contbr. articles to profl. jours. Mem. Cradle-to-Kindergarten Health Subcom., 1988-89, mem. task force and steering com., 1989-90; chair health care adv. com. Loretto Geriatric Ctr., 1989—, also mem. med. adv. com., bd. trustees; mem. long term care task force Ctrl. N.Y. Health Sys. Agy., 1989—, mem. capital investment com., 1989-92, mem. regional maternal and newborn svc. adv. com., 1990-92; mem. infant mortality coalition Women's Commn., Syracuse, 1990-94, mem. health task force, 1990-94; bd. dirs. Boys and Girl's Club of Syracuse, 1990—, mem. pers. com., 1991—, mem. pub. rels. com., 1991, mem. exec. dir. search, 1993, mem. devel. officer search, 1994; organizer, co-chair Ctrl. N.Y. Com. to Establish Nurse-Midwifery Ednl. Program, 1991—. Spl. Nurse fellow NIH, 1972-74; recipient Leadership award Ohio Nurses Assn., 1984, Program Excellence award Ohio Bd. Regents, 1986-87, Disting. Alumnus award U. Kans., 1990, Martha M. Borlick award U. Md., 1990. Fellow Am. Acad. Nursing; mem. ANA, Nat. League Nursing (mem. nat. rsch. com. 1981-83, accreditation visitor 1982-89, bd. rev. 1990-93), Am. Assn. Colls. Nursing (mem. membership com. 1980-81, mem. rsch. com. 1984-86, mem. edn. and credentialing com. 1989-91), N.Y. State Nurses' Assn. (chair coun. on nursing edn. 1992—, mem. ad hoc com. on recredentialing 1993—), N.Y. State Deans and Dirs. Colls. Nursing (treas. 1990-94), Sigma Theta Tau (mem. nat. rsch. com. 1979-83, Omicron chpt. 1987—). Home: 15 Arnold Park Rochester NY 14607-2001 Office: Syracuse U Coll Nursing 426 Ostrom Ave Syracuse NY 13210-2938

CHICKERING, HOWARD ALLEN, insurance company executive, lawyer; b. San Francisco, Mar. 21, 1942; s. Allen Lawrence and Caroline Cranford (Rogers) C.; m. Elizabeth Douglas Dalton, June 29, 1968; children: Philip Dalton, Caroline Howe. BS in Econs., U. Pa., 1966; JD, Stanford U., 1971. Bar: Calif. 1972. Assoc. Chickering & Gregory, San Francisco, 1971-76; sr. counsel Itel Corp., San Francisco, 1976-79; v.p., gen. counsel, bd. dirs. Clarendon Ins. Co. (Bermuda) Ltd., N.Y.C., 1979-81; pres. Clarendon Group Svcs. Inc., N.Y.C., 1981-85; exec. v.p., bd. dirs. Clarendon Ins. Group, N.Y.C., 1985-88; founder, pres., chief underwriting officer R.V.I. Guaranty Co., Ltd., Hamilton, Bermuda, 1989—; founder, pres. R.V.I. Am. Ins. Co., Stamford, Conn., 1994—. Spkr. in field. Contbr. articles to profl. publs. Co-author, acting campaign chmn. San Francisco Proposition C (Open Space), 1974; campaign sec. Proposition J (Open Space and Park Renovation), 1974; mem. San Francisco Open Space Citizens Adv. Commn., 1976-78; deacon Stanwich Congregational Ch.; leader, adminstr. Alpha Course on Basic Christianity. Lt. (j.g.) USNR, 1966-68, Vietnam. Mem. State Bar Calif., Soc. Colonial Wars, Soc. Mayflower Descs., Mil. Order Fgn. Wars, Order Founders and Patriots, Racquet and Tennis Club, N.Y. Yacht Club, Belle Haven Club (commodore 1996). Republican. Home: 80 Otter Rock Dr Greenwich CT 06830-7029 Office: RVI Am Ins Co 177 Broad St Ste 9 Stamford CT 06901-5003

CHICKERING, ROGER, history professor; s. Roger W. and Margaret Y. Chickering; m. Alison Baker, June 25, 1988; children: Roger, Max. PhD, Stanford U., 1968. Prof. history Georgetown U., Washington, 1993—, U. Oreg., Eugene, 1968—93. Author: (book) Imperial Germany and the Great War, Karl Lamprecht, We Men Who Feel Most German, Imperial Germany and a World Without War. Fellow, Guggenheim Found., 1980, Inst. for Advanced Study, Princeton U., 1991, Woodrow Wilson Ctr., 1996, Nat. Humanities Ctr., 2004, NEH, 2005. Mem.: Am. Hist. Assn. Office: BMW Ctr German and European Studies Georgetown Univ Washington DC 20057 Office Phone: 202-687-6701. Office Fax: 202-687-8359. E-mail: chickerr@georgetown.edu.

CHICOREL, MARIETTA EVA, publishing company executive, consultant; b. Vienna; came to U.S., 1939, naturalized, 1945; d. Paul and Margaret (Gross) Selby. AB, Wayne State U., 1951; MALS, U. Mich., 1961. Asst. chief libr. acquisitions divsn. U. Wash., Seattle, 1962-66; project dir. Macmillan Info. Scis., Inc., N.Y.C., 1968-69; pres. Chicorel Library Pub. Corp., N.Y.C., 1969-79, Am. Libr. Pub. Co., Inc., 1979—; pub. cons. Creative Solutions Co., 1986—. Asst. prof. dept. libr. sci. CUNY (Queens Coll.), 1986—; mem. edn. com. Gov.'s Commn. on Status of Women, Wash., 1963-65; instr. libr. scis. No. Ariz. U., Flagstaff, 1990; bd. dirs. Skills Devel. Tng. counseling; pub. cons. creative solutions. Chief editor: Ulrich's International Periodicals Directory, 1966-68; editor, pub.: Chicorel Indexes, 1969—; founding editor: Jour. Reading, Writing and Learning Disabilities International, 1985-90; contbr. chpt. on univs. to Library Statistics: A Handbook of Concepts, Definitions and Terminology, 1966. Mem. ALA (exec. bd. tech. svcs. divsn. 1965-68, chmn. libr. materials price index com. 1968-69, councillor 1969-73), Am. Assn. Profl. Cons., Am. Book Prodrs. Assn., Book League N.Y. (bd. govs. 1975-79), Am. Soc. for Info. Sci., Can. Libr. Assn., Pacific N.W. Libr. Assn., N.Y. Libr. Club, N.Y. Tech. Svcs. Librarians.

CHICOREL, RALPH, librettist, composer, playwright; b. Detroit, Dec. 4, 1930; s. Jacob and Judith (Louza) C.; m. Phyllis Philko, Feb. 3, 1957 (div. 1979); children: Steven Mitchell, Daniel Adam, Jacob; m. Debra Anne Lisch, Jan. 10, 1981; children: Matthew Aaron, Tyler William, Allison Anne. Grad., Am. Acad. Dramatic Arts, 1955. Performer various groups, Detroit, 1948-51; salesman Stein Ellbogen, Detroit, 1953-57; co-owner, entertainer Kenwood Restaurant and Lounge, Detroit, 1957-66; salesman Music Merchants, Detroit, 1966-67; co-owner Weight Watchers of Wis., Inc., Milw., 1968-92, also advt. spokesperson; pres. Chicorel Music Corp., Milw., 1970-92; co-owner Weight Watchers in Hawaii, Honolulu, 1989-91. Pres. Civic Music Assn., Milw., 1990-91. Producer, composer, lyricist 5 albums on Pleasure Records label, 1970-79; composer, lyricist (stage mus., album) Jean, 1973, 85, (CDs) C. Dickens' Great Expectations, 1995, Anna Karenina, 2002; composer: (songs) Milwaukee (premiere performance Milw. Symphony Orch. Feb. 1988); producer Lynn Redgrave and the World of Weight Watchers, The Milw. Auditorium, 1989; contbg. author: Milwaukee: The Best of All Worlds, 1991. Bd. dirs. Congregation Emanuel Bne Jeshurun Brotherhood, Milw., 1984-86, Comedy Sports Bd., Milw., 1992—, Jazz Unltd., 2005—. Served with USMC, 1951-53, Korea. Mem. Dramatists Guild, Song Writers Guild Am., ASCAP, Milw. Broadcasters Club. Sephardic. Avocation: collecting recordings of musical shows. Office: N64w14660 Poplar Dr Menomonee Falls WI 53051-5197

CHICQUOR, ISABEL, art educator, artist; b. NYC, July 6, 1943; d. Sydour and Sadie Chicquor; children: Daniel M Levitt, Jessica Knorr. BFA, Alfred U., 1967; MFA, Rochester Inst. Tech., 1995. Asst. prof., studio Baldwin-Wallace Coll., Berea, Ohio, 1973—76; prof. N.C. Ctrl. U., Durham, 1977—. Exhibitions include Delirious Rhythm (N.C Artists Fellowship Photography, 2003), Bajan Boy (Fayetteville Mus. Art, Hon. Mention, 2005), Sugar Cane Worker (NC Photographer's Competition, Meredith Coll., Raleigh, N.C., 2004). Juror front page awards Herald Sun Newspapers, Durham, NC, 1989—2005; chair spl. exhibitions Durham Art Guild, 1984—91; photographer Contemporary Art Mus., Raleigh, 1997—2005. Grantee, N.C. Humanities Coun., 1986. Mem.: Soc. Photographic Edn., Nat. Coun. Edn. Ceramic Art. Achievements include research in Faculty Research Grant-Structures of the Yucatan; UNC Board of Governors Award for Teaching Excellence. Avocations: travel, walking. Home: 346 Wesley Dr Chapel Hill NC 27516 Office: NC Ctrl U Lawson St Durham NC 27707 Office Phone: 919-530-7049. Personal E-mail: isartncrr@bellsouth.net. E-mail: ichicquor@nccu.edu.

CHIDA, JUNAID HASAN, lawyer; b. Lahore, Punjab, Pakistan, June 23, 1956; came to U.S., 1974; s. Noorul Hasan and Nazneen (Mohajir) C.; m. Rakhshan Mahmood, Jan. 16, 1986. BBA cum laude, U. Wis., Eau Claire, 1978, JD cum laude, 1983. Bar: Wis. 1983, N.Y. 1984, U.S. Dist. Ct. (so. dist.) N.Y. 1984, Calif. 1986. Ptnr., chmn. leasing fin. practice group Dewey Ballantine, N.Y.C., 1983—. Mem. Klanwatch project So. Poverty Law Ctr., Montgomery, Ala., 1987. Mem.: Calif. Bar Assn. Moslem. Office: Dewey Ballantine LLP 1301 Ave Of The Americas New York NY 10019-6092 Office Phone: 212-259-6308. Office Fax: 212-259-6333. Business E-Mail: jchida@dbllp.com.

CHIDGEY, GUY CLEMENT, real estate company executive; s. Francis Joseph and Isabelle Marie Chidgey; children: Guy, Mary. BSBA, MBA in Mktg. Lic. realtor 1956. CEO ChiDCo Inc., Colorado Springs, Colo., 1998—, ChiDCO Broker, Bakersfield, Calif., 2001—. Prodr. jazz radio show KIWI FM, Bakersfield; prodr. jazz radio show, host KMCL, McCall, Idaho. Prodr.: (concert) Red River Valley, Come Hell or High Water, CSUB's 2d annual jazz festival; author: Daddy, I Can't Wanna Do That, Tangents of a Mad Man; prodr.: (promotion) Travel the Californias. Corp. sponsorship chmn. Kern County Scottish Soc., Bakersfield, 2003—04. Mem.: Bakersfield Assn. Realtors, Calif. Assn. Realtors, Nat. Assn. Realtors. Avocations: travel, reading, swimming. Office: ChiDCo Broker PO Box 43262 Bakersfield CA 93384 Office Phone: 661-378-6600. Personal E-mail: gcchidgey@yahoo.com.

CHIECHI, CAROLYN PHYLLIS, federal judge; b. Newark, Dec. 6, 1943; BS magna cum laude, Georgetown U., 1965, JD, 1969, LLM in Taxation, 1971, LLD honoris causa, 2000. Bar: DC 1969, U.S. Dist. Ct. DC, U.S. Ct. Fed. Claims, U.S. Tax Ct., U.S. Ct. Appeals (5th, 6th, 9th, DC, and fed. cirs.), U.S. Supreme Ct. Atty. advisor to Hon. Leo H. Irwin U.S. Tax Ct., Washington, 1969-71; assoc. Sutherland, Asbill & Brennan, Washington, 1971—76, ptnr., 1976—92; judge U.S. Tax Ct., Washington, 1992—. Mem. bd. regents Georgetown U., Washington, 1988—2001, mem. nat. law alumni bd., 1986—93; mem. bd. govs. Georgetown U. Alumni Assn., 1994—2000; bd. dirs. Stuart Stiller Meml. Found., 1986—99; prin. Coun. for Excellence in Govt., 1990—92. Dept. editor: Jour. Taxation, 1986—92; contbr. articles to profl. jours. Fellow: Am. Coll. Tax Counsel, Am. Bar Found.; mem.: Am. Judicature Soc., Women's Bar Assn., DC Bar Assn., Fed. Bar Assn., Georgetown U. Law Alumni Assn. (Alumnae Achievement award 1994, Alumni Achievement award 1998). Office: US Tax Ct 400 2nd St NW Washington DC 20217-0002

CHIEF EAGLE, JOAN, secondary school educator; b. Pine Ridge, June 27, 1952; d. Eugene J. Chief Eagle, Alice V. Weasel Bear/Chief Eagle; children: Leslee M. McMath, Joelle M., Lorena L., Danielle J. McCane. AA, Standing Rock Coll., Ft. Yales, N.D., 1989; BA, Minot State U., N.D., 1991. Native Am. artist Five Nations Arts, Mandan, ND, 1987—; tchg. asst. Ft. Yates Pub. Sch. #4, Ft. Yates, 1993—97, fgn. lang. tchr., 1998—. Cons. for Native Am. lang. and art Ft. Yates Pub. Sch. #4, 1994—. With U.S. Army, 1970—71. Avocations: reading, sewing, culinary arts. Home: 179 Box 500 Sioux Village Fort Yates ND 58538 Office: Fort Yates Public Sch #4 105 Agency Ave Fort Yates ND 58538

CHIEGER, KATHRYN JEAN, recreational facility executive; b. Detroit, July 13, 1948; BA, Purdue U., 1970; MA, U. Mich., 1974; MBA, U. Denver, 1983. Libr. U. Mich., Ann Arbor, 1970-74; staff aide U.S. Sen. Gary Hart, Denver, 1974-79; dir. fin. rels. Petro-Lewis Corp., Denver, 1979-86; dir. investor rels. Kraft Inc., Glenview, Ill., 1987-89; v.p. corp. affairs Gaylor Container Corp., Deerfield, Ill., 1989-96; v.p. corp. and investor rels. Brunswick Corp., Lake Forest, Ill., 1996—. Mem. Nat. Investor Rels. Inst. (chpt. bd. dirs. 1979-84, v.p. mem. 1982-83, pres. 1983-84, nat. bd. dirs. 1984-88), Chgo. Execs. Club, Investor Rels. Assn. (vice chmn. membership), Chgo. Coun. Fgn. Rels., Sr. Investor Rels. Roundtable (mem. steering com.). Office: Brunswick Corp 1 N Field Ct Lake Forest IL 60045-4811 E-mail: kathryn.chieger@brunswick.com.

CHIEGO, WILLIAM J., museum director; b. Newark, Sept. 17, 1943; s. William Joseph and Rose Marie (Del Guercio) C.; m. Elizabeth Kimball Lee, July 3, 1971; children: Ruth Katharine, Rose Monica. BA in History with distinction, U. Va., 1965; MA in Art History, Case Western Reserve U., 1968, PhD in Art History, 1974. Asst. curator Toledo (Ohio) Mus. Art, 1973-74, assoc. curator European Paintings, 1974-76; curator Portland Art Mus., 1976-79, chief curator, 1979-82, N.C. Mus. Art, Raleigh, 1982-86; dir. Allen Meml. Art Mus. Oberlin (Ohio) Coll., 1986-91; dir. Marion Koogler McNay Art Mus., San Antonio, 1991—. Trustee Intermuseum Conservation Assn., Oberlin, 1986-91; mem., co-chmn. mus. liaison com. Midwest Art History Soc., 1987-91; mem. exhbn. adv. com. Am. Fedn. Arts, 1988-94; mem. conservation grant panel Inst. Mus. Svcs., 1991-93; chair membership com. Assn. Art Mus. Dirs., 1997-99, trustee, 2000-02; lectr. in field. Co-author, editor exhbn. catalog Sir David Wilkie of Scotland, 1987, An Eye for the Stage The Tobin Collection of Theatre Arts at McNay Art Mus., 2004; co-organizer, author intro. to French Paintings from The Chrysler Museum, 1986; coord. rsch. The N.C. Mus. Art Intro. to the Collections, 1983; author: Master Prints from the Gilkey Collection, 1980, From Oregon Private

Collections, 1977; organizer, author: (with others) Oberlin Alumni Collect Modern and Contemporary Art, 1989, Reginald Rowe: A Retrospective, 1996, Carl Rice Embrey: A Retrospective, 1997, O'Keeffe and Texas, 1998, César A. Martinez: A Retrospective, 1999; author/editor: Modern Art at The McNay, 2001; contbr. articles to profl. jours. Resident fellow Yale Ctr. for British Art, New Haven, Conn., 1982, Bingham Travel fellow Art History Case Western Reserve U., 1970-71, Univ. fellow Art History, 1969-70, Nat. Defense Edn. Act fellow Latin Am. History, 1965; Mus. Mgmt. Inst. scholar, 1981. Mem. Phi Beta Kappa. Office: Marion Koogler McNay Art Museum PO Box 6069 San Antonio TX 78209-0069 E-mail: william.chiego@mcnayart.org.

CHIEL, HILLEL JUDAH, biology and neuroscience educator; b. Fairfax County, Va., Aug. 21, 1954; s. Samuel and Jeanette (Eisenberg) C.; m. Elizabeth Karen Dreben, June 15, 1980; children: Benjamin Shalom, Joshua Robert. BA, Yale U., 1974; MS, Mass. Inst. Tech., 1976, PhD, 1980. Postdoctoral fellow Ctr. for Neurobiology & Behavior Columbia U., N.Y.C., 1980-85; cons. in neurobiology dept. molecular biophysics AT&T Bell Labs., Murray Hill, N.J., 1985-87; asst. prof. dept. biology Case Western Res. U., Cleve., 1987-92, asst. prof. dept. neuroscience, 1989-92, assoc. prof. depts. biology and neuroscience, 1992—99, prof. depts. biology, neuroscience, biomedical engring., 1999—. Contbr. more than 60 articles to profl. jours. Rsch. grantee NSF, 1988—, Office of Naval Rsch., 1990—, NIH, 1991—, fellow Inst. Physics, London, 2004; recipient Benjamin F. Barge prize in math., 1972, Carl F. Wittke award for Excellence in Undergraduate Edn., 2004. Mem. AAAS, Math. Assn. Am., Internat. Soc. Neuroethology, Soc. for Neuroscience, Sigma Xi. Democrat. Jewish. Achievements include patents for locomotion controller, peristaltic endoscopic, and soft gripper novel robotic devices. Avocations: reading, singing, walking. Office: Dept Biology Case Western Res U 2080 Adelbert Rd Cleveland OH 44106-2623

CHIEN, CHIA-LING, physics educator; b. China, Nov. 10, 1942; came to U.S., 1966; s. Ting and An-Hsiu (Wong) C.; m. Christina Yueh Wang, Apr. 15, 1972; children: David, Deborah. BS in Physics, Tunghai U., Taiwan, 1965; MS in Physics, Carnegie-Mellon U., 1968, PhD, 1972. Rsch. assoc. Johns Hopkins U., Balt., 1973-74, assoc. rsch. scientist, 1974-75, asst. prof., 1976-79, assoc. prof., 1979-83, prof., 1983—, dir. materials rsch. sci. and engring. ctr., 1997—, Jacob L. Hain prof. physics, 2002—. Vis. prof. Johns Hopkins U., Balt., 1975-76; hon. prof. Nanjing U. 2d lt. Air Force, 1965-66, Taiwan. Fellow Am. Phys. Soc.; mem. Materials Rsch. Soc. Office: Johns Hopkins U Dept Physics 3400 N Charles St Baltimore MD 21218-2680 Business E-Mail: clc@pha.jhu.edu.

CHIEN, JENNIE, sculptor; d. Linsan and Helen Ling Chien. AA Graphic Design, City Coll., San Francisco, Calif., 1972; BA Econ., Columbia U., N.Y., 1983; MBA, Stanford U., Palo Alto, Calif., 1985. Graphic designer Hisata Design, Steven Jacobs Design, Palo Alto, Calif.; art dir. Am. Express, CBS, Hakuhodo Advt., Leber Katz Ptnrs., Muir Cornelius Moore, N.Y.C., 1973—79; Fortune circulation mktg. mgr. Time Inc., 1985—87, Fortune Internat. subscription dir. Amsterdam, Netherlands, 1987—89; gen. mgr. Time Warner Inc., Editl. Svcs., N.Y.C., 1990—93; mktg. project mgr. Luna Inc., Nyack, 1994—2000; artist Luna A+D, 2000—. Treas., bd. dir. Asian Am. Arts Alliance, New York, 1992—97; panel mem., cmty. art grants Arts Coun. of Rockland County, Spring Valley, NY, 2003—05. Prin. works include Chien Noir: The Black Dog, The Guardian Angels, Open Heads, exhibitions include A. Houberbocken Old Ch. Cultural Ctr., Demerest, N.J., 2001, 2003, 2004, 2005. Com. mem. Rockland County Art in Pub. Places, 2003—05. Recipient Gold Medal, Silver Medal, Merit Award for Design Excellence, Western Art Dir. Club, 1975—77, Design Excellence award, San Francisco Art Directors Club, 1975—77, AIGA, 1979, Print Mag., 1980, Gold award, Folio Mag., 1986, Art and Industry award, Rockland Kitchen, Gamerville, N.Y., 2004, Mamaroneck Artists Guild award, Assocs. Show, 2005. Mem.: Hudson River Potters Assn., Phi Beta Kappa. Democrat. Office: Luna A+D 42 Village Gate Nyack NY 10960

CHIEN, NGUYEN TAM, ambassador; b. Nghe An Province, Vietnam, Jan. 20, 1948; married; 3 children. B in Elec. and Mech. Engring., Engring. U., former Soviet Union, 1972; M in Internat. Rels., Moscow Diplomacy Acad., 1984. With Vietnamese Embassy, Moscow, 1972—73; desk officer Dept. of Min. of Fgn. Affairs, Moscow, 1973—75, 1980—82; attache Vietnam Embassy, Moscow, 1975—80; policy planning dept. Min. of Fgn. Affairs, 1984—92, dep. dir. gen., 1988—90, dir. gen., 1990—92; amb. Extraordinary and Plenipotential of Vietnam to Japan, 1992—96; asst. min. of Fgn. Affairs, 1996—97; vice min. of Fgn. Affairs, 1997—2000; amb. Socialist Republic of Vietnam, 2000—; amb. Extraordinary and Plenipotentiary Socialist Republic of Vietnam to US, 2001—. Home: Embassy of Vietnam Ste 400 1233 20th St NW Washington DC 20036

CHIEN, SHU, physiology and bioengineering educator; b. Beijing, June 23, 1931; arrived in US, 1954, naturalized, 1971; s. Shih-liang and Wan-tu (Chang) C.; m. Kuang-Chung Hu, Apr. 7, 1957; children: May Chien Busch, Ann Chien Guidera. MB, Nat. Taiwan U., Taipei, 1953; PhD, Columbia U., 1957. Instr. physiology Columbia U. Coll. Physicians & Surgeons, N.Y.C., 1956-58, asst. prof. physiology, 1958-64, assoc. prof. physiology, 1964-69, prof. physiology, 1969-88, dir. div. circulatory physiology and biophysics, 1974-88; dir. Inst. Biomed. Scis. Academia Sinica, Taipei, 1987-88; prof. bioengring and medicine U. Calif.-San Diego, La Jolla, 1988—, bioengring. group coord., 1989-94, dir. Whitaker Inst. Biomed. Engring., 1991—, chmn. dept. bioengring., 1994-99, 2002—, prof., 2002—. Chmn. adv. com. Am. Bur. for Med. Advancement in China, N.Y.C., 1991-2003, Inst. Biomed. Scis., Academia Sinica, Taipei, 1991—, Nat. Health Rsch. Inst., Taipei, 1991—. Editor: Vascular Endothelium in Health and Disease, 1988, Molecular Biology in Physiology, 1989, Molecular Biology of Cardiovascular System, 1990; co-editor: Nuclear Magnetic Resonance in Biology and Medicine, 1986, Handbook of Bioengineering, 1986, Clinical Hemorheology, Applications in Cardiovascular and Hematological Disease, Diabetes, Surgery and Gynecology, 1987, Fibrinogen, Thrombosis, Coagulation and Fibrinolysis, 1990, Biochemical and Structural Dynamics of the Cell Nucleus, 1990, others; contbr. more than 400 sci. articles on physiology, bioengring. and related biomed. rsch. to profl. jours. Recipient Fahraeus award European Soc. for Clin. Haemorheology, London, 1981, Melville award ASME, 1990, 96, Zweifach award World Congress of Microcirculation, Louisville, 1991, Spl. Creativity Grant award NSF, 1985-88, Merit Grant award NIH, 1989-99, Nat. Health medal, Taiwan, 1998, Poiseuille Gold Medal, Internat. Congress Biorheology, 2002, Asian Am. Engr. of Yr. for Disting. Life Time Achievement, 2005. Mem. NAE, Academia Sinica (Taipei), Am. Physiol. Soc. (pres. 1990-91, Ray Daggs award 1999, Walter B. Cannon Lecture award, 2003), Biomed. Engring. Soc. (sr., ALZA award 1993, Disting. Svc. award 2001), Internat. Soc. Biorheology (v.p. 1983-89, pres. 2005-08), Microcirculatory Soc. (pres. 1980-81, Landis award 1983), N.Am. Soc. Biorheology (chmn. steering com. 1985-86), Fedn. Am. Socs. for Exptl. Biology (pres. 1992-93), Am. Inst. for Med. and Biol. Engring. (pres. 2000-01, Pierre Galletti award 2004), Inst. Medicine of NAS, Internat. Union Physiological Sci. (treas. 1997-2001, chair, Internat. Congr. 2005). Achievements include elucidation of the mechanism of red cell aggregation in terms of energy balance at cell surface; demonstration of the role of endothelial cell turnover in the transport of protein molecules into the artery wall; research on the molecular basis and physiological implications of blood cell deformability; studies on the effects of mechanicsl forces on endothelial cell gene expression, signal transduction, and remodeling. Office: U Calif San Diego Inst Biomed Engring 9500 Gilman Dr La Jolla CA 92093-0412 Office Phone: 858-534-5195. E-mail: shuchien@ucsd.edu.

CHIEN, SUFAN, surgeon, educator; b. Zhejiang Province, China, July 20, 1938; came to U.S., 1982; s. Jiaxing and Julian (You) C.; m. Lorrain Wilson; children: Samson, Lynn. MD, Shanghai 1st Med. Coll., 1962. Resident dept. gen. surgery Zhongshan Hosp. Shanghai 1st Med. Coll., 1962—66, attending gen. surgeon, 1975—79; supr. cardiopulmonary bypass Shanghai Inst. Cardiovasc. Diseases, 1975—82, attending surgeon cardiovasc. surgery, 1979—82; vis. scientist cardiovasc. divsn. Mayo Clinic, Rochester, Minn., 1982—84; vis. scientist physiology and biophysics La. State U. Med. Ctr., Shreveport, 1984—85; vis. scientist surgery, physiology and biophysics U. Ky. Med. Ctr., Lexington, 1985—87, asst. prof. divsn. cardio-thoracic surgery, 1987—93, assoc. prof., 1993—96; assoc. prof. surgery U. Louisville, 1996—2004, prof. surgery, 2004—. Invited lectr., presenter in field; mem. sci. rev. com. study sect. NIH. Author: Hibernation Induction Trigger for Organ Preservation, 1993; mem. editl. bd. Internat. Medicine Rev., 1979-84; contbr. articles and abstracts to med. jours., chpts. to books. Grantee NIH, VA, U.S. Army, AHA, Univ. Fellow Am. Coll. Angiology; mem. AHA, N.Y. Acad. Scis., Chinese Med. Assn., Chinese Surg. Assn., Chinese Soc. Thoracic Surgeons, Shanghai Med. Soc., Internat. Soc. Heart and Lung Transplantation. Office: U Louisville Sch Medicine Rudd Heart-Lung Ctr 1200 201 Abraham Flexner Way Louisville KY 40202-3841 Office Phone: 502-852-4418. Personal E-mail: sufanc@netscape.net.

CHIEN, YIE W., pharmaceutical science educator, academic administrator; b. Keelung, Taiwan, Oct. 20, 1938; came to U.S., 1967; s. Chou-lin and Ai-wen (Chen) C.; m. Margaret C. Chuang, Apr. 23, 1964; children: Steven, Linda. BSc in Pharmacy, Kaohsiung Med. Coll., Taiwan, 1963; PhD in Pharmaceutics, Ohio State U., 1972. Group leader, rsch. scientist Searle Lab., Skokie, Ill., 1972-78; sect. head Endo Lab. The Dupont Co., Garden City, N.Y., 1978-81; prof. pharmaceutics Coll. Pharmacy Rutgers U., Piscataway, N.J., 1981-86, prof. II, 1986-89, dept. chmn., 1982-88, Parke-Davis chair, 1989—; dir., founder Controlled Drug-Delivery Rsch. Ctr. Rutgers U., Piscataway, 1982-99; vis. prof. Nat. U. Singapore, 1999-2000; provost for univ. R & D Kaohsiung Med. U., 2000—. Cons. WHO, UN, 1988—; mem. editl. bd. several sci. jour., U.S., Spain, France, Taiwan, U.K., 1983—; com. of revision U.S. Pharmcopeial Conv., 1995-2000; bd. dirs. Nat. Health Rsch. Inst. Author: Novel Drug Delivery Systems, 1982, 2d rev. edit., 1992, Nasal Systemic Drug Delivery, 1989; editor: Transdermal Controlled Systemic Medications, 1987; editor-in-chief Ency. Drug Delivery, 2004—; contbr. more than 310 articles to profl. jours. Recipient Sci. and Tech. Achievement award, Bd. of Trustees award for rsch. excellence, Disting. Lecture Chair Parke-Davis Endowed chair. Fellow Acad. Pharm. Sci. Rsch./Am. Pharm. Assn., Am. Assn. Pharm. Scientists, Am. Inst. Chemists; mem. AAAS, Controlled Release Soc. (bd. dirs. 1984-87), Acad. Pharm. Rsch. and Sci., Parenteral Drug Assn., Fed. Internationale Pharmaceutique, Am. Chem. Soc. (polymeric materials scis. and engring. divsn.), Am. Assn. Coll. Pharmacy, Am. Found. for Pharm. Edn., N.Y. Acad. Scis., Sigma Xi, Rho Chi. Achievements include 25 patents for novel pharmaceutical delivery systems; for transdermal fertility control system and process; for programmable peptide/protein delivery; for oramucosal peptide delivery; for transdermal absorption dosage unit for estradiol and other estrogenic steroids; for transdermal estrogen/progestin dosage unit, system and process; transdermal iontotheraputic system, dosage unit and process. Office: Kaohsiung Med U R&D Office 100 Shih-Chuan 1st Rd Kaohsiung Taiwan Office Phone: (886) 7-312-1101. E-mail: yiechien@aol.com.

CHIEN-HALE, ELIZABETH, lawyer; d. Tony Tze-Chu Chien and Ni-Teh Ou; m. Roger Hale, May 19, 1985; children: Miranda, Morgan Lloyd. BS, U. Calif., Berkeley, 1983, MA, 1989; JD, U. Hawaii, 1994; LLM, Georgetown U., 1996. Bar: Hawaii 1994, D.C. 1996, Calif. 1998, U.S. Patent and Trademark Office 1998, registered: Hong Kong Law Soc. (fgn. lawyer) 2000; patent agt. Can. Intellectual Property Office. Patent liaison Zexel, Sunnyvale, Calif., 1996—97; assoc. Wilson Sonsini Goodrich & Rosati, Palo Alto, Calif., 1997—99, Fish & Richardson, Menlo Park, Calif., 1999—2000; sr. assoc. Baker & McKenzie, Hong Kong, 2000—01; pvt. practice Fremont, Calif., 2001—; dir. Inst. for Intellectual Property in Asia, Fremont, 2002—. Vis. scholar Peking U. Coll. Law, 1995; adj. prof. Northwestern Poly. U., Fremont, 2003—05. Contbr. articles to profl. jours. Elected mem. Neighborhood Bd., Honolulu, 1994; bd. dirs. Sunnyvale Ctr. for Innovations, Inventions and Ideas, Sunnyvale, Calif., 2004—05. Mem.: ABA (assoc.; com. chair 2002—, chair China task force intellectual property law sect. 2003—), Silicon Valley-China Wireless Tech. Assn. (dir. programs Silicon Valley 2004—), Am. Intellectual Property Law Assn. (assoc.), Am. Soc. Internat. Law (assoc.; interest group chair and vice chair 2003—05). Office: Inst for Intellectual Property in Asia 40087 Mission Blvd #367 Fremont CA 94539 Office Phone: 408-776-8719. Business E-Mail: ech@institute-ip-asia.org.

CHIGNOLI, C(ELSO) WILLIAM, health care center administrator; b. Santa Fe, Argentina, Apr. 19, 1938; MD, Universidad Nacional Cordoba, Argentina, 1961; MDiv, Eden Theol Sem., 1994. Telemedicine dir. Miami Children Hosp., 1985-89; pres. Global Outreach Network, Miami, 1989-93, Accion Social Comunitaria, St. Louis, 1993—; exec. dir. Am. Assn. of Family Counselors, 1999—. Founder, pres. Cross Cultural Studies Inst. Editor Family Counselor Jour., 1999. Sr. pastor Iglesia de la Nueva Comunidad/Sruggs U.M.C., 1995-2000; adv. mem. Nat. Coun. of the Chs. of Christ the USA, 1996-2000; conf. sr. min. The United Meth. Hispanic Ministry, 1995; bd. dirs. The Olive Br.-A Ctr. for Young Families, 1995-96; del. White House Conf. on Aging, Washington, 1995; mem. minority, elderly and disability com. State of Mo., 1994-95. Mem. NATAS, Am. Pub. Health Assn., Internat. Assn. for Cross-Cultural Psychology, Asociacion Para La Educacion Teologica Hispana, Internat. Teleconferencing Assn., Soc. of Satellite Profls. Internat., Nat. Religious Broadcasters, Am. Assn. of Christian Counselors, Health Scis. Comms. Assn., Assn. of Biomed. Communicators Dirs., Fla. Mortion Picture and TV Assn. Home: 9112 Desmond Dr Saint Louis MO 63126-2808 Office: Am Assn Family Counselors 3646 Fairview Ave Saint Louis MO 63116-4747 E-mail: cchignoli@aol.com.

CHIH, CHUNG-YING, physicist, consultant; b. Yuki, Fukien, China, Dec. 11, 1916; s. Lai Sui and Sung-Yee (Lin) C.; BSc, Nat. Tsing Hua U., Peking, China, 1937; PhD, U. Calif., Berkeley, 1954; m. Alice Yuen, Aug. 15, 1955; came to U.S., 1948, naturalized, 1962. Instr. physics Fukien Med. Coll., 1937-40; instr., then asso. prof. Fukien Tchrs. Coll., 1940-44; assoc. prof., then prof. physics Nat. Chi-Nan U., 1944-45; prof. physics Kiang-su Coll., 1945-48; physicist Radiation Lab., U. Calif., Berkeley, 1948-54, summer 1956; mem. faculty Middlebury (Vt.) Coll., 1954-68, prof. physics, 1966-68; sci. cons., Bridgeport, Conn., 1968— . NSF grantee, 1957-60. Mem. Am. Phys. Soc. Address: 3223 Main St Bridgeport CT 06606-4228

CHIH, LUKE, music educator, conductor; b. Taichung, Taiwan, July 2, 1957; s. Bob Chih and Mary Shau; m. Fanny Chen, Apr. 28, 1955; children: Grace, Samuel. MusM, Chinese Ch. Music Inst., 1987; MBA, Internat. Concordia U., 1994, Concordia U., M of Ch. Music, 1997. Mem. Glory Ministries, Taipei, Taiwan, 1981—; gen. editor Glory Music, Hayward, Calif., 1981—; assoc. pastor worship and music Taipei Internat. Ch., 1984—88; music dir. Grace Bapt. Ch., 1991—94; assoc. pastor worship and music Taipei Tabernacle Ch., 1996—97; CFO Media Group, Inc., Fremont, Calif., 1997—98; dir. outreach First United Presbyn. Ch., San Francisco, 2001—04; asst. prof. ch. music Truth Theol. Sem., Arcadia, 2004—, dir. ch. music dept., 2004—. Lecture Christ Coll., Taipei, 1994—96. Author: (book) Church Music Ministries, Today's High Tech and Church Administration; composer: (music) Concerto for Violin and Two Pianos (PCMC, 1985). Recipient Voting Mem. Grammy award, NARAS, 1988—. Fellow: NARAS; mem.: Choral Music Dir. Assn., Christian Music Pub. Assn., Chinese Composor League, Gospel Music Assn. Home: 21112 E Rimpath Dr Covina CA 91724 Office: Truth Theol Sem 141 E Durate Rd Arcadia CA 91006 Office Phone: 626-574-0770. Home Fax: 626-331-3598; Office Fax: 626-574-0497. Personal E-mail: lukechih@verizon.net. E-mail: lukechih@truthseminary.com.

CHIHARA, CHARLES SEIYO, philosophy educator; b. July 19, 1932; s. George I. and Mary N. (Fushiki) C.; m. Carol J. Rosen, June 14, 1964; 1 child, Michelle N. BS, Seattle U., 1954; MS, Purdue U., 1956; PhD, U. Wash., 1960. Instr. U. Wash., Seattle, 1961-62; asst. prof. U. Ill., Urbana, 1962-63, U. Calif., Berkeley, 1963-68, assoc. prof., 1968-74, prof. philosophy dept., 1974—2000, emeritus prof., 2000—. Author: Ontology and the Vicious-Circle Principle, 1973, Constructibility and Mathematical Existence, 1990, The Worlds of Possibility, 1998, A Structural Account of Mathematics, 2004. NEH fellow for ind. rsch., Paris, 1985-86, U. Calif., 1994-95; postdoctoral fellow Mellon Found., 1964-65, Humanities Rsch. fellow U. Calif., 1967-68; U. Calif. Pres.'s rsch. fellow in humanities, 1996-97. Office: Univ Calif Dept Philosophy Berkeley CA 94720-0001 Office Phone: 510-642-2722. Business E-Mail: charles1@socrates.berkeley.edu.

CHIKALLA, THOMAS DAVID, retired science facility administrator; b. Milw., Sept. 9, 1935; s. Paul Joseph and Margaret Ann (Dittrich) C.; m. Ruth Janet Laun, June 20, 1960; children: Paul, Mark, Karyn. BS in Metallurgy, U. Wis., 1957, PhD in Metallurgy, 1966; MS in Metallurgy, U. Idaho, 1960. Research scientist Gen. Electric Co., Richland, Wash., 1957-62; sr. research scientist Battelle Pacific N.W. Labs., Richland, 1964-72, sect. mgr., 1972-80, programs mgr., 1980-83, dept. mgr., 1983-86, assoc. dir., 1986-95; ret., 1995. Tchr. U. Wis., Madison, 1962-64. Contbr. articles to profl. jours. Fellow AEC. Fellow Am. Ceramic Soc. (counselor 1974-80); mem. AAAS, Am. Nuclear Soc., Sigma Xi. Clubs: Desert Ski (pres. 1958-59), Alpine. Republican. Roman Catholic. Avocations: skiing, golf, woodworking, mountain climbing. Home: 2108 Harris Ave Richland WA 99352-2021 E-mail: healey1828@aol.com.

CHIKLIS, MICHAEL, actor; b. Lowell, Mass., Aug. 30, 1963; m. Michelle Moran, June 21, 1992; children: Autumn, Odessa. BFA in acting, Boston U., 1986. Actor: (TV series) The Commish, 1991—95, St. Michael's Crossing, 1999, Daddio, 2000, Heavy Gear: The Animated Series (voice), 2001—02, The Shield (also prodr., 2003), 2002— (Emmy award for outstanding lead actor in a drama series, 2002, Golden Globe award for best performance by an actor in a TV series - drama, 2003); (TV films) The Commish: In the Shadow of the Gallows, 1995, The Three Stooges, 2000, numerous TV guest appearances; (films) Wired, 1989, The Rain Killer, 1990, Nixon, 1995, The Taxman, 1998, Soldier, 1998, Body and Soul, 1998, Carlo's Wake, 1999, Last Request, 1999, Do Not Disturb, 1999, Sen to Chihiro no Kamikakushi (voice), 2001, Fantastic Four, 2005; (Broadway plays) Defending the Caveman, (off-Broadway plays) Tracks, Return to Sender, The Fester and Rot Raw View, Ersatz Life, (regional theater) As You Like It, Romeo and Juliet, Streetcar Named Desire, You Can't Take It With You, The Rivals. Office: FX Networks LLC 1000 Santa Monica Blvd Los Angeles CA 90067*

CHIKLY, BRUNO JACQUES, physician; b. Paris, Feb. 10, 1961; arrived in U.S., 1995; s. Leon S. and Caroline Chikly; m. Alaya C. Ryan, Feb. 22, 1996. BS, Lycée Louis Le Grand, Paris, 1979; lic. in psychology, U. Paris XIII, 1984; MD, St. Antoine Hosp., 1989. Pres., lymph drainage therapist, founder, ptnr. Upledger Inst./Internat. Alliance Healthcare Educators, West Palm Beach, Fla., 1995—; pres. Internat. Health & Healing, Inc., Scottsdale, Ariz., 1995—. Cons. Riekes Ctr. for Human Enhancement, Calif., 1997—. Mem. adv. bd. Jour. Bodywork and Movement, U.K., 1998; contbr. articles to profl. jours. Mem. Am. Acad. Osteopathy (assoc.), Internat. Soc. Lymphology, Internat. Alliance Healthcare Educators, Cranial Acad. (assoc.), Upledger Inst. Achievements include invention of manual discovery of specific rythym of the lymphatic fluid, creation of manual lymphatic mapping technique, manual chik technique and lympho-facsia release technique (lfr). Avocations: sports, art. Home and Office: 28607 N 152nd St Scottsdale AZ 85262-6939

CHIKWENDU, SUNDAY C., engineering educator, mathematician; s. Joseph Chukwunwike and Cordelia Chikwendu; m. Eudora Ebitimi Kombo, May 25, 1968; children: Adaora Atonye Chikwendu-Henry, Zamafa Inodu, Meremu Ngozi, Azuka Biriye. BSE in Aerospace and Mech. Engring., Princeton U., 1966; postgrad., MIT, 1966—68; MS, U. Wash., 1969, PhD, 1971. Vis. asst. prof. math. UCLA, 1971—73; lectr., sr. lectr., assoc. prof. mech. engring. U. Nigeria, Nsukka, 1973—84; vis. asst. prof. U. Wash., Seattle, 1977—78, vis. prof. applied math., 1984—85; assoc. prof., prof. math. SUNY, New Paltz, 1985—, chair math. dept., 2000—03. Contbr. articles to profl. jours. Fellow Tchrs. for Africa, Ghana, Internat. Found. for Edn. and Self-Help, 1998—99; scholar African Scholarship Program of Am. Univs., Princeton U., African-Am. Inst., 1963—66; Du Pont fellow, MIT, 1966—67, Faculty Summer fellow, Smithsonian Instn., 1989. Mem.: ASME, AIAA, Math. Assn. Am., Am. Math. Soc., Phi Beta Kappa, Sigma Xi. Achievements include a perturbation method for hyperbolic equations with small nonlinearities; research in Slow-zone and N-zone models for contaminant dispersion in shear flows; diffusion analogy for stresses in granular soils. Office: SUNY-New Paltz 75 S Manheim Blvd New Paltz NY 12561

CHILCOAT, DALE ALLEN, artist, visual and performing arts educator; b. Phoenix, Ariz., Aug. 16, 1938; s. Robert Polk and Martha Viola (Barton) C.; m. Sharon Fernandez, Dec. 27, 1965; children: Jennifer Lee, Joshua Fernandez. BA, Ariz. State U., 1961; postgrad., U. Florence, 1963; MA, Calif. State U., Northridge, 1967. Cert. tchr., N.Y., Calif. Art tchr. Needles (Calif.) Pub. Schs., 1961-62; chmn. art dept. North Shore Schs., Glen Head, N.Y., 1962-70; chmn. dept. visual arts San Leandro (Calif.) High Sch., 1970-84; dir. collective antiques San Mateo (Calif.) Antique Corp., 1980-81; dir. visual and performing arts San Leandro Schs., 1986—. State mentor tchr. San Leandro Unified, 1984-94; cons. Greater Bay Area, San Mateo, 1981-94; chmn. art curriculum San Leandro Schs., 1988-94; arts dir. North Shore Sch., 1962-70. Author Calif. state art curriculum, 1989. Named Outstanding Artist Operation Democracy Am., 1963. Mem. Calif. Art Educators Assn. (no. state rep. 1994), San Leandro Tchrs. Assn., Nat. Tchrs. Assn. (rep. 1962). Republican. Presbyterian. Home: 62 Broadmoor Blvd San Leandro CA 94577-1818 Office: San Leandro Schs 14735 Juniper St San Leandro CA 94579-1222

CHILCOAT, RICHARD ALLEN, army officer, university president; b. Wilmerding, Pa., Sept. 16, 1938; s. Floyd Donald and Edna Bailey (Moles0 C.; m. Dixie Lowers, June 6, 1964; children: Michael, Sharon A. BS, U.S. Mil. Acad., 1964; MBA, Harvard U., 1974. Commd. 2d lt. US Army, 1964; speechwriter to Gen. John A. Wickham Jr., Office Chief of Staff, U.S. Army, Washington, 1984-87; comdr. Devil Troop Brigade, 5th Inf. Divsn. US Army, Ft. Polk, La., 1987-89, chief of staff, 3d Inf. Divsn. Germany, 1989-90; exec. asst. to Gen. Colin L. Powell, Joint Chiefs of Staff, Washington, 1990-92; dep. comdg. gen. US Army Tng. Ctr., Ft. Jackson, SC, 1993-94; comdt. US Army War Coll., Carlisle Barracks, Pa., 1994-97; pres. Nat. Def. U., Washington, 1997—2000; lt. gen. US Army (ret.), 2000; dean, George Bush Sch. Govt. & Public Svc. Texas A&M Univ., College Station, 2001—. Decorated DSM, Legion of Merit, Bronze Star with oak leaf cluster, Air medals. Mem. Assn. of U.S. Army, U.S. Mil. Acad. Assn. of Grads. Avocations: tennis, golf. Office: Bush Sch Govt Pub Svc 2132A Allen Building Texas A&M Univ College Station TX 77844 Office Phone: 979-862-8007. Business E-Mail: rchilcoat@tamu.edu.*

CHILCOTE, GARY M., museum director, reporter; b. St. Joseph, Mo., Nov. 2, 1934; s. Merrill and Mary Thelma C.; m. Mary Carolyn Abmeyer, April 2, 1958; children: Douglas A., Carolyn D. BA, Northwest Mo. State U., 1956. News-press spl. corr. St. Joseph News-Press/Gazette, 1954—2002; mus. dir. Patee House Mus. and Jesse James Home Mus., St. Joseph, 1963—. Vocat. tchr. Hillyard Tech. Sch., St. Joseph, 1964-91. Author, editor Pony Express Mail, 1972—. Staff sgt. Mo. Air Guard, 1957-63. Mem. Nat. Pony Express Assn. (nat. dir., nat. v.p. 1990—), Pony Express Hist. Assn. (bd. dirs., co-founder 1963), James-Younger Gang (nat. pres. 1997—, 98-99). Republican. Home: 1910 N 32nd St Saint Joseph MO 64506-2313 Office: Patee Ho Mus/Jesse James Ho Mus 1202 Penn St Saint Joseph MO 64503-2560 Office Phone: 816-232-8206.

CHILCOTE, LEE A., lawyer; b. Cleve., May 5, 1942; BA, Dartmouth Coll., 1964; BE, Thayer Sch. Engring., 1965; JD, U. Calif., San Francisco, 1972. Bar: Ohio 1972. With Arter & Hadden, Cleve. Bd. dirs., The Chilcote Co., sec., 1972—. Trustee Hough Housing Corp. 1972-88; bd. dirs. Cleve. Warehouse Dist. Local Devel. Corp., 1986—. Mem. ABA (real property and corp. sects.), Am. Coll. Real Estate Lawyers, Cleve. Bar Assn., Order of Coif, Thurston Soc. Office: The Chilcote Law Firm The Cedar Grandview Bldg 12434 Cedar Rd Ste No 1 Cleveland Heights OH 44106 Office Phone: 216-795-4117. E-mail: lee.chilcote@sbcglobal.net.

CHILCOTE, LUGEAN LESTER, retired architect, researcher; b. Oklahoma City, Jan. 14, 1929; s. Mark H. and Myrita A.J. (Lugeanbeal) C.; m. Clara Bernice Dudis, Dec. 18, 1953; children: Martin L., Frederick M., David L.(dec.), Bradley R. BArch, U. Ark., 1951. Registered architect, Ark., Mo.; cert. Nat. Coun. Archtl. Registration Bds. Designer, draftsman Ken Cole, Jr., Architect, Little Rock, 1953—54; architect Swaim & Allen Architects, Little Rock, 1954—58; architect, prin. Blass Chilcote Carter Gaskin Bogart Norcross (and predecessor firms), Little Rock, 1958. Gen. chmn. Gulf States Regional Conf., 1966; judge City Beautiful Commn., 1967-68; pres. Ark. State Bd. Architects, 1991-96; apptd. mem. bldg. code bd. of appeals, City of Little Rock, 1986-94. Co-author: 50 Years of Design, 1980; prin. works include First Christian Ch., 1962, Continental bldg., 1969, Main Toll and Dial bldg. Southwestern Bell Telephone Co., 1968, Bapt. Med. Center Complex, 1971-73, U. Ark. Med. Sci. Campus, 1973-99, U.S. Postal Svc. Gen. Mail Facility, Conv./Exhibit/Excelsior-Trust Hotel Complex, 1978-96, Ark. Children's Hosp., 1983-98, all Little Rock, U.S. Post Office and Courthouse, Pine Bluff, Ark., 1967, Nat. Center for Toxicological Research, Pine Bluff, 1973-90, Jefferson Reg. med. Ctr., Pine Bluff, 1985-96, White River Med. Ctr., Batesville, Ark., 1992-95, Drew Meml. Med. Ctr., Monticello, Ark., 1990-99. Mem. com. Ark. Art Festival, 1968, West Little Rock YMCA, 1969; mem. Ark. Arts Ctr., 1965—; bd. dirs., treas., mem. exec. com. Ark. Cmty. Found., 1972-85; bd. dirs. Ark. Hall of Fame, Quapaw coun. Boy Scouts Am., Pulaski County, Ark.; dist. chmn., mem. exec. bd. of coun. Boy Scouts Am.; mem. Little Rock Bldg. Bd. Appeals, 1986-96; v.p. Ark. Christian Men's Orgn.; mem. exec. com., chmn. bd., elder Ark. Christian Ch. Served to capt. USAF, 1951-53. Recipient Woodbadge Tng. award Boy Scouts Am., Little Rock, 1974, Dist. Award of Merit, 1981, Silver Beaver award, Pulaski County, 1976, Meritorious Svc. award Ark. Cmty. Found., 1985. Fellow AIA (pres. Ark. chpt. 1966-67, trustee ednl. endowment fund 1970-72, 83-95, gen. chmn. gulf states regional conf. 1966, nat. del. 1967, chmn. nat. profl. interest com. 1982-83, bd. dirs. nat. polit. action com. 1983-85, chmn. legis. affairs, chmn. Nat. Risk Mgmt. Com., chair 1997, profl. adv. bd. U. Ark. 1997, Gold Medal award Ark. chpt. 1996, bd. dir. 2000-2002); mem. Pleasant Valley Country Club Little Rock (bd. dirs., bd. govs.) Avocations: golf, fishing, hunting. Home: 806 Carywood Ln Little Rock AR 72205-2802 E-mail: lchilcote@aristotle.net.

CHILCOTE, SAMUEL DAY, JR., trade association administrator; b. Casper, Wyo., Aug. 24, 1937; s. Sam D. and Juanita C. (Cornelison) C.; m. Ellen Sheridan Spear, Nov. 11, 1966. BS, Idaho State U., 1959. Adminstrv. asst. Continental Oil Co., Glenrock, Wyo., 1960-63; asst. supt. public instrn., dir. Wyo. Surplus Property Agy., Wyo. Sch. Lunch Program, Cheyenne Wyo. Dept. Edn., Wyo., 1963-67; supr. North Ctrl. region Distilled Spirits Inst., Denver, 1967-71, exec. dir., COO North Ctrl. region Washington, 1971-73; exec. v.p., COO, Distilled Spirits Coun., Inc., Washington, 1973-77, pres., CEO, 1978-81; pres. Tobacco Inst., Washington, 1981-99; chmn. Chilcote Enterprises, Potomac, Md., 1999—; mng. ptnr. Tubac (Ariz.) Golf Resort and Spa, 2003. Adv. council consumer goods industry sect. Dept. Commerce. Pres. Sky Ranch Found. for Boys, 1975-81, pres. emeritus, 1981—; treas. Ford's Theatre, 1984-88, vice chmn., trustee, 1988-96, chmn., 1997-99; v.p. Santa Cruz County Citizens Assn., 2000-2005; treas. Santa Cruz County Tourism Coun., 2004—; bd. dirs., exec. com. Tubac Hist. Soc., 2004—; bd. dirs. St. Andrew's Children's Clinic, 2005, Art Barn, exec. com., Tukee Hist. Soc., 2005—; chmn. Awards Dinner Com., 1989-2000, USO Met. Washington, past pres. Capt. U.S. Army, 1959-60. Recipient Profl. Achievement award Idaho State U. Coll. Bus., 1986, Man of Yr. award Anti-Defamation league, 1986, Humanitarian of the Yr. award Tobacco and Confectionery Div. Dinner for the UJA-Fedn. 1991 campaign, Good Scout award Greater N.Y. Coun. Boy Scouts Am., 1996. Mem. Santa Cruz Citizen Assn. (v.p. 1999—), Georgetown Club, Congl. Country Club (past pres., exec. com., bd. govs.), Burning Tree Club, Nat. Press Club, Capitol Hill Club, City Club, F St. Club, TPC Avenel (Washington), Jefferson Islands Club (bd. govs.), Masons, Elks, Shriners. Mailing: PO Box 1235 Tubac AZ 85646-1235

CHILD, FRANK CLAYTON, economist, educator; b. Salt Lake City, Aug. 21, 1921; s. Charles William and Alveretta Gertrude (Clayton) C.; m. Eva Lorraine Clough, Sept. 22, 1948; children: Charles William, Matthew Daniel, Tracy, Suzanne. BA, U. Utah, 1941; MA, Stanford U., 1947, PhD, 1954. Instr. econs. Stanford U., 1950, Williams Coll., 1950-52; asst. prof. Pomona Coll., 1952-56; asst. prof., assoc. prof. econs. Mich. State U., 1956-59; adviser Mich. State U. Adv. Group, Saigon, Vietnam, 1959-61; vis. assoc. prof. econs. Stanford U., 1961-62; from assoc. prof. to prof. U. Calif.-Davis, 1962-82, chmn. dept., 1963-80; prof. econs. U. Calif.-Santa Cruz, 1983-90, prof. emeritus, 1990—, dean social sci. divsn., 1983-88. Econs. cons. UN Devel. Program, Sabah, Malaysia, 1965, AID, Pakistan, 1966; sr. economist, mission to Vietnam, Devel. and Resources Corp., 1967; research adviser Pakistan Inst. Devel. Econs. (Yale-Pakistan project), Karachi, 1967-69; vis. prof. Inst. for Devel. Studies, U. Nairobi, Kenya, 1972-73; also cons.; coordinator Agrl. Devel. Systems Project/Egypt, 1979-82; cons. Devel. and Resources Corp., Brazil, 1972, Pakistan Inst. Devel. Econs., Islamabad, 1975, 76; team leader agrl. sector rev. UN Devel. Program, Dhaka, Bangladesh, 1988-89. Author: Theory and Practice of German Exchange Control, 1958, Toward a Policy for Economic Growth (in Viet Nam), 1963, Small-Scale Industry in Rural Kenya, 1977; contbr. articles to profl. jours. Served from 2d lt. to capt. AUS, 1942-46. Decorated Bronze Star; Croix de Guerre France. Mem. Am. Econ. Assn. Home: 118 Limestone Ln Santa Cruz CA 95060-2058 E-mail: child@ucsc.edu.

CHILD, JOHN SOWDEN, JR., lawyer; b. Lansdale, Pa., July 22, 1944; s. John Sowden and Beatrice Thelma (Landes) C. BS in Polit. Sci., MIT, 1967; BSChemE, 1967; JD, U. Pa., 1973; BLit in Politics, Oxford U., 1974. Bar: Pa. 1974, N.Y. 1977, U.S. Dist. Ct. (ea. dist.) Pa. 1978, U.S. Dist. Ct. (ea. dist.) N.Y. 1978, U.S. Patent and Trademark Office 1978, U.S. Ct. Appeals (2d cir.) 1978, U.S. Ct. Appeals (fed. cir.) 1981, U.S. Ct.Appeals (3d cir.) 1986. Assoc. Davis Hoxie Faithfull & Hapgood, N.Y.C., 1974-78, Synnestvedt & Lechner, Phila., 1978-88; of counsel Dann, Dorfman, Herrell and Skillman, Phila., 1988—; arbitrator Pa. Ct. Common Pleas, Phila., 1979—, U.S. Dist. Ct., Ea. Dist.) Pa., Phila., 1983—. Firm coord. United Way Southeastern Pa., 1983-88. Mem. Am. Intellectual Property Law Assn., N.Y. Patent, Trademark and Copyright Law Assn., Phila. Bar Assn., Phila. Patent Law Assn. (chmn. program com. 1981-85, 94—, editor, co-editor newsletter 1980-90, gov. 1985-87, sec. 1987-89), Mil. Order Fgn. Wars, Com. of Seventy, Soc. Colonial Wars (treas. 1989-91, councilor 1991-97), English Speaking Union, Colonial Soc. Pa., Phila. Oxford and Cambridge Soc. (sec. 1985—). Republican. Mem. Soc. of Friends. Clubs: Union League, Phila. Club., Cricket (Phila.). Home: 8221 Seminole St Philadelphia PA 19118-3929 Office: Dann Dorfman Herrell & Skillman 1601 Market St Ste 720 Philadelphia PA 19103-2307

CHILDERS, BOB EUGENE, educational association executive; b. Cleveland, Miss., Sept. 16, 1930; s. William Nick and Allie Jeanette (Doty) C.; m. Jo Ann Roberts, May 1, 1953; children: William Frank, Robert Clayton, John Murry, Julia Ann. BA, Union U., 1953; MA, Memphis State U., 1958; EdD, U. Tenn., 1964. Cert. tchr., adminstr., Tenn. Field engr. RCA, El Paso, Tex., 1955-57; instr. USN, Memphis, 1957-60; prin. Halls H.S., Knoxville, Tenn., 1960-61, McMinn County H.S., Athens, Tenn., 1961-64; asst. commr. Tenn. State Dept. Edn., Nashville, 1964-66; regional dir. USOE, Vocat.-Tech. and Adult Edn., Atlanta, 1966-69; exec. dir. Commn. Occupl. Edn., Atlanta, 1969-82, So. Assn. Colls. and Schs., Atlanta, 1982-92. Cons. U.S. Dept. Edn., Washington, 1963-79, Fla. State Legislature, Tallahassee, 1979, Md. Values Edn. Commn., Annapolis, 1979-80; founder, pres. Childers-Childress Family Assn., 1982-88, 90-96. Editor SACS Procs., 1982-92. Bd. dirs. Boy Scouts Am., Atlanta, 1980-87, Ctr. for Citizenship Edn., Washington, 1978-81; bd. trustees YMCA, Nashville, 1964-66; v.p. Religious Heritage of Am., St. Louis, 1979-86; active Rotary, Atlanta, 1981-92. With U.S. Army, 1953-55. Mem. Am. Vocat. Assn. (life 1966, cons.), Am. Tech. Edn. Assn. (life 1978, pres.1984, v.p. 1983), Am. Vocat. Rsch. Assn., Am. Soc. Assn. Execs., Phi Delta Kappa (past treas. 1960-61, sec. 1960-61), Iota Lambda Sigma, Sigma Alpha Epsilon (pres. 1952). Democrat. Baptist. Avocations: geneology, vitaculture, gardening. Home and Office: 960 River Rd Woodruff SC 29388-9110

CHILDERS, CHARLES EUGENE, mining company executive; b. West Frankfort, Ill., Oct. 29, 1932; s. Joel Marion and Cora E. (Choate) C.; m. Norma A. Casper, June 8, 1952; children: Joel M., Katrina K. BS, U. Ill., 1955; LLD (hon.), U. Saskatchewan, 1994. With Duval Corp., Carlsbad, N.Mex., 1955-62, Internat. Minerals Corp. (IMC), 1963-77; v.p. Esterhazy oper. IMC, 1977-79; pres. IMC Coal, Lexington, 1979-81; v.p. potash oper. IMC, 1981-82, v.p. expansion and devel., 1982-87; pres., chief exec. officer Potash Corp. of Sask., Inc., Saskatoon, Can., 1987-90, chmn., pres., chief exec. officer, 1990-98, chmn., chief exec. officer, 1998-99, chmn., 1999—. Bd. dirs., past chmn. bd. Canpotex Ltd., Sask., Found. for Agronomic Rsch.; past chmn. bd. The Fertilizer Inst.; bd. dirs. Conf. Bd. Can., Battle Mountain Gold Corp.; past chmn. Potash and Phosphate Inst.; mem. fertilizer industry adv. com. to FAO. Dir. at large Jr. Achievement of Can. 1st lt. U.S. Army, 1955-57. Mem. AIME, Can. Inst. Mining and Metallurgy, Sask. Potash Producers Assn. (past. chmn.), Internat. Fertilizer Industry Assn. (past pres.). Republican. Baptist.

CHILDERS, ELSIE TRUSTY, recording studio owner; b. Henderson, Ky., Sept. 26, 1924; d. Enoch Bradshaw and Lola Pearl (Trusty) Arbuckle; widowed; children: Terry James, Jimmy Wayne. Student in bus., Midway Coll., 1942. Program clk. Hopkins County Agrl. Stabilization and Conservation Service Office, USDA, Madisonville, Ky., 1955-80; recording studio owner Trusty Tuneshop Recording Studio, Nebo, Ky., 1980—. Composer more than 400 songs; pub., editor Trusty Internat. Newsletter, 1992-96. Pianist, soloist Missionary Bapt. Ch., Nebo, 1959—. Recipient Leadership award King Eagle Awards Show, Nashville, 1996; named to Hon. Order Ky. Cols., Gov. of Ky., 1978, one of Am.'s Leading Execs., 1984. Mem. Country Music Assn., Nashville Songwriters Assn. Internat., Nat. Acad. Songwriters, Bus. and Profl. Women's Club of Madisonville, Rotary Club of Madisonville (sec. 1993-96), Hopkins Coutny/Madisonville C. of C. Democrat. Avocations: fishing, reading, watching tv. Home: 8781 Rose Creek Rd Nebo KY 42441-9766 Office: Trusty Tuneshop Rec Studio 8771 Rose Creek Rd Nebo KY 42441-9766 Office Phone: 270-249-3194.

CHILDERS, JOHN CHARLES, lawyer, civil engineer; b. Gallipolis, Ohio, Oct. 27, 1950; s. Frank W. and Bernice E. (Ziler) C.; m. Judith Marie Hughes, Jan. 1, 1976; children: Rachel Grace, Benjamin Hughes. BS in Civil Engring. cum laude, Ohio U., 1972; JD cum laude, Capital U., 1978. Bar: Ohio 1978, U.S. Supreme Ct. 1987. Pvt. practice, Carrollton, Ohio, 1978—; asst. pros. atty. County of Carroll, Carrollton, Ohio, 1981—89, 2001; ptnr. Childers and Smith, Attys., Carrollton, 1982—. Mem. Ohio Bar Assn. (coun. of dels. 1988-2005), Carroll County Bar Assn. (pres. 1984-2003). Office: Childers and Smith 70 Public Sq # 252 Carrollton OH 44615-1403

CHILDERS, MARY ANN, newscaster; m. Jay Levine. BS in Speech, Northwestern U., Evanston, Ill. Assoc. prodr. Phil Donahue Show, Chgo.; with WAVE-TV, Louisville, WTHR-TV, Indpls.; anchor, med. editor and reporter WLS-TV, Chgo., 1980—94, WBBM-TV, Chgo., 1994—, co-anchor 11am and 4pm and med. editor. Hon. bd. mem. Y-Me, Nat. Kidney Found. of Ill., Nat. Spinal Cord Injury Assn.; mem. Chgo. Cancer Rsch. Found.; mem. nat. adv. coun. Northwestern U. Sch. of Speech; mem. Chgo. Network. Recipient 3 Emmy awards. Office: WBBM-TV 630 McClurg Ct Chicago IL 60601

CHILDERS, PERRY ROBERT, psychology educator; b. Monticello, Ky., July 17, 1932; s. Charles T. and Leva M. (Spradlin) C.; children: William Charles, Richard Calvin, Linda Louise, Leva Catherine; m. Joyce Carolyn Irby Murray, May 14, 1988. BA, U. Ky., 1958; MA (Grad. fellow), U. Ga., 1961, EdD, 1963, PhD, 1966; JD, Woodrow Wilson Coll. Law (now Ga. State U.), 1978. Lic. psychologist, Wis. Asst. prof. psychology U. Ky., 1963-65; mgmt. psychologist Rohrer, Hibler & Replogle, Atlanta, 1966-67; assoc. prof. psychology U. Fla., 1967-68, U. Wis., 1968-73; dep. supt. edn. State of La., 1973; dir. evaluation and monitoring, social and rehab. svc. HEW, Atlanta, after 1974; dir. quality control Social Security Adminstrn., after 1977, state program officer, 1980-88; dep. commr. Tenn. Dept. Human Svcs., 1979-80; dir. work programs, refugee resettlement, spl. initiatives HHS, 1988-95; prof. psychology Gulf Coast Coll., Panama City, Fla., 1995—. Psychol. cons. to bus. mgmt.; cons. computer systems and med. psychology, 1996—. Office: 2905 Kings Dr Panama City FL 32405-1615

CHILDERS, TODD, graphic designer; b. Shelby, NC, Feb. 15, 1964; s. Norris Swain and Bobbie Childers; m. Jennifer Karches, June 23, 1994. B in environ. design, NC State U. Sch. of Design, 1982—87; MFA, Calif. Inst. of the Arts, 1991—93. Environ. graphic designer Graphic Dimensions, Inc., Garner, NC, 1987—88, Land Design Rsch., Inc., Columbia, Md., 1988—89; sr. corp. graphic designer Am. Yard Products, Inc., Orangeburg, SC, 1989—91; computer lab student Calif. Inst. of the Arts, 1992—93; assoc. prof. of graphic design Bowling Green State U. Sch. of Art, 1994—; vis. lectr. history of graphic design Western Carolina U., 1994. Interim chair graphic design divsn. Bowling Green State U. Sch. of Art, 2004; graphic designer Bowling Green State U. Coll. of Arts & Sciences; free-lance graphic designer BGSU Women's Studies, BGSU Fine Art Galleries, 1994—2005. Stationery design, Todd Childers Graphic Design stationery, poster, Women in the Zone, promotional video, BurnOut, stationery design, Tood Childers stationery (Hon. Mention from How Magazine's self promtional issue, 1989), font design, Ennis Brown, web site, Todd Childers Graphic Design web site, 70 graphic designs, Professional Portfolio (Selected for the Graphism collection at the Bibliothèque Nationale de France Réserve des Livres Rares Collection, 2003), poster, Out of the Mouths of Babes: The Power and Politics of Women's Humor, The Holocaust and the Moving Image (Merit Award from Portfolios.com First Ann. Graphic Design Competition, 2004), advertsing campaign, BGSU Make a Big Difference United Way 2000 (Gold Medal for Art & Graphics, 2001), font design, Usher Font Family (Hon. Mention in Garage Fonts Next Big Thing Font Design Competition, 1999), self promotional brochure, Todd Childers Graphic Design Self Promotional Brochure. Creative dir. Wood County Dem. Party, Bowling Green, Ohio, 2003—05. Coll. of Arts & Sciences Student Competitions grant, Bowling Green State U., 2005, TECS grant, 2003, Coll. of Arts & Sciences Faculty Devel. grant, 2003, 2000, Speed grant, 1995, 1996, 1999, 2003. Mem.: Soc. of Type Aficionados, United Coll. Designers Assn., Am. Inst. of Graphic Arts, Coll. Arts Assn. D-Liberal. Avocations: music, foreign and art films, thai food, basketball. Home: 407 N Main St Bowling Green OH 43402 Office: Bowling Green State Univ School of Art Fine Art Ctr Bldg BGSU Bowling Green OH 43403 Office Phone: 419-372-8374. Home Fax: 419-372-2544; Office Fax: 419-372-2544. Personal E-mail: btoddch@bgnet.bgsu.edu.

CHILD-OLMSTED, GISÈLE ALEXANDRA, retired language educator; b. Port-au-Prince, Haiti, Dec. 27, 1946; (parents Am. citizens); d. Daniel McGuire Child and Alice Dejean Child; m. Hans George Bickel, Sept. 1967 (div. Apr. 1984); children: Anna Kristina Villemez, Maia Selena Deubert; m. Jerauld Lockwood Olmsted, June 17, 1988. BA in French with honors, U. Md., 1970; MA in French, Johns Hopkins U., 1978, PhD in Romance Langs., 1981; cert. in translation, Georgetown U. Vis. instr. U. Md., College Park, 1980-81; instr. Johns Hopkins U., Balt., 1981-82; lang. instr. Holton-Arms Sch., Bethesda, Md., 1982-83; asst. prof. dept. modern langs. and lit. Loyola Coll., Balt., 1983-89, assoc. prof., 1989-98, chair dept. modern lang. langs. and lit., 1989-94, prof., 1998—2003; ret., 2003. V.p. faculty coun. Loyola Coll., 1998—2000, mem. steering com. Ctr. for Humanities, 1989—94; organizer, dir. Colloquia on Lang., Lit. and Soc., Balt., 1990, Balt., 95, Balt., 99, Balt., 2002. Author: Jean Genet: Criminalité et Transcendance, 1987; contbr. articles to profl. jours. Faculty Rsch. grant Loyola Coll., 1984, 89, Study grant French Embassy, 1986, 89; Gillman fellow, 1970-73, 79-80; visitor's scholar U. Cape Town, South Africa, 1995. Mem. MLA (del. Mid-Atlantic region 1992-94, 96-98), Am. Assn. Tchrs. French, Soc. Prof. Français et Francophones d'Amérique, Les Amis de Stendhal, Phi Beta Kappa. Avocations: painting, golf, antiques, classical music, flamenco dancing. Home: 7735 Arrowood Ct Bethesda MD 20817-2821

CHILDREE, ROBERT LAWRENCE, comptroller; BS in Acctg., U. Ala., 1973. State comptr. Fin. Dept., Ala., 1987—. Mem. Nat. Assn. Auditors, Comptrs., and Treas. (pres. 2001), Nat. Assn. State Comptrs. (pres. 1994, Pres.'s award 1997), Govt. Fin. Officers Assn. of Ala., Assn. Govt. Accts. (pres. Montgomery chpt. 1996-97, Pub. Adminstr. award 1992, Superior Performance award 1996-97, Membership Achievement award 1996-97). Office: Office State Comptroller 100 N Union St Ste 220 Montgomery AL 36130-3701

CHILDRESS, JOEL M., medical educator; b. Monroe, La., Mar. 18, 1955; s. Wilbur Theron and Monteal Finley Childress; m. Dee R. Robinson, Oct. 19, 1996; 1 child, Keely C. B in music edn., U. La., 1978, M in music edn., 1979; MA+30, various, 1981. Cert. Class A La., 1982. Assoc. dir. of bands West Monroe H.S., West Monroe, La., 1984—98; dir. of bands Pearl River Jr. High, Pearl River, La., 1998—2000, Mandeville Jr. High/Tchefuncte Mid. Sch., Mandeville, La., 2000—03, Tchefuncte Mid. Sch., Mandeville, 2003—. Coord. of instrumental music St. Timothy United Meth. Ch., Mandeville, La., 2003—. Author (presenter): (classroom tchr. workshop) The Planets Music Across the Curriculum; author: (article) Field Preparation Suggestions for the Young Director. Vice pres. greens chmn. Covington Country Club, Mandeville, La., 2000—03; pres. Versailles Property Owners Assn., Covington, La., 1999—2002. Recipient Commendation of Excellence, Ouachita Parish Sch. Bd., 1991, 1994. Mem.: Music Educators Nat. Conf., La. Music Educators Assn., Nat. Band Assn., Phi Beta Mu, Kappa Kappa Psi (life). R-Consevative. Meth. Avocations: golf, travel, biking. Home: 308 Ave Palais Royal Covington LA 70433 Office: St Tammany Parish Schs 1530 W Causeway Approach Mandeville LA 70471 Office Phone: 985-626-7118. E-mail: joel.childress@stpsb.org.

CHILDRESS, RICHARD THOMAS, international business consultant; b. Huntington, W.Va., Nov. 22, 1942; s. Grover Burgess and Zenna Belle C.; m. Elli Lisbeth, June 13, 1962; 1 child, Tyrone Richard. BA in Psychology, U. Cin., 1964; MA in Asian Studies, U. Ariz., 1976. Commd. 2d lt. U.S. Army, 1964, advanced through grades to col., 1984; gen. staff officer Asian affairs, exec. officer Dept. of Army, 1978—81; dir. Asian and polit. mil. affairs White House, Nat. Security Coun., 1981—89; pres. Asian Investment Strategies, 1989—; pres., co-founder Asian Energy Corp., Tulsa, Okla., 1992—. Sr. adv. Sec. of State, 1982-88; US del. Assn. Southeast Asian Nations, 1982-88; leader, participant US Policy Del., Vietnam, Laos, 1982-89; designated White House Surrogate Spkr. for Pres. US; NSC advisor to teo presdl. envoys; Rep. Nat. Comm., adv. bd. US-ASEAN Bus. Coun., Inc.; policy adv. Nat. League Prisoners of War, Missing in Action families, mem. U.S.-Philippine Bus. Com.; exec. com. US-Thailand Bus. Coun.; co-chair adv. com. Nat. Ctr. S.E. Asian Studies, Georgetown U.; Indochina forum Aspen Inst.; spkr. in field. Contbr. articles to profl. jours. Decorated Def. Disting. Svc. medal, Legion of Merit with Oak Leaf, Bronze Star, Vietnamese Cross of Gallantry, others; recipient Humanitarian awards Fgn. Govts., Nat. League Prisoners of War/Missing in Action Families, Svc. to Mankind, Pace award Dept. Army. Mem. Asia Soc., Thai-Am. Assn. Mailing: PO Box 104 Flat Rock NC 28731

CHILDRESS, ROBERT G., academic administrator, recreational sports specialist; b. Meridian, Miss., Jan. 26, 1951; s. Gordon Ricketts and Josephine (Huddleston) Childress; m. Bonita Moon, May 26, 1973; children: Bevin Anna, Blake Gordon. BA, U. Tex.-Austin, 1973, MEd, 1976. Cert. intramural recreational sports specialist. Tng. specialist Dir. Recreational Sports, Austin, 1973—76; recreational sports specialist UT-RecSports, Austin, 1976—77; asst. dir. RecSports, Austin, 1977—. Baseball umpire SBUA, Austin, 1986—; basketball official S.W. Basketball Officials Assn., Austin, 1992—2002; Tex. state dir. NIRSA, 1996—98. Bd. mem. Balcones Little League, Austin, 1990—95, v.p., 1995—96. Avocations: golf, reading, officiating HS baseball, walking, exercise. Office: The Division of Recreational Sports/UT Austin 2101 Speedway Austin TX 78712 Office Phone: 512-475-7180. Business E-Mail: bobc@mail.utexas.edu.

CHILDRESS, SCOTT JULIUS, medicinal chemist; b. Greenville, S.C., Apr. 6, 1926; s. Julius Dunford and Ola Irene (Scott) C.; m. Nelly Araxy Medzadour, Dec. 20, 1975 BS, Furman U., 1947; PhD, U. N.C., 1951. Research chemist Tenn. Eastman, Kingsport, 1951-52; research chemist Wallace & Tiernan, Belleville, N.J., 1952-58, Wyeth Labs., Radnor, Pa., 1959-62, mgr. medicinal chemistry, 1962-68, asst. to v.p. research and devel., 1968-73, asst. v.p. research and devel., 1973-85. Patentee in field; contbr. articles to profl. jours. Served with AUS, 1944-46 Fellow N.Y. Acad. Scis.; mem. Am. Chem. Soc. (treas. med. div. 1969-71, chmn. nat. med. chem. symposium 1968), Sigma Xi Home: 604 S Washington Sq Philadelphia PA 19106-4152

CHILDS, ALEX JOSEPH, gynecologist; b. Athens, Ga., Dec. 5, 1975; s. Larry and Gayle Childs; m. Julie Ann Johnson, May 22, 2001; children: Abigael, Emma, Andrew. BS, Mercer U., 1997; MD, Med. Coll. Ga., 2001. Lic. Practice Medicine Ga., 2002, Ala., 2004. Clin. fellow pelvic pain and advanced gynecologic laparoscopy C. Paul Perry Pelvic Pain Ctr. U. Ala. Birmingham, 2005; resident ob-gyn Meml. Health U. Med. Ctr., Savannah, Ga., 2001—. Chmn. Jr. fellow state sect. Am. Coll. Ob-Gyn, Savannah, 2004—, vice-chmn. jr. fellow state sect., 2003—04; v.p. acad. affairs Med. Coll. Ga., Augusta, 1999—2001. Contbr. articles to profl. jours. Vol. educator Boot Camp for New Dads, Savannah, 2004—05; vol. healthcare provider Beulah Grove Indigent Health Cmty. Clinic, Augusta, 1999—2001; vol. Habitat for Humanity, Macon, Ga., 1995—2001; educator Southside Bapt. Ch., Savannah, 2001—05. Recipient Physician's Physician Award, Med. Coll. Ga., 2001; Ednl. Grant for Hysteroscopic Rsch., ACMI, Inc., 2003, Acad. and Cmty. Svc. Scholarship, Ty Cobb Found., 1997—2001, Ednl. Scholarship, Jacques Found., 1997—2001, Freshman Scholar, AMA, 1997—98, Penfield Scholar, Mercer U., 1994—97. Mem.: Christian Med. And Dental Assn. (corr.), Internat. Pelvic Pain Soc. (assoc.), Am. Assn. Gynecologic Laparoscopic Surgeons (assoc.), Am. Coll. Ob-Gyn (assoc.; chmn. of state jr. sect. 2004—05), Phi Beta Sigma (corr.), Phi Kappa Phi (corr.), Alpha Omega Alpha (corr.). R-Consevative. Baptist. Avocations: tennis, travel, music. Office: C Paul Perry Pelul Pain Ctr Ste 402 2006 Brookwood Medical Ctr Dr Birmingham AL 35209 Office Phone: 205-397-9000. Personal E-mail: alex_j_childs@yahoo.com.

CHILDS, DAVID, architectural firm executive; Grad., Yale U., Yale Sch. Art and Architecture. Sr. designer Pennsylvania Ave. Commn., Washington, 1968—71; with Skidmore, Owings & Merrill, Washington, 1971—84, consulting design ptnr. N.Y.C., 1984—. Chmn. Nat. Capital Planning Commn., 1975—81, Commn. Fine Arts, 2002—; bd. dir. Am. Acad. in Rome; bd. dir., trustee Mus. Modern Art; bd. dir. Mcpl. Art Soc., Nat. Bldg. Mus. Prin. works include Washington Mall Master Plan and Constitution Gardens, Metro Ctr., U.S. News and World Report Hdqrs., Four Seasons, Park Hyatt and Regent Hotels, Bertelsman Tower at Time Square, AOL Time Warner Hdqrs. at Columbus Ctr., expansion of Dulles Internat. Airport main terminal, Washington, DC, U.S. Embassy, Ottawa, Can., T-3 Terminal, Changi Internat. Airport, Singapore, The Freedom Tower at the World Trade Center Site, Worldwide Plz., NY Mercantile Exch., JFK Internat. Arrivals Bldg., Bear Sterns Hdqs., Riverside So., Stuyvesant Sch. Bridge. Bd. mem. N.Y.C. Partnership. Fellow: AIA. Office: Skidmore Owings & Merrill 24th Fl 14 Wall St New York NY 10005*

CHILDS, JOHN DAVID, retired computer company executive; b. Washington, Apr. 26, 1939; s. Edwin Carlton and Catherine Dorothea (Angerman) C.; m. Margaret Rae Olsen, Mar. 4, 1966 (div.); 1 child, John-David. Student, Principia Coll., 1957—60; BA, Am. U., 1963. Jr. adminstr. Page Comms., Washington, 1962-65; account rep. Friden Inc., Washington, 1965-67; Western sales dir. Data Inc., Arlington, Va., 1967-70; v.p. mktg. Rayda, Inc., LA, 1970-73, pres., 1973-76, chmn. bd., 1976-84; v.p. sales Exec. Bus. Systems,

Encino, Calif., 1981—87, sr. v.p. sales and mktg., 1987—2001, ret., 2001; sr. assoc. World Trade Assn., Inc., 1976—2001. Pres. Coll. Youth for Nixon-Lodge, 1959-60, dir. state fedn.; mem. OSHA policy formulation com. Dept. Labor, 1967; polit. dir. Coun. 76, AFSCME, 2003–. Served with USAFR, 1960-66. Mem. Assn. Data Ctr. Owners and Mgrs. (chmn. privacy com. 1975, sec. 1972-74, v.p. 1974, sec. supr. com.). Democrat. Christian Scientist. Home: PO Box 460904 Denver CO 80246-0904

CHILDS, JOHN FARNSWORTH, retired bank executive; b. N.Y.C., Nov. 24, 1909; s. Albert Ewing and Amelia (McGraw) C.; m. Mary Elizabeth Cardozo, Apr. 21, 1950; 1 dau., Susan Elizabeth. BS, Trinity Coll., Hartford, Conn., 1931, MS, 1932; MBA, Harvard, 1933; LLB, Fordham U., 1946. Bar: N.Y. 1946. Analyst Dick & Merle-Smith, N.Y.C., 1935-40; sr. v.p., head corporate services div. Irving Trust Co., N.Y.C., 1941-74; sr. v.p. Kidder-Peabody Inc., 1974-94, Paine Webber Inc., N.Y.C., 1994-97. Mem. tech. adv. com. on fin. Fed. Power Commn., 1973-74; adj. prof. Columbia Grad. Bus. Sch.; cons. in field. Author: Long-Term Financing, 1961, Profit Goals and Capital Management, 1968, Earnings Per Share and Management Decisions, 1971, Encyclopedia of Long Term Financing and Capital Management, 1976, Corporate Finance and Capital Management for the Chief Executive Officer and Directors, 1979; Contbr. articles to profl. publs. Past treas., trustee Lenox Sch.; bd. dirs. N.Y. Council on Econ. Edn.; past bd. dirs. Sch. Book Fair Inc., Fla. Power Corp. Served as lt. comdr. USNR, World War II. Mem. Am. Mgmt. Assn. (pres. coun., past dir.), Atomic-Indsl. Forum (past dir.), N.Y. Soc. Security Analysts, Pine Valley Golf Club (Clementin, N.J.). Home: 15 Washington Pl New York NY 10003-6641

CHILDS, LARRY BRITTAIN, lawyer; b. Feb. 26, 1952; s. Don and Mattie Frances (Brittain) C.; m. Julie Truss; children: Lucy, Elizabeth, George. BA, U. Ala., 1974; JD, U. Va., 1977. Bar: Ala. 1977. Law clk. to sr. judge U.S. Dist. Ct. (no. dist.) Ala., Birmingham, 1977-78; assoc. Cabaniss, Johnston, Gardner, Dumas & O'Neal, Birmingham, 1978-83, ptnr., 1984-91, Walston, Wells, Anderson & Birchall, LLP, Birmingham, 1991—. Mem. ABA, Ala. Bar Assn., Birmingham Bar Assn. Presbyterian. Home: 2676 Alta Glen Dr Birmingham AL 35243-4508 Office: Walston Wells Anderson & Birchall LLP 1819 5th Ave North Ste 1100 Birmingham AL 35203-4628 Office Phone: 205-244-5200.

CHILES, MARY JANE, secondary school educator; b. Hampton, Iowa, Apr. 26, 1950; d. Thomas Donald and Grace Hermina (Bouvink) Stark; m. Stephen Eugene Chiles, July 8, 1972; 1 child, Samantha Kathryn Chiles Graef. BA, U. Iowa, 1972; postgrd., Morningside Coll., Sioux City, Iowa, 1974, Okla. State U., Stillwater, 1979-82. Tchr. 7th and 8th grade English Woodbury Ctrl. Sch., Moville, Iowa, 1974-75; tchr. 5-8th grade English Anderson Middle Sch., Sand Springs, Okla., 1979-80; tchr. 6th grade Anderson Elem. Sch., Sand Springs, 1980-81; tchr. 9th and 10th grade English Moore (Okla.) West Mid High, 1981-88; tchr. 9th grade English Moore West Jr. H.S., 1988—. Mem. Supt.'s Adv. Coun., Moore, 1997—, Supt.'s Patron Adv. Coun., Moore, 1997—, chair profl. devel. com., 1998-2000; field tester book Elements of Writing, 1993. 10 gallon donor Okla. Blood Inst., Oklahoma City, 1981—; mem. steering com. Educators of Moore PAC, 1983—90. Mem.: NEA (del. assembly 1985—, Western regional conf. 1990—, mem. elections com. 2003, 2005), Moore Assn. Classroom Tchrs. (profl. negotiations team 1982—2004, exec. com. 1985—86, sec. 1986—88, exec. com. 1988—, chair constn. com. 1989—90, chair resolutions com. 1992—94, v.p. 1996—98, chair constn. com. 1998—99, treas. 1999—, chmn. constn. com. 2004—05), Okla. Edn. Assn. (del. assembly 1983—, sec. resolutions com. 1984—97, standing rules com. 1997—98, resolutions com. 1998—2002, bd. dirs. 2003—, ESP com. 2003—), Moore C. of C. (edn. com. 2002—). Democrat. Avocations: travel, swimming. Home: 3201 Willow Lane Moore OK 73170-7912 Office: Moore West 9400 S Pennsylvania Ave Oklahoma City OK 73159-6903 Personal E-mail: chilly5@cox.net. E-mail: maryjanechiles@mooreschools.com.

CHILES, STEPHEN MICHAEL, lawyer; b. July 15, 1942; s. Daniel Duncan and Helen Virginia (Hayes) C.; m. Deborah E. Nash, June 13, 1964; children: Stephen, Abigail. BA, Davidson Coll., 1964; JD, Duke U., 1967. Bar: N.Y. 1970, Pa. 1978, Wis. 1981, Ill. 1986, U.S. Dist. Ct. (ea. dist.) Pa. 1978, U.S. Tax Ct. 1978, U.S. Supreme Ct. 1978. Officer trust dept. Irving Trust Co., N.Y.C., 1970-75, v.p., 1975-77; assoc. atty. Stassen Kostos & Mason, Phila., 1978-79, mem., shareholder, 1979-85; ptnr. McDermott, Will & Emery LLP, Chgo., 1986—2004, of counsel, 2005—. Contbr. articles to profl. jours. Served to capt. U.S. Army, 1967-69. Decorated Bronze Star, Army Commendation medal. Mem.: State Bar Wis., Landings Club, (Savannah, Ga.). Republican. Episcopalian. Office: McDermott Will & Emery 227 W Monroe St Ste 4700 Chicago IL 60606-5096 Business E-Mail: schiles@mwe.com.

CHILIVIS, NICKOLAS PETER, retired lawyer; b. Athens, Ga., Jan. 12, 1931; s. Peter Nickolas and Wessie Mae (Tanner) C.; m. Patricia Kay Tumlin, June 3, 1967; children— Taryn Tumlin, Nicole Tumlin, Nickolas Peter Tumlin. LL.B., U. Ga., Athens, 1953; LL.M., Atlanta Law Sch., Ga., 1955. Bar: Ga. 1952, U.S. Supreme Ct. 1965. Ptnr. Lester & Chilivis, Athens, Ga., 1953-58; ptnr. Erwin, Epting, Gibson & Chilivis, Athens, Ga., 1958-75; commr. of revenue State of Ga., Atlanta, 1975-77; ptnr. Powell, Goldstein, Frazer & Murphy, Atlanta, 1977-84, Chilivis & Grindler, Atlanta, 1984-95, Chilivis, Cochran, Larkins & Bever, Atlanta, 1995—2003. Adj. prof. U. Ga. Sch. Law, Athens, 1965-75. Author: Termination Settlement, 1955. Contbr. chpts. to books, articles to profl. jours. Bd. visitors U. Ga., Athens, 1983-85; trustee Skandalakis Found., Atlanta, 1984, Found. of the Holy Apostles; former trustee U. Ga. Found.; former mem. U. Ga. Rsch. Found. Bd.; pres. and sr. warden Ch. of Apostles. With USAFR, 1953-55. Recipient Archdiocesan medal Archbishop of North and South Am., 1980. Fellow Internat. Soc. Barristers, Am. Coll. Trial Lawyers, Am. Acad. Appellate Lawyers; mem. Am. Inns. of Ct. (emeritus, master), Old War Horse Lawyers Club, Lawyers Club Atlanta, Commerce Club, Heritage Club, (Atlanta), Pres.'s Club (U. Ga.), Elks. Avocations: handball, tennis, writing, lecturing. Home: 855 W Paces Ferry Rd NW Atlanta GA 30327-2655 Office: Chilivis Cochran Larkins & Bever Chilivis Bldg 3127 Maple Dr NE Atlanta GA 30305-2503 Office Phone: 404-233-4171.

CHILL, MYRTLE N., advertising copywriter, promoter; b. Indpls., Apr. 5, 1906; d. Henry and Mathilda (Kuhn) Newman; m. George F. Chill, June 28, 1932. BSJ, Northwestern U., Medill Sch. Journalism, 1927. Editor Armitage News, Chgo., 1927—28; mng. editor The Nor'wester, Chgo., 1928—29; asst. sales promotion editor Sears, Roebuck & Co., 1929—32; head copywriter Goldblatt Bros. Dept. Stores, Chgo., 1932—39; gen. mgr. Substantial Products Co., Chgo., 1939—65; part-time advt. work Edelstein-Nelson, Reich & Kahn; Chicago Bar and Restaurant Supply, Chgo., 1967—2001; promotion mgr. Barbara Newman Designs, Chgo., 2001—. Achievements include presently promoting a fused glass pin that with a necklace or cord becomes a pendant; updating her extensive 1992 Newman family medical history that now includes the fifth living generation; with medical research and care so specialized, it is important to know the allergies inherited from our genes.

CHILOW, BARBARA GAIL, social worker; b. Grand Forks, N.D., June 7, 1936; d. Alfred Thomas and Florence (Micken) Seeley; m. Steven Chilow, Aug. 15, 1987; children: John Mark Doss, Timothy Stephen Doss, Elizabeth De La Cruz, David Chilow. BS, UCLA, 1957; MSW, U. So. Calif., 1970; MPA, Calif. State U., Long Beach, 1985. Lic. social worker, Calif., Utah, marriage, family and child counselor, Calif. Social worker Dept. Pub. Welfare, San Diego, 1957, Dep. Pub. Assistance, Whitman, Mass., 1966-68; psychiat. social worker State of Calif., Pomona, 1971-73; clin. social worker Orange County Dept. Mental Health, Santa Ana, Calif., 1973-74, sr. clin. social worker, 1974-79; dep. dir. mental health Orange County Human Svcs. Agy., Santa Ana, Calif., 1979-80, dep. regional mgr., 1980-82, adminstrv. mgr. II, 1982-93; clin. coord. Brightway at St. George, Utah, 1993-2000; pvt. practice Newport Beach, Calif., 1977—93; owner, mgr., pvt. practice Desert Hills Therapeutic Svcs., St. George, 1998—2005; clin. coord. Lighthouse Behavioral Health Svcs., Inc., 2005—. Chmn. So. Calif. Case Mgmt. Coun., 1987-89, Orange County Bd. and Care Quality Com., Santa Ana, 1984-89. Pres. Winchester Hills Homeowners Assn., St. George, 1995-97; elected to Southwestern Spl. Svc. Dist. BD., 1997-, Leadership Dixie, 1998-99; trustee Music Hall Found.; gala bd. Cancer Soc., 2003-04. Mem. NASW, AAUW (v.p. 2002), DAR (Boston Tea Party chpt.), Alliance for Mentally Ill (pres. Orange County chpt. 1994-95), Phi Alpha Alpha, Gamma Phi Beta. Democrat. Presbyterian. Avocations: hiking, piano, reading, travel. Home: 1110 W 5830 N Saint George UT 84770-5944 Office: Lighthouse Behavioral Health Svcs Troon Park Plz 1240 E 100 S Ste 18B Saint George UT 84790-3001 Office Phone: 435-673-0050. Personal E-mail: bchilow@yahoo.com.

CHILSON, JOHN A., lawyer, military officer; s. Kenneth N. and Jean Kay Chilson; m. Donna Carol Mays, May 2, 1992; children: Matthew A., Cara N. BS, U.S. Naval Acad., 1991; JD, U. Mich., 1999. Bar: Mich. 1999, U.S. Ct. Appeals for the Armed Forces 1999, N.C. 2003, U.S. Dist. Ct. (ea. dist.) N.C. 2003, U.S. Dist. Ct. (mid. dist.) N.C. 2003, U.S. Dist. Ct. (we. dist.) N.C. 2003, U.S. Ct. Appeals (4th cir.) 2003. Commd. 2d lt. USN, advanced through grades to lt. comdr., 1991, surface warfare officer, engr. Charleston, SC, 1992—95, instr. leadership Newport, RI, 1995—97, atty. JAG Corps Pensacola, Fla., 1999—2003; atty. Womble Carlyle Sandridge & Rice PLLC, Winston-Salem, NC, 2003—04; lt. comdr. USNR, 2003—; atty. Ellis & Winters LLP, Greensboro, NC, 2004—. Editor: Mich. Jour. Law Reform (Louis Honigman Meml. award, 1999, Dykema Meml. award, 1998), Adelphia Law Jour. Naval acad. info. officer Naval Acad. Admissions Office, Clemmons, NC, 2003—; youth soccer coach YMCA, Clemmons, NC, 2003—; baseball coach Little League, Clemmens, NC, 2005—; nonresident dir. Navy Mut. Aid Assn., Arlington, Md., 1999—2003. Mem.: ABA, N.C. Bar Assn. (young lawyer's divsn. mil. liaison com. 2003—04, lawyer effectiveness and quality of life com. 2005—), Def. Rsch. Inst. (professionalism and ethics com. 2005—). Avocations: sports, teaching, coaching, studying. Office: Ellis & Winters LLP Ste 102 100 N Greene St Greensboro NC 27401 Office Phone: 336-217-4193. Office Fax: 336-217-4198. Business E-Mail: john_chilson@elliswinters.com.

CHILSTROM, ROBERT MEADE, lawyer; b. San Diego, July 1, 1945; s. Arne Oswald and Margaret Myra (Kippax) C.; m. Buena Lelia Hamlin, Aug. 24, 1968; children: Per Benjamin, Mikaela Lynn. BA, Princeton U., 1967; MA, Columbia U., 1969; JD, Yale U., 1973. Bar: N.Y. State 1975, U.S. Dist. Ct. (so. dist., ea. dist.) N.Y. 1975, U.S. Ct. Appeals (2d cir.) 1975. Assoc. Cravath, Swaine & Moore, N.Y.C., Paris, London, 1973-85, Skadden, Arps, Slate, Meagher & Flom LLP, N.Y.C., 1985-87, ptnr., 1987—. Office: Skadden Arps Slate Meagher & Flom LLP Rm 31-100 4 Times Sq New York NY 10036-6595 E-mail: rchilstr@skadden.com.

CHILTON, BRADLEY STEWART, law educator; b. Rockford, Ill., Oct. 28, 1955; s. Ermal Rural and Maybelle Rose (McNair) C.; m. Lisa Marie Hartmann, May 21, 1977. BA, Milton Coll., 1977; JD, U. Toledo, Ohio, 1980, MA, 1981, U. Wis., 1982; PhD, U. Ga., 1988; MLS, U. So. Miss., 1989. Instr. S.E. Mo. State U., Cape Girardeau, 1985-86; asst. prof. U. So. Miss., Hattiesburg, 1986-89, Wash. State U., Pullman, 1989-93; assoc. prof. U. Toledo, 1993-2000, U. North Tex., Denton, 2000—05; prof., chair dept. polit. sci. and criminal justice Appalachian State U., Boone, NC, 2005—. Pre-law advisor U. Toledo, 1993—99; fellow Tex. Ctr. for Digital Knowledge, U. North Tex. Author: Prisons Under the Gavel, 1991, Star Trek Visions of Law and Justice, 2003. Recipient Ann. Dissertation award NASPAA, 1988. Mem. Acad. Criminal Justice Sci., Am. Polit. Sci. Assn., Am. Soc. Criminology, Am. Soc. Pub. Adminstrn. Avocations: music, home design and building, religion. Office: Polit Sci and Criminal Justice Appalachian State U PO Box 32107 Boone NC 28608-2107 Office Phone: 828-262-3085. Business E-Mail: chiltonbs@appstate.edu.

CHILTON, ELIZABETH EASLEY EARLY, newspaper executive; b. Williamson, W.Va., Dec. 9, 1928; d. Carl Brooks and Susie Mason (Easley) Early; m. William Edwin Chilton III, Apr. 5, 1952 (dec. Feb. 1987); 1 child, Susan Carroll Chilton Shumate. Student, Hollins Coll., Va., 1946-48; AA in Primary Edn., Marjorie Webster Coll., Washington, 1950; LLD W.Va. State U. (hon.), 2004. Pub. rels. staff The Charleston (W.Va.) Gazette, 1952-87; v.p., treas. Daily Gazette Co., Charleston, 1987-91, pres., 1991—, also dir., 1994—, chmn. bd. dirs. Mgmt. com. The Charleston Newspapers, 1991-99; adv. bd. Eberly Coll. Arts and Scis., 1996. Editl. bd. The Charleston Gazette, 1987—. Chmn. W.Va. Gov.'s Mansion Preservation Found., Charleston, 1989—; bd. trustees U. Charleston, 1989-98, Marshall U.-Yeager Scholars, Huntington, W.Va., 1990-96, W.Va. State Coll. Found., Inst., 1988-96, WSWP-TV Pub. Broadcasting, 1980-94, Faculty Merit Scholars, 1991—, W.Va. Humanities Coun., 1994-2000; bd. dirs. BIDCO, 1996-98, Advantage Valley, Charleston, 1996-98, Greater Kanawha Valley Found., 1980-86, adv. bd., 1986—; bd. dirs. Childrens Express, 1987—, Charleston Renaissance, 1995—, Washington, 1997—, Gunston Hall Plantation, 1977-92, pres., 1989-92; bd. dirs., exec. com. Worth Bingham Prize Found., 1987—; bd. dirs. Nat. Youth Sci. Found., 1998; trustee W.Va. U., 2000—, Sulgrave Manor Found., 2001; bd. dirs. Clay Ctr. for Arts and Scis., 1998—. Recipient John Marshall medal for civic responsibility, Marshall U., 1997, Pres. Disting. Svc. award, W.Va. U., 2000, Second Century award for excellence in leadership, W.Va. State Coll., 2003. Mem. So. Newspaper Pubs. (journalism edn. com. 1992-94, minority affairs com. 1994—), Nat. Soc. of Colonial Dames of W.Va. (pres.), Internat. Press Inst. (dir. Am. com. 1994—), Newspaper Assn. Am. (com. mem. 1987—), Nat. Trust for Historic Preservation, Garden Club of Am. (chmn. libr., bd. dirs. 1989-92), Jr. League of Charleston, Edgewood Country Club of Charleston, Yale Club of N.Y.C., Sulgrave Club of Washington, Briar Hills Garden Club, Kanawha Garden Club, Sea Pines Country Club of Hilton Head. Democrat. Presbyterian. Avocations: travel, reading, golf, gardening. Home: 806 Cedar Rd Charleston WV 25314-1206 Office: The Charleston Gazette 1001 Virginia St E Charleston WV 25301-2895

CHILTON, KENNETH WAYNE, business research director, writer; b. St. Louis, Aug. 22, 1944; s. Thomas L. and Sadie I. (Smith) C.; m. Linda K. Bevirt, Aug. 23, 1965; children: Jennifer L., Thomas K. BS, Northwestern U., 1967, MS, 1968; MSBA, Washington U., 1992; PhD, 1994. Mgmt. sci. cons. McDonnell Douglas Corp., St. Louis, 1968-74; treas., dir. bus. planning Permaneer Corp., Maryland Heights, Mo., 1974-77; owner Auto Sell, Creve Coeur, Mo., 1977; asst. dir. Ctr. for the Study of Am. Bus., Wash. Univ., St. Louis, 1977-80, assoc. dir., 1980-91, dep. dir., 1991-95; dir., 1995—. Instr. Fontbonne Coll., Clayton, Mo., 1983-88, Washington U., 1988-91, 95. Co-editor: The Dynamic American Firm, Public Policy Toward Corporate Takeovers, American Manufacturing in a Global Market, Environmental Protection, Regulating for Results; contbr. articles to profl. jours. Mem. Pres. Reagan's Small Bus. Issues Task Force, 1980, Small Bus. Adv. Coun. Rep. Nat. Com., 1984. Recipient Spirit of Freedom award Discussion Club, St. Louis, 1988. Mem. AAAS, Nat. Assn. Bus. Econs., Acad. Mgmt., Assn. for Pvt. Enterprise Edn. Office: Washington U Ctr for Study Am Bus Saint Louis MO 63130-4899

CHILTON, LANCE ALIX, pediatrician; b. Akron, Ohio, Nov. 2, 1944; BA in Human Scis., Johns Hopkins U., 1966, MD, 1969. Diplomate American Board of Pediatrics. Intern U. Wash., Seattle, 1969—70; resident pediat. U. Pitts., 1972—74; clin. prof. pediat. U. N.Mex., 1975—; former pediatrician Gallup (N.Mex.) Indian Med. Ctr., Lovelace Pediat., Albuquerque, 1981—; pediatrician Lovelace Med. Ctr., N.Mex., 1981—, St. Vincent Hosp., N.Mex., 1995—. Columnist: Albuquerque Jour. Mem.: N.Mex. Pub. Health Assn., N.Mex. Pediat. Soc., Am. Acad. Pediat. (mem. first Indian child project adv. com., former chmn. com. on Native Am. child health, vice chair Dist. VIII, Native Am. Child Health Adv. award 2002). Office: Lovelace Pediat 5400 Gibson Blvd SE Albuquerque NM 87108-4763 Business E-Mail: lance.chilton@lovelacesandia.com.

CHILTON, WILLIAM DAVID, architect; b. Tulsa, Jan. 4, 1954; s. Horace Thomas Jr. and Betty Jane (Gray) C. BA in Architecture, Iowa State U., 1976; MArch, U. Minn., 1980. Registered arch., Minn., Conn., Calif., Va., Tex., Okla., Wash., Oreg., D.C., Mass. Designer CDG, Tulsa, 1976; assoc. architect Olson-Coffey Architects, Tulsa, 1977-78, The Leonard Parker Assocs., Mpls., 1980-81; sr. architect Conoco, Inc., Ponca City, Okla., 1981-89; v.p., project mgr. Ellerbe Becket, Inc., Mpls., 1989, v.p., sr. project mgr., 1990, v.p., project dir., 1991-93, sr. v.p., project dir., 1994-98; dir. The Ellerbe Becket Co., Mpls., 1995-99, pres. arch., mng. prin., 1998-99, mem. mgmt. com., 1997-99; mng. prin. Pickard Chilton, New Haven, 1999—. Bd. dirs. Rainier Tech., Mpls., 1998-2001; mem. architecture adv. coun. Iowa State U., 1994-99, chair, 1997-98, mem. advancement coun. Coll. Design Iowa State U., 2005— Prin. works include as project designer Milne Point (Alaska) Ops. Complex (award Best of Engring. News Record, 1986, Excellence in Arch. award North Ctrl. Okla. chpt. AIA, 1987, Honorable Mention Builder mag., 1985), Conoco Corp. Offices, Wilmington, Del. (Excellence in Arch. award North Ctrl. Okla. chpt. AIA, 1987), Conoco Office/Housing Facilities, Luanda, Angola, 1985—88, prin. works include as mng. prin. Dow Chem. Corp. Hdqrs. Master Plan, Midland, Mich., 1991, Dow Chem. Global Data Ctr., 1992, Sci. Mus. Minn., St. Paul, 1991—99, Kingdom Centre, Riyadh, Saudi Arabia, 1996—2002, CalPERS Hdqrs., Sacramento, 1999—. Bd. dirs. Children's HeartLink, Mpls., 1997-99; mem. nat. adv. bd. U. Minn. Coll. Architecture, 2004—. Recipient Design Achievement award Iowa State U., 1995. Mem. Conn. Soc. AIA (sec. North Ctrl. Okla. chpt. 1986, v.p. 1987, pres. 1988, bd. dirs. 1986-88, bd. dirs. Okla. Coun. 1987-88), Leadership Mpls., Inst. Dirs. (London), Interlachen Country Club (Edina, Minn.), Mpls. Club. Lutheran. Avocations: fly fishing, golf, reading, music. Home: 452 E River Rd Guilford CT 06437-2289 Office: Pickard Chilton 980 Chapel St New Haven CT 06510-2045 E-mail: wchilton@pickardchilton.com.

CHILUKURI, RAM, finance executive; s. Avadhani and Prasanna Chilukuri. B in Tech. with hons., Indian Inst. Tech., 1998; MS with hons., MIT, 2000. Assoc. Merrill Lynch, NYC, 2000—03, v.p. global equity derivatives, 2003—. Achievements include development of tradable VIX future in conjunction wth the Chicago Board Options Exchange. VIX futures started trading April 2004, and can be a key risk mitigating asset in any financial portfolio. Avocations: travel, poker, hiking, tennis. Office Phone: 212-449-5801.

CHILVERS, DEREK, insurance company executive; b. Torquay, Eng., Feb. 7, 1940; came to U.S., 1962; s. Reginald Charles and Selina Adelaide (Adamson) C.; m. Elizabeth Anne Locke, Aug. 25, 1968 (div. 1983); m. Cheryl Baker, Apr. 14, 1984; children: Justine, Derek Jr. BA, MA, Cambridge U., 1962. With John Hancock Life Ins. Co., Boston, 1962—, v.p. internat., 1980-85, sr. v.p. internat., 1985-2000, exec. v.p., 2001—04; chmn., CEO John Hancock Internat. Inc.

CHILVERS, ROBERT MERRITT, lawyer; b. Long Beach, Calif., Oct. 23, 1942; s. James Merritt and Elizabeth Louise (Blackburn) C.; m. Sandra Lee Rigg, Sept. 5, 1969; children: Jeremy Merritt, Jessica Rigg. AB, U. Calif., Berkeley, 1972; JD, Harvard U., 1975. Bar: Calif. 1975, U.S. Dist. Ct. (no. dist.) Calif. 1975, U.S. Ct. Appeals (9th cir.) 1980, U.S. Supreme Ct. 1980, U.S. Dist. Ct. (ctrl. dist.) Calif. 1981, U.S. Ct. Fed. Claims, 1984, U.S. Dist. Ct. (ea. dist.) Calif. 1987, U.S. Ct. Appeals (fed. cir.) 1987. Assoc. Brobeck, Phleger & Harrison, San Francisco, 1975-82, ptnr., 1982-93; spl. master U.S. Dist. Ct. (no. dist.) Calif., 1994-99; pres. Chilvers & Taylor, PC, San Rafael, Calif., 1996—. Neutral evaluator and mediator U.S. Dist. Ct. (no. dist.) Calif., 2001—; faculty U. Calif. Hastings Sch. Law, San Francisco, 1983-89, Emory U., Atlanta, 1984-90, fed. practice program U.S. Dist. Ct. (no. dist.) Calif., 1984-86, Nat. Inst. for Trial Advocacy, 1986—, Cardozo Law Sch., Yeshiva U., N.Y.C., 1993-99, Stanford U. Law Sch., 1994—, Widener U. Sch. Law, Wilmington, 1994-96, U. San Francisco Sch. Law, 1994—. Mem. Calif. Sch. Bds. Assn., 1985—89; trustee Mill Valley Sch. Dist., Calif., 1985—89, chmn., 1987—89; bd. dirs. Marin County Sch. Bds. Assn., Calif., 1985—86, Artisans, Mill Valley, Calif., 1999—2001. With USMC, 1964—71. Mem. Calif. Bar Assn. (commendation for Outstanding Contbns. to the delivery of vol. legal svcs. 1984), Marin County Bar Assn., Tau Beta Pi, Sigma Tau. Office: Chilvers & Taylor PC 83 Vista Marin Dr San Rafael CA 94903-5228 Office Phone: 415-444-0875.

CHIMA, FELIX O., social work educator; b. Aba, Imo, Nigeria, Oct. 10, 1953; came to U.S., 1976; s. Akposioha Okoye and Mkpokwo (Mercy) Onwubuariri; children: Christopher, Jerry Chike, Nena Jesica. BA in Bus. Adminstrn., Midland Luth. Coll., 1979; MBA, Atlanta U., 1981; MSW, Clark Atlanta U., 1988, PhD in Social Work Adminstrn., 1992. Sales mgr. Assoc. Industries, Aba, Imo, Nigeria, 1973-76; prodn. supr. Campbell Soup Co., Fremont, Nebr., 1976-79; account mgr. Greyhound Lines, Inc., Atlanta, 1979-84; rsch. asst. Atlanta U., 1984-87; prin. social worker City of Atlanta, 1987-90, dir. human svcs., 1990-93; prof. U. Ky., Lexington, 1993-99, Prairie View A&M U. Tex., 1999—, dir. social work program, 2003—. Ombudsman Tex. Dept. Aging. Contbr. articles to profl. jours. Bd. dirs. foster rev. Commonwealth of Ky., Lexington, 1995-99, cons. child welfare advocacy, 1994-99. Mem. NASW, Ky. Assn. Social Workers, Coun. on Social Work Edn., Assn. Baccalaureate Program Dirs Home: 13522 White Cliff Dr Houston TX 77065-3770 Office Phone: 936-857-2394.

CHIMPLES, GEORGE, lawyer; b. Canton, Ohio, Oct. 8, 1924; s. Mark and Katherine (Hines) C.; m. Eileen Mary Grumm, July 14, 2003; children: Alicia Candace, Mark II, John Hines, Katherine Hines. AB, Princeton U., 1951; LLB, Harvard Coll., 1954. Bar: Pa. 1955, U.S. Dist. Ct. (ea. dist.) Pa. 1955, U.S. Ct. Appeals (3d cir.) 1955, U.S. Ct. Claims, 1965, U.S. Tax Ct., 1965. Assoc. Stradley, Ronon, Stevens & Young, Phila., 1954-61, gen. ptnr., 1961-92; pvt. practice Wayne, Pa., 1993—. Adj. prof. law U. Pa., Drexel U. Grad. Sch. Bus.; co-authored establishment of overseas infrastructure for securities mktg. in Europe and the Antilles. Trustee Christ Ch. Preservation Trust; permament assoc. Phila. Mus. Art.; founding mem. Duxford (Eng.) Air Mus. Capt. USAAF, 1942-46, ETO. Decorated D.F.C., Air medal with four oak leaf clusters, Air Force Commendation medal, Victory medal, four Battle Stars; recipient Royal Air Force plaque, 1994. Mem. ABA (chmn. subcom. regulated investment cos.), Phila. Bar Assn. (tax sect.), Internat. Bar Assn., Internat. Fiscal Assn. (tax treaty sect.), Mid-Atlantic Coun., Newcomen Soc. U.S. (trustee emeritus, life mem.) Army and Navy Club (Washington chpt.), Penn Club (life, bd. dirs., historian) Athenaeum of Phila. (life), Libr. Co. of Phila. (life), Phila. Mus. Art (permanent assoc.), Phila. Club, Cannon Club (Princeton chpt.), Torresdale-Frankford Country Club. Home and Office: 1522 Overington St Philadelphia PA 19124-5808 Office Phone: 215-743-4070. E-mail: gchimples@aol.com.

CHIMSKY-LUSTIG, MARK EVAN, editor, consultant; b. Cin., Jan. 24, 1955; s. Matthew and Jean (Berger) C.; life ptnr. Robert Ira Lustig; 1 child, AJ. BA, Carnegie-Mellon U., 1976. Editor Anderson Pub. Co., Cin., 1977-79; copy editor Book-of-the-Month Club, Quality Paperback Book Club, N.Y.C., 1979-85; mng. editor Quality Paperback Book Club, N.Y.C., 1985-89, exec. editor, 1989-91; editor in chief Collier Books Macmillan Co., N.Y.C., 1991-94; dir. trade paperbacks Little, Brown and Co., N.Y.C., 1994-96; from exec. editor to editl. dir. Harper, San Francisco, 1996-98, exec. editor, 1998-99; editl. cons. Mark Chimsky Editl. Plus, Riverdale, N.Y., 1999—. Adj. instr. NYU, N.Y.C., 1999—; dir. NYU Summer Pub. Inst., N.Y.C., 2000, N.Y.C., 03, N.Y.C., 04. Contbr. essays and poetry to lit. jours. including Jour. AMA. Recipient New-Emerging Poet/Anna Davidson Rosenberg award, 1997. Office: Mark Chimsky Editorial Plus PO Box 630207 Bronx NY 10463-0802

CHIN, ALBERT KAE, research physician; b. Spokane, Wash., May 5, 1953; s. Ting H. and Beatrice Y. C.; m. Jeanne Yee, Aug. 6, 1977; children: Jennifer, Lisa, Stephanie. BSME, MIT, 1975; MSME, Stanford U., 1976; MD, U. Calif., San Francisco, 1983. Resident in gen. surgery U. Tex. Southwestern, Dallas, 1983-85; dir. rsch. Fogarty Rsch., Portola Valley, Calif., 1985-89; founder, v.p. rsch. Origin Medsystems, Inc., Menlo Park, Calif., 1989-99; v.p. rsch. divsn. cardiac and vascular surgery Guidant Corp., Santa Clara, Calif., 1994—. Cardiovascular cons. Baxter Edwards LIS Divsn., Irvine, Calif., 1988; expert witness Advanced Cardiovascular Systems, Santa Clara, Calif., 1989. Contbr. articles to profl. publs.; holder more than 130 patents in field. Bd. dirs. YMCA, Palo Alto, Calif., 1987-89. Mem. AMA, Soc. of Laparoendoscopic Surgeons, Internat. Soc. Endovascular Surgery, FF Fraternity (chmn. San Francisco lodge 1986). Avocations: piano, violin, organ, guitar, weightlifting. Office: Guidant Corp Cardiac Surgery Divsn 3200 Lakeside Dr Santa Clara CA 95054-2807

CHIN, BEVERLY ANN, language educator; b. Balt. BA in English, Fla. State U., 1970, MA in English Edn., 1971; PhD in Curriculum and Instrn., U. Oreg., 1975. Cert. lifetime tchg. secondary English Fla., Ariz., reading endorsement Fla. CC, Fla., Ariz. English tchr., adult edn. instr. Melbourne HS, Fla., 1971—73; dep. dir. field experience program Alt. Sch. Tchr. Edn. Program, Coll Edn., U. Mass., Amherst, 1972; grad. tchg. fellow U. Oreg. Coll. Edn., Eugene, 1973—75; asst. prof. elem. and secondary edn. U. New Orleans, 1976—77; asst. prof. English Ariz. State U., Tempe, 1977—78; adj. asst. prof. English Pinal CC, Mesa, Ariz., 1977—78; vis. asst. prof. edn. U. Oreg., Eugene, 1978; asst. prof. edn. U. Ctrl. Fla., Orlando, 1978—81; prof. English U. Mont., Missoula, 1981—. Chair Jt. Com. K-16 Composition Stds., 1999—2000; sr. advisor Mont. U. Sys., Writing Proficiency Admissions Stds.; cons. in field. Author: On Your Own: Writing Process, 1990, On Your Own: Grammar, 1991; editor: Chinese-American Literature, 1992, Dictionary of Characters in Children's Literature, 2001, How to Study for Success, How To Write a Great Research Paper, How to Ace Any Test, How to Build a Super Vocabulary, 2004; advisor Expanding the Canon: Teaching Multicultural Literature in High School, expert commentator, web writer, 2004, advisor Teaching Multicultural Literature: A Workshop for the Middle Grades, expert commentator, web writer, 2005, cons. Grammar for Writing, Grades 9-12, 2000, Glencoe Literature: The Reader's Choice, 2000; contbr. articles to profl. jours. Named Outstanding Young Women Am., 1980, Disting. Tchr., U. Mont., 1990, U. Disting. Alumni Coll. Edn., Fla. State U., 1995, Disting. Educator, Mont. Assn. Tchrs. English Lang. Arts, 2001. Mem.: ASCD, Conf. English Leadership (mem. at large 2003—), Conf. English Edn., Internat. Reading Assn., N.W. Regional Ednl. Lab. Assessment Adv. Coun., Nat. Coun. Tchrs. English (pres. 1995—96), Mont. Project Excellence (chair 1988—89), Mont. Assn. Tchrs. English Lang. Arts. (pres. 1984—85), Nat. Bd. Profl. Tchg. Stds. (mem. bd. 1995—2003), Phi Kappa Phi, Phi Delta Kappa, Kappa Delta Pi, Phi Beta Kappa. Office: U Mont Dept English Liberal Arts 133 Missoula MT 59812 Office Phone: 406-243-2463. Office Fax: 406-243-5130. Business E-Mail: beverly.chin@umontana.edu.

CHIN, CECILIA HUI-HSIN, librarian; b. Tientsin, China; came to U.S., 1961; d. Yu-lin and Ti-yu (Fan) C. BA, Nat. Taiwan U., Taipei, 1961; MSL.S., U. Ill., 1963. Cataloger, reference librarian Roosevelt U., Chgo., 1963; reference librarian, indexer Ryerson & Burnham Libraries, Art Inst. Chgo., 1963-70, head reference dept. indexer, 1970-75; acting dir. libraries Art Inst. Chgo., 1976-77, assoc. librarian, head reference dept., 1975-82; chief librarian Smithsonian Am. Art Mus. and Nat. Portrait Gallery, Smithsonian Inst., Washington, 1982—. Compiler: The Art Institute of Chicago Index to Art Periodicals, 1975 Recipient awards, Nat. Portrait Gallery, Smithsonian Instn., 1984, 1989, Smithsonian Instn. Libr., 2001. Mem. Art Librs. Soc., D.C. Libr. Assn., Washington Rare Book Group. Office: 750 9th St # 2100 Washington DC 20560-0975 Office Fax: 202-275-1929. Business E-Mail: chinc@si.edu.

CHIN, CHEN OOI, dean; b. Singapore; arrived in U.S., 1972; d. Sat-kai Chin and Piang-keow Lee; m. Charles Hsieh, Oct. 15, 1972; 1 child, Chih-Mao Hsieh. BA, Nat. Taiwan U., 1964, MA, 1966, Yale U., 1968; PhD, Ohio State U., 1976. Lectr. U. Singapore, 1968—72; asst. prof. U. Detroit, 1974—77; exec. dir. Chinese Am. Edn. and Cultural Ctr. of Mich., Ann Arbor, 1976—; adj. prof. Lawrence Technol. U., Southfield, Mich., 2000—; dean Ctr. for Cultural Diversity, Singapore, 2001—. Cons. Prudential, Chgo., 1999—, Internat. Oriental Resources, Chgo., 1999—, Berlitz Internat., Inc., NJ, 1999—, GMAC, Mich., 1999—. Prodr.(editor): (video) Twelve Years of Harvest, 1988. Asian Found. grantee, 1963—66, Fulbright-Hayes grantee, Malaysia, 1966, NEA grantee, 1977—94. Mem.: Acad. of Mgmt. Office: Chinese Am Ednl & Cultural Ctr 296 W Eisenhower Ann Arbor MI 48104 Home: 1826 Glenwood Ann Arbor MI 48104

CHIN, DENNY, federal judge; b. 1954; BA magna cum laude, Princeton U., 1975; JD, Fordham U., 1978. Law clerk Hon. Henry F. Werker, 1978-80; with Davis, Polk & Wardwell, N.Y., 1980-82, Campbell, Patrick & Chin, N.Y., 1986-90, Vladeck, Waldman, Elias & Engelhard, N.Y., 1990-94; dist. judge U.S. Dist. Ct. (so. dist.), N.Y., 1994—. Adj. prof. Fordham Law Sch. Mem. ABA, Asian Am. Bar Assn. N.Y. (pres. 1992-94), Assn. Bar of N.Y.C., Fordham Law Review Alumni Assn., N.Y. County Lawyers Assn. Office: U S Dist Ct 500 Pearl St Chambers 1020 New York NY 10007-1316*

CHIN, DER-TAU, chemical engineer, educator; b. Zhejiang, China, Sept. 14, 1939; came to U.S., 1963, naturalized, 1977; s. Tsu-Kang and Shou-Chen (Chen) C.; m. Lorna Fe Gencianeo, July 17, 1971; children: Janet G., Lynn G. BSChemE, Chungyuan Coll. Sci. & Enging, 1962; MSChemE, Tufts U., 1965; PhD in Chem. Enging., U. Pa., 1969. Plant engr. Lungyen Sugar Factory, 1962-63; sci. programmer USAF Cambridge (Mass.) Rsch. Lab., Lexington, Mass., 1965; sr. rsch. engr. rsch. labs. GM Corp., Warren, Mich., 1969-75; prof. Clarkson U., Potsdam, NJ, 1975—2004, prof. emeritus, 2004—. Vis. scientist Brookhaven Nat. Lab., Upton, N.Y., summers 1977, 80, U.S. Army Belvoir Research Devel. Ctr., Ft. Belvoir, Va., summer 1985, U.S. Army Electronics Tech. and Devices Lab., Ft. Mammouth, N.J., summer, 1986, Armstrong Lab. Tyndall Air Force Base, Fla., summer 1995; vis. prof. U. Calif., Berkeley, 1981, Swiss Fed. Inst. Tech., Zurich, 1981, Nat. U. Singapore, 1982, 87, Nat. Tsing Hua UNI, 1989, King Fahd U. Petroleum and Minerals, Dhahran, Saudi Arabia, 2000-2001; cons. Centro de Pesquisas do Energia Electrica, Rio de Janiero, Brazil, summer 1979. Fellow Electrochem. Soc. (Young Authors award 1971); mem. AIChE, Am. Electroplaters Soc., Am. Chem. Soc. Office: Clarkson U PO Box 5705 Potsdam NY 13699-5705 Office Phone: 315-268-7930. Business E-Mail: chin@clarkson.edu.

CHIN, MIAN, research scientist; m. Haili You, Sept. 1986; 1 child, Lida You. PhD, Ga. Inst. Tech., Atlanta, 1992. Postdoctoral fellow Harvard U., Mass., 1992—95; rsch. scientist U. Space Rsch. Assn., Md., 1995—97; rsch. scientist II Ga. Inst. Tech., Atlanta, 1997—2001, sr. rsch. scientist, 2001—03; phys. scientist NASA Goddard Space Flight Ctr., Greenbelt, Md., 2003—.

CHIN, MING W., state supreme court justice; b. Klamath Falls, Oreg., Aug. 31, 1942; m. Carol Lynn Joe, Dec. 19, 1971; children: Jennifer, Jason. BA in Polit. Sci., U. San Francisco, 1964, JD, 1967; LLD (hon.), Southwestern U. Sch. of Law, 1996, Golden Gate Un. Sch. of Law, 1997, U. San Diego Sch. of Law, 1998, Western State U. Sch. of Law, 1998. Bar: Calif. 1970, U.S. Fed. Ct., U.S. Tax Ct. Assoc., head trial dept. Aiken, Kramer & Cummings, Oakland, Calif., 1973—76, prin., 1976—88; dep. dist. atty. Alameda County, Calif., 1970—72; judge Alameda County Superior Ct., 1988—90; assoc. justice divsn. 3 Ct. Appeal 1st Dist., 1990—94; presiding justice 1st Dist. Ct. Appeal Divsn. 3, San Francisco, 1994—96; state supreme ct. assoc. justice Calif. Supreme Ct., San Francisco, 1996—. Capt. U.S. Army, 1967—69, Vietnam, Capt. USAR, 1969—71. Decorated US Army Commendation medal, Bronze Star; named Outstanding Judge of the Yr., So. Alameda County Bar Assn., 1989, Honoree for Service in Field of Law, Chinese Consolidated Benevolent Assn. & Chinese Women's Assn. of Am., 1997; recipient Learned Hand award, Am. Jewish Com., 1997, Legal Impact award, Asian Pacific Am. Legal Ctr. of So. Calif., 1997, Citizen of the Yr. award, Chinese Americans United for Self Empowerment, 1998, Public Service & Govt. Leadership award, Asian Bus. Assn., 1998, Trailblazer award, Nat. Asian Pacific Am. Bar Assn., 1999. Mem.: ABA, Asian Am. Bar Assn., San Francisco Dist. Atty.'s Commn. Hate Crimes, Alameda County Bar Assn., State Bar Calif., Calif. Judges Assn., Commonwealth Club of Calif. (pres. 1998), Alpha Sigma Nu. Office: Supreme Court Calif 350 McAllister St Fl 1 San Francisco CA 94102-4783 Office Phone: 415-865-7050. E-mail: ming.chin@jud.ca.gov.*

CHIN, NEE OO WONG, reproductive endocrinologist; b. Hong Kong, China, Nov. 27, 1955; came to U.S., 1958; s. Bing Leong and Din Sui (Gee) C.; m. Shelly Loraine Crumrine, June 25, 1977; children: Jason Lei, Taryn Mae. BA, U. Cin., 1977; MD, Ohio State U., 1981. Diplomate Am. Bd. Ob-Gyn. Resident Duke U. Med. Ctr., Durham, N.C., 1981-84, chief resident, 1984-85; fellow Ohio State U. Coll. Medicine, Columbus, Ohio, 1985-87; teaching staff Good Samaritan Hosp., Cin., 1987—; clin. asst. prof. U. Cin. Med. Ctr., 1987—; dir. assisted reproductive techs. The Christ Hosp., Cin., 1992—. Mem. High Sch. for the Health Profl. subcom., Cin., 1989—. Author: (with others) Current Therapy in Obstetrics, 1988; contbr. articles to profl. jours. Named to Honorable Order of Ky. Cols., Gov. Martha Collins of Ky., 1987. Fellow Am. Coll. Ob-Gyn.; mem. AAAS, Am. Fertility Soc., Soc. Assisted Reproductive Tech., Soc. for Immunology Repro., Cin. Ob-Gyn. Soc. (med. malpractice com. 1989—), Acad. Medicine Cin. Avocations: tennis, Karate. Office: 2814 Mack Rd Fairfield OH 45014 Office Phone: 513-326-4300. Personal E-mail: neeoowchinmd@aol.com.

CHIN, SUE SOONE MARIAN (SUCHIN CHIN), artist, photojournalist; b. San Francisco; d. William W. and Soo-Up (Swebe) C. Grad., Calif. Coll. Art, Mpls. Arts Inst.; scholar, Schaeffer Design Ctr.; student, Yasuo Kuniyoshi, Louis Hamon, Rico LeBrun. Photojournalist All Together Now Show, 1973, East-West News, Third World Newscasting, 1975-78, Sta. KNBC Sunday Show, L.A., 1975, 76, Live on 4, 1981, Bay Area Scene, 1981. Chmn. Full Moon Products; pres., bd. dirs. Aumni Oracle Inc. Graphics printer, exhbns. include: Kaiser Ctr., Zellerbach Pla., Chinese Culture Ctr. Galleries, Capricorn Asunder Art Commn. Gallery (all San Francisco), Newspace Galleries, New Coll. of Calif., L.A. County Mus. Art, Peace Pla. Japan Ctr., Congress Arts Comm., Washington, 1989; SFWA Galleries, Inner Focus Show, 1989—, Calif. Mus. Sci. and Industry, Lucien Labaudt Gallery, Salon de Medici, Madrid, Salon Renacimento, Madrid, 1995, Life is a Circus, SFWA Gallery, 1991, 94, UN/50 Exhibit, Bayfront Galleries, 1995, Somar Galleries, 1997, 2003 (Merit award 2003), Sacramento State Fair, 2000, Star Child, Women thru the Ages - Somarts Gallery, 2000, Kings Gallery, San Francisco, 2004, AFL-CIO Labor Studies Ctr., Washington, Asian Women Artists (1st prize for conceptual painting, 1st prize photography), 1978, Yerba Buena Arts Ctr. for the Arts Festival, 1994; represented in permanent collections L.A. County Fedn. Labor, Calif. Mus. Sci. and Industry, AFL-CIO Labor Studies Ctr., Australian Trades Coun., Hazeland and Co., also pvt. collections; author: (poetry) Yuri and Malcolm, The Desert Sun, 1994 (Editors Choice award 1993-94). Del. nat., state convs. Nat. Women's Polit. Caucus, 1977-83, San Francisco chpt. affirmative action chairperson, 1978-82, nat. conv. del., 1978-81, Calif. del., 1976-81. Recipient Honorarium AFL-CIO Labor Studies Ctr., Washington, 1975-76, Bicentennial award 1976; award Centro Studi Ricerche delle Nazioni, Italy, 1985; bd. advisors Psycho Neurology Found. Bicentennial award LA County Mus. Art, 1976, 77, 78, Mandalay Merit award Som Arts Gallery, 2003. Mem. Asian Women Artists (founding v.p., award 1978-79, 1st award in photography of Orient 1978-79, Merit award 2003), Calif. Chinese Artists (sec.-treas. 1978-81), Japanese Am. Art Coun. (chairperson 1978-84, dir.), San Francisco Women Artists, San Francisco Graphics Guild, Pacific/Asian Women Coalition Bay Area, Chinatown Coun. Performing and Visual Arts. Address: PO Box 421415 San Francisco CA 94142-1415

CHIN, SYLVIA FUNG, lawyer; b. NYC, June 27, 1949; d. Thomas and Constance (Yao) Fung; m. Edward G.H. Chin, July 10, 1971; children: Arthur F., Benjamin F. BA, NYU, 1971; JD, Fordham U., 1977. Bar: N.Y. 1978, U.S. Dist. Ct. (so. and ea. dists.) N.Y. 1979, U.S. Supreme Ct. 1990. Law clk. to dist. judge U.S. Dist. Ct. (so. dist.), N.Y.C., 1977-79; assoc. White & Case, N.Y.C., 1979-86, ptnr., 1986—. Adj. assoc. prof. law Fordham U., N.Y.C., 1979-81. Mem. editl. bd.: Bus. Law Today, 1996—2002. Mem.: ABA, Am. Law Inst., Am. Coll. Comml. Fin. Lawyers, Am. Coll. Investment Counsel (bd. dirs. 1999—, pres. 2002—03), Nat. Asian Pacific ABA (treas. 1997—98), Women's World Banking (bd. dirs.), Asian Am. Bar Assn. (bd. dirs. 1991—97, pres. 1994—96), NY County Lawyers Assn. (bd. dirs. 2004—), Assn. Bar City NY, Asian Am. Law Fund NY (treas.), Fordham Law Alumni Assn. (bd. dirs.). Office: White & Case LLP 1155 Ave of Americas New York NY 10036-2711 Office Phone: 212-819-8200. Business E-Mail: schin@whitecase.com.

CHIN, WILLIAM Y., law educator; m. Wing-Sze V. Chau-Chin. BS Polit. Sci., Portland State U., Portland, Oreg., 1990, MS Polit. Sci., 1996; J.D., Lewis & Clark Law Sch., Portland, Oreg., 1994. Bar: U.S. Supreme Ct. Mil. mem. USAF, San Antonio (basic tng.), Germany, 1982—87, Oreg. Air N.G., Portland, 1987—88, USAF Reserves, Portland, Oreg., 1988—89; law clk. U.S. Attys. Office, Portland, 1993—94; prosecutor Multnomah County D.A.'s Office, Portland, Oreg., 1994—95; mil. mem. Oreg. Army N.G., Portland, Oreg., 1994—97; legal writing prof. Lewis & Clark Law Sch., Portland, Oreg., 1996—. Co-chair Oreg. Minority Lawyers Assn., Portland, Oreg., 2002—02; v.p. Chinese Am. Citizens Alliance, Portland, Oreg., 2001—03; com. mem. Oreg. State Bar Uniform Criminal Jury Instrn. Com., Portland, Oreg., 2000—03; mem. Oreg. State Bar Ho. of Delegates, Portland, Oreg., 2002—, Legal Writing Inst., Seattle, 1996—; co-chair com. Remember Asian-Am. Veterans, 2003. Contbr. articles pub. to profl. jour. Mem. Orgn. of Chinese Am., Washington, 2002. Staff sgt. USAF, 1982—87, Germany, Okla. Decorated Commendation Medal USAF, Achievement Medal USArmy. Mem.: ABA, Scribes, Clarity, Oreg. State Bar, Asian Am. Youth Leadership Conf., Pi Sigma Alpha.

CHIN, YAN, pediatrician; b. Hong Kong, July 18, 1965; s. Fook Wah and Selena W.Y. Chin; m. Sylvia Chin. BA, Swarthmore, Pa., 1987; MPH, U. Calif., Berkeley, 1989; MD, U. Calif., Davis, 1995. Chief pediatrics San Francisco On Call Med. Group, 2004—. Office: San Francisco On Call Med Group 490 Post St Ste 710 San Francisco CA 94102 Office Phone: 415-732-7029.

CHINA, DANIEL WILLIAM, lawyer; b. Balt., Feb. 27, 1966; BA summa cum laude, Syracuse U., 1988; JD cum laude, U. Md., 1991. Bar: Ct. Appeals Md., U.S. Ct. Fed. Claims, U.S. Dist. Ct., Dist. Md. Ptnr., construction dept. and comml. litig. dept. Venable LLP, Towson, Md. Lectr. in field. Contbr. Chairperson Legis. Com. Cumberland Valley County, Assn. Builders and Contractors. Named one of Top Twenty Up-And-Coming Lawyers, Baltimore Mag., 2003; recipient Am. Jurisprudence Award. Mem.: ABA, Md. State Bar Assn., Bar Assn. Baltimore City, Phi Beta Kappa, Pi Sigma Alpha. Fluent in French. Office: Venable LLP 210 Allegheny Ave PO Box 5517 Towson MD 21204 Office Phone: 410-494-6204. Office Fax: 410-821-0147. E-mail: dwchina@venable.com.*

CHINANDER, KAREN R., business management educator; BA, Gustavus Adolphus Coll., 1989; MA, U. Pa., 1991, PhD, 1997. Asst. prof. U. Miami, Coral Gables, Fla., 1996—2003; asst. prof. bus. mgmt. Fla. Atlantic U., Jupiter, Fla., 2003—. Contbr. articles to profl. jours. Mem.: INFORMS (organizing com. 2005 ann. meeting 2003—05), Soc. for Judgment and Decision Making, Prodn. and Ops. Mgmt. Soc., Acad. Mgmt. (sec. ops. mgmt. divsn. 2002—05), Phi Beta Kappa. Office: Florida Atlantic Univ 5353 Parkside Dr Jupiter FL 33458 Office Phone: 561-799-8714. Business E-Mail: kchinand@fau.edu.

CHINARD, FRANCIS PIERRE, physiologist, consultant physician; b. Berkeley, Calif., June 30, 1918; s. Gilbert and Emma (Blanchard) C.; m. Josephine L. Wise, June 23, 1943; children: Suzanne F., Jeanne M., Marc F. AB, U. Calif., Berkeley, 1937; MD, Johns Hopkins U., 1941. Intern, jr. asst. resident in medicine Presbyn. Hosp., N.Y.C., 1941-42; asst. physician Hosp. Rockefeller Inst., N.Y.C., 1945-49; instr. to assoc. prof. medicine and physiol. chemistry Johns Hopkins Sch. Med., Balt., 1949-54; asst. prof. medicine U. Md., 1954-62, assoc. prof., 1962-63; physician Johns Hopkins Hosp., 1956-63; prof. exptl. medicine, dep. dir. med. clinic McGill U., Canada, 1963-64; prof. medicine NYU, 1964-68, adj. prof., 1968-70; career scientist N.Y.C. Health Rsch. Coun., 1964-68; prof. medicine, chmn. dept. U. Medicine and Dentistry N.J., Newark, 1968-75, prof. exptl. medicine, 1975-77, prof. rsch. medicine, 1977—, prof. physiology, 1978—, Disting. prof., 1989—, emeritus, 1996; physician-in-chief Balt. City Hosp., 1962-63; acting physician-in-chief Goldwater Meml. Hosp., N.Y.C., 1965-67; dir. med. svc. Martland Hosp., Newark, 1970-71; cons. physician VA Hosp., East Orange, NJ, 1971-79, 93-95. Mem. staff Balt. City Hosps., 1953-63; cons. in field; pres. Faculty Practice Svc. Corp., N.J. Med. Sch., 1986-88; vis. scientist Med. Rsch. Coun. Can., McGill U., Montreal, 1989-90; lectr. in field. Author: (With J.W. Bauman Jr.) Renal Function, 1975; editorial com.: Jour. Clin. Investigation, 1954-59, Jour. Applied Physiology, 1959-65, Am. Jour. Physiology, 1959-65, Circulation Research, 1967-72, Microvascular Research, 1981-89, Revue française des Maladies respiratoires, 1979-93, clin. and investigative medicine, 1985-96; contbr. articles on indicator-dilution techniques, membrane permeability and transport, pulmonary, renal function, free radicals and history of medicine, physiology, and med. ethical issues to med. jours. Mem. profl. adv. com. Martha's Vineyard Guidance Ctr., 1968-75; mem. pulmonary disease adv. com. Nat. Heart and Lung Inst., 1971-75, chmn., 1974-75, mem. bd. sci. counselors, 1976-80, chmn., 1978-80. Served to maj. M.C. USAAF, 1942-45. Decorated Legion of Merit; recipient Lucian award McGill U., 1989, Sir William Osler Humanitarian award N.J. Thoracic Soc., 1991, Laureate award N.J. chpt. Am. Coll. Physicians, 1993, Charles L. Brown award Alumni Assn. N.J. Med. Sch. Fellow: ACP, AAAS, N.Y. Acad. Scis.; mem.: Am. Chem. Soc., Am. Soc. Biochemistry and Molecular Biology, Am., Can. Socs. Clin. Investigation, Soc. Exptl. Biology and Medicine, Assn. Am. Physicians, Am. Physiol. Soc., Peripatetic Soc., Acad. Medicine NJ (trustee 1972—78), Am. Heart Assn. (rsch. com. NJ affiliate 1975—81), Inst Français Washington (trustee 1994—2005), Microcirculatory Soc. (Landis award), Am. Thoracic Soc., Soc. Scholars (Johns Hopkins), N.Y. Clin. Soc., Med. History Soc. NJ (pres. 1984—86), Am. Assn. History of Medicine (councilor), Harvey Soc., Interurban Clin. Club, Century Assn. Club (N.Y.C.), Charaka Club, Paris-Am. Club (N.Y.C.), Sigma Xi, Alpha Omega Alpha. Democrat. Achievements include research on chronic obstructive pulmonary disease, kidney and lung physiology, transcapillary water movement. Office: 40 Warren Pl Montclair NJ 07042-2534 Office Phone: 973-746-7847. Business E-Mail: chinard@umdnj.edu.

CHIN-BING, STANLEY ARTHUR, physicist, educator; b. New Orleans, La., Nov. 3, 1942; s. Arthur Joseph Chin-Bing and Adele Viola Peavy; m. Hilda Faye Taylor, Aug. 12, 1995 (dec. Aug. 12, 1997). BS, Tulane U., 1964; MS, U. New Orleans, 1966, PhD, 1973. Spl. lectr. U. New Orleans, 1973, asst. prof. of engring., 1975—79, adj. prof. of physics, 1988—; sys. analyst Martin Marietta Corp., New Orleans, 1974—75; advanced systems sr. engr. space divsn. Chrysler Corp., New Orleans, 1976—77; rsch. physicist Naval Ocean R & D Activity, Bay St. Louis, Miss., 1978—88; supervisory rsch. physicist Naval Oceanog. and Atmospheric Rsch. Lab., Bay St. Louis, 1988—92; head, acoustic simulation, measurements and tactics br. Naval Rsch. Lab., Stennis Space Center, Miss., 1992—. Contbr. more than 40 articles to sci. jours.; author: Procs. of Parabolic Equation Workshop II. Fellow: Acoustical Soc. Am. (assoc. editor 1996—2003); mem.: AAAS, Soc. Indsl. and Applied Mathematicians, NY Acad. of Sciences, Math. Assn. of Am., IEEE Ocean Engring. Soc., Am. Assn. of Physics Teachers, Optical Soc. of Am., Am. Phys. Soc., Sigma Pi Sigma. Home: 3619 Bauvais St Metairie LA 70001-5005 Office: Naval Rsch Lab 1005 Balch Blvd Stennis Space Center MS 39529-5004 Office Phone: 228-688-4798. E-mail: chinbing@nrlssc.navy.mil.

CHING, CHAUNCEY TAI KIN, agricultural studies educator, economist; b. Honolulu, July 25, 1940; m. Theodora Lam, July 7, 1962; children: Donna, Cory. AB in Econs., U. Calif., Berkeley, 1962; MS in Agrl. Econs., U. Calif., Davis, 1965, PhD in Agrl. Econ., 1967. Asst. prof. U. N.H., Durham, 1968-72; assoc. prof. U. Nev., Reno, 1972-77, prof., head div. agrl. and resource econs., 1977-80; prof., chmn. dept. agrl. and resource econs. U. Hawaii, Honolulu, 1980-84, prof. agrl. econs., 1992—, dir. Hawaii Inst. Tropical Agr. and Human Resources, 1984-92. Recipient Charles H. Seurferle award, U. Nev., Reno, 1977. Office: Hawaii Inst Tropical Agr 3050 Maile Way # 202 Honolulu HI 96822-2231 Office Phone: 202-262-6619. E-mail: cc@cching.com.

CHING, EDITH IRENE, librarian; b. Flushing, N.Y., Sept. 13, 1942; d. Norman and Edith (Crawford) Sprenger; m. Wallace Koon Leong Ching, Oct. 13, 1971; children: Alexander, Andrew, Christina. BA cum laude, Middleburg Coll., 1964; MAT, Harvard U., Cambridge, Mass., 1968; MLS, U.Md., College Park. Tchr. English Oyster Bay H.S., NY, 1965—67, Panahou Sch., Honolulu, 1967—70; edn. specialist Mitre Corp., McLean, Va., 1971—72; tng. specialist IRS, McLean, Va., 1972—75; English tchr. Montgomery Coll., Rockwell, Md., 1976—80, U. Md., College Park, 1985—91. Program chair Washington Childrens' Book List, DC, 2000—02; reviewer Booklist Mag., Chgo., 2004—; vol. Wahington Nat. Cathedral, DC, 1993—. Mem.: Washington Children's Book Guide. Achievements include Elected to 2007 Newberry Com. Home: 12805 Gaffney Ln Silver Spring MD 20904 Office: St. Albans Sch Mt St Alban Washington DC 20011

CHING, HO, surgeon; b. Kaoshung, Taiwan, Feb. 20, 1950; arrived in U.S., 1970; d. Feng Chih and Ai Hua Yin Ho; m. Stephen Jay Keller; children: Lisa, Michele. BS, Nat. U. Taiwan, Taipei, 1970; PhD, U. Cin., 1975, MD, 1984. Rsch. fellow Roche Molecular Biol. Inst., Nutley, NJ, 1975—76; Fogarty fellow Nat. Cancer Inst., NIH, Bethesda, Md., 1976—78; rsch. assoc. U. Cin., 1978—80; surg. resident Jewish Hosp., Cin., 1989, surgeon, 1989—91, Donna Stahl Assocs., Cin., 1991—2000; pvt. practice surgery Cin., 2000—. Assoc. dir. surg. resident program Jewish Hosp., 1992, mem. exec. com., 2001—03; chmn. women in medicine Acad. Medicine, 1998. Named one of Top Drs., Cin. Mag., 2001, 2003. Fellow: ACS; mem.: Am. Soc. Cell Biology. Avocations: yoga, travel. Office: Ching Ho MD Inc 4760 E Galbraith Rd Cincinnati OH 45236 Office Phone: 513-891-1200. E-mail: drho@fuse.net.

CHING, JAMES MICHAEL, artistic director opera company, composer, conductor; b. Honolulu, Hawaii, Sept. 29, 1958; BA summa cum laude, Duke U., 1980. Pianist, composer Houston Opera Studio, 1980-81; music adminstr. Fla. Grand Opera, 1981-85; mus. dir. Triangle Opera Theatre, 1987-88; asst. to gen. dir. Va. Opera, 1989-91, assoc. artistic dir., 1991-92; artistic dir. Opera Memphis, Tenn., 1992—. Mem. Phi Beta Kappa. Office: 6745 Wolf River Pkwy Memphis TN 38120 Office Phone: 901-257-3100. Business E-Mail: Michael@operamemphis.org.

CHING, SHIM, plastic surgeon; b. Kobe, Japan, June 2, 1969; s. Kai-Ming Ching and Marina Main-Jue Lok; m. Candice L. Naylor-Ching, July 7, 1996. BSc, McGill U., 1992, MSc, 1994; MD, U. B.C., Vancouver, 1998. Regional Med. Assn. scholar, McMaster U., Hamilton, Ont., Can., 1999—2000. Fellow: Royal Coll. Surgeons in Can. in Plastic Surgery; mem.: Can. Soc. Plastic Surgery. Office: 1329 Lusitana St 805 Honolulu HI 96813 Office Phone: 808-585-8855.

CHINN, ADAM, lawyer; b. London, Aug. 12, 1961; BA, Oxford U., 1982; CPE, Coll. Law England, 1983; JD cum laude, NYU Sch. Law, 1987. Bar: NY 1987. Ptnr. Wachtell, Lipton, Rosen & Katz, NYC. Editor NYU Law Review. Named one of 45 highest performing mem. pvt. bar under age of 45, Am. Lawyer. Office: Wachtell Lipton Rosen & Katz 51 W 52nd st New York NY 10019-6150 Office Phone: 212-403-1000.

CHINN, REX ARLYN, chemist; b. Bosworth, Mo., Apr. 5, 1935; s. Loren Herbert and Lima (Stanton) C.; m. Wanda June Williams, May 31, 1959 (dec.); children: Timothy Michael, Sharon Rose Chinn-Heritch, Jonathan Daniel; m. Victoria Loraine Hunter. BS in Chemistry, S.W. Mo. State Coll., 1961; grad., Cleve. Inst. Electronics. Lic. Bapt. minister. Rsch. asst. U. Mo. Med. Ctr., Columbia, 1961-65, William S. Merrell Co., Cin., 1965-67; lab. supr. U.S. Indsl. Chem. Co., Rsch. div., Cin., 1967-72; mgr. quality assurance Cloudsley Co., Cin., 1972-74; dir. tech. affairs Woodson Tenent Labs., Memphis, 1974-77; quality engr. Nat. Ind. for the Blind, Earth City, Mo., 1977-96; owner/mgr. The Master's Image, Maryland Hts., Mo., 1987—. Freelance field prodns. KNLC, Channel 24, St. Louis, 1987—; freelance audo rec. for ACTS Inc., 1996-2000; dir. video ops. Mission Gate Prison Ministry,

2000-2001; video cons.; environ. control sys. cons. Contbr. articles to profl. jours; producer/dir.: More Than a Fighting Chance, 1989. Founder, dir. Christian Alliance of Video Ministries, 2002—. With U.S. Army, 1954—56. Mem. Media Comms. Assn. Republican. Avocations: art, photography, electronics, motorcycling, guitar. Home and Office: The Masters Image 12079 Ameling Rd Maryland Heights MO 63043-4148

CHINNIS, C. CABELL, JR., lawyer; b. Washington, May 28, 1958; BA in Pub. Affairs, Princeton Univ.; Kennedy fellow, Harvard Univ., 1980—81; JD, Yale Univ., 1984. Bar: Pa. 1986, DC 1988, Calif. 2002, US Tax Ct. 1988. Law clk. Hon. John Minor Wisdom, US Ct. of Appeals (fifth cir.), 1984—85, Hon. Lewis F. Powell Jr., US Supreme Ct., 1985—86; atty. Latham & Watkins, Washington, 1986—93; pvt. practice, 1993—94; assoc. Mayer, Brown, Rowe & Maw LLP, Washington, 1994—97, ptnr., 1997—2001, Palo Alto, Calif., 2001—, now ptnr.-in-charge, Palo Alto office, 2003—. Mng. editor Yale Law Jour., 1984. Mem.: Phi Beta Kappa. Office: Mayer Brown Rowe & Maw LLP Ste 300 3000 El Camino Palo Alto CA 94306-2112 Office Phone: 650-331-2020. Office Fax: 650-331-2067. Business E-Mail: cchinnis@mayerbrownrowe.com.

CHINTAPALLI, MEENA, physician, social sciences educator, humanities educator, pediatrician; arrived in US, 1976; d. Krishnamurti and Syamala Bhadriraju; m. Kedar Nath Chintapalli, Aug. 15, 1975; children: Pallavi, Sumara. M.B.B.S., Gandhi Med., A.P., Hyderabad, 1972; intern, Gandhi Hosp., A.P., Hyderabad, 1974; degree, DC Gen. Hosp., Wash., 1976—78. Clin. instr. dept. pediat. Med. Coll. Wis., 1981—83; pvt. practice, 1984—94, 2001—; chair multi disciplinary meetings, dir. pediat. Bowling Green, San Antonio, 1989—91; pediatrician Mac Gregor Med. Assn., 1995, Quantum, 2000. Founder website edn. www.saiodo.org, 2000; pres. San Antonio A thru Z Pediat. P.A., 2001—; CEO San Antonio Internat. Inst. Educare, 2002—; chmn. physician adv. bd. NRCC, Tex., 2004; tchr. concepts neurobiology to parents, therapists, and tchrs. Author: Brain, Mind, Neuro Development & Behaviors, 2004; contbr. abtract and monographs to profl. jours. Worker Soc. Assistance Internat.,a 501c-3 tax exempt Orgn., for Health, Edn. and Social Welfare Without Borders, San Antonio, 1998, founder, 1998; with Traveler's Health Network, 1990—93, Humana Health Care Plans, 1992—95; vol. Battered Women's Shelter, Children's Ctr., Soup Kitchens, Bexar County Detention Programs, 1991; founder Satya Sai Ctr., San Antonio, 1991; organizer med. missions India, 1996—; founder Spiritual Ctr., San Antonio, 1991; mem. Satya Sai Orgn.; mem. steering com. Humana Women's Children's Hosp., 1992—93; mem. infectious disease com. South Tex. Meth. Children's Hosp., San Antonio, 1992—96, vice chair, 1998. Named Best Pediatrician in Town, Med. Gazette San Antonio, 1993; recipient Woman of Yr. award, Mayor's Commn. San Antonio, 1995; fellow U. Mich., Ann Arbor, 1978—80. Fellow: Am. Acad. Pediat. Avocation: community service. Office: San Antonio A thru Z Pediat PA 19016 Stone Oala San Antonio TX 78258 also: San Antonio A thru Z Pediat PA 7922 Ewing Halsell 360 San Antonio TX 78229 also: San Antonio A thru Z Pediat PA 13750 N San Pedro Ste 300 San Antonio TX 78232 Office Phone: 210-614-7500. Fax: 210-492-4172; Office Fax: 210-614-7540.

CHIODINI, JOHN ALLEN, musician, composer; s. Samuel Frank and Josephine Piti Chiodine; m. Virginia Dolores Meunier, Aug. 21, 1965; children: Carolyn Alexis Chiodini-Cable, Lauri Ann, Amy. Student, U. R.I., 1960—63, UCLA, 1999. Guitarist Boston Pops, 1975—77, Maynard Ferguson, 1978; guitarist, mus. dir. Peggy Lee, L.A., 1982—87; guitarist, prodr., arranger John Chiodini-Weightless album, 1987; guitarist, arranger Natalie Cole Take a Look Tour, 1993—97; guitarist Natalie Cole Stardust Tour, 1998, Natalie Cole Unforgetable Tour, 1991—93; guitarist, founding mem. Affinity, L.A., 1997, Polychrome, L.A., 2000; recording artist LA Studios for Motion Pictures, TV, Film and Records, 1980—. Prodr. various artists, L.A., 1970—; cons. mus. dir., composer Ind. Films, Award Winning Cable shows, prodr. Carolyn Chiodini Cable, Chatsworth, Calif., 1998—; cartoon orchestrator, arranger Nickelodean Network, L.A., 2003—; tchr. Head Start program, San Fernando Valley, Calif., 2000, R.I. H.S., East Providence, 2002, Mary Wheeler Sch., Providence, 1975; with Boudoir Prodns., Producer Amy Chiodini, 1983—90; owner Ginger Q Music Co., 1978—. Music contbr. (textbook and screenplay project) The Fame Game, 2001, copy editor Peggy Lee Autobiography, 1984, discography includes numerous albums for Peggy Lee, Al Jarreau, Shirley Horn, Dennis Rowland, Barry Manilow, Diane Schuur, Barbra Streisand, Nancy Wilson, numerous other artists; prodr.: (films) including Bioloxi Blues, Cats Don't Dance, Dukes of Hazard, Foul Play, Hanging Up, It Could Happen to You, Living out Loud, Mafia!, Oh God II, Yes Giorgio, Xanadu, When Dreams Come True, numerous others. Recipient Cable award, L.A. City Creative Learning Channel 36, 1999, Best Film, Action Film Festival, 1991, 1996. Democrat. Avocation: history. Office: Chiodini Prodns/Ginger Q Music PO Box 1063 Woodland Hills CA 91365

CHIOGIOJI, MELVIN HIROAKI, retired federal official, entrepreneur; b. Hiroshima, Japan, Aug. 21, 1939; came to U.S., 1939; s. Yutaka and Harumi (Yamasaki) C.; m. Pallas A. Chiogioji; children: Wendy A., Alan K. BS in Elec. Engring., Purdue U., 1961; MBA, U. Hawaii, 1968; DBA, George Washington U., 1972. Registered profl. engr., Hawaii. Head weapons gen. component div. Quality Evaluation Lab., Oahu, Hawaii, 1965-69; dir. weapons evaluation and engring. div. Naval Ordinance Systems Command, Washington, 1969-73; dir. Office Indsl. Analysis Fed. Energy Adminstrn., Washington, 1973-75; asst. dir., div. bldg. and community systems Dept. Energy, Washington, 1975-79, dir. fed. program div., 1980—, dep. asst. sec. state and local assistance program, 1980-85, dir. office of transp. systems, 1985-90; constrn. mgr. Office of New Prodn. Reactors, Washington, 1990-92; pres. EFC, Inc., 1980-99, Precision Auto Care, Inc., 1989-97, Intemco, 1993-96, Mele Assocs., Inc., 1999—. Prof. mgmt. sci. George Washington U., 1972—. Author: Industrial Energy Conservation, 1979, Energy Conservation in Commercial and Residental Buildings, 1982; contbr. articles to profl. jours. Mem. Md. State Adv. Com. on Civil Rights, 1976—; mem. Nat. Naval Res. Policy Bd., 1977—; vestryman Grace Episcopal Ch., Silver Spring, Md., 1982—; bd. dirs. Japanese Am. Nat. Mus., 1996—; chmn. Nat. Japanese Am. Meml. Found., 1995—. With USN, 1961-65; rear adm. USNR. Decorated Navy Commendation medal, Meritorious Svc. medal, Legion Merit medal. Mem. IEEE (sr.), NSPE, Acad. Mgmt., Naval Res. Assn., Assn. for Sci., Tech. and Innovation (pres. 1979-81), Soc. Am. Mil. Engrs., Armed Forces Mgmt. Assn., Seabee Meml. Scholarship Assn. (bd. dirs. 1973—), Triangle Fraternity Edn. Found. (bd. dirs. 1995—), Purdue U. Alumni Assn., Nat. Japanese Am. Meml. Found. (chmn.), Japanese Am. Nat. Mus. (bd. dirs.). Address: 15702 Thistlebridge Dr Rockville MD 20853-3226 Office: 14660 Rothgeb Dr Rockville MD 20850-5309 Office Phone: 240-453-6990. E-mail: mel@meleassociates.com.

CHIORAZZI, MARY LORRAINE, psychiatrist; b. New York; BS, Marymount Manhattan Coll., 1966; MD, Georgetown U., 1970. Diplomate Am. Bd. Psychiatry. Pvt. practice child, adolescent, adult psychiatry, Englewood, N.J., 1975—. Office: 163 Engle St Englewood NJ 07631-2530

CHIOU, PAUL C.J., statistician, educator; b. Tainan, Taiwan, Nov. 18, 1950; s. T.S. and H.C. Chiou; m. Peen-Peen Ma, Mar. 9, 1990; 1 child, Jonathan. BS, Nat. Chung Hsing U., 1974; MA, U. Tex., Arlington, 1980, PhD, 1984. Instr. U. Tex., Arlington, 1982—83; asst. prof. East Tex. State U., Commerce, 1983—88; from asst. prof. to assoc. prof. Lamar U., Beaumont, Tex., 1988—97, prof., 1997—. Assoc. editor: Jour. Statis. Rsch., 2003—, chief editor: Jour. Probability and Stats. Sci., 2002—; contbr. articles to profl. jours. Grantee Grad. Tchg. Assistantship grant, U. of Tex. at Arlington, 1978—83. Mem.: Inst. of Math. Stats., Am. Statis. Assn., Pi Mu Epsilon. Avocation: gardening. Office: Lamar University East Lavaca Beaumont TX 77710-0047 E-mail: chiou@math.lamar.edu.

CHIOU-TAN, FAYE, physician, educator; b. Hsin-Chu, Taiwan, Mar. 27, 1964; d. George and Tricia Chiou; m. Filemon Tan, Jr.; children: Filemon III, Michelle. AB, Princeton U., 1985; MD, Baylor U., 1990. Diplomate Am. Bd. Electrodiagnostic Medicine, Am. Bd. Phys. Med. Rehab. Asst. prof. Baylor Coll. Medicine, Houston, 1995—2003, assoc. prof., 2003—. Contbr. articles to profl. jours. Chief svc. phys. medicine and rehab. Harris County Hosp. Dist., Houston, 2000—, dir. electrodiagnosis, 1995—, dir. Ctr. for Trauma Rehab. Rsch., 2000—. Recipient Excellence in Rsch. Writing award Assn. Acad. Physiatrists/Am. Jour. Phys. Medicine and Rehab., 1999, 2000, 2003; named one of Am's Top Physicians, Consumer's Rsch. Coun. Am., 2003, 04. Mem.: Assn. Acad. Physiatrists (chair rsch. coun.), Am. Assn. Neuromuscular Electrodiagnostic Medicine (chmn. 2005, rsch. com.). Avocations: cooking, hiking, antiques. Office: Baylor Coll Medicine Dept PM&R 3601 N MacGregor Way Ste 240 Houston TX 77004

CHIPKIN, FREDERICK, textile designer, consultant; b. NYC, Mar. 11, 1963; s. Sidney and Pearl Chipkin; m. Rimma Zilman Chipkin, Feb. 28, 1985; children: Alexandra Elizabeth, Rebecca Tatiana. AS in Culinary Arts, Johnson and Wales Coll., 1983; BFA, Parsons Sch. of Design, 1989. Owner/designer Design Soc., Inc., NYC, 1987—90; textile designer Liz Claiborne, NYC, 1990—92, Bernard Chause, Inc., NYC; mgr., CAD dept. I. Appel, Inc., NYC, 1995—99; owner/designer Origin Inc., Textile Design Studio, 1999—. Author: ADOBE Photoshop for Textile Design, 2001—05. Home and Office: Origin Inc 117-14 Union Turnpike CD2 Kew Gardens NY 11415 Office Phone: 718-544-2754. Office Fax: 718-544-2754. Business E-Mail: design@origininc.com.

CHIPLIN, JOHN, medical company executive; b. 1958; BS in Pharmacy, U. Nottingham, Eng.; PhD in Biochemistry, U. Nottingham. CEO Superscape plc; with Molecular Design Ltd., Biosym Technologies, Inc.; co-founder, CEO, pres. GeneFormatics, Inc., San Diego. Mem.: Inst. of Dirs., Royal Soc. of Arts, The Pharm. Soc. Office: GeneFormatics Inc 10929 Technology Pl San Diego CA 92127-1811

CHIPMAN, DENNIS CLARENCE, JR., forensic psychiatrist, consultant; b. Seattle, Jan. 7, 1934; s. Dennis Clarence and Esther (Ränghild) Chipman; m. Karen Antoinette Ekern, Mar. 17, 1968 (div. Oct. 1982); children: Judith, Kimberly, Jason, Carolyn; m. Sandra Kay Woodell, Feb. 6, 1983. *Wife, Sandra Kay Woodell Chipman is a registered nurse and an attorney, in private law practice, in Anderson, S.C. Daughter, Judith, has a B.A. from Willamette University and operates a land development corporation with her husband, David, from Seattle W.A. Daughter, Kimberly, has a B.A. from Knox College and also an M.S. in Journalism from Northwestern; she works for Bloomberg media services in New York City. Son, Jason, has a B.A. from Mary Washington and a J.D. from the University of Virginia Law School; he is an Associate at Hogan & Hartson in Washington, D.C. Daughter, Carolyn, is a sophomore in College; she plans on studying architecture.* MD, U. Wash. Diplomate Am. Bd. Psychiatry and Neurology (subspecialty of forensic psychiatry), Am. Bd. Adolescent Psychiatry. Intern U. Nebr. Hosp., Omaha, 1959-60; resident U. Wash. Hosp. Sys., Seattle, 1960-63; pvt. practice Seattle, 1963-66; dir. Mental Health Ctr., Kingsport, Tenn., 1969-84; pvt. practice Kingsport, 1969-84, Hickory, NC, 1984-86; med. dir. Pinewood Hosp., Texarkana, Ark., 1986-89, Charter Hosp. Mobile, Ala., 1989-94; chief psychiatrist Patrick B. Harris Hosp., Anderson, SC, 1994—2001, sr. psychiatrist, 2001—; cons. forensic psychiatry, 1994—. Cons. Meth. Children's Home, Greenville, Tenn., 1969—75, Disability Determinations Divsn. Vocat. Rehab. Bd. dirs. Sheltered Workshop, Kingsport, 1973—80, Gateways Farm for Girls, New Boston, Tex., 1988—94, Home of Grace for Women, Mobile, 1990—94, New Haven Program, Mobile, 1990—94. Capt. U.S. Army, 1966—68. Named to Guide to America's Top Psychiatrists, Consumer Rsch. Coun. Am. Mem.: AMA, Internat. Soc. Philos. Enquiry, U.S. Chess Fedn., Am. Psychiat. Assn., Am. Mensa Ltd., Civtan Club, Rotary, Kappa Sigma. Libertarian. Baptist. Avocations: music, chess, reading, travel. Home: PO Box 5587 Anderson SC 29623-5587 Office Phone: 864-261-7872. Personal E-mail: c1219d@aol.com.

CHIPMAN, JACK, artist; b. LA, Oct. 31, 1943; s. George Geotz and June Naomi (Hanson) Chipman. BFA, Calif. Inst. Arts, 1966. Dealer Calif. pottery Calif. Spectrum, Redondo Beach, 1980-90. Cons. Schroeder Pub., Paducah, Ky., 1982—99. Author: Complete Collectors Guide Bauer Pottery, 1982, Collector's Encyclopedia California Pottery, 1992, 2d edit., 1998, Collector's Encyclopedia Bauer Pottery, 1997, Barbara Willis: Classic California Modernism, 2003, California Pottery Scrapbook, 2004; contbr. articles to profl. jours.; one-man shows include Oakland Mus., Calif., Long Beach (Calif.) Art Mus., U. Santa Clara (Calif.) Art Mus., Represented in permanent collections Oakland Art Mus., Long Beach Mus. Art, U. Santa Clara Art Mus.; editor: jour., 1990—93. Bd. dirs. Angels Gate Cultural Ctr., San Pedro, Calif. Avocation: pottery. Office: PO Box 1079 Venice CA 90294-1079 E-mail: jack@jackchipman.com.

CHIPMAN, JOHN SOMERSET, economist, educator; b. Montreal, Que., Can., June 28, 1926; s. Warwick Fielding and Mary Somerset (Aikins) C.; m. Margaret Ann Ellefson, June 24, 1960; children: Thomas Noel, Timothy Warwick. Student, U. Chile, Santiago, 1943—44; BA, McGill U., Montreal, 1947, MA, 1948; PhD, Johns Hopkins U., 1951; postgrad., U. Chgo., 1950—51; Doctor rerum politicarum honoris causa, U. Konstanz, Germany, 1991, U. Würzburg, 1998; D in Social and Econ. Scis., U. Graz, Austria, 2001. Asst. prof. econs. Harvard U., Cambridge, Mass., 1951-55; assoc. prof. econs. U. Minn., Mpls., 1955-60, prof., 1961-81, Regents' prof., 1981—. Fellow Ctr. for Advanced Study in Behavioral Scis., Stanford, Calif., 1972-73; Guggenheim fellow, 1980-81; vis. prof. econs. various univs.; permanent guest prof. U. Konstanz, 1985-91; bd. dirs. Leuthold Funds, Inc Author: The Theory of Intersectoral Money Flows and Income Formation, 1951; editor: (with others) Preferences, Utility, and Demand, 1971, Preferences, Uncertainty and Optimality, 1990, (with C.P. Kindleberger) Flexible Exchange Rates and the Balance of Payments, 1980; co-editor Jour. Internat. Econs., 1971-76, editor, 1977-87; assoc. editor Econometrica, 1956-60, Can. Jour. Stats., 1980-82; adv. bd. Jour. Multivariate Analysis, 1988-92. Recipient Humboldt Rsch. award for Sr. U.S. Scientists, 1992, 2003. Fellow AAAS, Econometric Soc. (coun. 1971-76, 81-83), Am. Statis. Assn., Am. Acad. Arts and Scis., Am. Econ. Assn. (disting.); mem. NAS (assoc., chair sect. econ. scis. 1997-2000, James Murray Luck award 1981), Internat. Statis. Inst., Am. Philos. Soc., Inst. Math. Stats., Can Econ. Assn., Royal Econ. Soc., History of Econs. Soc. Home: 2121 W 49th St Minneapolis MN 55409-2229 Office: U Minn Dept Econs 1035 Heller Hall 217 19th Ave S Minneapolis MN 55455-0400 Office Phone: 612-625-2816. Business E-Mail: jchipman@econ.umn.edu.

CHIRA, SUSAN, editor; married; 2 children. BA in History and East Asian Studies, Harvard U., 1980. Reporter The NY Times, 1982—84, Tokyo corr., 1984—89, dep. fgn. editor, 2004—. Author: A Mother's Place, 1998. Office: The New York Times 229 W 43rd St New York NY 10036-3959

CHIRIAC, VICTOR ADRIAN, aerospace engineer, researcher; b. Bucharest, Romania, Feb. 22, 1969; arrived in U.S., 1994; s. Florea Nicolae and Michaela Cornelia Chiriac; m. Raluca Olga Chiriac, June 30, 2000. BSc, Poly. U. Bucharest, 1992, MSc, 1993; PhD in Aero. and Mech. Engring., U. of Ariz., 1999. Registered Profl. Engr. Rsch. and tchg. asst. U. Ariz., Tucson, 1994—97; intern Motorola Inc., Tempe, Ariz., 1996—98, prin. staff engr., 1999—. Awareness sub.-com. Motorola Inc., 2001—02; session chair internat. congress INTERPACK 2003, Hawaii, ITHERM '04, Las Vegas; panel chmn. Internat. Congress Interpack, San Francisco, 2005. Contbr. articles to profl. jours. (Prize Paper Award, 2001). Mem.: ASME (k-16 com. mem. thermal divsn. 2002—), ASHRAE (corr.), Internat. Microelectronics & Packaging Soc. Orthodox. Achievements include patents for system and method for cooling using an oscillatory impinging jet; airbag circuit driver optimization. Avocations: tennis, swimming, hiking. Home: 15016 S 28th St Phoenix AZ 85048 Office: Freescale Semiconductor 2100 East Elliot Tempe AZ 85284 Office Phone: 480-413-6756. Personal E-mail: vchiriac@cox.net. Business E-Mail: victor.chiriac@freescale.com.

CHIRICO, ANTHONY (TONY), publishing executive; With Knopf Pub., NYC, 1986—, various mgmt. positions, 1988—2000, exec. v.p., COO, 2000—05, pres., 2005. Office: Knopf Publishing 1745 Broadway New York NY 10019-4305 Office Phone: 212-751-9600.

CHIRICO-ELKINS, URSULA, retired librarian; arrived in Can., 1958, arrived in U.S., 1961; d. Friedrich Winter and Gertrud Naake; m. John H. Elkins (dec.); children: Amadeus, Naomi, George, Tabitha; m. Francesco Chirico, Jan. 9, 2003. Student, Mercer County C.C., N.J.; diploma, Inst. Children's Lit., 1980, diploma, 1990. Libr. asst. Princeton (N.J.) U., 1978—81, libr. asst. David Sarnoff Rsch. Ctr., 1981—87, sr. libr. asst. David Sarnoff Rsch. Ctr., 1983—87; prin. asst. Rider U., Lawrenceville, NJ, 1987—89, 1990—93; ret., 1993. Author: A Celebration of Poets, 1998, Michelangelo's Creation of Adane, 1998, Falling Snow, 1998, Unending Love, 1999, Omnipotence, 1999, Universal Truth, 2000, Springtime, 2003, Freedom of Spirit, 2004, Let Not Your Heart Be Troubled, 2004, (anthology) Great Poems of the Western World, 2004. Vol. libr. Calvary Ch., Pemberton, NJ, 2000; literacy vol. Toms River, NJ, 1993—; vol. Samaritan Hospice, Moorestown, NJ, 1995—; mem. edn. coun. Indian Nations, Albuquerque, 2004; mem. coun. Am. Indian Edn. Found., Albuquerque, 2003—. Mem.: Am. Indian Edn. Found. (bd. dirs. 2004—), Internat. Soc. Poets (Disting. Mem.). Avocations: painting, classical music, literature, embroidery.

CHIRLS, RICHARD, lawyer; b. Newark, N.J., 1950; BS cum laude, U. Pa., 1973, JD, 1976; LLM in Taxation, NYU, 1979. Ptnr. Orrick, Herrington & Sutcliffe LLP, N.Y.C., ptnr. in charge-rates, billing & collection. Mem. ABA (chmn. tax exempt fin.com. 1989-91), Nat. Assn. Bond Lawyers (vice chmn. com. edn. 1985-86, bd. dirs. 1987-92, treasure & exec. com. 1988--1989, pres. 1990-91), N.Y. State Bar Assn. (co-chmn. tax exempt fin. com. tax 1984-86). Office: Orrick Herrington & Sutcliffe LLP 666 5th Ave New York NY 10103-1798 Office Phone: 212-506-5250. Business E-Mail: rchirls@orrick.com.

CHISARI, FRANCIS V., pathologist; BS, Fordham U.; MD, Cornell U., Ithaca, N.Y. Lic. Am. Bd. Internal Medicine with subspecialty in anatomic pathology. Faculty Scripps Rsch. Inst., LaJolla, Calif., 1975—, prof. dept. molecular and exptl. medicine, adj. prof., 1987—; rsch. fellow in virology NIH; fellow in immunology and mem. sci. faculty Scripps Clinic and Rsch. Found., 1973—; adj. prof. pathology U. Calif., San Diego. Mem. sci. adv. bd. Epimmune, 1998—; mem. disting. adv. com. U. Calif.-San ancer Ctr.; mem. sci. adv. bd. Ctr. for Study of HCV, Rockefeller U.; mem. internat. rsch. scholars program Howard Hughes Med. Inst. Contbr. articles to profl. jours. Recipient Rous-Whippple award, Assn. for Investigative Pathology, 1999, Ernst Jung-Preis for Medizin, 1997, Rsch. Career Devel. award, Merit award, NIH, Sheila Sherlock Liver Rsch. prize, U. Toronto; fellow, Fogarty Sr. Internat. fellow; scholar Fgn. scholar, Fondation pour la Recherche Medicale, France. Fellow: AAAS; mem.: Assn. of Am. Physicians, Am. . for Investigative Pathology, Am. Acad. Microbiology, Inst. Medicine, 2004 (life). Office: Scripps Rsch Inst Dept Molecular/Exptl Medicine 10550 N Torrey Pines Rd La Jolla CA 92037

CHISHOLM, ANDREA LYNNE, trade association administrator, foundation administrator; b. Waterloo, Iowa, Mar. 11, 1961; d. Delbert Eugene Brix and Lynne Larsen; m. Colin Alexander Joseph Chisholm, Nov. 3, 2001. BA, Iowa Lakes U., 1982. Dir. human resources Lord & Taylor, New York, 1986—98; dir. membership Stamford (Conn.) C. of C., 1998—. Dir., vice chmn. ARC, Stamford, 2000—02. Bd. dirs. Women in Mgmt., Stamford, 1999—2002. Mem.: Landmark Club. Republican. Avocations: yachting, deep water diving, golf, animal rescue. Office: Stamford C of C 7 33 Summer St Ste 104 Stamford CT 06901 Personal E-mail: achisholm@stamfordchamber.com. E-mail: achisholm@tcnnetworks.com.

CHISHOLM, DEAN D., lawyer; b. Missoula, Mont., Feb. 15, 1967; s. Richard L. and Marilyn R.W. Chisholm; m. Penni L. Chisholm, Sept. 4, 1993; children: Henry R., Ava P. BA, Colo. State U., 1989; JD, U. Mont., 1992. Bar: Mont. 1992, U.S. Dist. Ct. Mont. 1992, U.S. Ct. Appeals (9th cir.) 1992, Colo. 2001. Dep. county atty. Cascade County, Great Falls, Mont., 1992—94, acting county atty., 1994; ptnr. Lynch & Chisholm, P.C., Great Falls, Mont., 1995—96, Kaplan & Chisholm, P.L.L.P., Columbia Falls, Mont., 1996—2004, Chisholm & Chisholm P.L.L.P., Columbia Falls, Mont., 2004—; dep. city atty. Columbia Falls, 1998—; apptd. spl. prosecutor Mont. Supreme Ct. Commn. on Practice, 2001—02. Bd. mem. Fed. Law Enforcement Grant Bd., Great Falls, 1994—96. Bd. trustees Sch. Dist. 6, Mont., 2004—. Named one of Best Lawyers in Am., 2001—; recipient cert. of recognition for Nat. Mid. East Studies Symposium, Pa. State U., 1989, Am. Jurisprudence award for outstanding achievement in constl. law, 1991, Vol. Family of Yr., United Way, 2004. Mem.: Colo. Bar Assn., N.W. Mont. Bar Assn., Mont. Trial Lawyers Assn., Mensa. Avocations: literature, golf. Office: Chisholm & Chisholm PC PO Box 2034 Columbia Falls MT 59912 Office Phone: 406-892-4356. Business E-Mail: dean@chisholmlawfirm.com.

CHISHOLM, LIONEL DONALD JOHN, ophthalmologist; b. Montreal, Que., Can., July 9, 1935; s. Donald Munro and Isabelle Anne (Frizzell) C.; m. Ann Violet Webster, Feb. 12, 1960; children: Sarah Ann, John Webster. MD, U. Toronto, 1959. Retina fellow Retina Found., Mass. Eye and Ear Infirmary, Boston, 1964-66; asst. to assoc. prof. opthalmology U. Toronto, 1966-79, prof., 1979-93; ophthalmologist in chief Toronto Western and Toronto Hosp., 1979-93; prof., dir. of retina vitreous unit dept. ophthalmologyy W.Va. U., 1993—. W.Va. state rep. diabetes 2000 Am. Acad. Ophthalmology, 1994—. Fellow: Assn. for Rsch. in Vision and Ophthalmology, Schepens Internal Soc., Am. Acad. Ophthalmology, Royal Coll. Surgeons (Can.); mem.: Can. Med. Assn., Retina Soc. (founding mem.). Avocation: equestrian. Office: WVa U Eye Inst PO Box 9193 Morgantown WV 26506-9193

CHISHOLM, MALCOLM HAROLD, chemistry professor; b. Bombay, Oct. 15, 1945; came to US, 1972; s. Angus MacPhail and Gweneth (Robey) C.; m. Cynthia Ann Truax, May 1, 1982; children: Calum R.I., Selby Scott, Derek Adrian. BS in Chemistry, Queen Mary Coll., London, 1966, PhD in Chemistry, 1969; DSc (hon.), London U., 1981. Postdoctoral fellow U. Western Ont., London, 1969-72; asst. prof. Princeton (N.J.) U., 1972-78; assoc. prof. chemistry Ind. U., Bloomington, 1978-80, prof., 1980-85, Disting. prof. chemistry, 1985-99; disting. prof. math., phys. scis. Ohio State U., 2000—. Cons. in field. Editor: Polyhedron, Chem. Comm., Dalton Transactions; mem. editl. bd. Inorganic Chemistry, Organometallics, Inorganic Chimica Acta, Inorganic Syn. Inc., Jour. Cluster Sci., Chem. European Jour., Can. Jour. Chemistry, Chem. Record; contbr. over 500 rsch. articles to profl. jours. Recipient Basolo medal, Northwestern U. and Chgo. Am. Chem. Soc., 2004. Fellow AAAS, NAS, Am. Acad. Arts and Scis., Ind. Acad. Scis., Royal Soc. (London, Davy medal), Deutsche Akademie fuer Naturforch Leopoldina, Royal Soc. Chemistry (Corday Morgan medal 1981, award for Transition Metal Chemistry, Centenary Lectr. and medal, Mond Lectr. and medal), Am. Chem. Soc. (Akron sect. award 1982, Buck Whitney award 1987, Inorganic Chemistry award 1989, Disting. Svc. award 1999, Basolo medal Chgo. divsn. 2004). Home: 100 Kenyon Brook Dr Worthington OH 43085-3629 also: 38 Norwich St Cambridge CB2 1NE England Office: Ohio State U Dept Chemistry 100 W 18th Ave Columbus OH 43210-1185 Office Phone: 614-292-7216. Business E-Mail: chisholm.4@osu.edu.

CHISHOLM, MARGARET ELIZABETH, retired library director; b. Grey Eagle, Minn., July 25, 1921; d. Henry D. and Alice (Thomas) Bergman; children: Nancy Diane, Janice Marie Lane. BA, U. Washington, 1957, MLS, 1958, PhD, 1966. Libr. Everett (Wash.) C.C., 1961-63; from asst. to assoc. prof. edn. U. Oreg., Eugene, 1963-67; assoc. prof. edn. U. N.Mex., Albuquerque, 1967-69; prof., dean U. Md. Coll. Libr. and Info. Svcs., College Park, 1969-75; v.p. univ. rels. and devel. U. Washington, Seattle, 1975-81; dir., prof. Grad. Sch. Libr. and Info. Sci., U. Wash., Seattle, 1981-92; ret., 1992. Adv. com. White House Conf. on Libr. and Info. Sci., 1989-91, Pub. Broadcasting Svc. Archive; commr. Western Interstate Commn. Higher Edn., Colo., 1981-85. Author: Information Technology: Design and Applications (with Nancy Lane), 1990. Mem. USIA del. to Mexican-Am. Commn. on Cultural Coop., 1990. Civilian aide U.S. Army, 1978-88. Recipient Ruth Worden award U. Wash., Seattle, 1957, Disting. Alumni award St. Cloud (Minn.) U., 1977, Disting. Alumni award U. Wash., 1979, John Brubaker award Cath. Libr. Assn., 1987, Pres.'s award Wash. Libr. Assn., 1991. Mem. ALA (exec. bd. 1989-90, pres. 1988-89, v.p. 1986-87), Assn. Pub. TV Stas. (trustee 1975-84, 87-93), White House Conf. on Libr. and Info. Svcs. (adv. com. 1989-91), U. Wash. Retirement Assn. (v.p. 1995-96, pres. 1996-98). Home: 20900 Big Basin Way Saratoga CA 95070-5750

CHISHOLM, MAUREEN, academic administrator; d. Robert Kenneth and Jean Margaret Chisholm; children: Colleen Maria Haley, Meaghan Lyn Haley. AS, Aquinas Coll., Newton, Mass., 1974—76; BA in Bus. Adminstrn., Ea. Nazarene Coll., Quincy, Mass., 1990—92; MS in Mgmt., Lesley Coll., Cambridge, Mass., 1993—95; PhD in philosophy and human resource mgmt., LaSalle, Ky., 1998—2001. Cert. Myers Briggs Mass., 2003. Customer svc. New Eng. Tel., Boston, 1979—93; ops. manger Nynex, Malden, Mass., 1993—95; reimbursable engr. Bell Atlantic, Waltham, Mass., 1995—96; tng., devel. specialist Verizon Comm., Marlboro, Mass., 1996—2000, project mgr. dsl deployment Braintree, Mass., 2000—01; coord. mktg., enrollment, recruitment, and curriculum Ea. Nazarene Coll., adult edn. div., Quincy, Mass., 2002—. Instr. Jr. Achievement, Marlboro, Mass., 1998—2000. Mem.: Ea. Nazarene Coll. LEAD Alumni (pres. 1999—2003). Independent. Roman Catholic. Office: Ea Nazarene Coll 180 Old Colony Ave Quincy MA 02170 Business E-Mail: chisholm@enc.edu.

CHISHOLM, SALLIE WATSON, biological oceanography educator, researcher; b. Marquette, Mich., Nov. 5, 1947; BA, Skidmore Coll., 1969; PhD in biology, SUNY, 1974. Postdoctoral researcher biol. oceanography Scripps Instn. Oceanography, 1974-76; vis. scientist, biology dept. Woods Hole Oceanog. Instn., 1978—; prof., dept. civil and environ. engring. MIT, Cambridge, 1976—, Edgerton asst. prof., 1977—78, Doherty prof. ocean utilization, 1980—82, prof. dept. biology, 1993—, McAfee prof. engring. (endowed chair), 1995—2000, Lee & Geraldine Martin prof. environ. studies, co-dir., Earth Sys. Initiative, 2002—, co-dir., Terrascope, 2003—, Gordon and Betty Moore Found. investigator in marine sci., 2004—. MIT dir. MIT-Woods Hole Joint Program in Oceanography, 1988-95; steering com. U.S. Joint Global Flux Study, 1989-92; mem. ocean studies bd. NRC, 1990-93, com. on molecular biology, 1991-92; corp. mem. Bermuda Biological Station, 1992-96; vis. com. oceanography, Brookhaven Nat. Labs., 1995-98; mem. sci. adv. bd. Joint Genome Inst., Dept. Energy, 2000-, mem. policy bd., 2003; mem. adv. com. Carnegie Instn. Dept. Global Ecology, 2003-; mem. bd. trustees Inst. Ecosystem Studies, 2003-. Assoc. editor Jour. Phycology, 1983-87; mem. editorial bd. Jour. Marine Molecular Biology and Biotech., 1991—, Marine Ecology Progress Series, 1992—, Oceanus Mag., 1991-93, Environmental Microbiology, 1998-; subject editor Aquatic Microbiol Ecology, 1995-99; contbr. articles to profl. jours. Recipient Rosenstiel Award in Ocean Sciences, 1991; fellow, Am. Acad. of Arts and Sciences, 1992; Guggenheim fellow, 1997—98, Resident Scholar, Bellagio Ctr., Italy, 1998, elected, NAS, 2003. Mem.: Internat. Ecology Inst., Soc. of Analytical Cytology, AAAS, Ecological Soc. of Am., The Oceanography Soc., Am. Geophysical Union (fellow 1996), Phycological Soc. of Am., Am. Soc. Microbiology (fellow 1993), Am. Soc. Limnology and Oceanography, Sigma Xi. Office: MIT 3 Cambridge Center, NE20 Cambridge MA 02139

CHISHOLM, SALLY L., musician; b. Ponca City, Okla., Oct. 9, 1947; d. Louis Chisholm and Violet Rose; m. Eugene O. Purdue, Aug. 18, 1974. BA with highest honors, U. Okla., 1971; MusM with distinction, Ind. U., 1977. Violist Thovenel String Quartet, Midland/Odessa, Tex., 1977—91; violist, pro arte quartet U. Wis., Madison, 1991—. Violist, founding mem. Chamber Music Soc. Minn., St. Paul, 1991—; violist Festival Der Zukunft, Ernen, Wallis, Switzerland, 1993—. Recipient Commissioning award, Diesendruck, Fennelly, Koussevitzsky Found., Krenek Quartet; Consortium grant Carter, Powell, Babbitt Quartets, NEA, 1980, 1982. Mem.: Am. Viola Soc., Chgo. Viola Soc. Avocation: philosophy. Home: 5605 Old Middleton Rd Madison WI 53705 Office: 455 N Park St Madison WI 53706 Office Phone: 608-263-1935.

CHISHOLM, TOMMY, lawyer, utilities executive; b. Baldwyn, Miss., Apr. 14, 1941; s. Thomas Vandiver and Rubel (Duncan) C.; m. Janice McClanahan, June 20, 1964; children: Mark Alan (dec.), Andrea, Stephen Thomas, Patrick Ervin. BSCE, Tenn. Tech. U., 1963; JD, Samford U., 1969; MBA, Ga. State U., 1984. Registered profl. engr., Ala., Del., Ga., Ky., La., N.H., Miss., Pa., Tenn., S.C., Va., W.Va. Civil engr. TVA, Knoxville, Tenn., 1963-64; design engr. So. Co. Svcs., Birmingham, Ala., 1964-69, coord. spl. projects Atlanta, 1969-73, sec., house counsel, 1977-82, v.p., sec., house counsel, 1982-98; v.p., assoc. gen. counsel, sec. So. Co., Atlanta, 1998—, asst. to pres., 1973-75, sec., asst. treas., 1977—; mgr. adminstrv. svcs. Gulf Power Co., Pensacola, Fla., 1975-77; sec. So. Energy, Inc., Atlanta, 1981-82. Mem. ABA, State Bar Ala., Am. Soc. Corp. Secs., Am. Corp. Counsel Assn., Nat. Assn. Corp. Dirs., Phi Alpha Delta, Beta Gamma Sigma. Office: The Southern Co 270 Peachtree St NW BIN 912 Atlanta GA 30303-1247

CHISHOLM, WILLIAM DEWAYNE, retired contractor; b. Everett, Wash., Mar. 1, 1924; s. James Adam and Evelyn May (Iles) C.; m. Esther Troehler, Mar. 10, 1956; children: James Scott, Larry Alan, Brian Duane. BSChemE, BS in Indsl. Engring., U. Wash., 1949; MBA, Harvard U., 1955. Cert. profl. contracts mgr. Chemist, unit leader, tech. rep. The Coca-Cola Co., Atlanta and L.A., 1949-59; contract adminstr. Honeywell Inc., L.A., 1959-61, mktg. adminstr., 1961-64, contracts work dir., 1964-66, contracts mgr. Clearwater, Fla., 1966-73, contracts supr., 1973-75, sr. contract mgmt. rep., 1975-80, prin. contract mgmt. rep., work dir., 1980-82, contracts mgr., 1982-89; ret. Chmn. bd. Creative Attitudes, Inc., 1987-96; adj. faculty Fla. Inst. Tech., 1976-96. Contbr. articles to profl. jours. Trustee John Calvin Found., 1974-82; mem. budget adv. com. City of Clearwater, 1983-85; commr. to 196th gen. assembly Presbyn. Ch. (USA), 1984; sec. bd. trustees, treas. Presbytery of Tampa Bay, 1990-96, 99-2003, sec. coun., 1996-98, mem. rev., evaluation and planning com., 1996-98, treas. 1999-2003, elder session mem., 1964-65, 73-76, 77-80, 81-84, 86-90, 97-2000, 2001—, treas., 1994-96; Clearwater rep. on Long Ctr. bd. dirs., 1991-97, mem. exec. com., 1992-97, treas., 1992-93, v.p., 1993-95. With USN, 1944-46. Recipient Award of Distinction Fla. Inst. Tech. Grad. Ctr., 1987. Fellow Nat. Contract Mgmt. Assn. (chmn. S.E. region fellows 1985-87, past nat. dir., pres., v.p. Suncoast chpt.). Home: 1364 S Hercules Ave Clearwater FL 33764-3748 *We can't be too generous in sharing understanding and words of comfort, encouragement, and support to those facing adversity and challenge at various times in their lives.*

CHISM, SANDY L., artist, art educator; b. Great Bend, Kans., Dec. 7, 1957; d. Charles Ernst and Dorothy Elizabeth C.; m. Lane Douglas Ikenberry, Apr. 4, 1998. BFA, U. Kans., 1991; MFA, U. Ariz., 1993. Lectr. U. Kans. (Lawrence), 1994-96; asst. prof. Tulane U., New Orleans, 1996—; artist New Orleans, 1996—. One-woman shows include Sandy Chism exhbn., 1996, Change Anchors, 1998, Tender Scrutiny, 1999, Many As One, 1999, Sany Chism: A Survey, 2000, From Stillness to Frenzy, 2001, invitational exhbns., Drawn From Nature, 1998, Represented in permanent collections New Orleans Mus. Art. Recipient Purchase award Liquitex Paint, 1992; Materials grantee Liquitex Paint, 1993, summer rsch. grantee Tulane U., 1997. Office: Tulane University Newcomb Art Dept New Orleans LA 70118 E-mail: schism@tulane.edu.

CHISNELL, JANICE HOFFMAN, lawyer; b. Pitts., Oct. 11, 1960; d. Jack Edward and Mary Lou (Hazeltine) Hoffman; m. Dennis William Chisnell, Dec. 11, 1982. BA, Grove City Coll., 1982; JD, U. Pitts., 1988. Bar: Pa. 1988, U.S. Dist. Ct. (we. dist.) Pa. 1988. Legal asst. Buchanan Ingersoll, P.C., Pitts., 1982-85; law clk. Brennan Robins & Daley, Pitts., 1986-88; trust adminstr. Equibank, Pitts., 1989-90; lawyer sole practice, Pitts., 1990—. Recipient David Bookstaver award U. Pitts. Sch. Law, 1988, Robert Sisler Meml. award Grove City Coll., 1982. Avocations: photography, riding horses, sewing. Home: 140 Golden Gate Dr Verona PA 15147-2606

CHISU, IOAN, artist; b. Cluj-Napoca, Romania, Jan. 28, 1939; arrived in U.S., 88, naturalized, 96; s. Gheorghe and Hermina Chisu; m. Rodica Chisu, Mar. 24, 1961; children: Ioana, Daniel. M of Painting, Ion Andreescu Fine Arts Inst., Cluj-Napoca, 1963. Pres. Union Bd. Artists of Sibiu County, Romania, 1968-70, 80-89; mem. coun. Leadership Fine Arts Union Romania, 1980-89, mem., 1964-89. One-person shows include Sirius Gallery, Sibiu, 1965, 67, Apollo Gallery, 1970, Brukenthal Mus., Sibiu, 1973; exhibited in group shows Art Gallery, Brasov, 1964, 65-67, Art Movie Theater Show, Sibiu, 1965, Brukenthal Mus., Sibiu, 1964, 67, 68-70, 72, 88, Simu Mus., Bucharest, Romania, 1965, Dalles Gallery, Bucharest, 1965, 67-70, 73-88, Casa Armatei, Sibiu, 1966, 74, Sirius Gallery, Sibiu, 1967, 73-88, Mus. Art, Bucharest, 1968, Art Gallery Casa Artelor, Sibiu, 1971, 73-88, Culture's House, Medias, 1971, 74, Big Gallery, Cluj-Napoca, 1973, Ateneul Roman Gallery, Bucharest, 1976, Nat. Theater, Bucharest, 1977; exhibited in mus. Brukenthal Mus., Sibiu, Art Mus., Brasov, Art Mus., Tirgu Mures, Romania, Anchorage Mus. History and Art, Alaska, 1997-98; designs for monumental mosaic works: Tradition and Contemporary Times, Blaj, 1973, Homage to Human Creativity, Resita, 1980, Archways, Sibiu, 1981 Recipient Nat. Order of Cultural Merit for spl. artistic merits, Bucharest, 1968, Nat. Prize for Romania at 3d Internat. Festival of Painting, Cagnes-sur-Mer, France, 1971, 1st prize for painting Nat. Festival Art, Bucharest, 1985, 87, Grant award Cmty. Arts Assistance Program from City of Chgo. Dept. Cultural Affairs and Ill. Arts Coun. Access Program, 1993, 95. Home: 2417 N Alton Rd Mchenry IL 60050 Personal E-mail: ichisu2003@yahoo.com.

CHISUM, EMMETT DEWAIN, historian, researcher, archaeologist; b. Monroe, La., Mar. 19, 1922; BA in Social Sci., Northwestern State U., 1942; MA in Social Sci., La. State U., 1946; MA in History, U. Wyo., 1952, MA in Polit. Sci. an dAnthropology, 1961. Tchr. sci. Cameron (La.) Parish Sch. System, 1947-51; tchr. English Welsh (La.) High Sch., 1946-47; social sci. librarian U. Wyo., Laramie, 1954-77, prof. rsch. history, archeology, 1977—. Mem. faculty senate U. Wyo., 1986—. Author: (books) Guide to Library Research, 1969, Guide to Research in Political Science, 1970, Guide to Research in Education, 1974, Memories: University of Wyoming 1886-1986, 1987; contbr. articles to Ency. of Lir. and Info. Sci. (45 vols.), 1986—, profl. jours. Mem. AAAS, ALA, Am. Archeol. Soc., Western Pol. Sci. Assn., Am. Assn. for State and Local History for Wyo. Publs. (Agnes Milstead award for Outstanding Librarianship 1995). Home: 2032 Holliday Dr Laramie WY 82070-4803

CHITTY, ELIZABETH NICKINSON (MARY CHITTY), university historian; b. Balt., Apr. 27, 1920; d. Edward Phillips and Em Turner (Merritt) Nickinson; m. Arthur Benjamin Chitty, June 16, 1946; children: Arthur Benjamin, John Abercrombie, Em Turner, Nathan Harsh Brown. BA cum laude, Fla. State U., 1941, MA, 1942; DCL, U. of South, 1988. Tchr. Fla. Indsl. Sch. for Girls, Ocala, 1942-43; psychometrist neuropsychiat. dept. Sch. Aviation Medicine, Pensacola (Fla.) Naval Air Sta., 1943-46; assoc. editor Sewanee (Tenn.) Alumni News, U. of South, 1946-62; bus. mgr., mng. editor Sewanee Rev., 1962-65, dir. fin. aid and career svcs., 1970-80, assoc. univ. historiographer, 1980—. Freelance editor. Editor: (with H.A. Petry) Sewanee Centennial Alumni Directory, 1954-62, (with H.A. Petry and R.G. Dudney) Centennial Report of the Registrar of the University of the South, 1959; (with Arthur Ben Chitty) Too Black, Too White (Ely Green), 1970; author: (with Moultrie Guerry and Arthur Ben Chitty) Men Who Made Sewanee, 1981, (with A.B. Chitty and W. Givens) Ninety-Nine Iron, 1992; columnist Sewanee Mountain Messenger, 1985—. Bd. dirs. Sewanee Civic Assn., 1979-80, 86-88; CONTACT-Lifeline of Coffee and Franklin Counties, 1981-84; mem. adv. coun. St. Andrew's Sewanee Sch., 1988-98. Recipient Cmty. Svc. award Sewanee Civic Assn., 1996. Mem. Assn. Preservation Tenn. Antiquities (trustee 1985-88), AAUW (pres. Sewanee br. 1975-77), Fla. State U. Alumni Assn. (dir. 1941—, permanent pres. Class of 1941, Commitment to Excellence award, FSU Alumni Emeritus, 1997), Mortar Bd., Phi Beta Kappa, Phi Kappa Phi, Phi Alpha Theta, Kappa Delta. Democrat. Episcopalian. Office: Univ of South Sewanee TN 37385-1000 Home: 1344 Spring Lake Dr Orlando FL 32804-7127

CHITWOOD, JULIUS RICHARD, retired librarian; b. Magazine, Ark., June 1, 1921; s. Hoyt Mozart and Florence (Umfrid) C.; m. Aileen Newsom, Aug. 6, 1944. AB cum laude, Ouachita Bapt. Coll., Ark., 1942; M.Mus., Ind. U., 1948; MA, U. Chgo., 1954. Music supr. Edinburgh (Ind.) Pub. Schs., 1946-47; music and audiovisual librarian Roosevelt Coll., Chgo., 1948-51; humanities librarian Drake U., 1951-53; spl. cataloger Chgo. Tchrs. Coll., 1953; asst. circulation librarian Indpls. Pub. Library, 1954-57, coordinator adult services, 1957-61; dir. Rockford (Ill.) Pub. Library, 1961-79, No. Ill. Library System, Rockford, 1966-76; ret., 1979. Chmn. subcom. library system devel. Ill. Library Adv. Com., 1965—; adv. com. U. Ill. Grad. Sch. Library Sci., 1964-68; cons. in field, participant workshops Pres. Rockford Regional Academic Center, 1974-76; Mem. history com. Ill. Sesquicentennial Commn.; mem. Mayor Rockford Com. for UN, 1962-70; sect. chmn. Rockford United Fund, 1966-70; exec. Rockford Civic Orch. Assn., 1962-70. Served to maj., inf. AUS, 1942-45, ETO. Recipient Ill. Librarian of Year award, 1974 Mem. ALA (chmn. subcom. revision standards of materials, pub. library div. 1965-66, pres. bldg. and equipment sect. library adminstrn. div. 1967-68, chmn. staff devel. com. personnel adminstrn. sect., library adminstrv. div. 1964-68, pres. library adminstrn. div. 1969-70), Ill. Library Assn. (v.p. 1964-65, pres. 1965-66). Unitarian Universalist. Home: 3662 E Covenanter Dr Bloomington IN 47401-4681

CHITWOOD, JUSTIN CORY, music educator; b. Covington, Ky., Nov. 12, 1972; s. Patricia L. Heideman. MusB in Edn., Ea. Ky. U., 1994, MusM, 1996. Cert. Tchg. SC, 2001. Grad. asst. Ea. Ky. U., Richmond, Ky., 1995—96; choral music tchr. Walhalla Mid. Sch., Walhalla, SC, 1996—. Dir. No. Ky. Cmty. Chorus, Florence, Ky., 1994—95. Dir., instr. (summer drama workshops) Clemson Area Youth Theatre Summer Drama Workshops; dir.(actor): (one-man musical performance) Songs I'm Not Supposed To Sing, (choreographer) (theatre) The Boyfriend, (youth theatre) You're A Good Man, Charlie Brown. Recipient Tchr. Yr., Walhalla Mid. Sch., 2004—05. Mem.: Tri-M Music Honor Soc. (hon.), Delta Omicron (assoc.; life mem., dir. of music activities 1991—94, chpt. advisor 1995—96). Home: 36 Sirrine St Seneca SC 29678 Office Phone: 864-638-4575.

CHIU, DAVID TAK WAI, surgeon; b. Kwangtung, China, Oct. 23, 1945; s. Bud Yick and Lai Kwai (Lum) C.; m. Lilian Wah-Ying Shen, June 19, 1973; children: Vincent, Edmund, Jerome, Miranda. BA, U. Mo., St. Louis, 1969; MD, Columbia U., 1973. Diplomate Am. Bd. Plastic Surgery. Intern Barnes Hosp., St. Louis, 1973-74, resident in gen. surgery, 1974-77; resident in plastic surgery Columbia-Presbyn. Med. Ctr., 1977-79; fellow NYU Med. Ctr., N.Y.C., 1980, instr. surgery, 1981, asst. prof., 1981-89; supervisory attending Bellevue Hosp. Hand Clinic, N.Y.C., 1981-89; assoc. dir. plastic surgery, chief hand/microsurgery and replantation surgery divsn. plastic surgery Columbia Presbyn. Med. Ctr., N.Y.C., 1989-94, dir. microsurgery ctr., 1993, chief plastic surgery divsn. dept. surgery, 1994-97, prof. clin. surgery, 1990—2001, Thomas S. Zimmer prof., 1994-2000, Calvin F. Barber prof., 2000—01, dir. ctr. restorative surgery, 2000—; prof. plastic surgery NYU Med. Ctr., 2001—, dir. N.Y. Nerve Ctr., 2003—. Adj. prof. Coll. Physicians and Surgeons Columbia U., N.Y.C., 2001—. Author: Introduction to Microsurgery: A Lab Manual, 1985; mem. editorial bd. Jour. Reconstructive Microsurgery, 1990—. Recipient Alumni Fedn. Columbia U. medal, 1995. Fellow: ACS; mem.: AMA, World Soc. Reconstructive Microsurgery (founding mem.), Tissue Engring. Soc., Sunderland Soc., Am. Acad. Pediatrics (splty. fellow 1992), Internat. Soc. of Reconstructive Microsurgery, Northeast Soc. Plastic Surgery, Royal Soc. Medicine, Am. Soc. Peripheral Nerve Surgery (pres. 1999—2001, founding mem.), Am. Assn. Hand Surgery, Am. Soc. Plastic and Reconstructive Surgeons, Am. Soc. Surgery of Hand, Am. Soc. Reconstructive Microsurgery (pres. 1998—99), N.Y. Regional Soc. Plastic and Reconstructive Plastic Surgery (pres. 1997—98), Coll. Physicians and Surgeons Alumni Assn. (dir. 1984, pres. 2001—02, Bronze medal 1973, Gold medal 1997), Plastic Surgery Rsch. Coun., N.Y. Soc. Surgery of Hand (pres. 1996—97), N.Y. State Med. Soc., N.Y. County Med. Soc., Am. Assn. Plastic Surgeons, Chinese Am. Med. Soc. (dir. 1983—, pres. 1985—87, Presdl. medal 1987, Disting. Svc. award 1988, Scientific award 2001), Fedn. Chinese Am. and Chinese Can. Med. Socs. (founding trustee 2002—, founding pres. 2002—, Outstanding Achievement award 1994). Office: 900 Park Ave New York NY 10021-0231 Office Phone: 212-879-8880. Personal E-mail: dtwc@davidchiumd.com. Business E-Mail: office@davidchiumd.com, dtc1@columbia.edu.

CHIU, DOROTHY, retired pediatrician; b. Hong Kong, Aug. 8, 1917; came to U.S., 1946; d. Yan Tse Chiu and Connie Kwai-Ching Wan; m. Kitman Au; children: Katherine, Margo, Doris, James, Richard. BS, Lingnan U., 1939; MD, Nat. Shanghai Med. Coll., 1945. Diplomate Am. Bd. Pediats. Sch. physician L.A. Sch. Dist., 1954-55; pvt. practice Burbank, Calif., 1955—56, San Fernando, Calif., 1956—2000. Staff pediatrician Holy Cross Med. Ctr., Mission Hills, Calif., 1961-2000. Bd. dirs. Burbank Cmty. Concert, 1970-80. Fellow Am. Acad. Pediats.; mem. Calif. Med. Assn., L.A. County Med. Assn. Republican. Avocations: handicrafts, music, travel, reading, photography.

CHIU, HUNGDAH, law educator; b. Shanghai, Mar. 23, 1936; came to U.S., 1960; s. Han-ping and Ming-non (Yang) C.; m. Yuan-yuan Hsieh, May 14, 1966; 1 son, Wei-hsueh. LLB, Nat. Taiwan U., 1958; MA with honors, L.I. U., 1962; LLM, Harvard U., 1962, SJD, 1965. Assoc. in rsch. East Asian Research Center, Harvard U., 1964-65; assoc. prof. internat. law Nat. Taiwan U., 1965-66; rsch. assoc. in law Harvard U., 1966-70, 72-74; vis. prof. law Nat. Chengchi U., Taipei, Taiwan, 1970-72; assoc. prof. law U. Md., Balt., 1974-77, prof., 1977—2002, prof. emeritus, 2002—. Chmn. bd. dirs. Modern China Studies Quar., 2000—, Ctr. for Modern China, Princeton, NJ, 2000—; min. of state Exec. Yuan (Cabinet), Republic of China, Taiwan, 1993-94; mem. Presdl. Com. on Nat. Unification, Taiwan, 1995-2000, amb.-at-large, 1998-2000. Author: The Capacity of International Organizations to Conclude Treaties, 1966, The People's Republic of China and the Law of Treaties, 1972, (with J.A. Cohen) People's China and International Law, 2 vols, 1974 (certificate of merit Am. Soc. Internat. Law 1976), Normalizing Relations with China: Problems, Analysis and Documents, 1978, China and the Taiwan Issue, 1979, Agreements of the People's Republic of China, 1966-80, A Calendar of Events, 1981; (with S.C. Leng) China: 70 years after the 1911 Hsin-Hai Revolution, 1984, Criminal Justice in Post-Mao China, 1985, (with Y.C. Jao and Y.L. Wu) The Future of Hong Kong, 1987, (with G. Knight) International Law of the Sea: Cases, Documents and Readings, 1991; Hsian-t'ai Kuo-chi-fa (Modern International Law), 1995, rev. edit., 2005; (with Chun-i Chen) Hsien-tai Kuo-chi-fa Ts'an-kao Wen-chien (Reference Documents of Modern International Law), 1996, rev. edit., 2005, 1996 Case and Documentary Supplement for Knight and Chiu's International Law of the Sea, 1997; (with Hsing-wei Lee and Chih-Yu Wu) Implentationat Taiwan Relations Act: An Examination after Twenty Years, 2001; contbr. articles to profl. jours., chpts. to books; gen. editor: Contemporary Asian Studies, 1976—; editor in chief Chinese Yearbook of Internat. Law and Affairs, 1981—. Del. UN Conf. Law of the Sea, 1976—82; chmn. of the bd. Ctr. for Modern China, 2000—. Served to 2d lt. Chinese Army, 1958—60. Named One of 10 Outstanding Young Men, Jr. c. of C. of Republic of China, 1971; Social Sci. Rsch. Coun. fellow, 1968; recipient Cultural award Inst. Chinese Culture, 1980, Toulmin medal Soc. Am. Mil. Engrs., 1982, Nat. Reconstrn. award Chinese Profl. Assn. Mid-Am., 1980, Outstanding Achievement award Mid-Am. Chinese Sci. and Tech. Assn., 1991, 1st class Merit Svc. medal Exec. Yuan (Cabinet), Republic of China, 1994. Mem. Am. Soc. Internat. Law (panel on China and internat. order 1969-74, chmn. interest group on law Pacific region 1987-93), Assn. for Asian Studies (com. on Asian law 1976-89), Am. Assn. for Chinese Studies (v.p. 1982-84, pres. 1985-87), Assn. Am. Law Schs. (chair internat. legal exch. sect. 1986-88), Assn. Chinese Social Scientists, N.A. (pres. 1984-86), Chinese Soc. Internat. Law (pres. 1993-2000), Internat. Law Assn. (pres. 1998-2000, perm. v.p. 2000—). Home: 6168 Devon Dr Columbia MD 21044-3821 Office: U Md Law Sch 500 W Baltimore St Baltimore MD 21201-1786 Office Phone: 410-706-7579 3870. Business E-Mail: hchiu@law.umab.edu.

CHIU, JOHN TANG, physician; b. Macao, Jan. 8, 1938; s. Lan Cheong and Yau Hoon C.; m. Bonnie Doolan, Aug. 28, 1965 (div. Apr. 1986); children: Lisa, Mark, Heather; m. Karin Adams, Jan. 3, 2001. Student, U. Vt., BA, 1960, MD, 1964. Diplomate Am. Bd. Allergy & Immunology. Pres. Allergy Med. Group, Inc., Newport Beach, Calif., 1969-72, 1972—. Clin. prof. medicine U. Calif., Irvine, 1975—. Contbr. articles to profl. jours. Active Santa Ana Heights Adv. Commn., 1982-83; life mem. Orange County Sheriff's Adv. coun., 1987—. Recipient Freshman Chem. Achievement award Am. Chem. Soc., 1958. Fellow Am. Acad. Allergy Asthma and Immunology, Am. Coll. Allergy and Immunology, Am. Coll. Chest Physicians (sec. steering com. allergy 1977-81), Orange County Med. Assn. (chmn. comm. com. 1985-88, comm. com., mem. bull. editl. bd. 1995-01), Forensic Expert Witness Assn. Avocations: skiing, golf, aerobics, travels. Office: Allergy Med Group Inc 400 Newport Center Dr Newport Beach CA 92660-7601 Office Phone: 949-644-1422. Personal E-mail: chiuj@yahoo.com.

CHIU, YUN, electrical engineer, educator, researcher; b. GuanXian, SiChuan Province, China, Nov. 6, 1970; PhD, U. Calif. Berkeley, 2004. Grad. student rschr. UCLA, 1994—97; sr. staff mem. CondorVision Tech. Inc., Fremont, Calif., 1997—99; grad. student rschr. U. Calif. Berkeley, 1999—2004; prof. U. Ill., Urbana-Champaign, 2004—. Contbr. articles to profl. jours. Recipient Outstanding Overseas Student Award, Ministry of Edn., China; fellow, Intel Corp., 2001; Fgn. Scholar Award, UCLA, 1994, Regents' Fellowship, U. Calif. Berkeley, 1999, Cal View Tchg. Fellow Award, 2003. Mem.: IEEE. Achievements include patents for Improved CMOS gain-boosting scheme using pole-isolation technique, U.S. patent No. 6, 177, 838. Office: Univ Illinois 1308 W Main St Urbana IL 61801 Office Phone: 217-333-5693. Office Fax: 217-244-1946. Business E-Mail: chiu.yun@ieee.org.

CHIUSSI, FABIO MASSIMO, research and development company executive; married. BS in Elec. Engring., U. Padua, Italy, 1981—86, PhD in Computer Sci., 1988—91; MS in Engring. Mgmt., Stanford U., Calif., 1990—91, MS in Elec. Engring., 1987—88, PhD in Elec. Engring., 1988—93. Dir. Bell Labs., Lucent Technologies, Holmdel, NJ, 1993—2003; founder, CEO, pres. Invento Networks, Marlborough, Mass., 2004—. Contbr. articles to profl. jours. Fellow, Italian Elec. Assn., 1989. Mem.: IEEE. Achievements include patents in field. Personal E-mail: fabiochiussi@comcast.net.

CHIVERTON, PATRICIA ANN, nursing educator, dean; b. Rochester, N.Y., Nov. 21, 1947; d. Paul and Eleanor (Buyck) Gilmore; 1 child, Laura. BS, Ctrl. Mo. State U., 1970; MS, U. Rochester, 1980, EdD, 1990. Exec. dir. Alzheimer's Assn., Rochester, N.Y., 1987-89; clin. assoc. U. Rochester, 1987-89, clin. chief psychiat. mental health nursing, 1990-97, asst. prof. clin. nursing, 1994-95, interim chair health care sys. divsn., 1994-95, assoc. prof. clin. nursing, 1996—99, CEO cmty. nursing ctr., 1996—, assoc. dean clin. affairs Sch. Nursing and Med. Ctr., 1998—99, interim dean Sch. Nursing and Med. Ctr., 1999—2000, dean Sch. Nursing and Med. Ctr., 2000—. Judge Book of the Yr., Am. Jour. Nursing, 1999, reviewer, 1998—; cons. F.f. Thompson Continuing Care Facility, Canadaiguia, N.Y., 1997-99. Contbr. chpts. to books. in field. Rep. N.Y. State Alzheimer's Assn., 1985-88; bd. dirs. Health and Wellness Ctr., Livingston County, N.Y., Monroe County Long Term Care Agy., Rochester, 1997—. Mem. Am. Psychiat. Nurses Assn. (pres. Northwestern chpt. 1995-97, Excellence in Leadership award 1994), Ea. Nursing Rsch. Soc., Nat. Acads. Practice (Disting. Practitioner), Sigma Theta Tau. Office: U Rochester Sch Nursing 601 Elmwood Ave Rochester NY 14642-0001 E-mail: patricia_chiverton@urmc.rochester.edu.*

CHIVIAN, ERIC SETH, psychiatrist, environmental scientist, educator; b. Newark, June 10, 1942; children: Cybele, Dylan C., Judah B. AB, Harvard U., 1964, MD, 1968. Staff psychiatrist MIT, 1980—2000; asst. clin. prof. psychiatry Harvard Med. Sch., 1987—, dir. Ctr. for Health and the Global Environment, 1996—. Recipient Nobel Peace prize, 1985. Mem.: AAAS, Internat. Physicians Prevent Nuc. War (co-founder, treas. 1980—85), Physicians for Social Responsibility. Achievements include research in first large scale scientific survey of American and Soviet teenagers' attitudes about the future; US-USSR relations and nuclear war; health implications of species extinction and loss of biodiversity. Home: 136 Carter Pond Rd Petersham MA 01366-9728

CHIVUKULA, UPENDRA J., assemblyman, electrical engineer; b. Oct. 8, 1950; BEE, Coll. of Engring., Madras, India; MEE, CUNY City Coll. Councilman 5th Ward Franklin Twp., 1997—98, dep. mayor, 1998—2000, mayor, 2000—02; assemblyman NJ State Assembly, 2002—. Vice chair commerce and econ. devel. Environ. and Solid Waste Telecoms. and Utilities; mem. telecomm. and utilities com., transp. com. & world languages instruction com. NJ State Assembly, mem. bd. of election canvassers; mem. NJ Sci. and Techn. Commn., NJ Commerce and Bus. Growth Commn., CSG/Ea. States Conference on Energy and Environ.; mng. dir. Antarctica Group, NYC. Fellow Leadership NJ, 1998—, Flemming Inst., 2003—; nat. com. mem. Assn. of Indians in Am.; former pres. Asian Am. Polit. Coalition. Democrat. Office: NJ State Assembly 888 Easton Ave Somerset NJ 08873*

CHIZEN, BRUCE, electronics executive; BS, CUNY. Mgr. merchandising Mattel Electronics, 1980—83; dir. sales Microsoft Corp., 1983—87; mgr. Claris Corp., 1987—94; exec. v.p. Adobe Sys. Inc., San Jose, Calif., 1994—99, pres., 1999—2005, CEO, 2000—. Bd. dirs. Synopsys, Inc. Bd. dirs. Children's Discovery Mus., San Jose. Office: Adobe Systems Inc 345 Park Ave San Jose CA 95110-2704*

CHMELIR, LYNN KAY, academic librarian; b. Berwyn, Ill., Jan. 11, 1946; d. John Joseph and Dolores Margaret (Svehla) C.; m. John Philip Webb, June 12, 1976; 1 child, Lauren Jane Webb. AB, U. Ill., 1967, AM, 1970, MS in Libr. Sci., 1976. Catalog libr. Lewis and Clark Coll., Portland, 1976-78; tech. svcs. libr. Linfield Coll., McMinnville, Oreg., 1978-81, coll. libr., 1981-99; asst. dir. pub. svcs. Wash. State U., Pullman, 1999—2002, asst. dir. collections, 2002—04, asst. dir. collections and tech. svcs., 2004—. Chair Portals Coun. of Librs., Portland, 1995-96, Orbis Consortium, Eugene, 1997-98. Mem. ALA, Assn. of Coll. and Rsch. Librs. (com. chair, pres. Oreg. chpt. 1983-84, pres. Wash. chpt. 2001-02), Oreg. Libr. Assn. (pres. 1988-89), Alpha Lambda Delta, Beta Phi Mu. Office Phone: 509-335-8139. Business E-Mail: lchmelir@wsu.edu.

CHMELL, SAMUEL JAY, orthopedic surgeon; b. Chgo., Aug. 21, 1952; s. Samuel and Elsie (Wauterlek) C.; m. Nancy Jean Aumiller, June 22, 1974; children: Jessica, Carson, Alexis, Lesley, Samuel Jayson. BS, U. Notre Dame, 1974; MD, Loyola U., 1977. Diplomate Am. Bd. Orthop. Surgery. Intern Loyola U. Med. Ctr., Maywood, Ill., 1977-78, resident in orthop. surgery, 1980-84; emergency rm. physician USPHS Indian Health Svc., Chinle, Ariz., 1978-80; attending orthop. surgeon Hines (Ill.) VA Hosp., 1984-88, Shriners Hosp. for Crippled Children, Chgo., 1985-89, Gallup (N.Mex.) Indian Hosp., 1988-89, Humana-Michael Reese Hosp. and Health Plan, Chgo., 1989—99; chmn. sect. orthopaedic surgery Humana-Michael Reese Med. Ctr., Chgo., 1991—99; asst. prof. dept. orthopaedic surgery U. Ill., Chgo., 1991—. Clin. instr. in orthop. surgery Loyola U. Med. Ctr., Maywood, 1985-88; asst. prof. dept. orthop. surgery U. Ill., Chgo.; adv. coun. Coll. of Sci. U. Notre Dame. Contbr. articles to profl. jours. Active Olmsted Hist. Soc. Riverside, Ill. Sofield Travelling fellow Orthop. Rsch. Soc. Gt. Britain, 1985. Master: Alpha Omega Alpha; fellow: Am. Acad. Orthop. Surgeons, ACS; mem.: Founders' Cir. of Sorin Soc. U. Notre Dame, Notre Dame Orthop. Soc. Office: 23 Longcommon Rd Riverside IL 60546-2168 Office Phone: 708-447-3100. Business E-Mail: schmell@uic.edu. E-mail: samchmell@yahoo.com.

CHMIELINSKI, EDWARD ALEXANDER, retired electronics company executive; b. Waterbury, Conn., Mar. 25, 1925; s. Stanley ahd Helen Chmielinski; m. Elizabeth Carew, May 30, 1946; children: Nancy, Elizabeth, Susan Jean. BS, Tulane U., 1950; postgrad., Colo. U., 1965. V.p., gen. mgr. Clifton Products, Litton Industries, Colorado Springs, Colo., 1965-67; pres. Memory Products divsn. Litton Industries, Beverly Hills, Calif., 1967-69, Bowmar Instruments Can., Ottawa, Ont., 1969-73; gen. mgr. Leigh Instruments, Carleton Place, 1973—75; pres., CEO, dir. Lewis Engring. Co., Naugatuck, Conn., 1975—85, Liquidometer Corp., Tampa, Fla., 1975-85; pres. Lewis divsn. Colt Industries, 1985-90; ret., 1990. Pres. Acad. Water Bd., 1963-65; bd. dirs. United Way, Colorado Springs, 1965-67; fellow Tulane U. Served with USN, 1943-46. Mem. Air Force Assn., Navy League.

CHO, ALFRED YI, electrical engineer; b. Beijing, July 10, 1937; arrived in U.S., 1955, naturalized, 1962; s. Edward I-Lai and Mildred (Chen) Cho; m. Mona Lee Willoughby, June 16, 1968; children: Derek Ming, Deidre Lin, Brynna Ying, Wendy Li. BSEE, U. Ill., 1960, MS, 1961, PhD, 1968, D (hon.) Engring., 1999; DSc (hon.), City U. Hong Kong, 2000, Hong Kong Bapt. U., 2001, Hong Kong U. Sci. and Tech., 2003. Rsch. physicist Ion Physics Corp., Burlington, Mass., 1961—62; mem. tech. staff TRW-Space Tech. Labs., Redondo Beach, Calif., 1962—65, Bell Labs., Murray Hill, NJ, 1968—84, dept. head, 1984—87; dir. Materials Processing Rsch. Lab. AT&T Bell Labs., Murray Hill, 1987—90; semicondr. rsch. lab. v.p. Bell Labs. Lucent Techs. (formerly AT&T Bell Labs.), Murray Hill, 1990—2002; fellow Bell Labs., Lucent Techs. (formerly AT&T Bell Labs.), 1992—; rsch. asst. U. Ill., Urbana, 1965—68. Vis. prof. dept. elec. engring., vic. rsch. prof. coordinated sci. lab. U. Ill., Urbana, 1977—78, adj. prof. dept. elec. engring., adj. rsch. prof. coordinated sci. lab., 1978—; bd. dirs. Riber, Edison, NJ; trustee Coll. of N.J., 1996—2000. Contbr. over 590 articles to profl. jours. Named to, N.J. Inventors Hall of Fame, 1997; recipient Elec. and Computer Engring. Disting. Alumnus award, U. Ill., 1985, Disting. Achievement award, Chinese Inst. Engrs., USA, 1985, Internat. Gallium Arsenide Symposium award, 1986, Heinrich Welker Gold medal, 1986, The Coll. Engring. Alumni Honor award, U. Ill., 1988, World Materials Congress award, ASM Internat., 1988, Achievement award, Indsl. Rsch. Inst., Inc., 1988, Thomas Alva Edison Sci. award, N.J. Gov., 1990, Internat. Crystal Growth award, Am. Assn. for Crystal Growth, 1990, Asian Am. Corp. Achievement award, 1992, Chinese Am. Engrs. and Scientists Assn. So. Achievement award, 1993, Nat. Medal of Sci., NSF, 1993, Elliott Cresson medal, The Franklin Inst., 1995, Computer and Comm. prize, Japan, 1995, W.E. Lamb medal for laser sci. and quantum optics, 2000. Fellow: IEEE (Morris N. Liebman award 1982, IEEE Medal of Honor 1994, Third Millennium medal 2000), Am. Phys. Soc. (Internat. prize for new materials 1982); mem.: Third World Acad. Scis., Nat. Acad. Engring., U.S. Nat. Acad. Scis., Am. Acad. Art and Scis., Am. Philos. Soc., Chinese Acad. Scis., Academia Sinica (Taiwan), Materials Rsch. Soc. (Von Hippel award 1994), Electrochem. Soc. (electronic divsn. award 1977, Solid State Sci. and Tech. medal 1987), Am. Vacuum Soc. (Gaede-Langmuir award 1988), Sigma Tau, Eta Kappa Nu, Tau Beta Pi, Sigma Xi. Achievements include development of molecular beam epitaxy; 75 patents related to crystal growth and electronic and photonic devices. Fax: 908-582-2043. Office Phone: 908-582-2093. Business E-Mail: ayc@lucent.com. E-mail: alcho@aol.com. *I learned early in my life that hard work is a major ingredient for success. We can always do more than we think we are able to do. I drive myself to my utmost capacity so that I will not have regrets later that I did not try my best. My first love is art but I earn my living as an engineer. In my work as a research scientist, the secret for success is that I combine Oriental patience with Western technology. We should always try to enhance the best part of what we have and not be afraid to change.*

CHO, HO SOON MICHELLE L., adult education educator; m. Kyung Ku Peter Cho, Mar. 30, 1942; 1 child, Michael Michelle. BS, Tex. Woman's U., 1977, MS, 1981, PhD, 1996. RN Tex., 1974. Instr. ElCentro Coll., Dallas, 1981—96; assoc. prof. Tex. Woman's U., 1997—. Author: (novels) A Korean Dream. Adv. coun. mem. Dem. Unification of Korea, Seoul, 2003—05. Named Mem. of Yr., Parkland and Tex. Woman's U. Alumni Assn., 2002; recipient Disting. Alumni award, Gyungsang Nat. U., 2001. Master: Korean ANA (assoc.; v.p. 1982—84, Achievement award 1984), Gyungsang Nat. U. Can. and U.S. Alumni Assn. (assoc.; pres. 2003—05); mem.: North Tex. Korean ANA (bd. dirs. 1984—), Sigma Theta Tau (archivist 2000—05, sholar 1996, 2000, 2005). Roman Catholic. Achievements include patents for Papilla Gown. Home: 5217 Northmoor Dr Dallas TX 75229 Office: Texas Woman's U 1810 inwood Rd Dallas TX 75235-7299 Office Phone: 214-689-6532.

CHO, JANG-CHEON, microbiologist, researcher; b. Seoul, Dec. 26, 1969; m. Hoonshik Lee, Dec. 15, 1996; children: MinJoo, Jace M. PhD, Seoul Nat. U., 2000. Postdoctoral rschr. Seoul Nat. U.; faculty rsch. assoc. Oreg. State U., Corvallis, 2001—. Mem.: Am. Soc. for Microbiology (assoc.). Achievements include discovery of novel phylum in Kingdom Bacteria; uncultured Oligotrophic Marine Gammaproteobacteria in the ocean; at least 10 novel genus in Kingdom Bacteria; development of automated, continuous toxicity measuring system. Home: 109 NE Conifer #L Corvallis OR 97330 Office: Oreg State Univ Dept Microbiology NASH 222 Corvallis OR 97331 Office Phone: 1-541-737-0717. Office Fax: 1-541-737-0496. Personal E-mail: skycho@gmail.com.

CHO, LEE-JAY, social scientist, demographer; b. Kyoto, July 5, 1936; came to U.S., 1959; s. Sam-Soo and Kyung-Doo (Park) C.; m. Eun-Ja Chun, May 20, 1973; children: Kaia Nuy, Sang-Mun Ray, Han-Jae Jeremy. BA, Kookmin Coll., Seoul, Korea, 1959; MA in Govt., George Washington U., 1962; MA in Sociology, U. Chgo., 1964, PhD in Sociology, 1965; D in Econs. (hon.), Dong-A U., 1982; DSc in Demography, Tokyo U., 1983; D in Econs., Keio U., Tokyo, 1989; D in Econs. (hon.), Russian Acad. Scis., 2000. Statistician Korean Census Coun., 1958-61; research assoc., asst. prof. sociology Population Rsch. and Tng. Ctr., U. Chgo., 1965-66; assoc. dir. Cmty. and Family Study Ctr., 1969-70; sr. demographic adv. to Malaysian Govt., 1967-69; assoc. prof. U. Hawaii, 1969-73, prof., 1973-78; asst. dir. East-West Population Inst., East-West Ctr., Honolulu, 1971-74, dir., 1974-92; pres. pro tem East-West Ctr., 1980-81, v.p., 1987-98, sr. advisor, 1998—. Cons. in field; mem. NAS Com. on Population and Demography; mem. U.S. 1980 Census Adv. Com., Dept. Commerce. Author: (with others) Differential Current Fertility in the United States, 1970; editor: (with others) Introduction to Censuses of Asia and the Pacific: 1970-74, 1976, (with Kazumasa Kobayashi) Fertility Transition in East Asian Populations, 1979, (with Suharto, McNicoll and Mamas) Population Growth of Indonesia, 1980, The Own-Children Method of Fertility Estimation, 1986, (with R. Retherford and M. Choe) Economic Development of Republic of Korea: A Policy Perspective, 1989, (with Y.H. Kim) Korea's Political Economy: An Institutional Perspective, 1994, (with Yada) Tradition and Change in the Asian Family, 1994, (with Y.H. Kim) Hedging Bets on Growth in a Globalizing Industrial Order, 1997, (with Y.H. Kim) Korea's Choices in Emerging Global Competition and Cooperation, 1998, (with Y.H. Kim) Ten Paradigms of Market Economies and Land Systems, 1998, (with Y.H. Kim) The Multi-Lateral Trading System in a Globalizing World, 2000, Restructuring the National Economy, 2001, Restructuring the Korean Financial Market in a Global Economy, 2002, (with C.N. Kim and C.S. Ahn) A Changing Korea in Regional and Global Contexts, 2004; contbr. numerous articles on population and econ. devel. to profl. jours. Bd. dirs. Planned Parenthood Assn., Hawaii, 1976-77. Population Coun. fellow U. Chgo., 1963-64; Ford Found. grantee, 1977-79; Population Coun. grantee, 1973-75; Dept. Commerce grantee, 1974-78; recipient Award of Mugunghwa-Jang, govt. Republic of Korea, 1992, 4th N.E. Asia Niigata prize, 1996. Mem. Internat. Statis. Inst. (tech. adv. com. World Fertility Survey), Internat. Union Sci. Study Population, Population Assn. Am., Am. Statis. Assn., Am. Sociol. Assn., N.E. Asia Econ. Forum (founding chmn.). Home: 1718 Halekoa Dr Honolulu HI 96821-1027 Office: 1601 E West Rd Honolulu HI 96848-1601 *The survival and welfare of the future generations will depend largely upon what we do today to plan and manage human population growth and sustainable development.*

CHO, MARGARET (MORAN CHO), comedienne, actress; b. San Francisco, Dec. 5, 1968; d. Sueng-Hoon Cho and Young-Hie; m. Al Ridenour, 2003. Comedian, 1991—. TV appearances include All-American Girl, 1994—95, Life 360, 2001; films: Sweethearts, 1996, It's My Party, 1996, Fakin' Da Funk, 1997, Face/Off, 1997, The Rugrats Movie (voice), 1998, Can't Stop Dancing, 1999, Nobody Knows Anything!, 2003, Bam Bam and Celeste, 2005. Named Best Female Comedian Am. Comedy Awards, 1993.

CHO, MYEONG-JE, plant biologist, researcher; b. Taegu, Republic of Korea, Feb. 28, 1959; s. Sang-Soo Cho and Byeong-Soon Lee; m. Hyeon-Ok Ham, June 4, 1960; children: Yu-Ree, Yu-Na. BS with honors, Seoul Nat. U., 1984, MS, 1986; PhD, U. Ill., Urbana-Champaign, 1991. Rsch. assoc. U. Calif., Berkeley, 1994—98, asst. rschr., 1998—99, assoc. specialist, 1999—2004, specialist, 2004—. Hon. scientist Rural Devel. Adminstrn., Suwon, 1998—; cons. Ventria Biosci., Sacramento, 1999—99, Exelixis, Inc., San Francisco, 2000—01, Scigen Harvest, Seoul, 2000—01; v.p. Byotix, Inc., Richmond, Calif., 2001—; sci. advisor Genomine, Inc., Pohang, 2002—. Editor: In Vitro Application in Crop Improvement; contbr. articles to profl. jours. Mem. Berkland Bapt. Ch. Mem.: Amer. Soc. Plant Biol. Achievements include patents for plant transformation; gene expression systems; gene isolation and characterization. Home: 13 Ulster Pl Alameda CA 94502 Personal E-mail: myeongjecho@yahoo.com.

CHO, YONG HYO, educational association administrator; b. Sachon, Republic of Korea, Dec. 14, 1934; arrived in U.S., 60; s. Deuk Kyu Cho and Sue Nahm Park; m. Chung Soon Kim, May 6, 1960; children: Miyun Fellerhoff, Hearn Jay. PhD, Syracuse U., 1964. Prof. U. Nev., Las Vegas, 1964—67, U. Akron, 1967—89, San Francisco State U., 1989—97; dean Grad. Sch. Internat. Studies Sogang U., Seoul, 1997—2000; expert U.S. Dept. Edn., Washington, 2000—; sr. advisor Ctr. for Pub. Policy Edn., The Brookings Instn., Washington, 2002—. Author: The White House and the Blue House, 1997, Public Policy and Urban Crime, 1974, others. Nat. Conv. del. Dem. Party, Akron, Ohio, 1980. Recipient Diplomatic Svc. medal Govt. of Republic of Korea, 1998. Fellow Nat. Acad. Public Adminstrn. (life); mem. Am. Soc. for Pub. Adminstrn. (pres. 1996-97). Roman Catholic. Avocations: travel, golf. Home: 424 E Pine Lake Cir Vernon Hills IL 60061 Home Fax: (847) 362-7417. E-mail: yongcho@prodigy.net.

CHO, YONG-HO, engineer, researcher; b. Seoul, Republic of Korea, June 28, 1965; s. Kou-Sang Cho and Jae-Ock Yoon; m. Young-Ock Kim, Dec. 21, 1991; children: Hye-Jin, Hye-Jeong. PhD, Yonsei U., Seoul, 2004. Dir. Microfriend Inc., Republic of Korea, 1991—. 1st lt. Air Force, 1989—91, Republic of Korea. Mem.: AIAA (assoc.). Home: 1003-203 I-park apt 857 Sanghyun-dong Gyunggi-do Yongin 449-843 Republic of Korea Office: 324-14 Dangjung-Dong Gunpo-City 435-832 Republic of Korea Office Phone: 82-31-427-3205. Business E-Mail: 2852720@hanafos.com.

CHOATE, JEAN MARIE, historian, humanities educator; b. Syracuse, NY, Dec. 17, 1935; d. Max and Betty (Black) Molyneux; m. Woodrow Choate; children: Anne, Mike, Ruth, Susan. BA, Alma Coll., 1958; MA, U. Wis., 1962; MS, St. Cloud State U., 1972; PhD, Iowa State U., 1992. Instr. Open Bible Coll., Des Moines, 1983-85, Des Moines Area Coll., 1985-97; asst. prof. No. Mich. U., Marquette, 1992-99; prof. Coastal Ga. C.C., Brunswick, 1999—. Chair women's commn. No. Mich. U., 1996-97. Author: Disputed Ground: Farm Groups that Opposed New Deal Agricultural Programs, 2002, Eliza Johnson, Unknown First Lady, 2004; book reviewer Jour. of the West, 1996-2000; contbr. articles to profl. jours. Grantee No. Mich. U., 1993, Iowa Found., 1994; Everett Dirksen grantee, 1995, Franklin and Eleanor Roosevelt grantee, 1996, Carl Albert Libr. grantee, 1998, White House Hist. Assn. grantee, 2002. Mem. AAUW (v.p. 1995-97), Agrl. History, Women Historians of Midwest, Orgn. Am. Historians, Am. Hist. Assn., Social Sci. History Assn. Office: Coastal Ga C C Brunswick GA 31520 Business E-Mail: jchoate@cgcc.edu.

CHOBANIAN, ARAM, medical school dean, cardiologist; b. Pawtucket, R.I., Aug. 10, 1929; s. Van and Marina (Arsenian) C.; m. Jasmine Goorigian, June 5, 1955; children: Karin, Lisa, Aram. BA, Brown U., 1951; MD, Harvard U., 1955. Intern, resident Univ. Hosp., Boston, 1955-59, cardiovasc. rsch. fellow, 1959-62; from asst. prof. Sch. Medicine to prof. Sch. Medicine Boston U., 1964—70, prof. medicine, 1970—, dean Sch. Medicine, 1988—, provost Med. Campus, 1996—, interim pres., 2003—05, pres., 2005. Dir. Nat. Rsch. and Demonstration Ctr. in Hypertension, 1985-90; chmn. FDA Cardiovasc. and Renal Adv. Com., 1978-80, NIH Hypertension and Arteriosclerosis adv. com., 1977-78; chmn. Cardiovasc. Study Sect. B. NIH, 1982-84; chmn. Joint Nat. Com. on Hypertension, NIH, 1990-91, 2003; Sandoz lectr. Royal Coll. Physicians and Surgeons Can., 1989; mem. NIH Nat. Heart, Lung and Blood Adv. Coun., 1993-96; mem. bd. extramural advisers Nat. Heart, Lung and Blood Inst., 1999-2002. Author: Heart Risk Book, 1982; mem. editl. bd. New England Jour. Medicine, Hypertension, Jour. Hypertension, Jour. Vascular Biology, Hypertension Rsch., Cardiovasc. Pharmacology. Pres. Am. Heart Assn., Boston, 1974-75; bd. dirs. Armenian Culture Soc., WGBH, Jobs for Mass.; trustee Roger Williams Med. Ctr., Wolfson Found., Mass. Tech. Collaborative, New Eng. Healthcare Inst.; fellow trustee Armenian Assembly of Am. Capt. USAF, 1956-57. Recipient Cmty. Edn. and Disting. Svc. award Am. Heart Assn., Boston, 1975, 78, Eastman Kodak award Nat. Acad. Clin. Biochemistry, 1987, Abbott award Am. Soc. Hypertension. Fellow ACP, Am. Heart Assn. (chmn. coun. high blood pressure rsch. 1984-86, Corcoran lectr. 1989, award of merit 1990, Modern Medicine award 1990, Lifetime Achievement award in hypertension Bristol-Myers Squibb), Nat. Heart, Lung and Blood Inst. (Freis award 1997), Am. Soc. Clin. Investigation, Assn. Am. Physicians, Am. Physiol. Soc., New England Cardiovasc. Soc. (pres. 1985-86), Mass. Med. Soc. (mem. publs. com.), Phi Beta Kappa, Sigma Xi, Alpha Omega Alpha. Home: 5 Rathburn Rd Natick MA 01760-1011 Office: Boston U One Sherborn St Boston MA 02215 Business E-Mail: achob@bu.edu.

CHOBOTOV, VLADIMIR ALEXANDER, aerospace engineer, educator; b. Zagreb, Yugoslavia, Apr. 2, 1929; came to U.S., 1946; s. Alexander M. and Eugenia I. (Scherbak) C.; m. Lydia M. Kazanovich, June 22, 1957; children: Alexander, Michael. BSME, Pratt Inst., 1951; MSME, Bklyn. Poly. Inst., 1956; PhD, U. So. Calif., 1963. Dynamics engr. Sikorsky Aircraft, Bridgeport, Conn., 1951-53, Republic Aviation, Farmingdale, N.Y., 1953-57, Ramo-Wooldridge, Redondo Beach, Calif., 1957-62; mgr. The Aerospace Corp., El Segundo, Calif., 1962-93; adj. prof. Northrop U., L.A., 1982-91; instr. UCLA, 1984—. Cons. Univ. Space Rsch. Assn., Washington, 1984-85; ad hoc advisor USAF Sci. Adv. Bd., Washington, 1985-87; cons. NASA Space Sta. Adv. Com., Washington, 1990-91; course leader Space Debris, Washington, 1990-91. Author: Spacecraft Attitude Dynamics and Control, 1991; author, editor: Orbital Mechanics, 1991, 3d edit., 2002; contbg. author: Space Based Radar Handbook, 1989, Earth, Sea and Solar System, 1987; contbr. numerous articles and reports to profl. publs. Fellow AIAA (assoc., Achievement award 1993); mem. Internat. Acad. of Astronautics. Achievements include pioneering in the analysis and modeling of space debris. Office: The Aerospace Corp PO Box 92957 Los Angeles CA 90009-2957 E-mail: vladimir.chobotov@aero.org.

CHOCK, RAELENE, school system administrator; Bachelors, U. Hawaii; Masters, Columbia U.; EdD, Brigham Young U. Tchr., 1966—86; vice prin. Kaimuki H.S., 1986—88, Washington Mid. Sch., 1988—90; prin. Kuhio Elem. Sch., 1990—95, Kaimuki H.S., 1995—99; dep. supt. Honolulu Sch. Dist., 1999—2000, acting dist. supt., 2000—. Office: Honolulu Sch Dist 4967 Kilauea Honolulu HI 96816

CHOCOLA, CHRIS, congressman, lawyer; b. Jackson, Mich., Feb. 24, 1962; m. Sarah Chocola; children: Caroline, Colin. Degree in Bus. Adminstrn. and Polit. Economy summa cum laude, Hillsdale Coll., 1984; JD magna cum laude, Thomas Cooley Law Sch., 1988. Mgmt. trainee Soc. Nat. Bank, Cleve., 1984, fgn. exch. trader; credit mgr. Chocola Cleaning Materials; corp. counsel CTB Internat. Corp., Milford, Ind., 1988—94, CEO, 1994, chmn. bd. dirs., 1999; mem. U.S. Ho. Reps. from 2nd Ind. dist., 2003—, asst. majority whip, 2003—04, mem. ways and means com. Mem. coun. advisors South Bend Ctr. for the Homeless; bd. dirs. Oaklawn Psychiat. Ctr. Mem.: Rotary Club. Republican. Office: US Ho of Reps 510 Cannon Ho Office Bldg Washington DC 20515 also: Ste 330 100 E Wayne St South Bend IN 46601*

CHODOROW, NANCY JULIA, psychotherapist, psychoanalyst, educator; b. NYC, Jan. 20, 1944; d. Marvin and Leah (Turitz) C.; children: Rachel Esther Chodorow-Reich, Gabriel Issac Chodorow-Reich. BA, Radcliffe Coll., 1966; PhD, Brandeis U., 1975; grad., San Francisco Psychoanalytic, 1993. Cert. in Adult Psychoanalysis Am. Psychoanalytic Assn., 1993. From lectr. to assoc. prof. U. Calif., Santa Cruz, 1974-86, from assoc. prof. sociology to prof. Berkeley, 1986—2005, clin. faculty dept. psychology, 1999—, prof. emeritus, 2005. Faculty San Francisco Psychoanalytic Inst., 1994—. Author: The Reproduction of Mothering, 1978 (Jessie Bernard award Sociologists for Women in Soc. 1979, named one of Ten Most Influential Books of Past 25 Years, Contemporary Sociology 1996), 2nd edit., 1999, Feminism and Psychoanalytic Theory, 1989, Femininities, Masculinities, Sexualities, 1994, The Power of Feelings: Personal Meaning in Psychoanalysis, Gender, and Culture, 1999 (L. Bryce Boyer prize Soc. for Psychol. Anthropology 2000); contbr. articles to profl. jours. Fellow Russell Sage Found., NEH, Ctr. Advanced Study Behavioral Scis., ACLS, Guggenheim Found., Radcliffe Inst. for Advanced Study; recipient Contbn. to Women and Psychoanalysis award APA, L. Bryce Boyer prize Soc. for Psychol. Anthropology, 2000. Mem. Internat. Psychoanalytic Assn., Am. Psychoanalytic Assn., San Francisco Psychoanalytic Soc. Office: 5305 College Ave Oakland CA 94618 Office Phone: 510-547-5423.

CHODOSH, HYMAN LOUIS, neurologist; b. Newark, Mar. 6, 1925; s. Robert and Ida (Shapiro) C.; m. Leona Kovarsky, Mar. 6, 1948; children: Ellen Iris, Eliot Howard. MD, NYU, 1948. Diplomate Am. Bd. Psychiatry and Neurology. Intern Morrisania City Hosp., Bronx, N.Y., 1948-49, neurology resident, 1949-50, Bellevue Hosp., N.Y.C., 1950-51; psychiatry resident VA Hosp., Bronx, 1953-55; clin. asst. neurology Mt. Sinai Hosp., N.Y.C., 1955-57; cons. neurology Wayne (N.J.) Gen. Hosp., 1955—, Barnert Hosp., Paterson, N.J., 1955—, Chilton Meml. Hosp., Pompton Plains, N.J., 1955—; attending neurologist VA Hosp., East Orange, N.J., 1982—; clin. assoc. prof. N.J. Med. Sch., Newark, 1982—; med. dir. Alzheimer's Disease Day Care Program Daus. of Miriam Ctr. for Aged, Clifton, N.J., 1985—; neurologist North Jersey Neurologic Assn., Wayne, N.J., 1955—. Contbr. articles to profl. jours. Pres. bd. trustees Daus. of Miriam Ctr., Clifton, 1991-93; med. staff pres. Wayne Gen. Hosp., 1963-64; trustee Jewish Fedn. N.J., Wayne, 1993—. Capt. USAF, 1951-53, Korea. Recipient Profl. Svc. award Med. Staff Daus. of Miriam Ctr. for the Aged, 1985. Fellow Am. Acad. Neurology (life), Am. Psychiat. Assn.; mem. AMA, Med. Soc. N.J., Am. Geriatric Soc., Neuropsychiat. Assn. Jewish. Avocation: music.

CHOE, SEUNGHO, physicist, researcher; b. Iksan, Republic of Korea, July 1, 1967; s. Kyu-Jin Choi and Jung-Soon Kim. BS, Yonsei U., Republic of Korea, 1989, MS, 1992, PhD, 1997. Tchg. asst. Yonsei U., Seoul, Republic of Korea, 1990-94, rschr., 1992-97, 98—; lectr. Bucheon Tech. Coll., Republic of Korea, 1995-97; vis. post-doc Adelaide U., Australia, 1997-98; JSPS post-doc Hiroshima U., Japan, 1999—2001; rsch. sci. KAIST, Republic of Korea, 2002—04; postdoctoral fellow Johns Hopkins U., 2004—. Contbr. articles to profl. jours. Scholar Korean Air Lines, 1987-88; rsch. fellow Ctr. Theoretical Physics, 1997; fellow Korea Rsch. Found., 1997. Mem. Korean Phys. Soc., Korea Advanced Inst. Sci. and Tech., Japan Soc. Promotion Sci. Avocations: collecting stamps, playing soccer. Office Phone: 410-516-6238. Business E-Mail: seungho@jhu.edu.

CHOHAYEB, AIDA A., dentist, educator; DDS, Alexandria (Egypt) U., 1957; cert. in pediatric dentistry, Eastman Dental Hosp., London, 1958; cert. in orthodontics, Royal Dental Hosp., London, 1960; MS in Dentistry, U. Minn., 1968; cert. in clin. dentistry, NYU, 1978. Lic. dentist N.Y., Pa., D.C. Pvt. practice, Maadi, Egypt, 1961—66, 1968—74; chmn. dept. dentistry Geziera Hosp., Cairo, 1961—66, 1968—74; asst. dir. Gesundheightsamt, Pedodontic Clinic, Krefeld, Germany, 1974—76; pvt. practice Krefeld, Germany, 1974—76, N.Y.C., 1979—81; asst. dir. Inst. for Fgn. Trained Dentists NYU, N.Y.C., 1976—80, chief endodontic sect., 1976—80, asst. prof. dept. endodontics Coll. Dentistry, 1976—80, rsch. scientist dept. dental materials Coll. Dentistry, 1980—81; attending endodontist endodontics residency program Nassau County Med. Hosp., L.I., 1980—81; assoc. prof. Howard U. Coll. Dentistry, Washington, 1981—86, prof., 1986—. Guest scientist Am. Dental Assn. Health Found. Paffanburger Rsch. Ctr. NIST, Gaithersburg, Md., 1984—93; vis. prof. rsch. NYU Coll. Dentistry, N.Y.C., 2001—; guest scientist; cons. in field; presenter in field. Contbr. articles to profl. jours. Recipient Outstanding Svc. award, Am. Assn. Women Dentists,

1982, 1984, Lucy Hobbs Taylor award, 1987, Meritorious Svc. award to organized dentistry, 1989, D.C. Meritorious Pub. Svc. award, Mayor D.C., 1983, Outstanding and Valuable Contbn. to the Profession and to the Women in Dentistry award, Am. Assn. Women Dentists Md. State chpt., 1990, Dedicated Svcs. award, Am. Assn. for Dental Rsch.-Met. Washington sect., 1992. Fellow: Am. Coll. Dentists (numerous positions including chmn. Washington sect. 1992—94), Internat. Coll. Dentists, Acad. Dentistry Internat.; mem.: AAUP, ADA (reviewer Jour. ADA 1988—90), Am. Assn. Pub. Health Dentistry, Assn. Egyptian-Am. Scholars, Dist. Columbia Dental Soc., Fedn. Dentaire Internat., Am. Assn. for Dental Rsch. (numerous positions including 1998—99, mem. nat. affairs com. 1999—2002, mem. constn. and bylaws com. 1999—2002, ednl. rsch. group, sec.-treas. Met. Washington sect. 1982—83, v.p. Met. Washington sect. 1984, pres. Met. Washington sect. 1985, counselor Met. Washington sect. 1986—92), Internat. Assn. for Dental Rsch. (councilor Egyptian divsn. 1996—99, numerous positions including exec. com. ednl. rsch. group 1996—2001, mem. constn. and bylaws com. 1999—2002, chmn. various oral sessions), NYU Alumni Assn., Minn. Alumni Assn. Home: 15517 Grinnell Terr Rockville MD 20855

CHOI, BONNIE, musician, artist; d. Ping-loi Choi and Kam-Wan Ng; m. Robert Eidschun, June 25, 1994; 1 child, Erin Frances Eidschun. DMA, U. Mich., 1993. Lectr. Nazareth Coll., Rochester, NY, 1994—; aff. artist Syracuse U., 1997—. Artistic dir. Air de Cour, Victor, NY, 1995—. Musician (harpsichordist). Finalist Pro Musicis Competition, Pro Musicis, 1995; Arts grant, N.Y. State Arts and Cultural Coun., 2001, 2002. Office: Syracuse U 215 Crouse Coll Syracuse NY 13244 Office Phone: 585-389-2695. Personal E-mail: blchoi@naz.edu.

CHOI, DENNIS W., pharmaceutical executive, neurologist, educator; b. Ann Arbor, Mich., Sept. 26, 1953; three children. AB, Harvard Coll., 1974; MD, Harvard Med. Sch., 1978; PhD, Harvard U., 1978. Diplomate Am. Bd. Psychiatry & Neurology, Am. Bd. Clin. Neurophysiology, Am. Bd. Electrodiagnostic Medicine. Clin. fellow in medicine Harvard U., Boston, 1978-79, fellow in neurology, 1979-83; from asst. prof. to assoc. prof. Stanford (Calif.) U., 1983-91; prof., head dept. Washington U. Med. Sch., St. Louis, 1991—2002, adj. prof., Neurology, 2002—; exec. v.p. Merck Research Laboratories, 2002—. Mem. Am. Neurol. Assn. (v.p. 1996-97), Inst. Medicine, Soc. Neurosci. (pres. 1999—). Office: Merck & Co Inc 770 Sumneytown Pike PO Box 4 WP 14-2500 West Point PA 19486

CHOI, DOO-SUP, molecular biologist; b. Seoul, South Korea, Sept. 27, 1964; came to U.S., 1997; s. Byung-Man and Mi-Hong (Park) C.; m. Sun-Jung Lim, June 1, 1991; children: Ji-Won, Jung-Yeon, Jae-Hyun. BS, Yonsei U., Seoul, 1988, MS, 1990; PhD, Louis Pasteur U., Strasbourg, France, 1997. Rsch. assoc. Cheil Foods & Chems., Seoul, 1991-92; postdoctoral rschr. dept. biopharm. sci. U. Calif., San Francisco, 1997-98, staff rsch. scientist, 1998—2003, assoc. investigator, 2004—, asst. adj. prof., 2004—. Contbr. articles to profl. jours. Grantee Ctr. Nat. Rsch. Sci., France, 1993-97, NIH, 1997-98, State of Calif., 1998—. Fellow: Ctr. Internat. des Etudiants et Stagiares; mem.: Internat. Behavioral & Neural Genetics Soc., Soc. Neurosci., Serotonin Club. Christian Ch. Avocations: reading, travel, mountain climbing, tennis. Office: Gallo Rsch Ctr Univ of Calif-San Francisco 5858 Horton St Emeryville CA 94608 Office Phone: 510-985-3951. E-mail: choids@itsa.ucsf.edu.

CHOI, IN-SUP, radiologist; b. Pusan, Korea, July 22, 1947; came to U.S., 1975; s. Keun-Yoo and Jung-Sun (Han) C.; m. Hyung-kyung Cho, Nov. 14, 1974; children: Ellen, Philip. MD, Seoul Nat. U., 1972. Clin. asst. prof. NYU Sch. Medicine, 1981-82; asst. prof. radiology Mt. Sinai Sch. Medicine, N.Y.C., 1982-83; asst. prof. radiology Sch. Medicine NYU, 1984-92; assoc. prof. radiology Med. Sch. Harvard U., 1992—2004; prof. radiology Tufts U., Sch. Medicine, 2004—. Mem. Am. Soc. Neuroradiology, Am. Coll. Radiology, Radiol. Soc. N.Am., Am. Soc. Interventional & Therapeutic Neuroradiology (v.p.). Avocations: tennis, golf. Office: Lahey Clinic Med Ctr 41 Mall Rd Burlington MA 01805-0002 Office Phone: 781-744-3330. E-mail: in.sup.choi@lahey.org.

CHOI, JEE WOONG, research scientist; b. Jinhae, Gyeongsangnam-do, Republic of Korea, June 30, 1970; m. Yeon Sil You, Nov. 14, 1998. PhD, Hanyang U., Korea. Rsch. asst. Hanyang U., Ansan, Republic of Korea, 1996—2002, Underwater Acoustics Rsch. Ctr., Seoul Nat. U., 1997—2002; rsch. assoc. Applied Physics Lab., U. Wash., Seattle, 2002—. Contbr. articles to profl. jours. Petty officer Republic of Korea Navy, 1990—93. Recipient Postdoctoral award in Ocean Acoustics, Office Naval Rsch., 2002—04, Ocean Acoustics Spl. Rsch. award, 2004—. Mem.: Acoustical Soc. Korea, Acoustical Soc. Am. (underwater acoustics tech. com. 2004—). Home: 12508 Lake City Way NE #601 Seattle WA 98125 Office: Applied Physics Lab Univ of Washington 1013 NE 40th St Seattle WA 98105 Office Phone: 206-616-8597. Business E-Mail: choijw@apl.washington.edu.

CHOI, JEEYAE, nursing researcher; arrived in US, 1989; d. Moon-Ho Choi and Myung-Jung Yoon; m. Haigun Lee, Sept. 19, 1992; children: Jinjoo Rachel Lee, Hanjoo Richard Lee. BS, Seoul Nat. U., Republic of Korea, 1983, U. Ill., Chgo., 1995; MS, Boston U., 1998; post grad., Columbia U., N.Y.C., 2002—. RN Mass. Dept. Pub. Health, 1995. Nurse Seoul Nat. U. Hosp.; supr. Fairmount Oak Pk., Ill.; nurse Youvill Hosp. and Rehab., Cambridge, Mass., 1996—98; grad. tchg. asst. Boston U., 1997—98; rsch. asst. Decision Sys. Group, 1999—2001; grad. rsch. asst. Columbia U., N.Y.C., 2002—. Scholar, U. Ill. Chgo. Scholarship Assn., 1992; Korean Honor scholar, 1992, Women's scholarship, Boston U., 1997. Mem.: Sigma Theta Tau, Tau Beta Pi. Avocation: travel. Home: 35 Sylvia St Lexington MA 02421 Office: Columbia Univ GB335 617 West 168th St New York NY 10032 Office Phone: 212-305-6451. Personal E-mail: jc2293@columbia.edu.

CHOI, JOHN Y., neurologist, educator; s. Dai S. and Lisa E. Choi; m. Emily H. Hsu. MD, Hahnemann U., 1992. Diplomate Am. Bd. Neurology and Psychiatry, 1997. Fellow Washington U., St. Louis, 1996—98; mem. faculty Walter Reed Reed Army Med. Ctr, Washington, 1999—2003; asst. prof. U. Tex., Houston, 2003—. Maj. U.S. Army, 1999—2003. Mem.: Am. Stroke Assn. (mem. com. Tex. chpt. 2003—). Office: University of Texas HSC at Houston 6431 Fannin MSB 7124 Houston TX 77303 Office Phone: 713-500-7078. E-mail: john.y.choi@uth.tmc.edu.

CHOI, MICHAEL KAMWAH, aerospace engineer, mechanical engineer, researcher; b. Aug. 16, 1952; arrived in U.S., 1972, naturalized, 1987; s. Ying-Loi and Kan-Hau (Yuen) C.; m. Sophia Cheng; 1 child, Natalie. BSc in Engring. magna cum laude, Brown U., 1976; MSME, MIT, 1978, Engr's. Degree in Mech. Engring., 1979. Registered profl. engr., Va. Rsch. asst. dept. mech. engring. MIT, Cambridge, Mass., 1977-79; sr. rsch. engr. Sci. Applications Internat. Corp., McLean, Va., 1979-87; sr. engr. spacecraft thermal control sys. Fairchild Space and Defense Corp., Germantown, Md., 1987-90; project leader, mgr. NASA Goddard Space Flight Ctr., Greenbelt, Md., 1990—. Intrument thermal mgr. WIND and POLAR spacecraft Global Geospace Sci. Mission, 1990-92; thermal sys. mgr. Far Ultraviolet Spectroscopic Explorer Project, 1992-94; lead thermal engr. High Energy Solar Imager project, 1994-96; thermal sys. mgr. LANDSAT-7 mission, 1994-2000; lead thermal engr. electron reflectometer and magnetometer instruments on Lunar Prospector spacecraft, 1995-97, Next Generation Space Telescope, 1996-97, low energy neutral atom instrument on MIDEX IMAGE spacecraft, 1996-2000, Solar Probe Plasma Spectrometer Study, 1996-, Triana PlasMag instrument, 1999—, Swift Burst Alert Telescope instrument, optical bench and instrument module, 1999—; thermal architect Space Solar Power Exploratory Rsch. and Tech., 1999-2000, Instrument Synthesis & Analysis Lab. Thermal Lead, 2005-; cons. EO-1 Advanced Land Imager, 1997-2000, EO-1 Star Tracker thermal design, 2000, EO-1 obs. thermal vacuum & thermal vacuum test, 2000, MAP Star Tracker thermal design, 1999-2000, IRAC thermal cooldown, 2000, inFOCus Balloon instrument thermal design, 2001, STEREO SEP instrument thermal design, 2000; reviewer flight assurance office; organizer, chmn. spacecraft and instrument thermal control sessions 32d Intersoc. Energy Conversion Engring. Conf., 1997, chmn. spacecraft and aircraft thermal mgmt. sessions, 1998-2002, chmn. spacecraft and aircraft thermal mgmt. sessions, Internat. Energy Conversion Engring. Conf., 2003—, thermal mgmt. topical area coord., Internat. Engergy Conversion Engring. Conf., 2005-; contbr. solar heating and cooling program US Dept. Energy; spkr. nat. and internat. confs. Contbr. articles to profl. jours.; reviewer Solar Energy Jour., ASME Solar Energy Divsn., 1983-87. Fellow AIAA (assoc., Cert. Merit Best Paper in Aerospace Power Sys. 1996); mem. ASME, Soc. Automotive Engring., Sigma Xi, Tau Beta Pi. Home: 2237 Halter Ln Reston VA 20191-5824 Office Phone: 301-286-4707. Business E-Mail: michael.k.choi@nasa.gov.

CHOI, NAMOK, education educator; arrived in US, 1990; d. Chuntack and Bockran (Lee) Choi; m. Robert Roy Eagle, July 20, 2002. BA, Sungshin Womens U., Seoul, 1983; MS, Okla. State U., 1993, PhD, 1997. Tchr. Dept. Edn., Kwangwon, Republic of Korea, 1983—90; from rsch. asst. to tchg. asst. Okla. State U., Stillwater, 1991—97; asst. prof. Ga. So. U., Statesboro, 1997—2000, U. Louisville, 2000—04, assoc. prof., 2004—. Mem. editl. bd.: Jour. Social Psychology, 1999—, Jour. Counseling and Devel., 2004—, reviewer: Jour. Ednl. Psychology, 2003—; contbr. articles to profl. jours. Vol. St. John Homeless Ctr., Louisville, 2001—03; bd. dirs. Louisville Korean Sch., 2004—. Mem.: Am. Ednl. Rsch. Assn. (proposal reviewer 1998—, session chair 1999, 2004, textbook reviewer 2004, newsletter editor 2001—03, co-chair jur. faculty mentoring 2005). Democrat. Presbyterian. Avocations: literature, reading, gardening, tennis. Office: Univ Louisvile Coll Edn and Human Devel Louisville KY 40292 Business E-Mail: namok@louisville.edu.

CHOI, SEUNG-KYUM, researcher; b. Seoul, South Korea, Jan. 14, 1974; s. Soohong Choi and Jeongja Sun. PhD, Wright State Univ., 2005. EIT Human Resources Devel. Svc. of Korea, South Korea, 1995. Rsch. asst. Ajou U., Republic of Korea, 1995—96; engr., inteligence officer South Korea Army, Republic of Korea, 1996—99; rsch. asst. Wright State U., Dayton, Ohio, 2001—. Contbr. scientific papers (Young rschr. fellowship awarded by Second M.I.T. Conf., 2003). First lt. Engr. Brigade, 1996—99, Pocheon, South Korea. Recipient Graduation with honors, Ajou Univ. (South Korea), 1996, A citation for excellent performance, Engr. Brigade comdr. (South Korea), 1997, The comdr. of an army corps (South Korea), 1998; scholar Scholarship as an honor student, Ajou Univ. (South Korea), 1992-1995, Full scholarship for grad. studies, 1996, Dayton Area Grad. Studies Inst. (DAGSI) competitive scholarship, Dayton Area Grad. Studies Inst., 2003. Mem.: AIAA. Avocations: golf, photography, travel. Office: Wright State Univ 3640 Colonel Glenn Highway Dayton OH 45435 Office Phone: 937-775-5090.

CHOI, SOOK CHONG YOO, physiologist, educator; arrived in US, 1958; d. Dong-Sun Yoo and Kuan-Sum Kim; m. Paul W. Choi, Mar. 5, 1960; children: James Paul, William Augustine, Mary Anne. BSN, Seton Hall U., So. Orange, NJ, 1964; PhD, Rutgers U., 1973. Prof. biology Upsala Coll., East Orange, NJ, 1973—95; calman prof. biology Caldwell Coll., 1995—. Recipient Women of the Yr. award, Soroptimist Internat. of the Am., 1984, The Christian R. and Mary Lindback Found. award, Upsala Coll., 1986, Pres. Gala Honoree, Caldwell Coll., 2004. Mem.: Am. Physiol. Soc. (corr.). Roman Cath. Home: 8 Medford Rd Morris Plains NJ 07950 Office: Caldwell College 9 Ryerson Ave Caldwell NJ Office Phone: 973-618-3570. Office Fax: 973-618-3477. Business E-Mail: schoi@caldwell.edu.

CHOI, SOON CHAE, orthopaedic surgeon; b. Sept. 13, 1941; MD, Seoul Nat U., 1966. Diplomate Am. Bd. Orthopaedic Surgery. Intern Albert Einstein Med. Ctr., Phila., 1966—67; resident gen. surgery St. Peter's Med. Ctr., New Brunswick, NJ, 1967—69; resident orthop. surgery Columbia Presbyn. Med. Ctr., Harlem Hosp. Ctr., N.Y.C., 1969—73; chief orthop. surgery Muhlenberg Regional Med. Ctr., Plainfield, NJ, 1992—96; clin. asst. prof. orthop. surgery Robert Wood Johnson Med. Sch., U. Medicine and Dentistry N..J, 1975. Fellow Am. Acad. Orthopaedic Surgeons. Office: 1907 Park Ave South Plainfield NJ 07080-5530 Office Phone: 908-561-2122. E-mail: soonchoi@aol.com.

CHOI, YOUNGOK, information science educator; d. Seung-Chil Choi and Nam-Soo Lee; m. Sung-Ju Cho, Dec. 9, 1997; 1 child, Ashley Han-Hee Cho. Grad. magna cum laude, Ewha Womans U., 1988; PhD, U. Pitts., 2000. Asst. prof. SUNY, Oswego, 2001—. Program com. Internat. Assn. Sci. and Tech. for Devel., Calgary, Canada, 2004—. Contbr. articles to profl. jours. Recipient Margaret Corbett award, Sch. Info. Sci., U. Pitts., 2000; Eugene Garfield Doctoral Dissertation fellow, Beta Phi Mu, 1999. Mem.: Assn. Libr. and Info. Sci. Edn. (grantee 2005), Am. Soc. Info. Sci. and Tech., Assn. Computing Machinery.

CHOICE, PRISCILLA KATHRYN MEANS (PENNY CHOICE), retired international educational consultant; b. Rockford, Ill., Nov. 8, 1939; d. John Z. and Margaret A. (Haines) Means; m. Jack R. Choice, Nov. 14, 1964; children: William Kenneth, Margaret Meta. BA, U. Wis., 1963; MEd, Nat.-Louis U., 1990; MA, N.E. Ill. U., 1995. Field rsch. dir. Tatham-Laird and Kudner Advt., Chgo., 1964-69; drama specialist Children's Theatre Western Springs (Ill.), 1969-81; gifted teaching asst. Sch. Dist. 181, Hinsdale, Ill., 1980-84; tchr. Sch. Dist. 99, Cicero, Ill., 1984-85; gifted edn. program coord. Cmty. Consolidated Sch. Dist. 93, Carol Stream, Ill., 1985-99; coord. gifted edn. and fine arts Ednl. Svcs. Divsn., Lake County Regional Office Edn., Grayslake, Ill., 1999—2004; retired, 2004—. Drama specialist, cons. Choice Dramatics, Hinsdale and Clarendon Hills, Ill., 1976-2004; producing dir. Mirror Image Youth Theatre, Hinsdale, 1986-88; adj. prof. Coll. DuPage, Glen Ellyn, Ill., 1990-92, Nat.-Louis U., Evanston, Ill., 1991—, Aurora (Ill.) U., 1995—, Govs. State U., University Park, Ill., 1992-93; internat. cons. in gifted edn. and drama-in-edn., 1989—; co-chair advocacy com. Ill. Assn. Gifted Children, 2002-05, co-chair underserved populations, 05—; trustee Friends of the Lake Co. Discovery Mus., 2003—; chair arts divsn. Nat. Assn. for Gifted Children, 2003—; edn. dir. First Folio Shakespeare Festival, 2005— Contbg. author Gifted/Arts Resource Guide, 1990; contbg. editor Ill. Theatre Assn., Followspot News, 1992-95. 96-2002. Mem. gifted adv. com. Ednl. Svc. Ctr., Wheaton, Ill., 1987—90, 1992—95, Regional Office of Edn., Wheaton, 1995—99, Northeastern Ill. U.1993-95., Chgo., 1993—95; bd. dirs. Ill. Theatre Assn., Chgo., 1983—87; chair Arts Divsn. Nat. Assn. for Gifted Children, 2003—; co-chair advocacy Com. Ill. Assn. for Gifted Children, 2002—. Recipient Ill. State Bd. Edn. gifted edn. fellowship, 1988, AAUW continuing edn. scholarship, 1986, 90, Excellence award Ill. Theatre Assn., 1991, Excellence award Ill. Math. and Sci. Acad., 1990, 98, Recognition of Excellence, No. Ill. Planning Commn. Gifted Edn., 1990, Award of Excellence Ill. and Math. Sci. Acad., 1998. Mem. ASCD, World Coun. on Gifted Edn., Nat. Assn. Gifted Children, Ill. Assn. Gifted Children (membership chmn. 1992-94, advocacy com. 1995—, co-chair advocacy com. 2002—, co-chair underserved populations 2005—), Ill. Coun. Gifted, Am. Assn. Theatre in Edn., Ill. Theatre Assn. (bd. dirs. 1983-87, Outstanding Achievement award 1991), Inst. for Global Ethics, Ill. Alliance Arts Edn., Theatre Western Springs, Phi Delta Kappa. Avocations: swimming, walking, reading. Home and Office: 113 S Prospect Ave Clarendon Hills IL 60514-1422 Office Phone: 630-452-6675. E-mail: pennychoice@comcast.net.

CHOKEY, JAMES A., lawyer; b. Pitts., Sept. 2, 1943; AB, U. Pitts., 1965; JD, Duquesne U., 1969. Bar: Pa. 1969, U.S. Dist. Ct. (we. dist.) Pa., Wis. 1973. Atty. Westinghouse Electric Corp., 1972-73; v.p., gen. counsel, sec. Joy Mfg., 1973-87, RTE Corp., 1987-88, A.O. Smith Corp., 1989-91; v.p., gen. counsel Cooper Industries Inc., Houston, 1991—; v.p. corp. affairs, gen. counsel Beloit (Wis.) Corp.; exec. v.p., sec. and gen. counsel Joy Global (Harnischfeger Industries Inc.), Milw., 1997—. Mem. ABA, Am. Corp. Counsel Assn. (pres. we. Pa. chpt. 1985-86). Office: Joy Global PO Box 554 Milwaukee WI 53201-0554 E-mail: jchokey@HII.com.

CHOKSI, MARY, investment company executive; BA in French, U. Minn.; MA in Internat. Rels., John Hopkins U.; MPA, U. Minn. With pension devel. divsn. World Bank, sr. program officer South and S.E. Asia; mng. dir. Strategic Investment Ptnrs. Inc. and Emerging Markets Investors Corp., Arlington, Va., 1987—. Bd. mem. Emerging Markets South Asia Fund, Emerging Markets Quantitative Portfolio, HJ Heinz Co. Trustee Nat. Mus. Women in the Arts; bd. dirs. Beauvoir-The Nat. Cathedral Elem. Sch. Office: Strategic Investment Group 16th Fl 1001 19th St N Arlington VA 22209-1722

CHOKSY, JAMSHEED KAIRSHASP, historian, religious scholar, humanities educator, language educator; b. Bombay, Jan. 8, 1962; arrived in Sri Lanka, 1962; permanent resident, U.S. 1995, naturalized, 1999. s. Kairshasp Nariman and Freny Kairshasp (Cooper) C.; m. Carol Emma Burnside, Sept. 12, 1993; 1 child, Darius Jamsheed. AB in Mid.-Ea. Langs. and Culture, Columbia U., 1985; PhD in History and Religions, Harvard U., 1991. Tchg. fellow dept. anthropology and archaeology Harvard U., 1988, jr. fellow, 1988-91; vis. asst. prof. depts. history and internat. rels. Stanford U., 1991-93; from asst. prof. to prof. Ind. U., Bloomington, 1993—2001, prof. ctrl. Eurasian studies, history and religion, 2001—. Mem. Sch. Hist. Studies, Inst. for Advanced Study-Princeton, 1993—94; presenter in field; cons. in field. Author: Purity and Pollution in Zoroastrianism, 1989, Conflict and Cooperation, 1997, Evil, Good and Gender, 2002, Archeological Surveys in Pakistan, 1988-90, 1999-2001, Iran, 2003; contbr. numerous articles to profl. publs. Rsch. fellow Govt. India, Bombay, 1998; John Simon Guggenheim Meml. Found. fellow, 1996-97; resident scholar Ind. U., 1996-97, grantee 1994—, grantee Am. Acad. Religion, 1995-96, Andrew W. Mellon fellow, 1991-93, 2001-02. Fellow: NEH, Royal Asiatic Soc. Great Britain, Ireland, Ctr. for Advanced Study in the Behavioral Scis.; mem.: Mensa, Cosmos Club (Washington), Explorers Club (NY). Office: Ind U Dept Ctrl Eurasian Studies Goodbody Hall 157 1011 E 3rd St Bloomington IN 47405-7005 Office Phone: 812-855-8643. Business E-Mail: jchoksy@indiana.edu.

CHOLDENKO, GENNIFER, writer; married; 2 children. BA cum laude with honors, Brandeis Univ.; BFA in Illustration, RI Sch. Design. Author: (children's books) Moonstruck: The True Story of the Cow Who Jumped Over the Moon, 1997, Notes From a Liar and Her Dog, 2001, Al Capone Does My Shirts, 2004 (Newbery Honor Book, 2005, Am. Libr. Assn. Notable Book, 2005, Best Children's Book of Yr, Publisher's Weekly), Tales of a Second-Grade Giant, 2005. Mailing: c/o Penguin Group Putnam Publicity 345 Hudson St New York NY 10014

CHOLDIN, MARIANNA TAX, librarian, educator; b. Chgo., Feb. 26, 1942; d. Sol and Gertrude (Katz) Tax; m. Harvey Myron Choldin, Aug. 28, 1962; children: Kate and Mary (twins). BA, U. Chgo., 1962, MA, 1967, PhD, 1979. Slavic bibliographer Mich. State U., East Lansing, 1967—69; Slavic bibliographer, instr. U. Ill., Urbana, 1969—73, Slavic bibliographer, asst. prof., 1973—76, Slavic bibliographer, assoc. prof., 1976—84, head Slavic and East European Libr., 1982—89, head, prof., 1984—2002, dir. Russian and East European Ctr., 1987—89, C. Walter and Gerda B. Mortenson Disting. prof., 1989—2002, dir. Mortenson Ctr. for Internat. Libr. Programs, 1991—2002, prof. emerita, 2003—. Author: Fence Around the Empire: Russian Censorship, 1985; editor: Red Pencil: Artists, Scholars and Censors in the USSR, 1989, Books, Libraries and Information in Slavic and East European Studies, 1986. Chair Soros Found. Network Libr. Program Bd., 1997—2000. Recipient Pushkin gold medal for contbns. to culture, Russian Presdl. Coun. on Culture, 2000. Mem. ALA, Am. Assn. for Advancement of Slavic Studies (pres. 1995), Phi Beta Kappa. Jewish. Home: 888 S Michigan Ave #403 Chicago IL 60605 Personal E-mail: mcholdin@ameritech.net.

CHOLE, RICHARD ARTHUR, otolaryngologist, department chairman; b. Madison, Wis., Oct. 12, 1944; s. Arthur Steven and Wendy Elveyn (Danielczyk) C.; m. Cynthia Beiseker, Dec. 27, 1969; children: Joseph Michael, Timothy Thomas, Katharine, Melinda. Student, U. Calif., Berkeley, 1962-65; MD, U. So. Calif., 1969; PhD in Otolaryngology, U. Minn., 1977. Diplomate Am. Bd. Otolaryngology (sr. bd. examiner). Rotating intern U. So. Calif. Med. Ctr., 1969-70; med. fellow dept. surgery Sch. Medicine U. Minn., 1972-73, med. fellow dept. otolaryngology Sch. Medicine, 1973-77; asst. prof. dept. otolaryngology-head and neck surgery Sch. Medicine U. Calif., Davis, 1977-81, assoc. prof., 1981-84, prof., 1984-98, acting chmn. dept., 1985, chmn., 1985—98; chmn. dept. otolaryngology Washington U., St. Louis, 1998—. Mem. sci. rev. com. Deafness Rsch. Found., 1986—; mem. communicative disorders rev. com. Nat. Inst. Deafness and Communication Disorders, 1989—94; staff cons. Dept. Air Force, David Grant USAF Med. Ctr., Travis AFB, Calif., 1981—98; keynote spkr. 92d Japan Oto-Rhino-Laryngol. Soc. Meeting, Fukuoka City, Japan, 1990—; faculty mem. 4th Internat. Cholesteatoma Conf., Niigata City, Japan, 1992; bd. dirs. Am. Bd. Otolaryngology, 2000—; adv. coun. Nat. Deafness and Other Communication Disorders, 2001—; lectr. in field. Mem. editorial bd. Laryngoscope, 1985-87; mem. exec. editorial bd. Otolaryngology-Head and Neck Surgery, 1990—; contbr. numerous articles to profl. jours., book chpts., revs.; patentee in field. Mem. profl. edn. com. Am. Cancer Soc., 1977-78, Sacramento Noise Control Hearing Bd., 1977—, Greater Sacramento Profl. Standards Rev. Orgn., 1978-79; deacon 1st Bapt. Ch., Davis, 1979-82, elder, 1983-88. Recipient 1st pl. award Am. Acad. Ophthalmology and Otolaryngology, 1977, care recognition awards U. Calif., Davis, 1988-91; rsch. grantee NIH, Nat. Inst. Aging, Nat. Inst. Neurol. and Communicative Disorders and Stroke, Nat. Inst. on Deafness and Other Communication Disorders, Deafness Rsch. Found., Am. Otol. Soc., U. Calif., 1978-91. Mem. Collegeum Otorhinolaryngologicum Amicitiae Sacrum (U.S. group), Am. Acad. Otolaryngology-Head and Neck Surgery (Honors award 1984, com. on rsch. 1987—, rsch. coordinating coun. 1987—, continuing edn. com. 1991—), Am. Otol. Soc. (trustee rsch. fund 1986—, sec.-treas. 1989—, pres. 2001—), Assn. for Rsch. in Otolaryngology (pres. 1999-2000, award of merit com. 1988—), Am. Laryngol., Rhinol. and Otol. Soc., Am. Soc. for Bone and Mineral Rsch., Assn. Acad. Depts. Otolaryngology-Head and Neck Surgery (coun. 1986—), Calif. Med. Assn. (sci. adv. panel, sect. on otolaryngology-head and neck surgery 1986-98), Sacramento Soc. Otolaryngology and Maxillofacial Surgery, Soc. Univ. Otolaryngologists-Head and Neck Surgeons. Achievements include research in in experimental cholesteatoma, experimental otosclerosis, the aging auditory system, osteoclast cell biology. Office: Washington U Sch Med CB8115 660 S Euclid Ave # 8115 Saint Louis MO 63110-1010 E-mail: choler@msnotes.wustl.edu.

CHOLEWKA, PATRICIA ANNE, health facility administrator; m. Michael A. Cholewka; children: Maureen, Kathleen. Diploma in Nursing, Bellevue Sch. Nursing, 1967; BSN magna cum laude, Castleton State Coll., 1979; MPA in Pub. and Nonprofit Mgmt. Policy, NYU, 1987; EdD in internat. Edn. Devel., Columbia U., 1999; MA in Healthcare Informatics, NYU, 2005. RN; cert. nursing adminstrn. ANA; cert. Nat. Assn. Healthcare Quality. Mgr. med.-surg. clin. svcs. in acute and managed care orgns., 1967-95; educator, 1995—; rschr. healthcare policy and econ. mgmt., 1993—. Healthcare orgn. devel. cons. Razgrad Hosp., Bulgaria, 1993, Kaunas Med. Acad. Hosp., Lithuania, 1996-98, Lviv (Ukraine) Mcpl. Health Dept., 1998; reviewer curriculum med. quality mgmt., Am. Coll. Med. Quality, 2005. Author: Comparative Analysis of Two Post-Soviet Healthcare Organizations in Lithuania and Ukraine: Implications for Continuous Quality Improvement, 1999, Factors Affecting Sustainable Health Care Management Programs in Post-Soviet Transitional Economics; editor Jour. Healthcare Quality; guest editor Internat. Jour. Econ. Devel.; mem editl. bd Nursing Outlook, Jour. Nursing Scholarship, Jour. Transcultural Nursing. Mem. citizen emergency response team, Bay Ridge, 2004—; mem. cmty. coun., 2003—. Recipient Disting. Rsch. award, Columbia U., 1999, Fed. Nurse Traineeship award, NYU, 2003. Mem. Phi Delta Kappa, Sigma Theta Tau. Republican. Roman Catholic. Personal E-mail: pacholewka@verizon.net.

CHOMSKY, (AVRAM) NOAM (AVRAM CHOMSKY), linguistics and philosophy educator; b. Phila., Dec. 7, 1928; s. William and Elsie (Simonofsky) C.; m. Carol Doris Schatz, Dec. 24, 1949; children: Aviva, Diane, Harry Alan. BA, U. Pa., 1949, MA, 1951, PhD, 1955, DHL (hon.), 1984, U. Chgo., 1967, Loyola U., Chgo., 1970, Swarthmore Coll., 1970, Bard Coll., 1971, U. Mass., 1973, U. Maine, 1992, Gettysburg Coll., 1992, Amherst Coll., 1995, U. Rovira i Virgili, Catalonia, 1998; DHL (hon.), McGill U., 1998; DHL (hon.), U. Guelph, Can., 1999, Columbia U., 1999, U. Conn., 1999, U. Toronto,

2000, U. Western Ont., 2000; DHL (hon.), U. Nat. Comahue, Argentina, 2001; LittD (hon.), U. London, 1967; DHL (hon.), U. Nat. Bogota, Colombia, 2002, Vrije U., Brussels, 2003, Ctrl. Conn. State U., 2003, U. Florence, 2004, Ctrl. Conn. State U., 2004, U. Athens, 2004; LittD (hon.), Delhi (India) U., 1972, Visva-Bharati U., Santiniketan, West Bengal, 1980, Cambridge (Eng.) U., 1995; LittD (hon.), U. Calcutta, 2001; LLD (hon.), U. Buenos Aires, 1996; LLD, Harvard U., 2000; Doctorate (hon.), Scuola Normale Superiore, Pisa, Italy, 1999. Mem. faculty MIT, 1955—, prof. modern langs., 1961—, Ferrari P. Ward prof. modern lang. and linguistics, 1966—, Inst. prof., 1976—. Vis. prof. Columbia U., N.Y.C., 1957-58; mem. Inst. Advanced Study Princeton U., 1958-59; Linguistic Soc. Am. prof. UCLA, summer 1966; Beckman prof. U. Calif.-Berkeley, 1966-67; John Locke lectr. Oxford U., 1969; Bertrand Russell Meml. lectr., Cambridge, 1971; Nehru Meml. lectr., New Delhi, 1972; Huizinga lectr. U. Leiden, 1977; Woodbridge lectr. Columbia U., 1978; Kant lectr. Stanford U., 1979; Jeanette K. Watson disting. vis. prof. Syracuse U., 1982; Pauling Meml. lectr. Oreg. State U., 1995. Author: Syntactic Structures, 1957, Current Issues in Linguistic Theory, 1964, Aspects of the Theory of Syntax, 1965, Cartesian Linguistics, 1966, Topics in the Theory of Generative Grammar, 1966, (with Morris Halle) Sound Pattern of English, 1968, Language and Mind, 1968, American Power and the New Mandarins, 1969, At War with Asia, 1970, Problems of Knowledge and Freedom, 1971, Studies on Semantics in Generative Grammar, 1972, For Reasons of State, 1973, (with Edward Herman) Counterrevolutionary Violence, 1973, Peace in the Middle East, 1974, Logical Structure of Linguistic Theory, 1975, Reflections on Language, 1975, Essays on Form and Interpretation, 1977, Human Rights and American Foreign Policy, 1978, (with Edward Herman) The Political Economy of Human Rights, 2 vols., 1979, Language and Responsibility, 1979, Rules and Representations, 1980, Lectures on Government and Binding, 1981, Concepts and Consequences of the Theory of Government and Binding, 1982, Towards a New Cold War, 1982, Radical Priorities, 1982, Fateful Triangle, 1983, Turning the Tide, 1985, Barriers, 1986, Knowledge of Language, 1986, Pirates and Emperors, 1986, On Power and Ideology, 1987, Language and Problems of Knowledge, 1987, Language in a Psychological Setting, 1987, Generative Grammar, 1987, Culture of Terrorism, 1988, (with Edward Herman) Manufacturing Consent, 1988, Language and Politics, 1988, Necessary Illusions, 1989, Deterring Democracy, 1991, Chronicles of Dissent, 1992, What Uncle Sam Really Wants, 1992, Year 501, 1993, Rethinking Camelot, 1993, Letters from Lexington, 1993, The Prosperous Few and the Restless Many, 1993, Language and Thought, 1994, World Orders, Old and New, 1994, The Minimalist Program, 1995, Powers and Prospects, 1996, The Common Good, 1998, Profits Over People, 1998, The New Military Humanism, 1999, New Horizons in the Study of Language and Mind, 2000, Rogue States, 2000, A New Generation Draws the Line, 2000, Architecture of Language, 2000, 9-11, 2001, Propaganda and the Public Mind, 2001, Understanding Power, 2002, On Nature and Language, 2002, Pirates and Emperors, Old and New, 2002, Middle East Illusions, 2003, Hegemony or Survival, 2003. Recipient Disting. Sci. Contbn. award, APA, 1984, Kyoto prize, Kyocera Found., 1988, 2001, George Orwell award, Nat. Coun. Tchrs. English, 1987, 1989, James Killian Faculty award, MIT, 1992, Lannan Lit. award for nonfiction, 1992, Joel Seldin Peace award, Psychologists for Social Responsibility, 1993, Homer Smith award, NYU Sch. of Medicine, 1994, Loyola Mellon Humanities award, Loyola U. Chgo., 1994, Helmholtz medal, Berlin-Brandenburgische Akad. Wissenschaften, 1996, Benjamin Franklin Inst. award, 1999, Rabindranath Tagore Centenary award, Asiatic Soc. Calcutta, 2000, Rising Sun of Mehgarh award, Dawn Islamabad, 2001, Adela Dwyer St. Thomas Villanova Peace award, Villanova U., Phila., 2002, Peace award, Turkish Publishers' Assn., Istanbul, 2002, award, Kurdish Human Rights Assn., Dyarbakir, 2002, Soc. Writers and Artists award, UN, 2004, Carl-von-Ossietzky prize, Oldenburg, Germany, 2004; jr. fellow Soc. Fellows Harvard U., 1951—55. Fellow AAAS, Brit. Acad. (corr.), Brit. Psychol. Soc. (hon.), Royal Anthrop. Inst. Gt. Britain, Royal Anthrop. Inst. Ireland, Utrecht Soc. Arts and Scis. (hon.), Gesellschaft für Sprachwissenschaft (hon.), Am. Acad. Scis., Am. Acad. Philosophy, Royal Soc. Can. (fgn.), Am. Philos. Soc.; mem. APA (William James fellow 1990), NAS, Am. Acad. Arts and Scis., Linguistic Soc. Am., Deutsche Akademie der Naturforscher Leopoldina, Assn. for Edn. in Journalism and Mass Comm. (Profl. Excellence award 1991). Office: 77 Massachusetts Ave Cambridge MA 02139-4301 Office Phone: 617-253-7819. Business E-Mail: chomsky@mit.edu.

CHONG, CLAYTON ELLIOTT, lawyer; b. Hilo, Hawaii, July 6, 1950; s. Wing Kong and Ethel (Ishii) C. BS in Bus., Miami U., Oxford, Ohio, 1972, MBA, 1973; JD, Ohio No. U., 1977. Bar: U.S. Dist. Ct. Hawaii 1978, U.S. Ct. Appeals (9th cir.) 1978. Sole practice, Hilo, 1978-79; ptnr. Chong & Chong, Hilo, 1979—; pres. Island Designs Hawaii, LLC, 2000—. Named Outstanding Young Man of Am. U.S. Jaycees, 1989, YWCA Vol. of the Year, 1988-89, Hawaii Businessman of Yr., 2003. Mem. Hawaii State Bar Assn., Hawaii County Bar Assn., Miami U. Alumni Assn., Ohio No. U. Law Alumni Assn., Lehua Jaycees, Kuilima Jaycees (pres. 1989-90), Lions (pres. Hilo club 1986-87, Lion of Yr.), Delta Theta Phi (dist. chancellor 1983-2001, Hawaii State chancellor 2001—, Clarence W. Pierce award 1983, Chancellor's award 2003), Delta Sigma Pi (pres. Hawaii Alumni chpt. 1987-89, dist. dir. 1989-92, Silver Helmet award 1996, Hawaii Hall of Fame 1999). Avocation: rock collecting. Home and Office: PO Box 1483 Hilo HI 96721-1483 Office Phone: 808-935-5069. Personal E-mail: cechong@aol.com.

CHONG, DENNIS KHIN-HEUNG, physical medicine and rehabilitation specialist; b. Petaling Jaya, Selangor, Malaysia, June 12, 1965; m. Sweelin Alicia Wong, June 21, 1991; 2 children. MD, U. Calgary, 1988. Diplomate Am. Bd. Phys. Medicine and Rehab. Resident Meml. U. Nfld., 1988-90, McMaster U., Hamilton, Ont., Can., 1990-93; staff physician Rehab. Inst. of Mich., Detroit, 1993-96, med. dir., 1994-96; asst. prof., assoc. grad. faculty Wayne State U., Detroit, 1994—; clin. asst. prof. Oakland U., Rochester, Mich., 1995—; mem. active staff U. Pitts. Med. Ctr., Jefferson Hosp., McKeesport Hosp.; pvt. practice Pitts., 1996—97; assoc. med. dir. CIGNA, Freeport, Maine, 1997—99, v.p., regional med. dir. Seattle, 1999—. Adv. bd. Kessler Inst. Rehab., NJ, 1994; adj. faculty Duquesne U., Pitts., 1997; bd. mem. Assn. Wash. Healthplans, Wash.; cons. Highmark Blue Cross Blue Shield, Pitts., 1997. Contbr. articles to profl. jours. Con. physiatrist Internat. Cmty. Health, Seattle, 1999—; med. cons. Pitts. Youth Ballet, Pitts., 1997; mem. Pitts. leadership com. Nat. Osteoporosis Found., Pitts., 1997. Fellow: Am. Acad. Phys. Medicine and Rehab., Royal Coll. Physicians Can.; mem.: Am. Coll. Physician Execs. Protestant. Avocations: hiking, camping, fishing, skiing, reading. Office: Cigna HealthCare 701 Fifth Ave Ste 1900 Seattle WA 98104

CHONG, RICHARD DAVID, architect; b. Los Angeles, June 1, 1946; s. George and Mabel Dorothy (Chan) C.; m. Roze Gutierrez, July 5, 1969; children: David Gregory, Michelle Elizabeth. BArch, U. So. Calif., 1969; MArch, UCLA, 1974. Registered architect, Utah, Calif., Wyo., Wash. Assoc. Pulliam, Matthews & Assocs., Los Angeles, 1969-76; dir. Asst. Community Design Ctr., Salt Lake City, 1976-77; prin. Richard D. Chong & Assocs., Salt Lake City and L.A., 1977—. Planning cons. Los Angeles Harbor Dept., 1974-76; asst. instr. So. Calif. Inst. Architecture, Santa Monica, 1973-74; vis. design critic Calif. State Poly. U., Pamona, 1975, U. Utah, Salt Lake City, 1976-78; design instr. Calif. State Poly. U., 1975-76; adj. asst. prof. urban design, U. Utah, 1980-84; bd. dirs. Utah Housing Coalition, Salt Lake City; Salt Lake City Housing Adv. and Appeals Bd., 1976-80; presenter Rail-Volution Conf., Washington, 1996. Author: Design of Flexible Housing, 1974; prin. works include Airmen's Dining Hall, 1985 (1st Pl. Mil. Facility Air Force Logistics Command, 1986), Oddfellows Hall, 1984 (Heritage Found. award, 1986), Light Rail Sys. for Salt Lake City. Mem. Task Force for the Aged Housing Com. Salt Lake County, Salt Lake City, 1976-77; Salt Lake City Mortgage Loan Instns. Rev. Com., 1978; bd. dirs. Neighborhood Housing Svcs. of Fed. Home Loan Bank Bd., Salt Lake City, 1979-81, devel. com.; vice-chmn. Water Quality Adv. Coun., Salt Lake City, 1981-83; vice-chmn. Salt Lake City Pub. Utilities Bd., 1985-87; mem. adv. bd. Pub. Utilities Commn., Salt Lake City, 1985—; bd. dirs. Kier Mgmt. Corp.; bd. mem. Camp Kostopulos, Altro Nat. Risk Mgmt. Adv. Bd., 1996—, Ft. Douglas Social Adv. Bd., 1996—, Altro Nat. Safety Bd., 1996-01. Mem. AIA (jury mem. Am. Soc. Interior Designs Ann. awards 1981-82, treas. Salt Lake chpt. 1988-89, treas. Utah Soc. 1991, sec. 1992, pres.-elect AIA Utah 1993, pres. 1994-95), Am. Inst. Planning (juror Ann. Planning award 1984-85), Am. Planning Assn., Am. Arbitration Assn., Nat. Panel Arbitrators, Cottonwood Country Club. Democrat. Avocations: tennis, sailing, foreign travel. Office: Richard D Chong & Assocs 244 Edison St Salt Lake City UT 84111-2307 also: 714 W Olympic Blvd Ste 732 Los Angeles CA 90015-1439

CHONG, VERNON, retired surgeon, retired military officer; b. Fresno, Calif., Nov. 13, 1933; s. Seu Ling and Ruth (Lee) C.; m. Ann Sumiko Kawana, Sept. 7, 1957; children: Christopher Lee, Gerald Scott, Douglas James. BA, Stanford U., 1955, MD, 1958. Diplomate Am. Bd. Surgery. Intern Gen. Hosp. of Fresno (Calif.) County, 1958-59, resident in gen. surgery, 1959-63; commd. capt. USAF, 1963, advanced through ranks to maj. gen., 1987; chief gen. surgery svc. USAF Hosp., Scott AFB, Ill., 1963-65, staff surgeon, dir. edn. Tachikawa AFB, Japan, 1965-68; staff surgeon, instr. surgery David Grant USAF Med. Ctr., Travis AFB, Calif., 1968-70, dep. comdr., dir. hosp. svcs., 1976—78, comdr., 1978—81; surgeon, chief surgery, dir. hosp. svcs. USAF Acad. Hosp., Colorado Springs, Colo., 1970-74; dep. comdr. USAF Regional Hosp., March AFB, Calif., 1974—76; comdr. Malcolm Grow USAF Med. Ctr., Andrews AFB, Md., 1981-85; command surgeon Hdqrs., Mil. Airlift Command, Scott AFB, 1985-87; comdr. Wilford Hall USAF Med. Ctr., Lackland AFB, Tex., 1987-90, Joint Mil. Med. Command, San Antonio; command surgeon Hdqrs. Air Tng. Command, Randolph AFB, Tex., 1990-91, Hdqrs. U.S. European Command, 1991-94; ret., 1994; network dir. Vets. Integrated Svc. Network VA, Grand Prairie, Tex., 1995-2000; spl. asst. to network dir. Vets. Integrated Svc. Network-21, McClellan Clinic, Sacramento, 2000—03, ret., 2003. Bd. dirs. Alamo chpt. ARC, San Antonio, 1987-88, No. Calif. Retired Officers Cmty. Law, 2004; trustee Air Force Village Found., 1987-90; bd. dirs. San Antonio chpt. ARC, 1995—, No. Calif. Ret. Officers Cmty., 2004—; mem. Calif. Vets. Bd., 2004. Decorated D.S.M., Legion of Merit with bronze oak leaf cluster; recipient Order of Sword award USAF, 1989. Fellow ACS (gov. 1985-90); mem. Assn. Mil. Surgeons U.S. (bd. mgrs. 1997—, chmn. 2002—), Soc. Air Force Clin. Surgeons (bd. govs. 1971-73), Am. Coll. Physician Execs. Methodist. Avocation: physical fitness. Home: 1820 Starview Ln Lincoln CA 95648

CHONIN, NEIL HARVEY, lawyer; b. Bklyn., Dec. 30, 1936; s. Morris Joseph and Shirley (Goldberg) C.; m. Lynn Barbara Weinstein (div.); children: Mitchell, David, Loree; m. Patricia Lane Perrin, Aug. 13, 1972; children; Tiffany, Jason. BA in Govt., U. Fla., 1958, LLD, 1961. Bar: Fla. 1963, U.S. Dist. Ct. (so., mid. and no. dists.) Fla. 1963, U.S. Supreme Ct. 1975, U.S. Ct. Appeals (11th cir.) 1981; bd. cert. civil trial labor and employment law. Assoc. Dermer Rosen & Mofsky, Miami Beach, Fla., 1961-63; ptnr. Rosen & Chonin, Miami Beach, Fla., 1963-66, Goldstein, Franklin & Chonin, Miami Beach, Fla., 1966-72, Chonin & Sher, P.A., Coral Gables, Fla., 1972-92, Chonin, Sher & Navarette, Coral Gables, Fla., 1992—. Lectr. on trial advocacy. Contbr. articles to profl. jours. Pres. Legal Svcs. Greater Miami, 1974-76; chmn. 3d DCA Jud. Nominating Com., Miami, 1983-87. Named Man of Yr., ACLU, 1993, 94; recipient Tobias Simon Pro Bono award, 1984. Fellow Am. Acad. Matrimonial Lawyers (bd. mgrs. 1992), Am. Bd. Civil Trial Advs., Coll. Labor and Employment Law; mem. ATLA, Acad. Fla. Trial Lawyers, Family Inns of Ct. Office: Chonin Sher & Navarrete 95 Merrick Way Ste 100 Coral Gables FL 33134-5308

CHOO, ARTHUR C.S., structural engineer, consultant; b. Singapore, Oct. 19, 1927; s. Choo Siew Hong and Tham Sook Chee; m. Setsuko Tamashiro Choo, 1954 (div.); children: Arthur Jr., Victor. Student, U. Oreg., 1948—49; BSc in Engring., Oreg. State U., 1952; MS in Structural Engring., Yale U., 1954; MBA, Harvard U., 1956. Registered profl. engr., Mass., N.Y., Maine, R.I., Conn., Vt. Soil tester Ewart & Co., Singapore, 1947—48; draftsman Cornell, Howland, Hayes & Merryfield, Corvalis, Oreg., 1952—53; designer Cleverdon, Varney & Pike, Boston, 1953—56; engr. Linenthal and Becker, 1956—58, Hoyle, Doran & Berry, 1958—60; sr. engr. LeMessurier Assocs., 1960—64; pvt. practice, 1964—. Trustee Boston (Mass.) Evening Med. Ctr., 1980—, Arthur Choo Realty Trust, Keng Realty Trust, VAC Realty Trust, Am. Inst. Steel Constrn., Constrn. Specification Inst. Dir., trustee Boston (Mass.) Evening Clinic Found., 1985—, YMCA, South Cove, Mass., 1985—. Recipient Appreciation award, Gov. Mikael Dukakis, 1984, State of Mass., 1986. Mem.: ASCE, Am. Inst. Steel Constrn., Am. Concrete Inst. Home: 294 Rock Island Rd Quincy MA 02169 Office: Arthur Choo Assocs Inc 114 South St Boston MA 02111

CHOOK, PAUL HOWARD, publishing executive; b. N.Y.C., Oct. 17, 1929; s. Abraham and Etta (Cohen) C. BBA, CCNY, 1949; MS, Columbia U., 1950. Cons. quality control Philip Morris, Inc., N.Y.C., 1951-55; pres. media studies div. Alfred Politz Rsch., Inc., N.Y.C., 1955-66; v.p. rsch. Young & Rubicam, Inc., N.Y.C., 1966-74; pres. W.R. Simmons Rsch. Assocs., N.Y.C., 1974-75; exec. v.p. mktg. and circulation Ziff Davis Pub. Co., N.Y.C., 1975-84, sr. v.p. mktg., 1986-93; mktg. cons., 1993-95; exec. v.p. CBS Mags., N.Y.C., 1985; ind. mktg. cons., 1995—. Instr. CCNY, 1951-63. Sgt. N.Y. NG., 1948-56. Named Market Rsch. Coun. Hall of Fame, 1998. Mem. Advt. Rsch. Found. (bd. dirs. 1977-84), Am. Statis. Assn., Am. Mktg. Assn., Am. Assn. Pub. Opinion Rsch., Market Rsch. Coun. Jewish. Avocations: bridge, jogging. Home: 65-65 Wetherole St Flushing NY 11374-4764 Office Phone: 718-896-7097. E-mail: paulchook6@aol.com.

CHOPER, JESSE HERBERT, law educator, dean; b. Wilkes-Barre, Pa., Sept. 19, 1935; s. Edward and Dorothy (Resnick) C.; m. Mari Smith; children: Marc Steven, Edward Nathaniel. BS, Wilkes U., 1957, DHL, 1967; LLB, U. Pa., 1960. Bar: D.C. 1961. Instr. Wharton Sch. U. Pa., 1957-60; law clk. to Chief Justice Earl Warren U.S. Supreme Ct., 1960-61; asst. prof. U. Minn. Law Sch., 1961-62, assoc. prof., 1962-65; prof. Law Sch. U. Calif., Berkeley, 1965—, dean, 1982-92, Earl Warren prof. Pub. Law, 1991—. Vis. prof. Harvard U., 1970—71, Milan U., 1992, Autonoma U., Barcelona, 1996, Vrije U., Amsterdam, 1999, Fordham U., 1999, New South Wales U., 2002. Author: Constitutional Law: Cases-Comments-Questions, 9th edit., 2001, The American Constitution, Cases and Materials, 9th edit., 2001, Constitutional Rights and Liberties, Cases and Materials, 9th edit., 2001, Corporations, Cases and Materials, 6th edit., 2004, Judicial Review and the National Political Process, 1980, Securing Religious Liberty, 1995; contbr. articles to profl. jours. Mem. AAUP, Am. Law Inst., Am. Acad. Arts and Scis., Order of Coif. Jewish. Office: U Calif Sch Law Berkeley CA 94720-0001 Office Phone: 510-642-0339. Business E-Mail: choperj@law.berkeley.edu.

CHOPEY, NICHOLAS P., editor; b. N.Y.C., Dec. 22, 1932; s. Nicholas W. and Alice I. (Keshelak) C.; m. Katherine J. Heaney, Sept. 12, 1959; children: Nicholas, Michael, John, James. BChE, U. Va., 1955; MA in Econs., NYU, 1972. Process engr. Esso Standard Oil Co., Linden, NJ, 1955-56, 58-59; asst. assoc. editor McGraw-Hill, Inc., N.Y.C., 1960-67, sr. assoc. editor, 1967-72, mng. editor, 1972-78, exec. editor, 1978-82, editor-in-chief, 1982-87, 2000—, exec. editor, 1987-99, Chem. Week Assocs., 1999-2000, editor-in-chief, 2000—. Adv. com. Indsl. Energy Tech. Conf., Houston, 1992—. Editor: Handbook of Chemical Engineering Calculations, 1984, 3d edit., 2003; (reprint books) Environmental Engineering in the Process Plant, 1992, Fluid Movers, 1994. 1st lt. USAF, 1956-58. Mem. AIChE (past chair com.), Am. Soc. Engring. Edn., Knights of Malta, Roselle Golf Club, Tau Beta Pi. Roman Catholic. Office: Access Intelligence 110 William St New York NY 10038-3901

CHOPIN, L. FRANK, lawyer; b. New Orleans, Apr. 29, 1942; s. Alton Francis and Floretta (Thensted) C.; children: Philip, Alexandra, Christopher. BBA, Loyola U., New Orleans, 1964, JD, 1966; diploma in mil. law, Judge Adv. Gen.'s Sch., U. Va. Sch. Law, 1966; postgrad., Nat. Law Ctr., George Wash. U., 1967-68; LLM in Taxation, U. Miami, Fla., 1976; PhD in Law, Cambridge U., Eng., 1986. Bar: La. 1966, Fla. 1968, Iowa 1980, U.S. Dist. Ct. (so. dist.) Fla. 1968, U.S. Ct. Appeals (5th cir.) 1968. Ptnr. Chopin & Chopin, Miami, 1969-77; assoc. prof. law Drake U., Des Moines, 1979-80; ptnr. Cadwalader, Wickersham & Taft, Palm Beach, Fla., 1980-94, Chopin, Miller & Yudenfreund, Palm Beach, Fla., 1994-98, Chopin & Miller, Palm Beach, Fla., 2005—, L. Frank Chopin PLC, West Palm Beach, Fla., 2005—. Adj. prof. law U. Miami, 1982—96, U. Sherbrooke, Canada, 1982—94. Author: The New Residency Rules for Canadian Tax Considerations, 1985; also numerous articles in legal jours. Mem. Housing Fin. Authority; trustee Preservation Found., Palm Beach Community Chest, Inc. Served to capt. U.S. Army, 1966-68. Mem. ABA, Internat. Bar Assn., Fed. Bar Assn., Fla. Bar (tax sect.), Loyola U. Alumni Assn., U. Miami Alumni Assn., St. Thomas More Law Soc., Phi Alpha Delta (charter). Republican. Roman Catholic. Office: L Frank Chapin PLC PO Box 4297 West Palm Beach FL 33402 Office Phone: 561-655-9500.

CHOPIN, SUSAN GARDINER, lawyer; b. Miami, Fla., Feb. 23, 1947; d. Maurice and Judith (Warden) Gardiner; children: Philip, Alexandra, Christopher. BBA, Loyola U., New Orleans, 1966; JD cum laude, U. Miami, 1972; MLitt (Law), Oxford U., Eng., 1983. Bar: Fla. 1972, Iowa 1979. Sr. law clk. to judge U.S. Dist. Ct. (so. dist.) Fla., Miami, 1972-73; ptnr. Chopin & Chopin, Miami, 1973-77; assoc. prof. law sch. Drake U., Des Moines, 1979-80; pvt. practice law Palm Beach, Fla., 1981—; ptnr. Chopin & Chopin, 1999—2003, Chopin, Chopin & Chopin, 2003—, Chopin & Chopin, 2004—. Lectr. in family law. Editor (mem. editl. bd.): (jour.) Fla. Bar Jour., 1975; editor: (co-chair editl. bd.) Fla. Bar Family Law Commentator, 2000—01. Trustee Preservation Found. of Palm Beach, 1986-89. Mem.: Palm Beach County Bar Assn., Soc. Wig and Robe, Fla. Assn. Women Lawyers, Fed. Bar Assn., Iowa Bar Assn., Fla. Bar Assn., ABA, Phi Alpha Delta, Phi Kappa Phi. Office: Phillips Point West Tower 777 S Flager Dr Ste 800 West Palm Beach FL 33401 Office Phone: 561-651-7800. Office Fax: 561-651-7822. Business E-Mail: chopinlaw@bellsouth.net.

CHOPKO, MARK E., lawyer; b. Kingston, Pa., Nov. 4, 1953; s. Michael E. and Rose Ann C. (Gavlick) C.; m. Jane K. Chopko; children: Michael, Jessica, Laura, Sarah. BS summa cum laude, U. Scranton, 1974; JD cum laude, Cornell U., 1977. Bar: Pa. 1977, U.S. Supreme Ct. 1984, D.C. 1987. Gen. counsel U.S. Conf. Cath. Bishops, Washington, 1987—. Adj. prof. law Georgetown U. Law Ctr., 2004-; mem. religious liberty com. Nat. Coun. Chs., N.Y.C., 1987—. Mem. bd. editors Religious Freedom Reporter, N.C., 1987-2000; contbr. articles to profl. jours. Bd. advisors program on philanthropy and the law Sch. of Law, NYU, 1995-98; bd. dirs. Blessed Sacrament Sch., Alexandria, Va., 1986-88; legal advisor Ams. United for Life, Chgo., 1987-94; mem. legal scholars bd. DePaul Inst. for Ch.-State Studies, Chgo., 1988-2003; asst. coach basketball Cath. Youth Orgn., Alexandria, 1989-94. Recipient High Quality award U.S. Nuclear Regulatory Commn., 1982. Mem. ABA (vice chmn. religious, charitable and non-profit orgns. tort sect. 1990-92), Cath. Health Assn. (legal affairs com. 1988-96), Am. Corp. Counsel Assn. (com. on non-profit and profl. assn. law). Office: US Conf Cath Bishops 3211 4th St NE Washington DC 20017-1194

CHOPLIN, JOHN M., II, lawyer; b. Cedar Rapids, Iowa, Nov. 10, 1945; s. John M. and Joyce G. (Mickelsen) C.; m. Linda H. Kutchen, Feb. 14, 1969; children: Julie, John, James. BA, Drake U., 1967; JD, U. Mich., 1974. Bar: Ind. 1974, U.S. Dist. Ct. (so. dist.) Ind. 1974, U.S. Ct. Appeals (7th cir.) 1976, U.S. Supreme Ct. 1977, U.S. Ct. Appeals (6th cir.) 1983, U.S. Dist. Ct. (no. dist.) Ind. 1991. Assoc. Wilson, Tabor & Holland, Indpls., 1974-80; ptnr. Norris, Choplin & Schroeder, Indpls., 1980—. Committeeman precinct Carmel Reps., Ind., 1982-84. Served to capt. USAF, 1969-73. Mem. ABA, Ind. Bar Assn., Indpls. Bar Assn., 7th Fed. Cir. Bar Assn., Lawyers-Pilots Bar Assn., Ind. Trial Lawyers Assn., Assn. Trial Lawyers Am., Christian Legal Soc., Phi Beta Kappa, Omicron Delta Kappa. Baptist. Avocations: water sports, tennis, flying. Home: 8553 Twin Pointe Cir Indianapolis IN 46236-8903 Office: Norris Choplin & Schroeder 101 W Ohio St Ste 900 Indianapolis IN 46204-4213 Office Phone: 317-269-9330.

CHOPP, REBECCA S., academic administrator; m. Frederick H. Thibodeau; 3 children. BA, Kans. Wesleyan U., 1974; MDiv, St. Paul Sch. Theology, 1977; PhD, U. Chgo., 1983; DD (hon.), Lehigh U. Asst. prof. theology U. Chgo. Div. Sch., 1982—86; asst. prof. Candler Sch. and Grad. Divsn. Religion Emory U., Atlanta, 1986—89, assoc. faculty Inst. Liberal Arts, 1987, assoc. faculty Inst. for Women's Studies, 1987, dean of faculty and acad. affairs Candler Sch. of Theology, 1993—97, prof. theology Candler Sch. and Grad. Divsn. Religion, 1993, Charles Howard Chandler prof. theology Grad. Divsn., 1996, interim provost, v.p. acad. affairs, 1997—98, provost, exec. v.p. for acad. affairs, 1998—2001, dir. grad. studies Inst. for Women's Studies; dean, Titus Street prof. theology and culture Yale U. Div. Sch., 2001—02; pres., prof. philosophy and religion Colgate U., 2002—. Bd. dirs. Scholars Press; trustee Carnegie Found. Author: The Praxis of Suffering: An Interpretation of Liberation and Political Theologies, 1986, The Power to Speak: Feminism, Language, God, 1989, Saving Work: Feminist Practices of Theological Education, 1995; Co-editor: Differing Horizons: Feminist Theory and Theology, 1997, Reconstructing Christian Theology, 1999; theology editor Religious Studies Rev., 1989-93; editor-at-large Christian Century, 1989-95; editor Quar. Rev., 1998-; editl. bd. Emory Theol. Studies, Religion and Ideology, Jour. of Religion, Word and World, Internat. Jour. of Practical Theology; contbr. articles to profl. publs. Recipient Alumna Achievement award Kans. Wesleyan U., 1990, Disting. Alumna award St. Paul Sch. of Theology, 1991, Founder's Day award Baker U., 1995, Alumna of Yr. award U. Chgo. Divinity Sch., 1997. Mem. Am. Acad. of Religion (pres. southeastern divsn.), Am. Theol. Soc. (chair women in leadership project). Office: Colgate U 13 Oak Dr Hamilton NY 13346

CHOPPIN, GREGORY ROBERT, chemistry professor; b. Eagle Lake, Tex., Nov. 9, 1927; s. Gilbert P. and Nellie M. (Guidroz) C.; m. Ann M. Warner; children: Denise, Suzanne, Paul, Nadine. BS in Chemistry, Loyola U., New Orleans, 1949, DSc (hon.), 1969; PhD in Chemistry, U. Tex, 1953; DSc Tech. (hon.), Chalmers U., Göteborg, Sweden, 1985. Rsch. scientist Lawrence Radiation Lab., Berkeley, Calif., 1953-56; faculty Fla. State U., Tallahassee, 1956—, R.O. Lawton Disting. prof. chemistry, 1968—2001, prof. emeritus, 2001—. Vis. scientist Centre d'Etude Nucleaire Mol, Belgium, 1962-63; vis. prof. Sci. U. Tokyo, 1978; vis. scientist European Transuranium Inst., Karlsruhe, Germany, 1979-80, 95; cons. Argonne Nat. Lab., Los Alamos Nat. Lab., N.Mex., Lawrence Livermore Nat. Lab., Calif., Brookhaven Nat. Lab., N.Y., Sandia Nat. Lab., N.Mex., Kaiser-Hill Co., Archimedes Tech. Co.; served on panels and coms. of NRC, including bds. chem. sci. and tech. and radioactive waste mgmt. Co-author: Nuclear Chemistry: Theory and Applications, 1980, 2d edit., 1995, 3d edit., 2002; editor: Plutonium Chemistry, 1983, Actinide-Lanthanide Separations, 1985, Lanthanide Probes in Life, Chemical and Earth Sciences, 1989, Principles and Practice of Solvent Extraction, 1992, 2d edit., 2004, Separations of f-Elements, 1995, Chemical Separation Technologies and Related Methods of Nuclear Waste Management, 1999; mem. editl. bd. sci. jours. including Handbook on Physics and Chemistry of Rare Earths; co-discoverer of chemical element 101 Mendelevium; contbr. over 450 articles to sci. jours. Served to cpl. U.S. Army, 1946-48. Recipient Alexander von Humboldt Stiftung award, 1979, Chem. Mfrs. Assn. Edn. award, 1979, Seaborg Actinide Separations Sci. award, 1989, Presdl. citation, Am. Nuclear Soc., 1991, Scientist of Yr. award, Fla. Acad. Sci., 1992, Spedding award, N.Am. Rare Earth Rsch. Conf., 1996, Chem. Pioneer award, Am. Inst. Chemistry, 1997, Becquerel medal, Brit. Royal Soc. Chem., 2000, George Hevesy medal, Jour. Radiology and Nuc. Chem., 2005. Fellow AAAS; mem. Am. Chem. Soc. (award Fla. sect. 1973, So. Chemist award 1971, award in Nuclear Chemistry 1985, OESPER award Cin. sect. 1995), Royal Soc. Arts and Sci. (hon. fgn. mem.) (Sweden), Rare Earth Rsch. Conf. (pres. bd. 1981-83, chmn. 16th conf. 1983), Sigma Xi, Phi Beta Kappa. Avocations: sailing, racquetball. Home: 3290 Longleaf Rd Tallahassee FL 32310-6406 Office: Fla State U Dept Chemistry and Biochemistry Dittmer Bldg Tallahassee FL 32306-4390 Office Phone: 850-644-3875. Business E-Mail: choppin@chem.fsu.edu.

CHOPPIN, PURNELL WHITTINGTON, science administrator; b. Baton Rouge, July 4, 1929; s. Arthur Richard and Eunice Dolores (Bolin) Choppin; m. Joan Harriet Macdonald, Oct. 17, 1959; 1 child, Kathleen Marie. MD, La. State U., 1953; DSc (hon.), Emory U., 1988, La. State U., 1988; MD, MD, D Medicine, U. Cologne, 1988; DSc (hon.), Tulane U., 1989, Washington U., 1991, Med. U. S.C., 1995, U. Md., Baltimore County, 1995; DHL (hon.), Mt.

Sinai Sch. Medicine, 1996; DSc (hon.), U. Mass., 1999, Northwestern U., 1999; LLD (hon.), St. Francis Xavier U., 2000; DSc (hon.), Rockefeller U., 2000, Johns Hopkins U., 2002. Diplomate Am. Bd. Internal Medicine. Intern Barnes Hosp., St. Louis, 1953—54, asst. resident, 1956—57; fellow, rsch. assoc. Rockefeller U., N.Y.C., 1957—60, asst. prof., 1960—64, assoc. prof., 1957—60, prof., sr. physician, 1970—85, Leon Hess prof. virology, 1980—85, v.p. acad. programs, 1983—85, dean grad. studies, 1985; v.p., chief sci. officer Howard Hughes Med. Inst., Chevy Chase, Md., 1985—87, pres., 1987—99, pres. emeritus, 2000—; prin. Washington Adv. Group, 2000—. Chmn. sect. 43 microbiology and immunology NAS, 1989—92, chmn. class IV med. scis., 1983—86, mem. com. on reorganization structure, 1985—86, coun., 2000—, Inst. Medicine, 1987—92, exec. com., 1988—91; mem. virology study sect. NIH, 1968—72, chmn. virology study sect., 1975—78; bd. dirs. Royal Soc. Medicine Found. Inc., N.Y.C., 1978—93; mem. adv. com. fundamental rsch. Nat. Multiple Sclerosis Soc., 1979—84, chmn. adv. com. fundamental rsch., 1983—84; mem. adv. coun. Nat. Inst. Allergy and Infectious Diseases, 1980—83; mem. bd. scis., cons. Meml. Sloan-Kettering Cancer Ctr., N.Y.C., 1981—86, chmn. bd. scis., 1983—84; co-chair NRA Task Force Goals and Ops., 1999—2000; mem. commn. on life scis. NRC, Washington, 1982—87; mem. sci. rev. com. Scripps Clinic and Rsch. Found., La Jolla, Calif., 1983—85, chmn. sci. rev. com., 1984; mem. coun. for rsch. and clin. investigation Am. Cancer Soc., N.Y.C., 1983—85; mem. com. priorities for vaccine devel. Inst. Medicine, Washington; mem. governing bd. NRC, 1990—92. Contbr. articles to profl. pubs., chapters to books on virology, cell biology, infectious diseases, 1958; editor: Procs. Soc. Exptl. Biology and Medicine, 1966—69; assoc. editor: Virology, 1969—72; editor, 1973—86; assoc. editor: Jour. Immunology, 1968—72, Jour. Supramolecular Structure, 1972—75, mem. editl. bd.: Jour. Virology, 1972—85, Comprehensive Virology, 1972, mem. overseas adv. panel: Biochem. Jour., 1973—77. Capt. USAF, 1954—56, Japan. Named to alumni Hall of Distinction, La. State U., Baton Rouge, 1983; recipient Howard Taylor Ricketts award, U. Chgo., 1978, Waksman award for Excellence in Microbiology, NAS, 1984, Alumni Achievement award, Washington U. Sch. Medicine, 1990, Dean's medal, Harvard Med. Sch., 1992, Meml. Sloan-Kettering medal for outstanding contbns. to biomed. rsch., 1998, Spl. Recognition award, Assn. Am. Med. Colls., 1999, medal, U. Calif. San Francisco, 2000. Fellow: AAAS; mem.: NAS, Am. Soc. Virology (pres. 1985—86), Am. Clin. and Climatological Assn., Practitioners Soc. N.Y., Infectious Diseases Soc. Am., Soc. Cell Biology, Am. Assn. Immunologists, Harvey Soc., Am. Soc. Microbiology (chmn. virology divsn. 1977—79, divsn. group councilor 1983—85), Am. Soc. Clin. Investigation, Assn. Am. Physicians, Am. Philos. Soc. (coun. 1998—, v.p. 2000—), Am. Acad. Arts and Scis., Alpha Omega Alpha, Sigma Xi (chpt. pres. 1980—81). Office: Howard Hughes Med Inst 4000 Jones Bridge Rd Chevy Chase MD 20815-6789

CHOPPING, MARK, science educator; BA, U. of Exeter, Eng., 1981; MPhil, U. of Cambridge, Eng., 1995; PhD, U. of Nottingham, Eng., 1998. Post-doctoral fellow USDA, Agrl. Rsch. Svc., Beltsville, Md., 1999—2001, Las Cruces, N.Mex., 2001—02; asst. prof. Montclair State U., Montclair, NJ, 2002—. Prin. investigator Montclair State U., 2004—. Contbr. articles to profl. jours. Recipient Cert. of Merit For Outstanding Performance, USDA, Agrl. Rsch. Svc., 1999—2001; grantee, NASA grantee, 2004—. Mem.: NASA Land Cover Land Use Change Sci. Team, NASA Multiangle Imaging SpectroRadiometer Sci. Team, Am. Geophys. Union (mem. 2003—05), IEEE Geosci. and Remote Sensing Soc. (mem. 2002—05), The Remote Sensing and Photogrammetry Soc. (mem. 1994—2005, Best Master's Thesis 1996), Gamma Theta Upsilon (mem. 2002—05). Achievements include research in advancing earth observation in the solar wavelengths with BRDF modeling. Avocations: travel, classical guitar. Office Phone: 973-655-7384.

CHOPRA, DEEPAK, preventive medicine physician, writer; Medical dir. of edn. prog., CEO, founder The Chopra Center, La Costa Resort and Spa, 1995—. Author: Return of the Rishi, 1989, Quantum Healing, 1990, Perfect Health, 1990, Unconditional Life, 1991, Creating Health, 1991, Creating Affluence, 1993, Ageless Body, Timeless Mind, 1993, Restful Sleep, 1994, Perfect Weight, 1994, Journey Into Healing, 1994, The Seven Spiritual Laws of Success, 1995, Return of Merlin, 1995, Como Crear Abundancia/How to Create Wealth, 1999, Everyday Immorality: A Concise Course in Spiritual Transformation, 1999, How to Know God: The Soul's Journey into the Mystery of Mysteries, 2000, The Daughters of Joy: An Adventure of the Heart, 2002, Book of Secrets: Unlocking the Hidden Dimensions of Your Life, 2004, Peace Is the Way: Bringing War and Violence to an End in Our Time, 2005; (with David Simons, Vicki Abrams) Magical Beginnings, Enchanted Lives, 2005. Office: Chopra Ctr for Well Being 2100 Costa del Mar Rd Carlsbad CA 92009*

CHOPRA, DHARAM P., medical educator, researcher; b. Padhana, India, Feb. 2, 1944; arrived in U.S., 1971; BS, U. Delhi, 1963; MS, U. London, 1967; PhD, U. Newcastle Upon Tyne, 1971; MBA, Samford U., 1983. Asst. prof. Temple U., Phila., 1971—74; sr. scientist, sect. head So. Rsch. Inst., Birmingham, Ala., 1974—88; prof. Wayne State U., Detroit, 1988—. Grantee, NIH. Mem.: AAAS, Am. Assn. Cancer Rsch. Office: Wayne State U 2727 2d Ave #4000 Detroit MI 48201

CHOPRA, DHARAM VIR, statistician, educator; b. Oct. 15, 1930; s. Achhru and Vidya Wati (Sondhi) C.; m. Miran Devi Suri, Jan. 1969; 1 child, Sandeep K. MA, Panjab U., 1953; MS, U. Mich., 1961, MA in Psychology, 1963; PhD, U. Nebr., 1968. Lectr. math. M. Tech. Inst., Jalandhar, India, 1953—59; instr. math. U. Nebr., Lincoln, 1963—66; asst. prof. So. Colo. State U., Pueblo, 1966—67; asst. prof. stats. Wichita State U., Kans., 1967—71, assoc. prof., 1971—76, prof., 1976—, chmn. math. dept., 1985—. Contbr. articles to profl. jours. Mem.: Indian Statis. Assn., Indian Math. Soc., Internat. Assn. Survey Statisticians, Inst. Math. Stats., Am. Stats. Assn. Avocations: hiking, travel. Office: Wichita State U Dept Math and Stats Wichita KS 67260-0033 Office Phone: 316-978-3970. Business E-Mail: dharam.chopra@wichita.edu.

CHOPRA, INDER JIT, endocrinologist; b. Gujranwala, India, Dec. 15, 1939; came to U.S., 1967; s. Kundan Lal and Labhwati (Bagga) C.; m. Usha Prakash, Oct. 16, 1966; children: Sangeeta, Rajesh, Madhu. B of Medicine and BS, All India Inst. Med. Scis., New Delhi, India, 1961, MD, 1965. Intern All India Inst. Med. Scis., New Delhi, 1961-62, clin. resident, 1962-65, registrar in medicine, 1966-67; resident Queens Med. Ctr., Honolulu, 1967-68; fellow in endocrinology Harbor Gen. Campus UCLA Sch. Medicine, 1968-71; asst. prof. of medicine UCLA, 1971-74, assoc. prof., 1974-78, prof., 1978—. Mem. VA Merit Rev. Bd. in Endocrinology, 1988-91. Contbr. more than 280 rsch. articles, revs. and book chpts. to profl. lit. Recipient Rsch. Career Devel. award, NIH, 1972. Master Am. Coll. Physicians; mem. Endocrine Soc. (Ernst Oppenheimer award 1980), Am. Thyroid Assn. (Van Meter-Armour award 1977, Parke-Davis award 1988, Disting. Svc. award 1995), Am. Soc. Clin. Investigation, Assn. of Am. Physicians, Western Assn. Physicians, Am. Fed. for Clin. Rsch. Achievements include patent for radioimmunoassay for measurement of thyroxine and triiodothyonine. Office: UCLA Sch Medicine Ctr for Health Scis 24-130 Warren Hall 900 Veteran Ave Los Angeles CA 90024-2703 Office Phone: 310-825-2346. Business E-Mail: ichopra@mednet.ucla.edu.

CHOPRA, PARVEEN CHANDER, management consultant, educator, researcher, community activist; b. Punjab, India, May 2, 1941; came to U.S., 1970, naturalized, 1981; s. Om Parkash and Sumitra C.; m. Usha Bhatt, Sept. 6, 1970; children: Samir, Sachin. MA in Sociology with cert. of merit, Punjab U., India, 1966; MA with hons. in Pers. Mgmt. and Indsl. Rels., Tata Inst. Social Scis., India, 1968; BL, Bombay U., India, 1970; MBA, Baruch Coll., 1979; MPhil, CUNY, 1993, PhD in Bus. Adminstrn., 1997. Instr. mgmt. Hofstra U., Hempstead, N.Y., 1978-85, Rutgers U., Newark, N.J., 1977-78; asst. prof. mgmt. L.I. U., N.Y., 1985-86, Kean Coll., N.J., 1986-91. Adj. prof. Stevens Inst. Tech., N.J., 1981-84, Fordham U., 1985—; coord. L.I. Jewish Abbott House Project, 1973-75; cons. N.Y. State Legis. Inst., 1978-81; cons. on cultural diversity Mgmt. to Nassau County Med. ctr., 1997, Police Acad. 1999; mgr. adminstrn. Franco-Indian Pharms., Bombay, 1970; manpower mgmt. officer New India Assurance Co., Bombay, 1968-70; pers. mgr. Bofan Indian Textile Corp., Bombay, 1967-68; commr. human rights Nassau County, N.Y., 1989—; vice chmn. Human Rights Commn., Nassau County, 1996—, commr. planning 1996—; pres. Sunshine Mgmt. Svcs. Inc., 1998—. Author: Surveys on New York City Civil Servants, 1977, Corporate Crimes and Executive Liability: Analysis, Trends and Policy Guidelines, 1991; (with others) Organizational Communications, 1981-85; contbr. articles to profl. jours. Bd. dirs. Fedn. Indian Assns., N.Y., N.J., Conn., 1983—, pres. 1987-88; bd. dirs. Indian Assn. L.I., 1983—, pres. 1989-90; v.p. Indian-Am. Forum for Polit. Edn., 1990-92; bd. dirs. Nassau Arts Decentralization Consortium, 1991—; mem. exec. com. Martin Luther King Jr. Celebration Com., 1990—; convener World Conf. Internat. Punjabi Soc. N.Y., 1991; founding mem. Nassau County Diversity Seminar, 1995—; sec. Nargis Dutt Meml. Found., 1995-96, v.p. 1997—; apptd. mem. steering com. for Asian Am. for Bush-Quayle, 1992; at-large del. Nat. Rep. Party planning com., 1996—; co-chair Bus. Coun. Global Orgn. People of Indian Origin, 1999—. Recipient numerous honors. Mem. Nat. Fedn. Indian Am. Assns. (sec. 1992-94, exec. bd.), Jackson Heights Merchants' Assn. (N.Y., founder 1989—), Flushing Merchants' Assn. (N.Y., founder 1990—), Kiwanis Internat. (treas.), Baldwin Rep. Club (exec. bd.), Nassau County Rep. Party (committeeman election dists. in Baldwin), Ea. Acad. Mgmt., Acad. Mgmt. U.S.A., Indsl. Rels. Rsch. Assn. Avocations: marathon running, mountain climbing, indian dances. Office: PO Box 0165 Baldwin NY 11510-0165

CHOPRA, PRADEEP, physician, educator; m. Shalini Chopra, Dec. 12, 1994. MD, Harvard U., 2001. Diplomate Am. Bd. Anesthesiology, 2002, sub speciality cert. in pain mgmt. Am. Bd. Anesthesiology, 2002. Asst. prof. Boston U. Med. Sch., 2001—; dir. Pain Mgmt. Ctr., So. New Eng. Anesthesia and Pain Assocs., Providence, 2002—. Contbr. chapters to books, articles to profl. jours. Recipient John Hedley-Whyte prize in Critical Care Medicine, Harvard Med. Sch., 2000, Nancy E. Oriol prize in Obstetric Anesthesia, 2000. Mem.: Am. Soc. for Interventional Pain Physicians (dir. R.I. divsn. 2002—). Achievements include design of medical simulation model for a stuck expiratory valve. Office: Southern New England Anesthesia and Pain 102 Smithfield Ave Pawtucket RI 02860 Personal E-mail: painri@yahoo.com.

CHOPYK, DAN BOHDAN, language educator, poet; b. Beneva-Ternopol, Poland, Jan. 2, 1925; came to U.S., 1957; s. Gregory W. and Olga T. (Jankow) C.; m. Helen Nancy Sabin, June 28, 1956 (div. Nov. 1, 1977); children: Robin G., Mimi N., William B., Alexander R.; m. Aleksandra A. Kudryasheva, Dec. 19, 1990. Degree in philosophy, Ukrainian Theol. Sem., Hirschberg, Germany, 1947; B in Commerce, U. Birmingham, Eng., 1953; MA, U. Colo., 1962; LLB, Ukrainian Free U., Munich, 1963; PhD in Philology, Ukrainian Free U. and U. Colo., 1970; PhD, Internat. Info. Acad., 1998. Tchr. Jefferson County (Colo.) Pub. Schs., 1958-65; instr. Regis Coll., Denver, 1965; tchg. fellow U. Colo., Boulder, 1966-67; asst. prof., prof. U. Utah, Salt Lake City, 1969-96; pres. World Cossack Acad., N.Y.C., 1998—. Author: Guide to teaching, 1963, Navchania Movy, 1976, Movonavchania, 1997, Metodologia, 1994, G. Skovoroda His Life and Times, 1994, (poetry) Shlyakhy ta dumky, 1981, Zhyvy Zhyttya, 1983, 2000; Yar Slavutych Bohdan Chopyk-tvorchi dorohy vchenykh, 2004; Istorychni Hayku, 2004; poetry translations; co-editor: Nasha Mova Jour., 1975. Bd. dirs. Internat. Ctr. Nutrition and Health Rehab. Fellow Fullbright Found., 1986, NEH, 1983, 84. Mem. Internat. Franko Soc., Delta Tau Kappa. Democrat. Avocations: poetry, translating, cossackdom, travel. Home and Office: 106 Guadeloupe Dr Toms River NJ 08757

CHOQUETTE, PAUL JOSEPH, JR., construction company executive; b. Providence, July 24, 1938; s. Paul Joseph and Virginia Josephine (Gilbane) C.; m. Elizabeth Walsh, Aug. 18, 1962; children: Jeanne Marie, Denise Elizabeth, Suzanne, Christine Noell, Paul Joseph III. BA, Brown U., 1960; LL.B., Harvard U., 1963. Assoc. firm Edwards & Angell, Providence, 1963-65; gov.'s legal counsel State of RI, Providence, 1965-67; assoc. Edwards & Angell, 1967-69; gen. counsel Gilbane Bldg. Co., Providence, 1969-71, v.p., 1971-75, exec. v.p., 1975-81, dir., CEO, 1981—2004, chmn. Bd. dirs. FleetBoston Fin. Group, Ea. Utilities Assn., Carbide Corp., Carlisle Co.; chmn. bd. Gilbane Properties Inc. Dir. Nat. Football Found. and Coll. Hall of Fame; co-chmn. RI Econ. Policy Coun.; bd. trustee emeritus Brown U. Nat. Football Found. scholar, 1959; recipient Silver Ann. award NCAA, 1985. Mem. Greater Providence C. of C. (past pres., dir.) Clubs: Dunes, Hope, University. Roman Catholic. Office: Gilbane Bldg Co 7 Jackson Walkway Providence RI 02903

CHORBA, TIMOTHY A., former ambassador to Singapore; b. Yonkers, N.Y., Sept. 23, 1946; BA magna cum laude, Georgetown U., 1968; JD, Harvard U., 1972. Bar: N.Y. 1973, D.C. 1977, US Dist. Ct. (so. & ea. NY dist.), US Ct. Appeals (2d cir.). Legis. counsel to Hon. Jonathan B. Bingham U.S. Ho. of Reps., 1972-73; ptnr. Patton, Boggs & Blow, Washington, 1977—94; amb. to Singapore, 1994-97; ptnr., Public Policy & Bus. Law practices Patton Boggs LLP, Washington, 1998—. Bd. dir. Wolfcraft Inc. Fulbright scholar in Internat. Law and Internat. Rels., U. Heidelberg, West Germany, 1968-69. Mem. D.C. Bar, Phi Beta Kappa, Coun. Am. Ambs. Office: Patton Boggs LLP 2550 M St NW Washington DC 20037-1350 Office Phone: 202-457-6000. Office Fax: 202-457-6315. Business E-Mail: tchorba@pattonboggs.com.

CHORENGEL, BERND, international hotel corporation executive; b. Itzehoe/Holstein, Germany, 1944; Student, Columbia U., Cornell U. With Hilton Hotels, Bangkok, Manila, Hong Kong; exec. asst. mgr. food and beverage Hyatt Regency Hong Kong, 1969—70, resident mgr. then mgr., 1970—73; gen. mgr. Hyatt Singapore, 1973—79; v.p. S.E. Asia Hyatt Internat. Corp., 1979—82, sr. v.p. Europe, Africa and the Middle East, 1982, exec. v.p., COO, 1982—84, pres. Chgo., 1984—, also bd. dirs.; gen. mgr. Hyatt Carlton Tower, London, 1982. Bd. dirs. Hyatt Hotel Corp.; founding mem. Singapore Conv. Bur.; former dir. Singapore Indsl. Tng. Bd., former chmn. hotel and restaurant trade adv. com. Active Chgo.-Hamburg Sister Cities Program. Recipient Corp. Hotelier of the World award, 1990. Office: Hyatt Internat Hotels Corp Madison Plz 200 W Madison St Chicago IL 60606-3414

CHORIN, ALEXANDRE JOEL, mathematician, educator; b. Warsaw, June 25, 1938; came to U.S., 1962, naturalized, 1971; s. Joseph and Hannah (Judowicz) C.; m. Alice Louise Jones, Aug. 11, 1965; 1 son, Ethan Daniel. Diploma in engring., Swiss Fed. Inst. Tech., Lausanne, 1961; MSc, NYU, 1964, PhD, 1966; DSc (hon.), Israel Inst. Tech., 2003, Swiss Fed. Inst. Tech., 2005. Rsch. scientist NYU, 1966-69, asst. prof. math., 1969-71; assoc. prof. U. Calif., Berkeley, 1972-73, prof., 1973—, Miller rsch. prof., 1971-72, 82-83, Chancellor's prof., 1997-2000, Univ. prof., 2002—; sr. staff scientist Lawrence Berkeley Lab., 1980—; dir. Ctr. Pure and Applied Math. U. Calif., Berkeley, 1980—82, 1995—2004. Disting. vis. prof. Inst. for Advanced Study, Princeton, N.J., 1991-92; faculty rsch. lectr. U. Calif., Berkeley, 1999-00; vis. prof. Coll. France, 1992. Author: (with J. Marsden) A Mathematical Introduction to Fluid Dynamics, 1979, Computational Fluid Mechanics, selected papers, 1989, Vorticity and Turbulence, 1994; contbr. articles to profl. jours. Recipient Nat. Acad. Scis. award in applied math. and numerical analysis, 1989, Norbert Wiener prize Am. Math. Soc. and Soc. for Indsl. and Applied Math., 2000; fellow Sloan Found., 1972-74, Guggenheim Found., 1987-88. Fellow Am. Acad. Arts and Scis.; mem. NAS. Home: 1800 Spruce St Apt 201 Berkeley CA 94709 Office: U Calif Dept Math Berkeley CA 94720-0001 E-mail: chorin@math.berkeley.edu.

CHOROSINSKI, EUGENE CONRAD, writer, poet, author; b. Sienno, Poland, Jan. 1, 1930; came to the U.S., 1954, naturalized, 1961; s. Jozef Chorosinski and Weronika Religa; m. Anni Homeier, Mar. 23, 1959; children: Heidi Marie, Ramona Angela, Veronica Ann. LLB, Blackstone Sch. of Law, 1968; MLitt (hon.), World Acad. Letters, 2005. Chief field classification AMS, Ehiopia-U.S. Mapping Mission, Addis Ababa, 1965-67; intelligence analyst Combined Intelligence Ctr. Vietnam, 1968-69; sr. intelligence advisor DCAT 70, Lai Khe, South Vietnam, 1970-71; intelligance analyst 1st Armored Divsn., Support Command, Nuremberg, Germany, 1971-73; pvt. investigator Alexandria, Va., Md., Va., Washington, 1973-74; chief zoning review Dept. of Consumer and Regulatory Affairs, Govt. D.C., 1974-85; chmn. disaster damage assessment ARC, Ctrl. Fla. chpt., Orlando, Fla., 1995-96; freelance writer Eustis, Fla., 1996-99; ret., 1999. Author: (novels) Through the Years, 1995, Days Remembered, 1999, Eugene's Saga to Freedom, War and Poetry, 2001; co-author: (anthologies) The Nat. Libr. Poetry, Famous Poets Soc., Sparrowgrass Poetry Forum, Poetry Guild, Internat. Libr. Poetry; contbr. articles to profl. jours. Mem. Rep. Nat. com., 1994—; mem. Rep. Presdl. Trust; mem. City of Eustis Parks and Trees Commn., 1996—, chmn., 1998-99; vol. Orlando (Fla.) VA Healthcare Ctr., 2001—, literacy tutor, Lake County Libr. Sys., 2003—. Decorated Bronze star, Air medal, Joint Svc. Commendation medal, Army Commendation medal, Nat. DSM with bronze svc. star, Vietnam Svc. medal with silver star, others; recipient Editor's Choice award for Outstanding Achievement in Poetry Nat. Libr. of Poetry, Honor Award Spl. Citation for Exceptional Vol. Svc., ARC, 1994, Shakespeare Trophy of Excellence award, Eugene Conrad Chorosinski Poet of Yr. Medallion award, 2002; named Best Poet, 1995, 96; declared and selected as the Poet of the Millennium 2000, Internat. Poets Acad., Chennai-86, India, Excellence in World Poetry award, 2002; named to Famous Poets Soc., recipient Diamond Homer trophy, 1998; Internat. Poetry Hall of Fame; Internat. Peace Prize award, United Cultural Convention U.S.A., 2002, Voluntary Svc. medal Dept. Vets. Affairs, U.S.A., 2003. Mem. VFW, DAV, Internat. Soc. of Poets (life, Poet of Merit award 2001), Nat. Assn. Ret. Fed. Employees. Roman Catholic. Avocations: chess, travel, ping pong/table tennis. Home: 131 Madrona Dr Eustis FL 32726-2016

CHORPENNING, H. R., III, minister; b. Arlington Heights, Ill., Aug. 28, 1960; s. Harry R. and Margaret E. Chorpenning; m. Jean M. Sanfacon, May 7, 1988; children: Cameron Hayes, Christopher Eddy. Student, U. St. Andrews, Scotland, 1981—82; BA magna cum laude, U. Calif., Santa Barbara, 1983; MDiv with distinction, Iliff Sch. Theology, Denver, 1999. Ordained min. United Ch. of Christ. Dir. devel. comm. U. Calif., Santa Barbara, 1985—87; sr. writer Stanford (Calif.) U., 1987—89; owner Hal Chorpenning Comm., Boulder, Colo., 1989—99; assoc. conf. min. Conn. Conf. United Ch. of Christ, Hartford, 1999—2002; sr. min. Plymouth Congl. Ch., Fort Collins, Colo., 2002—. Bd. dirs. Elderly Housing Mgmt., Hamden, Conn., 1999-2002, Cmty. Housing Mgmt., 1999-2002, Iliff Religious Leadership Conf.; mem. Colo. Coun. Chs. Mem. The Coalition, Interfaith Alliance, Westar Inst., Clergy Leadership Network, Phi Beta Kappa. Avocations: sea kayaking, swimming, classical music. Office: Plymouth Congregational Church UCC 916 W Prospect Rd Fort Collins CO 80526

CHORY, JOHN H., lawyer; b. 1958; BS in computer sci. & psychology, with honors, U.S. Mil. Acad. West Point, 1980; MBA with honors, Golden Gate U., 1984; JD cum laude, Harvard Law Sch., 1988. Bar: Mass. 1988. Joined Wilmer, Culter, Pickering, Hale & Dorr LLP, Boston, 1988, ptnr., mem. Corp. dept., office ptnr.-in-charge Waltham, mem. exec. com.; chmn. Hale & Dorr Venture Group, Waltham. Teaching asst. Harvard Negotiation Project. Contbr. articles to profl. jours. USAR, 1978—88, intelligence officer U.S. Army. Named a Mass. Super Lawyer-securities & venture fin., Boston. Mag., 2004, High Tech All Star, Mass High Tech, 2002; named one of Boston's top lawyers, Boston Mag., 2002. Mem.: MIT Enterprise Forum (adv. bd.). Office: Hale & Dorr Venture Group Bay Colony Corporate Ctr 1100 Winter St Waltham MA 02451 Office Phone: 781-966-2001. Office Fax: 781-966-2100. Business E-Mail: john.chory@wilmerhale.com.

CHOU, CHARISSA J., staff scientist; d. Si-Ying and Chung Yi Kao. BA in acctg., Nat. Taiwan U., 1966; PhD in statistics, Kans. State U., 1972. CPA Pa., 1981. Statistician Kans. State U., Manhattan, Kans., 1972—73; asst. prof. Villanova U., Pa., 1974—81, assoc. prof., 1981—85; sys. analyst Rockwell Hanford Operations, Richland, Wash., 1985—88; principal scientist Westinghouse Hanford Co., Richland, 1988—93, prin. scientist, 1993—96; staff scientist V PAcific Northwest Nat. Lab., Richland, 1996—. Edtl. bd. Jour. of Environ. Monitoring and Assessment, Dordrecht, Netherlands, 2004—. Contbr. articles various profl. jours. and cptrs. in books. Recipient Outstanding Performance Svc. award, Pacific Northwest Nat. Lab., 2000, 2001, 2003, 2004, Women's Hist. Month Cert. of Honor award, 1998. Mem.: Nat. Rep. Com., Tri-Cities Chinese/Am. Assn. Achievements include development of liquid effluent monitoring program at the U.S. Dept. of Energy Hanford site. Avocations: gardening, travel, hiking. Office: Pacific Northwest Nat Lab PO Box 999 Battelle Blvd K6 75 Richland WA 99354 Office Fax: 509-376-2210. E-mail: charissa.chou@pnl.gov.

CHOU, CHIENTZU CANDACE, education educator; d. Kerpeng Chou and Guaiying Chiu; m. Stephen Philion, Apr. 12, 2001; 1 child, Langston Richard Chou Philion. PhD, U. of Hawaii at Manoa, 1995—2001. Asst. prof. U. of St. Thomas, Mpls., 2002—; assoc. dir. U. of Minn. Coll. of Liberal Arts Lang. Ctr., 2001—02; ednl. assoc. U. of Hawaii at Manoa, 2001; instrnl. designer Nat. Fgn. Lang. Resource Ctr., Manoa, Hawaii, 1994—2000; intern Sun Microsystem, Broomfield, Colo., 2000. Contbr. articles to profl. jours. Recipient Winner of First Ann. Campus Tech. Competition, U. of Hawaii-Manoa, 1996; Minn. Educators and Leaders Tech. Initiatives, Minn. Dept. of Edn., 2004, Improvement of Access to Computing, U. of Minn., 2001, Ednl. Enrichment, Bank of Hawaii, 2000, K.S. Cheng Meml. scholarship, U. of Hawaii, 1998. Mem.: Internat. Soc. for Tech. in Edn., Assn. for the Advancement of Computing in Edn., Assn. for Edn. and Communication Tech., Am. Ednl. Rsch. Assn., ASCD, Asia-Pacific Soc. for Computers in Edn. Achievements include design of first online chinese reading and writing course at the university of Hawaii.

CHOU, CHUNG-KWANG, bio-engineer; b. Chung-King, China, May 11, 1947; came to the U.S., 1969, naturalized, 1979; s. Chin-Chi and Yu-Lien (Hsiao) C.; m. Grace Wong, June 9, 1973; children: Jeffrey, Angela. BSEE, Nat. Taiwan U., 1968; MSEE, Washington U., 1971; PhD, U. Wash., 1975. Postdoctoral fellow U. Wash., Seattle, 1976-77, asst. prof., 1977-81, rsch. assoc. prof., 1981-85; rsch. scientist, head biomed. engring. sect. City of Hope Nat. Med. Ctr., Duarte, Calif., 1985-98, dir. dept. radiation rsch. divsn. radiation oncology, 1985-98; dir. Corp. RF Dosimetry Lab. Motorola, Inc., Plantation, Fla., 1998-2000; chief EME scientist, dir. Corp. EME Rsch. Lab. Motorola Inc., 2000—. Sci. adv. Mobile Mfrs. Forum, 2001—; sci. advisory bd. assoc. Motorola, 2005. Mem. editl. bd. IEEE EMC, MTT, 1999—; assoc. editor Jour. Bioelectromagnetics, 1987-2003; contbr. more than 180 articles to profl. jours. 2d lt. Army of Taiwan, 1968-69. Fellow: IEEE (subcoms. 1979—, com. on man and radiation 1990—2000, ad hoc task force on health care reform 1993—97, vice chmn. 1994—95, mem. med. tech. policy com. 1995—98, chmn. 1996—98, std. coordinating com.), Am. Inst. for Med. and Biol. Engring.; mem.: Internat. Radio Sci. Union, Electromagnetic Acad., Radiation Rsch. Soc., Bioelectromagnetics Soc. (bd. dirs. 1981—84, Curtis Carl Johnson Meml. award 1995), N.Am. Hyperthermia Soc., Internat. Microwave Power Inst. (1st Spl. Decade award 1981, Outstanding Paper award 1985), Nat. Coun. Radiation Protection and Measurements (subcom. vice chmn. 1995—2000, IEEE liaison 1997—99, coun. mem. 1998—2004), Commn. K., Tau Beta Pi, Sigma Xi. Office: Motorola Inc Fla Rsch Lab Plantation FL 33322 Office Phone: 954-723-5387. E-mail: ck.chou@motorola.com.

CHOU, CLIFFORD CHI FONG, research engineering executive; b. Taipei, Taiwan, Dec. 19, 1940; came to U.S., 1966, naturalized, 1978; s. Ching piao and Yueh li (Huang) C.; m. Chu hwei Lee, Mar. 23, 1968; children: Kelvin Lin yu, Renee Lincy. PhD, Mich. State U., 1972. Research asst. Mich. State U., East Lansing, 1967-70, Wayne State U., Detroit, 1970-72, research assoc., 1972-76; research engr. Ford Motor Co., Dearborn, 1976-81, sr. research engr., 1981-82, prin. research engr. assoc., 1982-89, prin. staff engr., 1989-93, sr. engring. specialist, 1993-95, staff tech. specialist, 1995—2003, tech. leader, 2003—. Adj. prof. Mich. Technol. U., 1997-2002, 2003—; lectr. to China under UN Devel. Program, 1987, 93, 95, lectr. to Taiwan under Automotive Rsch. and Test Ctr., 1991, 97, 98, 2005; organizer Safety Test Methodology, SAE session chair, 1997-2005, SAE fellow nom. com., 2004-, IBEC session chair 1999, 2000, 2004; coord. Detroit Automobile Tech. Conf., 1993, session chair, 1997; mem. safety and environ. systems planning com.

IBEC '98, 1997-2000, 01-03; indsl. acad. adv. to PhD Coms., U. Mich., 1995-98, Mich. Tchrs. U., 1997-2000, 1999—; tchr. in field; co-organizer 6th U.S. Nat. Conf. on Computational Mechs., crashworthiness session, Dearborn, 2001; mem. safety tech. com. China SAE, 2002—, mem. nomination com., 2004—. US regional editor Internat. Jour. Vehicle Safety, 2005-; contbr. chpts. to books, articles to profl. jours. Recipient Safety Engring. Excellence award Nat. Hwy. Traffic Safety Adminstrn., 1980, Best Paper award IBEC, 2002; grantee Soc. Automotive Engrs. Fellow: Soc. Automotive Engrs. (Forest R. McFarland award 2000); mem.: AIAA, ASME, Detroit Chinese Am. Assn., Mich. Chinese Acad. Profl. Assn. (bd. dirs. 1992—93, pres. 1993—94, advisor 1994—, seminar spkr. 2000), Ford Chinese Club (pres. 1991—92), Sigma Xi. Achievements include 7 patents. Avocations: travel, karaoke, ballroom dancing. Home: 28970 Forest Hill Dr Farmington MI 48331-2439 Office Phone: 313-594-2301. Business E-Mail: cchou@ford.com.

CHOU, ERWIN C., economist; b. San Francisco, July 12, 1952; s. George H. and Suet F. Chou. BA, U. Calif., Berkeley, 1974; PhD, Stanford U., 1986. Economist World Bank, Washington, 1977-84; internat. economist U.S. Treasury/IRS, San Francisco, 1987-94; mng. dir., sr. economist Price Waterhouse LLP, 1994-99; sr. economist EC Cons., San Francisco, 2000—. Economic cons. Pacific Gas & Electric Co., San Francisco, 1986-87. Mem. Am. Econ. Assn. Democrat. Home: 2921 Privet Dr Hillsborough CA 94010-6247 Office: Ecconsultants 4150 17th St Ste 2 San Francisco CA 94114-1995

CHOU, I-MING, geologist; b. Hsinchu, Taiwan, Republic of China, Apr. 6, 1945; s. Tsu-Chao and Fen Liao Chou; m. Chiu-Jung Tai, Aug. 8, 1971; children: Sophia Chou Dotton, Patricia. BS, Nat. Taiwan U., 1968; PhD, Johns Hopkins U., 1974. Scientist prin. Lockheed Electronic Co., Houston, 1978—79; geologist U.S. Geol. Survey, Reston, Va., 1979—. W.J. James prof. pure and applice sci. St. Francis Xavier U., Antigonish, NS, Canada, 1997. Contbr. articles to profl. publs. Gilbert fellow, U.S. Geol. Survey, 1990. Fellow: Mineral. Soc. Am.; mem.: Geochemical Soc. (assoc.), Am. Geophys. Union (assoc.). Office: US Geological Survey 12201 Sunrise Valley Dr Reston VA 20192 Office Phone: 703-648-6169. Office Fax: 703-648-6252. Business E-Mail: imchou@usgs.gov.

CHOU, LAISHENG, education educator; b. Shanghai, Nov. 8, 1952; s. Licheng Chou and Lanying Yang; m. Jialing Zhang, May 20, 1983; children: Sophia, Tina. DMD, Shanghai No. 2 Med. U., China, 1977; PhD, The U. of Brit. Columbia, Can., 1994. Diplomate Oral Pathology U. of Calif., 1987, Oral Medicine U. of Calif., 1989. Assoc. prof. biomaterials, assoc. prof. diagnostic scis., dir. oral aids clinic Boston U., 1994—2000, prof. biomaterials, prof. oral medicine, dir. divsn. of oral medicine, dir. oral aids clinic, 2000—. Hon. prof. China Med. U., Shengyang, 1993—; guest prof. China No. 4 Med. U., Xian, 2001—; sr. cons. The Chinese HIV/AIDS Found., Beijing, 2001—; sci. cons. The Chinese Acad. of Scis., Beijing, 2002—. Author: Over 100 sci. articles, abstracts, and book chpts. publ.; sci. reviewer The Jour. of Biomedical Materials Rsch., The Jour. of Dental Rsch., The Jour. of Biomaterials. Chmn. clin. investigation com. Am. Acad. of Oral Medicine, 2001, mem. membershp com., 2001; mem. awards and nominations com. Am. Soc. of Biomaterials Surface Scis.; mem. Boston U. Goldman Sch. of Dental Medicine Appointments and Promotions Com. Recipient The First Ann. award, The AU Found., 1988; fellow, Med. Rsch. Coun. of Can., 1992; grantee Grant award, NIH, 1988, Rsch. Grant, Calcitek Co., 1996, USBiomaterials Co., 1997, 1999, 2002, AIDS Edn. and Tng. Ctr. Grant, Dept. of Pub. Health and Svcs., 1998, 1999, 2000, 2001, 2002; grant, NIH, 1997, Zoller Meml. Fellow award, The U. of Chgo., 1989, Fellowship, The U. of Brit. Columbia, 1991. Mem.: Am. Soc. of Biomatrials Surface Scis., Soc. for Biomaterials, Am. Acad. of Oral Medicine (chmn., clin. investigation com. 2001), Internat. Assn. of Dental Rsch., ADA, Am. Acad. of Oral Pathology. Achievements include invention of Gold chloride enhanced cellular and molecular labeling system; Osteogenic elements of implant materilas; Novel scaffolds for human bone tissue engineering; Bioactive coating/implant materials for enhancement of bone attachment and regeneration; Novel materials for skin wound healing; discovery of Real earth filters for intraoral radiography with exposure reduction; Reduction of Langerhans' cells in smokeless tobacco-associated oral mucosal lesions; Oral mucosal Langerhans' cells as target, effector, and vector in HIV infection; first to Molecular biocompatibility of implant and tissue engineering scaffold materials. Office: Boston Univ 801 Albany St S207 Boston MA 02118 Business E-Mail: lchou@bu.edu.

CHOU, TING-CHAO, inventor, educator; b. Taiwan, Sept. 9, 1938; arrived in U.S., 1965, naturalized, 1976; s. Chao-Yun and Sheng-Mei (Chen) C.; m. Dorothy Tsui-chin Tseng, June 26, 1965; children: Joseph Hsin-I, Julia Hsin-Ya. *Spouse, Dorothy T.C. Tseng Chou, BS, 1961, MS 1964, National Taiwan University; Ph.D. 1970, Columbia University College of Physicians and Surgeons. Son, Joseph Hsin-I. Chou, BA, 1990, Harvard University, Summa cum Laude in biochemical sciences; MD, Ph.D. 2000, University of California San Francisco. Daughter, Julia Hsin-Ya Chou, BA, 1994, Harvard University, Cum Laude in general studies; MBA 2000, Wharton School, University of Pennsylvania. "Chou" is the family name which originated from the Chou Dynasty that ruled China for over 800 years about 3000 years ago. "Ting" is a generation name shared by cousins/siblings and "Chao" is the given name.* BS, Kaohsiung Med. Coll., Taiwan, 1961; MS, Nat. Taiwan U., 1965; PhD, Yale U., 1970. Tchg. asst. pharmacology Nat. Taiwan U., 1964-65; rsch. asst. pharmacology Yale U., 1969; postdoctoral fellow Johns Hopkins U., Balt., 1969-72; assoc. Sloan-Kettering Inst. Cancer Rsch., NYC, 1972-78, assoc. mem., 1978—88, mem., 1988-95, head lab. biochmn. pharmacology, 1988-98, dir. preclin. pharmacology core lab., 1995—. Asst. prof. Grad. Sch. Med. Sci. Cornell U., 1972—78, assoc. prof., 1978—88, prof. pharmacology, 1988—2000; vis. prof. Chinese Second Mil. Med. U., Shanghai, 1992—, Tonji Med. U., 1993—, Nanjing Med. U., China, 1994—; hon. prof. Chinese Acad. Med. Scis., Beijing, 1993—, Chinese Acad. Mil. Med. Scis., Beijing, 1995—; cons. in field. Author (with J. Chou): Dose Effect Analysis with Microcomputers, 1986; author: (with M. Hayball) CalcuSyn for Windows, Biosoft, 1996; author: (with N. Martin) CompuSyn for Drug Combinations, 2004; co-editor (with D. Rideout): Synergism and Antogonism in Chemotherapy, 1991; mem. editl. adv. bd.: Cancer Biochemistry Biophysics, 1984—, Jour. of the Nat. Cancer Inst., 1988—92, Kaohisung Jour. Med. Scis., 1992—, chmn. pub. bd.: Bio/Pharma Quar., 1995—2002; contbr. scientific papers over 340 articles on cancer, and AIDS chemotherapy and theoretical biology to profl. jours. Chmn. Lim-Wang Meml. Scholarship Fund, 1998—2003; mem. adv. bd. divsn. biotechnology and pharm. rsch. Nat. Health Rsch. Inst., Taiwan, 2001—02. Rsch. grantee Nat. Cancer Inst., Nat. Inst. of Allergy and Infectious Diseases, Elsa U. Pardee Found. and Am. Cancer Soc., 1975—. Mem. AAAS, Am. Assn. Cancer Rsch., Am. Soc. Pharmacology and Exptl. Therapeutics, Am. Soc. Preventive Oncology (founding mem.), Am. Soc. for Biochem. and Molecular Biol., Am. Bur. Med. Advancement in China (bd. dirs. 1991-2003, v.p. 1994-98), N.Y. Acad. Sci., Kaohsiung Med. Coll. Alumni Assn. Am. (bd. dir. 1968-91, pres. 1972), Harvey Soc., Sigma Xi. Achievements include 14 U.S. patents in anticancer agents including desoxyepothilones, ardeemins, ningalins and fludelone; creator median-effect equation, multiple drug effect equation, combination index, dose-reduction index and polygonogram. Office: 1275 York Ave New York NY 10021-6007 E-mail: chout@mskcc.org.

CHOU, WUSHOW, retired computer scientist; b. Shanghai, Kiangsu, China, Feb. 12, 1939; m. Lena Sun, Apr. 17, 1965; children: Warren, Wesley. BEE, Cheng Kung U., Tainan, Taiwan, 1961; MEE, U. N.Mex., 1965; PhD in Elec. Engring. and Computer Sci., U. Calif., Berkeley, 1968. Acting asst. prof. U. Calif., Berkeley, 1968-69; v.p. Network Analysis Corp., Glen Cove, NY, 1969-76; vis. prof. SUNY, Stony Brook, 1976; rsch. prof. George Washington U., Washington, 1975-76; prof. computer sci. dept. and elec. and computer engring. dept. NC State U., Raleigh, 1976—2003, prof. emeritus, 2003—, dir. computer studies, 1976-88; dep. asst. sec. for info. systems U.S. Dept. Treasury, Washington, 1994-97, chief info. officer, 1996-97; ret. Pres. ACK Computer Applications, Cary, NC, 1978—93; vis. prof. Poly. U., Bklyn., 1988—89; cons. AT&T, IBM, U.S. Govt., Singapore Govt., French Govt. Author, editor: Computer Communication, Vol. 1, 1984, Vol. 2, 1985, Advances in Telecommunications, 1985—86, editor-in-chief: Jour. Telecom., 1982—85, IT Profl., 1998—2001; chmn. adv. bd. IT Profl., 2002—; contbr. articles to profl. jours. Recipient award, GSA, Washington, 1988, Treasury Dept., 1997; Rsch. grantee, NSF, 1978, Army Rsch. Office, 1982, AT&T, 1987. Fellow: IEEE (award 2001, 2002), Assn. Computing Machines. Office: NC State U Dept Computer Sci PO Box 8206 Raleigh NC 27695-0001 E-mail: chou@ncsu.edu.

CHOUAI, ABDELLATIF, chemist, researcher; b. Taza, Morocco, June 16, 1971; s. Ahmed Chouai and Saadia Kenzouz; m. Amal Oukha, Aug. 24, 2000; 1 child, Anas Ahmed. PhD, U. Houston, 2003. Rsch. asst. U. Houston, 1998—2003; rsch. assoc. Tex. A&M U., College Station, 2003—, rsch. assoc. chemistry dept., 2003—. Rschr. Tex. A&M U., 2003—. Contbr. articles to profl. jours. Fellow, U. Houston, 1998—2002. Mem.: AAAS (assoc.), Am. Inst. Chemist, Nat. Postdoctoral Assn., NY Acad. Sciis. (assoc.), Am. Chem. Soc. (assoc.). Achievements include research in Design and synthesis of novel therapeutic agents for anticancer activities and photodynamic therapy. Home: 1411 D Airline Dr College Station TX 77845 Office: Tex A&M U Chemistry Dept PO Box 30012 College Station TX 77842-3012 Office Phone: 979-845-1966. Home Fax: 979-845-7177. Personal E-mail: achouai@mail.chem.tamu.edu.

CHOUDHARY, ADIL MUSHTAQ, gastroenterologist; b. Dec. 19, 1964; MB, BChir, U. Karachi, Pakistan, 1989. Diplomate Am. Bd. Internal Medicine. Intern medicine/gen. surgery Civil Hosp. and Dow Med. Coll., Karachi, 1990, resident internal medicine, 1991—93, NYU VA/Bellevue Hosp. Ctr., Manhattan, 1993—96; tchg. asst. medicine NYU Sch. Medicine, Manhattan, 1994—96; fellow gastroenterology Yale U. Gastroenterology Program at Bridgeport (Conn.) Hosp., 1996—99; advanced fellow therapeutic gastrointestinal endoscopy Tulane U. Med. Ctr., New Orleans, 1999; pvt. practice gastroenterology and internal medicine Rio Pecos Med. Assocs., Roswell, N.Mex., 1999—2000, Digestive Disease Inst., So. N.Mex. Med. Assocs., Roswell, 2001—; clin. asst. prof. medicine U. N. Mex. Sch. Medicine, 2003—. Vol. tchg. faculty family practice residency Ea. N.Mex. Med. Ctr., Roswell, mem. pharmacy and therapeutics com.; vol. pharmacy practice faculty U. N.Mex. Coll. Pharmacy, Albuquerque, 2001—02; mem. grad. med. edn. com. Ea. N.Mex. Family Practice Residency Program, 2001—; bd. dirs. Southeastern N.Mex. Physicians IPA, Inc.; presenter in field. Contbr. articles to profl. jours. Janssen Pharmaceutica USA scholar, World Congress Gastroenterology, Vienna, 1998. Mem.: AMA (Physician's Recognition award in continuing med. edn. 1998—2001, 1999—2002), ACP, Crohn's and Colitis Found. Am., Inc., Am. Assn. for the Study Liver Diseases, Am. Soc. for Gastrointestinal Endoscopy, Am. Coll. Gastroenterology (Cert. for outstanding contbn. to the field of gastroenterology and hepatology 1999, 1997), Am. Gastroenterol. Assn. Home: 5 Victoria Ct Roswell NM 88201 Office: 303 W Country Club Rd Roswell NM 88201 Office Phone: 505-623-1442.

CHOUDHURY, RAJ DEO, automotive executive; b. N.Y.C., 1969; s. Deo Chand and Annette Patricia Choudhury; m. Margarete Haeusler, 2002. BA, Princeton U., 1990; MA, Stanford U., 1993. Evaluation analyst Arco Ak. Inc., Anchorage, 1993—96; sr. planning analyst Atlantic Richfield Co., LA, 1996—99; mgr. fuel infrastructure and bus. devel. fuel cell activities GM Corp., Mainz Kastel, Germany, 1999—2003, mgr. ops. and policy Pub. Policy Ctr. Washington, 2003—. Contractor U.S. Army, 2004—. Author: On the Theory of Repeated Games, 1990; co-author: Well-to-Wheel Energy Use and Greenhouse Gas Emissions of Advanced Fuel-Vehicle Systems for North Am., 2001, Well-to-Wheel Energy Use and Greenhouse Gas Emissions of Advanced Fuel-Vehicle Systems for Europe, 2002. Mentor US Dept. Def. Dep. Sch., Wiesbaden, Germany, 1999—2002. Mem.: Am. Radio Relay League, Internat. Assn. for Energy Econs. (bd. dirs. Anchorage chpt. 1995—96), Nat. Hydrogen Assn. (bd. dirs.), Soc. Automotive Engrs., Princeton Club of Washington, Mountaineering Club Alaska, Sigma Xi. Avocations: photography, international travel, amateur radio, montaineering. Office: GM 1660 L St NW Ste 400 Washington DC 20036 Office Phone: 202-775-5033. E-mail: raj.choudhury@gm.com.

CHOUEIFATI, ANTOINE (TONY CHOUEIFATI), computer company executive; b. Sept. 14, 1946; s. Beatrice and Jim Choueifati; m. Sally Shar; children: Anthony, Angie. Bachelor in Computer Science, Sir George Williams, 1975. Western region ter. mgr. IBM Corp., Houston, 1983—; tech support mgr. Goldrus Drilling Co., Houston, 1980—83. Author: Sealed, 2002 (Marketing Excellence award, 1997), Incubus Immortal Seed. Mem.: Data Processing Mgmt. Assn. (cert.). Roman Catholic. Avocation: golf. Office Phone: 713-782-9147. Personal E-mail: tony1c@swbell.net.

CHOUEIR, BERTHE Y., computer scientist, educator; b. Kfarhata, Lebanon, Jan. 24, 1963; d. Yazid G. Choueiry and Salam M. Hamaty-Choveiry. MS in elec. engring., Swiss Federal Inst., Switzerland, 1986; PhD in computer sci., U. La., 1994. Rsch. assoc. EPFL, Switzerland, 1995—96; vis. scholar Stanford U., Calif., 1997—99; asst. prof. U. Nebr., Lincoln, Nebr., 1999—2003, assoc. prof., 2003—. Recipient Fritz-Kutter prize, 1995, Career award, NSF, 2002; Young Rschrs. fellowship, Swiss Nat. Salena Found., 1992—99, ABB fellowship, ABB, 1987—88. Mem.: IEEE, ACM, AAAF, Assn. Switzerland-Japan. Office: CSE U Nebr 256 Avery Hall Lincoln NE 68588 Office Phone: 402-472-5444. E-mail: choueiry@cse.uhl.edu.

CHOUERY, FARID ALEXANDRE, electrical engineer, structural engineer, consultant; b. Cairo, Feb. 2, 1951; arrived in U.S., 1969; s. Alexandre Choukri and Yvonne Emile Chouery; m. Bernice Joan Furdal Chouery, Aug. 18, 1978; 1 child, Alexis Kristina. BSEE, U. Wash., 1974, MSEE, 1979, MS in Structural Engring., 1984. Registered profl. engr., Wash. Design electronics engr. Nortec Corp., Tri-Cities, Wash., 1975—76; design elec. engr. Kenworth Truck Co., Kirkland, Wash., 1976—79; mgmt. in tng. GTE of the NW, Everett, Wash., 1979—80; cons. engr. Matrix Engring./DBM Inc., Federal Way, Wash., 1980—87; spl. assignment engr. ABKJ Inc., Seattle, 1988—91; testing engr. and proof reader Microsoft Corp., Redmond, Wash., 1993; pres., CEO and engr. FAC Systems Inc., Seattle, 1988—. Math tutor Seattle Ctrl. C.C., 1971—72. Composer: (15 minute symphony) The 21st Century. Scholar, Electric League of the Pacific NW, 1973—74. Independent. Christian. Achievements include patents in field; patents pending in field. Avocations: guitar, composing, poetry, photography, travel. E-mail: farid@facsystems.com.

CHOUGH, LEO Y., surgeon, orthopedist; b. Pullman, Wash., May 25, 1966; s. Kwang and Michiko Chough; m. Mimi Chough, July 30, 1998. BS Summa Cum Laude, U. Wash., Seattle, 1988; MD, Washington U., St Louis, 1993. Diplomate Am. Bd. Orthopedic Surgery, 2001. Intern in gen. surgery Barnes Hosp, St. Louis, 1993—94; resident in orthopedic surgery Barnes Jewish Hosp./ Washington U., St. Louis, 1994—98; fellow in sports medicine U. Pa. Hosp. Booth Bartolozzi, Balderston, Phila., 1998—99; orthop. surgeon Whidbey Orthop. Surgeons, Coupeville, Wash., 1999—2000, Ctrl. Lakes Med. Clinic, Crosby, Minn., 2000—. Fellow: Am. Acad. Orthop. Surgeons; mem.: Alpha Omega Alpha, Phi Beta Kappa (Book award 1984, scholarship 1988). Office: Ctrl Lakes Med Clinic 315 E Main St Crosby MN 56441

CHOUINARD, YVON, sportswear outfitter executive; b. Lewiston, Maine, Nov. 9, 1938; s. Gerard and Yvonne (Lizzotte) C.; m. Carol Lamb, 1962 (div. 1963); m. Malinda Pennoyer, Dec. 25, 1970; children: Fletcher, Claire. LHD (hon.), Yale U., 1995. Founder Chouinard Equipment, Burbank, Calif., 1957, Great Pacific Iron Works, Inc., Ventura, Calif., 1970, Lost Arrow Corp., Ventura, 1974—, Patagonia Inc., Ventura, 1976—. Author: Climbing Ice, 1978, Let My People Go Surfing, 2005. Active Surf Rider Orgn., various environ. orgns. worldwide. With U.S. Army, 1962-64, Korea. Mem. Am. Alpine Club. Democrat. Avocations: tennis, skiing, kayaking, sailing, surfing. Office: Lost Arrow Corp 259 W Santa Clara St Ventura CA 93001*

CHOUKAS-BRADLEY, JAMES RICHARD, lawyer; b. Hartford, Conn., Sept. 11, 1950; s. William Lee and Paula Ann (Elliott) Bradley; m. Melanie Rose Choukas, June 21, 1975; children: Sophia Crane, Jesse Elliott. BA cum laude, U. Vt., 1974; JD cum laude, Georgetown U., 1980. Bar: D.C. 1980, U.S. Ct. Appeals (D.C. cir.) 1981, U.S. Ct. Appeals (11th cir.) 1984, U.S. Ct. Appeals (10th cir.) 1985, U.S. Ct. Appeals (4th cir.) 1990, U.S. Ct. Appeals (6th cir.) 1993. Reporter, editor The Berlin (N.H.) Reporter, The Groveton (N.H.) News, The Northland News, 1973—74; editor, pub., creative dir. Ad Lib, Gorham, NH, 1974—75; asst. to city mgr. City of Berlin, 1975—77; contbg. reporter The Lewiston (Maine) Sun, 1976; legal intern Congl. Budget Office, Washington, 1978; rsch. assoc. Schlossberg-Cassidy & Assocs., Washington, 1978—80; assoc. Miller, Balis & O'Neil, P.C., Washington, 1980—84, mem., v.p., 1985—, exec. com., 1993—97. Legal advisor, 1st v.p. Sugarloaf Citizens Assn., Dickerson, Md., 1987—2000; counsel Mcpl. Gas Authority of Ga., Pub. Gas Ptnrs., Natural Gas Acquisition Corp. of City of Clarksville, Tenn., S.E. Ala. Gas Dist., Ala. Mcpl. Distbrs. Group, Tenn. Mcpl. Group, Mcpl. Gas Authority of Miss.; gen. counsel Tenn. Energy Acquisition Corp., Lower Ala. Gas Dist.; spkr. in field; pioneer in joint action and pub. financing in deregulated natural gas industry. Author: The Early Days, 1975; co-author: Report on Dynamics of Natural Gas Markets and Projected Gas Prices for 2005 and Beyond, 2005. Pres. D.C. Dukes Athletic Club, Washington, 1978-81, Montgomery Dukes, 1987-92; com. chmn. Berlin Bicentennial Commn., Berlin, 1975-76; youth soccer and flag football coach Seneca Sports Assn., 1999-. Regents scholar State of N.Y., 1968. Mem.: Hist. Medley Dist., Energy Bar Assn., For A Rural Montgomery, Nat. Youth Sports Coaches Assn., Sugarloaf Citizens Assn., Randolph Mountain Club, Phi Beta Kappa. Avocations: softball, guitar, songwriting, hiking, travel. Office: 1140 19th St NW Ste 700 Washington DC 20036 Home: 7100 Oakridge Ave Chevy Chase MD 20815 Office Phone: 202-296-2960. Business E-Mail: jchoukasbradley@mbolaw.com.

CHOUKAS-BRADLEY, MELANIE, writer, photographer; b. Jacksonville, N.C., Aug. 20, 1952; d. Michael Jr. and Juanita May (Crosby) Choukas; m. James Richard Bradley, June 21, 1975; children: Sophia Crane, Jesse Elliott. BA in English, U. Vt., 1974; student, Pierce Coll., Athens, 1971; postgrad., U.S. Dept. Agr. Grad. Sch., Chevy Chase, Md., 1995—. From reporter to news dir. Radio Sta. WBRL, Berlin, N.H., 1975-77; rsch. asst. subcom. on oversight and investigations Commerce Com., U.S. Ho. of Reps., Washington, 1978; writer, 1978—. Earth Day chmn. Sugarloaf Citizens Assn., Barnesville, Md., 1990-92, programs and edn. dir., Celebrate Rural Montgomery, 2005. Author: City of Trees, 1987, Sugarloaf: The Mountain's History, Geology and Natural Lore, 2003, An Illustrated Guide to Eastern Woodland Wildflowers and Trees, 2004; contbr. articles to Washington Post, Audubon Naturalist News, others. Dir. programs and edn. Celebrate Rural Montgomery Campaign, 2005; bd. dirs. Md. Native Plant Soc., 2005—. Grantee Am. Forest Inst., Nat. Forest Products Assn., Time Inc., Bendix, Union Camp Corp., 1978-81, naturalist lead field trips for Audubon Naturalist Soc., 2000—; grantee Sugarloaf Regional Trails, 1995, 2001. Mem. Authors Guild; Md. Native Plant Soc. (bd. dirs.). Democrat. Achievements include member Capitol Steps adult synchronized skating team, participant National Championships 2001 and 2002; member Capital Classics synchronized skating team, 2003-04, 04-05. Avocations: hiking, cross country skiing, synchronized figure skating, botany, ice dancing. Personal E-mail: choukas@erols.com.

CHOW, AMY, gymnast, Olympic athlete; b. San Jose, Calif., May 15, 1978; Student, Stanford U. Mem. USA Team, Hamamatsu, Japan, 1993, World Championships Team, Dortmund, Germany, 1994, Pan Am. Games Team, Mar del Plata, Argentina, 1995, U.S. Olympic Team, Atlanta, 1996. Placed 1st vault U.S. Gymnastics Championships, Ohio, 1992, 1st all around, vault, uneven bars, balance beam, 2d floor exercise, Mex. Olympic Festival, 1992, 3rd all around, vault, 1st floor exercise, USA/Japan Competition, Hamamatsu, Japan, 1993, 3rd vault Coca-Cola Nat. Championships, Nashville, Tenn., 1994, 1st vault, 2d uneven bars, 3rd all around Pan Am. Games, Mar del Plata, Argentina, 1995; recipient Gold medal Women's Gymnastics Team competition and Silver medal uneven bars, Olympic Games, Atlanta, 1996. Mem., U.S. Olympic Team, Sydney, 2000. Address: Octagon 2 Union St #300 Portland ME 04101-4295

CHOW, CHI-MING, retired mathematics professor; b. Tai-Yuan, Shansi, Republic of China, Nov. 15, 1931; arrived in U.S., 1959; s. Wei-Han Chow and Lu-Tsen Hsu. Cert. tech. officer, Chinese Air Force Tech. Inst., 1954; BS in Math., Ch. Coll. Hawaii, 1962; MS in Math., Oreg. State U., 1965. Tech. officer Chinese Air Force, China, 1954—59; prof. math. Oakland C.C., Mich., 1965—92, ret., 1992. Author (first author of the proof of the theorem): The sight area A of a moving body is inversely proportional to the square of the distance D between the body and observing point, i.e. A=C/(DxD), where C is a constant; contbr. articles to profl. jours. including The Math. Tchr., 1965. 1st Lt. Air Force of Republic of China, 1954-59. Mem.: Pi Mu Epsilon. Avocation: piloting aircraft. Home: PO Box 903 Novi MI 48376-0903

CHOW, GREGORY CHI-CHONG, economist, educator; b. Macau, South China, Dec. 25, 1929; arrived in US, 1948, naturalized, 1963; s. Tin-Pong and Pauline (Law) C.; m. Paula K. Chen, Aug. 27, 1955; children: John S., James S., Jeanne S. BA, Cornell U., 1951; MA, U. Chgo., 1952, PhD, 1955; hon. doctorate, Zhongshan U., 1986; LLD, Lingnan U., 1994. Asst. prof. MIT, 1955-59; assoc. prof. Cornell U., 1959-62, vis. prof., 1964-65; staff mem., mgr. econ. models IBM Research Center, Yorktown Heights, NY, 1962-70, prof., dir. econometric rsch. program, 1970-97; Class of 1913 prof. polit. economy Princeton U., 1979—. Adj. prof. Columbia U., 1965-70; vis. prof. Harvard U., 1967, Rutgers U., 1969; adviser Chinese Natural Sci. Found.; econ. adviser Shandong Provincial Govt. Author: Demand for Automobiles in the United States: A Study in Consumer Durables, 1957, Analysis and Control of Dynamic Economic Systems, 1975, Econometric Analysis by Control Methods, 1981, Econometrics, 1983, The Chinese Economy, 1985, Understanding China's Economy, 1994, Dynamic Economics: Optimization by the Lagrange Method, 1997; co-editor: Evaluating the Reliability of Macro-Economic Models, 1982, Asia in the 21st Century, 1997; co-author: The Demand for Durable Goods, 1960, Sower of Modern Economics in China: Interview of Gregory C. Chow (in Chinese)by Professor Liu Sufen, 1996, China's Economic Transformation, 2002, Knowing China, 2004; contbr. articles to profl. jours. Named Hon. Prof., Fudan U., Hainan U., The People's U., Zhongshan U., Shandong U., City U. Hong Kong, hon. pres., Lingnan U., Coll. at Zhongshan U., Naikai U. Fellow Econometric Soc., Am. Statis Assn.; mem. Academia Sinica, Am. Philos. Soc., Am. Econ. Assn., Soc. for Econ. Dynamics and Control (pres. 1979-80). Home: 30 Hardy Dr Princeton NJ 08540-1211 Business E-Mail: gchow@princeton.edu.

CHOW, HUMPHREY WAI, mechanical engineer; b. Hoi Ping, Guangzhou, China, Feb. 7, 1954; came to U.S., 1972; s. Lai and Ming-Kuen (Wong) C.; m. Joanna Qi Deng, Nov. 17, 1988; children: Genevieve Daisy, Daphne Jolie. BSME, U. Mass., Lowell, 1978; MS, Ga. Inst. Tech., 1984; PhD, Rensselaer Poly. Inst., 1993; MS in Engring. Mgmt., Tufts U., 2002. Product design engr. GE Medium Power Transformers, Rome, Ga., 1979-82; mech. design engr. GE Ordnance Sys., Pittsfield, Mass., 1984-85; rsch. asst. Rensselaer Poly. Inst., Troy, N.Y., 1985-87; sr. mech. design engr. GE Power Sys., Schenectady, NY, 1987—90; teaching asst. Rensselaer Poly. Inst., Troy, 1990-93; dynamic analysis engr. GE Naval & Drive Turbine Sys., Fitchburg, Mass., 1993-94; methods devel. engr. Knolls Atomic Power Lab., Schenectady, 1994-96; staff engr. GE Aircraft Engines, Lynn, Mass., 1996-98, 99—, GE Deutschland, Frankfurt, Germany, 1998-99. Contbr. articles to profl. jours. including European Jour. Mechanics. Mem.: AIAA, ASME, Am. Soc. for Engring. Mgmt. Achievements include patents for rotor coil connectors of turbine generators; design of propulsion turbine generator for the Navy integrated electric drive program; methods development for nuclear fuel and core design analysis in the Navy nuclear propulsion program; metal forming process modeling of compressor airfoils manufacturing for aircraft engines; qualification of high pressure compressor for USAF trainer aircraft. Office: GE Aircraft Engines 1000 Western Ave Lynn MA 01910-0001

CHOW, JACK C., international organization administrator; BA, U. Pa.; MBA, U. Chgo.; MS, U. Calif., Berkeley; MPA, Harvard U. Kennedy Sch. Govt.; MD, U. Calif., San Francisco. Sr. policy analyst White House Office of Sci. and Tech. Policy; asst. dir. for internat. rels. Forgarty Internat. Ctr., NIH; dep. asst. sec. for pub. health Dept. Health and Human Svcs.; staff mem. Ho. and Sen. Appropriations Coms., U.S. Congress; mgmt. cons. McKinsey & Co.; sr. advisor for global health policy to undersec. of state for global affairs U.S. Dept. State; dep. asst. sec. of state for health and sci. Bur. of Oceans and Internat. Environ. and Sci. Affairs, U.S. Dept. State; amb. Spl. Rep. of U.S. Sec. of State for HIV/AIDS; asst. dir.-gen., HIV/AIDS, TB, and Malaria WHO, Geneva, 2003—. Office: WHO Avenue Appia 20 1211 Geneva Switzerland

CHOW, JIMMY TAI-NIN, chemist; b. Hong Kong, Aug. 8, 1967; s. Ka Ho Chow and Chung Yue Ng; m. Lorena Lee. BS in Chemistry, U. Costa Rica, San Jose, 1991; MS in Chemistry, U. Tex.-Dallas, Richardson, 1995, D in Chemistry, 1998; postgrad., Kans. State U. Rsch. asst. Ctr. Investigacion de Tecnologia del Cuero, Sabanilla, Costa Rica, 1990-91; student intern Refineria Costarricense del Petroleo, Limon, Costa Rica, 1991; rsch. and tchg. asst. U. Tex.-Dallas, Richardson, 1992-95; chemist Rohm and Haas Tex., Inc., Deer Park, Tex., 1995-96; rsch. asst. U. Tex. and Carrington Labs., Inc., Richardson, 1997-98; postdoctoral chemist Carrington Labs., Inc., Irving, Tex., 1999; sr. chemist Bayer Corp., Baytown, Tex., 1999—. Tex. Pub. Ednl. Grant scholar, 1993-95, 97-98. Mem. AIChE, Am. Chem. Soc. E-mail: jimmy-chow@lycos.com.

CHOW, JUDY, librarian, educator; b. Taipei, Taiwan, Feb. 13, 1954; arrived in US, 1964; d. Charles and Lucy (Chu) C.; m. Steve Lee, July 3, 1982; children: Andrew Chow Lee, Mike Chow Lee. BA, UCLA, 1975, MLS, 1977. Prof. L.A. C.C., 1990—. Mem. Faculty Assn. of Calif. C.C. Spl. Interest Group. Sgi Buddhist. Avocations: drawing, painting, travel, music, reading. Personal E-mail: judychow@msn.com. Business E-Mail: chowjc@wlac.edu.

CHOW, POO, forester; b. Shanghai, Apr. 27, 1934; arrived in U.S., 1960, naturalized, 1971; s. Kai and Yung-Kwan (Hsieh) C.; m. Ai-Yu Kuo, July 17, 1965; children— Eugenia, Andrew E. MS in Forest Products, La. State U., 1961; PhD in Wood Sci. and Tech., Forestry, Mich. State U., 1969. Lab. dir. Pope and Talbot, Inc., Oakridge, Oreg., 1962-67; asst. prof. wood sci. U. Ill., Urbana, 1969-74, assoc. prof., 1974-80, prof., 1980—. Sr. Fulbright scholar, Fed. Republic Germany; cons. to industry; external examiner U. Ibadan, Nigeria; expert witness. Contbr. numerous articles to profl. jours.; patentee in field. Mem. ASTM, Forest Products Soc., Soc. Wood Sci. and Tech., Am. Railway Engrs. and Maintenance-of-Way Assn., Internat. Rsch. on Wood Preservation Group, German Wood Technology Soc., RR Tie Assn., Am. Wood Preservatives Assn., Xi Sigma Pi. Office: Univ Ill 1102 S Goodwin Ave Urbana IL 61801-4730

CHOW, RITA KATHLEEN, nursing consultant; b. San Francisco, Aug. 19, 1926; d. Peter and May (Chan) Chow. BS, nursing diploma, Stanford U., 1950; MS, Case Western Res. U., 1955; profl. diploma in nursing edn. adminstrn, Columbia U., 1961, EdD, 1968; B of Individualized Studies, George Mason U., 1983. Asst. in teaching Stanford U., Calif., 1951—52; instr., dir. student health Fresno (Calif.) Gen. Hosp. Sch. Nursing, 1952—54; instr. Wayne State U. Coll. Nursing, Detroit, 1957—58; rsch. assoc., project dir. cardiovasc. nursing rsch. Ohio State U., Columbus, 1965—68; commd. officer USPHS, 1968, advanced through grades to nurse dir. (capt.), 1974; spl. asst. to dep. dir. Nat. Ctr. Health Svcs. Rsch., Health Svcs. and Mental Health Adminstrn., HEW, Rockville, Md., 1969—73, dep. dir. manpower utilization br., 1970—73; dep. dir. Office Long Term Care; dep. chief nurse officer USPHS, Rockville, 1973—77; chief quality assurance br. div. long-term care Office Stds. and Certification, Health Standards and Quality Bur., Health Care Fin. Adminstrn., HHS, 1977—82; supervisory clin. nurse and spl. asst. to health systems adminstr. USPHS Indian Hosp., HRSA, HHS, Rosebud, SD, 1982—83; dir. patient edn., asst. dir. nursing G. W. Long Hansen's Disease Ctr., USPHS, Carville, La., 1984—89; dir. nursing Fed. Med. Ctr., Ft. Worth, 1989—95; pvt. cons., 1995—98; dir. Nat. Interfaith Coalition on Aging, Natl. Coun. on Aging, Washington, 1998—. Author: (book) Identifying Nursing Action with the Care of Cardiovascular Patients, 1967, Cardiosurgical Nursing Care: Understandings, Concepts and Principles for Practice, 1975; mem. editl. bd. Nursing and Health Care, 1983—95; contbr. articles to profl. jours. Served with Nurse Corps U.S. Army, 1954—57 USAR, 1957—68. Recipient Nursing Svc. award, Assn. Mil. Surgeons U.S., 1969, Commendation medal, USPHS, 1972, Meritorious Svc. medal, 1977, Disting. Svc. medal, 1987, citation for outstanding contbn. to cardiovascular nursing, Am. Heart Assn., 1972—79, award for disting. achievement in nursing rsch., Nursing Edn. Alumni Assn., Columbia U. Tchrs. Coll., 1973, Disting. Alumnus award, Case Western Res. U. Sch. Nursing, 1979, Women's Honors in Pub. Svcs. award, ANA, 1988, USPHS Commendable Svc. medal, U.S. Dept. Justice, Bur. Prisons, 1995, Holistic Nurse of the Yr. award, Am. Holistic Nurses Assn., 2001, Artist of Life First prize, Internat. Womens Writing Guild, 1987, Chief Nurse Officer award, USPHS, 2003; grantee, Sigma Theta Tau, 1966. Fellow: Gerontological Soc. Am., Nat. Gerontological Nursing Assn., Am. Assn. of Integrative Medicine (diplomate Coll. of Nursing 2003).

CHOW, TIMOTHY YI-CHUNG, mathematician, systems engineer; s. Daniel Tin-Wo and Nancy Yuk Chun Chow. AB in Math., Princeton U., 1991; PhD in Math., MIT, 1995. Asst. prof. math. U. Mich., Ann Arbor, 1995—98; rsch. engr. Tellabs Ops., Inc., Cambridge, Mass., 1998—2002; mem. tech. staff MIT Lincoln Lab., Lexington, Mass., 2002—. Contbr. articles to profl. jours. Grad. fellow, NSF, 1991—95, Postdoctoral fellow, 1995—98. Mem.: U.S. Othello Assn., Am. Math. Soc., Phi Beta Kappa. Achievements include patents pending for telecommunications network design. Avocations: composer and solver of puzzles and chess problems, Peanuts comic strip, Christian philosophy.

CHOW, TSE-TSUNG, foreign language and literature educator, humanities educator, poet, writer; b. Chiyang, Hunan, China, Jan. 7, 1916; s. P'eng-Chu and Ai-Ku (Tsou) C.; m. Nancy N.H. Wu; children: Lena Jane, Genie Ann. BA, Cheng-Chih U., 1942; MA, U. Mich., 1950, PhD, 1955; LLD (hon.), Hong Kong Bapt. U., 1997. Editor-in-chief New Understanding monthly, Chungking, China, 1942-43; dir. dept. rsch. and supervision Chungking Municipal Govt., 1943-44; editor-in-chief City Govt., monthly, 1943-44; editor New Critic monthly, 1945; dean Chungking Coll. Pub. Adminstrn., 1944; sec. to Pres. Govt. of China, 1945-47; rsch. asst. U. Mich., 1955; rsch. fellow Harvard U., 1956-60, rsch. assoc., 1961-62; vis. lectr. U. Wis., Madison, 1963, assoc. prof. depts. East Asian langs. and lit., and history, 1964-65, prof., 1966-94, chmn. dept. East Asian langs. and lit., 1973-79, prof. emeritus Madison, 1994—. Author: Election, Initiative, Referendum and Recall: Charter Provisions in Michigan Home Rule Cities, 1958, The May Fourth Movement: Intellectual Revolution in Modern China, 1960, 1998, 1999, 2004—, Research Guide to the May Fourth Movement, 1963, Hai-yen (Stormy Petrel) (collected poems), 1961, On the Chinese Couplet, 1964, A New Study of the Broken Axes in the Book of Poetry, 1969, An Index to Mathews' Chinese-English Dictionary with a New Method of Arranging Chinese Words, 1971, On Wang Kuo-wei's Tz'u Poetry, 1971, Ancient Chinese Wu Shamanistic Medicine and Poetry: A Study of the Origin of China's Romantic Literature, 1986, A Chinese Version of "The May Fourth Movement", 1996, Digested Writings of the Master of the Deserted Garden (Selected Writings on Chinese Literature, History, Culture and Philosophy), 1997, Hung-lou Meng An: Collected Essays on the Dream of the Red Chamber, 2000, Eighty-five Poems on Plum Blossoms, 1991, The White Jade Lyrics, 1991, A Chinese Palindrome, vol. 1, 1995; co-author: The May Fourth and China, 1979, Papers on Dream of the Red Chamber, 1982, Grand View of the Dream of the Red Chamber, 1987, Hu Shih and Modern China, 1991, Reminiscence, 1993; author, editor: Wen-Lin: Studies in the Chinese Humanities, vol. 1, 1968, vol. 2, 1989, Fifty Years After Graduation, 1993; Chinese transl. Rabindranath Tagore's Fireflies, 1971, rev. edit., 1994, Homer's Odyssey (1st part), 1972. Recipient medal of honor Chinese Govt., 1946; Ford Found./Carnegie Found. scholar, 1956-60; Guggenheim fellow, 1966-67; Disting. scholar fellow Am. Coun. Learned Socs./Am. Acad. Scis., 1982. Mem. MLA, Assn. Asian Studies, Island Soc. Singapore (hon. pres.). Home: 1101 Minton Rd Madison WI 53711-3140

CHOW, WINSTON, engineering research executive; b. San Francisco, Dec. 21, 1946; s. Raymond and Pearl C.; m. Lilly Fah, Aug. 15, 1971; children: Stephen, Kathryn. BSChemE, U. Calif. Berkeley, 1968; MSChemE, Calif. State U., San Jose, 1972; MBA cum laude, Calif. State U., San Francisco, 1985. Registered profl. chem. and mech. engr.; instr.'s credential Calif. Community Coll. Chem. engr. Sondell Sci. Instruments, Inc., Mountain View, Calif., 1971; mem. R & D staff Raychem Corp., Menlo Park, Calif., 1971-72; supervising engr. Bechtel Power Corp., San Francisco, 1972-79; sr. project mgr. water quality and toxic substances control program Electric Power Rsch. Inst., Palo Alto, Calif., 1979-89, program mgr., 1990-97, product line mgr. environ. market sector, 1997-99, indsl. and agrl. energy techs. and svcs. bus. area mgr., 1999—2001, exec. dir. Energy Ctrs. Network, 1999—2001, dept. mgr. energy utilization rsch. and devel., 2001—02. Mem. steering com. Indsl. Energy Tech. Conf., 1999-2002. Editor: Hazardous Air Pollutants: State-of-the-Art, 1993; co-editor: Clean Water: Factors that Influence Its Availability, Quality and Its Use, 1996; co-author: Water Chlorination, vols. 4, 6; co-editor 1997 Internat. Clean Water Conf.-Today's Sci. for Tomorrows Policies, The Environ. Profl., 1997; contbr. articles to profl. jours. Pres., CEO Directions, Inc., San Francisco, 1985-86, bd. dirs., 1984-87, chmn. strategic planning com., 1984-85; mem. industry com. Am. Power Conf., 1988-2002; with strategic long-range planning and restructuring com. Sequoia Union H.S. Dist., 1990-93, chmn. dist. ctrl. com., 1992-94. Recipient Grad. Disting. Achievement award, Calif. State U., San Francisco, 1985; Calif. Gov.'s Exec. fellow, 1982—83. Mem. ASME, AIChE (profl. devel. recognition award), NSPE, Calif. Soc. Profl. Engrs. (pres. Golden Gate chpt. 1983-84, v.p. 1982-83, state dir.), Water Environ. Fedn., Air and Waste Mgmt. Assn. (mem. electric utility com. 1990-2000), Calif. State U. Alumni Assn. (bd. dirs., treas. 1989-91), U. Calif. Alumni Assn., Beta Gamma Sigma.

CHOWDHURI, PRITINDRA, electrical engineer, educator; b. Calcutta, India, July 12, 1927; came to U.S., 1949, naturalized, 1962; s. Ahindra and Sudhira (Mitra) C.; m. Sharon Elsie Hackebeil, Dec. 28, 1962; children: Naomi, Leslie, Robindro, Rajendro. B.Sc. in Physics with honors, Calcutta U., 1945, M.Sc., 1948; MS, Ill. Inst. Tech., 1951; D.Eng., Rensselaer Poly. Inst., 1966. Jr. engr. lightning arresters sect. Westinghouse Electric Corp., East Pittsburgh, Pa., 1951-52; elec. engr. high voltage lab. Maschinenfabrik Oerlikon, Zurich, 1952-53; research engr. High Voltage Rsch. Commn., Daeniken, Switzerland, 1953-56; devel. engr. high voltage lab. GE, Pittsfield, Mass., 1956-59, elec. engr. research and devel. ctr. Schenectady, N.Y., 1959-62, engr. elec. investigations transp. systems div. Erie, Pa., 1962-75; staff mem. Los Alamos (N.Mex.) Nat. Lab., 1975-86; prof. elec. engring. Ctr. Elec. Power Tenn. Technol. U., Cookeville, 1986—. Lectr. Pa. State U. Behrend Grad. Ctr., Erie, 1969-75. Author: Electromagnetic Transients in Power Systems, 1996. Patentee in field. Fellow AAAS, IEEE, Instn. Elec. Engrs. (U.K.), N.Y. Acad. Scis. Democrat. Unitarian Universalist. Home: 690 Valley Forge Rd Cookeville TN 38501-1574 Office: Tenn Technol U Ctr Elec Power PO Box 5032 Cookeville TN 38505-0001 Office Phone: 931-372-3682. Business E-Mail: pchowdhuri@tntech.edu.

CHOWDHURY, ALI ASRAF, electrical engineer, researcher; b. Jaldi, Chittagong, Bangladesh, July 1, 1955; s. Hesamuddin Ahmed Chowdhury and Mahfuza Khatun Chowdhurani; m. Razia Khanam; 1 child, Fariha. MSEE with honors, Belarus Poly. Inst., 1980; MSEE, U. Sask., 1983, PhD in Elec. Engring., 1988; MBA, St. Ambrose U., 2002. Lic. profl. engr., Tex., registered Alta., Can., N.B., Can., chartered engr., Gt. Britain. Design engr. GE Mfg. Co., Chittagong, Bangladesh, 1980—81; reliability engr. Atlantic Nuclear Svcs. Ltd., Fredericton, Canada, 1987—90; sr. engr. Alta. (Can.) Power Ltd., Edmonton, 1990—99; sr. engring. reliability planning specialist MidAm. Energy Co., Davenport, Iowa, 1999—. Chmn. composite sys. reliability working group Mid-Continent Area Power Pool, St. Paul, 1999—; chmn. MidAm. Engring. Conf. MidAmerican Energy Co., Davenport, 2002; mem. Coun. Energy Advisors, USA, Davenport, 2001—; tech. advisor Electric Power Rsch. Inst., CA, Davenport, 2001—; industry advisor Power Sys. Engring. Rsch. Ctr., Davenport, 2000—; chmn. reliability task force Alta. Electric Utility Planning Coun., Calgary, 1990—95; chmn. coord. of reliability info. group Grid Co. Alta., Calgary, 1996—99; mem. tech. program com. Internat. Assn. Sci. and Tech. Devel., Calgary, 1991—99; mem. exec. com. Quad City Expo-Tech Orgn., Davenport, 1999, Quad City Engring. and Sci. Coun., Davenport, 1999—2002; advisor Jr. Achievement of No. Alta., Edmonton, 1990; mem. fund raising com. United Way of City of Edmonton, 1995; mem. organizing com., internat. tech. adv. com. 8th Internat. Conf. on Probabilistic Methods Applied to Power Sys., 2004. Contbr. over 90 technical papers in profl. jours. Mem. scholarship award com. Quad City Engring. and Sci. Coun., Davenport, 1999—2002. Recipient Best Paper award, Probabilistic Methods Applied Power Sys., 2004; scholar Talent Scheme scholar (7), Govt. Bangladesh, U. Sask., Can., 1965—88. Fellow: Instn. Elec. Engrs. U.K. (membership examiner 1999); mem.: IEEE (sr.; mem. several working groups 1995, chmn. Iowa-Ill. sect. 2004, Best Working Group award for IEEE Std. 762 2005, Best Paper award 1997, Region 4 Outstanding Engr. of Yr. 2003). Achievements include development of and advancement of innovative theories and application methodologis for power system reliability and value-based probabilistic planning in power industry applications. Avocations: travel, music, reading, writing, gardening. Office: MidAmerican Energy Co 106 East Second St Davenport IA 52801 Office Phone: 563-333-8142. Business E-Mail: aachowdhury@midamerican.com.

CHOWDHURY, ANWARUL KARIM, international organization official; b. Dhaka, Bangladesh, 1943; MA in History and Internat. Rels., U. Dhaka; D (hon.), Soka U. Permanent rep. of Bangladesh to UN, N.Y.C., 1996—2001; high rep. for least developed countries, landlocked developing countries and small island developing states UN, N.Y.C., 2002—; sec.-gen. UN Ministerial Conf. Landlocked and Transit Developing and Donor Countries, Almaty, 2003—, UN Internat. Meeting for Small Island Developing States, Mauritius, 2004—. Dir., Japan, Australia and New Zealand UNICEF, 1990—93; v.p., Econ. and Social Coun. UN, 1997—98, chmn. Fifth Com. Gen. Assembly, 1998—2000. Recipient U. Thant Peace Award, Gandhi Gold Medal for Culture of Peace, UNESCO.

CHOWDHURY, ARIF, civil engineer, researcher; s. Md. Mozammel Haque Chowdhury and Rashida Khatun; m. Anindita Ahmed, Jan. 25, 2004. BSCE, Bangladesh U. Engring. and Tech., Dhaka, 1993; MSCE, Tex. A&M U., 1999. Registered profl. engr. Tex. Jr. engr. Alcatel Contracting, Dhaka, 1994—95; asst. engr. Ministry of Edn., Dhaka, 1996—96; grad. asst. Tex. Transp. Inst., College Station, 1997—99, assoc. transp. rschr., 1999—; engring. asst. III Tex. Dept. Transp., Bryan, 1999. Mem. com. Transp. Rsch. Bd. Contbr. articles to profl. jours.;, author rsch. reports in field. Mem. Forum 86, Dhaka, 1988—2005; v.p. Bangladesh Student Assn., College Station, 1997—98, advisor, 2004—05. Recipient Chancellor award, Govt. of Bangladesh, 1984; scholar, Nat. Stone Assciation, 1998; Tech. scholar, Edn. Bd., 1986, Merit scholar, Bangladesh U. Engring. and Tech., 1992. Mem.: Assn. Asphalt Paving Technologist. Office: Texas Transp Inst Texas A&M University College Station TX 77843-3135 Office Phone: 979-458-3350. E-mail: a-chowdhury@tamu.edu.

CHOWDHURY, DHIMAN, physician, consultant; b. Chittagong, Bangladesh, Jan. 1, 1953; arrived in Can., 1996; s. Chitta Ranjan and Aruna Chowdhury; m. Smriti Chowdhury, Sept. 6, 1978; children: Muna, Chinmoy, Priyanka. MB, BS, Chittagong Med. Coll., 1975; Diploma in Child Health, U. Coll. Dublin, Ireland, 1983, Royal Coll. Surgeons, 1984. Intern Chittagong Med. Coll., 1975-76; med. officer Primary Health Care Ctrs., Chittagong, 1976-79; resident Arab Child Hosp., Baghdad, Iraq, 1979-80; gen. physician Suk Al-Shiukh Hosp., Thedar, Iraq, 1980-83; registrar Suleimania Children's Hosp., Riyadh, Saudi Arabia, 1984-90, cons. pediatrician, 1990-97, No. Regional Health Bd., Nova Scotia, Can., 1997; clin. assoc. IWK-Grace Health Ctr., Halifax, Novia Scotia, Can., 1997-99, cons. pediatrician, 1999—. Asst. prof. pediatrics Dalhousie U., 1999—; clin. asst. prof. King Saud U., Riyadh, 1993-97; program dir. Arab Bd. in Pediat. Residency Program, Riyadh, 1993-95, 96-97. Contbr. articles to profl. jours., chpt. to textbook. Fellow Royal Coll. Physicians (Edinburgh, U.K.); mem. Royal Coll. Physicians (Eng.), Saudi Pediat. Assn., N.Y. Acad. Sci., Bangladesh Med. Assn. Avocations: clinical photography, desert trips, travel, reading journals, fishing. Home: 967 Winwick Rd Halifax NS Canada B3H 4L5 Office: IWK Grace Health Ctr Dept Pediatric Medi PO Box 3070 Halifax NS Canada B3J 3G9 Office Phone: 902-428-8888. E-mail: d.chowdhury@dal.ca, dchowdhury@ns.sympatico.ca.

CHOWDHURY, DIPAK K., pharmaceutical executive, researcher; b. Chittagong, Bangladesh, Bangladesh, Dec. 1, 1956; s. Bimal Kanti and Srimitikana Chowdhury; m. Debjani Majumder, Sept. 1, 1965; children: Sudipa, Urvi. PhD, U. Sagar, 1984. Rsch. assoc. sch. pharmacy U. Mo., Kansas City, 1996—99; assoc. mgr. Murty Pharmaceuticals, Lexington, Ky., 1999—. Dept. pharmacy, assoc. prof. U. Dhaka, Bangladesh, 1989—96. Contbr. articles to internat. pharm. jours. Fellow, Ministry Edn., Govt. India, 1980—84, U. Mo., Kansas City, 1996; grantee, Nat. Inst. of Drug Abuse, NIH, 1999—2003. Mem.: Am. Assn. Pharm. Scientist (assoc.). Hinduism. Achievements include patents for Trasdermal delivery of tetrahydrocannabinol; patents pending for Sublingual Delivery For Tetrahydrocannabinol; In situ gel delivery for clindamycin; Microemulsion Delivery Of Tetrahydrocannabinol. Avocations: swimming, travel, reading. Home: 4321 Saron Dr Lexington KY 40515 Office: Murty Pharmaceuticals Inc 518 Codell Dr Lexington KY 40509 Personal E-mail: dipak56@hotmail.com. E-mail: dchowdhury@mpirx.com.

CHOWDHURY, MOHAMMED SHAMSUL, economics professor; b. Chittagong, Bangladesh; came to U.S., 1982. MA in Mgmt., Dhaka (Bangladesh) U.; MA in Econs., CUNY, 1988; DBA, Nova Southeastern U., 1997. Lectr. in mgmt. Govt. City Coll., Bangladesh; mgmt. cons. Bangladesh Mgmt. Devel. Ctr.; tchr. N.Y.C. Pub. Schs.; prof. Monroe Coll., Bronx, N.Y. Author: Economic and Commercial Geography, 1982; contbr. articles to profl. jours. Mem. Am. Acad. Mgmt. Avocations: reading, writing, fishing, gardening. Home: 8966 213th St Queens Village NY 11427-2328

CHOWDHURY, SUBIR, management consultant; came to U.S., 1991; s. Sushil Kumar and Krishna Keshi (Biswas) C.; m. Malini Guha, Feb. 26, 1997. BTech. in Aerospace Engring. with honors, Indian Inst. Tech., Kharagpur, India, 1989; MA in Indsl. Mgmt., Ctrl. Mich. U., 1993; PhD in Engring. (hon.), Mich. Tech. U., 2004. Software and sys. mgr. Ciproco Computers Ltd., Dhaka, Bangladesh, 1989-91; quality mgmt. cons. Gen. Motors Corp., Saginaw, Mich., 1993-97; exec. v.p. ASI, Livonia, Mich., 1997—2002, chmn., CEO, 2002—. Author: QS-9000 Pioneers, 1996, Robust Engineering, 1999, Management 21C, 2000, The Power of Six Sigma, 2001, Design for Six Sigma, 2002, The Talent Era, 2002, The Power of Design for Six Sigma, 2002, Organization 21C, 2002, Taguchi's Quality Engineering Handbook, 2004, Next Generation Business Handbook, 2004, The Ice Cream Maker: An Inspiring Tale About Making Quality The Key Ingredient in everything you do, 2005; editor-in-chief Automotive Excellence, 1997-99; founding editor Silicon mag., 1990. Fellow Royal Statis. Soc. (U.K.), Quality Soc. Australia; mem. Am. Soc. for Quality (sr., chair automotive divsn. 1999-2000, Philip Crosby medal 2003), Soc Mfg. Engrs. (sr., Gold medal 2002), Inst. Indsl. Engrs. (sr.), Soc. Automotive Engrs. (sr., Henry Ford II award of Excellence, 1996), World Innovative Found. (hon. 2003), Internat. Tech. Inst. (hon., inducted into the Hall of Fame for Engring., Sci. and Tech. 2004). Avocations: photography, music, writing, reading, surfing the internet. Office: ASI Cons Group LLC 38705 Seven Mile Rd Ste 345 Livonia MI 48152-3908

CHOWHAN, NAVEED MAHFOOZ, oncologist; b. Pakistan, Oct. 19, 1960; came to U.S., 1979; Student, Mao and Forman Christian Coll., Pakistan, 1979; MD cum laude, U Cetec, Dominican Republic, 1982. Bd. cert. internal medicine, 1986, hematology, 1992, oncology, 1993. Resident internal medicine Georgetown U. Svc., D.C. Gen. Hosp., Washington, 1983-86; fellowship oncology-hematology SUNY, Stony Brook, 1988-91, clin. asst. prof. dept. medicine divsn. oncology, 1992-94; pvt. practice New Albany, Ind., 1994—. Pvt. practice, South Bend, Ind., 1986—88; attending physician Meml. Hosp. and St. Joseph Med. Ctr., South Bend, 1987—88, Floyd Meml. Hosp., New Albany, 1994—, chair cancer conf., 1995—97, 2001, 03, dir. stem cell transplant unit, 1997—, chair cancer com., 1997—2000, sec. med. staff, 1998—2000, vice-chair staff, 2001, chair credentials com., 01, chmn. med. staff, 02; attending physician Clark Meml. Hosp., Jeffersonville, Ind., 1994—, mem. cancer com., 1995—, chair blood transfusion com., 1997, cancer liaison physician, 1999—2001; mem. Com. on Rsch. Involving Human Subjects, 1993—94; pioneer bone marrow transplant program SUNY, Stony Brook, 1994; investigator, rschr. and presenter in field. Contbr. articles to profl. jours. Named Physician of Yr., Nat. Rep. Congl. Com. Physician Adv. Bd., 2003; recipient Leadership award, 2002. Fellow ACP; mem. Am. Soc. Clin. Oncology, Am. Soc. Hematology, Am. Soc. Bone Marrow Transplantation. Office: 2210 Greenvalley Rd Ste 1 New Albany IN 47150-6809

CHOWNING, JOHN E., political scientist, educator, minister; s. Chattin D. and Elizabeth B. Chowning; m. Catherine Pence Chowning, Aug. 28, 1971; children: Kacey, Emily, Kaleb, Laura. AA, Lindsey Wilson Coll., 1971; BA, Transylvania U., 1973; MPA, Ea. Ky. U., 1977. Sch. tchr. Lincoln County Schs., Stanford, Ky., 1973—75; grad. asst. Ea. Ky. U., Richmond, 1975—76; dir. housing and cmty. devel. Lake Comb ADD, Russell Springs, Ky., 1977—80; dir. cmty. devel. City of Campbellsville, Ky., 1980—83; sr. cons., v.p. Pvt. Consulting, Lexington, Ky., 1983—95; dir. econ. devel. Congressman Ron Lewis, Elizabethtown, Ky., 1995—98; v.p., faculty polit. sci. Campbellsville U., 1998—. Pastor Saloma Bapt. Ch., Campbellsville; trustee, bd. chair Campbellsville U., 1990—98; chair Indsl. Devel. Authority, Campbellsville, 1998—2005; parliamentarian Ky. Bapt. Conv., Louisville, 2001—05; founder Ctr. Bivocational Ministry Campbellsville U., founder, dir. Ky. Heartland Inst. on Pub. Policy; bd. of institute Religion and Public Policy, DC; mem. Ctr. for Study of the Presidency; pres. Hopewell Acres, Inc.; chair Edn. Cabinet Transition Team for Ky., 2003, Commonwealth Marriage Initiative Task Force, 2002—05. Citizen mem. State Bd. Elections, Frankfort, 1991—2002; exec. bd. mem., former chair, vice chair Ctr. for Rural Devel., Somerset, Ky., 1996—2003; state exec. com. Rep. Party Ky., Frankfort, 1986—98. Named Citizen of Yr., Campbellsville C. of C., 1998, 2001, Man of Yr., BPW, Taylor County, 1999; recipient Econ. Devel. Leadership award, Gov. Ky., 1999. Mem.: Ky. Assn. of Econ. Devel., C. of C., Am. Soc. Pub. Adminstrn., Am. Polit. Sci. Assn. Avocations: reading, travel, public service, ministry. Home: 512 Fern Dr Campbellsville KY 42718 Office: Campbellsville Univ 1 University Dr UPO 1295 Campbellsville KY 42718

CHOY, HAK, oncologist; b. Seoul, South Korea, Jan. 17, 1958; MD, U. Tex. Med. Br., 1987. Cert. therapeutic radiology Am. Bd. Radiology, investigator Nat. Cancer Inst. Asst. prof. U. Tex. Health Sci. Ctr., San Antonio, 1991—92; clin. asst. prof. Brown U. Radiation Medicine, Providence, 1992—95; clin. dir., assoc. prof. Ctr. for Radiation Oncology Vanderbilt U. Med. Ctr., Nashville, 1995—98, prof. and vice chmn. Dept. Radiaion Oncology, 1998—2003; prof. and chmn. Dept. Radiation Oncology U. Tex. Southwestern Med. Ctr., Dallas, 2003—. Nancy B. and Jake L. Hamon disting. chair therapeutic oncology rsch. U. Tex. Southwestern Med. Ctr., Dallas, 2003—. Editor: (book series) Chemoradiation in Cancer Therapy for the Cancer Drug Discovery and Development; co author (book chpt.) The Role of Cyclooxygenase-2 Inhibitors in Combined Modality Therapy, Radiotherapy of Locally Advanced Non-Small Cell Lung Cancer, Potential for Combined Modality Therapy of Cyclooxygenase Inhibitors and Radiation, Basic Concepts of Chemotherapy and Irradiation Interaction; co-author: (book chpt.) Infusion Chemotherapy-radiation Interaction: Its Biology and Significancefor Organ Salvage and Prevention of Second Primary Neoplasms., Radiation Therapy for Non-Small Cell Lung Cancer; co author (book chpt.) Taxanes in Lung Cancer; co-author: (book chpt.) Taxanes and Radiation Therapy in Solid Tumors, The Role of Gemcitabine in Combined Modality Therapy, Chemoradition: Biological Principles and Perspectives; author (& co author): various editls., numerous jour. articles, numerous abstracts; reviewer numerous jours.

Mem. U. Tex. Southwestern Health Systems, Dallas, 2003. Mem.: Ea. Coop. Oncology Group, Nat. Cancer Inst., Internat. Assn. for the Study of Lung Cancer, Radiation Therapy Onocology Group, Am. Soc. Clin. Oncology, Am. Soc. Therapeutic Radiology and Oncology, Am. Cancer Soc. Achievements include patents for No. 6, 281, 223: Radioenhanced Camptothecin Derivative Cancer Treatments. Office: UT Southwestern Med Ctr 5801 Forest Park Rd Dallas TX 75390-9182 Office Fax: 214-645-7622. Business E-Mail: hak.choy@utsouthwestern.edu.

CHOYKE, PHYLLIS MAY FORD (MRS. ARTHUR DAVIS CHOYKE JR.), management executive, editor, poet; b. Buffalo, Oct. 25, 1921; d. Thomas Cecil and Vera (Buchanan) Ford; m. Arthur Davis Choyke Jr., Aug. 18, 1945; children: Christopher Ford, Tyler Van. BS summa cum laude, Northwestern U., 1942. Reporter City News Bur., Chgo., 1942-43, Met. sect. Chgo. Tribune, Chgo., 1943-44; feature writer OWI, N.Y.C., 1944-45; sec. corp. Artcrest Products Co., Inc., Chgo., 1958-88, v.p., 1964-88; pres. The Partford Corp., Chgo., 1988-90. Founder, dir. Harper Sq. Press div., 1966-90. Author: (under name Phyllis Ford) (with others) (poetry) Apertures to Anywhere, 1979; editor: Gallery Series One, Poets, 1967, Gallery Series Two, Poets—Poems of the Inner World, 1968, Gallery Series Three Poets: Levitations and Observations, 1970, Gallery Series Four, Poets, I am Talking About Revolution, 1973, Gallery Series Five/Poets—To An Aging Nation (with occult overtones), 1977; (manuscripts and papers in Brown U. Library). Bonbright scholar, 1942. Mem. DAR (corr. sec. Gen. Henry Dearborn chpt. 1991-92, treas. 1992-2003, regent, 2003-04), Soc. Midland Authors (bd. dirs. 1987—, treas. 1988-93, pres. 1993-95, membership dir. 1997-98, corr. sec. 1999—), Mystery Writers Am. (assoc.), Chgo. Press Vets. Assn., Arts Club Chgo., John Evans Club (Northwestern U.), Poetry Soc. Am. (N.Y.C.), Acad. Am. Poets (N.Y.C.). Home: 23 Windsor Dr Elmhurst IL 60126-3971

CHOYKE, WOLFGANG JUSTUS, physicist; b. Berlin, Ger., July 24, 1926; s. Frederick Samuel and Alice Sophia Amalia (Dessauer) C.; m. Helen Ruth Rubenfeld, June 19, 1949; children: Alice Mathea, Peter Lyle. BSc, Ohio State U., 1948, PhD, 1952. Rsch. physicist Westinghouse Rsch. Labs., Pitts., 1952-60, fellow physicist, 1960-63, adv. physicist, 1963-78, cons. physicst, 1978-88; adj. prof. physics U. Pitts., 1974-88, rsch. prof. physics, 1988—. Cons. Northrup-Grumman and Westinghouse Sci. & Tech. Ctr., Pitts., 1988-98; vis. prof. U. Erlangen-Nuremberg, 1990—. Contbr. over 390 articles to profl. jours. With U.S. Army Signal Corps, 1944-46. Recipient Westinghouse Order of Merit, 1983, Humboldt Rsch. prize, Bonn, 1990. Fellow: Am. Phys. Soc. (mem. com. applications physic 1977—86), AAAS; mem.: NRC (chmn. com. large band gap semiconductor devices 1993—95), Material Rsch. Soc. Achievements include fundamental studies and development of Silicon Carbide into what is presently the most promising high temperature semiconductor. Office: U Pitts Dept Of Physics Pittsburgh PA 15260 Office Phone: 412-624-9251. Business E-Mail: choyke@imap.pitt.edu.

CHRAI, SUGGY SINGH, pharmacist; b. Amritstar, India, Oct. 13, 1947; s. Sohan and Beant (Kaur) C.; m. Jane M. Limpert; children: Brian, Emily. BS in Pharmacy, Jadavpur U., Calcutta, India, 1969; MS, U. Wis., 1971, PhD, 1973; MBA, Fairleigh Dickinson U., 1977. Dir. pharm. tech. Bristol-Myers Squibb, New Brunswick, N.J., 1977-95; v.p. tech. affairs Mova Pharm. Corp., Cagaus, P.R., 1995; v.p. devel. Liposome Co., Plainsboro, N.J., 1995-97; v.p. tech. ops. Delsy's Pharm. Corp., Princeton, NJ, 1997—2001; CEO, pres. Chrai Assocs., Inc., Cranbury, NJ, 2001—. Contbr. articles to profl. jours. Active Boy Scouts Am., N.J., 1996—. Fellow Am. Pharm. Assn., Am. Assn. Indian Pharm. Scientists. Home: 16 Bodine Dr Cranbury NJ 08512-3159 Office: Chrai Assocs Inc 16 Bodine Dr Cranbury NJ 08512 Office Phone: 609-655-2573. E-mail: schrai@att.net.

CHREBET, WAYNE, professional football player; b. Garfield, N.J., Aug. 14, 1973; m. Amy Chrebet; children: Lukas Kane, Cade Jagger. BA in Criminal Justice, Hofstra U. Wide receiver NY Jets NFL, 1995—. Mem. AFC Ea. Championship team, 1998. Spokesman United Way, 1998—99; volunteer The Colleen Giblin Found. Office: NY Jets 1000 Fulton Ave Hempstead NY 11550-1030*

CHRETIEN, JANE HENKEL, internist; b. Jersey City, Mar. 24, 1941; m. Paul B. Chretien, Apr. 11, 1970; children: Jean Paul, Yves. AB, Barnard Coll., 1962; MD, N.J. Coll. Medicine, 1966; MPH, Harvard U., 1970. Diplomate Am. Bd. Internal Medicine, Am. Bd. Infectious Disease. Intern Cornell U. Med. Divsn-Bellevue Hosp. Ctr., N.Y.C., 1966-67; resident Meml. Hosp. Sloan Kettering Inst. Med. Ctr., N.Y.C., 1967-69; fellow Georgetown U. Hosp., Washington, 1970-72, clin. instr., staff physician student health svc., 1972-75, asst. dir. student health svc., 1975-87, med. dir., 1987-94, clin. asst. prof., 1975-79, clin. assoc. prof., 1979-94; assoc. prof. George Washington U., 1994-98, clin. assoc. prof., 1998—. Fellow ACP; mem. Internat. Soc. Travel Medicine. Office Phone: 301-656-4010.

CHRETIEN, PAUL BERNARD, oncologist, medical researcher; b. San Angelo, May 13, 1931; s. Joseph Rodney and Celeste Regina Chretien; m. Jane Susan Henkel, Apr. 11, 1970; children: Jean Paul, Yves Rene. BS, St. Louis U., Coll. Arts and Sci., 1953; MD, St. Louis U., Sch. Medicine, 1957. Diplomate Am. Bd. Surgery, lic. State of Md. From intern to chief resident, dept. surgery N.Y. U. Bellevue Hosp. Ctr., NY, 1957—62; nat. cancer inst. fellow, oncology Mem. Sloan-Kettering Cancer Cent., 1962—66; sr. investigator, asst. chief surgery br. Nat. Cancer Inst., 1966—72, chief, tumor immunology sect., surgery br., founding mem. immunotherapy contracts prog., 1972—80, coord., head, neck cancer contracts prog., div. cancer treatment, 1974—80; prof., dir. rsch., dept. surgery U. Md. Sch. of Medicine, 1983—93. Mem., sr. exec. svc. U.S. Civil Svc., 1976—80; co-originator, co-chmn. First Head and Neck Cancer Rsch. Workshop, 1980; cons., immunotherapy prog. Hoffmann-LaRoche Inc., 1980—92; v.p., med. affairs Alpha 1 Biomedicals Inc., 1982—94; originator, chmn. First Internat. Conf. Head and Neck Cancer, 1984. *Obtained sponsorship for the Conference by the Society of Head and Neck Surgeons and the American Society for Head and Surgery, with the expectation that their combined expertise would improve the treatment results of the malignancies and their interactions in the planning and execution of the Conference would lead to combining of the Societies. After the Conference, advised subsequent ones every four years. By the Sixth Conference, the Societies had formed the American Head and Neck Society and assumed sponsorship of the Research Workshops every four years, alternating every two years with the International Conferences.* Contbr. over 225 sci. abstract papers, articles, book chpts. Capt. Med. Corps. USAR, 1959—69. Mem.: Soc. Surg. Oncology, Clin. Immunology Soc., Am. Soc. Clin. Oncology, Am. Radium Soc., Am. Head Neck Soc., Am. Coll. Surgeons, Am. Fedn. Med. Rsch., Am. Assoc. Immunologists, Am. Assoc. Cancer Rsch., Am. Assoc. Advancement Sci. Achievements include assigned FDA IND 14,738 for first clin. trial of Thymosin alpa 1 (1978). Office: 10201 Grosvenor Pl Rockville MD 20852-4645 Office Phone: 301-493-6160. Business E-Mail: chretien.usa@erols.com.

CHRÉTIEN, RAYMOND A.J., retired ambassador; b. Shawinigan, Que., Can., May 20, 1942; s. Maurice and Cécile (Marcotte) C.; m. Kay Rousseau; children: Caroline, Louis-François. BA, Sém. de Joliette, 1962; LLL, U. Laval, 1965. Bar: Que. 1966. Mem. legal affairs div. Div. External Affairs Govt. of Can., 1966-67, policy dir. industry, investments and competition, asst. undersec. mfg., tech. and transp., insp. gen., assoc. undersec. state for external affairs, 1988-91, 3rd sec. permanent mission to UN N.Y.C., 1967-68, asst. sec. fed. and provincial rels. com. Privy Coun. Office, 1968-70, exec. asst. to sec., mem. treasury bd. Privy Coun. Office, 1970-71; exec. asst. to pres. Can. Internat. Devel. Agy., 1971-72; 1st sec. Can. Embassy, Beirut, 1972-75, 1st sec., counsellor Paris, 1975-78; Can. amb. to Zaïre, 1978-81; Can. amb. to Mexico, 1985-88; Can. amb. to Belgium and Luxembourg Brussels, 1991-94; Can. amb. to U.S. Washington, 1994—2000. Awarded Order of Aztec Eagle, Mex.

CHRISANT, ROSEMARIE KATHRYN, law library administrator; b. Chgo., Oct. 9, 1946; d. Theodore and Angeline Frances (Pawlik) Layne; 1 child, Paula Ellen Marie. BS in Edn., No. Ill. U., 1967; MLS, Rosary Coll., 1971. High sch. English tchr. Chgo. Sch. System, 1967-70; asst. libr. Akron (Ohio) Law Libr. Assn., 1971-76, libr. dir., 1976—. Cons. law firms, Akron. Contbr. articles to profl. jours. Mem. ABA, Am. Assn. Law Librs., Ohio Regional Assn. Law Librs. (Outstanding Svc. award 1986), Spl. Libr. Assn., Ohio Libr. Assn. Office: Akron Law Libr Assn Summit County Courthouse 209 S High St Rm 4 Akron OH 44308-1625 E-mail: allarkc@akronlawlib.org.

CHRISMAN, DIANE J., librarian; b. Lackawanna, N.Y., June 20, 1937; d. Floyd R and Elizabeth R (Nowakowski) Schutta. BA, U. Vt., 1959; MSL.S., Simmons Coll., 1960. Asst. head Crane br. Buffalo & Erie County Pub. Library, 1961-64, asst. head young adult dept., 1964-65, asst. head order dept., 1965-68, coordinator children div., 1968-79, dep. dir., 1979-98, dir., 2000—. Lectr SUNY, Buffalo, 1966—68, Buffalo, 1980, Buffalo, 1990—94. Contbr. articles to profl jours. Mem.: ALA, NY Library Asn, Zonta (past pres), Rotary. Avocations: skiing, golf. Home: 78 Rainbow Ter Orchard Park NY 14127-2517 Office: Buffalo & Erie County Pub Libr 1 Lafayette Sq Buffalo NY 14203-1823

CHRISMAN, RICHARD ALAN, minister, historian; b. Bismarck, Ill., Feb. 20, 1931; s. Merl Otis and Dorothy Louise (Boggess) Chrisman; m. Anna Marie Schlorff, July 1, 1951; children: Nancy Ann, Paul Alan, Gregory Scott, Stephen Lee. BA, Ill. Wesleyan U., 1953; BDiv, Garrott Theol. Inst., 1958; MA, Northwestern U., 1959. Pastor United Meth. Ch., Ill., 1951—92; historian Ill. Great Rivers Conf./United Meth. Ch., Bloomington, 1980—, archivist, 1992—2003, editor Hist. Messenger, 2004—. Office: United Meth Ch attn editor Bloomington IL 61702

CHRISMAN, WILLIAM HERRING, tax specialist, consultant; b. Evanston, Ill., June 28, 1932; s. Roswell Herring and Virginia Ruth (Haynes) C.; m. Margaret Baker Craig, Apr. 17, 1989; children: Katherine Anne, Emily Louise. AB, Harvard U., 1955. Media buyer Leo Burnett Co., Chgo., 1958-60; account exec. Lennen & Newell Inc., N.Y.C., 1960-63; subsidiary pres. Clairol Inc., N.Y.C., 1963-72; exec. v.p. Metalware Corp., Chandler, Ariz., 1973-75; pres. Chrisman Farms, Inc., Scottsdale, Ariz., 1975-80, E. Allen Mgmt. Corp., Phoenix, 1980-85; gen. mgr. Oasis Family Water Park, Phoenix, 1985; asset mgr. Evans Withycombe Inc., Phoenix, 1985-87; prin. Real Estate Valuation Cons., Phoenix, 1987—2002; ret., 2002—. Advt. instr. Katherine Gibbs Sch., N.Y.C., 1963-65. 1st lt. U.S. Army, 1955-57. Mem. Christmas Cove Improvement Assn., Spa at Camelback Inn. Democrat. Methodist. Home: 6235 E Catesby Rd Paradise Valley AZ 85253-3583

CHRISMER, RONALD MICHAEL, federal agency administrator; b. Washington, May 4, 1954; s. Michael Joseph and Phyllis Ann (Long) Chrismer; m. Dorothea May Shifflett, Sept. 20, 1986; 1 child, Jeffrey Ronald. BS magna cum laude, Towson State U., 1976; M in Gen. Adminstrn. and MIS, U. Md., 1987. Cert. purchasing mgr. Sr. proofreader Am. Assn. Life Ins., Washington, 1976-77; asst. supr. Coopers & Lybrand, CPAs, Washington, 1978-83, supr., 1983-85; purchasing mgr. APA, Washington, 1985-87; buyer U. Md., Balt., 1988; contract specialist IRS, Washington, 1988-98, contracting officer, 1994—2004, supr. contract adminstr., 1998—2004; supr. contract specialist, contracting officer Dept. Homeland Security, 2004—. Mem. telecom. adv. coun. Bell Atlantic, Washington, 1983—85. Mem. World Affairs Coun., Washington, 1983—85, Nat. Trust Hist. Preservation, Washington, 1983—85; block capt. Neighborhood Watch, Cardinal Forest Devel., 1987—; asst. den leader Cub pack Boy Scouts Am., 1996—98, scoutmaster troop, 1998—2003, asst. scoutmaster, 2003—, com. mem. venture crew, 2003—, mem. Order of Arrow, 2000—, com. mem. Indian Creek Dist., 2004—; com. mem. advanced jr. leader tng. Nat. Capital Area Coun., 2003—; mem. sch. bd. St. Mary's Sch., Laurel, Md., 1990—96, chmn., 1992—93, mem. parish coun., 1991—92; coach Cath. Youth Orgn., 1994—2000, Laurel Boys and Girls Club, 2001; min. children's liturgy St. Mary's, 1993—2000. Mem.: Inst. Supply Mgmt. (lifetime cert. 2003), Purchasing Mgmt. Assn. Washington, Purchasing Mgmt. Assn. Md. (chmn. edn. com. 1988), Nat. Assn. Purchasing Mgmt., KC (bd. dirs. club # 2203 1996—99, mem. Patuxent coun. 1996—, sec. 1997—99), Nat. Honor Soc., Psi Chi. Roman Catholic. Avocations: U.S. Civil War history, world history, music, art, literature. Home: 8810 Cardinal Ct Laurel MD 20723-1241

CHRISPEELS, MAARTEN JAN, biology professor; b. Kortenberg, Belgium, Feb. 10, 1938; married, 1966; 2 children. PhD in Agronomy, U. Ill., 1964. Rsch. asst. agronomy U. Ill., La Jolla, 1963-64; rsch. assoc. plant biochemistry Rsch. Inst. Advanced Studies, 1964-65, AEC, 1965-67; rsch. assoc. microbiology Perdue U., 1967, from asst. prof. to assoc. prof., 1967-79; prof. biology U. Calif., San Diego, 1979—. Program mgr. competitive rsch. grant office USDA, 1979. John. S. Guggenheim Found. fellow, 1973-74. Mem. AAAS, NAS, Am. Soc. Plant Physiologists (Stephen Hales prize 1996), Am. Soc. Cell Biologists. Office: U Calif at San Diego Div Biological Sci 9500 Gilman Dr La Jolla CA 92093-0116

CHRIST, CAROL TECLA, academic administrator; b. NYC, May 21, 1944; d. John George and Tecla (Bobrick) Christ; m. Larry Sklute, Aug. 15, 1975 (div. Dec. 1983); children— Jonathan, Elizabeth BA, Douglas Coll., 1966; M.Ph., Yale U., 1969, PhD, 1970. Asst. prof. English U. Calif., Berkeley, 1970-76, assoc. prof. English, 1976-83, prof. English, 1983—89, dean dept. English, 1985-88, dean dept. humanities, 1988, acting provost, dean, 1989-90, provost, dean Coll. Letters and Sci., 1990-94, vice chancellor, provost, 1994-2000; pres. Smith Coll., Northampton, Mass., 2002—. Former dir. summer seminars for secondary and coll. tchrs. NEH; former tchr. Bread Loaf Sch. of English; invited lectr. Am. Assn. Univs., Am. Coun. Edn. Author: The Finer Optic: The Aesthetic of Particularity in Victorian Poetry, 1975, Victorian and Modern Poetics, 1984; mem. editl. bd. Victorian Literature, The Victorian Visual Imagination, The Norton Anthology of English Literature; contbr. articles to profl. jours. Fellow Am. Acad. Arts & Sci.; mem. MLA. Office: Smith Coll College Hall 20 Northampton MA 01063*

CHRIST, DUANE MARLAND, retired computer systems engineer; b. Lakota, Iowa, Jan. 5, 1932; s. George Andrew and Esther Gertrude (Franke) C.; m. Lily Esther Shih, Sept. 14, 1963; 1 child, Wesley Anzo. BS, Iowa State U., 1953; MA, U. Minn., 1960; PhD, Rutgers U., 1998. Sci. programmer United Aircraft Corp., Hartford, Conn., 1960-63; computer sys. analyst IBM, N.Y.C., 1963-68, staff instr., 1968-76, adv. sys. engr., 1976-82, sr. sys. engr., 1982-87, prin., 1987—2003; ret., 2003. 1st lt. USAF, 1953-56. Recipient Ea. Regional Dir. award, 1983; named Area Specialist of Yr., 1986; IBM Resident Study fellow, 1966-68. Mem.: Assn. Computing Machinery, Inst. Ops. Rsch. and Mgmt. Scis., Math. Assn. Am., Am. Math. Soc., Soc. Indsl. and Applied Math. Home: 15 Tilton Dr Freehold NJ 07728-3359 Personal E-mail: christdm@msn.com.

CHRIST, KARYN LYNN, apparel designer, poet; b. Balt., Aug. 16, 1956; d. Robert John and Lois Mae Requard; m. Dale Robert Christ, Nov. 1, 1996. Diploma, Belair (Md.) H.S. Clothing designer Dress-Ups, Balt., 1974-86; master cutting contract designer Costume World, Pompano, Fla., 1994—; master designer, owner Jita Swim and Island Wear, 1987—; owner Hemp Hoggers, 2000—. Contract for swimwear designs and Spandex specialist; designer for theatrical prodns.; poet: A Journey Thru a Love, 1996. Fundraiser swim and fashion shows Cancer & Leukaemia in Childhood Trust, Bristol, Eng., 1993. Home: 1883 Jamaica Dr Navarre FL 32566 Office: 30 Papaya St Clearwater FL 33767 Office Phone: 850-939-5881. E-mail: jita@attglobal.net.

CHRIST, LILY ESTHER SHIH, mathematics professor; b. Korea, Sept. 19, 1936; came to U.S., 1955; d. Whan-Chang and Shin-Tze (Lin) Shih; m. Duane M. Christ, Sept. 14, 1963; 1 child, Wesley Anzo. BS, U. Minn., 1960; MA, Western Res. U., 1962; EdD, Columbia U., 1967. Tchr. Cleve. Pub. Schs., 1960-62; stats. lab. asst. Tchrs. Coll., Columbia U., N.Y.C., 1964-71; asst. prof. Coll. of Mt. St. Vincent, N.Y.C., 1966-68, John Jay Coll. Criminal Justice, CUNY, N.Y.C., 1969-73, assoc. prof., 1974—2005, HI-TECH PREP dir., 1993—, prof. emerita math., 2005—. Fulbright-Hays Sr. scholar, 1972. Mem. Math. Assn. Am. (gov. 1990-93, Cert. of Merit Svc. 1987, Disting. Coll. Tchg. Math award 2004), Am. Statis. Assn. (dist. 2 gov. 1990-91), Nat. Coun. Tchrs. Math. Office: CUNY John Jay Coll Criminal Justice 445 W 59th St New York NY 10019-1104 Office Phone: 212-237-8926. Business E-Mail: christle@jjay.cuny.edu.

CHRIST, ROXANNE E., lawyer; BA, UCLA, 1982; JD, Loyola Law Sch., 1985. Bar: Calif. 1985. With Paul, Hastings, Janofsky & Walker, Latham & Watkins, L.A., ptnr., 2001—. Office: Latham and Watkins LLC 633 W Fifth St Ste 4000 Los Angeles CA 90071

CHRISTAKIS, MICHAEL N., academic administrator; b. Rochester, N.Y., Aug. 2, 1977; s. Nikolaos M. and Vasiliki Christakis. BA in Polit. Sci. & History, Alfred U., 1999; MA in Pub. Policy, PhD, SUNY, 2001—. Resident asst. Alfred U., Alfred, NY, 1996—99; asst. residence hall dir. SUNY, Albany, NY, 1999—2001, residence hall dir., 2001—02. Co-coord. first yr. programs SUNY, 2001—02, asst. dir. residential life, 2002—; intern N.Y. State Edn. Dept., Albany, 2000—01. Congl. intern N.Y. 28th Congl. Dist., Rochester, NY, 1997—98. Mem.: Internat. Ldrop. Assn., Am. Soc. of Pub. Adminstrn., Omicron Delta Kappa (v.p. cir. std. 2002—, nat. student v.p. 2000—02, Meritorious Svc. award 2000). Greek Orthodox. Office: Department of Residential Life 1400 Washington Avenue Albany NY 12222-0001

CHRISTALDI, BRIAN, lawyer; b. Passaic, N.J., June 8, 1940; s. Peter Samuel and Helen (O'Brien) C.; m. Amy Edmonds, May 4, 1968; children: Kevin, Justin. BA, Amherst Coll., 1962; LLB, Harvard U., 1965. Bar: D.C. 1966, N.Y. 1967, Calif. 1988. Maxwell Pub. Svc. fellow, Papua, Guinea, 1965—66; with legal dept. Allied Chem. Corp., N.Y.C., 1967-69; assoc. then ptnr. Kelley Drye & Warren, N.Y.C., 1969-1995; counsel Kaye, Scholer, Fierman, Hays & Handler, LLP, N.Y.C., 1995-97; sr. comml. counsel, later asst. gen. counsel, then assoc. gen. counsel project fin. Overseas Pvt. Investment Corp., Washington, 1997—. Home: 4031 Oliver St Chevy Chase MD 20815-3432 Office: Overseas Pvt Investment Corp 1100 New York Ave NW Washington DC 20527-0001 E-mail: bchri@opic.gov.

CHRISTE, KARL OTTO, research chemist; b. Ulm, Fed. Republic Germany, July 24, 1936; s. Eugen A. and Elsa M. (Heller) C.; m. Brigitte F. Fischer, Jan. 27, 1962; children: Ralf, Mark, Tina. BS, Tech. U., Stuttgart, Fed. Republic Germany, 1957, MS, 1960, PhD, 1961; postgrad., U. Vienna, Austria, 1957-58. Sr. rsch. chemist Stauffer Chem. Co., Richmond, Calif., 1962-67; tech. staff Rocketdyne Divsn. Rockwell Internat., Canoga Park, Calif., 1967-78, mgr. rsch., 1978-94; sr. staff advisor Air Force Rsch. Lab., Edwards AFB, Calif., 1994—; prof. chemistry U. So. Calif., L.A., 1994—. Contbr. articles to profl. jours.; patentee in field. Recipient Apollo award NASA, 1969, Star Team award USAF, 1999, Prix Moissan award, Institution du Prix Moissan, Paris, 2000. Mem. AAAS, Am. Chem. Soc. (Creative Work in Fluorine Chemistry award 1986, Inorganic Chemistry award 2003), N.Y. Acad. Scis. Avocations: tennis, fencing, scuba diving. Home: 5645 Parkmor Rd Calabasas CA 91302-1036 Office: Loker Rsch Inst Univ So Calif Los Angeles CA 90089 Office Phone: 213-740-8957. E-mail: kchriste@usc.edu.

CHRISTEL, MARY TERESE, secondary school educator; b. Chgo., July 18, 1957; d. Walter L. and Isabel M. (Ritter) C. BSS, Northwestern U., 1979; MA, Columbia Coll., 1988. Tchr. Adlai E. Stevenson High Sch., Lincolnshire, Ill., 1979—. Co-editor Scriptor, 1991-94; co-author: Seeing and Believing; contbr. articles to profl. jours. Recipient fellowship NEH, Bloomington, Ill. 1989, Kenosha, Wis., 1990, Chgo., 1992; named Educator of Month Coca Cola Bottlers, Nov., 1992. Mem. NEA, Ill. Edn. Assn., Nat. Coun. Tchrs. of English (commn. on media edn. 1994), Ctr. for Media Literacy. Avocations: films, wines, travel. Office: 1 Stevenson Dr Lincolnshire IL 60069-2824

CHRISTEN, ARDEN GALE, dental educator, researcher, consultant; b. Lemmon, S.D., Jan. 25, 1932; s. Harold John Christen and Dorothy Elizabeth (Taylor) Deering; m. Joan Ardell Akre, Sept. 10, 1955; children: Barbara, Penny, Rebecca, Sarah. BS, U. Minn., 1954, DDS, 1956; MSD, Ind. U., 1965; MA, Ball State U., 1973. Lic. dentist, Ind. Commd. 1st lt. USAF, 1956, advanced through grades to col., 1972; base dental surgeon Zaragoza Air Base, Spain, 1970—73; dental surgeon, cons. preventive dentistry RAF Bentwaters, England, 1973—75; officer air force preventive dentistry Sch. Aerospace Medicine, Brooks AFB, Tex., 1978—80; prof., chmn. dept. preventive dentistry Ind. U., Indpls., 1981—93, dir. preventive/cmty. dentistry, 1993—2000, co-dir. nicotine dependence program, 1997—, acting chair oral biology, 2000—04, prof. emeritus oral biology, 2004—. Sr. med. svc. cons. Surgeon Gen., U.S. Air Force, U.S. and Eng., 1974-80; spl. cons. to asst. surgeon gen. for dental svcs., Washington, 1975-80. Co-author: Primary Preventive Dentistry, 4th edit., 1995; contbr. over 300 articles to profl. jours. Bd. dirs. Bexar County chpt. Am. Cancer Soc., San Antonio, 1976-80, Marion County chpt., Indpls., 1980—; mem. Ind. divsn. Pub. Edn. Standing Com., Indpls., 1980. Decorated Service medal with 2 oak leaf clusters, Legion of Merit. Fellow Am. Coll. Dentists; mem. ADA, Am. Acad. Oral Pathology, Internat. Assn. Dental Rsch., Am. Acad. History of Dentistry (v.p. 1984-85, pres. 1986-87). Presbyterian. Avocations: photography, classical music, travel, writing. Home: 7112 Sylvan Ridge Rd Indianapolis IN 46240-3541 Office: Ind U Sch Dentistry 1121 W Michigan St Indianapolis IN 46202-5186 Office Phone: 317-849-1152. Business E-Mail: achriste@iupui.edu.

CHRISTENBURY, LEILA, education educator; BA English, Hollins Coll., 1972; MA English, U. Va., 1973; EdD English Edn., Va. Tech., 1980. Tchr. English Roanoke Cath. High Sch., Va., 1973—75, William Fleming High Sch., 1975—78; asst. prof. dept. English lang. and lit. U. No. Iowa, Cedar Falls, 1979—80; asst. prof. English dept. James Madison U., Harrisonburg, Va., 1982—86; asst. prof., assoc. prof. Sch. Edn. Va. Commonwealth U., Richmond, 1968—95, prof. Sch. Edn., 1996—. Contbr. articles to profl. jours. Scholar, Va. Commonwealth U. Sch. Edn., 1993. Mem.: Va. Writers' Club, Va. Conf. English Educators, Va. Assn. Tchrs. English (treas., Frances Wimer award 2001), Assembly Women in Lit., Assembly Appalachian Lit., Assembly Lit. Adolescents, Nat. Conf. Rsch. Lang. and Lit., Nat. Coun. Tchrs. English (pres., Rewey Belle Inglis award Outstanding Women in English Edn. 1997), Omicron Delta Kappa, Phi Beta Kappa, Phi Kappa Phi, Phi Delta Kappa. Office: Va Commonwealth U Sch Edn PO Box 842020 Richmond VA 23284-2020

CHRISTENBURY, T. DANIEL, lawyer; b. 1959; BS, Lehigh Univ., 1981; MBA, JD, Univ. Richmond, 1985. Bar: Va. 1985, Pa. 1987, US Patent & Trademark Office. Ptnr., chmn. Patent Prosecution practice group DLA Piper Rudnick Gray Cary, Phila. Mem.: Am. Intellectual Property Law Assn., Phila. Intellectual Property Law Assn. Office: DLA Piper Rudnick Gray Cary One Liberty Pl Suite 4900 1650 Market St Philadelphia PA 19103 Office Phone: 215-656-3381. Office Fax: 215-656-2499. Business E-Mail: dan.christenbury@dlapiper.com.

CHRISTENSEN, ALLEN THOMAS, lawyer; b. Phila., Jan. 5, 1952; s. Erwin Henry and Joyce Diane (Thomas) C.; m. Pamela Jane Foster, Aug. 17, 1974; children: Grant Thomas, Lauren Elizabeth. BA, Ill. Wesleyan U., 1974; JD, U. Toledo, 1977; M of Law and Taxation, Coll. William and Mary, 1982. Bar: Ohio 1977, U.S. Dist. Ct. (no. dist.) Ohio 1978, U.S. Tax Ct. 1982. Labor atty. City of Toledo, 1977-81; assoc. Barkan & Robon, Toledo, 1982-87, ptnr., 1987-96, Marshall and Melhorn, LLC, 1996-2000, mem., 2001—. Pres. Toledo Estate Planning Coun., 2005 Mem. ABA, Ohio Bar Assn. (probate sect.), Toledo Bar Assn. (probate and tax com.). Methodist. Office: Marshall and Melhorn LLC Four Seagate 8th Flr Toledo OH 43604 E-mail: christensen@marshall-melhorn.com.

CHRISTENSEN, BETTY, artist; b. Collingdale, Pa., Apr. 11, 1915; d. Pasquale Grasso and Maria (Santella) Last; widowed, Mar. 1980. Cert., Phila. Coll. Art, 1936. Artist Al Paul Lefton Advt. Agy., Phila., 1940-48, McKee Albright Advt. Agy., 1948-50. Exhibited in group shows at Catherine Lorillard Wolfe Art Club, N.Y., Hudson Valley Art Assn., Conn. Watercolor Soc.; exhibited in permanent collections at Mattatuck Mus., Conn., Hoffman Fuel Co., Conn., Cyrenius Booth Libr., Conn.; illustrator: (book) A Few Thoughts on Trout, 1986. Recipient 1st prize in watercolor Richter Art Assn., 1997, Best in Show award Conn. Classic Arts, 1998, A. F. Harless Landscape award Hudson Valley Art Assn., N.Y., 1998, 1st prize in watercolor Housatonic Art League, 1998, Dorothy Watkeys Barberis Meml. award N.E. Watercolor Soc., 1999. Mem. Am. Watercolor Soc., Allied Artists of Am. (hon.), Hudson Valley Art Assn., N.E. Watercolor Soc. Evangelical. Avocation: gardening. Home: 25 West St Newtown CT 06470-2040 E-mail: bettycpaints@aol.com.

CHRISTENSEN, C. LEWIS, real estate developer; b. Laramie, Wyo., June 3, 1936; s. Raymond H. and Elizabeth C. (Cady) C.; m. Sandra Stadheim, June 11, 1960; children: Kim, Brett. BS in Indsl. Engring., U. Wyo., 1959. Mgmt. trainee Gen. Mills, Chgo., 1959, Mountain Bell, Helena, Mont., 1962—63, mgr. data comms. Phoenix, 1964—66, dist. mktg. mgr., so. Colo., 1970—73; seminar leader AT&T Co., Chgo., 1966—68, mktg. supr. N.Y.C., 1968—70; land planner and developer Village Assocs., Colorado Springs, Colo., 1973, exec. v.p., 1975—77; v.p. Cimarron Corp., Colorado Springs, 1974—75; pres. Lew Christensen & Assocs., Inc., Colorado Springs. Ptnr., gen. mgr. Briargate Joint Venture, 1977-82; pres. Vintage Comtys., Inc., 1982-95. Bd. dirs. Pikes Peak coun. Boy Scouts Am., Citizens Goals, Colo. Coun. on Econ. Edn., Cheyenne Mountain Zoo, U. Wyo. Found., engring. adv. bd.; chmn. Colorado Springs Econ. Devel. Coun., 1978, 89; bd. dirs., chmn. bd. Penrose St. Francis Hosp., chmn. 1999-2001. Served with USAF, 1959-62. Mem. Colorado Springs Home Builders Assn. (bd. dirs.), Urban Land Inst., Colorado Springs C. of C. (bd. dirs., chmn. bd.), Colorado Springs Country Club (bd. dirs.), Garden of Gods Club. Republican. Presbyterian. Achievements include development of 1,000-acre Peregrine planned community, south of USAF Academy; the 7,000 acre planned community of Briargate, just east of the USAF Academy. Office: Lew Christensen & Assocs Inc 2520 Stagsleap Pt Colorado Springs CO 80904-1192

CHRISTENSEN, DAN, painter; b. Lexington, Nebr., 1942; BFA, Kansas City Art Inst., 1964. Guest artist Whitney Mus. Sch., 1969, San Francisco Art Inst., 1971, Provincetown Workshop for Artists and Writers, 1972; instr. Ridgewood Sch. Art., 1975, 76, 77, Sch. Visual Arts, N.Y.C., 1976-82. Exhibited one-man shows, Noah Goldowsky Gallery, N.Y.C., 1967, Galerie Ricke, Cologne, Germany, 1968, 71, Andre Emmerich Gallery, N.Y.C., 1969, Nicholas Wilder Gallery, Los Angeles, 1970, Edmonton Art Gallery, Alta., 1973, Greenberg Gallery, St. Louis, 1974, Andre Emmerich Gallery, N.Y.C., 1975, Douglas Drake Gallery, Kansas City, 1976, 84, B.R. Kornblatt Gallery, Balt., 1977, Meridith Long Contemporary Gallery, N.Y.C., 1978, 79, 80, U. Nebr. at Omaha Art Gallery, 1980, Salander-O'Reilly Galleries Inc., N.Y.C., 1981, 82, 83, 84, Ivory Kimpton Gallery, San Francisco, 1982, Lincoln Ctr. Gallery, N.Y.C., 1983, Edward Thorp Gallery, 2005, group shows, Oberlin Coll., Ohio, 1966, Whitney Annual, N.Y.C., 1967, Whitney Mus. Am. Art, N.Y.C., 1968, 71, 72, 73, Galerie Ricke, Kassel, Germany, 1968, Corcoran Mus. Biennial, Washington, 1969, Guggenheim Mus., N.Y.C., 1969, Albright-Knox Gallery, Buffalo, N.Y., 1970, Balt. Mus. Art, 1971-72, Milw. Art Ctr., 1972, Boston Mus. Fine Arts, 1972, Aldrich Mus. Contemporary Art, Ridgefield, Conn., 1973, Greenberg Gallery, St. Louis, 1974, Museo Bellas Artes, Curacus, 1975, Lehigh U., Bethlehem, Pa., 1976, Edmunton Art Gallery, 1977, U. Nebr., Omaha, 1978, Zolla Liberman Gallery, Chgo., 1979, Carson-Sapiro Gallery, Denver, 1980, Mus. Modern Art, N.Y.C., 1981, Mus. Fine Arts, Houston, 1981, La Jolla Mus. Contemporary Art, Calif., 1981, Spl. Projects at PSI, N.Y.C., 1983; represented permanent collections, Albright-Knox Gallery, Boston Mus. Fine Arts, Chgo. Art Inst., Dayton Art Inst., Denver Mus. Art, Edmunton Art Gallery, Guggenheim Mus., Hirshhorn Mus. and Sculpture Garden, Washington, Houston Mus. Fine Arts, Wallraf-Richartz, Cologne, Germany, Met. Mus. Art, N.Y.C., Mus. Contemporary Art, Chgo., Mus. Modern Art, N.Y.C., St. Louis Art Mus., Toledo Mus., Whitney Mus. Am. Art. Recipient Nat. Endowment grant, 1968, Theodoron award, 1969; Guggenheim fellow, 1969, Gottlieb Found. grant, 1986, Pollock-Krasner Found. grant, 1996. Mem. Kansas City Art Inst. (gov. 1981)*

CHRISTENSEN, DAVID ALLEN, retired manufacturing executive; b. 1935; BS, S.D. State U., 1957. With John Morrell & Co., 1960-62, Raven Industries Inc., Sioux Falls, S.D., 1962—, product mgr., 1964-71, pres., chief exec. officer, 1971-2000; ret., 2000. Served with AUS, 1957-60. Office: Raven Industries Inc PO Box 5107 Sioux Falls SD 57117-5107

CHRISTENSEN, DAVID WILLIAM, mathematician, engineer; b. San Francisco, Jan. 19, 1937; s. Christopher Drost and Wilma (Hallowell) C.; m. Felicity Ann Bush, Nov. 2, 1963; children: Karen Anne, Paul Thomas. Student, MIT, 1954-58; BA, BS in Math., U. Calif., Santa Barbara, 1960; MIM in Internat. Mgmt. with honors, Am. Grad. Sch., Glendale, Ariz., 1973. Registered profl. engr., Calif. Project engr. North Am. Rockwell, Anaheim, Calif., 1963-70, Litton Ingalls Ships, Pascagoula, Miss., 1970-73; coord. of fin. Sonatrach Oil Co., Algiers, Algeria, 1975-78; revenue cons. Saudi Arabian Bechtel, Jubail, Saudi Arabia, 1978-80; sr. planner Arabian Am. Oil Co., Dhahran, Saudi Arabia, 1980-86; strategic planning and project controls Bechtel Power Corp., San Francisco, 1987—. Mem. (from Jubail) Saudi Royal Commn. Com. on Indsl. Devel., Riyadh, Saudi Arabia, 1978-80; lectr. U. Calif., Santa Barbara, 1964, citizens adv. group, subcom. Savannah River Site, S.C.; cons. DOE, U.S. Congress on tritium and plutonium projects. Contbr. articles to profl. pubs. Mem. Charcot-Marie-Toothe Assn., Balt., 1987—, Gertrude Herbert Art Inst., Augusta, Ga., 1990—, Jr. C. of C., Santa Barbara, Calif., 1960-64. Recipient Boit prize, 1957. Mem. NSPE (power group 1990), Soc. Am. Mil. Engrs. Republican. Episcopalian. Achievements include development with others of hydrocarbon and industrial resources in the Middle East (Algeria, Egypt, Saudi Arabia). Office: ETA-Z Inc 3408 Heather Dr Augusta GA 30909-2795 Personal E-mail: dchristx@mindspring.com.

CHRISTENSEN, DAWN MICHELLE, family practice nurse practitioner, consultant; b. Coatesville, Pa., June 28, 1970; d. John Richard Lebid; m. Scott Evan Christensen, Jan. 6, 1996; 1 child, Nicholas Scott. BSN, Temple U., Phila., 1992; MS, Pa. State U., 1997. FNP, Am. Nurses Credentialing Ctr., 1998, acute care nurse practitioner, ANCC, Pa., 1999. Staff nurse Pa. State Milton S. Hershey Med. Ctr., 1992—97, nurse practitioner, 1997—99, circulatory support coord., nurse practitioner, 1997—. Adj. faculty Pa. State U., Harrisburg, 2000—; clin. cons. Thoratec Corp., Pleasanton, Calif., 1999—2002, Novacor Inc., 2002—. Mem.: Pa. Nurses Soc. Dist. 15 (v.p. 1999), Am. Soc. Artificial Internal Organs, Internat. Soc. Heart and Lung Transplant, Am. Assn. of Critical Care Nurses. Home: 66 Cardinal Rd Pine Grove PA 17963 Office: Pa State Milton S Hershey Med Ctr 500 University Dr Hershey PA 17933 Office Phone: 717-531-4391. Business E-Mail: dchristensen@psu.edu.

CHRISTENSEN, DIETER, ethnomusicologist; b. Berlin, Apr. 17, 1932; PhD, Free U., Berlin, 1957. Curator, dir. Berlin Phonogramm Archiv, 1958-72; prof. Columbia U., N.Y.C., 1970—, dir. Ctr. for Ethnomusicology, 1971—2003; lectr. Free U., Berlin, 1962-70. Vis. prof. Wesleyan U., 1970, U. Hamburg, Germany, 1977, Hunter Coll.-CUNY, N.Y.C., 1978—80, U. Nova de Lisboa, 1992; sec. gen. Internat. Coun. for Traditional Music, UNESCO, 1981—2001; dir. The Universe of Music-A History, UNESCO, 1985—93. Author: Die Musik der Kate, 1957, Die Musik der Ellice-Inseln, 1964; co-author: El Anillo del Tlalocan, 1975, 1990, Dictionary of Traditional Music in Oman, 1994; editor: Yearbook for Traditional Music, 1981—2001, (compact disc) UNESCO Collection of Traditional Music, 1995—2000. Office: Columbia U Music Dept MC 1815 New York NY 10027 Business E-Mail: dc22@columbia.edu.

CHRISTENSEN, DONN WAYNE, insurance executive; b. Atlantic City, Apr. 9, 1941; s. Donald Frazier and Dorothy (Emily) Christensen; m. Marshella Abraham, Jan. 26, 1963 (div.); children: Donn Wayne, Lisa Shawn; m. Mei Ling Fill, June 18, 1976 (div.); m. Susan Kim, Feb. 14, 1987 (div.); m. Christina Yee, Dec. 2, 2000. BS, U. Santa Clara, 1964. West coast divsn. mgr. Ford Motor Co., 1964-65; agt. Conn. Mut. Life Ins. Co., 1965-68; pres. Christensen & Jones Inc., L.A., 1968—99; v.p. Rsch. Devel. Systems. Inc. Pres. Northern B.C. Enterprises Ltd., Misty Meadows Ranch Ltd., B.C., Can.; registered investment advisor, SEC. Pres. Duarte Cmty. Drug Abuse Coun., 1972-75; pres. Woodlyn Property Owners Assn., 1972-73; mem. L'Ermitage Found., 1985-90, Instl. Rev. Bd. White meml. Hosp., L.A., 1975-2000, Friend's Med. Rsch., 1992-2000; bd. dirs. Moberly Lake Cmty. Assn., 2002--; pres. Bd. of Moberly Lake Fire Dept., 2002--. Recipient Man of Yr. award L.A. Gen. Agts. and Mgrs. Assn. Mem. Nat. Life Underwriters Assn., Calif. State Life Underwriters Assn., Investment Co. Inst. (assoc.), Soc. Pension Actuaries, Foothill Cmty. Concert Assn. (pres. 1970-73). Office: 23801 Calabasas Rd Calabasas CA 91302 Office Phone: 250-788-9696. E-mail: wayne@moberlylake.com.

CHRISTENSEN, DOUGLAS D., school system administrator; BA, Midland Luth. Coll., 1965; MA, U. Nebr., 1970, PhD in Administration, Curriculum and Instruction, 1978. Tchr. Holdrege Sr. H.S., Nebr., 1965-70; h.s. prin. Bloomfield Cmty. Schs., Nebr., 1970-74, supt. of schs., 1974-76; county supt. of schs. Knox County Ctr., Nebr., 1975-76; supt. of schs. Colby Pub. Schs. Unified Sch. Dist. #315, Nebr., 1978-85, North Platte Pub. Schs., Nebr., 1985-90; assoc. commr. of edn. Nebr. Dept. of Edn., Lincoln, 1990-92, dep. commr. of edn., 1992-94, commr. edn., 1994—. Presenter, cons. in field. Contbr. articles to profl. jours. Chair North Platte Area Econ. Devel. Task Force, 1986-90, Coun. for Inter-Agy. Cooperation, 1986-90; liturgist First Luth. Ch., 1986-90, chair fin. com., 1988-90; bd. dirs. Mid-Nebr. Cmty. Found., 1989-90; bd. dirs. Mari Sandoz Soc., 1990—; mem. Nebr. Commn. for the Protection of Children, 1994—; advanced planning com. Southwood Luth. Ch., 1994—. Recipient Spirit of PTA award Nebr. PTA, 1997, 98, Cornerstone award Future Farmers Am., 1998, Walter Turner award Am. Assn. Ednl. Svc. Agys., 1998, David Hutchinson award U. Nebr., 1998, Burnham Yates award Nebr. Coun. Econ. Edn., 1999. Mem. ASCD (pres. Kans. affiliate 1984-85), Am. Assn. of Sch. Adminstrs. (Nebr. Supt. of Yr. 1990), Coun. Chief State Sch. Officers (bd. dirs. 1997—), Nebr. Coun. of Sch. Adminstrs., Rotary Internat. (pres. 1981-82), Nebr. Ctr. for Ednl. Excellence (chair 1985-90, bd. dirs. 1989-90), Midland Luth. Coll. Alumni Assn. (pres. 1992-93). Office: Commrs Office Dept of Edn PO Box 94987 Lincoln NE 68509-4987 also: 301 Centennial Mall S Lincoln NE 68509

CHRISTENSEN, HAYDEN, actor; b. Vancouver, BC, Canada, Apr. 19, 1981; s. David and Alie Christensen. Actor: (TV series) Family Passions, 1993; (films) Street Law, 1995, In the Mouth of Madness, 1995, Strike!, 1998, The Virgin Suicides, 1999, Life as a House, 2001, Star Wars: Episode II Attack of the Clones, 2002, Shattered Glass, 2003, Star Wars: Episode III Revenge of the Sith, 2005; (TV films) Love and Betrayal: The Mia Farrow Story, 1995, Harrison Bergeron, 1995, No Greater Love, 1996, Freefall, 1999, Trapped in a Purple Haze, 2000, R2-D2: Beneath the Dome, 2001, numerous TV guest appearances. Office: c/o The Gersh Agy 232 N Canon Dr Beverly Hills CA 90210*

CHRISTENSEN, HENRY, III, lawyer; b. Jersey City, Nov. 8, 1944; s. Henry Jr. and M. Louise (Brooke) C.; m. Constance L. Cumpton, July 1, 1967; children: Alexander, Gustavus, Elizabeth, Katherine. BA, Yale U., 1966; JD, Harvard U., 1969. Bar: N.Y. 1970, U.S. Tax Ct. 1973, U.S. Ct. Appeals (2d. cir.) 1973, U.S. Supreme Ct. 1975. Assoc. Sullivan & Cromwell, N.Y.C., 1969-77, ptnr., 1977—. Adj. assoc. prof. NYU, N.Y.C., 1985-88, U. of Miami Law Sch., 1997—. Author: International Estate Planning, 1999, ann. supplements, 1999—; contbr. articles to profl. jours. Chmn. Prospect Park Alliance, Bklyn., 1985—; trustee, 1st vice chmn. Peddie Sch., Hightstown, N.J., 1986—; trustee Am. Fund for the Tate Gallery, 1987—, Bklyn. Acad. Music, 1992—, Vincent Astor Found., 1993—, Alex Hillman Family Found., 2000—, Friends of the Prince's Trust, 2001—; dir., sec. Freedom Inst., N.Y.C., 1980—; dir., v.p. Am. Friends of Whitechapel Art Gallery Found., 1991—; trustee, mem. exec. com. Am. Ctr. Oriental Rsch. in Amman, 1993—. Fellow Am. Coll. Trust and Estate Counsel (chmn. internat. estate planning com. 2003-); mem. N.Y. State Bar Assn. (chmn. estate and gift tax com. 1983-84, chmn. exempt orgn. com. 1986, chmn. income taxation of trusts com. 1984-85, 87-89, exec. com. tax sect. 1983-89), Internat. Acad. Estate and Trust Law (v.p.). Home: 35 Prospect Park W Apt 8/9B Brooklyn NY 11215-2370 Office: Sullivan & Cromwell 125 Broad St Fl 29 New York NY 10004-2498 Office Phone: 212-558-3949.

CHRISTENSEN, JOHN WILLIAM, lawyer; b. Roselawn, Ind., Mar. 14, 1914; s. Henry Julius and Caroline Belle (Conrad) C.; m. Eleanor Schwerak, Sept. 2, 1939; children: William J., Amy Christensen Fox, Martha Christensen Rand, Nancy Christensen Couyoumjian; m. Beth Pinkley, Nov. 9, 1996. AB, DePauw U., 1935; JD, U. Ind., 1939. Bar: Ind. 1939, U.S. Supreme Ct., 1944, Ohio 1947. Acct. GE Co., Schnectady, N.Y., 1935-36; atty. SEC, Washington, 1939-44, spl. counsel utilities divsn., 1944-46; assoc., then ptnr. Dargusch, Caren, Greek & King, Columbus, Ohio, 1946-53; ptnr. Gingher & Christensen, Columbus, 1953-86; of counsel Baker & Hostetler, Columbus, 1986—98; gen. counsel Brodhead-Garrett Co., Cleve., 1955-86, also bd. dirs.; v.p., gen. counsel Columbus Mut. Life Ins. Co., 1962-84. V.p., gen. counsel, sec., bd. dirs. O.M. Scott & Sons Co., Marysville, Ohio, 1951-84; chmn., pres., CEO Nat. Extrusion and Mfg., Bellefontaine, Ohio, 1978-87; bd. dirs. State Automobile Mut. Ins. Co., United McGill Corp., Taylor Woodcraft Inc.; adj. prof. law Ohio State U., 1964-72. Trustee DePauw U., Greencastle, Ind., 1962—. With USCGR, 1943-45. Mem. ABA, Ohio Bar Assn., Columbus Bar Assn., Ind. U. Law Alumni Acad. of Fellows, Order of Coif, Phi Beta Kappa, Phi Delta Phi. Presbyterian. Home: 10401 W Charleston Blvd Apt A-305 Las Vegas NV 89135

CHRISTENSEN, KAREN KAY, lawyer; b. Ann Arbor, Mich., Mar. 9, 1947; d. Jack Edward and Evangeline (Pitsch) Christensen; m. Kenneth Robert Kay, Sept. 2, 1977; children: Jeffrey Smithson, Braden Kay, Bergen Kay. BS, U. Mich., 1969; JD, U. Denver, 1975. Bar: Colo. 1975, DC 1976, U.S. Supreme Ct. 1979. Atty., advisor office of dep. atty. gen. U.S. Dept. of Justice, Washington, 1975-76, trial atty. civil rights div., 1976-79; legis. counsel ACLU, Washington, 1979-80; staff atty. DC Pub. Defender Svc., Washington, 1980-85; asst. gen. counsel Nat. Pub. Radio, Washington, 1985-93; gen. counsel Nat. Endowment Arts, Washington, 1993-98, acting dep. chmn. for grants and partnership, 1997-98, dep. chmn. grants and awards, 1998—2001; arts cons., 2002—. Mem. DC Bd. Profl. Responsibility, 1990—98, chair, 1996—98. Bd. dirs. Corcoran Art Mus., 2001—03, Liz Lerman Dance Exch., 2002—05, Tucson Pima Arts Coun. Pub. Art Com., 2005—; vice chair bd. Mus. Contemporary Art, Tucson, 2005—; mem. pub. adv. com. KUAT-KUAZ (Pub. Radio/TV Com. Group), 2005—. Mem.: NCA/ACLU (mem. exec. bd. 1986—93, chair 1993), DC Bar Assn., Phi Beta Kappa. Personal E-mail: chriskk2@aol.com.

CHRISTENSEN, KATHLEEN ELIZABETH, foundation administrator; b. Madson, Wis., May 25, 1951; d. Norbert Martin and Janet Cull C.; m. John Joseph Murray III, May 25, 1990; children: Clare, Grace. BS summa cum laude, U. Wis., Green Bay, 1973; MS, Pa. State U., 1979, PhD, 1981. Policy analyst Urban Inst., Washington, 1973-75; from asst. prof. to prof. psychology CUNY, N.Y.C., 1981-91, prof., 1991-99; program dir. Alfred P. Sloan Found., N.Y.C., 1994—. Cons. in field. Author: Women & Home-based Work: The Unspoken Contract, 1988, Turbulence in the Workplace, 1990; editor: The New Era of Homebased Work, 1988, Contingent Work: American Employment Relations in Transition, 1998. Mem. adv. bd. Ctr. Work & Family Boston Coll., 1990-94. Humanities fellow NEH, 1977-79, Danforth fellow Danforth Found., 1979-81, Mellon fellow Aspen Inst., 1982. Mem. AAAS, Am. Sociol. Assn., Am. Anthropol. Assn. Office: Alfred P Sloan Found 630 Fifth Ave New York NY 10111 Office Phone: 212-649-1649. E-mail: christensen@sloan.org.

CHRISTENSEN, LAWRENCE O., historian, educator; b. Glasgow, Mont., Aug. 18, 1937; s. Andrew Lawrence and Orvella Sylvia (Oland) Christensen; m. Maxine Joyce Lahmann, Mar. 29, 1961. BS in Edn., Truman State U., 1960, MA in History, 1962; PhD in History, U. Mo., Columbia, 1972. Elem. sch. tchr., Columbia, Ill., 1957—58; tchr. William Chrisman HS, Independence, Mo., 1961—62, Westwood HS, 1963—64; secondary sch. tchr. Galesburg, Ill., 1960—61; instr. history Wis. U., Whitewater, 1968—69; instr. history to disting. tchg. prof. history U. Mo., Rolla, 1969—2000; program officer NEH, Washington, 1977—78; prof. U. Mo., Rolla, Mo., 1981—2000, Thomas Jefferson fellow, 1999, prof. emeritus, 2000—. Co-author: Missouri: The Heart of the Nation, 3 edits., 1981—2003, UM-Rolla: A History of MSM-UMR, 1982, The History of Missouri, vol. 4, 1875-1919, 1998 (Best Book award, 1998); co-editor: Dictionary of Missouri Biography, 1999 (award of merit Assn. for Study of State and Local History, spl. book award State Hist. Soc. Mo., 1999). Bd. dirs. Mo. Humanities Coun., St. Louis, 1989—91. P.f.c. USAR, 1955—61. Grantee, NEH, 1979. Mem.: State Hist. Soc. Mo. (pres. 1998—2001), So. Hist. Assn. (life), Orgn. Am. Historians (life). Democrat. Episcopalian. Avocations: reading, travel, fishing, wine. Home: 14190 State Rte Y Rolla MO 65401 Office: U Mo Rolla 131 Humanities Rolla MO 65401 E-mail: christen@umr.edu.

CHRISTENSEN, MADONNA DRIES, writer; b. Ashton, Iowa, Sept. 17, 1935; d. Frank Anton and Agnes Isabella (Guertin) Dries; m. Gary Lee Christensen, May 22, 1965; 1 child, Jill Christensen Buzby. Certs. in creative writing, U. Va., 1984, certs. in creative writing, 1988. Founder/facilitator Gulf Coast Writers, Sarasota, Fla., 1994—95; contbg editor Writer's Guidelines and News mag., Sarasota, Fla., 1998—2001, Jamaica, NY, 2001—02; contbg mem. Thema Lit. Soc., Metairie, La., 1992—. Contbr. chapters to books The Writer's Handbook; co-editor: (anthology) Tapestry; author: Swinging Sisters; contbr. anthology Mothers and Daughters: A Poetry Collection. Ct. monitor Mothers Against Drunk Drivers, Arlington County, Va., 1978—79; mem. Arlington County Fair Bd., Va., 1985—93; contest coord., editor Doorways, Sarasota, 1997—. Mem.: Gulf Coast Writers, Thema Lit. Soc., Internat. Women's Writing Guild, Emerald Coast Writers, West Coast Writers. Avocations: genealogy, reading, doll collecting.

CHRISTENSEN, MARGUERITE ALICE, librarian; b. Trout Lake, Wis., Aug. 24, 1917; d. Peter Carl and Alice (Cady) Christensen; B.A., U. Wis., 1938, B.L.S., 1939. Librarian, high sch. and Pub. Library, Bloomer, Wis., 1939-41; asst. librarian Wis. State U., Superior, 1941-43, Carroll Coll., Waukesha, Wis., 1943-45; asst. reference librarian U. Wis.-Madison, 1945-66, head gen. reference dept., 1967-82. Mem. ALA, Assn. Coll. and Research Libraries. Home: 4469 Hillcrest Dr Madison WI 53705-5020

CHRISTENSEN, MARVIN NELSON, venture capitalist; b. W. Branch, Iowa, July 15, 1927; s. Peter Ancher and Martha Henrietta (Neilsen) C.; m. Mary Lou Miller, Dec. 17, 1949 (dec. June 1999); children: Stephen R., Barbara; m. Virginia Thompson, 2001. BS, U. Iowa, 1950. Pvt. practice ins. and real estate, Iowa City, 1955-69; asst. to pres. Gen. Growth Cos., Des Moines, 1970-72; acquisitions dir. Life Investors of Iowa, Cedar Rapids, 1972-80; chmn., CEO Bus. Comml. Realty, Denver, 1980—, Colo. Internat. Devel., Colorado Springs, 1984—; chmn. Byers (Colo.) State Bank, 1987-89, Farmer's State Bank, Waubun, Minn., 1988-96. Founder, adminstr. Waubun Area Devel. Enterprises, 1988—. Columnist: View from My Window (monthly newspaper); contbr. many articles to nat. pubs. Lt. (j.g.) USNR, 1944-46. Mem. Am. Bankers Assn., Minn. Bankers Assn., Masons, Elks, Eagles, VFW. Avocations: writing, cabinet making, fishing. Home: RR 2 Waubun MN 56589-9802 also: 246 E Bain Dr Tidewater OR 97390

CHRISTENSEN, NIKOLAS IVAN, geophysicist, educator; b. Madison, Wis., Apr. 11, 1937; s. Ivan Rudolph and Alice Evelyn (Ethen) C.; m. Karen Mary Luberg, June 18, 1960; children— Kirk Nathan, Signe Kay. BS, U. Wis., 1959, MS, 1961, PhD, 1963. Rsch. fellow in geophysics Harvard U., Cambridge, Mass., 1963-64; asst. prof. geol. scis. U. So. Calif., 1964-66; prof. U. Wash., Seattle, 1966-83, Purdue U., Lafayette, Ind., 1983-97; Weeks disting. prof. U. Wis., Madison, 1997—. Mem. Pacific adv. panel Joint Oceanographic Instns. for Deep Earth Sampling, Seattle, 1973-75, mem. igneous and metamorphic petrology panel, 1973-75, mem. ocean crust panel, 1974-77; mem. adv. panel on oceanography NSF, 1976-78, mem. adv. panel on earth scis. 1994-97; mem. adv. panel on continental lithosphere NRC, 1979-83; mem. adv. panel Internat. Assn. Geodesy, 1980-88. Contbg. author: Geodynamics of Iceland and the North Atlantic Area, 1974; Contbr. numerous articles to profl. jours. NSF grantee, 1968—. Fellow Geol. Soc. Am. (chmn. geophysics divsn. 1984-86, assoc. editor Geology 1985-89, George P. Woollard award 1996), Am. Geophys. Union (assoc. editor Jour. Geophys. Rsch. 1998-2001). Achievements include research on nature of Earth's interior. Home: 11310 Marine Ln Anacortes WA 98221 Office: Dept Geology and Geophys U Wisc Madison WI 53706

CHRISTENSEN, PAUL WALTER, JR., gear manufacturing company executive; b. Cin., Jan. 31, 1925; s. Paul Walter and Lucy (Sickler) C.; m. Sarah Ernst, Nov. 22, 1947; children: Delle (Mrs. Edmund W. Jones), Sarah (Mrs. William McC. Reynolds), Lucy (Mrs. Craig M. Davis). BS in Mech. Engring., Cornell U., 1945. With Cin. Gear Co., 1946-87, v.p., 1947-58, pres., 1958-78, chmn. bd., 1978-87, ret., 1987; chmn. bd. Cin. Steel Treating Co., 1961-68, 87, pres., 1968-87, ret., 1987. Commr. Hamilton County Park Dist., 1980-93. Mem. Am. Gear Mfrs. Assn. (past pres.), Ohio Mfrs. Assn. (past pres.), Ocean Reef Club, Queen City Club, Commonwealth Club, Camargo Club, Comml. Club, Key Largo Anglers Club, Card Sound Golf Club. Home: 4660 Drake Rd Cincinnati OH 45243-4118

CHRISTENSEN, RAY RICHARDS, lawyer; b. Salt Lake City, July 7, 1922; s. E.R. and Carrie (Richards) C.; m. Carolyn Crawford, July 9, 1954 (dec. 1986); children: Carlie, Paul Ray, Joan, Eric.; m. Jeanne F. Pyke, June 24, 1989. LL.B., U. Utah, 1944. Bar: Utah 1944. Enforcement atty. OPA, 1946; law clk. to Utah Supreme Ct. Justice Wolfe, 1947-48; practice in Salt Lake City, 1949—; ptnr. Christensen & Jensen, P.C. (and predecessors), 1949—. Mem. Utah Bar Commn., 1963-66. Bd. dirs. Salt Lake City Jr. C. of C., 1949-53, v.p., 1950-52. Served with AUS, 1943-46. Fellow Internat. Acad. Trial Lawyers (bd. dirs. 1982-88), Am. Coll. Trial Lawyers (state chmn. 1984-85); mem. ABA (mem. council jr. bar conf. 1952-56, ho. of dels. 1966-68, 73-79, mem. council bar activities sect. 1967-70), Utah State Bar (pres. 1965-66, Utah Lawyer of Yr. 1981, Utah Trial Lawyer of Yr. 1993), Salt Lake County Bar Assn., Western States Bar Conf. (pres. 1969-70), Internat. Assn. Def. Counsel, Fedn. Defense and Corp. Counsel, Phi Eta Sigma, Phi Kappa Phi. Home: 992 Oak Hills Way Salt Lake City UT 84108-2022 Office: Christensen & Jensen PC 50 S Main St Ste 1500 Salt Lake City UT 84144-2044 Office Phone: 801-323-5000. Business E-Mail: ray.christensen@chrisjen.com.

CHRISTENSEN, RONALD E., physician; b. Seattle, Oct. 22, 1948; MD, U. Tenn., Coll. Medicine, 1975. Intern Riverside Gen. Co. Hosp., 1974—75; resident in family practice San Bernardino Co. Hosp., 1975—77; asst. assoc. clinical prof. U. Alaska, Coll. Nursing and Health Sci.; preceptor U. Wash. Trustee Am. Bd. Family Practice, 1999—2004, treas., 2002—03, pres., 2003—04. Mem.: Am. Acad. Family Physicians (bd. dirs. 1995—98). Avocations: fishing, skiing. Office: Independence Park Med Svc 9500 Independence Dr #900 Anchorage AK 99507-4600 Office Fax: 907-522-1343.

CHRISTENSEN, SHARLENE, artist; b. Fountain Green, Utah, Aug. 24, 1939; d. Frank Odell and Elaine (Nielsen) Huggins; m. Larry R. Christensen, Feb. 21, 1958; children: Tony Lamar, Craig G. Watercolor tchr. Salt Lake Art Ctr., Salt Lake City, 1972—83; artist-in-schs. Nat. Found. Arts and Utah Inst. Fine Arts, 1973—74; tchr. Christensen Workshops, Christensen Studio, Salt Lake City, 1975—. One-woman shows include Phillips Gallery, Salt Lake City, 1970, 1974, 1976, 1978, 1982, Artists-in-Action Galleries, Salt Lake City, 1981, Kimball Art Ctr., Park City, Utah, 1984, Southam Gallery, Salt Lake City, 1988, 1989, 1996, 1997, exhibited in group shows at Am.

Watercolor Soc., N.Y.C., 1977, Rocky Mountain Watermedia, Golden, Colo., 1978, Audubon Artists' Exhbn., N.Y.C., 1980, Watercolor West, Calif., 1980, San Diego Internat., 1981, Represented in permanent collections Am. Express Co., Salt Lake City, VA, 1st Interstate Bank, Salt Lake County Fine Arts, Leucadia Fine Arts, Salt Lake City, Salt Lake Conv. and Visitors Bur., others, watercolors include, What Brings Them Back? (Utah Watercolor Soc. Alpen Glow award of Excellence, 1974), Springtime-Central Park (Deseret News award of merit, 1978), Hilltop Aspen...Rooted Men (Utah State Fair award of merit, 1982), Winter Sounds (Utah State Fair award of merit, 1983), Winter's Own Shape (Purchase award Equitable Life Ins. Co., 1985). Mem.: Utah Watercolor Soc., Am. Watercolor Soc. (assoc.). Studio: Christensen Studio 3534 Dover Hill Dr Salt Lake City UT 84121-5527

CHRISTENSON, CHARLES JOHN, retired business educator; b. Chgo., Sept. 25, 1930; s. John Edward and Ethel Dagmar (Osterberg) C. BS, Cornell U., 1952; MBA, Harvard, 1954, D.BA, 1961. Mem. faculty Harvard Grad. Sch. Bus., 1957-58, lectr., 1959-61, asst. prof., 1961-63, assoc. prof., 1963-68, prof., 1968-74, Jesse Isidor Straus prof., 1974-79, Royal Little prof., 1980-96, prof. emeritus, 1996—. Prin. Auerbach Christenson Tagiuri, Inc., 1983-92; bd. dirs. Profile Techs., Inc. Author: Strategic Aspects of Competitive Bidding for Corporate Securities, 1965, (with J.L. Bower) Public Management: Cases and Readings, 1978, (with W.L. Berry and J.S. Hammond III) Management Decision Sciences: Cases and Readings, 1979. Bd. dirs. Boston Baroque, 1980—; trustee, chmn. Deep Springs Coll., 1986-94. With AUS, 1955-57. Mem. AAAS. Home: 1 Chauncy Ln Cambridge MA 02138-2401 Office: Harvard Bus Sch Soldiers Fld Boston MA 02163-1317 Office Phone: 617-495-6668. E-mail: cchristenson@hbs.edu.

CHRISTENSON, GORDON A., law educator; b. Salt Lake City, June 22, 1932; s. Gordon B. and Ruth Arzella (Anderson) C.; m. Katherine Joy deMik, Nov. 2, 1951 (div. 1977); children: Gordon Scott, Marjorie Lynne, Ruth Ann, Nanette; m. Fabienne Fadeley, Sept. 16, 1979. BS in Law, U. Utah, 1955, JD, 1956; SJD, George Washington U., 1961. Bar: Utah 1956, U.S. Supreme Ct. 1971, DC 1978. Law clk. to chief justice Utah Supreme Ct., 1956-57; assoc. firm Christenson & Callister, Salt Lake City, 1956-58; atty. Dept. of Army, N.G. Bur., Washington, 1957-58; atty., acting asst. legal adviser Office of Legal Adviser, U.S. Dept. State, Washington, 1958-62; asst. gen. counsel for sci. and tech. U.S. Dept. Commerce, 1962-67, spl. asst. to undersec. of commerce, 1967, counsel to commerce tech. adv. bd., 1962-67, chmn. task force on telecom. missions and orgn., 1967, counsel to panel on engring. and commodity stds., tech. adv. bd., 1963-65; assoc. prof. law U. Okla., Norman, 1967-70, exec. asst. to pres., 1967-70; univ. dean for ednl. devel., ctrl. adminstrn. SUNY, Albany, 1970-71; prof. law Am. U. Law Sch., Washington, 1971-79, dean, 1971-77; on leave, 1977-79; Charles H. Stockton prof. internat. law U.S. Naval War Coll., Newport, RI, 1977-79; dean, Nippert prof. law U. Cin. Coll. Law, 1979-85, univ. prof. law, 1985—98, prof. emeritus, dean emeritus, 1998—. Assoc. professorial lectr. in internat. affairs George Washington U., 1961-67; vis. scholar Harvard U. Law Sch., 1977-78, Yale Law Sch., 1985-86, Law Sch. U. Maine, Portland, 1997; Wallace S. Fujiyama vis. disting. prof. law Univ. Hawaii Law Sch., 1997; participant summer confs. on internat. law Cornell Law Sch., Ithaca, NY, 1962, 64; cons. in internat. law U.S. Naval War Coll., Newport, 1969; faculty mem., reporter seminars for experienced fed. dist. judges Fed. Jud. Ctr., Washington, 1972-77. Author: (with Richard B. Lillich) International Claims: Their Preparation and Presentation, 1962, The Future of the University, 1969; contbr. articles to legal jours. Cons. Ctr. for Policy Alternatives MIT, Cambridge, 1970-81; mem. intergovtl. com. on Internat. Policy on Weather Modification, 1967; v.p. Procedural Aspects of Internat. Law Inst., NYC, 1962-2001, trustee, 1962-. Served with intelligence sect. USAF, 1951-52, Japan. Fellow Grad. Sch. U. Cin. Mem. Am. Soc. Internat. Law (mem. panel on state responsibility), Utah Bar Assn., Cin. Bar Assn., Order of Coif, Lit. Club (Cin.), Cosmos Club (Washington), Phi Delta Phi, Kappa Sigma. Home and Office: 3465 Principio Ave Cincinnati OH 45208-4242 E-mail: christga@msn.com.

CHRISTENSON, GREGG ANDREW, bank executive; b. Kalamazoo, Mich., June 11, 1958; s. Elmer J. and Marie E. (Durrstein) C.; m. Karen Peterson. BA, Mich. State U., 1980. CPA. Auditor Price Waterhouse, N.Y.C., 1980-82; with Bankers Trust Co., N.Y.C., 1982-92, v.p., 1987-92; sr. v.p. Huntington Nat. Bank, Columbus, Ohio, 1992-2000, Troy, Mich., 2000—. Bd. dirs. Holy Family Regional Sch.; bd. trustees Mich. Interfaith Trust Fund, Venture, Inc. Mem. Mich. State Alumni Assn. Republican. Roman Catholic. Office Phone: 248-269-2034. Business E-Mail: gregg.christenson@huntington.com.

CHRISTENSON, LE ROY HOWARD, missions consultant; b. Rochester, N.Y., Oct. 28, 1948; s. Howard Le Roy and Sigrid (Anderson) Christenson; m. Pamala Jean Mattson, Jan. 26, 1974; children: Nathan Lee, David Wayne. BS, Valparaiso U., 1970; MS, Purdue U., 1972. CLU. Corp. actuary Western Life Ins. Co., St. Paul, 1972-84; v.p., reins. actuary Am. United Life Ins. Co., Indpls., 1984—99, exec. v.p., 1999—2000; pvt. practice cons. Fishers, Ind., 2001—02; Great Lakes assoc. dir. Advancing Chs. in Missions Commitment (ACMC), 2002—. Fin. cons. Mgmt. Assistance Program, Mpls., 1982. Bd. mem. Interserve, 1996—; mission conf. chmn. Faith Missionary Ch., Indpls., 1987—89, elder, 1991—93, 1999—2002, elder chmn., 1993, 2000—02, mission com. chmn., 1995—2000, vice chmn., 2003—, sr. pastor search team, 2003—04; bd. dirs. Lake Wapogasset Bible Camp, Mpls., 1982—83, Christian Businessman's Com., Indpls., 1985—88, Interserve, chmn. nominating com., 1999—2004, mem. exec. com., 1999—2001; age group leader Pioneer Club, Indpls., 1983, 1987. Fellow: Soc. Actuaries (chmn. audit working group reins. sect. 1985—88, vice chmn. reins. sect. 1988—89, 1995—96, chmn. 1989—90, 1996—97, sec.-treas. reins. sect. 1994—95); mem.: Indpls. Actuarial Club (pres. 1987—88), Tri-State Actuarial Club (Indpls. rep. 1984—90, chmn. 1989—90), Am. Acad. Actuaries. Avocation: Avocations: bible study, biking, motorcycling. Home and Office: 10955 Knightsbridge Lane Fishers IN 46037 Office Phone: 317-698-3224. E-mail: LeeChristenson@sbcglobal.net.

CHRISTENSON, SHEN, editor; b. Salt Lake City, Utah, Aug. 13, 1954; d. Nicholas G. and Isabelle Marion (Burrows) Smith; m. A. J. Martinez, Jan. 1, 1989; children: Chandra, Marissa, Karrilee, Nicholas, Jen, Claire, Jacob. BA, U. Utah, Salt Lake City, 1975, MA, 1987. Writer freelance, Salt Lake City, 1982—, editor, 1997—. Bd. dirs. Artvest, Salt Lake City, 1997—; cons. Three Orchids Press, Salt Lake City, 1999—. Contbr. short stories, articles in various literary jours. Story Mag., Quarterly, Black Ridge, Alaska Rev., Denver Rev., others. Recipient 1st Pl. award, Story Mag., 1996, Chgo. Mag., 1999, 2d Pl. award, Utah Fine Arts Coun., 1998. Mem.: Writers Guild. Achievements include raising children who had been abused, whose prognosis was poor to very poor; to make them feel secure and become loving adults who hold degrees from many universities.

CHRISTESEN, JOHN D., business educator; b. N.Y.C., July 16, 1936; s. Charles Nicholas and Mary Antoinette (Koza) Christesen. AB, CUNY, 1970; MBA with distinction, Pace U., 1975; postgrad., Columbia U., 1976—; D in Indsl. Mgmt. (hon.), U. Indsl. Mgmt. Credit mgr. Butler Lumber Co., 1961—62; fiscal comptroller, sales staff Lever Bros., 1962—67; contr., sales v.p. Cycle Circus, Inc., 1967—70; v.p. Putnam Bicycle Importers Co., 1970—73; curriculum chmn. bus adminstrn., prof. mgmt., dept. chmn. bus. adminstrn. & pub. svc. SUNY Westchester CC, Valhalla, NY, 1975—, dir. Mgmt. Inst., chmn. faculty devel. conf., v.p. Faculty-Student Assn., Joseph and Sophia Abeles Disting. chair of bus., 1994—. Vis. prof. econs. Mercy Coll., Dobbs Ferry, NY; adj. assoc. prof. mgmt. Iona Coll., New Rochelle, NY; adv. bd. U. Indsl. Mgmt.; cons. N.Y. State Bd. Regents, NY, N.Y. State Edn. Dept.; bd. dirs. Investment Properties Corp., Computweather Corp., Bio Med. Concepts, Inc. Author (with R. Wunsch): (book) The Complete Resume Handbook, 1967; author: Management Miscellany, 1978, 4th edit., 1990; author: (with Heinze Weirich) Instructor's Manual for Management, 1984; author: (films) Introduction to Business, 1980, Introduction to Finance, 1982; dir. editor: Honors Jour., 1995—. Chmn. Urban Devel. Corp., Lewisboro, NY, Town of Lewisboro Housing Com.; bd. dirs. Westchester Minority Devel. Corp., 1983—84. Recipient Medallion Edn. award, WCCF. Mem.: N.Y. State Assn. Two-Yr. Colls. (exec. bd. 1980—84), Assn. MBA Execs., Am. Acad. Polit. and Social Scis., Am. Inst. Higher Edn., Nat. Econs. Club, Am. Acad. Mgmt., Phi Theta Kappa, Nat. Bus. Honor Soc., Delta Mu Delta, Sigma Lambda, Alpha Beta Gamma (nat. chmn. 1978—79, nat. devel. chmn. 1980—81, CEO 1983—). Republican. Roman Catholic. Home: 1160 Midland Ave Apt 4C Bronxville NY 10708-6430 Office: Westchester CC 75 Grasslands Rd Valhalla NY 10595-1636 Office Phone: 914-606-6554. Business E-Mail: ceo@abg.org.

CHRISTIAN, BETTY JO, lawyer; b. Temple, Tex., July 27, 1936; d. Joe and Mattie Manor (Brown) Wiest; m. Ernest S. Christian, Jr., Dec. 24, 1960. BA summa cum laude, U. Tex., 1957, LL.B. summa cum laude, 1960. Bar: Tex. 1961, U.S. Supreme Ct. 1964, D.C. 1980. Law clk. Supreme Ct. Tex., 1960-61; atty. ICC, 1961-68, asst. gen. counsel Washington, 1970-72, assoc. gen. counsel, 1972-76, commr., 1976-79; ptnr. Steptoe & Johnson, Washington, 1980—. Atty. Labor Dept., Dallas, 1968-70 Fellow Am. Bar Found., Tex. Bar Found.; mem. ABA, FBA (Younger Fed. Lawyer award 1964), Tex. Bar Assn., Am. Law Inst., Am. Acad Appellate Lawyers, Adminstrv. Conf. U.S Office: 1330 Connecticut Ave NW Washington DC 20036-1704 Office Phone: 202-429-8113. Business E-Mail: bchristi@steptoe.com.

CHRISTIAN, CORA L.E, health facility administrator, physician; b. St. Thomas, VI, Sept. 11, 1947; d. Alphonso Augustine and Ruth Christian; m. Simon B. Jones-Hendrickson, Oct. 23, 1976; children: Nesha Christian-Hendrickson, Marcus Christian-Hendrickson. BS in Biology, Marquette U., 1967; MPH, Johns Hopkins U., 1975; MD, Jefferson Med. Coll., Phila., 1971. Diplomate Am. Coll. Forensic Examiners, Am. Bd. Quality Assurance and Utilization Rev., Am. Acad. Family Practice. Pvt. family-based practice, Frederiksted, 1975—; asst. commr. Dept. Health, St. Croix, 1977—91; educator, CEO, now med. dir. VI Med. Inst., Inc, St. Croix, 1978—; dir., prin. investigator US VI Household Survey, St. Croix, 1988; chief med. cons., med. dir. Hovensa, LLC, St. Croix, 1990—; cons. VI AIDS Edn. and Tng., NYC, 1992—2005. Pres. Caribbean Studies Assn., 2000—01; pres., exec. sec., treas. VI Med. Soc., St. Croix, 1995—. Contbr. articles to profl. jours., chapters to books. Bd. dirs. Am. Cancer Soc., St. Croix, 1991—2005. Named to Trail Blazers for Women's History, Women's Bus. Ctr., 2000; Paul Harris fellow, Rotary, 1997. Mem.: AARP (nat. bd. dirs. 2004—), Am. Acad. Family Physicians (com. mem. 1996—2005, pres. VI chpt. 1976—). Sgi/Buddhist. Avocation: dance. Home: PO Box 1338 Frederiksted VI 00841 Office: VI Med Inst Inc PO Box 5989 Christiansted VI 00823-5989 Office Phone: 340-712-2400. Office Fax: 340-712-2449. Personal E-mail: cchrisitian@aarp.org. E-mail: cchristi@viqio.sdps.org.

CHRISTIAN, EDWARD KIEREN, broadcasting station executive; b. Detroit, June 26, 1944; s. William Edward and Dorothy Miriam (Kieren) C.; m. Judith Dallaire, Nov. 25, 1966; children: Eric, Dana. BA, Wayne State U., 1966, postgrad.; MA, Cen. Mich. U., 1980. Mgr. John C. Butler Co., Detroit, 1968-69; nat. sales mgr. WCAR Radio, Detroit, WSUN Radio, St. Petersburg, Fla., 1969-70; v.p., gen. mgr., ptnr. WCER Radio, Charlotte, Mich., 1970-74; pres. Josephson Internat. Broadcast, 1975-86; pres., CEO Saga Comm., Inc., Detroit, 1986—. Pres., CEO, bd. dirs. Stas. WSNY-FM, WODB-FM, WJZA, WJZK, Columbus, Ohio, Sta. WNOR-FM, Norfolk, Va., Sta. WAFX, Norfolk, WJOI AM Norfolk, Stas. WKLH-FM, WLZR-FM, WJYI-AM, WFMR-FM, WJMR-FM Milw., Stas. KRNT, KSTZ-FM, KIOA-AM/FM, KAZR FM, KLTI FM, KPSZ AM, Des Moines, Stas. WLRW-FM and WIXY-FM, WCFF FM, Champaign, Ill., Stas. WYMG-FM, WQQL-FM, WDBR-FM, WABZ FM, WTAX-AM, Springfield, Ill., Stas. WGAN-AM/WMGX, WZAN-AM/WYNZ-FM, WPOR/FM, WBAE-AM, WVAE, Portland, Maine, Sta. WFEA-AM/WZID-FM, WQLL-FM, Manchester, N.H., Sta. WAQY-FM, WHNP-AM, Springfield, Mass., WHMP-AM, WLZX-FM, WRIS, Northampton, Mass., WHMQ-AM, WHAI-AM, WPVQ, Greenfield, Mass., KOAM TV, Joplin, Mo., WNAX-AM/FM, Yankton, S.D., KGMI, KISM-FM, Bellingham, Wash., KBAI-AM, KAFE FM, Bellingham, Wash., Victoria Tex., KUNU TV, KXTS TV, KAVU TV, KVCT TV, KMOL TV, Victoria, WXVT TV, Greenville, Miss., KICD AM-FM, KLLT, Spencer, Iowa, WKFN, WJQI, WZZP-FM, WCVQ-FM, WVVR-FM, Clarkesville, Tenn., KDXY-FM, KDEZ-FM, KJBX-FM, Jonesboro A.K., WKNE-FM, WKBK-AM, WZBK-FM, WUQL-FM, WINQ-FM, Keene, N.H., WKVT-AM/FM, WWRSY, Brattleboro, Vt., WHCU AM, WNYY AM, WQNY FM, WYXC, Ithaca, NY, WINA AM, WWWU FM, WQMZ FM, Charlottesville, Va., Mich. Radio Network, Ill. Radio Network, others; Mich. Farm Radio Network, Minn. Radio News Network; Bd. dirs., Nat. Assn. Broadcasters 2002-, bd. dirs., Broadcast Found. 2003-, chmn. Arbitron Radio Adv. Coun., 1978-79; bd. dirs. All Industry Music Licensing Com.; adj. prof. Ctrl. Mich. U. Bd. dirs. Am. Auto Immune Related Disease Found., 1995—; bd. mem. St. John Hosp.; consul Republic of Iceland for Mich., Ohio and Ind., 1996—. Mem. Alpha Epsilon Rho (nat. adv. coun. 1980—). Home: 21 Newberry Pl Grosse Pointe Farms MI 48236-3749 also: 3310 Sabal Cove Dr Longboat Key FL 34228-4154 Office: Saga Communications Inc 73 Kercheval Ave Grosse Pointe Farms MI 48236-3603 E-mail: echristian@sagacommunications.com.

CHRISTIAN, ELIOT JORDAN, federal agency administrator, computer specialist; b. Springfield, Mo., Aug. 17, 1952; s. Robert Aspel and Clara Mae (Hess) Smith; m. Marcia Bernadette FitzSimons Christian, July 4, 1976; children: Sikandra, Theresa, Sheila. BA in English, U. Wis., Milw., 1973. Dep. dir. field mgmt. svc. Office Data Mgmt. and Telecomm., VA, Washington, 1975-86; chief office mgmt. svcs. info. sys. divsn. geo. info. office U.S. Geol. Survey, Reston, Va., 1986—; key developer Common Alerting Protocol, 2002—; sys. arch. Global Earth Obs. Sys. of Systems, 2003—. Chmn. Spl. Interest Group on Wide Area Info. Servers, Washington, 1993—98; arch., leader Global Info. Locator Svc., 1995—. Author: fed. reports. Recipient Best Windows Application award, Windows World, 1993, Federal 100 award, Fed. Computer Week, 1995, 1996, Madison award for pub. right to know, ALA and AAAS, 1998. Democrat. Roman Catholic. Avocations: hiking, reading. Home: 2002 Lakebreeze Way Reston VA 20191-4006 Office: US Geol Survey 590 National Ctr Reston VA 22092-0001

CHRISTIAN, ERNEST SILSBEE, JR., lawyer; b. Gonzales, Tex., Jan. 15, 1937; s. Ernest Silsbee and Ruby Ruth (Hamon) Christian; m. Betty Jo Wiest, Dec. 24, 1960. LLB cum laude, U. Tex., 1961. Bar: Tex. 1961, D.C. 1961, U.S. Supreme Ct. 1978. Atty. Treasury Dept., Washington, 1970-72, tax legis. counsel, 1973-74, dep. asst. sec. treasury (tax policy), 1974-75; ptnr. Patton, Boggs & Blow, Washington, 1975-94, E.S. Christian, 1995—. Mem.: ABA, Am. Law Inst. Republican. Home: Willows Farm PO Box 1140 Union Bridge MD 21791-0582 Office: 800 Connecticut Ave NW Washington DC 20006-2709 Office Phone: 202-898-2090.

CHRISTIAN, FRANCIS JOSEPH, bishop; b. Peterborough, N.H., Oct. 12, 1942; s. Joseph Lucien and Dorothy May (Parent) C. BA, PhB, U. Ottawa, Can., 1964; MA in Theology, U. Louvain, Belgium, 1968, PhD in Religious Studies, 1975. Ordained priest Roman Cath. Ch., 1968. Asst. pastor Our Lady of Mercy Parish, Merrimack, N.H., 1968-71, St. Joseph Cathedral Parish, Manchester, N.H., 1971-72; asst. chancellor Diocese of Manchester, 1975-77, chancellor, sec. for adminstrn. canonical affairs Diocese Manchester, 1978—, vicar gen., 1996—, monsignor (prelate of honor), 1986—; aux. bishop of Manchester, 1996—. Roman Catholic. Office: Diocese of Manchester 153 Ash St Manchester NH 03104-4396 Office Phone: 603-669-3100.

CHRISTIAN, GARY D., chemistry professor; b. Eugene, Oreg., Nov. 25, 1937; s. Roy C. and Edna Alberta (Trout) Gonier; m. Suanne Byrd Coulbourne, June 17, 1961; children: Dale Brian, Carol Jean, Tanya Danielle, Tabitha Star. BS, U. Oreg., 1959; MS, U. Md., 1962, PhD, 1964; PhD (hon.), Chiang Mai U., 2005. Rsch. analytical chemist Walter Reed Army Inst. Rsch., Washington, 1961-67; asst. prof. U. Md., College Park, 1965-66, U. Ky., Lexington, 1967-70, assoc. prof., 1970-72; prof. chemistry U. Wash., Seattle, 1972—, acting chmn. dept., 1990, assoc. chmn., 1991-92, divisional dean sci. emeritus, 1993-2001. Vis. prof. Free U. Brussels, 1978-79; invited prof. U. Geneva, 1979; cons. Ames Co., 1968-72, Beckman Instruments, Inc., 1972-84, 88, Westinghouse Hanford Co., 1977-83, Tech. Dynamics, 1983-85, Porton Diagnostics, 1990-91, Bend Rsch., 1992-93, E.I. DuPont de Nemours, Inc., 1993; examiner Grad. Record Exam., 1985-90. Author: Analytical Chemistry, 6th edit., 2003, Instrumental Analysis, 1978, 2d edit., 1986, Atomic Absorption Spectroscopy, 1970, Trace Analysis, 1986, Problem Solving in Analytical Chemistry, 1988, Calculations in Pharmaceutical Sciences, 1993; editl. bd. Analytical Letters, 1971-2004, Can. Jour. Spectroscopy, 1974-96, Analytical Instrumentation, 1974-93, Talanta, 1980-88 (spl. editor USA honor issue, 1989), Analytical Chemistry, 1985-89, Critical Revs. in Analytical Chemistry, 1985—, The Analyst, 1986-90, Jour. Saudi Chem. Soc., 1995—; editor in chief Talanta, 1989—, Electroanalysis, 1988—, Jour. Pharm. and Biochem. Analysis, 1990-97, Fresenius' Z. Analytical Chem., 1991-93, Laborator Automation, 1992—, Quimica Analitica, 1993-2001; contbr. articles to profl. jours. Recipient Medal of Honor, Univ. Libre de Brussels, 1978, Talanta medal, Elsevier Sci., 1995, Commemorative medal, Charles U., 1999, Geoff Wilson medal, Deakin U., 2003, Sci. Honor medal, Japan Assn. for Analytical Chemistry, 2003, Sr. Scholar Silver award, Thailand Rsch. Fund, 2004; Fulbright Hays scholar, 1978—79. Mem. Am. Chem. Soc. (sect. chmn. 1982-83, chmn. elect divsn. analytic chemistry 1988-89, chmn. 1989-90, divsn. Analytical Chemistry award for Excellence in Tchg. 1988, Fisher award in analytical chemistry 1996), Soc. Applied Spectroscopy (sect. chmn. 1982), Spectroscopy Soc. Can., Am. Inst. Chemists (cert.), Soc. Electroanalytical Chemistry (bd. dirs. 1993-98). Republican. Home: PO Box 26 Medina WA 98039-0026 Office: Univ Wash Dept Chemistry Box 351700 Seattle WA 98195-1700 Office Phone: 206-543-1635. Office Fax: 206-685-3478. Business E-Mail: christian@chem.washington.edu.

CHRISTIAN, JAMES WAYNE, economist; b. Ft. Worth, Oct. 7, 1934; s. Nap B. and Daphne (Wright) Christian; m. Jo June Maples, June 5, 1952; children: Amy Joella, Nicole Denise. BA, U. Tex., Austin, 1962, MA, 1964, PhD, 1965. Dir. internat. div. Fed. Home Loan Bank Bd., Washington, 1972—74; sr. v.p., chief economist Nat. Savs. and Loan League, Washington, 1974—80, U.S. League Savs. Inst., Chgo., 1980—91; pres. James Christian Assocs., Fair Oaks Ranch, Tex., 1991; dir. Real Estate Ctr. at Tex. A & M Univ., 1993—95. Prof. econs. Iowa State U., 1965—74; dir. Nat. Housing Conf., 1980—84; cons. 23 developing country govts., 1970. Contbr. articles to profl. jour. Served with USN, 1952—55, served with USAF, 1955—59. Recipient Am. Legion award, 1949; univ. fellow, 1964, NSF fellow, 1965, Social Sci. Rsch. Coun. grant, 1968—69. Mem.: So. Econ. Assn., Am. Fin. Assn., Am. Econ. Assn., Cosmos, Phi Kappa Phi, Pi Sigma Alpha, Omicron Delta Epsilon, Phi Beta Kappa.

CHRISTIAN, JOHN CATLETT, JR., lawyer; b. Springfield, Mo., Sept. 12, 1929; s. John Catlett and Alice Odelle (Milling) C.; m. Peggy Jeanne Cain, Apr. 12, 1953; children: Cathleen Marie, John Catlett, Alice Cain. AB, Drury Coll., 1951; LLB, Tulane U., 1956. Bar: La. 1956, Mo. 1956, U.S. Supreme Ct. 1975. Assoc. Porter & Stewart, Lake Charles, La., 1956-58, Wilkinson, Lewis, Wilkinson & Madison, Shreveport, La., 1958-62, ptnr., 1962-64, Milling, Benson, Woodward, Hillyer, Pierson & Miller, New Orleans, 1964-92, of counsel, 1993-94. Pres. Sherburne Land Co., 1974-83, Pointe-Martin Mgmt., Inc., 1990-2000; dir. Emerald Land Corp. Pres. Kathleen Elizabeth O'Brien Found., 1963—. Served with USMCR, 1951-53. Fellow Am. Coll. Trial Lawyers; mem. ABA, Fed. Bar Assn., Mo. Bar, La. Bar Assn., La. Landowners Assn. (bd. dirs. 1983-2001), Boston Club, Beau Chene Country Club, Highlands Falls Country Club, Kappa Alpha Order, Omicron Delta Kappa, Phi Delta Phi. Home: 807 Tete Lours Dr Mandeville LA 70471-1774 Office: PO Box 1317 Mandeville LA 70470-1317 Office Phone: 985-845-4050. E-mail: jcchristiansr@aol.com.

CHRISTIAN, JOHN EDWARD, health science association administrator, educator; b. Indpls., July 12, 1917; s. George Edward and Okel Kandus (Waltz) C.; m. Catherine Ellen Spooner, July 23, 1948; 1 dau., Linda Kay. BS, Purdue U., 1939, PhD, 1944. Control chemist Upjohn Co., 1939-40; faculty Purdue U., Lafayette, Ind., 1940—, prof. pharm. chemistry, 1950-59, head dept. radiol. control, 1956-59, prof. bionucleonics, head dept., 1959-82; chmn. adminstrv. com. Trace Level Research Inst., 1960-88; dir. Inst. for Environmental Health, 1965-88; head Sch. Health Scis., 1979-82, Hovde Disting. prof., 1979-88, Hovde Disting. prof. bionucleonics and health scis. emeritus, 1988—. Vis. prof. radiation therapy Ind. U. Sch. Medicine, 1970-88; Harvey Washington Meml. lectr. Purdue U., 1955; Edward-Kremers Meml. lectr. U. Wis., 1956; vis. lectr. U. Tex., 1959, Taylor U. Ann. Sci. Lecture Series, Upton, Ind., 1960; Julius A. Koch Meml. lectr. U. Pitts., 1961 Assoc. editor Radiochem. Letters. Mem. revision com. U.S. Pharmacopeia, 1950-60, mem. adv. panel on radioactive drugs, 1960-70; adv. com. isotope distbn. AEC, 1952-58, mem. med. adv. com., 1967-75; mem. radiation and chem. def. sect. Ind. Dept. Civil Def., 1954—; vice chmn. Radiation Control Adv. Commn., Ind., 1958—; mem. exec. com. Ind. Comprehensive Health Planning Council, 1972-76; mem. adv. com. radiopharms. FDA, 1970-75; mem. Ind. Gov.'s Pesticide Council, 1970-73; Alumni research councilor Purdue Research Found., 1964-88; mem. Ind. Environmental Mgmt. Bd., 1972-87, Nat. Energy Policy Task Force, Dept. Energy, 1981-83; mem. Bd. Grants Am. Found. for Pharm. Edn., 1989—. Recipient award Chilean Iodine Ednl. Bur., 1956, Julius Sturmer award Phila. Coll. Pharmacy and Sci., 1958, Leather medal Purdue U., 1971, Hovde Faculty Purdue U. fellow, 1988. Fellow AAAS (past sec. and chmn. pharm. sci. sect., mem. council), Ind. Acad. Sci.; mem. AMA (spl. affiliate), AAUP, Am. Inst. Architecture (bd. dirs. 1998—, Gibson award 1999), Am. Assn. Colls. Pharmacy (past mem. exec. com., chmn. conf. tchrs., chmn. conf. grad. study and grad. tchrs., chmn. com. study grad. edn. in pharmacy), Am. Chem. Soc. (past chmn. Purdue sect.), Am. Pharm. Assn. (Ebert medal 1957, Justin L. Powers Research Achievement award 1963, past chmn. sci. sect.), Acad. Pharm. Sci. (past v.p.), Ind. Pharm. Assn., Am. Pub. Health Assn., Am. Nuclear Soc., Am. Soc. Bacteriology, Health Phys. Soc., Historic Landmarks Found. of Ind. (bd. dirs., exec. com. 1997—), Frank Lloyd Wright Bldg. Conservancy (Wright Spirit award 1997), Sigma Xi (past pres. Purdue chpt., research award Purdue chpt. 1950), Rho Chi, Phi Lambda Upsilon, Sigma Pi Sigma., Eta Sigma Gamma, Gamma Sigma Delta. Home: 1301 Woodland Ave West Lafayette IN 47906-2371 Office: Purdue U Sch Health Scis Civil Engring Bldg West Lafayette IN 47907

CHRISTIAN, JOHN KENTON, publishing executive, marketing professional, consultant; b. Pana, Ill., Nov. 6, 1927; s. Ben Ross and Ruth (Stevenson) C.; m. Marjorie Adair Pollock, Nov. 28, 1958; children—Jefrey, Dwane, Kevin. Student, Westminster Coll., 1945, Colo. Coll., 1948, Emerson Coll., 1949; BS, Boston U., 1951; student, Am. U., 1954-55. Relief editor, rep., columnist St. Louis Daily Record, 1950-51; reporter Commerce Clearing House, Washington, 1952; with U.S. News and World Report, 1953-68, regional sales mgr. Los Angeles, 1960-63, mktg. mgr. Washington, 1964-68; pub. Nation's Cities Mag., Washington, 1968-76; mem. U.S. Fed. Preparedness Agy. mission to Iran, 1975-76; pres. Internat. Center for Emergency Preparedness, Washington, 1977-80; also pub. Emergency Preparedness News, 1977-79; v.p. Nat. Radio Broadcasters Assn., 1979-84; pres. Communications Brokers, Inc., 1984-88; author, pub. and mktg. cons., 1988-92; mktg. dir. Marine Corps Assn., 1992-2000. Media and mktg. devel. cons., 2000—. Served with USAAF, 1945-48. Presbyterian. Home: 10867 Deborah Dr Potomac MD 20854-2716 Personal E-mail: JKChristian@erols.com.

CHRISTIAN, JOHN THOMAS, civil engineer; b. N.Y.C., Nov. 2, 1936; s. Thomas Douglas and Evelyn Catherine (Maestri) C.; m. Lynda Ballou Gregorian, June 8, 1960; children: Douglas Arthur, Shirin Lynda. BSCE, MIT, 1958, MSCE, 1959, PhD in Civil Engring., 1966. Registered profl. engr., Mass., Maine. Asst. prof. civil engring. MIT, Cambridge, 1966-70, assoc. prof. civil engring., 1970-73; cons. geotech. div. Stone & Webster Engring. Corp., Boston, 1973-76, cons. engr., 1976-80, sr. cons. engr., 1980-89, v.p., 1989—; exec. v.p. Stone & Webster Advanced Systems Devel. Svcs., Boston, 1989-92. Mem. engring. accreditation com. Accreditation Bd. for Engring. & Tech., N.Y.C., 1984—, chmn. 1990-91; mem. adv. bd. seismic group Electric Power Rsch. Inst., Palo Alto, Calif., Nat. Ctr. for Earthquake Engring. Rsch., Buffalo, N.Y., Mass. Bd. Bldg. Regulations and Standards, Boston; mem. vis. com. for civil engring. U. N.H., Durham, Princeton U., N.J., U. Tex., Austin.

Co-author, editor: Numerical Methods in Geotechnical Engineering, 1977, Productivity Tools For Geotechnical Engineers, 1997, Reliability and Statistics in Geotechnical Engineering, 2003; contbr. 100 articles to profl. jours. Vol. speaker Boston pub. schs., 1986—; reader Recordings for the Blind, Cambridge, 1990-1997. Lt. USAF, 1959-63. NSF fellow, 1963-66. Hon. mem. Am. Soc. Civil Engrs., 2001 (chmn. geotech. engring. div. 1985-86, various coms.); mem. Internat. Soc. Soil Mechanics and Found. Engring., Earthquake Engring. Rsch. Inst., Seismol. Soc. Am., Assn. for Computing Machinery, Boston Soc. Civil Engrs. (hon. mem., Desmond Fitzgerald medal 1973, chmn. computer group), NAE, 1999. Achievements include development of computer applications for geotechnical engineering, including finite element methods and scope stability; development of probabilistic methods for earthquake and geotechnical engineering. Home and Office: 23 Fredana Rd Waban MA 02468-1103

CHRISTIAN, JOSEPH RALPH, physician; b. Chgo., June 15, 1920; s. Ralph F. and Anna M. (Across) Co; m. Marcia Pomeroy, Sept. 25, 1944; children— Patricia Ann, Joseph Ralph. AA, U. Chgo., 1941; MD, Loyola U., Chgo., 1944. Diplomate: Am. Bd. Pediatrics. Intern Cook County Hosp., Chgo., 1944-45, resident, 1945-46, 48-49; faculty Stritch Sch. Medicine, Loyola U., Chgo., 1948-61; prof. Stritch Sch. Medicine, Loyola U. (pediatrics), 1957-61, chmn. dept., 1960-61; attending pediatrician Loyola Service at La Rabida Sanitarium, 1948-61; chmn. dept. pediatrics Mercy Hosp., 1960-61; chief pediatrics Lewis Meml. Maternity Hosp., 1951-61; chmn. dept. pediatrics Rush Presbyn.-St. Luke's Med. Center, Chgo., 1961-85; prof. pediatrics U. Ill. Coll. Medicine, Chgo., 1961-70; prof. Rush Med. Coll., Chgo., 1970-85, prof. emeritus, 1985—, chmn. dept. pediatrics, 1970-85. Sr. attending pediatrician children's div. Cook County Hosp., 1959-65 Editor: Pediatrics Digest, 1962-78; Mem. editorial bd.: Childcraft, 1963-87; Contbr. articles to med. jours. Chmn. poison control com. Chgo. Bd. Health, 1961-69; chmn. med. com. Infant Welfare Soc., Chgo., 1958-61; chmn. 9th Ill. Congress Maternal and Infant Health, 1962; chmn. bd. trustees Holy Cross Chgo., 1970-75. Served to capt. M.C. AUS, 1946-47. Recipient Clin. Faculty award Stritch Sch. Medicine, 1954, 57 Fellow Am. Coll. Chest Physicians, Am. Acad. Pediatrics (chmn. film rev. com. 1963-73, chmn. com. residency fellowships 1964-67), Am. Pub. Health Assn., A.C.P.; mem. A.M.A., Am. Fedn. Clin. Research, Am. Pediatric Soc., Am. Heart Assn., Ambulatory Pediatric Assn., Am. Assn. Poison Control Centers, Am. Assn. Maternal and Infant Health, Ill. Assn. Maternal and Infant Health (pres. 1964), Am. Pediatric Soc., Chgo. Pediatric Soc. (pres. 1964-65), Midwest Soc. Pediatric Research, Assn. Med. Sch. Pediatric Dept. Chairmen. Home: 3 Oakbrook Club Dr Apt E107 Oak Brook IL 60523-1330 Office Phone: 630-832-7648.

CHRISTIAN, LORI COFFELT, marketing professional; b. Houston, Dec. 5, 1960; d. Donald Warren and Charlotte Hollopeter Coffelt; m. John Catlett Christian, III, June 25, 1988 (div. Mar. 5, 2002); children: Charlotte Elizabeth, Camille Corinne, Catherine Catlett. BS, So. Meth. U., 1983; postgrad., U. Tex., 1984—86. Media planner Bozell Jacobs Kenyon and Eckhardt, Dallas, 1986—88; account exec. Levenson and Hill, Dallas, 1988—90; account exec., supr. Rubin Postaer and Assocs., Santa Monica, Calif., 1990—96; dir. brand mgmt. MediaOne, L.A., 1996—98; mng. dir., brand strategy Reliant Energy, Houston, 1998—99; CEO, ptnr DotDash, Inc., Houston, 1999—2003; chief mktg. officer Remedy Corp., Mountain View, Calif., 2000—01; v.p., innovation Pennzoil-Quaker State, Houston, 2002. Vol. Dem. Party, Calif., 1995—98; Sunday sch. tchr. St. Paul's United Meth. Ch., Houston, 1999—2000, Redondo Beach (Calif.) United Meth. Ch., 1993—96; Sunday sch. tchr., mem. adminstrv. bd. Oak Lawn United Meth. Ch., Dallas, 1986—88; Sunday sch. tchr., choir mem. United Meth. Ch., Kingwood, 2003. Mem.: River Oaks Dem. Women. Democrat. Methodist. Avocations: cooking, travel, reading, writing, gearhead. Personal E-mail: mslorichristian@aol.com.

CHRISTIAN, MILDRED STOEHR, health products executive; b. Phila., July 7, 1942; d. Harvey Edward and Alice Emily Stoehr. BS, Pa. State U., 1963, MS, 1965; PhD, Thomas Jefferson U., 1979. Sr. scientist McNiel Laboratories, a J and J Co., Fort Washington, Pa., 1965—79; pres. Argus Rsch. Laboratories, Horsham, 1979—89, Argus Internat., Inc., 1980—; sr. advisor sci. and compliance CRL - Argus Rsch., 1989—2003; chmn. and CEO Argus Health Products, LLC, 2004—. Dir. Pro-Pharmaceuticals, Inc., Newton, Mass., 2003—; founding editor, editor in chief Jour. Am. Coll. Toxicology, Washington, 1981—. Initiated hist. restoration of lamposts Franklin Lamposts, La., 2003—05; pres. Hist. Preservation Soc. - Restored 200 yr. old bldg., Phila., 2000—04; pres., bd. trustees Kensington M.E. Ch. (Old Brick), 1980—; donated children's libr. (Stoehr libr.) to Girard coll. Girard Coll., 2002—04. Recipient Lifetime Achievement award, ACT, 2004, Distinguished Scientists award, Genzyme Transgenics Corp., 2000, Outstanding Graduate award, Thomas Jefferson U., 1995. Mem.: Acad. Toxicologic Scientists (pres. 1999—2000), Teratology Soc. (pres. 1989—90), European Teratology Soc. (councilor 2002—), Am. Coll. Toxicology (pres. 1992—93), Soc. Quality Assurance (hon.), Plimsoll Club (state sec. 2000—), Patriotic Order Sons Am., Thomas Jefferson Alumni Soc. (pres. 1992—93). Conservative. Methodist. Avocations: piano, opera, travel. Office: Argus Health Products 933 Horsham Rd Horsham PA 19044 Office Phone: 215-672-8867.

CHRISTIAN, RALPH GORDON, agricultural research and animal health consultant; b. Lethbridge, Alta., Can., Apr. 17, 1942; s. Wesley Peel and Mary (Patterson) C.; m. Brenda Esther Kheong, 1976. DVM, U. Guelph, Ont., Can., 1966; Diploma in Vet. Pathology, U. Sask., Saskatoon, 1971. Cert. in vet. pathology Am. Coll. Vet. Pathologists. Instr. Vet. Sch. U. Melbourne, Australia, 1977; dir. animal health divsn. Alta. Dept. Agr., Edmonton, 1982-87; acting asst. dep. min. Alta. Agrl. Prodn. Sector, Edmonton, 1987; exec. dir. Alta. Agrl. Rsch. Inst., Edmonton, 1987—2000; exec. dir. rsch. divsn. Alta. Dept. Agr., Food and Rural Devel., Edmonton, 1987-2000; pres. Ralph Christian Cons., Inc., 2001—. Br. head pathology br. Alta. Agr. Vet. Lab., Edmonton, 1972-79, 79-82; lab. head Vet. Lab., Fairview, Alta., 1970-72; instr., resident pathology dept. Western Coll. Vet. Medicine, Saskatoon, 1969-70. Mem. Am. Coll. Vet. Pathologists, Can. Vet. Med. Assn. (chmn. specialization com. 1986-88), Alta. Vet. Med. Assn. (pres. 1981-82). Avocations: skiing, equine driving. Home and Office: RR 1 Edmonton AB Canada T6H 5T6 Personal E-mail: rbchristi@shaw.ca.

CHRISTIAN, RICHARD CARLTON, dean, former advertising agency executive; b. Dayton, Ohio, Nov. 29, 1924; s. Raymond A. and Louise (Gamber) C.; m. Audrey Bongartz, Sept. 10, 1949; children: Ann Christian Carra, Richard Carlton Jr. BS in Bus. Adminstrn, Miami U., Oxford, Ohio, 1948; MBA, Northwestern U., 1949; LLD (hon.), Nat.-Louis U., 1986; postgrad., Denison U., The Citadel, Biarritz Am. U. Mktg. analyst Rockwell Mfg. Co., Pitts., 1949-50; exec. v.p. Marsteller Inc., Chgo., 1951-60, pres., 1960-75; bd. dirs., exec. com. Young and Rubicam, Inc., 1979-84; chmn. bd. Marsteller Inc., 1975-84, chmn. emeritus, 1984—; assoc. dean Kellogg Grad. Sch. Mgmt. Northwestern U., 1984-91, assoc. dean Medill Sch. Journalism, 1991-99. Dir., chmn. Bus. Publs. Audit Circulation, Inc., 1969-75; spkr. in field. Trustee Northwestern U., 1970-74, Nat.-Louis U., Evanston, Ill., 1970-92, James Webb Young Fund for Edn., U. Ill., 1962-95; pres. Nat. Advt. Rev. Coun., 1976-77; bd. adv. coun. mem. Miami U.; mem. adv. coun. J.L. Kellogg Grad. Sch. Mgmt., Northwestern U.; v.p., dir. Mus. Broadcast Comm.; dir. Can. U.S. Ednl. Exch. (Fulbright Found.), 1988-92. With inf. AUS, 1942-46, ETO. Decorated Purple Heart, 1945; recipient Ohio Gov.'s award 1977, Alumni medal, Alumni Merit and Svc. awards Northwestern U.; named to the Advt. Hall of Fame, 1991. Mem. Am. Mktg. assn., Indsl. Mktg. Assn. (founder, chmn. 1951), Bus. Profl. Advt. Assn. (life mem. Chgo., pres. Chgo. 1954-55, nat. v.p. 1955-58, G. D. Crain award 1977), U. Ill. Found., Northwestern U. Bus. Sch. Alumni Assn. (founder, pres.), Am. Assn. Advt. Agys. (dir., chmn. 1976-77), Am. Acad. Advt. (1st disting. svc. award 1978), Northwestern U. Alumni Assn. (nat. pres. 1968-70), Mid-Am. Club, Comml. Club, Econ. Club Chgo., Kenilworth Club, Westmoreland Country Club, Alpha Delta Sigma, Beta Gamma Sigma, Delta Sigma Pi, Phi Gamma Delta. Baptist. Home: 2 Arbor Ln Apt 412 Evanston IL 60201

CHRISTIAN, ROBERT HENRY, retired architect; b. Cin., Feb. 28, 1922; s. Richard Dudley and Lillian Emma (Huber) C.; m. Marjorie Ann Ruff, Apr. 12, 1947; children— Carol Ann, Robert Alan. BS in Architecture, U. Cin., 1952. Color matcher Interchem. Corp., Cin., 1945-46; draftsman various cos., 1946-54; asso. architect Sullivan, Isaacs & Sullivan, Cin., 1954-62, L.P. Cotter & Assos., Cin., 1962-67, partner, 1967-72; v.p. devel. D.C. Peterson Co. Inc., Hilton Head Island, S.C., 1972-74; pres. Robert Christian Regimes Inc., 1981-88, Hilton Head/Beaufort Council Architects, 1976; ret., 1990. Mem. Hamilton County Regional Planning Commn., Cin., 1963-72; active Boy Scouts Am.; artist and archtl. rep. Cin. Archdiocesan Liturgical Commn., 1970-77; tech. adviser to Village Woodlawn, Ohio, 1963-70; mayor Village, 1957-63; Mem. Edgecliff Coll. Acad. Fine Arts Found., 1961-69, chmn., 1963-66. Served with USAAF, 1942-45. Mem. NRA, AIA, U.S. Tennis Assn. Tennis Umpires, Scarab, Am. Legion, KC (4th degree). Home: 7759 155th Rd N West Palm Beach FL 33418-1861

CHRISTIAN, SANDRA SVEC, retired state official; b. Evanston, Ill., Dec. 11, 1947; d. Joseph Francis and Martha Marjorie (Randau) Svec; m. Terry L. Yonker, June 28, 1969 (div. 1990); m. Bernard L. Christian, Aug. 20, 2001. BS in Meteorology, U. Wis., Madison, 1969. Sec., sales asst. Moore Bus. Forms Inc., Lansing, Mich., 1970-72; rsch. asst. Mich. Dept. Social Svcs., Lansing, 1972-74; adminstrv. analyst Mich. Pub. Svc. Commn., Lansing, 1974-79, supr. orgn. devel., 1980-84; program mgr. Gov.'s Energy Awareness Adv. Com., Lansing, 1979-80; labor rels. rep. Mich. Dept. Agr., Lansing, 1984-87, acting personnel dir., 1987-89, asst. to chief dep. dir., 1989-93, dir. EEO/affirmative action office, 1991-97, program mgr. human resources, 1997—2000; benefit analyst Human Resource Mgmt. Network, 1998—2002, ret., 2002. Bd. dirs. Lansing Area Advocates for Choice, 1991-93, Downtown Neighborhood Assn., Lansing, 1990-2004, v.p., 1992-95, sec., 1998-2000; vol. Radio Talking Book, East Lansing, Mich., 1974-93, Am. Cancer Soc. Relay for Life, 2003—; active Stratford (Ont., Can.), Shakespearean Festival, 1974—; Marshal vol. co-chair Oldsmobile Classic Ladies PGA event, East Lansing, 1993-96, Marshal vol., 1997-98, mdse. vol. co-team leader, 1999-2000; mem. Covenant Assn. United Ch. of Christ, Church and Ministry Com., 1992-96, chair, 1996. Mem.: Am. Bus. Women's Assn. (treas. Virgo chpt. 1998—2000, Woman of the Yr. award 1977), Friday Frolics, Grand Valley Corvette Assn. Avocations: golf, walking, community theater, conservation. Home: 1512 Settlers Hill Dr Lansing MI 48917-1284 Personal E-mail: kangaroo333@comcast.net.

CHRISTIAN, SHIRLEY ANN, journalist, author; b. Jan. 16, 1938; d. Herbert Walsh and Minnie Lucille (Acker) C. BA, Pittsburg (Kans.) State U., 1960; MA, Ohio State U., 1966. UN corr. AP, 1970-73, copy editor fgn. desk N.Y.C., 1974-77, chief of bur. Santiago, Chile, 1977-79; Latin Am. corr. Miami (Fla.) Herald, 1979-84; fgn. affairs reporter N.Y. Times, Washington, 1985-86, bur. chief Buenos Aires, 1986-91, bur. chief Ctrl. Am., 1991-93; pres. Hemisphere Bus. Books, 1994-97; publ. editor, sr. writer Stowers Inst. for Med. Rsch., Kansas City, Mo., 1998—2003. Adj. prof. journalism Columbia U., 1977. Author: Nicaragua: Revolution in the Family, 1985, Before Lewis and Clark: The Story of the Chouteaus, The French Dynasty that Ruled America's Froniter, 2004. Nieman fellow Harvard U., 1973-74; recipient Pulitzer prize for internat. reporting, 1981, George Polk Meml. award for fgn. reporting, 1981. Congregationalist. Home: 6836 Glenwood St Overland Park KS 66204-1453 Personal E-mail: schristian@everestkc.net.

CHRISTIAN, TERRY CLIFTON, lawyer; b. Welch, W.Va., Aug. 4, 1952; s. Samuel Clifton and Mary Jane Christian; m. Wendy Lee McCoy, Feb. 14, 1991. BA, U. Del., 1984; JD, Ind. U., Indpls., 1987. Bar: Fla. 1988, U.S. Dist. Ct. (mid. dist.) Fla. 1989, U.S. Ct. Appeals (11th cir.) 1990, U.S. Dist. Ct. (no. and so. dists.) Fla. 1996, U.S. Supreme Ct. 1996; cert. Bd. Legal Edn. and Specialization, Fla.; cert. Nat. Bd. Trial Advocacy. Asst. state atty. Office of State Atty., Ft. Myers, Fla., 1988-89; mng. ptnr. Christian & Assocs., P.A., Tampa, Fla., 1989—; U.S. Immigration Judge Detroit, 2003. Mem. criminal justice act panel U.S. Dist. Ct. for Mid. Dist. Fla., 1989—, for No. Dist., 1996—2000, for So. Dist., 1998—2005; spl. asst. pub. defender capital and RICO cases only, Tampa, 1989—. Author immigration and criminal law seminars. Bd. dirs. Humane Soc. Tampa Bay, 2002-03. Capt. U.S. Army Res., 1986-90. Mem.: FBA (exec. com. Tampa Bay chpt. 1996—2001, svc. award 1997—2001), Am. Inns of Ct. (exec. com. 2000—03, parliamentarian 2001, sec. 2002—03, svc. award 2002—03), Hillsborough County Assn. Criminal Def. Lawyers (sec. 1996—97, pres. 1997—98, bd. dirs. 1999—2002, svc. award 1998), Fla. Bar, Am. Immigration Lawyers Assn. (sec. Ctrl. Fla. chpt. 1992—94, treas. 1994—95, v.p. 1995—97, exec. com. 2005, bd. govs. 2005, svc. award 1995—97). Democrat. Roman Catholic. Avocations: reading, sports, exercise, weightlifting. Office: Christian & Assocs PA 620 E Twiggs St Ste 203 Tampa FL 33602 Business E-mail: tcclawpa@aol.com.

CHRISTIAN, THOMAS WILLIAM, lawyer; b. Tuscaloosa, Ala., Aug. 23, 1938; s. George William and Grace (Mandeville) C.; m. Dorothy Rosamond, Jan. 23, 1965; children: George, Ed, Delia. AB, U. Ala., 1960, LLB, 1965. Bar: Ala. 1965, U.S. Dist. Ct. (no. dist.) Ala. 1965, U.S. Ct. Appeals (5th and 11th cirs.) 1971, U.S. Supreme Ct. 1973. Ptnr. Balch & Bingham, Birmingham, Ala., 1965-81; firm Rives & Peterson, Birmingham, Ala., 1981-2000, Christian & Small, Birmingham, Ala., 2000—. Lt. U.S. Army, 1961-63. Fellow Internat. Acad. Trial Lawyers, Am. Bar Found., Am. Coll. Trial Lawyers; mem. ABA, Am. Bd. Trial Advocates, Ala. State Bar Assn., Birmingham Bar Assn. (pres. 1984), Ala. Def. Lawyers Assn. (pres. 1979), Internat. Assn. Ins. Counsel, Birmingham Country Club, Redstone Club. Presbyterian. Avocations: fishing, jogging, nautilis. Home: 4012 Old Leeds Ln Birmingham AL 35213-3235 Office: Christian & Small 1800 Financial Ctr Birmingham AL 35203-2696 E-mail: twchristian@csattorneys.com.

CHRISTIAN-CHRISTENSEN, DONNA MARIE, congresswoman; b. Teaneck, N.J., Sept. 19, 1945; d. Almeric L. Christian and Virginia Sterling; children: Rabiah Green, Karida Green; m. Chris Christensen; stepchildren: Lisa, Esther, Bryan, David. BS, St. Mary's Coll., Ind., 1966; MD, George Washington U., 1970; LLD (hon.), Morgan Coll. Pvt. medical practice, 1973—74; cmty. health physician U.S. V.I. Dept. Health; med. dir. Gov. Juan F. Luis Hosp., St. Croix; vice chairperson U.S. V.I. Dem. Territorial Com., 1980; mem. U.S. V.I. Bd. Edn., 1984; committeewoman Nat. Dem., 1984; apptd. U.S. V.I. Status Commn., 1988-92; del. Dem. Nat. Conv.; at large repr. from V.I. U.S. Ho. of Reps., 1997—; chair Congl. Black Caucus Health Braintrust, 1999—. Mem. Resources Com., Small Bus. Com.; mem. Select Com. Homeland Security; mem. Congl. Caucus Women's Issues; mem. Steering Com. Congl. Travel and Tourism Caucus; mem. Congl. Rural Caucus, Congl. Nat. Guard and Res. Caucus. Trustee, founding mem. Caribbean Youth Orgn. Recipient Disting. Alumni award, George Washington U., Disting. Svc. award, Howard U. Sch. Medicine. Mem. Nat. Med. Assn. (trustee), Caribbean Studies Assn., V.I. Med. Inst., V.I. Med. Soc. (pres., sec.), Women's Coalition St. Croix, St. Croix Environ. Assn. Democrat. Achievements include first to be the female delegate from U.S. Virgin Islands. Office: 1510 Longworth Ho Office Bldg Washington DC 20515-0001 E-mail: donna.christensen@mail.house.gov.*

CHRISTIANO, GREGORY JOHN, claims representative, writer; b. N.Y.C., Apr. 23, 1947; s. Ulderico Victorio (Emanuel) and Olympia (Circelli) Christiano; m. Kathleen Mary Schnaidt, Dec. 6, 1955; children: Jennifer, Theresa, Kevin. BA, Ctrl. U. Iowa, 1969. Editl. adminstr. Thomas Publ. Co., N.Y.C., 1971—74; dir. rsch. Hagstrom Co. Inc., N.Y.C., 1974—82; prodn. mgr. Tabard Press Corp., N.Y.C., 1982—84; print estimator Allied Graphic Arts, N.Y.C., 1984—85; prodn. mgr. Tabard/Copley Graphics, N.Y.C., 1985—94; claims adjuster SnowBird Corp., Jersey City, 1997—. Editl. asst. H. Wolf Book Mfg. Co., Inc., N.Y.C., 1970—71. Author: Collection of Poems, 2003, poetry anthologies and short stories, online essays, editorials and reviews. Vol., mem. Nat. Rep. Comm., Wash., DC, 2001—. Recipient Nettie and Carl Halpern Meml. best nostalgia piece, Bronx County Hist. Soc., 2002. Republican. Roman Catholic. Avocations: collector antique newspapers, books, maps, prints, ephemera. Office Phone: 201-451-4000 210. E-mail: falon@optonline.net.

CHRISTIANS, CLIFFORD GLENN, communications educator; b. Hull, Iowa, Dec. 22, 1939; s. Arnold and Verbena Janette (Geerdes) Christians; m. Priscilla Jean Kreun, June 13, 1961; children: Glenn Clifford, Ted Arnold, Paul Raymond. AB, Calvin Coll., 1961; ThM, Fuller Theol. Sem., 1965; MA, U. So. Calif., 1966; PhD, U. Ill., 1974. Dir. comms. Christian Ref. Home Ministries, Grand Rapids, Mich., 1966-70; rsch. asst. prof. comms. U. Ill., Urbana, 1974-80, rsch. assoc. prof. comms., 1980-87, rsch. prof. comms., 1987—. Rsch. fellow Calvin Ctr. for Christian Scholarship, Grand Rapids, 1983-84; vis. scholar in ethics Princeton (N.J.) U., spring, 1979; inst. fellow U. Chgo., 1986-87; Pew Evangel. scholar in ethics Oxford U., spring, 1995; dir. Inst. Rsch. Comms., Urbana, 1987—. Co-author: Jacques Ellul: Interpretive Essays, 1981, Good News: Social Ethics and The Press, 1993, Media Ethics: Cases and Moral Reasoning, 1998, Communication Ethics and Universal Values, 1997, Moral Engagement in Public Life: Theorists fro Contemporary Ethics, 2002; editor: Critical Studies in Mass Communication, 1992-95. Bd. dirs. Empty Tomb, Inc., Champaign, Ill., 1986—; elder Christian Ref. Ch., Champaign, 1974-82; bd. dirs. Univ. YMCA, Champaign, 1974-77, Judah Christian Sch., Champaign, 1984-90. Rsch. fellow, Program for Cultural Values and Ethics, 1990. Mem. Soc. for Philosophy and Tech., Assn. for Edn. in Journalism and Mass Comm. (chair qualitative studies divsn. 1980-81), Internat. Assn. Mass Comm. Rsch. (program co-chair 1991-94), Ellul Studies Forum, Nat. Comm. Assn. Democrat. Avocations: fishing, travel, reading. Home: U Ill Inst Comm Rsch 1002 W William St Champaign IL 61821 Office: U Ill Comm Dept 810 S Wright St Urbana IL 61801 Office Phone: 217-333-1549. Business E-Mail: cchrstns@uiuc.edu.

CHRISTIANS, KATHLEEN KAY, surgeon, education educator; b. Belmond, Iowa, Feb. 10, 1967; d. Ron and Virginia Christians. BA (hon.), Northwestern Coll., 1989; MD, Univ. Iowa, 1989—93; gen. surgery course, Cambridge Sch. Clin. Medicine, Eng., 1993; endoscopy and colonoscopy course, Warwick Dist.Gen. Hosp., Eng., 1996; post grad., Med. Coll. Wis., 1993—98; post grad. Sun Chieh Yeh Fellowship in hepatobiliary and pancreatic surgery, U. Hong Kong, 2002—03; post grad. ultrasound for surgeons, post grad. ultrasound in acute settings, ACS, Chgo., 2000; post grad. biostatistics I, Med. Coll. Wis., 2000, post grad. biostatistics II, 2002; post grad. ultrasound instr. course, ACS, Toronto, Can., 2001. Cert. BLS, 1993, ACS ACLS, 1993, ATLS Provider, 1993, lic. Wis., 1994, cert. ACS ATLS Instr., 1999, Am. Bd. of Surgery, 1999, ABS surg. critical care, 1999, Advanced Wilderness Life Support, Utah, 2000. Gen. surgery We. Gen. Hosp., Edinburgh, 1993; trauma and orthop. surgery Birmingham Accident and Emergency Hosp., England, 1993; resident Royal Coll. Surgery Eng., Warwick, 1996; clin. instr. Med. Coll. Wis., Milw., 1999—2000, asst. prof., 2000—. Author (with others) numerous referred med. jour. publ. and papers; contbr. scientific papers, chapters to books. Vol. physician Wis. First Ann. Camp for burn injured youth. Recipient Dean's List, Northwestern Coll.,Orange City, Iowa, 1985—89, Acad. Honor Scholarship, 1985—89, Gross Human Anatomy Tchg. Asst., Univ. Iowa, 1990—91, Robert E. Condon Golden Scalpel Award - Best Tech. Skills, Med. Coll. Wis., 1998; grantee Med. Student Rsch. Fellowship, Univ. Reading, Eng., 1990. Mem.: AMA, ACS, Internat. Coll. Surgeons, Soc. Surg. Oncology, Am. Hepata Pancreata Biliary Assn., Milw. GI Soc., Wis. Surg. Soc., Wis. State Med. Soc., Assn. Women Surgeons, Soc. for Critical Care, We. Surg. Assn., Assn. for Acad. Surgery. Avocations: rock climbing, bicycling, running. Office: Med Coll Wis 9200 W Wis Ave Milwaukee WI 53226 Office Phone: 414-805-8622. E-mail: kchristi@mcw.edu.

CHRISTIANSEN, ANDREW P., website designer, historic archives digitilizer; b. Barre City, Vt., July 9, 1953; s. Stanley Lee and Joyce (Rowland) C.; m. Jennifer Dow Zollner, 1987; 2 children. BA, BM, Lawrence U., 1976. Active Dem. Town Com., 1978-88; justice of peace East Montpelier, Vt., 1980-92; co-chmn. Vt. Rainbow Coalition, 1986-87; state rep. dist. 2 Vt. Ho. of Reps., 1987-97; owner Old Barn Vt. LLC, 1997—. Dairy farmer, East Montpelier, 1958-86; rschr. dept. psychology Lawrence U., Appleton, Wis., 1971-76; piano tchr., Ctrl. Vt., 1976—96; website designer. Mem. Danish Brotherhood Am., Am. Soc. Dowsers, Rural Vt., Vt. Hist. Soc. Address: 470 Hammett Hill Rd East Montpelier VT 05651-4034 Office Phone: 802-223-7858. E-mail: andy@oldbarnvt.com.

CHRISTIANSEN, COLLEEN M., physician assistant; d. Stephen Joseph and Lorraine Jane Colson; m. George R. Christiansen, Mar. 4, 2000; children: Johanna, Alexandra, Samantha. BSc cum laude, LI U., 1990; BSc Physician Asst., SUNY Stonybrook, 1993; cert. in Residency Surgery, Norwalk-Yale U., Norwalk, Conn., 1994; MA in Physician Asst. Studies, U. Nebr., 2000. Physician asst. Norwalk (Conn.) Hosp., 1994—95, Winthrop U. Hosp., Mineola, NY, 1995—, Good Samaritan Hosp., West Islip, NY, 1996—98, Mercy Med. Ctr., Rockville Ctr., NY, 1996—98; neurosurgical physician asst. Winthrop U. Hosp., 1995—, Huntington (N.Y.) Hosp., 1999—. Academic coord. Winthrop U. Hosp., 1996—98. Fellow: Am. Acad. Physician Assts.; mem.: Am. Coll. Clinicians, Am. Assn. Neurological Surgeons (assoc.), N.Y. State Soc. Physician Assts. (newsletter editor 1997—98, membership chmn. 1996—97). Republican. Roman Catholic. Home: 67 Jefferson Ave Islip Terrace NY 11752 Office: Winthrop Univ Hosp Neurosurgery 259 First St Mineola NY 11501 Office Phone: 516-663-3833. Personal E-mail: neurotek@optonline.net.

CHRISTIANSEN, DAVID K., health facility administrator; b. Logan, Utah, Sept. 10, 1952; s. John R. and Lucele (Kartchner) C.; m. Cynthia Ann Kutsko, July 28, 1982. BS, Brigham Young U., 1977; M in Health Care Adminstrn., U. Ala., 1979. Purchasing asst. McDonald Health Clinic, Provo, Utah, 1975—77; adminstrv. resident Bapt.-Montclair Hosp., Birmingham, Ala., 1978—79, adminstrv. asst., 1979—80; asst. adminstr. Lakeview Cmty. Hosp., Bountiful, Utah, 1980—83; adminstr. Shasta Gen. Hosp., Redding, Calif., 1983—84; CEO Knoxville (Iowa) Cmty. Hosp., 1984—89; COO Med. Ctr. Independence, Kansas City, Mo., 1989—92; CEO Newman Regional Hosp., Emporia, Kans., 1992—96; exec. v.p. MED/MAX Health Mgmt., San Diego, 1996—99; exec. dir. Salt Lake Sr. Clinic, 1999—2001; area adminstr. CHD-Meridan Healthcare Mgmt., 2001—03; CEO Mount Ogden Eye Ctr., 2003—. Cons. Ctr. Health Studies, Nashville, 1981—83; mem. faculty Ctr. Health Studies/Hosp. Cor. Am., Nashville, 1981—83. Explorer advisor Boy Scouts Am., Birmingham, 1977-80; campaign coord. United Way, Bountiful, 1983; exec. bd. dirs. Boy Scouts Am., Topeka, 1994-96. Named Outstanding Young Man of Am., U.S. Jaycees, 1982. Fellow Am. Coll. Healthcare Execs.; mem. Knoxville C. of C. (chmn. commerce com. 1986-87), Emporia Kans. C. of C. (bd. dirs. 1994-96), Rotary (membership chmn. Redding 1984, Knoxville bd. dirs. 1987-89).

CHRISTIANSEN, DONALD DAVID, electrical engineer, editor, publishing executive, consultant; b. Plainfield, NJ, June 23, 1927; s. David Carsten and Rita (Holmes) C.; m. Joyce Ifill, Jan. 1, 1951; children: Jacqueline, Jill. BEE, Cornell U., Ithaca, N.Y., 1950; postgrad., Mass. Inst. Tech., 1951, 54, U. Wis., Madison, 1966, 68, 71. Registered profl. engr., Mass. Engr. Philco Corp., Phila., 1948-50, CBS, Danvers, Lowell and Newburyport, Mass., 1950-62; solid-state editor Electronic Design, Hayden Pub. Co., N.Y.C., 1962-63; sr. editor EEE-Circuit Design Engring. Mactier Pub. Co., N.Y.C., 1963-66; sr. assoc. editor Electronics McGraw-Hill Pub. Co., N.Y.C., 1966, sr. editor, 1966-67, assoc. mng. editor, 1967-68, editor-in-chief, 1968-70, mgr. planning, devel. electronics publs., 1970-71; gen. mgr. Electronics in Medicine, 1971; editor and pub. Spectrum jour. of IEEE, N.Y.C., 1971-93, editor emeritus, 1993—, chmn. editorial bd., 1972-93; IEEE rep. to UN, 1974-87; pres. Informatica, Huntington, N.Y., 1993—. Lectr. Newark Coll. Engring., 1967, U. Mich., Ann Arbor, 1973, Walla Walla (Wash.) Coll., 1973, Ga. Inst. Tech., 1976, NASA Goddard Space Flight Ctr., 1981, Cornell U., 1982, Disting. lectr. Purdue U., 1986; cons. Bur. of Census, Dept. Commerce, NSF; mem. NRC Com. on Edn. and Utilization of the Engr.; elec. engring. adv. com. Worcester Poly. Inst.; mem. AIP mag. policy com., 1996-98; mem. AIP adv. com. on Indsl. Physicist, chmn., 2000-01; adv. bd. Encyclopedia Americana, 2000—; advisor Am. Inst. Physics Resources Ctr., 2000-01. Editor-in-chief: Electronics Engineers' Handbook, 4th edit., 1997; editor: Engineering Excellence, 1987, Standard Handbook of Electronic Engineering, 2005; publ. com. Cornell Alumni News mag., 1986-91; contbr. articles to profl. jours. Bd. dirs. YMCA, Newburyport, Mass., 1962, Broadband Info. Svcs., N.Y.C., 1970-87, L.I. Mus. Sci. and Tech., 1993-96. With USN, WWII. Recipient medal and citation for advancement of culture Flanders Acad. Art, Sci. and Lit., 1980, citation Folio mag., 1991. Fellow IEEE (co-founder, charter exec. com. chpt. 1958, Centennial medal, Gruenwald award), World Acad. Art and Sci., Radio Club of Am., 1987; mem. Nat. Press Club, N.Y. Acad. Sci., Cornell Soc. Engrs., Coun. Engring. and Sci. Soc. Execs., Am. Soc. Assn. Execs., Am. Soc. Mag. Editors, Soc. Nat. Assn. Publs. (dir. 1976-79, chmn. editl. com. 1976-79, pres. 1981-83), NY Bus. Press Editors (dir. 1978-79), Cornell Engring. Alumni Coun., Delta Club, Union Internat. de la Presse Radiotechnique et Electronique, Deadline Club, Nat. Conf. Electronics in Medicine (chmn. 1971), Soc. for History Tech., Soc. for Indsl. Archeology, Jovians, Antique Wireless Assn., Franklin Inst., Royal Instn., Newcomen Soc., Eta Kappa Nu (eminent mem., chmn., Outstanding Elec. Engr. award 1976-78, dir. 1982-84, chmn. Vladimir Karapetoff award 1991-2004, chmn. eminent mem. com. 1998—, Disting. Svc. award 2001), U.S. Naval Inst., Navy League of U.S. (life), USS San Jacinto Assn., Mu Sigma Tau, Sigma Delta Chi. Office: Informatica 434 W Main St Huntington NY 11743-3247

CHRISTIANSEN, JAY DAVID, lawyer; b. Slayton, Minn., Mar. 22, 1952; s. Holger K. and Dagny (Fjelstad) C.; children: Tyler, Carrie, Jayne. BA, Luther Coll., 1974; JD, Vanderbilt U., 1977. Ptnr. Faegre & Benson, Mpls., 1977—. Mem. ABA (chair 1997-99, health law sect., mem. ho. dels. 1999-2002), Am. Health Lawyers Assn., Order of Coif. Office: Faegre & Benson 90 S 7th St Minneapolis MN 55402-3901 E-mail: jchristi@faegre.com.

CHRISTIANSEN, KEITH ALLAN, lawyer; b. Madison, Wis., Dec. 14, 1943; s. Herman Louis and Faith Louise (Haase) C.; m. Sheila Irene Stangel, Apr. 11, 1966; children: Douglas, Jeffrey. BS, U. Wis., 1965, JD, 1968. Bar: Wis. 1968, Fla. 1973, U.S. Dist. Ct. (ea. dist.) Wis. 1968. Assoc. Foley & Lardner LLP, Milw., 1968-74, ptnr., 1975—. Co-author: Marital Property Law in Wisconsin, 1984, 3d edit., 2004. Active Potawatomi coun. Boy Scouts Am. 1975—, past pres.; v.p. Area 3 Ctrl. Region Boy Scouts. Am., 1992—. Fellow Am. Coll. Trust and Estate Counsel; mem. Mid-winter Estate Planning Clinic, Estate Counselors Forum. Republican. Office: Foley & Lardner LLP 777 E Wisconsin Ave Ste 3800 Milwaukee WI 53202-5306 Office Phone: 414-297-5746. E-mail: kchristiansen@foley.com.

CHRISTIANSEN, KENNETH ALLEN, biologist, educator; b. Chgo., June 24, 1924; s. Christian Peder and Ethel (Robinson) C.; m. Phyllis Jean Smith, June 7, 1947; children: Karen, Eric, Paula, Diane. BA, Boston U., 1948; PhD, Harvard, 1951. Teaching fellow Harvard, 1949-51; asst. prof. biology Am. U. Beirut, Lebanon, 1951-54; instr. zoology Smith Coll., 1954-55; faculty Grinnell (Iowa) Coll., 1955—, prof. biology, 1962-94, prof. emeritus, 1994—. Instr. Harvard Summer Sch., 1956, 59; vis. rschr. Le Lab. Souterrain, Moulis, France, 1962, 67-68; rschr. dept. biology U. Nat. Autonima Mex., Mexico City, 1995; vis. prof. biology Nanjing U., 1990; panelist NRC, EPA, 1995, 96, 97. Author: Collembola North America, 1980, revised 1998, Collembola Hawaii, 1992; contbr. articles to profl. jours. Mem. Iowa Gov.'s Sci. Adv. Coun. With AUS, 1942-45. Decorated Bronze Star with oak leaf cluster. Recipient award for merit Iowa Acad. Sci., 1976; rsch. grantee Sigma Xi, 1950-55; rsch. grantee Bache Fund, 1955; rsch. grantee Am. Philos. Soc., 1957; rsch. grantee NSF, 1957-78; rsch. grantee Whitehall Found., 1987-89; Iowa Gov.'s Sci. medal for sci. teaching, 1987; Grinnell C. of C. award. Fellow AAAS, Nat. Speleological Soc., Explorers Club, Soc. for Study Evolution; mem. Soc. Systemic Zoology, Internat. Soc. Soil Zoology, Am. Entomol. Soc., Cambridge Entomol. Soc., Mus. of Paris (corr.), Phi Beta Kappa, Sigma Xi. Home: 631 Park St Apt 101 Grinnell IA 50112-2283 Office Phone: 641-269-3032. Business E-Mail: christa@grinnell.edu.

CHRISTIANSEN, LYDIA R., pathologist; b. Broken Bow, Nebr., May 7, 1974; d. Duane Burdette and Genieve Suzane Christiansen; m. John Albert Stoysich, Apr. 25, 2003. BA, Azusa Pacific U., 1995; MD, U. Nebr., Omaha, 2002. Resident Med. U. S.C., Charleston, 2002—05, chief resident, 2005—. Small group moderator Med. U. S.C., Charleston, 2002—, on-call med. examiner, 2003—; S.C. resident del. Coll. Am. Pathologists, Charleston, 2004—, labarotory insp., Las Vegas, Nev., 2005. Illustrator: children's books Young Patriot Educational Series; contbr. articles to profl. jours. Vol. Habitat for Humanity, Azusa, Calif., 1992—95, Calif. AIDS Project, Azusa, 1992—95, Crisis Pregnancy Clinic, Azusa, 1992—95, Azusa Pacific U., 1993—94, Med. Outreach Clinics supported by U. Nebr. Med. Ctr., Omaha, 1998—2002. Presdl. Merit scholar, Azusa Pacific U., 1992—95, Edward O. Rejda Merit scholar, Edward O. Rejda Trust, 1998-2000. Mem.: S.C. Soc. Pathologists, S.C. Med. Assn., Am. Soc. Clin. Pathology, Coll. Am. Pathologists (state del. to the resident forum 2004—), Alpha Chi. Avocations: travel, painting, drawing, gardening, cooking. Office: Med U SC 165 Ashley Ave Ste 309 Charleston SC 29425 Office Phone: 843-792-4212.

CHRISTIANSEN, MARGARET LOUISE, law librarian, lawyer; d. James Birch and Elizabeth P. Dempsey; m. Phillip Edward Christiansen, June 1, 1996. BSBA in Econs., William Woods Coll., 1980; JD, Regent U., 1994; MS in Info. Sci., Fla. State U., Tallahassee, Florida, 2005. Bar: Va. 1996. Lectr. internat. trade Jiangsu Poly. Inst., Zhenjiang, China, 1990, Qingdao U., China, 1991; dir. career svcs. Regent U. Sch. Law, Virginia Beach, Va., 1994—95; faculty liaison Regent U. Law Libr., 1995—98, asst. libr., 1998—99, asst. dir., 1999—. Contbr. articles to profl. publs. Kids ch. leader Coastlands Cmty. Ch., Chesapeake, Va., 2004—05. Recipient Am. Jurisprudence award in Real Property, Lawyers Coop. Pub. Co. and Regent U., 1991. Mem.: Va. Assn. Law Librs. (co-editor newsletter 2002—04, chair membership com. 2005—), Southeastern Chpt. Am. Assn. Law Librs. (mem. scholarship com. 2005—), Am. Soc. for Info. Sci. and Tech., Focus on Christian Law Librarianship, Am. Assn. Law Librs. (centennial celebration com. 2004—), Va. Bar Assn. Conservative. Avocations: camping, backpacking, canoeing, animal training, missions/travel. Office: Regent Univ Law Libr 1000 Regent Univ Dr Virginia Beach VA 23464 Office Fax: 757-226-4451. E-mail: margchr@regent.edu.

CHRISTIANSEN, NORMAN JUHL, retired newspaper publisher; b. Isle, Minn., Apr. 30, 1923; s. Arthur Theodore and Ingeborg Hansena (Clemensen) C.; m. Margaret Eleanor Whorton, June 13, 1948; children— Gregory Lowell, Susan Joy. BA in Journalism, Drake U., Des Moines, 1947. Reporter Bloomington (Ill.) Pantagraph, 1947; spl. agt. FBI, 1948-54; mem. labor relations staff Am. Newspaper Pubs. Assn., 1954-59; with Gannett Newspapers, 1959-67; asst. gen. mgr. Westchester-Rockland Newspaper Group, 1965-67; with Knight-Ridder Newspapers, Inc., 1967-80, group v.p. ops. Miami, Fla., 1975-80; pres., pub. Wichita (Kans.) Eagle and Beacon, 1980-87. Bd. dirs. William Allen White Found. Served with AUS, 1943-45. Home: 1136 Cobblestone Ct Fort Collins CO 80525-2832

CHRISTIANSEN, PATRICK T., lawyer; b. Mpls., 1947; BSEE summa cum laude, U. Notre Dame, 1969; JD, Harvard U., 1972. Bar: Fla. 1972, Minn. 1974, U.S. Tax Ct. 1977, U.S. Supreme Ct. 1980. Mem. Akerman, Senterfitt & Eidson P.A., Orlando, Fla. Chmn. bd. Orlando Mus. Art; mem., bd. dirs. The Greater Orlando C. of C., Jobs and Edn. Partnership; chmn. Orange County Transp. Roundtable, BusinessForce, 2002--; mem. Orange County Blue Ribbon Commn., steering com., chmn. transp. com.; bd. dirs. United Arts Cen. Fla., Orlando Downtown Devel. Bd.; trustee, chmn. Orlando Repertory Theatre, 2002--, U. Ctrl. Fla. Found., 2001--; bd. trustees U. Ctrl. Fla.; mem. Orange County Arts & Cultural Affairs Adv. Com., chmn. advancement com., 2001--. Mem. ABA (sects. on bus. law, taxation, real property), Fla. Bar (trial lawyers sect., co-chmn. land trust com. real property, probate and trust law sect. 1978-82, dir. real property divsn. 1982-84, vice chmn. 1984-85, chmn. 1985-86, vice-chmn. UCC subcom. corp., banking and bus. law sect. 1979-84, bd. govs. young lawyers sect. 1981-83), Am. Coll. Real Estate Lawyers, Minn. State Bar Assn., Orange County Bar Assn. Office: Akerman Senterfitt & Eidson PA Citrus Ctr 17th Fl PO Box 231 255 S Orange Ave Orlando FL 32801-3445

CHRISTIANSEN, RAYMOND STEPHAN, librarian, educator; b. Oak Park, Ill., Feb. 15, 1950; s. Raymond Julius and Anne Mary (Fusek) Christiansen; m. Phyllis Anne Dombowski, Nov. 25, 1972; 1 child, Mark David. BA, Elmhurst Coll., 1971; MEd, No. Ill. U., 1974. Lic. lay min. Episcopal Ch., 1990. Dept. dir. Elmhurst Coll., Ill., 1971—73; asst. law libr. media svcs. Lewis U., Glen Ellyn, Ill., 1974—77; asst. prof. edn. Aurora U., Ill., 1977—90, assoc. prof., 1990—2003, emeritus prof., 2003—; media cons., 1977—; media libr. Aurora U., 1977—82, instnl. developer, 1982—89, dir. media svcs., 1985—2003, edn. and tech. libr., 2003—04; dir. libr. Kaneville Pub. Libr., Ill., 2005—. Author: (video series) Rothblatt on Criminal Advocacy, 1975, (book) Index to SCOPE the UN Magazine, 1977. Mem.: ASCD, Assn. Ednl. Comms. and Tech., Phi Eta Sigma, Alpha Psi Omega. Home: 424 S Gladstone Ave Aurora IL 60506-5370 Office: Kaneville Pub Libr 2 S 101 Harter Rd Kaneville IL 60144

CHRISTIANSEN, RICHARD DEAN, retired newspaper editor; b. Berwyn, Ill., Aug. 1, 1931; s. William Edward and Louise Christine (Dethlefs) C. BA, Carleton Coll., Northfield, Minn., 1953; postgrad., Harvard U., 1954; LHD (hon.), DePaul U., 1988. Reporter, critic, editor Chgo. Daily News, 1957-73, 74-78; editor Chicagoan mag., 1973-74; critic-at-large Chgo. Tribune, 1978-83, entertainment editor, 1983-91, chief critic, sr. writer, 1991—2002; ret., 2002. Author: A Theater of Our Own: A History and a Memoir of 1,001 Nights in Chicago, 2004. Served to cpl. U.S. Army, 1954-56. Recipient award Chgo. Newspaper Guild, 1969, 74, Joseph Jefferson award, 1996, Excellence in the Arts award DePaul U., 1998, Peter Lisagor award for criticism, 2002; named to Chgo. Journalism Hall of Fame, 1998. Mem. Am. Theatre Critics Assn., Chgo. Acad. TV Arts and Scis., Soc. Midland Authors, Headline Club Chgo. (Peter Lisagor award 2002), Arts Club Chgo. (dir.), Phi Beta Kappa, Sigma Delta Chi. Republican. Lutheran. Personal E-mail: rchris5568@aol.com.

CHRISTIANSEN, RICHARD LOUIS, orthodontist, educator, dean; b. Denison, Iowa, Apr. 1, 1935; s. John Cornelius and Rosa Katherine C.; m. Nancy Marie Norman, June 24, 1956; children— Mark Richard, David Norman, Laura Marie DDS, U. Iowa, 1959; MSD, Ind. U., Indpls., 1964; PhD, U. Minn., 1970; hon. doctorate, Nippon Dental U., Tokyo, 2000. Prin. investigator Nat. Inst. Dental Research NIH, Bethesda, Md., 1970-73, chief craniofacial anomalies program br., 1973-81, dir. extramural Nat. Inst. Dental Research, 1981-82; prof. dept. orthodontics U. Mich., Ann Arbor, 1982—, dean, Sch. Dentistry and dir. W.K. Kellogg Found. Inst., 1982—2001, prof., dean emeritus, 2001—. Organizer state-of-the -art workshops in field of craniofacial anomalies and other aspects of oral health; founder Internat. Union Schs. Oral Health, 1985; organizer oral health conf. in Poland, 1989, Jordan, 1995. Contbr. chpts. to books and articles to profl. jours. Chmn. Region III United Way, U. Mich., Ann Arbor, 1984; chmn., v.p. Trinity Luth. Ch., Rockville, Md., 1975; v.p. and chmn. planning task force Trinity Luth. Ch., Ann Arbor, chmn. bd. Sequois Sr. Housing; vice chmn., bd. dirs. Luth. Soc. Svcs. Mich., 1997—; with USPHS, 1959-82, mem. dental prof. adv. com., 2005. Recipient Commendation medal USPHS, 1980; Cert. of Recognition NIH, 1982, others. Fellow Internat. Coll. Dentists, Am. Coll. Dentists, Pierre Fauchard Acad.; mem. Am. Assn. Orthodontists, Am. Assn. Dental Sch., ADA (rsch. coun.), Mich. Dental Assn., Am. Assn. Dental Research (dir. craniofacial biology group 1975-79, v.p. 1979-80, pres. 1981-82), Omicron Kappa Upsilon (mem. numerous nat. and internat. coms. and bds.). Achievements include research in in craniofacial research and international oral health. Avocations: reading, jogging, tennis, sailing, econs. E-mail: vista@umich.edu.

CHRISTIANSEN, SUSAN PUTNAM, artist, educator, consultant; b. Fresno, California, Sept. 4, 1938; d. Murray and Iolene Lazelle (Lund) Putnam; m. Robert Lorenz Christiansen, June 23, 1962; children: Peter Putnam, John Robert (twins), Catherine Sara. BA in biology, art, Stanford U., 1960, MA in edn., 1961. Cert.: secondary tchr., Calif. Tchr. sci. and art Blach Sch., Los Altos, Calif., 1961-62; tchr. art appreciation Jefferson County Schs., Denver, 1963-68; docent Denver Art Mus., 1963-70; docent trainer, classroom aide Palo Alto (Calif.) Sch. Dist. and Cultural Ctr., 1973-84; art cons. Children's Hosp., Stanford, Calif., 1985-90; researcher Creative Svcs., Stanford Alumni Assn., 1989-92; docent Cantor Ctr. for Arts, Stanford U., 1982—. Castilleja Sch. tchr., 1985; freelance artist, illustrator, cons., 1973—; children's art tchr., painter, Hilo Art Ctr., Big Island, Hawaii, 1971-73. Illustrator: signs in Hawaii Volcanoes Nat. Pk., 1971-73; U.S. Geol. Survey, 1977; muralist Children's Hosp., 1979-84; painter, illustrator Stanford Centennial exhibit, 1991, portraits, Stanford Mgmt. Group and Alumni Assn. Chair Stanford Meml. Ch. docents. Mem.: Stanford Alumni Assn., Palo Alto Hist. Assn., Stanford Hist. Soc., Nat. Trust for Historic Preservation (v.p. spl. projects com. 1989—), Pacific Art League of Palo Alto. Democrat. Avocations: tennis, piano, gardening, cooking, family geneology. Home: 1118 Harker Ave Palo Alto CA 94301-3420

CHRISTIANSEN, WALTER HENRY, aerospace scientist, educator; b. McKees Rocks, Pa., Dec. 14, 1934; s. Walter Henry and Elizabeth (Miller) C.; m. Joan Marilyn Swisler, Aug. 5, 1960; children: Walter, Audrey. BS in Mech. Engring., Carnegie Inst. Tech., 1956; MS in Aero. Engring., Calif. Inst. Tech., 1957, PhD, 1961. Sr. scientist Jet Propulsion Lab., Pasadena, Calif., 1961-62, 1963-67; rsch. assoc. prof. aero. and aeronautics U. Wash., Seattle, 1967-70, assoc. prof., 1970-74, prof., 1974—2001, dept. chmn., 1992-98, prof. emeritus, 2001—. Cons. Boeing Sci. Rsch. Lab., 1967-69, Math. Scis. N.W., 1970-85, Spectra Tech., 1985-88, 91. Contbr. articles to profl. jours.; patentee in field. Com. mem. Directions for 70's Bellevue (Wash.) Sch. Dist., 1970. Served to capt. U.S. Army, 1961-63. Dept. Def. grantee, 1970-91, NSF grantee, 1977, 80, NASA grantee, 1980-89; Mesta Machine fellow, 1952-56, Convair fellow, 1958, Boeing fellow, 1960. Fellow AIAA (Pacific N.W. chpt. Sect. award 1972); mem. Am. Phys. Soc., Sigma Xi, Tau Beta Pi, Pi Tau Sigma, Theta Xi. Home: 9633 NE 28th St Bellevue WA 98004-1846 Office: Dept Aero & Astro Box 352400 Univ Wash Seattle WA 98195-0001 Business E-Mail: walt@aa.washington.edu.

CHRISTIANSON, ELIN BALLANTYNE, librarian, civic worker; b. Gary, Ind., Nov. 11, 1936; d. Donald B. and Dorothy May (Dunning) Ballantyne; m. Stanley David Christianson, July 26, 1959; children: Erica, David. BA, U. Chgo., 1958, MA, 1961, Cert. advanced studies, 1974. Asst. librarian, then librarian J. Walter Thompson Co., Chgo., 1959-68; libr. cons., 1968—; asst. prof. Grad. Libr. Sch., U. Chgo., 1981-90, Sch. Libr. and Info. Sci., Ind. U., 1982-95; editor The Libr. Quarterly Grad. Library Sch. U. Chgo., 1988-90. Chmn. Hobart Am. Revolution Bicentennial Commn., 1974-76; bd. dirs. Hobart Hist. Soc., 1973—, pres., 1980-85, 89—; pres. LWV, Hobart, 1977-79. Recipient Laura Bracken award Hobart Jaycees, 1976, Cert. Achievement Ind. Am. Revolution Bicentennial Commn., 1975; Woman of Yr. award Hobart Bus. and Profl. Women, 1985, Resident Recognition award Northwest Ind. Forum, 1988. Mem. AAUW, ALA, U. Chgo. Grad. Libr. Sch. Alumni Assn. (v.p. 1971-74, 76-77, pres. 1977-79). Unitarian. Author: Non-Professional and Paraprofessional Staff in Special Libraries, 1973; Directory of Library Resources in Northwest Indiana, 1976; Old Settlers Cemetery, 1976; New Special Libraries: A Summary of Research, 1980; Daniel Nash Handy and the Special Library Movement, 1980; co-author: Subject Headings in Advertising, Marketing and Communications Media, 1964; Special Libraries: A Guide for Management, 1981, rev. 3d edit., 1991, Growing Up in Hobart, 1994, Hobart Memories, 1996; mem. editorial adv. bd. New Standard Encyclopedia, 1986—. Home: 141 Beverly Blvd Hobart IN 46342-4346

CHRISTIANSON, GERYLD B., government agency administrator, consultant; b. Boyd, Minn., Dec. 31, 1934; m. Sue Singer, July 9, 1960; children: Stephen, Alexander. BA in Internat. Rels., U. Minn., 1957; postgrad., Johns Hopkins U., 1967-68. Fgn. svc. officer Dept. State, NATO Office, Bur. European Affaira, various fgn. locations, 1958-75; fgn. policy advisor Senator Claiborne Pell, Washington, 1975-81; minority staff dir. Senate Fgn. Rels. Com., Washington, 1981-87, staff dir., 1987-95; sr. counselor The Evans Group, Ltd., Washington, 1995, 97—; v.p. Jefferson Waterman Internat., Washington, 1995-97. With USAR, 1957—63. Mem. Coun. on Fgn. Rels., Internat. Inst. for Strategic Studies (London). Democrat. Episcopalian. Avocations: collecting political buttons, tennis. Home: 8716 Mary Lee Ln Annandale VA 22003-3659 Office Phone: 202-333-8777. Personal E-mail: geryld.christianson@verizon.net.

CHRISTIANSON, JEFFREY A., lawyer; b. 1957; BA, Whitman Coll.; JD, U. Wash. Bar: 1982. Gen. counsel, corp. sec. Heart Technology, Inc., 1993—96; sr. v.p. bus. devel., gen. counsel, corp. sec. Wizards of the Coast, Inc., 1996—2000; sr. v.p., gen. counsel, corp. sec. Western Wireless Corp., Bellevue, Wash., 2000—. Sec. bd. dirs. Bellevue Cmty. Coll. Found. Office: Western Wireless Corp 3650 131st Ave SE Ste 600 Bellevue WA 98006 Office Phone: 425-586-8700. Office Fax: 425-586-8666.

CHRISTIANSON, PAUL ALAN, music educator; b. Jan. 21, 1964; s. Donald Alan and Faye Lorraine (Jensen) Christianson; m. Denise Ellen Barber, June 26, 1993; children: Hannah, David, Mark. BA, N.W. Nazarene Coll., 1986; MusM, U. Idaho, 1988; D Mus. Arts, U. Ga., 1997. Vis. prof. music N.W. Nazarene Coll., Nampa, Idaho, 1989; assoc. prof. music Trevecca Nazarene U., Nashville, 1993—, chmn. cultural arts com., 2001—. Dir. worship Trinity Presbyn. Ch., Murfreesboro, Tenn., 2000—. Composer: (musical recordings) Rain on the Lake, 1991, Timeless, 1994, Music for 5 Vanderbilt Med. Ctr. videos, 1998—2000. Recipient 1st place award Collegiate Artists Piano Competition, Idaho Music Tchrs. Assn., 1987, Tchg. Excellence award, Trevecca Nazarene U., 2000. Mem.: Music Tchrs. Nat. Assn., Nashville Music Tchrs. Assn., Tenn. Music Tchrs. Assn. Nazarene. Avocations: reading, outdoor activities.

CHRISTIANSON, ROGER GORDON, biology professor, department chairman; b. Santa Monica, Calif., Oct. 31, 1947; s. Kyle C. and Ruby K. (Parker) Christianson; m. Angela Diane Rey, Mar. 3, 1967; children: Lisa Marie, David Scott, Stephen Peter. BA in Cell and Organismal Biology, U. Calif., Santa Barbara, 1969, MA in Biology, 1971, PhD in Biology, 1976. Faculty assoc. U. Calif., Santa Barbara, 1973-79, staff rsch. assoc., 1979-80; asst. prof. So. Oreg. U., Ashland, 1980-85, assoc. prof., 1985-93, prof., 1993—, coord. gen. biology program, 1980—, chmn. biology dept., 1996, 1997—2003. Instr. U. Calif. Santa Barbara, 1976, 78, 80. Contbr. articles to sci. and ednl. jours. Active Oreg. Shakespeare Festival Assn., Ashland, 1983—87; mem. bikeway com. Ashland City Coun., 1986—88; organizer Bike Oreg., 1982—92, Frontline HS Staff, 1985—2003; short-term mission work Mex. Orphanage, 1986—; ofcl. photographer Ashland H.S. Booster Club, 1987—92; coord. youth program 1st Bapt. Ch., Ashland, 1981—85, mem. ch. life commn., 1982—88, 2004—, chair ch. life commn., 2004—, bd. deacons, 1993—95, 2004—, mem. outreach commn., 1994, 1995; youth leader jr. and sr. H.S. students Grace Ch., Santa Barbara, 1973—80; bd. dirs. El Sauzal Found., 2004—, treas., 2004—. Mem.: AAAS (chair Pacific divsn. edn. sect 1985—2001, coun. Pacific divsn. 1985—, exec. com. Pacific divsn. 1998—, chair local organizing com. Pacific divsn. ann. meeting 2000, chair Pacific divsn. student awards com. 2001, exec. dir. Pacific divsn. 2002—, chair local organizing com. Pacific divsn. ann. meeting 2005), Assn. for Biology Lab. Edn., Oreg. Sci. Tchrs. Assn., Am. Mus. Natural History, Beta Beta Beta, Sigma Xi (chpt. membership com. 1998—2000). Republican. Avocations: sports, photography, youth work, multimedia presentations, amateur radio operator. Home: 430 Reiten Dr Ashland OR 97520-8762 Office: Southern Oregon U Dept Biology 1250 Siskiyou Blvd Ashland OR 97520-5010 Office Phone: 541-552-6747. E-mail: rchristi@sou.edu.

CHRISTIANSON, STANLEY DAVID, finance company executive; b. Chgo., Dec. 8, 1931; s. Stanley Olai and Emma Josephine (Johnson) D.; m. Elin J. Ballantyne, July 25, 1959; children: Erica Joanna, David Ballantyne. BS, U. Ill., 1954; MBA, U. Chgo., 1960. Auditor Price Waterhouse & Co., Chgo., 1956-58; asst. to controller Miehle-Goss-Dexter, Inc., Chgo., 1960-67, v.p. adminstrn. Goss Div., 1967-69; dir. mgmt. systems MGD Graphics Systems-N.Am. Rockwell (formerly Miehle-Goss-Dexter), Chgo., 1969-70; v.p. fin. Duchossois/Thrall Group (formerly Thrall Car Mfg. Co.), Chicago Heights, Elmhurst, Ill., 1970-83; vice chmn., bd. dirs. Thrall Enterprises, Inc., Chgo., 1983—. Bd. dirs. Midwestern U., 1992—, chmn., 1997-98. Bd. govs. Internat. House, U. Chgo., 1988-2000, chmn. 1997-2000; trustee Cmty. Theatre Guild, Valparaiso, Ind., 2001-, chmn., 2005—; mem. Hobart (Ind.) Plan Commn., 1986-92, pres., 1988-92. Capt. U.S. Army, 1954-56. Home: 141 Beverly Blvd Hobart IN 46342-4346 Office: Thrall Enterprises Inc 180 N Stetson Ste 3020 Chicago IL 60601-6223

CHRISTIE, CHRISTOPHER JAMES, prosecutor, lawyer; b. Mendham, N.J., 1963; m. Mary Pat Foster; children: Andrew, Sarah Anne, Patrick. BA, U. Del., 1984; JD, Seton Hall U., 1987. Bar: N.J. 1987, U.S. Dist. Ct. N.J. 1987. Atty. Dughi & Hewit, Cranford, NJ, 1987—93, ptnr., 1993—2002; U.S. atty. dist. NJ US Dept. Justice, 2002—. Bd. trustees Daytop Village-N.J., Mendham, 1998—2002; officer Christie Family Found., 2001—; chmn. Morris County Ins. Commn.; bd. dirs. United way Morris County, Family Svcs. Morris County, Morris County Bd. Social Svcs.; dir. bd. Morris County Bd. Chosen Freeholders, 1997—. Mem.: ABA, NJ State Bar Assn. Office: Peter Rodino Fed Bldg 970 Broad St Ste 700 Newark NJ 07102

CHRISTIE, DAVID GEORGE, insurance company executive; b. Glen Ridge, N.J., June 25, 1930; s. Francis Johnston and Catherine Fisher (Somes) C.; m. Diane Grace Wettyen, Mar. 23, 1950; children: Lindsey Diane, Mark Wettyen, Meredith Leigh. Student, Rutgers U., 1950-52. Asst. U.S. mgr., U.S. br. Union Re-ins. Co., Zurich, Switzerland, 1956-64; v.p. A.m Re-Ins. Co., N.Y.C., 1964—71, Towers, Perrin, Forster & Crosby, Inc., N.Y.C., 1971-78; sr. v.p., dir. Duncanson & Holt, Inc., N.Y.C., 1979-83; pres. Fester, Fothergill & Hartung Ltd., N.Y.C., 1984-89; sr. v.p. Willcox, Inc., Phila., 1989-91; chmn. Reinsurance Consultants of Princeton, Inc., NJ, 1991. With U.S. Army, 1953-54. Republican. Methodist. Home and Office: 2 Valencia Ct Skillman NJ 08558-2354 E-mail: dchris1001@aol.com.

CHRISTIE, GEORGE CUSTIS, lawyer, educator, writer; b. N.Y.C., Mar. 3, 1934; s. Custis and Sophie (Velimahitis) C.; m. Susan D. Monserud, Apr. 20, 1965 (div. July 1974); 1 child, Constantine George; m. Deborah D. Carnes, Dec. 20, 1974; children: Rebecca Sophia, Nicholas George. AB, Columbia U., 1955, JD, 1957; diploma in internat. law (Fulbright scholar), Cambridge (Eng.) U., 1962; S.JD, Harvard U., 1966. Bar: NY 1957, DC 1958. Assoc. Covington & Burling, Washington, 1958-60; Ford Found. fellow in law teaching Harvard U., 1960-61; assoc. prof. law U. Minn., Mpls., 1962-65, prof. law, 1965-66; asst. gen. counsel for Near E. and S. Asia, AID, Dept. State, 1966-67; prof. law Duke U., 1967-79, James B. Duke prof. law, 1979—. Vis. lectr. U. Witwatersrand, South Africa, 1980, Fudan U., China, U. Otago, New Zealand, 1985; fellow Nat. Humanities Center, 1980-81; scholar-in-residence McGuire, Woods & Battle, Richmond, Va., 1983, vis. Freda Alverson prof. law George Washington U., spring 1988; vis. prof. law Northwestern U., 1991-92, U. Athens, Greece, 2000; vis. fellow Rsch. Sch. Social Scis., Australian Nat. U., 2002. Author: Jurisprudence: Text and Readings on the Philosophy of Law, 1973, 2d edit. (with P. Martin), 1995, The Sum and Substance of the Law of Torts, 1980, Law, Norms & Authority, 1982, Cases and Materials on the Law of Torts, 1983, 2d edit. (with J. Meeks), 1990, 4th edit. (with others), 2004, The Notion of an Ideal Audience in Legal Argument, 2000, French edit., 2005, (with others) Cases and Materials on Advanced Torts, 2004. With U.S. Army, 1957. Mem. ABA, Am. Law Inst., Am. Soc. Internat. Law, Phi Beta Kappa. Democrat. Greek Orthodox. Home: 5212 Twin Pines Ln Durham NC 27705-8599 Office: Duke U Sch Law PO Box 90360 Durham NC 27708-0360 Office Phone: 919-613-7052. Business E-Mail: gcc@law.duke.edu.

CHRISTIE, HANS FREDERICK, retired utilities executive; b. Alhambra, Calif., July 10, 1933; s. Andreas B. and Sigrid (Falk-Jorgensen) C.; m. Susan Earley, June 14, 1957; children: Brenda Lynn, Laura Jean BS in Fin., U. So. Calif., 1957, MBA, 1964. Treas. So. Calif. Edison Co., Rosemead, 1970-75, v.p., 1975-76, sr. v.p., 1976-80, exec. v.p., 1980-84, pres., dir., 1984-87; pres., chief exec. officer The Mission Group (non-utility subs. SCE Corp.)., Seal Beach, Calif., 1987-89, ret., 1989, cons., 1989—. Bd. dirs. L.A. Ducommun

Inc., L.A., A.E. Com., L.A., Am. Mut. Fund, Inc., AMCAP, Am. Variable Ins., I.H.O.P. Corp., AECom Tech., L.A., Internat. House of Pancakes, Inc., Southwest Water Co., L.A., Smallcap World Fund, L.A., Bond Fund Am., Inc., L.A., Tax-Exempt Bond Fund Am., L.A., Ltd. Term Tax-Exempt Bond Fund Am., Am. High Income Mcpl. Bond Fund, Capital Income Builder, L.A., Capital World Bond Fund, L.A., Capital World Growth Fund, Capital World Growth and Income Fund, Intermediate Bond Fund Am., L.A., Intermediate Tax-Exempt Bond Fund Am., Capital World Growth 2d Income Fund, L.A.; trustee Cash Mgmt. Trust Am., New Economy Fund, L.A., Am. Funds Income Series, L.A., The Am. Funds Tax-Exempt Series II, Am. High Income Trust, L.A., Am. High-Inc Mun. Board Fund, Am. Variable Ins. Trust, U.S. Treasury Fund Am., L.A. Bd. councillor sch. policy, planning and devel. U. So. Calif., 1981—2001; trustee Occidental Coll., 1984—96, Idlwild Sch. Arts, 1998—2002, Chadwick Sch., Natural History Mus. Los Angeles County, 1984—2002. With U.S. Army, 1953—55. Named Outstanding mem. Arthritis Found., L.A., 1975, Outstanding Trustee, Multiple Sclerosis Soc. So. Calif., 1979 Mem. Pacific Coast Elec. Assn. (bd. dirs. 1981-87, treas. 1975-87), L.A. C. of C. (bd. dirs. 1983-87), Calif. Club. Republican. Avocations: swimming, horseback riding, bicycling. Home: 548 Paseo Del Mar Palos Verdes Estates CA 90274-1260 Office: PO Box 144 Palos Verdes Peninsula CA 90274-0144 Personal E-mail: hfc548@aol.com.

CHRISTIE, JASON DOUGLAS, medical educator, epidemiologist; s. Douglas Christie and Barbara Willows; m. Patricia Golino, July 1, 1995; children: Colin William, Grace Elizabeth. ScB, Brown U., 1989; MD, Columbia U., 1993; MS in Clin. Epidemiology, U. Pa., Phila., 2000. Asst. prof. medicine U. Pa. Sch. Medicine, Phila., 2001—, asst. prof. epidemiology, 2001—; sr. scholar Ctr. for Clin. Epidemiology and Biostatistics, Phila., 2001—. Office: Univ Pa 423 Guardian Drive 719 Blockley Hall Philadelphia PA 19038 Office Phone: 215-573-3209. Business E-Mail: jchristi@cceb.med.upenn.edu.

CHRISTIE, WILLIAM GARY, finance educator; b. Toronto, Sept. 22, 1955; s. Robert Louis and Margaret Elsa (Sparling) C.; m. Kelly Maureen McNamara, July 25, 1980. B in Commerce with honors, Queen's U., Kingston, Ont., Can., 1978; MBA in Fin., U. Chgo., 1980, PhD in Fin. and Econs., 1989. Fin. analyst Hewlett-Packard (Canada) Ltd., 1980-81, Ford Motor Co. of Canada Ltd., 1981-82; rsch. asst. in statistics and fin. U. Chgo., 1983-88; joined Owen Grad. Sch. Mgmt., Vanderbilt U., Nashville, 1989, asst. to assoc. prof. mgmt., assoc. dean faculty devel., 1999—2000, dean, Ralph Owen Prof. Mgmt. Fin., 2000—04, Frances Hampton Currey chair in fin. Econ. adv. bd. Nasdaq, 2000—03; bd. dirs. Grad. Mgmt. Admission Coun., 2002—. Contbr. articles to profl. jours. Fellow U. Chgo., 1982-89, Social Scis. and Humanities Rsch. Coun. Can., 1982-86, Ctr. for Rsch. in Securities Prices, 1983-84; recipient Irwin Disting. Paper award, 1994, Smith-Breeden award, 1995. Mem. Am. Fin. Assn., Southwestern Fin. Assn., Western Fin. Assn., Am. Econs. Assn., European Fin. Assn, Assn. to Advance Collegiate Schs. of Bus. (bus. com.), Fin. Mgmt. Assn. (academic dir.). Avocations: jogging, tennis, travel. Office: Vanderbilt U Owen Grad Sch 401 21st Ave S Nashville TN 37203

CHRISTIN, NICOLAS, computer scientist, researcher; b. Annemasse, France, June 5, 1977; s. Pierre and Christiane Christin. Diploma in engring., École Centrale Lille, 1999; MA in Computer Sci., U. Va., 2000, PhD in Computer Sci., 2003. Rsch. scientist U. Calif., Berkeley, 2003—05; sys. scientist, faculty Carnegie Mellon U., Pitts., 2005—. Mem.: Assn. Computing Machinery, IEEE. Achievements include discovery of technological solutions that could efficiently protect against illegal distribution of copyrighted works in peer-to-peer file sharing networks.

CHRISTISON, MURIEL BRANHAM, retired museum director, art educator; b. Mpls. d. Harold D. and Helen (Ferguson) Branham; children: Evelyn, Carolyn. BA, U. Minn., 1933, MA, 1940; diploma, U. Paris, 1936, U. Brussels, 1938. Grad. asst. dept. fine arts U. Minn., Mpls., 1933-36; curatorial rsch. asst. Mpls. Inst. Arts, Mpls., 1936-42, head edn., 1944-47; assoc. dir. Va. Mus. Fine Arts, Richmond, 1948-61; oper. and assoc. dir. Krannert Art Mus. U. Ill., Champaign, 1962-74, dir. Krannert Art Mus., 1975-82; ret., 1982; interim dir. Muscarelle Mus. Coll. William and Mary, Williamsburg, Va., 1984-85, 94-96, mem. vis. com., 1982-96, vis. prof. fine arts, 1983-98. Head grad. program mus. studies U. Ill., 1974—82; cons. U. Tex., Austin, Washington U., St. Louis, 1972—78, Ill. Arts Coun., 1968—82; v.p. Midwest Mus. Conf. Am. Assn. Mus., regional rep., 1972—82; examiner S.C. Arts Coun., 1984, 86, Ohio Arts Coun., 1986, Nat. Endowment for the Arts, 1973, 83, NEH, 1980. Author: numerous exhbn. catalogs; contbr. articles to mus. catalogues and other scholarly jours. Carnegie scholar Inst. Internat. Edn., 1936; CRB fellow Beligan-Am. Edn. Found., 1938; recipient Disting. Svc. award Midwest Mus. Conf., 1982, hon. nominee Va. Mus. Libr. Fund, 2003. Mem.: Colonial Williamsburg Fund, William and Mary Found., Coun. Va. Mus. Fine Arts, Assn. Preservation Va. Antiquities, Am. Assn. Museums (regional rep. 1972—82, coun. 1972—82, surveyor, examiner 1982—), Assn. Art Mus. Dirs. (emerita 1982, hon. 1982—), Cosmopolitan Club (N.Y.C.). Home: 257 Littletown Quarter Williamsburg VA 23185-5555 E-mail: mbchri@aol.com.

CHRISTMAN, ARTHUR CASTNER, JR., science administrator, consultant; b. North Wales, Pa., May 11, 1922; s. Arthur Castner and Hazel Ivy (Schirmer) C.; m. Marina Ilia Diterichs, Apr. 17, 1945; children: Candace Lee Christman Canto, Tatiana Marina Christman Harvey, Deborah Ann Christman Clark, Arthur C. III, Keith Ilia, Cynthia Ellen Christman Buckwalter. BS in Physics, Pa. State U., 1944, MS, 1950. Teaching asst. dept. physics Pa. State U., State College, 1943-44, grad. asst., 1946-48; instr. dept. physics George Washington U., Washington, 1948-51; cons. U.S. Navy, 1950-51; physicist ops. research office Johns Hopkins U., Chevy Chase, Md., 1951-58; sr. physicist SRI Internat., Menlo Park, Calif., 1958-62, head ops. research group, 1962-64, dept. mgr., 1965-67, dir. dept., 1968-71, dir. tactical weapons systems, 1971-75; sci. advisor to comdg. gen. and dep. chief staff combat devel. U.S. Army tng. and doctrine command Ft. Monroe, Va., 1975-87; cons. in field, 1988—. Bd. dirs. Cornerstone Affiliates, 2003—, mem. fin. com., 2004—. Author numerous publs. Pres. Valle Verde Continuing Care Retirement Cmty. Coun., 1991-93, 94-95, Am. Bapt. Homes of West Assn. of CCRC Resident Presidents, 1991-92; mem. bd. mgrs. fin. com. Valle Verde, 1988—; mem. Valle Verde Adv. Bd., 1997—, mem. fin. com., 1988—, chair environ. svcs. com., 1999—, mem. exec. com., 2002—; bd. dirs. Am. Bapt. Homes of the West, 1997—, mem. fin. and investment com., 1998—, mem. audit com., 1999, 2001—03, chair investment com., 2002—; bd. dirs. Ctrl. Coast Commn. for Sr. Citizens Area Agy. on Aging, 1993; mem. continuing care contract statutes rev. task force State of Calif., 1999-2000; umpire Palo Alto Little League, Calif., 1962-72. Lt. USNR, 1944-46, PTO. Decorated Meritorious Civilian Service award Dept. Army, 1983, Exceptional Civilian Service award Dept. Army, 1987; recipient Presdl. Rank, 1985, Governance award Am. Bapt. Homes of the West, 2002, Trustee of Yr. award Calif. Assn. Homes and Svcs. for the Aging, 2004. Fellow AAAS; mem. Am. Phys. Soc., Inst. for Ops. Rsch. and the Mgmt. Scis. (U.S. del. internat. confs. Operational Rsch., France 1960, Norway 1963, U.S. 1966, Ireland 1972), Santa Barbara Lawn Bowls Club (bd. dirs. 1990-93), MacKenzie Park Lawn Bowls Club. Sigma Xi, Sigma Pi Sigma, Delta Chi (chpt. pres.). Republican. Baptist (deacon, trustee). Avocations: golf, tennis, lawn bowling, photography. Home and Office: 1028 B Senda Verde Santa Barbara CA 93105-4407 Personal E-mail: achristman@abhow.com.

CHRISTMAN, BRUCE LEE, lawyer; b. Bethlehem, Pa., Apr. 1, 1955; s. Raymond J. Jr. and Irene May (Bowman) C.; m. Lynn Eloise Brodt, Oct. 11, 1980; children: Jennifer Lynn, Amy Nicole. BA, Coll. William and Mary, 1977; JD, U. Pa., 1980. Bar: Va. 1980, U.S. Ct. Appeals (4th cir.) 1980, U.S. Dist. Ct. (ea. dist.) Va. 1980. Assoc. Hunton & Williams, Richmond, Va., 1980-84; prin., ptnr. Reed Smith LLP, Fairfax, Va., 1984—. Adj. prof. George Mason Sch. Law. Mem. Leadership Fairfax Class of 1993, bd. dirs. 1997, 2000-02—. Mem. Va. State Bar Assn., Phi Beta Kappa, Omicron Delta Kappa, Kappa Sigma. Democrat. Avocations: tennis, basketball, swimming, bicycling, camping. Home: 13610 Flintwood Pl Herndon VA 20171-3331 Office: Reed Smith LLP 3110 Fairview Park Dr Falls Church VA 22042-4503 Office Phone: 703-641-4259.

CHRISTMAN, EDWARD ARTHUR, physicist; b. Lakewood, Ohio, Aug. 3, 1943; s. John N.H. and Mary Elizabeth (Fuller) C.; m. Florence T. Cua, July 21, 1979. MS, Rutgers U., 1975, PhD, 1977. Cert. Am. Bd. Health Physics. Mech. engr. missile systems div. AVCO Corp., Wilmington, Mass., 1966-72; instr. Rutgers U., New Brunswick, N.J., 1975-77, radiol. physicist, 1977-89, assoc. dir., 1989-91; dir. environ. health and safety Columbia U., N.Y.C., 1991-99; cons. Princeton, N.J., 1999—. Cons. in field, 1977—; assoc. faculty Rutgers U., 1978—; faculty Columbia U., 1991—. Mem.: NJ Tech. Coun., Health Physics Soc., Health Physics Soc. NJ (pres. 1989—90), Soc. for Risk Analysis, Am. Assn. Physicists in Medicine. Office: 443 Sayre Dr Princeton NJ 08540-5845 Office Phone: 609-919-0275. Personal E-mail: eac8@comcast.net.

CHRISTMAN, LUTHER PARMALEE, retired dean, consultant; b. Summit Hill, Pa., Feb. 26, 1915; s. Elmer and Elizabeth (Barnicoat) Christman; m. Dorothy Mary Black, Dec. 5, 1939; children: Gary, Judith, Lillian. Grad., Pa. Hosp. Sch. Nursing for Men, 1939; BS, Temple U., 1948, EdM, 1952; PhD, Mich. State U., 1965; LHD (hon.), Thomas Jefferson U., 1980; DSc (hon.), Grand Valley State U., 1998. Cons. Mich. Dept. Mental Health, Lansing, 1956—63; assoc. prof. psychiat. nursing U. Mich., 1963—67; rsch. assoc. Inst. Social Rsch., U. Mich., 1963—67; prof. nursing and sociology, dean nursing Vanderbilt U., Nashville, 1967—72; DON Vanderbilt U. Med. Ctr. Hosp., 1967—72; prof. sociology Rush Coll. Health Scis., Chgo.; sr. scientist Rush-Presbyn.-St. Luke's Med. Ctr.; prof. nursing, v.p. nursing affairs Coll. Nursing Rush U., 1972—87; dean Rush U. Coll. Nursing, 1972—87, dean emeritus, 1987—; sr. advisor to pres. Ctr. of Nursing, Am. Hosp. Assn., 1989; pres. Christman-Cornesky & Assocs., 1990—94. Chmn. planning com. 1st Midwest Conf. Psychiat. Nursing, Mpls., 1956; cons. cmty. svcs. and rsch. br. NIMH, 1963—66, mem. team to survey mental health facilities of Colo., 1982, mem. team to survey mental health facilities of Ga., 84; psychiat. rsch. project So. Regional Edn. Bd., 1964—67; mem., workshop leader White House Conf. on Children, 1970; nursing panel Nat. Commn. for Study Nursing and Nursing Edn., 1968—70; regional med. programs rev. com. dept. health, edn. and welfare Health Svcs. and Mental Health Adminstrn., 1968—72; cons. dept. medicine and surgery VA Ctrl. Office, 1968—71, 1974—77; panel nurse cons. to com. on nursing AMA, 1968—71; health svcs. adv. com. Am. Assn. Med. Colls., 1968—71; acting com. pub. health Am. Health Found., 1970—72; membership com. Inst. Medicine-NAS, 1972—76, com. on edn. in health professions, 1973—75; mem. S.D. Bd. Nursing, Tenn. Bd. Nursing; adj. prof. Vanderbilt U., 1991—; cons. in field. Contbr. numerous articles to profl. jours. Named Elinor Frances Reed Disting. Vis. Prof., U. Tenn., Memphis, 2000, Luther Christman Endowed scholar in his honor, Rush Coll. Nursing, 2002; named to Hall of Fame, Am. Nurses Assn., 2004; recipient Old Master, Purdue U., 1985, Coun. of Specialists in Psychiat. and Mental Health Nursing award, 1980, Hon. Recognition award, Ill. Nurses Assn., 1987, Edith Copeland Founders award for creativity, 1981, History Makers in Nursing award, Ctr. for Advancement of Nursing Practice, Beth Israel Hosp./Mass. Gen. Hosp., 1992, Lifetime Achievement award, Sigma Theta Tau, 1992, Disting. Alumnus award, Temple U., 1992, Rush U., 1997, Coll. Social Scis. Outstanding Alumnus award, Mich. State U., 1999, Hon. Recognition award, Nat. Academicians of Practice, 1996, Cert. of Appreciation, Marshall County Adult Edn., 1997, Lifetime Achievement award, Tenn. Nurses Assn., 2002. Fellow: AAAS, Soc. Applied Anthropology, Inst. Medicine Chgo., Am. Acad. Nursing (Living Legend award 1995); mem.: ANA (3d v.p., Jesse M. Scott award 1985, named to Hall of Fame 2004), AACN (life Margurite Rodgers Kinney award 2002), Nat. Acad. Practice (chmn. acad. nursing 1985—92, sec. 1992—96, Disting. Practitioner award 1985, Cert. of Appreciation 1995), Biomed. Engring. Soc., N.Y. Acad. Scis., Inst. Medicine, Soc. Gen. Sys. Rsch., Am. Sociol. Assn., Mich. Nurses' Assn. (pres. 1961—65), Alpha Kappa Delta, Alpha Omega Alpha (hon.). Home and Office: 5535 Nashville Hwy Chapel Hill TN 37034-2074 Personal E-mail: lchristman@united.net.

CHRISTMANN, EDWIN P., statistician, educator; b. Buffalo, Mar. 17, 1966; s. Edwin L. and Nina M. Christmann; m. Roxanne R. Christmann; children: Lauren A., E. Forrest, Alexandra Lee. EdB, Calif. U., Pa., 1988; EdM, Pa. State U., 1989; PhD, Old Dominion U., Norfolk, Virginia, 1995. Teaching Va., 1989. Prof. Slippery Rock U., Slippery Rock University, Pa., 1995—2004. Author Houghton Mifflin Pub., Boston. Co-editor science scope magazine. Sch. bd. dir. Slippery Rock Sch. Dist., Slippery Rock, Pa., 1997—2003. Fellow, U.S. Dept. of Energy, 1992. Mem.: NSTA (assoc.). Achievements include research in Research on Mathematics and Science Education. Home: 418 Franklin St Slippery Rock PA 16057 Office: Slippery Rock Univ 217 McKay Edn Bldg Slippery Rock PA 16057 Office Phone: 724-738-2319. Office Fax: 724-738-2880. E-mail: edwin.christmann@sru.edu.

CHRISTMAS, BOBBIE JAYE, freelance/self-employed writer; b. Columbia, SC, Sept. 18, 1944; d. Michael M. and Bernice (Mild) Rothberg; divorced, July 1983; 1 child, Sanford Lee Christmus. Student, U. S.C., 1962-64. Comm. specialist graphics dept. J.A. Jones Construction, Charlotte, N.C., 1974-76; editor Focus News, Greenville, S.C., 1976-78; account exec. Sta. WHYZ-AM, Greenville, 1978-83; supr. audio-visual dept. Leigh Mktg. Group, Greenville, 1983-84; coord. corp. comm. dept. Fluor Daniel, Greenville, 1984-87, asst. editor, reporter employee publs. dept., 1987-89, supr., editor employee publs. and media rels. dept., 1989-93; writer, editor, owner Zebra Comm., Atlanta, 1992—. V.p., dir. SC Writers Workshop, Columbia, 1991-92; founder Roswell (Ga.) Writers Workshop, 1994, Tri-County Writers Workshop, Worldwide Orgn., Writers Network Contbr. articles, photography to local publs.; editor Heartbeat newsletter Greenville Cen. Area Partnership, 1988-91 Recipient 1st Pl. Writing award United Way Greenville County, 1992, 1st Pl. Nonfiction award Reader's Digest Workshop, 1991, Sandhills Writers' Conf., 1989, 1st Pl. Color award Greenville Mag., 2d Pl. Black and White award Travelors Advisory newspaper, 1981, 2 Runners-up awards Greenville C. of C., 1989, 1st Pl. award Royal Palm Literary, 2004; named One of Upstate's Most Interesting People, Greenville Mag., 1986. Mem. Quest Soc. (dir. pub., rec. sec. 1989-92), Ga. Writers Inc. (bd. dirs. 1996-2004), Women's Nat. Book Assn., Ga. Freelance Writers Assn., Ga. Writers Assn. (past pres., 2d mem. adv. bd.) Office: 230 Deerchase Dr Ste B Woodstock GA 30188-4438 Office Phone: 770-924-0528. E-mail: bobbie@zebraeditor.com.

CHRISTMAS, GUY, actor; Student, Pa. State U., San Francisco State U., Los Medanos Coll.; studied drama with Marjorie Brown Thomas, studied acting with Al Valletta. Various positions Am. Marietta Co., Martin Marietta, Kaiser Gypsum Co.; dist. offices, asst. to v.p. & gen. mgr. New Enterprises Stone & Lime Co., Inc.; realtor Pa.; CEO Pub. Rels. Unlimited. Actor: (films) Perfect, Wisdom, Sid and Nancy, House II, Fatal Beauty, Split Decisions, True Crime, Sweet November; (TV series) Cagney and Lacey, General Hospital, Downtown, First and 10, Nash Bridges, The Division, The Henry Lee Project; (plays) The Silver Cord, 1776, Earth Angel, Cloud on a Candidate; writer, dir.: (documentaries) Keep America Singing. Wrestling coach, baseball coach So. Parkland Youth Assn. Recipient Editor's Choice award, Internat. Libr. Poetry. Mem.: AFTRA, SAG. Office: Talent Plus Agy 281 Moorpark Ave Ste 11 San Jose CA 95123 Home: 4220 Clayton Rd # 3115 Concord CA 94521

CHRISTMAS, MILLARD GUY, JR., entrepreneur; b. Wilkes-Barre, Pa., July 1, 1936; s. Millard Guy Christmas and Harriet Dawn McQuade; m. Frances Ann Belcastro, Mar. 4, 1962 (div. Dec. 1982); children: Guy Thomas, Timothy Roger(dec.). Student, San Francisco State U., Pa. State U. Lic. realtor assoc. Pa. Clk. Am.-Marietta Co., Chgo., 1956—58; office mgr. Martin Marietta Co., Chgo., 1958—60, sales engr., 1960—64; salesman New Enterprise (Pa.) Stone & Lime Co., Inc., 1964—66, asst. to v.p., gen. mgr., 1971—77; salesman Kaiser Gypsum Co., Oakland, Calif., 1966—71. Recipient Internat. Pub. Rels. award, SPEBSQA, Inc., Kenosha, Wis., 1968, citation, U.S. Def. Civil Preparedness, Washington, 1973. Mem.: SAG, Pub. Rels. Officers and Bull. Editors (internat. pres.), Media Access Officers, Performers with Disabilities, Masons. Republican. Episcopalian. Avocations: writing, singing, dramatics, movies, music. Office: Pub Rels Unltd Concord CA

CHRISTODOULATOS, CHRISTOS, environmental engineer, educator; b. Cephallonia, Greece, Feb. 5, 1958; s. Eric and Elpiniki Christodoulatos; m. Maria Kaouris, Mar. 13, 1983; children: Katherine, Eric, Jerry. PhD in environ. engring., Stevens Inst. Tech., 1991. Environ. engring. prof. Stevens Inst. Tech., Hoboken, NJ, 1991—. Author: (technical article) Correlations of Performance for Activated Slu (Founders Award, by the USA Nat. Com. Internat. Assn. on Water Quality for an outstanding paper in Water Rsch. by a US Author, 1994). Mem. NJ. Corp. for Advanced Tech., Bordentown, NJ. Achievements include patents for segmented electrode capillary discharge, non-thermal plasma apparatus and process for promoting chemical reactions; method and apparatus for treatment of wastewater. Office: Stevens Inst Tech Castle Point on the Hudson Hoboken NJ 07030 Office Phone: 201-216-5675. Office Fax: 201-216-8303. Personal E-mail: christod@stevens.edu.

CHRISTOFFEL, KATHERINE KAUFER, pediatrician, epidemiologist, educator; b. N.Y.C., June 28, 1948; d. George and Sonya (Firstenberg) Kaufer; children: Kevin, Kimberly. BA, Radcliffe Coll., 1969; MD, Tufts U., 1973; MPH, Northwestern U., 1981. Diplomate Am. Bd. Pediat., Nat. Bd. Med. Examiners. Intern Columbus (Ohio) Children' Hosp., 1972-73; resident then fellow Children's Meml. Hosp., Chgo., 1973-76; asst. prof. Sch. Medicine U. Chgo., 1976-79; asst. prof., then assoc. prof. Northwestern U. Med. Sch., Chgo., 1979-91, prof., 1991—; dir. Nutrition Evaluation Clinic Children's Meml. Hosp., Chgo., 1982-2000; med. dir. violent injury prevention ctr. Children's Meml. Med. Ctr., Chgo., 1993—2000, interim dir. Mary Ann and J. Milburn Smith Child Health Rsch. Program, 2000—03, interim co-dir. Children's Meml. Inst. for Edn. and Rsch., 2001—03, med. dir. Consortium to Lower Obesity in Chgo. Children, 2003—, dir. Ctr. for Obesity Mgmt. and Prevention, 2004—. Chmn. steering com. HELP Network, Chgo., 1993-99, pres. bd. dirs.; dir. then assoc. dir. Pediatric Practice Rsch. Group, Chgo., 1984-97; dir. statis. scis. and epidemiology program Children's Meml. Inst. for Edn. and Rsch., 1994-2000. Contbr. numerous articles to med. jours. Named one of 10 Most Powerful Women in Medicine in Chgo., Chgo. Sun Times, 2004; recipient M. Fay Spencer Disting. Woman Physician Scientist award, Nat. Bd. Hahnemann Med. Sch., 1997. Fellow Am. Acad. Pediat. (spokesperson on firearms 1985—, injury com. 1985-93, coun. on pediatric rsch. 1996-2000, chair adolescent violence task force 1994, 1st Injury Control award 1992); mem. APHA (Disting. Career award 1991), Am. Coll. Epidemiology, Soc. for Pediatric Rsch., Am. Pediat. Soc., Ambulatory Pediatric Assn. (bd. dirs. 2000-2003, Rsch. award 2000). Avocations: hiking, walking, creative writing, photography. Office: Childrens Meml Hosp 2300 N Childrens Plz #157 Chicago IL 60614-3394

CHRISTOFFERSEN, RALPH EARL, chemist, researcher; b. Elgin, Ill., Dec. 4, 1937; s. Arthur Henry and Mary C.; m. Barbara Hibbard, June 10, 1961; children: Kirk Alan, Rachel Anne. BS, Cornell Coll., 1959, LLD (hon.), 1983; PhD, Ind. U., 1963. Asst. prof. chemistry U. Kans., Lawrence, 1966-69, assoc. prof., 1967-72, prof., 1972-81, asst. vice chancellor for acad. affairs, 1974-75, assoc. vice chancellor for acad. affairs, 1976-79, vice chancellor for acad. affairs, 1979-81; pres. Colo. State U., Ft. Collins, 1981-83; exec. dir. Upjohn Co., 1983-85, v.p. biotech. and basic rsch. support, 1985-87, v.p. discovery rsch., 1987-89; v.p. rsch. SmithKline Beecham, King of Prussia, Pa., 1989-90, sr. v.p. rsch., 1990-92; CEO, pres. Ribozyme Pharms., Inc., Boulder, Colo., 1992-2001, chmn. bd., 2001; ptnr. Morgenthaler Ventures, 2001—. With Colo. BioSci. Assn.; bd. dirs. Serologicals Corp., GlobeImmune Corp., Replidyne Corp., Morphotek Corp., Threshold Pharms., Orexigen Corp., Avidia Corp. Contbr. articles to profl. jours. NIH fellow, 1962-63, 64-66. Fellow Sigma Xi, Phi Lambda Upsilon.

CHRISTOFORIDIS, A. JOHN, radiologist, educator; b. Greece, Dec. 24, 1924; s. John P. and Ada A. C.; m. Ann Dimitriadis, Nov. 11, 1961; children: John, Gregory, Alex, Jimmy. MD summa cum laude, Nat. U. Athens, Greece, 1949; M.M.Sc., Ohio State U., 1957; PhD, Aristotelian U., Greece, 1969. Instr. to prof. Ohio State U., Columbus, 1956-74, clin. prof., 1974—; chmn. dept. radiology Aristotelian U., Salonika, Greece, 1971; prof., chmn. dept. radiology Med. Coll. Ohio, Toledo, until 1982; prof., chmn. dept. Ohio State U., Columbus, 1982—. Researcher in chest and gastrointestinal radiology; cons. Greek Ministry Health, Batelle Meml. Inst., Columbus. Contbr. to textbook Atlas of Axial Sagittal and Coronal Anatomy with Computed Tomography and Magnetic Resonance; author: Radiology for Medical Students, 4th edit., 1988, Diagnostic Radiology-Thorax, 1989; contbr. several chpts. to books, over 100 articles to med. jours. Served to lt. M.C. Greek Army, 1950-52. Recipient Silver award Ohio Med. Assn., 1969, awards Heart Assn., 1960, awards Batelle Meml. Inst., 1965, awards Astra Co., 1967, awards Lung Assn., 1970-71; named Hon. Citizen City of Thessalonike, 1973; Ohio Geriatrics Med. grantee, 1980; NSF grantee, 1980 Fellow Am. Coll. Chest Physicians, Am. Coll. Radiology; mem. AAA, AMA, AAUP, Ohio Radiol. Soc., Assn. Univ. Radiologists, Radiol. Soc. N. Am., Soc. Chmn. Acad. Radiology Depts., Fleishner Soc. (charter), Am. Hellenic Ednl. Progressive Assn., Greek-Am. Progressive Assn., Acad. of Athens (corr. mem.). Greek Orthodox. Office: Ohio State U 410 W 10th Ave Columbus OH 43210-1240 Office Phone: 614-293-8315.

CHRISTOL, CARL QUIMBY, lawyer, political science professor; b. Gallup, SD, June 28, 1913; s. Carl and Winifred (Quimby) C.; m. Jeannette Stearns, Dec. 18, 1949 (dec.); children: Susan Quimby Christol-Deacon, Richard Stearns (dec.). AB, U. S.D., 1934, LLD (hon.), 1977; AM, Fletcher Sch. Law and Diplomacy, 1936; postgrad., Institut Universitaire des Hautes Etudes Internationales, Geneva, 1937-38, U. Geneva, 1937-38; PhD, U. Chgo., 1941; LLB, Yale U., 1947; postgrad., Acad. Internat. Law, The Hague, 1950. Bar: S.D. 1948, Calif. 1949. Assoc. firm Guthrie, Darling and Shattuck, Los Angeles, 1948-49; of counsel Fizzolio, Fizzolio & McLeod, Sherman Oaks, Calif., 1949-94; assoc. prof. polit. sci. U. So. Calif., 1949-59, prof., 1959-87, prof. emeritus, 1987—, chmn. dept. polit. sci., 1960-64, 75-77. Stockton chair internat. law U.S. Naval War Coll., 1962-63, cons., 1963-70; cons. World Law Fund; mem. L.A. Mayor's Adv. Com. Human Rels., Commn. to Study Orgn. of Peace; mem. adv. panel on internat. law Dept. State, 1970-76; v.p. Ct. of Man Found., 1971-77; scholar-in-residence Rockefeller Found. Bellagio Conf. and Study Ctr., Italy, 1980. Author: Transit by Air in International Law, 1941, Introduction to Political Science, 1957, 4th edit., 1982, Readings in International Law, 1959, The International Law of Outer Space, 1966, The International Legal and Institutional Aspects of the Stratosphere Ozone Problem, 1975, The Modern International Law of Outer Space, 1982, Space Law: Past, Present and Future, 1991, International Law and U.S. Foreign Policy, 2004; bd. editors: Western Polit. Quar, 1970-75, Internat. Lawyer, 1975-84, Space Policy, 1985—, Internat. Legal Materials, 1985—, Australian Internat. Law Jour., 1998—; contbr. articles to profl. jours. Bd. dirs. Los Angeles County Heart Assn., 1956-61. Served to lt. col. AUS, 1941-46; col. Res. ret. Decorated Bronze Star medal; recipient Dart award U. So. Calif., 1970, Assos. award for excellence in teaching, 1977, Raubenheimer award, 1982, Disting. Emeritus award, 1990, Rockefeller Found. fellow, 1958-59; Borchard Found. lectr., 2002. Mem. ABA, AIAA, LA Bar Assn., Am. Soc. Internat. Law (exec. coun. 1973-76), Internat. Studies Assn. (chmn. internat. law sect. 1977-78), Internat. Acad. Astronautics, State Bar Calif., UN Assn. LA (pres. 1961-63), Am. Polit. Sci. Assn., Internat. Inst. Space Law (pres. Am. br. 1973-75, Lifetime Achievement award 1998), Internat. Law Assn., UN Assn. U.S. (dir. 1967-69), Masons, Blue Key, Skull and Dagger, Phi Beta Kappa, Phi Kappa Phi (award 1987), Alpha Tau Omega. Republican. Presbyterian. Home: 327B W Figueroa St Santa Barbara CA 93101 Office: U So Calif Polit Sci Dept Los Angeles CA 90089-0044

CHRISTOPH, PETER RICHARD, historical editor, archivist; b. Albany, N.Y., Apr. 25, 1938; s. Hajo and Matilda Bertha (Haage) Christoph; m. Florence Anna Weaver, June 6, 1959; children: Daniel William, Richard Peter, AnnaLise Hall. BA, Hartwick Coll., N.Y., 1960; MA, SUNY, 1964, MLS,

1968. Secondary tchg. English N.Y. State Edn. Dept., 1960, Profl. Libr. N.Y. State Edn. Dept., 1968, Archival Adminstrn. U. of Denver, 1969. Asst. libr. cataloging N.Y. State Libr., Albany, 1967—68, sr. libr. manuscripts and history, 1968—72, assoc. libr., 1972—91; editor N.Y. Hist. Manuscripts, Albany, 1974—, sr. editor Selkirk, NY, 1991. Dir. New Netherland Project, Albany, NY, 1974—84, N.Y. Hist. Manuscripts, Selkirk, NY, 1988—. Editor: (document collection) The Kingston Papers, 1661-1775, 1976, Diary of Henry Edgar Whittelsey, Catskill Mountain Storekeeper, 1835-1836, 1999, (document collection) The Leisler Papers, 1689-1691, 2002, Administrative Papers of Governors Richard Nicolls and Francis Lovelace, 1664-1673, 1980, Books of General Entries of the Colony of New York, 1664-1688, 1982, Records of the People of the Town of Bethlehem, 1690-1880, 1982, Records of the Court of Assizes for the Colony of New York, 1665-1682, 1983, The Andros Papers, 1674-1680, 1989—91, The Dongan Papers,1683-1688, 1993—96; author: (biography) Albert Andriessen Bradt, 2004, (book) A Norwegian Family in Colonial America. Pres. Town of Bethlehem Hist. Assn., Cedar Hill, NY, 1980—82, trustee, 1989—92; mem. Bethlehem Rural Cemetery Assn., Selkirk, NY, 1995—2000; archivist First Luth. Ch., Albany, NY, 1983—2003, lay preacher, 1985—99; rep. Bd. of the Luth. Archives Ctr., Phila., 1988—2003; mem. com. on minutes and protocol Upstate N.Y. Synod, Syracuse, 1988—2003; mem., congl. coun. First Luth. Ch., Albany, NY, 1986—89, 2000—03; archivist Upstate N.Y. Synod, Evang. Luth. Ch. in Am., Syracuse, 1993—2003; mem. Friends of Schuyler Mansion, Albany, NY, 1988—96. Grantee, Nat. Endowment for the Humanities, 1992—94. Fellow: Holland Soc. of N.Y.; mem.: Luth. Hist. Conf., Friends of Tombstone (Ariz.), Friends of New Netherland, N.Y. Geneal. and Biog. Soc. Lutheran. Avocation: travel. Home: 181 Maple Ave Selkirk NY 12158 Personal E-mail: pchrist1@nycap.rr.com.

CHRISTOPHER, DANIEL ROY, lawyer; b. Denver, Apr. 10, 1947; s. Gordon Lawrence and Rita Marie (Gaulick) C.; m. Pamela Kay Frangos, Jan. 10, 1970; children: Peter Daniel, Stacy A. BS, U. Colo., 1969; MBA, Idaho State U., 1971; JD, U. Denver, 1974. Bar: Colo. 1974, U.S. Dist. Ct. Colo. 1974, U.S. Ct. Appeals (10th cir.) 1978, U.S. Supreme Ct. 1979. Law clk. Denver Dist. Ct., 1972-73; dep. dist. atty. Office of Dist. Atty., Denver, 1974-79; spl. pros. on police corruption Alamosa, Colo., 1979; asst. U.S. atty. Denver, 1979-81; ptnr. Kennedy & Christopher, P.C., Denver, 1981—. Spl. asst. atty. gen. State of Colo., 1991—; asst. clin. prof. legal medicine U. Colo. Health Scis. Ctr., 1991—, Faculty Fed. Advs.; bd. mem. Kids in Need of Dentistry, 2004—. Contbg. editor Dist. Atty. Evidence Manual, 1976; author: Risk Management for Health Care Professionals, 1992. Vol. Rep. party worker Arapahoe County Ct., 1980—; bd. dirs. U. Colo. at Denver, 1986-87, Holy Ghost Ch. Foodline for the Homeless, 1997—, Kids in Need of Dentistry, 2004— Recipient Am. Jurisprudence awrad 1974. Mem. ABA, Am. Bd. Trial Advocates, Colo. Bar Assn., Colo. Def. Lawyers Assn. (pres. 1995), Denver Bar Assn., Def. Rsch. Inst., Am. Health Lawyer's Assn., Faculty Fed. Advocates ((bd. dirs. 2000), Federalist Soc. Roman Catholic. Home: 5670 Big Canon Dr Greenwood Village CO 80111-3512 Office: Kennedy & Christopher PC 1050 17th St Ste 2500 Denver CO 80265-2080 Office Phone: 720-946-4749. Business E-Mail: dchristopher@kennedy-christopher.com.

CHRISTOPHER, DORIS K., consumer products company executive; m. Jay Christopher, 1967; children: Julie, Kelley. BS in Home Econs., U. Ill., 1967. Cert. in family and consumer svcs. H.S. home econs. tchr.; with U. Ill. Coop. Extension Svc.; founder, chmn. The Pampered Chef Ltd. (acquired by Berkshire Hathaway, 2002), Addison, Ill., 1980—. Appeared on various TV programs including Oprah Winfrey Show, NBC Weekend Today, CNBC, CNN. Author: Come to the Table: A Celebration of Family Life, 1999, The Pampered Chef: The Story of One of America's Most Beloved Companies, 2005. Recipient Torch award Marketplace Ethics, Better Bus. Bureau, Chgo. & No. Ill., 1998. Mem.: Direct Selling Assn. (bd. dirs. 1992—, past chairperson), Am. Assn. Family and Consumer Scis., America's Second Harvest, Com. of 200. Office: The Pampered Chef 1 Pampered Chef Lane Addison IL 60101-5630 Office Fax: 630-261-8522.*

CHRISTOPHER, IRENE, librarian, consultant; b. Greece, Nov. 17, 1922; arrived in US, 1923; d. George and Helen (Stephens) C. AB, Boston U., 1944; BLS, Simmons Coll., 1945. Gen. asst. Robbins Pub. Libr., Arlington, Mass., 1945-46, Boston U. Chenery Libr., 1946-47, head circulation dept., 1947-48, head reference dept., 1948-62; dir. libr. Emerson Coll., Boston, 1962-68; dir. Gordon McKay libr. Harvard U., Cambridge, Mass., 1968-70; chief libr. Boston U. Med. Ctr., 1970-92. Mem. AAUW, ALA (various coms. 1962-82, coun. 1970-74), Spl. Librs. Assn. (various coms. Boston chpt. 1952-75), Am. Soc. Info. Sci., Women's Nat. Book Assn., North Atlantic Health Scis. Librs., Med. Libr. Assn., New Eng. Online Users Group, Inc., Mass. Libr. Assn., Boston U. Women's Coun. Home: 790 Boylston St Apt 11C Boston MA 02199-7911

CHRISTOPHER, JAMES WALKER, architect, educator; b. Phila., Nov. 5, 1930; s. Arthur Bailey and Cornelia (Slater) C.; m. Carolyn Kennard, July 9, 1955; children: William W., Kathryn A., Kimberley, James S., Pamela W. BA, BS in Architecture, Rice U., 1953; M.Arch., MIT, 1956. Registered architect, Utah, Colo., Nev., Idaho, Wyo. Asst. prof. architecture U. Utah, Salt Lake City, 1956-60, adj. prof. architecture, 1983; archtl. designer various firms, Salt Lake City, 1960-63; founding prin. Brixen & Christopher Architects, Salt Lake City, 1963—. Architect, Phase I, Snowbird, Alta Canyon, Utah (AIA Western Mountain Region award 1971), Numemaker Place Chapel, Salt Lake City (AIA Western Mountain Region award 1977), Congregation Kol Ami, Salt Lake City (AIA Western Mountain Region award 1977), Block 53 Master Plan, Salt Lake City (Utah chpt. AIA award 1979). Mem. Utah Environ. Transp. Coun., Salt Lake City, 1970-77, vice chmn., 1970-75; mem. Big Cottonwood Citizens Planning Com., Salt Lake County, Utah, 1975, Salt Lake City Downtown Planning Com., 1981, Utah Transit Authority Transplan, Salt Lake City, 1982; trustee Utah Heritage Found., 2004-05. Served to lt. (j.g.) USNR, 1953-55. Fellow AIA (pres. Utah Soc. 1970 12 Utah Soc. Design awards, 12 Western Mountain Region Design awards 1968-83, 8 nat. Design awards 1975-83, Presdl. citation 1982, nat. design and planning com. 1976—, chmn. R/UDAT task group 1987-91, western mountain region Firm of the Yr. award 1987, Silver medal 1991, Utah Soc. Bronze medal 1999). Clubs: Alta. Episcopalian. Home: 2954 Millcreek Rd Salt Lake City UT 84109-3108 Office: Brixen & Christopher Architects 252 S 2nd E Salt Lake City UT 84111-2487

CHRISTOPHER, LIN, artist; b. Talladega, Ala., Dec. 23, 1948; d. Newman and Mary Anna (Stewart) White; m. William Jackson Christopher, July 16, 1975. BS, Auburn U., 1971. Artist, Roswell, Ga., 1975—. Bd. dirs. Roswell Artists' Studio Tour. Represented in permanent collections at IBM, Sunkist, Bell South, Citicorp, Norcom, Hyatt Hotels, Ball Stalker, Royal Caribbean Cruise Lines, Ridgeview Inst., United Va. Bank, Price Waterhouse, John Harland Co., Taiyo Elec. Co., Equitable Life Ins. Co., Coopers & Lybrand, Allen & Co., Kinder Care, Hilton Hotels, Crestar Bank, Ala. Power, Ven Der Groen, Sharp Industries, World Carpets, King & Spalding, Workman & Co., Bluff Park Art Assn., Ctrl. Ill. Light Co., SAFE, A.R.T. Sta., Trammel Crowe, Shaw Industries, Perimeter Mall Atlanta, The Landmark Group, Eastman Pharm., James Madison U., Meadows Meml. Hosp., Gainesville Arts Coun., USAF, Bus. Coun. Ga., Albany Mus. Art, Merrill Lynch, Bank of the South, Arthur Anderson, Creative Arts Guild, South Trust Bank, The Marcus Group, Fuqua Industries, North Ga. Coll., So. Engring. Co., Walt Disney World, Springfield (Ill.) Civic Assn., Universal Studios, M G M, Royal Caribbean Cruise Lines. Recipient over 100 awards. Mem. Nat. Assn. Ind. Artists, Am. Crafts Coun. Avocation: gardening. Home: 1534 Jones Rd Roswell GA 30075-2726 Office Phone: 770-992-4821.

CHRISTOPHER, MARY M., education educator, consultant; b. Post, Tex., Apr. 22, 1956; d. G. L. and Natalie C. Marable; m. Philip L. Christopher, Jan. 3, 1976; children: Jeremy Philip, Natalie Anne. BS in Edn., Tex. Tech. U., 1978, PhD in Curriculum and Instrn., 2003; EdM, U. Louisville, 1993. Cert. elem. edn., English, gifted and talented Tex., Okla., Ky. Classroom tchr. Trinity Valley Sch., Ft. Worth, 1979—81; classroom tchr., gifted and talented facilitator Ardmore (Okla.) City Sch. Dist., 1981—87; classroom tchr., gifted and talented tchr., tech. specialist Jefferson County Pub. Schs., Louisville, 1987—95; asst. prof., cert. officer Hardin-Simmons U., Abilene, Tex., 1995—. Edn. cons. in field, Tex., 1996—; with Tech. Leadership Inst. U. Tex., Austin, 2002; presenter in field. Mem. editl. bd.: Gifted Child Today, 1997—; contbr. articles to profl. jours. Mem. grant com. Cmty. Found. Abilene, Tex., 2000—; mem., grant com. Future Fund, Abilene, 2000—; mem. devel. coun. Baylor U., Waco, Tex., 2000—. Mem.: NAGC, Gifted and Talented Coords. Divsn., Tex. Assn. Gifted and Talented (regional dir. 1999—), Phi Kappa Phi. Baptist. Office: Hardin-Simmons U PO Box 16225 Abilene TX 79698 Office Phone: 325-670-1510.

CHRISTOPHER, NICHOLAS, poet, writer; b. N.Y.C., Feb. 28, 1951; m. Constance Barbara Davidson, Nov. 21, 1980. AB cum laude, Harvard Coll., 1973. Prof. Columbia U. Sch. Arts, Columbia U., 1988—. Author: On Tour with Rita, 1982, A Short History of the Island of Butterflies, 1986, The Soloist, 1986, Desperate Characters, 1988, In the Year of the Comet, 1992, 5 Degrees and Other Poems, 1995, Veronica, 1996, Somewhere in the Night: Film Noir and the American City, 1997, The Creation of the Night Sky, 1998, A Trip to the Stars, 2000, Atomic Field: Two Poems, 2000, Franklin Flyer, 2002, Crossing the Equator: New and Selected Poems, 1972-2004, 2004; editor: Under 35: The New Generation of American Poets, 1989, Walk on the Wild Side: Urban American Poetry Since 1975, 1994. Recipient Lavan award Acad. Am. Poets, 1991, Melville Cane award Poetry Soc. Am., 1993; NEA fellow, 1987, Guggenheim fellow, 1993, Amy Lowell fellow. Mem. PEN, Poetry Soc. Am. Office: Janklow & Nesbit Assocs 445 Park Ave New York NY 10022-2606 E-mail: nc11@nyu.edu.

CHRISTOPHER, RAY LOUIS, pilot, journalist, author; b. Louisville, Ky., Jan. 11, 1943; s. Joseph Raymond and Margaret Edith (Nalley) C.; m. Karen Lynn Christopher, June 25, 1964; children: Richard, Traci, Amanda, Wendi. Student in Journalism, Fla. State U., 1965; grad. (hon.), U.S. Army Flight Sch., 1971; Med. Svc. Officer, Acad. Health Sci., San Antonio, 1979; Aviation Safety Officer, Army Aviation Safety Sch., Ft. Rucker, Ala., 1980; grad. in Aviation Safety Tech., Embry-Riddle Aero. U., 1980. Cert. aviation safety insp., USASC and FAA, accident investigator, USASC and FAA; lic. airline transport pilot, FAA, flight instr. airplane/helicopter single and multi engine. Sgt. U.S. Army, 1971, advanced through grades to chief warrant officer, 1991; capt. ICH Corp., Louisville, 1985-90; dir. aviation safety U.S. Army ARCENT HQ, Dhahrain, Saudi Arabia, 1990-92; chief pilot ISAIR, Ft. Lauderdale, Fla., 1992-94, Wings for Christ, Louisville, 1994—. Author: The Ten Commandments of Aviation Safety, 1980, Personal Enhancement Manual, 1994, Pillars of Success, 1997, 66 Routes to Corvette City, 1998, The Ragged Ol' Flag, 1991, Aviating Prayers, 1995. Chmn. Pilots Assn. Ky., Somerset, 1981; dir. Ky. Aviation Assn., Frankfort, 1983; flight safety counselor, FAA, Louisville, 1983-87; show car judge Corvette Club Am., Bowling Green, Ky., 1996-99. Decorated Bronze star, 1991; recipient Silver Plate of Honor, Ind. State Police, 1978, Ky. Merit medal Office of Gov., Frankfort, 1982, Million Mile Pilot Safety award Nat. Bus. Aviation, 1983, 12000 Hour Pilot Safety award Nat. Bus. Aviation, 1994. Mem. Aero Club Am., VFW (Chaplain 1989-90), Quiet Birdmen Assn. (life), NRA (life, Disting. Life Mem. 1989), Disabled Am. Vets. (life). Republican. Roman Catholic. Avocations: corvette restoration, backpacking, sport shooting. Home: 8726 Running Fox Cir Fern Creek KY 40291 Office: Wings for Christ Bowman Field Louisville KY 40202 E-mail: chrisaire@aol.com.

CHRISTOPHER, RICHARD SCOTT, public relations executive, editor, advertising executive; b. Chgo., May 21, 1953; s. James J. and Geraldine A. (Kaulback) C.; m. Jacqueline D. Muter,Apr. 16, 1988; 1 child, Alyssa Lauren. B Journalism, U. Mo., Columbia, 1975. Gen. assignment reporter Salem (Mo.) News, 1975; news editor, tech. writer Am. Vet. Med. Assn., Schaumburg, Ill., 1975-77; sports reporter Daily Herald, Arlington Heights, Ill., 1977-78; assoc. editor, mktg. coord. Farm and Land Inst., Nat. Assn. Realtors, Chgo., 1978-80; mgr. project svcs. Kiwanis Internat., Chgo., 1980-82; account exec. Eckis Advt. & Design, Irvine, Calif., 1982-83; advt., pub. rels. exec. R.S. Christopher & Assocs., Newport Beach, Calif., 1983-86; pub. rels. account mgr., v.p. pub. rels. Basso & Assocs. Advt. Pub. Rels., 1986-92; mgr. internal comms. Nissan N. Am., Inc., 1992—2002, mgr. auto show events and news bur., 2002—. Editor, advt. mgr. Nat. Assn. Ind. Ins. Adjusters, Chgo., 1982—. Recipient Bronze award, Internat. Film and TV Festival N.Y., 1981, 1982, Helios award Excellence, 1992, Mercury award Gold winner, Internat. Film and TV Festival N.Y., 1992, Gold Quill, 1994, Advt. Design award Silver, 1997, CIPRA Intranet Devel. award, 1997. Mem. Internat. Assn. Bus. Communicators, Pub. Rels. Soc. Am., Kiwanis. Roman Catholic.

CHRISTOPHER, ROBERT, literature and language professor, researcher; b. NYC, Jan. 4, 1937; s. Constantine and Constance Christopher; m. Frima Yarmus Christopher; children: Nina, Noam. BA, City Coll. NY, 1960; MA, San Francisco State U., 1961; PhD, U. Calif., Berkeley, 1974. Instr. English U. Calif., Berkeley, 1967—69; asst. prof. English Pa. State U., University Park, 1969—74; prof. lit. Ramapo Coll., Mahwah, NJ, 1974—. Editl. bd. Jour. Basic Writing, NYC, 1993—99, Assn. Grad. Liberal Studies, 1999—. Recipient Outstanding Faculty Mem., Assn. Grad. Liberal Studies, 2001. Mem.: Assn. Intergraduate Studies, Assn. Can. Studies US. Avocation: art. Home: 245 W 107th St 14C New York NY 10025 Office: Ramapo Coll NJ 505 Ramapo Valley Rd Mahwah NJ 07430 Office Phone: 201-684-7418. Fax: 212-865-4118. Business E-Mail: rchristo@ramapo.edu.

CHRISTOPHER, ROBERT PAUL, retired physical therapist, educator; b. Cleve., Apr. 27, 1932; s. Walter Matthews and Charity Marie (Roberts) C.; m. Doreen Mary O'Leary, Apr. 28, 1962; children: Robert Jr., Judith, Mark. BS, Northwestern U., 1954; MD, St. Louis U., 1959. Diplomate Am. Bd. Physical Medicine and Rehab. Chief rehab. medicine V.A. Hosp., Ann Arbor, Mich., 1963-67; asst. prof. rehab. medicine U. Mich., Ann Arbor, 1964-67; assoc. prof. rehab. medicine U. Tenn., Memphis, 1967-71, prof. rehab. medicine, 1971-2001; ret., 2001. Med. dirs. Les Passees Children's Rehab. Ctr., Memphis, 1976-98, Le Bonheur Hosp. Rehab. Svcs., Memphis, 1981-2001, Regional Med. Ctr. Rehab. Svcs., Memphis, 1967-2001, assoc. med. dir. St. Joseph Rehab. Ctr., Memphis, 1981-98. Contbg. author: Seating the Cerebral Palsey Child, 1983; author: sound/slide program Systems of Physical Therapy in Cerebral Palsy, 1971; contbr. articles to profl. jours. Pres. Mid-South Health Systems Agy., Memphis, 1980; mem. Mayor's Adv. Council for Disabled, Memphis, 1977-98. Recipient Disting. Svc. Commn. on Accredited Rehab. Facilities, 1982. Fellow Am. Acad. Phys. Medicine and Rehab. (sec. 1982-88, v.p. 1992—, pres. elect 1993, pres. 1994), Am. Acad. Cerebral Palsy (pres. 1987); mem. AMA, Am. Congress Rehab. Medicine, So. Soc. Phys. Medicine and Rehab. (sec. 1976-2000), Am. Bd. of Phys. Medicine and Rehab. (vice chmn. 1992-98), East Memphis Cath. Club (bd. dirs. 1969-80), K.C. (Grand Knight 1969-70). Avocations: travel, swimming. Home: 818 Island Club Sq Vero Beach FL 32963-5505 E-mail: drbobchris1@aol.com.

CHRISTOPHER, RUSSELL LEWIS, baritone; b. Grand Rapids, Mich., Mar. 12, 1930; s. Russell Stewart and Violet (Jurewicz) C.; m. Gail B. Eldredge, Aug. 24, 1963 (div. 1985); 1 son, Russell Frederick. AA, Grand Rapids Jr. Coll., 1950; MusB, U. Mich., 1953, MusM, 1954. Music librarian NBC, N.Y.C., 1955-58. Elected U. Mich. Sch. Music Alumni Bd. Govs., 1997-2003. Prin. artist, N.Y.C. Opera Co., 1958-60, San Francisco Opera Co., 1962, 63, Met. Opera Assn., N.Y.C., 1963-91, soloist, L.A., Montreal, Chgo., Richmond symphony orchs., 1963—; sang role Maecenas in: world premiere Antony and Cleopatra at new, Met. Opera House, 1966; recs.: Carmen (Deutsche Grammophon), 1973, La Traviata (Electra Records), 1982, (CD) I'll Take Romance, 2002; numerous TV prodns. Live from the Met (Emmy award 1985); Miami Beach Symphony, Hollywood Bowl, Balt. Civic Opera, Central City Opera, Dayton Opera Assn., Phila. Lyric Opera Assn., Met. opera tour, Japan, 1975, 86; concert soloist, Spoleto (Italy) Festival, 1977. Mem. U. Mich. Sch. Music Alumni Bd., 1997. Recipient award Martha Baird Rockefeller Fund for Music, 1961; auditions winner Am. Opera, 1962; auditions winner Met. Opera, 1963; Mrs. Frederick K. Weyerhaeuser award, 1963; Disting. Alumni award Grand Rapids Jr. Coll., 1964, Alumnus of Yr. award U. Mich. Club of N.Y., 1978; recipient citation of merit award for outstanding contbns. to field of music, Alumni Bd., Sch. of Music, U. Mich., 1995. Mem. Am. Guild Musical Artists (nat. bd. govs. 1985-91, 94-99, exec. com. 1994-99).

CHRISTOPHER, SHARON A. BROWN, bishop; b. Corpus Christi, Tex., July 24, 1944; d. Fred L. and Mavis Lorraine (Krueger) Brown; m. Charles Edmond Logsdon Christopher, June 17, 1973. BA, Southwestern U., Georgetown, Tex., 1966; MDiv, Perkins Sch. Theology, 1969; DD, Southwestern U., 1990; DST, McMurray Coll., 1996. Ordained to ministry United Meth. Ch., 1970; elected bishop 1988. Dir. Christian Edn. First United Meth. Ch., Appleton, Wis., 1969-70, assoc. pastor, 1970-72; pastor Butler United Meth. Ch., Butler, Wis., 1972-76, Calvary United Meth. Ch., Germantown, Wis., 1972-76, Aldersgate United Meth. Ch., Milw., 1976-80; dist. supt. Ea. Dist. Wis. Conf. United Meth. Ch., 1980-85; asst. to bishop Wis. Conf. Wis. Conf. United Meth. Ch., Sun Prairie, Wis., 1986-88; bishop North Cen. jurisdiction United Meth. Ch., Minn., 1988-96, bishop Ill. area Ill. area, 1996—, resident bishop Ill. area Springfield, 1996—. Contbr. articles and papers to religious publs. Bd. dirs. Nat. Coun. Chs. of Christ, 1988—, United Meth. Ch. Bd. of Ch. & Soc., 1988-92, bd. discipleship, 1992—; trustee Hamline U., St. Paul, 1988-96; gen. and jurisdictional conf. del., 1976, 80, 84, 88; mem. N. Cen. Jurisdiction Com. on Episcopacy, 1984-88, Com. on Investigation, 1980-88, Gen. Bd. Global Ministries, 1980-88, chmn. Mission Pers. Resources Program Dept., 1984-88. Named one of Eighty for the Eighties, Milw. Jour., 1980.

CHRISTOPHER, WARREN MINOR, lawyer, former secretary of state; b. Scranton, ND, Oct. 27, 1925; s. Ernest W. and Catharine Anna (Lemen) Christopher; m. Marie Josephine Wyllis, Dec. 21, 1956; children: Lynn, Scott, Thomas, Kristen. Student, U. Redlands, 1942—43; BS magna cum laude, U. So. Calif., 1945; LLB, Stanford U., 1949; LLD (hon.), Occidental U., 1977, Bates Coll., 1981, Brown U., 1981, Claremont Coll., 1981. Bar: Calif. 1949, US Supreme Ct. 1953, DC 1972, NY 1984. Law clk. to Justice William O. Douglas US Supreme Ct., Washington, 1949—50; dep. atty. gen. US Dept. Justice, Washington, 1967—69; dep. sec. US Dept. State, Washington, 1977—81, sec., 1993—97; practice in LA, 1950—67, 1969—76, 1981—93, 1997—; mem. firm O'Melveny & Myers, LLP, 1950—67, 1969, ptnr., 1958—67, 1969—76, 1981—93, chmn. of the firm, 1982—92, sr. ptnr., 1997—. Spl. counsel to Gov. Calif., 1959; cons. Office Under Sec. State, 1961—65; mem. bd. bar examiners State Bar Calif., 1966—67; dir. So. Calif. Edison Co., First Interstate Bancorp, Lockheed Corp.; chmn. bd. trustee Carnegie Corp. NY; mem. Calif. Coordinating Coun. for Higher Edn., 1960—67, pres., 1963—65; vice chmn. Gov.'s Commn. on LA Riots, 1965—66; chmn. US dels. to US-Japan Cotton Textile Negotiations, 1961, Geneva Conf. on Cotton Textiles, 1961; spl. rep. sec. state for Wool Textile Meetings, London, Rome, Tokyo, 1964—64; mem. Trilateral Commn., 1975—77, 1981—88; mem. internat. adv. coun. Inst. Internat. Studies; chmn. Ind. Commn. on LA Police Dept., 1991; headed search for Gov. Clinton's running mate (Sen. Al Gore); served as dir. presdl. transition process. Author: In the Stream of History: Shaping Foreign Policy for a New Era, 1998, Chances of a Lifetime, 2001; co-author: American Hostages in Iran: The Conduct of a Crisis, 1985; pres. Stanford Law Review, 1947—48. Dir., vice chmn. Coun. on Fgn. Rels., 1982—91; mem. US-Korea Wisemen Coun., 1991—93; trustee Stanford U., 1971—77, 1981—93, pres. bd. trustees, 1985—88; dir. LA World Affairs Coun.; mem. exec. com. Am. Agenda, 1988. Lt. (j.g.) USNR, 1943—46. Decorated Medal of Freedom; recipient Harold Weill award, NYU, 1981, Louis Stein award, Fordham U., 1981, Jefferson award, Am. Inst. for Pub. Svc., UCLA medal, U. Va., Thomas Jefferson award in law, First Civic Medal of Honor, LA C. of C., 2003. Fellow: AAAS, Am. Coll. Trial Lawyers, Am. Bar Found.; mem.: ABA (ho. dels. 1975—77, chmn. standing com. fed. judiciary 1975—77), Am. Law Inst., LA County Bar Assn. (pres. 1974—75), Calif. Bar Assn. (gov. 1975—77), Chancery Club, Calif. Club, Order of Coif, Phi Kappa Phi. Achievements include negotiating the release of 52 American Hostages in Iran. Office: O'Melveny & Meyers LLP 1999 Avenue of Stars 7th Fl Los Angeles CA 90067-6035 Address: O'Melveny & Meyers LLP 400 South Hope St Los Angeles CA 90071-2899 Office Phone: 310-246-6750. Office Fax: 310-246-6779. Business E-Mail: wchristopher@omm.com.

CHRISTOPHER, WILLIAM GARTH, lawyer; b. Beaumont, Tex., Oct. 14, 1940; s. Garth Daugherty and Ollye Mittie (Harkness) C.; m. Kathleen S. Christopher; children: John William, David Noah, Michael O'Hara. BS in Engring., U.S. Mil. Acad., 1962; JD, U. Va., 1970. Bar: Va. 1970, D.C. 1970, U.S. Supreme Ct. 1975, Mich. 1977, Fla. 1988, Tex. 1989. Atty. Steptoe & Johnson, Washington, 1970-77; ptnr. Honigman MIller Schwartz & Cohn, Detroit, 1977-94, Holland & Knight, Tampa, Fla., 1994-95, Brown Clark Christopher & DeMay, P.A., Sarasota, Fla., 1995—2003, Gurley Dramis Lazo, Sarasota, 2003—. Contbr. articles to legal publ. Pres. Birmingham (Mich.) Hockey Assn., 1982-84; mem. Epsc. Diocese of Mich. Commn. on Ministry, 1983-88, co-chmn., 1987-88, standing com., 1988. Capt. C.E. U.S. Army, 1962-67. Mem.: Tex. Bar Assn., The Fla. Bar, Nat. Bd. Trial Advocacy, Sarasota County Bar Assn., Va. Bar, Order of Coif, Phi Delta Phi. Episcopalian. Office: Gurley Dramis Lazo 601 S Osprey Ave Sarasota FL 34236 Office Phone: 941-556-1485. Business E-Mail: wchristopher@gurleydramislazo.com.

CHRISTOPHERSON, ELIZABETH GOOD, broadcast executive; b. Cin. d. Walter R. and Jean S. Good; m. Paul C. Christopherson; 1 child, Katherine. BA, Wellesley Coll. Chmn., CEO NJ State Coun. Arts, 1989—91; exec. dir. NJ Pub. TV and Radio, Trenton, 1994—; pres. NJN Found., 1994—. Bd. dirs. PNC Bank N.J., PBS, Liberty Sci. Ctr., Wellesley Coll. Bus. Leadership Coun., NJ State Coun. Arts. Pres., bd. dirs. Leadership Am. Assn., Alexandria, Va., 1991—92; bd. dirs. N.J. Tech. Coun. Mem.: Internat. Woman's Forum (past pres. N.J. chpt.). Office: NJ Network PO Box 777 Trenton NJ 08625-0777

CHRISTOPHERSON, HOWARD M., artist; b. Duluth, Minn., 1955; m. Kristine Christopherson; 1 child, Emma. Represented in permanent collections Minn. Hist. Soc., AT&T, Mpls., Arthur Anderson Co., St. Paul, Schneider USA Plymouth, Minn., Lessors, Inc., U. Minn. Art Mus., Wlls Fargo, Minn., Dahl and Assoc., St. Paul, Heritage Ins. Co., Wis., Medtronic, Inc. Night Dance grant, Union Depot Place, 1985, Career Opportunity grant, Minn. State Arts Bd., 2002, Zoom Internat. Photographic Exhibition grant, 2004. Studio: Icebox Quality Framing and Gallery 1500 Jackson St NE Ste 443 Minneapolis MN 55413-1671 Office Phone: 612-788-1790. E-mail: icebox@bitstream.net.

CHRISTOPHERSON, MYRVIN FREDERICK, college president; b. Milltown, Wis., July 21, 1939; s. Fred J. and Inger J. (Haug) C.; m. Anne Christine Marking, June 10, 1967; children: Kirsten, Berit, Bjorn, Nisse. BA, Dana Coll., 1961; MS, Purdue U., 1963, PhD, 1965; DD (hon.), Wartburg Theol. Sem., 1998. Teaching asst., instr. Purdue U., West Lafayette, Ind., 1961-65; asst. prof. speech U. Wis., Madison, 1965-69, assoc. prof. communication Stevens Point, 1969-76, prof. communication, 1976-86, assoc. dean fine arts and communication, 1970-86; pres. Dana Coll., Blair, Nebr., 1986—2005, pres. emeritus, 2005—. Cons. Wis. Telephone, Milw., 1968-78, AT&T, N.Y.C., 1969-71, 1st Fin. Corp., Stevens Point, 1980-86; commr. Nebr. Coordinating Commn. for Post Sec. Edn., 1989-91; mem. N.E. jud. nominating commn. Ct. Appeals No. 3 Steering Com.; mem. adv. bd. Thrivent Fin. For Lutherans, 2002—. Author: Speaker's Trainer's Guide, 1970, The Company Speaker, 1979; editor: Jour. of the Wis. Communication Assn., 1978—80. Mem. adv. bd. The Lutheran, 1987—94, chmn., 1992—94; bd. dirs. Blair Cmty. Found., 1999—, Planned Giving Svcs., Nebr., chmn., 1992—94; ann. fund appeal chmn. Meml. Cmty. Hosp., 1994; trustee Palmer Chirpractic U., 1998—2004; mem. coun. pres. Evangel. Luth. Ch. in Am., 1999—, vice chmn., 1999—2000, chmn., 2000—, memls. com. churchwide assembly, 2001; mem. pastoral call com. First Luth. Ch., 1995, mem. ch. coun., 1999; mem. Nebr. Edni. Fin. Authority, 1991—, chmn., 1992—99, 2001, 2004—, vice chmn., 2002—03. Decorated knight Order of Dannebrog (Denmark); named A.T. Weaver Outstanding Comm. Tchr., 1979; recipient (with spouse) Blair Area Chamber Cmty. Svc. award, 2004, Acad. Achievement award, 2005; inducted into Wall of Honor, Unity High Sch., Polk County, Wis.; fellow Palmer Coll. Chiropractic, Palmer Coll. Chiropractic-West. Fellow: Found. for Ind. Higher Edn. (bd. dirs. 2003, sec. 2003—05); mem.: Coun. of Pres., Luth. Edn. Conf. N.Am. (vice chmn. 1994—95, chmn. 1995—96), Nebr. Ind. Coll. Found. (exec. com. 1990—92, vice chmn. 1992—93, chmn. 1994—95), Nebr. Bus. Higher Edn. Forum, Nat. Assn. Intercoll. Athletics (coun. of pres. 1999—2005), North Ctrl. Assn. Colls. and Schs. (cons.-evaluator 1997—2005, accreditation rev. coun. 2001—, team chair 2002—05), Nebr. Ednl. TV Coun. for higher Edn., Assn. Ind. Colls. Nebr. (chmn. 1992—93), Nat. Assn. Ind. Colls. and Univs. (bd. dirs. 1997—99, 2003—05, chmn.Great Plains athletic conf. coun. pres. 2004—05), Danish Brotherhood. Avocations: international travel, reading, writing, antique collecting and refinishing, study of theology. Office: Dana Coll Office of Pres Blair NE 68008 Office Phone: 402-426-3013. Business E-Mail: mchristo@dana.edu.

CHRISTOVICH, ALVIN RICHARD, JR., lawyer; b. New Orleans, Mar. 30, 1921; s. Alvin Richard Christovich and Elyria Kearney; m. Jane Elizabeth Pope, Dec. 7, 1943; children: Richard, David. BA, Tulane U., 1942, LLB, 1947. Ptnr. Christovich & Kearney, New Orleans, 1947—. 1st lt. U.S. Army Air Corps, 1943-45, Eng. Mem. Internat. Assn. Def. Counsel (former exec. com.), Def. Rsch. Inst. (former v.p., adminstrn.), La. State Bar Assn. (former bd. govs.), New Orleans Bar Assn. (former pres.), New Orleans Country Club, Pickwick Club. Roman Catholic. Office: Christovich & Kearney 601 Poydras St Ste 2300 New Orleans LA 70130-6078 Office Phone: 504-561-5700.

CHRISTY, ARTHUR HILL, lawyer; b. Bklyn., July 25, 1923; s. Francis Taggart and Catherine Virginia (Damon) C.; m. Gloria Garvin Osborne, Feb. 14, 1980; children by previous marriage: Duncan Hill, Alexandra. AB, Yale U., 1945; LL.B., Columbia U., 1949. Bar: N.Y. 1950. Assoc. firm Baldwin, Todd & Lefferts, N.Y.C., 1950-52; spl. asst. atty. gen. Saratoga Investigation, N.Y., 1952-53; asst. U.S. atty. So. Dist. N.Y., 1953-54; chief prosecutor spl. asst. atty. gen. Saratoga and Columbia County Investigations, 1954-55; asst. atty. gen. N.Y., 1955; chief criminal div. U.S. atty.'s Office, So. Dist. N.Y., 1955-57; chief asst. U.S. atty., 1957-58; U.S. atty., 1958-59; partner firm Christy & Viener (and predecessors), N.Y.C., 1959—. Spl. asst. to Gov. Rockefeller, 1959-61; apptd. 1st spl. prosecutor Under Ethics in Govt. Act of 1978 to investigate charges against White House Chief of Staff, 1979-80. Artist in scrimshaw. Trustee, vice chmn. Bklyn. Hosp., Cmty. Svc. Soc.; v.p., gen. counsel, mem. coun. N.Y. Heart Assn. Lt. USNR, 1944-46. Mem. ABA, N.Y. State Bar Assn., Fed. Bar Assn., Assn. Bar City N.Y. (chmn. exec. com. 1966-67, v.p. 1968-69), Am. Coll. Trial Lawyers, Century Assn., Rockefeller Luncheon Club, Univ. Club (N.Y.C.), Mastigouche Fish and Game Club (Que., Can.). Republican. Episcopalian. Home: 165 East 72nd St Apt 14N New York NY 10021 Office: 620 5th Ave New York NY 10020-2402 Office Phone: 212-632-5507. Business E-Mail: achristy@salans.com.

CHRISTY, CHARLES WESLEY, III, industrial engineering educator; b. Chester County, Pa., Apr. 29, 1942; s. Charles Wesley Jr. and Violet R. (Pierpont) C.; m. D. Jean Cullmann, Jan. 25, 1972; children: Richard Townsend, Charles Wesley IV, Michael Pierpont. BS, Widener U., 1973; MBA, Temple U., 1980. Chmn. indsl. engring. tech. Del. Tech. and C.C., Newark, 1970—. Pres. Pierpont Industries, Inc., Wilmington, Del., 1985—; adj. assoc. prof. U. Del., Newark, 1994; examiner Del. Quality Award, Wilmington, 1994. Bd. dirs., past pres. Opportunity Ctr., Inc., Wilmington, 1972—. Mem. Am. Inst. Indsl. Engrs. (bd. dirs. Del. chpt. 1970—, past pres.), Am. Soc. Quality Control. Home: 11 Harlech Dr Wilmington DE 19807-2507 Office: Del Tech & CC 400 Stanton Christiana Rd Newark DE 19713-2111 E-mail: cchristy@college.dtcc.edu.

CHRISTY, CINDY, telecommunications industry executive; m. Randy Christy; 4 children. BBA, Am. U. Joined AT&T Network Sys., 1988, various mgmt. positions in market rsch., market mgmt., sales, product planning, project mgmt. and product mgmt.; dir. CDMA/PCS Project Mgmt. Lucent Techs., Murray Hill, NJ, 1995—98, v.p. AMPS/PCS product mgmt. and mktg., 1998—2000, COO wireless networks group, 2001, COO mobility solutions group, 2002—03, pres. mobility solutions group, 2004—. Mem.: Cellular Telecom. Industry Assn. (bd. dirs., mem. exec. com.). Office: Lucent Techs 600 Mountain Ave Murray Hill NJ 07974

CHRISTY, JOHN GILRAY, diversified financial services company executive; b. Silver Creek, N.Y., Aug. 27, 1932; s. John Van Vlack and Ruth (Gilray) C.; m. Helen Llewellyn, 1991; children: Andrew, Jennifer. BA, Dartmouth Coll., 1954; MA in Asian Studies, U. Calif., Berkeley, 1960. Loan officer U.S. Devel. Loan Fund, 1960-61; with AID, New Delhi and Washington, 1961-65, chief extended risk guaranty divsn., 1965; with ITT, N.Y.C., 1965-72, treasury dept., 1965-68, v.p. internat. comm., 1968-69, asst. group exec. internat. comm., 1969-70; pres. ITT World Directories, Inc., N.Y.C., 1970-72; group v.p. land transp. IU Internat., Inc., Phila., 1972-76, exec. v.p., 1976-78; pres., COO IU Internat. Corp., 1978-80, chmn., pres., CEO, 1982-85, chmn., CEO, 1985-88; chmn. Chestnut Capital Corp., Phila., 1988—, First Fidelity Bank, Phila., 1991. Bd. dirs. 1838 Bond Debenture Trading Fund, Phila. Contributorship. Chmn. emeritus Fgn. Policy Rsch. Inst.; former trustee Colby Coll.; pres. coun. Eisenhower Exch. Fellowships Inc. Lt. USNR, 1958. Recipient Disting. Svc. award AID, 1965 Office: Chestnut Capital Corp PO Box 22 Flourtown PA 19031-0022 Office Phone: 215-233-3001. E-mail: jchristy@chapline.net.

CHRISTY, LARRY TODD, publisher; b. Tarentum, Pa., July 2, 1946; s. Todd Rowley and Eleanor Fern Christy; m. Kathleen Bernadette Braun, Nov. 26, 1976 (div. Feb. 1987); m. Lynn Elwell Sparrow, July 2, 1996. BA in Polit. Sci., Thiel Coll., 1968. Dir. Transact Corp., Geneva, 1972-76, pres. Pitts., 1976-96, Trendvest Corp., Virginia Beach, Va., 1978—, Thirders Found., Shelocta, Pa., 1989—; mgr. Trendvest Founders Ltd. Partnership Hedge Fund, 2000—, Trendvest Assocs. Ltd. Partnership, 2003—. Seminar speaker on Hedge Funds, Charles Schwab, Chgo., Phoenix, San Francisco, Pitts. and Columbus, 1989; publisher Internet World Wide Web Svc. for Investors, 1994—. Editor electronic investment svc./Trendvest Ratings, 1983—; author: Tax Trimmer Manual for Pennsylvania Corporations, 1980. Capt. mil. intelligence U.S. Army, Vietnam, Germany. Decorated Bronze Star. Mem. Thiel Coll. Alumni Assn. (pres. 1992-94, v.p. 1988-92, dir. 1983-95). Libertarian. Office: Trendvest Corp Ste 1805 923 First Colonial Rd Virginia Beach VA 23454 E-mail: larry@trendvest.com.

CHRISTY, NICHOLAS PIERSON, physician; b. Morristown, N.J., June 18, 1923; s. Leroy and Elizabeth (Baker) C.; m. Beverly Vairin Morris, June 21, 1947 (dec. Mar. 1997); children: Nicholas Pierson, Martha Vairin; m. Caroline P. Adams, June 26, 1999. AB, Yale, 1945; MD, Columbia, 1951. Diplomate: Am. Bd. Internal Medicine. Intern, asst. resident medicine, 1951—54; asst. vis. physician Delafield Hosp., N.Y.C., 1955-66, vis. physician, 1966-75; asst. vis. physician 1st med. div. Bellevue Hosp., N.Y.C., 1958-66; assoc. attending physician Presbyn. Hosp., N.Y.C., 1962-78, attending physician, 1978-93. Dir. med. svc. Roosevelt Hosp., N.Y.C., 1965-79; faculty Columbia Coll. Phys. and Surg., N.Y.C., 1956—, assoc. prof. medicine, 1962-65, assoc. clin. prof., 1965-67, clin. prof. medicine, 1967-71, prof. medicine, 1971-79, lectr. in medicine, 1979-88, sr. lectr. medicine, 1988-93, spl. lectr. in medicine, 1993—; mem. Columbia U. Health Scis. adv. coun., 1993—; prof. medicine, assoc. dean vets. affairs Health Sci. Ctr. at Bklyn., SUNY, 1979-88, prof. emeritus, 1988—; chief staff Bklyn. VA Med. Ctr., 1979-88; writer-in-residence, alumni writer Coll. Physicians and Surgeons, Columbia U., 1988—; assoc. Nat. Humanities Ctr., Research Triangle Park, N.C., 1979; cons. FDA, 1966, Bd. of Health, N.Y.C., 1965—, NIH Nat. Inst. Diabetes, Digestive and Kidney Diseases tng. grants divsn., 1969-72, endocrinology study sect., 1975-79; cons., bd. dirs. Royal Soc. Medicine Found., 1984-93. Editor, co-author: The Human Adrenal Cortex, 1971; editor-in-chief: Jour. Clin. Endocrinology and Metabolism, 1963-67; assoc. editor: Beeson-McDermott Textbook of Medicine, 1968-75; cons. editor, 1975-79; cons. Med. Dictionary (Dorland), 1988; adv. editor and contbr. Internat. Dictionary of Medicine and Biology (Endocrinology), 1986; mem. adv. bd.: Am. Jour. Medicine, 1971-88; contbr. numerous papers to profl. publs. Served to lt. (j.g.) USNR, 1943-46, PTO. Recipient Borden award, Joseph Mather Smith prize Columbia; John and Mary R. Markle scholar; NIH tng. grantee, 1959-65, endocrinology study sect. grantee, 1958-69; honoree St. Luke's Roosevelt Hosp. Alumni Assn., 2000. Fellow Am. Med. Writers Assn. (hon., Swanberg award 1989); mem. Harvey Soc., AAAS, Soc. Exptl. Biology and Medicine, Am. Soc. Clin. Investigation, Assn. Am. Physicians, Am. Fedn. Clin. Rsch., A.C.P., N.Y. Acad. Medicine, Laurentian Hormone Conf., Am. Physiol. Soc., N.Y. State Med. Soc., N.Y. County Med. Soc., Am. Clin. and Climatol. Assn. (recorder 1977-88, pres. 1990), Am. Assn. Study Liver Diseases, Endocrine Soc. (sec.-treas. 1978-89, Ayerst award 1986), N.Y. Clin. Soc., N.Y. Med. and Surg. Soc., Assn. Am. Physicians, Interurban Clin. Club, Hosp. Grads. Club, Peripatetic Soc., Practitioners Soc., Elizabethan (Yale), Colony (Yale), Century Assn. (pres. 1987-90, hon. 1995—). Home: 31 Reservoir Rd Killingworth CT 06419-1418 Office Phone: 860-663-0250.

CHRISTY, VICTOR JOSEPH, music educator; b. St. Louis, May 25, 1974; d. Dixie Kay Christy; m. Marisa Manie Brammer, June 24, 2000. MusB, Culver-Stockton Coll., Canton, Mo., 1996. Asst. music tchr., band dir. Clark County R-I Schs., Kahota, Mo., 1996—98; music tchr., dir. bands, vocal music, K-12 music world history LaPlata R-II Schs., Mo., 1998—, scholarship com. mem., 1999—2004. Democrat. Christian. Avocations: table tennis, farming, sports, reading, movies. Home: 516 E Sanders La Plata MO 63549 Office: La Plata R II Schools 201 W Moore La Plata MO 63549 Office Phone: 660-332-7001, 660-332-7003. Fax: 660-332-7656. Business E-Mail: vchristy@laplata.k12.mo.us.

CHRITTON, GEORGE A., theater producer; b. Chgo. s. George A. and Dorothea G. Chritton; m. Martha Gilman, Aug. 26, 1956; children: Stewart, Andrew, Douglas, Laura, Neil, Lyle. BA, Occidental Coll., 1955; postgrad., Princeton U., 1955-57. With CIA & various US govt. agys., 1960-89; gen. ptnr. Margeo Investment Co., LA, 1963-76; pres. Wildacre Prodns., Inc., LA, 1990—. Pres., CEO Fin. Svcs. Bancorp, Reno, 1990—; pres. Sycamore Prodns. Ltd., Nev., Calif., 1994—. Prodr.: (plays) Thornton Wilder's Youth, In Shakespeare and The Bible, A Ringing of Doorbells, The Rivers Under the Earth, 1999. Mem. Am. Fgn. Svc. Assn., Washington, 1960—; chmn. bd. dirs. Neighborhood Learning Ctr., Capitol Hill, Washington, 1985—87; vol. Options House, Hollywood, Calif.; vol. coord. Rebuild LA; spl. adv. Los Angeles County Juvenile Ct., 2000—. Maj. USAF, 1957—60. Princeton Nat. fellow, 1955—56, Vis. fellow, lectr., U. Calif., 1987—88. Mem.: SAG, AFTRA, Nat. Assn. Ind. Film & TV Prodrs., Am. Film Inst., LA World Affairs Coun., Princeton Club (So. Calif.), Phi Beta Kappa, Alpha Phi Gamma, Alpha Mu Gamma, Phi Gamma Delta. Office: Wildacre Prodns Inc PO Box 719 Beverly Hills CA 90213-0719 Business E-Mail: Chritton@alumni.Princeton.edu.

CHROMIZKY, WILLIAM RUDOLPH, accountant; b. Chgo., Jan. 21, 1955; s. Rudolph Joseph and Helen M. Chromizky; m. Laura Lee Lamoureux, Oct. 24, 1992. BS, No. Ill. U., 1977; M of Mgmt., Northwestern U., 1987. CPA, Ill. Sr. auditor Arthur Andersen & Co., Chgo., 1977-83; supr. internal audit AM Internat., Chgo., 1983-84, mgr. fin. reporting, 1984-85, dir. acctg., 1985; mgr. bus. analysis Premark Internat., Inc., Deerfield, Ill., 1985-87, dir. fin. reporting, 1987-2000; v.p., sec. and external reporting Aon Corp., Chgo., 2001—. Vol. CPAs for the Pub Interest, Chgo., 1990-92; mem. fin. com. Brother Rice H.S., 1995—, bd. dirs., 1999—. Mem.: AICPA, Fin. Execs. Inst. Avocations: skiing, tennis, bowling, competitive running. Office: Aon Corp 200 E Randolph St Chicago IL 60601 Office Phone: 312-381-3489. E-mail: william_chromizky@asc.aon.com.

CHROMOW, SHERI P., lawyer; b. N.Y.C., Aug. 27, 1946; d. Abe and Sara L. Pinsky. BA, Barnard Coll., N.Y.C., 1968; JD, NYU, 1971. Ptnr. Shearman & Sterling, N.Y.C., 1979—2001, Katten, Muchin, Rosenman LLP, N.Y.C., 2001—. Lectr. Practising Law Inst., N.Y. County Bar Assn., Urban Land Inst.; mem. exec. com. N.Y. dist. coun. U. L.I.; mem. adv. bd. Furman Real Estate Inst. NYU Law Sch.; mem. adv. bd. Ticor Title Ins. Co; award judge Real Estate Bd. N.Y., 2003, 04; bd. experts The Internat. Real Estate Trade Orgn. Bd. dirs. Bklyn. Philharm. Orch. Mem. Urban Land Inst. (former gen. counsel), Assn. Fgn. Investors in Real Estate, Pelham (N.Y.) Country Club Office: Katten Muchin Rosenman LLP 575 Madison Ave New York NY 10022 Office Phone: 212-940-8529. Business E-Mail: sheri.chromow@kattenlaw.com.

CHRONIS, HILDEGARD MARIA See TURKS, HILDEGARD

CHRONISTER, GREGORY MICHAEL, newspaper editor; b. York, Pa., Nov. 28, 1953; s. Francis Gilbert and Mary Jane (Hamberger) C. AB, Grove City (Pa.) Coll., 1975. Features editor The Ghent Press, Norfolk, Va., 1975, mng. editor, 1976; co-founder, editor Tidewater After Dark, Norfolk, 1977-79; asst. dir. New Va. Rev. Inc., Norfolk, 1979-80; editor univ. publs. Old Dominion U., Norfolk, 1980-85; assoc. editor Edn. Week, Washington, 1985-89, mng. editor, 1989—. Mem. Hist. Soc. Washington, Theodore Roosevelt Assn., Omicron Delta Kappa. Office: Edn Week 6935 Arlington Rd Ste 100 Bethesda MD 20814-5273 Home: 3001 Veazey Ter NW Apt 1434 Washington DC 20008-5409 Business E-Mail: gchron@epe.org.

CHRONLEY, JAMES ANDREW, real estate executive; b. Springfield, Mass., July 31, 1930; s. Robert Emmett and Eleanor Agnes (Sullivan) C.; m. Monique Mary Delpech, July 29, 1955; children: Mary Elizabeth, James Michael, Jean Louise, Patricia, Joseph Patrick, John Peter, Robert Emmett. AB, Brown U., 1952; diploma in real estate, U. R.I., 1963; MBA, Pepperdine U., 1991. With Arco Co., 1954-74, Ea. area mgr., until 1972; nat. real estate dir. Atlantic Richfield Co., L.A., 1972-74; v.p. restaurant real estate Marriott Corp., Washington, 1974-78; exec. v.p. Burger Chef Systems, Inc., Indpls., 1978—83, pres., 1983; sr. v.p. devel. Taco Bell, Irvine, 1983-94. Served with AUS, 1952-54. Mem. Nat. Assn. Corp. Real Estate Execs. (chpt. pres. 1979, chmn. bd. 1985-87, elected trustee 1987-92), Am. Arbitration Assn., Internat. Exec. Svc. Corps, Orange County Assn. Investment Mgrs. Roman Catholic. Office: Taco Bell 14602 Bel Aire St Irvine CA 92604-2201 Personal E-mail: moniqueusa@cox.net.

CHROPUFKA, MARK A., information technology executive, poet; b. West Islip, N.Y., Feb. 27, 1970; s. Edward and Regina (Abbatello) Seaman. BS in Mgmt., SUNY, Binghamton, 1992; MBA, St. John's U., 2001. Tech. and trade support Sanford Bernstein, N.Y.C., 1992-93; substitute prin., stenographer Wyandanch UFSD, N.Y., 1993-94; data analyst Pratt Inst., Bklyn., 1994-96, dir. info. mgmt., 1996-98; software analyst St. John's Univ., 1999—. Author of poems; Holly and OaK: A Crossroads in Life, 1996; prodr. TV spl. Crazy Dave's Magic Show, 1995; songwriter; creator, prodr. TV spl. Aggravated Cat!, 1999-2001. Guitarist, mem. music ministry Our Lady of Miraculous Medal Ch., Wyandanch, N.Y., 1999—; contbr. Friends of Karen Lavilla Fund, Purdys, N.Y., 1995, The Newman House, Binghamton, N.Y., 1992—; vol., participant Wyandanch Career Day, 1994; asst. coord. Wyandanch Book Fair, 1994; supporter, contbr. Manhattan Neighborhood Network, N.Y.C., 1995. Mem.: Beta Gamma Sigma. Avocations: writing, investing, biking, travel, independent tv production, guitar playing. Home: 11 Pearsall St Babylon NY 11702-2517 Office: St Johns University 8000 Utopia Pky Jamaica NY 11439-0002 E-mail: chropufm@stjohns.edu, mchropufka@aol.com.

CHRYSOSTOMOU, CONSTANTINOS, pediatrician, cardiologist; b. Limassol, Cyprus, Aug. 10, 1969; s. Demetris and Loretta Chrysostomou; m. Tatiana Milenka Zeballos, June 26, 2004. MD, U. Med. Sch. Debrecen, Hungary, 1996; subspecialty in Pediat., U. Minn., Minneapolis, 1998—2001; subspecialty in Pediatric Cardiology, U. Pitts., 2004. Pals Agh/ Pa, 2004, Atls Agh / Pa, 2004. Pre-medical student U. Med. Sch. Debrecen, Debrecen, Hungary, 1989—90, med. student, 1990—96; pediatrician U. Minn., Mpls., 1998—; fellow pediatric cardiology U. Miami, Fla., 2001—03; pediatric cardiologist U. Pitts., 2003—, pediatric cardiac intensivist, 2004—. Mem.: Pediatric Cardiac Intensive Care Soc. (assoc.), Soc. Critical Care Medicine (assoc.). Office: Children's Hosp Pitts 3705 Fifth Ave Pittsburgh PA 15213 Office Phone: 412-692-7366.

CHRYSSIS, GEORGE CHRISTOPHER, entrepreneur; b. Crete, Greece, May 21, 1947; came to U.S., 1966; naturalized U.S. citizen; s. Christopher and Ourania (Kamisakis) C.; m. Margo Sayegh, May 21, 1978; children: Rania, Lilian, Alexander. ASEE, Wentworth Inst., 1969; BEE, Northeastern U., 1972, MEE, 1977. Electronic engr. Orion Rsch., Boston, 1977-78; sr. engr. Datel, Inc., Mansfield, Mass., 1978-79; co-founder, v.p. ops. and engring. Power Gen. Corp., Canton, Mass., 1979-85; pres., founder, CFO Intelco Corp., Acton, Mass., 1985-90; pres., treas. G & M Enterprises, Inc., 1989-92; co-founder, chmn. Collegescape, Inc., 1997-98; pres. Arcadian Capital Mgmt., LLC, 1999—; founder, pub. The Hellenic Voice, 2001—02; founder, chmn. CEO Mistsoft Corp., 2003—. Pvt. investor, 1992-97; trustee Hellenic Coll./Holy Cross, 1989-97, 99— vice chmn., 2001—; trustee U. Crete Endowment Fund, 1992-97, Wentworth Inst., 1996—, Anatolia Coll., 1999-2002; chmn. NU Nat. Coun., 2001-2004; bd. dirs. Nat. Coun. Northeastern U., 1986—, Nat. Coun. Wentworth Inst., 1987—; corporator Wentworth Inst., 1990-96, chmn. fund campaign, 1989, trustee, 1996—; mem. Capital Campaign Cabinet, 1992-97; mem. Wentworth Inst. investment com., 1996—, chair long range planning com., 1999—; bd. dirs. Delphi Comms., Inc., Continuum Control Corp., EliteView Corp.; corporator Northeastern U., 1990, bd. overseers, 1995-2002, trustee 2002—, mem. indsl. advisory bd., 1997—, mem. long-range planning com. 1995—, audit com. 2002—, devel. com. 2002—; founding dir. Gorbachev Found. of N.Am., 1999—; adv. bd. NU Sch. of Entrepreneurship, 2000. Author: High Frequency Switching Power Supplies, 1984, 89, Echoes and Re-Echoes (poetry), 1993, Heliotropia (poetry), 1996, Short Poems of Homecoming, 1999, Medea, 2004; contbr. articles to profl. jours. Bd. dirs. St. Demetrios Ch., Weston, Mass., 1987-99, parish coun. pres. 1998-99, chmn. ways and means com., 1992-93, ch. svcs. com., 1989-90, stewardship com., 1994-2002; fellow Orthodox Steward of Boston Diocese, 1986—, Greek Orthodox Archdiocese Leadership One Hundred, 2000—, Archon Ecumenical Patriarchate, 2000; active numerous cmty. and civic orgns.; friends Univs. of Crete, 1995, Greek Inst., 1989, bd. dirs., 1998; mem. Am. Hellenic Inst., 1985, Mass. High Tech. Coun., 1986-90. Recipient New Englander award Smaller Bus. Assn. New Eng. (SBANE), 1989, Golden Leopard award Wentworth Inst., 1991, Arete award Greek Inst., 1996, Hellenic Leadership award, 1997, Ellis Island medal of honor award, 2000, Laity award, 2002, Minoan award, 2002, Hellenic Heritage award, 2004, W. Erwin Story citation Northwestern U. Alumni Assn., 2004; named finalist for Entrepreneur of Yr. Arthur Young Inc. and Inc. Mag., 1989; named Parishioner of Yr., Greek Orthodox Diocese, Boston, 1993. Mem.: Hellenic Scientists Assn., Internat. Soc. Poets (disting.), PanCretan Assn. Am. (pres. Boston chpt. 1987—89, co-chmn. 30th nat. conv. 1988, bd. govs. dist. I 1990—92, nat. pres. 1995—97, Minoan award 2002), Huntington Soc., President's Club, 500 Club of Northeastern U., Alpha Omega (coun. 1990—, treas. 1994—97). Greek Orthodox. Avocations: writing, tennis, travel. Office Phone: 781-890-7999.

CHRYSTAL, WILLIAM GEORGE, minister; b. Seattle, May 22, 1947; s. Francis Homer and Marjorie Isabell (Daubert) C.; m. Mary Frances King, Aug. 24, 1970; children: Shelley, Sarah, John, Philip. BA, U. Wash., 1969, MEd, 1970; MDiv, Eden Theol. Sem., 1978; MA, Johns Hopkins U., 1984. Ordained to ministry, United Ch. of Christ, 1977. Learning resources specialist Seattle C.C. Dist., 1970-71; dir. learning resources ctr. Whatcom C.C., Ferndale, Wash., 1971-73; minister St. Peter's United Ch. of Christ, Granite City, Ill., 1978-79; sr. minister 1st Congl. Ch., Stockton, Calif., 1979-83; minister Trinity United Ch. of Christ, Adamstown, Md., 1983-85; sr. minister Edwards Congl. Ch., Northampton, Mass., 1985-86, 1st Congl. Ch., Reno, Nev., 1991—. Hosp. chaplain Washoe Med. Ctr., Reno, 1993-99; host Thomas Jefferson Hour, on Nat. pub. radio stas. Author: Young Reinhold Niebuhr: His Early Writings, 1911-1931, 1977, 2d edit., 1982, A Father's Mantle: The Legacy of Gustav Niebuhr, 1982, The Fellowship of Prayer, 1987; author monographs; contbr. articles to profl. jours. V.p. Reno-Sparks Met. Ministry, Reno, 1994-97; Chautauqua scholar Great Basin Chautauqua, Reno, 1993, 94, 98, 99. Lt. comdr. USN, 1986-91, maj. Nev. Army N.G., 1992-96. Decorated (2) Meritorious Svc. medal. Mem. Am. Soc. Ch. History, Nev. Soc. Mayflower Descs. (past gov.), Am. Legion, Disabled Vets. (life), VFW (life), Rotary Club (Paul Harris fellow 1997). Home: 3820 Bluebird Cir Reno NV 89509-5601 Office: 1st Congl Ch 627 Sunnyside Dr Reno NV 89503-3515 Office Phone: 775-747-1414. Personal E-mail: williamgchrystal@yahoo.com. Business E-Mail: chrystal@intercomm.com.

CHRYSTIE, THOMAS LUDLOW, investor; b. N.Y.C., May 24, 1933; s. Thomas Witter and Helen (Duell) C.; m. Eliza S. Balis, June 9, 1955; children: Alice B., Helen S., Adden B., James McD. BA, Columbia U., 1955; MBA, NYU, 1960. With Merrill Lynch, Pierce, Fenner & Smith, Inc., N.Y.C., 1955-75, dir. investment banking divsn., 1970-75; sr. v.p. Merrill Lynch & Co., 1975-78, CFO, 1976-78; chmn. Merrill Lynch White Weld Capital Markets Group, 1978-81, Merrill Lynch Capital Resources, 1981-83; adv. on strategy Merrill Lynch & Co. Inc., 1983-88; pvt. investor Jackson, Wyo., 1988—. Bd. dirs. Jackson State Bank, Eeonyx Corp Trustee emeritus Columbia U.; trustee Nat. Mus. Wildlife Art. Capt. USAF, 1955-58. Mem. N.Y. Athletic Club, Teton Pines Tennis Club, Columbia Club. Home and Office: PO Box 640 Wilson WY 83014-0640 *Whatever you are involved in, see it as part of a larger picture.*

CHRZANOWSKI, LEYE JEANNETTE, publisher; b. Aug. 28, 1946; Student, Ctrl. Tex. Coll., 1978—79, Enterprise State Jr. Coll., 1982—83. Pres., founder Excel Networking Group, Inc., Va., 1991-94; v.p., exec. editor EKA Comms., Md., 1993-97; pres. Disability News Svc., Chantilly, Va., 1997—2000, Disability Press Assn., 2000—. Mem. Soc. Profl. Journalists, Investigative Reporters and Editors, Soc. Disability Studies, Washington Ind. Writers. Office: 13703 Southernwood Ct Chantilly VA 20151-3345 Office Phone: 703-861-2685. Business E-Mail: leyech@cox.net.

CHU, BENJAMIN K., hospital administrator; BA, Yale U., 1974; MD, NYU, 1978; MPH, Columbia Mailman Sch. Pub. Health, 1985. Diplomate Am. Bd. Internal Medicine, 1982. Intern, resident Kings County Hosp., 1978; assoc. prof. of clinical med., assoc. dean for clinical affairs NYU, 1994—2000; sr. assoc. dean Harlem Hospital Center, N.Y.C., 2000—02; sr. v.p. med. affairs N.Y.C. Health and Hosp. Corp., 2001—02, pres., CEO, 2002—. Office: NYC Health & Hospitals Corp 125 Worth St New York NY 10013

CHU, CHUNG KWANG, medicinal chemistry professor; b. Seoul, Republic of Korea, May 18, 1941; s. Jee Young Huh; children: Susan, Jackie. BS, Seoul Nat. U., 1964; MS, Idaho State U., 1970; PhD, SUNY, Buffalo, 1974. Rsch. assoc. Sloan-Kettering Cancer Inst., N.Y.C., 1974-80; asst. prof. Idaho State U., Pocatello, 1990-82; asst. prof. medicinal chemistry U. Ga., Athens, 1982-87, assoc. prof., 1987-89, prof., 1990-98, disting. rsch. prof., 1998—. Adv. bd. NIH, Pharmasset, Atlanta. Lt. (j.g.) Korean Navy. Mem. Am. Chem. Soc. (Rsch. grant 1988), Am. Assn. for Cancer Rsch., Am. Assn. Colls. Pharmacy, Internat. Soc. Antiviral Rsch. Achievements include patents for drug discovery field. Office: U Ga Coll Pharmacy Brooks Dr Athens GA 30602 Office Phone: 706-542-5379. Office Fax: 706-542-5381. Business E-Mail: dchu@rx.uga.edu.

CHU, DAVID S.C., federal agency administrator, economist; b. N.Y.C., May 28, 1944; s. H. T. and Esther Chu; m. Laura L. Tosi. BA in Economics and Mathematics magna cum laude, Yale U., 1964, PhD in Economics, 1972. Asst. dir. nat. security and internat. affairs Congl. Budget Office, Washington, 1978—81; dir. then asst. sec. def. for program analysis and evaluation Dept. Def., 1981—93; economist RAND, Santa Monica, Calif., 1970—78, sr. fellow Washington, 1993—94, dir. Washington rsch. dept., 1994—96, dir. Washington office, assoc. chmn. of rsch. staff, 1996—98; v.p. army rsch. divsn., dir. Arroyo Ctr., 1998—2001; under sec. defense for personnel and readiness US Dept. of Defense, 2001—. Capt. U.S. Army, 1968—70,

Vietnam. Decorated Bronze Star, Army commendation medal. Fellow: Nat. Acad. Pub. Adminstrn. (chmn., bd. trustees 1999—2001); mem.: Phi Beta Kappa. Office: 4000 Defense Pentagon Washington DC 20301-4000

CHU, ELLIN RESNICK, librarian, consultant; b. Bklyn., Nov. 23, 1932; d. David and Isobel (Janowitch) Resnick; m. Wallace Chu, Aug. 29, 1960 (div. Sept. 1979); children: Steven, Joshua, Amanda. BA in Modern European Hist. with honors, Ind. U., 1954, MA in Libr. Sci., 1956; postgrad., Columbia U., 1956-57. Young adult libr. Donnell br. N.Y. Pub. Libr., 1956-57; order libr. Nat. Indsl. Conf. Bd., 1957-58; reference libr. Columbia U. Reference Libr., 1958-59; libr. dir. Hillside Hosp., 1959-61, L.I. Jewish-Hillside Med. Ctr., 1972—; adult/young adult libr. Glen Cove (N.Y.) Pub. Libr., 1973-77; young adult cons. Rochester (N.Y.) Pub. Libr. Monroe County Libr. Sys., 1977-93, mgr. lit., religion and philosophy divsn., 1993-98, ret., 1998. Mem. nomination com. Glen Cove Interagy. Coun., 1976, chair youth recreation com., 1974-75, chair pre-screening com., info. and referral adv. bd. Nassau Libr. Sys., 1977; mem. libr. planning com. Rochester Sesquicentennial, 1984; mem. cen. libr. planning com. Rochester Pub. Libr., 1985-86; sec. Rochester Area Youth Dirs. Coun., 1980-81, mem. nominating com., 1987, profl. improvement com., 1987-89; presenter programming and svcs. for young adults Mid-Hudson Libr. Sys., Albany, N.Y., 1989-90; mem. On-line pub. catalog planning com. Monroe County Libr. Sys., 1986-92; libr. programming presenter and resource team mem. Learning Odyssey/SUNY Albany and New York State Divsn. Libr. Devel., 1989; active Brighton Cable Commn., 1980-93. Co-author: (chpt. to book) Our Family, Our Friends, Our World: An Annotated Guide to Significant Multicultural Books for Children and Teenagers, 1991; contbr. articles to profl. jours. Recipient 1st prize N.Y. Libr. Ad Hoc Com. on Women's Concerns, 1975; grantee Young Adult Libr. Instrn. Project, 1982-84; scholar Robert Flaherty Film Seminar, 1976, Lyman Langdon scholar Audubon Ecology Workshop, 1977. Mem. ALA (young adult svcs. divsn., chair high interest/low literacy level materials evaluation com. 1979-81, pub. liaison com. 1988-90, Margaret A. Edwards Author Award com. 1991-93), Ednl. Film Libr. Assn. (juror Am. Film Festival 1976-78, jury chair 1979-88), N.Y. Libr. Assn. (pres. youth svcs. sect. 1984, founding mem./sec. film/video roundtable 1977), Nassau County Libr. Assn. (founding mem. young adult sect. 1976).

CHU, ERNEST DAVID, medical products executive; b. N.Y.C., Sept. 15, 1946; s. Philip Mei Bao and Esther M. (Tang) Chu; m. Rosalind M. Hale, Feb. 13, 1972 (div.); children: Christopher James, Jonathan Peter; m. Diane Hom, May 28, 1983. Student, U. Delhi, India, 1966—67; BA cum laude, Amherst Coll., 1968; postgrad., Columbia U., 1968—69. Staff writer Wall St. Jour., Dow Jones News Svc., N.Y.C., 1968—69; account exec. Carter, Berlind & Weill, N.Y.C., 1969—71; spl. asst. to exec. com. Walters, Yeckes & Gallant Co., 1971—72, v.p., 1972—73; allied mem. N.Y. Stock Exch., N.Y.C., 1972—73; sr. v.p., dir. Danes Cooke & Keleher, Inc., N.Y.C., 1973—76; v.p., mem. exec. com. Roussel Capital Corp., N.Y.C., 1976—77; pres., chmn. bd. dirs. Ernest Chu & Co., Inc., 1976—. V.p. fin., treas. Haber Inc., Towaco, NJ, 1979, CFO, dir., 81, sr. v.p., 85, exec. v.p., 86; v.p., dir. Life Signs Inc., Towaco, 1979—; sec., dir. Silvertech Mines Inc.; dir. various cos.; cons. in field. Contbg. author: Guide to Venture Capital Sources, 4th edit.; author (with others): Winning Platform Tennis, Contemporary Platform Tennis, Understanding Tax Shelters; contbr. articles to profl. jours.; co-editor: Valley Review of Books, 1968. Bd. dirs. Nat. Com. Am. Fgn. Policy, 1979—82, Orgn. Chinese Ams., Inc., 1976—79, v.p., 1977—79; mem. alumni scholarship com. Amherst Coll. Mem.: Asian Mgmt. Bus. Assn. (chmn., CEO 1979—80), Am. Profl. Platform Tennis Assn. (pro adv. bd. 1977—79), Amherst Alumni Assn. (dir. 1975—80), Asia Soc., Shriners, Masons. Congregationalist. Office: Haber 470 Main Rd Towaco NJ 07082-1294

CHU, HAROLD, lawyer; b. Pine Bluff, Ark., Dec. 12, 1947; s. Yen and Lum (Ying) C.; m. Faye Watanabe, Aug. 27, 1972 (div. 1981); 1 child, Laura Yukiko. BA in Psychology with honors, Stanford U., 1971; JD, Northwestern U., 1974. Bar: Hawaii 1975, U.S. Ct. Appeals (9th cir.) 1975, U.S. Supreme Ct. 1979; lic. real estate broker. Assoc. Law Offices of Kenneth S. Robbins, Honolulu, 1975-78; ptnr. Robbins, Chu & Reilly, Honolulu, 1978-80; pvt. practice Honolulu, 1980—. Lectr. Kapioloni Community Coll. Paralegal Program, Honolulu, 1980—; mem. Ct. Arbitration Program, Honolulu, 1987-90. Mem. rules com. Dem. party, Honlulu, 1990; mem. Hawaii State Disciplinary Coun., Honolulu, 1988-90; mem. Com. for Unauthorized Practice Law, Honolulu, 1977-79; del. State Jud. Coun., Honolulu, 1989-90. Mem. ABA (litigation sect., real property, probate and trust law sect.), Nat. Assn. Realtors, Hawaii Assn. Realtors, Hawaii State Bar Assn. (publs. com. 1980-82). Avocations: photography, tennis, reading, theater. Office: Pacific Tower 1001 Bishop St Ste 1570 Honolulu HI 96813-3407 Fax: (808) 526-1231. E-mail: Hchulaw@worldnet.att.net.

CHU, HORN DEAN, chemical engineer; b. China, Sept. 9, 1933; s. Johnson S.T. and Daisy (Hsia) C.; m. Pik Yu Cheung, June 23, 1962. BS, Waseda U., Tokyo, 1959, MS, 1961, U. Pa., 1963; PhD, U. Ala., 1965. Project engr. Selas Corp., Dresher, Pa., 1965-71; asst. and adj. prof. Rutgers U., New Brunswick, N.J., 1971-79; sr. process engr. MacAndrews & Forbes Co., Camden, N.J., 1979-81; pres. Berkorp, Inc., Haddonfield, N.J., 1981—. Contbr. articles to profl. jours. Fellow Am. Inst. Chemists; mem. AIChE, Am. Chem. Soc., Inst. Food Technologists, AAAS, Sigma Xi. Office: Berkorp Inc 6-10S Haddon Ave Haddonfield NJ 08033-1860 Office Phone: 856-429-8886.

CHU, HSIEN-KUN, chemist, researcher; b. Shanghai, People's Republic of China, Oct. 14, 1947; came to U.S., 1971; s. Hwei-Teh and Yun-Hsiang (Chang) C.; m. Winnie K.S. Wong, Dec. 23, 1976; children: James C., Jason C. BS, Nat. Taiwan U., Taipei, Republic of China, 1970; PhD, Vanderbilt U., 1976. Vis. instr. U. Tex., Arlington, 1976-77; rsch. assoc. Tex. Christian U., Ft. Worth, 1977-80; rsch. specialist Dow Corning Corp., Midland, Mich., 1980-88; sr. scientist Loctite Corp., Rocky Hill, Conn., 1988—. Contbr. rsch. articles to sci. jours. Mem. Am. Chem. Soc., Sigma Xi. Achievements include patents on silicone sealants; research into mechanistic studies of organic reactions, silicone research. Home: 6 Harvest Hl Wethersfield CT 06109-2422 Office: Henkel Tech 1001 Trout Brook Xing Rocky Hill CT 06067-3910 E-mail: hk.chu@us.henkel.com.

CHU, JACK J. (JACK J. ZHU), electrical engineer; b. Shanghai, Jan. 26, 1938; arrived in U.S., 1980; s. Baoling Zhu(Chu), Zhi Yin Mo; m. Shannon Chongshan Sun, 1966; 1 child, Ling Zhu. BS in Automatic Control Engring., Tsinghua U., 1960, MS in Automatic Control Engring., 1962; MSEE, U. Minn., 1990. Sr. control sys. engr. Spectra Engring., Inc., Roseville, Minn., 1992—95, Innovex Engring., Inc., Hopkins, Minn., 1995—96, Quickie Design Inc., Fresno, Calif., 1996—97, Sunrise Med. Inc., Longmont, Colo., 1997—98, Kriton Med., Inc., Citrus Heights, Calif., 1998, Avery Dennison Inc., Ft. Wayne, Ind., 1999; sr. control sys., software engr. Balance Tech., Inc., Ann Arbor, Mich., 2000—01, Avionics Specialties Inc., Charlottesville, Va., 2001—. Contbr. articles to profl. jours. Recipient Nat. Merit Citation Class 2 in China, 1982. Achievements include development of microprocessor model reference adaptive control system; of adaptive thin-film sensor grinding system; of blood pump controller with indicator. Avocations: ping pong/table tennis, swimming, cooking, travel, chess. Personal E-mail: jackjchu@mybluelight.com.

CHU, JAMES, electronics executive; b. Taiwan; m. Lily Chu; children: Tina, Kevin. Various sales positions, Taiwan; pres. Taiwanese keyboard mfg. co., U.S., 1986; founder Keypoint Tech. Corp., 1987-90; reorganized Keypoint Tech. Corp. (now ViewSonic Corp.), 1990; CEO ViewSonic Corp., Walnut, Calif. Avocations: reading, tennis, exploring internet.

CHU, JEFFREY CHUAN, manufacturing executive, consultant; b. Tianjen, China, July 14, 1919; came to US, 1940; s. Yao and Vanyi (Tang) C.; m. Loretta Y. Tung, Feb. 9, 1928; children: Lynnet Helbig, Bambi Rae, Dashie Kocica. BSEE, U. Minn., 1942; MSEE, U. Pa., 1945. Rsch. assoc. Moore Sch., U. Pa., Phila., 1944-48; sr. engr. Reeves Instrument Co., NYC, 1948-50; chief sr. scientist Argonne Nat. Lab., Lemont, Ill., 1950-56; dir engring. Sperry Univac, Phila., 1956-62; v.p. asst., gen. mgr. Honeywell Info. Systems Inc., Waltham, Mass., 1962-72; sr. v.p. Wang Labs., Lowell, Mass., 1972-74; prin. advisor Nat. Sci. Commn., ROC, Taipei, Taiwan, China, 1974-77; chmn., chief exec. officer Santec Corp., Amherst, NH, 1980-85; chmn. Columbia Internat. Corp., Weston, Mass., 1985—. Adj. prof. Nankai U., Tanjen, Xinjiang U., Uremaqi; adj. prof., mem. U. Coun., Jiao Tong U., Shanghai; vis. prof. and mem. of the Univ. Coun., Qingdao U., Peoples Republic of China; advisor Com. for Higher Learning, Shandong U., Jinan; advisor office of pres. SRI Internat., 1986—; bd. dir. Interproject Corp., BTU Eng. Internat.; econ. advisor to Gov. Shandong Province, Peoples Republic of China. Mem. adv. bd. Wharton Sch. in China, U. Pa., Babage Inst., U. Minn.; hon. chmn. Inst. for Soft Sci. Studies, Shandong U., Jinan; bd. dirs. Fairbank Inst. Harvard U. Fellow IEEE (computer pioneer award 1981), Chinese Inst. Engrs.; hon. mem. Chinese Nat. Acad. Social Scis., Chinese Assn. Sci. Studies, Acad. Mil. Med. Sci., Beijing; mem. Sigma Xi (life). Avocations: tennis, skiing. Home: 10 Baldwin Cir Weston MA 02493-1520 Office: BTU Internat 23 Esquire Rd North Billerica MA 01862 Office Phone: 978-667-4111 x 411. Personal E-mail: chuanchu@comcast.net.

CHU, JENNIFER, hospital administrator, medical educator; d. Ah Chway Chu and Jane Shek; m. Waverly Stanford Andrews, Jan. 17, 1983; children: Justin Stanford Andrews, Jasmine Stanford Andrews. MD, Inst. Medicine, Rangoon, Burma, 1971. Cert. Nu Nu Yi Inst. Medicine, 1971. Dir. electrodiagnostic medicine Hosp. U. Pa., Phila., 1977—, dir. soft tissue comfort ctr., 2003—. Author: (book) Electrodiagnosis: An Anatomical and Clinical Approach; contbr. articles to profl. jours. Advisor Painfree Internat. Charitable Found., Ardmore, Pa., 2001. Fellow: Am. Acad. Phys. Medicine and Rehab. Achievements include patents for automated and electrical twitch obtaining intramuscular stimulation methods and devices; first to nerve related muscle pain treatments; invention of medical devices for eliciting deep muscle twitches. Office: Hosp Univ Pa 3400 Spruce St Ground White Bldg Philadelphia PA 19041 Office Phone: 215-662-3258. Home Fax: 215-662-4848; Office Fax: 215-662-4848.

CHU, JOHNSON CHIN SHENG, retired physician; b. Peiping, China, Sept. 25, 1918; arrived in U.S., 1948, naturalized, 1957; s. Harry S.P. and Florence (Young) Chu; m. Sylvia Cheng, June 11, 1949; children: Stephen, Timothy. MD, St. John's U., 1945. Intern Univ. Hosp., Shanghai, 1944-45; resident, research fellow NYU Hosp., 1948-50; resident physician in charge State Hosp. and Med. Ctr., Weston, W.Va., 1951-56; chief services, clin. dir. State Hosp., Logansport, Ind., 1957-84, ret., 1998. Active mem. Meml. Hosp., Logansport, Ind., 1968—. Research in cardiology and pharmacology; contbr. articles to profl. jours. Fellow: Am. Coll. Chest Physicians, Am. Psychiat. Assn.; mem.: AAAS, AMA, Cass County Med. Soc., Ind. Med. Assn. Office: Southeastern Med Ctr Walton IN 46994

CHU, JUDY MAY, assemblywoman; b. L.A., July 7, 1955; d. Judson and May C.; m. Michael Eng, Aug. 8, 1978. BA in Math., UCLA, 1974; MA in Clin. Psychology, Calif. Sch. Profl. Psychology, 1977, PhD, 1979. Lectr. UCLA, 1980-86; assoc. prof. L.A. City Coll., 1981-88; prof. East L.A. Coll., Monterey Park, 1988—2001; mem. Monterey Park City Council, 1988—2001, Calif. State Assembly, 2001—. Chair, select com. on hate crimes Calif. State Assembly, mem. select com. on language access, mem. rules, labor and employment com., environ. safety and toxic materials com., human svcs. com. & transportation com. Author, editor: Linking Our Lives: Chinese American Women in Los Angeles, 1984; contbr. articles profl. jours. Mem. city coun. City of Monterey Park, 1988—, mayor, 1990-91, 94-95; bd. dirs. Garvey Sch. Dist., 1985-88; chair Commn. for Sex Equity, L.A. Unified Sch. Dist., 1984-85; bd. dirs. Rebuild L.A.; mem. adv. com. U.S. Census Bur., 1994—; Bd. dirs. Gabriel Valley chpt. ARC; bd. dirs. Asian Youth Ctr., San Gabriel Valley United Way, West San Gabriel Valley Juvenile Diversion Project. Named One of 88 Leaders for 1988, L.A. Times, 1988, Dem. of Yr., 59th Assembly Dist. Dem. Com., 1989, Vol. of Yr. San Gabriel Valley chpt. United Way, 1989, L.A. Outstanding Founder, 1995; recipient Achievement award Asian Pacific Family Ctr., 1980, Pub. Svc. award Asian Pacific Legal Ctr., 1989, award for Excellence in Pub. Svc., UCLA Alumni, 1991, Leadership award West San Gabriel Valley chpt. ARC. Mem. Soroptimists. Office: Calif State Assembly PO Box 942849 Sacramento CA 94249 Business E-Mail: assemblymember.chu@asm.ca.gov.

CHU, KATHERINE K., music educator; arrived in U.S., 1983; d. James M. Chu and Lillian S. Yang. BA in Piano, Beijing Ctrl. Conservatory, 1982; BA in Profl. Music, Berklee Coll. Music, Boston, 1989; MS in Info. Sys., Northeastern U., Boston, 1992. Piano accompanist Children's Art Theater of China Welfare Soc., Shanghai, 1973—74; piano tchr. performance dept. Shanghai Drama Acad., 1974—78, Beijing Dance Acad., 1978—83; piano accompanist Boston Ballet, 1984—90; piano tchr., accompanist Boston Conservatory, 1985—91; piano tchr. KCHU Piano Studio, Boston, Phila. and Cupertino, Calif., 1985—. Bd. dirs. Steinway Soc. of the Bay Area, San Jose, Calif., 2002—04; participant 1st China-U.S. Dance Exch. Program, Boston Ballet, 1984. Mem.: Music Tchrs. Assn. Calif., Am. Coll. Musicians.

CHU, MARGARET S.Y., former federal agency administrator; b. Jan. 10, 1946; BS in Chemistry, Purdue U., 1967; PhD in Phys. Chemistry, U. Minn., 1973. Mem. tech. staff Sandia Nat. Labs., Albuquerque, 1980-86, disting. mem. tech. staff, 1986-91, tech. mgr., 1991-97, sr. mgr. nuclear waste mgmt., 1997-99, dir. nuclear waste mgmt., 1999—2002; dir. Civilian Radioactive Waste Mgmt. US Dept Energy, Washington, 2002—05. Contbr. numerous articles to sci. and profl. jours. Founding faculty mem. Albuquerque Chinese Sch., 1980. Mem. Am. Chem. Soc., N.M. Chinese Assn., Chinese Inst. Engrs. (bd. dirs., officer N.Mex. chpt. 1997-98).*

CHU, MORGAN, lawyer; b. N.Y.C., Dec. 27, 1950; s. Ju Chin and Ching (Chen) Chu; m. Helen M. Wong, Dec. 29, 1970. BA, UCLA, 1971, MA, 1972, PhD, 1973; MSL, Yale U., 1974; JD magna cum laude, Harvard U., 1976. Bar: Calif. 1976, admitted to practice: US Dist. Ct. (Ctrl. Dist.) Calif. 1977, US Dist. Ct. (No. Dist.) Calif. 1980, US Dist. Ct. Appeals (9th Cir.) 1980, US Dist. Ct. (So. Dist.) Calif. 1984, US Dist. Ct. (Ea. Dist.) Calif. 1986, US Ct. Appeals (Fed. Cir.) 1989, US Supreme Ct. 1991. Law clk. to Hon. Charles M. Merrill U.S. Ct. Appeals 9th Cir., San Francisco, 1976—77; assoc. Irell & Manella, LLP, LA, 1977-82, ptnr., 1982—, co-mng. ptnr., 1997—2003, exec. com., 1984—. Adj. prof. UCLA Sch. Law, 1979—82; judge pro tem LA Mcpl. Ct., 1980. Mem. editol. bd. Litigation News, 1981—84. Named Exec. of Yr. in Law, LA Bus. Jour., 1994, Best Intellectual Property Lawyer in Nation, Corp. Bd. Mem., 2001, Number One Intellectual Property Lawyer in Calif., Chambers Global, 2003—04, Top Super Lawyer in So. Calif., LA Mag., 2004; named one of 10 New Superstars, Legal Times of Wash., 1983, 100 Most Influential Lawyers in Am., Nat. Law Jour., 1994, 10 Top Trial Lawyers in Am., 1995, 100 Most Influential Lawyers in Am., 1997, 2000, Top 45 Lawyers Under 45, Am. Lawyer, 1995, Top 10 Most Influential Lawyers in Calif., Calif. Law Bus., 1999, 12 Superstars, Corp. Bd. Mem., 2001; recipient Significant Achievement award for excellence and innovation in alternative dispute resolution, Ctr. for Pub. Resources, 1987; fellow postdoctoral fellow, Yale U., 1974. Mem.: ABA (chmn. high tech. intellectual property and patent trials subcom. 1986—90, trial practice com., litigation sect.), LA Intellectual Property Law Assn. (bd. dirs. 1991—93, bd. dirs. pub. counsel 1993—, exec. com. bd. dirs. pub. counsel 1995—), LA County Bar Assn. (judiciary com. 1983—2001), Calif. Bar Assn. Office: Irell & Manella LLP Ste 900 1800 Avenue of the Stars Los Angeles CA 90067-4276 Office Phone: 310-277-1010. Office Fax: 310-203-7199. E-mail: mchu@irell.com.*

CHU, PAUL CHING-WU, physicist, educator; b. Hunan, China, Dec. 2, 1941; arrived in U.S., 1963; m. May P. Chern; children: Claire, Albert. BS, Cheng-Kung U., Taiwan, 1962; MS, Fordham U., 1965; PhD, U. Calif., San Diego, 1968; PhD (hon.), Fordham U., 1988, Northwestern U., 1988, Chinese U. of Hong Kong, 1988, Fla. Internat. U., 1989, SUNY, 1989, Whittier Coll., 1991, Hong Kong Bapt. U., 1999. 2d lt. Nationalist Chinese Air Forces, 1962—63; tchg. asst. Fordham U., Bronx, NY, 1963—65; rsch. asst. U. Calif., San Diego, 1965—68; tech. staff Bell Labs., Murray Hill, NJ, 1968—70; asst. prof. physics Cleve. State U., 1970—73, assoc. prof., 1973—75, prof., 1975—79; prof. physics U. Houston, 1979—, dir. magnetic info. rsch. lab., 1984—88, dir. Space Vacuum Epitaxy Ctr., 1986—88, dir. Tex. Ctr. for Superconductivity, 1987—2001, dir. NSF/materials rsch. sci. and engring. ctr., 1996—97; prin. investigator Lawrence Berkeley Nat. Lab., 1999—; convenor Heads of Univs. Com., Hong Kong, 2003—; pres. Hong Kong U. Sci. and Tech., 2001—; exec. dir. Ctr. Superconductivity, 2005—. Dir. Solid State Physics Program NSF, Washington, 1986—87; resident, rsch. assoc. Argonne (Ill.) Nat. Lab., 1972; vis. scientist Hansens Physics Lab., Stanford, 1973; vis. staff mem. Los Alamos (N.Mex.) Sci. Lab., 1975—80; chmn. organizing com. Internat. Conf. on High Pressure Low Temperature Physics, 1977; M.D. Anderson chair physics M.D. Anderson Found., 1987—89; T.L.L. Temple chair sci. T.L.L. Temple Found., 1987—; hon. prof. Zhongshan U., 1988, Chinese Acad. Scis. Physics Inst., 1979, Nankai U., 1991, Chinese U. Sci. and Tech., 1991, Nanjing U., 1996, Dongnan U., 2003; mem. internat. adv. bd. Materials Chemistry and Physics, 1992—; bd. dirs. Coalition for the Comml. Application of Superconductors, 1989—; co-chmn. solid state physics symposium Vereschagin Internat. Conf. on High Pressure Physics and Tech., Moscow, 1979; mem. White House ad hoc rev. panel on long-range plan for R & D of superconductivity, 1989; mem. rsch. adv. com. Inst. for Tech. and Strategic Rsch., 1989; adv. bd. Internat. Inst. Cond. Math., Physics U., Brasilia, 1993—; vis. Miller rsch. prof. U. Calif., Berkeley, 1991; mem. adv. com. to redesign the space sta. The White House, Washington, 1993; mem. sch. adv. bd. Ctr. Nanoscale Sci. and Tech., Rice U., 1995—; internat. adv. com. Hong Kong Bapt. U., 1995—; internat. adv. bd. China-Am. Tech. Corp., 1995—; mem. adv. com. on rsch. planning Higher Edn. Coordinating Bd., State of Tex., 1997—2000; invited contbr. Nat. Millenium Time Capsule, 2000; bd. dirs. S.S. Chern Found. Math. Rsch., 2000—; pres. Applied Superconductivity Corp., 2000—02; bd. dirs. Applied Superconductivity Conf., 2000—; mem. Academia Sinica Inst. Physics Acad. Adv. Com., 2001—; adv. Hong Kong Area of Excellence Project on "Chinese Med. Rsch. and Further Development", 2001—; mem. Academia Sinica Central Adv. Com., 2002—, Academia Sinica Coun., 2002—; chmn. ad hoc Com. on Future Nat. Energy, 2002—; dir. search com. Academia Sinica Ctr. Applied Sci. Engineering Rsch., 2002—; mem. Condensed Matter Experiment Screening Com. Nat. Acad. Scis., 2003—; mem. rsch. adv. bd. U. Tex., Dallas, 2004—; mem. adv. bd. Ctr. for Nanomagnetic Systems U. Houston, 2004—, mem. pres.'s exec. adv. coun., 2004—; mem. founding governing bd. Acad. Medicine, Engring. and Sci. Tex., 2004—; mem. program adv. com. Inst. Advanced Studies, Nanyung Tech. U., 2005—; cons. in field. Mem. editl. bd.: High Tech. Bus., 1988—, Modern Physics Letters B, 1988—, Applied Superconductivity, 1992—98, Indian Jour. Pure and Applied Physics, 1992—, News and Reviews of Physics in China Today, 1992—, Internat. Jour. Modern Physics, 1988—, Brazilian Jour. Physics, 1995—, Sci. in China, 1997—, Chinese Sci. Bull., 1997—, Applied Physics Rev. (Korea), 1998—2000; contbr. articles to profl. jours. Internat. adv. com. World Lab. Pan Am. Ctr. for Collaboration in Sci. and Tech., 1998—; bd. dirs. T.S. Chang Scholarship Found., 1999—. Named hon. citizen, State of Tex., 1987, City of Houston, 1987, Best Rschr. in U.S., U.S. News and World Report, 1990, one of 20th Century's 100 most intellectual people in gas and electric, Century of Power, Heat Energy, 2000, honoree, Alliance for Multicultural Cmty. Svcs., 2000; recipient Phys. and Math. Sci. award, N.Y. Acad. Sci., 1987, Leroy Randle Grumman medal, Grumman Corp., 1987, Achievement award, Chine Am. Acad. and Profl. Assn., 1987, Disting. Alumnus award, U. Calif., San Diego, 1987, Faculty Rsch. award, U. Houston, 1987, Sigma Xi Rsch. Excellence award, 1987, Achievement award, NASA, 1987, Nat. Medal Sci., Pres. of U.S., 1988, Disting. Alumnus award, Cheng-Kung U., 1988, Medal of Sci. Merit, World Cultural Coun., 1989, Founders' prize, Texas Instruments, 1990, St. Martin de Porres award, 1990, Superconductivity Excellence award in sci. accomplishments, World Congress on Superconductivity, 1994, Bernd Matthias prize, 4th Internat. Conf. on Materials and Mechanisms of Superconductivity, High Temperature Superconductors, 1994, Disting. Sci. Achievement award, Washington Met. Assn. Chinese Am. Profls., 1998, Houston Hall of Fame award, George Bush Internat. Airport, 1999, Sharif U., 1999, Esther Farfel award, U. Houston, 2000, Houston Hall of Fame award, Greater Houston Conv. and Vis. Bur., 1988, John Fritz medal, United Engring. Found., 2001. Fellow: Chinese Acad. Scis., Tex. Acad. Scis., Am. Phys. Soc. (teller divsn. Sol. St. Physics 1976, internat. prize com. 1988—89, Internat. prize for new materials 1988); mem.: NAS (mem. panel on High Temperature Superconductivity 1987, sect. co-chair 1992—95, selection com., Comstock award 1988, John J. Carty award for advancement of sci. 2005), AAAS, Russian Acad. Engring., State of Tex. Sci. and Tech. Coun., Electromagnetic Acad., Third World Acad. Scis., Academia Sinica (Taipei, mem. adv. com. Inst. Physics 1997—2000), Am. Acad. Arts and Scis., Royal Soc. Encouragement of Arts Mfrs. and Commerce. Office: U Houston Texas Ctr Superconductivity 202 Houston Science Center Houston TX 77204-5002 Office Phone: 713-743-8222. Business E-Mail: cwchu@uh.edu.

CHU, RICHARD CHAO-FAN, mechanical engineer; b. Beijing, Hopei, Peoples' Republic China, May 28, 1933; came to U.S., 1958, naturalized, 1968; s. Liang Hsi and Yun Hwa (Wang) C.; m. Theresa Sou-Chin Lee, Aug. 24, 1963; children: Banjamin, Benson, Benedict, Bonita. BSME, Nat. Cheng-Keng U., Tainan, Taiwan, 1958; MSME, Purdue U., 1960. Jr. assoc. engr. IBM Corp., Poughkeepsie, N.Y., 1960-64, sr. assoc. engr., 1964-65, project engr., mgr., 1965-67, devel. engr., mgr., 1967-69, sr. engr., mgr., 1969-75, program mgr., product technology, 1975-79, program mgr., engring. lab., 1979-83, fellow, 1983—; v.p. IBM Acad. Tech., 1990, pres., 1991. Author 2 books; patentee in field; contbr. articles to profl. jours. Pres. Mid-Hudson Chinese-Am. Civic Assn., Poughkeepsie, 1969. Recipient Disting. Alumnus award Purdue U., 1984, Outstanding Alumni award Nat. Cheng-Kung U., 1986. Fellow ASME (Heat Transfer Meml. award 1986), AAAS; mem. N.Y. Acad. Sci., Nat. Acad. Engring. Republican. Roman Catholic. Avocations: swimming, jogging, sailing, skiing, wind surfing. Home: 30 Saint Andrews Ln Hopewell Junction NY 12533 Office: IBM Corp P520/003 Poughkeepsie NY 12601 Office Phone: 845-433-5236. Business E-Mail: rcchu@us.ibm.com.

CHU, RODERICK GONG-WAH, educational administrator; b. N.Y.C., Jan. 17, 1949; s. Norton Yuen and Frances (Liang) C. BS, U. Mich., 1969; MBA with honors, Cornell U., 1971; D in Pub. Svc. (hon.), U. Rio Grande, 1999; D in Pub. Svc., Otterbein U., 2003; LHD (hon.), Youngstown State U., 1999, Cin, State Tech. and Cmty. Coll., 2001, Shawnee State U., 2004; assoc. of sci. (hon.), Edison Cmty. Coll., 2001; HHD (hon.), Capital U., 2003. Staff analyst Arthur Andersen and Co., N.Y.C., 1971-75, mgr., 1975-81, ptnr., 1981-83; commr. Taxation and Fin., pres. State Tax Commn. State of N.Y., Albany, 1983-88; ptnr. Andersen Cons., N.Y.C., 1988-95, worldwide mng. ptnr., state and local govt. practice, 1989-91, worldwide mng. ptnr., govt. practice, 1991-92; chancellor Ohio Bd. Regents, Columbus, Ohio, 1998—. Bd. dirs. Housing Fin. Agy., Med. Care Facilities Fin. Agy., Project Fin. Agy., Affordable Housing Corp., 1983-86, N.E. States Tax Ofcls. Assn., 1983-88, Fedn. Tax Adminstrs., 1985-88, Nat. Tax Assn.-Tax Inst. Am., 1986-88, mem. adv. bd. Coun. for Excellence in Govt., 1991-93, trustee, 1993-95, mem. N.Y.C. real property tax reform commn., 1993; mem. Ohio Workforce Devel. Bd., 1998-1999; bd. dirs. BEST (Bldg. Excellent Schs. for Today and the 21st Century), 1998—; mem. Ohio Commn. on African Am. Males, 1998-2003. Bd. dirs., bd. overseers Jacob's Pillow Dance Festival, Becket, Mass., 1984-97; mem. Cornell U. Coun., 1988-92, 94-98, 2001-05, mem. dean's alumni exec. coun. Johnson Sch. Grad. Mgmt., 1988-90, adv. coun., 1991-98, outdoor edn. adv. coun., 1992-98, strategic planning adv. bd., 1992-96; trustee SUNY, 1990-98, chmn. exec. compensation com., 1993-98; mem. pres.'s adv. coun. China Inst. Am., 1990-94; co-chair pres. circle The Asia Soc., 1994-97; mem. adv. bd. Barnard-Columbia Ctr. for Leadership in Urban Pub. Policy, 1994-98; mem. State Higher Edn. Exec. Officers, 1998-, treas., 2002, pres., 2003, Gov's Workforce Policy Bd., 1999-, MidWest Higher Edn. Commn., 2000-, Edn. Commn. of States, 2001-, exec. com., 2003-, steering com., 2004-, Ohio Third Frontier Commn., 2003-, Gov's Commn. on Higher Edn. and the Econ., 2003-04, Educators Standards Bd., 2004-, SchoolNet Commn., 2004; trustee The Coll. Bd., 2004-, Ohio Hist. Soc., 1998-. Recipient Man of Yr. award Chinese-Am. Planning Coun., 1984, N.Y.C. Police Dept., Asian Jade Soc., 1984, Disting. Achievement award United Chinese Am. League, 1985, Spl. Recognition award Asian Ams. for Affirmative Action, 1986, Champion of Excellence award Orgn. Chinese Am., 1986, Outstanding

Chinese Entrepreneur award Chinese Mgmt. Assn., 1991; Paul Harris fellow Rotary Internat., 1988, 92. Mem. Am. Soc. Pub. Adminstrn. (hon.), Cornell Club (N.Y.C.), Capital Club (Columbus), New Albany Country Club, Met. Opera Club, Cornell Asian Alumni Assn., Phi Kappa Phi. Republican. Avocations: skiing, photography, golf, fly fishing. Office: Ohio Bd Regents 30 E Broad St Fl 36 Columbus OH 43215-3414 Office Phone: 614-466-0887. Business E-Mail: schu@regents.state.oh.us.

CHU, SAMUEL C., history professor, writer; b. Shanghai, Mar. 25, 1929; arrived in U.S., 1941, naturalized, 1960; s. Shih-Ming and Grace Zia Chu; m. Lucy M. Kao, June 1, 1957; children: Elaine Fan, Laura Chu Stokes, Jonathan. AB, Dartmouth Coll., Hanover, N.H., 1951; MA, Columbia Univ., N.Y., 1953, PhD, 1958. Cert. East Asia Inst. Columbia Univ., 1953. Asst. prof. SUNY, New Paltz, NY, 1958, Bucknall Univ., Lewisburg, Pa., 1958—60; assoc. prof. Univ. Pitts., Pitts., 1960—69; prof., program dir. Ohio State Univ., Columbus, Ohio, 1969—95, prof. emeritus history, 1995—. Vis. prof. Dartmouth Coll., Hanover, NH, 1964, Univ. Mich., Ann Arbor, Mich., 1967—68, Georgetown Univ., Washington, 1982; chair fellowship com. Wang Am. Inst. Grad. Studies, Tewesbury, Mass., 1982—87; adv. com. ACLS, Prog. on Medicine China, N.Y., 1965. Author: Reformer in Modern China:Chang Chein 1853-1926, 1965; co-editor: Li Hung-Chang & China's Early Modernization, 1994, Passage to The Golden Gate, 1967; editor: Madame Chiang Kaishek and Her China, 2005; contbr. articles pub. to profl. jour. Pres. China Image Promotion Assn, Columbus, Ohio, 1970—72; maj. donor hosp., sch. religion groups; mem. orgn. of Wilbur Com. Columbus Univ., N.Y.C., 1998—2001; v.p. Dartmouth Club of Ctrl. Ohio, Columbus, Ohio, 2002—04. Grantee Fulbright and CSCPRC rsch. grant to China, 1981—82; scholar Fulbright Rsch. Scholar, Taiwan, 1961—62, ACLS, Japan, Korea, 1981. Mem.: Ohio Acad. of History, Midwest Conf. on Asian Affairs (Jackson Bailey award 2003), Assn. for Asia Studies, Am. Hist. Assn. Democrat. Protestant. Achievements include numerous occassions as invited speaker and at Inter-Am. Defense Coll. at Ft. McNair (DC), lectr. on China and Japan on many cruise ships, and with tourist groups. Avocations: public speaking, reading, sports. Home: 3553 Olentangy Blvd Columbus OH 43214 Office: Ohio State Univ 106 Dulles Hall 230 W 17th Ave Columbus OH 43210

CHU, STEVEN, physics professor, director; b. St. Louis, Feb. 28, 1948; s. Ju Chin and Ching Chen (Li) C.; children: Geoffrey, Michael. BS in Physics, AB in Math., U. Rochester, 1970; PhD in Physics, U. Calif., Berkeley, 1976. Post doctoral fellow U. Calif., Berkeley, 1976-78; mem. tech. staff Bell Labs., Murray Hill, NJ, 1978-83; head quantum electronics rsch. dept. AT&T Bell Labs., Holmdel, NJ, 1983-87; prof. physics and applied physics Stanford (Calif.) U., 1987—2004, Frances and Theodore Geballe prof. physics and applied physics, 1990—93, chmn. physics dept., 1999—2001; dir. Lawrence Berkeley Nat. Lab., Berkeley, Calif., 2004—. Morris Loeb lectr. Harvard U., Cambridge, Mass., 1987-88; vis. prof. Coll. de France, fall 1990; Richtmeyer Meml. lectr., 1990. Contbr. papers in laser spectroscopy and atomic physics, especially laser cooling and trapping, and precision spectroscopy of leptonic atoms, polymer and biophysics. Recipient Humboldt sr. scientist award, Sci. for Art prize, 1995; co-recipient King Faisal prize for sci., 1993, Nobel prize for physics, 1997; Woodrow Wilson fellow 1970, doctoral fellow NSF, 1970-74, postdoctoral fellow 1977-78, Guggenheim fellow, 1996. Fellow Am. Phys. Soc. (Herbert P. Broida prize for laser spectroscopy 1987, chair laser sci. topical group 1989, A.L. Schawlow prize 1994), Optical Soc. Am. (William F. Meggars award 1994), Am. Acad. Arts and Scis.; mem. NAS, Academica Sinica, Am. Philos. Soc., Chinese Acad. Sci. (fgn.), Korean Acad. Sci. and Tech. (fgn.). Achievements include development of methods to cool and trap atoms with laser light. Office: Lawrence Bekeley Nat Lab 1 Cyclotron Rd Mail Stop 50A4133 Berkeley CA 94720 Office Phone: 510-486-5111. Office Fax: 650-723-9173. Business E-Mail: SChu@lbl.gov. E-mail: schu@stanford.edu.*

CHU, TSANN MING, immunochemist, educator; b. Kaohsiung, Taiwan, Apr. 18, 1938; came to U.S., 1963, naturalized, 1971; s. Tsi Fa and Su Lian (Sun) C.; m. Bonnie Diane Covert, Sept. 28, 1967; children: Nancy, Daniel. BS, Nat. Taiwan U., 1961; MS, N.C. State U., 1965; PhD, Pa. State U., 1967; DSc (hon.), N.C. State U., 2001. Fellow Med. Found. Buffalo, 1967-69, Buffalo Gen. Hosp., 1969-70; assoc. chief cancer rsch. scientist, dir. diagnostic immunology and clin. chemistry Roswell Park Meml. Inst., Buffalo, 1970-76, dir. cancer rsch. in diagnostic immunology research and biochemistry, 1976-98; asst. prof. exptl. pathology SUNY, Buffalo, 1970-74, assoc. prof., 1974-77, prof., 1977-98, prof. emeritus, 1999—. Cons. nat. prostatic cancer project Nat. Cancer Inst., NIH, 1973-84, mem. com. cancer immunodiagnosis, 1978-79, mem. tumor immunology com., 1979-81; mem. immunology and immunotherapy com. Am. Cancer Soc., 1979-81; rsch. cons. Nat. Sci. Coun., Taiwan, 1976-94, vis. prof., 1986; adv. coun. Internat. Soc. Oncodevel. Biology and Medicine, 1978-94; mem. sci. rev. panel N.J. Commn. on Cancer Rsch., 1983-85, 87-99; cons. Merit Rev. Bd., VA, 1980-85, 94-98; mem. cancer therapeutic program rev. com. Nat. Cancer Inst., 1985-88; reviewers reserve NIH, 1988-92, 94-98; mem. scientific adv. coun. Internat. Acad. Tumor Marker Oncology, 1986-1998; mem. sci. coun. Swedish Cancer Found., 1988-1998; adv. com. Nat. Def. Med. Ctr. Cancer Rsch. Group, 1993-97. Mem. editorial bd. Tumor Biology, 1983-92, Jour. Clin. Lab. Analysis, 1985—, Jour. Tumor Marker Oncology, 1988-2003, Cancer Investigation, 1989-2003; contbr. over 300 articles to profl. jours. United Health Found. Western N.Y. fellow, 1968-69; recipient Presdl. Citation award Am. Urol. Assn., 1993, Am. Found. for Urologic Disease, 1993, Dornier Innovative Rsch. award, 1993, Roswell Park Cancer Inst. and Geritourinary Cancer Symposium award, 1993, Disting. Alumni award Pa. State U., 1994, N.C. State U., 1995, Abbott award Internat. Soc. Oncodevel. Biology and Medicine, 1996, Achievement in Health Care award D'Youville Coll., 1998, Honors award Pres. U.S., 1999, Western NY Pioneers of Sci. award, 2002; Alumni fellow Pa. State U., 1997. Mem. Am. Chem. Soc. (Jacob F. Schoellkopf medal 1997), Am. Assn. Clin. Chemists (Van Slyke award 1997), Am. Assn. Cancer Rsch. (cancer rsch. cover legend 1998), Am. Assn. Immunologists, Am. Urol. Assn. (hon.), Am. Soc. Biochem. and Molecular Biology, Am. Assn. Investigative Pathology, Biochem. Soc. (London), Am. Urological Assn. (hon.), Buffalo Urol. Soc., Phi Lambda Upsilon. Achievements include development of PSA test for early detection of prostate cancer. Office: Roswell Park Cancer Inst Elm And Carlton St Buffalo NY 14263-0001

CHU, VALENTIN YUAN-LING, author; b. Shanghai, Republic of China, Feb. 14, 1919; came to U.S., 1956, naturalized, 1961; s. Thomas V.D. and Rowena S.N. (Zee) Tsu; m. Victoria Chao-yu Tsao, Sept. 25, 1954; 1 child, Douglas Chi-hua. BA, St. John's U, Shanghai, 1940. Asst. Shanghai Mcpl. Coun., 1940-42; asst. mgr., pub., printer Thomas Chu & Sons, Shanghai, 1943-45; chief reporter China Press, Shanghai, 1945-49; pub. rels. officer Cen. Air Transport Corp., Hong Kong, 1949; Hong Kong corr. Time & Life mags., Hong Kong, 1949-56; with Time, Inc., N.Y.C., 1956-76; writer, asst. editor Time-Life Books, N.Y.C., 1968-76; assoc. editor Reader's Digest Gen. Books, N.Y.C., 1978-83. Lectr. on China. Author: Ta Ta, Tan Tan---Fight Fight, Talk Talk, 1963, Thailand Today, 1968, (with others) U.S.A., A Visitor's Handbook, 1969, The Yin-Yang Butterfly---Ancient Chinese Sexual Secrets for Western Lovers, 1993; contbr. articles to popular mags. Recipient spl. award UN Internat. Essay Contest, 1948. Mem. Authors League Am., Authors Guild, China Inst. in Am., Inst. Noetic Scis. Presbyterian. Home: 2934 Saklan Indian Dr Walnut Creek CA 94595-3911 Personal E-mail: valentinchu@aol.com.

CHU, WAI C., engineer, researcher; arrived in US, 1990; s. Suet Fung Chu and Suet King Lau; m. Le Quan Luong, Dec. 10, 2001. BS in electronics engring., Simon Bolivar U., Caracas, 1990; MSEE, Stevens Inst. Tech., Hoboken, NJ, 1992; PhD, Pa. State U., 1998. Field apps. engr. Tex. Instruments Hong Kong, 1993—94; mem. tech. staff Intervideo Inc., Fremont, Calif., 1999—2001; sr. rsch. engr. DoCoMo Comms. Labs. USA Inc., San Jose, Calif., 2001—; R & D engr. Digital Video Express, Herndon, Va., 1998—99. Author: (engring. textbook) Speech Coding Algorithms: Foundation and Evolution of Standardized Coders, 2003; contbr. articles to profl. jours. Mem.: IEEE, Audio Engring. Soc. Achievements include research in window optimization in linear prediction analysis; DCT-based image watermarking using subsampling; vector quantization of harmonic magnitudes in speech coding applications survey and new technique; vector quantization of neural networks. Personal E-mail: wcc2@ieee.org.

CHU, WEI-KAN, physicist, researcher; b. Kunming, China, Apr. 1, 1940; came to the U.S., 1963; s. Din Yuan and Y.C. (Wong) C.; m. Agnes Kuen, May 28, 1966; 1 child, Lawrence D. BS in Physics, Cheng-Kung U., 1962; MS, Baylor U., 1965, PhD, 1969. Postdoctoral fellow Baylor U., Waco, Tex., 1969-72; rsch. fellow, sr. rsch. fellow Calif. Inst. Tech., Pasadena, 1972-75; staff advisor, sr. engr. IBM, Hopewell Junction, N.Y., 1975-81; rsch. prof. physics U. N.C., Chapel Hill, 1981-88; disting. prof. physics U. Houston, 1989—2002, Robert A. Welsh prof. physics, 2002—. Panel mem. NSF, Washington, 1992, U.S. Dept. Energy, Washington, 1992, 93, 94, 97. Co-author: Backscattering Spectrometry, 1978; co-editor: HTS Materials, Bulk Processing and Bulk Applications, 1992, Procs. of the 6th U.S.-Japan Workshop on High Tc Superconductors, 1994, Procs. of the 10th Anniversary High Temperature Superconductors Workshop on Physics, Materials and Applications, 1996, Procs. of 6th Internat. Conf. Materials and Mechanisms of Superconductivity and High Temperature Superconductors, VI, 2000; contbr. chpts. to books and numerous articles to profl. jours.; holder 22 U.S. patents in field. Recipient Disting. Achievement award Baylor U., Waco, 1991, Assn. Am.-Chinese Profls., 1994, Superconductivity award of excellence for outstanding individual accomplishment World Congress on Superconductivity, 1994, Outstanding Alumni of Yr. Nat. Cheng-Kung U., 1997, 98. Fellow Am. Phys. Soc.; mem. Materials Rsch. Soc. Office: U Houston Tex Ctr Superconductivity Houston TX 77204-5002 Office Phone: 713-743-8252. Business E-Mail: wkchu@uh.edu.

CHU, XUEFENG, science educator; s. Baoyuan Chu and Hui Liu; m. Shuhong Yu, Jan. 3, 1990; 1 child, Yihang. BS (hon.), Inner Mongolia Agrl. U., Huhhot, China, 1984; MS, China U. of Geoscis., Beijing, 1991; PhD, U. Calif., Davis, 2002. Mem. faculty dept. environ. scis. China U. of Geoscis., Beijing, 1991—97; rsch. asst., postgrad. rschr. U. Calif., Davis, 1997—2002; asst. prof. Annis Water Resources Inst., Grand Valley State U., Muskegon, 2002—. Author: The Encyclopedia of Water, International Association of Hydrological Sciences. Grantee, U. Calif. Sys.-Wide Toxic Substances Rsch. and Tchg. Program, 2000—02, U.S. EPA CWA Sect. 319, Mich. Dept. of Environ. Quality, 2004—. Mem.: ASCE (EWRI groundwater mgmt. com.), Nat. Ground Water Assn., Internat. Assn. of Hydrological Scis., Am. Water Resources Assn. (hydrology and watershed mgmt. com.), Am. Geophys. Union. Achievements include development of three Windows-based hydrologic and environmental modeling software packages. Home: 3318 Nina Ln Muskegon MI 49441 Office: AWRI Grand Valley State U 740 W Shoreline Dr Muskegon MI 49441 Office Phone: 616-331-3987. Office Fax: 616-331-3864. Personal E-mail: chux@gvsu.edu.

CHUA, AMY, law educator; AB magna cum laude, Harvard U., 1984, JD cum laude, 1987. Law clk. to Hon. Patricia M. Wald US Ct. Appeals, DC Cir., 1987—88; assoc. Cleary, Gottlieb, Steen & Hamilton, 1988—93; assoc. prof. law Duke U., 1994—99, prof. law, 1999—2001; John M. Duff, Jr. prof. law Yale U., New Haven, 2001—. Vis. prof. law Columbia U., 1999, Stanford U., 2000, NYU, 2000. Author: World on Fire: How Exporting Free Market Democracy Breeds Ethnic Hatred and Global Instability, 2003; contbr. articles to law jours. Grantee Internat. Affairs Fellowship, Coun. Foreign Relations, 1998—99. Mem.: NY State Bar. Office: Yale Law Sch PO Box 208215 New Haven CT 06520 E-mail: amy.chua@yale.edu.

CHUANG, ALFRED S., information technology executive; BS in Computer Sci., U. San Francisco; MS in Computer Sci., U. Calif., Davis, Calif. Mgmt. positions in software product devel., network infrastructure, systems architecture & operations mgmt. Sun Microsystems, Inc., 1986—94; former founder, dir. Sun Intercontinental Operations; former corp. dir., chief scientist SunIntegration Svcs.; from founder (with Bill Coleman and Ed Scott) to pres., CEO BEA Sys., Inc., San Jose, Calif., 1995—2001, pres., 2001—, CEO, 2001—, chmn., 2002—. Bd. dir Tealeaf Tech. Trustee U. San Francisco. Office: BEA Systems Inc 2315 N First St San Jose CA 95131 Office Phone: 408-570-8000. Office Fax: 408-570-8901.*

CHUANG, TSU-YI, dermatologist, epidemiologist, educator; b. Amoy, China, May 21, 1946; arrived in U.S., 1976, naturalized, 1988; s. Hsi and Kia-Ling (Huang) C.; m. Lydia Ling-Chuan Lee, Dec. 22, 1973; children: Chester, Nancy. MB, Nat. Taiwan U., Taipei, 1971; MPH in Epidemiology, U. Wash., 1978. Diplomate Am. Bd. Dermatology, Am. Bd. Preventive Medicine. From asst. prof. to assoc. prof. dermatology U. Wis., Madison, 1984-92; chief dermatology svc. Middleton VA Med. Ctr., Madison, 1984-90; assoc. prof. dermatology Wright State U., Dayton, Ohio, 1990-95, dir. immunopathology lab., 1994-95; dir. dermatology clinic Frederick A. White Health Ctr., Dayton, 1995; prof. dermatology Ind. U., Indpls., 1995—2003, med. dir. melanoma program, 1996—2003, Arthur L. Norins prof., dir. dermatology clinic, 1999—2001; clin. prof. dermatology U. South Fla. Coll. Medicine, Tampa, 2004—. Vis. prof. Wright State U., Dayton, 1990, Nat. Taiwan U., Taipei, 1991-97; vis. scientist Mayo Clinic, Rochester, 1986-92, Moss lectr. Meriter Found., 2002; mem. guidelines/outcomes com., 1996-2001, melanoma guidelines task force, 1997-2001, melanoma/skin cancer com., 2004—. Co-author: Conn's Current Therapy, 1992, The Challenge of Dermato-Epidemiology, 1997, Sleisenger & Fordtran's Gastrointestinal and Liver Disease, 2002; ad hoc reviewer Arch Dermatol., Chgo., 1990-99, Jour. Am. Acad. Dermatology, 1986-2004, Internat. Jour. Dermatology, 2001-04; editor Dermatologica Sinica, Taipei, 1994-96; contbr. over 100 articles to profl. jours. Pres. Rochester (Minn.) Chinese Culture Assn., 1980-82; v.p. Orgn. of Chinese Ams., Madison, 1986-90; pres. Midwest Chinese Christian Assn., Dayton, 1993-94, Indpls., 1996-97, Indiana Chinese-Am. Profls. Assn., Indlps. 1998. Rsch. grantee U. Wis., 1985-89, Schering, Glaxo, Genentech, Amgen 1986-2004; VA merit rev. bd. grantee Dept. Vets. Affairs, 1986-88, 90-94; recipient Burdette-Kunkel award Mary Margaret Walther Program for Cancer Care Rsch., 1996-97, 21st Century Research & Technology Fund award, 2000-02, Fellow Am. Acad. Dermatology (editl. cons. Am. Acad. Dermatology jour. 1986-2001), Am. Soc. for Dermatol. Surgery; mem. Soc. for Investigative Dermatology, Am. Acad. Dermatology, Ind. Chinese Profls. Assn. (pres. 1998). Achievements include first historical cohort study of human papilloma virus infection in U.S. in a defined population, first historical cohort study of genital herpes virus infection in U.S. in a defined population, first incidence study of polymyalgia rheumatica in the U.S. in a defined population, first population-based incidence study of skin cancer in U.S. in two well-defined populations. Office: 6450 38th Ave N Ste 420 Saint Petersburg FL 33710 also: Advanced Dermatology 10875 Park Blvd Ste A Seminole FL 33772 Office Phone: 727-344-6851. Business E-Mail: chuang007@yahoo.com.

CHUANG, YII-DER, retired manufacturing executive, diplomat; b. Chekiang, China, July 1, 1934; came to U.S., 1964; s. W.C. Chuang and Y.F. Chang; m. Chung-hwa Lee, Jan. 6, 1968; children: David, Michael, Nancy. BS in Automotive Engring., Chung-Cheng Inst., 1957; MS in Metall. Engring., Mich. State U., 1966; PhD in Materials Sci., NYU, 1971. Dir. hot lab. Inst. Nuclear Energy Rsch. Atomic Energy Coun., Exec. Yuan, Taoyuan, Taiwan, 1972-82; sr. scientist sci and tech. adv. group Exec. Yuan, Taipei, Taiwan, 1980-84; dep. dir. prep. office materials rsch. lab. Indsl. Tech. Rsch. Inst., Hsinchu, Taiwan, 1981-82; dep. dir. materials rsch. and devel. ctr. Chung Shan Inst. Sci. and Tech., Taoyuan, Taiwan, 1982-84; dir. sci. divsn. Taipei Econ. and Cultural Office, Houston, 1984—86, San Francisco, 1986—92, Taipei Econ. and Cultural Rep. Office, Washington, 1992—2000; pres. H&Q Taiwan Co. Ltd., H&Q Asia Pacific, Taipei, 2000—02; ret., 2003. Exec. sec. materials steering com. Exec. Yuan, 1981-84; dir. Rep. Office Hsin-Chu Sci.-based Indsl. Park Adminstrn., Taiwan, 1986-92; patent reviewer Nat. Bur. Standards, Taiwan, 1973-83; exec. sec. Commn. Third Asian-Pacific Corrosion Control Conf., 1981-83. Editor: Nuclear Sci. Jour., 1978—79; contbr. over 38 articles to profl. jours. Disting. scholar NYU, 1972. Mem. Nuclear Energy Soc. of Rep. of China, Chinese Soc. Materials Sci. (editor Materials Sci. Quarterly 1972-78), Chinese Inst. Mining and Metall. Engrs., Chinese Soc. Mech. Engrs., Monte Jade Sci. and Tech. Assn., Alpha Sigma Mu. Home: 11F-5 No 70 Sec 2 An-He Rd Taipei 10680 Taiwan E-mail: ydchuang@ms77.hinet.net.

CHUAQUI, MIGUEL BASIM, composer, educator; b. Berkeley, Calif., Oct. 17, 1964; s. Rolando Basim Chuaqui and Kathleen Ellen Henderson; m. Lisa Marie Chaufty, May 10, 1996; children: Nicolas Basim, Anna Magdalena. BA in Math. and Music, U. Calif., Berkeley, 1987, MA in Music, 1989, PhD, 1994. Music lectr. dept. music San Francisco State U., 1992—93; music instr. dept. music Laney Coll. of Oakland, Calif., 1992—96; assoc. composer Ctr. for New Music and Audio Techs., Berkeley, Calif., 1994—96; asst. prof. U. Utah Sch. of Music, Salt Lake City, 1996—2002, assoc. prof., 2003—. Bd. dir.s Earplay New Music Ensemble, San Francisco, 1994—96; founding mem. Composers' Coalition, San Francisco, 1995; dir. Ussachevsky Electronic Music Studio, U. Utah Sch. of Music, Salt Lake City, 2002—. Composer: (songs) Melancolia en las Familias (De Lorenzo Prize for composition), Cuarteto Claroscuro, Juego (Eisner award, 1991), CRI: Exchange Latin America, (albums) Music By Miguel Chuaqui, 2005. Recipient commn., Fromm Found., Harvard U., 2001, Koussevitzky Found. at Libr. of Congress, 2004, award in Music, Am. Acad. of Arts and Letters, 2004; Charles Ives scholar, AAAL, 1994, Wellesley Composers Conf. fellow, 1997, Individual Artist grantrr, Utah Arts Coun., Nat. Endowment for the Arts, 2000, Aaron Copland rec. grantee, 2004. Fellow: Asociación Nacional de Compositores de Chile (life); mem.: Coll. Music Soc., Broadcast Music Inc., Am. Music Ctr., Phi Beta Kappa. Office: Univ Utah Sch of Music 1375 E Presidents Cir Salt Lake City UT 84112 Office Phone: 801-585-3720. Business E-Mail: m.chuaqui@utah.edu.

CHUBB, CHARLES RAY, physicist, researcher; b. Springfield, Mo., Apr. 18, 1931; s. Prosser Sylvester and Harriet Elizabeth Chubb; m. Jeanne R. C. (div. 1978); children: Alan C., Paula J. Mello, Thomas J., Lisa C. Rottler. BS in Engring. Physics, U. Ill., 1953; MS in Physics, U. Mo., 1958, PhD in Physics, 1963. Rsch. engr. N.Am. Aviation, L.A., 1953-54; mem. scientific and profl. pers. U.S. Army, Ft. Lee, Va., 1955-56; cons. McDonnell Douglas, St. Louis, 1957-62, group engr. to sr. tech. specialist, 1962-90; cons. Storz Instruments, St. Louis, 1990-91; rschr. C. Chubb Assocs., Ferguson, Mo., 1991—. Patentee in field of skin light exposure control methods. Recipient Optical Fiber Innovation award NASA, Houston, 1983. Mem.: Mo. Acad. Sci. (past exec. com., industry rep.), Am. Geophys. Union (charter mem.), St. Louis Met. (past pres.). Avocations: hiking, skiing. Home and Office: 438 Marie Ave Ferguson MO 63135-1904 Personal E-mail: c.r.chubb@sbcglobal.net.

CHUBB, STEPHEN DARROW, health products executive; b. Newton, Mass., Mar. 16, 1944; s. Phillip Darrow and Clarissa Stoddard (Nye) C.; m. Kathleen Alice Zimmerman, 1973. BS, U.S. Naval Acad., 1965; MBA, Northwestern U., 1974. CPA, Ill. With Am. Can Co., 1970—73, Baxter Labs., Deerfield, Ill., 1974—81; pres. Hyland Diagnostics, 1978—81; pres., chief exec. officer, dir. Cytogen Corp., 1981—84, T Cell Scis., Inc., 1984—86, Matritech Inc., 1987—; dir. Charles River Labs., 1994—, Compucyte, Cambridge, Mass., 1992—2001, I-Stat, Princeton, NJ, 1999—2002. Alumni adv. bd. Northwestern U., 1998. Bd. dirs. Sherwood Cmty. Assn., 1978-79, v.p., 1979-80; trustee Huntington Theatre Co., Boston, 1991-95, treas., 1992-95; trustee Mt. Auburn Hosp., Cambridge, 1995—; mem. Literacy Vols. Mass. With USN, 1965-70; capt., USNR (ret.). Recipient Meritorious Svc. medal, Combat Action Ribbon, U.S. Navy. Mem. AICPA, John Evans Club Northwestern U., U.S. Naval Acad. Alumni Assn. Avocation: deep sea diving. Office: Matritech Inc 330 Nevada St Newton MA 02460

CHUBB, TALBOT ALBERT, physicist, consultant; b. Pitts., Nov. 5, 1923; s. Charles F. and Mary Clare (Albert) C.; m. Martha Capps, Oct. 24, 1947 (dec. June 1990); children: Mary Carroll, Nancy Henderson, Talbot Spence, Constance Lamont. AB, Princeton U., 1944; PhD, U. N.C., 1950. Physicist, U.S. Naval Rsch. Lab., 1950-58, head upper air physics br., 1958-82; pres. Rsch. Systems, Inc., Oxon Hill, Md., 1982—2003, physicist cons., 2003—. Recipient Elisha Mitchell Soc. award U. N.C., 1951, E.O. Hulbert award Naval Research Lab., 1963, Pure Sci. award Naval. Research Lab.-Research Soc. Am., 1970, Disting. Civilian Service award Dept. Navy, 1978 Fellow Am. Geophys. Union, Am. Phys. Soc.; mem. Am. Astron. Soc. Achievements include rsch. on solar flare x-rays, x-ray stars, UV aurora, cosmology, solar thermal power, cold fusion theory. Home and Office: 5023 38th St N Arlington VA 22207-2845 Personal E-mail: tchubb@aol.com.

CHUBIN, ELLEN LISA, prosecutor; b. Phila., Pa., Apr. 12, 1968; d. Herbert Maurice and Selma (Parris) C. AB magna cum laude, Harvard-Radcliffe, 1990; JD cum laude, Harvard U., 1993. Bar: D.C. 1994, N.Y. 1994. Assoc. Covington and Burling, Washington, 1993—97; sr. trial atty. office of spl. investigations, criminal divsn. U.S. Dept. Justice, Washington, 1997—2001, asst. U.S. Atty., 2001. Mem. ABA, Internat. Assn. Jewish Lawyers and Jurists (bd. dirs., v.p. Washington chpt. 1994-2001), Bar Assn. DC (bd. dirs., sec. young lawyers sect. 1999-2002), Women's Bar Assn., Harvard Club Washington (bd. dirs., v.p. 1998-2002). Democrat. Jewish. Avocations: singing, violin. Office: US Attorney's Office for DC 555 4th St NW Washington DC 20530

CHUDLEIGH, G(ARY) STEPHEN, lawyer; b. Houston, Dec. 15, 1951; s. James Painter and Mary Lillian Chudleigh; m. Anna Marie Saldana, Oct. 29, 1977; children: Sky, Sabina, Dylan, Alexis. BA, U. Tex., 1973; JD, U. Houston, 1988. Bar: Tex. 1988, U.S. Dist. Ct. (so. dist.) Tex. 1989. Real estate broker, Temple, Tex., 1980-85; pvt. practice law Friendswood, Tex., 1988-93, Pasadena, Tex., 1993-97, League City, Tex., 1997—. Founding mem. League City C. of C. and Bus. Assn., 1997. Mem. ATLA, Tex. Bar Assn., Tex. Real Estate Commn. Roman Catholic. Avocation: soccer coach. Home: 2002 Sunny Bay Ct League City TX 77573-6964 Office: 122-C Michigan Ave League City TX 77573 E-mail: texlaw@gte.net.

CHUDOBIAK, WALTER JAMES, electronics executive; b. Gliechen, Alta., Can., Apr. 2, 1942; s. John and Clara (Suchy) C.; m. Mary Annetta Budarick, Oct. 11, 1969; children: Michael, Anne. BSc in Elec. Engring., U. Alta., Edmonton, 1964; MEng in Electronic Engring., Carleton U., Ottawa, Ont., Can., 1965, PhD in Electronic Engring., 1969. Rsch. officer Def. Rsch. Bd., Ottawa, 1965-69; group leader, rsch. scientist Comm. Rsch. Ctr., Dept. Comm., Ottawa, 1969-75; assoc. prof. Carleton U., 1975-81; pres., founder, dir. Avtech Electrosystems Ltd., Ottawa, 1975—. Contbr. numerous articles to profl. jours.; patentee in field. Mem. IEEE, Assn. Profl. Engrs. (Ont.). Home: 12 Timbercrest Ridge Nepean ON Canada K2R 1B4 Office: 55 Grenfell Cres Ste 205 Nepean ON Canada K2G 0G3 E-mail: info@avtechpulse.com, walter@avtechpulse.com.

CHUDZINSKI, MARK ADAM, lawyer; b. Chgo., Oct. 13, 1956; s. Brunon and Maria (Chmielinski) C.; m. Barbara Podkul, July 31, 1993; 1 child, Anna. BA, Northwestern U., 1977, MBA, JD, Northwestern U., 1981; diplome d'etudes approfondies, U. Paris, 1982. Bar: N.Y. 1982, Ill. 1990, U.S. Supreme Ct. 1994. Assoc. Coudert Bros., N.Y.C., 1982-85, London, 1985-88, Sydney, Australia, 1988-89; sr. assoc. Winston & Strawn, Chgo., 1990-95, ptnr., 1995-96; gen. counsel Ameritech Internat., 1996-99; sr. v.p., gen. counsel and sec. Eziaz Inc., Chgo., 2000—01; v.p., gen. counsel and sec. Callipso Corp., Santa Ana, Calif., 2003—. Articles editor Northwestern Jour. Internat. Law and Bus., 1981. Trustee Window To The World Comm., Inc. (Stas. WTTW-TV and WFMT-FM), Chgo., 1992-2004, Nat.-Louis U., Chgo., Kosciuszko Found., N.Y.C.; adv. bd. Sta. WBEZ-FM, Chgo., 1992-2002; mem. Chgo. com. Chgo. Coun. Fgn. Rels.; bd. dirs. Chgo. Legal Clinic, Inc., Polish Mus. Am., 1991-98, Polish Am. Congress, 1992-96. Austin scholar 1978; fellow Leadership Greater Chgo., 1990; U.S. Champ Jessup Moot Ct., 1979. Mem.: ABA, Am. Soc. Internat. Law, N.Y. State Bar Assn., U.S.-Poland C. of C. (founder, chmn. 1991—95). Roman Catholic. Office: Callipso Corp 2 MacArthur Pl 6th Fl Santa Ana CA 92707 Business E-Mail: mark.chudzinksi@callipso.com.

CHUEH, CHUN FEI, import/export company executive; b. Chaozhou, China; s. Yung Hsing and Ruu Mei Chueh; m. Cecilia Shih-mei Hsing, Apr. 15, 1961; children: Angelina Mary Kitten, Daniel Francis. BSChE, Nat. Taiwan U., 1954; MSChE, Kans. State U., 1957; PhD in Chem. Engring., Ga. Inst. Tech., 1962. Chem. engr. Sci. Design Co., N.Y.C., 1962—78; dir. devel. Halcon Internat., Inc., N.Y.C., 1978—86; gen. mgr. Haarmann & Reimer Cosfra, Ltd., Shanghai, 1987—97; pres. Elan Trading (Shanghai) Co., 1998—, Elan (Shanghai) Flavors & Fragrances Co., 2000—. Patentee in field. Home: 187-16 Cambridge Rd Jamaica NY 11432-2435 Office: Elan (Shanghai) Flavors & Fragrances Co #92 Ln 1129 Nanjing Rd W Shanghai 200041 China Office Phone: 86-21-62530204.

CHUGHTAI, RAANA LYNN, psychiatric nurse practitioner; d. Arshad Iqbal and Lynnette Janet Chughtai. BSN, U. Pitts., 2000. RN Pa., 2001. Crisis clinician Mercy Behavioral Health, Pitts., 2000—02, nurse/therapist Wexford, Pa., 2002—. Rsch. asst. U. Pitts., 1999—2000. Mem.: Grad. Nursing Student Orgn., Am. Psychiat. Nurses Assn., Three Rivers Rowing Assn., Golden Key.

CHUI, CHARLES K., mathematics professor; b. Macau, May 7, 1940; m. Margaret K. Lee, Aug. 22, 1964; children: Herman, Carie. BS, U. Wis., 1962, MS, 1963, PhD, 1967. Asts. prof. math. SUNY, Buffalo, 1967-70; assoc. prof. math. Tex. A&M U., College Station, 1970-74, prof. math., 1974-89, disting. prof. math., 1989—, dir. Ctr. for Approximation Theory, 1988-99, joint appointment in stats., computer sci. and electrical enging.; cons. prof. statistics Stanford U., 1997—; chief tech. officer TeraLogic, Inc., Mountain View, Calif., 1996-2000. Author: Multivariate Splines, 1988 (translated into Japanese and Chinese), An Introduction to Wavelets, 1992 (translated into Japanese and Chinese), Wavelets, A Mathematical Tool for Signal Analysis, 1997 (translated into Japanese); co-author: Elements of Calculus, 1983, 2nd edit., 1988, Kalman Filtering with Real-Time Applications, 1987, 2nd edit., 1991, 3d edit., 1997, Linear Systems and Optimal Control, 1988, Signal Processing and Systems Theory, Selected Topics, 1992, Hx Control, 1998; editor: Approximation Theory and Functional Analysis, 1991, Wavelets: A Tutorial in Theory and Applications, 1992 (translated into Japanese), (series) Wavelet Analysis and Its Applications, Approximations and Decompositions; co-editor: Approximation Theory II, 1976, Approximation Theory IV, 1983, Approxiamtion Theory V, 1986, Topics in Multivariate Approximation, 1987, Approximation Theory VI, vols. 1 and II, 1989, Multivariate Approximation Theory IV, 1989, Approximation Theory VII, 1992, Approximation Theory VIII, 1995; editor-in-chief Applied and Computational Harmonic Analysis: Wavelets, Signal Processing and Applications; editor: Wavelets: Theory, Algorithms, and Applications, Approximation Theory and Its Applications, Jour. Approximation Theory, Advances in Computational Math., Annals Numerical Math., Electronic Jour. Differential Equations, Advances in Computational Math., Neurocomputing; assoc. editor Jour. Math. Rsch. and Exposition, Revista de Matemáticas Aplicadas; patentee spline-wavelet signal analyses and methods for processing signals; patent pending method and apparatus for video image compression and decompression using boundary-spline-wavelets. Named. Hon. Prof., Ningxia U., China, 1987; Erskine fellow U. Canterbury, New Zealand, 1987; fellow Houston Advanced Rsch. Ctr., 1994. Fellow IEEE; mem. Am. Math. Soc., Math. Assn. Am., Soc. for Indsl. and Applied Math., Assn. Former Students Tex. A&M U. (Disting. Rsch. Achievement award 1981, 94). Roman Catholic. Avocations: music, fishing.

CHUI, CHI ON, electrical engineer, researcher; b. New Territories, Hong Kong, Jan. 23, 1977; s. Yu Chi Chui and Hau Ming Cheung; m. Hoi Yan Yiu, June 3, 2004. BEng in Elec. Engring., Hong Kong U. Sci. and Tech., 1999; MS in Elec. Engring., Stanford U., 2001, PhD in Elec. Engring., 2004. Doctoral rsch. asst. Stanford U., Calif., 2000—04, grad. tchg. asst., 2001—03; rschr.-in-residence Intel Corp., Santa Clara, Calif., 2004—. Reviewer Jour. of the Electrochem. Soc., 2002., Intel Corp. fellow, 2003, Microsoft Corp. grantee, 2003, Hong Kong Soc. Accts. scholar, 1996, Hong Kong Telecom Inst. of Info. Tech. scholar, 1998, Chiap Hua Cheng's Found. scholar, 1999, Hong Kong & Kowloon Elec. Appliances Mchts. Assn. scholar, 1999. Mem.: IEEE (reviewer, IEEE Electron Device Letters 2003—04), Materials Rsch. Soc. Achievements include patents pending for High-k dielectric for thermodynamically-stable substrate-type materials; MOS interface with reactive metal overlayers; Germanium substrate-type materials and approach therefor; first to Seminal contribution to incorporate high-permittivity gate dielectrics for germanium MOS field-effect device application; invention of Two low-noise photodetector architectures in Group IV semiconductor; A novel self-aligned MOS field-effect transistor fabrication process; development of Various germanium MOS technologies including three generations of gate dielectric, two generations of dopant incorporation, and three generations of MOS field-effect transistors. Home: 144 W Hillsdale Blvd San Mateo CA 94403 Office: Stanford Univ CIS 014 420 Via Ortega Stanford CA 94305 Office Fax: 650-725-6278. Personal E-mail: chion.chui@gmail.com. E-mail: chion@stanford.edu.

CHUKWU, ETHELBERT NWAKUCHE, mathematics professor; b. Mbano, Imo, Nigeria, Nov. 22, 1940; s. Nwachukwu Chukwu Uwaezuoke and Ihejere Theresa; m. Regina Chukwu Nyere, Dec. 26, 1966; children: Chika, Eze, Emeka, Uche, Obioma, Ndubuisi. BSc, Brown U., 1965; MSc, Nsukka U., Nigeria, 1973; PhD, Case Western Res. U., 1972. Asst. lectr. U. Nigeria, Nsukka, 1970; asst. prof. math. Cleve. State U., 1972-76, assoc. prof., 1976-78; prof. U. Jos, Nigeria, 1978-81, dean postgrad. studies, 1977-81; vice chancellor Fed. U. Tech., Yola, Nigeria, 1981-86; prof. math. N.C. State U., Raleigh, 1987—. Mem. Nat. UN Commn. on African Scholarship Program for Am. Univs. fellow, 1962-65. Author 6 books in field; assoc. editor Non-Linear Studies; contbr. 90 articles to profl. jours. Mem. AAAS, Nigerian Math. Soc. (v.p. 1980-82), Math. Assn. Nigeria (pres. 1981-82), Am. Math. Soc., Math Assn. Am., N.Y. Acad. Scis., Am. Assn. for Advancement of Sci., Internat. Fedn. Nonlinear Analysts (mem. global com.), Sigma Xi, Sigma Iota Rho. Roman Catholic. Address: NC State U Mathematics Dept Raleigh NC 27695-8205 Office Phone: 919-515-7442. E-mail: chukwu@math.ncsu.edu.

CHUKWUMEZIE, BEATRICE NKEM, research scientist; arrived in U.S., 1996; d. Anthony N. and Elizabeth O. Chukwumezie. B Pharmacy, Katholieke U. Leuven, Belgium, 1993; MS, Vrije U., Brussels, 1995, U. Notre Dame, 1998; PhD, Duquesne U., 2003. Lic. pharmacist Order of Pharmacy, Belgium. Rsch./tchg. asst. U. Notre Dame, South Bend, Ind., 1996—98, Duquesne U., Pitts., 1998—2003; pres. MEPHUDO, Rankin, Pa., 2001—; sr. scientist Shire Laboratories Inc., Rockville, Md., 2003—05, Biovail Tech., Chantilly, Va., 2005—. Treas. Nigerian Am. Assn. Pharm. Scientists, 2000—. Contbr. articles to profl. publs. Scholar, Vrije U. Brussels, 1994—95. Achievements include patents pending for Parkinson's disease therapy; attention deficit hyperactivity disorder therapy; controlled release pain therapy. Home: 118 Miller Ave Rankin PA 15104 Office: Mephudo 118 Miller Ave Rankin PA 15104 Office Phone: 703-480-5886. Office Fax: 412-271-0220. Personal E-mail: nkembc@yahoo.com.

CHUMACEIRO, ROLANDO JOSE MENDEZ, family practice physician; b. Orangestad, Aruba, Oct. 23, 1959; came to U.S., 1965; s. Rolando Jose and Regina Maria Chumaceiro; m. Cecilia Chumaceiro, Jan. 20, 1990; children: Jessica Marie, Emily Cristina. BS, Northeastern U., 1983; MD, U. Autonoma de Guadalajara, Mex., 1988. Bd. cert. family medicine. Attending physician (pvt. practice) So. Yonkers (N.Y.) Family Practice, 1993-95, Oxford Med. Group, Yonkers, 1996—; clin. faculty St. Joseph Med. Ctr., Yonkers, 1993—, med. dir. methadone maintenance program, 1994—. Med. bd. St. Josephs Med. Ctr., Yonkers, 1999—, Yonkers Gen. Hosp., 1999—; dir. 5th pathway program N.Y. Med. Coll. at St. Joseph Med. Ctr., Valhalla, N.Y., 1996—. Capt. med. team N.Y.C. Marathon, 1990—. Recipient Am. Heart Assn. award, 1992. Mem. AMA, Am. Acad. Family Practice, Spanish Am. Med. Soc. Republican. Roman Catholic. Avocations: tennis, golf, travel, camping, reading. Home: 1506 Pondcrest Ln White Plains NY 10607-1356 Office: Oxford Med Group 970 N Broadway Ste 305B Yonkers NY 10701-1311 E-mail: chuma1023@aol.com.

CHUMLEA, W. CAMERON, medical educator; BS, Wash. & Lee U., 1969; MA, U. Tex., 1976, PhD, 1978. Prof. of cmty. health and pediat. Wright State U. Sch. Medicine, Dayton, Ohio, 1978—. Cons. NIH, Bethesda, Md., U. Toulouse. Served with U.S. Army, 1969—73. Office: Lifespan Health Rsch Ctr 3171 Research Blvd Dayton OH 45420 Office Phone: 937-775-1428. Business E-Mail: cameron.chumlea@wright.edu.

CHUN, ANDREW, translator; b. Buryong-gun, Korea; arrived in U.S., 1973; s. Ly Hyon Chun and Jung Chuk Choe; m. Teresa Chun, Nov. 20, 1950; children: Agnese Lee, I Yup, John, Thomas. Student, Aoyama Coll., Tokyo, 1941—43. Acct. County Office, Puryung-gun, Republic of Korea, 1943—45; sect. chief U.S. Army Civil Aid Office, Pusan, Republic of Korea, 1947—49; transl. UN Civil Command, Pusan, 1951—54; radio monitoring transl. CIA, Seoul, Republic of Korea, 1955—68; mng. dir. Shin GmbH Trade Co., Seoul, 1968—73; ins. agt. Equitable Life Ins., L.A., 1974—79; tech. advisor Sunkyung Inc., Seoul; immigration documentation transl. L.S.A. Law Office, Lynnwood, Wash., 1998—2001. Patentee jet propulsion boat, roof and rain gutter cleaning tools, pedal-powered sailboat, exercycle mower. Home and Office: Peaceunion Co Ltd 8106 215th Pl SW Edmonds WA 98026 Fax: 425-775-8209. E-mail: a.chun@att.net.

CHUN, ASAPH Y., research scientist; s. YoungHee and Joseph Tok-Kyun Chun, Byung-Soon Lee; m. Myung-Joo P. Hong, May 4, 1991. BA, U. Mich., 1987, MA, 1989; ABD, U. Md., 2003. Data archivist Inst. Social Rsch., Ann Arbor, Mich.; instr. U. Md., College Park, 1991—94; pres., CEO Inst. Strategies and Reconciliation, Brookeville, 1998—; behavioral scientist U.S. Bur. Labor Stats., Washington; survey statistician U.S. Bur. Census, 1999—2000; sr. rsch. scientist Am. Insts. Rsch., 2000—. Dir. Inst. Strategies and Reconciliation, Brookeville, Md.; rschr. ednl. policy Am. Insts. Rsch.; rschr. survey methodology U.S. Bur. Labor Stats., 1991—2000. Founding mem. InterAction North Korea Working Com., Washington; chmn. Inst. Strategies and Reconciliation, Brookeville, Md., 1998—2005. Fellow, U. Mich., 1985—87; grantee, Inst. Social Rsch., Ann Arbor, 1987—89. Mem.: World Assn. Pub. Opinion Rsch., Am. Ednl. Rsch. Assn. Achievements include first to Led ISR to send over $25 million vaule of humanitarian aid to DPRK (North Korea) since 1998 with focus on helping people with disability, children, pregnant/nursing women; research in Have published scores of research papers in leading academic journals, and presented over 100 papers in national and int'l academic conferences; Provided research-based policy recommendations in American education, diplomacy and conflict resolution approaches to DPRK. Avocations: gardening, jogging, hiking, travel. E-mail: ychun@air.org.

CHUN, JACQUELINE CLIBBETT, artist, educator; d. Sydney H. and Hilda C. Moore; m. Edward W.C. Chun, Dec. 1967; children: Christine, Diana, David. Student, London Coll. Music, 1956—58; BA summa cum laude, U. Hawaii Manoa, 1992, MFA, 1997. Freelance musician, singer, songwriter, 1960—; pres. JCM Prodns., Honolulu, 1978—; lectr. painting Kapiolani C.C., Honolulu, 1999; faculty Kaimuki Cmty. Sch. Adults, Honolulu, 1988—; lectr. U. Hawaii Manoa, Honolulu, 1996—. Courtroom sketch artist KGMB TV, KHNL TV, Honolulu, 2000—; founder, dir. Girl Scout Band and Choir, 1987; poetry editor Hawaii Rev., 1992—93, asst. mng. editor, 1993—94, nonfiction editor, 1994—95; vice chair publs. bd. U. Hawaii at Manoa, 1988—89; mem. adv. bd. Kapiolani C.C., U. Hawaii. Author: (plays) By the Hand of a Woman, 1992; editor: The Touch of God, 1999, The Science of Happiness, 2000; composer: (songs) Official Theme Song for Girl Scout Coun. 75th Anniversary, Official Girl Scout Theme Song, 1988; co-author (artist, editor): Moiliili, The Life of a Community, 2005; contbr. articles to profl. jours. Band dir., choir dir. Girl Scout Coun. Pacific, Honolulu. Recipient Acquisition award, State Found. Culture and Arts, All USA Coll. Acad. First Team, USA Today, 1990, House Reps Resolution Ednl. Contribution award, State of Hawaii, Spirit award, Hawaii Rev., 1992, Gold award, 16th Ann. Shizuoka Friendship Postcard Art Contest, Japan, 2004. Mem.: ASCAP, Am. Fedn. Musicians, Acad. Am. Poets, Portrait Soc. Am., Nat. Music Pub. Assn., Musician's Assn. Hawaii, Phi Beta Kappa. Avocations: swimming, gardening, travel. Office: JCM Prodns PO Box 8363 Honolulu HI 96830-0363

CHUN, SHINAE, federal agency administrator; m. Kyong Chul Chun; 2 children. BA, Ewha Women's U., Seoul, Korea; MA in Edu. and Social Policy, Northwestern U.; fellowship, Harvard U. John F. Kennedy Sch. of Govt. Project dir. Title IX Multiethnic Training, Assistance and Dissemination Project; founding mem. Asian Am. Advisory Council to Gov. James R. Thompson State of Ill., 1982—84, special asst. on Asian Am. affairs to gov., 1984—87; dir. Dept. of Fin. Institutions, Chgo., 1988—90, Labor Dept., Chgo., 1991—99; dir. women's bur. US Dept. of Labor, Washington, 2001—. Author: From the Mountains of Masan to the Land of Lincoln, 1996, Korean Culture: A Passage Through Hermit Kingdom, 1980. Recipient Special Achievement for Leadership award, Bus. Women's Network, 2004. Office: US Dept Labor Women's Bur 200 Constitution Ave NW Washington DC 20210*

CHUNG, CAROLINE, marketing professional; b. Washington, Apr. 27, 1970; d. Jae Wan and Soojun Chung. BS, U. Wis., 1992; MBA, Vanderbilt U., 1997. Cert. Mad Dogg Spinning Instr., Aerobics and Fitness Assn. Am., Group Excercise Instr.; cert. Pilates instr. Mgr. ops. rsch. and statis. analysis Continental Airlines, 1997—99; mgr. product devel. US Airways, 1999—2001; ops. rsch. cons. Warden Assocs., 2001—03; fgn. svc. officer, 2d sec. U.S. Dept. State, 2003—05; sr. dir. mktg. MAXjet Airways, Inc., 2005—. Roman Catholic. Avocations: health and fitness, travel, reading, world maps, music. Office Phone: 571-246-4290. Personal E-mail: carolinechung1@gmail.com.

CHUNG, CHIA MOU (CHARLES CHUNG), former Oriental art business owner; b. Jiao Ling Hsien, Guangdong, China, Feb. 21, 1918; came to U.S., 1946; s. Kiu-Sin and Yee-Mui (Lee) C.; m. Sylvia E.E. Tuck, Jan. 16, 1955 (div. Jan. 1970); children: Wilma, Cathie, Vivian, Calvin; m. Betty Lee Sung, July 22, 1972; stepchildren: Tina, Cynthia, Victor, Alan Sung. Grad., Ctrl. Police U., Chungking, Sichuan, China, 1940, Nat. Cheng-Chi U., Chungking, 1943; BS, MS, Wash. State U., Pullman, 1948; postgrad., NYU, 1948-51. Editor Ctrl. Police U., 1941-43; profl. officer Exec. Yuan, Chungking, 1943-45; calligrapher, transl., reviser Secretariat UN, N.Y.C., 1948-79; pres. Jade and Oriental Arts, Inc., N.Y.C., 1961-99. Author: The Road for ROC (Taiwan) to be Readmitted to UN (in Chinese), 1994; co-editor: China Anthology (in English), 1996, Chung's Selected Essays (in Chinese), 1998; contbr. articles to Chinese newspapers and profl. pubs. Sr. advisor and pres. Chinese Chee-Yue Cmty. Assn., NYC, 1996-2004; bd. mem. Chinese Consol. Benevolent Assn., N.Y., 1996-2004. Recipient first prize Nat. Essay Contest on Police Sci. and Adminstrn. by Examination Yuan, 1941, Excellent Svc. award pres., Exec. Yuan, 1945, Chinese Rsch. Project award Tai-ti Found., 1951, Svc. award Sec. Gen. UN, 1985, Excellent Svc. award Ctrl. Police U. Alumni Assn., N.Am., 1993, Nat. Cheng-ta Alumni Assn. Ea. U.S., 1995, Svc. award Shanghai Tiffin Club, 1995. Mem. Ctrl. Police U. Alumni Assn. Eastern U.S. (chmn. 1991—, excellent svc. award 1996), Nat. Cheng-ta Alumni Assn. Eastern U.S. (exec. dir. 1991-94, hon. v.p. 1994-99, adviser 1999—), World Hakka Fedn. (pres. Ea. U.S. chpt. 1991-93, advisor 1993—), World Kwongtung Cmty. Assn. (advisor 1991—), ROC Nat. Devel. Assn. (mem. overseas com. 1991—), Taiwan Devel. Inst. (rsch. fellow 1993—), Chinese-Am. Jewelry Assn. (sr. adviser 1991—). Home (Winter): 3200 NE 36th St Apt 1520 Fort Lauderdale FL 33308 Home (Summer): 165 Park Row Apt 20F New York NY 10038

CHUNG, FUNG-LUNG, cancer research scientist; b. Keelung, Taiwan, Republic of China, Nov. 10, 1949; came to U.S., 1973; s. Tse-Yung and Carol (Cheng) C.; m. Judy Chu, Aug. 2, 1975; children: Christine, Christopher, Clifford. BS in Chemistry, Chung-Yuan U., Chung-Li, Taiwan, 1971; PhD, U. Utah, 1978. Postdoctoral fellow Columbia U., N.Y.C., 1979-80; rsch. assoc. Am. Health Found., Valhalla, N.Y., 1980-85, sect. head, 1985-89, assoc. chief, 1990-95, chief, 1995—. Mem. study sect. Nat. Cancer Inst., Washington, 1990-94; assoc. mem. Sloan-Kettering Cancer Inst., 1993—; mem. sr. adv. com. Am. Health Found., 1991—; program leader Am. Health Found. Cancer Ctr. Core Grant; adj. prof. N.Y. Med. Coll., 1998—. Editl. bd.: Chem. Rsch. in Toxicology, Oncology Reports; contbr. over 100 articles to profl. jours. Recipient Young Investigator award Nat. Cancer Inst., 1982, grantee, 1982—; featured on cover of Cancer Rsch., 1999. Mem. Am. Assn. Cancer Rsch., Am. Chem. Soc., Am. Soc. Preventive Oncology, The Oxygen Soc.

CHUNG, JENNIFER M., not-for-profit developer; d. Soo Kil and Soon Won Chung. BA in Bus. Adminstrn., Phila. Bibl. U., Langhorne, 2001; BS in Bible, Phila. Bibl. U., 2001. Payroll asst. Phila. Coll. of Bible, Langhorne, 1998; testing adminstr. asst. Law Sch. Admissions Coun., Newtown, Pa., 1999; ednl. outreach rsch. intern Rec. for the Blind and Dyslexic, Princeton, NJ, 2000; mgr. devel. comms. and rsch. Big Bros. Big Sisters of Am., Phila., 2001—04; program coord. exec. edn. Harvard Bus. Sch., Cambridge, Mass., 2004—. Mem.: Youth with a Mission, Students in Free Enterprise.

CHUNG, JIN SOO, ocean mining and ocean engineer; b. Seoul, Korea, Jan. 27, 1937; s. Hyun Mo and Soon Mo (Yoo) C.; m. Yang Ja Park, Aug. 11, 1967; children: Claude H., Christine M. BSE. in Naval Arch., Seoul Nat. U., 1961; MS, U. Calif., Berkeley, 1964; PhD in Engring. Mechanics, U. Mich., 1969. Sr. rsch. engr. Exxon Prodn. Rsch. Co., Houston, 1969—73; staff engr. Lockheed Missiles & Space Co., Sunnyvale, Calif., 1973—80; team leader advanced tech. Ocean Minerals Co., Mountain View, Calif., 1975—80; prof. Colo. Sch. Mines, Golden, 1980—2000; exec. dir. Internat. Soc. Offshore and Polar Engrs. (ISOPE), 1990—. Cons. hydrodynamics to Inter-Govtl. Maritime Consultative Orgn. UN, 1981; founder, editor, chmn. ISOPE Ocean Mining Symposium, 1995—. Sr. editor: Transactions Jour. Energy Resources Tech., 1980-85; editor: Internat. Jour. Offshore and Polar Engring., 1990—; assoc. editor: Applied Mechanics Rev., 1985-91; chmn., editor Proceedings 1st Offshore Mechanics/Arctic Engring. Symposium, New Orleans, 1981, 2nd Internat. Symposium, Houston, 1983, 3rd Internat. Symposium, New Orleans, 1984, 4th Internat. Symposium, Dallas, 1985, 5th Internat. Symposium and Exhibit, Tokyo, 1986, 7th Internat. Conf., Houston, 1988, 8th Internat. Conf., Hague, The Netherlands, 1989; contbr. articles to profl. jours. Rsch. grantee, Office Naval Rsch., 1967—69, NSF, 1986, 1988, 1992—2000. Mem.: ASME (policy bd. comm., tech. editor Trans. jour. 1981—85, editor various publs. 1981—, chmn. offshore mechanics com. 1982—84, founding chmn. offshore mechanics and arctic engring. divsn. 1985—89, Eugene W. Jacobson award Energy Tech. Conf. Houston 1978, Ralph James award 1980, Outstanding Achievement award 1987), Soc. Naval Archs. Japan, Internat. Soc. Offshore and Polar Engring. (co-founder 1989, chmn. editor Trans. jour. procs. ann. conf. 1991—, 1st elected pres. 1999—2000, Neptune award 1992, Jin S. Chung award 2002), Internat. Coun. Offshore Mechanics and Arctic Engring. (chmn. 1986—95, founder), Tau Beta Pi, Sigma Xi. Achievements include pioneering in advanced tech. devel. and position control simulation of deep ocean mining system; development of laser Doppler anemometer for turbulence in non-Newtonian fluids flow. Home: 11149 Sutherland Ave Cupertino CA 95014-4730 Office: Internat Soc Offshore & Polar Engrs PO Box 189 Cupertino CA 95015-0189 Office Phone: 650-254-1871. Business E-Mail: jschung@isope.org.

CHUNG, JONG-MOON, education educator; b. Lincoln, Nebr., June 30, 1969; s. Chin Wee and Young Cha Cho Chung; m. Seung-Won Han Chung, June 26, 1995; children: Yonhee, Yonju. BEE, Yonsei U., 1988—92, MEE, 1992—94; PhD electrical engring., Pa. State U., 1995—99. Rsch. asst. Info. and Telecom. Rsch. Inst., Yonsei U., Seoul, Korea (South), 1992—94, rschr., 1994—95; instr. Pa. State U., 1997—99, asst. prof. of elec. engring., 1997—99; asst. prof. Okla. State U., Stillwater, 2000—04, assoc. prof., 2004—. Dir., ACSEL and OCLNB laboratories Okla. State U., 2000—. Recipient Top Gun award, Shadowband Sys., 2003; grantee, Halliburton, Inc., Carrier Access Corp., LaLucha, LLC; grant, Nat. Sci. Found., Air Force Info. Assurance, Def. Advanced Rsch. Projects Agency, Dept. Edn. Mem.: IEEE (sr. Conf. Outstanding Paper, First Pl. award 2000). Catholic. Achievements include research in sailors wireless communication badge (SWCB) systems; hybrid wireless and wired network systems; Navy wireless audio/video/data headset; radio frequency identification micro memory module; golbal system for mobile communications network processor optimization; advanced broadband digital cable-TV set-top system and networkin; development of telecommunications & virtual laboratory; direct sequence spread spectrum (DSSS) wireless modem module. Avocations: basketball, golf. Office: Okla State U 202 Engineering South Stillwater OK 74078 Personal E-mail: jmc29@alumni.psu.edu. E-mail: jchung@okstate.edu.

CHUNG, JOSEPH SANG-HOON, economics professor; b. Unmun-myon, Chongdo-kun, Kyongbuk, Korea, Oct. 11, 1929; came to U.S., 1953; s. Anthony Doseng and Martha (Cho) C.; m. Louise Carol Guenther, Aug. 17, 1957; children: Vincent, Sara, Melissa. Student, Seoul Nat. U., Korea, 1949-51; BS in Econs., Marquette U., 1956, MA, 1958; PhD, Wayne State U., 1964. Lectr. in econs. Marquette U., Milw., 1958-60; from instr. to asst. prof. Kalamazoo Coll., 1962-63, 63-64; asst. prof. Ill. Inst. Tech., Chgo., 1964-68, chmn. dept. econs., 1975-82, assoc. prof., 1968-73, prof. econs., 1973-95, prof. emeritus, 1996—. Fulbright prof. Seoul Nat. U. Korea, 1966-68; cons. Hoover Instn., 1964-66, Def. Dept., 1969; assoc. Asia Sci. Rsch. Assocs., Menlo Park, Calif., 1968-85. Author: Evolution of the Japanese Electronics Industry, 1980, The North Korean Economy: Structure and Development, 1974; editor: Patterns of Economic Development: Korea, 1966. Social Sci. Rsch. Coun. fellow, 1962; Stanford U. Hoover Instn. grantee, 1964-65; Fulbright lectr. Dept. State, 1966-68; Gen. Electric Found. grantee, 1975 Mem. Am. Econs. Assn. Roman Catholic. Home: 22 W County Line Rd Barrington IL 60010 Personal E-mail: j1chung@aol.com.

CHUNG, KEA SUNG, television broadcasting executive; b. Pusan, Korea, Jan. 2, 1935; came to U.S., 1973; s. Tae In and Dou Kum (Lee) C.; m. Ok Soon Yang, June 20, 1958; children: Hee Sung, Yun Hee, Jaeh Hoon, Juneho. BS in Bus. Adminstrn., Cen. Mo. State U., 1957; D Bus. Mgmt., Calif. Internat. U., 1982; D Bus. Mgmt. (hon.), Kyung Nam U., 2002. Pres. Voice of Korea, Honolulu, 1975, Polynesian Fair, Inc., Honolulu, 1976—; pres., CEO KBFD, TV, Honolulu, 1984—; pres. The Asia Network, Honolulu, 1986—. Dir. Hawaii Korea Nat. Tourism Org., Honolulu, 1975—; pres. Korean TV Broadcasters Assn. of Am., 1993—. Past pres. Korean Cmty. Coun. Hawaii, Honolulu, 1980-82; chmn. Temple Constrn. of Dae Won Sa Buddhist Temple, Honolulu; hon. mem. adv. coun. Dem. and Peaceful Unification of Korea, 1984—. Recipient Merit Sus award Republic of Korea Ministry Culture and Info., 1978; Nat. Merit award Pres. Republic of Korea, 1990, Presdl. award, 1993. Mem. Am. Soc. Travel Agts. (past bd. dirs. 1975), Korea Tourist Bur. Inc. (pres. 1975), Hawaii TV Broadcasters Assn. (bd. dirs. 1992), Hawaii Korean C. of C. (past pres. 1979-80), Korean Athletic Assn. (past bd. dirs. 1977-79), Korean Press Club Hawaii (past pres. 1982-83), Lions (hon., charter pres. Honolulu 1987)(Zone Chmn 2003—). Avocation: golf. Office: KBFD TV 1188 Bishop St Ph 1 Honolulu HI 96813-3300 Office Phone: 808-521-8066. E-mail: ksc@kbfd.com.

CHUNG, KYUNG CHO, Korean specialist, educator, writer; b. Seoul, Korea, Nov. 13, 1921; s. Yang Sun and Kyung Ok (Peng) C.; m. Yosi S. Chung, Oct. 10, 1958; children: In Kyung, In Ja. Student, Waseda U., Tokyo, 1941-43; BA, Seoul Nat. U., 1947; postgrad., Columbia U., 1948-49; MA, N.Y. U., 1951; LL.D., Pusan Nat. U., 1965; Litt.D., Sungkyunkwan U., 1968; MA, Monterey Inst. Fgn. Studies, 1974. Mem. faculty U.S. Def. Lang. Inst., Monterey, Calif., 1951-92, Monterey Inst. Fgn. Studies, 1973-74, Hartnell Coll., Salinas, Calif., 1974-93. Pres. Korean Rsch. Coun.; adviser Korean Assn., Monterey, 1974—, Am.-Korean Found., Crossroads, Inc., 1992, Asia Devel. Inc.; treas. Korean Rsch. Bull.; hon. prof. Kunkuk U.; pres. South Carmel Hills Assn., 1962-99; hon. chmn. Inst. Far Eastern Studies Joint Rsch. Program U.S.-Russia-Korea-Japan-China, 1993—; chmn. Korea-Am. Assn. *Professor Chung's books have been highly praised by many critics throughout the world and translated into Korean and Japanese. He has joined the lofty ranks of outstanding scholars who write for encyclopedias and professional journals. His important and timely articles "Korean Unification Through Peaceful Means" (NYT Jan., 1971) and "Korean Unification" (NYT Dec., 1972) helped to generate the dialogue between South and North Korea toward Korean unification. A man of greatness of spirit, Dr. Chung is angered* *by injustice and the violation of high principles. He believes that every man is born with the right to live in liberty and peace.* Author: Korea Tomorrow, 1957, New Korea, 1962, Seoul (Ency. Americana), 1965, Naeil Hankuk, 1965, Sae Hankuk, 1968, Korea: The Third Republic, 1972, Korean Unification, 1973, Korea Reunion and Reunification, 1974, Kankuk Gaido, 1988, The Korea Guidebook: North and South Korea, 6th edit., 2002, Korea edit., 2002, Hankuk-chongran, 1999, East and West 1000 Munsun, 1995, Japanese Kangoku Gaizobuk, 2002. Recipient Superior Performance award, U.S. Govt., 1964, Recognition award of 40 Yrs. Svc., 1991, Excellency medal, 1992, Korean Prime Min. citation, 1965, cert. of achievement, U.S. Def. Lang. Inst., 1976, Outstanding Performance award, 1980, Commendation award, 1991, Olympic-Svc. Gold medal, Korean Pres., 1989, Spl. Commendation award, 1990, Fifa World Cup Svc. award, 2002, Spl. award medal, Korean Govt., 2002, Excellency Svc. award medal, Overseas Korean Found., 2003. Mem. AAUP, Am. Assn. Asian Studies, Am. Assn. Modern Langs., Am.-Korean Polit. Assn., Carmel Found., Korean Rsch. Coun. (pres. 2005-06). Democrat. Mem. Korean Ch. Home and Office: 25845 S Carmel Hills Dr Carmel CA 93923-8310 Office Phone: 831-624-4929. *Dedicate and contribute toward better relations among the nations and the lasting peace in the world, teaching other languages to meet the other nations half way by speaking the same language.*

CHUNG, PAUL MYUNGHA, mechanical engineer, educator; b. Seoul, Dec. 1, 1929; came to U.S., 1947, naturalized, 1956; s. Robert N. and Kyungsook (Kim) C.; m. E. Jean Judy, Mar. 8, 1952; children: Maurice W., Tamara P. BSME, U. Ky., 1952, MS, 1954; PhD, U. Minn., 1957. Asst. prof. mech. engring. U. Minn., 1957-58; aero. research scientist Ames Research Center, NASA, Calif., 1958-61; head fluid physics dept. Aerospace Corp., San Bernardino, Calif., 1961-66; prof. mech. engring. U. Ill., Chgo., 1966-95, head dept. energy engring., 1974-79, dean engring., 1979-94, prof., dean emeritus, 1995—. Mem. tech. adv. com. Ill. Inst. Environ. Quality, 1975-77; corp. mem. Underwriters Lab., 1983-95; cons. to industry, 1966—. Author: Electric Probes in Stationary and Flowing Plasmas, 1975, Russian edit., 1978, numerous papers in field; contbr. chpt. to Advances in Heat Transfer, 1965, Dynamics of Ionized Gasses, 1973. Bd. govs. YMCA, Redlands, Calif., 1965—67. Fellow AIAA (nat. tech. com. on plasmadynamics 1972-74, com. on propellants and combustion 1976-80); mem. AIChE (nat. com. on internat. activities 1992-94), Am. Soc. Engring. Edn. (exec. bd. engring. dean's coun. 1983-84), Sigma Xi, Tau Beta Pi, Pi Tau Sigma, Phi Kappa Phi. Home: 2003 E Lillian Ln Arlington Heights IL 60004-4215 Office: Univ Ill Off of Dean Chicago IL 60680 E-mail: jjpc2003@earthlink.net.

CHUNG, PING TSAI, education educator; b. Taipei, Taiwan, Republic of China; s. Tai-Der and Kun-Sen Lin Chung; m. Hsin-Hwa Hsiao Chung, Jan. 18, 1987; children: Rebecca, Timothy. PhD Computer Sci., Polytechnic U., 1998; M.S. Computer Sci., Stevens Instit. of Tech., 1986. Mem. tech. staff. Lucent Tech. Bell Lab., 1998—2000; software devel. AT&T Lab., 1997—98; asst. prof. dept. of computer sci. L.I. U., 2000—. Advisor computer sci. club L.I. U., Bklyn., 2001—04, chmn. computer sci. pers. com., 2002—04, chair computer sci. dept., 2004—; mem. program com. Internat. Multconf. in Computer Sci. and Engring., 2004—. Contbr. articles to profl. jours. Mem.: IEEE, Assn. for Computing Machinery. Office: Dept of Computer Sci Long Island U 1 University Plz Brooklyn NY 11201 Office Phone: 718-488-1073. Business E-Mail: pchung@liu.edu.

CHUNG, TONG SOO, lawyer; BA magna cum laude, Harvard U., 1977; MA in Public Affairs, Princeton U., 1980; JD, UCLA Sch. of Law, 1984. Financial analyst Exxon Corp., 1980—81; assoc. Whitman & Ransom, Los Angeles, Calif., 1984—86; co-founder, of counsel Lim, Ruger & Kim, LLP (formerly Kim, Chung & Lim), Los Angeles, Calif., 1986—; dir. export promotion & coord. Internat. Trade Administration, US Dept. Commerce, 1994, former dir. advocacy ctr., 1995—2000, former acting dep. asst. secy. for svc. industries & fin., 2000—01. Sr. advisor Sewon Telecom. Commr. Los Angeles County Private Industry Council, 1988—92; mem. Calif. Economic Develop. Advisory Com. on Asia, 1989—91; commr. Los Angeles Fire and Police Pension System, 1991—93, Calif. Postsecondary Ed. Commn., 1992—93; bd. dirs. Constitutional Rights Found.; founding mem. The Ethnic Coalition; founding pres. Korean Am. Coalition. Office: Lim, Ruger & Kim, LLP 1055 W Seventh St Ste 2800 Los Angeles CA 90017*

CHUNG, WHASUN OH, education educator; d. Oh; m. Samuel S. Chung. PhD, U. Wash., Seattle, Wash. Rsch. asst. prof. U. Wash., Seattle, 2003—. Grantee K22, NIH-NIDCR, 2004-2007. Office: Univ Wash Box 357132 Seattle WA 98195-7132 Office Phone: 206-543-4339. Office Fax: 206-685-3162. Business E-Mail: sochung@u.washington.edu.

CHUNG, WINGYAN, computer scientist, educator, information scientist, educator; arrived in U.S., 2005, permanent resident; s. Choi Chung and Yuk-ying Wu; m. Christina Hoiyin Leung, Dec. 22, 1996; children: Lydia Gimsin, Daniel Tinhang. BBA, Chinese U. Hong Kong, 1993; MS in Info. and Tech. Mgmt., The Chinese U. Hong Kong, 2000; PhD, U. Ariz., 2004. Network adminstr. Tucson Police Dept., 2003; registered tchr. Hong Kong Govt., 1998. Tchr. Ho Fung Coll., Hong Kong, 1993—94, CCC Tam Lee Lai Fun Meml. Secondary Sch., 1994—98; textbook rev. com. mem. commerce & bus. studies Curriculum Devel. Coun., Hong Kong Edn. Dept., 1997—99, com. mem. commerce & bus. studies, 1997—99; tchg. asst. Chinese U. Hong Kong, 1998—2000; grad. tchg. assoc. U. Ariz., Tucson, 2000—01, rsch. assoc. Artificial Intelligence Lab, 2001—04, instr., 2003—04; asst. prof. computer info. systems U. Tex., El Paso, 2004—. Acad. conf. reviewer Eighth Internat. Conf. Info. Visualization, 2004—04, European Conf. Digital Libraries, 2002—03, Internat. Conf. Asian Digital Libraries, 2001—03, Workshop Info. Tech. and Systems, 2003—03, Hawaii Internat. Conf. Sys. Scis., 2002—02, Internat. Conf. Digital Libr., Beijing, 2002—02; chmn. commerce and bus. studies subjects panel CCC Tam Lee Lai Fun Meml. Secondary Sch., Hong Kong, 1996—98; acad. conf. reviewer Internat. Conf. Info. Systems, 2002—02. Contbr. articles to profl. jours. Ch. deacon Christina and Missionary Alliance Tsing Yi Alliance Ch., Hong Kong, 1998—2000; bible class tchr. Christian and Missionary Alliance Tsing Yi Alliance Ch., 1996—2000. Recipient Young Investigators Initiative award, U.S. Def. Advanced Rsch. Projects Agys. Info. Processing Tech. Office, 2003; fellow, U. Tex., El Paso, 2004; grantee, NSF KDD Program, 2002, U. Tex., El Paso, 2004; scholar, Rotary Internat. Found., Hong Kong, 1999, U. Ariz., Dept. MIS, 2003, 2000—04. Mem.: IEEE, Assn. Info. Systems, Assn. Computing Machinery. Achievements include research in Developed and validated an automatic text mining framework for knowledge discovery on the Web. Conducted three empirical studies in the business intelligence domain to demonstrate its usability; Grant, "Discovering Business Intelligence from Stakeholders on the Web: A Knowledge Network Approach" funded by University Research Institute Grant Program, The University of Texas at El Paso, 2004; design of New course design on object-oriented programming in Java, UTEP, 2004; research in Developed and validated a new methodology on collecting and analyzing information of terrorist Web sites, 2005; Developed and validated a visual framework for knowledge discovery on the Web, 2005. Office Phone: 1-915-7475496.

CHUNG, YA-LI, music educator; b. Taoyan, Taiwan, June 4, 1962; arrived in U.S., 1999; d. Yung-Liang Chung and Yui-Chaio Lee; m. Tien-Un Yu, Aug. 12, 1990 (div. June 2001). B, Tun-Hai U, Taichung,Taiwan, 1986; M, Tex. Tech. U, 2001. Piano tchr. Yamaha Co., Chung-Lee, Taiwan, 1986—94; music tchr. Jr. HS, Chung-Lee, Taiwan, 1992, Taoyan, Taiwan, 1993—94; piano tchr. pvt. practice, Taoyan, Taiwan, 1986—99; accompany tchg. asst. Tex. Tech. U, Lubbock, Tex., 1999—2005, piano tchr., 2002—04. Composer (piano composition): Seasonal Songs, 2002; composer: Four Rhapsodies, 2004. Recipient Excellent Tchr. Award, Govt. of Taoyan City, 1989, 1996, 1997, 1998, Tchg. award, Steinbach Nat. Piano Competition, 1999. Mem.: MTNA - Music Tchr. Assn. (assoc.). Avocations: reading, composing, accompaniment, piano performance, travel. Home: 1612 Ave Y #210A Lubbock TX 79401 Office: School of Music in TTU MS 2033 18th St Boston Rd Lubbock TX 79409

CHUNG, YOUNG SIR, materials scientist; b. Cheongwon, Choongbuk, Republic of Korea, Dec. 10, 1960; arrived in U.S., 1989; s. In Ho Chung and Wan Sik Chae; m. Min Hye Park, June 7, 1990; children: Hugh Emanuel, Eugene Paul. BS, Hanyang U., Seoul, Republic of Korea, 1982, MS, 1986; PhD, Ariz. State U., Tempe, 1993. Rsch. scientist Korea Advanced Inst. Sci. And Tech., Seoul, 1984—89; prin. staff scientist Motorola Corp., Tempe, 1993—. Tech. com. mem. internat. symposium on semiconductor power devices and IC's IEEE, 2001—; invited spkr. Internat. Nano Ceramics/Crystal Forum & Internat. Symposium On Intermaterials, 2003, Tech. Symposium 2002; internat. adv. com. mem. Internat. Nano Ceramics/Crystal Forum & Internat. Symposium On Intermaterials, Seoul, 2003—; presenter at internat. symposia and confs. Author: IEEE Electron Device Letter; contbr. scientific papers. Prin. Global Mission Korean Sch., Tempe, Ariz., 2000—01. Recipient Gt. Contbn., 2003 Internat. Nano Ceramics/Crystal Forum & Internat. Symposium on Intermaterials, 2003, Best Paper award, 9th Internat. Conf. Mixed Designs of Integrated Circuits and Sys., 2002; scholar, Motorola, 1989—93. Mem.: IEEE. Achievements include discovery of temperature induced thermal snapback breakdown in semiconductor devices; surface reconstruction at specific alloy composition; invention of chemical probe field effect transistor; power copper tech. semiconductor performance enhancement; device and designs power dissipation enhancement; patents in field; invention of Electro Magnetic Sys. for ultra sensitive sensor tech; 3-D System-on-a-chip; intelligent power System-on-a-chip tech; magnetic embedded system-on-a-chip tech; ultra thin semiconductor tech. Avocations: natural science, golf. Home: 1283 E Saragosa St Chandler AZ 85225 Office: Freescale Semiconductor 2100 E Elliot Rd El709 Tempe AZ 85284 E-mail: young.chung@freescale.com.

CHUNGPAIBOONPATANA, SURASIT, government agency administrator, researcher, information technology manager; s. Seree J.K. Chungpaiboonpatana and Mukda W.D. Chungpaiboonapatana; m. Jane Y.J. Chen, July 29, 1974. DSc, Columbia U., 2001; PhD, U. Calif., 2005. Ems Duke U., 2003, Emba UCLA, 2005. Sec. U.S. Muay Thai Coun., Oxnard, Calif., 1993—; liason Fedn. of Brazilian Jujitsu Internat., Los Angeles, Calif., 1996—. Tech. HW&R Law Ptnr., Ltd., Laguna Hill, Calif., 2004—. Contbg. editor tech. jour. Sec. First Chinese Bapt. Ch., Irvine, Calif., 2002. 2d officer Army Med. Ctr., 1990—92, Taiwan. Recipient Goldwater Best Graduating Engr., Goldwater Fellowship, 1995, Outstanding Paper, IMAPS, 2003, Outstanding Presentation, IEEE, 2004, Outstanding Session Contbr., VMIC, 2004. Mem.: TMS (corr.; packaging 2000—05), IMAPS (corr.; interconnect process 1995—2005), IEEE (corr.; interconnects process 1999—2005), MRS (hon.; editl. bd. 1995—2005). Achievements include patents for Novel Direct Interconnect to Cu/Low-k; Forming Gas Distribution Interconnect Formation; RDL Design, Integrated Passive/Active Components in Semiconductor. Office Phone: 949-579-4098.

CHUNPRAPAPH, BOONMEE, physician, educator; b. Songkhla, Thailand, Nov. 23, 1938; came to U.S., 1966; s. Yen Hua Tseng and Chou Sou Chen; m. Kaysorn Suttajit, July 29, 1944; children: Benj, Kabin. MD, U. Med. Sci., Bangkok, 1964. Diplomate Am. Bd. Orthopedic Surgery. Rotating intern Samaritan Hosp., Troy, N.Y., 1966-67; pvt. practice gen. surgery Youngstown (Ohio) Hosp. Assn., 1967-68; pvt. practice specializing in orthopedic surgery Univ. Hosp., Mobile, Ala., 1968-71; assoc. prof. U. Ill., Chgo., 1980—. Contbr. articles to profl. jours. Fellow ACS, Internat. Coll. Surgeons; mem. AMA, Acad Orthopedic Surgeons, Am. Soc. Surgery of the Hand. Avocations: photography, gardening, tennis. Office: U Ill Coll Medicine 835 S Wolcott Ave Chicago IL 60612-7307 Office Phone: 312-996-7161. E-mail: boonc@uic.edu.

CHUPKA, WILLIAM ANDREW, chemical physicist, educator; b. Pittston, Pa., Feb. 12, 1923; s. William and Antoinette C.; m. Olive Augusta Pirani, May 21, 1955; children: Jocelyn Terese, Marc William. BS, U. Scranton, 1943; MS, U. Chgo., 1949, PhD, 1951. Instr. Harvard U., 1951-54; asso. physicist Argonne (Ill.) Nat. Lab., 1954-67; sr. physicist, 1967-75; prof. chemistry Yale U., 1975-96, prof. emeritus, 1996—. Research, numerous publs. in chem. physics. Served with U.S. Army, 1943-46. Guggenheim fellow, 1961-62 Mem. Am. Chem. Soc. Office: PO Box 208107 New Haven CT 06520-8107 Office Phone: 203-432-3989. Business E-Mail: william.chupka@yale.edu.

CHUPP, TIMOTHY EDWARD, physicist, educator, academic administrator; b. Berkeley, Calif., Nov. 30, 1954; AB, Princeton U., 1977; PhD in Physics, U. Wash., 1983. Instr., asst. prof. physics Princeton U., 1983-85; from asst. prof. to assoc. prof. physics Harvard U., 1985-91; assoc. prof U. Mich., Ann Arbor, 1991-94, prof. physics, 1994—. Fellow Alfred P. Sloan Found., 1987. Recipient Presdl. Young Investor award NSF, 1987. Fellow Am. Phys. Soc. (I.I. Rabi prize 1993). Achievements include research in low energy particle physics particularly by study of symmetries accessible with polarization; weak interactions: CP violation and time reversal violation; fundamentals of quantum mechanics; structure of nucleons; biomedical and technological applications of lasers and optical pumping. Office: U Mich Dept Physics Ann Arbor MI 48109

CHURCH, BARBARA RYAN, organizational psychologist; b. Vallejo, Calif. d. William Russell and Geraldine Hall (Hatcher) Ryan; divorced; children: Gabrielle Church Russell, Elizabeth Broward McGhie. BA, U. Fla., 1974; MA in Psychology, West Ga. Coll., 1981; EdD in Applied Psychology and Adult Edn., U. Ga., 1985. Pub. svc. dir., news editor, anchorwoman WJKS-TV, Jacksonville, Fla., 1969-71; dir. cmty. rels. Atlanta Assn. Ret. Citizens, 1977-78; coord. pub. info. Mental Health Assn., Atlanta, 1978-80; edn./testing specialist Federal Law Enforcement Tng. Ctr., Glynco, Ga., 1984-86; dir. evening coll., asst. prof. psychology Brewton-Parker Coll., Mt. Vernon, Ga., 1986-88; tng. rsch. analyst Federal Law Enforcement Tng. Ctr., 1988-90; researcher, edn. specialist U.S. Dept. Justice, Immigration & Naturalization Svc., Glynco, 1990-98, chief rsch. and evaluation, 1998—. Tchr., cons. adult edn. courses Ga. State U., Atlanta, 1978, Brunswick (Ga.) Coll., 1993; adj. prof. orgnl. behavior and Leadership, MBA Program, Sch. Bus. Adminstrn., Brenau U., 1997—. Convenor, cons. Kettering Found., 1987-88; mem. adv. bd. HRD degree, dept. adult edn. U. Ga. Recipient award for best campaign of non-profit orgn. Am. Mktg. Assn., 1978, ann. award for innovative programming Ga. Adult Edn. Assn., 1983; named communicator of yr. United Way, 1980. Mem. U. Ga. Lifelong Learning Assn., Ga. Adult Edn. Assn. (bd. dirs. 1989-91), Soc. Police & Criminal Psychology, Commn. Profs. of Adult Edn. Episcopal. Avocations: writing non-fiction, painting, travel, photography. Home: 257 Charlemagne Cir Ponte Vedra Beach FL 32082-2907

CHURCH, CHARLES CLAIR, biomedical acoustics researcher, consultant; b. Warren, Pa., Sept. 5, 1953; s. Charles Eugene and Edna Lorraine Church; m. Althea Webb, June 10, 1988; 1 child, Kathryn Louise Atkins. PhD, U. Rochester, 1983. Rsch. scientist Nat. Ctr. Physcial Acoustics, U. Miss., University, 1988—91, Molecular Biosystems, Inc., San Diego, 1992—95; prin. investigator Acusphere, Inc., Cambridge, Mass., 1995—2002; sr. rsch. scientist Nat. Ctr. Physcial Acoustics, U. Miss., 2002—; rsch. assoc. prof. physics U. Miss., 2003—. Mem. US Tech. Adv. Groups to Internat. Electrotechnical Commn. Tech. Com. 87 & Sci. Com. 62B, 1999—. Mem. Farmer's Market Bd., Oxford, Miss., 2005—05. Fellow: Am. Inst. Ultrasound Medicine (bd. govs. 2002—05); mem.: AAAS, IEEE, Internat. Soc. Therapeutic Ultrasound, Acoustical Soc. Am. (assoc. editor 2003—). Achievements include patents for System for treating blood processed in a cardiopulmonary bypass machine and ultrasound filtration apparatus; Polymer-lipid microencapsulated gases for use as imaging agents; Method for enhancing the echogenicity and decreasing the attenuation of microencapsulated gases. Avocations: gardening, reading, movies. Office: U Miss 1 Coliseum Dr University MS 38677 Office Fax: 662-915-5643. E-mail: cchurch@olemiss.edu.

CHURCH, CHARLOTTE, vocalist; b. Llandaff, Cardiff, Wales, Feb. 21, 1986; d. James and Maria Church. Contracted with Sony Music, 1997. Spokesperson Face of the Millennium campaign Ford Motor Co., 2000. Singer: (albums) Voice of an Angel, 1998, Charlotte Church, 1999, Dream a Dream, 2000, Enchantment, 2001, Prelude: The Best of Charlotte Church, 2002; singer: (duet with Josh Groban) (songs) The Prayer, 2001; singer: All Love Can Be, 2001, (TV spls.) Charlotte Church: Voice of an Angel. Achievements include appeared in command performances for England's Queen Elizabeth and Prince Charles and went on to sing in Washington, D.C. before the President of the United States; sang for Pope John Paul II at the Vatican.

CHURCH, DALE WALKER, lawyer; b. Portland, Oreg., Dec. 17, 1939; s. Floyd Walker and Lydia Belle (Barnette) C.; m. Mollie Ann Harper, Apr. 11, 1964; 1 child, Forrest Gregory. BS, Oreg. State U., 1961; JD, George Washington U., 1967. Bar: D.C. 1968, Calif. 1971. Contracting officer, exec. sec. contract rev. bd. CIA, Langley, Va., 1963-69; corp. gen. counsel, asst. sec. directory of contracts ESL, Inc., Sunnyvale, Calif., 1969-77; dep. under sec. rsch. and engring. U.S. Dept. Def., Washington, 1977-80; ptnr. Surrey and Morse, Washington, 1980-84, Seyfarth, Shaw, Fairweather & Geraldson, Washington, 1984-88, Pillsbury, Madison & Sutro, Washington, 1988-93, McDermott, Will & Emery, Washington, 1993-97; chmn., CEO Ventures & Solutions, LLC, Williamsburg, Va., 1998—, Mech. Tech., Inc., 2002—. Counsel def. mgmt. to pres.'s Blue Ribbon Commn.; cons. Def. Sci. Bd., Washington, 1980—; lectr. profl. orgns. and colls. Mem. task force on Industry-to-Industry Coop., AMC Commander's Exec. Round Table.; active Ctr. Strategic and Internat. Studies Def. Orgn. Project; trustee Oratorio Soc. Washington; co-founder, counsel, treas. Youth Engaged in Svc. Am. Mem. ABA, Am. Electronics Assn. (former gen. counsel, chmn. def. conversion com.), Nat. Def. Indsl. Assn. (bd. dirs., chmn. investments com.), Nat. Contracts Mgmt. Assn., Def. Sci. Bd. Acquisition Reform Task Force, Calif. Bar Assn., D.C. Bar Assn., Fed. Bar Assn., Soc. Logistics Engrs. (hon.), Delta Theta Phi, Sigma Phi Epsilon. Home: 9 Franklin St Alexandria VA 22314-3828 Office: Ventures & Solutions LLC 704 Fairfax Way Williamsburg VA 23185-8202 Office Phone: 703-519-0800.

CHURCH, DONNA B., speech pathology services professional; b. Biddeford, Maine, Apr. 18, 1958; d. Richard Courtney Bandlow and Geraldine Maria Ames; m. Edward Houghton Church III, Aug. 19, 1989; 1 child, Patrick Edward. BA in Comm. Disorders, U. Maine, Orono, 1980; MS in Comm. Disorders, U. N.H., Durham, 1989; post grad., Plymouth State Coll., N.H., 2000—. Lic. speech pathologist N.H., Vt., cert. Am. Speech and Hearing Assn. Speech therapist Greenville Sch. Dist., Maine, 1982—84, Maranarook Sch. Dist., Readfield, 1984—85, Fryeburg Sch. Dist., 1985—88; speech pathologist Mascoma Valley Sch. Dist., Enfield, NH, 1989—90, North County Edn. Svcs., Gorham, 1990—93, Stark, Pittsburg, Monroe and Stratford, 1990—2002, Berlin Sch. Dist., 2002—. Grad. asst. U. N.H., Durham, 1988—89; assoc. prof. Coll. Lifelong Learning, Berlin, 1991. Ski patrol Squaw Mountain, Maine, 1982—84; ski instr. Athtash Mountain, NH, 1985—89; whitewater rafting guide Kennebec, Pendercot and Eastern Rivers, Maine, 1993—94; cub scout leader Boy Scouts Am., Lancaster, NH, 2001—02; vol. Col. Town Recreation Program, 1995—, vol. coach basketball, 2001—02, vol. ski instr. Twin Mountain, 1999—2000; mem. PTO, Lancaster. Mem.: N.H. Speech Hearing Lang. Assn., Am. Speech and Hearing Assn. (clin. fellowship year supr. 1990—94), Alpha Lambda Delta. Avocations: camping, kayaking, skiing, outdoor activities. Office: Marston Sch Berlin Sch Dist 193 Pine St Berlin NH 03570-1889 Home: 20 Hartze Ave Lancaster NH 03584 Office Phone: 603-752-5068.

CHURCH, EUGENE LENT, physicist, consultant; b. Yonkers, N.Y., July 30, 1925; s. Wallace L. and Wilhelmina L. (Binger) C.; m. Anne Richardson Meirs, May 15, 1948; children— Rebecca Meirs, David Lent. AB, Princeton U., 1948; PhD, Harvard U., 1953. With U.S. Dept. Def., 1952-94; sr. phys. scientist Picatinny Arsenal, Dover, N.J., 1977-94; sr. physicist Frankford Arsenal, Phila., 1971-77. Guest physicist Argonne (Ill.) Nat. Lab., 1952-55, Brookhaven Nat. Lab., 1955-59, 61-71, 81—; vis. scientist Niels Bohr Inst., Copenhagen, 1959-61. Contbr. numerous articles to profl. jours. Served with USN, 1944-46 Recipient R&D-100 award, U.S. Army Achievement awards. Fellow AAAS, Am. Phys. Soc., Am. Optical Soc., Soc. Photo-Optical Instrumentation Engrs.; mem. IEEE (life sr.), St. Nicholas Soc. N.Y.C., Soc. Colonial Wars NJ, Holland Soc. Republican. Presbyterian. E-mail: echurch@ieee.org.

CHURCH, FRANK FORRESTER, minister, columnist; b. Boise, Idaho, Sept. 23, 1948; s. Frank Forrester and Bethine (Clark) C.; m. Amy Furth, May 30, 1970 (div. 1991); children: Frank Forrester, Nina Wynne; m. Carolyn Buck Luce, July 25, 1992. AB, Stanford U., 1970; MDiv, Harvard U., 1974, PhD, 1978. Sr. min. All Souls Unitarian Ch., N.Y.C., 1978—. Columnist The Chicago Tribune, 1987-88, The New York Post, 1989; vis. prof. Dartmouth Coll., Hanover, N.H., 1989. Author: Father and Son: A Personal Biography of Senator Frank Church of Idaho, 1985, The Devil and Dr. Church, 1985, Entertaining Angels, 1987, The Seven Deadly Virtues, 1988, Everyday Miracles, 1988, Our Chosen Faith: An Introduction to Unitarian Universalism, 1989, God and Other Famous Liberals, 1991, Life Lines, 1996, A Chosen Faith, 1998, Lifecraft, 2000, Bringing God Home, 2002, The American Creed, 2002, Freedom from Fear, 2004; translator: Greek Word-Building (Matthias Stehle), 1976; editor: Continuity and Discontinuity in Church History, 1978, The Essential Tillich, 1987, 2d edit., 1999, The Macmillan Book of Earliest Christian Prayers, 1988, The Macmillan Book of Earliest Christian Hymns, 1988, The Macmillan Book of Earliest Christian Meditations, 1989, One Prayer at a Time: A 12 Step Anthology, 1989, The Jefferson Bible, 1989, Without Apology: The Liberal Faith of A. Powell Davies, 1998, Restoring Faith: America's Religious Leaders Answer Terror With Hope, 2001, The Separation of Church and State: Writings on Religious Freedom by America's Founders, 2004; contbr. chapters to books; contbr. (articles) Harvard Theol. Rev., (speeches) Rep. Am. Speeches, 1983—84, 1986—87, 1987—88, 1989—90, 1992—93, 1995—96, 1997—98; contbr. articles to profl. publs. Bd. dirs. Union Theol. Sem., N.Y.C., 1992-98, Internat. Bridges Toward Justice, 2002; mem. exec. com. Franklin and Eleanor Roosevelt Inst., N.Y.C., 1990—; chmn. Coun. on Environment N.Y.C., 1995—; mem. svc. com. Unitarian Universalist Ch., 1978—; founder Lifelines Ctr., 1999 Montgomery fellow Dartmouth Coll., 1989. Mem. Unitarian Universalist Mins. Assn. Democrat. Home: 201 E 80th St New York NY 10021-0511 Office: All Souls Unitarian Church 1157 Lexington Ave New York NY 10021-0440 Personal E-mail: revchurch@aol.com.

CHURCH, GEORGE MILLORD, retired real estate company executive; b. Philadelphia, Miss., Sept. 21, 1924; s. George W. and Maggie (Smith) C.; m. Ruth Green, Nov. 12, 1948; children: Ray, Gary. Diploma in acctg., So. Bus. Coll., 1947; AA with honors, Meridian (Miss.) Jr. Coll., 1954; BA in History and Polit. Sci., Coll. of Ozarks, 1957; disting. grad., U.S. Army Noncommd. Officer's Acad., 1961; grad., Realtor's Inst., 1971; postgrad., U. Miss., 1976. Boatswain's mate 1st class USN, South Pacific, Aleutian's, 1942-46; shipfitter Ala. Dry Dock and Ship Bldg., Mobile, 1946; acct. Milton Supply Co., Meridian, 1948-50; staff sgt. USMC, Camp Pendelton, Calif., 1950-51, Meridian, 1953-54; chief acct. Meridian Grain and Elevator Co., 1951-52; cost acct. Flintkote Co., Meridian, 1952-53; enlisted U.S. Army, 1954, advanced through grades to command sgt. maj., 1968, served in Vietnam, retired, 1969; pres. Church Realty Co., Meridian, 1969—, ret., 2002. Instr. real estate, real estate math Meridain Jr. Coll. Chmn. Toys for Tots, Meridian, 1954; active Lauderdale County Planning Commn., 1980-84, past chmn.; charter mem. Rep. Presdl. Task Force, Washington, 1982—. Decorated 3 Bronze Star medals, Air medal, Gallantry Cross with Palm (Republic of South Vietnam), Gallantry Cross with Silver Star. Mem. Miss. Assn. Realtors (bd. dirs. 1972-73, 91, past chmn. profl. stds. com., FHA and VA liason officer), Meridian Bd. Realtors (pres. 1972-73, 91, bd. dirs. 1972-73, 91, chmn. legis. and polit. action com., bd. congl. coord., Realtor of Yr. 1973, 89), Realtors Polit. Action Com. (life), Navy League U.S. (life commodore), VFW (life, Nat. Home for Children), Am. Legion (life), NRA (life), SCV (life); comdr. Camp 1221, 1992, 93, chief of staff Miss. divsn. 1993-95, comdr./founder Camp 1649, 1994, brigade comdr., Miss. divsn. 1995-96, gen. exec. coun. 1998, comdr. Army of Tenn. Svc. 2000—), The Jefferson Davis Soc. (life, co-founder, sec.-treas. 1994-96, dir. 1997—), Order of So. Cross (life). Baptist. Avocations: hunting, fishing, travel, golf. Home: 4200 Pineview Dr Meridian MS 39305-3345 Office: Church Realty Co PO Box 224 Meridian MS 39302-0224

CHURCH, HERBERT STEPHEN, JR., retired construction company executive; b. Framingham, Mass., July 24, 1920; s. Herbert Stephen and Edith L. (Shaw) C.; m. Carol S. Orzech, Apr. 2, 1945; children: Carolyn, David, Kathryn, Patricia, Virginia. BS in Civil Engring, Northeastern U., Boston, 1943. Constrn. insp. N.Y., New Haven & Hartford R.R., 1940-43; with Turner Constrn. Co., 1943; from gen. supt. to v.p., gen. mgr. Chgo. terr., 1965-73; sr. v.p. Western region Chgo., 1974-80; sr. v.p. Central region, 1980-85. Dir., 1972-85 Trustee Nat. Commn. for Coop. Edn., 1981-90. Mem. Contractors Mut. Assn. (dir. 1974-84), Builders Assn. Chgo. (dir. 1969-74), Chgo. Club, Inverness Golf Club. Roman Catholic. Home: 811 W George St Arlington Heights IL 60005-1751

CHURCH, LILLIAN HAZEL See BROOKS, LILLIAN

CHURCH, MARTHA ELEANOR, retired academic administrator; b. Pitts., Nov. 17, 1930; d. Walter Seward and Eleanor (Boyer) Church. BA, Wellesley Coll., 1952; MA, U. Pitts., 1954; PhD, U. Chgo., 1960; DSc (hon.), Lake Erie Coll., 1975; LittD (hon.), Houghton Coll., 1980; LHD (hon.), Queens Coll., 1981, Ursinus Coll., 1981, St. Joseph Coll., 1982, Towson State U., 1983, Dickinson Coll., 1987, Coll. Notre Dame Md., 1995; LLD (hon.), Hood Coll., 1995; LHD (hon.), Ill. Coll., 2003. Instr. geography Mt. Holyoke Coll., South Hadley, Mass., 1953-57; lectr. geography Ind. U. Gary Ctr., 1958; instr., then asst. prof. geography Wellesley Coll., 1958—65; dean coll., prof. geography Wilson Coll., 1965-71; assoc. exec. sec. Commn. Higher Edn., Mid. States Assn. Coll. and Secondary Sch., 1971-75; pres. Hood Coll., Frederick, Md., 1975-95, pres. emerita, 1995—; sr. scholar Carnegie Found. for Advancement of Tchg., Princeton, 1995—97; interim pres. Ill. Coll., 2002—03; interim v.p. acad. affairs Holy Names U., Oakland, Calif., 2005—. Bd. dirs. Farmers and Mechanics Nat. Bank, 1982—2000, dir. emerita, 2000—; cons. Choice: Books for Coll. Librs.; co-chmn. nat. adv. panel Nat. Ctr. for Rsch. to Improve Postsecondary Tchg. and Learning, U. Mich., 1985—90; mem. bd. visitors Def. Intelligence Coll., 1988—91; mem. adv. bd. dirs. Automobile Club Md., 1991—2002; bd. dirs. AAA Mid-Atlantic, 1997—2002; mem. adv. bd. The Boyer Ctr. Messiah Coll., Grantham, Pa., 1997—. Author: The Spatial Organization of Electric Power Territories in Massachusetts, 1960; Co-editor: A Basic Geographical Library: A Selected and Annotated Book List for Am. Colls, 1966; cons. editor, Change mag., 1980-2001. Bd. dirs. Coun. for Internat. Exch. of Scholars, 1979-80, Japan Internat. Christian U. Found., 1977-91, Nat. Ctr. for Higher Edn. Mgmt. Sys., 1980-83; bd. dirs. Am. Coun. on Edn., 1976-79, vice chmn., 1978-79, mem. nat. identification panel, 1977-95, Nat. Rsch. Com., 1993-96; bd. advisors Fund for Improvement of Postsecondary Edn., HEW, 1976-79; mem. Sec. of Navy's Adv. Bd. on Edn. and Tng., 1976-80; chmn. Md. Commn. on Civil Rights, 1981-82; trustee Bradford Coll., Mass., 1982-87, Peddie Sch., N.J., 1982-98, chair acad. affairs com., 1987, 96-97, adv. trustee, 1998—, trustee; trustee Carnegie Found. for the Advancement of Tchg., 1986-96, vice chair, 1990-92, chair, 1992-94, immediate past chair, 1994-96; trustee Nat. Geog. Soc., 1989—, mem. com. for rsch. and exploration, 1998—, chair audit rev. com., 1993-98, chair mission, membership, medals and awards com., 2000—, mem. exec., audit and compensation coms.; trustee Nat. Geog. Soc. Edn. Found., 1989-96, 99—; chmn. bd. dirs. Medici Found., Princeton, N.J., 1985—; trustee United Bd. for Christian Higher Edn. in Asia, 1995-2004, sec. bd. trustees, 1998-2003, chmn. com. on trustees, 1997-2004, chmn East and Intra-Asia program subcom., 1996-97, exec. com., 1998-2004; mem. Md. Humanities Coun., 1985-86, Md. Jud. Disabilities Commn., 1985-94; commr. Edn. Commn. States, Md., 1981-99; exec. com. Campus Compact: Project for Pub. and Cmty. Svc., 1986-89—; trustee Internat. Partnership for Svc. Learning, 1999-2002. Mem. AAUW, Am. Assn. Advancement of Humanities (bd. dirs. 1979-81), Am. Assn. Higher Edn. (chmn. 1980-81, bd. dirs. 1979-83), Assn. Am. Geographers, Nat. Assn. Ind. Colls. and Univs. (bd. dirs. 1983-86), Md. Ind. Colls. and Univs. Assn. (pres. 1979-81, mem. exec. com. 1988-92), Assn. Am. Colls. and Univs. (mem. adv. com. project on status and edn. of women 1980-85), Women's Coll. Coalition (mem. exec. com. 1976-80, 87-89), Am. Conf. Acad. Deans (sec., editor 1969-71), Coun. Protestant Colls. and Univs. (bd. dirs. 1969-71), Soc. Coll. and Univ. Planning (mem. editl. bd. 1979-95), Cosmos Club (mem. jour. editl. bd. 1990-94), Inst. Ednl. Leadership (bd. dirs. 1982-87), Sigma Delta Epsilon, Delta Kappa Gamma (hon.). Home: 3124 Chartwell Crescent Ln Adamstown MD 21710-9643 Office Phone: 501-436-1004. Personal E-mail: marthachurch@edurostream.com. Business E-Mail: mchurch@hnv.edu.

CHURCH, PAMELA T., lawyer; b. Columbia, SC, Sept. 5, 1956; BA cum laude, Yale Univ., 1978; postgraduate, Univ. Bonn, Germany, 1978—79; JD, NYU, 1982. Bar: NY 1983. Ptnr., Global Mergers & Acquisition practice Coudert Bros. LLP, NYC, former mem. exec. bd. Contbr. articles to profl. jours. Mem.: ABA, Assn. Bar City of NY. Office: Coudert Bros LLP 1114 Ave of the Americas New York NY 10036 Office Phone: 212-626-4976. Office Fax: 212-626-4120. Business E-Mail: churchp@coudert.com.

CHURCH, PHILIP THROOP, retired mathematics professor; b. Conn., Mar. 18, 1931; s. Russell Frank and Margaret Church; m. Patricia Ethel Flynn, Sept. 1, 1954; children: Peter Thomas, Susan Elisabeth, Daniel Russell. BA, Wesleyan U., 1953; MA, Harvard U., 1954; PhD, U. Mich., 1959. Asst. prof. Syracuse U., NY, 1958-62, assoc. prof., 1962-65, prof., 1965-76, Francis H. Root prof. math., 1976—2001, Francis H. Root prof. emeritus, 2001—; mathematician Inst. for Def. Analyses, Princeton, N.J., 1962-63. Mem. Inst. for Advanced Study, Princeton, N.J., 1961, 65-66, summer 1977, summer 1978; vis. fellow Princeton U., N.J., spring 1976; disting. vis. prof. U. Alberta, fall, 1987 Contbr. articles to profl. jours. Fellow NSF, 1965-66, Danforth Found., 1953-57. Mem. Am. Math. Soc. (council 1973-77, 80, com. to monitor problems in communication, 1978-80, chmn. 1980, editor Trans. 1973-77, chmn. 1977); mem. Math. Assn. Am., AAUP, Sigma Xi, Phi Beta Kappa Methodist. Office: Syracuse U Dept Math Syracuse NY 13244-1150 Business E-Mail: ptchurch@syr.edu.

CHURCH, RANDOLPH WARNER, JR., lawyer; b. Richmond, Va., Nov. 6, 1934; s. Randolph Warner and Elizabeth Lewis (Gochnauer) C.; m. Lucy Ann Canary, July 4, 1970; children: Leslie R. Pennell, L. Weeks Kerr. BA with honors, U. Va., 1957, LLB, 1960. Bar: Va. 1960, U.S. Dist. Ct. (ea. dist.) Va. 1962, U.S. Ct. Appeals (4th cir.) 1981, U.S. Supreme Ct. 1999. Assoc. McCandlish, Lillard & Marsh, Fairfax, Va., 1960-63; ptnr. McCandlish, Lillard & Church and successor partnerships, Fairfax, 1963-84; city atty. Fairfax, 1968-72; mng. ptnr. McCandlish, Lillard & Church and successor partnerships, Fairfax, 1975-83, Hunton & Williams, Fairfax, 1984-99, mem. exec. com., 1988-94, sr. counsel, 2000—. Bd. dirs. George Mason Bank, George Mason Bankshares, Inc., George Mason Mortgage Co., 1991-98, Va. Found. for Rsch. and Econ. Edn., Inc., 1994-2000. Author: Appellate Civil Litigation, 1984; panelist: Lawyer Professionalism: Is Change in Order? 1988, Marketing Legal Services: What's Hot and What's Not, 1990, (with others) Equity Practice and Tips on Brief Writing. Active Fairfax Com. of 100, 1988—, bd. dirs., 1989-92; bd. visitors George Mason U., Fairfax, 1982-90, rector, 1983-86, chmn. adv. bd. Coll. Arts and Scis., 1999—; bd. dirs. Fairfax Symphony, 1991-2002, gen. counsel, exec. com., 1996-2002; bd. dirs. Fairfax Symphony Orch. Found., Inc., 1999-, Va. Found. for Humanities and Pub. Policy, 1993-99, vice chmn., 1997-99; active Va. Mus. of Fine Arts Found., 2000—, mem. exec. com., 2005—; pres. Fall for the Book, Inc., 2001-04, bd. dirs., 2001—. Fellow Va. Law Found., Am. Bar Found.; mem. Va. Bar Assn. (v.p. 1975), Country Club of Fairfax, U. Va. Club, Phi Beta Kappa. Home: 5114 Forsgate Pl Fairfax VA 22030-4507 Office: Hunton & Williams 1751 Pinnacle Dr Ste 1700 Mc Lean VA 22102-3836 Office Phone: 703-714-7420. E-mail: rchurch@hunton.com.

CHURCH, RICHARD DWIGHT, electrical engineer, scientist; b. Ogdensburg, NY, June 27, 1936; s. Dwight Perry and Carmeta Elizabeth (Walters) C.; m. Vernice Naomi Ives, Aug. 26, 1961; children: Joel, Benjamin. BEE, Clarkson Coll. Tech., 1963. Elec. design engr. IBM, Owego, NY, 1963-69; prin. engr., pres. ASL Systems, Inc., Afton, NY, 1969-94, chmn. bd. dirs.; sr. elec. design engr. Magnetic Labs., Inc., Apalachin, NY, 1980-82, power supply engrng. cons., 1982—; scientist Two Forty-Eight Co., Afton, 1994—2002, Norwood, NY, 2002—. Guest lectr. Afton Sch., Clarkson U. Co-author: Career Oriented Problems for Secondary Mathematics, 1974; contbr. articles to profl. jours.; patentee in field. Treas., trustee Candor Congl. Ch., 1972-84; vice chmn. Town Planning Bd. Candor, 1975-82; rep., mem. Candor Fire Co., 1972-87; bd. dirs., treas. Candor Cmty. Club, 1970-72; initiator endowed fund for Clarkson Theatre Co., Clarkson U., 1999. With USAF, 1955-59. Recipient Dr. Carl Michel award Clarkson Coll. Tech., 1960. Mem. IEEE (sr.), Assn. Energy Engrs. (sr.), Afton Bd. Fire Commrs. (fin. com. 1991-2002), Candor Coin Club (pres. 1978-81), Union of Concerned Scientists, The Cousteau Soc., NY Forest Owners Assn. (dir. 2003-), Am. Soc. Dowsers, Nat. Warplane Mus. Avocations: maple syrup production, maple tree farm development, singing, pyramid geometry, bicycling. Home: 516 Obrian Rd Norwood NY 13668 Office: PO Box 248 Norwood NY 13668 E-mail: rchurch248@cs.com.

CHURCH, ROBERT ARTHUR, retired publishing executive; b. Glendale, Ohio, Oct. 21, 1925; s. Arthur Joseph and Elizabeth Magdaline (Rosselot) Church; m. Mildred Sizemore, Apr. 21, 1950; children: Robert A. Jr., John W., Barbara A., Susan L. Student, U. Dayton, 1943, Washington U., 1944; BSBA, Xavier U., 1950, MBA, 1959. Real estate lic. Ohio. Product planner jet engine dept. GE, Evendale, Ohio, 1950—55, project supr. nuc. project dept., 1955—60, mem. mil. publs. staff jet engine dept., 1960—87. 2d lt. USAF, 1943—45. Mem.: KC, GE Elfun Soc. Home: 7483 Woodcroft Dr Cincinnati OH 45241

CHURCH, RUSSELL MILLER, psychologist, educator; b. N.Y.C., Dec. 24, 1930; s. Donald E. and Dee (Friedman) C.; m. Ruth Kutz, Apr. 4, 1954; children— Kenneth, Emily. BA, U. Mich., 1952; MA, Harvard U., 1954, PhD, 1956. Mem. faculty Brown U., 1955—, prof. psychology, 1965—, chmn. dept. psychology, 1980-83. Chair faculty exec. com. Brown U., 1995-96. Editor: (with E.E. Boe) Punishment: Issues and Experiments, 1968; editor (with B.A. Campbell) Punishment and Aversive Behavior, 1969. Fellow AAAS, Am. Psychol. Assn. (pres. div. exptl. psychology 1987-88, comparative and physiol. psychology 1991-92); mem. Ea. Psychol. Assn. (pres. 1991-92). Office: Brown U Dept of Psychology 89 Waterman St Providence RI 02912-9079 Business E-Mail: Russell_Church@Brown.edu.

CHURCH, THOMAS HAYDEN, actor; b. El Paso, Tex., June 17, 1961; Actor: (TV series) Wings, 1990—95, Ned and Stacey, 1995—97; (TV films) Fugitive Nights: Danger in the Desert, 1993, Mr. Murder, 1998; (films) Tombstone, 1993, Demon Knight, 1995, George of the Jungle, 1997, One Night Stand, 1997, Susan's Plan, 1998, Free Money, 1998, Goosed, 1999, The Specials, 2000, 3000 Miles to Graceland, 2001, Lone Star State of Mind, 2002, The Badge, 2002, Serial Killing 4 Dummys, 2004, Sideways, 2004 (Screen Actors Guild Award, outstanding performance by cast in motion picture, 2005), Spanglish, 2004; actor, dir., writer: Rolling Kansas, 2003; exec. prodr.: (films) Scotch and Milk, 1998; TV appearances include: 21 Jump Street, 1989; Cheers, 1989; China Beach, 1989; Booker, 1989; Flying Blind, 1992; Partners, 1995; Lucky, 2003; (voice) Teen Titans, 2004. Office: c/o Fox Searchlight Pictures 10201 W Pico Blvd Bldg 38 1st Fl Los Angeles CA 90035*

CHURCHILL, DAVID A., lawyer; b. Ft. Collins, Colo., May 13, 1952; s. A. Paul and Anna Marie Churchill; m. Barbara Jean Schultz, Sept. 15, 1972; children: Julia Marie, Heather E. BA, U. Colo., 1974; JD, Cornell U., 1979. Bar: D.C. 1979. Law clk. U.S. Ct. of Claims, Washington, 1979—80; ptnr. McKenna & Cuneo, Washington, 1980—2000, Jenner & Block LLP, Washington, 2000—. Mem.: ABA (chair contract law sect. 1998—99), Ct. Fed. Claims Bar Assn. (pres. 2004). Avocations: hiking, flying. Office: Jenner & Block LLP 601 13th St NW 1200 S Washington DC 20005 Office Phone: 202-639-6056. Business E-Mail: dchurchill@jenner.com.

CHURCHILL, DIANE, artist, educator; b. Bronxville, N.Y., Jan. 8, 1941; d. John and Amelia (Berry) C.; children: Tasha, Karina. BA, Wellesley Coll., 1962; postgrad., Bklyn. Mus. Art Sch., 1962-66; MA, Hunter Coll., 1972. Tchr. art dept. Jersey City State Coll., 1973-75; art tchr., chair art dept. Hudson Sch., Hoboken, N.J., 1978-86; art tchr. Fieldston Lower Sch., Bronx, N.Y., 1986—. One-woman exhibits include Soho 20 Gallery, N.Y., 1976, 78, 80, 02, 04, Light on Lyndon Gallery, Greensboro, NC, 2005, Interchurch Ctr., NY, 2004, Saint Peters Gallery at Citicorp, N.Y.C., 1984, Calif. State U. Gallery, San Luis Obispo, 1993, Hopper House, Nyack, N.Y., 1994, 93 South Gallery, Nyack, 1998, Interchurch Gallery, N.Y.C., 2004, Soho 20 Chelsea, N.Y.C., 2003; group shows include Flushing Town Hall, 1999, Rockland Ctr. for the Arts, 2000, Blue Bench Gallery, Piermont, N.Y., 2004, Hopper House, Nyack, N.Y., 2004. Painting fellow N.J. State Coun. on the Arts, 1979-80, 85-86; Wellesley Coll. Traveling fellow, 2005. Mem. Internat. Soc. for Edn. through Art, N.Y. Wellesley Artists. Home: 88 Clinton Ave Nyack NY 10960-4604 Office: Fieldston Rd Bronx NY 10471 E-mail: diane@dianechurchill.com.

CHURCHILL, JAMES GARTON, retired finance company executive; b. Bklyn., July 16, 1930; s. S. Garton and Mary Ellen (Peck) C.; m. Nancy Barrett Wickers, July 31, 1954 (dec. Jan. 1997); children: Glenn Garton, Bruce Barrett, Ellen Wickers; m. Ruth Mathews Leiter, Mar. 24, 2001. BA, Dartmouth Coll., 1952; MBA, Harvard U., 1954. Fin. analyst Mobil Oil Corp., N.Y.C., 1958-62; treas. Mobil Inner Europe, Geneva, 1962-65, Mobil Europe, London, 1965-68; fin. dir. Mobil Sekiyu, Tokyo, 1968-70; treas. internat. ops. Kaiser Aluminum & Chem. Corp., Oakland, Calif., 1970-81, treas., 1981-87; pvt. practice fin. cons. San Francisco, 1987-90. Served to lt. USNR, 1954-57. Avocations: history and french language study, reading. Home (Winter): 6333 Kennett Pl Mission KS 66202 Home (Summer): 2001 Grassy Ln Woodstock VT 05091 Personal E-mail: churchleit@earthlink.net.

CHURCHILL, JEAN FRANCES, secondary school educator, finance educator; b. Brockton, Mass., Aug. 16, 1949; d. Clyde Frederick McEnroe, Sr. and Gertrude Rita (Marchand) McEnroe; m. Daniel Wayne Churchill, Nov. 11, 1972. BS in Bus. Edn., Salem State Coll., 1973; MEd, Cambridge Coll., 1996. Cert. bus. tchr. State of Mass., 1973, instructional tech. specialist State of Mass., 1999. Secondary tchr. Silver Lake Regional HS, Kingston, Mass., 1973—77; bus. instr. Massasoit CC, Brockton, 1977, Fisher Jr. Coll., North Attleboro, 1977—86, Newbury Jr. Coll., Taunton, 1990—91; fin. literacy instr. Fabrizio McLaughlin Assocs., Washington, 2004; tchr. Oliver Ames HS, North Easton, Mass., 1977—. Sec. Found. Excellence in Edn. in Easton, Mass., 1994—; co-chair Easton Tech. Task Force, Mass., 1994—; chpt. advisor Future Bus. Leaders Am. Silver Lake Regional HS, 1973—77, Oliver Ames HS, 1977—; dir. spring leadership conf. Mass. Future Bus. Leaders Am. Author, photographer: H.H. Richardson Architectural Buildings, 1997; prodr.: (documentary) Portals of Easton, 1994—97 (Prodr. of Yr. award, 1997), A Tale of Two Buildings, 1996—97 (New England Cable TV award, 1997, Pub. Svc. award, 1997); prodr., videographer Hidden Gardens of Easton, 1996—97 (Pub. Rels. award, 1997). Program & publicity chmn. 300th Anniversary Founders Gala & Souvenir Booklet, 1994; judge Easton Film Festival, 2002; bd. dirs. Easton Garden Club, 1988—98; bd. dirs., sec. Easton Historical Soc., 1993—2000. Named Easton Educator of Yr., Town of Easton, 1979, 1993; grantee, Mass. Dept. Edn., 1999, Bell Atlantic, 1999, Insurance Education Inst., 2001. Mem.: Assn. Career and Tech. Edn., Mass. Tchrs. Assn., Nat. Bus. Edn. Assn., Ins. Edn. Found., Bristol County Educators Assn., Easton Educators Assn. Avocations: photography, gardening, travel, writing. Home: 16 Summer St North Easton MA 02356 Office: Oliver Ames HS 100 Lothrop St North Easton MA 02356 Office Phone: 508-230-3210.

CHURCHILL, JOHN HUGH, college academic administrator; b. Hector, Ark., Apr. 1, 1949; s. Olen Raymond and Mary Josephine (Cheek) C.; m. Jean Ann Hill, Aug. 19, 1972; children: William Houston, Mary Katherine Salisbury, Hugh Olen Hill. BA, Rhodes Coll., 1971; BA, MA, Oxford U., 1973; MA, MPH, PhD, Yale U., 1978. Asst. prof. philosophy Hendrix Coll., Conway, Ark., 1977—82, assoc. prof., 1982—92, prof., 1992—, dean of students, 1983—84, v.p. for acad. affairs, coll. dean, 1984—2001. Asst. Am. sec. The Rhodes Scholarship Trust, Middletown, Conn., 1974-77. Contbr. numerous articles to profl. jours. Mem. Rhodes Scholarship Com. Gulf Dist, 1977—, sec. Ark., 1980—. Recipient Rhodes scholarship Rhodes Trust, Oxford, Eng., 1971, NCAA Postgrad. scholarship, 1971. Mem. Soc. for Philosophy of Religion, Phi Beta Kappa (sec. 2001—), Omicron Delta Kappa. Democrat. Avocations: reading history, fiction, biography, and poetry, walking, cooking, canoeing. Office: 1606 New Hampshire Ave NW Washington DC 20009 Home: Apt 214 3133 Connecticut Ave NW Washington DC 20008-5104

CHURCHILL, MAIR ELISA ANNABELLE, medical educator; b. Liverpool, Eng., Nov. 28, 1959; BA in Chemistry, Swarthmore (Pa.) Coll., 1981; PhD in Chemistry, Johns Hopkins U., 1987. Lab. asst. Swarthmore Coll., 1979-81; teaching asst. Johns Hopkins U., Balt., 1981-83; non-clin. sci. staff grade I MRC Lab. Molecular Biology, Cambridge, Eng., 1987-93; asst. prof. biophysics U. Ill., Urbana, 1993-98; assoc. prof. biophysics U. Colo., Denver, 1998—. Contbr. numerous articles to profl. jours. Am. Cancer Soc. fellow, 1987-89, Cambridge U. fellow, 1988-91. Mem. Am. Chem. Soc., Sigma Xi (assoc.). Office: U Colo Health Scis Dept Pharm PO Box 6511 MS8303 Aurora CO 80045

CHURCHILL, MALCOLM HUGHES, retired diplomat, investment analyst; b. Cedar Rapids, Iowa, Sept. 29, 1937; s. Irving Lester and Kathryn Margaret (Hughes) Churchill; m. Bernardita Abueg Reyes, Dec. 22, 1962; children: Paul Reyes, Cristina Reyes. Student, Silliman U., Dumaguete, The Philippines, 1955—56; BA in Internat. Rels. cum laude, Dartmouth Coll., 1960; postgrad., Cornell U., 1960—61; MA in Econs., George Washington U., 1972. Fgn. svc. officer U.S. Dept. State, Washington, 1961—87; editor, owner The Insiders' Way, Washington, 1986—; resource person on Australia, New Zealand and the Philippines Lloyd Thomas & Ball, Inc., Washington, 1987—; analyst on Australia and New Zealand BERI, Inc., Washington, 1992—99. Treas. Philippine-Am. Edn. Found., Manila, 1973—76. Author: A Family Odyssey, Churchills the Ct, 1999; contbr. articles to profl. jours. Pres. Dartmouth Coll. Club Philippines, Manila, 1974—76, Manila Boat Club, 1975—76; pres., treas., bd. mem. Philippines Arts, Letters & Media Coun., Washington, 1993—2000. Mem.: Am. Fgn. Svc. Assn., Assn. for Asian Studies, Nat. Economists Club, Phi Beta Kappa. Avocations: rowing, bicycling, hiking, history, genealogy. Home and Office: The Insiders Way 4715 47th St NW Washington DC 20016 Office Phone: 202-364-8471.

CHURCHILL, MELVYN ROWEN, chemistry educator; b. London, June 2, 1940; came to U.S., 1964; s. Charles Rowen and Irene Lucy (Elms) C.; BSc, U. London, 1961, PhD, 1964; m. Charlotte Elizabeth Simmons, July 10, 1966; m. Gayle Frances Nason, July 12, 2003; children: Ronald Rowen, David George. Instr. chemistry Harvard U., Cambridge, Mass., 1964-67, asst. prof., 1967-70, assoc. prof., 1970-71; prof. U. Ill. at Chgo., 1971-75; prof. SUNY, Buffalo, 1975—, acting dept. chmn., 1981-82, 91-92; assoc. prof. U. Louis Pasteur, Strasbourg, France, 1982. Alfred P. Sloan Found. fellow, 1968-70, NSF grantee, 1965, 68, 70, 72, 74, 76-77, 79-80. Mem. Am. Chem. Soc. (Schoellkopf medal 2000), Am. Crystallographic Assn., Internat. Gilbert & Sullivan Assn. (sec., treas. Opera-Lytes), NY Acad. Scis., Royal Soc. Chemistry (Corday-Morgan medal 1976). Mem. United Ch. of Christ. Contbr. articles to profl. jours. Home: 670 Lebrun Rd Buffalo NY 14226-4221 Office: SUNY Chemistry Dept Buffalo NY 14260-3000 Office Phone: 716-645-6800 x2155. E-mail: chexray@buffalo.edu.

CHURCHILL, ROBERT WILSON, state legislator, lawyer; b. Waukegan, Ill., Apr. 10, 1947; s. George Oliver and Helga C. (Carlson) Churchill; children: Abigail Lee, Julia Aubrey, Christine Lizbeth. BA, Northwestern U., Evanston, Ill., 1969; JD, U. Iowa, 1972. Trustee Lake Villa (Ill.) Township, 1981-83; mem. Ill. Ho. Reps., 1983-99, 2003—; minority whip Ill. Gen. Assembly, 1987-89, asst. minority leader, 1989-91, dep. minority leader, 1991-94, 97-99; majority leader, 1995-97; chmn. Rep. Ctrl. Com. for Lake County, Ill., 1990-94. Co-chmn. Ill. Econ. and Fiscal Commn., Springfield, 1991-95, Space Needs Commn., 1997-99; mem. Ill. Prisoner Review Bd., 1999-2001; chief counsel, dir. legis. Ill. Ho. Reps., 2001-02. Del. Rep. Nat. Conv., 1980, 1992, 1996, 2004, alt. del., 1984. Mem. ABA, Lake County Bar Assn., Lake Villa Lions. Republican.

CHURCHILL, STUART WINSTON, chemical engineering educator; b. Imlay City, Mich., June 13, 1920; s. Howard Heenan and Faye Erma (Shurte) C.; m. Donna Belle Lewis, Feb. 22, 1946 (div.); children: Stuart Lewis, Diana Gail, Cathy Marie, Emily Elizabeth; m. Renate Ursula Treibmann, Aug. 3, 1974. BS in Math, BSChemE, U. Mich., 1942, MS, 1948, PhD, 1952; MA (hon.), U. Pa., 1972. Technologist Shell Oil Co., 1942-46; tech. supr. Frontier Chem. Co., 1946-47; mem. faculty U. Mich., 1949-67, prof. chem. engring., 1957-67, chmn. dept. chem. and metall. engring., 1962-67; mem. faculty U. Pa., 1967—, Carl V.S. Patterson prof. chem. engring., 1967-90, Carl V.S. Patterson prof. emeritus, 1990—; chmn. region 2 edn. and accreditation com. Engrs. Council Profl. Devel., 1961-65, mem. nat. council, 1965-71, exec. com., 1968-71; mem. bd. trustees Chemical Heritage Found., 1983-99, mem. bd. dirs., 1999-2001, mem. fin. com., 1987-2001. Cons. heat transfer and combustion. Recipient S. Reid Warren, Jr. award for disting. tchg. U. Pa., 1976, Max Jakob Meml. award for heat transfer ASME/Am. Inst. Chem. Engrs., 1979, medal for disting. achievement U. Pa., 1993, Alumni Merit award U. MIch., 2002; Japan Soc. for Promotion of Sci. grantee, 1977. Fellow AIChE (nat. coun. 1962-64, pres. 1966, Profl. Progress award 1964, William H. Walker award 1969, Warren K. Lewis award 1978, Founders award 1980, eminent chmn. engr. Diamond Jubilee 1983, heat transfer and energy conversion divsn. award 1997, inst. lectr. 1998); mem. Nat. Acad. Engring. (Founders award 2002), Combustion Inst., Am. Chem. Soc., Am. Soc. for Engring. Edn. (Corcoran award for best paper 1993), Verein Deutscher Ingenieure (corr. mem.), Sigma Xi, Phi Kappa Phi, Phi Lambda Upsilon (award U. Mich. chpt. 1961), Tau Beta Pi. Unitarian Universalist. Home: 137 Pole Cat Rd Glen Mills PA 19342-1301 Office Phone: 215-898-5579. Business E-Mail: churchil@seas.upenn.edu.

CHURCHILL, WARD L., social sciences educator, advocate; b. Urbana, Ill., Oct. 2, 1947; s. Jack Churchill and Maralyn L. (Allen) Debo; m. Leah R. Kelly, Aug. 8, 1995; 1 child, Jasmine Ann; m. Natsu Saito AA, Ill. Ctrl. Coll., 1972; BA, Sangamon State U., 1974, MA, 1975; LHD (hon.), Alfred U., 1992. Program dir. Boulder Valley Sch. Dist., Boulder, 1977-78, U. Colo., Boulder, 1978-90, assoc. prof., 1991-97, full prof., 1997—, chmn., Dept. Ethnic Studies, 1997—2005. Vis. prof. Alfred U., N.Y., 1990-91. Author: Pacifism as Pathology: Reflections on the Role of Armed Struggle, 1986, Struggle for the Land: Indigenous Resistance to Genocide, Ecocide and Expropriation in Contemporary North America, 1993, Indians Are Us?: Culture and Genocide in Native North America, 1994, Since Predator Came: Notes on the Struggle for American Indian Liberation, 1995, From a Native Son: Selected Essays in Indigenism, 1985-1995, 1996, A Little Matter of Genocide: Holocaust and Denial in the Americas 1492 to the Present, 1997, Fantasies of the Master Race: Literature, Cinema and the Colonization of American Indians, 1998, Struggle for the Land: North American Resistance to Genocide, Ecocide, and Colonization, 2002, Acts of Rebellion: The Ward Churchill Reader, 2002, Life in Occupied America, 2003, On the Justice of Roosting Chickens: Reflections on the Consequences on U.S. Imperial Arrogance and Criminality, 2003, Kill the Indian, Save the Man: The Genocidal Impact of American Indian Residential Schools, 2004; co-author (with Jim VanderWall) Agents of Repression: The FBI's Secret Wars Against the Black Panther Party and the American Indian Movement, 1988, The COINTELPRO Papers: Documents from the FBIÕs Secret War Against Domestic Dissent, 1991; editor: New Studies on the Left, 1987-94; contbg. editor: Z Magazine, 1987—, Issues in Radical Therapy, 1982-87, Dark Night Field Notes, 1992—. Mem. governing coun. Colo. AIM, Denver, 1993—, co-dir., 1982-93; comms. dir. Am. Indian Anti-Defamation Coun., Denver, 1992-94; mem. steering com. Yellow Thunder Camp, Rapid City, S.D.,

1981-85. Recipient Gustavus Myers award in writing Gustavus Myers Ctr., 1984. Avocation: films. Office: U Colo Dept Ethnic Studies Ketchum 30 Campus Pass 339 Boulder CO 80309*

CHURCHMAN, MICHAEL STEELE BRIGHT, educational consultant, educator; b. Indpls., Mar. 9, 1929; s. M. Steele and Luita Curtis Churchman; m. Jean Virginia Wood, Apr. 28, 1951; children: Jean Wood, Julia Churchman McCue, Diana Churchman Mason. BA, Wesleyan U, 1950; MA, U Mo., 1958; EdM, Harvard U, 1964. Tchr. The Barstow Sch., Kansas City, Mo., 1955—64; headmaster The Kent Sch., Denver, 1964—74, St. Catherine's, Richmond, Va., 1974—79, The Barstow Sch., 1979—85; dir. external affairs The Nelson-Atkins Mus. of Art, Kansas City, Mo., 1985—96, cons., 1996—. Trustee The Barstow Sch., Kansas City, Mo., 1999—2005, St. Paul's Episcopal Sch., Kansas City, Mo., 1994—2000, Episcopal Social Svcs., Kansas City, Mo., 2000—04. Author: The Kent Sch. 1922-1972, 1972, High Ideals and Aspirations: The Nelson-Atkins Museum of Art, 1993. Democrat. Episcopalian. Office: The Nelson Gallery Found 4525 Oak St Kansas City MO 64111 Office Phone: 816-751-1283. Business E-Mail: mchurchman@nelson-atkins.org.

CHURCHWELL, EDWARD BRUCE, astronomer, educator; b. Sylva, NC, July 9, 1940; s. Doris L. Churchwell; m. Dorothy S. Churchwell, June 24, 1964; children: Steven T., Beth M. BS, Earlham Coll., 1963; PhD, Ind. U., 1970. NASA fellow Ind. U., Bloomington, 1963; postdoctoral fellow Nat. Radio Astronomy Obs., Charlottesville, Va., 1970; Heinrich Hertz postdoctoral fellow Max Planck Inst. Radioastronomie, Bonn, Germany, 1970-72, staff scientist, 1972-77; asst. prof. U. Wis., Madison, 1977-79, assoc. prof., 1979-83, prof., 1983—, Alfred E. Whitford prof. astronomy, 2002—. Fellow NASA, 1985, Fulbright Rsch., 1988—89. Mem.: Union Concerned Scientists, Internat. Astron. Union, Am. Astron. Soc. Office: U Wis Washburn Observatory 475 N Charter St Madison WI 53706-1582

CHURGIN, AMY, publishing executive; Assoc. pub. Seventeen Mag., 1992—94; Pub. K III Mag. Corp. (now Primedia Corp.--N.Y. Mag.), N.Y.C., 1994—99; group pub., N.Y., Chgo. Automobile Mag., 1999; v.p., pub. Archtl. Digest, Condé Nast, L.A., 1999—. Organizer Architecture Days. Office: Architectural Digest Condé Nast 6300 Wilshire Blvd Ste 1100 Los Angeles CA 90048-9083*

CHURGIN, MICHAEL JAY, law educator; b. N.Y.C., Feb. 25, 1948; s. Raphael B. and Sylvia (Nussbaum) C. AB magna cum laude, Brown U., Providence, 1970; JD, Yale U., 1973. Bar: Conn. 1974, Tex. 1975. Supervising atty., teaching fellow Yale Law Sch., New Haven, 1973-75; asst. prof. U. Tex. Sch. Law, Austin, 1975-79, assoc. prof., 1979-81, prof., 1981-90, Raybourne Thompson prof., 1990—. Mem. adv. bd. Advocacy, Inc., Austin, 1985-90; vis. fellow Clare Hall, Cambridge, Eng., 1996; vis. fellow Wolfson Coll., Cambridge, Eng., 1992; Quatercentenary vis. fellow Emmanuel Coll., Cambridge, 2000. Co-author: Toward a Just and Effective Sentencing System, 1977; author: (monograph) Analysis of the Texas Mental Health Code, 1988, 2d edit., 1994; contbr. articles to profl. jours. Mem. pub. responsibility com. Austin Travis County MHMR, 1979-85; bd. dirs. Tex. Hillel, Austin. Fellow W.K. Kellogg Nat. Found., 1980-83. Mem. ABA (bar admissions com. 1998—), Am. Soc. for Legal History (chair com. 1987—), Phi Beta Kappa. Jewish. Home: 4006 N Hills Dr Austin TX 78731 Office: U Tex Sch Law 727 E Dean Keeton Austin TX 78705-3224 Office Phone: 512-232-1330. E-mail: mchurgin@law.utexas.edu.

CHURUKIAN, GEORGE ALLEN, retired education educator; b. Cleve., June 11, 1932; s. Giragos M. and Helen (Tootikian) C.; m. Carol Ann Jerjisian, July 5, 1958; children: Ann, Martha, Alice. BS, Millikin U., 1955; MS, Hofstra U., 1963; PhD, Syracuse U., 1970. Tchr. Patchogue-Medford Pub. Schs., Patchogue, N.Y., 1959-66; assoc. dir. urban tchr. prep. program Syracuse (N.Y.) U., 1969-71; dir. tchr. edn. Va. Wesleyan Coll., Norfolk, 1971-76; dir. secondary edn. Ill. Wesleyan U., Bloomington, 1976-79, dir. tchr. edn., 1979-90; cons. Bloomington, 1991-93; ret., 1993. Fulbright scholar Kuwait U., 1992.

CHUSED, RICHARD HARRIS, law educator; b. St. Louis, Jan. 31, 1943; s. Joseph and Marie Irene (Steinberg) C.; m. Elizabeth Langer, May 11, 1974; children: Benjamin Langer Chused, Samuel Chused Langer. BA, Brown U., 1965; JD, U. Chgo., 1968. Asst. prof. Sch. of Law, Rutgers U., Newark, 1968-71, assoc. prof., 1971-73, Georgetown U. Law Ctr., Washington, 1973-85, prof., 1985—. Author: Modern Approach to Property, 1978, Cases, Materials and Problems in Property, 1988, 2d edit., 1999, A Property Anthology, 1993, 2nd edit., 1997, Private Acts in Public Places: A Social History of Divorce in the Formative Era of American Family Law, 1994, A Copyright Anthology: The Technology Frontier, 1998; topic and comments editor U. Chgo. Law Rev., 1967-68; contbr. numerous articles to profl. jours. Bowman C. Lingle fellow, 1966-67; Brown U. Nat. Honor scholar, 1965-68, Fulbright scholar Hebrew U. Jerusalem, 2004-05. Mem. Soc. Am. Law Tchrs. (bd. govs. 1983-94), Am. Soc. Legal History, Am. Hist. Assn. Democrat. Jewish. Home: 3712 Ingomar St NW Washington DC 20015-1820 Office: Georgetown U Law Ctr 600 New Jersey Ave NW Washington DC 20001-2022 E-mail: chused@law.georgetown.edu.

CHUTORIAN, ABE M., pediatrician, educator; b. Winnipeg, Man., Can., Feb. 8, 1929; s. Morris and Rose (Cohen) C.; m. Helen Carol Olasker, Sept. 2, 1951; children: Leslie, Sandra, Tracy. MA, U. Man., 1952, MD, BSc (hon.), U. Man., 1957. Diplomate Am. Bd. Pediatrics, Neurology. Intern Winnipeg Gen. Hosp., 1957-58; resident L.A. Children's Hosp., 1958-60; from fellow of neurology to prof. pediatrics and neurology Columbia U., N.Y.C., 1960-90; prof. pediats. and neurology, chief dept. pediat. neurology Cornel U., N.Y. Hosp., 1990—. Adv. bd. Riverdale (N.Y.) Mental Health, 1985—. Mem. editl. bd. Pediatric Neurology Jour., 1992—; assoc. editor ACTA Neuropediatrica, 1996—; contbr. chpts. in books, articles and abstracts to profl. jours. Fellow Am. Acad. Pediatrics, Am. Acad. Neurology; mem. AMA, Am. Neurol. Assn., Internat. Chile Neurol. Soc., Child Neurology Soc., N.Y. State Med. Soc., N.Y. County Med. Soc. Avocations: chess, opera, ballet, cinema, travel. Office: NY Hosp/Cornell Univ Divsn Pediatric Neurology 525 E 68th St New York NY 10021-4870

CHVANY, CATHERINE VAKAR, foreign language educator; b. Paris, Apr. 26, 1927; m. 1948; 3 children. BA, Radcliffe Coll., 1963; PhD, Harvard U., 1970. Instr. Russian Wellesley Coll., 1966-67; instr. MIT, 1967-70, lectr., 1970-71, asst. prof., 1971-74, assoc. prof. Russian, 1974-83, prof., 1983-94, emerita, 1994—. Fellow Harvard Russian Rsch. Ctr., 1979—83; vis. prof. U. de. Paris 7, 1991; vis. lectr. Harvard U., 1995; Lindholm vis. prof. U. Oreg., 1999. Author: On the Syntax of BE-Sentences in Russian, 1975, Selected Essays, 1997; co-editor: Slavic Transformational Syntax, 1974, Morphosyntax in Slavic, 1980, Gertruda Vakar. Stikhotvorenija, 1984; New Studies in Russian Language and Literature, 1987; mem. editl. adv. bd. Essays in Poetics, Syntax; contbr. more than 100 articles on linguistics, poetics, Russian and Bulgarian langs. to profl. jours. Lilly postdoctoral teaching award fellow MIT, 1975-76; recipient Phi Beta Kappa, 1963; Disting. Scholarly Career award Assn. Tchrs. Slavic and East European Langs, 1991, Best Book prize 1997. Mem. Bulgarian Studies Assn. Office: MIT 77 Massachusetts Ave Rm 14n305 Cambridge MA 02139-4307 Business E-Mail: cvchvany@mit.edu.

CHWAST, SEYMOUR, graphic artist; b. N.Y.C., Aug. 18, 1931; Student, Cooper Union Sch., N.Y.C.; PhD (hon.), Parsons Sch. Design, 1992. Co-founder Push Pin Studios, 1954; dir., pres. The Pushpin Group Inc. Instr. Parsons Sch. of Design. One-man exhbns. include Royal Palm Gallery, Palm Beach, Fla., 1982, Galerie Delpire, Paris, 1974, Gutenburg Mus., Mainz, Germany, 1984, 35 yr. retrospective exhibition Cooper Union, 1986, Jack Gallery, N.Y., 1987, Mus. of Art, Sao Paulo, Brazil, 1989, Lustrare Gallery, N.Y., 1991, Ginza Graphic Gallery, Tokyo, 1992, Kunstschalter Gallery, N.Y.C., 1994, Sch. of Visual Arts Master Series, 1997, Warsaw Poster Mus., 2000; various group shows; work in permanent collections Mus. Modern Art, N.Y.C., Library of Congress, Washington, Met. Mus. Art, N.Y.C., Whitney Mus. Am. Art, N.Y. Recipient numerous awards including Saint-Gaudens medal, 1972; named to Art Dir.'s Hall of Fame, 1984. Mem. Am. Inst. Graphic Artists (former v.p., medal 1986), Art Dirs.' Club (v.p.), Alliance Graphique Internationale. Office: Pushpin Group 55 E 9th St Ste 1G New York NY 10003-3111 Office Phone: 212-529-7590. E-mail: seymour@pushpininc.com.

CHWAT, ANNE, food service executive; JD, NYU, 1987. Assoc. Clearly Gottlieb Steen & Hamilton, 1987—95; assoc. corp. counsel Joseph E. Seagram & Sons, Inc., 1995—2000; v.p. legal and bus. affairs BMG Music, N.Y.C., 2000—03, gen. counsel, sr. v.p. legal and bus. affairs, 2003—04, chief ethics and compliance officer; exec. v.p., gen. counsel Burger King Corp. Office: 5505 Blue Lagoon Dr Miami FL 33126 Office Phone: 305-378-7913. Business E-Mail: achwat@whopper.com.

CHYNOWETH, ALAN GERALD, retired telecommunications research executive, consultant; b. Harrow, Eng., Nov. 18, 1927; came to U.S. 1952; s. James Charles and Marjorie (Fairhurst) C.; m. Betty Freda Edith Boyce, Sept. 22, 1950; children: Trevor Alan, Kevin Ray. BS in physics, U. London Kings Coll., 1948, PhD, 1950. Demonstrator U. London Kings Coll., 1948-50; postdoctoral fellow NRC, Ottawa, 1950-52; mem. tech. staff Bell Labs., Murray Hill, N.J., 1953-60, dept. head, 1960-65, dir., 1965-76, exec. dir., 1976-83; v.p. applied rsch. Bellcore, Morristown, N.J., 1984-92; cons. R/D Strategy and Mgmt., 1993—. Mem. vis. com. Cornell U. Materials Sci. Ctr., 1973-76; cons. advanced study inst. and rsch. workshops com. NATO, Brussels, 1982-90; lectr. Electrochem. Soc., 1983; alt. dir. Microelectronics and Computer Tech. Corp., Austin, Tex., 1984-92; mem. The Conf. Bd. Internat. Coun. on Mgmt. of Innovation and Tech., 1990-97, mgr., 1995; dir. Optoelectronic Industry Devel. Assn., 1991-92; mem. adv. bd. dept. elec. engring. and computer sci. U. Calif., Berkeley, 1987-93; mem. natural sci. adv. bd. U. Pa., 1988-93; mem. adv. bd. dept. elec. engring. U. So. Calif., 1988-93; mem. Indsl. Rsch. Inst., 1980-92, dir., 1990-92, emeritus, 1993—; mem. indsl. and profl. adv. coun. elec. engring. dept. Pa. State U., 1993-98, chmn., 1995; mem. adv. task force on U.S. indsl. competitiveness U.S. Ho. of Reps., 1987; cons. European Commn. Telecom. Directorate, 1995; advisor to panel on high performance computing and comm. Office Sci. and Tech. Policy, The White House, 1991-92. Assoc. editor Solid State Communications, 1975-83; co-editor: Optical Fiber Telecommunications, 1979; contbr. articles to profl. jours.; patentee in field. Mem. Am. Mgmt. Assn. R & D Coun., 1989-93; chmn. tech. transfer merit program N.J. Commn. on Sci. and Tech., 1992-98. Fellow IEEE (chmn. device rsch. conf. 1963, mem. com. on U.S. competitiveness 1988-89, bd. adv. task force on new initiatives 1989-90, chmn. Marconi award com. 1987, mem. Alexander Graham Bell prize com. 1990-94, chmn. 1992-94, mem. Frederik Philips award com. 1998-02, W.R.G. Baker prize, 1967, Frederik Philips award 1992, engring. leadership recognition 1996, mem. corp. achievement award com. 1999-2003, chmn. 2001-02, mem. awards policies and planning com. 2003-05), Am. Phys. Soc. (indsl. affiliates com. 1984-87, editl. bd. Physics Today 1985-88, George E. Pake prize 1992), Inst. Physics and Phys. Soc. (London), Internat. Engring. Consortium; mem. NRC (survey dir. com. on survey of materials sci. and engring. 1970-74, panel chmn. com. on mineral resources and environ. 1973-75, panel chmn. materials sci. engring. study com. 1986-88, nat. materials adv. bd. 1976-80), Metall. Soc. of AIME (chmn. John Bardeen prize com. 1993-95), Materials Rsch. Soc., N.Y. Acad. Scis. Avocations: travel, boating. Home: 6 Londonderry Way Summit NJ 07901-2914 also: 17 Mill Close Fishbourne Chichester West Sussex PO19 3JW England E-mail: algchy@aol.com.

CHYTIL, FRANK, biochemist; b. Prague, Czechoslovakia, Aug. 28, 1924; came to U.S., 1965, naturalized, 1971; s. Frantisek and Ruzena (Vitouskova) C.; m. Lucie Scheinost, Nov. 26, 1949; children: Frank, Anna, Helena. MS, Sch. Chem. Tech., Prague, 1949, PhD, 1952; C.Sc., Czechoslovak Acad. Sci., Prague, 1956. Rsch. biochemist Charles U., Prague, 1949-51; rsch. fellow Inst. Human Rsch., Prague, 1952-63; sr. scientist Czechoslovak Acad. Sci., Prague, 1956-64; sr. rsch. fellow Brandeis U., Waltham, Mass., 1964, sr. rsch. assoc., 1965-66; head sect. enzymology S.W. Found. Rsch. and Edn., San Antonio, 1966-69; mem. faculty Vanderbilt U., 1969—2000, prof. biochemistry, 1975—2000, Gen. Foods Disting. prof. nutrition, 1984-89, Harvie Branscomb disting. prof., 1993-94, prof. emeritus, 2000—. Adj. assoc. prof. U. Tex., San Antonio, 1968—2000. Editor: Vitamins and Hormones, 1983; mem. editl. bd. Analytical Biochemistry, 1980-87, Jour. Biol. Chemistry, 1982-88, 96-99, Am. Jour. Clin. Nutrition, 1993-95; contbr. articles to profl. jours. Recipient Osborne-Mendel and Lederle awards; USPHS grantee, 1967-99. Fellow Am. Soc. Nutritional Scis.; mem. Am. Soc. Biochemistry and Molecular Biology, Endocrine Soc., Sigma Xi. Home: 914 Lynnwood Blvd Nashville TN 37205-4527 Office: Vanderbilt U Sch Medicine Dept Biochemistry Nashville TN 37232-0146 Personal E-mail: frank.chytil@comcast.net.

CHYUNG, CHI HAN, management consultant; b. Seoul, Republic of Korea, Jan. 27, 1933; arrived in U.S., 1954, naturalized, 1963; s. Do Soon and Boksoon (Kim) Chyung; m. Alice Yvonne Whorley, Dec. 23, 1961; children: Eric, Diana. BS, Kans. Wesleyan U., 1958; MBA, Mich. State U., 1960; postgrad., MIT. Opers. analyst Chevrolet divsn., GM, Detroit, 1959—61; economist Internat. Harvester Co., Chgo., 1961—63; sr. analyst, market divsn. Internat. Minerals & Chem. Corp., Skokie, Ill., 1963—66; mgr., market info. and planning Gulf & Western Industries, N.Y.C., 1966—68; dir., market planning and devel. Am. Standard, Inc., N.Y.C., 1968—71; pres. Oxytech Corp., Medcraft Industries, Inc.; mgmt. cons., internat. market devel. Darien, Conn., 1971—; dir. Korea Hapsum Co.; cons. Taisei Constrn. Co., Tokyo, Govt. of Republic of Korea. Contbr. articles to profl. jours. Served with Korean Army, 1951—53. Mem.: N.Am. Corp. Planning Soc., Am. Chem., Ops. Rsch. Soc., Am. Mktg. Assn., Inst. Mgmt. Scis., Beta Gamma Sigma. Office: Oxytech Corp 433 Boston Post Rd Darien CT 06820-3606

CIABARRA, LOUISE, secondary school educator, medical/surgical nurse; b. Phila., Jan. 28, 1940; d. Nick and Lillian Caruso; m. Mario Ciabarra, Sept. 25, 1965; children: Mimi, Anthony, Lilliana, Nicole, Christopher, Mario. BA, Temple U., 1965; MS, Villanova U., 1975. LPN, Pa.; tchr. chemistry and biology, Pa. Part-time nurse Holy Redeemer Hosp., Pa., 1981—92; tchr. H.S. Phila. Parochial Sch., 1966—. Camp nurse Phila. Diocesan Camp, Jamison, Pa., summers 1988-95, pvt. travel camp, Blue Bell, Pa., summers 1996-2005. Sunday sch. tchr. St. Raymond's Parish, 1976—. Named Tchr. of Yr., Diocesan Sch., Phila., 1987-88, Tchr. of Quarter, 2003; recognized by award "Hero in Edn." by Aktion Club, sponsored by Jenkintown & Glenside Kiwanis Clubs on May 6, 2003. Roman Catholic. Office: Archbishop Wood HS 655 York Rd Warminster PA 18974-2001 Office Phone: 215-672-5050. E-mail: lciabarra@archwood.org.

CIAGALA, KARENCIA LUCILLE, writer; b. Detroit, June 29; d. Rolland Michael and Lucille Mary Ciagala; m. Gary L. Kraatz, Oct. 29, 1968 (div. Jan. 13, 2001); children: Gary L. Jr., Michael L., Brian L., Bruce L., Joseph L. AS in legal assisting, PASCO/Hernando CC; BA in Criminology, St. Leo Univ., 2005. CPA cert. legal asst., Nat. Assn. of Legal Assts. Asst. br. mgr., officer First Fla. Bank, N.A., Brooksville, Fla., 1983-91; office mgr. E.C.I. Funeral Home, Spring Hill, Fla., 1991-98; legal asst. Pasco Hernando Cmty. Coll., 2000; pub. svc. officer City of Tampa, 2004—. Author: Great Poems of Our Time, 1991, In A Different Light, 1991, Listen With Your Heart, 1992, All My Tomorrows, 1992, Roses From Heaven "St. Theresa's Little Way", 1997; author song Roses From Heaven, 1992; newspaper columnist Hernando Today, 1996-2000. Dir. Brooksville Raid Festival Inc., 1985; aux. dep. Hernando County Sheriff's Dept., Brooksville, 1987; v.p. Rep. Woman's Club, Brooksville, 1990; sec., bd. dirs. State of Fla. HRS/Health and Human Svcs. Bd. Dist. 13, 1993-97; dir., treas. Hernando County Child Abuse Prevention Bd., 1990-93; mem. West Hernando Little League, 1992-94; bd. dirs. Health Com. for Children and Youth, 1992-93; appointed by Gov. Jeb Bush to S.W. Fla. Water Mgmt. Lacoochee River Basin Bd, 2000-2001; pub. svc. officer, 2004—; cmty. advisory bd. WEDV TV-PBS, Tampa, Fla., 2003-. Mem. Nat. Assn. Legal Assts., Friends of Libr. Republican. Roman Catholic. Avocations: writing poems, reading, politics. E-mail: karenoiatime@hotmail.com.

CIANCI, PHILIP JOESPH, broadcast engineer; b. White Plains, N.Y., Aug. 7, 1950; s. Philip and Rose Cianci; 1 child, Christopher. AS in Computer Sci., Dutchess C.C., 1985. Design tech. Honeywell, Pleasantville, NY, 1980—84; assoc. mem. rsch. staff Philips Rsch., Braircliff Manor, 1984—2001; broadcast engr. AT&T Broadband/Comcast, N.Y.C., 2002—03; broadcast media engr. ESPN, Bristol, Conn., 2003—. Composer: Matrix Dance Music, 1990, author of poems; contbr. articles to profl. jours.; exhibitions include Javitts Ctr., Jadite Galleries, Ward-Nasse Gallery, Z Gallery, Agora Gallery, The Nat. Arts Club, N.Y.C., Mari Galleries, Memaroneck, N.Y., Westbeth Gallery, N.Y.C., Boston Corp. Art, Hargis Unique Gallery, Calif., Represented in permanent collections Sarnoff Rsch. Inst., Princeton, N.J., Smithsonian Inst. HDTV Archive, Washington; editor: TV Trade web newsletter. Mem.: IEEE, Broadcast Music Inc., Soc. Motion Picture and TV Engrs., Soc. Broadcast Engrs. Avocations: golf, ballroom dancing.

CIANCIMINO, JOSEPH ANDREW, data processing executive; b. Austin, June 30, 1965; s. Joseph Ciancimino and Helen Kay Barbier; m. Melissa Kay McMahan, Mar. 7, 1989. Student aid North Harris Coll., Houston, 1985—86; mgr. Comics & Cards, 1988—96; self employed Spring, 1989—2001; with Altech Computers/Metals, Houston, 1996—97; telecomm. World Datacom, 1997—99; instr. North Harris Coll., 1999—2001; data comm. World Datacom, 2002—04; web server tech. Ev1servers.net, 2004—. Home: 22033 Jay Dr Spring TX 77373 Office Phone: 832-467-0307. E-mail: jciancimino@evl.net.

CIANCIO, GAETANO, transplant surgeon, urologist; b. Roccapiemonte, Salerno, Italy, June 15, 1956; s. Luigi and Maria Ciancio; m. Vivian Ramos; children: Anthony, Joseph. MD, Sch. of Medicine "Luis Razetti", UCV, 1982; MBA, U. Miami, 2001. Diplomate Am. Bd. of Urology 1997. Intern in gen. surgery Jackson Meml. Med. Ctr., U. Miami, Fla., 1986—87, resident in gen. surgery, 1987—89, resident in urology, 1989—92, chief resident urology, 1992—93, fellow in multiorgan transplantation, 1993—95; asst. prof. surgery (multiorgan transplantation) and urology U. Miami, 1995—98, assoc. prof., 1998—, assoc. dir. divsn. of kidney and kidney-pancreas transplantation, 2000—, dir. transplant edn., 2000—, dir. transplant urologic surgery, 2000—. Prof. surgery multiorgan transplantation U. Miami Sch. of Medicine, 2002—, prof. urology, oncology and gen. urology, 2002—. Author, contbr. Flow Cytometry: Advanced Research and Clinical Application, 1989 (Miracle Maker award, 1997); contbr. over 300 articles to profl. jours. Adv. bd. Nat. MOTTEP, Washington, 1997—98; vice chmn. adv. bd. Nat. MOTTEP Program, Washington, 1998—2001. Named The Person of the Mo., Italian Mag., 1998, Hon. Citizen, Comune di Roccapiemonte, Salerno, Italy, 2000, Atteding of the Yr., Award of Excellence for the outstanding dedication and commitment to patients, colleagues and residents, Dept. of Urologic Surgery, U. Miami, 1998—99; named to The Italians of Am., A tribute to America's most significant Italians, The Italians of Am., ed. Alfonso Panico, 1999; recipient Dean's Sr. Faculty Clin. Rsch. award, U. Miami Sch. Medicine, 1999—2000, Honoree, In recognition of extraordinary generosity and tireless dedication in support of organ donation and transplantation, Transplant Found., 2001, Dr. Martin Luther King Jr. Spirit award, Dr. Martin Luther King Festivities Com., Inc., 2002; fellow Surg. Rsch. fellow, VA Med. Ctr., Miami, 1984—86; scholar Exec. MBA Program scholar, University of Miami, 2000—01. Fellow: ACS; mem.: Soc. of Laparoendoscopic Surgeons, Soc. Univ. Surgeons, Am. Soc. of Transplant Surgeons, Urologic Soc. for Transplantation and Vascular Surgery, The Transplantation Soc., Am. Urol. Assn. Office: Univ Miami Sch Medicine 1801 NW 9th Ave Ste 517 Miami FL 33136 Business E-Mail: gciancio@med.miami.edu.

CIANI, ALFRED JOSEPH, language professional, associate dean; b. N.Y.C., June 29, 1946; s. Joseph Alfred and Aurora Smiles (VanOver) C.; m. Sharon Skolkey, Aug. 16, 1968 (div. 1979); children: Mieke Jo, Gabriel Wolf; m. Lesley Lockwood, Aug. 9, 1980; children: Joseph Alfred, Clinton Lockwood. BA, U. Albany, 1969; MA, Coll. of St. Rose, 1972; EdD, Ind. U., 1974. Tchr. Greater Amsterdam (N.Y.) Schs., 1969-72; rsch. asst. Ind. U., Bloomington, 1972-73, assoc. instr., 1973-74; vis. prof. U. Wis., Milw., 1980; asst. prof. U. Cin., 1974-79, assoc. prof., 1979—2002, assoc. dean, info. officer, 1988—2003, prof. emeritus, 2003—. Pres. Ohio Internat. Reading Assn., Columbus, 1981-82; outside cons. State of Miss., Jackson, 1982-84, State of Ky., 1996-99, State of W.Va., 1972-74, 97-98, City of N.Y. Pub. Schs.; cons., U. Oreg. Profl. Devel., Eugene, 1979-80, Nashville Schs., 1982-83, State of W.Va., N.Y.C. Pub. Schs.; mem. Dean's Cabinet; mem. Urban Schs. Task Force. Author: Motivating Reluctant Readers, 1981; editor: (book series) Reading in Content Areas, 1979-81; rev. editor: Rsch. in Mid. Level Edn., 1995—. Grantee Ford Found., 1990, IBM, 1990. Mem. AAUP, Internat. Reading Assn., Am. Edni. Rsch. Assn. (nat. coms.), Assn. Tchr. Educators (nat. coms.), Nat. Coun. Tchrs. English (nat. coms.), Nat. Mid. Sch. Assn. (nat. coms.), Nat. Reading Coun., Phi Delta Kappa, Kappa Delta Pi (counselor). Democrat. Roman Catholic. Avocations: reading, walking, family oriented activities. Office: U Cin Mail Location 02 Cincinnati OH 45221-0001 E-mail: alfred.ciani@uc.edu.

CIANI, JUDITH ELAINE, retired lawyer; b. Medford, Mass., July 24, 1943; d. A. Walter and Ruth Alice (Bowman) C.; m. Marion M. Smith, Sept. 29, 1982. Grad., Thayer Acad., Braintree, Mass., 1961; MA, Mt. Holyoke Coll., 1965; JD, Boston Coll., 1970. Bar: Calif. 1971, U.S. Dist. Ct. (no. dist.) Calif. 1971, U.S. Ct. Appeals (9th cir.) 1971. Aide/press sec. Rep. James A. Burke, Washington, 1965-67; atty. Pillsbury, Madison & Sutro, San Francisco, 1970-78, ptnr., 1978-90; ret., 1990. Del. Calif. Bar Conv., San Francisco, 1973-78, 83-85. Mem. San Francisco Police Commn., 1976-80, Juvenile Justice Task Force, San Francisco, 1981-83; bd. dirs. Bernard Osher Found., San Francisco, 1977—; pres. Common Fund for Legal Svcs., San Francisco, 1985—, Sinfonia San Francisco, 1985-86. Fellow Am. Bar Found.; mem. Bar Assn. San Francisco (bd. dirs., pres. Found. 1978—, bd. dirs. 1981-83, treas. 1987). Home: PO Box 960 Inverness CA 94937-0960 E-mail: jeciani@svn.net.

CIANNELLA, JOEEN MOORE, professional society administrator; b. Warren, Ohio, Mar. 20, 1948; d. Joseph Alvie and Elizabeth Dorthea Moore; m. Christopher M. Ciannella, July 31, 1976 (div. Jan. 1987); children: Bryce C., Tara E. BA in French, Denison U., 1970. Profl. staff U.S. Senate Rep. Policy Com., Washington, 1971-75; owner Jo Moore-Sophisticated Country, Park Ridge, NJ, 1984—; dist. dir. Congresswoman Marge Roukema U.S. Ho. Reps., Ridgewood, NJ, 1985—2002; exec. dir. Hermitage Mus., Hohokus, NJ, 2003—04; dir. devel. Helen Hayes Theatre Co., Nyack, NY, 2004—05; dir. external affairs Greater North Jersey Chpt. Nat. Multiple Sclerosis Soc., Paramus, NJ, 2005—. Mem. Nat. coun. Boy Scouts Am., 1995—98; trustee Greater Roles and Opportunities for Women N.J. GOP, 1997—2002; mem. Park Ridge Bd. Health, 1984—86; founding mem. Pioneer Women Bergen County, 1992—; mem. exec. bd. Bergen coun. Boy Scouts Am., 1991—98, co-chair Pascak Valley Dist. Luncheon, 1991—92, chair spl. events fin., 1993—94, mem. exec. com., 1993—98, vice chmn. fin., 1995—98, mem. exec. bd. No. N.J. coun., 1999—, vice chair fin., 2000—02; mem. exec. bd. Ramapo Coll. Found., 1991—, theme chairperson fundraiser, 1991—94, disting. citizen dinner com., 1991—, mem. bus. network com., 1994—97, chmn. pub. rels. and mktg. com., 1996—2000, mem. exec. com., 1996—, chmn. mktg./instl. rels., 2000—; com. mem. N.J. Network Found. Gala, 2000—02; bd. dirs. Helen Hayes Theater Co., Nyack, NY, 2001—, mem. devel. com. spl. events, 2002—, Day in the Garden, 2003; chairperson spl. effects West Bergen Mental Health 40th Anniversary Ruby Ball, 2003; founding mem. W. Bergen Mental Health Found., 2003—; active Bush for Pres. Campaign, 1988, 1992, Dole for Pres. Campaign, 1996; elected mem. Park Ridge County Com., 1983—, mcpl. chairperson, 1986—96; active Bergen County (N.J.) Rep. Com., 1983—, Park Ridge Rep. Orgn., 1983—, v.p., 1988—89; active N.E. Rep. Orgn. Dist. 39, NJ, 1984—, sec., 1990—91, treas., 1991—92, chairperson, 1992—93; ofcl. com. mem. N.J. GOP Conv.,

1991; charter mem. Women Leadership Summit Rep. Network to Elect Women, 1996—97. Recipient Mission award, Ramapo Coll. Found., 1999, Silver Beaver award, Boy Scouts Am., 1999. Mem.: Jr. League Bergen County (com. mem. Festival of Trees 1988), Ridgewood Unit Rep. Women, Bergen County Women's Rep. Club, N.J. Fedn. Rep. Women, Rep. Women of 90's State N.J., Rotary (mem. com. annual auction Park Ridge chpt. 1990—, chairperson holiday party 1991—). Avocations: gardening, antiques, sports, travel. Home: 34 Spring Valley Rd Park Ridge NJ 07656-1860 Office: Greater North Jersey Chpt Nat Multiple Sclerosis Soc 1 Kalisa Way Ste 205 Paramus NJ 07652 Personal E-mail: jciannella@optonline.net. Business E-Mail: joeen@njb.nmss.org.

CIAO, FREDERICK J., school system administrator, educator; b. Phila. married; 3 children. BA, LaSalle U., 1962; MEd, Temple U., 1965; MA, Villanova U., 1972; PhD, Southwest U., 1990. From tchr. to counselor to dept. chmn. N.E. Cath. High Sch., Phila., 1962-73; vice prin. Archibishop Wood High Sch., Warminster, Pa., 1973-85; prin. Bishop McDevitt H.S., Wyncote, Pa., 1985-93, pres., 1993—2003, Archbishop Wood H.S., Warminster, Pa., 2003—. Mem. adj. faculty St. Agnes Hosp. Nursing Sch., Phila., 1963-71, Spring Garden Coll., Phila., 1971-73, Gwynedd Mercy Coll., Gwynedd Valley, Pa., 1976-84, LaSalle U., 1980—; presentor Nat. Diffusion Network, 1992—. Mem. edn. advisor Phila. Orch., 1993—, Italian Lang. Preservation Found., 1999—. Named Man of the Yr., N.E. Cath. Alumni Assn., 1972, Educator of the Yr., Millay Club, 1986; named to Legion of Honor, Chapel of Four Chaplains, 1980; recipient John Neumann medal St. John Neumann High Sch., 1985. Mem. Nat. Assn. Secondary Sch. Prins., Nat. Cath. Edn. Assn., Nat. Coun. Tchrs. of Maths., Maths. Assn. Am., Nat. Assn. Curriculum Devel., Nat. Coun. for Self Esteem, Mid. States Assn. of Colls. (chair). Office: Archbishop Wood HS 655 York Rd Warminster PA 18974

CIARVELLA, DAVID R., music educator, plastics company executive; b. Rochester, N.Y., Aug. 29, 1970; s. Robert John Ciarvella and Donna Marie Dolan; m. Julie Mae Aarssen, July 28, 2001; stepchildren: Amber Lehman, Jessie Lehman, Marcie Lehman. BS Music Edn., Robert Wesleyan Coll., Rochester, N.Y., 2000. Prodn. mgr. Helvie Plastic Extrusions, Rochester, NY, 1991—2002; music tchr. Churchville-Chili H.S., Churchville, NY, 2000—02; adj. prof. Robert Wesleyan Coll., Rochester, 2002; music tchr. Chestnut Ridge Elem. Sch., Rochester, 2002—. Cpl. USMC, 1998—2001, Buffalo, N.Y. Republican. Free Methodist. Home: 28 Fitch St Churchville NY 14428 Mailing: PO Box 463 Churchville NY 14428

CIATTO, FRANK A., lawyer; b. Jersey City, July 25, 1966; BA cum laude, Georgetown U., 1988; JD, Georgetown U. Law Ctr., 1994. CPA NY, 1991; bar: NJ 1994, NY 1995, DC 1995. Auditor Coopers & Lybrand LLP (now PricewaterhouseCoopers LLP), NYC; ptnr., Bus. Trans. Dept. Venable LLP, Washington. Contbr. Bd. gov., Alumni Assn. Georgetown U., Washington, 2003—. Avocation: baseball. Office: Venable LLP 575 7th St NW Washington DC 20004 Office Phone: 202-344-8510. Office Fax: 202-344-8300. Business E-Mail: faciatto@venable.com.

CIBES, WILLIAM JOSEPH, JR., chancellor, educator; b. Newton, Kans., Aug. 25, 1943; s. William Joseph and Dorothy Beulah Cibes; m. Margaret Ann Collins, Sept. 2, 1967; 1 child, Julia Katherine. BA, U. Kans., 1965; PhD, Princeton (N.J.) U., 1975. Instr. to prof. Conn. Coll., New London, 1969-91; sec. Office of Policy and Mgmt., State of Conn., Hartford, 1991-94; chancellor Conn. State U. System, Hartford, 1994—. State rep. Conn. Gen. Assembly, Hartford, 1979-91. Democrat. Roman Catholic. Office: Conn State Univ System 39 Woodland St Hartford CT 06105-2337 Office Phone: 860-493-0010. Business E-Mail: cibesw@so.ct.edu.

CIBULSKI, DANA M., art educator, artist; b. New Orleans, Sept. 30, 1959; d. Floyd Edward and Earline Mouton Cibulski; m. Scott Bronstein; 1 child, Lucas Alphonse Bronstein. Student, U. Innsbruck, 1981; BA, U. New Orleans, 1982; MFA, CCNY, 1984. Instr. art CCNY, NYC, 1983—88; asst. registrar The Jewish Mus., 1983—85; dir. asst. gallery Atlanta Coll. Art, 1988—90, instr. art, 1990—96; contbg editor, paris corr. Art Papers Mag., 1996—2000. Chair, gallery com. Arts Exch., Atlanta, 1995—96; contbg. writer Sculpture Mag., Washington, 1995—; guest curator Lincoln Ctr. Performing Arts, NYC, 1986. Commission, atlanta airport, Kudzu Frieze. Chair, exhibitions com. Women's Caucus Art, NYC, 1985—86. Grantee, City of Atlanta, Bur. Cultural Affairs, 1990, Ga. Coun. Arts, 1991. Mem.: Coll. Art Assn., Women's Caucus Art (v.p. 1986—88, chair exhbns. com. 1985—86), City Coll. Art Art Alumni, Nat. Honor Soc. Democrat. Unitarian Universalist. Avocations: gardening, cooking, travel, reading, poetry. Home Fax: none.

CICCARELLI, CHICK, marketing professional; b. Oakland, Calif., Apr. 30, 1956; s. Wanda Bridges, Bernard Ciccarelli; m. Julia Barinova. Student, Calif. State U., Long Beach, 1976—78. Sr. art dir. Reeds, Farris & Lewis, Studio City, Calif., 1989—93; co-founder, exec. v.p. Theafilm Distribn. Network, Inc., Hollywood, Calif., 1993—95; pres. System X Entertainment, Hollywood, 1995—97; v.p. comm. Moviola, Hollywood, 1997—99, L.A. Digital Post, West Toluca Lake, Calif., 1999—2000; pres. Chick, Inc., Valley Village, Calif., 2000—. Creator (Online Digital Video Delivery System) Editvu, 2001. Recipient Cert. of Achievement, Voyager Flight, Smithsonian Inst., 1987, Cert. of Achievement, Design, Printing Industries of Am. Awards, 1985, 1986, 1988, Art Dirs. Club of L.A., 1987. Democrat. Roman Catholic. Avocation: traveling abroad.

CICCARONE, DANIEL, medical educator, researcher; b. NYC, Nov. 30, 1961; s. Pat and Joan Ciccarone; life ptnr. Kim Koester. MD, SUNY, 1987; MPH, U. Calif., Berkeley, 1998. Bd. cert. Am. Bd. Family Practice, 1992, Am. Bd. Preventive Medicine, 2003. Asst. prof. U. Calif., San Francisco, 2000—. Contbr. articles to profl. jours. Grantee Career Devel. award, NIH, 2004. Mem.: APHA, Am. Anthrop. Assn. Liberal. Avocation: bicycling. Office: U Calif 3180 18th St Ste 302 San Francisco CA 94110 Office Phone: 415-514-0275. Business E-Mail: ciccaron@fcm.ucsf.edu.

CICCARONE, RICHARD ANTHONY, financial executive; b. Akron, Ohio, June 15, 1952; s. Andrew and Marie Antoinette Ciccarone; m. Marilyn Douglas DeBorde, May 26, 1984. BA, Miami U., Oxford, Ohio, 1974; MA, U. Akron, 1978. Mcpl. bond analyst Harris Bank, Chgo., 1977-82, mcpl. rsch. mgr., 1982-83; v.p., dir. rsch., sr. analyst Van Kampen Merritt Investment Adv. Corp. (formerly Am. Portfolio), Lisle, Ill., 1983-89; sr. v.p., dir. fixed income rsch. Blunt Ellis & Loewi, Inc., Chgo., 1989-90; exec. v.p., dir. tax exempt fixed income rsch. Everen Securities Inc. (formerly Kemper Securities), Chgo., 1990-96; sr. v.p., co-dir. mcpl. investments, dir. mcpl. rsch., co-head fixed income dept. Van Kampen Inv. Adv. Corp. unit of Morgan Stanley, Oakbrook Terrace, Ill., 1996—2001; pres. Merritt Rsch. Svcs. LLC, Oakbrook Terrace, Ill., 2001—; mng. dir. McDonnell Investment Mgmt. LLC, Oakbrook Terrace, Ill., 2001—. Publisher MuniNet Guide Review, 1996—. Contbr. articles to profl. jours. and fin. pubs. Mem. exec. com., bd. dirs. Civic Fedn. Chgo.; mem. Village of Hinsdale Plan Commn., 1995-99; bd. trustees Village Hinsdale, 1999-2003; co-chair Am. Heart Assn., DuPage County Walkathon, 2000; bd. dirs. Hinsdale Libr. Found. Named All-Am Mcpl. Analyst (2d team), Global Guaranty, 1990, 91, The Bond Buyer, 1993, All-Am. Mcpls. Analyst, Generalist (2d team), 1993, Institutional Investor Mag., 1992, 94, Mcpl. Analyst Generalist (1st team), Institutional Investor Mag., 1995, 1st Team All-Star Smith's Rsch. and Ratings as Mcpl. Generalist, 1995, 96, 97, 98, 99, 1st Team All-Star Buyside Mcpl. Rsch. Dir., 1997, 98, 99, 2003, 04 Mem. Nat. Fedn. Mcpl. Analysts (nat. chmn. 1984-85, Disting. Svc. award 1988, Standards and Practices chair 1991-92, Long Term Planning Chair 1993-94, govt. acctg. standards adv. coun. 1996-99), Soc. Mcpl. Analysts (sec. treas. 2005—), Chgo. Mcpl. Analysts Soc. (pres. 1984), So. Mcpl. Fin. Soc., Miami (Ohio) U. Alumni Assn. (pres. Chgo. chpt. 1988-89), Com. of One Hundred (Hinsdale, Ill., pres. 1998-99), Omicron Delta Kappa. Roman Catholic. Home: 733 S Bodin St Hinsdale IL 60521-4316 Office: McDonnell Investment Mgmt LLC 1515 W 22d St 11th Fl Hinsdale IL 60523 Office Phone: 630-684-8697. Business E-Mail: ciccaroner@mcdmgmt.com.

CICCHERTI, DANTE, psychology professor; BS, U. Pitts., 1971; PhD, U. Minn., 1977. Lic. psychologist Mass., N.Y. Instr. dept. psychology U. Pitts., 1971—72; asst. prof. dept. psychology and social rels. Harvard U., Cambridge, Mass., 1977—82, dir. devel. risk rsch. project, 1978—85, dir. daycare and families project, 1978—85, assoc. prof. dept. psychology and social rels., 1982—83, Norman Tishman assoc. prof. psychology, mem. faculty Grad. Sch. Edn. Program in Human Devel., 1982—85; from assoc. prof. psychology and psychiatry to prof. psychology and psychiatry U. Rochester, NY, 1985—87, dir. Mt. Hope Family Ctr., 1985—, prof. psychology, psychiatry, and pediats., 1994—, prof. clin. and social scis. in psychology, psychiatry, and pediats., 1995—, Shirley Cox Kearns prof. psychology, psychiatry, and pediats., 2000—. Mem. Psychiat. Epidemiology Ctr. Harvard Med. Sch.; mem. Bush Ctr. in Child Devel. and Social Policy Yale U.; mem. ethics com. Am. Inst. for Rsch. in Behavioral Scis.; head Ad Hoc Com. on Emotionally Disturbed and Mentally Ill Children, Rochester; trainer intake and protective/preventive svc. workers Monroe County Dept. Social Svcs.; rsch. leader Surgeon Gen.'s Coun. on Interpersonal Violence; mem. nominating com. Joseph Zubin Award, 2000, 01; fellow Ctr. for Advanced Study of Behavioral Scis., Stanford U., 1992; mem. editl. bd. Devel. Psychology, 2004—, Attachment and Human Development, 1998—; mem. adv. bd. New Directions for Youth Development: Theory, Practice and Research, 2001—; founding editor Development and Psychopathology, 1988—; mem. editl. adv. bd. Zero to Three: National Center on Infants, Toddlers, and Families, 1997—; cons. editor Psychol. Bull., 1996—2002. Author papers to profl. jours. and chpts. to books. Recipient Young Scholars award in social and affective devel., Found. for Child Devel., 1982, Sci. Merit award, Nat. Inst. Mental Health, 1991—96, Outstanding Rsch. Study award, Am. Profl. Soc. on Abuse of Children, 1995, Rsch. Career Achievement award, 1997, John Romano award, Mental Health Assn., 2001. Fellow: APA (mem. divsn. 7, mem. rev. com. Nat. Ctr. on Child Abuse and Neglect, mem. selection com. Boyd McCandless Award divsn. 7 1991—93, chairperson Boyd McCandless Award Com. divsn. 7 1991—93, Boyd McCandless award 1983, Disting. Contbns. to Rsch. in Clin. Child Psychology award divsn. 12 1999, Nicholas Hobbs award divsn. 37 1999, Sr. Career award for disting. contbns. to psychology in pub. interest 2004)); mem.: Internat. Soc. for Rsch. on Emotions, Am. Acad. Psychoanalysis (mem. com. on children and adolescents), Soc. for Rsch. in Child Devel. (mem. planning com. for 1981 conv., chmn. on conv. info. and publicity). Office: U Rochester Mt Hope Family Ctr 187 Edinburgh St Rochester NY 14608

CICCOELLA, CHARLES S. (CHICK), federal agency administrator; BS, Auburn U.; MS, Ctrl. Mich. U. Dir. info. tech. policy, senate rules com. U.S. Senate, Washington; dep. asst. sec. for veterans US Dept. of Labor, Washington, acting asst. sec. for veterans employment & training, asst. sec., 2005—. Office: US Dept Labor 200 Constitution Ave NW Rm S1325 Washington DC 20210 Office Phone: 202-693-4700. Office Fax: 202-693-4754. E-mail: ciccolella.charles@dol.gov.*

CICCOLO, ANGELA, lawyer; b. Indpls., Aug. 12, 1961; BSFS, Georgetown U., 1983, JD, 1992. Bar: DC 1992, admitted to practice: US Dist. Ct. (DC) 1993. Asst. gen. counsel NAACP, interim gen. counsel, 2005—. Staff mem. Georgetown Internat. Environ. Law Rev., 1990—91, Writing Program Editor, 1991—92. Mem.: Women's Bar Assn., DC Trial Lawyers Assn., Bar Assn. DC. Democrat. Office: NAACP 4805 Mt Hope Dr Fifth Floor Baltimore MD 21215 Office Phone: 410-580-5792.

CICCONE, AMY NAVRATIL, art librarian; b. Detroit, Sept. 19, 1950; d. Gerald R. and Ruth C. (Kauer) Navratil. BA, Wayne State U., 1972; AM in Library Sci., U. Mich., 1973. Rsch. libr. Norton Simon Mus., Pasadena, Calif., 1974-81; chief libr. Chrysler Mus., Norfolk, Va., 1981-88; head libr. Architecture and Fine Arts Libr. U. So. Calif., L.A., 1988-97, acting asst. univ. libr. pub. svcs., 1993-95, ref. libr., 1997—2004, assoc. coord. collection devel., 2004—. Contbr. articles to profl. jours.; cons. editor Art Reference Svcs., 1990-98. Mem. Art Libraries Soc. N.Am. (moderator Decorative Arts Roundtable, 1991-93, facilities standards com. 1986-91, chmn. strategic planning task force 1994-96, vice-chmn. So. Calif. chpt. 1989, chmn. 1990, chmn. 2001 conf.), Rsch. Librs. Group, Art & Architecture Group (steering com. 1992-94). Office: U So Calif Libr Los Angeles CA 90089-1823 Office Phone: 213-740-1958. Business E-Mail: aciccone@usc.edu.

CICCONE, JOHN, information technology manager; At, Queens Coll., N.Y. Programmer and CICS support CBS, Inc., 1967—75, dir. sys. and programming records divsn., 1975—77, dir. apps. devel. and sys. software, 1977—81, dir. and sr. cons., 1981—85, dir. MIS engring. divsn., 1985—87, dir. MIS West Coast, 1987—94, dir. LAN ops., 1995—96, dir. tech. svcs. CBS Data Ctr., 1996—97; project mgr. and dir. tech. svcs. data ctr. Sys. Mgmt. Specialists, 1997—99; project mgr. AT & T Labs, 2000—. Address: 4 Oscar Way Yardville NJ 08620

CICCONE, MADONNA LOUISE VERONICA See MADONNA

CICCONI, JAMES WILLIAM, lawyer; b. Elmira, NY, June 8, 1952; s. Raymond Joseph and Doris Arlene (Strong) C.; m. Patricia Olivia Burgess, Aug. 10, 1974; children: Jill, Sara, Rachel. BA, U. Tex., 1974, JD, 1977. Bar: Tex. 1977, D.C. 1985. Issues dir. Jim Baker for Atty. Gen. campaign, Austin, Tex., 1977-78; adminstrv. asst. to the gov. State of Tex., Austin, 1979-80, gen. counsel to the sec. of state, 1980-81; spl. asst. to the pres., to the chief of staff The White House, Washington, 1981-85; sr. issues advisor Bush-Quayle '88 campaign, Washington, 1987-88; asst. to the pres., dep. chief of staff The White House, Washington, 1989-90; atty. Akin Gump Strauss Hauer & Feld, Washington, 1985-88, 91-98, ptnr., 1991—98; gen. counsel, exec. v.p. law and govt. affairs AT&T, Washington, 1998—. Issues dir. Bush-Quayle '92 Campaign; dep. dir. strategy Dole-Kemp '96 Campaign; dir. El Paso Electric Co., Am. Coun. Germany; cons. U.S. State Dept.; advisor Bush-Cheney transition. V.p. George Bush Presdl. Libr. Found., College Station, Tex., 1991—; del. Conf. Security Cooperation Europe (CSCE); mem. Adminstrv. Conf. U.S., U.S. Reform Observation Panel for UNESCO. Mem. D.C. Bar Assn., State Bar Tex. Republican. Roman Catholic. Avocations: baseball, tennis. Office: AT&T 1120 20th St NW Ste 1000 Washington DC 20036

CICERCHI, ELEANOR ANN TOMB, fundraising executive; b. Sayre, Pa., Dec. 11, 1944; d. William Horton and Brinton Elizabeth (Cauffiel) Tomb; m. Robert A. Weskerna, Nov. 19, 1966 (div. Feb. 1981); children: Amy Marie, Robert Campbell; m. Philip J. Cicerchi, July 1982. AB with great distinction, Mt. Holyoke Coll., 1966; MS, New Sch. Social Rsch., 1992. Cert. fundraising exec. Sr. mktg. rep. Group Health Plan, Guttenberg, N.J., 1976-79; dir. comty. rels. Burke Rehab. Ctr., White Plains, N.Y., 1979-84; exec. dir. Bergen comty. Coll. Fedn., Paramus, N.J., 1984-86; campaign counsel Brakeley John Price Jones, Inc., Stanford, Conn., 1986-88; v.p. instnl. advancement Marymount Coll., Tarrytown, N.Y., 1988-93; dir. maj. gifts Am. Found. for AIDS Rsch., N.Y.C., 1993-95, chief devel. officer, 1995-96; v.p. devel. and external affairs ORBIS Internat., Inc., N.Y.C., 1996-2000; assoc. v.p. devel. Save the Children, Westport, Conn., 2000—02; dir. devel. The Corning Mus. of Glass, 2002—. Faculty mem. Fundraising Sch., Ctr. Philanthropy, Ind. U., Indpls., 1989—; adj. grad. faculty mem. NYU, N.Y.C., 1990-97, New Sch. for Social Rsch., N.Y.C., 1995—, chmn. PR Group for Vision 2000: The Right to Sight, Geneva, 1998-99; bd. dirs. AMD Alliance, 1999-2001, devel. and marching com. Am. Assn. Mus. Author: Raid!, 1978, Anonymous Giving, 1991; co-author: The Earth Shook and the Sky Was Red, 1976, The Flower of the Virginian, 1980; editor: The Architecture of Bergen County, 1991. Bd. dirs., past chmn. Philharmonia Virtuosi, Dobbs Ferry, NY, 1985—2002; v.p. Orch. of the Finger Lakes, 2003—05, pres., 2005—, Dem. Club, River Vale, NJ, 1978—81; bd. dirs., sec. Am. Anorexia-Bulimia Assn., N.Y.C., 1984—99; bd. dirs. Planned Parenthood of the So. Finger Lakes, 2003—. Woodrow Wilson fellow, 1966; Sarah Williston scholar, 1964, Mt. Holyoke scholar, 1963. Mem. Am. Assn. Fundraising Profls. (Greater N.Y. chpt. v.p. 1993-95, 2004—, Finger Lakes chpt. bd. dirs., Finger Lakes chpt. Philanthropist of Yr. 2004), Assn. of Fundraising Profls. (Profl. Fundraiser of Yr., Finger Lakes chpt. 2004), Assn. for Rsch. on Nonprofit Orgns. and Voluntary Action, Phi Beta Kappa. Office: The Corning Museum of Glass One Museum Way Corning NY 14830 Office Phone: 607-974-5683. Business E-Mail: cicerchiet@cmog.org.

CICERO, CARMEN LOUIS, artist, educator; b. Newark, N.J., Aug. 14, 1926; s. Carmen and Mae C. BS in Fine Arts Edn., Newark State Coll., 1951; postgrad., Hunter Coll., N.Y.C., 1953; MFA, Montclair State College, 1991. Tchr. elem. sch., Paterson, N.J., 1951-54; tchr. secondary sch. Roselle Park, N.J., 1954-57; prof. Sarah Lawrence Coll., Bronxville, N.Y., 1959-68, Montclair Coll., N.J., 1969—. Participated in 34 solo exhbns. including various one-man shows New Orleans, 1969-71, N.Y.C., 1971-74, 1982, Los Angeles, 1978, Provincetown, Mass., 1979, 81, groups shows Rome-N.Y. Art Found., Premiere Bienale De Paris, France, Mus. des 20 Jahrunderts, Austria, Roosevelt House, New Delhi, N.Y. World's Fair; represented in permanent collections at 26 Mus., including Fogg Mus., Harvard U., Guggenheim Mus., N.Y.C., Mus. Modern Art, N.Y.C., N.J. State Mus., Trenton, Worcester Mus., Mass., Whitney Mus. Am. Art, N.Y.C., Art Gallery of Toronto, Can., Newark Mus., Larry Aldrich Mus., Conn., Mus. Boymaus Van Beuningen, Holland, Hirschhorn Mus., Washington, Neuberger Mus., Purchase, N.Y., Exeter Acad., N.H., Cornell U., Springfield Mus., Mass., Mint. Mus., Charlotte, N.C., Nat. Mus. Am. Art. Smithsonian Inst., Met. Mus., Long Point Gallery, Mass., June Kelly Gallery, N.Y.C., 6 anns., Whitney Mus. Am. Art. Guggenheim fellow, 1957, 63 Mem. Graham Gallery N.Y.C.

CICERO, J. DEBORAH, management consultant; b. Pitts., Mar. 24, 1948; d. James Francis and Margaret V. (Wuillmier) H. Diploma, Columbia Sch. Nursing, Pitts., 1969; BSN, La Roche Coll., Pitts., 1987; M in Pub. Mgmt./Healthcare, Carnegie Mellon U., 1988. Cert. med. staff coord., profl. in healthcare quality; RN Pa. Clin. asst. to exec. v.p. Forbes Health System, Pitts., 1983-88; dir. med. staff svcs. Monongahela Valley Hosp., Pitts., 1988-90; quality tracking mgr. Humana, Louisville, 1990-91, regional quality mgmt. dir., 1991-92; sr. cons. MetriCor, Inc., Louisville, 1992-94, mgr. accreditation svcs., 1994-95, HCIA-Sachs, Louisville, 1995-96, sr. quality mgmt. cons., JCAHO liaison, 1996-98; mgr. accreditation svcs. Performance Improvement, 1998-99; dir. accreditation svcs. and performance improvement Soluciant, LLC, 2000—03, PQC Enterprises, LLC, 2003—. Author study guide and publ. newsletter. Mem. Nat. Assn. Med. Staff Svcs., Nat. Assn. for Health Care Quality (study guide task force 1996-99), Ky. Assn. for Healthcare Quality (treas. 1996-99, pres. 2000-02), Am. Hosp. Assn., Pa. Assn. for Healthcare Quality. Avocations: exercising, biking, reading, music. Office Phone: 412-473-0104. Personal E-mail: dcicero01@comcast.net.

CICERONE, RALPH JOHN, foundation administrator, research scientist; b. New Castle, Pa., May 2, 1943; m. Carol Cicerone; 1 child, Sara. SB, MIT, 1965; MS in Elec. Engring. and Physics, U. Ill., Urbana-Champaign, 1967, PhD in Elec. Engring. and Physics, 1970. Physicist U.S. Dept. Commerce, 1967; rsch. asst. aeronomy U. Ill., 1967—70; assoc. rsch. scientist aeronomy space physics rsch. lab. U. Mich., Ann Arbor, 1970—78; assoc. rsch. chemist ocean rsch. divsn. U. Calif., San Diego, 1978—80, rsch. chemist Scripps inst. oceanography, 1980—81, Daniel G. Aldrich chair in earth system sci., prof. chemistry Irvine, 1989—94, dean Sch. Phys. Scis., 1994—98, chancellor, 1998—2005; sr. scientist, dir. atmospheric chemistry divsn. Nat. Ctr. Atmospheric Rsch., Boulder, Colo., 1980—89. Lectr., asst. prof. elec. engring. U. Mich., Ann Arbor, 1973—75. Assoc. editor: Jour. Geophysics Rsch., 1977—79; editor, 1979—83. Mem. adv. bd. Marian Koshland Sci. Mus. Recipient Bower award for Achievement in Sci., Franklin Inst., 1999, Albert Einstein World award of Sci., 2004. Fellow: AAAS, Am. Geophys. Union (Macelwane award 1979, Revelle medal 2002), Am. Meteorol. Soc., Am. Chem. Soc.; mem.: NAS (elected 1990, bd. sustainable devel. 1995—98, mem. coun. 1996—99, com. on a guide for recruiting & advancing women in sci. and engring. 2000—, chair com. on climate sci. 2001, pres. 2005—), Am. Philos. Soc., Am. Acad. Arts and Scis. Office: Nat Acad Scis 500 Fifth St NW Washington DC 20001

CICET, DONALD JAMES, lawyer; b. New Orleans, May 24, 1940; s. Arthur Alphonse and Myrtle (Ress) C.; m. Iona Perry. BA, Nicholls State U., 1963; JD, Loyola U., New Orleans, 1969. Bar: La. 1969, U.S. Dist. Ct. (ea. dist.) La. 1972, U.S. Dist. Ct. (mid. dist.) La. 1978, U.S. Dist. Ct. (we. dist.) La. 1979, U.S. Ct. Appeals (5th cir.) 1972, U.S. Supreme Ct. 1972. Pvt. practice, Reserve, La., 1969—88, LaPlace, La., 1988—; staff atty. La. Legis. Coun., 1972-73; legal counsel Nicholls State U. Alumni Fedn., 1974-76, 78-80; spl. counsel Pontchartrain Levee Dist., 1976—2001. Adminstrv. law judge La. Dept. Civil Svc., 1981—. Pres. Boys' State of La. Inc., 1990-92, bd. dirs., 1988—. With AUS, 1964, USNG, 1964-70. Recipient Am. Jurisprudence award Loyola U., 1968. Fellow La. Bar Found.; mem. ABA, La. Bar Assn. (ho. dels. 1973-77, 79-85), 40th Jud. Dist. Bar Assn. (pres. 1985-87). ATLA, La. Trial Lawyers Assn., Nicholls State U. Alumni Fedn. (exec. coun. 1972-76, 77-85, pres. 1982, James Lynn Powell award 1980), Am. Legion (post cmdr. 1976-77, dist. judge adv. 1975-95, judge adv. La. dept. 1990-92, 93-96, mem. La. dept. commn. on nat. security and govtl. affairs 1974-89, chmn. 1977-78, 79-81, 85-89, M.C. Gehr blue cap award 1983). Roman Catholic. Home: 263 Central Ave Reserve LA 70084-6003 Office: 197 Belle Terre Blvd La Place LA 70069-0461

CICHELLO, SAMUEL JOSEPH, architect; b. Syracuse, N.Y., June 19, 1931; s. Anthony John and Margaret (Stanziana) C.; m. Eileen Agnes O'Toole, Feb. 13, 1960; children: Mary, Teresa, Claire, Anthony, John, Michael, Paul. BArch, Syracuse U., 1954. Lic. architect, N.Y. Draftsman Pederson & Hueber, Syracuse, 1951-53, Hawley E. McAfee, Fayetteville, N.Y., 1954-55; project adminstr. Hueber Hares & Glavin, Syracuse, 1959-63; pvt. practice Weedsport, N.Y., 1963—. Editor: Environment of Educational Facilities, 1966. Town assessor Town of Brutus, 1972-95. With U.S. Army, 1955-56. Mem. AIA (award of merit 1967), N.Y. State Assn. Architects, Weedsport C. of C. (pres. 1965-68), Lions Club (pres. 1968-70). Republican. Roman Catholic. Avocation: woodworking. Office Phone: 315-689-7090.

CICILIONI, ORLANDO JOSEPH, plastic surgeon; b. Scranton, Pa., June 29, 1967; s. Orlando Joseph Cicilioni, Sr. and Carmella Maria Ciaglia; m. Lori Anne Vaughn, Oct. 19, 2002; children: Kelly, Kurt, Orlando III. BS, U. Scranton, 1988; MD, 1992. Diplomate Am. Bd. Surgery, 1997, Am. Bd. Plastic Surgery, 2001. Surgeon Fla. Hosp. Shares Found., Orlando, Fla., 2002—. Fellow: ACS. Office: Orlando Cosmetic Surgery LLC 1000 N Maitland Ave Ste B Maitland FL 32751 Office Phone: 407-681-3223. Office Fax: 407-681-0976.

CICILLINE, J. CLEMENT, mental health services professional, state legislator; b. Providence, Feb. 7, 1940; 6 children. AB, Providence Coll., 1962; MS, U. R.I., 1967. Mem. Newport (R.I.) Sch. Com., 1979-91, 92—, R.I. Senate, Dist. 50, Providence, 1992—2002; pres., CEO, Newport County Cmty. Mental Health Ctr., 1986—. Mem. Vols. in Newport Edn.; chair Dr. M.L. King Jr. State Holiday Commn.; chair Spl. Legis. Commn. to Study Svcs. to Mentally Ill Persons in Criminal Justice Sys.; vice chair Select Commn. on Race and Police Cmty. Rels.; mem. Gov.'s Commn. on Bias and Prejudice, Gov.'s Coun. on Mental Health. Mem. R.I. Coun. of Cmty. Mental Health Orgns., R.I. State Senate, 1992—, Senate Majority Pol. Leader; Forum Lodge Sons of Italy, Newport County Psychol. Soc. Democrat. Address: PO Box 3456 Newport RI 02840-0992

CICIO, ELIZABETH BUNTING, special education educator; b. St. Louis, Jan. 31, 1974; d. James T. and JoElla R. Harris; children: Kourtney Mackenzie, Dominic Joseph. AS, Belleville Area Coll., 1994; BS in Social Work, So. Ill. U., Edwardsville, 1998, BS in Spl. Edn., 2003. Adolescent substance abuse counselor Mid-America Behavioral Health, Belleville, Ill., 1998—99; social worker Granite City (Ill.) Sch. Dist., 1999—2000, spl. edn. tchr., 2003—; crisis counselor Phoenix Crisis Ctr., Granite City, 2000—02. Mem. Renaissance Com., Granite City, 2004—. Mem.: NASW. Avocations: reading, gardening, swimming. Office Phone: 618-451-5808.

CICIRELLI, VICTOR GEORGE, psychologist; b. Miami, Fla., Oct. 1, 1926; s. Felix and Rene (DeMaria) C.; m. Jean Alice Solveson, Aug. 9, 1953; children: Ann Victoria, Michael Felix, Gregory Sheldon. BS, Notre Dame U., 1947; MA, U. Ill., Urbana, 1950; M.Ed., U. Miami, 1956; PhD (Univ. fellow), U. Mich., 1964; PhD, Mich. State U., 1971. Asst. prof. ednl. psychology U. Mich., 1963-65; dir. student teaching for elem., secondary and M.A.T. programs U. Pa., 1965-67; assoc. prof. early childhood edn. Ohio U., 1967-68; dir. research Nat. Evaluation of Head Start Westinghouse Learning Corp. at Ohio U., 1968-69; Office Edn. postdoctoral fellow U. Wis. Inst. Cognitive Learning, 1969-70; prof. human devel. Purdue U., 1970-73, prof. devel./aging psychology, 1974—, dir. devel. psychology program, 1977-78, 80-81, 82-83, 92-93, 96, 99-2001. Vis. sci. fellow Max Planck Inst. for Human Devel. and Edn., Berlin, 1991; fellow Ctr. for Health Policy Rsch., J. Hillis Miller Health Sci. Ctr., Sch. Medicine, U. Fla., Gainesville, 1991; Petersen vis. scholar in gerontology and family studies Oreg. State U., 2004-05; rsch. adv. bd. Calif. Commn. for Tchr. Preparation and Licensing, 1973-78; scholar NSF Inst., Ohio U., 1956, Am. U., 1958, U. Fla., 1960; cons. in field. Author: Helping Elderly Parents: Role of Adult Children, 1981, Family Caregiving: Autonomous and Paternalistic Decision Making, 1992, Sibling Relationships Across the Life Span, 1995, Older Adults' Views on Death, 2002; mem. editl. bd.: Jour. Marriage and the Family, 1990—; contbr. articles to profl. publs. Bd. dirs. Nat. Com. on Prevention of Elder Abuse, 1988-91; mem. adv. com. Ind. Geriatric Edn. Ctr., U. Ind., 1991. Grantee OEO, 1968-69, 71-73, U.S. Office Edn., 1971-73; Nat. Inst. Edn., 1973-74, NIH, 1973-74, Office Child Devel., 1973-74, Nat. Ret. Tchrs. Assn./Am. Assn. Ret. Persons Andrus Found., 1978-82, 90-92, 95, Retirement Rsch. Found., 1984-85, 87-89; fellow Andrew Norman Inst. Advanced Study, Andrus Gerontology Ctr., U. So. Calif., 1984, Gerontology Soc., 1983-84. Fellow APA, Gerontol. Soc.; mem. Internat. Soc. Study Behavioral Deve., Am. Psychol. Soc., Am. Assn. Aging, Nat. Coun. on Family Rels. Soc. for Chaos Theory, Phi Kappa Phi. Roman Catholic. Home: 1221 N Salisbury St West Lafayette IN 47906-2415 Office: Purdue U Dept Psychol Sci West Lafayette IN 47907 Office Phone: 765-494-6925. Business E-Mail: victor@psych.purdue.edu.

CICOLANI, ANGELO GEORGE, research and development company executive, operating engineer; b. Norwood, Mass., Mar. 4, 1933; s. Luigi and Maria (Fossa) Cicolani; m. Marilyn Adell Griffith, June 4, 1955 (div. Jan. 1968); children: George, Susanne, Diana; m. Patricia Anne Kirsch, Nov. 1, 1979 (dec. July 1995); m. Christine Elizabeth Blair, Apr. 1, 2001. Student, Northeastern U., 1950; BS, U.S. Naval Acad., Annapolis, Md., 1955, Naval Postgrad. Sch., 1969. Commd. ensign U.S. Navy, 1955, advanced through grades to lt. comdr., 1975, chief reactor operator, 1958-62, exec. officer, 1963-67, sys. analyst for Strategic Sys. Project Office Arlington, Va., 1969-75; cons. Arlington, 1975-77; sr. rschr. R&D Assocs., Arlington, 1977-82, program mgr., sr. scientist, 1982-87, chief staff, tech. dir. Springfield Rsch. Facility, 1988—2003. Underwriter music commns., 1987—; mission vulnerability cons., 2003—. Author: The Role of Systems Analysis, 1974; contbr. numerous reports on command and control survivability rsch., 1978-86, numerous reports on underground mil. facilities rsch., 1987. Pres. emeritus bd. dirs. Dumbarton Concerts, Washington, 1982—. Mem.: Mineral Soc. DC (pres. 1972—77), Ops. Rsch. Soc. Am., Nature Conservancy, Mil. Officers Assn., Naval Submarine League, Naval Inst. Achievements include development of installation and underground facilities vulnerability assessment techniques and courses of instruction. Office Phone: 703-325-4273.

CIENCIALA, ANNA MARIA, history educator; b. Gdansk, Poland, Nov. 8, 1929; d. Andrew M. and Wanda M. (Waissmann) C.; came to U.S., 1965, naturalized, 1970; B.A., U. Liverpool, 1952; M.A., McGill U., 1955; Ph.D., Ind. U., 1962. Lectr. European history U. Ottawa, 1960-61, U. Toronto (Ont., Can.), 1961-65; asst. prof. history U. Kans., Lawrence, 1965-67, assoc. prof., 1967-71, prof. history and Soviet and Eastern European area studies, 1971-2002, ret., 2002. Recipient prize Pilsudski Inst. Am., 1968; Ford Found. fellow, 1958-60; Can. Council grantee, 1963; Fulbright-Hays fellow, 1968-69; U. Kans. gen. research grantee, 1965-75, 80-81; Am. Council Learned Socs. grantee, 1980, 83; Irex fellow, Poland, 1979-80, Russia 1993-94; NFH Poland 1993. Mem. AAUP, AAUW, Am. Assn. Advancement Slavic Studies, Am. Hist. Assn., Kosciuszko Found., PAU, Pilsudski Inst. Am., Polish-Am. Inst. Arts and Scis., Polish-Am. Hist. Assn., Hist. Preservation. Author: Poland and the Western Powers, 1938-39, 1968; From Versailles to Locarno, Keys to Polish Foreign Policy, 1919-25; editor: (with A. Headlam-Morley and R. Bryant) A Memoir of the Paris Peace Conference 1919, 1972; Jozef Beck Polska Polityka Zagraniczna, 1926-39, 1990; contbr. articles to profl. jours. Home: 3045 Steven Dr Lawrence KS 66049-3025 Business E-Mail: hanka@ku.edu.

CIENFUEGOS, MAURICIO, professional soccer player; b. San Salvador, El Salvador, Feb. 12, 1968; Profl. soccer player El Salvador's First Divsn., 1988—91, 1993—95, Mex. Nat. Team, 1991—93; midfielder L.A. Galaxy, 1996—. Three time MLS All-Star; named Galaxy's Most Valuable Player, 1997; one of six Galaxy players selected to 1996 All-Star game. Office: LA Galaxy 18400 Avalon Blvd 200 Carson CA 90746-2172

CIENNIWA, PAUL D., musician; b. Des Plaines, Ill., Jan. 6, 1972; s. Thomas F. Cienniwa and Marilyn C. Majewski; m. Audrey C. Sabattier, Mar. 4, 2001. BMusic DePaul U., 1995; MM, Yale U., 1997, MMA, DMusical Arats, Yale U., 1998. Dir. Newport Baroque Orch., RI, 2003—; dir. music Trinity Ch., Newport, 2003—. Lectr. U. Mass., North Dartmouth, 2000—. Scholar, Fulbright Found., 1998. Office: Newport Baroque Orch PO Box 584 Newport RI 02840 Personal E-mail: pcienniwa@newportbaroque.org.

CIESINSKI, KATHERINE ELIZABETH, singer, music educator, artist; b. Newark, Del., Oct. 13, 1950; d. Roman Anthony and Katherine Hansen Ciesinski. MusB, Temple U., 1972, MusM, 1973; diploma in opera, Curtis Inst. Music, Phila., 1976. Guest artist Sante Fe Opera, 1979, 1986, 1995, Met. Opera, NYC, 1988, 1989, 2002, San Francisco Opera, Chgo. Lyric Opera, Houston Grand Opera. Mem. Healing and Arts com. U. Tex. Sch. Pub. Health, Houston, 2002—05. Home Fax: 713-521-9942. Personal E-mail: katherine@katherineciesinski.com.

CIESLA, FRED JOHN, astrophysicist, researcher; b. Southbridge, Mass., Nov. 24, 1976; s. Vincent Bernard and Wendy Lee Ciesla; m. Carolyn Henley, May 10, 2003. BA in Physics, Cornell U., 1998; PhD in Planetary Scis., U. Ariz., 2003. Post doctoral rschr. U. Ariz., Tucson, 2003; assoc. NRC, Moffett Field, Calif., 2004—. Recipient Group Achievement award, NASA, 2002, Kuiper Meml. award, Lunar and Planetary Lab., U. Ariz., 2003. Mem.: Am. Astron. Soc. (divsn. planetary scis.), Meteorol. Soc. Avocations: reading, sports. Office: NASA Ames Rsch Ctr MS 245-3 Moffett Field CA 94035 Office Phone: 650-604-0328. E-mail: ciesla@cosmic.arc.nasa.gov.

CIEZADLO, JANINA A., art critic, educator; MFA in Printmaking, MA in Comparative Lit., Ind. U., Bloomington. Adj. prof., dept. liberal edn. Columbia Coll.; adj. asst. prof., dept. art and design U. Ill. at Chgo. Published (reviews, scholarly monographs, articles, poetry, exhibited art work), art critic Chgo. Reader, Afterimage, Jour. of Media Arts and Cultural Criticism. Mem.: Chgo. Art Critics Assn. Address: 7200 West Oak 4NE River Forest IL 60305 Office: U Ill at Chgo 106 Jefferson Hall MC036 Chicago IL 60612 Office Phone: 312-996-3337. Business E-Mail: janina@uic.edu.*

CIFELLI, JOHN LOUIS, lawyer; b. Chicago Heights, Ill., Aug. 19, 1923; s. Antonio and Domenica (Liberatore) C.; m. Irene Romandine, Jan. 4, 1948; children— Carla, David, John L., Bruce, Thomas, Carol. Student, Bowdoin Coll., 1943, Norwick Mil. Acad., 1943, Mt. Piliar Acad., 1943, U. Ill. Extension Ctr., 1946-47; LLB, DePaul U., 1950, JD (hon.), 1975. Bar: Ill. 1950, U.S. Supreme Ct. 1960. Ptnr. Piacenti, Cifelli & Sims, Chicago Heights, 1950-78; pres. John L. Cifelli & Assocs., Chicago Heights, 1978-85; sr. ptnr. Cifelli Baczynski & Scrementi Ltd. (now Cifelli & Scrementi), Chicago Heights, 1985—; spl. counsel City of Chicago Heights, 1961-72; village atty. Village of Richton Park, Ill., 1962-77, Village of Ford Heights, Ill., 1984-89. Counsel Maj. League Umpires Assn., 1973-78, Ill. High Sch. Baseball Coaches Assn., 1975-89. Sec. Bd. Fire and Police, Chicago Heights, 1959-65; co-founder Small Fry Internat. Basketball, 1969, pres., 1969—; coach, baseball coordinator Chicago Heights Park Dist., 1970-75; coach Babe Ruth League Baseball, 1972, 74, 75, asst. Ill. dir., 1973; dir. Ill. tournament, 1973. Served to 2d lt. USAAF, 1942-45, ETO. Mem. ABA, Ill. Bar Assn., Ill. Trial Lawyers Assn., Asns. Trial Lawyers Am., Justinian Soc. Lawyers, Isaac Walton League, Italo Am. Vets. Group, VFW (judge adv. 1951-72), Cath. War Vets. (judge adv. 1951-70), Am. Legion. Clubs: Chicago Heights Country (bd. dirs. 1972-76), Mt. Carmel; Pike Lake Fishing (Wis.). Lodges: Moose, Amaseno. Republican. Avocations: hunting, fishing, golf. Home: 879 Amico Dr Chicago Heights IL 60411 Office: Cifelli & Scrementi Ste 212 1010 Dixie Hwy Chicago Heights IL 60411-3555 Office Phone: 708-754-6200. E-mail: cifellilawfirm@msn.com.

CIFOLELLI, ALBERTA CARMELLA, artist, educator; b. Erie, Pa., Aug. 19, 1931; d. Charles and Adeline (Tonti) C.; m. Charles Perry Lamb, Jr., July 9, 1955; children: Mark Charles, John Jamison, Todd Vincent. Diploma in Painting, Cleve. Inst. Art, 1953; BS in Art Edn., Kent State U., 1955; MA in Communications, Fairfield U., 1975. Chmn. art Laurel Sch., Shaker Heights, Ohio, 1964-67; instr. painting and drawing Cleve. Inst. Art, 1967—70; arts adminstr. Conn. Commn. on Arts, Bridgeport, 1972—76; visual arts tchr. Interarts, 1972—76; assoc. prof. art Sacred Heart U., 1977—. Prof. art Grad. Sch., Coll. New Rochelle, N.Y., 1985—; co-dir. 31st Art of the N.E., Silvermine Guild Ctr. for Arts, Conn., 1982; keynote spkr. Pa. Art Educators Confs., 1999; co-curator About Paint Westport Arts Ctr. Conn., 2005; keynote spkr Pa. Art Educators, 1999. One woman shows Housatonic Mus. Art, 2002, Silvermine Guild Ctr. for Arts, New Canaan, Conn., 1978, Noho Gallery, N.Y.C., 1982, Artist's Signature Gallery, New Haven, 1982, Kaber Gallery, N.Y.C., 1983, Captiva Gallery, Fla., 1984, 1999 (Retrospective), Stamford Mus., Stamford, Conn., 1988, Conn. Gallery, Marlborough, 1988, Harmon-Meek Gallery, Naples, Fla., 1992, 93, 95, Reece Gallery, N.Y.C., Sacred Heart U., 1998, Art Place, 2001 (Artist of Yr.), Housatonic Mus. Art, 2003 (dir.'s choice), Silvermine Guild, 2003, PMW Gallery, Stamford, 2004, White Gallery, Lakeville, Conn., 2004; exhibited in group shows at Alice Nash Gallery, N.Y.C., Cleve. Inst. Art, 1967-69, Slater Meml. Mus., Norwich, Conn., 1977, Lyman Allyn Mus., Aldrich Mus. Contemporary Art, New London, Conn., 1983, Armstrong Gallery, N.Y.C., 1984, Aldrich Mus. Contemporary Art, Ridgefield, Conn., 1988, Portland (Maine) Mus. Art, 2002, Nat. Mus. Women i Arts, Washington, 1990, Bruce Mus., Greench, Conn.; residency to live and work at Djerassi Found., Woodside, Calif., May-June 1986; represented in permanent collections Nat. Mus. Women in the Arts, Reagan Libr., Simi Valley, Calif., Butler Inst. Am. Art, Youngtown, Ohio, Francis Lehman Loeb Arts Ctr., Vassar Coll., Poughkeepsie, N.Y., UN, N.Y., and numerous corp. and over 100 pub. collections. Co-campaign mgr., 1st selectman Democratic Orgn., Westport, Conn., 1977; mem. Westport Democrat Town Com., 1978-79. Recipient Best in Show award Ind. Artists, John Herron Art Mus., Indpls., 1959, Doris Kriendler award NAD, 1974, Salute to Women award Fairfield County YWCA, 1988; Conn. Commn. on Arts grantee, 1973-77; Outstandind Conn. Women award, 2003. Mem. Visual Art Steering Com. Westport Arts Ctr., Inst. Visual Arts (chairwoman 1988-89). E-mail: artistac@aol.com.

CIHAKOVA, DANIELA, medical researcher; b. Karlovy, Vary, Czech Republic, Feb. 25, 1973; arrived in U.S., 2000; d. Milan Pokorny and Dagmar Pokorna; m. Nicole Anne Cihakova. MD, Charles U., Czech Republic, 1998, PhD, 2004. Instr. U. Prague, Czech Republic, 1998—2000; vis. scientist U. Tampere, Finland, 2000, NIH, Bethesda, Md., 2002; postdoctoral fellow Johns Hopkins U., Balt., 2002—. Co-author: Methods of Mol Med, 2004. Mem.: Johns Hopkins Med. and Surg. Assn. Avocations: swimming, reading. Office: Johns Hopkins U Ross 648 720 Rutland Ave Baltimore MD 21205

CIKOVSKY, NICOLAI, JR., retired curator, art historian, educator; b. N.Y.C., Feb. 11, 1933; s. Nicolai and Hortense (Hilbert) C.; m. Sarah Eden Greenough, June 17, 1978; children— Emily Hilbert, Sophia Greenough. AB magna cum laude, Harvard Coll., 1955; A.M., Harvard U., 1958, PhD, 1965. Asst. prof. Skidmore Coll., Saratoga Springs, N.Y., 1961-63; chmn., assoc. prof. Pomona Coll., Claremont, Calif., 1964-68; vis. assoc. prof. U. Tex., Austin, 1969-70; dir. art gallery, assoc. prof. Vassar Coll., Poughkeepsie, N.Y., 1971-74; prof., chmn. dept. art U. N.Mex., Albuquerque, 1974-83; curator Am. and Brit. painting Nat. Gallery Art, Washington, 1983—2003, sr. curator Am. and Brit. painting, 1998—2003; ret., 2003. Author: Sanford Robinson Gifford, exhbn. catalogue, 1970; editor: Lectures on the Affinity of Painting with the Other Fine Arts (Samuel F.B. Morse), 1983; George Inness, 1971, The Life and Work of George Inness, 1977, Winslow Homer, 1990, Winslow Homer Watercolors, 1991, George Inness, 1993; contbg. author: exhbn. catalogues George Inness, 1985, Ansel Adams: Classic Images, 1985, William Merritt Chase: Summers at Shinnecock, 1987, Raphaelle Peale Still Lifes, 1988, William M. Harnett, 1992, James McNeill Whistler, 1994, Winslow Homer, 1995; also articles on William Merritt Chase, George Inness, Winslow Homer, Thomas Eakins, Am. landscape painting, Am. impressionism. Am. Council Learned Socs.-Smithsonian Instn. postdoctoral research fellow, 1968-69; Guggenheim fellow, 1978-79; Kress sr. fellow Nat. Gallery Art, 1983 Mem. Phi Beta Kappa. Clubs: Harvard (N.Y.C.). E-mail: nicolai.cikovsky@verizon.net.

CILELLA, SALVATORE GEORGE, JR., museum director; b. Chgo., Oct. 19, 1941; s. Salvatore G. and Mary Genevieve (LaRocque) C.; m. Mary Winifred Broucek, Aug. 29, 1970; children: Salvatore G. III, Peter Dominic. BA, U. Notre Dame, 1963, MA in Am. History, 1966; MA in Museum Adminstrn., Univ. N.Y., Oneonta, 1971. Community amb. Experiment in Internat. Living, Iran, 1965; exec. dir. No. Ind. Hist. Soc., South Bend, 1970-72; registrar, asst. dir. N.Y. State Hist. Assn., Cooperstown, 1973-76; exec. dir. Historic Bethlehem (Pa.) Inc., 1976-79; dir. devel. and membership Old Sturbridge (Mass.) Village, 1979-81; devel. officer Smithsonian Instn., Washington, 1981-87; exec. dir. Columbia (S.C.) Mus. Art, 1987-2001; pres., CEO Ind. Hist. Soc., Indpls., 2001—. Cons. various mus., 1979—; overseer Old Sturbridge Village, 1982-89; lectr. Seminar for Hist. Adminstrn., Williamsburg, Va., 1983—, Mus. Mgmt. Program, Boulder, Colo., 1993. Contbr. articles to profl. jours. Co-chmn. United Black Fund, 1999; chmn. search com. Hist. Columbia; vice chair Gov.'s Commn. on Heritage; bd. dirs. Indpls. Conv. and Visitors Assn. Decorated Army commendation medal, 1969. Mem.: Am. Assn. for State and Local History, Am. Hist. Print Collections Assn., Am. Assn. Mus. (chmn. devel. and membership com. 1984—89, bd. dirs. 1989—92), Univ. Club, Columbia Club. Roman Catholic. Avocations: collecting 18th and 19th century American prints and maps, antiques, Civil War artifacts and tribal rugs. Office: Ind Hist Soc 450 W Ohio St Indianapolis IN 46202-3269 E-mail: scilella@indianahistory.org.

CIMENT, JAMES D., writer, publisher; b. Montreal, Canada, May 12, 1958; arrived in US, 1960; s. Mortimer and Gloria Joyce Ciment; m. Irene Szeto Chow, Nov. 17, 2004. BA, UCLA, 1981; PhD, CUNY, 1992. Lectr. City Coll. NY, 1985—94; freelance writer, 1994—99; pres. East River Books, Marina Del Ray, Calif., 1999—. Editor: (book) Fury of American Immigration, 2001, Fury of the Great Depression and the New Deal, 2001. Home and Office: 20 Ironsides St #14 Marina Del Rey CA 90292

CIMENT, MELVYN, mathematician; b. Bronx, Sept. 23, 1941; s. Jack and Regina C.; m. Barbara Ann Kagan, July 3, 1966; children: Ethan J., Daniel I. BS, U. Miami, 1962; MS, NYU, 1964, PhD in Math., 1968; JD, Am. U., 1978. Mathematician Denver Rsch. Ctr., Marathon Oil Co., 1968-69; asst. prof. math. U. Mich., Tel-Aviv U. and NYU, 1967-72; applied mathematician Naval Surface Weapons Ctr., 1972-77; sr. applied mathematician Nat. Bur. Stds., Gaithersburg, Md., 1977-83, prog. analyst, 1981-82; Dept. Commerce, Sci. and Tech. congl. fellow U.S. Senate Com. on Commerce, Sci. and Transp., Washington, 1980-81; prog. dir. applied math. DMS, NSF, 1983-86, prog. dir. computational math., 1986; dep. dir. div. Adv. Sci. Computing, Computer, Info. Scis. NSF, Washington, 1986-90, coord. high performance computing and communications program, 1991, exec. officer Computer Info. Sci. and Engring., 1992-93, acting asst. dir., 1993-94, dep. asst. dir., 1993-99; dir. info. techs. Potomac Inst. for Policy Studies, Arlington, Va., 1999-2000; cons., sr. staff cons. Wash. Adv. Group, 2000—03. Mem. FCCSET Working Group on High Performance Computing, 1986-92, exec. com. high performance computing and comm. info. tech. subcom., 1993-94; vice chmn. com. info. and comm. Nat. Sci. and Tech. Coun., 1994, co-chmn. fed. info. svcs. and applications coun., com. computing, info. and comm., 1996-98; acting chmn. Fed. Networking Coun., 1993-94; vis. scientist U. Md., 1994-95; cons. Coun. on Competitiveness, 1994-95; sr. advisor Implementation Group, 2001-03; science adv. NSF EPSCOR Ctrs. Devel. Initiative, 2002-05, Wash. Office Soc. for Indsl. Applied Math., 2001-; mng. mem. CS Cubed Group, LLC, 2004-. Courant Inst. Math. Scis. fellow, 1962-66, others. Mem. Assn. for Computing Machinery, Soc. for Indsl. and Applied Math. (mem. coun. 1988-90, sr. advisor Washington office 2000-), D.C. Bar Assn., Fla. Bar Assn., Md. Bar Assn. Jewish. Avocations: reading, music, biking. Home: 12205 Kemp Mill Rd Silver Spring MD 20902-1720 E-mail: mel@ciment.com.

CIMINO, JOSEPH ANTHONY, preventive medicine physician, educator; b. N.Y.C., Jan. 1, 1934; m. Margaret Langan; children: Andrea, Laura, Lisa, Joseph, Linda, Margaret, John BA in Am. History, Harvard U., 1956, M.I.H., 1964, M.P.H., 1965; MS in Biology, Fordham U., 1958; MD, U. Buffalo, 1962. Diplomate: Am. Bd. Preventive Medicine. Intern Grasslands Hosp., Valhalla, N.Y., 1962-63; AEC fellow in environ. medicine Harvard U. Sch. Public Health, 1963-65; research asso., health officer N.Y.C. Dept. Health, 1965-66; dir. Bur. Community Safety and Occupational Health, 1968-71, dep. commr. health, 1971-72, commr. health, 1972-74; chief med. officer N.Y.C. Dept. Sanitation, 1966-69; med. dir. N.Y.C. Poison Control Center, 1966-72; dir. health and safety N.Y.C. Environ. Protection Adminstrn., 1968-71; commr. hosps. Westchester County, N.Y., 1974-78; pres., chief exec. officer N.Y. Med. Coll., 1978-81, prof. preventive medicine, 1976—, chmn. dept. preventive medicine, 1980—; pres. Occupational Medicine Assocs., 1978—. Assoc. prof. environ. medicine and pub. health NYU, 1971—76; prof. cmty. dynamics Pace U., 1977—78; adj. prof. pub. health and tropical medicine Tulane U., 1972—76; lectr. in pub. health Columbia U., 1973—76; vis. prof. cmty. health Albert Einstein Coll. Medicine, 1973—76, N.Y. State Pub. Health Coun.; pres. bd. Dominican Sisters Family Health Svcs., Inc. Author: Safety: Protection from Injury, 1969, Medical Service Manual, 1971, Drug Abuse Treatment Agencies in New York City, 1972; author numerous profl. monographs; contbr. articles to profl. publs. Chmn. Cath. Interracial Coun. of Westchester County; chief med. cons. N.Y.C. CSC, 1966-71. Civilian U.S. Army, 1964-65; mem. exec. com. Med.Bd. West Med. Ctr., chair greivance com., N.Y. med. Coll., mem. N.Y.S. Pub. Health Council. Recipient Ellis Island Honor award, 2005. Fellow Am. Coll. Preventive Medicine, N.Y. Acad. Medicine, Am. Coll. Occupational Medicine, N.Y. Acad. Sci.; mem. Am. Pub. Health Assn., N.Y.C. Pub. Health Assn., Indsl. Med. Assn., Assn. Govtl. Hygienists, Aerospace Med. Assn., Westchester County Med. Soc., N.Y. State Med. Assn., AMA, Am. Soc. Clin. Nutrition. Home: 50 Willard Ave Tarrytown NY 10591-1210 Office: NY Med Coll Dept Preventive Med Valhalla NY 10595 Office Phone: 914-594-4253. Fax: 914-594-4576. Business E-Mail: joseph_cimino@nymc.edu.

CIMPOERU, PETRE, archivist, educator; b. Gostinu, Romania, Nov. 29, 1939; s. Ion and Elena Cimpoeru; m. Lydia Nicola, Sept. 5, 1947; 1 child, Ligia Schaffer. MA in Libr. Sci., San Jose State U., Calif., 1992; MA in Nat. Security, Calif. State U., San Bernardino, 1988; MA in History and Romanian Lang., U. Bucharest, Romania, 1963; PhD in Internat. Studies, Preston U., Cheyenne, Wyo., 2004. Diploma West Point Mil. Acad., 1989. Bibliographer Nat. Libr., Bucharest, Romania, 1968—69; insp. Nat. Mil. Libr., Bucharest, Romania, 1970—73; history tchr. H.S., Bucharest, Romania, 1973—79; asst. prof. of history Calif. State U., San Bernardino, 1989—90, La Sierra U., Riverside, Calif., 1992—96; assoc. libr./asst. archivist Loma Linda U., Loma Linda, Calif., 1992—. Author: (book) Manual for Military Libraries; contbr. articles to profl. jours. Bd. dirs. Romanian Ministries Internat., Loma Linda, Calif., 1990—95. With Romanian Army, 1968—69. Named Safety Coord. of the Yr., Loma Linda U., 1995. Mem.: Am.-Romanian Acad. of Arts and Sci. (life; full mem. 1998—2004), The Acad. of Polit. Sci. (assoc.; mem. 2003—04). R-Conservative. Seventh-Day Adventist. Achievements include development of Automation of Romanian SDA Seminary Library. Avocations: sports, classical music, archaeology, politics, theology. Home: 25522 Nicks Ave Loma Linda CA 92354 Office: Loma Linda University 11072 Anderson St Loma Linda CA 92354 Office Phone: 909-558-4942. Office Fax: 909-558-0381. Personal E-mail: pcimpoeru@adelphia.net.

CINBERG, JAMES ZUBOW, otolaryngologist, educator; b. N.Y., June 19, 1945; BA, Dartmouth Coll.; MD, Columbia U., 1970. Intern Mt. Sinai Hosp., N.Y.C., 1970—71, resident in surgery, 1971—72; resident in otolaryngology Columbia-Presbyn. Med. Ctr., N.Y.C., 1972—75; fellow in otolaryngology Lenox Hill Hosp., N.Y.C., 1975; otolaryngologist St. Barnabas Hosp., NJ, St. James Hosp., NJ. Clin. asst. prof. Seton Hall Postgrad. Med. Sch. Recipient Ira Tresley award, 1985, honor award Am. Acad. Otolaryngology, 1985. Mem.: ACS, Soc. Head and Neck Surgeons, Am. Acad. Otolaryngology-Head and Neck Surgery. Unitarian-Universalist. Office: 219 S Broad St Elizabeth NJ 07202-3453 Office Phone: 908-527-1717. Personal E-mail: balancecontrol@aol.com.

CINELLI, BETHANN, school health educator; b. Norristown, Pa., Apr. 23, 1958; d. Anthony and Donna (George) C. BS, Ind. U. of Pa., 1980; MEd, Temple U., 1982; EdD, Pa. State U., 1986. Cert. health edn. specialist. Health edn. instr. Pa. State U., State College, 1982-86; asst. prof. health edn. West Chester (Pa.) U., 1987—. Pres. Healthcor Assoc., Exton, Pa., 1989—. Contbr. articles to profl. jours. Com. HIV/AIDS Edn. Pa. Acad. Profession of Teaching, Harrisburg, 1990, comprehensive sch. health Pa. Dept. Health, Harrisburg, 1990. Mem. Am. Sch. Health Assn. (bd. dirs. 1989-90), Pa. Sch. Health Assn. (pres. 1990). Office: West Chester U Dept Health West Chester PA 19383-0001

CINK, STEWART, professional golfer; b. Huntsville, Ala., May 21, 1973; m. Lisa Cink; children: Connor Stewart, Reagan Braswell. Degree in mgmt., Ga. Inst. Tech. Winner Mexican Open, 1996, 1999, Canon Greater Hartford Open, 1997, MCI Classic, 2000, MCI Heritage, 2004, WGC-NEC Invitational, 2004. Mem. Presidents Cup team, 2000, Ryder Cup team, 2002, 04. Avocations: roller hockey, hiking. Office: c/o PGA Tour 112 PGA Tour Blvd Ponte Vedra Beach FL 32082

CINO, MARIA, federal agency administrator; b. Buffalo, Apr. 19, 1957; d. Richard J. and Lucy M. (Tripi) C. BA in Polit. Sci., St. John Fisher Coll. Project supr. Rep. Nat. Com., 1981-82, dir. local programs, 1983-84, exec. asst. field dir., 1985-86, dep. chmn. polit. and congl. rels., 2000—01, dep. chmn., 2003—05; rsch. analyst Am. Viewpoint, Inc., 1986-88; adminstrv. asst. Rep. L. William Paxon, 1989-93; exec. dir. Nat. Rep. Congl. Com., 1993—97; sr. advisor Wiley, Rein & Fielding, 1997—99; nat. polit. dir. Bush for Pres., 1999—2000; asst. sec. and dir. general, U.S. comml. svc. U.S. Dept. Commerce, Washington, 2001—03; dep. sec. US Dept. Transport., Washington, 2005—. Mem. Ho. Adminstrv. Assts. Assn. Republican. Avocations: antiques, travel, golf. Office: US Dept Transport 400 7th St SW Rm 10200 Washington DC 20590

CIOCAN, RAZVAN MARIAN, science educator, researcher; b. Roman, Romania, Sept. 8, 1963; s. Ioan and Elena C.; m. Eugenia Lazaroniu, July 2, 1988; 1 child, Mihai. BS, U. Bucharest (Romania), 1988; MS, Case Western Res. U., Cleve., 2000; Dr. Candidate, U. Akron (Ohio), 2003. Cert. Ndt Level III, 1988. Scientist Inst. Nuc. Rsch., Pitesti, Romania; rsch. asst. Case Western Res. U., Cleve., 1999—2000; tchg. and rsch. asst. elec. engring. dept. U. Akron, 2000—. Adj. assoc. prof. Ovidius U., Constanta, Romania, 1997—98; cons. U. Pitts., 2002—; presenter in field. Contbr. articles. Fellow, Internat. Atomic Agy., Chalk River Labs., Ont., 1995, Student Travel Contingency grant, SPIE-Internat. Soc. Optical Engring., 2002. Mem.: IEEE, Am. Soc. Non-Destructive Testing (fellowship award for postgrad. rsch. 2001).

Achievements include patents for equipment and method for ultrasonic imaging of nuclear fuel. Office: U Akron Dept Elec Engring 302 Buchtel Common Akron OH 44325-3904 Personal E-mail: razvanc1@yahoo.com. E-mail: rc17@uakron.edu.

CIOCHETTY, JOHN BRYAN, protective services official; b. Parkersburg, W.Va., June 17, 1955; s. John Joseph and Mary Ann Ciochetty. BA, Marshall U., W.Va., 1980, MS, 1988. Polit. sci. instr. Marshall U., Huntington, W.Va., 1976—86; dep. sheriff Wood County Sheriff's Dept., Parkersburg, 1986—88; jud. officer probation svcs. W.Va. Supreme Ct., Charleston, 1988—90; sociology, criminology instr. W.Va. Univ. Ch., Parkersburg, 1990—91; loss prevention investigator Meijer Corp., Columbus, Ohio, 1995—2000; pub. safety campus police Ohio Wesleyan U., Delaware, 2001—. Mgmt. devel. v.p. Jr. C. of C., Parkersburg, W.Va., 1986—92; chief probation officer Marysville Mcpl. Ct., Ohio, 1991—92; custom protection officer and investigator Wackenhut Corp., Columbus, Ohio, 1992—95; patrolman, investigator Statewide Bur. Investigations, Parkersburg, W.Va., 1975—. Author: Nuclear Biological and Chemical Defense, 1986. Adv. bd. mem. Big Brothers/Big Sisters of Am., Parkersburg, W.Va., 1980—83; mem. Nat. Performance Rev. Office of U.S. V.P. Al Gore, 1993—2000. Lt. USAR, 1980—88. Avocations: horseback riding, writing, computers, travel, Karate, Aikido. Home: 166 Muirwood VillageDr Delaware OH 43015 Office: Ohio Weslyan Univ Pub Safety 61 S Sandusky St Delaware OH 43015 E-mail: darkknightjc_007@msn.com.

CIOFFARI, ANGELINA GRIMALDI, retired foreign languages educator; b. Port Chester, N.Y.; d. Samuel Ludwig and Mary Grace (Corigliano) Grimaldi; B.A., Coll. of New Rochelle, 1935; M.A., Columbia U., 1940; m. Vincent Cioffari, Dec. 27, 1937; 1 son, Vincent Grimaldi. Asst. prof. Romance langs. U. Iowa, 1943-44; asst. dir. modern langs. project War Dept., N.Y.C., 1944-45; lectr. Romance langs. Boston U., 1957-61; vis. prof. Harvard U., 1961-62; assoc. prof. modern langs. Mass. Bay Community Coll., Wellesley Hills, 1965-80. Sec., Circolo Italiano Boston, 1960-62. Mem. Modern Lang. Assn., AAUP, Italian Tchrs. Assn., Mass. Tchrs. Assn., Dante Soc. Am. Roman Catholic. Clubs: Watertown Yacht; Windsor; Cornell of N.Y.; Harvard Faculty. Author: Italian Operatic Arias, 1951; Beginning Italian I, 1958, II, 1958 (with others) Graded Italian Reader, 1979, 91, Graded Italian Reader, Seconda Tappa, 1984. Home: 45 Amherst Rd Newton MA 02468-2301

CIOFFI, FRANK LOUIS, language educator; b. Bklyn., Sept. 5, 1951; s. Louis Frank and Agnes (Russell) C.; m. Kathleen McCutcheon, Jan. 5, 1974. BA, Northwestern U., 1973; MA, Ind. U., 1976, PhD, 1980. Assoc. instr. English dept. Ind. U., Bloomington, 1976-78; assoc instr. Prison Edn. Devel. Project, Bloomington, 1978-79, dir., 1979-80; asst. prof. Eastern N.Mex. U., Portales, 1980-84; Fulbright sr. lectr. U. Gdansk (Poland), 1984-87; asst. prof. Cen. Wash. U., Ellensburg, 1987—. Author: Formula Fiction?, 1982; editor: (anthology) Unlocking Shackled Minds, 1980; contbr. articles to profl. jours. Pilot grantee Nat. Endowment for the Humanities, 1979. Mem. MLA, No. Pacific Popular Culture Assn. Avocations: classic cars, biking, swimming, running, weight-lifting. Office: Cen Wash U English Dept Ellensburg WA 98926 Home: PO Box 95 Kingston NJ 08528-0095

CIOFFI, MICHAEL LAWRENCE, lawyer; b. Cin., Feb. 2, 1953; s. Patrick Anthony and Patricia (Schroeder) C.; children: Michael A., David P., Gina M. BA magna cum laude, U. Notre Dame, 1975; JD, U. Cin., 1979. Bar: Ohio 1979, U.S. Dist. Ct. (so. dist.) Ohio 1980, U.S. Dist. Ct. (no. dist.) Ohio 1983, U.S. Ct. Appeals (6th cir.) 1985. Asst. atty. gen. Ohio Atty. Gen., Columbus, 1979-81; from assoc. to ptnr. Frost & Jacobs, Cin., 1981-87; staff v.p., asst. gen. counsel Penn Cen. Corp., Cin., 1988-93; v.p., asst. gen. counsel Am. Fin. Group, Cin., 1993-2000; ptnr. Blank Rome LLP, Cin., 2000—. Adj. prof. law U. Cin. Coll. Law, 1983—. Author: Ohio Pretrial Litigation, 1991, 2d edit., 1998; co-author: Sixth Circuit Federal Practice Manual, 1993, 2d edit., 1999. Bd. dirs. Charter Com. of Greater Cin., 1985—88. Recipient Goldman Prize for Tchg. Excellence U. Cin. Coll. Law, 1995, Nicholas Longworth Disting. Alumni award, 1996, Adj. Faculty Tchg. Excellence award, 2000. Mem. ABA, Fed. Bar Assn. (mem. exec. com., pres.1994), Ohio Bar Assn., Cin. Bar Assn. Avocations: tennis, travel. Office: Blank Rome LLP 201 E 5th St Cincinnati OH 45202

CIOFFI, PATRIZIA, soprano, voice educator, arts consultant; b. Bloomfield, N.J., Feb. 9, 1946; d. Raphael and Musette (Recchia) C.; children: Regina, Jennifer. BA cum laude, Mt. Holyoke, 1998; cert. lang. proficiency, Inst. Lorenzo de Medici, Florence, Italy. Bus. mgr. Whole Theatre Co., Montclair, N.J., 1972-75; founder, exec. dir. New Sch. for Arts/N.J. Opera Inst., Montclair, 1975-92; pvt. tchr. voice, Montclair, 1987—; artistic dir. le voci internazionali, Montclair, 1998—. Freelance on-site evaluator, writer, panel mem., cons. Nat. Endowment for Arts, Washington, 1983—; freelance writer, arts cons. to several artists and orgns., N.Y.C., 1991—; tchr. voice Mt. Holyoke Coll., South Hadley, Mass., 1996; career devel. cons. Pro Arte Internat., N.Y.C., 1997—, others; author: le donne che non sorridono mai, the Women Who Never Smile, 1997. Well-known for high vocal range and rendering of heroic Puccini, Verdi, Wagner music, In Questa Reggia, Turandot, Brunhilde's Battle Cry; recorded Petit Messe Solenelle, 1993. Mem. Nat. Italian-Am. Found., leader in preservation of the indigenous style in Italian singing. Fellow Nat. Endowment for Arts, 1982; Mary Vance Young and Frances Perkins scholar Mt. Holyoke Coll., 1995-97; various vocal study grants for study La Scala, Milan, Covent Garden, London, Mrs. Franco Corelli, N.Y.C., 1986—; scholar Lee Strasberg Theatre Inst. Mem. Nat. Assn. Tchrs. Singing, Nat. Opera Assn. Roman Catholic. Avocations: swimming, horseback riding, bike riding, advocate for singer over 35. Office: le voci internazionali 197 Grove St Montclair NJ 07042-4216 Fax: 973-744-2292.

CIONEK, EDMUND, composer, educator; b. Amsterdam, N.Y., Nov. 26, 1950; s. Edmund and Stella Cionek. BS in music, Ball State U., 1972; M in music composition, U. Mich., Ann Arbor, 1977, D in music composition, 1981. Lectr. Purchase Coll., White Plains, NY, 1995—, N.Y.U., N.Y., 1998—; composer-in-residence Bar Harbor Music Festival, 1995—; resident artist Mabou Mines Theatre, N.Y., 2003—04; composer Tri Sci Fi. Bd. dirs. League of Composers- Internat. Soc. Contemporary Music, N.Y., 1982—85. Composer: (chamber music) Ghost Rhapsodies, 1981, (large orchestra) Burnin' Rubber/ Visions of Vivaldi, 1995, (string orchestra) Serenade, 2000; co-creator: (musical revue, off-Broadway) Streakin', 2003; composer: Attack of the 50 Foot Walt Whitman, 2004. Recipient Meet the Composer award, Quintet of Ams.; grantee, A.S.C.A.P., N.Y., 2003.

CIOPPA, ROBERT, architectural firm executive; BArch, Pratt Inst., 1967; grad. Sch. Bus. Exec. Program, Stanford U., 1967. Joined Kohn Pedersen Fox Assocs., N.Y.C., 1976—, ptnr., 1979, mng. prin. design and constrn. of govt., corp. hdqrs., corp. interior fit-out and investment office bldgs., ptnr. fin., 1995—. Juror Seattle/Tacoma and Ohio chpts. AIA; participant Archtl. Record Round Table on Archtl. Edn.; lectr. in field. Fellow: AIA. Office: KPF Assocs 111 W 57th St New York NY 10019

CIPARICK, CARMEN BEAUCHAMP, state appeals court judge; b. NYC, 1942; m. Joseph Damian Ciparick; 1 child. Grad., Hunter Coll., 1963; JD, St. John's U., 1967. Staff atty. Legal Aid Soc., NYC, 1967—69; asst. counsel Office of Jud. Conf. State of NY, 1969—72; chief law asst. NYC Criminal Ct., 1972—74; counsel Office of NYCAdminstrv. Judge, 1974—78; judge NYC Criminal Ct., 1978—82, NYC Supreme Ct, 1982—94; assoc. judge NY State Ct. Appeals, NYC, 1994—. Former mem. N.Y. State Commn. Jud. Conduct. Trustee Boricua Coll.; bd. dirs. St. John's U. Sch. of Law Alumni Assn. Named to Hunter Coll. Hall of Fame, 1991. Office: NY State Ct Appeals 122 E 42nd St New York NY 10168-0002 Address: State NY Court of Appeals 20 Eagle St Albany NY 12207-1095

CIPITI, JOHN DAVID, music educator; b. Port Clinton, Ohio, Feb. 17, 1957; s. Santo Thomas and Martha Zelma Cipiti; m. Sally Lee Clemons, June 6, 1998; children: Brando Lewis Reyna, Tara Kinney Reyna. MusB, Heidelberg Coll., Tiffin, Ohio, 2002; MusM in Composition, Bowling Green State U., 2002. Archtl. drafstman Don C. Waggoner, P.E., Inc., Port Clinton, Ohio, 1986—92; office mgr. and sales Frank Sales Inc., Port Clinton, Ohio, 1993—2004; music educator Terra State C.C., Fremont, Ohio, 2004—. Freelance guitarist, pianist, percussionist, composer, 1972—. Composer: (symphony orch.) Pentacles, (brass quintet) Sanctius, (two pianos) Looking Glass Aberations, (piano and voice) Two Songs On Texts By W. B. Yeats, (choral) Eight O'clock, (ascension) String Quartet, (electronic tape) Distillations. Trustee Playmakers Civic Theatre, Port Clinton, Ohio, 1990—92. Undergrad. Rsch. scholarship, Pepsi Corp., 2002. Mem.: Alpha Sigma Lambda, Tau Mu Sigma. Office: Terra State CC 2830 Napoleon Rd Fremont OH 43420 Office Phone: 419-334-8400. Personal E-mail: jdcipiti@adelphia.net.

CIPLIJAUSKAITE, BIRUTE, humanities educator; b. Kaunas, Lithuania, Apr. 11, 1929; came to U.S., 1957; d. Juozas and Elena (Stelmokaite) C. BA, Lycée Lithuanien Tubingen, 1947; MA, U. Montreal, 1956; PhD, Bryn Mawr Coll., 1960. Permanent mem. Inst. Rsch. in Humanities U. Wis., Madison, 1974, asst. prof., 1961-65, assoc. prof., 1965-68, prof., 1968-73, John Bascom prof., 1973—. Author: Solitude and Spanish Contemporary Poetry, 1962, Poetry and the Poet, 1966, Baroja, a style, 1972, Plenitude as Commitment: The Poetry of Jorge Guillén, 1973, The Generation of 1898 and History, 1981, The Unsatisfied Woman: Adultery in Realist Novel, 1984, Contemporary Women's Novel (1970-85), 1988, Literary Sketches, 1992, Of Signs and Significations. I: Games of the Avant-Garde, 1999, Carmen Martín Gaite, 2000, Guilleniana, 2002, Construction of the Feminine I in Literature, 2004; editor: (Luis de Góngora), Complete Sonnets, 1969, 75, 79, 81, 85, 99, critical edit., 1989, Jorge Guillén, 1975, (with C. Maurer) The Will to Humanism. Homage to Juan Marichal, 1990, Novísimos, postnovísimos, clásicos: Poetry of the 80s in Spain, 1991; translator: (Juan Ramón Jiménez), Platero and I, 1982, (María Victoria Atencia), Trances of the Holy Virgin, 1989, Voices Within Silence: Contemporary Lithuanian Poetry, 1991, Birute Pukeleviciute, Lament, 1994, (with Nicole Laurent-Catrice) Twenty Lithuanian Poets of Today, 1997, (Vidmante Jasukaityte), The Miraculous Grass Along the Fence, 2002, (J. Degutyté and B. Pukelevićiute) Between the Sun and Dispossession, 2002, (Mercè Rodoreda) The Girl of the Doves, 2002, (Nijole Miliauskaité) Forbidden Room, 2003, others. Guggenheim fellow, 1968 Mem. Assn. For Advancement Baltic Studies (v.p. 1981), Asociación Internacional de Hispanistas, Order Alfonso X elSabio (named commdr. Spain, 2003) Office: U Wis Inst Rsch in Humanities 1401 Observatory Dr Madison WI 53706-1209

CIPOLLA, MARK, lawyer; b. Bklyn., Sept. 20, 1964; BS, St. John's U., 1986, JD, 1992. Bar: NY 1993. Asst. dist. atty., Kings County, NY, 1992—98; ptnr. Wilson, Elser, Moskowitz, Edelman & Dicker LLP, NYC. Mem.: Assn. Trial Lawyers of Am. Office: Wilson Elser Moskowitz Edelman & Dicker LLP 23rd Fl 150 E 42nd St New York NY 10017-5639 Office Phone: 212-490-3000 ext. 2526. Office Fax: 212-490-3038. Business E-Mail: cipollam@wemed.com.

CIRASUNDA, ESTHER BOND, librarian; b. Richmond, Va., July 10, 1950; d. Hobart Genues and Beulah Ann (Neal) Bond; m. Gary Lee Musser, June 3, 1977 (div. 1989); children: Laura Beth Musser, Jessica Lynn Musser; m. Francis Peter Cirasunda, July 4, 1990. BS, Madison Coll., Harrisonburg, Va., 1972; MS, Radford U., 1983. Sch. libr. Botetourt County Pub. Schs., Fincastle, Va., 1972-74, Roanoke (Va.) City Pub. Schs., 1974—2003; ret., 2003; pvt. tutor; owner Motivation Plus, 2005—. Del. Gov.'s Conf. on Libr. and Info. Svcs., Richmond, 1990; teaching homebound students and private tutoring, 2003; spkr. Motivation Plus, 2005—. Author poems. Mem. NEA (del. conv. 1993, vice-chair libr. info. tech. caucus), Va. Edn. Assn., Roanoke Edn. Assn. (v.p. instrn. 1992-93, Polit. Action Com chair 1994-95, pres. 1996-98, dist. 5 pres. 1998-2000), Roanoke City Ret. Tchrs.'s Assn. (v.p. 2005-2007), Roanoke Valley Reading Coun., Va. Ednl. Media Assn. (workshop presenter 1986), Phi Kappa Phi. Avocations: continuing education, working with women on survival skills. Home and Office: 5066 Dan Robin Rd Salem VA 24153 Office Phone: 540-797-1798. Personal E-mail: ecirasun@yahoo.com.

CIRAULO, DOMENIC ANTHONY, psychiatrist, educator; 3 children. BA, U. Hartford, 1971; MD, Georgetown U., 1975. Diplomate in psychiatry with added qualification in addiction psychiatry Am. Bd. Psychiatry and Neurology. Med. resident Inst. Living, Hartford, 1975—77; chief resident psychiatry Mass. Mental Health Ctr., Boston, 1977—78; clin. fellow psychiatry Harvard Med. Sch., Boston, 1977—78, clin. instr., 1978—79, lectr. psychiatry, 2002—; asst. prof. psychiatry U. Conn. Sch. Medicine, Farmington, 1979—84; from asst. prof. to assoc. prof. psychiatry Tufts U. Sch. Medicine, 1984—92, prof. psychiatry, 1992—96, lectr. pharmacology, 1993—; chief psychiatry svc. VA Med. Ctr./Outpatient Clinics, Boston, 1995—2001; psychiatrist in chief Boston Med. Ctr., 1996—; prof., chmn. divsn. psychiatry Boston U. Sch. Medicine, 1996—. Chair R&D com. VA Outpatient Clinic, Boston, 1987—94; mem. exec. com. dept. psychiatry Tufts U. Sch. Medicine, Boston, 1989—93, mem. addiction medicine com., 1989—96; sr. cons. Norcap Addictions Program, Norfolk, Mass., 1990—96; mem. dean's com. VA Med. Ctr., Boston, 1996—; mem. exec. com. Boston U. Sch. Medicine, 1996—, com. mem., 2001—02; gen. clin. rsch. ctr. adv. com. Boston U. Med. Ctr., 1997—; sci. adv. com. Boston U. Cmty. Tech. Fund, 1997—2000. Author: (book) Drug Interactions In Psychiatry, Clinical Manual of Chemical Dependence; contbr. chapters to books. Grantee, Nat. Inst. On Drug Abuse, 1995—, Nat. Inst. On Alcoholism and Alcohol Abuse, 1997—, Nat. Inst. On Drug Abuse, 2002—, 2002—, 2002—. Fellow: Am. Psychiat. Assn. (disting. fellow); mem.: AMA (ad hoc com. on physicians health 1996), FDA Adv. Bd., Am. Bd. Psychiatry and Neurology (examiner), Mass. Med. Soc., Mass. Psychiatry Soc. (com. on alcohol and addiction 1984—). Office: Boston Univ Sch Medicine Ste 914 720 Harrison Ave Boston MA 02118

CIRCEO, LOUIS JOSEPH, JR., research scientist, civil engineer; b. Everett, Mass., Aug. 31, 1934; s. Louis Joseph and Matilda (Marotta) C.; m. Brigitta H. Rockstroh, Jan. 26, 1961 (dec. 1986); children: Renata B., Craig L. BS in Engring., U.S. Mil. Acad., West Point, 1957; MS in Soils Engring., 1961; PhD in Civil Engring., Iowa State U., 1963. Registered profl. civil engr., DC. Commd. 2d lt. U.S. Army, 1957, advanced through grades to col., 1987; rsch. assoc. Lawrence Radiation Lab., Livermore, Calif., 1962-64; civil engr. Bangkok Bypass Road, Thailand, 1965—66; instr. dept. engring. and mil. sci. U.S. Army Engr. Sch., Ft. Belvoir, Va., 1966—68; civil engr. advisor Vietnamese Nat. Mil. Acad., Dalat, Vietnam, 1968-69; rsch. tech. mgr. Def. Atomic Support Agy., Washington, 1969-72; comdr. 20th Engr. Bn., Ft. Campbell, Ky., 1973-75; ops. rsch. analyst nuclear activities br. SHAPE, NATO, Mons, Belgium, 1975-79; dir. U.S. Army Constrn. Engring. Rsch. Lab., Champaign, Ill., 1979-83; dir. Nuclear Survivability, Security and Safety Directorate, Hdqrs. Def. Nuclear Agy., Washington, 1983-87; ret., 1987; dir. Constrn. Rsch. Ctr., Ga. Inst. Tech., Atlanta, 1987—98; prin. rsch. scientist Ga. Tech Rsch. Inst., Atlanta, 1998—. Mem.: ASCE, Soc. Am. Mil. Engrs., Assn. U.S. Army, Sigma Xi. Roman Catholic. Achievements include patents for recovery of fuel products from carbonaceous matter using plasma arc; in-situ plasma soil stabilization method and apparatus; in-situ plasma remediation and vitrification of contaminated soils, deposits and buried materials. Avocations: reading, travel. Home: 4245 Navajo Trl NE Atlanta GA 30319-1532 Office: Ga Tech Rsch Inst Atlanta GA 30332-0837 Office Phone: 404-894-2070. Business E-Mail: lou.circeo@gtri.gatech.edu. *It is important that an individual does the most with his God-given talents for the betterment of mankind.*

CIRELLO, JOHN, utility and engineering company executive; b. Bound Brook, N.J., Apr. 17, 1943; s. Fiore Avanti and Assunta Cirello; m. Sherron Anne Thomas, July 31, 1965; children: Sueann, Elizabeth Rose, Sherron Marie. BS, Rutgers U., 1965, MS, 1971, PhD, 1975. Registered profl. engr., N.J., Pa. Engr. Calif. Dept. Water, L.A., 1965-66, U.S. Army Corps of Engrs., Ft. Belvoir, Va., 1966-68, Balt. Gas and Elec., 1968-69; rschr. Rutgers Water Resources Inst., New Brunswick, N.J., 1969-71; asst. prof. Rutgers U., New Brunswick, 1971-80; pres. Princeton Aqua Sci., Edison, N.J., 1980-85; v.p. IT Corp., Edison, N.J., 1985-88; v.p. ea. region Chem. Waste Mgmt., Inc., Princeton, N.J., 1988-92; pres. Metcalf & Eddy Svcs., Inc., Branchburg, N.J., 1992-95; with Environ. Engring. Svcs. Inc., 1995-96; pres., CEO Fla. Water Svcs. Corp., 1995—2002; exec. v.p. Allete Corp., Duluth, Minn., 1995—2002; pres. Resource Ventures Inc., 2002—; v.p. WRF Ga. LLC, 2002—. Editor (tng. manuals) Land Application of Effluents & Sludges, 1976, Ultimate Disposal of Organic and Inorganic Sludges, 1976, Water and Wastewater Polishing and Rennovation Techniques, 1976; co-editor (tng. manual) Construction and Environmental Inspectors Training Manual, 1977; contbr. articles to profl. jours. Mem. Bd. Adjustment, Bound Brook, N.J., 1976-81; councilman, pres., Bound Brook Town Coun., 1981-87; chmn. Dem. com. Bound Brook, 1982-86; Grad. Leadership Fla. Class XVI. Capt. U.S. Army Engr. Corps, 1966-68. Recipient award N.J. Water Pollution Control Assn., 1990. Mem.: ASCE, Fla. Water Wks. Assn. (bd. dirs. 1997—2002), Am. Chem. Soc., Water Environ. Fedn., Fla. State C. of C. Roman Catholic. Avocations: antique and classic cars, golf. Home: 540 Winding Creek Pl Longwood FL 32779-6119

CIRESE, ROBERT CHARLES, economist, real estate consultant; b. Oak Park, Ill., Feb. 25, 1938; s. Ferd Louis and Ruth (Olson) Cirese; m. Sarah Jane Williams, Apr. 3, 1965 (div. 1973); children: Lesley Mesarchik, Jeffrey Robert. BS, DePaul U., 1961; MS, U. Ill., 1963; postgrad., U. Calif., Berkeley, 1964. Lic. real estate broker Calif., cert. coll. tchr. Calif. Economist State of Calif. Employment Divsn., San Francisco, 1965—67; assoc. prof. Golden Gate U., San Francisco, 1967—72; v.p. Larry Smith & Co., San Francisco, 1972—77; dir. PricewaterhouseCoopers, San Francisco, 1977—79; v.p. Rubloff Inc., San Francisco, 1979—85; pres. Cirese Assocs., Sausalito, Calif., 1985—; concession mgr. bus. mgmt. divsn. Nat. Pk. Svc. Dept. Interior, San Francisco, 1994—. Guest lectr.; spkr. in field; econ., fin. and real estate investment counselor corps., govt. agys., pvt. insts. Contbr. articles to profl. jours. Active Stanford U. Buck Fund, U. Calif. Berkeley Bear Backer, Berkeley Repertory Theater, Calif. Shakespeare Festival; bd. dirs. San Francisco Camp Fire, Inc., 1988—92; mem. San Francisco Ballet Assn., Am. Conservatory Theater, San Francisco Opera, San Francisco Symphony, Friends of Filoli, Sierra Club, San Francisco. With Ill. N.G., 1956—63. Mem.: Urban Land Inst., San Francisco Planning and Urban Rsch. Assn., Am. Soc. Real Estate Counselors (past chmn. No. Calif. chpt. 1988—89, bd. dirs. 1986—), U. Calif. Berkeley Alumni Assn., Stanford Alumni Assn., San Francisco Commonwealth Club. Avocations: hiking, theater, sports, humor writing. Home: 54 Buckelew St Sausalito CA 94965-1120 Office: Fort Mason Bldg 201 San Francisco CA 94123 Office Phone: 415-561-4943. Personal E-mail: bob.cirese@sbcglobal.net. Business E-Mail: robert_cirese@nps.gov.

CIRESI, MICHAEL VINCENT, lawyer; b. St. Paul, Apr. 18, 1946; s. Samuel Vincent and Selena Marie (Bloom) Ciresi; m. Ann Ciresi; children: Carolina, Dominic, Adam. BBA, U. St. Thomas; JD, U. Minn.; LLD, Southwestern U., 2001. Bar: Minn. 1971, U.S. Dist. Ct. Minn. 1974, U.S. Ct. Appeals (8th cir.) 1971, U.S. Supreme Ct. 1981, U.S. Ct. Appeals (2d cir.) 1986, U.S. Ct. Appeals (9th cir.) 1987, U.S. Ct. Appeals (10th cir.) 1990, NY 1995, Fed. Cir. 1998, U.S. Ct. Appeals (5th cir.) 1999. Assoc. Robins, Kaplan, Miller & Ciresi, Mpls., 1971—78, ptnr., 1978—, exec. bd., 1983—, chmn. exec. bd., 1995—. Adv. bd. Ctr. Advanced Litig. Nottingham (Eng.) Law Sch. Trustee U. St. Thomas; candidate U.S. Senate, 2000; bd. dirs. U. St. Thomas, bd. dirs. Sch. Law; bd. dirs. Inst. Jud. Adminstrn. Sch. Law NYU; bd. dirs. Lawyers' Com. Civil Rights Under Law, The Guthrie Theater, Ordway Ctr. Performing Arts. Named Product Liability Lawyer of Yr., Australian Nat. Consumer Law Assn., 1989, Trial Lawyer of Yr., Trial Lawyers for Pub. Justice Found., 1998; recipient Ellis Island Medal of Honor, Nat. Ethnic Coalition of Orgns. Found., 2002. Mem.: ATLA, ABA, Am. Coll. Trial Lawyers, Am. Acad. Trial Lawyers, Internat. Acad. Trial Lawyers, Trial Lawyers for Pub. Justice, Inner Cir. of Advocates, Internat. Bar Assn., Am. Bd. Trial Advocates, Ramsey County Bar Assn., Hennepin County Bar Assn., Minn. State Bar Assn. Roman Catholic. Avocations: sports, U.S. history. Home: 1247 Culligan Ln Saint Paul MN 55118-4151 Office: Robins Kaplan Miller & Ciresi 2800 Lasalle Plz Minneapolis MN 55402 Office Phone: 612-349-8533. Business E-Mail: mvciresi@rkmc.com.

CIRILLO, JEANNINE L., pharmacist; d. Willie Gedeon and Lottie Clara Vadenais; m. Francis E. Cirillo, June 29, 1957; children: Sharlene Jean, Leslie Frances, Alison Jane. BS in Pharmacy, U. R.I., 1955; DPharm, U. Ill., Chgo., 1994. Cert. pharmacist R.I., Mass. With Gagne Pharmacy, Bellingham, Mass., 1955—76; staff pharmacist St. Elizabeth Cmty. Health Ctr., Lincoln, Nebr., 1977—82, Overlook Hosp., Summit, NJ, 1983—94, Owen Healthcare, Wareham, Mass., 1994—97, Oaks Bluff, Mass., 1997—. Mem. adv. coun. and edn. com. N.J. Drug Info. and Poison Control Ctr., 1989—94; various positions N.J. Soc. Health Sys. Pharmacists, 1990—93; del. People to People Internat., Germany, 1993, Hungary, 93; N.J. del. ann. meeting Am. Soc. Health Systems Pharmacist. Bd. dirs. Hunterdon (N.J.) Mental Devel., 1988—94. Avocations: sailing, crafts, bicycling, bridge, knitting. Home: 14 Quamhasset Rd Buzzards Bay MA 02532-5608

CIRILLO, RICHARD ALLAN, lawyer; b. N.Y.C., Feb. 7, 1951; s. Paul F. and Edith A. (Flanagan) C.; m. Kathleen V. Rossi, Aug. 23, 1975; children: Benjamin F., Theodore T., Amanda K. BA, Yale U., 1972; JD cum laude, Fordham U., 1975. Bar: N.Y. 1976, U.S. Dist. Ct. (so. dist.) N.Y. 1977, U.S. Dist. Ct. (no. dist.) N.Y. 1990, U.S. Ct. Appeals (5th and 10th cirs.) 1978, U.S. Ct. Appeals (2d cir.) 1982, U.S. Ct. Appeals (9th cir.) 1984, U.S. Ct. Appeals (11th cir.) 1994, U.S. Tax Ct. 1984, U.S. Supreme Ct. 1983. Assoc. Rogers & Wells, N.Y.C., 1975-83, ptnr., 1983—99, King & Spalding, N.Y.C., 1999—. Bd. dirs. MIM Corp. Editor: Fordham Law Rev.; contbr. articles to profl. jours. Trustee Colony Found., New Haven, 1982-84. Republican. Presbyterian. Home: 246 E 33d St New York NY 10016 Office: King & Spalding LLP 1185 Ave of the Americas Ste 3400 New York NY 10036

CIRILLO, VINCENT J., medical historian, consultant; b. New Haven, Conn., Sept. 21, 1937; s. Joseph Oscar and Mary (Venezia) Cirillo; m. Annette Vellaccio, July 2, 1960; children: Vincent J. Cirillo Jr., Paul L. BA, U. Conn., 1959, MS, 1961; PhD, Rutgers U., 1999. Asst. dir. clin. rsch. Merck & Co., Inc., Rahway, NJ, 1962—93; assoc. Inst. for Health, Health Care Policy and Aging Rsch. Rutgers U., New Brunswick, NJ, 1999—. Cons. Target Rsch., Scotch Plains, NJ, 1993, Transcend Therapeutics, Cambridge, Mass., 1995, N.J. Vets. Mus., East Orange, 1999—2001. Author: Bullets and Bacilli: The Spanish-American War and Military Medicine, 2004; contbr. articles to profl. jours. Recipient Margaret Hastings and Margaret Judson fellowship, Rutgers U., 1994—95. Mem.: History of Sci. Soc., Am. Assn. for History of Medicine, Med. History Soc. N.J. (pres. 1986—88, David L. Cowen award 2005), Red-Headed League N.J. Avocation: book collecting. Home: 1387 Joseph St North Brunswick NJ 08902-1509 Personal E-mail: vjcirillo@worldnet.att.net.

CIRILO, AMELIA MEDINA, educational consultant; b. Parks, Tex., May 23, 1925; d. Constancio and Guadalupe (Guerra) Cirilo; m. Arturo Medina, May 31, 1953 (div. June 1979); children: Dennis Glenn, Keith Allen, Sheryl Amelia, Jacqueline Kim. BS in Chemistry, U. North Tex., 1950; MEd, U. Houston, 1954; PhD in Edn. and Nuc. Engring., Tex. A&M U., 1975; cert. in radioisotope tech., Tex. Woman's U., Denton, 1962; cert. in pub. speaking, Dale Carnegie, 1993. Cert. in supervision, bilingual Spanish Tex., permanent profl. tchr. Tex. Tchr. sci. dept. Starr County Schs., Rio Grande City, Tex., 1950—53; elem. tchr. San Benito-Brownsville, Tex., 1953—54, Kingsville (Tex.) Schs., 1954—56; tchr. sci. dept. head chem. physics LaJoya (Tex.) Pub. Schs., 1956—70; tchg. asst. Tex. A&M U., College Station, 1970—74; instr. fire chemistry Del Mar Jr. Coll., Corpus Christi, Tex., 1974—75; exec. dir. Hispanic Ednl. Rsch. Mgmt. Analysis Nat. Assn., Inc., Corpus Christi, 1975—79; head dept. chem. physics San Isidro (Tex.) HS, 1979—82; tchr. chemistry W.H. Adamson HS, Dallas, 1982—84; ednl. cons. Skyline HS, 1992—, tchr. high intensity lang. sci., 1984—86, chmn. faculty adv. com., 1983—84, chemistry tchr., 1986—92. Mem. core faculty Union Grad. Coll., Cin., P.R., Ft. Lauderdale and San Diego, 1975—79; mathematician Well Instrument Devel. Co., Houston, 1950—85; panelist, program evaluator Dept. of Edn., Washington, 1977—79; program evaluator, Robstown, Tex., 1975—79; tchr., trainer Edn. 20 and 2 Region Ctrs., Corpus Christi and San Antonio, 1975—79; rschr., writer Coll. Edn. and Urban Studies Harvard U., Cambridge, Mass., 1978—80; vis. prof. bilingual dept. East Tex. State Coll.,

Commerce, 1978; ednl. cons. and supr. Adult Basic Edn. Dallas Pub. Schs., 1994—99, kindergarten tchr., 1999—2000, tchr. elem. sci. and math., 2000—02, newcomers ESL tchr., 2002—; conf. presenter program evaluation, 1977—79. Author, rschr. Comparative Evaluation of Bilingual Programs, 1978 (named one of best US books), (poetry) Reflections, 1983; contbr. chapters to books. Mem. Srs. Active in Life adv. com. Dallas City Parks and Recreation; Brazos County advisor Tex. Constl. Revision Commn., 1973—74; sec. Goals for Corpus Christi Com. of 100; Corpus Christi rep. Southwestern Ednl. Authority, Edinburg, Tex., 1977—79; pres. Elem. PTA, 1972—75; mem. Women's Polit. Caucus, Mex. Am. Dems.; exec. bd. Nat. Com. Domestic Violence, 1978—80; bd. trustees Sci. Cluster Skyline HS, 1994—; bd. dirs. Meth. Home for Elderly, Weslaco, Tex., 1968, Am. Cancer Soc. fund drive, College Station, 1971—74; co-founder, bd. dirs. Women's Shelter, Corpus Christi, 1977—78. Named Educator of Yr., Literary Couns. of Greater Dallas, 1997—98; recipient Sr. Salute award for achievements in edn., City of Dallas and NYL Care, 1996; grantee, NSF, The Women's U., 1963—65. Mem.: AAUW, NEA, Metroplex Educators Sci. Assn., Rocky Mountain Sociol. Assn., So. Sociol. Assn., Chem. Soc., Tex. Assn. Bilingual Educators, Tex. Tchrs. Assn., League United Latin Am. Citizens (pres. College Station 1973—74, past dist. dir. Corpus Christi), Pan Am. Round Table, Fiesta Bilingual Toastmasters. Avocations: ballroom dancing, comedy. Home and Office: 5005 Oak Trl Dallas TX 75232-1643

CIRINCIONE, ROSS JOSEPH, mathematician, educator; b. Cleve., Apr. 8, 1948; s. Charles Ignatius and Mary Italia Cirincione. BA, Dartmouth Coll., 1970; MS, Harvard U., 1972; PhD, U. Calif., Berkeley, 1979. Radar sys. analyst Hughes Aircraft Co., El Segundo, Calif., 1981—83, stats. quality control instr., 1983—86; instrnl. asst. El Camino CC, Torrance, Calif., 1996—98; math. lectr. Case Western Res. U., Cleve., 2000—. Author: (company manual) Concepts in Experimental Design, 1985. Mem.: Am. Math. Soc., Dartmouth Alumni Assn. Avocation: photography. Office: Case Western Res Univ 10900 Euclid Ave Cleveland OH 44106 Business E-Mail: rjc13@case.edu.

CIRINO, NICK MARIO, lab administrator, research scientist; b. Cleve., Ohio, Mar. 22, 1965; s. Dominic Mario Cirino and Ellen Louise Shelgren; m. Rebecca Eleanor Bergen, Sept. 9, 1989; children: Riley Catherine, Bailey Elizabeth, Sidney Victoria, Alexander Dominic. BA, Earlham Coll., 1983—87; PhD, Case Western Res. U., 1990—95. Rsch. fellow Los Alamos Nat. Lab., Los Alamos, N.Mex., 1997—99; microbial sciences team leader Battelle Meml. Inst., Columbus, Ohio, 1999—2002; biodefense lab. dir. Wadsworth Ctr., NYSDOH, Albany, NY, 2002—. Asst. prof. SUNY Albany Sch. of Pub. Health, 2003—. Tech. adv. boards for biodefense, 2003—. Recipient Outstanding Innovations, U. of Calif., 2001, Pub. Health Response, NYS Health Commr., 2004. Achievements include 5 patents focused on therapies for infectious diseases. Office: Wadsworth Center NYSDOH 120 New Scotland Ave Albany NY 12201 Office Phone: 518-474-1838. Office Fax: 518-486-7971. E-mail: ncirino@wadsworth.org.

CIRMINELLO, AMY L., school system administrator; b. Bayonne, N.J., May 27, 1974; d. Richard and Dorothy Cirminello. BS, U. Scranton, 1996; MA, Montclair (N.J.) State U., 2003. Cert. elem. sch. tchr. NJ, prin. NJ, supr. NJ, sch. adminstr. NJ. H.s. job coach Occupl. Ctr. of Hudson County, Jersey City, 1996—97; basic skills tchr. grades K-3 Bayonne Bd. of Edn., 1997—98; tchr. grades 1, 2 and 4 Elizabeth (N.J.) Bd. Edn., 1998—2004, vice prin., 2004—. Sch. leadership coun. chairperson Madison-Monroe Elem. Sch. #16, Elizabeth, 1999—2004. Mem.: ASCD, N.J. Prin. and Supr. Assn. Avocations: travel, skiing. Home: 1221 Magie Ave Apt 10C Union NJ 07083 Office: Marquis de Lafayette Sch #6 1071 Julia St Elizabeth NJ 07201 Office Phone: 908-436-5603. Office Fax: 908-436-5618. Personal E-mail: amycirminello@comcast.net. E-mail: cirminam@elizabeth.k12.nj.us.

CIRONE, WILLIAM JOSEPH, educational administrator; b. Bklyn., Dec. 27, 1937; s. Joseph Nicholas and Marie Ann (Basile) C.; m. Barbara Jane Skirkie, Dec. 22, 1962; 1 child, Peter Craig. BA, Providence Coll., 1959; MA, NYU, 1960; adminstrv. cert., U. Calif., Santa Barbara, 1977. Tchr. N.Y.C. Pub. Schs., 1960-68; dir. product devel. ednl. divsn. Mead Corp., Atlanta, 1968-70, dir. mktg., 1970-73; founder, dir. Ctr. Cmty. Edn. and Citizen Participation, Santa Barbara, Calif., 1973-82; supt. schs. Santa Barbara County, 1983—. Vis. fellow Chisholm Inst. Tech., Melbourne, Australia, 1986; vis. scholar Ctr. for excellence Tenn. State U., 1986. Host (cable talk shows) Education On-Line-A Line to Learning, Cirone on Schools. Bd. dirs., chair student aide com. Santa Barbara Cmty. Found., bd. dirs., 1998—, bd. chmn., 2003—04; bd. dirs. Cmty. Action Commn., 1973—81, Cmty. Resource Info. Svc., 1978—82, Fin. Crisis Mgmt. Assistance Team, 1993—, Nat. Partnership in Edn., 1998—, S.B. Fightnig Balk, 1994—, chmn., 2002—, Calif. Alliance for Arts Edn., 1999—, Santa Barbara Anti-Defamation League, 2001—; bd. dirs., sec. Pvt. Industry Coun., Santa Barbara, 1999—; bd. dirs. Industry Edn. Coun., Santa Barbara, 1983—, pres., 1990, 1999; bd. dirs. Coun. of Alcoholism and Drug Abuse, 1998—, Santa Barbara Lung Assn., 1983—87, Philip Francis Siff Ednl. Found., 1986—, Impact II, 1989—, pres., 1993—99; bd. dirs. Nat. Comm. Edn. Assn., 1989—92, pres., 1990; regional chair Calif. County Supt. Assn., 1990—96, bd. dirs. media and values, 1989—92; hon. bd. dirs. So. Coast Spl. Olympics; mem. Gov.'s Commn. on Earthquake Hazards, 1981; mem. state bd. Common Cause, 1974—77; organizer and 1st state chmn. Ga., 1970—73; mem. voter accessibility adv. bd. Santa Barbara County, 1986—; mem. adv. bd. CALM, Peace Resource Ctr., Marymount Sch., Women's Cmty. Bldg., Jodi House, Girl Scouts U.S.; comdrs. cmty. liaison com. Vandenberg AFB; mem. Access Theatre, Hon. Commn. for Goleta Hosp.; mem. campaign cabinet Santa Barbara United Way, 1991, 1998; adv. bd. Santa Barbara Brand Opera Assn., 1996—; co-chair State Supts. Statewide Arts Task Force, 1997; pres.-elect Nat. Ctr. for Learning and Citizenship, 2004, 2005. Recipient Smallheiser award United Fedn. Tchrs., 1968, Hon. Svc. award 15th Dist. PTA, 1979, 81, Intercongregation Orgn. Project Action award, 1995, Anti-Defamation League Santa Barbara Disting. Svc. award, 1996, Meritorious Svc. award Cmty. Action Com., Santa Barbara, 1981, Ind. Living Resource Ctr., 1985, Hon. Svc. award Calif. State PTA, 1995, 99 for '99 award, Santa Barbara C. of C., 1993-99, Profl. Publ. award Calif. County Supts. Assn., Comm. Achievement award Toastmasters Internat., 1999, Santa Barbara Wildlife Care Network award, 2000, Excellence in Svc. award South Coast Bus. and Tech., 2000, Vanguard award, 2002, Calif. Outstanding Art Educators' award Calif. Art's Comm., Emmanus Disting. Cmty. Svc. award, 2002-, Easy Lift Van Guard award, 2002, Lifetime Achievement award, Santa Barbara News Press, 2004; named Calif. Cmty. Educator of Yr., Calif. Cmty. Edn. Assn., 1984, Pub. Servant of Yr., Santa Barbara County, 1987. Mem. World Future Soc. (life), Am. Assn. Sch. Adminstrs., Assn. Calif. Sch. Adminstrs. (Region XIII Adminstr. of Yr. award 2002), So. Coast Coord. Coun. (past chmn., past exec. com.), Nat. Soc. Fundraising Execs., Automobile Assn. Am. (So. Calif. adv. bd.), Phi Delta Kappa. Democrat. Unitarian Universalist. Home: 218 Valhalla Dr Solvang CA 93463-9608 Office: PO Box 6307 Santa Barbara CA 93160-6307

CIRULLI, MICHELLE ELIZABETH, literature and language educator; b. Reading, Pa., Sept. 16, 1981; d. Jack Richard and Suzanne Louise Cirulli. BS in English, Millersville (Pa.) U., 2003. Tchr. Penn Manor H.S., Millersville, 2003—04, Twin Valley H.S., Elverson, Pa., 2004—. Dance club organizer, advisor Twin Valley H.S., 2004—, choreographer benefit talent show, 2005—. Editor: The Critical Approach to Arthur Miller, 2005. Leader People to People Student Ambassadors, 2004—05; student trustee Millersville U., 2002—03. Mem.: NEA, Nat. Coun. Tchrs. English. Democrat. Lutheran. Avocations: swimming, reading, travel, hiking. Home: 407 Parkside Ave Reading PA 19607 Office: Twin Valley Sch Dist 4897 N Twin Valley Rd Elverson PA 19520-9340 Office Phone: 610-286-8600. Personal E-mail: michellecirulli@hotmail.com. E-mail: mcirulli@twinval.k12.pa.us.

CIRULNICK, ARTHUR E., lawyer; b. Bklyn., June 20, 1954; BA, U. Calif. Santa Barbara, 1975; JD magna cum laude, U. San Francisco, 1979. Bar: DC 1979. Ptnr., Corp. Fin. & Securities Dept. Venable LLP, Washignton, DC. Adj. prof. George Washington U. Law Ctr., Washington, 1985—; lectr. in field. Contbr. Mem.: DC Bar. Office: Venable LLP 575 7th St NW Washington DC 20004 Office Phone: 202-344-8511. Office Fax: 202-344-8300. Business E-Mail: aecirulnick@venable.com.

CISKOWSKI, MICHAEL S., energy executive; BBA, MBA in Fin., Ctrl. State U. Okla. Pos. in fin. and planning Williams Exploration Co., Getty Oil Co.; various pos., including investor rels. dir., fin. planning dir., mgr. fin. planning Valero Energy Corp., San Antonio, exec. v.p., CFO, 2003. Office: Valero Corp Hdqrs One Valero Place San Antonio TX 78212-3186*

CISLOWSKI, JOSEPH A., non-profit association executive; b. L.A., Mar. 11, 1960; s. Al and Bela C.; m. Ruth Ellen Reaven, May 25, 1997; 1 child, Bailey Solomon. AB, U. Calif., L.A., 1981; M in Pub. Policy, Harvard U., 1984. Legis. aide Calif. Legislature, Sacramento, 1981-82; program analyst NIH, Bethesda, Md., 1983; analyst in social legis. Libr. of Congress, Washington, 1984-88; cons. Nat. Acad. Scis., Washington, 1989; policy analyst Nat. Commn. on Children, Washington, 1989-91; prin. The Generation Group, L.A., 1991-96; exec. dir. Ctr. for Health Care Rights, L.A., 1996-99, So. Calif. Leadership Network, L.A., 1999—. Faculty Ctr. Nonprofit Mgmt. So. Calif., L.A., 1994—. Commr. County of L.A. Pub. Libr., 1999—; trainer United Way Greater L.A., 1994-99; dir. Jewish Cmty. Rels. Com., L.A., 1994-2003; mem. Calif. State Democratic Ctrl. Com., 1979-81, 93—; elector Calif. Electoral Coll., 2000; bd.d irs. Calif. Assn. Leadership Programs, 2000—. Recipient Spl. Achievement award Librarian of Congress, Washington, 1985, Marilyn Gilbert award UCLA Internship Program, L.A., 1990, Achievement award UCLA Dept. Pediats., 1993, Dem. of Yr. award L.A. County Dem. Party, 1998; fellow Calif. State Assemby, Sacramento, 1981. Mem. UCLA Alumni Assn. (life), Harvard-Radcliffe Club So. Calif., Phi Beta Kappa. Jewish. Avocation: photography. Office: 5757 Wilshire Blvd Ste 315 Los Angeles CA 90036 Office Phone: 323-857-5200. Personal E-mail: jcislowski@sbcglobal.net.

CISNEROS, EVELYN, dancer; b. Long Beach, Calif., 1958; Mem. San Francisco Ballet Co., 1977—99. Performances include Scherzo, Mozart's C Minor Mass, Romeo and Juliet, Medea, The Tempest, 1980, Stars and Stripes, In the Night, A Midsummer Nights Dream, Cinderella, A Song for Dead Warriors, 1984, Confidences, 1986, Sleeping Beauty, 1992, Swan Lake, 1993. Office: San Francisco Ballet 455 Franklin St San Francisco CA 94102-4471

CISNEROS, HENRY G., homebuilding executive, broadcast executive, former federal official; b. San Antonio, June 11, 1947; s. J. George and Elvira (Munguia) C.; m. Mary Alice Perez; children: Teresa Angelica, Mercedes Christina, John Paul. BA, Tex. A&M U., 1969, M. Urban and Regional Planning, 1970; MPA, Harvard U., 1973; D. Public Adminstrn., George Washington U., 1975. Adminstrv. asst. to city mgr., San Antonio, 1968, Bryan, Tex., 1969-70; asst. dir. dept. model cities San Antonio, 1969-70; asst. to exec. v.p. Nat. League Cities, Washington, 1970-71; White House fellow asst. Sec. of HEW, Washington, 1971-72; teaching asst. dept. urban studies and planning M.I.T., 1972; mem. City Coun., San Antonio, 1975-81; mayor City of San Antonio, 1981-89; chmn. Cisneros Asset Mgmt., 1989-93; sec. U.S. Dept. HUD, Washington, 1993-97; pres., COO, Univision Comm., Inc., L.A., 1997-2000; chmn., CEO Am. CityVista, San Antonio, 2000—. Chmn. Nat. Civic League; vice chair New Am. Alliance; bd. mem. KB Home, The Entprise Found. Recipient Thomas Jefferson award for pub. architecture AIA, 1995. Office: Am CityVista 454 Soledad St Ste 300 San Antonio TX 78205-1555 Fax: 210-228-9906.*

CISNEROS, SANDRA, poet, short story writer, essayist; b. Chgo., Dec. 20, 1954; BA, Loyola U., 1976. College recruiter, counselor Loyala U., Chicago; literature dir. Guadalupe Cultural Arts Center, San Anto, Tex.; artist-in-residence Foundation Michael Karolyi, France. Guest prof. Calif. St. U., U. Calif., Berkeley, U. Mich., U. N.M. Author: (books) The House On Mango Street, 1984 (Am. Book award Columbus Found. 1985), Woman Hollering Creek and Other Stories, 1991, (children's) Hairs=Pelitos, 1994, (poetry) Bad Boys, 1980, The Rodrigo Poems, 1985, My Wicked, Wicked Ways, 1987, Loose Women, 1994, La Casa en Mango Street, 1994, El Arroyo de la Llorona, 1996, Caramelo, 2002. Fellow NEA, 1982, 87, MacArthur fellow, 1995; recipient Lannan Found. Lit. award, 1991. Home and Office: Susan Bergholz Literary SvcsAgy 17 W 10th St # 5 New York NY 10011-8746

CISSELL, JAMES CHARLES, lawyer; b. Cleve., May 29, 1940; s. Robert Francis and Helen Cecelia (Freeman) C; children: Denise, Helene-Marie, Suzanne, James. Student, Sophia U., Tokyo, 1961; AB, Xavier U., 1962; JD, U. Cin., 1966; postgrad., Ohio State U., 1973-74; D. Tech. Letters, Cin. Tech. Coll., 1979. Bar: Ohio 1966, U.S. Dist. Ct. (so. dist.) Ohio 1967, U.S. Ct. Appeals (6th cir.) 1978, U.S. Supreme Ct. 1980, U.S. Dist. Ct. (ea. dist.) Ky. 1981. Pvt. practice law, 1966—78, 1982—2003; asst. atty. gen. State of Ohio, 1971-74; first v.p. Cin. Bd. Park Commrs., 1973-74; vice mayor City of Cin., 1976-77; U.S. atty. So. Dist. Ohio, Cin., 1978-82. Adj. instr. law No. Ky. U., 1982-86; pres. Nat. Assn. Former U.S. attys., 2001—02. Author: Oil and Gas Law in Ohio, 1964, Federal Criminal Trials, 6th edit., 2003; editor: Proving Federal Crimes. Gen. chmn. amateur pub. links championship U.S. Golf Assn., 1987; mem. coun. City of Cin., 1974-78, 85-87, 89-92; clk of cts., Hamilton County, 1992-2003; judge Hamilton County Probate Ct., 2003-; commr. Recreation Bd. Cin., 1974, Planning Bd. Cin., 1977; pres. Ohio Clk. of Cts. Assn., 1998; mem. Ohio Bicentennial Commn., 1998-2003; mem. Ohio Cts. Futures Commn., 1998-2000; mem. Ohio Supreme Ct. Adv. Com. on Tech. and the Cts., 2000—, privacy of access subcom. of Supreme Ct. adv. com. on tech. of the Cts. Recipient Econ. Opportunity award, Dr. Martin Luther King Jr. Holiday Commn., 2002; fellow, Ford Found., 1973—74. Mem. Ohio Bar Assn., Cin. Bar Assn., Fed. Bar Assn., Former U.S. Attys. Assn. (pres. 2002-03), Greater Cin. Golf Assn. (pres. 2003-). Avocation: golf. Office: William Howard Taft Law Ctr 230 E 9th St 10th Fl Cincinnati OH 45202 Office Phone: 513-946-3535. Business E-Mail: jcissell@cms.hamilton-co.org.

CITRANO-CUMMISKEY, DEBRA MOIRA, chemist, network technician; b. Glen Cove, NY, Feb. 23, 1957; d. Helen Marie and Roy Maurice Citrano; 1 child, Nikki Marie Cummiskey. Student, Hofstra U.; BS in Edn., BS in Chemistry, Almeda U., 2004. A+ Certification Computer Career Ctr., 2002. Raw materials auditor Hi-Tech Pharm., Amityville, NY, 2003—; qc raw materials chemist Kos Pharmaceuticals, Edison, NJ, 2003—03. Corp. reference std. coord. DuPont Pharmaceuticals, Garden City, NY, 1978—2001. Mem.: Am. Chem. Soc. American Independent. Roman Catholic. Avocations: dance, swimming. Office: Hi-Tech Pharmacal Co Inc 369 Bayview Avenue Amityville NY 11701 Personal E-mail: corporatewoman@msn.com.

CITRIN, JAMES MICHAEL, executive search consultant; b. Great Neck, N.Y., Nov. 2, 1959; s. Harold Lee and Glenna (Green) C.; m. Gail Sarner, Aug. 14, 1988; children: Theodore, Oliver. AB, Vassar Coll., 1981; MBA with distinction, Harvard U., 1986. Fin. analyst Morgan, Stanley & Co., Inc., NYC, 1981-84; assoc. Goldman, Sachs & Co., NYC, 1986-87; sr. engagement mgr. McKinsey & Co., Stamford, Conn., 1987-92; dir. corp. planning Reader's Digest Assn., Inc., Pleasantville, NY, 1992-94; dir. Spencer Stuart, Stamford, Conn., 1994—. Co-author (with James Citrin): Lessons from the Top, 1999; co-author: (with James Citrin and Catherine Fredman) You're in Charge-- Now What: The 8-Point Plan, 2005. Founder, chmn. Vassar Coll. 21st Century Com., 1987-91. Mem. Phi Beta Kappa. Avocations: triathlon (world championship 1987), marathons, golf. Home: 740 West Rd New Canaan CT 06840-2517 Office: Spencer Stuart 3 Landmark Sq 695 Main St Ste 2 Stamford CT 06901-2150 Office Phone: 203-326-3753.

CITRON, BEATRICE SALLY, law librarian, lawyer, educator; b. Phila., May 19, 1929; d. Morris Meyer and Frances (Teplitsky) Levinson; m. Joel P. Citron, Aug. 7, 1955 (dec. Sept. 1977); children: Deborah Ann, Victor Ephraim. BA in Econs. with honors, U. Pa., 1950; MLS, Our Lady of the Lake U., 1978; JD, U. Tex., 1984. Bar: Tex. 1985; cert. sch. libr., tchr. Tex. Claims examiner Social Security Adminstrn., Pa., Fla. and N.C., 1951-59; head libr. St. Mary's Hall, San Antonio, 1979-80; media, reference and rare book libr., asst. and assoc. prof. St. Mary's U. Law Libr., San Antonio, 1984-89; asst. dir. St. Thomas U. Law Libr., Miami, Fla., 1989-96, assoc. dir./head pub. svc., 1996-99, acting dir., 1997-98. Law libr. cons., 2000—. Mem.: ABA, South Fla. Assn. Law Librs. (treas. 1992—94, v.p. 1994—95, pres. 1995—96), S.E. Assn. Law Librs. (newsletter, program and edn. coms. 1991—98), S.W. Assn. Law Librs. (continuing edn. com. 1986—88, chmn. local arrangements 1987—88), Am. Assn. Law Librs. (publs. com. 1987—88, com. on rels. with info. vendors 1991—93, bylaws com. 1994—96).

CITRON, DIANE, lawyer; b. Cin., Oct. 9, 1953; d. Carl and Georgia (Reid) C. BA, Franklin and Mareshall Coll., 1975; JD, Case Western Res. U., 1978. Bar: D.C. 1978, Calif. 1985. Assoc. Wasserman, Orlow, Ginsberg & Rubin, Washington, 1978-80; staff atty. SEC, Washington, 1980-83; sr. counsel Freddie Mac, Washington, 1983-84; assoc. Orrick, Herrington & Sutcliffe, San Francisco, 1984-85, Brown & Wood, San Francisco, 1985-87; spl. counsel Skadden, Arps, Slate, Meagher & Flom, San Francisco, 1987-92; ptnr. Mayer, Brown Rowe & Maw LLP, N.Y.C., 1992—. Adj. prof. law real estate LLM program John Marshall Law Sch. Real Estate, Chgo., 1995—. Mem. ABA (subcom. securitization real property sect.), FBA, Women's Art Assn. D.C., Bar Assn. D.C., Pi Gamma Mu. Democrat. Jewish. Office: Mayer Brown, Rowe & Maw LLP 1675 Bdwy New York NY 10019 Office Phone: 212-506-2520. E-mail: dcitron@mayerbrownrowe.com.

CITRON, JEFFREY A., telecommunications industry executive; b. Staten Island, Sept. 5, 1970; m. Suzanne Citron; 2 children. Clerk to day trader Datek Securities, 1987—92; pres. Christian Klein and Cogburn; founder The Island ECN (acquired by Instinet Group for $503 million), 1995; co-founder, CEO Datek Online Brokerage Services (acquired by Ameritrade Holdings for $1.3 billion), 1996—99; co-founder, chmn., CEO Vonage Holdings Corp., 2001—. Co-founder (with Suzanne Citron) The Charles LaFitte Found., 1999—; bd. dirs. Montclair Art Museum. Achievements include first to develop trading system (with Joshua Levine) to automate daily brokerage operations in 1989; co-founder Vonage, one of the first companies to offer voice-over-Internet-protocol, the technology known as VoIP, that allows people to make telephone calls over the Internet. Office: Vonage 2147 Route 27 Edison NJ 08817 Office Phone: 732-528-2600. Office Fax: 732-287-9119.

CITRON, RICHARD IRA, management consultant; b. Chgo., Apr. 1, 1944; s. Irving I. and Ruth (Katz) C.; m. Phyllis Sarah Kalifey, Dec. 26, 1971; children: Brian Todd, Dana Ann. BS, Roosevelt U., Chgo., 1966; MS, Ill. Inst. Tech., 1968, PhD, 1972. Enrolled Actuary. Consulting prin. A.S. Hansen, Inc., Chgo., 1972-79, mng. prin. N.Y.C., 1979-82; exec. v.p. Frank B. Hall Consulting Co., N.Y.C., 1982-86; pres., CEO W F Corron, Inc., Stamford, Conn., 1986-92; pres. Benefit Svcs. div., exec. v.p., dir. Hogg Robinson, Inc., N.Y.C., 1992-95; CEO Penn Gen. Svcs. Corp., Inc., N.Y.C., 1992-95; chmn. Hogg Robinson Consulting Group, Inc., N.Y.C., 1992-95, Group Plan Cons., Inc., N.Y.C., 1992-95; corp. dir. worldwide benefits Campbell Soup Co., Inc., Camden, NJ, 1996—2002; CEO Nortic Cons., LLC, 2002—. Chmn., CEO Citron & Assocs., Inc.; bd. dirs. Employee Benefit Rsch. Inst., Washington, HRI, Inc., N.A; adv. bd. mem. Am. Benefits Coun., 1998—. Author articles in profl. jours. Trustee Optometric Ctr. of N.Y., mem. Coll. Council of SUNY; cons. State of Ill. Pension Laws Commn. 1974-78 Recipient: Blum-Kolver Found. grant 1963-66, Nat. Sci. Found. grant 1968-70. Mem. Am. Acad. of Actuaries, Internat. Found. Employee Benefits (chmn actuaries com. 1981-82), Assn. of Private Pension and Welfare Plans, Am. Soc. for Advancement of Sci., Boardroom, Landmark, Elmwood Country Club. E-mail: mardino@aol.com.

CITTADINI, PETE, reporting applications platform company executive; BA in Liberal Arts, Boston Coll. Held sales mgmt. and tech. positions at Applied Data Rsch., CSC Infonet and MacMillan, Inc.; v.p., NE divsn. Oracle, 1986—92; with Interleaf, Inc., 1992—95; CEO, pres. Actuate Corp., South San Francisco, Calif., 1995—. Office: Actuate Corp 701 Gateway Blvd South San Francisco CA 94080-7084 Office Phone: 650-837-2000. Office Fax: 650-827-1560.

CIULLO, JAMES ANTHONY, special education services professional, writer; b. Pittsfield, Mass. s. George and Loretta DiNicola Ciullo. BA, Boston (Mass.) Coll., 1969; MEd, U. Mass., 1974. Vol. Peace Corps., Puerto Orduz, Venezuela, 1969—71; dir. Big Bros. Pittsfield, 1972; tchr. Educentro, Madrid, 1973; coord. youth Berkshire United Way, Pittsfield, 1974—76; mental retardation profl. Mass. Dept. Mental Retardation, Pittsfield, 1976—98; freelance cons., writer Pittsfield, 1998—. Guardian ad litem Ct. Appointed Spl. Advocates, Pittsfield, 1998—. Author: A Tango in Tuscany, 2002. Writer telegrams Amnesty Internat., Pittsfield, 1990—. Mem.: Order Sons Italy in Am. Roman Cath. Avocations: sports, politics, travel. Home: 125 Birch Grove Dr Pittsfield MA 01201

CIUPARU, DRAGOS MIHAEL, research scientist, educator; b. Ploiesti, Prahova, Romania, July 6, 1967; s. Dumitru and Zinovia Ciuparu; m. Alina Madalina Vasile, Oct. 27, 1990; children: Andrei Catalin, Georgiana Eugenia. MSc, Petrol-Gaze U., Ploiesti, 1991; PhD, Denis Diderot U., Paris, France, 1999. Lectr. Petrol - Gaze U., Ploiesti, Romania, 1996—99; assoc. prof. Petrol - Gaze U, 2003—; postdoctoral assoc. Yale U., 1999—2001, rsch. scientist, 2001—. Contbr. articles to profl. jours. Grantee PhD fellowship, French Ministry of Superior Edn., 1996-1999, TEMPUS-PHARE, European Union, 1998, Tng. grant, USAID, 1995. Mem.: Am. Chem. Soc., North Am. Catalysis Soc., AIChE. Achievements include design of first synthesis of pure boron single wall nanotubes and synthesis of controlled diameter single wall carbon nanotubes. Office: Yale University 9 Hillhouse Ave Mason Laboratory 310 New Haven CT 06520-8286 Office Phone: 203-432-4383. E-mail: dragos.ciuparu@yale.edu.

CIVEROLO, KEVIN LAWRENCE, research scientist; s. Edwin and Mary Civerolo; m. Stacey Rattner; 1 child, Tari. BS, Va. Tech U., 1990; PhD, U. Md., 1996. Rsch. assoc. SUNY Rsch. Found., Albany, NY, 1996—97; rsch. affiliate Health Rsch. Inc, 1998—98; rsch. scientist NY State DEC, 1998—; adj. asst. prof. SUNY, 2004—. Mem.: Am. Geophys. Union. Office Phone: 518-402-8383.

CIVIELLO, MARY, correspondent; Bachelor, Master, U. Mo. Reporter L.A. Times, 1974-77; anchor, reporter Sta. WEAU-TV, Eau Claire, Wis.; reporter various stas., Sta. WNBC-TV, N.Y.C., 1982-98; corr. CNBC, Ft. Lee, N.J., 1998—; pres., chmn. Civiello Comm. Group, Bronxville, N.Y. Recipient 3 Emmy awards, N.Y. Press Club Byline award, Deadline Club Sigma Delta Chi award. Office: Civiello Comm Group 5 Woodland Ave Bronxville NY 10708

CIVILETTI, BENJAMIN RICHARD, lawyer, former United States attorney general; b. Peekskill, NY, July 17, 1935; m. Gaile Lundgren Civiletti; 3 children. AB, Johns Hopkins U., 1957; LLB, Columbia U. and U. Md., 1961; LLD (hon.), U. Balt., 1978, NY Law Sch., 1979, Tulane U., 1979, St. John's Coll., 1979, U. Notre Dame, 1980, U. Md., 1983; LHD (hon.), Towson State U. Bar: Md. 1961, US Supreme Ct. 1965, DC 1981. Law clk. to the Hon. W. Calvin Chesnut US Dist. Ct. for Md., 1961-62; asst. US atty. dist. Md., 1962-64; assoc. Venable, Baetjer & Howard, Balt., 1964—68, ptnr., 1969—77, head litig. dept., 1971—77; asst. atty. gen. criminal divsn. US Dept. Justice, Washington, 1977-78, dep. atty. gen., 1978-79, atty. gen., 1979-81; now ptnr., firm chmn. Venable LLP, Balt. Founding chair Md. Legal Services Corp., 1982—86; mem. legal adv. bd. Lexis-Nexis/Martindale-Hubbell, 1990—; mem. lawyers com. Nat. Ctr. for State Courts, 2004—; dir. MBNA Corp., MBNA Internat.; mem. Matthew Bender & Co., Inc. Mem. bd. editors Fed. Litig. Guide Reporter; contbr. articles to profl. jours. Trustee Johns Hopkins U., 1980—98. Named Knight-Comdr., Order of Merit of the Italian Republic; recipient Herbert H. Lehman Ethics Award, Am. Jewish Theol. Sem., Disting. Alumnus Award, Johns Hopkins Alumni Assn., Equal Justice Award, Balt. Urban League, 1997. Fellow Am. Bar Found., Am. Law Inst., Am. Coll. Trial Lawyers; mem. ABA (mem. ho. dels. 1990-, Commn. on

Am. Jury, chmn. Task Force on Internat. Criminal Ct., rep. to UN), FBA, Md. Bar Assn., DC Bar Assn., Bar Assn. Balt. City, Am. Judicature Soc., Omicron Delta Kappa, Phi Alpha Delta., Order of Coif. Office: Venable LLP 1800 Merc Bank & Trust Bldg 2 Hopkins Plz Ste 2100 Baltimore MD 21201-2982*

CIVISH, GAYLE ANN, psychologist; b. Lynnwood, Calif., Sept. 29, 1948; d. Leland and Arline (Frazer) Civish; children: Nathan Morrow, Shane Morrow. BA, U. Nev., Reno, 1970; MA, U. Colo., 1973, PhD, 1983; student in Theology, ILiff Sch., 2001—. Lic. psychologist, Colo., Pa.; cert. sch. psychologist, Colo. Sch. psychologist Jefferson County (Colo.) Schs., 1983-89; psychologist in pvt. practice Lakewood, Colo., 1983-99, Boulder, Colo., 1999—. Cons. charter schs. integrated spl. edn., 1998. Contbr. articles to profl. jours. and books. Mem. APA (editor newsletter regional divsn.), Colo. Psychol. Assn. (bd. dirs. 1990-93), Pa. Psychol. Assn., Colo. Women Psychologists (past external liaison), Am. Soc. Clin. Hypnosis, Feminist Therapy Inst. (steering com. 1994-99), Assn. for Women in Psychology, Phi Kappa Phi, Phi Delta Kappa. Democrat. Office: #8 2885 Aurora Ave Ste 14 Boulder CO 80303-2251 Office Phone: 303-443-9570.

CLAASSEN, W(ALTER) MARSHALL, employment company executive; b. St. Paul, Jan. 16, 1943; s. Walter Marshall and Marie Christine (Petersen) C.; m. Nancy Rector Alcock, Mar. 2, 1974; children: Katherine, Walter. BA, BJ, U. Mo., 1966. Sr. adminstr. Honeywell, Inc., Chgo., 1968-74; pers. dir. Lyon-Healy, div. of CBS, Inc., Chgo., 1974-78; mgr., corp. placement CF Industries, Long Grove, Ill., 1978-82; mgr. of recruiting Newark Electronics, Chgo., 1983-84; dir. human resources Swift, div. of Reichold Chem., Downers Grove, Ill., 1984-86, ECM, Inc., Schaumburg, Ill., 1986-87; pres. GBX, Inc., dba Express Personnel Svcs., Vernon Hills, 1988—. Bd. dirs. Elk Grove-Schaumburg Mental Health Ctr., 1975-77, Pvt. Industry Coun. of Lake County, Waukegan, Ill., 1990-96, chmn., 1994-96; bd. dirs. Pvt. Industry Coun. Found., 1992—, Lake County Workforce Investment Bd., 2000—. Lt.(j.g.) USNR, 1966-68. Recipient Circle of Excellence award, 1992—. Mem. Libertyville-Vernon Hills C. of C., Lake County C. of C., Lincolnshire C. of C., Arlington Heights C. of C., Univ. Mo. Alumni Assn., Phi Delta Theta. Republican. Quaker. Avocations: fly fishing, scuba diving. Office: Express Personnel Svcs 977 Lakeview Pkwy Ste 190 Vernon Hills IL 60061-1429 Office Phone: 847-816-8422. E-mail: marshall.claassen@expresspersonnel.com.

CLACK, JERRY, classics educator; b. N.Y.C., July 22, 1926; s. Christopher Thrower and Mildred Taylor (VanDyke) C. AB, Princeton U., 1946, MA, 1958; PhD, U. Pitts., 1962; MA, Duquesne U., Pitts., 1977. Documents officer U.S. Nat. Commn. for UNESCO, 1946-52; exec. dir. Allegheny County chpt. Nat. Found., Pitts., 1953-68; asst. prof. dept. classics Duquesne U., Pitts., 1968-71, assoc. prof., 1971-75, prof., 1975—, chmn. dept., 1973-75, 80-83, mem. preprofl. health com., 1970-76, mem. univ. library com., 1979-93, mem. univ. due process, core curriculum, arts and scis. curriculum coms., 1986-94, mem. univ. promotion and tenure com., 1988-90. Editor: The Classical World, 1977-93, Anthology of Hellenistic Poetry, 1982, Meleager: The Poems, 1992, Asclepiades of Samos and Leonidas of Tarentum: The Poems, 1999, Dioscorides and Antipater of Sidon: The Poems, 2001; mem. editl. bd. Duquesne Univ. Press, 1991-94; author books, articles, revs. in field. Pres. We. Pa. Pub. Health Conf., 1967; v.p. We. Pa. chpt. Citizens for Global Solutions, 1965—88, treas. We. Pa. chpt., 1987—; U.S. del. 3d UNESCO Gen. Conf., Florence, Italy, 4th UNESCO Gen. Conf., Paris; bd. dirs. Pitts. Opera Theater, treas., 2003—. Mem. Classical Assn. Pitts. and Vicinity (treas. 1970-78, 85—, sec. 1988—), Pa. Classical Assn. (treas. 1977-99), Classical Assn. Atlantic States (pres. 1987, exec. com. 1974—, 2d v.p. 1975, 1st v.p. 1976, exec. dir. 1993-2001, archivist 2001—), Am. Philol. Assn. (chmn. working group editors classical jours. 1982-93, chmn. com. regional classical orgns. 1986-95), Vergilian Soc. Am. (trustee 1985-87), Phi Sigma Iota, Delta Phi Alpha, Alpha Epsilon Delta, Phi Alpha Theta. Home: Apt 512 5850 Centre Ave Pittsburgh PA 15206 Office: Duquesne U Dept Classics Pittsburgh PA 15282-0001 Office Phone: 412-396-6452. E-mail: clack@duq.edu.

CLAES, DANIEL JOHN, physician; s. John Vernon and Claribel Claes; m. Gayla Christine Claes, Jan. 19, 1974. AB magna cum laude, Harvard U., 1953, MD cum laude, 1957. Intern UCLA, 1957-58; Bowyer Found. fellow rsch. in medicine LA, 1958-61; pvt. practice specializing in diabetes, 1962—. V.p. Am. Eye Bank Found., 1978—83, dir. rsch., 1980—, pres., 1983—, chmn., CEO, 1995—; pres. Heuristic Group, 1981—, Cavendish Assocs., 2002—; biotech. cons. SIRA Techs., 1995—. Contbr. articles to profl. jours. Mem. LA Mus. Art, 1960—. Mem.: AAAS, AMA, Cell Transplantation Soc., Diabetes Tech. Soc., Am. Math. Soc., Internat. Pancreas and Islet Transplant Assn., Internat. Diabetes Fedn. Am. Diabetes Assn. (profl. coun. on immunology, immunogenetics and transplantation), Los Angeles County Med. Assn., Calif. Med. Assn., Royal Commonwealth Club (London), Harvard and Harvard Med. Sch. So. Calif. Club. Achievements include research in supercomputer bioinformatics in medicine, computational chemistry, molecular modeling, quantum chemistry, genomics, proteomics and preventive care. Office: Am Eyebank Found 15237 W Sunset Blvd Ste 108 Pacific Palisades CA 90272-3690

CLAES, GAYLA CHRISTINE, writer, editor, consultant; b. L.A., Oct. 17, 1946; d. Henry George and Glorya Desiree Blasdel; m. Daniel John Claes, Jan. 19, 1974. AB magna cum laude, Harvard U., 1968; postgrad., Oxford (Eng.) U., 1971; MA, McGill U., Montreal, 1975. Adminstrv. asst. U. So. Calif., L.A., 1968-70; teaching asst. English lit. McGill U., Montreal, 1970-71; editorial dir. Internat. Cons. Group, L.A., 1972-78; v.p. Gaylee Corp., L.A., 1978-81, CEO, 1981-88; writer, cons. L.A. and Paris, 1988—. Dir. pub. rels. Ctr. Internat. for the Performing Arts, Paris and L.A., 1991—2000. Author: (play) Berta of Hungary, 1972, (novel) Christopher Derring, 1990; contbr. articles to lit. and sci. jours. Co-founder White Swan Awards, ann. benefit for Crippled Children's Soc. dba AbilityFirst, 1999. Mem. Harvard-Radcliffe Club of So. Calif., Royal Commonwealth Soc. (London).

CLAEYS, JEROME JOSEPH, III, investment company executive; b. South Bend, Ind., Oct. 23, 1942; s. Jerry F. and Evadna (Shoemaker) Claeys; m. Barbara Lauman, May 4, 1974; children: Elizabeth Anne, Matthew Jerome, Andrew Francis, Katherine Ellen. BS, Georgetown U., 1965; MBA, U. Notre Dame, 1969. First v.p. White Weld & Co., N.Y.C., 1969—76; exec. v.p. JMB Realty Corp., Chgo., 1977—89; chmn. JMB Instnl. Realty Corp. (JMB Instnl. Realty Corp. and JMB Properties Co. merged with Heitman Financial in 1999), Chgo., 1990—94, Heitman Capital Mgmt., 1994; chmn, CEO Heitman Financial LLC, 1999—2002, chmn., 2002—. Served with U.S. Army, 1965—67. Decorated Bronze Star with oak leaf cluster. Mem.: Nat. Assn. Indsl. and Office Parks, Internat. Assn. Shopping Ctr. Developers. Roman Cath. Office: Heitman Financial 191 N Wacker Dr Ste 2500 Chicago IL 60606*

CLAFLIN, ARTHUR CARY, lawyer; b. Bowling Green, Ohio, July 7, 1950; s. Edward Scott and Mona Sophia (Cretney) C.; m. Gretchen Elaine Anders, May 31, 1975; children: Rachel Anders, Emily Anders. BA magna cum laude, Wesleyan U., 1972; JD, Yale U., 1975. Bar: Wash. 1975, U.S. Dist. Ct. (we. dist.) Wash. 1975, U.S. Dist. Ct. (ea. dist.) Wash. 1981, U.S. Ct. Appeals (9th cir.) 1979, U.S. Ct. Appeals (5th cir.) 1982. Assoc. Bogle & Gates, Seattle, 1975-81, ptnr., 1981-99, Claflin & Christensen, Seattle, 1999-2000; mem. Hall, Zanzig, Zulauf, Claflin, McEachern, Seattle, 2000—. Mem. Phi Beta Kappa. Presbyterian. Office: Hall Zanzig Zulauf Claflin McEachern 1200 5th Ave Ste 1414 Seattle WA 98101-3106 Office Phone: 206-292-5900.

CLAFLIN, BRUCE, communications company executive; BA in Polit. Sci., Pa. State U. Formerly with IBM Corp.; gen. mgr. IBM PC Co., 1989-93; pres. PC Co. Americas, 1993-94, gen. mgr. products and brand mgmt., 1994-97; former sr. v.p. and gen. mgr. sales and mktg. Digital Equipment Corp., 1997-98; pres., COO 3Com Corp., Santa Clara, Calif., 1998—2001, pres., CEO, 2001—. Bd. dirs. Advanced Micro Devices, Time Warner Telecom. Mass. Bus. Roundtable. Alumni fellow Pa. State U., 1998. Office: 3Com Corp 5400 Bayfront Plz Santa Clara CA 95054-3601

CLAFLIN, JAMES ROBERT, pediatrician, allergist; b. Apr. 30, 1946; m. Marcee Claflin; children: James Sean (dec.), Brian Scott (dec.), Susan Nicole, Timothy Lynn. Student, Northwestern State Coll.; MD, U. Okla., 1971. Diplomate Am. Bd. Pediatrics, Am. Bd. Allergy Immunology. Intern U. Tex. Med. Br., Galveston, 1971-72; advanced through grades to lt. col. USAF, 1969-84, chief pediatric svcs. Goodfellow AFB, 1972-73, 75-77, chief pediatric svcs. and hosp. svcs. RAF Upper Heyford, 1977-80, chief allergy and clin. immunology Carswell AFB, 1982-84; fellow allergy/immunology Willford Hall USAF Med. Ctr., Lackland AFB, Tex., 1980-82; ret. USAF, 1984. Clin. asst. prof. pediatrics, Oklahoma U.; presenter in field. Contbr. articles to profl. jours. Advisor child welfare com. Tom Green County, 1976-77; mem. child welfare com. RAF, Upper Heyford, Eng., 1978-80; mem. sch. and pub. health com. Tarrant County Med. Soc., 1984-85, chmn., 1986-87, publs. com., 1988-89, religion and meml. com., 1989; mem. quality assurance and infectious disease coms. Cook-Ft. Worth Children's Hosp., 1986-89; v.p. Brenham State Sch. Parent Assn., 1987-88; pres. Parents Assn. for the Retarded of Tex., 1987-88; chmn. cmty. conscience com. Wedgwood Bapt. Ch. Recipient Svc. award Am. Diabetes Assn., 1976. Fellow Am. Acad. Pediatrics, Am. Coll. Allergy (mem. com. on allergic rhinitis, mem. com. on adverse reactions to food 1991-96), Am. Acad. Allergy; mem. AMA (alt. del.), Am. Coll. Allergy, Asthma and Immunology (spkr. ho. of dels. 2001-03), Oklahoma County Med. Soc. (pres.-elect 2003-04), Okla. State Med. Assn. (sec.-treas. 2003-05, v.p., 2005-), Okla. Allergy and Asthma Soc. (pres. 1998-2000). Home: 750 NE 13th St Oklahoma City OK 73104-5051

CLAGETT, BRICE MCADOO, lawyer, writer, genealogist; b. Washington, July 6, 1933; s. Brice and Sarah Fleming (McAdoo) Clagett; m. Virginia Lawrence Parker, Sept. 18, 1965 (div.); children: John Brice, Ann Calvert Brooke; m. Diana Wharton Sinkler, July 26, 1987. AB summa cum laude, Princeton U., 1954; postgrad., U. Allahabad, India, 1954-55; JD magna cum laude, Harvard U., 1958. Bar: D.C. 1958, U.S. Supreme Ct. 1962. Assoc. Covington & Burling, Washington, 1958-67, ptnr., 1967-2000, sr. counsel, 2000—02. Jud. counsellor Cambodian del. Internat. Ct. Justice, 1960—62; legal advisor Transition Team U.S. Dept. State, 1980—81; mem. nat. steering com. U.S. Iran Claimants Com., 1982—99; adv. bd. Inst. Transt. Arbitration, 1989—2000; mem. lawyers com. Ctr. Individual Rights, 1992—; trustee Wentz Holdings, Inc., Charitable Remainder Unitrust, 2001—. Co-author: (book) The Valuation of Property in International Law, vol. 4, 1987, An Illustrated History of St. Albans School, 1981; bd. editors: Harvard Law Rev., 1956—58; contbr. articles to legal, geneal. and hist. jours. Trustee Md. Hist. Trust, 1971—78, chmn., 1972—78; trustee Md. State Ho. Trust, 1972—76, Md. Environ. Trust, 1978—, vice chmn., 1981—85, chmn., 1985—89; bd. dirs. Chester-Sassafras Found., 1985—89; trustee New Eng. Hist. Geneal. Soc., 1989—92, 1995—98, Tudor Place Found., 1992—96, Found. Preservation Hist. Georgetown, 2000—; bd. advisors Nat. Trust Hist. Preservation, 1978—81; Clagett family com. Chesapeake Bay Found., 1982—; mem. Human Rights Law Group del. to Romania, 1990; counselor to the Pres. Gen. Soc. Cin., 1988—89, solicitor, 1998—; mem. adv. coun. Accokeek Found., 1989—91, trustee, 1991—94; comdr. Royal Order Cambodia, 1962. Recipient Cert. Disting. Citizens, State of Md., 1978. Mem.: So. Md. Soc., Federalist Soc., Washington Inst. Fgn. Affairs, Internat. Law Assn., Am. Law Inst., Am. Soc. Internat. Law, Mil. Order Stars and Bars, City Tavern Club (D.C.), Radnor Hunt Club (Pa.), Marlborough Hunt Club (Upper Marlboro, Md.), Met. Club (D.C.), Soc. Cin. Md., Sons Confederate Vets., Phi Beta Kappa. Republican. Episcopalian. also: 3331 O St NW Washington DC 20007-2814 Office: Covington & Burling PO Box 7566 1201 Pennsylvania Ave NW Washington DC 20044 Office Phone: 202-662-5316. Business E-Mail: bclagett@cov.com.

CLAGETT, VIRGINIA PARKER, state official; b. Washington, July 18, 1943; d. William Merrick and Virginia (Lawrence) Parker; m. Brice McAdoo, Sept. 18, 1965; children: John Brice, Ann Brooke. Student, U. Geneva, 1963-64; BA, Smith Coll., 1965. Asst. reporter Triangle Stas., Phila., 1966-68; county councilwoman County of Anne Arundel, Annapolis, Md., 1974-94, council chmn., 1984-91; mem. Md. Gen. Assembly Ho. of Dels., 1994—. Vice chmn. Balt. Regional Planning Coun., 1984—; trustee Hammond-Harwood Ho., 1978—, Chesapeake EPA, 1976—; mem. Alcohol and Drug Abuse Adv. Com., 1985—; mem. Anne Arundel County Agrl. Adv. Com., 1978—; bd. dirs. Historic Annapolis, Inc. Mem. Am. Bus. Womens Assn., Md. Assn. Counties (legis. com.). Democrat. Episcopalian. Avocations: tennis, gardening, horseback riding. Home: PO Box 1 West River MD 20778-0001 Office: Ho of Dels Md Gen Assembly 212 Lowe Office Bldg 84 College Ave Annapolis MD 21401 Office Phone: 410-841-3216. E-mail: virginia_clagett@house.state.md.us.

CLAGUE, CHRISTOPHER K(ARRAN), economics professor; b. Washington, May 28, 1938; s. Ewan and Dorothy Clague; m. Monique Weston, June 9, 1960 (div. 1982); children: Holly Weston, Heather Whipple. BA, Swarthmore Coll., 1960; PhD, Harvard U., 1966. Instr. Harvard U., Cambridge, Mass., 1965-67; sr. staff economist Coun. Econ. Advisers, Washington, 1967-68; asst. prof. U. Md., College Park, 1968-71, assoc. prof., 1971-79, prof. econs., 1979-98; lectr. in econs. San Diego State U., 1999—. Dept. chmn., 1980-82; cons. World Bank, Washington, 1977-80, 83, 95-96; dir. rsch. IRIS, 1990-97. Co-author: Capital Utilization, 1981; editor: Institutions and Economic Development, 1997; co-editor: The Emergence of Market Economics in Eastern Europe, 1992; bd. editors So. Econ. Jour., 1977-79. Mem. Am. Econ. Assn., Conf. on Income and Wealth (exec. com. 1983-87). Democrat. Office: San Diego State Econs Dept 5500 Campanile Dr San Diego CA 92182-0001 Home: PO Box 267 Descanso CA 91916 Business E-Mail: cclague@mail.sdsu.edu.

CLAGUE, DAVID A., geologist; b. Phila., Aug. 3, 1948; married; 1 child. PhD in Earth Sci., Scripps Inst. Oceanography, 1974. With nat. rsch. coun. U.S. Geol. Survey, 1974-75, rsch. geologist, 1979-96; asst. prof. geology Middlebury Coll., 1975—79; scientist-in-charge Hawaiian Volcano Obs., 1991-96; dir. rsch. an devel. Monetary Bay Aquarium Rsch. Inst., 1996-99, sr. scientist, 1999—. Fellow Geol. Soc. Am., Am. Geophys. Union, Calif. Acad. Sci. Office: Monterey Bay Aquarium Rsch Inst 7700 Sandholdt Rd Moss Landing CA 95039-9644 E-mail: clague@mbari.org.

CLAIBORNE, LIZ (ELISABETH CLAIBORNE ORTENBERG), fashion designer; b. Brussels, Mar. 31, 1929; came to U.S., 1939; d. Omer Villere and Louise Carol (Fenner) C.; m. Arthur Ortenberg, July 5, 1954; 1 son by previous marriage, Alexander G. Schultz. Student, Art Sch., Brussels, 1948-49, Academie, Nice, France, 1950; DFA, R.I. Sch. Design, 1991. Asst. Tina Lesser, N.Y.C., 1951-52, Omar Khayam, Ben Reig, Inc., N.Y.C., 1953; designer Juniorite, N.Y.C., 1954-60, Dan Keller, N.Y.C., 1960-76, Youth Guild Inc., N.Y.C., 1976-89; designer, pres., chmn. Liz Claiborne Inc., N.Y.C., 1985-89, pres., 1976-89, chmn., chief oper. officer, until 1989; chmn. Liz Claiborne Cosmetics, 1985-89, cons. Guest lectr. Fashion Inst. Tech., Parsons Sch. Design; bd. dirs. Coun. of Am. Fashion Designers, Fire Island Lighthouse Restoration Com. Recipient Designer of Yr. award Palciode Hierro, Mexico City, 1976, Designer of Yr. award Dayton Co., Mpls., 1978, Ann. Disting. in Design award Marshall Field's, 1985, One Co. Makes a Difference award Fashion Inst. Tech., 1985, award Coun. Fashion Designers, 1986, Gordon Grand Fellowship award Yale U., 1989, Jr. Achievement award Nat. Bus. Hall of Fame, 1990, Frederick A.P. Barnard award Barnard Coll., 1991, Hon. Doctorate, R.I. Sch. of Design, 1991; named to Nat. Sales Hall of Fame, 1991. Mem. Fashion Group. Roman Catholic.*

CLAIR, JOHN J., JR., lawyer; BA, Brown Univ., 1968; JD, Univ. Pa., 1972. Bar: Calif. 1973. Various mgmt. positions Latham & Watkins, LA, 2000—04, mng. ptnr., 2004—, and mem. tax dept. Mem.: ABA, State of Calif. Bar Assn., LA County Bar Assn. Office: Latham & Watkins Ste 4000 633 W Fifth St Los Angeles CA 90071-2007 Business E-Mail: john.clair@lw.com.

CLAIR, KATHLEEN SUSAN, educational association administrator; b. Phila., Apr. 19, 1958; d. Edward Franklin and Margaret Mary Clair. BA magna cum laude, Wellesley Coll., 1980; MA, U. Oxford, 1985; MA with distinction, Arcadia U., 1997. Bar: Pa. 1986; cert. leadership U. Pa., 2001, instructional II Pa., 2000, secondary prin. Pa., 2001. Atty. Schnader, Harrison, Segal and Lewis, Phila., 1986—89, Abramson, Cogan, Kogan, Freedman and Thall, Phila., 1989—90, Sidkoff, Pincus and Green, Phila., 1990—91, White and Williams, Phila., 1991—96; tchr., adminstr. Interboro Sch. Dist., Prospect Pk., Pa., 1997—. Adv. Nat. Constitution Ctr., Phila., 2001—; cons. McGraw/Hill Co., N.Y.C., NY, 2003—; v.p. Pennsbury Sch. Bd., Fallsington, Pa., 1992—97; with Supreme Ct. Inst., Adv. Civics Inst. Contbr. articles to profl. jours. Fellow, James C. Ackerman Ctr., Purdue U. Mem.: 25th Reunion Wellesley Coll., Oxford Soc., Phi Delta Kappa. Avocation: masters swimming. Home: 2300 Armstrong Ave Holmes PA 19043 Office: Interboro Sch Dist 900 Wash Ave Prospect Park PA 19076 Office Phone: 610-237-6410. Office Fax: 610-237-8103. E-mail: clairks@interborosd.org.

CLAIR, THEODORE NAT, educational psychologist; b. Stockton, Calif., Apr. 19, 1929; s. Peter David and Sara Renee (Silverman) C.; m. Laura Gold, June 19, 1961; children: Shari, Judith. AA, U. Calif., Berkeley, 1949, AB, 1950; MS, U. So. Calif., 1953, MEd, 1963, EdD, 1969. Tchr., counselor L.A. City Schs., 1957-63; psychologist Alamitos Sch. Dist., Garden Grove, Calif., 1963-64, Arcadia (Calif.) Unified Sch. Dist., 1964-65; head psychologist Wiseburn Sch. Dist., Hawthorne, Calif., 1966-69; asst. prof. spl. edn., coord. sch. psychology program U. Iowa, Iowa City, 1969-72; dir. pupil pers. svcs. Orcutt (Calif.) Union Sch. Dist., 1972-73; adminstr. Mt. Diablo Unified Sch. Dist., 1973-77; program dir., psychologist San Mateo County Office Edn., Redwood City, 1977-91; assoc. prof. John F. Kennedy U. Sch. Mgmt., 1975-77; pvt. practice as ednl. psychologist specializing in Attention Defecit Disorders Menlo Park, 1978—; pvt. practice marriage and family counselor specializing in Attention Defecit Disorders, 1978—. Dir. Peninsula Vocat. Rehab. Inst., 1978—; psychologist Coll. Counseling Svc., Menlo Park, 1992-2001, Calif. Pacific Hosp., San Francisco, 1993—; mem. adv. bd. Kitty Petty ADD/LD Inst., Palo Alto. Author: Phenylketonuria and Some Other Inborn Errors of Amino Acid Metabolism, 1971; editor Jour. Calif. Ednl. Psychologists, 1992-94; contbr. articles to profl. jours. Served with USNR, 1952-54. Mem. Am. Assn. Marriage & Family Therapy (Calif. divsn.), Calif. Assn. Marriage and Family Therapists, Palo Alto B'nai B'rith Club (pres.), Stanford Club Palo Alto. Home and Office: 56 Willow Rd Menlo Park CA 94025-3654 Office Phone: 650-323-2212. E-mail: cnatusc2@aol.com, tedclair@sbcglobal.net.

CLAIRE, JUDITH SUSAN, lawyer; b. Phila., Dec. 29, 1950; d. Martin and Gertrude Gantshar; m. Robert Walter Van Every, June 20, 1976; children: Alison Beth, Benjamin Harris. BA, U. Mass., 1972; JD, SUNY, Buffalo, 1975. Bar: N.Y. 1976, U.S. Dist. Ct. (we. dist.) N.Y. 1978. Health planning counsel N.Y. Govs. Commn. Health Planning, Albany, 1975-76; atty. Mental Health Info. Service, Ogdensburg, N.Y., 1976-78; ptnr. Van Every & Claire, Falconer, N.Y., 1978-91; matrimonial referee, confidential law clk. Supreme Ct. Chautauqua County; family ct. judge Chautauqua County, 1999—. Bd. dirs., v.p. Palace Civic Ctr.; past chmn. Route 60 Orgn.; former chmn. Lenna Civic Ctr.; bd. dirs. Family Svcs. Girl Scouts U.S.A., H.S. Compact Team; mem. B.O.C.E.S. Adv. Coun., Workforce Youth Coun. Named Outstanding Young Woman of Am., 1980. Mem. N.Y. Bar Assn., Jamestown Bar Assn., Jamestown Bus. and Profl. Womens Club (pres. 1983-85), Erie County Bar Assn. Office: Family Ct PO Box 149 Mayville NY 14757-0149

CLAIRMONT, WILLIAM EDWARD, real estate developer; b. Walhalla, N.D., Jan. 2, 1926; s. Emil O. and Mae E. (Bisenius) C.; m. Patricia Ann Filben, Oct. 7, 1950; children: Stephen, Julie, Cynthia, Nancy. Student, N.D. State U., 1948-49. Founder William Clairmont, Inc., Bismarck, N.D., 1949, owner, 1949—. Chmn. bd. First Southwest Bank, Mandan, N.D., 1975-89, Grant County State Bank, Carson, N.D., 1981-85; land developer, Bismarck; owner farm, N.D. Mem. City Council, Walhalla, 1955-56; owner ranch, irrigation farm, Costa Rica, 1975-83; owner, pres. Country West Real Estate, 1978—; trustee, mem. bd. regents U. Mary, Bismarck, chmn. bd., 1980-81; trustee Bismarck State Coll. Found.; bd. dirs. Theodore Roosevelt Medora Found., 2000—. Served with USMCR, 1944-46. Mem. N.D. Assn. Gen. Contractors (dir. 1964-72, pres. 1971). Office: 1720 Burnt Boat Dr Bismarck ND 58503-0806

CLAMAR, APHRODITE J., psychologist; b. Hartford, Conn. d. James John and Georgia (Panas) Clamar; m. Richard Cohen, June 24, 1973. BA, CCNY, 1953; MA, Columbia U., 1955; PhD, NYU, 1978; student, S. Adler Conservatory Acting, 1987-91. Mgmt. cons., psychologist Milla Alihan Assocs., N.Y.C., 1957-62; rsch. psychologist coord. Inst. Devel. Studies N.Y. Med. Coll., N.Y.C., 1964; intern psychologist Bellevue Psychiat. Hosp., N.Y.C., 1964-66; assoc. prof. Fashion Inst. Tech., N.Y.C., 1966-69; supervising psychologist Lifeline Ctr. Child Devel., N.Y.C., 1966-67; chief psychologist I Spy Health Program Beth Israel Med. Ctr., N.Y.C., 1967-70; dir. community-sch. mental health programs Soundview Community Svcs., Albert Einstein Coll. Medicine Yeshiva U., N.Y.C., 1970-73; dir. treatment program court-related children, dept. child psychiatry Harlem Hosp.; mem. faculty dept. psychiatry Coll. Physicians and Surgeons Columbia U., N.Y.C., 1973-76; pvt. practice psychotherapy, N.Y.C., 1976—; co-founder, pres. Richard Cohen Assocs. Pub. Rels. Agy., N.Y.C., 1979—99; prof. John Jay Coll., CUNY, 2000—. Cons. to pub. health and mental health agys., N.Y.C., 1976-91; mem. faculty Lenox Hill Hosp. Psychoanalytic Psychotherapy Tng. Program, 1982-88; theater producer, artistic dir. Tom Cat Cohen Prodns., Inc., 1990—. Author: (with Budd Hopkins) Missing Time, 1981; contbr. articles to profl. jours. Fellow AAAS; mem. APA, Authors Guild. Democrat. Greek Orthodox. Home: 155 W 68th St Apt 1618 New York NY 10023-5829 Office Phone: 212-724-1091.

CLAMPITT, SANDRA LYNN, music educator, director; b. Seoul, Republic of Korea, Sept. 17, 1959; arrived in U.S., 1960; d. Thomas Richard, Jr. and Louanna Jacqueline Clampitt. B in Music Edn., Midwestern State U., Wichita Falls, Tex., 1996. Tchr. Acad. Kids, Wichita Falls, 1994—96; choral dir. Burkburnett (Tex.) Mid. Sch., 1998—. Musician: Backdoor Theatre, 1982—. Scholar, Musicians Club, 1988. Mem.: NEA, Tex. Choral Dirs. Assn., Tex. Music Educators Assn. Avocations: music composition, travel. Home: 4709 Taft # 602 Wichita Falls TX 76308-5009 Office: Burkburnett Mid Sch 108 S Ave D Burkburnett TX 76354

CLANCY, BRIAN PAUL, music educator; b. Manhasset, NY, Sept. 22, 1962; s. Paul Michael and Maureen Egan Clancy; m. Kristin Donna LaFauci, June 30, 2000; children: Jessie Ann, Megan Tracey, Michael Brian. AAS, Nassau Cmty. Coll., 1982; MusB, Potsdam Coll., 1985, MusM, 1987. Music tchr. Deer Pk. Sch., NY, 1987—90, Hauppauge Pub. Sch., NY, 1990—. Exec. bd. mem. Suffolk County Music Educators Assn., NY, 1990—97; edn. com. Percussive Arts Soc., Lawton, Okla., 1994; presenter NY State Music Assn. Winter Conf. Avocations: woodworking, carpentry, gardening. Home: 19 Balsam Dr Medford NY 11763 Office: Hauppauge Pub Sch 500 Lincoln Blvd Hauppauge NY 11788

CLANCY, CAROLYN M., social services administrator, former science foundation director; Grad., Boston Coll., U. Mass. Fellow Henry Kaiser Family Found. U. Pa.; clin. assoc. prof. dept. health care scis. George Washington U. Sch. Medicine; asst. prof. dept. internal medicine Va. Commonwealth U./Med. Coll. Va.; dir. Ctr. Primary Rsch. Agy. Healthcare Rsch. and Quality, HHS, dir., Ctr. Outcomes and Efffectiveness Rsch. (COER), 1997—2002, acting dir., 2002—03, dir., 2003—. Rschr. in field. Sr. assoc. editor Health Svcs. Rsch.; mem. editl. bd.: Am. Jour. Pub. Health; Jour. Evaluation in Clin. Practice, Jour. Gen. Internal Medicine, Med. Care Rsch. and Rev.; contbr. articles in peer-reviewed jours. Recipient award, APHA Women's Caucus . Mem.: Soc. Gen. Internal Medicine. Office: Agcy for Healthcare Research & Quality 540 Gaither Rd Rockville MD 20850-6649

CLANCY, MARGUERITE ALINE (MEG CLANCY), librarian; b. Holyoke, Mass., July 8, 1961; d. Robert Elmer and Constance Aline (Hubert) Clancy; 1 child, Aaron Hubert Soule. AA, Holyoke C.C., 1981; BA, U. Mass., 1983; MLS, So. Conn. State U., 1994. Cert. libr. Mass., 1994. Adminstrv. asst. South Hadley Pub. Libr., Mass., 1986—96, youth svcs. libr., 1996—. Mem. statewide steering com. Mass. Summer Reading Program, 1998—2000. Sec. South Hadley Dem. Town Com., 1994—; register of voters, 1999—. Mem.: New Eng. Libr. Assn., Mass. Libr. Assn. (sec. exec. bd. 2002—03, mem. legis. com. 1989—2003, mem. youth svcs. sect. 1998—2003), Am. Libr. Assn. Office: South Hadley Pub Libr 27 Bardwell St South Hadley MA 01075 Office Phone: 413-538-5045. E-mail: mclancy@cwmars.org.

CLANCY, PATRICIA, state representative; b. Cin., Aug. 10, 1952; BS, U. Cin. State rep. dist. 29 Ohio Ho. of Reps., Columbus, 1996—2004, mem. fin. and appropriations, rules and reference, and state govt. coms., mem. agr. and devel., and ethics and elections subcoms., majority fl. leader; state senator Ohio Senate Dist. 8, Columbus, 2005—, mem. fin. and fin. instns. com., mem. health, human svcs. and aging com., mem. hwys. and transp. com., mem. ins., commerce and labor com., vice chair judiciary and criminal justice com. Mem. Hamilton County Solid Waste Dist. Task Force, Colerain Ave. Task Force; past pres., trustee Colerain Twp. Mem.: Hamilton County Twp. Assn. (sec.-treas.), Colerain Twp. Hist. Soc., Colerain Twp. Rep. Club (sec.), Hamilton County Rep. Club. Republican. Office: Ohio Senate Statehouse Rm 143 Columbus OH 43215

CLANCY, PATRICK L., lawyer; b. Washington, Mar. 17, 1958; BA, U. Md., 1982, JD with honors, 1987. Bar: Md. 1987, DC 1988, admitted to practice: US Dist. Ct. (Dist. Md.) 1988, US Dist. Ct. (DC) 1988, US Ct. Appeals (4th Cir.) 1994. Lectr. in field. Exec. editor Venable's Workplace Labor Updade. Bd. dir. Our Lady of Good Counsel High Sch., Wheaton, Md. Mem.: Md. Ct. Appeals (character com.), Fed. Bar Assn., DC Bar Assn. (Labor Sect., Employment Law Sect.), Md. State Bar Assn., ABA, Montgomery County Bar Assn., Order of Coif. Office: Venable LLP One Church St Ste 500 PO Box 1906 Rockville MD 20850-4129 Office Phone: 301-217-5612. Office Fax: 301-217-5617. Business E-Mail: plclancy@venable.com.

CLANCY, THOMAS L., JR., novelist, producer; b. Balt., Apr. 12, 1947; m. Wanda Thomas, Aug. 1969 (div. 1998); children: Michelle, Christine, Tom, Kathleen; m. Alexandra Marie Llewellyn, July 26, 1999. BA, Loyola Coll., 1969. Ins. agent, Balt., Hartford, until 1973, O. F. Bowen Agy., Owings, Md., 1973-80, owner, from 1980; formed Red Storm Entertainment, Morrisville, NC, 1997; co-owner Baltimore Orioles. Author: (novels) The Hunt for Red October, 1984, Red Storm Rising, 1986, Patriot Games, 1987, The Cardinal of the Kremlin, 1988, Clear and Present Danger, 1989, The Sum of All Fears, 1991, Without Remorse, 1993, Debt of Honor, 1994, Executive Orders, 1996, Balance of Power, 1998, Rainbow Six, 1998, The Bear and the Dragon, 2000, Red Rabbit, 2002, The Teeth of the Tiger, 2003, (non-fiction) Submarine, 1993, Armored Cav, 1994, Fighter Wing, 1995, Marine, 1996, Airborne, 1997, Into the Storm, 1997, Every Man a Tiger, 1999; co-author: Battle Ready, 2004; co-creator Tom Clancy's OP Center, 1995—97, (video game series) Ghost Recon, 2001, Tom Clancy's Splinter Cell, 2002; exec. prodr.: (films) The Sum of All Fears, 2002; (TV miniseries) Tom Clancy's OP Center, 1995; exec. prodr., creator Tom Clancy's NetForce, ABC, 1999; author (screen adaptations): (films) The Hunt for Red October, 1990, Patriot Games, 1992, Clear and Present Danger, 1994, The Sum of All Fears, 2002, (TV miniseries) Tom Clancy's OP Center, 1995, Netforce, 1999. Roman Catholic.

CLANIN, DOUGLAS EDWARD, editor, researcher; b. Anderson, Ind., May 5, 1940; s. Howard Paul and Sarah Elizabeth (Weatherford) C.; m. Rebecca Suzanne Flowers, Aug. 9, 1970 (div. Dec. 1974); children: Christopher Lee, David Matthew. BS, Purdue U., 1963; MA, Ind. U., 1964. Social studies tchr. Whitewater-Fountain City H.S., Ind., 1964—65; asst. editor history U. Wis., Madison, 1970—80; editor publs. divsn. Ind. Hist. Soc., Indpls., 1980—2005. Editor: Papers of William Henry Harrison 1800-1815, 1993, 1999, Papers of Lew and Susan Wallace, 2005; asst. editor: Documentary History First Federal Elections, 1976, Documentary History Ratification of Constitution, 1976—81. Staff sg. USAF, 1965-69. Mem. Assn. for Documentary Editing, Ind. Assn. Historians, Soc. for Historians Early Am. Rep., Am. Legion, Svc. Club Indpls. Methodist. Avocations: conducting oral history interviews, travel, classical music.

CLANTON, WENDY MCCARLEY, elementary school educator; b. Pascagoula, Miss., Mar. 9, 1970; d. Aubry Lee McCarley, Sr. and Linda Gail McCarley; m. Darrin Hayden Clanton, Feb. 28, 1998; children: Stephen Craig Henry, Ashlyn Brooke, Lauren Elizabeth. BS in Elem. Edn. summa cum laude, Auburn U., 1996; M in Ednl. Leadership, U. South Ala., 2002; postgrad., Nova Southeastern U., 2003—. Tchr. grade 3 Calvary Christian Sch., Mobile, Ala., 1997—98, tchr. grade 5, 1999—2000; math./sci. tchr. grad 5 East Ctrl. Upper Elem., Hurley, Miss., 1998—99; tchr. grade 5 Indian Springs Elem., Mobile, 2000—01; tchr. grade 3 Eichold-Mertz Elem., Mobile, 2001—04, reading coach, 2004—. Pub. rels. rep. Eichold-Mertz Elem., Mobile, 2003—. Rep. Student Govt. Assn., Troy, Ala., 1999. Leadership scholar, Troy State U. Mem.: Alpha Gamma Delta. Home: 8550 Bay Leaf Dr Eight Mile AL 36613 Office: Nova Southeastern Univ 1750 NE 167th St North Miami Beach FL 33162-3017

CLAPHAN (KESTER), LAVADA JEAN, counseling administrator, educator; b. Memphis (Hall), Tex., Aug. 25, 1960; d. Willie Elmer Kester and Betty Jean Kester (White), Leon Don Crouch (Stepfather); m. Larry D. Claphan, Oct. 2, 1992; children: McKenzie Laren Claphan, Meghan Janae Claphan. BA in Psychology, Northeastern State U., 1982, MEd in Spl. Edn., 1987, MS in Counseling Psychology, 2004. LaVada Claphan Okla. State Dept. Edn., 1984. Educator Zion Sch., Stilwell, Okla., 1984—; psychometrist, 2002—. Mem.: NEA, APA, Okla. Edn. Assn., Okla. Sch. Psychology Assn., Nat. Sch. Psycholgy Assn.

CLAPMAN, PETER CARLYLE, lawyer, finance company executive; b. N.Y.C., Mar. 11, 1936; s. Jack and Evelyn (Clapman); m. Barbara Posen, May 8, 1966; children: Leah, Alice. AB, Princeton U., 1957; JD, Harvard U., 1960. Bar: N.Y. 1961, Conn. 1972. Assoc. Sage, Gray, Todd & Sims, N.Y.C., 1961-63; asst. counsel Stichman Comm., N.Y.C., 1964; legal cons. OEO, Washington, 1965—72; sr. v.p., chief counsel investments Tchrs. Ins. and Annuity of Am., Coll. Ret. Equities Fund, N.Y.C., 1972—. Chmn. Internat. Corp. Govt. Network; past bd. dirs. Nat. Com. for Quality Assurance; bd. dirs. Investor Responsibility Rsch. Ctr. Author: Fiduciary Responsibilities of Institutional Managers on Proxy Issues, Iowa Law Jour., 1994, SEC Market 2000 Report, London Stock Exchange Primary Market Report, 1994; co-author: Notre Dame U. Law Rev., 1981. Mem. ABA, Assn. Bar City N.Y. (com. on securities regulation spl. com. on mergers), Am. Law Inst. Home: 3 Valley Rd Scarsdale NY 10583-1123 Office: Tchrs Ins & Annuity Assn Am 730 3rd Ave New York NY 10017-3206 Business E-Mail: pclapman@computer.net.

CLAPP, ALLEN LINVILLE, electric supply and communications utility consultant, mediator/arbitrator; b. Raleigh, N.C., Oct. 8, 1943; s. Byron Siler and Alene Linville (Hester) C.; m. Anne Stuart Calvert, Dec. 18, 1966. BS in Engring. Ops., N.C. State U., 1967, M in Econs., 1973. Lic. profl. engr., N.C., N.J. Asst. engr. Booth-Jones and Assocs., Raleigh, 1965-67, assoc., 1969-71; chief ops. analysis N.C. Utilities Commn., Raleigh, 1971-77, engring. and econs. advisor to commrs., hearing examiner, 1977-82; dir. tech. assessment N.C. Alterative Energy Corp., Rsch. Triangle Park, 1982-85; pres. Clapp Rsch. Assocs., P.C., Clapp Rch. Inc., Raleigh, N.C., 1985—, Utility Bookstore, 2000—. Pvt. practice elec. safety cons., Raleigh, 1971—; mem. nat. Elec. Safety Code Com., 1971—, chmn., 1984—93; lectr. in field. Editor: National Electric Safety Code Handbook, 1984, 91, 92, 96, 2001, Assembly and Testing of Aerial Mines, 1968, Practical Utility Safety, 1999; editor, pub. Danesc Update Newsletter; contbr. to McGraw-Hill Std. Handbook for Elec. Engrs.; contbr. articles to profl. jours. Past co-chmn. Brookhaven/Deblyn Park Action Com., Raleigh. With U.S. Army, 1968-69. Recipient Cert. of Recognition and Appreciation Aerial Mine Lab., 1969. Mem. NSPE (past bd. dirs.), IEEE (stds. bd. 1989, 90), Profl. Engrs. N.C. (pres. 1980, Disting. Svc. award ctrl. Carolina chpt. 1978), N.C. Assn. Professions (pres. 1981), Power Engring. Soc., Nat. Safety Coun., Am. Soc. Safety Engrs., Soc. Cable TV Engrs., Indsl. Applications Soc., Am. Nat. Stds. Inst. (chair Z535.2 std. on environ. and facility safety signs). Republican. Baptist. Avocations: leather carving, golf, engraving, photography, raising orchids. Office: Clapp Rsch Assocs 6112 Saint Giles St Raleigh NC 27612-7043

CLAPP, DAVID FOSTER, library administrator; b. Birmingham, Ala., July 17, 1952; s. Merwin Bailey and Katherine Lorraine (Aderholt) C.; m. Sara Louise Stephan, Sept. 18, 1982. BA in Classical Langs., Tulane U., 1975; MS in LS, U. Ill., 1980; cert. advanced study in info. mgmt., U. Chgo., 1987. Asst. mgr. Kroch's & Brentano's Bookstore, Chgo., 1976-79; libr. I acquisitions dept. Chgo. Pub. Libr., 1980-82, libr. II, 1st asst. Walker br., 1982-83, libr. II, head Clearing br., 1983-84, libr. III, head Rogers Park br., 1984-89; asst. dir. for ext. svcs. Chattanooga-Hamilton County Bicentennial Libr., 1989—2002, dir., 2002—. Recipient Outstanding Pub. Svc. award Friends Chgo. Pub. Libr., 1987; Josie B. Houchens fellow U. Ill., 1979. Mem. ALA, Pub. Libr. Assn., Libr. Adminstrn. and Mgmt. Assn., Tenn. Libr. Assn. (exec. bd. 1991-92), Chattanooga Area Libr. Assn. (pres. 1991-92), Mensa, Beta Phi Mu. Avocations: genealogy, history, development and philosophy of religions, ancient history. Office: Chattanooga Pub Libr 1001 Broad St Chattanooga TN 37402-2620 Office Phone: 423-757-5320. Business E-Mail: clapp_david@lib.chattanooga.gov.

CLAPP, GORDON, actor; b. North Conway, NH, Sept. 24, 1948; s. Bill Clapp and Janet Knowlton; m. Deborah Taylor (div. 1999); 1 child, William. BA in Theatre, Williams Coll. Co. mem. Nat. Arts Ctr., Ottowa, Canada. Contrbr. New York Post, Los Angeles Golf mag., Variety mag. (Los Angeles Press Club award); actor: (TV series) NYPD Blue, 1993—2005 (Emmy award, best supporting actor in a drama series, 1998); (plays) Trafford Tanzi (nominee, Dora Moore award), Spring Awakening, Of Mice and Men, Ah Wilderness, The Snowball; (Broadway plays) Glengarry Glen Ross, 2005— (nominee, Tony award, best featured actor in a play, 2005, Theatre World award, 2005); actor & exec. prodr. (films) Fast Cars & Babies, 2003, Bananas, 2004; actor: (films) Splendor Falls, 1999, The Rage: Carrie 2, 1999, Skeletons in the Closet, 2000, Rules of Engagement, 2000, Sunshine State, 2002, Moonlight Mile, 2000, The Sure Hand of God, 2004, Flatbush, 2005.*

CLAPP, KENT W., insurance company executive; b. Montpelier, Ohio; BS in Acctg., Tri-State Univ., Angola, Ind.; graduate Advanced Mgmt. Program, Harvard Sch. Bus.Adminstrn., 1989. CPA 1972. Corp. controller Blue Cross, NW Ohio (merged into Medical Mutual), 1976—89; sr. v.p. Medical Mutual of Ohio, Cleve., 1989—92, COO, 1992—97, pres., 1992—, CEO, 1997—, chmn., 1997—. Graduate Leadership Cleve., 1992; bd. dir. Harvard Bus. Club, Cleve., United Way Greater Cleve. Named Bus. Exec. Yr., Sales & Mktg. Execs, Cleveland, 2002; named an honoree at NE Ohio Multiple Sclerosis Soc. Dinner of Champions, 2002; recipient Franklin Delano Roosevelt Humanitarian award, March of Dimes, 2000. Office: Medical Mutual Ohio 2060 E Ninth St Cleveland OH 44115 Office Phone: 216-687-6514. Office Fax: 216-687-7632.*

CLAPP, ROGER HOWLAND, retired publishing executive; b. Scarsdale, N.Y., May 11, 1928; s. Kenneth John and Louise (Allen) Clapp; m. Patricia Anne Townshend, June 26, 1954 (dec. Nov. 18, 1998); children: Roger Howland Jr., Georgia Louise, Sarah Townshend. BA cum laude, Amherst Coll., 1954. V.p. Benton & Bowles, Inc., N.Y.C., 1954-67, Rumrill-Hoyt, Inc., N.Y.C., 1967-72; v.p., advt. dir. Richmond (Va.) Newspapers, Inc., 1972-93. Counselor Svc. Corps of Ret. Execs.; bd. dirs. Richmond chpt. Better Bus. Bur., 1986—88, ARC, 1987—93. With USN, 1948—52, Korea. Recipient Silver medal, Am. Advt. Fedn., 1980. Mem.: Internat. Newspaper Advt. and Mktg. Execs. (pres. 1988). Home: 15470 Cedarwood Ln # 103 Naples FL 34110-8638

CLAPP, STEPHEN HENRY, dean, violinist; b. Nov. 27, 1939; MusB, Oberlin Conservatory Music, 1961; MusM, Juilliard Sch. Music, 1965. Mem. Beaux-Arts String Quartet, N.Y.C., 1965-67; asst. assoc. prof. violin Peabody Coll., Nashville, 1967-72; concertmaster Nashville Symphony, 1968-69; 1st violinist Blair String Quartet, Nashville, 1968-72; concertmaster Aspen (Colo.) Chamber Symphony, 1971-79; violinist, faculty Aspen Music Festival, 1971—94; assoc. prof. U. Tex., Austin, 1972-79; prof. Oberlin (Ohio) Conservatory Music, 1978-90; assoc. dean The Juilliard Sch., N.Y.C., 1991-94; faculty Juilliard Sch. Music, N.Y.C., 1987—, dean, 1994—. Master classes, recitals and concerts nationwide, 1970—; mem. The Oberlin Trio, 1982—; trustee Aspen Music Festival, Aspen and N.Y.C., 1978-90; concertmaster Austin Symphony, 1972-77. Rec. artist Orion, Advance Amplitude labels. Sr. warden Christ Episcopal Ch., Oberlin, 1986-88; vestry mem. Christ Episcopal Ch., Greenwich, Conn., 1993-96; sr. warden St. John's Episc. Ch., Stamford, Conn., 2004— Recipient 1st Chamber Music award Walter W. Naumburg Found., 1965. Mem. Violin Soc. Am. (bd. dirs. 1987-91), Music Tchrs. Nat. Assn., Am. String Tchrs. Assn. (contbr. articles to assn. jour. 1978-81), Chamber Music Am. Democrat. Avocations: tennis, restoring old houses. Office: The Juilliard Sch 60 Lincoln Center Plz New York NY 10023-6588 Office Phone: 212-799-5000.

CLAPPER, JAMES R., JR., federal agency administrator; BS, U. Md., 1963; MS in Polit Sci., St. Mary's U., San Antonio, 1970; Grad., Armed Forces Staff Coll., Norfolk, 1975; student, Nat. War Coll., 1978—79; PhD in Strategic Intelligence (hon.), Joint Mil. Intelligence Coll. Advanced through grades to lt. gen. USAF, 1991, ret., 1995; analytic branch chief Air Force Spl. Comm. Ctr., Kelly AFB, Tex., 1964—65; watch officer & air def. analyst 2nd Air Divsn., Son Nhut Air Base, 1965—66; aide to the comdr. & command briefer Air Force Security Svc., Kelly AFB, Tex., 1966—70; comdr. Detachment 3 6994th Security Squadron, Nakhon Phanom Royal Thai AFB, Thailand, 1970—71; mil. asst. to dir. Nat. Security Agy., Ft. George G. Meade, Md., 1971—73; aide to the comdr. & intelligence staff officer Air Force Systems Command, Andrews AFB, Md., 1973—74; chief, signal intelligence branch, J-23 US Pacific Command, Camp H.M. Smith, Hawaii, 1975—76, chief signal intelligence branch, J-23, 1976—78; Wash. area rep. for electronic security command Ft. George G. Mead, Md., 1979—80; comdr. 6940th Electronic Security Wing, Ft. George G. Meade, Md., 1980—81; dir. intelligence plans & systems Office Asst. Chief of Staff for Intelligence, USAF, Washington, 1981—84; commdr., Air Force Technical Applications Ctr. USAF, Patrick AFB, Fla., 1984—85, asst. chief of staff intelligence U.S. Forces Korea, dep. asst. chief of staff intelligence Repubic of Korea & US Combined Forced Command Seoul, Republic of Korea, 1985—87, dir. intelligence US Pacific Command Camp H.M. Smith, Hawaii, 1987—89, dep. chief of staff intelligence Strategic Air Command Offutt AFB, Nebr., 1989—90, asst. chief of staff intelligence Washington, 1990—91; dir. Def. Intelligence Agy., Washington, 1991—95; exec. v.p. Vredenburg, Inc., Reston, Va., 1995—98; exec. dir. mil. intelligence programs Booz-Allen & Hamilton, 1995—98; v.p., dir. intelligence programs SRA Internat., Inc., 1998—2001; dir. Nat. Geospatial-Intelligence Agy. (formerly Nat. Imagery and Mapping Agy.), Bethesda, Md., 2001—. Vice chair Adv. Panel to Assess Domestic Response Capabilities for Terrorism Involving Weapons of Mass Destruction, 2000. Recipient Def. Disting. Svc. medal, Disting. Svc. medal, Def. Superior Svc. medal, Legion of Merit with two oak leaf clusters, Bronze Star medal with oak leaf cluster, Def. Meritorious Svc. medal, Air medal with oak leaf cluster, Joint Svc. Commendation medal, Air Force Commendation medal, French Order of Nat. Merit, ROK Order of Nat. Security of Merit, Nat. Intelligence Disting. Svc. medal. Office: Nat Geospatial-Intelligence Agy 4600 Sangamore Rd Bethesda MD 20816-5003

CLAPPER, MARIE ANNE, magazine publisher; b. Chgo., Nov. 21, 1942; d. Chester William and Hazel Alice (Gilso) Reinke; m. William Neil Petersen, Aug. 17, 1963 (div. 1975); children: Elaine Myrtice Petersen, Edward William Petersen; m. Lyle N. Clapper, Jan. 1, 1980; children: Jeffrey Leland, Anne Reinke stepchildren: John Scott, Susan Louise Clapper Kashmier. Student, Augustana Coll., Rock Island, Ill., 1960-63; EdB, Northeastern U., 1964. Writer Pack-o-Fun mag., Park Ridge, Ill., 1976-77, editor Des Plaines, Ill., 1977-78, pub., 1990—; asst. to pub., circulation dir. Crafts 'n Things mag., Des Plaines, Ill., 1978-82, pub., 1982—, Decorative Arts Painting mag., Des Plaines, 1990—, The Cross Stitcher mag., Des Plaines, 1991—, 101 Bridal Ideas mag., Des Plaines, 1991—; pub., pres. Clapper pub. Host TV show The Crafts 'n Things Show, 1984-86, Crafting for the 90s, 1990-94; author: EveryDay Matters, 1996. Mem. TEC, Mag. Pubs. Am. (bd. dirs.), Hobby Industry Am. (bd. dirs., treas. 1998-99). Office: Crafts 'n Things 2400 E Devon Ave Ste 375 Des Plaines IL 60018-4618

CLAPTON, ERIC, musician; b. Ripley, Surrey, Eng., Mar. 30, 1945; s. Edward Fryer and Patricia Molly Clapton; 1 child (with Yvonne Kelly), Ruth; 1 child (with Lory Del Santo), Conor (dec.); M. Patricia Anne Boyd, 1979 (div. 1988); m. Melia McEnery; children: Julie Rose, Ella Maw, Mary. Student, Kingston Art Sch. Former mem. rock music groups Yardbirds, John Mayall's Bluesbreakers, Cream, Blind Faith, Delaney & Bonnie & Friends, Derek & the Dominos; performer: (films) A Concert for Bangladesh, 1972 (Grammy award Album of Yr.), Tommy, 1975, Music Communion, 1989; composer: Badge, Let It Rain, Layla; musician: (albums) Eric Clapton, 1970, Rainbow Concert, 1973, 461 Ocean Boulevard, 1974, There's One in Every Crowd, 1974, EC Was Here, 1975, No Reason to Cry, 1976, Slowhand, 1977, Backless, 1978, Just One Night, 1980, Another Ticket, 1981, Money and Cigarettes, 1983, Behind the Sun, 1985, August, 1987, Crossroads (retrospective), 1988, Time Pieces/Best of Eric Clapton, 1988, Time Pieces II/Live in the Seventies, 1988, One Moment in Time, 1988, Journeyman, 1989, 24 Nights, 1991, Unplugged, 1992 (Winner of 6 Grammy awards including Album of Yr., Record of Yr.), From the Cradle, 1994 (Grammy award Best Traditional Blues Album), Pilgrim, 1998, Chronicles, 1999, Riding With the King, 2000 (Grammy award Best Trad. Blues Album), Reptile, 2001 (Grammy award Best Pop Instrumental Perf.), One More Car, One More Rider, 2002, Me and Mr. Johnson, 2004; prodr. (with Rod Stewart) Beginnings, 2004; wrote songs: BBC miniseries Edge of Darkness, 1986; composer film score Homeboy, 1988, Lethal Weapon, 1986, Lethal Weapon 2, 1989, The Van, 1996, Nil by Mouth, 1997; co-composer film score: Lethal Weapon 3, 1992. Named into Rock & Roll Hall of Fame, (as mem. of Yardbirds), 1992, (as mem. of Cream), 1993, (as solo artist), 2000; recipient Silver Clef Award Outstanding Achievement in World of British Music, presented by Princess Michael of Kent, 1983, Lifetime Achievement Award, British Phonographic Inst., 1987, presented with silver model of a Fender Stratocaster by Prince Charles to commemorate 25th yr. in music industry, 1988, Best Guitarist Award, Internat. Rock Awards, 1989, Living Legend Award, 1990, W.C. Handy Award For Blues, 16th Annual Ceremony, 1995, Man of Yr. Award music: solo artist, GQ Mag., 1999, Stevie Ray Vaughan, Music Assistance Program, 1999. Achievements include minor planet named "(4305) Clapton" in his honor, 1990; first triple inductee into Rock & Roll Hall of Fame. Office: c/o Warner Bros Records 3300 Warner Blvd Burbank CA 91505-4632

CLARE, GEORGE, safety engineer, systems safety consultant; b. Apr. 8, 1930; s. George Washington and Hildegard Marie (Sommer) C.; m. Catherine Saidee Hamel, Jan. 12, 1956; children: George Christopher, Kristine Ren.è. Student, U. So. Calif., 1961, U. Tex., Arlington, 1963-71, U. Wash., 1980. Cert. product safety mgr. Enlisted USN, 1948, advanced through grades to comdr., 1968, naval aviator, 1951-70; served in Korea; comdr. Res., 1963-70; ret., 1970; mgr. sys. safety missiles divsn. LTV Missiles and Electronics Group, Dallas, 1963-90. Mem. Nat. Rep. Com., Rep. Senatorial Com., Rep. Congl. Com., Rep. Senatorial Com., Rep. Congl. Com., Tex. Rep. Com., Citizens for Republic. Decorated Air medal with gold star, others. Mem. AIAA, Am. Security Coun., Internat. Soc. Air Safety Investigators, Sys. Safety Soc., Am. Def. Preparedness Assn., Naval Aviation, Ret. Officers Assn., Air Group 7 Assn. (pres.) Roman Catholic. Home and Office: 7358 Peterson Ln Pensacola FL 32506-6507

CLARE, KENNETH GUILFORD, economist, consultant; b. Dallas, Wis., June 13, 1918; s. Hans and Josie Bertina (Jacobson) C.; m. Elizabeth Rae Padfield, Oct. 5, 1945 (div. 1959); children: Raymond, Loren; m. Anne Worth Liesmann, Aug. 27, 1961; children: Steven, Janice, Keith. PhB in Economics, U. Wis., 1941; MA in Economics, U. So. Calif., 1946, PhD in Economics, 1950. Asst. prof. U. So. Calif., L.A., 1947-50, 56-59, U. Utah, Salt Lake City, 1950-51; dist. economist Office Price Stabilization, Boise, Idaho, 1951-53; economist CIA, Washington, 1953-56; sr. economist Stanford Rsch. Inst., Menlo Park, Calif., 1959-65; v.p. Westwood Rsch., Inc., L.A., 1965-72; sr. economist World Bank, Washington, 1972-83, cons., 1983—2000; ret., 2000. Asst. prof. UCLA, 1960-62; cons. various govtl. bodies, several locations. Author: Southern California Regional Airport Study, 1962, Area Study of Korea, 1969, (with others) Persian Gulf States, 1985, (hist. novel) Promises, Promises, 2003, Restless Man, A Memoir, 2003, (hist. novels) Escape from Johnson's Island, 2004, Intrepid Sloopers, 2005. Mem. Transp. Rsch. Forum (Internat. chpt. pres. 1990—), Omicron Delta Epsilon. Presbyterian. Avocations: reading, art collecting, genealogy. Home: 1763 Royal Oaks Dr, N C12 Bradbury CA 91010

CLAREY, DONALD ALEXANDER, government affairs consultant; b. Johnson City, N.Y., Feb. 8, 1950; s. James Roger and Dorothy (Wait) C. BA, Union Coll., Schenectady, 1972; M.P.A., Harvard U., Cambridge, Mass., 1977. Exec. asst. to dir. for Congl. affairs FEA, Washington, 1973-76; program assoc. to majority leader N.Y. State Senate, Albany, 1977-79, adminstrv. asst. to majority leader, 1979-82; cons. Dept. State, Washington, 1983; assoc. dir. cabinet affairs The White House, Washington, 1983-85, spl. asst. to Pres. of U.S., 1985-87; dep. adminstr. SBA, 1987-88; cons. govt. affairs, v.p. Strategic Mgmt. Assocs., Washington, 1989-96; pres. Minerva Group, 1996—. Republican candidate for N.Y. State Assembly, 1980, 82. Republican. Roman Catholic. Avocations: skiing, golf. Home: 234 Lenox Ave Albany NY 12208-1408 Office: PO Box 459 Albany NY 12201-0459

CLAREY, JOHN ROBERT, personnel director; b. Waterloo, Iowa, June 5, 1942; s. Robert J. and Norma (Knox) C.; m. Kathleen Ann Kingsley, June 5, 1965; children: Sharon Diane, Suzanne Marie. BSBA, Iowa Sate U., 1965; MBA, U. Pa., 1972. Fin. analyst Ford Motor Co., Dearborn, Mich., 1972-74; cons. Price Waterhouse, Chgo., 1974-75, mgr., 1975-76; assoc. Heidrick & Struggles, Chgo., 1976-81, v.p., ptnr., 1981-82; pres. Clarey, Andrews & Klein, Inc., Northbrook, Ill. Served to lt. USN, 1965-70, Vietnam. Mem. Stick and Rudder, Assn. Exec. Search Cons., Lifeline Pilots, Mid-Am. Club (Chgo.), Sunset Ridge Country Club (Northbrook). Republican. Roman Catholic. Avocations: flying, microcomputers, tennis. Home: 1347 Hillside Rd Northbrook IL 60062-4612 Office: Clarey Andrews & Klein Inc 1200 Shermer Rd Ste 108 Northbrook IL 60062-4563 Personal E-mail: jackclarey@ameritech.net. Business E-Mail: jack@clarey-a-klein.com.

CLAREY, PATRICIA, state official; BS, Union Coll., Schenectady, NY, 1975; MPA, Harvard U. John F. Kennedy Sch. of Govt., Cambridge, Mass., 1983. Govt. affairs rep. Chevron Corp., San Francisco; govt. rels. position Ashland Oil, Inc.; dep. dir. legis. affairs Nat. Park Svc., Washington; congl. liaison US Dept. of Interior, Washington, 1986—89; dep. chief of staff (for 8 yrs.) former Calif. Gov. Pete Wilson; v.p. public affairs Transamerica Corp., San Francisco, 1999—2001; pres. Transamerica Found., San Francisco, 1998; v.p. govt. rels. Health Net, Inc. (formerly known as Foundation Health Sys., Inc.), LA, 2001—03; ran primary campaign for Gov.-elect Arnold Schwarzenegger; chief of staff Calif. Gov. Arnold Schwarzenegger, Sacramento, 2003—. Former bd. dir. Calif. Found. on the Environ. and the Economy; mem. joint pub. adv. com. Commn. for Environ. Cooperation of N.Am., 2003—. Office: Chief of Staff Office of Gov Schwarzenegger State Capitol Bldg Sacramento CA 95814 Office Phone: 916-445-5106. Business E-Mail: Pat.Clarey@gov.ca.gov.*

CLAREY, TIMOTHY LEE, geologist, educator; b. Midland, Mich., Oct. 9, 1960; s. Harlan Dale and Betty Lou Clarey; m. Renee Lynn Atwood, Sept. 4, 2004; children: Ryan, Ashley, Hailey, Erin. BS in Geology, Western Mich. U., 1982, MS in Geology, 1993, PhD, 1996; MS in Geology, U. Wyo., 1984. Cert. profl. geologist. Exploration geologist Chevron USA, Denver, 1984—92; prof. geology Delta Coll., University Center, Mich., 1995—. Author: Introduction to Dinosaurs, 2001, Physical Geology Lab Book, 2002; contbr. articles to profl. jours. Named Endowed Tchg. Chair, Delta Coll., 2000; recipient Bergstein Tchg. award, 1998, Scholarly Achievement award, 2002. Mem.: Geol. Soc. Am., Am. Assn. Petroleum Geologists, Sigma Xi (chpt. pres.). Avocations: archaeology, running. Office: Delta Coll 1961 Delta Rd University Center MI 48710 Office Phone: 989-686-9252. Business E-Mail: tlclarey@delta.edu.

CLARIDGE, ELMOND LOWELL, retired engineering educator; b. Delaplaine, Ark., June 5, 1917; s. Elmond Lee and Irene Cynthia Gates (Compton) Claridge; m. Zola Ruth McDowell, Jan. 1, 1939 (dec. Oct. 9, 1990); children: David Elmond, Jonathan McDowell; m. Mary Lasley Moore, Feb. 11, 1995 (dec. Feb. 16, 1999). BSChemE, U. Mo., 1939, MSChemE, 1941; PhD in Chem. Engring., U. Houston, 1979. Registered profl. engr., Tex. Rsch. chemist Shell Oil Co., Wood River, Ill., 1941—43, technologist, 1943—48, asst. chief rsch. Houston, 1948—55, 1957—60, sr. head technologist office N.Y.C., 1960—64; group leader Royal Dutch Shell, Amsterdam, 1955—57; sr. rsch. assoc. Shell Devel. Co., Houston, 1964—79; assoc. prof. chem. engring. dept. U. Houston, 1979—91, dir. petroleum engring. grad. program, 1979—87; ret., 1991. Cons. Gulf Univs. Rsch. Consortium, Houston, 1979—85, TCA Reservoir Engring. Svcs., Houston, 1979—2000. Author: PE 506, Miscible Processes, 1992; contbr. articles to profl. jours. Recipient Disting. Life award, St. Luke's United Meth. Ch., 1990. Mem.: AAAS, AIChE, Soc. Petroleum Engrs. (editor reprint book Surfactant/Polymer Chemical Flooding vols. I, II 1982, Enhanced Oil Recovery Pioneer 1980), Petroleum Soc./Can. Inst. Mining, Metallurgy and Petroleum, Am. Petroleum Inst. (rsch. adv. bd. prodn. divsn. 1978—81), Am. Chem. Soc., Sigma Xi, Alpha Chi Sigma. Achievements include patents in field. Personal E-mail: eclaridge@sbcglobal.net.

CLARIE, THOMAS CASHIN, II, librarian; b. Providence, Dec. 21, 1943; s. T. Emmet and Gertrude Clare (Reynolds) C.; m. Rosemary Dorr Hamilton, Nov. 16, 1985. BS in History, Coll. of Holy Cross, 1965; MS in Libr. Sci., So. Conn. State U., 1972; MA in History, U. Conn., 1973. Reference libr. Hamden (Conn.) Libr., 1967-69; head libr. Avon (Conn.) Old Farms Sch., 1969-71; reference libr. U. Conn., Storrs, 1973; head reference libr. So. Conn. State U., New Haven, 1973-97. Author: Occult Bibliography, 1978, Occult/Paranormal Bibliography, 1984, Just Rye Harbor, 2005; creator various ednl. card games, 1991 (Parents' Choice mag. award 1992). Recipient Best Reference Book Idea award Carrollton Press, 1978. Mem. ALA, AAUP, UN Assn. of U.S.A. Roman Catholic. Avocations: golf, theater, tennis. Home: 1 Huckleberry Ln Hampton NH 03842 Office: So Conn State U Buley Libr New Haven CT 06515 E-mail: TomClarie@aol.com.

CLARK, ALAN FRED, physicist; b. Milw., June 29, 1936; BS in Physics, U. Wis., Madison, 1958, MS in Nuclear Engring., 1959; PhD in Nuclear Sci., U. Mich., Ann Arbor, 1964. NAS-NRC postdoctoral assoc. Nat. Bur. Standards, Boulder, Colo., 1964-66, physicist, 1966-78, chief cryogenic properties of solids, 1978-80, group leader supercondr. and magnetic measurements, 1981-87; liaison scientist Office Naval Rsch., London and Europe, 1987-89; group leader fundamental elec. measurements Nat. Inst. Stds., Gaithersburg, Md., 1989-92, 95-98, sr. scientist electricity divsn., 1992-94, dep. chief optoelectronics divsn. Boulder, Colo., 1998-2001, chief magnetic tech. divsn., 2001—. Chmn., founder Internat. Cryogenic Materials Conf. Bd., Boulder, Colo., 1975—; mem. Internat. Cryogenic Engring. Conf. Bd., 1982—. Contbr. over 150 articles to profl. jours.; editor Cryogenics Jour., 1982-94, IEEE Trans. Applied Superconductivity, 1994-98, 8 conf. proceedings, 4 books. Recipient Superior Rsch. Nat. Bur. Standards, 1967, 74, 82, 83, 84, 85, 86, 93-97. Fellow IEEE, Am. Phys. Soc.; mem. ASTM (chmn. superconductor com. 1980-89), IEEE Superconductivity Com. (chmn. 1989-94), Internat. Acad. Electrotech. Scis. Office: Nat Inst Standards & Tech MS 816 00 325 Broadway Boulder CO 80305 E-mail: aclark@boulder.nist.gov.

CLARK, ALICIA GARCIA, political party official; b. Vera Cruz, Mex. arrived in US, 1970; d. Rafael Garcia Aully and Maria Luisa (Cobos) Garcia; m. Edward E. Clark, Oct. 20, 1970; 1 child, Edward E. MSChemE, Nat. U. Mex., Mexico City, 1951. Chemist Celanese Mexicana, Mexico City, 1951—53, lab. mgr., 1953—60, sales promotion mgr., 1960—65, sales promotion and advt. mgr., 1965—70; nat. chmn. Libertarian Party, Houston, 1981—83, coord. coun. state chairs, 1987—95. Pres. San Marino (Calif.) Guild of Huntington Hosps., 1981-82, chmn. Celebrity Series, 1989-91. Pres. bd. dirs. LA Opera League, 1990-96; founder, co-chair Hispanics for LA Opera, 1991-99; bd. dirs. Guild Opera Co., 1994-96, Club 100, 1996-99; mng. dir. L.A. Opera, 1995—; opera panel Nat. Endowment for Arts, 1997; active Redcat Theater Coun. Recipient award La Mujer de Hoy mag., 1969, Heroes LA award Hispanic Traditions and Heritage Coun., 1995, Star of Our Culture award Mex. Cultural Inst. LA, 1998, Placido Domingo award, 2000, Zachary Soc. Ann. award, 2001. Mem. Fashion Group (treas. 1969-70, award 1970). Home Fax: 626-796-3485.

CLARK, ANNE LOUISE, music educator, musician; b. Columbus, Ohio, Nov. 7, 1949; d. James Daniel and Donna Grace (Click) Schaffner; m. William Louis Clark, Mar. 17, 1986; 1 child, Elizabeth Anne stepchildren: Annie Kathleen Baker, Lindy Marie Coyle. BA English, U. Mo., St. Louis, 1971; MM, So. Ill. U., Edwardsville, 1979; D of Musical Arts, U.Tex., Austin, 1988. Cert. Tchr. (lifetime) State of Mo., Tchr. Kans. Bd. Edn. Adj. instr. Southwestern U., Georgetown, Tex., 1982—84, Southwest Tex. State U., San Marcos, 1982—84; asst. prof. cello Northeast Mo. State U., Kirksville, 1984—86; founder, dir. Junction City/ Ft. Riley Strings., Junction City, Kans., 1989—95; tchr. orch. Unified Sch. Dist. 379, Clay Ctr., Kans., 1989—2004; dir. and founder Cmty. Chamber Orch., Morganville, Kans., 1997—; adj. instr. music Kans. State U., Manhattan, 2005—. Section cellist Fla. Symphony, 1974—75; prin. cellist Jacksonville Symphony, Ill., 1978—79; asst. tchr. U. Tex. String Project, Austin, 1980—81; cellist Radio Kans. FM, 1987—; artist-in-residence Kans. Arts Commn., 1989—90; bd. dirs. Clay County Arts Coun., Clay Ctr., Kans., 1998—; cellist Pernambuco String Quartet, 2001—; section cellist Salina Symphony, Kans., 2003—05; cellist Kans. Touring Program, Kans. Arts Commn., 2004—. Author: (book) Recommended List of Easy Level String Chamber Music, 1982, Expandable Chamber Music at Various Levels, 1982; contbr. articles to profl. jours.; musician (cello player): (CD) Works of the Romantic Era, 2003; editor: Endpin, 1988—91. Founder, dir. Congress of Strings at USC, L.A., 1967, Congress of Strings at Aspen Music Sch., 1968, Communiversity of UMSL, 1972. Recipient Grad. Rsch. award, U. Tex., 1983. Mem.: Chamber Music Am., Clay County Arts Coun. Methodist. Avocations: gardening, historical restoration, writing, christian missionary support. Home: 454 23rd Rd Morganville KS 67468-9117

CLARK, ANTHONY EUGENE, education educator, researcher; b. Eugene, Oreg., Mar. 12, 1967; s. James Edward Clark III and Shirley Ann Cockrum; m. Amanda Catherine Roth, Aug. 16, 1997; 1 child, Cassandra Marie. BA, Univ. Oreg., Eugene, Oreg., 1999, PhD, 2005. Instr. Univ. Oreg., Eugene, Oreg., 1999—. Instr., asst. adminstr. Oreg. Sys. of Higher Edn., Eugene, Oreg., 1998. Contbr. encyclopedia entry, articles pub. to profl. jour., academic papers. Fulbright Scholar, Dept. of State, Taiwan, 2001—02, NSEP Fellowship, Dept. of Defense, Taiwan, 2001—02. Mem.: Soc. for the study of Early China, Assn. for Asian Studies, Am. Oriental Soc., Phi Beta Kappa. Roman Cath. Avocations: taiji, book collecting, Chinese art collecting. Office: EALL U Oreg 1248 U Oreg Eugene OR 97405

CLARK, ARTHUR WATTS, insurance company executive; b. Seattle, Nov. 28, 1922; s. Irving Marshall and Nell (Watts) C.; m. Mary Dick Cannon, Nov. 21, 1942; children: Arthur Watts, Claiborne Marshall, Johnston Jewell. AB, U. N.C., 1943; MA, U. Calif., 1948. With Home Security Life Ins. Co., Durham, N.C., 1948-50, 52-85, pres., 1967-75, chmn., chief exec. officer, 1975-85, also dir.; chmn., chief exec. officer Peoples Life Ins. Co. of Washington, D.C., 1983-85; chmn., pres., chief exec. officer Peoples Security Life Ins. Co., 1985-86, chmn. bd., 1986-88. Mem. Res. Forces Policy Bd., Office Sec. Def., 1975-78. Treas. Research Triangle Regional Planning Commn., 1959-63; mem. N.C. Health Ins. Adv. Bd., 1966-70; chmn. bd. dirs. N.C. Ctrl. U. Found., Zool. Coun., 1994-96, chmn., 1996-2002; vice-chmn. bd. dirs. N.C. Med. Found.; chmn. Greater Triangle Cmty. Found., 1992-94, The Explorer's Club, 1999—. With USAAF, 1942-46, USAF, 1952, maj. gen. USAF, ret. Decorated D.S.M., Legion of Merit with oak leaf cluster, Bronze Star. Mem. Am. Life Conv. (dir. 1972), Am. Life Ins. Assn. (dir. 1973-75), Life Office Mgmt. Assn. (dir. 1973-76), Am. Council Life Ins. (dir. 1976), Life Insurers Conf. (exec. com. 1972-75, 1983-86), Assn. N.C. Life Ins. Cos. (chmn. 1986-87), Phi Beta Kappa, Sigma Xi. Office: 194 Finley Golf Course Rd Ste 100 Chapel Hill NC 27517 Home: 100 Cedar Berry Ln Chapel Hill NC 27517 Personal E-mail: artwclark@aol.com.

CLARK, BETH, minister; b. Bradford, N.H., Apr. 15, 1914; d. John Scott and Bessie (Murdock) Pendleton; m. John Guill Clark, June 20, 1940 (dec. June 1955); children: John Guill Jr. (dec. 1999), Beverly Estelle Clark Daggett. BA, Colby Coll., 1935; BD, Andover Newton Theol. Sch., 1938; MDiv, Ea. Bapt. Theol. Sem., 1967; D Ministry, Lancaster Theol. Sem., 1981; postgrad., U. Athens, 1970, Jungian Inst., Zurich, 1980, Mansfield Coll., Oxford, Eng., 1982, 85, Caribbean Inst., 1989. Ordained to ministry United Ch. of Christ, 1967. Exec. dir. YWCA, Bristol, Tenn., 1955-59, Asheville, N.C., 1959-60; dean of women Anderson (S.C.) Coll., 1960-61, Eastern Coll., St. Davids, Pa., 1961-65; vol. rsch. coord. Selinsgrove (Pa.) State Sch., 1965-78; interim min. various chs. Pa. Ctrl. Conf., United Ch. of Christ, Harrisburg, 1968-96. Author: Grief in the Loss of a Pastor, 1981; editor: Meditations on the Lord's Supper (John G. Clark), 1958. Bd. mgr. Bethany Children's Home, Womelsdorf, Pa., 1982-88; mem. adv. com. Sun Home Nursing Svcs., Northumberland, Pa., 1982-95, sec. bd. dirs., 1989-96; mem. stewardship coun. United Ch. of Christ, 1997—. Mem. Interim Network (steering com. 1978-80), Assn. Ret. State Employees, Alban Inst., Interagy. Club (pres. 1966-68), Triangle Club (v.p. 1970-74, pres. 1996-98), Phi Mu. Democrat. Home: 8 Pine St Augusta ME 04330 E-mail: bethpclark@aol.com. *Our world is crying out for honesty, for absolute truth. Communication is impossible without belief and trust in the sincerity of the other person. Better the bitter truth than favor catering deception.*

CLARK, BEVERLY ANN, lawyer; b. Davenport, Iowa, Dec. 9, 1944; d. F. Henry and Arlene F. (Meyer) C.; m. Richard Floss; children: Amy and Barry (twins); stepchildren: Heather, Gretchan. Student, Mich. State U., 1963—65; BA, Calif. State U., Fullerton, 1967; MSW, U. Iowa, 1975, JD, 1980; grad., Iowa Massage Inst., 1999. Bar: Iowa 1980; lic. social worker, Iowa; nat. cert. lic. massage therapist. Probation officer County of San Bernardino, San Bernardino, Calif., 1968, County of Riverside, Riverside, Calif., 1968-69; social worker Skiff Hosp., Newton, Iowa, 1971-73, State of Iowa, Mitchellville, 1973-74, planner Des Moines, 1976-77, law clk., 1980-81; corp. counsel Pioneer Hi-Bred Internat., Inc., Des Moines, 1981-2000; atty. Jasper County Legal Aid, 2002—03; pvt. practice, 2000—. Instr. Des Moines Area C.C., Ankeny, Iowa, 1974—75, 2001—; adj. prof. Drake Law Sch., 1993—96, Buena Vista U., 2002—; pub. Sweet Annie Press; past owner Annie's Place, The B&B Connection Gift Catalog. Editor: Proceedings: Bicentennial Symposium on New Directions in Juvenile Justice, 1975; author monthly column Wellfem-In-Law; contbr. articles to prof. jours. Founder Mother of Twins Club, Newton, 1971; co-chmn. Juvenile Justice Symposium, Des Moines, 1974-75; mem. Juvenile Justice Com., Des Moines, 1974-75; mem. Nat. Offender Based State Corrections Info. Sys. Com., Iowa rep., 1976-78; incorporator, dir. Iowa Dance Theatre, Des Moines, 1981; mem. Pesticide User's Adv. Com., Fort Collins, Colo., 1981-88; co-developer Iowa Migrant Ombudsmen Project, Pioneer, Inc. and Proteus, Inc. Recipient Disting. Alumni award U. Iowa, 1990, Nat. award Ctr. for Pub. Resources. Mem.: DAR, ABA (termination-at-will subcom. 1982—2000, subcom. on devel. individual rights in work place), Iowa Bar Assn., Iowa Orgn. Women Attys. (bd. dirs., sec. 2001). Office Phone: 641-417-0020. E-mail: clarklaw@pcpartner.net.

CLARK, BEVERLY JEAN, lawyer, mediator; b. Detroit, May 21, 1939; d. Harry and Evelyn Blanche (Mabin) C. BA, U. Mich., 1961, MA, 1963; JD, Wayne State U., 1972. Bar: Mich. 1973, U.S. Dist. Ct. (ea. dist.) Mich. 1973, U.S. Dist. Ct. (we. dist.) Mich. 1990, U.S. Ct. Appeals (6th dist.) 1973. Pvt. practice, Detroit, 1973—. Bd. dirs. Mich. Indian Legal Services, Traverse City, 1976-, chair, 1999. Co-founder Mich. Women's Campaign Fund, Detroit; mem. Mich. Civil Rights Commn., 1981-91, chmn., 1991. Named Ford Scholar, Ford Motor Co., 1957-61. Fellow Am. Acad. Matrimonial Lawyers; mem. Assn. for Conflict Resolution; mem. Mich. Trial Lawyers Assn. (pres. 1983-84), Women's Lawyers Assn. (pres. 1978-79, First in Leadership 1987), Mich. Coun. for Family and Divorce mediation (pres. 1996-98), Mediation Works (dir.) Democrat. Office Phone: 313-331-0048. Personal E-mail: bev.clark@worldnet.att.net.

CLARK, BRUCE BUDGE, humanities educator; b. Georgetown, Idaho, Apr. 9, 1918; s. Marvin E. and Alice (Budge) C.; m. Ouida Raphiel, Nov. 7, 1946; children— Lorraine, Bradley, Robert, Jeffrey, Shawn, Sandra. BA, U. Utah, 1943, PhD, 1951; MA, Brigham Young U., 1948. Teaching fellow Brigham Young U., 1946-47, U. Utah, 1947-50; asst. prof. Brigham Young U., 1950-55, assoc. prof., 1955-58, prof., 1959—, dir. humanities program, 1958-60, chmn. dept. English, 1960-65; dean Coll. Humanities, 1965-81. Author: The Spectrum of Faith in Victorian Literature, 1966, The Challenge of Teaching, 1966, Romanticism through Modern Eyes, 1968, Oscar Wilde, A Study in Genius and Tragedy, 1970, Brigham Young on Education, 1970, Idealists in Revolt, 1975, History of the Brigham Young U. Coll. Humanities, 3 vols., 1984, Family History, 3 vols., 1998, Selected Essays and Other Writings, 1998; Editor: Richard Evans Quote Book, 1971; anthology (Out of the Best Books, vol. I, 1964, vol. II, 1966, vol. III, 1967, vol. IV, 1968, vol. V, 1969, Great Short Stories for Discussion and Delight, 1979; Contbr. articles to profl. jours. Served with AUS, 1944-46. Recipient Karl G. Maeser Teaching Excellence award, 1972, David O. McKay Humanities award, 1983, Brigham Young U. Presdl. citation for disting. svc., 1994. Mem. MLA, Nat. Coun. Tchrs. English, Rocky Mountain Modern Lang. Assn., Coll. Conf. on Composition and Communications, Phi Kappa Phi. Mem. Lds Ch. Home: 365 E 1655 S Orem UT 84058-7903

CLARK, BRUCE E., lawyer; b. NYC, 1946; AB, Holy Cross, 1967; JD, Harvard U., 1970. Bar: NY 1971, US Supreme Ct., Court of Claims. Clk. to Hon. Edward C. McLean US Dist. Ct. So. Dist. NY, 1970—71; assoc. Sullivan & Cromwell, NYC, 1975—80, ptnr., 1980—. Capt. USAF, 1971—75. Mem.: Assn. of the Bar of the City of NY (former mem. bankruptcy com.), State Bar NY (mem. com. bankruptcy law), ABA (mem. subcom. on letters of credit, com. uniform comml. code). Office: Sullivan & Cromwell 125 Broad St New York NY 10004-2498

CLARK, BRUCE F., lawyer; b. Jacksonville, Fla., May 17, 1946; s. Charles H. and Martha Jean Clark; m. Monika Weidner, May 30, 1970; children: Thomas, Stephen, Benjamin. BSBA, Western Ky. U., 1968; JD, U. Of Ky., 1976. Bar: Ky. 1976. Atty. Stites & Harbison, Pllc, Frankfort, Ky., 1976—. Chmn. Frankfort C. of C., 1992—93. Capt. U.S. Army, 1968—71, Germany/Vietnam. Avocation: golf. Office: Stites & Harbison Pllc 421 West Main St Frankfort KY 40602-0634 E-mail: bclark@stites.com.

CLARK, BRUCE ROBERT, geologist, consultant; b. Pitts., June 17, 1941; s. Harold Thomas and Florence (Miller) Clark; m. Karen Pelton Heath, Dec. 30, 1967; children: Adam, Andrea. BS, Yale U., 1963; PhD, Stanford U., 1967. Asst. prof. U. Mich., Ann Arbor, 1968-73, assoc. prof., 1973-77; v.p. Leighton and Assocs., Inc., Irvine, Calif., 1977-85, pres., 1986—2002, CEO, 1988—2002, sr. cons., 2002—. Contbr. articles to profl. jours. Commr. Calif. Seismic Safety Commn., 2000—, chmn., 2001—03; chmn. bd. dirs. YMCA Orange County, Calif., 1999—2002. Fellow: Geol. Soc. Am.; mem.: Seismol. Soc. Am., Assn. Engring. Geologists, Am. Geophys. Union, Earthquake Engring. Rsch. Inst. (bd. dirs. 2002—). Office: Leighton and Assocs Inc 17781 Cowan Irvine CA 92614-6009 Business E-Mail: bclark@leightongeo.com. E-mail: bruce-clark@cox.net.

CLARK, BURTON ROBERT, sociologist, educator; b. Pleasantville, N.J., Sept. 6, 1921; s. Burton H. and Cornelia (Amole) C.; m. Adele Halitsky, Aug. 31, 1949; children: Philip Neil (dec.), Adrienne. BA, UCLA, 1949, PhD, 1954; Doctorate (hon.), U. Strathclyde, 1998, U. Turku, Finland, 2000. Asst. prof. sociology Stanford (Calif.) U., 1953-56; rsch. assoc., asst. prof. edn. Harvard U., 1956-58; assoc. prof., then prof. edn. and assoc. rsch. sociologist, then rsch. sociologist U. Calif., Berkeley, 1958-66; prof. sociology Yale U., 1966-80, chmn. dept., 1969-72, chmn. higher edn. rsch. group, 1973-80; Allan M. Carter prof. higher edn. UCLA, 1980-91, prof. emeritus, 1991—. Author: Adult Education in Transition, 1956, The Open Door College, 1960, Educating the Expert Society, 1962, The Distinctive College, 1970, The Problems of American Education, 1975, Academic Power in Italy, 1977, The Higher Education System, 1983, The Academic Life, 1987, Places of Inquiry, 1995, Creating Entrepreneurial Universities, 1998, Sustaining Change in Universities, 2004; co-author: Students and Colleges, 1972, Youth: Transition to Adulthood, 1973, Academic Power in the United States, 1976, Academic Power: Patterns of Authority in Seven National Systems of Higher Education, 1978; editor: Perspectives on Higher Education, 1984, The School and The University, 1985, The Academic Profession, 1987, The Research Foundations of Graduate education, 1993; co-senior editor: Encyclopedia of Higher Education, 1992. Served with AUS, 1942-46. Recipient Comenius medal UNESCO, 1998. Fellow Brit. Soc. for Rsch. in Higher Edn.; mem. Am. Sociol. Assn., Am. Ednl. Rsch. Assn. (Am. Coll. Testing award 1979, Divsn. J. Disting. Rsch. award 1988, Outstanding Book award 1989), Assn. Study Higher Edn. (pres. 1979-80, Rsch. Achievement award 1985, Howard Bowen Disting. Svc. award 1997), Am. Assn. Higher Edn., Nat. Acad. Edn. (v.p. 1989-93), Consortium Higher Edn. Rschrs., European Assn. for Instnl. Rsch. (disting. mem.) Home: 201 Ocean Ave 1710B Santa Monica CA 90402 Office: UCLA Dept Edn Los Angeles CA 90095-1521

CLARK, CALEB MORGAN, political scientist, educator; b. Washington, June 6, 1945; s. Tanner Morgan and Grace Amanda (Kautzman) C.; m. Janet Morrissey Sentz, Sept. 28, 1968; children: Emily Claire, Grace Ellen, Evelyn Adair. BA, Beloit Coll., 1966; PhD, U. Ill., 1973. Lectr. N.Mex. State U., Las Cruces, 1972-75, asst. prof., 1975-78, assoc. prof. govt., 1978-81; assoc. prof. polit. sci. U. Wyo., Laramie, 1981-84, prof., 1984-92, U. Auburn, 1992—, prof., head polit. sci. Co-author: Comparative Patterns of Foreign Policy and Trade, 1976, Development's Influence on Yugoslav Political Values, 1976, Taiwan's Development, 1989, Women in Taiwan Politics, 1990, Foresight, Flexibility and Fortuna in Taiwan's Devel., 1992; mng. editor IS Notes, 1984-92; co-editor: North/South Relations, 1983, State and Development, 1988, Polit. Stability and Economic Development, 1988, Polit. Stability and Economic Development, 1991, The Evolving Pacific Basin, 1992, Technological Change and Rurdal Development in Poor Countries, 1994, Beyond the Developmental State, 1998, The ROC on the Threshold of the 21st Century, 1999, Democracy and the Status of Women in East Asia; cons., assoc. editor Soviet Union, 1974-77, World Affairs, 1975-84, Social Sci. Jour., 1978-80; contbr. articles to profl. jours. NDEA fellow, 1966-69; Woodrow Wilson dissertation fellow, 1969-70; grantee N.Mex. Humanities Coun., 1975, Wyo. Coun. for Humanities, 1982, U.S. Dept. Edn., 1983-85, Pacific Cultural Found., 1984-86, Am. Coun. Learned Socs., 1976, Met. Life Edn., 1978-80, NEH, 1978, NSF, 1981, Chiang Ching-Kuo Found., 1993-95. Mem. Am. Polit. Sci. Assn., Am. Assn. Chinese Studies (exec. coun. 1995-97), Western Polit. Sci. Assn., Assn. Asian Studies, Southern Polit. Sci. Assn., Internat. Studies Assn. (exec. dir. West 1981-84), Ala. Polit. Sci. Assn. (v.p. 1993-94, pres. 1994-95), Phi Beta Kappa (treas. 1983-91), Pi Eta Sigma, Phi Kappa Phi, Phi Beta Delta. Office Phone: 334-844-6460. Business E-Mail: clarkcm@auburn.edu.

CLARK, CAROLYN COCHRAN, lawyer; b. Kansas City, Mo., Oct. 30, 1941; d. John Rogers and Betty Charleton (Holmes) Cochran; m. L. David Clark, Jr., Dec. 29, 1967; children: Gregory David, Timothy Rogers. BA, U. Mo., 1963; LLB, Harvard U., 1968. Bar: N.Y. 1968, Fla. 1979. Assoc. Milbank, Tweed, Hadley & McCloy, N.Y.C., 1968-76, ptnr., 1977—2001, cons. ptnr., 2002—. Mem. deferred giving com., former regional chmn. major gifts com. Harvard Law Sch. Fund; mem. vis. com. Harvard Law Sch., 1982-88; mem. com. on trust and estate gift plans Rockefeller U.; trustee Madison Ave. Presbyn. Ch., 1984-86, N.Y. Bot. Garden, 1993-96, Vis. Nurse Assn. N.Y. and Vis. Nurse Health Care, 1991-96, Riverdale Country Sch., 1994-98, Milbank Meml. Fund, 1996—, The Woodlawn Cemetery, 1999—; del. John D. Rockefeller Conf. Philanthropy in the 21st Century, N.Y., 1989; bd. advisors NYU program Philanthropy and the Law; chmn. program taxation exempt orgns. NYU Tax Inst. Recipient Disting. Alumna award U. Mo., 1989. Fellow Am. Coll. Trust and Estate Counsel (ind. regent, chmn. com. on charitable giving and exempt orgns.), N.Y. Bar Found., Am. Bar Found.; mem. ABA (chmn. subcom. income taxation of charitable trusts 1976-78, chmn. com. charitable instns. 1989-94), Assn. Bar City of N.Y. (chmn. com. on non-profit orgns. 1986-89, sec. com. philanthropic orgns. 1976-82, mem. com. trusts, estates and surrogates cts. 1977-80, 85-86), N.Y. State Bar Assn. (com. estate planning, trusts and estates sect. 1978-89), Am. Law Inst., Practising Law Inst. (lectr.), Harvard U. Law Sch., Assn. Greater N.Y. (trustee 1978-80, v.p. 1980-81, pres. 1981-82), NYU Tax Inst. (chmn. conf. tax planning charitable orgns. 1993-95), Nat. Harvard Law Sch. Alumni Assn. (exec. com. 1978-80, v.p. 1986-90, pres. 1990-92), Soc. Colonial Dames Am. in Mo., Maidstone Club. Home: 161 E 79th St New York NY 10021-0480 Office: Milbank Tweed Hadley Et Al 46th Fl 1 Chase Manhattan Plz New York NY 10005-1401 E-mail: cclark@milbank.com.

CLARK, CELIA RUE, lawyer; b. N.Y.C., Aug. 16, 1951; d. Edward Frank and Rosemary (Reddick) Clark, Jr.; m. Edgar Crawford Gentry, Jr., Aug. 11, 1979; children: Diana Marron, Carl Edgar. BA with distinction, U. Wis., 1974; JD, U. Chgo., 1979; LLM, NYU, 1988. Bar: N.Y. 1980. Mng. editor Heldref Publs., Washington, 1974-78; assoc. Rogers & Wells, N.Y.C., 1979-84; adj. asst. prof. law Yeshiva U., 1985; assoc. Weitzner, Levine & Hamburg, N.Y.C., 1988-92; counsel Pirro, Collier, Cohen, Crystal & Block, White Plains, NY, 1992—96; ptnr. Smith, Buss & Jacobs, L.L.P., N.Y.C., 1996—2002; pvt. practice N.Y.C., 2002—. Co-author: Wealth Protection M.D., 2004; contbg. author: Asset-Based Financing, 1984; contbr. articles to profl. jours. Mem. planned giving coun. Am. Cancer Soc.; chair NY chpt. Arthritis Found., bd. govs., chair planned giving coun. NY chpt.; bd. dirs. Louis R. Cappelli Found. Mem. ABA. Democrat. Office: Law Offices of Celia R Clark 100 Park Ave 33d Fl New York NY 10017 Office Phone: 212-370-4220. Business E-Mail: cclark@cclarklaw.com.

CLARK, CHARLES M., JR., medical school administrator; b. Greensburg, Ind., Mar. 12, 1938; s. Charles Malcolm and Mary Louise (Christian) C.; m. Julia Berg Freeman, Jan 27, 1963 (div. 1982); children: Margaret Louise, Brian Alexander; m. Eleanor DeArman Kinney, June 25, 1983; 1 child, Janet Marie Clark. BA, Ind. U., 1960, MD, 1963. From asst. prof. to prof. medicine Ind. U., Indpls., 1969—, from asst. prof. to prof. pharmacology, 1970—; assoc. chief staff rsch. and devel. VA Hosp., Indpls., 1988—2002; dir. Diabetes Rsch. and Tng. Ctr., Indpls., 1977—2002; co-dir. Regenstrief Inst., Indpls., 1993-97; assoc. dean Ind. U. Sch. Medicine, Indpls., 2002—. Chmn. Safety and Quality com. DCCT, 1982-93, Nat. Diabetes adv. bd., 1987-88; chair Nat. Diabetes Edn. Program, 1995-2002; vis. prof. Facultad de Ciencias Medicas, U. Nacional de la Plata, Argentina, 1999-2000. Editor Diabetes Care, 1996-2001; contbr. numerous articles to profl. jours. Lt comdr. USPHS, 1967-69. Fulbright scholar, 2004—05. Mem. ACP, Am. Soc. Clin. Investigation, Internat. Diabetes Fedn., Am. Diabetes Assn. (Banting award 1989, J.K. Lilly award 2003). Office: 714 N Senate Ave EF 200 Indianapolis IN 46202 Office Phone: 317-274-0104. E-mail: chclark@iupui.edu.

CLARK, CHARLES T(ALIFERRO), retired statistician; b. Danville, Ill., Mar. 18, 1917; s. Charles A. and Kathryn S. (Gentry) C.; m. Pearl W. DuBose, Oct. 6, 1943; children: Charles A., Mary D., Robert S. BBA, U. Tex., 1938, MBA, 1939, PhD, 1956. Asst. mgr. Austin C. of C., Tex., 1940-41; dir. personnel U. Tex., Austin, 1946-59, asst. prof. bus. stats., 1959-60, assoc. prof., 1961-79, prof., 1979-91, Mary Lee Harkins Sweeney Centennial prof. emeritus in bus., 1991—. Bd. dirs. Tex. Student Publs., Austin, 1964-69, Tex. Union, Austin, 1969-83, Univ. Fed. Credit Union, Austin, 1976-84, Univ.

Coop. Soc., Austin, 1980-84. Author numerous text books; (with L.L. Schkade) textbooks Statistical Analysis for Adminstrative Decision, 1969, 4th edit., 1983, (with John R. Stockton) Introduction to Business and Economic Statistics, 1971, 3d edit., 1980; contbr. articles to profl. jours. Served to 2d lt. USAAC, 1941-46, PTO. Recipient 11 teaching awards U. Tex., 1960-80 Mem. Coll. and Univ. Personnel Assn. (pres. 1959), Austin Personnel Assn. (pres. 1950), Austin Stat. Assn. (pres. 1975) Home: 4106 Farhills Dr Austin TX 78731-2812 Office: U Tex Dept Mgmt Sci & Info Systems Austin TX 78712 Personal E-mail: ctclark@orotech.net.

CLARK, CHRISTINE MAY, editor, author; b. Peoria, Ill., Apr. 25, 1957; d. Darrell Ronald and Alice Venita (Burkitt) French. BA, Judson Coll., 1978. Assoc. editor David C. Cook Pub., Elgin, Ill., 1978-80; editor Humpty Dumpty, 1980-94, Jack and Jill, 1983-86, Turtle mag., 1990—; editl. dir. Children's Better Health Inst., Indpls.; assoc. editor Highlights for Children, Honesdale, Pa., 1994-96, mng. editor, 1996—2001, v.p. editl., 1997—, editor, 2001—, also bd. dirs. Recipient Journalism award EDPRESS, 1986, 87, 88, 89, 90, 92, Outstanding Reporting award Soc. Profl. Journalists, 1990; Aurora Found. scholar, 1975. Mem. Am. Soc. Mag. Editors, Soc. Children's Book Writers and Illustrators, Ednl. Press Assn., Judson Coll. Alumni Assn. Reorganized Ch. of Jesus Christ of Latter-day Saints. Avocations: piano, travel. Office: Highlights for Children 803 Church St Honesdale PA 18431-1895

CLARK, CHRISTOPHER ROY, music educator; b. Akron, Ohio, Nov. 18, 1966; s. Lester Kent and Loretta Irene Clark; m. Tami Lynne Clark, Aug. 4, 1990; children: Benjamin Roy, Jacob Edward, Alice Catherine. MusB, U. Akron, 1989. Music tchr. Open Door Christian, Elyria, Ohio, 1990—2005. Mem.: Assn. of Christian Sch. Internat., Ohio Music Edn. Assn. Avocations: reading, running. Home: 2217 E 32d St Lorain OH 44055 Office: Open Door Christian Schools 8287 West Ridge Rd Elyria OH 44035 Office Phone: 440-322-6386. Personal E-mail: clark2217@hotmail.com.

CLARK, CLIFFORD EDWARD, JR., history professor; b. BayShore, N.Y., July 13, 1941; s. Clifford Edward and Helen C.; m. Grace Williams, Aug. 20, 1966; children: Cynthia Williams, Christopher Allen, Susan McGrath. BA, Yale U., 1963; MA, Harvard U., 1964, PhD in Am. Civilization, 1968. History tutor Harvard U., Cambridge, Mass., 1966-67; instr. Amherst (Mass.) Coll., 1968-69, asst. prof., 1969-70; from asst. to assoc. prof. Carleton Coll., Northfield, Minn., 1970-80, prof. history, 1980—, M.A. and A.D. Hulings prof. Am. studies, 1982—, dir. summer acad. programs, 1984—2002, chmn. history dept., 1986-89. Cons. Minn. Humanities Commn., Mpls., 1976—, Minn. Hist. Soc., Mpls., 1982—; Northfield Sch. Bd., 1978-87; editl. cons. Winterthur Portfolio, Del., 1983-92. Author: Henry Ward Beecher, Spokesman for a Middle-Class America, 1978, The American Family Home, 1800-1960, 1986, (with others) The Enduring Tradition, 5th edit. 2004; editor: Minnesota in a Century of Change: The State and Its People Since 1900, 1989. Mem. Northfield Heritage Preservation Commn., 1986—. Fellow Woodrow Wilson Found., 1964, 67; Demonstration grantee NEH, 1978, sr. fellow NEH, 1980; recipient Younger Humanist Summer Stipend, NEH, 1973. Mem. Am. Studies Assn., Am. Hist. Assn., Orgn. Am. Historians, Northfield Hist. Soc. Episcopalian. Avocations: woodworking, squash. Home: 718 4th St E Northfield MN 55057-2316 Office: Carleton Coll Dept History One N College St Northfield MN 55057 Office Phone: 507-646-4208. Business E-Mail: cclark@carleton.edu.

CLARK, CLIFTON BOB, physicist; b. nr. Fort Smith, Ark., July 8, 1927; s. Clifton Breckenridge and Coly (Stroud) C.; m. Sue Magruder, Sept. 1, 1950; children— Carol Jane, Charles Brian, Richard Thomas. BA, U. Ark., 1949, MA, 1950; PhD, U. Md., 1957. Asst. prof. sci. Florence State Tchrs. Coll., 1950-51; asst. prof. physics U.S. Naval Acad., 1951-55; asso. prof., 1956-57; physicist U.S. Naval Research Lab., 1955-56; asso. prof. physics So. Meth. U., Dallas, 1957-61, prof., 1961-65, head dept., 1962-65; physicist, head dept. U. N.C., Greensboro, 1965-75, prof., 1965-94, prof. emeritus, 1994—. Vis. prof. physics Fla. State U., 1975-76 Served with USNR, 1945-46. Mem. Am. Assn. Physics Tchrs. (pres. South Atlantic Coast sect. 1974-75, 77-78, pres. N.C. sect. 1996-97), Am. Phys. Soc. (treas. S.E. sect. 1973-91), N.C. Acad. Sci., Phi Beta Kappa, Sigma Xi, Sigma Pi Sigma, Pi Mu Epsilon, Kappa Mu Epsilon, Omicron Delta Kappa. Home: Apt 3208 6100 W Friendly Ave Greensboro NC 27410-4085 Office: U NC Dept Physics and Astronomy PO Box 26170 Greensboro NC 27402-6170 *I believe people who are happy are those who accept doing things they do not enjoy as the price they pay for getting to do the things they enjoy. The most pleasant of experiences is the completion of a task which demanded extremely hard work. The most unhappy people I have known are those who cheated themselves of this satisfaction, because they tired of hard work and quit before they completed an endeavor.*

CLARK, COLIN WHITCOMB, mathematics professor; b. Vancouver, B.C., Can., June 18, 1931; s. George Savage and Irene (Stewart) C.; m. Janet Arlene Davidson, Sept. 17, 1955; children: Jennifer Kathleen, Karen Elizabeth, Graeme David. BA, U. B.C., 1953; PhD, U. Wash., 1958; DSc (hon.), U. Victoria, 2000. Instr. math. U. Calif., Berkeley, 1958-60; asst. prof. math. U. B.C., 1960-65, assoc. prof., 1965-68, prof., 1968-94, acting dir. Inst. Applied Math., 1983-86, prof. emeritus, 1994—. Vis. prof. math. N.Mex. State U., 1970-71; vis. scientist Fisheries and Oceanography div. C.S.I.R.O., Cronulla, Australia, 1975-76, Ecology and Evolutionary Biology, U. Ariz., 1992; Regents lectr. U. Calif., Davis, 1986; vis. prof. Biol. Scis. Cornell U., 1987; vis. prof. Princeton U., 1997. Author: The Theoretical Side of Calculus, 1972, Mathematical Bioeconomics, 1976, 2d edit., 1990, Elementary Mathematical Analysis, 1982, Bioeconomic Modelling and Fisheries Management, 1985, (with J. Conrad) Resource Economics: Notes and Problems, 1987, (with M. Mangel) Dynamic Modeling in Behavorial Ecology, 1988, (with J. Yoshimura, eds.) Adaption in Stochastic Environments, 1993, (with M. Mangel) Dynamic State Variable Models in Ecology, 2000; contbr. articles to profl. jours. Fellow Royal Soc. Can., Royal Soc. (U.K.); mem. Can. Applied Math. Soc. (pres. 1981-83), Resource Modeling Assn. (pres. 1988-90). Office: Univ BC Dept Math Vancouver BC Canada V6T 1Z2 Personal E-mail: colin_clark@shaw.ca.

CLARK, CORNELIA, lawyer; b. Johannesburg, South Africa, Feb. 2, 1966; arrived in U.S., 96; d. Carel Johannes and Maria Magaretha Jarrard; m. William Robert Clark, Oct. 7, 1995; children: Carlene, Charlize. BA in Law, U. Stellenbosch, Cape Town, South Africa, 1986, LLB, 1988. Article clk. Mazahams Attys., Johannesburg, 1989—91; pvt. practice, Johannesburg, 1991—95; assoc. Roger Knowles Attys., Durban, South Africa, 1995; pvt. practice Law Offices of Cornelia Clark, Seattle, 1998—. Office: 7200 S 180th St Ste 101 Seattle WA 98188 Home: 13013 SE 261st Pl Kent WA 98030 Business E-Mail: attorney@seanet.com.

CLARK, CYNTHIA ZANG FACER, federal agency administrator; b. Sterling, Colo., Apr. 1, 1942; d. Joseph Elmer and Flora Burnell Zang; m. Glenn Willett Clark, Aug. 20, 1963; children: Randall, Drew, Ariel Silver, Allison, Timothy, Emily BA in Math., Mills Coll., Oakland, Calif., 1963; MS in Math., U. Denver, 1964; MS in Stats., Iowa State U., 1973, PhD in Stats., 1977. Instr. dept. maths. U. Denver, 1963-66, Drake U., Des Moines, 1971-72; mathematical statistician Statistical Rsch. Divsn. Bur. Census, 1977-79; econ. statistician Office Fed. Statistical Policy and Standards Dept. Commerce, 1979-81; statistical policy analyst Statistical Policy Office Office Info. and Regulatory Affairs Office Mgmt. & Budget, 1981-83; asst. divsn. chief for rsch. & methodology Agriculture Divsn Bur. Census, 1983-90, dir. rsch. and applications divsn., 1990-92; dir. survey mgmt. divsn. Nat. Agrl. Statistics Svc. Dept. Agriculture, 1992-96; assoc. dir. methodology and standards Bur. Census Dept. Commerce, Washington, 1996—2004; dir. methodology Office of Nat. Stats. U.K., London, 2004—. Contbr. articles to profl. jours. Recipient Sr. Exec. Svc. bonus award, 1994, 1995, 1997—2003. Fellow Am. Statistical Assn. (mem. InterCASIC 1996 conf. planning com., past pres. sect. govt. statistics, bd. dir.); mem. Am. Assn. Pub. Opinion Rsch., Washington Statis. Soc. (pres.), Internat. Assn. Survey Stats., Sr. Exec. Assn. (Dept. Agr. chpt. pres. 1993-95), Caucus for Women in Stats. (past pres.), Natural Resource Conservation Svc. (blue ribbon panel on info. and data mgmt. 1996), Internat. Stats. Inst. (chair com. on women in stats. 2003—) Mem. Ch. of Jesus Christ of Latter Day Saints. Avocations: family history, geneaology, ice skating, cultural activities, travel. Office: Office for National Statistics 1 Drummond Gate London SW1V 2QQ England Home: Hugh St 32 Royal Belgrave House London SW1V 1RR England

CLARK, DAVID EDWARD, lawyer; b. N.Y.C., Apr. 19, 1960; s. Edward White Clark and Croll Margaret; m. Jessica Ruth Towne, Sept. 3, 1988; children: Phoebe Merrill, Gordon Allistair. BA, SUNY, Fredonia, 1981; JD, U. Ga., 1989. Bar: Ga. 89. Assoc. Boyce, Thompson & O'Brien, Norcross, Ga., 1989—91; ptnr. Clark & Towne P.C., Lawrenceville, Ga., 1991—. Contbr. column to Atlanta Jour.-Constitution. Mem. Dems. of Gwinnett County, Lawrenceville, 2001—. Mem.: Ga. DODD DUI Group (Lawyer of Yr. 1999), Ga. Assn. Criminal Def. Lawyers. Office: Clark & Towne PC 600 Perry St Lawrenceville GA 30045 E-mail: dclark@clarktowne.com.

CLARK, DAVID WILLIAM, lawyer, councilman; b. Manchester, Eng., Jan. 27, 1954; s. Chandler Kinney and May Clark; m. Sally Catherine Clark, June 27, 1987; children: Hilary Alexandra, Gillian Noelle. AB in History, Princeton U., 1975; JD, Duke U., 1978. Bar: Calif. 1978, Colo. 1990, Fla. 1992. Assoc. Thelen, Marrin, Johnson & Bridges, L.A., 1978-84; counsel Ultrasys. Inc. (later Hadson Corp.), Irvine, Calif., 1984-89, Oxbow Corp., West Palm Beach, Fla., 1989—2003, 2004—, FPL Energy, LLC, Juno Beach, Fla., 2003—04. Councilman City of Palm Beach Gardens, Fla., 1993—2004, mayor, 1994-95; bd. dirs. Palm Beach County chpt. ARC, West Palm Beach, 1998-2001. Mem. State Bar Calif., Colo. Bar Assn., Fla. Bar Assn. Republican. Avocations: reading, history, ships and the sea. Office: Oxbow Corp 1601 Forum Pl Ste 1202 West Palm Beach FL 33401 Home: 14689 Crazy Horse Ln Palm Beach Gardens FL 33418 Office Phone: 561-640-8709. E-mail: Dave_Clark@oxbow.com.

CLARK, DAVID WRIGHT, lawyer; b. West Point, Miss., May 19, 1948; s. Douglas Earl and Sarah Evelyn (Wright) C.; m. Victoria Baugher, Oct. 16, 1976; children: Alexander, Nicholas, Peter. BA with high honors, Millsaps Coll., 1970; MA, Harvard U., 1971; JD, U. Mich., 1974. Bar: Ill. 1974, Miss. 1978, U.S. Dist. Ct. (no. dist.) Ill. 1974, U.S. Ct. Appeals (7th cir.) 1974, U.S. Dist. Ct. (so. and no. dists.) Miss. 1978, U.S. Ct. Appeals (5th cir.) 1978. Adj. prof. Miss. Coll. Sch. Law, Jackson, 1978-82; assoc. Wildman, Harrold, Allen & Dixon, Chgo., Friedman & Koven, Chgo., 1974-78; shareholder Wise Carter Child & Caraway, P.A., Jackson, 1978-96; ptnr. Lake Tindall, LLP, Jackson, 1996-2001, Bradley Arant Rose & White LLP, Jackson, 2001—. Pres. Miss. Bar Rev., 1979—. Mem. Miss. Constitution Study Commn., Jackson, 1985-87; bd. dirs. Miss. First, Inc., Jackson, 1983-87; pres. U.S.A. Internat. Ballet Competition, Jackson, 1990-98; mem. Leadership Jackson, 1989-90. Mem. ABA (Miss. Bar del. to ho. dels. 1998—, sect. litigation, dir. divsn., com. chmn. and task force chmn. 1987-2000, chmn. gun violence coord. com. 1998-2002), Miss. Bar Assn. (chmn. litigation sect. 1994-95), Am. Law Inst., Charles Clark Am. Inn of Ct. Avocations: musicals, opera. Home: 110 Olympia Fields Jackson MS 39211-2509 Office: Bradley Arant Rose & White LLP One Jackson Pl Ste 450 Jackson MS 39201 E-mail: dclark@bradleyarant.com.

CLARK, DAYLE MERITT, civil engineer; b. Lubbock, Tex., Sept. 5, 1933; s. Frank Meritt and Mamie Jewel (Huff) C.; m. Betty Ann Maples, Apr. 11, 1968; 1 child, Alison. BS, Tex. Tech U., 1955; MS, So. Meth. U., 1967. Registered profl. engr.; registered profl. land surveyor. Field engr. Chgo. Bridge & Iron Co., 1955; mgr. L.K. Long Construction Co., 1958-64; prof. U. Tex. Arlington, 1964-99. Cons. AID, 1966, NSF, 1967-68; expert witness in court cases. Editor Tex. Civil Engr., 1967-71; contbr. articles to profl. jours. Served to capt. USAF, 1955-57. Fellow ASCE (pres. Dallas br. 1987, pres. Tex. sect. 1992-93, Profl. Svcs. award 1991, Award of Honor 1998), Tex. Soc. Profl. Engrs. (achievement award in civil engring. Dallas chpt. 1995), Rotary (pres. Arlington-West 1986, Paul Harris fellow, Rotarian of Yr. 1987). Office: PO Box 185 Arlington TX 76004-0185

CLARK, DEANNA DEE, volunteer; b. Cedar Rapids, Iowa, June 1, 1944; d. Cyrus Dean and Isabelle Esther Thomas; m. Glen Edward Clark, July 16, 1966; children: Andrew Curtis, Carissa Jane. AA, Coll. of the Desert, 1964; BA, Coe Coll., 1966. Fund devel. chmn. Nat. Assistance League, 1992—94; resource devel. writer and trainer, 1992—2002; convenor U.S. Internat. Youth Exch. Initiative Cmty. Network, Utah, 1984—94; human svcs. subcom. child advocacy project, social justice and peacemaking min. unit Presbyn. Ch. U.S.A., 1992—93; pres. Provo-Jordan River Pkwy. Found., 1993—95; sustaining mem. Jr. League Salt Lake City, 1976—, Assistance League Salt Lake City, 1986—; bd. dirs. Friends of Libr., U. Utah, 1991—94; moderator, nominating com. Synod of the Rocky Mountains, 1999—2002; numerous civic coms. and found. Utah, 1992—; sec., vice-chmn. City of Holladay Interfaith Coun., 1999—; info practices com. Utah Legislature, 1990; exec. com. of Gen. Assembly Coun., Presbyn. Ch. (U.S.A.), 1993—97; elder Presbyn. Ch., 1983—; mem. coun. Presbytery of Utah, 1985—2001, moderator, 2000—01. Mem. LWV (Utah pres. 1981-83), P.E.O. (historian Utah chpt. 1992-95, chpt. H pres. 1995-97, Utah chmn. Gump and Ayers Scholarship Com. 1998-99). Home: PO Box 711098 Salt Lake City UT 84171-1098

CLARK, DONALD MALIN, professional association executive; b. Buffalo, Feb. 11, 1929; s. Jack Merritt Malin and Louise Mary C.; m. Joan Marie Coyle, Dec. 27, 1958; children— Kevin Malin, Michael John, Elizabeth Anne. BS magna cum laude, Canisius Coll., Buffalo, 1950, MA, 1952; Ed.D., SUNY, Buffalo, 1961; grad., U.S. Army Advanced Armor Sch., Ft. Knox, Ky., 1964, U.S. Army Command and Gen. Staff Coll., 1969, U.S. Army War Coll., 1975. Administrv. asst. Traveler's Ins. Co., Buffalo, N.Y., 1950-57; mem. faculty Orchard Park (N.Y.) Sr. High Sch., 1957-66; dir. Ctr. Econ. Edn. SUNY, Buffalo, 1966-70; exec. dir. Industry-Edn. Coun., Niagara Falls, N.Y., 1970-79; pres., CEO, Nat. Assn. Industry-Edn. Cooperation, Buffalo, 1979—. Radio and TV pub. info. news commentator, 1962-78; adj. prof. Canisius Coll. Grad. Sch., Buffalo, 1962-63, Lemoyne Coll. Sch. Mgmt., Syracuse, N.Y., 1973-79, Rochester Inst. Tech., 1983-84; adj. prof. Mt. Carmel Coll., Niagra Falls, Ont., Can., 1966; summer faculty Nat. War Coll., Washington, 1967-68; pres. Consumer Credit Counseling Svc., Buffalo, 1973, edn. chmn.; dir. Industry Edn. Coun. Calif., 1992-94; mem. Econ. Forum, Buffalo, 1994-2000; mem. editl. adv. bd. for Business Ethics, 1988-92; selected by People to People Internat.'s Citizen Amb. Program as del. leader for industry and edn. leaders in U.S. to visit Russia, Latvia, 1993, to China, 1995, South Africa, 1996, U.K., 1997, Australia/New Zealand, 1998, China, 1999; cons. (on site) to Ministry of Ed., Koror, Rep. of Palau, Micronesia, 1996; profl. pianist pvt. functions, spl. occasions for agencies and orgns., 1986—. Author: Meeting the Challenge of a Free Society, 1965; writer editls.: Buffalo News and Business First, also newsletters, handbooks, articles, guides for nat. publs.; prodr.: film on industry-edn. cooperation; contbr. articles over 100 articles to nat. and Can. publs. Apptd. by Pres. Reagan to Nat. Adv. Coun. on Ednl. Rsch. and Improvement, 1988-90; bd. dirs. N.Y. State Coun. Econ. Edn., 1980-84, Amherst (N.Y.) Symphony Orch., 1997-98; lectr. St. Michael's Roman Cath. Ch., Buffalo; mem. cmty. adv. coun. SUNY, Buffalo, 1981—; mem. adv. com. ERIc Clearinghouse adult, career, and vocat. edn. Ohio State U., 1982-84; mem. adv. bd. Erie C.C., Williamsville, N.Y., 1995-97. With U.S. ANG, col. USAR, 1948-83; held position of chief of the Western/East European Divsn., Directorate of Fgn. Intelligence, Dept. Army, 1980-83, instr. U.S. Army Intelligence Sch., Fy. Holabird, Md., 1963-70; rev. panleist U.S. Dept. Edn.'s Nat. Elem. Sch. program, 1985-86, Secondary Sch. Recognition program, 1988-89. Recipient Kazanjian Found. Coll. Econs. Tchg. award, 1968, Freedoms Found. medal, 1965, Presdl. Citation for Pvt. Sector Initiatives, 1985, Cert. of Recognition, U.S. Dept. Edn. for contbns. of time and talent toward adult literacy, 1984, Canisius Coll. Disting. Alumni award 1996; fellow NAM, 1965. Mem. ASTD, Western N.Y. Export Coun. (assoc.), U.S. Dept. Commerce, Active Corps Execs., U.S. SBA, Mil. Officers Assn. of Am., Amherst Dance Club (pres. 1987-88), Am. Assn. Career Edn. (Disting. Mem. award 2005), Phi Delta Kappa (rsch. award 1996). Republican. Roman Catholic. Achievements include complete studies at the foriegn svc., Dept. of State, Washington, 1973, 1977 and 1982, and at the Naval amphibious warfare sch., Colo., Calif., 1974, 1983. Avocations: piano, writing, ballroom dancing, reading, correspondence. Home: 235 Hendricks Blvd Amherst NY 14226-3304 Office Phone: 716-834-7047. E-mail: dmalin@adelphia.net. *Being in the vanguard of change has been the most exciting aspect of my professional career. To participate in effecting change, particularly in education and human resources, economic development requires risk taking and the determination to gain support for one's ideas.*

CLARK, DONALD OTIS, lawyer; b. Charlotte, N.C., May 30, 1934; s. Otis and Ruby Lee (Church) C.; m. Jo Ann Hager, June 15, 1957 (div. 1980); children: Deborah Elise, Stephen Merritt; m. Anja Maria Smith, Nov. 5, 1983. AB, U. S.C., 1956, JD cum laude, 1963; MA, U. Ill., 1957. Bar: S.C. 1963, Ga. 1964, D.C., 1999. Practice law, Atlanta, 1963-83; mem. Candler, Cox, McClain & Andrews, 1968-70, McClain, Mellen, Bowling & Hickman, 1970-75; ptnr. King & Spalding, 1975-78; sr. ptnr. Hurt, Richardson, Garner, Todd & Cadenhead, 1978-83; ptnr. Bishop, Liberman, Cook, Purcell & Reynolds, Washington, 1983-86, Kaplan Russin & Vecchi, Washington, 1986-92, Whitman & Ranson (merged with Breed Abbot & Morgan 1993), Washington, 1992-93; sr. ptnr. Whitman Breed Abbott & Morgan, Washington, 1993-95; ptnr. Keck, Mahin & Cate, Washington, 1995-97, Reed Smith LLP, Washington, 1997—. Mem. dist. export council U.S. Dept Commerce, 1974—; adj. prof. law Emory U., 1970—, U.S.C., 1974; lectr. Ga. State U., 1972; lectr. numerous internat. trade seminars and workshops Author: German govt. study on doing bus. in Southeastern U.S., 1974; editor-in-chief: S.C. Law Rev., 1963; contbr. articles to profl. jours. Served to capt. USAF, 1957-60. Decorated knight Order St. John of Jerusalem, Knights of Malta, knight Order St. Stanislas, knight and minister of justice Order of New Aragon, Sungrye medal Korea; recipient Nat. Leadership medal Air Force Assn., 1956, Coll. award Am. Legion, Outstanding Sr. award U. S.C., 1956, hon. consul Republic of Korea, 1972—. Mem. Atlanta Bar Assn., ABA, S.C. Bar Assn., Ga. Bar Assn., D.C. Bar Assn., Lawyers Club Atlanta, Am. Judicature Soc., Am. Soc. Internat. Law, Atlanta C. of C., Ga. C. of C. (exec. com. Internat. Councils), Inst. Internat. Edn. (chmn. Southeastern regional adv. bd. 1974—, nat. trustee), So. Consortium Internat. Edn. Inc. (dir.), Wig & Robe, Sigma Chi (pres. 1956 Province Balfour award), Omicron Delta Kappa, Kappa Sigma Kappa, Phi Delta Phi (pres. 1963 Province Grad. of Yr. award) E-mail: andon_6971@msn.com.

CLARK, DONNA M., elementary school educator; b. Roseville, Mich., Sept. 15, 1939; d. Granville Raymond Jewel and Evelyn Marie Steiger-Jewel; m. Buddy Lee Clark, Dec. 30, 1979; children: Thomas, Douglas Lee Jewel, Nancy Gruber, Barbara Merkle. BS in Elem. Edn., Olivet U., 1962; M in Elem. Edn., St. Francis Coll., 1970. First grade tchr. VanDyke Pub. Sch., Warren, Mich., 1969; upper elem. tchr. DeKalb County Ea. Cmty. Sch. Dist., Butler, Ind., 1969—2005. Upper elem. dept. chair DeKalb County Ea., Riverdale Elem., Saint Joe, Ind., 1984—2005; summer sch. coord. DeKalb County Ea. Cmty. Sch. Dist., 1980—82. State field rep. Ind. Jr. Hist. Soc., Indpls., 1971—79; county pres. DeKalb County Hist. Soc., Auburn, Ind., 1977—78. Mem.: Delta Dappa Kamma (assoc.; v.p. 1980—82), DAR (chmn. radio, tv and movie com. 1990—93, state libr. 1994—97, state chaplain 1997—2000). Home: 7093 County Rd 59A Spencerville IN 46788

CLARK, DORIS ELLEN, music educator; b. Montpelier, Ohio, Nov. 8, 1930; d. Lowell Adolphus and Mabel Mae (Cox) Millard; m. Vernon Nelson Clark, Sept. 3, 1953; children: Valeda Murr, Virginia Johnson, Vaughn, Victor, Valerie Biasini. BA in music magna cum laude, Lincoln Christian Coll., 1950—55. Substitute music tchr. Elem. Sch., Ashland, Kans., 1974—76; with U.S. Census, 1980, 1990; substitute music tchr. Jr. High and Sr. High, Marlow, Okla., 1992. Performed at local nursing homes (singing and playing), Madison, Kans., 1997—2004. Mem.: Northeast Kans. Music Teachers Assn. (sec. 2003—04), Topeka Music Teachers Assn. (sec. 2001—05), Flint Hills Genealogists (sec. 2001—). Republican. Christian Ch. Avocations: art, genealogy, piano, singing, writing. Home: 220 W Sherman St Madison KS 66860

CLARK, DOUGLAS H., JR., lawyer; b. Phoenix, July 17, 1941; s. Douglas H. Clark and Virginia Lee Russel; m. Kathryn Lewis (div. 1973); children: Gregory R., Devon A. Glasco. BS, JD, LLB, U. Ariz., 1966. Bar: Ariz. 1966, U.S. Dist. Ct. Ariz. 1966. Atty. Mesch, Marquez & Rothschild, Tuscon, 1967—73; ptnr. Mesch, Marquez, Clark & Rothschild, PC, Tuscon, 1973—83, Mesch, Clark & Rothschild, PC, Tuscon, 1983—. Mem.: ATLA, ABA, Ariz. State Bar, Ariz. Trial Lawyers Assn. Republican. Avocations: water-skiing, handball. Office: Mesch Clark and Rothschild 259 N Meyer Tucson AZ 85701 Business E-Mail: dclark@mcrazlaw.com.

CLARK, EARNEST HUBERT, JR., tool company executive; b. Birmingham, Ala., Sept. 8, 1926; s. Earnest Hubert and Grace May (Smith) C.; m. Patricia Margaret Hamilton, June 22, 1947; children: Stephen D., Kenneth A., Timothy R., Daniel S., Scott H., Rebecca G. BS in Mech. Engring, Calif. Inst. Tech., 1946, MS, 1947. Chmn., chief exec. officer Friendship Group, Baker Hughes, Inc. (formerly Baker Oil Tools, Inc.), L.A., 1947-89, v.p., asst. gen. mgr., 1958-62, pres., chief exec. officer, 1962-69, 75-79, chmn. bd., 1969-75, 79-87, 87-89, ret., 1989; chmn. The Friendship Group, Newport Beach, Calif., 1989—. Bd. dirs. Regenesis Inc. Past chmn., bd. dirs. YMCA of U.S.A.; past chmn. bd. YMCA for Met. L.A.; mem. nat. coun. YMCA; trustee Harvey Mudd Coll. With USNR, 1944-46, 51-52. Mem. AIME, Am. Petroleum Inst., Petroleum Equipment Suppliers Assn. (bd. dirs.), Tau Beta Pi. Office: Friendship Group 3822 Calle Ariana San Clemente CA 92672-4502 E-mail: ehclarkjr@cox.net.

CLARK, EDGAR SANDERFORD, insurance broker, consultant; b. Nov. 17, 1933; s. Edgar Edmund, Jr., and Katharine Lee (Jarman) C.; m. Nancy E. Hill, Sept. 13, 1975; 1 child, Schuyler; children by previous marriages: Colin, Alexandra, Pamela. Student, U. Pa., 1952-54; BS, Georgetown U., 1956; JD, 1958; postgrad., INSEAD, Fountainbleu, France, 1969, Golden Gate Coll., 1973, U. Calif. Berkeley, 1974. Staff asst. U.S. Senate, Washington, 1958-59; underwriter Ocean Marine Dept. Fireman's Fund Ins. Co., San Francisco, 1959-62; mgr. Am. Fgn. Ins. Assn., San Francisco, 1962-66; with Marsh & McLennan, 1966-72; mgr. for. Europe resident dir. Brussels Belgium, 1966-70; asst. v.p., mgr. captive and internat. div. San Francisco, 1970-72; v.p., dir. Risk Planning Group. Inc., San Francisco, 1972—75; v.p., dir. global constrn. group Alexander & Alexander Inc., San Francisco, 1975-94; exec. dir. The Surplus Line Assn. Calif., 1995-97; CEO Capital Risk Solutions Corp., 1997—. Lectr. in field.; guest lectr. U. Calif., Berkeley, 1973, Am. Grad. Sch. Internat. Mgmt., 1981-82, Golden Gate U., annually 1985-91; dir. Soc. Ins. Brokers, 1991-94; del. Calif. Agts. and Brokers Legis. Coun., 1992-95; pres. Ins. Forum of San Francisco. Mem. editl. bd. Risk Mgmt. Reports, 1973—76. With USAF, 1956—58. Mem. Am. Mgmt. Assn., Am. Risk and Ins. Assn., Internat. Insurance Soc., Chartered Ins. Inst., Am. Soc. Internat. Law, Soc. Calif. Pioneers San Francisco, Meadow Club, Fairfax, Calif., World Trade San Francisco. Republican. Episcopalian. Personal E-mail: snarkclark@worldnet.att.net.

CLARK, EDWARD EMERSON, lawyer; b. Middleboro, Mass., May 4, 1930; s. Fletcher Jr. and Marguerite (Swift) C.; m. Alicia Garcia Cobos, Oct. 20, 1970; 1 child, Edward Emerson. AB, Dartmouth Coll., 1952; JD, Harvard U., 1957. Bar: N.Y. 1950, Calif. 1965. Assoc. Donovan Leisure Newton & Irvine, N.Y.C., 1957-64; mergers and acquisitions Sausalito, Calif., 1964-65; sr. atty. Atlantic Richfield Co., L.A., 1967-70, antitrust counsel, 1970-73, assoc. gen. counsel, 1973-79, dep. gen. counsel, 1979-94; pvt. practice Sausalito, 1965-67. Trustee Plaza de la Raza, L.A., 1988-94, dir. U.S. Baltic Found., 1995—; co-founder, dir. Hispanics for L.A. Opera, 1990—. Author: A New Beginning, 1980. Candidate for Gov. of Calif., 1978; Libertarian candidate for Pres. of U.S., 1980. Served with USN, 1952-54. Mem. Calif. Bar Assn. E-mail: balticed@aol.com.

CLARK, ELOISE ELIZABETH, biologist, educator; b. Grundy, Va., Jan. 20, 1931; d. J. Francis Emmett and Ava Clayton (Harris) C. BA, Mary Washington Coll., 1951; PhD in Zoology, U. N.C., 1958; DSc, King Coll., 1976; postdoctoral rsch., Washington U., St. Louis, 1957-58, U. Calif. at

Berkeley, 1958-59. Rsch. asst., then instr. U. N.C., 1952-55; instr. physiology Marine Biol. Lab., Woods Hole, Mass., 1958-62; from instr. to asst. prof. Columbia U., 1959—65, assoc. prof. biol. sci., 1966-69; with NSF, Washington, 1969-83, head molecular biology, 1971-73, div. dir. biol. and med. scis., 1973-75, dep. asst. dir. biol., behavioral and social scis., 1975-76, asst. dir. biol., behavioral and social scis., 1976-83; v.p. acad. affairs Bowling Green State U., Ohio, 1983—96, prof. biol. sci. to trustee prof. emeritus, 1983—2002, trustee prof. emeritus, 2002—. Contbr. articles to profl. jours. and congl. hearings. Mem. alumnae bd. Mary Washington Coll., U. Va., 1967—70; bd. regents Nat. Libr. of Medicine, 1973—83; mem. policy group competitive grants program U.S. Dept. Agr.; mem. White House Interdepartmental Task Force on Women, 1978—80, Task Force for Conf. on Families, 1980, Com. on Health and Medicine, 1976—80; vice chmn. Com. on Food and Renewable Resources, 1977—80; mem. selective excellence task force Ohio Bd. Regents, 1984—85; mem. Ohio Adv. Coun., Coll. Prep. Edn., 1983—84, Ohio Inter-Univ. Coun. for Provosts, 1983—96, chmn., 1984—85, 1995—96; nat. adv. rsch. resources coun. NIH, 1987—89; mem. informal sci. edn. panel NSF, 1986—88, adv. com., social, behavioral and econ. scis., 1997—2000; program adv. coun. sci., tech. and pub. policy Harvard U., 1988—90, mem. editl. bd. Forum, 1997—2001; mem. governing bd. OhioLink, 1990—96, vice chair, 1992, chair, 1993—94. Named Disting. Alumnus Mary Washington Coll., 1975; Wilson scholar, 1956; E.C. Drew scholar, 1956; USPHS postdoctoral fellow, 1957-59; recipient Disting. Svc. award NSF, 1978 Mem. AAAS (coun. 1969-71, bd. dirs. 1978-82, pres.-elect, 1992, pres., 1993, chmn. bd. 1994), Soc. Gen. Physiology (sec. 1965-67, coun. 1969-71), Biophys. Soc. (coun. 1975-76), Am. Soc. Cell Biology (coun. 1972-75), Am. Inst. Biol. Scientists, Marine biol. Lab. (trustee 1993), NASULGC (higher edn. and tech. com. 1988-93, com. on info. tech. 1994-96), Consortium of Social Sci. Assn. (bd. dirs. 1993-96), Ohio Coun. rsch. and Econ. Devel., Assn. Women in Sci. (bd. dirs. 1998-2001), Phi Beta Kappa (com. on qualifications 1985—, chair 1998-2004, senate 1996—, exec. com. 1997-2003), Sigma Xi, Omicron Delta Kappa. Home: 1222 Brownwood Dr Bowling Green OH 43402-3503 Office: Bowling Green State U Dept Biol Scis Bowling Green OH 43403-0001 Office Phone: 419-372-9390.

CLARK, EMORY EUGENE, diversified financial services company executive; b. Opelika, Ala., Jan. 24, 1931; s. Bunk Henry and Dorothy (Bolt) C.; m. Jean F. Reed, Sept. 30, 1951; children: Steven E., Michael E. Grad. pubs. schs. CLU, CFP. With Mgrs. Life Ins. Co., 1956-74, agt. supr. L.A., 1956-60, mgr. Hawaii br., 1960-65, mgr. Pitts. br., 1965-68, mgr. Houston br., 1968-74; with Jefferson Std. Life Ins. Co., Fort Worth, 1974-82; fin. planner E.F. Hutton & Co., Inc., 1983-90; v.p. investments A.G. Edwards & Sons, Inc., Ft. Worth, 1990-99, sr. v.p. investments, 1999—. 1st lt. Inf. AUS, 1950-56. Mem. Fort Worth Life Underwriters Assn., Am. Soc. Life Underwriters, Fort Worth Soc. Life Underwriters, Ft. Worth Securities Dealers Assn., Inst. Cert. Fin. Planners (cert., registered practitioner). Home: 8109 Meadowbrook Dr Fort Worth TX 76120-5309 Office: AG Edwards & Sons Inc 420 Throckmorton Ste 1000 Fort Worth TX 76102 Office Phone: 817-302-1432. E-mail: emoryclark@sbcglobal.net.

CLARK, ERIC C., state official; b. Smith County, Miss. s. Mr. and Mrs. John S. C.; m. Karan C.; children: Charles, Catherine. BA, Millsaps Coll.; MA, U. Miss.; PhD in History, Miss. State U. Prof. history and govt. Miss. Coll., 1989-95; mgr. family tree farm Smith County; mem. Miss. Ho. of Reps., 1980-96; sec. of state State of Miss., 1996—. Democrat. Baptist. Address: PO Box 136 401 Mississippi St Jackson MS 39205-0136

CLARK, EUGENIE, zoologist, educator; b. N.Y.C., May 4, 1922; m. Hideo Umaki, 1942; m. Ilias Konstantinou, 1949; 4 children; m. Chandler Brossard, 1966; m. Igor Klatzo, 1969; m. Henry Yoshinobu Kon, 1997. BA, Hunter Coll., 1942; MA, NYU, 1946, PhD (Pacific Sci. Bd. fellow 1949), 1950; DSc (hon.), U. Mass., Dartmouth, 1990, U. Guelph, 1995, U. South Hampton, 1995. Rsch. asst. in ichthyology Scripps Instn. Oceanography, 1946-47; with N.Y. Zool. Soc., 1947-48; research asst. in animal behavior Am. Museum Nat. History, N.Y.C., 1948-49, research assoc., 1950-80; instr. Hunter Coll., 1954; exec. dir. Cape Haze Marine Lab., Sarasota, Fla., 1955-67; asso. prof. biology City U. N.Y., 1966-67; asso. prof. zoology U. Md., 1968-73, prof. zoology, 1973-92, prof. emerita, sr. rsch. scientist, 1992—. Vis. prof. Hebrew U., 1972; sr. rsch. scientist, dir. emerita Mote Marine Lab., Sarasota, Fla., 1999—. Author: Lady with a Spear, 1953, The Lady and the Sharks, 1969, Desert Beneath the Sea, 1991; subject of biographies Shark Lady (Ann McGovern), 1978, Adventures of the Shark Lady (Ann McGovern), 1998, Eugenie Clark, Adventures of a Shark Scientist (Ellen R. Butts, Joyce R. Schwartz), 2000, Fish Watching with Eugenie Clark (Michael E. Ross), 2000, America's Shark Lady (Ann McGovern), 2004, Eugenie Clark, (Ronald A. Reis) Marine Biologist, 2005. Recipient Myrtle Wreath award in sci. Hadassah, 1964, Nogi award in art Underwater Soc. Am., 1965, Dugan award in aquatic sci. Am. Littoral Soc., 1969, Diver of Yr. award Boston Sea Rovers, 1978, David Stone medal, 1984, Stoneman Conservation award, 1982, Gov. of S. Sinai medal, 1985, Lowell Thomas award Explorers Club, 1986, Wildscreen Internat. Film Festival award, 1986, medal Gov. Red Sea, Egypt, 1988, Nogi award in Sci., 1988, Women's Hall of Fame award State of Md., 1989, Women Educators award, 1990, Alumnae award, Franklin Burr award Nat. Geographic Soc., 1993; named to Hunter Coll. Hall of Fame, 1990, DEMA Hall of Fame, 1993, BUEI Hall of Fame, 2004, Wyland ICON award, 2005; Fellow AEC, 1950; Saxton fellow, 1952; Breadloaf Writer's fellow; Fulbright scholar Egypt, 1951. Fellow: AAAS; mem.: Am. Elasmobranch Soc. (disting. fellow 1999), Am. Littoral Soc. (v.p. 1970—89), Nat. Pks. and Conservation Assn. (vice chmn. 1976), Internat. Soc. Profl. Diving Scientists, Soc. Woman Geographers (Gold medal 1975, U. Md. Pres.'s medal 1993), Israeli Zool. Soc. (hon.), Am. Soc. Ichthyology and Herpetology (life). Achievements include special research in ecology and behavior of tropical sand fishes, morphology and taxonomy marine fishes, isolating mechanisms poecillid fishes and behavior deep sea sharks. Office: Ctr Shark Rsch Mote Marine Lab 1600 Ken Thompson Pkwy Sarasota FL 34236 Office Phone: 941-388-4441. Business E-Mail: yoppe@mote.org.

CLARK, EVE VIVIENNE, linguist, educator; b. Camberley, U.K., July 26, 1942; arrived in U.S., 1967; d. Desmond Charles and Nancy (Aitken) Curme; m. Herbert H. Clark, July 21, 1967; 1 child, Damon Alistair. MA with honors, U. Edinburgh, Scotland, 1965, PhD, 1969. Rsch. assoc. Stanford (Calif.) U., 1969-71, from asst. prof. to assoc. prof., 1971-83, prof., 1983—. Author: Ontogenesis of Meaning, 1979, Acquisition of Romance, 1985, The Lexicon in Acquisition, 1993, First Language Acquisition, 2003; co-author: Psychology and Language, 1977. Fellow Ctr. for Advanced Study in the Behavioral Scis., 1979-80, Guggenheim Found., 1983-84. Mem. Dutch Acad. Scis. (fgn.). Business E-Mail: eclark@psych.stanford.edu.

CLARK, FRANK M., utilities executive; degree in bus. adminstrn., JD, DePaul U. Joined ComEd, 1966, various positions, 1966—2001, pres. Chgo., 2001—. Office: ComEd 37th Flr 10 S Dearborn St Chicago IL 60690*

CLARK, FRED, writer, editor; b. Limón, Costa Rica, Dec. 12, 1930; came to U.S., 1968; s. Thomas and Irene (Penney) C.; m. Dorothy Hyacinth James, Aug. 4, 1956; children: Paul, Fred Jr., Lydia Ramona. Student, Ctrl. Am. Acad., 1944-49; BLitt, U. Costa Rica, 1951; postgrad., Stafford Coll., 1956-57; barrister-at-law, Inner Temple, London, 1960. Bar: Eng. 1960, Jamaica 1960; cert. in law Coun. Legal Edn. Master of langs. Merl Grove Sch., 1951-55; trust officer Govt. of Jamaica, 1960-61; pvt. law practice Kingston, Jamaica, 1961-67; legal editor Corp. Trust Co., N.Y.C., 1968-69; sr. legal editor Prentice-Hall, Inc., Englewood Cliffs, N.J., 1969-91. Cons. commonwealth law. Editor The Corp. Jour., 1968-69. Trustee United Ch. of Christ, 1970-78; spl. advisor U.S. Congl. Adv. Bd.; nat. adv. bd. Am. Security Coun. Recipient Disting. Leadership award, 1984, Presdl. medal of merit, 1986. Mem. Am. Mgmt. Assn., Internat. Platform Assn., Internat. Commn. Jurists, Am. Mus. Natural History, Nat. Geog. Soc., N.Y. Acad. Scis., Am. Ballet Theater, Met. Opera Guild, U.S. Naval Inst., Freeport Bus. Promotion (bd. dirs.), U.S. Power Squadron (asst. sec.), Inter-Am. Soc., Rosicrucians. Home: PO Box 291 Bergenfield NJ 07621-0291

CLARK, GAIL THEROUX, artist; b. Framingham, Mass., Aug. 27, 1954; d. William Henry Theroux and Francis Regina La Salle; m. Gordon Hostetter Clark Jr., July 23, 1988; 1 child, Adam Arthur. BFA in Painting, U. Mass., 1976; MA in Painting, Edinboro U. Pa., 1994. Art tchr. King Philip Regional Sch. Dist., Wrentham, Mass., 1977-78, Holliston (Mass.) Pub. Schs., 1978-81, 87-88; dir. children's programs, adminstrv. asst. Newport Harbor Art Mus., Newport Beach, Calif., 1981-83; art tchr. Millis (Mass.) Pub. Schs., 1984-87; co-owner N.H. Artists Guild Gallery, Laconia, 1988-90; artist, owner Royal River Art Studio, Yarmouth, Maine, 1995—. Juror Fort Williams Arts Festival, New Eng. Exhibit, South Portland, Maine, 1996, 97. Bd. mem. Erie (Pa.) Art Mus., 1991-93, Florence Krittenon Home, Erie, 1991-92; vice chair Yarmouth Sch. Bd., 1997-99. Works exhibited at U. Ctrl. Fla., Orlando, 1989 (1st place award 1989), Lakes Region Festival of the Arts, Laconia, 1990 (1st place award 1990), So. Vt. Art Ctr., 1992, Chantauque (N.Y.) Arts Nat., 1993, Westmoreland Arts Nats., Latrobe, Pa., 1993, 94 (Heritage award 1994), Kennebeck Valley Art Assn., 1998. Democrat. Avocations: running, tennis, mountain climbing, gardening. Home: 10 Park St Yarmouth ME 04096-7757 Office: Royal River Art Studio 161 E Elm St Yarmouth ME 04096-7109 E-mail: RyeRvrArt@aol.com.

CLARK, GARY CARL, lawyer; b. Flippin, Ark., Mar. 4, 1947; m. Jane W. Clark; children: Ross, Lauren. BS in Agrl. Edn., Okla. State U., 1969, MS, 1972; JD with honors, U. Tex., 1975. Bar: Okla. 1975, U.S. Dist. Ct. (no. dist.) Okla. 1975, U.S. Ct. Appeals (10th cir.) 1979. Tchr. Laverne H.S., Okla., 1969—70; assoc. Conner, Winters, Ballaine, Barry & McGowen, 1975—81, ptnr., 1981, Baker & Hoster, Tulsa, 1981—97; dir. Crowe & Dunlevy, PC, Tulsa, 1997—2004; v.p., gen. counsel Okla. State U. Found., Stillwater, 2004—. Lawyer-staffed Panel of Ct. Appeals, 1991; speaker in field. Vol. Legal Svcs. Ea. Okla., 1993—; trustee Okla. State Univ., Tulsa, 1999-2001; mem. bd. regents Okla. State Univ. and A&M Colls., 1993-2001, chmn., 1997-98; past v.p. Jane Addams Elem. Sch. PTA, sch. vol.; chair site adv.; mem. Okla. Jud. Evaluation Com., 1999—. Recipient Silver Beaver award Boy Scouts Am., 1996. Fellow Am. Coll. Trust and Estate Coun., Am. Bar Found., Okla. Bar Found. (trustee); mem. Okla. Bar Assn. (pres. 2002, bd. govs. 1997-99, 2001-2003, John Shipp Ethics award 1999, chair estate planning and probate sect. 1988-89, vice chair probate code com. 1991, bd. dirs. young lawyers divsn., mem. real property sect.), Tulsa County Bar Assn. (pres. 1993-94, Golden Rule award 1993, Outstanding Sr. Lawyer 1996), Tulsa County Bar Found. (pres. 1994-95, treas. 1995-99, charter fellow), Tulsa Title and Probate Lawyers Assn. (pres. 1989-90), Okla. State U. Alumni Assn. (life), FFA Alumni Assn. (life), Order of Coif, Alpha Gamma Rho Alumni Assn. (Okla. chpt. dir., past pres.), Phi Delta Phi. Home: 5505 S 97th West Ave Sand Springs OK 74063-4726 Office: OSU Found 400 S Monroe Stillwater OK 74076 Office Phone: 405-385-5146. Business E-Mail: gclark@osuf.org.

CLARK, GARY R., newspaper editor; b. Cleve., June 27, 1946; s. Dale Francis and Mary Louise (Rozeski) C.; m. Caryn Elaine Helm, Dec. 18, 1976; children: Jessica Lynn, Brian Michael. BA, Ohio State U., 1973, MA, 1978. Reporter Chronicle-Telegram, Elyria, Ohio, 1973-77, The Plain Dealer, Cleve., 1978-88, state editor, 1988-89, nat. editor, 1989, city editor, 1989-90, mng. editor, 1990—2000; city editor The Columbus Dispatch, 2000—02; mng. editor for news The Denver Post, 2003—. Tchg. assoc. Ohio State U., Columbus, 1977-78; juror, Pulitzer Prize, 1996. Sgt. USMC, 1966-69, Vietnam. Recipient Best of Show award, Ohio Soc. Profl. Journalists, 1999. Mem. AP Mng. Editors, Am. Soc. Newspaper Editors, Investigative Reporters and Editors, Cleve. City Club. Office: Mng Ed Denver Post 1560 Broadway Denver CO 80202

CLARK, GERDA MARGARETE, special education educator; d. Rudolf Weiner and Anna Maria Bader; 1 child, John Thomas. Diploma, Moody Bible Inst., 1969; MA, Northeastern Ill. U., 1992. Cert. learning and behavior specialist I Ill. State Bd. Edn., adminstrv. type 75 Ill. State Bd. Edn. German tchr. Gordon Tech. H.S., Chgo., 1975—89; learning disability tchr. and physically disabled facilitator Harvey (Ill.) Sch. Dist. 152, 1996—97; spl. edn. tchr. Chgo. Bd. of Edn., 1997—. Recipient Outstanding H.S. Tchr. award, U. Chgo., 1980, Tutoring award, Northeastern Ill. U., 1995; scholar Fortbildungskurs für Lehrer, Goethe Inst. of Chgo., 1980; Robert Bosch scholar, U. Ill. at Chgo., 1975, gifted fellow, Ill. State Bd. Edn., 1990—91. Mem.: ASCD, Am. Ednl. Rsch. Assn., Chgo. Bot. Garden. Home: 3716 N Richmond St Chicago IL 60618 Personal E-mail: clark6905@sbcglobal.net.

CLARK, GLEN EDWARD, judge; b. Cedar Rapids, Iowa, Nov. 23, 1943; s. Robert M. and Georgia L. (Welch) C.; m. Deanna D. Thomas, July 16, 1966; children: Andrew Curtis, Carissa Jane. BA, U. Iowa, 1966; JD, U. Utah, 1971. Bar: Utah 1971, U.S. Dist. Ct. Utah 1971, U.S. Ct. Appeals (10th cir.) 1972. Assoc. Fabian & Clendenin, 1971-74, ptnr., 1975-81, dir., chmn. banking and comml. law sect., 1981-82; judge U.S. Bankruptcy Ct. Dist. Utah, Salt Lake City, 1982-86, chief judge, 1986—. Bd. govs. nat. Conf. Bankruptcy Judges, 1988-94; mem. com. on bankruptcy edn. Fed. Jud. Ctr., 1989-92; vis. prof. U. Utah, Salt Lake City, 1977-79, 83; pres. Nat. Conf. Bankruptcy Judges, 1992-93; chair bd. trustees Nat. Conf. Bankruptcy Judges Endowment for Edn., 1990-92; vis. assoc. prof. law Univ. Utah; instr. adv. bus. law Univ. Utah. Articles editor: Utah Law Review. With U.S. Army, 1966-68. Finkbine fellow U. Iowa. Fellow Am. Coll. Bankruptcy (charter, mem. bd. regents 1995-2000, dir. found. 2002-03); mem. Jud. Conf. U.S. (mem. com. jud. br. 1992-99, 10th cir. bankruptcy appellate panel 1996—), Utah Bar Assn., Order of Coif. Presbyterian. Office: 365 US Courthouse 350 S Main St Salt Lake City UT 84101-2106

CLARK, GORDON HOSTETTER, JR., physician; b. New Haven, Aug. 5, 1947; s. Gordon Hostetter and Elizabeth Master (Mapes) C.; m. Gail Marie Theroux, July 23, 1988; children: Emily Blakeslee Clark Ehl, Christopher Robert, Heather Mays Richmond, Adam Arthur. BA, Yale U., 1970; MDiv, Pacific Sch. Religion, 1973; MD, George Washington U., 1977. Diplomate Am. Bd. Psychiatry and Neurology, Am. Bd. Med. Mgmt., Am. Coll. Physician Execs.; cert. in adminstrv. psychiatry, APA, 1992; cert. physician exec. Commn. in Med. Mgmt., 1998. Intern, then resident, then fellow Dartmouth-Hitchcock Med. Ctr., Hanover, N.H., 1977-81; staff psychiatrist Lakes Region Med. Health Ctr., Laconia, N.H., 1981-82, med. dir., 1982-86; dir. psychiat. unit Lakes Region Gen. Hosp., Laconia, 1986-89; med. dir. behavioral svcs. St. Vincent Health Ctr., Erie, Pa., 1990-93; dir. med./profl. adminstrn. Deerfield Mgmt. Group, Erie, Pa., 1991-94; pres. Deerfield Profl. Assocs., 1992-94; med. advisor Deerfield Behavioral Health Network, 1994-95; sr. psychiat. cons. Med. Groups Divsn. Maine Harvard Cmty. Health Plan, Portland, Maine, 1995-96; pres., med. dir. Integrated Behavioral Healthcare, Portland, Maine, 1995—; med. dir. Behavioral Health Network of Maine, 1995-99, Augusta (Maine) Mental Health Inst., 1995-96; assoc. med. dir. Maine Dept. Mental Health and Mental Retardation, Augusta, 1995-96; med. dir. med.-psychiat. program Westbrook (Maine) Comty. Hosp., 1996-97; sr. physician advisor CMG Healthsource Maine, Maine, 1996-97. Adj. asst. prof. clin. psychiatry Dartmouth Med. Sch., Hanover, 1983-90; clin. asst. prof. psychiatry U. Pitts. Sch. Medicine, 1990-96; clin. assoc. prof. psychiatry U. Vt. Med. Sch., 1996—2004; chmn. com. psychiatrists in NH Cmty. Mental Health Ctrs., Concord, 1982-86; med. liaison to Pa. Office Mental Health and Mental Retardation and Erie County Office Mental Health and Mental Retardation, 1991-94; bd. dirs. Med. Network, Inc., credentials com. 1995-98, med. mgmt. com. 2002—, med. dir. depression mgmt. program, 2002—; New Eng. region adv. com. Cigna Behavioral Health Care, 2000-2001; New Eng. region pharmacy and therapeutics com. Cigna Health Care, 2000, nat. pharmacy and therapeutics com., 2001; depression work group MaineHealth, 2002—; mem. provider adv. com., quality mgmt. improvement com. Anthem Behavioral Health, 2004—. Exec. v.p. Erie Phiharm., 1991—92. Recipient Exemplary Psychiatrist award Nat. Alliance for Mentally Ill, 1992; recipient Benjamin Manchester award George Washington U., 1977. Fellow: Am. Coll. Physician Execs., Am. Assn. Social Psychiatry (mem. coun. 1993—99), Am. Coll. Mental Health Adminstrn., Am. Psychiat. Assn. (disting.) (examiner oral part of exams. cert. adminstrn. psychiatry 1993—96, com. on stds. and survey procedures 1998—2001, APA/Bristol-Myers Squibb fellowship selection com. 1999—2002, task force develop guidlines psychiat. practice mental health ctrs., com. state and cmty. psychiatry sys., com. chronically mentally ill, Falk fellow 1979—81); mem.: Maine Psychiat. Assn. (chair program com. 1996—97), We. Pa. Psychiat. Soc. (pres. elect 1992—94), Psychiat. Physicians Pa. (fed. legis. rep. pbu. psychiatry com. 1993—94, treas. 1994, coun., govt. rels. com.), Nat. Psychiatric Alliance (chmn. med. staff com. 1992—94, exec. com. 1992—95), Am. Coll. Psychiatrists, Am. Assn. Psychiat. Adminstrs. (coun. 1996—97, pres.-elect 1997—99, pres. 1999—2001), Am. Assn. Cmty. Psychiatrists (founding pres. 1984—90, bd. dirs. 1984—92, com. psychiat. practice in cmty. mental health ctrs. guideline devel., Disting. Svc. award 1990). Avocations: skiing, biking, hiking, golf. Home: 10 Park St Yarmouth ME 04096-7757 Office: Integrated Behavioral Healthcare 1 Forest Ave Portland ME 04101-2810 Office Phone: 207-761-4761.

CLARK, H. WESTLEY, health facility administrator; BA, Wayne State U., 1969; MD, MPH, U. Mich., 1974; JD, Harvard U., 1981. Diplomate Am. Bd. Psychiatry and Neurology. Past chief assoc. substance abuse programs VA Med. Ctr., San Francisco; dir. Ctr. Substance Abuse Treatment, Rockville, Md., 1998—. Sr. program cons. Robert Wood Johnson Substance Abuse Policy Program; assoc. clin. prof. psychiatry U. Calif., San Francisco; adv. bd. Treatment-on-Demand Planning Coun., San Francisco. Contbr. articles to profl. jours., chpts. to books. Grantee Nat. Inst. Drug Abuse. Mem. Am. Soc. Addiction Medicine (cert., nat. bd. dirs.). Office: Ctr Substance Abuse Treatment 5600 Fishers Ln Rockwall II Ste 618 Rockville MD 20857-0001

CLARK, HATTIE GILES, real estate broker, real estate appraiser; b. Meridian, Miss., Apr. 2, 1938; d. Willie and Luida (Lockett) Giles; m. William Clark, Aug. 8, 1960; children: William, Reginald. AS, Bishop State Jr. Coll., Mobile, Ala., 1959; BS, Ala. State U., 1961; MLS, Atlanta U., 1967. Cert. fund raising exec. Nat. Soc. Fund Raising. Libr., tchr. Mobile County Pub. High Sch., 1961-70; instr. libr. sci. Bishop State Jr. Coll., 1970-81, dir. tng. and devel., 1981-84, dir. alumni affairs, 1981-89; founder Property Realty Inc., Mobile, 1974—2003. Bd. dirs. Mobile United, 1981-83, Mobile Mental Health, 1982-2004, Mobile Mental Health Found., 1983-85. Mem. Coalition 100 Black Women, Delta Sigma Theta (Delta of Yr. award 1978). Democrat. Baptist. Avocations: tennis, reading, gardening. Home: 711 S Atmore Ave Mobile AL 36612-1901 Office: Property Realty Inc 1556 St Stephens Rd Mobile AL 36603-5033 Office Phone: 251-438-1547. E-mail: clark2587@bellsouth.net.

CLARK, HOWARD LONGSTRETH, JR., finance company executive, director; b. N.Y.C., Feb. 1, 1944; s. Howard Longstreth and Elsie (Dancaster) C.; m. Karen K. Burke, July 25, 1992; 1 child by previous marriage, Howard Longstreth III. BSBA, Boston U., 1967; MBA, Columbia U., 1968. Exec. v.p., chief fin. officer Am. Express Co., N.Y.C., 1981-90; vice chmn. Lehman Bros., Inc. Bd. dirs. The Maytag Co., White Mountains Ins. Group, Ltd., Walter Industries, Inc., United Rentals, Inc. Mem.: River, Racquet and Tennis, Round Hill, Blind Brook, Links, Seminole, Jupiter Island, Nantucket Golf. Episcopalian. Home: 404 Round Hill Rd Greenwich CT 06831-2637 Office: Lehman Bros Inc 745 7th Ave Fl 20 New York NY 10019 Office Phone: 212-526-6255. E-mail: hclark@lehman.com.

CLARK, I. E., publisher; b. Schulenburg, Tex., Dec. 9, 1919; s. Harvey Robert and Annie Ruby (Miekow) C.; m. Lila Rhea Norwood, Sept. 1, 1945; children: Candace Ann, Robin Rhea. BA, U. Tex., 1941, MA, 1945. Rancher, 1945-95; tchr., theatre dir., publs. dir., lang. arts coord. Schulenberg Pub. Schs., 1945-77; founder, owner I.E. Clark, Publs. pub. plays and books for theatre, 1959—. Tchr. Newspaper Fund seminars U. Tex. at Austin, summers, 1961-66; regional observer for Nat. Observer, 1961; mem. Tex. Edn. Agy. Commn. for Lang. Arts Curriculum Revision, 1958-59, State Com. Devel. of Speech-Drama Publ. of Tex. Edn. Agy., 1960-61. Author: (plays) Twelve Dancing Princesses, 1969, Hansel and Gretel, 1970, It's A Dungaree World, 1974, Once Upon a Texas, 1985; also several one-act plays including The Christmas Dream, transl. into Spanish, produced TV, Ecuador, 1973; (Tex. Sesquicentennial pageant) Fate of Fayette, 1986. Mem. Fayette County Hist. Survey Com., 1969—; founder, artistic dir., bd. dirs., officer Backstage, Inc., Fine Arts Coun. for South Ctrl. Tex., 1969—; adv. dir. 1st Nat. Bank of Schulenburg, 1974-80; Dem. precinct chmn. Fayette County Dem. Exec. Com., 1955-80; county campaign chmn. Lyndon B. Johnson, 1949, 55; area campaign chmn. Tex. Lt. Gov. Bill Hobby, 1972; bd. dirs. Schulenberg Hist. Soc. Recipient Finest Journalism Tchr. in Tex. award U. Tex. Interscholastic League, 1967, Outstanding Citizen award Colorado Valley Coun. on Drug and Alcohol Abuse, 1990; Order Golden Quill, 1977; named Hon. State Farmer, Future Farmers Am., 1956; Newspaper Fund fellow, 1959. Mem. Am. Theatre Assn. (nat. chmn. play publs. panel 1977, editor Secondary Sch. Theatre Jour. 1982-83), S.W. Theatre Assn. (hon., life), Dramatists Guild, Am. Alliance for Theatre and Edn., Tex. Secondary Theatre Conf. (dir., Newsletter editor 1966-69, mem. Interscholastic League adv. com.), Tex. Ednl. Theatre Assn. (Founders award 1985), Modern Music Masters (hon., life), Masons, Phi Beta Kappa, Delta Tau Delta, Sigma Delta Chi, Phi Eta Sigma. Methodist. Home and Office: PO Box 246 Schulenburg TX 78956-0246 Office Phone: 979-743-3232. E-mail: email@ieclark.com.

CLARK, JACK, retired health facility administrator; b. Munford, Ala., Feb. 23, 1932; s. Raymond E. and Ora (Camp) C.; m. Louise Omega Lackey, Jan. 30, 1951; 1 son, Terry Wayne. BS, Springhill Coll., Mobile, Ala., 1960. Staff acct. Max E. Miller, C.P.A., Mobile, 1960-62; comptr. Mobile Gen. Hosp., 1962-67; assoc. adminstr. fin. Univ. Med. Ctr., Mobile, 1967-74; regional mgr. Humana Inc., Mobile, 1974-75, v.p., 1975-80, sr. v.p., 1980-84, exec. v.p., 1984-93, Galen Health Care, Mobile, 1993-94; ret. Columbia-HCA Healthcare, 1994. Trustee Mid-South region Humana hosps., 1974-87, Southwestern region, 1987-89, region IV, 1989-91, region 2, 1991-93, Regional Hosps., Columbia/HCA, 1994—. Bd. dirs. Agape S. Ala., Mobile, 1983, Rainbow Omega, 2000—; trustee Faulkner U., Montgomery, Ala., 1993—. Served in USAF, 1952-56, Korea. Mem. Hosp. Fin. Mgmt. Assn. (assoc.), Am. Hosp. Assn., Ala. Hosp. Assn., Ala. Hosp. Assn. Accts. (pres. so. council, dir. 1967-68), Mobile C. of C. Democrat. Mem. Ch. of Christ. Home: 6449 Canebrake Rd Mobile AL 36695-3817

CLARK, JACK IVOR, civil engineer, researcher; BSc, Acadia U., 1955; B Engring., Tech. U. N.S., Can., 1957; PhD in Civil Engring., NS Tech. Coll., Can., 1970; MSc, U. Alta., Can., 1961; DEng honoris causa, Tech. U. NS, 1993; DSc (hon.), Laurentian U., 1998. With major civil engring. projects, 1957—; dir. Ctr. for Cold Ocean Resources Engring. Meml. U. Nfld., St. John's, Can, 1984-91, 1st pres., CEO, Ctr. for Cold Ocean Resources Engring., 1991-97, prin. cons. Ctr. for Cold Odean Resources Engring., 1997—. Past editor Can. Geotech. Jour. Decorated officer Order of Can.; recipient R.M. Hardy keynote address, 1996, Roger J.E. Brown award, 1996, Queen's Golden Jubilee Anniversary medal, 2002; Karl Terzaghi fellow Norwegian Tech. Inst., 1997, MMS Corp. Leadership award Minerals Mgmt. Svc., USDA, 1999, 25th Anniversary Achievement award Nfld. Ocean Industries Assn., 2002, Gold Medal award Can. Coun. Profl. Engrs., 2005. Fellow Engring. Inst. Can. (Julian C. Smith medal 1987), Can. Soc. Civil Engrs.; mem. Can. Acad. Engring., Nat. Scis. and Engring. Coun. (v.p., exec. com. for coun. 1988-94), Can. Geotech. Rsch. Bd. (chmn. 1991-94), Founds. for Offshore Structures (chmn. Can. Stds. Assn. Com. S472), Can. Geotech. Soc. (G. Geoffrey Meyerhof award 1995). Office: C-CORE Saint John's NL Canada A1B 3X5 E-mail: Jack.Clark@c-core.ca.

CLARK, JAMES ALLEN, lawyer, educator; b. Canton, Ill., Nov. 13, 1948; s. Howard R. and Helen (McElwain) C. BS in Edn., BA in Polit. Sci., Miami U., Oxford, Ohio, 1971; MS in Urban Studies, Cleve. State U., 1974; JD, Case Western Res. U., 1977. Bar: U.S. Dist. Ct. (no. dist.) Ohio 1977, U.S. Ct. Appeals (6th cir.) 1978, U.S. Dist. Ct. (no. dist.) Ill. 1979, U.S. Ct. Appeals (7th cir.) 1980, U.S. Supreme Ct. 1981, U.S. Ct. Appeals (D.C. cir.) 1985, U.S. Dist. Ct. (ea. dist.) Wis. 1986, U.S. Ct. Appeals (8th cir.) 1994. Law clk. U.S. Dist. Ct., Cleve., 1977-79; assoc. Schiff Hardin & Waite, Chgo., 1979-85, ptnr., 1985-; prof. De Paul U. Law Sch., Chgo., 1985—. Mem. Order of the Coif. Office: Schiff Hardin & Waite 7200 Sears Tower Chicago IL 60606 Business E-Mail: jclark@schiffhardin.com.

CLARK, JAMES BENTON, retired rail transportation executive; b. Sweetwater, Tenn., Jan. 3, 1914; s. John Edgar and Nancy Ella (Webster) C.; m. Maxine Jeanette Butcher, Oct. 14, 1939; children— Diana Clark Hudgens, Sylvia Clark Pulliam. BS, U. Tenn., 1937; grad. transport course, Northwestern U., 1959. Registered profl. engr. Ky. Coop. student Bur. Pub. Rds., 1934-36; with Louisville & Nashville R.R., 1937-74, asst. dir. personnel, 1955-59, chief engr., 1959-69, asst. v.p. personnel and labor relations, 1969-73, v.p. personnel and labor relations, 1973-74; v.p. ops. Seaboard Coast Line R.R., Jacksonville, Fla., 1974-76, v.p. exec. dept., 1976; cons. Louisville, 1976-81, Franklin, Ky., 1982—. Pvt. industry council Barren River Area Devel. Dist., 1985-91; mem. Nat. Ry. Labor Conf., Southeastern Carriers Conf. Com., 1969-73. Chmn. bd. trustees Simpson County Libr. Dist., 1989-92; mem. Simpson County (Ky.) Solid Waste Mgmt. Bd., 1990-93, chmn., 1993. Mem. Am. Ry. Engrng. Assn. (life, bd. dirs. 1965-68, v.p. 1969), Franklin-Simpson County C. of C. (pres. 1986), Chi Epsilon. Baptist. Home: 305 Hillcrest St Franklin KY 42134-2374 Personal E-mail: jimclark@bowlinggreen.net.

CLARK, JAMES COVINGTON, journalist, historian; b. Washington, May 22, 1947; s. William Edward and Louise (Covington) C.; children: Randall Healy, Kevin Healy. BA, Lenoir-Rhyne Coll., 1975; MA, Stetson U., 1986; PhD, U. Fla., 1998. Reporter UPI, Washington, 1967, Columbia (S.C.) Record, 1968, AP, Charlotte, N.C., 1969-70, Phila., 1972-73, Hickory (N.C.) Daily Record, 1974-75; regional editor Tampa (Fla.) Tribune, 1976-77; asst. exec. editor The Orlando (Fla.) Sentinel, 1977-98; syndicated columnist UP Syndicate, 1997-99; editor, pub. Orlando mag., 2000—. Instr. U. Ctrl. Fla., Orlando, 1986—. Author: Last Train South, 1984, Faded Glory: Presidents Out of Power, 1985, The Murder of James Garfield, 1994, Trips Through Florida History, 2000. Recipient George Polk award L.I. U., 1983, Gerald Loeb award, L.A., 1983, Arthur Thompson prize Fla. Hist. Soc., Gainesville, 1989. Mem. Authors Guild, Orgn. Am. Historians, Am. Hist. Assn. Personal E-mail: clarknews@aol.com.

CLARK, JAMES E., lawyer; b. Washington, Sept. 2, 1948; AB, Brown U., 1970; JD, U. Chgo., 1976. Bar: Ill. 1976. Ptnr. comml. law Sidley Austin Brown & Wood LLP (formerly Sidley & Austin), Chgo. Mem. faculty Practicing Law Inst., 1989. Lt. USN, 1970-72. Mem. ABA (chmn., subcom. acquisition fin. commercial fin. svcs. com. Bus law sect. 1990—94), Chgo. Bar Assn., Ill. State Bar Assn., Fellow Am. Coll. Comml. Fin. Lawyers, Phi Beta Kappa. Office: Sidley Austin Brown & Wood LLP Bank One Plz 10 S Dearborn St Chicago IL 60603 Office Phone: 312-853-7776. Office Fax: 312-853-7036. Business E-Mail: jclark@sidley.com.

CLARK, JAMES H., former software company executive, real estate company executive; b. Ft. Worth, Tex., 1944; BS in Physics, U. New Orleans, 1970; MS in Physics, Louisiana State U., 1971; PhD in Computer sci., U. Utah, 1974, DSc (hon.), 1995. Assoc. prof. Stanford U.; founder, chmn. bd. Silicon Graphics, Inc., 1981—94; co-founder (with Marc Andreessen), chmn. Netscape Communications (formerly Mosaic Comm. Corp.), 1994—2001; chmn. & founder myCFO, Mountain View, Calif., 1999—2002; co-chair WebMD (formerly Healtheon/WebMD), 1999—2000; chmn. Shutterfly, 2000, Neoteris, 2001—02; with Hyperion Devel. Group, Fla., 2003—. Bd. dirs. Paracomp. Author: Netscape Time: The Making Of The Billion-Dollar Start-Up That Took On Microsoft. Fellow Am. Acad. Arts & Sci.; mem. NAE. Office: Hyperion Devel Group 724 NE 2nd Ave Miami FL 33132*

CLARK, JAMES JOSEPH, lawyer; b. SI, Dec. 5, 1954; s. James J. and Patricia A. (Bruns) C.; m. Cynthia Ann Jorgensen, Aug. 29, 1980 (div.); 1 child, Caroline; m. Cristina Maria Arico, Nov. 29, 1997. BS, Stonehill Coll., 1976; JD, Albany Law Sch., 1979. Bar: NY 1980, Calif. 1987. Assoc. Cahill Gordon & Reindel LLP, NYC, 1979—87, ptnr., 1987—. Editor-in-chief Albany Law Rev., 1978-79. Mem. ABA, NY State Bar Assn. Republican. Roman Catholic. Avocation: sports. Office: Cahill Gordon & Reindel LLP 80 Pine St New York NY 10005 Office Phone: 212-701-3849. Office Fax: 212-378-2169. E-mail: JClark@cahill.com.

CLARK, JAMES KERMIT, JR., real estate executive; b. Atlanta, Nov. 17, 1942; s. George W. and Jean (Scutaro) K. BBA, U. Ga., 1965; grad., Realtor Inst. Ga., 1973. Lic. real estate broker, Ga. Chief appraiser First Fed. Savs. & Loan Assn., Atlanta, 1965-67; comml. appraiser Draper-Owens Co., Atlanta, 1967-69; pres. Tri-City Comml. Sales, Inc., College Park, Ga., 1969—2002; exec. v.p. Group VI Corp., Peachtree City, Ga., 1993—. Dir. Student Leadership Univ. Dir. Second Wind Ministries; advisor Bible Tng. Ctr. for Pastors; lead lay counselor First Bapt. Ch., Atlanta. Mem. Nat. Assn. Realtors, Ga. Assn. Realtors, Atlanta Bd. Realtors (comml. adv. coun., comml. dir. and ethics com., chmn. equal opportunity com. 1986-90), Million Dollar Club (active life; Phoenix award, Silver Phoenix award), Atlanta C. of C. (Southside devel. task force 1972), Phi Kappa Alpha, Rho Epsilon Real Estate Fraternity. Republican. Baptist. Office: 900 W Park Dr Ste 300 Peachtree City GA 30269-3521

CLARK, JAMES MILFORD, retired college president; b. Mich., Apr. 11, 1930; s. Roy Wesley and Florence (Grice) C.; m. Patricia Ann Haynes, Mar. 11, 1960; children— Pamela, Matthew, Timothy. BA, U. Mich., 1952, PhD (Horace H. Rackham fellow), 1962; MA, U. Philippines, 1955; Doctor (hon.), U. North London, 1993; Dr. (hon.), Capital Normal U., Beijing, 1994. Fulbright travel grantee, France, 1955-56; teaching fellow U. Mich., 1957-59; asst. prof. polit. sci. U. Maine, Orono, 1960-64, asso. prof., 1964-79, asst. to pres., 1966-68, v.p. for acad. affairs, 1968-79; pres. SUNY Coll., Cortland, 1979-95; ret., 1995. Fulbright lectr. U. Toulouse (France), 1965-66; mem. Com. on Internat. Exchange Scholars, 1988-92. Author: Teachers and Politics in France, 1967. Chmn. Maine Health Planning Coun., 1970-72, mem. exec. com., 1972-76; bd. dirs. Penobscot Valley United Fund, 1972-77, Cortland County United Way, 1979-85, Eden Alternative, Inc., 2002-05; bd. overseers Rockefeller Inst. Govt., 1988-91; mem. N.Y. State Citizens com. on Bicentennial of French Revolution, 1988-90; mem. Tioughnioga Waterfront Devel. Commn., 2000--, Cortland Rural Cemetary Found. (mem. bd. dirs 2002-); With U.S. Army, 1952-55. Mem. Nat. Assn. State Univs. and Land-Grant Colls. (exec. com. council for acad. affairs 1971-76, sec. council 1974-76), Am. Assn. State Colls. and Univs. (N.Y. rep. 1979-81), Phi Beta Kappa, Phi Kappa Phi, Phi Eta Sigma, Pi Sigma Alpha, Sigma Phi Epsilon.

CLARK, JAMES RICHARD, lawyer; b. Madison, Wis., Mar. 30, 1946; s. James F. and Gloria J. Clark; m. Martha C. Conrad, Mar. 18, 1950; children: Lindsey Kelley, Chad. BA, Ripon Coll., 1968; JD, U. Wis., 1971. Bar: Wis. 1971, U.S. Dist. Ct. (we. and ea. dists.) Wis. 1972, U.S. Ct. Appeals (7th cir.) 1973, U.S. Dist. Ct. (no. dist.) Ill. 1974, U.S. Supreme Ct. 1976. Assoc. Foley & Lardner, Milw., 1971-78, ptnr., 1978—. Editor-in-chief Wis. Law Rev., 1971. Trustee Ripon Coll., 1985—. 1st lt. U.S. Army, 1971. Mem. ABA, Am. Coll. Trial Lawyers, Am. Bd. Trial Advs., Def. Rsch. Inst., 7th Cir. Bar Assn., Wis. Bar Assn., Ripon Coll. Alumni Assn. (past pres.), Milw. Athletic Club, Tripoli Country Club, Order of Coif, Phi Beta Kappa. Home: 9719 N Dalewood Ln Mequon WI 53092-6210 Office: Foley & Lardner Firstar Ctr 777 E Wisc Ave Milwaukee WI 53202 Office Phone: 414-297-5543. Business E-Mail: jclark@foley.com.

CLARK, JANET EILEEN, political scientist, educator; b. Kansas City, Kans., June 5, 1940; d. Edward Francis and Mildred Lois (Mack) Morrissey; m. Caleb M. Clark, Sept. 28, 1968; children: Emily Claire, Grace Ellen, Evelyn Adair. AA, Kansas City Jr. Coll., 1960; AB, George Washington U., 1962, MA, 1964; PhD, U. Ill., 1973. Staff US Dept. Labor, Washington, 1962-64; instr. social sci. Kans. City Jr. Coll., Kans., 1964-67; instr. polit. sci. Parkland Coll., 1970-71; asst. prof. govt. N.Mex. State U., Las Cruces, 1971-77, assoc. prof., 1977-80; assoc. prof. polit. sci. U. Wyo., 1981-84, prof., 1984-94; prof. polit. sci., head dept. U. West Ga., Carrollton, 1994—. Co-author: Women, Elections and Representation, 1987, The Equality State, 1988, Women in Taiwan Politics: Overcoming Barriers to Women's Participation in a Modernizing Society, 1990; editor Women and Politics, 1991-2000; contbr. articles to profl. jours. Wolcott fellow, 1963-64, NDEA Title IV fellow, 1967-69. Mem. Internat. Soc. Polit. Psychology (gov. coun., 1987-89), NEA (pres. chpt. 1978-79), Am. Polit. Sci. Assn., We. Polit. Sci. Assn. (exec. coun. 1984-87), Western Social Sci. Assn. (exec. coun. 1978-81, v.p. 1982, pres. 1985), Women's Caucus for Polit. Sci. (treas. 1982, pres. 1987), LWV (exec. bd. 1980-83, 2002-2003, treas. 1986-90, pres. 1991-93, 2004-06), Women's Polit. Caucus, Beta Sigma Phi (v.p. chpt. 1978-79, sec. 1987-88, treas. 1988-89, v.p. 1989-90, pres. 1990-91), Phi Beta Kappa Chi Omega (prize 1962), Phi Kappa Phi. Home: 2507 Waterford Rd Auburn AL 36832-4113 Office: U West Georgia Dept Polit Sci Carrollton GA 30118-0001 Office Phone: 678-839-6504. Business E-Mail: jclark@westga.edu.

CLARK, JEANIE HALL, mathematics educator; d. James Cecil and Barbara Willard Hall; m. Katelynn Marie Clark, June 6, 1954; children: Randall Wayne, Matthew Kyle Romer. BS in Math., 1990, M of Curriculum and Instrn., 1995. Sec. acctg. Soails Ins., Stuard, Va., 1984—90; tchr. math. Henry County Schs., Martinsville, 1990—96, Patrick County High Sch., Stuart, 1997—2005. Head math dept. Patrick County High Sch., 2000—05. Mem.: Beta Ro. Home: 692 Dominion Valley Ln Stuart VA 24171 Office: Patrick County High Sch 215 Cougar Ln Stuart VA 24171

CLARK, JEFFREY RAPHIEL, research and development company executive; b. Provo, Utah, Sept. 29, 1953; s. Bruce Budge and Ouida (Raphiel) C.; m. Anne Margaret Eberhardt, Mar. 15, 1985; children: Jeffrey Raphiel, Mary Anne Elizabeth, Edward William Eberhardt. BS, Brigham Young U., 1977, MBA, 1979. CPA, Tex. Fin. analyst Exxon Coal USA, Inc., Houston, 1979-83; constrn. mgr. Gen. Homes, Inc., Houston, 1983-84; controller Liberty Data Products, Houston, 1984-86; v.p. Tech. Rsch. Assocs., Inc., Salt Lake City, 1987—2001, also dir., 1987—2001; contr. Internat. Sports Broadcasting, LLC, 2001—03, Masterbuilt Cos., Inc., Fairfax, Va., 2003—04, Gen. Sci. Corp., 2004—. Scoutmaster Boy Scouts Am., Salt Lake City, 1989-91. Mem. AICPA, Utah Inst. CPAs, Salt Lake C. of C. (legis. action com.), Salt Lake Country Club. Republican. Mem. Lds Ch. Avocations: skiing, golf, mountain climbing. Office: PO Box 708039 Sandy UT 84070-8039 Home: 329 E St SE #3 Washington DC 20003-4230

CLARK, JENNIE L., lawyer, webmaster; b. Spokane, Apr. 17, 1966; BS, Portland State U.; JD, U. Calif., San Francisco, 1997. Bar: Oreg. 2000. Pvt. practice, Portland, Oreg., 2000—. Office: Jennie L Clark Atty at Law LLC 1906 SW Madison St Portland OR 97205 Office Phone: 503-238-1010. Personal E-mail: trialanterayclark@yahoo.com. Business E-Mail: jennie@jennieclark.com.

CLARK, JENNIFER BABBIN, lawyer; b. N.Y.C., June 1, 1961; d. Malcolm J. and Fredlyn (Goodman) Babbin; m. William M. Clark, May 5, 1991; c. Benjamin Frederic, Stephanie Rae. BA, Brandeis U., 1983; JD, Boston U., 1986. Bar: N.Y. 1987, Mass. 1988. Assoc. Weil, Gotshal & Manges, N.Y.C., 1986-88, Sullivan & Worcester LLP, Boston, 1988-94, ptnr., 1994—99; v.p., gen. counsel Reit Mgmt. & Rsch., Newton, Mass., 1999—. Office: Reit Mgmt Rsch 400 Centre St Newton MA 02458

CLARK, JERE WALTON, economics professor, researcher; b. Rex, Ga., Jan. 31, 1922; s. Grover Cleveland and Jessie Beatrice (Butler) C.; m. Juanita Stone, June 13, 1947; children: Merrilyn, Melissa Clark Vickers. Student, Berry Coll., 1941-43; BBA, U. Ga., 1947, MA, 1949; PhD, U. Va., 1953. Asst. prof. W.Va. U., Morgantown, 1952-55; assoc. prof. U. Chattanooga, 1955-62; prof. econs. So. Conn. State U., New Haven, 1962-91, prof. emeritus econs., 1991—, chmn. econs. dept., 1962-71, 85-91. Dir. Ctr. for Interdisciplinary Creativity, 1966-91; pres. Quality Optimizer Assocs., 1991—; mem. Nat. Blue-Ribbon Expert Panel of Interdisciplinarians (Merit Commn. on Sci. Edn., New Mex.), 1992-93. Author: 10 book chpts., 1965-89; co-author: Full Circle...of Unified Science, 1974, (with Juanita S. Clark) The Joy Imperative, 2003; editor nat. yearbook Enterprising Teachers, 1963, 64, 65; mem. editorial bd. Jour. Creative Behavior, 1967-93, Gen. Systems Bull., 1968-72, Internat. Assns., 1970-72; contbr. articles to profl. jours. Moderator 12 TV panels on edn. Nat. League of Nursing, Chattanooga, 1961; author, narrator 60 radio econ-o-grams Nat./Joint Coun. Econ. Edn., New Haven, 1966; chmn. internat. task force on Gen. Systems Edn., SGSR, 1967-72. With U.S. Army, 1943-45, ETO. Recipient Best Coll. Course in Econs. for Tchrs. award Nat./Joint Coun. on Econ. Edn., 1965, 1st statewide Acad. Freedom Award in pub. higher edn. in Conn., 1992; grantee Kazanjian Found. (5), 1967-80, USOE/HEW, 1975-76. Mem.: Internat. Cooperation Coun. (mem. gen. adv. bd. 1976—78, charter), Conn. Consotium on Gen. Sys. (founding dir. 1968—75), World Future Soc. Conn. (pres. 1975—76), New Eng. Bus. Adminstrn. (bd. dirs. 1987—), Am. Econs. Assn., Creative Edn. Found. (colleague 1957—).

CLARK, JESSIE DONA, social worker; b. Rochester, N.Y., Feb. 28, 1922; m. James Governeau Banks, Jan. 23, 1943 (div. Nov. 1972); children: James Governeau Banks, Franklin Frazier Banks, David Robert Banks; m. Paul Andrews Clark, Jan. 21, 1973. BA, Howard U., 1947, MSW, 1960. Psychiat. social worker St. Elizabeths Hosp., Washington, 1960-65; family relocation officer D.C. Redey, Land Agy., 1965-73; supr. social worker Dept. Community Mental Health, St. Thomas, V.I., 1975; spl. asst. to comptroller V.I. Housing Auth., St. Thomas, 1975-85. Evaluator, vice chmn. Operation Sisters United, St. Thomas, 1975-83; cons. V.I. Labor Mgmt. Com., St. Thomas, 1984—; cons. human resources dept. U. V.I., 1992—; People to People amb. abroad.; mem. cmty. planning group HIV prevention V.I. Proper to People amb. del. ednl. exch. programs, Russia, 1991, South Africa, 1995, India and Nepal, 1997, China and Hong Kong, 1996, Cuba, 2002, 2003. Bd. dirs. YWCA (Phyllis Wheatley Br.), Washington; commr. Youth Coun., Washington, Vis. Nurses Assn., Washington, Ptnrs. for Health, St. Thomas (editor mo. newsletter 1988-89); mem. Bd. for HIV Prevention, 1999—. Recipient Disting. Lady award Plymouth Congl. Ch., 1967, Outstanding Performance award D.C. Redevelopment Agy., 1971; NIMH fellow 1957-60. Mem. Internat. Assn. Pers. Mgrs. (v.p.), Nat. Assn. Housing and Renewal Ofcls., NASW (pres. V.I. chpt. 1985-87, Social Worker of Yr. award 1983, V.I. Pioneer award 1998), Eta Phi Beta (v.p. 1988-89). Home: PO Box 8485 St Thomas VI 00801-1485

CLARK, JIM, communications executive; b. Plainview, Tex., 1945; BS in Physics, La. State U., MS in Physics, 1971; PhD in Computer Sci., U. Utah, 1974. Asst. prof. U. Calif., Santa Cruz, 1974-78; assoc. prof. Stanford (Calif.) U., 1979-82; founder, chmn. Silicon Graphics, 1982-94, myCFO; co-founder, chmn. Netscape Comms. Corp., Mountain View, Calif., 1994—; co-founder, bd. dir. Healtheon/WebMD, 1996—. Author: (book) Netscape Time: the Making of the Billion-Dollar Start-Up that Took Microsoft. Office: AOL Netscape Comm 466 Ellis St Mountain View CA 94043-4042 Office Phone: 650-254-1900. Office Fax: 650-528-4129.

CLARK, JOAN HARDY, retired journalist; b. Toronto, Ont., Can., Apr. 17, 1934; came to the U.S., 1960; d. Henry Robert Hardy and Irene Elsie Stevens; children: Lisa Anne Hanson, Anthony David Stuart Hanson. BA, Carleton U., Ottawa, Can., 1954; postgrad., Sarah Lawrence Coll., 1973-75. Co-chmn. internat. coun. World Monuments Fund, 2004—; bd. dirs. N.Y. Pub. Libr., N.Y.C., 1996—, chmn. coun. conservators, 1986—2001, hon. chmn., 2001—; mem. exec. com. Whitney Nat. Com., 2003—; bd. dirs. Whitney Mus., N.Y.C., 1984—2003. Mem. Cosmopolitan Club. Home: 1 Gracie Sq New York NY 10028-8001 also: Deer Meadow Farm Andover VT 05143

CLARK, JOHN, corporate financial executive; Asst. contr. Avnet, Inc., Culver City, Calif., 1983, held various positions such as customer contracts mgr. and mgr. of budget and sales admin. Calif., ops. mgr. sales office Chatsworth, Calif., ops. mgr. for the S.W. area Calif., dist. sales mgr., Huges Aircraft sales and support team, dir. kitting ops.; running of the corp. adminstrn. orgn. Avnet Electronics Mktg.; v.p. and dir ops., computer mktg. group Avnet Computers Mktg.; apptd. to head up the Total Quality Mgmt. efforts Avnet, EM, 1992—95; group fin. officer Avnet, CM, 1997—2003; named v.p., dir. of N. Am. credit and collection Avnet, Inc., 2003. Moved admin. ops. to it's new home in, Phoenix, 1996. Office: Avnet Inc 2211 S 47th St Phoenix AZ 85034

CLARK, JOHN F., aerospace engineering educator; b. Reading, Pa., Dec. 12, 1920; s. John F. Clark and Edith Dix (Long) Guenther; m. June Teubner Schweiger, July 14, 1974; children from previous marriage: Linda J. Marks, James C. BSEE with honors, Lehigh U., 1942, EE, 1947; MS in Math., George Washington U., 1946; PhD in Physics, U. Md., 1956. Registered profl. engr., N.J. Electronic engr. Naval Rsch. Lab., 1942-47, physicist, atmospheric electricity br. head, 1948-58; asst. prof. elec. engring. Lehigh U., 1947-48; dir. physics and astronomy programs NASA, 1958-63, dep. assoc. adminstr. space sci. and applications (scis.), 1963-65, chmn. space sci. steering com., 1963-65; dir. Goddard Space Flight Center, 1965-76; dir. space applications and tech. RCA Corp., Princeton, N.J., 1976-86; part-time cons. Gen. Electric Astro Space Div., 1987-88; NAVSPACE rsch. prof. U.S. Naval Acad. aerospace engrng. dept., Annapolis, Md., 1988-90; dir. grad. studies, prof. space sytems Fla. Inst. Tech. Spaceport Grad. Ctr., 1990—. Part-time lectr. math. George Washington U., 1956-58; part-time cons. rsch. Grad. Coun., 1960-66; part-time lectr. physics U. Md., 1958; mem. indsl. and profl. adv. coun. Pa. State U., 1963-65; mem. vis. com. physics Lehigh U., 1966-74; mem. Com. on Fed. Labs., 1971-75, Md. Gov.'s Sci. Adv. Coun., 1972-76, N.J. Gov.'s Sci. Adv. Com., 1980-86, Am. Geophys. Union-URSI Bd. Radio Sci., 1974-78; mem. study panel Office Telecommunications, Nat. Assembly Engring., 1976-77; chmn. adv. com. FCC, 1981-83; mem. U.S. del. to Internat. Telecommunication Union Conf., Regional Adminstrv. Radio Conf., 1983, World Adminstrv. Radio Conf., 1985; chmn. Direct Broadcast Satellite Assn., 1986; mem. spectrum planning adv. com. U.S. Dept. Commerce, 1986-92; bd. dirs. ECON Inc.; mem. Calif. Inst. Tech. Jet Propulsion Lab.'s Mars Observer Program Rev. Bd., 1986-93. Contbr. numerous articles to profl. jours.; cons. editor space tech. McGraw-Hill Ency. Sci. and Tech, 1977—. Recipient NASA medals for Disting. Service, Outstanding Leadership, Exceptional Service, Collier trophy Nat. Aero. Assn. Fellow Am. Astron. Soc., AIAA (gen. chmn. Communications Satellite System Conf. 1984, v.p. pub. policy 1986-90), IEEE, Explorers Club; mem. Am. Geophys. Union, Am. Meterol. Soc., Satellite Broadcasting and Communications Assn. (chmn. 1987, chmn.'s coun. 1989-90, 1st Pres.'s award 1993), Internat. Soc. Satellite Profls. (bd. dirs. 1985-89), Internat. Acad. Astronautics, Phi Beta Kappa, Sigma Xi, Pi Mu Epsilon, Tau Beta Pi, Sigma Phi Epsilon, Sigma Pi Sigma. Achievements include patents in electronic circuits and systems. Home: 947 Loggerhead Island Dr Satellite Beach FL 32937-3863 Office Phone: 321-773-2071. Business E-Mail: jfclark@fit.edu.

CLARK, JOHN J., economist, finance educator; b. N.Y.C., June 21, 1924; s. John J. and Mary E. (Taylor) Clark; m. Margaret T. Norton, July 1, 1965; 1 child, Patricia Ann. BBA magna cum laude, St. John's U., 1948; MBA, CCNY, 1950; PhD, NYU, 1959. Prof. econs. Coll. Bus. Adminstrn., St. John's U., 1950-69, chmn. dept., 1959-62, dean, 1962-70; Royal H. Gibson Sr. prof. bus. adminstrn. Drexel U., Phila., 1971-90, prof. emeritus, 1990—, dir. doctoral studies LeBow Coll. Bus. Lectr. econs. Bklyn. Poly. Inst., 1954—58. Co-author: (book) The Impact of the Foundation Reports on Business Education, 1963, Business Fluctuations, Growth and Economic Stabilization, 1963, Professional Education for Business, 1964, The New Economics of National Defense, 1966, Financial Management: A Capital Market Approach, 1976, Management of Capital Expenditures, 1979, 3d rev. edit., 1989, Lease/Buy Decision, 1980, A Statistics Primer for Managers, 1980, Business Mergers and Acquisition Strategies, 1985, Restructuring Corporate America, 1996; contbr. articles to profl. jours.; editor: (book) Business and the Liberal Arts, 1962; contbg. editor: Fin. Mgmt. Jour., 1972—82. Mem. Borough Pres.'s Planning Com., Queens County, N.Y.C., 1964—69; economist joint legis. com. banking law N.Y. State Legislature, 1965—68. Recipient Mil. Rev. award, U.S. Army Command and Gen. Staff Coll., 1964. Mem.: Royal United Svc. Inst. Def. Studies, Ea. Fin. Assn. (exec. dir. 1974—77), Am. Econ. Assn., Phila. Maritime Mus. (advisor), U.S. Naval Inst. (medal 1969), Omicron Delta Epsilon, Delta Mu Delta, Beta Gamma Sigma. Home: White Horse Village 535 Gradyville Rd # V101 Newtown Square PA 19073-2815 Office: Coll Bus Adminstrn Drexel U Philadelphia PA 19104

CLARK, JOHN M., III, lawyer; b. Memphis, Feb. 27, 1950; BA, Rice U., 1972; JD, Stanford U., 1975. Bar: Calif. 1975. Law clk. U.S. Dist. Ct., L.A., 1975-77; European counsel Nat. Semiconductor Corp., Santa Clara, Calif., 1979-82, corporate counsel, 1982-85, assoc. gen. counsel, 1985-86, v.p., assoc. gen. counsel, 1986-92, sr. v.p., gen. counsel, sec., 1992—. Office: Nat Semiconductor Corp 2900 Semiconductor Dr Santa Clara CA 95051-0606 Office Phone: 408-721-6529. Office Fax: 408-739-9803. E-mail: john.clark@nsc.com.

CLARK, JOHN PETER, III, engineer, consultant; b. Phila., May 6, 1942; s. John Peter Jr. and Victoria Mary (McQuaide) C.; m. Nancy Ann Lapin, June 22, 1968; children: Shannon John, Hannah Marie. BSChemE, Notre Dame U., 1964; PhD, U. Calif., Berkeley, 1968. Registered profl. engr., Va., Ill. Rsch. engr. Agrl. Rsch. Svc., USDA, Berkeley and Washington, 1968-72; from asst. to assoc. prof. Va. Poly. Inst. and State U., Blacksburg, 1972-78; dir. R & D, ITT Continental Baking, Rye, N.Y., 1978-81; pres. Epstein Process Engring. Inc., Chgo., 1981-94; pvt. practice, engring. cons., Oak Park, Ill., 1994-95; v.p. tech. Fluor Daniel, Inc., 1995-98. Co-author: Food Processing Operations and Scale-up, 1991; editor: Exercises in Process Simulation, 1977; contbg. editor Food Tech.; contbr. articles to profl. jours.; patentee (with C.J. King) in field for sys. for freeze drying. Fellow: AIChE (divns. chmn. 1982, award in chem engring. 1998); mem.: Inst. Food Technologists (divns. chmn. 1984). Roman Catholic. Avocations: reading, folk music, Indian art. Home and Office: 644 Linden Ave Oak Park IL 60302-1661 Office Phone: 708-848-2205. Personal E-mail: JPC3@worldnet.att.net.

CLARK, JOHN RUSSELL, marine biologist; b. Seattle, Apr. 11, 1927; s. Donald Hathaway and Mildred (Taylor) C.; m. Catherine Lochner; children: John M., Jeffry R., George K., Linda J., Kerry S., Karen M. BS, U. Wash., Seattle, 1949. Research biologist Woods Hole (Mass.) Fishery Lab., Dept. Interior, 1950-59; asst. dir. Sandy Hook (N.J.) Marine Lab., Dept. Interior, 1960-70; dir. Narragansett (R.I.) Marine Lab., Dept. Interior, 1971; dir. water programs Conservation Found., Washington, 1972-81; mgr. coastal programs internat. affairs office Nat. Park Svc., Washington, 1982-87; sr. rsch. assoc. U. Miami Sch. Marine Sci., Fla., 1988—. Adj. scientist Mote Marine Lab, Sarasota, Fla., 1994—. Author: Through the Fish's Eye, 1973, Shark Watch, 1975, Coastal Ecosystems Management, 1977, The Sanibel Report, 1977, Wetland Functions and Values, 1979, Coastal Environment Management, 1980, Wetlands of Bottomland Hardwood Forests, 1981, Snorkeling: A Complete Guide, 1985, Integrated Management of Coastal Zones, 1992, Coastal Zone Management Handbook, 1996, Coastal Seas, 1998, Marine Protected Areas, 2000. Served with USNR, 1945-46. Named Conservationist of Year Am. Motors Corp., 1968; recipient Meritorious Publ. award U.S. Fish and Wildlife Service, 1969 Mem. Am. Littoral Soc. (founder, dir., past pres.) Office: Mote Marine Lab Field Office PO Box 420313 281 W Indies Dr Ramrod Key FL 33042-5462 E-mail: JohnRClarkX@cs.com.

CLARK, JOHN WALTER, JR., water transportation executive; b. Mobile, Ala., Oct. 21, 1919; s. John Walter and Mae (Kappner) C.; m. Evelyn Ruth Hamilton, Aug. 29, 1941 (dec.); children: Ann Clark (dec.), Ruth Clark Day, Susan Clark Wells; m. Sandra L. Sharp, June 21, 1977; stepchildren: Kirsten J. Acomb, Heidi J. Qualey. Grad., U.S. Mcht. Marine Acad., 1940; postgrad., Tulane U., 1950-55. Served as officer, master mariner U.S. Mcht. Marine, 1940-46; mgr. Argentina, Brazil, West Africa and Europe Delta Steamship Lines, Inc., 1946-50, asst. to pres. New Orleans, 1950-53, v.p., 1953-59, pres., 1959-79, chmn. bd., 1979-80; pres. Clark Maritime Assocs., Inc., 1979—. Bd. dirs. Panama Canal Commn., 1978-82; past pres., mem. exec. com., bd. dirs. World Trade Ctr. of New Orleans; maritime arbitrator New Orleans Bd. of Trade; commr., pres. Port of New Orleans, 1978-82; exec. dir. Miss. State Port Authority, 1982-85; nat. vice chmn. Coun.of Ams., 1974-80. Rear adm. U.S. Maritime Svc. Decorated Order of Crown of Belgium; Order of Star of Africa

Liberia; Order of So. Cross Brazil; Comendador de la Orden de Mayo Argentina; Orden de Isabel La Catolica Spain; named Maritime Man of Year Port of New Orleans, 1965. Mem. U.S. Mcht. Marine Acad. Alumni Assn. (Alumnus of Yr. 1975, named to Hall of Fame 1998). Clubs: Plimsoll, So. Yacht, Pickwick, Pass Christian Yacht, Pass Christian Isles Golf. Methodist. Office: Clark Maritime Assocs Inc 23322 Woodland Way Pass Christian MS 39571-5711

CLARK, JONATHAN MONTGOMERY, lawyer; b. Bklyn., Oct. 20, 1937; s. Russell Inslee and Lillian (Longmore) C.; m. Priscilla M. Jorgensen, Sept. 24, 1960; children: Jonathan M. Jr., Christopher D. BA, Yale U., 1959; LLB, U. Va., 1964. Bar: N.Y. 1965. Assoc. Davis Polk & Wardwell, N.Y.C., 1964-71, ptnr., 1971-93; gen. counsel, mng. dir. Morgan Stanley & Co., Inc., N.Y.C., 1993—98; sr. counsel Davis Polk & Wardwell, N.Y.C., 1999—. Advisor mission to Poland, Fin. Svcs. Vol. Corps, 1990, 92; cons. Warren Commn., Washington, 1965; bd. dirs. Greenwich Hosp. Assn., 1990-98, Prentice Cup Com. bd. dirs. Caramoor Ctr. Music & the Arts. 1st lt. USMC, 1959-61. Mem. ABA, N.Y. State Bar Assn., Assn. Bar City N.Y., Securities Industry Assn. (bd. dirs., 1995-96), N.Y. Stock Exchange Legal Adv. Com. Republican. Episcopalian. Avocations: golf, fly fishing, birding. Office: Davis Polk & Wardwell 450 Lexington Ave New York NY 10017 Business E-Mail: jonathan.clark@dpw.com.

CLARK, JOSHUA MAKER, publishing executive; s. Robert Brewster and Betsy Gambrill Clark. BA in Econs., Yale U., 1998. Pres., founder Light of New Orleans Pub., LLC, 2000—. Freelance graphic designer, New Orleans, 2002—05; freelance travel writer, New Orleans, 2003—; editor Scat Mag., New Orleans, 2003—; trustee La. Writers Found., New Orleans, 2003—05, New Orleans Writers Mus., 2004—05; mem. Kohlmeyer bd. Ogden Mus. So. Art, New Orleans, 2003—05. Author short stories; editor: French Quarter Fiction, 2001 (Book of Yr. in Gulf South, 2002), Southern Fried Divorce, 2003. Mem.: New Orleans Gulf South Booksellers Assn., Pub. Mktg. Assn., Faulkner Soc. Avocations: bodybuilding, running, nutrition, pool. Office: Light of New Orleans Pub Ste 307 828 Royal St New Orleans LA 70116

CLARK, KAREN ELAINE, secondary school educator; b. Mitchell, S.D., Aug. 26, 1950; d. Willard John and Mary Edna Clark. BA, Dakota Wesleyan U., 1972; MEd, S.D. State U., 1987; MA Teaching, English, No. State U., 1992. Tchr. English, libr. Ethan Sch. Dist., SD, 1973—75; tch. English, speech Kimball Sch. Dist., 1976, Stickney Sch. Dist., 1977—84, Corsica Sch. Dist., 1985—91, Chamberlain Sch. Dist., 1992—2000. Chair Chamberlain Hish Sch. NCA Steering Com., 1999—2002. Named Tchr. of Yr., S.D. Reading Coun., 1998. Mem.: S.D. Coun. Tchrs. English, Mid-Dakota Reading Coun., Delta Kappa Gamma. Republican. Avocations: reading, gardening, travel. Home: 300 East 15th Ave Mitchell SD 57301 Office: Chamberlain High Sch 301 E Kellan Chamberlain SD 57325

CLARK, KAREN HEATH, lawyer; b. Pasadena, Calif., Dec. 17, 1944; d. Wesley Pelton and Lois (Ellenberger) Heath; m. Bruce Robert Clark, Dec. 30, 1967; children: Adam Heath, Andrea Pelton. Student, Pomona Coll., Claremont, Calif., 1962—64; BA, Stanford U., 1966; MA in History, U. Wash., 1968; JD, U. Mich., 1977. Bar: Calif. 1978. Instr. Henry Ford C.C., Dearborn, Mich., 1968-72; assoc. Gibson, Dunn & Crutcher LLP, Irvine, Calif., 1977-86, ptnr., 1986—2003, adv. counsel, 2004—. Bd. dirs. Dem. Found. Orange County, 1989-91, 94—, Planned Parenthood Orange County, Santa Ana, Calif., 1979-82, New Directions for Women, Newport Beach, 1986-91, Human Options, 2001-03; bd. dirs. Women in Leadership, chair, 1995-99; trustee Newport Beach Pub. Libr., 2001—; mem. deans adv. coun. Sch. Humanities, U. Calif., Irvine. Recipient Choice award Planned Parenthood of Orange & San Bernardino Counties, 1996. Mem. Women in Leadership (founder 1993). E-mail: kclark@gibsondunn.com.

CLARK, KAREN MICHAEL KYAME, conservator, archivist; b. New Orleans, Mar. 10, 1957; d. Michael John and Marie Kyame; m. Terry Lee Clark, Nov. 12, 1989. BA in Spl. Edn., U. New Orleans, 1981. Conservator Jessica Hack Textile Conservation, New Orleans, Gentle Arts, 1994—2004, Aikaterina Textile Conservation, 2005—. Vol. Living Witness, 1995—2005, Greek Orthodox Monasteries, 2002—05; cons. hist. artifacts Holy Trinity Greek Orthodox Cathedral, 1990—. Ednl. grant Iconography, Holy Trinity Greek Orthodox Cathedral, 2003, Angels grant, Am. Inst. Conservation, 2004, Profl. Devel. scholarship, Found. Am. Ins. Conservation, 2004. Mem.: La. Assn. Mus., La. Art Conservation Alliance, Costume Soc. of Am., Am. Inst. Conservation, Philoptochos, Daughters of Penelope. Eastern Orthodox Christian. Avocations: iconography, Eastern Orthodox vestment making, art, needlecrafts, writing. Home: 5750 Cameron Blvd New Orleans LA 70122-4148 Office: Aikaterina Textile Conservation 5750 Cameron Blvd New Orleans LA 70122-4148

CLARK, KATHLEEN MULHERN, foreign language and literature educator; b. Phila., Oct. 10, 1948; d. John Joseph Jr. and Rosalie (Callahan) Mulhern; m. Robert Lee Clark, Oct. 7, 1972; children: Matthew, Kelly. AB, Immaculata U., 1970; MA, Villanova U., 1981; postgrad., U. Laval, Que., Can., 1969, Ecole Francaise des Attachés de Presse, Paris, 1991. Cert. French tchr. French tchr. Great Valley H.S., Devault, Pa., 1971-72, Conestoga Sr. H.S., Berwyn, Pa., 1970-71, 72-78; lectr. fgn. lang. Immaculata (Pa.) U., 1973-89, prof. fgn. lang., lit., 1989—, dept. chmn., 1997—. Translator Burroughs Corp., Paoli, Pa., 1976-78; translator, cons. Smith, Kline Animal Health Products, West Chester, Pa., 1985; co-developer, designer Leadership Core Curriculum, Immaculata, 1990—. Class rep. Immaculata U. Alumnae Assn., 1970-98, bd. govs. 1996-2002. Recipient grant U. Laval, 1969, Pew Meml. Trust, 1990. Mem. AAUP, Pa. State MLA (exec. bd. dirs., 1999-2002), Am. Assn. Tchrs. French (v.p. Phila. chpt.), Am. Coun. on Tchg. of Fgn. Langs., Pa. Soc. Tchg. Scholars, Alliance Française, Pi Delta Phi, Lambda Iota Tau. Roman Catholic. Avocations: travel, music. Home: 65 Rossiter Ave Phoenixville PA 19460-2509

CLARK, KATHRYN, government agency administrator; m. Robert Ike. MA, PhD, U. Mich. Faculty dept. anatomy and cell biology U. Mich., 1993; dep. dir. NASA Comml. Space Ctr., 1996—98; space sta. chief scientist NASA Office Space Flight, Washington, 1998—. Grantee, NIH, Nat. Inst. Aging, Am. Fedn. for Aging Rsch., NSF, NASA. Mem.: Internat. Soc. Women Pilots, Internat. Soc. for Gravitational and Space Biology, Am. Soc. for Gravitational and Space Biology, Soc. for Neurosci., Am. Coll. Sports Medicine. Avocations: bicycling, swimming, skiing. Office: NASA Hdqs Bldg HQ Rm 4022 Washington DC 20546-0001

CLARK, KEVIN P., medical products executive; BA, MBA, Mich. State U. Fin. exec. Chrysler Corp.; treas. Fed.-Mogul Corp.; from asst. treas. to v.p., contr. Fisher Sci., Hampton, NH, 1995—2001, v.p., CFO, 2001—. Office: Fisher Sci Internat Liberty Ln Hampton NH 03842

CLARK, KIM BRYCE, academic administrator, former dean; b. Salt Lake City, Mar. 20, 1949; s. Merlin and Helen Mar (Hickman) C.; m. Sue Lorraine Hunt, June 14, 1971; children: Bryce, Erin, Jonathan, Andrew, Michael, Julia, Jennifer. BA in economics, Harvard U., 1974, MA in economics, 1977, PhD in economics, 1978. From asst. prof. to prof. Harvard Bus. Sch., Boston, 1978-89, Harry E. Figgie prof. bus. adminstrn., 1989-95, dean, 1995—2005; pres. Brigham Young U., Rexburg, Idaho, 2005—. Bd. dirs. Ceramics Process System Corp., Milford, Mass., Analysis Group, Belmont, Mass., Automotive Industries, Inc. Co-author: Industrial Renaissance, 1983, Dynamic Manufacturing, 1988, Product Development Performance, 1991, Revolutionizing Product Development, 1992, Leading Product Development, 1995, Design Rules: The Power of Modularity, 2000; editor: The Uneasy Alliance, 1985; co-editor: The Perpetual Enterprise Machine, 1994; contbr. articles to profl. jours. Coord. Belmont Youth Basketball, 1983—. Mem. IEEE (assoc. mem.), Am. Econ. Assn., Inst. Mgmt. Sci. Avocations: golf, jogging. Office: Brigham Young U 525 S Ctr St Rexburg ID 83460

CLARK, KIMBERLY, music educator; b. Seoul, Republic of Korea, May 16, 1979; d. William and Mildred Clark. BME, Evangel U., Springfield, Mo., 2001; ME, William Woods U., Fulton, Mo., 2004. Cert. Mo. Tchg. Mo., 2001. Band/orch. dir. Springfield Pub. Schs., Springfield, Mo., 2001—04; band/orch. sales Hoover Music Co., Inc., Springfield, Mo. Music tchr. Self Employed, Springfield, 2001—. Home: 3126 E Valley Water Mill Rd Apt 5507 Springfield MO 65803 Office: Hoover Music Co Inc 440 S Jefferson Ave Springfield 65806 Personal E-mail: kimberlykclark@gmail.com. Business E-Mail: hoovermusicco@yahoo.com.

CLARK, LAVERNE HARRELL, writer; b. Smithville, Tex., June 6, 1929; d. James Boyce and Belle Bunte Harrell; m. L.D. Clark, Sept. 15, 1951. BA, Tex. Women's U., 1950; student, Columbia U., 1951-54; MA, U. Ariz., 1962, MFA, 1992. Reporter, libr., photographer Ft. Worth Press, 1950-51; with sales and advt. depts. Columbia U. Press, N.Y.C., 1951-53; asst. promotion-news Episcopal Diocese Bull., N.Y.C., 1958-59; founding dir. U. Ariz. Poetry Ctr., Tucson, 1962-66, photographer, 1966-99. Author, photographer: They Sang for Horses, 1966 (award U. Chgo. 1967), rev. edit., 2001, Revisiting the Plains Indian Country of Mari Sandoz, 1977, Focus 101, 1979, The Deadly Swarm and Other Stories, 1985, 87, Keepers of the Earth, 1997, 2d edit., 2002 (1st Novel award Western Writers of Am. 1998), Mari Sandoz's Native Nebraska, 2000; editor, photographer: The Face of Poetry, 1976, 2d edit., 1979. Recipient 19 awards Nat. League Am. Pen Women, 1967-96, Disting. Alumna award Tex. Woman's U., Denton, 1973; grantee Am. Philos. Soc., 1967, 69. Mem. PEN, Western Writers of Am., Westerners Internat., Women Writing the West, Sandoz Heritage Soc. (hon. mem. adv. bd. 1989-2002), Tex. Inst. Letters. Democrat. Episcopalian. Avocations: travel, bicycling, showing slides. Home: 604 Main St Smithville TX 78957 Office Phone: 512-237-2796. Personal E-mail: lhldclark@aol.com.

CLARK, LAWRENCE JAMES, minister; b. Greensboro, N.C., Feb. 1, 1957; s. Henry Walker and Katherine Margaret Clark; m. Kathryn E. Clark (div.); 1 child, Tyler James Little Eagle. AA, City Coll. Chgo., 1988; BBA, McKendree Coll., 2001; postgrad., Hood Theol. Sem., Salisbury, N.C. EMT. Tank comdr. U.S. Army, 1975—96; intern New Mt. Vernon United Meth. Ch., Winston-Salem, NC, 2001—; min., student Bethany United Meth. Ch., Liberty, NC, Staley United Meth. Ch. Actor: (films) The Patriot, Shake Rattle and Roll, Juwana Man, Black Knight; (TV series) Dawson's Creek, 2 NASCAR commls. Soccer coach Optimist Club, Winston-Salem, 1997; county rep. Piedmont Fatherhood Initiative, Greensboro, NC, 2001; Rep. candidate for Pres., 1998—99; Libertarian candidate for gov. State of N.C., 1999; Libertarian candidate for senate, 2000; vol. chaplain Randolph County Honor Guard; sr. deacon, 2003—04; jr. warden, 2004—. Named Ky. Col., Gov. John Y. Brown; recipient Order of St. George, US Armor Assn., 1995. Fellow: Am. Legion (local comdr. 1999—2000), Greensboro Lodge (jr. deacon 2001—02, sr. deacon 2003—, jr. warden 2004—); mem.: Optimist Club (v.p. 1985—86). Republican. Methodist. Avocations: boating, bowling, coaching sports, sports, walking. Home: 423 Back Creek Ter Asheboro NC 27205-2311 E-mail: larryclark27408@yahoo.com.

CLARK, LEROY D., law educator; b. 1934; BA, CCNY, 1956; LLB, Columbia U., 1961. Bar: N.Y. 1961. Staff atty. Office of N.Y. Atty. Gen., 1961-62; asst. cousnel NAACP Legal Def. and Edn. Fund, Inc., N.Y.C., 1962-68; prof. law NYU Law Sch., N.Y.C., 1969-79, Cath. U., 1981—. Gen. counsel EEOC, 1979-81; arbitrator Am. Arbitration Assn., Fed. Mediation and Conciliation Svc. Author: The Grand Jury: The Use and Abuse of Political Power, 1975, Employment Discrimination Law--Cases and Materials, 5th edit., 2000. Office: Law School Catholic Univ Am 3600 John Mccormack Rd NE Washington DC 20064-0001 Office Phone: 202-319-5158. Business E-Mail: clarkl@law.cua.edu.

CLARK, LLOYD, historian, writer, educator; b. Belton, Tex., Aug. 4, 1923; s. Lloyd C. and Hattie May (Taylor) C.; m. Jean Reeves, June 17, 1950; children: Roger, Cynthia, Candyce. BSJ, So. Meth. U., 1948; B in Fgn. Trade, Am. Grad. Sch. Internat. Mgmt., Thunderbird, 1949; MPA, Ariz. State U., 1972. String corr. AP, Dallas, 1941-42; reporter Dallas Morning News, 1947; editor, pub. Ex-Press, Arlington, Tex., 1945-48; publicity mgr. Advt. Counselors Ariz., Phoenix, 1949; reporter Phoenix Gazette, 1949-65; asst. pub. Ariz. Weekly Gazette, 1965-66; founder Coun. on Abandoned Mil. Posts-USA, 1966, Papago Trackers, 1985; project cons. City of Prescott, Ariz., 1971-72; dep. dir. adminstrv. svcs. No. Ariz. Coun. Govts., Flagstaff, 1972-73; regional adminstr. South Eastern Ariz. Govts. Orgn., Bisbee, 1973-75; local govt. assistance coord. Ariz. Dept. Transp., Phoenix, 1975-80, program adminstr., 1980-83; history instr. Rio Salado C.C., Phoenix, 1983-89, Ariz. State U.-West, Sun City, 1995-98; proprietor LC Enterprises, 1993—; columnist Daily News-Sun, Sun City, 1995—. Editor, pub. Clark Biog. Reference, 1956-62, mem. spkrs bur. Ariz. Humanities Coun., 1998-99. Author: Lloyd Clark's Scrapbook, Vol. 1, 1958, Vol. 2, 1960, Here's Looking at You, 1997, The Usual Suspects, 1998, You Must Remember This, 1999. Bd. dir. Friends of Channel 8, 1984-86; mem. transit planning com. Regional Pub. Transit Authority, 1988; bd. dir. Friends of Ariz. Hwys. Mag., 1989-92; mem. Ariz. State Geographic and Historic Names Bd., 1994—. Lt. AUS, 1942-46, maj., 1966-70, col. Res. Recipient Ariz. Press Club's exemplary gen. news coverage award, 1960, outstanding news reporting, 1961; Lloyd Clark Journalism scholarship named in honor U. Tex. at Arlington Alumni Assn., 1992. Mem. Ariz. Press Club (pres. 1962), Soc. Profl. Journalists (pres. Valley of Sun chpt. 1964), Am. Grad. Sch. Internat. Mgmt. Alumni Assn. Thunderbird (pres. Phoenix chpt. 1965), Ariz. Hist. Soc. (bd. dir. cen. Ariz. chpt. 1992-93, state bd. dir. 1993-95), Sharlot Hall Hist. Soc. (life), Res. Officers Assn. (life), Ex-Students Assn. No. Tex. Agrl. Coll. Arlington (pres. 1946-48), U. Tex. Arlington Alumni Assn. (life, bd. dir. 1994—, Disting. Alumni Svc. award 1997, Mil. Sci. Dept. Hall of Honor 1998), The Westerners (sheriff Phoenix Corral 1986-88), University Club (Phoenix) Address: PO Box 1537 Surprise AZ 85378-1537

CLARK, LUTHER THEOPOLIS, physician, educator, researcher; b. Bradenton, Fla., Oct. 21, 1949; m. Camille C. Jackson; children: Jason Myles, Monica Marie. AB, Harvard U., 1971, MD, 1975. Intern, resident, chief residency internal medicine Roosevelt Hosp., N.Y.C., 1975-79, fellow cardiology, 1978-80; dir. preventive cardiology Health Sci. Ctr. SUNY, Bklyn., 1992-95, chief divsn. cardiovascular medicine Health Sci. Ctr., 1995—, prof. clin. medicine Health Sci. Ctr. Fellow ACP, Am. Coll. Cardiology; mem. Nat. Med. Assn. Avocations: tennis, jogging. Office: SUNY Health Sci Ctr Box 1199 450 Clarkson Ave Brooklyn NY 11203-2056 E-mail: ltclarke@downstate.edu.

CLARK, MARIAN WILSON, writer; b. Hereford, Tex., Sept. 8, 1934; d. Robert Lee and Mabel Faulkner Wilson; m. Kenneth K. Clark, Dec. 29, 1963; children: Rebecca, Kevin. BS in Vocat. Home Econs. Edn., Tex. Tech. U., 1957. Home svc. advisor Tex. Elec., Ft. Worth, 1958—59; tchr. McCamey (Tex.) Pub. Schs., 1959—61, Odessa (Tex.) Pub. Schs., 1961—63. Spkr. various Rt. 66 groups, nationwide, 1993—; writer Rt. 66 Mag. and Rt. 66 Fedn. Newsletter, 1993—. Author: Southwestern Heritage Cookbook, 1989, Route 66 Cookbook, 1993, 2000, Main Street of America, 1997, Hogs on 66: Best Food for Road Trips on Route 66, 2004. Pres., bd. dirs. Camp Fire Girls, Tulsa, Okla., 1981—82. Recipient Gulick award, Camp Fire Girls, Tulsa, 1983. Mem.: Green Country Home Economists (pres.), Mortar Bd., United Meth. Women (pres.), Salvation Army Aux., Phi Upsilon Omicron. Methodist. Avocations: travel, aerobics. Home: 3019 S Madison Ave Tulsa OK 74114 Personal E-mail: mclark66@sbcglobal.net.

CLARK, MARILYN SUZANNE, secondary mathematics educator; b. Pontiac, Ill., Jan. 15, 1935; d. Rollin Kenneth and Lucille Hortense (Myer) Snethen; m. Ralph Ernest Clark, Jr., June 2, 1956; children: Robert Ian, Wendy Heather. BS, Tex. Tech, 1956; MA, U. Colo., 1985. Cert. secondary math. educator. Tchr. L.A. Pub. Schs., 1957-60, Abraham Lincoln High Sch., Denver, 1961-65, Adams County Schs., Westminster (Colo.) High Sch., 1980—. Curriculum writer, inservice presenter in field; adv. com. Westminster High Sch., 1989—. Contbr. articles to profl. jours. Recipient Focus on Excellence award Adams County Schs., 1989. Mem. NEA, Colo. Edn. Assn., Colo. Coun. Tchrs. Math., Nat. Coun. Tchrs. Math., WEA. Republican. Presbyterian. Avocations: photography, weaving. Home: 1651 Old Squaw Pass Rd Evergreen CO 80439-4734

CLARK, MARK LEE, lawyer; b. Muskegon, Mich., July 13, 1953; s. Alva Lee and Esther Luella (Bellinger) C.; m. Jane Ellen Lyons, Sept. 3, 1983; children: Zachary, Caitlin. BA with high honors, Mich. State U., 1975; JD with honors, Wayne State U., 1978. Bar: Mich. 1978, U.S. Dist. Ct. (ea. dist.) Mich. 1982. Assoc. McLean & Mijak, Romeo, Mich., 1978-82; ptnr. McLean, Mijak & Clark, P.C., Romeo, 1982—; mcpl. atty. City of Richmond, Mich., 1993—. Mcpl. atty. Village of Romeo, 1985—. Pres. bd. trustees, bd. dirs. Romeo Dist. Library, 1981-85. Mem. Mich. Bar Assn., Macomb County Bar Assn. Avocations: running, golf. Home: 268 W Saint Clair St Romeo MI 48065-4662 Office: McLean Mijak & Clark P C 137 W Saint Clair St Romeo MI 48065-4657 Office Phone: 586-752-2097.

CLARK, MARY HIGGINS, writer, communications executive; b. NYC, Dec. 24, 1929; d. Luke J. and Nora C. (Durkin) Higgins; m. Warren Clark, Dec. 26, 1949 (dec. Sept. 1964); children: Marilyn, Warren, David, Carol, Patricia; m. John J. Coheeney, Nov. 3, 1996. BA, Fordham U., 1979; hon. doctorate, Villanova U., 1983, Rider Coll., 1986, Stonehill Coll., 1992, Marymount Manhattan Coll., 1992, Chestnut Hill, 1993, Manhattan Coll., 1993, St. Peter's Coll., 1993; 7 additional hon. doctorates. Advt. asst. Remington Rand, 1946; stewardess Pan Am., 1949-50; radio scriptwriter, prodr. Robert G. Jennings, 1965-70; v.p., ptnr., creative dir., prodr. radio programming Aerial Communications, N.Y.C., 1970-80; chmn. bd., creative dir. D. J. Clark Enterprises, N.Y.C., 1980—. Author: Silent Night, Aspire to the Heavens, A Biography of George Washington, 1969 (NJ Author award 1969), Where Are the Children?, 1976 (NJ Author award 1977), A Stranger Is Watching, 1978 (N.J. Author award 1978), The Cradle Will Fall, 1980, A Cry in the Night, 1982, Stillwatch, 1984, Weep No More, My Lady, 1987, While My Pretty One Sleeps, 1989, The Anastasia Syndrome and Other Stories, 1989, Loves Music, Loves to Dance, 1991, All Around the Town, 1992, I'll Be Seeing You, 1993, Remember Me, 1994, The Lottery Winner, 1994, Bad Behavior, 1995, Let Me Call You Sweetheart, 1995, Moonlight Becomes You, 1996, Pretend You Don't See Her, 1997, The Plot Thickens, 1997, You Belong to Me, 1998, All Through the Night, 1998, We'll Meet Again, 1999, Before I Say Good-Bye, 2000, Deck the Halls, 2000, Daddy's Little Girl, 2002, Silent Night/All Through the Night, 2002, On the Street Where You Live, 2002, Kitchen Privileges, 2002, The Second Time Around, 2003, Nighttime is My Time, 2004 (Publishers Weekly paperback bestseller list, 2005), No Place Like Home, 2005 (NY Times Bestseller list, Publishers Weekly Bestseller list); (with Thomas Chastain and others) Murder in Manhattan, 1986; editor: Murder on the Aisle: The 1987 Mystery Writers Anthology, 1987. Recipient Grand Prix de Litterature Policiere, France, 1980, Horatio Alger award, 1997, Gold Medal of Honor, Irish-Am. Hist. Soc., Spirit of Achievement award, Albert Einstein Coll. of Med., Yoshiva Univ., Nat. Arts Club Gold Medal in Edn., Grand Master award, Mystery Writers of Am., 2000. Mem. Mystery Writers Am. (pres. 1987, dir.), Authors League, Am. Soc. Journalists and Authors, Acad. Arts and Scis. Republican. Roman Catholic.

CLARK, MATT, writer; b. Chgo., Feb. 3, 1930; s. Matthew and Kathryn Clark; m. Ellen Ann Mitchell, Aug. 23, 1952 (dec. 1978); children: Thomasin, Geoffrey Beach, Douglas Mitchell; m. Phyllis Malamud, Nov. 9, 1986. Grad., Hill Sch., 1947; AB, Wesleyan U., Middletown, Conn., 1951. Reporter Boston Traveler, 1953-56, sci. editor, 1956-58; writer Med. News, N.Y.C., 1958- 61; medicine editor Newsweek mag., 1961-88; free-lance sci. writer, 1958—. Served with USNR, 1951-53. Recipient Albert Lasker Med. Journalism award, 1964, 67, Howard W. Blakeslee award Am. Heart Assn., 1965, 68, 73, 83, Penney-Mo. mag. award in health, 1967, 71, 75, med. journalism award AMA, 1969, Claude Bernard Sci. Journalism award Nat. Soc. Med. Rsch., 1971, Page One award Newspaper Guild N.Y., 1974, 83, Media award (mag.) Am. Cancer Soc., 1976, N.Y. Deadline Club award 1977, James T. Grady award Am. Chem. Soc., 1983, Am. Med. Writers Assn.-Searle Labs. journalism award, 1983. Fellow AAAS; mem. Nat. Assn. Sci. Writers, Century Assn., Coffee House Club (N.Y.C.).

CLARK, MATTHEW HARVEY, bishop; b. Troy, N.Y., July 15, 1937; s. M. Harvey and Grace (Bills) C. Student, Coll. Holy Cross, Worcester, Mass.; BA, St. Bernard's Sem., Rochester, N.Y.; STL, N. Am. Coll., Rome; JCL, Gregorian U., Rome. Priest Roman Catholic Ch., 1962. Vice chancellor Diocese of Albany, NY; Cath. chaplain Albany Law Sch.; mem. faculty Vincentian Inst.; chmn. pers. bd. Diocese of Albany; spiritual dir. N. Am. Coll.; bishop Diocese of Rochester, Rochester, NY, 1979—. Office: Chancery Office 1150 Buffalo Rd Rochester NY 14624-1823*

CLARK, MAURA J., oil, gas industry executive; CFO Clark Refining & Mktg. Inc.(now Premcor), Glen Ellyn, Ill., 1995—2000; v.p., fin. No. Am. Life Assurance Co.; sr. v.p., strategy and M&A Direct Energy, Toronto, Canada. Office: Direct Energy Atria III 4th Fl 2225 Sheppard Ave E Toronto ON M2J 5C2 Canada*

CLARK, MAXINE, retail executive; b. Miami, Fla., Mar. 6, 1949; d. Kenneth and Anne (Lerch) Kasselman; m. Robert Fox, Sept. 1984. B.A. in Journalism, U. Ga., 1971. Exec. trainee Hecht Co., Washington, 1971, hosiery buyer, 1971-72, misses sportswear buyer, 1972-76; mgr. mdse. planning and research May Dept. Stores Co., St. Louis, 1976-78, dir. mdse. devel., 1978-80, v.p. mktg. and sales promotion Venture Stores div., 1980-81, sr. v.p. mktg. and sales promotion Venture Stores div., 1981-83, exec. v.p. mktg. and softlines, 1983-85; exec. v.p. apparel Famous-Barr, St. Louis, 1985-86; v.p. mdsing. Lerner Shops div. Limited Inc., N.Y.C., 1986-88; exec. v.p. Venture Stores, St. Louis, 1988-92; pres. Payless ShoeSource, Topeka, 1992-96; founder, CEO Smart Stuff, Inc. children's retail concept devel. firm and the Build-A-Bear Workshop, 1996—; bd. dirs. Earthgrains Co., Tandy Brands Accessories Co., Wave Techs., Inc., Dept. 56, J.C. Penney Co., Inc., 2003-. Sec., Lafayette Sq. Restoration Com., 1978-79; mem. com. 200 Nat. Coun. Coll. Arts and Scis. Washington U., St. Louis; trustee U. Ga. Found., 1995—; mem. nat. adv. coun. Girl Scouts U.S.A., 1995-97. Office: Build A Bear Workshop 1960 Innerbelt Business Center Overland MO 63114-5760

CLARK, MAYREE CARROLL, investment banking executive; b. Norman, Okla., Mar. 9, 1957; d. Benton C. Clark and Joan M. (Harris) Richards; m. Jeffrey P. Williams, Apr. 28, 1984; two children. BS, U. So. Calif., 1976; MBA, Stanford U., 1981. Econ. analyst Nat. Econ. Rsch., LA, 1976-79; assoc. Morgan Stanley, NYC, 1981-84, v.p., 1985-87, prin., 1987-89, mng. dir., 1990—, global rsch. dir., 1994—2001, head newly merged (Internat. Private Client Group and its Private Wealth Mgmt. bus.) private wealth businesses for wealthy individuals, 2002—03, head internat. individual investor businesses, 2003—05. Adj. prof. Columbia U., N.Y.C., 1988-89. Chmn. Student Sponsor Partnership, N.Y.C., 1996-99. Republican. Office: Morgan Stanley and Co 1585 Broadway Fl 14 New York NY 10036-8200*

CLARK, MELVILLE, JR., physicist, consultant, electrical engineer; b. Syracuse, N.Y., Dec. 19, 1921; s. Melville and Dorothy Drew (Speich) C. BS, MIT, 1943, postgrad., 1943-44, U. N.Mex., 1945-46, Princeton U., 1946; MA, Harvard U., 1947, PhD, 1949. Registered profl. engr., Mass. Mem. staff Radiation Lab. MIT, Cambridge, Mass., 1942-45; mem. staff Manhattan dist. U. Calif., Los Alamos, N.Mex., 1945-46; physicist Brookhaven Nat. Lab., Upton, N.Y., 1949-53; dir. 416 South Salina St. Corp., Syracuse, NY, 1957—66, pres., 1965—66; mem. staff Radiation Lab. U. Calif., Livermore, 1953-55; dir. Clark Music Co., Syracuse, N.Y., 1948-60, v.p., 1957-60; pres. Meldor Corp., Cazenovia, N.Y., 1960-66; sr. engrng. specialist Sylvannia Electric Products, Waltham, Mass., 1962-64; sr. cons. scientist AVCO, Wilmington, Mass., 1964-67; sr. scientist NASA, Cambridge, 1967-70; sr. devel. engr. Thermo Electron, Waltham, 1970-73; sr. cons. engr., sr. tech. strategist Combustion Engring., Windsor, Conn., 1973-83; pres. Melville Clark Assocs., Wayland, Mass., 1949—. Cons. Raytheon Mfg. Co., Waltham, 1955-58, United Shoe Machinery Co., Beverly, Mass., 1956, Arthur D. Little,

Cambridge, 1957-58, Aerodyne Rsch., Inc., Billerica, Mass., 1983-84; tech. expert witness Pennie and Edmonds, N.Y.C., 1984—; trustee Inst. Sci. Rsch. in Music, Wayland, Mass., 1990—; assoc. prof. nuclear engring. MIT, Cambridge, 1955-62; adviser Congressman Robert Drinan. Author: (with Rose) Plasmas and Controlled Fusion, 1961, (with Hansen) Numerical Methods of Reactor Analysis, 1964; translator, editor: (with B. Daniel) Introduction to the Theory of Ionized Gases, 1960; contbr. articles to profl. jours.; patentee in field. MIT scholar, 1939-43; NRC predoctoral fellow Harvard U., 1946-49, NRC predoctoral and Hercules Powder Co. fellow Princeton U., 1946. Mem. AAAS, IEEE, Am. Phys. Soc., Am. Inst. Physics, Fusion Power Assocs., Acoustical Soc. Am., Assn. Computing Machinery (Greater Boston chpt.), Soc. Music Perception and Cognition, Sigma Xi. Home and Office: 8 Richard Rd Wayland MA 01778-4099 Office Phone: 508-655-0906. Fax: 508-651-0602. E-mail: mclarkjr@gis.net.

CLARK, MELVIN EUGENE, chemical company executive; b. Ord, Nebr., Oct. 2, 1916; s. Ansel B. and Ruth Joy (Bullock) C.; m. Virginia May Hiller, Sept. 16, 1938; children— John Robert, Walter Clayton, Dale Eugene, Merry Sue. BSChemE cum laude, U. Colo., 1937; grad. exec. program, Columbia U., 1952; grad. advanced mgmt. program, Harvard U., 1961. Asst. editor Chem. Engring., McGraw-Hill, N.Y.C., 1937-41; mktg. staff Wyandotte Chem. Corp., Mich., 1941-53; chief program br. War Prodn. Bd., Washington, 1942-44; v.p. mktg. Frontier Chem. Co., Wichita, 1953-69; exec. v.p. chems. div. Vulcan Materials Co., Birmingham, Ala., 1969-81, v.p. planning, chems. and metals group, 1981-82; cons., 1982—. Pres. Chlorine Inst., 1977-80 Contbr. numerous articles to profl. jours. Recipient U. Colo. Alumni Recognition award, 1972; named Chem. Market Rsch. Assn. Man of Year, 1963, Disting. Engring. Alumnus, U. Colo., 1985, Centennial medalist Coll. of Engring., U. Colo., 1994, Geroge Norlin award U. Colo., 2005 Mem. AIChE, Comml. Devel. and Mktg. Assn., Am. Chem. Soc., Boulder Country Club, Tau Beta Pi, Pi Mu Epsilon. Republican. Mem. Christian Ch. Home and Office: 7145 Cedarwood Cir Boulder CO 80301-3716 E-mail: meclark1@aol.com.

CLARK, MERRELL EDWARD, JR., lawyer; b. Bklyn., Apr. 30, 1922; s. Merrell Edward and Eleanor Everest (Wild) C.; m. Hollis Logan, May 22, 1943; children: Julie Clark Goodyear, Kenyon Wild. BA, Yale U., 1943, LLB, 1948. Bar: N.Y. 1948, U.S. Dist. Ct. (so. dist.) 1949, U.S. Ct. Appeals (2d cir.) 1949, U.S. Tax Ct. 1951, Conn. 1952, U.S. Dist. Ct. (ea. dist.) N.Y. 1952, U.S. Dist. Ct. (ea. dist.) N.Y. 1952, U.S. Supreme Ct. 1956, U.S. Ct. Appeals (6th cir.) 1965, U.S. Ct. Appeals (8th cir.) 1973, U.S. Ct. Appeals (4th cir.) 1974, U.S. Dist. Ct. (no. dist.) N.Y. 1982, U.S. Dist. Ct. (we. dist.) N.Y. 1982. Assoc. Winthrop, Stimson, Putnam & Roberts, N.Y.C., 1948-55, ptnr., 1956-91; sr. counsel Pillsbury Winthrop Shaw Pittman LLP, 1992—. Editor Yale Law Sch. Jour., 1947-48. Mem. Town Meeting, Greenwich, Conn., 1953-56, com. on jud. appointments (Appelate Div. 1st Dept.), 1978-82, 2d cir. jud. conf. evaluation com., 1980-87; dir.; trustee Perrot Meml. Library, Old Greenwich, Conn., 1956-63, Pomfret (Conn.) Sch., 1966-74, Richard Found., N.Y.C., 1965-2002, William Nelson Cromwell Found., N.Y.C., 1979—, Steep Rock Assn., Washinton, Conn., 1993-2004, Internat. Coll. Hospitality Mgmt., 1994-2002; adviser women's rights project ACLU, 1976-90; mem. N.Y.C. Bd. Ethics, 1987-89; chair N.Y.C. Conflicts of Interest Bd., 1989-90, N.Y.C. Hardship Appeals Bd., 1993-2001; bd. dirs. N.Y. Legal Aid Soc., 1985-88. Served to capt. AUS, 1943-46. Decorated Bronze Star with two battle stars. Mem. ABA (ho. of dels. 1985-89), Assn. of Bar of City of N.Y. (pres. 1978-80), Am. Law Inst., Am. Coll. Trial Lawyers, River Club (N.Y.C.), Washington Club (Conn.). Office: Pillsbury Winthrop Shaw Pittman LLP 1540 Broadway New York NY 10036 Office Phone: 212-888-1969. Personal E-mail: htgclark@aol.com. Business E-Mail: clarkm@law.com.

CLARK, MERRELL MAYS, management consultant; b. Clifton Springs, NY, Feb. 8, 1935; s. Arthur Tillotson and Ruthanna Frame (Anderson) C.; m. Lynne Ruth Butcher, June 14, 1957; children: Elisabeth Lynne Clark Jenks, Aimee Ruthanna Clark Peterson, Catherine Merrell Clark Seda. BA, Yale U., 1957, MA in Religion, 1970. Asst. to advt. mgr. Armstrong Rubber Co., West Haven, Conn., 1959—60; mktg. analyst SSC & B, N.Y.C., 1960—62, account exec., 1962—64, v.p., account supr., 1964—68, v.p. mgmt. supr., 1968—70; prin. Knight, Gladieux & Smith, N.Y.C., 1970—72; v.p. Edna McConnell Clark Found., N.Y.C., 1972—77; exec. v.p. Acad. for Ednl. Devel., N.Y.C., 1977—81; prin. Clark Co., Scarsdale, NY, 1981—. Contbr. articles to profl. jours. Bd. dirs. Westchester Cmty. Svcs. Coun., White Plains, 1965-72, Elderhostel, Boston, 1977-98, Scarsdale Adult Sch., Scarsdale Cmty. Ctr.; pres. Elderworks, Scarsdale, 1978—, Nat. Sch. Vol. Program, Alexandria, Va., 1977-89, chmn. nat. adv. bd., 1977-1989, Scarsdale Adult Sch., 2002—, Coun. for Arts in Westchester, White Plains, 1978-83, Scarsdale Found., 1981-90; advisor Nat. Exec. Svc. Corps, N.Y.C., 1977-87, United Way Scarsdale-Edgemont, 1989-97; treas. Greenacres Assn. Scarsdale, Inc. 1993-97; active Scarsdale Arts Coun., 2002— Mem. Fox Meadow Tennis Club, Yale Club N.Y.C., Yale Westchester Alumni Assn (treas. 1995-2001, pres. 1997-03, chmn. bd. dirs., chmn. scholarship com. 2003—), Town and Village Civic Club (bd. dirs. edn. found. 2003-) Republican. Presbyn. Avocations: piano, organ, painting. Office: PO Box 1385 Scarsdale NY 10583-9385

CLARK, MICHAEL, artist; m. Felicity Hogan, Dec. 1995. BA, Corcoran Sch. Art. Founder & co-dir. Mus. Contemporary Art, Washington, 1991—. Represented in permanent collections, Nat. Gallery Art, DC, exhibitions include Clark & Hogan: Paintings & Collaborations, Barry Gallery, 2002—03, Clark in Context: Day of the Revolutionary, Mus. Contemporary Art, 2003. Office: Mus Contemporary Art 1054 31st St Washington DC 20007*

CLARK, MOIRA REGINA, writer, consultant; b. Hazlet, N.J., Apr. 17, 1964; d. Regina Diane and James Francis Dorsey; m. Kenneth Howard Clark, Nov. 1, 2001; 1 child, Matthew Charles Gibson. Myotherapy & exercise therapist Myotherapy Assocs., Stockton, Calif., 1985—88; registered prosthetic & orthotic technician Palo Alto Orthopedics, Calif., 1988—91; med. billing mgr. E. Carolina U., Greenville, NC, 1991—93; hosp. accounts mgr. U. Va. Med. Ctr., Charlottesville, 1993—95; med. auditor Qual Choice Va., Charlottesville, 1995—2001, Horizon Mercy Blue Cross, West Trenton, NJ, 2002—03; med. auditor, asst. adminstr. Cascade Corp., Cape May Court House, NJ, 2004—. Author: (novel) Leaving the Nest, You May be Stressed Out If, The Adventures of Maynard B. Roman Catholic. Avocations: travel, sports, reading, writing. Home: 7 Country Village Dr Cape May Court House NJ 08210 Office: Cascade Corp 1419 Rte 9 North Cape May Court House NJ 08210 Office Phone: 609-465-2260. Personal E-mail: mosie64@comcast.net. E-mail: moira.clark@easternshorenursing.com.

CLARK, MORTON HUTCHINSON, lawyer; b. Norfolk, Va., Apr. 21, 1933; s. David Henderson and Catharine Angelica (Hutchinson) C.; m. Lynn Harrison Adams, Aug. 12, 1961; children: Allison Adams, David Henderson, Susan West, Julia Dixon. BA in English, U. Va., 1954, LLB, 1960. Bar: Va. 1960, U.S. Dist. Ct. (ea. dist.) Va. 1960, U.S. Ct. Appeals (4th cir.) 1976, U.S. Ct. Appeals (1st cir.) 1993, U.S. Supreme Ct. 1993. Assoc. Vandeventer Black LLP, Norfolk, 1960-65, ptnr., 1965—. Co-editor: The Virginia Lawyer, 1991-93. Chmn. Va. Commn. for Children and Youth, Richmond. Fellow Am. Coll. Trial Lawyers, Va. Law Found.; mem. Maritime Law Assn. (exec. com. 1984-87), Hoffman I'Anson Am. Inns of Ct. (exec. com. 1993-95), The Harbor Club (pres.), Town Point Club. Episcopalian. Avocations: off shore racing, cruising. Home: 103 Rivers Edge Kingsmill Williamsburg VA 23185-8930 Office: 295 McLaws Cir Ste 1 Williamsburg VA 23185 Office Phone: 757-258-9515. E-mail: clarklaw2@verizon.net.

CLARK, NANCIE M., writer; b. Savannah, Ga., Oct. 9, 1948; d. Asa and Rebecca (Stein) Meddin; m. Fred S. Clark, Dec. 27, 1970; children: Jonathan, Alison, Robert. Student, Syracuse U.; BA in journalism, U. S.C., 1969. Intern reporter Savannah Evening Press; columnist Westside Weekly News; dir. pub. rels. Darvoe Advt. Agy.; propr., former owner Software Store, Savannah; tchr. computer applications EOA, Seniornet. Author The Forgotten Tunnel, A Savannah Mystery; editor (cookbook) The Kosher Palette, Savannah Style; contbr. articles to various newspapers. Vol. United Way, Heart Fund, Nat. Cancer Soc., JEA Children's and Teens Commns., Hebrew Women's Aid, Am. Lung Assn., Savannah Sci. Mus., Ga. Hist. Soc. (Dor L'dor com.); docent Mickve Israel Synagogue. Recipient award Vol. Action Coun. Mem. Savannah Bar Aux., B'nai B'rith Women, Hadassah, Theta Sigma Phi Home: 318 Early St Savannah GA 31405-5641 E-mail: nancieclark@yahoo.com.

CLARK, NANCY LUCINDA BROWN, retired music educator; b. Akron, Ohio, Dec. 11, 1946; d. Gardner Lane Brown and Ruth Marie Thomas; m. Eugene Ernest Zielinski, Aug. 1968 (div. Mar. 1989); children: Ruth Karlotte Zielinski Hansen, Jennifer Jane Zielinski Webber; m. Douglas Napier Clark, Mar. 11, 1989. Student, Kent State U., 1964-66; BS in Mus. Edn., U. Ill., 1968; postgrad., Nazareth Coll., 1981-82. Music tchr. pre-kindergarten and kindergarten Diocese of Rochester, N.Y., 1970s; tchr., supr. Muzak Cranford (N.J.) Mid. Sch., 1982-87; asst. music dir. First Presbyn. Ch., Maplewood, N.J., 1984-89; music min. Salem Bapt. Ch., Lexington, Ga., 1990-96, ret., 1996. Cons. Nat. Postal Mus., 2004—. Author: (book chpt.) Nantucket Postmarks to 1890, 1989, Philatelic Congress Book Maine Fancy Cancels, 2000; host (internet radio program) APS Stamp Talk with Nancy Clark; contbr. articles to profl. jours. Pres. Olymphilex 96, Atlanta, 1992—96; mem. Barnstable County Hist. Pres. Commn., 2001—; juror, team leader Juvalux 98, Luxembourg, 1998, Bangkok, 2000, Olymphilex, Greece, 2004; chmn. 1st Nat. Youth in Philately Symposium, 2002; v.p. Barnstable County Hist. Pres. Commn., 2002—03, chair, 2003—; dir. edn. Stamp Camp USA, 2003—04, co-chair, 2003—04; bd. dirs. Oglethorpe County Libr., Lexington, 1989—98, Athens-Clarke County Regional Libr., 1992—98. Recipient Internat. Gold award ROCPEX Taipei, China, 1981, Polska, 1997, Grand Stamporee award, Palm Beach, Fla., 1996. Mem.: Mass. Postal Rsch. Soc. (bd. dirs. 2003—), Mobile Post Office Soc. (bd. dirs. 2004—), Aux. Markings Club (pres. 2003—), Cape Cod Area Philatelic Group (bd. dirs. 2001—03, pres. 2004), Am. Assn. Philatelic Exhibitors, Boston Philatelic Group (sec.-treas. 2004—), Collectors Club N.Y., Am. Philatelic Soc.

CLARK, NOREEN MORRISON, behavioral science educator, researcher; b. Glasgow, Scotland, Jan. 12, 1943; arrived in US, 1948; d. Angus Watt and Anne (Murphy) Morrison; m. George Robert Pitt, Dec. 3, 1982; 1 child, Alexander Robert. BS, U. Utah, 1965; MA, Columbia U., 1972, MPhil, 1975, PhD, 1976. Rsch. coord. World Edn. Inc., N.Y.C., 1972-73; asst. prof. Sch. Pub. Health Columbia U., N.Y.C., 1973-80, assoc. prof., 1980-81, Sch. Pub. Health U. Mich., Ann Arbor, 1981-85, prof., chmn. dept. health behavior and health edn., 1985-95, Marshall H. Becker prof. of pub. health, 1995—2005, dean, 1995—2005, dir. ctr. mng. chronic disease, 2005—; prof. pediatrics and com. diseases U. Mich. Medical Sch., Ann Arbor, 2003—. Adj. prof. health adminstrn. Sch. Pub. Health Columbia U., 1988—; prin. investigator NIH, 1977—; adv. com. pulmonary diseases Nat. Heart, Lung & Blood Inst., Rockville, Md., 1983-87, adv. com. for prevention, edn. and control, 1987-91, coord. com. Nat. Asthma Edn. Program, 1991—; assoc. Synergos Inst., NYC, 1987-99; nat. adv. environ. health scis. coun. NIH, 1999-2002; task force on preventive cmty. svc. CDC, 2002-05 Co-author: Evaluation of Health Promotion, 1984; editor Health Edn. and Behavior, 1985-97; assoc. editor Ann. Rev. of Pub. Health, 2002-05; mem. editl. bd. Women in Health, Advances in Health Edn. and Promotion, Home Health Care Services Quar.; contbr. articles to profl. jours. Bd. dirs., adv. Aaron Diamond Found., 1989-96, Family Care Internat., NYC, 1987—, Internat. Asthma Coun., 1996-2000, Am. Lung Assn., NYC, 1988—, World Edn., Inc., 1998-. Mem. Soc. Pub. Health Edn. (pres. 1985-86, Disting. Fellow award 1987), APHA (chair health edn. sect. 1982-83, Derryberry award in behavioral sci. 1985, Disting. Career award 1994), Am. Thoracic Soc. (Health Edn. Rsch. award Nat. Asthma Edn. Program 1992, Healthtrac Found. Health Edn. award, 1997), Internat. Union Health Edn., Soc. Behavioral Medicine, Coun. Fgn. Rels., Inst. Medicine of NAS, Pi Sigma Alpha. Office: U Mich Sch Pub Health 109 Observatory St Ann Arbor MI 48109-2029

CLARK, PAT ENGLISH, lawyer; b. Austin, Tex., Feb. 26, 1940; s. Pat Wheeler and Jennie Bell (Lagrone) C.; m. Peggy Arnold Gray, March 16, 2002; 1 child, Susan Louise Beisert. BA, JD, U. Tex. Bar: Tex. 1963, U.S. Ct. Mil. Appeals 1964, U.S. Dist. Ct. (so. and no. dists.) Tex. Staff atty. Phillips Petroleum Co., Houston, 1967-69; atty. Amoco Production Co., Houston, 1969-75; ptnr. Vinson & Elkins, Houston, 1975-95, Borrego & Clark, 1996-99. Capt. JAGC, U.S. Army, 1964-67. Methodist. Office: 9809 Villa Maria Cove Austin TX 78759 Business E-Mail: pclark8@austin.rr.com.

CLARK, PATRICIA RUTH, foreign language educator; b. Lincoln, Nebr., Sept. 26, 1945; d. Martin and Virginia (McDowell) Dunklau; m. Neil B. Clark, Nov. 20, 1965; children: Scott B., Todd B. BA, U. Nebr., 1968. Cert. tchr., Conn. French tchr. Norris H.S., Courtland, Nebr., 1968-69, Canton (Conn.) H.S., 1970; French and Spanish tchr. Renbrook Sch., West Hartford, Conn., 1975—, head of lang. dept., 1980—. Workshop presenter Mid. Sch. Conf., West Hartford, 1991, 93, Advocates of Lang. Learning, Mpls., 1988, Conn. Coun. Lang. Tchrs., 1993-94. Mem. Shelterworks, Bloomfield, 1989-94, bd. dirs., 1994. Recipient Staff Pedagogique award Amb. de France, 1994. Mem. Am. Coun. Tchrs. Fgn. Langs., Conn. Coun. Lang. Tchrs. (Helen Amaral award 1993), Orgn. Progressor Educators, Nat. Network Elem. Lang., Alliance Francaise. Avocations: bicycling, gardening, dance. Office: Renbrook Sch 2865 Albany Ave Hartford CT 06117-1899

CLARK, PETER BRUCE, retired publishing executive; b. Detroit, Oct. 23, 1928; s. Rex Scripps and Marian (Peters) C.; m. Lianne Schroeder, Dec. 21, 1952 (dec. Jan. 1996); children: Ellen Clark Brown, James. BA, Pomona Coll., 1952, LL.D. (hon.), 1972; M.P.A., Syracuse U., 1953; PhD, U. Chgo., 1959; H.H.D., Mich. State U., 1973, Lawrence Inst. Tech., 1982; LL.D. (hon.), U. Mich., 1977. Research assoc., then instr. polit. sci. U. Chgo., 1957-59; asst. prof. polit. sci. Yale U., 1959-61; with Evening News Assn., Detroit, 1960-86, corp. sec., 1960-61, v.p., 1961-63, pres., 1963-86, chmn. bd., chief exec. officer, dir., 1969-86; pub. Detroit News, 1963-81, also dir.; dir. Gannett Co., Inc., 1986-99. Regent's prof. UCLA Grad. Sch. Mgmt, 1987; chmn. Fed. Res. Bank Chgo., 1975-77, former chmn. br. Fed. Res. Bank Detroit. Served with AUS, 1953-55. Mem.: Am. Soc. Newspaper Editors, Am. Newspaper Pub. Assn. (dir. 1966—74), Ironwood Country Club.

CLARK, PETER S., II, lawyer; b. Alexandria, Va., Feb. 13, 1957; s. Seymour Garland and Joan (Smith) Clark; m. Stacy Ellen West, June 19, 1988. BA in pub. policy & economics, Duke U., 1979; JD, Wash. U., 1982. Bar: Pa. 1982, NY 2004. Assoc. to ptnr. Duane Morris, Phila., 1982—2000; ptnr. Reed Smith LLP, Phila., 2000—, practice group leader corp. restructuring & bankruptcy group. Mem. editl. adv. bd. Jour. of Corp. Renewal. Mem. editl. bd.: Jour. Bankruptcy Law. Mem.: ABA (mem. com. on bus. bankruptcy, mem. com. on comml. fin. services), Comml. Law League of Am., Am. Bankruptcy Inst., Turnaround Mgmt. Assn. Office: Reed Smith LLP 2500 One Liberty Pl 1650 Market St Philadelphia PA 19103 Office Phone: 215-851-8142. Office Fax: 215-851-1420. Business E-Mail: pclark@reedsmith.com.

CLARK, PHILLIP LLOYD, JR., lawyer; b. New Castle, Pa., Feb. 6, 1954; s. Phillip Lloyd and Pauline Elizabeth (Burgess) C.; m. Alice McDowell, Sept. 8, 1984; children: Lindsey, Ashley, Emily. BA, U. Pitts., 1976, JD, 1979. Bar: Pa. 1979, U.S. Dist. Ct. (we. dist.) Pa. 1980, U.S. Supreme Ct. 1983. Ptnr. Keller, Pomericl, Leymarie, Clark & Puntureri, Ellwood City, Pa., 1980-94, Balph, Nicolls, Mitsos, Flannery & Clark, New Castle, Pa., 1994—. Pres. New Castle Parou Ballet Co., 1996—, dir., 1992—; spl. dep. atty. gen. Pa. Atty. Gen.'s Office, 1994—. Mem. Western Pa. Trial Lawyers Assn. (bd. govs. 1994—), Penna. Trial Lawyers Assn. (bd. govs.). Democrat. Roman Catholic. Avocations: skiing, ballet. Home: RR 4 Box 585 New Castle PA 16101-9645 Office: Balph Nicolls Mitsos Flannery & Clark 300 Sky Bank Bldg 14 N Mercer St New Castle PA 16101

CLARK, R. KERRY, manufacturing executive; b. Ottawa, Ont., Can., Apr. 29, 1952; B in Commerce, Queen's U., 1974. Brand asst. P&G Can. Procter & Gamble, 1974—75, asst. brand mgr. P&G Can., 1975—76, brand mgr. P&G Can., 1976—80, assoc. advt. mgr. P&G Can., 1980—84, assoc. advt. mgr. P&G Far East (Japan), 1984—85, advt. mgr. P&G Far East (Japan), 1985—87, gen. mgr. hard surface cleaners Cin., 1987—91, v.p., gen. mgr. laundry products Procter & Gamble USA, 1991—95, pres. laundry and cleaning products-U.S., Procter & Gamble N.Am., group v.p., 1995—97, pres. laundry and cleaning products-N.Am., Procter & Gamble N.Am., group v.p., 1997—98, exec. v.p. The Procter & Gamble Co., pres. Asia, Procter & Gamble Asia, 1998—99, pres.-Asia, 1999, pres. global feminine protection and Asia, 1999—2000, pres. global market devel. orgn., 2000—01, pres. global market devel. and bus. ops., 2001—02, vice chmn. bd. dirs., pres. global market devel. and bus. ops., 2002—. Mem. mgmt. bd. GS1; bd. dirs. EAN Internat.; past mem. Am. C. of C. in Japan; past vice chairperson The Soap and Detergent Assn., NY. Chmn. bd. dirs. Cin. Zoo and Bot. Gardens; mem. Leadership Cin., Class XIX; past mem. Greater Cin. United Way Cabinet. Mem.: Bacchus Soc. Am., Indian Hill Club, Queen City Club, Kenwood Country Club, The Commonwealth Club. Office: The Procter & Gamble Co 1 Procter & Gamble Plz Cincinnati OH 45202

CLARK, RAMSEY, lawyer, former United States attorney general; b. Dallas, Dec. 18, 1927; s. Thomas Campbell and Mary (Ramsey) Clark; m. Georgia Welch, Apr. 16, 1949; children: Ronda Kathleen, Thomas Campbell III. BA, U. Tex., 1949; MA, JD, U. Chgo., 1950. Bar: Tex. 1951, US Supreme Ct. 1956, DC 1969, NY 1970. Assoc. to ptnr. Clark, Reed and Clark, Dallas, 1951-61; asst. atty. gen. lands divsn. US Dept. Justice, 1961-65, dep. atty. gen., 1965-67, atty. gen., 1967-69; atty. Paul, Weiss, NYC, 1969—73; pvt. practice lawyer, 1973—; founder Internat. Action Ctr., NYC, 1991, Internat. ANSWER (Act Now to Stop War and End Racism), DC, 2001. Adj. prof. Howard U., 1969—72, Bklyn. Law Sch., 1973—81. Author: Crime in America, 1970, The Fire This Time: US War Crimes in the Gulf War, 1991. Served to cpl. USMC, 1945-46. Office: 36 E 12th St Fl 6 New York NY 10003-4692

CLARK, RANJANA B., bank executive; arrived in U.S., 1987; BA in Econs., MA in Mktg. and Sales. With Deutsche Bank, Bombay, 1982; joined Wachovia Bank as product mgr. capital markets divsn. Charlotte, NC, 1989; sr. v.p. - group exec. Treas. Svcs. Divsn., 1999—2001; exec. v.p., head Treas. Svcs. Divsn. Charlotte, NC, 2001—. Named One of Most Powerful Women in Banking, U.S. Banker Mag., 2003. Office: Wachovia Bank 301 South College St Charlotte NC 28288-0570

CLARK, RAYMOND S., architectural firm executive; With Skidmore, Owings & Merrill, Chgo.; pres. DeStefano & Ptnrs., 2000—03; mng. prin. Chgo. DeStefano Keating Ptnrs. Ltd., 2003—. Office: DeStefano Keating Ptnrs Ltd Ste 250 445 E Illinois St Chicago IL 60611

CLARK, RIC, real estate company executive; Bus. Degree, Ind. U. Pa. Various positions including COO, exec. v.p., dir. leasing Brookfield Fin. Properties, 1984—; pres., CEO U.S. comml. ops. Brookfield Properties Corp., N.Y.C., 2002—; also bd. dirs. Mem. bd. govs. Real Estate Bd. N.Y.; mem. Lincoln Ctr. Real Estate and Constrn. Coun. Office: Brookfield Properties Corp One Liberty Plaza 165 Broadway 6th Fl New York NY 10006

CLARK, RICHARD EUGENE, music educator; b. Wenatchee, Wash., Apr. 16, 1930; s. Raymond Otto Clark and Maude Myrtle Bass. BA, We. Wash. U., 1952, MA, 1970; MDiv, Am. Bapt. Sem. of West, 1955; MA, Calif. State U., Carson, 1989; postgrad., Wycliffe Coll., 1960—61. Nat. cert. tchr. music. Instr. sociology Coll. of Ozarks, Point Lookout, Mo., 1970—71, S.W. Mo. State U., Springfield, 1971—72, Whatcom C.C., Bellingham, Wash., 1972—73; cmty. planner Whatcom County Opportunity Coun., Bellingham, 1973—76; itinerant prof. sociology and religion Chapman U., Orange, Calif., 1977—83; journalist, former editor Rec.-Jour. Newspaper, Ferndale, Wash., 1984—90; instr. piano Wash. State Music Tchrs. Assn.-Bellingham chpt., Blaine, 1990—. Editor The Clarion Wash. State Music Tchrs. Assn., 1994—97, pres. Bellingham chpt., 1997—99. Author: Point Roberts, USA: The History of a Canadian Enclave, 1980, Sam Hill's Peace Arch: Remembrance of Dreams Past, 2003; editor: The Last Diary of Andrew JAckson Laomis, 2005. Founder Pacific Arts Found.; vicar Ch. Holy Nativity, Calgary, Canada, 1961—67; pastor First Bapt. Ch., Pincher Creek, Canada, 1955—59. Named to Wash. State Music Tchrs. Assn. Hall of Fame, 2004; recipient Dyson Hague Meml. Liturgics First prize, 1960, Bob Robbins Performing Arts award, Close Up Found. & No. Light Newspaper, 1999, Thomas L. George hon. lifetime achievement award, Record-Jour. Newspaper, 2004, Hon. Lifetime Achievement award, Internat. Peace Arch Assn., 2005. Mem.: Internat. Peace Arch Assn. (hon. Lifetime Achievement award 2005), Old Main Soc. Office Phone: 360-332-5175. Personal E-mail: dclark30@peoplepc.com.

CLARK, RICHARD T., pharmaceutical company executive; BA in Liberal Arts, Washington and Jefferson Coll., 1968; MBA, Am. Univ., 1970. Quality control insp., indsl. engr., quality control analyst, lead supr. pharm. prodn. MSD, 1972—78, sr. new products planner, 1978—81, prodn. mgr. Elkton Pharm. Labs., 1981—83, mgr. indsl. engring., 1983—84; sr. mgr. indsl. engring. MPMD, 1984—85, dir. ops. improvement, 1985—86; sr. dir. mgmt. engring. Merck Sharp & Dohme/MPMD, 1986—89; exec. dir. mgmt. engring. Merck Pharm. Mfg. Divsn., 1989—91; v.p. materials mgmt. and mgmt. engring. MMD, 1991—93, v.p. procurement and materials mgmt., 1993—94, v.p. N.Am. ops., 1994—96, sr. v.p. N.Am. ops., 1996—97; exec. v.p., COO Merck-Medco Managed Care, 1997—2000; chmn., pres., CEO Merck Medco Health Solutions, Inc. (formerly Merck-Medco Managed Care, L.L.C.), 2000—02; chmn. Merck Medco Health Solutions, Inc., 2002—03; sr. v.p. quality comml. affairs Merck Mfg. Divsn., 1997, pres., 2003—05; pres., CEO Merck & Co. Inc., 2005—. Lt. U.S. Army, 1970—72. Office: Merck & Co Inc One Merck Dr Whitehouse Station NJ 08889-0100

CLARK, RICHARD WALTER, education consultant; b. Mt. Pleasant, Iowa, Apr. 14, 1936; s. Samuel Richard and Floreine Eunice (Walz) C.; m. Rosemary Helma Savage, June 10, 1958; children: Melissa O'Neal, Cameron Clark. BA, U. Wash., 1957, MA, 1963, PhD, 1970. Cert. tchr., prin., supt., Wash. Lectr., grad. asst. U. Wash., Seattle, 1960-61; tchr. Bellevue (Wash.) Pub. Schs., 1961-65, adminstr., 1965-91, dep. supt., to 1991; sr. assoc. Ctr. for Ednl. Renewal, U. Wash., Seattle, 1987—, Inst. for Ednl. Inquiry, Seattle, 1992—; exec. dir. Nat. Network Ednl. Renewal, 2001—04. Cons. Pew Charitable Trusts, Phila., 1988-2001, MacArthur Found., Chgo., 1991-92, Coalition of Essential Schs., Brown U., Providence, 1990-97, Ednl Commn. of the States, Denver, 1990-91, Calgary (Alta., Can.) Bd. Edn., 1990-91, others. Author: Effective Speech, 1982, 3d edit., 1994, (with others) Glencoe English 10, 11, 12, 1981, 2nd edit., 1985, (with others) Kids and School Reform, 1997, Effective Professional Development Schools, 1999; contbr. articles to profl. jours., chpts. to books. Pres. Youth Eastside Svcs., Bellevue, 1972. Capt. USMC, 1957-63. Recipient Outstanding Performance Pub. Svc. award Seattle King County Mcpl. League, 1987; named Educator of Yr., Lions Club, 1991. Mem.: Nat. Soc. Study of Edn., Wash. Assn. Sch. Adminstrs., Am. Edn. Rsch. Assn., Phi Delta Kappa. Methodist. Home and Office: 209 140th Ave Bellevue WA 98005 Personal E-mail: clarkd@msn.com.

CLARK, ROBERT ARTHUR, mathematician, educator; b. Melrose, Mass., May 3, 1923; s. Arthur Henry and Persis (Kidder) C.; m. Jane Burr Crofut Kinder, June 25, 1966. Student, Colo. Coll., 1940-42; BA, Duke, 1944; MA, MIT, 1946, PhD, 1949. Instr., research asso. MIT, 1946-50, vis. asst. prof., 1956-57; faculty Case Inst. Tech. (now Case Western Res. U.), Cleve., 1950—, prof. math., 1964-85, prof. emeritus, 1985—, acting head dept. math., 1960-61, assoc. chmn. dept. math., 1974-79, 82-84, exec. officer, 1981-82. Vis. mem. U.S. Army Math. Research Center, Madison, Wis., 1961-62 Mem. AAAS, Am. Math. Soc., Math. Assn. Am., Soc. Indsl. and Applied Math., Phi Beta Kappa, Sigma Xi. Achievements include spl. research asymptotic integration theory of differential equations and theory thin elastic shells. Home: 7469 Sherman Rd Gates Mills OH 44040-9769 Office: Case Western Res Univ Dept Math Cleveland OH 44106

CLARK, ROBERT CHARLES, law educator; b. New Orleans, Feb. 26, 1944; s. William Vernon and Edwina Ellen (Nuessly) Clark; m. Kathleen Margaret Tighe, June 1, 1968; children— Alexander Ian, Matthew Tighe. BA in Theology, Maryknoll Coll., 1966; PhD in Philosophy, Columbia U., 1971; JD, Harvard U., 1972. Bar: Mass. 1972. Assoc. Ropes & Gray, Boston, 1972-74; asst. prof. Yale Law Sch., New Haven, 1974-76, assoc. prof., 1976-77, prof., 1977-78; vis. prof. Harvard Law Sch., Cambridge, Mass., 1978—79, prof., 1979—, Royall prof. law, 1989—2003, Harvard U. disting. svc. prof., Austin Wakeman Scott prof. law, 2003—, dean, 1989—2003. Bd. dirs. Collins & Aikman Corp., 1994—, Omnicon Group Inc., 2002—, Time Warner, Inc., 2004—; trustee Teachers Ins. Annuity Assn., 1988—. Contbr. articles to profl. jours. Mem.: ABA. Office: Harvard Law Sch 1563 Massachusetts Ave Cambridge MA 02138*

CLARK, ROBERT HENRY, JR., finance company executive; b. Manchester, N.H., Mar. 4, 1941; s. Robert Henry and Elva C. (Stearns) C.; m. Rosalie Foster Case, Dec. 21, 1963; children: Robert Henry III, Hilary Eagan, Hadley Case. BSBA, Boston U., 1964. Mcpl. bond underwriter Merrill Lynch, Pierce, Fenner & Smith, N.Y.C., 1964-70; v.p. Case, Pomeroy & Co., Inc., N.Y.C., 1971-75, exec. v.p., 1975-83, pres., 1983—, CEO, 1993—, chmn., 1999—; v.p. fin. Felmont Oil Corp., 1972-79, exec. v.p., 1979-84. Trustee Boston U., 1984-87. Mem. Sigma Alpha Epsilon Office: Case Pomeroy & Co Inc 521 5th Ave 36th Flr New York NY 10175

CLARK, ROBERT KING, communications educator, consultant, actor, model; b. Springfield, Mass., Apr. 12, 1934; s. Harry Robert and Alice (McClure) C.; m. Suzanne Chapin, Apr. 9, 1966; children— Jennifer, Jeffrey, Anne Elizabeth BA, U. Wyo., 1956; MA, U. Tenn., 1960; PhD, Ohio State U., 1971. Instr. journalism U. Tenn., Knoxville, 1958; instr. speech Westminster Coll., New Wilmington, Pa., 1959-61; faculty Bowling Green State U., Ohio, 1963—, prof. radio-TV film, 1980-84, prof. emeritus, 1985—; gen. mgr. Sta. WBGU-FM, 1976-85. Cons. in field; lectr. in field; seminar leader in field; yoga instr./therapist. Contbr. articles to profl. jours. Presbyterian. Office: 1064 Village Dr Bowling Green OH 43402-1231 Personal E-mail: rkclark@wcnet.org.

CLARK, ROBERT LLOYD, JR., librarian; b. McAlester, Okla., Sept. 12, 1945; s. Robert Lloyd and Ruth Fairel (Nelson) C.; children: Roberta, Johnathan, Kathryn; m. Audrey Lynn Wolfe, 1987. BA, U. Okla., 1968, M.L.S., 1969. Dir. div. archives and records Okla. Dept. Librs., Oklahoma City, 1968-72, data processing coord., 1972-73, dir., 1976—2001; libr. emeritus Okla. State, 2001—. Asst. dir. pub. services Jackson (Miss.) Met. Library System, 1973-74; dir. Mid-Miss. Regional Library, Kosciusko, 1974-76; sec. Okla. Archives and Records Commn., 1976—; ex officio sec. Okla. Arts and Humanities Council, 1976-81; sec. adv. council Library Services and Constrn. Act., 1976—; adv. bd. Okla. Hist. Records, 1979—; adv. council U. Okla. Sch. Library and Info. Sci., 1985-88, 95—; adv. council State regents for Higher Edn. on Ednl. Outreach, 1985-88; cons. in field. Author: Archive-Library Relations, 1976; contbr. articles to library pubs. Mem. adv. com. State Regents for Higher Edn., 1984-88. Robert L. Clark, Jr. Day proclaimed by Gov. of Okla., Nov. 15, 1982 Mem. ALA (chmn. pub. library assn. interlibrary coop. com. 1974-77, mem. standards com. 1979-82), Okla. Library Assn., Southwestern Library Assn. (pres. 1980-82), Amigos Bibliog. Council (exec. bd. 1977-80), Assn. State Libraries (bd. dirs. 1977-80), Assn. Chief Officers of State Library Agys. (chmn. legis. com. 1979-81, chmn. 1982-84), Western Coun. State Librs. (pres. 2000). Office: Okla State Libr Emeritus 1300 Wildrose Trl Edmond OK 73034

CLARK, ROBERT MUREL, JR., lawyer; b. Dallas, Mar. 7, 1948; s. Robert M. Sr. and Dorrace Helen (Schaerdel) C.; m. Kimberly Ann Kerss, Oct. 25, 1986; 1 child, Ashley Pendleton. BBA, U. Tex., 1972; MBA, So. Meth. U., 1978; JD, Oklahoma City U., 1982. Bar: Tex. 1982, U.S. Dist. Ct. (no. dist.) Tex. 1982, U.S. Ct. Appeals (5th cir.) 1982, U.S. Supreme Ct. 1988; cert. in civil trial law Tex. Bd. Legal Specialization; cert. trial specialist Nat. Bd. Trial Advocacy. Ptnr. Eddleman & Clark, Dallas, 1989—. Author: The Evangelical Knights of Saint John, 2003; contbr. articles to profl. jours. Del. state conv. Tex. Rep. Party, 1970, 72, 74, 82, 90; bd. dirs. Haile Selassie Fund for Ethiopian Children in Need; sec., bd. dirs. Dallas Goethe Ctr., Tex. Conf. of Chs. Decorated grand officer Order of Ethiopian Lion, hon. Knight of Justice, Order of Vitez (Hungary), knight Order of St. John (Brandenburg), Order of Francis I; recipient Grand Cross, Rwandan Order of the Lion, 2000. Fellow Tex. Bar Found. (life), Soc. Antiquaries (Scotland); mem. State Bar Tex., Am. Bd. Trial Advs. (Dallas chpt.), Oak Cliff Bar Assn. (pres. 1990), Am. Soc. Legal History, Soc. of the Cin., Aztec Club, Sons Republic of Tex., Founders and Patriots Am. (atty. gen.), Nat. Huguenot Soc. (former coun. gen. and 3d v.p. gen.), St. Nicholas Soc., Johanniterorden-Bailiwick of Brandenburg, Johanniter Hilfsgemeinschaften (pres., bd. dirs., Tex.), Army and Navy Club (Washington), City Tavern Club (Washington), Phi Delta Phi, Phi Delta Theta. Episcopalian. Office: 4627 N Central Expy Dallas TX 75205-4022 Office Phone: 214-528-2400. Personal E-mail: rmkkclark@aol.com.

CLARK, ROBERT NEWHALL, electrical and aeronautical engineering educator; b. Ann Arbor, Mich., Apr. 17, 1925; s. Ellef S. and Esther (Baker) C.; m. Mary Quiatt, Aug. 20, 1949; children: Charles W., John R., Timothy J., Franklin T. BSEE, U. Mich., 1950, MSEE, 1951; PhD, Stanford U., 1969. Registered profl. engr., Wash., Minn. Rsch. engr. Honeywell, Inc., Mpls., 1951-57; lectr. Stanford U., 1968; prof. elec. engring. U. Wash., Seattle, 1957—, prof. aeronautics and astronautics, 1986-94, prof. emeritus, 1994—. Vis. scientist Fraunhofer Gesellschaft, Karlsruhe, W. Germany, 1976-77; guest prof. U. Duisburg, W. Germany, 1983-84; cons. analyst Boeing Aerospace Co., Seattle, 1971-92. Author: Introduction to Automatic Control Systems, 1962, Fault Diagnosis in Dynamic Systems, 1989, Control System Dynamics, 1996, Issues of Fault Diagnosis for Dynamic Systems, 2000, An American Family, 2003. With USMC, 1943-46. NSF fellow, 1966-68. Fellow IEEE (life), AIAA (assoc.). Home: 3900 50th Ave NE Seattle WA 98105-5238 Office: U Wash PO Box 352500 Seattle WA 98195-2500 Office Phone: 206-523-1685.

CLARK, ROBERT PHILLIPS, editor, consultant; b. Randolph, Vt, Dec. 3, 1921; s. James S. and Gladys M. (Phillips) C.; m. Jeanne Orr Rice, Dec. 14, 1949; children: Patricia Orr Clark Roy, Elizabeth Phillips Clark Christiansen. AB, Tufts U., 1942; MA, U. Mo., 1948. Reporter Owensboro Messenger & Inquirer, Ky., 1948-49; reporter, sci. writer Courier-Jour., Louisville, 1949-62, Washington corr., 1958; mng. editor Louisville Times, 1962-71; exec. editor Courier-Jour. and Louisville Times, 1971-79; editor Fla. Times-Union and Jacksonville Jour., 1979-82; v.p news Harte-Hanks Newspapers, 1983-86; co-chmn. rsch. com. Newspaper Readership Project, 1982-83; news, editorial cons., 1987—. Disting. vis. prof. Baylor U., 1990-92, Slippery Rock U., 1990; mem. accrediting com. Accrediting Coun. on Edn. in Journalism and Mass Comm., 1986-89. Author: Success Stories: What 28 Newspapers Are Doing to Gain and Retain Readers, 1988, Keys to Success: Strategies for Newspaper Marketing in the '90s, 1989; also numerous articles. Bd. dir. Louisville Presbyn. Theol. Sem., 1968-73, past sec.; trustee S.W. Sch. of Art and Craft, 1993-96; bd. dir. San Antonio Bot. Soc., 1996—2004; Pulitzer Prize juror, 1968, 69, 88, 89. Served to capt. US Army, WWII, PTO. Decorated Bronze Star, Purple Heart; Nieman fellow Harvard U., 1960-61; named Editor of Yr., Nat. Press Photographers Assn., 1967. Mem. Am. Soc. Newspaper Editors (pres. 1985-86, v.p. Found. 1980-81, 85-86, contbr. Am. Editor), Soc. Profl. Journalists (contbr. Quill Jour.), AP Mng. Editors Assn. (pres. 1974-75, chmn. regents 1979-80), Internat. Press Inst. (bd. dir. Am. com. 1981-87), Soc. Mayflower Descs. (capt. San Antonio colony 1999-2003, elder 2003—05), Club Giraud, Torch Club (San Antonio, pres. 1997-98, contbr. The Torch), Harvard Club, Delta Tau Delta. Democrat. Presbyterian. Home: 3506 Elm Knoll San Antonio TX 78230-2706

CLARK, ROGER EARL, lawyer; b. New Orleans, Oct. 23, 1946; s. Earl B. and Erma Le (Chambers) C.; m. Barbara Jo Columbus, Dec. 23, 1971; 1 dau., Kelly Elizabeth. B.A., Rice U., 1968; J.D., Harvard U., 1971. Bar: Ill. 1971, Colo. 1973. Assoc. Pope, Ballard, Shepard and Fowle, Chgo., 1971-73, Hammond and Chilson, Loveland, Colo., 1973-76; assoc. Lynn A. Hammond Law Offices, Loveland, Colo., 1976-80, ptnr. Hammond, Clark and White, 1980-97, ptnr. Hammond and Clark, 1997, now ptnr. Clark Williams and Matsunaka LLC, Loveland; Bd. dirs. Hospice of Larimer County, 1994—, pres. 1997-98, bd. dirs. Loveland Econ. Devel. Coun., 1992-94. Mem. ABA, Colo. Bar Assn. (exec. council young lawyers sect. 1977-83, chmn. 1982-83, bd. of govs. 1985-87, 96—, chmn. gen. practice sect. 1985-87, v.p. 1986-87, pres.-elect 2004), Larimer County Bar Assn. (pres. 1984-85), Colo. Trial Lawyers Assn., Loveland C. of C. (bd. dirs. 1983—, pres.-elect 1987, pres. 1988). Democrat. Methodist. Club: Loveland Sertoma (pres. 1980-81). Home: 1220 W 6th St Loveland CO 80537-5347 Office: Clark Williams and Matsunaka LLC Suite 1-2881 N Monroe Ave PO Box 801 Loveland CO 80539

CLARK, ROSS BERT, II, lawyer; b. Lafayette, Ind., Dec. 23, 1932; s. Ross Bert and Pauline Frances (Wilkinson) C.; m. Madge Logan, Dec. 27, 1959; 1 stepchild, George W. Johnson III. BA in History, U. of the South, 1954; JD, U. Tenn., 1960. Bar: Tenn. 1961, U.S. Dist. Ct. (we. dist.) Tenn. 1961, U.S. Dist. Ct. (no. dist.) Miss. 1981, U.S. Dist. Ct. (ea. dist.) Ark. 1996, U.S. Ct. Appeals (6th cir.) 1962. Law clk. to presiding judge U.S. Dist. Ct. (we. dist.) Tenn., Memphis, 1961-62; assoc. Rupert & Ewing, Memphis, 1962-64, Laughlin, Watson, Garthright & Halle, Memphis, 1964-68; ptnr. Laughlin, Halle, Clark, Gibson, McBride, Memphis, 1968-84, McKnight, Hudson, Lewis, Henderson & Clark, Memphis, 1985-91, Apperson, Crump, Duzane & Maxwell, Memphis, 1991-96, Armstrong Allen PLLC, Memphis, 1996—. Instr. med. and dental jurisprudence U. Tenn., Memphis, 1963-72; asst. city atty. City of Memphis, 1972-78. Tenn. commr. Nat. Conf. Commrs. on Uniform Laws, 1998—; chmn. bd. dirs. Memphis Heart Assn., 1971—72; mem. adv. coun. U. Tenn. Law Sch., 1983—90, chmn. adv. coun., 1986—88; trustee U. of the South, 1992—95, 1998—2004. Fellow: Tenn. Bar Found. (trustee 1989—98, chmn. 1996—97), Am. Bar Found.; mem.: Memphis Bar Assn. (treas. 1981, sec. 1982, v.p. 1983, pres. 1984), Tenn. Bar Assn. (ho. of dels. 1986—88, bd. govs. 1988—94), Tenn. Supreme Ct. Hist. Soc. (bd. dir. 2002—, pres. 2004—05), Rotary (sec. 1988, bd. dir. 1988—90, 2002—, Paul Harris fellow 2002). Republican. Episcopalian. Office: Armstrong Allen PLLC Brinkley Plz Ste 700 80 Monroe Ave Memphis TN 38103-2481

CLARK, R(UFUS) BRADBURY, lawyer, director; b. Des Moines, May 11, 1924; s. Rufus Bradbury and Gertrude Martha (Burns) C.; m. Polly Ann King, Sept. 6, 1949; children: Cynthia Clark Maxwell, Rufus Bradbury, John Atherton. BA, Harvard U., 1948, JD, 1951; diploma in law, Oxford U., Eng., 1952; D.H.L., Ch. Div. Sch. Pacific, San Francisco, 1983. Bar: Calif. 1952. Assoc. O'Melveny & Myers, L.A., 1952-62, sr. ptnr., 1961-93; mem. mgmt. com., 1983-90; of counsel O'Melveny & Myers LLP, L.A., 1993—. Bd. dirs. Econ. Resources Corp., Brown Internat. Corp., Brown Citrus Sys., Inc., Avoco Internat. Corp., John Tracy Clinic, also pres. 1982-88, Tracy Family Hearing Ctrs., Ch. Charitable Found. Episcopal Diocese L.A., 2000—. Editor: California Corporation Laws, 7 vols, 1976-2005. Chancellor Protetant Episcopal Ch. in the Diocese of L.A., 1967-2005, chancellor emeritus, hon. canon, 1983—. Capt. U.S. Army, 1943-46. Decorated Bronze Star with oak leaf cluster, Purple Heart with oak leaf cluster; Fulbright grantee, 1952. Mem.: ABA (com. law and acctg., task force on audit letters 1976—93, com. on opinions 1988—92), L.A. County Bar Assn., State Bar Calif. (chmn. drafting com. on gen. corp. law 1973—81, drafting com. on nonprofit corp. law 1980—84, exec. com. bus. law sect. 1977—78, 1984—87, sec. 1986—87, com. nonprofit orgns. 1991—, task force and standing com. on opinions 1999—), Alamitos Bay Yacht Club (Long Beach, Calif.), Chancery Club, Harvard Club. Republican. Office: O'Melveny & Myers LLP 400 S Hope St Los Angeles CA 90071-2899 Business E-Mail: bclark@omm.com.

CLARK, SHARON ANN, educational consultant, music educator; b. Lowell, Mass., Aug. 3, 1961; d. William K. and Dorothy A. (McNamara) Clark; m. Eric J. Mortenson, July 11, 1998. MusB, U. of Mass. at Lowell, Lowell, MA, 1983; MED, Fitchburg State Coll., Fitchburg, MA, 1988; EdD, Nova Southeastern U., Ft. Lauderdale, Florida, 2003. Cert. tchr. Mass., 1983. Ednl. cons. Edn. Performance Systems, Inc., Woburn, Mass., 2000; instrnl. specialist Lowell Pub. Schools, Mass., 2001—. Music specialist Lowell Pub. Schs., Mass., 1998—2005. Choir mem. St. Margaret Ch., Lowell, Mass., 1997—. Vis. scholar Comprehensive Sch. Reform grant, Mass. Dept. of Edn., 2002; Lighthouse Tech. grant, 1999, Jordan Fundamentals grant, Michael Jordan Found. - NIKE, 2001, Creative Schools grant, Mass. Cultural Coun., 2002. Mem.: Lowell Sch. Adminstrs. Assn., Am. Fedn. Tchrs., Music Educators Nat. Conf., Nat. Staff Devel. Coun. Avocations: biking, painting, travel. Home: 18 Crestwood Dr Hudson NH 03051 Office: BFButler Mid Sch Tech 1140 Gorham St Lowell MA 01852 Office Phone: 978-970-5494. Personal E-mail: shadotclark@earthlink.net. E-mail: sharonclark@lowell.k12.ma.us.

CLARK, SHARON JACKSON, private school administrator; b. Istanbul, Turkey, Feb. 3, 1939; d. John Warren and Maxine Jett (Brient) Jackson; m. Ronald Eugene Clark, June 6, 1959; children: Kristen Anne, Kevin Brooks, Jeffrey Kimball. BFA, Calif. Coll. Arts and Crafts, 1968; MS in Edn., Wheelock Coll., 1978; student, Moore Coll. Art. Co-founder Jowanio, Syracuse, NY, The Thoreau Sch., Salt Lake City, Glen Urquhart Sch., Beverly, Mass.; head, founder Clark Sch. for Creative Learning, Danvers, Mass. Mem. Gifted/Talented Educators North Shore (bd. dir.), Danvers Hist. Soc. (bd. dir.). Home: 502 Locust St Danvers MA 01923-1252 Office Phone: 978-777-4699. E-mail: clarkschool@clarkschool.com.

CLARK, SHERMAN J., law educator; Grad., Towson State U.; JD, Harvard U. Atty. Kirkland & Ellis; prof. law U. Mich Law Sch., Ann Arbor, 1995—. Contbr. articles to law jours. Office: U Mich Law Sch 300F Legal Research 625 S State St Ann Arbor MI 48109-1215 Office Phone: 734-747-4039, 734-764-8309. E-mail: sjclark@umich.edu.

CLARK, STANFORD E., accountant; b. Farmington, Utah, Sept. 21, 1917; m. Merrial Jane Knight Mackay, Nov. 16, 1942 (dec. July 1993); m. Evelyn Harrow, Nov. 3, 1995. Student, LDS Bus. Coll., Salt Lake City, 1935. With Utah Constrn. Co., Riverton, Wyo., 1955-57; rancher Riverton, 1948-55; office mgr. Superior Bit Svc., Riverton, 1958-68; v.p., sec., treas. Allied Nuclear Corp., Riverton, 1957-69, Western Std. Corp., Riverton, 1957-83, pres., treas., dir., 1989—; also bd. dirs. Treas.; v.p., sec., bd. dirs. Snow King Resort Mgmt. Inc., Jackson, 1992-, Jackson Hole Springs Water Co., 1995—; treas. S.K. Land Ltd. Liability Co., 1992—; v.p., treas., bd. dirs. Snow King Resort Ctr., Inc., 1999—, Snow King Resort, Inc., 1999—; sec., treas., bd. dirs., 1991-99; pres. Western Recreation Corp., 1957—. With USCG, 1942-45. Republican. Office: Western Standard Corp 205 S Broadway Ave Riverton WY 82501-4331

CLARK, STEVEN J., plastic surgeon, consultant; b. Bklyn. s. Ruben and Mildred Clark; m. Donna Lucy Abate, July 15, 1987; children: Alexandra, Benjamin, Jacob. BS in Biomed. Scis., CCNY, 1974—77; DMD, U. Pa., Phila., 1977—81; MD, Hahnemann U., Pa., 1988—90. Diplomate Nat. Bd. Med. Examiners, 1991, cert. Am. Bd. Oral and Maxillofacial Surgery, 1998, diplomate Am. Bd. Plastic Surgery, 2001. Resident Hackensack Med. Ctr., NJ, 1981—82; maxillofacial surg. resident Columbia U., N.Y.C., 1982—85; intern and resident, gen. surgery St. Barnabas Med. Ctr., Livingston, NJ, 1990—93; fellow, plastic and reconstructive surgery U. Chgo., 1993—95; breast and cosmetic fellow Charlotte Plastic Surgery Ctr., U. N.C., Chapel Hill, 1998—99; med. dir., emergency med. svcs. and tng. Eglin Regional Med. Ctr., Eglin AFB, Fla., 1995—98, breast reconstructive surgeon, 2001—; assoc. attending Presbyn. Hosp., 1998—99, Carolina Med. Ctr., 1998—99, Sacred Heart Med. Ctr., Emerald Coast, 2002—, N. Okaloosa Med. Ctr., 1999—, Twin Cities Hosp., Niceville, Fla., 1999—2003, chief, dept. surgery, 2003—. Instr., head and neck anatomy Sch. Dental Medicine, Columbia U., N.Y.C., 1984, clin. instr., 1984—85; surg. attending, dept. surgery Harlem Hosp. Ctr., NY, 1986; asst. clin. prof. Sch. Dental Medicine, Fairleigh Dickinson U., 1986—87; assoc. attending, dept. maxillofacial surgery St. Barnabas Med. Ctr., Livingston, NJ, 1985—87. Fellow: ACS, Am. Soc. Dental Anesthesiology; mem.: AMA, Med. Soc. N.J., Okaloosa County Med. Soc., Fla. Med. Assn., Am. Soc. Maxillofacial Surgeons, S.E. Soc. Plastic and Reconstructive Surgeons, Am. Soc. Plastic Surgeons. Avocations: music, boxing, collecting classic cars, art. Office: Bluewater Plastic Surgery & Cosmetic Ctr 4400 E Hwy 20 Ste 501 Niceville FL 32578

CLARK, SUSAN (NORA GOULDING), actress; b. Sarnia, Ont., Can., Mar. 8, 1940; d. George Raymond and Eleanor Almond (McNaughton) Clark; m. Alex Karras; 1 child, Katie Karras. Student, Toronto (Ont.) Children's Players, 1956-59; student (Acad. scholar), Royal Acad. Dramatic Art, London. Ptnr. Georgian Bay Prodns. Actor: (stage prodn.) Appearances to the Contrary, 2000, Glass Menagerie, 2002, Sisters Rosensweig, 2002, BiCoastal Woman, 2003, Dancing at Lughnasa, 2003, Importance of Being Earnest, 2004, The Body, 2004; (TV series) Webster, 1983, Emily of New Moon, 1998; (films) Nobody's Perfekt, 1981, Porky's, 1981, Butterbox Babies, 1995; (TV films) Babe, 1975 (Emmy for oustanding lead actress in a drama, 1975), Sherlock Holmes: The Strange Case of Alice Faulkner, 1981, The Choice, 1981, Maid in America, 1982, Tonya & Nancy: The Inside Story, 1994, Snowbound: The Jim and Jennifer Stolpa Story, 1994. Mem. ACLU, Am. Film Inst. Office: Ste 308 13400 Riverside Dr Sherman Oaks CA 91423-2541

CLARK, SUSAN MATTHEWS, psychologist; b. Newton, Kans., Aug. 5, 1950; d. Glenn Wesley Matthews and Jane Buckles; m. S. Bruce Clark, Aug. 14, 1971; children: Casandra Jane, Ryan Matthews. BME, Wichita State U., 1971, MME, 1975, MA, 1982; PhD, North Tex. State U., 1985. Elem. tchr. Derby (Kans.) Pub. Schs., 1972-74; profl. musician Amarillo (Tex.) Symphony, 1974-77; psychol. cons. Achenbach Ctr., Hardtner, Kans., 1983-85; psychologist intern VA Med. Ctr., Wichita, Kans., 1984-85; psychologist St. Francis Acad., Inc., Salina, Kans., 1986-89, Psychiat. Clinic Wichita, 1989-93; gen. mgr. Affiliated Psychiat. Svcs., Wichita, 1993-95; psychologist Charter Clinic, Wichita, Kans., 1995-99. Bd. dirs. Salina Coalition for the Prevention of Child Abuse, 1986-87. Author: Grant, 1987 Bd. deacons Plymouth Congl. Ch., Wichita, 1989-92. Recipient: Phi Kappa Phi, Mu Phi Epsilon, Psi Chi. Mem. APA, Nat. Acad. Neuropsychology, Kans. Psychol. Assn., Children with Attention Deficit Disorder. Republican. Congregationalist. Avocations: stained glass, photography, bridge, tennis, reading. Office: 242 Courtleigh St Wichita KS 67218-1712 Home: PO Box 252 Derby KS 67037-0252 Fax: 316-788-5013/316-291-6928.

CLARK, SYLVIA DOLORES, business educator; b. NYC, June 5, 1959; d. Barna and Eva Anna (Beniczky-Gabriel) Csuros. BBA, Bernard Baruch Coll. CUNY, 1979, MPhil, 1993, PhD, 1994; MBA, NYU, 1982. Rsch. analyst Kornhauser and Calene and predecessor firm, N.Y.C., 1979-80; project coord. Gen. Foods, Inc., White Plains, N.Y., 1980-82; rsch. assoc. Lord, Geller, Federico, Einstein, Inc., N.Y.C., 1982-83; instr. Coll. of S.I. CUNY, 1984-93, asst. prof., 1994-97; instr. Wagner Coll., S.I., 1993-94; asst. prof. Queensborough C.C. CUNY, 1997-98, St. John's U., Jamaica, NY, 1998—2004, assoc. prof., 2004—. Becker Family Fund scholar, 1978, Baruch Coll. Alumni Assn. scholar, 1979. Mem.: Am. Statis. Assn., Am. Mktg. Assn., Phi Beta Kappa, Beta Gamma Sigma (past exec. bd.). Home: 62 Renwick Ave Staten Island NY 10301-4216 Office: St John's U Spellman Hall TCB 300 Howard Ave Staten Island NY 10301-4496 Office Phone: 718-390-4552. E-mail: clark1094@aol.com.

CLARK, TERRI, country singer; b. Montreal, Can., Aug. 5, 1968; d. Les Sauson and Linda Clark. Previous jobs include work at restaurants, Gilley's, the Wax Mus., Nashville. Albums: Terri Clark, 1995, Just the Same, 1996, How I Feel, 1998, Fearless, 2000, Pain to Kill, 2003. Named Top New Female Country Artist Billboard mag., 1995; recipient Album of Yr. award Country Music Assn., 1996, Song of Yr., 1996, Vista Rising Star award, 1996, Canadian County Music Assoc. best single, 2003.

CLARK, TERRY DEE, political scientist, educator; b. Washington, D.C., Dv. Nov. 6, 1951; s. DeLair Aubrey and Sally Ethel Clark; m. Bonnie M. Guy, July 31, 1954; 1 child, Jessica Renelle Barron. PhD, U. of Ill., Urbana-Champaign, Illinois, 1985—92; B.S., US Mil. Acad., West Point, NY, 1969—73. Prof. of polit. sci. Creighton U., Omaha, Nebr., 1993—. J. william fulbright sr. scholar peer rev. com. for ctrl. eurasia CIES, Washington, D.C., DC. Author: (books) 1) books: a) Unity or Separation: Center-Periphery Relations in the Former Soviet Union (Praeger, 2002), b) Going Beyond Post-Communist Studies (ME Sharpe, 2002), (journal articles) Slavic Review (two articles), (articles) Nationalities Papers (two articles), (journal article) European Politics and Society (EEPS), PS: Politics and Political Science, (journal articles (three articles) Journal of Baltic Studies, (journal article) Economic Development and Cultural Change (EDCC), Journal of Policy Studies. Capt. US Army, 1973—85, Goeppingen, Germany. Recipient Dean's Award for Excellence in Tchg., Creighton Coll. of Arts and Sciences, 1988; fellow Fulbright Scholar, Fulbright, 1999-2000; grantee IREX Advanced Individual Rsch. Grant, Internat. Rsch. Exch. Bd. (IREX), 1996, APSA Small Rsch. Grant, Am. Polit. Sci. Assn., 2003-2004. Mem.: Lithuanian Polit. Sci. Assn. (LPSA), Assn. for the Advancement of Slavic Studies (AAASS), Am. Polit. Sci. Assn. (APSA). R-Consevative. Charismatic Protestant. Avocations: hiking, international travel, writing. Office: Creighton University Department of Political Science Omaha NE 68178 Office Phone: 402-280-4712. E-mail: tclark@creighton.edu.

CLARK, THOMAS B., SR., real estate broker; b. Ann Arbor, Mich., Jan. 21, 1943; s. Thomas W. and Helen (Sheldon) Clark; m. Dianne Stribley, Dec. 4, 1970; children: Thomas B. Jr., Andrea Lynn. BA, U. Mich., 1964. Dir. rec. U. Mich., Ann Arbor, 1965-70; sr. auditor Touche Ross (now Deloitte and Touche), Detroit, 1970-72; acctg. mgr. E.R.I.M., Ann Arbor, 1972-75; owner/developer Clark Apts., Ann Arbor, 1975—; owner Irish Hills Golf Club and Banquet Ctr., Onsted, Mich. Bd. dirs. Kenitis Corp. Mem.: Ann Arbor Apt. Assn. (bd. dirs.). Avocation: golf. Address: PO Box 7822 Ann Arbor MI 48107-7822 Office: 621 S Forest Ave Ann Arbor MI 48104-3123 Office Phone: 734-996-2836. Personal E-mail: tcapts@aol.com.

CLARK, THOMAS CARLYLE, banker; b. Barbourville, Ky., Dec. 1, 1947; s. Buford Thomas and Eleanor Randolph (Owens) C. AB, Duke U., 1969; MBA, Harvard U., 1971; LLD, Cumberland Coll., 1991, Union Coll., 2004. Officer Chem. Bank, N.Y.C., 1975-78; divsn. pres., mng. dir. U.S. Trust Co. N.Y., N.Y.C., 1978—. Pres. emeritus bd. dirs. Lubovitch Dance Co.; chmn. emeritus bd. trustees Union Coll., Ky.; bd. dirs. Concert Artists Guild, past pres.; bd. dirs. Svc. Mems. Legal Def. Network; trustee Duke U. With USN, 1971—75. Mem. Risk Mgmt. Assn. (past chmn. pvt. lending com.), Lincoln's Inn Soc. (alumni coun.), Duke U. Met. Alumni Assn. (past pres.), Am. Banking Assn. (past chair exec. com. for pvt. banking, alumni coun.), Kentuckians N.Y. Club, Met. Opera Club (bd. dirs.), Duke U. Alumni Assn. (bd. dirs., pres.-elect). Republican. Methodist. Office: Divsn Pres US Trust One Pickwick Plz Greenwich CT 06830

CLARK, THOMAS P., JR., lawyer; b. N.Y.C., Sept. 16, 1943; AB, U. Notre Dame, 1965; JD, U. Mo., Kansas City, 1973. Bar: Calif. 1973. Shareholder Stradling, Yocca, Carlson & Rauth P.C., Newport Beach, Calif., 1978—. Editor-in-chief The Urban Lawyer, 1972-73; contbr. articles to profl. jours. Capt. USMC, 1966-70. Mem. State Bar Calif., Orange County Bar Assn., Phi Kappa Phi. Office: Stradling Yocca Carlson & Rauth PC 660 Newport Center Dr Ste 1600 Newport Beach CA 92660-6458 E-mail: tclark@sycr.

CLARK, TOM JAY, science educator; b. Grand Rapids, Mich., Sept. 4, 1963; s. Tom Jay and Mary Ann Clark; m. Marit Ettersti Clark, Nov. 25, 2002; children: Lisa E. Blumenfeld, Camilla E. BS in Natural Resource Planning, Humboldt State U., 1989; postgrad., San Francisco State U., 1995. Tchr. sci. Benicia High Sch., Calif., 1995—2000, Berkeley High Sch., 2000—02, Tammalpais High Sch., Mill Valley, 2002—. Vol. U.S. Peace Corps, Niamey, Niger, 1990—93. Democrat. Avocations: backpacking, mountain climbing, bicycling, running, skiing. Office: Tamalpais High Sch 700 Miller Ave Mill Valley CA 94941

CLARK, TRUDY H., career officer; BA in sociology with honors, U. Md., 1972; student, Comm. Electronics Officer Sch., 1973—74; MS in guidance and counseling, Troy State U., 1987; disting. grad., Squadron Officer Sch., Maxwell AFB, 1980, Air Command and Staff Coll., 1987, Armed Forces Staff Coll., 1992, Air War Coll., Maxwell AFB, 1993. Second lt. USAF, 1973, first lt., 1975, cptn., 1977, major, 1985, lt. col., 1989, col., 1994, brigadier gen., 1999, maj. general, 2003; dir. command, control, comm. and computer sys. US Strategic Command, Offutt AFB, Nebr., 1999—2001; deputy dir. Defense Threat Reduction Agency (DTRA), Ft. Belvoir, Va., 2003—; chief tel. installations 392nd Comm. Group, Vandenberg AFB, Calif., 1974—76; chief programs mgmt. div. 2006th Comm. Group, Incirlik AFB, Turkey, 1976—79; chief comm. branch Joint Studies Group, Nellis AFB, Nev., 1979—81; chief threat analysis 4440th Tactical Fighter Training Group, Red Flag, Nellis AFB, Nev.; chief facilities operation branch 2146th Comm. Group, Osan AB, Republic of Korea, 1981—82; chief telecom. div. Langley AFB, Va., exec. officer, Hdqs. Tactical Comm. Div., 1982—84; comdr. 1880th Info. Systems Squadron, Tonopah Test Range, Nev., 1984—86; chief tactical command and control comm. sys. Hdqs. USAF, Washington, directorate, programs and evaluation, exec. officer for dep. dir. of programs and evaluation, 1987—89; comdr. staff support unit White House Comm. Agy., Washington, presdl. comm. officer, 1989—92; comdr. 60th comm. group Hdqs. 15th Air Force, Travis AFB, Calif., chief comm. div., 1993—94. Office: 8725 John J Kingman Rd MSC 6201 Fort Belvoir VA 22060-6201

CLARK, TUDY, art association administrator; b. Columbia, S.C., Mar. 26, 1947; d. Jason Leon Brown and Mary Lauren DeVore; m. Robert Clark; 1 child, Jamie Melissa Brus. MS, U. of S.C., 1986. Cert. Teacher SC. State dept. of Edn., 1969. Sch. program coord. Columbia Mus. of Art, Columbia, SC, 1998—; mus. divsn. coord. S.C. Art Edn. Assn., Columbia, SC, 2000—. Advisor CMA-Northeast, Columbia, SC, 2004—05. Mem.: ABC Steering Com., S.C. Arts Alliance, S.C. Fedn. of Mus., Nat. Art Edn. Assn., S.C. Art Edn. Assn. (bd. 2000—05, Outstanding Performance in Mus. Edn. award 2002, Pres. award 2003). Conservative-R. Episcopalian. Achievements include Numerous exhibitions of artwork. Avocations: painting, golf, travel. Office: Columbia Museum of Art PO Box 2068 Columbia SC 29202 Office Phone: 803-343-2199.

CLARK, VERNON E., retired military officer; b. Sioux City, Iowa, Sept. 7, 1944; Commd. ensign USN, advanced through ranks to adm., 2004; various assignments to vice-adm., dir. for opers., J-3 Joint Staff/The Pentagon, Washington; comdr. Second Fleet/Striking Fleet Atlantic, Norfolk, Va., 1999—2000; chief of naval ops. USN, Washington, 2000—05. Decorated Defense Distinguished Service medal, Distinguished Service medal, Legion of Merit, Defense Meritorious Service medal, Meritorious Service medal, Navy Commendation medal.

CLARK, VERONICA ANN WILDS (RONNI PATRIQUIN CLARK), journalist; b. St. Louis, May 22, 1943; d. Charles Ernest, Jr. and Marie Elizabeth (Perabo) Wilds; m. Guy Albert Luno, Jr., Aug. 10, 1961 (div. Nov. 1967); children: Judith Wilds Luno Adams, Guy Albert Luno III; m. Francis David Patriquin, Dec. 23, 1972 (dec. Apr. 1982); m. Farris Laray Clark, Jr., Nov. 25, 1995. Student, La. State U., 1961, N.E. La. U., 1964—67. Soc. editor Monroe News Star, La., 1964; news reporter Monroe Morning World, 1967; news dir. Televisual News, Baton Rouge, 1972—73; capital corr. Clarion Ledger, Jackson, Miss., 1974—76; chief capital bur. Shreveport Jour., Baton Rouge, 1976—91; polit. writer Gannett News Svc., Tallahassee, 1991—92; sr. reporter Mobile Register, Ala., 1992—2000, asst. city editor, 2000—. Pres. Capital Corrs. Assn., Baton Rouge, 1979-80, Mobile Gridiron, 1993; judge Loyola U. Silver Scribe Competition, New Orleans, 1985-90. Pres. Hist. Spanish Town Civic Assn., Baton Rouge, 1982-85; mem. Hist. Dist. Commn., Baton Rouge, 1984-85. Recipient numerous 1st Pl. AP awards Miss., Ala., La., 1974-97, Best Coverage Gov. award La. Press Assn., 1986, 88, Media Environ. award Organized Fisherman Fla., 1992, Edward J. Meeman Nat. Journalism award Scripps Howard Found, 1993. Mem. Mobile Press Club (News & Excellence award 1992, 98, Gen. Excellence/Cmty. Svc. award 1998), Soc. Profl. Journalists (pres. 1993-94). Roman Catholic. Avocations: canoeing, biking, gardening, reading, travel. Office: The Mobile Register 304 Government St Mobile AL 36602-2600 Office Phone: 251-219-5710. Business E-Mail: rpatriquin@mobileregister.com.

CLARK, VICKY JO, artist; b. Lamesa, Tex., Sept. 14, 1937; d. John and Betty Lee (McCleskey) T.; m. Bobby Claude Clark, Jan. 2, 1960; children: John Mark, James Matthew, Ginger. Student, Abilene Christian U., 1956-59. Instr. pastel workshops and pastel demonstrations. Exhibited in shows at The Pastel Soc. Am. Show, N.Y.C., 1987, 88, 89, 91, The Salmagundi Nonmember Show, N.Y.C., 1988-91, The Catharine Lorillord Wolfe Show, N.Y.C., 1988-90, Shades of Pastel, Balt., 1989-90, Westcoast Pastel Soc. Show, Carmichael, Calif., 1988, 89, 91, Midwest Pastel Show, Chgo., 1989-91, Kans. Pastel Soc. Show, Wichita, 1986, 89-91, Degas Pastel Soc. Show, New Orleans, 1990, Nat. Miniature Show, La Lus, N. Mex., 1986-88, Floral Inspirations, 1997, others; paintings published in the Best of Pastels Book. Recipient Southeastern Pastel Soc. Show 1st Pl. award, Atlanta, 1989, Shades of Pastel 89 Show Matthew and Mary Lou Fenton Portrait award, Balt., Nat. Miniature Show Best of Show award La Luz, N.Mex., 1987, Salmagundi-Pastel Soc. Am. NOA Mem. Show award. Mem. Pastel Soc. Am. (A&A Guffoni award), Catharine Lorillord Wolfe Art Club N.Y.C. Home: 607 SW Avenue I Seminole TX 79360-5313

CLARK, VICTORIA, actress; b. Dallas, Oct. 10, 1959; 1 child. B in Music, Yale Univ. Actor: (Broadway plays) Sunday in the Park With George, 1985, Guys and Dolls, 1992—93, A Grand Night for Singing, 1993—94, Titanic, 1997—99, Cabaret, 1999—2000, Urinetown, 2003, Bye Bye Birdie, 2004, The Light in the Piazza, 2005 (Tony award for best performance by a leading actress in a musical, 2005, Drama Desk award, outstanding actress in a musical, 2005, Outer Critics Circle award, outstanding actress in a musical, 2005, Joseph Jefferson award, 2005); (films) Cradle Will Rock, 1999; (TV series) Law and Order, 1998, Law and Order: SVU, 2003, (TV spl.) Sweeney Todd: The Demon Barber of Fleet Street in Concert, 2002; dir.: (numerous operas); tchr. (voice). Mailing: c/o Vivian Beaumont Theatre Lincoln Ctr 150 W 65th St New York NY 10003*

CLARK, WALLACE LEE, JR., physicist; b. St. Joseph, Mo., June 12, 1944; s. Wallace Lee and Muriel Elizabeth (Landree) C.; m. Beryl Fay Walker, Feb. 14, 1980; stepchildren: Valerie, Mark, Erich. BA in Physics, U. Colo., 1967. Physicist Nat. Bur. Stds., Boulder, Colo., 1967, ESSA, 1967—70; physicist aeronomy lab. NOAA, 1967—2003; asst. rsch. scientist Coop. Inst. for Rsch. in the Environ. Sci., U. Colo., 2003—. Recipient silver medal Dept. Commerce, 1979. Mem. Am. Meteorol. Soc., Am. Geophys. Union. Office: NOAA R/AL3 325 Broadway St Boulder CO 80305-3337 Office Phone: 303-497-3101. E-mail: wallace.clark@noaa.gov.

CLARK, WESLEY KANNE, emergency management executive, retired military officer; b. Little Rock, Ark., Dec. 23, 1944; m. Gertrude Kingston, 1966; 1 child, Wesley. Grad., U.S. Mil. Acad., West Point, 1966; M in philosophy, politics, and econs., Oxford U., 1966—68; grad., Nat. War Coll., Command and Gen. Staff Coll., Armor Officer Adv. and Basic Courses, Ranger and Airbourne Sch. Fellow White House, 1975—76, special asst. to dir. office mgmt. and budget, 1975—76; instr. to asst. prof. social sci. U.S. Mil. Acad.; comdr. 1st Battalion, 77th Armor, 4th Infantry Divsn. US Army, 1980—82; chief plans integration divsn. Office Deputy Chief of Staff Oper. and Plans, US Army, Washington, D.C., 1983; chief army's study group Office Chief of Staff of Army, Washington, D.C., 1983—84; comdr. oper. group US Army, 1984—86, comdr. 3rd Brigade, 4th Infantry Divsn., 1986—88, comdr. Nat. Tng. Ctr., 1989—91; deputy chief staff for concepts, doctrine, and developments US Army Tng. and Doctrine Command, Fort Monroe, Va., 1991—92; comdr. 1st Cavalry Divsn. US Army, Fort Hood, Tex., 1992—94, dir. strategic plans and policy, JR, the Joint Staff, 1994—96, comdr.-in-chief - U.S. So. Command Panama, 1996—97, comdr.-in-chief - U.S. European Command, 1997—2000; supreme allied comdr.- Europe NATO, 1997—2000; ret. US Army, 2000; mng. dir. merchant banking Stephens Group Inc., Little Rock, 2000—03; chmn., CEO Wesley K. Clark & Associates, LLC, Little Rock; vice chair & sr. advisor James Lee Witt Assoc., LLC, Washington, 2004—. Military analyst CNN, 2001—03. Author: Waging Modern War: Bosnia, Kosovo and the Future of Combat, 2001, Winning Modern Wars: Iraq, Terrorism and the American Empire, 2003. Decorated Defense Disting. Svc. Medal (three awards), Disting. Svc. Medal, Silver Star, Legion Merit (four awards), Bronze Star Medal (two awards), Purple Heart, Meritorious Svc. Medal (two awards), Army Commendation Medal (two awards); recipient Presidl. Medal of Freedom, 2000; Rhodes scholar, Oxford U., 1966—68. Achievements include led mil. negotiations for the Bosnian Peace Accords at Dayton; commanded three companies to combat in Vietnam. Office: James Lee Witt & Associates, LLC 1201 F St NW Ste 850 Washington DC 20004 Office Phone: 202-585-0780. Business E-Mail: wclark@wittassociates.com.

CLARK, WESLEY M., manufacturing executive; b. 1952; BA magna cum laude in Philosophy, U. Calif., LA, Calif., 1974; MBA, Stanford U. With Cummins Engine Co.; mem. sr. mgmt. team Granite Rock, 1984—91; from mgr. to pres., COO W.W. Grainger, Inc., Lake Forest, Ill., 1992—2001, pres., 2001—, COO, 2001—. Bd. dir. W.W. Grainger, Inc. Bd. dir. Mex. Fine Arts Ctr. Mus.; bd. trustees The Lincoln Found. Bus. Excellence, Am. Second Harvest Nat. Food Bank Network, Preserve to Enjoy. Mem.: Econ. Club Chgo., Exec.'s Club Chgo. Office: WW Grainger Inc 100 Grainger Parkway Lake Forest IL 60045-5201

CLARK, WILLIAM, JR., government agency administrator; b. Oakland, Calif., Oct. 12, 1930; s. William and Mary Edith (Coady) C.; m. Judith Lee Riley, Sept. 11, 1954; 1 child, Jared Riley. BA, San Jose State U., 1955; postgrad., Columbia U., 1967—68; diploma with distinction, Nat. War Coll., 1977; LittD (hon.), Calif. State U., 1992. Dir. liaison dept. U.S. Civil Adminstrn., Naha, Japan, 1970-72; U.S.-Japan Trade Officer Am. Embassy, Tokyo, 1972-74, minister, 1981-85, polit. counselor Seoul, Republic of Korea, 1977-80, minister Cairo, 1985-86, charge d'affaires, 1986; dir. spl. trade activities Dept. of State, Washington, 1974-76, dir. Japanese Affairs, 1980-81, dep. asst. sec. state, 1986-89; ambassador to India, 1989-92; asst. sec. of state East Asian and Pacific affairs Dept. of State, Washington, 1992-93; Japan chair, sr. advisor Ctr. for Strategic and Internat. Studies, Washington, 1993-95; pres. Japan Soc., N.Y.C., 1996—2003; mng. dir. Hills & Co., 2004—. Chmn. Japan Am. Student Conf., 2003—05. Lt. (j.g.) USN, 1950-53. Recipient Superior Svc. award Dept. Army, 1971, Outstanding Svc. award Dept. Army, 1972, Disting. Svc. award Pres. U.S., 1985, Meritorious Svc. award Pres. U.S., 1987, 89, Disting. Honor award Dept. State, 1989, Charles E. Cobb award Dept. State, 1991, Disting. lectr. Fgn. Svc. Inst., 1995, Order of the Sacred Treasure, Gold and Silver Star, Emperor of Japan, 2000. Mem.: Coun. Fgn. Rels., Am. Japan Soc. (bd. dirs. 1981—85), Japan Am. Soc. (bd. dirs. 1994—2000), Asia Soc. (bd. adv.), Am. Fgn. Svc. Assn., Am. C. of C. (hon. mem. Tokyo 1981—85, Cairo 1985—86), Cosmos Club (Washington), Gizira Club (Cairo), Chevy Chase Club (Washington), Pres.'s Estate Polo Club (New Delhi), Tokyo Am. Club. Episcopalian. Avocations: tennis, riding, skiing, golf. Office Phone: 202-822-4700. E-mail: jlnwclark@aol.com.

CLARK, WILLIAM ALFRED, federal judge; b. Dayton, Ohio, Aug. 27, 1928; s. Webb Rufus and Dora Lee (Weddle) C.; m. Catherine C. Clark, Apr. 5, 1952; children: Mary Clark Youra, Jennifer Clark Kinder, Cynthia S., Andrea G. AB, U. Mich., 1950, JD, 1952. Bar: Ohio 1952, Mich. 1953. Pvt. practice, Dayton, 1954—57; assoc. Frank J. Svoboda, Dayton, 1957—73; ptnr. Legler, Lang & Kuhns, Dayton, 1973-82, Pickrel, Schaeffer & Ebeling, Dayton, 1982-85; judge so. dist. Ohio U.S. Bankruptcy Ct., Dayton, 1985-99, chief judge, 1993-99; apptd. recalled bankruptcy judge, 1999—. Judge Montgomery County Ct., Dayton, 1958-62; trial counsel in eminent domain Asst. Atty. Gen. Ohio, Dayton, 1963-70; tchr. bus. law Dayton chpt. Cert. Property and Casualty Underwriters, 1963-83; arbitrator Montgomery County Common Pleas Ct., Am. Arbitration Assn., Better Bus. Bur. Contbr. to Ohio Practice and Procedure Handbook, 1962. Lt. USAF, 1952-54. Named Alumnus of Yr., U. Mich. Club, Dayton, 1965. Mem. ABA, Ohio State Bar Assn. (chmn. eminent domain 1979-82), Dayton Bar Assn. (treas. 1964-65), Nat. Conf. Bankruptcy Judges, Lawyers Club. Republican. Avocations: tennis, other sports, reading, travel. Office: US Bankruptcy Ct Federal Bldg 120 W 3rd St Dayton OH 45402-1872

CLARK, WILLIAM H., JR., lawyer; b. Phila., Apr. 10, 1951; s. William H. and Alice Kimes (Metts) C.; m. Cristine D. Merkel, Aug. 18, 1973; children: Matthew, Alison, Daniel. BA summa cum laude, Amherst Coll., 1973; MA in Religion, Westminster Sem., 1979; JD magna cum laude, Temple U., 1983. Bar: Pa. 1983. Assoc. Morgan, Lewis & Bockius, Phila., 1983-89; ptnr. Klett Lieber Rooney & Schorling, Pitts., 1989-98, Phila., 1998-99; ptnr., bus. fin. dept. Drinker Biddle & Reath LLP, Phila., 1999—. Chmn. corp. bur. advisory com. Pa. Dept of State, 1991—; cons. rules disciplinary bd. Supreme Ct. Pa., Harrisburg, 1983—. Fellow Am. Bar Found.; mem. ABA (com. on corp. laws, com. on bus. courts), Pa. Bar Assn. (draftsman, lobbyist, corp. law com. 1984—, coun. sect. corp. banking and bus. law 1989-93, officer 1993-2001), Allegheny County Bar Assn. (coun. sect. corp. banking and bus. law 1991-97, officer 1997-98), Phila. Bar Assn. (coun. bus. law sect. 1998—2003, officer 2004-), Am. Law Inst., Phi Beta Kappa. Republican. Presbyterian. Office: Drinker Biddle & Reath LLP One Logan Sq 18th & Cherry Sts Philadelphia PA 19103-6996 Office Phone: 215-988-2804. Office Fax: 267-402-4629. Business E-Mail: william.clark@dbr.com.

CLARK, WILLIAM HARTLEY, political science professor; b. Pitts., Apr. 29, 1930; s. Arthur Tillotson and Ruthanna Frame (Anderson) C.; m. Barbara Jean Rockne, June 27, 1953; children— Heather Anderson, Jill Eleanor, Robert Hartley, Edward Kirtland. BA, Carleton Coll., 1952; MA, N.Y. U., 1955, PhD, 1960. Researcher for Carnegie Endowment for Internat. Peace, Brookings Instn., N.Y. U., 1953-54; instr. polit. sci. Western Coll., Oxford, Ohio, 1954-55; instr. internat. relations Carleton Coll., 1955-60, asst. prof., 1960-66, assoc. prof., 1966-70, prof., 1970-92, prof. emeritus, 1992—, chmn. dept. polit. sci., 1972-76, Frank B. Kellogg prof. internat. rels., 1973-92. Lectr. U. Minn., 1970; dir. Geneva Seminar on Internat. Instns., 1975-91; pres. Clark Assocs., 1992—. Author: The Politics of the Common Market, 1967; contbr. articles and revs. to profl. publs. Fulbright research fellow, 1961-62; Ford Found. research fellow, 1967; NSF research fellow, 1970, 71, 79; von Humbolt-Stiftung fellow, 1961. Mem. Coun. Fgn. Rels. (St. Paul-Mpls. com. fgn. rels.), UN Assn. Home: 216 Nevada St Northfield MN 55057-2343 Personal E-mail: clark@carleton.edu.

CLARK, WILLIAM NORTHINGTON, lawyer, retired military officer; b. Meridian, Miss., Jan. 16, 1941; s. Oliver Watson and Mildred Catherine (Northington) C.; m. Faye Virginia Baker, Feb. 1, 1964; children: Helen Catherine Smith, William Northington Jr. BS, U.S. Mil. Acad., 1963; JD, U. Ala., 1971. Bar: Ala. 1971, U.S. Ct. Appeals (5th and 11th cirs.), U.S. Supreme Ct. Law clk. to Judge Walter P. Gewin U.S. Ct. Appeals (5th cir.), 1971—72; assoc. Rogers Howard Redden & Mills, Birmingham, Ala., 1972-74, ptnr., 1974-79, Redden Mills & Clark, Birmingham, 1979—. Adj. prof. evidence U. Ala. Sch. Law, 1979, adj. prof. criminal procedure, 2000, adj. prof. bus. fraud, 01; mem. Ala. Supreme Ct. Advisory Com. on Criminal Procedure, 1979—94. Bd. dirs. Boys and Girls Club of Cen. Ala., Birmingham, 1987—, Metro YMCA of Birmingham, 1989—, chmn., 1992-94. Capt. U.S. Army, 1963—68, Vietnam, ret. maj. gen. AUS. Mem. Ala. State Bar Assn. (chmn. com. on indigent defense 1975-81, chmn. Fed. judiciary liaison com. 1983-85, pres.-elect 2002-03, pres. 2003-04) Birmingham Bar Assn. (sec., treas. 1987-88, pres.-elect 1992, pres. 1993), Ala. Law Inst. (chmn. children's code com. 1986-93), Nat. Assn. Criminal Def. Lawyers. Methodist. Office: Redden Mills & Clark 940 Financial Ctr 50520th St N Birmingham AL 35203-3288 Office Phone: 205-322-0457. E-mail: wmc@rmclaw.com.

CLARK, WILLIAM ROBERT, JR., lawyer; b. Des Moines, Aug. 1, 1951; s. William Robert and Dorothy Virginia (Peterson) C.; m. Nancy Ann Welsh, June 10, 1972; 1 child, William Robert III. BA, Drake U., 1973, JD with honors, 1975. Bar: Iowa 1976, Ill. 1976, U.S. Dist. Ct. (so. and no. dists.) Iowa 1979, U.S. Ct. Appeals (8th cir.) 1979. Atty. Electronic Engring. Co., Des Moines, 1976; law clk. to judge Iowa Ct. Appeals, Des Moines, 1976-78; assoc. Herrick, Landgon & Langdon, Des Moines, 1978-81, ptnr., 1982—. Mem. Des Moines Estate and Fin. Planners (pres. 1989-90), Mason (33 degree), Shriner (legal counsel Des Moines 1985—), Order of Coif, Royal Order of Jesters (dir. 1998, treas. 1999—). Republican. Methodist. Avocations: tennis, sporting events. Office: Herrick Langdon & Langdon Financial Ctr Ste 1550 Des Moines IA 50309-3914 Office Phone: 515-282-8150.

CLARKE, ANNE-MARIE, lawyer; b. St. Louis; d. Thomas P. and Mary Ann (Vincent) C.; m. Richard K. Gaines. BA in Polit. Sci., N.W. Mo. State U.; JD, St. Louis U. Bar: Mo. Past rschr. Arthur D. Little, Inc., Cambridge, Mass.; past asst. corp. sec. N.E. Utilities, Hartford, Conn.; past staff counsel Bi-State Devel. Agy., St. Louis; pvt. practice St. Louis. Hearing officer St. Louis City Juvenile Ct., 1986-98; bd. mem. The Bar Plan, St. Louis, 1985-98. Bd. mem. St. Louis Office for Mentally Retarded and Developmentally Disabled, St. Louis, 1984-91, pres., 1989-91; mem. St. Louis Bd. Police Commrs., 1993-98, pres. 1994-98. Mem. Mo. Bar (bd. govs. 1986-90, 91-95), Mound City Bar Assn. (pres. 1981-83). Avocations: travel, exercise. Home: 3439 Longfellow Blvd Saint Louis MO 63104-1630 Office: 10 N Tucker Divsn 14A Saint Louis MO 63101 Office Phone: 314-641-8303.

CLARKE, SIR ARTHUR CHARLES, author; b. Minehead, Somerset, Eng., Dec. 16, 1917; s. Charles Wright and Norah (Willis) C.; m. Marilyn Mayfield, June 15, 1953 (div. 1964). B.Sc. in Physics and Math. with 1st class honors, King's Coll., London, 1948; D.Sc. (hon.), Beaver Coll., 1971, U. Moratuwa, 1979; D.Litt. (hon.), U. Bath, Eng., 1988, U. Liverpool, 1995, U. Hong Kong, Beijing, 1996. Auditor British Civil Service, His Majesty's Exchequer and Audit Dept., London, 1936-41; asst. editor Science Abstracts Inst. of Elec. Engineers, London, 1949-50; lectr., author, 1951—; chancellor U. Moratuwa, Sri Lanka, 1979—2002; Vikram Sarabhai prof. Phys. Rsch. Lab., Ahmedabad, India, 1980. Underwater explorer, photographer Great Barrier Reef of Australia and coast of Ceylon, 1954-64; commentator with Walter Cronkite Apollo missions, 1968-70; dir. Rocket Pub. Co., Underwater Safaris, Sri Lanka; founder Arthur C. Clarke Centre for Modern Technologies, Sri Lanka, 1984—; trustee Inst. Integral Edn.; fellow Franklin Inst., 1971, King's Coll., 1977, Inst. of Robotics, Carnegie-Mellon U., 1981; lectr. U.S. and Britain, 1957-74; bd. dirs. Nat. Space Soc., Space Generation Found., Internat. Astronomical Union, Planetary Soc., Rocket Pub. Co., Eng., Underwater Safaris, Sri Lanka; chmn. Second Internat. Astronautics Congress, London, 1951; moderator "Space Flight Report to the Nation", N.Y., 1961; fgn. assoc. Nat. Acad. Engring. (U.S.); mem. adv. coun. Internat. Sci. Policy Found., Fauna Internat., Sri Lanka, Earth Trust. Author: (non-fiction) Interplanetary Flight, 1950, The Exploration of Space, 1951 (Internat. Fantasy award 1952), The Young Traveller in Space, 1953 (pub. as Going Into Space, 1954), (with R.A. Smith) The Exploration of the Moon, 1955, The Coast of Coral, 1956, The Making of a Moon, 1957, The Reefs of Taprobane, 1957, The Scottie Book of Space Travel, 1957, (with Mike Wilson) Boy Beneath the Sea, 1958, Voice Across the Sea, 1958, The Challenge of the Spaceship, 1959, The Challenge of the Sea, 1960; (with Wilson) The First Five Fathoms, 1960, Indian Ocean Adventure, 1961, Profiles of the Future, 1962, The Treasure of the Great Reef, 1964, Indian Ocean Treasure, 1964; (with editors of Life mag.) Man and Space, 1964, Voices from the Sky, 1965, The Promise of Space, 1968; (with astronauts) First on the Moon, 1970, Report on Planet Three, 1972; (with Chesley Bonestell) Beyond Jupiter, 1972, The View from Serendip, 1977; (with Simon Welfare and John Fairley) Arthur C. Clarke's Mysterious World, 1980, Ascent to Orbit, 1984, 1984: Spring-A Choice of Futures, 1984, (with Welfare and Fairley) Arthur C. Clarke's World of Strange Powers, 1984, (with Peter Hyams) The Odyssey File, 1985, Arthur C. Clarke's July 20, 2019: Life in the 21st Century, 1986, Arthur C. Clarke's Chronicles of the Strange and Mysterious, 1987, Astounding Days, 1989, Opus 700, 1990, How the World Was One, 1992, (with Welfare and Fairley) Arthur C. Clarke's A-Z of Mysteries, 1993, By Space Possessed, 1993, The Snows of Olympus, 1994, Front Line of Discovery: Science on the Brink of Tomorrow, 1994, Greetings, Carbon-based Bipeds, 1999; (fiction) The Sands of Mars, 1951, Prelude to Space, 1951, Islands in the Sky, 1952, Against the Fall of Night, 1953, Childhood's End, 1953, Expedition to Earth, 1953, Earthlight, 1955, Reach For Tomorrow, 1956, The City and the Stars, 1956, Tales from the White Hart, 1957, The Deep Range, 1957, The Other Side of the Sky, 1958, Across the Sea of Stars, 1959, A Fall of Moondust, 1961, From the Oceans, from the Stars, 1962, Tales of Ten Worlds, 1962, Dolphin Island, 1963, Glide Path, 1963, Prelude to Mars, 1965, The Nine Billion Names of God, 1967, (with Stanley Kubrick) 2001: A Space Odyssey, 1968, The Final Odyssey, 1997, The Lion of Comarre and Against the Fall of Night, 1968, The Wind from the Sun, 1972, Of Time and Stars, 1972, The Lost Worlds of 2001, 1972, Rendezvous with Rama, 1973 (Nebula award Sci. Fiction Writers Am. 1973, Hugo award World Sci. Fiction Conv. 1974, John W. Campbell Meml. award Sci. Fiction Rsch. Assn. 1974, Jupiter award Instructors of Sci. Fiction in Higher Edn. 1974), The Best of Arthur C. Clarke, 1973, Imperial Earth, 1975, The Fountains of Paradise, 1979 (Nebula award Sci. Fiction Writers Am. 1980, Hugo award World Sci. Fiction Conv. 1980), 2010: Odyssey Two, 1982, The Sentinel, 1983, Selected Works, 1985, The Songs of Distant Earth, 1986, 2061: Odyssey Three, 1988, (with Gentry Lee) Cradle, 1988, A Meeting with Medusa, 1988, (with Lee) Rama II, 1989, Tales from Planet Earth, 1989, (with Gregory Benford) Beyond the Fall of Night, 1990, Ghost from the Grand Banks, 1990, (with Lee) Garden of Rama, 1991, More Than One Universe, 1991, The Hammer of God, 1993, (with Lee) Rama Revealed: The Ultimate Encounter, 1994, (with Mike McQuay) Richter 10, 1996, 3001: The Final Odyssey, 1997, (with Mike-Kube-McDowell) Trigger, 1999, (with Stephen Baxter) The Light of Other Days, 2000, (with Stephen Baxter) Time's Eye, 2004, (with Stephen Baxter) Sunstorm, 2005; screenwriter: (films) (with Stanley Kubrick) 2001: A Space Odyssey, 1968 (Academy award nomination best original screenplay 1968, Second Internat. Film Festival Spl. award 1969); writer, host: (TV series) Arthur C. Clarke's Mysterious World, 1980, Arthur C. Clarke's World of Strange Powers, 1984, Mysterious Universe, 1994; actor: (films) Beddagama, 1979; editor: Time Probe: The Science in Science Fiction, 1966, The Coming of the Space Age, 1967, Three for Tomorrow, 1972, The Science Fiction Hall of Fame Vol. III, 1982. With Lindbergh Award Noms. Com. Served to flight lt. RAF, 1941-46; mem. adv. bd. Science Fiction Mus. and Hall of Fame. Recipient Presdl. award U. Ill., 1997. Fellow Royal Astron. Soc., Royal Soc. Arts; mem. Brit. Interplanetary Soc. (chmn. 1947-50, 53), Internat. Council Integrative Studies, AIAA, Inst. Engrs. Sri Lanka (named hon. fellow 1983), Sri Lanka Astron. Soc., Royal Astron. Soc., Assn. Brit. Sci. Writers (life), Internat. Acad. Astronautics, World Acad. Art and Sci., Nat. Space Inst. (dir.), Brit. Sci. Fiction Assn. (pres.), Royal Soc. Arts, Brit. Sub-Aqua Club, Brit. Astron. Assn., H.G. Wells Soc. (hon. v.p.), Sci. Fiction Writers Am., Internat. Sci. Writers Assn., Sci. Fiction Found., Soc. Authors (mem. coun.), Am. Astronautical Assn., Am. Assn. for Advancement of Sci., Nat. Acad. Engring., Third World Acad. of Scis. (assoc. fellow), Sri Lanka Animal Welfare Assn., Sri Lanka Assn. Advancement Sci., Sri Lanka Nat. Inst. Paraplegics, Astron. Soc. Haringey, Soc. Satellite Profls. (hon. chmn., Hall of Fame 1987), Nat. Space Soc. (bd. dirs., R.A. Heinlein Meml. award 1990), Royal Asiatic Soc., Astron. Soc. Pacific, Nat. Acad. Engring. (fgn. assoc.). Office Phone: 9411 2699757.

CLARKE, BETTY ANN, librarian, minister; b. Townsend, Va., Nov. 9, 1947; d. Joshua Samuel and Queenie Victoria (Morris) Spady; m. Kenneth Clarke, June 30, 1972; 1 stepchild, Cynthia Clarke Rhinehart. BA in Polit. Sci., Norfolk State U., 1970; postgrad., N.J. Conf. Ministerial INst., 1979—84; MA, Rowan U., 1995. Cert. libr. N.J. Sr. libr. Atlantic County, Mays Landing, NJ, 1978—; pastor St. Mark African Meth. Episcopal Ch., Lindenwold, NJ, 1987—. Chaplain trauma unit Cooper Hosp., Camden, NJ, 1990—98. Recipient Jarena Lee award, Harrisburg Dist. African Meth. Episcopal Ch., 1992, African Am. Women's Network Bronze Star, Delaware Valley Humanity Field Health, 1996, Woman Making A Difference award, Bethel African Meth. Episcopal Ch., 2002. Democrat. Avocations: reading, travel, writing, bowling. Home: 14 Jefferson Ave Browns Mills NJ 08021 Office: St Mark AME Ch 929 Walnut & Taylor Aves Lindenwold NJ 08021 Office Phone: 609-625-2776 ext. 6328.

CLARKE, CHARLES FENTON, lawyer; b. Hillsboro, Ohio, July 25, 1916; s. Charles F. and Margaret (Patton) C.; m. Virginia Schoppenhorst, Apr. 3, 1945 (dec. July 1989); children: Elizabeth, Margaret, Jane, Charles Fenton, IV; m. Lesley Wells, Nov. 13, 1998. AB summa cum laude, Washington and Lee U., 1938; LLB, U. Mich., 1940; LLD (hon.), Cleve. State U., 1971. Bar: Mich. 1940, Ohio 1946. Pvt. practice, Detroit, 1942, Cleve., 1946—; ptnr. firm Squire, Sanders & Dempsey, 1957—, adminstr. litigation dept., 1979-85. Trustee Cleve. Legal Aid Soc., 1959-67; pres. Nat. Assn. R.R. Trial Counsel, 1966-68; life mem. 6th Circuit Jud. Conf.; chmn. legis. com. Cleve. Welfare Fedn., 1961-68; master bencher Celebrezze Inn of Ct., 1991—; bd. dirs. Wheeling and Lake Erie R.R. Co. Pres. alumni bd. dirs. Washington and Lee U., 1970-72; pres. bd. dirs. Free Med. Clinic Greater Cleve., 1970-86; trustee Cleve. Citizens League, 1956-62, Cleve. chpt. ACLU, 1986-93; bd. dirs. citizens adv. bd. Cuyahoga County (Ohio) Juvenile Ct., 1970-73; bd. dirs. George Jr. Republic, Greenville, Pa., 1970-73, Bowman Tech. Sch., Cleve., 1970-91; vice chmn. Cleve. Crime Commn., 1973-75; exec. com. Cuyahoga County Rep. Orgn., 1950—; councilman Bay Village, Ohio, 1948-53; pres., trustee Cleve. Hearing and Speech Ctr., 1957-62, Laurel Sch., 1962-72, Fedn. Cmty. Progress, 1984-90; mem. planning commn. Cleveland Heights, 1994-2003. Fellow Am. Coll. Trial Lawyers; mem. Greater Cleve. Bar Assn. (trustee 1983-86), Cleve. Civil War Round Table (pres. 1968), Cleve. Zool. Soc. (dir. 1970), Phi Beta Kappa. Clubs: Skating, Union (Cleve.); Tavern, Rowfant. Presbyterian. Home: 2262 Tudor Dr Cleveland Heights OH 44106-3210 Office: Squire Sanders & Dempsey 4900 Key Tower 127 Public Sq Cleveland OH 44114-1304 Office Phone: 216-479-8551. Business E-Mail: cclarke@ssd.com.

CLARKE, CLAIRE DIGGS, academic counselor; b. Long Branch, N.J. d. Jeremiah and LeeBertha (Smith) Diggs; m. David C. Clarke Jr.; 1 child: Caroletta. Student, Livingston Coll., 1948-51; BA, Knoxville Coll., 1955; postgrad., Columbia U., 1961-63; MA in Edn., Hofstra U., 1968; postgrad., U. N.H., Durham, New England Coll., Concord, N.H., 1981. Cert. tchr. English, physical edn. and health edn., counselor edn. Tchr. Charles M. Hall Sch., Alcoa, Tenn., 1955-59, Gilbert Sch., Bklyn., 1959-61; caseworker Bur. Child Welfare of N.Y., 1961-63; tchr., cons. pub. sch. #192, Hollis, N.Y., 1963-69; guidance counselor Winnisquam Regional Sch. Dist., Tilton, NH, 1969—92, specialist assessment intellectual functioning, 1981—. State rep. N.H. House Rep., 2000—. Mem. Merrimack Valley Sch. Bd., 1983-98; police commr. Boscawen Police Dept., 1980—; trustee Boscawa Congregation Ch., 2003—. Mem. N.H. Council Vocat. Tech. Edn. (sec. 1976—), Assn. Supervision Curriculum Devel. Lodges: Zonta Internat. (pres. 1979-81). Avocations: fishing, reading, travel, gardening, gourmet cooking. Home: 437 Daniel Webster Hwy Boscawen NH 03303-2411

CLARKE, CORDELIA KAY KNIGHT MAZUY, management consultant, artist; b. Springfield, Mo., Nov. 22, 1938; d. William Horace and Charline (Bentley) Knight; m. Logan Clarke, Jr., July 22, 1978; children by previous marriage— Katharine Michelle Mazuy, Christopher Knight Mazuy. AB in English with honors, U. N.C., 1960; MS in Stats., N.C. State U., 1962; BFA in Painting, Lyme Acad. Coll. Fine Arts, 2005. Statistician Research Triangle Inst., Durham, NC, 1960—63; statis. cons. Arthur D. Little, Inc., Cambridge, Mass., 1963—67; dir. mktg. planning and analysis Polaroid Corp., Cambridge, 1967—70; dir. mktg. and bus. planning Transaction Tech. Inc., Cambridge, 1970—72; pres. Mazuy Assos., Boston, 1972—73; v.p. Nat. Shawmut Bank, Boston, 1973—74; sr. v.p., dir. mktg. Shawmut Corp., 1974—78; sr. v.p., dir. retail banking Shawmut Bank, 1976—78; v.p. corp. devel. Arthur D. Little, Inc., 1978—79; v.p. Conn. Gen. Life Ins. Co., 1979—85; pres. CIGNA Securities, 1983—85; exec. v.p. McGraw-Hill Inc., 1988-90; chmn. Templeton, Inc., 1985—92, 1995—; pres. micromarketing divsn. ADVO, 1990—95. Faculty Williams Sch. Banking; adv. com. Bur. of Census, 1978-84; bd. dirs. Guardian Life Ins. Co., Berkshire Life Ins., Providence Jour. Co.; tchr. Amos Tuck Grad. Sch. Bus., Dartmouth Coll., 1964-65, exec.-in-residence, 1978, 80; bd. overseers, 1979-85; exec.-in-residence Wheaton Coll., 1978; vis. prof. Simmons Grad. Sch. Mgmt., 1978; mem. schs. adv. coun. Bank Mktg. Assn., 1976-78; mem. corp. adv. bd. Hartford Nat. Bank & Trust Co., 1980-87. Columnist Am. Banker, 1976-78. Mem. Mass. Gov.'s Commn. on Status of Women, 1977-79; bd. corporators Babson Coll., 1977-80; adv. bd. Boston Mayor's Office Cultural Affairs, 1977-79; bd. dirs. McGraw-Hill, Inc., 1976-88, Blue Shield of Mass., 1976-79, Greater Hartford Arts Coun., 1979-93, Cybex Internat. Inc., 1996-2000; trustee Children's Mus. Hartford, 1980-82; corporator Inst. of Living, 1981-92; regent U. Hartford, 1982—; bd. dirs. Hartford Art Sch., 1982-94, Hartford Stage Co., 1985-99, Manhattan Theatre Club, 1988-91, Inst. for Future, 1988-92, N.Y. Internat. Festival of Arts, 1988-91, Goodspeed Opera, 1990—, Inst. Design, 1990-98, Aeroflex Found., 1972—. Mem. Artists Assn. Nantucket (elected), Lyme Art Assn. (assoc.), Essex Art Assn. (assoc.), Internat. Womens Forum, Power 10, Phi Beta Kappa, Phi Kappa Phi, Kappa Alpha Theta. Home and Office: 89 River Rd East Haddam CT 06423-1462 Office Phone: 860-526-3368.

CLARKE, DAVID H., industrial products executive; b. 1941; married. Vice chmn. bd. Hanson Pub. Ltd. Co., 1965-83; dep. chmn., pres., CEO Hanson Industries N.Am. (subs. Hanson Trust PLC, London), 1978-95, also bd. dirs.; chmn., CEO US Industries Inc., 1995—, Jacuzzi Brands, 1995—. Office: Ste 1100 W 777 S Flagler Dr West Palm Beach FL 33401 Office Phone: 561-514-3838.

CLARKE, DOUGLAS E., lawyer; b. Houston, 1948; BA, Wash. & Lee U., 1970; JD, U. Houston, 1973. Bar: Tex. 1973; cert. estate planning & probate law Tex. Bd. Legal Specialization. Ptnr., Probate Dept. Andrews & Kurth LLP, Houston. Assoc. editor Houston Law Rev., 1972—73, probate editor Tex. State Bar News (for Real Estate Probate & Trust Sect.), 1986—91. Mem.: Houston Estate Forum, State Bar Tex. (Real Estate, Probate & Trust Law Counsel 1993—97), Houston Bar Assn. (Probate, Trust & Estate Sect.). Office: Andrew Kurth LLP 600 Travis St Ste 4200 Houston TX 77002-3090 Office Phone: 713-220-4474. Office Fax: 713-238-4285. Business E-Mail: dclarke@andrewskurth.com.

CLARKE, EDWARD NIELSEN, engineering science educator; b. Providence, Apr. 25, 1925; s. Edward O.A. and Edith (Nielsen) C.; m. Vivian Constance Bergquist, July 23, 1949; children— Sandra J., David E., Allan R., Jeffrey B. BS, Brown U., 1945, PhD, 1951; MS, Harvard U., 1947, M in Engring. Sci., 1948. Mem. tech. staff, sect. head for semiconductors, physics lab. Sylvania Electric Products Co., Bayside, NY, 1950-56; group head for rsch. Sperry Semiconductor divsn. Sperry Rand Corp., Norwalk, Conn., 1956-59; v.p. ops. and dir. Nat. Semiconductor Corp., Danbury, Conn., 1959-65; assoc. dean faculty, assoc. dean grad. studies, dir. rsch. Worcester Poly. Inst., 1965-86, prof. engring. scis., 1968-94, dir. Ctr. Solar Electrification, 1986-94, prof. emeritus, 1995—; tri-coll. coord. rsch. Clark U.-Holy Cross Coll.-Worcester Poly. Inst., 1974-85. Co-founder Nat. Semiconductor Corp.; founder solar electrification ctr. Worcester Poly. Inst.; disting. vis. prof. Nichols Coll., 2002, lectr. history of semiconductors and hybrid-electric cars, 1995—. Trustee Upsala Coll., East Orange, N.J., 1971-74. Served with USNR, 1943-46. Recipient Brown U. Engring. Alumni medal, 1998. Mem. IEEE, Am. Phys. Soc., Torch Club (Worcester), Sigma Xi (past chpt. pres.), Tau Beta Pi. Lutheran. Achievements include patents and inventions in semiconductor technology; pioneering development of solar powered racing car. Home: 85 Richards Ave Paxton MA 01612-1123 Personal E-mail: encvcc@aol.com. *Helping others to achieve has been my own principal achievement. Retain mobility and be willing to use one's skills wherever they are needed. Do not become too comfortable and secure. Move on to find new challenges. Stay young with variety in one's life and a healthy use of the out-of-doors.*

CLARKE, EDWARD OWEN, JR., lawyer; b. Balt., Dec. 19, 1929; s. Edward Owen and Agnes Oakford C.; m. P. Rhea Parker, Dec. 18, 1954; children: Deborah Jeanne, Catherine Ann, Carolyn Agnes, Edward Owen III. AB magna cum laude, Loyola Coll., Balt., 1950; JD with honors, U. Md., 1956. Bar: Md. 1956, U.S. Dist. Ct. Md. 1956. Law clk. U.S. Dist. Ct. Md., 1956-57; assoc. Smith, Somerville & Case, Balt., 1957-62, ptnr., 1962-71, Piper & Marbury, Balt., 1971-94, mem. policy and mgmt. com., 1981-94, mng. ptnr., 1987-90, co-chmn. bus. div., 1991-94. Mem. Gov.'s Com. to Study Blue Sky Law, 1961; mem. Md. Commn. on Revision Corp. Law, 1965-66. Bd. dirs. Bon Secours Hosp., 1964-73, sec., 1968-73; bd. dirs. Hosp. Cost Analysis Svc., 1966-81; bd. pres. exec. coun. Md. Hosp. Assn., 1968-74, chmn. com. on legislation, 1971-73, treas., 1973; trustee St. Mary's Coll. Md., 1983-94, chmn. bd., 1988-94; trustee St. Mary's Sem., U. Balt., 1986-89, Loyola H.S., Balt., 1984-90, Hannah More Ctr., 1980-83; bd. dirs. Helix Health Sys., Inc., 1995-98, Med Star Health, 1998—; active Md. Higher Edn. Commn., 1994-2004, chmn. 1995-2000. Lt. USNR, 1952-55. Recipient Alumni Laureate award Loyola Coll. in Md., 2001. Mem. ABA, Md. State Bar Assn. (mem. sect. coun. corp., banking and bus. law sect. 1968-71, chmn. 1970-71), Wednesday Law Club (sec., treas. 1984-88, v.p. 1988-89, pres. 1990), Center Club (Balt., bd. govs. 1988-94), Order of Coif, Order of the Ark and the Dove, Phi Beta Kappa, Alpha Sigma Nu, Tau Kappa Alpha.

CLARKE, FLORA CLAIBORNE, counselor; d. Paul Mason and Otis Batte Claiborne; m. Ervin Bernard Clarke, June 1, 1975; children: Shannan, Ashley. BS, Va. State U., 1973, MEd, 1987. Cert. tchr. Dept. Edn., Va., 1973. Tchr. Northside Elem. Sch., Dinwiddie, Va., 1973—74; employment interviewer Va. Employment Commn., Petersburg, Va., 1975—80; mgr. employment and recruitment Va. State U., Ettrick, Va., 1980—89; guidance counselor Rohoic Elem. Sch., Dinwiddie, Va., 1989—. Sec. Safe and Drug-Free Schs., Dinwiddie, 2000—02, cmty. adv. bd., 2000—02. Composer (musician): (albums) Never Alone; musician Potpourri. Mem.: Va. Sch. Counselor Assn., Am. Sch. Counselor Assn. Baptist. Office: Rohoic Elementary School 23312 Airport Street Petersburg VA 23803 Office Phone: 804-863-4150. Office Fax: 804-863-4154. E-mail: fclarke@dcpsnet.org.

CLARKE, FRANK WILLIAM, communications executive; b. Quebec, Que., Can., Apr. 16, 1942; came to U.S., 1946; s. William Frank Clarke and Tolly (English) Wing; m. Barbara Jean Dreher, Mar. 1966 (div. Sept. 1975); children: Kathleen Julienne Clarke Smith, Lori Christine Clarke Genovese; m. Vera Gretel Thol, Nov. 14, 1977; stepchildren: Teo Capriles, Gretel Capriles Saade. Student, U. Va., 1958-61; BS in Commerce, NYU, 1964; MS in Journalism, Northwestern U., 1965. Staff asst., then asst. account exec. Grey Advt. Inc., N.Y.C., 1969-70, account exec., 1970-73, account dir. Caracas, Venezuela, 1973-75, v.p. account svcs., 1975-78, v.p., area dir., 1978-82, N.Y.C., 1982-88, sr. v.p., area dir., 1988-93, exec. v.p., area dir., 1993-99; sr. cons. Strategy XXI Group Ltd., N.Y.C., 1999-2000, ptnr., 2001—. Mem. product mktg. com. U.S. Fund for UNICEF, N.Y.C., 1989-93, nat. adv. coun., 1991-93, bd. dirs., 1994-2000, mem. exec. com., 1996-2000; bd. dirs. Street Law, Inc., Washington, 1999—, chmn. 2001-. Capt. U.S. Army, 1966-69. Mem. Racquet and Tennis Club N.Y. Republican. Avocations: gardening, cross country skiing. Office: Strategy XXI Group Ltd 515 Madison Ave New York NY 10022-5403

CLARKE, GARRY EVANS, composer, educator, academic administrator, musician; b. Moline, Ill., Mar. 19, 1943; s. Clarence Henderson and Gladys Arlene (Hokinson) C.; m. Melissa Jane Naul, May 24, 1975; children: Catharine van Gelder, Margaret Elizabeth Jane. MusB summa cum laude, Cornell Coll., Mount Vernon, Iowa, 1965; MusM, Yale U., 1968; LittD (hon.), Washington Coll., 1988. Asst. prof. music Washington Coll., Chestertown, Md., 1968-73; assoc. prof., 1973-79; prof. Washington Coll., Chestertown, 1979—, dean coll., 1977-83, acting pres., 1981-82. Am. liaison Harrison & Harrison Ltd., Durham, Eng. Composer symphonic, chamber, vocal, piano and organ music and opera; lectr. and recitalist (U.S., Europe): Am. music; condr. piano workshops; opera coach; organist and choir master, St. Paul's Episcopal Parish, Centerville, Md., 1975-88; Chester Parish, Chestertown, Md., 1988—; author: Essays on American Music, 1977; contbr. articles, revs. to profl. jours.; co-editor: Varied Air and Variations (Ives), 1971; editor: Charles Ives. Soc. publs. Trustee Coun. Econ. Edn. Md.; bd. dirs. Talbot Chamber Orch., Ea. Shore Chamber Music Festival. Ford Found. fellow, 1965, Woodrow Wilson fellow, 1965; Carnegie Found. rsch. grantee, 1964, NEH rsch. grantee, 1970; recipient Bronze medal Coun. for Advancement and Support of Edn., 1993. Mem. AAUP, Soc. Music Theory, Assn. Anglican Musicians, Sonneck Soc., Council Higher Edn. in Music, Am. Conf. Acad. Deans, Nat. Assn. Schs. Music, Am. Assn. Higher Edn., Yale Sch. Music Alumni Assn. (exec. com. 1975-80), Assn. Yale Alumni, Yale Club (N.Y.C.), Order of Omega, Pi Kappa Lambda, Omicron Delta Kappa, Phi Delta Theta. Episcopalian. Home: Fairways 7775 Waterview Ln Chestertown MD 21620-4746 Office: Washington Coll 300 Washington Ave Chestertown MD 21620-1197 Office Phone: 410-778-7838. E-mail: gclarke2@washcoll.edu.

CLARKE, HENRY LEE, foreign service officer, ambassador; b. Ft. Benning, Ga., Nov. 15, 1941; s. Edwin Lee and Jane Iredell (Jones) C.; m. Kathleen Ann Smith, May 19, 1973 (div. 1996); children: Ann Marie, Edwin Lee; m. Elena Anatolyevna Fedyai, Jan. 8, 1997; children: Yuliya Chikerenda, Christopher Lee. AB, Dartmouth Coll., 1962; MPA, Harvard U., 1967. U.S. fgn. svc. officer Dept. State, 1967-99; econ. counselor Am. Embassy, Moscow, 1982-85, dep. chief Bucharest, Romania, 1985-89, econ. counselor Tel Aviv, 1989-92, amb. to Uzbekistan, Tashkent, 1992-95; internat. affairs advisor Nat. War Coll., Washington, 1995-98; sr. advisor for property restitution in Europe, Dept. State, Washington, 1998-2000; dep. high rep. for Bosnia and Brcko Supr., 2001—03. Chmn. bd. Am. Sch., Bucharest, 1985-89, Tashkent Internat. Sch., 1994-95.

CLARKE, JAMES WESTON, political science professor, writer; b. Elizabeth, Pa., Feb. 16, 1937; s. Alonzo Peterson and Beatrice (Weston) C.; m. Jeanne Nienaber; children— Julianne, Michael BA, Washington and Jefferson Coll., 1962; MA, Pa. State U., 1964, PhD, 1968. Asst. prof. Fla. State U., 1967-71; assoc. prof. U. Ariz., Tucson, 1971-76, prof. polit. sci., 1976—, chmn. dept., 1973-78, univ. disting. prof., 2000. Author: American Assassins: The Darker Side of Politics, 1982, Last Rampage: The Escape of Gary Tison, 1988, On Being Mad or Merely Angry: John W. Hinckley Jr. and Other Dangerous People, 1990, The Lineaments of Wrath: Race, Violent Crime, and American Culture, 1998. Served with USMC, 1955-58 Recipient James Gillespie Blaine prize Washington and Jefferson Coll., 1962, Matthew Brown Ringland prize, 1962, Burlington Northern Found. award for excellence in tchg., 1987, Golden Key Nat. Honor Soc. award for tchg., 1989, Social and Behavioral Scis. award for outstanding tchg., 1991, 96; Udall fellow, 1993; Fulbright scholar, Ireland, 1999. Mem. Am. Polit. Sci. Assn. (Outstanding Tchg. in Polit. Sci. 2000). Home: 855 E Placita Leslie Tucson AZ 85718-1960 Office: U Ariz 315 Social Sci Bldg Tucson AZ 85721-0001 Office Phone: 520-621-7600. E-mail: jclarke@u.arizona.edu.

CLARKE, JANET MORRISON, marketing executive; b. Springfield, Mass., Feb. 2, 1953; d. Morton and Shirley (Harkinson) Morrison, m. Frederick G.E. Clarke, Oct. 4, 1980. BA in Architecture, Princeton U., 1976. Sales rep. Sci. Press, Ephrata, Pa., 1977-78, R.R. Donnelley & Sons Co., Chgo., 1978, various positions including sr. v.p. Information Technol. and dir. venture capital fund, 1978—97; mng. dir., global database mktg. Citibank, 1997—2000; chmn., CEO KnowledgeBase Marketing, Inc., 2000—01; exec. v.p. Young & Rubicam, Inc, 2000—01; chief mktg. officer DealerTrack, Inc., 2002—03; founder Clarke Littlefield LLC, 2001—, pres., 2001—02, 2003—. Bd. dirs. Cox Communications, 1995—, Asbury Automotive Group, ExpressJet Holdings Inc., 2002—, eFunds Corp., 2000—, Forbes.com Inc., Gateway Computers, 2005—. Charter trustee, Princeton U.; bd. dirs. YWCA, Westbrook, Conn., 1984—; mem., regional chmn. Nat. Ann. Giving Com. Princeton (N.J.) U., 1985—. Mem.: Princeton (N.Y.C.); Landmark (Stamford, Conn.). Republican.

CLARKE, JOHN, physics professor; b. Cambridge, Eng., Feb. 10, 1942; came to U.S., 1968; s. Victor Patrick and Ethel May (Blowers) C.; m. Grethe Fog Pedersen, Sept. 15, 1979; 1 child, Elizabeth Jane. BA, Cambridge U., 1964, MA, PhD, Cambridge U., 1968, ScD (hon.), 2003. Postdoctoral scholar U. Calif.-Berkeley, 1968-69, asst. prof. physics, 1969-71, assoc. prof., 1971-73, prof., 1973—, faculty rsch. lectr., 2005; chair exptl. physics Luis W. Alvarez Meml., 1994—. Contbr. numerous articles to profl. jours. Recipient Charles Vernon Boys prize Brit. Inst. Physics, 1977, award Soc. Exploration Geophysics, 1979, Outstanding Tchg. award U. Calif., 1983, Fritz London award for low temperature physics, 1987, Fed. Lab. Consortium award for excellence in technology transfer, 1992, divsn. materials scis. award in solid state physics Dept. Energy, 1986, 92, IEEE U.S. Activities Bd. Electrotechnology Transfer award, 1995, Comstock prize Physics NAS, 1999, Coun. on Superconductivity award IEEE, 2002, Olli V. Lounasmaa prize Finnish Acad. Sci. and Letters, 2004; fellow Sloan Found., 1970-72, Miller Inst. for Basic Rsch., 1975-76, 94-95; Guggenheim fellow, 1977-78; named Calif. Scientist of Yr., 1987, One of 50, Scientific Am., 2002. Fellow AAAS, Royal Soc. London (Hughes medal 2004), Am. Phys. Soc. (Joseph F. Keithley Advances in Measurement Sci. award 1998), Brit. Inst. Physics, Christ's Coll. (hon.). Office: U Calif Dept Physics Berkeley CA 94720-7300

CLARKE, JOHN CLEM, artist; b. Bend, Oreg., June 6, 1937; s. Eugene and Wilma Mary (Owen) C. BS, U. Oreg., 1960; student, Oreg. State U., U. Mexico, Mexico City Coll. Exhbns. include Whitney Mus., N.Y.C., 1967-73, Realism Now, N.Y. Cultural Center, Tokyo Biennale, Mus. Modern Art, N.Y.C., USA Bicentennial, U.S. Dept. Interior; represented in permanent collections, Whitney Mus. Am. Art, Met. Mus., Mus. Modern Art, Dallas Mus. Fine Arts, Va. Mus. Fine Arts, William Rockhill Nelson Gallery Art, Kansas City, Mo., Balt. Mus. Fine Arts, Hirshorn Mus., Washington, Utrecht Mus., The Netherlands, Bklyn. Mus., Milw. Arts Ctr., Indpls. Mus. Art, Fort Worth Art Ctr., Fogg Mus., Boston, L.A. County Mus. Art, Akron (Ohio) Art Inst., U. Calif., Berkeley, Flint (Mich.) Inst., Sch. of Art, Syracuse (N.Y) U., U. Ga. at Atlanta, Security Pacific Nat. Bank, N.Y.C., Security Pacific Nat. Bank, World Hdqrs., L.A., Chase Manhattan Bank, N.Y.C., Post Keyes Garner, Inc., Chgo., Wichita State U., Westmoreland County Mus., Greenburg, Pa., Kresge Co., Detroit, Am. Republic Ins. Co., Des Moines, Lewis and Clark Coll., Portland, Oreg.

CLARKE, JOHN PATRICK, retired newspaper publisher; b. Mattoon, Ill., Oct. 29, 1930; s. Patrick Joseph Clarke and Lucille (Hennebry) Stoeckinger; m. Roberta June Steiner, July 25, 1959 (div. 1984); children: Shannon, Dana; m. Sheila Cordill, June 24, 1995. BS, Ind. U., 1958; MBA, Harvard U., 1962. With contr.'s staff Ethyl Corp., N.Y.C., 1958-60; bus. mgr. State Jour.-Register, Springfield, Ill., 1962-68, pub., 1968-96; ret., 1996. Sec., bd. dirs. Ill. Ambassadors, 1986—; mem. Atty. Registration and Disciplinary Commn., 1987—; chmn bd. dirs. State Farm Rail Classic (LPGA tour). With USN, 1949-50, 52-54. Mem. Am. Newspaper Pubs. Assn., Inland Daily Press Assn., Kensington Golf and Country Club, Sangamo Club (pres. 1978-79). Avocations: sailing, golf. Home: 4301 Gulf Shore Blvd N Apt 504 Naples FL 34103-3477

CLARKE, JUDY, lawyer; b. Asheville, N.C., 1953; m. Speedy Rice. B in Psychology, Furman U., 1974; JD, U. S.C., 1977. Trial atty. Fed. Defenders San Diego, Inc., exec. dir., 1983—91; pvt. practice, 1991-92; exec. dir. Fed. Defenders of Ea. Washington & Idaho. Mem. faculty Nat. Criminal Def. Coll., Macon, Ga., bd. regents, 1985—, pres. Nat. Assn. Criminal Def. Lawyers, 1996-97 Author: Federal Sentencing Manual; contbr. articles to profl. jours. Mem. NACDL (pres. 1996-97). Office: Fed Pub Defenders Office 10 N Post St Ste 700 Spokane WA 99201-0705*

CLARKE, KATHLEEN BURTON, federal agency administrator; b. Utah; BA in Polit. Sci., UT State U. From dir. constituent svcs. to exec. dir. Office of Congressman James V. Hansen, 1987—93; dep. dir. Utah Dept. Natural Resources, 1993—98, exec. dir., 1998—2001; dir. Bur. Land Mgmt. U.S. Dept. Interior, Washington, 2001—. Office: US Dept Interior Bur Land Mgmt 1849 C St NW Washington DC 20240

CLARKE, KENNETH KINGSLEY, retired electronics executive; b. Miami, Fla., June 7, 1924; s. Kenneth Kingsley and Mary (Coffin) Clarke; m. Nona Nelme, Sept. 15, 1945; 1 child, Kenneth Stephen. Student, Cornell U., 1941—42; MSEE, Stanford, 1948; DEE, Bklyn. Poly. Inst., 1959. Rsch. fellow Bklyn. Poly. Inst., 1949-50, faculty, 1955-69, prof. elec. engring., 1965-69, dir. grad. elec. engring. divsn., 1967-69; asst. prof. Madras (India) Inst. Tech., 1950-52; lectr. U. Ceylon, Colombo, 1952-54; asst. prof. Clarkson Coll. Tech., Potsdam, NY, 1954-55; pres. Clarke-Hess Comm. Rsch. Corp., N.Y.C., 1969-99. Cons. in field; vis. prof. Mid. E. Tech. U., Ankara, Turkey, 1961—62; dir. Julie Rsch. Labs., 1966—71. Author (with M. V. Joyce): Transistor Circuit Analysis, 1961; author: (with D. T. Hess) Communication Circuit Analysis, 1971; author: Spoken Speech and the Invention of Writing, 2004. 2d lt. AC U.S. Army, 1943—46. Recipient Svc. award, Parlar Found., 1992. Fellow: IEEE (life), Instrument and Measurement Soc. (mem. adminstrv. com. 1993—96, mem. visitor accreditation bd. 1983—88, bd. dirs. Instrumentation/Measurement Tech. Conf., tech. program chmn. 1995); mem.: AAAS, AAUP, Sigma Xi, Tau Beta Pi. Achievements include co-inventor frequency locked loop. Home: 300 Riverside Dr New York NY 10025-5279 Personal E-mail: ken1924@ix.netcom.com.

CLARKE, KIT HANSEN, radiologist; b. Louisville, May 24, 1944; d. Hans Peter and Katie (Bird) Hansen; m. John M. Clarke, Feb. 14, 1976; children: Brett Bonnett, Blair Hansen, Brandon Chamberlain; stepchildren: Gray Campbell, Jeffrey William John M. AB, Randolph-Macon Woman's Coll., 1966; MD, U. Louisville, 1969. Diplomate Am. Bd. Radiology. Intern Louisville Gen. Hosp., 1969—70; resident in internal medicine and radiology U. Tenn., Knoxville, 1970—73; resident in radiology U.S. Fla., Tampa, 1973—74; staff radiologist Palms of Pasadena, St. Petersburg, Fla., 1974—, chmn. radiology dept., 1992—. Active Fla. Competitive Swim Assn. of Amateur Athletics Union. Fellow Am. Coll. Radiology; mem. AMA, Fla. West Coast Radiology Soc., Radiol. Soc. N.Am., Fla. Med. Assn., Pinellas County Med. Soc., Fla. Radiology Soc., Am. Horse Show Assn. (hunter, jumber divsn.). Episcopalian. Home: 7171 9th St S Saint Petersburg FL 33705-6218 Office: 6550 1st Ave N Saint Petersburg FL 33710 Office Phone: 727-341-7552. E-mail: khclarke@tampabay.rr.com.

CLARKE, LAMBUTH MCGEEHEE, retired academic administrator; b. Salisbury, Md., Oct. 4, 1923; s. Hawes Palmore and Jessie Lee (Ham) C.; m. Alice Royall Acree, July 16, 1955; children: Leighton Krips, Palmore, Jessica, Virginia Hitch. BA, Randolph-Macon Coll., 1944, LLD (hon.), 1969; MA, Johns Hopkins U., 1948; postgrad., U. Birmingham, 1948, Harvard U., 1982; LHD (hon.), Va. Wesleyen Coll., 2002. English instr. Randolph-Macon Coll., Ashland, Va., 1948-51, asst. to pres., 1951-58, v.p. devel., 1958-66; pres. Va. Wesleyan Coll., Norfolk, 1966-92, pres. emeritus, 1992—, also trustee; acting pres. Randolph-Macon Womans' Coll., 1993-94. Bd. dirs. Va. Symphony, Norfolk, 1970-88, trustee, 1990—; bd. dirs. Leigh Meml. Hosp., later Med. Ctr. Hosps., 1970-82, Norfolk Forum, 1970-80, World Affairs Coun., 1972-76, YMCA, Norfolk, 1972-78, Sta. WHRO-TV, 1972-76, Greater Norfolk Corp., 1978-92, Com. of 101-Future of Hampton Rds., Norfolk, 1983-92, Order of Cape Henry 1607, Norfolk, Va. Eye Found., Norfolk, 1973-92, Va. Coun. Chs., 1978-82; trustee Va. Found. Ind. Colls., Richmond, 1982-92, vice-chmn., 1990-92, assoc., 1992-97; trustee Randolph-Macon Womans Coll., 1992-97, hon. trustee, 1997—; univ. senate United Meth. Ch., Nashville, 1988-92, bd. dirs., gen. bd. higher edn., 1980-88, del. jurisdictional conf., 1976-96, gen. conf., 1980-92; adv. bd. DePaul Med. Ctr., Norfolk, 1988-96; bd. dirs. Lee's Friends, 1993-99, adv. bd., 1999—; bd. dirs. Tidewater Scholarship Found., 1994-2000, Westminster-Canterbury of Hampton Rds., 1995-2003, Norfolk Sr. Ctr., Portsmouth Mus. Found., Inc., 1997-2000, Norfolk Bot. Gardens Found.; chmn. adminstrv. bd. Larchmont United Meth. Ch., 1993. Lt. (j.g.) USNR, 1943-46. Recipient Brotherhood citation NCCJ, 1991, John Wesley Disting. Educator award, 1991, Francis Asbury Educator award, 1995, Jerry G. Bray Dist. Svc. medal Va. Wesleyan Coll., 1997, Lambuth M. Clarke Acad. Ctr. of Va. Wesleyan Coll., 1999. Mem. Soc. Alumni Randolph-Macon Coll. (bd. dirs. 1993-99), Soc. of the Cin., Rotary Club Norfolk, Phi Beta Kappa, Omicron Delta Kappa, Phi Kappa Phi, Lambda Chi Alpha. Methodist. Avocations: volunteerism, reading, music, art and church architecture, stamp collecting/philately. Personal E-mail: acclmc@aol.com.

CLARKE, LEWIS JAMES, landscape architect; b. Eng., Mar. 10, 1927; s. Roland and May (Pringle) C.; children: Lewis Nigel, Jennifer Kay, Rachel May, Lisa Elaine. Dip. Arch., Sch. Architecture, Leicester, Eng., 1950; Dip. L.D., Kings Coll, U. Durham, 1951; M.L.A., Harvard U., 1952. Prof. Sch. Design N.C. State Univ., Raleigh, 1952-68; sr. partner Lewis Clarke Assos., Raleigh, 1952—. Served with Corps Royal Engrs., 1946-49. Smith Mundt fellow, Fulbright fellow, 1951-52. Fellow Inst. Landscape Architects, Am. Soc. Landscape Architects; mem. Royal Inst. Brit. Architects. Home and Office: Lewis Clarke Assocs 1701 Glen Eden Dr Raleigh NC 27612-4335

CLARKE, LOGAN, JR., management consultant; b. Atlanta, May 28, 1927; s. Leonard Warner Moore and Marion (Ray) C.; children: Logan III, Jeffrey Reed, Jonathan, Lisa Beth; m. Cordelia Kay Knight Mazuy. Student, U. Okla., 1944; La., State U., 1945; Stonier Grad., Sch. Banking, 1960; BA, U. Pa., 1949; MS, Hartford Grad. Center, 1981. Salesman Liberty Mut. Ins. Co., Boston, 1949-52; with Nat. Shawmut Bank Boston, 1952-70, asst. v.p., 1955-58, v.p., 1958-70; exec. v.p. County Bank NA, Cambridge, Mass., 1970-71, pres., dir., 1971-75; pres. Shawmut Bank of Boston, N.A.; pres., dir. Shawmut Corp., 1976-78; alt. dir. Atlantic Internat. Bank Ltd., London; alt. rep. Internat. Monetary Conf., 1976-78; lectr. Hartford (Conn.) Grad. Center, 1979-86, dean Sch. Mgmt., 1983-85; exec. v.p. Soc. for Savings, Hartford, 1986-90; acting pres. Hartford Coll. for Women, 1990-91; pres. Templeton Inc., 1991—. Trustee Lyme Acad. Fine Art, 1997—; cons. Arthur D. Little, Inc., 1979-85. Mem. Town Meeting Lexington, Mass., 1961-70, appropriations com., 1960-66, sch. com., 1966-70; bd. overseers Children's Hosp. Med. Ctr., Boston, 1967-87; trustee Lesley Coll., Cambridge, 1971-86, Hartford Coll. for Women, 1985-92; chmn. bd. Govs. Higher Edn., Conn., 1992-97, chmn., 1994-97; corporator Northeastern U., Boston, 1976-85. Recipient Outstanding Young Man award Boston Jr. C. of C. Mem. Masons. Episcopalian. Home: 89 River Rd East Haddam CT 06423-1462 E-mail: lclarke4@mindspring.com.

CLARKE, MILTON CHARLES, lawyer; b. Chgo., Jan. 31, 1929; s. Gordon Robert and Senoria Josephine (Carlisa) C.; m. Dorothy Jane Brodie, Feb. 19, 1955; children: Laura, Virginia, Senoria K. BS, Northwestern U., 1950, JD, 1953. Bar: Ill. 1953, Mo. 1956, U.S. Dist. Ct. (we. dist.) Mo. 1961, U.S. Ct. Appeals (8th cir.) 1961. Assoc. Swanson, Midgley, Gangwere, Clarke & Kitchin, Kansas City, Mo., 1955-61, ptnr., 1961-91; of counsel Olsen & Talpers, P.C., Kansas City, 1994—. Served with U.S. Army, 1953-55. Mem. Rotary. Office: Olsen and Talpers PC 2100 City Center Square 1100 Main St Kansas City MO 64105-2125 Office Phone: 816-421-2050. Personal E-mail: miltonclarke@hotmail.com.

CLARKE, PAMELA JONES, headmaster; b. Boston, Jan. 11, 1945; d. Gilbert Edward and Jean (Morse) Jones; children: Jean, Henry David. BA in Ancient Greek, Vassar Coll., 1966; MA in Classics, Yale U., 1967; MEd in Counseling and Consulting Psych., Harvard U., 1979. Dir. curriculum Groton (Mass.) Sch., 1972-90; head of sch. The Masters Sch., Dobbs Ferry, NY, 1990—2000, St. Paul Acad. & Summit Sch., St. Paul, 2000—05, Trevor Day School, NYC, 2005—. Cons. The Mead Sch., Greenwich, Conn., 1970-72; site dir. CTY Johns Hopkins, Balt. and Carlisle, Pa., 1988, 89; tchr. winter term, Lenk, Switzerland, 1989; alumnae trustee Coll. Yr. in Athens, 1966-70. Contbr. articles to jours., newspaper. Treas. Town Soccer Bd., Groton, 1985-89; mng. Adult Ice Hockey Program, Groton, 1986-90; fund raiser The Shipley Sch., Vassar Coll. Mem. Coun. for Women in Ind. Schs. (mem. task force 1984-90). Democrat. Episcopalian. Avocations: travel, tennis, reading, skiing. Office: Trevor Day Sch 11 E 89th St New York NY 10128*

CLARKE, PAULA KATHERINE, anthropologist, researcher, social studies educator; b. Berkeley, Gloucestershire, Eng., July 27, 1946; d. Percy George and Grace Anne C.; m. Warren Ted Hamilton. BA, U. Calif. Berkeley, 1982; PhD, U. Calif. San Francisco, 1991. Prof. anthropology and sociology Columbia Coll., Sonora, Calif., 1997—. Spkr. 3d Internat. Conf. on Gender and Equity, Bangkok, 2001. Contbr.: Men and Masculinities: A Social, Cultural, and Historical Encyclopedia, 2003; contbr. articles to ednl. jours. (Nominated-Kathleen Gregory Klein Award by Women's Caucus/Popular and Am. Culture Assn. for best unpublished article on feminism and popular culture, 1999). Creator Future Promise Award scholarship Columbia Coll., Sonora, 2001. Recipient Excellence in Tchg. award, Tuolumne County Bd. Edn., 2002. Office: Columbia Coll 11600 Columbia College Dr Sonora CA 95370 Office Phone: 209-588-5356. Business E-Mail: clarkep@yosemite.cc.ca.us.

CLARKE, PETER, communications and health educator; b. Evanston, Ill., Sept. 19, 1936; s. Clarence Leon and Dorothy (Whitcomb) C.; m. Karen Storey, June 4, 1962 (div. 1984); 1 child, Christopher Michael. BA, U. Wash., 1959; MA, U. Minn., 1961, PhD, 1963. Dir., asst. prof. Comm. Rsch. Ctr. U. Wash., Seattle, 1965-68, assoc. prof. Sch. Comm., 1967-72, dir. Sch. Comm., 1971-72; prof. dept. journalism U. Mich., Ann Arbor, 1973-74, chmn., prof. dept. journalism, 1975-78, chmn., prof. dept. comm., 1979-80; dean, prof. Annenberg Sch. Comm., U. So. Calif., L.A., 1981-92, prof., 1993—; prof. preventive medicine U. So. Calif. Keck Sch. Medicine, L.A., 1985—. Co-dir. From the Wholesaler to the Hungry, 1991—; dir. Ctr. for Health and Med. Comm., 1997—; cons. for various fed. and state govt. commns. on mass media and social problems. Co-author: (with Susan H. Evans) Covering Campaigns: Journalism in Congressional Elections, 1983, Surviving Modern Medicine: How to Get the Best from Doctors, Family and Friends, 1998; editor: New Models for Communication Research, 1973; co-editor: (with Susan H. Evans) The Computer Culture, 1985; contbr. articles to profl. jours. Numerous Fed., corp., pvt. founds. grants. Office: U So Calif Annenberg Sch Comm 3502 Watt Way Los Angeles CA 90089-0054 Office Phone: 213-740-0940. E-mail: chmc@usc.edu.

CLARKE, RICHARD ALAN, former federal official; b. Dorchester, Mass., 1950; BA, U. Pa., 1972; MS, MIT, 1978. Nuclear weapons & European security analyst Office Sec. Def., 1973-77; sr. analyst Pacific Sierra Rsch. Corp., 1978-79, Bur. Politico-Mil. Affairs, U.S. Dept. State, Washington, 1979-85; dep. asst. sec. for intelligence U.S. Dept. State, 1985-89, asst. sec. for politico-mil. affairs, 1989-92; spl. asst. to Pres. for global affairs Nat. Security Coun., Washington, 1992—98, nat. coord. for security, infrastructure protection, & counter-terrorism, 1998—2001, spl. adviser for cyberspace security, 2001—03; chmn. Good Harbor Consulting, LLC, Arlington, Va., 2003—. Chair Critical Infrastructure Protection Bd., 2001—03. Author: (non-fiction) Against All Enemies: Inside America's War on Terror, 2004, (novels) The Scorpion's Gate, 2005. Address: care Bruce Nichols Free Press Simon & Schuster 1230 Ave of Americas New York NY 10020

CLARKE, RICHARD LEWIS, health science association administrator; b. Indpls., Sept. 9, 1948; s. John Richard and Opal (Emmons) C.; m. Linda DeMattia, Aug. 12, 1972; children: John, Laura, R. Bradley. BS, Bradley U., 1971; MBA, U. Miami, 1972. Bus. mgr. Jackson Meml. Hosp., Miami, 1973-76; controller Palmetto Gen. Hosp., Hialeah, Fla., 1976-80; sr. v.p. fin. Swedish Med. Ctr., Englewood, Colo., 1980-86; pres. Healthcare Fin. Mgmt. Assn., Westchester, Ill., 1986—. Bd. dirs., treas. Colo. Hosp. Assn. Trust, Denver. Fellow Healthcare Fin. Mgmt. Assn.; mem. Am. Soc. Assn. Execs., Econ. Club of Chgo. Avocations: sailboat racing, skiing. Office: Healthcare Fin Mgmt Assn 2 Westbrook Corp Ctr Ste 700 Westchester IL 60154

CLARKE, ROBERT EARLE (BOBBY CLARKE), hockey executive; b. Flin Flon, Manitoba, Can., Aug. 13, 1949; m. Sandy Clarke; children: Wade, Lucas, Jody, Jakki. Player Flin Flon Bombers, Phila. Flyers, NHL, 1969-84, asst. coach, 1979—82, gen. mgr., 1984-90; gen. mgr., v.p. Minn. North Stars, NHL, 1990-92; gen. mgr. Fla. Panthers, 1993—94; now pres., gen. mgr. Phila. Flyers, 1993—. Winner West Divsn. Rookie of Yr., 1970, Player of Yr. West Divsn. Sporting News, 1972-73, Bill Masterton Meml. trophy, 1972, Hart Meml. trophy, 1973, 75, 76, Player of Yr. Comp. Conf. Sporting News, 1974-75, Player of Yr. Sporting News, 1975-76, Lester B. Pearson trophy, 1973, Frank J. Selke trophy, 1983, NHL Exec. of Yr. Sporting News, 1993-94, 94-95; co-winner Lester Patrick award, 1981; named to NHL Hall of Fame, 1987. Office: Phila Flyers First Union Ctr 3601 S Broad St Philadelphia PA 19148-5250

CLARKE, ROBERT F., utilities company executive; b. Oakland, Calif. BA, U. Calif., Berkeley, 1965, MBA, 1966. Pres., CEO, chmn. Hawaiian Electric, Honolulu, 1991—. Office: Hawaiian Electric Industries Inc 900 Richards St Honolulu HI 96813-2919*

CLARKE, ROBERT LOGAN, lawyer; b. Tulsa, Okla., June 29, 1942; s. Ralph Logan and Faye Louise (Todd) C.; m. Jean (Puddin) Barrow Talbert, Sept. 23, 1967; 1 child, Robert Logan Jr. BA Econs., Rice U., 1963; LLB, Harvard U., 1966. Bar: N.Mex. 1966, Tex. 1967. Legis. asst. to U.S. Senator Edwin L. Mechem, Washington, 1964; assoc. Hinkle, Bondurant, Cox, Eaton & Hensley, Roswell, N.Mex., 1966, Bracewell & Patterson, Houston, 1968-73, ptnr., 1973-85, ptnr., head fin. svcs. sect., 1992—; comptr. of currency Washington, 1985-92; dir. FDIC, Washington, 1985-92, Resolution Trust Corp., Washington, 1989-92. Bd. dirs. Cmty. Bancorp. N.Mex., Inc., Cmty. Bank, Eagle Materials, Inc., First Investors Fin. Svcs., Inc., Stewart Info. Svcs. Corp., Encore Trust Co.; sr. advisor to pres. Nat. Bank Poland, 1992-2000; advisor to bank suprs. in Ea. Europe, Mexico, Argentina, Brazil and Kazakhstan. Precinct chmn. Harris County Reps., 1970-74, 76-85, legal counsel, 1984-85; trustee Mus. N.Mex. Found., 1992—, Southwestern Grad. Sch. Banking Found., 1993—, Internat. Folk Art Found., 1995-2002; dir. Santa Fe Chamber Music Festival, 2003—; founding dir. Houston Rep. Club, 1982-85; bd. dirs. Houston Polit. Action Com., 1983-85; trustee Trout Unlimited, 1997—; adv. com. Harris County Reagan-Bush campaign, 1984; asst. scoutmaster Boy Scouts Am., Houston, 1980-85; deacon 1st Presbyn. Ch. Houston. Capt. U.S. Army, 1966-68. Recipient Disting. Svc. medal U.S. Treasury Dept., 1992, Banking Leadership award Western States Sch. Banking, Albuquerque, 1993. Mem. Houston Bar Assn., Houston Bar Found., State Bar Tex., State Bar N.Mex., Rice U. Alumni Assn. (chmn. area club com. 1984-85, mem. exec. bd. dirs. 1987-89, Disting. Alumnus award 1992), River Oaks Country Club, Chevy Chase Club, Houston Club, Coronado Club, Houston City Club, Rotary (trustee student's ednl. fund). Avocations: tennis, fishing, hiking. Office: Bracewell & Patterson Pennzoil South Tower 711 Louisiana St Ste 2300 Houston TX 77002-2781

CLARKE, ROY, physicist, researcher; b. Bury, Lancashire, England, 1947; BSc in Physics, U. London, PhD, 1973. Rsch. assoc. Cavendish Lab., Cambridge, U.K., 1973-78; James Franck fellow U. Chgo., 1978-79; prof. U. Mich., Ann Arbor, 1979-86; dir. applied physics program, 1986—2002. Co-founder k-Space Assocs. Inc. Editor: Synchrotron Radiation in Materials Research, 1989. Fellow Am. Phys. Soc. Achievements include development of novel methods for real-time x-ray and electron diffraction studies; patents for quasiperiodic optical coatings and epitaxial spin-valve devices. Office: U Mich Randall Lab Ann Arbor MI 48109-1040

CLARKE, S. GORDON, clergyman; b. Charleston, W.Va., Mar. 3, 1931; s. Leonard Gordon and Marguerite (Lyons) C.; m. Martha Thompson, Nov. 3, 1950; children: Daniel Gordon, David Allen (dec.)./ AB in Religion, Marion (Ind.) Coll., 1959, ThM, 1962; DD (hon.), Colo. Theol. Sem., 1965. Ordained to ministry Friends Ch., 1959. Dir. Creative Ministries, Indpls., 1959-69; regional exec. sec. Am. Bible Soc., Chgo., 1959-77; pastor Forsuth Friends Ch., Winston-Salem, NC, 1977—79; sr. pastor Garden Grove (Calif.) Friends Ch., 1979-99; vol. chaplain Wayne County Sheriff Office, 1996—; pastor New Hope Friends Ch., Goldsboro, N.C., 1999—, Rhodes Friends Ch., Mt. Olive, NC. Chaplain Garden Grove Police Dept., Wayne County Sheriff Dept.; chmn. Bd. Spiritual Life Friends United Meeting, chmn. program meeting 1987, mem. meeting ministries commn.; mem. exec. com. bd. adminstrn. S.W. Yearly Meeting, chmn. spiritual life com.; pres. bd. trustees Calif. Friends Homes; founder Chaplain-on-Call. Mem. Spl. Task Force of Religious Well Being for White House Conf. on Aging; mem. Gov.'s Commn. on Aging, Gov.'s Commn. on Tourism, Gov.'s Com. on Migrant Labor. Sgt. USAF, 1950-55. Mem. Coll. Chaplains Am. Protestant Hosp. Assn., Correctional Chaplains Assn., Internat. Platform Assn., Nat. Assn. Religious Broadcasters. Leisure Fellowship Ministry. Home: 102 Woods Mill Rd Goldsboro NC 27534-9122 Office: Garden Grove Friends Ch 4451 US 70 E Goldsboro NC 27534 E-mail: gmclrk2@aol.com.

CLARKE, STEPHAN PAUL, retired language educator, writer; b. Watertown, N.Y., Jan. 18, 1945; s. Albert John and Marjory Ruth (Grieb) Clarke; m. Mary Elizabeth Hawley, May 23, 1970; 1 child, Erin Elizabeth. BS in Edn., SUNY, Geneseo, 1966; MA, Bowling Green State U., 1968. Cert. secondary tchr. N.Y. Dept. Edn. Tchr. English E. J. Wilson HS, Spencerport, NY, 1970-99; ret., 1999. Spkr. N.Y. State Edn. Dept. Writer's Conf., Albany, 1982, Albany, 87. Author: (book) The Lord Peter Wimsey Companion, 1985 (Edgar Allan Poe Spl. award, Mystery Writers of Am.), The Lord Peter Wimsey Companion, rev. edit., 2002, Crimes and Clues, 1977. Chmn. supr. com. Spencerport Fed. Credit Union, 1985—2003, bd. dirs., sec. bd., 1999—2004; rec. sec. Ch. and Ministry Com. Genesee Valley Assn. United Ch. of Christ, Rochester, 1983—88. Lt. USNR, 1968—70. Recipient Excellence in Secondary Sch. Tchg. award, U. Rochester Grad. Sch. Edn. and Human Devel., 1991. Mem.: SAR (bd. mgrs. Rochester chpt. 1997—, chpt. historian 1999—2004, chpt. pres. 2001—, War Svc. medal 1996, Silver Good Citizenship medal 1997), Rochester Geneal. Soc. (spkr. 2002, 2003), USN Meml. Found., Dorothy L. Sayers Soc. U.K. (spkr. 1985, 2003), Stratford Shakespearean Festival Found. Can., Sons Union Vets Civil War, U.S. Naval Inst. (life). Democrat. Avocations: reading, travel, photography, model railroads, genealogy. Home: 148 Greenway Blvd Churchville NY 14428-9210 Personal E-mail: sclarke@rochester.rr.com. *Live with the realization that the greatest success is that in which the world partakes, the indestructable good you leave behind.*

CLARKE, STEVEN GERARD, chemistry professor; b. L.A., Nov. 19, 1949; BA in Chemistry/Zoology magna cum laude, Pomona Coll., 1970; PhD in Biochemistry & Molecular Biology, Harvard U., 1976. NIH undergrad. fellow Glynn Rsch. Labs., Bodmin, Eng., summer 1969; NSF predoctoral fellow Harvard U., 1970-73, biochemistry and molecular biology instr., 1973-74; Miller Inst. fellow U. Calif., Berkeley, 1976-78; asst. prof. chemistry and molecular biology UCLA, 1978-83, assoc. prof. chemistry and biochemistry, 1983-87, prof. chemistry and biochemistry, 1987—, dir. Molecular Biology Inst., 2001—. Vis. fellow molecular biology Princeton (N.J.) U., 1986-87; mem. sci. com. 1st Internat. Symposium on Post-Translational Modifications of Proteins and Aging, Lacco Ameno d'Ischia, Naples, Italy, 1987; chair, symposium organizer ann. meeting Am. Soc. for Biochemistry and Molecular Biology, Atlanta, 1991; mem. adv. bd. nutrition and metabolism sect. biol. aging Nat. Inst. Aging, NIH, 1993; co-chair Fedn. Am. Socs. for Exptl. Biology summer rsch. conf., Vt., 1995; dir. Molecular Biology Inst., U. Calif., L.A., Calif., 2001— Assoc. editor Protein Sci., 1995-98, mem. editl. adv. bd., 1994-95; mem. editl. bd. Jour. Biol. Chemistry, 1994-98; contbr. more than 200 articles to profl. jours. Woodrow Wilson fellow, 1970; grantee Am. Heart Assn., 1984-85, 85-86, 87-88, 89, NSF, 1989, 90, 91, NIH, 1995. Mem. Am. Chem. Soc. (Ralph F. Hirschmann award 1996), Am. Soc. Biochemistry and Molecular Biology, The Protein Soc., Assn. Med. and Grad. Depts. Biochemistry, Phi Beta Kappa, Alpha Chi Sigma. Office: UCLA Dept Chemistry & Biochem 607 Charles E Young Dr East Los Angeles CA 90095-1569 Office Phone: 310-825-8754. Business E-Mail: clarke@mbi.ucla.edu.

CLARKE, TERENCE MICHAEL, public relations and advertising executive; b. Altoona, Pa., Apr. 9, 1937; s. Robert Ewing and Louise Mercedes (Eckley) C.; m. Judith Ann Lawson, Oct. 15, 1966; children: Lawson Robert, Penn Terence. Student, U. Pitts., 1955-57; cert., Inst. Far Ea. Langs., Yale U., 1958; BS, Boston U., 1963, MS, 1989. Pub. rels. mgr. Pepsi-Cola Co., N.Y.C., 1963, H.P. Hood & Sons, Boston, 1964-66; pres. The Taggart Co., Chgo., 1966-70; dir. pub. rels. Creamer, Trowbridge, Case & Basford, Boston, 1970; v.p., dir. Johnson, Raffin & Clarke Inc., Boston, 1971-76; assoc. prof. Boston U., 1976-77; chmn. Clarke Goward Advt. Inc., Boston, 1977—; chmn., CEO Clarke & Co. Inc., Boston, 1997—2004, Red 98 Interactive, 1999—2003. Bd. dirs. EPROPSHOP, Inc. Chmn. planning, site, constrn. com. Hingham (Mass.) Sch., 1971-86; exec. com. Coll. Comm., Boston U., 1987—; bd. dirs. Mass. Soc. for Prevention of Cruelty to Children, 1980-94; mem. Hingham Police Sta. Constrn. Com., 1987-90; trustee Belmont (Mass.) Hill Sch., 1988-2003, Boston U., 1995-97; bd. overseers Huntington Theatre Co., Boston, 1992-2004. With USAF, 1957-60. Recipient L.E. Sissman award Greater Boston Advt. Club, 1984. Mem. Greater Boston Advt. Club (bd. dirs. 1980-83), Soc. for Preservation of Barber Shop Quartet Singing in Am. (internat. quartet champions 1980), Boston U. Alumni (pres. 1995-97, Disting. Alumni award Coll. Comms.1984), Algonquin Club, Univ. Club. Republican. Presbyterian. Avocation: barbershop quartet singing. Office: Clarke Goward Advt and Pub Rels 535 Boylston St Boston MA 02116-3720

CLARKE, THOMAS E., apparel executive; b. Binghamton, N.Y., Aug. 8, 1951; married. MS, U. Fla., 1977; D in Biomechanics, Pa. State U., 1980. Rschr. Sports and Rsch. Lab NIKE, Inc., Exeter, N.H., various to dir. product devel., corp. v.p. of mktg., 1983-94, pres. Beaverton, Oreg., 1994-2000, co-CFO, pres. new bus. ventures, 2000—. Avocation: running (competitive marathon runner). Office: Nike Inc One Bowerman Dr Beaverton OR 97005-6453

CLARKE, THOMAS HAL, lawyer; b. Atlanta, Aug. 10, 1914; s. James Caleb and Mary Cox (DeSaussure) C.; m. Mary Louise Hastings, July 12, 1951; children: Thomas Hal Jr., Katie Clarke Hamilton, Rebecca DeSaussure Morrison. LLB, Washington and Lee U., 1938. Bar: Ga. 1939, U.S. Dist. Ct. (no. dist.) Ga., U.S. Ct. Appeals (5th cir.), U.S. Supreme Ct., 1973. Ptnr. Clarke & Anderson, Atlanta, 1948-60, Mitchell, Clarke, Pate & Anderson, Atlanta, 1960-69, 73-85; of counsel Gambrell, Clarke, Anderson & Stolz, Atlanta, 1985-92. Copyright trustee Gone With the Wind and sequels, 1983—. Mem. Fed. Home Loan Bank Bd., Washington, 1969-73; past pres., bd. dirs. Atlanta Hist. Soc.; past bd. visitors Emory U.; trustee emeritus Washington and Lee U.; mem. Hibernian United Service Club, Dublin, Ireland. Served with USNR, 1942-46, ETO, PTO. Mem. Internat. Bar Assn. (past chmn. savs. and bldg. socs. com.), ABA (chmn. savs. and loan com. 1970-73, chmn. corp. banking and bus. law sect. 1973-74, mem. ho. of dels. 1974-80, editor The Business Lawyer 1972), Ga. Bar Assn., Atlanta Bar Assn., Am. Law Inst., Atlanta Lawyers Club (past pres.), Selden Soc., English Speaking Union (past pres., chmn. bd.), Metropolitan Club (Washington D.C.), Commerce Club, Piedmont Driving Club (Atlanta). Presbyterian. Home: 186 15th St NE Atlanta GA 30309-3511

CLARKE, WILLIAM A. LEE, III, lawyer; b. Balt., May 7, 1949; s. William Anthony Jr. and Eileen Sheila (Walsh) C.; m. Dara Ford, May 8, 1994. Student, John Carroll U., 1969-72; JD magna cum laude, U. Balt., 1975. Bar: Md. 1975, U.S. Dist. Ct. Md. 1975, U.S. Supreme Ct. 1979, U.S. Ct. Appeals (4th cir.) 1981. Trial atty. Tenn. Valley Authority, Knoxville, 1975-76; pvt. practice Salisbury, Md., 1977—. Vis. lectr. criminal law U. Md. Eastern Shore, Princess Anne, 1989. Pres. Wicomico County Dems., Salisbury, 1981-83; commr. Md. Human Rels. Commn., Balt., 1983-85. Served to cpl. USMC, 1967-69, Vietnam. Mem.: Nat. Bd. Trial Adv. (cert. criminal trial advocate 1987—2002), Md. Criminal Def. Attys. Assn. (bd. dirs. 1984—93), Salisbury Jaycees (legal counsel 1977—79). Office: 30644 Brandywine Ct Salisbury MD 21804-2558 Office Phone: 410-219-5899. Business E-Mail: walc@clarkelaw.com.

CLARKIN, JOHN FRANCIS, health care management executive; b. Atlantic City, Dec. 30, 1936; s. John Francis and Agnes (Winterholer) C.; m. Dorothy Louise Piffath, 1 son, John F. BSBA, Rider Coll., 1959; postgrad., Temple U. Cert. mgmt. cons. Inst. Mgmt. Cons., 1968. Mktg. rep. Scott Paper Co., Indpls., 1960-62; systems and mktg. rep. Burroughs Corp., Phila., 1962-67; dir. Mid-Atlantic health care ops. mgmt. practice Coopers & Lybrand, Phila., 1967-92; v.p. corp. fin. svcs. Crozer-Keystone Health Sys., Upland, Pa., 1992-97; pres. The Clarkin Group, West Chester, Pa., 1997-98; v.p. bus. svcs. Thomas Jefferson U. Hosp., Phila., 1998—. Lead instr., spkr. numerous profl. meetings and seminars. Author: Topics in Health Care Financing, 1982; (with others) Handbook of Health Care Accounting and Finance, 1982, 89, Billing Systems, 2 vols., 1982, 89, Managing Accounts Receivable, 1990; contbr. articles to profl. jours. Mem. Grand Oak Run Civic Assn., 1970—. With U.S. Army, 1959. Grantee Rotary Club, 1955—59. Mem. Inst. Mgmt. Cons., Hosp. Mgmt. Systems Soc., Hosp. Fin. Mgmt. Assn., Med. Group Mgmt. Assn., Am. Hosp. Assn., Vesper Club, Pickering Racquet Club. Republican. Roman Catholic. Home: 1421 Grand Oak Ln West Chester PA 19380-5951 Office: Thomas Jefferson U Hosp Bus Svcs 170 S Independence Sq W Philadelphia PA 19106 Office Phone: 215-955-6403.

CLARK-JOHNSON, SUSAN, publishing executive; b. Mount Kisco, NY, Feb. 21, 1947; d. Emile Schurmacher and Elizabeth Woolf; m. Samuel Brooks Johnson. BA in history, SUNY, Binghamton, 1967. With Niagara Gazette, NY, 1970—83; pub. Binghamton Press & Sun-Bulletin, 1983—84; v.p. N.E. region Gannett Co. Inc., 1984—85; pres., pub. Reno Gazette-Jour., 1985—2000; pres. Gannett West Gannett Co. Inc., 1985—94, sr. group pres. Pacific Newspaper Group, 1994—2005; chmn. & CEO Phoenix Newspapers, 2000—05; pub. Ariz. Republic, 2000—05; pres. Gannett Co. newspaper divsn., McLean, Va., 2005—. Bd. dirs. Harrah's Entertainment, Inc.; bd. visitors John S. Knight Fellowships for Profl. Journalists, Stanford U. Office: Gannett Co Newspaper Divsn 7950 Jones Branch Drive Mc Lean VA 22101*

CLARK-LANGAGER, SARAH ANN, curator, academic administrator; b. Lynchburg, Va., May 14, 1943; m. Craig T. Langager, 1979. BA in Art History, Randolph-Macon Woman's Coll., 1965; postgrad., U. Md., 1968; MA in Art History, U. Wash., 1970; PhD in Art History, CUNY, 1988. Assoc. edn. dept., lectr. Yale U. Art Gallery, New Haven, 1965-67, Albright-Knox Art Gallery, Buffalo, 1967-68; asst. to dir. Richard White Gallery, Seattle, 1969-70; curatorial asst. to curators painting and sculpture San Francisco Mus. Modern Art, 1970; assoc. edn. dept., lectr. Seattle Art Mus., 1971-73, 74-75; asst. curator, and then assoc. curator modern art, lectr. Seatle Art Mus., 1975-79; curator 20th century art, lectr. Munson-Williams-Proctor Inst., Utica, NY, 1981-86; asst. prof. art history, dir. Univ. Art Gallery, U. North Tex., Denton, 1986-88; dir. Western Gallery, curator outdoor sculpture collection Western Wash. U., Bellingham, 1988—, mem. adj. faculty, 1988—. Lectr., cons. in edn. NY Cultural Ctr., NYC, 1973-74; editl. asst. October, MIT Press, NYC, 1980; lectr. art history South Seattle C.C., 1975; lectr. 20th century art Cornish Inst. Fine Arts, Seattle, 1977-78; sole rep. for N.Y. State, Art Mus. Assn. Am., 1984-86; bd. dirs. Wash. Art Consortium, v.p., 1989-90, pres., 1990-93, acting pres., 1996, pres. 1990-93, 1999-2001, v.p. 1989-90, 2001-2003; cons. State of Wash. Save Outdoor Sculpture, 1994-2000, others. Contbr. articles to profl. jours.; curator exhbns., 1970—, including Rodney Ripps traveling exhbn., 1983, Sculpture Space: Recent Trends, 1984, Order and Enigma: American Art Between the Two Ward, 1984, Stars over Texas: Top of the Triangle, 1988, Master Works of American Art from the Munson-Williams-Proctor Institute, 1989, Public Art/Private Visions, 1989, Drawing Power, 1990, Audiophone Tour for Sculpture Collection-20 Interviews, 1991, Focus on Figure, 1992, Chairs: Embodied Objects, 1993, Northwest Native American and First Nations People's Art, 1993, New Acquisitions, 1995, Stars and Stripes: American Prints and Drawings, 1995, Photographs from America, 1996, (catalog introduction) Metalcrafts, 1998, Western Gallery, NW Artists' Books, 1999, Decades of Giving: Virginia Wright and Sculpture at Western, 1999, Surface Tension, 2003, A Sofa and..., 2003, Noguchi & Dance, 2005, others; author: The Outdoor Sculpture Collection: The Development of Public Art at Western, 2000 The Italian Period in Susan Bennerstoom, 2000, Sculpture in Place: A Campus as Site, 2002, Isamu Noguchi: Beyond Red Square, 2004. Recipient Woman of Merit in Arts award Mohawk Valley C.C. and YWCA, Utica, 1985; Kress Found. fellow U. Wash., 1970; Helena Rubenstein Found. scholar CUNY Grad. Ctr., 1980. Office: Western Wash U Western Gallery Fine Arts Complex Bellingham WA 98225-9068 Business E-Mail: sarah.clarklangager@wwu.edu.

CLARKSON, ADRIENNE, Governor General of Canada; b. Hong Kong, 1939; m. John Ralston Saul. BA with honours, MA in English Lit., U. Toronto; postgrad., Sorbonne, Paris. Host, writer, prodr. CBC TV, 1965-82; first agt.-gen. for Ont. Paris, 1982-87; pres, pub. McClelland & Stewart, 1987-88; exec. prodr., host, writer Adrienne Clarkson's Summer Festival, Adrienne Clarkson Presents, 1988-98; gov. gen. Govt. of Can., 1999—. Chair, bd. trustees Can. Museum of Civilization, Hull, Que.; pres. exec. bd. IMZ, Vienna; active numerous arts and charitable orgns. Exec. prodr., host CBC TV program Something Special, others; writer, dir. several films, Can. Named Officer of the Order of Can., 1992, Chancellor and Prin. Companion of the Order of Can., 1999. Office: Rideau Hall 1 Sussex Dr Ottawa ON Canada K1A OA1

CLARKSON, CHARLES ANDREW, real estate investment executive; b. Grove City, Pa., Sept. 1, 1945; s. Harold William and Jean Henrietta (Jaxtheimer) C.; m. Patricia Holt, June 14, 1969; children: Thomas Byerly, Blair Elizabeth, John Holt. AB, Princeton U., 1967; JD, George Washington U., 1972. With N.Y. Urban League, 1967—68; real estate negotiator Safeway Stores, Washington, 1968-69; mortgage banker J.W. Rouse Co., Washington, 1970-73; pres. Alex Brown Realty, Balt., 1973-76; founder, pres. The Clarkson Group, Jacksonville, Fla., 1976—. Bd. dirs. Ramgow, Inc.; chmn. Intelligenxia, JCCI. Chmn. bd. dirs. Jacksonville Urban League, 1987, Cmtys. in Schs.; hon. trustee UNF Found.; mem. Environ. Land Mgmt. Study Com III, Fla.; chmn. bd. trustees WJCT-TV; mem. Commn. on Future of the South, 1998; mem. Bd. Govs. FCCJ Found. Mem. River Club, Sawgrass Club, The Lodge at Ponte Vedra. Office: The Clarkson Co Ste 200 3100 University Blvd S Jacksonville FL 32216-2727

CLARKSON, CHERYL LEE, healthcare executive; b. Chgo., Apr. 14, 1953; d. George Mendenhall and Carol Ann (Fertig) C.; m. Daniel J. Townsend; children: Drew Scott Clarkson-Townsend, Danielle Ann Clarkson-Townsend. BA in Sociology, Ariz. State U., 1975; MS in Mgmt., MIT, 1990. Sales rep. Am. Hosp. Supply, Inc., Phoenix, 1975-78, area sales mgr. Dallas, 1978-79, Edison, N.J., 1979-81, regional mgr. Boston, 1981-83, dir. sales Evanston, Ill., 1983-85; v.p. sales, mktg. Rudolph Beaver, Inc., Waltham, Mass., 1985-88; pres. Beaver Steriseal, Inc., Waltham, 1987-88, Clarkson and Assocs., 1988-90, Abiodent, Inc., Danvers, Mass., 1990-92; CEO, COO, bd. dirs. Peer Review Analysis, Inc., Boston, 1992-95; CEO, pres. SkinHealth, Inc., Wellesley, Mass., 1999—. Bd. overseers Boston U. Med. Ctr. Hosp., 1993-1997; bd. dirs. NMT Med. Inc., Boston. Trustee Kingsley Montessori Sch., Boston, 1996—99; bd. dirs. Northeastern U. Sch. of Bus., 1998—; trustee Mass. Eye and Ear Infirmary, Boston, 1998—; mem. global rsch. coun. Children's Hosp. of Boston, 2005—. Mem. Algonquin Club (Boston). Avocations: travel, golf, horseback riding. Office: SkinHealth Inc 251 Washington St Wellesley Hills MA 02481 Office Phone: 781-431-0454.

CLARKSON, ELISABETH ANN HUDNUT, volunteer; b. Youngstown, Ohio, Apr. 20, 1925; d. Herbert Beecher and Edith (Schaaf) Hadnut; m. William M. E. Clarkson, Sept. 23, 1950; children: Alison H., David B., Andrew E. AB, Wilson Coll., 1947, LHD, 1985; MA, SUNY, 1973, postgrad. With J. L. Hudson Co., Detroit, 1947-50; writer Minute Parade daily Sta. WGR, Detroit, 1948-50. Author: (book) You Can Always Tell a Freshman, 1949, An Adirondack Archive: The Trail to Windover, 1993; contbr. articles to profl. jours. Trustee Wilson Coll., Chambersburg, Pa., 1970—83, chmn. bd. trustees, 1979—82; collector, curator Graphic Controls Corp. art collection, 1976—83; active N.Y. State Mus., 1985—90; past chmn. jr. group Albright Knox Art Gallery; mem. Buffalo Art Commn., 1983—, chmn., 1990—96; sustainer Jr. League, 1983—; mem. exec. bd. arts adv. coun. SUNY, Buffalo, 1985—95; mem. cmty. adv. panel Niagara Frontier Transp. Authority, 1991—94; trustee Clarkson Ctr. Human Svcs., 1995—2000, Irish Classical Theatre Co., 1998—2004; mem. adv. bd. Tannery Pond Cmty. Ctr., North Creek, NY, 2002—; mem. Trinity Episcopal Ch., 1950—, Trinity Vestry, 1996—99, mem. cultural leadership group, 1994—96, 1998—2000; mem. racism commn. Episcopal Diocese of Western N.Y., 1989—92; mem. Companion of the Holy Cross, 1971—, companion-in-charge soc., 1985—90; bd. dirs. Buffalo Mus. Sci., 1972—87, 1990—96, Bischoff Clarkson Hudnut Corp., North Creek, NY, 1973—83, Windover Corp., 1997—, pres., 1998—2001; bd. dirs. N.Y. State Mus. Assn., Albany, 1985—90; adv. bd. dirs. North Creek R.R. Mus., 2003—. Recipient Trustee award for disting. svc., Wilson Coll., 1983, award in the arts, NCCJ, 1998. Mem.: Buffalo Club (art and archives com. 2004—), Sloane Club (London), Buffalo Tennis and Squash Club, Garret Club (bd. dirs. 2000—03, pres. 2001—02). Home: 156 Bryant St Buffalo NY 14222-2003: Log house Windover North Creek NY 12853

CLARKSON, JOHN G., academic administrator, ophthalmologist; m. Diana Teasdale; children: Paige, David. BS, Princeton U.; MD, Miami Sch. Medicine, 1968. Intern U. Hosp., Boston; resident ophthalmology U. Miami/Jackson Meml. Med. Ctr., Fla.; opthalmic pathology, retinal and vitreous surgery fellow Johns Hopkins U., Balt.; chmn. dept. ophthalmology, dir. Bascom Palmer Eye Inst., 1991—96; sr. v.p. med. affairs, dean Sch. Medicine U. Miami, 1995—. Mem.: Macula Soc., Retina Soc., Am. Ophthalmol. Soc., Am. Acad. Ophthalmology, Am. Bd. Ophthalmology (bd. dirs.), Club Jules Gonin. Office: U Miami Sch Medicine PO Box 016099 (R699) 1600 NW 10th Ave Miami FL 33136-1090

CLARKSON, JULIAN DERIEUX, retired lawyer; b. Coral Gables, Fla., Mar. 12, 1929; s. Julian Livingston and Hazel (Lamar) C.; m. Joan Combs, Dec. 24, 1950, children— James L., Julian L., Joanna D., Melinda C.; m. 2d, Shirley Lazonby, Nov. 8, 1979; 1 child, Shirley Lamar. B.A., U. Fla., 1950, LL.B., 1955, J.D., 1967. Bar: Fla. 1955, U.S. Ct. Appeals (5th cir.) 1961, U.S. Supreme Ct. 1964, U.S. Ct. Appeals (11th cir.) 1981, D.C. 1983. Ptnr., Henderson, Franklin, Starnes & Holt, Ft. Myers, Fla., 1955-76; sole practice, Ft. Myers, 1976-77; ptnr. Holland & Knight, Ft. Myers, 1977-79, Tampa, 1979-82, Tallahassee, 1982—; ret., 1993; lectr. in field. Chmn. Fla. Supreme Ct. Jud. Nominating Commn., 1976-78. Served to 1st lt. U.S. Army, 1950-53. Decorated Purple Heart, 1951; named Outstanding Grad. Province V Phi Delta Phi, 1955. Mem. Am. Coll. Trial Lawyers, Am. Acad. Appellate Lawyers, Fla. Blue Key, Order of Coif, Phi Beta Kappa. Democrat. Episcopalian. Author: Let No Man Put Asunder— Story of a Football Rivalry, 1968, Golden Era II, 1994. Home: 4957 Southern Wood Dr Sarasota FL 34241-6227

CLARKSON, KELLY BRIANNE, singer; b. Burleson, Tex., Apr. 24, 1982; d. Steve Clarkson, Jeanne and Jimmy Taylor (Stepfather). Winner inaugural Am. Idol contest, 2002; 2d place World Idol contest, 2004. Singer: (songs) Before Your Love/A Moment Like This, 2002, (albums) Thankful, 2003 (Reached #1 on the Billboard Charts, 2004), Breakaway, 2004; actor: (films) Issues 101, 2002, From Justin to Kelly, 2003; singer: (films) Love Actually, 2003, Ella Enchanted, 2004, The Princess Diaries 2: Royal Engagement, 2004. Recipient Best Female Video and Best Pop Video for Since U Been Gone, MTV Video Music Awards, 2005. Office: RCA Records 1540 Broadway New York NY 10036

CLARKSON, LAWRENCE WILLIAM, air transportation executive; b. Grove City, Pa., Apr. 29, 1938; s. Harold William and Jean Henrietta (Jaxtheimer) Clarkson; m. Barbara Louise Stevenson, Aug. 20, 1960; children: Michael, Elizabeth, Jennifer. BA, DePauw U., 1960; JD, U. Fla., 1962. Counsel Pratt & Whitney, West Palm Beach, Fla., 1967-72, program dep. dir., 1972-75, program mgr., 1974-75, v.p., mng. dir. Brussels, 1975-78, v.p. mktg. West Palm Beach, 1978-80, v.p. contracts Hartford, Conn., 1980-82, pres. comml. products div., 1982-87; sr. v.p. Boeing Comml. Airplanes Group, Seattle, 1988-91; corp. v.p. planning and internat. devel. Boeing Co., Seattle, 1992-93, sr. v.p., 1994-99; pres. Boeing Enterprises, Seattle, 1997-99; sr. v.p. Project Internat., Seattle, 2000—. Chmn. Hitco Carbon, 2002—, Interturbine NV, 2000—02; bd. dirs. Partnership for Improved Air Travel, Washington, 1988—91, Atlas Air, Avnet Inc. Trustee DePauw U., Greencastle, Ind., 1987—, vice chmn., 1996—2002; trustee Embry Riddle Aero. U., Daytona Beach, Fla., Seattle Opera, 1990—, chmn., 1991—2002; overseer Tuck Sch. Dartmouth, Hanover, NH, 1993—99; corp. counsel Interlochen (Mich.) Ctr. Arts, 1987, trustee, 1988—, chmn., 1996—2001; pres. Japan-Am. Soc., Wash., 1993, Wash. State China Rels. Com., 1992—93; chmn. Nat. Bur. Asia Rsch., Coun. Fgn. Rels., U.S. Pacific Econ. Corp. Coun., 1993—2000. Mem.: Am. Inst. Contemporary German Studies (bd. dirs. 1997—99), Nat. Assn. Mfrs. (bd. dirs. 1993—99), The Pilgrims of the U.S., Wings Club (bd. govs. 1987—91), Met. Club DC, N.Y. Yacht Club, Order St. John (bd. govs., Knight). Episcopalian. Home: 10127 NE 66th Ln Kirkland WA 98033-6870 Office Phone: 206-979-7001. Personal E-mail: lwc42938@aol.com.

CLARKSON, PATRICIA, actress; b. New Orleans, Dec. 29, 1959; d. Buzz and Jackie Clarkson. Student, La. State U.; B in Theatre Arts, Fordham U., 1982; MFA, Yale U. Actor: (films) The Untouchables, 1987, The Dead Pool, 1988, Rocket Gibraltar, 1988, Everybody's All-American, 1988, Tune in Tomorrow, 1990, Jumanji, 1995, Pharaoh's Army, 1995, High Art, 1998, Playing by Heart, 1998, Simply Irresistable, 1999, Wayward Son, 1999, The Green Mile, 1999, Joe Gould's Secret, 2000, Falling Like This, 2000, The Pledge, 2001, Wendigo, 2001, The Safety of Objects, 2001, Welcome to Collinwood, 2002, Far from Heaven, 2002, Heartbreak Hospital, 2002, The Baroness and the Pig, 2002, Pieces of April, 2003 (Acad. award nomination for best supporting actress, 2004), All the Real Girls, 2003, The Station Agent, 2003, Dogville, 2003, Miracle, 2004; (TV films) The Old Man and the Sea, 1990, Legacy of Lies, 1992, An American Story, 1992, Four Eyes and Six-Guns, 1992, Blind Man's Bluff, 1992, Caught in the Act, 1993, She Led Two Lives, 1994, London Suite, 1996, Wonderland, 2002, Carrie, 2002; (TV series) Davis Rules, 1991, Murder One, 1995—96; (TV miniseries) Queen, 1993, (TV guest appearance) Six Feet Under, 2001—05 (Emmy for outstanding guest actress in a drama series, 2002), Frasier, 2001, (stage appearances) A Cheever Evening, 1993, Raised in Captivity, 1995, Three Days of Rain, 1997, The Maiden's Prayer, 1998, Streetcar Named Desire, 2004.*

CLARKSON, ROBERT T., lawyer; b. Yakima, Wash. AB with distinction and honors, Stanford Univ., 1975; JD, UCLA, 1982. Bar: Calif. 1982. Atty. Wilson Sonsini Goodrich & Rosati; various exec. positions to COO CKS Group; ptnr.-in-charge Menlo Park office Jones Day, Calif. Bd. dir. Symmetricom Inc. Mem.: Order of Coif. Office: Jones Day Ste 240 2882 Sand Hill Rd Menlo Park CA 94025-7057 Office Phone: 650-739-3996. Office Fax: 650-739-3900. Business E-Mail: rtclarkson@jonesday.com.

CLARKSON, THOMAS WILLIAM, toxicologist, educator; b. Eng., Aug. 1, 1932; came to U.S., 1957; s. William and Olive (Jackson) C.; m. Winifred Browne, Mar. 4, 1957; children: Ian, Jean, Ann. BSc, U. Manchester, 1953, PhD, 1956; Dr Medicine (hon.), U. Umea, Sweden, 1986. Sci. officer tox research unit Med. Research Council U.K., Carshalton, Surrey, 1962-64; sr. fellow polymer sci. Weizmann Inst. Sci., Rehovot, Israel, 1964-65; mem. faculty U. Rochester (N.Y.) Med. Sch., 1958—, prof. toxicology, 1971—, head div., 1980-86, J. Lowell Orbison Disting. Svc. Alumni prof., 1983—, dir. Environ. Health Scis. Ctr., 1986-98; chmn. Dept. Environ. Medicine, 1992-98. Dir. NASA Ctr. Rsch. and Tng. in Space Environ. Health, 1991-95. Mem. editorial bds. profl. jours.; author articles in field. Recipient Founders' award CIIT, 1997, Arthur Kornberg Rsch. award U. Rochester, 1999. Mem. Inst. Medicine of NAS, Permanent Commn. Internat. Assn. Occupational Health, Soc. Toxicology (Arnold J. Lehman award 1993, Merit award 1999), Brit. Pharm. Soc., Am. Soc. Pharmacology and Exptl. Therapeutics, Internat. Soc. for Trace Element Rsch. in Humans, Ramazzini Collegium, Polish Toxicology Soc. (hon.), La Academia Nacional de Medicina de Buenos Aires (hon. mem.). Office: Dept Environ Medicine U Rochester Med Sch Rochester NY 14642-0001

CLARY, BRADLEY G., lawyer, educator; b. Richmond, Va, Sept. 7, 1950; s. Sidney G. and Jean B. Clary; m. Mary-Louise Hunt, July 31, 1982; children: Benjamin, Samuel. BA magna cum laude, Carleton Coll., 1972; JD cum laude, U. Minn., 1975. Bar: Minn. 1975, US Dist. Ct. Minn. 1975, US Ct. Appeals (10th cir.) 1977, US Ct. Appeals (8th cir.) 1979, US Ct. Appeals (6th cir.) 1980, US Ct. Appeals (7th cir.) 1981, US Supreme Ct. 1986, US Ct. Appeals (4th cir.) 1989, US Ct. Appeals (9th cir.) 1991. Assoc. Oppenheimer Wolff & Donnelly, St. Paul, 1975-81, ptnr., 1982-2000; from legal writing dir. Law Sch. to clin. prof. U. Minn., 1999—2004, Vaughan G. Papke clin. prof. law, 2004—, dir. applied legal instrn., 2004—. Adj. prof. Law Sch. U. Minn., Mpls., 1985-99; adj. instr. William Mitchell Coll. Law, St. Paul, 1995-96, 98, adj. prof., 1997, 99. Author: Primer on the Analysis and Presentation of Legal Argument, 1992; co-author: Advocacy on Appeal, 2001, 2d edit., 2004, Successful First Depositions, 2001, Successful Legal Analysis and Writing: The Fundamentals, 2003. Vestryman St. John Evangelist Ch., St. Paul, 1978-81, 98-00, pledge drive co-chmn., 1989-90, sr. warden, 2000-2002; mem. alumni bd. Breck Sch., Mpls., 1981-85, 89-96, exec. com., 1991-96, dir. emeritus, 1996—; mem. adv. bd. Glass Theatre Co., West St. Paul, Minn., 1982-87; mem. antitrust adv. panel dept. health State of Minn., 1992-93. Mem. ABA (adv. group antitrust sect. 1987-89, corp. counseling com.), Minn. Bar Assn. (program chmn. antitrust sect. 1986-87, treas. 1987-88, vice-chmn. 1989-90, co-chmn. 1990-92, governing coun. appellate practice sect. 2001-03, 2003—), Phi Beta Kappa Avocations: tennis, sailing. Office: U Minn Law Sch 229 19th Ave S Rm 444 Minneapolis MN 55455-0400

CLARY, RICHARD WAYLAND, lawyer; b. Tarboro, N.C., Oct. 10, 1953; s. S. Grayson and Jean (Beazley) C.; m. Suzanne Clerkin, July 21, 1991; children: Grayson Edward, Taryn Fenner. BA magna cum laude, Amherst Coll., 1975; JD magna cum laude, Harvard U., 1978. Bar: N.Y. 1981, U.S. Dist. Ct. (so. and ea. dists.) N.Y. 1981, U.S. Dist. Ct. (no. dist.) Calif. 1982, U.S. Ct. Appeals (9th cir.) 1983, U.S. Supreme Ct. 1989, U.S. Ct. Appeals (3d cir.) 1990, U.S. Ct. Appeals (2d cir.) 1994, U.S. Ct. Appeals (fed. cir.) 1995, U.S. Dist. Ct. (no. dist.) N.Y. 1998, U.S. Ct. Appeals (11th cir.) 1999, U.S. Ct. Appeals (6th cir.) 2000, U.S. Dist. Ct. D.C. 2002, U.S. Ct. Appeals (5th cir.) 2003. Law clk. to judge U.S. Ct. Appeals (2d cir.), N.Y.C., 1978-79; law clk. to Justice Thurgood Marshall U.S. Supreme Ct., Washington, 1979-80; assoc. Cravath, Swaine & Moore LLP, N.Y.C., 1980-85, ptnr., 1985—, mng. ptnr. litigation, 1997—. Bd. dirs. Legal Aid Soc., 1998—(vice chair, 2003-) John Woodruff Simpson fellow Amherst Coll., 1975-76. Mem. ABA, Fed. Bar Found. (bd. dirs. 1998-2001), N.Y. State Bar Assn., Assn. Bar City N.Y., Fed. Bar Coun., Phi Beta Kappa. Roman Catholic. Office: Cravath Swaine & Moore LLP Worldwide Plz 825 8th Ave New York NY 10019-7475 Office Fax: 212-474-3700. E-mail: rclary@cravath.com.

CLARY, RONALD GORDON, insurance agency executive; b. Moultrie, Ga., May 2, 1940; s. Ronald Ward and Hazel (Collins) C.; m. Adrian Irene Baker; children: Lynn, Beth, Lindsay, Baker. Student, Young Harris Coll., 1958-60; BBA in Ins., U. Ga., 1963; LLB, Woodrow Wilson Coll. Law, 1966. Registered rep. fin. planner. Field rep. Comml. Union Ins. Cos., 1962-67; ind. ins. agt., 1967—; ins. agt., sec. of agy. Day, Reynolds & Parks, Gainesville, Ga., 1970-93, pres., 1993—. Fin. planner, registered rep. Am. Express Fin. Advisors, Inc. Mem. Profl. Ins. Agts. Am., Ga. Assn. Ind. Ins. Agts., Gainesville Assn. Ind. Ins. Agts. (past pres.), Young Agts. Com. Ga. (past chmn.), Am. Legion, Elks, Rotary. Republican. Baptist. Avocations: tennis, sailing. Office: American Express 1184 Cumberland Valley Rd Gainesville GA 30501-1807 Fax: 770-754-9690.

CLARY, ROSALIE BRANDON STANTON, timber farm executive, civic worker; b. Evanston, Ill., Aug. 3, 1928; d. Frederick Charles Hite-Smith and Rose Cecile (Liebich) Stanton; m. Virgil Vincent Clary, Oct. 17, 1959; children: Rosalie Marian Hawley, Frederick Stanton, Virgil Vincent, Katheleen Elizabeth. BS, Northwestern U., 1950, MA, 1954. Tchr. Chgo. Pub. Schs., 1951-61; faculty Loyola U., Chgo., 1963; v.p. Stanton Enterprises, Inc., Adams County, Miss., 1971-89; timber farmer, trustee Adams County, Miss., 1975—. Author Family History Record, geneaology record book, Kenilworth, Ill., 1977—. Lectr. Girl Scouts U.S., Winnetka, Ill., 1969-71, 78-86, Cub Scouts, 1972-77; badge counselor Boy Scouts Am., 1978-87; election judge Rep. Com., 1977—; vol. Winnetka Libr. Geneaology Projects Com., 1995—. Mem. Nat. Soc. DAR (Ill. rec. sec. 1979-81, nat, vice chmn. program com. 1980-83, state vice regent 1986-88, state regent 1989-91, rec. sec. gen. 1992-95, state parliamentarian 1999—), Am. Forestry Assn., Forest Farmers Assn., North Suburban Geneal. Soc. (governing bd. 1979-86, 99—, pres. 1997-99), WInnetka Hist. Soc. (governing bd. 1978-90, 95—), Internat. Platform Assn., Delta Gamma (mem. nat. cabinet 1985-89). Roman Catholic. Home: 509 Elder Ln Winnetka IL 60093-4122 Office: PO Box 401 Kenilworth IL 60043-0401

CLARY-WILSON, CHRISTINA LYNN, music educator; b. Cabool, Mo., Mar. 19, 1958; d. Earnest Eugene Clary and Sharon Lee Odle; m. Charles Michael Smith, Mar. 20, 1999; children: Andrew Robert Gathright, Patrick Benjamin Wilson. BS, William Woods U., 1976—80. Vocal music dir. Ferguson Florissant Sch., Florissant, Mo., 2000—; children and youth worship leader Morning Star Meth. Ch., Lake St. Louis, Mo., 2002—. Choreographer, Mo., 1980—; safe sanctuary trainer Mo. Meth. Ch., Columbia, Mo., 2002—. Lay spkr. Mo. Meth. Ch., Lake St. Louis, Mo., 2004—05. Recipient Outstanding Faculty Mem., Ferguson Florissant Schools, 1999, 2000, 2002, Performance Carnegie Hall, Mid-America Productions, 1993, 1996. Mem.: Mo. Music Educators Assn. (vocal v.p. 1992—94). United Methodist. Avocations: golf, hiking, camping, tennis, dance. Home: 540 Quarter Horse Trail Saint Peters MO 63376 Office Phone: 314-524-3877. Personal E-mail: charles_and_christy@charter.net.

CLASSON, ROLF ALLAN, pharmaceutical company executive; b. Nassjo, Sweden, Aug. 20, 1945; s. Allan K.E. and May Britt (Lagerquist) C.; m. Birgitta Larsson, Feb. 3, 1968; children— Peter, Karin, Erik. M in Bus. Econs., Gothenburg U., 1969. Personnel mgr. Pharmacia, Uppsala, Sweden, 1969-74; mgmt. cons. Asbjorn Habberstad, Stockholm, 1974-77; mktg. mgr. Pharmacia, Uppsala, 1977-80; div. gen. mgr. Tarkett, Ronneby, 1980; pres. Pharmacia Infusion, Uppsala, 1981-84, Pharmacia Devel. Co. Inc., Piscataway, N.J., 1984-90; pres., chief oper. officer Pharmacia Biosystems AB, 1990—91; exec. v.p. Bayer Corp., 1995—2002, exec. v.p., worldwide mktg., sales & services, group diagnostics, 1991—92, pres., group diagnostics, 1995—2002, sr. v.p., sales & services, group diagnostics, 1992—95, chmn. exec. comm., health care div., 2002—; interim pres., CEO Hillenbrand Industries, 2005—. Bd. dirs. Pharmacia Deltec, Inc., Pharmacia/LKB Biotech., Inc, Hillenbrand Indus. Office: c/o Hillenbrand Industries 700 State Route 46 East Batesville IN 47006*

CLASTER, JILL NADELL, academic administrator, history educator; d. Harry K. and Edith Lillian Nadell; m. Millard L. Midonick, May 24, 1979; 1 child from previous marriage, Elizabeth Claster (dec.). BA, NYU, 1952, MA, 1954; PhD, U. Pa., 1959. Instr. history U. Pa., 1956-58; instr. ancient and medieval history U. Ky., Lexington, 1959-61, asst. prof., 1961-64; adj. asst. prof. classics NYU, N.Y.C., 1964-65, asst. prof. history, 1965-68, assoc. prof., 1968-84, prof., 1984—, acting undergrad. chmn. history, 1972-73, dir. M.A. in liberal studies program, 1976-78; assoc. dean Washington Sq. and Univ. Coll., 1978, acting dean, 1978-79, dean, 1979-86; dir. Hagop Kevorkian Ctr. for Near Eastern Studies, NYU, 1991-96. Appointee N.Y.C. Commn. on Status of Women. Author: Athenian Democracy: Triumph or Travesty, 1967, The Medieval Experience, 1982; Contbr. articles to profl. jours. Danforth grantee, 1966-68; Fulbright grantee, 1958-59 Mem. Am. Hist. Assn., Medieval Acad. Am. Home: 161 W 15th St New York NY 10011-6720 Office: NYU Dept History 53 Washington Sq S Dept History New York NY 10012-1098 Office Phone: 212-998-8611. E-mail: jill.claster@nyu.edu.

CLASTER, WILLIAM D., lawyer; b. Apr. 9, 1952; BA, Stanford Univ., 1973; JD, UCLA, 1976. Bar: Calif. 1976, US Supreme Ct., Ct. of Appeals (9th cir.). Joined Gibson Dunn & Crutcher LLP, Irvine, Calif., 1976—, now ptnr. labor and employment dept. Orange County office. Mem. exec. com. Gibson Dunn & Crutcher. Mng. editor UCLA Law Rev., 1975—76, contbg. author Wrongful Employment Termination Practice, 1987, California Practice Guide: Employment Litigation, 2000. Mem.: ABA, Orange County Bar Assn., Calif. Bar Assn. Office: Gibson Dunn & Crutcher LLP Jamboree Ctr Ste 1400 4 Park Plz Irvine CA 92614-8557 Office Phone: 949-451-3804. Office Fax: 949-475-4629. Business E-Mail: wclaster@gibsondunn.com.

CLATWORTHY, CATHERINE LYNN, educational trainer, graphics designer; b. Chatham, Ont., Can., June 10, 1963; d. John Ferguson Clatworthy and Patricia Anne (Maynard) Clatworthy. A.O.C.A., Ont. Coll. Art and Design, Toronto, 1985. Graphic designer Burton Kramer Assocs., Toronto, 1985—87; co-owner/mgr. The Allery, Toronto, 1987—98; tng. ctr. instr. Larson-Juhl Co., Atlanta, 1998—2003; v.p., mktg. mgr. Dakota Framing Specialties, Inc., Watertown, SD, 2000—02; propr., cons. LilyCrest, Huron, SD, 2002. Com./facilitator Color Mktg. Group, Alexandria, Va., 2000—; mem. Visual Arts Ont., Toronto, 1985—; educator/lectr. Profl. Picture Framers Assn., Jackson, Mich., 1996—; mem. Can. Conservation Inst., Ottawa, 1998—, Am. Inst. Conservation, Washington, 2002—. Author: The Art of Colour & Design for the Art and Framing Industry, 1999; contbr. mags., newspapers, and interviews in field. Mem.: Visual Arts Ont., Profl. Picture Framers Assn., Color Mktg. Group. Avocations: art, antiques, travel, photography, cooking. Office: LilyCrest PO Box 906 Huron SD 57350 E-mail: lilycrest@hur.midco.net.

CLAUSELL, ARLENE MIDGET, retired elementary school educator; d. James and Ollie Elaine Midget; m. Paul L. Clausell, Mar. 2, 1974; children: Christopher Paul, Eric Scott. BS in Elem. Edn., W.Va. State U., 1968; MA in Reading, W.Va. U., 1973, postgrad., 2004—. Cert. prin. elem. and jr. h.s. 1-9, prin. mid.-jr. h.s./sr. h.s. 5-12, supt. K-12, supr. gen. instr. K-12, vocat. adminstrn. 5-12, tchr. elem. edn. 1-8, tchr. English and social studies 1-9, reading specialist K-12. Tchr. remedial lang. Steubenville Pub. Schs., 1969; substitute tchr. Hancock County Bd. Edn., Weirton, W.Va., 1968, tchr. 4th grade, 1969—74; elem. classroom tchr., reading specialist Monongalia County Bd. Edn., Morgantown, W.Va., 1974—2004; ret., 2004. Diversity officer W.Va. English Lang. Arts, 1994—2000. Contbr. articles to profl. publs. Game Day vol. Relay for Life, Am. Cancer Soc., 2002—05; literacy vol. Ruby Meml. Hosp. Named Vol. of Month, Ruby Meml. Hosp., 2000; recipient All-Am. Scholars award, 1997, Nat. Writing Project award, 1997, A Picture Is Worth a Thousand Words award, 1997, Golden Apple award, Ashland Oil, 1998, Esteemed Colleague award for outstanding svc., W.Va. English Lang. Arts Coun., 1997. Mem.: Nat. Coun. Tchrs. English (rep.-at-large 1999—2001), Phi Delta Kappa. Avocations: reading, travel. Home: 1 Catalpa St Morgantown WV 26505

CLAUSELL, DEBORAH DELORIS, artist; b. Mobile, Ala., July 16, 1951; d. Stephen Joseph and Estell Abney Clausell. BA in Sociology, U. Mobile, 1976; cert., Barbizon Modeling Sch., 1984. Movie extra Century Casting, Santa Monica, Calif., 1984—85; libr. Mobile Pub. Libr., 1996-97. Exhibited in group shows Greater Gulf State Fair, Mobile, 1990, 96 (3d, 2d and 1st prize ribbons), 97 (3rd prize ribbon), 99, Mercy Med. Gallery, Daphne, Ala., 1993, Mus. of City of Mobile, 1993, Fine Art Mus. of the South, Mobile, 1993, Spring Hill Art, Mobile, 1993, Greater Gulf State Fair Exhibit Fine Arts, 1999, Monticello-Thomas Jefferson Meml., 1993; pvt. collection The White House, Heritage Hall, 2000 and Art Auction, Energen Corp. Artpark Exbhn., 2001. Mem. Smithsonian Inst., 2001, USS Constn. Mus., 2002, U.S. Border Control, 2003. 2d lt. USAF, res. Recipient Gold Eagles and Stars Letters from U.S. President Bush, 2001. Mem. VFW, Internat. Platform Assn., Nat. D-Day Mus., U.S. Naval Inst., Libr. Congress Assn., Nat. Trust for Hist. Preservation, Civil War Trust, Mt. Vernon Ladies Assn., Navel League, Preservation Alliance. Democrat. Roman Catholic. Avocations: classic guitarist, harmonica, swimming, vocal singing, reading. Home: 5859 Reams Dr N Mobile AL 36608-3652 Office Phone: 251-341-1217.

CLAUSEN, ANDREW CHRISTOPHER, lawyer; b. Mobile, Ala., Jan. 7, 1955; s. Harry Donald, Jr. and Juanita Gay (Christopher) C.; 1 child, Christopher Scott Clausen. BA in Criminal Justice, U. Ala., 1977, JD, 1986. Bar: Ala., La. Owner, mgr. Clausen & Co., Mobile, 1974-83; assoc. Adams & Reese, New Orleans, 1986-91; ptnr. Pierce, Carr, Alford, Mobile, 1991-96, Carr, Alford, Clausen & McDonald, LLC, Mobile, 1996—. Mem. ABA, Def. Rsch. Inst., Ala. Def. Lawyers Assn. Baptist. Office: Carr Alford Clausen & McDonald LLC One St Louis Ctr # 5000 Mobile AL 36602

CLAUSEN, HUGH JOSEPH, retired army officer; b. Mobile, Ala., Dec. 25, 1926; s. Hugh Martin and Elizabeth Hazel (Orrell) C.; m. Betty Sue Richards, June 7, 1949; children: Melinda, Joseph. LL.B., U. Ala., 1950; grad., Advanced Mgmt. Program, Harvard U., 1970. Bar: Ala. 1950, U.S. Supreme Ct. 1959, U.S. Ct. Mil. Appeals 1959. Commd. 1st lt. U.S. Army, 1951, advanced through grades to maj. gen.; various assignments, 1951-62; asst. staff judge adv. (8th Army), Korea, 1962-64; judge adv. U.S. Disciplinary Barracks, Fort Leavenworth, Kans., 1964-66; instr. U.S. Army Command and Gen. Staff Coll., 1966-68; staff judge adv. 1st Inf. Div., Vietnam, 1968-69; assigned Office Legis. Liaison, Dept. Army, Washington, 1969-71; chief mil. justice div. Office JAG, 1971-72, exec. officer, 1972-73; staff judge adv. III Corps and Ft. Hood, Tex., 1973-76; chief judge U.S. Army Ct. Mil. Rev., Falls Church, Va., 1976-78; asst. judge adv. gen. for mil. law Dept. Army., 1978-79, asst. judge adv. gen., 1979-81, judge adv. gen., 1981-85. Vice pres. for adminstrn., sec. bd. trustees Clemson U., S.C., 1985-92, v.p. emeritus, 1992—. Decorated Disting. Service Medal, Bronze Star with 3 oak leaf clusters, Meritorious Service medal, Legion of Merit with oak leaf cluster, Air medal with oak leaf cluster, Army Commendation medal with oak leaf cluster; RVN Honor medal; RVN Gallantry Cross with palm; RVN Civic Action Honor medal with palm. Mem. Ala. Bar Assn., Phi Alpha Delta. Address: 107 Hermitage Mooring Dr Seneca SC 29672-9138 Personal E-mail: hughclausen@nuvok.net.

CLAUSEN, JEANNE LORRAINE, musician; b. L.A., Calif., Oct. 16, 1944; BA, Sarah Lawrence Coll., 1967; MusM, Cleve. Inst. Music, 1972. Mem. Calif. New Musictack, L.A., 1975—78; mem. trio in residence Claremont (Calif.) Grad. Sch., 1976—79; concert mistress Ensemble Concerto, dir. Roberto Gini, Milan, 1983—86; mem. Amsterdam Baroque Orch., dir. Ton Koopman, Netherlands, 1986—87; founder, 1st violin La Cetra, San Francisco, 1982—. *La Cotra has performed at teatro Litta, Milan and Chiesa di San Maurizio, Milan among other prestigious venues. It has been included in the Milano Estate concert series and also Musica e Poesia di Chiesa San Maurizio. La Cotra has been honored to Maborate with colleagues Monica Huggett, Guido Morini and Paolo Rizzi.* Author: Something Has Been Lost In the Passage of Time, (video) The Rhapsodic Art Of The Ancients. Esoteric Christian. Achievements include Research on 16th century stringed instrument lira da braccia. Avocations: hiking, swimming, reading, good conversation, enjoying the mystical beauty of nature. Home: PO Box 2603 Nevada City CA 95959 Office Phone: 530-477-2206. E-mail: jeannelc@earthlink.net.

CLAUSEN, JERRY LEE, psychiatrist; b. Wausau, Wis., Nov. 5, 1939; s. Douglas William and Florence Jean (Amidon) Clausen; m. Nancy Eileen Longdon, Aug. 3, 1962; children: Keith Rusell, Pamela Dawn. BA, Wesleyan U., Middletown, Conn., 1961; MD, Albany Med. Coll., N.Y., 1965. Diplomate in psychiatry and addiction psychiatry Am. Bd. Psychiatry and Neurology, 1994, cert. Am. Soc. Addiction Medicine. Psychiatry intern Upstate Med. Ctr., Syracuse, 1965-66, psychiat. resident, 1966-67, 69-71, asst. attending, 1971-72, attending, 1972-80; staff psychiatrist Onondaga Mental Health Clinic, Syracuse, 1971-72; courtesy staff Benjamin Rush Psychiatric Ctr., Syracuse, 1971-84, active staff, 1984—2004; pvt. practice psychiatry Syracuse, 1971—2004; clin. asst. prof. SUNY, 1972—. Staff psychiatrist Onondaga Pastoral Counseling Ctr., Syracuse, 1971—72, Syracuse, 1981—97, psychiat. dir., 1973—81; cons. psychiatrist Loretto Rest Geriatric Ctr., Syracuse, 1972—74. Tchr. 1st Universalist Ch., Syracuse, 1966—. Lt. comdr. USN, 1967—69. Fellow: Am. Psychiat. Assn. (life; chmn. ins. mktg. com. 1979—88); mem.: N.Y. State Med. Soc., Onondaga County Med. Soc. Avocations: walking, tennis, cross country skiing. Office Phone: 315-727-9263. E-mail: jclausen@twcny.rr.com.

CLAUSEN, JØRGEN MADS, engineer, business executive; b. Havnbjerg, Denmark, Sept. 23, 1948; s. Mads and Bitten (Hinrichsen) C.; m. Anette Nohr Nielsen, June 21, 1975; children: Mads, Marcus. Degree in Elec. Engring., Denmarks Engring. Acad., Copenhagen, 1971; MBA in Fin., U. Wis., 1975. Corp. rsch. dir. Danfoss Nordborg, Denmark, 1981-91, exec. v.p., 1991-96, pres., CEO, 1996—. Mem. Danfoss exec. com., 1991-; chmn. Riseo Nat. Lab., 2000-;chmn., Sauer-Danfoss Inc.; chmn. of Young Enterprise Europe. Mem. Danish Acad. Tech. Sci. Avocation: flying jets. Office: Danfoss DK-6430 Nordborg Denmark*

CLAUSEN, ROBERT A., chemicals executive; BSBA, U. Mo. With Inernat. Harvester Co., 1968; various mgmt. positions Monsanto's Comml. Products Co., dir. results mgmt., 1977—79; controller Monsanto Polymer Products Co., 1979—83; bur. dir. Rubber Chems., 1983—85, asst. treas., 1985—87; dir. fin. Monsanto Europe-Africa, 1987—91, Monsanto L.Am., 1991—92; v.p. asset mgmt. Monsanto, 1992—94; pres. Monsanto Bus. Svcs., 1994—97; vice chmn., CEO, chief adminstrv. officer Solutia Inc., 1997—. Mem. CFO's exec. com. The Conf. Bd.; mem. adv. bd. St. Louis U. Boeing Inst. Internat. Bus.; bd. trustees Maryville U.; mem. adv. bd. Orgn. Cons. Svcs. Mem.: Fin. Execs. Inst., Am. Chem. Soc. Office: Solutia Inc PO Box 66760 Saint Louis MO 63166-6760 also: Solutia Inc 575 Maryville Ctr Dr Saint Louis MO 63141

CLAUSEN, WENDELL VERNON, retired classics educator; b. Coquille, Oreg., Apr. 2, 1923; s. George R. and Gertrude (Johnson) C.; m. Corinna Slice, Aug. 20, 1947; children: John, Raymond, Thomas; m. Margaret W. Woodman, June 19, 1970. AB, U. Wash., 1945; PhD, U. Chgo., 1948; A.M. (hon.), Harvard U., 1959. Mem. faculty Amherst Coll., 1948-59, assoc. prof. classics, 1955-59; prof. Greek and Latin Harvard U., 1959-82, Victor S. Thomas prof. Greek and Latin, 1982-88, Pope prof. Latin lang. and lit., 1988-93, prof. comparative lit., 1984-93, prof. emeritus, 1993—, chmn. dept. classics, 1966-71; ret., 1993. Vis. prof. Univ. Coll., London, 1971; Sather prof. U. Calif., Berkeley, 1982; vis. prof. I Tatti, Florence, Italy, 1989. Author: Virgil's Aeneid and the Tradition of Hellenistic Poetry, 1987, A Commentary on Virgil's Eclogues, 1994, Virgil's Aeneid: Decorum Allusion and Ideology, 2002, articles in classical philology; editor: Persius, 1956, Persius and Juvenal, 1959, rev. edit., 1992, Appendix Vergiliana, 1966, Harvard Studies in Classical Philology, 1990—92; editor, contbr. The Cambridge History of Latin Literature, 1982, Premio Internazionale Virgilio, 1994, assoc. editor Am. Jour. Philology, 1976—81, Style and Tradition: Studies in Honor of Wendell Clausen, 1998. William Rainey Harper scholar U. Chgo., 1946-48; fellow Am. Acad. in Rome, 1952-53, Am. Council Learned Socs., 1962-63, fellow commoner Peterhouse, Cambridge. Fellow Am. Acad. Arts and Scis.; mem. Am. Philol. Assn., Cambridge Philol. Soc., Signet Soc., Phi Beta Kappa. Home: 8 Kenway St Cambridge MA 02138-4724 Office: Harvard U 204 Boylston Hall Cambridge MA 02138

CLAUSER, DONALD ROBERDEAU, musician; b. Fort Worth, Mar. 2, 1941; s. Donald Milton and Selina Almira (Sizer) C. B.F.A., U. N.M., 1962; Mus.M., Boston U., 1964; diploma, Curtis Inst. Music, 1967. Mem. viola sect., Phila. Orch., 1966—2004. Home: 1609 Chanticleer Cherry Hill NJ 08003-4820 *It is my conviction that music is a universal medium of communication— a factor which is surely of distinct value in these troubled times. Keeping this in mind has constantly been uppermost in the pursuit of my career, wherever this may have led me.*

CLAUSMAN, GILBERT JOSEPH, retired medical librarian; b. Los Angeles, Nov. 8, 1921; s. Pete John and Lila (Mason) C. AB, Willamette U., 1947; BS, Columbia U., 1948, MS, 1952. Med. librarian N.Y. Acad. Medicine, N.Y.C., 1948-55; med. librarian NYU Med. Ctr., N.Y.C., 1955-86, librarian emeritus, 1987—. Cons. Milton Helpern Library Legal Medicine, 1963-88. Served with USN, 1942-45 Mem. Med. Libr. Assn. (pres. 1977-78), Archons of Colophon, N.Y. Acad. Medicine, Acad. Health Info. Profls. (Disting. mem. emeritus). Home: 6 Cobble Hill Rd Westport CT 06880-2915

CLAUSON, SHARYN FERNE, consulting company executive, educator; b. Phila., Oct. 4, 1946; d. Eugene and Gertrud Jayn (Besser) C. BA in English, Temple U., 1968; MEd in Psychology, Arcadia U. (formerly Beaver Coll.), 1979; MBA in Marketing, Drexel U., 1982; postgrad. in law, Temple U., 1987. Market analyst Epstein Rsch., Bala, Pa., 1967-69; cons. Ednl. Testing Svc., Princeton, N.J., 1979-80; CEO CCX, Narberth, Pa., 1978-79; mem. faculty Cheltenham Twp. Sch. Dist., Elkins Park, Pa., 1969—2003; dir. Sharyn Clauson Bus. Comm., Narberth, Pa., 1975-85; pres. S. Clauson & Assocs., Inc., King of Prussia, Pa., 1985—; dir. Execuwriter, King of Prussia, 1985—. Mem. adj. faculty Drexel U., Phila., 1979-96, Phila. U., 1985-89, St. Joseph's U., Phila., 1986-92, Phila. Ctr. of Gt. lakes Coll. Assn., 1988; mem. adv. bd. Ergodyne, Inc., 1995-96; talk show host Sta. WDVT-AM, Phila., 1985; bd. dirs. Site Selex, Inc., Doylestown, Pa., dir. comm. and pub. rels., 1988-95. Editor: Curriculum for Optacon Music Reading, 1984; mem. editorial adv. bd. Bus. Communications and Concepts, 2d edit., 1985 Mem. com. Women's Polit. Caucus, Phila.; mem. Phila. Art Alliance; mem. exec. bd., arts and scis. alumni bd. Temple U. Women's Law Caucus; sec., v.p. bd. dirs. VFTW Coun., 2000-02, 2004—, sec. 2000-2001, v.p., 2001-2002, 2004—. Golden Hearts honoree, 1999; recipient U.S. Congl. award, 1999. Mem. ASCD, AAUW, Am. Mktg. Assn., Nat. Spkrs. Assn. (chairperson 1985), Nat. Assn. Profl. Saleswomen (honoree 1982—), Nat. Coun. Tchrs. of English, Delaware Valley Writing Coun., Wallenberg Communicators, Phi Delta Kappa. Office: 21036 Valley Forge Circle King Of Prussia PA 19406 E-mail: Sfc1210@aol.com.

CLAUSS, PETER OTTO, lawyer; b. Knoxville, Tenn., Sept. 23, 1936; s. Alfred and Jane (West) C.; m. Elizabeth Mary Lou Percival, Apr. 28, 1962; children: Andrew Bradford, Victoria Johns. AB, U. Chgo., 1955; LLB, Yale U., 1958. Bar: Pa. 1959, U.S. Dist. Ct. (ea. dist.) Pa. 1959, U.S. Tax Ct. 1959, U.S. Ct. Appeals (3d cir.) 1959, U.S. Supreme Ct. 1963, U.S. Ct. Claims 1960, U.S. Ct. Customs 1962. Assoc. Clark, Ladner, Fortenbaugh & Young, Phila., 1958-65, ptnr., 1966-96, mem. exec. com., 1967-76, mng. ptnr., 1968-72, sr. ptnr., chmn. corp. and bus. dept., 1983-96; sr. ptnr. Pepper, Hamilton LLP, Phila., 1996—2004, of counsel, 2004—. Past dir. Norcross, Inc., Nutrion Corp., Helicrane Constrn. Corp., Mannion Co., Henry Cantor, Inc., Keystone Helicopter Corp., Interactive Graphics, Inc.; asst. sec. Masland Corp., 1974-86, 91-96; adj. prof. law Villanova U., 2002—; lectr. in field. Contbr. articles to legal jours. Sec., mem. vestry, mem. Outreach Com., stewardship com., search com., Christ Ch., Ithaca; past coach Little League Baseball; past treas. Ithan Sch. PTA; past treas. Boy Scouts Am., Ithan, Pa. Ford Found. fellow, 1952-55; chmn. 50th reunion class gift com., U. Chglo., 2004-05. With USNG, 1959-67. Mem. ABA (past chmn. sales, exchanges and basis com. tax sect.), Phila. Bar Assn. (past chmn. unpopular causes com., past vice chmn. pub. svc. com.), Pa. Bar Assn., Juristic Soc. of Phila. (past bd. govs.), Yale Law Sch. Assn. for Ea. Pa. (pres. 1974-82), Assn. Yale Alumni (Phila. del. 1982-84, gen. counsel ednl. com. 1999—), Phi Gamma Delta (nat. sec., bd. dirs., 1982-88, gen. counsel, 1972-82), Phi Delta Phi, Yale of Phila. Club (past pres.), Phila. Club, Racquet of Phila. Club, First Troop Phila. City Calvary Club, Univ. Barge Club, Merion Cricket Club, Orpheus Club, First Monday Club (past pres.), Ocean Point and Ocean Creek Golf Club (Fripp Island, S.C.), Dataw Island Golf Club (S.C.). Republican. Episcopalian. Home: 758 Darby Paoli Rd Newtown Square PA 19073-2609 Office: 3000 Two Logan Sq 18th & Arch Sts Philadelphia PA 19103-2799 Office Phone: 215-981-4541. Business E-Mail: claussp@pepperlaw.com.

CLAUSS-EHLERS, CAROLINE S., psychologist, educator, columnist; b. Manhasset, N.Y., July 17, 1967; d. Harold Wilson and Carole (Page) Clauss; m. Julian Charles Edward Clauss-Ehlers; 1 child, Isabel S. BA with honors, Oberlin Coll., 1989; MA, Columbia U., 1992, EdM, 1993, PhD, 1999. Bilingual clinician Henry St. Settlement, Cmty. Consultation Ctr., N.Y.C., 1992-96; clin. interviewer N.Y. State Psychiat. Inst., N.Y.C., 1995-98; predoctoral intern in clin. psychology NYU Med. Ctr./Bellevue Hosp., N.Y.C., 1996-97; columnist HOY, 2002—; psychologist pvt. practice, 2000—. Adj. asst. prof. psychology and edn. Tchr. Coll., Columbia U., 1998—2001; asst. prof. counseling psychology Rutgers U. Grad. Sch. Edn., 2001—; media cons., 1999—. Co-editor: Community Planning to Foster Resilience in Children, 2004; contbr. articles to profl. jours. Oberlin Alumni scholar, 1992; Tchrs. Coll. scholar, 1994-96; Leopold Schepp Found. fellow, 1994-97; Rosalynn Carter fellow for mental health journalism, 2004-05. Mem. APA, N.Y. State Psychol. Assn., Assn. Hispanic Mental Health Profls. Office: Rutgers U 10 Seminary Pl New Brunswick NJ 08901

CLAUSSEN, EILEEN BARBARA, environmental services administrator, former federal agency administrator; b. N.Y.C., June 9, 1945; d. Louis and Elsie (Young) Lerner; children: Hillary Anne, Geoffrey David. BA, George Washington U., 1966; MA, U. Va., 1967. Systems analyst USN, Washington, 1967-68; cons. Booz, Allen & Hamilton, Inc., Washington, 1968-69; asst. dir. ctr. for comml. devel. Boise Cascade Corp., Washington, 1969-72; various mgmt. positions Office of Solid Waste U.S. EPA, Washington, 1972-83, dir. characterization and assessment div., 1984-87, dir. atmospheric & indoor air programs, 1987-93, acting dep. asst. adminstr. air & radiation, 1988-89, dep. asst. adminstr. Office Air & Radiation, 1990—91; spl. asst. to Pres., sr. dir. global environ. affairs NSC, Washington, 1993—96; asst. sec. oceans, internat. environment & science affairs US Dept. State, Washington, 1996—98; pres. Pew Ctr. on Global Climate Change, Arlington, Va., 1998—. Bd. dirs. Environ. Law Inst., Coun. Fgn. Rels., China Coun. for Internat. Cooperation on Environ. & Devel.; commr. Pew Ocean Commn. Recipient Career Achievement award, US Dept. State, Meritorious Exec. award for Sustained Superior Accomplishment, Disting. Exec. award for Sustained Extraordinary Accomplishment, Fitzhugh Green award for Outstanding Contributions to Internat. Environ. Protection. Office: Pew Ctr on Global Climate Change 2101 Wilson Blvd Ste 550 Arlington VA 22201*

CLAVER, ROBERT EARL, television producer, director; b. Chgo., May 22, 1928; s. Louis E. and Sara M. (Sosna) C.; 1 child, Nancy Beth. BS in Journalism, U. Ill., 1950. Prodr.-writer: first 1000 Captain Kangaroo shows (Sylvania award, Peabody award); prodr., dir.: (TV shows) Here Comes the Brides, 1968-70, The Interns, 1970-71, Partridge Family, 1970-74, Gloria, CBS-TV, 1982-83, Small Wonder, 1985, New Love American Style, 1985, New Leave It to Beaver, 1986-87, Charles in Charge, 1987, Out of This World, 1987-91, numerous other series; dir.: (TV shows) Welcome Back Kotter, ABC-TV, 1977-78, All's Fair, CBS-TV, Housecalls, CBS-TV, 1979-80, Mork and Mindy, ABC-TV, 1981-82. With U.S. Army, 1951-53. Mem. Dirs. Guild Am.

CLAVERIE, PHILIP DEVILLIERS, lawyer; b. New Orleans, June 29, 1941; s. Louis Barbot and Viola Aimee (Schlegel) C.; m. Laura Lynn McCampbell, Apr. 27, 1974; children: Philip deVilliers Jr., Stephanie McCampbell. AB, Princeton U., 1963; JD, Tulane U., 1966. Bar: La. 1966. Assoc. Phelps Dunbar, New Orleans, 1966-70, ptnr., 1970—. Contbr. articles to profl. jours. Trustee Children's Hosp. New Orleans, 1978-, pres. 1985-87; mem. bd. govs. Isidore Newman Sch., 1982-2000, chmn. 1995-98; mem. exec. bd. New Orleans Police Found., 1998—, hon. consul of Finland; bd. dirs. World Affairs Coun. New Orleans, 2004—. Served to lt. comdr. JAGC, USNR, 1973-79. Fellow Am. Bar Found., La. Bar Found.; mem. ABA, La. State Bar Assn., New Orleans Bar Assn., Assn. Bar City N.Y., Am. Law Inst., Am. Judicature Soc., La. State Law Inst., World Trade Ctr., Pickwick Club, Stratford Club. Home: 14 Versailles Blvd New Orleans LA 70125-4114 Office: Phelps Dunbar LLP Ste 2000 365 Canal St New Orleans LA 70130-6534 Office Phone: 504-584-9223. E-mail: claverip@phelps.com.

CLAWSON, CURTIS J., manufacturing executive; MBA, Harvard U. Various positions Allied Signal, Arvin Industries; pres. Beverage Cans Am. Bus. Unit Am. Nat. Can Group Inc., 1998—99, pres., COO Chgo., 1999—2000; chmn. Hayes Lemmerz, Northville, Mich., 2001—, pres., 2001—, CEO, 2001—. Office: Hayes Lemmerz 15300 Centennial Dr Northville MI 48167*

CLAWSON, DAVID KAY, orthopedic surgeon; b. Salt Lake City, Aug. 8, 1927; s. David J. and Elva (Gundry) C.; m. Janet Dorothy Smith, June 1, 1952; children: Kim Debra, David Roger. Student, U. Utah, 1944-45, 47-48; MD, Harvard U., 1952. Diplomate: Am. Bd. Orthopedic Surgery. Intern Stanford U. Hosp., 1952-53, resident gen. surgery, 1953-54; resident orthopedic surgery Stanford U. Hosp., also San Francisco City and County Hosp., 1954-57; fellow in orthopedics Nat. Found. Infantile Paralysis, 1955-58; hon. sr. registrar Royal Nat. Orthopedic Hosp., London, Eng., 1957-58; asst. prof. UCLA Med. Sch., 1958; asst. prof. surgery, head div. orthopedic surgery U. Wash. Med. Sch., 1958-61, assoc. prof. surgery, head div. orthopedic surgery, 1961-65, prof., 1964-83, chmn. dept. orthopedics, 1964-75; dean Coll. Medicine, U. Ky., 1975-83, vice chancellor for clin. profl. services, 1982-83; exec. vice chancellor U. Kans. Med. Ctr., Kansas City, 1983-94, cons. to chancellor, 1994; prof. surgery/orthopaedics U. Ky., 1994—, cons. to dean, 1994—. Mem. Accreditation Coun. for Grad. Med. Edn., 1977-88; chmn. residency rev. com. on structure and functions, 1987-88; chmn. coun. of deans Assn. Am. Med. Coll., 1985-86, chmn. of the assembly, 1988-89, immediate past chmn., 1989-90, disting. svc. rep. to exec. coun., 1992-95; active Am. Orthopaedic Soc. for Sports Medicine, 1972-87, founder, 1972; active Assn. Orthopaedic Chmn., 1971-73, founder, 1971. Contbr. med. jours.; mem. editorial bd.: Clin. Orthopedics and Related Research, 1964—. Mem. Heart of Am. coun. Boy Scouts Am., 1989—, mem. adv. bd., 1989-92, Regional Task Force and Edn. Found., 1972—. With USNR, 1945-46. Exchange fellow Am. Orthopedic Assn., 1967 Mem. AMA (coun. for med. affairs 1998—), Am. Acad. Ortho. Surgeons (coun. on health policy 1990-95), Am. Orthopaedic Assn., Assn. Acad. Health Ctrs., Assn. Am. Univs., Assn. Bone and Joint Surgeons (pres. 1977), Harvard Med. Sch. Alumni Assn. (pres. 1984-85). Home: 3785 Jamaica Ct Lexington KY 40509-9506 also: 10 E Roanoke St Seattle WA 98102-3257 Personal E-mail: dkcjd@msn.com. *Look to the past only for the lessons we can learn, live today for the joy of being alive, plan to the future to insure that what should be, will be.*

CLAWSON, HARRY QUINTARD MOORE, retired business executive; b. N.Y.C., Aug. 8, 1924; s. Harry Marshall and Marguerite H. (Burgoyne) C.; m. Annemarie Korntner, Dec. 1967 (dec. 1988); m. Mary Louise Kirkland, July 1989 (dec. 2004). Student, NYU, 1951-52, New Sch. for Social Rsch., 1953. Supr. transp., liaison with U.S. Army ARC, 1945-46; asst. to dir. pers. UNESCO, Paris, 1947; resident rep. Tex. Co., Douala, French Cameroun, West Africa, 1948-50; asst. dir. overseas bus. svc. McGraw-Hill Pub. Co., 1951-58; dir. client svcs. Internat. Rsch. Assocs., N.Y.C., 1958-61; v.p., sec. Frasch Whiton Boats, Inc., 1961-63; gen. mgr. Sailboat Tng. Facility, 1961-63; pres. Harry Q.M. Clawson & Co., Inc., N.Y.C., 1961-76, Charleston, S.C., 1978-2000; dir. planning and adminstrn. splty. chems. div. Essex Chem. Corp., 1976-78; pres. Trident Seafarms Co., Charleston, 1980-85. Contbr. articles to profl. jours. With U.S. Army, 1943-45, ETO. Decorated Bronze Star. Mem. Soc. Colonial Wars, Ex-Mems. Assn. Squadron A., Carolina Yacht Club, 112 Infantry Regiment Assn. Home: 2 1/2 Legare St Charleston SC 29401-2337

CLAWSON, JAMES F., JR., judge, arbitrator, mediator; b. Coryell County, Tex., Aug. 31, 1923; s. James F. and Julia Josephine (Doolittle) C.; m. Mary Louise Forester, May 4, 1945; children: Marylou Bowen, Cathy Jo Young. JD, Baylor U., 1948. Bar: Tex. 1948, U.S. Dist. Ct. (so. dist.) Tex. 1995. Atty. Clawson, Jennings & Clawson, Houston, 1948-59; banker, trust officer First Nat. Bank of Temple, Tex., 1959-67; county judge Bell County, Belton, Tex., 1967-69; presiding judge 3d Adminstrv. Jud. Region of Tex., Belton, 1985-90; dist. judge 169th Jud. Dist. of Tex., Belton, 1969-85, sr. judge, 1985—. Chmn. Bd. Regional Judges of Tex., 1985-90; chmn. Ctrl. Tex. Coun. Govts., belton, 1967-69. Served to capt. USAF, 1942-46, 51-53. Named Outstanding Citizen of Yr., Temple (Tex.) Jaycees, 1966. Fellow Tex Bar Found.; mem. State Bar Tex. (mem. exec. com. jud. sect. 1972-82, chmn. jud. sect. 1982-83). Home: 1211 N Pea Ridge Rd Temple TX 76502-4917 E-mail: clawson@stonemedia.com.

CLAWSON, JOHN ADDISON, investment company executive, retired chemicals executive; b. Monaco, Pa., June 4, 1922; s. Ralph S. and Elsie (Winnett) C.; m. Patricia Harmon, July 5, 1947; children: Christine Brandwie, Hunter Winnett. BS, Miami U., 1943, LLD, 1979; postgrad., Harvard U., 1968. Vice pres., nat. mgr. bus. and labor reports div. Prentice-Hall, N.Y.C., 1948-55; with DuBois Chems. div. Chemed Corp., Cin., 1955-78, dist. mgr. N.Y.C., 1955-60, regional mgr. Ea. div., 1960-64, divisional mgrs. v.p., 1964-66, exec. v.p., dir. sales, 1966-70, gen. mgr., 1968-70, pres., chief exec. officer, 1970-79, group exec., 1975-79; v.p. Chemed Corp., 1971-77, exec. v.p., 1978-79, ret., 1979. Chmn. Whitehall Mgmt. Corp., Cin.; bd. dirs. Suburban Fed. Savs. & Loan Assn. Trustee Providence Hosp., 1974-76; dean's assoc. Miami U., 1973— . Lt. (j.g.) USNR, 1943-46. Mem. Cin. C. of C. (city and county planning com. 1971-74), Soap and Detergent Assn. (vice-chmn. bd. 1971-73, chmn. bd., chief exec. officer 1974-75, mem. exec. com., bd. dirs. 1976-79), Delta Sigma Phi, Sigma Alpha Epsilon. Clubs: Queen City (Cin.), Kenwood Country (Cin.); John's Island (Fla.), Cat Cay, Ltd., Commodore (Bahamas). Presbyterian. Home: Johns Island 301 Island Creek Dr Vero Beach FL 32963-3306

CLAXTON, REBECCA LYNNE, journalist, consultant; b. Georgetown, Ky., Oct. 13, 1962; d. Frank Russell Smith and Judith Louise Cutler; m. Michael James Claxton, Jan. 5, 1965; children: Marshall David, Gabrielle Catherine, Bryce Michael. BA, Franklin Coll., 1985. Copy editor The Wash. Times/Insight Mag., Washington, 1985—86, The Indpls. Star, 1986—88; book editor Benchmark Press, Indpls., 1988—89; copy editor The Shelbyville (Ind.) News, 1991—2001, The Daily Jour., Franklin, Ind., 2001—; cons. WordPro Pub. Co., Shelbyville, 2000—. Editor Shelby County C. of C. Directory, Shelbyville, 1996—97, writer, 1999—2000. Editor: (resource manual) Sports and Recreation for the Disabled: A Resource Manual, 1989, (textbook) One Rep Max: A Guide to Beginning Weight Lifting, 1989. Chmn. ann. festival St. Joseph Cath. Ch., Shelbyville, 2002—; bd. mem., sec. Trinicon Outreach Ministries, Greensburg, Ind., 1997—99; bd. mem. Shelby County Heart Assn., Shelbyville, 1994—96; founding mem., first pres. Mainstreet Shelbyville, 1997—98. Recipient Third Pl. headline writing, AP Mng. Editors, 1989, 1992, 1992, Third Pl. deadline news reporting staff, 1993, Third Pl. headline writing, 1993, Third Pl. deadline news reporting staff, 1994, Second Pl. headline writing, Soc. Profl. Journalists, 1994, First Pl. deadline news reportingn staff, 1994, First Pl. best spot news category, Nat. Newspaper Assn. Better Newspaper Contest, 1993. Mem.: Daughters of Isabella (rec. sec. 2003—04), Delta Delta Delta (alumna adviser). Conservative. Roman Catholic. Avocations: needlepoint, reading, photography, camping, scrapbooks. Home: 202 W Broadway Shelbyville IN 46176 Office Phone: 317-736-7101.

CLAY, BRYAN EZRA, Olympic track and field athlete; b. Austin, Tex., Jan. 3, 1980; m. Sarah Smith. BA in Social Work, Azusa Pacific U., 2003. Decathlete Team USA, Athens Olympic Games, 2004. Achievements include NAIA Champion, 2000; Won World Indoor Silver medal, Budapest, Hungary, 2004. Office: c/o USOC One Olympic Plz Colorado Springs CO 80909

CLAY, CAROL SUE, reading specialist; b. Davenport, Iowa, Jan. 6, 1953; d. George Ross Campbell and Marian Lois Wirtz; m. Craig Allen Clay, Dec. 9, 1977; children: Cayce, Caitlyn. BA in Edn., Marycrest Coll., 1975; MS in Edn. and Reading, We. Ill. U., 1980. Cert. K-12 lang. arts specialist Ill. State Bd. Edn., 1983, K-12 reading specialist Ill. State Bd. Edn., 1988. Title I specialist Rock Island (Ill.) Sch. Dist., 1975—, reading recovery tchr., 1993—, lang. arts. tchr., 2002—04. Auditions chair Quad City Music Guild, Moline, Ill., 1992—95, usher, 2000—. Recipient We. Ill. Master Tchr. award, 1992. Mem.: Internat. Reading Assn., Alpha Delta Kappa, Alpha Kappa (pres. 1999—2000). Avocations: music, travel, sports. Home: 1327 W 53rd Davenport IA 52806 Office: Rock Island Dist #41 1998 6th Ave Rock Island IL 61201

CLAY, CASSIUS MARCELLUS See ALI, MUHAMMAD

CLAY, CHARLES COMMANDER (CHUCK CLAY), lawyer, former state senator; m. Sara Murphree; 1 child, Erin. Degree, U. N.C.; JD, U. Ga. Asst. dist. atty. Cobb County, Ga.; ptnr. Brock & Clay, P.C.; senator 37th dist. Ga. State Legislature, 1988-99; ptnr. Brock Clay Calhoun Wilson & Rogers P.C., Marietta, Ga., 1999—. Senate minority leader, vice chmn. banking and fin. instns. com., mem. appropriations and rules coms., ethics and jud. coms., senate study com. on local edn. fin. rev., chmn. Gen. Assembly's World

Congress Ctr. Overview Com. Ga. State Senate. Grad. Leadership Cobb, Ga.; mem. adv. bd. Cobb Justice Found., North Ctrl. Ga. Police Acad., Open Gate Child Abuse Ctr.; bd. dirs. Kennesaw Mountain Nat. Battlefield Pk., U. Ga. Law Sch. Assn.; mem. Cobb County Commn., 1986-88; tchr. Sunday sch. St. James Episcopal Ch., Marietta. Recipient Disting. Svc. award Ga. Mid. Sch. Assn., 1992-93, Outstanding Legislator award Ga. Coun. on Aging. Mem. Kiwanis (Marietta chpt.), Cobb Landmark Soc., Phi Beta Kappa. Republican. Office: Brock Clay Calhoun Wilson & Rogers PC 49 Atlanta St SE Marietta GA 30060-8611

CLAY, CLARENCE SAMUEL, acoustical oceanographer; b. Kansas City, Mo., Nov. 2, 1923; s. Clarence Samuel and Mary Else (Hall) C.; m. Andre Jane Edwards, Mar. 27, 1945; children: Arnold, Jo, David, Michael. BS, Kans. State U., 1947, MS, 1948; PhD in Physics, U. Wis., 1951. Asst. prof. U. Wyo., Laramie, 1950-51; physicist Carter Oil Co., Tulsa, 1951-55; rsch. scientist Columbia U., Dobbs Ferry, N.Y., 1955-67; prof. dept. geol. geophysics U. Wis., Madison, 1967-89, emeritus prof., 1989—. Author: Elementary Exploration Seismology, 1990, (with I. Tolstoy) Ocean Acoustics, 1966, (with H. Medwin) Acoustical Oceanography, 1977, Fundamentals of Acoustical Oceanography, 1997; (with I. Tolstoy) Ocean Acoustics, 1987. Fellow Acoustical Soc. Am. (Silver medal in Acoustical Oceanography, 1993); mem. Sigma Xi. Home: 5109 St Cyr Rd Middleton WI 53562 Office: U Wis Weeks Hall 1215 W Dayton St Madison WI 53706-1600

CLAY, CYNTHIA JOYCE, writer, editor-in-chief; b. Cedar Falls, Iowa, Aug. 4, 1957; d. James Hubert and Delight Clay; m. Guillermo Jose Ramon, Jan. 7, 1987. Attended, Nat. Theater Inst., 1978; BA cum laude, Brandeis U., 1979; MFA, U. Ga., 1979. Editor-in-chief Oestara Pub. LLC, Key Biscayne, Fla., 2004—. Author: (book) Vector Theory and the Plot Structures of Literature and Drama, (novels) Zollocco: A Novel of Another Universe (Eppie Sci. Fiction finalist, 2001), The Romance of the Unicorn, (short stories) New Myths of the Feminine Divine; actor: The First Loebner Prize Competition Touring Test, Lulu, Marriage of Figaro, Has Washington Got Legs?. Pagan priestess /webmistress betweenplace.com, Key Biscayne, 2003—. Mem.: Electronically Pub. Internet Connection. Democrat. Avocations: travel, swimming, reading. Home: 575 Sabal Palm Dr Key Biscayne FL 33149 Personal E-mail: cynthia@oestarapublishing.com.

CLAY, ERIC L., federal judge; b. Durham, NC, Jan. 18, 1948; BA, U. N.C., 1969; JD, Yale U., 1972. Bar: Mich. 1972, U.S. Dist. Ct. (ea. dist.) Mich. 1972, U.S. Supreme Ct. 1977, U.S. Ct. Appeals (6th cir.) 1978, U.S. Dist. Ct. (we. dist.) Mich. 1987, U.S. Ct. Appeals (DC cir.) 1994. Law clk. to Judge Damon J. Keith U.S. Dist. Ct. (ea. dist.) Mich., 1972—73; atty., shareholder, dir. Lewis, White & Clay, P.C., Detroit, 1973—97; judge U.S. Ct. Appeals (6th cir.), Detroit, 1997—. Hearing panelist Atty. Discipline Bd., State of Mich., 1985—97. Fellow John Hay Whitney, Yale U. Mem.: ABA, Wolverine Bar Assn., Detroit Bar Assn., Nat. Assn. Railroad Trial Counsel, Nat. Bar Assn., U.S. Sixth Jud. Conf. (life), Phi Beta Kappa. Office: Potter Stewart US Cthse 100 E 5th St Cincinnati OH 45202-3988*

CLAY, JOHN PETER, investment company executive; b. Paterson, N.J., June 26, 1934; s. Harold Peter and Mary D. (Cox) C.; m. Rosanagh Mary Maurice, June 20, 1958 (div. Apr. 1972); children: Teresa, Lalage, Xanthe; m. Jennifer Mary Coutts, Aug. 9, 1972. BA, Oxford U., 1957, MA, 1982. Dep. chmn. Vickers da Costa, London, 1957-81; co-chmn. Clay Finlay Inc., N.Y.C., 1981—2000, dir. and chmn. emeritus, 2000—. Hon. fellow Oxford U., 1998. Mem. Tuxedo Club N.Y.C., Sky Club N.Y.C., City London Club, Queens Club London. Republican. Episcopalian. Office: Clay Finlay Inc 200 Park Ave New York NY 10166-0005 Office Phone: 212-557-7022. E-mail: jclay@clayfinlay.com.

CLAY, ORSON C., insurance company executive, director; b. Bountiful, Utah, July 26, 1930; s. George Phillips and Dorothy (Cliff) C.; m. Dianne Jones, June 13, 1961; children: Orson Cliff, Charles Kenneth, Elizabeth Temple. BS, Brigham Young U., 1955; MBA with distinction, Harvard U., 1959. With Continental Oil Co., various locations in, U.S.; mng. dir. Conoco A.G., Zug, Switzerland, 1962-63; dir. econs. divsn. Continental Oil Co. Ltd., London, Eng., 1964-65; gen. mgr. adminstrn. and ops. Continental Oil (U.K.) Ltd., London, 1965-66; asst. mgr. marine transp. Continental Oil, N.Y.C., 1966-68; exec. asst. fin. Pennzoil United, Inc., Houston, 1968-70; exec. v.p. fin., treas. Am. Nat. Ins. Co., Galveston, Tex., 1970-73, sr. exec. v.p., treas., 1973-76, pres., 1977-95, CEO, 1978-91, also bd. dirs., ret., 1995. Past mem. nat. adv. coun. mgmt. Brigham Young U. Past trustee United Way Galveston; past bd. dirs. Tex. Rsch. League; active LDS Ch., missionary in Can., 1951-53. 1st lt. USMCR, 1955-57. Donald Kirk David fellow Harvard U., 1959. Mem. Life Officers Mgmt. Assn. (bd. dirs. 1993-95). Home: 5682 169th Pl SE Bellevue WA 98006-5514

CLAY, PHILLIP L., academic administrator; married; 1 child. AB with honor, U. NC, Chapel Hill, 1968; PhD in City Planning, MIT, 1975. Faculty MIT, Cambridge, Mass., 1975, assoc. dept. head, 1990—92, head, dept. urban svcs., 1992—94, assoc. provost, office of provost, 1994—2001, prof. of city planning, chancellor; asst. dir., Joint Ctr. for Urban Studies MIT and Harvard, 1980—84. Chair Mass. Inst. Tech. Coun.; mem. bd. Media Lab Europe, Cambridge-Mass. Inst. Tech. Author: (books) Neighborhood Renewal: Middle-class Resettlement and Incumbent Upgrading in American Neighborhoods; co-author (with Rob Hollister): Neighborhood Politics and Planning. Founding mem. Nat. Housing Trusts; vice pres. bd. Com. Builders; sr. adv. on project in several areas that include pub. housing, cmty. capacity bldg., and urban job initiatives; bd. trustees Roxbury Cmty. Coll.; mem., policy and rsch. adv. coun. Fed. Nat. Mortage Assn. (Fannie Mae); cons. to numerous fed. and state agencies and found. Avocation: gardening. Office: Office of Chancellor Rm 10-200 Mass Inst Tech 77 Mass Ave Cambridge MA 02139-4307 Office Phone: 617-253-9742. Office Fax: 617-258-6261.

CLAY, TONYA J., artist, consultant; b. Champaign, Ill., Mar. 21, 1975; d. Ernest H. and Gloria J. Clay; 1 child, Elijah David Clay-Chapman. BFA, U. Ill., Urbana, 1997; MFA, SUNY, Stony Brook, 2000. Graphic designer 3TV, Stony Brook, NY, 1998—2000; galery mgr. Chappell Gallery, N.Y.C., 2000—01; prof. representational drawing and figure painting Ringling Sch. Art & Design, Sarasota, Fla., 2002—03; design cons. Bradenton, 2004—. Participant Coll. Arts Assn. Conf., Atlanta, 2005. Prin. works include Birth, Conception and the Annunciation of the Last Moment (the moment before) (2000 award, 2004), exhibitions include Tampa Mus. Art, 2004. Recipient Purchase award, Dorothy Peiper Meml. Found., 2000. Mem.: Coll. Arts Assn. Home: 2400 Ave C Bradenton Beach FL 34217

CLAY, WILLIAM LACY, JR., congressman; b. St. Louis, July 27, 1956; s. William L. and Carol Ann (Johnson) C.; m. Ivie Lewellen, Jan. 24, 1992. BS in Polit. Sci., U. Md., Coll. Park, 1983. Cert. paralegal; lic. real estate salesman, Mo. Mem. Mo. Gen. Assembly, Jefferson City, 1983—90, Mo. State Senate, 1991—98, U.S. Congress from 1st Mo. dist., 2001—; mem. fins svcs. com. and govt. reform com. Chmn. Mo. Jesse Jackson 1988 Presdl. Campaign; Jackson del. to 1988 Dem. Nat. Conv.; committeeman to Dem. Nat. Com.; bd. dirs. William L. Clay Scholarship and Rsch. Fund. Mem. Ams. Dem. Action (Outstanding Legis. Mo. chpt. 1985, 86). Democrat. Roman Catholic. Office: US Ho of Reps 131 Cannon HOB Washington DC 20515*

CLAYBROOK, MARJORIE ANNETTE, fiber artist; b. Corpus Christi, Tex., Aug. 13, 1940; d. Walter Bert and Nona (O'Neal) Walger; m. James Russell Claybrook, 1963. BS in Organic Chemistry, U. Tex., 1962; student, Toledo Mus. Sch., 1970, 76-78, Arrowmont, 1985-93. Asst. scientist U. Tex., Austin, 1961-63; assoc. scientist U. Ill., Champaign, 1966-68. Solo exhbns. include Etherridge Ctr. U. S.C., 1989, Francis Marion U., Florence, S.C., 1989, 92, Cotton Exch. Gallery, Augusta, Ga., 1990, West Ga. Coll., Carrolton, 1991, The Atrium, Augusta, 1991, Berry Coll., Rome, Ga., 1991, Colquitt Art Ctr., Moultrie, Ga., 1993, Del. Ctr. Contemporary Art, 1994; group exhbns. include Toledo Mus. Art, 1979-85, Tweed Mus., 1981, Duluth Art Inst., 1981, Am. Craft Mus. II, N.Y.C., 1983, ODC Galleries, Columbus, Ohio, 1987, Albany Mus. Art, 1990, 94, Decatur House, Washington, 1990, 91, Vanderbilt U., 1990, Miss. Mus. Art, 1991, U. Fla., 1989, Kimball Mus., Utah, 1993, others; studio artist-tchr., Augusta, 1987—; presenter workshops in field. Recipient various awards nat. exhbns., 1979-89; Ga. Arts Coun. Individual Artist grantee, 1991-92, 94-95; Arrowmont Sch. Arts and Crafts work-study fellow, 1992; Bus. and Profl. Women scholar, 1958-62. Mem Surface Design Assn., Peidmont Craftsmen Guild, Women's Caucus for Art, Jr. League, Inc. (sustaining), VMFA Council. Republican. Avocation: gardening. Home: 5010 W Seminary Ave Richmond VA 23227-3408 E-mail: maclaybrook@aol.com.

CLAYCOMB, CECIL KEITH, biochemist, educator; b. Twin Falls, Idaho, Oct. 19, 1920; s. Cecil R. and Frilla E. (Reams) C.; m. Elizabeth Jane Gregg, Mar. 10, 1943; children: John K., Mary E. BS, U. Oreg., 1947, MS, 1948, PhD, 1951. Prof., head dept. biochemistry Dental Sch. U. Oreg., Portland, 1951-82, dir. minority recruitment, 1971-74, asst. to pres./dir. minority student affairs, 1974-84, coordinator basic sci. curriculum, 1951-77, chmn. admissions com., 1959-69, emeritus, 1985—; emeritus prof. biochemistry Oreg. Health and Sci. U., 1986—. Contbr. articles to sci. jours. Served to 1st lt. AUS, 1943-46. Scholar dental bd. New South Wales, Sydney, Australia, 1970 Mem. Am. Chem. Soc., Internat. Assn. Dental Research, AAAS, Res. Officers Assn., Sigma Xi. Home: 3326 SW 13th Ave Portland OR 97239-2922

CLAYCOMB, HUGH MURRAY, lawyer, writer; b. Joplin, Mo., May 19, 1931; s. Hugh and Fern (Murray) C.; m. Jeanne Cavin, May 5, 1956; children: Stephen H., Scott C. BS in Bus., U. Mo., 1953, JD, 1955; LLM, U. Miss., 1969. Bar: Mo. 1955, Ark. 1957, U.S. Tax Ct. 1956, U.S. Dist. Ct. (ea. dist.) Ark. 1957, U.S. Supreme Ct. 1979. Asst. staff judge advocate USAF, 1955-57; law clerk Ark. Supreme Ct., Little Rock, 1957-58; ptnr. Gregory & Claycomb, Pine Bluff, Ark., 1958-69; partner Haley, Claycomb, Roper & Anderson, Warren, Ark., 1969—. Dir. The Strong Co., Inc., Pine Bluff, Ark., bd. dirs. Ark. Cmty. Found. Author: Arkansas Corporations, 1967, 82, 92. Pres. Jefferson County Bar Assn., Pine Bluff, 1969, Warren YMCA, 1973-75, S.E. Ark. Legal Inst., 1980-81, Ctrl. Ark. Estate Planning Coun., 1963-64, pres. Bradley County YMCA Found.; spl. assoc. justice Ark. Supreme Ct., 1978, 87. Lt. USAF, 1955-57. Recipient Pres.'s award Ark. Trial Lawyers Assn., 1985. Fellow Am. Bar Found.; mem. Ark. Bar Found. (pres. 1990), Ark. Bar Assn. (sec.-treas. 1998-2000, pres. 2002-03, C.E. Ransick award 1996), Warren Rotary (pres. 1972, Paul Harris fellow). Episcopalian. Home: 619 E Cedar St Warren AR 71671-3001 Office Phone: 870-226-2681.

CLAYPOOL, DAVID L., lawyer; b. Springfield, Ill., 1946; BA in History, Ill. Coll., 1968; JD with high distinction, U. Iowa, 1975. Bar: Iowa 1975. Ptnr., pub. fin. practice and ptnr.-in-charge Dorsey & Whitney, LLP, Des Moines. Editor notes and comments Iowa Law Review, 1974-75. Capt. U.S. Army, 1968-72 Mem. Iowa State Bar Assn., Pol County Bar Assn., Nat. Assn. Bond Lawyers, Iowa Mcpl. Attys. Assn., Order of Coif. Office: Dorsey & Whitney LLP 801 Grand Ave Ste 3900 Des Moines IA 50309-2790 Office Phone: 515-283-1000. Business E-Mail: claypool.david@dorsey.com.

CLAYTON, CAROL A., lawyer; b. Aug. 11, 1958; BA, Univ. Utah, 1979; JD, Univ. Va., 1982. Bar: DC 1982. Ptnr., environ. law practice Wilmer Cutler Pickering Hale & Dorr, Washington, asst. mng. ptnr., mem. mgmt. com. Editor (articles): Va. Jour. Natural Resources Law; contbr. chapters to books; co-author: Environ. Auditing Handbook. Office: Wilmer Cutler Pickering Hale & Dorr 2445 M St NW Washington DC 20037 Office Phone: 202-663-6650. Office Fax: 202-663-6363. Business E-Mail: carol.clayton@wilmerhale.com.

CLAYTON, CLAUDE F., JR., lawyer; b. Tupelo, Miss., June 15, 1948; s. Claude F. and Bronson (Munday) C.; children from a previous marriage: Frances, Claude III; m. Tacey Clark, July 25, 1997. Student, Stanton Mil. Acad., 1966; BA, Tulane U., 1971; JD, U. Miss., 1973. Bar: Miss. 1973. Mem. judiciary com. U.S. Senate, Washington, 1968; ptnr. Mitchell, Voge, Clayton and Beasley, Tupelo, 1973-85, Mitchell, McNutt & Sams, Tupelo, 1985—2001; pres. Mitchell, NcNutt & Sams, Tupelo, 1995—97; ptnr. Clayton Law Firm, PLLC, 2001—03, Clayton, O'Donnell, Walsh & Davis, PLLC, 2003—. Mem. complaints tribunal Supreme Ct. Miss., 1990-93; speaker Miss. Jud. Coll., also various trial practice and ethics seminars; special justice Miss. Supreme Ct., 2000. Mem. ABA (young lawyers div., chmn. justice dept. liaison com. 1978-79), Miss. State Bar (pres. fellows of young lawyers 1990-91, co-chmn. specialization com. 1990-92, chmn., 1980-82, lawyer econs. com. 1988-89, ethics com. 1982-85, co-chmn. continuing legal edn. com. 1980-81, law jour.-law sch. liaison com. 1974-76, various coms. young lawyers sect. 1985-90, bd. dirs. 1975-80), Miss. Def. Lawyers Assn. (bd. dirs. 1992-95), Def. Rsch. Inst., Internat. Assn. Def. Counsel. Office: Clayton O'Donnell Walsh & Davis PLLC 115 N Broadway PO Box 755 Tupelo MS 38802-4869 Office Phone: 662-620-7938. Business E-Mail: cclayton@northmslaw.com.

CLAYTON, DANIEL LOUIS, lawyer; b. Chgo., Mar. 11, 1963; s. James D. and Betty (Brisendine) C.; m. Stacy Elizabeth Johnson, June 29, 1985; children: Amy Brooke, Hannah Margaret, Kay Ellen, Christopher, Dalton BA, David Lipscomb Coll., Nashville, 1984; JD, U. Tenn., 1987. Bar: Tenn. 1987, U.S. Dist. Ct. (mid. and we. dists.) Tenn. 1987, U.S. Ct. Appeals (6th cir.) 1991. Ptnr. Kinnard & Clayton, Nashville, 1987—. Mem. faculty Law Seminars Internat., Seattle, 1991. Elected mem. Franklin Spl. Sch. Dist. Bd. Edn., 1994-97. Recipient Lewis F. Powell, Jr. medal for excellence in advocacy. Mem. Tenn. Bar Assn., Tenn. Trial Lawyers Assn. (bd. govs. 1998—. v.p. mid. region 2004—), Nashville Bar Assn Mem. Ch. of Christ. Avocations: golf, tennis. Office: The Woodlawn 127 Woodmont Blvd Nashville TN 37205-2240

CLAYTON, DAVID A(LVIN), biology professor; b. Joliet, Ill., Feb. 5, 1944; m. Lauretta Swanson, 1965; children: Lindsay, Ryan, Megan. BS, No. Ill. U., 1965; PhD in Biophysics and Chemistry, Calif. Inst. Tech., 1970. Asst. prof. pathology Stanford U., 1970—76, assoc. prof., 1976—82, prof., 1982—89, prof. devel. biology, 1989—; sr. sci. officer Howard Hughes Med. Inst., 1996—99, v.p. sci. devel., 2000—02, v.p., chief scientific officer, 2002—. Mem. adv. com. nucleic acids and protein synthesis, Am. Cancer Soc., 1976-80; mem. molecular biology study sect., NIH, 1982-86, chmn., 1984-86; mem. sci. rev. bd. Howard Hughes Med. Inst., 1993-96; mem. nat. adv. bd. Gen. Med. Sci. Coun., 1996-99; Fisher lectr. So. Ill. U., 1989. Recipient Warner-Lambert/Parke Davis award, 1982. Mem. Inst. Medicine Nat. Acad. Sci., Am. Soc. Biochemistry and Molecular Biology.

CLAYTON, DONALD DELBERT, astrophysicist, nuclear physicist, educator; b. Shenandoah, Iowa, Mar. 18, 1935; s. Delbert Homer and Avis (Kembery) C.; children: Donald, Devon, Alia, Andrew; m. Nancy McBride. BS, So. Meth. U., 1956; PhD, Calif. Inst. Tech., 1962. Rsch. fellow in physics Calif. Inst. Tech., 1961-63; faculty Rice U., Houston, 1963-65, assoc. prof. physics and space sci., 1965-69; prof. physics and space sci., faculty assoc. Wiess Coll., 1969-77, Andrew Hays Buchanan prof. astrophysics, 1975-89; prof. physics and astronomy Clemson (S.C.) U., S.C., 1989—, centennial prof., 1996—. Vis. assoc. physics Calif. Inst. Tech., 1966-67; vis. fellow Inst. Theoretical Astronomy, Cambridge, summers 1967-72. Author: Principles of Stellar Evolution and Nucleosynthesis, 1968, The Dark Night Sky, 1975, The Joshua Factor, 1986, Photo Archive for History of Nuclear Astrophysics, 2000, A Walking Tour of Residential Seneca, 2001, Handbook of Isotopes in the Cosmos, 2003; contbr. over 200 articles to profl. jours. Recipient Humboldt award Max Planck Inst., Heidelberg, 1977, 82, Exceptional Sci. Achievement medal NASA, 1992, Disting. Alumni award So. Meth. U., 1993, S.C. Gov.'s award for sci. excellence, 1994, Jesse Beams award, 1998; Sloan fellow, 1966-70, Fulbright fellow, Heidelberg, 1979-80. Fellow Am. Phys. Soc. (Jesse W. Beams medal 1998), Meteoritical Soc. (Leonard medal 1991), Am. Acad. Arts and Scis.; mem. AAAS, Am. Astron. Soc., Royal Astron. Soc. (G.H. Darwin lectr. 1981), Cosmos Club (Washington), Phi Beta Kappa, Sigma Xi. Office: Clemson U Dept Physics Astronomy Clemson SC 29634-0978 E-mail: cdonald@clemson.edu. *My life centers on love of nature. As a cosmologist studying the universe, I find the truth to be stranger than fiction, and the commonplace to be the spectacular. To share this joy with laymen, I wrote a personal memoir, The Dark Night Sky, and a scientific novel, The Joshua Factor.*

CLAYTON, JAMES EDWIN, journalist; b. Johnston City, Ill., Nov. 14, 1929; s. John Herman and Vinnie Ethel (Black) C.; m. Elise Brookfield Heinz, June 3, 1961; children— Jonathan Brown, David Lake. BS, U. Ill., 1953; MPA, Princeton, 1956. Reporter So. Illinoisan, Carbondale, Ill., 1951-52; reporter Washington Post, 1956-64, asst. mng. editor, 1964-67, 72-74, editorial writer, 1967-72, assoc. editor, 1974-82; assoc. dir. Reporter's Com. for Freedom of Press, 1984; sr. fellow Airlie Found., 1984-94. Vis. lectr. Northwestern U., 1966-67, Johns Hopkins, 1970. Author: The Making of Justice, 1964; editor: The Rights of Free Men, 1984. Chmn. bd. trustees Sofia Am. Schs., Inc. Served to 1st lt. AUS, 1951-52. Recipient Interpretive Reporting awards Washington Newspaper Guild, 1959, 62, 63, Distinguished Washington Correspondence award Sigma Delta Chi, 1960, Worth Bingham prize, 1970, George Polk Meml. award for editorial writing, 1970 Mem.: Princeton (Washington, N.Y.C.). Baptist. Home: 2728 N Fillmore St Arlington VA 22207-4936

CLAYTON, JON KERRY, insurance company executive; b. Cin., Dec. 29, 1945; s. Lawrence and Charlotte Marie (Miller) C.; m. Mary-Paige Royer, Aug. 27, 1983; 1 child from previous marriage: Margaret Allyn; children: Thomas Barry, Timothy Jon. B.I.E., Ga. Inst. Tech., 1968; MBA, Harvard U., 1970. Asst. treas. Am. Security Ins. Co., Atlanta, 1970-76, treas., 1976-78; v.p., treas. Am. Security Inc. Co., Atlanta, 1978-80; v.p. fin. Fortis, Inc., NYC, 1980-83, sr. v.p., 1983-85; pres. Fortis Benefits Ins. Co., 1985-93; exec. v.p. Assurant Inc., NYC, 1993—99, pres., 2000—05, CEO, 2000—. Served to 1st lt. U.S. Army, 1970. Office: Assurant Inc 1 Chase Manhattan Plz New York NY 10005-1401*

CLAYTON, JOSEPH P., broadcast executive; b. 1949; MBA in Mktg. and Mgmt., Indiana U., Bloomington; BA in Bus. Admin., Bellarmine U., Louisville. Various mgmt. positions RCA Consumer Electronics, 1973—86; senior v.p. TV div. Thomson Consumer Electronics, 1987—92, exec. v.p. mktg. and sls. Am. & Asia, 1992—97; pres., CEO Frontier Corp. (aquired by Global Crossing Ltd.), Rochester, NY, 1997—99; pres. N. Am. region, vice chmn. Global Crossing Ltd., 1999—2001; pres., CEO SIRIUS Satellite Radio, NYC, 2001—04, chmn., 2004—. Former mem. bd. dirs. Global Crossing, Frontier Corp., E.W. Scripps; mem. bd. dirs. Transcend Services, Atlanta, Sirius Satellite Radio, NYC; former chmn. Consumer Electronics Assn.; mem. bd. dirs., bd. govs. Electronics Industry Assn. Mem. Dean's Advisory Bd. Indiana U. Kelley Sch. of Bus.; mem., former vice chmn. NY State Office of Science, Tech. and Academic Rsch. Advisory Council; trustee Bellarmine U., Louisville, Rochester Inst. of Technology., Rochester, NY. Office: SIRIUS Satellite Radio 1221 Ave of the Americas New York NY 10020 Office Phone: 212-584-5100.

CLAYTON, JULIA B., academic administrator, musician; b. Salt Lake City, Oct. 27, 1942; d. Ivan Miles and Violet P. Bryson; m. Archer Robert Clayton, Dec. 5, 1963; children: Ned William, April Diane, Christopher Michael; 1 child, Laura Furst. MusM, U. Utah, 1984. Assoc. dir., office of fin. aid and scholarships U. Utah, Salt Lake City, 1988—97, dir. fin. aid and scholarships, 1997—98; dir. student fin. svcs. SUNY Downstate Med. Ctr., Bklyn., 1998—. Cons., website rev. bd. Thompson Pub., Washington, 1995; adv. coun. Utah Higher Edn. Assistance Authority, Salt Lake City, 1990—97. Mem. editl. bd.: Jour. Fin. Aid, 1996—98. Organist, pianist, choir dir., arranger, performer LDS Ch., 1952—2003. Scholar, U. Utah, 1960—64. Mem.: Rocky Mtn. Assn. Fin. Aid Adminstrs., Utah Assn. Fin. Aid Adminstrs. (student newsletter editor, pub. 1992—94), NY Assn. Fin. Aid Adminstrs., Nat. Assn. Fin. Aid Adminstrs. (governance com., profl. devel. com., history com., editl. bd. Transcript mag. 1999), Mu Phi Epsilon, Phi Kappa Phi. Office: SUNY Downstate Med Ctr 450 Clarkson Ave Brooklyn NY 11203-2098 Business E-Mail: julia.clayton@downstate.edu.

CLAYTON, KEVIN E., elementary school educator, music educator; b. Spokane, Dec. 30, 1975; s. Mel and Kathy Clayton; m. Katherine Nicole Kelley, July 15, 2000. BA, B of Music, U. Wash., 1998. Dir. band Ctrl. Kitsap Jr. High Sch., Silverdale, Wash., 1999—2000; dir. band, orch. Bothell High Sch., 2000—. Mem.: Wash. Music Educators Assn., Music Educators Nat. Conf. Home: 21030 42d Ave SE Bothell WA 98021 Office: Bothell High Sch 18125 92d Ave NE Bothell WA 98011-3398

CLAYTON, MARK J., architecture educator; b. New Orleans, La. BArch, Va. Poly. Inst. and State U., 1983; MArch, UCLA, 1987; PhD, Stanford U., 1998. Project arch. Arch. Michael L. Oxman & Assocs., Sterling, Va., 1984—86; grad. tchg. asst. Grad. Sch. Arch. and Urban Planning UCLA, 1987; lectr. Coll. Arch. and Environ. Design Calif. Poly. State U., 1988—91; grad. tchg. asst. Sch. Engring. Stanford U., 1992—93; asst. prof. Coll. Arch. Tex. A&M U., College Station, 1995—2001, assoc. prof. dept. arch., 2001—, exec. assoc. dean Coll. Arch., 2001—. Contbr. articles to profl. jours. Mem. bd. adjustments City of College Station, 2000—. Recipient Commend award, Va. Soc. AIA. Mem.: Assn. for Computer Aided Design in Arch. (v.p.), Phi Kappa Phi, Tau Sigma Delta. Achievements include research in computer-aided design in architecture. Office: Tex A&M Univ Coll Arch Dept Arch A202 Langford A College Station TX 77843-3137

CLAYTON, MICHAEL F., lawyer; b. Mar. 2, 1954; BA, Wake Forest U., 1977; JD, U. Va. Sch. Law, 1980. Bar: D.C. 1980, Va. 1981, registered: U.S. Supreme Ct. 1988. Ptnr., intellectual property trademark/copyright practice group leader Morgan, Lewis & Bockius LLP. Pro bono gen. counsel Women in Mil. Svc. Am. Meml.; lectr. U. Va. Sch. Law. Recipient Elizabeth D. & Richard A. Merrill Endowment Lectr. Law, U. Va. Office: Morgan Lewis & Bockius LLP 1111 Pennsylvania Ave NW Washington DC 20004 Office Phone: 202-739-5215. Office Fax: 202-739-3001. Business E-Mail: mclayton@morganlewis.com.

CLAYTON, ORVILLE WOOLFORD, surgeon; b. Ft. Payne, Ala., May 30, 1921; s. Olney Walker Clayton and Flora Pauline Wheeler; m. Dorothy Nell Meadows, June 20, 1944; children: Stephen W., Kathy L. Stockham, Shelley E. BA, U. Ala., Tuscaloosa, 1943; B in Medicine, Northwestern U., 1945, MD, 1946. Post surgeon U.S. Army, Huntsville, Ala., 1946-48; chief resident in surgery Univ. Hosp., Birmingham, Ala., 1948; chief surgery Bapt. Med. Montclair, Birmingham, 1969-74, pres. staff, 1982; clin. assoc. prof. surgery U. Ala., Birmingham, 1973-91. Bd. dirs. Am. Pulmonary Inst., Birmingham, 1973—91. Capt. U.S. Army, 1946—48. Fellow: ACS, So. Thoracic Soc. Avocations: gardening, genealogy. Home: 3133 Ryecroft Rd Birmingham AL 35223-2715

CLAYTON, RAYMOND EDWARD, municipal official; b. Saskatoon, Sask., Can., Nov. 6, 1942; m. Joan Ann Snodgrass, Sept. 21, 1963; children: Grant, Sheila, Matthew, Daniel. B. of Commerce, U. Sask., 1964; MA in Econs., 1965. Dir. rsch. Dept. Mcpl. Affairs, Govt. Sask., Regina, 1965-67, Dept. Edn., Govt. Sask., Regina, 1967-69, dir. ednl. adminstrn., 1969-77, dep. minister, 1979-84; dir. taxation and fiscal policy Dept. Fin., Govt. Sask., Regina, 1977-78; dep. minister Dept. Urban Affairs, Govt. Sask., Regina, 1978-79; chmn. Govt. Fin. Comm., Regina, 1984-86; asst. dep. minister Dept. Energy & Mines, Govt. Sask., Regina, 1986-94, dep. minister, 1994—2002; pres. Sask. Property Mgmt. Corp., Regina, 2002—04, Sask. Transp. Co., Regina, 2004—. E-mail: rclayton@stcbus.ca.

CLAYTON, RICHARD REESE, retired diversified financial services company executive; b. St. Louis, Aug. 26, 1938; s. Lester Cox and Gladys Caroline (Reese) C.; m. Leigh Ila Smith, Feb. 25, 1961; children: Mark, Catherine, Christine. BS in Indsl. Econs., Purdue U., 1960. With Trane Co., 1960-73, mng. dir. Sydney, Australia, 1970-73; pres. Hallowell div. Standard Pressed Steel Co., Hatfield, Pa., 1973-77; exec. v.p. domestic ops., dir. SPS Technologies Inc., Jenkintown, Pa., 1977-84; pres., CEO, dir. Vermont

Castings, Inc., Randolph, Vt., 1984-87; exec. v.p., chief adminstrv. officer Ea. Enterprises (formerly Ea. Gas & Fuel Assocs.), Weston, Mass., 1987-89, exec. v.p., COO, 1990-91, pres., COO, 1991-98. Baptist.

CLAYTON, ROBERT NORMAN, chemist, educator; b. Hamilton, Ont., Can., Mar. 20, 1930; came to U.S., 1952, naturalized, 1995; s. Norman and Gwenda (Twist) C.; m. Cathleen Shelburne, Jan. 30, 1971; 1 dau., Elizabeth Jane. B.Sc., Queens U., 1951, M.Sc., 1952; PhD, Calif. Inst. Tech., 1955. Research fellow Calif. Inst. Tech., 1955-56; mem. faculty Pa. State U., 1956-58, U. Chgo., 1958—, prof. chemistry and geochemistry, 1966—. Fellow AAAS, NAS, Royal Soc. (London), Royal Soc. Can., Am. Acad. Arts Scis., Am. Geophys Union, Meteoritical Soc. Achievements include research distbn. stable isotopes of light elements in nature, application to problems in geology. Home: 5201 S Cornell Ave Chicago IL 60615-4207 Office Phone: 773-702-7777. Business E-Mail: r-clayton@uchicago.edu.

CLAYTON, VERNA LEWIS, retired state legislator; b. Hamden, Ohio, Feb. 28, 1937; d. Matthews L. and Yail (Miller) Lewis; m. Frank R. Clayton, Feb. 4, 1956; children: children: Valerie S., Barry L. Office mgr. Village of Buffalo Grove, Ill., 1972-78, village clk., 1971-79, village pres., 1979-91; mem. Ill. Ho. of Reps., Springfield, 1993-99. Bd. dirs. Savannah Lakes Property Owners Assn., 2000, pres., 2004. Mem. Lake County Solid Waste Planning Agy., chmn. tech. com., chmn. agy., Nat. League of Cities, chmn. transp. and comms. steering com.; bd. govs. SC Patients Compensation Fund, 2005—; mem. Rep. Com. McCormick County; dist. legis. officer U.S. Power Squadrons. Recipient Disting. Svc. award Amvets, 1981; named Libr. Legislator of the Yr. 1997. Mem. N.W. Mcpl. Conf. (pres. 1983-84), Chgo. Area Transp. Study Coun. Mayors (vice chmn. 1981-83, chmn. 1985-91), Mcpl. Clks. Ill. (treas. 1978-79), Mcpl. Clks. Lake County (pres. 1977-78), Ill. Mcpl. League (bd. dirs., v.p. 1985-90, pres. 1989-90), Buffalo Grove Rotary Club (hon. mem.), Buffalo Grove C. of C. (bd. dirs.). Republican. Methodist. Home: 11 Overlook Pt Mc Cormick SC 29835-2850 E-mail: vclayton@wctel.net.

CLAYTOR, KATHERINE W. MOSS, secondary school educator; b. Richlands, Va., Dec. 9, 1959; d. Robert Lincoln Moss and Katherine Kiser Gillespie Huffman. BEd, Radford (Va.) U., 1984. Phys. sci. tchr. Tazewell County Pub. Schs., Tazewell, Va., 1986—. Sci. fair coord. Richlands Tazewell (Va.) Middle Sch, 1989—. Mem. NEA, Va. Edn. Assn., Tazewell Edn. Assn., Nat. Middle Sch. Assn. Avocations: horseback riding, camping, horse showing. Office: Tazewell Middle Sch 100 Bulldog Ln Tazewell VA 24651-9765

CLAYTOR, RICHARD ANDERSON, retired federal agency administrator; b. Roanoke, Va., Sept. 4, 1927; s. William Graham and Gertrude (Boatwright) C.; m. Mary Lee Leary, June 18, 1949; children: Gale Catherine, Douglas Gordon, Richard Anderson Jr. BS, U.S. Naval Acad., 1949; BS in Marine Engring., MS in Naval Architecture, Webb Inst. Naval Architecture, 1956. Registered profl. engr., N.J., Calif. Commd. ensign USN, 1949, advanced through grades to capt., 1969; served in various ships, 1949-53; project mgr. nuclear power div. USN Bur. Ships, Washington, 1956-63; asst. mgr. Pitts. Naval Reactors Office, AEC, 1963-73; ret., 1973; v.p., asst. to pres. Burns and Roe, Inc., Oradell, N.J., 1973-79; pres. Burns and Roe-Humphreys & Glasgow Synthetic Fuels, Inc., Oradell, 1979-81, Burns and Roe Pacific Co., L.A., 1981-90; asst. sec. for def. programs U.S. Dept. Energy, Washington, 1990-93; ind. cons. Decorated Legion of Merit. Mem. ASME, Soc. Naval Engrs., Am. Nuclear Soc., Army-Navy Club. Episcopalian. Avocations: golf, bridge, canoeing, painting.

CLAYTOR, WILLIAM MIMMS, lawyer; b. Nashville, Mar. 31, 1941; s. George White and Dorothy (Mimms) C.; m. Anne Edwards, June 1, 1968; children: Justin H., Graham F. BA in Econs. and Math., Truman U., 1963; MA in Econs. and Math., Univ. Memphis, 1964, JD, 1969. Bar: N.C., Tenn. Estate tax atty. IRS, Charlotte, 1970-72; ptnr. Baucom, Claytor, Benton, Morgan & Wood, Charlotte, 1973—. Bd. trustees Ctrl. Piedmont C.C., 1977-93, chmn. 1982-93; past bd. dirs. Goodwill Industries of So. Piedmont Inc., mem. exec. com.; past chmn., bd. deacons St. John's Bapt. Ch.; bd. dirs. Met. YMCA; bd. dirs. Habitat for Humanity of Charlotte; bd. dirs. Alzheimer's Assn. Mem. ABA, N.C. Bar Assn., 26th Jud. Bar Assn., Mecklenburg Bar Assn., Mecklenburg County Bar Assn. (pres. 1996-97), Mecklenburg Bar Found. (vice chmn. 1992), Mecklenburg County Bar Found. (chmn. capital funds drive 1990), Charlotte C. of C., Omicron Delta Kappa. Office: Baucom Claytor Benton Morgan & Wood PO Box 35246 Charlotte NC 28235-5246

CLEAGE, PEARL MICHELLE, writer, playwright, journalist; b. Springfield, Mass., Dec. 7, 1948; d. Albert B. Clege Jr. and Doris (Graham) C.; m. Michael Lomax, 1969 (div. 1979); 1 child, Deignan Njeri Lomax; m. Zaron W. Burnett Jr., 1994. Student, Howard Univ., Washington, DC; BA in Drama, Spelman Coll., Atlanta, 1971. Faculty Spelman Coll.; press secy. speechwriter Mayor Maynard Jackson, Atlanta. Contbr. articles to Atlanta Jour. Constitution, Atlanta Tribune; co-founder, editor Catalyst, literary journ.; author (self-published vol.): Mad at Miles: A Blackwoman's Guide to Truth, 1990; author: The Brass Bed, 1991, (collection of essays) Deals with the Devil and Other Reasons to Riot, 1993, (novels) What Looks Like Crazy on an Ordinary Day, 1997 (NY Times Bestseller list, Oprah Book Club selection, 1998, BCALA Lit. award), I Wish I Had a Red Dress, 2001, Some Things I Thought I'd Never Do, 2003, Babylon Sisters, 2005, (plays) Blues for an Alabama Sky, 1995, Flyin' West, 1992, Bourbon at the Border, 1997. Recipient Bronze Jubilee award for lit., 1983, Outstanding Columnist award, Atlanta Assn. Black Journalists, 1991. Office: Spelman College 350 Spelman Ln SW Atlanta GA 30314*

CLEAR, ALBERT F., JR., retired hardware manufacturing company executive; b. N.Y.C., June 9, 1920; s. Albert F. and Edna (Coyle) C.; m. Jeanne Posselt, Aug. 7, 1947; children: Geoffrey Posselt, Gregory Stuart. BS, MIT, 1942; MBA, Harvard U., 1948. V.p., mgr. Mallory div. John B. Stetson Co., Danbury, Conn., 1948-57; mng. assoc. Booz-Allen & Hamilton, N.Y.C., 1957-65; v.p., gen. mgr. hardware div. Stanley Works, New Britain, Conn., 1965-69, v.p. consumer group, chmn. European ops., 1967-69, exec. v.p., 1969-76, pres., 1977-80, vice chmn., 1980-82. Chmn. Ansonia (Conn.) Copper & Brass, 1999-2001; bd. dirs. The Stanley Works, New Britain, Stanley Home Products, Westfield, Mass., Barden Corp., Danbury, Curtis Corp., Sandy Hook, Constructive Workshop, Inc., New Britain, D&L Corp., Danbury; adv. dir. Conn. Nat. Bank. Vice chmn. MIT Ctr. N.Y., 1965; bd. dirs. Danbury chpt. ARC, 1953; trustee Hartford Grad. Ctr., Hartford Coll. for Women, Housatonic Valley Assn., 1976-80. Capt. AUS, 1942-46. Mem. Builders Hardware Mfrs. Assn. (exec. com.), Danbury C. of C. (pres. 1954), New Britain C. of C. (dir. 1967-69, 72-80, pres. 1977). Home: 344 Westmont West Hartford CT 06117-2938

CLEAR, GLORIA LEWIS, elementary school educator; b. Ft. Edward, N.Y., Aug. 8, 1927; d. Gerald Sidney and Anne Amelia (Brown) Lewis; m. George P. Clear, Apr. 14, 1976 (dec. Dec. 1980); 1 child, Ellen McEntee. BE, Oneonta (NY) State Tech. Coll., 1948; postgrad., U. N.Y., Plattsburg, U. of N.Y., Oneonta. Cert. tchr. Tchr. elem., Ft. Edward, 1948-54, Rochester, N.Y., 1954-55, Hudson Falls (N.Y.) Cen. Sch., 1957-93; ret., 1993. Sec., team leader Widowed Person's Svcs., Glen Falls, N.Y., 1989-99, v.p. bd.; vol. RSVP, South Glens Falls, Moreau Cmty. Ctr., South Glens Falls. Mem. AARP, Hudson Falls Tchrs. Assn. (com. concerning dropouts 1979, math. com. 1987, sci. com. 1989-90, report card com. 1990), N.Y. State Tchrs.' Retirement System. Republican. Episcopalian. Home: 28 Circle Dr South Glens Falls NY 12803

CLEAR, JOHN MICHAEL, lawyer; b. St. Louis, Dec. 16, 1948; s. Raymond H. and Marian (Clark) Clear; m. Isabel Marie Bone, May 10, 1980; 1 child, Thomas Henry. BA summa cum laude, Washington U., St. Louis, 1971; JD with honors, U. Chgo., 1974. Bar: Mo. 1974, D.C. 1975, U.S. Ct. Appeals (5th and D.C. cirs.) 1975, U.S. Supreme Ct. 1977, U.S. Ct. Appeals (3d cir.) 1978, U.S. Ct. Appeals (8th cir.) 1980, U.S. Ct. Appeals (9th cir.) 1990, U.S. Dist. Ct. (so. dist.) Ill. 1995, U.S. Ct. Appeals (7th cir.) 1997. Law clk. to judge U.S. Ct. Appeals (5th cir.), Atlanta, 1974-75; assoc. Covington & Burling, Washington, 1975-80; jr. ptnr. Bryan, Cave, McPheeters & McRoberts, St. Louis, 1980-81, ptnr., 1982—. Mem. ABA, Mo. Bar Assn., D.C. Bar Assn., St. Louis Met. Bar Assn., Am. Law Inst., Order of Coif., Racquet Club, Noonday Club, Fox Run Golf Club, Phi Beta Kappa. Office: Bryan Cave LLP One Metropolitan Sq Saint Louis MO 63102-2750 Office Phone: 314-259-2283. Business E-Mail: jmclear@bryancave.com.

CLEARFIELD, HARRIS REYNOLD, physician; b. Phila., Aug. 8, 1933; s. Samuel and Rae (Lewis) C.; m. Louise Libby, June 30, 1957; children: Andrea, Jonathan. BS, Franklin and Marshall Coll., 1955; MD, Jefferson Med. Coll., 1959. Intern Grad. Hosp. U. Pa., Phila., 1959-60, resident in internal medicine, 1960-62, resident in gastroenterology, 1962-63, mem. staff, 1963-72, Episcopalian Hosp., Phila., 1967-72, head sect. gastroenterology, until 1972; sr. attending physician Phila. Gen Hosp., 1972-77; mem. faculty U. Pa. Med. Sch., Phila., 1963-72; clin. asst. prof. medicine Temple U. Med. Sch., Phila., 1967-72; dir. div. gastroenterology Hahnemann Hosp., Phila., 1972—, prof. medicine, 1972—. Lectr., cons. Naval Regional Med. Ctr., Phila., 1976-78; sr. cons. Phila. Gen. Hosp., 1972-74; mem. gov.'s adv. com. of ACP, 1980-88; dir. Krancer Ctr. for Inflamatory Bowel Disease Rsch., 1985—. Author: (with Dinoso) Gastrointestinal Emergencies, 1979, (with Borowsky) Case Studies in Gastroenterology, 1989; editorial cons. Am. Jour. Proctology, 1976-86; contbr. articles to profl. jours. Chmn. sci. adv. bd. Nat. Found. Ileitis and Colitis, 1976-80, trustee, 1990—. Recipient Lindback award Phila. chpt. Nat. Found. Ileitis and Colitis, 1979, named Physician of Yr., 1980, Janssen award, 1998. Fellow ACP (mem. bd. regents 1999-2003, chmn. coun. subspecialty socs. 1999-2003), Phila. Coll. Physicians; mem. Am. Gastroenterologic Assn., Bockus Internat. Soc. Gastroenterology (trustee, v.p., pres. 1993-95), Phila. Gastroenterology Group (pres. 1974-75), Am. Coll. Gastroenterology (Master; gov. Ea. Pa. 1990-92, trustee 1992-96), Pa. Soc. Gastroenterology (pres. 1993-95), Delaware Valley Soc. Gastrointestinal Rsch. Forum, Pa. Med. Soc. (commn. on accreditation 1986-92), Phila. Med. Soc. (bd. dirs. 1996—, sec. 1998—, v.p. 1999-, pres. 2001-02), Musical Fund Soc. Phila. (physician, 2003—). Home: 720 Oxford Rd Bala Cynwyd PA 19004-2112 Office: 219 N Broad St Philadelphia PA 19102-1121 Office Phone: 215-762-6070. Personal E-mail: harris.clearfield@drexel.com.

CLEARY, BEVERLY ATLEE (MRS. CLARENCE T. CLEARY), writer; b. McMinnville, Oreg., Apr. 12, 1916; d. Chester Lloyd and Mable (Atlee) Bunn; m. Clarence T. Cleary, Oct. 6, 1940; children: Marianne Elisabeth, Malcolm James. BA, U. Calif., 1938; BA in Librarianship, U. Wash., 1939; LHD (hon.), Cornell Coll., 1993. Children's librarian Pub. Libr., Yakima, Wash., 1939-40; post librarian U.S. Army Regional Hosp., Oakland, Calif., 1942-45. Author: Henry Huggins, 1950, Ellen Tebbits, 1951, Henry and Beezus, 1952, Otis Spofford, 1953, Henry and Ribsy, 1954, Beezus and Ramona, 1955, Fifteen, 1956, Henry and the Paper Route, 1957, The Luckiest Girl, 1958, Jean and Johnny, 1959, The Real Hole, 1960, Hullabaloo ABC, 1960, 98, Two Dog Biscuits, 1961, Emily's Runaway Imagination, 1961, Henry and the Clubhouse, 1962, Sister of the Bride, 1963, Ribsy, 1964, The Mouse and the Motorcycle, 1965, Mitch and Amy, 1967, Ramona the Pest, 1968, Runaway Ralph, 1970, Socks, 1973, (play) The Sausage at the End of the Nose, 1974, Ramona the Brave, 1975, Ramona and Her Father, 1977 (Newbery Honor Book award ALA 1978), Ramona and Her Mother, 1979, Ramona Quimby, Age 8, 1981 (Newbery Honor Book award ALA 1982), Ralph S. Mouse, 1982, Dear Mr. Henshaw, 1983 (ALA Notable Book citation 1984, John Newbery medal 1984), Ramona Forever, 1984, Lucky Chuck, 1984, The Ramona Quimby Diary, 1984, Beezus and Ramona Diary, 1986, Janet's Thingamajigs, 1987, The Growing Up Feet, 1987, A Girl from Yamhill: A Memoir, 1988, Muggie Maggie, 1990, Strider, 1991, Petey's Bedtime Story, 1993, My Own Two Feet: A Memoir, 1995, Ramona's World, 1999. Recipient Disting. Alumna award U. Wash., 1975, Laura Ingalls Wilder award ALA, 1975, Regina medal Cath. Libr. Assn., 1980, De Grummond award U. Miss., 1982, U. So. Miss. medallion, 1982, Hans Christian Andersen medal nominee, 1984, Nat. Medal of the Arts, 2003, Libr. of Congress Living Legent medal, 2003. Mem. Authors Guild of Authors League Am. Office: c/o Harper Collins Children's Books 1350 Sixth Ave New York NY 10019-4702

CLEARY, DAVID MICHAEL, composer, critic, library assistant; b. Chelsea, Mass., Nov. 11, 1954; s. Robert Joseph and Sally Ann (Deuker) C.; m. Janice Tucker Rhoda, Jan. 21, 2001. MusB, New Eng. Conservatory Music, 1976; MusM, U. Hartford, 1978; MusD, U. Cin., 1982. Asst. to composition dept. New Eng. Conservatory Music, Boston, 1974-76; tchg. asst. in music theory U. Hartford, Conn., 1976-78, U. Cin., 1978-80, rotating instr. in music theory, 1980-81; libr. asst. Harvard U., Cambridge, Mass., 1984—. Assoc. prodr. The Composers Show, Sta. WGBH-FM, Boston, 1974-75; co-dir. Composers in Red Sneakers, 1994-2000, pres., 1997-2000. Compositions include Seven Bagatelles for Piano, 1975, Five Character Studies, 1979, A Gathering of Quokkas, 1985 (commd. Dinosaur Annex Ensemble), Lake George Overture, 1988, String Quartet no. 1, 1988, Gryllus, 1988-89, Cruikshank Fantasy, 1989 (commd. Alea III), Woodwind Quintet no. 2, 1990 (commd. Arcadian Winds), String Quartet no. 2, 1991 (commd. Artaria Quartet Boston), Linsner Sextet, 1992 (commd. Northwestern U. Trombone Ensemble), Western Wind Fragments, 1993-94 (commd. Eos Ensemble), Fanfares for Teddy Roosevelt, 1994-95, The Deeper Magic, 1995-96 (commd. Duo Renard), Fourteen Movie Characters, 1996-97 (commd. Am. Composers Forum Boston Area chpt.), Postcards from Annaghmakerrig, 1998, One Chord Wonders, 1999 (commd. Quincy Symphony), composer piano accompaniments ABCs of Strings Method Series, 2001—, Crosscultural Variations, 2002 (commd. Continental Harmony/Am. Composers Forum), SICPP Fantasies, 2002 (commd. SICPP Festival), Woodwind Quintet No. 3, 2003 (commd. Equinox Chamber Players); contbg. music writer (website) All-Music Guide, 1997—; (book) All Music Guide to Rock, 2d edit., 3d edit., 4th edit.; contbg. music critic New Music Connoisseur, 1999—, The Enterprise, 1999—, 21st Century Music, 2000—, Living Music, 2003—, Boston Herald, 2003—; contbr. articles to profl. jours.; recs. on Centaur, Vienna Modern Masters, New Ariel, Musicians Showcase CD labels. Mem. fellows coun. Va. Ctr. for the Creative Arts, 1999-02; bd. advisors Kalvos and Damian's New Music Bazaar, 1999—. Recipient 1st pl. Rosenberger Meml. Comm. Competition, Cin., 1989, Harvey Gaul Composition Competition, 1990; ASCAP grantee U. Hartford, 1978, grantee Somerville Arts Coun., 1987, 90, Meet the Composer, 1990, ASTRAL grantee Nat. Found. for Advancement in Arts, 1994; rsch. fellow U. Cin., 1980, Douglas W. Bryant fellow, 1988, fellow Va. Ctr. for Creative Arts, 1988-89, Yaddo fellow, 1988, Cummington fellow, 1989, Millay fellow, 1990, fellow Ella Lyman Cabot Trust, 1990, Ragdale fellow, 1992, MacDowell fellow, 1995, Tyrone Guthrie Ctr. fellow, 1998, Djerassi fellow, 2002. Mem. BMI, Am. Music Ctr., Am. Composers Forum, Soc. Composers, Electronic Music Found. Home: 7 Arlington St Apt 34 Cambridge MA 02140-2736 Office: Harvard U Biolabs Libr 16 Divinity Ave Cambridge MA 02138-2020 E-mail: dcleary@fas.harvard.edu.

CLEARY, EDWARD WILLIAM, retired diversified forest products company executive; b. Sergeant Bluff, Iowa, May 21, 1919; s. Edward D. and Laura Helen (Rich) C.; m. Arita Louise Hefferan, June 12, 1946; children: John William, Kathryn Louise, Patricia Jane. BA, DePauw U., 1941; BSc, Ohio State U., 1947. Sr. acct. Price Waterhouse & Co., Portland, Oreg., 1947-53; treas., contr. Nat. Hosp. Assn., Portland, 1953-55, Valsetz Lumber Co., Portland, 1955-60; asst. compt. Boise Cascade (Idaho) Corp., 1960-63, compt., 1963-68, v.p., compt., 1968, v.p., treas., 1968-80, v.p., 1980-82, ret., 1982. Chmn. bd. dirs. Farmers & Merchants State Bank, 1993-2002. Mem. Pacific N.W. Area coun. YMCA, 1967-70; mem. exec. com. Boise United Fund, 1966-69, chmn. budget com., 1966-69; pres., bd. dirs. YMCA, 1967-69; bd. dirs. Idaho Blue Cross Hosp. Assn., 1969-75, Discovery Ctr. of Idaho, 1990-99; past pres. Bogus Basin Recreation Assn., bd. dirs. 1973-91. With AUS, 1941-42, USNR, 1942-46. Mem. AICPA, Nat. Assn. Accts. (past pres. Boise chpt., past nat. dir.), Idaho Soc. C.P.A.'s, Hillcrest Country Club (past dir., past v.p.). Home: Apt 408 3110 Crescent Rim Dr Boise ID 83706 Personal E-mail: ecleary1@mindspring.com.

CLEARY, JOHN JOSEPH (JACK), lawyer; b. Boston, Nov. 24, 1946; s. John Joseph and Mildred Kathleen (Bell) C.; m. Nancy Jean Miller, June 1, 1968; children: Nina Dorothy, Eric John. BS, MIT, 1968; MPhil, Yale U., 1970; JD magna cum laude, Harvard U., 1974. Bar: Mass. 1974. Assoc. Goodwin, Procter & Hoar, Boston, 1974-81; ptnr., employee benefits practice group Goodwin Procter LLP (formerly Goodwin, Procter & Hoar), Boston, 1981—. Dir. N.E. Employee Benefits Coun., Wellesley, Mass., 1988-94. Mem. Needham (Mass.) Youth Commn., 1984-86; dir. Cath. Meml. High Sch., West Roxbury, Mass., 1987-95. Mem. ABA, Mass. Bar Assn., Boston Bar Assn. (past co-chmn. ERISA com. 1987-89), Dedham Country and Polo Club. Roman Catholic. Avocations: golf, theater, travel. Office: Goodwin Procter Exchange Pl Boston MA 02109-2881 Office Phone: 617-570-1199. Office Fax: 617-523-1231. Business E-Mail: jcleary@goodwinprocter.com.

CLEARY, MANON CATHERINE, retired artist, educator; d. Frank and Crystal (Maret) C. Attended, U. Valencia, Spain, Cocoran Sch. Art; BFA, Washington U., St. Louis, 1964; MFA, Temple U., 1968. Instr. fine arts SUNY, Oswego, 1968-70; from instr. to assoc. prof. D.C. Tchrs. Coll., Washington, 1970-78; from assoc. prof. to prof. art U. DC, Washington, 1978—2004, 2005, ret., 2005. One woman shows include Mus. Modern Art Gulbenkian Found., Lisbon, Portugal, 1985, Iolas/Jackson Gallery, NYC, 1982, Osuna Gallery, Washington, 1974, 77, 80, 84, 89, Univ. D.C., 1987, Tyler Gallery SUNY at Oswego, 1987, J. Rosenthal Fine Arts, Washington, 1991, Addison/Ripley Gallery, Washington, 1994, 99, Md. Arts Pl., 1997, Kramer Book Afterwords, 1998, Pass Gallery, Washington, 2000, others; group exhibits include Twentieth Century Am. Drawings: The Figure in Context, Traveled Nat. Acad. Design, 1984-85, Butler Inst. Am. Art, Youngstown, Ohio, 1987, Art Inst. Chgo., 1999-00, Huntsville (Ala.) Mus., 1987, Boca Raton (Fla.) Mus. Art, 1987, Corcoran Gallery Art, Washington, 1987, 96, Dimock Gallery, Washington, 1987, Tretyakov Gallery, Moscow, 1990, Nohra Haime Gallery, N.Y.C., 1994, Holter Mus., Helena, Mont., 1996, Gallery Stendahl, NYC, 1996, Alt. Mus., NYC, 1996, Kasteyev Mus., Almaty, Kazakstan, 1996, Alouan Gallery, Almaty, 1997, Art Inst. Chgo., 1999-2000, RAP, Rockville, Md., 2000-01, Nat. Mus. Women in the Arts, Washington, 2000, others; artist-in-residence Herning Hojskole, Denmark, 1980, Ucross Found., Wyo., 1984, Bridge Assn., Creative Lab. Project, Almaty, 1996, 97. Recipient Mayor's 14th ann. award for excellence in an artistic discipline, 1998; individual artist grantee D.C. Commn. on the Arts, 2000-01. Mem. Coll. Art Assn., Pi Beta Phi. Personal E-mail: manonart@aol.com.

CLEARY, PAUL DAVID, sociomedical educator; b. Toronto, May 14, 1948; s. Frank C. and Janet E. (Sweeney) Cleary; m. Cynthia F. Barnett, May 20, 1982; children: Janet A., Barnett D. BS in Physics, U. Wis., 1970, MS in Sociology, 1973, PhD in Sociology, 1980. Lectr. dept. sociology U. Wis., 1976-77; asst. rsch. prof. grad. sch. of social work Rutgers U., 1979-81, assoc. rsch. prof., 1981-82; asst. prof. dept. social medicine and health policy Harvard Med. Sch., 1982-87, assoc. prof. dept. health care policy and social medicine, 1988-92, prof. dept. health care policy and social medicine, 1993—; lectr., prof. dept. behavioral scis. Harvard Sch. of Pub. Health, 1983—2000; vis. assoc. prof. dept. sociomed. scis. Columbia U. Sch. of Pub. Health, 1988—. Rsch. assoc. dept. medicine Beth Israel Hosp., Boston, 1982—; assoc. epidemiologist dept. medicine, Brigham and Women's Hosp., Boston, 1987—; cons. Marshfield Rsch. Found., 1978-80, Hershey Med. Sch., Nat. Heart, Lung, and Blood Inst., Bundesgesundheitsamt, West Berlin, 1983-85, Harvard Inst. for Internat. Devel. Applied Diarrheal Disease Rsch. Project; mem. study sect. NIMH, 1980, 81, 85-89; study sect. sci. adv. com. Am. Found. AIDS Rsch., 1987-92; mem. program rev. panel Mass. AIDS Office, 1988-91; local adv. com. VIII Internat. Conf. on AIDS, 1989-92, co-chair social sci., policy, and law track, 1990-92; mem. faculty coun. Harvard Med. Sch., 1991-93, com. promotions, reappointments and appointments, 1993-96; vis. prof. Dept. Sociology, U. Stockholm, Sweden, 1982. Author: The Three Mile Island Nuclear Accident, 1988; author: (with others) Heart Disease and Rehabilitation, 1979, Handbook of Health, Health Care and the Health Professions, 1983, Heart Disease and Rehabilitation, 1986, Illness Behavior: A Multidisciplinary Model, 1986, Taking Care: Understanding and Encouraging Self-Protective Behavior, 1987, Gender and Stress, 1987, AIDS: The Safety of Blood and Blood Products, 1987, Evaluating Family Programs, 1988, The Future of Mental Health Services Research, 1989, AIDS and The Health Care System, 1990, Depression in Primary Care: Screening and Detection, 1990, Effectiveness and Outcomes in Health Care, 1990, International Law and AIDS: International Responses, Current Issues and Future Directions, 1992; assoc. editor: Jour. of Health and Social Behavior, 1983—86, 1989—92; editor: The Milbank Quar., 1992—2000. Mem.: AAAS, Inst. of Medicine, Assn. of Health Svcs. Rsch., Am. Sociol. Assn. (med. sociology sect. nominations com. 1985—86, 1989—90). Office: Harvard Med Sch Dept Health Care Policy 180 Longwood Ave Boston MA 02115-5821

CLEARY, ROBERT EMMET, gynecologist, infertility specialist; b. July 17, 1937; s. John J. and Brigid (O'Grady) C.; m. June 10, 1961; children: William Joseph, Theresa Marie, John Thomas. MD, U. Ill., 1962. Diplomate Am. Bd. Ob-Gyn, Am. Fertility Soc. Intern St. Franis Hosp., Evanston, 1962-63, resident, 1963-66; practice medicine specializing in gynecology and infertility Chgo., 1970—. Head Sect. of Reproductive Endocrinology and Infertility, Chgo. Lying-In Hosp., U. Chgo., 1968-70; head Sect. of Reproductive Endocrinology and Infertility, Ind. U. Med. Center, Indpls., 1970-80; prof. ob-gyn Ind. U., Indpls., 1976-80, clin. prof. ob-gyn, 1980—2003, prof. emeritus, 2004—. Contbr. articles to profl. jours. Recipient Meml. award pacific Coast Obstetrical and Gynecol. Soc., 1968. Fellow ACOG, Am. Soc. Reproductive Medicine; mem. Endocrine Soc., Soc. Gynecol. Investigation, Pacific Coast Fertility Soc., Soc. Reproductive Endocrinologists, Soc. Reproductive Surgeons, N.Y. Acad. Scis., Sigma Xi. Roman Catholic. Home: 7036 Dubonnet Ct Indianapolis IN 46278-1541

CLEARY, SEAN MICHAEL, risk management consultant; b. Somerset West, South Africa, Oct. 26, 1948; s. Thomas Stanislaus and Isobel Forsyth Cranston (Bell) C.; m. Sophia Natalie Smit, June 5, 1971; children: Sean Michael, Mary Siobhan. BA, U. South Africa, 1969; MBA, Brunel U., England, 1999. Vice consul, consul SA Consulate Gen., Tehran, Iran, 1971-75; deputy head econ. & fin. rels. divsn. Min. Fgn. Affairs, Pretoria, South Africa, 1976—77, head tng. divsn., 1978; polit. counsellor South African Embassy, Washington, 1978-82; consul gen. SA Consulate Gen., Beverly Hills, Calif., 1982-83; chief dir. Office of Adminstr. Gen., Windhoek, Nambia, 1983-85; mng. dir. Strategic Concepts Ltd., Johannesburg, 1985—. Guest lectr. Grad. Sch. Bus., UNISA, Johannesburg, 1986—, Witwatersrand Bus. Sch., Johannesburg, 2002, Henley Mgmt. Coll., England, 2002—; faculty mem. Italy and Germany Parmenides Found. Grad. Inst. Mgmt. and Tech., Johannesburg, 1996—; faculty mem. Internat. Ctr. for Mgmt. Devel., Johannesburg, Gordon Inst. Bus. Sci.; forum fellow World Econ. Forum; vice chmn. Meridian Worldwide LLC, 1998—; mng. dir. Ctr. Advanced Governance; mgmt. bd. Think Tools AG, 1999—2003, supervisory bd., 2003—, RedIT AG, 2004—; mem. facilitating and prep. com. Nat. Peace Accord, 1992; chair Working Group on Code of Conduct for Polit. Parties/Orgn.; mem. bd. Lead Internat. Contbr. articles to profl. jours. Mem. Africa Task Force, World Econ. Forum, South African Inst. Internat. Affairs, Africa Inst. South Africa, Soc. Advancement Socio-Econs. Avocations: fishing, riding, writing, music. Home: The Lodge Silverhurst Silverhurst Est Constantia 7806 Cape Town South Africa Office Phone: +271 3154600. Personal E-mail: sean.cleary@thinktools.com. Business E-Mail: scleary@stratconcepts.co.za.

CLEARY, THOMAS CHARLES, technology company executive; b. Chgo., Nov. 15, 1921; s. Thomas Harold and Mary Margaret (Russell) C.; m. Barbara Winnifred Johnson, Dec. 18, 1948; children: Thomas Robert, Margaret Mary Cleary Nurmia, Mary Ann Cleary Robitaille. BS in Mech. Engring., UCLA, 1949. Pres., gen. mgr. Whittaker Corp., Denver, 1950-63; dir. program mgmt. Litton Industries, Woodland Hills, Calif., 1963-65; asst. gen. mgr. Teledyne Sys., Inc., 1965-66; v.p., CEO Viking Industries, Chatsworth, Calif., 1966-67; v.p. Power Conversion, Inc., Long Beach, Calif., 1967-68; chmn. bd. dirs., mng. dir. TRW Electronic Comp. Co., Taiwan,

Republic of China, 1968-69; pres., CEO Deutsch Relays, Inc., East Northport, NY, 1969-89, Struthers Dunn-Hi G, Pitman, NJ, 1989-91; chmn., CEO G&H Tech., Inc., Camarillo, Calif., 1992—. Author: Dynamic Management System, 1990, Management By Intent, 1991. Fundraiser Meml. Sloan-Kettering Cancer Ctr., N.Y., 1989—; mem. chancellor's assocs. UCLA, 1992—, mem. exec. com., dean's coun., sch. engring., 1992—; mem. bd. councillors UCLA Found., 1997. Capt. inf. U.S. Army, 1942-50, PTO. Named Entrepreneur of Yr. in mfg. Greater L.A. Area, 1997. Republican. Roman Catholic. Achievements include patents in the gyroscope and relay areas. Office: G&H Tech Inc 750 W Ventura Blvd Camarillo CA 93010-8382

CLEARY, TIMOTHY FINBAR, professional society administrator; b. Cork, Ireland, Sept. 30, 1925; s. John Francis and Nora (Riordan) C.; m. Patricia Agnes Hanley, June 21, 1947; children: Timothy F. X., Maureen P., Therese A., Richard S., Gail P., Eileen P. BS, Fordham U., 1955, JD, 1959. Bar: N.Y. 1959, D.C. 1980. Atty. N.Y.C. Police Dept., 1959-67; asst. counsel Fair Labor Standards div. U.S. Dept. Labor, Washington, 1967-71, chief counsel, 1971-73, mem., 1973-85; cons. in occupational safety and health, 1985—; exec. dir. Nat. Trust for Tng., Edn. and Research in Constrn., 1987-1991; internal campaign contbn. administrator Internat. Brotherhood Elec. Workers. Chmn. U.S. Occupational Safety and Health Rev. Commn., Washington, 1977-81; mem. Adminstrv. Conf. U.S.; cert. arbitrator Nat. Mediation Bd.; lectr. labor law Practising Law Inst., U. Wis., Washington and Lee U., Cumberland Sch. Law, Ohio No. U., Brookings Instn., AFL-CIO Center for Labor Studies, Gompers-Murray Inst.Trade Assc., numerous others. Contbr. articles to profl. jours. Served with USN, 1943-45. Mem.: Friendly Sons St. Patrick, D.C. Home and Office: 5709 Cheshire Dr Bethesda MD 20814-2207 Office Phone: 301-530-6570.

CLEARY, WILLIAM JOSEPH, JR., lawyer; b. Wilmington, NC, Aug. 14, 1942; s. William Joseph and Eileen Ada (Gannon) C. AB in History, St. Joseph's U., 1964; JD, Villanova U., 1967. Bar: N.J., 1967, Calif. 1982, U.S. Ct. Appeals (3d cir.) 1969, U.S. Ct. Appeals (9th cir.) 1983, U.S. Dist. Ct. (ctrl. dist.) Calif. 1983, U.S. Supreme Ct. 1992. Law sec. to judge N.J. Superior Ct., Jersey City, 1967-68; assoc. Lamb, Blake, H&D, Jersey City, 1968-72; dep. pub. defender State of N.J., Newark, 1972-73; 1st asst. city corp. counsel Jersey City, N.J., 1973-76; assoc. Robert Wasserwald, Inc., Hollywood, Calif., 1984-86, Gould & Burke, Century City, Calif., 1986-87; pvt. practice Hollywood, 1989—. Mem. ABA, FBA, N.J. State Bar Assn., Calif. Bar Assn., L.A. County Bar Assn. (appellate cts. com.), Nat. Jesuit Hon. Soc., Alpha Sigma Nu. Democrat. Roman Catholic. Office: 1853 1/2 Canyon Dr Los Angeles CA 90028-5607 Office Phone: 323-856-0436. E-mail: jmclaw42@aol.com.

CLEAVE, MARY L., environmental engineer, former astronaut; b. Southampton, N.Y., Feb. 5, 1947; BS in Biol. Scis., Colo. State U., 1969; MS in Microbiol. Ecology, Utah State U., 1975, PhD in Civil and Environ. Engring., 1979. Mem. rsch. staff Utah State U., 1971-80; astronaut NASA, Lyndon B. Johnson Space Ctr., Houston, 1980-90, mission specialist STS 61-B, 1985, mission specialist STS-30, 1989; now dep. project mgr. NASA Ocean Color Satellite Program, Greenbelt, Md. Mem. Tex. Soc. Profl. Engrs., Water Pollution Control Fedn., Sigma Xi, Tau Beta Pi. Office: NASA Headquarters 300 E St SW Washington DC 20024-3202

CLEAVER, EMANUEL, II, congressman, former mayor, minister; b. Waxahachie, Tex., Oct. 26, 1944; s. Lucky and Marie (McKnight) Cl; m. Dianne Donaldson, June 1970; children: Evan Donaldson, Emanuel III and Emiel Davenport (twins), Marissa Dianne. BA, Prairie View (Tex.) A&M Coll.; ThM, St. Paul Sch. Theology, Kansas City, Mo.; DD (hon.), Baker U., 1988. Ordained to ministry United Meth. Ch. Pastor St. James-Paseo United Meth. Ch.; council mem. City of Kansas City, 1979—91, mayor pro-tem, 1987-91, mayor, 1991—99; mem. U.S. Ho. Reps., 109th Congress, 5th Dist. Mo., 2005—. Lectr. to chs., schs., civic and social orgns. nationwide. Councilman Fifth Dist. City, 1979-91; chmn. City Coun. Plans and Zoning Com., 1984-87, Policy and Rules Com., 1987-91; mid-cen. regional v.p. So. Christian Leadership Conf., Drum Major for Justice award, 1991; founder, co-chair Kansas City Harmony In A World of Difference. Recipient Centurions Leadership award Greater Kansas City C. of C., 1987, William Yates Disting. Svc. Medallion William Jewel Coll., 1987, Pub. Svc. award Am.-Jewish Com., 1991, Junteenth Man of Yr. award Black Archives of Mid-Am. Inc., 1991, Disting. Citizen award Greater Kansas City Urban Affairs Coun., 1991, Community Svc./Leadership award Webster U., 1991, Disting. Svc. award Park Coll., 1991, Drum Major of Justice award Nat. SCLC, 1991, Friend of Youth award Boys & Girls Clubs, 1991, Outstanding Contbns. to Black Cmty. award Concerned Citizens Black Clergy of Atlanta, 1991, Rainbow award, 1992, 100 Most Influential Kansas Citians award Kansas City Globe, 1991, 92, 93, Bridge Builders award Kansas City Globem 1992, Harold L. Holiday Sr. Civil Rights award NAACP, 1992, Disting. Grad. award St. Paul Sch. Theology, 1993, Kansas City Anti-Apartheid award, 1993, James C. Kirkpatrick Excellence for Govt. award, 1993, Disting. Citizen of Midwest award NCCJ, 1993, Gov. award for local elected ofcl. of yr. State of Mo., 1994. Mem. NAACP, Greater Kansas City C. of C. (Centurions Leadership award 1987), Alpha Phi Alpha. Founder and co-chmn., Harmony In A World of Difference program. Democrat. Office: 1641 Longworth House Office Bldg Washington DC 20515-2505 Office Phone: 202-225-4535.*

CLEAVER, JAMES EDWARD, radiologist, educator; b. Portsmouth, England, May 17, 1938; came to the U.S., 1964; s. Edward Alfred and Kathleen Florence (Cleveley) C.; m. Christine J. Cleaver, Aug. 8, 1964; children: Jonathan, Alison. BA, St. Catharine's Coll., 1961; PhD, U. Cambridge, 1964. Rsch. fellow Mass. Gen. Hosp., Boston, 1964-66; asst. rsch. biophysicist lab. radiobiology environ. health U. Calif., San Francisco, 1966-68, asst. prof. radiology, 1968-70, assoc. prof. radiology, 1970-74, prof. radiology, 1974—; vis. prof. Imperial Cancer Rsch. Fund, London, 1973-74, prof. radiology, 1975-96, prof. dermatology, 1996—. Contbr. over 350 articles to profl. jours. Recipient Lila Gruber award Am. Acad. Dermatology, 1976, Sr. Investigator award Am. Soc. Photobiology, 1995, Luigi Provasoli award Phycol. Soc. Am., 1992, J. Little award for radiation rsch. Harvard U., 2003. Mem. NAS, Nat. Coun. on Radiation Protection, Radiation Rsch. Soc. (councillor 1982-84, Rsch. award 1973).

CLEAVES, PETER SHURTLEFF, foundation administrator; b. Washington, Dec. 4, 1943; s. Richard Delaplane and Margaret Grant (Shurtleff) C.; m. Dorothy Barchan, Aug. 31, 1968; children: Geoffrey, Rachel. AB, Dartmouth Coll., 1966; MA, Vanderbilt U., 1968; PhD, U. Calif., Berkeley, 1972. Escort interpreter U.S. Dept. State, Washington, 1966-68; assoc. rep. for Peru, Ecuador and Bolivia, Ford Found., Lima, Peru, 1972-76, rep. for Mex. and C.Am., Mexico City, 1977-82; vis. scholar Yale U., New Haven, 1976-77; v.p. 1st Nat. Bank Chgo., 1982-90; prof. U. Tex., Austin, 1990-99, dir. Inst. Latin Am. Studies, 1990-95, dir. Ctr. for Study Western Hemisphere Trade, 1995-97; exec. dir. Avina Found., Hurden, Switzerland, 1997—2004. Cons. UN U., Tokyo, 1977, various corp. and non-profit orgns. in Latin Am., 1990—. Author: Bureaucratic Politics and Administration in Chile, 1974, Agriculture, Bureaucracy and Military Government in Peru, 1980, Profession and the State, The Mexican Case, 1987, Latin America in the 21st Century, 2003; also numerous articles. Chmn., trustee Internat. Sch. Panama, Panama City, 1984-86; advisor on L.Am. policy position papers Nat. Dem. Com., Washington, 1988, 92, 96. William Hill Meml. fellow Dartmouth Coll., 1966, NDEA Title VI fellow U. Calif., 1968, Doherty rsch. fellow Doherty Found., 1970, Fulbright-Hays fellow, 1971. Mem. L.Am. Studies Assn., Barton Creek Country Club. Episcopalian. Avocations: tennis, languages. Office: AVINA 1015 Beecave Woods Rd Ste 203 Austin TX 78746-6752 Fax: 512-329-5016. Office Phone: 512-327-9393. E-mail: pcleaves@drgconsultants.com.

CLEESE, JOHN MARWOOD, writer, comedian; b. Weston-Super-Mare, Eng., Oct. 27, 1939; s. Reginald and Muriel Cleese; m. Connie Booth, Feb. 20, 1968 (div. 1978); 1 child, Cynthia; m. Barbara Trentham, Feb. 15, 1981 (div. 1990); 1 child, Camilla; m. Alyce Faye Elchelberger, Dec. 28, 1992. Student, Clifton Coll., Bristol, Eng.; MA, Cambridge (Eng.) U.; LLD (hon.), St. Andrews U. Andrew D. White prof.-at-large Cornell U., 1999—. Writer, performer (TV series) The Frost Report, 1966, At Last the 1948 Show, others; actor: (TV series) Monty Python's Flying Circus, Fawlty Towers, Third Rock from the Sun, 1998 (Emmy nomination), The Human Face, 2001; (TV films) The Taming of the Shrew, 1981, (guest appearance): (TV series) Cheers (Emmy award for Outstanding Guest Performer in a Comedy Series, 1987),: (films) Interlude, 1968, The Magic Christian, 1970, The Rise and Rise of Michael Rimmer, 1970, And Now for Something Completely Different, 1972, Monty Python and the Holy Grail, 1975, Romance with a Double Bass, 1975, Life of Brian, 1979, The Secret Policeman's Ball, 1979, Time Bandits, 1981, Monty Python Live at the Hollywood Bowl, 1982, The Secret Policemen's Other Ball, 1982, Privates on Parade, Yellowbeard, 1983, The Meaning of Life, 1983, Silverado, 1984, Clockwise, 1986, Erik the Viking, 1988, Splitting Heirs, 1992, Mary Shelley's Frankenstein, 1994, Jungle Book, 1994, The Out-of-Towners, Isn't She Great, 1998, The World is Not Enough, 1999, Rat Race, 2000, Harry Potter and the Sourcerer's Stone, 2001, Die Another Day, 2002, Harry Potter and the Chamber of Secrets, 2002, Scorched, 2003, Charlie's Angels: Full Throttle, 2003, (voice) Shrek 2, 2004, Around the World in 80 Days, 2004, (voice) Valiant, 2005, Complete Guide to Guys, 2005; actor, writer: A Fish Called Wanda, 1988; actor(voice actor): Fierce Creatures, 1997; co-author: (book) The Strange Case of the End of Civilization as We Know It, 1977, Monty Python's Big Red Book, 1975, Families and How to Survive Them, 1983, Life and How to Survive It, 1993, The Human Face, 2001; founder, former dir. Video Arts Ltd., London, 1979—91 (Queen's award for Exports, 1982), creator TV and radio commls. Office: care David Wilkinson 115 Hazlebury Rd London SW6 2LX England*

CLEGG, JAMES STANDISH, physiologist, biochemist, educator; b. Aspinwall, Pa., July 27, 1933; divorced; 3 children; m. Eileen Clegg; 1 stepchild. AA in Biology, Coffeyville Coll., 1953; BS in Zoology, Pa. State U., 1958; PhD in Biology, Johns Hopkins U., 1961. Rsch. assoc. biologist Johns Hopkins U., 1961-62; asst. prof. zoology U. Miami, 1962-64, from assoc. prof. biology to prof., 1964-70; prof. sect. molecular and cellular biology U. Calif., Davis, 1986—, dir. Bodega Marine Lab., 1986-98. With CNRS Thias France, 1983; pres. Nat. Assn. Marine Labs., 1992-94. With U.S. Army, 1953—55. Recipient Fulbright Sr. Rsch. award U. London, 1978, U. Ghent, 1999; Wilson fellow, 1958-59. Fellow AAAS; mem. Am. Soc. Zoologists, Am. Soc. Cell Biology, Biophys. Soc., Soc. Cryobiology, Sigma Xi. Independent. Achievements include research in comparative biochemistry and biophysics; mechanisms of cryptobiosis; properties and role of water in cellular metabolism; cytoplasmic organization. Office: U Calif Bodega Marine Lab PO Box 247 Bodega Bay CA 94923-0247 Office Phone: 707-875-2010. Business E-Mail: jsclegg@ucdavis.edu.

CLEGG, KAREN KOHLER, lawyer; b. Junction City, Kans., Jan. 7, 1949; d. John Emil and Delores Maxine (Letkeman) Kohler; m. Stephen J. Clegg Jr., Mar. 28, 1970. BS, Emporia State U., 1970; JD, U. Kans., 1975; MBA, Rockhurst Coll., 1989. Bar: Kans. 1975, U.S. Dist. Ct. Kans. 1975, Mo. 1977, U.S. Dist. Ct. (we. dist.) Mo. 1977. Asst. atty. gen. State of Kans., Topeka, 1975-77; atty. The Bendix Corp., Kansas City, Mo., 1977-81, sr. atty., 1981-84; counsel Allied Corp. (now Allied Signal, Inc.), Kansas City, 1984-90, v.p. adminstrn., 1990—93, v.p. field svcs. Columbus, Md., 1994—95, v.p. ops. Kansas City, 1995—2001; pres. Honeywell Fed. Mfg. and Technologies Honeywell Internat., 2001—02, v.p. def. and space programs, Honeywell Aerospace; ret. Mem. council human resources mgmt. adv. bd. Commerce Clearing House, Chgo., 1985-88. Sec. Assn. Greater Devel. Coll. Blvd., Shawnee Mission, Kans., 1986-87; bd. dirs. adv. council Avila Coll. Bus., Kansas City, 1984—, Dimension's Unltd., Kansas City, 1985-86. Mem. ABA, Mo. Bar Assn., Am. Soc. Personnel Adminstrn. (v.p., bd. dirs. EEO 1985, profl. services 1986-87), Greater Kansas City C. of C. (centurian leadership program). Avocations: music, theater, art, reading, travel. Office: Honeywell 2000 E 95th St Kansas City MO 64131-3030 Home: 6909 Burnt Sienna Cir Naples FL 34109-7828

CLEGG, ROGER BURTON, lawyer; b. Odessa, Tex., Apr. 18, 1955; s. Joe Dunn and Margaret Elisabeth (Blau) C.; m. Joann Ruth Catalfamo, June 15, 1985; 1 child, Paul. BA magna cum laude, Rice U., 1977; JD, Yale U., 1981. Bar: D.C. 1981. Grad. fellow Office Gen. Counsel, CIA, Langley, Va.; mem. staff editorial and research div. Republican Nat. Com., Washington, 1980; law clk. to presiding judge U.S. Ct. Appeals, Washington, 1981-82; atty.- adviser office of legal policy U.S. Dept. Justice, Washington, 1982, spl. asst. to atty. gen., 1982-83, dep. asst. atty. gen., 1983-84, acting asst. atty. gen., office legal policy, 1984, assoc. dep. atty. gen., 1984-85, spl. litigation counsel, civil div., 1985, asst. to solicitor gen., 1985-87, dep. asst. atty. gen. civil rights div., 1987-91, dep. asst. atty. gen. env. div., 1991-93; v.p., gen. counsel Nat. Legal Ctr. for Pub. Interest, Washington, 1993-97, Ctr. for Equal Opportunity, Washington, 1997—. Editor-in-chief Yale Studies in World Public Order, 1979-80. Mem.: D.C. Bar, Federalist Soc., Phi Beta Kappa. Republican. Methodist. Home: 9703 Flintridge Ct Fairfax VA 22032-1712 Office: Ste 500 14 Pidgeon Hill Dr Sterling VA 20165 Office Phone: 703-421-5443.

CLEGHORN, JOHN EDWARD, bank executive; b. Montreal, July 7, 1941; m. Pattie E. Hart; children: Charles, Ian, Andrea. B in Commerce, McGill U., Montreal, 1962; DCL (hon.), Bishop's U., 1989; LLD (hon.), Wilfrid Laurier U., 1991; DCL (hon.), Acadia U., 1996. Chartered acct. Articled with Clarkson Gordon, chartered Accts., Montreal, 1962-64; sugar and futures trader St. Lawrence Sugar Ltd., Montreal, 1964-66; with Citibank, NY, Montreal, Winnipeg & Vancouver, 1966—74; with Royal Bank of Canada, Montreal, Toronto & Vancouver, 1974—86, pres., 1986-90; pres., COO RBC, 1990—94; CEO Royal Bank of Can., Montreal, 1994-95, chmn., CEO, 1995—2001; chmn., bd. dirs. SNC Lavalin Group, Inc., 2001—. Bd. dirs. Finning Internat. Inc., Nortel Networks, Can. Pacific Ry. Ltd., Molson Inc, McGill U; chmn. internat. adv. bd. McGill Faculty Mgmt.; dir. Can. Spl. Olympics Found.; chancellor emeritus Wilfrid Laurier U. Chmn. Hist. Found. of Can. Fellow Order of Chartered Accts. Quebec, Inst. Chartered Accts. Ont.; mem. Can. Inst. Chartered Accts. Office: Ste 3115 31st Flr S Tower 200 Bay St Royal Bank Plz Toronto ON Canada M5J 2J5 Business E-Mail: john.cleghorn@rbc.com.

CLEGHORN, JOHN MICHAEL, communications executive; b. Atlanta, Jan. 15, 1962; s. George Reese and Gwendolyn Michael C.; m. Ellison Kelly Johnston; children: Ellison, Sophie. BA, Washington and Lee U., 1984. Journalist Charlotte (N.C.) Observer, 1984-90; chief speech writer Bank of Am., Charlotte, 1990-97, issues mgmt. exec., 1995-2000, corp. affairs exec. consumer and comml. banking, 2001—03, exec. communications mgr., 2003—. Dir. Issues Mgmt. Coun., Washington. Editor: Words That Mattered: The Speeches of Hugh L. McColl, Jr., 1990-2000, 2001. Dir. Washington and Lee U. Bd. Alumni, Lexington, Va., 2000; bd. advisors U. N.C. Sch. Social Work, Charlotte, 1998—2002; elder, past clk. session Covenant Presbyn. Ch., Charlotte; participant Leadership Charlotte; chair, bd. dirs. Family Ctr., Charlotte, 1994-95; vice chair Annual Fund Washington and Lee U., exington, Va.; dir. Seversville Ptnrs. Inc., Charlotte, 1987-92; bd. dirs. Novello Festival Press, 2002-. Recipient Disting. Young Alumnus Washington and Lee U., 1989, Outstanding Grad. in Journalism Simga Delta Chi, 1984, Excellence in Consumer Edn. award Nat. Assn. Consumer Agy. Adminstrs., 1998, Sch. Bell award for excellence in edn. reporting N.C. Assn. Educators, 1986. Mem. Am. Bankers Assn. Presbyterian. Office: Bank Am 101 S Tryon St Charlotte NC 28255

CLEINO, EDWARD H., music educator; b. Rolla, Mo. s. Henry and Lula Pharess Cleino; m. Elizabeth Anne White, Mar. 7, 1943; children: Anne Witt, William Henry, Jeanne Perkins, Elizabeth Allaway, Barbie. BS in Edn., Southeast Mo. State, Cape Girardeau, 1938; MA in Music Edn., George Peabody Coll. (now Vanderbilt U.), Nashville, 1940, PhD in Music Edn., 1958. Tchr. secondary music, New Madrid, Mo., 1938—39; dir. choral music and band George Peabody Coll. (now Vanderbilt U.), Nashville, 1939—42; prof. music and music edn. U. Ala., Tuscaloosa, 1949—79, prof. emeritus, 1979—. Percussionist/timpanist St. Louis Symphony Orch., 1933—35, Nashville Symphony Orch., 1946—49, Birmingham Symphony Orch., Ala., 1949—51; mentor freshman music students U. Ala., Tuscaloosa, 1980—2003. Capt. USAF, 1942—46, PTO. Recipient Educator of Yr., Druid Arts, 2004, Algernon Sidney Sullivan award, U. Ala., 2005. Mem.: Ala. Music Educators Assn. (sec. 1980—90, editor Ala. Breve mag. 1980—90), So. Assn. Music Educators Nat. Conf. (pres. 1968—70), Music Educators Nat. Conf. (life). Independent. Episcopalian. Home: 7 Hickory Hill Tuscaloosa AL 35404 Office Phone: 205-553-7735.

CLELAND, CHARLES CARR, psychologist, educator; b. Murphysboro, Ill., May 15, 1924; s. Homer W. and Stella (Carr) C.; m. Betty Lou Woodburn, July 18, 1948 BS, So. Ill. U., 1950, MS, 1951; PhD, U. Tex., 1957. Lic. psychologist, Tex. Chief psychologist Lincoln State Sch., Ill., 1956-57; chief psychologist Austin State Sch., 1957-59; supt. Abilene State Sch. Tex., 1959-63; prof. spl. edn. and ednl. psychology U. Tex.-Austin, 1963—. Author: Mental Retardation, 1969, 2d edit., 1978, Handbook for Widowers, 1997, Profound Retardation, 1979, Exceptionalities, 1982; contbr. articles to profl. jours.; patentee in field Bd. dirs. Child Guidance Ctr., Austin, 1966-67. Served with USAAF, 1943-46, PTO Recipient Disting. Psychologist award Tex. Psychol. Assn., 1980, Edn. award Am. Assn. Mental Deficiency, 1978 Fellow AAAS, Am. Psychol. Assn., Am. Assn. for Mental Deficiency (v.p. psychology div. 1973); mem. Tex. Psychol. Assn. (pres. 1962-63) Republican. Presbyterian. Office: U Tex E Db408A Austin TX 78712

CLELAND, JOSEPH MAXWELL (MAX CLELAND), federal official, former senator; b. Atlanta, Ga., Aug. 24, 1942; s. Joseph Hugh and Juanita (Kesler) C. BA, Stetson U., Deland, Fla., 1964, LLD (hon.), 1979; MA, Emory U., 1968, hon. degree. Mem. Ga. Senate, Atlanta, 1971-75; cons. Com. on Vets. Affairs, U.S. Senate, Washington, 1975, profl. staff mem., 1975-77; adminstr. VA, Washington, 1977-81; sec. of state State of Ga., Atlanta, 1982-95; U.S. senator from Ga, 1997—2003; mem. armed svcs. com., govtl. affairs com., small bus. com.; disting. adj. prof. Am. Univs. Washington Semester Program, 2003—. Mem. commerce com. U.S. Senate, 1999-2003; strategic cons. The Carmen Group, 2003—, mem. Export-Import Bank of the US, 2003- Author: Strong at the Broken Places, 2000, Going for the Max!: 12 Principles for Living Life to the Fullest, 2002. Candidate U.S. Senate, Ga., 1996. Capt. U.S. Army, 1965-68, Vietnam. Decorated Bronze Star, Silver Star; fellow Ctr. for Congrl. and Presdl. Studies, 2003—; recipient Disting. Alumnus award Stetson U., 1972, Gt. Georgian award WSB Radio, award for gallantry Easter Seal Soc., 1973, Outstanding Handicapped Citizen in Ga. award, 1973, Jefferson award for greatest pub. service by individual under 35 Am. Inst. Pub. Service, 1977, Inspiration award Assn. U.S. Army, Atlanta, 1978, AMP of Yr. award, 1978, Life Inspiration award Religious Heritage Am., 1978, Golden Key award Am. Assn. Sch. Adminstrs., 1978, Gold medallion Chapel of Four Chaplains, 1979, Am. Patriot's medal Valley Forge Freedom's Found., 1979, J.O. Wright award, 1979, Neal Pike award, 1979, Citizen of Yr. award Nat. Conf. Citizenship, 1986; named One of Five Outstanding Young Men in Ga. Ga. Jaycees, Outstanding Disabled Vet. DAV, one of 100 most influential people in Ga. by Ga. Trend mag. Democrat. Office: Export-Import Bank of the US 811 Vermont Ave NW Washington DC 20571

CLELAND, SHERRILL, college president; b. Galion, Ohio, Sept. 21, 1924; s. Fred Burr and Doris Louise (Gregg) C.; m. Betty Irene Chorpenning, July 6, 1946 (dec. June 1986); children: Ann Denise Cleland Feldmeier, Douglas Stewart, Sarah McDermott Cleland Allen, Scott Cameron; m. Diana Ashley Drake, Sept. 3, 1988; stepchildren: Cynthia Rush, Allison Abizaid, Linda Wiener, Carol Abizaid, Amanda Abizaid, Richard Abizaid. AB, Oberlin Coll., 1949; MA, Princeton U., 1951, PhD in Econs., 1957; LLD (hon.), Marietta Coll., 1989. Instr. econs. Princeton U., 1951-55; asst. prof. U. Richmond, 1955-56; mem. faculty Kalamazoo Coll., 1956-73, acad. v.p., 1964-67; prof. econs., pres. Marietta Coll., Ohio, from 1973, now prof. emeritus. Econs. adviser Hashemite Kingdom Jordan, 1963-64; Ford Found. vis. prof. econs. and devel. adminstrn. Am. U. Beirut, Lebanon, 1967-69, hon. prof. Southwestern U. Fin. and Econs., Chengdu Peoples Republic China, 1985; cons. examiner North Ctrl. Assn. Colls., 1960-90; dir. Cleve. Fed. Res. Bank, Cin. br., 1980-85. Co-editor, author: Continuity and Change in the World Oil Industry, 1970; contbg. author: Linear Programming and Theory of Firm, 1962; contbr. to profl. jours. Pres. Kalamazoo chpt. Human Rels. Coun., 1958-60; bd. dirs. Tuition Exch., Inc., 1975—; chmn. Student Loan Funding Corp., 1991-97; bd. dirs. AHEAD Corp., Amideast, Inc.; past pres. Ohio Coll. Assn.; chmn. East Ctrl. Coll. Consortium, Ind. Colls., Univs. Ohio; trustee Oberlin Coll., 1976-82, Mt. Vernon Coll., 1992-97; Trustee Knowledge Works Found., Cin., 1997—. With AUS, 1944-46. Decorated Bronze Star, Purple Heart.; recipient Kazanjian Found. teaching award econs., 1971; Leadership tng. fellow N. Central Assn. Colls., 1959 Fellow Middle East Studies Assn.; mem. Am. Econ. Assn., UN Assn. (past pres. Kalamazoo chpt.), Ohio Assn. for Freedom to Die. Presbyterian. Home: 4489 Highland Oaks Cir Sarasota FL 34235-5175 Home (Summer): 67 Birch Tree Ln Waitsfield VT 05673 Personal E-mail: dadcleland@aol.com.

CLELAND, THOMAS ANDREW, neurobiologist; b. Seattle, Oct. 6, 1965; s. Robert Erskine and Mary Love Cleland; m. Christiane Linster, Oct. 3, 1998; children: Linsey, Haley. BA cum laude in Biology, Whitman Coll., 1987; postgrad., U. Mich., 1988—90; PhD in Neurobiology, U. Calif., San Diego, 1997. Rschr. neurosci. Tufts U., Boston, 1997—99; rschr. psychology Boston U., 1999—2000; rsch. assoc. Cornell U., Ithaca, NY, 2000—05, sr. rsch. assoc., 2005—. Grant reviewer Army Rsch. Office, NSF; presenter in field; instr., lectr. U. Calif., San Diego, 1991—92, tchr. lab. asst. immunology, 1995, asst. neurobiology lab., 94, asst. mammalian physiology, 92; guest lectr. Boston U., 1999, Cornell U., 2003, instr., course developer, 05. Editl. bd.: Jour. Electronic Lectures, 2004—, Am. Jour. Alzheimer's Disease and Other Dementias, 2004—, mng. editor: Mich. Discussions in Anthropology, 1989—90, prodn. editor:, 1988—89, editl. cons.: Behavioral Neurosci., Biol. Bull., Bull. Math., Biology, Chem. Senses, Ethology, Jour. Computational Neurosci., Jour. Neurophysiology, Molecular and Cellular Neurosci., Proceedings of Nat. Acad. Sci.; contbr. chapters to books. Recipient Nat. Rsch. Svc. award, Nat. Inst. on Deafness and Other Communication Disorders, 1999, Nat. Inst. of Defense and other Comm. Disasters, 2002—05; fellow, U. Mich., 1988—90, NSF, 1991—94; Nat. Merit scholar, Whitman Coll., 1983—87, Young Scholars' Inst. fellow, German Am. Acad. Coun., 1996—97. Mem.: Soc. Neurosci. USA, N.Y. Acad. Sci., Molecular and Cellular Cognition Soc., Internat. Brain Rsch. Orgn., Internat. Behavioral and Neural Genetics Soc., Assn. Chemoreception Sci., Phi Beta Kappa. Avocations: backpacking, theater. Office: Cornell Univ Dept Neurobiology and Behavior W249 Mudd Hall Ithaca NY 14853

CLELAND, THOMAS EDWARD, JR., secondary school educator; b. Holyoke, Mass., Nov. 4, 1943; s. Thomas Edward and Hazel (Mitchell) C.; m. Patricia Helen Deitz, Apr. 10, 1965; children: David T., Donna J., Todd R. BA in Liberal Arts, U. Mass., 1965; MS in Guidance, Troy State U., 1976. Cert. tchr. Ark., Mass., USAF. Commd. 2d lt. USAF, 1965, advanced through grades to col., 1986, ret., 1991; dir. aerospace sci. Pine Bluff (Ark.) H.S., 1991-93; chmn. aerospace sci. dept. Ctrl. H.S., Springfield, Mass., 1993—. Author: (manual) Guide for Instructor Supervisors, 1978, AFJROTC Cadet Guide, 1992. Deacon, trustee United Congrl. Ch., Holyoke, 1994—; mem. Vets. Activities Com., Sprinfield, 1996, pastoral search com., Holyoke, 1994—. Recipient 13 Air medals, Letter of Appreciation Pres. Bush, 1991; named Western Mass. Tchr. of Yr., 2006. Mem. Air Force Assn., Am. Legion, Ret. Officers Assn., Aircraft Owners & Pilots Assn., Red River Valley Fighter Pilots Assn., Springfield Tchrs. Assn., Order of Daedalians (flight capt.). Avocations: aviation history, running. Home: 36 Roosevelt Ave South Hadley MA 01075-2337 Office: Springfield Ctrl HS 1840 Roosevelt Ave Springfield MA 01109-2437 E-mail: flytec@aol.com.

CLELAND, W(ILLIAM) WALLACE, biochemistry educator; b. Balt., Jan. 6, 1930; s. Ralph E. and Elizabeth P. (Shoyer) C.; m. Joan K. Hookanson, June 18, 1967 (div. Mar. 1999); children: Elsa Eleanor, Erica Elizabeth. AB summa cum laude, Oberlin Coll., 1950; MS, U. Wis., 1953, PhD, 1955. Postdoctoral fellow U. Chgo., 1957-59; asst. prof. U. Wis., Madison, 1959-62, assoc. prof., 1962-66, prof., 1966—, M.J. Johnson prof. biochemistry, 1978—, Steenbock prof. chem. sci., 1982—2002. Contbr. articles to profl.

biochem. and chem. jours. Served with U.S. Army, 1957-59. Grantee NIH, 1960—, NSF, 1960-94; recipient Stein and Moore award Protein Soc., 1999. Mem. NAS, Am. Acad. Arts and Scis., Am. Soc. Biochemistry and Molecular Biology (Merck award 1990), Am. Chem. Soc. (Alfred R. Bader Bioinorganic or Bioorganic Chem. award 1993, Repligen award 1995). Achievements include development of dithiothreitol (Cleland's Reagent) as reducing agent for thiol groups; development of application of kinetic methods for determining enzyme mechanism. Office: Enzyme Inst 1710 University Ave Madison WI 53726-4087 Office Phone: 608-262-1373. E-mail: cleland@biochem.wisc.edu.

CLEM, ALAN LELAND, retired political scientist, educator; b. Lincoln, Nebr., Mar. 4, 1929; s. Remey Leland and Bernice (Thompson) Clem; m. Mary Louise Burke, Oct. 24, 1953; children: Andrew, Christopher, Constance, John, Daniel. BA, U. Nebr., 1950; MA, Am. U., 1957, PhD, 1960. Copywriter, rsch. dir. Ayres Advt. Agy., Lincoln, 1950-52; press sec. to Congressman Carl Curtis of Nebr., 1953-54; press sec. to Congressman R. D. Harrison of Nebr., 1955-58; info. specialist Fgn. Agrl. Svc., Dept. Agr., 1959-60; from asst. prof. to assoc. prof. polit. sci. U. S.D., Vermillion, 1960—64, prof., 1965—; assoc. dir. Govtl. Rsch. Bur., 1962-76, chmn. dept. polit. sci., 1976-78; ptnr. Opinion Survey Assocs., 1964-88, ret., 1996. State analyst Comparative State Elctions Project, U. N.C., 1968—73; dir. Mt. Rushmore Presdl. Inst., 1970—71; mem. adv. com. state and local govt. stats. U.S. Census Bur., 1970—74. Author: (book) Prairie State Politics: Popular Democracy in South Dakota, 1967, The Making of Congressmen: Seven Campaigns of 1974, 1976, American Electoral Politics: Strategies for Renewal, 1981, Law Enforcement: The South Dakota Experience, 1982, The Government We Deserve, 1985, 5th edit., 1995, Congress: Powers, Processes and Politics, 1989, Government by the People? South Dakota Politics in the Last Third of the 20th Century, 2002; editor: Contemporary Approaches to State Constitutional Revision, 1969; contbr. articles to profl. jours. Mem. Vermillion City Coun., 1965—69; sr. warden St. Paul's Episcopal Ch., Vermillion, 1971—73, treas., 1996—. Recipient Alumni Achievement award, U. Nebr. Coll. Arts and Scis., 1998; Nat. Conv. faculty fellow, 1964. Mem.: Am. Polit. Sci. Assn., Midwest Polit. Sci. Assn. (mem. exec. coun. 1970—72, mem. editl. bd. Am. Jour. Polit. Sci. 1971—72), Mensa, Vermillion Golf Assn. (pres. 1986—87), Phi Beta Kappa, Sigma Delta Chi, Pi Sigma Alpha (mem. nat. coun. 1986—89), Phi Alpha Theta. Republican. Home: 608 Colonial Ct Vermillion SD 57069 *Avoid haste, anxiety, contentiousness, and self-centeredness. Care, clarity, persistence, honesty, and grace will prevail in the long run.*

CLEM, HARRIET FRANCES, library director; b. Akron, Ohio, Nov. 8, 1940; d. Paul Milton and Mary Eva (Koppes) Miller; m. Ross Lynn Clem, June 23, 1979. BA cum laude, Kent State U., 1963, MLS, 1965. Teletype operator Babcock & Wilcox Co., Barberton, Ohio, 1958-59; bookmobile libr. Wadsworth (Ohio) Pub. Libr., 1963-64; head ext. dept. Rodman Pub. Libr., Alliance, Ohio, 1965-68, libr. dir., 1969—. Instr. children's lit. Mt. Union Coll., Alliance, 1970—71; instr. libr. sci. Kent (Ohio) State U., 1975—77. Trustee YMCA, Alliance, 1974-84; pres. ARC, Alliance, 1975-77; bd. dirs. Leadership Stark County, Canton, Ohio, 1997-2003. Named Boss of Yr., Assn. Secs., Alliance, 1982; honoree Stark County Bicentennial Wall of Fame, 2003. Mem. Ohio Libr. Coun. (founder acctg. divsn.), Alliance C. of C. (pres. 1983, 93, Athena award 1990), Greater Alliance Devel. Corp. (pres. 2000), Beatrix Potter Soc., C.S. Lewis Soc., Alliance Women's Club (pres. 1977), Alliance Country Club, Coterie (pres. 2004), Sorosis, Beta Phi Mu (nat. coun. 1978-80). Episcopalian. Avocations: travel, cooking. Home: 13484 Louisville St NE Paris OH 44669-9713 Office: Rodman Pub Libr 215 E Broadway St Alliance OH 44601-2650 Office Phone: 330-821-2665.

CLEM, JOHN RICHARD, physicist, educator; b. Waukegan, Ill., Apr. 24, 1938; s. Gilbert D. and Bernelda May (Moyer) Clem; m. Judith Ann Paulsen, Aug. 27, 1960; children: Paul Gilbert, Jean Ann. BS, U. Ill., 1960, MS, 1962, PhD, 1965. Rsch. assoc. U. Md., College Park, 1965-66; vis. rsch. fellow Tech. U., Munich, 1966-67; from asst. prof. to assoc. prof. physics Iowa State U., Ames, 1967—75, prof., 1975—, disting. prof. in liberal arts and scis., 1989—, chmn. dept. physics, 1982-85. Vis. staff mem. Los Alamos Nat. Lab., 1971—83, cons., 1997—2001, Argonne Nat. Lab., Ill., 1971—76, Brookhaven Nat. Lab., Upton, NY, 1980—81, Oak Ridge (Tenn.) Nat. Lab., 1981, Allied-Signal, Torrance, Calif., 1990—92, Am. Superconductor Corp., Westborough, Mass., 1996—97, Pirelli Cable Corp., Lexington, SC, 1996—97; guest prof. U. Tuebingen, Germany, 1978; cons. IBM Watson Rsch. Ctr., Yorktown Heights, NY, 1982—85, vis. scientist, 1985—86, Electric Power Rsch. Inst., Palo Alto, Calif., 1992—93; vis. prof. applied physics Stanford U., 1992—93. Editor: Virtual Jour. Applications Superconductivity; sci. editor: newsletter High-Tc Update, 1987—2003; contbr. articles to profl. jours. Recipient award for sustained outstanding rsch. in solid state physics, U.S. Dept. Energy; Fulbright Sr. Rsch. fellow, 1974—75, NATO grantee, 1979—82. Fellow: Am. Phys. Soc. (chair divsn. condensed matter physics 1994—95); mem.: AAUP, Iowa Acad. Sci., Sigma Xi, Phi Kappa Phi, Tau Beta Pi. Democrat. Presbyterian. Achievements include patents in field. Avocation: singing. Home: 2307 Timberland Rd Ames IA 50014-8251 Office: Iowa State Univ A517 Zaffarano Ames IA 50011-3160 Business E-Mail: clem@ameslab.gov.

CLEM, RALPH S., career officer, educator; BA in Geography with honors, San Diego State Coll., 1965; MA in Geography and Soviet Studies, Columbia U., 1972, PhD in Geography and Soviet Studies with distinction, 1976; student, Air Command and Staff Coll., 1987, Air War Coll., 1989. Commd. 2d lt. USAF, 1965, advanced through grades to maj. gen., 2000; spl. agt. detachment 101 Off. Spl. Investigations, Hartford, 1965-68, spl. agt. dist. 51 Bangkok, 1968-69, supervising case officer hdqs. Washington, 1969-70; chief intelligence 915th Airborne Early Warning and Control Group, Homestead AFB, Fla., 1976-78, 93rd Tactical Fighter Squadron, Homestead AFB, 1978-83, 482d Tactical Fighter Wing, Homestead AFB, 1983-90; intelligence staff officer, sr. strategic air ops. analyst Off. Mil. Forces, Nat. Security Agy., Ft. George G. Meade, Md., 1990-93; mobilization asst. to asst. dep. dir. ops. Nat. Security Agy., Ft. George G. Meade, 1993-96; mobilization asst. to comdr. Hdqs. Air Intelligence Agy., Kelly AFB, Tex., 1996-98; dep. chief Air Force Res. Hdqs. USAF, Washington, 1998-2000; aide to chief of Air Force Res. 482nd Tactical Fighter Wing, Homestead AFB, Fla., 2000—; prof., internat. rels. Fla. Internat. Univ., Miami, Fla., and dir., Ctr. for Transnat. and Comparative Studies. Contbr. articles to profl. jours. Decorated Rep. Vietnam Campaign medal. Office: Dept Internat Relations DM 367A Florida Internat Univ 11200 SW 8th St Miami FL 33199

CLEMA, JOE KOTOUC, computer scientist; b. Omaha, Sept. 23, 1938; s. Joseph Arthur and Sylva Marie (Kotouc) C.; m. Maria Estela Cobos, Apr. 1, 1960; children: Jennifer, Arta. Student, U.S. Mil. Acad., 1957—60; BS, U. Nebr., 1963; MS, U. Miami, 1969; PhD, Colo. State U., 1973. Systems analyst Gen. Electric, Louisville, 1969-70; head sci. applications Colo. State U., Ft. Collins, 1970-73; project engr. Gen. Dynamics, Ft. Worth, 1973-77; sr. mgr. Simulation Tech., Inc., Dayton, Ohio, 1977-79; program mgr. Pratt and Whitney, West Palm Beach, Fla., 1979-82; dept. mgr. CACI, Dayton, 1982-83; dir. spl. projects Systems and Applied Scis., Vienna, Va., 1983-85; chief software engr. IIT Rsch. Inst., Annapolis, Md., 1985-90; cons. to IBM with, pres. Neurosystems, Inc., Bethesda, Md., 1991-98; cons. on IRS tax system modernization TRW, Merriefield, Va., 1993-95, cons. simplified tax & wage sys., 1995-96; mgr. Sys. Resources Corp., 1997-98, Houston Assocs., Inc., Arlington, Va., 1998—2002; dir. Nat. Tech., Inc., McLean, Va., 2002—04; sr. scientist 1st IO Commd., Ft. Belvoir, 2004—. Contbr. articles to profl. jours. Sustaining mem. Rep. Nat. Com., Washington, 1983—. Served to capt. U.S. Army, 1963-67. First Ann. Simulation Symposium Rsch. grantee, 1972; recipient Outstanding Svc. award Ann. Simulation Symposium Bd. Dirs., 1980. Mem.: ACM (nat. lectr. 1978—83), IEEE (sr.), Internat. Platform Assn., Ann. Simulation Symposium (chmn. bd. dirs. 1979), Spl. Interest Group on Simulation (chmn. 1979—81), Mid Atlantic Electronic Commerce Network (bd. dirs. 1995—98), Soc. Computer Simulation (bd. dirs., program chmn. 1988—96), Nat. Def. Indsl. Assn., Herndon C. of C., Toastmasters, No. Va. Tech. Coun., Armed Forces Comm. and Elec. Assn., Worldgate Athletic Club, Hidden Creek Country Club. Republican. Avocations: bridge, tennis. Home: 301 Missouri Ave Herndon VA 20170-5426 Office: 1st IO Commd Fort Belvoir VA E-mail: jkclema@istiocmd.army.mil, joeclema2@cs.com.

CLEMANS, M. PATRICIA, elementary school educator; d. William H. and Dolores A. Gleich; m. Craig A. Clemans, Oct. 14, 1985; 1 child, Chelsea Anne. BA in Edn., Capital U., 1982; M, Ashland U., 2002. Tchr. third grade Gahanna Jefferson Schs., Gahanna, Ohio, 1984—. Sci. curriculum devel. com. Gahanna Jefferson Schs. Independent. Office: Gahanna Jefferson Schs 515 Havens Corner Gahanna OH 43230 Office Phone: 614-478-5555.

CLEMEN, JOHN DOUGLAS, lawyer; b. Mineola, N.Y., Dec. 18, 1944; s. John Douglas and Amy Gertrude (Ackerson) Clemen; m. Judith Anne Davis, June 3, 1967; children: Elizabeth, Jennifer. BA, Hobart Coll., 1966; JD cum laude, Seton Hall U., 1974. Bar: N.J. 1974, U.S. Dist. Ct. N.J. 1974, U.S. Ct. Appeals (3d cir.) 1980, U.S. Supreme Ct. 1982, N.Y. 1984, U.S. Dist. Ct. (so. dist.) N.Y. 1985, U.S. Dist. Ct. (ea. dist.) N.Y. 1989, U.S. Ct. Appeals (2d cir.) 1989. Law sec. to assoc. justice N.J. Supreme Ct., Trenton, 1974-75; assoc. Shanley & Fisher, P.C., Newark, 1975-83, ptnr., 1983-99; founding ptnr. Hooker, Pucciarelli, Clemen & Tibbs (and predecessor firm), Woodcliff Lake, NJ, 1999—2003; pvt. practice River Vale, NJ, 2003—. Guest lectr. Acad. Medicine N.J., 1980—82; arbitrator U.S. Dist. Ct. N.J., 1985—, N.J. Superior Ct., Morristown, 1986—, Hackensack, 2002—. Contbg. editor: Seton Hall Law Rev., 1973—74. Bd. dirs. Acad. Decathalon N.J., 1997—2001; mem. mass disaster response team ARC, 1997—. Capt. USAF, 1966—71, Vietnam. Mem.: ABA, Commerce and Industry Assn. N.J. (bd. dirs. 1986—2005, counsel 1988—92), Bergen County Bar Assn., Trial Attys. N.J., Assn. Bar City of N.Y. (mem. aeronautics com. 1992—2001), N.Y. State Bar Assn., N.J. Bar Assn. (chmn. aviation sect. 1992—94). Home: 574 Colonial Rd Rivervale NJ 07675-6107 Office: Law Office of John D Clemen 574 Colonial Rd River Vale NJ 07675-6107 E-mail: jdclemen@aol.com.

CLEMENCE, ROGER DAVIDSON, landscape architect, educator; b. Worcester, Mass., Jan. 20, 1936; s. Luther Davidson and Dorothy (Kay) C.; m. Margaret Ann Weinandy, Aug. 19, 1961; children: Peter, Benjamin, Ellsabeth. AB, Amherst Coll., 1957; MArch, U. Pa., 1960, M in Landscape Architecture, 1962. Registered landscape architect, Minn. Instr., asst. prof. Coll. Architecture and Design U. Mich., Ann Arbor, 1962-66; assoc. prof. Sch. Architecture and Landscape Architecture U. Minn., Mpls., 1966-73, dir. Urban Edn. Ctr., Sch. Architecture and Landscape Architecture, 1970-77, interim head Sch. Architecture and Landscape Architecture, 1984, mem. urban studies faculty Coll. Liberal Arts, 1973—97, mem. Am. studies faculty Coll. Liberal Arts, 1986—97, dir. grad. studies in architecture Sch. Architecture and Landscape Architecture, 1978-85, prof. dept. architecture, 1973, assoc. dean Coll. of Architecture and Landscape Architecture, 1989-95, acting dean, spring 1993, interim dean, 1995-96. Landscape arch., planner, Mpls., 1963; collegiate program leader Minn. Ext. Svc., 1993-97, prof. emeritus, summer 1997—. Co-creator 10-part TV series The Meanings of Place, 1986. Mem. Minn. Com. on Urban Environment, 1979-88, Designer Selection Bd., 1980-85, chmn., 1983-84; mem. Mpls. Fed. Cts. Master Plan Com., 1991-92. Recipient Morse-Alumni Disting. Tchg. award, 1974, Pub. Svc. award Minn. Soc. Landscape Architects, 1982, Lob Pine award, 1996, CALA Disting. Svc. award, 1995; T.P. Chandler fellow U. Pa. Grad. Sch. Fine Arts, 1960-62; HWS Cleveland Vis. scholar U. Minn., 2000-03. Fellow Am. Soc. Landscape Architects; mem. AIA (prof. affiliate Minn. chapt. 1979), MASLA, Tau Sigma Delta. Democrat. Mem. Unitarian Universalist Assn. Avocations: photography, writing, golf, reading, gardening. Office: U Minn CALA 89 Church St SE Minneapolis MN 55455-0109

CLEMENDOR, ANTHONY ARNOLD, obstetrician, gynecologist, educator; b. Port-of-Spain, Trinidad, Nov. 8, 1933; came to US, 1954, naturalized, 1959; s. Anthony Arnold and Beatrice Helen (Stewart) C.; m. Elaine Browne, May 31, 1958 (dec. May, 1991); children: Anthony Arnold, David Alan; m. Janat Jenkins, Sept. 23, 1993. AB, NYU, 1959; MD, Howard U., 1963. Diplomate Am. Bd. Ob-Gyn. Intern USPHS, S.I., NY, 1963-64; resident Met. Hosp. Ctr., N.Y.C., 1964-68; chief outpatient dept. ob-gyn Metro. Hosp. Ctr., 1969-73; med. dir. family planning Human Resources Adminstrn., 1973-74; assoc. dean student affairs, dir. office minority affairs N.Y. Med. Coll., Valhalla, 1974-97, assoc. clin. prof. dept. ob-gyn, 1978-90, prof. clin. ob-gyn, 1990-98, clin. prof. ob-gyn., 1998—. Bd. dirs. Elmcore, Caribbean-Am. Ctr. N.Y.C., Nat. Assn. Minority Med. Educators, Inc., 1978-88, Empire State Med. Sci. and Ednl. Found., Inc., Caribbean Am. Ctr. N.Y., 1988-91; mem. Nat. Urban League, N.Y. Urban League; life mem. NAACP. Fellow ACOG, APHA; mem. AMA (survey team liaison com. on med. edn. 1989—, del. N.Y. State 1998—, liaison com. on med. edn. 1989-97), Am. Fertility Soc., Nat. Med. Assn., Med. Soc. State of N.Y. (treas. PAC 1997, councilor 1999-2002, asst. sec. 2002, treas. 2004-05), N.Y. County Med. Soc. (sec. 1989, v.p. 1990, pres. elect 1991, pres. 1992-93, bd. trustees, chmn. bd. trustees 1997-98), N.Y. Acad. Medicine, N.Y. Gynecol. Soc. (v.p. 1986, pres. 1988) Personal E-mail: aclemendor@aol.com.

CLEMENS, DAVID ALLEN, minister; b. Camden, NJ, Aug. 8, 1941; s. Arleigh and Mae C.; m. Janice, Feb. 13, 1965; children: Stephen David, Daniel Lee. BA magna cum laude, Houghton Coll., 1963; MA, Nat. Christian U., 1972; ThD, Clarksville Sch. Theology, 1980; PhD, Christian Bible Coll., 1990. Ordained to ministry Ind. Bapt. Ch., 1963. Missionary Pocket Testament League, Argentina, Paraguay, Chile, Peru, Bolivia, 1963-66; min. Richfield (Pa.) Mennonite Ch., 1966-67; itinerant Bible tchr. Bible Club Movement Inc., Upper Darby, Pa., 1968-2000, nat. rep., 1971-77, dir. Family Adult Ministries dept., 1977-80, min. at large, 1980-99, missionary, Bible tchr., 1999-2000; pres., Bible tchr. David Clemens Bible Tchg. Ministries, Inc., Marlton, 2000—. Preaching and tchg. tours Eng., Scotland, The Netherlands, Belgium, Sweden, Spain, Ireland, Can., Middle East, The Philippines, Zimbabwe, Poland, Cuba, Italy, Germany, Switzerland, Zambia, Guyana. Author: Steps to Maturity, Vols. I-III, 1973-79, How to Get Along With Impossible People, 1978. Mem. Nat. Home Missions Fellowship. Home and Office: 72 Knox Blvd Marlton NJ 08053-2921 E-mail: drdavidclemens@aol.com. *To know, love, and serve God (as revealed in Jesus Christ) is the highest privilege of life.*

CLEMENS, JASON WESLEY, music educator; b. Painesville, Ohio, Sept. 22, 1981; s. Wesley Louis and Susan Marie Clemens; m. Heidi Elizabeth Barth, July 12, 2003. MusB, Heidelberg Coll., Tiffin, Ohio, 1999—2003. Music tchr. Ledgemont Local Schs., Thompson, Ohio, 2003—. Children's ch. dir. Willoughby Bapt. Ch., Ohio, 2004. Mem.: NEA, Ohio Music Edn. Assn., Music Educators Nat. Conf. Avocations: reading, travel, music.

CLEMENS, KEVIN M., music educator; b. Altoona, Pa., Feb. 5, 1955; s. William Brooks Clemens and Marian Cecilia (Roesch) Clemen. BS in music edn., Pa. State U., 1977; M in ch. music, Kent State U., 1988. Cert. CAGO The Am. Guild of Organists. Dir. music Cathedral of the Blessed Scrament, Altoona, Pa., 1977—82; elem. vocal, instrumental tchr. Springfield Sch. Dist., Akron, Ohio, 1983—92; dir. music St. Timothy's Episc. Ch., Massillou, Ohio, 1983—92, St. Ursula Roman Cath. Ch., Balt., 1992—; instr. of piano Harford C. C., Bel Air, Md., 2003—. Pipe organist recitals in Md., NY, Ohio and Pa. Mem.: Chorrsters Guild, Nat. Assn. Pastoral Musicians (chpt. dir. 2004—), Am. Guild of Organists (dean 1999—2001). Republican. Cath. Avocations: jogging, dog breeding, clocks, historic pipe organs. Home: 711 Ct Sq Way Edgewood MD 21040 Office: St Ursula RC Ch 8801 Harford Rd Parkville MD 21234 Office Phone: 410-661-0600. Office Fax: 410-665-0758.

CLEMENS, MICHAEL TERRENCE, furniture manufacturing representative; b. Dubuque, Iowa, Apr. 7, 1950; s. William Michael and Mary Ellen (Degear) C.; m. Christine Marie Busalacchi, May 17, 1975; children: James William, Anthony Michael, Jennifer Lee. BBA, Loyola U., New Orleans, 1972. Mfr. rep. Flexsteel Industries, Inc., Dubuque, Iowa, 1973-79, Wis., Mich., 1980—; asst. golf profl. Fort Dodge (Iowa) Country Club, 1972. Mem. Northville (Mich.) Jaycees, 1980, Flexsteel 1989 All-Star Sales Team. Mem. Mich. Home Furnishings Reps. Assn., Wis. Home Furnishings Reps. Assn. (pres. 1978), Internat. Home Furnishings Reps. Assn., Home Furnishing Reps. of Mich. (treas.), Flexsteel Seven Million Dollar Sales Club, Nat. of Evansville Million Dollar Club (charter), Walnut Creek Country Club, Beta Gamma Sigma, Alpha Sigma Nu. Avocations: golf, water-skiing, photography. Office: Flexsteel Industries 42128 Crestview Cir Northville MI 48167-2205

CLEMENS, RICHARD GLENN, lawyer; b. Chgo., Oct. 8, 1940; s. James Ralston and Jeanette Louise (Moellering) C.; m. Judith B. Clemens, Aug. 19, 1967; 1 child, Kathleen. BA, U. Va., 1962, JD, 1965. Bar: Ill. 1965. Assoc. Sidley Austin Brown & Wood LLP, Chgo., 1965—66, Washington, 1968—71, Brussels, 1972—73, ptnr. Chgo., 1973—. Served to capt. U.S. Army, 1966-68. Mem. ABA, Chgo. Bar Assn., Lawyers Club, Mid-Day Club. Office: Sidley Austin Brown & Wood LLP 10 S Dearborn St Chicago IL 60603 Office Phone: 312-853-7642. Business E-Mail: rclemens@sidley.com.

CLEMENS, ROBERT, instruments executive; b. Kitchener, Ont., Can., Mar. 22, 1963; s. Adam Alphonse and Carolyn May (Weber) C.; m. Julia Hodgson, July 17, 1984. Diploma, Chgo. Sch. Violin Making, 1986; postgrad. study with, Zenon W W. Petesh, 1987-89. Profl. violin maker supplying instruments to Kenneth Warren and Son, Ltd., Chgo., William Moennig and Son, ltd., Phila., Gengakki Duo Co., Tokyo, 1987-91; founder, ptnr. Clemens Violins, Violas and Violoncellos, St. Louis, 1991—. Can. Arts Coun. grantee, 1984-85, 85-86. Mem. Chamber Music Am. Avocations: sculpting, painting. Address: 6353 Clayton Rd Saint Louis MO 63117-1808

CLEMENS, ROGER (WILLIAM ROGER CLEMENS), professional baseball player; b. Dayton, Ohio, Aug. 4, 1962; m. Debbie Lynn Godfrey, May 27, 1963; children: Koby Aaron, Kory Allen, Kacy Austin, Kody Alec. Student, San Jacinto North Jr. Coll., Houston, 1980—81, U. Tex., 1981—83. Baseball player Boston Red Sox, 1984—96, Toronto Blue Jays, 1997—98, N.Y. Yankees, 1998—2003, Houston Astros, 2004—. Named Major League Player of Yr., Sporting News, 1986, Pitcher of Yr., 1986, 1991, 1997—98, 2001; named to Am. League All-Star Team, 1986, 1988, 1990—92, 1997—98, 2001, 2003, Nat. League All-Star Team, 2004—05, MLB All-Century Team, 1999; recipient Cy Young award, Am. League, 1986, 1987, 1991, 1997, 1998, 2001, Cy Young Award, Nat. League, 2004, Am. League MVP, 1986, MLB All-Star Game MVP, 1986. Achievements include holds MLB record for strikeouts in a single game (20); recorded 300th career win and 4,000 career strikeouts, June 13, 2003; mem. World Series Champion New York Yankees, 1999, 2000; holds MLB record for Cy Young Awards (7), 2004; holds MLB record for oldest player to win Cy Young Award (age 42), 2004. Office: c/o Houston Astros PO Box 288 Houston TX 77001

CLEMENS, ROSEMARY A., health facility administrator, foundation administrator; m. Mitchel Greenfield Garren, Aug. 30, 1985. BA, St. John's U., 1966; MA, NYU, 1968, PhD, 1973. Assoc. prof. Fordham U. Sch. Social Work and Edn., NYC, 1973—83; dir. strategic planning and mktg. NY Hosp., 1983—88; clin. instr. Cornell Med. Coll., Dept. Pub. Health, 1983—88; dir. AIDS and adolscent awareness project Women's City Club, 1988—92; dep. dir. NY State Inst. Basic Rsch. Devel. Disabilities, S.I., 1992—96; devel. and program dir. Skin Cancer Found., N.Y.C., 1996—98; pres., CEO N.Y. divsn. Prevent Blindness Am., N.Y.C., 1998—2001; CEO N.Y.Children's Vision Coalition, N.Y.C., 2001—. Author: (book) Lessons to be Learned - Adolescents and AIDS (Cmty. Achievement Award - NYS Optometric Assn, 2004). Bd. mem. Cmty. Bd. #1, Women's City Club, UN Assn., NYC, 1975—2005; rsch. assoc. Gov. Nelson A. Rockefeller Presdl. Campaign, 1968—69, Mayor John Lindsay's Adminstrn., N.Y.C., 1973—75; dir. decentralization studies State Sen. Roy M. Goodman Commn. on N.Y.C. Governance, 1975—77; rsch. asst. Ford Found., 1968. Mem.: Cosmopolitan Club of NY (pub. affairs com. 1997—99). Avocations: travel, reading, gardening, theater, interior decorating. Home: 7 Lexington Ave New York NY 10010 Office: NY Children's Vision Coalition 33 West 42nd St New York NY 10036 Home: 110 Atlantic Ave Palm Beach FL 33480 Office Phone: 212-997-3550. Office Fax: 212-780-4949. Personal E-mail: rosemaryclemens@aol.com.

CLEMENS, T. PAT, manufacturing executive; b. Hibbing, Minn., July 26, 1944; s. Jack LeRoy and Mildred (Coss) C.; m. 1966 (div. 1992); children: Patrick Michael, Heather Kristen. BS in Econs. and Mgmt., St. Cloud State U., 1968; student of theology, Coll. St. Thomas, 1985-87. Sales adminstr. Transistor Electronics Co., Eden Prarie, Minn., 1969; head instnl. sales Chiquita Brands, Edina, Minn., 1970; dist. sales mgr. Menley & James Labs., Phila., 1971-75; owner, pres. T.P. Clemens Labs., Eagan, Minn., 1975—. Instr community edn. Rosemount, Minn., 1977-78; bd. dirs. Rosemount Hockey, 1977-78, Relocation Assistance Assn. Am., 1984-85; v.p. Sch. Dist. #196 Booster Club, 1984-85; lectr. econs. to corps., high schs. and colls. in U.S., Scotland, Ireland, and Jamaica, 1979—. Author, editor: How Prejudice and Narcissism Control Economics of the United States and the World, 1979. Mem. Rosemont Cmty. Edn. Bd., 1985, chmn., 1986-87; chmn. speakers bur. Citizens Steering Com., 1984-85; coach Little League, 1970-82, 88-91; coach high sch. weight lifting team, 1975-95; vol. worker with comatose children, 1975-96, 97—. Recipient letter of recognition for stopping armed robbery Dakota County Atty.'s Dept., 1979, 93. Mem. Internat. Platform Assn., Kids-N-Kinship Program 1988-92. Home and Office: 1276 Wildmark Dr Eagan MN 55123-2801 Office Phone: 651-454-6746. E-mail: tpatclemens@cs.com.

CLEMENT, DANIEL EVAN, lawyer; b. N.Y.C., Mar. 15, 1961; s. Stanton J. and Lorraine Clement; m. Michelle Sue Schwartz, Oct. 24, 1998. BA, SUNY, Albany, 1983; JD, Bklyn. Law Sch., 1986. Bar: N.J. 1986, N.Y. 1987, U.S. Dist. Ct. N.J. 1986, U.S. Dist. Ct. (so. and ea. dists.) N.Y. 1987, U.S. Ct. Appeals (2d cir.) 1991. Sole practitioner, N.Y.C., 1996—; of counsel Wallman Gasman & McKnight, LLP, N.Y.C., 1996—. Arbitrator N.Y.C. Small Claims Ct. Mem. Assn. Bar City N.Y. Office: 350 5th Ave Ste 3000 New York NY 10118-3022 E-mail: oclebent@clementlaw.com.

CLEMENT, DANIEL ROY, IV, accountant; b. Kirtland, Ohio, Apr. 2, 1943; s. Roy A. Jr. and Evelyn Violet (Hale Chase) C.; m. Jennifer Ilean Handley, July 10, 1965 (div. 1975); children: Elizabeth Ann Clement Baitt, Catherine Lynn Clement Holder; m. Barbara Jane Griffiths, Dec. 10, 1985. Student, Fenn Coll., 1961-63, Alexander Hamilton Inst., 1963-67, Am. Inst. of Banking, 1963-65, Lakeland Coll., 1965-70, Case Western Res. U., 1970-73, Lake Erie Coll., 1973-85, Auburn Career Ctr., 1987—; PhD, Case Western Res. U., 1999. Notary public Ohio, 1967. Shipping and cost acctg. Mentor (Ohio) Products, 1961; acctg. asst. N.Y. Ctrl. Transport, Cleve., 1963—65; acct. mgr. Am. Soc. Metals, Novelty, 1965—67; corp. fleet mgr. Addressograph Multigraph, Euclid, 1967—72; treas. Debevec Salo & Assocs., Ohio, 1972—74; with sales Pontiac Cadillac-Record Shack, Mentor, 1974—78; asst. plant mgr. Ajax Mfg., Euclid, 1978—82; tax preparer H&R Block, 1978—2005; home care pvt. duty nurse, 1987—; server restaurant and lodge Geneva State Pk., 2004—; with Geneva Ohio Shipping Line Assembly, 2005—. Home care pvt. duty nurse, 1967—. Active Jr. C. of C., Mentor, Willoughby, Brunswick, Novelty, Lake County, 1965-75; mem. Congl. Task Force Pres. Bush, 1981-94; notary public, 1967- Republican. Methodist. Avocations: gardening, dogs, cats, tropical fish, camping. Home: 5724 Lake Rd E #C Geneva OH 44041-9485 Office Phone: 440-466-9402. Personal E-mail: danielroyc@alltel.net.

CLEMENT, EDITH BROWN, federal judge; b. Birmingham, Ala., Apr. 29, 1948; d. Erskine John and Edith (Burrus) Brown; m. Rutledge Carter Clement Jr., Sept. 3, 1972; children: Rutledge Carter III, Catherine Lanier. BA, U. Ala., 1969; JD, Tulane U., 1972. Bar: La. 1973. Law clk. to Hon. Herbert W. Christenberry U.S. Dist. Ct., New Orleans, 1973-75; ptnr. Jones, Walker, Waechter, Poitevent, Carrere & Denegre, New Orleans, 1975-91; judge U.S. Dist. Ct. (ea. dist.) La., New Orleans, 1991—2001, U.S. Ct Appeals (5th cir.), New Orleans, 2001—. Fellow La. Bar Found. (life); mem. Am. Law Inst., La. Bar Assn., Federalist Soc. Advisory Bd. Louisiana Chpt., Maritime Law Assn.

U.S., Fed. Bar Assn., Am Inn Ct., Com. Admin. Office of the Judicial Conference of the U.S., 5th Cir. Judicial Coun. Office: US Ct Appeals 5th Cir 600 Camp Street Rm 200 New Orleans LA 70130-3313*

CLEMENT, EVELYN GEER, library educator; b. Springfield, Mass., Sept. 1, 1926; d. Elihu and Helen (Schenck) Geer; m. J.R. Clement, Sept. 9, 1946 (div. 1972); children: James Randall, Timothy B., Susan Henson, Marc W., Audrey Ethriedge. BA with honors, U. Tulsa, 1965; MLS, U. Okla., 1966; PhD, Ind. U., 1975. Librarian Tulsa City-County Library, 1960-66; learning resources librarian Oral Roberts U., Tulsa, 1966-68; spl. instr. U. Okla., Norman, 1966-70; prof., chmn. library sci. Memphis State U., 1972-85, dir. Ctr. for Instructional Service and Research, 1985-95, ret., 1995; regional trustee Geer Family Assn., chmn. acad. senate, 1979-80, mem. faculty tenure and promotion appeals com., 1980-82, mem. standing univ. com. on libraries, 1975-80, 86-87, chmn. women's task force, 1984-85; dir. media consortium Tenn. Regents, 1993-95. Editor: Bibliographic Control of Nonprint Media, 1972; contbr. articles to profl. jours. Doctoral fellow U.S. Office Edn., Title II-B, Ind. U., 1968-71. Mem. ALA, Afghanistan Preceivers, Red Hat Soc., Pi Gamma Mu, Phi Alpha Theta, Beta Phi Mu. Republican. Avocations: microcomputer, needlepoint, exercise, reading. Home: 5206 S Harvard Ave #336 Tulsa OK 74135-3591 E-mail: erren@aol.com.

CLEMENT, FRANCES ROBERTS, lawyer, consultant, nurse, mediator; b. Columbia, S.C., Oct. 1, 1945; d. Ralph Winfred and Frances Lucille (Harter) Roberts; m. Tom F. Clement; children: Everett Hudson Smith, Armenta Harter Smith. BS in Biology, U. Ala., 1967; MS in Counseling, Fla. State U., 1970; AA in Nursing, Victoria Coll., Tex., 1978; JD with honors, Jones Sch. Law, Montgomery, Ala., 1986. Bar: Ala. 1987, U.S. Supreme Ct. 1997. Staff nurse Citizen's Meml. Hosp., Victoria, Tex., 1978-81, DeTar Hosp., Victoria, Tex., 1981, Bapt. Med. Ctr., Montgomery, 1982-84; adminstr sch. nurse Bloomington (Tex.) Sch. Dist., 1981-82; supr. Humana Hosp., Montgomery, 1985; legal asst. Kaufman, Rothfeder & Blitz, Montgomery, 1985-87; assoc. Powers & Willis, Montgomery, 1987-88; pvt. practice Montgomery, 1988-90, 2001—; with Office of Atty. Gen., 1990-2001; mediator, 1999—. Adj. prof. U. Houston, Victoria, 1980, Auburn U., Montgomery, 1988-90. Mem. Montgomery County Bar Assn. Methodist. Avocation: computers. Home: 3502 Bankhead Ave Montgomery AL 36111-2018 Office: 312 Scott St Montgomery AL 36104 Office Phone: 334-262-4887. Personal E-mail: FrClement@aol.com.

CLEMENT, HENRY JOSEPH, JR., diversified building products executive; b. New Orleans, May 14, 1942; s. Henry Joseph Sr. and Margaret (Dowd) C.; m. Kathleen Erin Shean; children: Colleen and Collette (twins). BS, Loyola U., 1973. Sales rep. GE, New Orleans, 1972-77, mgr. product planning Louisville, Ky., 1977-79, mgr. internat. market Tyler, Tex., 1979-83; v.p. internat. sales Phillips Industries, Inc., Dayton, Ohio, 1983-84, pres. internat. div., 1984-88; pres. internat. group Tomkins Industries, Dayton, 1988-94; pres. Crescent Group, Inc., Dublin, Ohio, 1994—. Vice chmn., bd. dirs. Shaanxi-Hytec, Ltd., Xian, Chila, 1988-89. Loan exec. United Way, New Orleans, 1974, Tyler, 1979. Mem. Miami Valley (Ohio) Internat. Trade Assn. (trustee), Blue Key (Cross Key Svc. award 1973). Republican. Roman Catholic. Home: 4666 Chatham Ct Dublin OH 43017-8607 E-mail: cresgroup@cs.com.

CLEMENT, HOPE ELIZABETH ANNA, retired librarian; b. North Sydney, N.S., Can., Dec. 29, 1930; d. Harry Wells and Lana (Perkins) Clement. BA, U. of King's Coll., 1951; MA, Dalhousie U., 1953; BLS, U. Toronto, 1955; D of Civil Law (hon.), U. King's Coll., 1992. With Nat. Library of Can., Ottawa, Ont., 1955-92, chief nat. bibliography div., 1966-70, asst. dir. research and planning br., 1970-73, dir. research and planning br., 1973-77, assoc. nat. librarian, 1977-92; ret., 1992. Editor: Canadiana, 1966—69. (Outstanding Svc. to Librarianship award 1992), Internat. Fedn. Libr. Assns. (medal 1991).

CLEMENT, JACLYN, oceanographer; b. Jackson, Tenn., Jan. 19, 1978; MS in Biol. Oceanography, U. Tenn., 2002. Rsch. assoc. Naval Postgrad. Sch., Monterey, Calif., 2002—. Republican. Achievements include research in Oceanography of the Bering Sea. Office: Naval Postgrad Sch Dept Oceanography 833 Dyer Rd Monterey CA 93943

CLEMENT, JOHN EDWARD STRAUSZ, retired minister, retired religious organization administrator; b. Enid, Okla., Jan. 9, 1934; s. Joseph Alvis and Sarah Evelyn (Brown) C.; m. Judith A. Strausz-Clement; children: Stephen W., Paul E., Catherine K., Christopher S. Clark, Karen L. Clark. BA, Oberlin Coll., 1956; MDiv, Union Theol. Sem., 1960. Ordained to ministry Presbyn. Ch., 1960. Pastor, Williamsport, Pa., 1960-65, Wilmington, Del., 1965-69; project leader S. Cen. Ministry, Minn., 1969-74; mission enabler Los Ranchos Presbytery, Long Beach, Calif., 1974-78; exec. presbyter Cayuca-Syracuse Presbytery, Syracuse, N.Y., 1978-91, Pitts. Presbytery, 1991-95; interim exec. presbyter Carlisle Presbytery, Camp Hill, Pa., 1995-96, gen. presbyter Blackhawk Presbytery, Oregon, Ill., 1996—2001, ret., 2001. Mem. Ecumenical Execs. of No. Ill., 1996—2001, Campus Ministry Com. of Synod of Lincoln Trails, 1998-2000, Nat. Cooperative Com. on Partnership Funding, Presbyn. Ch. (USA), 1998—2001. Organizing mem. Habitat for Humanity, Syracuse, N.Y.; chmn. ecumenical exec. cabinet and v.p. Syracuse Interreligious Coun., 1985-87; ch.-wide adminstrv. coord. cabinet Presbyn. Ch. (USA), 1986-88, 91-92; chmn. pers. com. N.Y. State Coun. of Chs., 1989-91; chmn. Synod of N.E. Ecumenical Cabinet, 1987-91; mem. AIDS Task Force of Ctrl. N.Y.; mem. nat. com. Bicentennial Fund Campaign, Presbyn. Ch. (USA), 1988-92; organizing mem. Christian Leaders Fellowship, Pitts., 1991-95; exec. com. Coun. of Christian Assocs. of Western Pa., 1991-95; mem. coun. judicatory execs. Ill. Conf. Chs., 1996-200; mem. Downtown Chs. Ecumenical Com., Sante Fe, 2003-04, N.Mex. Conf. Chs. Faith and Order Task Force, 2003—; chair Presbytery of Sante Fe Task Group on Korean Fellowship, 2003-04. E-mail: johnesclement@comcast.net. *I believe God loves our world and has become one of us to redeem us and guide us toward a new humanity. I see our ministry standing on the side of the poor and oppressed as well as loving the oppressor.*

CLEMENT, MEREDITH OWEN, economist, educator; b. Colusa, Calif., June 7, 1926; s. Eldon Wilford and Lillian (Ohm) C.; m. Jacqueline Parker, Apr. 10, 1955; children— William, Christopher. Student, Yuba Coll., Marysville, Calif., 1946-48; BS, U. Calif. at Berkeley, 1950, PhD, 1958. Rsch. economist CIA, 1954-56; mem. faculty Dartmouth Coll., Hanover, N.H., 1956—, prof., 1967-96, prof. emeritus, 1996—. Vis. asst. prof. U. Calif. at Berkeley, 1961-62; Brookings research prof. Brookings Instn., 1964-65; Fulbright lectr. Robert Coll., Istanbul, Turkey, 1969-70; vis. scholar U. New S. Wales, 1988-89. Author: (with others) Theoretical Issues in International Economics, 1967, An Economic Evaluation of the Federal Grant-in-Aid Programs in New England, 1961, also articles. Served with USMCR, 1944-46. Mem. Am., So. econ. assns., Royal Econ. Soc., Econometric Soc. Unitarian Universalist. Home: PO Box 767 Etna NH 03755-0767 Office: Dartmouth Coll Dept Econs Hanover NH 03755

CLEMENT, OMDSHILE OLAJIDE, application developer; arrived in U.S., 1996; s. Emmanuel Fusho Clement and Abiodun Mercy Ige; m. Olayinka Abosede Ogunlabi, Aug. 10, 1990; children: Tobi, Yeni. BS, U. Ibadan, 1985, MS, 1987, Queen's U., 1991, PhD, 1995. Rsch. asst. Queen's U., Kingston, 1990—95; scientist Molecular Simulations, San Diego, 1998—99; product mgr. Accelrys, Inc., 2000—03, sr. product mgr., 2003—. Rsch. cons. prof. U. Md., Balt., 2003—. Contbr. articles to profl. jours., chapters to books. Fellow, PNNL, Richland, Wash., 1996—98. Mem.: Am. Chem. Soc. Office: Accelrys Inc 10188 Telesis Ct San Diego CA 92121

CLEMENT, PAUL D., federal agency administrator, lawyer; b. Milw., June 24, 1966; BSFS summa cum laude, Georgetown U., 1988; MPhil with distinction, Cambridge U., Eng., 1989; JD magna cum laude, Harvard Law Sch., 1992. Intern Office of U.S. Sen. Robert Kasten, Washington, 1985-86; intern White House, Office of Pub. Liaison, Washington, 1987; summer assoc. McGuire, Woods, Battle & Boothe, Washington, 1990, Covington & Burling, Washington, 1991, Gibson, Dunn & Crutcher, Washington, 1992; teaching fellow Harvard U., 1990-92; law clk. to Hon. Laurence H. Silberman U.S. Ct. Appeals (D.C. cir.), Washington, 1992-93; law clk. to Assoc. Justice Hon. Antonin Scalia U.S. Supreme Ct., Washington, 1993-94; assoc. Kirkland & Ellis, Washington, 1994-97; chief counsel U.S. Senate Subcom. on Constitution, Washington, 1997—99; head, appellate div. King & Spalding LLP, Washington, 1999—2001; prin. dep. solicitor gen. US Dept. Justice, Washington, 2001—04, acting solicitor gen., 2004—05, solicitor gen., 2005—. Adj. prof. Georgetown U. Law Ctr., 1998—; acad. tutor for 1st yr. students Harvard Law Sch., 1991-92. Recipient Olin fellowship in law and econs. Harvard Law Sch., 1991-92, Harvard Law Review, U.K. Fgn. Office scholarship Cambridge U., 1989, Humes Jr. fellowship in diplomacy, Notz medal, Nevils medal Georgetown U., 1988. Mem. Phi Beta Kappa. Office: US Dept Justice Robert F Kennedy Bldg 10th St & Constitution Ave NW Rm 5143 Washington DC 20530

CLEMENT, PAUL PLATTS, JR., performance technologist, educator; b. Geneva, Ill., Aug. 30, 1935; s. Paul P. and Vera Elizabeth (Dahlquist) C.; m. Susan Alice Aikins, June 7, 1958; children: Paul P. IV, Kathleen Elizabeth. BA in Math., Coe Coll., 1957. Sales tech. rep. Burroughs Corp., Chgo., 1960-63; mgr. EDP, Harding-Williams Corp., Chgo., 1963-65; edn. coord. Standard Oil Co., Chgo., 1965-69; mgr. product planning Edutronics Systems Internat., Chgo., 1969-71; interactive video instrn. specialist Advanced Systems Inc., Chgo., 1971-88; ind. cons. in tng., media use, computers Downers Grove, Ill., 1988; prin. instr., developer UNISYS Corp., Lisle, Ill., 1988-89; mgr. employee devel. CNA Ins. Cos., Chgo., 1990-91; cons. media tng. Internet Systems Corp., Chgo., 1990-93; prin. Clement Consulting Group, Downers Grove, 1993—. Part-time data processing faculty Coll. of DuPage and Coll. extension, Harper Coll., Ill., DeVry Inst., Joliet Jr. Coll.; invited spkr. numerous computer and tng. confs., nat. and internat. assns.; developer, presenter workshops in field; mem. adv. bd. Northeastern Ill. U., Chgo. Developer and pub. 12 animated films with supplementary texts, 84 videotapes, 17 interactive videodiscs and over 7000 pages of expository texts; collaborator 100 other videotapes with supplementary texts; prin. developer micro-computer based People Compatability System, 1983; developer Decision Table Algorithms, 1986, 94th Inf. Div. Assn. Info. System, 1977, Basic Computer Programmer Tng. Curriculum for Eng. Govt., 1979, computerized Data Processing Curricula Devel. System, 1973, Early COBOL Lang. precompiler, 1967, AutoMagic Glossary, 1992; contbr. articles to Datamation Mag., Data Tng. Mag. Capt. USAF, 1958-60. Recipient Silver award WPC, 1996, Gold award, 1998. Home and Office: 4942 Linscott Ave Downers Grove IL 60515-3537 Office Phone: 630-969-7957. E-mail: paulclementjr@peoplepc.com.

CLEMENT, RICHARD JOSEPH, retired obstetrician, gynecologist; b. Crowley, La., Apr. 10, 1937; m. Emily S. Clement. MBA in Bus. Adminstrn. and Statis., McNeese State U., 1959; MD, La. State U., 1963. Diplomate Am. Bd. Ob-Gyn. Intern Charity Hosp., New Orleans, 1963-64, resident in ob-gyn. and anesthesiology, 1964-67; pvt. practice, 1963—97; chief of staff Lake Charles Meml. Hosp., 1993-94; ret. Chmn. bd. Walter O. Moss Regional Hosp., 1994—; clin. asst. prof. La. State U. Sch. Medicine, New Orleans, 1974. Col. U.S. Army. Fellow ACOG, Am. Fertility and Sterility Soc., Soc. for Colposcopy and Colpomicroscopy, Internat. Coll. Surgery; mem. AMA, La. State Med. Soc., Calcasieu Parish Med. Soc., Am. Coll. Obstretics & Gynecology, New Orleans Parish Med. Soc., La. State U. Postgrad. Ob-Gyn. Soc. (pres.), Royal Soc. Medicine. Home: 517 S Ryan St Lake Charles LA 70601-5724

CLEMENT, RICHARD WOLCOTT, librarian, educator; b. Phila., Aug. 28, 1951; s. Danforth and Patricia (Harshman) C.; m. Susanne Kofod, Aug. 24, 1974; children: Kristina Alexandra, Elizabeth Wolcott. BA, U. Nev., 1975, MA, 1977; AM, U. Chgo., 1984. Asst. prof. English Ill. State U., Normal, 1981-84; rare book cataloger U. Chgo. Libr., 1985-86; assoc. spl. collections libr. Spencer Libr., U. Kans., Lawrence, 1996-2000, spl. collections libr., head, 2000—. Author: The Book in America, 1996, Books in the Frontier: Print Culture in the American West 1763-1875, 2003; editor: Iberia and the Mediterranean, 1989, Greece and the Mediterranean, 1990, Spain and the Mediterranean, 1992, RBM: A Jour. of Rare Books, Manuscripts, and Cultural Heritage, 2003—. Summer fellowship NEH, 1983, fellowship Newberry Libr., Chgo., 1982, Andrew W. Mellon Found., St. Louis U., 1982. Mem. ALA, Mediterranean Studies Assn. (bd. dirs. 1994--, pres. 1994-98), Medieval Acad. of Am., Soc. for the History of Authorship, Reading and Publishing. Avocations: travel, reading, music, building houses. Home: 2205 Riviera Dr Lawrence KS 66047-1990 Office: Spencer Rsch Libr U Kans Lawrence KS 66045-7616 Fax: 785-864-5803. E-mail: rclement@ku.edu.

CLEMENT, ROBERT LEBBY, JR., lawyer; b. Charleston, S.C., Dec. 14, 1928; m. Helen Mathilda Lewis, Nov. 26, 1954; children: Jeanne Marie, Robert Lebby III, Thomas L.T. AB, The Citadel, 1948; JD, Duke U., 1951. Bar: N.C. 1951, S.C. 1954. Practiced in Charlotte, N.C., 1951-53; ptnr. Cornish, Clement & Horlbeck, Charleston, 1955-60, Hagood, Rivers & Young, 1960-65, Young, Clement, Rivers LLP, 1965-93, of counsel, 1994—. Pres. Charleston Automotive Parts, Inc., 1969-84, Charleston Mus., 1980-83; mem. adv. bd. Bank of Am., 1960-2001; asst. city atty., Charleston, 1960; judge Mcpl. Ct., Charleston, 1961-63. Mem. Charleston County Coun., 1983-86, chmn., 1985-86. With JAGD, USAF, 1953-55. Mem. ABA, N.C. Bar Assn., S.C. Bar Assn., Charleston County Bar Assn. (pres. 1990-91), Rotary. Presbyterian. Office: Young Clement Rivers LLP PO Box 993 Charleston SC 29402-0993 Office Phone: 843-724-6624.

CLEMENT, ROBERT WILLIAM, retired air force officer; b. Columbus, Ohio, Aug. 8, 1927; s. Coleman Clay and Leola Marie (Barnett) C.; m. Leila Ann Cameron, Dec. 27, 1950 (dec. Nov. 1998); children: Susan Lee, Robert William (dec.), Sandra Gay, Randall Clay; m. Elizabeth deGaris Atherton, June 1999. Student, Yale U., 1945-46; BS, U.S. Mil. Acad., 1950; MS in Aero. Engring., U. Colo., 1957; postgrad., Army War Coll., 1966-67. Commd. 2d lt. USAF, 1950, advanced through grades to maj. gen., 1978; vice comdr. 12th Air Force, Tactical Air Command, Bergstrom AFB, Tex., 1976; dep. chief staff for ops. and intelligence USAF in Europe Ramstein Air Base, Federal Republic of Germany, 1978-80; comdr. 16th Air Force, Torrejon AB, Spain, 1980-84; ret., 1984; asst. prof. math U.S. Air Force Acad., 1956-59. Decorated Air Force DSM, Legion of Merit with 3 oak leaf clusters, DFC with one oak leaf cluster, Bronze Star, Air medal with 9 oak leaf clusters. Mem. Haines City Citrus Growers Assn. (pres. 1990-92). Home: PO Box 2207 Haines City FL 33845-2207

CLEMENTE, CARMINE DOMENIC, anatomist, educator; b. Penns Grove, N.J., Apr. 29, 1928; s. Ermanno and Caroline (Friozzi) Clemente; m. Juliette Vance, Sept. 19, 1968. AB, U. Pa., 1948, MS, 1950, PhD, 1952; postdoctoral fellow, U. London, 1953—54. Asst. instr. anatomy U. Pa., 1950—52; mem. faculty UCLA, 1952—, prof., 1963—95, chmn. dept. anatomy, 1963—73, dir. brain rsch. inst., 1976—87, prof. pathology, neurobiology and anatomy, 1995—, Disting. prof. neurobiology and anatomy, 2004—; prof. surg. anatomy Charles R. Drew U. Medicine and Sci., LA, 1974—. Hon. rsch. assoc. Univ. Coll., U. London, 1953—54; vis. scientist Nat. Inst. Med. Rsch., Mill Hill, London, 1988—89, London, 1991; cons. VA Hosp., Sepulveda, Calif., 1956—96, NIH; mem. med. adv. panel Bank Am.-Giannini Found., 1963—98; chmn. sci. adv. com., bd. dirs. Nat. Paraplegia Found.; bd. dirs. Charles R. Drew U., 1985—94. Author: Aggression and Defense: Neurol Mechanisms and Social Patterns, 1967, Physiological Correlates of Dreaming, 1967, Sleep and the Maturing Nervous System, 1972, Anatomy: An Atlas of the Human Body, 1975, 5th edit., 2004, Clemente's Anatomy Dissector, 2001; editor: Gray's Anatomy, 1973, 30th Am. edit., 1985; editor-in-chief: Exptl. Neurology, 1973—86, assoc. editor: Neurol. Rsch., Jour. Clin. Anatomy; contbr. articles to sci. jours. Recipient award for merit in sci., Nat. Paraplegia Found., 1973, 23rd Ann. Rehfuss Lectr. and medal, Jefferson Coll., 1986, award for excellence in med. edn., UCLA, 1996, Award of Extraordinary medit, UCLA Med. Alumni Assn., 1997, Significant Early Contributor award, Sleep rsch. Soc., 2003; fellow John Simon Guggenheim Meml. Found., 1988—89. Mem.: NAS (mem. com. on neuropathology, mem. BEAR coms.), Soc. for Neurosci., Japan Soc. Promotion of Sci. (Rsch. award 1978), N.Y. Acad. Scis., Med. Rsch. Assn. Calif. (bd. dirs. 1976—87), AMA-Assn. Am. Med. Colls. (mem. liason com. on med. edn. 1981—87), Internat. Brain Rsch. Orgn., Biol. Stain Commn., Assn. Anatomy Chairmen (pres. 1972), Nat. Bd. Med. Examiners (bd. dirs. 1978—84, mem. anatomy test com. 1980—84), Coun. Acad. Socs. (mem. adminstrv. bd. 1973—81, chmn. 1979—80), Assn. Am. Med. Colls. (mem. exec. com. 1978—81, disting. svc. mem. 1982), Am. Neurol. Assn., Am. Assn. Clin. Anatomists (Honored Mem. of Yr. 1993), Am. Acad. Neurology, Am. Assn. Anatomists (v.p. 1972, pres. 1976—77, Henry Gray award 1993), Am. Physiol. Soc., Brain Rsch. Inst. (dir. 1976—87), Pavlovian Soc. N.Am. (pres. 1972, Ann. award 1968), Inst. Medicine of NAS (mem. sci. adv. bd.), Am. Acad. Cerebral Palsy (hon.), Alpha Omega Alpha, Sigma Xi. Democrat. Home: 11737 Bellagio Rd Los Angeles CA 90049-2158 Office: UCLA Sch Medicine Dept Neurobiology Los Angeles CA 90095-0001 E-mail: cdclem@ucla.edu.

CLEMENTE, CELESTINO, physician, surgeon; b. Penns Grove, N.J., June 11, 1922; s. Ermanno and Caroline (Friozzi) C.; m. Marie Ann Strangio, Nov. 16, 1946; children: Jeffrey, Roderick, Mark, Laurie Ann, Jonathan. BS, Rutgers U., 1942; MD, U. Pa., 1945. Diplomate Am. Bd. Surgery. Intern Jersey City Med. Ctr., 1945-46; resident in gen. surgery Martland Med. Ctr., 1950-53; practice medicine specializing in gen. surgery Newark, 1953—; dir. surgery Children's Hosp., Newark, 1962-70, St. Vincent's Hosp., Montclair, N.J., 1972-83; trustee United Hosps. Med. Ctr., Newark, 1972-88, v.p. med. affairs, 1975-88. Assoc. clinic prof. surgery N.J. Med. Sch., Newark, 1975—; dir. surgery Roseland (N.J) Surg. Ctr., 1983—, also chmn. bd. Rep. candidate for U.S. Ho. of Reps, N.J., 1968; active Nat. Ad Council/HEW, 1970-74. Served to lt. USNR, 1946-48. Fellow ACS, Internat. Coll. Surgeons; mem. AMA, AAAS, Essex Club (Newark). Home and Office: 364 Ridgewood Ave Glen Ridge NJ 07028-1513 Office: 556 Eagle Rock Ave Roseland NJ 07068-1500 Office Phone: 973-743-5188. E-mail: ccmdnj@aol.com.

CLEMENTE, LILIA CALDERON, capital company executive; b. Manila, Philippines, Feb. 21, 1941; d. Jose Damocles and Belen-Dimatulac (Fabros) Calderon; m. Leoploldo Manalac Clemente, June 24, '964. BSBA, U. Philippines, 1960; MA, ABD in Econs., U. Chgo., 1962. Investment analyst, portfolio mgr. CNA Fin. Corp., Chgo., 1967-69; dir. of investments, rsch. and asst. treas. The Ford Found., N.Y.C., 1969-76; 1st v.p., chief investment officer, internat. investments Paine Webber Inc. Mitchell Hutchins Asset Mgmt., N.Y.C., 1983-86; chmn., chief exec. officer Clemente Capital Inc., N.Y.C., 1976—. Asian cons. Am. Can, Greenwich, Conn., 1982-83; cons. on Asian portfolio Eberstadt Internat. Fund; cons. on Japanese and Asian portfolio Capital Rsch., L.A., Geneva, 1976-78; cons. Montreal Investment Mgmt., Can., 1978, Vilas Fischer Assocs., 1978-82, Yasuda Trust Internat. Dept., 1978; mem. U.S. Export Devel. Mission to Japan, 1978; del. Fin. Analysts Fed., 1976-78; chmn. Philipine Am. Found. Bd. trustees Manhattan Coll., 1987—. Named Most Outstanding Overseas Filipino Presdl. award Rep. of the Philippines, 1990; recipient Excellence 2000 award U.S. and Asian C. of C., 1989, Outstanding Alumni, U. Philippines. Roman Catholic. Avocations: writing, poetry, gardening, painting. Office: Clemente Capital Inc 575 Madison Ave New York NY 10022

CLEMENTE, PATROCINIO ABLOLA, secondary school educator; b. Manila, Apr. 23, 1941; arrived in U.S., 1965; s. San Jose Elpidio and Amparo (Ablola) Clemente. BSE, U. Philippines, 1960; MA, Ball State U., 1966, EdD, 1969; postgrad., U. Calif., Riverside, 1970, Calif. State Coll., Fullerton, 1971—72. H.S. tchr. gen. sci. and biology Divsn. City Schs., Quezon City, Philippines, 1960—65; doctoral fellow dept. psychology Ball State U., Muncie, Ind., 1966—67, dept. spl. edn., 1967—68, grad. asst. dept. gen. and exptl. psychology, 1968—69; tchr. educable mentally retarded H.S. level Fontana Unified Sch. Dist., Calif., 1969—70, intermediate level, 1970—73, dist. sch. psychologist, 1973—79, bilingual edn. counselor, 1979—81; resource specialist Morongo Unified Sch. Dist., Calif., 1981—83, spl. day class tchr., 1983—90, tchr. math, sci., Spanish, English, 1990—. Adj. assoc. prof. Chapman Coll., Orange, Calif., 1982—91. Adult leader mem. sch. bd. Blessed Sacrament Sch., Twentynine Palms, Calif. State bd. scholar Ball State U., 1965 Girl Scouts of Philippines, 1963—65; mem. sch. bd. Blessed Sacrament Sch., Twentynine Palms, Calif. State bd. scholar, Ball State U., 1965—66. Mem.: NEA, ASCD, Smithsonian Instn., Morongo Tchrs. Assn., Calif. Tchrs. Assn., Nat. Geog. Soc., Assn. for Children with Learning Disabilities, Found. Exceptional Children, Nat. Assn. of Sch. Psychologists, Am. Assn. on Mental Deficiency, Coun. for Exceptional Children. Roman Catholic. Home: PO Box 637 Twentynine Palms CA 92277-0637

CLEMENTS, BUDDY NEAL, music educator; b. Inglewood, Calif., Apr. 30, 1955; s. Rena Lee Clements. MusB in Music Performance, MusM in Performance, U. Redlands, 1985; MusD, Claremont (Calif.) U., 2002. Lic. tchr. Calif. Dir. band and orch. Walnut (Calif.) H.S., 1984—98; dir. band Cal-Poly Pomona (Calif.) U., 1998—. Assoc. condr., musician Crystal Cathedral Orch., Graden Grove, Calif., 1986—98. Composer: (songs) I Will Fight No More Forever, Concerto for Jazz Trumpet and Orchestra, Spirit Dances, Escapades for Woodwind Quintet, If My Lover Calls Me, Opus Blue & Sunny, Little Child. Mem.: Film Music Soc., Music Educator Nat. Conf., Am. Soc. Composers, Authors and Pubs., Nat. Assn. Rec. Arts and Scis. (assoc.). Office: Walnut High School 400 N Pierre Rd Walnut CA 91789 Office Phone: 909-594-2263. Office Fax: 909-444-3602. Personal E-mail: buddytuba@aol.com. E-mail: buddyclements.com.

CLEMENTS, GREGORY LELAND, physics professor; b. Lincoln, Nebr., Apr. 5, 1949; BS, U. Iowa, 1971, MS, 1976, PhD, 1978. Asst. prof. Dickinson Coll., Carlisle, Pa., 1978-82; systems mgr. SofTec, Iowa City, Iowa, 1982-83; prof. Midland Coll., Fremont, Nebr., 1983—. Mem. Am. Assn. Physics Tchrs. (state pres. 1991). Office: Midland Luth Coll 900 N Clarkson St Fremont NE 68025-4254

CLEMENTS, KIMBERLY DAWNE, school counselor; b. Honolulu, Hawaii, Aug. 26, 1971; d. John O. and Dorothy J. Clements. BA summa cum laude, U. South Fla., Tampa, 1994, MA, 1998; PhD, Barry U., Miami Shores, Fla., 2004. Cert. ednl. leadership (all levels) Fla. Dept. Edn., guidance and counseling (pre-kindergarten through 12th grades) Fla. Dept. Edn., sch. counselor. Part-time rsch. asst. U. South Fla., Tampa, 1996; child life intern Children's Hosp. S.W. Fla., Fort Myers, 1996; sch. counseling practicum U. South Fla., Fort Myers, 1997, sch. counseling intern, 1998; sch. counselor Lee County Sch. Dist., Fort Myers, Fla., 1998—. Contbr. profl. essay and articles to jour. and bull. in field. Health program vol. Lee County Breast Screening Program, Fort Myers, 1991; classroom vol. Lee County Sch. Dist., Fort Myers, 1992, 1995; hosp. vol. Children's Hosp. S.W. Fla., Fort Myers, 1995—96. Mem.: NEA, Am. Sch. Counseling Assn., Acad. Human Resource Devel., Am. Edn. Rsch. Assn., Assn. Supervision, Curriculum, Devel. Avocations: writing, reading. Office: Tanglewood Riverside Sch 1620 Manchester Blvd Fort Myers FL 33919

CLEMENTS, LINDA L., materials engineer, educator, journalist; b. Phoenix, Oct. 6, 1945; d. Howard Abner Clements and Louella Tooley; m. John Laurence Crowley; children: Timothy Crowley, Colin Crowley. BS, Stanford U., 1967; MS Engring., U. Pa., 1971; PhD, Stanford U., 1974. Engr. Lawrence Livermore Lab., Livermore, 1974—78, program mgr., 1977—78; project dir. Advanced Rsch. and Applications Corp., Sunnyvale, Calif., 1978—81, NASA-Ames Rsch. Ctr., Moffett Field, Calif.; assoc. prof., materials engring. San Jose State U., 1981—85, full prof., materials engring., 1985—91; dir. of materials R& D TFI Inc., Pacifica, Calif., 1989—98; adj. prof. U. of Nev., Reno, 1995—99; nat. adj. faculty ASM Internat., Materials Park, Ohio, 1984—2002; instr. Soc. for the Advancement of Material and Process Engring., Covina, Calif., 1995—; adj. faculty Western Nev. C.C., Carson City, Nev., 1999—2002; dir. of materials r & d 2Phase Technologies, Inc., Dayton, Nev., 1998—; pres. C & C Technologies, Dayton, 1991—. Faculty advisor student chpt. Soc. of Women Engineers San Jose State U., 1980—86, San Jose State U. SAMPE, 1985—91; reviewer ASM Internat., Materials Park, Ohio, 1983—99, Technomic Pub. Co., Lancaster, PA.,

1999—2000; peer rev. bd. Jour. of Advanced Materials, Covina, 1999—; steering com. Composites Fabrication mag., Arlington, 2000—; reviewer NSF Grad. Fellowships, 1995, DOE Integrated Manufacturing Fellowships, 1997, Ford Found. Fellowships for Minorities, 2004. Mem. editl. bd.: SAMPE Jour., 2000—, correspondant: Advanced Composites Bull., 1999—2000, contbg. editor: High-Performance Composites Mag., 1998—2000, Composites Fabrication Mag., 2000—. Mem. engring. adv. bd. Western Nev. C.C., Carson City, 1998—, chair engring. adv. bd., 2001—03. Recipient Clements award named in her honor, Western Nev. Cmty. Coll., 2004; fellow, Ford Found., 2004; grantee (3), Northrop Corp., 1986—90. Mem.: ASTM (d-30 com. sec. 1976—78), Soc. of Plastics Engineers, Am. Chem. Soc., ASM Internat., Soc. for the Advancement of Materials and Process Engring. (internat. com. chmn. 1986—2003, chpt. dir. 1996—, internat. sec. 2003—, internat. v.p. 2005—, bd. dirs. 1984—2003), Dayton (Nev.) Hist. Soc. (bd. dirs. 2002—), Friends of the Dayton Valley Libr. (life; pres. 1995—2000, sec. 2000—02, bd. dirs. Do-Mor Dayton 2002—, Vol. of the Yr. 2002), Dayton (Nev.) Mus. Hist. Soc. (bd. dirs. 2003—), Phi Kappa Phi, Tau Beta Pi, Phi Beta Kappa. Avocation: genealogy, historic preservation, science fiction, camping, sewing. Office: 2Phase Techs Inc PO Box 730 Dayton NV 89403 Business E-Mail: lclements@2phasetech.com.

CLEMENTS, LYNN, elementary school educator, reading specialist; b. Honolulu, Nov. 6, 1957; d. Harold E. and Nona J. Downey; m. Mark Evan Clements, Aug. 15, 1988; children: Kevin J., Christopher R. AA, Pasadena City Coll., 1978; BA, Calif. State U., 1979, MA in Edn., 1981. Tchr. Temple City Schs., Calif., 1979—89; reading specialist Pasadena City Schs., 1986—89; instr. reading Pierce Coll., L.A., 1989; reading specialist Soledad Sch. Dist., 1989—96; instr. reading Chapman U., Monterey, 2000—; reading specialist Pacific Grove Unified Sch., 1997—. Site coord. Monterey County Reads, 2000—05. Co-chair numerous coms. Jr. League Monterey, 1992—2004; vol. guide Monterey Aquarium, 1990—91; sec. sch. site coun. bd. Pacific Grove Sch., 1996—97; sec. mem. chair David Ave. PTA, 1996—98. Named Vol. of Yr., Jr. League Monterey, 1993; recipient Golden Bell award, Calif. Sch. Bd. Assn., San Francisco, 2004. Mem.: Calif. Reading Assn., Internat. Reading Assn. Presbyterian. Avocations: travel, reading, cooking, skiing.

CLEMENTS, LYNNE FLEMING, marriage and family therapist, application developer; b. Bklyn., Aug. 8, 1945; d. Daniel Gillies and Dorothy Frances (Zitzmann) Fleming; m. Louis Myrick Clements, Feb. 19, 1972; children: Ryan Louis, Glenn Fleming. BA in Sociology, Bradley Univ., 1967; MSW, Fordham Univ., 1973; post grad. studies, Columbia Univ., 1970-71; cert. in family therapy, Inst. for Mental Health Edn., 1990. LCSW NJ, cert. social work mgr. Computer programmer Employer's Comml. Union Group Ins. Co., Boston, 1967-69, Harvard Bus. Sch., Cambridge, Mass., 1969-70, Volkswagon of Am., Englewood Cliffs, NJ, 1971; psychiat. social worker Associated Cath. Charities Family and Children's Svc., Paramus, NJ, 1973-74, Christian Health Ctr., Wyckoff, NJ, 1976; owner, mgr. Wicker Wagon, Bergenfield, NJ, 1977-85; psychotherapist The Psychotherapy Counseling Ctr., Bergenfield, NJ, 1982-89; programmer analyst Atlas Computing Svc., Secaucus, NJ, 1984-86; program coord., family therapist Divsn. Family Guidance, Hackensack, NJ, 1986-91; pres. Corp. Family Resources, Ridgewood, NJ, 1989—; family therapist cons. Family Recovery of Valley View, White Plains, NY, 1992-94, Furman Clinic, Fair Lawn, NJ, 1995-96, Van Ost Inst. for Family Living, Englewood, NJ, 1996; cert. social work mgr., 1997—. Part time family therapist NJ Ctr. Psychotherapy Inc., Ridgefield Pk., NJ, 1990. Chmn. curriculum enhancement com. Bergen County Acad. Advancement Sci. and Tech., NJ, 1992—96; chmn. entertainment Bergen County Children's Festival, 1993; founder, chmn. Bergenfield Coun. of the Arts, 1993; chmn., designer Bergenfield Coun. Arts, 1993—99, chmn. author and poet program, 1996—, Bergenfield Coun. of the Arts, 1996—; mem. fundraising com., arts programming chmn. Bergenfield Cmty. Ctr., 2000—; co-chmn. Bergenfield Film Festival, 2004—; sec. Mayor's Beautify Bergenfield Com., NJ, 1991—95; chmn. bd. cmty. play ctr. All Saints Ch., 1977—78, Sunday sch. tchr., 1982—89, 1994—; mem. Twin Boro Youth Ministry Coun., 1989—. Recipient First and Second Pl. awards, Bergenfield Art Contest, 1980, Best Practice Award for Author/Poet Program, N.J. Dept. Edn., 2003; grantee NIMH, 1973. Mem.: NASW, AAUW, N.J. Coalition Mental Health Profl., N.J. Soc. Clin. Social Workers (bd. dir., chmn. mktg. and vendor 1999—2003, membership chmn. 2003—), N.J. Commerce and Indsl. Assn. (child care com. 1990—, human resources com. 1990—), Fordham U. Alumni Assn., Am. Orthopsychiatric Assn., Acad. Cert. Social Workers, Gifted Child Soc. (parent workshop coord. 1989—, bd dir.), Women of Accomplishments (founder, pres. 1990—, chmn. women's coalition conf. 1993—), Zonta (Amelia Earhart chmn. 1987—88, chmn. status women com. 1993—94, lit. com. 1995—). Episcopalian. Avocations: walking, art, music, crafts, boating, acting. Home: 148 Harcourt Ave Bergenfield NJ 07621-1917 Office: Corp Family Resources 15 Godwin Ave Ste 1 Ridgewood NJ 07450-3739 Office Phone: 201-670-0269. Personal E-mail: lynne.clements@att.net.

CLEMENTS, MARY LOU, epidemiologist, educator; BA, Tex. Tech U., 1968; MD, U. Tex., 1972; DTMH, U. London, Eng., 1975; MPH, Johns Hopkins U., 1979. Diplomate Am. Bd. Internal Medicine, subspecialty of infectious diseases. Intern, resident in internal medicine Temple U. Hosp., Phila., 1972-75; spl. epidemiologist WHO, Uttar Pradesh, India, 1975-77; corrd. accreditation self-study Sch. Hygiene and Pub. Health Johns Hopkins U., Balt., 1978, asst. faculty mem. Sch. Medicine, 1979-81, assoc. prof. dept. internat. health Sch. Hygiene and Pub. Health, 1985-90, mem. med. staff Sch. Medicine, 1986—, dir. Ctr. Immunization Rsch., 1986—, prof., head divsn. vaccine scis. dept. internat. healthSch. Hygiene and Pub. Health, 1990—, prof., head dept. immunology and infectious diseases Sch. Hygiene and Pub. Health, 1991—; dir. home health care program, staff internist E. Balt. Med. Plan, 1978-79; mem. med. staff dept. medicine Johns Hopkins Hosp., Balt., 1979-81, 86—; asst. prof. dept. medicine, chief clin. studies sect. Ctr. Vaccine Devel. Sch. Medicine, U. Md., 1979-84, asst. prof. dept. epidemiology and preventative medicine, 1983-85, assoc. prof. dept. medicine, 1984-85; mem. med. staff Francis Scott Key Med. Ctr., 1986—. Mem. com. for AIDS Rsch. Johns Hopkins Med. Instns., 1990—; mem. adv. com. on immunization practices Ctrs. for Disease Control and Prevention, 1990—; mem. com. on The Children's Vaccine Initiative: Strategies towards full U.S. Participation, Inst. Medicine, 1991—; active U.S. AID/PHS Consultative Group on Vaccine Devel., 1991-93, Data and Safety Monitoring Bd. for Respiratory Syncytial Virus Immunoglobulin Treatment Trials, 1991—; med. cons. to numerous med. orgns. including WHO, APHA, NIH. Contbr. chpts. to books; contbr. articles to profl. med. jours. Fellow Am. Infectious Disease Soc. Am.; mem. Am. Soc. Microbiology. Am. Soc. Virology, Delta Omega (alpha chpt.). Office: Johns Hopkins U Ctr Immun Res Sch Pub Health 624 N Broadway Baltimore MD 21205-1900

CLEMENTS, MICHAEL CRAIG, health services consulting executive, retired renal dialysis technician; b. Cin., Sept. 17, 1945; s. Marvin Hubert and Mildred Helen (Rabe) C.; m. Minnie Faye Pospisil, Dec. 1, 1972; children: Melissa Ayn, Michael Aaron. Student, U. Cin., 1968-70; EMT/paramedic, Good Samaritan Health Ctr., 1980. Cert. renal dialysis technician. Hemodialysis technician Christ Hosp., Cin., 1968-79; tech. svcs. dir. Dialysis Clinic, Inc., Cin., 1980-91; pres. Critical Care Svcs., Inc., Mason, Ohio, 1987—. Firefighter/paramedic Mason Vol. Fire Co., 1978-85, EMS tng. officer, 1984, EMS capt., 1985; coop employers environ. and sci. lab. tech. programs Cin. State Coll. Contbr. articles to profl. jours. Mem. Mason Environ. Adv. Commn., 1990—, vice chmn., 1992-93, bus. and parent curriculum review com. Mason City Schs., 1992; employer advisor coop. program Cin. Tech. Coll. Biomed. Engring. Tech., 1986-91; with U.S. Naval Sea Cadet Corps, 2002—, exec. officer Cin. divsn., 2003—. With USN, 1964-70. Mem. Assn. for Advancement of Med. Instrumentation, Ohio Acad. Sci. Mem. Ch. of Christ. Office: Critical Care Svcs Inc 7562 Central Parke Blvd Mason OH 45040-6816 Office Phone: 513-573-9901. Business E-Mail: michael.clements@criticalcareservicesinc.com.

CLEMENTS, ROBERT, insurance executive; b. Chgo., Sept. 7, 1932; s. John and Mildred L. (Chapman) C.; m. Marilyn Trexler, Dec. 27, 1955; children: Paula J., John, Jeffrey, Ben T. BA, Dartmouth Coll., 1954. Underwriter Royal Ins. Co., N.Y.C., 1956—59; sr. v.p. Marsh & McLennan, Ltd., Toronto, Canada, 1959—75; chmn. Marsh & McLennan Inc., N.Y.C., 1975—92; pres. Marsh & McLennan Cos., Inc., N.Y.C., 1992-94; founder, chmn. MMC Capital Corp., 1994-96; chmn. Risk Capital Holdings, Inc., 1996—2000, Arch Capital Group Ltd., 2000—05. Chmn. Island Heritage Holdings, 2002-, Integro Ltd., 2005-; chmn. bd. trustees Risk Found.; chmn. emeritus Coll. Ins. Bd. overseers emeritus Inst. for Civil Justice. With U.S. Army, 1954-56. Democrat. Office: Arch Capital Group Sound Shore Dr Greenwich CT 06830 Office Phone: 203-862-4343.

CLEMENTS, WILLIAM ELLSWORTH, II, lawyer; b. Cin., Dec. 17, 1953; s. William E. and Margaret A. (Green) Clements; m. Radne F. Roff; children: Sarah Margaret, Anne K., Julia P. BA, Miami U., 1976; JD, U. Cin., 1979. Bar: Ohio 1979, U.S. Dist. Ct. (so. dist.) Ohio 1979, U.S. Ct. Appeals (6th cir.) 1979. Assoc. Kondritzer Gold & Frank, Cin., 1979-88; ptnr. Clements, Mahin & Cohen, Cin., 1988—. Mem. ABA, ATLA, Ohio State Bar Assn. Ohio Acad. Trial Lawyers, Cin. Bar Assn., Hamilton County Trial Lawyers Assn. Avocations: motorcycling, golf. Office: Clements Mahin & Cohen 35 E 7tn Ste710 Cincinnati OH 45202-2022 Office Phone: 513-721-6500. Business E-Mail: wec@cmclawyers.com.

CLEMENTZ, DAVID M., information technology executive; BS, U. Ariz.; MS, Purdue U.; MBA, Pepperdine U.; PhD, Mich. State U.; attended, INSEAD Advanced Mgmt. Program, Fontainebleau. France. Cert. engr., Alberta Assn. Petroleum Engineers. Pres. Chevron Petroleum Tech. Co., 1994—97, Chevron Info. Tech. Co., 1997—2001, Chevron eBusiness Devel. Co., 2000—01; enterprise chief info. officer, pres. ChevronTexaco Info. Co., 2001—03; exec. v.p. svc. delivery EDS, Plano, Tex., 2003—. Prin. Walking Liberty Ventures; former bd. dir. upstreaminfo.com, PetroCosm; past chair exec. com. info. mgmt. and tech. Am. Petroleum Inst.; keynote spkr. and lectr. numerous forums and conf. Mem. Am. Grad. Sch. Internat. Mgmt.; industry advisory bd. Thunderbird; advisory bd. Coll. Sci. and Engring., San Francisco State U.; past pres. La Habra Area C. of C., Calif. Infantry officer USMC, 1969—71, Vietnam and Camp Pendleton, Calif. Mem.: Soc. Petroleum Engr. Office: EDS Corp HQ 5400 Legacy Dr Plano TX 75024 Office Phone: 972-604-6000. Office Fax: 972-605-6033.

CLEMETSON, CHARLES ALAN BLAKE, physician; b. Canterbury, Eng., Oct. 31, 1923; came to U.S., 1961, naturalized, 1972; s. Charles Harold and Gwendoline Maude Winefred (Blake) C.; m. Helen Cowan Forster, Mar. 29, 1947 (dec. Nov. 2002); children: Claudia, Charles, David (dec.), Andrew. B.M.,B.Ch., Oxford (Eng.) U., 1948. Lic. physician, La., U.K. Research asst. Obstetric Hosp., Univ. Coll. Hosp., London, 1950-52; Nichols research fellow Royal Soc. Medicine, 1951-52; house surgeon obstetrics W. Middlesex Hosp., 1952-53; resident med. officer obstetrics Queen Charlotte's Hosp., 1953; house surgeon gynaecology Hammersmith Hosp., 1953-54; obstetric and gynecol. registrar Lake Hosp., Ashton-under-Lyne, Lancashire, Eng., 1954-56; lectr. ob-gyn. Univ. Coll. Hosp., London, 1956-58; asst. prof. Univ. Hosp., Saskatoon, Sask., Can., 1958-61, U. Calif., San Francisco, 1961-67; dir. dept. ob-gyn. Meth. Hosp., Bklyn., 1967-81, Huey P. Long Meml. Hosp., Pineville, La., 1981-91; assoc. prof. SUNY, Bklyn., 1967-72; prof. Downstate Med. Ctr., SUNY, 1972-81, Tulane U., 1981-91, prof. emeritus, 1991. Mem. obstetric adv. com. N.Y.C. Dept. Health, 1968; cons. in field; mem. med. adv. com. Planned Parenthood N.Y.C., 1971; mem. physicians rev. com. Blue Cross-Blue Shield N.Y.C., 1975; lectr. maternal health U. Calif., Berkeley, 1964-65 Author: Vitamin C, 3 vols., 1989; contbr. articles to med. jours. Served in RAF, 1948-50. Recipient Rsch. Career Devel. award NIH, 1965-67. Fellow ACOG, Royal Coll. Obstetricians and Gynaecologists, Royal Coll. Physicians and Surgeons Can.; mem. Bklyn. Gynecol. Soc. (pres. 1977-78). Personal E-mail: mogee2000@yahoo.com. *Certainty of knowledge is the antithesis of progress.*

CLEMMENSEN, LARRY P., former investment company executive; Grad., Calif. State U., Fresno, 1969. V.p., corp. contr. Pertec Computer Corp., 1979; CEO Capital Group Cos., L.A. Named Outstanding Alumni, Calif. State U., Fresno, 2001. Office Fax: (213) 486-9217.

CLEMMER, DAN ORR, librarian; b. Etowah, Tenn., Dec. 28, 1938; s. Dan Orr and Nancy Elizabeth (Haney) C.; m. Elizabeth Louise Campbell, Aug. 25, 1962; children: Nancy Day, Helen, Stephen. BA, Davidson Coll., 1961; MA Teaching, Brown U., 1964; MS Libr. Svc., Columbia U., 1967. Intern Libr. of Congress, Washington, 1967-68, asst. head African-Asian exchange, 1968-70; asst. to librarian Smithsonian Inst. Libr., Washington, 1970-72, asst. chief access svc., 1972-73; chief, reader svcs. U.S. Dept. State Libr., Washington, 1973-92, chief librarian, 1992—2002; ret., 2002. Mem. Depository Libr. Coun., 1994-98. Contbr. articles to profl. jours. Mem. ALA (pres. Fed. Librs. Roundtable 1993-94, exec. bd. of Fed. Libr. and Info. Ctr. com.); mem. D.C. Libr. Assn. (pres. 1995-96). Home: 5527 Trent St Chevy Chase MD 20815-5511

CLEMMER, DAVID E., chemistry professor, researcher; b. 1965; BS, Adams State Coll., 1987; PhD in Chemistry, U. Utah, 1992. Postdoctoral fellow Himeji Inst. of Tech., Japan, 1992—93; postdoctoral rsch. assoc. Northwestern U., 1993—95; prof. chemistry Indiana U., 1995—, Robert & Marjorie Mann chair chemistry. Mem. U.S. Defense Sci. Study Group. Author: (over 80 scientific articles including) Gas-phase DNA: Oligothymidine Ion Conformers, 1997, Magic Number Clusters of Serine In The Gas Phase, 2001, Coupling Ion mobility Separations, Collisional Activation Techniques, and Multiple Stages of MS For Analysis of Complex Peptide Mixtures, 2002. Named one of Brilliant 10, Polular Sci. mag., 2002; recipient Early Career award, Nat. Sci. Found., 1996, Finnegan award, Am. Soc. for Mass Spectrometry, 1997, Alfred P. Sloan Rsch. Fellowship, 1998—2000, TR-100 Rsch. Innovation award, MIT Tech. Review Mag., 1999, Arthur F. Findeis award, Am. Chemical Soc., 1999, Eli Lilly Analytical Chemistry award, 2000, Pittcon Achievement award, 2002. Office: Indiana U Chemistry Dept 800 E Kirkwood Ave Bloomington IN 47405-7102

CLEMMER, LEON, architect, space designer; b. Phila., Feb. 11, 1926; s. Leon and Mary Colton (Steele) C.; m. Mary Jane Bertolet, 1955, Nov. 19, 1955; children: Catherine C. Pickell, Leon Jr. BArch, U. Pa., 1951. Registered architect, Pa., N.J., Fla. Architect Vincent G. Kling, FAIA, Phila., 1951-56, Nolen & Swinebure, Phila., 1957-58, Gleeson & Mulrooney, Phila., 1958-62; pvt. practice Leon Clemmer Arch., Phila./Jenkintown, 1962--. Author: One God, 16 Homes, The Steele Idea, The history of Horsham Township. Vice-chmn. Abington Township Planning Commn.; mem. Phila., Glenside, Jenkintown C. of C., Independence Hall Assn.; mem. bd. of mgrs. Abington YMCA; bd. dirs. Friends of Historic Rittenhouse Town, Historic Bartram Gardens. With USN, 1943-46, PTO. Recipient Disting. Bldg. award Pa. Soc. Architects, MacArthur award Carpenters' Co. of Phila., 1988, Juvenile Justices Penna/'s Best, 1990, Juvenile Justices Nation's Best, 1991. Mem. AIA, Pa. Soc. Architects (bd. dirs.), Engrs. Club, Found. for Architecture, Carpenters Co. City and County Phila. (pres.), Am. Soc. Planning Ofcls., Am. Soc. Ch. Architecture, Nat. Trust for Hist. Preservation, Soc. for Indsl. Archaeology (bd. dirs.), Pa. Hist. Soc., Old York Road Hist. Soc. (bd. dirs., pres.), Victorian Soc., Union League Phila. (bd. dirs.), Mennonite Historians Ea. Pa., Clinkers Club, Huntingdon Valley Kennel Club (pres.), Rotary. Republican. Episcopalian. Avocations: watercolorist, historian. Home: 324 Chestnut Lane Ambler PA 19002 Personal E-mail: leonclem@comcast.net.

CLEMMONS, DAVID ROBERT, internist, educator; b. Nashville, May 19, 1947; s. Robert Starr and Beatrice (Winter) C.; m. Kathy Silverman, Nov. 27, 1971; children: Amy Elizabeth, Anna Katherine. Student, Vanderbilt U., 1965-66; BS, Davidson Coll., 1969; MD, U. N.C., 1974. Diplomate Am. Bd. Internal Medicine. Intern in medicine Mass. Gen. Hosp., Boston, 1974-75, jr. and sr. resident in medicine, 1975-77; fellow in endocrinology Harvard U., Boston, 1977-79; asst. prof. medicine U. N.C., Chapel Hill, 1979-83, assoc. prof., 1983-87, prof. medicine, 1987—, div. chief endocrinology and metabolism, 1990—, assoc. chmn. dept. medicine, 1997—, Kenan prof. medicine, 1999—. Assoc. dir. clin. rsch. unit N.C. Meml. Hosp., Chapel Hill, 1979—; cons. Monsanto Inc., St. Louis, 1982—, Celltrix Inc., Santa Clara, Calif., 1991—, Genentech, Inc., So. San Francisco, 1991—; mem. cell biology and Physiology study sect. NIH, 1986-90. Contbr. articles to profl. jours. Chmn. adminstrv. bd. Univ. Meth. Ch., Chapel Hill, 1986, lay leader, 1987. Research grantee Nat. Inst. Aging, 1980, 83, 87, 92, 97, Nat. Heart, Lung and Blood Inst., 1980, 84, 86, 91, 96, Am. Heart Assn. Fellow ACP; mem. Am. Soc. Clin. Investigation, Am. Fedn. Clin. Research, Assn. Am. Physicians (young investigator award 1986), Endocrine Soc. Democrat. Office: U NC Dept Medicine CB 7170 6111 Thurston Bowles Chapel Hill NC 27599-0001

CLEMMONS, EVELYN YVONNE, administrative assistant; b. Toledo, Ohio, Oct. 14, 1939; d. Larry Rogers and Blondella Mims; m. Lucius Eugene Clemmons (dec.); children: Christa Dee, Christina Louise; m. James C. Kiner; children: Michelle A. Kiner, Stephen J Kiner, Carolyn L Kiner. Administrative Assistant Certification SUNY Buffalo EOC, 1995. Gs-5 sec. Soil Conservation Svc., Albany, NY, 1989—89; sr. corp. support clk. Computer Task Group, Buffalo, 1995—99; admin. asst. EPA, Atlanta. Contact person Computer Task Group, Buffalo, 1995—99. Author: (poetry book) Lessons. Officer VFW Aux. Post 2851, Fremont, Ohio, 1983—85; listing names Wall of Tolerance, Montgomery, Ala., 2002—02; pres. Bissel Ave. Block Club, Buffalo, 1981—81. Mem.: Internat. Soc. of Poets. Avocations: knitting, crocheting, sewing, dance, cooking.

CLEMMONS, JOHN B., bank executive, director, retired mathematics educator; b. Rome, Ga., Apr. 11, 1916; s. Lewis Isaac Clemmons and Bessie Turner; m. Mozelle Dailey; children: John B. Jr., Sheila Mozelle. BS, Morehouse Coll.; MS, Atlanta U.; postgrad., U. So. Calif. Prin. Harlan (Ky.) H.S., 1941—43; asst. prin. Carver H.S., Cumberland, Md., 1943—47; dept. head Savannah (Ga.) State U., 1947—87; chmn. bd. dirs. Carver Bank, Savannah. Bd. dirs. Goodwill, 1975—2001. Recipient Silver Beaver award, Boy Scouts Am., 1963; fellow Mention, Boule Found., 1996—, Russell, 2000; grantee, Ford Found., 1951, NSF, 1960. Mem.: Am. Math. Assn., Masons (32d degree), Beta Kappa Chi, Alpha Kappa Mu. Home: 2201 E Victory Dr Savannah GA 31404 Office: Carver Bank PO Box 2769 Savannah GA 31498-1201

CLEMMONS, NANCY WASHINGTON, library administrator, educator; b. Sept. 6, 1947; m. W. Ronald Clemmons. BS in Chemistry, Birmingham So. Coll., 1968; MLS, U. Ala., 1973. Grad. sci. libr. Samford U., Birmingham, Ala., 1973-76; sr. libr. govt. docs. La. State U., Baton Rouge, 1976-77; reference libr. Lister Hill Libr. U. Ala., Birmingham, 1977-81, vision sci. libr., 1981-82, head reference svcs., 1983-89, head info. and instrnl. svc., 1989-92, acting dir., assoc. prof., 1992-95, dep. dir., 1995—, prof., 1999—. Mem. regional adv. coun. Southeastern Atlantic Med. Library Svcs., Balt., 1994—96; mentor Acad. Health Info. Profls., 1995—; mem. adv. bd. HealthInfoNet, Jefferson County, Ala., 2000—. Author: (with others) Reference and Information Services Quarterly, 1994; mem. edtl. bd. Med. Ref. Svcs. Quar., 1990—; various book reviews; contbr. articles to profl. jours. Mem. adopt a troop com. Boy Scouts Am., 1988-92. Mem.: Ala. Health Librs. Assn. (pres. 1983—84), Med. Libr. Assn. (chair pub. svcs. sect. 1988—89, chair mem. com. 1988—89, chair awards com. 1993—94, chpt. coun. rep. 1994—97, chair so. chpt. 1997—98, chair Lucretia McClure Excellence in Edn. Award Jury 2000—01, mem. nominating com. 2000, bd. dirs. 2003—, sr. assoc. editor jour. 2000—05), Acad. Health Info. Profls. (disting. mem.), Beta Phi Mu. Office: U Ala at Birmingham Lister Hill Libr HealthScis 251C 1530 3d Ave S Birmingham AL 35294-0013 Office Phone: 205-934-5460. Business E-Mail: nclemmon@uab.edu.

CLEMONS, JANE ANDREA, state legislator; b. Poughkeepsie, N.Y., Apr. 2, 1946; d. Mary (Longendyke) Martin; m. Michael R. Clemons, Oct. 15, 1966; children: Bret, Nick, Benjamin. Student, Moore Gen. Hosp., Grasmere, N.H., 1966. Nurse various orgns., Nashua, N.H., 1967-89; mem. N.H. Ho. of Reps., Dist. 31, Nashua, 1990—, dep. Dem. House leader, 2005; dep. Dem. leader N.H. Ho. of Reps.; 2nd vice chair N.H. Dem. State Party, 2005—; ranking dem. election law com. N.H. Ho. of Reps. Sponsor Sr. Citizen Computer Health Care Program, Nashua, 1983-84; ward chair Dem. City Com., Nashua, 1988; del. Dem. State Conv., Nashua, 1988; vol. Merrimack (N.H.) Friars Club, 1990-92; del. State Dem. Pary, 1993, Dem. Nat. Conv., 2004; chmn. Nashua Dem. City Com. Greek Orthodox. Avocations: gardening, reading, camping. Home: 177 Kinsley St Nashua NH 03060-3649 Office: NH House Reps State House Concord NH 03301 E-mail: JCSR119@aol.com.

CLEMONS, JOHN ROBERT, lawyer; b. Oak Park, Ill., June 9, 1948; BA, U. Iowa, 1970; JD, DePaul U., 1975. Asst. village mgr. Village of Riverside, Ill., 1970-72; co-dir. dist. 208 Youth Ctr., Riverside, 1970-73; area dir. S.W. area Cook County OEO, 1972-73; clk., legal researcher Klein, Thorpe & Jenkins, attys., Chgo., 1974-75; asst. state atty.'s Jackson County, Murphysboro, Ill., 1975-80, state's atty., 1980-88; adj. prof., lectr. So. Ill. U., Carbondale, 1978—; ptnr. Clemons & Hood, 1991—; pres. Mt. Joy Enterprises, Inc. Home: 375 Mount Joy Rd Murphysboro IL 62966-4464 Office: 813 W Main St Carbondale IL 62901-2537 Office Phone: 618-529-4000.

CLEMONS, KAY K., librarian; b. Peru, Ind., Jan. 17, 1937; d. Ellis Allen and Ferne (Bowman) Metzger; widow; 1 child, Wayne Ellis Shafer. Diploma, Marion (Ind.) Bus. Coll., 1985. Mem. Grant County Genealogy Club (sec. 1994-99, rschr. 1994—, v.p. 2001—). Avocations: geneological and family history research, crosswords, jigsaw puzzles, collecting reader's digest condensed books, collecting unusual bookmarks. Home: 1200 S Hendricks Ave Trlr 27 Marion IN 46953-1283 Personal E-mail: ckaykay4706@aol.com.

CLEMONS, MAGGIE RUTH, retired elementary school educator; b. Lafayette, La., Dec. 1, 1945; d. Clarence Darrell and Rita Miles; 1 child, Justina Maria Clemons. BA, So. U., 1969; MEd, Trinity Coll., Washington, 1979. Tchr. Paul Breaux Elem. Sch., Lafayette, La., 1969-70, Woodvale Elem., Lafayette, 1970-72, Myrtle Pl. Elem., Lafayette, 1972-75, Benjamin Franklin, Miami, 1975-76, Sacred Heart Sch., Washington, 1976-81, Plantation Elem., Lafayette, 1981—2000; retired, 2000. Author: (poetry) Thoughts by Mag, 1998; appeared on Acadicana Open TV Channel, 1997, 98; contbr. poems to books. Recipient Nat. Inventive Thinking-Winner's Tchr. Weekly Reader, 1991. Mem. Retired Tchrs. Assn., La. State Poetry Soc., Alpha Kappa Alpha (new reporter 1989-92, asst. sec. 1993). Roman Catholic. Avocations: crocheting, writing, poetry, short stories.

CLEMONS, WILLIAM ERIC, psychiatrist, educator; b. DeQueen, Ark., Aug. 14, 1973; s. Warren William and Bertha Enid Clemons; m. Alison Ruwet Clemons, Sept. 11, 1999; 1 child, Tate Carolina. BA in Microbiology, U. Ark., 1995; MD, U. Tenn., 1999. Resident psychiatry W.Va. U., Morgantown, W.Va., 1999—2003; fellow sleep medicine U. Mich., Ann Arbor, Mich., 2003—04, asst. prof., 2004—.

CLENDENEN, WILLIAM HERBERT, JR., lawyer; b. New London, Conn., Dec. 2, 1942; s. William H. and Ethel L. (Clifford) Clendenen; m. Corinna P. Clendenen; children: William, Patrick, Allison, Derek, Luke. BA, Providence Coll., 1964; JD, Cath. U. Am., 1967. Bar: Conn. 1967, U.S. Dist. Ct. Conn. 1971, U.S. Dist. Ct. (so. dist.) N.Y. 1977, U.S. Dist. Ct. R.I. 1977, U.S. Ct. Claims 1977, U.S. Ct. Appeals (2d cir.) 1971, U.S. Supreme Ct. 1976. Reginald Heber Smith Cmty. Lawyer fellow U. Pa., Phila., 1967—68; staff atty. New Haven Legal Assistance Assn., Inc., 1966—73; prin. William H. Clendenen Jr., PC, New Haven, 1973—2002; mng. mem. Clendenen & Shea LLC, New Haven, 2002—. Supervising atty. Yale Law Sch., 1981; alt. pub. mem. Conn. State Bd. Mediation and Arbitration, 1976—78; co-chmn. U.S. Dist. Ct. Conn. Spl. Masters Com., New Haven, 1985—89. Fellow: Am. Coll. Trial Lawyers, Conn. Bar Found. (life; dir. 1991—2004, treas. 1992—2004); mem.: ATLA, ABA, New Haven County Bar Found. (dir. 1993—2003), Conn. Trial Lawyers Assn., New Haven County Bar Assn. (sec.

1986—87, treas. 1987—88, v.p. 1988—89, pres. 1989—90), Conn. Bar Assn. (chmn. consumer law sect. 1974—78, chmn. lawyer referral com. 1987—89, jud. independence task force 1998—99). Home: 102 River Edge Farms Rd Madison CT 06443-2756

CLENDINEN, CRAIG P., lawyer; b. Savannah, Fla., Mar. 11, 1961; s. Norman W. and Virginia L. Clendinen; m. Cynthia Creel (div. Aug. 1998); 1 child, Anissa Nicole; m. Carolyne Anne Clendinen, July 17, 1999. BA in Econs. and Polit. Sci., Fla. So. Coll., 1983; JD with honors, Fla. State U., 1986. Bar: U.S. Dist. Ct. (mid. and so. dists.) Fla. 88, U.S. Ct. Appeals (11th cir.) 89, Fla. 96. Assoc. Trenam, Simmons, Kemker et al, Tampa, Fla., 1986—91, Stearns Weaver Miller, Tampa, 1992—94, Bales Weinstein, Tampa, 2001—; gen. counsel, v.p. Fla. Employers Safety Assn., Lakeland, 1991—92; asst. states atty. Hillsborough County States Atty., Tampa, Fla., 1994—2001. Bd. dirs. Bay Area Legal Svcs., Tampa, Samaritan Counseling Ctrs., Tampa; mem. adv. bd. temermarketing fraud Am. Prosecutors Rsch. Inst., Washington, 1998—2000; lectr. in field. Author: Commercial Arbitration, 1990, Creditors Right in Florida, 1993. Pres., dist. gov. Sertoma, Tampa, 1993; chmn. Tampa Drug Nuicance Bd., 1989—91; pres. Human Devel. Ctr., Tampa. Named Sertoman of Yr., Sertoma, 1993; grantee, Dept. Justice. Master: Tampa Bay Inn of Ct. (sec. 1991—99); mem.: Hubert Goldbert Criminal Inn of Ct. (barrister). Avocations: tennis, sailing, hiking, canoeing. Home: 10605 Coquita Ln Tampa FL 33618 Office: Bales Weinstein 625 E Twiggs Tampa FL 33602

CLERGUE, LUCIEN GEORGES, photographer; b. Arles, France, Aug. 14, 1934; s. Etienne and Jeanne (Grangeon) C.; m. Yolande Wartel, Jan. 10, 1963; children: Anne, Olivia. Dr. es Letters in Photography, U. Provence, 1979. Tchr. workshops New Sch., N.Y.C., Art Ctr., Pasadena, Osaka U., Japan, other U.S. univs. and colls. Freelance photographer, 1959—; artistic dir. Arles Festival, 1971-75, 86-88; founder, Rencontres Internat. de la Photographie, Arles, 1969, art dir. XXVth anniversary, 1994; one-man shows include Kunstgewerbe Mus., Zurich, 1958, 63, Mus. Modern Art, NYC, 1961—, Musèe d'Arts Decoratifs, Paris, 1962—, Moderna Museet, Stockholm, 1969—, Art Inst. Chgo., 1970—, Kunsthalle, Düsseldorf, Fed. Republic Germany, 1970—, Gallery Witkin, NYC, 1972-79, Bruxelles Musee d'Ixelles, 1974—, Israel Mus., Jerusalem, 1974—, Ctr. Pompidou, Paris, 1980—, Mus. d'Art Moderne Paris, 1984, George Eastman House, Rochester, 1985, ICP, NY, 1986, Amos Anderson Mus., Helsinki, 1987, Real Maestranza Sevilla, 1991, Houston Photo Fest, 1992, Milw. Art Mus., 1993, Calif. Mus. Photography, Riverside, 1997, Centro de la Imagen, Mexico, 1997, Kunstmuseum Dortmund, 1999, John Stevenson Gallery, NY, 2000, 02, 05, Gallery B. Lebon, Paris, 2000, Vitoria, Spain, 2002, Bernheimer Gallery, Munich, 2004, Arles 35th RIP, 2004; works rep. books, movies; represented in permanent collection Fogg Mus., Harvard U., Cambridge, Mass., Mus. Modern Art, NYC, Met. Mus., NYC; films include Picasso War Love and Peace; books include Footprints of the Gods, 1988, Picasso my Friend, 1993, Grands Nus, 1999, Poesie Photographique, 2003; contbr. articles to profl. jours. Decorated chevalier Nat. Order Merit, Legion of Honor; recipient Louis Lumière prize, 1966, Grand Prix of Higashikawa Photo Fest, 1986, 3rd prize World Press Photo Internat., Amsterdam, 1997, Prix Polyedre, Aix, France, 1998. Mem. Ste. des Amis Jean Cocteau, Ste des Amis de La Fond, St. J. Perse, Aix en Provence, Rencontres Internat. de la Photographie Arles, Memoire 2000, Union des Photographes Createurs. Roman Catholic. Home: 19 Rue Aristide Briand 13200 Arles France Office Phone: 33 4 90520704.

CLERKIN, EUGENE PATRICK, physician, educator; b. N.Y.C., Feb. 22, 1931; s. Eugene and Nance (Fitzsimmons) C.; m. Nancy Lucille Oshirak, Aug. 16, 1958; children: Eugene J., Brian A., Lucille A., Kathryn M. BS, Manhattan Coll., 1952; MD, NYU, 1956. Diplomate Am. Bd. Internal Medicine and Endocrinology. Physician Lahey Clinic Found., Burlington, Mass., 1963—, chmn. dept. internal medicine, 1970-91, also bd. govs., 1981-91; asst. clin. prof. medicine Harvard Med. Sch., Boston, 1976-99; assoc. clin. prof. Tufts Med. Sch., 1999—. Mem. corp. N.E. Deaconess Hosp., 1980-93. Lt. USNR, 1958-60. Fellow ACP; mem. AMA, Endocrine Soc., Am. Diabetes Assn., Mass. Med. Soc. Roman Catholic. Avocations: tennis, hiking. Office: Lahey Clinic Med Ctr 41 Mall Rd Burlington MA 01805-0002

CLERMONT, KEVIN MICHAEL, law educator; b. N.Y.C., Oct. 25, 1945; s. William Theodore and Rita Ruth (Healy) C.; m. Emily Sherwin; 2 children, Adrienne Shaine, Jian Louise. AB summa cum laude, Princeton U., 1967; postgrad., U. Nancy, France, 1967-68; JD magna cum laude, Harvard U., 1971. Bar: Mass. 1971, N.Y. 1974, U.S. Dist. Ct. (so. and ea. dists.) N.Y. 1974, U.S. Ct. Appeals (2d cir.) 1974. Law clk. to judge U.S. Dist. Ct. (so. dist.) N.Y., 1971-72; assoc. Cleary, Gottlieb, Steen & Hamilton, N.Y.C., 1972-74; asst. prof. Sch. Law Cornell U., Ithaca, N.Y., 1974-77, assoc. prof., 1977-80, prof., 1980-89, Flanagan prof. law, 1989—. Vis. prof. Sch. Law Harvard U., Cambridge, 1991. Co-author: Law: Its Nature, Functions, and Limits, 3d edit., 1986, Civil Procedure: Territorial Jurisdiction and Venue, 1999, Res Judicata: A Handbook on Its Theory, Doctrine, and Practice, 2001, Materials for a Basic Course in Civil Procedure, 8th edit., 2003, Civil Procedure Stories, 2004, Principles of Civil Procedure, 2005; editor: Harvard Law Rev., 1969—71. Fulbright scholar, 1967-68. Mem. ABA, Assn. Am. Law Schs., Order of Coif, Phi Beta Kappa, Sigma Xi. Home: 100 Iroquois Rd Ithaca NY 14850-2223 Office: Cornell U Sch Law Myron Taylor Hall Ithaca NY 14853 Office Phone: 607-255-5189. Business E-Mail: kmc12@cornell.edu. E-mail: kevin-clermont@postoffice.law.cornell.edu.

CLERMONT, YVES WILFRID, anatomy educator, researcher; b. Montreal, Que., Can., Aug. 14, 1926; s. Rodolphe and Fernande (Primeau) C.; m. Madeleine Bonneau, June 30, 1950; children— Suzanne, Martin, Stephane B.Sc., U. Montreal, 1949; PhD, McGill U., 1953. Lectr. anatomy McGill U., Montreal, 1953-56, asst. prof., 1956-60, assoc. prof., 1960-63, prof., 1963-97, prof. emeritus, 1997—, chmn. dept., 1975-85. Mem. Nat. Bd. Med. Examiners, Phila., 1979-82; mem. rsch. grant com. Med. Rsch. Coun., Ottawa, 1970-97; cons. WHO, NIH, Ford Found., Fonds pour la formation de chercheurs et l'aide à la recherche, Quebec; sec. Artur Lucian Award Com. for Rsch. in Circulatory Diseases, 1983-97, hon. mem., 1997-2000. Contbr. chpts. to books, numerous articles to profl. jours. Recipient Ortho prize Can. Soc. Study Fertility, 1958, Prix Scientifique Govt. of Que., 1963, S.L. Siegler award Am. Soc. Study Fertility, 1966, Van Campenhout award Can. Fertility and Andrology Soc., 1986, Osler Teaching award McGill U., 1990. Fellow: Royal Soc. Can.; mem.: Can. Assn. Microscopy (v.p. 1982—83), Am. Assn. Andrology (Disting. Andrologist award 1988, Serono award lectureship 1992), Can. Assn. Anatomists (hon. J.C.B. Grant award 1986), Soc. Study of Reprodn., Am. Assn. Anatomists (v.p. 1970—73). Home: 567 Townshend St Saint Lambert PQ Canada J4R 1M4 Office: McGill U Dept Anatomy Cell Biol 3640 University St Montreal PQ Canada H3A 2B2 Business E-Mail: yves.clermont@mcgill.ca.

CLEVELAND, HARLAN, public information officer; b. NYC, Jan. 19, 1918; s. Stanley Matthews and Marian Phelps (Van Buren) Cleveland; m. Lois W. Burton, July 12, 1941; children: Zoë, Melantha, Alan Thorburn. Grad. cum laude, Phillips Acad., Andover, Mass., 1934; AB in Politics with high honors, Princeton U., 1938; recipient 22 hon. degrees. Intern Office of U.S. Senator Robert M. LaFollette, Jr., 1939-40; writer info. div. Farm Security Adminstrn., Washington, 1940-42; ovcl. Bd. Edn. Warfare and successor Fgn. Econ. Adminstrn., Washington, 1942—44; exec. dir. econ. sect. Allied Control Commn., Rome, 1944-45; mem. U.S. del. 3d session UNRRA Coun., London, 1945; acting v.p. in charge econ. sect. Allied Commn., Rome, 1945-46; dept. chief of mission UNRRA Italian Mission, Rome, 1946-47; dir. China office UNRRA, Shanghai, 1947-48; dir. China program ECA, Washington, 1948-49, dept. asst. adminstr., 1949-51; asst. dir. for Europe Mut. Security Agy., 1952-53; exec. editor The Reporter, N.Y.C., 1953-56, pub., 1955-56; prof. polit. sci., dean Maxwell grad. sch. citizenship and pub. affairs Syracuse U., 1956-61; chmn. Citizens for Kennedy, Central N.Y., 1960; asst. sec. for internat. orgn. affairs Dept. State, 1961-65; chmn. Cabinet Com. on Internat. Cooperation Yr., 1965; U.S. amb., rep. to NATO, 1965-69; prof. polit. sci., pres. U. Hawaii, Honolulu, 1969-74, pres. emeritus, 1974—; dir. program in internat. affairs Aspen Inst. Humanistic Studies, Princeton, N.J., 1974-80, disting. fellow, 1988—; chmn. U.S. Weather Modification Adv. Bd., 1977-78; disting. vis. Tom Slick prof. world peace LBJ Sch. Public Affairs, U. Tex., Austin, 1979; prof. pub. affairs and planning Hubert H. Humphrey Inst. Public Affairs, U. Minn., Mpls., 1980-88, prof. emeritus, 1988—, dean, 1980-87. Hon. chmn. The Am. Forum for Global Edn., Vols. in Tech. Assistance; bd. dirs. Vols. of Am., Mertz-Gilmore Found., Am. Refugee Com.; nat. adv. coun. World Learning; del. from N.Y. Dem. Nat. Conv., 1960; electronic faculty Western Behavioral Scis. Inst., 1983—91; faculty Connected Edn., 1987—96; hon. trustee The Atlantic Coun. Author: The Obligations of Power, 1966, NATO: The Transatlantic Bargain, 1970, The Future Executive, 1972 (Louis Brownlow award 1975), China Diary, 1976, The Third Try at World Order, 1977, The Knowledge Executive, 1985, The Age of Choice, 1990, The Global Commons, 1990, Birth of a New World, 1993, Leadership and the Information Revolution, 1997, Nobody in Charge, 2002; co-author: Next Step in Asia, 1948; The Overseas Americans, 1960, Humangrowth, 1978; editor: The Promise of World Tensions, 1961, The Management of Sustainable Growth, 1980, Energy Futures of Developing Countries, 1980; gen. editor: Readings for Leaders (series), 1988; co-editor: The Art of Overseasmanship, 1957, The Ethic of Power, 1962, Ethics and Bigness, 1962, Bioresources for Development, 1980, Prospects for Peacemaking, 1988. Decorated U.S. Medal of Freedom, gold star Order Brilliant Star (China), gran ufficiale Order of Merit (Italy); recipient Woodrow Wilson award, Princeton U., 1968, Prix de Talloires, 1981, Leader for Peace award, U.S. Peace Corps, 1985, Rhodes scholar, Oxford U., 1938—39. Fellow: Internat. Leadership Forum, World Bus. Acad., World Acad. of Art and Sci. (pres. 1991—2000); mem.: ASPA (pres. 1970—71, Dwight Waldo award 1988, Elmer Staats Lifetime Achievement award 2003), Coun. on Fgn. Rels., Am. Polit. Sci. Assn., Century Club (N.Y.C.), Phi Beta Kapp. Home: 46891 Grissom St Sterling VA 20165-3593 E-mail: harlancleve@cs.com. *If you try too carefully to plan your life, the danger is that you will succeed—succeed in narrowing your options, closing off avenues of adventure that cannot now be imagined, perhaps because they are not yet technologically possible. When a student asks me for career advice, I can only suggest that he or she opt for the most exciting "next step" without worrying where it will lead, and then work hard on the job in hand, not pine for the one in the bush. When your job no longer demands of you more than you have, go and do something else. Always take by preference the job you don't know how to do. If you build into your life enough variety of experience, you will be training for leadership in the role I have called The Public Executive.*

CLEVELAND, LILA VIRGINIA, lawyer; b. Mobile, Ala., Nov. 15, 1968; d. Henry Brooks and Marjorie Virginia Cleveland; m. Gregory Wayne Boyington, Aug. 24, 1999. BA in Polit. Sci. and History, Auburn U., 1991; JD, Auburn U. Birmingham Sch. Law, 1995. Bar: Ala., U.S. Dist. Ct. (mid. and so. dists.) Ala. 1996, U.S. Ct. Appeals (11th cir.) 1996. Pvt. practice, Mobile, Ala., 1996—. Instr. U. South Ala., Mobile, 1998—. Mem.: ABA, Ala. Criminal Def. Lawyers Assn., Nat. Assn. Criminal Def. Lawyers. Avocation: reading. Office: 312 N Joachim St Mobile AL 36603

CLEVELAND, MICHAEL F., music educator, musician; b. Elmira, N.Y., Jan. 20, 1952; s. Wendell V. and Eleanor A. Cleveland; children: Christopher, Kathleen. MusB, Ithaca (N.Y.) Coll., 1974. Tchr. music Utica (N.Y.) City Sch. Dist., 1974—75, Whitesboro (N.Y.) Ctrl. Sch. Dist., 1975—, chmn. Dept. Music, 1998—. Adj. prof. violin Colgate U., Hamilton, NY, 1996—, concertmaster violin, 1996—, concertmaster orch., 1996—; concertmaster Utica (N.Y.) Symphony Orch., 1983—89; adv. Whitesboro (N.Y.) Chpt. Nat. Jr. Hon. Soc., 1978—96. Musician: Glimmerglass Opera Orch., 1975—. Named Outstanding Music Educator, Whitesboro (N.Y.) Ctrl. Sch. Dist., 1986—87; recipient Outstanding Music Educators award, Kids Ednl. Youth Svcs., 2003. Mem.: Oneida County Music Educators Assn., N.Y. State Schs. Music Assn. Republican. Roman Catholic. Avocations: running, golf, hiking, skiing. Home: 7011 Ives Rd Marcy NY 13403 Office: Whitesboro Ctrl Sch Dist 6000 Route 291 Marcy NY 13403 also: Colgate U 13 Oak Dr Hamilton NY 13346

CLEVELAND, PETER WATKINS, lawyer; b. Gulfport, Miss., Apr. 30, 1955; s. C. Hal and Marjorie (Ragsdale) C.; m. Faye Carole Sibley, June 9, 1979; children: Katherine Saunders, William Peter. BBA, U. Miss., Oxford, 1978, JD, 1982. Bar: Miss. 1982, U.S. Dist. Ct. (no. dist.) Miss. 1982, U.S. Ct. Appeals (5th cir.) 1982, U.S. Dist. Ct. (so. dist.) Miss. 1995. Staff atty. Hancock Bank, Gulfport, 1983; law clk. to presiding justice U.S. Dist. Ct., Aberdeen, Miss., 1983-84; assoc. Threadgill, Smith, Sanders & Jolly, Columbus, Miss., 1984-89, Compton, Crowell & Hewitt, Biloxi, Miss., 1990, Minor & Guice, Biloxi, 1990-92; atty. at law Gulfport, 1992-95; asst. city atty., 1995-97; pvt. practice, 1997-2000; spl. asst. atty. gen. Office of Atty. Gen., Jackson, Miss., 2000—. Pres. Ole Miss. Coll. Reps., Oxford, 1977. Mem. ABA, Miss. Bar Assn. (ethics com. 1988-90), Miss. Trial Lawyers Assn., Lowndes County Bar Assn. (sec.-treas. 1984-86), Harrison County Bar Assn., Centaurus Club, Century Club, Rotary, Phi Delta Phi. Republican. Methodist. Avocations: tennis, swimming, chess. Home: 8 53rd Cir Gulfport MS 39507-4550 Office: PO Box 220 Jackson MS 39205-0220

CLEVELAND, SUSAN ELIZABETH, library administrator, researcher; b. Plainfield, N.J., Mar. 14, 1946; d. Robert Astbury and Grace Ann (Long) Williamson; m. Stuart Craig Cleveland, Aug. 21, 1971; children: Heather Elizabeth, Catherine Elisa. BA, Douglass Coll., Rutgers U., 1968; MLS, Rutgers U., 1969. Acquisitions libr. Jefferson U., Phila., 1970-71; biomed. libr. VA Hosp., Hines, Ill., 1972; med. cataloger U. Ariz., Tucson, 1973-74; dir. U. Pa. Hosp. Libr., Phila., 1974-87; exec. dir. Cleveland, Lamb, Urban Assocs., 1987-89; libr. dir. Mt. Sinai Hosp., Phila., 1989, West Jersey Health System (now Virtua Health Sys.), Voorhees, NJ, 1990—2002, Our Lady of Lourdes Med. Ctr., Camden, NJ, 2002—. Cons. in field, Phila. USPHS fellow, Detroit, 1969-70; recipient Chapel of 4 Chaplains Legion of Honor. Mem. Med. Libr. Assn. (Phila. chpt.), Spl. Libr. Assn., Basic Health Sci. Libr. Consortium, So. N.J. Consortium for Health Info. Svcs., Health Scis. Libr. Assn. N.J., Acad. Health Info. Profls., Caravan Club. Home: 9 Sylvan Ct Laurel Springs NJ 08021 Office Phone: 856-757-3548. Business E-Mail: clevelands@lourdesnet.org.

CLEVENGER, RAYMOND CHARLES, III, federal judge; b. Topeka, Kans., Aug. 27, 1937; s. Raymond and Mary Margaret (Ramsey) Clevenger; m. Celia Faulkner, Sept. 6, 1961 (div. Mar. 1987); children: Winthrop, Peter. BA, Yale U., 1959, LLB, 1966. Law clerk to Justice Byron S. White U.S. Supreme Court, Washington, 1966—67; ptnr. Wilmer Cutler & Pickering, Washington, 1967—71, 1972—90; special assist. to gen. counsel John W. Barnum US Dept. of Transp., Washington, 1971—72; judge U.S. Ct. Appeals (Fed. Cir.), Washington, 1990—. Bd. dir. Markle Found. Mem.: ABA, Bar of Supreme Ct. of US, Bar of US Customs Ct., DC Bar Assn. Office: Howard T Markey Nat Ct Bldg 717 Madison Pl NW Washington DC 20439-0002*

CLEVENGER, ROY EDWARD, credit and collections manager; b. Kansas City, Kans., Nov. 24, 1953; s. Roy J. and Rosa E. (Johnson) C.; m. Judith Ann Elizabeth Kowalski, Aug. 25, 1976; 1 child, Judith Ann. BJ, U. Kans., 1975. Exec. dir., trustee Washington Crossing (Pa.) Found., 1973-76; with credit and collections dept. Milton Roy Co., Ivyland, Pa., 1979-82; asst. credit mgr. McGraw-Hill Publs., Hightstown, N.J., 1982-83, mgr. credit and collections, 1984-89, Wood Textures, Inc., Edison, N.J., 1989-91; mgr. collections div. HIAS Inc., N.Y.C., 1991—. Vol. Independence Nat. Hist. Park, Phila., 1983-92. Mem. Media Credit Assn., Nat. Assn. Credit Mgmt., Ea. Nat. Park and Monument Assn. Avocations: stamp collecting/philately, geology, history. Home: PO Box 33 Washington Crossing PA 18977-0033

CLEVENGER, SARAH, botanist, computer technician, consultant; b. Indpls., Dec. 19, 1926; d. Cyrus Raymond and Mary Beth (Stevens) C. AB, Miami U., 1947; PhD, Ind. U., 1957. Tchr sci. Radford Sch., El Paso, Tex., 1949-51, Hillsdale Sch., Cin., 1951-52; asst. prof. Berea (Ky.) Coll., 1957-59, 61-63, Wittenberg U., Springfield, Ohio, 1959-60, Eastern Ill. U., 1960-61, Ind. State U., Terre Haute, 1963-66, assoc. prof., 1966-78, prof., 1978-85, prof. emerita, 1985—. Mem. Am. Inst. Biol. Sci., Am. Soc. Plant Taxonomists, Bot. Soc. Am., Internat. Assn. Plant Taxonomy, Phytochem. Soc. N.Am. (past sec.). Home: 717 S Henderson St Bloomington IN 47401-4838 Personal E-mail: sclevenger@iquest.net.

CLEVER, LINDA HAWES, physician; b. Seattle; d. Nathan Harrison and Evelyn Lorraine (Johnson) Hawes; m. James Alexander Clever, Aug. 20, 1960; 1 child, Sarah Lou. AB with distinction, Stanford U., 1962, MD, 1965. Diplomate Am. Bd. Internal Medicine, Am. Bd. Preventive Medicine in Occupl. Medicine. Intern Stanford U. Hosp., Palo Alto, Calif., 1965—66, resident, 1966—67, fellow in infectious disease, 1967—68; fellow in cmty. medicine U. Calif., San Francisco, 1968—69, resident, 1969—70; med. dir. Sister Mary Philippa Diagonostic and Treatment Ctr. St. Mary's Hosp., San Francisco, 1970—77; chmn. dept. occupl. health Calif. Pacific Med. Ctr., San Francisco, 1977—. Clin. prof. medicine U. Calif. Med. Sch., San Francisco; NIIH rsch. fellow Sch. Medicine, Stanford U., 1967—68; mem. nat. adv. panel Inst. Rsch. on Women and Gender, 1990—, chair panel, 1998—2000; mem. San Francisco Comprehensive Health Planning Coun., 1971—76; bd. dirs., mem. Calif.-OSHA Adv. Com. on Hazard Evaluation Sys. and Info. Svc., 1979—85, Calif. Statewide Profl. Stds. Rev. Coun., 1977—81, San Francisco Regional Commn. on White House Fellows, 1979—81, 1983—89, 1992, 95, chmn., 1977—81, 2001—02; bd. sci. counselors Nat. Inst. Occupl. Safety and Health, 1995—. Editor We. Jour. Medicine, 1990—98; contbr. articles to profl. jours. Trustee Stanford U., 1972—76, 1981—91, v.p., 1985—91; pres. RENEW, 2000—; bd. dirs. Sta. KQED, 1976—83, chmn., 1979—81; bd. dirs. Ind. Sector, 1980—86, vice chmn., 1985—86; bd. dirs. San Francisco U. H.S., 1983—90, chmn., 1987—88; active Womens Forum West, 1980—, bd. dirs., 1992—93; mem. Lucile Packard Children's Hosp. Bd., 1993—97, Lucile Packard Found. Children, 1997—99; mem. policy adv. com. U. Calif. Berkeley Sch. Pub. Health, 1995—, chair, 1995—2000; bd. dirs. The Redwoods Retirement Cmty., 1996—2001, Buck Inst. for Rsch. in Aging, 2000—; bd. govs. Stanford Med. Alumni Assn., 1997—2002, 2003—, pres., 2003—05; bd. dirs. No. Calif. Presbyn. Homes and Svcs., 2000—. Master: ACP (gov. No. Calif. region 1984—89, chmn. bd. govs. 1989—90, regent 1990—96, vice chair bd. regents 1994—95); fellow: Am. Coll. Occupl. and Environ. Medicine; mem.: APHA, We. Assn. Physicians (pres. 2003), We. Occupl. Medicine Assn., Calif. Acad. Medicine, Calif. Med. Assn., Inst. Medicine NAS, Stanford U. Women's Club (bd. dirs. 1971—80), Chi Omega. Office: 2340 Clay St Ste 106 San Francisco CA 94115-1931 Office Phone: 415-600-3321. E-mail: lclever@itsa.ucsf.edu.

CLEVER, MARCIA SUE, psychiatrist; b. Natrona Heights, Pa., Aug. 13, 1956; d. John Stacy and Marjorie Mae (DeBay) Clever; m. James Paul Hickey, June 27, 1987; 1 child, Blair. BS, U. Pitts., 1977; MD, Cornell U., 1981. Diplomate Am. Bd. Psychiatry and Neurology. Intern in surgery U. Calif.-Davis Med. Ctr., Sacramento, 1981-82, resident in surgery, 1982-83, resident in psychiatry, 1983-85; sr. resident in geropsychiatry U. Calif.-San Francisco, Langley Porter Neuropsychiat. Inst., 1985-86; assoc. psychiatrist Timberlawn Psychiat. Hosp., Dallas, 1986-87; pvt. practice Johannesburg, S.Africa, also Rome, 1987—; asst. clin. prof. U. Ill., Chgo., 1989; med. dir. psychiat. emergency screening svc. Kimball Med. Ctr., Lakewood, NJ, 1992-95; asst. clin. prof. psychiatry U. Medicine and Dentistry N.J., Piscataway, 1995—. Psychiat. cons. U.S. Dept. State, Johannesburg, 1987-89. Burroughs-Wellcome fellow, 1984-86. Mem. Am. Psychiat. Assn. Avocations: boating, reading. Office: 25 Bridge Ave Ste 205 Red Bank NJ 07701 Office Phone: 732-345-9100.

CLEWELL, DON B., microbial geneticist, educator; b. Dallas, Sept. 5, 1941; AB, Johns Hopkins U., 1963; PhD, Ind. U., Indpls., 1967. Cert. molecular biologist, microbiologist. From asst. prof. to assoc. prof. schs. dentistry and medicine U. Mich., Ann Arbor, 1970-77, prof., 1977—2004, prof. emeritus, 2004—. Burroughs Wellcome vis. prof. U. Rochester, N.Y., 1982; found. lectr. Am. Soc. for Microbiology, 1985-86; mem. recombinant DNA adv. com. NIH, Bethesda, Md., 1986-90. Mem. editl. bd.: Jour. Bacteriology, 1974—80, Plasmid, 1977—87, Infection and Immunity, 1985—96; contbr. over 200 articles to profl. jours., chapters to books. Recipient Rsch. Career Devel. award USPHS, 1975-80, Disting. Faculty Achievement award U. Mich., 2002, Disting. Faculty Lectureship award Biomed. Rsch. U. Mich. Med. Sch., 2003. Mem.: Am. Acad. Microbiology. Achievements include discovery and characterization of bacterial sex pheromone systems and conjugative transposons. Office: U Mich Sch Dentistry Biol and Materials Scis Ann Arbor MI 48109-1078 Office Phone: 734-763-0117. E-mail: dclewell@umich.edu.

CLEWETT, KENNETH VAUGHN, college official; b. Pomona, Calif., June 3, 1923; s. Heber Hovey and Thelma Lela (Sikes) C.; m. Margery Marie Haas, July 10, 1949; children: Richard A., Bruce D., Curtis L., Janet M. AA, Pomona Jr. Coll., 1943; student naval tng., U. Redlands, 1943-44, Columbia U., 1944; BA, Stanford U., 1947. Gen. clk. So. Counties Gas Co., Pomona, 1947; pers. examiner Calif. Pers. Bd., Sacramento, 1947-50; asst. pers. officer Calif. Dept. Mental Hygiene, Sacramento, 1950-52; pers. dir. Sonoma State Hosp., Eldridge, Calif., 1952-60, hosp. adminstr., 1960-72, Fairview State Hosp., Costa Mesa, Calif., 1972—76; acting exec. dir. Patton (Calif.) State Hosp., 1975-76, exec. dir., 1976-78; bus. mgr. So. Calif. Coll., 1978-82, dir. planning and corp. rels., 1982-84; v.p. adminstrn., dir. external affairs Kona campus U. of the Nations (formerly Pacific and Asia Christian U.), 1985—. Preceptor George Washington U., Grad. Sch. Health Care Adminstrn., 1962-78, Northwestern U. Grad. Sch. Mgmt., 1975-78, U. Minn. Program Mental Health Adminstrn., 1976-78. Pres. Sonoma Valley C. of C., 1964; v.p. Sonoma-Mendocino coun. Boy Scouts Am., 1968—71, bd. dirs., 1965—72; v.p. Sonoma County United Crusade, 1969—70; chmn. Sonoma Valley Coun. Edn. Com., 1969—71; founding chmn. bd. dirs. Sonoma Valley United Crusade, 1969—70, bd. dirs., 1969—72; vice chmn. bd. dirs. Big Sisters Orange County, Calif., 1975—77; bd. dirs. Ctrl. Sonoma County ARC, 1956—60, So. Calif. Coll., 1977—78, Goodwill Industries Ctrl. Calif., 1951—52, Goodwill Industries Inland Counties, 1978, West Hawaii Housing Found., 1988—2004, vice chmn., 1994—2004, Cmty. Orgn.for Edn. Devel., 1995—, Bridge Ho. Rehab. Ctr., 1997—2000, Kona Pacific Condo Owners Assn., 1990—2001, pres., 1992—93, 1998—2001; mem. sch./cmty.-based mgmt. coun. Konawaena H.S., 1992—95, Kealakehe H.S., 1998—; mem. adv. bd. Orange County Rescue Ctr., 1980—84, Hawaii County Decisions, 1988—91, Salvation Army Kona, 1991—99, chmn., 1995—98; mem. adv. bd. West Hawaii Food Bank, 1994—, vice chair, 1998—99; mem. adv. coun. Kona Hosp., 1996—2001, 2003—, West Hawaii ARC, 1988—; mem. West Hawaii adv. com. Hawaii Health Sys. Corp., 1997—, chair, 2001—03; trustee Sonoma Valley Unified Sch. Dist., 1971—72; pres. Redwood Empire Hosp. Conf., 1967, bd. dirs., 1966—68; founding co-chair West Hawaii Coalition on Homeless Concerns, 1991—92; founding chair Meet 'N Eat feeding program, 1992—, Kona Area Coun. of Svc. Clubs, 1993—; bd. dirs. Greater Kona Cmty. Coun., 1991—92, vice chmn., 1992; elder United Presbyn. Ch. in U.S.A., 1949—74; deacon Newport-Mesa Christian Ctr., Costa Mesa, Calif., 1975—76, 1979—84. Lt. (j.g.) USNR, 1943—46, PTO. Recipient Citizens award of Year Valley Moon Tchrs. Assn., 1970, Outstanding Svc. award Redwood Empire Hosp. Conf., 1972, Rotarian Club Mem. of Yr., 1996, Clara Barton vol. award ARC, 1999. Fellow: Assn. Mental Health Adminstrs. (pres. 1976, bd. dirs. 1967—72, 1974—77), Royal Soc. Health (bd. dirs. 1989—95); mem.: Kona-Kohala C. of C., Christian Mgmt. Assn., Am. Assn. Mental Retardation, Rotary (pres. Kona 1993—94, Club Mem. of Yr. 1996), Alpha Gamma Sigma (hon.; life). Home: 75-5787 Kakalina St Kailua Kona HI 96740-1909 Office Phone: 808-326-4447. Personal E-mail: kenclewett@cs.com. *Each additional personal achievement further confirms the weakness of depending upon myself alone and that real success is dependent upon truly following the leading of God, our heavenly Father.*

CLEWETT, RAYMOND WINFRED, mechanical design engineer; b. Upland, Calif., Nov. 7, 1917; s. Howard Jasper and Pansy Gertrude (Macy) C.; m. Hazel Royer, June 11, 1938; children: Alan Eugene, Patricia Gail, Charles Raymond, Richard Howard, Beverly Lynn. Student, Chaffey Jr. Coll., 1937. Exptl. mechanic Douglas Aircraft Co., Santa Monica, Calif., 1937-51; shop foreman, exptl. designer Lear, Inc., Los Angeles, 1945-51; design engr., shop mgr. The RAND Corp., Santa Monica, Calif., 1951-83; mech. designe cons. Pacific Sierra Rsch. Corp., Santa Monica, Calif., 1981—99; also design cons. The RAND Corp., Santa Monica, Calif.; owner, mgr. HY-TECH Engring. and Devel. Lab., Malibu, Calif., 1983—2001. Works include mech. design of JOHNNIAC early model electronic computer; designer various computer input/output devices, 1953-70; developer low vision reading aids for the blind, 1970-75; design and constrn. spl. equipment for sci. and research, 1983-99; stone sculptor, 1994-2001; exhbns. include Malibu Art Festival, 1998, Art Affair XIII, Pacific Palisades, Calif., 1998; patentee in field. Republican. E-mail: ray_clewett@juno.com.

CLEWIS, CHARLOTTE WRIGHT STAUB, retired mathematics educator; b. Pitts., Aug. 20, 1935; Student, Memphis State Coll., 1953-54, U. Wis., 1957-59; BA, Newark State Coll., 1963; MAT, Loyola Marymount U., 1974. Asst. dir., housemother Leota Sch. & Camp, Evansville, Wis., 1957—59; tchr. math. Rahway (N.J.) Jr. HS, 1963-70, Torrance (Calif.) Unified Sch. Dist., 1970-95, coord. math. dept., 1977; mem. instrnl. materials rev. panel State of Calif., 1986; instr. weekend coll. Marymount-Palos Verdes, 1985—95, math. teams coach; ret., 1995. Treas. adult leaders YMCA, Metuchen, NJ, 1967—89; sec., pres. Larga Vista Property Owners Assn., 1975—84, treas., 2001—04; mem. Rolling Hills Estates City Celebration Com., 1975—81; bd. dirs. Peninsula Symphony Assn., 1978—84, sec., 1993—97; commr. Rolling Hills Estates Pks. and Activities, 1981—, chmn., 1985, 1990, 1996, 2003; vol. Iditarod Dog Sled Race, 1996—. Recipient Appreciation award, PTA, 1984, Hon. Svc. award, 1986. Fellow: Soc. Antiquaries of Scotland; mem.: Clan MacIntyre Assn., Clan of the Highlands (treas. 2004—), Clan MacLeod Soc. U.S.A. Pacific Region. Avocations: camping, reading, computers. Home: 1 Gaucho Dr Rolling Hills Estates CA 90274-5113 E-mail: jclewis2@earthlink.net.

CLIBURN, VAN (HARVEY LAVAN CLIBURN JR.), concert pianist; b. Shreveport, La., July 12, 1934; s. Harvey Lavan and Rildia Bee (O'Bryan) C. Studied music with, mother, 1937-51; studied with, Mme. Rosina Lhevinne; grad. (Frank Damrosch scholar), Juilliard Sch. Music, 1954; MFA, Moscow Conservatory, 1989; HHD (hon.), Baylor U., 1958; D (hon.), The Juilliard Sch. of Music, 1998; D (hon.), Loyola U., Texas Christian U., Michigan State U., U. Cincinnati, Louisiana State U., Southern Methodist U., Boston U., Moscow Conservatory. Helped establish the Van Cliburn Foundation, 1958, first Van Cliburn Internat. Piano Competition, Forth Worth, TX, 1962. Pub. appearances, Shreveport, 1940, debut, Houston Symphony Orch., 1947; appeared with Dallas Symphony Orch., 1952, N.Y. Philharm. Orch., Carnegie Hall, 1954, 58; concert pianist on tour, U.S. & Europe, 1955-78, Soviet Union, 1960-72; retired in 1978; came out of retirement to perform at White House, 1987; on tour U.S., 1994-. recs. RCA Victor; guest TV shows, concert with Symphony of the Air, Carnegie Hall, 1958, concert Brussels Fair, Belgium, 1958, other appearances: Phila., Chgo., Hollywood, Denver, London, Amsterdam, Paris, Athens, Monaco, The Hague, Copenhagen, Stockholm, Bucharest, Oslo, La Scala, Moscow, Leningrad, Kiev, Boston, Washington, Dallas, Rio de Janeiro, Mexico City, Tokyo, Berlin, Munich, Zurich, Geneva, Madrid, Barcelona, Lisbon, Vienna, Tel Aviv; extensive recs. of works by Rachmaninoff, Chopin, Beethoven, others; composer classical music; recordings include My Favorite Encores-Works by Chopin, et. al., A Romantic Collection, World's Favorite Piano Music. Recipient Tex. State prize, 1947; Nat. Music Festival award, 1948; G.B. Dealy award Dallas, 1952; Kosciuszko Found. Chopin award, 1952; grantee Olga Samaroff Found., 1953; 1st place Juilliard Concerto concert, 1953; Edgar M. Leventritt Found. award, 1954; Carl M. Roeder Meml. award Juilliard Sch. Music, 1954; 1st prize Internat. Tchaikovsky Piano Competition Moscow, 1958; citation Am. Assn. Sch. Adminstrs., 1959; U. Mich. Musical Soc. First Disting. Artist award, 1996; Arturo Toscanini award, Classical Music Broadcaster's Assn., 1998, Lifetime Achievement award Texas Cultural Trust, 2001, Kennedy Ctr. Honors Medallion, 2001, President's Merit award Nat. Academy of Recording Arts & Sciences, 2002, Presidential Medal of Freedom, 2003; named number one in classical field Top Artists on Campus Poll (album sales), 1968. Mem. Am. Guild Mus. Artists. Clubs: Thespian (Kilgore, Tex.) (pres.), Rotary (hon.), Lotos (life), Shreveport, Ft. Worth. Baptist. Achievements include performed for numerous US Presidents, royalty and heads of state in Europe, Asia, and South America; inducted into Am. Classical Music Hall of Fame, 2001. Office: Van Cliburn Found 2525 Ridgmar Blvd Ste 307 Fort Worth TX 76116-4583*

CLIETT, CHARLES BUREN, retired aeronautical engineer, retired educator, retired academic administrator; b. Montpelier, Miss., July 10, 1924; s. James Thomas and Sallie Lou (Saul) C.; m. Grace Holland Campbell, Dec. 25, 1946; children— Susan Marie, Charles Buren. BS in Aero. Engring, Ga. Inst. Tech., 1945, MS in Aero. Engring, 1950; DSc (hon.), Miss. State U., 2003. Registered profl. engr., Miss. Faculty Miss. State U., 1947—, prof. aero. engring., 1957-91, prof. emeritus, 1991—, chmn. dept., 1960-91; ret., 1991. Lt. (j.g.) USNR, 1943—46. Recipient Spl. Achievement award Miss. State U. Alumni Assn., 1987, Faculty award for Career Achievement Faculty of Coll. Engring., Miss. State U., 1988. Mem. AIAA, NSPE, Am. Soc. Engring. Edn., Miss. Engring. Soc., Aerospace Dept. Chairpersons Assn. (pres. 1979), Am. Legion, Tau Beta Pi, Sigma Gamma Tau. Methodist. Home: 638 Commerce St West Point MS 39773-3016 Office: Engring Rsch Ctr Miss State PO Box 6176 Mississippi State MS 39762-6176

CLIFF, JOHNNIE MARIE, mathematics and chemistry educator; b. Lamkin, Miss., May 10, 1935; d. John and Modest Alma (Lewis) Walton; m. William Henry Cliff, Apr. 1, 1961 (dec. 1983); 1 child, Karen Marie. BA in Chemistry, Math., U. Indpls., 1956; postgrad., NSF Inst., Butler U., 1960; MA in Chemistry, Ind. U., 1964; MS in Math., U. Notre Dame, 1980; postgrad., Martin U., 2000. Cert. tchr. Ind. Rsch. chemist Ind. U. Med. Ctr., Indpls., 1956-59; tchr. sci. and math. Indpls. Pub. Schs., 1960-88; tchr. chemistry, math. Martin U., Indpls., 1989—, chmn. math. dept., 1990—, divsn. chmn. depts. sci. and math., 1993—. Adj. instr. math. U. Indpls., 1991, Ivy Tech State Coll., Indpls., 2002. Contbr. rsch. papers to sci. jours. Grantee NSF, 1961-64, 73-76, 78-79, Woodrow Wilson Found., 1987-88; scholarship U. Indpls., 1952-56, NSF Inst. Reed Coll., 1961, C. of C., 1963. Mem. AAUW, NAACP, NEA, Assn. Women in Sci., Urban League, N.Y. Acad. Scis., Am. Chem. Soc., Nat. Coun. Math. Tchrs., Am. Assn. Physics Tchrs., Nat. Sci. Tchrs. Assn., Am. Statis. Assn., Am. Assn. Ret. Persons, Neal-Marshall-Ind. U. Alumni Assn., U. Indpls. Alumni Assn., U. Notre Dame Alumni Assn., Ind. U. Chemist Assn., Notre Dame Club Indpls., Kappa Delta Pi, Delta Sigma Theta. Democrat. Baptist. Avocations: gardening, sewing. Home: 405 Golf Ln Indianapolis IN 46260-4108 Office: Martin U 2171 Avondale Pl Indianapolis IN 46218-3878 Office Phone: 317-543-3235.

CLIFF, NORMAN, psychology educator, consultant, writer; b. Royal Oak Township, Mich., Sept. 1, 1930; s. Charles Benjamin and Dorothy Cliff; m. Rosemary Hayes, July 1, 1956; children: Lawrence, Roger, Paul. BS Wayne State U., 1953; PhD, Princeton U., 1957. Rsch psychologist US Pub. Health Svc., Washington, 1956—58, Ednl. Testing Svc., Princeton, NJ, 1958—62; prof. psychology U. So. Calif., LA, 1962—95, chmn., 1973—77, emeritus prof. psychology, 1995—. Faculty senate bd. U. So. Calif., LA, 1980—85; cons. in field. Editor: (rsch. jour.) Psychometrika, 1980—84; author: Analyzing Multivriate Data, 1987, Ordinal Methods for Behavioral Data Analysis, 1996; contbr. more than 100 to rsch. jours. Recipient Best Paper Yr., Multvariate Behavioral Rsch., 1996; grantee Ednl. Testing Svc. Psychometric fellow, Princeton U., 1953—56, L. L. Thurstone Disting. Vis. fellow, U. NC, 1969—70, James McKeen Cattell fellow, 1978—79, Macquarrie U. Vis. fellow, Australia, 1985. Fellow: AAAS; mem.: Psychometric Soc. (pres. 1978—79, bd. trustees), Friends of Albuquerque Museum, Friends of Rio Grande Nature Ctr., Soc. for Multivariate Exptl. Psychology (pres. 1983—84), APA (divsn. 5 exec. bd. 1982—85, pres. 1983—84). Avocations: bridge, gardening, reading, tour guide. Home and Office: 1323 Camino Ecuestre Albuquerque NM 87107 E-mail: nrcliff2@nmia.com.

CLIFF, STEVEN BURRIS, engineering executive; b. Knoxville, Tenn., Mar. 30, 1952; s. Edgar Burris and Otella (Patterson) C.; m. Sharon Grace Davis, Sept. 11, 1971; children: Sarah Elizabeth, Susan Rebecca, Steven John. BS in Engring. Sci., U. Tenn., 1974, MS in Engring. Sci., 1976; postgrad., So. Sem., 1974-75. Rsch. asst. U. Tenn., Knoxville, 1972-75, asst. rsch. prof., 1975-76; program analyst Oak Ridge (Tenn.) Nat. Lab., 1976-77, rsch. engr., 1977-79; chief tech. officer Computer Concepts Corp., Knoxville, 1979-81; pres. Productive Programming Inc., Knoxville, 1981-82; v.p. R&D Control Tech. Inc., Knoxville, 1982-98, sr. v.p. R&D, 1998-2001, corp. sec., 1991-2001; sr. embedded systems software engr. Remotec/Northrop Grumman, 2001—05, program tech. leader, 2002—05. Ptnr. Middlebrook Indsl. Properties, 1985-2003, Cliff Bros. Investments, 1988-2000. Contbr. articles to profl. jours. Deacon West Knoxville Bapt. Ch., 1984—87, Loveland Bapt. Ch., Knoxville, 1976—82; mem. Bearden United Meth. Ch., 2001—04, tchr., 2001—04; exec. bd. Rocky Hill PTO, Knoxville, 1987, 1991—97, pres., 1994—95; bd. dirs. Rocky Hill Baseball League, 1995—2000. U. Tenn. scholar, 1970. Mem. Soc. Mfgs. Engrs. (sr.), Nat. Electronic Mfg. Assn. (chmn. com. 1987-94, seminar spkr. 1988-94), Am. Assn. for Artificial Intelligence, Instrument Soc. Am., Open DeviceNet Vendors Assn. (com. chair 1998-2001), ControlNet Internat. (com. chair 2000-2001), PT Cruiser Club (Tenn. dir. 2000-03), Oak Ridge Sportsman Assn. Avocations: photography, gun sports, fishing, bluegrass guitar. Home: 8210 Northshore Dr SW Knoxville TN 37919-8711

CLIFF, WALTER CONWAY, lawyer; b. Detroit, Jan. 2, 1932; s. Frank V. and Virginia L. (Conway) C.; m. Ursula McHugh, Nov. 5, 1960; children: Walter C., Mary F., Catherine C. BS, LL.B., U. Detroit, 1955; LL.M., NYU, 1956. Bar: Mich. 1956, N.Y. 1958. Assoc. firm Cahill Gordon & Reindel, N.Y.C., 1958-66, ptnr., 1966-2000; sr. counsel, 2000—. Bd. dirs. Florence Gould Found., N.Y.C., 1983—; bd. dirs. Austen Riggs Center, Stockbridge, Mass., 1983-89, Geoffrey Hughes Found., 1992—; mem. Collections com. Harvard U. Art Mus., 1992—. Served with U.S. Army, 1956-58. J.K. Lasser fellow NYU, 1955-56. Mem. ABA, Assn. of Bar of City of N.Y., N.Y. Bar Assn., Stockbridge Golf Club. Democrat. Roman Catholic. Office: Cahill Gordon & Reindel 80 Pine St Fl 17 New York NY 10005-1790 Business E-Mail: wcliff@cahill.com.

CLIFFORD, EUGENE THOMAS, lawyer; b. Utica, N.Y., July 15, 1941; s. James Anthony and Mary Margaret (Ellard) C.; m. Joyce Victoria Siwinski, Sept. 4, 1965; children: Michael Sean, Elizabeth Joyce, Thomas More. BA, Boston Coll., 1963, LLB, 1966. Bar: N.Y. 1967, U.S. Dist. Ct. (we. dist.) N.Y. 1967. Assoc. Chamberlain, D'Amanda, Bauman, Chatman & Oppenheimer, Rochester, N.Y., 1967-72, Lamb, Webster, Walz, Telesca & Donovan, Rochester, 1972-76; ptnr. Webster, Sullivan, Santoro & Clifford, Rochester, 1976-86, Fulreader, Rosenthal, Sullivan, Clifford, Santoro & Kaul, Rochester, 1986-2001, Davidson, Fink, Cook, Kelly & Galbraith, 2001—. Bd. dirs. N.Y. state divsn. Am. Cancer Soc., Syracuse, 1972-78, 82-88, 90-97, chmn. bd. dirs., 1982-83, nat. bd. dirs., 1991-97; bd. dirs. Urban League of Rochester, 1988-91. Recipient Nat. Bronze award N.Y. state divsn. Am. Cancer Soc., 1984, Hope award Monroe County unit, 1983. Mem.: ABA, Nat. Acad. Elder Law Attys., N.Y. State Bar Assn., Monroe County Bar Assn. (pres. 2002—03). Office: 28 Main St E Ste 1700 Rochester NY 14614 Office Phone: 585-546-6448. E-mail: eclifford@dfckg.com.

CLIFFORD, GEORGE WHEELER, college administrator; b. Rome, N.Y., Aug. 18, 1952; s. George William Clifford and M. Elizabeth Wheeler. BS, SUNY, Oneonta, 1974; MPA, SUNY, Albany, 1978, PhD with distinction, 1992. Dir. grants mgmt. AIDS program N.Y. Dept. Health, N.Y.C., 1987; dir. contracts and grants N.Y.C. Human Resources Adminstrn., 1987-89; AIDS coord. N.Y. Office Mgmt. and Budget, N.Y.C., 1989-90; adminstr. AIDS program Albany (N.Y.) Med. Ctr., 1991—. Cons. HIV Health and Human Svc. Planning Coun., N.Y.C., 1990-91. Author: The AIDS Epidemic: 1980-1989, 1991. Bd. dirs. Support Ministries, Waterford, N.Y., 1992-94, Names Project of the Capital, Albany, 1997—; co-chmn. bd. dirs. N.E. N.Y. Ryan White Steering Com., Albany, 1995-97. Grantee N.Y. State Dept. Health, 1996, 97, 98, 99, 2000, Health Rsch., Inc., 1997, 98, 99, 2000, U.S. HHS/HRSA, 1998. Mem. APHA, ASPA, Am. Polit. Sci. Assn. Home: 1 North St Delmar NY 12054-1017 Office: Albany Med Coll 47 New Scotland Ave Albany NY 12208-3412 E-mail: cliffog@mail.amc.edu.

CLIFFORD, GERALDINE JONCICH (MRS. WILLIAM F. CLIFFORD), education educator; b. San Pedro, Calif., Apr. 17, 1931; d. Marion and Geraldine Joncich; m. William F. Clifford, July 12, 1969 (dec. 1993). AB, UCLA, 1954, M.Ed., 1957; Ed.D., Columbia U., 1961. Tchr., San Lorenzo, Calif., 1954-56, Maracaibo, Venezuela, 1957-58; researcher Inst. Lang. Arts, Tchrs. Coll., Columbia, 1958-61; asst. prof. edn. U. Calif., Berkeley, 1962-67, asso. prof., 1967-74, prof., 1974-94, assoc. dean, 1976-78, chmn. dept. edn., 1978-81, acting dean Sch. Edn., 1980-81, 82-83, dir. edn. abroad program, 1988, 89, prof. grad. sch. Berkeley, 1994—97. Author: The Sane Positivist: A Biography of Edward L. Thorndike, 1968, The Shape of American Education, 1975, Ed Sch: A Brief for Professional Education, 1988, Lone Voyagers: Academic Women in Coeducational Universities, 1870-1937, 1989, Equally in View: The University of California, Its Women, and The Schools, 1995. Macmillan fellow, 1958-59, Guggenheim fellow, 1965-66, Rockefeller fellow, 1977-78; recipient Willystine Goodsell award for Contbns. to Women in Edn. Mem. History Edn. Soc., Am. Ednl. Rsch. Assn., Phi Beta Kappa, Pi Lambda Theta. Home: Apt 733 1661 Pine St San Francisco CA 94109-0420

CLIFFORD, LISA MARY, marketing and sales professional; b. Albany, NY, Nov. 23, 1969; d. John Rocco and Kathleen Mary Fedele; m. Timothy Stephen Clifford, Sept. 16, 1995; children: Christian Gerard, John Anthony. BS in Fin., St. John Fisher Coll., Rochester, N.Y., 1991. Pension consulting assoc. First Albany Corp., 1992—94; assoc. v.p. mktg. First Albany Asset Mgmt., 1994—2000; v.p., dir., mktg. and bus. devel. Curran Investment Mgmt., Albany, 2000—. Mem. Capital Leadership Class 2004 Albany-Colonie C. of C., 2003; treas. Wildwood Found., Albany, 2002—. Recipient recipient 40 Under Forty award, Albany Bus. Rev., 2004. Mem.: Investment Mgmt. Consultants Assn. Office: Curran Investment Mgmt 30 S Pearl St Albany NY 12207

CLIFFORD, PATRICK G.D., music educator; b. Oklahoma City, Nov. 20, 1963; s. James Daniel Clifford and Lee Clifford Bonnie; m. Belen Maria Guitart, June 15, 1999; children: Nathaniel Owen, Joanna Beth. MusB, Cleve. Inst. Music, 1989; MusM, Frost Sch. Music U. Miami, Coral Gables, Fla., 2000. Prof. violin Sch. Music and Fine Arts Palm Beach Atlantic U., West Palm Beach, 2000—. Pres. Stringendo Sch. Strings, Inc., West Palm Beach, Fla., 2000—. Office: Palm Beach Atlantic Univ 901 S Flagler West Palm Beach FL 33416 Office Phone: 561-803-2407. Office Fax: 561-803-2424. E-mail: patrick_clifford@pba.edu.

CLIFFORD, BROTHER PETER, academic administrator, religious studies educator; b. NYC, Feb. 17, 1925; s. Peter and Mary (Lynch) C. AB, Manhattan Coll., 1950; MA, Fordham U., 1957; EdD, Harvard U., 1970; EdD (hon.), St. Mary's Coll., Winona, Minn., 1987. Cert. sch. supt., N.Y. Tchr., prin. Cath. schs., N.Y.C., 1947-57; dean De La Salle Coll., Manila, 1957-61; asst. prin. Bishop Loughlin High Sch., Bklyn., 1962-64; assoc. supt. schs. Diocese Bklyn., 1968-71; exec. sec. Nat. Cath. Edn. Assn., Washington, 1971-74; assoc. dean edn. St. John U., N.Y.C., 1974-76; pres. St. Mary's Coll., Winona, Minn., 1976-84; provincial Bros. Christian Schs., Narragansett, RI, 1984-87; staff asst. higher edn. U.S. Cath. Conf., Washington, 1987-89; pres. St. Mary Coll., Leavenworth, Kans., 1989-94; dir. fin. Narragansett Christian Bros. Ctr., 1994-99; v.p. Metanoia St. Mary's U., Winona, Minn., 2000—02; dir. accreditation studies Ocean Tides Sch., 2002—. Mem. Leavenworth Area Devel., 1989-94; trustee Christian Bros. Investment Svcs., 1994—, Christian Bros. Svcs., 1994-2000; mem. bd. regents La Salle Acad., Providence, 1994-96; mem. diocesan sch. bd. Diocese of Providence, 1994-2000; v.p. Metanoia Group, St. Mary's U. of Minn., 2000-02. Recipient Avila award Coll. St. Teresa, Winona. Mem. Am. Fundraising Profls., Kans. Ind. Coll. Assn., Kans. Ind. Coll. Fund, Bros. of the Christian Schs (Christian Bro. 1943—). E-mail: clifford@smumn.edu.

CLIFFORD, ROBERT WILLIAM, state supreme court justice; b. Lewiston, Maine, May 2, 1937; s. William H. and Alice (Sughrue) C.; m. Clementina Radillo, Jan. 18, 1964; children: Laurence M., Matthew P. BA, Bowdoin Coll., 1959; LLB, Boston Coll., 1962; LLM, U. Va., 1998. Bar: Maine 1962, U.S. Dist. Ct. Maine 1965. Ptnr. Clifford & Clifford, Lewiston, 1964-79; justice Maine Superior Ct., Auburn, 1979-83, chief justice, 1984-86; assoc. justice Maine Supreme Ct., Auburn, 1986—. Mem. Lewiston City Coun., 1968-70, mayor, 1971-72; mem. Maine State Senate, 1973-76; chmn. Lewiston Charter Commn., 1978-79; mem. Maine Probate Law Revision Commn., 1973-79; bd. trustees St. Joseph's Coll. Maine, 2000—. Mem. Maine Bar Assn., Androscoggin County Bar Assn., Am. Judicature Soc. Roman Catholic. Office: Maine Supreme Jud Ct 2 Turner St PO Box 3488 Auburn ME 04212-3488 Office Phone: 207-783-5425. Business E-Mail: robert.w.clifford@maine.gov.

CLIFFORD, STEVEN FRANCIS, science administrator, director; b. Boston, Jan. 4, 1943; s. Joseph Nelson and Margaret Dorothy (Savage) C.; children from previous marriage: Cheryl Ann, Michelle Lynn, David Arthur; m. Theresa Kavanagh, Aug. 1996. BSEE, Northeastern U., Boston, 1965; PhD, Dartmouth Coll., 1969. Postdoctoral fellow NRC, Boulder, Colo., 1969-70; physicist Wave Propagation Lab., NOAA, Boulder, 1970-82, program chief, 1982-87, dir. environ. tech. lab., 1987—2001; sr. rsch. scientist emeritus U. Colo., 2001—. Mem. electromagnetic propagation panel, NATO, 1989-93; vis. sci. closed acad. city Tomsk, Siberia, USSR; apptd. mem. NAS Bd. on Atmospheric Sci. and Climate, 1999—. Author: (with others) Remote Sensing of the Troposhpere, 1978; contbr. 130 articles to profl. jours.; patentee in acoustic scintillation liquid flow measurement, single-ended optical spatial filter, acoustic sensor of surface ocean current and waves, high resolution GPS scatterometer. Recipient 5 Outstanding publs. awards Dept. Commerce, 1972, 75, 89, 96, Outstanding Career Performance, U.S. Presidental award, 1998; inducted NAE, 1997. Fellow: Acoustical Soc. Am., Optical Soc. Am. (editor atmospheric optics 1978—84, advisor atmospheric optics 1982—84); mem.: NRC (bd. atmospheric sci. and climate, chair panel on FAA weather forecasting accuracy, study team on homeland security), NAE, IEEE (sr.), Am. Geophys. Union, Internat. Radio Sci. Union. Avocations: running, cross country skiing. Office: CIRES/NOAA Environ Tech Lab 325 Broadway St Boulder CO 80305-3337 Office Phone: 303-497-6291.

CLIFFORD, STEWART BURNETT, banker, director; b. Boston, Feb. 17, 1929; s. Stewart Hilton and Ellinor (Burnett) C.; m. Cornelia Park Woolley, Apr. 26, 1952; children: Cornelia Lee Wareham, Rebecca Lyn Mailer-Howat, Jennifer Leggett Danner, Stewart Burnett Jr. AB, Harvard U., 1951, MBA, 1956. Asst. cashier Citibank, N.A., N.Y.C., 1958-60, asst. v.p., 1960-63; exec. v.p., gen. mgr. Merc Bank, Montreal, Canada, 1963-67, v.p. planning Overseas div., 1967-68; v.p., adminstr. comml. banking group Citibank, N.Y.C., 1969-72, v.p. head world corp. dept. London, 1973-75, sr. v.p. domestic energy N.Y.C., 1975-80, sr. v.p., head pvt. banking and investment divsn., 1981-87, div. exec., head investment divsn., 1987-93; sr. banker Pvt. Bank U.S., 1993-94; cons. MB Investment Ptnrs., N.Y.C., 1995—. Elder Brick Ch.; trustee Presbyn. Ch. Found., 1996—2001; bd. dirs. Nat. Inst. Social Scis., N.Y.C.; trustee emeritus Princeton Theol. Sem.; mem. com. univ. resources Harvard Coll.; bd. dirs. Monumental Corp., Balt., 1974—89; pres. 120 East End Ave. Corp, Woolley-Clifford Found.; vice chmn. Asphalt Green. 1st lt. U.S. Army, 1951—54. Mem.: Ocean Reef Club (Key Largo, Fla.), Harvard Club (N.Y.C.), Union Club (N.Y.C., pres.), Bath and Tennis Club (Palm Beach), Duxbury Yacht Club (Mass.), Pilgrims (N.Y.C.). Republican. Avocations: squash, tennis. Home: 120 E End Ave New York NY 10028-7552 Office: MB Investment Ptnrs 31st Fl 825 3d Ave New York NY 10022 Office Phone: 212-370-7300.

CLIFT, ELEANOR, news correspondent, writer; b. Bklyn., July 7, 1940; d. Erk and Inna Roeloffs; m. William Brooks Clift Jr., 1964 (div. 1981); children: Edward, Woodbury, Robert; m. Tom Brazaitis, Sept. 30, 1989 (dec. Mar. 30, 2005). Student, Hofstra U., Hunter Coll. Former sec. to nat. affairs editor Newsweek, NYC, former reporter Atlanta bur., former White House corr., named dep. Washington bur. chief, 1992, contbg. editor, 1994—; with Washington bur. LA Times, 1985—86. Regular panelist The McLaughlin Group, 1983—; polit. analyst Fox News Network; column Capitol Letter appears weekly on Newsweek-MSNBC website; co-chair bd. dirs. Internat. Women's Media Found. Co-author (with Tom Brazaitis): War Without Bloodshed: The Art of Politics, 1996, Madam President: Shattering the Last Glass Ceiling, 2000; author: Founding Sisters and the 19th Amendment, 2003. Office: Newsweek Washington Bur 1750 Pennsylvania Ave NW Washington DC 20006-4502 E-mail: eclift@newsweek.com, eclift@aol.com.

CLIFT, W.E., telecommunications industry executive; BS in Elec. Engring., Tenn. Tech. U.; MBA, U. Memphis. Dir., engring. BellSouth Mobility, 1991—92, dir., engring. and opers., 1992—96, gen. mgr., 1996—98, regional v.p., gen. mgr., Am. Cellular's Ind. markets, 1998—2000; pres. Am. Cellular Comm. Corp. and BellSouth Mobility DCS, 2000—; chief tech. officer Cingular Wireless, 2000—. Office: Cingular Wireless Glenridge Highlands Two 5565 Glenridge Connector Atlanta GA 30342

CLIFTON, BRETT, academic administrator, political scientist; BS, BA, U. Conn.; MA, Ph.D., Brown U. Postdoctoral rsch. assoc. Brown U., 2002—03, adminstrv. rsch. assoc., 2003—. Co-dir.:. Office: Brown University Taubman Ctr Public Policy Box 1977 Providence RI 02912 Personal E-mail: brett_clifton@brown.edu.

CLIFTON, DOUGLAS C., newspaper editor; b. Bklyn., July 14, 1943; s. Norman Stanton and Anne Frances (Montesano) C.; m. Margaret E. Clifton, Dec. 18, 1965; children: Amy Elizabeth Clifton Gallup, Clay Norman. BA in Polit. Sci., Dowling Coll., 1965. Positions including reporter, city editor, dep. mng. editor Miami Herald, 1970-87; news editor Washington bur. Knight Ridder, 1987-89; mng. editor Charlotte Observer, NC, 1989-91; sr. v.p., exec. editor Miami Herald, 1991-99; editor Plain Dealer, 1999—. Lt. U.S. Army, 1966-69, Vietnam. Named Editor of Yr., Editor & Pub. Mag., 2003. Mem.: Am. Soc. Newspaper Editors (freedom of info. com. 2003—). Office: Plain Dealer 1801 Superior Ave E Cleveland OH 44114-2198 E-mail: dclifton@plaind.com.*

CLIFTON, JAMES ALBERT, physician, educator; b. Fayetteville, NC, Sept. 18, 1923; s. James Albert Jr. and Flora M. (McNair) Clifton; m. Katherine Rathe, June 25, 1949; children: Susan M.(dec.), Katherine Y., Caroline M. BA, Vanderbilt U., 1944, MD, 1947. Diplomate Am. Bd. Internal Medicine (mem. 1972-81, mem. subsplty. bd. gastroenterology 1968-75, chmn. 1972-75, mem. exec. com. 1978-81, chmn. 1980-81). Intern U. Hosps., Iowa City, 1947—48, resident dept. medicine, 1948—51; staff dept. medicine Thayer VA Hosp., Nashville, 1952—53; asst. clin. medicine Vanderbilt Hosp., Nashville, 1952—53; cons. physician VA Hosp., Iowa City, 1965—93; assoc. medicine dept. internal medicine Coll. Medicine, U. Iowa, 1953—54, chief divsn. gastroenterology, 1953—71, asst. prof. medicine, 1954-58, assoc. prof., 1958—63, prof., 1963—91, prof. emeritus, 1991—, traveling fellow, 1964, vis. prof. dept. physiology, 1964, vice chmn. dept. medicine, 1967—70, chmn. dept. medicine Coll. Medicine, 1970—76, Roy J. Carver prof. medicine, 1974—91, Roy J. Carver prof. emeritus, 1991—, dir. James A. Clifton Ctr. Digestive Diseases, 1985—90, interim dean, 1991—93. Investigator Mt. Desert Isle Biol. Lab., Salisbury Cove, Maine, 1964; vis. faculty mem. Mayo Found. and Mayo Clinic, 1966; vis. prof. dept. medicine U. N.C. Chapel Hill, 1970; cons. gastroenterology and nutrition tng. grants com. Nat. Inst. Arthritis and Metabolic Diseases, NIH, 1964—68, chmn., 1965—68; mem. Nat. Adv. Arthritis and Metabolic Diseases Coun., 1970—73; mem. gastroenterology tng. com. VA, Washington, 1967—71, chmn. tng. grants com., 1971—73; mem. med. adv. bd. Digestive Disease Found., 1969—73; vis. prof. gastroenterology U. London (St. Marks Hosp.), 1984—85; mem. sci. adv. com. Ludwig Inst. Cancer Rsch., Zurich, 1984—95. Internat. editl. bd. Italian Jour. Gastroenterology, 1970—90, Gastroenterology, 1964—68. Recipient Disting. Alumnus of Yr. award, Vanderbilt U. Sch. Medicine, 1984, Disting. Alumnus of Yr. Achievement award, U. Iowa Coll. Medicine, 2000,

Disting. Mentoring award, 2002, Disting. Alumni award, U. Iowa Alumni Assn., 2004; fellow, NIH, USPHS, 1955—56, Evans Meml. Hosp., Mass. Meml. Hosps., also Boston U. Sch. Medicine, 1955—56; Phi Connell scholar, Vanderbilt U., 1943—44. Fellow: ACP (bd. regents 1972—79, pres. 1977—78, Alfred Stengel award 1984, Laureate award 1989); mem.: AAUP, AAAS, AMA (liaison com. grad. med. edn. 1976—77), Internat. Soc. Internal Medicine (exec. com. 1978—80), Assn. Profs. Medicine (councillor 1972—73, sec.-treas. 1973—75), Assn. Am. Med. Colls., Am. Physiol. Soc., Soc. Exptl. Biology and Medicine, Assn. Am. Physicians, Am. Clin. and Climatol. Assn. (v.p. 1984), Am. Fedn. Clin. Rsch., Am. Soc. Internal Medicine (Internist of Yr. award Iowa chpt. 1986), Am. Assn. Study Liver Disease, Am. Heart Assn., Am. Gastroent. Assn. (pres. 1970—71), Inst. Medicine NAS, U. Iowa Assn. Emeritus Faculty (pres. 1999—2000), U. Iowa Retirees Assn. (pres. 1999—2000). Home: 39 Audubon Pl Iowa City IA 52245-3437 Office: U Iowa Hosp and Clinics 4 JCP Hawkins Dr Iowa City IA 52242 Office Phone: 319-356-1771. Personal E-mail: zylumjim@mchsi.com. Business E-Mail: james-clifton@uiowa.edu.

CLIFTON, JAMES K., market research company executive; m. Susan Clifton; children: Nicole, Jonathan, Jackie. DHL (hon.), Medgar Evers Coll., Jackson State Univ.; DComm (hon.), Bellevue Univ. Chmn., CEO Gallup Org., Washington, 1988—. Chmn. Thurgood Marshall Scholarship Fund. Office: Gallup Organization 901 F St NW Washington DC 20004*

CLIFTON, LINDA JANE, elementary school educator, editor-in-chief, poet; b. July 31, 1940; BA, U. Wash., 1962, MA, 1983, PhD, 1989. Cert. tchr., Wash. Tchr. English Stanwood (Wash.) Sch. Dist., 1963-66, Ephrata (Wash.) Sch. Dist., 1966-83, Northshore Sch. Dist., Bothell, Wash., 1984-98; co-dir. Puget Sound/Wash State wroting project, asst. prof. U. Wash., Dept. of English, Seattle, 1983-94; founder, editor Crab Creek Rev., Seattle, 1983-95. Cons. to schs. and sch. dists., Puget Sound region, 1985—. Contbr. articles to profl. jours., poetry to various publs. Cand. Wash. State Legislature, 1976, 78; trustee, 1st woman to serve as chair bd. trustees Cen. Wash. U., Ellensburg, 1977-82; pres. Wash. Women United, 1980-82; com. woman King County Dem. Ctrl. Com. Named State Woman of Achievement, Wash. State Bus. and Profl. Women, 1975. Mem. Nat. Coun. Tchrs. English, Wash. State Coun. Tchrs. English (publs. bd.). Avocations: gardening, opera, jazz.

CLIFTON, LUCILLE THELMA, author; b. Depew, N.Y., June 27, 1936; d. Samuel Louis and Thelma (Moore) Sayles; m. Fred James Clifton, May 10, 1958 (dec. Nov. 1984); children: Sidney, Fredrica (dec. 2000), Channing (dec. 2004), Gillian, Graham, Alexia. Student, Howard U., 1953-55, Fredonia (N.Y.) State Tchrs. Coll., 1955; DL (hon.), Dartmouth Coll., 2005. Prof. literature and creative writing U. Calif., Santa Cruz, 1985-90; dist. prof. humanities St. Mary's Coll. Md., 1990—, Hilda C. Landers endowed chair in liberal arts, 2000—. Poet-in-residence, Coppin State Coll., Balt., 1972-76, Jenny Moore vis. writer, George Washington U., 1982-83. Author: Good Times, 1969, Good News About The Earth, 1972, An Ordinary Woman, 1974, Generations, 1976, Two-Headed Woman, 1980, Sonora Beautiful, 1981, Next, 1987, Good Woman, 1987, Quilting, 1991, The Book of Light, 1993, Blessing the Boats, 2000 (Nat. Book award); Everett Anderson books and other books for children; co-author: Free to Be You and Me, 1974 (Emmy award), Free To Be A Family. Named Poet Laureate, State of Md., 1979; recipient Discovery award Poetry Center, 1969, winner Nat. Book Award, 2000; YMHA grantee, 1969; Nat. Endowment Arts grantee, 1970, 72 Fellow Am. Acad. Arts and Scis.; mem. Authors League, Author Guild, P.E.N., Acad. Am. Poets (chancellor), Poetry Soc. Am. (bd. dirs., Lila Wallace/Reader's Digest award 1999). Office: St Marys Coll of Maryland Divsn Arts and Letters Montgomery Hall 126 Saint Marys City MD 20686

CLIFTON, NELIDA, social worker; b. Buenos Aires, Aug. 16, 1944; arrived in U.S., 1968; d. Juan Antonio and Zaira Elizabeth (Vera) Tovar; m. Mark Earl Jolls, Nov. 8, 1968 (div. July 1984); children: Patricia Elizabeth, Michael Thomas, Diana Marie Kathleen; m. Anthony Gene Clifton, June 19, 1993. BA in Bus. Adminstrn., Nat. Sch. Commerce, Tucuman, Argentina; BA in Psychology magna cum laude, Fairleigh Dickinson U., 1986; postgrad., William Paterson Coll., 1988—89. Cert. diplomate Am. Psychotherapy Assn.; lic. cert. social worker Bd. Social Work Examiners, N.J.; cert. bilingual. Social worker Bergen County Bd. Social Svcs., Rochelle Park, N.J., 1987—. Crisis intervention counselor; phone counselor; cmty. resources referral profl. Mem. APA, NASW, Am. Assn. Christian Counselors, Phi Zeta Kappa, Phi Omega Epsilon, Psi Chi Nat. Honor Socs. Republican. Avocations: reading, chess, tennis, gardening. Home and Office: PO Box 8581 Saddle Brook NJ 07663-8581

CLIFTON, RICHARD RANDALL, federal judge; b. Framingham, Mass., Nov. 13, 1950; s. Arthur Calvin and Vivian Juanita (Himes) C.; m. Teresa Morano Aleshire, Oct. 15, 1988; children: David Madison, Katherine Kaleilani. AB, Princeton U., 1972; JD, Yale U., 1975. Bar: Ill. 1975, Hawaii 1976, U.S. Dist. Ct. Hawaii 1976, U.S. Ct. Appeals (9th cir.) 1976, U.S. Ct. Appeals (2d cir.) 1979, U.S. Supreme Ct. 1982. Law clk. to judge U.S. Ct. Appeals (9th cir.), Honolulu, 1975-76; from assoc. to ptnr. Cades, Schutte, Fleming & Wright, Honolulu, 1977—2002; judge U.S. Ct. of Appeals (9th cir.), 2002—. Adj. prof. law U. Hawaii, Honolulu, 1979-89. Co-author: The Shreveport Plan: An Experiment in the Delivery of Legal Services, 1974. Mem. dist. com. Nancy J. Stivers Meml. Fund, Honolulu, 1984—; bd. dirs. Hawaii Pub. Radio, Honolulu, 1991—, chmn., 1995-2000; mem. Hawaii State Jud. Conf., 1987-90; 1st vice chmn. Hawaii Rep. Party, 1989-93, chmn. rules com., 1987-90, gen. counsel, 1993-2001; bd. dirs. Hawaii Women's Legal Found., 1987—, Ninth Jud. Cir. Hist. Soc., 1996—; mem. Hawaii State Reapportionment Com., 1991-92. Mem. ABA, Hawaii Bar Assn., Am. Law Inst. Office: US Court of Appeals 999 Bishop St #2010 Honolulu HI 96813

CLIFTON, RUSSELL B., banking and mortgage lending consultant, retired mortgage company executive; b. Maroa, Ill., Jan. 16, 1930; s. Russell Thomas and Clara Leoda (Luckenbill) C.; m. Mary Joyce Hartline, Oct. 10, 1948; 1 son, Steven Shawn. BA, Mich. State U., 1957. Bank auditor Arthur Andersen & Co., Detroit, 1957-59; v.p. Mich. Nat. Bank, Lansing, 1959-65; sr. v.p. Assoc. Mortgages Co., Kansas City, Mo., 1965-69; v.p. Fed. Nat. Mortgage Assn., Washington, 1969-85, ret., 1985; pres., chief exec. officer First Chesapeake Mortgage, Inc., Beltsville, Md., 1985-86, also bd. dirs.; cons. banking and mortgage lending, 1986—. Mem. adv. com. Home Owner's Warranty Corp., Washington, 1978-81; bd. dirs., mem. exec. com., treas. Nat. Acad. Conciliators, Washington, 1979-91; bd. dirs. Lincoln Savs. & Loan (now Seasons Savs. Bank), Richmond, Va., 1987-89; bd. dirs., treas. Nat. Ctr. for Dispute Settlements, Washington, 1987-91. Served with U.S. Army, 1952-54. Named disting. fellow Nat. Assn. Cert. Mortgages Bankers, 1975 Mem. Phi Kappa Phi, Beta Alpha Psi, Beta Gamma Sigma, Tau Sigma. Methodist.

CLIFTON, THOMAS E., academic administrator, minister; m. Audrey Vought; children: Sandra, Jill Clifton Mallard. Student, Duke Divinity Sch.; M in Divinity, Crozer Theol. Sem., Rochester, N.Y.; MS in Personnel Counseling, Wright State U., Dayton; D in Ministry, Princeton Theol. Sem. Pastor First Bapt. Ch., Perry, Ohio, 1967-70, Sidney, Ohio, 1970-73; assoc. pastor Binkley Bapt. Ch., Chapel Hill, N.C., 1973-77; pastor First Bapt. Ch., Lafayette, Ind., 1977-85, Penfield, N.Y., 1985-93; pres. Ctrl. Bapt. Theol. Seminary, Kansas City, Kans., 1993—2003. Writer: Bapt. Leader, Capitol Report; (curriculum) Judson Press. Office: Ctrl Bapt Theol Sem 741 N 31st St Kansas City KS 66102-3964

CLIJSTERS, KIM, professional tennis player; b. Bilzen, Belgium, June 8, 1983; Profl. tennis player WTA, 1999—. Winner numerous tennis tournaments including Luxembourg, 1999, Hobart, Leipzig, 2000, Stanford, Leipzig, Luxembourg, 2001, Hamburg, Filderstadt, Luxembourg, 2002, Sydney, Indian Wells, Rome, Rosmalen, Stanford, Los Angeles, Filderstadt, Luxembourg, 2003, Paris, Antwerp, 2004, Indian Wells, Miami, Eastbourne, Stanford, Los Angeles, Toronto, 2005, US Open, 2005; finalist Bratislava, 1999, Filderstadt, 2000, Roland Garros, Indian Well's, Hertogenbosch, 2001. Office: Ste 1500 1 Prospect Plaza Saint Petersburg FL 33701-1500*

CLIMAN, RICHARD ELLIOT, lawyer; b. NYC, July 19, 1953; s. David Arthur and Mary (Vitale) C. AB cum laude, Harvard U., 1974, JD cum laude, 1977. Bar: Calif. 1977. Assoc. Pettit & Martin, San Francisco, 1977-83, ptnr., 1984-94; ptnr., head mergers and acquisitions group Cooley Godward LLP, Palo Alto, San Francisco, Calif., 1994—. Co-chair Doing Deals Practising Law Inst., 1997-2002, Tech. Mergers and Acquisitions Inst. Glasser Legal-Works, 1999-2001; adv. bd. BNA Mergers & Acquisitions Law Report; exec. com. Securities Reg. Inst., Corp. Counsel Ctr., Sch. Law Northwestern U.; lectr. and panelist in field. Contbr. articles to profl. jours. Mem. ABA (sect. bus. law, chair com. on negotiated acquisitions 2002—, co-chair Nat. Inst. on Negotiating Bus. Acquisitions 2003—). Home: 1 Tulip Ln San Carlos CA 94070-1551 Office: Cooley Godward LLP 5 Palo Alto Sq 3000 El Camino Real Palo Alto CA 94306-2120 Office Phone: 650-843-5174. E-mail: rcliman@cooley.com.

CLINARD, KEITH A., lawyer; b. High Point, NC, Feb. 25, 1954; BA cum laude, Wake Forest U., 1976, JD cum laude, 1979. Bar: NC 1979, US Dist Ct. Mid. Dist. NC, US Dist. Ct. We. Dist. NC, US Ct. Appeals 4th Cir. Mem. Womble Carlyle Sandridge & Rice PLLC, Winston-Salem, NC, chair product liability litig. practice group. Mem.: ABA, NC Assn. Def. Attorneys (bd. dirs. 1989—92), Forsyth County Bar Assn., NC Bar Assn. Office: Womble Carlyle Sandridge & Rice PLLC PO Box 84 Winston Salem NC 27102 Office Phone: 336-721-3631. Office Fax: 336-733-8376. Business E-Mail: kclinard@wcsr.com.

CLINARD, ROBERT NOEL, lawyer; b. Welch, W.Va., Nov. 1, 1946; s. Vernon Carlos and Mary Elizabeth (Noel) C.; m. Margaret Hawthorne Higgins, May 21, 1977; children: Elizabeth Kercheval, Edward Noel, Margaret Graham Robinson, Kathryn Moir. BA, Washington & Lee U., 1968, JD, 1976. Bar: N.Y. 1977, Va. 1978, U.S. Dist. Ct. (so. dist.) N.Y. 1977, U.S. Dist. Ct. (ea. dist.) Va. 1978, U.S. Ct. Appeals (4th cir.) 1986, U.S. Supreme Ct. 1990. Assoc. Winthrop, Stimson, Putnam & Roberts, N.Y.C., 1976-78, Hunton & Williams, Richmond, Va., 1978-86, ptnr., 1986—. Sec. Va. Cultural Laureate Soc., Richmond, 1981-86, bd. dirs., 1981-90. Served to lt. USNR, 1969-72. Mem. ABA (antitrust sect., franchising and healthcare coms.), Va. State Bar (vice chmn. antitrust com. health law sect. 1985-86, chmn. 1986-87, bd. govs. antitrust sect. 1989-95, vice chmn. antitrust sect. 1992, chmn. 1993), Nat. Health Lawyers Assn., Coun. of Franchise Suppliers, Internat. Franchise Assn., Order of Coif, Phi Beta Kappa, Omicron Delta Kappa. Republican. Episcopalian. Avocations: boating, saltwater fishing, house renovation. Home: 6010 York Rd Richmond VA 23226-2737 Office: Hunton & Williams Riverfront Plaza East Tower 951 E Byrd St Richmond VA 23219-4074

CLINCH, NICHOLAS BAYARD, III, pharmaceutical executive; b. Evanston, Ill., Nov. 9, 1930; s. Nicholas Bayard Jr. and Virginia Lee (Campbell) C.; m. Elizabeth Wallace Campbell, July 11, 1964; children: Virginia Lee, Alison Campbell. Student, N.Mex. Mil. Inst., Roswell, 1948-49; AB, Stanford U., 1952, LLB, 1955. Bar: Calif. 1959. Expedition leader First Ascent, Gasherbrum I (26,470 ft.), Pakistan, 1958, First Ascent, Masherbrum (25,660 ft.), Pakistan, 1959-60; assoc. Voegelin, Barton, Harris & Callister, L.A., 1961-68; pvt. practice Washington, 1968-70; v.p., counsel Lincoln Savs. & Loan Assn., L.A., 1970-74; exec. dir. Sierra Club Found., San Francisco, 1975-81; environ. cons. Fluor Corp., Grass Valley, Calif., 1981-84; v.p., sec. CCA, Inc., Denver, 1984—. Bd. dirs. Growth Stock Outlook Inc., Potomac, Md.; mem. adv. bd. Lowell Obs. Author: A Walk in the Sky, 1982. Leader Am. Antarctic Mountaineering Expdn., Sentinel Range, 1966-67; co-leader Chinese Am. Ulugh Muztagh Expdn., Kun Lun Range, Xinjiang, 1985, Am. Expdns. to Kang Karpo Range, Yunnan-Tibet border, 1988, 89, 92, 93; co-founder, trustee Calif. League Conservation Voters, San Francisco, 1972-97; bd. dirs. Environ. Law Inst., 1981-86, Recreational Equipment Inc., 1985-91, 93-2001. 1st lt. USAF, 1956-57. Recipient John Oliver La Gorce medal Nat. Geog. Soc., Washington, 1967. Fellow Royal Geog. Soc., Explorers Club; mem. ABA, Am. Alpine Club (hon., pres. 1967-70), Appalachian Mountain Club (hon.), State Bar Calif., Roxburghe Club of San Francisco, Alpine Club (hon. London), Chinese Assn. Sci. Expdns. (hon.). Republican. Episcopalian. Avocations: mountain climbing, skiing, book collecting. Home: 2001 Bryant St Palo Alto CA 94301-3714 Office: CCA Inc 220 Josephine St 200 Denver CO 80206

CLINE, ANDREW HALEY, lawyer; b. Fountain Hill, Pa, Nov. 30, 1951; s. William Matthew and Eleanor Mary (Bosich) m. Sharon (Harlan) C.; children: Haley Andrea, Catherine Anne. BA, Guilford Coll., 1973; JD, U. Ala., 1978. Bar: Pa. 1978, U.S. Dist. Ct. (mid. dist.) Pa. 1982, U.S. Dist. Ct. (ea. dist.) 1989, U.S. Ct. Appeals (3rd cir.) 1988, U.S. Supreme Ct. 1990. Law clk. Commonwealth Ct. Pa., Harrisburg, 1978—80; asst. counsel Dept. Transp., Harrisburg, 1980—86; assoc. dep. gen. counsel Gov. Office, Harrisburg, 1986—87, dep. gen. counsel, 1987—89; assoc. Kirkpatrick & Lockhart, LLP, Harrisburg, 1989—91, ptnr., 1992—2001; dep. gen. counsel Gov. Office, Harrisburg, 2001—02; dep. chief counsel Dept. Transp., Harrisburg, Pa., 2003. Editor-in-chief Ala. Law Rev., 1978. Named one of Outstanding Young Men Am. Jaycees, 1978. Mem. Fed. Bar Assn. (pres. Ctrl. Pa. chpt. 1994-95, nat. del. 1995-97), Pa. Bar Assn., Dauphin County Bar Assn. (chmn. continuing legal edn. com. 1992-95, bd. dirs. 1993-95, chmn. govt. law sect. 1994, sec. 1996), Bench and Bar Soc., Am. Inns of Ct. (master emeritus J.S. Bowman chpt.), St. Thomas More Soc. (bd. dirs. 1997-98), Omicron Delta Kappa. Avocation: photography. Office: Office Chief Counsel PO Box 8212 Harrisburg PA 17105-8212 Office Phone: 717-787-5473. Business E-Mail: acline@state.pa.us.

CLINE, BOBBY JAMES, insurance company executive; b. Floydada, Tex., Mar. 12, 1932; s. Howard O. and Carrie (Tomlinson) C.; m. Martha Nolen, May 29, 1954; children: Carolyn, Pamela, Millie, Robert, Sean. BBA, U. Tex., 1954. Casualty underwriter Ins. Co. N.Am., Dallas, 1956-59; account exec./ptnr. Munger-Moore & Assocs., Dallas, 1959-68; ptnr. Harris-Moore & Assocs., Dallas, 1968-70; sr. v.p. Alexander & Alexander Inc., Dallas, 1970-72, exec. v.p., 1972-77, pres., 1977-96, vice chmn. bd.; exec. v.p. Aon Risk Svcs. Tex., Dallas, 1997-2000. Chmn. bd. Texas Banc Ptnrs. Inc., 2000—05; bd. dirs. Oaks Bank. Served with USN, 1954-56. Mem. Soc. CPCUs (dir.), U. Tex. Ex-Students Assn. (past pres.), Salesmanship Club, Preston Trail Golf Club, Dallas Club, Dallas Athletic Club, Garland Toastmasters, Riverhill Country Club. Baptist. Avocations: golf, hunting. Home: 1944 Wynn Joyce Rd Garland TX 75043-2542 Office: Texas Banc Partners 9304 Forrest Ln Suite 245N Dallas TX 75243 Office Phone: 972-445-8803. Personal E-mail: bobbyjcline@yahoo.com.

CLINE, CELESTE ANN, primary school educator; b. Phila., Jan. 10, 1954; d. Eugene Francis and Ida Mary Rizzo; m. Raymond L. Cline, Feb. 14, 1976; children: Evelyn Danielle, Raymond L. III, Gina Marie, Maria Nicole, Shannon Marie. B, Holy Family U., 1975. Tchr. All Saints Cath. Sch., Phila., 1972—78, Little Learners, 1979—81, Incarnation Our Lord, 1981—. Capt. Block Captains Am., Phila., 1993—96; dir. adult religious edn. St. William's Cath. Ch., 2000—04; pres. Incarnation Home and Sch. Assn., 1989—92. Mem.: NEA (assoc.). Democrat. Roman Catholic. Avocations: cooking, reading, writing, music, walking. Home: 4715 North Second St Philadelphia PA 19120-4201 Office: Incarnation Our Lord Cath Sch 425 West Lindley Ave Philadelphia PA 19120-4201 Office Phone: 215-457-2779. Personal E-mail: each14@libertasconsulting.net.

CLINE, DAVID BRUCE, physicist, researcher; b. Kansas City, Kans., Dec. 7, 1933; s. Andrew B. Cline and Ella M. Jacks; children: Heather, Bruce, Richard, Yasmin, Daphne. BS, MS, Kansas State Univ., 1960; PhD, Univ. Wis., 1965. Asst. prof. physics Univ. Wis., Madison, 1965-66, assoc. prof. physics, 1966-68, prof. physics, 1969; prof. physics and astronomy UCLA, 1969—. Vis. appts. U. Hawaii, Lawrence Berkeley (Calif.) Lab., Fermilab, CERN; mem. various high energy physics adv. panels and program coms., theory and lab. astrophysics panel, panel on particles NRC Astronomy & Astrophysics Survey Com.; past co-dir. Instit. for Accelerator Physics at U. Wis.; founder Ctr. for Advanced Accelerators, UCLA, 1987. Editor numerous books. With U.S. Army, 1956-58. Recipient Sloan fellow A.P. Sloan Found., 1967. Fellow N.Y. Acad. Scis.; mem. AAAS, Am. Inst. Physics, Phi Beta Kappa. Democrat. Achievements include first search for weak neutical currents that charge flavor; co-discovery of Weak Neutral current at FNAL (HPWF exp) early evidence for charm particle; devise of the antiproton-proton collider; liquid xenon; co-discovery of the W and Z intermediate boson at CERN, Geneva; discovery of B 0 - Bo mixing; patentee for PET medical imagery technique. Office: UCLA Dept Physics 405 Hilgard Ave Los Angeles CA 90095-9000

CLINE, FRED ALBERT, JR., retired librarian, conservationist; b. Santa Barbara, Calif., Oct. 23, 1929; s. Fred Albert and Anna Cecelia (Haberl) C. AB in Asian Studies, U. Calif., Berkeley, 1952, MLS, 1962. Resident Internat. House, Berkeley, 1950-51; trainee, officer Bank of Am., San Francisco, Düsseldorf, Fed. Republic Germany, Kuala Lumpur, 1954-60; adminstrv. reference libr. Calif. State Libr., Sacramento, 1962-67; head libr. Asian Art Mus. San Francisco, 1967-93; ret., 1993. Contbg. author: Chinese, Korean and Japanese Sculpture in the Avery Brundage Collection, 1974; author, editor: Ruth Hill Cooke, 1985; contbr. articles and book revs. on AIDS to various publs. Bd. dirs. Tamalpais Conservation Club, 1990-94, 98-99; dissident AIDS activist. Sgt. M.C., U.S. Army, 1952-54. Mem. Metaphys. Alliance (sec., bd. dirs. San Francisco chpt. 1988-91), Sierra Club. Democrat. Avocations: hiking, music, reading. Home: 825 Lincoln Way San Francisco CA 94122-2369 Personal E-mail: facpat@comcast.net.

CLINE, JAMES E., music educator; b. Welch, W.Va., Mar. 13, 1977; s. Tenna M. Collins. BA, Concord Coll., 2000. Provisional music educator cert. Va. Choir dir. Parry McCluer H.S., Buena Vista, Va., 2001—02, Buffalo Gap H.S., Swoope, Va., 2002—. Mem.: VMEA, ACDA, Music Educators Nat. Conf. Personal E-mail: jecline@space.com.

CLINE, JANICE CLAIRE, education educator; b. Wausau, Wis., Aug. 22, 1945; d. George Leroy and Irma Olga (Brummond) Cline; m. Brent Buell, Jan. 28, 1979. BS, U. Wis., 1967; MA, NYU, 1972; student of Eli Siegel, 1978; student of Ellen Reiss, Aesthetic Realism Found., N.Y.C., 1977—2001; student of Aesthetic Realism Teaching Method, 1977—2002. Tchr. Hyde Park HS, Chgo., 1967-69; instr. JOB tng. program Chase Manhattan Bank, N.Y.C., 1969-71; adj. lectr. N.Y.C. CC CUNY, Bklyn., 1971-72, lectr. York Coll. Jamaica, 1972—; evaluator title I evaluation team York Coll., Jamaica, 1972. Lectr. Aesthetic Realism Fedn., N.Y.C., 1977—2001; guest spkr. WVON, Chgo., 1980. Contbr. articles to profl. jours. Coord. Conf. Support Liberation South Africa and Namibia York Coll., Jamaica, 1985, coord. Student/Faculty Consortium Ctrl. Am., 1986. Recipient Outstanding Contbn. award, Conf. African People, 1986. Mem.: AAUP, Nat. Action Network, Nat. Coun. Tchrs. English, Am. Fedn. Tchrs. (del. 2000—), Internat. Reading Assn., Profl. Staff Congress (sr. coll. officer, mem. exec. com. 2002—, chpt. chmn.), CUNY Women's Coalition. Office: CUNY York Coll Dept English 94-20 Guy R Brewer Blvd Jamaica NY 11451-0001

CLINE, JOHN CARROLL, clinical psychologist; b. Staunton, Va., Sept. 6, 1955; s. Carroll Hubert and Naomi Edith (Hevener) C.; m. Diane Jeannette Goudreau, May 21, 1983; 1 child, Virginia Goudreau Cline. BA, U. Va., 1977; PhD, U. Toledo, 1984. Lic. psychologist, Conn.; cert. biofeedback; clin. assoc. Am. Bd. Med. Psychotherapists; diplomate Am. Acad. Pain Mgmt. Psychology intern U. Toledo, 1980-81; predoctoral intern VA Med. Ctr., West Haven, Conn., 1981-82, attending psychologist, 1984-85; clinician Alcohol Svcs. Orgn., New Haven, 1982-85; team leader, staff psychologist Elmcrest Hosp., Portland, Conn., 1985-86, asst. unit chief, 1986, dir. behavioral medicine svc., 1986-90; pvt. practice psychologist Hamden, Conn., 1986-94; dir. adult outpatient svcs. Inst. of Living, Hartford, Conn., 1990-93; psychol. svcs. cons. Hamden, Conn., 1994—; clin. dir. dept. counseling and psychiat. svcs. Grove Hill Med. Ctr., New Britain, Conn., 1994-2000, chair quality assurance & outcomes mgmt. dept. psychiat. svcs., 1995-2000; psychologist Gaylord Hosp., Wallingford, Conn., 2000—; cons. Conn. Edn. Svcs., Middletown, 2000—; pvt. practice Affiliated Clin. Therapists, Middletown, 1999—2002. Clin. affiliate Yale Psychol. Svcs. Clinic, Yale U., New Haven, 1985—; cons. psychologist VA Med. Ctr., West Haven, 1985—91; asst. prof. clin. psychiatry U. Conn. Med. Sch., Farmington, Conn., 1991—94; adj. asst. prof. phys. therapy, orthop. phys. therapy program Sch. Grad. and Continuing Edn. Quinnipiac U., Hamden, Conn., 1992—; sr. cons. network devel. Inst. of Living, Hartford, 1993—94; affiliate clin. faculty, Grad. Inst. Profl. Psychology U. Hartford, Conn., 1997—99, 2001—; asst. prof. clin. psychiatry, dept. psychiatry Yale U. Sch. Medicine, New Haven, 2002—. Mem. mission study com. 1st Presbyn. Ch., New Haven, 1990-91; mem. Conn. Coun. Mental Health Providers, 1993-96, chair, 1993-94. Mem. AAAS, APA (coun. rep. 1997-99), Conn. Psychol. Assn. (chair hosp. practice com. 1990-92, practice directorate coord. 1993, pres.-elect 1994, pres. 1995-96, past pres. 1997), Conn. Behavior Therapy Assn. (mem. exec. com. 1992-96), N.Y. Acad. Scis., Assn. Psychiat. Clinics of Conn. (mem. polit. com. 1993-94, mem. edn. com. 1993-94), Soc. Behavioral Medicine, Am. Pain Soc. Avocations: microcomputers, fitness walking, fatherhood. Home: 4 Lamkin St Hamden CT 06517-3309 Office: Gaylord Hosp Dept Psychology PO Box 400 Gaylord Farm Rd Wallingford CT 06492-7048 Office Phone: 203-741-3474. Personal E-mail: jccline@netscape.net.

CLINE, JUDITH SALISBURY, marketing consultant, writer; b. Plainfield, N.J., Aug. 5, 1940; d. James Donald and Gladys Maybelle (Scull) S.; m. Leonard Gordon Hartsoe, July 9, 1966 (div. 1982); 1 child, Allison Lynn Hartsoe; m. James M. Cline, Sr., Sept. 26, 2000. BA in English, Vassar Coll., 1962; MA, Ind. U. Pa., 1972. Cert. paralegal; lic. real estate broker and broker/appraiser, Pa.; cert. secondary sch. tchr., N.J., Pa. Tchr. Greater Johnstown (Pa.) Pub. Schs., 1967-68, Altoona (Pa.) Area Pub. Schs., 1968-71; instr. Pa. State U., Altoona, 1970-72, C.C. Allegheny County, Pitts., 1973-84; realtor Greater Pitts. Bd. Realtors, 1973-91; instr. La Roche Coll., Pitts., 1974-75; owner Salisbury Mktg. Assocs., Evans City, Pa., 1991—; mktg. mgr. TRI-V, Inc., 1994-97; freelance writer Pitts. Post-Gazette, 1996—; sales rep. Marshall Electronics, Pitts., 1988-90; owner The Memoir Writer, 1998—; real estate appraiser, broker Nicklas King McConahy, Cranberry Twp., 1999—2000. Staff writer Butler (Pa.) Eagle, 1993-94; sales rep. Future Electronics Corp., Westborough, Mass., 1984-87. Vol. Peace Corps, Sierra Leone, West Africa, 1962-64, Butler County Literacy, 1991-94, Neighborhood Legal Svc., Butler, 1993, Butler County Hospice, 1990-94, Red Cross Disaster Team, 2001--; telephone bank coord. Campaign for State Rep., Butler County, 1992; active pub. rels. LWV, Butler County, 1990-91, AAUW, Pa., 1990-91. Recipient Andron Epiphanon award Greater Pitts. Bd. Realtors, 1975-77, Pa. Gov.'s award Pennserve, 1991; named Top 25 Realtors North Suburban Multi-List, 1974. Mem. Internat. Toastmasters (v.p. pub. rels. 1993-94), West. Pa. Press Club, Returned Peace Corps Vols. Episcopalian. Avocations: genealogy research, history, needlecrafts, poetry, writing memoirs and fiction.

CLINE, PHILIP LEE, business and economics educator; b. Oklahoma City, Okla., July 10, 1945; s. Maurice Lee and Natha Louise (Craig) C.; m. Julia Ann Semtner, June 8, 1968; children: Benjamin Lee, Susan Elizabeth. BA, Washington and Lee U., 1967; MS, Okla. State U., 1973, PhD, 1975. Assoc. systems engr. IBM, Tulsa, Okla., 1967-69, mktg. rep., 1969-70; rsch. assoc. Okla. State U., Stillwater, 1970-75; from asst. prof. to prof. econs. Washington and Lee U., Lexington, Va., 1975—, head dept. mgmt., 1990-95, The Lewis Whitaker Adams prof. econs. and mgmt., 1995—. Cons. Resources for the Future, Washington, 1975, USDA, Washington, 1975; North River Assocs., Lexington, 1986; bd. dirs Lexington Golf and Country Club. Contbr. articles to profl. jours. Vol. Rockbridge Area Habitat for Humanity. Recipient Outstanding Faculty award Va. Coun. Higher Edn.; grantee Ford Found., 1974, John M. Glenn, 1976, '82, NSF, 1977, '78; Fulbright Sr. Fellow, Trinidad, Tobago, 2000. Mem. Am. Statis. Assn., Am. Mgmt. Assn., Am. Econs. Assn., Beta Gamma Sigma, Omicron Delta Epsilon, Phi Kappa Phi. Office: Washington Lee U Lexington VA 24450

CLINE, ROBERT STANLEY, retired air freight company executive; b. Urbana, Ill., July 17, 1937; s. Lyle Stanley and Mary Elizabeth (Prettyman) C.; m. Judith Lee Stucker, July 7, 1979; children: Lisa Andre, Nicole Lesley, Christina Elaine, Leslie Jane. BA, Dartmouth Coll., 1959. Asst. treas. Chase Manhattan Bank, N.Y.C., 1960-65; v.p. fin. Pacific Air Freight Co., Seattle, 1965-68; exec. v.p. fin. Airborne Express (formerly Airborne Freight Corp.), Seattle, 1968-78, vice chmn., CFO, dir., 1978-84, chmn., CEO, dir., 1984—2002. Bd. dirs. Safeco Corp., Esterline Techs. Corp. Trustee Seattle Repertory Theatre, 1974-90, chmn. bd., 1979-83; trustee Children's Hosp. Found., 1983-91, 96—, Corp. Coun. of Arts, 1983-2002; bd. dirs. Washington Roundtable, 1985-2002, chmn. 1995-96; chmn. bd. dirs. Children's Hosp. Found., 1987-89; trustee United Way of King County, 1991-93. With U.S. Army, 1959-60. Home: 1209 39th Ave E Seattle WA 98112-4403 Office: Airborne Express PO Box 662 Seattle WA 98111-0662

CLINE, RUTH ELEANOR HARWOOD, translator, historian; b. Middletown, Conn., Oct. 31, 1946; d. Burton Henry and Eleanor May (Cash) Harwood; A.B., Smith Coll., 1968; M.A., Rutgers U., 1969; Ph.D., Georgetown U., 2000; cert. translation from French, Georgetown U., 1978; m. William R. Cline, June 10, 1967; children: Alison, Marian. Reviewer, U.S. Dept. State, Washington, 1979-94. Former v.p. Smith Coll. Class of 1968; rsch. assoc. dept. history Georgetown U., 2002-. Mem. Am. Translators Assn. (cert. in French, Spanish and Portuguese), MLA, Internat. Arthurian Soc. Episcopalian. Translator English verse: Yvain; or the Knight with the Lion (Chretien de Troyes), 1975; Perceval; or the Story of the Grail (Chretien de Troyes), 1983, Lancelot or the Knight of the Cart (Chretien de Troyes), 1990 (Lewis Galantiere Prize 1992), Erec and Enide (Chretien de Troyes), 2000, Cliges (Chretien de Troyes), 2000. Home: 5315 Oakland Rd Chevy Chase MD 20815-6638

CLINE, STARR, elementary school educator; b. Bklyn., Feb. 27, 1937; d. Albert and Any (Barocas) Funess; B.A. magna cum laude, Molloy Coll., 1974; postgrad. Hofstra U., 1977; Ed.D., Columbia U., 1985; m. Jerome Z. Cline, Apr. 27, 1957; children— Adam, Larry. Tchr., Oceanside (N.Y.) Public Schls., 1974-81, tchr. gifted elem. program, Herricks Public Schs., 1981—; coordinator Inst. on Gifted and Talented, Columbia U. for Three Village Sch. Dist., Setauket, L.I., 1978, asst. coordinator summer inst., 1978; field reader U.S. Dept. HEW, 1978; adj. instr. Molloy Coll., Hofstra U., C.W. Post Coll., Adelphi U.; regional coordinator Advocacy for Gifted and Talented Edn., 1984, state coordinator, 1985; leader delegation U.S. Amb. Program to Moscow and Siberia, 1991; lectr., cons. in field. Pres., Ocean Lea Civic Assn., 1977; adv. com. N.Y.C. Gifted Ed., 1979. Winner 1st, 3d prizes Creative Problem Solving Inst., Buffalo, 1979; Pub. Service TV Tri-State award, N.Y., N.J., Conn., 1980, others. Mem. Advocacy Gifted and Talented Edn. (dir., treas., pres.), World Council Gifted and Talented Children, Nat. Assn. Gifted Children, Nat. Alliance State Assns. for Gifted Edn. (chair 1993), L.I. Soc. Gifted and Talented, Assn. for Supervision and Curriculum Devel. Clubs: Kiwanettes (trustee 1982, pres. 1985). Author: Independent Study, 1980, Teaching for Talent, 1984, The Independent Learner, 1986, What Would Happen If I Said Yes?, 1989; contbr. articles to profl. jours. Home: 14 Saint James Pl Lynbrook NY 11563-2618

CLINE, STEPHANIE E., food service executive; 2 children. V.p. sys. devel. Jack in the Box Inc., San Diego, 1994—2000, v.p., chief info. officer, 2000—. Named IT Operator of Yr., Hospitality Tech. mag., 2001. Office: Jack in the Box Inc 9330 Balboa Ave San Diego CA 92123

CLINE, STEWART M., real estate executive; BS in Civil Engring., U. Del., 1971; MBA in Fin., Loyola Coll., Balt., 1974. Supr. Ryland Homes, 1972-83, pres. midwest and ctrl. areas, 1983-88, pres., 1989-91; exec. v.p. Ryland Bldg. Co., Md., 1992; pres. S.W. region The Ryland Group, 1992-94; pres., CEO, Morrison Homes, Alpharetta, Ga., 1994—. Office: Morrison Homes 3655 Brookside Pkwy #400 Alpharetta GA 30022-1430 E-mail: scline@morrisonhomes.com.

CLINE, THOMAS WARREN, geneticist, educator; b. Oakland, Calif., May 6, 1946; married, 1986. AB, U. Calif. Berkeley, 1968; PhD in Biochemistry, Harvard U., 1973. Fellow devel. genetics Helen Hay Whitney Found., U. Calif. Irvine, 1973-76; from asst. to prof. biology Princeton U., 1976-90; prof. genetics and devel. U. Calif. Berkeley, 1990—. Recipient Molecular Biology award NAS, 1992. Fellow AAAS, Am. Acad. Arts and Scis.; mem. U.S. Nat. Acad. Scis., Genetics Soc. Am. Achievements include research in development regulation of gene expression in Drosophila melanogaster with emphasis on oogenesis, sex determination, and X-chromosome dosage compensation. Office: U Calif 16 Barker Hall MC 3204 Berkeley CA 94720-3204 Office Phone: 510-643-5632.

CLINE, THOMAS WILLIAM, real estate leasing company executive, management consultant; b. Flint, Mich., Oct. 17, 1932; s. Leo D. and Helen (Wolohan) C.; m. Joanne Greiner, July 18, 1959; children: Robert Arthur, Thomas John, Mary Elizabeth. BS, U. Detroit, 1954, JD, 1956. Bar: Mich. 1957. Gen. atty. Wickes Corp., Saginaw, Mich., 1958-61, sec., gen. counsel 1961-69, sr. v.p., gen. counsel, 1969-71, sr. v.p., sec., 1971-80, dir., 1964-70, 74-80; sr. v.p., group officer, dir. Wickes Cos. Inc., Saginaw, 1980-83; pres. Cline Mgmt. Co., Saginaw, 1983—; pres., COO Signature Corp., Chgo., 1984-85; exec. v.p., COO Seitner Bros. Inc., Saginaw, 1986—2004. Bd. dirs. Mid-Am. Life Assurance Co., Mich. Nat. Bank, Saginaw, Can. West Fin. Svcs.(U.S.) Inc., Aristar Inc. Chmn. fin. com. Diocese of Saginaw, 1970-72; chmn. Saginaw Cath. Schs. Study Com., 1969, Nat. assn. Boys Clubs Am.; bd. dirs. San Diego Symphony Assn., 1975-78, Econ. devel. Corp. San Diego County, 1975-78, also vice-chmn., Saginaw Japanese Cultural Ctr. and Tea House; vice chmn. Boys Clubs San Diego, 1975-77; trustee Saginaw Gen. Hosp. Assn., 1971-72, 73-75; trustee, fin. chmn. Saginaw Coop. Hosp. Inc., 1972; trustee, v.p. United Way of Saginaw County; bd. fellows Saginaw Valley Coll., 1973-75, chmn. bus. fund dr., 1978; mem. adv. bd. Delta Coll., U. San Diego, 1975-78, San Diego State U. Bus. Sch., 1975-78, Saginaw Art Mus., 1986-94; mem. instnl. rev. bd. Saginaw Valley State U., 2002--; mem. fin. com. Diocese San Diego, 1975-78; bd. dirs. Mich. State C. of C., 1973-75, Saginaw Symphony Assn. 1984-88, also v.p.; chmn. Saginaw Met. Area Nat. Alliance of Bus., 1979-80; bd. dirs. San Diego C. of C., 1976-77; ann. programs fund stategic advisor Rotary Found., 2001-03; pres. Big Creek Fishing Lodge, 2000-03; bd. dirs. Saginaw Hall of Fame, 2005—, Saginaw Valley State U. Humanities Series. With U.S. Army, 1956-58. Mem. Mich. Bar Assn., Mich. Mfrs. Assn. (bd. dirs. 1980-88), U.S. C. of C. (adv. com.), Saginaw Club (bd. dirs., v.p. 1991), Serra Club Saginaw County (pres., bd. dirs.), Rotary (pres. Saginaw 1990-91, dist. gov. 1994-95, chair dist. found.1996-2000, del. coun. on legis. 1998, nat. advisor to Rotary Found. 2001-03), Blue Key Soc., Delta Sigma Pi, Beta Alpha Psi, Delta Theta Pi. Home and Office: 4640 Ashland Dr Saginaw MI 48603-4605

CLINE, WILLIAM CHAMBERS, automotive executive; b. Elmhurst, Ill., June 15, 1949; s. William Herbert and Polly (Stevens) C.; m. Linda Blair, July 3, 1971; children: Polly Hayes, Sarah McGavock, William Crockett, Blair Chambers. AB, Duke U., 1971; MM, Northwestern U., 1974. CPA, Ill. Audit staff Arthur Young, Chgo., 1974-79, audit mgr., 1979-82; mgr. Borg-Warner, Chgo., 1982-85, asst. controller, 1985-93; v.p., contr. Borg-Warner Automotive, Inc., Chgo., 1993—. Mem. AICPAs, Ill. Soc. CPAs, Chgo. Athletic Assn. Avocations: horse racing, golf. Office: Borg-Warner Corp 200 S Michigan Ave Ste 1700 Chicago IL 60604-2460

CLINE, WILLIAM RICHARD, economist, educator; b. Denver, Oct. 30, 1941; s. John Russell and Marian Alice (Franklin) C.; m. Ruth Eleanor Harwood, June 10, 1967; children: Alison Margaret, Marian Harwood. AB Pub Affairs summa cum laude, Princeton U., Princeton U., 1963; MA in Econs., Yale U., 1964, PhD, 1969. Lectr. Princeton U., 1967-69, asst. prof., 1969-70; Ford Found. vis. prof. Brazilian Planning Ministry and U. Sao Paulo, 1970-71; dep. dir. trade and devel. research U.S. Treasury Dept., Washington, 1971-73; sr. fellow Brookings Instn., Washington, 1973-81, Inst. for Internat. Econs., Washington, 1982—; pres. Econs. Internat., Inc., Washington, 1981—; dep. mng. dir., chief economist Inst. Internat. Fin., Washington, 1996—2001; sr. fellow Ctr. for Global Devel., Washington, 2002—. Professorial lectr. Johns Hopkins Sch. Internat. Studies, 1981-82, 84; vis. lectr. Princeton U., 1983, 85; vis. prof. Aoyama Gakuin U., Tokyo, 1992-94; adv. bd. U.S. Export-Import Bank, 1986-87. Author: Economic Consequences of a Land Reform in Brazil, 1970, Potential Effects of Income Redistribution, 1972, Trade Negotiations in the Tokyo Round, 1978, World Inflation and the Developing Countries, 1981, International Debt: Systemic Risk and Policy Response, 1984, The U.S.-Japan Economic Problem, 1985, Exports of Manufactures From Developing Countries, 1984, The Future of World Trade in Textiles and Apparel, 1987, Informatics and Development, 1987, United States External Adjustment and the World Economy, 1989, The Economics of Global Warming, 1992, International Economic Policy in the 1990s, 1994, International Debt Reexamined, 1995, Trade and Income Distribution, 1997, Trade Policy and Global Poverty, 2004. Woodrow Wilson fellow, 1964, Ford Found. fellow, 1965; recipient Harold and Margaret Sprout award Internat. Studies Assn., 1993. Mem. Am. Econ. Assn., Council Fgn. Relations. Episcopalian. Home: 5315 Oakland Rd Chevy Chase MD 20815 Office: Inst Internat Econs 1750 Massachusetts Ave NW Washington DC 20036-1903

CLINEFELTER, RUTH ELIZABETH WRIGHT, historian, educator; b. Akron, Ohio, Nov. 2, 1930; d. Cyril and Ruth Elizabeth (Dresher) Wright. BA, U. Akron, Ohio, 1952, MA, 1953; MLS, Kent State U., Kent, Ohio, 1956. Serial libr. U. Akron, Akron, Ohio, 1953-61, social sci. rsch. libr., 1961-76, humanities rsch. libr., 1977-83, social sci. humanities bibliographer, 1983—. Lectr. in gen. studies U. Akron, 1960, instr. bibliography, 1956-59, asst. prof. bibliography, 1959-77, assoc. prof. bibliography, 1977-84, prof. bibliography, 1984-99, prof. emeritus, 2000—; resource person NEH, Ohio; mem. joint study com. Am. History Rsch. in Ohio, Ohio Hist. Soc., 1969-70; mem. acad. affairs com. Ohio Faculty Senate, 1971-72; mem. hist. abstracts bibliographic svc. ABC Clio Users Bd., 1978-79. Contbr. articles to profl. jour. Trustee, Akron Area Women's History Project, Summit County Hist. Soc., 1997—, bd. mem. Humane Soc. Greater Akron, Nat. Trust for Hist. Preservation, Progress Through Preservation Recipient Pioneer award for contbns. to women Mortar Board, 1997; named Woman of the Yr., Akron Area NOW, 2001, Organizational Woman of the Yr., History Project, 1993, 1998 Mem. AAUP, Am. Hist. Assn., Assn. for Bibliography of History, North Am. Conf. British Studies, Cascade Locks Park Assn.(bd. dirs.) Democrat. Episcopalian. Home: 1377 Hadden Cir Akron OH 44313-6505 Office: U Akron Bierce Libr Akron OH 44325-0001

CLINKENBEARD, JAMES HOWARD, principal; b. Alexandria, Va., Apr. 1, 1950; s. Howard Samuel and Ethel Jane (Schwager) C.; m. Janelle Darlene Turner, May 27, 1972; children: Adam James, Nathan Linton, Evan Joel. BS, Murray State U., 1977; MEd, Xavier U., 1985, postgrad., 1986—87, postgrad., 1989—92. Cert. tchr. and adminstr., Ky. Tchr. art Newport (Ky.) Ind. Schs., 1978-88, chief negotiator, 1985-88, asst. prin., 1988-91, 92-96, dir. Title V, 1991-92, acting prin., 1992, 94-95, prin., 1996—; freelance artist, designer Bellevue, Ky., 1977—. Juror various sch. and profl. art shows; speaker pub. sch. in-service programs. Featured in Kentucky Artist and Craftsman mag., 1977, Inside Kentucky Schools, Ky. Ednl. T.V., 2001; author various documents, ednl. reports. State advisor Ky. Imagination Celebration, 1984—85; advisor Ky. Task Force for Comprehensive Arts, 1984, Ky. Task Force on Acad. Competition, 1985; active Ft. Thomas and Newport PTAs, Bellevue Civic Assn.; chmn. Citizens for Bellevue Schs., 1980—81, Arts Subcom, Coun. on Higher Edn., 1985—86, Ky. Foster Care Rev. Bd., 1991—97; mem. select panel Ky. Disting. Educators Program; chmn. Sch. Based Decision Making Coun., 1996—; chair com. Troop 70 Boy Scouts Am., 1997—2001, Ky. Rewards Category Sch., 1996—98, 1998—2000; deacon First Christian Ch., Ft. Thomas, 1976—, chmn. bd., 1982—83, Sunday sch. tchr., 1976—97, 1999—2000; bd. dirs. Ky. Citizens for the Arts in Edn., 1983—85. Recipient commendation Ky. Supt. Pub. Instrn., 1984. Mem.: ASCD, NEA, Washington Evening Star Cartoonists Guild, Newport Adminstrs. Assn. (pres. 1994—97, 2001—), Newport Tchrs. Assn. (sec. 1982—83, vice chmn. polit. action com. 1984, treas. 1985—88, pres. 1988), Ky. Edn. Assn. (svcs. com. 1985—87, del. 1986—88, task force 1987—88), Ky. Art Edn. Assn. (various offices including pres. 1983—84, Project Art Tchr. award 1980), Nat. Art Edn. Assn. (Ky. del. 1976—77, 1981), Ft. Thomas Swim Club (bd. dirs. 1994—2000, pres. 1995—2000), Alpha Tau Omega (chpt. advisor 1987—91, chpt. housing corp. pres. 1993—, chpt. trustee 1995—). Republican. Mem. Christian Ch. (Disciples Of Christ). Avocations: reading, sports, working with children. Home: 30 Kathy Ln Fort Thomas KY 41075-1914 Office: Newport Ind Schs 101 E 4th St Newport KY 41071-1615 E-mail: jclink.nky@fuse.net.

CLINKENBEARD, JANELLE DARLENE, elementary school educator; b. Akron, Ohio, Dec. 6, 1951; d. Lee J. Sr. and Felica (Genet) Turner; m. James H. Clinkenbeard, May 17, 1972; children: Adam, Nathan, Evan. BS, Murray State U., 1973, MAEd, 1977. Tchr. Sault Area Pub. Sch., Sault Ste. Marie, Mich., 1973-75; tchr. learning disabilities Trigg County Bd. Edn., Cadiz, Ky., 1975-78, Bellevue (Ky.) Bd. Edn., 1978-85; tchr. Ft. Thomas (Ky.) Bd. Edn., 1985—. Team mem. So. Assn. Sch. Accreditation; dist. math. cluster leader, dist. writing cluster leader, intern tchr. supr. Recipient Golden Apple award Ky. Post, 1992, Lions Club Tchr. of the Yr., 1997, Rotary Club Tchr. of the Yr., 1997, Mrs. Ky., Mrs. Am. Beauty Pageant, 1980. Mem.: NEA, Ft. Thomas Edn. Assn. (bldg. rep., rec. sec., past v.p.), Ky. Edn. Assn., Phi Delta Kappa, Delta Kappa Gamma (pres. 2005—), Alpha Delta Pi. Home: 30 Kathy Ln Fort Thomas KY 41075-1914 Office: Highland Mid Sch 2400 Meml Pkwy Fort Thomas KY 41075-1609

CLINKSCALE, MARTHA, music educator, researcher; b. Akron, Ohio, June 16, 1933; d. Joseph John and Ophia May Novak; m. Alfred Thorpe Loeffler, Jr., Apr. 7, 1955 (div. Oct. 1966); children: Alfred Thorpe Loeffler III, Lise Morrison Loeffler-Welton; m. Edward Henry Clinkscale, Mar. 4, 1968 (dec. July 1994). MusB in Piano Performance, U. Louisville, 1953; MusM in Piano Performance, Yale U., 1955; PhD in Musicology, U. Minn., 1970. Music libr., accompanist Chaffey Coll., Alta Loma, Calif., 1965—68; vis. lectr. Calif. State U., San Bernardino, U. Redlands, Calif.; lectr. piano, fortepiano, chamber music U. Calif., Riverside, 1979—96; vis. lectr. Calif. State Poly. U., Pomona, 1989—90; adj. prof. fortepiano emerita So. Meth. U., Dallas, 1998—2004. Presenter in field. Author: Makers of the Piano 1700-1820, 1993, Makers of the Piano 1820-1860, 1999; editor: Jour. of the Am. Musical Instrument Soc., 1993—96; contbr. articles to profl. jours. Mem.: Royal Mus. Assn., Soc. for Seventeenth-Century Music, Galpin Soc., Midwestern Hist. Keyboard Soc., Internat. Musicol. Soc., Internat. Coun. on Museums, Com. Internat. des Musées et Collections d'Instruments de Musique, Am. Musicol. Soc. (treas. Pacific S.W. chpt. 1985—87, v.p. Pacific S.W. chpt. 1990—92, mem. nat. chpt. fund com. 1991—94, pres. Pacific S.W. chpt. 1992—96, chair nat. chpt. fund com. 1993—94), Am. Musical Instrument Soc. (bd. govs. 1991—95), Am. Inst. Verdi Studies, Southeastern Hist. Keyboard Soc. (bd. mem. 1998—2003, chair nominating com. 2003—04, mem. jour. oversight com. 2003—04, treas. 2004—), Sigma Alpha Iota, Pi Kappa Lambda. E-mail: marthaclinkscale@yahoo.com.

CLINTON, BARBARA MARIE, director, social worker; b. Bklyn., May 21, 1947; d. Lawrence Joseph and Kathleen Byrne C.; m. James Edward Selin, Sept. 12, 1981; children: Greta Maureen, Caitlin Carol. Auditor's cert., U. Tunis, Tunisia, 1968; BS, State U. Coll., Buffalo, 1971; student, SUNY, Buffalo, 1970-71; MSW, U. Ga., 1979. Child care worker Gateway United Meth. Youth Ctr., Williamsville, N.Y., 1970; caseworker Erie County Dept. Social Svcs., Buffalo, 1975-76; social worker Orchard Park (N.Y.) Nursing Home, 1976-77; group counselor Erie Med. Ctr., Buffalo, 1976-77; therapist Buffalo Children's Hosp., 1977-78; intern N.E. Ga. Community Mental Health Ctr., Athens, 1980-81; assoc. dir. ctr. health svcs. Vanderbilt U., Nashville, 1981-87, acting dir. ctr. health svcs., 1987-88, dir. ctr. health svcs., 1988—. Lectr. sch. medicine SUNY, Buffalo, 1977-78; gov.'s intern State of Ga., 1978, 79; dir. Maternal Infant Health Outreach Worker Project, 1982-90; adj. lectr. community health sch. nursing Vanderbilt U., 1986—; expert panelist Nat. Resource Ctr. Children Poverty Columbia U., 1987-89, Save The Children Fedn., Westport, Conn., 1992-93, cons.; evaluation advisor Tenn. Commn. Aging, 1991-92; mem. adv. bd. Vanderbilt U. Women's Ctr., 1992-94; presenter in field. Author: (with Mary Porter) Postnatal Home Visit Guide: The Second Year of Life, 1986, (with Toby Barnett) The Emotional Development of Infants: A Discussion Guide for Outreach Workers, 1987; contbr. articles to profl. jours. Active Bring Urban Recycling Nashville Today, Woodbine Community Orgn.; mem. steering com. S.E. Women's Employment Coalition, Lexington, Ky., 1988-91, bd. dirs., 1989-91; bd. dirs. Tenn. Coalition Def. Battered Women, 1990—, Vanderbilt Women's Ctr., 1992—, U. Ky. Coalition on Cancer, Lexington, 1992—. Regents scholar State of N.Y., 1965, 66, 68, 69; grantee Ford Found., 1982-88, J.C. Penny Found., 1983, Robert Wood Johnson Found., 1983-89, van Leer Found., 1986-93, Pub. Welfare Found., 1989-93, Unitarian Universalist Veatch Fund, 1988-93. Mem. APHA, NASW, Nat. Women's Health Network, Internat. Childbirth Edn. Assn., Tenn. Primary Care Assn., Acad. Cert. Social Workers. Home: 313 Peachtree St Nashville TN 37210-4925 Office: Vanderbilt U Ctr Health Svcs Sta 17 Nashville TN 37232-0001

CLINTON, BILL (WILLIAM JEFFERSON CLINTON), 42nd President of the United States; b. Hope, Ark., Aug. 19, 1946; s. Virginia Dell Cassidy and William Jefferson Blythe IV; m. Hillary Rodham, Oct. 11, 1975; 1 child, Chelsea Victoria. BS in Internat. Affairs, Georgetown U., 1968; postgrad., Oxford U., 1968-70; JD, Yale U., 1973. Prof. U. Ark. Sch. Law, Fayetteville, 1973-76; pvt. practice law, 1973-76; atty. gen. State of Ark., Little Rock, 1977-79, gov., 1979-81, 83-92; of counsel Wright, Lindsey & Jennings, Little Rock, 1981-82; pres. US, Washington, 1993-2001; spl. envoy for tsunami reconstruction UN, 2005—. Chmn. So. Growth Policies Bd., 1985-86. Author: (memoir) My Life, 2004 (Grammy Award for Spoken Word Album, 2005, Publishers Weekly Bestseller, NY Times Bestseller, Biography of Yr., Brit. Book Awards, 2005, Audiobook of Yr., Audio Publ. Assn., 2005). Chmn. Edn. Commn. of the States, 1986-87, mem. steering com.; mem. Task Force on Adolescent Edn., Carnegie Found.; chmn. Dem. Leadership Coun., 1990-91. Rhodes scholar Univ. Coll., Oxford U., 1968-70; named one of most influential people, TIME mag., 2005. Mem. ABA, Ark. Bar Assn., Nat. Govs. Assn. (vice chmn. 1986, chmn. 1986-87, exec. com., fin. com., com. on human resources, com. on internat. trade and fgn. rels., task force on rural devel., co-chmn. task force for edn. 1990-92). Democrat. Address: 55 W 125th St New York NY 10027*

CLINTON, HILLARY RODHAM, senator, lawyer, former First Lady of United States; b. Chgo., Oct. 26, 1947; d. Hugh Ellsworth and Dorothy (Howell) Rodham; m. William J. Clinton, Oct. 11, 1975; 1 child, Chelsea Victoria. BA with high honors, Wellesley Coll., 1969; JD, Yale U., 1973; LLD (hon.), U. Ark., Little Rock, 1985, Ark. Coll., 1988, Hendrix Coll., 1992, U. Sunderland, 1993, U. Pa., 1993, U. Mich., 1993, U. Ill., 1994, U. Minn., 1995, San Francisco State U., 1995, U. Ulster, 2004; LLD, Marymount Manhattan Coll., 2005, Rensselaer Poly. Inst., 2005; D Pub. Svc. (hon.), George Washington U., 1994, U. Md., College Park, 1996; DHL (hon.), Drew U., 1996, Ohio U., 1997, Pace Univ., 2003, Manhattanville College, 2004. Bar: Ark. 1973, US Dist. Ct. Ea. and We. Dists. Ark. 1973, US Ct. Appeals 8th Cir. 1973, US Supreme Ct. 1975. Atty. Children's Def. Fund, Cambridge, Mass. and Washington, 1973-74; legal cons. Carnegie Coun. on Children, New Haven, 1973-74; counsel, impeachment inquiry staff Judiciary Com. US Ho. of Reps., Washington, 1974; asst. prof. law, dir. Legal Aid Clinic U. Ark. Sch. Law, Fayetteville, 1974-77, asst. prof. law Little Rock, 1979-80; ptnr. Rose Law Firm, Little Rock, 1977-92; First Lady of the US, 1993—2001; chair Presdl. Task Force on Nat. Health Care Reform, 1993; mem. US Senate from NY, 2001—. Author: Handbook on Legal Rights for Arkansas Women, 1977, 87, It Takes a Village: And Other Lessons Children Teach Us, 1996, Dear Socks, Dear Buddy: Kids' Letters to the First Pets, 1998, An Invitation to the White House, 2000, Living History, 2003; syndicated columnist Talking It Over, 1995—; contbr. articles to profl. journals. Bd. dirs. Childrens Def. Fund, Washington, 1976-92, chair, 1986-91, Legal Svcs. Corp., Washington, 1977-81, chair, 1978-80; founder, pres., bd. dirs. Ark. Advs. for Children and Families, 1977-84; bd. dirs. Child Care Action Campaign, 1986-92, Nat. Ctr. on Edn. and the Economy, 1987-92, Ark. Children's Hosp., 1988-92, Franklin and Eleanor Roosevelt Inst., 1988-92, Children's TV Workshop, 1989-92, Public/Private Ventures, 1990-92; chmn. Ark. Edn. Stds. Com., 1983-84; mem. commn. on quality edn. So. Regional Edn. Bd., 1984-92; chair ABA Commn. on Women in the Profession, 1987-91; former hon. pres. Girl Scouts of Am.; mem. adv. bd. HIPPY, 1988-92, bd. dirs.; former hon. chair Pres.' Com. on the Arts and Humanities, US Del., UN Fourth World Conf. on Women, 1995; hon. mem. The Pen and Brush, 1996—. Named Outstanding Layman of Yr. Phi Delta Kappa, 1984, Health Educator of Yr., Ryan White Found., 1995; recipient Lewis Hine award Nat. Child Labor Law Com., 1993, Albert Schweitzer Leadership award Hugh O'Brian Youth Found., 1993, Iris Cantor Humanitarian award UCLA Med. Ctr., 1993, Friend of Family award Am. Home Econs. Assn., 1993, Charles Wilson Lee Citizen Svc. award Com. for Edn. Funding, 1993, Claude D. Pepper award Nat. Assn. for Home Care, 1993, Commitment to Life award AIDS Project LA, 1994, Disting. Svc., Health Edn. and Prevention award Nat. Ctr. for Health Edn., 1994, First Ann. Eleanor Roosevelt Freedom Fighter award, 1994, Brandeis award U. Louisville Sch. of Law, 1994, Social Justice award United Auto Workers, 1994, Ernie Banks Positivism trophy Emil Verban Meml. Soc., 1994, Humanitarian award Alzheimer's Assn., 1994, Elie Wiesel Found., 1994, Internat. Broadcasting award Hollywood Radio and TV Soc., 1994, Ellen Browning Scripps medal Scripps Coll., 1994, Disting. Pro Bono Svc. award San Diego Vol. Lawyer Program, 1994, HIPPY USA award, 1994, C. Everett Koop medal Am. Diabetes Assn., 1994, Women's Legal Def. Fund award, 1994, Martin Luther King, Jr. award Progressive Nat. Bapt. Conv., 1994, 30th Anniversary Women at Work award in Pub. Policy, Nat. Commn. on Working Women, 1994, Greater Washington Urban League award, 1995, Servant of Justice award NY Legal Aid Soc., 1995, Presdl. award Bklyn. Coll., 1995, Outstanding Mother award Nat. Mother's Day Com., 1995, Dedication, Annual Survey Am. Law, NYU, 1995, Nat. Breast Cancer Coalition Leadership award, 1995, Faith in Humanity award Nat. Coun. Jewish Women, 1996, NICHE Humanitarian award, 1996, Nat. Assn. Elem. Sch. Prins. Dist. Svc. award, 1996, Grammy award, 1997, Bully Pulpit award Nat. Coun. for Adoption, 1997, Nat. Family Advocate award Parents' Plus Newspaper, 1997, Disting. Svc. to Edn. award Coll. Bd., 1997, Disting. Svc. award Columbia U. Ctr. of Addiction and Substance Abuse, 1997, Commitment to Children award The Elizabeth Glaser Pediat. AIDS Found., 1997, Eleanor Roosevelt Living World award Peace Links, 1997; Paul Harris fellow Rotary Found., 1996; named one of Most Powerful Women, Forbes mag., 2005. Fellow Am. Bar Found.; mem. Ark. Bar Assn., Ark. Trial Lawyers Assn., Ark. Women Lawyers Assn., Am. Trial Lawyers Assn., Pulaski County Bar Assn. Democrat. Meth. First First Lady elected to the US Senate and the first woman elected statewide in NY. Office: 476 Russell Senate Office Bldg Washington DC 20510*

CLINTON, JACK W., dean; DMD, Oreg. Health and Sci. U. Sch. Dentistry, 1964. Assoc. dean clin. affairs Oreg. Health and Sci. U. Sch. Dentistry, interim dean, 2003—04, dean, 2004—. Mem.: ADA, Internat. Coll. Dentists (vice regent), Am. Assn. Dental Schools, Am. Assn. Dental Examiners. Office: Oreg Health and Sci U Sch Dentistry 611 SW Campus Dr Portland OR 97239

CLINTON, JAMES W., military professor; s. Patrick Wiliam Clinton; m. Shirley Rae Powers; children: Shari, Cyndi, Vicki, Wendy, Lisa. BS, Columbia U., 1950; MBA, U. Wash., 1961; PhD, St. Louis U., 1973. Instr., navigator U.S. Air Force, 1951—75; analyst OJCS, Pentagon, Wash., 1975—77; asst. prof. U. Wis., Whitewater, 1977—80; prof. U. Colo., Greeley, 1980—99. Author: Loyal Opposition, 1995; contbr. articles to profl. jours. Candidate for mayor City of Greeley, 1990, 1992. Lt. col. USAF, 1951—77. Fulbright scholar, Fulbright Assn., Ho Chi Minh City, Vietnam, 1996. Avocations: genealogy, writing. Home: 1720 Highland Dr SE Puyallup WA 98372-5106

CLINTON, LAWRENCE PAUL, psychiatrist; b. Lubbock, Tex., Apr. 27, 1945; s. Lewis Paul Clinton and Dorothy E. (Higgins) Clinton-Billingslea; m. Bonnie Gail Orenstein, June 22, 1969; children: Kerry Elizabeth, Andrew James, Alexander Geoffrey, Kaylin Lee. BA with honors, So. Conn. State

Coll., 1966; postgrad., Ohio State U., 1966-68; MD, Hahnemann U., 1972. Diplomate Am. Bd. Psychiatry and Neurology, Am. Bd. Forensic Examiners, Am. Acad. Experts in Traumatic Stress, Am. Bd. Psychotherapy, 2000, Am. Psychiat. Assn. Teaching asst. Ohio State U., Columbus, 1966-68, research fellow, 1966-68; clin. instr. psychiatry Hahnemann U., Phila., 1975-82, asst. clin. prof., 1982—. Chief exec. officer Bldg. Mgmt. Group, Vineland, NJ, 1986—; psychiat. dir. James Guiffre Med. Ctr., Phila., 1976-79; med. dir. PSI Group, 1990-2003; cons. Superior Ct. NJ, 1975—, Ranch Hope, Alloway, NJ, 1989-92. Contbr. articles to profl. jours. Mem. Am. Security Coun., 1975—, Rep. Senatorial Com., 1978—, Rep. Nat. Com., 1978, The Pres. Club, 1990—. Recipient awards Am. Security Coun., 1982, Buena Regional Sch. Dist., NJ, 1983, Vineland Parent Support and Adv. Group, 1990, Rep. Presdl. Legion of Merit medal, 1992; decorated Chevalier Comdr. Ordre Souverain et Militaire de la Milice du Saint Sepulcre, 1990—, The DaVinci Diamond award, Cambridge Eng., 2004 Fellow Am. Bd. Forensic Examiners, Phila. Coll. Physicians and Surgeons, Am. Psychiat. Assn. (disting.); mem. AMA, Internat. Assn. Group Psychotherapy, NJ Psychiat. Soc., Med. Club Phila., World Fedn. Mental Health, InterAm. Coll. Physicians and Surgeons, Hahnemann Undergrad. Rsch. Soc. (treas. 1971-72), Confedn. of Chivalry, Am. Chem. Soc., Soc. d'Chemie (pres. 1965-66), South Jersey Psychiat. Soc. (sec.-treas. 1994-2001, pres. 2001-03), Internat. Churchill Soc., The Heritage Found., SPQR Club (pres. 1961-62) (Milford, Conn.), Union League Phila., Union League Phila. Yacht Club, Phi Lambda Kappa (v.p. 1972). Avocations: gardening, art collecting, book collecting, historical biography, golf, sailing. Office: 1138 E Chestnut Ave Bldg 6 Vineland NJ 08360-5053 Office Phone: 856-696-2660.

CLINTON, MARIANN HANCOCK, educational association administrator; b. Dyersburg, Tenn., Dec. 7, 1933; d. John Bowen and Nell Maurine (Johnson) Hancock; m. Harry Everett Clinton, Aug. 25, 1956; children—Carol, John Everett. BMus, Cin. Conservatory Music, 1956; BS, U. Cin., 1956; MMus, Miami U., Oxford, Ohio, 1971. Tchr. music public schs., Hamilton County, Ohio, 1956-57; tchr. voice and piano Butler County, Ohio, 1964—; instr. music Miami U., 1972-75; exec. dir. Music Tchrs. Nat. Assn., Cin., 1977-86. Mng. dir. Am. Music Tchr., 1977-86. Mem. adminstrv. bd. Middletown (Ohio) 1st United Methodist Ch., 1968-72; bd. dirs. Friends of the Sorg Opera House; concert presenter Friends of Music of Charlotte County (Fla.). Mem. Music Educators Nat. Conf., Am. Ednl. Research Assn., Am. Soc. Assn. Execs., Nat. Fedn. Music Clubs, Pi Kappa Lambda, Kappa Delta Pi, Mu Phi Epsilon, Phi Mu. Republican. Home: 714 Macedonia Dr Punta Gorda FL 33950-8013 *I have found that a consideration for the interrelatedness of all parts so necessary in the presentation of music and a warm regard for the feelings of others which is implicit in the practice of good manners in daily observance create success in one's personal and professional lives.*

CLINTON, RICHARD M., lawyer; b. Milw., June 25, 1941; s. William J. and Idella (Loftis) C.; m. Barbara Lynch, June 14, 1969; children: Amanda, Camille, Rebecca. BS, U. Wis., 1963, JD, 1967; LLM, George Washington U., 1971. Bar: Wis. 1967, Wash. 1971, U.S. Ct. Appeals (9th cir.) 1972, U.S. Dist. Ct. (ea. dist.) Wash. 1975. Instr. legal writing U. Wis. Law Sch., Madison, 1966-67; trial atty. antitrust div. U.S. Dept. Justice, Washington, 1967-71; assoc. Bogle & Gates, Seattle, 1971-75, mem., 1975-99; ptnr., sr. trial atty., litig., and co-chmn., anti-trust practice Dorsey & Whitney LLP, Seattle, 1999—. Fellow Am. Coll. Trial Lawyers; mem. ABA, Wash. Bar Assn. (pres. antitrust sect. 1982-83), Fed. Bar Assn. (pres. 1986-87), Wash. Athletic Club, Columbia Tower Club. Roman Catholic. Avocations: sailing, skiing, fishing, hiking, travel. Office: Dorsey & Whitney LLP Ste 3400 US Bank Centre 1420 5th Ave Seattle WA 98101-4010 Office Phone: 206-903-8851. Office Fax: 206-903-8820. E-mail: clinton.richard@dorsey.com.

CLINTON, STEPHEN MICHAEL, academic administrator; b. Wichita, Kans., Aug. 21, 1944; s. Thomas Francis and Bettie Lee (Harrison) C.; m. Virginia Ann Schoonover, Aug. 30, 1964; children: Matthew, Michael, Shanna. MA in Philosophy, Trinity Evang. Div. Sch., Deerfield, Ill., 1969, MDiv, 1970; PhD in Theology, Calif. Grad. Sch. Theology, 1979; postgdoc. in philosophy, U. Calif., Riverside, 1985-87, PhD in Edn., 1997; MA in Counseling, Internat. Sch. Theology, San Bernardino, Calif., 1987; MA in Edn., Calif. State U., San Bernardino, 1988. Ordained to ministry Evang. Free Ch. Am., 1973; cert. gifted edn. tchr., Calif. Pastor Lake Zurich (Ill.) EFC, 1967-69, Faith Presbyn. Ch., Wichita, Kans., 1972-74, Highlander Evang. Free Ch., 1974—78, East Cmty. Ch., Orlando, Fla., 1993-94, First Bapt. Ch., St. Cloud, Fla., 1999-2000; dir. extension degree programs Internat. Sch. Theology, 1974-86, assoc. prof., 1978-86; dir. Internat. Leadership Coun., 1986—; pres. Orlando (Fla.) Inst., 1991—, prof. edn. and religion, 1992—; dir. EdD program Iberia-Am. U. Leadership, 1998—2004; exec. dir. Vision Orlando, 2005—. Pres. Ministry Devel., Inc., San Bernardino, 1978-86; chmn. bd. dirs. Masterlife Internat., 1999-2000; bd. dirs. Vision Orlando, 1992—, exec. dir., 2005-; bd. reference Am. All Stars, 2000—; prof. Belhaven Coll., 2000-01; adj. prof. Moody Bible Inst., Phoenix U., Valenia C.C., Asbury Theol. Sem. Author: The Doctrine of the Christian Life, 1981, Cultural Apologetics, 1983, Calvinism and Arminianism, 1985, The Everlasting God, 1989, Movements Which Changed History, 1993, Theistic Realism, 1998, The Role of the Holy Spirit in Spiritual Development, 2001; also 40 articles. Pres. Advs. for Gifted and Talented Edn., San Bernardino, 1979-85; chmn. state parent coun. Calif. Assn. for Gifted, 1978-83; pres. advocates for gifted and talented edn. San Bernardino Unified Sch. Dist., 1984-87; chmn. bd. dirs. Ctr. for Individuals with Disabilities, San Bernardino, 1984-88; Maitland C. of C., bd. dirs., 2002—, pres. elect, 2005. Mem. Evang. Philos. Soc. (editor 1979-81, 84-98, pres. 1983), Evang. Free Ch. Ministerial Assn., Evang. Theol. Soc. (chmn. 1982, 03), John Dewey Soc., Philosophy of Edn. Soc. Office: Orlando Inst 100 Lake Hart Dr Ste 3000 Orlando FL 32832 E-mail: sclinton@toi.edu.

CLIPPARD, RICHARD F., prosecutor; Graduate, U. Miss., 1976; JD, U. Miss. Law Sch., 1980. Private practice Butler, Lackey, Holt and Snedeker, 1980—83; special asst. US atty. US Small Bus. Adminstrn., 1983—88; asst. US atty. US Atty. Office, Nashville, 1988—2000, chief of Civil Division, 2000—01; interim U.S. atty. Middle Dist., Tenn., 2001—02; U.S. trustee for Tenn. & Ky. Exec. Off. for U.S. Trustees, 2003—. Office: 200 Jefferson Ave Ste 400 Memphis TN 38103*

CLIPPERT, CHARLES FREDERICK, lawyer; b. Detroit, May 21, 1931; s. Harrison Frank and Ethelyn (Reuss) C.; m. Lynne Davison, June 6, 1959; children: Martha G. Shannon, Charles Frederick III, Thomas Harrison. BA, U. Mich., 1953, LLB, 1959. Bar: Mich. 1959. Assoc. Dickinson, Wright, Moon, Van Dusen & Freeman, Bloomfield Hills, Mich., 1959-67, ptnr., 1967-97, mem. exec. com., 1986-89; mem. Dickinson Wright PLLC, Bloomfield Hills, Mich., 1998-2000, cons. mem., 2001—. Commr. City of Birmingham, Mich., 1964-70, mayor, 1969-70; gov. Cranbrook Schs., Bloomfield Hills, 1978-99; trustee Cranbrook Ednl. Community, Bloomfield Hills, 1980-98, sec., 1989-93. Lt. (j.g.) USNR, 1953-56; mem. endowment com. The Consortium of Endowed Episcopal Parishes, 1998—. Fellow Am. Bar Found., Mich. Bar Found.; mem. ABA, State Bar Mich. (real property law coun. 1980-85, mem. select com. on professionalism 1992-99, mem. alternate dispute resolution coun. 1999—), Oakland County Bar Assn. (bd. dirs. 1985-91, pres. 1990-91), Orchard Lake Country Club (gov. 1986-92, pres. 1991-92), Am. Arbitration Assn. (panel of neutral arbitrators 1997—), Pi Sigma Alpha. Office: Dickinson Wright PLLC Ste 2000 38525 Woodward Ave Bloomfield Hills MI 48304-2971 Mailing: PO Box 509 Bloomfield Hills MI 48303-0509 Office Phone: 248-433-7212. Business E-Mail: cclippert@dickinson-wright.com.

CLIZBE, JOHN ANTHONY, psychologist, social services administrator; b. Council Bluffs, Iowa, June 28, 1942; s. Harold George and Margaret Jane (Fariday) C.; m. Rebecca Rose Maddox, Jan. 30, 1965; children: Mark Andrew, Diane Christine. BA, William Jewell Coll., Liberty, Mo., 1964; PhD, Washington U., St. Louis, 1967. Clin. psychology resident Norfolk (Nebr.) State Hosp. and Northeast Mental Health Clinic, 1967-68; cons. psychologist Nordli, Wilson Assocs., Worcester, Mass., 1968-97, gen. ptnr., 1975-97, resident mgr., 1978-83, mng. ptnr., 1983-93, sr. ptnr., 1993-97; v.p. disaster svcs. ARC, Falls Church, Va., 1997—2002, interim exec. dir. Triangle Area chpt., 2003, interim CEO Price George's County chpt., 2003; emergency planner City of Alexandria Health Dept., Va., 2004—. Pres. PCMS, Inc., 1984-97; dir., treas. PSI, Inc., 1983-97, Human Interface Group, Inc., 1986-97; dir., v.p., treas. Student Achievement Inst., Worcester, 1973-97. Columnist Bus. Times. Dir., treas., pres. Nat. Psychol. Cons. to Mgmt.; mem. bd. edn. Town of Madison, Conn., 1980-86; trustee Calvin K. Kazanjian Econ. Found., Inc., 1986—; dist. chmn. 101st Assembly Dist., 1992-97, Conn. Party, 1992—; chmn. Conn. Red Cross Disaster Mental Health Com., 1992-97, Nat. Bd. Emergency Ford and Shelter Program, 1997—; facilitator Vision Project City of New Haven, 1994; coord. Mental Health Svcs., 1995, Spl. Olympics World Games; mem. exec. com. Nat. Hurrican Conf., 1997—; chmn. waterfront com. City of New Haven Vision Project; others; nat. chmn. disaster svcs. ARC, 1995-97; mem. exec. com. Internat. Conf. on Disaster Mgmt., 2000; mem. adv. com. Natural Hazards Rsch. and Applications Ctr., 1998—; chmn. bioterrorism emergency planners subcom. Washington Area Coun. Govts. NDEA fellow Washington U., 1967. Mem. APA (membership com. div. 14), Mass. Psychol. Assn., Am. Mgmt. Assn. (faculty President's Assn. 1987-97), New Haven C. of C. (bd. dirs. 1989-95), Sigma Xi, Pi Gamma Mu, Pi Kappa Delta. Home: 607 Queen St Alexandria VA 22314-2514 Office: ARC 8111 Gatehouse Rd Falls Church VA 22042-1203 Office Phone: 703-838-4400. Business E-Mail: john.clizbe@udh.virginia.gov.

CLODFELTER, DANIEL GRAY, state legislator, lawyer; b. Thomasville, N.C., June 2, 1950; s. Billy G. and Marie Lorene (Wells) C.; m. Elizabeth Kay Bevan, Aug. 20, 1974; children: Julia Elizabeth, Catherine Gray. BA, Davidson Coll., 1972; AB, Oxford U., Eng., 1974; JD, Yale U., 1977. Bar: N.C. 1977, U.S. Dist. Ct. (we. dist.) N.C. 1977, U.S. Dist. Ct. (ea. dist.) N.C. 1979, U.S. Ct. Appeals (4th cir.) 1984, U.S. Dist. Ct. (mid. dist.) N.C. 1985. Law clk. to presiding judge U.S. Dist. Ct., Charlotte, N.C., 1977-78; assoc. Moore & Van Allen, Charlotte, 1978-82, ptnr., 1983—. Mem. N.C. Senate, 1999—. Mem. Charlotte City Coun., 1987-93, Charlotte-Mecklenburg Planning Commn., 1984-87, chmn., 1986-87; state sec. Rhodes Scholarship Trust, N.C., 1986-97; trustee Z. Smith Reynolds Found., Inc., Winston-Salem, N.C., 1983—; bd. dirs. N.C. Ctr. for Pub. Policy Rsch., 1994-96. Rhodes scholar, 1972. Mem. N.C. Bar Assn. (antitrust law com., bankruptcy sect. coun.). Office: Moore & Van Allen 100 N Tryon St 4700 Charlotte NC 28202-4003 E-mail: clodfelter@mvalaw.com.

CLODIUS, ROBERT LEROY, retired economist; b. Walla Walla, Wash., Mar. 10, 1921; s. Hans Friedrich and Emma (Wellman) C.; m. Joan Elizabeth Coyle, Aug. 27, 1949; children: Catherine, Mark. Student, Whitman Coll., 1938-40, LLD, 1970; BS, U. Calif., Berkeley, 1942, PhD, 1950. Lectr. econs. U. Calif., 1949-50; mem. faculty U. Wis., 1950-90, prof. agrl. econs., 1958-90, chmn. dept., 1960-62, v.p. univ., 1962-71, acting pres., 1970, prof. agrl. econs. emeritus, 1990—, prof. econs., 1971-90, prof. econs. emeritus, 1990—, prof. ednl. adminstrn., 1971-90, prof. ednl. administr. emeritus, 1990—, prof. univ., 1971-90, prof. univ. emeritus, 1990—, v.p. univ. emeritus, 1990—; pres. Nat. Assn. State Univs. and Land Grant Colls., 1979-91, pres. emeritus, 1992—. Vis. assoc. Harvard Bus. Sch., 1954; lectr. Am. Coun. Edn., Inst. Coll. and Univ. Adminstrs.; State Dept. specialist in South Am., 1961; cons. Dept. Agr., 1961; mem. com. agr. scis. to Sec. Agr., 1961-69; cons. Rockefeller Found., 1963-67; adviser U. East Africa, 1963-67; chmn. Com. Instnl. Coop., 1968; cons. Ford Found., Philippines, 1970; chmn. exec. bd. commn. instns. higher edn. North Ctrl. Assn., 1972-74; v.p. Midwest Univs. Consortium Internat. Activities, Inc., 1964-70, chmn. bd., 1970-71; mem. Commn. on Higher Edn., Govt. Sierra Leone, 1969; adminstr. Indonesian Higher Agr. Edn. Project, 1971-77; adv. commr. Edn. Commn. of the States, 1980-91; mem. Nat. Commn. on Higher Edn. Issues, 1981-82, chmn. adv. com. Nat. Ctr. Food and Agrl. Policy, Resources for the Future, 1984-89; nat. adv. com. Adult Learning Svc. PBS, 1987-91, Debt for Devel. Coalition, Inc., 1988-92, chmn., 1988-91, chmn. adv. com., 1992-97; cons. U.S. Info. Agy., 1991-94; v.p. WM Acad. Search Cons. Internat. Inc., 1991-94. Author articles, monographs, chpts. in books; editor: Jour. Farm Econs, 1958-60. Bd. dirs. Univ. Corp. Atmospheric Rsch., 1962-67, Ctr. for Rsch. Librs., 1969-71, Argonne Univ. Assocs., 1978-84, USN Meml. Found., 1995-2000, sec., 1998-2000, trustee, 2001-05; docent Navy Mus., Washington Navy Yard, 1997-2000; mem. adv. bd. Rockford Coll. Music Acad., 2002—; docent Andersen Japanese Gardens, 2002—. Lt. USNR, 1942-55. Decorated Commendation medal; recipient Kiekhofer Teaching award U. Wis., 1953. Mem.: AAUP (pres. U. Wis. 1957), Am./Schleswig Holstein Heritage Soc. (adv. com. 1999—), U.S.-Indonesian Soc. Washington, Am. Agrl. Econs. Assn. (v.p. 1960), Navy Club of USA-Ship 1 (chaplain 2002—), Rotary Internat., Phi Beta Kappa, Phi Kappa Phi, Alpha Zeta. Home: 1909 Shaw Woods Dr Rockford IL 61107-1729

CLOGAN, PAUL MAURICE, English language and literature educator; b. Boston, July 9, 1934; s. Michael J. and Agnes J. (Murphy) C.; m. Julie Sydney Davis, July 27, 1972 (dec. 1982); children: Michael Rodger, Patrick Terence, Margaret Murphy. BA, Boston Coll., 1956, MA, 1957; PhD, U. Ill., 1961; F.A.A.R., Am. Acad. in Rome, 1966; MDiv, Blessed John XXIII Sem., 1999. Asst. prof. Duke U., 1961-65; assoc. prof. Case Western Res. U., Cleve., 1965-72; prof. English U. North Tex., Denton, 1972—. Vis. prof. U. Keele, Eng., 1965, U. Pisa, Italy, 1966, U. Tours, France, 1978; vis. mem. Inst. Advanced Study, Princeton, N.J., 1970, 77; cons. Library of Congress, Ednl. Testing Service, NEH, Nat. Acad. Scis., NRC Commn. Human Resources, Nation Rsch. Council Com. for the Study of Rsch.-Doctorate-Programs in the U.S., Am. Council Learned Socs., Nat. Enquiry into Scholarly Communication, Chilton Research Services; mem. Am. Arts Assn., Inst. Internat. Edn., nat. screening com. 1984-88. Author: The Medieval Achilleid of Statius, 1968, Social Dimensions in Medieval and Renaissance Studies, 1972, In Honor of S. Harrison Thomson, 1970, Medieval and Renaissance Studies in Review, 1971, Medieval and Renaissance Spirituality, 1973, Medieval Historiography, 1974, Medieval Hagiography and Romance, 1975, Medieval Poetics, 1976, Transformation and Continuity, 1977, Byzantine and Western Studies, 1984, Fourteenth and Fifteenth Centuries, 1986, The Early Renaissance, 1987, Literary Theory, 1988, Spectrum, 1992, Columbian Quincentenary, 1992, Renaissance and Discovery, 1993, Breaching the Boundaries, 1994, Convergences, 1994, Diversity, 1995, Historical Inquiries, 1997, Transitions, 1998, Civil Strife and National Identity in the Middle Ages, 1999, Literacy and the Lay Reader, 2000, Ethnicity and Self-Identity, 2002, Papal Letters, Manual for Confessors and Romance, 2003, Humanist Educational Theory, Gregory the Great, and Culinary Comedy, 2004 Reengagement with History, 2005; editor: Medievalia et Humanistica, Studies in Medieval and Renaissance Culture, 1970—; contbr. articles to profl. jours. Grantee Duke Endowment 1961-62, Am. Coun. Learned Socs., 1963-64, 70-71, 88, Am. Philos. Soc., 1964-69, U. North Tex., 1972-75, 80-81, 89; sr. Fulbright-Hays postdoctoral rsch. fellow, Italy, 1965-66, France, 1978, fellow Prix de Rome, 1966-67, Bollingen Found., 1966, NEH, 1969-70, 86, 90-91. Mem. Internat. Assn. Univ. Profs. English, MLA (exec. com. 1980-86, del. assembly 1981-86), Internat. Comparative Lit. Assn., Internat. Arthurian Soc., Modern Humanities Research Assn., Medieval Acad. Am. (nominating com. 1975-76, John Nicholas Brown Prize com. 1981-83), Internat. Assn. for Neo-Latin Studies, The New Chaucer Soc., Fulbright Assn. Democrat. Roman Catholic.

CLOHESY, WILLIAM WARREN, philosopher, educator; b. Chgo., July 31, 1946; s. John Cecil and Mary Evelyn (Ahern) Clohesy; m. Stephanie June Jagucki, June 19, 1971. BS, Loyola U., Chgo., 1964-68; MA, So. Ill. U., 1968-71; PhD, New Sch. Social Rsch., N.Y.C., 1981. Instr. Loyola U., Chgo., 1967, asst. prof., 1982-83; tchg. asst. So. Ill. U., Carbondale, 1969; adj. prof. Montclair State Coll., Upper Montclair, NJ, 1981-82; asst. prof. Rochester (N.Y.) Inst. Tech., 1983-86, rsch. assoc., 1986-87; lectr. U. Belgrano, Buenos Aires, 1987; asst. prof. U. No. Iowa, Cedar Falls, 1987-93, assoc. prof., 1993—. BSN adv. com. Allen Coll., Waterloo, Iowa, 1991—2002; instnl. rev. bd. U. No. Iowa, 2002—. Editor: (book) Ethics at Work, 1992; contbr. articles to profl. jours. Recipient Kurt Riezler Meml. award, New Sch. for Social Rsch., 1982, Faculty Excellence award, Iowa Bd. Regents, 2001; fellow Fulbright fellowship to Argentina, 1987; grantee W.K. Kellogg Found., 1995—2001, Iowa Humanities Bd., 1991—92, NEH, 1991—92. Mem.: Soc. Advancement Am. Philosophy, N.Am. Kant Soc., N.Am. Soc. Social Philosophy, Hume Soc., Am. Philos. Assn., Internat. Soc. 3d Sector Rsch. Democrat. Roman Catholic. Avocation: Irish language, literature, and music. Office: U No Iowa Dept Philosophy & Religion Cedar Falls IA 50614-0501 Office Phone: 319-273-6123. E-mail: william.clohesy@uni.edu.

CLONEY, TERENCE J., lawyer; b. Chgo., Oct. 29, 1953; s. John Edward and Helen (Junginger) C.; m. Katherine Giam, 1985; children: Sean Christopher, Michael Brendan. AB, Columbia U., 1975; JD, NYU, 1979. Bar: N.Y. 1980, Ill. 1989. Assoc. Milbank, Tweed, Hadley & McCloy, N.Y.C., 1979-83, Hong Kong, 1983-86, Singapore, 1986-89; ptnr. Gardner, Carton & Douglas, Chgo., 1989-97, Altheim & Gray, Chgo., 1997—. Bd. dirs. Juvenile Diabetes Found., Chgo., 1993-2001, mem. exec. com., 1994-96. Mem. ABA. Home: 421 Concord Ln N Barrington IL 60010-2207

CLONINGER, CLAUDE ROBERT, psychiatrist, researcher, epidemiologist, educator; b. Beaumont, Tex., Apr. 4, 1944; s. Morris Sheppard and Marie Concetta (Mazzagatti) Cloninger; m. Sharon Lee Rogan, July 11, 1969; children: Bryan Joseph, Kevin Michael. BA, U. Tex., 1966; MD, Washington U., St. Louis, 1970; hon. degree, U. Umea, Sweeden, 1983. Diplomate Am. Bd. Psychology and Neurology. Instr. psychiatry Washington U., St. Louis, 1973—74, asst. prof., 1974—78, assoc. prof., 1978—81, prof., 1981—, prof. genetics, 1978—, prof. psychology, 1989—, Wallace Renard prof. psychiatry, 1991—, head dept. psychiatry, 1989—94, dir. ctr. psychobiology personality, 1994—. Psychiatrist-in-chief Barnes and Renard Hosps., St. Louis, 1989—94; vis. prof. U. Hawaii, Honolulu, 1978—79, U. Umea, Sweden, 1980; chmn. NIMH Psychopathology Rev. Com., Washington, 1980—84; cons. WHO, Geneva, 1981—, Am. Psychiat. Assn., Washington, 1978—, Nat. Inst. on Alcohol Abuse and Alcoholism, 1984—99, Inst. Medicine, 1986; chmn. genetics initiative schizophrenia NIMH, 1989—97; mental health commr. State of Mo., 1990—95. Author: Feeling Good: The Science of Weel-Being, 2004, others; editor: Jour. Behavior Genetics, 1980—86, Am. Jour. Human Genetics, 1980—83; assoc. editor Genetic Epidemiology, 1983—92, Human Heredity, 1989—, mem. editl. bd. Arch. Gen. Psychiatry, Comprehensive Psychiatry, Neuropsychopharmacology, Jour. Comprehensive Psychiatry, Jour. Psychiat. Rsch., Jour. Med. Genetics; contbr. articles to profl. jours. Recipient Rsch. Scientist award, NIMH, 1975, 1980, 1985, Strecker award, Inst. Pa. Hosp., 1988, James B. Isaacson award, ISBRA, 1992, Lifetime Achievement award, Am. Soc. Addiction Medicine, 2000, Finnish Psychiatry Assn. Annual medal, Lifetime Achievement award, Internat. Soc. Psychiat. Genetics, 2003. Fellow: AAAS, Am. Psychopathol. Assn. (treas. 1984—89, v.p. 1990, pres. 1991—93, sec. 1994—96, Samuel Hamilton award 1993), Am. Psychiat. Assn. (Adolph Meyer award 1993); mem.: Rsch. Soc. Alcoholism (bd. dirs. 1987—90), Inst. Medicine of NAS, Behavior Genetics Assn. (editl. bd. 1980—), Am. Soc. Human Genetics (editl. bd. 1980—83). Avocations: gardening, reading, travel. Home: 7100 Delmar Blvd Saint Louis MO 63130-4303 Office: Washington U Dept Psychiatry 4940 Childrens Pl Saint Louis MO 63110-1002 Office Phone: 314-362-7005. Business E-Mail: clon@tci.wustl.edu.

CLONINGER, DALE OWEN, finance educator; b. Clearwater, Fla., Aug. 30, 1940; s. Raymond and Mary E. (Ewing) C.; m. Judy Branson Parrish, Mar. 20, 1961; children: Bret B., Eric O. BS in Indsl. Mgmt., Ga. Inst. Tech., 1962; MBA, Emory U., 1965; DBA, Fla. State U., 1973. Field engr. Gen. Telephone of Fla., 1962-64; instr. econs. U. South Fla., Tampa, 1965-68, asst. prof., 1969-74; assoc. prof. fin. and econs. U. Houston - Clear Lake, 1974-80, prof. fin. and econs., 1980—, dir. programs in acctg. and fin., 1982-85, assoc. dean Sch. Bus., 1985-87, pres. faculty senate, 2004—05. Interim dean Dean Sch. Bus. and Pub. Adminstrn., 1997-98; cons. So. Bell Telephone, Atlanta, 1964-65, Fla. Fed. Savs., St. Petersburg, Fla., 1969-71, Fla. State Legislature, Tallahassee, 1967, 68, 69, various law firms, Houston, 1977—; tax and edn. cons. Fla. State Legislature, 1967-69; designer bus. and econ. activity index Fla. Fed. Savs. and Loan, 1971-74; econ. and fin. evaluator, expert testimony in civil suits of personal injury, lost profits and asset evaluations, 1977—; mem. accreditation teams So. Assn. Colls. and Schs., 1984-90; presenter in field. Author: Income, Employment and the Retired, 1967, The Economics of Crime and Law Enforcement, 1975, 2nd edit., 1980; author: (with Kim Q. Hill) Death on Demand, 1985, 5th edit., 2005; contbr. numerous articles to profl. jours.; referee: Am. Jour. Econs. and Sociology, Contemporary Policy and Issues, Fin. Rev., Jour. Applied Econs., Jour. Econ. Behavior and Orgn., Jour. Econ. Edn., Social Scis. Urban Studies Quar. Recipient Best Paper J. Risk & Ins., 1981; fellow Am. So. Engring. Edn. fellow, NASA, 1976; Emory U. fellow, 1964. Mem. Am. Fin. Assn., Am. Econ. Assn., Fin. Mgmt. Assn., So. Fin. Assn., So. Econ. Assn., Beta Gamma Sigma. Methodist. Avocations: writing, tennis, running. Home: 1011 Live Oak Ln Taylor Lk Vlg TX 77586-4528 Office: U Houston Clear Lake 2700 Bay Area Blvd Houston TX 77058-1002 Office Phone: 281-283-3210. Business E-Mail: cloninger@uhcl.edu.

CLONINGER, KRISS, III, insurance company executive; b. Houston, Oct. 21, 1947; s. Kriss and Jewel JoAnn (Jones) C.; m. Lisa L. Welch; children: Laura Kay, Kriss Alan; stepchildren: J. Tanner Prewit, Presley N. Lanier. BBA, U. Tex, 1969, MBA, 1971. Actuary KPMG Peat Marwick, Dallas, 1973-74, Atlanta, 1977-92, Rudd & Wisdom, Austin, Tex., 1974-77; CFO AFLAC Inc., 1992—, sr. v.p. Columbus, Ga., 1992—93, exec. v.p., 1993—2001, pres., 2001—, bd. dirs. Columbus, Ga., 2001—. Bd. dirs. Tupperware Corp., Total Sys. Svcs., Inc. Served to 1st lt. USAF, 1971-73 Fellow Soc. Actuaries; mem. Am. Acad. Actuaries Home: 612 Front Ave Columbus GA 31901-2924 Office: AFLAC Ctr 1932 Wynnton Rd Columbus GA 31999-0002 E-mail: kcloninger@aflac.com.

CLONTS, GEORGE GARY, packaging company executive; b. Alton, Ill., Mar. 22, 1940; s. George William and Fern Lorene (Miller) C.; m. Charlotte Joann Shelburn, Feb. 28, 1960; children: George Randall, Gary Deneal. Aero. engring. student, USAF, 1957-1961. Flight engr. USAF, Fairbanks, Alaska, 1957-61; prodn. worker Hoerner Boxes, Inc., Springfield, Mo., 1961-64, office mgr. Denver, 1964-69; sales rep. Hoerner Waldorf, Inc., Denver, 1969-72, South West Packaging, Oklahoma City, 1972-77, gen. mgr., 1977-87, Green Bay Packaging, Oklahoma City, 1987-88; pres., chief exec. officer Tech Pack, Inc., Oklahoma City, 1988—2001; pres., gen. ptnr. TPA-L.C., Oklahoma City, 2001—. Active Rep. Presdl. Task Force, Washington, 1982—. With USAF, 1957-61. Mem. Petroleum Club Okla., Gaillardia Golf and Country Club. Avocations: golf, antique automobiles, history. Home: 14908 Gaillardia DR Oklahoma City OK 73142-1832 E-mail: ggcinvest@aol.com.

CLOONAN, JAMES BRIAN, investment company executive; b. Chgo., Jan. 28, 1931; s. Bernard V. and Lauretta D. (Maloney) C.; m. Edythe Adrianne Ratner, Mar. 26, 1970; children: Michele, Christine, Mia; stepchildren: Carrie Madorin, Harry Madorin. Prof. Sch. Bus. Loyola U., Chgo., 1966-71; pres. Quantitative Decision Sys., Inc., Chgo., 1972-73; chmn. bd. Heinold Securities, Inc., Chgo., 1974-77; prof. grad. sch. bus. DePaul U., Chgo., 1978-82; chmn. Investment Info. Svcs., 1981-86; pres. Mktg. Sys. Internat. Inc., 1985-87, Analytics Sys. Inc., 1987—. Bd. dirs., chmn. Mktg. Svcs. Internat., Inc. Author: Estimates of the Impact of Sign and Billboard Removal Under the Highway Beautification Act of 1965, 1966, Stock Options-The Application of Decision Theory to Basic and Advanced Strategies, 1973, An Introduction to Decision Making for the Individual Investor, 1980, Expanding Your Investment Horizons, 1983, A Lifetime Strategy for Investing in Common Stocks, 1988, Maximum Return Minimum Risk, 2003. Mem.: Am. Assn. Individual Investors (pres. 1979—92, chmn. 1992—), Am. Mktg. Assn. Home: 1242 N Lake Shore Dr Chicago IL 60610-2361 Office: Am Assn Individual Investors 625 N Michigan Ave Chicago IL 60611-3110 Office Phone: 312-280-0170. E-mail: jbcaaii@aol.com.

CLOONEY, GEORGE, actor; b. Lexington, Kentucky, May 6, 1961; s. Nick Clooney; m. Talia Blasam, Dec. 15, 1989 (div. Sept. 1993). Student, No. Ky U. Actor: (TV series) E/R, 1984—85, The Facts of Life, 1985—86, Roseanne, 1988—89, Sunset Beat, 1990, Baby Talk, 1991, Sisters, 1992—94, ER, 1994—99; (films) Return of the Killer Tomatoes, 1988, Red Surf, 1990,

Unbecoming Age, 1992, One Fine Day, 1996, Batman & Robin, 1997, From Dusk Till Dawn, 1996, The Peacemaker, 1997, The Thin Red Line, 1998, Out of Sight, 1998, Three Kings, 1999, (voice) South Park: Bigger, Longer and Uncut, 1999, O Brother, Where Art Thou, 2000 (Golden Globe award for Best Peformance by an Actor in a Motion Picture, 2001), The Perfect Storm, 2000, Ocean's Eleven, 2001, Spy Kids, 2001, Solaris, 2002, Spy Kids 3-D: Game Over, 2003, Intolerable Cruelty, 2003; actor, dir. (films) Confessions of a Dangerous Mind, 2002, actor, exec. prodr. Ocean's Twelve, 2004, (TV films) Fail Safe, 2000, prodr., writer (films) Kilroy, 1999; exec. prodr.: (films) Rock Star, 2001, Insomnia, 2002, Welcome to Colinwood, 2002, Far From Heaven, 2002, The Jacket, 2005; prodr.: Criminal, 2004; exec. prodr.: (TV series) K Street, 2003; dir.: Unscipted, 2005—. Recipient SAE awards, 1998, 99; named one of 50 Most Powerful People in Hollywood, 2003-05. Office: Creative Artist Agy 9830 Wilshire Blvd Beverly Hills CA 90212-1804*

CLORE, LAWRENCE HUBERT, lawyer; b. Tulsa, July 31, 1944; s. Hubert Charles and Jessie Louada (Fowler) C.; m. Carol Jean Roegelein, June 3, 1967 (div. 1981); children: Robert William, James Lawrence; m. Martha Jo Lawyer; children: Kathryn Denise, Michael Hubert. BBA, Tex. Christian U., 1966; JD, U. Tex., 1969. Bar: Tex. 1969. Assoc. Fulbright & Jaworski, Houston, 1971-77, ptnr., 1977—. Capt. U.S. Army, 1969-71, Vietnam. Mem. ABA, Tex. Bar Assn. (labor and employment sect., coun. 1990-93, vice chair 1993-94, chair 1994-95), Indsl. Rels. Rsch. Assn., Houston Mgmt. Lawyers Forum (chmn. 1976-77). Republican. Methodist. Avocations: hunting, fishing, golf. Office: Fulbright & Jaworski 1301 Mckinney St Ste 5100 Houston TX 77010-3031 Office Phone: 713-651-5403. Business E-Mail: lclore@fulbright.com.

CLOS, LYNNE MOBLEY, magazine publisher, paleontologist; b. Baton Rouge, Sept. 2, 1955; d. Ralph C. and Theodora A. Mobley; m. Christopher J. Clos, Sept. 14, 1979; children: Allison Lee, Mattie Michelle. BSME with dept. honors, Oakland U., 1978; M Basic Sci. in Mus. Studies, U. Colo., 1991. Corrosion engr. GM Proving Ground, Milford, Mich., 1979-81; product engr. Rockwell Internat., Golden, Colo., 1981-87; paleontology demonstrator Denver Mus. Natural History, 1989; free-lance writer Boulder, 1990-97; editor, pub. Fossil News, Boulder, 1998—. Author: Field Adventures in Paleontology, 2003; contbr. numerous articles on paleontology to sci. jour., including Jour. Vertebrate Paleontology, Fossil News; costume designer Kinetic Sculpture Challenge, 1984-89. Vol. paleontology dept. Denver Mus. Natural History, 1988-96; vol. Ross Perot Campaign, Boulder, 1992; guest spkr. on paleontology to local schs., Boulder, 1994—; paleontology mentor for jr. high and high sch. students over internet, 1999. Recipient award for ednl. excellence in web site, Field Adventures/Study Web, 1999. Mem. Soc. Vertebrate Paleontology, Western Interior Paleontol. Soc. (bd. dirs. 1988-89, 98-00, newsletter editor 1994-00), Cycad Soc. (bd. dir. 1990-2001), Tau Beta Pi. Avocations: mac computers, horticulture (cycads), reading, travel, tropical fish. Office: Fossil News 1185 Claremont Dr Boulder CO 80305-6601 Business E-Mail: lynne@fossilnews.com.

CLOSE, BETSY L., state representative; b. Shelton, Wash., May 4, 1950; m. Chris Close; 4 children. BA, Wash. State U., 1972, Ctrl. Wash. U., 1974; MS, Oreg. State U., 1978. Tchr. Wash. State Pub. Schs., 1974—76; grad. tchg. asst. Oreg. State U., Corvallis, 1976—78; instr., job devel. Benton County, 1978—79; tchr. Albany Pub. Schs., 1979—81; mem. Oreg. Ho. of Reps., 1998—. Chair Benton County Rep. Party, 1996—98; bd. dirs. Palestine Rural Fire, 1997—. Republican. Office: 900 Court St North East H-493 Salem OR 97301

CLOSE, CHUCK (CHARLES THOMAS CLOSE), artist; b. Monroe, Wash., July 5, 1940; s. Leslie Durwood and Mildred Emma (Wagner) C.; m. Leslie Rose, Dec. 24, 1967; children: Georgia Molly, Maggie Sarah. BA, U. Wash., 1962; BFA, Yale U., 1963, MFA, 1964; postgrad. (Fulbright grantee), Akadamie der Bildenen Kunste, Vienna, Austria, 1964-65; ArtsD (hon.), Art Inst. of Boston, 1992, U. Mass., 1995; LHD (hon.), Skidmore Coll., 1992; DFA (hon.), Colby Coll., 1994. Faculty U. Mass., 1965-67, Sch. Visual Arts, N.Y.C., 1967-71, N.Y.U., 1970-73. Mem. Bykert Gallery, NYC, 1969-74, Pace Gallery, NYC, 1977— One-man shows include Los Angeles County Museum, 1971, Mus. Contemporary Art, Chgo., 1972, 81, Mus. Modern Art, NYC, 1973, San Francisco Mus. Art, 1975, Balt. Mus. Art, 1976, Georges Pompidou Centre/Musée Nationale d'Art Moderne, Paris, 1979, Univ. Art Mus., Berkeley, Calif., 1982, Richard Gray Gallery, Chgo., 1982-83, Milw. Art Mus., 1984, Contemporary Arts Mus., Houston, 1985, Fuji Gallery, Tokyo, 1985, Aldrich Mus., Yokohama Museum of Art, Japan 1989, Pace Gallery, NYC, 1991, others; retrospective Walker Art Center, Mpls., 1980, St. Louis Art Mus., 1981, Whitney Mus., NYC, 1981, Aldrich Mus., Art Inst. Chgo., 1989, Butler Inst., Youngstown, Ohio, 1989, Mus. Modern Art, NYC, 1991, Kunsthalle Baden Baden, Germany, 1994, Lenbachhaus House, Munich, 1994, Cartier Found., Paris, 1994, Photographs by Chuck Close, Worcester Mus. of Art, 1999, 2000, traveling exhibition originating in Mus. Modern Art, NYC, 1998-99, Chuck Close Prints: Process and Collaboration, Met. Mus. of Art, 2004; group shows include, Whitney Mus., NYC., 1969, 70, 72, 77, 79, 91, Whitney Biennial Exhbn., Documenta 5 & 6, Kassel, Fed. Republic Germany, 1972, 77, Tokyo Biennale, 1974. Trustee Whitney Mus. Am. Art, NYC. Recipient Showhegan medal Nat. Acad. Arts and Letters, 1991, Infinity award Internat. Ctr. of Photography, 1990, Skowhegan medal, 1991, Acad. and Inst. of Arts and Letters prize, 1991; Nat. Endowment for Arts grantee, 1973 Office: Pace Wildenstein 32 E 57th St Fl 3 New York NY 10022-2513*

CLOSE, GLENN, actress; b. Greenwich, Conn., Mar. 19, 1947; d. William and Bettine Close; m. Cabot Wade 1969 (div. 1971); m. James Marlas, 1984 (div. 1987); 1 child, Annie Maude Starke. BA in drama and anthropology, Coll. William and Mary, 1974. Joined New Phoenix Repertory Co., 1974. Co-owner The Leaf and Bean Coffee House, Bozeman, Montana, 1993-94. Actor: (Broadway debut) Love for Love, 1974; (Broadway plays) The Rules of the Game, 1974, The Member of the Wedding, 1975, Rex, 1976, Barnum, 1980—81 (Tony award nomination for best featured actress in a musical, 1980), The Real Thing, 1984—85 (Tony award for best actress in a play, 1984), Benefactors, 1985—86, Death and the Maiden, 1992 (Tony award for best actress in a play, 1992), Sunset Boulevard, 1994—95 (Tony award for best actress in a musical, 1995), (other theatre appearances include) Uncommon Women and Others, The Singular Life of Albert Nobbs, 1982, Childhood, 1985, Joan of Arc at the Stake, 1985, Sunset Boulevard (LA), 1993—94, The Vagina Monologues, 1998; (films) The World According to Garp, 1982, The Big Chill, 1983, Greystoke: The Legend of Tarzan, Lord of the Apes (voice), The Natural, 1984, The Stone Boy, 1984, Jagged Edge, 1985, Maxie, 1985, Fatal Attraction, 1987, Gandahar (voice), 1988, Dangerous Liaisons, 1988, Immediate Family, 1989, Reversal of Fortune, 1990, Hamlet, 1990, Meeting Venus, 1991, Hook, 1991, The House of the Spirits, 1993, The Paper, 1994, Mary Reilly, 1996, 101 Dalmations, 1996, Mars Attacks!, 1996, Paradise Road, 1997, Air Force One, 1997, Cookie's Fortune, 1999, Tarzan (voice), 1999, Things You Can't Tell Just by Looking at Her, 2000, 102 Dalmations, 2000, The Safety of Objects, 2001, Pinocchio (voice), 2002, Le Divorce, 2003, The Stepford Wives, 2004, Nine Lives, 2005, Heights, 2005, The Chumscrubber, 2005; (TV films) The Rules of the Game, 1975, Too Far to Go, 1979, Orphan Train, 1979, The Elephant Man, 1982, Something About Amelia, 1984, Stones for Ibarra, 1988, She'll Take Romance, 1990, In the Gloaming, 1997, The Lion in Winter, 2003 (Golden Globe Award for best actress in a mini-series or TV movie, 2005, Screen Actors Guild Award for best actress in a TV movie or miniseries, 2005), Strip Search, 2004; (TV series) The Shield, 2005—; actor, exec. prodr. (TV films) Sarah, Plain and Tall, 1991, Skylark, 1993, Serving in Silence: The Margarethe Cammermeyer Story, 1995 (Emmy award for best actress in a miniseries or special, 1995), Sarah, Plain and Tall: Winter's End, 1999, Baby (voice), 2000, The Ballad of Lucy Whipple, 2001, South Pacific, 2001; exec. prodr.: (TV films) Journey, 1995. Recipient Woman of Yr. Award Hasty Pudding Theatricals, Harvard U., 1990, Dartmouth Film Award, 1990. Mem. Phi Beta Kappa. Office: Creative Artists Agy 9830 Wilshire Blvd Beverly Hills CA 90212-1804*

CLOSE, LANNY GARTH, otolaryngologist, educator; b. San Antonio, Aug. 13, 1946; s. James Garth and Nona Lee (Galbraith) C.; m. Sharron Maredith Smith, Nov. 22, 1980; children: Hunter, Maredith. BA summa cum laude, Tex. Tech. U., 1968; MD cum laude, Baylor Coll. Medicine, 1972. Diplomate Am. Bd. Otolaryngology. Resident in surgery Johns Hopkins Hosp., Balt., 1972-74; resident in otolaryngology Baylor Affiliated Hosps., Houston, 1974-77; asst/assoc. prof. otolaryngology U. Tex., Houston, 1977-82; asst. surgeon dept. head & neck surgery M.D. Anderson Hosp., Houston, 1978-79; from assoc. prof. to prof. otolaryngology U. Tex. Southwestern Med. Sch., Dallas, 1982-94; prof., chmn. dept. otolaryngology/head and neck surgery Columbia U., N.Y.C., 1994—. Guest examiner Am. Bd. Otolaryngology, 1993, 94, 96, 97; pres.-elect Columbia-Presbyn. Med. Bd. Contbr. numerous articles to profl. jours. Fellow ACS, Am. Laryngological Assn., The Triological Soc., Am. Rhinological Assn., Am. Broncho Esophageal Assn., Am. Soc. for Head & Neck Surgery, Soc. of Head and Neck Surgery; mem. Johns Hopkins Soc. Scholars, Alpha Omega Alpha. Office: Coll Physicians & Surgeons Columbia U 630 W 168th St New York NY 10032-3702 Office Phone: 212-305-5820. Business E-Mail: lgc6@columbia.edu.

CLOSE, MICHAEL JOHN, property manager, lawyer; b. Sandusky, Ohio, Jan. 24, 1943; s. Robert J. and Mary Lee (Graefe) C.; m. Nancy L. Schelp, June 18, 1995; children: Christina C., Karen L. AB in History, Lafayette Coll., Easton, Pa., 1965; JD cum laude, U. Mich., 1968. Assoc. Dewey, Ballantine, Bushby, Palmer & Wood, N.Y.C., 1968-76; ptnr. Dewey Ballantine, N.Y.C., 1976-96; pres., CEO Balmer Parc LLC, N.Y.C., 2003—. Chmn. Tax Rev., N.Y.C. Author: Tax Aspects of Oil and Gas Drilling Funds, 1972, Drilling Funds: The 1977 Perspective, 1977, Special Allocations in Oil and Gas Ventures, 1982, The Final Section 704 (b) Regulations: Special Allocations Reach New Heights of Complexity, 1986, Fringe Benefit Regulation and the New York Law Firm Culture: A New Era, 1989, Off Balance Sheet Financings, 1994; contbr. articles to profl. jours. Bd. dirs., adminstrv. vice-chmn. Conn. Swimming, Inc., 1992-99; chmn. ad-hoc com. on by-laws USA Swimming, Inc., 1995-96; bd. dirs. Sharks Swim Team, Inc., 1991-94, pres., 1992-94. Mem. ABA (mem. tax sect. com. on partnerships), Assn. of Bar of City of N.Y., N.Y. Law Inst. (life mem.), N.Y. State Bar Assn. (mem. tax sect. com. partnerships), Ohio State Bar Assn., Real Estate Bd. N.Y.(assoc.), India House (N.Y.C.), Burning Tree Country Club (Greenwich), Meadows Country Club (Sarasota, Fla.), Phi Delta Phi, Theta Chi. Republican. Home: 4951 Windsor Park Sarasota FL 34235-2610 Office: Balmer Parc LLC 16th Fl 445 Park Ave New York NY 10022 Office Phone: 212-486-8500. Personal E-mail: thecloses@comcast.net. Business E-Mail: mclose@dakotarealtyny.com.

CLOSE, THOMAS JAMES, school administrator; b. Adrian, Mich., Oct. 9, 1935; s. James Thomas and Katherin Bellenir Close; m. Beatrice L. Close, July 26, 1961 (div. Feb. 1990); m. Sandra Lee McAnaleen, Aug. 9, 1993; children: Thomas James, Jonathon D., Julia S. AB, St. Joseph Coll., 1958; MA, Cen. Mich. U., 1969, EdS, 1973; EdD, Calif. Coast U., 1999. LPC, Mich. Tchr. Kalkaska (Mich.) Pub. Sch., asst. prin., A.D., sch. counselor, sch./cmty. adminstr.

CLOSE, TIMOTHY, museum director; Exec. dir. Albany Mus. Art, Ga., Boise Art Museum, Boise, Idaho. Office: Boise Art Museum 670 S Julia Davis Dr Boise ID 83702-4168 E-mail: Tim@boiseartmuseum.org.*

CLOSEN, MICHAEL LEE, retired law educator; b. Peoria, Ill., Jan. 25, 1949; s. Stanley Paul and Dorothy Mae (Kendall) Closen. BS, MS, Bradley U., 1971; JD, U. Ill., 1974. Bar: Ill. 1974. Instr. U. Ill., Champaign, 1974; jud. clk. Ill. Appellate Ct., Springfield, 1974-76, 77-78; asst. states atty. Cook County, Chgo., 1978; prof. law John Marshall Law Sch., Chgo., 1976—2003; notary pub. State of Fla., 2004—, State of Ill., 1990—2003. Reporter Ill. Jud. Conf., Chgo., 1981—2002; arbitrator Am. Arbitration Assn., Chgo., 1981—2003; lectr. Ill. Inst. Continuing Legal Edn., Chgo., 1981—2002, BRI, 1985—; vis. prof. No. Ill. U., 1985—86, adj. prof., 1990, St. Thomas U., 1991, Loyola U., Chgo., 1999—2002; vis. prof. U. Ark., 1993, 96; arbitrator Cook County Cir. Ct. Mandatory Arbitration Program, 1990—2002, Will County Cir. Ct. Mandatory Arbitration Program, 1996—2002; dir. Ctr. for Legal Edn., Ltd., 1995—96. Author: (casebook) Agency and Partnership Law, 1984, Agency and Partnership Law, 3d edit., 2000; author: (with others) Contracts, 1984, Contracts, 3d edit., 1992, AIDS Cases and Materials, 1989, AIDS Cases and Materials, 3d edit., 2002, Notary Law and Practice, 1997, Contract Law and Practice, 1998; co-author: (book) The Shopping Bag: Portable Art, 1986, AIDS Law in a Nutshell, 2d edit., 1996, Legal Aspects of AIDS, 1991; contbr. articles to profl. jours. Named One of Outstanding Young Men in Am., 1981; recipient Svc. award, Am. Arbitration Assn., 1984—85, 5-Yr. Cmty. Achievement award, Ill. Politics Mag., 1998. Mem.: Nat. Notary Assn. (cons. 2004—, Achievement award 1998). Home: 1243 Motorcoach Polk City FL 33868-5101

CLOSIUS, PHILLIP J., dean, law educator; BA, U Notre Dame; JD, Columbia U. Atty. Kelley Drye & Warren, New York, NY; faculty mem. U. Toledo Sch. Law, 1979—, dean, prof. law, 1999—. Contbr. articles to law jours.; pub. in fields of Sports Law, Constl. Law and Law and Lit. Mem.: ABA, Toledo Bar Assn., Ohio State Bar Assn., Assn. Am. Law Sch. Office: U Toledo Sch Law 2801 W Bancroft Toledo OH 43606 Office Phone: 419-530-2379. Office Fax: 419-530-4526. E-mail: Phillip.Closius@utoledo.edu.

CLOTFELTER, CHARLES T., economics professor; b. Birmingham, Ala., Aug. 20, 1947; s. James Hodson and Caroline (Postelle) C.; m. Theresa Newman; children: James, John. AB, Duke U., 1969; AM, Harvard U., 1972, PhD, 1974. Asst. prof. econs. U. Md., College Park, 1974-79; fin. economist U.S. Treasury, Washington, 1978-79; assoc. prof. pub. policy and econs. Duke U., Durham, 1979-85, prof. pub. policy and econs., 1985-96, prof. pub. policy, econs. and law, 1996—, vice-provost, 1983-85, 93-94, vice-chancellor, 1985-88. Co-author: (with Philip Cook) Selling Hope: State Lotteries in America, 1989, (with Ronald Ehrenberg, Malcolm Getz, John Siegfried) Economic Challenges in Higher Edn., 1994; author: Federal Tax Policy and Charitable Giving, 1995, Buying the Best: Cost Escalation in Elite Higher Education, 1996; The Rise and Retreat of School Desegregation, 2004. Mem. Am. Econ. Assn., So. Econ. Assn. (v.p. 1982-83, pres. 1991-92), Assn. Policy Analysis and Mgmt., Nat. Tax Assn. United Ch. of Christ. Office: Duke U PO Box 90245 Durham NC 27708-0245 Office Phone: 919-613-7361.

CLOTHIER, JEFFREY LANE, neuropsychiatrist, educator; b. Plainview, Tex., Mar. 18, 1957; s. Gale Joseph and Mary Jo Clothier; m. Risa McSpadden, Dec. 29, 1956; children: Amy Nicole, Matthew Travis. MD, U. Tex., 1982. Diplomate Diplomate Am. Bd. Psychiatry and Neurology, 1989. Assoc. prof. U. Ark. for Med. Scis., Little Rock, 1990—; acting assoc. chief staff for mental health Ctrl. Ark. Veterans Healthcare Sys., 2001—. Mem. UAMS Founder's Soc., Little Rock, 1996—2002. Recipient Emil Eckart award, UAMS Dept. Psychiatry, 1992, Golden Apple Tchg. award, UAMS, 1996, 2000, Tchr. Yr. award- Region 7, Assn. for Academic Psychiatry, 1997, Robert Shannon, M.D. award, UAMS Dept. of Psychiatry, 2000, 2001. Mem.: Ark. Psychiat. Soc. (disaster com. chmn. 2002), Assn. Convulsive Therapy, Am. Psychiat. Assn. Avocations: golf, cooking, gardening. Office: Ctrl Ark Vets Adminstrn 2200 Fort Roots Dr North Little Rock AR Office Phone: 501-257-3094. Personal E-mail: clothier@swbell.net. E-mail: clothier.jeffreyl@med.va.gov.

CLOTWORTHY, JOHN HARRIS, oceanographic consultant; b. Balt., Mar. 23, 1924; s. Harris A. and Violet (Klein) C.; m. Martha D. Wilson, Mar. 22, 1947; 1 son, John S. B.E.E., U. Va., 1946; certificate, Harvard Bus. Sch., 1956. Registered profl. engr., Md. With Westinghouse Electric Corp., 1948-67, v.p. def. and space center, gen. mgr. underseas div., 1963-67; chmn. div. ocean engrng. U. Miami, Fla., 1967-68; cons. to oceanographic industry, 1967-68; founder, pres. Oceans Gen., Inc., Miami, 1968-71; dir. office congl. and legislative affairs NOAA, Washington, 1971-78; v.p., gen. mgr. Joint Oceanographic Instns. Inc., Washington, 1978-88, cons., 1988—. Sec., v.p. Oak Bldg. & Savs. Assn., 1946-56; Bd. govs. Va. Engrng. Found., 1965-68, 72-78 Trustee, co-chmn., bd. advisors Mare Nostrum Found., 1986-88. Fellow Marine Tech. Soc. (founding mem., bd. dirs. 1966-69, chmn. silver anniversary com. 1986-88, Lockheed award for ocean sci. and engring. 1992); mem. AAAS, Am. Geophys. Union, Am. Guild Organists, Nat. Oceanography Assn. (pres. 1966-69), Internat. Club of Annapolis (pres. 1995-96), Annapolis Yacht Club, Atlantic City Convention Hall Organ Soc. (sec., treas. 1998—), Alpha Tau Omega. Home: 2014 Gov Thomas Bladen Way Apt #201 Annapolis MD 21401 E-mail: jclotwor@comcast.net.

CLOUD, BRUCE BENJAMIN, SR., construction company executive; b. Thomas, Okla., Feb. 15, 1920; s. Dudley R. and Lillian (Sanders) C.; m. Virginia Dugan, June 5, 1944; children: Sheila Marie Cloud Kiselis, Karen Susan, Bruce Benjamin, Deborah Ann Cloud McKenzie, Virginia Ann Cloud Treadwell. BCE, Tex. A&M U., 1940. Registered profl. engr., Tex. With H.B. Zachry Co., San Antonio, 1940-42, 55-99, exec. v.p., 1963-87, pres., 1987-93, vice chmn., 1993-94, sr. corp. advisor, 1995-99, adv. dir., 1999—2004; ptnr., bd. dirs. Dudley R. Cloud & Son, Constrn., San Antonio, 1946-55; owner Cloud Enterprises, San Antonio; ret. Mem. adv. bd. dirs. Capitol Cement Co./Aggregate Co., 1999-2004. Mem. adv. coun. Boysville Inc., 1978-79; bd. dirs. Tex. State Tech. Coll. Found., 1983-97, 98—, hon. life bd. mem. Lt. col. C.E. AUS, 1942-46, ETO. Recipient Pro Deo Et Juventute award Nat. Coun. Cath. Youth, Soyr Svc. award, 2003. Mem. AIM, NSPE, KC (3d degree), Tex. Assn. Gen. Contractors (life, dir. hwy. and heavy br. 1947-48, 72-76, pres. 1974, chmn. corps engrs. joint com. 1989-90), Am. Concrete Paving Assn. (v.p. 1970-74, bd. dirs., 1st v.p. 1975, pres. 1976), Nat. Asphalt Paving Assn., Tex. Hotmix Paving Assn. (bd. dirs. 1972), Nat. Assn. Gen. Contractors (bd. dirs. 1976-88, life dir., exec. com. 1978-79, bur. reclamation com. 1968-97, corps engrs. com. 1988-97, equipment mgmt. com. 1978-97, Nat. AGC Outstanding Com. chmn., 1997, chmn. heavy divsn. 1979, environ. com, 1971-76, energy and materials 1976-86, fin. com. 1979, engring. documentation rev. com. 1985, ethics rules legis. com. 1979, water and power resource com. 1980-81, transp. policy com. 1980-95, quality in constrn. com. 1993-96), San Antonio Livestock Assn. (life), Tex. Soc. Profl. Engrs., Tex. Good Rds.-Transp. Assn. (dir. 1974-79, exec. com. 1975-81, 85-89), Am. Mgmt. Assn., San Antonio C. of C. (chmn. better rds. task force 1978-79, 85-93, bd. dirs. 1993-94), Tex. Transp. Inst. (adv. bd. 1993-97), Tex. Engrng. Ext. Svc. (adv. bd. 1995-97), Cons. Contractors Coun. Am. (chmn. 1989), Holy Name Soc. (v.p. 1962-63), Nocturnal Adoration Soc.

CLOUD, JOHN M., diplomat; married; 2 children. BA, U. Conn., 1975; MA in Internat. Affairs, George Washington U., 1977. Mem. US Dept. State, Washington, 1988—91, economic counselor, Am. Embassy in Bonn Germany, 1991—95, Am. dep. chief in Warsaw, 1996—99, Am. dep. chief to EU, 1999—2001; spl. asst. to pres., sr. dir. internat. affairs NSC, Washington, 2001—03; Am. dep. chief in Berlin US Dept. State, Berlin, 2003—, chargé d'affaires ad interim, 2005. Recipient Superior Honor award, US State Dept. Office: 5090 Berlin Pl Washington DC 20521-5090*

CLOUD, MARK F., film director, film editor, film producer, musician; b. Culver City, Calif., Sept. 17, 1955; s. Wade and Maxine Esther Cloud; m. Cheryl L. Sorensen, Jan. 22, 1977 (dec. Aug. 3, 1995); children: Rory S., Jaren S. AA, San Bernardino Valley Coll., 1975; BA, Calif. State Fullerton, 1978. Lic. fed. Comm. Commn., 1978. Mgr. corp. comm. Sav-On Drugs, Anaheim, Calif., 1983—85; owner Cloud Productions, Murrieta, Calif., 1985—. Instr. Santa Ana C.C., Calif., 1985—87. Musician (producer): (cd) Hard Choices, 1994, Wings of Silver, 1996, Live at the Emu Farm, 1998, From the Cobwebs of Our Minds, 2001, Joyous Songs of Sorrow, 2001; prodr.: (cd) Legacy by Cheryl Cloud, 2001, Songs of Christmas by Cheryl Cloud, 2002, On the Street, 2005. Song leader Avaxat Elem. Sch., Murrieta, Calif., 1995—2000. Recipient Award of Excellence, Calif. Parks and Recreation Soc., 1990. Non-Partisan. Avocations: mountain biking, camping, skiing. Office: Cloud Prodns PO Box 1109 Murrieta CA 92564-1109 Office Phone: 951-696-7640. Personal E-mail: markcloud@uncommonlyround.com.

CLOUD, ROBERT ROYCE, surgeon; b. Houston, Feb. 12, 1954; s. Albert Hadden and Emily Ann (Royce); m. Karen Sue Mooneyham, June 5, 1982; children: Kyle, Ashley, Tyler. BS, Northeast La. U., 1976; MD, Tulane, 1980. Intern gen. surgery Baylor Med. Ctr., Dallas, 1980-81, resident gen. surgery, 1981-85, fellow colon rectal surgery, 1985-86; private practice Dallas, 1986—. Mem. staff Med. City Hosp., Dallas, 1986—, Baylor Hosp., 1986—, Presbyn. Hosp., Dallas, 1988—. Bd. dirs. Wednesday's Child, Am. Cancer Soc. Fellow ACS, Am. Soc. Colon Rectal Surgeons; mem. Tex. Surgical Soc., Tex. Med. Assn., Tex. Soc. Colon Rectal Surgeons, Dallas County Med. Soc. Avocations: golf, tennis. Office: 12200 Park Central Dr Ste 100 Dallas TX 75251-2102

CLOUD, STANLEY WILLS, journalist, writer, editor, reporter; b. Los Angeles, Nov. 4, 1936; s. Wade and Esther Maxine (Sowers) C.; m. Nancy Jean Fuller, June 22, 1962 (div. 1979); children: Michael Sean, David Stanley, Matthew Wade; m. Christina Lynne Olson, Jan. 5, 1980; 1 child, Caroline Wills. BA, Pepperdine Coll., Los Angeles, 1958; postgrad. in Russian lang., Def. Lang. Inst., Monterey, Calif., 1961-62. Editorial clk. Los Angeles Times Mirror Syndicate, 1954-58; reporter Monterey Peninsula Herald, Calif., 1964-66; editor The Advocate, Monterey, 1966-68; corr. Time Mag., San Francisco, 1968-69, Moscow, USSR, 1969-70, bur. chief Bangkok, Thailand, 1970-71, Saigon, Vietnam, 1971-72, Senate corr. Washington, 1972-74, polit. corr., 1974-76, White House corr., 1976-78, news services editor, 1978-79, dep. Washington bur. chief, 1987-89, Washington bur. chief, 1989-93, Washington contbg. editor, 1993-94; contbributor, 1994; asst. mng. editor Washington Star, 1979-80, mng. editor, 1980-81; exec. editor Los Angeles Herald Examiner, 1982-86; freelance journalist Alexandria, Va., 1986-87; writer, author, 1995—. Co-author: The Murrow Boys, 1996, A Question of Honor, 2003; playwright: The Murrow Boys, God and Emma Goldman. Exec. dir. The Citizens Election Project, 1995-96. Served to lt. USNR, 1958-64. Mem. Cosmos Club. Personal E-mail: stancloud@mac.com.

CLOUDSLEY, DONALD HUGH, retired library administrator; b. Buffalo, Jan. 11, 1925; s. James Rowland and Helen Margaret (Macgregor) C. BA, Bethany Coll., W.Va., 1948; MLS, Carnegie Inst. Tech., 1949. Jr. librarian Buffalo Pub. Library, 1949-52; sr. librarian I Erie County Pub. Library, Buffalo, 1952-58; sr. librarian II Buffalo and Erie County Pub. Library, 1958-59, dep. dir., 1974-83, dir., 1983-95; reference librarian Grosvenor Library, Buffalo, 1959-61; head Brighton br. Tonawanda Library, N.Y., 1961-65; dir. Tonawanda Library, 1965-73; trustee West N.Y. Libr. Resources Coun., Buffalo, 1983-93, treas., 1976-89. Mem. N.Y. State Regent's Adv. Coun. on Librs., 1988-93, chmn., 1990-91; mem. adv. com. on pub. librs. Online Computer Libr. Ctr., 1991-94. Mem. citizens adv. coun. SUNY-Buffalo, 1983-95. Named Boss of Yr., Am. Bus. Women's Assn., Buffalo, 1984; recipient Alumni Achievement award Bethany Coll., 1991, Buffalo (N.Y.) News Citizen of Yr. award, 1992. Mem. ALA, N.Y. Libr. Assn., N.Y. State Pub. Librs. Assn. (cert. com. 1971-75), Rotary (treas. Kenmore, N.Y. club 1975-76), Beta Theta Pi. Methodist. Home: 152 Hidden Ridge Cmn Williamsville NY 14221-5765

CLOUES, EDWARD BLANCHARD, II, lawyer; b. Concord, NH, Dec. 28, 1947; s. Alfred Samuel and H. Jeannette (Callas) C.; m. Mary Anne Matthews, Aug. 21, 1971; children: E. Matthew, M. Elizabeth. BA, Harvard U., 1969; JD, NYU, 1972. Bar: Pa. 1972, U.S. Dist. Ct. (ea. dist.) Pa. 1973. Law clk. to hon. judge James Hunter III U.S. Ct. Appeals (3d cir.), Phila. and Camden, NJ, 1972-73; assoc. Morgan, Lewis & Bockius LLP, Phila., 1973-79, ptnr., 1979-98; chmn., CEO K-Tron Internat., Inc., Pitman, NJ, 1998—. Bd. dirs. K-Tron Internat., Pitman, N.J., vice chmn. bd., 1987-94; bd. dirs. Amrep Corp., chmn., 1995—; bd. dirs. Penn Va. Corp., Penn Va. Resource Ptnrs., L.P. Republican. Lutheran. Avocations: travel, reading. Office: K-Tron Internat Inc PO Box 888 Rtes 55 & 553 Pitman NJ 08071 Office Phone: 856-256-3310. Business E-Mail: ecloues@ktron.com.

CLOUGH, GERALD WAYNE, academic administrator; b. Douglas, Ga., Sept. 24, 1941; married; 2 children. BSCE, Ga. Inst. Tech., 1964, MSCE, 1965; PhD, U. Calif., Berkeley, 1969. Registered prof. engr., Calif., Va. Assoc. prof. to prof. civil engring. Stanford U., Calif., 1974—82; prof. civil engring., coord. geotech. program Va. Polytechnic Inst. and State U., 1982—83, prof. civil engring., head dept. civil engring., 1983—90, dean Coll. Engring., 1990—93; provost, prof. civil engring. U. Wash., Seattle, 1993—94; pres. Ga. Inst. Tech., Atlanta, 1994—. Bd. dirs. Noro-Moseley Ptnrs., TSYS, Columbus, Ga., Nat. Sci. Bd.; spl. cons. San Francisco Bay Area Rapid Transit Sys.; apptd. Pres. Coun. Adv. on Sci. & Tech., 2001—; chmn. nanotechnology task force. Contbr. articles to profl. jours., chapters to books. Trustee Ga. Rsch. Alliance; chmn. Gov. Perdue's Telecomm. Task Force; mem. exec. com., co-chair Nat. Innovation Initiative U.S. Coun. Competitiveness; mem. exec. com. Metro Atlanta C. of C. Named one of 100 Most Influential People in Ga., Ga. Trend Mag.; recipient George Westinghouse award, Am. Soc. Engring. Edn., 1986, Nat. Engring. award, Am. Assn. Engring. Societies, 2001, Norman Medal, 1982, 1996. Mem.: NAE (chmn., Engr. of 2020 project), ASCE (hon. OPAL award Lifetime Achievement in Edn. 2004), Metro Atlanta C. of C. (exec. com.). Home: Ga Inst Tech Office of the Pres 225 N Ave NW Carnegie Bldg Atlanta GA 30332-0325*

CLOUGH, RAY WILLIAM, JR., civil engineering educator; b. Seattle, July 23, 1920; s. Ray William and Mildred (Nelson) Clough; m. Shirley Claire Potter, Oct. 30, 1942; children: Douglas Potter, Allison Justine, Meredith Anne. BSCE, U. Wash., 1942; MS, Calif. Inst. Tech., 1943; SM, MIT, 1947, ScD, 1949; D.Tech. (hon.), Chalmers U., Goteborg, Sweden, 1979; D.Tech. (hon.), Norges Tekniske Høgskole, Trondheim, Norway, 1982. Registered engr., Wash. Faculty U. Calif.-Berkeley, 1949—, prof. civil engring., 1959—, chmn. div. structural engring. and structural mechanics, 1967—70, dir. Earthquake Engring. Rsch. Ctr., 1973—76, Nishkian prof. structural engring., 1983—87, prof. emeritus, 1987—. Cons. in field; adv. com. NAS-NAE Environ. Sci. Svcs. Adminstrn., 1967—70; mem. U.S. C.E. Structural Design Adv. Bd., 1967—79. Capt. USAF, 1942—46. Named Hon. Rschr., Lab. Nat. De Engenharia Civil Lisbon, 1972; recipient Sr. Rsch. award, Am. Soc. for Engring. Edn., 1986, Congress medal, Internat. Assn. Computer Mechanics, 1986, citation, U. Calif., 1987, A.C. Eringen medal, Soc. of Engring. Sci., 1992, U.S. Nat. Medal of Sci., presented by Pres. William J. Clinton, 1994, Prince Philip medal, Royal Acad. Engring., 1997, George W. Housner medal, Earthquake Engring. Rsch. Inst., 1996; fellow Fulbright, Rsch. Inst., 1956—57, Overseas fellow, Cambridge (Eng.) U. Fellow: ASCE (hon.; chmn. engring. mechanics divsn. 1964—65, Rsch. award 1960, Howard award 1970, Newmark medal 1979, Moissieff medal 1980, T. VonKarman medal 1980), Inst. Water Conservation and Hydroelectric Power Rsch. (hon.); mem.: NAE, NAS (dynamics panel adv. bd. on hardened electric power sys. 1964—70), Seismol. Soc. Am. (bd. dirs. 1970—73), Structural Engrs. Assn. No. Calif. (bd. dirs. 1967—70). Home: PO Box 4625 Sunriver OR 97707-1625 Office Phone: 541-593-5064. Office Fax: 544-593-2823.

CLOUGHER, JAIME LOUISE, director; b. Neptune, NJ, Nov. 24, 1979; d. Sharon Clougher. BA, Lynchburg Coll., Va., 2003; MEd, Ind. U., Bloomington, 2005. Resident asst. Lynchburg Coll., 1999—2002, asst. hall dir., 2000—01, hall dir., 2001—03; grad. hall dir. Ind. U. Purdue U. Indpls., 2003—, interim asst. dir. housing and residence life, 2003; program coord. Va. Govs. Sch. Math., Sci., and Tech., Lynchburg, 2001—02. Named Leader of Yr., Lynchburg Coll., 2001-2002; recipient Nat. BACCHUS and GAMMA Outstanding Student award, BACCHUS and GAMMA, 2002, Options Providing Enjoyable Nights Minded award, Lynchburg Coll., 2003. Mem.: Gt. Lakes Assn. Coll. and U. Housing Officers (mem. awards and recognition com. 2003—04), Assn. Coll. and U. Housing Officers Internat., Ind. Student Affairs Assn. (conf. com. 2004—05), Am. Coll. Pers. Assn., Kappa Delta Pi (life), Order of Omega (life), Alpha Sigma Alpha (chpt. pres. and stds. 2001—03).

CLOUSE, JERRY ALLAN, architectural historian; b. Carlisle, Pa., Aug. 20, 1950; s. Elmer Ellsworth Clouse and Bessie Virginia Warner. BA, U. Ky., 1972; MA, Pa. State U., 1993. Archtl. rschr. Cumberland County Hist. Soc., Carlisle, 1987—88; preservation specialist Pa. Hist. & Mus. Commn., Harrisburg, 1988—95; archtl. historian McCormick, Taylor & Assocs., Inc., Harrisburg, 1995—. Mem. tours com. Vernacular Architecture Tours, 2000—. Author: The Whiskey Rebellion, 1994, Gayman Tavern: A Study of a Canal-Era Tavern in Dauphin Borough, 2003; co-author: Perry County: A Pictoral History, 1978, Briner Family History, 1984. Bd. dirs. The Perry Historians, pres., 1990—92, 1997—98, v.p., 1992—97. Republican. Lutheran. Avocations: genealogy, collecting stoneware, watercolors. Home: 118A S Railroad St Hummelstown PA 17036

CLOUSE, JOHN DANIEL, lawyer; b. Evansville, Ind., Sept. 4, 1925; s. Frank Paul and Anna Lucille (Frank) C.; m. Georgia L. Ross, Dec. 7, 1978; 1 child, George Chauncey. AB, U. Evansville, 1950; JD, Ind. U., 1952. Bar: Ind. 1952, U.S. Supreme Ct. 1962, U.S. Ct. Appeals (7th cir.) 1965. Assoc. Firm of James D. Lopp, Evansville, 1952-56; pvt. practice Evansville, 1956—. Guest editorialist Viewpoint, Evansville Courier, 1978—86, Evansville Press, 1986—98, Focus, Radio Sta. WGBF, 1978—84; 2d asst. city atty. Evansville, 1954—55; mem. Com. for Implementation of Criminal Justice Act of 1964, 1965; mem. appellate rules sub-com. Ind. Supreme Ct. Com. on Rules of Practice and Procedure, 1980. Pres. Civil Svc. Commn. Evansville Police Dept., 1961-62, v.p., 1988; pres. Ind. War Memls. Com., 1963-69; mem. jud. nominating com. Vanderburgh County, Ind., 1976-80; dir. Ind. Fed. Cmty. Defender Project, Inc., 1993-98. With inf. U.S. Army, 1943-46. Decorated Bronze Star; named one of World's Most travelled Man Guinness Book of Records, 1993, Most Travelled Man, 1995-2001. Fellow Ind. Bar Found.; mem. Internat. Wood Collector's Soc., Evansville Bar Assn. (v.p. 1972, James Bethel Gresham Freedom award 1997), Ind. Bar Assn. (chmn. com. on civil rights 1991-92), 87th Inf. Divsn. Assn., Internat. Wood Collectors Soc., Club Internat. Des Grand Voyageurs, Travelers Century Club (L.A.), Pi Gamma Mu. Republican. Methodist. Office: 123 NW 4th St Ste 317 Evansville IN 47708-1712 Office Phone: 812-424-6671. Personal E-mail: jdcmjs@aol.com.

CLOUSE, VICKIE RAE, biologist, paleontologist, educator; b. Havre, Mont., Mar. 28, 1956; d. Olaf Raymond and Betty Lou (Reed) Nelson; m. Gregory Scott Clouse, Mar. 22, 1980; 1 child, Kristopher Nelson. BS in Secondary Sci. Edn., Mont. State U. N., Havre, 1989, MEd in Sci., 2002; postgrad., Mont. State U., Bozeman, 1991—94. Tchg. asst. biology/paleontology, asst. prof. biology and earth scis. Mont. State U.-N., Havre, 1986-90; asst. prof. biology and earth scis. Mont. State U. Northern, Havre, 1990—; rsch. asst. dinosaur eggs and embryos Mus. the Rockies, Bozeman, 1992-95. Dir. Dinosaur Rsch. Expdns. Bd. Trustees H.E. Clack Mus., Havre, 1991—97, H.E. Clack Mus. Found., Havre, 1991—97; dir. Mont. Bd. Regents Higher Edn., Helena, 1989—90, Mont. Higher Edn. Student Fin. Assistance Corp., Helena, 1989—90; mem. Ea. Mont. Hist. Soc., 1993—; adj. prof. biology and paleontology Mont. State U. N., Havre. Named Young Career Woman of Yr., Bus. and Profl. Woman's Club, 1986. Mem.: AAAS, Mont. Geol. Soc., Soc. Vertebrate Paleontologists. Avocations: collecting vertebrate fossils, directing dinosaur excavations for laypersons, boating. Address: PO Box 7751 Havre MT 59501 Office Phone: 406-265-3759, 406-265-3700 ext. 3759. Office Fax: 406-265-3759. E-mail: clousev@msun.edu.

CLOUSER, SHANNON CASSANDRA, language educator; b. Coaldale, Pa., Sept. 19, 1976; d. Ralph Leonard and Patti Lavona Clouser. BA, Cedar Crest Coll., Allentown, Pa., 1997. Cert. tchr.- Spanish K-12 Pa., 1997. Coord. Internat. Programs Cedar Crest Coll., Allentown, Pa., 1997—98; tchr. Spanish Jim Thorpe (Pa.) HS, 2000—. A.C.E. Advisor Jim Thorpe Area Jr. HS, Jim Thorpe, 2000—. Mem.: Am. Coun. of Tchrs. Fgn. Langs., Alpha Mu Gamma. Lutheran. Avocations: cooking, crafts, reading, travel. Office: Jim Thorpe Area HS 1100 Center St Jim Thorpe PA 18229 Home: 728 N Cooper Ave Ottumwa IA 52501-2802 Personal E-mail: sclouser@jtasd.k12.pa.us.

CLOUSTON, ROSS NEAL, retired food and related products company executive; b. Montreal, Que., Can., Sept. 13, 1922; came to U.S., 1965, naturalized, 1973; s. Alan Roy and Maude (Neal) C.; m. Brenda Kerson, Feb. 12, 1944; children: Robert, Brendan. B.Sc., McGill U., 1949; MBA, Harvard U., 1951. With fisheries plant, N.S., Can., from 1940; founder LaSalle Foods Ltd., 1953, Blue Water Sea Food Ltd., Montreal, 1959, Blue Water Sea Food Ltd. (merged into Gorton Corp., 1963, merged into Gen. Mills, Inc. 1968); pres. Gorton Group div. Gen. Mills, Inc., 1969-86, chmn., 1986-87, corp. v.p. parent co., 1970-87; v.p. Gen. Mills Can. Ltd. Pres. Nat. Fisheries Inst., 1975, Fisheries Council Can., 1962. Served with RCAF, 1941-45. Decorated Royal Norwegian Order of Merit; recipient Man of Yr. award Nat. Fisheries Inst., 1985. Mem. The Oaks.

CLOUTMAN, EDWARD BRADBURY, III, lawyer; b. Lake Charles, La., Dec. 8, 1945; s. Edward Bradbury Jr. and Evelyn (Daniel) C.; m. Kathryn Sue Robinson, Aug., 1967 (div. 1974); children: Michael Edward, Chad Edward; m. Elizabeth Katherine Julian, June 11, 1976; 1 child, Edward Bradbury IV. JD, La. State U., 1969. Bar: La. 1969, U.S. Dist. Ct. (we. dist.) La., U.S. Ct. Appeals (5th cir.) 1970, Tex. 1971, U.S. Dist. Ct. (no., we., and ea. dists.) Tex., U.S. Supreme Ct. 1973, U.S. Ct. Appeals (10th cir.) 1974, U.S. Ct. Appeals (6th cir.) 1980, U.S. Ct. Appeals (11th cir.) 1982. Reginald Heber Smith fellow CENLA Legal Aid Soc., Alexandria, La., 1969-70, Dallas Legal Svcs. Found., 1970-71; ptnr. Johnston, Polk, Larson, Cloutman & Dixon, Dallas, 1971-73; assoc. Mullinax, Wells, Mauzy and Baab, Inc., Dallas, 1973-74; ptnr. Mullinax, Wells, Baab and Cloutman, P.C., Dallas, 1975-90; pvt. practice Dallas, 1990—. Adj. prof. So. Meth. U. Sch. Law, 1990-98. Mem. ABA, Inns of Ct. (master 1990—). Democrat. Office: 3301 Elm St Dallas TX 75226-2562 Office Phone: 214-939-9222. E-mail: crawfish11@prodigy.net.

CLOVIS, SAMUEL HARVEY, academic administrator; b. Salina, Kans., Sept. 18, 1949; s. Samuel Harvey and Mildred Marie (Baize) C.; m. LaVeta Roos, Nov. 27, 1971 (div. Mar. 2000); children: Travis Justin, Matthew Allen; m. Charlotte Anne Chase, July 21, 2000; 1 stepson, Robert Khan Rosenberger. BS in Polit. Sci., USAF Acad., 1971; MBA, Golden Gate U., 1984; postgrad., U. Ala., Tuscaloosa, 1998—. Commd. 2d lt. USAF, 1971, advanced through grades to col., 1992, ret., 1996; mgr. tech. support Betac Corp., Colorado Springs, Colo., 1996-97; mgr. strategic solutions divsn. Logicon Inc., Herndon, Va., 1997-2000; assoc. dean, dir. of faculty Coll. Working Adults William Penn U., Oskaloosa, Iowa, 2000—02, founding dean Coll. of Bus. and Mgmt. Sci., 2002—. Mem. affiliate faculty Regis U., Denver, 1995—; cons. Rand Corp., Santa Monica, Calif., 1996—. Mem. ASPA, Am. Polit. Sci. Assn., Assn. of Grads. USAF Acad. Avocations: fishing, golf, weightlifting. Office: William Penn U 201 Trueblood Ave Oskaloosa IA 52577

CLOW, LEE, advertising agency executive; With Chiat/Day, LA, 1972—, Formerly exec. v.p., creative dir., pres., chief creative officer; chmn, worldwide chief creative dir. TBWA/Chiat/Day, LA, 1995. Bd. dir. Oakley Inc., 2002—. Named to One Club Hall of Fame, Art Dir. Hall of Fame, Advt. Hall of Fame, Mus. Modern Art; recipient Lifetime Achievement Award, Clio Awards Fest., 2004. Office: TBWA Chiat/Day 5353 Grosvenor Blvd Los Angeles CA 90066*

CLOWER, WILLIAM DEWEY, retired trade association executive; b. Salem, Va., Oct. 9, 1935; s. Alton Oliver and Addie Vane (Young) C.; m. Shirley Carol Tuttle, Sept. 1, 1956; children— Candice Denise, Michael DeWayne, Catherine Dione. BS, U. Va., 1958. Applications engr. ITT, Nutley, N.J., 1958-60; regional mktg. mgr. Litton Industries, Washington, 1960-61; propr. W.D. Clower Co., Gt. Falls, Va., 1961-70; spl. asst. to Pres. of U.S., 1970-75; exec. v.p. CISPI, Washington, 1975-76; pres. Food Processing Machinery and Supplies Assn., Washington, 1976-86; dir. Food Processors Inst., 1977-80; propr. Clower Assocs., Great Falls, Va., 1986-88; pres., CEO NATSO, Inc., Alexandria, Va., 1988—2003. Dir. Small Bus. Legis. Coun., 1991—92; chmn. Found. for Internat. Meetings, 1993; mem. Pres.'s adv. coun. Peace Corps, 1982—85; mem. Industry Policy Adv. Coun. for Export Policy, 1982—86; pres. The NATSO Found., 1991—2003; mem. campaign svcs. steering com. Rep. Nat. Com., 1977. With USAF, 1959—60. Va. Gen. Assembly scholar, 1954-58 Mem.: Am. Soc. Assn. Execs., Aircraft Owners and Pilots Assn., Fawn Lake County Club, Country Club at Two Rivers, Sertoma (pres. 1963—64), Capitol Hill Club, Gamma Delta Epsilon. Presbyterian. Home: Fawn Lake 11701 General Wadsworth Dr Spotsylvania VA 22553

CLOWES, GARTH ANTHONY, electronics executive, consultant; b. Didsbury, Eng., Aug. 30, 1936; came to U.S., 1957; s. Eric and Doris Gladys (Worthington) C.; m. Katharine Allman Crewdson, July 29, 1950 (dec. Jan. 1998); children: John Howard Brett, Peter Miles, Vicki Anne. BSc, Stockport Coll., Cheshire, Eng., 1953; postgrad., UCLA, 1965-66; higher nat. cert., Birmingham (Eng.) Coll. Tech., 1955-56. Gen. mgr., v.p., dir. Eldon Industries, Inc., El Segundo, Calif., 1962-69; CEO, founder Entex Industries, Inc., Compton, Calif., 1969-83; pres., founder Entex Electronics, Inc., Camano Island, Calif., 1983—. Pres., founder TTC, Inc., Carson, Calif., 1984-86; pres. Universal Telesis Electronics, Inc., Carson, 1986-87; gen. mgr. Matchbox Toys (U.S.A.) Ltd., Moonachie, N.J., 1987-88; dir. gen. Matchbox Spain, S.A., Valencia, 1988-89; cons. Matchbox Internat. Ltd., worldwide, 1986-89; spkr. in bus. field. Inventor electronic voice recognition devices, numerous others. Mem. pres.'s com. UNICEF, N.Y., 1972-74, Senate Adv. Bd., Washington, 1982-83; cons. Interracial Coun., L.A., 1967-69; mem. adv. bd. Santa Rosa Coll., 1993-99. Decorated Knight of Malta. Avocations: antiques, gardening, art, breeding scotch highland cattle. Home: 68 W Cross Island Rd Camano Island WA 98282-6667 E-mail: sonoma@webtv.net.

CLOWES, JOHN HOWARD, lawyer; BA, Univ. Calif., Santa Barbara, 1976; JD, Univ. Calif., Berkeley, 1982. Bar: Calif. 1982. Ptnr., co-chmn. Emerging Growth & Venture Capital practice group DLA Piper Rudnick Gray Cary, San Francisco. Named a No. Calif. Super Lawyer, San Francisco mag., 2004. Mem.: ABA. Office: DLA Piper Rudnick Gray Cary Suite 800 153 Townsend St San Francisco CA 94107 Office Phone: 415-836-2510. Office Fax: 415-836-2501. Business E-Mail: howard.clowes@dlapiper.com.

CLOYD, G. GIL, information technology executive; Joined Proctor & Gamble Co., 1970—; v.p. Proctor and Gamble Distributing Co., Cin.; global v.p. for consumer products, v.p. corporate R&D in Asia; chief technology officer Proctor and Gamble Co., 2000—. Named Technology Leader of Yr., Industry Week, 2004. Office: Proctor and Gamble 1 Proctor & Gamble Plz Cincinnati OH 45202 Office Phone: 513-983-1100. Office Fax: 513-562-4500.*

CLOYD, J. TIMOTHY, academic administrator; m. Rebecca Davis Cloyd; 2 children. BA in Philosophy and Polit. Sci. magna cum laude, Emory and Henry Coll., 1985; MA in Polit. Sci., U. Mass., 1990, PhD in Polit. Sci., 1991. Rsch. fellow Inst. for the Study of World Politics, Washington, 1990—91; mem. polit. sci. faculty, coord. program in social and polit. thought Vanderbilt U., 1991—94; mgr. U.S. Senate Race, Tenn., 1994; exec. dir. devel. and alumni rels. U. Ark., Little Rock, 1994—97; from asst. prof. to prof. politics Hendrix Coll., Conway, Ark., 1997—, v.p. for devel. and coll. rels., 1997—2001, pres., 2001—. Chair exec. com. So. Collegiate Athletics Conf., 2004—. Author: The Gulf War and Just War: A Study Guide on the Persian Gulf War; co-editor: (collection of essays) Politics and the Human Body, 1995. Office: Hendrix Coll 1600 Washington Ave Conway AR 72032 Office Phone: 501-450-1351. E-mail: cloyd@hendrix.edu.

CLUBB, BRUCE EDWIN, retired lawyer; b. Blackduck, Minn., Feb. 6, 1931; s. Ernest and Abigail (Gordy) Clubb; m. Martha Lucia Trapp, Dec. 19, 1954 (dec. Nov. 2001); children: Bruce Allen, Christopher Wade. BBA, U. Minn., 1955, LL.B. cum laude, 1958. Bar: DC 1959. Atty. Covington & Burling, 1958-61, Devel. Loan Fund, 1961-62, Chapman, DiSalle and Friedman, 1962-67; commr. U.S. Tariff Commn., 1967-71; ptnr. firm Baker & McKenzie, Washington, 1971-96; disting. lawyer in residence U. Minn. Law Sch., 1981-82. Chmn. bd. dirs. Sunrise Properties, Inc., 1989—99. Author: (treatise) United States Foreign Trade Law (2 vols.), 1991; contbr. law revs. Served with U.S. Army, 1952—54. Mem. D.C. Bar Assn., Am. Arbitration Assn. (arbitrator 1994-2000), Order of Coif, Cosmos Club (pres. 1986), Met. Club, Army Navy Club. Republican. Personal E-mail: bclubb2@aol.com.

CLUFF, LLOYD STERLING, earthquake geologist; b. Provo, Utah, Sept. 29, 1933; s. Colvin Sterling and Melba Cluff; m. Janet L. Peterson, Dec. 21, 1976; children: Tanya, Sasha, Branden. BS in Geology, U. Utah, 1960. Registered profl. geologist, Calif.; cert. engring. geologist, Calif. Jr. geologist El Paso Natural Gas Co., Salt Lake City, 1957-59; tchg. asst. dept. geology U. Utah, Salt Lake City, 1958-60; geologist Lottridge Thomas & Assocs., Salt Lake City, 1960; v.p., prin. geologist Woodward-Clyde Cons., San Francisco, 1960-85; assoc. prof. geology and geophysics U. Nev., Reno, 1967-73; dir. dept. geoscis. Pacific Gas and Electric Co., San Francisco, 1985—. Cons. Trans-Alaska Pipeline Siting Study, 1972-74; Aswan High Dam seismic safety evaluation, Govt. of Egypt, 1982-86; mem. com. Nat. Earthquake Hazards Reduction Program, Washington, 1987, Decade for Natural Disaster Reduction, Washington, 1989; advisor Venezuela Pres.'s Earthquake Safety Com., 1967-72; advisor Joint Legis. Com. on Seismic Safety, State of Calif., 1970-74; chmn. seismic rev. panel Calif. Pub. Utilities Commn., San Francisco, 1980-81; mem. Calif. Seismic Safety Commn., 1985-99, chmn., 1988-90, 95-97; adv. bd. So. Calif. Earthquake Ctr., 1996-2001; chmn. Tech. Adv. Bd. on Earthquake Risk, Israel, 1996—; mem. adv. panel on earth scis. NSF, 1992-95; chmn. com. on practical lessons from the Loma Prieta Earthquake, 1994; mem. organizing com. for Pub. Policy Partnership 2000-White House Confs. on Natural Disaster Loss Reduction, 1997-98; com. on assessing costs of natural disasters NAS, 1998-99, bd. Natural Disasters NAS, 1997-2000, Natural Disaster Roundtable, 2000—; nat. pre-disaster mitigation program adv. panel FEMA, 1998-99; external adv. panel for Pacific Earthquake Engring. Rsch. Ctr., 1998-99, implementation adv. bd., 1999—; natural disaster panel Heinz Ctr. Inst. for Natural Disasters, 2000-02; chmn. sci. earthquake studies adv. com. USGS Nat. Earthquake Hazards Reduction Program, 2002—. Recipient Hogentagler award ASTM, 1968, Alfred E. Alquist medal, Calif. Earthquake Safety Found., 1998, John Wesley Powell award, USGS, 2000, William Joyner Meml. Lecture award Seismol. Soc. Am. and Earthquake Engring. Rsch. Inst., 2003; named Woodward lectr., San Francisco, 1979. Fellow Calif. Acad. Scis.; mem. NAE, Seismol. Soc. Am. (pres. 1982-83), Assn. Engring. Geologists (pres. 1968-69), Earthquake Engring. Rsch. Inst. (hon., pres. 1993-95, chmn. Internat. Conf. on Seismic Zonation, Nice, France 1995), Geol. Soc. Am., Structural Engrs. Assn. No. Calif. (H.J. Degenkolb award 1992), Nat. Acad. Delegation Islamic Rep. of Iran, 2000. Republican. Avocations: photography, skiing, mountain climbing, hiking, bicycling. Office: Pacific Gas & Elec Co 245 Market St San Francisco CA 94105-1797 Office Phone: 415-973-2791. E-mail: lsc2@pge.com.

CLUMP, MICHAEL ADEN, psychologist, educator; s. Aden H. and Dee Wagner Clump; m. Keli Braitman, Aug. 2, 2001. BA, Wabash Coll., 1997; PhD, So. Ill. U., 2001. Asst. prof. psychology Boise (Idaho) State U., 2001—03, Marymount U., Arlington, Va., 2003—, chair undergrad. psychology program, 2004—. Vis. asst. prof. psychology St. Mary's Coll., Notre Dame, Ind., 2001. Contbr. articles to profl. jours. Mem.: APA, Am. Psychol. Soc., Eastern Psychol. Assn., Midwestern Psychol. Assn., Coun. Tchrs. Undergrad. Psychology, Phi Beta Kappa, Psi-Chi (pres. 1995—97). Avocations: travel, hiking, soccer, collecting Native American artifacts, golf. Office: Marymount U Dept Psychology 2807 N Glebe Rd Arlington VA 22207 Business E-Mail: michael.clump@marymount.edu.

CLUMPNER, KRISTA ELLIS, library science educator; b. La Crosse, Wis., Oct. 26, 1956; d. Rudolph Odine and Marion Haugen Ellis; m. James Joseph Clumpner, Sept. 1, 1984; children: Ellisa Antoinette, Joseph Ellis. BA in Art History, U. Wis., 1980, MALS, 1981. Cataloger U.S. newspaper project State Hist. Soc. Wis., Madison, 1983, coord. conversion project, 1984-85; project coord. Marquette U., Milw., 1983-84; cataloger, supr. Iowa Hist. Soc., Iowa City, 1985-86; tech. svcs. libr. Clarke Hist. Libr., Cen. Mich. U., Mt. Pleasant, 1986-90, interim dir., 1989-90; asst. prof., head tech. svcs. and systems Olson Libr., No. Mich. U., Marquette, 1991—95, assoc. prof., 1995—. Contbr. articles to profl. jours. Mem.: ALA, Mich. Libr. Assn. (preservation roundtable historian sec. 1991), N. Am. Serials Interest Group, Libr. Info. Tech. Assn. Office: Olson Libr No Mich U 1401 Presque Isle Ave Marquette MI 49855 E-mail: kclumpne@nmu.edu.

CLUTE, ROBERT EUGENE, political science professor; b. Earlville, Iowa, July 12, 1924; s. Henry and Leta (Allen) C.; m. Doris Reams, 1947; children: Robert Eugene, Andrea Reams. BA, U. Ala., 1947; MA, George Washington U., 1948; PhD, Duke U., 1957. Selector U.S. Displaced Persons Commn., Frankfurt, Fed. Republic Germany, 1948-50; analyst USAF, Austria, 1950-54; rsch. assoc. Duke U., Durham, N.C., 1957-58; vis. asst. prof. Tulane U. La., New Orleans, 1958-59; asst. prof. U. Nev., 1959-62; assoc. prof. U. Ga., Athens, 1962-68, prof. polit. sci., 1968—, head dept. polit. sci., 1972-75, grad. coord., 1975-88, chmn. social scis. div., 1982-93, prof. emeritus, 1993—. Am. specialist to Anglophone Africa, Cultural Affairs div. U.S. Dept. State, 1977. Author: The International Legal Status of Austria, 1962; (with others) The International Law Standard and Commonwealth Developments, 1966, De lege pactorum, 1970, Law and Justice, 1970; contbr. articles to profl. jours. With U.S. Army, 1943-46. Fulbright scholar 1967-68; Danforth assoc. 1972. Mem. Am. Soc. Internat. Law, Am. Polit. Sci. Assn., Ga. Polit. Sci. Assn., So. Polit. Sci. Assn., Internat. Studies Assn., African Studies Assn., Phi Kappa Phi, Phi Alpha Theta, Pi Sigma Alpha, Phi Beta Delta. Democrat. Episcopalian. Home: Ste 214 Arbor Terr 3736 Atlanta Hwy Athens GA 30606-3159 Office: U Ga Dept Polit Sci Athens GA 30602 *It is important for me to have career opportunities which help people. The preservation, analysis and dissemination of the knowledge of the past is as essential as the creation of new knowledge. Practical application of knowledge is extremely important. One must be loyal to one's colleagues and the institutions in which one participates.*

CLYBURN, JAMES E., congressman; b. Sumter, S.C., July 21, 1940; m. Emily England; children: Mignon, Jennifer, Angela. Grad., S.C. State Coll., 1962; LHD (hon.), Winthrop Coll., 1987; DSc (hon.), Coll. of Charleston, 1992, Med. U. S.C., 1993; LHD (hon.), St. Augustine Coll., 1994; LLD (hon.), Claflin Coll., 1995; LHD (hon.), S.C. State U., 1995; LLD (hon.), Voorhees Coll., 1996. Teacher Charleston County Pub. Sch. System; counselor S.C. Employment Security Commn.; dir. Charleston County Neighborhood Youth Corps/New Careers Projects; exec. dir. S.C. Comm. Farmworkers Inc.; staffer for Gov. John C. West, Charleston, S.C., 1971-74; commr. S.C. Human Affairs Commn., Columbia, 1974-92; mem. 103rd Congress from 6th S.C. dist., D.C., 1993—; transp. & infrastructure com. Congressional Black Caucus 106th Congress. Pres. Nat. Assn. Human Rights Workers, 1980-81, Internat. Assn. Official Human Rights Agys., 1985-87. Active Southern Regional Coun., Atlanta; bd. dirs. Wofford Coll., Spartanburg, Allen U., Columbia, Brookgreen Gardens Murrell's inlet, James R. Clark Sickle Cell Anemia Found., Ctr. for Cancer Treatment and Rsch., S.C. Literacy Assn. Recipient ann. award for disting. svc. to state gov. Nat. Govs. Assn.; named Pub. Adminstr. of Yr. Am. Soc. Pub. Adminstrn. S.C. chpt. Mem. NAACP (life), Masons, Shriners, Omega Psi Phi. Democrat. Office: 319 Cannon House Office Bldg Washington DC 20515-4006 E-mail: jclyburn@mail.house.gov.*

CLYBURN, LUTHER LINN, real estate broker, real estate appraiser; b. Evansville, Ind., May 17, 1942; s. Luther and Robbie (Cobb) C.; children: Lisa Michelle, Luther Brent. Grad., Am. Savs. and Loan Inst., 1970; ABA, Pontiac (Mich.) Bus. Inst., 1972; BS, Detroit Coll. Bus., 1972; M of Bus. Mgmt., Ctrl. Mich. U., 1983. Lic. merchant marine; cert. scuba instr.; cert. Profl. Assn. Dive Instrs. Chief loan officer First Fed. Savs. and Loan Assn. Oakland, Pontiac, 1964-74; assoc. broker Bateman Real Estate Corp., Pontiac, 1975-77; regional rep. United Guaranty Residential Ins., Troy, Mich., 1977-83; sr. account mgr. Investors Mortgage Ins. Co., Boston, 1983-87; real estate broker, appraiser White Lake, Mich., 1977—, Clyburn Appraisal Svcs., White Lake, 1987—; project dir. Norwood Project, 2004. Dir. sea ops. Mirek

Standowicz shipwreck recovery expedition, Lake Mich., 2001, Drowned River project, Straits of Mackinac, 2001; project dir. sea ops. Norwood Project, 2004; founder, pres. Noble Odyssey Found. Inc., 2002-. Project dir., capt.: (documentary film) Angels of the Sea, 1982 (N.Y. Film Festival award 1983); photographer for Tundra Tours 25th anniversary of Alaska's Iditarod dog sled race, 1997, 2000; contbr. articles to profl. jours. Capt., comdr. Noble Odyssey Tng. Ship, Mt. Clemens, Mich., 1977-89; dir., comdr. U.S. Naval Sea Cadet Corps Great Lakes div., Mt. Clemens, Mich., 1973—; nat. bd. dirs. U.S. Naval Sea Cadet Corps, 1988; project dir. Interseas Inc., Pontiac, 1982; ship capt. Great Lakes Botanical Island research project for Cranbrook Inst. Sci. (Thunder Bay Islands, Lake Huron, 1987, Islands of Green Bay, 1989, 90); dir. of Underwater Cinitofu; capt. Pride of Mich., 1989—; capt. Great Lakes Island Rsch. Project for Oakland U., Fox Islands, 1996; project dir. In Search of the Griffin, Great Lakes Rsch. Bd., Pride of Mich., 1998—; founder, pres. Inter-Seas Exploration Ltd., 1999—. Recipient Cert. Appreciation award Southfield Bicentennial Commn., 1976, Letter of Commendation award Sec. of Navy, 1983, Quality People award Meritorious Cmty. Svc., 1993, Oakland County Q2 award, 1993, Unsung Hero award Mich. Ho. of Reps., 1994. Mem. Internat. Ship Masters Assn., Navy League of U.S., Am. Soc. Appraisers, Mich. Assn. Real Estate Appraisers, Detroit Lodge Internat. Ship Masters Assn. Home and Office: 9000 Gale Rd White Lake MI 48386-1411 Office Phone: 248-666-9359. E-mail: lclyburn@aol.com.

CLYDE, LARRY FORBES, banker; b. Heber, Utah, Nov. 19, 1941; s. Don and Kathryn (Forbes) C.; m. Barbara Eliason, Dec. 23, 1963 (div. Jan. 1985); children: Lynne, Karen Lee; m. Katharyn L. Decker, July 3, 1986. BA, Utah State U., 1963, MS, 1965. With Pitts. Nat. Bank, 1965-68; with Crocker Nat. Bank, San Francisco, 1968-86, mgr. investment banking, 1973-75, mgr. capital markets divsn., 1975-86, sr. v.p., 1976-78, exec. v.p., mem. policy com., 1978-86; mng. dir., chief exec. US capital markets activities Midland Bank Group, NYC, 1986-87; CEO Midland Montagu Govt. Securities, Midland Montagu Mcpl. Securities, Midland Montagu Trust Co., 1986-87, American Express Bank, 1987—88; exec. v.p., mgr. capital mkts., mem. sr. mgmt. com. Mellon Bank N.A., Pitts., 1988—2000. Mem. govt. borrowing com. Pub. Securities Assn., 1981-87, vice chmn., 1981, chmn., 1982; treas., dir. No. Calif. chpt. Invest-In-Am., 1975-87; bd. dirs. Am. Banker Assn., Fed. Farm Credit Funding Corp.; vice chmn. Farm Credit Sys. Audit Com., 2000—, chmn. funding corp. audit com., 2004— Mem. Am. Bankers Assn. (vice chmn. bank investment and funds mgmt. divsn. exec. com. 1982, chmn. exec. com. 1983), Dealer Bank Assn. (bd. dirs. 1986-87), San Francisco Bond Club, Club Las Campanas. Office: 12 Mustang Mesa Santa Fe NM 87506-7702

CLYDE, ROBERT ALLAN, computer software engineer; b. Salt Lake City, June 9, 1959; s. Allan Roy and Janet (Wright) C.; m. Lisa Marie DeFranco, July 14, 1981; children: Elizabeth, Julie. BS in Computer Sci., Brigham Young U., 1984. V.p. engring./mktg. Clyde Digital Systems, Orem, Utah, 1981-91; v.p., gen. mgr. Security Products divsn. Raxco, Orem, 1991-94; v.p. security svcs. Axent Techs., Orem, 1994-96; v.p., gen. mgr. Security Mgmt. Bus. unit Axent, Orem, 1996—2000; v.p., chief tech. officer Symantec Corp., Cupertino, Calif., 2001—. Author: (software product) Contrl, Audit, KBlock; inventor systems for parallel monitoring. Mem. IEEE, Info. Security Assn., EDP Auditors Assn., Assn. for Computing Machinery. Avocations: fishing, camping. Office: Symantec Corp 20330 Stevens Creek Blvd Cupertino CA 95014

CLYMER, ADAM, columnist; b. NYC, Apr. 27, 1937; s. Kinsey and Eleanor (Lowenton) Clymer; m. Ann Wood Fessenden, June 3, 1961; 1 child, Jane Emily (dec.). AB, Harvard U., 1958; postgrad., U. Cape Town, South Africa, 1959; LHD (hon.), U. Vt., 2005. Reporter Virginian-Pilot, Norfolk, Va., 1960—62, Balt. Sun, 1963—76, N.Y. Daily News, Washington, 1977; reporter, editor N.Y. Times, N.Y.C. and Washington, 1977—90, asst. Washington editor, 1991—97, Washington editor, 1997—99, Washington corr., 1999—2003. Vis. scholar Annenberg Pub. Policy Ctr., 2003—. Author: (book) Edward M. Kennedy: A Biography, 1999; co-author: Reagan: The Man, The President, 1981; editor: N.Y. Times Yr. in Rev., 1986—87. Mem. Harvard Crimson Grad. Bd., Cambridge, Mass., 1958—, chair, 2005—; bd. dirs. Washington Press Club Found., 1995—, pres., 2000—03. With U.S. Army, 1961—62. Recipient Everett Dirksen award, Dirksen Congl. Rsch. Ctr., 1994, Carey McWilliams award, Am. Polit. Sci. Assn., 2003. Mem.: Nat. Press Club, Delhi Golf Club (India) (life). Avocation: fly fishing. Office: 2022 Columbia Rd NW #302 Washington DC 20009 Office Phone: 202-549-7161. E-mail: adam.clymer@earthlink.net.

CLYMER, BRIAN WILLIAM, diversified financial services company executive, retired state official; b. Camden, N.J., May 16, 1947; s. Howard Young and Jean (Hatch) C.; children: Kathleen Norris, Richard Hatch; m. Valerie Clymer; children: Caitlin, Emily, Daniel Scott. AA in Bus., Mitchell Coll., 1968; BS in Bus. and Econs., Lehigh U., 1969; DSc in Commerce (hon.), Drexel U., 1999. CPA, Pa. Ptnr. Clymer, Merves & Amon, CPAs, 1982-89; adminstr. Fed. Transit Adminstrn., Dept. Transp., Washington, 1989-93; pres., CEO Railway Systems Designs Inc., 1993-94; treas. State of N.J., 1994-97; v.p. external affairs Prudential Fin., 1997—. Vice chmn. Southeastern Pa. Transp. Authority, 1981—89; exec. com. Am. Pub. Transit Assn., 1993—95; bd. dirs. Longport, Inc., N.J. Alliance Action, N.J. Ind. Coll. Fund. With Pa. N.G., 1970-76. Mem. AICPA, Pa. Inst. CPA, N.J. Soc. CPA. Republican. Presbyterian. Avocations: fishing, golf. Home: 62 Brookville Hollow Rd Stockton NJ 08559-2006 Office: Prudential Fin 751 Broad St Newark NJ 07102-3777 Office Phone: 973-367-2510.

CLYMER, JUDITH ELAINE, elementary school educator; b. Defiance, Ohio, June 3, 1957; d. Lester Earl and Ruth Annabelle (Desgrange) Brinkman; m. Jack David Rishel, Aug. 14, 1982 (div. Jan. 1986); m. Burley Benjamin Clymer, Apr. 30, 1994; children: Mark, Robin, Ben, Terri. BA, Ohio No. U., 1978; MA, Bowling Green State U., 1988. Tchr. grade 2 Cory-Rawson Local Sch., Rawson, Ohio, 1978-82, 84—; substitute tchr. Calhoun County Pub. Schs., Battle Creek, Mich., 1982-84, math tchr. grades 1& 2, 1984—. Young author liaison U. Findlay, Ohio, 1992, Mazza enthusiast, 1992—; math. curriculum model writing team mem Ohio Dept. Edn., 2004-05. Mem. Am. Fedn. Tchrs., Ohio Fed. Tchrs., Cory-Rawson Edn. Assn. (bargaining team 1986—). Republican. Mennonite. Avocations: walking, bicycling, gardening. Home: 12038 Township Road 130 Findlay OH 45840-9009 E-mail: bbjec94@bright.net.

CLYNCH, EDWARD JOHN, political science professor, public information officer; b. South Bend, Ind., Nov. 30, 1942; s. James Harpster and June May (Roberts) C.; m. Barbara Meadow, Aug. 22, 1970; children: Barnaby Patrick, Jennifer Sarah. BA, Hillsdale (Mich.) Coll., 1965; MA, Ball State U., 1968; PhD, Purdue U., 1975. Tchr. Penn H.S., Mishawaka, Ind., 1967; instr. Elizabethtown (Ky.) C.C., 1968-70; asst. prof. polit. sci. U. New Orleans, 1974-78, Kans. State U., 1978-81; assoc. prof. Miss. State U., Mississippi State, 1981-87, prof., 1987—, head. dept. polit. sci., 1983-94, grad. coord., 1995—. Co-author: (with Tom Lauth) Governors, Legislators and Budgets: Diversity Across the American States, 1991; contbr. articles to profl. jours. Pres. Miss. Pub. Mgmt. Grad. Edn. Coun., 1985—; mem. Oktibbeha County Dem. Conv., 1984. Mem. Nat. Assn. Sch. Pub. Affairs and Adminstrn. (mem. exec. coun. 1984-86, chair polit. sci. based program of nation sect. 1987-89, mem. commn. on peer rev. and accreditation 1988-91, 2003-2005), S.E. Conf. Pub. Adminstrn. (chair 1989 meeting), Am. Soc. Pub. Adminstrn. (pres. Miss. chpt. 1984-85, mem. pub. adminstrn. edn. nat. coun. sect. 1988—, pub. adminstrn. program evaluator 1990—, pres. pub. adminstrn. edn. sect. 1992-94), Am. Poli. Sci. Assn., So. Polit. Sci. Assn., Starkville C. of C. (mem. govtl. affairs com. 1987—), Rotary (Starkville v.p. 2004-05, pres., 2005), Epsilon Delta Alpha, Omicron Delta Kappa, Pi Alpha Alpha, Pi Sigma Alpha, Phi Kappa Phi. Democrat. Presbyterian. Home: 401 Colonial Cir Starkville MS 39759-4213 Office: Miss State U Dept Polit Sci and Pub Adminstrn PO Drawer PC Mississippi State MS 39762 Office Phone: 662-325-7852. Business E-Mail: eve1@ps.msstate.edu.

COADY, PHILIP JAMES, JR., retired naval officer; b. Boston, Aug. 25, 1941; s. Philip James and Helen (Mowles) C.; m. Judith Mary Greene, July 11, 1964; children: Meredith, Philip, Adrienne. AB, Tufts U., 1963; MS, Naval Postgrad. Sch., 1972. CLU, ChFC. Commd. ensign USN, 1963, advanced through grades to rear adm., comdg. officer USS Conolly, 1981-83, dir. command and tactics dept. Newport, R.I., 1983-86, comdg. officer USS Antietam, 1986-89; dir. polit. and mil. policy and current plans div. Chief of Naval Ops. Washington, 1989-91; comdr. Cruiser-Destroyer Group Five, 1991-93; dir. surf warfare divsn. Chief of Naval Ops., 1994-95; pres. Navy Mut. Aid Assoc., Arlington, Va., 1995—. Author: (monograph) Shipbuilding: Perspective for the '80s, 1980. Nat. v.p. Surface Navy Assn., 1998—2002; treas. world bd. govs. USO, 2001—03. Decorated D.S.M., Legion of Merit with 5 gold stars. Mem.: Army and Navy Club. Roman Catholic. Office: Henderson Hall 29 Carpenter Rd Arlington VA 22204-4584

COAKER, JAMES WHITFIELD, mechanical engineer; b. Boston, Nov. 12, 1946; s. George W. and Margaret N. Coaker; m. Ruth Johnson, May 17, 1969; children: James W., John A., Stephen D. BSME, Lafayette Coll., 1968; MSB, Va. Commonwealth U., 1976. Registered profl. engr., Va. Application engr. pump and condenser div. Ingersoll-Rand Co., Richmond, Va., 1972-76; project mgr. Reco Industries, Inc., Richmond, Va., 1976-77, asst. mgr. engring., 1977-79, mgr. engring., 1979-83; systems engr., program mgr. Advanced Tech., Inc., Arlington, Va., 1983-87; program mgr. Boiler and Elevator Safety U.S. Postal Svc., Washington, 1987—2002; prin. Coaker & Co. P.C., Fairfax, Va., 2002—. Lectr. and educator in field. Capt. ED USNR, ret. Fellow ASME (life, elevator and escalator safety code com., past nat. chmn. Plant Engring. and Maintenance Divsn., mem. bd. profl. devel. 1990-96, sr. v.p. codes and stds., 2002-2005, v.p. bd. safety codes and stds. 1996-99, bd. govs., 2005-), Nat Coun. Examiners Engring. and Surveying (affiliate), Naval Res. Assn. (life). Home: 11675 Captain Rhett Ln Fairfax Station VA 22039-1236 E-mail: coakerandco@aol.com.

COAKES, MICHELLE DENISE, artist, potter; b. Ft. Worth, Dec. 10, 1959; d. Raynor Eugene and Shirley Ann (Johnson) C. BFA in Ceramics, No. Ill. U., 1982, MA in Ceramics, 1985, MFA in Ceramics, 1987; postgrad., Wichita State U., 1987-88. Apprentice Eckel's Pot Shop, Bayfield, Wis., 1982-83; instr. Highland C.C., Freeport, Ill., 1986-87; ceramics technician Wichita (Kans.) State U., 1988-89; artist-in-residence Fla. Gulf Coast Art Ctr., Belleair, 1989-91; asst. prof. art, mem. honors and grad. faculties Western Ky. U., Bowling Green, 1991-95; instr. Waubonsee C.C., Sugar Grove, Ill., 1995-97; asst. prof. art, mem. grad. faculty U. Louisville, 1997—. Demonstrating artist Artrain Nat. Travelling Art Mus., 1986; studio asst. Penland (N.C.) Sch., 1988; studio asst. Arrowmont Sch. Arts and Crafts, Gatlinburg, Tenn., summers 1989-90, instr., 1992; juror scholastic art awards Regional High Sch. Exhbn., Tampa, Fla., 1990; curator Nat. Exhibit Fla. Craftsmen Gallery, St. Petersburg, 1990, Nat. Crafts Invitational Fine Arts Gallery, Western Ky. U., 1993, Ky. Mus., Bowling Green, 1993; monitor Haystack Mountain Sch. Crafts, Deer Isle, Maine, 1992. One-woman show Fine Arts Gallery, Bowling Green, 1993; exhibited in group shows, including Arrowmont Sch. Arts and Crafts, 1990, Everson Mus. Art, Syracuse, N.Y., 1990, San Angelo (Tex.) Mus. Fine Art, 1990, 91, Miss. Mus. Art, Jackson, 1991, Wichita Falls (Tex.) Art Mus., 1991, Auckland (New Zealand) Inst. and Mus., 1992, Newport Harbor Art Mus., Newport Beach, Calif., 1993, Evansville (Ind.) Art Mus., 1993, Headley-Whitney Mus., Lexington, Ky., 1993, Nat. Ceramics Exhbn., New Haven, Conn., 1993; author: Creative Pottery; A Step by Step Guide and Showcase, 1998. Vol. Meals on Wheels, Largo, Fla., 1990-91. Recipient purchase award TransFinancial Art Exhibit, Bowling Green, 1993; artist grantee Pinellas County Arts Coun., Clearwater, Fla., 1991. Mem. Nat. Coun. on Edn. for Ceramic Arts, Am. Craft Coun. Democrat. Office: U Louisville Hite Art Inst Louisville KY 40292-0001

COAKLEY, THOMAS PATRICK, education educator; b. Danville, Pa., July 4, 1947; s. Thomas Maurice and Catherine Cecilia C.; m. Katheine Irene Stroh Coakley, June 14, 1969; children: Katrina G., Thomas F., Suzanna C., Rebekka A. BA, Villanova (Pa.) U., 1969; MA, U. Tex. at San Antonio, 1977; PhD, The Pa. State U., State College, 1983. Exec. officer USAF, Chanute AFB/IL, 1970-71, squadron commdr., 1971-73, flight commdr. Lackland AFB/TX, 1973-77; prof. USAF Acad., Colorado Springs, 1977-88; sr. rsch. fellow Nat. Def. U., Washington, 1988-92; rsch. affiliate Harvard U., Cambridge, Mass., 1988-92; prof., chairperson Mt. Aloysius Coll., Cresson, Pa., 1992—. Cons. Word One Assocs., Inc., Colorado Springs, 1994—. Editor: Issues of Command and Control, 1991; author: Command and Control for War and Peace, 1992. Recipient Frank J. Seiler Award for Rsch. Excellence, 1991, Excellence in Writing award Def. Intelligence Agy., 1992; grantee Yossarian at the Acad. Conf. Colrado Endowment for the Humanities, USAF Acad./CO, 1986. Office: Mount Aloysius Coll 7373 Admiral Peary Hwy Cresson PA 16630-1902 Fax: 814-886-2978. E-mail: tcoakley@mtaloy.edu.

COALTER, MILTON J., JR., library director, educator; b. Memphis, July 5, 1949; s. Milton J. and Jewel (Mitchel) C.; m. Linda M. Block, May 20, 1973; children: Martha Claire, Siram Jacob. BA, Davidson Coll., 1971; MDiv, Princeton Theol. Sem., 1975, ThM, 1977; PhD in Religion, Princeton U., 1982. Asst. prof. Am. religion N.C. State U., Raleigh, 1981-82; pub. svcs. libr. The Iliff Sch. Theology, Denver, 1982-84, acting libr. dir., 1984-85; libr. dir., prof. bibliography and rsch. Louisville Presbyn. Theol. Sem., 1985—, acting pres., 2002—03; libr. dir., prof. bibliography and rsch. Union Theol. Sem.-PSCE, Richmond, Va., 2004—. Bd. dirs. Louisville Inst., Scholars Press; gen. assembly coun. task force on ch. membership growth Presbyn. Ch., Louisville, 1989-91. Author: (with John M. Mulder) The Letters of David Avery, 1979, Gilbert Tennent, Son of Thunder, 1986; (with John M. Mulder and Louis B. Weeks) The Presbyterian Presence in the Twentieth Century, 7 vols., 1989-92, Vital Signs, 1996, Resources for American Christianity, 2002, website for religion divsn. Lilly Endowment, 2000--; editor: (with Virgil Cruz) How Shall We Witness?, 1995; contbr. articles to profl. jours. Mem. Gen. Assembly Theol. Task Force on Peace, Unity and Purity of the Ch., 2001—. Recipient Jonathan Edwards award Princeton U., 1977-80, Tchg. award Assn. Princeton Grad. Alumni, 1979-80, Francis Makemie award Presbyn. Ch. Dept. History; Lilly Endowment grantee, 1987-90, 99—, N.J. Hist. Commn. grantee, 1979-80, Pew Charitable Trust grantee, 1990-93; Princeton U. Whiting fellow, 1980-81. Mem. Am. Theol. Libr. Assn. (bd. dirs. 1997-2003, pres. 1998-2000), Am. Soc. Ch. History. Presbyterian. Office: William Smith Martin Libr Union Theol Sem-PSCE 3401 Brook Rd Richmond VA 23227 Office Phone: 804-278-4311.

COAN, PATRICIA A., judge; b. N.Y.C., July 21, 1945; 2 children. BSN, Georgetown U., 1967; JD, U. Denver, 1981. Bar: Colo. 1982; RN N.Y., Conn., Mont. Pvt. practice, Denver, Colo., 1982-96; magistrate judge U.S. Dist. Ct. for Dist. Colo., Denver, 1996—. Bd. dirs. Colo. Lawyers Health Program. Mem. FBA, Women's Bar Assn., Am. Soc. Law and Medicine, Colo. Bar Assn., Denver Bar Assn., Sigma Theta Tau, Alpha Sigma Nu. Office: 901 19th St Denver CO 80294-1929 Office Phone: 303-844-4892.

COAN, RICHARD WELTON, psychologist, educator; b. Martinez, Calif., Jan. 24, 1928; s. Otis Welton and Esta Dorothy (Wilson) C.; children: Lisa Cooper, Cynthia, Angela Lambert, Abbie. BA in Psychology, U. Calif., Berkeley, 1948, MA in Psychology, 1950; PhD in Psychology, U. So. Calif., 1955. Psychology instr. L.A. City Coll., 1950-55; rsch. assoc. psychology U. Ill., Urbana, 1955-57; from asst. prof. to prof. psychology U. Ariz., Tucson, 1957-89, prof. emeritus, 1989—. Author: The Optimal Personality, 1974, Hero, Artist, Sage, or Saint?, 1977, Psychologists: Personal and Theoretical Pathways, 1979, Psychology of Adjustment, 1983, Human Consciousness and Its Evolution, 1987, A Princess for Larkin, 2001, Shaul of Tarsos, 2004. Democrat. Avocations: musical composition, writing novels and poetry. Home: 2992 W Royal Copeland Dr Tucson AZ 85745 E-mail: rwcoan@cox.net.

COAR, RICHARD JOHN, mechanical engineer, aerospace transportation executive, consultant; b. Hanover, N.H., May 2, 1921; s. Herbert Greenleaf and Anne (Langille) C.; m. Cecilie Berle, 1942 (dec. 1971); children—Gregory, Candace, Andrea, Kenneth; m. Lucille Hicks, 1972. BS in Mech. Engring., Tufts U., 1942. Engr. Pratt & Whitney Aircraft, East Hartford, Conn., 1942-56; chief engr. Fla. Research and Devel. Ctr., 1956-70, asst. gen. mgr., 1970—72; v.p. engring. Pratt & Whitney Aircraft, East Hartford, 1972—76, exec. v.p., 1976-83, pres., 1983-84; sr. v.p. United Techs., Hartford, 1983-84, exec. v.p., 1984-86. Patentee aircraft engines and controls Corporator Hartford Hosp., 1983; bd. dirs. Hartford Symphony, 1985-87. Recipient Franklin W. Kolk Air Transp. Progress award Soc. Automotive Engrs., 1985, Daniel Guggenheim medal for contbns. to aeronautic and space propulsion sys., 1998. Mem. ASME (George Westinghouse Gold medal 1986), NAE, Am. Soc. Metals (disting. life mem.), Tau Beta Pi, Water's Edge Country Club. Avocations: sailing, golf. Home and Office: 105 Blackwater Cir Penhook VA 24137-5260

COASE, RONALD HARRY, economist, educator; b. Willesden, Eng., Dec. 29, 1910; arrived in U.S., 1951; s. Henry Joseph and Rosalie (Giles) Coase; m. Marian Ruth Hartung, Aug. 7, 1937. B of Commerce, London Sch. Econs., 1932; DSc in Econs., U. London, 1951; D Rer. Pol. (hon.), Cologne U., Germany, 1988; D of Social Sci. (hon.), Yale U., 1989; LLD (hon.), Washington U., St. Louis, 1991, U. Dundee, Scotland, 1992; DSc (hon.), U. Buckingham, Eng., 1995; DHL (hon.), Beloit Coll., 1996; PhD (hon.), U. Paris, 1996; DHum (hon.), Clemson U., 2003. Sir Ernest Cassel Travelling scholar, 1931—32; asst. lectr. Dundee Sch. Econs., 1932—34, U. Liverpool, England, 1934—35; from asst. lectr. to lectr. to reader London Sch. Econs., 1935—51; prof. U. Buffalo, 1951—58, U. Va., Charlottesville, 1958—64, U. Chgo., 1964—, now Clifton R. Musser prof. emeritus, sr. fellow in law and econs. Law Sch. Statistician, then chief statistician Ctrl. Statis. Office, Offices War Cabinet, England, 1941—46. Author: British Broadcasting, A Study in Monopoly, 1950, The Firm, the Market and the Law, 1988, Essays on Economics and Economists, 1994; editor: Jour. Law and Econs., 1964—82. Mem. hon. com. Eurosci. Named Rockefeller fellow, 1948; recipient Nobel prize in econs., 1991, Innovations award, The Economist, 2003; fellow Ctr. for Advanced Study Behavioral Scis., 1958—59; Sr. Rsch. fellow, Hoover Instn., Stanford U., 1977, hon. fellow, London Sch. Econs. Fellow: European Acad., Am. Econ. Assn. (disting.), Brit. Acad. (corr.), Am. Acad. Arts and Scis.; mem.: Internat. Soc. for New Instnl. Econs. (founding pres. 1997), Mont Pelerin Soc., Royal Econ. Soc. Office: U Chgo Laird Bell Law Quadrangle 1111 E 60th St Chicago IL 60637-2776 Home: The Hallmark 2960 N Lake Shore Dr Chicago IL 60657 Office Phone: 773-702-7342.

COATES, DIANNE KAY, retired social worker; b. Adrian, Mich., Jan. 4, 1945; Student, Jackson Bus. U., 1962-63; AA with honors, Macomb C.C., Warren, Mich., 1977; BA with high distinction, Madonna Coll., 1979; MSW, Wayne State U., 1982; postgrad., Internat. Grad. Sch., 1984, Ea. Mich. U., 1989. Cert. social worker, Mich. Nat. svc. officer Mil. Order of the Purple Heart, Detroit, 1973-80; psychology technician VA Med. Ctr., Allen Park, Mich., 1980-84; clin. cons. HOMEBASE, Detroit, 1983-85; clin. social worker Cmty. Counseling Assocs., Adrian, 1983, Roseville, Mich., 1983-87, Ypsilanti (Mich.) Regional Psychiat. Hosp., 1987-90, Southgate (Mich.) Regional Ctr. for the Developmentally Disabled, 1990-92, 92-96, Lafayette Clinic, 1992; from intake/admissions/discharge coord. to dir. social work svcs. Southgate Ctr., 1996—2001; clin. social worker Northville Psychiat. Hosp., 2001—02, acting dir. social svcs., 2002—03; clin. social work mgr. Walter Reuther Psychiat. Hosp., 2003—05; ret., 2005. Group counselor Survivors of Homicide, Detroit, 1981-82; vol. HAVEN, Pontiac, Mich., 1986-87; internat. exch. counselor Edn. Found. Fgn. Study, 1987-92; field instr. Wayne State U., 1988—; ind. contract therapist Renaissance West Cmty. Mental Health Svcs. Clinic, Detroit, 1988-89, Caknipe-Kovach Assocs., 1988-92; area rep. Ednl. Resource Devel. Trust, 1991-94 Recipient Ann. Disting. Svc. award LA MOPH Dept. of Mich., 1992. Mem. NASW (bd. cert. diplomate), Acad. Cert. Social Workers, Assn. State Employed MSW's (v.p. 1991-93), Mich. Mental Health Assn., Mich. Assn. Mental Health Profls., Social Work Assn. Madonna Coll. (co-founder), Wayne State U. Alumni Assn., Bus. and Profl. Women, VietnamVets. Am. (hon. life assoc. mem.), Met. Svc. Officers Assn. (pres. 1990-92), Ladies Aux. Mil. Order of Purple Heart (region 2 v.p. 1985-86, nat. membership officer 1995-96), Ladies Aux. VFW, DAV Aux. Home: 1502 Elias St Westland MI 48186-4919 Personal E-mail: coatesd@sbcglobal.net.

COATES, DONALD ROBERT, geologist, educator; b. Grand Island, Neb., July 23, 1922; s. Frank Jefferson and Harriet (Ferris) C.; m. Jeanne Louise Grandison, Mar. 18, 1944 (dec. Jan. 1993); children: Cheryl D., Donald Eric, Lark J.; m. Marilyn Hilton Williams, Jan. 12, 1998 (dec. Jan. 2004). BA, Coll. Wooster, 1944; MA, Columbia U., 1948, PhD, 1956. Faculty Earlham Coll., Richmond, Ind., 1948—51; geologist, project chief U.S. Geol. Survey, Tucson, 1951—54; faculty Harpur Coll. (now Binghamton U./SUNY), 1954—90, chmn. dept. geology, 1954—63, prof., 1963—90; prof. emeritus SUNY Binghamton, 1990—; rsch. geologist U.S. Geol. Survey, Vestal, NY, 1958—61; vis. geoscientist Am. Geol. Inst., 1963—85; cons. Engring. Corps U.S. Army, 1965—86. Cons. Empire State Electric Energy Rsch. Corp., Consol. Edison N.Y., Niagara Mohawk Power Corp., Mohonk Preserve Corp., Protector Pine Oak Woods Inc., U.S. Army C.E., Town of Islip, N.Y. State Dept. Environ. Conservation, N.Y. State Electric & Gas Corp., N.Y. State Dept. Transp., N.Y. State Atty. Gen., N.Y. State Power Authority, N.Y. Low Level Nuc. Waste Siting Commn., Town of Vernon, N.Y., Broome County, Chemung County, Town of Vestal, N.Y., Town of Trenton, N.Y., Town of Deerfield, N.Y., Town of Norwich, Adastra West Pubs., 1999, Facts on File, Inc., 1987, 99, also pvt. cos.; assoc. program dir. NSF Found., 1963-64; vis. prof. Ind. U., 1955, U. Ill., 1963, Guangdong Seismol. Bur., China, 1987; vis. scholar Chinese Acad. Sci., 1995. Editor: Geology of South-Central New York, 1963, Environmental Geomorphology and Landscape Conservation, 3 vols., Coastal Geomorphology, Glacial Geomorphology, Geomorphology and Engineering, Landslides, (with John Vitek) Threshholds in Geomorphology, Urban Geomorphology, Environmental Geomorphology, 1971, Environmental Science Workbook, 1972, (with Charles Higgins) Ground Water Geomorphology, 1990; editor, author: Environmental Geology; author: Geology and Society; contbr. to Science - A Process Approach, 1965; also articles, reports. Lt. USN, 1943—46, lt. USNR, 1946—54. Recipient award for Sustained Superior Performance NSF, 1964; Rsch. grantee NSF, U.S. Dept. Commerce, U.S. Geol. Survey, N.Y. State Atomic and Space Devel. Authority, Rsch. Found. SUNY, 1958-61. Fellow AAAS, Geol. Soc. Am. (Merit cert. engring. geology divsn. 1980, E.B. Burwell Jr. award 1995); mem. Assn. Engring. Geologists, Nat. Assn. Geology Tchrs. (pres. Ea. sect. 1962, Ralph Digman award 1972, Coll. Tchr. of Yr. award 1971), Am. Inst. Profl. Geologists, N.Y. State Geol. Assn. (pres. 1963, 81), Phi Beta Kappa. Home: 6608 17th Ave Court West Bradenton FL 34209 Office: Binghamton U SUNY Dept Geol Scis Binghamton NY 13902 Personal E-mail: profcoates@earthlink.net.

COATES, GLENN RICHARD, lawyer; b. Thorp, Wis., June 8, 1923; s. Richard and Alma (Borck) C.; m. Dolores Milburn, June 24, 1944; children—Richard Ward, Cristie Joan Student, Milw. State Tchrs. Coll., 1940-42, NMA and MA, 1943-44; LLB, U. Wis., 1949, SJD, 1953. Bar: Wis. 1949. Atty. Mil. Sea Transp. Service, Dept. Navy, 1951-52; pvt. practice Racine, Wis., 1952—. Sec., gen. counsel Racine Federated Inc.; lectr. U. Wis. Law Sch., 1955-56. Author: Chattel Secured Farm Credit, 1953; contbr. articles to profl. publs. Chmn. bd. St. Luke's Meml. Hosp., 1973-76, bd. dirs., 1990-91; pres. Racine Area United Way, 1979-81; bd. curators State Hist. Soc. Wis., 1986-2001, pres., 1995-97; bd. dirs. Racine County Area Found., 1983-89; bd. dirs. Wis. History Found., Inc., 1983-99, Hist. Sites Found., Inc., 1987-89, St. Luke's Hosp./St. Mary's Med. Ctr. Healthcare Found., 1992-96. With U.S. Army, 1943-46. Fellow Am. Bar Found. (life); mem. ABA, State Bar Wis. (bd. govs. 1969-74, chmn. bd. 1973-74), Wis. Jud. Coun. (chmn. 1969-72), Am. Law Inst. (life), Racine Country Club, Masons, Order of Coif. Methodist (chmn. fin. com. 1961-67). Home: 2830 Michigan Blvd Racine WI 53402-4254

COATES, JOHN C., IV, law educator; b. Lynchburg, Va., Sept. 15, 1964; BA in History, U. Va., 1986; JD, NYU, 1989. Bar: NY 1989. Assoc. Wachtell, Lipton, Rosen & Katz, NYC, 1989—97, ptnr., 1997; asst. prof. law Harvard

Law Sch., Cambridge, Mass., 1997—2001, prof., 2001—. Office: Harvard Law Sch 1563 Massachusetts Ave Cambridge MA 02138 Office Phone: 617-496-4420. Office Fax: 617-496-5156. Business E-Mail: jcoates@law.harvard.edu.

COATES, JOHN PETER, technical executive; b. Coventry, Eng., Apr. 4, 1946; came to U.S., 1978; s. Harry and Barbara Joan (Snape) C.; m. Laura Frances Curran, July 28, 1979; children: Jonathan Edmund, Kristen Elizabeth, Ross James. BS/MS in Chemistry, Slough Coll. of Tech. now Thames Valley Univ., Eng., 1972; PhD in Chemistry, Brunel U., London, 1987. Analytical chemist Castrol Oil Co., Bracknell, Eng., 1964-73; sr. chromatographer Burmah Oil, Bromboro, Eng., 1973-74; sr., chief chemist Perkin-Elmer Ltd., Beaconsfield, Eng., 1974-78; sr. staff scientist Perkin-Elmer Corp., Norwalk, Conn., 1978-85; dir. mktg. Spectra-Tech Inc., Stamford, Conn., 1985-88; dir. analyzer div. Nicolet Instrument Corp., Madison, Wis., 1988-92; dir. mktg. real time systems divsn. (PAI) Perkin-Elmer, Norwalk, Conn., 1992-96; prin. cons. Coates Cons., Newtown, Conn., 1996—; dir. techs. Global Technovations, Inc., Atlanta, 1998—2002; interim dir. MCEC, U. Tenn., Knoxville, 1999—2001; ptnr. Personal Instruments, LLC, Sentelligence Corp. Co-author: (with L.C. Setti) Oils, Lubricants and Petroleum Products--Characterization by Infrared Spectra, 1985; patentee in field; contbr. chpts. to books and articles to profl. jours. Fellow Royal Soc. Chemistry; mem. Am. Chem. Soc., Instrument Soc. Am., Soc. Automotive Engrs., Soc. Applied Spectroscopy. Avocations: writing, photography, music, computers. Office: Coates Cons PO Box 3176 Newtown CT 06470-3176 Office Phone: 203-426-8495. Personal E-mail: JohnC79051@aol.com.

COATES, PAMELA MARIE, principal; b. Middletown, Ohio, July 25, 1949; d. Charles Ray Blanton and Martha Louise Blenton; m. Gary Michael Coates, Aug. 14, 1970; 1 child, Nathan Paul. BS in Edn., U. Dayton, 1971; MEd in Curriculum & Supervision, Wright State U., 1983, MEd Adminstrn., 1989. Tchr. elem. sch. Little Miami Sch. Dist., Blanchester, Ohio, 1971—2000, prin., 2000—. Recipient Master Tchr. award, Martha Holden Jennings Found., 1999; grantee, Ohio Edn. Dept., 2001. Mem.: ASCD, Nat. Assn. Elem. Sch. Prins. Avocation: reading. Home: 346 Summit St Lebanon OH 45036 Office: Butlerville Elem Sch 8276 St Rt 132 Blanchester OH 45107

COATES, ROBERT JAY, retired electronics executive; b. Lansing, Mich., May 8, 1922; s. Archie Louis and Ruth Agnes (Hutchings) C.; m. Gladys Buchhorn, Aug. 17, 1946; (dec.); 1 child, Bonnie; m. H. Regina Thorsen, Oct. 17, 1999. BSE.E., Mich. State U., 1943; MSE.E., U. Md., 1948; PhD in physics, Johns Hopkins U., 1957. Radio engr. U.S. Naval Research Lab., Washington, 1943—46, electronic scientist, 1946—49, 1952—59; instr. physics Johns Hopkins U., Balt., 1949—52; from assoc. chief Tracking Sys. Divsn. to mgr. Crustal Dynamics Project Goddard Space Flight Ctr. NASA, Greenbelt, Md., 1959—79, mgr. Crustal Dynamics Project Goddard Space Flight Ctr., 1979—88, ret., 1988. Cons. in field Vol. Habitat for Humanity, 1996-99. Served with USN, 1944-45. Recipient Outstanding Performance award NRL, 1959, Group Achievement award NASA, 1973, 1968, 1986, Apollo Achievement award, 1969, Exceptional Performance award Goddard Space Flight Center, 1971, Exceptional Service medal, 1986; Outstanding Leadership medal NASA, 1989. Fellow IEEE; mem. Am. Phys. Soc., Am. Geophys. Union, AAAS, Sigma Xi, Phi Kappa Phi, Tau Beta Pi. Home: 529 Whittingham Dr Silver Spring MD 20904-6330

COATES, THOMAS J., medical association administrator; BA in Philosophy, San Luis Rey Coll., 1968; MA in Psychology, San Jose State U., 1971; PhD in Counseling Psychology, Stanford U., 1977. Mem. faculty Stanford Heart Disease Prevention Program; with Johns Hopkins U.; dir. behavioral medicine unit div. gen. internal medicine U. Calif., San Francisco, 1984—, mem. med. attending staff, 1984—, prof. div. gen. internal medicine dept. medicine, 1990—, dir. Ctr. AIDS Prevention Studies, 1991—. Spl. advisor family health internat.'s AIDS prevention project USAIDS; chair global programme on AIDS steering com. social and behavioral studies unit WHO. Contbr. articles to profl. jours. Mem.: NAS (mem. Inst. Medicine). Office: UCLA Dept Med Divsn Infectious Dis Prevention & Policy Rsch 10940 Wilshire Blvd Ste 1220 Los Angeles CA 90024-7320

COATES, TIMOTHY JOEL, historian; s. Charles Kedron and Barbara Coates. BA, U. Ariz., 1974; MA, U. Minn., 1991, PhD, 1993. Vis. asst. prof. Brown U., Providence, 1993-95; assoc. prof. Coll. of Charleston, S.C., 1995—. Author: Degredados e Orfas, 1998, Convicts and Orphans, 2001, The Conversions of the King of Bissau, 2001, Commander Order of St. James (Portugal); assoc., book rev. editor Portuguese Studies Rev., 1997—. Calouste Gulbenkian Found. fellow, Portugal, 1990, Fundação Oriente fellow, Macau, 1997; grantee Am. Inst. Indian Studies, India, 1991, Luso-Am. Devel. Found., Portugal, 1997. Mem. Am. Hist. Assn., Soc. for Spanish and Portuguese Hist. Studies, Soc. for the History of Discoveries, Hakluyt Soc., James Ford Bell Libr. Office: Coll of Charleston Dept History 66 George St Charleston SC 29424-1407 E-mail: coatest@cofc.edu.

COATES, WINSLOW SHELBY, lawyer; b. Bayville, N.Y., Mar. 4, 1929; s. Winslow Shelby and Jane (Brush) C.; m. Frances Ward White, Feb. 16, 1959; children: Susan F. White, Trevor D. BA, Yale U., New Haven, Conn., 1952; LLB, U. Va., Charlottesville, 1959. Bar: N.Y. 1961, U.S. Dist. Ct. (so. dist.) N.Y. 1962. Assoc. Dow & Stonebridge, N.Y.C., 1961-67; pvt. practice N.Y.C., 1967-77; ptnr. Miller, Montgomery, Sogi, Brady & Taft, N.Y.C., 1977-80; shipping exec. Oceanic Fleet Carriers S.A., N.Y.C., 1980-86; pvt. practice Oyster Bay, N.Y., 1986—. Founder Trident Maritime Svcs., Ld., Oyster Bay, 1994—. Author: Maritime Product Liability, 1979; contbr. articles to local newspapers. Co-founder Friends of the Bay, 1988; active Bd. Zoning Appeals, Matinecock, N.Y. Lt. USN, 1953-56. Mem. Maritime Law Assn. of the U.S., Piping Rock Club, Army and Navy Club. Republican. Avocations: chess, tennis, reading literature on history, travel, yachts. Home: 200 Piping Rock Rd Locust Valley NY 11560-2509 Office: 115 South St Oyster Bay NY 11771-0186 Office Phone: 516-674-1556.

COATS, ANDREW MONTGOMERY, dean, lawyer, former mayor; b. Oklahoma City, Okla., Jan. 19, 1935; s. Sanford Clarence and Mary Ola (Young) C.; m. Linda M. Zimmerman; children— Andrew, Michael, Jennifer, Sanford BA, U. Okla., 1957, JD, 1963. Assoc. Crowe and Dunlevy, Oklahoma City, 1963-67, ptnr., 1967-76, sr. trial ptnr., 1980—96; dist. atty. Oklahoma County, Oklahoma City, 1976-80; mayor City of Oklahoma City, 1983-87; dean U. Okla. Coll. Law, 1996—2004; dir. IBC Bank Okla., 2004—. Pres. Okla. Young Lawyers Conf., 1968-69; dir. Local Okla. Bank, Oklahoma City. Democratic nominee U.S. Senate, 1980; pres. Oklahoma County Legal Aid Soc., 1972-73. Served to lt. USN, 1960-63 Named Outstanding Lawyer in Okla., Oklahoma City U., 1977, Phi Beta Kappa of Yr., 2003, U. Okla. Coll. Law named in honor of Andrew M. Coats. Fellow Am. Coll. Trial Lawyers (pres. 1996-97, 10th Cir. regent 1992-96), Am. Bd. Trial Advocates (charter pres. Okla. 1986), Am. Bar Found., Internat. Acad. Trial Lawyers; mem. ABA, U.S. Supreme Ct. Hist. Soc. (trustee), Okla. Bar Assn. (pres. 1992-93), Okla. County Bar Assn. (pres. 1976-77), Am. Bd. Trial Advs. (charter pres. Okla. Chap.) Order of Coif, Oklahoma City Golf and Country Club (bd. dirs. 1977-80, 93-96), Petroleum Club (pres. 1995), Phi Beta Kappa (pres. 1975), Pi Kappa Alpha (pres. 1956), Phi Delta Phi (pres. 1962). Clubs: Oklahoma City Golf and Country, Petroleum. Democrat. Episcopalian. Avocations: music, golf. Office: Crowe and Dunlevy 20 N Broadway Ave Ste 1800 Oklahoma City OK 73102-8273 also: U Okla Coll Law 300 Timber Dell Rd Norman OK 73019-5081 Office Phone: 405-235-4720. E-mail: acoats@ou.edu.

COATS, CHARLES F., physics and mathematics educator; b. LaJunta, Colo., Oct. 31, 1949; s. Robert Harold and Edna Lucille (Varner) C. BS in Math., Physics, Southeastern State Coll., 1970; MA in Math., U. Okla., 1977, MS in Physics, 1979, PhD in Physics, 1982. Asst. prof. McPherson (Kans.) Coll., 1979-80, U. Pitts., Bradford, 1980-86, Southeastern Okla. State U., Durant, 1987-89; asst. prof. physics and math. U. Montevallo, Ala., 1989-94, Laredo (Tex.) C.C., 1995—. Prin., Coats Photographic Svcs., Durant, Okla., 1986-89. With U.S. Army, 1971-73. Mem. AAUP, Am. Assn. Physics Tchrs., Math. Assn. Am., Tex. C.C. Tchrs. Assn., Sigma Xi, Kappa Mu Epsilon, Pi Mu Epsilon. Office: Laredo CC Laredo TX 78040

COATS, DANIEL RAY, lawyer, former ambassador, former senator; b. Jackson, Mich., May 16, 1943; s. Edward R. and Vera E. C.; m. Marcia Crawford, Sept. 4, 1965; children: Laura, Lisa, Andrew. BA, Wheaton (Ill.) Coll., 1965; JD cum laude, Ind. U., 1971. Bar: Ind. 1972. Asst. v.p., counsel Mutual Security Life Ins. Co., Ft. Wayne, Ind., 1969—75; Dist. rep. U.S. Congressman Dan Quayle, 1976-80; mem. 97th-100th Congresses from 4th Dist. Ind., Washington, 1981-89; U.S. senator from Ind., 1989-99; lobbyist Pharm. Rsch. and Mfrs. of Am.; spl. counsel Verner, Liipfert, Bernhard, McPherson and Hand, 1999—2001; U.S. amb. to Germany U.S. Dept. State, Berlin, 2001—05; sr. counsel King & Spaulding LLP, Washington, 2005—, co-chmn. govt. rels. group, 2005—. Mem. Armed Svcs. Com., Labor and Human Resources Com., Intelligence Com.; bd. dirs. IPALCO. Lear Siegler Svcs., Inc., Internat. Repub. Inst., The Empowerment Network. Pres., Big Bros./Big Sisters of Am., Ind. Served with U.S. Army, 1966-68. Office: King & Spaulding LLP 1700 Pennsylvania Ave NW Washington DC 20006 Office Phone: 202-731-6262. Business E-Mail: dcoats@kslaw.com.

COATS, NATHAN B., state supreme court justice; m. Mary Ricketson; 1 child, Johanna. BA in Econs., U. Colo., 1971, JD, 1977. Assoc. Hough, Grant, McCarren and Bernard, 1977-78; asst. atty. gen. Appellate Sect., Colo., 1978-83, dep. atty. gen., 1983-86; adj. prof. U. Colo., Colo., 1990; chief appellate dep. dist. atty. 2d Jud. Dist., Denver, 1986-2000; justice Colo. Supreme Ct., 2000—. Chief reporter Erickson Commn. on Officer-Involved Shootings, 1996-97; lectr. Denver Police Acad., 1986-97; reporter Govs. Columbine Commn., 1999-2000; mem. Colo. Supreme Ct. Criminal Rules Com., 1983-2000, chmn., 1997-2000, Colo. Bd. Law Examiners, 1984-94, Colo. Supreme Ct. Appellate Rules Com., 1985-2000, Colo. Supreme Ct. Civil Rules Com., Colo. Supreme Ct. Criminal Pattern Jury Instructions Com., 1987-2000, Colo. Supreme Ct. Jury Reform Pilot Project Com., 1998-2000, Colo. Dist. Attys. Coun. Legis. Com., 1990-2000. Office: Colo State Supreme Ct Judicial Bldg 2 E 14th Ave Denver CO 80203-2115*

COATS, TERESA L., internist, researcher; b. Denver City, Tex., Nov. 28, 1957; d. David and Camilla Coats; m. David M. Marquez, May 4, 1985; children: Daniel C. Marquez, Elena C. Marquez. MD, Tex. Tech U., Lubbock, 1985. Cert. internal medicine Am. Bd. Internal Medicine, 2001. Physician Ctrl. Austin Internists, Austin, Tex., 1996—; principle investigator Benchmark Rsch., Austin, Tex., 1999—. Clin. asst. prof. U. Tex. Med. Br., Galveston, 1999—. Fellow: ACP. Office: Ctrl Austin Internists Ste 309 1015 E 32nd Austin TX 78705 Office Phone: 512-472-6791.

COATS, WARREN L., JR., economist; b. Bakersfield, Calif., May 19, 1942; s. Warren L. and Sara Jane C.; m. Louise Wilkinson, Feb. 15, 1968 (div. June 1980); children: Brandon, Daylin. BA in Econs., U. Calif., Berkeley, 1965; MA in Econs., U. Chgo., 1967, PhD in Econs., 1972. Instr. econs. Ill. Inst. Tech., Chgo., 1966-67, 68-70; asst. prof. econs. U. Hawaii, Honolulu, 1968, U. Va., Charlottesville, 1970-76, asst. dep. chmn., 1972-74, dir. honors program, 1974-76; economist, sr. economist ctrl. banking dept. Internat. Monetary Fund, Washington, 1976-81, chief SDRs and divsn. treas. dept., 1982-88, advisor treas. dept., 1989-91, advisor monetary and exch. affairs dept., 1992-99, asst. dir. monetary and exch. affairs dept., 1999—2003; dir. Cayman Island Monetary Authority, 2003—. Tech. asst., advisor ctrl. banks Afghanistan, Bangladesh, Bosnia, Bulgaria, Croatia, Czech Republic, Egypt, Hungary, Kazakhstan, Kosovo, Kyrgyz Republic, Malta, Moldova, Slovakia, Turkey, Iraq, Yugoslavia, Iraq, Israel, West Bank Gaza Strip and other countries; presenter in field; sr. monitary policy advisor Ctrl. Bank of Iraq. Co-author: The World Development Report, 1989, The Simple Analytics of Digital Money: Finance in Cyberspace, 1996; editor: Inflation Targetting in Transition Economics: The Case of the Czech Republic, 2000; co-editor: Money and Monetary Policy in Less Developed Countries: Survey of Issues and Evidence, 1980; contbr. articles to profl. jours. Mem. Am. Econ. Assn., We. Econ. Assn. Internat. (past mem. exec. com.), Order of the Golden Bear, Phil. Soc. (past bd. dirs.), Mt. Peleron Soc., Alpha Tau Omega (past pres.). Home: PH 7 1300 Crystal Dr Arlington VA 22202-3234

COBB, BRIAN ERIC, broadcast executive; b. Berlin, N.H., Jan. 3, 1945; s. Everett Bryan and Eleanore (Bouchard) C.; m. Denise Leclair, Sept. 20, 1986; children: Jennifer, Heather. BS, U. Nev., 1967. Gen. sales mgr. Sta. WNGE-TV, Nashville, 1972, mktg. mgr., 1973-76, v.p., gen. mgr., 1977, Sta. WSIX AM/FM, Nashville, 1977, Gen. Electric Broadcasting of Colo., stas. KOA-AM, KOAQ, KOA-TV, Denver, 1978-81; v.p. TV Chapman Assocs., Washington, 1982-87; ptnr. Media Venture Ptnrs., Naples, Fla., 1987-2001; pres. Cobb Corp., N.Y.C., 2001—. Cons. Denver Broncos, 1982—2000; pres. Media Ventur Mgmt., Biltmore Broadcasting. Comml. chmn. Mile-Hi United Way, 1980; bd. dirs. Vanderbilt Children's Hosp., 1973-76; founder, chmn. Naples Children and Edn. Found.; trustee Fla. Gulf Coast U., 2001—. Named an Outstanding Young Man of Yr., Nashville Jaycees, 1978. Mem. Nat. Assn. Broadcasters, Nat. Assn. TV Program Execs., Tenn. Assn. Broadcasters (bd. dirs. 1975-77), Nat. Assn. Media Brokers (pres. 1993-95), Rotary. Republican. Roman Catholic. Avocations: golf, reading. Office: Cobb Corp LLC Ste 210 800 Laurel Oak Dr Naples FL 34108-7512 Office Phone: 202-478-3737. E-mail: briancobb@cobbcorp.tv.

COBB, CALVIN HAYES, JR., lawyer; b. San Diego, Aug. 2, 1924; s. Calvin Hayes and Frances King (Halm) Cobb; m. Olive Latimer Watson, Mar. 19, 1955; children: Alice Cobb Parte, Joan Cobb Pettit, Calvin Hayes III, Robert Watson, Olive Latimer Waxter. BS with distinction, U.S. Naval Acad., 1944; LLB, Georgetown U., 1950. Bar: DC 1950, Md. 1950, U.S. Supreme Ct. 1953. Assoc. Law Offices Elisha Hanson, Washington, 1950-55; ptnr. Hanson, Cobb & O'Brien, Washington, 1955-69, Steptoe & Johnson, Washington, 1969—. Leading article editor: Georgetown Law Jour., 1949; contbr. articles to law revs. and profl. jours. Trustee Found. Mid. East Peace, 1969—, Naval Hist. Found., 1983—2003; chmn. Found. Mid. East Peace, 2004—. Lt. (j.g.) USN, 1944—47. Recipient Disting. Pub. Svc. award, U.S. Sec. of Navy, 1979, 1991, Pub. Svc. award, USCG, 1991. Mem.: Soc. Cin., U.S. Naval Acad. Alumni Assn. (trustee 1955—58), Navy League U.S. (nat. judge adv. 1975—89, bd. dirs. 1975—, sr. v.p. 1988—89, pres. 1989—91, Nat. Pres.'s award 1976, 1983, 1986), Naples Athletic Club, Forum Club (bd. dirs. 2000—03), Barristers Club (pres. 1974), Naples Bath and Tennis Club, Royal Poinciana Golf Club (pres. 2003—05), Gibson Island Club, Chevy Chase Club (pres. 1974—75), Lawyers Club. Republican. Roman Catholic. Avocations: tennis, golf, bridge. Office: 1330 Connecticut Ave NW Washington DC 20036-1704 Office Phone: 202-429-8105. Personal E-mail: chcobbjr@aol.com. Business E-Mail: ccobb@steptoe.com.

COBB, CHARLES KENCHE, JR., lawyer, real estate broker; b. Canton, Ga., Aug. 23, 1934; s. Charlie Kench and Alice (Enloe) Cobb; m. Carolyn Webb, Aug. 31, 1963; children: Charlie Kenche III, Catherine Elizabeth Fryman. BS, Ga. Tech., 1956; MBA, Harvard U., 1962; postgrad., Emory U., 1963, Georgetown U., 1959; LLD, Woodrow Wilson, 1968. Bar: Ga. 1969. Pres. C. Cobb Properties, Atlanta, 1969—, Sterling Land Co., Atlanta, 1973—; dir. Canton Textile Mills, Inc., 1991—. Mem. exec. com. Ga. Tech. Wesley Found., Atlanta, 1983—2003; former treas., sec., trustee Reinhardt Coll., Waleska, Ga., 1974—; bd. dirs. Ga. Tech. YMCA, Atlanta, 1976—89; lay leader Northside United Meth. Ch., Atlanta, 1978. Served to 1st lt. USAF, 1956—59, ETO. Mem.: Ga. Assn. Exchangors (former pres., Ga. Exchangor of Yr. 1971, 1990), Atlanta Bd. Realtors (bd. dirs. 1983—90, Outstanding Transaction of Yr. award 1986), Ga. Bar Assn., Ga. Tech. Alumni Assn. (trustee 1976—79), Ga. Hist. Trust, Buckhead 50 Club (pres. 1997), Canton Golf Club, Shriner Lodge, Mason Lodge. Home: 2851 Howell Mill Rd NW Atlanta GA 30327-1333 Office: 1 Northside 75 NW Ste 102 Atlanta GA 30318-7715 Office Phone: 404-355-0889.

COBB, DAVID KEITH, accountant; b. Calhoun City, Miss., Mar. 2, 1941; s. Bayne and Frances (Clements) C.; m. Dorothy Hill, June 15, 1963; children: Paul J., John D., Mark F. BS, U. So. Miss., 1963. Nat. mng. ptnr. fin. svcs. KPMG Peat Marwick, N.Y.C., 1963-95; CEO, vice chmn. Alamo Rent A Car, Inc., 1995-97. Bd. dirs. RHR Internat., Inc., BankAtlantic Bancorp, Alliance Data Sys., Inc., BFC Fin. Corp. Bd. dirs. United Way of Broward County, Nova Southeastern U. Grad. Sch. Bus. Republican. Presbyterian. Home and Office: 2521 Del Lago Dr Fort Lauderdale FL 33316-2303 E-mail: kcobb@cobbcorner.com.

COBB, EDWARD RAY, actor; b. Reidsville, N.C., July 6, 1957; s. Robert Edward and Mary Elizabeth Cobb; life ptnr. David M. Glaser, Oct. 9, 1981. Student, Greensboro Coll., 1975—78. Actor: (plays) Picture Me, Picture You, 1985, Lady L, 1986, Untold Decades, 1988, On Tina Tuna Walk, 1989 (Robby award for best actor in a comedy Frontiers After Dark, 1989), Bud O'Connor's Coconut Angel Pies, 1990, Body and Soul, 1991. Bd. mem. The Espoir Found., N.Y.C., 1985—94. Mem.: SAG, Actors Equity Assn.

COBB, G. ELLIOTT, JR., lawyer; b. Franklin, Va., July 11, 1939; s. Gardner E. and Thelma L. (Whitley) C.; m. Betty Minor, July 15, 1961; children: Polly, Susan, Gardner. BS, U. Va., 1960, LL.B., 1966. Bar: Va. 1966, Supreme Ct. U.S 1974. Asso. counsel Union Camp Corp., Wayne, N.J., 1967-74, counsel, mgr. adminstrn., 1974-76, gen. counsel, asst. sec., 1976, v.p., gen. counsel, sec., 1976-78; ptnr. Moyler, Rainey & Cobb, Franklin, 1978—. Mem. adv. bd. SunTrust Bank, Franklin. Mem. Franklin City Coun., 1980-88; vice mayor of Franklin, 1982-84, mayor, 1984-88; bd. dirs. SFranklin Southampton Charieies. Served with USMC, 1960-61. Mem. Va. Bar Assn., Southampton-Franklin Bar Assn. Clubs: Cypress Cove Country, Rotary. Episcopalian. Home: 913 Clay St Franklin VA 23851-1306 Office: Moyler Rainey & Cobb 506 N Main St Franklin VA 23851-1438

COBB, GEORGE EDWARD, surgeon; b. Oklahoma City, Aug. 10, 1930; MD, Harvard U., 1955. Diplomate Am. Bd. Surgery. Intern Johns Hopkins Hosp., Balt., 1955-56, resident in surgery, 1956-57, San Francisco USPHS Hosp., 1958-61; staff Providence Hosp., Calif., Merritt Hosp., John Muir Med. Ctr. Hosp., Calif., Mt. Diablo Hosp., Concord, Calif., Summit Hosp., Oakland, Calif., Walnut Creek Hosp. Mem. AMA, Am. Coll. Surgeons, Calif. Med. Assn., ACCMA. Office: 3501 School St Lafayette CA 94549-4505 Office Phone: 925-284-5522. Personal E-mail: gecblue@aol.com.

COBB, HENRY NICHOLS, architect; b. Boston, Apr. 8, 1926; s. Charles Kane and Elsie Quincy (Nichols) C.; m. Joan Stewart Spaulding, June 5, 1953; children: Sara Quincy, Emma Trow, Pamela Codman. AB, Harvard U., 1947, MArch, 1949; DFA (hon.), Bowdoin Coll., 1985; D Tech. Scis (hon.), Swiss Fed. Inst. Tech., 1990. Designer in office Hugh Stubbins, 1949-50; mem. archtl. divsn. Webb & Knapp, Inc., 1950-60; ptnr. Pei Cobb Freed & Ptnrs. (formerly I.M. Pei & Ptnrs.), N.Y.C., 1960—. Vis. critic Yale U., 1963-66, Bishop vis. prof. architecture, 1973, 78, Davenport vis. prof., 1975; studio prof., chmn. dept. architecture Harvard U. Grad. Sch. Design, Cambridge, Mass., 1980-85. Prin. works include Pl. Ville Marie, Montreal, Can., 1962; acad. ctr. and residence halls State U. Coll., Fredonia, N.Y., 1967, John Hancock Tower, Boston, 1972, Collins Place, Melbourne, Australia, 1976, Wilson Commons, U. Rochester, 1976, World Trade Ctr., Balt., 1977, Dallas Ctr., 1979, Johnson & Johnson World Hdqrs., New Brunswick, N.J., 1981, 16th St. Mall, Denver, 1982, Mobil Rsch. Lab., Farmers Branch, Tex., 1983, Portland (Maine) Mus. Art, 1983, Arco Tower, Dallas, 1984, hdqrs. Pitney Bowes Corp., Stamford, Conn., 1985, Fountain Place, Dallas, 1986, Columbia Sq., Washington, 1986, Commerce Sq., Phila., 1987, First Interstate World Ctr., L.A., 1989, Anderson Grad. Sch. Mgmt. UCLA, 1994, AAAS Hdqrs., Washington, 1997, U.S. Courthouse, Boston, 1998, World Trade Ctr., Barcelona, 1999, Head Office ABN-AMRO Bank, Amsterdam, 1999, Coll.-Conservatory of Music, U. Cin., 1999, Tour EDF, Paris, 2001, 2099 Pennsylvania Ave., Washington, 2001, Friend Ctr. for Engring. Edn., Princeton U., 2001, U.S. Courthouse, Hammond, Ind., 2002, World Trade Ctr. and Grand Marina Hotel, Barcelona, 2002, Nat. Constn. Ctr., Phila., 2003. Trustee Am. Acad. in Rome, 1972-90, Brearley Sch., 1975-80. Served with USNR, 1944-46. Recipient Topaz medallion for excellence in archtl. edn. Assn. Collegiate Schs. of Architecture/AIA, 1995. Fellow AIA (medal of honor N.Y. chpt. 1982), Am. Acad. Arts and Scis.; mem. AAAL (Arnold W. Brunner Meml. prize in architecture 1977), NAD. Office: Pei Cobb Freed & Ptnrs 88 Pine St New York NY 10005

COBB, HOWELL, federal judge; b. Atla., Dec. 7, 1922; s. Howell and Dorothy (Hart) C.; m. Torrance Chalmers (dec. 1963); children: Catherine Cobb Cook, Howell III, Mary Ann Cobb Walton; m. Amelie Suberbielle, July 3, 1965; children: Caroline Cobb Ervin, Thomas H., John L. Student, St. John's Coll., Annapolis, Md., 1940-42; LLB, U. Va., 1948. Assoc. Kelley & Ryan, Houston, 1949-51, Fountain, Cox & Gaines, Houston, 1951-54, Orgain, Bell & Tucker, Beaumont, 1954-57, ptnr., 1957-85; judge U.S. Dist. Ct. (ea. dist.) Tex., Beaumont, 1985—. Mem. jud. coun. U.S. Ct. Appeals (5th cir.), 1994-97; mem. adv. com. East Tex. Legal Svcs., Beaumont. Pres. Beaumont Art Mus., 1969, bd. dirs., 1967-68; mem. vestry St. Stephens Episcopal Ch., Beaumont, 1973; mem. bd. adjustment City of Beaumont, 1972-82; trustee All Saints Episcopal Sch., Beaumont, 1972-76. 1st lt. USMC, 1942-45, PTO. Mem.: ABA, Maritime Law Assn. U.S., Am. Bd. Trial Advs., Am. Judicature Soc., Jefferson County Bar Assn. (sec. 1960, bd. dirs. 1960—61, 1967—68), State Bar Tex. (grievance com. 1970—72, chmn. 1972, admissions com. 1974—, bd. dirs. 1993—94, adv. mem.). Office: US Dist Ct 118 US Courthouse PO Box 632 Beaumont TX 77704-0632 Business E-Mail: howell_cobb@txed.uscourts.gov.

COBB, HUBBARD HANFORD, magazine editor, writer; b. N.Y.C., Aug. 5, 1917; s. Frank I. and Margaret Hubbard (Ayer) C.; m. Elizabeth Youngblood Simon, Feb. 6, 1954. Grad., Avon Old Farms Sch., Conn., 1936. Bldg. editor Am. Home mag., 1952-61, editor, 1961-69; author syndicated column home problems, 1946-60; condr. radio program home bldg., 1947-54; contbg. editor Woman's Day mag., 1972-84. Author: How to Build Your Dream House, 1948, Home Handyman's Guide, 1949, Homeowners Guide to Remodeling, 1950, Complete Homeowner, 1965, The Dream House Encyclopedia, 1970, How to Buy and Remodel the Older House, 1972, How to Paint Anything, 1972; (with Betsy Cobb) Vacation Houses--All You Should Know Before You Buy or Build, 1973, City People's Guide to Country Living, 1973, Preventive Maintenance for Your House or Apartment, 1975, Improvements That Increase the Value of Your House, 1976, Woman's Day Homeowners Handbook, 1976, (with Betsy Cobb) Your Barn House, 1991, American Battlefields, 1995. With USAAF, World War II. Mem. Authors Guild. Home: 60 Main St Apt 203 Deep River CT 06417

COBB, JEANNE BECK, education educator, researcher, consultant; b. Thomasville, N.C., Apr. 5, 1948; d. Howard Paul and Thelma Lorene (Clanton) Beck; m. James Paul Cobb, June 10, 1974; children: James Alexander, Rebecca Jeanne. BS in Elem. Edn., West Carolina U., 1970; MS in Elem. Edn. and Reading, U. Tenn., 1971, EdD in Reading and Lang. arts, 1992. Cert. tchr. Tex., reading specialist Tex. Title one tchr. Decatur (Ga.) City Schs., 1976-80; grad. tchg. asst. U. Tenn., Knoxvlle, 1989-92, asst. dir. Reading Ctr., 1991-92; adj. prof. U. North Tex., Denton, 1992-93, lectr., site coord. Evers Park Profl. Devel. Sch., 1995-99, from lectr. to asst. prof., 1993—2002, TAMS selection com., 1995-96, dir. reading clinic, dir. Am. Reads, dir. reading svcs. child and family resource clinic; assoc. prof. reading Ea. N.Mex. U., Portales, 2002—. Adj. prof. Tex. Wesleyan U., Ft. Worth, 1992-93; cons. Greenhill Sch., Dallas, 1995; reviewer Multicultural Edn., 1995—. Contbr. articles to profl. jours. Dir. Sat. sch. scholars First Christian Ch., Ft. Worth, 1997-99; teams vol. L.D. Bell H.S., Hurst, Tex., 1996-97; active PTA Ga., Tenn., Tex., 1985-96; band boosters fundraiser HEB Parent Assn., Hurst, 1996—; asst. chair clinical divsn. nat. reading conf. Coll. Reading Assn., 2001-03, chair clin. divsn., 2003—. Mem. Internat. Reading Assn. (corr. sect. 1971—), Nat. Coun. on Rsch. in Lang. and Literacy, Assn. Childhood Edn. Internat., Internat. Listening Assn. (edn. task force 1994-2001), Phi Kappa Phi, Alpha Delta Kappa. Democrat. Avocations: reading, hiking, camping, collecting children's china and old basal readers. Mailing:

4336 Tiffani Amarillo TX 79109 Home: 1401 W 17th St Portales NM 88130 Office: Eastern NMex Univ Sch Edn Station 25 Portales NM 88130 Office Phone: 505-562-2201. E-mail: jbcobb2940@hotmail.com.

COBB, JOHN BOSWELL, JR., clergyman, educator; b. Kobe, Japan, Feb. 9, 1925; s. John Boswell and Theodora Cook (Atkinson) C.; m. Jean Olmstead Loftin, June 18, 1947; children: Theodore, Clifford, Andrew, Richard. MA, U. Chgo. Div. Sch., 1949, PhD, 1952. Ordained to ministry United Meth. Ch., 1950. Pastor Towns County Circuit, N.Ga. Conf., 1950-51; faculty Young Harris Coll., Ga., 1950-53, Candler Sch. Theology and Emory U., 1953-58, Sch. Theology, Claremont, Calif., 1958-90; Avery prof. Claremont Grad. Sch., 1973-90; ret., 1990; mem. commn. on doctrine and doctrinal standard United Meth. Ch., 1968-72; mem. commn. on mission, 1984-88. Author: A Christian Natural Theology, 1965, The Structure of Christian Existence, 1967, Christ in a Pluralistic Age, 1975, (with Herman Daly) For the Common Good, 1989. Dir. Ctr. for Process Studies. Fulbright prof. U. Mainz, 1965-66; fellow Woodrow Wilson Internat. Ctr. for Scholars, 1976 Mem. Am. Acad. Religion, Am. Metaphys. Soc. Business E-Mail: cobbj@cgu.edu.

COBB, JOHN CANDLER, medical educator; b. Boston, July 8, 1919; s. Stanley and Elizabeth Mason (Almy) C.; m. Helen Imlay-Franchot, July 27, 1946; children: Loren, Nathaniel, Bethany, Julianne. BS in Astronomy cum laude, Harvard U., 1941, MD, 1948; MPH, Johns Hopkins U., 1954. Diplomate Nat. Bd. Med. Examiners, Am. Bd. Preventive Medicine and Pub. Health; lic. physician, Conn., Md., N.Mex. Intern Yale New Haven Hosp., 1948-49, fellow in pediatrics, 1949-50; jr. asst. resident Yale Psychiatric Clinic, 1950-51; instr. pediatrics Johns Hopkins U., 1951-56, asst. prof. hygiene, 1954-56; cons. Indian Health divsn. USPHS, Albuquerque, 1956-60; prof. preventive medicine U. Colo., Denver, 1965-85, emeritus prof., 1985—, chmn. dept., 1966-73. Dir. med. social rsch. project on population Govt. of Pakistan, 1960-64; cons. Am. Friends Svc. Com., Algeria, 1964; short term cons. WHO, Indonesia and Western Pacific Region, 1969, 70-73, USAID, Togo and Niger, 1979; exch. prof. Guangxi Med. Coll., Nanning, China, 1985-86; coord. ethics seminars U. Health Scis. Ctr., 1980-85; pres. World Hand Assocs., 1985--; cons. in field. Contbr. numerous articles to profl. jours. Bd. dirs., pres. Am. Assn. Planned Parenthood Physicians, 1966-67; chmn. Task Force for Preparing 314(b) Agy. Grant Application, 1969; mem., chmn. health com. of Gov. Lamm and U.S. Congressman Wirth's Task Force on Rocky Flats Nuc. Weapons Plant, Denver, 1974-75; mem. Gov.'s Task Force on Health Effects of Air Pollution, 1978-79; commr. Air Pollution Control Commn. of Colo., 1976-79; mem. air quality policy com. Denver Regional Coun. of Govts., 1978-80, environ. council, U. Colo., 1970-75, Gov.'s Sci. adv. Counc., Colo., 1973-80, Gov.'s Blue Ribbon Task Force on Transp., Colo., 1977; bd. dirs. ROMCOE Ctr. for Environ. Problem Solving, 1978-81, Colo. Coalition for Full Employment, 1978-80; mem. Am. Friends Svc. Com. Adv. Group on Rocky Flats/Nuclear Weapons Project, 1979-85; owning mem. Chaordic Commons. Recipient Florence Sabin award Colo. Pub. Health Assn., 1979, Jack Gore Meml. Peace award Am. Friends Svc. Com., 1980; U.S. EPA grantee, 1975-82. Mem. AAAS, WHO, Internat. Solar Energy Soc., Am. Solar Energy Soc., Internat. Physicians for Prevention of Nuclear War (del. to Congresses in Moscow and Montreal), Appropriate Rural Tech. Assn. (bd. dirs. 1987-2002, v.p. 1991-92), Nat. Resources Def. Coun. (bd. advisors 1991-92), N.Mex. Solar Energy Assn. (bd. dirs. 1995-98), Physicians for Human Rights, Physicians for Social Reponsibility. Home and Office: # 4320 10501 Lagrima De Oro NE Albuquerque NM 87111

COBB, KAY BEEVERS, judge, retired state senator; b. Quitman County, Miss., Feb. 28, 1942; m. Larry Cobb; children: Barbara Cobb Murphy, Elizabeth Cobb DeBusk. BS, Miss. U. Women; JD, U. Miss. Atty. priv. practice, Oxford, Miss., 1978—84; dir. prosecutors prog. U. Miss. Law Sch.; atty. Miss. Bureau of Narcotics, 1984—88; various positions including coord. SWEEPS anti-drug prog. Office of Miss. Atty. Gen., 1988—92; senator State of Miss., 1992—96; atty. priv. practice, Oxford, 1996—99; assoc. justice Miss. Supreme Ct., 1999—, presiding justice, 2004—. Former mem. President's Commn. on US Model State Drug Laws, Nat. Alliance for Model State Drug Laws. Mem. Miss. Bar Assn. (Chief Justice award 2003), Vets. Aux., C. of C. Baptist. Office: Miss Supreme Ct PO Box 117 450 High St Jackson MS 39205 Home: PO Box 604 Oxford MS 38655-0604 Office Phone: 601-359-2099.

COBB, MICHAEL, principal; s. Sherman Joseph and Anita Joan (Gamache) Cobb; m. Regina Ann Cobb, Apr. 11, 1992; children: Jeff Wiler, Andrew Wiler. BA in Humanities, St. Joseph's Coll., Mountain View, Calif., 1986; STB cum laude, Gregorian U., Rome, 1989; MA in Pastoral Theology magna cum laude, U. St. Thomas, Rome, 1990; post grad. in Edn., U. Calif., Riverside, 2000—. Credential tchg. with bilingual cross-cultural lang. acad. devel. emphasis Calif., 1995, adminstrv. svc. Calif., 1998, 1st degree black belt Jin Mu Hapkido, 2001. Bi-lingual elem. tchr. Pomona Unified Sch. Dist., Calif., 1992—93, Rowland Unified Sch. Dist., LaPuente, 1993—99, program specialist Rowland Heights, 1999—2000, bilingual tchr., 2000—01; asst. prin. elem. Fontana Unified Sch. Dist., 2001—02, dist. coord., 2002—03, asst. prin. elem., 2003—04; prin. elem. sch. Pomona Unified Sch. Dist., 2004—. Religious edn. tchr. baptism team Our Lady of Assumption Ch., Claremont, Calif., 1993—2003; mem. St. Mark's Ch., Upland, 2003—. 2d lt. Res. USAF, 1989—94. Recipient Key Clubber of Yr. (Calif., Nev., Hawaii), Key Club Internat., 1976. Mem.: ASCD, Nat. Assn. Elem. Sch. Prins., Assn. Calif. Sch. Adminstrs., Am. Ednl. Rsch. Assn. Democrat. Episcopalian. Avocations: martial arts, travel.

COBB, MILES ALAN, retired lawyer; b. Salt Lake City, May 8, 1930; s. Miles Cobb and June (Ray) Cobb Wilson; children: Jennifer, Melissa, Mary. BS, U. Calif.-Berkeley, 1953, LL.B., 1958. Bar: Calif. 1958. Assoc. Bronson, Bronson & McKinnon, San Francisco, 1958-65, ptnr., 1965-76, 78-84; gen. counsel FDIC, Washington, 1976-78; pres. Bell Savs & Loan Assn., San Mateo, Calif., 1984-85. Author: Federal Regulation of Depository Institutions, 1984. Served to 1st lt. U.S. Army, 1953-55; Korea Democrat. Avocations: photography, golf, gardening. E-mail: macobb@sbcglobal.net.

COBB, NATHAN KNIGHT, physician; MD, Boston U. Sch. of Medicine, 1997—2001. Diplomate Internal Medicine Am. Bd. of Internal Medicine, 2004. Chief med. officer QuitNet Inc, Boston, 2001—. Mem.: Am. Med. Informatics Assn., Soc. for Rsch. on Tobacco and Nicotine, Mass. Med. Soc. Office: QuitNet Inc 1 Appleton St Jamaica Plain MA 02116 E-mail: nate@quitnet.com.

COBB, ROWENA NOELANI BLAKE, real estate broker; b. Kauai, Hawaii, May 1, 1939; d. Bernard K. Blake and Hattie Kanui Yuen; m. James Jackson Cobb, Dec. 22, 1962; children: Shelly Ranelle Noelani, Bret Kimo Jackson. BS in Edn., Bob Jones U., 1961; broker's lic., Vitousek Sch. Real Estate, Honolulu, 1981. Lic. real estate broker, Honolulu; cert. residential specialist, 1995-. Med. supr. Hawaii Med. Svc. Assn., 1964-65, 66-68; bus. mgr. Micronesian Occupl. Ctr., Koror Palau, 1968-70; prin. broker Cobb Realty, Lihue, Hawaii, 1983—; sec. Neighbor Island MLS Svc., Honolulu, 1985-87, vice chmn., 1987-88; chmn. MLS Hawaii, Inc., Honolulu, 1988-90. Assoc. editor Jour. Entymology, 1965-66. Sec. Koloa Cmty. Assn., 1981-98, pres., 1989, bd. dirs. 2002-04, dir., 05—; mem. Hoi'Ke Pub. TV, 1998—, treas., 1999, v.p., 2002, pres. 2000-2002, 2003-04; vice chair Kauai Schs. Adv. Coun., 1995-98, pres., 2000; mem. adv. bd. KKCR Radio, 2000; bd. dirs. Kekahu Found, 1999-2001, Kauai United Way, 2003-04, 05—; chmn. Kauai Ctr. Arts, Edn. and Tech., 2003, 04, 05. Mem. Nat. Assn. Realtors (grad. Realtors Inst., cert. residential specialist), Hawaii Assn. Realtors (cert. tchr., state bd. dirs. 1984, v.p. 1985, dir. 1995-96, 2004—), Kauai Bd. Realtors (v.p. 1984, pres. 1985, bd. dirs. 1995-97, treas. 1999, Realtor Assoc. of Yr. award 1983, Realtor of Yr. award 1986), Kauai C. of C., Soroptomists (bd. dirs. Lihue chpt. 1986-89, treas. 1989). Avocations: reading, music, travel. Office: PO Box 157 Koloa HI 96756-0157 Office Phone: 808-742-9497. Business E-Mail: ro@jrcobb.net.

COBB, RUTH, artist; b. Boston, Feb. 20, 1914; d. Charles Edward and Bessie (Cohen) C.; m. Lawrence Kupferman, Apr. 29, 1937; children: Nancy Rose, David. Diploma, Mass. Coll. Art, 1935. One-woman shows include Shore Galery, Boston, 1958, 60, 63, 65, 70, DeCordova Mus., Lincoln, Mass., 1955, Art Unlimited Gallery, San Francisco, 1961, Cober Gallery, N.Y.C., 1962, 65, 67, McNay Mus., San Antonio, 1966, Phila. Art Alliance, 1962, Galerie Moos, Montreal, Que., Can., 1969, Witte Mus., San Antonio, 1967, Harold Ernst Gallery, Boston, 1974, 75, 76, Midtown Gallery, N.Y.C., 1981, 82, Foster Harmon Gallery, Sarasota, 1984, Francesca Anderson Gallery, Boston, 1984, 87, Cen. Pl. Galleries, Bangor, Maine, 1988, Thayer Acad., Braintree, Mass., 1994, Cataumet (Mass.) Art Ctr., 1997, A.R.A. Gallery, Hamilton, Mass., 1999, Women Studies Rsch. Ctr. Brandeis U.; featured in exhbn. Boston's Honored Artists, Danforth Mus., Framingham, Mass., 1995; represented in permanent collections Boston Mus. Fine Arts, Brandeis U., Butler Inst. Am. Art, Munson-Williams-Proctor Inst., Addison Gallery Am. Art, Va. Mus. Fine Arts, DeCordova Mus., Tufts U.; featured in TV program Artist At Work, 1981; work featured in Am. Artist mag., 1979, Newton mag., 2004. Recipient awards Pa. Acad. Fine Arts, 1967, awards Allied Artists N.Y.C., 1966 Mem. Am. Watercolor Soc. (award), New Eng. Watercolor Soc., Allied Artists Am. (award), NAD (award)*

COBB, STEPHEN A., lawyer; b. Moline, Ill., Jan. 27, 1944; s. Archibald William and Lucile Bates C.; m. Nancy L. Hendrix, Dec. 18, 1971. AB cum laude, Harvard U., 1966; MA in Sociology, Vanderbilt U., 1968, PhD in Sociology, 1971, JD, 1977. Bar: Tenn. 1978, U.S. Dist. Ct. (mid. dist.) Tenn. 1978. Asst. prof. Tenn. State U., Nashville, 1970-74, dept. head, 1972-74; mem., chair edn. oversight com. Tenn. Ho. Reps., Nashville, 1974-86; pvt. practice law Nashville, 1978-86; with Waller Lansden Dortch & Davis, Nashville, 1986-90, ptnr., 1990—2005. Fulbright Jr. lectr. U. Caen, France, 1977—78; lectr. dept. sociology Fisk U., 1981—86. Former pres. Sister Cities of Nashville, Inc.; mem. So. Regional Edn. Bd., former vice chmn commn. ednl. quality. Decorated officer Ordre des Palmes Academiques (France); recipient Paul Simon Internat. award, 1990, Edwin Cudeki Internat. Bus. award, 1992; NDEA fellow, NIMH fellow, 1966-70. Mem. ABA, Am. Immigration Lawyers Assn., Tenn. Bar Assn., Tenn Fgn. Lang. Inst., Nashville Bar Assn., Fedn. Alliances Francaises (former pres.), Order of Coif. Home: 1929 Castleman Dr Nashville TN 37215-3901

COBB, SUE MCCOURT, diplomat, lawyer, educator; b. Aug. 18, 1937; d. Benjamin Arnold and Ruth (Griffin) McCourt; m. Charles E. Cobb Jr., Feb. 28, 1959; children: Christian McCourt, Tobin Templeton. BA, Stanford U., 1959; JD, U. Miami, 1978. Bar: US Supreme Ct., Fla. 1978, Colo., DC 1989. Tchr. Crystal Springs Sch. for Girls, Hillsborough, Calif., 1960—68; CEO Fla. Dept. Lottery; founding ptnr. pub. fin. dept. Greenberg-Traurig Law Firm; US Amb. to Jamaica, 2001—05; ptnr. Cobb Ptnrs., Ltd., Coral Gables, Fla. Chmn. bd. Fed. Res. Bank, Miami br., 1984, 1986, 1988; chmn. Dade County Super Bowl Authority, 1982—87; bd. dirs. Ransom-Everglades Sch., 1976—86; dir. United Way, Dade County; founder, sponsor Dept. of State's Cobb Award for Initiative and Success in Trade Devel. Recipient Order of the Falcon, Grand Cross Knight, Iceland, Humanitarian of Yr. award, Red Cross, Silver Medallion award, Nat. Conf. Christians and Jews. Achievements include being the first female US Chief of Mission at Embassy Kingston. Avocations: scuba diving, skiing, tennis. Office Phone: 305-441-1700. Business E-Mail: scobb@cobbpartners.com.

COBB, TY, lawyer; b. Great Bend, Kans., Aug. 25, 1950; s. Grover Cowling and Elizabeth Anne (McCleary) C.; m. Leigh Elliott Stevenson, Aug. 21, 1976; children: Chance Wyatt, Chelsea Leigh, Brady Elliott, Chloe Elizabeth. AB, Harvard U., 1972; JD, Georgetown U., 1978. Bar: D.C. 1979, U.S. Dist. Ct. D.C. 1979, U.S. Dist. Ct. Md. 1979, U.S. Ct. Appeals (4th and D.C. cirs.) 1979, U.S. Ct. Internat. Trade 1980, U.S. Ct. Appeals (3d cir.) 1987, U.S. Supreme Ct. 1986, Md. 1987, Colo. 1998, U.S. Ct. Appeals (10th cir.) 1999. Legis. adminstrv. asst. U.S. Ho. of Reps., Washington, 1974-75; law clk. to fed. judge U.S. Dist. Ct., Balt., 1978-79; assoc. Collier, Shannon, Rill & Scott, Washington, 1979-81; asst. U.S. atty. Office of U.S. Atty., Balt., 1981-86; chief criminal cases Office U.S. Attorney, Balt., 1984-86; mid-Atlantic regional coord. Organized Crime Drug Enforcement Task Force U.S. Dept. Justice, Balt., 1985—86; ptnr. Hogan & Hartson LLP, Washington and Balt., 1988-98, mng. ptnr. Denver, 1998—, dir. litig. practice group. Spl. trial counsel Office of Ind. Counsel HUD, 1994-95; instr. U.S. Atty. Gen.'s Adv. Inst., U.S. Dept. Justice, 1983-86; mem. Jud. Conf. of U.S. Ct. Appeals (4th cir.); trustee Grand Canyon Trust, 2004—. Contbr. articles to profl. jours. Chmn. Md. lawyers Dole for Pres., 1986-87; counsel Forest Glen Park Civic Assn., Montgomery County, Md., 1981-84, Colo. Fed. Jud. Selection Com., 2001—; bd. trustees Grand Canyon Trust, 2004—. Fellow Am. Coll. Trial Lawyers (com. on fed. criminal procedure); mem. ABA, Internat. Bar Assn., Harvard Alumni Assn. (bd. dirs. 1990-92), Congress of Fellows Ctr. for Internat. Legal Studies. Republican. Office: Hogan & Hartson LLP 555 13th St NW Ste 800 E Washington DC 20004-1161 also: Hogan & Hartson LLP One Tabor Ctr 1200 17th St Ste 1500 Denver CO 80202-5835 Office Phone: 202-637-6437, 303-899-7300. Office Fax: 202-637-5910. Business E-Mail: tcobb@hhlaw.com.*

COBB, VIRGINIA HORTON, artist, educator; b. Oklahoma City, Nov. 23, 1933; d. Wayne and Ruth (Goodale) Horton; m. Bruce L. Cobb, Dec. 30, 1951 (div. 1985); children: Bruce Wayne, Juliann, William Stuart, M. Jerrold Friedman, 1988. Student, U. Colo., 1966-67, Community Coll., Denver, 1967; student of, William Schimmel, Ariz., 1965-66, Edgar Whitney, N.Y.C., 1966, Chen Chi, 1974. Comml. artist and designer Ruth Horton Studios, Oklahoma City, 1954-63; instr. seminars, 1974—, N.Mex. Watercolor Soc., Albuquerque, 1976, Okla. Mus. Art, Oklahoma City, 1976, Upstairs Gallery Workshops, Arlington, Tex., 1977, 78, 79, 80, St. Louis Art Guild, 1980, Alaska Water Color Soc., Anchorage, 1981, Needham (Mass.) Art Center, 1981, N.C. Watercolor Soc., Charlotte, 1981, San Diego Watercolor Soc., 1981, S.C. Water Color Soc., Florence, 1981, Hawaii Water Color Soc., 1989, Trillium Workshops, Toronto, 1989, 90, Baffin Island, 1992, Maui, Hawaii, 1993, Vancouver Island, 1990, 91. Guest instr. Crafton Hills Coll. Master Seminars, Yucaipa, Calif., 1979, 80, 81, U. Alaska, Anchorage, 1981, Master Class/Santa Fe Painting Workshops/Friedman Cobb Studios, 1989—; guest lectr. Watermedia 2000, Houston; lectr. Sta. KRDO-TV, 1977, Francis Marion Coll., Florence, 1981, Sta. KAKM, Anchorage, 1981. Author: Discovering The Inner Eye, 1988; author (with Jerrold Friedman) Alice...on bristol, 1996, (with Polly Hammett) Designsense, 2003; contbr. articles to art publs.; one-woman shows of watercolor paintings, Jack Meier Galleries, Houston, 1979-81, 83-85, One Artist: San Juan Coll., 1995, Art Resources, St. Paul, 1988, Sturh Mus., Grand Island, Nebr., 1982; group shows include recent acquisitions of the Nat. Acad., 1982, layering, an art of time and space, 1985, NAD, N.Y.C., 1978, 79-81, San Bernardino (Calif.) County Mus., 1978, Nat. Watercolor Invitational, Rochester, N.Y., 1981, Rocky Mountain Nat. Watermedia Exhbt., Golden, Colo., 1978, 79, 81, Albuquerque Mus. Art, 1985, Am. Watercolor Soc., 1985; invitational exhbns. include Internat. Waters: A Touring Exhibit, Canada, 1991, USA, 1992, Great Britain, 1992, Scotland, 1993; represented in permanent collections, NAD, Jefferson County (Colo.) Public Library, Foothills Art Center, Golden, Colo., St. Lawrence U., Canton, N.Y., N.Mex. Watercolor Soc., Albuquerque, Santa Fe Mus. Fine Arts. Recipient Foothills Art Ctr. award, 1976, Edgar Fox award Watercolor U.S.A., 1973, Denver award Rocky Mountain Nat. Exhbn., 1981, Am. Artist Achievement award, 1994. Mem. NAD (Walter Biggs Meml. award 1978, 81), Nat. Watercolor Soc. (Strathmore Paper Co. award 1975), Am. Watercolor Soc. (Paul B. Remmey Meml. award 1974,. Arches Paper Co. award 1977, Edgar Whitney award 1978, Mary Pleishner Meml. award 1980, High Winds medal 1981, Silver medal of Honor 1983, guest demonstrator 1980, nat. juror 1981, Dolphin fellow 1982, juror Watercolor West 1990, Juror award 1999), N.Mex. Watercolor Soc. (hon.), Rocky Mountain Watermedia Soc. E-mail: veacobb@yahoo.com.

COBB, WILLIAM C., Internet company executive; BSc, U. Pa.; MBA, Northwestern U. From v.p. new bus. to sr. v.p., chief mktg. officer Tricon Restaurants Internat. PepsiCo, sr. v.p., chief mktg. officer Tricon Restaurants Internat.; sr. v.p. global mktg. eBay Inc., San Jose, Calif.; pres. eBay N. Am., San Jose, Calif., 2005—. Office: eBay Inc 2145 Hamilton Ave San Jose CA 95125-5905

COBB, WILLIAM THOMPSON, environmental and agricultural consultant; b. Spokane, Wash., Nov. 10, 1942; s. Elmer Jean and Martha Ella (Napier) C.; m. Sandra L. Hodgson, Aug. 29, 1964 (div. 1988); children: Mike, Melanie, Megan, Bill II. BA, Ea. Wash. U., 1964; PhD, Oreg. State U., 1973. Cert. profl. agronomist, profl. plant pathologist, crop advisor, environ. inspector. Mgr., agronomist Sun Royal Co., Royal City, Wash., 1970-74; sr. scientist Lilly Rsch. Labs., Kennewick, Wash., 1974-87; environ. and agrl. cons. Cobb Cons. Svcs., Kennewick, Wash., 1988—. Bd. dirs. Bentech Labs., Portland, Oreg., 1989; dir. spl. projects Bioremediation, Inc., Lake Oswego, Oreg., 1990-92; adv. bd. Adv. Coun. Tri-Cities, Wash., 1991. Contbr. articles to profl. jours. 1st lt. U.S. Army, 1964-67. Mem. Am. Phytopath. Soc., Weed Sci. Soc. Am., We. Soc. Weed Sci., Am. Soc. Agronomy, N.W. Assn. Environ. Profls., Nat. Assn. Environ. Profls., N.Y. Acad. Scis., Environ. Assessment Assn., Sigma Xi. Republican. Home and Office: Cobb Cons Svcs 815 S Kellogg St Kennewick WA 99336-9369

COBBAN, WILLIAM AUBREY, paleontologist; b. Anaconda, Mont., Dec. 31, 1916; s. Ray Aubrey and Anastacia (McNulty) C.; m. Ruth Georgina Loucks, Apr. 15, 1942; children: Georgina, William, Robert. BA, U. Mont., 1940; PhD, Johns Hopkins U., 1949. Geologist Carter Oil Co., Tulsa, 1940-46; paleontologist U.S. Geol. Survey, Washington, 1948-92, emeritus scientist, 1992—. Contbr. numerous articles to profl. jours. Recipient Meritorious Svc. award Dept. Interior, 1974, Disting. Svc. award U.S. Dept. Interior, 1986; honoree 6th Internat. Symposium, Cephalopods--Recent and Past, 2004. Fellow AAAS, Geol. Soc. Am.; mem. Soc. Econ. Paleontologists and Mineralogists (hon.; Disting. Pioneer Geologist award 1985, Raymond C. Moore Paleontology medal 1990), Rocky Mountain Assn. Geologists (hon.), Mont. Geol. Soc. (hon.), Wyo. Geol Assn. (hon.), Paleontol. Soc. Am. (Paleontol. medal 1985), Assn. Petroleum Geologists, Paleontol. Rsch. Inst. (Gilbert Harris award 1996), Rocky Mountain Assn. Geologists (Outstanding award 2001), Phi Beta Kappa, Sigma Xi. Republican. Mem. United Ch. of Christ. Office: US Geol Survey Federal Ctr PO Box 25046 # 980 Denver CO 80225 Office Phone: 303-236-5670.

COBBE, JAMES HAMILTON, economics professor; b. July 24, 1946; arrived in U.S., 68, naturalized, 85; s. Clifford James and Beatrice Aileen (Blake) Cobbe; m. Louise Grant Barrett, June 14, 1969; 1 child, Andrew van Leer. BA, U. Cambridge, 1968; MPhil, Yale U., 1970, PhD, 1977. Fellow Yale U., New Haven, 1968—72; rsch. economist Carnegie Endowment for Internat. Peace, N.Y.C., 1971; lectr. in econs. London Sch. Econs. and Polit. Sci., 1972—73, U. Botswana, Lesotho and Swaziland, 1973—76; asst. prof. econs. Fla. State U., Tallahassee, 1976—81, assoc. prof., 1981—86, prof. econs., 1986—, assoc. dean Coll. Social Scis., 1985—91, dir. interdisciplinary program social sci., 1985—89, interim dean Coll. Social Scis., 1986—87, dir. grad. program in econs., 1992—97, chmn. dept. econs., 1997—, vice chmn. faculty sen. steering com., 2002—05, pres., faculty senate and trustee, 2005—. Invited rsch. fellow Inst. So. African Studies Nat. U. Lesotho, 1981—82; cons. in field. Author: Governments and Mining Companies in Developing Countries, 1977, Lesotho: Dilemmas of Dependence in Southern Africa, 1985; contbr. articles to profl. jours., chpts. to books. Mem.: Soc. Internat. Devel., African Studies Assn., So. Econ. Assn., Am. Econ. Assn., Fla. Economic Club, Leander Club (Henley, Eng.), Hawks Club (Cambridge, Eng.). Democrat. Home: 2012 E Randolph Cir Tallahassee FL 32308-3354 Office: Fla State U Dept Econs Tallahassee FL 32306-2180 Office Phone: 850-644-7091. E-mail: jcobbe@mailer.fsu.edu.

COBBLE, JAMES WIKLE, chemistry professor; b. Kansas City, Mo., Mar. 15, 1926; s. Ray and Crystal Edith (Wikle) C.; m. Margaret Ann Zumwalt, June 9, 1949 (dec.); children— Catherine Ann, Richard James. Student, San Diego State Coll., 1942-44; BA, No. Ariz. U., 1946; MS, U. So. Calif., 1949; PhD, U. Tenn., 1952. Chemist Oak Ridge Nat. Lab., 1949-52; postdoctoral research asso. U. Calif., Berkeley, 1952-55, instr. dept. chemistry, 1954; asst. prof. dept. chemistry Purdue U., Lafayette, Ind., 1955-58, asso. prof., 1958-61, prof., 1961-73; prof., dean Grad. div. San Diego State U., 1973—; v.p. rsch., dean Grad. divsn. San Diego State U., 1997—. Cons. in field. Contbr. articles to sci. publs. Mem. bd. visitors USAF Air Univ., 1984—92, chmn., 1988—90; vpres. San Diego State Univ. Found., 1975—; trustee Calif. Western Law Sch., 1987—93; mem. Joint Grad. Bd., 1973—78; Lt. (j.g.) USNR, 1945—46. Recipient E.O. Lawrence award U.S. AEC, 1970, Disting. Svc. award USAF, 1992; Guggenheim fellow, 1966; Robert A. Welch Found. lectr., 1971. Fellow Am. Inst. Chemists, Am. Phys. Soc.; mem. Am. Chem. Soc., Sigma Xi, Phi Kappa Phi, Alpha Chi Sigma, Phi Lambda Upsilon. Home: 1380 Park Row La Jolla CA 92037-3709 Office: San Diego State Univ Grad & Rsch Affairs San Diego CA 92182-8020

COBBS, PRICE MASHAW, social psychiatrist; b. LA, Nov. 2, 1928; s. Peter Price and Rosa (Mashaw) C.; m. Evadne Priester, May 30, 1957 (dec. Oct. 1973); children: Price Priester, Marion Renata; m. Frederica Maxwell, May 26, 1985 AB, U. Calif.-Berkeley, 1953; MD, Meharry Med. Coll., 1958. Intern San Francisco Gen. Hosp., 1958-59; psychiat. resident Mendocino State Hosp., Talmage, Calif., 1959-61, Langley Porter Neuro-Psychiat. Inst., San Francisco, 1961-62; pres., CEO Pacific Mgmt. Systems, San Francisco, 1967—; CEO Cobbs, Inc. Mgmt. cons. in workforce diversity numerous cos., govt. agys. and community projects; conducted seminars UN, Dept. State; guest lectr. leading colls. and univs.; chair 1st Ann. Nat. Diversity Conf., San Francisco, 1991; speaker 1st Internat. Diversity Conf., Johannesburg, South Africa, 1991; vis. cons., lectr. workforce diversity, South Africa, 1993; co-founder, pres. Renaissance Books, Inc.; adv. bd. Black Scholar. Author: My American Life: From Rage to Entitlement, 2005, (with William H. Grier) Black Rage, 1968, The Jesus Bag, 1971, (with Judith L. Turnock) Cracking the Corporate Code: From Survival to Mastery, 2000; contbr. State of Black America 1988, 89. Bd. dirs. Lucille Packard Found. for Children's Health; founding mem. Diversity Collegium. Served to cpl. U.S. Army, 1951-53 Recipient Pathfinder award Assn. Humanistic Psychology, 1993. Fellow Am. Psychiat. Assn.; mem. Nat. Med. Assn., NAACP (life), Nat. Acad. Scis.; charter mem. Nat. Urban League. Achievements include pioneering in discipline of ethnotherapy to understand differences in race, culture and ethnicity. Office: Pacific Mgmt System 3528 Sacramento St San Francisco CA 94118-1850*

COBEN, HARLAN, writer; b. Newark; m. Anne Armstrong-Coben; 4 children. BS in Polit. Sci., Amherst Coll., 1984. Author: (novels) Drop Shot, 1996, Back Spin, 1997, One False Move, 1999 (Fresh Talent award, W.H. Smith booksellers, UK), The Final Detail, 1999, Darkest Fear, 2000, Deal Breaker, 2000, Tell No One, 2001 (NY Times, London Times, Le Monde, Publishers Weekly, LA Times, San Francisco Chronicle bestseller lists, nominee Edgar award, nominee Macavity award, nominee Anthony award, nominee Barry award, recipient Le Grand Prix des Lectrics de Elle for fiction, France), Gone For Good, 2002 (NY Times, London Times, Le Monde, Publishers Weekly, LA Times, San Francisco Chronicle bestseller lists, Thumping Good Read award, W.H. Smith, UK), No Second Chance, 2003 (NY Times, London Times, Le Monde, Publishers Weekly, LA Times, San Francisco Chronicle bestseller lists, Internat. Book of the Month Club pick), Fade Away, 2004, Just One Look, 2004 (NY Times, London Times, Le Monde, Publishers Weekly, LA Times, San Francisco Chronicle bestseller lists), The Innocent, 2004 (Publishers Weekly bestseller list, 2005), (short stories) A Simple Philosophy (nominee Anthony award, nominee Macavity award, nominee Agatha award), The Key to My Father. Recipient Edgar Allan Poe award, Mystery Writers of Am., Anthony award, World Mystery Conf., Shamus award, Private Eye Writers of Am. Office: c/o Dutton Books Penguin Group USA 375 Hudson St New York NY 10014 Personal E-mail: me@harlancoben.com.*

COBEY, RALPH, industrialist; b. Sycamore, Ohio, Aug. 15, 1909; m. Hortense Kohn, Feb. 28, 1944; children: Minnie, Susanne. ME, Carnegie Inst. Tech., 1932; D.Sc. (hon.), Findlay Coll., 1958. Pres. Perfection Steel Body Co., Galion, Ohio, 1945-70, Perfection-Cobey, Co., Galion, Ohio, 1949-70, Eagle Crusher Co., 1954-90, chmn. bd., 1990—; pres. Philips-Davies Co., 1965-70, Cobey Co., 1946-70, Diamond Iron Works, 1972-90, Austin-Western Crusher Co., 1974-90, Scoopmobile Co., 1978-90, Madsen Co., 1979-90, World Wide Investment Co., 1950—. Aide in preparation of prodn. and design of Army tanks OPM, 1939-42. Mem. contbg. com. NCCJ, 1951-55, now area chmn. spl. gifts com.; founder, pres. Harry Cobey Found.; area chmn. U.S. Savs. Bonds; mem. pres.'s adv. coun. for devel. Ashland Coll., Ohio, mem. Ohio Gov.'s Citizens' Task Force on Environ. Protection, 1971-72, Pres.'s Tax Com., 1962-66; pioneer chaplain svcs. in indsl. plants; mem. Ohio Expns. Commn., 1964, Radio Free Europe Com.; chmn. Cmty. Heart Fund Campaign, 1971-72; pres., spl. gifts chmn. Crawford County Heart Fund, 1972-78; mem. Ohio fin. bd. Heart Fund, 1973—; mem. Ohio Rep. Fin. Com.; mounted dep. sheriff, Morrow County (Ohio), 1974-84; bd. dirs., chmn. long range planning com. Johnny Appleseed Area coun. Boy Scouts of Am.; hon. life mem. Galion Cmty. Ctr.; trustee Galion City Hosp. Found. Bd.; mem. pres.'s coun. Ohio State U.; chmn., founder Minnie Cobey Meml. Libr.; founder, chmn. bd. trustees Louis Bromfield Malabar Farm Found.; bd. dirs. Morrow County United Appeals; State of Ohio amb. of natural resources; numerous other civic activities. Capt. USAAF, 1942-46, 51, Korea. Baden-Powel World fellow King Carl Gustaf of Sweden, 1992; recipient Disting. Citizen of Yr. award Heart of Ohio Coun., Boy Scouts Am., 1995, Lifetime Commitment to Humanitarianism award from Rep. Joan Lawrence, Ohio Ho. Reps., 1996, award Louis Bromfield Soc., 2001, resolution from Ohio Dist. 5 Agy. on Aging, Cert. of Appreciation USDA, 2003; inductee Ohio State Fair Hall of Fame, 1992, Ohio Agrl. Hall of Fame, 1999, Ohio Natural Resources Hall of Fame, 2001, Ohio Sr. Citizens Hall of Fame, 2002, N. Ctrl. Ohio Entrepreneural Hall of Fame, 2003; Ralph Cobey Day in City of Galion, 1995, City of Bucyrus, 1999. Mem. NAM, Nat. Assn. 4-H Clubs, Future Farmers Am., U.S. C. of C. (mem. taxation, fgn. affairs, labor rels. coms.), Masons (32 degree), Shriners (sec.-treas.). Home: 4270 State Route 309 Galion OH 44833-9618 Office: Eagle Crusher Co Inc PO Box 537 Galion OH 44833-0537

COBLE, ALYSSA GANGAROSA, music educator, conductor; d. Clara Amalfi Gangarosa; m. John Thomas Coble; m. John Thomas Coble, Aug. 6, 1988. MusB in Edn., Augusta State U., 1987; MusM in Edn., Fla. State U., 1990. Kodaly Certification Ind. U., 1997. Dir. of adult and children's choirs Ctrl. Christian Ch., Augusta, Ga., 1986—88; band dir. Columbia Mid. Sch., Appling, Ga., 1987—88; music dir. First United Meth. Ch., Bainbridge, Ga., 1989—91; choral and gen. music tchr. Hutto Mid. Sch., 1990—91; choral, handbell, and gen. music tchr. Clay Jr. H.S., Carmel, Ind., 1994—95; asst. dir. Columbus Ind. Children's Choir, Columbus, Ind., 1996—2002, Indpls. Children's Choir, Indpls., 1995—2002; music tchr. Bunker Hill Elem. Sch., 1991—94, 1995—2002; music specialist Kemp Elem. Sch., Powder Springs, Ga., 2002—; artistic dir. Ga. Young Singers of KSU, Marietta, Ga., 2003—. Guest condr. Ga. Music Educators' Assn. Statewide Elem. Honor Chorus, Ga., 2003; guest condr., workshop clinician So. Wash. and Oreg. Kodaly Educators' Honor Choir, Portland, Oreg., 2004; guest condr. Midwest Kodaly Educators of Am. Region Conv. Honor Choir, Indpls., 2004; choral dir. U. of Mich. Flint Jr. Acad. of Music, Flint, Mich., 1999—; guest condr., Tex., 2005—. Pres. Augusta Coll. Concert and Jazz Bands, Augusta, Ga., 1985—87. Recipient Ga. All-State Coll. Band, Ga. Music Educators Assn., 1986 and 1987; Maxwell Music scholar, Augusta State U., 1983-1987. Mem.: Music Educators Nat. Conf., Am. Choral Dirs. Assn., Orgn. of Am. Kodaly Educators, Pi Kappa Lambda Nat. Music Honor Soc., Pi Kappa Lambda. Office: Kemp Elem Sch 865 Corner Rd Powder Springs GA 30127 Office Phone: 678-594-8158. Office Fax: 678-594-8160. E-mail: alyssa.coble@cobbk12.org.

COBLE, FREDERICK CHARLES, retail executive; b. Sanford, Fla., Mar. 22, 1961; s. Joseph Henry and Alicia Alejandro Coble; m. Gayle Coble, May 20, 1989. BS, U. Va., 1982. CPA, Va. Audit mgr. KPMG LLC, Norfolk, Va., 1982—87; internal audit mgr. Royster Co., Norfolk, 1987—89; contr. K&K Toys, Inc./Only One Dollar Inc., Norfolk, 1989-91; v.p., contr. Dollar Tree Stores, Inc., Norfolk, 1991—97, CFO Chesapeake, Va., 1997—2004, sr. v.p., corp. sec., 2004—. Mem. AICPA, Va. Soc. CPAs, Beta Alpha Psi, Beta Gamma Sigma. Office: Dollar Tree Stores Inc 500 Volvo Pkwy Chesapeake VA 23320

COBLE, JOHN HOWARD, congressman, lawyer; b. Greensboro, N.C., Mar. 18, 1931; s. Joseph Howard and Johnnie (Holt) C. Student, Appalachian State U., 1949-50; AB in History, Guilford Coll., 1958; JD, U. N.C., 1962. Bar: NC 1966. Field claim rep., supt. State Farm Mut. Ins., 1961-67; asst. county atty. Guilford County, N.C., 1967-69; mem. N.C. Ho. of Reps., Raleigh, 1969, 1979—83; asst. U.S. atty. U.S. Dist. Ct. (mid. dist.) N.C., 1969-73; sec. N.C. Dept. Revenue, Raleigh, 1973-77; atty. Turner, Enochs & Sparrow, Greensboro, 1979-84; mem. U.S. Congress from 6th N.C. dist., Washington, 1985—; mem. judiciary com., transp. and infrastructure com. Served to capt. USCG, 1952-56, comdg. officer USCGR. Mem. N.C. Bar Assn., Greensboro Bar Assn., Masons (33 degree; master Mason), Am. Legion, VFW, Lions, SAR. Republican. Presbyterian. Office: US Ho of Reps 2468 Rayburn Ho Office Bldg Washington DC 20515-3306 Office Phone: 202-225-3065.*

COBLE, MISTIE LINKER, elementary school educator; d. Larry Charles and Barbara Jones Linker; m. Todd Andrew Coble, Nov. 20, 1999; 1 child, Landri Noel. BA in Elem. Edn., Mars Hill Coll., 1996; M of Elem. Edn., Wingate U., 1999. Tchr. 1st and 2d grades Stanly County Schs., Albemarle, NC, 1996—. Tchr. Sunday sch. Big Lick Bapt. Ch., Oakboro, NC, 1999—, children's leader, 1996—2000, mem. choir, 1990—. Avocations: writing, reading, scrapbooks, photography.

COBLE, PAUL ISHLER, advertising agency executive; b. Indpls., Mar. 17, 1926; s. Earl and Agnes Elizabeth (Roberts) C.; m. Marjorie M. Trentanelli, Jan. 27, 1951; children: Jeffery Mansfield, Sarah Anne Davis, Douglass Paul Coble. AB, Wittenberg U., 1950; postgrad., Case-Western Res. U., 1950-53. Reporter Springfield (Ohio) Daily News, 1944; reporter, feature writer Rockford (Ill.) Register-Republic, 1947-48; account exec. Fuller & Smith & Ross, Inc., Cleve., 1949-57; dir. sales promotion McCann Erickson, 1957-63; dir. sales devel. Marschalk Co., 1963-65, v.p., 1965-70, sr. v.p., 1970-73; pres. Coble Group, 1973—; chmn. bd., sec.-treas. Hahn & Coble, Inc., advt., mktg. and pub. relations, 1977—. Pub. Islander mag., Hilton Head Island, S.C., 1973-83; asst. prof. advt. W.Va. U., 1982-83. Chief instr. Cleve. Advt. Club Sch., 1961-73. Contbr. articles to profl. pubs. Active fund raising drives for various charitable and youth orgns.; bd. dirs. The Deep Well Project Inc. Served with AUS, 1944-46. Mem. Sales and Marketing Internat., Assn. Indsl. Advertisers, Cleve. Advt. Club, Newcomen Soc., Woodside Country Club, Sea Pines Country Club, Cleve. Rotary. Home: 106 Longwood Green Ct Aiken SC 29803-2751 E-mail: picoble@aol.com.

COBLE, YANK DAVID, JR., internist, endocrinologist; b. Burlington, NC, 1937; m. Shereth Landrum; 2 children. MD, Duke U., 1962; degree in clin. medicine of the tropics, London Sch. Hygiene and Tropical Medicine; DHL (hon.), U. North Fla., 2003. Diplomate Am. Bd. Internal Medicine, Am. Bd. Endocrinology. Intern N.Y. Hosp.-Cornell Med. Ctr., N.Y.C., 1962-63, resident, 1963-64; resident in internal medicine London Sch. Trop Medicine Hygiene, 1966-67; resident in endocrinology NIH, Bethesda, Md., 1967-68; fellow in endocrinology Vanderbilt Med. Sch., Nashville, Tenn., 1968-69; pvt. practice; clin. prof. medicine U. Fla., Jacksonville, chair dept. cmty. health and family medicine, prof. medicine and family medicine. Hosp. staff Univ. Hosp., 1970—, St. Luke's Hosp., 1970—, Bapt. Med. Ctr., 1970—, St. Vincents Med. Ctr., Jacksonville, Fla., 1970—; bd. dirs. Blue Cross/Blue Shield of Fla., Inc.; chmn. FLAMEDCO, Inc., Fla. Med. Ins. Trust; bd. dirs., exec. com. Fla. Physicians Ins. Co., Koger Equity Co.; dirs. adv. com. NIH; mem. nat. guidelines clearing house policy bd. AHRQ; advisor to U.S. delegation to WHO, 2003—. Pres. Jacksonville Cmty. Coun.; bd. dirs. Leadership Jacksonville, Big Bros., Arts Assembly, Jacksonville Enterprise Ctr. for Health Care Tech., Wesley Manor Retirement Village; bd. dirs. Rsch.! Am., 2001—, Nat. Osteoporosis Found., 2001—, Hospice NEF, 2001—04; roundtable on environ. health scis. Inst. Medicine, 2003—. Named Disting. Alumnus, Duke U., 2003. Master ACP (pres. emeritus), Am. Coll. Endocrinology (pres.); mem. AMA (trustee 1994-2004, pres. 2002-03, commr. joint commn. on accreditation of healthcare orgns., chair practice parameters partnership, clin. quality improvement forum governing bd., sec.-treas. bd. trustees, pres. edn. and rsch. found. 1995-97, chair audit com., fin. com., EVP search, town and gown com., continuing med. edn. adv. com. 1986-88, vice chair/chair coun. sci. affairs 1988-94), Fla. Med. Assn. (past pres., Cert. of Merit), Am. Assn. Clin. Endocrinologists (1st pres.), Jacksonville C. of C., World Med. Assn. (pres. 2004—), Am. Clin. and Climatol. Assn. Business E-Mail: ycoble@aace.com.

COBOS, PATRICIO, music educator; s. Henry A. and Maria V. Cobos; m. Andrea Marie Dean, Mar. 22, 1997. MusM in performance, Violin, Fla. State U., 1969. Violinist Atlanta Symphony, Atlanta, 1961—62; concert master Chattanooga Symphony, Chattanooga, 1962—66; prof. violin Winthrop U., Rock Hill, SC, 1969—74; concert master Charlotte Symphony, Charlotte, NC, 1971—75; artist in residence U. N.C., Charlotte, NC, 1973—75, SUNY, Buffalo, 1975—79; first violinist with profl. string quartet Rowe Quartet, 1973—83; coll. prof. violin Akron U., Akron, Ohio, 1980—83; prof. violin Columbus State U., Columbus, Ga., 1983—. Assoc. music dir. Nat. Symphony of Chile, Santiago, Chile, 1991—95; artistic dir., condr. Lago Ranco Music Festival, Lago Ranco, Chile, 1996—98; music dir., condr. LaGrange Symphony Orch., LaGrange, Ga., 2001—; concert master Macon Symphony Orch., Macon, Ga., 1984—; assoc. concert master Columbus Symphony Orch., Columbus, Ga., 2001—. Toured as first violinist with a profl. string quartet U.S. State Dept. Recipient Peabody Award, George Foster Peabody, 1977, Silver Medal, N.Y. Film Festival, 1977, Award in Performing Arts, Nat. Assn. of TV Program Executives, 1977, Gabriel Award, 1977;, Rockefeller Found., 1961, Fellowship in Violin, Koussevitzky Found., 1968. Mem.: Phi Mu Alpha (life). Achievements include New York debut as first violinist of the Rowe Quartet in 1977 at the Lincoln Center, returned to perform at the Lincoln Center in 1978; Served on the Faculty of Switzerland's Sommer Musikowochen; Founded the University of North Carolina-Charlotte Orchestra; Toured Spain and Italy as a violinist with the Atlanta Virtuosi; Violin soloist in Japan and Germany 1996 - 1997; Performed with the Garth Newel Chamber Players in France in 1998. Home: 6901 Sandstone Ct Columbus GA 31907 Office: Columbus State University 4225 University Ave Columbus GA 31907

COBURN, ANDREW, writer; b. Exeter, N.H. s. Andrew and Georgiana (Nedeau) C.; m. Geraldine Knapp, 1951 (div. 1954); m. Bernadine Casey, 1955; children: Cathleen, Krista, Lisa, Heather. Student, Suffolk U., 1954-58; LittD (hon.), Merrimack Coll., 1987. City editor Lawrence (Mass.) Eagle-Tribune, 1963-73; copy editor, book reviewer Boston Globe, 1973-78; columnist Mass. newspapers, 1978-82. Author: The Trespassers, 1974, paperback edit., 1980, The Babysitter, 1979, paperback edit., 1980 (also several translations), Off Duty, 1980, paperback edit., 1983 (German and French transl.), Company Secrets, 1982 (German transl.), Widow's Walk, 1984 (French transl.), Sweetheart, 1985 (German, Japanese, Swedish, Norwegian, Czech, French transl.), Lovenest, 1987 (German transl.), Goldilocks, 1989 (German transl.), No Way Home, 1992 (Japanese and French transl.), Voices in the Dark, 1994, Birthright, 1997 (Polisy transl.); (movies) Toutes Peines Confondues, 1992 (based on Sweetheart), Noyade Interdite, 1989, Un Dimanche de Flics, 1985 (based on Off Duty). Eugene Sexton fellow Harper & Row, 1966. Democrat. Home: 3 Farrwood Dr Andover MA 01810-5206

COBURN, ANDREW F., research scientist educator; AB, Brown U., 1972; EdM, Harvard U., 1975; PhD, Brandeis U., 1981. Cons. Maine Dept. Human Svcs., 1977-81; chair policy bd. Bingham Cortium for Health Rsch., 1988; dir. Health Policy Ctr., 1981-88; assoc. prof. Edmund S. Muskie Inst. of Public Affairs, 1986—, assoc. dir. for rsch. programs, 1986—. Mem. gov.'s task force on maternal and child health, 1979-80; mem. Cumberland County Child Abuse and Neglect Coun., 1980-82; steering com. Nat. Acad. for State Health Policy, Washington, 1988—. Reviewer Med. Care, Policy Studies Jour., Social Sci. and Medicine, Jour. of Health Politics, Policy and Law, Health Care Financing Rev.; contbr. numerous articles to profl. jours. Office: University of Southern Maine Edmund S Muskie Inst of Pub Aff 96 Falmouth St Portland ME 04103-4864

COBURN, D(ONALD) L(EE), playwright; b. Balt., Aug. 4, 1938; s. Guy Dabney and Ruth Margaret (Somers) C.; m. Nazlee Joyce French, Oct. 24, 1964 (div. Sept. 1971); children: Donn Christopher, Kimberly; m. Marsha Woodruff Maher, Feb. 22, 1975. Student pub. schs., Balt. Propr. Don Coburn & Assocs., Balt., 1966-70; with Stanford Agy., Dallas, 1970-73; propr. Donald L. Coburn Corp. Cons., Dallas, 1973-75; ind. playwright, 1975—. Playwright: The Gin Game, 1977 (Pulitzer prize in drama 1978, Tony award nomination 1978, Golden Apple 1978), Bluewater Cottage, 1979, The Corporation Man, 1981, Currents Turned Awry, 1982, Guy, 1983, Noble Adjustment, 1986, Anna-Weston, 1988, Return to Blue Fin, 1991; (screenplays) Flights of Angels, 1987, A Virgin Year, 1992; (teleplay) Hollywood Presents: The Gin Game, 2002. Served with USNR, 1958-60. Mem. Authors League Am., Writers Guild Am., Tex. Inst. Letters, Soc. des Auteurs et Compositeurs Dramatiques. Office Phone: 212-445-0160. E-mail: playwright@earthlink.net.

COBURN, JAMES LEROY, academic administrator; b. Oak Park, Ill., Nov. 21, 1933; s. Forest Edward and Myrtle Emmaline (Clarke) C.; m. Julianne Whitty, Sept. 3, 1955; children: James, Gregory, Julie, Cheryl. BA, North Cen. Coll., Naperville, Ill., 1956; MS, No. Ill. U., 1965; EdD, Vanderbilt U., 1983. Cert. tchr., guidance counselor, supt., Ill. Tchr. Luther South High Sch., Chgo., 1956-58, Maine Township High Sch. East, Park Ridge, Ill., 1958-61, dean, counselor, 1961-64; dir. student pers. svcs. Maine Twp. High Sch. South, Park Ridge, 1964-67; asst. prin. for staff Maine Twp. High Sch. West, Des Plaines, Ill., 1967-73, prin., 1973-97; ret., 1997. Cons. Pitts. Pub. Schs., 1965; chmn. Ill. Blue Ribbon Com. on Edn., Bloomington, 1988; spkr. Internat. Edn!. Symposium, South Korea, 1996. Editor: Growth through Reading, 1960, 61. Pres. Inter-Suburban Assn.; chmn. judges 4th of July Parade, Des Plaines, 1980-86; mem. Des Plaines Beautification Com., 1987, Des Plaines Mayor's Adv. Com., 1989—; Ill. state commr. North Ctrl. Assn., 1992-95; pres. Des Plaines chpt. United Way, 1995—; twp. sch. trustee Maine, 1996—; pres. Twp. Sch. Bd. Caucus, 2002. Recipient Those Who Excel award Ill. Bd. Edn., 1977, Disting. Educator's award Idea Inst., 1984. Mem. Nat. Assn. Secondary Sch. Prins., Am. Assn. Sch. Adminstrs., Ill. Prins. Assn., Intersuburban Assn. Prins. (pres. 1986—), Des Plaines C. of C. (bd. dirs 1980-85, 92-95), Rotary (pres. Des Plaines 1976-77, Most Valuable Mem. award 1979, Paul Harris fellow 1989, John Vaughin excellence in edn. award 1997). Lutheran. Avocations: reading, travel, recreational sports, gardening. Home: 1843 Locust St Des Plaines IL 60018-2326 E-mail: jim0181@comcast.net.

COBURN, LEWIS ALAN, mathematics professor; b. Austin, Tex., Aug. 16, 1940; s. Nathaniel and Ann (Block) C.; m. Charlaine Elizabeth Ackerman, June 19, 1966; 1 child, Elinor Nadia. BS, U. Mich., 1961, MS, 1962, PhD, 1964. Asst. prof. NYU, N.Y.C., 1964-65, Purdue U., West Lafayette, Ind., 1965-66, Yeshiva U., N.Y.C., 1966-68, assoc. prof., 1968-72, prof. math., 1972-79; prof. SUNY, Buffalo, 1979—, chmn. dept. math., 1979-97. Mem. editorial bd. Jour. Integral Equations and Operator Theory, 1978—; contbr. over 40 articles to math. rsch. jours. NSF grantee, 1966—. Mem. Am. Math. Soc. Office: SUNY Dept Of Math Buffalo NY 14260-0001 Office Phone: 716-645-6284. Business E-Mail: lcoburn@buffalo.edu.

COBURN, MARJORIE FOSTER, psychologist, educator; b. Salt Lake City, Feb. 28, 1939; d. Harlan A. and Alma (Ballinger) Polk; m. Robert Byron Coburn, July 2, 1977; children: Robert Scott, Kelly Anne; children: Polly Klea Foster, Matthew Ryan Foster. BA in Sociology, UCLA, 1960; Montessori Internat. Diploma with honors, Washington Montessori Inst., 1968; MA in Psychology, U. No. Colo., 1979; PhD in Counseling Psychology, U. Denver, 1983. Lic. clin. psychologist. Probation officer Alameda County, Oakland, Calif., 1960—62; dir. Friendship Club, Orlando, Fla., 1963—65; probation officer Contra Costa County, El Cerrito, Calif., 1966, Fairfax County, Va., 1967; tchr. Va. Montessori Sch., Fairfax, 1968—70; spl. edn. tchr. Leary Sch., Falls Church, Va., 1970—72, sch. administr., 1973—76; tchr. Aseltine Sch., San Diego, 1976—77, Coburn Montessori Sch., Colorado Springs, 1977—79; pvt. practice psychotherapy Colorado Springs, 1979—82, San Diego, 1982—. Cons. in field. Author (with R.C. Orem): Montessori: Prescription for Children with Learning Disabilities, 1977; contbr. articles to profl. jours. Mem.: APA, Mensa, The Charter 100, San Diego Psychol. Assn., Calif. Psychol. Assn., Coun. Exceptional Children, Phobia Soc., Am. Orthopsychiat. Assn., Rotary. Episcopalian. Office: 836 Prospect St Ste 101 La Jolla CA 92037-4206 Office Phone: 858-456-5065.

COBURN, RICHARD JOSEPH, company executive, electrical engineer; b. N.Y.C., Nov. 4, 1931; s. Elmer Roswell and Marie Veronica (Greenan) C.; m. Catherine Elizabeth Wilkinson (div. 1992); children: Jenifer, Catherine, Steven; m. Elizabeth A. Semmler, Jan. 1993. BSEE, Yale U., 1954. Devel. engr. Hamilton Standard, Windsor Locks, Conn., 1954-59; chief engr. Dynamic Controls Corp., South Windsor, Conn., 1959-66; mgr. digital logic Fairchild Industries, Germantown, Md., 1966-68; co-founder, pres. Scan Optics, East Hartford, Conn., 1968-72; pres. Coburn Tech., East Hartford, 1972-77, KCR Tech., East Hartford, Conn., 1977-91; co-founder, chmn. Accent Color Sciences, Inc., East Hartford, Conn., 1993—2001; mgr. SentryTec, LLC, Bloomfield, Conn., 2001—. Mgr. Iconical Sys. LLC, 2004—. Mem. Yale Club, Franklin & Eleanor Roosevelt Inst. Republican. Roman Catholic. Achievements include invention of electronic back pressure control, radio noise free switch, apparatus for image reproduction. Home: 15 Stratford Park Bloomfield CT 06002-2143 Office Phone: 860-206-7017. Personal E-mail: dickacs@aol.com.

COBURN, ROBERT CRAIG, philosopher, educator; b. Mpls., Jan. 25, 1930; s. William Carl and Esther Therice C.; m. Martha Louise Means, July 12, 1974. BA, Yale U., 1951; B.D., U. Chgo., 1954; MA, PhD, Harvard U., 1958. Asst. prof. philosophy U. Chgo., 1960-65, assoc. prof., 1965-68, prof., 1968-71; prof. philosophy U. Wash., Seattle, 1971—. Vis. assoc. prof. philosophy Cornell U., 1966, U. Bergen, Norway, spring 1986; condr. NEH summer seminar, 1983; cons. ERDA. Author: The Strangeness of the Ordinary: Issues and Problems in Contemporary Metaphysics, 1989; contbr. articles to philos. jours., chpts. to books. Ordained elder Rocky Mountain Conf. United Methodist Ch. Andrew Mellon postdoctoral fellow in philosophy U. Pitts., 1961-62; NSF grantee, 1968-69 Mem. Am. Philos. Assn. (exec. com. Pacific div. 1973-74), AAUP, Soc. Values in Higher Edn., Phi Beta Kappa. Home: 6852 28th Ave NE Seattle WA 98115-7145 Office: Univ Wash Dept Philosophy Seattle WA 98195-3350 Office Phone: 206-543-5873.

COBURN, RONALD MURRAY, ophthalmologist, surgeon; b. Detroit, Aug. 25, 1943; s. Sidney and Jean (Goldberg) C.; m. Barbara Joan Levy, Feb. 21, 1969; children: Nicholas Scott, Lauren Joy. BS, Wayne State U., 1965, MD, 1969; postgrad., Kresge Eye Inst., 1971—74. Diplomate Am. Bd. Ophthalmology, Am. Bd. Eye Surgery (surg. examiner). Dir. The Coburn Clinic, Dearborn, Mich., 1976—; chief ophthalmology Straith Hosp. for Spl. Surgery, Southfield, Mich., 1985—2000; dir. Cataract Specialty Surgery Ctr., Berkley, Mich., 2003—. Cons. CooperVision, Inc., Bellevue, Wash., 1985-88, Alcon Surg., Inc., Ft. Worth, 1988—. Co-author: Lens-Stat Intraocular Lens Modeling System; editorial advisor Phaco and Foldables, 1990. Trustee Straith Hosp. for Spl. Surgery, 1986—. Capt. Mich. N.G., 1969-76. Fellow ACS, Internat. Coll. Surgeons, Soc. Eye Surgeons, Royal Soc. Medicine (London), Leadership Soc. ACS, Soc. for Excellence in Eye Care; mem. AAAS, Am. Soc. Cataract and Refractive Surgery, Am. Diabetes Assn., Mich. Ophthal. Soc., Wayne County Med. Soc., Rsch. To Prevent Blindness, N.Y. Acad. Scis., Internat. Assn. Ocular Surgeons, Internat. Eye Found., Soc. Geriatric Ophthalmology, Internat. Glaucoma Congress, Phi Beta Kappa. Achievements include design of Am. Med. Optics PC19LB intraocular lens, CILCO CPLU CP20 intraocular lenses, CooperVision CP10BG posterior chamber intraocular lens, Alcon CZ20BD intraocular lens. Home: 1490 W Long Lake Rd Bloomfield Hills MI 48302-1340 Office Phone: 313-561-4225. Personal E-mail: roncoburn45@hotmail.com.

COBURN, STEVEN D., composer, musicologist, educator, pianist; b. Albany, N.Y., Aug. 7, 1955; s. Richard and Nancy Coburn; m. Lynn K. Ostro, May 14, 1989; 1 child, Maxwell R. MusB, SUNY, Potsdam, 1978; MA, NYU, 1992, PhD, 2002. Adj. instr. Pace U., N.Y.C., 2003—. Asst. dir., accompanist The Pk. Slope Singers, Bklyn., 2000—; accompanist The Cmty. Chorus Bklyn., Bklyn., 2002—; piano instr. BrooklynPianoLessons.com; music dir. Stageworks Summer Repertory Theatre. Author: (book) Mahler's Tenth Symphony: Form and Genesis, Essential Exercises for the Development of Piano Technique; composer: (choral) Aspects of Prospect Park, Four Bird Songs, Alleluia, Jubilation, Motet, (chamber) String Quartet, Scherzo for Septet, Brass Quartet, Trumpet Sonata, Prelude and Allegro for Clarinet and Piano, (orchestral) Fantasy. Mem.: Soc. for Music Theory, Am. Musicol. Soc. Avocation: painting. Personal E-mail: stevendcoburn@aol.com.

COBURN, TOM (THOMAS ALLEN COBURN), senator; b. Casper, Wyo., Mar. 14, 1948; m. Carolyn Denton; 3 children. BS in Acctg., Okla. State U., 1970; MD, U. Okla., 1983. Mfg. mgr. ophthalmic divsn. Coburn Optical Industries, 1970-78; resident surgery St. Anthony's Hosp., 1983-84; resident in family practice U. Ark. Area Health and Edn. Ctr., 1984-86; family practice physician, obstetrician, 1986—94; mem. U.S. Congress from 2d Okla. dist., 1995-2001; commerce and sci. com.; co-chmn. Presidential Advisory Coun. on HIV & Aids, Wash., DC, 2002—; U.S. senator from Okla., 2005—. Mem. judiciary, energy & power, health & environment, oversight & investigations coms.; bd. dirs Optical Mfrs. Assn., 1973-74, Better Vision Inst., 1976-77, Family Rsch. Coun., Saxon Pub. Cp. Author (with John Hart): Breach of Trust: How Washington Turns Outsiders Into Insiders, 2003. Recipient Spl. Legis. award, OK Psychol. Assn., 1999. Republican. Office: US Senate 172 Russell Senate Office Bldg Washington DC 20510*

COCANOUGHER, ARTHUR BENTON, academic administrator; b. Lubbock, Tex., July 6, 1938; s. Arthur Clifton and Bonnie Odell (Ford) C.; m. Dianne Esther Reisenauer, May 27, 1967; children: Carolyn, David. Mgr. Gen. Electric Co., N.Y.C., 1962-67; asst. prof. U. So. Calif., Los Angeles, 1970-72; assoc. prof. So. Meth. U., Dallas, 1972-73; prof. mktg. U. Houston, 1973-75, chmn. dept., 1975-76, dean Coll. Bus., 1976-85, sr. v.p., provost, 1985-87; dean Tex. A&M U. Coll. Bus., College Station, 1987-2001, emeritus, disting. prof., 2001—; interim chancellor Texas A&M U. System, 2003—04. Trustee Investment Series Smith Barney, Citibank Mutual Fund-s;cons. in field. Contbr. articles to profl. jours. Bd. dirs. Better Bus. Bur., Houston, 1979-87, West Houston Assn., 1984-87. Served to 1st lt. U.S. Army, 1960-62. Recipient Nicholas Salgo award So. Meth. U., 1973, Outstanding Service award U. Houston Alumni Assn., 1982, Disting. Alumnus award Coll. Bus. U. Tex.-Austin, 1981. Mem. Am. Mktg. Assn., Acad. Mktg. Sci. Home: 4409 Nottingham Ln Bryan TX 77802-5904 Office: Tex A&M U Coll Bus Coll Bus 4112 Tamu College Station TX 77843-4112

COCCA, WILLIAM P., music educator; b. Buffalo, Jan. 24, 1952; s. William Anthony and Carmella Cocca; m. Wendy Sutton, July 18, 1981; children: Christina, William Lyle. BA in Music Edn., SUNY, Fredonia, 1974; MA in Music Edn., Ithaca Coll., 1987; cert. in ednl. adminstrn., SUNY, Fredonia, 1993. Music tchr. grades 7-12 LeRoy (NY) Ctrl. Sch., 1974—76, Greene (NY) Ctrl. Sch., 1976—85; mucis tchr. grades 9-12 Springville (NY) Griffith Inst., 1985—, music coord., 1993—. Mem.: Erie County Music Educators Assn. (mem. exec. bd. 1996—2000), NY State Sch. Music Assn. (Zone I rep. 2003—, ass-state brass judge 1990—), Kiwanis. Office: Springville Griffith Inst 290 N Buffalo St Springville NY 14141

COCCO, MARIE ELIZABETH, journalist; b. Malden, Mass., Jan. 15, 1956; d. Morris Alfred and Dorothy Anne (Colameta) C.; m. Thomas Neal Burrows, Sept. 4, 1982; children: Matthew C. Burrows., Michael C. Burrows. BA, Tufts U., 1978; MS, Columbia U., 1979. Journalist Daily Register, Shrewsbury, N.J., 1979-80, Newsday, L.I., N.Y., 1980—. Nat. syndication through The Washington Post Writers Group, 2002. Recipient Nat. Reporting award Sigma Delta Chi, 1991, Excellence in Editorial Writing award N.Y. State Pubs. Assn., 1992, N.Y. State AP award, 1997, 99. Mem. White House Corrs. Assn. (Barnet Nover award 1991), Nat. Press Club (Washington Corr. award 1991). Office: Newsday Washington Bur 1730 Pennsylvania Ave NW Washington DC 20006-4706

COCHÉ, JUDITH, psychologist, educator; b. Phila., Sept. 2, 1942; d. Louis and Miriam (Nerenberg) Milner; m. Erich Coché, Oct. 16, 1966 (dec. 1991); 1 child, Juliette Laura; m. John Anderson, Jan. 1, 1994. BA, Colby Coll., 1964; MA, Temple U., 1966; PhD, Bryn Mawr Coll., 1975. Diplomate Am. Bd. Profl. Psychology, lic. psychologist Pa., Md., N.J., Fla., cert. in group psychotherapy Nat. Registry Group Psychotherapists. Rsch. asst. Jefferson Med. Coll., 1965-66; diagnostician Law Ct., Aachen, Germany, 1967-68; staff psychologist N.E. Community Mental Health Ctr., Phila., 1969-74; family clinician Inst. Pa. Hosp., 1974-76; instr. psychology Drexel U., 1976-77; lectr. Med. Coll. Pa., 1977-78; asst. clin. prof. Hahnemann Med. Coll., Phila., 1979—; pvt. practice Phila., 1974—, N.J., 1985—; assoc. prof. psychiatry U. Pa., 1985—, clin. coord. Psychology, 1999—; assoc. clin. prof. psychology in psychiatry U. Pa. Med. Coll., 1986—; mem. faculty Family Inst. of Phila., 1990—; sr. cons. Phila. Child Guidance Clinic, 1992-96; assoc. clin. prof. psychology in psychiatry U. Pa. Med. Coll., 1986—. Clin. cons. Hilltop Prep Sch., 1977—86; clin. supr. Am. Assn. Marriage and Family Therapy. Co-author: Couples Group Psychotherapy, A Clinical Practice Model, 1990, Powerful Wisdom: Voices of Distinguished Women Psychotherapists, 1993; contbr. chapters to books, articles to profl. jours. Bd. dirs. Whitemarsh Art Ctr., 1977-78, Please Touch Museum, 1982-89; mem. prof. adv. bd. Parents Without Ptnrs., 1977-86; mem. adv. com. Pa. Ballet/Shirley Rock. Named Women of Distinction, Phila. Bus. Jour., 2004; grantee, Del. Children's Bur. Bryn Mawr Coll., 1974—75, Pa. Hosp., 1975—77. Fellow Am. Group Psychotherapy Assn.; mem. APA, Am. Assn. Marriage and Family Therapy (approved supr.), Am. Family Therapy Assn., Phila. Soc. Clin. Psychologists (pres. 1980-81), Family Inst. Phila., Pa. Psychol. Assn. (chmn. legis. com. 1982), Soc. Rsch. in Psychotherapy, Women's Exec. Forum (Phila.). Address: Acad House 1420 Locust St Ste 410 Philadelphia PA 19102-4202 also: Price Waterworks Bldg Ste 3023 359 96th St Stone Harbor NJ 08247 Office Phone: 215-735-1908.

COCHETTI, ROGER JAMES, international communications and internet company executive; b. Albany, N.Y., Apr. 11, 1950; s. Roger Peter and Mary Ann Cochetti; m. Mary Remmers. BS in Fgn. Svc., Georgetown U., 1972; postgrad., Johns Hopkins U., 1975; cert., Cambridge U., 1976, U. Va., 1986. Dir. Washington office UN Assn. of U.S.A., 1972-77; asst. dir. for legis. and pub. affairs U.S. Internat. Devel. Coop. Agy., Washington, 1978-81; dir. pub. and investor rels. Communications Satellite Corp., Washington, 1981-85, dir. investor and internat. rels., 1985-87, v.p. maritime bus. planning and devel., 1987-88, v.p. mobile bus. planning and devel., 1989-93; author, cons., lectr., 1993—; program dir. Internet policy and bus. planning IBM Corp., 1994-2000; sr. v.p. policy Network Solutions, Inc., 2000; sr. v.p. Veri Sign, 2001—03; cons. to Internet and technology industries, 2003; group dir. pub policy CompTIA Computing Tech. Industry Assn., 2004—. Cons. to John D. Rockefeller III, N.Y.C., 1975; bd. dirs. Truste, Inc., Internet Law and Policy Forum, Internet Edn. Found., Internet Content Rating Assn., Electronic Authentication Partnership, The Pub. Affairs Coun., Inc. Author: Mobile Satellite Handbook, 1994. N.Y. State Regents scholar, 1968. Mem. Pacific Telecommn. Coun., Nat. Press Club (Washngton), Princeton Club (N.Y.C.). Democrat. Roman Catholic. Office Phone: 703-812-1333. E-mail: roger@cochetti.us.

COCHRAN, CARA, dean; d. William H. and Jo Ann Dillard Cochran. BA, BS, So. Wesleyan U., 1986; MM, U. S.C., 1987; PhD, M of Theology, MDiv, MA, New Orleans Bapt. Theol. Sem., 2005. Lic. profl. counselor Divsn. Health Related Bds., Tenn., 2005, marital and family therapist Divsn. Health Related Bds., Tenn., 2004. Counselor intern Counseling Svcs. New Orleans, New Orleans, 2001—03; dir. clin. pastoral edn. program SE La. Hosp., Mandeville, 2002—03; asst. acad. dean, asst. prof. of counseling and psychology Psychol. Studies Inst., Chattanooga, 2004—, marital & family therapist, 2004—, individual & exec. coach, 2004—. Adj. instr. New Orleans Bapt. Theol. Sem., 2003. Contbr. book. Mem. adv. bd. women's individual outpatient program Pickens County Behavioral Health Svcs., SC, 1995—97. Fellow, New Orleans Bapt. Theol. Sem., 1999—2003. Mem.: Am. Assn. Marriage and Family Therapists, Christian Assn. Psychol. Studies. Office: Psychological Studies Inst 1815 McCallie Ave Chattanooga TN 37404 Office Phone: 423-266-4574.

COCHRAN, CAROLYN, library director; b. Tyler, Tex., July 13, 1934; d. Sidney Allen and Eudelle (Frazier) C.; m. Guy Milford Eley, June 1, 1963 (div.). BA, Beaver Coll., 1956; MA, U. Tex., 1960; MLS, Tex. Woman's U., 1970. Libr. Canadian (Tex.) High Sch., 1970-71; rep. United Food Co., Amarillo, Tex., 1971-72; libr. Bishop Coll., Dallas, Tex., 1975-76, St. Mary's Dominican, New Orleans, 1976-77, DeVry Inst. Tech., Irving, Tex., 1978-98, libr. dir. emeritus, 1998—. With Database Searching Handicapped Individuals, Irving, 1983—; vol. bibliographer Assn. Individuals with Disabilities, Dallas, 1982-85. Mem. Am. Coalition of Citizens with Disabilities, 1982-85, Assn. Individuals with Disabilities, 1982-86, Vols. in Tech. Assistance, 1985—, Radio Amateur Satellite Corp., 1985-86; sponsor 500, Inc., 1988-95. Reviewer Libr. Jour., 1974, Dallas Morning News, 1972-74, Amarillo Globe-News, 1970-71. Mem. Dallas regional adv. com. Tex. Commn. for the Blind, 2001. HEW fellow, 1967; honored Black History Collection, Dallas Morning News, Bishop Coll., Dallas, 1973. Mem. ALA, Spl. Libr. Assn., Am. Coun. of Blind (sec. Dallas chpt. 1997-99), Toastmistress Club (pres. 1982-83) (Irving). Personal E-mail: mabelhain2003@sbcglobal.net.

COCHRAN, FIELDING B., III, lawyer; b. Corpus Christi, Tex., Nov. 14, 1949; BA, So. Meth. U., 1971; JD, U. Tex., 1975. Bar: Tex. 1975. Ptnr. Vinson & Elkins LLP, Houston. Mem.: ABA, Houston Bar Assn., Tex. Bar Assn. Office: Vinson & Elkins LLP First City Tower 1001 Fannin St, Ste 2300 Houston TX 77002 Office Phone: 713-758-2817. E-mail: fcochran@velaw.com.

COCHRAN, GEORGE CALLOWAY, III, retired bank executive, lawyer; b. Dallas, Aug. 29, 1932; s. George Calloway and Miriam (Welty) C.; m. Jerry Bywaters, Dec. 9, 1961; children: Mary, Robert BA, So. Meth. U., 1954; JD, Harvard U., 1957; cert., La. State U. Sch. Banking, 1969. Bar: Tex. 1957. Assoc. Leachman, Gardere, Akin and Porter, Dallas, 1960-62; with Fed. Res. Bank of Dallas, 1962-76, sr. v.p., 1976-92, ret., 1992. Adv. com. Bank Ops. Inst., Tex. A&M U., Commerce, 1982—2003; mem. task force on truth in lending regulation Bd. Govs. of Fed. Res. Sys., Washington, 1968—69; bd. dirs. Am. Inst. Banking, Dallas, 1986—90; bd. dir. The Dance Coun., Dallas, 2004—. Hist. landmark survey task force City of Dallas, 1974-78. Capt. USAF, 1958-60 Recipient Warner award for svc. to dance The Dance Coun., Dallas, 1999. Mem. State Bar Tex., Phi Beta Kappa (pres. North Tex. Assn. 1998-2000), Harvard Club. Methodist. Home: 3541 Villanova St Dallas TX 75225-5008 Personal E-mail: ccjbc@earthlink.net.

COCHRAN, GEORGE MOFFETT, retired judge; b. Staunton, Va., Apr. 20, 1912; s. Peyton and Susie (Robertson) C.; m. Marion Lee Stuart, May 1, 1948; children— George Moffett, Harry Carter Stuart. BA, U. Va., 1934, LLB, 1936; LLD (hon.), James Madison U., 1991. Bar: Va. 1935, Md. 1936. Asso. law firm, Balt., 1936-38; partner firm Peyton Cochran and George M. Cochran, Staunton, 1938-64, Cochran, Lotz & Black, Staunton, 1964-69; justice Supreme Ct., Richmond, Va., 1969-87. Pres. Planters Bank & Trust Co., Staunton, 1963-69 Chmn. Woodrow Wilson Centennial Commn. Va., 1952-58, Va. Cultural Devel. Study Commn., 1966-68, Frontier Culture Mus. Va., 1986-98; mem. Va. Commn. Constl. Revisi on, 1968-69, Jud. Coun. Va., 1963-69, Va. Ho. Dels., 1948-66, Va. Senate, 1966-68; chmn. bd. dirs. Stuart Hall, 1971-86; mem. bd. visitors Va. Poly. Inst., 1960-68; trustee Mary Baldwin Coll., 1967-81, U. Va. Law Sch. Found., 1975-89, Woodrow Wilson Birthplace Found., 1955-93. Lt. comdr. USNR, 1942-46. Recipient Algernon Sydney Sullivan award Mary Baldwin Coll., 1981. Mem. ABA, Va. Bar Assn. (pres. 1965-66), Raven Soc., Soc. of Cin., Phi Beta Kappa, Phi Delta Phi, Beta Theta Pi. Episcopalian. Home and Office: 24 Ridgewood Dr Staunton VA 24401-2424

COCHRAN, GLORIA GRIMES, retired pediatrician; b. Washington, June 24, 1924; d. Paul DeWitt and Muriel Ann (Quackenbush) Grimes; m. Winston Earle Cochran, June 10, 1950 (dec. June 19, 2003); children: Edith Ann, Winston Earle, Jr., Donald Lee, Robert Edward. BS in Zoology, Duke U., 1945; MD, 1949; MPH, Johns Hopkins Sch. Hygiene, Balt., 1979. Diplomate Nat. Bd. Med. Examiners, 1950, Am. Bd. Pediatrics, 1958. Asst. resident Pathology Boston Children's Hosp., Boston, 1949—50, asst. resident Pediatrics, 1950—51; chief resident Pediatrics Charlotte Memorial Hosp., Charlotte, NC, 1952—53; clinic pediatrician, sch. med. advisor health dept. Montgomery County, Md., 1955—65; fellow in pediat. habilitation St. Christopher Hosp. for Children, Phila., 1965-66; assoc. dir. Child Development Clinic Baylor Med. Sch., Tex. Children's Hosp., 1966-72; dir. Northern Va. Child Devel. Field Svcs. Bur. Child Health State Health Dept. Commonwealth Va., 1972-76; coord. Handicapped Svcs. Children's Hosp. Nat. Med. Ctr., Washington, 1976-78; acting chief Divsn. of Svcs. to Children with Spl. Needs Bur. Sch. Health Svcs., Washington, 1982-89; retired, 1989. Cons. Head Start Program, Md., Va., Tex., Pa., D.C., 1965-89; bd. mem. Ctrs. for Handicapped, Silver Spring, Md., 1982-89; Child Health com. Med. Soc. D.C., Washington, 1976-91. Producer, editor: (teaching film) Challenge for Habilitation: The Child with Congenital Rubella Syndrome, 1976. Steering com. Rock Days Inter-Church Camp, Washington, 1978-82; bd. mem. Open Door Cmty. Ctr., Columbus, Ga., 1993-94; co-chair curriculum com. Columbus Coll. Acad. of Life Long Learning, Columbus, 1994. Mem. Am. Assn. Mental Retardation, Am. Med. Women's Assn., Assn. for Retarded Citizens, Am. Acad. Cerebral Palsy, Am. Acad. Pediatrics, Phi Beta Kappa, Delta Omega. Democrat. Methodist. Avocations: travel, gardening. Home: 800 Canadian Trails Dr Apt 147 Norman OK 73072-7658 Office Phone: 405-447-8207.

COCHRAN, J. GUYTON, JR., corporate financial executive; BBA, U. Ga., 1988; MBA, Ga. State U., 1995. Wire and cable controller bus. process design team Southwire, 1995—99, dir. fin., 1999—2000, v.p. fin., 2000—03, chief fin. officer, 2003—. Mem.: AICPA, Alumni Club Ga. State U., Alumni Club U. Ga. Office: Southwire 1 Southwire Dr Carrollton GA 30119

COCHRAN, JAMES ALAN, mathematics professor, department chairman; b. San Francisco, May 12, 1936; s. Commodore Shelton and Gwendolyn Audrey (Rosenau) C.; m. Katherine Koehler Kern, Sept. 6, 1958; children: Cynthia Royal, Sarah Lynn. BS in Physics, Stanford U., 1956, MS in Physics, 1957; PhD in Math., Stanford U., 1962. Mem. tech. staff, supr. applied math. Bell Telephone Labs. Inc, Whippany, N.J., 1962-72; prof. math. Va. Poly. Inst. and State U., Blacksburg, 1972-78; prof., chmn. dept. math. Wash. State U., Pullman, 1978-84, prof., 1978-89, campus exec. officer and founding dean tri-cities Richland, Wash., 1989-98, prof. math., 1999—2003, prof. emeritus, 2003—; staff assoc. First Presbyn. Ch., Kennewick, Wash., 2001—. Vis. prof. math. Stanford U., 1968-69, Wash. State U., 1977, U. NSW, Sydney, Australia, 1985, Southeast U., Nanjing, China, 1994; fgn. scholar math. and mechanics Nanjing Inst. Tech., 1984; vis. fellow Deakin U., Victoria, Australia, 1985, 87. Author: Analysis of Linear Integral Equations, 1972, Applied Mathematics: Principles, Techniques, and Applications, 1982, Advanced Engineering Mathematics, 1987; also articles. Mem. nat. coun. Boy Scout Am., 1973-76, 99-2001, mem. local coun., 1974-77, 82-84, 93—, coun. pres., 1999-2001, mem. western region, 1996-02; chmn. bd. commrs. Morris County (N.J.) Area Libr. Sys., 1971-72; mem. bd. dirs. Tri-Cities Sci. and Tech. Park Assn., 1990-2003, chmn., 1990-93; bd. dirs. Wash. Environ. Industry Assn., 1990-95, TRIDEC, 1996-2001; dir. state bd. Math. Engring. Sci. Achievement, 1992-2001; mem. Am. Pub. TV Stas. Bd., 1992-96; exec. com. Tri-Cities Commercialization Partnership, 1993-97; mem. Hanford Adv. Bd., 1994-2003; sr. advisor Tri-Cities Corp. Coun. for the Arts, 1991-2000; bd. trustees Tri-Cities Prep Found., 2003—. Recipient Silver Beaver award Boy Scouts Am., 1997, Disting. Eagle Scout award, 1997, Founders award Wash. State U., Tri Cities, 2003, God and Svc. award Presbyn. Ch. U.S.A., 2004; Gordon vis. fellow, Deakin U., Victoria, Australia, 1985. Mem. Am. Math. Soc., Math. Assn. Am., Soc. Indsl. Applied Math., Nat. Eagle Scout Assn. (young man pres. 1957-58, adviser 1958-71, Disting. Service award 1976), Phi Beta Kappa, Sigma Xi, Golden Key, Alpha Phi Omega. Republican. Presbyterian. Home: 1927 Cypress Pl Richland WA 99352-2414 Office: First Presbyn Ch 2000 W Kennewick Ave Kennewick WA 99336 E-mail: bigjim@jkms.com.

COCHRAN, JAMES KIRK, dean, oceanographer, educator, geochemist; BS summa cum laude, Fla. State U., 1973; M in Philosophy, Yale U., 1975, PhD in Geochemistry, 1979. Rsch. staff geochemist Yale U. dept. geology and geophysics, New Haven, 1979-81; asst. scientist dept. chemistry Woods Hole (Mass.) Oceanographic Instn., 1981-83; asst. prof. marine scis. SUNY, Stony Brook, 1985-90, assoc. prof., 1985-90, prof., 1990—, assoc dir. for rsch., 1990-92; assoc. dean for rsch. Marine Scis. Rsch. Ctr., SUNY, Stony Brook, 1992-94, dean, dir., 1994-98; rsch. assoc. dept. invertebrate paleontology Am. Mus. Natural History, N.Y.C., 1986—. Invited lectr., UCLA, 1979, vis. scholar, Dept. Oceanography, U. Wash., Seattle, 1982, vis. scientist Ctr. des Faibles Radioactivités CNRS, Gif sur Yvette, France, 1989; vis. fellow Program in Oceanic and Atmospheric Scis., Princeton (N.J.) U., 1990, vis. prof. Inst. di Geol. Marina, Bologna, Italy, 1992, 98; assoc. rschr. European Ctr. for Environ. Geoscis., Aix-en-Provence, France, 1998, 2000, 04, vis. scientist Internat. Atomic Engr. Agency, Monaco, 1999; mem. Group of Experts on Sci. Aspects of Marine Pollution and Internat. Atomic Energy Agy. working group to formulate an oceanographic model for dispersion of wastes disposed in the deep sea, 1980-82; sci. rep. to Phys. Oceanography Task Group of the Internat. Seabed Working Group, 1983-87; mem. Alvin Rev. Com., 1984-87, Joint Global Ocean Flux Steering Com., 1990-93; dir. summer course Processes in the Coastal Ocean, Bologna, Italy, 2000. Contbr. more than 100 articles to profl. jours. Mem. Am. Geophys. Union, Geochem. Soc., Oceanography Soc., Sigma Xi. Office: SUNY at Stony Brook Marine Sciences Rsch Ctr Stony Brook NY 11794-0001

COCHRAN, JOHN EUELL, JR., aerospace engineer, educator, lawyer; b. Dawson, Ala., May 22, 1944; s. John Euell and Beatrice Ann (Raley) Cochran; m. Gladys Carol Holdbrooks, Dec. 26, 1965; children: Christopher, Jonathan. BAE., Auburn U., 1966, MS, 1967; PhD, U. Tex.-Austin, 1970; JD, Jones Law Inst., 1976. Registered profl. engr., Ala.; bar: Ala. 1977. Asst. prof. aerospace engring. Auburn (Ala.) U., 1970-75, assoc. prof., 1975-78, alumni assoc. prof., 1978-80, alumni prof., 1980-81, prof., 1981—, assoc. athletic dir., 1981-84, interim head aerospace engring., 1992-93, head aerospace engring., 1993—. Cons. Northrup Svcs., Huntsville, Ala., 1970—71, U.S. Army Missile Command, Redstone Arsenal, Ala., 1975—82, SRS Tech., Huntsville, 1984—89, Dept. Justice, 1996—97, Boeing Co., 1998, others; pres. Eaglemark, Inc.; legal cons. Sigmatech, Inc. Assoc. editor: Jour. Guidance Control and Dynamics, 1989—91; contbr. articles to profl. jours. Tau Beta Pi fellow, 1965, Nat. Coll. Athletic Assn. fellow, 1965, NSF fellow, 1968. Fellow: AIAA, Am. Astronautical Soc.; mem.: NSPE, ABA, Ala. Soc. Profl. Engrs. (v.p. Auburn chpt. 1985, pres. 1986, Young Engr. of the Yr. 1980), Am. Helicopter Soc. Methodist. Achievements include (with others) analysis, simulation and reconstruction of aircraft accidents; research in areas of dynamics and control, spacecraft altitude dynamics and control; stability and control of aircraft including towed vehicles; missile launcher dynamics; simulation of aerospace and transportation systems; short courses/seminars on engineering topics and engineering law and ethics. Home: 1887 Prim Dr Auburn AL 36830-7545 Office: Auburn U 211 Aerospace Engring Buil Auburn AL 36849 Office Phone: 334-844-6800. Business E-Mail: jcochran@eng.auburn.edu.

COCHRAN, JOHN P., economics professor; b. Ft. Collins, Colo., Dec. 22, 1949; s. Ira Williams and Elizabeth Ann C.; m. I. Ann Cochran, Aug. 23, 1977. BA in Econs., Met. State Coll. of Denver, 1978; MA in Econs., U. Colo., 1981, PhD in Econs., 1985. Intern as sr. economist Colo. Pub. Utility Commn., summer 1986; asst. prof. econs. Met. State Coll. of Denver, 1986-90, chair of econs., 1990-94, assoc. prof. econs., 1990-96, prof. econs., 1996-97, chair and prof. econs., 1997—2003, interim dean sch. bus., 2004—. Vis. lectr. econs. Met. State Coll. of Denver, 1981-82, vis. asst. prof., 1982-86, dir. Ctr. for Econ. Edn., 1997-2003; adj. asst. prof. econs. Regis U., Denver, 1986-90; adj. scholar Ludwig von Mises Inst., 1997—; vis. prof. U. Colo., Boulder, 2001-2003; Mises Meml. lectr. at Austrian Scholars' Conf. 9, Ludwig Von Mises Inst., 2003; mem. faculty Young Am.'s Rd. to Freedom: The Friedrich Hayek Seminar at the Reagan Ranch Ctr., 2003; presenter in field. Co-author: (book) The Hayek-Keynes Debate: Lessons for Current Business Cycle Research, 1999; mem. editl. bd. Quar. Jour. Austrian Econ., 2004—; mem. editl. adv. bd. Indian Jour. Econs. and Bus., 2002—; contbr. articles to profl. jours.; editor books/publs. in field. Mem.: Golden Key Honor Soc. (Outstanding Scholar/Rsch. award 2002). Office Phone: 303-556-3218. Business E-Mail: cochranj@mscd.edu.

COCHRAN, JOHN R., III, bank executive; b. 1951; married. Graduate, Loyola College. Sr. v.p. MBNA Am. Bank Nat. Assn., Newark, Del., 1985-87; bd. dirs. MBNA Am. Bank N.A., Del., 1986—, exec. v.p., 1987-91, CEO, 1990-91; exec. v.p. MBNA Corp., Del., 1991; vice-chmn. bd. MBNA Am. Bank N.A., Del., 1991, chmn., CEO, 2003—. Office: MBNA Am Bank NA 1100 N King St Wilmington DE 19884

COCHRAN, KENNETH WILLIAM, toxicologist; b. Chgo., Nov. 2, 1923; m. Martha Louise Wells, May 10, 1945; children: Kenneth W. III, Kimberley W. Cochran Nelson (dec.). SB, U. Chgo., 1947, PhD, 1950. Rsch. asst. to instr., toxicity lab. and dept. pharmacology U. Chgo., 1946-52; from rsch. assoc., instr. to prof. emeritus U. Mich., Ann Arbor, 1952—. Contbr. articles to profl. jours. 1st lt. U.S. Army, 1943-46. Fellow AAAS; mem. Am. Soc. for Microbiology, Am. Soc. for Pharmacology and Exptl. Therapeutics, Mycol. Soc. of Am., N.Am. Mycol. Assn. (exec. sec. 1988-97). Home: 3556 Oakwood St Ann Arbor MI 48104-5213 Office Phone: 734-971-2552. Personal E-mail: kwcee@umich.edu.

COCHRAN, MARY LEFFLER, volunteer; b. May 4, 1921; d. Shepherd and Nora Elizabeth Leffler; m. John A. Cochran, July 10, 1943; children: Jacquelyn, Cynthia Cochran Johnston, Catherine Cochran Berg. Tchr. math. and history Anita (Iowa) H.S., 1942—43; timekeeper supr. Pratt-Whitney Aircraft, Kansas City, Mo., 1943—45; tchr. Ames (Iowa) H.S., 1945—46; psychometrist Boston U. Counseling Svc., 1947—49; prs. Delta Gamma Bldg. Corp., U. Ill., Urbana, 1953—56. Editor: (calendar) The Gardener's Year for 1980, 81; author: Fulfilling the Dreams, The Story of National Garden Clubs, Inc. 1929-2004, 2004. Sec. U. Ill. Commerce Wives, 1955—56; pres. So. Ill. U. Women's Club, Carbondale, 1961—62, newcomer's chmn., 1963—64; pres. Ariz. State U. Faculty Wives Club, Tempe, 1967—68; products chmn. Cactus-Pine coun. Girl Scouts U.S.A., 1967—68; pres. Salt River Panhellenic (Ariz.), 1973—75; sec. Ariz. State U. Lyric Opera Guild, 1976; asst. sutdio dir. Phoenix Studio Rec. for Blind, 1978—79; docent Desert Bot. Garden, Phoenix, 1987—, pres. vols., 1991—93, exec. com., 1993—. Mem.: P.E.O., Ariz. Fedn. Garden Clubs (rec. sec. 1976—79, pres. 1981—83, Pub. Rels. award 1979, Presdl. citation 1986), Nat. Garden Clubs (personnel chmn. 1983—85, corr. sec. 1985—87, rec. sec. 1987—89, historian 1993—2001, 2003—04, bd. dirs., Presdl. citation 1989, 1993, 1997, 1999, 2004, 2005), Desert Designers Club (pres. 1983—85), Tempe Garden Club (pres. 1977—79), Mortar Bd., Delta Gamma (chmn. Ariz. State U. adv. bd. 1965—67), Pi Lambda Theta, Pi Kappa Delta, Kappa Delta Pi. Home: 116 E Greentree Dr Tempe AZ 85284-3147 Personal E-mail: Leaflets@aol.com.

COCHRAN, MONA SHEINFELD, economics professor, consultant; b. Phila., Dec. 3, 1934; d. Samuel and Sara (Baram) Sheinfeld; m. Kendall Pinney Cochran, Dec. 19, 1975; children: Paula, Susan, Kenneth, Hersh BA, Rutgers U., New Brunswick, N.J., 1956; MA, Temple U., Phila., 1968; PhD, So. Meth. U., Dallas, 1966. Systems analyst RemingtonRand UNIVAC, Phila., 1956-58; rsch. analyst Coopers & Lybrand, N.Y.C., 1958-60; tchg. asst. So. Meth. U., Dallas, 1961-65; vis. rsch. scholar London Sch. Econs., 1981-82; acad. visitor U. York, Eng., 1981-82; prof. econs. Tex. Woman's U., Denton, Tex., 1965-91, prof. emerita, 1991—. Avocations: travel, sewing, entertaining. Home: 3765 Weeburn Dr Dallas TX 75229-2716

COCHRAN, RADEEN M., librarian; b. Gallup, N.Mex., Mar. 3, 1955; d. Elton W. and Maxine Elizabeth (Horton) Mann; m. Frederick Hayden Cochran, July 19, 1980. BS in Edn., Millersville State U., 1976, MS in Elem. Edn., 1982; student, Pa. State U., King of Prussia, Wilkes Coll. Cert. libr.; reading specialist. With Lancaster (Pa.) Catholic High Sch.; libr., elem. reading specialist Perkiomen Valley Sch. dist., Schwenksville, Pa.; libr. jr. high Northeastern Sch. Dist., Manchester, Pa.; libr. elem. Upper Perkiomen Sch. Dist., East Greenville, Pa. Upper Perkiomen Sch. Dist. grantee. Mem.: Upper Perkiomen Edn. Assn. (sec.), Pa. State Edn. Assn.

COCHRAN, REBECCA SUE, accountant; b. Decatur, Ind., Feb. 27, 1959; d. Robert Junior and Ola Berniece (Kistler) Sheets; m. Kevin James Cochran, Aug. 2, 1980; children: Matthew Steven, Douglas Robert, Crystal Marie. BS in Bus. with distinction, Ind. U., 1981. CPA, Ind. Staff acct. T.L. Brehm, Decatur, Ind., 1981-85; ptnr. Brehm & Cochran, CPAs, Decatur, 1985-91; sole propr. Rebecca S. Cochran, CPA, Decatur, 1991—. Vol. Adams County unit Am. Cancer Soc. Mem. Ind. CPA Soc., Ind. U. Alumni Assn., Decatur C. of C. (bd. dirs.), Bus. and Profl. Women. Methodist. Home: 4D 4460 N 200 E # 4D Decatur IN 46733-8095 Office: Rececca S Cochran CPA 165 N 2nd St Decatur IN 46733-1608

COCHRAN, STEVE, lawyer; b. LA, Mar. 18, 1957; BA, U. Calif., Santa Cruz, 1979; JD, U. Calif., Berkeley, 1982. Bar: Calif. 1982, US Dist Ct. 1983, Ctrl. Dist. Calif., US Ct. Appeals, Ninth Cir. 1986, US Dist. Ct., Ea. Dist. Calif. 1991. Law clerk to Hon. William P. Gray Ctrl. Dist. of Calif.; extern clerk to Hon. Cecil F. Poole US Ct. Appeals, 9th Cir.; ptnr. Katten Muchin Rosenman, LA, 1991—. Mem. adv. bd. Nat. Circuit Judicial Conf. Mem.: LA Criminal Cts. Bar Assn., Calif. Attys. Criminal Justice, State Bar of Calif. Office: Katten Muchin Rosenman Ste 2600 2029 Century Park E Los Angeles CA 90067-3012 Office Phone: 310-788-4455. Office Fax: 310-712-8455. Business E-Mail: steve.cochran@kmzr.com.

COCHRAN, SUSAN MILLS, research librarian; b. Grinnell, Iowa, Nov. 21, 1949; d. Lawrence Omen and Louise Jane (Morgan) Mills; m. Stephen E. Cochran, July 1, 1972; children: Bryan, Jeremy. Libr. Iowa Geneal. Soc., Des Moines, 1987-96; rsch. libr. Royal Gorge Regional Mus. & History Ctr. (formerly Local History Ctr., Canon City Pub. Libr.), Colo., 1997—. Editor: Mingo, Iowa 1884-1984, 1984; contbr. articles to profl. jours. Past mem. Jasper County Cemetery Commn., Newton; mem. Jasper County His. Soc.; past bd. dirs. Jasper County Libr., Newton, Iowa. Mem. Iowa Geneal. Soc., Jasper County Geneal. Soc., State Assn. for the Preservation of Iowa Cemeteries (charter), Fremont County Geneal. Group (coord.), Colo. Coun. Geneal. Socs. Avocations: genealogy, history, birding. Office: Royal Gorge Regional Mus & History Ctr 612 Royal Gorge Blvd Canon City CO 81212 Address: PO Box 1460 Canon City CO 81215 Office Phone: 719-269-9036. E-mail: historycenter@canoncity.org.

COCHRAN, THAD (WILLIAM THAD COCHRAN), senator; b. Pontotoc, Miss., Dec. 7, 1937; s. William Holmes and Emma Grace (Berry) C.; m. Rose Clayton, June 6, 1964; children: Thaddeus Clayton, Katherine Holmes. BA, U. Miss., 1959, JD cum laude, 1965; postgrad. (Rotary Found. fellow), U. Dublin, Ireland, 1963-64. Bar: Miss. 1965. Practiced in Jackson, 1965-72; assoc. firm Watkins & Eager, 1965-72; mem. 93d-95th congresses from Miss., 1973—78; U.S. senator from Miss., 1978—; chmn. Rep. conf. 104th Congress, 1995. Mem. agr. nutrition and forestry com., appropriations com., govtl. affairs com., rules and adminstrn. com., senate Rep. conf. com. Mem.

exec. bd. Andrew Jackson council Boy Scouts Am., 1973-. Served to lt. USNR, 1959-61. Named Outstanding Young Man of Jackson, 1971, One of Three Outstanding Young Men of Miss., 1971, Conservation Achievement award, Nat. Wildlife Fedn., Conservationist of the Year, Dicks Unlimited, 1994, Congl. Leadership award, Airports Coun. Internat. N. Am., 2004; Named Honored Cooperator Nat. Cooperative Bus. Assn., 2003 Mem. ABA, Miss. Bar Assn. (pres. young lawyers sect. 1972-73), Omicron Delta Kappa, Phi Kappa Phi, Pi Kappa Alpha. Clubs: Rotarian. Republican. Baptist.*

COCHRAN, THOMAS BRACKENRIDGE, physicist; b. Washington, Nov. 18, 1940; s. Robert Samuel and Amelia (Weaver) C.; m. Carol Frances Jeter, July 10, 1971; children: Jaquelin Marie, Carolyn Michelle. BEE cum laude, Vanderbilt U., 1962, MS in Physics, 1965, PhD in Physics, 1967. Asst. prof. physics U.S. Naval Postgrad. Sch., Monterey, Calif., 1967—69; group supr. Mellonics divsn., Litton Industries, Fort Ord, Calif., 1969—71; sr. rsch. assoc. Resources for the Future, Washington, 1971—73; sr. staff scientist Natural Resources Def. Coun., Washington, 1973—; dir. nuc. program Natural Resources Defense Coun., Washington, 1993—. Mem. energy rsch. adv. bd. Dept. Energy, Washington, 1978-82; mem. adv. bd. Three Mile Island Health Fund, Phila., 1981-93, Doe Environ. Mgmt. adv. bd., DOE Nuclear Energy Rsch. adv. bd., 1999—. Author: The Liquid Metal Fast Breeder Reactor: An Environmental and Economic Critique, 1974, (with others) Nuclear Weapons Databook, Volume I: U.S. Nuclear Forces and Capabilities, 1984, Volume II: U.S. Nuclear Warhead Production, 1987, Volume III: U.S. Nuclear Warhead Facility Profiles, 1987, Volume IV: Soviet Nuclear Weapons, 1989, Making the Russian Bomb: From Stalin to Yeltsin, 1995; contbr. articles to Bull. of Atomic Scientists, SIPRI Yearbook, Environ. Mag., Phys. Rev. Lt. USNR, 1962-69. Fellow AAAS, Am. Phys. Soc. (Szilard award 1987), Fedn. Am. Scientists (coun. 1985-88, Pub. Svc. award 1987), Am. Nuc. Soc., Health Physics Soc., Sigma Xi. Democrat. Home: 4836 30th St N Arlington VA 22207-2716 Office: Natural Resources Def Coun 1200 New York Ave NW Ste 400 Washington DC 20005-3929 Office Phone: 202-289-2372.

COCHRAN, WENDELL ALBERT, science editor; b. Carthage, Mo., Nov. 29, 1929; s. Wendell Albert and Lillian Gladys (Largent) C.; m. Agnes Elizabeth Groves, Nov. 9, 1963; remarried Corinne Des Jardins, Aug. 25, 1980. AB, U. Mo., Columbia, 1953, A.M. in Geology, 1956, B.J., 1960. Geologist ground-water br. U.S. Geol. Survey, 1956-58; reporter, copyeditor Kansas City (Mo.) Star, 1960-63; editor Geotimes and Earth Sci. mags., Geospectrum newsletter, Alexandria, Va., 1963-84; v.p. Geol. Survey Inc., Bethesda, Md., 1984-86; freelance editor, tech. editor Okla. Geol. Survey, 1998—. Co-author: Into Print: A Practical Guide to Writing, Illustrating, and Publishing, 1977; sr. editor: Geowriting: A Guide to Writing, Editing and Printing in Earth Science, 1973; contbr. articles to profl. jours. and encys. Mem. geol. socs. Washington, London, Assn. Earth Sci. Editors (award Outstanding Contbns. 1982), Dog in the Night-time. Home: 4351 SW Willow St Seattle WA 98136-1769 Office Phone: 206-932-8227. E-mail: atrypa@eskimo.com.

COCHRAN, WILLIAM MICHAEL, librarian; b. Nevada, Iowa, May 6, 1952; s. Joseph Charles and Inez (Larson) Cochran; m. Diane Marie Ohm, July 24, 1971. BLS, U. Iowa, 1979, MA with distinction in Libr. Sci., 1983; MA in Pub. Adminstrn., Drake U., 1989. Dir. Red Oak (Iowa) Pub. Libr., 1984; patron svcs. libr. Pub. Libr. of Des Moines, 1984-87; LSCA program coord. State Libr. of Iowa, Des Moines, 1987-88, dir. libr. devel., 1988-89, asst. state libr., 1989-90; dir. Parmly Billings Libr., 1990—. Mem. White House Conf. on Libr. and Info. Svcs. Mem.: Mont. Ctr. for Book Adv. Com., Libr. Adminstrn. and Mgmt. Assn., Pub. Libr. Assn., Mont. Gov.'s Blue Ribbon Telecommunications Task Force, Mont. Libr. Assn. (chair, pub. libr. divsn. 1991—92, legis. com. chair 1992—93, pres. 1998—99, named Libr. of Yr. 1998), ALA, Beta Phi Mu. Office: Parmly Billings Libr 510 N Broadway Billings MT 59101-1156

COCHRANE, BETSY LANE, former state senator; b. Asheboro, NC; d. William Jennings and Bobbie (Campbell) Lane; m. Joe Kenneth Cochrane, 1958; children: Lisa, Craig. BA cum laude, Meredith Coll., 1958. Tchr. Winston-Salem (NC) Sch. Sys., Highland Presbyn. Ch. Sch.; mem. NC Ho. of Reps., Raleigh, 1980-88, house minority leader, 1985-88; mem. NC Senate, Raleigh, 1988-2001, chmn. Commn. on Aging, 1989-99, vice chmn. higher edn. com., 1991-92, senate minority whip, 1993-94, senate minority leader, 1995-96, vice chmn. senate appropriations, 1995—2000, vice chmn. senate commerce commn., 1995—2000, ranking minority mem. senate agr., 1995—2000. Mem. Nat. Rep. Platform Com., Order of LongLeaf Pine, 1992, Joint Legis. Ethics Com., 1989—2000, chmn., 1989—90; mem. NC Parks Commn., 1989—96, Retail Mchts. Adv. Bd., 1989—2000, Govtl. Ops., 1989—97, Select Com. on Redistricting, 1991, 92, 94, Revenue Law, 1992—2000, Environ. Rev. Com., 1997—2001, Utility Rev. Com., 1997—2001, Gov.'s Advocacy Coun. on Children and Youth, 1990—2001. Trustee Davie County Hosp.; bd. advisors Z. Smith Reynolds Found., 1996—99, Meredith Coll., chmn. pres.'s adv. coun., 1999—2001, govs. adv. budget com., 1989—93, pub. sch. forum, 1985—99; mem. Davie County Schs. Task Force on Facilities, 2001—02, So. Regional Edn. Bd., 1987—2001; bd. dirs. Davie County Sch. Mebane Challenge, 2004—; del. GOP Nat. Conv., 1976, 1988, 1992, 1996; mem. Bible Study Fellowship, discussion leader, 2003—; mem. Faith Works Task Force, 2005—; bd. dirs. Forks of the Yadkin Mus., 2002—, vice chmn., 2004—. Named Disting. Citizen of Yr., N.C. Libr. Dirs., 1991, Legislator of Yr., N.C. Divsn. Aging, 1991, N.C. Assn. for Home Care, 1992, N.C. Health Facilities Assn., 1993, N.C. Wildlife Fedn., 1995, Autism Found., 1995, Disting. Alumnae of the Yr., Meredith Coll., 1996; named one of 10 Outstanding Legislators in Nation, 1987; named to N.C. GOP Hall of Fame, 2001, GOP Hall of Fame, Davie County, 2003; recipient Woman in Govt. award, N.C. Jaycees, 1985, Myers-Honeycutt award for excellence in pub. svc., 1996, Dr. Ewald W. Busse award, Aging Advocates of N.C., 1997, Women Achievement award, FWC N.C., 2002. Baptist. Home and Office: 331 Orchard Pk Dr Advance NC 27006-9582 Personal E-mail: betsycochrane@triad.rr.com. Business E-Mail: betsyc@ncleg.net.

COCHRANE, JAMES LOUIS, economist; b. Nyack, N.Y., Aug. 31, 1942; s. Thomas and Anna (Yaroscak) C.; m. Katherine Prince Schirmer, Mar. 24, 1984; 1 child. BA, Wittenberg U., 1964; PhD, Tulane U., 1968. Instr. Tulane U., New Orleans, 1967-68; asst. prof. U. S.C., Columbia, 1968-70, assoc. prof., 1970-72, prof., 1972-77; sr. staff mem. NSC, Washington, 1978-79; directorate of intelligence CIA, Washington, 1980-83; sr. v.p., chief economist Tex. Commerce Bancshares Inc., Houston, 1984-88, N.Y. Stock Exch., 1988—. Assoc. staff Brookings Instn., Washington, 1972-76, 76-78; 1st v.p. So. Econ. Assn., U. N.C., 1976-77; vis. prof. U. Melbourne, Australia, 1972, U. Tex., Austin, 1973-74; mem. adv. bd. White Ctr. Fin. Rsch., U. Pa., Fin. Markets Rsch. Ctr., Vanderbilt U.; mem. bd. advisors N.Y. Assembly; bd. dirs. Catalyst Inst., Columbia U. Ctr. Law and Econ. Studies; mem. emerging econs. program bd. U. Pa. Wharton Sch.; mem. deans adv. bd. Hofstra U. Sch. Bus.; mem. study equities markets Pace U.; mem. internat. adv. com. Ctr. for Internat. Affairs, Harvard U., U.S. Nat. Com. for Pacific Econ. Cooperation. Author: Macroeconomics Before Keynes, 1970, Macroeconomics Analysis and Policy, 1974, Industrialism and Industrial Man in Retrospect, 1977; editor: Multiple Criteria Decision Making, 1975; mem. editl. bd. History Polit. Economy, Duke U., 1974-80, So. Econ. Jour., U. N.C., 1976-79. Mem. History of Econs. Soc. (treas. 1974-80), Asia Soc. (adv. dir. 1986), Am. Econ. Assn., Western Fin. Assn. Avocations: tennis, singing, writing. Office: NY Stock Exch 11 Wall St Fl 7 New York NY 10005-1974

COCHRANE, PAUL HOLLIS, general practice physician; b. Boston, Oct. 23, 1953; s. Joseph Xavier and Bernadette Anne (Abbott) C.; m. Meryle Roberta Lee, Aug. 10, 1978; children: Gregory, Jennifer, Amanda, Casey. BA, U. Mass., 1974; OD, N.Eng. Coll. Optometry, 1979; D Naturopathy, Clayton Sch. Natural Healing, Birmingham, Ala., 1986; D Chiropractic, Palmer Coll. Chiropractic, 1988; A in Paralegal Sci., Southland U., 1983; DO, New England Coll. Osteopathic Medicine, 1992; JD, Monticello U., 1997. Pvt. practice, Arlington, Mass., 1980—; resident in osteopathy Community Hosp. R.I., Cranston, 1992-93; med. examiner Nicholas County, W.Va., 1995-96. Real estate developer, Mass., 1981—; instr. diagnosis Palmer Coll. Chiropractic, Davenport, Iowa, 1986-88; instr. U. N.Eng. Coll. Osteopathic Medicine, Biddeford, Maine, 1990—. Coord. glaucoma, pediatric eye screenings, Lions Club, Arlington, 1980— (disting. svc. award 1984); player, coach pro baseball Bangor Blue Ox Northeast League, 1996. Fellow Internat. Acad. Clin. Acupuncture; mem. Am. Osteopathic Assn., Am. Acad. Osteopathy, Am. Coll. Osteopathic Family Physicians, Mass. Osteopathic Soc., N.Eng. Coll. Osteopathic Medicine. Democrat. Roman Catholic. Avocations: sports, reading, boston red sox. Office: 347 Massachusetts Ave Arlington MA 02474-6718 Home: 34 Snow Creek Dr Hyannis MA 02601

COCHRANE, ROBERT LOWE, biologist; b. Morgantown, W.Va., Feb. 10, 1931; s. Thomas Joseph and Isabelle Durston (Lowe) C. BA, W.Va. U., 1953; MS, U. Wis., 1954, PhD, 1961. Rsch. asst. genetics U. Wis., Madison, 1953—55, rsch. asst. zoology, 1957—60; with Fur Animal Exptl. Sta., Petersburg, Alaska, 1955; agt. in animal husbandry U.S. Dept. Agr., Madison, Wis., 1955—61; biologist FDA, Washington, 1961—62; sr. research fellow dept. anatomy U. Birmingham (Eng.), 1962—65; project assoc. dept. physiology U. Pitts., 1965—66; sr. endocrinologist Eli Lilly & Co., Indpls., 1966—80; rsch. assoc. G.D. Searle & Co., Skokie, Ill., 1980—81; with Short's Fur Farm, Granton, Wis., 1981—83; rsch. assoc. Marshfield (Wis.) Med. Found., 1983—84; biologist Northwood Fur Farms, Inc., Cary, Ill., 1984. Cons. for FAO to Wildlife Inst. India, Dehra Dun, 1985; adj prof. div. animal and vet. sci., W.Va. U., Morgantown, 1987—. Ad hoc reviewer (various sci. jours.); ad hoc reviewer: grants U.S. Dept. of Agr. Competitive Rsch. Grants; participant Internat. Mink Show, Wis., 1976—2005, W. Va. State Fox Show, Morgantown, 1989. Rsch. bd. advisors The Am. Biog. Inst., 1988-98; mem. adv. coun. Internat. Biog. Centre, 1989-98; mem. Golden Horseshoe Reunion Com., W.Va. Homecoming '96. Recipient Knight of Golden Horse Shoe award W.Va. Pub. Sch. System, 1945, W.Va. Boy's State, 1948; U. Birmingham (Eng.) sr. rsch. fellow, 1962-65. Mem. AAAS, Am. Inst. Biol. Scis., Soc. Exptl. Biology and Medicine, Soc. for Reprodn. and Fertility, Soc. Study of Reprodn., Am. Soc. Animal Sci., Endocrine Soc., N.Y. Acad. Sci., Soc. Endocrinology, Coun. Agrl. Sci. and Tech., Internat. Platform Assn., NRA (life), Sigma Xi, Pi Kappa Alpha, Gamma Sigma Delta. Presbyterian. Achievements include discovery of the ovarian hormonal requirements for ova-implantation and embryonic diapause in the rat, the elucidation of the role played by prostaglandins in corpus luteum function, parturition and ductus arteriosus closure in the rat; discovery of timing, duration and pattern of reproductive cycles in martens; development of steroid synthesis inhibitors for controlling reproduction in mammals; rsch. in the successful raising of ruffed grouse in captivity, dissemination of scientific information on fur farming and raising ruffed grouse to the commercial trade and public. Home: 404 Junior Ave Morgantown WV 26505-2208 Office Phone: 304-293-2406 ext 4408. Business E-Mail: rcochra2@wvu.edu.

COCHRANE, SHIRLEY GRAVES, writer, educator; b. Chapel Hill, N.C., Mar. 5, 1925; d. Thornton Shirley and Margaret (White) Graves; m. William McWhorter Cochrane, June 3, 1945; children: William Daniel, Thomas McWhorter. AB with honors, Agnes Scott Coll., 1946; MA, Johns Hopkins U., 1970. Editor U. N.C. Press, 1946-50, 51-52; tchr. various univs. including Am. U., Georgetown U., Cath. U., Washington, 1974—. Instr., mem. Writer's Ctr., Bethesda, Md., 1978—. Author: Everything That's All, 1991, Letters to the Quick/Letters to the Dead, 1998; contbr. short stories and poems to lit. mags., anthologies, etc.; free-lance editor, Duke U. Press, Yale U. Press, Shakespeare Quar., others, 1951-73; work represented in Libr. of Congress Archive of Recorded Poetry and Lit. Recipient awards including PEN award for Syndicated Fiction, others. Mem. Writers Ctr. Bethesda, Phi Beta Kappa. Democrat. Presbyterian.

COCHRANE, WALTER E., academic administrator, conductor, music supervisor, clarinet soloist; b. Phila. s. Earl and Martha (Binder) C. BS, MS, U. Pa., Phila.; grad. study, Columbia U., 1959-60. Cert. sch. dist. adminstr., N.Y., Pa., N.J., Mass., Maine, Va.; cert. music supr., N.Y., Pa., Va.; supt. schs., N.Y., Mass.; sch. prin., N.Y., Pa., Mass. Clarinet soloist Phila. Brahms Cycle, 1950; dir. bands Upper Darby Pa. Schs., 1950-51; prof. clarinet and chamber music Phila. Musical Acad., 1950-52; solo clarinetist Phila. Symphonic Band, 1950-58; dir. music Alexandria Va. City Schs., 1951—58; clarinet soloist Alexandria String Quartet, 1952; dist. music dir. Sch. Dist. II, L.I., NY, 1958-60; supr. music N.Y. State Edn. Dept., Albany, 1960-67; conductor NY State Bands, 1960-67; v.p. Found. Am. Art Song, Albany, 1965-70; supr. music Hartford (Conn.) City Schs., 1967-69; faculty music edn. U. Hartford, 1967—69; asst. supt. Sch. Dist. 5, L.I., N.Y., 1970-78; supt. schs. Maine Sch. Adm. Dist. 19, Lubec, Maine, 1978-80; v.p. and dean Inst. Security and Tech., Phila., 1980-87; corp. dir. edn. PTC Career Insts., Phila., 1987; pres. Career Guidance Corp., 1988-91, dir. GED home study program N.Y. State, 1992—. Founder, dir. Stony Brook Conservatory Music, L.I., 1958—61. Author: GED Home Study Program, 2000, Meet The Great Composers, 2000, The Gulf War, 1994, World Wars I and II, Mathematics Mastery Manual, 1998, Science Mastery Manual, 1997, Understand Music, 1990, Women Composers, 1991, Literature Mastery Manual, 1997, Who Was the Killer Composer?, 1992, Clarinet Curriculum, 1951, Flute Curriculum, 1951, Graded Music for Wind and String Chamber Music, 1952, Graded Music for Brass Instruments, 1960, Public Schools Can Help You, 1960, The AAA Method in American Education-Analysis, Action and Alleviation of Attrition, 1960, CATP: Cooperative Analysis of Teacher Performance, 1966, Non-Traditional Employment for Women, 1982, A Philosophy and Basic Procedures for Supervision, 1982, Understanding Students for the Improvement of Learning, 1983, Encyclopedia of Conductors, 2001. Recipient Humanitarian award Chgo. PTC, Music Edn. Svc. award, NY State Sch. Music Assn, 1999. Mem. ASCD, NEA, SAR, N.Y. State Sch. Music Assn. (adjudicator, all-state conductor, Svc. to Music Edn. award), Nat. Assn. of Secondary Sch. Prin., Am. Assn. Sch. Adminstrs., Music Educators Nat. Conf., Nat. Assn. Trade and Tech. Schs. (adminstrv. advancement com. 1981), N.Y. ASCD, Phila. Musical Soc.

COCHRUN, JOHN WESLEY, financial consultant; b. Spencerville, Ohio, May 4, 1918; s. Paul Wesley and Laura Edna (McClure) C.; m. Almut Boesel-Michaud, Aug. 26. 2000; children: Timothea Jourdan, David Wesley. BS, Purdue U., 1940; diploma, U.S. Army Command and Gen. Staff Coll., 1944; MS in Fin. Svcs., Am. Coll., 1985. CLU, chartered fin. cons. Spl. apprentice Bendix-Westinghouse A.A.B. Co., Pitts., 1940-41, asst. svc. mgr. Elyria, Ohio, 1945-50; mgr. customer svc. DeVilbiss Co., Toledo, 1950-58; exec. v.p. Elec. Products R & D Co., Toledo, 1958-60; spl. agt. Northwestern Mut. and other ins. cos., Toledo, 1961-81, St. Petersburg, Fla., 1981-87, Las Cruces, N.Mex., 1987-97. Registered investment adviser SEC, State of N.Mex., 1989-95; pres. Cochrun Inc., Sylvania, Ohio, 1976-81, Seminole, Fla., 1981-87. Author: Service of the Piece, 1945, Avoid Financial Shocks in Your Family's Future, 1976, Wills, Trusts, and Life Insurance Settlement Options, 1995. Pres. Community League Sylvania, 1954; lobbyist Ohio Pub. Expenditure Coun., Sylvania, 1955, Fed. Transp. Commn., Washington, 1947-50. Lt. col. U.S. Army, 1941-45. Mem. Am. Soc. CLU and ChFC, Million Dollar Round Table (life), Res. Officers Assn., Phi Kappa Psi. Republican. Avocations: gardening, canoeing. Home and Office: 1615 Thunderbird Las Cruces NM 88011-9123

COCKBURN, ALEXANDER, journalist; b. Scotland; arrived in US, 1973, permanent resident; Grad, Oxford Univ, 1963. Former editor New Statesman, Times Literary Supplement; editor CounterPunch mag; columnist The Nation. Author: Corruptions of Empire, 1987; co-author: The Fate of the Forest, Developers, Destroyers and Defenders of the Amazon; contbr. columns in newspapers. Office: CounterPunch PO Box 228 Petrolia CA 95558*

COCKCROFT, ANN JONES, writer; b. Greenport, N.Y., Aug. 23, 1934; d. Corbett Tralon Jr. and Adele Mary (Bumble) Jones; m. George Powers Cockcroft; children: Corbett, Powers, Chris. RN, Bkln. Hosp. Sch. Nursing, 1955. Author: Pirate's Promise, 1984, River Jewel, 1985, Beloved Pirate, 1984; (poetry) Brush Strokes, 1977. Democrat. Roman Catholic. Avocations: painting, gardening. Home and Office: Rte 295 Canaan NY 12029

COCKE, WILLIAM MARVIN, JR., plastic surgeon, educator; b. Balt., Aug. 2, 1934; s. William M. and Clara E. (Bosley) C.; m. Sue Ann Harris, Apr. 25, 1981; children: Gregory William, Laura Marie, Julie Ann; children by previous marriage: William Marvin III, Catherine Lynn, Deborah Kay, Brian Thomas. BS with honors in Biology, Tex. A&M U., 1956; MD, Baylor U., 1960. Diplomate: Am. Bd. Plastic Surgery (guest examiner 1978). Intern surgery Vanderbilt U. Hosp., Nashville, 1960-61; fellow gen. surgery Ochsner Clinic and Found. Hosp., New Orleans, 1961-64; chief resident surgery Monroe (La.) Charity Hosp., 1963-64; resident reconstructive surgery Roswell Park Meml. Inst., Buffalo, 1965-66; chief resident plastic surgery VA Hosp., Bronx, N.Y., 1966; practice medicine specializing in plastic surgery Nashville, 1968-75, Sacramento, 1976-79; pvt. practice medicine specializing in plastic surgery Bryan, Tex., 1980-92; prof. surgery, head div. plastic/reconstructive surgery Marshall U. Sch. of Medicine, Huntington, W.Va., 1992—. Mem. staff St. Mary's Hosp., Cabell-Huntington Hosp., Huntington Vets. Med. Ctr.; asst. prof. plastic surgery Vanderbilt U. Sch. Medicine, Nashville, 1968-69, asst. clin. prof. plastic surgery, 1969-75; assoc. prof. plastic surgery Ind. U. Sch. Medicine, Indpls., 1975-76; chief plastic surgery service Wishard Meml. Hosp., Ind. U., 1975-76; assoc. prof. surgery U. Calif. Sch. Medicine, Davis, 1976-79, chmn. dept. plastic surgery, 1976-79; prof. surgery, chief div. plastic surgery Tex. Tech. U. Sch. Medicine, Lubbock, 1979-80, dir. Microsurg. Research Lab., 1979-80; clin. prof. surgery Tex. A&M U. Sch. Medicine, 1983-92; prof. plastic surgery, 1986-89; chief plastic surgery svc., dept. surgery, Olin Teague VA Med. Ctr., Temple, Tex., 1986-92; prof. head surgery divsn. plastic and reconstruction Marshall U. Sch. Medicine, 1992—. Author textbooks on plastic surgery; contbr. articles to profl. jours. Served with M.C. USAF, 1966-68. Recipient Dean Echols award Ochsner Hosp. Found., 1963 Mem. ACS, Am. Assn. Plastic Surgeons, Soc. Head and Neck Surgeons, Assn. for Acad. Surgery, Alton Ochsner Surg. Soc. Episcopalian. Home: 45 Olde Farm Rd Ona WV 25545-9747 Office: Marshall U Sch Medicine Dept Surgery 1600 Medical Center Dr Huntington WV 25701-3656

COCKER, BARBARA JOAN, marine artist, interior designer; b. Uxbridge, Mass. AA, Becker Jr. Coll., 1943; student, Mt. St. Mary Coll., 1944-45, Clark U., 1945, N.Y. Sch. Interior Design, 1965-67. Owner, operator Barbara J. Cocker, Interior Design, Rumson, N.H., 1966—; owner Barbara J. Cocker Paintings of the Sea Gallery, Nantucket, Mass., 1975-99; tchr. adult edn. courses in interior design, 1965-68; artist, pvt. instr. marine art; pres. Maximus Praetorius Corp., Nantucket, 1979—. One-woman shows marine paintings at Little Gallery, Barbizon, N.Y., 1971, Old Mill Assn., 1971, Pacem en Terris Gallery, N.Y.C., 1972, Ctrl. Jersey Bank & Trust Co., Rumson, 1971, 72, 74, 77, 79, Little Gallery, Nantucket Art Assn., 1975, 77, 79, 81, 84, 87, 89, 91, 92, 95, Caravan House Galleries, N.Y.C., 1975, 179, Guild of Creative Art, Shrewsbury, N.J., 1976, 81, 85, 88, 93, 85, IBM Corp., N.J., 1977, South St. Seaport Mus., N.Y., 1977, 80, Provident Nat. Bank, Phila., 1978, Gallery 100, Princeton, 1978, Bell Telephone Rsch. Labs., 1982, 866, AT&T, 1987, Midlantic Bank, N.J., 1988, 93, 94, 95, Art Alliance N.J., 1983, 91, Gilpin House Gallery, Va., Swain Art Art Gallery, N.J., 1984, Oceanic Libr., N.J., 1989, 91, 93, 99, Red Bank Libr., N.J., 1989, 91, Captiva (Fla.) Civic Assn., 1994, Captiva Cmty. Ctr., 1994-97, Suntrust Bank, Sanibel, Fla., 1997, Pen and Brush Club, 1996, PNC Bank, Red Bank, 1997, Oceanic Libr., N.J., 1998, Monmouth (N.J.) City Libr., 1999, Monmouth Beach Cultural Ctr., 2002, 03, Sea Bright Libr., NJ, 2004; group shows include Composers Authors and Artists Am. NAD, Monmouth Coll. Festival of Arts, Pen and Brush Club, N.Y.C., Lever House Galleries, N.Y.C., Nat. Arts Club, N.Y.C., Ocean County Artists Guild N.J., Chelsea Gardens Gallery, Fla., Frank Lewis, Killarney, Ireland; painting selected for publ. Clean Ocean Action, N.J., 1994. Named Woman of Yr. Zonta Internat., 1986. Mem. Composers, Authors and Artists Am., Allied Artists Am., Monmouth Arts Found, So. Vt. Artists Inc., Pen and Brush Club (N.Y.C., Big Arts Ctr., Sanibel, Fla.), Sanibel-Captiva Art League. Address: 3 Rumson Rd Rumson NJ 07760-2005

COCKERHAM, KIMBERLY PEELE, ophthalmologist, educator; b. Bellevue, Wash., Apr. 10, 1961; d. Fred Arthur and Dorothy Anne (Cooper) Piontkowski; m. Glenn Cooper Cockerham, Feb. 22, 1997. BA in Biology, U. Calif., San Diego, 1983; MD, George Washington U., 1987. Commd. 2nd lt. U.S. Army, 1983, advanced through grades to maj.; surg. intern Letterman Army Ctr., San Francisco, 1987-88; chief emergency svcs. McDonald Army Hosp., Newport News, Va., 1988-89; neuro-opthalmology cons. Fitzsimons Army Med. Ctr., Denver, 1993-94; resident in ophthalmology Walter Reed Army Med. Ctr., Washington, 1989-92, neuro-ophthalmology fellow, 1992-93, mem. neuro-ophthlamology staff, 1993-94, 95—; orbital disease fellow Allegheny Gen. Hosp., Pitts., 1994-95; dir. orbital disease and oculoplastics Walter Reed Army Med. Ctr., Washington, 1995-98; ret., 1998; ophthalmologist Cockerham Eye Cons., Lock Haven, Pa., 1997—; dir. oculoplastics, orbital disease and reconstrn. Allegheny Gen. Hosp., Pitts., 1999—2002; dir. neuro-ophthalmology and orbital oncology Allegheny Cancer Ctr., Pitts., 2002—. Asst. clin. prof. Uniformed U. Health Scis., Bethesda, Md., 1992-98; instr. neuro-ophthalmology Harvard's Lancaster, U. Houston's Stanford basic ophthalmology courses, 1994—; asst. clin. prof. Drexel U. Sch. Medicine, 2000—; oral bd. examiner Acad. Ophthalmology, 1998—; cons. surg. neuro-ophthalmology U. Pitt. Med. Ctr.; bd. dirs. Vision Svcs.; team opthalmologist Pitts. Pirates baseball team. Author: Practical Diagnois & Management of Orbital Disease, 2001; assoc. editor Jour. of Allegheny Med. Soc.; contbr. articles to profl. jours., chpts. to books. Eye camp doctor Charitable Trust, New Delhi, India, 1996; mem. Surg. Eye Expedition Internat., 1997-99. Fellow ACS, Am. Acad. Ophthalmology, Am. Soc. Ophthalmic Plastic and Reconstructive Surgeons, Am. Soc. Oculofacial Plactics Reconstrn.; mem. N.Am. Soc. Neuro-Ophthalmology, Assn. Rsch. in Vision and Ophthalmology, Orbital Soc., Pa. Med. Soc. (alt. del.), Orbital Soc., Rotary Internat., Alpha Omega Alpha. Avocations: running, writing, tennis, gardening, cooking. Office: Allegheny Ophthalmic & Orbital Assocs 320 E North Ave Ste 116 Pittsburgh PA 15212-4756

COCKERHAM, SIDNEY JOE, professional society administrator; b. Waxahachie, Tex., Aug. 17, 1951; s. Sidney Julius and Joan (Barlow) C. BS in Biology, U. Tex., Arlington, 1973. Cert. tchr., Tex. Tchr. Tex. Pub. Schs., Waxahachie, 1973-77; dir., founder U.S. Nat. Tennis Acad., Dallas, 1982—. Lt. USN, 1977-82. Avocation: tennis. Home and Office: 3523 McKinney Ave # 208 Dallas TX 75204 Office Phone: 214-887-5999. E-mail: sjcntx_sohw@yahoo.com.

COCKING, SUSAN CAROLINE, writer; b. High Point, N.C., Aug. 4, 1954; d. Ronald William and Olivia Martin C. BA, Am. U., 1976. News dir. WKNE-AM Radio, Keene, NH, 1976—78; anchor, reporter WPOC-FM Radio, Balt., 1978—79; news dir. WKWF-AM Radio, Key West, Fla., 1979—81; news reporter WK12-AM Radio, Key West, 1982—87; news anchor WIOD-AM Radio, Miami, 1987—88; outdoors writer Miami Herald, 1994—. Charter boat capt., Key West, 1982—87. Contbr. articles, photographs. Mem.: Fla. Outdoor Writers Assn. Presbyterian. Avocations: skiing, running, fishing, scuba diving, hiking. Home: 4201 N Ocean Dr # 305 Hollywood FL 33019

COCKLIN, KIM ROLAND, lawyer; b. Massillon, Ohio, Apr. 13, 1951; s. Roland and Jacqueline Lou (Cope) C.; m. Crystal Elaine Chandler; children: Ross, Toben, Brooke. BS, Wichita State U., 1973, M in Adminstrn. Justice, 1975; JD, Washburn U., 1981. Bar: Colo. 1981, D.C. 1984, U.S. Appeals Ct. (5th, 8th and 10th cirs.) 1984. Instr. Wichita (Kans.) State U., 1974-81; atty. Colo. Interstate Gas Co., Colorado Springs, 1981-84, Tex. Gas Transmission Corp., Owensboro, Ky., 1984-85, gen. counsel, 1985-87, v.p., gen. counsel, 1987-89, sr. v.p., gen. counsel, 1989; sr. v.p. Planning, Rates and Regulatory, and Bus. Devel. Williams Gas Pipeline, Owensboro, Ky.; sr. v.p., gen. counsel, chief compliance officer Piedmont Natural Gas, Charlotte, NC, 2003—. Bd. dirs. Big Brothers and Big Sisters of Greater Charlotte. Mem. ABA, Fed. Energy Bar Assn., Colo. Bar Assn., Ky. Bar Assn., D.C. Bar Assn., Daviess Bar Assn., Am. Gas Assn. (legal com.), Phi Kappa Phi. Avocations: fishing, golf, family. Office: Piedmont Natural Gas PO Box 33068 1915 Rexford Rd Charlotte NC 28233

COCKRAM, SUZANNE M., elementary school educator; d. Joseph and Kathleen Rabedeaw; m. Donald R. Cockram, June 13, 1981; children: Joshua, Jason. BS, Ea. Mich. U., 1977, M in Reading, 1982. Cert. in reading recovery Mich. Tchr. Hillsdale (Mich.) Cmty. Schs., 1977—, reading recovery tchr., 1996—2001; tchr. literacy tng. Hillsdale Ind. Sch. Dist., 2002—. Den leader Boy Scouts Am., Hillsdale, coun. mem.

COCKRELL, KENNETH DALE, astronaut; b. Austin, Tex., Apr. 9, 1950; s. Dale and Jewell Cockrell; 2 children. BSc in Mech. Engring., U. Tex., 1972; MSc in Aeronautical Sys., U. W. Fla., 1974. Commd. lt. USN, 1972, naval aviator Pensacola, Fla., 1974—75; served on USS Midway, 1975—78; various assignments naval air test ctr. USN, 1979—82; comdr. USS Ranger Naval Sta., San Diego, 1982—85; aerospace engr., rsch. pilot Ellington Field, Houston, 1987—90; astronaut NASA, Houston, 1991—. Astronaut Discovery, 1993, Endeavour, 1995, Columbia, 1996, Atlantis, 2001, Endeavour, 2002. Decorated Humanitarian Svc. medal USNR, Def. Meritorious Svc. medal, Disting. Flying Cross; scholar, Alcoa Found., 1968. Mem.: Assn. Space Explorers, Soc. Exptl. Test Pilots. Avocations: sport flying, skiing, tennis, water-skiing. Office: Astronaut Office CB NASA Johnson Space Center Houston TX 77058

COCKRELL, PEARL HAND, writer; m. Harold R. Cockrell; children: Pamela C. White, Jan C. Mitchell, Donis C. Schweizer. Author: (poems) Sing On, America, 1976, Of Men and Seasons, 1978, The Song Within, 1989, Poems on Music, 1997, Hoots 'n Hollers, 1998, Introspection, 1999, Garden Therapy, 2000, Transcending bonds, 2001, Beyond the Altar Vows, 2003, Poems for the Family, 2004, A World of Wonders, 2005; contbr. to mags. including Sci. of Mind, Home Life, Modern Maturity, Music Ministry, Grit, Vol. Gardener, Tenn. Voices, The American, A Potpourri of Verse, 2002. Progressive Farmer, Nat. Daffodil Jour., Missionary Messenger, Am. Camellia Jour., Poet's Monthly, Encore, Pen Woman, Old Hickory Rev., Pegasus, The Sampler, Prizepoems Nat. Fedn. State Poetry Socs., Clover Collection Verses, Sandcutters, RoseGarden, Garden Prayers, Alalitcom, Power for Living, Mature Living, Nat. Enquirer, Wall Street Journal, Saturday Evening Post; weekly columnist So. Democrat, 1973-80; pub. (booklet) A World of Wonders, 2005 Recipient Tenn. Fedn. Carden Clubs, Inc. Poet Laureate award, 1973, 74, 75, 76, 77, Am. Legion award, 1974, Freedom Found. at Valley Forge award, 1976, 1st pl. poetry awards Nat. Fedn. State Poetry Socs., 1974 (2), 79, Authors and Artists Club Chattanooga, 1972, Ala. Writers Conclave Lit. Competition, 1975, 77, 78, Mid S. Poetry Festival, 1976, 77, 78 (2), 80, 81 (2), 84, Nat. Contest Ky. State Poetry Soc., 1976, Nat. Contest Utah State Poetry Soc., 1977, Deep S. Writers and Artists Assn., 1978, Dalton Creative Arts Guild, Ga., 1981, Nat. Contest Fla. State Poets Assn., 1985, 1st pl. prize Ann. Contest Poetry Soc. Tenn., 1986 (2), 1987 (2), 1st pl. award Reading Poetry Affiliates, 1988, 1st pl. award Poets Study Club, 1989, 1st pl. award Lake Placid Poets, 1989, 1st pl. award Funtastic, 1991 (2), 92, 93, 1st place Mid-South Writers Assn., 1994, numerous other awards. Me. Nat. League Am. Pen Women (historian Chickasaw br., Tenn. State Letters awards 1975, 77, 81), Tenn. Writers Guild (past v.p.), Cleve. Creative Arts Guild (1st place awards 1973, 74 (2), 79, Catriona Dow plaque 1974). Home and Office: 1615 Summit Dr Apt 8 Columbus GA 31906

COCKRELL, SANFORD ALONZA, III, accountant; b. Raleigh, N.C., Feb. 2, 1959; s. Sanford Alonza Jr. and Vivian Mercer Cockrell; m. Louise Heath, Dec. 5, 1960; children: L. Heath, Morgan. M. BSBA, U. N.C., 1982. CPA, N.Y. Staff acct. Rackley & Parker CPAs, Raleigh, N.C., 1982-84; mgr. Deloitte Haskins & Sells, Raleigh, 1984-89; sr. mgr. Deloitte & Touche, N.Y.C., 1989-93, ptnr., 1993—, bd. dirs., 2001—. Mem. bd. dirs. Deloitte Touche Thmatsu, 2003—; Grad. Leadership Raleigh I, Greater Raleigh C. of C., 1985-86; pres., treas. N.C. Soc. N.Y., 1996—, chmn. fin. com.; chmn. Younger Mem.'s Activities Com.; mem. Coun. Nominating Com., The Univ. Club, mem. exec. com. coun.; adv. bd. U. N.C., Inst. for Arts and Humanities, Chapel Hill, N.C., 1999—; co-chair cons. adv. bd., Youth, Inc.; coun. mem. U. N.C. Chapel Hill Nat. Devel. Coun., 1995—; coach girls' basketball and T-ball Yorkville Youth Athletic Assn., N.Y.C., 2000—; elder, deacon Brick Presbyn. Ch., N.Y.C., 1994-2000; 2d v.p., N.Y. area dir. U. N.C., Chapel Hill Gen. Alumni Assn. Bd. Dirs., 1996-2000; mem. reunion gift com. U. N.C., Chapel Hill, 1991-92. Recipient Mac Disting. Alumni award, Kenan-Flager Bus. Sch., 2004. Mem. N.C. Soc. CPAs (chmn. com. on taxation 1986-88), Coral Beach Club (Bermuda), Rockaway Hunting Club, Lawrence Beach Club. Presbyterian. Avocations: golf, running, sailing, travel, reading. Office: Deloitte Tax LLP 1633 Broadway New York NY 10019 Home: 359 Mansfield Ave Darien CT 06820-2113 Home Fax: 203-655-0731; Office Fax: 212-492-3881. E-mail: scockrell@deloitte.com.

COCKRILLE, STEPHEN, art director, business owner; b. Washington, Jan. 19, 1945; s. Donald Herbert and Dorothy Charolette (Hoover) C.; m. Éva Vágréti, May 17, 1987; children: Christopher Lewis, Micki Lee. BA, W.Va. State Coll., 1968; MA, U. N.D., 1972. Grad. tchg. asst. U. N.D., Grand Forks, 1971; design asst. Thomas Clayton Printing, N.Y.C., 1974-75; art dir. West Side Printing & Graphics, N.Y.C., 1975-76; studio mgr. Graphic Concern, Inc., N.Y.C., 1976-78; ind. art dir. N.Y.C., 1978-84; pres. Textart, Inc., N.Y.C., 1984-97; ind. art dir. Woodland Park, Colo., 1997—2004; pres., mng. dir. Vision Miro, Inc., Colorado Springs, 2004—. Judge New Eng. Book Show, Boston, 1987; selected for presentation to the Jordanian Min. of Edn. and staff on the U.S. textbook industry, N.Y.C., 1995. Prodr. numerous basal ednl. programs for nat. distbn., 1984-97. With Ctrl. Intelligence Ctr., U.S. Army, 1968-70, Vietnam. Recipient hon. mention New Eng. Book Show, Boston, 1992, Pupil's Edit. and Theme Posters, Boston, 1992, bronze award Dimensional Illustrators Awards Show, N.Y.C., 1992, 1st place award Ednl. Sch. Divsn. N.Y. Book Show, N.Y.C., 1994. Republican. Avocations: painting, reading, skiing. Home: 1150 Kings Crown Rd Woodland Park CO 80863-7731 Office Phone: 719-624-5222. Personal E-mail: scockrille@visionmisd.net.

COCKROFT, JEANNETTE WIMMER, historian educator; b. Bad-Hersfeld, Germany, Mar. 17, 1957; d. Charles Samuel and Elaine D. (Bouchard) Wimmer; m. Ronald D. Cockroft, Nov. 26, 1986. Student, U. Maine, 1975—78; BA in East Asian Langs. & Cultures, U. Pa., 1980; MA in Polit. Sci., U. Kans., 1989; PhD of History, Tex. A&M U., 2000. Adminstrv. asst. Christian Assn., U. Pa., 1978—80; tutor Supportive Ednl. Svcs., U. Kans., 1981; adj. faculty Blinn Coll., Bryan, Tex., 1992—96; grad. tchg. asst. dept. history Tex. A&M U., College Station, 1995—2001; asst. prof. History and Polit. Sci. Schreiner U., Kerrville, Tex., 2002—. Dir. Joint Lang. Inst. Suzhou U. - Marshall U., China, 2001—. Vol. VISTA Capitol Area Food Bank, Austin, Tex., 1986-87; nursing home visitor, Bryan, Tex., 1991—. Mem. Phi Kappa Phi, Phi Alpha Theta, Pi Sigma Alpha, Alpha Lambda Delta. Avocations: knitting, reading, collecting books. Home: 600 Meadowview Ln Apt 204 Kerrville TX 78028 Office Phone: 830-792-7262. E-mail: ronellewimmer@hotmail.com.

COCKROFT, KEVIN M., neurosurgeon; MD, Cornell U.; MSc, Penn State U. Bd Cert/ Am. Bd. of Neurol. Surgery. Dir. of cerebrovascular and endovascular neurosurgery Dept. of Neurosurgery, Penn State - M.S. Hershey Med. Ctr., Hershey, 2004—. Contbr. articles to profl. jours., chapters to books. Fellow: ACS; mem.: Congress of Neurol. Surgeons, Am. Assn. of Neurol. Surgeons, Am. Stroke Assn. Office: Penn State - MS Hershey Medical Center 500 University Dr Hershey PA 17033 Office Phone: 717-531-8807.

COCKRUM, DAVID SCOTT, medical educator; b. Sault Ste. Marie (Kincheloe AFB), Mich., May 15, 1966; s. Donald Joseph and Joann Cockrum. BA, Abilene Christian U., 1988; MD, Tex. Tech U. Sch. of Medicine, 1994; MPH, Uniformed Svcs. U. of Health Scis., 2004. Family Physician Am. Bd. of Family Medicine, 1997. Resident in family practice John Peter Smith Hosp., Fort Worth, Tex., 1994—97; family physician 374th Airlift Wing, Yokota Air Base, Japan, 1997—99, 422d Air Base Squadron, RAF Croughton, England, 1999—2001; flight surgeon 92d Aerial Refueling Wing, Fairchild AFB, Wash., 2001—03; resident, aerospace medicine USAF Sch. of Aerospace Medicine, Brooks City-Base, Tex., 2004—. Med. student mem., bd. of trustees AMA, Chgo., 1993—94. Author: (profl. pub.) Initial Experience With Mass Immunization as a Bioterrorism Countermeasure (Journal of the American Osteopathic Association). Mem. Coun. of Ch., Lubbock, Tex., 1990—92; founding mem. Fourth on Broadway, Lubbock, Tex., 1991. Maj. USAF, 2004—. Decorated Meritorious Svc. medal USAF, Aerial Achieve. medal, Air Force Commendation medal, Air Force Achieve. medal, Air Force Commendation medal. Mem.: Assn. of Mil. Surgeons of the US, Soc. of USAF Flight Surgeons, Aerospace Med. Assn., Uniformed Svcs. Acad. of Family Physicians, Am. Acad. of Family Physicians. Avocation: travel. Office Phone: 210-536-2845.

COCKRUM, WILLIAM MONROE, III, investment banker, educator; b. Indpls., July 18, 1937; s. William Monroe C. II and Katherine J. (Jaqua) Moore; children: Catherine Anne Cockrum Dean, William Monroe IV AB with distinction, DePauw U., 1959; MBA with distinction, Harvard U., 1961. With A.G. Becker Paribas Inc., L.A., 1961-84, mgr. nat. corp. fin. div., 1968-71, mgr. pvt. investments, 1971-74, fin. and adminstrv. officer, 1974-80, sr. v.p., 1975-78, vice chmn., 1978-84; prin. William M. Cockrum & Assocs., L.A., 1984—; faculty Northwestern U., 1961—63. Vis. lectr. Anderson Grad. Sch. Mgmt. UCLA, 1984—88, adj. prof., 1988—; vis. prof. Warwick U., England, 2004—. Mem. Deke Club (NYC), UCLA Faculty Club, Alisal Golf Club (Solvang, Calif.), Bel-Air Country Club (LA), Delta Kappa Epsilon. E-mail: bcockrum@anderson.ucla.edu.

COCKS, GEORGE GOSSON, retired chemical microscopy professor; b. Sioux City, Iowa, Mar. 22, 1919; s. George Green and Nellie Patricia (Gosson) C.; m. Marian L. Singer, May 11, 1942; children: Gary, Kathleen (Mrs. Thomas Sadlowski), Francis, Kenneth. BS in Chemistry, Iowa State U., 1941; PhD in Chem. Microscopy, Cornell, 1949. Researcher Battelle Meml. Inst., Columbus, Ohio, 1949-64; prof. chem. microscopy Cornell U., 1964-81, prof. emeritus, 1981—; cons. Los Alamos (N.Mex.) Nat. Lab., 1980-81, staff mem., 1981-90; ret., 1990. Scoutmaster Central Ohio council Boy Scouts Am., 1956-64. Served to lt. comdr. USNR, 1942-45. NSF grantee to study crystallization inorganic materials in polymers, 1966-68, to study biomed. uses collagen, 1972—, DOE grantee in hot dry rock geothermal energy project, 1981-90. Fellow AAAS (coun. 1970-75); mem. Am. Optical Soc., Am. Chem. Soc., Microscopy Soc. Am. (exec. sec. 1964-76), Sigma Xi, Phi Kappa Phi. Achievements include patents in field. Home: 1719 Hyland St Bayside CA 95524-9302

COCKWELL, JACK LYNN, finance company executive; b. East London, South Africa, Jan. 12, 1941; s. William Henry and Daphne (Cound) C.; children: Linda, Lorie, Leslie, Tessa, Malcolm, Gareth. M.Com., U. Cape Town, 1964, postgrad. with distinction, 1966. Chartered Acct. Mgr. Touche Ross & Co., Cape Town and Montreal, 1959-67; exec. v.p., chief oper. officer Edper Enterprises Ltd., Toronto, Ont., Can., 1968-90, Brascan Corp., Toronto, 1979-91, pres. and CEO, 1991—2002, group chmn., 2002—. Bd. dirs. Falconbridge Inc., Noranda Inc., Norbord, Inc., Fraser Papers, Inc., Great Lakes Power, Inc., Brookfield Properties, Inc., Astral Media Inc. Chmn. bd. trustees Royal Ont. Mus.; bd. dirs. C.D. Howe Inst. Office: Brascan Corp Ste 300 181 Bay St PO Box 762 Toronto ON Canada M5J 2T3 E-mail: dhorton@brascancorp.com.

COCO, SAMUEL LOUIS, music educator, musician, composer; b. Johnstown, Pa., May 7, 1950; s. Sam and Anna Grace Coco; m. Kathleen Marie Bombatch, Aug. 10, 1974. BS in Music Edn., Indiana U. of Pa., 1973. Cert. educator Pa. Tchr., choral condr. Forest Hills Mid. and H.S., Sidman, Pa., 1973—. Asst. condr., condr. Johnstown Youth Symphony, 1981—90; guest condr. Cambria County Chorus Festivals, Pa.; double bassist Johnstown Symphony, 1968—73, percussionist, 1976—89; asst. hockey coach Forest Hills H.S., golf coach, 1982—84. Composer: (folk song) Flight to the Coast, Nine For Nine, (choral composition) Vision of a Holy Night, (organ composition) Prelude in F minor. Mem. Johnstown Symphony Opera Festival Com., chmn., 1996—2000; chmn. student devel. com. Johnstown Symphony Opera Festival. Sgt. Pa. N.G., 1971—77. Mem.: Music Educators Nat. Conf., Pa. Music Educators Assn., Moose. Avocations: skiing, hockey, golf. Office: Forest Hills Sch Dist 487 Locust St Sidman PA 15955 Office Phone: 814-487-7613. E-mail: samcoc@mail.fhsd.k12.pa.us.

COCOVES, ANITA PETZOLD, psychotherapist; b. Princeton, N.J., June 2, 1957; d. Charles Bernard and Kathleen Marie (McDonald) Petzold; m. Nicholas John Cocoves, Oct. 11, 1997; 1 child, Nicholas Euthymius. AS in Bus., Indian River C.C., Fla., 1986; BS in Liberal Studies, Barry U., 1988; MS in Human Svcs. Adminstrn., Nova U., 1989, postgrad., 1989—91; PhD in Human Svcs. Adminstrn., LaSalle U., 1994. Lic. mental health counselor, Fla.; cert. addictions prevention profl.; internat. cert. alcohol and drug abuse counselor; nat. cert. counselor; cert. employee assistance counselor; nat. cert. clin. mental health counselor; nat. cert. addictions counselor; cert. DUI instr.; cert. family and county ct. mediator. Admissions coord. Palm Beach Inst., West Palm Beach, Fla., 1985—86; dir. admissions Heritage Health Corp., Jensen Beach, Fla., 1986—89; coord. rug abuse strategy Martin County Bd. of County Commrs., Stuart, Fla., 1989—2001; adminstr. health and human svcs. Martin County Bd. of County Commr., Stuart, 2001—. Mem. Drug Resource Team for the 12th Congl. Dist., Fla., 1990—, Juvenile Justice Assn. of the 19th Jud. Ct., Fla., 1993—, vice chmn. 1999—; grant writer in field. Vol. Hist. Soc. Martin County, Stuart, 1986—; mem. United Way Martin County, Stuart, 1993; mem. bd. dirs. Cmty. AIDS Adv. Project, Stuart, 1993; chmn. treatment com. Martin County Task Force on Substance Abused Children, Stuart, 1993; chmn. Legis. Subcom. Martin County Juvenile Justice Com., 1998—. Recipient Outstanding Cmty. Svc. award United Way Martin County, Stuart, 1993. Mem. NASW, Am. Mental Health Counselors Assn., Nat. Criminal Justice Assn., Nat. Assn. Alcoholism and Drug Abuse Counselors, Nat. Consortium Treatment Alternatives to St. Crime Programs, Am. Coll. Addiction Treatment Adminstrs., Am. Labor-Mgmt. Adminstrs., Fla. Alcohol and Drug Abuse Assn. Republican. Roman Catholic. Avocations: walking, reading. Office: Martin County Bd County Commrs 400 SE Osceola St Stuart FL 34994-2504 E-mail: acocoves@martin.fl.us.

COCOZZOLI, GARY RICHARD, library director; b. Detroit, Oct. 27, 1951; s. Berto and Yolanda Virginia Cocozzoli. BA in Geography, Wayne State U., Detroit, 1973, MLS, 1974. With serials and interloan dept. Lawrence Inst. Tech., Southfield, Mich., 1975-81; dir. libr. Lawrence Tech. U., Southfield, 1981—. Mem. exec. bd. Mich. Libr. Consortium, 1994-97. Author: (with others) German-American History and Life, 1980, Japan's Economic Challenge, 1988; reviewer: Am. Reference Books Annual, 1985—. Pres. Cambridge Village Assn., Southfield, 1987—. Recipient Disting. Alumnus award libr. sci. program Wayne State U., 1990, Marburger Exellence in Achievement award, Adminstr. of Yr. award, 1998. Mem. ALA, Mich. Libr. Assn. (acad. divsn. bd. 1986-88, continuing edn. com. 1992-94, bd. mgmt. and adminstrv. divsn. 1998-2000), Spl. Librs. Assn. (career devel. com. 1987-88), S.E. Mich. League Librs. (chair 1988-90, bd. dirs. 1996-98), Coun. on Resource Devel. (chmn. Oakland County, Mich. 1990-91, sec. coun. resource devel. 1996-97), Mich. Libr. Exch. (steering com. 2001—), Data Rsch. Users Group (v.p. 2005—), Toastmasters. Office: Lawrence Tech U 21000 W Ten Mile Rd Southfield MI 48075-1058 Office Phone: 248-204-3000. E-mail: grc@ltu.edu.

CODDING, FREDERICK HAYDEN, lawyer; b. Hopewell, Va., Dec. 13, 1938; s. Francis Chadwick and Ruthcille Sharon (Craven) C.; m. Judith Willis Hawkins, Apr. 30, 1966; children: Forrest Hayden, Judith Chadwick, Cally Willis, Clare Catharine. AB, Coll. William and Mary, 1962; JD, Georgetown U., 1966. Bar: Va. 1966, D.C. 1968, U.S. Supreme Ct. 1979. Legal asst. VA, Washington, 1963-65; Capitol Hill reporter, editor Congressional Monitor, Washington, 1966; law clk. to chief judge D.C. Ct. Appeals, 1966-68; individual practice law Va. and Washington; v.p., counsel Nat. Assn. Miscellaneous, Ornamental and Archtl. Products Contractors, Fairfax, Va., 1970—; counsel, dir. Nat. Assn. Reinforcing Steel Contractors, Fairfax, 1970—. Editor pub. legis., adminstrv., bldg. and constrn. industry newsletters, reports. Mem. federally established rev. bds. for constrn., OSHA and industry; counsel, pres. Fairfax Police Youth Club; appointee Fairfax City Sch. Bd., 1983-88. Mem. ABA, D.C. Bar Assn., Va. Bar Assn., Fairfax Bar Assn., Nat. Coun. Erectors, Fabricators and Riggers, Sigma Nu. Office: Law Office 10382 Main St Fairfax VA 22030-2412

CODDING, MITCHELL ALLAN, museum director, cultural organization administrator; b. Bartlesville, Okla., Sept. 20, 1954; m. Amparo Gonzalez, Aug. 10, 1983. BA in Spanish, U. Okla., 1954; PhD in Spanish, U. Ky., 2000. Vis. asst. prof. U. Calif., Riverside, 1983-84; asst. dir. The Hispanic Soc. Am., N.Y.C., 1984-95, dir., 1995—. Lectr. in field. Co-author: Maps, Charts, Globes: Five Centruies of Exploration, 1992, Defining the Americas: Accounts and Images of Latin America fromthe European Encounter through Independence, 1997; co-editor: Coastal Charts of the Americas and West Africa from the School of Luis Teixeira, circa 1585, 1993, Facsimiles from an Illuminated Hebrew Bible of the Fifteenth Century at The Hispanic Society of America, 1993. Edward Larocque Tinker fellow The Hispanic Soc. Am., 1982, John Carter Brown Libr. fellow Brown U., 1982. Office: Hispanic Soc Am 613 W 155th St New York NY 10032-7501*

CODELKA, MAUREEN, music educator, theater educator, conductor; b. Balt. MusM in Vocal Performance, Cath. U. Am., 1975. Instr. Trinity Coll., Washington, 1974—75; assoc. prof. musical theatre Cath. U. Am., 1975—. Asst. chorus dir., choir dir., condr. Cath. U. Am., Washington, 1975—2000; asst. condr. Summer Opera Theatre, Washington, 1978—90; music dir., accompanist Mark Forrest, Internat. Irish Tenor, 1990—; condr., music dir. Surflight Theatre, Beach Haven, NJ, 2000—, York Theatre Musicals, N.Y.C., 2000—; music dir. Mandela, N.Y.C., 2000—03; condr., music dir. Seacoast Repertory Theatre, Portsmouth, NH, 2001—01; chorus condr. Smithsonian Instn., Washington; condr., music dir., stage dir. Shaker Mountain Opera, Pittsfield, Mass., Amalfi Coast Music Festival, Italy; music dir., accompanist U. S. DOD Overseas Tours, Washington. Composer/music director/accompanist: musical theatre Reflections on the Heart of a Woman, Electric Blue. Office: Catholic Univ America 620 Michigan Ave NE Washington DC 20064 E-mail: codelka@cua.edu.

CODERE, HELEN FRANCES, anthropologist, educator, university dean; b. Winnipeg, Man., Can., Sept. 10, 1917; came to U.S., 1919, naturalized, 1924; d. Charles Francis and Mabelle (Prosser) C. BA summa cum laude, U. Minn., 1939; PhD, Columbia, 1950. Instr. Vassar Coll, 1946-50, asst. prof., 1951-53, asso. prof., 1955-57, prof., 1958-63; vis. lectr. anthropology U. B.C., 1954-55, Northwestern U., winter 1963; mem. faculty Bennington Coll., 1963-64; prof. anthropology Brandeis U., 1964-82; dean Brandeis U. (Grad. Sch. Arts and Scis.), 1975-77, retired, 1982; anthrop. fieldwork Kwakiutl Indians of, B.C., 1951-55, Rwanda, Africa, 1959-60. Mem. adv. panel on anthropology Nat. Sci. Found., 1968-71 Author: Fighting with Property: A Study of Kwakiutl Potlatching and Warfare, 1792-1930, 1950, The Biography of an African Society, Rwanda 1900-1960; also articles.; Editor: Kawkiutl Ethnography (Franz Boas), 1966. Faculty fellow Vassar Coll., 1956; Social Sci. Research Council fellow, 1956, 62-63; Guggenheim fellow, 1959-60 Fellow Am. Anthrop. Assn. (exec. council 1966-69), AAAS; mem. Am. Ethnol. Soc. (pres. 1972-73), Northeastern Anthrop. Assn. (pres. 1973), Phi Beta Kappa. Home: 100 Newbury Ct Ste 609 Concord MA 01742

CODEY, RICHARD JAMES, acting governor, former state legislator; b. Orange, N.J., Nov. 27, 1946; m. Mary Jo Rolli, Nov.28, 1981; children: Kevin, Christopher. Student Trenton Jr. Coll.; BA in Edn., Fairleigh Dickinson U., 1981. Mem. N.J. Gen. Assembly, Trenton, 1974—81, chmn. Assembly State Govt Com.; mem. NJ State Senate (dist. 27), Trenton, 1982—; chmn. Senate Institutions, Health and Welfare Com NJ State Senate, 1982—92, asst. minority leader, 1992—98, minority leader, 1998—2001, Dem. Senate pres. Trenton, 2002—03, pres., 2004—; acting gov. State of NJ, Trenton, 2002, 2004—. Pres. Olympic Insurance Agy., 1983—. Recipient Svc. award N.J. Mental Health Assn., Svc. award N.J. Prosecutor's Assn.; named Citizen of Yr., N.J. Psychiat. Assn. Mem. Nat. Assn. Funeral Dirs., State Assn. Funeral Dirs. Democrat. Office: NJ Senate PO Box 099 State Capitol Trenton NJ 08625

CODINHA, J. WILLIAM, lawyer; b. NYC, 1947; BA, Ohio Wesleyan U., 1969; JD, Boston U., 1972. Bar: Mass. 1972, DC 1994, Fed. Dist. Ct. Mass., First Cir. Ct. Appeals. First asst. dist. atty., chief trial div. Middlesex County Dist. Atty.'s Office; spl. asst. atty. gen. Ward Commn., 1980—81; mem. Nixon Peabody LLP, Boston, 1981—, ptnr., practice group co-leader. Chief counsel US Senate Select Com. on POW/MIA Affairs, 1991—93, US Senate Com. on Banking, Housing and Urban Affairs (Whitewater Investigation), 1994. Mem.: DC Bar Assn. Office: Nixon Peabody LLP 100 Summer St Boston MA 02110 Office Phone: 617-345-1325. Office Fax: 866-947-1684. E-mail: jcodinha@nixonpeabody.com.

CODISPOTI, ANDRE JOHN, allergist, immunologist; b. Bklyn., Apr. 27, 1938; s. Bruno Mario and Antoinette (Savarese) C.; m. Miranda Babini, June 14, 1967; children: Rita, Elisa, Andrew. BA, Coll. of Holy Cross, 1959; MD, U. Bologna, Italy, 1965. Diplomate Am. Bd. Pediatrics, Am. Bd. Allergy and Immunology. Rotating intern Long Island Coll. Hosp., Bklyn., 1966, resident in pediatrics, 1967-69, fellow in allergy and immunology, 1971-73; pvt. practice Suffern, N.Y., 1972—. Maj. M.C., U.S. Army, 1969-71. Fellow Am. Coll. Allergy, Asthma and Immunology, Am. Acad. Allergy, Asthma and Immunology. Republican. Roman Catholic. Avocations: reading, music, travel, tennis, skiing. Office: 7 Hemion Rd Suffern NY 10901-4903 also: 70 Gilbert St Monroe NY 10950-1538 E-mail: acodispotimd@aol.com.

CODRON, MICHAEL VICTOR, theatrical producer; b. June 8, 1930; s. I.A. and Lily (Morganstern) C. Ed., St. Paul's Sch.; MA, Worcester Coll., Oxford U. Mem. adv. coun. Hampstead Theatre; adminstr. Aldwych Theatre; Cameron Mackintosh prof. contemporary theatre Oxford U., Eng., 1993, emeritus fellow St. Catherine's Coll., 2003—. Prodns. include: Breath of Spring, 1957; The Birthday Party, 1958; Pieces of Eight, 1959; The Caretaker, 1960; The Tenth Man, 1961; Rattle of a Simple Man, 1962; Next Time I'll Sing to You, Private Lives, The Lovers and the Dwarfs, Cockade, 1963; Poor Bitos, The Formation Dancers, Entertaining Mr. Sloane, 1964; Loot, The Killing of Sister George, Ride a Cock Horse, 1965; Little Malcolm and His Struggle Against the Eunuchs, The Anniversary, There's a Girl in My Soup, Big Bad Mouse, 1966; The Judge, The Flip Side, Wise Child, The Boy Friend, 1967; Not Now Darling, The Real Inspector Hound, 1968; The Contractor, Slag, The Two of Us, The Philanthropist, 1970; The Foursome, Butley, A Voyage Round My Father, The Changing Room, 1971; Veterans, Time and Time Again, Crown Matrimonial, My Fat Friend, 1972; Collaborators, Savages, Habeas Corpus, Absurd Person Singular, 1973; Knuckle, Flowers, Golden Pathway Annual, The Norman Conquests, John Paul George Ringo-...and Bert, 1974; A Family and a Fortune, Alphabetical Order, A Far Better Husband, Ashes, Absent Friends, Otherwise Engaged, Stripwell, 1975; Funny Peculiar, Treats, Donkey's Years, Confusions, Teeth 'n' Smiles, Yahoo, 1976; Dusa Stas, Fish & Vi, Just Between Ourselves, Oh, Mr. Porter, Breezeblock Park, The Bells of Hell, The Old Country, 1977; The Rear Column, Ten Times Table, The Unvarnished Truth, The Homecoming, Alice's Boys, Night and Day, 1978; Joking Apart, Tishoo, Stage Struck, 1979; Dr. Faustus, Make and Break, The Dresser, Taking Steps, Enjoy, 1980; Hinge & Bracket, Rowan Atkinson in Revue, House Guest, Quartermaine's Terms, 1981; Season's Greetings, Noises Off, Funny Turns, 1982, The Real Thing, 1982; The Hard Shoulder, 1983; Look, No Hans!, Benefactors, 1984; Jumpers, Who Plays Wins, Clockwise (film), 1985, Made in Bangkok, 1986, Woman in Mind, 1986; Hapgood, Uncle Vanya, Re Joyce!, The Sneeze, Henceforward, 1988; The Cherry Orchard, 1989; Man of the Moment, Look, Look, Hidden Laughter, Private Lives, 1990, What the Butler Saw, 70 Girls 70, The Revengers Comedies, 1991, The Rise and Fall of Little Voice, 1992, Time of My Life, 1993, Jamais Vu, 1993, Dead Funny, 1994, Arcadia, 1994, The Sisters Rosensweig, 1994, Indian Ink, 1995, The Killing of Sister George, 1995, Dealer's Choice, 1995, The Shakespeare Revue, 1995, A Talent to Amuse, 1996, Tom and Clem, 1997, Silhouette Heritage, 1997, Things We Do For Love, 1998, Elton John's Glasses, 1998, Alarms and Excursions, 1998, The Invention of Love, 1998, Copenhagen, 1999 (Tony award, 2000),

Quartet, 1999, Comic Potential, 1999, Peggy For You, 2000, Blue/Orange, 2001, Life After George, 2002, Bedroom Farce, 2002, Damsels in Distress, 2002, My Brilliant Divorce, 2003, Dinner, 2003, Democracy, 2004, Ying Tong, 2005, Losing Louis, 2005. Recipient Michael Victor Codron CBE. Mem.: Garrick Club. Office: Aldwych Theatre London WC2B 4DF England

CODY, ALDUS MORRILL, retired editor, journalist, typographer; b. Somerville, Mass., Jan. 11, 1915; s. Luther Morrill and Josephine Belle (Morrill) C.; m. Dorothy Gifford, Dec. 25, 1936; 1 child, Raymond Gifford; m. Bertha Hood Carnahan, June 1, 2002. BA in Journalism, U. Fla., 1936. Editor Suwannee Dem., Live Oak, Fla., 1936-37, Williamson County News, Franklin, Tenn., 1937, Marion County News, Ocala, Fla., 1938-39, Kissimmee (Fla.) Gazette, 1939-41, Share Your Knowledge Rev. (later Rev. Graphic Arts), Cin., 1970-80, The High Twelvian, St. Louis, 1989-95; mng. editor Ocala Morning Banner, 1937-38; editor, pub. The Fla. Cattleman, Kissimmee, 1940-45; founder, CEO, Cody Publs., Kissimmee, 1946-77; editor News of Masonic Cmty., Kissimmee, 1989-96; ret., 1996; editor The Quadrangle, Good Samaritan Retirement Village, Kissimmee, 1996—2000. Author: (with Robert Cody) Osceola County—First 100 Years, 1996; editor The Connector, 1st United Meth. Ch., 2001—. Former commr. and mayor City of Kissimmee. Mem. Internat. Assn. Printing House Craftsmen (dist. gov. 1968-70, nat. editor 1970-80), Fla. Assn. Square Dancers (founder, pres.), Masons (past master), Shriners, Rotary (past pres. Kissimmee). Democrat. Methodist. Avocation: genealogy. Address: 1660-02 Westgate Dr Kissimmee FL 34746-6446 E-mail: aldus@kua.net.

CODY, FRANK JOSEPH, secondary school educator, education educator, consultant; b. Detroit, Sept. 13, 1940; s. Burns J. and Margaret (Dowley) C.; m. Shirley Black, May 16, 1992. AB, Loyola U., 1962, PhD, 1965, MA, 1966, MDiv, 1975; PhD, Ohio State U., 1980. Cert. tchr., prin., supr., Ohio, Mich. Headmaster St. Ignatius H.S., Cleve., 1977-81; dir. Chapel Sch., Sao Paulo, Brazil, 1981-83, U. Detroit Ctr. Econ. Edn., 1988-91; assoc. prof., tchr. adminstrv. edn. U. Detroit, 1983-91; adminstr. Grand Rapids Cath. Secondary Schs., 1991-95; headmaster Woodside Priory Sch., Portola Valley, Calif., 1995-97; tchr. Kalamazoo Ctrl. H.S., 1997—2005, asst. prin., 1998-99; dir. Small Learning Cmtys. Project, 2002—03; instr., acad. coord. Spring Arbor U., 2005—; cons. Prosouc, Inc., Sao Paulo, Brazil, 2005—. Trustee Wheeling Coll., 1980-82, mem. Coun. Entrance Svcs. Coll. Bd., 1978-81; mem. Mich. Supt.'s Com. on Accreditation, 1984-88; commr. Nat. Assn. Secondary Sch. Prins./Carnegie Found. Commn. on Future of Am. H.S., 1994-96; dir. rsch. English lang. studies Unified Coll. Guarulhos, Sao Paulo, Brazil, 1998-2002; faculty U. Phoenix, 2005—. Co-author: Manual of Educational Risk Management, Escola e Communidade: Uma Parceria Necessaria, O Professor Do Terceiro Milenio; contbr. articles to profl. jours. Trustee Trinity Sch., Menlo Park, Calif., 1996-97; commr. planning commission City of Kalamazoo, 2003—; mem. Kalamazoo Cath. Unified Sch. Bd., 2004—. Roman Catholic. Office: Kalamazoo Ctrl High Sch 2432 N Drake Rd Kalamazoo MI 49006-1361 E-mail: buffcody@ameritech.net.

CODY, HIRAM SEDGWICK, JR., retired telecommunications industry executive; b. Nov. 1, 1915; s. Hiram Sedgwick and Harriett Mary (Collins) C.; m. Mary Vaughn Jacoby, Oct. 4, 1941; children: Margaret Vaughn, Harriett Mary, Hiram Sedgwick III, Henry Jacoby, William Collins. BS cum laude, Yale U., 1937, JD, 1940. Bar: NC 1940. With Western Electric Co., Inc., 1946-71, regional mgr. engrng. and installation Chgo., 1961-64, dir. orgn. planning N.Y.C., 1964-65, sec., treas., 1965-71; asst. treas. AT&T, N.Y.C., 1971-80; ret., 1980. V.p. Morris-Sussex coun. Boy Scouts of Am., 1970-80; vice-chmn. Zoning Bd. Adjustment Mountain Lakes, N.J., 1968-80; boro councilman, Mountain Lakes, 1960-61; trustee, treas. Asheville (N.C.) Sch., 1974-84; trustee Asheville Symphony Orch., 1981-91, Asheville Cmty. Concert Assn., 1981-91; bd. advisors Warren Wilson Coll., 1983—, chmn., 1987-90. With USN, 1941-45, MTO, comdr. USNR, 1946. Mem. N.C. State Bar, Tel. Pioneers Am. (v.p. 1969-71, treas. 1971-78), Tau Beta Pi. Home: HIghland Farms 200 Tabernacle Rd Unit H-214 Black Mountain NC 28711

CODY, JUDITH, composer, writer; Student, U. Calif., Berkeley, 1977, Foothill Coll., Los Altos Hills, Calif., 1972—75; pvt. student in Japanese culture and music, 1966—68. Editor: Resource Guide on Women in Music, 1981; author: Vivian Fine: A Bio-Bibliography, 2001; (poems) Eight Frames Eight, 2002; author numerous poems; composer: Trio for flute, classical guitar and poem, 1974, Firelights: Variations for classical guitar, 1976-77, City and Country Themes in G, 1976, Dances, opus 8, 1977, Nocturne, opus 9, 1977, classical guitar Seven Concert Etudes, opus 7, 10, 11, 13, 14, 15 & 18, 1977, classical guitar, Christmas Theme, opus 17, 1977, Opus 16, flute & guitar, 1977, Trio, opus 21, two flutes and guitar, 1978, Three Songs of Middle English, opus 26, voice and guitar, 1978, Sonata, opus 22, flute and guitar, 1978, Theme and Variations, opus 27, piano, 1978, Three Patterns, opus 29, piano, 1978, Two Patterns, opus 30, piano, 1978, Flute Poems, opus 19, 1978, Meditation for Four Hands, duet, steel string and classical guitars, 1983, Rain on the Face of Buddha at Kamakura, classical guitar, 1984, Three Haiku Love Songs, piano and soprano, 1986, Danger Dance, piano and soprano, 1986, Whales' Song, piano, 1986, Swan River, piano, 1986, Looking Under Footprints, voice and classical guitar, 1986, Two Songs, piano, 1999, Heart-Blood-Heart, piano, 1999, Death of a Small Animal, piano, 1999, Earth of Ukraine, piano, 1999, Song Cycle: Updated History of the Universe, classical guitar, flute ensemble, voice, 2003. Founder steering com., mem. 1st Bay Area Congress on Women in Music, San Francisco State U., 1980—81. Recipient 1st Prize poem Amelia Mag., 1993, music composition winner New Times Concerts, La. State U., 1979, winner Atlantic Monthly Poetry Contest, 1973, Hon. Mention Emily Dickinson Poetry award, 2003; poetry in permanent collection Smithsonian Instn., Washington, 1978. Mem. PEN, Am. Music Ctr., Poets and Writers, Inc., Bay Area Congress on Women in Music (founding Steering Com. mem.). Achievements include First to discover and document composer's creative explosions in youth and old age, 2001; first woman engineering drafter in city and county of San Francisco Power and Utilities Engineering Bureau. Avocations: soprano in opera chorus, classical guitar. Personal E-mail: poeticsethisc-whoswho@yahoo.com.

CODY, PETER MALCOLM, economist, development, management consultant; b. Paris, July 30, 1925; s. Edward Morrill C. and Frances (Ryan) Millington; m. Rosa Maria Alatorre, Jan. 28, 1957; children: Cornelia Francisca, Cecilia Leonor, Michael Peter, William Ryan, Peter Malcolm. BA in Internat. Rels., Yale U., 1947, MA in Econs., 1948, postgrad., 1949-50. Instr. econs. Yale U., 1948—50; economist Fed. Res. Bd., Washington, 1950—54; program economist U.S. Agy. Internat. Devel., Mexico, 1954—57, program officer, 1957—59, Laos desk officer, 1959—61, dep. dir., U.S. aid, 1961—64, dep. dir., 1965—67, dir. U.S. aid, 1967—71, dir. U.S aid, 1971—75, dir. ops.appraisal staff Washington, 1975—76, dir. U.S. aid Philippines, 1976—79, dir., 1979—80, Office Vietnam Affairs, Washington, 1964—65; freelance econ. and social devel. and mgmt. cons. Haiti, Mauritania, Liberia, Egypt, Sudan, Zaire, Kenya, El Salvador, Guatemala, Bolivia and South Pacific, 1980—. Sch. bd. Am. Sch. Laos, Vientiane, Laos, 1965-67, Am. Sch. Paraguay, Asunción, Paraguay, 1967-71, Paraguay Nat. Cultural Ctr. Bd., Asunción, 1964-71. Lt. USN, 1943—46. Recipient Orden Nacional del Merito Pres. of Paraguay, 1971, Meritorious Svc. award US AID, 1981. Mem. Am. Fgn. Svc. Assn., Cosmos Club (Washington). Avocations: computers, reading, tennis, skiing, hiking. Home: 5600 Wisconsin Ave Apt 606 Chevy Chase MD 20815-4410

CODY, RICHARD A., career military officer; b. Montpelier, Vt., Aug. 20, 1950; m. Vicki Lyn Cody; children: Clint, Tyler. BS, U.S. Mil. Acad., 1972. Master army aviator. Commd. 2d lt. U.S. Army, 1972, advanced through grades to gen., 2004; comdr. 1st bn., 101st aviation regt. 101st Airborne Divsn., Operation Desert Storm; bn. exec. officer, co. comdr. Attack Helicopter Bns.; asst. divsn. comdr. for maneuver 4th Inf. Divsn. (Mechanized), Ft. Hood, Tex., 1998—2000; comdr. 101st Airborne Divsn., Ft. Campbell, Ky., 2000—02; dep. chief of staff, G-3 U.S. Army, Washington, 2002—04, vice chief of staff, 2004—. Decorated Legion of Merit with 2 oak leaf clusters, DFC, Bronze Star medal, Air medals, others. Office: 200 Army Pentagon Washington DC 20310-0200

CODY, THOMAS GERALD, management consultant, writer; b. Holyoke, Mass., Feb. 18, 1929; s. John Francis and Mary Gertrude (Scanlon) C.; m. Kathleen Mary Maguire, Nov. 17, 1956 (dec. June 2004); children—Kathleen, Joseph. AB, Coll. of Holy Cross, 1950; postgrad., Boston Coll., 1950—52; MBA, Harvard U., 1957. Various corp. mgmt. positions, 1955—62; cons., prin., v.p. Fry Cons., Inc., Chgo., L.A., Washington, 1962—72; exec. dir. U.S. EEOC, Washington, 1972—74; asst. sec. for adminstrn. HUD, Washington, 1974—76; Washington v.p. L.B. Knight & Assoc., Inc., 1976—79; pres. Lester B. Knight Mgmt. Cons. Group, 1979—81, Thomas Cody & Assoc., Annapolis, Md., 1981—84; v.p. human resources Baxter Travenol Labs. Inc., Deerfield, Ill., 1984—86, corp. v.p., 1985—87; exec. v.p., Chgo. office Jannotta Bray & Assoc. Inc., 1987—, ptnr. Washington office, 1989—96; prin. The Washington Group, 1996—. Author: Management Consulting: A Game Without Chips, 1986, Strategy of a Megamerger, 1990, Innovating For Health, 1994. Mem. U.S. Arch. and Transp. Barriers Compliance Bd., 1974-76, Anne Arundel Commn. on Women, 1977-79, U.S. Comptr. Gen. Adv. Panel, 1983-88; bd. dirs. Found. for Jr. Blind, L.A., 1968-70, Baxter Am. Found., 1986-88, Suburban Cook County Area Agy. on Aging, 1988-89; trustee St. Mary of the Woods Coll., Terre Haute, Ind., 1987-90; mem. panel on employers and working families NAS. 1st lt. USMC, 1953-55. Mem. Harvard Club of N.Y.C. Home: 5450 Whitley Park Ter Apt 303 Bethesda MD 20814-2054 Personal E-mail: thomas-cody@hotmail.com.

CODY, THOMAS GERALD, lawyer; b. N.Y.C., Nov. 4, 1941; s. Thomas J. Cody and Esther Mary Courtney; m. Mary Ellen Palmer, Nov. 26, 1966; children: Thomas Jr., Mark, Amy, Anne. BA in Philosophy, Maryknoll Coll., 1963; JD, St. John's U., 1967; LLD (hon.), Cen. State U., Wilberforce, Ohio, 1985. Bar: N.Y. 1967. Assoc. Simpson Thacher & Bartlett, N.Y., 1967-72; asst. prof. law sch. St. John's U., N.Y., 1972-76; sr. v.p., gen. counsel, sec. Pan Am. Airways, N.Y., 1976-82; sr. v.p. law and pub. affairs Federated Dept. Stores, Cin., 1982-88, exec. v.p. legal & human resources, 1988—2003, vice chmn. legal, human resources and external affairs, 2003—. Trustee Xavier U., Cin., Children's Hosp. Med. Ctr., Cin; bd. dirs. Cin. USA Regional Chamber Mem. ABA, Bankers Club, Queen City Club, Hyde Park Country Club, Commonwealth Club of Cin. Roman Catholic. Office: Federated Dept Stores Inc 7 W 7th St Cincinnati OH 45202-2424 Office Phone: 513-579-7768.*

CODY, WALTER JAMES MICHAEL, lawyer, retired state attorney general; b. Memphis, Mar. 13, 1936; s. Walter James and Bess Lou (Hill) C.; m. Suzanna Marten; children; Jane BArton, Michael, Mia. BA, SouthwesternU., Memphis, 1958; JD, U. Va., 1961; LLD, Rhodes Coll., Memphis, 1989. Bar: Tenn. 1961. Ptnr. Burch, Porter & Johnson, Memphis, 1961-77, 81-84, 89—; U.S. atty. Western Dist. Tenn., Memphis, 1977-81; atty. gen. State of Tenn., 1984-88; ptnr. Bass, Berry and Sims, Nashville, 1988-89. Lectr. LeMoyne-Owen Coll., Memphis State U. Law Sch.; instr. polit. sci. Southwestern U., Memphis; adj. prof. law Vanderbilt U.; mem. bd. profl. responsibility Tenn. Supreme Ct., 1990-92; bd. dirs. Nat. Civil Rights Mus. Contbr. to: You Can't Eat Magnolias, 1972. Pres. L.Q.C. Lamar Soc., 1970-71; chmn. Shelby County Dem. Party, 1972-74; mem.-at-large Memphis City Coun., 1975-77; trustee, mem. exec. com. Memphis Acad. Arts; chmn. Tenn. Sports Festivals, 1989-92. 1st lt. U.S. Army Res., 1961-67. Recipient Sam A. Myer Meml. award, 1976 Fellow Am. Coll. Trial Lawyers, Am. Bar Found.; mem. ABA, Fed. Bar Assn., Tenn. Bar Assn., Memphis and Shelby County Bar Assn. (co-founder neighborhood legal service project), Nat. Assn. Former U.S. Attys., Memphis and Shelby County Legal Services Assn. (dir.). Democrat. Episcopalian. Office: Burch Porter & Johnson PLLC 130 N Court Ave Memphis TN 38103-2288

CODY, WILLIAM BERMOND, political science professor; b. Brunswick, Ga., Jan. 15, 1949; s. Bermond Hamp and Dorothy Jane (Satterfield) C.; m. Mildred Ann McInnis, Sept. 5, 1970; children: Margaret Jae, Elizabeth Joelle. AB, U. Ga., 1971, MA, 1973, JD, 1986; PhD, New Sch. Social Rsch., 1980. Bar: Ga. 1986. Student advisor New Sch. Social Rsch., N.Y.C., 1978-79; asst. to pres. Robeal Mgmt. Co., Charleston, S.C., 1983-85; assoc. Carr, Tabb & Pope, Atlanta, 1987; legal asst. Ga. Ct. Appeals, Atlanta, 1987-89; asst. prof. polit. sci. U. Ga., Athens, 1989-90; asst. prof. Oxford (Ga.) Coll. Emory U., 1990-93; assoc. prof. Oxford (Ga.) Coll. Emory U., 1993—. Adj. instr. Coll. New Rochelle, N.Y., 1978-79; vis. asst. prof. Clemson (S.C.) U., 1980-83; mem. Emory U. Senate, 1995-97, pres.-elect, 1996-97, pres., 1997-98. Vestryman St. Bede's Episcopal Ch., Atlanta, 1988-92, jr. warden, 1990, sr. warden, 1991; bd. dirs. Interfaith, Inc., Atlanta, 1989-90. Mem. ABA, Am. Polit. Sci. Assn., Ga. Polit. Sci. Assn., So. Polit. Sci. Assn., Am. Hist. Assn., Acad. Polit. Sci., Ga. Bar Assn. Democrat. Office: Polit Sci Dept Oxford Coll Emory U Oxford GA 30054 E-mail: bcody@emory.edu.

CODY, WILMER ST. CLAIR, educational policy researcher; b. Mobile, Ala., Jan. 1, 1937; s. Wilmer St. Clair and Madeline (Maygarden) C.; m. Caroline Marie Burns, Aug. 16, 1958; children: David Marshall, Alison Marie. AB, Harvard U., 1959, EdM, 1960, EdD, 1968. Tchr. Newton (Mass.) Schs., 1960, Mobile County Schs., 1960-62, prin., 1962-64; dir. tchr. edn. Atlanta Schs., 1966-67; supt. Chapel Hill (N.C.) Schs., 1967-71; sr. rsch. assoc. Nat. Inst. Edn., 1971-73; supt. Birmingham (Ala.) City Schs., 1973-83, Montgomery County Schs., Rockville, Md., 1983-87; dir. nat. assessment project Council Chief State Sch. Officers, 1987-88; supt. edn. State of La., 1988-92; exec. dir. Nat. Edn. Goals Panel, Washington, 1992-93; dir. Nat. Faculty/So. Region, New Orleans, 1993-95; commr. edn. State of Ky., Frankfort, 1995-99; pres. Cody Assocs., Inc., 1999—. Cons. in field; mem. Nat. Assessment Governing Bd., 1998-02, Smithsonian Nat. Bd. Contbr. articles to ednl. jours. Mem. Nat. Adv. Com. on Juvenile Justice and Delinquency Prevention, 1976-78; bd. dirs. Comty. Chest, Campfire Girls; trustee Nat. Coun. Econ. Edn., So. Assn. Colls. and Schs., 1990-92; chmn. Nat. Assessment Edn. Policy Com., 1983-87; dir. S.W. Edn. Devel. Lab., 1988-92; steering com. Edn. Commn. of the States, 1990-92, So. Region Edn. Bd., 1990-92, 96-99; exec. bd. Nat. Coun. for Accreditation of Tchr. Edn., 1990-92, 96-98, chair 1998; pres. Coun. Chief State Officers, 1997-98. Named Educator of Yr. ALA, 1977. Mem. Am. Assn. Sch. Adminstrs., Am. Edn. Research Assn., Phi Delta Kappa. Methodist. Home: 1535 Eleonore St New Orleans LA 70115-4242

COE, ANNE ELIZABETH, artist; b. Henderson, Nev., Feb. 27, 1949; d. Percy Ellis and Mary Ernest (Jackson) Coe; m. Dennis Neal Barr, Sept. 13, 1970 (div. May 1973); 1 child, Laurye; m. Robert Patrick Horvath, Apr. 11, 1992. BA cum laude, Ariz. State U., Tempe, 1970, MFA cum laude, 1980. Artist in residence Ariz. Commn. for the Arts, Phoenix, 1982. Illustrator: (children's book) Here is the Southwestern Desert, 1995; exhibited in solo shows at Harry Wood Gallery/Ariz. State U., 1980, Elaine Horwitch Galleries, 1987, 89, 92, 94, Anne Reed Gallery, Sun Valley, Idaho, 1991, 92, Horwitch Newman Gallery, Scottsdale, 1995, 96, Joseph Gross Gallery/ U. Ariz., 1998, Moynihan Gallery, Jackson, Wyo., 1995, others; group shows include Suzanne Brown Gallery, Scottsdale, The White House, Washington, Segal Gallery, N.Y.C., Bruce Mus., Greenwich, Conn., White Tops Gallery, Palm Desert, Calif., Elaine Horwitch Galleries, Soho West, Denver, Americana Mus., El Paso, Ariz. Mus. for Youth, MARS Artspace, Phoenix, Martin Harris, Jackson, Wyo., numerous others; included in collections at Eiteljorg Mus., Indpls., Whitney Mus. Western Art, Cody, Wyo., Centro de Arte Moderna, Guadalajara, Mex., Mus. of N.D., Grand Forks, Sky Harbor Internat. Airport, Phoenix, Smithsonian Instn., Washington, Ariz. State U., Tempe, Scottsdale Ctr. for the Arts, numerous others; subject of numerous articles. Mem. adv. bd. Ctrl. Ariz. Land Trust, 1994—; chmn. superstition area land trust Apache Junction Sch. Dist., 1995-96; mem. Gov.'s Exec. Task Force for the Ariz. Preserve Initiative, 1995; mem. State Land Conservation Adv. Com., 1996-99. Avocations: land use issues, hiking, the environment. Home: PO Box 1701 Apache Junction AZ 85217-1701

COE, BENJAMIN PLAISTED, retired state official; b. Long Beach, Calif., Aug. 24, 1930; s. Benjamin and Mary Plaisted (Ricker) C.; m. Margaret Jane Butler, Sept. 5, 1953; children: Benjamin B., Elizabeth C., Mary Susan, Margaret Jane. AB, Bowdoin Coll., 1953; BS, Ch.E., MIT, 1953. Lic. profl. engr., N.Y. With silicone products dept. Gen. Electric Co., Waterford, N.Y., 1953-65, process econs. engr., 1963-65; exec. dir. Vols. for Internat. Tech. Assistance, Schenectady, 1965-68, exec. dir. U.S.A. div., 1969-73, v.p., 1971-73; exec. dir. Tug Hill Commn., N.Y. State, 1973-93; ret. Tug Hill Commn., 1993. Vestry Trinity Episcopal Ch., 1978-81, warden, 1981-86, 93-96; bd. dirs. Schenectady Symphony, 1969; chmn. pub. svc. divsn. Jefferson County United Way, 1982-84, bd. dirs., 1985-88, 2d v.p., 1988-89, 1st v.p., 1990-91, pres., 1992-94; pres. Vol. Ctr. Jefferson County, 1994-96, 98—. Named Exec. of Yr. Watertown Profl. Secs. Internat., 1978-79; recipient Ageless Achievers award, N.Y. State, 2002. Mem. AIChE (chmn. N.E. N.Y. sect. 1965), Rotary (pres. Watertown 1989-90, dist. gov. 1996-97, Citation for Meritorious Svc. 2002), Phi Beta Kappa, Sigma Xi, Tau Beta Pi. Home: 627 Stone Cir Watertown NY 13601 *I have come to think that success should be measured internally, between man and his maker, rather than by external signs. My goals are to involve myself with mankind in a worthwile way and at the same time keep my family fed, healthy, and in a position to work toward their own goals.*

COE, CHRISTOPHER LANE, psychology researcher; b. N.Y.C., Jan. 4, 1951; s. Samuel Peter and Katherine (Diamond) C.; m. Lyn Bromley, Aug. 25, 1980; children: Ian Andrew, Kieran Michael. BA, CCNY, 1971; PhD, SUNY, Bklyn., 1976. Postdoctoral fellow Stanford U. Med. Sch., Calif., 1977; asst. dir. Stanford Primate Facility, 1977-79; rsch. assoc. dept. psychiatry, 1979-81; asst. prof. dept. psychiatry, 1981-85; assoc. prof. U. Wis., Madison, 1985-87; chmn. Wis. Primate Lab., 1985—; prof., 1988—. Outside reviewer NSF and NIH, Washington, 1982—. Author: Handbook of Squirrel Monkey Research, 1985; assoc. editor Am. Jour. Primatology; cons. editor Brain Behavior and Immunity, Developmental Psychobiology; contbr. numerous articles to profl. jours., chpts. to books. Biomed. rsch. grantee NIH, 1983; NIMH grantee, 1983—. Mem. Can. Inst. for Advanced Rsch. (assoc.), Acad. Behavioral Medicine Rsch. (elected), Psychoneuroimmunology Rsch. Soc. Home: 5525 Varsity Hl Madison WI 53705-4651 Office: U Wis Dept Psychology 22 N Charter St Madison WI 53715-1239

COE, DONALD KIRK, retired academic administrator; b. Tuscaloosa, Ala., Nov. 21, 1934; s. Glen Dale and Hazel Mae (Coley) C.; m. Frances Ellen Truman, May 31, 1958; children: Mark William, Sandra Elizabeth, Bonnie Lee. BA, U. Ala., 1957. Wire editor Xenia (Ohio) Daily Gazette, 1958-59; reporter, county editor Sharon (Pa.) Herald, 1959-61; asst. wire editor Pitts. Press, 1961-66; in public relations and fund raising Carnegie-Mellon U., Pitts., 1966-70; editorial writer St. Petersburg (Fla.) Times, 1970-75; chief editorial writer Chgo. Sun-Times, 1975-84; univ. dir. pub. affairs U. Ill., 1984-98, spl. asst. to pres., 1998-2000; ret., 2000. Pres. Nat. Conf. Editorial Writers Found., 1989-91. Capt. USAR, 1958-68. Recipient Ill. UPI award, 1977 Mem. Sigma Delta Chi (pres. coll. chpt. 1957) Presbyterian. Home: 723 Bonnie Brae Pl River Forest IL 60305-1930

COE, FREDRIC L., internist, educator, medical researcher; b. Chgo, Dec. 25, 1936; s. Lester J. and Lillian (Chaitlen) C.; m. Eleanor Joyce Brodny, May 5, 1965; children: Brian, Laura. AB, U. Chgo., 1955, MS, 1957, MD, 1961. Diplomate Am. Bd. Internal Medicine. Intern Michael Reese Hosp., Chgo., 1961-62, resident, 1962-65, U. Tex. S.W. Med. Sch., 1967-69; chmn. nephrology Michael Reese Hosp., 1972-82; prof. medicine U. Chgo., 1977—, prof. physiology, 1979—; chmn. nephrology A.M. Billings Hosp., Chgo., 1982—; founder, pres. Litholink Corp., 1995—. Author: Nephrolithiasis, 1978, 2d edit. (with J. Parks), 1987, (with B. Brenner and F.C. Rector) Renal Physiology, 1986, Clinical Nephrology; editor: Renal Therapeutics, 1978, Nephrolithiasis, 1980, Hypercalciuric States, 1983, (with M. Favus) Disorders of Bone and Mineral Metabolism, 1993, 2d edit., 2001; editor-in-chief Yearbook of Nephrology, 1991-96; editor: (with others) Kidney Stones: Medical and Surgical Management, 1996. Served to capt. USAF, 1961-67. Recipient Belding Scribner medal for lifetime achievement in clin. rsch. Am. Soc. Nephrology, 2000; Univ. of Chgo. Distingguished Svc. Award, 2001; grantee NIH, 1977-. Fellow ACP; mem. Am. Soc. Clin. Investigation, Am. Physiol. Soc., Assn. Am. Physicians Jewish. Achievements include first evidence for hyperuricosuria as cause of calcium renal stones; discovery of nephro calcin a protein inhibitor of crystal growth; first demonstration that human idiopathic hypercalciuria is hereditary. First evidence that apatile plaque begins inthe basement membranes of the renal thin limbs of Henle's loop. Home: 5490 S Shore Dr Chicago IL 60615-5984 Office: U Chgo Med Ctr 5841 S Maryland Ave Chicago IL 60637-1463 Office Phone: 773-702-1475.

COE, HENRY CHITTENDEN, artist; b. Balt., Oct. 23, 1946; s. Ward Baldwin Jr. and Diana Chittenden Coe; m. Pamela Karen Salsbury, Nov. 27, 1999; children: Julia Sibyl, Matthew Chittenden. BA in English, Roanoke Coll., 1969; MFA in Painting, Md. Inst. Coll. Art, 1972. Artist residency Rochefort-en-Terre (France) Residency Program, 1994, Les Amis de la Grande Vigne, Dinan, France, 1998, 2004. Visual arts grantee, Md. State Arts Coun., 1992. Home and Studio: 3300 Gibbons Ave Baltimore MD 21214

COE, LAURIE LYNNE BARKER, photojournalist, artist; b. Miami, Fla., Nov. 26, 1954; d. George Felton Barker and Dorita Maria Comas; m. James Woodrift Coe, Sept. 29, 1980 (div. Apr. 2005); children: Blake Alexander, Alexandra Noelle. Profl. photography, N.Y. Inst. Photography, 1994; grad., Ringling Sch. Art & Design, 2004. Cert. in digital filmmaking, specializing in documentaries. Photographer Marie Selby Botanical Gardens, Sarasota, Fla., 1997—99; corr. North Port Rev., Englewood, Fla., 1997—99; pres. Artistic Endeavours, North Port, Fla., 1998—. Author: In The Beauty of the Morning, 2001; photographer to profl. mags., calendars, postcards, books, Sarasota, A Photographic Portrait, 2000, Greater Miami, a Photographic Portrait, 2002. Photographer Sun Coast Humane Soc., Sarasota, 1998, North Port, 2000—01; bd. mem. Arts and Culture Alliance, Sarasota, 2002—. Recipient Muses award, Arts and Cultural Alliance, 2003, Wall of Tolerance, 2003. Mem.: N.Am. Nature Photographer Assn., North Port Area Art Guild (chairwoman all shows 1998—2001, chair ways and means 1998—2001, v.p. 1999—2001, photographic tchr. childrens summer workshop 2000—01). Achievements include recognition in Cambridge, England Living Legends. Avocations: mentor fo high schools, natural healing, gardening, music. Home and Studio: 2651 Colonade Ln North Port FL 34286 Office Phone: 941-626-1928. Personal E-mail: toadcoe@comcast.net.

COE, LINDA MARLENE WOLFE, marketing development, photographer; b. Logan, Ohio, Apr. 5, 1941; d. Kenneth William and Mary Martha (Eddy) Wolfe; m. Frederic Morrow Coe, Sept. 15, 1962; children: Christopher, Jennifer, Peter, Michael. BFA, Columbus Coll. of Art and Design, 1978. Freelance photographer, Columbus, 1978—; sec., receptionist Plaza Dental, Columbus, 1983; sec. Worthington (Ohio) Dental Group, 1983-85; mktg. and devel. adminstr. Custom Corp. Gift Svc., Worthington, 1985-92, Grandparents Living Theatre, 1993, Premiums & Promotions, Inc., 1995-96; ret., 1996. Trustees Met. Women's Ctr., Columbus, 1986-87. Docent trainee Columbus Mus. Art, 1982-83; mem. Worthington Arts Coun., 1982, 83, 85, 87, 89-93, 94. Mem. Zephrus League, Phoenix Soc. (mem. exec. bd.), Nat. Soc. Fund Raising Execs., Women's Bus. Bd., Columbus Bus. and Profl. Women, Columbus C. of C., Columbus Coll. Art and Design Alumni Assn. Republican. Roman Catholic. Avocations: photography, reading, gardening, sailing. Home: Heron Bay 15240 Shoreline Dr Thornville OH 43076-8855

COE, MICHAEL DOUGLAS, anthropologist, educator; b. NYC, May 14, 1929; s. William Rogers and Clover (Simonton) C.; m. Sophie Dobzhansky, June 5, 1955; children: Nicholas, Andrew, Sarah, Peter, Natalie. AB, Harvard, 1950, PhD, 1959. Asst. prof. U. Tenn., 1958-60; mem. faculty Yale U., 1960—, prof. anthropology, 1968-90, Charles J. MacCurdy prof. anthropology, 1990-94, prof. emeritus, 1994—. Adviser Robert Woods Bliss Collection Pre-Columbian Art, Dumbarton Oaks, Harvard, 1963-80. Author: La Victoria, An Early Site on the Pacific Coast of Guatemala, 1961, Mexico, 1962, The Jaguar's Children: Pre-Classic Art of Central Mexico, 1965, The Maya, 1966, (with Kent V. Flannery) Early Cultures and Human Ecology in South Coastal Guatemala, 1967, America's First Civilization, 1968, The Maya Scribe and His World, 1973, Classic Maya Pottery at Dumbarton Oaks, 1975, Lords of the Underworld, 1978, (with Richard A. Diehl) In the Land of the Olmec,

1980, Young Lords and Old Gods, 1982, (with Dean R. Snow and Elizabeth P. Benson) Atlas of Ancient America, 1986, Breaking the Maya Code, 1992, (with Sophie D. Coe) The True History of Chocolate, 1996, (with Justin Kerr) The Art of the Maya Scribe, 1998, (with Mark Van Stone) Reading the Maya Glyphs, 2001, Angkor and the Khmer Civilization, 2003; contbr. articles to profl. jours. Chmn. bd. Planting Fields Found., 1985—; pres. Heath Hist. Soc., Mass., 1984-90. Fellow Royal Anthrop. Soc.; mem. NAS, Am. Anthrop. Assn., Conn. Acad. Arts and Scis., Conn. Acad. Scis. and Engring., Limestone Trout Club, The Anglers Club of N.Y., Sigma Xi. Home: 376 St Ronan St New Haven CT 06511-2251 Personal E-mail: olmecC@aol.com.

COE, ROBERT CAMPBELL, retired surgeon; b. Seattle, Nov. 14, 1918; s. Herbert Everett and Lucy Jane (Campbell) C.; m. Josephine Austin Weiner, Mar. 24, 1942; children: Bruce Everett, Virginia Austin, Matthew Daniel. BS, U. Wash., 1940; MD, Harvard U., 1950. Diplomate: Am. Bd. Thoracic Surgery, Am. Bd. Surgery. Intern Mass. Gen. Hosp., Boston, 1950-51, asst. resident, 1951-54, chief surg. resident, 1955, chief surg. clinics, 1956; instr. surgery Med. Sch. Harvard U., 1956; pvt. practice medicine specializing in thoracic and vascular surgery Seattle, 1957-84. Hon. mem. staff Children's Hosp.; attending surgeon Swedish Hosp.; cons. thoracic surgeon Firland Sanitarium, Seattle, 1957-68, Children's Hosp. Tumor Clinic, 1968-84; mng. ptnr. Invex & Inpark med. offices, Seattle, 1970-88; clin. prof. U. Wash., 1973-2000; mem. Wash. State Med. Disciplinary Bd., 1981-86; chmn. med. adv. bd. Physio-control. div. Eli Lilly, 1979-85; pres. 1st Mercer (Wash.) Corp., 1969-73, 80-91, treas., 1973-80; owner, operator Hidden Valley Guest Ranch Cle Elum, Wash., 1969-93; developer Kula Estate, Maui, Hawaii; treas. 13th Internat. Cancer Congress. Editor: King County Med. Soc. Bull, 1964-70; mem. adv. bd. Pacific N.W. Mag. 1968-85; contbr. articles to profl. jours. Mem. Mayor's Harbor Adv. Com., 1958-61; chmn. bd. N.W. Seaport, Inc., hist. mus. Seattle, 1974-75; mem. Mercer Island City Coun., 1988-92. With USNR, 1941-46. Decorated Bronze Star, Presdl. Unit citation. Fellow ACS; mem. North Pacific Surg. Assn. (sr. mem.), Pacific Coast Surg. Assn. (sr. mem.), King County Med. Soc. (jud. coun. 1972-78, chmn. 1976-78), Seattle Surg. Soc. (pres. 1969), Psi Upsilon, Seattle Yacht Club, Cruising of Am. Club (bd. govs. 1992-95). Episcopalian. Home and Office: 7260 N Mercer Way Mercer Island WA 98040-2132

COE, RODNEY MICHAEL, medical educator; b. Marquette, Mich., Nov. 10, 1933; s. Roy Arthur and Renee Adelaide (Reeder) C.; m. Elaine Elwell, Sept. 6, 1954; children: Kevin Elwell, Curtis Daniel, Andrea, Douglas Arthur. BS, Iowa State Coll., 1955; MA, So. Ill. U., 1959; PhD, Wash. U., 1962. From asst. to assoc. prof. Wash. U., St. Louis, 1962-70; from assoc. prof. to prof. St. Louis U., 1970—, chmn. cmty. and family medicine, 1989—, prof. emeritus, 1999. Exec. dir. Med. Care Rsch. Ctr., St. Louis, 1963-73; vis. prof. L.Am. Faculty Social Scis., Santiago, Chile, 1969-70; cons. Chilton Rsch. Svcs., Radnor, Pa., 1970-79, NIH, Bethesda, Md., 1976—. Author: Sociology of Medicine, 1970, and eighteen others; contbr. articles to profl. jours. Mem. Health Care for the Homeless, St. Louis, 1985—; mem., past pres. SSM Rehab. Inst., St. Louis, 1968—. Capt. U.S. Army, 1956-58. Recipient Geriatric Leadership Acad. award NIH, 1986-92; grantee NIH, Dept. Vets. Affairs, pvt. founds. Avocations: swimming, golf.

COE, SUE, artist, journalist; b. Tamworth, England, 1951; Grad., Royal College of Art, London, 1973. Illustrator Time Magazine, N.Y. Times. Exhibitions include All Over Manhattan, Thumb Gallery, 1979, Drums of the Night, Moira Kelly Fine Art (London), 1982, P.P.O.W. Gallery, 1982, Oppression & Expression, Contemporary Art Center, 1986, The Malcolm X Series, Phyllis Kind Gallery, 1986, Police State, Anderson Gallery, Commonwealth U., Knight Gallery, Portland Art Musuem, Wesleyan U., Contemporary Arts Museum, Ohio State U., San Francisco Art Institute, 1987, European Tour, City Gallery of Contemporary Art, 1988, Porkopolis - Animals an Industry, Galerie St. Etienne, 1989, Brody's Gallery, 1990, The Road to the White House, Galerie St. Etienne, 1992, Current Events, Maryland Art Place, 1993, Recent Work, Galerie St. Etienne, 1994, Non-Fiction, Brody's Gallery, 1994, Directions, Hirshhorn Museum, 1994, Mesa Coll. Gallery, 1995, Ship of Fools, Galerie St. Etienne, 1996, We All Fall Down, Salt Lake City Art Ctr., 1996, Heel of the Boot, Nelson Fine Arts Center, 1996, The Pit: The Tragical Tale of the Rise and Fall of a Vivisector, Galerie St. Etienne, 1999, The Tragedy of War, 2000—01, The Pit, Lewis and Clark U., William Benton Mus. of Art, 2000—01, One Hand Washes the Other: Prints and Drawings 1985-2001, Tyler Art Gallery, 2002, Commitment to the Struggle, David Winton Bell Gallery, 2002, AIDS Portfolio, Ctr. Contemporary Art, 2003, The Tragedy of War: A Print Cycle, Fairbanks Gallery, Oreg., 2004, Overtones Gallery, Calif., 2004, Sheep of Fools, Gallery St. Etienne, N.Y., 2005, exhibited in group shows at Portraits, Am. Inst. of Graphic Arts, 1977, European Illustrators, Georges Pompidou Ctr., 1978, People's Art, U.N. HQ, 1980, exhibitions include New Portraits, P.S.1 LI, 1984, exhibited in group shows at Art as Social Conscience, Avery Arts Ctr., 1984, Biennale 111, San Francisco Museum of Art, 1984, 57th Between A and D, Holly Solomon Gallery, 1985, East Village Situation '85, Museum of Modern Art (Italy), 1985, 75th Am. Exhibition, Art Institute of Chicago, 1986, The New Avant-Garde, L.A. County Museum of Art, 1987, Committed to Print, Museum of Modern Art (New York), 1988, Art of the 1980's, Duke U., 1991, Thinking Print: Books to Billboards, Museum of Modern Art (New York), 1996, Political Illustration of the Late Twentieth Century, 2001, Represented in permanent collections, Galerie St. Etienne, exhibited in group shows, others, —; author: (books) How to Commit Suicide in South Africa, 1983, Paintings and Drawings, 1985, X (The Life and Times of Malcom X), 1986, Dead Meat, 1996, Pits Letter, 2000, Bully: Master of the Global Merry-Go-Round, 2004, Sheep of Fools... A Song Cycle for 5 Voices, 2005, (exhibition catalogue) Police State, 1987. Named National Academician, 1994. Office: Galerie St Etienne 24 West 57th Street New York NY 10019

COELHO, SANDRA SIGNORELLI, secondary school educator, consultant; b. Torrington, Conn., Oct. 19, 1940; d. Ernest J. and Linda M. (Zanolli) Signorelli; m. Walter S. Coelho, July 11, 1964. BS, Cen. Conn. State U., 1962, MS, 1969, postgrad; Intermediate Administration Certification, Cen. Conn. State, 1980- 6th year certificate. Tchr. Torrington Bd. Edn., 1962-65; K-12 tech./math. coord. East Windsor (Conn.) Bd. Edn., 1965—2002; cons. Enfield Town Hall, 2002, Conn. Acad., 2003—04, PIMMS, 2003—; assoc. dir. math PIMMS Wesley U., 2004—. Mem. assistive tech. task force State of Conn.; presenter C.A.B.E.; cons. Town of Enfield, Conn. Acad. Chmn. townwide curriculum com. East Windsor; chmn. East Windsor Tech. Com. Recipient Golden Apple award; BEST Mentor-Assessor; Apple Computer scholar; PIMMS fellow. Mem. NEA, Conn. Edn. Assn., Conn. Educators Computing Assn. (adviser), Conn. Coun. Leaders Math. (co-pres.), East Windsor Edn. Assn. (past pres.), Atomic (sec. exec. bd., past chmn. ann. meeting), Pi Lambda Theta, Phi Delta Kappa (exec. bd.), Delta Kappa Gamma (past v.p. Rho chpt., cons. edn. & tech.) Home and Office: 50 Smalley Rd Windsor Locks CT 06096-1134 Office Phone: 860-685-6466. Personal E-mail: sandrac101@aol.com. Business E-Mail: scoelho@wesleyan.edu. *Think about what you do before you decide to do it. People are most important. Try to do what you believe in and proceed in a respectful manner on your own merits and not at the expense of others.*

COEN, ADRI STECKLING See ADRI

COEN, ETHAN, film director, writer; b. Saint Louis Park, Minn., Sept. 21, 1957; married. Student in Philosophy, Princeton U. Former statis. typist Macy's, N.Y.C. Screenwriter: (with Joel Coen) Crime Wave (formerly XYZ Murders); prodr., screenplay, editor as Roderick James) Blood Simple, 1984, Raising Arizona, 1987, Miller's Crossing, 1990, Barton Fink, 1991 (Palme D'Or and Best Dir. awards, Cannes Internat. Film Festival 1996), The Hudsucker Proxy, 1994, Fargo (Oscar award Best Writing 1997, CFCA award Best Screenplay 1997, Golden Satellite award Best Motion Picture 1997, Ind. Spirit award Best Feature 1997, Best Screenplay 1997, WGA Screen award Best Screenplay 1997), Big Lebowski, 1998, The Naked Man, 1998, writer, dir., prodr.: O Brother, Where Art Thou?, 2000, The Man Who Wasn't There, 2001, Intolerable Cruelty, 2003, The Ladykillers, 2004; exec. prodr. Down From the Mountain, 2000, writer A Fever in the Blood, 2002, Bad Santa, 2003. Office: care UTA c/o Jim Berkus 9560 Wilshire Blvd Beverly Hills CA 90212-2427

COEN, JOEL, film director, writer; b. Saint Louis Park, Minn., Nov. 29, 1954; s. Ed and Rena C.; divorced. Student, Simon's Rock Coll.; student in film, NYU. Writer, dir. The Man Who Wasn't There, 2001, Intolerable Cruelty, 2003; asst. editor Fear No Evil, Evil Dead,; worked with rock video crews; screenwriter: (with Ethan Coen) Crime Wave (formerly XYZ Murders); dir., screenwriter, Blood Simple, 1984, Raising Arizona, 1987, Miller's Crossing, 1990, Barton Fink (Palme D'Or and Best Dir. awards, Cannes Internat. Film Festival), 1991, The Hudsucker Proxy, 1994, Fargo (Best Dir. award, Cannes Internat. Film Festival, 1996, Acad. award for best writing screenplay written for the screen 1997), The Big Lebowski, 1998, O Brother, Where Art Thou?, 2000; exec. prodr. Down From the Mountain, 2000, Bad Santa, 2003; writer, producer, director, the LadyKillers, 2004. Office: United Talent Agy c/o Jim Berkus 9560 Wilshire Blvd Fl 5 Beverly Hills CA 90212-2400

COERPER, MILO GEORGE, lawyer, priest; b. Milw., May 8, 1925; s. Milo Wilson and Rose (Schubert) C.; m. Lois Hicks, Apr. 11, 1953; children: Milo Wilson, Allison Lee, Lois Paddock. BS, U.S. Naval Acad., 1946; LLB, U. Mich., 1954; MA, Georgetown U., 1957, PhD, 1960. Bar: D.C. 1954, Md. 1960, N.Y. 1980. Since practiced in, Washington; asso. firm Wilmer & Broun, 1954-60; firm Coudert Bros., 1961-63, mem. firm, 1964-96, retired ptnr., 1996—; ordained deacon Episcopal Ch., 1978, priest, 1979. Cathedral chaplain Washington Nat. Cathedral, 1986—. Contbr. articles to profl. jours. Trustee, vice chmn. for U.S., Canterbury Cathedral Trust in Am., 1982-97, acting chmn., 1991, 97; mem. coun. The Friends of Canterbury Cathedral in U.S., 1999—. Ensign USN, 1946-49; to lt. 1951-53. Mem.: ABA, Internat. Assn. for Protection of Indsl. Property, Am. Soc. Internat. Law, Am. Law Inst., Md. State Bar Assn., Bar Assn. DC, Chevy Chase Club, Met. Club (pres. 1986), Army and Navy Club. Home: 7315 Brookville Rd Chevy Chase MD 20815-4057 Office: Coudert Bros 1627 I St NW Washington DC 20006-4007 Office Phone: 202-736-1860. Business E-Mail: coerperm@coudert.com.

COETZER, AMANDA, professional tennis player; b. Hoopstad, South Africa, Oct. 22, 1971; Profl. tennis player, 1996—; winner tournament title WTA Tour Family Circle Championship, 1998; winner Budapest Ladies Open, 1997; mem. South African Fed Cup Team, 1992—93, 1995—97, South African Olympic Team, 1992, 1996, 2000. Named Most Improved Player and recipient Diamond ACES award and Karen Krantzcke Sportsmanship award, 1997; title holder Benelux Open, 2000. Office: WTA Tour 1 Progress Plz Ste 1500 Saint Petersburg FL 33701-4335

COFER, JONATHAN H., career officer; b. Pa., July 13, 1950; Commd. 2d lt. U.S. Army, 1972, advanced through grades to brig. gen., 1998; dir. joint rear area coord. U.S. Ctrl. Command, MacDill AFB, Fla., 1998—2000; dep. dir. ops., combating terrorism U.S. Army, Washington, 2000—02; sr. exec. v.p. MZM Inc., Washington, 2002—. Office: MZM Inc 1523 New Hampshire Ave NW Washington DC 20036*

COFFEE, JOHN ÇOLLINS, JR., legal educator; b. Albany, N.Y., Nov. 15, 1944; s. John Collins and Mary E. (Morse) C.; 1 dau., Megan Purcell. BA, Amherst Coll., 1966; LLB, Yale U., 1969; LLM in Taxation, NYU, 1976. Bar: N.Y. 1970, U.S. Dist. Cts. (so. and ea. dists.) N.Y. 1974, U.S. Ct. Appeals (2d cir.) 1974, D.C. 1980. Assoc. Cravath, Swaine & Moore, N.Y.C., 1970-76; assoc. prof. law Georgetown U. Law Ctr., Washington, 1976-79; vis. prof. U. Va. Law Sch., Charlottesville, 1978, U. Mich. Law Sch., 1979; Adolph A. Berle prof. law Columbia U. Law Sch., N.Y.C., 1980—; vis. prof. Harvard Law Sch., 2001. Vis. prof. St.anford U. Law Sch., Palo Alto, Calif., 1987. Author: (with others) Knights, Raiders, and Targets: The Impact of the Hostile Takeover, 1988, Business Origanization and Finance, 5th edit., 1995, Cases and Materials on Securities Regulation, 8th edit., 1998, Cases and Materials on Corporations, 4th edit., 1995. Contbr. articles to legal jours. Mem. panel on sentencing research Nat. Acad. Scis., 1980-83; mem. SEC Adv. Com. on Capital Formation, 1995-96, Subcoun. on Capital Markets, U.S. Competitiveness Policy Coun., 1994, Standong Com. On Law and Justice Nat. Rsch. Coun., 1992-95; legal adv. com. N.Y. Stock Exch., NADS, 1996—; gen. coun. Am. Econ. Assn.; mem. legal advb. bd. NASD; mem. market regulation com. NASD Regulation, Inc.; mem. adv. bd. LENS, Inc.; mem. standong com. on law and justice NAS. Reginald Heber Smith fellow, 1969-70. Fellow AAAS, Am. Bar Found.; mem. Am. Law Inst. (reporter project on corp. governance), ABA (reporter minimum standards for criminal justice), Am. Assn. law Sch. (chmn. sect. on bus. assns. 1981-82, chmn. com. on sects. 1984-85, chmn. audit com.), Assn. Bar City of N.Y. (com. on securities laws 1981-92). Office: Columbia U Sch Law 435 W 116th St New York NY 10027-7201 E-mail: jcoffee@law.columbia.edu.

COFFEE, JOSEPH DENIS, JR., retired college chancellor; b. Glens Falls, N.Y., Dec. 8, 1918; s. Joseph Denis and Kathryne Grace (Dwyer) C.; m. Margaret Mary Jennings, Oct. 7, 1941 (dec. Aug. 1998); children: John Allan (dec.), James Jennings, Mary Joyce Coffee, Barbara Grace Coffee Wolf, Matthew Brian, Margaret Erin Coffee Giovannini, Ann Ellen Coffee Beach. AB, Columbia U., 1941. Asst. to gen. sec. Columbia U., N.Y.C., 1946-50, dir. devel., 1950-60, founder corp. matching gift program of alumni support, 1953, assoc. dean, 1959-60, asst. to pres. for alumni affairs, 1960-66; v.p. Eisenhower Coll., Seneca Falls, N.Y., 1966-69, exec. v.p., 1969-76, acting pres., 1975-76, pres., 1976-80, chancellor, 1980-81, chancellor emeritus, 1981—. Dir. scholarship program Joint Industry Bd., Elec. Industry of N.Y., 1947-81; exec. sec. Com. for Corporate Support Am. Univs., 1962-64 Chmn. March Dimes campaign, Closter, N.J., 1953; active Boy Scouts Am.; former treas., dir. Anglo-Am. Hellenic Bur. Edn.; pres. Seneca County United Way, 1973-75; Chmn. Teaneck Polit. Assembly, 1967-68; Trustee Teaneck Bd. Edn., 1961-64, 65-68, Columbia U., 1978-84; bd. dirs. Nat. Women's Hall of Fame. Served from ensign to lt. comdr. USNR, 1941-46. Mem.: Seneca Falls Hist. Soc. (past trustee), Rotary (past pres. Seneca Falls, Paul Harris fellow 1988, 2002). Roman Catholic.

COFFEE, VIRGINIA CLAIRE, civic worker, former mayor; b. Alliance, Nebr., Dec. 8, 1920; D. James Maddigan and Adelaide Mary (Forde) Kennedy; M. Bill Brown Coffee, June 21, 1942; children: Claire, Sara, Virginia Anne, Sue. BS, Chadron State Coll., 1942. Prin. Whitman (Nebr.) H.S., 1942; bookkeeper Coffee & Son, Inc., Harrison, Nebr., 1965—, officer, 1967, pres., 1987-97, v.p., 1998—; dir. Friends of Agate Fossil Beds, Inc., Harrison, 1988, v.p., 1988-2001. Chmn. compilation com. book Sioux County Memoirs of Its Pioneers, 1967; coord. Harrison sect. book Nebraska Our Towns, 1988. Mayor City of Harrison, 1978-80; leader Girl Scouts U.S.A., 1953-63; mem. Harrison Elem. Sch. Bd., 1958-64, liason com. Chadron State Coll., 1975, pub. rels. chmn. Nebr. Cowbelles, 1968; hon gov. Nebr. Centennial, 1967; sec. NW Stock Growers, 1971-73; corp. officer Ft. Robinson Centennial, 1973-88; officer Gov's Ft. Robinson Centennial Commn., 1973-75; chmn. Sioux County Bicentennial, 1973-77; trustee Nebr. State Hist. Soc. Found., 1975—, Village of Harrison, 1973-80; bd. dirs. Chadron State Coll. Found., 1996—, sec., 2003; bd. dirs. Harrison Cmty. Club, Inc., 1983-86, officer, 1984-86; bd. dirs. Running Water Ranching Coalition, 2005—; apptd. Sioux County Vis. Com. 1989-2003, adm. Nebr. Navy, 1992; mem. com. for marker to honor Harrison Centennial 1985-86; mem. Sioux County History Book Com. 1985-86 Recipient Disting. Svc. award, Chadron State Coll., 1994. Mem. Nebr. State Hist. Soc. (life, dir. 1979-85, 2d v.p. 1982-84, 1st v.p. 1984-85), Wyo. State Hist. Soc., Sioux County Hist. Soc. (life, bd. dirs. 1975-81, 83-84, 87-90, 97-2003, pres. 1988-90, co-pres., 2d v.p.), Nebr. Cattle Women, Harrison Cmty. Inc., Cardinal Key. Roman Catholic. Address: PO Box 336 Harrison NE 69346-0336

COFFEL, PATRICIA K., retired social worker; b. Bismarck, N.D., Sept. 14, 1934; m. Raymond A. Kobe, 1956; children: Anne, Elizabeth, Colleen, Denise, Tim, Heidi; m. Mitchel D. Coffel, 1983. Student, U. N.D., 1954-55; BA in Sociology, Coll. St. Benedict, 1956; MSW, Wayne State U., 1981. Diplomate in clin. social work; cert. social worker, Mich. Dir. social svcs. dept. Pontiac Nursing Ctr., 1978-84; dir. of med. social work dept. Advanced Profl. Home Health Care, Troy, Mich., 1985-86; med. social worker Visiting Nurses of Met. Detroit, 1987; family worker, therapist Camp Oakland Youth Svcs., Oxford, Mich., 1987-89; client svcs. case mgr. Macomb-Oakland Regional Ctr., Mt. Clemens, Mich., 1989-90; clin. social worker, case mgr. Oakdale Regional Ctr., Lapeer, Mich., 1990-91; clin. social worker Clinton Valley Ctr., Pontiac, Mich., 1991-96; retired, 1996. Counselor Suicide Prevention, Inc., St. Louis, 1971-72, Macomb County Crisis Ctr., Warren, Mich., 1973-74; geriatric counselor Beverly Enterprises, Pontiac and Novi, Mich., 1981-83; grief and loss counselor Hospice SE Mich., Southfield, 1982-83. Grad. profl. scholar Wayne State U. Sch. Social Work, 1980. Mem. NASW (qualified clin. social worker), Acad. Cert. Social Workers. Avocations: antique silver collecting, needlepoint, videotape collecting. Home: 645 Oakwood Rd Ortonville MI 48462-8589

COFFEY, BARBARA JANE, psychiatrist; b. Schnectady, N.Y., Jan. 24, 1949; AB, U. Rochester, 1971; MD, Tufts U., 1975; MS, Harvard U., 2000. Diplomate Am. Bd. Psychiatry and Neurology, Child Psychiatry. Dir. Child Psychiatry Clin. Tufts - New Eng. Med. Ctr., Boston, 1980-87, dir. tng. for child psychiatry, 1987-92; dir. pediatric psychopharmacology McLean Hosp., Belmont, Mass., 1992—. Fellow Am. Acad. Child and Adolescent Psychiatry; mem. Am. Psychiat. Assn.

COFFEY, CHARLES MOORE, communication research professional, writer; b. Chgo., July 8, 1941; s. Charles Adams and Helen Marie (Moore) C. BA in Econs., Beloit Coll., 1963; postgrad., Purdue U., 1980. WDBJ radio and TV reporter Times-World Corp., Roanoke, Va., 1964-65; reporter, anchor, prodr. WHAS AM FM TV, Louisville, 1967-72; asst. to chancellor Ind. U. S.E., New Albany, 1972-77; dir. spl. events Ind. U., Bloomington, 1977-82; dir. alumni affairs Ind. U.-Purdue U., Indpls., 1982-88; comm. advisor Bayh-O'Bannon Campaign, Indpls., 1988; comm. asst. Lt. Gov. of Ind., Indpls., 1989-97; dir. comm. rsch. Ind. Dept. Adminstrn., Indpls., 1997—2005. Lt. gov.'s rep. Intelenet Commn., Indpls., 1990-97, gov.'s rep., 1997-2004; gov.'s rep. Enhanced Data Access Rev. Com., Indpls., 1997-2005 Contbr. articles to profl. jours. Pres. Coun. for Retarded Children, Clark County, Ind., 1975—76, Bloomington Restorations, 1982; founding chmn. Clark-Floyd Conv. Bur., Jeffersonville, Ind., 1977; bd. dirs. YMCA Greater Indpls., 1989—95, 1997—98, 2000—03, 2004—05, sec. bd., 1998—2000, trustee, 1999—2004. With USAF, 1963. Recipient AP award for comprehensive reporting Va. AP Broadcasters, 1964-65. Mem. Internat. Assn. Protocol Cons., Rotary Club Indpls. Democrat. Home: 3922 Alsace Pl Indianapolis IN 46226-5413 Personal E-mail: ccoffey2@indy.rr.com.

COFFEY, DAVID ALAN, history professor, writer; s. Jerry Garvin and Carole Coffey. BA in History, Tex. Christian U., 1994, MA in History, 1996, PhD, 1999. Asst. prof. McMurry U., Abilene, Tex., 2000—01; chair, dept. of history and philosophy U. of Tenn., Martin, 2001—. Author: (non-fiction book) Soldier Princess: The Life and Legend of Agnes Salm-Salm in North America, 1861-1867, John Bell Hood and the Struggle for Atlanta; editor: (reference book) Encyclopedia Of American Military History (three volumes), Encyclopedia of the Vietnam War; author: (non-fiction book) Historic Abilene. Mem.: Soc. of Civil War Historians, Souther Hist. Assn., Phi Kappa Phi, Phi Alpha Theta (chpt. pres. 1996—98). Home: PO Box 57 Martin TN 38237 Office: Univ Tenn 322 Humanities Building Martin TN 38238 Office Phone: 731-881-7342. Office Fax: 731-881-7584. Personal E-mail: dcoffey@utm.edu.

COFFEY, DEBORAH S. FINDLEY, elementary school educator; b. Cincinatti, Ohio, Jan. 30, 1952; d. William Hinton and Bonnie Ezzell Findley; children: Melissa Chaney, Amelia, Melinda, Brian. BS in elem. edn., Bowling Green State U., 1994, MA in curriculum and tchg., 2003. Tchr. Sandusky City Schools, Ohio, 1999—2005; christian edn. coord. Grace Episcopal Ch., Sandusky, Ohio, 1975—; ednl. buyer Creative Tchg., Sandusky, 1983—2000. Bd. mem. Kinship, Sandusky, 2000. Leader Girl Scouts, Sandusky, 1979—84, Boy Scouts Am., 1993—98; mem. and pres. Madison Sch. Parent Coun., 1978—98. Recipient Educator of the Yr., Erie County C. of C., 2003. Mem.: Nat. Edn. Assn., Ohio Edn. Assn., Sandusky Edn. Assn. Avocations: reading, computers. Office: Osborne Elem Sch 920 W Osborne St Sandusky OH 44870

COFFEY, JOHN LOUIS, federal judge; b. Milw., Apr. 15, 1922; s. William Leo and Elizabeth Ann (Walsh) Coffey; m. Marion Kunzelmann, Feb. 3, 1951; children: Peter, Elizabeth Mary Coffey-Robbins. BA, Marquette U., 1943, JD, 1948; MBA (hon.), Spencerian Coll., 1964, D (hon.) in Bus., 1973. Bar: Wis. 1948, U.S. Dist. Ct. 1948, U.S. Supreme Ct. 1980. Asst. city atty. City of Milw., 1949—54; judge Civil Ct., Milw. County, 1954—60, Milw. County Mcpl. Ct., 1960—62; judge criminal divsn. Cir. Ct., Milw. County, 1962—72, sr. judge criminal divsn., 1972—75, chief presiding judge criminal divsn., 1976, judge civil divsn., 1976—78; justice Wis. Supreme Ct., Madison, 1978—82; cir. judge U.S. Ct. Appeals (7th cir.), Chgo., 1982—; mem. Wis. Bd. Criminal Ct. Judges, 1960—78, Wis. Bd. Circuit Ct. Judges, 1962—78. Mem. adv. bd. St. Mary's Hosp., 1964—70; mem. Milw. County coun. Boy Scouts Am., 1970—78; chmn. vol. svcs. adv. com. Milw. County Dept. Pub. Welfare, 1970—72; chmn. St. Eugene's Sch. Bd., 1967—70; pres. St. Eugene's Ch. Coun., 1974; bd. dirs., mem. exec. bd. Milw.-Waukesha chpt. ARC; chmn. adv. bd. St. Joseph's Home for Children, 1958—65. With USNR, 1943—46. Named Outstanding Young Man of Yr., Milw. Jr. C. of C., 1951, 1 of 5 Outstanding Young Men of Yr., Jr. C. of C., Wis. State, 1957; recipient Outstanding Law Alumnus of Yr. award, Marquette U., 1980, Merit award, Marquette U. Alumni Assn. disting. profl. achievement, 1985, Alumni Merit award, Marquette U. HS, 2001. Fellow: Am. Bar Found.; mem.: State Bar Assn. Wis., Ill. State Bar Assn., 7th Cir. Bar Assn., Marquette U. Law Alumni Assn. (Disting. Profl. Achievement Merit award 1985), Marquette U. M Club (former dir.), Nat. Lawyers Club, Am. Legion (Disting. Svc. award 1973), Alpha Sigma Nu (Marquette U. chpt.), Phi Alpha Delta (hon.). Roman Catholic. *I have tried to the best of my ability to render justice to all and remember that "We are a country of laws, not of men" and while protecting the individual's rights I have not lost sight of the common good of all mankind and cautioned each and every one who appeared before me that with every right there is a corresponding obligation.*

COFFEY, JOHN P. (SEAN), lawyer; b. Bronx, NY, July 15, 1956; BS with merit, U.S. Naval Acad., Annapolis, 1978; JD magna cum laude, Georgetown Univ., 1987. Bar: NY 1988, NJ 1999, US Dist. Ct. (so. dist. NY 1989, we. dist. NY 1995, ea. dist. NY 1998, NJ 1999), US Ct. Appeals (2d cir. 1992). Asst. U.S. atty. US Dept. Justice, so. dist. NY, 1991—95; ptnr., litigation Latham & Watkins; ptnr., class action litigation, securities litigation Bernstein Litowitz Berger & Grossmann LLP, NYC. Adj. prof. Fordham Univ. Law Sch., 1993—94. Editor (articles): Georgetown Law Jour.; frequent commentator in news media. Served USN, 1978—86, served to Capt. USNR, 1986—2004. Mem.: ABA, Assn. Bar City of NY, Order of the Coif. Office: Bernstein Litowitz Berger & Grossmann LLP 1285 Ave of the Americas New York NY 10019 Office Phone: 212-554-1409. Office Fax: 212-554-1444. Business E-Mail: sean@blbglaw.com.*

COFFEY, JOHN WILLIAM, museum curator; b. Raleigh, N.C., Mar. 12, 1954; s. John Nelson and Martha Caroline (Snow) C.; m. Ann Patricia Roth. BA, U. N.C., Chapel Hill, 1976; MA, Williams Coll., 1978. Asst. to dir. Williams Coll. Mus. Art, Williamstown, Mass., 1978-79, acting dir., 1979-80, instr. history of art, 1979-80; curator of collections Bowdoin Coll. Mus. Art, Brunswick, Maine, 1980-88; curator of Am. and modern art, N.C. Mus. of Art., Raleigh, 1988—, chief curator, 1993-2005, dep. dir. for collections and programs, 2001-05, dep. dir. for art, 2005. Trustee, Williamstown Regional Art Conservation Lab., 1979-80; trustee Maine Festival of Arts, 1981-85, v.p., 1982-83, pres., 1983-84; mem. visual arts adv. panel Maine State Com. on Arts and Humanities, 1982-85; mem. adv. com. Vinalhaven Workshop and

Press, 1984-86, Baxter Gallery, Portland Sch. Art, 1985-88; adv. coun. Maine Coast Artists Gallery, 1986-92; mem. visual arts panel N.C. Arts Coun., 1990-91; exhbns. rev. panel Nat. Endowment for the Arts, 1992; dir. N.C./Israel Cultural Exch., 1994-97; mem. internat. com. N.C. State Bd. Sci. and Tech., 1996-98; mem. material arts anchor orgn. rev. panel Mich. Coun. for Arts and Cultural Affairs, 1997; mem. steering com. N.C. Global Partnership, 1997-98; bd. dirs. N.C. Global Ctr., 1998-2000. Author: American Posters of World War One, 1978, Four Artists, 1982, Yvonne Jacquette: Tokyo Nightviews, 1986, Twilight of Arcadia: American Landscape Painters in Rome, 1830-1880, 1987, Lucy Sallick: In the Vicinity of Self, 1987; introduction to Christine Woelfle: Sculptor, 1987, Referees: Dotty Attie, Christopher Hewat, John O'Reilly, 1990, Making Faces: Self-Portraits by Alex Katz, 1990, Finding the Forgotten: Landscape Paintings by John Beerman, 1991, Moshe Kupferman: Between Oblivion and Remembrance, 1991; co-author: The Landscapes of Louis Remy Miznor: A Southern Painter Abroad, 1996; contbr. articles to profl. jours. Office: NC Mus of Art 2110 Blue Ridge Rd Raleigh NC 27607-6494 Office Phone: 919-664-6759. Business E-Mail: jcoffey@ncmamail.dcr.state.hc.us.

COFFEY, JOSEPH IRVING, political scientist, educator; b. St. Louis, Feb. 13, 1916; s. Joseph Aloysius and Catherine Elizabeth (Burns) C.; m. Marjorie Ann Strode, Nov. 15, 1939 (div. 1963); m. Rosemary Klineberg, June 28, 1963 (div. 1976); m. Maryann Bishop, May 13, 1978; children: John Patrick, Catherine Elizabeth, Judith Ann, Megan Forbes, Susan Fox, James Odell; 1 stepchild, Janet Lynn Bishop. BS, U.S. Mil. Acad., 1939; postgrad., Columbia U., 1943-45; PhD in Internat. Relations, Georgetown U., 1954. Asst. dir. programs, spl. studies project Rockefeller Bros. Fund, 1956-57; exec. asst. to spl. asst. to Pres. for security ops. coordination, Washington, 1958-60; mem. staff Pres.'s Com. on Info. Activities Abroad, White House, 1960; research analyst Inst. for Def. Analyses, Washington, 1960-63; chief office of nat. security studies Bendix Systems div., Ann Arbor, Mich., 1963-67; prof. public and internat. affairs U. Pitts., 1967-80, Disting. Service prof., 1980-82, prof. emeritus, 1982—, dir. Ctr. for Internat. Security Studies, 1975-81; sr. research fellow Univ. Ctr. Internat. Studies, 1981-90; vis. prof. internat. peace and security studies Carnegie-Mellon U., 1986-91. Adj. prof. Carnegie Mellon U., 1991—92; sr. vis. fellow Ctr. for Internat. Studies Princeton U., 1990—91, sr. rsch. assoc., 1993—95, vis. lectr. Woodrow Wilson Sch., 1992; cons. AID, ACDA, Dept. Def. Dept. State, Internat. Comm. Agy.; dir. program on religion and conflict resolution Tanenbaum Ctr. Interreligious Understanding, 1999—2001. Author/editor books in field including Strategic Power and National Security, 1971, Arms Control and European Security, 1977, Allied Perceptions of Threat, 1983, Deterrence and Arms Control: American and West German Perspectives on INF, 1985, The Atlantic Alliance and the Middle East, 1989, Defense and Détente: U.S. and West German Perspectives on Defense Policy, 1989, Germany, the EU and the Future of Europe, 1995, The Future Role of NATO, 1997, Religion, Law and the Role of Force, 2002. Served to col. U.S. Army, 1939-60. Internat. Inst. Strategic Studies rsch. assoc., 1972-73; Stockholm Internat. Peace Rsch. Inst. fellow, 1977, NATO rsch. fellow, 1981, 89 Mem. Coun. Fgn. Rels., Istituto Affari Internat. Home: 102 Marten Rd Princeton NJ 08540 Office Phone: 609-497-2882. E-mail: mbricec@aol.com.

COFFEY, KENDALL BRINDLEY, lawyer; b. Merced, Calif., Dec. 5, 1952; s. John Brindley and Valerie Althea (Kendall) C.; m. Joni Beth Armstrong, Jan. 28, 1984; 1 child, Meredith Armstrong. BS in Broadcasting, U. Fla., 1975, JD, 1978. Bar: Fla. 1978, U.S. Ct. Appeals (9th and 11th cirs.) 1982. Law clk. U.S. Ct. Appeals (5th cir.), Newnan, Ga., 1978; assoc., bd. dirs. Greenberg, Traurig, Askew, Hoffman, Lipoff, Rosen & Quentel, P.A., Miami, Fla., 1978-88; founding mem. Coffey, Aragon, Martin & Burlington, P.A., Miami, 1988-93, also bd. dirs.; U.S. atty. U.S. Dept. of Justice, Miami, Fla., 1993-96; ptnr. Coffey& Wright, LLP, Miami, 1996—. Lectr. in field. Contbr. articles to profl. jours. Named Outstanding Young Dem. in Fla., Fla. Dem. Women's Clubs, 1975. Mem. Dade County Bar Assn. (pres. 1990-91), U. Fla. Law Rev. Alumni Assn. (pres. 1986-88, Most Productive Young Lawyer in Fla.). Office: Coffey & Wright LLP 2665 S Bayshore Dr PH-IIB Miami FL 33133-5448

COFFEY, MATTHEW B., trade association executive; b. Cumberland, Md., Jan. 20, 1941; s. Francis Wade and Mary Agnes (Stegmaier) C.; m. Sharon Harriet West, May 20, 1971; children: Julia Katherine West, Francis Matthew West. AA, Potomac State Coll., 1960; BS, W.Va. U., 1962, MBA, 1969. Investigator U.S. CSC, Washington, 1964-65; staff asst. to Pres. Johnson The White House, Washington, 1965-69; dir. planning Corp. for Pub. Broadcasting, Washington, 1969-73; dir. recruiting Carter-Mondale Transition, Washington, 1976-77; pres. Assn. of Pub. Radio Stas., Washington, 1973-77; sr. v.p. Nat. Pub. Radio, Washington, 1977; exec. v.p. Nat. Alliance of Bus., Washington, 1977-78; dir. Washington Office Textron, Inc., Washington, 1978-79; v.p., CFO Bridgeport-Textron, Bridgeport, Conn., 1979-83; exec. dir. Nat. Assn. Counties, Washington, 1983-85; pres. Nat. Tooling and Machining Assn., 1985—2005, Coffey & Co., 2005—. Bd. dirs. Coun. for Adult and Experiential Learning, 1996-97; co-chmn. Commn. on Workforce Skills in Indsl. Found. Firms, 1992-94; mem. Nat. Alliance Bus. Coun. on Work Force Excellence, 1992-97; mem. industry adv. bd. D.O.E. Labs., 1993-96. Author: Toward a Clinical Method of Executive Selection, 1969; pub. Precision Mag., 1992-96; contbr. articles to profl. jours. Chmn., bd. dirs. Pub. Interest Groups, Washington, 1985; bd. dirs. Bridgeport Econ. Devel. Corp., 1981-83, Naugatuck Valley Indsl. Devel. Com., 1980-83; chmn. Pvt. Industry Coun., Bridgeport, 1981-83; bd. govs. Nat. Cathedral Sch., 1988; mem. bldg. com. Washington Nat. Cathedral, 1989—, co-chair long range planning task group, 1994-98, chmn. bldg. com., 1998—; trustee Protestant Episcopal Cathedral Found., 1998-; prin. Ctr. for Excellence in Govt., 1988-98; bd. mem. Small Bus. Legis. Coun., 1990—, chmn., 1998-99. Fellow Nat. Acad. Pub. Adminstrn., Congl. Country Club, Univ. Club. Home: PO Box 367 Marshall VA 20116 Office: 3602 Massachusetts Ave NW Washington DC 20007-1449 Office Phone: 202-329-2340. Personal E-mail: mattcoffey@earthlink.net. Business E-Mail: coffey&compnay@msn.com.

COFFEY, NANCY, real estate broker; b. Palm Springs, Calif. d. Arthur Johnson and Joan (Hunter) Coffey. BA, Stanford U., 1967, MS in Engring., 1977. Indsl. real estate broker Coldwell Banker, Houston, 1977-79, comml. broker San Francisco, 1980-87, Cushman & Wakefield, N.Y.C., 1987-90; model Gilla Roos, N.Y.C., 1991-96; real estate broker, 1990-96; comml. real estate broker The Rolfe Group, N.Y.C., 1997-98, Cushman & Wakefield, Inc., N.Y.C., 1998-2000, Halstead Property, NYC, 2001—. Active Jr. League, San Francisco, 1981—87, N.Y.C., 1987—2000, sustainer, 1999—2000, Palo Alto Jr. League, 2000—01, N.Y. Jr. League, 2001—; mem. exec. com. spl. projects bd., vice chair thrift shop com. Meml. Sloan Kettering Cancer Ctr., N.Y.C.; vice chair membership com., vice chair Thrift Shop, Soc. Meml. Sloan Kettering, 1999—2000, mem. adminstrv. bd., 2002—; v.p. Class of 1967 Stanford U.; parish life com. mem. St. James Ch., 1997—2000. Mem.: River Club NY, Rockaway Hunting Club. Home: Smoke Tree Ranch Palm Springs CA 92264 Office Phone: 212-381-3355.

COFFEY, PAUL, professional hockey player; b. Weston, Ont., Can., June 1, 1961; With Edmonton (Can.) Oilers, 1980-87, Pitts. Penguins, 1987-92, L.A. Kings, 1992, Detroit Red Wings, 1993-97, Philadelphia Flyers, 1997—98, Chicago Blackhawks, 1998, Carolina Hurricanes, 1998—2000, Boston Bruins, 2000—01. Mem. Team Canada, Canada Cup, 1984, 87, 91, Team Canada, World Cup of Hockey, 1996. Recipient James Norris Meml. trophy, 1984-86, 1995; named to NHL All-Star game, 1982-1986, 1988-1994, 1996-1997, NHL Second All-Star team, 1982, 83-84, 1990, NHL First All-Star team, 1985, 86, 89, 1995; inducted to Hockey Hall of Fame, 2004 Achievements include mem. Stanley Cup Champion Edmonton Oilers, 1984, 1985, 1987, Pittsburgh Penguins, 1991.

COFFEY, SUSANNA JEAN, art educator, artist; b. New London, Conn. d. Edwin Raymond and Magel C. (Willingham) C. BFA magna cum laude, U. Conn., 1977; MFA, Yale U., 1982. Tchg. asst. Yale U., 1982—; F.H. Sellers prof. painting Sch. of the Art Inst. of Chgo., Oxbow, Mich., 1985—. Vis. artist various schs., 1983—; adj. assoc. prof. U. Ill, 1983; vis. critic Royal Coll. Art, London, 1995, Vt. Studio Ctr., 1994; panel mem. Harvard Ctr. for Religious Studies, 2001. Illustrator: The H Hymn to Demeter, 1989, Monovassia (Eleni Fourtouni), 1979; one-woman shows include The Cultural Ctr. of the Chgo. Pub. Libr., 1986, Weatherspoon Gallery, Greensboro, N.C., 1993, Alpha Gallery, 1995, 2001, 04, Galeria Alejandro Sales, Barcelona, 1995, Tibor De Nagy Gallery, 1996-97, 2001, 2003, others; represented in permanent collections Northwestern U., Evanston, Ill., Art Inst. Chgo., Mpls. Mus. Art, Bryn Mawr (Pa.) Coll., Boston Mus. Fine Arts, Weatherspoon Gallery, and pvt. collections. Individual Artists grant Conn. Commn. on the Arts, 1980, Chgo. Artists Abroad grant, 1990, Ill./Arts Coun. grant, 1985, 92, Studio Program grant Marie Walsh Sharpe Found., 1992, Nat. Endowment for the Arts grant, 1993; Guggenheim fellow, 1996; recipient Louis Comfort Tiffany Found. award, 1993, Acad. award in art Am. Acad. of Arts and Letters, 1995; named to Nat. Acad. Design, 2001. Office: Sch of the Art Inst of Chgo 37 S Wabash Ave Chicago IL 60603-3002

COFFEY, THOMAS FRANCIS, JR., retired writer; b. Walthourville, Ga., Feb. 14, 1923; s. Thomas Francis and Julian (Bacon) C.; m. Mary Corley, Apr. 6, 1946 (dec. July 1988); 1 child, Mary Cynthia Smith; m. Marjorie Kinsner Guice, Nov. 11, 1989. Student Am. Press Inst., Columbia U., 1964; student program for urban execs., MIT, 1970. Reporter Savannah (Ga.) Eve. Press, 1940-42, asst. city editor, sports editor, 1945-55, city editor, 1960-64, mng. editor, 1964-67; dir. civilian pub. relations U.S. Army, Camp Stewart, Ga., 1942; news dir. Sta. WSAV-TV, Savannah, 1955-57; sports editor Savannah Morning News, 1957-60, mng. editor, 1967-69, assoc. editor, 1974-87, editor, 1987-89, columnist, 1989-98; ret., 1998. Commentator WJCL-TV, Savannah, 1990-99. Author: Working for God, 1992, Only in Savannah, 1995, Savannah Lore and More, 1997. Asst. city mgr., City of Savannah, 1969-74; Bd. dirs. United Way of Savannah. Served with AUS, 1943-45. Decorated Bronze Star, Purple Heart. Mem. Ga. A.P. News Coun., Greater Savannah Hall Fame Assn. (pres. 1969), Internat. City Mgmt. Assn., Nat. Conf. Edit. Writers, Nat. Soc. Newspaper Columnists, Midway Soc. Ga. (pres. 1985), SR (pres. Ga.), Am. Legion, Sigma Delta Chi. Republican. Episcopalian (lic. lay reader). Club: Am. Business (past pres. Savannah chpt.). Home: 6401 Habersham St Unit 1B Savannah GA 31405-5632 Office: Savannah News Bldg 1375 Chatham Pkwy Savannah GA 31405 *Dedication to the task at hand/Compassion and concern for others/Gratitude to those who have built this nation/Faith in God.*

COFFEY, TIMOTHY, physicist; b. Washington, June 27, 1941; s. Timothy and Helen (Stevens) C.; m. Paula Marie Smith, Aug. 24, 1963; children: Timothy, Donna, Marie. BS in Elec. Engring. (Cambridge scholar 1958), MIT, 1962; MS in Physics, U. Mich., 1963, Evening News Assn. fellow, 1964, PhD, 1967. Rsch. physicist Air Force Cambridge Rsch. Lab., 1964; theoretical physicist EGG, Inc., Boston, 1966-71; head plasma dynamics br., then supt. plasma physics div. Naval Rsch. Lab., Washington, 1971-80, assoc. dir. rsch. for gen. sci. and tech., 1980-83, dir. rsch., 1983—2001; sr. rsch. scientist U. Md., Coll. Pk., 2001—. Recipient award Naval Rsch. Lab., 1974, 75, Disting. Civilian award Dept. Defense, 1991, Robert Dexter Conrad medal Dept. of Navy, 2000. Fellow Am. Phys. Soc., Washington Acad. Scis.; mem. AAAS, Franklin Inst. (com. for sci. and arts, Delmar S. Fahrney medal 1991), Am. Phys. Soc. Office: Univ Md 2133 Lee Bldg College Park MD 20742

COFFIELD, SHIRLEY ANN, lawyer, educator; b. Portland, Oreg., Mar. 31, 1945; BA, Willamette U., 1967; MA, U. Wisc.-Madison, 1969; JD, George Washington U., 1974. Bar: D.C. 1975. Clk. Stitt, Hemmendinger and Kennedy, Washington, 1973-74; asst. gen. counsel Office U.S. Trade Rep., Washington, 1975-79; ptnr. Reaves & Coffield, Washington, 1979-82; sr. counsel to dep. asst. sect. textiles and apparel U.S. Dept. Commerce, Washington, 1982-85; spl. counsel Skadden, Arps, Slate, Meagher and Flom, Washington, 1985-87; ptnr. Piper & Marbury, Washington and Balt., 1987-90, Baker & Hostetler, Washington, 1990-94, Keller and Heckman, L.L.P., Washington, 1994-98, Duane, Morris & Heckscher, 1998-2000, Coffield Law, Washington, 2000—. Adj. prof. internat. econ. law Georgetown U. Law Sch., 1982—. Mem. Fed. Bar Assn., Am. Soc. Internat. Law, D.C. Bar, Pi Gamma Mu, Phi Delta Phi. Office: Coffield Law Ste 315 666 11th St NW Washington DC 20001-4530 Office Phone: 202-331-3097. Personal E-mail: coffieldlaw@yahoo.com.

COFFIN, ANNE GAGNEBIN, arts administrator, editor; d. Albert Paul and Genevieve (Hope) G.; m. John Devereux Coffin, Apr. 7, 1962; children: Samuel Devereux, Thomas Huguenin. BA, Smith Coll. Asst. editor, feature writer Look mag., N.Y.C., 1961-71; N.Y. rep. Villa I Tatti, Harvard U. Ctr. for Italian Renaissance Studies, Florence, 1984-92; dir. Internat. Print Ctr., N.Y.C., 2000—. Curator, exhbn. organizer Am. Art: The Last 4 Decades, London, 1977. Bd. dirs N.Y. Landmarks Conservancy, N.Y.C., 1981—; bd. dirs. Chamber Music Soc. Lincoln Ctr., N.Y.C., 1984—, Leopold Schepp Found., 1991—, Brit.-Am. Arts Assn., 1985—; co-chmn. Contemporary Arts Coun., Mus. of Modern Art, N.Y.C.; mem. Art Table, Villa I Tatti Coun., 1992—. Mem.: The Century Assn., Cosmopolitan Club. Mailing: 20 E 9th St 3AB New York NY 10003

COFFIN, BEATRIZ DE WINTHUYSEN, landscape architect; b. Madrid, July 20, 1930; came to U.S., 1952; d. Javier de Winthuysen and Maria Hector; m. Laurence E. Coffin Jr., Jan. 4, 1958; children: Thomas A., Alisa W. BS, Furman U., Greenville, S.C., 1954; M in Landscape Arch., Harvard U., 1957. Cert. landscape architect, Md., Va. Landscape architect A. Carl Stelling, N.Y.C., 1957-58, Vorhees-Walker-Smith-Haines Architects, N.Y.C., 1958-60; ptnr. Coffin & Coffin, Washington, 1963—. Landscape architect USN, Washington, 1968; instr. George Washington U., 1974, U. Md., 1985; pres. Internat. Inst. Site Planning, Washington, 1976—; lectr. U. Guanajuato, Mex., 1989, 92; lectr., cons. City of Quito, Ecuador (sponsored by USIA), 1990, 1994, 99, La Paz, Bolivia (sponsored by USIA), 1995. Co-author: A Maryland New Town Turns 50, Arquitectura Paisajista, Quito, Conceptos y diseños, 1991, Lexicon 2001 Multi-Lingual Dictionary of Landscapes and Urban Planning, 2001; contbr. numerous articles to profl. publs. Mem. design adv. steering com. D.C. Commn. on the Arts and the Humanities, 1986-94; bd. dirs. The World Charter Pub. Sch., Washington, 1998-2001. Fellow Am. Soc. Landscape Archs.; mem. Latin Am. Mgmt. Assn. (treas. 1990-95), Grupo Cultural San Gil. Office: Internat Inst Site Planning 715 G St SE Washington DC 20003-2853 Office Phone: 202-546-2322. Personal E-mail: iisitep@aol.com.

COFFIN, DAVID FRANK, pastor, educator; b. Washington, July 18, 1952; s. David Frank and Edith Davis Coffin; m. Jennifer Pauline Quie, Aug. 17, 1974; children: Andrew Marshall, Rebecca Elizabeth, Sarah Jacqueline. BA magna cum laude, St. Vincent Coll., Pa., 1978; PhD, Westminster Theol. Sem., Pa., 2003. Ordination Potomac Presbytery, Presbyn. Ch. in Am., 1990. Legislative asst. Cook, Purcell, Henderson & Zorack, Washington, 1980—84; writer Prison Fellowship, Reston, Va., 1984—85; lectr. in theology Chesapeake Theol. Sem., Linthicum, Md., 1983—93; dir. Berea Ctr. for Bibl. and Theol. Studies, Mitchellville, Md., 1982—90; pastor New Hope Presbyn. Ch., Fairfax, Va., 1990—. Mem., ad hoc com. on nuc. arms and deterrence Gen. Assembly Presbyn. Ch. in Am., Atlanta, 1984—87, mem., ad interim com. on govt. and structure, 1985—88, chmn., ad interim com. on jud. procedures, 1993—96, adv. mem., strategic planning com., 2004—. Contbr. book. Mem.: Va. Hist. Soc., Presbyn. Hist. Soc. Avocations: canoeing, hiking, reading, films, genealogy. Office: New Hope Presbyn Ch PO Box 705 Fairfax VA 22030-0705 Office Phone: 703-385-9056. E-mail: newhope@nhpca.org.

COFFIN, DWIGHT CLAY, retired grain company executive; b. Evansville, Ind., Aug. 21, 1938; s. Dwight DeWitt and Ruth Robertson (Clay) Coffin; m. Carol Ann Elsaesser, Dec. 27, 1986; 1 child from previous marriage, John Charles. Student, DePauw U., 1959—61; BA, U. Pitts., 1963; MBA, NYU, 1970; postgrad., Harvard U., 1976; cert. in counseling, Postgrad. Ctr. Mental Health, N.Y.C., 2001. With Chase Manhattan Bank, N.Y.C., 1964-72, employee rels. officer, 1968-70, mgmt. svcs. officer, 1970-72; dir. employment and tng. Continental Grain Co., N.Y.C., 1972-73, dir. internat. pers. Paris, 1973-75, v.p. pers. N.Y.C., 1975-85, v.p., sec., 1985-86, v.p. human resources, 1986-99; ret., 1999. Mem global adv coun Am Grad Sch Int Mgt, 1986—. Pres Bishop's Fund for Children; dir Greenwich Found; pres Greenwich chpt English Speaking Union; warden St Barnabas Episcopal Ch, 1992—; bd dirs St Luke's Life Works, Stamford, 1989—. Mem.: SAR (treas Capt Mead chpt), Human Resource Planning Soc, Nat Foreign Trade Coun (chmn mgt resources comt 1984), Innis Arden Golf Club. Republican. Home: 115 Oak Tree Pl Santa Barbara CA 93108 Personal E-mail: dwightcc@sover.net.

COFFIN, FRANK MOREY, federal judge; b. Lewiston, Maine, July 11, 1919; s. Herbert Rice and Ruth (Morey) Coffin; m. Ruth Ulrich, Dec. 19, 1942; children: Nancy, Douglas, Meredith, Susan. AB, Bates Coll., 1940, LLD, 1959; postgrad. indsl. adminstrn., Harvard U., 1943, LLB, 1947; LLD, Bates Coll., 1959, U. Maine, 1967, Bowdoin Coll., 1969; degree (hon.), Colby Coll., 1975. Bar: Maine 1947. Law clk. to fed. judge Dist. of Maine, 1947—49; engaged in practice Lewiston, 1947—52; with Verrill, Dana, Walker, Philbrick & Whitehouse, Portland, Maine, 1952—56; mem. 85th-86th Congresses from 2d Dist. Maine, House Com. Fgn. Affairs; mng. dir. Devel. Loan Fund, Dept. State, Washington, 1961; dep. adminstr. AID, 1961—64; U.S. rep. devel. assistance com. Orgn. Econ. Coop. and Devel., 1964—65; judge 1st circuit U.S. Ct. Appeals, 1965—, chief judge, 1972—83, sr. judge, 1989—; chmn. com. jud. br. U.S. Jud. Conf., 1984—90. Adj. prof. U. Maine Sch. Law, 1986—89. Author: Witness for Aid, 1964, The Ways of a Judge-Reflections from the Federal Appellate Bench, 1980, A Lexicon of Oral Advocacy, 1984, On Appeal, 1994. Emeritus Bates Coll.; dir. The Governance Inst., 1987—; mem. emeritus The Examiner; chair Maine Justice Action Group, 1996—2001. Lt. USNR, 1943—46. Recipient Edward J. Devitt Disting. Svc. to Justice award, 2001. Mem.: ABA, ABA (co-chmn. com. on loan forgiveness and repayment 2001—02), Am. Acad. Arts and Sci., Am. Acad. Arts and Sci. Office: US Ct Appeals 156 Federal St Portland ME 04101-4152

COFFMAN, EDWARD MCKENZIE, retired history professor; b. Hopkinsville, Ky., Jan. 27, 1929; s. Howard Beverly and Mada (Wright) C.; m. Anne Nelson Rouse, June 30, 1955; children: Anne Wright, Lucia Page, Edward McKenzie. AB, U. Ky., 1951, MA, 1955, PhD (So. Faculty fellow), 1959. Instr., asst. prof. Memphis State U., 1957-61; research asso. George C. Marshall Research Found., 1960-61; asst. prof., assoc. prof., prof. history U. Wis., Madison, 1961-92, prof. emeritus, 1992—. Dwight D. Eisenhower vis. prof. Kans. State U., 1969-70; vis. prof. mil. history U.S. Mil. Acad., 1977-78; disting. vis. prof. USAF Acad., 1982-83; Harold K. Johnson vis. prof. U.S. Army Mil. History Inst., 1986-87; mem. adv. com. Dept. Army Mil. History Program, 1971-76, 87-89, chair, 1989-93; mem. Nat. Hist. Publs. and Records Commn., 1972-76; John F. Morrison vis. prof. U.S. Army Command and Gen. Staff Coll., 1990-91. Author: The Hilt of the Sword: The Career of Peyton C. March, 1966, The War to End All Wars: The American Military Experience in World War I, 1968, The Old Army: A Portrait of the American Army in Peacetime, 1784-1898, 1986, The Regulars: The American Army, 1898-1941, 2004; mem. editl. bd. Mil. Affairs, 1974-77, Arno Press series The American Military Experience and The George C. Marshall Papers; chmn. editl. bd. Jour. Mil. History, 1995-99. Served with U.S. Army, 1951-53. Recipient Outstanding Civilian Svc. medal Dept. Army, 1978, Comdr.'s Pub. Svc. award, 1987, Disting. Civilian Svc. medal, 1991; Guggenheim fellow, 1973-74; Harmon Lectr. USAF Acad., 1976; Am. Philos. Soc. grantee, 1960; named U. Ky. Disting. Alumnus, 1995. Mem. Soc. for Mil. History (pres. 1983-85, Samuel Eliot Morison prize 1990, Moncado prize 1995, Disting. Book award, 2005), U.S. Commn. Mil. History, So. Hist. Soc., Phi Beta Kappa. Democrat. Home: 1089 Lakewood Dr Lexington KY 40502-2523

COFFMAN, HAROLD EMERSON, retired agricultural products supplier, retail merchant; b. Lafayette, Ind., Sept. 5, 1927; s. Russell Ambrose and Irene Elizabeth (Wiggins) Coffman; m. Marrie Christine Nelson, Oct. 3, 1953. BS, Morningside Coll., Sioux City, Iowa, 1948—53; attended, U. Ill., Chgo., 1962—63. Asst. dir. mfg. budgets Oliver Corp., Chgo., 1955, sales analyst, Ter. mgr., market rsch. analyst; sales promotion mgr. Oliver Corp., White Farm Equip., Chgo., 1977; dir. dealer devel. White Farm Equip., Omaha; gen. sales mgr. White Outdoor Equip., Oak Brook, Ill.; shop owner Framing Loft, Sun City, Ariz., 1977—97, ret., 1997—. Pres. Prof. Picture Framing Assn., Ariz. Chpt., Phoenix, 1980—81. Author: This is Our Forest, 2002. Quarter master 3 USN, 1946—47, Pacific, ensign USNR, 1956, retired LTJG USN, 1963. Recipient 1st pl. creative framing, needlework, Prof. Picture Frames Assn., 1989. Avocations: stained glass, golf, writing, reading. Home: 10533 W Wheatridge Dr Sun City AZ 85373-1978 E-mail: coff2@juno.com.

COFFMAN, JAMES RICHARD, academic administrator, veterinarian, educator; b. Lyndon, Kans., July 19, 1938; s. Harry Thomas and Eleanor Louise (Lowe) C.; m. Sharon Sue Neill, June 10, 1960; children: David Neill, Michael James, Scott Thomas. BS, Kans. State U., 1960, DVM, 1962, MS, 1969. Pvt. practice equine vet., Wichita, Kans., 1962-65, Oklahoma City, 1969-71; inst. vet. medicine Kans. State U., Manhattan, 1965-69, prof., head dept. surgery and medicine, vet. medicine, 1981-84, prof. vet. medicine, dean, 1984-87, provost, 1987—2004; assoc. prof. vet. medicine and surgery U. Mo., Columbia, 1971-75, prof., 1975-81, dir. Equine Ctr., 1973-78; prof., head dept. surgery and medicine Sch. Vet. Medicine Kans. State U., Manhattan, 1981-84, prof., dean, 1984-87, provost, 1987—2004, provost emeritus vet. clin. sci., 2004—. Chair Nat. rsch. Coun., Bd. on Agr. subcom., 1999. Author: Equine Chemistry and Pathophysiology, 1991; equine editor Compendium on Continuing Edn. 1980-83, mem. editorial bd., 1980-85; editor in chief Equine Sportsmedicine, 1981-85; mem. editorial bd. Jour. Equine Medicine and Surgery, 1979-80; adv. bd. Equine Vet. Jour., 1980—; contbr. numerous articles to profl. jours. Bd. dirs. St. Mary Hosp., Manhattan, 1989—. Recipient Disting. Tchr. award Norden Labs., 1969. Mem. Am. Coll. Vet. Internal Medicine (diplomate, pres. 1978-79, chmn. bd. regents 1979-80), Am. Assn. Equine Practitioners (dir. at large 1982-83, v.p. 1984, pres. 1986-87), Am. Vet. Med. Assn. (trustee profl. liability ins. trust 1978-85, chmn. 1980-82), Nat. Acads. Practice Vet. Medicine (exec. bd. 1985-87, founding com. mem. 1985—), Kans. Vet. Med. Assn., Nat. Assn. State Univs. and Land Grant Colls. (coun. chief acad. officers 1987—, exec. coun. on acad. affairs), Rotary (bd. dirs. 1989-90), Phi Kappa Phi, Gamma Sigma Delta, Phi Zeta. Avocation: painting. Home: 200 Waterbridge Rd Manhattan KS 66503-2512

COFFMAN, JAY DENTON, internist, educator; b. Quincy, Mass., Nov. 17, 1928; s. Frank David and Etta (Kline) C.; m. Louise G. Peters, June 29, 1955; children: Geoffrey J., Joanne K., Linda J., Robert B. AB, Harvard U., 1950; MD, Boston U., 1954. Diplomate Am. Bd. Internal Medicine. Med. intern Univ. Hosp., Boston, 1954-55, asst. resident in medicine, 1955-56, chief resident in medicine, 1957-58, fellow in cardiovascular disease, 1956-57, sect. head peripheral vascular dept., 1960—; asso. in medicine Boston U. Med. Sch., 1960-65, mem. faculty, 1965—, prof. medicine, 1970—. Author: Raynaud's Phenomenon, 1989; co-author: Ischemic Limbs, 1973, Peripheral Arterial Disease, 2002. Trustee Solomon Carter Fuller Mental Health Center, Boston, 1975-81. Served to capt. M.C. USAR, 1958-60. Mem. ACP, Am. Soc. Clin. Investigation, Am. Fedn. Clin. Rsch., Am. Heart Assn., Begg's Soc., Phi Beta Kappa, Alpha Omega Alpha. Office: 88 E Newton St Boston MA 02118-2308

COFFMAN, JENNIFER BURCHAM, judge; b. 1948; BA, U. Ky., 1969, MA, 1971, JD, 1978. Ref. libr. Newport News (Va.) Pub. Libr., 1972-74, U. Ky. Libr., 1974-76; atty. Law Offices Arthur L. Brooks., Lexington, Ky., 1978-82; ptnr. Brooks, Coffman and Fitzpatrick, Lexington, 1982-92, Newberry, Hargrove & Rambicure, Lexington, 1992-93; judge U.S. Dist. Ct. (ea. dist. and we. dist.) Ky., 1993—. Adj. prof. Coll. Law, U. Ky., 1979-81. Elder Second Presbyn. Ch., 1993—96; bd. dirs. YWCA Lexington, 1986—92, Shepherd Ctr., 2000—. Mem. Ky. Bar Assn., Fayette County Bar Assn., U. Ky. Law Sch. Alumni Assn. Office: 306 US Courthouse 101 Barr St Lexington KY 40507-1313 Office Phone: 859-233-2453.

COFFMAN, MICHAEL S., international organization official, ecologist; b. 1943; m. Susan Coffman; children: Jonathan, Tamera. BS in forestry, No. Ariz. U., 1966, MS in biology, 1967; PhD in forest sci., U. Idaho, Moscow,

1970. Faculty Mich. Tech. U.; former mgr. Champion Internat. (now Internat. Paper), Stamford, Conn.; pres. Environmental Perspectives, Inc.; and exec. dir. Sovereignty Internat. Pub. Discerning the Times Digest, 1999—. Author: Saviors of the Earth. Nazarene. Office: Environmental Perspectives Inc 6 Heather Rd Bangor ME 04401

COFFMAN, ROY WALTER, III, publishing company executive; b. Detroit, May 27, 1943; s. Roy Walter and Adele Ruth (Carlson) C.; m. Brenda Lynn Spies, June 27, 1964; children: Christa Ruth, Eric Ross. Student, U. Okla., 1967-70. Enlisted USAF, 1960, advanced through grades to tech. sgt., 1968, resigned; sales mgr. Christian Sci. Monitor, Boston, 1968-75; v.p. Logos Internat., Plainfield, N.J., 1975-77; promotion mgr. Aspen Systems Corp., Germantown, Md., 1977-78; v.p. Christianity Today, Inc., Carol Stream, Ill., 1978-85, sr. v.p., 1985-96, pub. Campus Life mag., 1989-95; area dir. Spl. Olympics, 2000—. Dir. internat. tng. The Upper Room, 1996-98; bd. dirs. Evang. Christian Pubs. Outreach; dir. internat. ministries The Upper Rm., 1998; pub. Sojourners Mag., 1998-99; pub. cons., 2000. Current area dir. Spl. Olympics, 2000—; trustee Wheaton (Ill.) Christian H.S., 1987—90. Mem. Evang. Christian Pubs. Assn. (bd. dirs. 1986-92). Home: 13673 N Pima Spring Way Tucson AZ 85737-7199

COFFMAN, TERRENCE J., retired academic administrator; b. 1945; m. Wallis Coffman. Student, Corcoran Coll. Art and Design, Lacoste Sch. Arts. Dean then pres. Md. Coll. Art and Design, Silver Spring, 1973—83; pres. Milw. Inst. Art & Design, 1983—2003; ret., 2003. Instr. Smithsonian Instn., Washington; artist-in-residence Milw. Inst. Art & Design. Author: A Walk Through the Wheatfields: The Missing Journals of Vincent van Gogh. Recipient Milw.'s Frank Kirkpatrick award, 2001. Avocation: playing acoustic guitar. Office: Milw Inst Art & Design 273 E Erie St Milwaukee WI 53202-6003

COFFMAN, VANCE D., aerospace company executive; b. Kinross, Iowa, Apr. 3, 1944; BS in Aerospace Engring., Iowa State U., 1967; MS in Aeronautics/Astronautics, PhD in Aeronautics and Astronautics, Stanford U., 1974; D of Aerospace Engring. (hon.), Embry-Riddle U.; LLD (hon.), Pepperdine U. George L. Graziadio Sch. Bus. and Mgmt. Guidance and control sys. analyst Space Sys. divsn. Lockheed Martin, 1985—87, divsn. v.p., 1987—88, gen. mgr., 1988, pres. Space Sys. divsn., 1988—92, pres., COO Space & Strategic Missiles sector, 1995, pres., 1996—97, 1999—2000, exec. v.p., 1996, CEO and vice chmn. bd. dirs., 1997-98, chmn., CEO, 1998—2004, chmn. bd. dirs., 2004—. Bd. dirs. Bristol-Myers Squibb, 3M, United Negro Coll. Fund, John Deere; chmn. President's Nat. Security Telecommunications Adv. Com., Aerospace Industries Assn. Recipient Profl. Progress in Engring. award Iowa State U., 1989, Disting. Achievement award Iowa State U., 1999, Bob Hope Disting. Citizen award Nat. Def. Indsl. Assn. L.A. chpt., Exec. of Yr., Nat. Mgmt. Assn., 2002. Fellow AIAA, Am. Astron. Soc.; mem. NAE, Am. Def. Preparedness Assn., Nat. Security Indsl. Assn., Security Affairs Support Assn. Office: Lockheed Martin 6801 Rockledge Dr Bethesda MD 20817-1877

COFIELD, JUDITH MARA, lawyer; b. N.Y.C., Jan. 5, 1949; d. Kenneth Harvey and Naomi (Comenentz) Schwartz; m. Harvey Harmon Zeigler (div.); m. William Rodney Cofield, Oct. 1970; 1 child, Brandon Harvey Zeigler. BA cum laude, Coll. William & Mary, 1975; JD, Marshall-Wythe Sch. Law, 1978. Bar: Va., 1978, U.S. Dist. Ct. (ea. dist.) Va., U.S. Ct. Appeals (4th cir.), U.S. Supreme Ct. Assoc. Steingold & Chovitz, P.C., Norfolk, Va.; atty. Guy, Cromwell, Betz & Lustig, P.C., Virginia Beach, Va., Shuttleworth, Ruloff & Giordano, P.C., Virginia Beach; ptnr. Stallings & Richardson, P.C., Virginia Beach. Apptd. commr. chancery, 1993-96, 96—; participant Sec. Def. 57th Joint Civilian Orientation Conf., 1994; instr. Marshall-Wythe Sch. Law, 1994-95; spkr. in field. Polit. steering com. mem. Sen. Sonny Stallings, Del. Gelnn Croshaw, candidate Scott Carnes; tutor Laubach Soc. Mem. ABA, Assn. Trial Lawyers Am., Va. State Bar Assn. Va. Women's Bar Assn. (bd. dirs. 1980), Norfolk/Portsmouth Bar Assn. (exec. com. 1985), Virginia Beach Bar Assn. (exec. com. 1995-97). Avocations: skeet shooting, pool. Office: Stallings & Richardson PC 2101 Parks Ave Ste 801 Virginia Beach VA 23451-4160 Home: 3436 Archer Ct Virginia Bch VA 23452-5911

COFIELD, PHILIP THOMAS, educational association administrator; b. Monmouth, Ill., July 3, 1951; s. Earl Crescant and Vera (Shunick) C.; divorced; children: Calla, Megan. BA in English, St. Ambrose U., 1973. Dir. Jr. Achievment of Quad Cities, Davenport, Moline, Iowa, Ill., 1980-83; account exec. Jr. Achievment Inc., 1983-85; pres., CEO Jr. Achievment of Utah, Salt Lake City, 1985—. Established Utah Bus. Hall of Fame, 1991; bd. dirs. Utah Partnership for Ednl. and Econ. Devel. Mem. Utah Coun. on Economic Edn. (bd. dirs.), Salt Lake area C. of C., Rotary Club, (com. co-chmn. Salt Lake City). Office: Jr Achievement of Utah 182 S 600 E Salt Lake City UT 84102-2060

COFIELD, ROBERT HAHN, orthopedic surgeon, educator; b. Cin., Oct. 24, 1943; s. Robert Hedrick and Virginia (Hahn) C.; m. Pamela Joyce Haarbauer, Aug. 12, 1967; children: Robert, Stacey, Virginia. BA, Washington and Lee U., 1965; MD, U. Ky., 1969; MS, Mayo Grad. Sch. Medicine, 1976. Diplomate Am. Bd. Orthopedic Surgery. Intern Charity Hosp./Tulane U., New Orleans, 1970; cons. Mayo Clinic, Rochester, Minn., 1975—; from instr. to assoc. prof. Mayo Med. Sch., Rochester, 1975-88, prof., 1988—; vice chmn. dept. orthopedics Mayo Clinic, Rochester, 1992-97, Frank R. and Shari Caywood prof. orthopedic surgery, 1993, chmn. dept. orthopedics, 1997—2005; assoc. dean Mayo Grad. Sch., Rochester, 1992-94, dean, 1994-98; pres. Am. Bd. Orthopaedic Surgery, Chapel Hill, 1999-2000. Editor-in-chief Jour. Shoulder and Elbow Surgery, 1990-96; contbr. chpts. to books, more than 175 articles to profl. jours.; co-inventor humeral resect. guide; co-designer Cofield total shoulder sys. Lt. comdr. USNR. Mem. ACS, AMA, Am. Acad. Orthopedic Surgery, Am. Bd. Orthopedic Surgery (dir. 114—), Am. Orthopedic Assn., Am. Shoulder and Elbow Surgeons (founding sec.-treas. 1982-87, pres. 1988-89). Republican. Presbyterian. Office: Mayo Clinic 200 1st Ave NW Rochester MN 55901-3004

COFOID, PAUL BRIAN, physician; b. LaSalle, Ill., Mar. 25, 1945; s. Harry Edwin and Doris Mae (Phelps) C.; m. Kathleen Frances Hobnecj Moore, June 29, 1968 (div. Feb. 1993); children: Steven M., Melyssa B.; m. Pamela Sue Weaver, Apr. 2, 1993; children: Stephanie Zimmer, Beau Zachary Smith. BS in Zoology, U Ill., 1967; MD, St. Louis U., 1971. Physician Graves-Gilbert Clinic, Bowling Green, Ky., 1993—; also bd. dirs. Bd. dirs. Cmty. Health Plan, Bowling Green; spkr. in field. Bd. dirs. Salvation Army, Pekin, Ill., 1988-93, Am. Cancer Soc., Pekin, 1990-93. Col. USAF, 1967-87. Fellow Am. Coll. Physicians; mem. Am. Diabetes Assn., Nat. Osteo. Assn., The Endocrine Soc. Avocations: skiing, scuba diving, sailing, racquetball. Office: Graves-Gilbert Clinic 201 Park St Bowling Green KY 42101-1708

COFONI, PAUL M., computer company executive; BS in Math., U. R.I., 1970; student in Sr. Exec. Program, MIT, 1989. With Gen. Dynamics, 1974—91; from v.p. Tech. Mgmt. Group Ea. Region to v.p., pres. Fed. Sector Computer Scis. Corp., El Segundo, Calif., 1991—2001, v.p., 2001—05, pres. Fed. Sector, 2001—05; pres. CACI Internat. Inc.-Federal, Arlington, Va., 2005—. With U.S. Army, 1970—74. Mem.: AIAA, Info. Tech. Assn. Am. (bd. dirs.), Armed Forces Comms. and Electronics Assn. (bd. dirs.), Nat. Def. Indsl. Assn. (bd. dirs.), The Bus. Roundtable. Office: CACI Internat Inc-Federal 1100 N Glebe Road Arlington VA 22201*

COGAN, JOHN FRANCIS, JR., lawyer; b. Boston, June 13, 1926; s. John Francis and Mary (Galligan) C.; m. Mary T. Hart, May 1, 1951 (div.); m. Mary L. Cornille, June 24, 1989; children: Peter G., Pamela E., Jonathan C., Gregory M. AB cum laude, Harvard U., 1949, JD, 1952. Bar: Mass. 1953. Ptnr. Hale and Dorr, Boston, 1957—2000, mng. ptnr., 1976—84, chmn., 1984—96, of counsel, 2000—04, Wilmer, Cutler, Pickering, Hale, and Dorr, Boston, 2004—; dep. chmn. Pioneer Global Asset Mgmt., SpA, Milan, 2000—; non-exec. chmn. Pioneer Investment Mgmt., USA, Inc., Boston, 2000—. Trustee various Pioneer Funds, Inc., Boston, 1963—; pres. Pioneer Group, Inc., Boston, 1963—2000; chmn. bd. dirs. Teberebie Goldfields, Inc., 1986—2000; chmn. exec. com. bd. dirs. Pioneer Western Corp., 1968—79; sr. v.p., bd. dirs. Western Res. Life Assurance Co., Ohio, 1968—79; chmn. bd. dirs. ICI Mutual Ins. Co., 1987—94, bd. dirs., Harbor Global Co. Trustee Boston Symphony Orch., 1989—, overseer, 1984—92, chmn., 1989—92, vice chmn., 2003—; overseer Mus. Fine Arts, 1989—90, trustee, 1990—, chmn., 1994—98; trustee Boston Ballet, 1986—89; mem. Mass. Dem. State Com., 1968—80; trustee Univ. Hosp., Boston, 1965—95, chmn. bd., 1972—89; trustee Boston Med. Ctr., 1995—; bd. dirs. Wendell P. Clark Meml. Assn., Walker Home for Children, 1972—, Brigham Surg. Group, Inc., 1981—95, The Med. Found., 1986—90; trustee Boston U. Med. Ctr., 1973—90; bd. govs. Investment Co. Inst., 1971—74, 1975, 1981, 1982, chmn. bd. govs., 1978—80, 1982—85, 1986—89, 1991—. Served with USNR, 1944—46. Mem. ABA, Internat. Bar Assn., Mass. Bar Assn. (chmn. corp. banking and bus. law com. 1973-76), Boston Bar Assn. (past chmn. profl. svcs. sect., mem. bench-bar com.), Boston Estate and Bus. Planning Coun. (past pres.), Boston Probate and Estate Planning Forum (sec. 1958-73), Nat. Assn. Security Dealers (bd. dirs. 1983-86, legal adv. bd. 1988-94). Home: 975 Memorial Dr Apt 802 Cambridge MA 02138-5755 Office: Pioneer Investment Mgmt USA Inc 60 State St Boston MA 02109-1820 Office Phone: 617-422-4802.

COGAN, JOHN P., JR., lawyer; b. Baton Rouge, La., Jan. 14, 1944; s. John P. and Stell E. (Greene) C.; m. Jean M. Wilson, May 2, 1970; children: John, Malcolm, Elizabeth, James, Victoria, Charles. BA cum laude, U. Tex., 1965, LLB, 1968. Bar: Tex. 1968. Assoc. Baker Botts, LLP, Houston, 1969-76, ptnr., 1977-94, sr. ptnr., 1995-97; ptnr. Baker & McKenzie, Houston, 1997-99, King & Spalding, Houston, 2000—04, Akin Gump Strauss Hauer & Feld LLP, Houston, 2004—, London, 2004—, chair firm global projects practice, 2004—. Pres. parish coun. St. Anne Ch., 1984-85, mem. fin. com., 1986-87; mem. sch. bd. St. Anne Sch., 1983-87; mem. Mayor's Com. for a Houston World Trade Ctr., 1985; bd. dirs., mem. exec. com. HoustonWorld Trade Assn., 1983—, pres., 1980-82; intermediate league coord. Inner S.W. Youth Baseball Assn., 1984; adv. dir. Inst. for Internat. and Comparative Law; adv. dir., chmn. fin. com. Duchesne Acad. of Sacred Heart, 1975-82, bd. dirs., 1988-95, corp. sec., 1990-95; mem. N.Y. adv. bd. Coun. of the Ams.; chmn. bd. trustees Broadacres Civic Assn., 1983-85, chmn. deed restrictions com., 1985—; adv. dir. Asia Soc., 1988—. Lt. JAG, USNR, 1971-77, with Tex. N.G., 1968. Fellow Tex. Bar Found., Houston Bar Found.; mem. ABA, State Bar Tex. (mem. coun. internat. law sect. 1986-89, chmn. internat. banking and fin. com. 1988-89), Houston Bar Assn. (sec. internat. law com. 1969), Am. Soc. Internat. Law. Office: Akin Gump Strauss Hauer & Feld LLP 1111 Louisiana St 44th Flr Houston TX 77002-5200 Office Phone: 713-220-5885. Office Fax: 713-236-0822. E-mail: jcogan@akingump.com.*

COGAN, NANCY ADAMS, chaplain, poet; b. Ishpeming, Mich., Feb. 22, 1935; d. John Woodard and Mabel Eva Adams; m. Max Cogan, June 28, 1959 (dec. Jan. 1988); children: Charles, Deirdre, Elin, Dana, Tasha, Caitlin. BA, Carleton Coll., 1957; MA, Columbia U., 1958; Cert., Ch. Divinity Sch. Pacific, Berkeley, Calif., 1987. Lay assoc. Assn. Profl. Chaplains. Speech and lang. clinician Head Start N.E. Mo. Comty. Action, 1979-85, 88-90; chaplain U. Iowa Hosps. and Clinics, Iowa City, 1990—. Author: (poetry) Snap Shots, 1995, In Strange Places, Overtime. Bd. dirs. LWV, Kirksville, Mo., 1969—90; com. mem. Cmty. Betterment, Kirksville, 1980—86; leader La Leche League, Kirksville, 1968—80. Episcoplian. Avocations: camping, watercolor, sketching. Office: Dept Pastoral Svcs U of Iowa Hosps & Clinics Iowa City IA 52242

COGBILL, JOHN VALENTINE, III, lawyer; b. Munich, Jan. 30, 1948; m. Janet Mary Cogbill; children: John, Jamie, Chrissy. BS in Engring., USMA, 1970; JD, U. Richmond, 1979. Bar: Va. 1979, admitted to practice: US Fed. Ct. 1979. Joined McGuireWoods LLP, Richmond, Va., 1987, ptnr., real estate & environ. dept., mng. ptnr. Richmond office. Mem. Commonwealth Transp. Bd., 1995—99, Richmond Met. Authority Bd., 1995—99; chmn. Nat. Capital Planning Commn., 2001—; bd. trustees The Henricus Found., 2001—. Served U.S. Army, 1970—76. Fellow: Va. Law Found.; mem.: Urban Land Inst., Chesterfield-Colonial Heights Bar Assn., Am. Coll. Real Estate Lawyers, Richmond Bar Assn., Va. Bar Assn., Greater Richmond C. of C. (bd. dirs. 1998—2002, Bernard L. Savage Cmty. Svc. Award 2003). Office: McGuireWoods LLP One James Ctr 901 E Cary St Richmond VA 23219-4030 Office Phone: 804-775-4383. Office Fax: 804-698-2031. Business E-Mail: jcogbill@mcguirewoods.com.

COGDILL, KEITH W., librarian, educator; b. Huntsville, Ala., July 15, 1967; s. Thomas J. and Patricia Cogdill. BA, U. of the South, Sewanee, Tenn., 1989; MLS, Univ. Ala., Tuculossa, Ala., 1992; PhD, Univ. N.C., Chapel Hill, 1998. Libr. Univ. Ill., Chgo., 1992—95; asst. prof. Univ. Md., Coll. Pk., Md., 1999—2002; outreach libr. Nat. Libr. of Medicine, Bethesda, Md., 2002—. Contbr. articles to profl. jour. Recipient Phi Beta Kappa, 1989; inform. fellow, Nat. Libr. of Medicine, 1994—95, Goldsmith Scholarship, Hebrew Univ., Jerusalem, 1989—90. Mem.: Med. Libr. Assn (editl. bd. 1994—97, 1999—2002). Office: Nat Libr of Medicine 8600 Rockville pike Bethesda MD 20894

COGEN, RICHARD M., lawyer; b. NYC, 1955; BA cum laude, U. Rochester, 1976; JD, Cornell U., 1979. Bar: NY 1980. Ptnr. Nixon Peabody LLP, Albany, NY. Mem.: ABA, Albany County Bar Assn., Environ. Auditing Roundtable, Inst. Environ. Auditing (mem. bd. dirs. 1985—94), Air and Waste Mgmt. Assn. (chmn. Legal Com. 1990—92, vice chair Environ. Auditing Com. 1995—98), NY State Bar Assn. Office: Nixon Peabody LLP Omni Plaza 30 S Pearl St Albany NY 12207-3425 Office Phone: 518-427-2665. Office Fax: 866-947-1278. E-mail: rcogen@nixonpeabody.com.

COGGAN, PATRICIA CONNER, elementary school educator; d. Leslie Lynn and Grace Hartnell Conner; m. Leland Latrill Coggan, Jr., July 26, 1958; children: Robert Leslie, Sharon Coggan McBride. BS, U. Okla., 1958; M in Humanities, U. Dallas, 1983. Life tchg. cert. Tex., std. tchg. cert. Okla. 1st grade tchr. Dallas Ind. Sch., 1958—60; elem. tchr. The Hockaday Sch., Dallas, 1976—. Devel. tester Gesell Inst., New Haven, 1978—; trained tchr. Met. Opera-Creating Original Opera, N.Y.C., 1996—; trained evaluator All Kinds of Minds, Raleigh, NC, 1999—. Dallas host com. Rep. Conv., 1984; Presbyn. Women pres. Highland Pk. Presbyn. Ch., 1974; pres. Kappa Alpha Theta Alumnae, Dallas, 1970—71. Named hon. life mem., Presbyn. Women, 1974, hon. alumnae, Hockaday Alumnae Assn., 2003; Curriculum Writing grantee, Hockaday Bd. Trustees, 2002. Mem.: Nat. Coun. for Social Studies, Ela Hockaday Cum Laude Soc. (past pres. 1976—), Michael Stoner DAR (charter), Dallas Craft Guild, Tex. Old Missions and Forts Restoration Assn. Avocations: gardening, book binding, book reviewer. Office: The Hockaday Sch 11600 Welch Rd Dallas TX 75229

COGGIN, CHARLOTTE JOAN, cardiologist, educator; b. Takoma Park, Md., Aug. 6, 1928; d. Benjamin and Nanette (McDonald) C. BA, Columbia Union Coll., 1948; MD, Loma Linda U., 1952, MPH, 1987; DSc (hon.), Andrews U., 1994. Diplomate Am. Bd. Pediatrics. Intern L.A. County Gen. Hosp., 1952-53, resident in medicine, 1953-55; fellow in cardiology Children's Hosp., L.A., 1955-56, White Meml. Hosp., L.A., 1955-56; rsch. assoc. in cardiology, house physician Hammersmith Hosp., London, 1956-57; resident in pediatrics and pediatric cardiology Hosp. for Sick Children, Toronto, Ont., Can., 1965-67; cardiologist, asst. prof. medicine, co-dir. heart surgery team Loma Linda (Calif.) U., 1961-73, assoc. prof., 1973-91, prof. medicine, 1991—. Asst. dean. Sch. Medicine Internat. Program, 1973—75; v.p. for global outreach Loma Linda U. Health Scis. Ctr., 1998—; assoc. .dean. Sch. Medicine Internat. Program, 1975—, spl. asst. to univ. pres. for interat. affairs, 1991; co-dir., cardiologist heart surgery team missions to, Pakistan and Asia, 63, Greece, 67, Greece, 69, Saigon, Vietnam, 1974—75, Saudi Arabia, 1976—87, China, 1984, China, 1989—91, Hong Kong, 1985, Zimbabwe, 88, Zimbabwe, 93, Kenya, 88, Nepal, 92, China, 92, Myanmar, 95, North Korea, 96. Author: Atrial Septal Defects, motion picture (Golden Eagle Cine award and 1st prize Venice Film Festival 1964); contbr. articles to med. jours. Recipient award for service to people of Pakistan City of Karachi, 1963, Medallion award Evangelismos Hosp., Athens, Greece, 1967, Gold medal of health South Vietnam Ministry of Health, 1974, Charles Elliott Weinger award for excellence, 1976, Wall Street Jour. Achievement award, 1987, Disting. Univ. Svc. award Loma Linda U., 1990; named Honored Alumnus Loma Linda U. Sch. Medicine, 1973, Outstanding Women in Gen. Conf. Seventh-day Adventists, 1975, Alumnus of Yr., Columbia Union Coll., 1984, Outstanding Achievement in Edn., Adventist Alumni Achievement award, 1999. Mem. AAUP, AAUW, Am. Coll. Cardiology, AMA (physicians adv. com. 1969—), Calif. Med. Assn. (com. on med. schs., com. on member svcs.), San Bernardino County Med. Soc. (chmn. comm. com. 1975-77, mem. comm. com, 1987-88, editor bull., 1975-76, William L. Cover, M.D. Outstanding Contbn. to Medicine award 1995), Am. Heart Assn., Med. Rsch. Assn. Calif., Calif. Heart Assn., Am. Acad. Pediatrics, World Affairs Coun., Internat. Platform Assn., Calif. Museum Sci. and Industry MUSES (Outstanding Woman of Yr. in Sci. 1969), Am. Med. Women's Assn., Loma Linda Sch. Medicine Alumni Assn. (pres. 1978), Alpha Omega Alpha, Delta Omega. Democrat. Home: 25052 Crestview Dr Loma Linda CA 92354-3415 Personal E-mail: jcoggin@verizon.net.

COGGINS, EILEEN M., lawyer; b. 1964; BA, West Chester U., 1987; JD, Widener U., 1992. In house counsel Keystone Care Group, Media, Pa.; asst. gen. counsel to gen. counsel, sr. v.p. Genesis Health Ventures, Kennett Square, Pa., 1998—2003; gen. counsel, sr. v.p. corp. compliance Genesis HealthCare, Kennett Square, Pa., 2003—. Mem.: Del. County Bar Assn., Am. Health Lawyers Assn., Pa Bar Assn., Guy G. deFuria Inn of Ct. Office: Genesis HealthCare 101 E State St Kennett Square PA 19348

COGGINS, PAUL EDWARD, JR., lawyer; b. Hugo, Okla., May 21, 1951; s. Paul E. and Rebecca (Cates) C.; m. Regina T. Montoya, June 12, 1976; 1 child, Jessica Chandler. BA in Polit. Sci. summa cum laude, Yale U., 1973; BA with honors, Oxford U., 1975; JD cum laude, Harvard U., 1978. Bar: Tex. 1978. Tchr. Project New Gate N.Mex. State Penitentiary, 1973; law clk. Mass. Ct. Appeals, 1978-79; fed. prosecutor U.S. Attys. Office, Dallas, 1980-83; assoc. Johnson & Swanson, Dallas, 1979-80, ptnr., 1983-86, Meadows, Owens, Collier, Reed & Coggins, Dallas, 1986-93; U.S. atty. U.S. Dept. of Justice, Dallas, 1993-2001; prin. Fish & Richardson PC, Dallas, 2001—. Mem. adv. com. Magnet Sch. in Dallas, 1984—. Author: The Lady is the Tiger, 1987; co-author: Out of Bounds, 1992. Pres. bd. dirs. Dem. Forum, Dallas, 1985—. Named a Rhodes scholar, 1973—76; named one of Best Lawyers in Dallas, D Mag., 2005. Mem. ABA, CASA (pres. elect, 2004), Dallas Bar Assn. (mem. pro bono panel), Greater Dallas Crime Commn. (chair, 2004), Dallas County Hist. Found., Town and Gown (pres., 2003-04). Office: Fish & Richardson PC 5000 Bank One Ctr 1717 Main St Dallas TX 75201 Fax: 214-747-2091. Office Phone: 214-292-4003. Business E-Mail: coggins@fr.com.

COGHLAN, JOHN PHILIP, corporate financial executive; b. San Francisco; life ptnr. Tina Vindum; children: Kearney, Callan. BA in Psychology, with honors in social thought, Stanford U.; MA in Economics and Public Policy, Princeton U.; MBA, Harvard U. Founder, COO San Francisco Grocery Express. Ltd.; joined Charles Schwab & Co., 1986, gen. mgr. Schwab Instl., 1992—97, exec. v.p., 1992—2005, enterprise pres. retirement plan services, 1997—2001, enterprise pres. services for investment managers, 1998—2001, enterprise pres. Schwab Instl., 2001—02, vice chmn., 1999—2005, enterprise pres. individual investor's bus., 2002—05; pres. CEO Visa USA, 2005—. Bd. dirs. Success Metrics, San Francisco, CollectAmerica, Denver. Pres. bd. dirs. San Francisco Lighthouse for the Blind; bd. dirs. Glide Meml. Ch. Mem.: Internat. Bd. of Practices and Standards for Certified Financial Planners (Nat. Advisory Coun.). Office: Visa USA 900 Metro Center Blvd Foster City CA 94404*

COGHLAN, KELLY JACK, lawyer; b. Longview, Tex., Sept. 3, 1952; s. Howard and Peggy Coghlan. BBA with honors, So. Meth. U., 1975, JD cum laude, 1978. Bar: Tex. 1978, U.S. Dist. Ct. (so. dist.) Tex. 1979, U.S. Tax Ct. 1981, U.S. Ct. Appeals (5th cir.) 1981, U.S. Supreme Ct. 1984. Law clk. to presiding judge Finis E. Cowan U.S. Dist. Ct. (so. dist.) Tex., 1978-79; assoc. Vinson & Elkins, Houston, 1979-84; equity ptnr. Dotson, Babcock & Scofield, Houston, 1984-88, chmn. risk mgmt. com., head gen. litigation group, 1987-88; pvt. practice, Houston, 1988—. Bd. dirs. Sta. KSBJ, Houston, sec., 1990-93, chmn. long range planning com., 1989-93, mem. exec. com., 1990-97, v.p., 1994-97. Mem. So. Meth. U. Law Sch. Southwestern Law Jour. Mem. steering com. Palmer Drug Abuse Program, Houston, 1980-82; vol. jr. high and H.S. youth programs, 1990—, 2d Bapt. Ch., Houston, 1990—; mem. 1st Meth. Ch., Longview, Tex., 1962—; youth min., Wesley United Meth. Ch., Longview, 1972-77. Recipient So. Meth. U. M award, 1975, Russell Baker Moot Ct. 1st pl. award So. Meth. U. Law Sch., 1976; named Players of 1999, Tex. Lawyer. Fellow Houston Bar Found., Coll. State Bar Tex., Pro Bono Coll. State Bar Tex.; mem. ABA, Tex. Bar Assn., Houston Bar Assn., Houston Young Lawyers Assn. (chmn. com. on consumer rights 1981-82), Nat. Eagle Scout Assn. (life), So. Meth. U. Student Found. (hon.), Order of Coif (hon.), Am. Mensa, Gulf Coast Mensa, Blue Key Soc. (hon., pres. 1974-75), Beta Gamma Sigma (hon.), Phi Delta Phi (hon.), Lambda Chi Alpha. Avocations: drumming, singing, youth work. Office: 505 Lanecrest Ln Ste 1 Houston TX 77024-6716 Office Phone: 713-973-7475.

COGLIANO, DAN, tax specialist, accountant; b. Bklyn., Aug. 20, 1952; s. Angelo and Adelaide Cogliano; m. Debra Hayden Barrett, Mar. 19, 1978 (div. Oct. 21, 1991); children: Daniel, David, Dustin. BBA in Acctg., Hofstra U., 1974. Tax acct., Ozone Park, NY, 1975—; jr. acct. ABC Radio Network, N.Y.C., 1978—80; v.p. internat. mktg. Merrill Lynch, N.Y.C., 1980—2003. Income maintenance screener Suffolk County Dept. Social Svcs., Amityville, NY, 1975—77. Author: (book) Thick Skinned, 2003. Actor West Side Repertory Theater, N.Y.C., 1977—93, treas., 1989—92; mem. Mens Sr. Baseball League, L.I., 1993—, mgr., player, 1999—2001; baseball player Legends of Baseball Tournament, Cooperstown, NY, 2000—. Avocations: baseball, writing, acting. Home: Apt 19H 340 E 80th St New York NY 10002 E-mail: coglida@aol.com.

COGNETTA, ARMAND BENNET, dermatologist; b. Stamford, Conn., Sept. 13, 1952; s. Armand Bennet and Mary Teresa Cognetta; m. Suzanne Doumar; children: Armand Bennet, Dominique, Marco. BS in Biochemistry, Columbia Coll., 1975; MD, U. Conn., 1979. Diplomate Am. Bd. Family Practice, 1982, Am. Bd. Dermatology, 1985. Intern, resident Tallahassee Meml. Hosp., 1975—82; resident U. Ala., Birmingham, 1982—85; dermatologist Dermatology Assocs. Tallahassee, 1985—. Assoc. prof. U. Fla., Gainesville, 1990—, Fla. State U., Tallahassee, 2005—. Co-author: Color Atlas of Dermatoscopy, Dermoscopy and New Imaging Techniques, Dermatologic Clinics; medical co-director (automated melanoma detection) Melafind. Bd. mem. Boys and Girls Town USA, Tallahassee, 1990. Recipient Spirit of Youth award, Girls and Boys Town USA, 2005; fellow, U. Ala., 1990—91. Fellow: Am. Coll. Mohs Micrographic Surgery and Cutaneous Oncology; mem.: Fla. Soc. Dermatology (pres. 2001—02). Avocations: tennis, sailing, bicycling. Office: Dermatology Assocs 1707 Riggins Rd Tallahassee FL 32308 Office Phone: 850-877-4134. Office Fax: 850-877-7870. E-mail: cognetta@ix.netcom.com.

COGSWELL, JOHN HEYLAND, retired telecommunications industry executive, financial consultant; b. Southampton, N.Y., Oct. 18, 1933; s. John W. and Lucy A. (McCurdy) C.; m. Patricia A. Morrissey, June 18, 1955; children: Julie A., Catherine J. AB, Dartmouth Coll., 1955, MS, 1956. Registered profl. engr., Mass. Engr. New Eng. Telephone Co., Boston, 1956-61, planning engr., Pittsfield, Mass., 1961-63, staff acct., Boston, 1963-65, constrn. program engr., 1969-71, div. mgr. fin., 1971-83, sec.-treas., 1983-90; engr. Am. Telephone Co., N.Y.C., 1965-68, mgr. econs., 1968-69. Treas., bd. dirs. Neighborhood Health Plan, Boston, 1986-88, 90-98, pres. 1988-90. Mem. Needham Bd. Selectmen, 1996—, Needham Town Meeting, 1975—; pres. bd. dirs. Health Action Forum, Greater Boston, 1992—97, treas., 1983—92, 1997—98; treas., bd. dirs. Muscular Dystrophy Assn., Greater Boston, 1978—91, Needham Hist. Soc., Inc., Mass., 1975—95, trustee, 1995—; treas., bd. dirs. Cmty. Health Ctr. Capital Fund, 1992—99;

chmn. Needham Planning Bd., 1977—87; mem. Needham Bd. Appeals, 1987—91; chmn. Needham Bd. Selectmen, 1998, 2001; bd. dirs. Pathway Health Networks, 1995—96, Care Group, 1996—, Health Agys. of Mass., 1996—99, Cmty. Health Charities, 1999—2005, pres., 2001; bd. dirs. Mass. Hosp. Assn., 2000—03, Bridgewater Goddard Park Med. Assocs., 2000—02, chmn., 2000—02; bd. dirs. Combined Health Appeal of Mass., 1991—96, pres., 1993—95; chmn. bd. dirs. Provider Svc. Network, 2003—05; bd. dirs. Ctr. Cmty. Responsive Care, 1994—98, treas., 1994—95; trustee Deaconess-Glover Hosp., 1991—99, vice-chmn., 1992—94, chmn., 1994—99; bd. dirs. Mass. Health Data Consortium, 1991—96, treas., 1994—96; bd. dirs. HealthPoint, 2001—04, Deaconess-Waltham Hosp., 2002, New Eng. Health Care Found., 1992—96; bd. dirs., treas. Cogswell Family Assn., 1989—. Recipient Class of 1955 award Dartmouth Coll., 2003; named Vol. of Yr., Combined Health Appeal Am., 1992. Mem. Fin. Mgmt. Assn. (bd. dirs. 1977-79), Fin. Exec. Inst. (bd. dirs. 1988-90), Treas.'s Club Greater Boston (pres. 1987-88), Republican Club (New Providence, N.J.; pres. 1966-68). Episcopalian. Avocations: gardening, golf. Home and Office: 1479 Great Plain Ave Needham MA 02492-1217 Personal E-mail: j.cogswell@verizon.net.

COHAN, CHRISTOPHER J., professional sports team executive; b. Salinas, Calif., 1951; s. Helen; m. Angela Cohan; 3 children. BA, Ariz. State U., 1973. With Feather River Cable TV Corp., Orinda, Calif., 1973-77; founder, owner Sonic Comm., 1977—98; owner, CEO Golden State Warriors, NBA, Calif., 1995—. Adv./fin. com. NBA Bd. Governors. Founder Warriors Found., 1997—; established Annual Angela and Christopher Cohan Cmty. Svc. Award, 2000. Office: Golden State Warriors 1221 Broadway Fl 20 Oakland CA 94612*

COHAN, GEORGE SHELDON, advertising and public relations executive; b. Oak Park, Ill., May 30, 1924; s. Charles and Ann (Holt) C.; m. Natalie Holmes, Dec. 14, 1974; children— Barry, Gail, Charles, Victoria. Student, Colo. Sch. Mines, 1941-42, Ind. U., 1942-43; BS in Mech. Engring, U. Cin., 1948; postgrad., John Marshall Law Sch., 1954-56. Certified bus. communicator. Field engr. Indsl. Erectors, Inc., Chgo., 1948-50; sales engr. Fairbanks-Morse & Co., Chgo., 1950-56; v.p., account supr. Hoffman & York Advt. Agy., Milw., 1956-62, Tobias & Olendorf, Chgo., 1962-65; sr. v.p., gen. mgr. Bozell & Jacobs, Inc., Chgo., 1965-74; chmn. bd., pres. Cohan & Paul, Inc., Chgo., 1975-84; pres. Fletcher, Mayo & Assocs., Chgo., 1984-87, Doremus & Co., Chgo., 1987-89, George Cohan Co., Chgo., 1989—; chmn. Cohan Seafood Co., San Francisco, 1988—. Bd. dir. Forest Labs., N.Y.C., Universal Gift Cert., Inc. Author: (play) Black Mutiny, 1948; contbr. articles to profl. jours. Mem. Cen. Ind. coun. Boy Scouts Am., 1965-69; mem. exec. com. March of Dimes, 1965-69, ANTA, 1948-51. 1st lt. C.E. AUS, 1943-45, CBI. Recipient Outstanding Merit award 8th Pan Am. Ry. Congress, 1954, 1st pl. Nat. Lithographic Soc., 1955, 15th ann. G.D. Crain award, 1981, gold award Chgo. Assn. Direct Mktg., 1979, 80, Pres.'s Cup award, 1986; named to Advt. Hall of Fame, 1981. Mem. ASME, Bus. and Profl. Advertisers Assn. (internat. pres. 1976-77, Best Seller award 1954, Best of Show 1962, Best of Show Indpls. 1966-67, ABP award 1971, Addy Gold award 1979, Profl. Excellence award 1978, Gold medal 1979, 80, Pro-Com. Gold award, 1981, 83, 84, Career of Excellence Spl. award 1989, Lifetime Career of Excellence award 1989), Pub. Rels. Soc. Am., Screen Actors Guild. Unitarian Universalist. Avocations: flying, cooking, fishing, opera, acting. Home: 2048 Foxfire Ct Henderson NV 89012-2190 Office Phone: 702-260-4244. E-mail: geocoh@aol.com.

COHAN, JAMES, art gallery director; b. 1960; m. Jane Cohan. B, Washington Univ., St. Louis; intern., New Mus., NYC. With John Weber Gallery; dir. Paula Cooper Gallery; sr. dir. Anthony d'Offay Gallery, 1991—99; owner, dir. James Cohan Gallery, NYC, 2000—. Office: James Cohan Gallery 533 W 26th St New York NY 10001 Office Phone: 212-714-9500. Office Fax: 212-714-9510. Business E-Mail: jcohan@jamescohan.com.*

COHAN, LEON SUMNER, lawyer, retired electric company executive; b. Detroit, June 24, 1929; s. Maurice and Lillian (Rosenfeld) C.; m. Heidi Ruth Seelmann, Jan. 22, 1956; children: Nicole, Timothy David, Jonathan Daniel. BA, Wayne State U., 1949, JD, 1952. Bar: Mich. 1953. Pvt. practice, Detroit, 1954-58; asst. atty. gen. State of Mich., Lansing, 1958-61, dep. atty. gen., 1961-72; v.p. legal affairs Detroit Edison Co., 1973-75, v.p., 1975-79, sr. v.p., gen. counsel, 1979-93; counsel Barris, Sott, Denn & Driker, Detroit, 1993—. Bd. dirs. Oakland Commerce Bank. Trustee Mich. Cancer Found.; bd. dirs. Concerned Citizens for Arts in Mich., U. Mich. Musical Soc.; mem. arts commn. Detroit Inst. Arts; mem. Race Rels. Coun. Met. Detroit. With U.S. Army, 1952-54. Recipient Disting. Alumni award Wayne State U. Law Sch., 1972, Disting. Svc. award Bd. Govs., Wayne State U., 1973, Judge Ira W. Jayne award NAACP, 1987, Israel Histadrut Menorah award, 1987, Knights of Charity award Pontifical Inst. for Fgn. Missions, 1989, Fellowship award Am. Arabic and Jewish Friends of Met. Detroit, Judge Learned Hand Human Rels. award, 1991, Gov.'s Arts award for Civic Leadership in the Arts, Michiganian of Yr. award Detroit News, 1993. Mem. ABA, Detroit Bar Assn., State Bar Mich. (Champion of Justice award 1993), Mich. Gen. Counsel Assn., Detroit Club. Democrat. Jewish. Home: 17 Eastbury Ct Ann Arbor MI 48105-1402 Office: Barris Sott Denn & Driker 15th Fl 211 W Fort St Lbby 15 Detroit MI 48226-3244 E-mail: icohan@aol.com.

COHANE, HEATHER CHRISTINA, publishing executive, editor; b. Camberley, Surrey, Eng. came to U.S., 1982; d. William Willoughby and Naomi Mary (Winder) Fausset; m. John Philip Cohane, May 13, 1961 (dec. Dec. 1981); children: Alexander, Candida, Ondine; m. Ossian Kare Berga, Nov. 2, 1985. (dec. Oct. 2000). Student pvt. schs., Isle of Wight, Eng. and Neuchatel, Switzerland. Founding editor, pub. Quest mag., N.Y.C., 1987—; exec. v.p. Gotham Mag., N.Y.C., 1999—2001; editor-at-large Avenue Mag., 2002—04. Personal E-mail: hcohane@aol.com.

COHELEACH, GUY JOSEPH, artist; b. N.Y.C. s. Gaetan Guy and Flavia Marie (Aymong) C.; m. Patricia Arlene McGauley; children: George G., Coleen P., Hugh G., Guy G. (dec.), Elizabeth P. (dec.). Grad., Cooper Union; D.Arts (hon.), Coll. William and Mary, 1975. Bd. dirs. Soc. Animal Artists. One-man shows include over 100 exhbns. from N.Y. to L.A. including L.A. County Mus., 1991, Carnegie Mus., Pitts., 1995-96, Newark (N.J.) Mus., 1996, West Valley Art Mus., Phoenix, 2000; group shows include Bird Artists of World, Tryon Gallery, London, Mammal Artists of World, Nairobi, Kenya, Bird Artists of Am., Graham Gallery, N.Y.C., Am. Mus. Natural History, Denver Mus., Nat. Collection of Fine Art, Washington, Corcoran Gallery, Washington; represented in permanent collections, White House, Nat. Wildlife Fedn. Gallery, Am. Mus. Natural History, Nat. Audubon Soc. Gallery; master artist from Leigh Yawkee Woodson Art Mus., 1983, Nat. History Mus. of L.A., 1991, R.W. Norton Art Gallery Glassmere Wildlife Park, 1992, Cin. Mus. of Natural History, 1992, Cultural Ctr. Gallery, Stuart, Fla., 1993, Ctrl. Park Gallery, N.Y.C., 1993, Internat. Wildlife Mus., Tucson, 1993, Dayton Mus., 1994, Houston Mus., 1994, Cleve. Mus., 1994, Blauvelt Art Mus., 1995, Carnegie Mus., 1995, Newark Mus., 1996, John James Audubon Mus., 1997, Roger Tory Petersen Inst., 1997, Haley Mus., 1997, Ft. Worth Zoo Mus., 1998, Nebel Pub. Mus., Green Bay, Wis., 1998, Michelson Mus., Marshall, Tex., 1999, Burpee Mus., Rockford, Ill., 1999, West Valley Art Mus., Surprise, Ariz., 2000, Cultural Ctr., Stuart, Fla., 2001, RT Peterson Inst., Jamestown, N.Y., 2002, Wildlife Experiences Mus., Parker, Colo., 2003, RW Norton Gallery, Shreveport, La., 2003, Vero Beach (Fla.) Art Mus., 2004. Served with AUS. Recipient Mzuri Safari Internat. Wildlife Artist's Magnum Opus award, 1974; Conservation award African Safari Club, 1976; blue ribbon award Printing Industries Am., 1969-81; named Artist of Yr., Gt. Lakes Art Festival, Milw., 1985 Fellow Explorers Club; mem. Soc. Animal Artists (v.p., 8 awards of excellence, 1980—), Nat. Audubon Soc. (life), Nat. Wildlife Fedn. (life, Artist of Yr. 1985), East African Profl. Hunters Assn. (hon.), Adventurers Club, Boone and Crocket Club, Campfire (N.Y.), Pres.'s Club (U. Tenn.), Phila. Gun Club. Prints of work American Eagle chosen by Dept. State as gifts for vis. fgn. heads of state. Office: Pandion Art PO Box 96 Bernardsville NJ 07924-0096 *I believe anyone can attain a very high degree of success in any field as long as he or she loves his chosen field and is not afraid of work.*

COHEN, AARON MITCHELL, television producer, publisher, columnist, writer; b. West Palm Beach, Fla., Aug. 12, 1948; s. Seymour Benjamin and Frances Rhoda (Bachman) Cole; life ptnr. Jeffrey Greathouse BA, Boston U., 1970, MEd, 1997. Psychiat. milieu therapist Human Resource Inst. Boston, 1970-73; dir. prodn. Videograf Inc., Needham, Mass., 1972-74; assoc. prodr., asst. to founder Regional Arts Found., West Palm Beach, Fla., 1977-81; adj. instr. Palm Beach Atlantic Coll., West Palm Beach, 1980-82; exec. v.p., exec. prodr., artistic dir. Leonard Davis Ctr. for Arts CUNY, N.Y.C., 1982-90; project dir. model libr. of future project Lenox (Mass.) Libr. Assn., 1993-95; program dir. Peter F. Drucker Found. Nonprofit Mgmt., N.Y.C., 1997-98; pub. Democracy Chronicle, 1998—2001; dir. tng. 2000 Census Palm Beach County, Fla., 2000; pres. CreatorsUSA and TwoCreators.com, 2004—. Exec. prodr., cons., Boston, West Palm Beach, N.Y.C., 1974-82, 90-96; columnist Palm Beach Post, Palm Beach Daily News, West Palm Beach, 1976-78, 81-82; co-exec. prodr. Nat. Town Meeting with Nelson Mandela ABC-TV Ted Koppel Prodns., 1990; program dir. Peter F. Drucker Live by Satellite, 1997; adj. instr. Williams Coll., Williamstown, Mass., 1993, 96; co-founder WHRS FM, 1976-80, WHRS TV, 1976-80; dir. devel. Free Speech TV, 2003-05; pres. creators website, 2005—; pub. website, 2005—; cons. in field Author: The Golden Anniversary Book of Congregation Beth El, 1976; author, dir. (documentary) And the Wilderness Shall Bloom: The Story of Henry Morrison Flagler and the East Coast of Florida, 1980; pub., editor The Democracy Chronicle, 2000-01; artist (group shows) Southeastern Ctr. for Contemporary Art, Norton Mus., Boston U., 1975-82. Exec. com. N.Y.C. Arts Coalition, 1988-90; bd. dirs. Lenox Libr. Assn., 1992-94. Recipient Scarlet key Boston U., 1970, First Pl. ADDY award Am. Advt. Fedn., 1980; winner internat. poster design competition Palm Beach Festival, 1981; Joseph Laffan Morse Found. scholar, 1966-70; Nat. Endowment Arts and NEH project grantee, 1980-90, 94; fellow Fla. Atlantic U. Internat. Inst. for Creative Comm., 1980-82. Mem. Dramatists Guild, Nat. Alliance for Media Arts and Culture. Avocations: writing, art, musical composition, teaching, web design. Home and Office: PO Box 270272 Louisville CO 80027

COHEN, ABBY JOSEPH, investment company executive; b. NYC, Feb. 29, 1952; d. Raymond and Shirley (Silverstein) Joseph; m. David M. Cohen. AB in Econs., Cornell U., 1973; MA in Econs., George Washington U., Washington, 1976. CFA. Economist Fed. Res. Bd., Washington, 1973-76; economist/analyst T. Rowe Price Assocs., Balt., 1976-83; investment strategist Drexel Burnham Lambert, NYC, 1983-90, Goldman, Sachs & Co., NYC, 1990—, mng. ptnr., 1998—. Trustee/fellow Cornell U.; bd. overseers Cornell Med. Sch. Named one of Most Powerful People, Forbes mag., 2005; named to top 50 in Global Fin., 1996; recipient Woman Achiever (Woman of Yr.), YWCA, NYC, 1989, Wall St. Week Hall of Fame, 1998. Mem. Nat. Assn. Bus. Economists, Inst. Chartered Fin. Analysts (chair), N.Y. Soc. Security Analysts (mem. bd. govs.), Nat. Economists Club (bd. govs.), Assn. for Investment Mgmt. and Rsch. (chair bd. govs. 1997-98). Office: Goldman Sachs & Co 85 Broad St New York NY 10004-2456*

COHEN, ALAN, investment banker; b. N.Y.C., N.Y., Jan. 1, 1945; s. Harold and Edith (Schneider) Cohen; m. Carolyn Zacks, Jan. 3, 1970; children: Davi Melissa, Michael Jarrett. BA in Econs., Bklyn. Coll., 1967; postgrad, NYU. Commodity broker Reynolds Securities Inc., N.Y.C., 1977—78; v.p., regional commodity mgr. Loeb Rhoades Hornblower, N.Y.C., 1978—79; v.p., regional commodity dir. E.F. Hutton Co., N.Y.C., 1979—80; v.p., nat. commodities sales mgr., ltd. ptnr. and assoc. dir. Bear, Stearns & Co., N.Y.C., 1980—91; sr. mktg. dir. Stamford Co., N.Y.C., 1991—. Home: 7 Hemlock Ln Marlboro NJ 07746-1212 Office: Independence Cmty Bank Corp 182 Atlantic Ave Brooklyn NY 11201-5604

COHEN, ALAN BARRY, researcher, educator; b. Bklyn., Nov. 3, 1952; s. Max B. and Blanche (Katz) C.; m. Helaine Francine Hartman, Dec. 22, 1973; children: Jeremy Todd, Bradley Daniel, Melanie Ann, Brandon Adam. BA, U. Rochester, 1973; MS, Harvard U., 1975, ScD, 1983. Rsch. asst. Beth Israel Hosp. and Harvard Med. Sch., Boston, 1974-75; sr. analyst Urban Systems Rsch. & Engring. Inc., Cambridge, Mass., 1975-79; rsch. assoc. Harvard Sch. Pub. Health, Boston, 1979-81, Johns Hopkins Sch. Hygiene and Pub. Health, Balt., 1981-82, asst. prof., 1982-84; assoc. dir. John Hopkins Ctr. for Hosp. Fin. and Mgmt., Balt., 1983-84; program officer Robert Wood Johnson Found., Princeton, NJ, 1984-87, sr. program officer, 1987-88, v.p., 1988-92; rsch. prof. Heller Grad. Sch. Brandeis U., 1992-94; prof. health policy and mgmt. Boston U. Sch. Mgmt., 1994—, dir. health care mgmt. program, 1994—2003; exec. dir. Health Policy Inst. Boston U., 2003—; prof. health svcs. Boston U. Sch. Pub. Health, 2004—. Nat. program dir. Robert Wood Johnson Found. Scholars in Health Policy Rsch. Program, 1992—; mem. nat. adv. com. Robert Wood Johnson Found. Info. for State Health Policy Program, 1994-98; cons. NJ Dept. Health, 1993; chmn. commr.'s cardiac svc. com. State of NJ, Trenton, 1990-92; mem. Inst. Medicine, Tech. Monitoring Panel on Access to Care, 1989-91; cons. DC State Health Planning and Devel. Agy., 1984, Nat. Ctr. Health Svc. Rsch., 1984. Mem. editl. bd. Inquiry, Health Affairs; contbr. articles to profl. jours. Recipient Charles F. Wilinsky award Harvard Sch. Pub. Health, 1979; Kaiser fellow in health policy and mgmt., 1973-74; Dissertation grantee Nat. Ctr. Health Svc. Rsch., 1979-80. Fellow Acad. Health; mem. APHA, Am. Econ. Assn., Am. Polit. Sci. Assn., Nat. Acad. Social Ins., Health Tech. Assessment Internat., Zeta Beta Tau (pres. Gamma Pi chpt. 1972-73, treas. 1970-72), Beta Gamma Sigma. Jewish. Avocations: reading, travel, cinema, basketball, gardening. Office: Boston U Health Policy Inst 53 Bay State Rd Boston MA 02215

COHEN, ALAN M., investment company executive; Assoc. Debevoise & Plimpton, 1981—82; asst. US atty. (So. dist.) NY, 1982—91; ptnr. O'Melveny & Meyers, LLP, LA, 1991—2004; exec. v.p. The Goldman Sachs Group, 2004—, global head compliance, 2004—. Office: The Goldman Sachs Group Inc 85 Broad St New York NY 10004

COHEN, ALAN SEYMOUR, internist; b. Boston, Apr. 9, 1926; s. George I. and Jennie (Laskin) C.; m. Joan Elizabeth Prince, Sept. 12, 1954; children: Evan Bruce, Andrew Hollis, Robert Adam AB magna cum laude, Harvard Coll., 1947; MD magna cum laude, Boston U., 1952. Intern Harvard Med. Svc., Boston City Hosp., 1952-53, resident, 1953-55; exch. registrar in medicine Dundee Royal Infirmary and U. St. Andrews, Scotland, 1955-56. Rsch. and clin. fellow in rheumatology Mass. Gen. Hosp., Boston, 1956-58; instr. Med. Sch. Harvard Coll. and Mass. Gen. Hosp., 1958-60; head arthritis and connective tissue disease sect. Evans dept. clin. rsch. Mass. U. Hosp., Boston, 1960-72; Conrad Wesselhoeft prof. medicine Sch. Medicine Boston U., 1972-93, prof. pharmacology, 1974-92, disting. prof. medicine in rheumatology, 1993—; dir. Arthritis Ctr., 1977-94; dir. divsn. medicine Boston City Hosp., 1973-93; dir. Thorndike Meml. lab., 1973-93; bd. dirs. Hemagen Diagnostics Inc.; scientific bd. Neurochem. Inc., Can., 1997—. Editor: Laboratory Diagnostic Procedures in the Rheumatic Diseases, 1967, rev. edit., 1975, 3d edit., 1985, (with others) Symposium on Amyloidosis, 1968, (With R. Friedin and M. Samuels) Medical Emergencies: Diagnostic and Management Procedures from Boston City Hospital, 1977, (with J. Combes and H. Koh) 2d edit., 1983, Rheumatology and Immunology, 1979, (with J.C. Bennett) 2d edit., 1986, Progress in Clinical Rheumatology, 1984, (with D. Goldenberg) Drugs in the Rheumatic Diseases, 1986, Amyloidosis, 1986, Clinical Problems in Acute Care Medicine (J.J. Heffernan, R.A. Witzburg, A.S. Cohen), 1989; founder, editor-in-chief Amyloid Jour. Protein Folding Disorders, 1994—; contbr. more than 700 articles to profl. jours. Trustee Arthritis Found., Atlanta, 1976-82, trustee Mass. chpt., 1966-85, vice chmn., 1971-84, pres., 1981-94; vice sec. for N.Am., mem. exec. com. Pan Am. League Against Rheumatism, 1982-85; chmn. Boston City Hosp. Physician Alumni Reunion Com., 1992; pres. Boston City Hosp. Fund for Excellence, 1992. Served to surg. USPHS, 1953-55. Recipient Outstanding Alumnus award Boston U. Sch. Medicine, 1975, Purdue Frederic Arthritis award, 1979, James H. Fairclough Jr. award for disting. svc. to Mass. chpt. Arthritis Found., 1981, Alumni award for spl. distinction Boston U., 1981, Jan Van Bremeen Gold medal Dutch Rheumatism Soc., 1990, Commrs. Disting. Physician award Boston City Hosp., 1991, Gold medal Am. Coll. Rheumatology, 1994, Dr. Marian Ropes award Arthritis Found., 1995, Socius Honoris Causa, Hungarian Amyloid Soc., 2001, Hero award Arthritis Found., 2001. Master Am. Coll. Rheumatology (pres. 1978-79); fellow ACP; mem. Internat. Soc. Amyloidosis (bd. dirs. 2004), Am. Soc. Clin. Investigation, Assn. Am. Physicians, Am. Fedn. Clin. Rsch., Am. Soc. Exptl. Pathology, Soc. Exptl. Biology and Medicine, Electron Microscopy Soc. Am., New Eng. Soc. for Electron Microscopy, Am. Soc. Cell Biology, N.Y. Acad. Sci., AMA, Mass. Med. Soc., New Eng. Rheumatism Assn. (past pres.), Italian Rheumatism Soc. (hon.), Spanish Rheumatism Soc. (hon.), Finnish Rheumatism Soc. (hon.), Brazilian Rheumatism Soc. (hon.), Irish Soc. Rheumatism and Rehab. (hon.), Italian Soc. Amyloidosis (hon.), Boston U. Sch. Medicine Alumni Assn. (past pres.), Harvard Club (Boston), Wightman Tennis Ctr. (Weston, Mass.), Interurban Clin. Club, Boulders Club (Carefree, Ariz.), Phi Beta Kappa, Alpha Omega Alpha. Jewish. Office: Boston U Sch Medicine Amyloid Program 715 Albany St Bradston 204 Boston MA 02118-2307 Office Phone: 617-638-8900. Business E-Mail: jlienert@bu.edu.

COHEN, ALBERT, musician, educator; b. N.Y.C., Nov. 16, 1929; s. Sol A. and Dora Cohen; m. Betty Joan (Berg), Aug. 28, 1952; children: Eva Denise, Stefan Berg. BS, Juilliard Sch. Music, 1951; MA, NYU, 1953, PhD, 1959; postgrad., U. Paris, 1956-57. Mem. faculty U. Mich., Ann Arbor, 1960-70, assoc. prof. music, 1964-67, prof., 1967-70; prof. music, chmn. dept. SUNY, Buffalo, 1970-73, Stanford U., 1973-87, William H. Bonsall prof. music, 1974—, prof. emeritus, 2000—. Editor: Broude Bros. Ltd., N.Y.C., Info. Coordinators, Detroit. Author: Treatise on the Composition of Music, 1962, Elements or Principles of Music, 1965; (with J.D. White) Anthology of Music for Analysis, 1965; (with L.E. Miller) Music in the Paris Academy of Sciences, 1666-1793, An Index, 1979, Music in the French Royal Academy of Sciences, 1981, Music in the Royal Society of London 1660-1806, 1987; editor: J.B. Lully, Ballet de Flore, 2001; contbr. articles to profl. jours. Guggenheim fellow, 1968-69; NEH fellow, 1975-76, 82-83, 85-89 Mem. Internat. Musical Soc., Am. Musical Soc., French Musical Soc., Music Libr. Assn. Office: Stanford U Dept Music Stanford CA 94305

COHEN, ALBERT DIAMOND, retail executive; b. Winnipeg, Man., Can., Jan. 20, 1914; s. Alexander and Rose (Diamond) C.; m. Irena Kankova, Nov. 6, 1953; children: Anthony Jan, James Eduard, Anna-Lisa. LLD (hon.), U. Man., 1987. Pres. Gendis Inc., Winnipeg, 1953-87; chmn., chief exec. officer Winnipeg, 1987-99; chmn., 1999—. Chmn. exec. com. Gendis Realty Inc., Winnipeg, 1961-88 Author: The Entrepreneurs (Cert. of Merit Nat. Bus. Book award 1986), The Story of SAAN, 2002. Past pres. Winnipeg Clin. Rsch. Inst., 1975-80, Paul H.T. Thorlakson Rsch. Found., 1978-80, Man. Theatre Ctr., 1968-71, 76-81; past hon. chmn. St. John's Ravenscourt Sch., 1984-94; commr. Metric Bd. Ottawa, 1978. Named mem. Order of Can., 1983, promoted to officer, 1995; recipient Internat. Disting. Entrepreneur award U. Man., 1983, Man. of Yr. award Sales and Advt. Club, Winnipeg, 1974, Commemorative medal 125th Ann. Can. Fedn., 1992, Sony Lifetime Achievement award, 2000; inducted into Can. Bus. Hall of Fame, 1994. Office: Gendis Inc PO Box 9400 1370 Sony Pl Winnipeg MB Canada R3C 3C3 E-mail: finance@gendis.ca.

COHEN, ALLAN RICHARD, broadcast executive; b. Bklyn., Dec. 27, 1947; s. Ike and Fae C.; m. Roberta Segal, July 12, 1970; children: Evan, Stacie. BS, Hofstra U., 1970; MM, Poly. Inst. Bklyn., 1976. Electronics engr. Sperry Systems Mgmt. Div., Great Neck, N.Y., 1970-74; with CBS/Viacom, 1974—; dir. planning and adminstrn. WCBS-TV, 1977-79; v.p. personnel CBS Broadcast Group, 1979-80; v.p., gen. mgr. Sta. KMOX-TV, St. Louis, 1980-86, Sta. KMOV-TV, St. Louis, 1986—. Lectr. in comm. and journalism Washington U., St. Louis; mem. affiliates adv. bd. CBS. Restaurant critic, travel editor St. Louis Bus. Jour. Vice chmn. bd. dirs. St. Louis Symphony; bd. dirs. Paraquad, Jewish Hosp., United Way, Variety Club; mem. adv. bd. Nat. Coun. Jewish Women, St. Louis. Recipient Flair awards, Emmy awards. Mem. NATAS (v.p. St. Louis chpt. 1987-88, pres. 1989-91), Mo. Broadcasters Assn. (bd. dirs.), Ill. Broadcasters Assn., Nat. Assn. Broadcasters, St. Louis Jr. League (adv. bd.), Westwood Club, St. Louis Variety Club (bd. dirs.).

COHEN, ANDREW, news analyst, lawyer; b. Montreal; BA, Boston U., 1988, JD, 1991. Assoc. Gorsuch Kirgis, Boston, 1991; legal analyst, commentator CBS News Radio, 1997—, CBS News, CBS 4, Denver, Gavel to Gavel law column. Recipient S.P.J. Award for Best Spot News coverage. Office: CBS 4 1044 Lincoln St Denver CO 80203*

COHEN, ANDREW DAVID, language educator, applied linguist; b. Washington, Mar. 14, 1944; s. Harold Jack and Rena (Alpert) C.; m. Sabina Rose Alpert, Mar. 31, 1968; children: Judy Naomi, Daniel Moshe. BA, Harvard U., 1965; MA, Stanford U., 1971, PhD, 1973. Tchg. fellow Stanford U., Calif., 1970—72; asst. prof. UCLA, 1972—75; assoc. prof. Hebrew U., Jerusalem, 1975—91; prof. ESL U. Minn., Mpls., 1991—. Dir. Ctr. for Applied Linguistics Rsch., Hebrew U., 1981-91, sr. lectr., 1975-79; coord. English lang. placement UCLA, 1972-75; Fulbright lectr., rschr. Cath. Pontifical U., São Paulo, Brazil, 1986-87; dir. Nat. Lang. Resource Ctr., Mpls., 1993-2004, Inst. Linguistics and Asian and Slavic Langs. and Lits., 1993-2000, Inst. Linguistics, ESL and Slavic Langs. and Lits., 2000—; Disting. lectr. Temple U., Japan, 1988, scholar of coll. Coll. Liberal Arts, U. Minn., 2002-05; vis. prof. Dept. Applied Lang. Studies and Linguistics U. Auckland, New Zealand, 2004-2005. Author: A Sociolinguistic Approach to Bilingual Education, 1975, Describing Bilingual Education Classrooms, 1980, Language Learning, 1990, Assessing Language Ability in the Classroom, 1994, Strategies in Learning and Using a Second Language, 1998; co-editor Interfaces Between Second Language Acquisition and Language Testing Research, 1998, Studying Speaking to Inform Second Language Learning, 2004 Rural cmty. devel. vol. Peace Corps., Bolivia, 1965-67. Sgt. U.S. Army, 1968-74. Mem. Studies in Second Lang. Acquisition (editl. bd. 1985-95), Am. Assn. for Applied Linguistics (sec.-treas. 1993—), Minn. TESOL, Am. Coun. Tchg. Fgn. Langs., Tchrs. English Fgn. Lang. (rsch. award com.), Internat. Assn. Applied Linguistics (sec. gen. 1996-2002). Democrat. Jewish. Avocations: squash, music, trumpet, language learning. Office: Univ Minn Dept ESL 214 Nolte Ctr 315 Pillsbury Dr SE Minneapolis MN 55455 Office Phone: 612-624-3806. Business E-Mail: adcohen@umn.edu.

COHEN, ANDREW JAY, lawyer; b. Springfield, Mass., Apr. 7, 1967; s. Michael and Judith Cohen; m. Ruth Cohen, Oct. 10, 1993; children: Rachel, Jenna, Rebecca. BA, Tufts U., Medford, Mass., 1989; JD, Georgetown, Washington, 1993. Bar: Minn. 1993, Conn. 1995, 8th Cir. Ct. Appeals: U.S. 1994. Assoc. Dorsey & Whitney, Mpls., 1993—95, Shipman & Goodwin, Hartford, Conn., 1995—97; gen. counsel Disability Mgmt. Svcs., Springfield, Mass., 1997—. Dir. Disability Mgmt. Svcs., Springfield, Mass., 1998—, Psychiat. Disability Cons., Springfield, Mass., 1999—. Chmn. bd. Southend Cmty. Svcs., Hartford, Conn., 2001—04, bd. mem., 1997—2004, Bushnell Pk. Found., Hartford, Conn., 1997—2000. Avocations: football, golf, jogging. Office: Disability Mgmt Svcs Inc 1350 Main St Springfield MA 01103 Business E-Mail: andy_cohen@di-mgmt.com.

COHEN, ANN ELLEN, librarian; b. Binghamton, N.Y., June 11, 1949; d. Leonard Francis and Shirley Frances (Greenhouse) C. Student, Elmira Coll., 1967-69; BA, George Washington U., 1971; MSLS, Syracuse U., 1972. N.Y. State Librarian's Cert. Br. libr. Binghamton Pub. Libr., 1973-77, info. services libr., 1977-84, Broome County Pub. Libr., Binghamton, 1985-88; asst. div. head Rochester (N.Y.) Pub. Libr., 1988—. Dir. Temple Israel Libr., Binghamton, 1982-85, cons., 1982—, cons. children's libr., 1985-86. Author book revs., Libr. Jour., 1983-97, Booklist's Reference Books Bulletin, 1989—. Mem. 123d Dist. of N.Y. State Assembly's Edn. Aid Task Force, 1986-88, Broome County (N.Y.) Com. of U.S. Commn. for Bicentennial Celebration of U.S. Constn., 1987; bd. dirs. Jewish Cmty. Ctr., Binghamton, 1982-85, Temple Beth Am, Henrietta, N.Y., 1996—. Mem. AAUW, ALA (affiliates coun. rep. jr. mems. round table 1984-86, editl. bd. reference books bulletin 1989-92), N.Y. Libr. Assn. (pres. jr. mems. round table 1985-86), Hadassah, Jewish Genealogy Soc. of Greater Rochester. Office: Rochester Pub Libr 115 South Ave Rochester NY 14604-1896

COHEN, ARNOLD NORMAN, gastroenterologist; b. N.Y.C., Nov. 5, 1949; s. Norman and Edna Clara (Arnold) C.; m. Colleen Ruth Carey; children: Eric Arnold, Leslie Carey. BA summa cum laude, Hobart Coll., 1971; MD, Harvard U., 1975. Diplomate Am. Bd. Internal Medicine, Am. Bd. Gastroenterology. Resident internal medicine U. Pa., Phila., 1975-78, asst. instr. medicine, 1977-78; fellow gastroenterology, instr. medicine Northwestern U., Chgo., 1978-80; asst. clin. prof. medicine U. Wash. Med. Sch., Seattle, 1980—; mem. faculty Spokane (Wash.) Family Medicine Residency, 1980—; pvt. practice gastroenterology Spokane, 1980—. Mem. various coms. St. Lukes-Deaconess Hosp., Spokane, 1980—; pres. med. staff St. Lukes Hosp., 1985-86. Contbr. articles to profl. jours. and textbooks. Fellow ACP, Am. Coll. Gastroenterology; mem. Am. Soc. Gastrointestinal Endoscopy, Am. Gastroent. Soc., Wash. Med. Soc., Spokane Internal Med. Soc., Phi Beta Kappa, Alpha Omega Alpha. Avocations: shooting sports, martial arts, swimming. Home: 3514 S Jefferson St Spokane WA 99203-1441 Office: Spokane Digestive Disease Ctr 801 W 5th Ave Spokane WA 99204-2823 Office Phone: 509-747-5145.

COHEN, ARTHUR MORRIS, artist; b. N.Y.C., Jan. 2, 1928; s. Morris Aaron and Flora (Hasson) C.; m. Elizabeth Copstein, Jan. 15, 1972; 1 son, Ezekiel. Student, Cooper Union, 1947-49, Art Student's League, N.Y.C., 1951, 60. Mem. faculty Studio Art Sch. of the Agean, Greece, 1987. Represented in permanent collections Met. Mus. Art, N.Y.C., Hirshhorn Mus., Washington, Bklyn. Mus., N.Y.C., Boston Mus., Mus. City N.Y., N.Y. Hist. Soc., Everson Mus., Syracuse, Cooper Hewitt Mus., N.Y.C.; group shows include Everson Mus., Syracuse, Nat. Acad. Design, N.Y.C., 1976, 82, 83, David Findlay Gallery, N.Y.C., 1983, Hirshhorn Mus., Washington, 1979-80, Bklyn. Mus., N.Y.C., 1983, Cooper Hewitt Mus., N.Y.C., 1983, Albany Inst. History and Art, N.Y., 1985-86, East End Gallery, Provincetown, 1986, Lillian Kornbluth Gallery, 1987, Provincetown (Mass.) Art Assn., 1987, Forum Gallery, 1993; one-man shows at Blue Mountain Gallery, N.Y.C., 1980, 83, 85, Swansborough Gallery, Wellfleet, Mass., 1980, 83, Peter Rose Gallery, N.Y.C., 1982, Munson Gallery, Chatham, Mass., 1981, 85, 89, 90, East End Gallery, Provincetown, 1986, 87, Forum Gallery, N.Y.C., 1976, 90, Roko Gallery, N.Y.C., 1970, Ellen Harris Gallery, Provincetown, 1985, Lillian Kornbluth Gallery, Fairlawn, N.J., 1986, Phoenix Gallery, Provincetown, 1988, New East End Gallery, Provincetown, 1989, Forum Gallery, N.Y.C., 1990, East End Gallery, Provincetown, Mass., 1991, 92, Munson Gallery, Chatham, Mass., 1990, Wellfleet (Mass.) Fine Arts Gallery, 1990, Gallery Beshert, Montclair, NJ, 2004, Gallery Beauregard, Rumson, NJ, 2004; exhbns. yearly at East End Gallery, Provincetown, Mass., Berta Walker Gallery, Provincetown. 1993; contbr. articles to various periodicals. Served with U.S. Army, 1946-47. Named N.Y. State grantee, 1977, Ingram Merill grantee, 1979, Guggenheim grantee, 1981, Pollack Krasner grantee, 1993; recipient Pollock-Krasner award, 1986, 93, Adolf Gottlieb award, 1987, William Palmer prize Nat. Acad. Design, 1993. Jewish. Home: 55 Tiemann Pl New York NY 10027-3332

COHEN, ARYELL, music educator; b. Bronx, NY, Aug. 20, 1952; s. Aaron Moses Cohen and Phyllis Novik; m. Maxine Judith Hersh (div.); children: Michelle, Erica. BA in Music, Calif. State U., 1978. Tchg. credential Calif., 2000. Tchr. Sinai Temple, L.A., 1970, organist, choir dir., 1975—; tchr. L.A. Unified Sch. Dist., 1995—. Mem. Music Educators Nat. Conf. Mem.: Guild Temple Musicians, Am. Choral Directors Assn., Am. Guild Organists. Democrat. Jewish. Office: Sinai Temple 10400 Wilshire Blvd Los Angeles CA 90024 Office Phone: 310-474-1518. Business E-Mail: acohen@sinaitemple.org.

COHEN, BARTON POLLOCK, lawyer; b. Kansas City, Kans., Dec. 11, 1930; s. Joseph Cohen and Margaret Pollock; m. Mary Davidson, Dec. 30, 1989; children: Thomas M., Margo, John. BA, Yale U., 1952; JD, Harvard U., 1955. Bar: Kans. 1955, U.S. Dist. Ct. Kans., U.S. Supreme Ct., U.S. Ct. Appeals (10th cir.). Assoc., ptnr. Cohen, Schnider, Shamberg, Kansas City, Kans., 1957-66; ptnr. Cohen, Benjamin, Comer, Overland Park, Kans., 1966-88, Blackwell Sanders Matheny Weary Lombardi, Overland Park, 1988-96; of counsel Blackwell Sanders Peper Martin LLP, Overland Park, 1997—. Pres. Metcalf BancShares Inc., Overland Park, 1980—; dir., vice-chmn., gen. counsel Metcalf Bank, Overland Park, 1968—, dir. Rosedale Bank, Kansas City, Kans., 1958-80. Councilman City of Prairie Village, Kans., 1964-69; bd. chmn. Johnson County Mental Health Ctr., Johnson County, 1974; bd. dirs. Johnson County Libr., Wyandotte County Hist. Soc. and Mus. With U.S. Army, 1955-57; mem Johnson County Heritage Trust Fund Grant Review Bd, 2002-2003. Fellow Johnson County Bar Found. (treas.); mem. Nat. Assn. Security Dealers (arbitrator), Kans. State Hist. Soc. (bd. dirs.), Temple Congregation Bnai Jehulah Endowment Com (chmn. 2003—), Rep. Jewish Coalition (bd. dirs.). Republican. Jewish. Avocations: golf, travel. Home: 12617 Briar Dr Leawood KS 66209-3169 Office: Blackwell Sanders Peper Martin LLP 9401 Indian Creek Pkwy Ste 1200 Overland Park KS 66210-2020 Fax: 913-696-7070. E-mail: bcohen@blackwellsanders.com.

COHEN, BENJAMIN JERRY, political economy educator; b. Ossining, N.Y., June 5, 1937; s. Abraham and Rachel (Grossman) C.; m. Jane DeHart, Sept. 20, 1986. BA, Columbia U., 1959, PhD, 1963. Economist Fed. Res. Bank N.Y., 1962-64; asst. prof. econs. Princeton (N.J.) U., 1964-71; assoc. prof. Tufts U. Fletcher Sch. of Law and Diplomacy, Medford, Mass., 1971-78; William L. Clayton prof. Internat. Econ. Affairs Fletcher Sch. Law and Diplomacy Tufts U., Medford, Mass., 1978-91; Louis G. Lancaster prof. Internat. Polit. Economy U. Calif., Santa Barbara, 1991—. Author: Organizing the World's Money, 1976, Banks and the Balance of Payments, 1981, In Whose Interest?, 1986, Crossing Frontiers, 1991, The Geography of Money, 1998, The Future of Money, 2004. Mem. Am. Econ. Assn., Am. Polit. Sci. Assn., Coun. Fgn. Rels., Internat. Studies Assn., Pacific Coun. Internat. Policy. Jewish. Office: U Calif Dept Polit Sci Santa Barbara CA 93106-9420 Office Phone: 805-893-8763. Business E-Mail: bjcohen@polsci.ucsb.edu.

COHEN, BERNARD LEONARD, physicist, researcher; b. Pitts., June 14, 1924; s. Samuel and Mollie (Friedman) C.; m. Anna Foner, Mar. 30, 1950; children: Donald, Judith, Frederick, Ernest. BS, Case Inst. Tech., 1944; MS, U. Pitts., 1948; PhD, Carnegie Inst. Tech., 1950. With Oak Ridge (Tenn.) Nat. Lab., 1950-58; prof. physics U. Pitts., 1958-94, prof. emeritus, 1994—, adj. prof. chemistry, chem. engring., radiation health, environ. and occupl. health; dir. Sarah Mellon Scaife Nuc. Physics Lab., 1965-78. On leave with Gen. Atomic Lab., San Diego, 1959-60, Inst. for Def. Analysis, Washington, 1962, Brookhaven Nat. Lab., 1965, Los Alamos Sci. Lab., 1969, Inst. Energy Analysis, Oak Ridge, 1974-75, Electric Power Rsch. Inst., 1975, Argonne Nat. Lab., 1978-79; cons. numerous govtl. agys. and pvt. corps. Author: Heart of the Atom, 1967, Concepts of Nuclear Physics, 1971, Nuclear Science and Society, 1974, Before It's Too Late: A Scientist's Case for Nuclear Power, 1983, A Homeowner's Guide to Radon, 1987, The Nuclear Energy Option: Alternative For The Nineties, 1990; contbr. numerous articles to profl. jours. Fellow AAAS, Am. Phys. Soc. (chmn. divsn. nuc. physics 1974-75, Bonner prize for nuc. physics 1981); mem. NAE, Am. Assn. Physics Tchrs. (nat. coun. 1973-78), Am. Nuc. Soc. (chmn. divsn. environ. scis. 1980-81, Pub. Info. award 1984, Walter Zinn award 1996, Spl. award 1996), Soc. Risk Analysis, Health Physics Soc. (Disting. Sci. Achievement award 1992). Home: 307 S Dithridge St Apt 204 Pittsburgh PA 15213-3514 Office Phone: 412-624-9245. Fax: 412-624-9163. Business E-Mail: blc@pitt.edu.

COHEN, BERNARD S., lawyer; b. Bklyn., Jan. 17, 1934; s. Benjamin and Fannie Linda (Davis) C.; m. Rae Rose, Dec. 21, 1958; children: Bennett Alan, Karen Linda. BBA, CCNY, 1956; JD, Georgetown U., 1960. Cert. civil trial advocate, Nat. Bd. Trial Advocacy; bar: Va. 1961. Labor economist and labor law advisor U.S. Dept. Labor, Washington, 1956-61; ptnr. Cohen, Dunn, Curcio, Keating & Rohrstaff, PC, Alexandria, Va., 1961-98; mem. Va. Ho. of Dels., Richmond, 1980-95. Co-author: Environmental Rights and Remedies, 1971. Chmn. Alexandria (Va.) Dem. Com., 1967; alt. del. Nat. Dem. Conv., N.Y.C., 1980. Mem. ABA, Va. State Bar Assn. Trial Lawyers of Am., Va. Trial Lawyers Assn., B'nai B'rith. Democrat. Jewish. Office: Law Office of Bernard S Cohen PC 221 S Alfred St Alexandria VA 22314-3647

COHEN, BRAM, web programmer; b. 1975; Graduate, Stuyvesant High Sch., NYC, 1993; attended, SUNY, Buffalo. Software engr. Earthweb Inc., 1996; programmer db-Centric Corp., 1997; chief software developer Signet Assurance Co., 1997—99; software engr. MojoNation, 2000—01, Valve Software, 2003—04; software developer BitTorrent Inc., Bellevue, Wash., 2001—. Named one of World's 100 Most Influential People, Time Mag., 2005. Achievements include development of BitTorrent, software for downloading & sharing large files. Mailing: BitTorrent Inc #152 227 Bellevue Way NE Bellevue WA 98004*

COHEN, BRETT I., health products executive; b. Bronx, N.Y., Aug. 13, 1962; s. Gilbert Victor and Phyllis C. (Strassberg) C.; m. Elissa Bloom, Aug. 23, 1986; children: Harley Lennon, Jake Aaron. BS, SUNY, Albany, 1984, PhD in Chemistry, 1987. Postdoctoral fellow Rutgers U., New Brunswick, NJ, 1988; CEO, v.p. dental rsch. Essential Dental Systems, South Hackensack, NJ, 1989—2003. Mem. dental magnets subcom. Am. Dental Assn./ISO Specification No. 81 Magnets and Keepers, 1993—. Contbr. articles to profl. jours.; patentee in field. Mem. Am. Chem. Soc., Soc. for Dental Materials, Soc. for Lasers, Am. Soc. Quality Control. Avocations: reading, running, movies. Office: Essential Dental Systems 89 Leuning St South Hackensack NJ 07606-1326 Business E-Mail: eds@pipeline.com.

COHEN, BRUCE MICHAEL, psychiatrist, educator, scientist, health facility administrator; b. Univ. Heights, Ohio, Sept. 1, 1947; s. Herschel and Natalie (Marshall) C.; m. Marian A. Oliner, July 11, 1970; children: Matthew, Laura. BS, MIT, Cambridge, Mass., 1969; MD, Case Western Res. U., Cleveland, Ohio, 1975; PhD, Case Western Res. U., Dept. Biology, Cleveland, Ohio, 1975. Diplomate Am. Bd. Psychiatry and Neurology, 1979, Nat. Bd. Med. Examiners, 1976, Mass. Lic., 1976. Resident in psychiatry McLean Hosp., Belmont, Mass., 1975-78; clin. fellow in psychiatry Harvard Med. Sch., Boston, 1975—78; chief resident in psychiatry McLean Hosp., Belmont, Mass., 1977-78; instr. in psychiatry Harvard Med. Sch., Boston, 1978-81, asst. prof. psychiatry, 1981-85; asst. psychiatrist McLean Hosp., Belmont, Mass., 1978—83, assoc. psychiatrist, 1984—88, chief clin. biochem. lab. Mailman Rsch. Ctr., 1981-85, assoc. dir. mental health clin. rsch. ctr., 1981-85, chief clin. and molecular pharmacology lab., Mailman Rsch. Ctr., 1985—; assoc. prof. psychiatry Harvard Med. Sch., Boston, 1985-95, prof. psychiatry, 1995—; spec. asst. to the gen. dir./psychiatrist-in-chief McLean Hosp., Belmont, Mass., 1987—88, assoc. gen. dir., 1988-94, psychiatrist, 1988—, dir., residency tng. program, 1993—97, sr. v.p. Rsch. and Tng., 1994-97; dir. combined Mass. Gen. Hosp./McLean Hosp., Belmont, Mass., 1995—97; pres., psychiatrist in chief McLean Hosp., Belmont, 1997—; pres. McLean Health Svcs., Belmont, Mass., 1998—99, dir., CEO, 1999—; head dept. psychiatry Med. Sch. Harvard U. McLean Hosp., Belmont, 1997—, dir. Brain Imaging Program, 1993—97, 1997—. Vis. physician Clin. Rsch. Ctr., MIT, 1979-85, vis. scientist, 93-; asst. chief, Clin. Rsch. Ctr., Mailman Rsch. Ctr., Belmont, Mass., 1979-81, assoc. chief, 1981-85; cons. psychiatrist Westwood (Mass.) Lodge, 1986-88; lectr. in field. Contbr. numerous sci. articles and abstracts to peer-reviewed jours.; author 20 book chpts.; adv. editor, Psychopharmacology, 1980-2002; assoc. editor Am. Jour. of Psychiatry, 2000- Laureate investigator Nat. Alliance for Rsch. on Schizophrenia and Depression, 1989. Predoctoral fellow NSF, Case Western Res. U., 1971-73, Ethel duPont Warren fellow in psychiatry Harvard Med. Sch., McLean Hosp. 1977-78, fellowship, Scottish Rite Schizophrenia Rsch. Program, NMJ, USA, 1978-80, recipient 6 grants NIMH, 3 grants Scottish Rite Schizophrenia Program, 7 projects program grants NIMH. Fellow Mass. Psychiatric Soc., Soc. Magnetic Resonance, Am. Psychiat. Assn., Am. Coll. Neuropsychpharmacology; mem. AAAS, AMA, Soc. Biological Psychiatry Office: McLean Hosp Adminstrn bldg Rm 118 115 Mill St Belmont MA 02478-1048 Office Phone: 617-855-3227. Office Fax: 617-855-3670. Business E-Mail: cohenb@mclean.harvard.edu.

COHEN, BURTON A., radiologist; MD, NY Med. Coll., 1975. Cert. Diagnostic Radiology 1979. Intern Brookdale Hosp., Bklyn., 1975—76; resident, diagnostic radiology Mt. Sinai Hosp., N.Y.C., 1976—79; radiologist Mt. Sinai Med. Ctr., N.Y.C., 1979—85; assoc. clin. prof., radiology Mt. Sinai Sch. Medicine, N.Y.C., 1982—. Office: 1 E 82d St New York NY 10028-0302 Office Phone: 212-535-9770. E-mail: drburtoncohen@aol.com.

COHEN, BURTON DAVID, food service executive, lawyer; b. Chgo., Feb. 12, 1940; s. Allan and Gussy (Katz) C.; m. LInda Rochelle Kaine, Jan. 19, 1969; children: David, Jordana. BS in Bus. and Econs., Ill. Inst. Tech., 1960; JD, Northwestern U., 1963. Staff atty. McDonald's Corp., Oak Brook, Ill., 1964-69, asst. sec., 1969-70, asst. gen. counsel, 1970-76, asst. v.p., 1976-78, dep. dir. legal dept., 1978-80, v.p. franchising, asst. gen. counsel, asst. sec., 1980-89, sr. v.p., chief franchising officer, 1989-98. Adv. dir., 1992-93, McDonald's Corp., 1992—; adv. bd. La. State U. Franchise U.; dir. Goodwill Enterprises Devel. Corp.; franchise mediator CPR Inst. for Dispute Resolution; adj. prof. Kellogg Grad Sch. Mgmt., Northwestern U.; bd. dirs. Dwyer Group, Valet Today; cons. Exec. Svc. Corps. Chgo.; sr. cons. Ifranchise Group; lectr., cons. in field. Author: Franchising: Second Generation Problems, 1969. With AUS, 1963-64. Mem. ABA, Ill. Bar Assn., Chgo. Bar Assn., Internat. Franchise Assn. (lectr.), Assn. Nat. Advertisers, Chgo. Coun. Fgn. Rels., Execs. Club (Chgo.), Tau Epsilon Phi, Phi Delta Phi. Office: 300 Cedar Ave Highland Park IL 60035

COHEN, CARL I., psychiatrist, educator; b. N.Y.C., Aug. 7, 1947; s. Louis and Louise Cohen; m. Katherine A. Henry, Sept. 12, 1987; children: Sara, Zachary. BA, CUNY, 1967; MD, SUNY, Buffalo, 1971; MA, NYU, 1974. Diplomate Am. Bd. Psychiatry and Neurology, Am. Bd. Psychiatry and Neurology with Added Qualifications in Geriatric Psychiatry. Intern Med. Coll. Pa., 1971-72; resident NYU Bellevue Med. Ctr., 1972-74; fellow NYU Med. Ctr., 1974-75, asst. prof., dir. social and cmty. psychiatry N.Y.C., 1976-81; prof. psychiatry, dir. divsn. geriatric psychiatry SUNY Health Sci. Ctr., Bklyn., 1981—. Dir. Downstate Mental Hygiene Assocs., Bklyn., 1983—, Bklyn. Alzheimer's Disease Assistance Ctr., 1988—; mem. adv. b.d L.I. Alzheimer's Found., N.Y., 1998—; spl. advisor White House Conf. on Aging, Washington, 1980; advisor to various coms. NIMH, 1985-99; presenter N.Y.C. Mayor's Conf. on Alzheimer's Disease, 1992-99. Author: Old Men of the Bowery, 1989, Schizophrenia Into Later Life, 2003; mem. editl. bd. Jour. Geriat. Psychiatry, London, 1983—99, Am. Jour. Geriat. Psychiatry, 1994—2000, spl. editor Cmty. Mental Health Jour., 1993; contbr. over 150 articles to med. jours., chapters to books. Bd. dirs. St. Francis Friends of Poor, N.Y.C., 1983—. Named Disting. Alumnus, CUNY Bklyn. Coll., 2004; named one of Best Drs. in N.Y., N.Y. Mag., 1996, 1998, 2001; over 40 grants, including, NIMH, N.Y. State Dept. Health, pvt. founds. Fellow Am. Psychiat. Assn.; mem. Am. Assn. Geriatric Psychiatry, Am. Assn. Cmty. Psychiatrists (Psychiatrist of Yr. award 1991), Internat. Assn. Geriatric Psychiatry. Avocation: handball. Office: SUNY Health Sci Ctr Bklyn 450 Clarkson Ave # 1203 Brooklyn NY 11203-2056 Office Phone: 718-287-4806. E-mail: cohen_c@hscbklyn.edu, cohenhenry@aol.com.

COHEN, CARMEL, oncologist; b. New Orleans, 1932; MD, Tulane U. Sch. Medicine, 1958. Cert. obstetrics and gynecology 1967, gynecologic oncology 1974. Intern to resident Mt. Sinai Med. Ctr., N.Y.C., 1958—60, resident to fellow, 1962—65; prof. ob-gyn Mt. Sinai Sch. of Medicine; oncologist, gynecology Mt. Sinai Med. Ctr., 1965—2004; prof. clin. gynecology and obstetrics Columbia U., N.Y.C., 2004—. Mem.: Ovarian Cancer Rsch. Fund (chmn. bd. dirs., chmn. scientific adv. com.), Am. Cancer Soc. Nat. Assembly and Gynecological Cancer Adv. Group, Am. Cancer Soc. (v.p. N.Y.C. divsn., bd. dirs. Eastern divsn., pres. ea. divsn. 2004—), Internat. Gynecologic Cancer Soc. (founding mem.), Soc. Pelvic Surgeons (pres.), Soc. Gynecologic Oncologists (pres.), NY Obstetrical Soc. (Pres.). Office: Columbia U Herbert Irving Pavilion 161 Ft Washington Ave Fl 8 New York NY 10032 Office Phone: 212-305-3410. Business E-Mail: cc2438@columbia.edu.

COHEN, CAROLYN ALTA, healthcare educator; b. Boston, Aug. 25, 1943; d. Haskell Mark and Sarah (Siegal) Cohen. BS, Boston U., 1965; postgrad., Boston State Coll., U. Mass., 1978, Boston Leadership Acad., 1989, Boston Leadership Inst., 1997. Health and phys. edn. tchr., coach, girls athletic coord. Roslindale H.S., Boston, 1965—76; health and phys. edn. tchr., coach, athletic coord. West Roxbury H.S., Boston, 1976—87; asst. dir. health phys. edn. athletics Madison Park Campus, Boston, 1979—87; health educator dept. phys. edn./athletics West Roxbury H.S., Boston, 1989—90, 1990—, lead tchr., 1995—2000; commr. girls' basketball Boston Pub. Schs., 1979—. Cheerleading judge various orgns., 1963, 64, 65, 70, 74, 80, 69-74; coach recreational programs N.E. Deaconess Hosp. Sch. Nursing, 1962-64, Beth Israel Hosp. Sch. Nursing, 1961-64; basketball ofcl. Bay State League, Pvt. Sch. League, Cath. H.S., 1961-80; coach phys. edn. dept. Boston U., 1962-65, 65-68; ofcl. Boston Park and Recreation Dept., 1962-75, summer playgrounds instr., 1961-65; instr. garening, athletic specialist agr. dept. Boston Schs., 1965-76. Trustee Adaptic Environ. Ctr., Boston, 1986—, treas., mem. exec. bd., 1990—; trustee Friends of Boston Harbor Islands, Inc.; instr. ARC, 1965—; rep. Office Children-Area IV, Roslindale, Boston, 1974—76; liaison West Roxbury H.S. and Cmty. Sch. New Move Unlimited Theatre, Boston, 1981—84; liaison spl. arts project West Roxbury H.S., 1993—94. Named to Boston U. Scarlet Key Soc., 1998, N.E. New Agenda Hall of Fame, 2003; recipient Spl. Citation, Boston U. Sargent Coll. Alumni Assn., 1980, Cert. of Appreciation, ARC Mass. Bay, 1986, New Agenda award, Boston Salute to Women in Sport, 1993, Disting. Svc. to Alma Mater award, Boston U., 1994, Citation, Mass. Celebration Women in Sports Day, 2002, citation, Mil. Order of World Wars, 2002, Youth Patriotic & Leadership, 2002, Patrick Henry award, YPAL Program of Officier's of World Wars, 2004. Mem.: Sargent Coll. Alumni Assn. (class sec., editor class newsletter 1965—, Spl. Citation 1980, Black Gold award 1995), Boston U. Nat. Alumni Coun., Boston U. Alumni Assn. (v.p. 1980—82, 1987—89, v.p. cmty. 1995—97, sec. 1997—, named to North East New Agenda Hall Fame 2003), Mass. Assn. Health, Phys. Edn., Recreation and Dance (state and exec. com. 1969—74, treas. 1981—94, coord. registration ann. state conv. 1975—94, Honor award recognition 1978, Presdl. Citation 1988, Joseph McKenney award 2002), AAHPERD (bud. mgr. nat. conv. 1988—89), Boston U. Women's Grad. Club (v.p. for scholarship 1981—83, 1985—). Home: 100 Corey St West Roxbury MA 02132-2330 Office Phone: 617-635-8917.

COHEN, CHARLES EMIL, art historian, educator; b. N.Y.C., July 11, 1942; s. Philip and Hannah (Abramson) Cohen; m. Sondra Eileen Cohen, Sept. 27, 1964; children: Joshua K., Jonathan E. BA, Columbia U., 1963; MFA, Princeton U., 1965; PhD, Harvard U., 1971. Tutor Harvard U., Cambridge, Mass., 1967-68, head teaching fellow, 1969-70; asst. prof. art U. Chgo., 1970-75, assoc. prof., 1975-80, chmn. art dept., 1985—89, Resident Master Pierce Hall, Mary L. Block prof. art, 1980—, chmn. com. visual arts. Curator of drawings Pordenone 500th Anniversary, 1984; resident master Pierce Hall U. Chgo. Author: I Disegni di Pomponio Amalteo, 1975, Drawings of Giovanni Antonio da Pordenone, 1980, Art of Giovanni Antiorio da Pordenone: Between Dialect & Lang.; contbr. articles to profl. jours. Fellow Guggenheim Found., 1983, Am. Coun. Learned Socs., 1980, Gladys Krieble Delmas Found., 1989, NEH, summer 1983; Univ. fellow NEH, 1989-90. Mem.: Renaissance Soc. Am., U. Chgo. Renaissance Seminar, Midwest Art History Soc., Coll. Art Assn. Am. Jewish. Office: U Chgo Dept Art 5540 S Greenwood Ave Chicago IL 60637-1506 Office Phone: 773-702-5880. E-mail: cac5@uchicago.edu.*

COHEN, CHRISTOPHER B., lawyer; b. Washington, July 10, 1942; m. Judith Calder; 2 children. BA, U. Mich., 1964, JD, 1967. Bar: Ill. 1968, Wis. 1986, D.C. 1972, U.S. Dist. Ct. D.C. 1969, U.S. Dist Ct. (no. dist.) Ill. 1968, U.S. Ct. Mil. Appeals 1977, U.S. Supreme Ct. 1974; lic. real estate broker, cert. real estate continuing edn. instr., Ill. Clerk, lawyer Legal Aid Bur.-United Charities of Chgo., 1967-68; adminstrv. asst. to pres. Cook County Bd. Commrs., 1969-71; hearing officer Liquor Commn. Cook County, Chgo., 1970-71; alderman 46th ward Chgo. City Coun., 1971-77; atty. Schwartzberg, Barnett & Cohen, Chgo., 1973-77; midwest regional dir. U.S. Dept. HHS, Chgo., 1977-81; atty. Hinshaw, Culbertson, Moelmann, Hoban & Fuller, Chgo., 1981-82, Cassiday, Shade & Gloor, Chgo., 1982-85; ptnr. Holleb & Coff, Chgo., 1985-98; of counsel Buyer & Rubin, Chgo., 1998—; prin. Cohen Law Firm, Chgo., 1998—. Lectr. Northwestern U., 1973, DePaul U., Chgo., 1981, U. Ill., Chgo., 1981, 82; adult edn. tchr. Francis Parker Sch., Chgo., 1979, 80, 81; bd. dirs. State of Ill. Hosp. Licensing Bd., 1987-97; bd. dirs. State of Ill. Med. Ctr. Commn., 1985-90; mem. fed. regional coun. 1977-81; nursing home adv. coun. Office of Ill. Atty. Gen., 1988-94; Dem. candidate U.S. Ho. Reps., 10th Congressional Dist. Ill., 1999. Contbr. articles to profl. jours. and nat. newspapers. Field organizer Humphrey for Pres., Chgo., 1968; asst. to Ill. field dir. Jimmy Carter for Pres., Chgo., 1976; active spl. projects, polit. unit Clinton/Gore Campaign, Little Rock, 1992; mem. govt. affairs com. Jewish Fedn. Met. Chgo., 1988—; mem. U. Mich. Law Sch. Alumni Fund, Glenview Concert Band; fin. exec. bd. New Trier Township Dem. Orgn., 1993-98; bd. dirs. UNICEF Chgo., 1996-97. Mem. ABA (adminstrv. law and regulatory practice sect. 1990-95), Ill. State Bar Assn. (founding mem., chair health care sect. coun. 1986-87, mem. legis. com. 1988-90, assembly 1991-97, local govt. sect.), Chgo. Bar Assn. (vice chair urban affairs com. 1991, chair health law com. 1983, mem. real estate tax com.), D.C. Bar Assn., State Bar Wis. Office: Cohen Law Firm 185 Franklin Glencoe IL 60022-1259

COHEN, CLAIRE GORHAM, investment company executive; b. St. Johnsbury, Vt., May 9, 1934; d. John David and Muriel (Somers) Gorham; m. Richard D. Cohen, Nov. 26, 1959; 1 son, James H. Student, U. Vt., 1953—54; BA, Radcliffe Coll., 1956. Proofreader Dun & Bradstreet, Inc., 1956, mcpl. bond analyst, 1957-64, sr. state analyst, 1965-66, sr. analyst, 1970-71, Moody's Investors Svc. Inc., N.Y.C., 1971-75; v.p., assoc. dir. rsch. Mcpl. Bond Rsch. Divsn., N.Y.C., 1975-86, v.p. mng. dir. state ratings, 1986-89; exec. mng. dir. govtl. fin. Fitch Investors Svc., Inc., N.Y.C., 1989-91, exec. v.p., 1991-94, vice chmn., 1994-97, Fitch IBCA, N.Y.C., 1997—2004; cons., 2005—. Mem. Govt. Acctg. Stds. Adv. Bd., 1999-2002; mem. Fed. Acctg. Stds. Adv. Bd., 2002—; mem. Task Force on N.Y. State Pub. Authorities, 1974-75. Mem. N.Y. Harvard-Radcliffe Schs. Com.; 1952 class agt. St. Johnsbury Acad., 1981-86; 1956 class agt. Radcliffe Coll., 1981-86. Recipient Disting. Svc. award State Debt Mgmt. Network, 1999. Mem. Mcpl. Forum N.Y. (Career Svc. award 2002), Mcpl. Analysts Group N.Y. (treas. 1983-84, chmn. 1984-85, Career Achievement award 2004), Nat. Fedn. Mcpl. Analysts (bd. govs. 1984-86, chmn. awards com. 1984-85, Career Achievement award 1991), Soc. Mcpl. Analysts, India House Club (bd. govs. 2003—). Office: Fitch IBCA One State St Plz New York NY 10004-2614 Office Phone: 212-908-0552.

COHEN, CLAUDIA, journalist, television reporter; b. Englewood, N.J., Dec. 16, 1950; d. Robert B. and Harriet (Brandwein) C.; 1 child, Samantha. BA, U. Pa., 1972. Mng. editor The Daily Pennsylvanian; with More Mag., N.Y.C., 1973-76; mng. editor, 1976-77; reporter N.Y. Post, N.Y.C., 1977-78; editor, author Page Six column, 1978-80; daily columnist I, Claudia N.Y. Daily News, N.Y.C., 1980-81; tv entertainment reporter Live with Regis and Kathie Lee, 1983—; reporter Eyewitness News WABC, 1984—89. Bd. overseers Sch. Arts and Scis. U. Pa.; mem. adv. bd. N.Y. Hosp. Cornell Med. Ctr. Honoree Sarah Herzog Meml. Hosp. Centennial, 1995, Rita Hayworth Gala Benefit for Alzheimers, 2000. Office: Sta WABC 7 Lincoln Sq New York NY 10023-5900

COHEN, CORA, artist; b. N.Y.C., Oct. 19, 1943; d. George and Anne (Lenarsky) C. BA, Bennington Coll., 1964, MA, 1972. Vis. artist U. Pa., 1969-70, U. Chgo., 1983-95, Art Inst. Sch. Chgo., 1983-85, 97, Boston Mus. Sch. Fine Arts, 1994-95, U. Minn., 1996, Kunsthögskolan, Stockholm, 1996, Corcoran Mus. Sch. Art, 2000, Washington U., St. Louis, Mo., 2003; vis. prof. Art Inst. Sch. Chgo., 1992-93; adj. faculty NYU, 1990-2000, Rutgers U., Newark, N.J., 2004; assoc. prof. art, U. N.C., Greensboro, 1998-2003, Vt.

Studio Ctr., 1999-2002; nat. focus artist Emory and Henry Coll., Emory, Va., 2003-04; guest lectr. New Sch., 2004; 4th yr. adviser Md. Inst. Coll. Art, 2005. One-person shows include Everson Mus. Art, Syracuse, N.Y., 1974, Max Hutchinson Gallery, N.Y.C., 1979-80, 84, Wolff Gallery, 1988, Holly Solomon Gallery, 1990, New Arts Program, Kutztown, Pa., 1993, Jason McCoy Gallery, N.Y.C., 1993-94, David Beitzel Gallery, N.Y.C., 1994, Sarah Moody Gallery Art, Tuscaloosa, Ala., 1996, Joslyn Art Mus., Omaha, 1996, Hering Raum, Bonn, Germany, 1997-98, Rena Bransten Gallery, San Francisco, 1997, Jason McCoy Gallery, N.Y.C., 1997, Belvedere Strasse, 1999, Bentley Gallery, Scottsdale, Ariz., 1999, 2002, 05, Stefanie Hering, Berlin, 2000, McCoy Chelsea, 2001, Emory (Va.) and Henry Coll., 2003-04, Jason McCoy Inc., N.Y.C., 2004, Abaton Garage, Jersey City, 2005; exhibited in group shows at Baxter Art Gallery, Pasadena, Calif., 1985, Am. Acad. and Inst. Arts and Letters, N.Y.C., 1987, Barbara Krakow Gallery, Boston, 1987, Pamela Auchincloss Gallery, Contemporary Surfaces, N.Y.C., 1992, A/C Project Room, An Esemplastic Shift, N.Y.C., 1992, Sandra Gering Gallery, 1992, Piccolo Spoleto Festival, Charleston, S.C., 1992, The Fetish of Knowledge, A/C Project Room, N.Y.C., 1992, Daniel Weinberg Gallery, L.A., 1989, Wolff Gallery, N.Y.C., 1991, Feigen Gallery, 1991, Sytsema Galleries, Baarn, Holland, 1992, Jason McCoy Gallery, N.Y.C., 1993, The Painting Ctr., N.Y.C., 1993, White Columns, N.Y.C., 1993, Bill Maynes Contemporary Art, N.Y.C., 1994, Penine Hart Gallery, N.Y., 1994, Trans Hudson Gallery, Jersey City, Out of the Blue Gallery, Edinburgh, Scotland, 1994, Cepa Gallery, Buffalo, 1995, 2000, the Smart Fair, Stockholm, 1995, NYU, N.Y.C., 1995, Newhouse Ctr. Contemporary Art, S.I., N.Y., 1997, Galleri Mariann Ahnlund Umea, Sweden, 1996, Accrochage, Hering Raum, Bonn, 1996, Galerie Brigitte Schenk, Köln, Germany, Köln Art Fair, 1997, Cepa Gallery, Buffalo, Galleri Mariann Ahnlund, Stockholm, Stalke Out of Space, Copenhagen, Barbara Davis Gallery, Houston, 1998, Oppenhoff & Rädler, Leipzig, Stockholm Art Fair, Hunter Coll., Times Square Gallery, N.Y., The Art Fair, The 69th Regiment Armory, N.Y., 1999, 2002, 04, McCoy, Kansas City, 2000, Open Studio to Benefit the Coalition for the Homeless, N.Y., 2000, U. Ariz. Mus. Art, Tucson, 2001, The Five and Dime Series, Jan Van de Donk, NY, 2001, Cynthia Broan Gallery, N.Y., 2002, Painting Painting N3 Project Space, Williamsburg, Brooklyn, N.Y., 2003, Sheldon Art Galleries, St. Louis, 2003; photgrapher: Cohen, Cora: The Record, The Death, The Surprise, 1999. Recipient N.Y. Found. Arts Gottlieb Found. award, 1990, Pollock Krasner award, 1998, Kohler Fund award U. N.C., 1999; Painting fellow Nat. Endowment for the Arts, 1987; Yaddo Residence grantee, 1982, 95, New Faculty grantee U. N.C., 1999. Mem. Simon Wiesenthal Ctr., Coll. Art Assn. Jewish. Home: 287 Broadway New York NY 10007-2004 Office Phone: 212-267-9430. Personal E-mail: ccohen287@earthlink.net.

COHEN, CYNTHIA MARYLYN, lawyer; b. Bklyn., Sept. 5, 1945; AB, Cornell U., 1967; JD cum laude, NYU, 1970. Bar: N.Y. 1971, U.S. Ct. Appeals (2nd cir.) 1972, U.S. Dist. Ct. (so. and ea. dists.) N.Y. 1972, U.S. Supreme Ct. 1975, U.S. Dist. Ct. (ctrl. and no. dists.) Calif. 1980, U.S. Ct. Appeals (9th cir.) 1980, U.S. Dist. Ct. (so. dist.) Calif. 1981, U.S. Dist. Ct. (ea. dist.) Calif. 1986. With Paul, Hastings, Janofsky & Walker, LLP, L.A., N.Y.C. Lawyer del. 9th Cir. Jud. Conf. Bd. dirs. N.Y. chpt. Am. Cancer Soc., 1977-80; active Pres.'s Coun. Cornell Women; lawyer del. Ninth Cir. Jud. Conf. Recipient Am. Jurisprudence award for evidence, torts and legal instns., 1968-69; John Norton Pomeroy scholar NYU, 1968-70, Founders Day Cert., 1969. Mem. ABA, Assn. Bar City N.Y. (trade regulation com. 1976-79), Assn. Bus. Trial Lawyers, Fin. Lawyers Conf., N.Y. State Bar Assn. (chmn. class-action com. 1979), State Bar Calif., Los Angeles County Bar Assn., Order of Coif, Delta Gamma. Avocations: tennis, bridge, rare books, wines. Home: 4531 Dundee Dr Los Angeles CA 90027-1213 Office: Paul Hastings Janofsky & Walker LLP 515 S Flower St 25th Fl Los Angeles CA 90071 Office Phone: 213-683-6000. Business E-Mail: cynthiacohen@paulhastings.com.

COHEN, D. ASHLEY, clinical neuropsychologist; b. Omaha, Oct. 2, 1952; d. Cenek and Dorothy A. (Bilek) Hrabik; m. Donald I. Cohen, 1968 (div. 1976); m. Lyn J. Mangiameli, June 12, 1985. BA in Psychology, U. Nebr., Omaha, 1975, MA in Psychology, 1979; PhD in Clin. Psychology, Calif. Coast U., 1988; PhD in Neuropsychology, Pacific Grad. Sch., 2000. Lic. psychologist, Calif.; lic. marriage and family therapist, Nev. Family specialist Ea. Nebr. Human Svcs. Agy. Consultation & Edn., 1979-80; psychotherapist Washoe Tribe, Gardnerville, Nev., 1980; therapist Family Counseling Svc., Carson City, Nev., 1980-93; mental health dir. Alpine County Mental Health, Markleeville, Calif., 1981—93, dir., 1990-93; psychologist Golden Gate Med. Examiners, San Francisco, San Jose, Calif., 1993-97; prin., owner CogniMetrix, San Jose, Calif., 1997—. Site coord. nat. standardization Kaufmann brief intelligence test A.G.S., 1988-90, nat. standardization WISC-IV, WPPSI-III Bayley Scales of Infant Development; examiner criminal cts. San Mateo and Santa Clara (Calif.) County; test reviewer Buros' Mental Measurements Yearbooks; conf. presenter and spkr. in field. Vol. EMT, Alpine County, 1983-93. Recipient Svc. to Youth award Office Edn., 1991. Mem. Internat. Soc. Study Individual Differences, Nat. Acad. Neuropsychology, Coalition Clin. Practioners Neuropsychology, Soc. Personal Assessment, Intelligence Rsch. Soc. Avocations: astronomy, adventure travel, target shooting. Office: 320 S 3d St # 201 San Jose CA 95112 Office Phone: 408-832-8329. E-mail: dac@cognimetrix.com.

COHEN, DANIEL EDWARD, writer; b. Chgo., Mar. 12, 1936; s. Milton M. and Sue Greenberg C.; m. Susan Lois Handler, Feb. 2, 1958; 1 child, Theodora (dec.). BA in Journalism, U. Ill., 1958. Mng. editor Sci. Digest mag., N.Y.C., 1959-68; writer, 1968—. Author: Myths of the Space Age, 1967, Secrets from Ancient Graves, 1968, Vaccination and You, 1968, The Age of Giant Mammals, 1969, Animals of the City, 1969, Mysterious Places, 1969, A Modern Look at Monsters, 1970, Night Animals, 1970, Conquerors on Horseback, 1970, Talking with Animals, 1971, Superstition, 1971, A Natural History of Unnatural Things, 1971, Ancient Monuments and How They Were Built, 1971, Masters of the Occult, 1971, Voodoo, Devils, and the New Invisible World, 1972, Watchers in the Wild, 1972, In Search of Ghosts, 1972, The Magic Art of Foreseeing the Future, 1973, How Did Life Get There?, 1973, Magicians, Wizards and Sorcerers, 1973, How the World Will End, 1973, reissued as Waiting for the Apocalypse, 1983, Shaka: King of the Zulus, 1973, ESP: The Search Beyond the Senses, 1973, The Black Death, 1974, The Magic of the Little People, 1974, Curses, Hexes, and Spells, 1974, Intelligence: What Is It?, 1974, Not of the World, 1974, Human Nature, Animal Nature, 1974, The Far Side of Consciousness, 1974, The Mysteries of Reincarnation, 1975, The Greatest Monsters in the World, 1975, The Body Snatchers, 1975, The Human Side of Computers, 1975, Monsters, Giants, and Little Men from Mars, 1975, The New Believers, 1975, The Spirit of Lord, 1975, Animal Territories, 1975, Mysterious Disappearances, 1976, The Ancient Visitors, 1976, Dreams, Visions, and Drugs, 1976, Gold, 1976, Biorhythms in Your Life, 1976, Supermonsters, 1977, Ghostly Animals, 1977, The Science of Spying, 1977, Real Ghosts, 1977, Meditation, 1977, What Really Happened to the Dinosaurs?, 1977, Creativity: What Is It?, 1977, Ceremonial Magic, 1978, The World of UFO's, 1978, The World's Most Famous Ghosts, 1978, Young Ghosts, 1978, rev. edit., 1994, Frauds, Hoaxes, and Swindles, 1979, Missing, 1979, Mysteries of the World, 1979, What's Happening to Our Weather, 1979, Dealing with the Devil, 1979, Famous Curses, 1979, Great Mistakes, 1979, Close Encounters with God, 1979, The Monsters of "Star Trek", 1980, Monsters You Never Heard Of, 1980, The Tomb Robbers, 1980, Bigfoot: America's Number One Monster, 1980, Everything You Need to Know about Monsters and Still Be Able to Sleep, 1981, Ghostly Terrors, 1981, The Headless Roommate and Other Tales of Terror, 1981, The Last Hundred Years' Medicine, 1981, The Great Airship Mystery, 1981, Re-Thinking, 1982, America's Very Own Monsters, 1982, How to Buy a Car, 1982, Horror in the Movies, 1982, How to Test Your ESP, 1982, Real Magic, 1982, The Last Hundred Years' Household Technology, 1982, Monster Hunting Today, 1983, The Encyclopedia of Monsters, 1983, The Simon and Schuster Question and Answer Book on Computers, 1983, Southern Fried Rat and Other Gruesome Tales, 1983, Monster Dinosaur, 1983, The Restless Dead, 1983, The Encyclopedia of Ghosts, 1984, Musicals, 1984, Horror Movies, 1984, Hiram Bingham and the Dream of Gold, 1984, Masters of Horror, 1984, America's Very Own Ghosts, 1985, Henry Stanley and the Quest for the Source of the Nile, 1985, The Encyclopedia of the Strange, 1985; (with Susan Cohen) The Kids' Guide to Home Computers, 1983, Teenage Stress, 1984, The Kids' Guide to Home Video, 1984, Screen Goddesses, 1984, Hollywood Hunks and Heroes, 1985, Rock Video Superstars, 1985, Wrestling Superstars, Vol. 1, 1985, Vol. 2, 1986, Heroes of the Challenger, 1986, A Six-Pack and a Fake ID, 1986, The Encyclopedia of Movie Stars, 1986, A History of the Oscars, 1986, ESP: The New Technology, 1986, Strange and Amazing Facts About Star Trek, 1986, (with Susan Cohen) Wrestling Superstars II, 1986, Teenage Competition, 1986, Hollywood's Newest Superstars, 1987, The Encyclopedia of Unsolved Crimes, 1988, UFO's: The Third Wave, 1988, (with Susan Cohen) What Kind of Dog is That, 1989, Zoo Superstars, 1989, When Someone You Know is Gay, 1989, Ancient Egypt, 1990, The Ghosts of War, 1990, Ancient Greece, 1990, The Magical World of Monsters, 1991, Beverly Hills 90210: Meet the Stars, 1991, (with Susan Cohen) Going for the Gold: Medal Hopefuls for Winter '92, 1991, Zoos, 1992, Where to Find Dinosaurs Today, 1992, Ancient Rome, 1992, Ghostly Tales of Love and Revenge, 1992, Prophets of Doom, 1992, Ghosts of the Deep, 1993, Ghost in the House, 1993, Animal Rights, 1993, Dinosaur Discovery, 1993, The Beheaded Freshman and Other Nasty Rumors, 1993, The Ghost of Elvis and other Celebrity Spirits, 1994, Cults, 1994, 101 of the World's Strangest Mysteries, 1994, Into The Darkness, 1994, Real Vampires, 1995, The Phantom Hitchhiker, 1995, Riddle of the Stones, 1995, Prohibition, 1995, The Modern Ark, 1995, Gus the Bear, The Flying Cat and the Lovesick Moose, 1995, Allosaurus and Other Jurassic Meat Eaters, 1995, Stegosaurus and Other Jurassic Plant Eaters, 1995, Tyrannosaurus Rex and Other Cretaceous Meat Eaters, 1995, Triceratops and Other Cretaceous Plant Eaters, 1995, Werewolves, 1996, The Alaska Purchase, 1996, Joseph McCarthy: The Misuse of Political Power, 1996, Ghostly Warnings, 1996, Dangerous Ghosts, 1996, Screaming Skulls: 101 of the World's Great Ghost Stories, 1996, (with Susan Cohen) Gold Medal Glory: The Story of America's 1996 Women's Gymnastics Team, 1996, Hollywood Dinosaur, 1997, Great Conspiracies and Elaborate Cover-ups., 1997, Raising the Dead, 1997, The Millennium, 1997, Watergate: Deception in the White House, 1998, Cloning, 1998, The Alien Files 1, 1998, Contact, 1998, The Alien Files 2, Conspiracy, 1998, Are You Ready, The Best and Worst Predictions for the Millennium, 1998, The Manhattan Project, 1999, Prophets of Doom, The Millennium Edition, 1999, Wrestling Renegades, Civil War Ghosts, 1999, The Impeachment of William Jefferson Clinton, 1999, Yellow Journalism, 2000, George W. Bush, 2000, Apatosaurus, 2000, Pteranodon, 2000, Velociraptor, 2000, Stegosaurus, 2000, Triceratops, 2000, Tyrannosaurus, 2000, (with Susan Cohen) PanAm 103, 2000, rev. edit., 2001, Jesse Ventura, 2001, Hauntings and Horrors, 2002, Ankylosaurus, 2002, Brachiosaurus, 2002, Diplodocus, 2002, Ichythosaurus, 2002, Iguanoden, 2002, Allosaurus, 2002, Spinosaurus, 2003, Miasaurus, 2003, Pachcephalosaurus, 2003, Parasauiolophus, 2003, Trodon, 2003, Sarcosuchus imperator, 2003. Mem. Authors Guild, Watson's Erroneous Deductions Club, The Wodehouse Soc. (editor Plum Lines), Chapter One, The Capers of Sherlock Holmes Club, Clumber Spaniel Club Am. Avocation: dogs. Home and Office: 877 W Hand Ave Cape May Court House NJ 08210-1865 E-mail: bladgscast@aol.com.

COHEN, DANIEL MORRIS, museum director, marine biologist, researcher; b. Chgo., July 6, 1930; s. Leonard U. and Myrtle (Gertz) C.; m. Anne Carolyn Constant, Nov. 4, 1955; children— Carolyn A. Leech, Cynthia S. BA, Stanford U., 1952, MA, 1953, PhD, 1958. Asst. prof., curator fishes U. Fla., Gainesville, 1957-58; systematic zoologist Bur. Comml. Fisheries, Washington, 1958-60; dir. systematics lab. Nat. Marine Fisheries Service, Washington, 1960-81, sr. scientist Seattle, 1981-82; chief curator life scis. Los Angeles County Mus. of Natural History, 1982-93, dep. dir. rsch. and collections, 1993-95; emeritus, 1995—. Adj. prof. biology U. So. Calif., 1982-98. Contbr. numerous articles to profl. jours. Mem. adv. coun. Cordell Bank Nat. Marine Sanctuary. Fellow AAAS, Calif. Acad. Sci. (rsch. assoc.); mem. Am. Soc. Ichthyologists and Herpetologists (v.p. 1969, 70, pres. 1985, Gibbs award 1997), Biol. Soc. Washington (pres. 1971-72), Soc. Systematic Biology (mem. coun. 1976-78). Avocations: gardening, cooking, reading, hiking. Home: PO Box 192 Bodega Bay CA 94923-0192 E-mail: dmco@monitor.net.

COHEN, DAVID BLAIR, lawyer; b. Glen Ridge, NJ, Mar. 27, 1958; BA, U. Tex., 1980, JD, 1983. Bar: Tex. 1983, DC 1989. Ptnr., co-head Bus. & Internat. Sect. Vinson & Elkins LLP, Washington, DC. Office: Vinson & Elkins LLP Willard Office Bldg 1455 Pennsylvania Ave NW, Ste 600 Washington DC 20004 Office Phone: 202-639-6566. E-mail: DCohen@velaw.com.

COHEN, DAVID HARRIS, neuroscientist, educator, academic administrator; b. Springfield, Mass., Aug. 26, 1938; s. Nathan Edward and Sylvia (Golden) C.; m. Arline Wyler, June 17, 1960 (div. Aug. 1980); children: Bonnie, Daniel, Ian; m. Anne Helena Remmes, Jan. 17, 1981; 1 child, Kaitlin. BA, Harvard U., 1960; PhD, U. Calif., Berkeley, 1963. Postdoctoral fellow UCLA, 1963—64; asst. prof. physiology Western Res. U., Cleve., 1964—68; assoc. prof. to prof. physiology U. Va. Med. Sch., Charlottesville, 1968—79; prof., chmn. neurobiology SUNY, Stony Brook, 1979—86; v.p. rsch., dean grad. sch. Northwestern U., Evanston, Ill., 1986—91, provost, 1992—95, prof. neurobiology and physiology, 1986—95; v.p. arts and scis., dean of faculty emeritus Columbia U., N.Y.C., 1995—2003, prof. biol. scis. and psychiatry, 1995—. Mem. adv. com. directorate biol., behavioral and social scis. NSF, 1982-89; mem. life scis. rsch. adv. bd. Air Force Office Sci. Rsch., 1985-91; mem. bd. govs. Argonne Nat. Lab., 1986-92; bd. dirs. Zenith Electronics, Inc., 1990-95, Rsch. Librs. Group, 1993-97, 2001—, Columbia U. Press, 1996—, Thuris Corp., 2000—, Trevor Day Sch., 2000—, Socratic Arts, 2003—, KLi, 2004—; mem. adv. bd. Knowledge Investment Ptnrs., 2003—, Identity Theft 911, 2004—. Mem. various editl. bds. profl. jours.; contbr. articles to profl. jours. Bd. overseers Fermi Nat. Accelerator Lab., Batavia, Ill., 1987-94; exec. com. Ill. Gov.'s Sci. Adv. Com., 1989-95; mem. Liaison Com. Med. Edn., 1987-89; bd. dirs. N.Y. Structural Biology Ctr., 1999-2003. Mem. Soc. Neurosci. (pres. 1981-82), Pavlovian Soc. (pres. 1978-79), Assn. Neurosci. Depts. and Programs (pres. 1981-82), Nat. Soc. Med. Rsch. (v.p. 1984-85), Nat. Assn. Biomed. Rsch. (bd. dirs. 1985-87), Coun. Acad. Socs. (adminstrv. bd. 1982-87, chmn. 1985-86), Assn. Am. Med. Colls. (exec. coun. 1984-91, chmn. 1989-90), Internat. Brain Rsch. Orgn. (ctrl. coun. 1978-82). Jewish. Home: 445 Riverside Dr Apt 72 New York NY 10027-6801 Office: Columbia Univ 669 Schermerhorn Ext Mail Code 5545 New York NY 10027 Business E-Mail: dhc14@columbia.edu.

COHEN, DAVID JOEL, medical educator; b. New Haven, Conn., Nov. 2, 1960; AB summa cum laude, Harvard U., 1982, MD, 1986, MSc, 1994. Diplomate Am. Bd. Internal Medicine; lic. physician, Mass. Intern then resident Brigham and Women's Hosp., Boston, 1986-89; clin. rsch. fellow Beth Israel Hosp., Boston, 1989-94, now asst. dir. interventional cardiology; fellow Harvard Sch. Pub. Health, Boston, 1992-94, instr. health policy and mgmt., 1995—; instr. medicine Harvard Med. Sch., Boston, 1993-96, asst. prof., 1996—. Asst. dir. invasive cardiology sect. Beth Israel Hosp., 1994—. Contbr. chpts. to books and numerous articles to profl. jours. Grantee Johnson and Johnson, 1993-94, Am. Heart Assn., 1995—. Mem. Phi Beta Kappa. Home: 29 Reservoir Ave Chestnut Hill MA 02467-1329

COHEN, DAVID K., education educator; BA in hist. polit. sci., Alfred U., 1956; PhD in European intellectual his., U. Rochester, 1961. Asst. prof. Case Western Reserve U., 1961—66; cons. to gen counsel NAACP, 1964—66; cons. United Presbyn. Ch., United Ch. of Christ, 1964—65; dir. US Commn. on Civil Rights, 1966—67; vis. assoc. Joint Ctr. for Urban Studies, Mass. Inst. Tech., Harvard U., 1967—68; assoc. fellow Metro. Applied Rsch. Ctr., NYC, 1968—70; lectr. to sr. rsch assoc. to assoc. prof. to prof. Harvard Grad. Sch. Edn., 1968—86; pres. Huron Inst., Cambridge, Mass., 1971—86; vis. prof. Yale U., 1976—77; vis. prof. to dist. prof. to interim dean Mich. State U., 1984—91; prof. edn. U. Mich., 1993—. Contbr. articles various profl. jours. Mem.: Nat. Acad. Edn., Math. Scis. Edn. Bd, Nat. Rsch. Coun., Nat. Acad. Scis., Coun. Behavorial Social Sci. Office: U Mich Sch Edn 610 E U Ann Arbor MI 48109-1259 also: 10815 Boyce Rd Chelsea MI 48118 E-mail: dkcohen@umich.edu.

COHEN, DAVID LEON, physician; b. St. Louis, Feb. 2, 1947; s. Benjamin David and Hannah (Finfer) C.; m. Sheila Zeisel, July 2, 1974; children: Robin, Lori, Jonathan, Jennifer. BS, Roosevelt U., 1967; MS, Chgo. Med. Sch., 1972; MD, Mt. Sinai Sch. Medicine, 1976. Diplomate Am. Bd. Dermatology. Intern in internal medicine Michael Reese Hosp., Chgo., 1976-77; resident Mt. Sinai Hosp., N.Y.C., 1977-80; pvt. practice Hewlett and Jamaica, NY, 1980—. Clin. instr. dept. dermatology Mount Jinm Sch. Medicine, NYC, 1980—. Office: 1800 Rockaway Ave Ste 208 Hewlett NY 11557-1645 also: 86-75 Midland Pkwy Jamaica NY 11432 Office Phone: 516-887-4343.

COHEN, DAVID WALTER, academic administrator, educator, periodontist; b. Phila., Dec. 15, 1926; s. Abram and Goldie (Schlein) C.; m. Betty Axelrod, Dec. 19, 1948 (dec. Mar. 1992); children: Jane Ellen, Amy Sue, Joanne Louise. DDS, U. Pa., 1950; DSc (hon.), Boston U., 1975; PhD (hon.), Hebrew U., Jerusalem, 1977, U. Athens, 1979; Dr Honoris Causa, U. Louis Pasteur, Strasbourg, France, 1986; DHL (hon.), U. Detroit, 1989. Diplomate: Am. Bd. Periodontology (chmn. 1972). Research fellow pathology and periodontia Beth Israel Hosp., Boston, 1950-51; mem. faculty U. Pa. Sch. Dentistry, Phila., 1951—, prof. periodontics, 1962-86, chmn. dept., 1962-73; dean Sch. Dental Medicine U. Pa., Phila., 1972-83; dean emeritus U. Pa. Sch. Dentistry, Phila., 1983—; pres. Med. Coll. Pa., 1986-93; chancellor Allegheny U. of Health Scis., 1993-98; chancellor emeritus Coll. Medicine Drexel U., 1998—; mem. staff Albert Einstein Med. Center, Phila., Children's Hosp., Phila.; pres. Jewish Publ. Soc., 1993-96. Vis. prof. Boston U. Sch. Grad Dentistry, 1972—; nat. cons. periodontics USAF, 1965-70; bd. govs. Hebrew U., Jerusalem, Betty and Walter Cohen chair in periodontal rsch., 1986; D. Walter Cohen endowed chair in periodontics U. Pa., 1995. Author: (with H.M. Goldman) Periodontia, 1957, (with others) An Introduction to Periodontia, 1959, Periodontal Therapy, 1960, (with R. Genco and Goldman) Contemporary Periodontics, 1990, (with Genco, L. Rose and B. Mealey) Periodontal Medicine, 1999, Periodontics, Medicine Surgery and Implants, 2001; also numerous articles and chpts. V.p. Jewish Publ. Soc., 1985-89, pres., 1993-96; pres. Nat. Mus. Am. Jewish History, Phila., 1996—. Served with USN, 1944-45. Named to Ctrl. H.S. Hall of Fame, 1976; 1st Presdl. scholar U. Calif., San Francisco, 1985-86; named for him Hebrew U. Betty and D. Walter Cohen Chair in Periodontal Rsch., 1986, U. Pa. D. Walter Cohen Endowed Chair in Periodontics, 1995; D. Walter Cohen Mid. East Ctr. for Dental Edn. dedicated by Hebrew U. of Jerusalem, 1997. Fellow AAAS, Am. Acad. Oral Pathology, Am. Acad. Periodontology, Inst. of Medicine of Nat. Acad. Scis.; mem. Am. Soc. Periodontists (pres. 1967), Friends of Nat. Inst. Dental Rsch. (pres. 1998—). Office: Med Coll Pa 3300 Henry Ave Philadelphia PA 19129-1191

COHEN, DOV JOSEPH, education educator, researcher; s. Harold Jay and Ronna Ellen Cohen, Kent Patterson Talcott (Stepfather); m. Andrea Aguiar; 1 child, Ilana Aguiar. BA, U. Mich., 1988, MA, 1991, PhD, 1994. Freelance journalist; asst. prof. U. Ill., Champaign, 1995—99, assoc. prof., 2002—, U. Waterloo, Canada, 1999—2002. Co-organizer Ont. Symposium on Culture and Social Behavior. Co-author: Culture of Honor, 1996; reviewer Am. Jour. Sociology, Criminal Justice Rev.; co-editor: Handbook of Cultural Psychology, 2005, Annotated Bibliography for The Positive Cmty., 2005, Culture and Social Behavior, 2005; mem. editl. bd. Jour. Personality and Social Psychology, 2004; contbr. articles to profl. jours., chapters to books. Recipient Best Presentation by a Young Investigator, Internat. Soc. Rsch. Aggression, 1994; grantee, U. Mich., 1994—95, U. Waterloo, 1999—2002, NSF, 1998—2000, U. Ill., 1998—99, 2004—, Social Scis. and Humanities Rsch. Coun. Can., 2001—04; Fellowship, U. Mich. Culture and Cognition program, 1994—95. Mem.: Am. Psychol. Soc. Office: U Ill 603 E Daniel Champaign IL 61820 Office Phone: 217-244-5830. Business E-Mail: dcohen@s.psych.uiuc.edu.

COHEN, EDMUND STEPHEN, lawyer; b. Newark, June 25, 1946; s. Louis William and Edna (Medresch) C.; m. Lisa Beth Sonenthal, June 30, 1968; children: Ellen Paige, Paul Lawrence. BA cum laude, Dartmouth Coll., 1968; JD cum laude, Harvard U., 1971; LLM in Taxation, NYU, 1975. Bar: N.Y. 1972, U.S. Ct. Appeals (2d cir.) 1972, U.S. Ct. Claims, 1973, U.S. Tax Ct. 1973, U.S. Dist. Ct. (so. dist.) N.Y. 1975. Assoc. Davis Polk & Wardwell, NYC, 1971-78; ptnr. Cole & Deitz, NYC, 1978-81, Coudert Bros. LLP, NYC, 1981—2005; ptnr., chmn. Global Tax practice Winston & Strawn, NYC, 2005—. Adj. prof. law grad. tax program NYU Law Sch., 1977-86; chmn. seminars World Trade Inst., N.Y.C., 1977—, Practicing Law Inst., N.Y.C., 1977—, NYU Fed. Tax Inst. Contbr. articles to profl. jours. Mem. ABA, N.Y. State Bar Assn., Assn. Bar City N.Y., Internat. Fiscal Assn. Office: Winston & Strawn LLP 200 Park Ave Fl 41 New York NY 10166 Office Fax: 212-294-4700. Business E-Mail: ecohen@winston.com.

COHEN, EDWARD BARTH, lawyer; b. Washington, Oct. 13, 1949; s. Stanley Edward and Marjorie Cohen; m. Charlene Barshefsky, Jan. 25, 1976; two children. BA with acad. honors, U. Wis., 1971; JD, Georgetown U., 1974. Bar: D.C. 1975, U.S. Ct. Appeals (D.C. and 9th cirs.) 1981, U.S. Supreme Ct. 1981, U.S. Ct. Internat. Trade 1982, U.S. Tax Ct. 1983. Mem. profl. staff, counsel commerce com. U.S. Senate, Washington, 1971-77; gen. counsel U.S. Office Consumer Affairs, Washington, 1977-79; dep. spl. asst. Pres. Jimmy Carter, Washington, 1979-81; assoc. Davis, Wright & Jones, Washington, 1981—93; ptnr. Davis Wright Tremaine (and predecessor firm Davis, Wright & Jones), Washington, 1983-94; counselor to Sec. of Interior U.S. Dept. Interior, Washington, 1994-95, dep. solicitor, 1995-2000; v.p. govt. & industry rels. Honda North Am. Inc., Washington, 2000—. Mem. Bar of D.C. Office: Honda N Am Inc 1001 G St NW Ste 950 Washington DC 20001

COHEN, EDWARD HERSCHEL, lawyer; b. Lewistown, Pa., Sept. 30, 1938; s. Saul Allen and Barbara (Getz) C.; m. Arlene Greenbaum, Aug. 12, 1962; children: Fredrick, James, Paul. AB, U. Mich., 1960; JD, Harvard U., 1963. Bar: N.Y. 1964. Assoc. Katten Muchin Zavis Rosenman, N.Y.C., 1963-72, ptnr., 1972—86, 1988—2002, counsel, 1987, 2003—; v.p., gen. counsel, sec. Phillips-Van Heusen Corp., N.Y.C., 1987. Mem. Fenway Golf Club (Scarsdale, N.Y.), Ventana Golf and Racquet Club (Tucson). Republican. Jewish. Avocations: golf, travel. Office: Katten Muchin Zavis Rosenman 575 Madison Ave New York NY 10022-2585 Home: 45 Club Pointe Dr White Plains NY 10605

COHEN, EDWIN SAMUEL, lawyer, educator; b. Richmond, Va., Sept. 27, 1914; s. LeRoy S. and Miriam (Rosenheim) C.; m. Carlyn Labenberg, June 27, 1936 (dec. 1942); m. Helen Herz, Aug. 31, 1944; children: Edwin C., Roger, Wendy. BA, U. Richmond, 1933; JD, U. Va., 1936. Bar: Va. 1935, N.Y. 1937, D.C. 1973. Assoc. Sullivan & Cromwell, N.Y.C., 1936-49; ptnr. Root, Barrett, Cohen, Knapp & Smith (and predecessor firm), N.Y.C., 1949-65; counsel Root, Barrett, Cohen, Knapp & Smith, 1965-69; prof. law U. Va., Charlottesville, 1965-68, Joseph M. Hartfield prof., 1968-69, 73-85, prof. emeritus, 1985—, professorial lectr. law, 1994—; asst. sec. treasury for tax policy, 1969-72; under sec. treasury, 1972-73; of counsel Covington & Burling, Washington, 1973-77, ptnr., 1977-86, sr. counsel, 1986—. Vis. prof. Benjamin N. Cardozo Sch. Law, Yeshiva U., 1987-92, U. Miami Law Sch., 1993, 95-99, chmn. grad. program in taxation and estate planning, 1995-98; mem., counsel adv. group on corp. taxes ways and means com. U.S. Ho. of Reps., 1956-58; spl. cons. on corps. fed. income tax project Am. Law Inst., 1949-54; mem. adv. group Fed. Estate and Gift Tax Project, 1964-68; mem. Va. Income Tax Conformity Study Commn., 1970-71; cons. Va. Income Tax Conformity Study Commn., 1966-68; mem. adv. group to commr. IRS, 1967-68. Author: A Lawyer's Life Deep in the Heart of Taxes, 1994. Recipient Alexander Hamilton award Treasury Dept. Mem. Am. Judicature Soc., ABA (chmn. com. on corporate stockholder relationships 1956-58, mem. council 1958-61, chmn. spl. com. on substantive tax reform 1962-63, chmn. spl. com. on formation tax policy 1977-80, Disting. Svc. award taxation sect. 1997), Va. Bar Assn., D.C. Bar Assn., N.Y. State Bar Assn., Va. Tax Conf. (planning com. 1965-68, 85-95, trustee emeritus 1995—), C. of C. of U.S. (bd. dirs., chmn. taxation com. 1979-84), Assn. Bar City N.Y., N.Y. County Lawyers Assn., Am. Law Inst., Am. Coll. Tax Counsel, Order Coif, Raven Soc., Colonnade Club, Boar's Head Club, Farmington Club, City Club,

Phi Beta Kappa, Omicron Delta Kappa, Pi Delta Epsilon, Phi Epsilon Pi (Nat. Achievement award - A Living Legend) Home: 104 Stuart Pl Ednam Forest Charlottesville VA 22903 Office Phone: 202-662-5326. Business E-Mail: ec4n@virginia.edu.

COHEN, ELAINE HELENA, pediatrician, cardiologist, educator; b. Boston, Oct. 14, 1941; d. Samuel Clive and Lillian (Stocklan) C.; m. Marvin Leon Gale, May 7, 1972; 1 child, Pamela Beth Gale. AB, Conn. Coll., 1963; postgrad., Tufts U., 1963—64; MD, Woman's Med. Coll. Pa., 1969. Diplomate Am. Bd. Pediat. Pediat. intern Children's Hosp. of L.A., 1969-70, resident in pediat., 1970-71; fellow in pediat. cardiology UCLA Ctr. Health Scis., 1971-72, L.A. County/U. So. Calif. Med. Ctr., LA, 1972-74; pediatrician Children's Med. Group of South Bay, Chula Vista, Calif., 1974—. Clin. instr. dept. pediat. UCLA Sch. Medicine, 1971-72, U. So. Calif., L.A., 1972-74; asst. clin. prof. dept. pediat. U. Calif., Calif. Sch. Medicine, San Diego, 1974-98, preceptor dept. pediat., 1992—, assoc. clin. prof. dept. pediat., 1998—. Fellow Am. Acad. Pediat.; mem. Calif. Med. Assn., San Diego County Med. Soc. Avocations: sketching, design. Office: Children's Med Group South Bay 280 E St Chula Vista CA 91910-2945 Office Phone: 619-425-3951.

COHEN, ERIC, optometrist; b. Balt., July 9, 1949; s. Isadore Rael and Frieda Rose Cohen; m. Lindalou Silverman Cohen, Aug. 19, 1971; children: Natalie Yve, Ira Charles. BA, U. Md., 1970; BS, Pa. Coll. Optometry, 1971, OD, 1974. Resident pediat. optometry Pa. Coll. Optometry, Phila.; pvt. practice Md. Optometric Assn., Balt., 1974—. Asst. prof. Howard C.C., Ellicott City, Md., 1980-83; pediat. optometrist Katzen Eye Group, Balt., 1988-98. Author: Renazicatative Techniques in Binocular Dysfunction, 1974. Mem. Am. Optometric Assn., Md. Optometric Assn. (treas., v.p., pres.-elect, pres., Optometrist of Yr. 1998). Democrat. Jewish. Avocations: tennis, golf. Home: 11006 Valley Heights Dr Owings Mills MD 21117 Office: 6660 Security Blvd Baltimore MD 21207-4012 E-mail: e.cohe@bcpl.org.

COHEN, ERIC I., lawyer; b. NYC, Oct. 19, 1958; BA cum laude, Brandeis U., 1980; JD magna cum laude, Yeshiva U., 1983. Bar: NY 1984, DC 1990. Assoc. Robinson Silverman Pearce Aronsohn & Berman LLP (now Bryan Cave LLP), NYC, 1983—92, ptnr., 1992—98; sr. v.p., gen. counsel, sec. Terex Corp., Westport, Conn., 1998—. Mem.: Bar of the DC Ct. Appeals, NY State Bar Assn. Office: Terex Corp 500 Post Rd E Ste 320 Westport CT 06880

COHEN, EZECHIEL GODERT DAVID, physicist, researcher; b. Amsterdam, Holland, Jan. 16, 1923; came to U.S., 1963; s. David Ezechiel and Sophia Louisa (de Sterke) C.; m. Marina Arnoldina Linnekamp, Apr. 19, 1950; children: Michael Benjamin, Andrea Margaret. BS in Math., Physics and Astronomy, U. Amsterdam, 1947, PhD, 1957. First asst. U. Amsterdam, 1950-61, assoc. prof., 1961-63; research assoc. U. Mich., 1957-58, Johns Hopkins, 1958-59; prof. Rockefeller U., 1963-93, prof. emeritus, 1993—. Vander Waals prof. U. Amsterdam, 1969; Lorentz prof. U. Leiden, 1979; vis. prof. Coll. de France, 1969, 72, 79, 83, 90, Inst. for Advanced Studies, Australian Nat. U., Canberra, 1982, 88, 92, 96, 99, U. Florence, Italy, 1999, 2000; Donders prof. U. Utrecht, 1988; Francqui prof. interuniversitaire U. Brussels and U. Leuven, 1997. Editor: Fundamental Problems in Statistical Mechanics, Vol. I, 1961, Vol. II, 1968, Vol. III, 1975, Vol. IV, 1978, Vol. V, 1980, Vol. VI, 1985, Statistical Mechanics at the Turn of the Decade, 1971, The Boltzmann Equation, Theory and Applications, 1973. Recipient Royal Decoration as Knight, Order of Dutch Lion, 2004. Fellow Am. Phys. Soc.; mem. Royal Dutch Acad. Scis., Johns Hopkins Soc. of Scholars, Mexican Acad. Molecular Engring. (corr.), Internat. Union of Pure and Applied Physics (Triann. Boltzmann Medal of the Commn. on Statis. Physics 2004). Home: 450 E 63rd St New York NY 10021-7957 Office: Rockefeller U 1230 York Ave New York NY 10021-6399

COHEN, EZRA HARRY, lawyer; b. Macon, Ga., Mar. 13, 1942; s. Harry M. and Rena C. Cohen; m. Bonnie E. Cohen, Feb. 1, 1969 (div. Mar. 1988); children: Aaron M., Eileen R.; m. Katherine C. Meyers, June 18, 1989. BA, Columbia U., 1964; JD, Emory U., 1969. Bar: Ga. 1969. Ptnr. Troutman, Sanders, Lockerman & Ashmore, Atlanta, 1969-76, 79—; judge U.S. Bankruptcy Ct., U.S. Dist. Ct. (no. dist.) Ga., Atlanta, 1976-79. Dir. S.E. Bankruptcy Law Inst., Atlanta. Contbg. author: Cowan's Bankruptcy Laws & Practices, 1979. Mem. Emory U. Law Sch. Coun., Atlanta, 1988—. With U.S. Army, 1964-66, ETO. Fellow Am. Coll. Bankruptcy; mem. Ga. Bar Assn. (chmn. bankruptcy law sect.), Assn. Former Bankruptcy Judges (bd. dirs.), Nat. Assn. Bank Judges (assoc.), Atlanta Bar Assn. (bd. dirs. 1988-90), Lawyers Club of Atlanta. Home: 546 W Wesley Rd Atlanta GA 30305-3534 Office: Troutman Sanders 600 Peachtree St NE Ste 5200 Atlanta GA 30308-2216 E-mail: ezra.cohen@troutmansanders.com.

COHEN, FELIX ASHER, lawyer; b. Pitts., Aug. 11, 1943; s. Alex Harry and Audrey Gwen (Williams) C.; m. Nancy Ann Wills, July 24, 1971; children: Timothy Asher, Blair Wills Lavey. AB, Princeton U., 1965; JD, U. Pitts., 1971. Bar: Pa. 1972, U.S. Dist. Ct. (we. dist.) Pa. 1972, U.S. Tax Ct. 1972. Systems engr. IBM Corp., Pitts., 1965-68; law clk. U.S. Dist. Ct., Pitts., 1971-72; assoc. Buchanan Ingersoll, Pitts., 1972-75; sr. v.p., sec., counsel, bd. dirs. Signal Fin. Corp., Pitts., 1975-92; counsel CoreStates Fin. Corp., Phila., 1994-98; ptnr. Wolf Block Schorr & Solis-Cohen, Phila., 1999—. Mem. ABA, Pa. Bar Assn., Allegheny County Bar Assn., Phila. Bar Assn., Del. State Bar Assn. Home: 3 Black Rock Rd Chadds Ford PA 19317-9271

COHEN, FLORENCE EMERY, retired financial services executive; b. Paterson, N.J., Mar. 6, 1944; d. Claude John and Esther (Belber) Emery; m. Harvey H. Cohen, Sept. 5, 1965; children: John Aaron, Jason Matthew. AB in History, Temple U., 1965; MA in Social Scis., U. Chgo., 1970. Product planning mgr. Penn. Mut. Ins. Co., Phila., 1970-77; dir. mktg. sys. Prudential Co., Newark, 1978-80, v.p. mktg. analysis, 1980-82, v.p. tax adminstrn., 1983-84, v.p. market devel., 1984-88, v.p. enterprise planning, 1988-90; sr. v.p. individual pensions Pruco Life Co., 1990-93, v.p., Prudential annuity svcs. exec., 1993—94; ret. Lectr. numerous industry assns.; mem. exec. coun. Jersey City (N.J.) State Coll., 1985; mem. bd. visitors St. Andrew's Presbyn. Coll., N.C. grad. study fellow U. Del., 1965, Temple U., 1965, U. Chgo. 1970. Rep. committeewoman West Windsor; elder First Presbyn. Ch. Dutch Neck, mission com., deacon; bd. dir. Project Freedom; chmn. Affordable Housing Com., West Windsor; pres. Welcoming Svcs., L.L.C., 1999—. Recipient Prudential Cmty. Champions award, 2001, 02, 03, 04, Project Freedom Spirit award, 2000, 03. Fellow Life Office Mgmt. Assn., Limra Life Inst.; mem. Am. Soc. CLUs, Soc. Advancement Mgmt. (N.J. chpt., exec. of yr. 1986), Rotary (Princeton Corridor), Friends of West Windsor Open Space, West Windsor Hist. Soc. Republican. Avocations: cooking, gardening, swimming. Home: 3 Stonelea Dr Princeton Junction NJ 08550 also: 1621 A Spoonbill Ln Naples FL 34105

COHEN, FRED HOWARD, lawyer, investment company executive; b. Pitts., Mar. 22, 1948; s. Morris and Sylvia (Kalickman) C.; m. Katherine Jane Litman, July 12, 1970; children: Julia Jackson, Joseph Litman. BA, Stanford U., 1970; MA, York U., Toronto, Ont., Can., 1971; postgrad., Princeton U., 1971-72; JD, Harvard U., 1976. Bar: Calif. 1976. Assoc. Latham & Watkins, L.A., 1976-82, ptnr., 1983-85; v.p. Salomon Bros. Inc., N.Y.C., 1985-86, dir., 1986-88; v.p. Goldman Sachs & Co., N.Y.C., 1988-89; ptnr. Shearman & Sterling, N.Y.C., 1989-94; mng. dir. Salomon Bros. Inc., N.Y.C., 1994-98; with Cohen Fin. Advisors, 1998-99; mng. dir., head global high yield and leveraged fin. Bank Am. Securities, 2000—. Mem. Phi Beta Kappa. Home: 86 Kellogg Hill Rd Weston CT 06883-2640

COHEN, GEORGE LEON, lawyer; b. Covington, Ga., June 20, 1930; s. Leon and Callie (Harrison) C.; m. Jacqueline Lanier Edwards, Nov. 17, 1951 (dec. May 2001); children— George Leon, Gardner Edwards; m Martha Starr Daniels, Nov 20, 2004. AB, Va. Mil. Inst., 1951; LLB, U. Va., 1956. Bar: Ga. 1957, U.S. Ct. Appeals (11th cir.). Assoc. Sutherland, Asbill & Brennan, Atlanta, 1956-62, ptnr., 1962—. Editorial bd. Va. Law Rev., 1954-56 Mem.: ABA (various coms.), Am. Law Inst. (advisor to corp. governance project), Lawyers Club Atlanta, Atlanta Bar Assn., Ga. State Bar (chmn. corp. and banking law sect. 1968—69, chmn. Ga. bus. corp. code revision com. 1986—89, various coms.), Peachtree Club, Omicron Delta Kappa, Order of Coif. Office: Sutherland Asbill & Brennan 999 Peachtree St NE Ste 1950 Atlanta GA 30309-3996 Office Phone: 404-853-8035. Business E-Mail: george.cohen@sablaw.com.

COHEN, GEORGE MEREDITH, law educator; b. Bklyn., 1960; BA summa cum laude, Yale U., 1982; JD, U. Pa., 1986, PhD in Economics, 1992. Bar: NJ 1987, NY 1988. Winston fellow Inst. Law & Economics U. Pa. Law Sch., 1986—87; law clk. to Hon. Walter K. Stapleton US Ct. Appeals 3rd Cir., Wilmington, Del., 1987—88; asst. prof. U. Pitts. Sch. Law, 1988—93; assoc. prof. U. Va. Sch. Law, 1993—95, prof., 1995—, Edward F. Howrey prof. law, 2001—04. Vis. asst. prof. U. Va. Sch. Law, 1992—93. Mem.: Am. Law & Economics Assn. Office: U Va Sch Law 580 Massie Rd Charlottesville VA 22903-1789 Office Phone: 434-924-3814. E-mail: gmc3y@virginia.edu.

COHEN, GLORIA ERNESTINE, elementary education educator; b. Bklyn., July 6, 1942; d. Victor George and Marion Theodosia (Roberts) C. BS in Edn., Wilberforce U., 1965; MA in Elem. Edn., Adelphi U., 1975; Profl. Diploma in Edni. Adminstrn., L.I. U., 1984; MS in Edn., Bklyn. Coll., 1986. Tchr. Bd. Edn., Bklyn., 1965—; case worker Dept. Welfare, Bklyn., 1965—. Mem. comprehensive sch. improvement program Pub. Sch. 149, 1990—91, mem. open corridor planning com., 1990—91, mem. consultation com., 1990—; tchr. in charge of after sch. reading and math. tutorial program, 1995—96; dean grades 4-6, 1996—98; supr. Sat. Acad.; tchr. in charge of Read Extended Day program, 1997—98; cons. tchr. for 4th grade class, 1999; tchr. in charge of food and nutrition distbn. Maxwell H.S., Bklyn., 1999, P.S. 64 Dist. 27, Queens, 2000; tutorial tchr. Pub. Sch. 149, 2001—02; tutorial reading tchr. P.S. 149, Bklyn., 2004; tchr. in charge of food and nutrition distbn. P.S. 174 Dist. 19, Bklyn., 2001—04, Dist. 27, Pub. Sch. 60, Bklyn., 2005. Mem.: U.S. Tennis Assn., Hempstead Lake Tennis Club, Rockville Racqhet Club, Kappa Delta Pi, Zeta Phi Beta. Democrat. Roman Catholic. Avocations: tennis, skiing, swimming.

COHEN, GORDON M., chemist, researcher; b. Chgo., Jan. 7, 1948; s. Arthur and Ruth Cohen; m. Adele S. Schneider, July 2, 1978; children: Jeffrey, Brian, Adrienne. BS in Chemistry with honors, McGill U., Montreal, Can., 1969; AM, Harvard U., 1970, PhD, 1974. Rsch. chemist DuPont Elastomer Chems., Wilmington, Del., 1974—80; sr. rsch. chemist DuPont Polymer Products, Wilmington, 1980—83; sr. rsch. assoc. DuPont Ctrl. R&D, Wilmington, 1983—. Bd. mem. Congregation Beth T'Fillam, Phila., 1996—2000. Mem.: Am. Chem. Soc. Achievements include patents in field. Home: 627 Greythorne Rd Wynnewood PA 19096

COHEN, HARLEY, engineering educator; b. Winnipeg, Man., Can., May 12, 1933; s. Joseph and Ettie (Gilman) C.; m. Estelle Brodsky, Dec. 25, 1956; children: Brent, Murray, Carla. B.Sc. hons., U. Man., 1956; Sc.M., Brown U., 1958; PhD, U. Minn., 1964. Registered profl. engr., Man. Research engr. Boeing Co., Seattle, 1958-60; sr. research scientist Honeywell, Inc., Mpls., 1960-64; asst. prof. aero. and engring. mechanics U. Minn., Mpls., 1965-66; assoc. prof. civil engring. U. Man., Winnipeg, 1966—, prof., 1968-89, disting. prof., 1983—, head dept., 1984-89, prof. applied math., 1989-94, dean faculty of sci., 1989-94, prof. applied math. and civil engring., 1994-98, disting. prof. math. emeritus, 1998—. J.L. Record prof. U. Minn.; invited vis. prof. U. Pisa, Italian Rsch. Coun., 1987; bd. dirs. Man. Rsch. Coun., 1989-94, Tri-Univ.-Meson Facility, U. B.C., 1989-94, Premier's Econ. Innovation and Tech. Coun., 1989-94. Co-author: Theory of Psuedo-Rigid Bodies, 1988; contbr. over 100 articles to profl. jours. Killam scholar, 1982; Brit. sci. fellow, 1985 Fellow Am. Acad. Mechanics (bd. dirs. 1988-91); mem. Soc. Natural Philosophy, Soc. Engring. Sci. Home: 55 Tanoak Park Dr Winnipeg MB Canada R2V 2W6 Office: U Man Dept Applied Math Faculty of Sci Winnipeg MB R3T 2N2 Canada R3T 2N2 E-mail: hcohen@cc.umanitoba.ca.

COHEN, HARRIS L., diagnostic radiologist, consultant; b. Bklyn., Sept. 18, 1951; s. Samuel G. and Lola Estera (Altman) C.; m. Sandra Wilensky, Oct. 18, 1979; children: David Matthew, Lauren Elizabeth, Benjamin Adam. BA cum laude in Chemistry, CUNY, Bklyn., 1969—73; MD in Medicine, SUNY, Bklyn., 1972—76. Diplomate Am. Bd. Radiology, Nat. Bd. Med. Examiners; cert. added qualifications in pediatric radiology Am. Bd. Radiology. Asst. prof. radiology SUNY Health Sci. Ctr., Bklyn., 1981-88; asst. chief of imaging Brookdale Hosp. Med. Ctr., Bklyn., 1983-85; med. dir. diagnostic med. imaging program Coll. Health Related Professions, SUNY Health Sci. Ctr., Bklyn., 1985—88, 1994—; assoc. prof. radiology Cornell U. Med. Coll., NYC, 1988-93; chief pediatric CT and ultrasound North Shore U. Hosp.-Cornell, Manhasset, NY, 1988-93, assoc. dir. divsn. CT/ultrasound/magnetic resonance imaging, 1988-93; assoc. dir. radiology Kings County Hosp., Bklyn., 1993-2000; prof. radiology SUNY Health Sci. Ctr., Bklyn., 1993-2000, assoc. chmn. acad. affair and clin. rsch., 1998-2000; vis. prof. radiology, dir. divsn. pediat. imaging Johns Hopkins U., Balt., 2000—02; prof. radiology, vice chmn. dept. radiology, dir. divsn., body imaging, chief pediatric body imaging SUNY, Stony Brook, 2002—, dir. abdominal imaging fellow program, 2003—. Dir. divsn. ultrasound U. and Kings County Hosps., Bklyn., 1985-88, 93-2000, dir. divsn. pediat. radiology, 1999-2000; cons. ultrasound and pediatric imaging Brookdale Hosp. Med. Ctr., Bklyn., 1988—; cons. diagnostic radiology Med. Mut. Liability, N.Y.C., 1992—. Author (author, editor/co-editor): Ultrasonography of the Prenatal and Neonatal Brain, 1996, 2d edit., 2002, Spanish transl., 2002, Obstetrics & Gynecology (Ultrasound), 1997, Fetal and Pediatric Ultrasound, 2001, Chinese Transl., 2003, Spanish Transl., Ecografia Fetal y Pediatrica, 2004, Gastrointestinal Disease VI, 2004; mem. editl. bd.: Jour. Diagnostic Med. Sonography, 1985—, Radiographic, 1991— (Editors cert. recognition, 1990-2003), appropriateness criteria/ exam standards for AIUM, ACR, —, Ultrasound in Ob-Gyn., —; contbr. articles articles to profl. jours.; singer (mem. editl. bd.): Radiology; Journal of Ultrasound in Medicine, —; contbr. chapters to books; co-dir.:. Recipient Master Tchr. award in radiology SUNY Health Sci. Ctr. at Bklyn. Alumni Assn., 1996. Fellow Soc. Radiologists in Ultrasound (chmn. constitution com. 1996-98, program cmty, 2004-), Am. Coll. Radiology (stds. and accreditation com. 1992-98, commn. ultrasound edn. com. 1998—, mem. task force on disaster planning 2001—, disting. cmty. svc. award, 1998, 2004), Am. Acad. Pediatrics (chmn. radiology sect. 1992-94), Am. Inst. Ultrasound in Medicine (chmn. ctrl. program com. 1995-97, chmn. pediatrics sect. 1994-95, bd. dirs. 1999-2002, co-chair emergency ultrasound 2001—04, bd. govs. 1999-2002); mem. Soc. Pediatric Radiology (liaison to Am. Acad. Pediatrics 1993-94, liaison to Am. Inst. Ultrasound in Medicine 1995, program cmty., 2004), Soc. Radiology in Ultrasound (program com. 2004—), Radiologic Soc. N.Am. (audiovisual com. 1992-96, editl. fellow 2004-05), SUNY-Downstate Alumni Assn. (councillor, bd. mgrs. 1998-2001), Alpha Omega Alpha. Avocations: computers and computer education, basketball, sports, american and jewish history. Home: 78 Grove Ave Cedarhurst NY 11516-2311 Business E-Mail: harris.cohen@stonybrook.edu. E-mail: hcohenmb@optonline.net.

COHEN, HARRIS S., academic administrator; b. Neptune, N.J., Aug. 29, 1941; s. Meyer and Henrietta (Gershman) C.; m. Zipora Milner, June 21, 1964; children: Aaron M., Miriam S., David P., Hannah E. BA, Bklyn. Coll., 1962; postgrad., Kollel Gur Aryeh Inst., Bklyn., 1963-65; MA, New Sch. Social Rsch., 1965; PhD, NYU, 1970. Lectr. in polit. sci. Bklyn. Coll., 1967-68; rsch. assoc. dept. psychiatry Georgetown U., 1968-70; analyst Nat. Ctr. for Health Svcs. Rsch./HEW, Rockville, Md., 1970-72; chief polit. and legal analysis br. HEW, Rockville, 1972-74; chief, health resources branch, office policy devel. Office Asst. Sec. Health U.S. Dept. Health Human Svcs., Washington, 1974-82; v.p. Brochers Trading Corp., N.Y.C., 1982-89; sr. exec. L & B Industries, N.Y.C., 1989-94; assoc. dean, sch. career and applied studies Touro Coll., Bklyn., 1994-96, dean, 1996—2000, Gamla Coll., Bklyn., 2000—04; v.p. acad. stds. and rsch. NY Coll. Health Professions, Syosset, NY, 2004—. Lectr. in Talmud Woodside Synagogue, Silver Spring, Md., 1969-82. Co-author: Developments in Health Manpower Licensure, 1973, Credentialing Health Manpower, 1977; author: Sefer Maadanei Chaim: Analytical Notes and Essays on the Talmud, 1999; mem. editl. bd. Jour. Health Politics, Policy and Law, 1976-82; author numerous articles on health care, public policy, Talmudic law. Recipient Meritorious Svc. award HEW, 1972, Spl. Recognition award, 1977. Mem. Phi Beta Kappa. Home: 43 Stevens Pl Lawrence NY 11559-1328 Office: NY Coll Health Professions 6881 Jemond Tpke Syosset NY 11791 E-mail: hcohen@nycollege.edu.

COHEN, HARVEY JAY, geriatrician, hematologist, oncologist, educator; b. Bklyn., Oct. 21, 1940; s. Joseph and Anne (Margolin) C.; m. Sandra Helen Levine, June 1964; children: Ian Mitchell, Pamela Robin. BS, Bklyn. Coll., 1961; MD, Downstate Med. Coll., Bklyn., 1965. Diplomate Am. Bd. Internal Medicine, Am. Bd. Hematology. Intern, then resident internal medicine Duke U. Med. Ctr., Durham, NC, 1965-67, fellow hematology and oncology, 1969-71; chief hematology-oncology VA Med. Ctr., Durham, NC, 1975-76, chief med. service, 1976-82, assoc. chief of staff-edn., 1982-84, now dir. geriatric research, edn. and clin. ctr.; assoc. prof. medicine Duke U. Med. Ctr., Durham, 1976-80, now prof. medicine, chief geriatric divsn., also dir. Ctr. for Study of Aging, interim chair dept. medicine, 2002—03, vice chair faculty devel. and acad. affairs, 2004. Chair bd. sci. counselors Nat. Inst. Aging, 1999—2003. Author: Medical Immunology, 1977; co-author: (with H.G. Koenig) The Link Between Religion and Health: Psychoneuroimmunology and the Faith Factor, 2002, Taking Care After 50, 2000; editor: Cancer I and II, 1987, Jour. Gerontology: Med. Scis., 1988-92, Geriatric Medicine, 1997; contbr. articles to profl. jours. Served as surgeon USPHS, 1967-69. Fellow ACP, Am. Geriat. Soc. (bd. dirs. 1987-96, chair bd. dirs. 1995-96, sec. 1991-93, ethics com. 1992-96, pres. 1994-95, Dennis W. Jahnigen Meml. award 2005), Gerontology Soc. Am. (clin. sec., rsch. com. 1987-92, chair publs. com. 1996-98, program chair 1994, pres. 2000); mem. Am. Soc. Clin. Oncology, Am. Soc. Hematology, Am. Assn. Cancer Rsch. (cancer and acute leukemia group B, chair cancer in the elderly com.), Assn. Am. Physicians, Internat. Soc. Geriat. Oncology (bd. dirs. 2000-, pres. 2004-). Home: 2811 Friendship Cir Durham NC 27705-5521 Office: Duke U Med Ctr for Study Aging & Human Devel Box 3003 Durham NC 27710-0001 Office Phone: 919-660-7502. Business E-Mail: cohen015@mc.duke.edu.

COHEN, HARVEY JOEL, pediatric hematology and oncology educator; b. N.Y.C., July 4, 1943; s. Phillip and Ida (Teitel) C.; m. Ilene Verne Bookseger, Aug. 15, 1965; children: Philip Jason, Jonathan Todd. BS, Bklyn. Coll., 1964; MD, PhD, Duke U., 1970. Intern Children's Hosp., Boston, 1970-71, resident, 1973-74; instr. pediatrics Harvard U. Med. Sch., Boston, 1974-76, asst. prof., 1976-79, assoc. prof., 1979-81; assoc. prof. pediatrics U. Rochester (N.Y.) Med. Ctr., 1981-84, prof., 1984-93, assoc. chmn. dept., 1987-93, chief pediatric hematology and oncology, 1981-93; prof., chmn. dept. pediatrics Stanford (Calif.) U. Sch. Medicine, 1993—; chief staff Lucile Salter Packard Children's Hosp. at Stanford, 1993—. Med. advisor Montgomery Med. Ventures, San Francisco, 1984—97; sci. advisor St. Jude Children's Rsch. Hosp., Memphis, 1985—90, 2001—; chmn. hematology study sect. NIH, Washington, 1986—88. Editor: Hematology: Basic Principles and Practice, 1991, 94, 99, 2005. Med. dir. Camp Good Days and Spl. Times, Rochester, 1981—93, Monroe County chpt. Am.Cancer Soc., Rochester, 1983—93; med. dir. Rochester br. Cooley's Anemia Found., 1984—93; bd. dirs. Lucile Pakcard Children's Hosp., 1993—97, 2000—, Ronald McDonald House of Palo Alto, Calif., 1995—2005, Children's Health Coun., 1996—2005, Lucile Packard Found. for Children's Health, 1997—2000. Tng. grantee Nat. Inst. Gen. Med. Scis., 1983-90, Nat. Inst. Child Health and Human Devel., 1990-94. Mem. Soc. for Pediatric Rsch. (pres. 1988-89), Am. Soc. for Clin. Investigation, Am. Pediatric Soc. Democrat. Jewish. Achievements include research in on continuous assay for superoxide production, effect of selenium on synthesis of glutatnione peroxidase; relationship of in vitro and in vivo killing of leukemic cells by asparaganse clinical trials in childhood leukemia; comparative proteomics in pediatric diseases. Office: Stanford U Sch Medicine Dept Pediatrics Rm H-310 Stanford CA 94305 Office Phone: 650-723-6134. Business E-Mail: punko@stanford.edu.

COHEN, HENRY RODGIN, lawyer; b. Charleston, W.Va, May 7, 1944; s. Louis W. and Bertie (Rodgin) C.; m. Barbara Latz, Aug. 31, 1969; children: Sarah Abigail, Jonathan David. BA, Harvard U., 1965, LLB, 1968; LLB (hon.), U. Charleston, 1998. Bar: W.Va. 1968, NY 1970. Assoc. Sullivan & Cromwell, NYC, 1970-77, ptnr., 1977—, vice chmn., 1999-2000, chmn., 2000—. Contbg. editor Fin. Svcs. Regulation Newsletter, 1985; bd. advisors Banking Law Rev.; mem. nat. bd. contbrs. Am. Lawyers Newspaper Group. Trustee NY Presbyn. Hosp.; trustee Hampton Coll., Econ. Club, Hackley Sch. With U.S. Army, 1968—70. Office: Sullivan & Cromwell 125 Broad St Fl 28 New York NY 10004-2489 also: Sullivan & Cromwell 1701 Pennsylvania Ave NW Washington DC 20006-5805 Office Phone: 212-558-3534, 202-956-7500. Business E-Mail: cohenhr@sullcrom.com.

COHEN, HERBERT JESSE, pediatrician, educator; b. NYC, Apr. 27, 1935; s. Barnet and Edith (Lepolstat) C.; m. Marion E. Finger, Aug. 29, 1960; children— Linda Elizabeth, Gerald Daniel, Seth Michael. BA (Ford Found. scholar), Columbia, 1955; MD, State U. N.Y., 1959. Intern Bellevue Hosp., N.Y.C., 1959-60; resident N.Y. Hosp., N.Y.C., 1960-62; asst. instr. Cornell Med. Sch., 1961-62; instr. Tulane Med. Sch., 1962-64; NIH fellow Albert Einstein Coll. Medicine, 1964-66, asst. prof. pediatrics and rehab. medicine, 1966-71, assoc. prof., 1971-76, prof., 1976—; dir. Children's Evaluation and Rehab. Ctr., Rose F. Kennedy Center for Mental Retardation and Human Devel., Bronx, N.Y., 1968-74, 78—, Bronx Developmental Services, N.Y. State Dept. Mental Hygiene, 1971-80, Rose F. Kennedy Univ Ctr. for Excellence in Devel. Disabilities Tng. Svcs. and Rsch., 1974—, dir. div. child devel. and devel. disabilities, dept. pediatrics, 1981—. Vice chmn. Pres.'s Com. on Mental Retardation, 1978-81; mem. study sect. human devel. NIH, 1978-82; mem. profl. adv. bd. various founds. and profl. orgns. Author 4 books; also contbr. over 80 articles to profl. pubs. Served with USPHS, 1962-64. Recipient Disting. Humanitarian Research and Devel. awards Mental Retardation Service Orgns.; United Cerebral Palsy Research and Edn. Found. fellow, 1966-68 Fellow Am. Acad. Pediatrics (chmn. child devel. sect., chmn. com. on children with disabilities, Arnold J. Capute award sect. on children with disabilities 2004); mem. AAAS, Am. Acad. Cerebral Palsy, Am. Assn. Univ. Affiliated Facilities (pres. 1980-81, dir. 1977-84), Am. Assn. Mental Retardation (Leadership award 1996). Office: R F Kennedy Ctr 1410 Pelham Pky S Bronx NY 10461-1101 Office Phone: 718-430-8522. Business E-Mail: hcohen@aecom.yu.edu.

COHEN, HERMAN NATHAN, private investigator; b. Bklyn., June 3, 1949; s. Stanley and Hannah (Persky) C.; m. Carolyn P. Grillo, Jan. 8, 1989. BA, Bklyn. Coll., 1970; MS in Ednl. Adminstrn., Hofstra U., 1975. Investigator IRS, N.Y.C., 1970-72, adminstrv. intern Washington, 1972-73, employee devel. specialist Uniondale, N.Y., 1973-75, br. chief Bklyn., 1975-79; pers. officer Home Ins. Co., N.Y.C., 1979-81; asst. v.p. City Investing Co., N.Y.C., 1981-85; prin. H.N. Cohen Enterprises, Inc., N.Y.C., 1985-86; human resources dir. Empire Blue Cross Blue Shield, N.Y.C., 1986-89; v.p. adminstrn. ASPCA, N.Y.C., 1989-90, sr. v.p., 1990, exec. v.p., 1990-91, chief adminstrv. officer, 1991-92, chief law enforcement, 1992-94; CEO, pvt. investigator Due Diligence Plus, Amherst, N.Y., 1994—, pvt. investigator West Hartford, Conn., 1994—; chief oversight U.S. Dept. Vets. Affairs, Washington, 2000—. Arbitrator Am. Arbitration Assn., 1986—; bd. dirs. Ashfield Corp.; adj. faculty Conn. Criminal Law Found. Bd. dirs. Owen Sch.; adjutant, dir. at large Centennial Legion of Hist. Mil. Commands; mem. amb.'s coun. Wadsworth Atheneum, Conn., 1st co. Gov. Foot Guard, Conn.; vol. Montgomery County (Md.) Police Dept. Mem. Internat. Assn. Chiefs of Police (chmn. pvt. security com.), Conn. Police Chiefs Assn., Vet. Corps. Arty., Nat. Assn. Investigative Specialists, World Affairs Coun., Mensa, Ancient Free and Accepted Masons, Am. Soc. Indsl. Security, Md. Police Chiefs Assn. Democrat. Jewish. Office: US Dept Vets Affairs 810 Vermont Ave NW 264C Washington DC 20420 E-mail: cyberpi@msn.com.

COHEN, HIYAGUHA RACHELLE, language educator, writer; b. N.Y., Oct. 10, 1951; d. David Cohen and Fay Goldsmith; m. David Sudheya Rosenberg, Aug. 10, 1980. M of Social Work, Smith Coll., 1980; MFA, Southampton Coll., 2000. Instr. in english Southampton Coll., Southampton, NY, 1999—2001; tchr. Ross Sch., Easthampton, NY, 2001—; instr. in english

Dowling Coll., Oakdale, NY, 2002—. Judge James Jones Novel Competition, N.Y., 2002; cons. Learning Solutions Group, Hampton Bays, NY, 1997—. Author: (book) Boldly Live as You've Never Lived Before, 1996; co-editor: Bodly Live as You've Never Lived Before, 1996; contbr. articles to profl. jour. (see below); author, co-editor: No-Pain Resume Workbook, 1992; co-author, co-editor: Grassroots: The Writer's Workbook, 1997. Recipient Steinbeck Contest, First Prize for Fiction (Elaine Benson Prize), Elaine Benson Found./Southampton Coll., 2000, Best Article Award, Nat. Bus. Employment Weekly, 1990. Mem.: Nat. Writers Union. Avocations: dogs, travel, writing, meditation, marathons. Personal E-mail: hiyaguha@optonline.com.

COHEN, IRA, legislative staff member; b. Chgo., Sept. 6, 1947; With Rep. Danny K. Davis, Washington, 1979—, issues and comm. dir., 1996—. Office: Office of Rep Danny K Davis 3333 W Arthington St Ste 130 Chicago IL 60624-4102

COHEN, IRA MYRON, aeronautical and mechanical engineering educator; b. Chgo., July 18, 1937; s. Harry Nathan and Esther (Lenchner) C.; m. Linda Barbara Einstein, June 12, 1960; children: Susan Ellen Bolstad, Nancy Beth Cavanaugh. B in Aero. Engring., Poly. Univ., Bklyn., 1958; MA, Princeton U., 1961, PhD in Aero. Engring., 1963; MA (hon.), U. Pa., 1971. Mem. tech. staff Sandia Labs., Albuquerque, summers 1971, 74, 77; asst. prof. engring. Brown U., Providence, 1963-66; asst. prof. mech. engring. U. Pa., Phila., 1966-67, assoc. prof., 1967-76, prof., 1976—, chmn. dept., 1992-97. Guest prof. Technische Hochschule Aachen, Germany, 1966; cons. fluid mechanics related problems to industry, 1966—, attys., 1966—; mem. bd. The Sch. in Rose Valley, Moylan, Pa., 1969-74 Author: (with P.K. Kundu) Fluid Mechanics, 2d edit., 2002, 3d edit., 2004; contbr. articles to various publs. Travel grant, Fulbright, 1966. Fellow AIAA (sect. sec. 1977-80, 85—), ASME; mem. AAUP, Am. Phys. Soc., Sigma Xi. Office: U Pa Dept Mech Engring & Applied Mechanics 233 Towne Bldg Philadelphia PA 19104-6315 Business E-Mail: imcohen@seas.upenn.edu. *Persistent hard work and uncompromising high standards will eventually overcome greed, corruption, and evil. Never forget to treat every human being with dignity, respect, kindness, and compassion. A loving mate is a lifelong inspiration.*

COHEN, IRVING ELIAS, real estate executive; b. Bklyn., Nov. 7, 1946; s. Daniel Arthur and Shirley B. (Kanner) C.; 1 child, Jonathan D. BA in Psychology, CCNY, 1968; MBA in Fin., NYU, 1973, 68. Mut. fund cashier Investors Funding Corp., Inc., 1968-69; syndication cashier Eastman Dillon, Union Securities, Inc., 1969-70; registered rep. Steiner, Rouse & Co., Inc., N.Y.C., 1970-72; instl. rep. Shearson Hayden Stone, Inc., N.Y.C., 1972-74; exec. v.p. Howard P. Hoffman Assos., Inc. subs. Lehman Bros. Kuhn Loeb, Inc., N.Y.C., 1974-81; sr. v.p. Security Pacific Realty Adv. Group, 1981-83; exec. v.p. E.F. Hutton Properties Inc., 1983-87; trustee, chmn. investment com. Mellon Participating Mortgage Trust, 1988-89; mng. dir. Real Estate Cons. Svcs. Group, Price Waterhouse, N.Y.C., 1989-90; mng. ptnr. Fuller Corp. Realty Ptnrs., 1990-94; pres. TimeMinder Ltd., N.Y.C., 1994-96; mng. dir., chief acquisition officer Dames & Moore/Brookhill LLC, N.Y.C., 1996-97; mng. dir. Cherokee Investment Ptnr. LLC, NYC, 1997—2003; mng. mem. Greeneagle LLC, NYC, 2003—. Mem. Am. Soc. Real Estate Counselors, Urban Land Inst., Nat. Brownfield Assn. Jewish. Office: Greeneagle LLC 433 W 34th St Ste 14G New York NY 10001 Office Phone: 212-904-0705. Business E-Mail: icohen@greeneagle.us.

COHEN, IRWIN, economist; b. Bronx, NY, Feb. 29, 1936; s. Samuel and Gertrude (Levy) C. BS in Acctg., NYU, 1956, MBA in Fin., 1964, MA in Econs., 1969; BS in Math., CCNY, 1970. Fin. analyst U.S. SEC, N.Y.C., 1965-67, Fed. Res. Bank N.Y., N.Y.C., 1967-72, Prudential Ins. Co. Am., 1973-74, SEC, 1974—98; ret. Mem. Internat. Platform Assn. (life), Math. Assn. Am., Am. Fin. Assn., Econ. History Assn. Home: 372 Central Park Ave Apt #2K Scarsdale NY 10583-1308

COHEN, JAY M., career military officer; Grad., U.S. Naval Acad., 1968; MS in Marine Engring. and Naval Arch., MIT. Commd. ensign USN, 1968, advanced through grades to rear adm., 1997; dir. SEALAB Group, San Diego; supply and weapons officer USS Diodon, San Diego; with engring. dept. USS Nathanal Greene, New London; engr. officer USS Nathan Hale, Bremerton, Wash.; staff Comdr. Submarine Force, U.S. Atlantic Fleet; exec. officer USS George Washington Carver, New London; comdr. USS Hyman G. Rickover, New London; sr. mem. nuclear propulsion examining bd. Comdr. in Chief, U.S. Atlantic Fleet; dir. operational support Dir. Naval Intelligence, Pentagon, Washington; comdr. USS L.Y. Spear, 1991—93; dep. chief Navy Legis. Affairs SECNAV; dep. dir. ops. Joint Staff SECNAV, dir. Navy Y2K Project Office; chief, Naval Rsch. Naval Rsch. Lab., Washington, 2000—; dir., test and eval. tech. requirements Office of Chief of Naval Ops., 2000—; dep. commandant for sci. and tech. U.S. Marine Corps., 2000—. Decorated Legion of Merit, Def. Superior Svc. medal, Meritorious Svc. medal. Office: Office of Naval Rsch Ballston Ctr Tower One 800 N Quincy St Arlington VA 22217-5660

COHEN, JEFF, editor; b. Cheyenne, Wyo. m. Kathryn M. Kase. Degree in journalism, U. Tex., 1976. Sports and feature writer San Antonio Light, 1976—89, mng. editor, 1989—93; spl. projects editor new media Hearst Newspaper Divsn., NYC, 1993—94; editor Times Union, Albany, NY, 1994—2002; exec. v.p., editor Houston Chronicle, 2002—. Juror Pulitzer Prize, 1999, 2000. Fellow Multicultural Mgmt. Program, U. Mo. Sch. Journalism, 1987, Newspaper Mgmt. Ctr., Kellogg Grad. Sch. Mgmt., Northwestern U., 1990. Office: Houston Chronicle 801 Texas Ave Houston TX 77002*

COHEN, JEFFREY, lawyer; b. Bklyn., Jan. 31, 1956; s. Fred and Ann (Piel) Cohen. AB in Politics and Philosophy with departmental honors magna cum laude, Brandeis U., 1977; JD, Bklyn. Law Sch., 1980. Bar: NY 1981, Colo. 1981. Assoc. Freedman & May, NYC, 1980—81, Alter, Zall & Haligman, Denver, 1981—82; ptnr. Quiat & Dice, Denver, 1982—84, Koransky, Friedman & Cohen, P.C., Denver, 1984—89, Cohen & Kenney, Denver, 1989—. Recipient Am. Jurisprudence award, 1977; Rose Meml. scholar, 1977. Mem.: ABA (bus. bankruptcy com.), Denver Bar Assn., Colo. Bar Assn., Colo. Mountain Club. Republican. Jewish.

COHEN, JEFFREY ALLEN, neurologist, educator; b. July 3, 1951; BA with honors, Tulane U., 1973; MD, U. Okla., 1977; MA, U. Denver, 1993. Diplomate Am. Bd. Psychiatry and Neurology. Intern in internal medicine Mt. Sinai Hosp., N.Y.C., 1977—78, resident, chief resident neurology, 1978—81; fellow neurology Mass. Gen. Hosp., Boston, 1981—82, Mayo Clinic, Rochester, Minn., 1985—86; asst. prof. Mt. Sinai Sch. Medicine, N.Y.C., 1982—85; assoc. prof. U. Colo. Sch. Medicine, Denver, 1986—91, clin. prof., 1991—2000; assoc. prof. Dartmouth Med. Sch., Lebanon, NH, 2000—04, assoc. chief neurology, 2000—, prof., 2004—. Recipient Svc. award, Am. Diabetes Assn., 1996;, Tulane U. scholar, 1970—73. Fellow: ACP, Am. Bd. Electrodiagnostic Medicine, Am. Acad. Neurology; mem.: Am. Neurol. Assn. Office: Dartmouth-Hitchcock Clinic 1 Medical Center Lebanon NH 03756 Office Phone: 603-650-5000. E-mail: Jeffrey.A.Cohen@Dartmouth.edu.

COHEN, JEFFREY E., lawyer; b. NYC, Feb. 14, 1951; AB, Princeton Univ., 1972; JD, Harvard Univ., 1982. Bar: NY 1983. Ptnr., head of Global Securities practice Coudert Bros., NYC. Mem.: ABA. Office: Coudert Bros LLP 1114 Ave of the Americas New York NY 10036 Office Phone: 212-626-4936. Office Fax: 212-626-4120. Business E-Mail: cohenj@coudert.com.

COHEN, JEFFREY MICHAEL, lawyer; b. Dayton, Ohio, Nov. 13, 1940; s. H. Mort and Evelyn (Friedlob) C.; m. Betsy Z. Zimmerman, July 3, 1966; children: Meredith Sue, Seth Alan. AB, Colgate U., 1962; JD, Columbia U., 1965. Bar: Fla. 1965, U.S. Supreme Ct. 1969; cert. civil trial lawyer Fla. Bar Bd. Cert.; diplomate Nat. bd. Trial Advocacy. Asst. pub. defender Dade County (Fla.), 1968-70, asst. state's atty., 1970-72, spl. asst. state's atty., 1973; ptnr. Fromberg Fromberg Gross Cohen Shore & Berke, P.A., 1972-84, Cohen, Berke, Bernstein, Brodie & Kondell, P.A., Miami, Fla., 1984-2000, Carlton Fields, 2000—. Adj. prof. litigation skills U. Miami Sch. Law, 1989—, adj. prof. trial skills Nova Southeastern U. Law Sch.; chair bd. of legal specialization and edn. Fla. Bar. Trustee Miami-Dade County Alliance for Ethical Govt. Mem. ABA, Dade County Bar Assn. (bd. dirs.), Acad. Fla. Trial Lawyers, Assn. Trial Lawyers Am., Am. Judicature Soc., Nat. Inst. Trial Advocacy (chair and faculty mem.), Fla. Criminal Def. Attys. Assn. Home: 3628 Saint Gaudens Rd Miami FL 33133-6533 Office: 4000 Internat Pl 100 SE 2d St Miami FL 33131 Office Phone: 305-530-0050. E-mail: jmcohen@carltonfields.com.

COHEN, JOEL EPHRAIM, biologist, educator, demographer, sociologist; b. Washington, Feb. 10, 1944; s. Hymen Ezra and Alice. C.; children: Zoe, Adam. BA, Harvard U., 1965, MA, 1967, MPH, PhD, Harvard U., 1970, DrPH, 1973; MA (hon.), Cambridge U., 1974. Jr. fellow in math. biology and sociology Soc. of Fellows Harvard U., 1967-71, asst. prof. biology, 1971-72, assoc. prof., 1972-75; prof. populations Rockefeller U., N.Y.C., 1975—, Abby Rockefeller Mauzé prof., 1996—; prof. populations Columbia U., N.Y.C., 1995—; dir.'s visitor Inst. for Advanced Study, Princeton, 1989-90. Chmn. bd. Societal Inst. Math. Scis., 1973—88; mem. ednl. adv. bd. John Simon Guggenheim Meml. Found., 1985—2001, mem. com. selection of fellows, 1990—99; mem. Mayor's Commn. for Sci. and Tech. City of N.Y., 1984—90; mem. sci. adv. bd. Inst. Sci. Interchange, Torino, Italy, 1991—; mem. bd. math. scis. NRC, 1991—92, mem. exec. com, panel on sci., tech. and law, 2000—, mem. governing bd., 2001—05; mem. bd. The Nature Conservancy, Arlington, Va., 2000—; trustee N.Y. Nature Conservancy, 2001—; mem. exec. com. Tyler Prize for Environ. Achievement, 2001—04, 2005—; mem. adv. bd. Sci. for Judges Project Bklyn. Law Sch., 2002—. Author: A Model of Simple Competition, 1967, Casual Groups of Monkeys and Men, 1971, Food Webs and Niche Space, 1978, Community Food Webs, 1990, Absolute Zero Gravity, 1992, How Many People Can the Earth Support?, 1995, Comparisons of Stochastic Matrices, 1998, Plants and Population: Is There Time?, 1999, Forecasting Product Liability Claims in the Manville Asbestos Case, 2004; mem. edit. bd.: American Scholar, 1994—99. Trustee Russell Sage Found., 1989-99, vice chmn. bd., 1996-99; trustee Black Rock Forest Preserve, 1989—, Population Reference Bur., Washington, 2004—. Recipient Mercer award Ecol. Soc. Am., 1972, disting. statis. ecologist award 6th Internat. Congress of Ecology, 1994, Olivia Nordberg award for excellence in writing on population scis. Population Coun., N.Y.C., 1997, Fred L. Soper award Pan Am. Health & Edn. Found., Washington, 1998, Tyler prize Environ. Achievement, 1999, N.Y.C. Mayor's award for excellence in sci. and tech., 2002; fellow Ctr. for Advanced Study in Behavioral Scis., Stanford, 1981-82, John Simon Guggenheim Meml. fellow, 1981-82, MacArthur Found. fellow, 1981-86. Fellow AAAS, Am. Acad. Arts and Scis. (mem. coun. 2000—04), Am. Statis. Assn.; mem. Population Assn. Am. (Mindel Sheps award for math. demography 1992), Cambridge Philos. Soc., Am. Soc. Naturalists, Am. Philos. Soc., U.S. Nat. Acad. Scis. (mem. coun. 2001—04). Office: Rockefeller U 1230 York Ave Ste 20 New York NY 10021-6399

COHEN, JOEL J., lawyer, investment banker; b. N.Y.C., Feb. 8, 1938; s. David M. and Eva (Weinstein) C.; m. Lillian Zeisel, June 30, 1963; children: Peter, Andrew Daniel, Nancy Elizabeth. BBA, CCNY, 1959; JD, Harvard U., 1962. Bar: N.Y. 1963. Assoc. Davis, Polk & Wardwell, N.Y.C., 1963-69, ptnr., 1969-87; mng. dir. investment banking, co-head global mergers and acquisitions Donaldson, Lufkin & Jenrette Securities Corp., N.Y.C., 1989-2000; chmn. bd. dirs. Chubb Corp., Warren, NJ, 2002—03; chmn., co-CEO Sagent Advisors Inc., N.Y.C., 2003—. Bd. dirs. Maersk Inc., Madison, N.J., Chubb Corp., Warren, N.J., Fed. Ins. Co., Warren, Borders Group Inc., Ann Arbor, Mich.; gen. counsel Presdl. Task Force on Market Mechanisms, 1987-88. Served with USAR, 1962-68. Mem. Assn. of Bar of City of N.Y. Office Phone: 212-904-9450. Business E-Mail: jcohen@sagentadvisors.com.

COHEN, JON STEPHAN, lawyer; b. Omaha, Nov. 9, 1943; s. Louis H. and Bertha N. (Goldstein) C.; children: Carolyn, Sherri, Barbara, Shayna, Jordan; m. Cheryl A. Jiroux, Oct. 7, 1994. Student, London Sch. Econs., 1963-64; BA, Claremont Men's Coll. (now Claremont McKenna Coll.), 1965; JD, Harvard U., 1968. Bar: Ariz. 1968. Assoc. Snell & Wilmer, Phoenix, 1968-73, ptnr., 1973—. Bd. dirs. Vika Corp., Phoenix, Ariz. Tech. Coun., Phoenix, Ariz. Sci. Ctr., Phoenix. Bd. dirs. Kronos Rsch. Inst., Phoenix. Fellow Ariz. Bar Found.; mem. ABA, Ariz. Bar Assn., Maricopa County Bar Assn., Village Athletic Club. Avocations: record collecting, skiing, racquetball. Home: 6901 E Northern Ave Paradise Valley AZ 85253 Office: Snell & Wilmer One Arizona Ctr Phoenix AZ 85004-0001 Office Phone: 602-382-6247. E-mail: jcohen@swlaw.com.

COHEN, JONATHAN LITTLE, investment banker; b. N.Y.C., Feb. 18, 1939; s. Reuben and Marjorie (Little) C.; children: Gregory David, Suzanne Elizabeth; m. Allison B. Morrow, 1998. AB, Dartmouth Coll., 1960, MBA, 1961. Asst. v.p. Irving Trust Co., N.Y.C., 1963-68; assoc. Goldman, Sachs & Co., N.Y.C., 1969-73, v.p., 1973-84, gen. ptnr., 1984-96; ltd. ptnr. The Goldman Sachs Group, L.P., N.Y.C., 1996-99, adv. dir., 1999—. Former trustee 1st Presbyn. Ch., N.Y.C.; trustee Wildlife Conservation Soc., N.Y.C., 2000—; former trustee Oberlin Coll.; bd. overseers Amos Tuck Sch. Bus. Adminstrn., Dartmouth Coll., 1991—2004, chmn., 1995—2001; bd. overseers Hopkins Ctr. and Hood Mus. Art, Dartmouth Coll., 2001—; mem. pres.'s leadership coun. Dartmouth Coll., 1998—, former mem. coun. alumni, 1983—86; former mem. sch. com. Friends Sem., N.Y.C., 1985—91; trustee Pa. Acad. Fine Arts, 1998—. Lt. USN, 1961—63. Mem.: Coral Beach and Tennis Club (Bermuda), Bond Club, Bellport Bay Yacht Club, India House. Office: Goldman Sachs & Co 22nd Fl 85 Broad St New York NY 10004-2456 Business E-Mail: jonathan.cohen@gs.com.

COHEN, JORDAN JAY, medical association executive; b. St. Louis, June 18, 1934; s. Bernard and Gladys (Brauer) C.; m. Carole Goldstein, Aug. 26, 1956; children: Deborah, Joel, David. BA, Yale U., 1956; MD, Harvard U., 1960; DSc, George Washington U. Sch. Med., and Health Scis., 1995, SUNY Health Sci. Ctr., Syracuse, 1996, Wake Forest U., 1997; LHD, Chgo. Med. Sch., 1998; DSc, U. Med. and Dental, N.J., 1998; DH Sci., Boston U., 1998; DSc, Thomas Jefferson U., 2001. Diplomate Am. Bd. Internal Medicine (mem. critical care medicine test and policy com. 1985-87, chmn. 1987-89, mem. subspecialty com. on nephrology 1981-86, chmn. 1986-88, chmn. com. on evaluation of clin. competency 1987-92, bd. dirs. 1986-94, mem. exec. com. 1990-94, chmn. 1993-94). Intern, asst. resident Boston City Hosp., 1960-62, sr. resident, 1964-65; rsch. fellow in renal medicine New Eng. Med. Ctr. Hosp., Boston, 1962-64; tchg. fellow Harvard U. Med. Sch., Boston, 1964-65, instr. in medicine, 1968-74, lectr. in medicine, 1974-82; asst. prof. med. scis. Brown U., Providence, 1965-68, assoc. prof. med. scis., 1968-71; assoc. prof. medicine Tufts U. Sch. Medicine, Boston, 1971-75, prof. medicine, 1976-82; prof., assoc. chmn. medicine Pritzker Sch. Medicine, U. Chgo., 1982-88; dean sch. medicine, prof. medicine SUNY, Stony Brook, 1988-94; dir. Univ. Med. Ctr., Stony Brook, 1993-94; pres. Assn. Am. Med. Colls., Washington, 1994—; clin. prof. dept. medicine Georgetown U. Sch. Medicine, 1995—. Dir. divsn. renal disease R.I. Hosp., Providence, 1965-71; chief renal svc. New Eng. Med. Ctr. Hosp., Boston, 1971-82, pres. med. staff, 1975-76, physician-in-chief and chmn., dept. medicine Michael Reese Hosp. and Med. Ctr., Chgo., 1982-88; pres. med. staff Univ. Hosp., Stony Brook, N.Y., 1988-94. Co-author: (textbooks) Acid-Base, 1982, Nephrology Forum, 1983, Repairing Bodily Fluids, 1989; author chpts. to books; editor Nephrology Forum, 1978—, Tufts Family Health Guides, 1979-82; manuscript reviewer Am. Jour. Physiology, Annals Internal Medicine, Jour. Clin. Investigation, Kidney Internat., New England Jour. Medicine; contbr. articles to profl. jours. Lt. col. M.C., U.S. Army, 1969-71. Recipient Scroll of Merit, Nat. Med. Assn., 1997. Master: ACP (mem. coun. on subsplty. socs. 1978—84, chmn. coun. 1981—82, nominating com. 1983—84, chmn. edn. policy com. 1983—89, bd. regents 1983—89, vice chmn. 1988—89, rep. to Coun. Med. Splty. Socs. 1991—94, chmn. search com. for assoc. exec. v.p. for edn., mem. nephrology com. med. knowledge self-assessment program, chmn.); fellow: Royal Soc. Medicine; mem.: Rsch. Am., Partnerships for Quality Edn., Edn. Commn. Fgn. Med. Grads., Coalition for Health Svc. Rsch., Carl J. Shapiro Inst. for Edn. and Rsch., Am. Bd. Internal Med. Found., Internat. Soc. Nephrology, Ctrl. Soc. Clin. Rsch., Nat. Med. Fellowships, China Med. Bd., Assn. Program Dirs. in Internal Medicine (mem. coun. 1984—90, pres. 1988—89), Assn. Am. Physicians, Soc. Med. Adminstrs., Nat. Kidney Found. (mem. task force on nephrology manpower 1987—89), Am. Soc. Nephrology (rep. to CSS 1978—82, chmn. manpower task force 1980), Am. Soc. Clin. Investigation, Am. Heart Assn., Am. Geriat. Soc. (mem. program com. 1985—88), Am. Fedn. Clin. Rsch. (chmn. Ea. sect. 1975), Am. Clin. and Climatol. Assn., Inst. Medicine of NAS, Qatar Found. Edn., Sci. and Cmty. Devel., Josiah Macy Found., Dept. Vets. Affairs, Cosmos Club, Midwest Salt and Water Club, Sigma Xi, Phi Beta Kappa. Home: 1819 Kalorama Sq NW Washington DC 20008-4021 Office: Assn Am Med Colls 2450 N St NW Washington DC 20037-1127 Office Phone: 202-828-0400.

COHEN, JOSHUA, political science professor; BA, MA, Yale Univ, 1973; PhD, Harvard Univ, 1979. Asst prof MIT, 1979—84, assoc prof, 1984—90, prof, 1990—2001, Leon & Anne Goldberg prof, 2001—. Vis assoc prof Univ Wis, 1989, Princeton Univ, 1989; pres Boston Critic, Inc, 1991—; bd mem & treas Inst for Defense & Disarmament Studies. Editor (in chief): Boston Review, 1991—; editor: (assoc) Philosophy & Public Affairs, 1991—; co-author (with Joel Rogers): On Democracy, 1983, Inequity and Intervention: The Federal Budget and Central America, 1986, Rules of the Game, 1986, Associations and Democracy, 1995; contbr. articles to prof jours, columns in newspapers. Mem.: Am Philos Assn, Am Polit Sci Assn, Phi Beta Kappa. Office: Dept of Political Science MIT E53-473 Cambridge MA 02139 Business E-Mail: jcohen@mit.edu.*

COHEN, JOSHUA ROBERT, lawyer; b. East Patchogue, N.Y., Aug. 20, 1963; s. Abraham Cohen and Elizabeth Joan Caufield; m. Robin Renee Conlon, Feb. 28, 1967. BA, Hartwick Coll., 1985; JD, Fordham U., 1991. Bar: Conn. 1991, N.Y. 1992, U.S. Dist. Ct. (so. and ea. dists.) N.Y., 1992. Sr. assoc. Belair & Evans LLP, N.Y.C., 1991-99; ptnr. Garson, Gerspach, DeCorato & Cohen, LLP, N.Y.C., 1999—. Office: Garson Gerspach De Corato & Cohen LLP 110 Wall St New York NY 10005 Office Phone: 212-742-8700. E-mail: cohen@ggdc.com.

COHEN, JUDITH ANN, child psychiatrist, educator; b. Knoxville, Tenn., Dec. 7, 1953; d. Bernard L. and Anna (Foner) C.; children: Shari, Aren, Lauren. BA, Bowdoin Coll., 1974; MD, U. Pitts., 1978. Diplomate in gen. and child psychiatry Am. Bd. Psychiatry and Neurology. Pediatric intern Mercy Hosp., Pitts., 1978-79; resident and fellow in psychiatry and child psychiatry Western Psychiat. Inst., Pitts., 1979-83, med. dir. Ctr. for Children and Families, 1986-88, med. dir. Child and Adolescent Sexual Abuse Clinic, 1988-94; asst. prof. child psychiatry U. Pitts. Sch. Medicine, 1983-94, cons. Student Health Svc., 1986-94; assoc. prof. psychiatry MCP-Hahnemann Sch. Medicine, 1994-98, prof., 1998—; med. dir. Ctr. for Traumatic Stress in Children & Adolescents, 1994—. Cons. Karma House Drug and Alcohol Ctr., Pitts., 1981-82, Asklepieion Juvenile Offenders Program, Pitts., 1983, Alternatives Drug and Alcohol Ctr., Pitts., 1983-85. Contbr. articles to med. jours., chpts. to books. Cons. Allegheny County Task Force on Child Sexual Abuse, Pitts., 1983-84. Grantee NIMH, 1986-89, 90—, NCCAN, 1990-95. Fellow APA (disting.); mem. AMA, Am. Psychiat. Assn., Am. Acad. Child and Adolescent Psychiatry, Pitts. Regional Orgn. Child and Adolescent Psychiatry, Am. Profl. Soc. on the Abuse of Children (bd. dirs. 1994-2001), Inernat. Soc. for Trauma Stress Studies. Avocation: running. E-mail: jcohen1@wpahs.org.

COHEN, JULES, former dean, internist, educator; b. Bklyn., Aug. 26, 1931; s. Samuel S. and Dora (Goldstein) C.; m. Doris Eidlin, Mar. 25, 1956; children: Stephen E., David E., Sharon C. Anisfeld. AB, U. Rochester, 1953, MD, 1957. Intern Beth Israel Hosp., Boston, 1957-58; resident, fellow in medicine U. Rochester (N.Y.) Strong Meml. Hosp., 1958-60, mem. faculty, 1963—, prof. medicine, 1973—; NIH research asso. Bethesda, Md., 1960-62; research fellow Postgrad. Med. Sch., London, 1962-63; physician in chief Rochester Gen. Hosp., 1976-82; sr. asso. dean med. edn. U. Rochester Sch. Medicine, 1982-97. USPHS research grantee, 1963-69; USPHS research grantee, 74-77; recipient USPHS Research Career Devel. award, 1970-75; Am. Heart Assn. grantee-in-aid, 1969-71 Fellow ACP, Am. Coll. Cardiology; mem. Am. Physiol. Soc., Am. Heart Assn. (fellow coun. on clin. cardiology), Monroe County Med. Soc., N.Y. State Med. Soc., Rochester Acad. Medicine. Home: 152 Burkedale Cres Rochester NY 14625-1704 Office: U Rochester Sch Medicine and Dentistry 601 Elmwood Ave Rochester NY 14642-0001 Office Phone: 585-273-4536. Business E-Mail: Jules_Cohen@urmc.rochester.edu.

COHEN, KARL PALEY, nuclear energy consultant; b. NYC, Feb. 5, 1913; s. Joseph M. and Ray (Paley) C.; m. Marthe H. Malartre, Sept. 20, 1938; children: Martine-Claude Lebouc, Elisabeth M. Brown, Beatrix Josephine Cashmore. AB, Columbia U., 1933, MA, 1934, PhD in Phys. Chemistry, 1937; postgrad., U. Paris, 1936—37. Rsch. asst. to Prof. H. C. Urey Columbia U., 1937-40; dir. theoretical divsn. SAM Manhattan Project, 1940—44; physicist Std. Oil Devel. Co., 1944-48; tech. dir. H.K. Ferguson Co., 1948-52; v.p. Walter Kidde Nuc. Lab., 1952-55; cons. AEC, sr. sci. Columbia U., 1955; mgr. advance engring. atomic power equipment dept. GE, 1955-65, gen. mgr. breeder reactor devel. dept., 1965-71, mgr. strategic planning, nuc. energy divsn., 1971-73, chief scientist, nuc. energy group, 1973-78; cons. prof. Stanford U., 1978-81. Author: The Theory of Isotope Separation as Applied to Large Scale Production of U-235, 1951; contbr. articles to profl. jours. Recipient Energy Rsch. prize Alfried Krupp Found., 1977 Fellow AAAS, Am. Nuc. Soc. (pres. 1968-69, bd. dirs.), Am. Inst. Chemists (Chem. Pioneer award 1979); mem. NAE, IEEE, Am. Phys. Soc., Phi Beta Kappa, Sigma Xi, Phi Lambda Upsilon. Home and Office: 928 N California Ave Palo Alto CA 94303-3405 Office Phone: 650-858-0565. Personal E-mail: karlpc@earthlink.net.

COHEN, KENNETH P., oil industry executive, lawyer; BA, Northwestern U.; JD, Baylor U. Law Sch.; LLM, Yale Law Sch. Law dept. Exxon USA, 1977, pub. affairs; law dept. Exxon Co. Internat.; gen. counsel Exxon Chem. Co., 1995—99; v.p. pub. affairs ExxonMobil Corp., 1999—. Editor-in-chief Baylor Law Rev. Office: ExxonMobil Corp 5959 Las Colinas Blvd Irving TX 75039-2298

COHEN, LARRY, film director, producer, screenwriter; b. Chgo., Apr. 20, 1947; TV writer: (series) Kraft Mystery Theatre, The Defenders, Arrest and Trial, NYPD Blue, 87th Precinct Ice, Heatwave; (movies) Cool Million, 1972, Shootout in a One-Dog Town, 1974, Man on the Outside, 1975, Desperado: Avalanche at Devil's Ridge, 1988; creator: Branded, 1965-66, The Invaders, 1967-68; film writer: The Return of the Seven, 1966, Daddy's Gone A-Hunting, 1969, El Condor, 1970, I, The Jury, 1982, Best Seller, 1987, Deadly Illusion, 1987, Guilty as Sin, 1993, Phone Booth, 2003; dir., prodr., writer: Bone, 1972, Black Caesar, 1973, Hell in Harlem, 1973, It's Alive, 1974, Demon, 1976, The Private Files of J. Edgar Hoover, 1978, It Lives Again, 1978, Full Moon High, 1982, Q, 1982, Perfect Strangers, 1984; story: Success, 1979, The Man Who Wasn't There, 1983, Scandalous, 1984, Body Snatchers, 1984; dir., writer: Special Effects, 1984, The Ambulance, 1990; exec. prodr., dir., writer: The Stuff, 1985, It's Alive III: Island of the Alive, 1987, Return to Salem's Lot, 1987, Wicked Stepmother, 1989; prodr., writer: Maniac Cop II, 1990.; writer, dir.: As Good As Dead, 1996; dir.: Original Gangstas. 1997.

COHEN, LAWRENCE ALAN, health facility administrator; b. N.Y.C., Nov. 29, 1953; s. Irwin Wolf Cohen and Ernestine Jacqueline (Rosenbloom) Chaut; m. Ilene Beth Rosen, May 27, 1979; children: Bari, Kerri, Andrew. BBA in Acctg., George Washington U., 1975; JD, St. Johns U., 1979; LLM in Taxation, NYU, 1982. Bar: N.Y.; CPA. Assoc. Rogers & Wells, N.Y.C., 1979-82, Battle Fowler, N.Y.C., 1982-84; 1st v.p. VMS Realty Ptnrs., N.Y.C., 1984-88; exec. v.p. PaineWebber Properties Inc., N.Y.C., 1989-90, pres., CEO, 1991-96; vice chmn., CFO Capital Sr. Living Corp., N.Y.C., 1996-98,

CEO, 1999—. Mem. Nat. Realty Com. (exec. com. 1990—), Nat. Multi Housing Coun. (exec. com. 1992—), Am. Srs. Housing Assn. (exec. bd. dirs. 1992—). Jewish. Office Phone: 212-551-1770. E-mail: lcohen@capitalsenior.com.

COHEN, LAWRENCE BARUCH, neurobiologist, educator; b. Indpls., June 18, 1939; s. Gabriel Murel and Helen (Aronovitz) C.; children: Daniel, Avrum, Lily Rachel. BS, U. Chgo., 1961; PhD, Columbia U., 1965. Asst. prof. Yale U., New Haven, 1968-71, assoc. prof., 1971-79, prof. physiology, 1979—. Recipient Elizabeth R. Cole award, Biophys. Soc., 1987, McMaster Award, Columbia U., 1965; named Dist. Lectr., Am. Physiol. Soc., 1998. Office: Yale U Sch Medicine 333 Cedar St New Haven CT 06520 Office Phone: 203-785-4047. Business E-Mail: lawrence.cohen@yale.edu.

COHEN, LAWRENCE EDWARD, sociologist, educator, criminologist; b. L.A., July 20, 1945; s. Louis and Florence (White) C. BA, U. Calif., Berkeley, 1969; MA, Calif. State U., 1971; PhD, U. Wash., 1974; postdoctorate study, SUNY, Albany, 1973-75. Rsch. assoc. Sch. of Criminal Justice, SUNY, Albany, 1973-76; asst. prof. U. Ill., Urbana, 1976-80; assoc. prof. U. Tex., Austin, 1980-85; prof. Ind. U., Bloomington, 1985-88, U. Calif., Davis, 1988—. Cons. editor Social Forces, 1981-84, Jour. Criminal Law and Criminology, 1982-2000, Am. Sociol. Rev., 1982-84, Am. Jour. Sociology, 1990-98, Criminology, 1996-98; contbr. numerous articles to profl. jours. Sgt. USMC, 1963-66, Vietnam. Grantee NIMH, 1978-80, NSF, 1983-89. Mem. Am. Sociol. Assn., Am. Soc. Criminology, Acad. Criminal Justice Scis., Soc. for Study Social Problems. Office: U Calif Dept Sociology Davis CA 95616 Business E-Mail: lecohen@ucdavis.edu.

COHEN, LAWRENCE SOREL, internist, educator; b. N.Y.C., Mar. 27, 1933; s. Max and Fannie (Cooper) C.; m. Jane Abramson, Aug. 5, 1961; children: Melanie, Wendy. AB, Harvard U., 1954; MD, N.Y. U., 1958; MA (hon.), Yale U., 1970. Diplomate: Am. Bd. Internal Medicine, Sub Bd. Cardiovascular Diseases. Intern, then resident in medicine Yale-New Haven Hosp., 1958-60, 64-65; asst. in medicine Harvard U. Med. Sch., 1962-64; sr. investigator Nat. Heart, Lung and Blood Inst., 1965-68, mem. task force on arteriosclerosis, 1978-80, chmn. clin. trials rev. com., 1984-85, 87-89; assoc. prof. medicine U. Tex. Med. Sch., Dallas, 1968-70; prof. medicine Yale U. Med. Sch., 1970-81, Ebenezer K. Hunt prof. medicine, 1981—, dep. dean, 1991-95, spl. advisor to dean, 1995—. Mem. editorial bd. Circulation, Am. Jour. Cardiology, Am. Heart Jour.; contbr. over 160 articles to med. jours. Active Am. Heart Assn., chpt. pres., 1980-81, affiliate pres. Conn. chpt., 1984-86. With USPHS, 1960-62. Recipient Francis Gilman Blake award for Teaching of Med. Scis., 1973 Fellow ACP, Am. Coll. Cardiology (trustee 1978-83, mem. editorial bd. jour.); mem. Assn. Univ. Cardiologists (pres.-elect 1990, pres. 1991), Brit. Cardiac Soc., Ombudsman Assn., Interurban Clin. Club (pres. 1988), Alpha Omega Alpha. Home: 633 Whitney Ave New Haven CT 06511-2218 Office: Yale U Sch Medicine 333 Cedar St I-207 New Haven CT 06510-3289 Office Phone: 203-785-4683. Business E-Mail: lawrence.s.cohen@yale.edu.

COHEN, LEE STEVEN, psychiatrist; b. Bklyn., June 22, 1959; s. Seymour and Carol C.; m. Correy Hope Kustin, Aug. 19, 1984; children: Spencer Ari, Hayden Lev. BS in Biomed. Scis., CUNY, 1980; MD, SUNY, Stony Brook, 1982. Lic. psychiatrist, N.Y.; diplomate Am. Bd. Psychiatry and Neurology, Nat. Bd. Med. Examiners. Resident in pediatrics Mt. Sinai Hosp., N.Y.C., 1982-83, resident in psychiatry, 1983-85; fellow Columbia U., N.Y.C., 1985-86, chief fellow Coll. physicians and Surgeons, 1986-87, rsch. psychiatrist Coll. Physicians and Surgeons, 1987—, instr. clin. psychiatry Coll. Physicians and Surgeons, 1987—, asst. clin. prof. psychiat. Coll. Physicians and Surgeons, 1992—; team leader The Holliswood (N.Y.) Hosp., 1987-90, dir. rsch., 1990-94; dir. psychiatry clin. neurosci. ctr. St. Luke's/Roosevelt Hosp., N.Y.C., 1999—. Lectr. N.Y.C. Bd. Edn., 1989—, SUNY Sch. Medicine, Queens, N.Y., 1989—. Contbr. articles to profl. jours. Mem. AMA, Am. Psychiat. Assn., N.Y. County Psychiat. Assn., N.Y. State Psychiat. Assn. Office: 623 Warburton Ave Hastings On Hudson NY 10706-1523 Office Phone: 914-478-1330.

COHEN, LEONARD (NORMAN COHEN), poet, writer, musician; b. Montreal, Que., Can., Sept. 21, 1934; s. Nathan B. and Masha (Kline) C. BA, McGill U., 1955; postgrad., Columbia.; LLB (hon.), Dalhousie U., 1971; LLD (hon.), McGill U., 1992. Author: (poetry) Let Us Compare Mythologies, 1956, The Spice Box of Earth, 1961, Flowers for Hitler, 1964, Parasites of Heaven, 1966, Selected Poems, 1956-68, 1968, The Energy of Slaves, 1972, Death of a Lady's Man, 1979, Book of Mercy, 1984, Stranger Music: Selected Music and Songs, 1993, Dance Me to the End of Love, 1995, (novels) The Favorite Game, 1963, Beautiful Losers, 1966, also articles, songs including music for McCabe and Mrs. Miller, 1971, Natural Born Killers, 1994; rec. artist for Sony Music; albums include I'm Your Man, 1988, The Future, 1992, Cohen Live, 1993, More Best Of, 1997, Field Commander Cohen: Tour of 1979, 2001, Ten New Songs, 2001, Dear Heather, 2004. Decorated Order of Can.; recipient McGill Lit. award, 1956, Que. Lit. award, 1964, Gov. Gen.'s Performing Arts award, Can., 1993. Office: care Core Mgmt Co 345 N Maple Dr Ste 304 Beverly Hills CA 90291 E-mail: cohensings@aol.com.

COHEN, LEWIS CARROLL, sculptor, educator; b. Mpls., Apr. 19, 1936; s. Irving and Celia (Tolchiner) C.; m. Adrianne Luther; children: Julia, Aaron. Student, U. Minn., 1952-53; postgrad., Ecole des Arts Decoratif, Paris, 1962-63; diploma with honors, Mus. Sch., Boston, 1962; MFA, Claremont (Calif.) Coll., 1976. Instr. Boston U., 1964-67; lectr. Calif. State U., Long Beach, 1970-87; instr. Laguna Beach (Calif.) Coll. Art, 1973-85; asst. prof. Scripps Coll., Claremont, 1974-75; assoc. prof., then prof. Coll. of William and Mary, Williamsburg, Va., 1987—. Interim dir. Laguna Beach Sch. Art, 1980. Exhibited sculpture in solo exhbns. Four Oaks Gallery, Pasadena, Calif., 1985, Twentieth Century Gallery, Williamsburg, 1988, Martin Sumers Gallery, N.Y.C., 1990, Muscarelle Museum of Art, Williamsburg, 1993; commd. works include Portrait of Henry Mudd, Harvey Mudd Coll., sculpture of Reverand James Blair, Tercentenary of Coll. of William and Mary, 1993. Recipient Prix de Rome Am. Acad. in Rome, 1967-70; named National Academician, 1992. Mem. Nat. Acad. Design. Office: Coll of William and Mary Dept Fine Arts Williamsburg VA 23185*

COHEN, LEWIS ISAAC, lawyer; b. N.Y.C., July 27, 1932; s. Benjamin and Jeannette (Klotzko) C.; m. Sheila Lipman, Sept. 8, 1957; children— Leslie, Bruce, Wendy. BA, U. Calif. at Los Angeles, 1953; LL.B., Columbia, 1958. Bar: N.Y. State bar 1959, D.C. bar 1964, U.S. Supreme Ct. bar 1966. Atty. FCC, Washington, 1959-64; 1995practiced in Washington, 1964—95; ptnr. Cohen & Berfield, 1964-95. Served with AUS, 1954-56. Mem. Fed., D.C. bar assns., FCC Bar Assn. Home: 45 Sunset Ct Edinburg VA 22824 E-mail: lihcohen@shentel.net.

COHEN, LORI G., lawyer; b. Boston, May 18, 1965; BA cum laude, Duke U., 1987; JD with distinction, Emory U., 1990. Bar: Georgia, Am. Bar Assoc. Ptnr., medical malpractice def. litig. Alston & Bird LLP, Atlanta, 1990—2005; ptnr., litig. products liability, life sciences Greenberg Traurig LLP, Atlanta. Editor Medical Malpractice & Strategy, Product Liability Law & Strategy, Pharmaceutical and Medical Device Law Bulletin. Recipient Top Defense Wins Award, Nat. Law Journal, 1999—2000. Mem.: Product Liability Advisory Council, Defense Research Institute. Office: Greenberg Traurig LLP Ste 400 The Forum 3290 Northside Pkwy Atlanta GA 30327 Office Phone: 678-553-2100. Office Fax: 678-553-2212.

COHEN, LOUIS RICHARD, lawyer; b. Washington, Nov. 28, 1940; s. Milton Howard and Rowna (Chaffetz) C.; m. Bonnie Rubenstein, Aug. 29, 1965; children: Amanda Carroll, Eli Augustus. AB, Harvard U., 1962, LLB, 1966; student, Wadham Coll., Oxford, Eng., 1962-63. Bar: DC. Law clk. to Hon. John M. Harlan U.S. Supreme Ct., Washington, 1967-68; assoc. Wilmer Cutler Pickering LLP, Washington, 1968—74, ptnr., 1974—86, 1988—2004; dep. solicitor gen. U.S. Dept. Justice, Washington, 1986—88; ptnr. Wilmer Cutler Pickering Hale and Dorr LLP, Washington, 2004—. Vis. prof. Stanford (Calif.) Law Sch., 1981; lectr. law Harvard Law Sch., Cambridge, Mass., 1986. Author: Book Review Michigan Law Review, 1993. Chair Harvard Law Sch. Fund, 1993-96; mem. overseers com. to Visit Harvard Law Sch., 1986-92; bd. dirs. Woolly Mammoth Theatre Co., Washington, 1988-91, 96—; bd. of dir. Ptnrs. for Sacred Places, 2002--. Mem.: Telluride Soc. for Jazz (bd. dir. 2001—), Am. Law Inst., Am. Acad. Appellate Lawyers, Supreme Ct. Hist. Soc. Jewish. Avocation: hiking. Office: Wilmer Cutler Pickering Hale and Dorr LLP 2445 M St NW Ste 500 Washington DC 20037-1420 Office Phone: 202-663-6700. Business E-Mail: louis.cohen@wilmerhale.com.

COHEN, LYOR, recording industry executive; b. N.Y.C. married; 1 child. B in Mktg. and Fin., U. Miami. Road mgr. Run DMC; with Rush Mgmt.; ptnr. Phat Fashions LLC, 1992—2004; pres. Def Jam records, 1988—99; co-pres. Island Def Jam Music Group, 1999—2004; chmn, CEO, U.S. Recorded Music Warner Music Group, 2004—; interim chmn. Elektra Entertainment Group, 2004, The Atlantic Group, 2004. Office: Warner Music Group 75 Rockefeller Pl New York NY 10019

COHEN, MALCOLM MARTIN, psychologist, researcher; s. Nathan and Esther C.; m. Marilyn Jerrow, Jan. 2, 1959 (dec. 1967); m. Eleanor Johnson, June 30, 1969 (div. 1988); m. Suzana Gal, Feb. 14, 1988. BA, Brandeis U., 1959; MA, U. Pa., 1961, PhD, 1965. Lic. psychologist, Pa., 1974. Asst. instr. U. Pa., Phila., 1961-63; rsch. psychologist Naval Air Engring. Ctr., Phila., 1963-67; supervisory rsch. psychologist Naval Air Devel. Ctr., Warminster, Pa., 1967-82; asst. chief biomed. rsch. divsn. NASA-Ames Rsch Ctr., Moffett Field, Calif., 1982-85, chief neuroscis. br., 1985-88, rsch. scientist, 1988—, chief human info. processing rsch., 2000—. Lectr. dept. aeros. and astronautics Stanford U., lectr. human biology program, 1994—95, consulting assoc. prof. human biology program, 1995—98, cons. prof. human biology program, 1998—2003. Assoc. editor Habitation Jour., 2004-; contbr. articles to profl. jours. Founding mem. Common Cause of Phila., 1973. Recipient Exceptional Sci. Achievement medal, NASA 1994. Fellow AIAA (assoc.), Aerospace Med. Assn. (editl. bd. Aviation Space and Environ. Medicine 1985-93, assoc. editor 2001-03, Environ. Sci. award 1985, William F. Longacre award 1989), Environ. Sci. award 1985), Aerospace Human Factors Assn. (pres. 1992); mem. AAAS, NY Acad. Scis., Psychonomics Soc., Sigma Xi. Jewish. Achievements include patents for light bar to monitor human acceleration tolerance. Avocations: scuba diving, photography, chess. Office: NASA Ames Rsch Ctr Mail Stop 262-2 Moffett Field CA 94035 E-mail: malcolm.m.cohen@nasa.gov.

COHEN, MALCOLM STUART, economist; b. Mpls., Jan. 17, 1942; s. Jack Alvin and Lorraine Ethel (Hill) Cohen; m. Judith Ann Arenson, Sept. 25, 1965; children: Laura, Randall, Ilona. BA in Econs. summa cum laude, U. Minn., 1963; PhD in Econs., MIT, 1967. Labor economist U.S. Bur. Labor Stats., Washington, 1967-68; lectr. U. Md., College Park, 1968; asst. to v.p. state rels. and planning U. Mich., Ann Arbor, 1968-70, various tchr. positions, 1968-85, co-rsch. dir. Inst. Labor and Indsl. Rels., 1973-80, dir. Inst. Labor and Indsl. Rels., 1980-93; cons. Corp. Pub. Broadcasting, 1994-97; lectr. indsl. rels. ctr. U. Minn., 1994-96; pres. Employment Rsch. Corp., Ann Arbor, 1997—. Project dir. various projects, Washington, 1968—92; expert witness discrimination and econ. loss various clients, 1982—; cons. Mich. Senate Fiscal Agy., Lansing, 1988, U.S. Dept. Labor, 1995—2001, EEOC, 1996—. Co-author: A Micro Model of Labor Supply, 1970, Global Skill Shortages, 2002; author: Labor Shortages: As Am. Approaches the 21st Century, 1995; contbr. articles to profl. jour. Mem.: Internat. Indsl. Rels. Assn., Labor and Employment Rels. Assn., Nat. Assn. Forensic Economists. Avocations: jogging, geneology. Office: Employment Rsch Corp Ste 250 3820 Packard Rd Ann Arbor MI 48108-3348 Office Phone: 734-477-9040. E-mail: malco@umich.edu, mc@employmentresearch.com.

COHEN, MARC, physician, consultant; b. Cairo, Mar. 3, 1953; came to U.S., 1958; MD, NYU Sch. of Medicine, New York, New York, 1973—77. Prof. of medicine MCP Hahnemann Sch. of Medicine, Philadelphia, Pa., 1995—; dir. of clin. rsch. Hahnemann U. Hosp., Philadelphia. Author: (medical research) The ESSENCE Trial, 1997 (Simon Dack Tchg. Award, 1991). Fellow ACP, Am. Coll. Cardiology; mem. Am. Heart Assn. Office: MCP Hahnemann School of Medicine Mail Stop 119 Broad and Vine Streets Philadelphia PA 19102-1192

COHEN, MARCIA FAN BALTIMORE, writer, psychologist; b. Scranton, Pa., July 7, 1931; d. Harry Moshkowitz and Annabel Baltimore Smiley; m. Richard Tampol; m. Joseph Cohen, Mar. 29, 1953 (dec.); children: Sharryn, William. BS in Biology, Syracuse U.; M in Psychology, U. Scranton; EdD, U. So. Calif. Tchr. Torrance Unified Sch. Dist., Calif.; adminstr. L.A. Unified Sch. Dist., psychologist. Grant writer L.A. Unified Sch. Dist. Author: The Making of a Mistress, 2002, Inner City Angels, 2005. Fellow: U. So. Calif. Libr. Assn. Home: 5535 W 64th St Los Angeles CA 90056

COHEN, MARK HERBERT, broadcasting company executive; b. Boston, Mar. 27, 1932; s. Henry I. and Francis C.; m. Mary Jane Pitman, July 30, 1961; children: Patricia Beth, H. Jonathan, Cathy Ann. BA in Bus. Adminstrn., U. Maine, 1954; MS in TV Prodn, Syracuse U., 1958. Announcer Sta. WGUY-AM-FM, Bangor, Maine, 1954, Sta. WGAN-AM-TV, Portland, Maine, 1954-55; various positions in sales, planning and station clearance ABC-TV network, N.Y.C., 1958-68, v.p. sales planning, 1967-70, v.p., assoc. dir. planning, bus. and fin. analysis, 1970-76, sr. v.p. fin. and planning, 1976-77, sr. v.p., 1977-85; v.p. Am. Broadcasting Cos. Inc., 1981-83, sr. v.p., 1983-85, exec. v.p. broadcast group, 1985-86; bd. dirs. ESPN, 1983—85; exec. v.p. ABC Network Div., 1986-88; v.p. Capital Cities/ABC, 1986-88; pres. distbn. and prodn. co. D.L. Taffner Ltd., N.Y.C., 1990-91; broadcasting cons., 1991—. Mem. exec. com. of alumni coun. U. Maine, 1980-86. Mem. adv. bd. Newhouse Sch., Syracuse U., 1985-88; mem. exec. com. of pres.'s coun. U. Maine, 1988, vice chmn. of pres.'s coun., 1992-93, chmn., 1993-95, vice chmn. Campaign for Maine, 1991-96. 1st lt. inf. U.S. Army, 1954—57. Fellow Nat. Acad. Arts and Scis. (pres. internat. coun. 1984-85, exec. com. 1986-92); mem. Internat. Radio and TV Soc. (gov. 1980-81, v.p. 1983-85), Whipporwill Club. Personal E-mail: mhc001@aol.com.

COHEN, MARK N., publishing executive; b. Camden, N.J., July 14, 1947; s. Morris and Esther (Sobel) C.; m. Rhoda Posner, Dec. 19, 1971; children: Michele Rebecca, Gregory Leighton. BS, U. Mo., Kansas City, 1969; postgrad., N.Y. Med. Coll., 1969-70; MS, Am. Western U., Tulsa, 1972, PhD, 1976. Cert. state advisor U.S. Congl. Adv. Bd. Founder, pres., chmn. Nat. Recall Alert Ctr., Marlton, N.J., 1973—; founder Acad. Guidance Svcs., Marlton, 1975-88; founder, pres., chmn. Nat. Corp. Svcs., Marlton, 1977—, Nat. Pub. Corp., Marlton, 1979—. Pres. Am. Bus. Opportunity Commn., N.J., 1975; bd. dirs., chmn. Health Sytems Agy., Bellmawr, N.J., 1982; treas., bd. dirs. Perinatal Coop./South N.J., Camden, 1983; mem. bd. advisors Free Enterprise, Marlton, 1985; pres. Cohenterprises, Inc., Marlton, 1986, Am. Profl. Copy-Quick Printing Corp., Marlton, 1985, Nationwide Wats Telephone Answering Service, Inc., Marlton, 1985-88, Slim Scents, Inc., 1993, On Air-Everywhere, Inc., 1994, In-Press Express, Inc., 1994. Author: 100 Best Spare Time Business Opportunities Today, 1990, Win Your Weight, Loss War, 1998, Mindstrings and How to Pull Them, 1998. Bd. dirs. Beth Israel Synagogue; trustee Cooper Found./Cooper Hosp. U. Med. Ctr.; assoc. advisor post 65 Explorer Scouts. Recipient Young Exec. of Yr. award Jim Walter Corp., Tampa, Fla., 1972, Disting. Leadership award Am. Security Council Found., 1984, Annual Register award Esquire mag.; named one of 50 Bus. People to Watch, N.J. Bus. Jour. Mem. Am. Hosp. Assn., U.S. C. of C., Am. Assn. Fin. Profls., Nat. Council on Patient Info. and Edn., Nat. Health Lawyers Assn., N.J. Assn. Commerce and Industry (chmn. 1974), Am. Assn. Sch. Adminstrs., Am. Assn. Univ. Adminstrs., Am. Assn. Indiv. Investors, Internat. Coun. Computers Edn., MENSA. Republican. Jewish. Home: 6 Alluvium Lakes Dr Voorhees NJ 08043-4816

COHEN, MARK STEVEN, dentist; b. N.Y.C., Dec. 10, 1948; s. Lawrence and Yetta (Grossman) C.; m. Arlene Debbie Deutsch, Aug. 23, 1970 (div. May 1984); 1 child, Aaron Philip; m. Donna Lynn Poissonnier, Nov. 27, 1985. BS, CCNY, 1971; DDS, Columbia U., 1975, cert. in Pedodontics, 1976. Practice dentistry, Yonkers, N.Y., 1975-76, Bristol, Conn., 1976-79, Brookfield, Conn., 1977—. Dir. dental service N.Y. Inst. for the Edn. Blind, Bronx, 1976-78; assoc. attending dentist Danbury (Conn.) Hosp., 1976-82, Blythdale Children's Hosp., Valhalla, N.Y., 1986-87; assoc. clin. prof. dentistry Columbia U., N.Y.C., 1976—, mem. quality assurance com., 1982-85. Patentee in field. Active Dental Guidance Council for Cerebral Palsy, N.Y.C., 1976-81. Chemistry fellow NSF, Washington, 1969-71, research fellow NIH, 1971, United Cerebral Palsy, 1975-76. Mem. ADA, Conn. State Dental Assn., Greater Danbury Dental Soc., Am. Dental Vols. for Israel, OKU Dental Honor Soc. Democrat. Jewish. Avocations: travel, photography, biking, collecting antiques. Office: Mark S Cohen 940 Federal Rd Brookfield CT 06804-1144 Office Phone: 203-775-5533. Personal E-mail: mscddspc@aol.com, mscddspc@mindspring.com.

COHEN, MARLENE LOIS, pharmacologist; b. New Haven, May 5, 1945; d. Abraham David and Jeanette (Bader) C.; m. Jerome H. Fleisch, Aug. 8, 1976; children: Abby Fleisch, Sheryl Fleisch. BS, U. Conn., 1968; PhD, U. Calif., San Francisco, 1973. Registered pharmacist, Calif., Conn. Postdoctoral fellow Roche Inst. of Molecular Biology, Nutley, N.J., 1973-75; sr. pharmacologist Eli Lilly & Co., Indpls., 1975-80, rsch. scientist, 1980-85, sr. rsch. scientist, 1985-89, rsch. advisor, 1989-94, Lilly Rsch. fellow, 1994—2002; co-founder Creative Pharmacol. Solutions LLC, Carmel, Ind., 2002—. Adj. asst. prof. dept. pharmacology and toxicology Ind. U. Sch. Medicine, Indpls., 1976-82, adj. assoc. prof., 1982-86, adj. prof., 1987—; rsch. asst. Pfizer Labs., Groton, Conn., 1967; cons. Drug Dependence Inst., Yale U., New Haven, 1974. Mem. editl. bd. Jour. Clin. and Exptl. Hypertension, 1978—99, Procs. of the Soc. for Exptl. Biology and Medicine, 1979-84, Life Sci., 1984—, Jour. Pharmacology and Exptl. Therapeutics, 1987—, Current Drugs: Serotonin 1992—, Current Topics in Pharmacology, 1994—;, Molecular Interventions Adv. Bd., 1999-; ad hoc reviewer for profl. jours.; author: (with others) Principles of Medicinal Chemistry, 1974, 3d edit., 1989, New Antihypertensive Drugs, 1976, The Serotonin Receptors, 1988, The Peripheral Actions of 5-Hydroxytryptamine, 1989, Central and Peripheral 5-HT3 Receptors, 1992; contbr. articles to profl. jours. Recipient Disting. Alumni award, U. Conn. Sch. Pharmacy, 2002. Mem. Soc. for Exptl. Biology and Medicine, Am. Soc. for Pharmacology and Exptl. Therapeutics (chair subcom. on women in pharmacology 1984-89, chairperson nominating com. 1984, com. on profl. affairs 1984-89, membership com. 1989-92, bd. publs. trustees 1989—95, pres. 2001), Serotonin Club (councilor 1987-90, nomenclature com. 1988—2000), Alpha Lambda Delta, Phi Kappa Phi, Rho Chi. Office: Creative Pharmacol Solutions LLC 10532 Coppergate Ste 101 Carmel IN 46032 E-mail: marlenelcohen@aol.com.

COHEN, MARTIN BRUCE, physician; b. Bayshore, N.Y., Nov. 2, 1954; BA, Brandeis Univ., 1976; MD, SUNY, 1980. Diplomate Am. Bd. Internal Medicine, Am. Bd. Cardiovasc. Disease. Attending physician Westchester County Medical Ctr., Valhalla, N.Y., 1985—. Fellow Am. Coll. Cardiology, mem. Medical Soc. State N.Y. Office: Cardiology Cons Westchester Westchester County Med Ctr Valhalla NY 10595

COHEN, MARVIN A., writer; b. N.Y.C., Feb. 3, 1932; s. Phillip and Minnie Cohen; m. Mary Catherine Quinn-Cohen, Feb. 17, 1982; children: Lauren Bufi, Dina. BA, Bklyn. Coll., 1958; MA, Columbia U., 1963. Cert. ednl. and vocat. counselor N.Y. Bd. Edn. English tchr., counselor N.Y.C. Bd. Edn., 1959—87; instr. psychology Mercy Coll., Dobbs Ferry, NY, 1982—89, Elmira (N.Y.) Coll., 1995—99; writer, presenter sales workshops Broome C.C., Binghamton, NY, 1997—99. Author: Dodgers-Giants Rivalry: 1900-1957, 1999, An Innocent Murderer, Doc Farrell's Odyssey, (plays) Baseball in Broome County, Hockey in Broome County, Why Not Marlow?. Home: 416 Main St Vestal NY 13850-1536

COHEN, MARY ANN, federal judge; b. Albuquerque, July 16, 1943; d. Gus R. and Mary Carolyn (Avriette) C. BS, UCLA, 1964; JD, U. So. Calif., 1967. Bar: Calif. 1967. Ptnr. Abbott & Cohen, P.C. and predecessors, L.A., 1967-82; judge U.S. Tax Ct., Washington, 1982—, chief judge, 1996-2000. Mem. ABA (sect. taxation), Legion Lex. Republican. Office: US Tax Ct 400 2nd St NW Washington DC 20217-0002

COHEN, MELANIE ROVNER, lawyer; b. Chgo., Aug. 9, 1944; d. Millard Jack and Sheila (Fox) Rovner; m. Arthur Wieber Cohen, Feb. 17, 1968; children: Mitchell Jay, Stephanie Tomasky, Jennifer Sue, Jason Canel. AB, Brandeis U., 1965; JD, DePaul U., 1977. Bar: Ill. 1977, U.S. Dist. Ct. (no. dist.) Ill., U.S. Ct. Appeals (7th cir.). Law clk. to Justice F.J. Hertz U.S. Bankruptcy Ct., 1976-77; ptnr. Antonow & Fink, Chgo., 1977-89, Altheimer & Gray, Chgo., 1989—2003, Quarles & Brady, Chgo., 2003—. Mem. Supreme Ct. Ill. Atty. Registration and Disciplinary Commn. Inquiry Bd., 1982-86, Hearing Bd., 1986-94; instr. secured and consumer transactions creditor-debtor law DePaul U., Chgo., 1980-90; bd. dirs. Bankruptcy Arbitration and Mediation Svcs., 1994-96; instr. real estate and bankruptcy law John Marshall Law Sch. LLM program, Chgo., 1996-98, 2004-05. Contbr. articles to profl. jours. Panelist, spkr., bd. dirs., v.p. Brandeis U. Nat. Alumni Assn., 1981-90; life mem. Brandeis Nat. Women's Com., 1975—, pres. Chgo. chpt., 1975-82; mem. Glencoe (Ill.) Caucus, 1977-80; chair lawyers com. Ravinia Festival, 1990-91, chmn. sustaining com., 1991, mem. annual fund, 1991—. Brandeis U. fellow. Fellow: Am. Coll. Bankruptcy; mem.: ABA (co-chair com. on enforcement of creditors' rights and bankruptcy), Internat. Women's Insolvency and Restructuring Confederation, Internat. Fedn. Insolvency Profls., Internat. Insolvency Inst., Turnaround Mgmt. Assn. (pres. Chgo./midwest chpt. 1990—92, internat. bd. dirs. 1990—2004, mem. mgmt. com. 1995—2003, pres. internat. bd. dirs. 1999—2000, chmn. internat. bd. dirs. 2000—01), Comml. Fin. Assn. Edn. Found. (bd. govs.), Ill. Trial Lawyers Assn., Comml. Law League, Chgo. Bar Assn. (chmn. bankruptcy reorgn. com. 1983—85), Ill. State Bar Assn. Home: 167 Park Ave Glencoe IL 60022-1351 Office: Quarles & Brady 500 W Madison Ave Ste 3700 Chicago IL 60661 Office Phone: 312-715-5050. Business E-Mail: mcohen@quarles.com.

COHEN, MELVIN IRWIN, retired communications systems and technology executive; b. N.Y.C., June 25, 1936; s. Alexander and Fannie (Becker) C.; m. Elaine Chesin; children: Daniel Marc, Martha Rachel. SB, MIT, 1957, SM, 1958; PhD, Rensselaer Poly. Inst., 1965. Engr. Pratt & Whitney Aircraft, East Hartford, Conn., 1958-61; mem. tech. staff, supr. Bell Telephone Labs., Murray Hill, N.J., 1964-72; asst. dir. Western Elec. Co., Princeton, N.J., 1972-79; dept. head AT&T Bell Labs., Murray Hill, 1979-82, dir. Whippany, N.J., 1982-87, Murray Hill, 1987, v.p. mfg. R&D Princeton, 1987-88, exec. dir., 1988-90, exec. dir. electronics and photonics div. Breinigsville, Pa., 1990-93, v.p. rsch. effectiveness Murray Hill, N.J., 1993-96, Bell Labs/Lucent Techs., Murray Hill, 1996-2000; ret., 2000. Mem. panel on assessment of Nat. Inst. Standards and Tech. Programs, NRC, 1990-96; trustee AT&T Found., 1993-96; mem. sci. policy bd. Rutgers U., Newark, 1993-96. Patentee in laser tech. Trustee Temple Sinai Summit, N.J., 1977-79, N.J. Prison Complex, Trenton, 1975-83; bd. advisors Rahway Lifers Program, 1979-83; mem. deptl. adv. bd. Rensselaer Poly. Inst., 1988-92, mem. exec. bd. Anderson Ctr. for Innovation in Undergrad. Edn., 1992-98. Named Key Exec., Rensselaer Poly. Inst., 1986-99, chmn. Key Exec. Program, 1994-95; recipient Clarence E. Davies medal for engring. achievement, 1993, Fellow award Rensselaer Poly. Inst. Alumni Assn., 1993. Fellow IEEE (3d Millennium medal), Optical Soc. Am.; mem. AAAS, IEEE Lasers and Electrooptics Soc. (pres. 1989, Disting. Svc. award 2000). Home: 188 High Tor Dr Watchung NJ 07069-5412 Personal E-mail: micohennj@aol.com.

COHEN, MELVIN R., physician, educator; b. Chgo., May 24, 1911; s. Louis M. and Anna S. (Friedman) C.; m. Miriam, May 19, 1946; children: Nancy, Alan BS, U. Ill., 1931, MS in Pathology, 1933, MD, 1934. Diplomate: Am. Bd. Ob-Gyn. Practice medicine specializing in infertility, Chgo.; sr. attending physician Michael Reese Med. Ctr., Chgo., Northwestern Meml. Hosp.,

Chgo.; founder, dir. Fertility Inst. Ltd., Chgo.; prof. Northwestern U. Med. Sch., Chgo., prof. emeritus; guest vis. prof. first Martin Clyman postgrad. course in infertility Mount Sinai Hosp., N.Y.C., 1982. Author: Laparoscopy, Culdoscopy and Gynecography: Technique and Atlas, 1970; contbr. numerous chpts. in med. books and articles to med. jours. on infertility, endometriosis and Spinnbarkeit. Dir., producer: 8 teaching films on infertility; video films during surgery; ektochrome slides established world-wide technique. Pioneer use of Pergonal for stimulating ovulation. Served with MC, AUS, 1942-45. Co-recipient Gold Medal for Infertility exhibit AMA, 1951; recipient award for film on endometriosis 10th World Congress of Fertility and Sterility, Madrid, Spain, 1980, Lifetime Achievement award for contbns. to gynecologic endoscopy and women's health care Internat. Congress of Gynecologic Endoscopy, 1994; named honoree Internat. Soc. Gynecologic Endoscopy for pioneering work in laparoscopy, 1996, named Father of Modern American Laparoscopy, 1974. Fellow Chgo. Gynecol. Soc. (life); mem. AMA, Am. Fertility Soc., Am. Coll. Ob-Gyn., Am. Assn. Gynecol. Laparoscopists (Lifetime Achievement award Internat. Congress 1994), Internat. Fertility Assn., Internat. Family Planning Research Assn., Ill. State Med. Soc., Chgo. Gynecol. Soc., Kansas City Gynecol. Soc. (hon.), Los Angeles Gynecol. Soc., Inst. Medicine Chgo., Midwest Bio-Laser Inst., Indian Assn. Gynecol. Endoscopists (hon.), Soc. Reproductive Surgeons, Chgo. Assn. Reproductive Endocrinologists (pres. 1984-85), Sigma Xi, Alpha Omega Alpha. Address: 990 N Lake Shore Dr # 26C Chicago IL 60611-1366

COHEN, MICHAEL PAUL, statistician; b. San Mateo, Calif., July 8, 1947; s. Herman Charles and Evadna Fern (Tull) C. BA, U. Calif. San Diego, La Jolla, 1969; MA, UCLA, 1971, PhD, 1978. Math. statistician Bur. Labor Stats., Washington, 1978-87; math. statistician, cons. Nat. Ctr. Edn. Stats., Washington, 1987-2000, Bur. Transp. Stats., Washington, 2000—, asst. dir. for survey programs, 2002—. Reviewer Inst. for Statis. Math., Tokyo, 1988-92, Jour. Bus. and Econ. Stats., Washington, 1988, Annals of Stats., Hayward, Calif., 1991, Survey Methodology, 1998-2003 Jour. Ofcl. Stats., 1998-2003; tech. adv. bd. Nat. Ctr. Edn. Stats., Washington, 1987-2000; invited spkr. Internat. Stats. Inst., Seoul, Republic of Korea, 2001. Assoc. editor: Jour. Ofcl. Stats., 2003—, Jour. Am. Stats. Assn., 2004—; contbr. articles to profl. jours. Recipient cash awards U.S. Dept. Edn., 1987, 89, 90, 92, 93, 97, 98, 99, Quality Step Increases, U.S. Dept. Edn., 1988, 91, 94, 96, U.S. Dept. Transp., 2003. Fellow Washington Acad. Scis. (bd. mgrs. 1996—, sec. 1997-2000, pres.-elect 2002-03, pres. 2003—); mem. Inst. Math. Stats., Am. Statis. Assn., Am. Math. Soc., Am. Assn. Pub. Opinion Rsch. (assoc. treas. D.C. chpt. 2003, treas., 2004), Soc. Indsl. and Applied Math., Washington Statis. Soc. (bd. dirs. 1990—, Pres. award 1999), Calif. State Soc., Capital PC Users Group, Philos. Soc. of Washington (bd. dirs. 1999-2003), Washington Acad. Scis. (bd. mgrs. 1996—), Am. Assn. Pub. Opinion Rsch. (assoc. treas. D.C. chpt. 2003, treas. 2004-). Achievements include significant statistical contributions to index aggregation and expenditure weights, consumer price index revision; proof of admissibility of empirical distribution function. Office: Bur Transp Stats 400 7th St SW # 4432 Washington DC 20590-0001 E-mail: mcohen@cpcug.org.

COHEN, MICHAEL R., health facility administrator, pharmacist; Degree, Temple. U. Sch. Pharmacy. Pres. Inst. for Safe Medication, Huntingdon Valley, Pa., 1994—. Mem. Sentinel Event Adv. Group, Joint Commn. on Accreditation of Healthcare Orgns.; mem. Drug Safety and Risk Mgmt. Adv. Panel FDA; mem. Nat. Quality Forum's Evidence-Based Practices Steering Com. Author: Medication Errors, 1999; co-editor: ISMP Medication Safety Alert!; assoc. editor Hosp. Pharmacy jour., mem. editl. bd. Jour. Intravenous Nurse Soc., Healthcare Risk Control, Joint Commn. Jour. on Quality Improvement. Named Am. Druggist Top 50, 1997, 1998; recipient Prof. Anthony J. Amadio Disting. Lecture Award, Duquesne U., 1994, Nicholas Tucci Memorial Lecture Award, U. Pittsburgh, 1996, 1999, Sr. M. Gonzales Duffy Award, Penn. Society of Health-System Pharmacists, 1997, Am. Druggist Top 50, 1999, Award for Achievement, Sustained Contbn.- Lit. Pharmacy Practice in Health Systems, Am. Society of Health-System Pharmacists, 1998, Pharmacist of the Year, Am. Druggist, 1999. Office: Inst Safe Medication Practices 1800 Byberry Rd Ste 810 Huntingdon Valley PA 19006

COHEN, MILDRED THALER, art gallery director; b. NYC, Oct. 30, 1921; d. William and Dora (Snow) Intner; m. Seymour R. Thaler, June 17, 1945 (dec. 1976); children: Frederic I., Joan Thaler Zimmer; m. Sidney Cohen, Mar. 20, 1982. BA, Hunter Coll., 1942; BLS, Pratt Inst., 1943. Libr. Queens Borough Pub. Libr., NYC, 1943-44, Mus. of French Art, French Inst., NYC, 1944-46; dir. Marbella Gallery, Inc., NYC, 1971—. Author: (catalogues) Women Students of William Merritt Chase, 1973, Robert Hallowell, 1983, Eliot Clark, 1990, Tonalism, America's Gift to Landscape Painting, 1993, (brochures) Ethel Paxson, 1976, Three Generations of Wiggins, 1981, Samuel Rothbart, 1989, Rachel V. Hartley, 1991, Frank Kleinholz, 1992, Anthony Springer, 1996, Joseph Margulies, 1997, Allen Blagden, 1998, Hildegarde Hamilton, 1999, Samuel Brecher, 1999, 2003, James Bowman Consor, 2001, 2004. Bd. dirs. Lenox Hill Settlement House, NYC, 1955—77. Mem. Appraisers Assn. Am., Hunter Coll. Alumni (pres. Queens chpt. 1951-54, past bd. dir., pres. scholarship and welfare fund 1958-60, mem. coll. art adv. com., named to Hall of Fame 1973). Democrat. Jewish. Home and Office: 28 E 72nd St New York NY 10021-4234 Office Phone: 212-288-7809. E-mail: marbella_gallery@aol.com.

COHEN, MILLARD STUART, diversified manufacturing company executive; b. Chgo., Jan. 17, 1939; s. Lawrence Irmas and Myra Paula (Littmann) C.; m. Judith E. Michel, Aug. 2, 1970 (dec. Dec. 1995); children: Amy Rose, Michele Lauren. BSEE, Purdue U., 1960. Design engr. GTE Automatic Electric Labs., Northlake, Ill., 1960-66; chief elec. engr. Nixdorff Krein Industries, St. Louis, 1966-68, dir. data processing, 1968-72, treas., 1970—, v.p., 1980-85, pres., 1985—, exec. v.p. Nixdorff Chain, 1972-76, pres. Grape Expectations, 1976, also bd. dirs. Mem. Mo. Wine Adv. Bd., 1980—, vice chmn., 1983, 93; mem. St. Louis County Restaurant Commn., 1979—, Augusta (Mo.) Wine Bd., 1981—. Dist. commr. Boy Scouts Am., 1968-72; judge Mo. State Fair; trustee Congl. Temple Israel. Recipient award of merit French Wine Commn., 1972. Mem. IEEE, Assn. for Computing Machinery, Internat. Wine and Food Soc. (gov. Ams. 1985—), Mensa, Les Amis du Vin, Chaine des Rotisseurs, Commanderie de Bordeaux, St. Louis Club. Home: 11233 Ladue Rd Saint Louis MO 63141-8318 E-mail: millardcohen@cs.com.

COHEN, MITCHELL S, political science professor; b. NYC; PhD, Columbia Univ. Prof Weissman Sch, Baruch Col, NYC. Co-editor: Dissent Mag; author: The Wager of Lucien Goldmann, 1994, Zion and State, 1987; editor: Princeton Readings in Political Thought, 1995, Rebels and Reactionaries: An ANthology of Great Political Stories, 1992; contbr. articles in prof jours, columns in newspapers. Office: Dissent magazine Suite 1201 310 Riverside Dr New York NY 10025 E-mail: mitchellcohen@aol.com.*

COHEN, MORREL HERMAN, physicist, biologist, educator; b. Boston, Sept. 10, 1927; s. David and Rose (Kemler) C.; m. Sylvia Zwein, June 18, 1950; children: Julie, Robert, Daniel, Lisa. BS in Physics, Worcester Poly. Inst., 1947, DSc (hon.), 1973; MA in Physics, Dartmouth Coll., 1948; PhD in Physics, U. Calif., Berkeley, 1952. Faculty U. Chgo., 1952-57, assoc. prof. physics, 1957-60, prof., 1960-72, prof. theoretical biology, 1968-72, Louis Block prof. physics and theoretical biology, 1972-81, com. developmental biology, 1973-74, publs. bd., 1969-70; acting dir. James Franck Inst., 1965-66, dir., 1968-71; dir. materials rsch. lab. NSF, 1977-81; sr. sci. advisor Corp. Rsch. Lab. Exxon Rsch. and Engring. Co., 1981-96. Cons. govt. and industry, 1953-81, 96—; vis. scientist NRC, Can., 1960, Xerox Corp., 1975, 78; disting. vis. scientist Rutgers U., 1998-99, dist. scientist 1999—; disting. scientist Princeton U., 2003—; vis. fellow Clare Hall U., Cambridge, 1972-73; Shrum lectr. Simon Fraser U., 1973; assoc. Clare Hall U. Cambridge, Eng., 1973-85; vis. prof. U. Va., 1976, Kyoto U., 1979; mem. adv. panel electrophysics NASA, 1962-66; mem. adv. com. Nat. Magnet Lab., 1963-66; mem. rev. com. solid state sci. and metallurgy div. Argonne Nat. Lab., 1964-67, chmn., 1966, bd. govs., 1982-89, sci. & tech. adv. com., 1983-91; chmn. Gordon Conf., 1968, 4th Internat. Conf. Armorphous and Liquid Semicondrs., 1971; mem. adv. com. Inst. Amorphous Studies, 1982—; mem. Army Basic Research Com., 1979-85, mem. steering com., 1980-85; adv. com. dept. physics U. Tex., Austin, 1982-91; chmn. vis. com. dept. Physics Colo. Sch. of Mines, 1987-94; vice chmn. IUPAP commn. on stats. mechanics, 1987-93; van der Waals prof. U. Amsterdam, 1991-92; panelist Doe Workshop on Effective Utilization of Solar Energy, 2005. Contbr. articles on physics of solids, liquids, gases, theoretical and developmental biology, geophysics, materials sci., chem. physics, chem. engring. and econophysics; assoc. editor Jour. Chem. Physics, 1960-63; mem. editl. bd. advanced physics monograph series McGraw-Hill Co., 1963-70; mem. editl. bd. The Physics of Condensed Matter, 1962-74, Advances in Chem. Physics, 1960-93; mem. publs. bd. U. Chgo., 1969-70; bd. editors Jour. Statis. Physics, 1970-75. AEC fellow, 1951-52, Guggenheim fellow, 1957-58, NSF sr. postdoctoral fellow Rome, 1964-65, Spl. fellow NIH, 1972-73. Fellow AAAS, Am. Phys. Soc. (divsn. coun. 1978-82, exec. com. solid state physics divsn. 1968-71, chmn. 1970, mem. panel on pub. affairs, 2002-05); mem. AAUP, Am. Inst. Physics, Nat. Acad. Scis. (class mem. com. 2003), N.Y. Acad. Scis., Sigma Xi (nat. lectr. 1966). Home: 1100 Crim Rd Bridgewater NJ 08807-1872 Office: Dept Physics and Astronomy Rutgers The State Univ NJ 136 Frelinghuysen Rd Piscataway NJ 08854-8019 E-mail: mhcohen@prodigy.net.

COHEN, MORRIS LEO, retired law librarian, educator; b. N.Y.C., Nov. 2, 1927; s. Emanuel and Anna (Frank) C.; m. Gloria Weitzner, Feb. 1, 1953; children— Havi, Daniel Asher. BA, U. Chgo., 1947; LLB, Columbia U., 1951; MLS, Pratt Inst., 1959. Bar: N.Y. bar 1951. Pvt. practice, N.Y.C., 1951-58; asst. law librarian Rutgers U. Law Sch., 1958-59, Columbia Law Sch., 1959-61; law librarian, assoc. prof. law State U. N.Y. at, Buffalo, 1961-63; Biddle law librarian, prof. law U. Pa. Law Sch., Phila., 1963-71; law librarian, prof. law Harvard U. Law Sch., 1971-81, Yale U. Law Sch., New Haven, 1981-91; prof. emeritus, 1991—. Lectr. Drexel Inst. Sch. Libr. Sci., 1964-70, Columbia Sch. Libr. Svc., 1965-70; vis. prof. Simmons Coll. Libr. Sch., 1977-80; mem. exec. bd. Phila. chpt. ACLU; bd. visitors Columbia U. Law Sch., 1977-95. Author: Legal Research in a Nutshell, 1968, 8th edit., 2003, How to Find the Law, 9th edit., 1989, Law and Science: A Selected Bibliography, 1980, Finding the Law, 2d edit., 1989, Law: The Art of Justice, 1992, A Guide to the Early Reports of the Supreme Court of the United States, 1995, The Bench and Bar: Great Legal Caricatures from Vanity Fair, 1997, Bibliography of Early American Law, 1998. Mem. Am. Antiquarian Soc. NEH grantee. Mem. ABA, ALA (chmn. law and polit. sci. sect. 1967-69), AAUP (pres. U. Pa. chpt. 1966-67), Am. Assn. Law Librs. (pres. 1970-71), Am. Soc. Legal History (hon. fellow), Jewish Publs. Soc. (v.p. 1975-80), Bibliog. Soc. Am., Internat. Assn. Law Librs., Grolier Club, Yale Club of N.Y.C. Jewish. Office: Yale U Sch Law PO Box 208215 New Haven CT 06520-8215 Office Phone: 203-432-4024. Business E-Mail: morris.cohen@yale.edu.

COHEN, MYRON, lawyer, educator; b. Paterson, N.J., Feb. 4, 1927; s. Jacob B. and Rose (Stone) C.; m. Nancy Kamin, Nov. 4, 1951 (div. 1960); m. Barbara Levitov, May 12, 1963; children: Peter Fredric, Lee Susan. BEE, Cornell U., 1948; LLB, Columbia U., 1951. Bar: N.Y. 1951, U.S. Dist. Ct. (so., ea. dists.) N.Y. 1955, U.S. Ct. Appeals (2nd cir.) 1960, U.S. Ct. Appeals (Fed. cir.) 1984, U.S. Supreme Ct. 1974. Staff atty. Union Switch and Signal, Swissvale, Pa., 1952-54; assoc. Levisohn, Niner & Cohen, N.Y.C., 1954-56; sr. ptnr. Hubbell, Cohen, Stiefel & Gross, N.Y.C., 1956-85, Cohen, Pontani, Lieberman & Pavane, N.Y.C., 1985—. Adj. prof. N.Y. Law Sch., 1970-2003; vis. lectr. Peking U. Law Sch., 2000—; bd. dirs. Tri Magna Corp.; sec. Medallion Funding Corp., N.Y.C., 1979-86, 86-96. Author: U.S. Patent Law and Practice, 1976, Recent Developments in U.S. Law of Intellectual Property, 1985. Chmn. Mayor's Subway Watchdog Commn., N.Y.C., 1974-76. Lt. j.g. USNR, 1944-57. Mem. ABA, N.Y. State Bar Assn., Assn. Bar City N.Y., N.Y. Intellectual Property Law Assn., Internat. Trademark Assn. Democrat. Jewish. Avocation: skiing. Home: Two Fifth Ave New York NY 10011 Office: Cohen Pontani Lieberman & Pavane 551 5th Ave Rm 1210 New York NY 10176-0091 Office Phone: 212-687-2770. E-mail: myron@cplplaw.com.

COHEN, N. JEROLD, lawyer; b. Pine Bluff, Ark., June 13, 1935; s. Maurice and Gertrude L. Cohen; children: Pamela, Lindsey L., Giles T. BBA, Tulane U., 1957; LLB magna cum laude, Harvard U., 1961. Bar: N.Y. 1962, Ga. 1966, D.C. 1966. Assoc. Cleary, Gottlieb, Steen and Hamilton, N.Y.C., 1961-65, Sutherland, Asbill, and Brennan, Atlanta, Washington, 1965, ptnr., 1968-79, 81—; chief counsel IRS, 1979-81, adv. coun., 1999-2000, chmn. Former pres., former mem. nat. bd. dirs. ACLU Ga.; chmn. Atlanta Cmty. Rels. Commn., 1976-79; trustee Am. Tax Policy Inst. 1st lt. U.S. Army, 1958. Recipient Gen. Counsel's award U.S. Dept. Treasury, Commrs. award IRS. Fellow Am. Bar Found.; mem. ABA (past chair tax sect.), FBA, Am. Law Inst., Am. Coll. Tax Counsel (regent, chair). Office: Sutherland Asbill & Brennan 999 Peachtree St NE Ste 2300 Atlanta GA 30309-3996 Office Phone: 404-853-8038. Business E-Mail: jerry.cohen@sablaw.com.

COHEN, NEAL S., former air transportation executive; BA, MBA, U. Chgo. Various positions in internat. fin., banking, planning GM, N.Y.C., 1984-91; dir. corp. planning Northwest Airlines Corp., St. Paul, 1991, from dir. mkt. planning to v.p. fin. and contr., 1992-99, sr. v.p., treas., 1999—2000; exec. v.p., CFO Budget Group Inc., 2000, Sylvan Learning Systems, 2000—01, Conseco Fin., 2001—02; exec. v.p., fin., CFO U.S. Airways, Inc., Arlington, Va., 2002—04.

COHEN, NELSON CRAIG, lawyer; b. Harrisburg, Pa., Nov. 8, 1947; s. Raymond and Rhea (Jaschik) C. BS in Acctg., Pa. State U., 1969; JD, George Washington U., 1973. Bar: Md. 1973, D.C. 1974. Assoc., ptnr. Levitan Ezrin West & Kerxton, Bethesda, Md., 1973-84; ptnr. Kerxton & Cohen Chartered, Bethesda, 1984-87, Zuckerman Spaeder LLP, Washington, 1987—. Speaker on bankruptcy matters. Mem. ABA (bus. banking sec.), Bankruptcy Bar Assn. Md., Montgomery County Bar Assn., Md. State Bar Assn. Republican. Jewish. Avocation: golf. Office: Zuckerman Spaeder LLP 1201 Connecticut Ave NW Washington DC 20036-2605 Office Phone: 202-778-1823. E-mail: ncohen@zuckerman.com.

COHEN, NERI MESHIVLAM, cardiologist; b. Washington, Feb. 21, 1961; s. Miamon Moses and Barbara (Milgrome) C.; m. Ilene Marcia Gudelsky, June 8, 1986; children: Dena Michal, Joel Alexander. BA with honors, MS with honors, Northwestern U., 1982; PhD, U. Md., 1987, MD, 1989. Intern Va. Commonwealth U., Richmond, 1989-90, resident, 1990-96, fellow cardiothoracic surgery, 1996—. Contbr. articles to profl. jours. Mem. AAAS, Am. Coll. Cardiology (affiliate), Am. Heart Assn. (affiliate), Am. Coll. Surgeons. Office: Va Commonwealth U Dept Surgery Box 980068 1200 E Broad St Richmond VA 23298-5025

COHEN, NICHOLAS, immunologist, educator; b. N.Y.C., Nov. 20, 1938; s. Saris and Frances (Pakett) C.; m. Jayne Sevin Rogal, July 1, 1962 (div. 1972); children: Jaime Anne, Jessica Sevin; m. Catharina Johanna van der Harst, Oct. 23, 1974; children: Misha Thomas, Mark Sebastian. AB, Princeton U., 1959; PhD, U. Rochester, 1965. Asst. prof. microbiology and immunology Sch. Medicine and Dentistry U. Rochester, NY, 1967-73, assoc. prof., 1973-80, prof. microbiology, immunology and psychiatry, 1980—2004, dir. divsn. immunology, 1980—2004, prof. oncology, 1997—2004, prof. emeritus, 2004—; assoc. dir. Ctr. for Psychoneuroimmunology Rsch., Rochester. Vis. prof. Agrl. U., Wageningen, The Netherlands, 1982-83; mem. Basel Inst. for Immunology, Switzerland, 1975-76; mem. peer rev. bds. NIH, 1976-80; cons. NIH study sects., NIMH study sects., NSF. Co-author: Monograph; assoc. editor Brain, Behavior and Immunity Jour., Devel. Comparative Immunology; editor 5 books; contbr. articles to profl. jours. Postdoctoral scholar in immunology UCLA, 1965-67, Fulbright scholar, 1982-83; grantee NIH, NIMH, NSF, 1967—; recipient Rsch. Career Devel. award NIH, 1974-78, NIH Merit award, 1987-97. Mem. Am. Soc. Zoologists (chmn. divsn. comparative immunology 1977-79), Transplantation Soc., Am. Soc. Immunologists, Brit. Soc. Immunology, Internat. Soc. Devel. and Comparative Immunology (v.p. the Americas 1994-2000), Psychoneuroimmunology Rsch. Soc. (councilor 1993-97). Democrat. Avocations: music, travel. Home: 211 Highland Pkwy Rochester NY 14620-2544

COHEN, NOEL LEE, otolaryngologist, educator; b. N.Y.C., Sept. 20, 1930; s. Victor Max and Esther Lily (Schonfeld) C.; m. Baukje Philippina Boersma, June 1, 1957; 1 child, Mark Bennett. AB, NYU, 1951; MD, U. Utrecht, The Netherlands, 1957; MD with honors, U. Freiburg, 2002. Intern Stads-en Academi Ziekenhuis, Utrecht, 1955-57; resident in otolargyngology Bellevue Med. Ctr. NYU, N.Y.C., 1959-62, instr. Sch. Medicine, 1962-64, asst. prof., 1964-69, assoc. prof., 1969-73, clin. prof., 1973-80, prof. otolargyngology, 1980—, chmn. dept. otolaryngology, 1981—2003, interim dean, provost Sch. Medicine, 1997-98, vice dean for clin. affairs, 1998-99, sr. advisor to dean, 2000—, Mendik Found. prof., 1999—2003, prof. otolaryngology, 2003—; pres. NYU Hosp. Ctr., 1998. Bd. dirs. League for Hard of Hearing, Am. Auditory Soc.; mem. adv. bd. Self Help for Hard of Hearing People, 1995, Alexander Graham Bell Assn., Acoustic Neuroma Assn.; sci. adv. bd. Sci. Deafness Rsch. Found., 2000—. Mem. editl. bd. Jour. of Otology & Neurotology, 1986-2004, Otolaryngology-Head and Neck Surgery, Internat. Cochlear Implant Jour., 1999—; reviewer articles and books for profl. jours.; contbr. numerous articles to profl. jours.; author chpts. in books. Lt. USNR, 1957—59. Fellow: ACS; mem.: N.Y. Acad. Scis., N.Y. Otol. Soc. (pres. 1998—99), Soc. Acad. Depts. Otolaryngology, Soc. Univ. Otolaryngologists, Am. Neuro-Otol. Soc., N.Am. Skull Base Soc., N.Y. Head and Neck Soc. (charter mem., pres. 1984), N.Y. State Soc. Otolaryngology-Head and Neck Surgery (pres. 1988—89), N.Y. Acad. Medicine, Am. Otol. Soc., Am. Bronchoesophagol. Assn., Am. Soc. Head and Neck Surgery, Rhinol. and Otol. Soc., Am. Laryngol., Am. Acad. Otolaryngology-Head-Neck Surgery (Honor award 1985, Disting. Svc. award 2001). Democrat. Avocations: tennis, skiing, gardening, carpentry. Office: NYU Med Ctr 530 1st Ave New York NY 10016-6402 Office Phone: 212-263-7373. Business E-Mail: noel.cohen@med.nyu.edu.

COHEN, NORM, chemist; b. NYC, Dec. 13, 1936; s. Moshe and Yetta (Pickman) C.; m. Anne Elizabeth Billings, July 11, 1959 (div. 1987); children: Alexandra Elizabeth Rachel, Carson Benjamin; m. Verni Greenfield, Feb. 6, 1987; 1 child, Matthew Jonathan Greenfield. BA in Chemistry, Reed Coll., 1958; MA in Math., U. Calif., Berkeley, 1960, PhD in Chemistry, 1963. Mem. tech. staff Aerospace Corp., El Segundo, Calif., 1963—72, head dept. chem. kinetics, 1972—84, sr. scientist, 1984—94; adj. asst. prof. chemistry U. Portland, 1995—99, Portland C.C., 1995—. Exec. sec. John Edwards Mem. Forum, LA, 1969—94. Author: Long Steel Rail, 1981, 2d edit., 2000 (Chgo. Folklore prize 1982, Deems Taylor award ASCAP 1982, Botkin prize Am. Folklore Soc. 1983), Traditional Anglo-American Folk Music: An Annotated Disography of Published Recordings, 1994, A Finding List of American Secular Songsters Published 1860-99, 2002, Folk Music: A Regional Exploration, 2005; editor: Ozark Folk Songs, 1982, John Edwards Meml. Forum Quar., 1966-83, 85-86; asst. editor Internat. Jour. Chem. Kinetics, 1977-83, editor, prodr. album Minstrels and Tunesmiths, 1982 (Grammy nomination 1982); contbr. articles and revs. to chemistry and folk, music jours. Grantee NEA, NEH, DOE, EPA, NIST. Mem.: Am. Chem. Soc., Assn. for Recorded Sound Collections, Soc. Am. Music. Democrat. Jewish. Achievements include research and publications in combustion chemistry, atmospheric chemistry, thermochemistry, chemistry of high energy chemical lasers. Home: 3001 Grant St Vancouver WA 98660-2053 E-mail: ncohen@teleport.com.

COHEN, NORTON JACOB, lawyer; b. Detroit, Nov. 5, 1935; s. Norman and Molly Rose (Natinsky) C.; m. Lorelei Freda Schuman, June 16, 1957 (dec. Jan. 1998); children: Debrah Anne, Sander Ivan. Student, U. Mich., 1953-55, U. Detroit, 1955-56; JD, Wayne State U., 1959. Bar: Mich. 1959, Tex. 1962, U.S. Dist. Ct. (ea. dist.) Mich. 1963, U.S. Ct. Appeals (6th cir.) 1966, U.S. Supreme Ct. 1970. Law clk. to presiding justice Mich. Supreme Ct., Lansing, 1959; assoc. Zwerdling, Miller, Klimist & Maurer, Detroit, 1963—68; legal dir. ACLU of Mich., Detroit, 1968—69; sr. dir. Miller, Cohen, Martens, Ice & Geary, P.C., Southfield, Mich., 1971—97, Miller Cohen, P.L.C., Detroit, 1997—. Chmn. Southfield (Mich.) Dem. Party, 1965-67; co-chair Robert F. Kennedy for Pres., Oakland County, Mich., 1968; mem. exec. bd. Met. Detroit ACLU, 1969-93, chmn., 1972-74; vice chair Equal Justice Coun., Detroit, 1970-74; spl. counsel workers compensation Mich. AFL-CIO, 1983-86; mem. dir.'s adv. coun. Workers Compensation Bur., Mich. Dept. Labor, 1986-1999. Served to capt. JAGC, U.S. Army, 1960-63. Decorated Army Commendation medal; recipient Spirit of Detroit award Detroit Common Coun., 1982; elected to Mich. Workers' Compensation Hall of Fame, 2000. Mem. ABA (labor co-chair workers compensation com. sect. labor and employment law 1989-96, 2005—), Fed. Bar Assn., B'nai B'rith, Am. Jewish Com. Jewish. Office: Miller Cohen PLC 600 W Lafayette Blvd Fl 4 Detroit MI 48226-3125 Office Phone: 313-964-4454. Business E-Mail: yourlawyers@millercohen.com.

COHEN, PAUL JOSEPH, mathematician; b. Long Branch, N.J., Apr. 2, 1934; Student, Bklyn. Coll., 1950—53; M, U. Chgo., 1954, PhD, 1958. Instr. U. Rochester, 1957—58, MIT, 1958—59; fellow Inst. Advanced Study, Princeton U., 1959—61; faculty Stanford (Calif.) U., 1961—, prof. math., 1964—, named Marjorie Mhoon Fair prof. Quantitative Sci. Recipient Bôcher Meml. prize, Am. Math. Soc., 1964, Fields medal, Internat. Congress Math., Moscow, 1966, Nat. medal Sci., 1967. Mem.: NAS. Achievements include a technique called forcing to prove the independence in set theory of the axiom of choice and of the generalised continuum hypothesis. Office: Stanford U Dept Math Bldg 380 Rm 383T Stanford CA 94305-2125*

COHEN, PERRY D., management consultant; b. Atlanta, May 27, 1946; s. Bernard W. and Rae Alice Cohen; m. Rosalie Mandelbaum, Aug. 16, 1975; children: Shayna K., Jonah B. BS, Carnegie-Mellon U., 1968; MS, MIT, 1971, PhD, 1979. Assoc. engr. Lockheed Ga. Co., Marietta, 1968-69; rsch. analyst Blue Cross-Blue Shield of Mass., Boston, 1971-72; instr. bus. MIT, Cambridge, 1972-75; rsch. assoc. Assn. Am. Med. Colls., Washington, 1975-77; sr. assoc. Urban Systems Rsch., Washington, 1977-79; pres. Perry Cohen Assocs., Washington, 1979—, Unison Corp., Bethesda, 1987-89. Adj. assoc. prof. U. Md., 1991—; dir. health svcs. rsch. Parkinsons Disease Found., 1998—. Contbr. articles to profl. jours. Trustee Group Health Assn., Washington, 1986-92, Consumer Health Found., 1995-96, Medstar Rsch. Inst., 1998-2001; trustee Nat. Capital chpt., Am. Parkinson's Disease Assn., 1996-98, v.p., 1997-98. MIT Spl. Rsch. fellow, 1972-75; grantee NIH, 1986-87, Nat. Cancer Inst., 1985-86. Mem. Am. Pub. Health Assn., Manpower Analysis and Planning Soc. (from v.p. to prs. 1981-83), Assn. Health Svcs. Rsch., Acad. Mgmt., Soc. for Health Care Planning and Mktg. Home: 3914 Harrison St NW Washington DC 20015-1938

COHEN, PHILIP HERMAN, accountant; b. Bklyn., Dec. 4, 1936; s. David J. and Toby (Jaeger) C.; m. Susan Rudd; children: Davina Ellen, Tobias Samuel Dory. BS, NYU, 1957. From acct. to ptnr. Touche Ross & Co., N.Y.C., 1957-81; exec. v.p. fin., CFO Integrated Resources, Inc., N.Y.C., 1981-86, sr. exec. v.p. fin., CFO, 1986-90; fin. and real estate cons. Philip H. Cohen & Co., Cedarhurst, N.Y., 1990—. Chmn. bd. dirs., pres., CEO FRMT Ltd. (A Bermuda Mut. Ins. Co.), 1996—99; bd. dirs. FMRT Ltd. (A Bermuda Mut. Ins. Co.); chmn. exec. com. FRMT Ltd. (A Bermuda Mut. Ins. Co.), 1999—2001; bd. dirs. Diwal Corp., Mitcor Corp., Odin Mgmt. Corp., Sy Sims Sch. Bus. Yeshiva U.; chmn. bd. dirs. Fraternity Risk Mgmt. Trust, 1994—99, chmn. exec. com., 1999—2000. Bd. dirs. Alpha Epsilon Pi Found., Inc., 1976—, Nat. Interfrat. Conf., 1975-86, Nat. Interfrat. Found., 1996—, State of Israel Bonds, N.Y.; bd. dirs. Sutton Pl. Synagogue, 1984-99, v.p., 1993-99; bd. dirs. joint purchasing com. Fedn. Jewish Philanthropies, 1977-78; mem. Cmty. Bd. Manhattan, N.Y., 1992—; internat. bd. dirs. Hillel Found. for Jewish Student Campus Life, 1999—. Recipient State of Israel Bond Peace award 1983, Accts. Bankers and Fin. award Am. Jewish Congress, 1984, Gold medal Nat. Interfraternity Conf., 1994, Disting. Svc. award Fraternity Exec. Assn., 1999. Mem. Found. Acctg. Edn., Am. Inst. CPA's (real estate com. 1987-90), N.Y. State Soc. CPA's (admissions com. 1968-69, chmn. fin. and leasing com. 1972-74, com. on rels. with the bar 1974-76, com. on real estate acctg. 1976-79, com. ins. 1980-81, fin. acctg.

standards com. 1983-86, chmn. mem.-in-industry com. 1981-83, chief fin. officers com. 1984-86, furtherance com. 1986, annual conf. com. 1985-87, com. on ops. 1987-88, bd. dirs. 1983-86, v.p. 1985-86, Outstanding CPA in Industry award 1986), Fin. Execs. Inst., Am. Acctg. Assn., Nat. Assn. Accts., Soc. Ins. Accts., Alpha Epsilon Pi (supreme gov. 1966-73, nat. pres. 1974-76, mem. fiscal control bd. 1977-81, vice chmn. 1981-92, chmn. 1992—), Beta Alpha Psi, Areopagus Clubs: N.Y. Alumni of Alpha Epsilon Pi. Lodges: Masons. Jewish. Home: 30 Beekman Pl New York NY 10022-8060 Office: 123 Grove Ave Cedarhurst NY 11516-2302 Office Phone: 516-371-5215.

COHEN, PRESTON SCOTT, architecture educator; BFA, RISD, 1982, BArch, 1983; MArch, Harvard U. With Contects Cons. and Archs., Austin, Tex., 1978, Kinney and Stone, Archs., Austin, 1979, Albert Ledner, Arch., New Orleans, 1980, Peter Eisenman, Arch., N.Y.C., 1984, Hardy Holzman Pfeiffer Assocs., N.Y.C., 1986—87, Prentice and Chan, Ohlhausen Archs., N.Y.C., 1988; design critic in arch. Harvard Grad. Sch. Design, Cambridge, Mass., 1989—92, asst. prof. arch., 1992—95, assoc. prof. arch., 1995—2001, prof. arch., 2002—03, Gerald M. McCue prof. arch., 2003—, dir. MArch Degree Programs Harvard Design Sch., 2003—. Mem. dean's adv. acad. rev. com. Harvard Design Sch., Cambridge, 2000—; vis. faculty European Honors Summer Program in Rome RISD, 1993—; vis. assoc. prof. arch. Princeton (N.J.) U. Sch. Arch., 1997; adj. asst. prof. arch. Ohio State U., 1997. Exhibitions include Grad. Sch. Design, 1990, 1994, 1996, 1997, Archtl. League N.Y., 1992, Boston Ctr. for the Arts, 1993, Archtl. Assn., London, 1996, VI Venice Biennale Internat. Exhbn. Arch., 1996, Gallery Joe, Phila., 1998, Rensselaer Poly. Inst., 1998, Phila. Art Alliance, 1999, Internat. Exhbn. Arch., Glasgow, 1999, Armand Hammer Mus. Art, UCLA, 1999, Walker Art Ctr., Mpls., 1999, MAK, Vienna, 1999, Mus. Modern Art, N.Y., 1999, Mucsarnok/Kunsthalle, Budapest, 1999, Columbia U., 2000, Heinz Archtl. Ctr., Carnegie Mus. Art, Pitts., 2001, 3rd Internat. Archtl. Conf., Orleans, France, 2001, Mus. Art and Tech., N.Y., 2001, Thomas Erben Gallery, 2001, Represented in permanent collections Mus. Modern Art, Heinz Archtl. Ctr., Carnegie Mus. Art, Pitts. Recipient Young Archs. award, Archtl. League N.Y., 1992, Progressive Arch. award in arch., 1998, 2000. Office: Harvard Grad Sch Design 48 Quincy St Cambridge MA 02138

COHEN, RACHELLE SHARON, journalist; b. Phila., Oct. 21, 1946; d. Hyman and Diane Doris (Schultz) Goldberg; m. Stanley Martin Cohen, June 22, 1968; 1 child, Avril Heather. BS, Temple U., 1968. Editor Somerville (Mass.) Jour., 1968—70; reporter Lowell (Mass.) Sun, 1970—72, AP, Boston, 1972—79; state house bur. chief Boston Herald Am., 1979—80, editl. page editor, 1980—82; editl. page editor, columnist Boston Herald, 1982—. Mem.: Mass. Assn. Mental Health (bd. dirs. 1993—), Mass. Bar Assn. (bench, bar, press com.). Office: Boston Herald 1 Herald St Boston MA 02118-2200

COHEN, RAYMOND, mechanical engineer, educator; b. St. Louis, Nov. 30, 1923; s. Benjamin and Leah (Lewis) C.; m. Katherine Elise Silverman, Feb. 1, 1948 (dec. May 1985); children: Richard Samuel, Deborah Elise, Barbara Beth; m. Lila Lakin Cagen, Nov. 30, 1986. BS, Purdue U., 1947, MS, 1950, PhD, 1955. Instr. mech. engring. Purdue U., 1948-55, asst. prof., 1955-58, assoc. prof., 1958-60, prof., 1960-98, asst. dir. Ray W. Herrick Labs., 1970-71, dir., 1971-93, acting head Sch. Mech. Engring., 1988-89, Herrick prof. engring., 1994-99, Herrick prof. emeritus engring., 1999—. Cons. to industry. Departmental editor: Ency. Brit., 1957-62; editorial bd. Jour. Sound and Vibration, 1971-87; editor Internat. Jour. of Heating, Ventilating, Air Conditioning and Refrigerating Rsch., 1994-98. Served as sgt. inf. AUS, 1943-46. Recipient Kamerlingh Onnes gold medal, 1995; NATO sr. fellow in sci., 1971 Fellow ASME, ASHRAE; mem. NSPE, Am. Soc. Engring. Edn., Soc. Exptl. Mechanics, Internat. Inst. Refrigeration (chmn. U.S. nat. com. 1992-95, U.S. del. 1992-99, Merit medal 2003), Acoustical Soc. Am., Inst. Noise Control Engring. (pres. 1990), Sigma Xi, Pi Tau Sigma, Tau Beta Pi. Home: 2501 Spyglass Dr Valparaiso IN 46383 Office: Purdue U Ray W Herrick Labs 140 S Intramural Dr West Lafayette IN 47907-2031 Personal E-mail: rcohen81@comcast.net.

COHEN, RICHARD MARTIN, journalist; b. N.Y.C., Feb. 6, 1941; s. Harry Louis and Pearl (Rosenberg) C.; m. Barbara Stubbs, May 3, 1969 (div.); m. Leslie Feely, July 17, 1992; 1 son, Alexander Prescott. BS, N.Y. U., 1967; MS in Journalism, Columbia U., 1968. With UPI, 1967-68; gen. assignment reporter Washington Post, 1968-76, syndicated columnist, 1976—. Author: A Heartbeat Away, 1973. Office: Washington Post Co 251 W 57th St New York NY 10019-1802 Office Phone: 212-445-4901. E-mail: cohenr@washpost.com.

COHEN, RICHARD NORMAN, insurance executive; b. NYC, Oct. 28, 1923; s. Norman M. and Janet (Goldsmith) C.; m. Ann Robertson, Oct. 25, 1975; children: Daniel Hays, James Matthew; 1 stepchild, Mark Thompson. Grad., Phillips Exeter Acad., 1941; BA, Yale U., 1945. Salesman Cohen, Goldman & Co., N.Y.C., 1947-50; mens fashion editor Fawcett Publs., N.Y.C., 1951-52; life ins. broker Mass. Mut. Life Ins. Co., N.Y.C., 1954—; account exec. John M. Riehle, Inc., N.Y.C., 1961-63, v.p., 1963-83, Leonard Newman Agy. Inc., White Plains, N.Y., 1984-94, Arthur Gallagher & Co., White Plains, 1994-2000; dir. Silver Hill Hosp., New Canaan, Conn., 1997—2004. Dir. NY Times, 1960—72, Silver Hill Hosp., 1996—2002. Served to 2d lt. USAAF, 1943-45. Mem. Country Club of New Canaan, Yale Club (N.Y.C.), Century Country Club (White Plains, N.Y.), Beta Theta Pi. Republican. Jewish. Home: 1062 Ponus Rdg New Canaan CT 06840-3420 Personal E-mail: RNCI@optonline.net.

COHEN, ROBERT ABRAHAM, retired physician; b. Chgo., Nov. 13, 1909; s. Ezra Harry and Catherine (Kurzon) C.; m. Mabel Jean Blake, Mar. 21, 1933 (dec. Oct. 1972); children— Donald Edward, Margery Jean; m. Alice L. Muth, Mar. 31, 1974. BS, U. Chgo., 1930, PhD, MD, 1935. Intern Michael Reese Hosp., Chgo., 1936-37; resident Henry Phipps Psychiat. Clinic Johns Hopkins U., 1937-38; resident Sheppard-Pratt Hosp., Towson, Md., 1938-39, 40-41; sr. fellow Inst. Juvenile Research, Chgo, 1939-40; pvt. practice psychiatry Washington, 1946-48; clin. dir. Chestnut Lodge, Rockville, Md., 1948-53, dir. psychotherapy, 1981-91; dir. clin. investigations NIMH, Bethesda, Md., 1953-69, dir. div. clin. and behavioral research, 1969-81, dep. dir. intramural research program, 1969-81. Pres. Washington Sch. Psychiatry, 1973-82; bd. dirs. Founds. Fund for Rsch. in Psychiatry, 1960-63, chmn. bd., 1962-63; trustee William Alanson White Psychiat. Found. Served from lt. (j.g.) to comdr. M.C. USNR, 1941-46. Recipient HEW Disting. Svc. award, 1970, Salmon medal N.Y. Acad. Scis., 1978, Fromm-Reichmann award Am. Acad. Psychoanylsis, 1979, Woodley House award, 1982. Fellow Am. Psychiat. Assn. (disting. life); mem. Am. Psychoanalytical Assn., Am. Psychopathol. Assn., Assn. Rsch. in Nervous and Mental Disease, Washington Psychoanalytic Soc. (pres. 1951-53), Washington Psychiat. Soc. (pres. 1958-59), Washington Psychoanalytic Inst. (chmn. edn. com. 1955-59), Washington Acad. Medicine, Cosmos Club. Home: 5216 Elsmere Ave Bethesda MD 20814-5734 Personal E-mail: alibob@starpower.net.

COHEN, ROBERT EDWARD, chemical engineering professor, consultant; b. Oil City, Pa., Jan. 21, 1947; s. David M. and Minnie E. Cohen; m. D. Jane Woodman, Nov. 18, 1978; children: Genevieve Elizabeth, Eliot Lee. BS with distinction, Cornell U., 1968; MS, Calif. Inst. Tech., 1970, PhD, 1972. Postdoctoral rsch. fellow Calif. Inst. Tech., Pasadena, 1972; ICI rsch. fellow Oxford (Eng.) U., 1972-73; asst. prof. chem. engring. MIT, Cambridge, 1973-75, Harold and Esther Edgerton asst. prof., 1975-77, assoc. prof., 1977-82, prof., 1982—, founding dir. program in polymer sci. and tech., 1985-88, Bayer prof. chem. engring., 1988-95, St. Laurent prof. chem. engring., 1995—, assoc. chmn. of faculty, 1989-91, chem. engring. grad. officer, 1992-01, founding dir. PhD in Chem. Engring. Practice degree program; co-dir. DuPont-MIT Alliance, 2000—. Vis. appt. Sandia Nat. Labs., Albuquerque, summer 1979, Istituto Guido Donegani, Novara, Italy, 1981-82; vis. prof. dept. chemistry Harvard U., 1989; co-founder, bd. dirs., cons. MatTek Corp., Ashland, Mass., 1985—; bd. dirs. Kiser Rsch., Inc., Washington, 1992-94; chmn. sci. adv. bd. William and Mary Greve Found., NYC, 1988—, bd. dirs., 1997—; chair Nominations Com., 2005-. Co-editor: Jour. Polymer Engring.; mem. editorial adv. bd. Jour. Applied Polymer Sci., 1989—, Chemistry of Materials, 1989-93; cons. editor AIP Series on Polymers and Complex Fluids, 1992-97; contbr. articles to profl. jours.; patentee in field. Bd. trustees The Advent Sch., Boston, 1996-99. Recipient Camille and Henry Dreyfus Tchr. Scholar award Dreyfus Found., 1977; Robert W. Vaughan Meml. lectr. Calif. Inst. Tech., 1984, Shell Disting. lectr. dept. materials sci. Northwestern U., 1996. Mem. AIChE (program chair materials divsn. polymer sect. 1993-97, dir. materials divsn. 1998-2001, Charles M.A. Stine award 2000), Am. Chem. Soc., Materials Rsch. Soc., Soc. Rheology, N.Y. Acad. Scis. Jewish. Avocation: golf. Office: MIT Dept Chem Engring Bldg 66 Rm 554 Cambridge MA 02139

COHEN, ROBERT SONNÉ, physicist, philosopher, educator; b. NYC, Feb. 18, 1923; m. Robin Gertrude Hirshhorn, June 18, 1944; children: Michael, Daniel, Deborah. BA, Wesleyan U., Middletown, Conn., 1943, LHD, 1986; MS, Yale U., 1943, PhD (NRC fellow), 1948. Instr. physics Yale U., 1943-44, instr. philosophy, 1949-51; sci. staff, war research div. Columbia U. and Communications Bd., U.S. Joint Chiefs Staff, 1944-46; asst. prof. physics and philosophy Wesleyan U., 1949-57; assoc. prof. physics Boston U., 1957-59, prof. physics and philosophy, 1959-93, chmn. dept. physics, 1959-73, chmn. dept. philosophy, 1986-88, prof. emeritus, 1993—; acting dean Coll. Liberal Arts, 1971-72. Chmn. Boston U. Center for Philosophy and History Sci., 1970-93, chmn. emeritus, 1993—; vis. lectr. humanities and philosophy of sci. Mass. Inst. Tech., 1958-59, 61-62; vis. prof. history of ideas Brandeis U., 1959-60; lectr. history and philosophy of sci. Am. U., Washington, summers 1958-68; vis. fellow Polish and Yugoslav Acad. Sci., 1963, Hungarian Acad. Sci., 1964; vis. prof. philosophy U. Calif., San Diego, 1969, Yale U., 1973; rsch. fellow history of sci. Harvard U., 1974; mem., chmn. U.S. Nat. Com. for Internat. Union History and Philosophy of Sci., 1969-75; trustee Wesleyan U., 1968-84, emeritus, 1984—; trustee Tufts U., 1984-93, emeritus, 1993—. Author, editor articles, books and jours. in field.; Editor: Boston Studies in Philosophy of Sci., Vienna Circle Collection, Sci. in Context. Trustee Bill of Rights Found. Am. Council Learned Soc. fellow philosophy and sci., 1948-49, Ford faculty fellow Cambridge, Eng., 1955-56, fellow Wissenschaftskolleg zu Berlin, 1983-84, Inst. fur Wissenschaften dem Menschen, Vienna, 1994; papers collected in Robert S. Cohen Collection at Howard Gotlieb Archival Rsch. Ctr., Boston U. Fellow AAAS (chmn. sect. L history and philosophy of sci. 1978-79), Am. Phys. Soc.; mem. AAUP, Am. Assn. Physics Tchrs., Am. Philos. Assn. (exec. com. 1988-91), History Sci. Soc., Philosophy Sci. Assn. (v.p. 1972-75, pres. 1982-84), Nat. Emergency Civil Liberties Com. (mem. nat. coun.), Am. Inst. Marxist Studies (chmn. 1964-82), Fedn. Am. Scientists (nat. coun. 1967-70), Inst. for Unity of Sci. (exec. com. 1960-74). Home: 44 Adams Ave Watertown MA 02472-1391 Office: Boston U Dept Philosophy 745 Commonwealth Ave Boston MA 02215-1401 Personal E-mail: robertscohen@hotmail.com.

COHEN, ROBERT STEPHAN, lawyer; b. N.Y.C., Jan. 14, 1939; s. Abraham and Florence C.; children: Christopher, Ian, Nicholas; m. Stephanie J. Stiefel, Jan. 29, 1998. BA, Alfred U., 1959; LLB, Fordham U., 1962. Bar: N.Y. 1963, U.S. Dist. Ct. (so. and ea. dists.) N.Y. 1964, U.S. Ct. Appeals (2d cir.) 1965. Sr. ptnr. Cohen Lans LLP and predecessor firms, N.Y.C., 1968—. Lectr. U. Pa. Law Sch., 2003-; mem. faculty Am. Acad. Psychiatry and the Law, 1984-2003. Author: Reconcilable Differences, 2002; contbr. articles to legal jours. 1st lt. JAG USAR, 1965—67. Fellow Am. Coll. Family Trial Lawyers; mem. ABA, N.Y. State Bar Assn., N.Y.C. Bar Assn., N.Y. Acad. Matrimonial Lawyers, Univ. Club (N.Y.C.). Office: Cohen Lans LLP 885 3d Ave New York NY 10022 Office Phone: 212-326-1701. Business E-Mail: rscohen@cohenlans.com.

COHEN, ROBERTA JANE, think-tank associate; b. N.Y.C., Feb. 5, 1940; d. George H. and Ethel (Israel) Cohen; m. David A. Korn, Apr. 8, 1981; stepchildren: Marie Korn, David Korn, Philip Korn, Stephen Korn. BA, Barnard Coll., 1960; MA, Johns Hopkins U., 1963. Exec. dir. Internat. League for Human Rights, N.Y.C., 1971-78; sr. adviser to U.S. del. to UN and human rights officer Dept. of State, Washington, 1978-80, dep. asst. sec. state for human rights, 1980-81; head pub. affairs office U.S. Embassy, Addis Ababa, 1982-85; hon. sec. Parliamentary Human Rights Group, London, 1985-86; sr. advisor to refugee policy group Washington, 1989-96; sr. advisor NAS Com. on Human Rights, Washington, 1991-95; sr. advisor on internally displaced to rep. UN Sec.-Gen., 1994—; co-dir. project on internal displacement Brookings Instn., Washington, 1994—, sr. fellow, 2001—. Cons. World Bank, various govt. and non-govt. orgns., 1991—94; chmn. task force on human rights UN Assn., Washington, 1993—94; chair task force on China Internat. Human Rights Law Group, Washington, 1997—99, vice chair, 1992—96; bd. dirs. Jacob Blaustein Inst. for Advancement Human Rights; mem. adv. com. Human Rights Watch/Africa, RFK Meml. on Human Rights, Internat. League Human Rights, Acad. on Human Rights and Humanitarian Law, Am. Univ. Washington Coll. Law, Trinity Coll. Human Rights Program; mem. Coun. Fgn. Rels., Women's Fgn. Policy Group, Fund for Peace, Human Rights Bus. Roundtable; commr. Women's Commn. on Refugee Women & Children. Author: People's Republic of China: The Human Rights Exception, 1987; co-author (with Francis Deng): Masses in Flight: The Human Rights Exception, The Global Crisis of Internal Displacement, 1998; co-editor: The Forsaken People, 1998; co-editor: The Guiding Principles on Internal Displacement and the Law of the South Caucasus: Georgia, Armenia and Azerbaijan, 2003. Pub. mem. U.S. del. UN Commn. on Human Rights, 1998, Orgn. for Security and Cooperation in Europe, 2003. Co-recipient The Grawemeyer award for Ideas Improving World Order, U. Louisville, 2005; recipient Superior Honor award, USIA, Addis Abada, 1985, Human Rights award, UN Assn., 1994, Fiftieth Ann. award for Exemplary Writing on Fgn. Affairs and Diplomacy, Diplomats and Consular Officers Ret., 2002, Disting. Alumna award, Barnard Coll., 2005. Mem.: Cosmos Club.

COHEN, RONALD S., accountant; b. Lafayette, Ind., July 13, 1937; s. William and Stella (Fleischman) C.; m. Nancy Ann Plotkin, May 29, 1960; children: Philip, Douglas. BS in Acctg., Ind. U., 1958. CPA Ind. Staff acct. Crowe, Chizek & Co., South Bend, Ind., 1958—65, ptnr., 1965—2003, mng. ptnr., 1982—94, chmn. bd. dirs., 1994—2000. Chmn. Horwath Internat., 1999—; mem. dean's adv. coun. Ind. U. Sch. Bus., 1996—. Commr. Housing Authority of South Bend, 1976-85, also vice-chmn.; pres. Jewish Fedn., 1979-82; bd. dirs. United Way of South Bend, 1987-90. Served to lt. USAR, 1958-66. Mem. AICPA (bd. dirs. 1990-97, vice-chmn. 1994, chmn. 1995), Ind. Soc. CPAs, Ind. U. Sch. Bus. Alumni Assn. (bd. dirs. 1992-95). Democrat. Jewish. Office: Crowe Chizek & Co PO Box 7 330 E Jefferson Blvd South Bend IN 46601-2366 Office Phone: 574-236-8677. E-mail: rcohen@crowechizek.com.

COHEN, SANFORD IRWIN, physician, educator; b. N.Y.C., Sept. 5, 1928; s. George A. and Gertrude (Slater) C.; m. Jean Steinbruecker, Nov. 30, 1952; children— Jeffrey, Debra, John, Robert. AB magna cum laude, N.Y. U., 1948; M.B., MD, Chgo. Med. Sch., 1952. Intern Jackson Meml. Hosp., Miami, Fla., 1952-53; resident psychiatry U. Colo. Med. Center, 1953-54; resident Duke Med. Center, 1954-55, 57-58, mem. faculty, 1956-68, prof. psychiatry, 1964-68, head div. psychosomatic medicine and psychophysiol. research, 1964-68, lectr. psychology, 1960-68; instr. Washington Psychoanalytic Inst., 1964-68; cons. VA Hosp., Durham, N.C., 1957-65, NIMH, 1963-66; prof. psychiatry Boston U. Med. Sch., 1970-86, chmn. dept., 1970-86; vis. research scientist health and behavior br., div. basic scis. NIMH, 1986-88; prof. psychiatry U. Miami (Fla.) Sch. Medicine, 1988-2000, vice chmn. dept., 1990-2000, prof. emeritus, 2000—. Markle scholar med. sci., 1957-62; Commonwealth fellow, Czech Republic and USSR, 1966. Contbr. articles to profl. jours., chpts. to books. Recipient Robert Morse award excellence in sci. writing, 1965 Fellow Am. Psychiat. Assn. (disting. life), Am. Coll. Clin. Pharmacology (life); mem. AAAS, Am. Psychosomatic Soc., Acad. Behavioral Medicine Rsch. Home: 15110 Rollinmead Dr Darnestown MD 20878-3906 Office Phone: 305-355-9106. Business E-Mail: scohen@med.miami.edu.

COHEN, SANFORD NED, pediatrician, educator, academic administrator; b. N.Y.C., June 12, 1935; s. George M. and Fannie Leah (Epstein) C.; m. Judith Luskind, June 22, 1958 (div. 1984); 1 child, Andrew B.; m. Elizabeth Prevot(div. 1991); m. Sandra Hoffmann, June 13, 1992. AB, The Johns Hopkins U., 1956, MD, 1960. Diplomate Am. Bd. Pediat. Intern in pediat. Johns Hopkins Hosp., 1960-61, resident, 1961-63; instr. to assoc. prof. NYU Sch. Medicine, N.Y.C., 1965-74; chmn., prof. pediat. Wayne State U. Sch. Medicine, Detroit, 1974-81, assoc. dean, 1981-86, sr. v.p. for acad. affairs, provost, 1986-91, prof. pediat., 1991-98, prof. emeritus, 1998—. Dir. Wayne State U. Devel. Disability Inst., 1983-86, Child Rsch. Ctr., Detroit, 1975-81; pediatrician-in-chief Children's Hosp. Mich., Detroit, 1974-81; adj. faculty U. Mich. Sch. Pub. Health, Ann Arbor, 1980-90; chair steering com. NIH Network of Pediat. Pharmacology Rsch. Units, 1994-98, mem. adv. com., 1999-2002; reviewer Inst. of Medicine Nat. Acad. Sci.; mem. profl. adv. coun. Children's Med. Rsch. Inst., Oklahoma City, 1999—; vol. cons. Lee Meml. Health Sys., Ft. Myers, Fla., 2000—; mem. Adv. Bd. Children's Hosp. of SW Fla., 2003-; co-pres. Temple Judea. Editor: Progress in Drug Therapy in Children, 1981; contbr. articles to profl. jours. Mem. bd. health, Leonia, N.J., 1972-74; mem. Bd. Police Commrs., Detroit, 1995-99, chmn., 1997-98. John and Mary R. Markle scholar acad. medicine, 1968-74. Mem.: Soc. Pediat. Rsch. (v.p. 1980—81), Sr. & Ret. Physicians Assn. (pres. 2001—), Midwest Soc. Pediat. Rsch. (pres. 1979—80), Am. Pediat. Soc. Avocations: reading, golf. Office: Children's Hosp Mich 3901 Beaubien St Detroit MI 48201-2119 Office Phone: 313-745-5214. E-mail: scohen@med.wayne.edu.

COHEN, SANTIAGO, artist, illustrator, animator; b. Mexico City, June 28, 1954; s. Arié and Lillian Cohen; m. Ethel Cesarman; children: Diego, Cohen Isabel. MS, Pratt Inst., 1986. Creative dir. Ink Tank, N.Y.C., 1985—2001. Animated series, Troubles the Cat, 1995, book, It's Magic- Troubles the Cat-Golden Books, 1997, book/graphic novel, The Fifth Name, 2001 (Xeric Found. grantee, 2000); dir.: (HBO- children programming animated) Thank You Lord, 1996 (Emmy, 1997), (HBO- children programing) Hush Little Baby, 2000 (Emmy, 2001). Active Friends of the Hoboken (N.J.) Pub. Libr., 2001—02. Recipient Bronze award/ Comedy Central Brochure, Broadcast Designer Assn., 1992, Bronze award/ Comedy Central Logo, 1992, Bronze award, 1997, second place Animation, Asifa East, 1997, First place in Animation, 1998.

COHEN, SASHA (ALEXANDRA PAULINE COHEN), ice skater; b. Westwood, Calif., Oct. 26, 1984; d. Roger and Galina Cohen. Winner Junior Grand Prix, Stockholm, 1999; 2nd place U.S. Championships, 2000; winner Pacific Coast Sectional, 2000; 3rd place Troph?Lalique, 2001; Silver medalist U.S. Nats. Championship, 2001—02; 2nd place U.S. Championships, 2002; 4th place World Championships, 2002, Olympic Winter Games, 2002; 2nd place Hersheys Kisses Challenge, 2002; 4th place Campbells Classic, 2002; 1st place Skate Can., 2002, Trophee Lalique, 2002; 2nd place Cup of Russia, 2002; 1st place Crest White Strips Challenge, 2002; bronze medalist Nats., 2003; 4th place Worlds, 2003; champion Grand Prix Finals, 2003; 1st place Trophy Lalique, 2004, Skate CAn., 2004, Skate Am., 2004, Campbells Soup, 2004; silver medalist World Championships, 2004—05. Recipient Gardena Winter Trophy, 1999, Finlandia Trophy, 2001. Avocations: art, jewelry making, reading, designing costumes. Office: 9 Journey c/o Ice Palace Aliso Viejo CA 92656

COHEN, SAUL BERNARD, retired academic administrator, geographer; b. Malden, Mass., July 28, 1925; s. Barnett and Anna (Kaplinsky) C.; m. Miriam Friederman, June 11, 1950; children: Deborah Fae, Louise Esther. AB, Harvard U., 1947, AM, 1949, PhD, 1955; DSc (hon.), LLD (hon.), CUNY, 1986; DSc (hon.), Clark U., 1991; DPhil (hon.), Haifa (Israel) U., 2004, Clark U., 2004. From instr. to prof. geography Boston U., 1952-65; vis. prof. U.S. Naval War Coll., 1957; prof. geography, dir. Grad. Sch. Geography, Clark U., Worcester, Mass., 1965-78; dean Grad. Sch. Geography, Clark U. (Grad. Sch.), 1967-70, chmn. faculty, 1973-76, 77-78; pres. Queens Coll., Flushing, N.Y., 1978-85; univ. prof. geography Hunter Coll., N.Y., 1986-96, univ. prof. emeritus, 1996—. Vis. prof. Hebrew U., Jerusalem, 1971, 74, 75; adj. prof. Haifa U., 1977; cons. social sci. div. NSF, 1966-74, U.S. Office Edn., 1966-77; mem. U.S. nat. delegation Internat. Geog. Union, 1966-69; chmn. com. geography Nat. Acad. of Scis.-NRC, 1966-69. Author: Geography and Politics in a World Divided, 1963, rev. edit., 1973, Problems and Trends in American Geography, 1967, Experiencing the Environment, 1976, Resources and Human Networks, 1977, Jerusalem-Bridging the Four Walls, 1977, Jerusalem Undivided, 1980, Israel's Defensible Borders: A Geopolitical Map, 1983, The Geopolitics of Israel's Border Question, 1987, Geopolitics of the World System, 2003, also articles; geog. editor The Oxford World Atlas, 1973; geog. advisor New Columbia Ency., 1991, 93; editor-in-chief Columbia Gazetteer of the World, 1998. Chmn. N.Y.C. Early Childhood Commn., 1985-86; co-chmn. N.Y. State Sch. and Bus. Alliance, 1986-94; mem. Temp. State Commn. on N.Y.C. Sch. Governance, 1989-91; at-large mem. N.Y. State Bd. Regents, 1993—, chmn. Regents Telecom. Policy Commn., 1994-97, Regents Elem., Secondary and Continuing Edn. Com., 1995-98, Regents Higher Edn. and Profession com., 1999-2003, co-chmn. critical issues workgroup, 2004-05, chmn. quality com., 2005-; mem. N.Y. State Archives Partnership Trust, 1994—; chmn. vis. com. N.Y. State Mus., 1997—. Mem. Consortium Profl. Assns. (chmn. 1965-71), Assn. Am. Geographers (exec. officer 1964-65, del. Am. Coun. Learned Socs. 1964-66, mem. coun. 1966-70, chmn. com. coll. geography 1965-67, v.p. 1988-89, pres. 1989-90, past pres. 1990-91, chmn. com. on geog. curriculum internat. exch. 1990-96), Am. Geog. Soc. (coun. 1970-79). Home: 82 Taymil Rd New Rochelle NY 10804-2802 Personal E-mail: sbcohen1@optonline.net.

COHEN, SAUL G., chemist, educator; b. Boston, May 10, 1916; s. Barnet M. and Ida (Levine) C.; m. Doris E. Brewer, Nov. 27, 1941 (dec. July 1971); children— Jonathan Brewer, Elisabeth Jane; m. Anneliese F. Kissinger, June 1, 1973. AB summa cum laude, Harvard U., 1937, MA, 1938, PhD, 1940; ScD, Brandeis U., 1986. Research fellow Harvard, 1939-40, 41-43, instr., 1940-41; NRC fellow, lectr. U. Calif. at Los Angeles, 1943-44; research chemist Pitts. Plate Glass Co., 1944-45, Polaroid Corp., 1945-50, cons., 1950—98; with Brandeis U., 1950—, prof. chemistry, 1952—, Univ. prof., 1974-86, prof. emeritus, 1986—, chmn. Sch. Sci., 1950-55, dean faculty, 1955-59, chmn. dept. chemistry, 1959-66, 68-72; vis. prof. Havard Med. Sch., 1965, Hebrew U., Jerusalem, 1972. Contbr. articles on reaction mechanisms, free radicals, photochemistry, enzymology to profl. jours. Bd. overseers Harvard U., 1983-89; mem. Joint Com. on Appointments, 1984-89. Fulbright sr. scholar, 1958-59; Guggenheim fellow, 1958-59; Centennial medalist Harvard Grad. Sch. Arts and Scis., 1992. Fellow Am. Acad. Arts and Scis. (council), AAAS; mem. Am. Soc. Biol. Chemists, Am. Chem. Soc. (James F. Norris award 1972, trustee Northeastern sect. 1976-84), Chem. Soc. London, AAUP, Fedn. Am. Scientists, Phi Beta Kappa, Sigma Xi. Achievements include patents in polymers, hyroxylamines as photographic developers, heterocyclic silver solvents, dye-developers, diagnostic assays. Home: 90 Commonwealth Ave Apt 7 Boston MA 02116

COHEN, SELMA, librarian, researcher; b. N.Y.C., Mar. 14, 1930; d. George and Rose (Cohen) Unger; m. Irwin H. Cohen, Nov. 19, 1950; children: Barbara Katzeff, Joel. Grad., William Howard Taft HS, 1948. Asst. bookkeeper acctg. dept. Severud, Perrone et al, N.Y.C., 1970—75, Russell Reynolds Assoc., Inc., 1976—77, rsch. asst., 1977—, reference libr., 1985—. Chairwoman Scott Tower Charity Com., Bronx, NY, 1976-84, Scott Tower Property Improvement Com., Bronx, 1983-84. Home: 3400C Paul Ave # 10H Bronx NY 10468-1042 Office: Russell Reynolds Assocs 200 Park Ave New York NY 10166-0005 Office Phone: 212-351-2032.

COHEN, SEYMOUR I., lawyer; b. NYC, Apr. 15, 1931; s. Fred and Nettie (Sederer) C.; m. Rhoda Goldner, July 22, 1956; children: Cheryl Lynn, Marcy Ann, Lori Beth. BBA cum laude, CCNY, 1951; LLB, Bklyn. Law Sch., 1954, JD, 1967; MBA, NYU, 1960. Bar: N.Y. 1954, U.S. Tax Ct. 1954, Calif. 1973, U.S. Ct. Appeals (9th cir.) 1973, U.S. Supreme Ct. 1976; CPA, Ohio, Calif. Staff acct. S.D. Leidesdorf, N.Y.C., 1958-61; mgr., acct. Rockwell, L.A., Columbus, Ohio, 1961-69; mgr. contracts Logicon, L.A., 1970-71; mgr. internal audit Daylin, 1971-72; contr. NYSE Co., 1972-73; pvt. practice Torrance, Calif., 1973—. Mem. AICPA, L.A. County Bar Assn. (appellate ct. com. 1979—, svcs. com. 1981-82), Compton Bar Assn. (pres. 1998), South Bay Bar Assn. (pres. 1986-87, chmn. referral svc. 1977-81), State Bar Calif.

(client trust fund commr. 1983, 84), Ohio Inst. CPAs, N.Y. Inst. CPAs, Calif. Inst. CPAs, Inst. Mgmt. Accts., L.A. Trial Lawyers Assn. Jewish. Republican. Home: 30691 Via La Cresta Palos Verdes Peninsula CA 90275-5353 Office: 18411 Crenshaw Blvd Ste 411 Torrance CA 90504-5081 Office Phone: 310-329-6384. Personal E-mail: cohensy@aol.com.

COHEN, SEYMOUR MARTIN, oncologist, hematologist, educator; b. N.Y.C., Dec. 19, 1936; s. Harry and Rose (Ehrlich) C.; m. Carole J. Pomerantz, Aug. 16, 1976; children: Roger, Michael. BA, Bklyn. Coll., 1957; MD, U. Pitts., 1962. Diplomate Am. Bd. Internal Medicine and Subspecialty in Med. Oncology. Intern Montefiore Hosp., N.Y.C., 1962-63, asst. resident in medicine, 1963-64; resident in medicine Mt. Sinai Hosp., N.Y.C., 1964-65, Am. Cancer Soc. fellow in hematology, 1965-66, mem. staff, 1969—. Fellow in hematology L.I. Jewish Hosp., 1968-69; pvt. practice medicine specializing in med. oncology and hematology, N.Y.C., 1969—; clin. assoc. in medicine Mt. Sinai Med. Sch., 1969-73, sr. clin. asst. physician in medicine, 1969-73, asst. clin. prof. medicine, 1973-78, assoc. clin. prof. medicine, 1979—; bd. dirs. Cmty. Oncology Alliance, 2004—. Assoc. editor Cancer Investigation, 1993-2002; contbr. articles to profl. publs., research on malignant melanoma. Mem. exec. com. Jewish Am. Polit. Action Com., 1975-79, v.p., 1979-81, pres., 1981-83; bd. govs. State of Israel Bonds, 1979-92. Capt. M.C., USAF, 1966-68. Fellow A.C.P.; mem. AMA, Am. Soc. Clin. Oncology, Internat., Am. Socs., Hematology, N.Y. Cancer Soc. (sec. 1983-86, v.p. 1987, pres. 1989), N.Y. State Soc. of Med. Oncologists and Hematologists (pres. 1989-92), N.Y. Alliance of Physicians and Surgeons (bd. dirs. 1988-89, co-chmn. 1990—), New York County Med. Soc. Office: 1045 5th Ave New York NY 10028-0138 Office Phone: 212-249-9141. Business E-Mail: smonc@aol.com.

COHEN, SEYMOUR STANLEY, biochemist, educator; b. N.Y.C., Apr. 30, 1917; s. Herman and Lena (Tanz) Cohen; m. Elaine Pear, July 12, 1940; children: Michael, Sara. BS, CCNY, 1936; PhD in Biol. Chemistry, Columbia U., 1941; Dr.h.c., U. Louvain, Belgium, 1972, U. Kuopio, Finland, 1982. NRC fellow Rockefeller Inst., 1941—42; mem. faculty U. Pa., 1943—71, prof. biochemistry in pediatrics, 1954—71, Charles Hayden-Am. Cancer Soc. prof. biochemistry, 1957—71, Hartzell prof., chmn. dept. therapeutic research Sch. Medicine, 1963—71; Am. Cancer Soc. prof. microbiology U. Colo. Sch. Medicine, Denver, 1971—76; distinguished prof., Am. Cancer Soc. prof. pharm. scis. State U. N.Y., Stony Brook, 1976—85, prof. emeritus, 1985—. Chmn. council analysis and projection Am. Cancer Soc., 1972—74, adviser research, 1974—76; Guggenheim fellow Pasteur Inst., Paris, 1947—48; Jesup lectr. Columbia U., 1967; guest investigator Institut du Radium, Paris, 1967—68; vis. prof. Collège de France, Paris, 1970; vis. fellow Smithsonian Instn., 1973—74, 1986; vis. prof. U. Tokyo, 1974, Hadassah Med. Sch., 1974, Zuckerman lectr. tropical disease, 79; Guggenheim and Lady Davis fellow Faculty Agr., Israel, 1983; fellow Nat. Humanities Ctr., NC, 1982—83, NC, 1985; research assoc. history of sci. Smithsonian Instn., 1986; presdl. scholar U. Calif., San Francisco, 1988; lectr. Academia Sinica, Taiwan, 1989; trustee Marine Biol. Lab., Woods Hole, Mass.; bd. sci. cons. Sloan-Kettering Inst. Author: Virus-Induced Enzymes, 1968, Introduction to the Polyamines, 1971, Guide to the Polyamines, 1998, Biography of Thomas Cooper, 1999; editl. bd.: Virology, 1954—59, Jour. Biol. Chemistry, 1959—65, Jour. Cell Physiology, 1966—71, Bacteriol. Revs, 1969—73, Hist., Philos. Life Scis., 1985. Named Fogarty scholar, NIH, 1973—74; recipient cert. for war research, OSRD, 1945, War Manpower Commn., 1945, War Research medal, Columbia U., 1943, Eli Lilly award and medal, Am. Soc. Bacteriology, Immunology and Pathology, 1951, 1st Mead Johnson award, Am. Acad. Pediatrics, 1952, medal, Soc. de Chimie Biologique France, 1964, Borden award, Am. Assn. Med. Colls., 1967, Passano award, 1974, Townsend Harris medal, CCNY Alumni Assn., 1978, Forster award, German Acad. Sci. and Letters, Mainz, 1978. Master: Am. Acad. Arts and Scis.; fellow: AAAS (Newcomb Cleveland award 1955), Am. Acad. of Microbiology; mem.: NAS, Am. Assn. Cancer Rsch. (bd. dirs. 1974—77), French Soc. Microbiology (hon.), Inst. Medicine, Soc. Gen. Physiologists (councilor, pres. 1967—88), Phi Beta Kappa. Home: 10 Carrot Hill Rd Woods Hole MA 02543-1206

COHEN, SHELDON GILBERT, physician, historian, immunologist; b. Pittston, Pa., Sept. 21, 1918; s. Samuel H. and Dorthy (Goldberg) C. Grad., Wyo. Sem., 1936; student, Syracuse U., 1936-37; BA, Ohio State U., 1940; MD, NYU, 1943; DSc (hon.), Wilkes U., 1976. Diplomate Am. Bd. Allergy and Immunology. Intern Bellevue Hosp., N.Y.C., 1944; resident internal medicine Ft. Howard VA Hosp., Balt., 1947-48; resident in allergy VA Hosp., Aspinwall, Pa., 1948-49, U. Pitts. Med. Ctr., 1948-49; rsch. fellow U. Pitts. Sch. Medicine, 1949-50; rsch. assoc. U. Pitts., 1950-51; attending physician Allergy Clinic, Falk Clinics, 1950-51; chief of allergy Mercy Hosp., Wilkes-Barre, 1951-72; attending physician in allergy VA Hosp., Wilkes-Barre, 1951-60, cons. in internal medicine and rsch., 1960-72; assoc. prof. biol. rsch. Wilkes U., Wilkes-Barre, 1952-62, prof. biol. rsch., 1962-68, prof. exptl. biology, 1968-72, adj. prof. immunology, 1991—; cons. extramural programs Nat. Inst. Allergy and Infectious Diseases, 1972-73, chief allergy and immunology br., 1973-76, dir. immunology, allergic and immunologic diseases program, 1977-88, sci. advisor div. of intramural rsch. office of dir., 1988—; bd. sci. advisors Allergy and Immunology Inst. of Internat. Life Scis. Inst., 1989-97; sr. staff physician NIAID-NIH Clin. Ctr., 1974—. Adj. prof. medicine Northwestern U., 1988-98; scholar Nat. Libr. Medicine, 1988-99, vis. scholar history of medicine, 1999--; regional med. cons. Children's Asthma Research Inst. and Hosp., Denver, 1969-72; mem. medico adv. bd. CARE, 1977-89; cons. to Ministry Public Health, State of Kuwait, 1981-83; mem. expert adv. panel on immunology WHO, Geneva, Switzerland, 1979-2004, dir. WHO Collaborating Ctr. for Allergy, 1985-89; bd. dirs. Asthma and Allergy Found. Am., 1969-81, mem. com. public edn., 1976-81; bd. dirs. Lupus Found. Am., 1978-85, exec. v.p., 1981-85, mem. med. council, 1978-93; mem. aeroallergens com. NRC, 1976-80. Author: Excerpts from Classics in Allergy, 2d edit., 1992, Asthma Among the Famous, 1995—2002; mem. editl. bd. Jour. Devel. and Comparative Immunology, 1976—81, Allergy Proc., 1983—93; editor: Hist. Notes, Allergy and Asthma Proc., 1988—93, Allergy Archives, Jour. Allergy and Clin. Immunology, 2001—; cons. editor Am. Jour. Rhinology, 1986—93; contbr. articles to profl. jours., chapters to books. Trustee Marywood Coll., Scranton, Pa., 1983-89; bd. govs. adv. coun. Wilkes U., Wilkes-Barre, 1991-92. Capt. M.C., USAF, 1944-46. Recipient Disting. Svc. award Wyo. Sem., 1978, Asthma and Allergy Found. Am., 1981, Clemens von Pirquet award Georgetown U., 1981, NIH Centennial award, Terri Gottheif Lupus Rsch. Inst., 1987, NYU Med. Alumni Achievement award in health sci., 1988, Achievement award Internat. Assn. Allergology and Clin. Immunology, 1988, Spl. Recognition award Am. Acad Allergy and Immunology, 1989, 2002, recognition citation ILSI Allergy and Immunology Inst., 1992. Fellow: Am. Acad. Allergy (chmn. rsch. coun. 1963—66, historian 1963—69, v.p. 1979—80, Disting. Svc. award 1971), ACP, Coll. Physicians Phila., Am. Coll. Allergists (hon.); mem.: Washington Soc. History of Medicine (v.p. 1993—94, pres. 1994—96), Am. Assn. History of Medicine, Am. Fedn. Clin. Rsch., Collegium Internat. Allergologicum, Soc. Exptl. Biology and Medicine, Am. Coll. Rheumatology, Clin. Immunology Soc., Assn. Am. Physicians, Am. Assn. Immunologists, Cosmos Club, Alpha Omega Alpha (NYU alumni), Sigma Xi. Home: 5500 Friendship Blvd Apt 1927N Chevy Chase MD 20815-7272 Office: NIH NIAID MSC 6611 6610 Rockledge Dr Rm 2014 Bethesda MD 20892-7600 also: Nat Libr Medicine Bldg 38 HMD Room 1 E21 Bethesda MD 20892 Office Phone: 301-402-0269. Business E-Mail: scohen@niaid.nih.gov.

COHEN, SHELDON IRWIN, lawyer; b. Newark, July 25, 1937; BS in Ceramic Engring., AB in Humanities, Rutgers U., 1959; LLB, Georgetown U., 1964. Bar: Va. 1964, D.C. 1964, U.S. Ct. Appeals (D.C. and 4th cirs.) 1964, U.S. Supreme Ct. 1967. Assoc. Chapman, Disalle & Friedman, Washington, 1964-70; pvt. practice law Washington, Arlington, Va., 1970—. Author: Security Clearances and the Protection of National Security Information, Law and Procedure, 2000. Vice chmn. Arlington Dem. Com., l968-70; mem. Va. Dem. Cen. Com., l969-70. Capt. USAR, l959-67. Mem. ABA (chmn. govt. pers. com. 1986-89, chmn. nat. security interests com. 1990-95), D.C. Bar Assn. (chmn. civil svc. law com. 1984-86). Democrat. Office: 2009 14th St N Ste 708 Arlington VA 22201-2514 Office Phone: 703-522-1200. E-mail: sicohen@sheldoncohen.com.

COHEN, SHELDON STANLEY, lawyer; b. Washington, June 28, 1927; s. Herman and Pearl (Jaffe) C.; m. Faye Fram, Feb. 21, 1951; children: Melinda Ann Cohen Goetzl, Laura Eve Cohen Apelbaum, Jonathan Adam, Sharon Ruevena Cohen Liebman. AB with spl. honors, George Washington U., 1950, JD with highest honors (Charles W. Dorsey scholar), 1952; DLit (hon.), Lincoln Coll.; LLD (hon.), George Washington U., 2003. Bar: D.C. 1952, U.S. Dist. Ct. D.C. 1952, U.S. Ct. Appeals (D.C. cir.) 1952, U.S. Claims Ct. 1956, U.S. Tax Ct., 1956, U.S. Supreme Ct. 1956, U.S. Ct. Appeals (fed. cir.) 1986; CPA, Md. Acct., 1950-52; legis. atty. Office Chief Counsel, IRS, Dept. Treasury, 1952-56, chief counsel, 1963-65, commr. internal revenue, 1965-69; assoc. Paul, Weiss, Rifkind, Wharton & Garrison, 1956-60; ptnr. Arnold, Fortas & Porter, Washington, 1960-63, Cohen & Uretz, Washington, 1969-85, Morgan, Lewis & Bockius, Washington, 1985—2005; Disting. prof. in residence George Washington U. Sch. Pub. Policy and Pub. Mgmt., 2005—. Lectr. Howard U. Law sch., 1957-58; professorial lectr. George Washington U. Law Sch., 1958-81; adj. prof. U. Miami Law Sch., Fla., 1974-85; mem. adv. com. Inst. Estate Planning, U. Miami Law Ctr., 1969-86; chmn. exec. compensation com. U.S. Pay Bd., 1971-72; cons. Commn. for Revision of Tax Laws, 1969-71; cons. Filer Commn. on Pvt. Philanthropy and Pub. Needs, 1975-76; mem. Commn. on Founds. and Pvt. Philanthropy, 1969-70; mem. adv. group to commr. IRS, 1969-70; chmn. steering com. Adminstrv. Conf. U.S., 1974-84; mem. exec. com. Washington Lawyer's Com. for Civil Rights Under Law, 1975—, co-chmn., 1988-90; mem. Jimmy Carter Tax Task Force, 1976; advisor on tax and econs. Walter F. Mondale Campaign, 1984, Albert Gore campaign, 2000, John Kerry campaign, 2004; mem. cons. panel to controller gen. U.S. Gen. Acctg. Office, 1982-2000, chmn. Audit Adv. Com, 1995—; pres. Am.-Israel Tax Found., 1969-80; mem. coun. Sch. Govt. and Bus. Adminstrn. George Washington U., 1969-79, mem. commn. on governance, 1970, trustee, 1980-2002, chmn. bd. of trustees, 2000-02, chmn. emeritus, 2003; pres. Law Assn., 1978-79; rapporteur CIAT Conf. in Can., 1987; adv. bd. The Lincoln Legals, 1988—; v.p. presdl. Inaugural Found., 1992-93; bd. dirs. Supreme Ct. Hist. Soc., treas. 1995—; adv. bd. mem. Sch. of Public Affairs & Public Policy, Geo. Washington U., 2004—. Editorial and bus. sec.: George Washington U. Law Rev, 1952; case notes editor, 1951-52; bd. editors Nat. Law Jour., 1978—85; editorial bd. advisors Corporate Taxation. Sec., tax counsel Ctr. for Nat. Policy, 1981—2000; mem. adv. com. D.C. Ct. Appeals Admission Com., Lincoln Bicentennial Commn., 2003—; counsel Project Judaica Found., Inc., 1980—; bd. regents Omar N. Bradley Found., U.S. Army Hist. Collection, 1970—73; v.p. Am. Jewish Hist. Soc., 1980—92, chmn., 1993—2000, hon. chair, 2001—; v.p. trustees Walter Mondale;s Blind Trust, 1976—81; treas. Nat. Jewish Dem. Coun., 1991—; spl. tax counsel Dem. Nat. Com., 1969—72, gen. counsel, 1972—77; v.p. Presdl. Inaugural Found., 1992—93; past pres. Jewish Social Service Agy., Washington; chmn. endowment steering com. Coun. Jewish Fedns., 1991—2000, Am. Jewish Hist. Soc., 1993—; past v.p. Jewish Cmty. Ctr. Greater Washington; bd. overseers Jewish Theol. Sem. Am., 1972—; trustee United Jewish Endowment Fund, 1980—2002, trustee emeritus, 2003—; bd. dirs., past v.p. Jewish Cmty. Found.; trustee B'nai B'rith Found. of U.S.; bd. dirs. Adas Israel Congregation, Jewish Welfare Bd., United Synagogues Am., Common Cause, Nat. Council for a Responsible Firearms Policy, Inc., Nat. Found. for Jewish Culture, 1968-72, Am. Jewish Joint Distbn. Com., United Jewish Appeal Found. of D.C., 1969—2002, Supreme Ct. Hist. Soc., 1993—, treas., 1997—; bd. dirs., chmn. devel. com. Cmty. Found. Greater Washington, 1982—90; bd. dirs. Am. Assocs. Ben-Gurion U. of the Negev, Israel, v.p., 1988—90; bd. dirs. Gomez Found. for Mill House, 1982—95, Ulysses S. Grant Assn., 1976—, v.p., 1994—; bd. dirs. B'nai B'rith, 1979—85. With USNR, 1945—46. Recipient Young Person Under 40 in Govt. award, Downtown DC Jr. C. of C., 1964, Alumni Achievement award George Washington U., 1965, Arthur Flemming award, 1966, Alexander Hamilton award U.S. Treasury Dept., 1969, Joseph Ottenstein community service award Jewish Social Agy., 1976. Ourisman award for comm. svc. 1999. Mem. Nat. Acad. Pub. Adminstrn. (chmn. com. on energy 1978-79, trustee, sec. 1983-90, com. on ethics), ABA (chmn. spl. com. on retirement benefits legis. tax csect. 1972-73), Fed. Bar Assn. (coun. tax sect.), D.C. Bar Assn. (bd. dirs. 1969-72), D.C. Bar (Unified) (bd. govs. 1972-75, tax counsel 1972-, chair Iolta Study), Am. Coll. Tax Counsel, Am. Law Inst., J. Edgar Murdock Am. Inn of Ct. (counselor 1988—), D.C. Inst. CPAs (hon.), Inter-Am. Ctr. for Tax Adminstrs. (pres. 1967-68), Am.-Israel C. of C. (chmn. tax com.), Cosmos Club, Tournament Players Assn., Golf Avenel Club, Masons. Home: 5518 Trent St Bethesda MD 20815-5512 Office: Morgan Lewis & Bockius 1111 Penna Ave NW Washington DC 02004-5802 Business E-Mail: sscohen@morganlewis.com.

COHEN, SIDNEY MAXIMILIAN, neurologist; b. Morristown, N.J., May 26, 1919; s. Abraham Isaac and Shaina Rachel C.; m. Lea Ostrojinsky, Feb. 26, 1955; children: Ron, Navah, Oren. BS, Columbia U., 1939; MD, L.I. Med. Coll., Bklyn., 1943; DMS, Columbia U., 1952. Diplomate Am. Bd. Psychiatry and Neurology. Rotating intern Cumberland Hosp., Bklyn., 1943, asst. resident medicine, 1944; resident in neurology Mt. Sinai Hosp., N.Y.C., 1947; asst. resident neurology Neurol. Inst., N.Y.C., 1948; fellow dept. neurology Columbia U., N.Y.C., 1949-54; attending neurologist Roosevelt/St. Luke's Hosp., N.Y.C., 1952-91; sr. attending neurologist Roosevelt St. Luke's Hosp., 1991—; assoc. neurologist Neurol. Inst., 1952—. Contbr. articles to profl. jours. Capt. M.C., U.S. Army, 1944-46. Recipient Scroll of Honor United Jewish Appeal, 1971. Fellow Am. Acad. Neurology; mem. Am. Psychiat. Assn., Assn. for Rsch. Nervous & Mental Diseases. Avocations: art, coin and antique collecting, ballet, opera, theater. Office: 1213 Park Ave New York NY 10128-1703 Office Phone: 212-876-2522.

COHEN, STANLEY, pathologist, educator; b. N.Y.C., June 4, 1937; s. Herman Joseph and Eva (Lapidus) C.; m. Marion Doris Cantor, Aug. 30, 1959; children: Laurie Ellen, Ronald Nelson, Kenneth Stuart. AB, Columbia U., 1957, MD, 1961. Diplomate Am. Bd. Pathology (mem. immunopathology com.). Intern Albert Einstein Med. Ctr., Bronx, N.Y., 1961-62; resident Mass. Gen. Hosp., 1962-64; fellow NYU Med. Ctr., 1964-66; prof. pathology SUNY, Buffalo, 1968-74; acting dir. Ctr. for Immunology, Buffalo, 1973-74; prof. pathology U. Conn. Health Ctr., Farmington, 1974-87, assoc. chmn., 1976-80; prof., chmn. bd. Hahnemann U., Phila., 1987-94; prof., chmn. U. Medicine Dentistry-N.J. Med. Ctr., 1994—. Mem. study sect. allergy and immunology, 1981-85; chair study sect. tumor immunology ahd therapy TRDRP, 1992-94; co-chmn. 3d, 4th and 5th Internat. Lymphokine Workshops, 1982, 84, Congress on Cytokines, 1987, UCLA colloquium: molecular pathways of cytokines, 1990—, Keystone Symposium, 1992. Author: Mechanisms of Cell-Mediated Immunity, 1974, Mechanisms of Tumor Immunity, 1976, Mechanisms of Immunopathology, 1978, Biology of the Lymphokines, 1979, Interleukins, Lymphokines and Cytokines, 1983, Molecular Basis of Lymphokine Action, 1987, Role of Lymphokines in the Immune Response, 1989; assoc. editor-in-chief Clin. Immunology and Immunopathology; mem. editorial bds. 8 profl. jours.; contbr. more than 195 articles to profl. jours. Served to capt. U.S. Army, 1966-68. Recipient Kinne award, 1954, Borden award, 1961, Parke-Davis award in Exptl. Pathology, 1977, Outstanding Investigator award Nat. Cancer, Inst., 1986; Witobsky Meml. lectr., 1995. Mem.: Pluto Soc., Am. Soc. Exptl. Biology (fin. com. 2001—), Am. Soc. Investigative Pathology (sec.-treas. 2001—), Clin. Immunol. Soc. (councilor), Am. Assn. Immunologists, Am. Assn. Pathologists. Home: 79 Ettl Cir Princeton NJ 08540-2334 Office: UMDNJ Med Sch Newark NJ 07103 Business E-Mail: cohenst@umdnj.edu.

COHEN, STANLEY, retired biochemistry educator; b. Brooklyn, N.Y., Nov. 17, 1922; s. Louis and Fannie (Feitel) C.; m. Olivia Larson, 1951 (div.); children: Burt Bishop, Kenneth Larson, Cary; m. Jan Elizabeth Jordan, 1981. BA, Bklyn. Coll., 1943; MA, Oberlin Coll., 1945, PhD, 1989; PhD in Biochemistry, U. Mich., 1948; PhD, U. Chgo., 1985, Washington U., 1993. Instr. dept. biochemistry and pediatrics U. Colo., Denver, 1948-52; Am. Cancer Soc. fellow in radiology Washington U., St. Louis, 1952-53, assoc. prof. dept. zoology, 1953-59; asst. prof. biochemistry, sch. medicine Vanderbilt U., Nashville, 1959-62, assoc. prof., 1962-67, prof. biochemistry, 1967-86, disting. prof., 1986-2000, disting. prof. emeritus, 2000—. Charles B. Smith vis. rsch. prof. Sloan Kettering, 1984; Feodor Lynen lectr. U. Miami, 1986, Steenbock lectr. U. Wis., 1986. Mem. editorial bd. Abstracts of Human Developmental Biology, Jour. of Cellular Physiology. Cons. Minority Rsch. Ctr. for Excellence. Recipient Research Career Devel. award NIH, 1959-69, William Thomson Wakeman award Nat. Paraplegia Found., Earl Sutherland Research Prize Vanderbilt U., 1977, Albion O. Bernstein MD award Med. Soc. State N.Y., 1978, H.P. Robertson Meml. award Nat. Acad. Sci., 1981, Lewis S. Rosentiel award Brandeis U., 1982, Alfred P. Sloan award Gen. Motors Cancer Research Found., 1982, Louisa Gross Horwitz prize Columbia U., 1983, Disting. Achievement award UCLA Lab. Biomed. and Environ. Scis., 1983, Lila Gruber Meml. Cancer Research award Am. Acad. Dermatology, 1983, Bertner award MD Anderson Hosp. U. Tex., 1983, Gairdner Found. Internat. award, 1985, Fred Conrad Koch award Endocrine Soc., 1986, Nat. Medal Sci., 1986, 89, Albert and Mary Lasker Found. Basic Med. Research award, 1986, Nobel prize in physiology or medicine, 1986, Tennessean of Yr. award Tenn. Sports Hall of Fame, 1987, Franklin Medal, 1987, Albert A. Michaelson award Mus. Sci. and Industry, 1987. Fellow Jewish Acad. Arts and Sci.; mem. Nat. Acad. Sci., Am. Soc. Biol. Chemists, Am. Chem. Soc., AAAS, Internat. Inst. Embryology, Internat. Acad. Sci. (hon. internat. coun. for sci. devel.).*

COHEN, STANLEY, commercial real estate developer; b. Cin., Jan. 4, 1929; s. Robert Lieb and Celia (Gordon) C.; m. Rae A. Cohen, Aug. 28, 1960; children: Gordon Alan, Gary Louis, Sharon Diann. BA, U. Cin., 1950. Promotion assoc. Ziv TV Programs, Inc., Cin., 1953-57; program dir. WDSU-TV, New Orleans, 1957-64; pres. Royal Street Devel. Co., Inc., Newport Beach, Calif., 1965-73, Mission Hills Ranch, Inc., Newport Beach, 1969-73; vice chair Greater Park City Co., Inc., Park City, Utah, 1971-74; sr. v.p. E.M. Warburg, Pincus & Co., Inc., Newport Beach, 1973-75; mng. ptnr. Stanley Cohen/Crocker/Pacific Assocs., Newport Beach, 1978-85, Shoreline Sq. Assocs., Newport Beach, 1985-94; owner Stanley Cohen & Assocs., Costa Mesa, Calif., 1975—. Bd. dirs. Flowline, Inc., Los Alamitos, Calif.; mem. exec. com. The Olson Co., Seal Beach, Calif., 1995—; guest lectr. UCLA Grad. Sch. Bus., U. So. Calif. Grad. Sch. Bus., U. Calif. San Diego Grad Sch. Bus. Contbr. articles to L.A. Times, Orange County Register. Bd. dirs. Calif. State U. Found., Long Beach, 1987-95; trustee St. Mary Med. Ctr., Long Beach, 1984-90; chmn. ednl. resources adv. com. Newport-Mesa Unified Sch. Dist., Newport Beach, 1982-83. Recipient Disting. Achievement award U. Cin., 1993, Disting. Bus. and the Arts award Pub. Corp. for the Arts, Long Beach, 1989, Outstanding Achievement award Long Beach Area C. of C., 1983, Outstanding Leadership award Newport Harbor Coun. PTA Pres., 1983, Outstanding Leadership award Newport-Mesa Unified Sch. Dist. Bd. Edn., 1983. Mem. Nat. Assn. TV Program Execs. (hon. life; founding pres. 1963-65), Lincoln Club of Orange County. Home: 1501 Antigua Way Newport Beach CA 92660-4917 Office: Stanley Cohen and Assocs 2183 Fairview Rd Ste 219 Costa Mesa CA 92627-5674

COHEN, STANLEY ALVIN, land use planner; b. Bklyn., Apr. 7, 1929; s. Moe and Bessie Cohen. BEE, CCNY, 1951; MEE, Poly. Inst. Bklyn., 1954. Registered Profl. engr., N.Y. Lectr. CCNY, 1958—65; group leader IT Rsch. Inst., Annapolis, Md., 1965—73; cons. Conic Rsch., Bethesda, Md., 1973—78, dir., 1973—78; staff engr. Applied Physics Lab. Johns Hopkins U., Laurel, Md., 1978—92. Staff engr. E-Sys. Inc., Greenville, Tex., 1976—77; project leader Space divsn. GE, Valley Forge, Pa., 1977—78. Contbr. articles to profl. jours. Mem.: IEEE (sr.), Md. Soc. Profl. Engrs. (pres. Annapolis chpt. 1973—74), Eta Kappa Nu, Sigma Xi (assoc.). Achievements include invention of fields of radar and electronics. E-mail: ConicRes@consultant.com.

COHEN, STANLEY NORMAN, geneticist, educator; b. Perth Amboy, N.J., Feb. 17, 1935; s. Bernard and Ida (Stolz) Cohen; m. Joanna Lucy Wolter, June 27, 1961; children: Anne, Geoffrey. BA, Rutgers U., 1956; MD, U. Pa., 1960, ScD (hon.), 1995, Rutgers U., 1994. Intern Mt. Sinai Hosp., N.Y.C., 1960-61; resident Univ. Hosp., Ann Arbor, Mich., 1961-62; clin. assoc. arthritis and rheumatism br. Nat. Inst. Arthritis and Metabolic Diseases, Bethesda, Md., 1962-64; sr. resident in medicine Duke U. Hosp., Durham, N.C., 1964-65; Am. Cancer Soc. postdoctoral rsch. fellow Albert Einstein Coll. Medicine, Bronx, 1965-67, asst. prof. devel. biology and cancer, 1967-68; mem. faculty Stanford (Calif.) U., 1968—, prof. medicine, 1975—, prof. genetics, 1977—, chmn. dept. genetics, 1978-86, K.-T Li Prof., 1993—. Mem. com. recombinant DNA molecules NAS-NRC, 1974; mem. com. on genetic experimentation Internat. Coun. Sci. Unions, 1977—96. Trustee U. Pa., 1997—2002. With USPHS, 1962—64. Named to Nat. Inventors Hall of Fame, 2001; recipient Burroughs Wellcome Scholar award, 1970, Mattia award, Roche Inst. Molecular Biology, 1977, Albert Lasker basic med. rsch. award, 1980, Wolf prize, 1981, Marvin J. Johnson award, 1981, Disting. Grad. award, U. Pa. Sch. Medicine, 1986, Disting. Svc. award, Miami Winter Symposium, 1986, Nat. Biotech award, 1989, de la Vie prize, LVMH Inst., 1988, Nat. Medal Sci., 1988, City of Medicine award, 1988, Nat. Medal of Tech., 1989, Spl. award, Am. Chem. Soc., 1999, Lemelson MIT Prize, MIT, 1996, Albany Med. Ctr. prize in medicine and biomedical rsch., 2004, The Shaw prize in Life Sci. and Medicine, 2004; Guggenheim fellow, 1973, faculty scholar, Josiah Macy, Jr., 1975—76. Fellow: AAAS, Am. Acad. Microbiology; mem.: NAS (chmn. genetics sect. 1988—91), Inst. Medicine, Assn. Am. Physicians, Am. Soc. Clin. Investigation, Am. Soc. Pharmacology and Exptl. Therapeutics, Am. Soc. Microbiology (Cetus award 1988), Genetics Soc. Am., Am. Soc. Biol. Chemists, Phi Beta Kappa, Sigma Xi, Alpha Omega Alpha. Achievements include obtaining, with Herbert Boyer, first patent in the field of recombinant deoxyribonucleic acid (DNA), 1980. Office: Stanford U Sch Med Dept Genetics Rm M-322 Stanford CA 94305

COHEN, STEPHEN FRAND, political scientist, writer, historian, educator, commentator; b. Indpls., Nov. 25, 1938; s. Marvin Stafford and Ruth (Frand) C.; m. Katrina vanden Heuvel; children: Andrew, Alexandra, Nicola. BS, Ind. U., 1960, MA, 1962; PhD, Columbia U., 1969; cert., Russian Inst., 1969. Instr. Columbia U., N.Y.C., 1965-68; asst. prof. politics Princeton (N.J.) U., 1968-73, assoc. prof., 1973-80, prof., 1980-98, prof. emeritus, 1998—, dir. Russian studies, 1973-80, 88-94; prof. Russian studies and History NYU, 1998—. Cons. on Russia, CBS news TV commentator, 1989—; corr., chief cons. PBS WNET films on Russia, 1994-2001; adv. coun. U.S. Acad. Scis., Washington, 1979-82. Author: Bukharin and the Bolshevik Revolution, 1973 (Nat. Book Award nominee 1974, Bukharin prize 1989), Rethinking the Soviet Experience, 1985, Sovieticus: American Perceptions and Soviet Realities, 1985 (Page One award 1985), Failed Crusade: America and the Tragedy of Post-Communist Russia, 2000, 2d edit., 2001; editor: (with Robert C. Tucker) The Great Purge Trial, 1965, (with Rabinowitch and Sharlet) The Soviet Union Since Stalin, 1980, An End to Silence, 1982, (with Katrina vanden Heuvel) Voices of Glasnost: Interviews with Gorbachev's Reformers, 1989; mem. editl. bd. Slavic Rev., 1977-82, Post-Soviet Affairs, 1992-2002; assoc. editor World Politics, 1972-88; columnist The Nation Mag., 1982-87; contbg. editor, 1994-; mem. editl. coun. Svobodnaya Mysl (Moscow), 2004-. Bd. dirs. NYU Ctr. for the Media; mem. ednl. adv. bd. Guggenheim Meml. Found., 2003-. Recipient Page One award Column Writing, 1985, Ind. U. Disting. Alumn award, 1998, Columbia U. Harriman Inst. Alumnus of Yr. award, 2002; fellow Am. Coun. Learned Socs., 1971, 72-73; fellow John Simon Guggenheim Found., 1976-77, 88-89, Rockefeller Found., 1980-81; NEH fellow, 1985-86; Fulbright-Hays fellow, 1988-89. Mem. Coun. Fgn. Relations, Am. Polit. Sci. Assn., Am. Hist. Assn., Am. Assn. for Advancement Slavic Studies. Home: 340 Riverside Dr Apt 8B New York NY 10025-3436 Office Phone: 212-998-8289.

COHEN, STEPHEN IRA, lawyer, state legislator; b. Memphis, May 24, 1949; s. Morris David and Genevieve (Goldsand) C. BA, Vanderbilt U., 1971; JD, U. Memphis, 1973. Bar: Tenn. 1974. Sole practice, 1974-75; legal advisor Memphis Police Dept., 1975-78; mem. Shelby County Commn., 1978-80; sole practice Memphis, 1978—; mem. Tenn. Senate, 1982—, deputy spkr., 2000—, chair, Senate State & Local Govt. Comm., 1991, mem., Senate Judiciary, Transp. & Fiscal Review Comm. Interim judge Gen. Sessions Ct., 1980; v.p. Tenn. Constnl. Conv., 1977; del. Democratic Nat. Conv., 1980, 92; chair lottery info. and recommendation com.; mem. coun. state govts. exec. com., 2002, exec. com. Nat. Conf. State Legislators. Trustee Memphis Coll. Art, 2000, bd. trustees, 1988-2002; mem. Redbirds Found., Memphis Shelby County Center City Commn, Memphis Zoological Soc., 1998-, (bd. dirs.

1988-). Recipient Public Leadership award, Tenn. Human Rights Campaign, 2002, Legislator of the Year, Boys & Girls Clubs of Tenn., 2003, Leadership Award, Gov.'s Awards in the Arts. Mem. Memphis Bar Assn., Shelby County Charter Commn. Democrat. Home: 349 Kenilworth Pl Memphis TN 38112-5405 Office: Legislative Plz Ste 8 Nashville TN 37243-0030

COHEN, S(TEPHEN) MARSHALL, philosophy educator; b. N.Y.C., Sept. 27, 1929; s. Harry and Fanny (Marshall) C.; m. Margaret Dennes, Feb. 15, 1964; children: Matthew, Megan. BA, Dartmouth Coll., Hanover, N.H., 1951; MA, Harvard U., 1953, Oxford U., 1977. Jr. fellow, Soc. of Fellows Harvard U., Cambridge, Mass., 1955-58, asst. prof. philosophy and gen. edn., 1958-62; asst. prof. U. Chgo., 1962-64, assoc. prof., 1964-67, acting chair Coll. Philosophy, 1965-66; assoc. prof. Rockefeller U., N.Y.C., 1967-70; prof. philosophy Richmond Coll. (now Coll. of S.I.), 1970-83; exec. officer program in philosophy Grad. Ctr. CUNY, 1975-83; prof. philosophy and law U. So. Calif., L.A., 1983—98, dean divsn. humanities, 1983-94, interim dean Coll. Letters, Arts and Sci., 1993-94, Univ. prof. philosophy and law emeritus, 1998—, dean emeritus Coll. Letters, Arts and Sci., 1998—. Lectr. Lowell Inst., Boston, 1957-58; vis. fellow All Souls Coll., Oxford, Eng., 1976-77; mem. Inst. for Advanced Study, Princeton, N.J., 1981-82. Editor: The Philosophy of John Stuart Mill, 1961, Philosophy and Public Affairs, 1970-99, Philosophy and Society series, 1977-83, Ethical, Legal and Political Philosophy series, 1983-99; co-editor: Film Theory and Criticism, 1974, 79, 85, 92, 98, 2004, War and Moral Responsibility, 1974, The Rights and Wrongs of Abortion, 1974, Equality and Preferential Treatment, 1977, Marx, Justice and History, 1980, Medicine and Moral Philosophy, 1982, What Is Dance?, 1983, International Ethics, 1985, Punishment, 1995. Rockefeller Found. humanities fellow, 1977, Guggenheim fellow, 1976-77. Mem. Am. Philos. Assn., Am. Coun. Learned Socs. (bd. dirs. 1987-91, 93-2004), Coun. on Internat. Ednl. Exch. (bd. dirs. 1991-94). Democrat. Jewish. Office: U So Calif Law Sch Los Angeles CA 90089-0071 Office Phone: 213-740-4794. Business E-Mail: mcohen@law.usc.edu.

COHEN, STEPHEN PHILIP, social sciences educator, researcher; b. Chgo., Mar. 9, 1936; s. Saul and Bess (Passovoy) C.; m. Roberta Sue Brosilow, June 22, 1958; children: Edward, Jeffrey, Peter, Benjamin, Tamara, Susan. BA, U. Chgo., 1958, MA, 1959; PhD, U. Wis., 1967. Prof. emeritus U. Ill., Urbana, 1998—; sr. fellow Fgn. Policy Studies program Brookings Instn., Washington, 1998—. Mem. policy planning staff for South Asia, Dept. State, 1985-87; vis. prof. Keio U., Tokyo, 1974, Andhra U., India, 1977-78; co-founder Program Arms Control, Disarmament and Internat. Security, U. Ill., 1978-85 cons. U.S. State Dept., Ford Found., Lawrence Livermore Nuclear Lab., Dept. State, Rand Corp., Asia Soc. Author: The Indian Army, 2d edit., 1990; co-author: (with C.V. Raghavulu) The Andhra Cyclone of 1977, 1980, The Pakistan Army, 1984, (with others) Brasstacks and Beyond: Perception and Management of Crisis in South Asia, 1995, India: Emerging Power, 2001, The Idea of Pakistan, 2004; editor: The Security of South Asia, American and Asian Perspectives, 1987, Nuclear Proliferation in South Asia: The Prospects for Arms Control, 1991, South Asia After the Cold War, 1993. Ford Found. scholar in residence, India, 1992-93. Mem. Internat. Inst. Strategic Studies, Psi Upsilon. Jewish. Home: 2501 Virginia Ave NW Apt 912N Washington DC 20037-1903 Office: Brookings Instn 1775 Massachusetts Ave NW Washington DC 20036-2103 E-mail: scohen@brook.edu. *The central challenge facing mankind is a competition between self-destructive violence and reasoned restraint. My professional activities as a researcher, teacher, consultant and government official are devoted to understanding—and ameliorating— the institutions and forces which now have us moving along the edge of catastrophe.*

COHEN, STEVEN A., investment company executive; b. 1956; m. Alexandra Cohen; 7 children. BS in econ., U. Pa. Wharton Sch. Trader Gruntal & Co., 1978—92; chmn., founder SAC Capital Adv., 1992—. Bd. mem. Michael J. Fox Found.; co-founder Steven and Alexandra Cohen Found.; mem. painting & sculpture com. Mus. Modern Art. Named one of top 200 collectors, ARTnews Mag., 2004. Achievements include ranked by Forbes as one of the Worlds Richest People, 2004. Avocation: collector of impressionism, modern & contemporary art. Office: SAC Capital Adv 72 Cummings Pt Rd Stamford CT 06902 Office Phone: 203-614-2000.*

COHEN, STEVEN CHARLES, geophysicist; b. New Kensington, Pa., Aug. 27, 1947; s. Reuben and Rose Edith (Gordon) Cohen; m. Davria Eileen Millstone, Aug. 15, 1970; children: Amber, Phillip. BS, Drexel U., 1970; MS, U. Md., 1972, PhD, 1973. Physicist, Laser Tech. Br. Goddard Space Flight Ctr., Greenbelt, Md., 1970—76, geophysicist Lab. Terrestrial Physics, 1976—, sr. scientist, 1984—, asst. head geodynamics br., 1993—; U.S. del. geodynamics Working Group on U.S.-China Cooperation in Space Sci. and Tech., 1984—86; project scientist Geodynamics Laser Ranging System, 1986—90; vis. scholar U. Tex., 1991—92, Inst. of Geol. and Nuclear Sci., New Zealand, 1996—97, 2000; mem. Whitten medal award com. Am. Geophys. Union, 1998—2000. Del. Workshop on the interdisciplinary role of space geodynamics, 1988. Author (contbg.): Advances in Geophysics, Vol. 41; editor: AGU Geophysical Monograph: Slow Deformation and Transmission of Stress in the Earth, 1988—89; editor: (guest) Jour. Geophys. Rsch., 1985. Recipient Earth Sci. Spl. Achievement award, Goddard Space Flight Ctr., NASA, 1979., 1979. Mem.: Am. Geophys. Union, Sigma Xi, Pi Mu Epsilon, Sigma Pi Sigma, Phi Kappa Phi. Avocations: history, golf. Office: Goddard Space Flight Ctr Geodynamics Br Greenbelt MD 20771-0001

COHEN, STEVEN HOWARD, allergist, immunologist, educator; b. Akron, Ohio, May 15, 1946; s. Julius Abraham and Goldie Rebecca (Katzman) C.; m. Esta Rachel Ashrey, June 14, 1970 (dec. Aug. 1987); children: Hal, Beth; m. Deborah Mendeloff, Apr. 6, 1989. BS, Akron U., 1968; MD, Ohio State U., 1972. Intern Med. Coll. Wis.-Milwaukee County Hosp., 1972-73, resident internal medicine, 1973-75, fellow allergy and immunology, 1975-77; asst. prof. medicine Med. Coll. Wis., Milw., 1977-84, clin. assoc. prof. medicine, 1984—; physician Allergic Diseases S.C., Milw., 1984—, St. Lukes Hosp., Milw. Pres. Anshe Sfard Kehillat Torah, 1995-98. Mem. ACP, Am. Thoracic Soc., Am. Acad. Allergy Asthma and Immunology (ethics com. 1982-84), State Med. Soc. Wis. (ethics commn. 1994-2001). Office: 11121 W Oklahoma Ave Milwaukee WI 53227-4033 Office Phone: 262-545-1111. E-mail: scgolf@aol.com.

COHEN, STEVEN MICHAEL, radiologist; b. Bronx, N.Y., Oct. 2, 1958; s. Martin and Zeena Cohen; m. Karen Sue Sturtz, June 28, 1981; children: Dana, Alyssa. BA in Biology, SUNY Binghamton, 1979; MD, N.Y. Med. Coll., 1983. Diplomate Am. Bd. Radiology. Instr. radiology Albert Einstein Coll. Medicine, Bronx, 1987—88; fellow Thomas Jefferson U. Hosp., Phila., 1988—89; asst. prof. radiology Jefferson Med. Coll., Phila., 1989—90; radiologist Stamford Health Sys., Conn., 1990—96, radiologist-in-chief, 1997—. Clin. asst. prof. radiology Columbia Coll. Physicians and Surgeons, N.Y.C., 2000—. Mem.: Radiol. Soc. Conn. (exec. com. 1999—, treas. 2002—), Radiol. Soc. N.Am., Am. Coll. Radiology, Alpha Omega Alpha. Jewish. Avocations: golf, tennis, travel. Office: Stamford Radiol Assocs 76 Progress Dr Stamford CT 06880 Office Phone: 203-359-0130.

COHEN, STEVEN PAUL, anesthesiologist, researcher; b. Phila., Dec. 9, 1963; s. Allen Theodore Cohen and Harriet Ruth Hershfeld; m. Eun-Kyung Im, July 7, 2001; children: Berklee Kordell, Zared Orion. BA, SUNY, Stony Brook, 1985; MD, Mt. Sinai U., 1989. Diplomate Am. Bd. Anesthesiology. Intern Beth Israel Med. Ctr., N.Y.C., 1990—93; resident in anesthesia Presbyn. Hosp. Columbia U., N.Y.C., 1993; commd. 2d. lt. U. S. Army, 1993; asst. chief anesthesia & operavice svc. 121st Gen. Hosp., Seoul, Republic of Korea, 1993—95; chief anesthesia & operative svc. Wverzburg (Germany) MEDDAC, 1995—96, 121st Gen. Hosp., Seoul, Republic of Korea, 1996—99; fellow in pain mgmt. Mass. Gen. Hosp./Harvard Med. Sch., Boston, 1999—2000; dir. acute pain svc. Walter Reed Army Med. Ctr., Washington, 2000—; dir. inpatient pain svcs. NYU Med. Ctr., N.Y.C., 2002—04; assoc. prof. Divsn. Pain Medicine Sch. Medicine Johns Hopkins U., Balt., 2004—. Assoc. prof. NYU Sch. Medicine, N.Y.C., Walter Reed Army Med. Ctr., Washington, 2004—. Contbr. articles to profl. jours and newspapers. Lt. col. USAR. Recipient 1st pl., U.S. Army Photography Contest, 1998, 2d. pl., U.S. Army Forces Photography Contest, 1998, 2d ranked in black belt form N.Y./N.J. region, Karate Illustrated Mag., 1984. Mem.: N.Y. Acad. Scis., Am. Soc. Anesthesiologist, Am. Pain Soc. Avocations: martial arts, photography, writing, travel. Office: Johns Hopkins Divsn Pain Management 550 N Broadway Ste 301 Baltimore MD 21205 Office Phone: 410-955-1818.

COHEN, STUART F., software development company executive; BS in Quantitative Bus. Analysis, Ariz. State U. Sr. positions in US sales and mktg. divsn., IBM Personal Computer Co. and Networking Divsn. IBM; v.p. worldwide mktg., corp. officer InFocus Corp.; v.p. mktg. and bus. devel. RadiSys Corp.; CEO Open Source Devel. Labs, Beaverton, Oreg., 2003—. Office: Open Source Devel Labs 12725 SW Millikan Way Ste 400 Beaverton OR 97005 Office Phone: 503-626-2455. Office Fax: 503-626-2436. Business E-Mail: stuartcohen@osdl.org.

COHEN, SUSAN LOIS, writer; b. Chgo., Mar. 27, 1938; d. Martin and Ida Handler; m. Daniel E. Cohen, Feb. 2, 1958; 1 child, Theodora (dec.). BA, New Sch. for Social Rsch., 1960; MA in Social Work, Adelphi U., 1962. Social worker, N.Y.C., 1962-67; various social work positions in N.Y.C., 1962-68. Author: The Liberated Couple, 1969, reassued under title Liberated Marriage, 1973; (under name Elizabeth St. Clair) Stonehaven, 1974, The Singing Harp, 1975, Secret of the Locket, 1975, Provenance House, 1976, Mansion in Miniature, 1977, Dewitt Manor, 1977, The Jeweled Secret, 1978, Murder in the Act, 1978, Sandcastle Murder, 1979, Trek or Treat, 1980, Sealed with a Kiss, 1981; (with Daniel Cohen) The Kids' Guide to Home Computers, 1983, The Kids' Guide to Home Video, 1984, Teenage Stress, 1984, Screen Goddesses, 1984, Rock Video Superstars, 1985, Wrestling Superstars, Vol. 1, 1985, Vol. 2, 1986, Hollywood Hunks and Heroes, 1985, Heroes of the Challenger, 1986, A Six-Pack and a Fake ID, 1986, The Encyclopedia of Movie Stars, 1986, A History of the Oscars, 1986, Teenage Competition: A Survival Guide, 1987, Young and Famous: Hollywood's Newest Superstars, 1987, Going for the Gold, 1987, What You Can Believe about Drugs, 1988, What Kind of Dog is That, 1989, When Someone You Know Is Gay, 1989, Zoo Superstars, 1989, Zoos, 1992, Where to Find Dinosaurs Today, 1992, Going for the Gold: Medal Hopefuls for Winter '92, 1992, Gold Medal Glow: The Story of America's Women's Gymnastic Team, 1996, Pan Am 103, 2000, rev. edit. 2001, Hauntings and Horrors, 2002. Mem.: Wodehouse Soc. (pres.), Watson's Erroneous Deductions, Chapter One, The Capers of Sherlock Holmes, Clumber Spaniel Club of Am. Avocation: cats. Address: 877 W Hand Ave Cape May Court House NJ 08210-1865 Personal E-mail: blndyscast@aol.com.

COHEN, TAMMY SUSAN, pharmacist, educator; b. Orange, Calif., Sept. 8, 1972; d. Thomas Joseph and Catherine Doris Shallow; m. Brian Adam Cohen, Oct. 8, 1974; 1 child, Allyson Nicole. BS in Biology, Ill. State U., 1994; MS in Pharmacy Adminstrn., U. Kans., 1999; PharmD, U. Ill., Chgo., 2001. Registered pharmacist Kans. State Bd. Pharmacy, 1999, Tex. State Bd. Pharmacy, 2003. Pharmacy clin. practice mgr. U. Kans. Hosp., Kansas City, 2001—03; pharmacy asst. dir. Tex. Children's Hosp., Houston, 2003—. Peer reviewer Am. Jour. Health-System Pharmacists, Bethesda, Md., 1999—; adj. clin. prof. U. Kans., Lawrence, 2001—, pharmacy practice mgmt. residency preceptor, Kansas City, 2002—03; liason U. Health-System Consortium, Chgo., 2002—02. Named Outstanding Leader, Pfizer Pharmaceuticals, 1999; recipient Cmty. Pharmacy award, Ill. Assn. Cmty. Pharmacy, 1998, Innovative Clin. Practice award, Bd. Kans. Soc. Health-System Pharmacist, 2001, Bd. Kans. Soc. Health Sys. Pharmacists, 2001; ACCP Meeting scholar, Aventis Pharmaceuticals, 2000. Mem.: Gulf Coast Soc. Health Sys. Pharmacists (assoc.; com. mem. 2003—03), Tex. Soc. Health Sys. Pharmacists (assoc.; com. mem. 2003—03), Ill. Coun. Health Sys. Pharmacists (assoc.; student pres., v.p., coms. 1995—98), Kans. Soc. Health-System Pharmacists (assoc.), Inst. for Healtcare Improvement (assoc.), U. Health-System Consortium (assoc.), Am. Soc. Health Sys. Pharmacists (assoc.; coun. mem. 1997—98, Outstanding Student Leadership award 1998, 1999), Phi Lambda Sigma. Office: Texas Children's Hosp 6621 Fannin Houston TX 77030 Personal E-mail: drsbtcohen@earthlink.net. E-mail: tscohen@texaschildrenshospital.org.

COHEN, TED, philosopher, educator; b. Danville, Ill., Dec. 13, 1939; s. Sam and Shirley E. Cohen; m. Julie Simon, Apr. 18, 1940 (div. 1992); children: Shoshannah, Amos; m. Ann Rutherfurd Collier Austin, 1994. AB, U. Chgo., 1962; MA, Harvard U., 1965, PhD, 1972. Prof. philosophy U. Chgo., 1967—, chmn. dept. philosophy, 1974-79. Author: Jokes, 1999, Korean transl., 2002; editor: Essays in Kant's Aesthetics, 1982, Pursuits of Reason, 1993; contbr. articles to profl. jours. Bd. dirs. Ctr. Rehab. and Tng. Disabled, B'nai Brith Hillel Found. of U. Chgo., KAM Isaiah Israel Congregation, Chgo., 1980—, mem. faculty religious sch.; chmn. com. gen. studies humanities U. Chgo., 1991—. Named William R. Kenan Jr. Disting. Prof. Humanities, Coll. William and Mary, 1986—87; grantee, Am. Coun. Learned Socs., 1980, 1985. Mem.: Am. Philos. Assn. (v.p. 2005, pres.-elect 2005), Am. Soc. Aesthetics (pres. 1997—), Phi Beta Kappa (vis. scholar 2000—01). Avocation: baseball theory and practice. Office: U Chgo Dept Philosophy 1050 E 59th St Chicago IL 60637-1559 Home: 5816 S Blackstone Ave Chicago IL 60637 Office Phone: 773-702-8506. Business E-Mail: tedcohen@midway.uchicago.edu.

COHEN, VINCENT HAMILTON, SR., lawyer; b. Bklyn., Apr. 7, 1936; s. Victor George and Marion T. (Roberts) C.; m. Diane LaRue Hasbrouck, Aug. 19, 1962; children: Robyn Elaine, Traci Marie, Vincent Jr. BA, Syracuse U., 1957, JD cum laude, 1960. Atty. Consol. Edison, N.Y.C., 1960-62; trial atty. U.S. Dept. Justice, Washington, 1962-67; atty. Ohio Bell Telephone Co., Cleve., 1967; dir. compliance U.S. EEOC, Washington, 1968-69; ptnr. Hogan & Hartson, Washington, 1969—2003. Editor Syracuse Law Rev., 1956-57. Rep. ward 4 D.C. Dem. State Com., Washington; trustee Group Health Assn., Washington, 1985—. Mem.: ABA, Washington Convention Ctr. Authoruty, Justinian Law Soc. (chmn. 1999—2003), Am. Coll. Trial Lawyers, Nat. Bar Assn., N.Y. State Bar Assn., D.C. Bar Assn. (bd. govs. 1985—), Scabbard and Blade, Order of Coif, Pi Sigma Alpha. Office: Hogan & Hartson 555 13th St NW Ste 800E Washington DC 20004-1161

COHEN, WALTER STANLEY, financial consultant; b. Bklyn., Oct. 24, 1936; s. Harry and Ruth (Spitz) Cohen; m. Barbara Lee Cooper, June 18, 1960; children: Howard H, Andrea Sue. BS, U. Buffalo, 1958; postgrad., NYU, 1960-64. Jr. acct. Morris, Sherwood & May (CPAs), N.Y.C., 1958-59; semi-sr. acct. H. Merdinger & Co. (CPAs), 1960-61; sr. acct. Skillman & Michaels (CPAs), N.Y.C., 1961-62; with Blessings Corp., N.Y.C., 1962-84, sr. acct., 1962-66, asst. contr., 1966-69, asst. sec., 1969-70, sec., 1970-79, sec.-treas., 1979-84; v.p. fin. Sketchley Am., Inc., 1984-86; fin. cons. Thomson-McKinnon Securities, 1987-89; assoc. v.p. investments Prudential Securities, Bridgewater, N.J., 1989-94; assoc. v.p. Morgan Stanley Dean Witter, Somerville, NJ, 1994—2003; retired, 2003. With AUS, 1959—60. Mem.: B'nai B'rith, Kappa Nu (v.p. 1956—57, treas. 1955—56). Republican. Jewish. Home: 9 Hazeltine Ln Jackson NJ 08527 Office Phone: 732-928-7298. Personal E-mail: waltbarb@optonline.net.

COHEN, WARREN I., history professor; b. Bklyn., June 20, 1934; s. Murray and Fay (Phillips) C.; m. Janice Prichard, June 22, 1957 (div. Mar. 1986); children: Geoffrey Scott, Anne Leslie; m. Nancy Bernkopf Tucker, June 12, 1988. AB, Columbia U., 1955; A.M., Fletcher Sch. Law and Diplomacy, Tufts U., 1956; PhD, U. Wash., 1962. Lectr. U. Calif.-Riverside, 1962-63, asst. prof., 1963-67, assoc. prof., 1967-71; prof. history Mich. State U., East Lansing, 1971-93, univ. disting. prof., 1990-93, dir. Asian Studies Ctr., 1979-89; disting. univ. prof. U. Md., Baltimore County, 1992—. Vis. prof. Nat. Taiwan U., Taipei, 1964-66, Columbia U., N.Y.C., 1971, Fgn. Affairs Coll., Beijing, 1986; mem. Com. on Am.-East Asian Rels., Balt., 1973—; mem. adv. com. on hist. diplomatic documentation Dept. State, 1986-90, chmn., 1988-90; scholar-in-residence Assn. for Diplomatic Studies and Tng., 1994-95; acting dir. Asia program Wilson Ctr., 1995-99. Author: The American Revisionists, 1967, America's Response to China, 1971, The Chinese Connection, 1978, Dean Rusk, 1980, Empire without Tears, 1987, East Asian Art and American Culture, 1992, America in the Age of Soviet Power, 1945-1991, 1993, East Asia the the Center, 2000, Asian American Century, 2002, America's Failing Empire, 2005; editor Diplomatic History, 1979-82, New Frontiers in American-East Asian Relations, 1983, (with Akira Iriye) Japan and the United States in the Postwar World, 1988, Great Powers in East Asia, 1953-60, 1990, (with Nancy Bernkopf Tucker) Lyndon Johnson Confronts the World, 1994, Pacific Passage, 1996, (with Li Zhao) Hong Kong Under Chinese Rule, 1997. Bd. dirs. Mich. China Council, East Lansing, 1978-92; exec. sec. Gov's Mich. and China Com., Lansing, 1982-84; mem. Gov's Commn. on China, 1984-88; bd. dirs. Japan Council, 1979-92. Served to lt. (j.g.) USNR, 1956-59, PTO. Fulbright lectr. Tokyo, 1969-70; rsch. grantee Am. Coun. Learned Socs., 1968, Ford Found., 1976-77, Henry Luce Found., 1983-84; recipient Disting. Faculty award Mich. State U., 1988; Wilson Ctr. fellow, 1990-91, sr. scholar, 1999—; Presdl. rsch. scholar UMBC, 2001--. Mem. ACLU, Coun. on Fgn. Rels., Orgn. Am. Historians, Soc. for Historians of Am. Fgn. Rels. (v.p. 1983, pres. 1984, Graebner prize 2004). Democrat. Jewish. Office: U Md Balt County Dept History Baltimore MD 21250-0001 also: 11500 S Glen Rd Potomac MD 20854-1852 Office Phone: 410-455-2312. Business E-Mail: wcohen@umbc.edu.

COHEN, WAYNE R., lawyer; b. 1966; m. Jill F. Cohen. BBA with distinction, U. Mich., 1988; JD cum laude, U. Miami, 1991. Admitted: 1991. Founder, mng. ptnr. Cohen & Cohen, PC, Washington. Assoc. professorial lectr. law George Washington U. Sch. Law, 1993—; appointed to peer review comm. Atty. Grievance Commn. Md., 2002—04. Named Washington's Top Lawyers, Washingtonian Mag., 2004; named one of Top 50 Lawyers in Washington, 2002, Top 75 Best Lawyers in Washington, 2002, Washington's Top Trial Lawyers. Mem.: DC Bar Assn. (former chmn., litig. sect., former chair, injury to persons and property), Assn. Trial Lawyers Am., Trial Lawyers Assn. Metropolitan Washington, DC (immediate past pres., former bd. gov.). Office: Cohen & Cohen PC 1717 K St NW Ste 502 Washington DC 20006 Office Phone: 202-955-4529. Business E-Mail: wrc@cohenandcohen.net.

COHEN, WENDY E., neurologist; b. Long Island, N.Y., Mar. 23, 1944; BA, NYU, 1966; MD, N.Y. Med. Coll., 1970. Resident in neurology Flower Fifth Ave.-Met. Hosps., N.Y.C., 1970-74; pvt. practice Englewood, N.J., 1974—. Office: PO Box 588 Englewood NJ 07631-0588

COHEN, WILLIAM, law educator; b. Scranton, Pa., June 1, 1933; s. Maurice M. and Nellie (Rubin) C.; m. Betty C. Stein, Sept. 13, 1952 (div. 1976, dec. 2000); children: Barbara Jean, David Alan (dec. 1995), Rebecca Anne; m. Nancy M. Mahoney, Aug. 8, 1976; 1 dau., Margaret Emily. BA, UCLA, 1953, LLB, 1956. Bar: Calif. 1961. Law clk. to U.S. Supreme Ct. Justice William O. Douglas, 1956-57; from asst. prof. to assoc. prof. U. Minn. Law Sch., 1957-60; vis. asso. prof. UCLA Law Sch., 1959-60, mem. faculty, 1960-70, prof., 1962-70, Stanford (Calif.) Law Sch., 1970—, C. Wendell and Edith M. Carlsmith prof. law, 1983-99, Carlsmith prof. emeritus, 1999—. Vis. prof. law European U. Inst., Florence, Italy, fall 1977; Merriam vis. prof. Ariz. State U. Law Sch., Spring 1981 Author: Constitutional Protection of Expression and Conscience: The First Amendment, 2003; co-author: The Bill of Rights, a Source Book, 1968, Comparative Constitutional Law, 1978, Constitutional Law Cases and Materials, 1981, 7th edit., 2005, Constitutional Law: The Structure of Government, 1981, Constitutional Law: Civil Liberty and Individual Rights, 1982, 4th edit., 2002, The First Amendment: Constitutional Protection of Expression and Conscience, 2003. Home: 698 Maybell Ave Palo Alto CA 94306-3819 Office: Stanford Law Sch Nathan Abbott Way Stanford CA 94305 Business E-Mail: wcohen@stanford.edu.

COHEN, WILLIAM ALAN, marketing educator, author, consultant; b. Balt., June 25, 1937; s. Sidney Oliver and Theresa (Bachman) C.; m. Janice Dawn Stults, Jan. 3, 1963 (div. Jan. 1966); 1 child, William Alan II; m. Nurit Kovnator, May 28, 1967; children— Barak, Nimrod. BS, U.S. Mil. Acad., 1959; MBA, U. Chgo., 1967; MA, Claremont Grad. Sch., 1978; PhD, Indsl. Coll. of the Armed Forces, 1989. Registered profl. engr., Israel. Project mgr. Israel Aircraft Industries, 1970-73; mgr. rsch. and devel. Sierra Engring. Co., Sierra Madre, Calif., 1973-76; pres. Global Assocs., 1973—2003; mgr. advanced tech. mktg. McDonnell-Douglas Co., Huntington Beach, Calif., 1976-78; prof. mktg. Calif. State U., L.A., 1979—2002, dir. bur. bus. and econ. rsch., 1979-83, chmn. mktg. dept., 1986—89; pres. Calif. Am. U., L.A., 2002—03, Inst. of Leader Arts, L.A., 2003—; prof. bus. adminstrn. Touro Univ. Internat., 2003—. Bd. dir. Inst. Bus. Devel.; cons. Fortune 500 cos. Author: The Executives Guide to Finding a Superior Job, 1978, 83, Principles of Technical Management, 1980, Successful Marketing for Small Business, 1981, How to Sell to Government, 1981, The Entrepreneur and Small Business Problem Solver, 1983, 89, Direct Response Marketing, 1984, Building a Mail Order Business, 1982, 85, 91, 96, Making It Big as a Consultant, 1985, 90, 2001, Winning on the Marketing Front, 1986, High Tech Management, 1986, Developing a Winning Marketing Plan, 1987, The Students Guide to Finding a Superior Job, 1987, 93, The Practice of Marketing Management, 1988, 91, The Entrepreneur and Small Business Financial Problem Solver, 1989, The Art of Leader, 1990, The Entrepreneur and Small Business Marketing Problem Solver, 1991, Get a Great Job Fast, 1993, The Paranoid Corporation and Eight Other Ways Your Company Can Be Crazy, 1993, The Marketing Plan, 1994, 98, 2001, Making It!, 1994, Model Business Plans for Service Businesses, 1995, Model Business Plans for Product Businesses, 1995, The Stuff of Heroes: The 8 Universal Laws of Leadership, 1998, The New Art of the Leader, 2000, Marketing Your Small Business Made E-Z, 2000, The Wisdom of the Generals, 2001, Break the Rules, 2001, The Art of the Strategist, 2004; contbr. numerous articles to profl. jours. Maj. USAF, 1959-70, maj.-gen. USAFR, ret. Decorated Disting. Svc. Medal, Legion of Merit, D.F.C. with 3 oak leaf clusters, Meritorious Svc. medal with 2 oak leaf clusters, Air medal with 11 oak leaf clusters, numerous other U.S. and fgn. awards; named Disting. Grad. Indsl. Coll. Armed Forces, 1989; recipient Ministry Def. award State of Israel, 1976, Outstanding Svc. award Nat. Mgmt. Assn., 1979, Pres.'s award West Point Soc., 1982, Outstanding Prof. award, 1983, Chgo. Tribune Gold medal, George Washington medal Freedoms Found. at Valley Forge, 1986, CSULA Statewide Outstanding Prof., 1996, Great Tchr. in Mktg. award Acad. of Mktg. Sci., 1999. Fellow Acad. Mktg. Sci.; mem. Direct Mktg. Assn. (fellow 1980, 83), World Mktg. Congress (del. N.S. 1983), Direct Mktg. Club So. Calif. (bd. dirs., grantee 1981), Am. Mktg. Assn. (award 1982), West Point Soc. (pres., bd. dirs. 1981-82), Beta Gamma Sigma, Phi Sigma Phi. Republican. Jewish.

COHEN, WILLIAM MARK, lawyer; b. N.Y.C., May 22, 1951; s. Martin and Annabelle (Turner) C.; m. Melinda Pauline Salomon, Aug. 3, 1975; children: Jessica, Adam. AB, Rutgers U., 1973; JD, Georgetown U., 1976. Bar: Tenn. 1976, U.S. Dist. Ct. (mid. dist.) Tenn. 1976, U.S. Ct. Appeals (6th cir.) 1977, U.S. Supreme Ct. 1980. Law clk. to chief judge U.S. Dist. Ct. (mid. dist.) Tenn., Nashville, 1976-78; asst. U.S. atty. U.S. Atty.'s Office, 1978—83, 1st asst. U.S. atty., 1983—92, chief criminal divsn., 1992—98, asst. U.S. atty., 1998—2002, 2003—05, sr. litigation counsel, 2002—03, 2005—; adj. prof. law Vanderbilt U. Law Sch., 2003—. Home: 6021 Foxland Dr Brentwood TN 37027-5733 Office: US Attys Office 110 9th Ave S Ste A961 Nashville TN 37203-3870

COHEN, WILLIAM NATHAN, radiologist; b. Balt., Dec. 10, 1935; s. Herbert and Lillian (Goldberg) C.; m. Sylvia Weinstein, Feb. 9, 1964; children: Elaine, Shirah, Jonathan. Student, Johns Hopkins U., 1952—55; MD, U. Md., 1959. Intern U. Mich. Hosp., Ann Arbor, 1959-60; resident in radiology Mallinckrodt Inst., Washington U., St. Louis, 1960-63; chief radiology sect. Gallup Indian Hosp., USPHS, 1963-65; asst. prof. radiology U. Iowa, Iowa City, 1965-69, asso. prof., 1969-73, prof., 1973-76; prof. radiology SUNY Health Sci. Ctr., Syracuse, 1976-83, clin. prof. radiology, 1983—. Attending radiologist Crouse Hosp., Syracuse; vis. prof. radiology Hebrew U., Jerusalem, 1971-72; examiner Am. Bd. Radiology, 1981-87. Contbr. articles in field to med. jours. Fellow Am. Coll. Radiology; mem. Radiol. Soc. N. Am., Am. Roentgen Ray Soc., Am. Inst. Ultrasound in Medicine (sr.), Alpha Omega Alpha. E-mail: wcohen@twcny.rr.com.

COHEN, WILLIAM SEBASTIAN, consultant, former Secretary of Defense; b. Bangor, Maine, Aug. 28, 1940; s. Reuben and Clara (Hartley) C.; children: Kevin, Christopher. AB cum laude, Bowdoin Coll., 1962; LLB cum laude, Boston U., 1965; LLD, St. Joseph's Coll., Windham, Maine, 1974; LL.D., U. Maine, 1975, Western New Eng. Coll., 1975, Bowdoin Coll., 1975, Nasson Coll., 1975, Thomas Coll., 1988, Colby Coll., 1988. Bar: Maine, Mass., D.C. Ptnr. Paine, Cohen, Lynch, Weatherbee & Kobritz, Bangor, 1966-72; instr. U. Maine, 1968-72; asst. county atty. Penobscot County, Maine, 1968-70; U.S. Senator from Maine, 1979-96; sec. US Dept. Def., Washington, 1997-2001; chmn., CEO The Cohen Group, Washington, 2001—. Mem. Bangor Sch. Com., 1970-71, Bangor City Council, 1969-72, mayor, Bangor, 1972; Trustee Unity Coll.; bd. overseers Bowdoin Coll., 1973-85; trustee and counselor Ctr. Strategic and Internat. Studies, Washington, 2001—; chmn. bd. advisors MIC Industries Author: Of Sons and Seasons, 1978, Roll Call, 1981, Getting the Most Out of Washington, 1982, A Baker's Nickel, 1986, One-Eyed Kings, 1991, (with Gary Hart) The Double Man, 1985, (with George Mitchell) Men of Zeal, 1988, (with Thomas B. Allen) Murder in the Senate, 1993. Recipient Alumni award for disting. pub. service Boston U., 1976; named to N.E. Hall of Fame Basketball Team, 1962, Silver Anniversary award Nat. Collegiate Athletic Assn., 1987; Outstanding Young Man of Yr. Nat. Jaycees, 1975; James Bowdoin scholar, 1961-62; Alumni Fund scholar, 1962, selected for Balfour Silver Anniversary All-Am. Team, Nat. Assn. Basketball Coaches U.S., 1987. Republican. Office: The Cohen Group 1200 19th St NW Ste 400 Washington DC 20030

COHEN-DEMARCO, GALE MAUREEN, pharmaceutical executive; b. Rochester, N.Y., June 4, 1947; d. Maurice Cohen and Florence Michaels; m. David Earl McCarty, June 16, 1975 (div. Nov. 1979); 1 child, Brock Adam; m. Peter Francis DeMarco, Aug. 3, 1984. BA, U. Rochester, 1969; MA, SUNY, Buffalo, 1971. Various pharm. cos.; hosp. rep., dirs. mgr., med. liason Glaxo Pharms., 1987—97; regional bus. mgr. Axcan Pharma, 1997—2003, sr. regional account mgr., 2003—. Grantee, NIH, 1969; scholar, N.Y. State Regents, 1964. Democrat. Jewish. Avocations: environmental activities, charity organizations. Home: 27621 W Lakeview Dr N Wauconda IL 60084-2362 Office: Axcan Pharma 22 Inverness Ctr Pkwy Ste 310 Birmingham AL 35242 Office Phone: 800-950-8085. Personal E-mail: jap19472002@yahoo.com.

COHEN-STRONG, ELAYNE BARBARA, director, educator; b. Detroit, Jan. 29, 1952; d. Lawrence Cohen and Rae Sarah Saulles; m. Leroy Strong, Jr., May 16, 1987; 1 child, Kacie Leah Strong. BA, Mich. State U., 1974; student, Oakland C.C., Farmington Hills, Mich., 1969—71, Calif. State U., Long Beach, 1995. Cert. assistive tech. applications Calif. State U. Northridge, multi-subject tchg. credential Calif., Clear credential in spl. edn.-visually handicapped Calif. Med. technician Henry Ford Hosp., Detroit, 1975—85; adminstrv. asst. Hosp. Homecare of Orange County, Santa Ana, Calif., 1985—87; pvt. billing office asst. Doctors and Nurses, Newport Beach, Calif., 1987—91; dir. youth outreach dept. and tech., tchr. for the visually impaired Blind Children's Learning Ctr., Santa Ana, 1991—. Contbr. mag. Individuals with Disabilities News, newspaper In Focus, L.A. Times. Named Tchr. of the Yr., Wal-Mart, 1996. Mem.: PTA (assoc.; historian 2002—03), CEC (assoc.), Assn. for the Edn. and Rehab. of the Visually Impaired (assoc.), Calif. Transcribers and Educators of the Visually Impaired (assoc.). Avocations: swimming, travel, ceramics. Home: 6478 New Gate Way Yorba Linda CA 92886 Office: Blind Children's Learning Ctr 18542-B Vanderlip Santa Ana CA 92705 Office Phone: 714-573-8888. Personal E-mail: teachem45@pacbell.net. Business E-Mail: elayne.strong@blindkids.org.

COHEN-VADER, CHERYL DENISE, municipal official; b. Ft. Bragg, N.C., Mar. 23, 1955; BA, Princeton U., 1977; MBA, Columbia U., 1983. Treas. internat. divsn. commodity import-export financing Bank of N.Y., N.Y.C., 1977-81; v.p. Citicorp Securities Markets, Inc. Citicorp, N.Y.C., 1983-90; v.p. Weldon, Sullivan, Carmichael & Co., 1990-92; asst. v.p. Kirkpatrick Pattis, 1993-95; mgr. revenue dept. City of Denver, 1996—, dep. mayor, 2003—04. Mem. Mcpl. Securities Rulemaking Bd., 1998-2001. Bd. dirs. Mile High chpt. ARC, Colo. Episcopal Found., 1998-2001; bd. dirs. Black Ch. Intitiatives, 1998—. Recipient Consortium of Grad. Mgmt. Edn. fellowship, 1981-83, Recognition of Achievement award Five Points Bus. Assn., Inc., 1995, Leadership Denver award Denver C. of C., 1994; honored in Living Portraits of African-Am. Women Nat. Coun. Negro Women, 1997. Mem. Govt. Finance Officers Assn. Office: City Denver Revenue Dept McNichols Bldg Rm 300 144 W Colfax Ave Denver CO 80202-5391

COHILL, MAURICE BLANCHARD, JR., federal judge; b. Pitts., Nov. 26, 1929; s. Maurice Blanchard and Florence (Clarke) C.; m. Suzanne Miller, June 27, 1952 (dec. May 1986); m. Anne D. Mullaney, May 26, 2005; children: Cynthia Cohill Plattner, Jonathan, Jennifer Cohill O'Connor, Victoria. AB, Princeton U., 1951; LLB, U. Pitts., 1956. Bar: Pa. 1957. Judge family div. Common Pleas Ct., Allegheny County, Pitts., 1965-76; judge U.S. Dist. Ct. Pa. (we. dist.), 1976-94, chief judge, 1985-92, sr. judge, 1994—. Bd. dirs. Pa. George Jr. Republic, Grove City; chmn. bd. fellows Nat. Ctr. for Juvenile Justice. Served to capt. USMCR, 1951-53. Mem. ABA, Pa. Bar Assn. Allegheny County Bar Assns., Nat. Coun. Juvenile Ct. Judges (past v.p.), Pa. Coun. Juvenile Ct. Judges (past pres.), Phi Delta Phi. Republican. Presbyterian. Office: US Dist Ct US Courthouse 700 Grant St 8th Fl Rm 803 Pittsburgh PA 15219 Office Phone: 412-208-7380.

COHLER, BERTRAM JOSEPH, social sciences educator, psychologist; b. Chgo., Dec. 3, 1938; s. Jonas Robert and Betty (Cahn) C.; m. Anne Meyers, June 11, 1962 (dec. Dec. 1989); children: Jonathan Richard, James Joseph. BA, U. Chgo., 1961; PhD, Harvard U., 1967; cert. in adult analysis, Inst. Psychoanalysis, 1989. Diplomate Am. Bd. Psychoanalysis, Am. Bd. Examiners in Profl. Psychology. Lectr. social relations Harvard U., Cambridge, Mass., 1967-69; assoc. dir. Sonia Shankman Orthogenic Sch., 1969-72, 94-96; dir. Orthogenic Sch. U. Chgo., 1969-72, 94—; asst. prof. U. Chgo., 1969—75, assoc. prof., 1975—81, William Rainey Harper dept. chair, 1977—, prof. depts. psychology, edn. and psychiatry, 1981—. Co-dir. Univ. Ctr. Health anf Aging Soc., 1987—; sci. and profl. staff dept. psychiatry Michael Reese Hosp., Chgo., 1980-90; cons. The Tresholds, Chgo., 1972-81, Inst. Psychoanalysis, Chgo., 1972—, Ill. State Psychiat. Inst., Chgo., 1977-82; pres. bd. Ctr. Religion and Psychotherapy, Chgo. Author (with H. Grunebaum et al.): Mentally Ill Mothers and Their Children, 1975, 1982, Mothers, Grandmothers and Daughters, 1981; author: (with others) Parenthood as an Adult Experience, 1983, The Invulnerable Child, 1987, Handbook of Clinical Research on Adolescence, 1993; author: (with R. Galatzer-Levy) The Essential Other, 1993; author: The Course of Gay and Lesbian Lives, 2000; author: (with R. Galatzer-Levy) The Psychoanalytic Study of Lives Over Time, 1999; author: (with others) Rethinking Psychoanalysis and the Homosexualities, 2002. Bd. dirs. Horizons Cmty. Svcs., Chgo.; mem. initial rev. group in aging NIMH, Washington, 1982—86, Mental Health Spl. Projects, 1988—2003. Recipient Quantrell prize for disting. tchg. U. Chgo., 1975, 99, Lily Gondor award Postgrad. Ctr. for Mental Health, 2000; fellow Inst. Medicine, 1975. Fellow Gerontol. Soc., Soc. Projective Techniques Am. Orthopsychiat. Assn. (bd. dirs. 1981-84, pres. elect 1991, pres. 1992), Am. Psychol. Assn. (chmn. profl. affairs com. divsn. 39 1981-83, editor Psychoanalytic Psychology 1987-97, pres. sect. II 1992); mem. Am. Sociol. Assn., Am. Anthrop. Assn., Am. Assn. Psychiat. Svcs. to Children (Alexander Gralnick award), Soc. Rsch. in Child Devel., Chgo. Assn. Psychoanalytic Psychology (pres. 1983-84), Am. Psychoanalytic Assn. Home: 5408 S Blackstone Ave Chicago IL 60615-5407 Office: U Chgo 5730 S Woodlawn Ave Chicago IL 60637-1603 Office Phone: 773-702-3574. E-mail: bert@midway.uchicago.edu. *Emphasis on community services has been an important tradition in my family for several generations. This concern includes making knowledge and skills available to others, providing leadership and giving of time where needed. Teaching, writing, and research and clin. svc. are all involved in making the world better for my having been a part of it. My own goal has been to improve the human condition and to inspire my students to carry on this concern for the welfare of others.*

COHN, AARON I., anesthesiologist, educator; b. L.A., Sept. 8, 1959; s. Alan Franklin and Louise Christine (Huff) C.; m. Nicola Ann Bernau, July 1984 (div. Aug. 1986). BS, U. Calif. Riverside, 1980; MA, Rice U., 1984; MD, U. Tex. Galveston, 1987. Diplomate Am. Bd. Anesthesiology. Med. intern Montefiore/Univ. Hosp., Pitts., 1987-88; postdoctoral fellow Ctr. for Med. Informatics, Yale U. Med. Sch., New Haven, 1988-90; resident in anesthesiology Yale-New Haven Hosp., New Haven, 1990-91, St. Elizabeth's Med. Ctr., Boston, 1991-93; asst. prof. dept. anesthesiology U. Tex. Med. Br., Galveston, 1993-96; anesthesiologist North Tex. Anesthesia, Dallas, 1996-97; asst. prof. dept. anesthesiology U. Okla., Oklahoma City, 1997-99, U. Colo., Denver, 1999—. Member biomed. computing and health informatics study section (formerly SSS-9), NIH, Bethesda, Md., 1993-2004; reviewer Jour. Clin. Anesthesia, 1998-99. Contbr. articles to profl. jours. Mem. Internat. Anesthesia Rsch. Soc., Am. Soc. Anesthesiologists. Republican. Jewish. Avocations: bicycling, pistol shooting, computers, scuba diving, underwater photography. Home: 939 Jersey St Denver CO 80220-4592 Office: U Colo Dept Anes CB B113 4200 E 9th Ave Denver CO 80262-0001 Office Phone: 303-372-6306. Personal E-mail: aaron_cohn@cyberdude.com. Business E-Mail: aaron.cohn@uchsc.edu.

COHN, ALBERT LINN, lawyer; b. Paterson, NJ, June 18, 1928; s. David and Rose (Yolken) C.; m. Sylvia J. Jacoby, June 14, 1959; children: Melissa Lynn, Joshua Peter, Priscilla Betsy, Liza-Faith Michaelis, Thaddeus Augustus David. BS, Georgetown U., 1948; JD, Harvard U., 1951. Bar: D.C. 1951, N.J. 1954, cert.: (civil trial atty.). Assoc. David Cohn, Paterson, 1954—59; ptnr. David & Albert L. Cohn, 1959—66; sr. ptnr. Cohn & Lifland, Saddle Brook, NJ, 1967—. Adj. prof. law Rutgers U., Newark, 1979—, Inst. Cont. Legal Edn., 1980, 1982—, chmn. curriculum adv. com., 1984—85; vis. instr. Mass. Cont. Legal Edn., Nat. Inst. Trial Advocacy, Harvard U. Law Sch., 1981; trustee N.J. Inst. Cont. Legal Edn., chair, 1993—; master Arthur T. Vanderbilt Inn. Ct., 1988—90, Morris Pashman Inn of Ct., 1990—98, mem. coord. com., 1992—98. Mem. editl. bd. Divorce Litigation, 1996—; contbr. articles. Pres. Temple Shomrei Emunah, 1968—70. 1st lt. USAF, 1951—53. Named Superlawyer, N.J. Monthly, 2005; recipient Alfred O. Clapp award, NJ Inst. Continuing Legal Edn., 1994. Fellow: Am. Bar Found.; mem.: ABA, Harvard Law Sch. Assn. N.J. (pres. 1998), Saddle Brook C. of C. (past pres., trustee), Million Dollar Advs. Forum, Trial Attys. N.J., Soc. Med. Jurisprudence, N.J. State Bar Assn., Bergen County Bar Assn., Passaic County Bar Assn. (trustee 1978—86), Hamilton Club (Paterson), Harvard Club (N.Y.C.). Home: Llewellyn Park 74 Mountain Ave West Orange NJ 07052 Office: Cohn & Lifland 1 Park 80 Plz W Saddle Brook NJ 07663-5830 Office Phone: 201-845-9600. Business E-Mail: alc@njlawfirm.com.

COHN, ANDREW HOWARD, lawyer; b. N.Y.C., Jan. 17, 1945; s. Maurice John and Margaret Ethel (Gordon) C.; m. Marcia Bliss Leavitt, July 10, 1977; children: Marisa Leavitt, David Herman. BA, U. Pa., 1966; AM, Harvard U., 1970, PhD, 1972; JD, Yale U., 1975. Bar: Mass. 1975, U.S. Dist. Ct. Mass. 1976, U.S. Ct. Appeals (1st cir.) 1976. Law clk. to presiding justice U.S. Ct. Appeals (1st cir.), Providence and Boston, 1975-76; assoc. Hill & Barlow, Boston, 1976-80; sr. ptnr. Hale and Dorr, Boston, 1980—. Chmn. exec. com. Hale and Dorr, 1990-91, real estate dept., 1991-97, energy group, 1992—; cons. for juvenile justice standards project ABA and Inst. for Judicial Adminstrn., N.Y.C., 1973-74; rsch. fellow MIT-Harvard U. Joint Ctr. for Urban Studies, Cambridge, Mass., 1969-71, Univ. Coll., Nairobi, Kenya, 1968. Contbr. articles to profl. jours.; note and project editor Yale Law Jour., New Haven, 1974-75. Advisor Newton (Mass.) Community Schs. Found., 1987—88. Named Law and Social Sci. fellow, Russell Sage Found., 1972—74. Mem. ABA (environ.controls com., bus. law sect.), Am. Coll. Real Estate Lawyers, Boston Bar Assn. (chmn. real estate sect. 95-97), Yale Law Sch. Assn. Mass. (treas. 1985-87). Democrat. Jewish. Office: Wilmer Cutler Pickering Hale & Dorr LLP 60 State St Boston MA 02109-1816 Office Phone: 617-526-6218. Business E-Mail: andrew.cohn@wilmerhale.com.

COHN, AVERN LEVIN, district judge; b. Detroit, July 23, 1924; s. Irwin I. and Sadie (Levin) C.; m. Joyce Hochman, Dec. 30, 1954 (dec. Dec. 1989); m. Lois Pincus Cohn, June 1992; children: Sheldon, Leslie Cohn Magy, Thomas. Student, John Tarleton Agrl. Coll., 1943, Stanford U., 1944; JD, U. Mich., 1949. Bar: Mich. 1949. Practiced in, Detroit, 1949-79; mem. firm Honigman Miller Schwartz & Cohn, Detroit, 1961-79; sr. judge U.S. Dist. Ct., 1979—. Mem. Mich. Civil Rights Commn., 1972-75, chmn., 1974-75; Mem. Detroit Bd. Police Commrs., 1975-79, chmn., 1979; bd. govs. Jewish Welfare Fedn., Detroit, 1972—. Served with AUS, 1943-46. Mem. ABA, Mich. Bar Assn., Am. Law Inst. Office Phone: 313-234-5160. E-mail: avern_cohn@mied.uscourts.gov.

COHN, BERTRAM JOSIAH, investment banker; b. Newark, Sept. 12, 1925; s. Julius Henry and Bessie Ruth (Einson) C.; m. Barbara Biard, June 20, 1956; children: Daniel, Susan, Diana. AB cum laude, Harvard, 1949; MBA, NYU, 1957. Vice pres. Decatur Iron & Steel Co., Ala., 1951-67; chmn. bd. Schuylkill Lead Corp., Baton Rouge, 1968-70, DPF, Inc., Hartsdale, N.Y., 1970—, Interstate Bakeries Corp., 1970-82. Mem. internat. adv. com. Cohn Inst. for History and Philosophy Sci., Tel Aviv U. Trustee Washington Inst. for Near East Policy. With AUS, 1943-46. Mem. Wilderness Soc. (governing coun.). Home: 125 Woodbine Ave Larchmont NY 10538-3523 Office: First Manhattan Co 437 Madison Ave New York NY 10022-7001

COHN, BRADLEY M., lawyer; b. Chgo., July 5, 1953; s. Charles M. and Marian Cohn; m. Janet M. Minow, Mar. 25, 1995; children: Robert M., Eliana M. BA, U. Iowa, 1975; JD, U. Miami, 1978. Assoc. Hanson & Shire, P.C., Chgo., 1978-88; ptnr. Thrun, Tallman & Cohn, Ltd., Mt. Prospect, Ill., 1988—. Dir., pres. Ctr. Enriched Living, Riverwoods, Ill., 1989—. Office: Thrun Tallman and Cohn Ltd 111 E Busse Ave Ste 504 Mount Prospect IL 60056-3248 Office Phone: 847-255-6355.

COHN, BRUCE, film and television company executive; b. San Francisco, Apr. 8, 1931; s. Theodore and Rosebud Enid (Schmulian) C.; 1 child, Mitchell Barry. M of Journalism, U. Calif., Berkeley, 1954. Writer, producer Clete Roberts News Sta. KTLA-TV, Hollywood, Calif., 1957-62; west coast producer Huntley-Brinkley and Today Show NBC, Burbank, Calif., 1962-63; news dir. Sta. KNBC-TV, Burbank, 1963-66; Washington producer ABC Evening News, 1966-68; west coast producer Los Angeles, 1968-71; exec. producer Nat. Pub. Affairs Ctr. for TV Pub. Broadcasting System, Washington, 1971-73; ind. producer, writer various film studios, Burbank, 1973-75, 1973—; pres. Bruce Cohn Prodns., Inc., Mill Valley, Calif., 1975—. Instr. US history, critical thinking Fashion Inst. for Design and Merchandising, San Francisco, 2004. Screenwriter: Good Guys Wear Black, 1979; writer, producer (TV documentary) 1968-A Crack in Time, 1978, Secret Files of J. Edgar Hoover, 1990; producer (documentary series) Time Was, 1980; producer, dir. (documentary series) Rember When, 1981; writer, producer, dir. (documentary) Kisses with Lauren Bacall, 1991; writer, producer (documentary) Tom Clancy Presents John Ehrlichman In the Eye of the Storm, 1998, Couples, 2000. Recipient Cable Ace award, 1979, 81, 2 Gold medals N.Y. Internat. Film Festival, 1981, Gold plaque Chgo. Internat. Film Festival, 1982, Emmy award NATAS, 1984, 97. Mem. Writers Guild Am., Am. Film Inst. Home and Office: 125 Via Lerida Greenbrae CA 94904-1211 Personal E-mail: bcp333@aol.com.

COHN, DANIEL ROSS, physicist; b. Berkeley, Calif., Nov. 28, 1943; s. Roy Wolfsohn and Betty (Black) C.; m. Helen Desfosses, Aug. 25, 1967 (div. 1974); 1 child, Adam Robsohn; m. Joanne Brecker, June 10, 1978. BA, U. Calif., Berkeley, 1966; PhD, MIT, 1971. Rsch. scientist, gp. leader Francis Bitter Nat. Magnet Lab., MIT, Cambridge, Mass., 1971-80; divsn. head Plasma Fusion Ctr., MIT, Cambridge, 1980—; sr. rsch. scientist Nuc. Sci. and Engring. Dept., MIT, Cambridge, 1980—; acting asst. dir. plasma fusion ctr. MIT, Cambridge, 1992-96; pres., CEO Integrated Environ. Techs., 1996—2000. Cons. in field. Editor Jour. of Fusion Energy, 1984-92; contbr. more than 150 articles to profl. jours. Recipient Discover award for Technol. Innovation, Discover Mag., 1999. Fellow Am. Phys. Soc.; mem. Am. Nuc. Soc., Phi Beta Kappa. Achievements include holder of more that 20 U.S. patents on environmental, energy and monitoring technology; devel. of new energy and environmental technology. Home: 26 Walnut Hill Rd Chestnut Hill MA 02467-3125 Office: MIT Plasma Fusion Ctr 167 Albany St Cambridge MA 02139-4213 Business E-Mail: cohn@psfc.mit.edu.

COHN, DANIELLE BURD, writer, translator; b. Renton, Va., July 16, 1963; d. Richard Leroy Burd and Leone Lucille Burger; m. Alan Stephen Cohn, Oct. 6, 1996 (div. Nov. 6, 2001). BS in Polit. Sci., U. Calif., Irvine, 1987; MFA in Creative Writing, Antioch U., Marina del Rey, 2000. Office mgr. Trade Show Data Corp., Culver City, Calif., 1987—88; writer Walt Disney Imagineering, Glendale, Calif., 1988—2000; freelance writer, edicotr L.A., 2000—. Poetry workshop leader Juvenile Justice Sys., Tujunga, Calif., 1999. Contbr. poems; editor, translator: The Making of Disneyland Paris, 2001; translator: poems. Avocations: motorcycling, music, skydiving, backpacking, belly dancing. E-mail: nomdeplume8@aol.com.

COHN, DAVID STEPHEN, lawyer; b. Richmond, Va., June 19, 1945; s. Alfred Jerome and Jane Shaffer Cohn; m. Jane Boyle, Nov. 22, 1970; children: Elizabeth, Sarah. AB, U. Pa., 1967; JD, Harvard U., 1971. Bar: Pa. 1971, U.S. Dist. Ct. (ea. dist.) Pa. 1971, U.S. Ct. Appeals (3d cir.) 1971, Va. 1973. Assoc. Schnader, Harrison, Segal & Lewis, Phila., 1971-73; asst. prof. law T.C. Williams Sch. Law, U. Richmond, 1973-75; counsel Hunton & Williams, Richmond, 1975-84; mem., chmn., real estate dept. Browder, Russell, Morris & Butcher, P.C., Richmond, 1984-89; ptnr. Troutman Sanders LLP, Richmond, 1989—. Arbitrator Am. Arbitration Assn., 1972—; lectr. Marshall Wythe Sch. Law, Coll. William and Mary, Williamsburg, Va., 1977—81; mem. Va. Gov.'s Regulatory Reform Adv. Bd., 1983—85, Va. Gov.'s Com. on Efficiency in Govt., Richmond, 1985—87; chmn. Va. com. Harvard Law Sch. Fund, Cambridge, Mass., 1986—88, 2002—03. Editor: (book) The Residential Real Estate Transaction, 1975. Bd. dirs., pres. Sci. Mus. Va. Found., 1987—2002; mem. Va. Hist. Landmarks Bd., 1988—89; chmn., pres. Richmond Goodwill Industries, Inc., 1988—2002, 2004—; mem. Va. Vol. Formulary Bd., 1989—2003; mem. adv. coun. Va. Gov.'s Sch. Govt. and Internat. Studies for Gifted, 1991—93; mem. regulatory climate subcom. Va. Gov.'s Econ. Recovery Coun., 1991—92; mem. orgnl. structure team Gov.'s Commn. on Efficiency and Effectiveness, 2002; bd. dirs. Va. Nonprofit Housing Coalition, 1990—, sec., 1990—; mem. state ctrl. com. Va. Dem. Party, Richmond, 1985—93; assoc. trustee U. Pa., Phila., 1984—94; bd. dirs. Better Housing Coalition, 1988—99; chmn. trustees Sci. Mus. Va., 2002—. Mem.: ABA (chmn. govtl. assistance for real estate programs com. 1989—93), Va. State Bar (mem. bd. govs. real estate sect. 1984—87), Va. Bar Assn. (chmn. real estate com. 1985—87), Am. Coll. Real Estate Lawyers (chmn. affordable housing com. 1991—97). Jewish. Office: Troutman Sanders LLP Troutman Sanders Bldg 1001 Haxell Point Richmond VA 23219 Office Phone: 804-697-1470. Business E-Mail: david.cohn@troutmansanders.com.

COHN, DAVID V(ALOR), biochemist, educator; b. NYC, Nov. 8, 1926; s. Ralph and Clara (Schenkman) C.; m. Evelyn Turner, 1947; children: Robert Warren, Emily. BS, CCNY, 1948; PhD, Duke U., 1952; postgrad., Western Res. U., 1953. Faculty U. Kans. Sch. Medicine, Kansas City, 1953-82, prof. biochemistry, assoc. dean rsch., 1974-82; assoc. chief staff for rsch. VA Med. Ctr., Kansas City, Mo., 1953-82; prof. biochemistry U. Mo., Kansas City, 1971-82; v.p. R&D Immuno Nuc. Corp., Stillwater, Minn., 1982; chmn. bd. sci. advisors Endotronics Corp., Mpls., 1983-85; rsch. prof. oral biology and biochemistry U. Louisville Sch. Medicine, Sch. Dentistry, 1984—2002, emeritus prof., 2002—, chmn. dept. oral health, 1989-91, chmn. dept. biol. and biophys. scis., 1992-97, univ. dir. tech. devel., 1996-99; asst. to v.p. rsch. U. Louisville, 1992-95, asst. v.p. econ. devel. and indsl. rels., 1999—2002; CEO, pres. Biomed. Rsch. Cons., Louisville, 2002—. Mem. bd. sci. counselors Nat. Inst. Dental Rsch., Bethesda, Md., 1980-84; bd. dirs. Cambridge Med. Tech., Inc., 1985-86; cons. VA, Washington, 2000—. Editor: Hormonal Control of Calcium Metabolism, 1981, Endocrine Control of Bone and Calcium Metabolism, 1984, Calcium Regulation and Bone Metabolism: Basic and Clinical Aspects, 1987, Calcium Regulating Hormones and Bone Metabolism: Basic and Clinical Aspects, vol. II, 1992; editor in chief Bone and Mineral, 1986-94; contbr. articles to profl. jours. With USN, 1945—46. Grantee USPHS, 1957—, Am. Cancer Soc., 1959-60, VA, 1975-82, Ky. Heart Assn., 1991-93. Mem. AAAS, AAUP (pres. Louisville chpt. 2000—), Internat. Bone and Mineral Soc. (pres.), Am. Soc. Molecular Biology and Biochemistry, Am. Chem. Soc., Gordon Rsch. Conf. Chem. and Biol. of Bones and Teeth (chmn. 1974). Achievements include research on calcium metabolism, parathyroid gland parathormone/chromogranin biosynthesis and secretion, bone cell growth, differentiation and hormone responsivity, economic development, entrepreneurship, history of science and medicine. Home and Office: 5709 Apache Rd Louisville KY 40207-1715 E-mail: cohndv@attglobal.net, dvcohn@louisville.edu.

COHN, DEREK, marketing executive; b. N.Y.C., Apr. 3, 1947; s. Sol H. and Sylvia (Berg) C.; m. Regina Ross, Feb. 14, 1974; children: Casey S., Kylie M. BA in Psychology, Syracuse U., 1967. Asst. account exec. Compton Advt., N.Y.C., 1972-76; acct. exec. Grey Advt., N.Y.C., 1976-78; asst. product mgr. CPC Internat., Englewood, N.J., 1978-80; product mgr. ITT Continental Baking, Rye, N.Y., 1980-82; sr. v.p. mktg. and sales Internat. Plastics Co., N.Y.C., 1982—. Served to capt. Med. Service Corps, U.S. Army, 1967-71, Vietnam. Jewish. Office: Internat Plastics Co 1950 3rd Ave New York NY 10029-4024

COHN, GARY DENNIS, journalist; b. Bklyn., Mar. 9, 1952; s. Morton J. and Claire Cohn; m. Sally Denton, 1980 (div. 1983); 1 child, Jacob Max Cohn. BA in Psychology and Polit. Sci., SUNY, Buffalo, 1974; postgrad., U. Calif., Berkeley, 1974-75. Reporter Jack Anderson Column, Washington, 1975-80, Lexington (Ky.) Herald-Leader, 1980-84, Miami bur. Wall St. Jour., N.Y.C., 1984-86, Phila. Inquirer, 1986-93, Balt. Sun, 1993—2001, LA Times, 2003—. Atwood chair dept. journalism and pub. comm. U. Alaska, Anchorage, 2001—03; adj. prof. Sch. Journalism U. So. Calif., 2004—. Recipient Edward W. Scripps 1st Amendment award, 1980, Inter-Am. Press Assn. award, 1996, Overseas Press Club of Am. award, 1995, 97, Selden Ring award, 1996, 98, 1st Amendment award Soc. Profl. Journalists, 1997, 1st prize for investigative reporting Sigma Delta Chi, 1997, Investigative Reporters and Editors award, 1997, George Polk award, 1997, Pulitzer Prize for Investigative Reporting, 1998, finalist, Pulitzer Prize for Public Svc., 1996, finalist, Pulitzer Prize for Nat. Reporting, 2002. Office: LA Times 202 W First St Los Angeles CA 90012 Office Phone: 213-237-6476. Business E-Mail: gary.cohn@latimes.com.

COHN, HOWARD, retired magazine editor; b. N.Y.C., Nov. 1, 1922; s. Morris and Vivian (Siegel) C.; m. Regina Levy, Apr. 2, 1949; children—Steven B., Robert D. BA, Am. U., 1947. Assoc. editor Sportfolio mag., 1947-48; assoc. editor, then mng. editor Am. Lawn Tennis mag., 1948-50; assoc. editor Quick mag., 1950-51, Collier's mag., 1951-56; freelance writer, 1957-59; articles editor Pageant mag., 1959, exec. editor, 1959-63; mng. editor True mag., 1964-68, Med. World News mag., 1968, exec. editor, 1968-75, editor, 1975-77; exec. editor McGraw-Hill Newsletter Center, 1977-79; sr. staff editor McGraw-Hill Pub. Co., N.Y.C., 1979-81; editor-in-chief Graduating Engr. mag., 1981-88. Served with AUS, 1943-46. Home: 750A Heritage Hls Somers NY 10589-4009

COHN, IAN J., architect; b. Phila., Jan. 9, 1950; s. Isidore Jr. and Jacqueline (Heymann) C.; m. Vicki Hertzberg, June 23, 1973; children: Kevin Aton, Adrian Kirrin. Grad., The Gunnery, Washington, Conn.; BA, Washington U., St. Louis, 1971, MArch, 1974. Registered arch., N.Y. Staff arch. Howell, Killick, Partridge & Amis, London, 1974-76, George Nelson & Co., N.Y.C., 1977; assoc. Perkins & Will, N.Y.C., 1977-80; founding ptnr. Ian-Aaron Archs., N.Y.C., 1980-89, Ian-Aaron Architects Internat. (in assn. with Sheehan & Barry, Dublin, Ireland), Dublin, Ireland, 1985-89; prin. Diversity: Architecture & Design, N.Y.C., 1989—. 1st vis. young artist-in-residence The Gunnery Sch., 1989, vis. prof., 1992. Author: Structures: A Rule of Thumb Handbook, 1973; designs exhibited in mus. and mags. Bd. dirs. Kids of NYU Found., Inc.; chair comm. com. Ctrl. Synagogue, N.Y., 1997-2000. Mem. The

Gunnery Alumni Assn. Democrat. Jewish. Avocations: photography, tennis, travel, wine, gourmet foods. Office: Diversity: Architecture & Design 250 E 87th St Apt 22A New York NY 10128-3101 E-mail: ddiversity@aol.com.

COHN, ISIDORE, JR., surgeon, educator; b. New Orleans, Sept. 25, 1921; s. Isidore and Elsie (Waldhorn) C.; m. Jacqueline Heymann, July 4, 1944 (div. Aug. 1971); children: Ian Jeffrey, Lauren Kerry; m. Marianne Winter Miller, Jan. 3, 1976. MD, U. Pa., 1945; M.Med. Sci. in Surgery, 1952, DMS in Surgery, 1955; LHD (hon.), U. S.C., 1995. Diplomate Am. Bd. Surgery (bd. dirs. 1969-75). Intern Grad. Hosp. U. Pa., 1945-46, resident in surgery, 1949-52; fellow dept. surg. rsch. U. Pa., 1947-48; vis. surgeon Charity Hosp., New Orleans, 1952-62, sr. vis. surgeon, 1962-2000, hon. sr. vis. surgeon, 2000—; surgeon in chief La. State U. Svc., Charity Hosp., New Orleans, 1962-89; prof. surgery La. State U. Sch. Medicine, New Orleans, 1959-2000, emeritus chmn., emeritus prof. surgery, 2000—. Cons. surgeon VA Hosp., New Orleans, Touro Infirmary, New Orleans; instr. surgery La. State U. Sch. Medicine, New Orleans, 1952-53, asst. prof., 1953-56, assoc. prof., 1956-59, prof., 1959-2000, chmn. dept. surgery, 1962-89; mem. surg. rsch. rev. com. VA, Washington, 1967-68; dir. Nat. Pancreatic Cancer Project, 1975-84; mem. Soc. Surg. Chairmen, 1962-89. Mem. editl. bd. Am. Surgeon, 1963-87, Current Surgery, 1964-90, Am. Jour. Surgery, 1968-96, emeritus, 1997—, Digestive Diseases and Scis., 1978-82, Surg. Gastroenterology, 1982—, Cancer, 1992—2002, Digestive Surgery, 1995—. Bd. dirs. New Orleans Met. Conv. and Visitors Bur., 1998-2000, New Orleans Mus. Art, 2004—. Served to capt. M.C., AUS, 1946-47. Isidore Cohn, Jr. Professorship named in his honor at La. State U., 1987, Isidore Cohn, Jr., M.D. Student Learning Ctr. at La. State U. Health Sci. Ctr. Sch. Medicine dedicated in his honor, 2002, Spirit of Charity award Med. Ctr. La., 2003; named Outstanding Alumnus, Isidore Newman Sch., New Orleans, La., 2003. Fellow ACS (exec. com., bd. govs. 1987-91, vice-chmn. 1989-90, chmn. 1990-91, 1st v.p. 1993-94); mem. AMA, Am. Surg. Assn., So. Surg. Assn. (1st v.p. 1979-80, treas.-recorder 1981-82, pres. 1982-83), La. Surg. Assn. (pres. 1968), So. Med. Assn., La., Orleans Parish med. socs., Soc. Univ. Surgeons, Southeastern Surg. Congress (chmn. forum on progress in surgery 1967-69, councillor for La. 1967-73, pres. 1972), Surg. Biology Club II, Assn. Acad. Surgery, James D. Rives Surg. Soc., Internat. Surg. Soc., Am. Gastroenterol. Assn., Bockus Soc. Gastroenterology, Soc. Surgery Alimentary Tract (trustee 1969-80, recorder 1973-76, pres. 1976-77, chmn. bd. 1977-78, Founders medal 2004), Am. Soc. Microbiologists, Soc. Surg. Oncology, N.Y. Acad. Scis., Am. Assn. Cancer Research, Southeastern Cancer Research Assn. (pres. 1975), Collegium Internationale Chirurgiae Digestivae, Am. Cancer Soc. (vice chmn. clin. investigation adv. com. 1969, chmn. clin. investigation adv. com. 1969-73), Tex. Surg. Soc. (hon.), Sigma Xi, Phi Beta Kappa, Alpha Omega Alpha, Omicron Delta Kappa. Office: La State U Med Sch New Orleans LA 70112 E-mail: icohn@lsuhsc.edu.

COHN, JAY N., cardiologist, educator; b. Schenectady, N.Y., July 6, 1930; s. Morris Mandel and Rose (Gold) C.; m. Syma Cheris, June 14, 1953; children: Cynthia, Lauren, Joshua. BS, Union Coll., 1952; MD, Cornell U. Med. Coll., 1956. Diplomate Am. Bd. Internal Medicine. Intern Beth Israel Hosp., Boston, 1956-57, asst. resident in medicine, 1957-58; rsch. fellow in medicine Georgetown U. Med. Ctr., Washington, 1960-61; chief resident in medicine VA Hosp., Washington, 1961-62, clin. investigator, 1962-65, chief hypertension and clin. hemodynamics divsn., chmn. rsch. and edn. com., 1965-74; asst. prof. medicine Georgetown U. Sch. of Medicine, Washington, 1965-68, assoc. prof. medicine, 1968-72, prof., 1972-74, co-dir. cardiovascular rsch. divsn., 1972-74, mem. exec. com. dept. medicine, 1972-74; prof. medicine, head cardiovascular divsn. U. Minn. Med. Sch., Mpls., 1974-96, prof. medicine, 1996—. Mem. cardiovascular studies merit rev. bd. VA Ctrl. Office, Dept. VA, 1970-75, chmn. VA Cooperative Study on Vasodilator Therapy of Acute Myocardial Infarction, 1974-81, VA Cooperative Studies-Vasodilator-Heart Failure Trials, 1980—; mem. cardiovascular and renal adv. com. FDA, 1977-81, chmn., 1979-81, mem. congrl. commn. fed. drug approval process, 1981-82; co-chair Coun. Hypertension and Atherosclerosis Edn., 1990-94; mem. subcom. Nat. Bur. Info. Coronary and Heart Disease Risk, 1996; mem. sci. adv. com. Victor Chang Cardiac Rsch. Inst., Sydney, Australia, 1997; mem. task force hypertension edn., steering com. WHO, 1994—, coun. geriatric cardiology, task force heart failure edn., 1994—, coun. geriatric cardiology, task force cardiac rehab. edn., 1995—; mem. numerous coms. NIH. Guest editor various jours.; contbr. over 600 articles to profl. jours., chpts. to textbooks. With USPHS, 1958-60. Scholar N.Y. State Coll., N.Y. State Med. Sch.; recipient Ann. award N.Y. State Arthritis and Rheumatism Found., 1955, Arthur S. Flemming award Fed. Govt. Svc., 1969; named one of 400 Best Drs. in Am., Good Housekeeping, 1992, 96, one of 250 Top Drs. in Twin City Area, Mpls.- St. Paul Mag., 1992, Arrigo Recordati Internat. prize for sci. rsch., 2003, others. Fellow AAAS, ACP, Am. Coll. Cardiology (Disting. Scientist award Clin. Svc. 2005), Am. Heart Assn. (bd. dirs. 1979-85, coun. circulation, coun. high blood pressure rsch., coun. basic sci., Disting. Svc. award 1982, Sci. Coun. Disting. Achievement award 1998, Novartis Award in Hypertension Rsch. Coun. on High Blood Pressure Rsch. 2000, James B. Herrick award 2003); mem. Am. Fedn. Clin. Rsch. (chmn. eastern sect. 1969-70), Assn. Am. Physicians, Assn. Univ. Cardiologists, Assn. Profs. Cardiology (councilor 1992-94), Am. Soc. Hypertension (pres.-elect 1988-90, pres. 1990-92, chmn. intersocietal affairs com. 1995—, sci. awards com. 1996—, William S. Harvey award 1987), Am. Physiol. Soc., Am. Soc. Clin. Investigation, Am. Soc. Clin. Pharmacology and Therapeutics (chmn. program com. 1971-72, v.p. 1973-74, chmn. cardiopulmonary sect. 1976—), Am. Soc. Pharmacology and Exptl. Therapeutics, Internat. Soc. Hypertension (v.p. 1994-96, organizing com. 18th Sci. Meetings Year 2000, Chgo. chpt. 1994—, pres.- elect 1995-96, pres. 1996-98), Internat. Soc. Cardiovascular Pharmacotherapy (chmn. 5th Congress, Mpls. 1993), Heart Failure Soc. Am. (pres. 1995-98), Ctrl. Soc. Clin. Rsch. (chmn. cardiovascular subsect. 1980-81, mem. coun. 1987-89), Alpha Omega Alpha. Office: U Minn Med Sch Cardiovascular Divsn 420 Delaware St SE Minneapolis MN 55455-0374 Business E-Mail: cohnx001@umn.edu.

COHN, JONATHAN ALLEN, education educator, physician, researcher; b. N.Y., N.Y., Dec. 22, 1951; s. Bertram D. and Arline Cohn; m. Anita H. Hashem, June 14, 1992; children: Julia G., Ellen M. AB, Harvard Coll., Cambridge, Mass., 1972; MD, Cornell Univ. Med. Coll., N.Y., 1978. Cert. Internal Medicine A.B.I.M., Pa., 1981, Gastroenterology A.B.I.M., Pa., 1983. Postdoctoral fellow Yale Univ. Schl. Med., New Haven, 1981—84; asst. prof. medicine Wash. Univ. Sch. Med., St. Louis, 1984—87; asst. and assoc. prof. medicine Duke Univ. Med. Ctr., Durham, NC, 1988—2002, prof. medicine, 2002—. Home: 13 Charrington Pl Chapel HIll NC 27517 Office: Duke Univ Med Ctr Durham NC 27710 Office Phone: 919-684-6879. Personal E-mail: cohn0001@mc.duke.edu.

COHN, JOSEPH DAVID, surgeon; b. NYC, Jan. 26, 1937; s. Samuel Theodor and Gertrude (Emsheimer) C.; m. Barbara Ester Forst, July 27, 1966; children: Michael, Russell. SB, MIT, 1957; MD, NYU, 1961; MBA, Rutgers U., 1993. Diplomate Am. Bd. Surgery, Am. Bd. Thoracic Surgery, Am. Bd. Critical Care Surgery. Intern Duke Hosp., Durham, N.C., 1961-62; surg. resident Bronx Mcpl. Hosp. Ctr., N.Y., 1962-67; thoracic surgery resident U. Calif., San Diego, 1969-71; from asst. dir. surgery to dir. St. Barnabas Med. Ctr., Livingston, N.J., 1971-83; thoracic surgeon Northfield Surg. Assn., Livingston, 1978-99; mem. staff Santa Rosa Meml. Hosp. Sutter Med. Ctr., Santa Rosa, Calif., 2001—. Clin. asst. prof. surgery UMDNJ, Newark, 1972—79, assoc. prof., 1979—90, prof., 1990—99. Editor sci. jours.; author software programs, 1988; contbr. articles to profl. jours. Capt. USAF, 1967-69. Fellow Am. Heart Assn. 1966-67, NIH 1964-66. Fellow ACS, Am. Coll. Critical Care Medicine; mem. Sigma Xi, Phi Lambda Upsilon, Alpha Omega Alpha. Avocations: scuba, flying. Office: 5773 Shiloh Ridge Road Santa Rosa CA 95403-7802 Office Phone: 707-578-6714. Business E-Mail: jcohn@alum.mit.edu.

COHN, LAWRENCE H., cardiothoracic surgeon; b. San Francisco, Mar. 11, 1937; s. Harold Edward and Dorothy Harriet (Cohen) C.; m. Roberta Lee Cohn, June 26, 1960; children— Leslie Anne, Jennifer Lynne BA, U. Calif., Berkeley, 1958; MD, Stanford U., 1962. Diplomate Am. Bd. Surgery, Am. Bd. Thoracic Surgery. Sr. cardiothoracic surgeon Brigham & Woman's Hosp., Boston, 1980-87, chief div. cardiac surgery, 1987—; prof. surgery Harvard Med. Sch., Boston, 1980—. Chmn. bd. regents Nat. Libr. Medicine, 1991-92; chmn. Physicians Orgn., Brigham & Women's Hosp., 2000-04. Served to lt. comdr. USPHS, 1964-66. Fellow Am. Coll. Cardiologists, Am. Coll. Chest Physicians (pres. 1987), Soc. Thoracic Surgeons, Am. Assn. Thoracic Surgery (pres. 1999), Am. Surg. Assn., Soc. Office: Brigham Womens Hosp 75 Francis St Boston MA 02115-6106 Office Phone: 617-732-7678. Business E-Mail: lcohn@partners.com.

COHN, MARJORIE F., law educator, legal association administrator; b. Pomona, Calif., Nov. 1, 1948; d. Leonard L. and Florence Cohn; m. Pedro López children: Victor, Nicolas; m. Jerome P. Wallingford. BA, Stanford U., 1970; JD, Santa Clara U., 1975. Bar: Calif. 1975, U.S. Dist. Ct. (so. dist.) Calif. 1982, U.S. Dist. Ct. (no. dist.) Calif. 1983. Staff atty. Nat. Lawyers Guild, San Francisco, 1975-76, Agrl. Labor Rels. Bd., Sacramento, 1976-78, Appellate Defenders, Inc., San Diego, 1987-91; dep. pub. defender Fresno County Pub. Defender's Office, Fresno, Calif., 1978-80; pvt. practice Monterey and San Diego Counties, San Diego, 1981-87; prof. law Thomas Jefferson Sch. Law, San Diego, 1991—. Legal analyst on TV, radio and in print media. Co-author: Cameras in the Courtroom: Television and the Pursuit of Justice, 1998; editor-in-chief Guild Practitioner, 1994—. Mem. adv. bd. Support Com. for Maquiladora Workers, 1996—. Recipient Golden Apple award Student Bar Assn., Thomas Jefferson Sch. Law, 1995-98. Mem. Nat. Lawyers Guild (nat. exec. com. 1996—, exec. v.p.), Calif. Attys. for Criminal Justice, Phi Alpha Delta. Office: Thomas Jefferson Sch Law 2121 San Diego Ave San Diego CA 92110-2986 Office Phone: 619-297-6923. Business E-Mail: marjorie@tjsl.edu.

COHN, MICHAEL S., corporate financial executive; BA in Econ., Rutgers U., 1981; MBA in Fin., U. Pa., 1984. V.p., trader fixed income dept. Goldman Sachs and Co., 1984—89; dir. treasury divsn. Kleinwort Benson, 1989—91; dir., head proprietary trading, OTC bond options trading Merrill Lynch Internat., London, 1991—92; founding ptnr., trader Panther Capital Mgmt., 1992—99; CFO, exec. v.p. fin. Fairways Internat. Clubs, Greenwich, Conn., 1999—2003; with global pvt. client divsn. Merrill Lynch, NYC, 2003—. Interim dir. rsch. and trading analysis Old Bailey Alumni Ptnrs., 2005—. Home: 7 Edgewood St Unit B Norwalk CT 06854

COHN, MILDRED, biochemist, educator; b. NYC, July 12, 1913; d. Isidore M. and Bertha (Klein) Cohn; m. Henry Primakoff, May 30, 1938; children: Nina, Paul, Laura. BA, Hunter Coll., 1931, DSc (hon.), 1984; MA, Columbia U., 1932, PhD, 1937; DSc (hon.), Women's Med. Coll., 1975, Radcliffe Coll., 1978, Washington U., St. Louis, 1981, Brandeis U., 1984, U. Pa., Phila., 1984, U. N.C., 1985; PhD (hon.), Weizmann Inst. Sci., 1988; DSc (hon.), U. Miami, 1990. Rsch. asst. biochemistry George Washington U. Sch. Medicine, 1937—38; rsch. assoc. Cornell Med. Coll., 1938—46, Washington U. Sch. Medicine, 1946—58; assoc. prof. biol. chemistry Washington U., 1958—60; assoc. prof. biophysics and phys. biochemistry U. Pa. Med. Sch., 1960—61, prof., 1961—71, prof. biochemistry and biophysics, 1971—82, Benjamin Rush prof. physiol. chemistry, 1978—82, prof. emerita, 1982—; sr. mem. Inst. Cancer Rsch., Phila., 1982—85; chancellor's vis. prof. biophysics U. Calif., Berkeley, 1982; vis. prof. biol. chemistry Johns Hopkins U. Med. Sch., 1985—91. Rsch. assoc. Harvard U. Med. Sch., 1950—51; established investigator Am. Heart Assn., 1953—59; career investigator, 1964—78; vis. prof. chemistry Yale U., 1973. Mem. editl. bd. Jour. Biol. Chemistry, 1958—63, 1967—72. Recipient Hall of Fame award, Hunter Coll., 1973, Disting. Alumni award, 1975, Cresson medal, Franklin Inst., award, Internat. Assn. Women Biochemists, 1979, Humboldt award, Germany, 1980, 1982, Nat. Medal Sci., 1983, award, Am. Acad. Achievement, 1984, Chandler medal, Columbia U., 1986, Women in Sci. award, N.Y. Acad. Sci., 1992, Gov.'s award for excellence in sci., Pa., 1993, Founders medal, Magnetic Resonance in Biology, 1994, Stein-Moore award, Protein Soc., 1997. Mem.: NAS, Inst. de Biologie Physico-Chimique, Coll. Physicians of Phila. (Disting. Svc. award 1987), Am. Biophys. Soc., Am. Soc. Biochemistry and Molecular Biology (pres. 1978—79), Harvey Soc., Am. Chem. Soc. (chmn. divsn. biol. chemistry 1975—76, Garvan medal 1963, Remsen award Md. sect. 1988, Cinn. sect. Oesper award 2000), Am. Philos. Soc. (v.p. 1994—2000, sec. 2005—), Am. Acad. Arts and Scis., Iota Sigma Pi (hon. nat. mem. 1988), Sigma Xi, Phi Beta Kappa. Office: U Pa Med Sch 242 Anat Chem Bldg Dept Biochemistry & Biophys Philadelphia PA 19104-6059 Business E-Mail: cohn@mail.med.upenn.edu.

COHN, NATHAN, retired lawyer; b. Charleston, S.C., Jan. 20, 1918; s. Samuel and Rose (Baron) C.; 1 child, Norman; m. Carolyn Venturini, May 18, 1970. JD, San Francisco Law Sch., 1947. BAr: Calif. 1947, U.S. Supreme Ct. 1957. Pvt. practice law, San Francisco, 1947—2004; ret., 2004. Judge pro tem Mcpl. Ct., Superior Ct. Columnist, San Francisco Progress, 1982-86; contbr. and author seminars in field. Mem. Calif. State Recreation Commn., 1965-68; former mem. Dem. State Ctrl. Com. Served to 1st lt. USAF, 1950-55. Named to San Francisco Law Sch. Hall of Fame, 2000. Fellow Am. Bd. Criminal Lawyers (founder, past pres.), Am. Bd. Trial Advs. (diplomate; chpt. pres. 1984), Internat. Acad. Law and Sci., San Francisco Trial Lawyers (past pres., Lifetime Achievement award 2000), Criminal Trial Lawyers Assn. No. Calif., Irish-Israeli-Italian Soc. (co-founder, co-pres.), Internat. Footprinters Assn., Regular Vets. Assn. (national judge advocate), Calamari Club, Godfathers Club (past pres.), St. Vincent Sch. for Boys, Press Club (life), Masons (32 deg.), Shriners, South of Market Boys (past pres.), Ancient Order Hibernians Am. (hon. life). Jewish. Office: 2 Corte Las Casas Tiburon CA 94920

COHN, ROGER, editor; m. Patricia Leigh Brown; children: Jacob, Gabriel. Grad, Yale Univ, 1973. Reporter Philadelphia Inquirer, 1977—87; editor Audubon mag, 1992—99, Mother Jones mag, 1999—. Contbr. columns in newspapers. Grantee Alicia Patterson Found Fellowship, 1984. Office: Mother Jones Magazine 6th Fl 222 Sutter St San Francisco CA 94108*

COHN, SALOMON, hypnotherapist; b. Rabat, Morocco, Jan. 1, 1942; s. Abraham Albert and Mazel Cohn; children: Ari Lawrence, Ilana Margot. B of Clin. Hypnotherapy, Am. Inst. of Hypnotherapy, Anaheim, Calif., 1998; PhD summa cum laude, Harrington U., London, 2000; postgrad. in Clin. Hypnotherapy, Am. Inst. of Hypnotherapy, Anaheim, Calif., 1998—2002. Cert. healing and pain control therapist Hypnotherapy Tng. Inst. of L.A., 1999; diploma piano repair San Francisco Sch. of Piano Repair, 1996, diploma piano tuning San Francisco Sch. of Piano Tuning, 1996, cert. deep massage therapy practitioner Health Massage Inst., Haifa, Israel, 1988, reflexology practitioner Health Massage Inst., Haifa, Israel, 1989, clin. hypnotherapy practitioner Am. Inst. of Hypnotherapy, Calif., 1993, Reiki Master Unltd. Reiki Sys., Calif., 1995, cert. palmistry practitioner Acad. of Ancient Wisdom, Calif., 1996, voyager tarot tchr. Wanless Tarot Inst., Calif., 1997, metaphysical and tarot instr. Amron Metaphysical Ctr., Calif., 1997, time line therapy practitioner Time Line Therapy Assn., Calif., 2000, palm therapist Moshe Zwang, Instr., Calif., 2001, Feng Shui instr. Am. Inst. of Hypnotherapy, Calif., 2002. Healer, rschr. Visionary Quantum Healing, San Francisco, 1985—. Author: (book) The Complete Guide to Visionary Quantum Healing. Chief sgt. Israeli Mil., 1960—63. Decorated Hero Army of Israel, Six Day War. Master: Am. Coun. of Hypnotherapy, Internat. Brotherhood of Magicians (sr. officer 1970—2004, Magician 1971), Masons (3d degree 1969, 33d degree 1971); fellow: Shriners (Noble 1971); mem.: Am. Coun. of Hypnotherapy Examiners, San Francisco, Calif. Acad. Scis., Am. Bd. of Clin. Hypnotherapy, Am. Coun. Examiner Hypnotherapy, Commonwealth Club of Calif., Amnesty Internat., Sierra Club. Judaism. Achievements include patents pending for Pain Relieving and Healing Device, EAC2 Duotech Prototype. Avocations: antiquity, art collector, painter, writer, inventor. Office Phone: 415-751-9777.

COHN, SHERMAN LOUIS, lawyer, educator; b. Erie, Pa., July 21, 1932; s. Jacob and Bella (Kaufman) C.; m. Lucy Diaz, July 5, 1998 (dec. Sept. 2003); children by previous marriage: Ronald Bruce, Jerald Seth, Joshua Biber, Steven David, Leah Sura Guihen. BS in Fgn. Svc. summa cum laude, Georgetown U., 1954, JD, 1957, LLM, 1960, M of Acupuncture (hon.), 1993. Bar: Va. 1957, D.C. 1957, Md. 1978. Law clk. to Judge Burton R. Laub Erie County Ct., Pa., 1955, Walton H. Hamilton, 1957, Judge Charles Fahy, U.S. Ct. of Appeals for D.C. Circuit, 1957-58; staff atty. Appellate sect. Civil divsn. Dept. Justice, Washington, 1958-62, asst. chief, 1962-65; prof. law Georgetown U. Law Ctr., Washington, 1965—, dir. continuing legal edn., 1977-84. Lectr. Cath. U. Law Sch., 1963-65; vis. prof. Am. U. Law Sch., 1969-78, 92-95; adminstr. Preview of U.S. Supreme Ct. Cases, 1975-79; cons., litigation counsel Select Com. on Presdl. Campaign Activities U.S. Senate, 1973-74; mem. Jud. Conf. D.C. Circuit, 1965-73, 75, 77-78, 86, Jud. Conf. D.C. Ct. Appeals, 1979-81; reporter Nat. Conf. on Appellate Justice, San Diego, 1976. Contbr. articles to profl. jours. Pres. H.M. and A.E. Himmelfarb Found., 2002—, Charles Fahy Am. Inn of Ct., 1985—86, Traditional Acupuncture Found., 1984—88; chmn. Nat. Accredited Commn. Schs. and Colls. Acupuncture and Oriental Medicine, 1983—93; dir. Jewish Coun. for the Aging, bd. dirs., 2003—, Nat. Acupuncture Found., 2000—, pres., 2004—; trustee Am. Inns of Ct. Found., pres., 1985—98; trustee Tai Sophia; bd. dirs. Acupuncture and Oriental Medicine Alliance, 1999—2003; chmn. bd. dirs. Tai Hsuan Found., 1998—2001, mem. bd. overseers, 2003—; trustee Rule of Law Found., 2002—. Recipient A. Sherman Christensen award Am. Inns of Ct., 1990, Younger Fed. Lawyer award for outstanding service to U.S., 1964, Civil Justice award Am. Bd. Trial Advocates, 1993. Mem. ABA, D.C. Bar Assn., Am. Law Inst., Internat. Assn. Jewish Lawyers and Jurists (pres. Am. sect. 1983-87, dep. pres. internat. 1985-91), Jewish Law Assn. (pres. 1998-2002), Soc. Am. Law Tchrs., Georgetown U. Alumni Assn. (chmn. alumni fund 1985-87, Presdl. citation 1978, 87, John Carroll award 1980) Lodges: B'nai B'rith. Office: Georgetown U Law Ctr 600 New Jersey Ave NW Washington DC 20001-2075 Office Phone: 202-662-9069. Business E-Mail: cohn@law.georgetown.edu.

COHN, STEPHEN M., composer, music producer; s. Morris E. and Bernice Cohn. BS, Calif. State U., Northridge; postgrad., UCLA. Composer Arditti Quartet, London, 1991—95, RCA/Columbia, L.A., At Peace Media, Conn., 2000—05, KTLA, L.A. Instr. UCLA Ext., L.A., 1997—2003; composer in residence Internat. Mus. Encounters of Catalonia, 1996. Composer: (film score) Dying With Dignity (Emmy award for Outstanding Achievement in Music, 1989), Edith Ann's Christmas (Peabody award for prodn., 1998), Hunger in the Promised Land (Emmy award for prodn., 1987), (music for CD rec.) Two Together, An Amercian Folk Music Suite (Parents' Choice Gold award, 2003), (string quartet for CD rec.) Eye Of Chaos. Grantee, Anne and Gordon Getty Found., Harris Found., 1996, Am. Composers Forum, 2002; grantee for commn. to compose string quartet, Joan Palevsky, 1996. Mem.: ASCAP, Profl. Musicians, Am. Composers Forum (adv. bd. 2004—05). Personal E-mail: scohnmusic@earthlink.net.

COHN, STEVEN FREDERICK, sociology educator, consultant; b. Chgo., Sept. 5, 1939; s. William Wolf and Sylvia Ann (Wechsler) C.; m. Kathleen Marie Cusick, May 8, 1968 (div. Jan. 1974); 1 child, Iain. BA, Dartmouth Coll., 1961; PhD, Columbia U., 1975. Lectr. U. Strathclyde, Glasgow, Scotland, 1968-69, U. Glasgow, 1969-71; asst. prof. U. Maine, Orono, 1971-77; policy analyst NSF, Washington, 1978-79; assoc. prof. U. Maine, Orono, 1980-85, prof., 1986—. Cons. ACTION, Washington, 1970-72, The Royal Soc., London, 1984. Contbr. articles to profl. jours. Fulbright fellow Coun. for Internat. Exch. Scholars, 1984. Mem. Am. Sociol. Assn. (sect. program com. 1995-96), Ea. Soc. Assn. (publs. com. mem. 1990), Phi Beta Kappa. Jewish. Home: 99 N Main Ave Orono ME 04473-4430 Office: U Maine 201 Fernald Orono ME 04469-0001 Business E-Mail: steve.cohn@umit.maine.edu.

COHN, THEODORE ELLIOT, optometry educator, optometrist; b. Highland Park, Ill., Sept. 5, 1941; s. Nathan and Marjorie Cohn; m. Barbara Adler, Nov. 29, 1975; children: Avery Simon, Adrienne Leah, Harris Samuel. SB in Elec. Engring., MIT, 1963; MS in Bioengring., U. Mich., 1965, MA in Math., 1966, PhD in Bioengring., 1969. Asst. prof. U. Calif., Berkeley, 1970-76, assoc. prof., 1976-84, prof., 1985—. Vis. fellow John Curtin Med. Sch., Australian Nat. U., Canberra, 1977; vis. scholar U. Calif., San Diego, 1981-90; chair grad. group in bioengring. U. Calif., Berkeley/U. Calif., San Francisco, 2000—03; vice chair grad. affairs, dept. bioengring., U. Calif. Berkeley, 1999—. Author, editor: Visual Detection, 1993. Bd. dirs. Berkeley-Richmond Jewish Cmty. Ctr., 1995-2002. Recipient Appreciation award, Aerospace Lighting Inst., 1999. Fellow Optical Soc. Am. (chairvision tech. group 1984-86); mem. IEEE (sr. mem.), Vision Scis. Soc., Human Factors and Ergonomics Soc., Sigma Xi. Office: U Calif Sch Optometry 360 Minor Hall Berkeley CA 94720-2020 E-mail: tecohn@berkeley.edu.

COHOAT, MATTHEW A., real estate company executive; BS in Acctg., Purdue U., 1982. CPA Ind. With Ernst & Young, 1982—90; contr. Duke Realty Corp., Indpls., 1990, sr. v.p., corp. contr., exec. v.p., CFO, 2004—. Treas. bd. dirs. Cathedral H.S.; pres. bd. dirs. Cath. Youth Orgn., Indpls.; bd. dirs. Goodwill Indpls. Found.; coach various youth basketball and baseball teams. Mem.: Ind. Evans Scholar Alumni Assn. (past pres.). Office: Duke Realty Corp Ste 100 600 E 96th St Indianapolis IN 46240

COHON, JARED L., academic administrator; m. Maureen Cohon; 1 child, Hallie. BA in Civil Engring., U. Pa., 1969; MA in Civil Engring., MIT, 1972, PhD in Civil Engring., 1973. Legis. asst. for energy and environment U.S. Senator Daniel P. Moynihan, 1997—98; from faculty to assoc. dean engring. to vice provost rsch. Johns Hopkins; prof. environ. systems analysis, dean Sch. Forestry and Environ. Studies Yale U., 1992—97; pres. Carnegie Mellon U., Pitts., 1997—; apptd. chmn. by Pres. Clinton Nuclear Waste Tech. Review Bd., 1997—2002. Bd. dir. Mellon Fin. Corp. Recipient Joan Queneay Hodges award, Nat. Audubon Soc. and Am. Assn. Engring. Scis., Pareto-Edgeworth award, Multiple Criteria Decision Making Soc. Mem.: Am. Soc. of Civil Engr., Am. Water Resources Assn., Inst. for Ops. Research and Mgmt. Sci., Am. Geophysical Union, Sigma Xi, Tau Beta Pi. Office: Carnegie Mellon Univ 5000 Forbes Ave Pittsburgh PA 15213-3890*

COIFMAN, RONALD R., mathematician, educator; b. Tel Aviv; PhD, U. Geneva, 1965. Former prof. U. Chgo., Washington U.; prof. math. and computer sci. Yale U., New Haven, 1980—, chair math dept., 1986—89, Phillips prof. math., 1998—. Vis. prof. Tel Aviv U., Israel, U. Chgo. Co-author 3 books; contbr. articles and papers to profl. jours. Recipient State of Conn. medal of Sci., Gov. John G. Rowland, 1996, Nat. medal of Sci., 1999. Fellow: NAS; mem.: Conn. Acad. Sci. and Engring., Am. Acad. Arts and Scis. Office: Yale U Dept Math PO Box 208285 New Haven CT 06520-8283 Office Phone: 203-432-1213.*

COILE, RUSSELL CLEVEN, electrical engineer, consultant; b. Washington, Mar. 11, 1917; s. Cecil Roy and Gunda Cristoffersen Coile; m. Ruth Ledig, 1942 (div. 1951); children: Russell Cleven Jr., Christopher Christoffersen, Benjamin Paul; m. Ellen Miller Coile, Dec. 27, 1951; children: Jennifer Norah Miller, Jonathan Roy Miller, Andrew Cleven Miller. SB, MIT, 1938, SM, 1939, EE, 1950; PhD, City U., London, 1978; Grad., Naval War Coll., 1959, Air War Coll., 1964. Registered profl. engr., Pa., 1947, DC, 1951, lifetime instr. credential in engring., Calif. Cmty. Colls., 1989; cert. emergency mgr. Internat. Assn. Emergency Mgrs., 1993, lic. pvt. pilot FAA. Rsch. asst. Elec. Engring. Rsch. Lab., MIT, Cambridge, 1938—39; magnetician Cargnegie Instn. Wash./Huancayo (Peru) Magnetic Obs., 1939—42; engr. Colton & Foss, Inc., Washington, 1946—47; ops. rsch. scientist Ops. Evaluation Group, MIT, Washington, 1947—62; dir. rsch. Ops. Rsch. Group, Office Naval Rsch., Washington, 1953—57; dir. marine corps ops. analysis group Ctr. For Naval Analyses, Franklin Inst., Washington, 1962—67; ops. rsch. analyst Ctr. for Naval Analyses, U. Rochester, Arlington, Va., 1967—78; sr. rsch. analyst Ketron, Arlington, 1978—81; dep. exec. dir./chief scientist Planning Rsch. Corp., Fort Ord, Calif., 1982—87; sr. analyst Evaluation Tech. Inc., Monterey, Calif., 1988—90; disaster coord./emergency program mgr. Pacific Grove Fire Dept., Pacific Grove, Calif., 1990—2000; adj. prof. Inst. for Joint Warfare Analysis, Naval Postgraduate Sch., Monterey, 1998—2000; dir. disaster svcs. Carmel Chpt., ARC, Carmel-by-the-Sea, Calif., 2000—01; disaster cons., 2002—. Lectr. U.S. Naval War Coll., 1949, 56, 59, Anthropol. Soc. Hawaii, Honolulu, 1951, U.S. Naval Postgrad. Sch., 1951, 54, Japanese Maritime Def. Force Staff Coll., 1956, NATO Sci. Affairs Conf., London,

1964, U.S. Naval Postgrad. Sch., 1984—86; expert witness FCC Broadcast Station Hearing, 1946; Am. del. Internat. Fedn. Operational Rsch. Socs., Oslo, 1963; mem. small arms adv. com. Advanced Rsch. Projects Agy., Dept. Def., Washington, 1968—70; cons. Pres. Sci. Adv. Counsel, 1965, IEEE, 1966—67, Purdue U., Lafayette, Ind., 1978, NSF, Washington, 1997, Fed. Emergency Mgmt. Agy., Washington, 2000—02, Assn. Monterey Bay Area Govts., Marina, Calif., 2002—; instr. Neighborhood Emergency Response Teams, Pacific Grove, 1994—97; mem. Nat. Civil Def./Emergency Mgmt. Monument Commn., 2001—02. Asst. editor: Quality Control and Applied Statistics Abstracts, 1956—57, mem. editl. adv. bd.: Hungarian Acad. Scis. Internat. Jour. Scientometrics, 1978—97; contbr. articles to profl. jours. Chmn. cmty. working group Global Disaster Info. Network Conf., Mexico City, 1999, Ankara, Turkey, 2001. Commd. 2nd lt. U.S. Army, 1938, active duty, 1942—46, WWII, with U.S. Army, 1945, advanced through grades to col. USAF, 1962, ret., 1977. Recipient Exemplary Practices in Emergency Mgmt. award, Fed. Emergency Mgmt. Agy., 1998, 1999, 2000; Rschr. Exch. Travel fellow to visit Chinese Acad. of Scis., NSF, 1997. Fellow: Inst. Civil Def. and Disaster Studies; mem.: IEEE (life; cons. 1955), Am. Soc. Profl. Emergency Planners, Internat. Test and Evaluation Assn. (bd. dirs. 1985—88), U.K. Emergency Planning Soc., Inst. for Ops. Rsch. and the Mgmt. Scis., Am. Soc. for Info. Sci., Internat. Emergency Mgmt. Soc., Internat. Assn. Emergency Mgrs. (cert. emergency mgrs. comm. 1998—2003, assessor Emergency Mgmt. Accreditation Program 2003—), Island Sailing Club (Cowes, Eng.), Marine Meml. Club (San Francisco). Achievements include world speed record holder for flight from Washington to Rome, NY. Avocations: sailing, amateur radio. Home: 970 Egan Ave Pacific Grove CA 93950-2406 Office: Sand City Police Dept 1 Sylvan Park Sand City CA 93955 Office Phone: 831-394-1451. Personal E-mail: russell@coile.com.

COJBASIC, IVANA R., pianist, music educator; arrived in U.S., 1992; d. Rafailo S. and Marija M. Cojbasic; m. Michael Van Waldrop, Aug. 23, 2000. BA in Piano performance, U. Belgrade, 1986, MA in Piano performance, 1990; diploma in piano performance, State Conservatory of Music L. Cherubini, Florence, Italy, 1990; D Mus. Arts in Piano performance, U. North Tex., 1998. Piano collaborator Sch. Music Kornelije Stankovic, Belgrade, 1986—92; tchg. fellow in piano U. North Tex., Denton, 1993—96; asst. prof. piano U. Belgrade, 1998—2001; lectr. music Mesa State Coll., Grand Junction, Colo., 2001—04. Numerous performances as piano soloist and chamber musician in Europe, U.S. and Mexico. Recipient 1st prize internat. piano competition, Music Assn. Frederick Chopin, Rome, 1990; scholar for specialization in music, Hungarian Govt., 1988. Mem.: Music Tchrs. Nat. Assn., Nat. Guild Piano Tchrs. (adjudicator). Avocations: literature, languages, fine arts.

COKELET, GILES ROY, biomedical engineering educator; b. N.Y.C., Jan. 7, 1932; s. Roy S. and Anna M. (Trippel) C.; m. Sarah Drew, June 15, 1963; children: Becky, Bradford BS, Calif. Inst. Tech., 1957, MS, 1958; ScD, MIT, 1963. Rsch. engr. Dow Chem. Co., Williamsburg, Va., 1958-60; asst. prof. Calif. Inst. Tech., Pasadena, 1964-68; assoc. prof. Mont. State U., Bozeman, 1969-76, prof., 1976-78, U. Rochester, N.Y., 1978-98; rsch. prof. Mont. State U., Bozeman, 1998—. Contbr. articles to profl. jours. With U.S. Army, 1954-55, Japan. Recipient Sr. U.S. Scientist award Humboldt-Stiftung, Bonn, Fed. Republic Germany, 1981-82, 88. Fellow AAAS; mem. Biomed. Engring. Soc., Microcirculatory Soc., No. Am. Soc. Biorheology, Internat. Soc. Biorheology (past pres., Poiseuille medal 1999). Avocations: stamp collecting/philately, hiking. Office: Mont State U Dept Chem and Biol Engring Bozeman MT 59717-0001 Office Phone: 406-994-7048. Business E-Mail: giles_c@coe.montana.edu.

COKER, CLAYTON, ionospheric scientist, researcher; b. Oklahoma City, Okla., Feb. 5, 1962; s. Warren and Kathy Coker; m. Debbie Etheredge, Aug. 8, 1992; children: Logan, Alex, Makenzie. BS, Baylor U., Waco, TX, 1984; MA, U. of Tex., Austin, 1986. Rsch. scientist asst. U. of Tex., Applied Rsch. Laboratories, Satellite and Geophysics Divsn., Austin, Tex., 1984—86; rsch. scientist assoc. III U. of Tex., Applied Rsch. Laboratories, Electromagnetics Group, Austin, Tex., 1986—97; rsch. scientist assoc. IV U. of Tex., Applied Rsch. Laboratories, Space and Geophysics Lab, Austin, Tex., 1997—2001, engring. scientist, 2001—02; ionospheric scientist Praxis Inc., Naval Rsch. Lab., Washington, 2002—. Contbr. articles to profl. jours. Chorus mem. Austin Lyric Opera, Austin, Tex., 1987—91; rnc del. Rep. Party, Philadelphia, Pa., 2000—00; bd. of trustees Crestview Bapt. Ch., Austin, Tex., 1994—99; liaison bd. mem. Rawson-Saunders Sch., Austin, Tex., 1996—2000. Mem.: Internat. Union of Radio Sci., Assn. of Old Crows, Am. Geophys. Union. Achievements include development of early space weather instrument using Global Positioning System; Developed techniques for identifying auroral activity using satellite signals; Developed data fusion techniques for ionospheric tomographic imaging; research in ionospheric measurements from ultraviolet Earth limb imaging; First observations of conjugate storm-enhanced density in ionosphere. Avocations: singing, volleyball. Home: 11208 Lakeview Dr Dunkirk MD 20754 Office: Naval Rsch Lab - Praxis Inc 4555 Overlook Av SW Washington DC 20375 Office Phone: 202-404-3976. Personal E-mail: clayton@coker.net. E-mail: clayton.coker@nrl.navy.mil.

COKER, HOWARD COLEMAN, lawyer; b. Jacksonville, Fla., Apr. 30, 1947; B in Journalism, U. Fla., 1969, JD, 1971. Bar: Fla. 1972. Asst. state atty. Fourth Jud. Cir., 1972; assoc. Howell, Kirby, Montgomery, D'Aiuto & Dean, P.A., 1973-76; pres., dir. Coker, Myers, Schickel, Sorenson & Green, Jacksonville, Fla., 1976—. Guest lectr. more than 40 CLE seminars on litig. and trial matters throughout Fla., for Fla. Bar Assn., Acad. Fla. Trial Lawyers; advisor mock trial team U. Fla. Law Sch., 1991-98; adj. prof. U. North Fla. Chair ednl. adv. coun. U. North Fla., 1992-94, chair adv. bd. for paralegals, 1990-92. Fellow Am. Bar Found., Internat. Soc. Barristers; mem. ABA (ho. of dels., jud. qualifications commn.), ATLA, Am. Arbitration Assn. (panel arbitrators 1983—), Fla. Bar Assn. (pres. 1998-99, bd. govs. 1994-99, exec. com. 1995-97, all bar fconf. del. 1990-92, 94, 96, 97, budget com. 1995-97, bd. rev. coml. on profl. ethics chair 1995-96, disciplinary rev. com. 1994-95, jud. qualification screen com. 1994-95, legis. com. 1994-95, profl. retreat chair 1996, program evaluation com. chair 1996-97, 4th jud. cir. grievance com. reviewer 1994-97, coun. sects. 1991-94, chair 1993-94, sect. leadership conf. chair 1995, trial lawyers sect. exec. coun. 1987-94, bd. govs. liaison 1996, chair 1992-93, exec. co. 1989-93, legis. com. 1988-93), Am. Bd. Trial Advocates (pres. Jacksonville chpt. 1988—, media rep. 1988, exec. com. 1988—, diplomate), Am. Judicature Soc., Chester Bedell Meml. Found. (trustee 1996-2001), First Coast Trial Lawyers Assn., Acad. Fla. Trial Lawyers (bd. dirs. 1995—, pres. 2002-2003, Eagle sponsor 1990—), Fla. Lawyers Assn. for Maintenance of Excellence (bd. dirs. 1995-97), So. Trial Lawyers, Nat. Conf. Bar Presidents, Fla. Supreme Ct. Hist. Soc., Jacksonville Bar Assn., Roscoe Pound Found., U.S. Supreme Ct. Hist. Soc., Internat. Acad. Trial Lawyers, Fla. Conservation Assn. (pres. 1993-94), Fla. Ducks Unltd. (Sportsman of Yr. 1994), Fla. Wildlife Fedn., Seminole Club (bd. dirs. 1988, pres., 1989), U. Fla. Nat. Alumni Assn. (pres.'s coun. 1992-2001), Sigma Alpha Epsilon, Phi Delta Phi. Office: PO Box 1860 136 E Bay St Jacksonville FL 32201 Home: 4931 River Point Rd Jacksonville FL 32207 Office Phone: 904-356-6071. E-mail: hcoker@cokerlaw.com.

COKER, KELLER W., music educator; b. Salem, Oreg., Dec. 4, 1965; s. Gary Lynn Coker and Diane Pamela Bachmeier. MusB in Jazz Studies, U. So. Calif., 1988, MusM, 1990, MusD in Hist. Performance, 1996. Assoc. prof. We.Oreg. U., Monmouth, Oreg., 1999—. Home: 2090 Frost St NE Salem OR 97303 Office: Western Oregon Univ 345 N Monmouth Ave Monmouth OR 97361

COKUSLU, LYNDA ELIZABETH MCCORD, physician assistant; b. Atlanta, June 11, 1956; d. Joseph Adair and Yvonne (Champagne) McCord; m. Fethi Cokuslu, Aug. 24, 1985; children: Sasha, Sedef, Samantha. Cert. med. asst., Bryman Sch., 1975. Cert. med. asst. Casualty/liability claims processor Continental Ins./UAC, Atlanta, 1978—82; nutrition asst. Fayette County Edn., Peachtree City, Ga., 2001—03. Mem. adv. bd. CCSU. Host benefit Hapeville (Ga.) Hist. Soc., 1988; officer PTA, Hapeville, 1997; catechist Youth/Adult Sch. Religion, Hapeville, 1996—2002, Fayetteville, 2003—04. Mem.: Am. Health Info. Mgmt. Assn., Am. Med. Asst. Assn., Travelers Protective Assn., Midtown Bus. Assn., Internat. Poet Soc. Roman Catholic. Avocations: travel, collector, gardening, guitar, archaeology. Home: 105 Buckeye Ln Fayetteville GA 30214 Office: Audvi Elecs 140 A Robinson Dr Fayetteville GA 30214

COLA, PHILIP ANDREW, research administrator; b. Cleve., Nov. 14, 1965; s. Augustine Daniel and Elaine Theresa C.; m. Diane Marie Piskos, Oct. 12, 1991; children: Adam Denton, Samantha Marie. BA in Psychology, Cleve. State U., 1987, MA in Exptl. Psychology, 1994. Adminstrv. dir., lab. of biol. psychiatry Case Western Res. U., Cleve., 1989-96; dir. grants and contracts office U. Hosps. of Cleve., 1996—, dir. ctr. for clin. rsch., 2002—. Reviewer, UHC grant rev. com. U. Hosps. of Cleve., 1998—, IRB adminstv. office head, 1999—. Contbr. articles to profl. jours. Religious edn. instr. Saint Bartholomew Parish, Middleburg Heights, 1996—; vol. instr. Juvenile Detention Ctr. Sch., Cleve., 1996; vol. Am. Suicide Found., N.E. Ohio chpt., 1992-96. Mem. Soc. for Am. Baseball Rsch., Soc. of Rsch. Adminstrs., Applied Rsch. Ethics Nat. Assn. Democrat. Roman Catholic. Avocations: baseball history and research, psychology/psychiatry history, reading, sports publications. Office: U Hosps Cleve 11100 Euclid Ave Cleveland OH 44106-7061 E-mail: Philip.Cola@UHHS.com.

COLABELLA, GEORGE MICHAEL, management consultant, not-for-profit fundraiser; b. Yonkers, N.Y., Sept. 27, 1948; s. Vincent and Concetta (Onorato) C.; m. Linn Margaret Stanton, Nov. 4, 1995. BA in Psychology, Canisius Coll., 1970; MA in Psychology, Hunter C.U.N.Y., 1975. Mgmt./devel. cons. Grace Ch. Cmty. Ctr., White Plains, 1995-97; devel. cons. Westchester Ctr. Arts, Mt. Kisco, NY, 1997—2001; mgmt. cons. Family Svc. Soc. Yonkers, N.Y., 1998—; mgmt./fund raising cons. Westchester/Putnam Legal Svcs., White Plains, NY, 1997—, Project Children, N.Y.C., 2002—, Victims Assistance Svcs., Elmsford, NY, 1999—; devel. cons. UGC Found., New Rochelle, NY, 2001—. Adj. prof. Pace U., White Plains, NY, 1993—; columnist Mental Health News, New Rochelle, 1999—; devel. cons. Victims Asst. Svcs., 2000—; devel., mgmt. cons. Batoto Yetu Dance Co., 2000—, Project Kids Worldwide, 2002—; lectr. in field. Bd. dirs. Westchester Vol. Ctr., 1993—. Mem. Nat. Soc. Fund Raising Execs. Home: 30 Priscilla Ave Yonkers NY 10710-3606 Office: Colabella Assocs 30 Priscilla Ave Yonkers NY 10710-3606 E-mail: galluppe@aol.com.

COLAIANNI, JOSEPH VINCENT, judge; b. Detroit, Mar. 19, 1935; s. Pasquale and Marie D. (Mastrantonio) C.; m. Rita Milena Roll, Oct. 13, 1962; children: Marie Elena, Joseph Vincent, Michael Philip, Vincent Gerard. BEE, U. Detroit, 1956; postgrad., Wayne State U., 1956—58; JD with honors, George Washington U., 1961. Bar: Mich. 1962, Ohio 1963, Washington 1964. Assoc. firm Fay and Fay, Cleve., until 1965; trial atty. civil divsn. Dept. Justice, Washington, 1965-70; commr. U.S. Ct. Claims, Washington, 1970-73, trial judge, 1973-77; judge U.S. Ct. Claims D.C., 1977-84; mng. ptnr. Pennie & Edmonds, Washington, 1984-98; chair intellectual property Patton Boggs LLP, Washington, 1998—. Sci. liaison com. Sci. Ct., 1976-84; prof. grad. sch. Patent Resources Inst.; adj. prof. Am. U., 1984-87, Cath. U. Sch. Law, 1997—; adv. com. patents and trademarks U.S. Dept. Commerce, 1987-89; sr. adviser U.S. Claims Ct. Adv. Coun., 1984—; adv. com. U.S. Patent and Trademark Office. Adv. bd. Patent, Trademark and Copyright Jour., 1984-91. District Heights (Md.) Recreation Coun., 1969-70; bd. dirs. Henson Valley Montessori Sch.; pres. Tilden PTA, 1979-81; pres. Lido Civic Club, 1981, bd. dirs., 1982-90, 2000—; trustee Western Coll. Medicine, 1982-85; adv. bd. Holy Rosary, Washington, 1984-; co-pres. U. Md. at College Park Parents Assn., 1991-97; mem. pres. cabinet U. Detroit Mercy, 1982—, commn. on future Coll. Engring., 1995-96. Mem. Am., Fed. Bar Assns., Patent Office Soc., Mich., Ohio, Washington Bars, Phi Delta Phi, Eta Kappa Nu, Omicron Delta Kappa, Phi Delta Kappa, George Washington U. Law Rev. (1960-61). Office Phone: 202-457-6174. Business E-Mail: jcolaianni@pattonboggs.com.

COLAIZZI, JOHN LOUIS, dean; b. Pitts., May 10, 1938; s. Peter Richard and Lena M. (Sebastian) C.; m. Maria Rose Santoro, Aug. 12, 1967; children: James J., Patricia R., John Louis. BS, U. Pitts., 1960; MS, Purdue U., 1962, PhD, 1965. Asst. prof. Sch. Pharmacy, W.Va. U., Morgantown, 1964—65; asst. prof., assoc. prof. Sch. Pharmacy, U. Pitts., 1965—76, prof., chmn., assoc. dean, 1976—78; prof., dean Sch. Pharmacy Rutgers U., Piscataway, NJ, 1978—, acting v.p. acad. affairs, 2003. Bd. dirs. Rahway Hosp., N.J., 2003—; bd. dirs. Robert Wood Johnson Univ. Hosp., New Brunswick, N.J., 1984—, chmn., 1997-2000; mem. Medicaid Drug Utilization Rev. Bd. N.J., 1996-97; bioavailability cons. Drug Utilization Rev. Coun. N.J., 1997-2000. Mem. Am. Pharm. Assn., Am. Assn. Pharm. Scis., Am. Soc. Health-Sys. Pharmacists, Am. Assn. Coll. Pharmacy, Pharm. Care Mgmt. Assn. (dean's adv. coun. 1998-2003), Am. Inst. History of Pharmacy, Rho Chi, Alpha Zeta Omega, Sigma Xi. Democrat. Roman Catholic. Home: 21 Jason Dr East Brunswick NJ 08816-3342 Office: Rutgers U Sch Pharmacy 160 Frelinghuysen Rd Piscataway NJ 08854-8020 Office Phone: 732-445-2675. Personal E-mail: j.colaizzi@comcast.net. Business E-Mail: jlcolaiz@rci.rutgers.edu.

COLAIZZI, ROGER A., lawyer; b. Rochester, Pa., June 16, 1958; BA, Dickinson Coll., 1980; JD, Widener U., 1983. Bar: Pa. 1983, Md. 1984, DC 1988, NY 1991, Va. 1991, US Dist. Ct. (ea. dist.) Va. 1991, US Dist. Ct., DC 1992. Prosecutor honors prog. Civil Rights Div. Employment Litig. Sect., US Dept. Justice, 1983—87; spcl. asst. US Atty. for DC, 1986—87; ptnr. Intellectual Property Litig. Dept. Venable LLP, Washingotn, DC, 1992—. Mem. No. Va. Tech. Coun. Recipient Del. Law Forum Award. Mem.: ABA (mem. Litig. Sect.), Alexandria Bar Assn., NY Bar Assn., Pa. Bar Assn., Va. Bar Assn., Md. Bar Assn., DC Bar Assn. Office: Venable LLP 575 7th St NW Washington DC 20004 Office Phone: 202-344-8051. Office Fax: 202-344-8300. E-mail: racolaizzi@venable.com.

COLANDER, DAVID CHARLES, economist, educator; b. Jamestown, N.Y., Nov. 16, 1947; s. Fred J. and Elsie J. (Clauson) C. Student, U. Birmingham, Eng., 1968-69; BA, Columbia U., 1970, MPhil, PhD, 1976. Policy fellow Brookings Instn., Washington, 1977-78; cons. U.S. Govt., Washington, 1977-82; assoc. prof. U. Miami, Coral Gables, Fla., 1979-82; Christian A. Johnson Disting. prof. Middlebury (Vt.) Coll., 1982—; Kelley profl. disting. tchr. Princeton U., 2001—02. Author: (with Harry Landreth) The Coming of Keynesianism to America, 1989, (with Abba Lerner) MAP: A Market Anti-Inflation Plan, 1980, Macroeconomic Theory and Policy, 1986, (with Elgin Hunt) Social Science, 1984, 87, 90, 93, 96, 99, (with Harry Landreth) History of Economic Thought, 1988, 93, 2000, 2004, (with Arjo Klamer, The Making of an Economist, 1990, Why Aren't Economists as Important as Garbagemen?, 1991, Economics, 1993, 96, 98, 2001, 2004, (with Dewey Dane) The Art of Monetary Policy, 1994, (with Ed Ganber) Macroeconomics, 2002, The Lost Art of Economics, 2000; contbr. articles to profl. jours. With U.S. Army, 1970. Mem. Am. Econ. Assn., Ea. Econ. Assn. Avocation: biking. Office: Middlebury Coll Dept Econ Munroe 215 College St Middlebury VT 05753 Office Phone: 802-443-5302. E-mail: colander@middlebury.edu.

COLANGELO, BRYAN, professional sports team executive; BS in Bus. Mgmt. and Applied Econ., Cornell U., 1987. Scout Phoenix Suns, 1990-92, asst. dir. player personnel, 1992-95, v.p. adminstrn., gen. mgr., 1995-97, exec. v.p., 1997—99, gen. mgr., 1997—, pres., 1999—. Alt. gov. bd. govs. NBA; tournament dir. NIKE Desert Classic; pres. Phoenix Arena Sports; bd. dirs. Ariz. Sports Coun., Phoenix Suns Charities, Home Base Youth Svcs. Bd. dirs. Phoenix C. of C., vice chmn. econ. devel., mem. exec com. Named one of top 25 Valley Bus. Leaders, Ariz. Bus. Jour., 1995, NBA Exec. of the Year, The Sporting News, 2005 Office: Phoenix Suns 201 E Jefferson St Phoenix AZ 85004-2412

COLANGELO, CARMON, artist, printmaker, educator; b. Toronto, Oct. 29, 1957; came to U.S., 1981; s. Patrick and Coreen (Ciciretto) C.; m. Susan Jane Berry, Oct. 6, 1984; children: Jessica Lynn, Ashley Coreen, Chelsea Michelle. BFA in printmaking & painting, U. Windsor, Ontario, Can., 1981; MFA in printmaking, La. State U., 1983. Instr. La. State U., Baton Rouge, 1984; asst. prof. art W.Va. U., Morgantown, 1984-88, assoc. prof., 1988—94, dir. grad. studies in art, 1989—, assoc. chair div. art, 1993, chair, prof. art, 1993—97; dir. & distinguished rsch. prof. Lamar Dodd Sch. Art, U. Ga., Athens, Ga., 1999—; art prof. Lamar Dodd Sch. Art, Athens, Ga.; dir., prof. art Lamar Dodd Sch. of Art, U. Ga., Athens, 1997—; disting. rsch. prof. U. Ga., 2003—; grad. coord. W. Va. U., 1986—99. Founding dir. Ideas for Creative Exploration, U. Ga. Exhibited prints in shows U.S.-Korea Internat., 1989, Boston Printmakers 42d, 1990, Silvermine Internat., 1992, New World Contemporary Prints, Balt., 1993; solo exhbns.: Laura Mesaros Gallery, W.Va., 2004, Phantasmasoria, Scuola Internat. di Grafica, Venice, Italy, 2003, Phantasmasoria, Maseo de Pueblos, Guanajuato, Mex., 2004, Street Gallery, Liverpool Contemporary Biennial, Eng., Fountain of Age, Sandler-Hudson Gallery, Atlanta, 2002, Re-tracings, John and Jane Allcott Gallery, U. Chapel Hill, NC, 2001; represented in collections Nat. Mus. Am. Art, Wash. DC, Whitney Mus. of Am. Art, Fla. State Art Mus., Musco Nat. del Grabado, Buenos Aires, Kennedy Mus. Art, Butler Mus. Am. Art, Fogg Art Mus., Bibliotechue Internat. Recipient Clemson Nat. award, 1993, 65th Nat. SAGA Purchase award, N.Y., 1993; featured in Printmaking: A Primary Form of Expression, 1992, Sr. Rsch. Fine Arts grant, U. Ga., 1998, Disting. Rsch. Prof., U. Ga., 2003. Mem. Boston Printmakers, L.A. Printmaking Soc., Phila. Print Club, Mo. Print Consortium, Coll. Art Assn, Coll. Art Assn. (bd. mem.), Nat. Coll. Art Adminstrs., Ga. Mus. Art (bd. mem.), So. Graphics Coun. (bd. mem., 1995-1997), Art Papers (bd. mem, 1998). Avocation: sports. Office: University of Georgia Lamar Dodd School Art 100 B Visual Arts Athens GA 30602 Office Phone: 706-542-1511. E-mail: ccola@uga.edu.

COLANGELO, JERRY JOHN, professional sports team executive; b. Chicago Heights, Ill., Nov. 20, 1939; s. Larry and Sue (Drancek) C.; m. Joan E. Helmich, Jan. 20, 1961; children: Kathy, Kristen, Bryan. BA, U. Ill., 1962. Ptnr. House of Charles, Inc., 1962—63; assoc. D.O. Klein & Assocs., 1964—65; dir. merchandising Chgo. Bulls, 1966—68; gen. mgr. Phoenix Suns, 1968—87, now also exec. v.p., 1987, pres., chief exec. officer, 1987—; CEO Arizona Diamondbacks, Phoenix, 1998—2004, team exec. emeritus, 2004—. Mem. Basketball Congress Am. (exec. v.p., dir.), Phi Kappa Psi. Clubs: University, Phoenix Execs. Republican. Baptist. Office: Phoenix Suns 201 E Jefferson St Phoenix AZ 85004-2412

COLANTUONO, ANTHONY D., art history educator; b. Somerville, N.J., May 5, 1958; s. Frank Joseph and Flora Assunta (Pasquale) C. BA, Rutgers Coll., 1980; MA, Johns Hopkins U., 1982, PhD, 1987. Vis. asst. prof. Kenyon Coll., Gambier, Ohio, 1986-88, Wake Forest U., Winston-Salem, N.C., 1986-89; asst. prof. Vanderbilt U., Nashville, 1989-90; asst. prof. art history U. Md., College Park, 1990—. Contbr. articles to profl. publs. Am. Acad. in Rome fellow, 1983-85; NEH grantee, 1990. Mem. Phi Beta Kappa, Delta Phi Alpha. Avocations: painting, drawing, music, writing short stories and novels. Office: U md Dept Art History & Archeol College Park MD 20742-0001

COLANTUONO, THOMAS PAUL, prosecutor, former state legislator; b. Newton, Mass., Oct. 4, 1951; m. Pamela E. Chaloge. BA, Duke U., 1973; JD, Boston Coll., 1976. Bar: N.H. 1976. Assoc. Hamblett & Kerrigan, Nashua, N.H., 1976-78; asst. atty gen. N.H. Atty. Gen.'s Office, 1978-81; pvt. practice Derry, 1981—2001; state senator State of N.H., 1990-96; vice chmn. exec. dept., adminstrn. coms.; exec. councilor State of N.H., 1999—2001; U.S. atty. dist. N.H. U.S. Dept. of Justice, NH, 2002—. Former chmn ways and means com., N.H. Senate, mem. capitol budget, fin., judiciary, ins. coms., vice chmn. exec. dept., adminstrn. coms. Mem. ABA, N.H. Bar Assn., Derry Rotary, Londonderry and Hudson C. of C. Office: 55 Pleasant St Rm 352 Concord NH 03301

COLASURD, RICHARD MICHAEL, lawyer; b. Navarre, Ohio, Apr. 1, 1928; s. Michael and Adeline (Manack) C.; m. Jane Cooley, Dec. 20, 1986; children: Steven Michael, David Gerard, Cathie Marie. AB, U. Notre Dame, 1950; JD, Harvard U., 1953. Bar: Ohio 1953. Practice in, Toledo, 1960-99; spl. agt. FBI, 1953-56; asst. U.S. atty. charge Northwestern Ohio, 1956-60; mem. firm Shumaker, Loop & Kendrick, 1960-64; asst. city law dir. Toledo, 1964; mem. firm Mulholland, Hickey & Lyman, 1964-73; U.S. commr., 1963-67. Mem. Ohio Bar Assn., Toledo Bar Assn., Soc. Former Spl. Agts. FBI, Lexington C.C., Rotary. Roman Catholic. Home: 16133 Edgemont Dr Fort Myers FL 33908-3651

COLBERN, STEVEN GARRETT, chemist, researcher; s. Robert John and Mildred Elaine (Garrett) Colbern; m. Heather Noel Ebersole, Dec. 20, 1997; 1 child, Garrett James. BS in Chemistry, UCLA, 1994. Hazardous materials cert. Calif. Specialized Tng. Inst. Electronics technician USN, Ft. Magu, Calif., 1978—79; owner exotic animal bus., Glendale, Calif., 1984—89; biotech. rschr. L.A. Neuropsychiat. Inst., 1989—92, Cedars-Sinai Inst., Beverly Hills, Calif., 1992—94; owner vitamin bus., Oxnard, Calif., 1994—97; chemist, rschr. Applied Silicates, Ventura, Calif., 1997—98, YTC Am., Camarillo, Calif., 1998—. Patentee in field. Mem.: Internat. Soc. Optical Engrs., Am. Chem. Soc., Exptl. Aircraft Assn. Libertarian. Roman Catholic. Achievements include development of sol-gel process for the manufacture of ultra-pure, fluorinated silica glass; high and low pressure drying processes for sol-gel materials and monoliths. Avocations: model building, scuba diving, weightlifting.

COLBERT, ALICE TAYLOR, history educator; b. Atlanta, May 11, 1955; d. Codie Artez and Fay (Waits) Taylor; m. James Early Colbert Jr., May 18, 1991. BA, Shorter Coll., 1977; MA, Emory U., 1983, PhD, 1988. Adminstrv. asst. Atlanta Hist. Soc., 1980-81, mus. asst., 1981-83; contract curator Gulf Islands Nat. Seashore, Nat. Pk. Svc., Fla. and Miss., 1983-84; prof. history, dir. mus. Shorter Coll., Rome, Ga., 1984—, dean Sch. Edn. and Social Scis., 2002—. Mus. cons. Chieftains Mus., Rome, 1986—; project dir. Ga. Women Meeting Challenges symposium. Editor Jour. Cherokee Studies, 1988—, Jour. Ga. Assn. Historians, 1995-2002; regional coord. New Ga. Guide, 1993-96; contbr. articles to profl. jours. Mem. Ga. Rev. Bd. for Nat. Register of Historic Places, 1995—98, Ga. Hist. Records Adv. Bd., 2001—. Exhibit and program grantee Ga. Humanities Coun., 1987, 88, 93. Mem. Am. Studies Assn., So. Hist. Assn., Ga. Assn. Historians (exec. coun. 1991-94, pres. 1997-98), Ga. Assn. Mus. and Galleries (sec. 1987-88), Pi Gamma Mu (sec. 1985—). Avocations: public speaking, historical research. Office: Shorter Coll 315 Shorter Ave Rome GA 30165-4267

COLBERT, DEBORA A., director; d. Neil R. Montgomery; m. Jonathan L. Colbert; children: Robert N., Kathryn L., Curtis L. M in Mgmt., Regis U., 1999; PhD in Ednl. Leadership, Colo. State U., 2003. Cert. program planner LERN, 2002, program planner cert. programs LERN, 2004. Cmty. edn. coord. Nat. Technol. U., Fort Collins, Colo., 1996—2000; dir. distance degrees Colo. State U. Continuing Edn., Fort Collins, 2000—. Mem. Leadership Ft. Collins, 2004—05. Mem.: U. Continuing Edn. Assn., Nat. U. Degree Consortium (v.p. 2004—05). Office: Colorado State Univ Continuing Edn Spruce Hall Campus Delivery 1040 Fort Collins CO 80523-1040 Office Phone: 970-491-2645. Business E-Mail: dcolbert@learn.colostate.edu.

COLBERT, JAMES W., III, lawyer; b. N.Y.C., Sept. 1, 1945; AB magna cum laude, Yale U., 1967; JD magna cum laude, Harvard U., 1970. Bar: Calif. 1971. Law clk. to Hon. Shirley M. Hufstedler U.S. Ct. Appeals (9th cir.), 1970-71; mem. O'Melveny & Myers, L.A. Mem. L.A. County Bar Assn. Office: O'Melveny & Myers 400 S Hope St Los Angeles CA 90071-2899

COLBERT, JEAN MARIA, elementary school educator; b. Waynesboro, Pa., May 29, 1953; d. Florence M. C. BS in Edn., Shippensburg (Pa.) U., 1975, MEd, 1979. Cert. instructional level II. Tchr. Greencastle (Pa.) Antrim Sch. Dist., Chambersburg (Pa.) Area Sch. Dist.; coach Faust Jr. High Sch., Chambersburg. Coach eighth grade girl's basketball. Mem. NEA, Pa. Edn. Assn., Chambersburg Area Edn. Assn. Home: 42 W Commerce St Chambersburg PA 17201-1114

COLBERT, MARVIN JAY, retired internist, educator; b. Spokane, Wash., Nov. 6, 1923; s. John B. and Elizabeth (Peters) C.; m. Eleanor Ruth Rott, June 2, 1951 (dec. July 2000); children: Janet Lynn, James Lee, Lawrence Jay. Student, U. Utah, 1940-43; BS, Yale U., 1946; MD, Boston U., 1949. Diplomate: Am. Bd. Internal Medicine. Intern, resident in internal medicine Presbyn. Hosp., Chgo., 1949-50, VA Hosp., Boston, 1953-54, U. Ill. Rsch. and Ednl. Hosp., 1954-55; pvt. practice internal medicine Belmond, Iowa, 1955-56; mem. faculty U. Ill., Chgo., 1956-58; dir. health svc. Med. Ctr., 1959-78, prof. medicine, 1969-78; dir. employee health svcs. Evang. Hosp. Assn., Oak Brook, Ill., 1978-86. Cons. internal medicine radiol. and environ. rsch. div. Argonne (Ill.) Nat. Lab., 1978-79. Pres. Hillcrest PTA, Downers Grove, Ill., 1960-62; Parent-Tchrs. Group Chiengmai Co-Ednl. Ctr., Thailand, 1965-66. Capt. M.C. AUS, 1943-46, 50-52. Fellow ACP; mem. Assn. for Advancement of Automotive Medicine (dir. 1969-76). Home: 1700 Robin Ln #544 Lisle IL 60532 Office Phone: 630-969-1139. Personal E-mail: ERColbert@aol.com. *While on leave from The University of Illinois, Marvin Jay Colbert was a Visiting Professor of Internal Medicine. Between the years of 1965-66 he taught at The Chiengmai Medical School and Hospital in Chiengmai, Thailand.*

COLBERT, STEPHEN, comedian, actor; b. Charleston, S.C., May 13, 1964; m. Evelyn McGee; 3 children. Grad., Northeastern U., 1986. Performer Second City, Chgo., Annoyance Theatre, Chgo. Actor: (films) Snow Days, 1999, Nobody Knows Anything, 2003, Bewitched, 2005, (voice): (TV series) Harvey Birdman, Attorney at Law, 2001—, Crank Yankers, 2002, Tough Crowd with Colin Quinn, 2002—; actor, writer: Exit 57, 1995—96; The Dana Carvey Show, 1996; (co-creator and voice of Ace, The Ambiguously Gay Duo) Saturday Night Live, 1996—; actor: (TV series) The Daily Show with Jon Stewart, 1997—; writer: TV series The Daily Show with Jon Stewart, 2003—; actor, writer: (TV films) Strangers with Candy: Retardation, a Celebration, 1998; actor, writer, co-prodr.: (TV series) Strangers with Candy, 1999—2000; co-author (with Amy Sedaris and Paul Dinello): Wigfield, 2003. Office: The Daily Show 513 W 54th St New York NY 10019*

COLBERT, THOMAS, state supreme court justice; b. Oklahoma City, Okla., Dec. 30, 1949; m. Doretha Guion; 3 children. Grad., Eastern Okla. State Coll., 1970; BS, Ky. State U., 1972, MA in Ed., 1976; JD, U. Okla. Coll. of Law, 1982. Asst. dean Marquette U. Law Sch., 1982—84; asst. dist. atty. Okla. County, 1984—86; atty. Miles-LaGrange & Colbert, 1986—89, Colbert and Associates, 1989—2000, Okla. Dept. Human Services, 1988—89, 1999—2000; judge Okla. Ct. of Civil Appeals, 1999—2004, chief judge, 2004; justice Okla. Supreme Ct., 2004—. Served in criminal investigation div. U.S. Army, 1973—75. Mem.: ABA, Nat. Bar Assn., Tulsa County Bar Assn., Okla. Bar Assn. Office: Okla Supreme Ct Rm 204 State Capitol Bldg Oklahoma City OK 73105

COLBERT, VIRGIS W., food products executive; m. Angela Colbert; three children. BS in Indsl. Mgmt., Ctrl. Mich. U. Mfg. gen. supt. Chrysler Corp.; asst. to plant mgr. Miller Brewing Co., Reidsville, N.C., 1979-80, prodn. mgr. Ft. Worth, 1980-81, profn. mgr. Milw., 1981, plant mgr., 1981-87, asst. dir. can mfg., 1987-88, dir. can mfg., 1988, dir. container and support mfg., 1988-89, v.p. materials mfg., 1989-90, v.p. plant ops., 1990-93, sr. v.p. ops., 1993-95, sr. v.p. worldwide ops., 1995-97, exec. v.p., 1997—, also bd. dirs. and exec. com. Bd. dirs. Weyco, Inc., Delphi Corp., Manitowoc Co.; bd.d irs. The Stanley Works. Past chmn. bd. Thurgood Marshall Scholarship Fund; past chmn. bd. trustees Fisk U., Nashville; bd. dirs. Bradley Sports and Entertainment Corp. Ctr., Greater Milw. Open; exec. adv. com. Nat. Urban League's Black Exec. Exch. Program. Recipient various awards Jarvis Christian Coll., Tyler, Tex., So. U., New Orleans, N.C. AT&T, Greensboro, Clark Coll., Atlanta, Grambling (La.) State Coll., Fla. Meml. Coll., Miami, U. N.C., Greensboro, Young Program of Nat. Alliance Bus., Svc. award Nat. Urban Leage, Trumpet award Turner Broadcasting Sys., 1996, Exec. Leadership Coun. Achievement award, 1998; named Harlem YMCA Black Achiever, Milw. YMCA Black Achiever, Phi Beta Sigma Fraternity Black Achiever, one of 50 Top Black Execs. in Corp. Am., Ebony Mag., 1992, one of 24 To Watch in '94, Ebony Mag., 1994, one of 12 Most Powerful Blacks in Corp. Am., Ebony Mag., 1998, one of Am.'s 40 Most Powerful Black Execs., Black Enterprise Mag., 1993, One of 50 Top Black Execs. in Corp. Am., Black Enterprise Mag., 2000, Beverage Exec. of Yr., Beverage Industry Mag., 2001, One of 50 Most Powerful Balck Execs. in Am., Fortune Mag., 2002, One of 75 Most Powerful African Ams. in Corp. Am., Black Enterprise Mag., 2005; inductee Scott H.S. Hall of Fame, Toledo, 1987. Mem. NAACP (life, Svc. award), 100 Black Men of Am. (hon.), Omega Psi Phi. Office: Miller Brewing Co 3939 W Highland Blvd Milwaukee WI 53201

COLBERT, VIRGIS WILLIAM, food products executive; b. Jackson, Miss., Oct. 13, 1939; s. Quillie and Eddi Colbert. BS, Ctrl. Mich. U. With Toledo Machining Plant Chrysler Corp., 1966—79, foreman, 1968—70, gen. foreman, 1970—73, mfg. supt., 1973—77, gen. mfg. supt., 1977—79; asst. to plant mgr. Miller Brewing Co., Reidsville, NC, 1979—80, prodn. mgr. Ft. Worth, 1980—81, plant mgr. Milw. Container Plant, 1981—87, asst. dir. can mfg., 1987—88, dir. container and support mfg., 1988—90, v.p. materials mfg. and plant ops., 1990—91, v.p. plant ops., 1991—93, sr. v.p. ops., 1993—95, sr. v.p. worldwide ops., 1995—97, exec. v.p., 1997—. Bd. dirs. Delphi Corp., The Stanley Works, Manitowoc Co., Inc., Miller Brewing Co., Milw., Bradley Ctr., Sports and Entertainment Corp. Mem.: NAAPC, Frontiers Internat. Club, Shriners, Masons, Sigma Pi Phi, Omega Psi Phi. Office: Miller Brewing Co 3939 W Highland Blvd Milwaukee WI 53208-2866

COLBERT-CORMIER, PATRICIA A., secondary school educator; b. Lake Charles, La., Nov. 12, 1943; 4 children. BS in Biology, U. La., 1965, MS in Microbiology, 1975. Edn. specialist cert. in reading 1978. Tchr. biology dept. Lafayette (La.) H.S., 1975—, mem. health acad. com., 2003—. Mem. editl. adv. panel Cold Spring Harbor Labs. DNA Learning Ctr. Mem. Nat. Academics Tchrs. Adv. Group; past bd. dirs. Nat. Bd. Profl. Tchg. Stds. Finalist, Nat. Tchr. Hall Fame; DuPont fellow, 1994, Albert Einstein fellow, NASA, Washington, 2000—01, Disney Ch. Am. Tchr. and Tandy Tech. scholar, 1996. Office: Lafayette HS Biology Dept 3000 W Congress St Lafayette LA 70506 Office Phone: 337-984-5284. Personal E-mail: p53colbert@aol.com.

COLBORN, GENE LOUIS, anatomy educator, researcher; b. Springfield, Ill., Nov. 23, 1935; s. Adin Levi and Grace Downey (Tucker) C.; divorced; children: Robert Mark, Adrian Thomas, Lara Lee Colborn Russell; m. Sarah Ellen Crockett, Aug. 14, 1976; children: Jason Matthew, Nathan Tucker. BA with honors, Ky. Christian Coll., 1957; BS with honors, Milligan Coll., 1962; MS in Anatomy, Wake Forest U., 1964, PhD in Anatomy, 1967. Postdoctoral fellow U. N.Mex. Sch. Medicine, Albuquerque, 1967—68; asst. prof. U. Tex. Health Sci. Ctr., San Antonio, 1968—72, assoc. prof., 1972—75; assoc. prof. anatomy Med. Coll. Ga., Augusta, 1975—88, prof. anatomy, 1988—2000, prof. surgery, 1993—2000, emeritus prof. anatomy and surgery, 2000—, dir. Ctr. for Clin. Anatomy, 1987—2000, dir. med. gross anatomy, 1975—2000, cons. dept. surgery, 1977—2000; clin. prof. surgery Emory U. Sch. Medicine, Atlanta, 1996—; chmn. divsn. anat. scis. Ross U. Sch. Medicine, Dominica, 2000—01; prof. Am. U. Caribbean Sch. Medicine, St. Maarten, Netherlands Antilles, 2002—04, chmn. anatomy, 2002—04. Pres. Ga. State Anat. Bd., 1983-93; cons. Eisenhower Army Med. Ctr., 1990-96; founder Gelco Med. Pub. Co., 2004. Author: Practical Gross Anatomy, 1982, Surgical Anatomy, 1987, Hernias, 1988, Musculoskeletal Anatomy, 1989, Workbook of Surgical Anatomy, 1990, Clinical Gross Anatomy, 1993, Modern Hernia Repair, 1996, The Embryological and Anatomical Basis of Surgery, 2002; mem. editl. bd.: Clin. Anatomy Jour.; contbr. numerous articles on cardiac conduction, nervous sys., primate anatomy, cell culture and clin. and surg. anatomy to profl. jours. Active San Antonio Symphony Mastersingers, 1970-75, Augusta Opera, 1975—, Augusta Choral Soc., 1975-95; judge Regional Sci. Fairs, Augusta, 1978-90. Recipient Golden Apple award, U. Tex. Health Sci. Ctr., 1975, Outstanding Med. Educator award, Med. Coll. Ga., 1976, 1977, 1978, 1982, 1987, 1988, 1990, 1991, 1997, Disting. Faculty award, 1978, 2000, Excellence in Tchg. award, 1997, 1999, Regents' award in tchg., 1998, others. Mem. AAUP, Am. Assn. Clin. Anatomists (membership chmn. 1982-86, mem. editl. bd. Jour. Clin. Anatomy 1994—), Am. Assn. Anatomists, Columbia County Choral Soc. (founding mem.), KC (4th degree). Republican. Avocations: opera, chorales, chess, tennis, camping. Address: 178 Creekview Ct Martinez GA 30907 E-mail: glcolb@yahoo.com.

COLBORN, NANCY WOOTTON, school librarian; b. Emporia, Kans., Aug. 29, 1959; d. Calvin Richard and Linda Jean Wootton; m. James Randall Colborn; children: Elizabeth Milhander, Tyler. BS, Kans. State U., 1981; MLIS, Ind. U., 1993. Asst. libr. ref. Franklin D. Schurz Libr., Ind. U. South Bend, Ind., 1994—98, assoc. libr. ref., coord. pub. rels. and staff develop., 1998—2002, assoc. libr., coord. libr. instr. and staff devel., 2002—. Contbr. articles to profl. jours. Mem.: ALA (mem. machine-assisted ref. sect. of user access svc. com. 1998—2002, chair machine-assisted ref. sect. of user access svc. com. 1999—2000, occasional papers subcom. 2002—), Assn. Coll. Rsch. Librs., Ind. Acad. Libr. Assn. (exec. bd. 1997—2005, sec./treas. 2001—02, vice chmn. 2002—03, chmn. 2003—04), Ind. Libr. Fedn. (exec. bd. 2003—, sec. 2004—), Beta Phi Mu (Chi chpt. exec. bd. 1999—2000). Office: Franklin D Schurz Library IUSB 1700 Mishawaka Ave PO Box 7111 South Bend IN 46634 Business E-Mail: ncolborn@iusb.edu.

COLBOURN, TREVOR, retired academic administrator, historian; b. Armidale, New South Wales, Australia, Feb. 24, 1927; came to U.S., 1948; s. Harold Arthur and Ella Mary (Henderson) C.; m. Beryl Richards Evans, Jan. 10, 1949; children: Katherine Elizabeth, Lisa Sian Elinor. BA with honors, U. London, 1948; MA, Coll. William and Mary, 1949, Johns Hopkins, 1951, PhD, 1953. From instr. to asst. prof. Pa. State U., 1952-59; from asst. prof. to prof. Am. history Ind. U., 1959-67; dean Grad. Sch., prof. history U. N.H., 1967-73; v.p. for acad. affairs San Diego State U., 1973-77, acting pres., 1977-78; pres. U. Central Fla., Orlando, 1978-89. Author: The Lamp of Experience, 1965, 2d edit., 1998, The Colonial Experience, 1966, (with others) The Americans: A Brief History, 1972, 4th edit., 1985; co-editor: (with others) The American Past in Perspective, 1970; editor: (with others) Fame and the Founding Fathers, 1974, 2d edit., 1998. Mem. Orgn. Am. Historians, Am. Assn. State Colls. and Univs. Office: U Cen Fla Office Pres Emeritus Orlando FL 32816-1110 Office Phone: 407-823-2373. Business E-Mail: colbourn@mail.ucf.edu.

COLBURN, DAVID DUNTON, brokerage house executive; b. San Mateo, Calif., Aug. 18, 1958; s. Richard Dunton and Joan Francis (Garber) C.; m. Carolyn Louise Hadley, Sept. 30, 1989; children: Margaret Hadley, Ethan Dunton. BA, Harvard U., 1980; MBA, U. Pa., 1989. V.p. Bank of Am., L.A., 1981-87; investment mgr. CED Mgmt. Svcs. Inc., Northbrook, Ill., 1989-91; mng. ptnr. Lincolnshire Assocs., Ltd., 1991—, Miranda Investors, LLC, Northbrook, 2000—. Trustee R.L. Stevenson Sch., 2003—. Mem. Young Pres. Orgn. Office: 555 Skokie Blvd Ste 555 Northbrook IL 60062-2854 E-mail: davidcolburn@mac.com.

COLBURN, DAVID R., academic administrator; BA, MA, Providence Coll.; PhD, U. N.C., 1971. Joined U. Fla., Gainesville, 1972, chairperson dept. history, 1981—89, assoc. dean Coll. Liberal Arts and Scis., 1989—95, provost, 2000—. Author: Government in the Sunshine State: Florida Since Statehood, 1999, African American Mayors: Race, Politics and the American City, 2000, Florida's Megatrends: Critical Issue Facing Florida in the Twenty-First Century with Lance deHaven-Smith, 2001; contbr. chapters to books, articles to profl. jours., to newspapers. With U.S. Army, 1966, Vietnam. Office: Univ Fla 235 Tigert Hall PO Box 113175 Gainesville FL 32611

COLBURN, DONALD EUGENE, protective services official; b. Atlanta, Oct. 22, 1954; s. Dillard Eugene and Juanita Kuykendall C.; divorced; children: Allison, Lindsey, Kyle, Madelyn. Student, Clayton State Coll., Valencia State Coll. Ordained to ministry Bapt. Ch., 1988. Maintenance Eggo Frozen Foods, Atlanta, 1972-75; police officer City of Palmetto, Ga., 1975—76; detective Clayton County Police SWAT Dept., Jonesboro, Ga., 1976-81; police officer, SWAT team Dekalb County Police Dept., Decatur, Ga., 1981—83; lt. comdr. narcotics Clayton County Dist. Attys. Office, 1983—95, capt., 1995—98; asst. comdr. narcotics Clayton County Drug Enforcement Task Force, 1998-99; with Clayton County Sheriff Office, 1983—99; investigator III Clayton County Dist. Attys. Office, Jonesboro, Ga., 1999—2002; capt. spl. ops., comdr. vice unit, gang unit, K-9 unit, street narcotics unit, intell unit, homeland def. terrorist task force Clayton Police Dept., 2002—. Firearms instr.; std. tng. instr. Ga. P.O.S.T.; sr. instr. Clayton County Police Acad., Ga. P.O.S.T. Sr. Instr., Clayton County Dist. Atty. Office. Former asst. pastor, pastor and youth min. First Freewill Bapt. Ch. Mem. Ga State Power Engrs., Internat. Narcotics Officers Assn., Police Benevolent Assn., Ga. Assn. Law Enforcement Firearm Instrs., Ga. Narcotics Officers Assn., Nat. Narcotics Officer Assn., Ga. State Intell Network, Ga. Gang Investigators Office: Spl Ops Unit Clayton County Police Dept 7911 N McDonough St Jonesboro GA 30236 Office Phone: 770-477-3609. E-mail: donald.colburn@co.clayton.ga.us.

COLBY, ANNE, psychologist, educator; b. Galveston, Tex., Feb. 10, 1946; d. Malcolm Young and Emily Jane (Armacost) C.; m. William V.B. Damon; 1 child, Caroline Colby. BA, McGill U., Montreal, Que., Can., 1968; PhD, Columbia U., 1972. Lic. psychologist, Mass. Rsch. assoc., lectr. Harvard U., Cambridge, Mass., 1972-80; dir. Henry A. Murray Rsch. Ctr., Radcliffe Coll., Cambridge, 1980-98; sr. scholar Carnegie Found. for Advancement of Tchr., Stanford, Calif., 1997—. Vis. prof. Haas ctr. Stanford U., 1994-95; cons. prof. Stanford U., 1997—. Author: The Measurement of Moral Judgment, 1987, Some Do Care, 1992, Ethnography and Human Development, 1996, Competence and Character through Life, 1998, Looking at Lives, 2002, Educating Citizens, 2003. Grantee NIMH, NSF, John D. and Catherine T. MacArthur Found., Mellon Found., W.T. Grant Found., Spencer Found., Social Sci. Rsch. Coun., Inst. Noetic Scis., Surdna Found., Walter and Elise Haas Fund, Carnegie Corp., Hewlett Found., Ford Found Office: Carnegie Found Advancement Tng 51 Vista Ln Stanford CA 94305-8703 E-mail: colby@carnegiefoundation.org.

COLBY, DAVID C., healthcare management company executive; BA in Biophysics, Columbia U., 1975; MBA, Tulane U., 1978, MHA, 1979. CPA. Healthcare cons. Touche Ross & Co. (now Deloitte & Touche; sr. v.p., CFO, Meth. Hosp., Houston; sr. v.p., CFO, then sr. v.p. and treas. Columbia/HCA Healthcare Corp.; exec. v.p., CFO, bd. dirs. Am. Med. Response, urora, Colo., until 1997; exec. v.p., CFO, WellPoint Health Networks Inc., Woodland Hills, Calif., 1997—. Bd. dirs. Blyth Holdings, 2 Connect, Inc. Office: Wellpoint Health Networks One WellPoint Way Thousand Oaks CA 91362-3809 Office Phone: 805-557-6767. E-mail: david.colby@wellpoint.com.*

COLBY, FRANK GERHARDT, scientific consultant; b. Mulhausen, Germany, Apr. 10, 1915; came to U.S., 1946; s. Fritz and Paula (Oppenheimer) Cohn; m. Renee Hiller, Oct. 15, 1952 (dec. Mar. 1995); children: Audrey B., Leonard F. ChemE, U. Geneva, 1939, DSc, 1941. Pvt. practice various cos., Havana, Cuba, 1941-46; rsch. chemist Indsl. Tape Corp., New Brunswick, N.J., 1946-47; chem. lit. specialist Comml. Solvents Corp., Terre Haute, Ind., 1947-51; from dir. rsch. info. to assoc. dir. sci. issues R.J. Reynolds Tobacco, Winston-Salem, N.C., 1951-83; sci. cons. rsch. analysis and product liability N.Y.C., 1983—. Fellow AAAS; mem. Am. Chem. Soc.

COLBY, GEORGE VINCENT, III, electronics executive; b. Ft. Huachuca, Ariz., May 24, 1957; s. George Vincent Jr. and Barbara Colby; m. Celina Paratore, Sept. 27, 1986; children: George Nicholas, Celina Marie. BSBA, Suffolk U., Boston, 1982; MBA, Bentley Coll., 1985. Materials mgr. Craig Sys., Inc., Amesbury, Mass., 1985-88, Summit Technology, Inc., Waltham, Mass., 1988-93, Madison Cable Corp., Worcester, Mass., 1994; v.p. logistics Elec. Americas, FCI USA Inc., Manchester, N.H., 1994—. Com. mem. Holy Cross Ch., Derry, N.H., 1999. Mem. Nat. Assn. Purchasing Mgrs., Am. Prodn. and Inventroy Control Soc. (past pres. Granite State chpt.). Avocations: kayaking, cross country skiing. Home: 4 Cyril Rd Derry NH 03038 Office: FCI USA Inc 47 E Industrial Park Dr Manchester NH 03019

COLBY, JAMES D., art gallery director, curator; b. Erie, Pa., Apr. 22, 1950; s. Robert Dale and Agnes Lois Colby; children: Robert Anderson, Erika Ann. BS, SUNY, Brockport, 1973; MFA, SUNY, Buffalo, 1980. Aquatics dir. Byron-Bergen (N.Y.) Ctrl. Sch., 1973—78; owner, cons. Colby Photographics, Jamestown, NY, 1980—86; assoc. prof., curator Jamestown C.C., Olean, NY, 1983—96, dir. exhbns. and galleries, 1996—. Artist-in-residence N.Y. State Coun. on the Arts, Jamestown, 1990, mem. visual arts panel; founder, dir. Mus. Without Walls and the Global Collection of Photography Weeks Gallery, Jamestown C.C. Exhibitions include Weeks Gallery, 1983—2005; creator, editor (website) Weeks Gallery, 2004—05; contbr. articles to profl. jours. Mus. outreach Jamestown and Southwestern pub. schs., 2000—05. Mem.: Soc. for Photographic Edn. (sec., treas., chair, newsletter editor N.E. region 1993—96, portfolio reviewer 1995—2005). Avocations: fitness, gardening, motorcycling, skiing. Office: Weeks Gallery Jamestown CC 525 Falconer St Jamestown NY 14702-0020 Business E-Mail: jimcolby@mail.sunyjcc.edu.

COLBY, JENNIFER LOUISE, artist; b. Oxnard, Calif., Mar. 9, 1957; d. John III and Janet Gay (Fiske) C.; m. Mark Eric Newman, Sept. 17, 1983; children: Sarah Jean Colby Newman, Rebekah Lynn Colby Newman. BA in Biology/Art, U. Calif., Santa Cruz, 1980; MA in Art, Calif. State U., Fresno, 1985; MA in Theology, Grad. Theol. Union, Berkeley, Calif., 1987. Instr. Gavilan Coll. Comm. Edn., Gilroy, Calif., 1989-95; faculty Hartnell Coll., Salinas, Calif., 1992-94, Chapman U., Monterey, Calif., 1989-96, Santa Catalina Sch., Monterey, 1995-96; dir./owner Galeria Tonantzin, San Juan Bautista, Calif., 1992-97; art. coord. Bade Mus./Pacific Sch. Religion, Berkeley, 1991—. Adj. faculty Pacific Sch. of Religion, Berkeley, 1994-97; curator Women's Caucus for Art, Monterey, 1992-94. Exhbns. include Face to Face, 1987, Border Crossings, 1985; curator: (exhibit) Flyways: Women and Ecology, 1992; contbr. articles to profl. jours. Pres. Monterey Bay Women's Caucus for Art, 1990-93. Recipient Ina Gregg Meml. award Calif. State U., Fresno, 1984, Best of Show award IFRA, 1987; artist-in-residence, Calif. Arts Commn., Sacramento, 1991-92. Mem. Monterey Bay Women's Caucas for Art (pres. 1990-93). Avocations: swimming, hiking, music, sewing. Home: PO Box 264 Aromas CA 95004-0264 Office: Galeria Tonantzin PO Box 606 San Juan Bautista CA 95045-0606

COLBY, JOY HAKANSON, critic; b. Detroit; d. Alva Hilliard and Eleanor (Radtke) Hakanson; m. Raymond L. Colby, Apr. 11, 1953; children: Sarah, Katherine, Lisa. Student, Detroit Soc. Arts and Crafts, 1945; BFA, Wayne State U., 1946; DFA (hon.), Coll. for Creative Studies, 1998. Art critic Detroit News, 1947—; originator exhibit Arts and Crafts in Detroit, 1906-1976; with Detroit Inst. Arts, 1976. Author: (book) Art and A City, 1956; contbr. articles to art periodicals. Mem. visual arts adv. panel Mich. Coun. Arts, 1974—79; mayor's appointment Detroit Coun. for the Arts, 1974; mem. Bloomfield Hills Arts Coun., 1974. Recipient Alumni award, Wayne State U., 1967, Art Achievement award, 1983, Headliner award, 1984, award arts reporting, Detroit Press Club, 1984, Art Leadership award, Coll. for Creative Studies, 1989. Office: 615 W Lafayette Blvd Detroit MI 48226-3124 Business E-Mail: jcolby@detnews.com.

COLBY, KAREN LYNN See WEINER, KAREN

COLBY-HALL, ALICE MARY, language educator; b. Portland, Maine, Feb. 25, 1932; d. Frederick Eugene and Angie Fraser (Drown) C.; m. Robert A. Hall, Jr., May 8, 1976 (dec. 1997); stepchildren: Philip, Diana Hall Goodall, Carol Hall Erickson. BA, Colby Coll., 1953; MA, Middlebury Coll., 1954; PhD, Columbia U., 1962. Tchr. French, Latin Orono (Maine) HS, 1954-55; tchr. French Gould Acad., Bethel, Maine, 1955-57; lectr. French Columbia U., 1959-60; instr. Romance lit. Cornell U., Ithaca, NY, 1962-63, asst. prof., 1963-66, assoc. prof., 1966-75, prof. Romance studies, 1975-97, prof. emerita, 1997—, chmn. Romance studies, 1990-96. Author: The Portrait in Twelfth Century French Literature: An Example of the Stylistic Originality of Chrétien de Troyes, 1965; mem. editl. bd. Speculum, 1976-79, Olifant, 1974—. Fulbright grantee, 1953-54; NEH fellow, 1984-85; recipient Médaille des Amis d'Orange, 1985; decorated chevalier de l'Ordre des Arts et Lettres, 1997. Mem. Modern Lang. Assn., Medieval Acad. Am. (councillor 1983-86), Internat. Arthurian Soc., Société Rencesvals, Académie de Vaucluse, Phi Beta Kappa. Republican. Congregationalist. Home: 308 Cayuga Heights Rd Ithaca NY 14850-2107 Office: Cornell U Dept Romance Studies Ithaca NY 14853 Business E-Mail: amc12@cornell.edu.

COLDEWEY, JOHN CHRISTOPHER, English literature educator; b. Beloit, Wis., June 13, 1944; s. George Henry and Frances Mary (McLoughlin) C.; m. Carolyn Culver (div.); children: Christopher, Devin; m. Christine May Rose, Sept. 9, 1989. BA, Lewis U., 1966; student, U. London, Eng., 1966; MA, No. Ill. U., 1967; PhD, U. Colo., 1972. Acting asst. prof. English U. Wash., Seattle, 1972-73, asst. prof. English, 1973-79, assoc. prof. English, 1979-91, prof. English, 1991—, dir. grad. studies, 1995-99; postdoctoral rsch. fellow Nottingham (Eng.) U., 1979-80; Fulbright exchange prof. U. East Anglia, Norwich, Eng., 1986-87. Lectr., speaker and reader in field. Author: Pseudomagia: A 17th Century Neo-Latin Tragicomedy by William Mewe, 1979, Renaissance Latin Drama in England, Vol. IV, 1987, Vol. 14, 1991, Contexts for Early English Drama, 1989, Early English Drama: An Anthology, 1993, Drama: Classical Through Contemporary, 1998, rev., 2001; editor: Modern Lang. Quar., 1983-93; contbr. chpts. to books, articles to profl. jours. Bd. dirs. Friends U. Wash. Libr., 1991-99 (pres. 1995-97); hon. advisor Brit. Univs. Summers Schs. Program, 1977-94. Fellow Medieval Acad. Am., 1974-75; grantee Am. Coun. Learned Socs., 1974-75, 1976-77, 86-87, 89-90, grantee NEH, 1979-80, 82-83, 92-93, fellow, 1999-2000. Mem. Coun. Editors Learned Jours. (pres. 1992-94, v.p. 1990-92, sec.-treas. 1989-90), Medieval and Renaissance Drama Soc. (exec. coun. 1997-98, v.p. 1998-00), Medieval European Drama Coun. (Am. rep. 1997-99). Avocations: skiing, mountain travel, running, biking. Home: 333 35th Ave E Seattle WA 98112-4923 Office: U Wash Dept English Box 354330 Seattle WA 98195-0001 Office Phone: 206-543-2183. E-mail: jcjc@u.washington.edu.

COLDITZ, GRAHAM, research scientist; MBBS, U. Queensland, 1979, MD, 1998; D of pub. health, Harvard U., 1986. Prof. medicine Harvard Med. Sch.; prof. epidemiology Harvard Sch. Pub. Health; dir. edn. Harvard Ctr. Cancer Prevention, 1994—2004, exec. dir., 2004—. Author: Handbook of Cancer Risk Assessment and Prevention, 2004. Recipient AACR-DeWitt S. Goodman Meml. Lectureship, 2003. Fellow: Royal Australian Coll. Physicians; mem.: Am. Cancer Soc. (dir. New England divsn., Clin. Rsch. Professorship 2003). Office: Harvard Sch Pub Health Dept Epidemiology Channing Lab 181 Longwood Ave Boston MA 02115

COLDREN, LARRY ALLEN, electrical engineering educator, consultant; b. Lewistown, Pa., Jan. 1, 1946; s. Roscoe Calvin and Mary (Hutchinson) C.; m. Donna Kauffman, Sept. 4, 1966; children: Christopher William, Bret Allen. BS, AB, Bucknell U., 1968; MS, Stanford U., 1969, PhD, 1972. Registered profl. engr., N.J. Mem. tech. staff Bell Labs., NJ, 1968-84, supr., 1984; prof. U. Calif., Santa Barbara, 1984—; chmn., chief tech. officer Agility Commns., 1998—. Contbr. over 500 papers to tech. jours.; patentee in field. Recipient John Tyndall award, 2004. Fellow IEEE (mem. ad com. 1988-94), Optical Soc. Am., IEE; mem. NAE, Phi Beta Kappa, Tau Beta Pi, Pi Mu Epsilon, Sigma Pi Sigma. Presbyterian. Avocation: flying. Home: 4665 Via Vistosa Santa Barbara CA 93110-2333 Business E-Mail: coldren@ece.ucsb.edu.

COLDWELL, MARIA V., art association administrator; b. Troy, N.Y., Dec. 4, 1952; d. John and Agnes (Reck) Vedder; m. Charles P. Coldwell, Oct. 16, 1982; 1 child, Thomas J. BA, PhD, Yale, New Haven, Conn., 1974. Vis. prof. Univ. Chgo., Chgo., 1981; coll. prof. Yale Univ., New Haven, 1979—83; exec. dir. Seattle Camerata, Seattle, 1989—91, Early Music Guild of Seattle, Seattle, 1991—99, Early Music Am., Seattle, 2002—. Bd. pres. Seattle Barogue Orchestra, Seattle, 2004—; bd. mem. The Tudor Chair, Seattle, 2000—. Recipient Noah Greenberg, Am. Musicological Soc., 1981. Episc. Office: Early Music Am 2366 Eastlake Ave E #429 Seattle WA 98102

COLDWELL, PHILIP EDWARD, financial consultant; b. Champaign, Ill., July 20, 1922; s. Montgomery Ian and Donna Clare (Rose) C.; m. Norma Elaine Abels, June 1, 1947; children: Douglas Michael, Cameron Iliff. BA, U. Ill., 1946, MS, 1947; PhD, U. Wis., 1952. Teaching asst. U. Ill., at Urbana, 1947; instr. Southwestern La. Inst., Lafayette, 1947-48, asst. prof., 1950-51; instr. Mont. State U., 1949-50; research economist Fed. Res. Bank, Kansas City, 1951-52, economist, officer Dallas, 1952-62, 1st v.p., 1962-68, pres., 1968-74; mem. bd. govs. Fed. Res. System, Washington, 1974-80; fin. cons., 1980—. Lectr. Southwestern Sch. Banking, Dallas, 1962-74; dir. Maxus Energy Corp., 1987-93. Trustee Austin Coll., 1977-89; dir. Temp Fund, Fed Fund, Muni Fund, 1980-99. Pilot USNR, 1942-46. Mem. Am. Econ. Assn., So. Finance Assn., Phi Delta Theta. Presbyn. (elder). Club: Economists (Dallas) (founder, 1st pres.). Home: 3330 Southwestern Blvd Dallas TX 75225-7653

COLE, ANDREW JAMES, neurologist, educator; b. N.Y.C. AB magna cum laude, Dartmouth Coll., 1979, MD, 1982. Lic. physician, N.Y., Md., Mass.; cert. specialist, Que.; diplomate Am. Bd. Psychiatry and Neurology, Am. Bd. Clin. Neurophysiology; cert. added qualification in clin. neurophysiology Am. Bd. Psychiatry and Neurology. Intern in internal medicine U. Hosps. Cleve., Case Western Res. U., Cleve., 1982-83; resident in neurology Mont. Neurol. Inst., McGill U., Que., Can., 1983-85, chief resident in neurology, 1985-86, chief fellow lab. clin. neurophysiology and electroenceph., 1986-87; rsch. fellow dept. neurosci., fellow dept. neurology Johns Hopkins U. Sch. Medicine, Balt., 1987-88, active med. staff dept. neurology, 1988-92; assoc. attending mem., active med. staff divsn. neurology Sinai Hosp., Balt., 1991-92; asst. neurologist Mass. Gen. Hosp., Boston, 1992-98, dir. epilepsy svc., 1992—. From instr. to asst. prof. dept. neurology Johns Hopkins U. Sch. Medicine, Balt., 1988-92; asst. prof. neurology Harvard Med. Sch., Boston, 1992-98, assoc. prof. neurology, 1999—; cons. neurologist Monson Devel. Ctr., Palmer, Mass., 1993—; cons. epileptologist Fernald State Sch., Waltham, Mass., 1994—; courtesy staff Emerson Hosp., Concord, Mass., 1996—; assoc. neurologist Brigham and Women's Hosp., Boston, 1998—, Mass. Gen. Hosp., Boston, 1999—; ad hoc reviewer Med. Rsch. Coun., Can., 1992, New Zealand Neurol. Found., 1997—, referee, 1995—; vis. clinician Mayo Clinic Found., Rochester, Minn., 1995; invited prof. Am. Brit. Cowdray Hosp., Mexico City, 1996; vis. prof. Barrow Neurol. Inst., Phoenix, 1999, Zayad Mil. Hosp., Abu Dhabi, United Arab Emirates, 2000; presenter in field. Ad hoc reviewer: (jours.) Neurology, Neurosci., Epilepsia, Brain Rsch., Exptl. Neurology, others. Recipient Clin. Investigator Devel. award Nat. Inst. Neurol. Disease and Stroke, 1989; Whitehall Found. Rsch. grantee, 1996, rsch. grantee Epilepsy Found. Am., 1992; Klingenstein fellow in neurosci., 1989, rsch. fellow Am. Acad. Neurology Neuropharmacology, 1988. Fellow Royal Coll. Physicians Can.; mem. Am. Neurol. Assn., Am. Acad. Neurology, Can. Neurol. Soc., Assn. for Rsch. in Nervous and Mental Diseases, Am. Epilepsy Soc. (mem. com. on med. student edn. 1993—, mem. ann. meeting program com. 1994-96, mem. com. on rsch. funding 1994—, mem. ann. course com. 1998—, leader clin. database devel. task force 1998—), Soc. for Neurosci. Office: Mass Gen Hosp Epilepsy Svc VBK-830 Boston MA 02114 Fax: (617) 726-9250. E-mail: cole.andrew@mgh.harvard.edu.

COLE, ANN HARRIET, psychologist, consultant; b. Phila., Feb. 27, 1949; d. Albert and Deborah (Mann) Brawerman; m. Stephen Cole, June 4, 1969 (div. June 18, 1987); children: Richard David, Robert Walter; m. Allan J. Besbris, Aug. 4, 1998. BA, SUNY, Stony Brook, 1971, MA, 1975. Dir. field rsch. Opinion Rsch. Assocs., 1974-76; v.p. Social Data Analysts, Inc., 1976-86; rsch. assoc. Jay Schulman, Inc., N.Y.C., 1986-87; cons. Litigation Scis., Inc., N.Y.C., 1988-90, Stanley S. Arkin, P.C., N.Y.C., 1990, Chadbourne & Parke, N.Y.C., 1990-91; pres. Ann Cole Opinion Rsch. and Analysis, 1991—. CBS news cons., 1994-95. Mem. Am. Soc. Trial Cons. (bd. dirs. 1994-99, v.p. 1996-97, pres. 1997-99), Qualitative Rsch. Cons. Am. Office: Ann Cole Opinion Rsch and Analysis 8913 Pennystone Ave Las Vegas NV 89134 Office Phone: 212-302-1650, 702-363-0390. E-mail: ahcole@acoraweb.com.

COLE, BRAD, mayor; b. Decatur, Ill., Nov. 27, 1971; s. Neal and M. Sue Cole. BA, So. Ill. U., Carbondale, 1994. Commr. Ill. Student Assistance Commn., Springfield, 1993-95; asst. dir. So. Ill. U. Alumni Assn., Carbondale, 1995-99; city councilman City of Carbondale, 1999—2003; asst. dep. chief of staff Office of Gov., Stat of Ill., Springfield, 1999—2001; dep. chief of staff Office of the Gov., State of Ill., Springfield, 2002—03; mayor City of Carbondale, 2003—. Dir. Lower Miss. Delta Devel. Ctr., Memphis, Tenn., 2000—. Trustee Carbondale Pub. Libr., 1997-99; commr. Carbondale Pk. Dist., 1997-99. Named one of Outstanding Young Men of Am., 1996, 98. Mem. So. Ill. U. Alumni Assn., Rotary (Club Rotarian of Yr. 1998), Masons (sec. lodge 2000— grand orator 2003—, Delta Chi (ritual com. 1997-), So. Ill. Mayor's Assn. (pres. 2005—). Home: PO Box 1071 Carbondale IL 62903 Office: City of Carbondale 200 S Illinois Ave Carbondale IL 62901

COLE, BRIAN, music educator; b. Manchester, Iowa, July 25, 1978; s. Jim and Carol Cole. MusB in Edn., Wartburg Coll., Iowa, 2000. Dir. of bands East Buchanan Cmty. Sch. Dist., Winthrop, Iowa, 2000—. Mem.: KC (warden 2004—). R-Consevative. Catholic. Home: 444 4th St N Winthrop IA 50682 Office: East Buchanan Cmty Sch Dist 414 5th St N Winthrop IA 50682 Office Phone: 319-935-3367. Office Fax: 319-935-3615. Personal E-mail: bcole@netins.net. E-mail: bcole@east-buc.k12.ia.us.

COLE, BRUCE MILAN, federal agency administrator, art historian; b. Cleve., Aug. 2, 1938; s. Jerome I. and Selma (Kaufman) C.; m. Doreen Luff, July 15, 1962; children: Stephaine Wren, Ryan Lawrence. BA, Western Res. U., 1962; MA, Oberlin Coll., 1964; PhD, Bryn Mawr Coll., 1969. Asst. prof. U. Rochester, 1969-73; assoc. prof. Ind. U., Bloomington, 1973-77, prof., 1973-88, disting. prof. fine arts, 1988—2001; chmn. Nat. Endowment for the Humanities, Washington, 2001—. Author: Giott and Florentine Painting 1280-1575, 1976, paperback edit., 1977, Agnolo Gaddi, 1977, Italian Majolica from Midwestern Collections, 1977, Masaccio and the Art of Early Renaissance Florence, 1980, Sienese Painting from Its Origins to the Fifteenth Century, 1969, The Renaissance Artist at Work, 1983, London, John Murray, 1983, Sienese Painting in the Age of Renaissance, 1985, Italian Art 1250-1550: The Relation of Renaissance Art to Life and Soc., 1987, Art of the Western World, Piero della Francesca, 1991, Giotto: The Scrovegni Chapel, Padua, 1993, Studies in Italian Art 1250-1550, 1996, Titian and Venetian Painting, 1450-1590, 1998, The Informed Eye, 1999. Recipient Pres.' award Am. Assn. Italian Studies, 1987; NEH fellow, 1972, Guggenheim Found. fellow, 1975, Am. Coun. Learned Socs. fellow, 1981. Fellow Accademia Senese degli Intronati; mem. Nat. Coun. on the Humanities, 1992-99. Avocation: walking. Office: Nat Endowment for the Humanities 1100 Pennsylvania Ave NW Washington DC 20506 Office Phone: 202-606-8310. E-mail: bcole@neh.gov.

COLE, CAROLYN, photojournalist; b. Boulder, Colo., Apr. 24, 1961; BA in Photojournalism, U. Tex., 1983. Staff photographer El Paso Herald Post, 1986—88, San Francisco Examiner, 1988—90; freelance photographer Mexico City, 1990—92; staff photographer Sacramento Bee, 1992—94, L.A. Times, 1994—. Contbr. (photographs) Holy Lands, Life Books, Time Inc., The American Spirit, Life--The Year in Pictures, 2002. Recipient Pictures of the Year, newspaper portrait/personality award of excellence, U. Mo., 1986, first place, feature pictures story for "Cadet McKeag: Wentworth Academy's Only Female", Calif. Press Photographers Assn., 1993, Mark Twain Award, first place picture story for "Haiti: Crisis in the Caribbean", AP News Execs. Coun., 1994, best spot news photo or photographic series for "Haiti: Crisis in the Caribbean", LA Times Editl. Award, 1994, best feature photo or photographic series for "Health Crisis in Russia", LA Time Editl. Award, 1995, first place, newspaper feature picture & newspaper feature story award of excellence, Pictures of the Year, U. Mo., 1994, issue reporting picture story award of excellence for "California's Fragile Future", 1996, third place issue reporting, 1998, Journalist of the Year Award, Times Mirror Corp., 1998, Pulitzer Prize, breaking news for LA Times team coverage of the North Hollywood shootout, 1998, newspaper feature story, second place for "In the Shadow of War", Pictures of the Year, U. Mo., 1999, global news picture story, award of excellence for "No Winners in War, 1999, general news picture award of excellence for "Face of Conviction", 2000, newspaper photographer of the year, Nat. Press Photographers Assn., 2002, Mark Twain Award for best of show, AP News Execs. Coun., 2002, first place, people in the news for "Church of the Nativity", World Press Photo, 2003, first place, mag. news story editing & second place, feature picture story for "Church of the Nativity", Pictures of the Year, U. Mo., 2003, Robert Capa Award for courage in photography for covering the siege at the Church of the Nativity, Bethlehem, Overseas Press Club, 2003, Newspaper Photographer of Yr., U. Mo., 2003, Nat. Press Photographers Assn., 2003, award for news photography for church of the nativity, Sigma Delta Chi, 2003, Pulitzer Prize for feature photography, 2004, George Polk award for photojournalism, 2004, Robert Capa award for courage in photography for Iraq war and civil conflict in Liberia, 2004, award for news photography Iraq war, Sigma Delta Chi, 2004, 2d pl. people in the news Iraq War, 3d pl. for civil conflict in Liberia, World Press Photo, 2004. Office: LA Times 2 Park Ave New York NY 10016

COLE, CAROLYN JO, brokerage house executive; b. Carmel, Calif. d. Joseph Michael Jr. and Dorothea Wagner (James) C. AB, Vassar Coll., 1965. Sr. v.p. UBS Painewebber, Inc., N.Y.C., 1975—95; exec. v.p. Tucker Anthony, Inc., Boston, 1995—97; chmn. Inst. Econ. & Fin., Inc., N.Y.C., 1997—98; mng. dir. Citigroup, N.Y.C., 1998—. Guest lectr. Harvard U. Bus. Sch.; lectr. Securities Industry Inst., Wharton Sch. U. Pa.; past chmn. bd. dirs. N.Y. Women's Bldg.; bd. dirs. Women's Venture Fund. Named to YWCA Acad. Women Achievers. Mem. NOW, DAR, N.Y. Soc. Security Analysts (past bd. dirs.), The CFA Inst., Soc. Fgn. Analysts, Aspen Inst. Humanistic Studies, Fin. Women's Assn., Women's Econ. Roundtable, Econ. Club N.Y., Women in Need (past bd. dirs.), Vassar Club. Democrat. Office: Citigroup Private Equity 388 Greenwich St New York NY 10013-2339 Office Phone: 212-816-4766. Business E-Mail: cali.cole@citigroup.com.

COLE, CHARLES DEWEY, JR., lawyer; b. Lower Merion Twp., Pa., Aug. 12, 1952; s. Charles Dewey and Margaret Ann (Leach) C. AB, Columbia U., 1974; JD, St. John's U., Jamaica, N.Y., 1979; ML Info. Sci., U. Tex., 1982; LLM, NYU, 1988; LLM in Environ. Law, Pace U., 1993; LLM in Trial Advocacy, Temple U., 1999; LLM in Advanced Litigation, Nottingham Trent U., 2003. Bar: N.Y. 1980, Tex. 1980, N.J. 1986, D.C. 1988, U.S. Dist. Ct. (we. and ea. dists.) Tex. 1980, U.S. Dist. Ct. (so. and ea. dists.) N.Y. 1980, U.S. Dist. Ct. (no. dist.) Tex. 1982, U.S. Dist. Ct. (no. dist.) N.Y. 1983, U.S. Dist. Ct. (we. dist.) N.Y. 1984, U.S. Dist. Ct. N.J. 1986, U.S. Dist. Ct. D.C. 1994, U.S. Ct. Internat. Trade 1980, U.S. Tax Ct. 1984, U.S. Ct. Appeals (5th and 11th cirs.) 1981, U.S. Ct. Appeals (Fed. cir.) 1982, U.S. Ct. Appeals (2d cir.) 1984, U.S. Ct. Appeals (D.C. cir.) 1987, U.S. Ct. Appeals (3d cir.) 1993, U.S. Supreme Ct. 1984; solicitor, Eng. and Wales, 1995; Higher Rights of Audience (civil procs.) Qualification, 2002. Law clk. to chief judge U.S. Dist. Ct. (ea. dist.), Beaumont, Tex., 1979-80, U.S. Ct. Appeals (5th cir.), Austin, Tex., 1981-82; assoc. Moore, Berson, Lifflander & Mewhinney, Garden City and N.Y.C., NY, 1982-85; assoc. and ptnr. Newman Schlau Fitch & Burns P.C., N.Y.C. and Mineola, NY, 1985-88; assoc. Meyer, Suozzi, English & Klein, P.C., Mineola and N.Y.C., 1988-95; of counsel, ptnr. Newman Fitch Altheim Myers, P.C., N.Y.C. and Newark, 1995—. Instr. trial techniques program Hofstra Law Sch., 1994—2000; instr. intensive trial advocacy program Widener Law Sch., 1999—. Author: Law Books as a Charitable Contribution, 1975, The EPA Lender Liability Regulations: EPA's Questionable Authority to Promulgate the Regulations as Part of the National Contingency Plan, 1993, Charging the Jury on Damages in Personal-Injury Cases: How New York Can Benefit from English Practice, 2004; contbr. book revs. to profl. publs. Mem.: Legal Writing Inst., Solicitors Assn. of Higher Ct. Advs., Coll. of State Bar Tex., State Bar Tex., Selden Soc., Supreme Ct. Hist. Soc., Soc. Advanced Legal Studies, Osgoode Soc. for Can. Legal History, Brit. and Irish Assn. Law Librs., Law Libr. Assn. Greater N.Y., Am. Assn. Law Librs., Fed. Bar Coun., Bar Assn. 5th Fed. Cir., Maritime Law Assn. U.S. (proctor), N.Y. County Lawyers Assn. (com. on fed. cts.), DC Bar, N.Y. State Bar Assn. (exec. and co-chmn. appellate practice coms., comml. and fed. litigation sect.), Law Soc. (reference group on multi-party actions), Clarity, Scribes (dir., brief-writing competition com.). Republican. Home: 16 94th St Apt 3B Brooklyn NY 11209-6643 Office: Newman Fitch Altheim Myers PC 14 Wall St New York NY 10005-2101 Office Phone: 212-619-4350. Business E-Mail: dcole@nfam.com.

COLE, CHARLES EDWARD, lawyer, state attorney general; b. Yakima, Wash., Oct. 10, 1927; married; 3 children. BA, Stanford U., 1950, LLB, 1953. Law clk. Vets. Affairs Commn. Territory of Alaska, Juneau, 1954, Territorial Atty. Gen.'s Office, Fairbanks, Alaska, 1955-56, U.S. Dist. Ct. Alaska, Fairbanks, 1955-56; city magistrate City of Fairbanks, 1957-58; pvt. practice law, 1957-90; atty. gen. State of Alaska, 1990-94; pvt. law comml. litigation, 1995—. Profl. baseball player, Stockton, Calif. and Twin Falls, Idaho, summers of 1950, 51, 53. With U.S. Army, 1946-47. Mem. Calif. State Bar, Washington State Bar Assn., Alaska Bar Assn. Office: Law Dept State of AK Office of Atty Gen PO Box 110300 Juneau AK 99811-0300 also: Law Offices of Charles E Cole 406 Cushman St Fairbanks AK 99701-4632

COLE, CHARLES GLASTON, lawyer; b. Washington, Jan. 17, 1952; s. Alan Y. and Gloria G. (Glaston) C.; m. Linda Martin, June 6, 1976; children: Elizabeth, Laura, Alan. BA, Yale U., 1973; JD, Harvard U., 1976. Bar: D.C. 1976, U.S. Dist. Ct. D.C. 1977, U.S. Ct. Appeals (D.C. cir.) 1977, U.S. Supreme Ct. 1982. Law clk. U.S. Ct. Appeals, Washington, 1976-77, U.S. Supreme Ct., Washington, 1977-78; assoc. Steptoe & Johnson, Washington, 1978-83, ptnr., 1983—. Mem. ABA (chair coun. appellate lawyers), Nat. Assn. R.R. Trial Counsel, Am. Bankruptcy Inst. Office: 1330 Connecticut Ave NW Washington DC 20036-1704

COLE, CHARLES LEE, marriage and family therapist, educator; b. Hobbs, N.Mex., Aug. 24, 1944; s. Artie Lee and Margaret Ellen (Black) C.; m. Anna L. Cole, June 4, 1971. BA, Tex. Wesleyan U., 1967; MA, Tex. Christian U., 1968; PhD, Iowa State U., 1973. Asst. prof. U. Ark., Little Rock, 1968-70, Denison U., Granville, Ohio, 1972-76; assoc. prof. Iowa State U., Ames, 1976—. Contbr. numerous articles to profl. jours. Mem. Am. Assn. for Marriage and Family Therapy (clin. mem., approved supr.), Nat. Coun on Family Rels. (chair family action sect., bd. mem., cert. family life educator, Outstanding Student award 1973), Iowa Assn. Marriage and Family Therapy (Disting. Leadership Svc. award 1983). Democrat. Mem. Soc. Of Friends. Avocations: golf, running.

COLE, CLARENCE RUSSELL, college dean; b. Crestline, Ohio, Nov. 20, 1918; s. Arthur Leroy and Anita Emma (Stephan) C.; m. Mary Piper, Mar. 15, 1945; children: Carole Ann, Larry Lee, Pamela Sue. Student pre-med., Otterbein Coll., Westerville, Ohio, 1937-39; DVM, Ohio State U., 1943, MS, 1944, PhD, 1947. Instr. dept. vet. pathology Coll. Vet. Medicine Ohio State U., Columbus, asst. prof., 1947-49, chmn. dept., 1947-67, assoc. prof., 1949-54, prof., 1954-67, asst. dean Coll. Vet. Medicine, 1960-67, dean Coll. Vet. Medicine, 1967—, prof. pathology Coll. Medicine, 1952—, prof. comparative pathology Grad. Sch., 1954—, now prof. emeritus. Regents prof. Ohio Bd. Regents, 1966—; chmn. Mershon Ctr. Nat. Security, Ohio State U., 1965-67; mem. U. Coun. Rsch., 1960-67; adminstr. cons. Vet. Rsch., Archtl. Engring. Planning, Animal Med. Ctr., N.Y.C.; cons. nat. adv. rsch. resources coun. NIH, 1972—, NIH Health Manpower Grants Br; mem. nat. adv. com. Nat. Ctr. for Primate Biology, 1967-70; mem. com. on comparative pathology NRC, NAS, 1971—; mem. fellowship com. NATO. Recipient Herzfeld lectr. award Auburn U.; 1st award sci. exhibit Ohio State Med. Assn., 1956; 2nd award AMA. Mem. Men and Women of Sci., Internat. Acad. Pathology (mem. exec. coun.), Internat. Toxoplasmosis Com. (vice-chmn. 1959—), AVMA (Gold award, chmn. adv. bd. vet. med. spltys. 1960-75), Am. Coll. Vet. Pathologists (Disting. citation 1967, pres. 1957, Disting. Mem. 1989), Assn. Am. Vet. Med. Colls. (sec.-treas. 1969—), Sigma Xi, Phi Zeta, Omega Tau Sigma. Clubs: Torch Internat. Address: 1925 Coffey Rd Columbus OH 43210-1005

COLE, DANIEL, retired music educator, conductor, clinician; b. Portland, Oreg., May 22, 1946; s. John Virgle and Barbara Jean (Johnson) Cole; 1 child, Erika Kristine. BA in Music, Marylhurst Coll., 1984; MMus in Conducting, U. Portland, 1987; MAT, Lewis and Clark Coll., 1996; PhD in Music Edn., Hamilton U., 1999. Cert. music tchr., Oreg., Wash., N.Mex., Ariz. Music instr., orch. condr. Clark Coll., Vancouver, Wash., 1975-89; music instr. Marylhurst (Oreg.) Coll., 1985-94; prof. music edn., dir. bands Warner Pacific Coll., Portland, Oreg., 1993-97; condr., music dir. Pacific Crest Wind Ensemble, Marylhurst, 1988-97; prof. music U. Ala., Fairbanks, 1997-98; cons. music edn., conducting, 1998—; fine arts chair dir. of bands Newcomb High Sch., Newcomb Mid. sch, N.Mex., 2000—03. Guest condr. Pres.'s USCG Band, 1994, Mercer U. Band, 1996; dir. bands Newcomb H.S./Middle Sch. Author: Marsdan Guitar Method, 1979; editor Oreg. Music Educators Assn. mag., 1994-97. With USAR, 1966-73. Recipient Clark County Theater Art award, 1988, Disting. Svc. to Music Edn. award Oreg. Music Educators, 1994. Mem. Music Educators Nat. Conf., World Assn. Symphonic Bands and Ensembles, Coll. Music. Soc., Coll. Band Dirs. Nat. Assn., Nat. Band Assn., Phi Mu, Tau Kappa Epsilon. Avocations: horseback trail riding, golf. E-mail: drdanielusa@yahoo.com.

COLE, DAVID EDWARD, automotive executive, educator; b. Detroit, July 20, 1937; s. Edward Nicholas and Esther Helen (Engman) C.; m. Carol Hutchins, July 9, 1965; children: Scott David, Christopher Carl. BS in Mech. Engring. and Math., U. Mich., 1960, MS in Mech. Engring., 1961, PhD, 1966. Engr. GM, Detroit, 1960—65; prof. U. Mich., Ann Arbor, 1967—, dir. Office for Study of Automotive Transp., 1978—2000; entrepreneur 6 cos., 1975—95; pres. Ctr. Auto Rsch. and Mgmt., ptnr. The Altarum Inst. Mich, 2000—03; chmn. Ctr. for Automotve Rsch. (ind. not for profit), 2003—. Bd. dirs. MSX Internat., Detroit, Saturn Electronics, Aurburn Hills, Mich., Plastech, Dearborn, R.L. Polk, Southfield, Mich., Campfire Interactive, Ann Arbor, Mich., Mich. Econ. Devel. Corp., Lansing, Mich. Tech., Tri-Corridor Steering Com.; mem. energy engring. bd. NRC, 1989-94; select panel U.S.-Can. Free trade Pact, 1988-91. Author: Elementary Vehicle Dynamics, 1972; contbr. articles to profl. jours. Bd. trustees Hope Coll., 1994—; mem. exec. com., Mich. Economic Devel. Corp.; bd. dirs. Automotive Hall of Fame, Dearborn. Fellow Soc. Automotive Engrs. (dir. 1980-83, 85-88, Teetor award 1969), Engring. Soc. Detroit (Horace H. Rackham medal 2000); mem. Chevalier of the Nat. Order of Merit from France, 1999, Soc. Mktg. Execs. (Mktg. Educator of Yr. 1998, Rene Dubos Environ. award 1998), Nat. Auto Dealers Assn. Found. (Freedom of Mobility award 1993), Swedens Royal Order of the Polar Star. Republican. Presbyterian. Avocations: hunting, fishing, boating, running, golf. Office: Ctr Auto Rsch 1000 Victors Way Ste 200 Ann Arbor MI 48108 Office Phone: 734-662-1287. E-mail: dcole@cargrop.org.

COLE, DAVID MACAULAY, journalist, consultant; b. Richmond, Calif., Feb. 17, 1954; s. Frederick George and Norma Ann C. Student, San Francisco State U., 1972-77. Mng. editor Feed/Back Mag., San Francisco, 1974-78, exec. editor, 1978-83; asst. music editor Rolling Stone Mag., San Francisco, 1976-77; from copy editor to asst. mng. editor The San Francisco Examiner, 1979-87, asst. mng. editor, 1987-89; prin., owner The Cole Group, Pacifica, Calif., 1989—. Editor, publisher The Cole Papers, 1989—, NewsInc., 1997—; author: Cole's Notes--Profiles in Pagination, 1996, Cole's Guide to Publishing Systems, 1994, 95, 96, 97; contbg. editor Presstime Magazine, 1994—, TechNews Mag., 1994—2003; columnist, Publish Mag., 1997. Trustee Jr. Statesman Found, San Mateo, Calif., 1997—, exec. com., 2001—. Mem. Nat. Press Photographers Assn., Soc. News Design, Soc. Profl. Journalists (v.p. local chpt. 1979). Avocation: steam train preservation. Office: The Cole Group PO Box 719 Pacifica CA 94044-0719 Fax: 650-557-9696. E-mail: dmc@colegroup.com.

COLE, DAVID W., information technology executive; MS in math., Western Wash. U., 1986. V.p. Internat Client and Collaboration Divsn., Microsoft, Redmond, Wash., v.p. Web Client and Consumer Experience Divsn., v.p. Consumer Windows Divsn., 1999, sr. v.p. Consumer Svcs. Divsn., 1999—2000, sr. v.p. Svcs. Platform Divsn., 2000—01, sr. v.p. MSN and Personal Svcs. Group, 2001—. Mem. Bus. Leadership Team, Microsoft.

COLE, DOUGLAS, retired English literature educator; b. N.Y.C., July 25, 1934; s. Ronald and Helen Elizabeth (Bladykas) C.; m. Virginia Ann Ford, Nov. 28, 1957; children: David, Stephen, Karen, Kristin. BA, U. Notre Dame, Ind., 1957; MA, U. Chgo., 1957; PhD, Princeton U., 1961. Instr. English, Yale U., New Haven, 1960-64, asst. prof., 1964-67, assoc. prof., 1967-69; prof. Northwestern U., Evanston, Ill., 1969-98, prof. emeritus, 1998—, chmn. dept. English, 1974-77, acting chmn., 1993, master Humanities Residential Coll., 1981-84, dir. major program in drama, 1980-93, 95-97. Author: Suffering and Evil in the Plays of Christopher Marlowe, 1962, Christopher Marlowe and the Renaissance of Tragedy, 1995; editor: 20th Century Views of Romeo and Juliet, 1970, Renaissance Drama XI: Tragedy, 1980; contbr. numerous articles to profl. jours. Morse fellow, 1966-67; Woodrow Wilson fellow, Danforth fellow Princeton U., 1957-61. Office: Northwestern U English Dept Evanston IL 60208-0001 E-mail: d-cole@northwestern.edu.

COLE, ELSA KIRCHER, lawyer; b. Dec. 5, 1949; d. Paul and Hester Marie (Pellegrom) Kircher; m. Roland J. Cole, Aug. 16, 1975; children: Isabel Ashley, Madeline Aldis. AB in History with distinction, Stanford U., 1971; JD, Boston U., 1974. Bar: Wash. 1974, U.S. Supreme Ct. 1980, Mich. 1989, Kans. 1997, Ind. 1999. Asst. atty gen., rep. dept. motor vehicles State of Wash., Seattle, 1974-75, asst. atty. gen., rep. dept. social and health svcs., 1975-76, asst. atty. gen., rep. U. Wash., 1976-89; gen. counsel U. Mich., Ann Arbor, 1989-97, NCAA, Indpls., 1997—. Presenter ednl. issues various confs. and workshops. Contbr. articles to profl. jours. Fellow: Nat. Assn. Coll. and Univs. Attys. (mem. nominations com., mem. site selection com. 1987—88, co-chair student affairs sect. 1987—88, program 1988—89, mem. fin. com., articles com., by-laws com. 1988—89, co-chair student affairs sect. 1988—89, bd. dirs. 1988—91, program 1989—90, chair profl. devel. com. 1990—91, program 1991—92, honors and awards, ethics com. 1991—92, program 1992—93, bd. ops. 1992—93, mem. nominations com., mem. site selection com. 1995—96, CLE com. 1995—96, program 1995—96, CLE com. 1996—97, pub. com. 1996—97, CLE com. 2000—02, honors and awards com. 2002—03, named NACUA fellow 1998); mem.: Nat. Sports Law Inst. (bd. advisors 2001—), Sports Lawyers Assn. (bd. dirs. 2001—), Indpls. Bar Assn. (sports and entertainment sect. bd. dirs. 2001—), Seattle-King County Bar Assn., Wash. Women Lawyers (pres. Seattle-King County chpt. 1986, state chair candidate endorsement com. 1987, v.p. membership, state bd. dirs. 1987—88, state chair candidate endorsement com. 1988), Wash. State Bar Assn. (chair law sch. liaison com. 1988—89). Office: NCAA PO 6222 Indianapolis IN 46206-6222 E-mail: ecole@ncaa.org.

COLE, EMRIED DARGAN, JR., lawyer; b. Hattiesburg, Miss., Nov. 6, 1945; m. Wandaleen Poynter. BA in History with high honors, Emory U., 1967; JD, Harvard U., 1970. Bar: Md. 1990, US Ct. Appeals (5th, 6th, 7th, 11th and DC cir.) 1974, US Supreme Ct. 1974. Assoc. Powell, Goldstein, Frazer and Murphy, Atlanta, 1970—73; asst. gen. atty., asst. gen. solicitor Louisville and Nashville R.R. Co., Louisville, 1973—77; gen. atty. Seaboard System R.R., Jacksonville, 1977—83, gen. solicitor, 1983—86; v.p. law and risk mgmt. CSX Transp.-Equipment Group, Balt., 1986—90; of counsel, ptnr. Venable LLP, Balt., 1990—. Adj. faculty Johns Hopkins Univ. Sch. of Profl. Studies in Bus. and Edn., 2002; adj. faculty, dir. Luth. Theol. Sem., Gettysburg, 2004. Contbr. articles to profl. jours. Trustee, bd. pensions Evangelical Luth. Ch. in Am., 2003—; chair bd. dirs. Biakon Luth. Soc. Ministries; cabinet mem. Cmty. Investment Vision, United Way, Ctrl. Md. Mem.: ABA, Assn. Transp. Practitioners (chmn. com. profl. ethics 1982—84), State Bar Ga., Nat. Assn. R.R. Trial Counsel, Fla. Bar Assn. Office: Venable LLP 1800 Mercantile Bank & Trust Bldg 2 Hopkins Plz Baltimore MD 21201-3805 also: 575 7th St NW Washington DC 20004 Office Phone: 410-224-7787, 202-344-4887. Office Fax: 410-244-7742, 202-334-8300. Business E-Mail: edcole@venable.com.

COLE, G. MARCUS, law educator; b. 1961; BS in Applied Economics, Cornell U., 1989; JD, Northwestern U., 1993. Bar: Ill. 1993, US Dist. Ct. No. Dist. Ill., US Ct. Appeals 8th Cir., US Ct. Appeals 7th Cir., US Ct. Appeals Fed. Cir. Law clk. to Hon. Morris Sheppard Arnold US Ct. Appeals 8th Cir., 1993—94; assoc. in comml. litig. Mayer, Brown & Platt, 1994—97; asst. prof. law Stanford Law Sch., 1997—2000, assoc. prof., 2000—03, prof., 2003—, Helen L. Crocker faculty scholar, 2003—, assoc. dean curriculum and academic affairs, 2003—. Vis. prof. law Northwestern U., 2001—02. John M. Olin Fellow, U. So. Calif. Law Ctr., 1998, Jr. Faculty Fellow, The Polit. Econ. Rsch. Ctr., Mont. State U., 1999, Nat. Fellow, The Hoover Instn. on War, Revolution and Peace, 2002—03. Mem.: ABA (vice chair sect. bus. law com. bankruptcy 2002—), Am. Bankruptcy Inst., Am. Law & Economics Assn. Office: Stanford Law Sch Crown Quadrangle 559 Nathan Abbott Way Stanford CA 94305-8610 Office Phone: 650-723-0615. Business E-Mail: gmcole@stanford.edu.*

COLE, GEORGE ARTHUR, marketing professional; b. Spokane, Wash., July 12, 1943; s. Russell W. and Ruth J. (Connick) C.; m. Susan Merie Bickell, July 3, 1965; children: Francine Tageant, Spencer Cole. BA, U. Mont., 1965; Grad. Cert. in Internat. Bus., U. San Diego, 1996. Cert. mediator. Pres. Media West, Inc., Spokane and Ferndale, Wash., 1978—, San Diego, 1978—; internat. bus. advisor USAID/Global Tech. Network, Washington and San Diego, 1996-99; econ. devel. dir. City of Imperial Beach, Calif., 1993-96; asst. dir. comms. San Diego State U., 1989-92. Cons. Pacific Southwest Airlines, San Diego, 1980-86. Author: (oral history) Chet Huntley: Reflections, 1972; screenwriter/dir.: (films and videos) Smokin', 1982 (Chgo. Internat. Film Festival award 1983), Community Colleges of Spokane, 1983 (CASE Regional Video awards/Spokane Advt. Fedn. award 1984); anchor/prodr.: (radio series) On the Move, 1972-72 (Sigma Delta Chi award 1971-72). Commr., chair Spokane Housing Authority, 1978-87; bd. dirs. Wash. State ACLU Seattle and Spokane, 1978-79, Spokane Pub. Broadcasting Assn., 1971-74, 78-87. Recipient U.S. Presdl. commendation Pres. Richard Nixon, 1973, Wash. State Gov.'s Cmty. Svc. award, Spokane, 1973. Mem. Internat. Exec. Svc. Corps. (internat. bus. advisor), U. Mont. Alumni Assn. (del. 1990-91). Democrat. Unitarian Universalist. Avocations: running, hiking, travel, writing. Office: PO Box 430 Alpine CA 91903-0430

COLE, GEORGE THOMAS, lawyer; b. Orlando, Fla., Mar. 14, 1946; s. Robert Bates and Frances (Arnold) C.; m. Peggy Ellen Stimson, May 23, 1981; children: Leslie Elizabeth, Ashley Ellen, Robert Warren. AB, Yale U., 1968; JD, U. Mich., 1975. Bar: Ariz. 1975. With Fennemore, Craig, von Ammon, Udall & Powers, Phoenix, 1975-81; ptnr. Fennemore Craig, P.C., Phoenix, 1981—. Mem. Ariz. State U. Coun. for Design Excellence. Served to lt. (j.g.) USN, 1968-71. Fellow: Ariz. Bar Found. (founding); mem.: Maricopa Bar Assn., Ariz. Bar Assn. (coun. real property sect. 1985—88, chmn. 1987—88), Cmty. Assns. Inst., Nat. Golf Found. (assoc.), ULI (cmty. devel. coun. 1995—2001, 2003—), Ariz. Assn. Home Bldrs., Nat. Assn. Home Bldrs., White Mountain Country Club (Pinetop, Ariz.), Paradise Valley Country Club (Phoenix), Yale Club (pres. 1984). Republican. Methodist. Home: 5102 E Desert Park Ln Paradise Valley AZ 85253-3054 Office: Fennemore Craig 3003 N Central Ave Ste 2600 Phoenix AZ 85012-2913 Office Phone: 602-916-5308. E-mail: gcole@fclaw.com.

COLE, GEORGE WILLIAM, foundation administrator; b. Denver, Oct. 1, 1955; s. Herbert Merril and Frances Jane (Buchanan) C. Grad. high sch., Denver. Cert. real estate investment counselor. Owner Jayhawker Investment Co., Inc., 1965--95; pres. Herb Cole Real Estate, Inc., Denver, 1969-95. Bd. dirs. Cos. West Group, Inc., Denver, Jayhawker Investment Co., Denver; cons. Bus. Concepts Corp., Denver, 1981-84, Centennial Growth Equities Corp., 1981-82; pres. Co. West Group, 1982-93; exec. dir. Cole Found., 1993-2001; bd. mem. Varied Media Group, Inc.; co-owner Timeline Films; founder Purple Mountain Cos. Author: Real Estate Investing for the Future, 1981, Mom: A Study in Grieving Grace, 1990; pub.: (newsletter) Encouraging Words, 1986-92. Deacon Baptist Ch., 1987; bd. dirs. World Wide Leadership coun., Compa Food Mins., others. Grace Lay Min. Sch. fellow. Republican. Avocations: history, photography, fishing, travel, dance. Home and Office: 3270 E Virginia Ave Denver CO 80209-3523 Office Phone: 303-777-1368.

COLE, GLEN DAVID, minister; b. Tacoma, Dec. 21, 1933; s. Ray Milton and Ruth Evelyn (Ranton) C.; m. Mary Ann Von Moos, June 6, 1953; children: Randall Ray, Ricky Jay. BA in Theology, Cen. Bible Coll., 1956; DD, Pacific Coast Bible Coll., 1983. Assoc. pastor Bethel Temple, Dayton, Ohio, 1956—57; pastor Assembly of God, Marion, Ohio, 1957-60, Maple Valley, Wash., 1960-65; assoc. pastor Calvary Temple, Seattle, 1965-67; sr. pastor Evergreen Christian Ctr., Olympia, Wash., 1967-78, Capital Christian Ctr., Sacramento, 1978-95, pastor emeritus, 1995—; dist. supr. Assemblies of God, Sacramento, 1997—. Exec. presbyter Assemblies of God, Springfield, 1985-95; bd. mem., ch. extension plan, Salem, Oreg., 1997-; bd. mem. fin. svcs. group, Assemblies of God, Springfield, Mo., 1998-; trustee Bethany Bible Coll., Santa Cruz, Calif., 1979—; bd. dirs. Cen. Bible Coll., Springfield, Mo., 1988-99; bd. dirs. Calif. Theol. Sem., Fresno, 1985-90. Mem. Rotary (pres. Olympia chpt. 1977-78). Republican. Mem. Assemblies Of God Ch. Office: Assemblies of God 6051 S Watt Ave Sacramento CA 95829-1304 *It seems that the people God uses most are not those with greater ability, or more education, or superior talent but those who become totally dependent on him.*

COLE, HEATHER ELLEN, librarian; b. Rochester, N.Y., Nov. 7, 1942; d. Donald M. and Muriel Agnes (Kimball) C.; m. Stratis Haviaras; 1 child, Elektra Maria Muriel BA, Cornell U., 1964; MS, Simmons Coll., 1973. Mgr. Brentano's, Boston, 1968-70; intern Harvard Coll. Libr., Cambridge, Mass., 1970-73, reference libr., 1973-77, libr., 1977—, Hilles Libr., 1977—2005, The Lamont Libr., 1977—2005. Mem.: AAUW, ALA, Am. Soc. Info. Sci. (New Eng. chpt.), Assn. Coll. Rsch. Librs. Democrat. Episcopalian. Avocation: gardening. Home: 19 Clinton St Cambridge MA 02139-2303 Office: Harvard Coll Lamont Library Cambridge MA 02138

COLE, HENRY PHILIP, educational psychology educator; b. Buffalo, Jan. 5, 1937; s. Raymond James and Hannah Christina (Shapleigh) C.; m. Marion Margaret Montgomery, Aug. 19, 1961; children: Mark Douglas, David Arthur, Debra Lynn. BS in Chemistry, Nasson Coll., 1958; MEd, SUNY, Buffalo, 1966, EdD, 1968. Chemistry technician WASCO Chem. Co., Sanford, Maine, 1957-58; tchr. physics and sci. Holland (N.Y.) Ctrl. Sch., 1958-59; med. rsch. technician Buffalo Gen. Hosp., 1959-61; tchr. sci. Griffith Inst. and Ctrl. Sch., Springville, N.Y., 1961-65; instr. ednl. psychology SUNY, Buffalo, 1966-68; ednl. psychologist Ea. Regional Inst. for Edn., Syracuse, N.Y., 1968-71; prof. ednl. psychology U. Ky., Lexington, 1971—, prof. preventive medicine, 1990—, head behavioral rsch. aspects safety-health group (BRASH), 1984-97. Vis. prof. Syracuse U., 1968-70; rsch. psychologist U.S. Bur. Mines, Pitts., 1988-89; U.S. del. MINESAFE Internat. Conf., Western Australia, 1993; behavioral safety expert ILO, China, 1993. Author: Measuring Learning in Continuing Education for Engineers and Scientists, 1984; contbr. more than 200 tech. reports, articles to profl. jours., chpts. to books. Cubmaster Boy Scouts Am., Lexington, 1975-77, round table commr., 1976-78; v.p., team. rep. Little League Baseball, Lexington, 1975-78. With U.S. Army, 1959-61. Recipient Disting. Author award Jour. Allied Health, 1981, Best Paper award Am. Soc. Engring. Edn., 1985, Pub. of Yr. award Bur. of Mines-Pitts. Rsch. Ctr., 1987, Tech. Transfer award, 1989, Unsung Hero's award for outstanding rsch. contbns. U. Ky., Exceptional Achievement award for Rsch., Tchg., and Svc. Coll. of Edn., U. Ky., 2000, 03. Mem. APA, APHA, Am. Ednl. Rsch. Assn., Am. Soc. Agrl. Engrs. Republican. Presbyterian. Avocations: jogging, bicycling, reading natural science, farming. Office: University Kentucky Dept Preventive Medicine 1141 Red Mile Rd Ste 102 Lexington KY 40504-9842 Office Phone: 859-323-5202. Business E-Mail: hcole@uky.edu.

COLE, JACK ELI, physician; b. Matamoras, Pa., Jan. 7, 1915; s. Eli Martin and Louise (Henneberg) C. m. Evelyn Gaston Darragh, Apr. 26, 1941; children: Jack Eli, Thomas, Beverly, Martin, Robert, Leslie, Christopher, Candace, Champa. BS, Pa. State U., 1937; MD, U. Pa., 1941. Diplomate Am. Bd. Family Practice. Intern Wilkes-Barre (Pa.) Gen. Hosp., 1941-42; practice medicine, specializing in family practice Matamoras, Pa., 1946-47; staff St. Luke's Hosp., Bethlehem, Pa., 1948—; practice medicine, specializing in family practice Bethlehem, 1952-68, 1973-89; sec. dept. family practice St. Luke's Hosp., Bethlehem, 1973-88; incorporator, mem. med. staff Muhlenberg Hosp., Bethlehem, 1960—, pres. med. staff, 1961-62; student health physician Lehigh U., Bethlehem, 1948-52; physician Peace Corps, Afghanistan, Swaziland, India, 1968-73; leader mission med. team United Ch. Christ, Honduras, 1987; preceptor Temple U. Med. Sch., Phila., 1978-86. Author: Wandering Voices, 1999, Richard and Sabina, 2001; contbr. poetry to anthologies, children's stories and articles to profl. publs. Charter mem. mission partnership com. N.E. Pa. conf. United Ch. of Christ, 1984. With U.S. Army, 1942-45 Decorated Purple Heart, Combat Medic badge; recipient Recognition award Temple U. Med. Sch., 1979; Boss of Yr. award Allentown Bus. Womens Assn., 1975. Fellow Am. Acad. Family Physicians; mem. AMA, Northampton County Med. Soc., Pa. Med. Soc., Lehigh Valley Acad. Family Physicians (v.p. 1979-81, pres. 1981-83), Pa. Acad. Family Physicians, Am. Acad. Family Physicians. Democrat. Avocation: opera. Home: 782 Barrymore Ln Bethlehem PA 18017-2522 Personal E-mail: jackcolesr@aol.com.

COLE, JAMES S., dean, dental educator; b. Mpls., Minn. m. Barbara Cole. BS, Stephen F. Austin State U., 1967; DDS, Baylor Coll. Dentistry, 1975. Instr., restorative sciences Baylor Coll. Dentistry, Texas A&M U., Dallas, 1977—81, v.p., dir. computer services, 1981—92, prof., restorative sciences, 1992—, interim pres. and dean, 1990, exec. v.p., assoc. dean, CFO, COO, vice dean, interim dean, 1999—2000, dean, 2000—; pres., treas. Baylor Oral Health Found., 1997—99; interim pres. Tex. A&M U. Sys. Health Sci. Ctr., 2000—01. Lt. USN, 1967—71. Recipient Dentist of Yr., Dallas County Dental Soc., 2000. Fellow: Internat. Coll. Dentists, Am. Coll. Dentists. Office: 3302 Gaston Ave Dallas TX 75246

COLE, JAMES YEAGER, foundation administrator; b. Cleve., Sept. 20, 1957; s. Charles and Nancy Cole. JD, Blackstone Sch. Law, Dallas, 1980, U. N.C., 1989; MA, M.C.I., London, 1981; PhD, N.W. London U., 1981. CEO Cole Corp., Tallahassee, 1979-81; judge Inst. Advanced Law Study, Las Vegas, 1981-84; cons., sentencing adv. Cullowhee, NC, 1984-2001. Decorated Knight Comdr. Royal Knights Justice, London, Venerable Order of Knigths of Michael the Archangel Knight Chevalier; recipient Presdl. medal of Merit, U.S. Pres. Ronald Reagan, Washington, 1980, Disting. Leadership award, ABA jud. divsn., 1997. Mem.: N.C. Fraternal Order Police, N.C. Sheriff's Assn., Nat. Sherriff's Assn., Am. Fedn. Police, Internat. Bar Assn., Nat. Judges Assn., World Judges Assn., Am. Judges Assn., Maggic Valley C. of C., Island Found., Human Rights Inst., Haywood County C. of C., Heirs, Inc. Avocations: swimming, skiing, volleyball, tennis, movies. Home and Office: 389 Chestnut Walk Dr Waynesville NC 28786 Office Phone: 828-301-8117. Business E-Mail: judge.cole@abanet.org.

COLE, JESSIE MAE, nursing assistant, freelance/self-employed writer; b. McGehee, Ark., Nov. 19, 1925; d. Alonso Smith and Estelle Hursey; m. Amos Burns, May 15, 1942; children: Bobbie D., Joyce R.; m. Mose Eddie Cole (div. Nov. 1972). AA, Fresno City Coll, 1985; BA, Charter Oak State Coll., 1999. Cert. tchr. Calif., 1979. Beautician Beauty Culture, Chgo., 1956—76; nursing asst. Hope Manor Facility, Fresno, Calif., 1983—. Pvt. piano tchr., Fresno, 1981—. Author: (website) How to Read Sheet Music, 1997. Mem. Wall of Tolerance Nat. Campaign for Tolerance, 2002—03; bible study instr. Coll. Ch. of Christ, Fresno, 1975—. Mem.: Nat. Assn. Black Journalists. Home: 3749 N Fruit Apt C Fresno CA 93705 Office Phone: 559-228-1440.

COLE, JOAN HAYS, social worker, clinical psychologist; b. Pitts., Sept. 4, 1929; d. Frank L. Wertheimer and Edith H. Einstein; m. Robert M. Wendlinger, June, 1984; children: Geoffrey F., Douglas R., Peter Hays. BA, Western Res. U., 1951; MSSA in Social Work, Case Western Res. U., 1962; PhD, Wright Inst., 1975. Cert. clin. social worker; diplomate Am. Bd. Orthopsychiat. Social group worker Alta House Settlement House, Cleve., 1958-59; housing dir. Cleve. Urban League, 1961-62; dir. Citizens for Safe Housing, Cleve., 1963; housing dir. United Planning Orgn., Washington, 1963-68; asst. prof. cmty. orgn. U. Md. Sch. Social Work and Cmty. Planning, Balt., 1968—72; assoc. prof. Lone Mountain Coll., San Francisco, 1975-78; psychotherapist, supr., orgnl. cons., Berkeley, Calif., 1977—. Cons. various pub. and vol. social welfare, health and housing agys., 1969—; mem. adj. faculty Union Grad. Sch. and Antioch West Coll., 1978-80; lectr. U. Calif. Sch. Social Welfare, Berkeley, 1980-84; mem. faculty Berkeley Psychotherapy Inst., 1981—, pres., 1983-85; clin. faculty Inst. Clin. Social Work, Berkeley, 2004. Grantee NIMH, 1971-72, Sr. Social Work Career Devel. grantee, 1973-75. Fellow Soc. Clin. Social Work (diplomate), Am. Orthopsychiat. Assn.; mem. NASW, ACLU, Soc. for Study Social Issues, Acad. Cert. Social Workers, Nat. Conf. on Social Welfare and Psychotherapists for Social Responsibility. Office: 6239 College Ave Oakland CA 94618-1384 Office Phone: 510-654-5151. Personal E-mail: jhcole@earthlink.net.

COLE, JOHN, controller; BS in Econ., Villanova Univ., 1964. CPA 1970. Auditor Seidman and Siedman, CPA, 1965—70; fin. officer for the video comm. group Avnet, Inc., Phoenix, 1974—82; v.p. and dir. of fin. Fannon Courier Corp., 1982—85; chief fin. officer for the electrical and ind. group Avnet, Inc., Phoenix, 1985, corp. contr., 1993—; contr. Christmas Club Corp., 1971—73. Mem.: AICPA, Nat. Investor Rels. Inst., N.Y. State Soc. CPA. Office: Avnet Inc 2211 S 47th St Phoenix AZ 85034

COLE, JOHN ADAM, insurance executive; b. Odessa, Tex., May 6, 1951; s. Alling and Millicent (McWilliam) C.; m. Karen Elisabeth Jones, June 28, 1974 (dec. May 2002); children: J. Adam Jr., Robert H., Kathryn E. A in Occupational Studies in Acctg., Busi.i, Utica (N.Y.) Sch. Commerce, 1973; postgrad., New Sch. Social Rsch., 1984, Am. Coll., Bryn Mawr, Pa. ChFC, CLU. Sales mgr. Mohawk Frozen Foods, Marcy, N.Y., 1973-77; sole propr. From the C's, Inc., Rome, N.Y., 1975-77; agt., dist. asst. Equitable Fin. Svcs., Rome, 1978-83; advanced mktg. specialist Farm Family Ins. Cos., Albany, N.Y., 1984, dir. agt. and mgr. devel., 1985-87, dir. devel. and advanced life sales, 1987-96, dir. advanced markets, 1996-97, dir. life sales, 1997—2003, dir. life and fin. svcs., 2003—; v.p. life ops. Farm Family Ins. Co., 2004—; mem. mktg. com. Farm Bur. Bank, 1998—. Adj. instr. various profl. tng. orgns., Rome, Utica and Albany, 1981—. Pres. Rome Cmty. Concerts Assn., 1978-80, Voorheesville (N.Y.) Ctrl. Sch. Bd., 1990—; cubmaster Boy Scouts Am.; mem. Holland Patent (N.Y.) Ctrl. Sch. Bd., 1982-85; mem. parents adv. bd. Pine Bush Little League, New Scotland Pop Warner, Guilderland Babe Ruth League; coach Ea. N.Y. State Champions team Babe Ruth Allstars, 1995; found. dir. Voorheesville Cmty. Schs. Found., 1999—. Mem. Ea. N.Y. Soc. CLUs & ChFCs (bd. dirs. 1986-91), Ea. N.Y. Soc. Fin. Svcs. Profls. (bd. mem. 2003—), Albany Assn. Life Underwriters (bd. dirs. 1987-92), Mohawk Valley Life Underwriters (pres., chmn. 1980-84), Kiwanis, N.Y. State Newsletter award 1992), Masons. Republican. Methodist. Office: Farm Family Ins Co PO Box 656 Albany NY 12201-0656 E-mail: jcole002@nycap.rr.com.

COLE, JOHN POPE, JR., lawyer; b. Washington, Jan. 12, 1930; s. John Pope and Helen (Gorman) C.; m. Patsy Nan Moss, Mar. 20, 1960; children—John Moss, Nina Gorman. BS, Auburn U., 1953; LL.B., George Washington U., 1956. Bar: D.C. 1956, Md. 1956, Ga. 1961. Atty. FCC, Washington, 1956-57; ptnr. Smith & Pepper, Washington, 1957-66, Cole, Raywid & Braverman, Washington, 1966—; staff U.S. Ho. Reps., Washington, 1961-62. Served with USAF, 1948-49. Home: 5309 Portsmouth Rd Bethesda MD 20816-2930 Office: Cole Raywid & Braverman 1919 Pennsylvania Ave NW Washington DC 20006-3458 Office Phone: 202-659-9750. Business E-Mail: jcole@crblaw.com.

COLE, JOHNNETTA BETSCH, academic administrator, educator; b. Jacksonville, Fla., Oct. 19, 1936; d. John Thomas and Mary Frances (Lewis) Betsch; m. Robert Eugene Cole (div. 1982); children: David, Aaron, Ethan; m. Arthur J. Robinson, Jr. (div. 2002). Student, Fisk U., 1953; BA in Sociology, Oberlin Coll., 1957; MA in Anthropology, Northwestern U., Evanston, Ill., 1959, PhD, 1967. Instr. UCLA, 1964; dir. black studies Wash. State U., Pullman, 1969-70; prof. anthropology U. Mass., Amherst, 1970-83, assoc. provost undergrad. edn., 1981-83; vis. prof. Hunter Coll., N.Y.C., 1983-84, prof. anthropology, 1983-87, dir. Inter-Am. Affairs Program, 1984-87; pres. Spelman Coll., Atlanta, 1987-97, pres. emeritus, 1997—; pres. Bennett Coll. for Women, Greensboro, NC, 2002—. Corp. bd. dirs. Merck & Co., Inc.; presdl. disting. prof. anthropology, women's studies and Afro-Am. studies Emory U., 1998-2001. Author, editor: Anthropology for the Eighties, 1982, All American Women, 1986, Anthropology for the Nineties, 1988, Conversations: Straight Talk with America's Sister President, 1993, Dream the Boldest Dreams, 1998; author: (with Beverly Guy-Sheftall) Gender Talk: The Struggle for Women's Equality in African American Communicies, 2003; mem. editl. bd. The Black Scholar. Chair bd. trustees United Way. Am. Recipient numerous hon. degrees. Fellow Am. Anthrop. Assn.; mem. Am. Acad. Arts and Scis., Assn. Black Anthropologists (past pres.). United Methodist. Office: Bennett Coll for Women 900 E Washignton St Greensboro NC 27401 Office Phone: 336-517-2225. Business E-Mail: jcole@bennett.edu.

COLE, KATHLEEN ANN, advertising executive, social worker; b. Nov. 22, 1946; d. James Scott and Kathryn Gertrude (Borisch) Cole; m. Brian Brandt, Mar. 21, 1970. BA, Miami U., 1968; MSW, U. Mich., 1972; MM, Northwestern U., 1978. Social worker Hamilton County Welfare Dept., Cin., 1969—70, Lucas County Children Svcs. Bd., Toledo, 1970—74, East Maine Sch. Dist., Niles, Ill., 1974—77; account supr. Leo Burnett Advt. Agy., Chgo., 1978—93; primary therapist Lifeline, Chgo., 1994—95; acct. dir. Green-House Comm., 1995—2001; program coord. North Shore Sr. Ctr., 2004—. Field instr. Loyola U., Chgo., 1976—77. Mem. North Shore United Meth. Congregation. Mem.: NASW (chair pub. rels. task force), Kellogg Alumni Assn., Northwestern U. Prof. Women's Assn., Miami U. Alumni Assn. (dir. 1976—78), Acad. Cert. Social Workers. Home: 414 Kelling Ln Glencoe IL 60022-1113 Office: 1779 Winnetka Rd 60093 Personal E-mail: colemarketing@comcast.net.

COLE, K.C., journalist, writer; BA, Barnard Coll. Writer, editor Saturday Rev., San Francisco; editor Newsday; sci. commentator Pasadena Pub. Radio (KPCC); sci. writer L.A. Times, 1994—. Adj. prof. UCLA; tchr. sci. writing Yale U., Wesleyan U.; mem. Jour. Women Symposium; dir. PEN West. Author: (book) The Hole in the Universe: How Scientists Peered Over the Edge of Emptiness and Found Everything, The Universe and the Teacup: The Mathematics of Truth and Beauty, First You Build a Cloud: Reflections on Phyics as a Way of Life, Mind Over Matter: Conversations with the Cosmos, 2003; contbg. writer: The New Yorker, The New York Times, Washington Post, Newsday, Esquire, Newsweek, others. Recipient Writing prize, Am. Inst. Physics, Edward R. Murrow award, Skeptics Soc., Elizabeth A. Wood Sci. Writing award, Am. Crystallographic Assn., 2001; fellow Math. Sci. Rsch. Inst., Exploratorium. Office: LA Times 202 W First St Los Angeles CA 90012 Office Phone: 213-237-7354. Office Fax: 213-237-4712. Business E-Mail: kc.cole@latimes.com.

COLE, KENNETH D., footwear and accessories company executive; b. 1954; Sr. exec. El Greco, Inc., 1976-82; CEO, pres., chmn. bd. dirs. Kenneth Cole Prodns., Inc., N.Y.C., 1982—. Bd. dirs. Am. Found. for AIDS Rsch., 1985-, H.E.L.P., 1987-. Recipient Spotlight award for dedication to increasing public awareness, Creative Coalition, Media Spotlight award, Amnesty International, 1992, Award for Humanitarian Excellence, Coun. Fashion Designers Am., 1996, Extraordinary Voice award, Mother's Voices for his continued efforts in AIDS awareness, Humanitarian Leadership award, Coun. on Foundations, 1996, Fashion Medal of Honor award, Fashion Footwear Assn. NY (FFANY), 1997; named Humanitarian of Yr., Divine Design, footwear industry's highest honor as Footwear News' Person of Yr. Office: Kenneth Cole Prodns Inc 630 West 50th St New York NY 10019 Fax: (212) 713-6666. Office Phone: 212-265-1500. Office Fax: 212-830-7422.

COLE, KENNETH DUANE, architect; b. Ft. Wayne, Ind., Jan. 23, 1932; s. Wolford J. and Helen Francis (McDowell) Cole; m. Carolyn Lou Meyer, Apr. 25, 1953; children: David Brent, Denelle Hope, Diana Faith, Dawn Love. Student, Ft. Wayne Art Inst., 1950-51; BS in Architecture, U. Cin., 1957. Draftsman/intern Humbrecht Assocs., Ft. Wayne, 1957-58; ptnr., arch. Cole-Matott, Archs./Planners, Ft. Wayne, 1959-94, Cole & Cole Archs., Ft. Wayne, 1995—. Mem. adv. bd. Gen. Svcs. Adminstrn., Region 5, 1976, 78. Prin. works include Weisser Pk. Jr. HS, 1963, Brandt Hall, 1965, Bonsib Bldg., 1967, Lindley Elem. Sch., 1969, Young Elem. Sch., 1972, Study Elem. Sch., 1975, Old City Hall Renovation, 1978, Peoples Trust Bank Adminstrv. Svcs. Ctr., 1979, Cole Residence (Design award, 1988), Ossian Office Old 1st Nat. Bank, 1988, Perimeter Security Wall, Ind. State Prison. Bd. dirs. Ft. Wayne Art Inst., 1969—74, Izaak Walton League Am., Ft. Wayne, 1970—76, Arch, Inc., Ft. Wayne, 1975—77, Downtown Ft. Wayne Assn., 1977—82, Hist. Soc. Ft. Wayne and Allen County, 1982—88. Mem.: AIA (bd. dirs. No. INd. 1971—74, pres. 1974), Am. Arbitration Assn. (panel arbitrators 1980—96), Ft. Wayne Soc. Archs. (pres. 1970—71), Ind. Soc. Archs. (bd. dirs. 1973—76, sec. 1976, citation for remodeling Bonsib Bldg. 1978), Ft. Wayne C. of C. Lutheran. Home: 11602 Stellhorn Rd New Haven IN 46774-9775 Office: Cole and Cole Archs 903 W Berry St Fort Wayne IN 46802-3917 E-mail: kennethcole@grinsfelderarchitects.com.

COLE, KENNETH W., automotive executive; Reg. dir. pub. govt. affairs Amoco Corp.; v.p. pub. affairs Allied Corp., 1981; corp. v.p. Allied Signal Inc., 1983; v.p. govt. rels. GM Corp., 2001—. Mem.: Nat. Assn. Bus. Polit. Action (past pres.), Business-Govt. Rels. Coun. (past pres.), Congl. Inst. (bd. dirs.), European Inst. (bd. dirs.), Coun. Pub. Affairs Execs. (bd. dirs.), Pub. Affairs Coun. (bd. dirs.), Nat. Fgn. Trade Coun. (bd. dirs.), U.S. Capital Hist. Soc. (bd. dirs.), Wolf Trap Found. (bd. dirs.). Office: GM Corp 1660 L St NW Washington DC 20036 also: 300 Renaissance Ctr PO Box 300 Detroit MI 48265-3000*

COLE, LEWIS GEORGE, lawyer; b. N.Y.C., Mar. 9, 1931; s. Ralph David and Emma (Balterman) C.; m. Sara Livingston, June 22, 1952; children: Elizabeth, Peter. BS in Econ., U. Pa., 1951; LLB, Yale U., 1954. Bar: N.Y. 1954. Ptnr. Stroock & Stroock & Lavan, LLP, N.Y.C., 1958—. Bd. dirs. Ametek, Inc. Served as 1st lt. U.S. Army, 1954-57. Mem. ABA, Assn. Bar City N.Y., N.Y. State Bar Assn. Office: Stroock & Stroock & Lavan LLP 180 Maiden Ln New York NY 10038-4925 Office Phone: 212-806-6050.

COLE, LUTHER FRANCIS, former state supreme court associate justice; b. Alexandria, La., Oct. 25, 1925; s. Clem and Catherine (Wiley) C.; m. Juanita Barton, Mar. 9, 1945; children: Frances Jeannette, Jeffrey Martin, Christopher Warren. Student, La. Tech. U., 1943-44; JD, La. State U., 1950. Ptnr. Cole, Mengis & Durant, Baton Rouge, 1950-66; judge 19th Jud. Dist., Baton Rouge, 1966-75, chief judge, 1975-79; judge Ct. Appeals, Baton Rouge, 1979-86; assoc. justice Supreme Ct. La., New Orleans, 1986-92. Chmn. Jud. Budgetary Control Bd., 1990-92; mem. La. Bd. Ethics for Elected Ofcls., 1994-95, La. Comm. on Law Enforcement and Adminstrn. of Criminal Justice, 1996—2004. Rep. La. Legis., Baton Rouge, 1964-66; v.p. Merchants Assn., Baton Rouge, 1954; chmn. awards Boy Scouts Am., Baton Rouge, 1956; mem. Civic Ctr. com., Baton Rouge, 1971-74; bd. dirs. Blundon Home, Baton Rouge, 1984-86. Served to lt. (j.g.) USN, 1943-46. Mem. ABA (ann. meeting 1991, Jury Standards award 1991), La. Bar Assn., Baton Rouge Bar Assn. (pres. 1966), La. Dist. Judges Assn. (pres. 1972-73). Clubs: Exchange (Baton Rouge) (pres. 1954). Democrat. Baptist. Avocations: hunting, cooking. Home: 9213 Hilltrace Ave Baton Rouge LA 70809-2614

COLE, MAURICE YOUNGMAN, JR., lawyer; b. Atlantic City, Jan. 26, 1928; s. Maurice Y. and Rachel S. C.; m. Linda Stewart, Dec. 3, 1949; children— Jeffrey, Daniel, Laurie. A.B., Dartmouth Coll., 1949; LL.B., Cornell U., 1952, J.D., 1952. Bar: N.J. 1952. Pres., Cole and Cole, Atlantic City, 1952—; v.p., dir. Central Pier Co., Atlantic City, Mary A. Riddle Co. of Del., Atlantic City; mem. com. on unauthorized practice of law N.J. Supreme Ct., 1966—; atty. Brigantine Planning Bd., 1966-82. Atty. Brigantine Bd.

Edn., 1982—; bd. dirs. United Way Atlantic County. Served as 1st lt. JAGC, U.S. Army, 1952-55. Mem. Internat. Assn. Ins. Counsel, Am. Judicature Soc., ABA, N.J. Bar Assn., N.J. Def. Assn., Def. Research Inst., Trial Attys. Am., Trial Attys. of N.J., Atlantic County Bar Assn. (pres. 1970). Republican. Presbyterian. Club: Kiwanis (pres. 1970). Home: 403 Morton Ave Absecon NJ 08201-1407 Office: 1000 Atlantic Ave Atlantic City NJ 08401-7405

COLE, MAX, artist; b. Hodgeman County, Kans., Feb. 14, 1937; BA, Fort Hays State U., 1961; MFA, U. Ariz., 1964. One-man shows include Louver Gallery, LA, 1978, 80, Sidney Janis Gallery, NYC, 1977, 80, Zabriskie Gallery, NY, 1987, Haines Gallery, San Francisco, 1988, 93, 96, 98, Galerie Schlegl, Zurich, 1990, 96, 99-2000, Mus. Folkwang, Essen, Germany, 1993, Kunstraum Kassel (Germany), 1992, Roswell (N.Mex.) Mus. and Art Ctr., 1996, Stark Gallery, NY, Galerie Michael Strum, Stuttgart, 1997, 99, Mus. Modern Art, Otterndorf, Germany, 1998, Haus Konstructive und Konkrete Kunst, Zurich, 2001, Walter Storms Gallery, Munich, 2002, Kunstverein, Aschaffenberg, Germany, 2002, Diozesan Museum, Cologne, 2004; exhibited in group shows including LA County Mus. Art, 1976, Corcoran Gallery Art, Washington, 1977, La Jolla Mus., 1980, Santa Barbara Mus., 1980, Mus. Fine Arts of N.Mex., 1984, Neuberger Mus., Purchase, NY, 1984, Marilyn Pearl Gallery, NYC, 1985, Pratt Manhattan Ctr. Gallery, 1985, UCLA, 1988, Nat. Gallery Modern Art, New Delhi, 1988, Panza Found., Verese, Italy, 1995, Aagauer Kunsthaus, Aarau, Switzerland, 1995, Trento (Italy) Mus., 1996, Galerie Schlegl, Zurich, 1996, Manif, 1997, Internat. Art Forum, Seoul, 1997, Mus. Modern Art, Otterndorf, Germany, 1998, Haines Gallery, San Francisco, 1998; represented in permanent collections LA County Mus. Art, Newport Harbor Mus. Art, La Jolla Mus. Contemporary Art, Mus. N.Mex., Dallas Mus. Art, Santa Barbara Mus., Everson Mus., Tel Aviv Mus., La. Mus., Van Der Heyt Mus., Wuppertal, Germany, Denmark, Panza Collection, Italy, Diozesan Mus., Cologne, Chiat Found., NY, Panza Collection, Italy, Lembach Haus, Munich, Ingolstaadt Mus., Germany. Address: PO Box 56 Ruby NY 12475

COLE, MICHAEL STEVEN, physician; b. Harrison, Ark., Apr. 28, 1955; s. Billy Maynard and Freda Belle (Stuckey) C.; m. Mary Jean Johns, Aug. 16, 1975; children: Angelique Diane Cole Moses, Michael Steven II. BS in Chemistry, Harding U., 1976; MD, U. Ark., 1980. Diplomate Am. Bd. Family Practice. Commd. ensign USN, 1976, advanced through grades to lt. comdr., 1984, resigned, 1987; resident in family practice U. Ark., Ft. Smith, 1980-83; family physician Roland (Okla.) Family Med. Clinic, 1987—2003; mem. staff Sparks Regional Med. Ctr., 1987—. Mem. Sparks Hosp. pub. adv. com., 1997—; mem. Ptnrs in Progress Med. Mission team to Guyana, 1991, annual team leader, 1991—. Elder Ch. of Christ, 2000—. Fellow Am. Acad. Family Physicians; mem. Ark. Geneal. Soc. (life). Republican. Mem. Ch. of Christ. Avocation: genealogy. Office: Sparks South Clinic 8600 S 36th Terr Fort Smith AR 72908 Office Phone: 479-709-7465. Business E-Mail: mcole@sparks.org.

COLE, MONROE, neurologist, educator; b. N.Y.C., Mar. 21, 1933; s. Harry and Sylvia (Firman) C.; m. Merritt Ellen Frindel, June 15, 1958; children: Elizabeth Anne, Victoria, Scott Frindel, Pamela Catherine. AB cum laude, Amherst Coll., 1953; MD magna cum laude, Georgetown U., 1957. Diplomate Am. Bd. Psychiatry and Neurology. Intern in medicine Seton Hall Coll. Medicine, Jersey City, 1957-58, asst. resident in medicine, 1958-59; asst. resident in neurology Mass. Gen. Hosp., Boston, 1959-60, rsch. fellow in neuropathology, 1960-61, rsch. fellow in neurology, 1961-62; teaching fellow in neurology Harvard U., Cambridge, Mass., 1959-60, 61-62, teaching fellow in neuropathology, 1960-61; clin. instr. in neurology Georgetown U., Washington, 1962-65; asst. prof. neurology, assoc. in anatomy Bowman Gray Sch. Medicine, Wake Forest U., Winston-Salem, N.C., 1965-69, assoc. prof., assoc. in anatomy, 1969-70; assoc. prof. neurology Case Western Res. U., Cleve., 1970, clin. assoc. prof., 1972—, assoc. prof., 1989-93, prof., 1993—2000; chief neurology Highland View Hosp., Cleve., 1970-72; neurologist U. Hosps. Cleve.; prof. emeritus Case Western Res. U., Cleve., 2000—. Contbr. chpts. and articles to med. publs. Served to capt. U.S. Army, 1962-65 Fellow ACP, Am. Acad. Neurology, AHA Stroke Coun.; mem. N.Y. Acad. Scis., Acad. of Aphasia, Assn. for Rsch. in Nervous and Mental Disease, Am. Assn. Neuropathologists (assoc.), Am. Neurol. Assn., Alpha Omega Alpha Office: Univ Hosps Cleve Dept Neurology 11100 Euclid Ave Cleveland OH 44106-1736 E-mail: mcole@nacs.net.

COLE, NANCY STOOKSBERRY, educational research executive; b. Brenham, Tex., Nov. 29, 1942; d. Joe Brady and Grace Darling (Pyburn) S.; m. James W.L. Cole, June 4, 1966; 1 child, David Leverett. BA, Rice U., 1964; MA, U. N.C., 1967, PhD, 1968. Rsch. psychologist Am. Coll. Testing Program, Iowa City, 1968-71, dir. test devel., 1971-73, asst. v.p., 1973-74; from assoc. prof. to prof. U. Pitts., 1975-85; prof., dean edn. U. Ill., Champaign, 1985-89; exec. v.p. Ednl. Testing Svc., Princeton, N.J., 1989-93; pres., 1994-2000; sr. advisor, 2000—04; ret., 2004. Contbr. articles on ednl. testing to profl. jours. Fellow Am. Psychol. Assn.; mem. Nat. Acad. Edn., Nat. Coun. on Measurement in Edn. (pres. 1983-84), Am. Ednl. Rsch. Assn. (pres. 1988-89).

COLE, NATALIE MARIA, singer; b. LA, Feb. 6, 1950; d. Nathaniel Adam and Maria (Harkins) Cole; m. Marvin J. Yancy, July 31, 1976 (div. 1980); 1 child, Robert Adam; m. Andre Fischer, Sept. 16, 1989 (div. 1995); m. Rev. Kenneth Dupress, Oct. 12, 2001 (div. 2004). BA in Child Psychology, U. Mass., 1972. Rec. singles and albums, 1975—; albums include Dangerous, 1985, Everlasting, 1987, The Natalie Cole Collection, 1987, Inseparable, Thankful, Good To Be Back, 1989, Unforgettable, 1991 (4 grammys, 3 grammys 1992), Too Much Weekend, 1992, I'm Ready, 1992, I've Got Love On My Mind, 1992, Take A Look, 1993 (Grammy award nominee best jazz vocal 1994), Holly and Ivy, 1994, Stardust (2 Grammy awards), Magic of Christmas, 1999, Snowfall on the Sahara, 1999, Greatest Hits, 2000, Ask a Woman Who Knows, 2002; television appearances include Big Break (host), 1990, Lily in Winter, 1994; appeared in TV movies The Wizard of Oz in Concert (as Glinda), 1995, Always Outnumbered, 1998, Freak City, 1999; co-author: Angel on My Shoulder, 2000; composer Easter Egg Escapade, 2005. Recipient Grammy award for best new artist, 1975, best Rhythm and Blues female vocalist 1976; recipient 1 gold single, 3 gold albums; recipient 2 Image awards NAACP 1976, 77; Am. Music award 1978, other awards. Mem.: Nat. Assn. Rec. Arts & Scis., AFTRA, Delta Sigma Delta. Baptist. Office: c/o Jennifer Allen 8500 Wilshire Blvd Ste 700 Beverly Hills CA 90211

COLE, NIKKI JO, music educator; b. Mansfield, Pa., July 29, 1971; d. Clifton Thomas and Phyllis Eleanor Griffin; m. John Arthur Cole, July 23, 1994. MusB in Music Edn., U. Pa., Mansfield, 1993; MusM in Music Edn., Ithaca Coll., 1999. Lic. music educator N.Y. State, 1993. Instrumental music educator Elmira (N.Y.) City Sch. Dist., 1993—2000, Bath (N.Y.) Ctrl. Sch. Dist., 2000—. Workshop presenter on assessment in music edn. various sch. dists., NY, 1996—; mentor, cooperating tchr. U. Pa., Mansfield, Pa., 1997—. Contbr. Music- A Resource Guide for Standards-Based Instrn. Recipient Commissioner's Acad. for Tchg. and Learning award, N.Y. State Edn. Dept., 2000. Mem.: N.Y. State Band Dir.'s Assn., N.Y. State Sch. Music Assn., Music Educator's Nat. Conf. Avocation: flutist.

COLE, NORA, actor; b. Louisville, Sept. 10, 1953; d. Lattimore Walls and Mary Lue (Bradford) Cole. BFA, Art Inst. Chgo., Goodman Sch. Drama, 1978; postgrad., Beloit Coll.; studies acting with Wynn Handman, Am. Pl. Theatre. Actor: (plays) Alice in Wonderland, 1965, The Ups and Downs of Theophilus Maitland, 1976, Movie Buff, 1977, Boogie-Woogie Rumble, 1982 (Theatre Renewal award), Medwa, 1987, Tamer of Horses, 1987, Joe Turner's Come and Gone, 1989—90, Birdsend, 1990—91, A Christmas Carol, 1990—91, The Good Times Are Killing Me, 1991, Groundhog, 1992, Avenue X, 1992, Olivia's Opus, 1993, I Have A Dream, On The Town, 1996, The Colored Museum, 1997, Love, Langston, 1988 (nominee Conn. Critics award); (Broadway plays) Runaways, 1978, Inacent Black, 1981, Your Arms Too Short to Box Gold, 1982, Jellys Last Jam (nominee Joseph Jefferson award); (plays) Alice, I'm Laughin' but I Ain't Tickled, El Hajj Malik, Cartoons for a Lunch Hour, The Peanut Man, Trojan Women, The Wiz, When Hell Freezes Over I'll Skate, 1984, The All-Night Strut, 1984—85; (TV series) The Cosby Mysteries, numerous soap operas. Mem.: Am. Guild Variety Artists, Screen Actors Guild, Am. Fedn. Television and Radio Artists, Actors' Equity Assn. Mailing: c/o Schiowitz Clay Rose Inc 165 W 46th St Ste 1210 New York NY 10036

COLE, PAULA, pop singer, songwriter; b. Rockport, Mass. Student, Berklee Sch. Music, Boston. Back-up singer Melissa Etheridge, Sarah McLachlan, Peter Gabriel; rec. artist Imago Records, 1992; rec. artist Harbinger, 1992, This Fire, 1996, Amen, 2000, I Believe in Love, 2003.

COLE, PETER DAVID, pediatrician, oncologist, educator; b. N.Y., May 24, 1967; m. Lisa Brier, Apr. 25, 1967; children: Sally Lauren, Ethan Henry. MD, Cornell U., 1993, BS in neurobiology. Diplomate in pediatric hematology/oncology Am. Bd. Pediat., 2000. Intern, pediat. Mount Sinai Med. Sch., N.Y.C., NY, 1993—96; fellow, pediat. hematology/oncology Meml. Sloan-Kettering Cancer Ctr., N.Y.C., NY, 1996—99; asst. prof. pediat. Robert Wood Johnson Med. Sch., New Brunswick, NJ, 1999—. Grantee, Damon Runyon Cancer Rsch. Found., 2003—. Mem.: Am. Assn. Cancer Rsch. Avocation: ice hockey. Office: The Cancer Institute of New Jersey 195 Little Albany St New Brunswick NJ 08901 Office Phone: 732-235-8076. Office Fax: 732-235-8234.

COLE, PHILLIP ALLEN, lawyer; b. Washington, Mar. 3, 1940; s. Gordon Harding and Dorothy Barbara (Jugel) C.; m. Mary Jo Ruff, July 2, 1994; children: Jennifer Leigh, Christopher Harding, Catherine Anne. BA, U. Md., 1961; JD, Georgetown U., 1964. Bar: Md. 1964, Minn. 1968, U.S. Supreme Ct. 1967, U.S. Ct. Appeals (8th cir.) 1968, U.S. Dist. Ct. Minn. 1965, U.S. Ct. Mil. Appeals 1965; cert. civil trial specialist. Assoc. Beatty & McNamee, Hyattville, Md., 1968; founder, sr. mem. Lommen, Nelson, Cole & Stageberg, Mpls., 1969—. Spl. counsel Md. Ho. of Dels., 1968. Contbr. articles to profl. jours. Capt. USMC, 1965—67. Mem. ATLA, Am. Bd. Profl. Liability Attys., Internat. Assn. Def. Counsel. Avocations: golf, reading. Office: Lommen Nelson Cole & Stageberg 2000 IDS Ctr Minneapolis MN 55402 Office Phone: 612-339-8131. E-mail: phil@lommen.com.

COLE, R. DENO, lawyer; b. St. Louis, Mo., Aug. 7, 1971; s. Robert Reland Cole and Cynthia Lamperson Azari. BA in English, The Citadel, 1993; JD, Touro Law Ctr., 1997. Bar: 1997. Atty. Law Offices of Felicia Pasculli, Bayshore, NY, 1996—97, Yancey, Cooper, Simpson and Cole, Knoxville, 1997—2001, McGehee, Newton, Stewart, Cole, Dupree and Boswell, 2001—. Moot ct. judge ATLA, Knoxville, 2004; judge, H.S. moot ct. competition Knoxville Bar Assn., 2000—04, coach, H.S. moot ct. competition, 2002. Bd. dirs. Boy Scouts Am., Knoxville, 2000—; active mem. atty. Knoxville Pro Bono Project. Mem.: ATLA, ABA, Knoxville Bar Assn., Knoxville Optimist Club (pres. 2004—05). Republican. Episcopal. Avocations: hiking in the Smoky Mountains and enjoying mountain home., aviation, travel. Office: McGehee, Newton, Stewart, Cole, Dupree and Boswell 709 Market St Suite 2 Knoxville TN 37902 Office Phone: 865-281-8400. Personal E-mail: denocole@aol.com.

COLE, RACHEL P., science educator; b. McKenney, Va., Sept. 24, 1942; d. Alex Luther and Fannie Wynn Parham; m. Moses Cole, Sept. 20, 1969; 1 child, Marsha Lynn. BS in Biology, Va. State U., Petersburg, 1964; BA in Biology, NYU, 2002. CLU; ChFC, cert. Notary Pub. Sci. tchr. Franklin City Schs., Va., 1964—66; pension cons. Equitable Life, N.Y.C., 1966—91; sub. tchr. Bd. of Edn., N.Y.C., 1992—98; tchr. Aux. Svc. High Schs., N.Y.C., 1998—. Pres. Black Tchrs. Who Care, N.Y.C., 2000—; chairperson Scholarship Commn., N.Y.C., NY, 1993—; pres. Wynn's Family Reunion; treas. Fitts, Parham, Walker Family Reunion. Mem.: NAUW (fin. sec., named Woman of Yr.), Va. State U. Alumni Assn. Democrat. Baptist. Avocations: reading, watching basketball, tennis.

COLE, RANSEY GUY, JR., federal judge; b. Birmingham, Ala., May 23, 1951; s. Ransey Guy and Sarah Nell (Coker) Cole; m. Kathleine Kelley, Nov. 26, 1983; children: Justin Robert Jefferson, Jordan Paul, Alexandra Sarah. BA, Tufts U., 1972; JD, Yale U., 1975. Bar: Ohio 1975, D.C. 1982. Assoc. Vorys, Sater, Seymour and Pease, Columbus, Ohio, 1975—78, ptnr., 1980—86, 1993—95; trial atty. U.S. Dept. Justice, Washington, 1978—80; judge U.S. Bankruptcy Ct., Columbus, 1987—93, U.S. Ct. Appeals (6th cir.), Cinn., 1995—. Mem.: ABA, Columbus Bar Assn., Nat. Bar Assn. Office: US Courthouse 85 Marconi Blvd Rm 127 Columbus OH 43215-2823 also: US Court of Appeals 6th Circuit 532 Potter Stewart US Courthouse 100 E Fifth St Cincinnati OH 45202

COLE, RICHARD A., retired lawyer; b. Syracuse, N.Y., Feb. 21, 1951; s. Victor and Marie (Pogacar) C.; m. Lois Hallonquist, Sept. 27, 1975. AB, Brown U., 1973; JD, Cornell U., 1976. Bar: Ill. 1976, U.S. Dist. Ct. (no. dist.) Ill. 1976. Assoc. Mayer, Brown, Rowe & Maw, Chgo., 1976—82, ptnr., 1983—2002. Trustee U. Notre Dame, London, 1981-2002. Avocation: travel. Home: 29 Beverley Rd London SW 13 England E-mail: rlcole@blueyonder.co.uk.

COLE, RICHARD CARGILL, language educator; b. Kansas City, Kans., Apr. 16, 1926; s. Horace Richard and Iris Verner (Cargill) C.; m. Florence Adaline Mason, June 27, 1956; children: Celia Elizabeth Cole Shaw, Paul Richard. BA, Hamilton Coll., 1950; MA, Yale U., 1951, PhD in English, 1955. English tchr. Manlius (N.Y.) Sch., 1951-52; asst. to dean of freshmen Yale U., New Haven, 1953-54; instr. English U. Tex., Austin, 1954-57; assoc. prof. Radford Va. Coll. (now Univ.), 1957-59, prof. English, 1959-61, Davidson (N.C.) Coll., 1961-93, prof. emeritus, 1993—. Author: Irish Booksellers and English Writers, 1740-1800, 1986; author, editor: Robert Colvill's Atalanta and Savannah, 1987, John Singleton's Grand Tour, 1815-1817, 1988, The General Correspondence of James Boswell, 1766-1767, 1993, Thomas Mante, Writer, Soldier, Adventurer, 1993, The General Correspondence of James Boswell, 1768-1769, 1997; contbr. articles to profl. jours. Sgt. USAAF, 1944-46, ETO. Robert Warnock rsch. fellow Yale U., 1975-76, rsch. fellow Yale U. Div. Sch., 1978; rsch. grantee Bd. Higher Edn., Presbyn. Ch., 1968, Piedmont U. Ctr. N.C., 1968; grantee Am. Coun. Learned Socs., 1976, Nat. Endowment for the Humanities grantee, 1985, 89. Mem. Phi Beta Kappa. Republican. Presbyterian. Home: 400 Avinger Ln Apt 101 Davidson NC 28036-9700

COLE, RICHARD CHARLES, lawyer; b. Albany, N.Y., Apr. 23, 1950; s. Charles Stanley and Doris Jean (Hatch) C.; m. Margaret O'Leary; children: Jack Patrick, Charles Michael. BA magna cum laude, Cornell U., 1972; JD, Harvard U., 1975. Bar: N.Y. 1976, U.S. Dist. Ct. (so. and ea. dits.) N.Y. 1977, U.S. Ct. Apeals (D.C. cir.) 1980, U.S. Ct. Appeals (2d and 5th cirs.) 1981, U.S. Dist. Ct. (no, ea., so. and ctrl. dists.) 1989, U.S. Supreme Ct. 1995. Assoc. LeBoeuf, Lamb, Leiby & MacRae, N.Y.C., 1975-83, ptnr., 1984-89, LeBoeuf, Lamb, Greene & MacRae, San Francisco, 1989-95; pvt. practice Mill Valley, 1996—. Mem. ABA. Avocations: woodwind instruments, school volunteering. Office: 111 Stanford Ave Mill Valley CA 94941-3562

COLE, RICHARD JOHN, marketing executive; b. N.Y.C., Oct. 18, 1926; s. Arthur and Anna C.; m. Birgitta Ofling, Aug. 26, 1961; children— Catherine Ann, Richard Arthur, John Eric, Christopher Arne. BA, Yale U., 1946. Pres. Richard J. Cole, Inc., N.Y.C., 1954-61; gen. mgr. Dynasty of Hong Kong, N.Y.C., 1961-67; CEO, M.I. Group div. Manhattan Industries, Inc., 1967-83; mng. dir. B. Barclay Internat., Inc., 1983-87; prin. Sources Unltd., 1991—, R.&R. Internat., Inc., N.Y.C., 1995—. Served with USNR, 1943-46, 52-53. Congregationalist. Home and Office: 72 Main St Newtown CT 06470 Office Phone: 917-756-0972. E-mail: rcole054@earthlink.net.

COLE, RICHARD LOUIS, political scientist, educator; b. Dallas, Jan. 25, 1946; s. Louis Ray and Mary (Steely) C.; children: Jonathan, Ashley. BA, North Tex. State U., Denton, 1967, MA, 1968; PhD, Purdue U., 1973. Asst. prof. George Washington U., 1973-78, assoc. prof., 1978-79; research scholar Yale U., New Haven, Conn., 1979-80; prof. polit. sci., dean Sch. Urban and Pub. Affairs U. Tex., Arlington, 1980—; acting dean Coll. Liberal Arts, 2001—. Cons. Office Revenue Sharing Rand Corp. Author: Citizen Participation, 1974, Revenue Sharing, 1976, Introduction to Political Inquiry, 1980, Urban Life in Texas, 1986, Texas Politics and Public Policy, 1987, The Politics of American Government, 1994, Introduction to Political and Policy Research, 1996; mem. editl. bd. Am. Politics Quar., 1977-88, Jour. Cmty. Action, 1981—, Pub. Adminstrn. Rev., 1986-89, Jour. Urban Affairs, 1988—; contbr. articles to profl. jours. Mem. Leadership Arlington. Mem. Am. Soc. Pub. Adminstrn. (pres. N. Tex. chpt. 1989-90), S.W. Polit. Sci. Assn. (v.p. 1983-84, pres.-elect 1990, pres. 1991-92), Am. Polit. Sci. Assn. Democrat. Methodist. Home: 614 Portofino Dr Arlington TX 76012-2759 Office: Inst Urban Studies U Tex PO Box 19588 Arlington TX 76019-0001 E-mail: cole@uta.edu.

COLE, RICHARD RAY, university dean; b. Forney, Tex., Apr. 20, 1942; s. Richard W. and G. Gladys C.; m. Lynda F. Painter, May 31, 1968. BJ, U. Tex., 1964, MA, 1966; PhD, U. Minn., 1971. Asst. city editor The News, Mexico City, 1966-67; freelance writer, 1966-67; reporter Harrow Observer, Harrow-on-the-Hill, Eng., 1968; asst. prof. W.Va. U., 1967-68; instr. U. Minn., 1968-71; mem. faculty U. N.C., Chapel Hill, 1971—, prof. journalism, 1979—, John T. Kerr Jr. disting. prof., 2002—, dean Sch. Journalism and Mass Comm., 1979—. Nat. scholarship com. Freedom Forum, 1980-86, chmn., 1987-93; chief judge H.L. Mencken Nat. Writing Award Competition, 1983-90; mem. journalism awards program steering com. William Randolph Hearst Found., 1981—, chmn., 1991—; chmn. accrediting teams U.S. journalism schs.; mem. faculty adv. com. World Press Inst.; mem. Nat. Accrediting Coun. on Edn. in Journalism and Mass Comm., 1987-96, v.p., 1989-95; cons. in field; creator cooperative programs with univs. in Mexico City, Santiago, Chile, Brazil, State of Parana, Havana, Cuba, United Arab Emirates; apptd. adh., coun. facultad comunicaciones Pontificial Cath. U. Chile, 1999—. Co-author: Gathering and Writing The News: Selected Readings, 1975; editor: Communication in Latin America: Journalism, Mass Communication, and Society, 1996; asst. editor Journalism Quar., 1973-85; contbr. articles to profl. jours. Chmn. U. N.C. Bicentennial Observance Planning Com., 1986-87; mem. Bicentennial Policy Com., 1988-94. Recipient Excellence award in undergrad. tchg. Amoco Found., 1978, Freedom Forum medal for lifetime accomplishments in journalism-mass comm. adminstrn., 1992, Earl Gluck award for disting. svc. to broadcasting, 2004, Dist. Svc. medal UNC-Chapel Hill General Alumni Assn., 2005, named to NC Journalism Hall of Fame, 2005; grantee U. Minn., U. N.C. Dept. State, Internat. Comm. Agy., Internat. Media Fund, U.S. AID, others; Fulbright fellow, Brazil, 2001. Mem. Assn. Edn. Journalism and Mass Communication (exec. com. 1977-79, 81-84, chmn. coms. 1974-75, 77-79, pres. 1982-83, nat. task force on future mass communication of edn. 1983-84), Internat. Assn. Mass Communication Rsch. (coun. 1980-88, v.p. 1984-88), Assn. Schs. Journalism and Mass Communication (exec. com. 1983-88, 1992-93, pres. 1986-87, mem. nat. steering com. to select 1st journalist in space NASA 1985-86), Inter Am. Press Assn., Order of Golden Fleece, Sigma Delta Chi, Kappa Tau Alpha. Office: U NC Sch Journalism & Mass Communication PO Box 3365 Chapel Hill NC 27599-0001 Office Phone: 919-843-8289. Business E-Mail: richard_cole@unc.edu.

COLE, RICHIE THOMAS, musician, composer, educator; b. Trenton, N.J., Feb. 29, 1948; s. Thomas and Emily Cole; m. Rise Cole, July 4, 1999; children: Amy Marrazzo, Shawn Shaw. Degree in Saxaphone, Berklee Coll. Music, 1969. Musician Alto Madness Music, Pensacola, Fla., 1969—2005. Cons., arranger, composer, educator Alto Madness Music, Pensacola, Fla., 1969—. Composer over 5000 musical compositions. Mem.: United Fedn. Musicians, Chamber Music Assn., Rec. Acad., Internat. Assn. Jazz Educators (Lifetime Jazz Educator award 2003), Nat. Jazz Svc. Orgn. (assoc.). Achievements include spreading a colorblind musical vision throughout the world of americas only artform, jazz. Home: 209 Nancy Ln Trenton NJ 08638 Office: Alto Madness Music 4870 Manolete Pensacola FL 32504 Office Phone: 305-495-1809. Home Fax: 609-882-2078; Office Fax: 609-882-2078. Personal E-mail: richiecolealtomadness@yahoo.com.

COLE, ROBERT K., diversified financial services company executive; MBA, Wayne State Univ. Pres. NBD Bancorp and Pub. Storage, Triple Five Inc., real estate devel., 1990—94; pres., COO-fin. Plaza Home Mortgage Corp., 1994—95; chmn., CEO, co-founder New Century Fin. Corp., Irvine, Calif., 1995—. Bd. dir. Option One Mortgage Corp. (subs. Plaza Home Mortgage), 1994—95, New Century Mortgage, 1995—. Office: New Century Fin Corp Ste 1000 18400 Von Karman Ave Irvine CA 92612 Office Phone: 949-440-7032.*

COLE, ROBERT THEODORE, lawyer; b. Bklyn., Mar. 16, 1932; s. Harold I. and Bella (Weissman) C.; m. C. Margaret Hall, Oct. 25, 1959; children: Elizabeth, Tanya, Judith Amy. BS, U. Pa., 1953; LLB magna cum laude, Harvard U. Law Sch., 1956; diploma in law, London Sch. Econs., 1958. Bar: N.Y. 1956, D.C. 1972. Assoc. Law Office Frank Boas, Brussels, 1960-62, Nixon Mudge Rose et al, N.Y.C., 1962-67; atty. U.S. Treasury Dept., Washington, 1967-73, internat. tax counsel, 1971-73; ptnr. Cole Corette & Abrutyn, Washington, 1973-96; ptnr., sr. counsel, internat. tax group Alston & Bird LLP, Washington, 1997—, chmn. internat. tax group, 1997—2000; co-owner The Little Gym, No. Va. Lectr. on internat. tax. Editor, prin. author Practical Guide U.S. Transfer Pricing; contbr. articles on internat. taxes to legal jours. Capt. USAF, 1957-59. Recipient exceptional svc. award U.S. Treasury Dept., 1973. Fellow Am. Coll. Tax Counsel; mem. Assn. Bar City N.Y., Nat. Fgn. Trade Coun. (vice-chair tax com. 1989-95), Harvard Club (N.Y.C.). Avocations: hiking, theater. Office: Alston & Bird LLP 10th fl N Bldg 601 Pennsylvania Ave NW Washington DC 20004-2601 Office Phone: 202-756-3306. Business E-Mail: rcole@alston.com.

COLE, SOLON ROBERT, pathologist, educator; b. McComb, Miss., Sept. 18, 1937; s. Robert Walter and Thelma Rebecca (Price) C. BS, Tulane U., 1959, MD, 1962. Diplomate Am. Bd. Pathology. Intern St. Vincent's Hosp., N.Y.C., 1962-64; resident in pathology Boston City Hosp., 1964-67; rsch. fellow Harvard Med. Sch., Boston, 1967-69; pathologist pulmonary sect. Armed Forces Inst. Pathology, Washington, 1970-72; sr. pathologist Hartford Hosp., 1972—2002, dir. electron microscopy, 1972—. Assoc. prof. pathology U. Conn. Health Ctr., Farmington, 1974-2003, prof., 2004—; with Hartford Pathology Assocs., 1992—; com. on nomenclature of lung disease WHO, Geneva, Switzerland, 1978—; lung pathology cons. Regional Hosps., Hartford, 1972—. Contbr. chapters to books. Bd. dirs. Hartford Symphony Orch., 1985. Royal Hort. Soc. fellow, London, 1985; grantee HEW, 1976, Nat. Heart and Lung Assn., 1978, Combined Hosp. Fund, 1983; named one of the Top Doc. in Am., 2001, 02, Internat. Scientist of Yr., 2003. Fellow: Coll. Am. Pathologists; mem.: Soc. Pulmonary Pathologists, New Eng. Cancer Soc., Electron Microscopy Soc. Am., Internat. Acad. Pathology, Sigma Xi. Democrat. Avocation: landscaping. Home: 1 Gold St Apt 23E Hartford CT 06103-2932 Office: Dept Pathology Hartford Hosp 80 Seymour St Hartford CT 06115-2701 Personal E-mail: solonc@snet.net.

COLE, SUSAN A., academic administrator, language educator; m. David Cole, two children. BA in English and Am. Lit., Columbia U., 1962; MA in English and Am. Lit., Brandeis U., 1964, PhD in English and Am. Lit., 1972. Tchg. asst. Clark U., 1964-65; assoc. prof. CCUNY-N.Y.C. Tech. Coll., 1968-77; assoc. dean for acad. affairs Antioch U., 1977-80; v.p. for univ. adminstrn. and pers. Rutgers U., New Brunswick, N.J., 1980-92; pres., prof. English Met. State U., Mpls. and St. Paul, 1993-98; pres. Montclair State U., Upper Montclair, N.J., 1998—. Guest adj. assoc. prof. Pace U., fall 1977; vis. sr. fellow in acad. adminstrn. Office Acad. Affairs, CUNY, 1991-93; bd. dirs. Western State Bank; presenter in field. Contbr. articles to profl. jours. Chmn. edn. resolutions sessions, coord. edn. panels N.Y. State meeting Internat. Women's Year, Albany, 1977; agy. mem. N.J. Gov.'s Mgmt. Improvement Program, 1982; v.p., bd. dirs. Bklyn. Ecumenical Coops., 1988-90; mem. cmty. health care policy task force Robert Wood Johnson Univ. Hosp., New Brunswick, 1991; mem. blue ribon task force Mpls. Pub. Libr., 1994-95; mem. steering com. Greater St. Paul Tomorrow, 1994—; trustee Twin Cities Pub. TV, 1994—, Sci. Mus. Minn., 1994; bd. dirs., mem. exec. com. St. Paul Riverfront Corp., 1994—; v.p., founding bd. dirs. St. Paul Pub. Schs. Found.,

1995—; bd. dirs. St. Paul Found., 1995—. Mem. Am. Assn. State Colls. and Univs. (urban and met. steering com. 1993—), Am. Coun. on Edn. (Commn. on Women in Higher Edn. 1993—), Greater Mpls. C. of C. (enterprise devel. task force 1994—). Office: Montclair State U Office of Pres 1 Normal Ave Montclair NJ 07043-1624

COLE, SUSAN STOCKBRIDGE, retired theater educator; b. San Francisco, Jan. 26, 1939; d. Elmer Leroy Stockbridge and Martha Louise Rosenauer; m. John Michael Day, June 28, 1965 (div. May 1968); m. Willie Robert Cole, June 12, 1976. AB, Stanford (Calif.) U., 1960, MA, 1961; PhD, U. Oreg., 1972. Asst. prof. theatre Bakersfield (Calif.) Coll., 1962-69; grad. tchg. fellow U. Oreg., Eugene, 1969-72; asst. prof. theatre Keuka Coll., Keuka Park, N.Y., 1972-75; prof. Appalachian State U., Boone, NC, 1975—2005, dept. chair theatre and dance, 1989—2005; ret., 2005. Cons. Dept. Pub. Instrn., Raleigh, N.C., 1980—2005, N.C. Arts Coun., Raleigh, 1989-93. Author: American National Biography, 1999, Notable Women in American Theatre, 1990; designer more than 100 play prodns., 1962—; dir. more than 60 play prodns. Recipient Outstanding Svc. award, Coll. Fine and Applied Arts, 2005. Mem.: Am. Soc. for Theatre Rsch., Assn. for Theatre in Higher Edn., N.C. Theatre Conf. (pres. 1991—92, Svc. award 1997), Southeastern Theatre Conf. (pres. 1998—99, Suzanne Davis award 2002), Lions Club Internat. (dist. officer 1997—2003, treas. 1999—2004, past pres.), Alpha Psi Omega (pres. 1997—2002, Outstanding Svc. to fine and applied arts 2005). Democrat. Episcopalian. Avocation: reading. Home: PO Box 220 Todd NC 28684-0220 Personal E-mail: coless@appstate.edu.

COLE, TERRENCE M., historian, educator; b. Quakertown, Pa., Sept. 23, 1953; s. William P. and Anne E. Cole; m. Marjorie K. Cole, Dec. 20, 1977 (div. Oct. 1997); children: Henry L., Desmond E.; m. Eugenia F. Salisbury, Aug. 9, 2003. BA in Geography, U. Alaska, 1976, MA in History, 1978; PhD in History, U. Wash., 1983. Editor Alaska N.W. Pub. Co., Edmonds, Wash., 1980—88; prof. history U. Alaska, Fairbanks, 1988—, dir. office public history, 2004—. Author: Nome: City of Golden Beaches, 1984, The Cornerstone on College Hill: History of the University of Alaska, 1992, Crooked Past, 1991, Banking on Alaska, 2000; contbr. articles to profl. jours. Mem. Fairbanks North Star Borough Libr. Commn., 1991—. Recipient Bullock Award for Svc., U. Alaska Found., 1998, Usibelli award for tchg., 1994. Mem.: Alaska Hist. Soc. (v.p. 1986—88, Alaska Historian of the Yr. 1986). Office: U Alaska-Fairbanks Office Pub History Fairbanks AK 99775 Office Phone: 907-474-6995. Business E-Mail: fftmc@uaf.edu.

COLE, THOMAS AMOR, lawyer; b. Phila., Nov. 2, 1948; s. George Lough and Elizabeth (Bush) C.; m. Carol L. Owen, Dec. 27, 1969 (div. 1979); children: Kirsten E., Lauren E.; m. Constance J. Ward, Nov. 17, 1979; children: Lindsay W., Emily C. BA with honors, Johns Hopkins U., 1970; JD with honors, U. Chgo., 1975. Bar: Ill. 1975, U.S. Dist. Ct. (no. dist.) Ill. 1975. Assoc. Sidley & Austin, Chgo., 1975-81; v.p. law Northwest Industries, Chgo., 1982-85; ptnr. Sidley & Austin, Chgo., 1981—, mgmt. com., 1988—, chair exec. com., 1998—2001, Sidley Austin Brown & Wood LLP, Chgo., 2001—. Adj. prof., U. Chgo. Law Sch.; chmn. exec. com. Northwestern U. Sch. Law, Garrett Corp., Securities Law Inst.; co-chair Tulane Corp. Law Inst., Practising Law Inst., Northwestern U. Kellogg Grad. Sch. Mgmt.; bd. dirs. U. Chgo., Northwestern Meml. Hosp., Chgo. Coun. Fgn. Rels. U. Chgo.; adv. com. to bd. of NYSE. Bd. dirs. Ravinia Festival; Joffrey Ballet. Mem. ABA, Chgo. Bar Assn., Am. Law Inst., Chgo. Club, Econ. Club, Comml. Club, Law Club of Chgo., Order of Coif, Phi Beta Kappa. Democrat. Mem. Soc. Friends. Office: Sidley Austin Brown & Wood Bank One Plz 10 S Dearborn St Chicago IL 60603-2000 Office Phone: 312-853-7473. Office Fax: 312-853-7036. Business E-Mail: tcole@sidley.com.

COLE, TODD GODWIN, management consultant transportation; b. Coushatta, La., Mar. 5, 1921; s. Ira and Lucie (Triche) C.; m. Inez Hamilton, Feb. 9, 1953 (div. 1974); children: Michael H., Diane Cole Janusz (dec. 1994); m. Josephine Giovanetti, Oct. 1974 (dec. 1985); m. Pamela Wilds, Mar., 1987. Student, La. State U., 1935—37; LLB, Woodrow Wilson Coll., 1947. CPA, Ga. With Delta Airlines, 1940-63, dir., exec. v.p. adminstrn., 1955-63; sr. v.p. fin. and adminstrn., dir. Ea. Airlines, 1963-67, vice chmn., chmn. fin. com., dir., 1967-69; v.p., asst. to pres., dir. C.I.T. Fin. Corp., N.Y.C., 1969, v.p. fin., 1969-71, mem. exec. com., 1970-86, exec. v.p., 1971-73, pres., chief adminstrv. officer, 1973-80, pres., COO, 1980-83, pres., CEO, 1984-86; CEO, bd. dirs. Frontier Air Lines D.I.P., 1987-89; vice chmn., dir. Ea. Air Lines D.I.P., 1989-91; mng. dir. Simat, Hellesen & Eichrer, Inc., 1992-96; pres. Cole & Wilds Assocs., Miami, 1996—; vice chmn. Hawaiian Airlines, Inc., 2002—03; founding dir. Coral Gables Trust Co., 2004. Chmn. Arrow Air, Inc., 1997-98; bd. dirs. Kaiser Ventures, LLC. Mem. Ga. Bar Assn. Office: Todd G Cole 60 Edgewater Dr #14E Coral Gables FL 33133-6975 Office Phone: 305-666-8136. Personal E-mail: coletg@bellsouth.net.

COLE, TOM, congressman; b. Shreveport, La., Apr. 28, 1949; s. John D. and Helen Gale Cole; m. Ellen Decker; 1 child, Mason. BA, Grinnell Coll., 1971; MA, Yale U., 1974; PhD, U. Okla., 1984. Fellow Yale U., 1974; instr. U. Okla., 1975-78, Okla. Bapt. U., 1981; exec. dir. Okla. Rep. Com., 1980-81; dir. dist. svcs. congressman Mickey Edwards U.S. Congress, 1982-84; exec. dir. Reagan-Bush Campaign, Okla., 1984; chmn. Okla. State Rep. Party, 1985-89; mem. Okla. State Senate, 1988—91; pres. Cole, Hargrave, Snodgrass & Assocs., 1989—; sec. of state State of Okla., 1995-99; chief of staff Republican Nat. Com., Wash., 1999—; mem. U.S. Ho. of Reps. from 4th Okla. dist., 2003—. Lectr. Grinnell Coll., 1977, 79; mem. Cleve. County Rep. Exec. Com., 1979-85, Okla. County Rep. Exec. Com., 1983-85; campaign mgr. Helen Cole for State Rep., 1978, 80, 82, Helen Cole for State Senate, 1984, Ken Wilson for County Commr., 1981, Evelyn Orth for County Commr., 1981; dep. campaign mgr. Daxon for Gov., 1981-82. Fullbright fellow U. London; Watson felow Inst. Hist. Rsch., London; recipient Robert A. Taft award Okla. Rep. Party, Guardian Small Bus. award Nat. Fedn. Ind. Bus. Mem. Am. Hist. Assn., Inst. Hist. Rsch., Soc. Study Labor History, Ea. London Hist. Soc., Okla. C. of C., Phi Alpha Theta. Republican. Methodist. Office: 501 Cannon Ho Office Bldg Washington DC 20515-3604*

COLE, VINCENT J., lawyer; b. Binghamton, N.Y., Nov. 25, 1956; s. Joseph F. and Allene J. (Van Gordon) C.; m. Lenore Ymer, May 14, 1994; children: Joseph, Chrisopher, Lisa. BA in polit. sci. & philosophy, Syracuse U., 1978, JD, 1981. Bar: N.Y. 1982, U.S. Dist. Ct. (so. dist.) N.Y. 1982. Assoc. Cahill Gordon & Reindel, N.Y.C., 1981-91; corp. counsel Lexmark Internat., Inc., Greenwich, Conn., 1991-96, asst. gen. counsel, sec., 1996, v.p., gen. counsel, sec. Lexington, Ky., 1996—. Office: Lexmark Internat Inc 740 W New Circle Rd Lexington KY 40550-0001

COLE, WAYNE STANLEY, historian, educator; b. Manning, Iowa, Nov. 11, 1922; s. Roy Eldon and Gladys Evelyn (Granseth) Cole; m. Virginia Rae Miller, Dec. 24, 1950; 1 child, Thomas Roy. BA with high honors, Iowa State Tchrs. Coll., 1946; MS, U. Wis., 1948, PhD, 1951. From instr. to asst. prof. history U. Ark., 1950-54; from asst. prof. to prof. Iowa State U., 1954-65; prof. U. Md., College Park, 1965-92, Disting. scholar tchr., 1989-90, prof. history emeritus, 1992—; Fulbright lectr. U. Keele, England, 1962-63. Author: (book) America First, 1953, Senator Gerald P. Nye and American Foreign Relations, 1962, An Interpretive History of American Foreign Relations, 1968, An Interpretive History of American Foreign Relations, 2d edit., 1974, Charles A. Lindbergh and the Battle Against American Intervention in World War II, 1974, Roosevelt and the Isolationists 1932-1945, 1983, Norway and the United States, 1905-55, 1989, Determinism and American Foreign Relations During the Franklin D. Roosevelt Era, 1995, A Life in Twentieth Century America, 2002. Served to 1st lt. USAAF, 1943—45. Fellow Woodrow Wilson Internat. Ctr. for Scholars, 1973, NEH, 1978—79. Mem.: Soc. Historians Am. Fgn. Rels. (pres. 1973, Graebner award 1994). Lutheran. Home: 10203 Mcgovern Dr Silver Spring MD 20903-1612 Business E-Mail: wc14@umail.umd.edu. *Work hard. Give your best. Never give up. Empathize with those who are different. Remember you stand on shoulders of those who came before. Leave the world a better place than it was. Never forget that you could be wrong.*

COLE, WILLIAM EDWARD, economics educator, consultant; b. Mineola, Tex., Feb. 5, 1931; s. Isaac Harry and Anna Belle (Davis) C.; m. Evelyn Mallory Taylor, June 9, 1967 (div. 1977); 1 child, Mary Kathleen; m. Mary Elizabeth Riddle, Nov. 21, 1978. BA, U. Tex., 1952, PhD, 1965. Auditor Procter and Gamble, Cin., 1955-61; from asst. to assoc. prof. econs. U. Tenn., Knoxville, 1965-70, prof., 1972—; gen. ptnr. Tenn.-Tex. Assocs.; head dept. U. Tenn., Knoxville, 1983-86; indsl. devel. specialist UN Indsl. Devel. Orgn., Vienna, 1970-72. Cons. World Bank, Internat. Labor Orgn., TVA, People's Republic of China, 1989, Fgn. Ministry of Japan, 1990; adminstr. UN Productivity Quality Project in Brazil, 1990. Author: Steel and Economic Growth in Mexico, 1967, The Economics of Total Quality Management, 1995; editor: Economic Policy in Mexico, 1987; contbr. articles to profl. jours. Served to 1st lt. U.S. Army, 1952-55, Korea. NDEA fellow Dept. HEW, Washington, 1962-65, Fulbright fellow Dept. HEW, Washington, 1964; grantee Tinker Found., N.Y.C., 1987. Mem. Am. Econ. Assn., N.Am. Econs. and Fin. Assn. (bd. dirs. 1984—), Assn. Evolutionary Econs., Latin Am. Studies Assn. Democrat. Avocation: travel. Office: Univ of Tenn Dept Economics Knoxville TN 37916

COLE, WILLIAM KAUFMAN, retired lawyer; b. Hartford, Conn., Oct. 5, 1914; s. Francis Watkinson and Grace (Kaufman) C.; m. Julia Emily Kistler, May 29, 1942 (div. 1955); children: David Brockway, Frank Kistler; m. Marion Beach, June 22, 1957 (dec. July 1990); m. Ula Tenney Duncan, May 9, 1992. BA, Yale U., 1936, LLB, 1939. Bar: Conn. 1939, U.S. Supreme Ct. 1954. Tchr. Laguna Blanca Sch., Santa Barbara, Calif., 1940-42; assoc. firm Robinson, Robinson & Cole, Hartford, 1942-48, partner, 1949-79, ret. ptnr., 1980—. Pres. Legal Aid Soc., Hartford County, 1955-62, YMCA Greater Hartford, 1964-66; trustee McLean Fund, Simsbury, Conn., 1967-89, chmn., 1980-89, trustee emeritus, 1989-2000; adv. dir. Hartford Hosp., bd. dirs., 1958-85, vice chmn., chmn., 1961-76; chmn. bd. trustees Conn. Hosp. Assn., 1977-78; bd. dirs. Westchester and So. Conn. Cmty. Health Plans, 1980-82, chmn., 1980-81; mem. Southbury Bd. Selectmen, 1987-94. bd. dirs. Regional Hospice Western Conn., Inc., 1990-93. With S.C. AUS, 1942-45. Fellow Am. Bar Found. (state chmn. 1978-82); mem. ABA, Conn. Bar Found. (bd. dirs. 1973-92, pres. 1975-76), Am. Law Inst., Conn. Bar Assn. (pres. 1974-75), Hartford County Bar Assn. (pres. 1963-64), Hartford Club, Yale Club (N.Y.C.). Republican. Congregationalist. Office: 1 Commercial Plz Hartford CT 06103-3509 Home: 777 Main St Hartford CT 06115-2303

COLE, WILLIAM L., lawyer; b. L.A., May 13, 1952; AB magna cum laude, U. Calif., Irvine, 1974; JD, Stanford U., 1977. Bar: Calif. 1977. Atty. Mitchell, Silberberg & Knupp, L.A., mng. ptnr., 1991—97, mem. exec. com., 1997—. Mem. ABA (co-chair sports and entertainment com.), State Bar Calif., Los Angeles County Bar Assn. (mem. exec. com. labor law sect. 1989-90), Order of Coif, Phi Beta Kappa. Office: Mitchell Silberberg & Knupp 11377 W Olympic Blvd Los Angeles CA 90064-1625 Office Phone: 310-312-2000. Business E-Mail: wlc@msk.com.

COLE, WILLIE, artist; b. Somerville, N.J., 1955; Student, Boston U., 1974—75; BFA, Sch. Visual Arts, N.Y., 1976; student, Art Students League, N.Y., 1976—79. Artist-in-residence Studio Mus., Harlem, NY, 1989, The Contemporary, Balt., 1994, Pilchuck Glass Sch., Seattle, 1994, Capp St. Project, San Francisco, 1995. One-man shows include Ednl. Testing Svc. Corp., Princeton, N.J., 1986, Inst. Contemporary Arts, L.I., 1990, Peter Miller Gallery, Chgo., 1991, 1993, Newark Mus., 1992, St. Louis Art Mus., 1992, Brooke Alexander, N.Y., 1992, 1994, Balt. Mus. Industry, 1994, Capp St. Project, San Francisco, 1995, U. Arts, Phila., 1995, Fabric Workshop Mus., 1995, Alerie Almine Rech, Paris, 1997, Alexander and Bonin, N.Y., 1997, John Berggruen Gallery, San Francisco, 1998, Mus. Modern Art, N.Y.C., 1998, Birmingham (Ala.) Mus. Art, 1998, Morris Mus., Morristown, N.J., 1999, Alexander and Bonin, 2002, exhibited in group shows at Littlejohn-Smith Gallery, N.Y., 1986, Robeson Ctr. Gallery, Rutgers U., 1987, Palais Exposition, Nice, France, 1988, Artworks, Princeton, 1989, Art in General, N.Y., 1990, Brooke Alexander, 1991; author: Brooke Alexander, 1993; Exhibited in group shows at Weatherspoon Art Gallery, Greensboro, N.C., 1992, Tokushima Modern Art Mus., Japan, 1992—94, Newark Mus., 1993, 1997, N.J. Ctr. Visual Arts, Summit, 1994, 1996, Josh Baer Gallery, N.Y., 1994, Neuberger Mus. Art, Purchase, N.Y., 1994, 1997, Mus. Modern Art, N.Y.C., 1995, 1996, K&E Gallery, N.Y., 1995, Whitney Mus. Am. Art, Champion, 1995, City Gallery Chastain, Atlanta, 1996, Rhona Hoffman Gallery, Chgo., exhibited in group shows, N.Y., 1998, exhibited in group shows, Paine Webber Art Gallery, N.Y., 1998, Alexander and Bonin, 1998—99, Represented in permanent collections Bronx Mus. Art, Mus. Contemporary Art, Chgo., Dallas Mus. Art, Milw. Art Mus., Newark Mus. Art, N.J. Mus. Modern Art, N.Y.C., Whitney Mus. Am. Art, N.Y., St. Louis Art Mus., State Mus., Trenton, N.J., Nat. Gallery Art, Washington, FRAC Lorraine, Metz. Recipient Joan Mitchell Found. award, 1996; fellow Rutgers Ctr. Innovative Printmaking fellow, Rutgers U., 1991; Penny McCall Found. grantee, 1991, Wheeler Found. grantee, 1994, Louis Comfort Tiffany Found. grantee, 1995. Office: c/o Alexander & Bonin 132 10th Ave New York NY 10011-4727*

COLELLA, ANTONIA KLARA, reading specialist, educator, writer; b. Auburn, N.Y., Oct. 20, 1948; d. Lucian Milton and Stella Dorothy Colella; 1 child, Luke Peter. BA in Edn., Rosary Hill Coll., Buffalo, N.Y., 1970; MA in Urban Edn., George Washington U., Washington, 1976; MS in Reading and Lang. Arts, Syracuse U., N.Y., 1980. Elem. tchr. D.C. Pub. Schs., Washington; reading specialist Hawaii Prep. Acad., Kamuela, Cornell U., Ithaca, NY; adj. instr. SAT Cayuga Cmty. Coll., Auburn; reading specialist Auburn H.S., State St. Sch., Skaneateles, NY. Creator of N.Y. State Newberry Quiz Bowl. Author: Now We're Talking...The Story of Theodore W. Case and Sound on Film, 2003. Sec. bd. trustees Coyoga Mus. History and Art; mem. St. Mary's Choir, 1990—. Mem.: Fingerlakes Ski Club. Democrat. Roman Catholic. Avocations: tennis, walking, yoga, classic cinema.

COLELLA, LOUIS MICHAEL, music educator, musician; b. New Castle, Pa., Dec. 14, 1935; s. Louis and Giovanina DeVivo Colella; m. Jeanette L. Giovanelli, June 17, 1961; children: Louis V., Mark R., Christopher J. B of Music Edn., Youngstown State U., 1961; M of Music Edn., Duquesne U., 1968. Woodwind instr. U.S. Naval Sch. of Music, Washington, 1961—63; music tchr. Hubbard (Ohio) Sch. Dist., 1963—67, Farrell (Pa.) Area Sch. Dist., 1967—93; adj. prof. Westminster Coll., New Wilmington, Pa., 1979—, Grove City (Pa.) Coll., 1988—. Clarinet and saxophone performer, Pa. and Ohio, 1950—; condr., Pa. and Ohio, 1961—. With U.S. Army, 1961—63. Mem.: Am. Fedn. Musicians, Music Educators Nat. Conf. Avocations: gardening, music performance. Home: 444 Patt Dr Farrell PA 16121

COLELLA, PHILIP, mathematician; BS, MS, PhD, U. Calif. Head applied numerical algorithms group Lawrence Berkeley Nat. Lab. Recipient Sidney Fernbach award, IEEE, 1998, SIAM/ACM prize for computational sci. and engring., 2003. Mem.: Nat. Acad. Scis. (mem. bd. math. scis. and their applications). Office: Lawrence Berkeley Nat Lab 1 Cyclotron Rd MS 50A-1148 Berkeley CA 94720

COLEMAN, ARLENE FLORENCE, retired pediatrics nurse; b. Braham, Minn., Apr. 8, 1926; d. William and Christine (Judin) C.; m. John Dunkerken, May 30, 1987. Diploma in nursing, U. Minn., 1947, BS, 1953; MPH, Loma Linda U., 1974. RN, Calif. Operating room scrub nurse Calif. Luth. Hosp., L.A., 1947-48; indsl. staff nurse Good Samaritan Hosp., L.A., 1948-49; staff nurse Passavant Hosp., Chgo., 1950-51; student health nurse Moody Bible Inst., Chgo., 1950-51; staff nurse St. Andrews Hosp., Mpls., 1951-53; pub. health nurse Bapt. Gen. Conf. Bd. of World Missions, Ethiopia, Africa, 1954-66; staff pub. health nurse County of San Bernadino, Calif., 1966-68, sr. pub. health nurse, 1968-73, pediatric nurse practitioner, 1973—. Contbr. articles to profl. jours. Mem. bd. dist. missions Bapt. Gen. Conf., Calif., 1978-84; mem. adv. coun. Kaiser Hosp., Fontana, Calif., 1969-85, Bethel Sem. West, San Diego, 1987—; bd. dirs. Casa Verdugo Retirement Home, Hemet, Calif., 1985—; active Calvary Bapt. Ch., Redlands, Calif., 1974—; mem. S.W. Bapt. Conf. Social Ministries, 1993—. With Cadet Nurse Corps USPHS, 1944-47. Calif. State Dept. Health grantee, 1973. Fellow Nat. Assn. Pediatric Nurse Assocs. and Practitioners; mem. Calif. Nurses Assn. (state nursing coun. 1974-76). Democrat. Avocations: gardening, travel, reading. Home: 622 Esther Way Redlands CA 92373-5822

COLEMAN, BARBARA MCREYNOLDS, artist; b. Omaha, Neb., May 5, 1956; d. Zachariah Aycock and Mary Barbara (McCulloh) McR.; m. Stephen Dale Dent, Mar. 12, 1983 (div. Dec. 20, 1992); children: Madeleine Victoria, Matthew Stephen; m. Ross Coleman, Oct. 16, 1993; 1 child, Mia Jeanne Coleman. Student, U. N.Mex., 1979, MA in Cmty. and Regional Planning, 1984. Lectr. U. N.Mex. Sch. Arch., Albuquerque, 1979—82, 1991—2000; assoc. planner, urban designer planning divsn. City of Albuquerque, 1982-84, city planner, urban designer N.Mex. redevel. divsn., 1984-88; v.p. Hydra Aquatic, Inc., Albuquerque, 1997—. Cons. City of Albuquerque Redevel. Dept., 1987-88; urban design cons. Southwest Land Rsch., Albuquerque, 1991, instr. at Ctr. for Action and Contemplation, Albuquerque, NM, 1999-present. Columnist for Kids and Art, 1990-92; author: Coors Corridor Plan (The Albuquerque Conservation Assn. Urban Design award 1984), Electric Facilities Plan, Downtown Core Revitalization Strategy and Sector Development Plan; contbg. author: Anasazi Architecture and American Design, 1994; contbr. articles to profl. jour.; invited artist Florence Biennale Internat. Exhbn., 2005; exhibited in shows and solo exhbns. at Dartmouth St. Gallery, Albuquerque, 2000-05, Chimayo (N.Mex.) Trade and Mercantile, JoAnne Chappel Gallery, San Francisco, Southwest Arts Festival, Albuquerque, Act I Gallery, Taos, N.Mex., Nat. Arts Club, NYC, Hermitage Mus., Norfolk, Va., Schimmel Ctr. for the Arts, Pace U., NYC, Musée Granet, Aix-en-Provence, France, Fine Arts Gallery, Albuquerque, 1999 (1st pl.); invited artist Florence Biennial Internat. Art Exhibit, 2005. Vol. art tchr. A. Montoya Elem. Sch., Roosevelt Mid. Sch., Albuquerque, 1989-97. Recipient First Pl. for pastels N.Mex. Art League, 1991, Merit award Pastel Soc. of S.W., 1989, 1st pl. award N.Mex. State Fair Fine Arts Gallery, Albuquerque, 1999; finalist Nat. Cath. Reporter Jesus 2000 contest. Mem. Pastel Soc. of Am. (signature mem.), Pastel Soc. N.Mex. (pres. 1991-92, Best of Show 1990 award, 4th pl. Am. Artist Mag. award 1999). Democrat. Episc. Avocations: hiking, skiing, running. Office: U NMex Sch Architecture Albuquerque NM 87131-0001

COLEMAN, BERNELL, physiologist, educator; b. Jefferson County, Miss., Apr. 26, 1929; s. Percy and Julia (Nailor) C.; m. Annie C. Richardson, Jan. 30, 1962; children— Rochelle, Ronald. BS, Alcorn A&M Coll., 1952; PhD, Loyola U., 1964. Rsch. asst. in biochemistry U. Chgo., 1956-57; rsch. in cancer Hines (Ill.) VA Hosp., 1957-59; instr. St. Louis U. Sch. Medicine, 1963-65, asst. prof. physiology, 1965-67; asst. prof. Chgo. Med. Sch., 1967-69, assoc. prof., 1969-76, prof., 1976, Howard U. Coll. Medicine, Washington, 1976—, chmn. dept. physiology and biophysics, 1979—. Lectr. Cook County Grad. Sch. Medicine, U. Ill. Med. Sch.; vis. prof. Rush Med. Coll.; external examiner Godfrey Huggins Sch. Medicine, U. Zimbabwe, Salisbury, 1981; mem. cardiovasc. and pulmonary study sect. Nat. Heart, Lung and Blood Inst./NIH, 1982-83, rsch. tng. rev. com., 1990-94. Peer rev. com. Am. Heart Assn., 1988-93, 95—, rsch. com., 1993—. With U.S. Army, 1953-56, Korea. Recipient rsch. award Chgo. Med. Sch. Bd. Trustees, 1975; NIH rsch. fellow, 1960-61; NIH grantee, 1966-68, 69-74, 74-76, 79—; USPHS fellow, 1961-63; Univ. fellow Loyola U., 1964; Dept. Def. grantee, 1965-67 Mem.: AAAS, AAUP, Heart Failure Soc. Am., Am. Soc. Hypertension (charter), N.Y. Acad. Scis., Internat. Soc. of Hypertension in Blacks, Assn. Black Cardiologists, Fedn. Am. Socs. Exptl. Biology (vis. scientist for minority instns. programs 1982—83, 1989—90), Am. Heart Assn. (basic sci. coun.), Am. Physiol. Soc. (cardiovascular fellow 1985), Phi Rho Sigma, Sigma Xi. Democrat. Achievements include research numerous publs. in cardiovascular physiology. Home: 14200 Myer Ter Rockville MD 20853-2350 Office: 520 W St NW Washington DC 20001-2337 Office Phone: 202-806-6330. Business E-Mail: bcoleman@howard.edu.

COLEMAN, BRIAN, voice educator; b. Dayton, Ohio, Oct. 25, 1971; s. William A. and Sheila M. Coleman; 1 child, W. Alexander. MusB in Edn., Bowling Green State U., Ohio, 1994. Tchg. Lic. Ohio, 2002. Vocal music tchr. West Carrollton City Schs., West Carrollton, Ohio, 1997—, Cardington Lincoln Local Schools, Cardington, Ohio, 1995—97. Dir.: (musical theatre production) Seussical, Little Shop of Horrors, Pajama Game. Precint leader Move On PAC, Kettering, Ohio, 2004—05. Mem.: Am. Choral Dirs. Assn., Ohio Edn. Assn., Ohio Music Edn. Assn. (dist. 12 pres. elect 2004—). Avocations: reading, travel, theater. Office: West Carrollton City Sch 5833 Student St West Carrollton OH 45449 Office Phone: 937-859-5121. Personal E-mail: brian.coleman@mac.com.

COLEMAN, BRITTIN TURNER, lawyer; b. Tuscaloosa, Ala., Dec. 12, 1942; s. Jefferson Jackson and Rose Wallace (Turner) C.; m. Johanna M. Nicol, June 1963 (div. 1967); 1 child, Anna M. Shields; m. Jane M. Kirkman, June 27, 1970; children: Mary Elizabeth, Emily Jane. BA in Am. Studies, U. Ala., 1964, LLB, 1967. Bar: Ala. 1967, U.S. Dist. Ct. (no. dist.) Ala. 1972, U.S. Ct. Appeals (5th cir.) 1975, U.S. Ct. Appeals (11th cir.) 1981, U.S. Dist. Ct. (mid. and so. dists.) Ala. 1986. With Bradley, Arant, Rose & White, Birmingham, Ala., 1971—, ptnr., 1976—. Adj. prof. law, coach Nat. Mock Trial teams Cumberland Sch. Law, 1979-84 (2 Nat. Championships); former mem. faculty Ala. Def. Lawyers Assn. Trial Acad., 1992; former mem. Ala. Pattern Jury Instructions Com.; mem. ct.'s adv. group No. Dist. Ala., 1997; mem. Product Liability Adv. Coun. Bd. dirs. Downtown YMCA, 1993-99; active Canterbury United Meth. Ch. Capt. JAGC, U.S. Army, 1967-71. Decorated Bronze Star with first oak leaf cluster, Army Commendation medal with first oak leaf cluster, Vietnam Svc. medal, Vietnam Campaign medal, Vietnam Civil Action Honor medal. Master: Birmingham Inn of Am. Inns of Ct.; fellow: Ala. Law Found., Am. Bar Found.; mem.: ABA, Farrah Law Soc., Def. Rsch. Inst., Ala. Def. Lawyers Assn., Am. Bd. Trial Advocates, Ala. Law Inst., Birmingham Bar Found. (bd. dirs. 2000—02), Birmingham Bar Assn. (chmn. grievance com. 1989, exec. com. 1992—94, pres.-elect 1998, pres. 1999, past chmn. civil cts. com., past chmn. CLE com., past chmn. ins. com., past Liberty Bell award com., past chmn. election com., past exec. com. young lawyers sect., past chmn. long range planning com.), Am. Judicature Soc., Ala. Law Sch. Found. (pres. 1994—96, exec. 1997—), The Summit Club, The Club, Ala. Alumni of Order of Coif (pres. 1992—94). Office: Bradley Arant Rose & White One Federal Pl 1819 5th Ave N Birmingham AL 35203 Business E-Mail: bcoleman@bradleyarant.com.

COLEMAN, CAROLYN QUILLOIN, association executive; b. Savannah, Ga. 1 child. BS in History, Savannah State Coll.; MS in Adult Edn. and C.C. Adminstrn., N.C. A&T State U. Nat. staff mem. NAACP, N.C. state exec. dir., so. voter edn. dir., dir. voter registration/voter edn./voter turnout campaign in the South, 1989—92, coord. voter registration, 1990, 1991, mem. nat. bd. dirs.; dir. James B. Hunt Jr. campaign for gov., 1992; spl. asst. for cmty. affairs to Gov. James B. Hunt Jr., 1993—. Mem.: Nat. Assn. Negro Bus. and Profl. Women, Greensboro Br. NAACP, Wildacres Leadership Initiative, Women's Polit. Forum, Delta Sigma Theta (Greensboro Alumnae chpt.). Baptist. Office: NAACP 4805 Mt Hope Dr Baltimore MD 21215

COLEMAN, CATHERINE G., astronaut; b. Charleston, S.C., Dec. 14, 1960; d. James J. Coleman and Ann L. Doty; m. Josh Simpson. BS in Chemistry, MIT, 1983; D in Polymer Sci. and Engring., U. Mass., 1991. Commd. 2nd lt. USAF, 1983, advanced through grades to lt. col.; rsch. chemist materials directorate Wright Lab., Wright Patterson AFB; astronaut NASA Johnson Space Ctr., Houston, 1992—, with astronaut office mission support br., spl. asst. to ctr. dir., with astronaut office payloads and habitability br., mission specialist on STS-73, 1995, mission specialist on STS-83, lead mission specialist on STS-93, 1999. Surface analysis cons. for Long Duration Exposure Facility; vol. test subject centrifuge program Crew Sys. Directorate Armstrong Aeromedical Lab. Mem. ACS, AAUW, Soc. Photo-Optical Instrumentation Engrs., Internat. Womens' Air and space Mus. Avocations: flying, scuba diving, sports, music. Office: NASA Lyndon B Johnson Space Ctr Houston TX 77058

COLEMAN, CHARLES CLYDE, physicist, educator; b. York, Eng., July 31, 1937; arrived in U.S., 1941; s. Jesse C. and Geraldine (Doherty) C.; m. Sharon R. Slutsky, Aug. 12, 1976; children: Jeffrey Andrew, Matthew Casey. BA, UCLA, 1959, MA, 1961, PhD, 1968. Asst. prof. physics Calif. State U., LA, 1968-71, assoc. prof, 1971-76, prof., 1976—2002, prof. emeritus, 2002—. Cons. Gen. Dynamics Corp., 1975-77, China Lake Naval Rsch. Labs., 1981; dir. Csula Accelerator Facility; exec. dir. Csula Applied Physics Inst., 1978-83; sr. rsch. fellow Darwin Coll., Cambridge (Eng.) U., 1975-76; project specialist Chinese Provincial Univs. Devel. Project of World Bank, 1987-90; vis. prof. physics U. Istanbul, Turkey, 1969, 72, U. Sydney, Australia, 1977, Arya Mar U., Iran, 1976, U. Natal, South Africa, 1977, UCLA, 1990-91, U. Leicester, U.K., 1995-2001, Hubei U., Wuhan, China, 2002; mem. NASA rev. panel, 1992. Contbr. articles to sci. publs.; referee Solid State Electronics, Phys. Rev., Phys. Rev. Letters, Jour. Phys. Chem. Solids, Jour. Solid State Chem., Jour. Optical Materials. Trustee Calif. State U. LA Found., 1981-85. Grantee NSF, 1976-, Rsch. Corp., 1987-91; NATO Collaborative Rsch. grantee, 1991—; NATO Sr. Rsch. fellow Cavendish Lab. (U.K.), 1983-84, Am. Chem. Soc. Rsch. Faculty fellow, 1990. Fellow Brit. Interplanetary Soc., Royal Philatelic Soc. (London); mem. Am. Phys. Soc., Am. Radio Relay League, Sigma Xi, Phi Kappa Phi, Phi Beta Delta, Sigma Pi Sigma. Office: Calif State U Dept Physics Los Angeles CA 90032 Office Phone: 323-343-2134. E-mail: ccolema@calstatela.edu.

COLEMAN, CHARLES PAYSON, JR., (PAYSON COLEMAN), lawyer; b. NYC, May 9, 1950; C. Payson and Mimi (Wainwright) C.; m. Catherine C. Coleman, June 23, 1972; children: Charles P. III, Avery W., Phillips Reed. BA, Williams Coll., 1972; JD, Hofstra U., 1976. Bar: N.Y. 1976. Assoc. Winthrop, Stimson, Putnam & Roberts, NYC, 1976-84, ptnr., 1985—2001, Pillsbury Winthrop LLP, NYC, 2001—05; ptnr., Fin., Aviation practices, mem. finance com. Pillsbury Winthrop Shaw Pittman LLP, NYC, 2005—. Mem. aviation working group Cape Town Convention. Articles editor Hofstra Law Rev., 1975-76. Trustee Greenwood Cemetery, Bklyn., 1982—, North Shore Univ. Hosp., Manhasset, N.Y., 1993. Named Best of the Best among Aviation lawyers, Expert Guide to the World's Aviation Lawyers, 2004. Mem.: ABA (mem. sub-com. on aircraft financing). Office: Pillsbury Winthrop Shaw Pittman LLP 1540 Broadway New York NY 10036 Office Phone: 212-858-1426. Office Fax: 212-858-1500. Business E-Mail: payson.coleman@pillsburylaw.com.

COLEMAN, CHASE, music educator, musician; b. Oakland, Calif., May 7, 1962; s. Hawes and Natalie Coleman; m. Meredith Nichols, May 20, 1999. MusB, Boston (Mass.) U., 1985; MusM, U. Mass., 1992. Pianist Artie Shaw Orch., Boston, 1989, Copley Plz. Hotel, Boston, 1989—91; adj. faculty Boston (Mass.) Conservatory, 1991—94; prin., owner Coleman Wynne Music LLC, Flagstaff, Ariz., 1997—, tchr. piano, 1997—. Rehearsal pianist Fairfield County Student Operetta Workshop, Wilton, Conn., 1978—81; concerto soloist YMF Orch., L.A., 1987—87; leader, pianist Sole Agents Jazz Orch., Boston, 1988—93; dir. musical Boston (Mass.) Children's Theatre, 1983—85, La Canaille Dramatique, Lowell, Mass., 1990—91; pianist New Eng. Philharm., Cambridge, Mass., 1990—92; dir. musical La Mama Etc., N.Y., 1991, Wheelock Family Theatre, Boston, 1992, New London (N.H.) Barn Playhouse, 1992; bandleader Radisson Seven Seas Cruises, Fort Lauderdale, Fla., 1995—96; concerto soloist Timberline (Colo.) Symphony, 1997—98; pianist Longmont (Colo.) Symphony Orch., 1997—98; concerto soloist Sedona (Ariz.) Chamber Orch., 2000, Coconino Coll. Orch., Flagstaff, Ariz., 2001, Verde Valley Chamber Orch., Sedona, Ariz., 2004; dir. Coconino C.C. Jazz Ensemble, Flagstaff, 2004—; concerto soloist Coconino Coll. Orch., 2005; adj. faculty Boston (Mass.) Conservatory, 1991—94, Northeastern U., Boston, 1997; assoc. faculty Coconino C.C., Flagstaff, 2004—. Composer (lyricist, author): (plays) Your Place or Mine, 1994. Recipient Carnegie Recital Hall Performance winner, N.Y. Music Tchrs. League, 1980, Chopin Competition First prize, Schubert Club Fairfield County, Conn., 1979, Third prize, Performers Conn., Westport, CT, 1980; scholar, U. Mass., Lowell, Mass., 1985—87; Shirley R. Koffler Piano scholarship, Schubert Club Fairfield County, Conn., 1980. Master: No. Ariz. Music Tchrs. Assn. (pres. 1999—2000); mem.: Ariz. State Music Tchrs. Assn. Independent. Avocations: acting, snorkeling, nature, history. Home: 1235 West Saturn Way Flagstaff AZ 86001 Office: Coconino Community College 2800 South Lone Tree Road Flagstaff AZ 86001-2701 Personal E-mail: chase@npgcable.com. E-mail: chase.coleman@coconino.edu.

COLEMAN, CLAIRE KOHN, public relations executive; b. New Castle, Pa., Nov. 19, 1924; d. Louis and Florence (Frank) Kohn; m. Frederick H. Coleman, Mar. 10, 1957; children: Franklin, Elliot. BA, Pa. State U., 1945. Market editor Fairchild Publs., N.Y.C., 1945—48; asst. home editor N.Y. Times, 1949—50; pub. rels. dir. United Wallpaper, Chgo., 1950—53, Assoc. Am. Artists, N.Y.C., 1953—54; dir. Wallpaper Info. Bur., N.Y.C., 1954; dept. head Roy Bernard, Inc., N.Y.C., 1955—58; pub. rels. dir. Siesel Co., N.Y.C., 1972—, sr. v.p., 1988; pres. Tisch Trask Comm. Resources Pub. Rels. Group, 1988—89; sr. v.p. Anthony M. Franco, N.Y.C., 1989—90; pres. Coleman Comm., N.Y.C., 1990—. Ctrl. steering com. Sch. Dist. Critical Assessments, New Rochelle, NY, 1969—71; active Mayor's Adv. Coun. on Aging, 1966, Mayor's Adv. Coun. on Bd. Edn. Appts., 1969; v.p. Coun. of PTAs, 1969—70; chmn. women's divsn. United Jewish Appeal, New Rochelle, 1971; v.p. Found. Women Execs. Pub. Rels., 1992—93, pres., 1993—94, bd. dirs., 1998—; bd. dirs., v.p. Beechmont Assn., 1969—74, adv. bd., 1990—. Fellow: Internat. Furnishings and Design Assn. (founder 1947, exec. chmn. 1947, pres. 1947, v.p. 1948—50, v.p. Chgo. chpt. 1950—53, nat. treas. 1977—78, nat. pres. 1980—81, v.p. N.Y. chpt. 1994, nat. v.p. mktg. 1998—2000, Cir. of Excellence award 1994, Internat. Hon. Recognition award 1998); mem.: Women Execs. Pub. Rels. (bd. dirs. 1983—84, sec. 1986—87, pres.-elect 1994—95, pres. 1996—97). Fax: 914-576-6885. Office Phone: 914-633-6914. E-mail: ckcpr@aol.com.

COLEMAN, COURTNEY STAFFORD, mathematician, educator; b. Ventura, Calif., July 19, 1930; s. Courtney Clemon and Una (Stafford) C.; m. Julia Wellnitz, June 26, 1954; children: David, Margaret, Diane. BA, U. Calif., Berkeley, 1951; PhD, Princeton U., 1955. Asst. prof. Wesleyan U., Middletown, Conn., 1955-58; from asst. prof. to full prof. Harvey Mudd Coll., Claremont, Calif., 1959-98. Lectr. Princeton (N.J.) U., 1954-55; rsch. in field. Author, editor: Differential Equations Models, 1983; editor, translator: Local Methods in Nonlinear Differential Equations, 1988; author: (with others) Differential Equations, 1987, Differential Equations Laboratory Workbook, 1992 (EDUCOM award for best math./computer course materials), Ordinary Differential Equations: A Modeling Perspective, 1998, 2d edit., 2004, ODE Architect, 1999 (award of excellence and Gold medal for best CD-ROM in edn.); mem. editl. bd. Jour. of Differential Equations, 1964—, UMAP Jour., 1980—. Mem. Am. Math. Soc., Math. Assn. Am., Soc. Indsl. Applied Math. Office: Harvey Mudd Coll Math Dept 1250 N Dartmouth Ave Claremont CA 91711 E-mail: coleman@hmc.edu.

COLEMAN, D. JACKSON, ophthalmologist, educator; b. Waverly, N.Y., Dec. 1, 1934; s. Max Elliot and Frances Agnes (Henton) C.; m. Jane Marie Holmes, July 6, 1963; children: Jeffrey, Jonathan, Jeremy. BS, Union Coll., 1956; MD, U. Buffalo, 1960. Intern Columbia Med. Div., Bellevue Hosp., N.Y.C., 1960-61; lt. comdr. USPHS Bur. State Services Heart Disease Control Program, Washington, 1961-64; resident in ophthalmology Edward S. Harkness Eye Inst., Columbia Presbyn. Med. Center, N.Y.C., 1964-67, mem. faculty, staff, 1967-79; John Milton McLean prof. Cornell U. Med. Coll., N.Y.C., 1979—; chmn. dept. ophthalmology N.Y. Hosp.-Cornell Med. Ctr., 1979—, ophthalmologist-in-chief, 1979—. Sr. author: Ultrasonography of Eye and Orbit, 1977; contbr. articles to med. jours. Recipient Wacker award of Club Jules Gonin Internat. Retina Soc., 1976, Lucien Howe medal, 1988; NIH grantee. Fellow ACS, Am. Acad. Ophthalmology; mem. Am. Inst. Ultrasound Medicine (bd. govs. 1970-73), Am. Ophthamolgy Soc., Am. Retina Soc. (v.p. 1989-91, pres. 1991-93), Assn. Rsch. Ophthamology (Weisenfeld award 1996), Societas Interationalis de Diagnostic Ultrasonica in Ophthalmology (exec. bd. 1971-81), World Fedn. Ultrasound Medicine and Biology (exec. bd. 1973-82, sec.treas. 1973-77, treas. 1977-82), Am. Intraocular Lens Soc. (sci. advisor 1976-79), Am. Soc. Ophthalmic Ultrasound (bd. govs. 1976—), AMA, N.Y. County Med. Soc., Am. Eye Study Club, Jules Gonin Club (exec. com. 1992—, v.p. 1993-98, pres. 1998-2004). Republican. Methodist. Office: NY Presbyterian Hosp-Weill-Cornell Med Ctr 525 E 68th St New York NY 10021-4870 Office Phone: 212-746-5588. E-mail: djceye@aol.com.

COLEMAN, DAVID CECIL, financial executive; b. Topeka, Sept. 7, 1937; s. Merrill Orda and Cecil Jennie (Warders) C. BS in Fin., Kans. U., 1959; PhD in Bus. Adminstrn., Calif. Western U., 1979. Registered investment advisor. Cost acct. Am. Electronics, Inc., Orange, Calif., 1963-65; fin. mgr. Univ. Calif. San Diego, La Jolla, 1965-67; v.p. fin. Aero Titanium Products, San Diego, 1967-69; contr. Gen. Tire, Tustin, Calif., 1969-70; fin. mgr., satellite telecom. analyst Hughes Aircraft, El Segundo, Calif., 1970-76; proprietor Concept Pub., York, N.Y., 1976—. Realtor assoc. Mitchell Pierson Jr., Realtor, Mendon, N.Y., 1980-92; instr. MBA prog. Rochester (N.Y.) Inst., 1982-86. Author: Management of the Firm, 1977, For the Long Term Investor, 1979, Consistency in Market Forecasting, 1982, How to Collect Bad Checks, 1989, Tax Tricks for the Proprietor, 1990, Starting a Business for the Proprietor, 1992, How to Avoid Audit for the Proprietor, 1992, Asset Protection for the Small Firm, 1995. Fin. mgr. York (N.Y.) Hist. Soc., 1988; mem. com. Orgn. to Regain States' Rights per U.S. Constitution, N.H. 1st Lt. USMC, 1959-63. Home: PO Box 500 York NY 14592-0500 Office: Concept Pub 2682 Main St York NY 14592 Office Phone: 585-243-3148. Fax: 585-243-4214. E-mail: conceptpublishing@hotmail.com.

COLEMAN, DEBORAH ANN, lawyer; b. Chgo., July 19, 1951; d. Louis J. and Gloria (Bryskier) C.; m. Dan A. Polster, May 29, 1977; 3 children. AB magna cum laude, Radcliffe Coll., 1973; JD, Harvard U., 1976. Bar: Ohio 1976, U.S. Dist. Ct. (no. dist.) Ohio, 1976, U.S. Ct. Appeals (6th cir.) 1982. Assoc. Hahn Loeser & Parks, Cleve., 1976-83, ptnr., 1984—. Mem. task force on rules of profl. conduct Ohio Supreme Ct. Contbr. articles to legal jours. Mem. ABA (chair standing com. on ethics and profl. responsibility 1997-98), Ohio Bar Assn., Cleve. Bar Assn. (past chair profl. ethics com.). Office: Hahn Loeser & Parks LLP 3300 BP Tower 200 Public Sq Ste 3300 Cleveland OH 44114-2303 Office Phone: 216-274-2220.

COLEMAN, DENNIS M., lawyer; b. Mar. 5, 1953; AB, Brown Univ., 1975; JD, Georgetown Univ., 1978. Bar: R.I. 1979, US Dist. Ct. (Fed. dist.). Assoc. Ropes & Gray, Boston, 1988—93, ptnr. corp. dept., 1993—, head sports law practice group. Pres. Brown Univ. Hall of Fame; incorporator Kent Meml. Hosp. Mem.: ABA (sports & entertainment forum), R.I. Black Lawyers Assn., Boston Bar Assn., Sports Lawyers Assn. Office: Ropes & Gray 1 International Pl Boston MA 02110-2624 Office Phone: 617-951-7361. Office Fax: 617-951-7050. Business E-Mail: dennis.coleman@ropesgray.com.

COLEMAN, EARL MAXWELL, publishing company executive; b. N.Y.C., Jan. 9, 1916; s. Samuel Sidney and Rose (Ensleman) C.; m. Frances Louise Allan, Mar. 23, 1942 (div. Mar. 15, 1965); children: Allan Douglass, Dennis Scott; m. Ellen Schneid, Aug. 19, 1973. Student, NYU, 1933-34, CCNY, 1934-35, Columbia U., 1946. Founder, pres. Plenum Pub. Corp. (and predecessors), N.Y.C., 1946-77, chmn. bd. dirs., 1960-77, cons., 1977—. Founder Earl M. Coleman Enterprises, Inc. (Pubs.), 1977—; pres. Nat. Pubs. The Black Hills Inc., 1984-89; cons. Prentice Hall Coll. div., 1989-90. Contbr. poems, short stories to mags. Served with USAAF, 1941-45. Mem. Info. Industry Assn. (dir. 1971—), Assn. Am. Publishers (exec. com. tech.-sci.-med. div. 1970—), Sci. Tech. Med. Publishers (Holland). Home: 131 Ridge Dr Montville NJ 07045-9473 *Do whatever you do passionately. Never be astonished at the fact that literally all the worldly affairs with which humans busy themselves and into which they pour so much energy, are games, sometimes bloody games, but games. Not only does the passionate player have a greater chance to get ahead in the game, he also enjoys it more than the passive player. Only the person who is willing to be stark naked before his own eyes, which can be the cruelest of mirrors, gets to savor his life to the fullest. Here too, passion serves, for ruthless honesty with self is key to an honest appraisal of anything else.*

COLEMAN, ELIZABETH, college president; b. N.Y.C., Nov. 23, 1937; d. Lewis and Sophie (Brantman) Ginsburg; m. Aaron Coleman, June 14, 1959; children: Daniel, David. BA, U. Chgo., 1958; MA, Cornell U., 1959; PhD, Columbia U., 1965; Doctorate (hon.), Hofstra U.; LLD (hon.), U. Vt. Instr. humanities SUNY, N.Y.C., 1960-65; assoc. dean faculty New Sch. Social Research, N.Y.C., 1966-76, dean Coll. Arts and Scis., 1977-84, prof. literature and humanities, 1984-87; pres. Bennington (Vt.) Coll., 1987—. Vis. lectr. Hebrew U., 1972, SUNY-Stony Brook, 1975; curriculum cons. Howard U., 1973; chmn. outside evaluating com. CUNY, 1976 Contbr. articles to profl. pubs. Mem. nat. adv. coun. Woodrow Wilson Found., 1990; bd. dirs. Ctrl. Vt. Pub. Svc. Corp., 1990-96; bd. trustees Inst. Ecosystem Studies, 1994. Fellow Ford Found., 1954-58; Woodrow Wilson fellow, 1958-59; F.J.E. Woodbridge fellow Columbia U., 1963-64; Pres.'s fellow Columbia U., 1964-65 Mem. MLA, Am. Assn. Colls. Home and Office: Bennington Coll Office of Pres Rte 67A Bennington VT 05201

COLEMAN, FAY, literature and language educator, director; b. Detroit, May 8, 1949; d. Hiter Carrington and Etta Jewel (Roberts) Coleman. *Fay and her family value the importance of education. Brother, Homer, PhD in Education, University of Michigan, Ann Arbor, has 36 years in education. Niece, Susan, CPA, has a BS in Business Administration from Wayne State University, Detroit, Michigan. Nephew, Jonathan, has a BS in Civil Engineering from Lawrence Technological University, Southfield, Michigan. Nephew, Robert, has a BS in Computer Science and wife, Kelly, has a BS in Nursing, from University of Michigan, Ann Arbor. Nephew, Ray V. Jr., has a BS in Biology, and wife, Stephanie, has a BS in Chemical Engineering from University of Michigan, Ann Arbor. Ray Jr. has 11 years in Education.* BS in English and History, Ea. Mich. U., 1971, MA in English Lit. and Langs., 1972. Tchr. adult edn. Melvindale High Sch., Mich., 1973—84; substitute tchr. Taylor Pub. Schs., Mich., 1974—77; tchr. English, history Taylor Ctr. HS, 1977—80, tchr. English, yearbook advisor, 1993—97; tchr. English, history West Jr. HS, Taylor, 1984—85, Brake Jr. HS, Taylor, 1985—93; tchr. English, dept. chair John F. Kennedy HS, Taylor, 1997—. Social chair Brake Jr. High Sch., 1985—92, union rep., 1991—92. *In 1994-1997, Fay received a sizable grant for the disadvantaged students at Taylor Center High in Taylor, Michigan. In 1999-2000, at Kennedy High in Taylor, she participated in a job-shadowing program for career awareness in the hospitality industry and received a Golden Apple Award from Wayne County Regional Service Agency. In 1999-2001, she co-authored and designed a career awareness planner for the students at Kennedy. In 1998-2003, she served on the North Central Accreditation Steering Committee and presented at the NCA State Conference in 1999. In 1999-2001 she was class advisor for the Class of 2003. She has also participated in conferences on chemical dependency in the school, family, and community, education and reproductive health.* Baptist. Avocations: travel, gardening, sewing. Home: 21609 Bayside Saint Clair Shores MI 48081 Office: John F Kennedy High Sch 13505 Kennedy Dr Taylor MI 48180

COLEMAN, FRANCES MCLEAN, secondary school educator; b. Jackson, Miss., Feb. 17, 1940; d. Robert Beatty and Dorothy Trotter (Witty) McLean.; m. Thomas Allen Coleman, Aug. 29, 1964; children: James Plemon, Robert McLean, Dorothy Witty McLean, Josiah Dennis, Leonidas McLean. BA, U. Miss., Oxford, 1962; MS, U. Miss., Jackson, 1964, PhD, 1970. Cert. tchr., Miss.; cert. in young adult/adolescent sci., Nat. Bd. Prof. Tchg. Stds. Adolescent/Young Adult Scis. Coord. Title I ESEA Choctaw County, Ackerman, Miss., 1970-73; instr. anatomy and physiology Wood Jr. Coll., Mathiston, Miss., 1977-78; instr. math. Miss. State U., Starkville, 1978-81; tchr. Choctaw City Sch. Dist., Ackerman, 1982—2003, dist. tech. coord., 1995—2003; facilitator PBS Teacherline, 2002—. Adj. faculty Lesley U., Cambridge, Mass., 2002—; cons. JBHM Edn. Group, LLC, 2003—. Contbr. articles to profl. jours. including Surgery, T.H.E. Jour., Learning and Leading with Tech. Active Miss. State Bd. of Health, Jackson, 1980-94. Recipient Presdl. award for excellence in sci. teaching NSF, 1990, Sci. Tchr. awards Disney, 1993; named to Women Hall of Master Tchrs. Miss. U., 1994; named Educator of Yr. Milken Family Founds., 1991; Tandy scholar, 1991; Tapestry grantee, 1995; Coun. for Basic Edn. Sci.-Math. fellow, 1994, Access Excellence fellow Genentech, 1995, Am. Physiol. Soc. fellow, 1995, Einstein Disting. Educator fellow Dept. of Energy, 2000. Mem. Nat. Sci. Tchrs. Assn., Am. Assn. German Tchrs., Am. Assn. French Tchrs., Am. Assn. Physics Tchrs., Nat. Assn. Biology Tchrs., Miss. Edn. Computer Assn. (Miss. Computer Educator of Yr. 1990, pres.-elect 1995, pres. 1996), Miss. Fgn. Lang. Assn. (pres. secondary sect. 1992-94). Episcopalian. Avocations: reading, travel. Home: PO Box 268 Ackerman MS 39735-0268 Office: Choctaw County Sch Dist PO Box 398 Ackerman MS 39735-0398 Personal E-mail: fcoleman@telepak.net. *We advise students to do what they like in life. Perhaps we should advise them that with imagination and hard work they can transform almost any job so that they like what they do.*

COLEMAN, FRANCIS J., JR., lawyer; b. McCook, Nebr., Jan. 28, 1945; BA, Rice U., 1966; JD (with hons.), U. Tex., 1972. Bar: Tex. 1972. City atty. City of Houston, Tex., 1982-84; ptnr. Vinson & Elkins LLP, Houston, co-head Pub. Fin. Sect. Office: Vinson & Elkins 2300 1st City Tower 1001 Fannin St Houston TX 77002-6760 Office Phone: 713-758-2222. E-mail: hcoleman@velaw.com.

COLEMAN, GARY L., insurance company executive; V.p., chief acctg. officer Torchmark Corp., Birmingham, Ala., 1994—99, exec. v.p., CFO, 1999—. Office: Torchmark Corp 2001 3rd Ave S Birmingham AL 35233

COLEMAN, GARY WILLIAM, elementary school educator; b. Davenport, Iowa, Dec. 16, 1945; s. Robert Earl and Mildred Margaret (Mast) C.; m. Janice Marie Coleman, Dec. 29, 1973; children: Heidi Marie, Sean Robert. BS in Elem. Edn., U. S.D., 1987; BSBA, Ariz. State U., 1969. Cert. elem. tchr., S.D. Tchr. Marty (S.D.) Indian Sch., 1987-91, Parkston (S.D.) Elem. Sch., 1991-2000; acct./bookkeeper Ulland Bros Constrn., Austin, Minn.; realtor assoc. Myre-Sorenson Real Estate, Albert Lea, Minn.; bldg. constrn. contractor, landscaper, Alcester, S.D.; site mgr. Heritage Ct. Apts., Oak Leaf Real Estate Mgmt. Ltd., 2001—03; preschool tutor South Ctrl. Edn. Coop., 2002—03; tutor Avon Elem. Sch., SD, 2003—04; human resources coord. Boys and Girls Club, Wagner, SD, 2003—04; tchr. Marty (S.D.) Elem. Sch., SD, 2005—. E.M.T., 1982—2003. Sgt. USAF, 1969-73. Mem. NEA, Parkston Edn. Assn. (v.p. 1995-96, pres. 1996-97, founder scholarship fund 1997), Am. Legion (vice-comdr. S.D. 7th Dist. 2003-05, comdr. 2005—).

COLEMAN, GEORGE EDWARD, vocalist, musician; b. Memphis, Mar. 8, 1935; s. George Edward and Indiana (Lyle) C.; m. Gloria Bell, Aug. 3, 1959; children: George, Gloria; m. Carol Ann Hollister, Sept. 7, 1985. Grad. high sch., Memphis. Ind. saxophonist with numerous jazz combos, 1952-74; leader George Coleman Quartet/Quintet/Octet, 1974—. Cons. Lenox (Mass.) Jazz Sch. Music, 1958, L.I. U., 1984—, NYU, 1987—, New Sch. Social Rsch., 1987—, Thelonious Monk Inst., 1996, New Eng. Conservatory, 1998; judge Thelonious Monk Inst. Internat. Jazz Competition, Washington, 2002; pvt. instr. Saxophonist B.B. King Band, 1952-53, 55, Max Roach Quintet, 1958-59, MIles Davis quintet, 1963-64, Lionel Hampton Orch., 1965-66, Lee Morgan quintet, 1969, Elvin Jones Quartet, 1970; composer, arranger mus. shows, films: Sweet Love Bitter, 1970, Comedie (French), 1985, Freejack, 1991, The Preacher's Wife, 1996. Grantee NEA, 1975, 81, 85; recipient award for contbns. to music Beale St. Assn., 1977, Tip of the Derby awards, 1978, 79, NY Jazz Audience award, 1979, Gold Note Jazz award, 1985, Key to the City of Memphis, 1991, Lifetime Achievement award Jazz Found. Am., 1997, Concertgebow Jazz award, 2002, Excellence in Jazz award Manhattan Assn. Cabarets and Clubs, 2005; selected by Internat. Jazz Critics Poll, 1958; named Artist of Yr., Record World mag., 1969. Address: 63 E 9th St New York NY 10003-6302 Personal E-mail: biggeorgecoleman@aol.com.

COLEMAN, GERALD CHARLES, judge, law educator; b. Phila., Apr. 23, 1935; s. Francis Eugene and Mary Veronica Coleman; m. Mary Lou Coleman, Sept. 3, 1960; children: Margaret Mary, Miriam, Christine. BS in econ., Villanova U., 1957; JD, Georgetown U. Law Ctr., 1963, LLM, 1976; MA in internat. rels., Boston U., 1971; MS in sys. mgmt., U. So. Calif., 1983. Bar: Va. 1963, Pa. 1991, Supreme Ct. US 1970. Apptd. mil. law judge, 1970; law educator Rutgers U., Camden, NJ, 1992—95; adminstrv. law judge Commonwealth Pa., Phila., 1995—. Contbr. articles to profl. jours. Legacy mem. Nat. Constn. Ctr., Phila., 2003; founding supporter Kimmel Ctr. Performing Arts, Phila., 2003. Officer U.S. Army, 1964—92, lt. colonel U.S. Army, 1963—92, Vietnam, Japan, Germany. Decorated Bronze Star US Army, Phan Rang, Vietnam, Master Parachute Wings US Army, Ft. Bragg, NC, Legion Merit US Army, Tokyo. Mem.: Federalist Soc., Am. Soc. Internat. Law. Avocations: mountain climbing, boating. Home: 233A Bainbridge St Philadelphia PA 19147 Office: Bureau Hearings and Appeals Commonwealth of Pa State Office Bldg 1400 Spring Garden St Philadelphia PA 19130

COLEMAN, GINA ALBERTA, language educator; b. Washington, D.C., May 8, 1964; d. Paul Norman Tester, Ruth Mae (Thomas) Tester; m. Henry Faine Coleman III, June 2, 1991. Ba in Biology and Chemistry, Gallaudet U., 1989; MA in Deaf Edn., Western Md. Coll., 1991; postgrad. Am. Sign. Lang., We. Md. Coll., 2000. Cert. Am. sign lang. specialist. Tchr. secondary/spl. edn. Ala. Sch. for Deaf, Talladega, 1989—92; tchr. mid. sch./spl. edn. Tenn. Sch. for Deaf, Knoxville, 1992—95; tchr. secondary Ind. Sch. for Deaf, Indpls., 1995—96, Franklin Cmty. H.S., Franklin, Ind., 1996—. Named Tchr. of Yr., WalMart, Franklin, 2002. Mem.: NEA, Nat. Assn. of Deaf, Nat. Am. Sign Lang. Tchr. Assn., Harley Owner Group (life). Avocations: motorcycling, scuba diving, travel, camping. Home: 13650 Brooks School Rd Noblesville IN 46060 Office: Franklin Cmty High Sch 625 Grizzly Cub Dr Franklin IN 46131

COLEMAN, GREGORY G., former magazine publisher; V.p., gen. mgr. Readers Digest, 1995—97; pub. Reader's Digest mag., Pleasantville, N.Y., Readers Digest, U.S. edit., 1991—97; sr. v.p., worldwide pub. Reader's Digest mag., 1997—2001; exec. v.p. North Am. Ops, Yahoo! Inc., 2001—. Office: Yahoo! Inc 701 1st Ave Sunnyvale CA 94089

COLEMAN, HENRY EDWIN, art educator; b. Charlottesville, Va., Oct. 26, 1938; s. Albin Clayton and Mary Louise (Nay) C.; m. Charlotte Heyne, Dec. 29, 1962 (dec. 1984); children: Edwin Randolph, Mary Clayton; m. Leslie W. Rose, Jan. 4, 1993; 1 stepson, John A. Rose. AB in Fine Arts, Coll. William and Mary, 1961; MA, U. Iowa, 1963. Instr. art Lawrence Coll., Appleton, Wis., 1963-64; mem. faculty Coll. William and Mary, Williamsburg, Va., 1964-99, prof. fine arts, 1989—91, chair dept. fine arts, 1987—91. Cons. for purchasing CSX Corp. Art Collection, Richmond, Va., 1985. Illustrator: Oscar Wilde's Remarkable Rocket, 1974; one-man shows include Radford Coll., Va., 1975, Gallery II West, St. George, Utah, 1984, U. Maine, Presque Isle, 1989, Andrew & Laura McLain Mus., Florenceville, N.B., Can., 1989, Muscarelle Mus. of Art, William & Mary Coll., Williamsburg, Va., 1999, exhibited in group shows at Patio Show, Iowa City, 1962, 1963, Des Moines Art Ctr., 1963, Lawrence Coll., Appleton, 1964, 20th Century Gallery, Williamsburg, 1964, 1965, 1966, Chrysler Mus., Norfolk, Va., 1972, So. Ill. U. at Carbondale, 1975, Peninsula Art Ctr., Newport News, Va., 1980, Nat. Small Image Exhbn., Spokane, Wash., 1984, Am. Drawing Biennial Muscarelle Mus. of Art, Coll. William and Mary, Williamsburg, 1988, 1990 (Honorable Mention award), 1992, Internat. Cultural Exch. Art Exhibit, Neyagawa, Japan, 1988, Bowery Gallery, N.Y.C., 1988, Invitational D'Art Ctr., Norfolk, 1991, Peninsula Fine Arts Mus., Newport News, 1995, 1996, 2001. Commr. Williamsburg Arts Commn., 1985-91; bd. dirs. Yorktown (Va.) Arts Found., 1989-93; juror Occasion for the Arts, Williamsburg, 1988, 27th Regional Art Exhbn., W.C. Rawls Libr. & Mus., Courtland, Va., 1990; commr. archtl. rev. bd., City Williamsburg, 1994-2000. Summer Rsch. grantee Coll. William & Mary, 1976, Semester Faculty grantee, 1985, Faculty Rsch. grantee, 1991-92. Office: Coll William and Mary Andrews Hall Williamsburg VA 23185

COLEMAN, HUGH VICTOR, retired surgeon; b. Columbia, S.C., Apr. 30, 1928; MD, Med. Coll. S.C., 1952. Cert. MRO. Intern U. Tex. Med. Br. Hosp., Galveston, 1952-53; resident surgery Columbia VA Hosp., 1953-57; surgeon

Marion (S.C.) Meml. Hosp.; ret. Med. dir. S.C. Recovering Profls. Program, 1998—. Recipient, Order of Palmetto, 2003. Fellow ACS, SSC; mem. AMA. Home: PO Box 1070 Marion SC 29571-1070 Personal E-mail: hipocates@aol.com.

COLEMAN, JACQUELYN LYNZETTA, public service representative; b. Columbus, Miss., Dec. 2, 1966; d. Royal Bailey and Maxine Hall; m. Bennie Ray Coleman, Aug. 3, 1991; children: Brelana Danielle, Benjamin Jalon. BA in Bus. Info. Sys. and Quantatative Analysis, Miss. State U., 1988. Account rep. Omnova Solutions, Columbus, Miss., 1990—2002; pub. svc. rep. Social Security Adminstrn., Columbus, Miss., 2002—; adminstrv. asst. Charity Ch. of Aberdeen (Miss.), 2003—. Author: Back to Basics, 2001, The Father's Daughters, 2002. Sunday Sch. curriculum writer Full Gospel Bapt. Ch. Fellowship, New Orleans, 1998. Baptist. Avocations: reading, play writing. Office Phone: 662-369-0270. E-mail: benblessed@juno.com.

COLEMAN, JAMES H., JR., lawyer, former state supreme court justice; b. Lawrenceville, VA, May 4, 1933; s. James H. Sr. and Neda Coleman; m. Sophia Coleman, May 12, 1962; 2 children. BA cum laude, Va. State U., 1956, LLD (hon.), 1995; JD, Howard U., 1959. Bar: N.J. 1960, U.S. Dist. Ct. N.J. 1960, U.S. Supreme Ct. 1963. Asst. and/or cons. various N.J. commns. and divs., 1960-64; pvt. practice law Elizabeth and Roselle, N.J., 1960-70; judge N.J. Workers' Compensation Ct., 1964-73, Union County Ct., 1973-78, Law div. N.J. Superior Ct., 1978-81; mem. spl. three-judge resentencing panel N.J. Superior Ct., 1979-81; judge Appellate div. N.J. Superior Ct., 1981-87, presiding judge, 1987-94; assoc. justice Supreme Ct. of N.J., Springfield, 1994—2003; atty. Porzio, Bromberg & Newman, Morristown, 2004—. Mem. various Supreme Ct. coms.; lectr. in field. Chmn. Elizabeth Good Neighbor Coun.; mem. Elizabeth Adv. Bd. on Urban Renewal; incorporator, bd. dirs. Union County Legal Svcs., Elizabeth Anti-Poverty Program; v.p., bd. dirs., counsel to Urban League of Union County; counsel to Elizabeth NAACP; v.p. Scotch Plains-Fanwood Human Rights Coun.; Mem. N.J. Com. on Hiring the Handicapped; mem. Union County Coordinating and Adv. Com. on Higher Edn.;mem. Essex County Coll. Equal Edn. Opportunity Fund Bd., others. Fellow ABA; mem. Nat. Bar Assn. (judicial coun.), N.J. Bar Assn., Union County Bar Assn., Am. Law Inst., Am. Judicature Soc., Garden State Bar Assn., Omega Psi Phi. Baptist. Avocations: tennis, gardening. Office: Porzio Bromberg & Newman 100 Southgate Pkwy PO Box 1997 Morristown NJ 07962-1997 Office Phone: 973-889-4088. E-mail: jhcoleman@pbnlaw.com.

COLEMAN, JAMES J., electrical engineer, educator; b. Chgo., Il, May 15, 1950; s. Harry A. and Lorita Marie (Kelly) C.; m. Teresa Ann Stoerger, Mar. 10, 1984; children: Amelia, Harry T., Lucy. BSEE, U. Ill., 1972, MSEE, 1973, PhD, 1975. Fellow U. Ill., Urbana, 1975-76; tech. staff Bell Labs., Murray Hill, N.J., 1976-78, Rockwell Internat., Anaheim, Calif., 1978-82; from assoc. prof. to prof. elec. and computer engring. U. Ill., 1982—, Intel Alumni Endowed Chair Electrical and Computer Engineering, 2003—. Pres. Bd. Edn. Monticello (Ill.) Bd. Edn., 1997—. Fellow IEEE, AAAS, Optical Soc. Am., Am. Phys. Soc. Achievements include patents in field. Office: U Ill Dept Elec & Computer Engring 208 N Wright St Urbana IL 61801-2355

COLEMAN, JAMES JULIAN, lawyer; b. New Orleans, May 5, 1915; s. William Ballin and Millie (Davis) C.; m. Dorothy Louise Jurisich, July 30, 1940; children: James Julian, Thomas Blaise, Peter Dee, Dian Judith. BA, Tulane U., 1934, JD, 1937; LL.D. (hon.), Hampden-Sydney Coll., 1982. Bar: La. 1937. Sr. ptnr. Coleman, Johnson, Artigues & Jurisich, New Orleans. Past pres. Internat. Trade Mart, New Orleans Philharmonic Symphony; hon. consul gen. Republic of Korea; chmn. La. Jud. Compensation Commn. Past pres. New Orleans C. of C., Jr. Achievement New Orleans, Adult Edn. Ctr.; past bd. dirs. U.S. C. of C., Internat. House, Fed. Rels. Assn.; past chmn. New Orleans coordinating com. NASA; founder Peoples League; trustee emeritus Principia Coll.; past chmn. Tulane U. Bus. Sch. Coun.; chmn. bd. trustees Crimestoppers. Decorated Order of Oranje-Nassau Diplomatic Service Merit Republic Korea; recipient Nat. Achievement award Jr. Achievement, Loving Cup award New Orleans Times-Picayune, 1980, Joseph W. Simon, Jr. award, 1981, Disting. Alumnus award Tulane U., 1982, New Orleans Activist award, 1984, C. Alvin Bertel award, 1985; named to Bus. Hall of Fame, 1984; named Pres. Emeritus, World Trade Ctr., N.Y.C., Chmn. Emeritus, The City Energy Club, Humanitarian of Yr. ARC, 2000; recipient Benemerenti Papal Honor, 1989. Mem. ABA, Internat. Bar Assn., La. Bar Assn., New Orleans Bar Assn., Am. Judicature Soc. (past dir.), Beta Gamma Sigma (hon.) Christian Scientist (1st reader 1953-56). Home: 10 Audubon Pl New Orleans LA 70118-5526 Office: 321 Saint Charles Ave New Orleans LA 70130-3145 *Success in Family Enterprises depends on an inbred family loyalty supported by love, compassion and understanding for and between family members and their spouses from generation to generation.*

COLEMAN, JAMES JULIAN, JR., lawyer, industrialist, real estate company executive; b. New Orleans, May 7, 1941; s. James Julian Sr. and Dorothy Louise (Jurisich) C.; m. Carol Campbell Owen, Dec. 19, 1970 (dec. Sept. 1979); 1 child, James Owen; m. Mary Olivia Cochrane Cushing, Oct. 12, 1985. BA, Princeton U., 1963; postgrad. in law, Oxford (Eng.) U., 1963-65; JD, Tulane U., 1968. Bar: La. 1969, U.S. Supreme Ct. 1969. Chmn. Internat.-Matex Tank Terminals, New Orleans, 1969—; pres. Coleman Devel. Co., New Orleans, 1969—, IMTT, Quebec, 1993—, Nfld. Transhipment Terminal Inc.; ptnr. Coleman, Johnson & Artigues, New Orleans, 1972—; chmn. DownTown Parking Service, New Orleans, 1978—; pres. City Ctr. Properties, New Orleans, 1980—. Mng. ptnr. Windsor Court Hotel, New Orleans Hilton Hotel, Exxon Bldg., Chevron Bldg., Freeport Cooper Gold Bldg., Internat. River Ctr.; chmn. East Jersey R.R. and Terminal Co., 1993; trustee Loving Found., New Orleans, R.L. Blaffer Found., Houston; dir., v.p. U.S. Coast Guard Found., pres. Natl. Coast Guard Museum Assn. 2001—. Author: Gilbert Antoine de St. Maxent: The Spanish Frenchman of New Orleans, 1975. Mem. history coun. Princeton U., 1982—; mem. N.J. Commn. on Sci. and Tech., 1992—, chmn. 2003—; bd. dirs. Hampden Sydney Coll., 1982-92, Liberty Sci. Ctr., Liberty State Park, N.J., 1999—; bd. overseers N.J. Inst. Tech., 1999—. Named H.M. Hon. Brit. Consul for La., Brit. Consulate, New Orleans, 1975—, to Order of Brit. Empire, Queen Elizabeth II, London, 1986. Mem. ABA, La. Bar Assn., N.Y. Yacht Club, N.Y. Racquet Club, Newport Reading Room, So. Yacht Club, New Orleans Lawn Tennis Club, USN League (bd. dirs. New Orleans), Union League Club. Office: Coleman Johnson & Artigues 321 St Charles Ave 10th Fl New Orleans LA 70130-3145 Office Phone: 504-586-8300. E-mail: jjcjr@imtt.com.

COLEMAN, JAMES SCOTT, environmental research executive; b. Pitts., Dec. 30, 1960; s. Morton and Greta Bernice Coleman; m. Adele Ruth Johnson, June 25, 1999. BS, U. Maine, 1982; MS, MPhil, PhD, Yale U., 1987. Postdoctoral scholar Stanford (Calif.) U., 1987-88; postdoctoral fellow Harvard U., Cambridge, Mass., 1988-90; prof. biology Syracuse (N.Y.) U., 1990-97; program dir. NSF, Arlington, Va., 1995-96; exec. dir. bio. scis. ctr. Desert Rsch. Inst., Reno, 1997-99; dir. State of Nev. NSF EPSCoR program U. and C.C. Sys. Nev., Reno, 1998—; v.p. rsch. and bus. devel. Desert Rsch. Inst., Reno, 1999—. Mem. bd. dirs. Nev. Tech. Coun., Reno, Nat. EPSCoR Coalition, Washington, Internat. Arid Lands Consortium, Tucson; councilor Oak Ridge (Tenn.) Associated Univs., 2000-01. Mem. editl. bd. Ecology and Ecol. Monographs, 1996-99, Internat. Jour. Plant Sci., 1998—; contbr. numerous articles to profl. jours. Recipient grant NSF, 1992-96, 98—, Young Investigator award NSF, 1993-99, grant Andrew W. Mellon Found., 1993—, grant USEPA, 1999—, grant U.S. Dept. Energy, 2000—. Mem. AAAS, Ecol. Soc. Am. (pres. physiol. ecology sec. 1997-2000), Bot. Soc. Am., Western Indsl. Nev., Nev. Tech. Coun. (chair tech. adv. bd. 2000). Avocations: guitar, hiking, dogs, basketball. Office: Desert Rsch Inst 2215 Raggio Pky Reno NV 89512 Fax: 775-673-7421. E-mail: jcoleman@dri.edu.

COLEMAN, JEFFREY PETERS, lawyer; b. Providence, Nov. 21, 1959; s. Gerard Giles and Molly Claire (Armbrecht) C.; m. Vonnie Lynn Hendrickson, July 11, 1981; children: Chelsea Adelle, Rebecca Rose, Martin Daniel, Angelyn Marie. BA in Psychology, Davidson (N.C.) Coll., 1981; postgrad., Exeter (Eng.) U., 1984; JD, Coll. of William and Mary, 1985. Bar: Fla. 1985, U.S. Dist. Ct. (mid. dist.) Fla. 1986, U.S. Supreme Ct. 2005. Assoc. Harris, Barrett, Mann & Dew, St. Petersburg, Fla., 1985-86; ptnr. Bonner, Hogan & Coleman, P.A., Clearwater, Fla., 1986-97; pres. Coleman Law Firm, 1997—. Author: Spotting Those Bad Apples: Investment Fraud in the New Millenium, 1999. Counsel Pinellas County (Fla.) Habitat for Humanity, 1989, Boy Scouts Am. Pinellas County; advisor Phiomont Expdn., 2002, troop com. chmn., 2005; mem. adv. coun. Pinellas County Schs., 2005; worship leader Heritage United Meth. Ch. Mem. Fla. Bar Assn., Clearwater Bar Assn. (pres. young lawyers divn., coord. pub. rels. com. 1989-90), Publ. Investors Arbitration Bar Assn. (chmn. 1999 Fla. mid-year conf., presenter ann. meeting 2000-2005), Nat. Assn. Securities Dealers (arbitrator 2000), Am. Trial Lawyers Assn. (nat. chmn. securities litigation sect.). Democrat. Avocations: scuba diving, camping, boating, swimming. Office: Coleman Law Firm 581 S Duncan Ave Clearwater FL 33756 Fax: 727-461-7474. E-mail: jeff@colemanlaw.com.

COLEMAN, JOEL CLIFFORD, lawyer; b. Reading, Pa., Nov. 6, 1930; s. Thomas and Lee (Jason) Iscovitz; m. Lois M. Schulman, Feb. 4, 1960; children: Teri, Thomas. BS in Econs., U. Pa., 1952, LLB cum laude, 1955. Bar: N.Y. 1956. Assoc. Kaye, Scholer, Fierman, Hays & Handler, N.Y.C., 1955-67; atty. Twentieth-Century Fox Film Corp., N.Y.C., 1967-69; gen. counsel Internat. Playtex, Inc., N.Y.C. and Stamford, Conn., 1969-86, sec., 1975-86, v.p., 1980-86, also dir.; v.p., gen. counsel, sec. Playtex Inc., 1986-88, Playtex Family Products Corp., 1989-94, Playtex Products, Inc., 1994, assoc. gen. counsel, asst. sec., 1994-95. Editor U. Pa. Law Rev., 1953-55, case editor, 1954-55. Trustee Larchmont (N.Y.) Temple, 1973-75; bd. dirs. Jewish Home for the Elderly of Fairfield County, 1996-2005, Bruce Mus., Greenwich, Conn., 1997-2004, 05—. Mem. Order of Coif. Home and Office: 61 Ridgeview Ave Greenwich CT 06830-4755

COLEMAN, JOHN JAMES, III, lawyer, educator; b. Birmingham, Ala., Apr. 10, 1956; s. John James Jr. and Yonceil Oden (Foster) C.; m. Lizabeth Gaines, Aug. 24, 1985; 1 child, John J. IV. AB in History and Econs. magna cum laude, Duke U., 1978, JD, 1981. Bar: Ala. 1981, U.S. Dist. Ct. (no. and mid. dists.) Ala., U.S. Ct. Appeals (4th and 11th cirs.) 1982, U.S. Supreme Ct. 1987, Ga. 2000, Tex. 2001. Law clerk Judge Donald Russell, U.S. Ct. Appeals 4th cir., Richmond, Va., 1981-82; assoc. Balch & Bingham, Birmingham, 1982-88, ptnr., 1989-2000, Burr & Forman LLP, Birmingham, 2000—. Adj. instr. Cumberland Sch. Law, Birmingham, 1990—, Birmingham Sch. Law, 1994—; v.p. Indsl. Rels. Rsch. Assn., Birmingham, 1990-91; bd. dirs. Indsl. Health Coun. of Ala., Inc., Birmingham, 1991—. Author: Employment Discrimination in Alabama, Supplement to Employment Discrimination in Alabama, 1991, Disability Discrimination in Employment, 2001; co-author: (guide publ.) Workers Compensation Practice, 1994; contbr. articles to profl. jours. Ballot security atty. Rep. Party, Ala., 1988, 92, 94; co-chmn. Kidschance Scholarship, Birmingham, 1992. Mem. ABA (labor and employment law sect. OSHA com.), Am. Arbitration Assn. (mem. panel arbitrators), Ala. State Bar (exec. com. labor and employment sect. treas. 1995-96, vice chmn. 1996-97, chmn. 1997-98), Shades Mountain Sunrise Rotary Club (treas. 1994-96), Redstone Club. Republican. Roman Catholic. Avocations: tennis, bicycling, riding, writing. Home: 10 Peachtree St Birmingham AL 35213-3018 Office: Burr & Forman LLP 3100 SouthTrust Tower 420 N 20th St Birmingham AL 35203 Fax: (205) 458-5100. E-mail: jcoleman@burr.com.

COLEMAN, JOHN JOSEPH, III, surgery educator; b. Boston, Nov. 15, 1947; Grad., Harvard U., 1969, MD, 1973. Intern Emory U. Affiliated Hosp., Atlanta, 1973-74, resident in gen. surgery, 1974-78, resident in plastic surgery, 1978-80; fellow in surg. oncology U. Md., Balt., 1980; prof. surgery Ind. U., Indpls., 1980—86; chief plastic surgery Ind. U. Med. Ctr., Indpls., 1980—86, James E. Bennett prof. of plastic surgery & Wadley R. Glenn chair in surgery, 1986—91, prof. of surgery & chmn. plastic surgery, 1991—. Mem.: Am. Head and Neck Soc., Am. Bd. of Plastic Surgery (chmn. 2002—03). Office: U Plastic Surg Assocs 235 Emerson Hall 565 Barnhill Dr Indianapolis IN 46202-5112

COLEMAN, JOHN MICHAEL, lawyer, consumer products company executive; b. Boston, Dec. 28, 1949; s. John Royston Coleman and Mary Norrington Irwin; m. Susan Lee Lavine, Oct. 29, 1978; children: William L., Anne H. L. BA, Haverford (Pa.) Coll., 1975; JD, U. Chgo., 1978. Bar: N.Y. 1978, Pa. 1979, U.S. Ct. Appeals (3rd and 4th cirs.) 1979, U.S. Dist. Ct. (ea. dist.) Pa. 1979, U.S. Dist. Ct. (so. dist.) N.Y. 1981, U.S. Supreme Ct., 1982, N.J. 1988. Law clk. to judge U.S. Ct. Appeals, Richmond, Va., 1978-79; law clk. to chief justice Warren Burger U.S. Supreme Ct., Washington, 1980-81; assoc. Dechert Price & Rhoads, Phila., 1981-86, ptnr., 1986-89; v.p., gen. counsel Campbell Soup Co., Camden, N.J., 1989-90, sr. v.p. law and pub. affairs, 1990-97; sr. v.p., gen. counsel The Gillette Co., Boston, 1997-99; mng. dir., CEO, Cambridge (Mass.) Capital Ptnrs. LLP, 1999-2000, chmn., CEO, 2000—. Adj. prof. law U. Pa., Phila., 1985-88; bd. dirs. CDI Corp. Contbr. articles to profl. jours. Chmn. bd. trustees Campbell Soup Found., 1990-97; trustee N.J. State Aquarium, 1991-94, Food and Drug Law Inst., 1991-98, Inst. for Law and Econs., 1993-97, Am. Judicature Soc., 1995—; mem. vis. com. U. Chgo. Law Sch., 1993-95; mem. corp. Haverford Coll., 1994—; bd. dirs. The Guidance Ctr., treas., 2000—. Mem. Am. Law Inst., Order of the Coif, Phi Beta Kappa. Mem. Religious Soc. of Friends.

COLEMAN, JOHN ROYSTON, writer; b. Copper Cliff, Ont., Can., June 24, 1921; came to U.S., 1946, naturalized, 1954; s. Richard Mowbray and Mary Irene (Lawson) C.; m. Mary N. Irwin, Oct. 1, 1943 (div. 1966); children: John M., Nancy J., Patty A., Stephen W. BA, U. Toronto, 1943; MA, U. Chgo., 1949, PhD, 1950; LLD (hon.), Beaver Coll., 1963, U. Pa., 1968, Gannon Coll., 1975; L.H.D. (hon.), Manhattanville Coll., 1975, Emory and Henry Coll., 1977, Green Mountain Coll., 1984; DLitt (hon.), Haverford Coll., 1980, Elizabethtown Coll., 1987; D.Litt. (hon.), Marlboro Coll., 1991; DSL (hon.), U. Toronto Victoria Coll., 1994. Rsch. assoc. U. Chgo., 1947-49; instr. econs. Mass. Inst. Tech., 1949-51, asst. prof., 1951-55; asso. prof., asst. head dept. econs. Carnegie Inst. Tech., 1955-60, prof., head dept. econs., 1960-63, dean div. humanities and social sci., 1963-65; assoc. dir. econ. devel. and adminstrn. Ford Found., 1965-66, program officer in charge social devel., 1966-67; pres. Haverford Coll., Pa., 1967-77, Edna McConnell Clark Found., N.Y.C., 1977-86; chmn. Coleman Assocs. Inc., 1985-97; pres. Home Town Press, Inc., 1995-2001. Chmn. bd. dirs. Fed. Res. Bank Phila., 1973-76; labor arbitrator, cons., 1953-85; cons. indsl. rels. rsch. Ford Found. in India, 1960-61; tchr. Am. Economy CBS-TV, 1962-63 Author: Goals and Strategy in Collective Bargaining, 1951, Readings in Economics, 1952, 55, 58, 64, 67, Labor Problems, 1953, 59, Working Harmony, 1955, The Changing American Economy, 1967, Comparative Economic Systems, 1968, Blue Collar Journal, 1974, The Ballad of Clarence Adams, 1992, Pieces from the Quilt, 1993, The Play of the Three Kings, 1995, Takeoff at the North Pole, 2002; contbr. numerous articles to mags. Justice of peace, chmn. bd. civil authority Town of Chester, Vt., 1991—; prodr., dir. Chester Players Guild, 1991—; dir. Green Mountain Union H.S. Bd., 1998—; v.p. So. Windsor United Way, 1997-2003; chmn. Reparative Parole Bd., Springfield, Vt., 1997—. Lt. Royal Can. Navy, Vol. Res., 1943-46. Mem. Religious Soc. of Friends. Home: PO Box 995 Chester VT 05143-0995

COLEMAN, JOHN WILLIAM, urologist; b. Jersey City, Jan. 26, 1939; s. John William and Marion Cecille (McAuliffe) Coleman; m. Rosemary Elizabeth Romano, July 13, 1963 (div. 1984). AB, Georgetown U., 1960, MD, 1964. Diplomate Am. Bd. Urology. Intern, resident in surgery N.Y. Hosp., 1964-66, resident in urology, chief resident in urology, 1968-72, asst. attending surgeon urology, 1972-75, assoc. attending urologist Cornell Med. Ctr., 1975—. Assoc. prof. urology Cornell Med. Coll., 1975—; cons. Rockefeller U. Hosp., N.Y.C., 1985—, Vets. Gen. Hosp., Taipei, Taiwan, 1987; bd. dirs. Am. Bur. Med. Advancement China. Bd. dirs. Kidney and Urology Found. Am., sec. urology coun., 2003—04; bd. dirs. Nat. Kidney Found. Greater NY. Chief med. officer USN, 1966—68, Vietnam. Recipient John K. Lattimer award, 1997, N.Y., N.J. sect. Nat. Kidney Found. award, 1997. Fellow: ACS, Am. Acad. Pediat.; mem.: Soc. Urologie Internat., Soc. Pediat. Urology, Chinese Am. Med. Soc., Asian Surg. Soc. Roman Catholic. Avocations: golf, study of Southeast Asia. Office: 407 E 70th St #2 New York NY 10021-5302 Office Phone: 212-535-4545.

COLEMAN, JOSEPH MICHAEL, truck lease and logistics consultant; b. Washington, Mar. 6, 1945; s. Francis Thomas and Helen (Hile) C.; m. Dorothy Burke, Feb. 14, 1976; children: Caroline Dalton, Joseph Michael Jr., Elizabeth O'Keefe. BSBA, Georgetown U., 1971. Asst. to pres. Leaseway Transp. Corp., Cleve., 1971-73; pres. Leaseway Transp. Mktg. Corp., N.Y.C., 1973-77; v.p. Colorlab Corp., Rockville, Md., 1977-78; area dir. Hertz Corp., N.Y.C., 1978-82; nat. account exec. Hertz Penske Truck Leasing, Reading, Pa., 1982-86; v.p. Indsl. Fleet Mgmt., Towson, Md., 1986-88; pres. Friedman, Fuller & Coleman, Inc., Rockville, Md., 1988—, Joseph M. Coleman & Assocs. Ltd., Bethesda, Md., 1992—. Mem. Am. Truck Hist. Soc., Washington Hist. Soc., Md. Motor Truck Assn., Soc. of Friendly Sons of St. Patrick, Gentleman Afield Sporting Club, Traffic Club (Balt.), Kenwood Country Club, Assn. of the Oldest Inhabitants of Washington. Republican. Roman Catholic. Office: Coleman & Assocs 7625 Wisconsin Ave Bethesda MD 20814 E-mail: jmc45@georgetown.edu.

COLEMAN, JULES L., law educator; b. 1947; BA, Brooklyn Coll., 1968; PhD, CUNY, 1972; MSL, Rockefeller U., 1976. Asst. prof. U. Calif., Santa Barbara, 1972-73; assoc. prof. of philosophy U. Wis., 1976-81; vis. prof. jurisprudence and social policy U. Calif., Berkeley, 1977-78; prof. philosophy U. Ariz., 1981-84, prof. of philosophy and law, 1984-86; vis. prof. Yale U., New Haven, 1985-86, prof. of law and political sci., 1986—, Garver prof., 1992—98, Wesley Newcomb Hohfeld Professor of Jurisprudence and prof philosophy, 1998—. Clarendon lectr. Oxford U., 1998, Austin lectr., 1998—99. Guggenheim Fellow, 1988—89. Mem.: Econ. Scis. Assn., Am. Philosophy Assn. Office: Yale Law Sch PO Box 208215 New Haven CT 06520 E-mail: jules.coleman@yale.edu.*

COLEMAN, KATHRYN ANNE, lawyer; b. July 19, 1959; BA magna cum laude, Pomona Coll., 1980; JD, Univ. Calif., Berkeley, 1983. Bar: Calif. 1983. Law clk. Judge Martin Pence US Dist. Ct. Dist of Hawaii, 1983—84; joined Gibson Dunn & Crutcher LLP, San Francisco, 1986—, now ptnr. bus. restructuring and reorganization practice group, and ptnr.-in-charge Palo Alto office. Assoc. editor Calif. Law Rev., 1981—82, sr. articles editor, 1982—83. Mem.: Calif. State Bar Assn. (past mem. Uniform Comml. Code Com.), Phi Beta Kappa, Order of Coif. Office: Gibson Dunn & Crutcher LLP Ste 3100 One Montgomery St San Francisco CA 94104 Office Phone: 415-393-8265. Office Fax: 415-374-8417. Business E-Mail: kcoleman@gibsondunn.com.

COLEMAN, LORING W., artist; b. Boston, 1918; Grad., Middlesex School, Scott Carbee School of Art, Boston. Prof., painting, sculpture Middlesex School; represented Francesca Anderson Find Art, Lexington, Mass. Exhibitions include Retrospective, Concord Art Assoc., Francesca Anderson Fine Art, St. Botolph Club, Central Place Galleries, Shore Galleries, exhibited in group shows, Am. Watercolor Soc., Knickerbocker Artists, High Art Museum, Munson Gallery, Milton College, Museum of Fine Arts, Addison Gallery of Am. Art, Represented in permanent collections, Salmagundi Club, Museum of Fine Arts, Butler Institute of Am. Art, Parrisch Art Museum, Canton Art Institute, Fitchburg Art Museum, Concord Public Library. Named National Academician, 1994; recipient Strathmore Paper Co Award, Elizabeth K. Ellis Artists Fellowship Award, Salmagundi Club, Lifetime Achievement Award, New England Watercolor Soc. Office: c/o Francesca Anderson Fine Art 56 Adams Street Lexington MA 02420*

COLEMAN, LYNN R., lawyer; BA, Abilene Christian Coll., 1961; LLB with honors, U. Tex., 1964. Bar: Tex. 1964, DC 1973. Ptnr. Vinson & Elkins, Houston; law clerk to the Hon. John R. Brown US Ct. of Appeals, Fifth Cir., 1964—65; gen. counsel, dep. sec. US Dept. Energy, 1978—81; dir. Tricentrol, Ltd., London, 1981—86; ptnr., practice leader legislative/lobbying, energy matters and legislation Skadden, Arps, Slate, Meagher & Flom, LLP, Washington. Mem. Adminstrv. Conf. US, 1979—81; chair President's Task Force on Coal Exports, 1980—81; mem., govt. rels. adv. coun. Mobil Corp., 1997—98; spkr. at energy conferences and seminars. Editor: Tex. Law Review, 1963—64. Order of the Coif; Chancellor. Mem.: Tex. Law Assn. (pres.), ABA (spl. com. on energy law 1980—85). Office: Skadden Arps Slate Meagher & Flom LLP 1440 New York Ave NW Washington DC 20005 Office Phone: 202-371-7600. Office Fax: 202-661-8211. Business E-Mail: lcoleman@skadden.com.

COLEMAN, MARSHALL DONALD, psychiatrist, psychoanalyst; b. Utica, N.Y., Dec. 27, 1925; s. Jacob and Lucille (Smith) C.; m. Beverly Sitrin, June 28, 1949; children: Charles Theodore, Jacqueline Sue. BA, Harvard Coll., 1947; MD, Harvard Med. Sch., 1952. Diplomate Am. Bd. Psychiatry and Neurology. Intern Mass. Meml. Hosps., Boston, 1952-53; resident Boston Psychopathic Hosp., Boston, 1953-56; tchg. fellow Med. Sch. Harvard U., Boston, 1953-56; instr. Albert Einstein Sch. Medicine, Bronx, N.Y., 1956-57, asst. prof., 1957-63, asst. clin. prof., 1963—; sr. vis. staff Jacobi Hosp., Bronx, N.Y., 1962—; pvt. practice Mamaroneck, N.Y., 1968—. Dir. walk-in psychiat. clinic Albert Einstein Sch. Medicine, 1956; pres. N.Y. State Psychoanalytic Coordinating Com., 1988-2005. Author: Winston S. Churchill: Overcoming Childhood Adversities Help Form the Heroic Character of the Statesman, 1994; contbg. editor: Generations of Holocaust, 1982; editor articles on psychiat. walk-in clinics, brief psychotherapy and agoraphobia. Co-chairperson mental health profls. N.Y. area United Jewish Appeal, 1990-2003, chmn. emeritus, 2003—. With U.S. Army, 1944-46, ETO. Recipient M. Jucovy Lifetime Achievement award, 2000. Fellow Am. Psychiat. Assn. (life); mem. N.Y. Psychoanalytic Soc., Internat. Psychoanalytic Soc., Westchester Psychoanalytic Soc. (pres. 1978-79), Internat. Psychoanalytic Soc. Office: 1030 Greacen Point Rd Mamaroneck NY 10543-4609

COLEMAN, MARTHA ANN, literature educator, social studies educator; b. Danville, Ill., Nov. 21, 1949; d. William Robert and Ruth Prince Coleman; m. Miceal Aidan Cinnsela Tobi, July 23, 1975 (dec. July 28, 1976). BS in Edn., Miami U., Oxford, Ohio, 1970. Lic. tchr. Vt. Standards Bd. Dir. gender fair project Am. Friends Svc. Ctr, Dayton, Ohio, 1978—80; ind. cons. Wilmington, Ohio, 1980—82; cons. equity and desegregation Vt. Dept. Edn., Montpelier, Vt., 1982—83, evaluation specialist, 1984—86, chief R&D, 1987—91; tchr. Green Mountain Tech. & Career Ctr., Hyde Park, Vt., 1991—, curriculum coord., 1991—. Sec. Vt. Vocat. Assn., Montpelier, Vt., 1996—2000; adult tng. com. mem. Girl Scouts of Am., Burlington, Vt.; curriculum & evaluation cons. Cin. Pub. Schools, Cincinnati, Ohio, 1979—82, Jefferson County Pub. Schools, Louisville, 1980—82; conf. coord. Nat. Coalition for Sex Equity in Edn. Editor: Women & Education. Vol. Nat. Women's Polit. Caucus, Cin., 1980; mem. com. Religious Soc.Friends, Bloomington, Ind., 1976—78. Mem.: ASCD (assoc.), Nat. Croquet Assn. Am. (assoc.), Girls Scouts Am. (life), Croquet Club of Vt. (assoc.), Sigma Sigma Sigma (life). Republican. Soc. Friends. Avocations: sailing, croquet, lacemaking, travel. Home: 190 Northwood Dr D7 Plainfield VT 05667 Office: Green Mountain Technology & Career Ctr PO Box 600 Route 15 West Hyde Park VT 05655 Office Phone: 802-888-4447 255. Office Fax: 802-888-7838. Personal E-mail: moirec@aol.com. E-mail: moirec@gmtcc.k12.vt.us.

COLEMAN, MARY H., state legislator; b. Noxapater, Miss., July 25, 1946; m. Cayle Coleman, children Marcus, Crystal, Arqullas. Student, L.A. Trade-Tech. Coll., Tougaloo Coll. Mem. Miss. Ho. of Reps., 1987—; mem. edn., ins., pub. bldgs., pub. health coms.; mem. ways and means com. Exec. asst. to State Auditor, 1987-92; pres. Nat. Black Caucus of St. Legislators. Mem. NAACP, NOW, SCLC, Women in Govt., Alpha Kappa Alpha (Beta Delta Omega chpt.). Democrat. Baptist. Home: 308 Lynwood Ln Jackson MS 39206-3931 Office: State Capitol Bldg PO Box 1018 Jackson MS 39215-1018

COLEMAN, MARY SUE, academic administrator; b. Richmond, Ky, Oct. 2, 1943; m. Kenneth Coleman; 1 child, Jonathan. BA, Grinnell Coll., 1965; PhD, U. N.C., 1969; DSc (hon.), Dartmouth Coll., 2005. NIH postdoctoral fellow U. N.C., Chapel Hill, 1969—70, U. Ky., 1971—72, instr., rsch. assoc. depts. biochemistry and medicine, 1972—75, asst. prof. dept. biochemistry, 1975—80, assoc. prof. dept. biochemistry, 1980—85, prof. dept. biochemistry, 1985—90; prof. dept. biochemistry and biophysics U. N.C., Chapel Hill, 1990—93; provost, v.p. for academic affairs, prof. biochemistry U. N.Mex.,

1993—95; pres., prof. biochemistry, prof. biol. scis. U. Iowa, Iowa City, 1995—2002; pres. U. Mich., 2002—. Pres. Iowa Health Sys., 1995—2002; vice chancellor grad students and rsch. U. N.C., 1992—93, assoc. provost, dean rsch., 1990—92; trustee U. Ky., 1987—90, assoc. dir. rsch. L.P. Markey Cancer Ctr., 1983—90, dir. grad. studies biochem., 1984—87; acting dir. basir rsch. U. Ky. Cancer Ctr., 1980—83; NSF summer trainee Grinnell Coll., 1962; scientific cons. Abbott Labs., 1981—85, Collaborative Rsch., 1983—88, Life Techs., Inc., 1992; bd. trustees Univs. Rsch. Assn., 1998—; mem. rsch. accountabolity task force Am. Assn. Univs., 2000—, chair undergrad. edn. com., 1997—, mem. exec. com., 2001—; mem. task force on tchrs. edn. Am. Coun. Edn., 1998—; bd. dirs. Meredith Corp., Am. Coun. Edn.; mem. Big Ten Coun. Pres.'s, 1995—2002; mem. stds. success adv. bd. Am. Assn. Univs. and he Pew Charitable Trusts, 2000—; co-chair Inst. Medicine Com. on Consequences of Uninsurance, 2000—; mem. Gov.'s Strategic Planning Coun., 1998—2000, Imagining Am. Pres.'s Coun., 1999—, Bus.-Higher Edn. Froum, 1999—, Knight Commn., 2000—01; presenter in field; mem. bd. dirs. Johnson & Johnson, 2003—. Mem. editl. bd.: Jour. Biol. Chemistry, 1989—93; contbr. articles to profl. jours. Trustee Crinnell Coll., 1996—; mem. bd. govs. Warren G. Magnuson Clin. Ctr., NIH, 1996—2000, State of Iowa Gov.'s ACCESS Edn. Commn., 1997; bd. dirs. United Way, Albuquerque, 1995. Fellow postdoctiral fellow, Clayton Found. Biochem. Inst., U. Tex., 1970—71. Fellow: AAAS, Am. Acad. Arts and Scis.; mem.: Nat. Coll. Athletic Assn. (bd. dirs. 2002—), Nat. Assn. State Univs. ans Land Grant Colls. Coun. Cchief Acad. Officers (exec. com. 1993—95), Am. Soc. Biochem. and Molecular Biology, Am. Assn. Cancer Rsch.*

COLEMAN, MICHAEL B., mayor; s. John and Joan Coleman. Student, U. Cin.; JD, U. Dayton, 1980. Pvt. practice; mem. City Coun. Columbus, Ohio, 1992—99; mayor Columbus, Ohio, 2000—. Pres. Columbus (Ohio) City Coun., 1997—99. Office: Mayors Office 90 W Broad St Rm 247 2nd Fl Columbus OH 43215-9014 Office Phone: 614-645-7671. Office Fax: 614-645-5818. Business E-Mail: mac@columbus.gov.*

COLEMAN, MICHAEL DORTCH, nephrologist; b. Jackson, Tenn., June 19, 1944; s. Ivery R. and Kathleen (Campell) C; children: Michael Dortch, Christopher Matthew, Cassandra Sherean. BA in Chemistry, U. Ark., 1966; MD, Duke U., 1970. Diplomate Am. Bd. Internat. Medicine. Intern Duke U. Med. Sch., Durham, N.C., 1970-71, resident internal medicine, 1971-72; practice medicine specializing in nephrology Durham, 1972-74, Kannapolis, N.C., 1973-74, Dr. Smith, Ark., 1974—. Nephrology cons. Cabarras County Hosp., Kannapolis, 1973; chief dept. nephrology Holt Krock Clinic, Ft. Smith, 1974-99, Cooper Clinic, 1999—; dir. dialysis Holt Krock Dialysis Ctr., 1974-99; dir. dialysis Sparks Regional Med. Ctr., Ft. Smith, 2000—, chief medicine, 1994-96; dir. dialysis St. Edward's Mercy Med. Ctr., Ft. Smith, 1980—, Ft. Smith Regional Dialysis Ctr.; assoc. prof. medicine U. Ark., Ft. Smith, 1976—; mem. med. rev. bd. Ark. Kidney Disease Commn., 1974—; mem. exec. com. and med. rev. bd. Ark.-Okla. Endstage Renal Disease Coun., 1977—. Contbr. articles to profl. jours. Bd. dirs. Ark Tennis Assn., Jr. Tennis Coun., Holt Krock Clinic, Ft. Smith; bd. dirs., mem. fin. com. Holt Krock Clinic, Cooper Clinic, 1999—. Nephrology fellow Duke U. Med. Sch., 1972-74. Mem. AMA, Ark. Med. Assn., Sebastian County Med. Assn., Intenat. Soc. Nephrology, Renal Physician Assn., Am. Soc. Nephrology, Am. Heart Assn., St. Smith Racquet Club (bd. dirs., pres.), Town Club Ft. Smith, Hardscrabble Country Club, Alpha Ometa Alpha. Office: 1500 Dodson Ave Fort Smith AR 72901-5128

COLEMAN, MICHAEL MURRAY, polymer science educator; b. Herne Bay, Eng., Jan. 24, 1938; s. Ronald and Winifred L. (Legg) C.; m. Mary Jane Ogorek, June 25, 1977; 1 child, David Spencer. BSc in Polymer Sci., Borough Poly., London, 1968; MS in Macromolecular Sci., Case Western Res. U., 1971, PhD in Macromolecular Sci., 1973. Analytical chemist Rhokana Corp. Ltd., Nkana, Zambia, 1955-61, Johnson-Mathey Ltd., Wembley, Eng., 1963-64; rsch. chemist Revertex Ltd., Harlow, Eng., 1968-69, E.I. du Pont de Nemours & Co., Wilmington, Del., 1973-75; asst. prof. polymer sci. Pa. State U., 1975-78, program chmn. polymer sci., 1976-84, assoc. prof., 1978-82, prof., 1982—2002, head, dept. materials sci. and engring., 1983-91, prof. emeritus, 2002—. Author: (with others) The Theory of Vibrational Spectroscopy and its Application to Polymeric Materials, 1982, Specific Interactions and the Miscibility of Polymer Blends, 1991, Fundamentals of Polymer Science, 1994, 2d edit., 1997; contbr. over 200 tech. articles to profl. jours. Fellow Am. Phys. Soc. (high polymer physics divsn.); mem. Am. Chem. Soc. (polymer and polymeric materials sci. and engring. divsns.), Soc. Plastics Engrs. Office: Pa State Univ 330 Steidle Bldg University Park PA 16802-5007 Fax: (814) 865-2917. Office Phone: 814-865-3117. E-mail: MMC4@psu.edu.

COLEMAN, M.L. (MICHAEL LEE), artist; b. Livingston, Mont., May 11, 1941; s. Lee Lambert and Alma Phylis (Samson) Coleman; m. Sheri Donita Short, Dec. 31, 1981; m. Linda Kay Savage (div.); children: Diane Marie Ehlert, Kimberly Ann. BS, U. Wyo., Laramie, 1963. CPA Colo. Staff acct. Arthur Andersen, Denver, 1965—69; mgr. Arthur Anderson, 1969—73; self-employed artist Big Fork, Mont., 1973—81, Sedona, Ariz., 1982—. Exhibitions include Cattleman's Found. Art Show and Auction, Calgary, Can., 1981 (Best of Show). Bd. dir. Sedona Arts Festival, Ariz., 1998—2001, Marilyn Sunderman Found., Sedona, Ariz., 2002—04. Capt. U.S. Army, 1963—65. Avocation: travel. Home and Studio: Sunset Pass Studios 650 Sunset Pass Rd Sedona AZ 86351-9515 Office Phone: 928-284-5803.

COLEMAN, MORTON, oncologist, educator, hematologist; b. Norfolk, Va., Sept. 15, 1939; s. Isadore and Bessie (Levin) C.; m. Joyce Goodman, May 26, 1968; children: Ingrid Alexandra, Benjamin Lee, Abigail Rachael. AA, Coll. William and Mary, 1958; BA, Johns Hopkins U., 1959; MD, Med. Coll. Va., 1963. Diplomate Nat. Bd. Med. Examiners, Am. Bd. Internal Medicine, Am. Bd. Hematology, Am. Bd. Clin. Oncology. Intern Grady Meml. Hosp.-Emory U. Med. Ctr., Atlanta, 1963-64, resident, 1964-65, N.Y. Hosp.-Cornell U. Med. Ctr., N.Y.C., 1967-68; NIH fellow in hematology Cornell U. Med. Coll., 1968-70, asst. prof. medicine, 1970-74, assoc. prof., 1974-86, clin. prof., 1986—; asst. attending N.Y. Hosp., N.Y.C., 1970-74, assoc. attending, 1974-86, attending, 1986—99, assoc. dir. oncology svc., 1974-86; assoc. program dir. Nat. Cancer Inst. Clin. Chemotherapy Program Cancer Control, 1974-80; attending N.Y. Presbyterian Hosp., 1999—. Dir. Ctr. for Lymphoma and Myeloma, divsn. hematology-oncology, 1997—; attending staff Manhattan Eye and Ear Hosp., 1972—82, Doctors Hosp., 1973—90, Beth Israel NorthMed. Ctr., 1990—94, New Rochelle Med. Ctr., 1980—91; chmn. new agts. com. Cancer and Leukemia Group B, 1975—82; chmn. bd. dirs. Fund for Blood and Cancer Rsch., 1975—; sci. advisor United Leukemia Fund, 1976—82; program chmn. N.Y. Cancer Soc., 1993—94, sec., 1994—95, treas., 1995—96, v.p., 1996—97, pres.-elect, 1997—98, pres., 1998—99, coun. of advisors, 2002—, 2002—; bd. dirs. Cure for Lymphoma Found., 1997—2001, chmn. med. affiliates bd., 2000—01; chmn. lymphoma/Hodgkins' diseases symposium com. Internat. Union Against Cancer Congress, 1993—94; co-chmn. clin. rsch. rev. com. Israel Cancer Rsch. Fund, 1988—93; chmn. bd. dirs. Affiliated Physicians Network, Inc., 1996—2001; Internat. Adv. Cancer Care Trust and Rsch. Found., India, 1995—; mem. sci. adv. com. Lymphoma Rsch. Found., 1998—, bd. dirs., 2001—, chmn. med. affiliates bd., 2001—; bd. dirs. Immunomedics, Inc., 1999—, BML Pharms., 2000—02. Assoc. editor: Cancer Investigation, 1987—; mem. editl. adv. bd. Hem/Onc Today, 1999—, internat. adv. bd. Indian Jour. Med. and Pediatric Oncology, 1994—; contbr. articles to rsch. publications on blood and cancer. V.p. alumni coun. Cornell U. Med. Ctr., 1992-94, pres., 1994-96. Lt. comdr. USN, 1965-67. Recipient Disting. Alumni award, Old Dominion U., 1994, Together award, Cure for Lymphoma Found., 2000, 2001. Fellow: ACP; mem.: AMA, AAAS, N.Y. County Med. Soc., N.Y. State Med. Soc., Soc. Study of Blood, N.Y. State Soc. Med. Oncology and Hematology (mem. exec. com. 1991—99), N.Y. Acad. Sci., Internat. Soc. Hematology, Harvey Soc., Cornell U. Med. Ctr. Alumni Assn., Am. Soc. Hematology, Am. Soc. Clin. Oncology (mem. clin. practice com. 1997—2001, mem. pub. com. 2001—04, chmn. policy and procedures subcom. 2002—04, mem. program com. 2001—03, chmn. hematol. malignancy subcom. 2002—03), Am. Radium Soc., Am. Fedn. Clin. Rsch., Am. Assn. Cancer Rsch., Explorers Club, Sigma Zeta, Alpha Omega Alpha. Office: 407 E 70th St 3rd fl New York NY 10021-5302 also: NY Presbyn Hosp-Weill Cornell U Med Ctr Div Hematology-Oncology 525 E 68th St New York NY 10021-4870 Office Phone: 212-517-5900. Personal E-mail: mortoncolemanmd@aol.com.

COLEMAN, NORMAN, JR., senator, former mayor; b. Bklyn., Aug. 17, 1949; m. Laurie Casserly; children: Jacob, Sarah. BA in Political Sci., Hofstra U., 1971; JD, U. Iowa, 1976. Bar: Minn. Criminal prosecutor, civil litig. supr., chief lobbyist Minn. Atty. Gen.'s Office, 1976—86, asst. atty. gen., chief prosecutor & solicitor. gen., 1986—92; mayor City of St. Paul, 1994—2002; US senator from Minn., 2003—; mem. fgn. rels. com. US Senate. Active in creation of Minn. Drug Abuse Resistance Edn. program, also The Partnership for a Drug Free Minn.; adj. prof., William Mitchell Coll. Law, 1983-92. Humphrey fellow U. Minn.; award for Pub. Svc Woodrow Wilson Internat. Ctr. for Scholars, award of Excellence in Pub.-Pvt. Partnerships US Conf. Mayors, 2001, Mondale award Japan-Am. Soc. of Minn., 2001, Urban Innovator award Ctr. for Civic Innovation, The Manhattan Inst., 2001. Republican. Office: 320 Hart Senate Office Building Washington DC 20510*

COLEMAN, PAUL DAVID, neurobiology educator, researcher; b. N.Y.C., Dec. 2, 1927; s. A. Barnett and Martha L. (Michaels) C.; m. Zinia J. Cereska, Mar. 13, 1955 (div. Sept. 1978); children: Laura A., Paul David; m. 2d Dorothy G. Flood, Feb. 26, 1983. AB, Tufts U., 1948; PhD, U. Rochester, 1953. Asst. prof., research assoc. Tufts U., Medford, Mass., 1956-59; assoc. Computer Ctr. MIT, Cambridge, 1957-59; spl. fellow Johns Hopkins Sch. Medicine, Balt., 1959-62; assoc. prof. Sch. Medicine U. Md., Balt., 1962-67; prof. neurobiology and anatomy Sch. Medicine, U. Rochester, N.Y., 1967—. Editor in chief Neurobiology of Aging, 1988—; contbr. articles to profl. jours. 1st lt. U.S. Army, 1953—56. Recipient award for leadership and excellence in Alzheimer's disease Nat. Inst. Aging, NIH, 1990, Pioneer award Alzheimers Assn., 2000; Rsch. grantee NSF, 1958-67, NIH, 1963—; NIH spl. fellow Johns Hopkins U. Sch. Medicine, 1959-62. Mem. Soc. for Neurosci., Am. Assn. Anatomists, AAAS, Gerontol. Soc., Am. Psychol. Assn., Sigma Xi. Clubs: Yacht (Rochester, N.Y.) (bd. dirs. 1971-72). Home: 7 Durham Way Pittsford NY 14534

COLEMAN, PAUL JEROME, JR., physicist, researcher; b. Evanston, Ill., Mar. 7, 1932; s. Paul Jerome and Eunice Cecile (Weissenberg) C.; m. Doris Ann Fields, Oct. 3, 1964; children: Derrick, Craig. BS in Engring. Math., BS in Engring. Physics, U. Mich., 1954, MS in Physics, 1958; PhD in Space Physics, UCLA, 1966. Rsch. scientist Ramo-Wooldridge Corp. (name now Northrop Grummson), El Segundo, Calif., 1958-61; instr. math. U. So. Calif., L.A., 1958-61; mgr. interplanetary scis. program NASA, Washington, 1961-62; rsch. scientist UCLA, 1962-66, prof. geophysics, space physics, 1966—; asst. lab. dir., mgr. Earth and Space Scis. divsn., chmn. Inst. Geophysics and Planetary Physics Nat. Lab., Los Alamos, N.Mex., 1981-86; dir. Inst. Geophysics and Planetary Physics UCLA, 1989-92; dir. Nat. Inst. for Global Environ. Change, 1994-96; pres. Univs. Space Rsch. Assn., Columbia, Md., 1981-2000, Girvan Inst. Tech., 2002—. Bd. dirs. Axcess Inc., Dallas, Knowledge Vector, Inc., Durham, N.C., others; mem. adv. bd. San Diego Supercomputer Ctr., 1986-90, chmn., 1987-88, others; trustee Univs. Space Rsch. Assn., Columbia, Md., 1981-2000, Am. Tech. Alliances, 1990-2002, Internat. Small Satellite Orgn., 1992-96; vis. scholar U. Paris, 1975-76; vis. scientist Lab. for Aeronomy Ctr. Nat. Rsch. Sci., Verrieres le Buisson, France, 1975-76; com. mem. numerous sci. and ednl. orgns., cons. numerous fin. and indsl. cos. Co-editor: Solar Wind, 1972; co-author: Pioneering the Space Frontier, 1986; mem. editorial bd. Geophysics and Astrophysics Monographs, 1970—; assoc. editor Cosmic Electrodynamics, 1968-72; contbr. revs. to numerous profl. jours. Apptd. to Nat. Commn. on Space, Pres. of U.S., 1985, apptd. to Space Policy Adv. Bd., Nat. Space Coun., v.p. of U.S., 1991; bd. dirs. St. Matthew's Sch., Pacific Palisades, Calif., 1979-82, v.p., 1981-82. 1st lt. USAF, 1954-56, Korea. Recipient Exceptional Sci. Achievement Medal NASA, 1970, 1972, spl. recognition for contributions to the Apollo Program, 1979; Guggenheim fellow 1975-76, Fulbright scholar, 1975-76, Rsch. grantee NASA, NSF, Office Naval Research, Calif. Space Inst., Air Force Office Sci. Research, U.S. Geol. Survey. Mem. Internat. Acad. Astronautics, Bel Air Bay Club (L.A.), Birnam Wood Golf Club (Monteceito, Calif.), Cosmos Club (Washington), Valley Club (Montecito, Calif.), Eldorado Country Club (Indian Wells, Calif.), Tau Beta Pi, Phi Eta Sigma. Avocations: flying, skiing, racquetball, tennis, golf. Home: 1323 Monaco Dr Pacific Palisades CA 90272-4007 Office: UCLA Inst Geophysics & Planetary Physics 405 Hilgard Ave Los Angeles CA 90095-9000 Office Phone: 310-825-1776.

COLEMAN, PHYLLIS, law educator; b. Bronx; d. Harvey and Amy Davis Gallub. BS in Journalism, U. Fla., 1970, MEd, 1975, JD, 1978. Bar: Fla. 1978, Fla. Supreme Ct. 1978. Reporter, news editor Gwinnett Daily News, Lawrenceville, Ga., 1972—73; assoc. Broad & Cassel, Bay Harbor, Fla., 1978—79; from asst. to full prof. law Nova Southeastern U., Fort Lauderdale, Fla., 1979—. Editor: Family Law: Text and Commentary (annual), 1997—; co-author: (casebook) Sports Law: Cases and Materials, 1999, Bush v. Gore: The Fight for Florida's Vote, 2001; contbr. articles to profl. jours., chapters to books. Mem. Broward County Managed Care Ombudsman Com., Fort Lauderdale, 2002; selection com. Hall of Fame Ind. Fla. Alligator, Gainesville, Fla., 2003—05; founding mem. animal law com. Fla. Bar, 2003—05. Named Outstanding Faculty Mem., Black Law Students, Nova Southeastern U., 1994, Prof. of Yr., Student Bar Assn., Nova Southeastern U., 2004—05; named to Hall of Fame, U. Fla., 1971, Alligator Hall of Fame, Ind. Fla. Alligator, 1999. Liberal. Jewish. Avocation: scuba diving. Office: Nova Southeastern U 3305 College Ave Fort Lauderdale FL 33314-7721 Office Phone: 954-262-6166. Office Fax: 954-262-3835. E-mail: colemanp@nsu.law.nova.edu.

COLEMAN, REXFORD LEE, lawyer, educator; b. Hollywood, Calif., June 2, 1930; s. Henry Eugene and Antoinette Christine (Dobry) C.; m. Aiko Takahashi, Aug. 28, 1953 (dec.); children: Christine Eugenie, Douglass Craig; m. Sucha Park, June 15, 1978. Student, Claremont McKenna Coll., 1947-49; AB, Stanford U., 1951, JD, 1955; M. in Jurisprudence, Tokyo U., 1960. Bar: Calif. 1955, Mass. 1969. Mem. faculty Harvard U., 1959-69; mem. firm Baker & McKenzie, 1969-83, income ptnr., 1971-73, capital ptnr., 1973-83, mng. ptnr. Tokyo office, 1971-78; sr. ptnr. The Pacific Law Group, L.A., 1983—. Adj. prof. McGeorge Sch. Law, U. Pacific, 1989—; lectr. Gray's Inn, The Inns of Ct. Sch. Law, London, 1989; cons. U.S. Treasury Dept., 1961-70; counselor Japanese-Am. Soc. for Legal Studies, 1964—; guest lectr. Ford Seminar on Comparative History, MIT, 1968; lectr. Legal Tng. and Research Inst., Supreme Ct., Japan, 1970-73; guest lectr. Colloguium Scholars, Calif. Luth. U., 1989; chmn. fgn. bus. customs consultative com. Bur. Customs, Ministry of Fin., Govt. of Japan, 1971-72; chmn. fgn. bus. consulatative commn. Japanese Ministry of Internat. Trade and Industry, 1973-76; mem. U.S. Del., U.S.-Japan Income Tax Treaty Negotiations, 1961, internat. bd. advisors, McGeorge Sch. Law, U. Pacific, 1989—. Author: Am. Index to Japanese Law, 1961, Standard Citation of Japanese Legal Materials, 1963, The Legal Aspects Under Japanese Law of an Accident Involving a Nuclear Installation in Japan, 1963, An Index to Japanese Law, 1975; editor: Taxation in Japan, World Tax Series, 1959-70; founding chmn. bd. editors: Law in Japan: An Ann., 1964-67; mem. bd. editors Stanford Law Rev., 1954-55, Japan Ann. Internat. Law, 1970-92; mem. Internat. Adv. Bd., The Transnational Lawyer, 1988—; contbr. articles to profl. jours. Participant in Japanese-Am. Program for Cooperation in Legal Studies, 1956-60; co-chmn. Conf. on Internat. Legal Protection Computer Software, Stanford Law Sch., 1986, Tokyo, Japan, 1987. Served to 1st lt., Inf. AUS, 1951-53; lt. col. Ret. Ford Found. grantee, 1956-60. Mem. ABA, State Bar Calif., Mass. Bar Assn., Japanese-Am. Soc. for Legal Studies, Internat. Fiscal Assn. Japan, Res. Officers Assn. (v.p. army dept. Far East 1974-75), Ret. Officers Assn., Internat. House Japan (Tokyo), Stanford U. Alumni Assn., Gakushi Kai (grads. of former Japanese Imperial Univs. Assn.), Internat. Law Assn. Japan, Japan-Western Assn., Pacific Basin Econ. Council, (U.S. exec. com. 1985-87), Nihon Shiho Gakkai, Nihon Kokusai Ho Gakkai, Nihon Kokusai Shiho Gakkai, Sozei Ho Gakkai, Phi Alpha Delta Episcopalian (vestryman 1966-69, del. Conv. Episcopal Diocese Mass. 1968, Conv. Episcopal Diocese L.A., 1989-91, Bishop's com. 1983-87, 91-93). Clubs: Tokyo Am; Harvard (N.Y.C.), North Ranch Country. Home: 32314 Blue Rock Rdg Westlake Village CA 91361-3912 Office: The Pacific Law Group 12121 Wilshire Blvd Ste 205 Los Angeles CA 90025-1164

COLEMAN, RICHARD WILLIAM, retired lawyer; b. Brookline, Mass., Dec. 9, 1935; s. Michael John and Mary Ellen (Motherway) C.; m. Mary M. Kilcommins, June 3, 1961; children: Lauren, Christopher. BS, Boston Coll., Newton, Mass., 1957; JD, Boston Coll., Brighton, Mass., 1960. Bar: Mass. 1960, U.S. Dist. Ct. Mass. 1961, U.S. Ct. Appeals (1st cir.) 1981. Field atty. NLRB, Newark, 1960-61; assoc. Segal & Flamm, Boston, 1961-69; labor rels. advisor Scott Paper Co., Phila., 1969-70; labor rels. mgr. Harvard U., Cambridge, Mass., 1970-72; ptnr. Segal, Roitman & Coleman, Boston, 1972-93; pres. Richard W. Coleman, P.C., Needham, 1994—2002; ret. Contbg. editor Development of Law Under National Labor Relations Act, 1988. Bd. dirs. Little Bros. of St. Francis, 1998-2001. Recipient Cushing award Cath. Labor Guild Boston, 1976. Mem. ABA, Am. Prepaid Legal Svcs. Inst. (bd. dirs. 1997—), Indsl. Rels. Rsch. Assn., Mass. Bar Assn., Boston Bar Assn., AFL-CIO Lawyers Coord. Com. Democrat. Roman Catholic. Avocations: golf, reading, choir singing. E-mail: rcolegolf@aol.com.

COLEMAN, ROBERT D., music critic, educator; b. Logan, Utah, Jan. 11, 1953; s. Denton H. and Beverly H. Coleman; m. Janie L. Peterson, Sept. 30, 1976; 1 child, Amy L. BA, Utah State U., 1977. Band tchr. South Ogden (Utah) Jr. H.S., 1977—; free-lance music critic. V.p. for jr. high/mid. schs. Utah Music Edn. Assn., 2004—. Recipient Rookie of Yr. award, Utah Music Edn. Assn., 1978. Home: 5084 S 150 E Ogden UT 84405 Office: South Ogden Jr HS 4300 Madison Ave Ogden UT 84403 Office Phone: 801-452-4460. E-mail: rcoleman@weber.k12.ut.us.

COLEMAN, ROBERT GRIFFIN, geology educator; b. Twin Falls, Idaho, Jan. 5, 1923; s. Lloyd Wilbur and Frances (Brown) C.; m. Cathryn J. Hirschberger, Aug. 7, 1948; children: Robert Griffin Jr., Derrick Job, Mark Dana. BS, Oreg. State U., 1948, MS, 1950; PhD, Stanford U., 1957. Mineralogist AEC, N.Y.C., 1952-54; geologist U.S. Geol. Survey, Washington, 1954-57, Menlo Park, Calif., 1958-80; prof. geology Stanford U., Calif., 1981-93, prof. emeritus, 1993—. Vis. petrographer New Zealand Geol. Survey, 1962-63; br. chief isotope geology U.S. Geol. Survey, Menlo Park, 1964-68, regional geologist, Saudi Arabia, 1970-71, br. chief field geochemistry and petrology, Menlo Park, 1977-79; vis. scholar Woods Hole Oceanographic Inst., Mass., 1975; vis. prof. geology Sultan Qaboos U., Oman, 1987, 89; cons. geologist, 1993—; instr. geobotany field sch. Siskiyou Inst., Oreg., 1998-99. Author: Ophiolites, 1977, Geologic Evolution of the Red Sea, 1993, Ultrahigh Pressure Metamorphism, 1995; contbr. articles to profl. jours. Named Outstanding Scientist, Oreg. Acad. Sci., 1977; Fairchild scholar Calif. Inst. Tech., Pasadena, 1980; recipient Meritorious award U.S. Dept. Interior, 1981 Fellow AAAS, Geol. Soc. Am. (coun.), Am. Mineral Soc. (coun., editor), Am. Geophys. Union; mem. Nat. Acad. Scis., Russian Acad. Sci. (fgn. assoc.). Republican. Avocations: wood carving, art. Home: 2025 Camino Al Lago Atherton CA 94027-5938 Business E-Mail: coleman@pangea.stanford.edu.

COLEMAN, ROBERT J., lawyer; b. Phila., Dec. 24, 1936; s. Francis Eugene and Mary Veronica (McCullough) C.; m. Mary Patricia Coleman, June 26, 1955; children: Debra, Robert P., Linda, Martin S. AB, Villanova U., 1959; JD, Temple U., 1964. Bar: Pa., U.S. Dist. Ct. (ea. dist.) Pa., 1964, U.S. Ct. Appeals (3d cir.), U.S. Supreme Ct., 1973. With First Pa. Bank, Phila., 1955-57; underwriter Employer's Mut. Co., Phila., 1957-59; claim adjuster Safeco Ins. Co., Phila., 1959-62; claim supr. Gen. Accident Ins., Phila., 1962-64; assoc. Rappaport & Lagakos, Phila., 1964; trial atty. Allstate Ins. Co., Phila., 1964-67; chmn., CEO Marshall, Dennehey, Warner, Coleman & Goggin, Phila., 1967—. Chmn. hearing com. Pa. Disciplinary Bd., Phila., 1986-94; mem. Pa. Bd. Law Examiners, 1997-2003; bd. dirs. Republic First Bancorp, 2003. Assoc. editor Phila. County Reporter, 1984-96; contbr. articles to legal publs. Bd. dirs. Ins. Soc. Phila., HERO Scholarship Fund Delaware County; bd. vis. Temple U. Law Sch. With USAR, 1954-62. Mem. ABA, Pa. Bar Assn., Phila. Bar Assn., Phila. Bar Found. (trustee), Pa. Def. Inst., Internat. Assn. Def. Lawyers, Def. Rsch. Inst. Republican. Roman Catholic. Avocations: tennis, boating, travel. Home: 908 Penn Valley Rd Media PA 19063-1652 Office: Marshall Dennehey Warner Coleman & Goggin 1845 Walnut St Philadelphia PA 19103-4797 Office Phone: 215-575-2600. Business E-Mail: rcoleman@mdwcg.com.

COLEMAN, ROBERT J., literature and language educator; b. Trenton, N.J. s. Robert F. and Elsie M. Coleman; m. Christine Coleman, Feb. 29, 1984; 1 child, Robert S. stepchildren: Brigette Beers, David Beers. BA, Haverford Coll., Pa., 1980, Trenton State U., N.J., 1983. English tchr. Elizabeth H.S., NJ, 1984—85, Marlboro H.S., NJ, 1985—2003; chmn., English dept. Piscataway H.S., NJ, 2003—. Mem.: Nat. Coun. Tchrs. English, Assn. for Supr. & Curriculum Devel. Home: 945 Central Ave Plainfield NJ 07060 Office: Piscataway HS 100 Behmer Rd Piscataway NJ 08854

COLEMAN, ROBERT LEE, retired lawyer; b. Kansas City, Kans., June 14, 1929; s. William Houston and Edna Fay (Smith) C. B of Music Edn., Drake U., 1951; LLB, U. Mo., 1959. Bar: Mo. 1959, Fla. 1973. Law clk. to judge U.S. Dist. Ct. (we. dist.) Mo., Kansas City, 1959-60; assoc. Watson, Ess, Marshall & Enggas, Kansas City, 1960-66; asst. gen. counsel Gas Svc. Co., Kansas City, 1966-74; v.p., corp. counsel H & R Block, Inc., Kansas City, 1974-94; retired, 1994. With U.S. Army, 1955-57. Mem.: ABA.

COLEMAN, ROBERT WINSTON, lawyer; b. Oklahoma City, Mar. 1, 1942; s. Clint Sheridan and Genevieve (Ross) C.; m. Judith Moore, Sept. 7, 1963; children: Robert Winston, Jr., Claire Elizabeth. BA, Abilene Christian Coll., 1964; JD with hons., U. Tex., 1968. Bar: Tex. 1968, Ga. 1970. Law clk. to presiding justice U.S. Ct. Appeals (5th cir.), Montgomery, Ala., 1968-69; assoc. Kilpatrick, Cody, Rogers, McClatchey & Regenstein, Atlanta, 1969-75; ptnr. Meyers, Miller, Middleton, Weiner & Warren and predecessor, Dallas, 1975-80, Jones, Day, Reavis & Pogue, Dallas, 1981-85; dir. Baker, Glast and Middleton, P.C., Dallas, 1985-92; ptnr. Vial, Hamilton, Koch & Knox, LLP, Dallas, 1992-2000, Brown McCarroll LLP, Dallas, 2000—. Mem. exec. com. Dallas County Dem. Com., 1980-87. Mem. ABA, Dallas Bar Found., Dallas Bar Assn., Tex. Bar Assn., Ga. Bar Assn., Am. Judicature Soc. Office: Brown McCarroll LLP 2000 Trammell Crow Ctr 2001 Ross Ave Dallas TX 75201 Office Phone: 214-999-6100. E-mail: RColeman@mailbmc.com.

COLEMAN, RODERICK FLYNN, lawyer; b. Washington, Pa., Sept. 20, 1958; s. Harry Sullivan and Marlyn Hope (McAninch) C.; m. Gale Faith Zeisel, July 28, 1984; children:, Tara, Lindsey. BA, Oglethorpe U., 1980; JD, Stetson U., 1983. Bar: Fla. 1983, U.S. Dist. Ct. (so. dist.) Fla. 1984, U.S. Ct. Appeals (11th cir.) 1984, U.S. Dist. Ct. (mid. dist.) Fla. 1988. Assoc. Law Offices of Richard Ralph, Miami, Fla., 1983-85, Schwartz and Assocs., Miami, 1986-87; ptnr. Marlow, Connell, Valerius, Abrams, Lowe & Adler, Miami, 1988-96, Stettin & Coleman, P.A., Miami, 1996-97, Coleman & Assocs., P.A., Coral Gables, Fla., 1997—. Mem. ABA, Fla. Bar, Dade County Bar Assn., Fla. Trial Lawyers Assn., Am. Judicature Soc., Riviera Country Club, Kiwanis. Republican. Avocations: golf, sailing. Home: 1470 Mendavia Ave Coral Gables FL 33146-1608 Office: 122 Minorca Ave Coral Gables FL 33134-4510 E-mail: lawcoleman@mobile.att.net.

COLEMAN, RODNEY ALBERT, political scientist, consultant; b. Newburgh, N.Y., Oct. 12, 1938; s. Samuel and Rebecca (Belden) Coleman; children: Terri Lynn, Stephen Anthony. BArch, Howard U., 1963; grad. exec. devel. program, U. Mich., 1988. Commd. 2nd lt. USAF, 1963, advanced through grades to capt., separated, 1973; White House fellow Washington, 1970-71; exec. asst. to chmn. D.C. City Coun., Washington, 1973-78; archtl. design cons. Pennsylvania Ave. Devel. Corp., Washington, 1978-80; dir. govt. rels. Gen. Motors, Detroit, 1980-85, dir. mcpl. govt. affairs, 1985-90, exec. dir. urban and mcpl. affairs, 1990-94; asst. sec. of Air Force for manpower, Res. affairs, installations, and environ. Dept. of Air Force, Washington,

1994-98; exec. v.p. ICF Kaiser Internat., Fairfax, Va., 1998-99; ptnr. Alcalde & Fay, Arlington, Va., 1999—. Chmn. bd. adv. Mus. Aviation of Ga., 1998—; trustee Air Force Aid Soc., 1998—; bd. dirs. Washington Hosp. Ctr., 2002—. Decorated Bronze Star medal, Air Force Commendation medal Republic of Vietnam, Honor medal First Class, Air Force Meritorious Svc. medal; recipient Disting. Alumni award for postgrad. achievement in corp. and govt. svc. Howard U., 1996, Disting. Alumnus award Newburgh Free Acad., 1994, Black Engr. of Yr. dean's award, 1996, Lt. Gen. Benjamin O. Davis Jr. Disting. Achievement award of The Tuskegee Airmen, 1996, decoration for exceptional civilian svc. Dept. of Air Force, 1997, Eagle award Nat. Guard Bur., 1998. Mem. White House Fellows Assn., Exec. Leadership Coun, Air Force Assn., Tuskegee Airmen. Methodist. Avocation: golf. Home: 1200 Crystal Dr Arlington VA 22202-4320 Office Phone: 703-841-0626. Personal E-mail: honrc@aol.com. Business E-Mail: coleman@alcalde-fay.com.

COLEMAN, RONALD D., lawyer; b. Queens, N.Y., Mar. 11, 1963; s. Gerald and Teresa (Buznicki) C.; m. Jane Golberg, Dec. 26, 1989; children: Mordecai, Israel Asher, Moses, Abraham. AB, Princeton U., 1985; JD, Northwestern U., Chgo., 1988. Bar: N.J. 1989, N.Y. 1989, U.S. Dist. Ct. N.J. 1989, U.S. Dist. Ct. (so. dist.) N.Y. 1990, U.S. Dist. Ct. (ea. dist.) N.Y. 1990, U.S. Ct. Appeals (3d cir.) 1993. Assoc. Kaye, Scholer, Fierman, Hays & Handler, N.Y.C., 1990-92, Lowenstein, Sandler, Kohl, Fisher & Boylan, Roseland, N.J., 1992-94, Pitney, Hardin, Kipp & Szuch, Morristown, N.J., 1996-2000; gen. counsel Solomnet, Inc., Clifton, 2000; mem. Gibney, Anthony & Flaherty, N.Y.C., 2000—03; of counsel Coleman Law Firm P.C., 2004—; gen. counsel Media Bloggers Assn., 2005—. Adv. trustee Princeton Broadcasting Corp. PC, 1994—; lectr. Aish Hatorah Coll. Jewish Studies, N.Y.C., 1995-97; adj. prof. law Seton Hall U., Newark, 1995. Author: The Princeton Review Pre-Law Companion, 1996, ABA Guide to Consumer Law, 1997; editor: Latino Literacy, 1997; contbr.: West's Business and Commercial Litigation in the Federal Courts, 1998, ABA Family Legal Guide, 1994, ABA Legal Guide for Small Business, 2000; pub. weblog www.likelihoodofconfusion; contbr. articles to profl. jours. Mem. Jewish Commn. on Law and Pub. Affairs, 1988-91. Kollel fellow Yeshiva Rabbi Chaim Berlin Rabbinical Acad., Bklyn., 1990. Mem. Federalist Soc. Law and Pub. Policy Studies (vice chmn. E.J. Wiegand Practice Group, vice chmn. publs. 1996-2004), N.J. State Bar Assn., N.Y. State Bar Assn., Assn. Bar City of N.Y. (mem. trademark and unfair competiton com. 2002—), Computer Law Assn., Agudath Israel Am., Internat. Trademark Assn. (mem. online use subcom. internet com.). Avocations: talmud study, public speaking. Office: Coleman Law Firm PC 410 Park Ave 15th Fl New York NY 10022 Office Phone: 212-752-9500. Business E-Mail: rcoleman@coleman-firm.com.

COLEMAN, RONALD LEE, insurance claims executive; b. Danville, Va., June 10, 1941; s. Raymond Lee and Mildred Sue (Floyd) C.; m. Stephanie Walther Barton Ewalt; children: Ronald Lee, Christopher Brent. BSBA summa cum laude, Va. Poly. Inst. and State U., 1964; BS in Pub. Adminstrn. summa cum laude, U. Richmond, 1964, postgrad., 1971; postgrad. law sch., U. Va., 1980. Pres. Johnson & Coleman, Ltd., Richmond, 1974-79, Ron Coleman & Assocs., Ltd., Richmond, 1981—; v.p. Schnell, Johnson & Coleman, Ltd., Richmond, Va., 1979-81. Adj. prof. U. Tex., Austin, Pa. State U., State College; adv. coun. Pamplin Bus. Sch., Va. Tech. Author: Investigation and Handling of Aviation Claims, 1981, Presentation of Evidence in Accident Reconstruction Cases, 1989, others; editor-in-chief Claimsman mag., 1971-76; contbr. articles to profl. jours. Mem. U.S. Senatorial Bus. Adv. Bd., 1988; mem. adv. coun. Paplin Coll. Bus., Va. Tech.; mem. Rep. Presdl. Task Force, 1988; mem. Va. Rep. Com., Chesterfield County, 1984; mem. The Pres.'s Coun., 1990, Pres. Club Rep. Party; bd. dirs. Va. Tech. Found., Va. Tech. Athletic Fund., Va. Tech. Athletic Bd.(exec. com.). Mem. ABA (exec. bd.; exec. com., torts and ins. practice sect.), Richmond Claims Assn. (pres. 1971-72, Man of Yr. award 1971), Va. Claims Assn. (Bob Anderson Humanitarian award), Def. Law Inst., Atlanta Claims Assn., Profl. Claims Assn. Richmond, Truck Ins. Def. Assn., 1872 Soc. at Va. Poly. Inst. and State U., Assn. Lloyds Mems. (London), Pilon Soc. at Va. Poly. Inst. and State U., Ut Prosim Soc. at Va. Poly. Inst. and State U., Va. Tech. Found., 1789 Soc. at Hampden-Sydney Coll., Soc. of Founders Hampden-Sydney Coll., Va. Hist. Soc., Rotunda Soc. U. Va., Reform Club (London), St. James Club (London), Salisbury Country Club, Hurlingham Club (London), Sloane Club (London), Quinnipiack Club (New Haven), Yale Club N.Y.C., Pilon Soc., Va. Tech. Methodist. Avocations: jazz, golf.

COLEMAN, SHANNON DESHAE, lawyer, educator; b. Middlesboro, Ky., Apr. 21, 1975; d. James Emory and Judy Carol Coleman. BA in English, Lincoln Meml.U., 1996; JD, U. Tenn., 1999. Bar: Tenn. 1999, US Dist. Ct. (ea. dist. Tenn.) 2000, US Tax Ct. 1999. Assoc. Gentry, Tipton & McLemore, PC, Knoxville, 1999—2005, Holifield & Assocs., P.C., Knoxville, 2005—. Adj. prof. law U. Tenn., 2003—; lectr. in field. Mem. Rotary Club Knoxville, 2002—. Mem.: ABA, Knoxville Bar Assn., Tenn. Bar Assn., Am. Health Lawyers Assn. Avocations: skiing, running, reading, travel. Home: 6656 Bay Circle Dr Knoxville TN 37918 Office: Holifield & Assocs PC 8351 E Walker Springs Ln Ste 303 Knoxville TN 37923 Office Phone: 865-566-0115. Office Fax: 865-566-0119. Business E-Mail: scoleman@hapc-law.com.

COLEMAN, STEVEN ANDREW, surveyor; b. Columbus, Ga., Aug. 29, 1958; s. Jim, Jr. and Jackie Coleman; m. Deborah Louise Jones, June 10, 1979; children: Stefanie Lynn, Jessica Ann, James Andrew. Cert., Mid. Ga. Coll., 1990. Registered land surveyor Ga. State Bd. Registration for Profl. Engrs., 1996, broker Ga. Real Estate Bd., 1994. V.p. Mercer Land Surveying, Inc., Forsyth, Ga., 1985—95; dir. of constrn. Ocmulgee Fields, Inc., Macon, Ga., 1996—97; pres., owner Steve Coleman & Assoc., Inc., Forsyth, 1997—. Mem. Mary Persons H.S. Coun., Forsyth, 2001—03; bd. dir. Monroe County Recreation Bd., Forsyth, 1995—97. Recipient Torch award for Marketplace Ethics, BBB of Mid. Ga., 2002. Mem.: Nat. Soc. Profl. Surveyors, Am. Congress on Surveying and Mapping, Surveying and Mapping Soc. Ga., Forsyth-Monroe County C. of C. (bd. dirs. 1996—2001, Golden Nail award 2000), Jaycees (bd. dirs. 1982—83), Mary Persons Touchdown Club (v.p. 2000—01, pres. 2002—03), Forsyth Golf Club (bd. dirs. 1999—2002), Rotary (bd. dirs. Forsyth-Monroe county chpt. 1996—97, charter mem.). Avocations: my family, my community, outdoor sports. Office: Steve Coleman & Assoc Inc 38 EJohnston St PO Box 892 Forsyth GA 31029-0892 Office Phone: 478-992-9900. Business E-Mail: steve@steve-coleman.com.

COLEMAN, STUART H., lawyer; b. NYC, Nov. 24, 1954; BA magna cum laude, Wesleyan Univ., 1976; JD cum laude, NYU, 1979. Bar: NY 1980. Co-mng. ptnr., mem. operating exec. com. Stroock & Stroock & Lavan LLP, NYC. Mem.: ABA (Task Force on Fund Director's Guidebook, Task Force on Independent Dir. Counsel), Assn. Bar City NY (chmn., investment mgmt. com.), Order of Coif. Office: Stroock & Stroock & Lavan LLP 180 Maiden Ln New York NY 10038-4982 Office Phone: 212-806-6049. Office Fax: 212-806-9049. Business E-Mail: scoleman@stroock.com.

COLEMAN, TERRY LEWIS, state legislator; b. Dodge County, Ga., Dec. 5, 1943; m. Carol Cofield Coleman; 2 children. AA, Reinhardt Coll.; BS, Brenau Coll., 1981; JD, Woodrow Wilson Coll. Law, 1981. Rep. 144th dist. Ga. Ho. of Reps., 1973—, spkr., 2003—04. Chmn. pub. safety com. Ga. Ho. Reps., 1978—86, chmn. natural resources com., 1987—88, chmn. ways and means com., 1989—90, chmn. appropriations com., mem. budget conf. com., chmn. joint com. budget responsibility oversight com., 1991—2002; pres. Coleman & Co. Benefits; bd. dirs. Bank Dodge County, Colony Bank Corp. Mem. Eastman Vol. Fire Dept.; pres. C. of C., 1985—87; bd. govs. Mercer Med. Sch., 1990—2002. With Ga. N.G. Mem.: Million Dollar round Table, Pacific Mutual Nat. Leaders Club. Democrat. Home: PO Box 157 Eastman GA 31023-0157 Office: Rm 436 18 Capitol Sq Atlanta GA 30334 Office Phone: 478-374-5594. Business E-Mail: tcoleman@legis.state.ga.us.

COLEMAN, THOMAS YOUNG, lawyer; b. Richmond, Va., Jan. 6, 1949; s. Emmet Macadium and Mary Katherine (Gay) C.; m. Janet Clare Norris, Aug. 30, 1980; children: Dana Alicia (dec.), Amanda Gay, Blair Norris. BA, U. Va., 1971, JD, 1975. Bar: Va. 1975, U.S. Dist. Ct. (we. dist.) Va. 1975, U.S. Ct. Appeals (4th cir.) 1976, Calif. 1977, U.S. Dist Ct. (no. dist.) Calif. 1977. Law clk. to Hon. James C. Turk, chief judge U.S. Dist. Ct. (we. dist.) Va., Charlottesville, 1975-76; assoc. Morrison & Foerster LLP, San Francisco, 1976-79; v.p., counsel Calif. 1st Bank (now Union Bank of Calif.), San Francisco, 1979-85; of counsel Orrick, Herrington & Sutcliffe LLP, San Francisco, 1985-86, chmn. profl. devel. com., ptnr., 1987—, gen. counsel, ptnr. in charge profl. devel. Speaker in field; vis. atty. Clifford-Turner Solicitors (now Clifford Chance), London, 1984. Mem. bus. gifts com. San Francisco Symphony. Mem. Internat. Bankers Assn. in Calif. (co-counsel). Office: Orrick Herrington & Sutcliffe LLP 405 Howard St San Francisco CA 94111-2669 Office Phone: 415-773-5870. Office Fax: 415-773-5759. Business E-Mail: tycoleman@orrick.com.

COLEMAN, WADE HAMPTON, III, management consultant, mechanical engineer, retired banker; b. Tuscaloosa, Ala., June 24, 1932; s. Wade Hampton, Jr. and Margaret Pauline (James) C.; m. Kate Shannon Stabler, June 2, 1958 (div. 1966); children— Shannon Hunter, Wade Hampton IV; m. Eileen Marie Lincoln, Dec. 23, 1967; 1 child, Lydie Elizabeth BA, U. N.C., 1954; BS and BSM.E., U. Ala., 1960; MSI.E., Lehigh U., 1965. Registered profl. engr., Pa. Rsch. engr. Western Electric Co., Princeton, N.J., 1960-65; tech. staff mem. MITRE Corp., Arlington, Va., 1965-66; mgmt. cons. Booz, Allen & Hamilton, Washington, 1967-70; prin. Auerback Corp., Phila., 1970-72; spl. asst. to sec. HEW, Washington, 1972-73; sr. v.p. Citibank, NA, N.Y.C., 1973-85; chmn., chief exec. officer Asbestos Claims Facility Inc, Princeton, N.J., 1985-87; pres. ELW Devel. Group, Lawrenceville, N.J., 1987-89, Coleman & Evans Inc., Princeton, 1989—. Mem. Civic Assn., Lawrenceville, N.J., 1973—, bd. dirs. Lower Eastside Services Ctr., N.Y.C., 1978—, pres. 1986-90; bd. dirs. Capstone Found., Tuscaloosa, 1980— . Served with USN, 1954-57, lt. comdr. res. ret. Mem. Nat. Soc. Profl. Engrs., Am. Bankers Assn., Sigma Pi Sigma, Tau Beta Pi, Delta Kappa Epsilon Republican. Episcopalian. Home: 4 Monroe Ave Lawrenceville NJ 08648-1606

COLEMAN, WILBUR JOHN, economics professor; b. Wahiawa, Hawaii, Feb. 20, 1959; s. James Andrew and Anna Magaretha Coleman; m. Maria Glock, June 12, 1982; children: Blake Ann, Corey Barbara. PhD, U. Chgo., 1987. Economist Bd. Govs. of the FRS, Washington, 1987—92; prof. econs. Duke U., Durham, NC, 1992—. Office: Fuqua Sch Bus Duke Univ Durham NC 27708

COLEMAN, WILLIAM THADDEUS, JR., lawyer, former secretary of transportation; b. Germantown, Pa., July 7, 1920; s. William Thaddeus and Laura Beatrice (Mason) Coleman; m. Lovida Hardin, Feb. 10, 1945; children: William Thaddeus III, Lovida Hardin Jr., Hardin L. AB summa cum laude, U. Pa., 1941; LLB magna cum laude, Harvard U., 1943. Bar: Pa. 1947, DC 1977. Law sec. Judge Herbert F. Goodrich, U.S. Ct. of Appeals, 3d Cir., 1947—48, Justice Felix Frankfurter (assoc. justice Supreme Ct. U.S.), 1948—49; assoc. Paul, Weiss, Rifkind, Wharton & Garrison, N.Y.C., 1949—52, Dilworth, Paxson, Kalish, Levy & Green, Phila., 1952—56; ptnr. Dilworth, Paxson, Kalish, Levy & Coleman, 1956—75; sec. US Dept. Transp., Washington, 1975—77; sr. counselor, sr. ptnr. O'Melveny & Myers, Hong Kong, Shanghai, Beijing, China, Brussels, Belgium, Great Britain, 1977—. Spl. counsel for transit matters City of Phila., 1952—63; rep. atty. gen. Pa. and Commonwealth of Pa. in litig. to remove racial restrictions at Girard Coll., 1965; mem. Pres.'s Com. on Govt. Employment Policy, 1959—61; cons. ACDA, 1963—74; sr. cons., asst. counsel Pres.'s Commn. on Assassination of Pres. Kennedy, 1964; co-chmn. planning sessions White House Conf. to Fulfill These Rights, 1965—66; mem. U.S. del. 24th Session UN Gen. Assembly, 1969; mem. legal adv. com. Coun. on Environ. Quality, 1970; pub. mem. Pres.'s Nat. Commn. on Productivity, 1970; commr. Price Commn., 1971—72, Phila. Fairmount Pk. Commn., 1967—75, White House Commn. Aviations Safety and Security, 1996—97; mem. Gov.'s Commn. on Constl. Revision, 1963—65; mem. mil. tribunal, appellate, maj. at Guantanamo Bay, Cuba, 2004—. Contbr. articles to profl. jours. Former chmn. bd. NAACP Legal Def. and Ednl. Fund; v.p., trustee, mem. exec. com. Phila. Art Mus.; trustee Brookings Instn., Nat. Gallery Art, 1999; mem. Trilateral Commn.; mem. exec. com. Lawyers Com. for Civil Rights Under Law; bd. overseers Harvard U., 1975—81; bd. dirs., adv. dir. NY City Ballet. Decorated officer French Legion of Honor; recipient Joseph E. Beale prize, 1946, Presdl. Freedom medal, Pres. Clinton, 1995, NAACP Legal Def. Fund Thurgood Marshall Lifetime Achievement award, 1997, Marshall Wythe medallion, 2003, Chief Justice John Marshall award, ABA, Lifetime Achievement award, The Am. Lawyer, 2004; Langdell fellow, 1946—47. Fellow: Am. Coll. Trial Lawyers; mem.: Coun. Fgn. Rels., Am. Arbitration Assn. (gov.), Am. Acad. Arts and Scis., Am. Philos. Soc., Phila. Bar Assn. (past chmn. jud. com.), Am. Law Inst. (coun., Henry J. Friendly medal 2000), Am. Acad. Appellate Lawyers, Met. Club (Washington), Jr. Legal Club (Phila.), Alfalfa Club, Cosmos Club, Order of Coif, Harvard Law Sch. Club, Pi Gamma Nu (Wickersham award 1997, The Fordham-Stein prize 2000), Phi Beta Kappa. Office: O'Melveny & Myers 1625 I St NW Washington DC 20006-4001 Office Phone: 202-383-5325. Office Fax: 202-383-5325.

COLEMAN, WINIFRED ELLEN, academic administrator; b. Syracuse, NY, Oct. 3, 1932; d. Peter Andrew and Josephine (Fahey) C. BA, Le Moyne Coll., Syracuse, N.Y., 1954; MA, Marquette U., 1956; DHL (hon.), Le Moyne Coll., 1993. Dean of students Cazenovia (N.Y.) Coll., 1957-70, Trinity Coll., Washington, 1970-80; exec. dir. Nat. Coun. Catholic Women, Washington, 1980-85; pres. Cashel House, Ltd., Syracuse, NY, 1985—, St. Joseph Coll., West Hartford, Conn., 1991—. Trustee LeMoyne Coll., Syracuse, 1995—, The Mark Twain House, Hartford; trustee emerita Loretto Geriatric Ctr., Syracuse, N.Y.; pres. Assn. Mercy Coll. Presidents, 1993-97, Hartford Consortium for Higher Edn., 1993-97; bd. dirs. Conn. Higher Edn. Student Loan Adminstrn., Hartford Mutual Funds. Bd. dirs. St. Francis Hosp. and Med. Ctr. Hon. membership Trinity Coll. Alumnae, Washington, 1978, Cazenovia (N.Y.) Coll. Alumnae, 1961, Naming of Winifred E. Coleman Student Union, Cazenovia Coll., 1963; recipient Chantal Award, Catholic Woman of the Yr., 1965. Mem.: Nat. Jesuit Honor Soc. for Women, Gamma Pi Epsilon. Roman Catholic. Avocations: reading, composing lyrics. Home: 6010 Bay Hill Cir Jamesville NY 13078 Office: St Joseph Coll 1678 Asylum Ave West Hartford CT 06117-2764

COLEMAN-PERKINS, CAROLYN, medical/surgical nurse; b. Kansas City, Kans., Nov. 15, 1947; d. Samuel Coleman and Theorist Vernice Osborne-Coleman; m. Carl Edward Mitchell, June 1968 (div. Oct. 1973); 1 child, Vicki Lynn Mitchell; m. Charles Talmadge Perkins, July 20, 1977; 1 child, Cynthia Perkins. Diploma in nursing, 1966. Sales clk. J.C. Penney Dept. Store, Kansas City, Mo., 1964—65; nurse Bapt. Meml. Hosp., 1966—68, San Francisco Blood Bank, 1968—71, Kaiser Permanente Med. Ctr., 1972—. V.p. Local 250 SEIU - United Healthcare Workers West, Oakland, Calif., 1988—. Democrat. Baptist. Avocations: football, walking. Home: 2208 89th Ave Oakland CA 94605-3928 Office: SEIU - UHW West 560 Thomas L Berkeley Way Oakland CA 94612 Office Phone: 415-833-3224.

COLEN, FREDERICK HAAS, lawyer; b. Pitts., May 16, 1947; married, 1972. BSChemE, Tufts U., 1969; JD, Emory U., 1975. Bar: Pa. 1975, Ga. 1975, U.S. Patent Office 1976, U.S. Dist. Ct. (we. dist.) Pa. 1975, U.S. Dist. Ct. (no. dist.) Ga. 1975, U.S. Ct. Appeals (fed. and 3d cirs.) 1975, U.S. Supreme Ct. 1980. Chem. engr. Shell Oil Co., New Orleans, 1969-71; san. engr. USPHS, Morgantown, W.Va., 1971-73; patent atty. Mobay Chem. Corp., Pitts., 1975-79; assoc. Reed Smith, LLP, Pitts., 1979-86, ptnr., 1986—. Contbr. articles to profl. jours. Mem. ABA, Allegheny County Bar Assn., Pa. Bar Assn., Ga. Bar Assn., Am. Intellectual Property Law Assn. Home: 4940 Ellsworth Ave Pittsburgh PA 15213-2807 Office: Reed Smith LLP 435 6th Ave Pittsburgh PA 15219-1886 Office Phone: 412-288-4164. Business E-Mail: fcolen@reedsmith.com.

COLEN, HELEN SASS, plastic surgeon; b. Bytom, Poland, Jan. 9, 1947; came to the U.S., 1963; d. Karl Julius and Sabina (Orgel) Sass; m. Stephen Robert Colen, Mar. 25, 1972; children: Kari, Michael. BA, NYU, 1968, MD, 1972. Diplomate Am. Bd. Plastic Surgery. Intern Jefferson U. Hosp., 1972-74; gen. surgeon U. Colo., Denver, 1974-79; plastic surgeon U. Columbia-St. Lukes, N.Y.C., 1979-81; microsurgeon Bellevue Hosp., N.Y.C., 1981-82; practice medicine specializing in plastic surgery N.Y.C., 1982—. Fellow ACS; mem. Am. Soc. Plastic Surgeons, Am. Soc. Aesthetic Plastic Surgery, Phi Beta Kappa. Office: 742 Park Ave New York NY 10021-3553 Office Phone: 212-772-1300. Business E-Mail: hscsurg@colenmd.com.

COLEN, STEPHEN R., plastic and reconstructive surgeon; b. N.Y.C., Feb. 11, 1947; s. Leslie Colen and Ruth Mintz; m. Helen Sass, Mar. 25, 1972; children: Kari, Michael. Bachelor's degree, St. Lawrence U., 1967; DDS, NYU, 1971; MD, Hahnemann U., 1974. Surgeon NYU Hosp., N.Y.C., 1982—; clin. asst. plastic surgery Bellvue Hosp., N.Y.C., 1982—; attending physician plastic surgery N.Y. Vets. Hosp., N.Y.C., 1983—; attending surgeon Manhattan Eye, Ear & Throat, N.Y.C., 1983—, Beth Israel North Hosp., N.Y.C., 1994—; assoc. prof. plastic surgery NYU Med. Ctr., 2003—; chief dept. plastic surgery Hackensack U. Hosp., 2003—. Attending N.Y. Eye and Ear Infirmarmy, N.Y.C., 1983—; mem. surg. case rev. com. NYU Med. Ctr., N.Y.C., 1987—, mem. ednl. com., 1988—; mem. utilization rev. com. Bellvue Hosp., N.Y.C., 1984—. Mem. Am. Assn. Plastic Surgeons, Am. Soc. Plastic Surgeons, N.Y. Regional Med. Soc., Westchester Country Club, Olde Fla. Golf Club, Univ. Club. Office: 742 Park Ave New York NY 10021 Office Phone: 212-988-8900. E-mail: scolen47@aol.com.

COLES, ANNA LOUISE BAILEY, retired dean, nurse; b. Kansas City, Kans., Jan. 16, 1925; d. Gordon Alonzo and Lillie Mai (Buchanan) Bailey; children: Margot, Michelle, Gina. Diploma, Freedmen's Hosp. Sch. Nursing, 1948; BSN, Avila Coll., Kansas City, Mo., 1958; MSN, Cath. U. Am., 1960, PhD in Higher Edn., 1967. Instr. VA Hosp., Topeka, 1950—52, supr. Kansas City, Mo., 1952—58; asst. dir. in-service edn. Freedmen's Hosp., Washington, 1960—61, adminstrv. asst. to DON, 1961—66, assoc. dir. nursing services, 1966—67, DON, 1967—69; dean Howard U. Coll. Nursing, Washington, 1968—86, dean emeritus, 1986—; pvt. practice Kansas City, Kans.; dir. minority devel. U. Kans., 1991—95. Pres. Nurses Examining Bd., 1967—68; cons. Gen. Rsch. Support Program, NIH, 1972—76; mem. Inst. Medicine, NAS, 1974—; cons. VA Ctrl. Office continuing edn. com., 1976—; mem. D.C. Health Planning Adv. Com., 1967—68, Tri-State Regional Planning Com. for Nursing Edn., 1969, Health Adv. Coun., Nat. Urban Coalition, 1971—73; bd. dirs. Hilton Grand Vacation CLub Seaworkd Internat. Ctr. Contbr. articles to profl. jours. Trustee Cmty. Group Health Found., 1976—77, cons., 1977—; bd. regents State Univ. Sys. Fla., 1977; adv. bd. Am. Assn. Med. Vols., 1970—72; bd. dirs. Iona Whipper Home for Unwed Mothers, 1970—72, Nursing Edn. Opportunities, 1970—72. Recipient Sustained Superior Performance award, HEW, 1962, Meritorious Pub. Svc. award, Govt. of D.C., 1968, medal of honor, Avila Coll., 1969, Disting. Alumni award, Howard U. Nat. Assn. for Equal Opportunity in Higher Edn., 1990, Cmty. Svc. award, Black Profl. Nurses Kansas City, 1991, Lifetime Achievement award, Assn. Black Nursing Faculty in Higher Edn., 1993, Svc. award, Midwest Regional Conf. on Black Families and Children, 1994. Mem.: ANA, Am. Assn. Colls. Nursing (sec. 1975—76), Am. Congress Rehab. Medicine, Nat. League Nursing, Societas Docta (charter, pres. 1996—99), Freedmen's Hosp. Nursing Alumni Assn., Alpha Kappa Alpha, Sigma Theta Tau. Home: 15107 Interlachen Dr Apt 315 Silver Spring MD 20906-5627

COLES, BERTHA SHARON GILES, information scientist; b. Paris, Tenn., Aug. 13, 1949; d. Charles Ray and Etter Bell (Lightfoot) Giles. Student, Profl. Edn. Divsn. Dallas, 1979, Dynamic Graphics Ednl. Found., 1980, No. Va. C.C., 1981. Typesetter, illustrator Def. Printing, Washington, 1979-83; editl. asst. Exec. Office of Pres., Washington, 1983; visual info. specialist Naval Media Support Ctr., Washington, 1983—. Design, layout, paste-up specialist for various publs., including USN Medicine, 1981, 83, Bull., 1983, Playbook 1995; cover design July 1996 issue All Hands Mag.; design, layout Posture Statement Mag., 1997; cover design USN-(Joint Civilian Orientation Conf.)-Dept. Def.; cover design and layout of Dept. Navy Posture Statement, 1998. Bd. dirs. London Woods Cmty. Assn., Capitol Heights, Md., 1995. Democrat. Avocations: painting, gardening, interior decorating, collector. Home: 5634 Onslow Way Capitol Heights MD 20743-3059 Office: Navy Media Support Ctr 2713 Mitscher Rd SW Washington DC 20373-5819

COLES, DONALD EARL, retired engineering educator; b. St. Paul, Feb. 8, 1924; s. Courtney J. and Lorna (Addison) C.; m. Ellen Searight, Sept. 11, 1947; children: Christopher Lee, Elizabeth Anne, Kenneth Spencer, Janet Jacqueline. B.Aero. Engring., U. Minn., 1947; MS, Calif. Inst. Tech., 1948, PhD, 1953. Research engr. Jet Propulsion Lab., Pasadena, Calif., 1950-53; research fellow Calif. Inst. Tech., Pasadena, 1953-56, mem. faculty, 1953-96, prof. aeros., 1964-96; ret., 1996. Cons. to industry, 1954—; mem. Nat. Com. Fluid Mechs. Films, 1960 Producer ednl. film Channel Flow of a Compressible Fluid, 1966. Served with AUS, 1943-46. Fellow AIAA (Lawrence Sperry award 1953, Dryden medal 1985), Am. Phys. Soc. (Otto Laporte award 1996); mem. Nat. Acad. Engring., Sigma Xi. Home: 1033 Alta Pine Dr Altadena CA 91001-1409

COLES, GRAHAM, conductor, composer; b. London, May 7, 1948; arrived in Canada, 1951; s. Walter Harold and Phyllis Irene Gwendoline (Conn) C. MusB, U. Toronto, 1972, MusM, 1974, EdB, 1991. Music dir. Kitchener-Waterloo (Ont.) Chamber Orch., 1985—; rental agt. Berandol Music Ltd. Mem. coll. of examiners Royal Conservatory of Music, Toronto. Composer numerous instrumental and vocal compositions. Mem. Can. League Composers, Can. Music Ctr. (assoc. composer), Assn. Can. Orchs. Home: 86 Weber St E Kitchener ON Canada N2H 1C7 Office Phone: 519-744-3828. E-mail: kwchamberorchestra@on.aibn.com.

COLES, LAVERANUES, professional football player; b. Jacksonville, Fla., Dec. 29, 1977; Degree, Fla. State U. Wide receiver N.Y. Jets, 2000—02, 2005—, Washington Redskins, 2003—04. Named Player in Pro Bowl, 2003. Office: 1000 Fulton Ave Hempstead NY 11550

COLES, ROBERT, child psychiatrist, educator, writer; b. Boston, Mass., Oct. 12, 1929; s. Philip and Sandra (Young) C.; m. Jane Hallowell; children— Robert, Daniel, Michael. AB, Harvard U., 1950; MD, Columbia U., 1954; MD (hon.), Temple U., Notre Dame U., Bates Coll., 1972, Wayne State U., 1973, Western Mich. U., Holy Cross Coll., 1974, Hofstra U., 1975, Coll. William and Mary, Bard Coll., U. Lowell, U. Cin., 1976, Stonehill Coll., Lesley Coll., Rutgers U., 1977, Wesleyan U., Columbia Coll., Knox Coll., Cleve. State U., Wooster Coll., 1978, U. N.C., Manhattan Coll., St. Peter's Coll., Coll. New Rochelle, Pratt Inst. and Sch. Design, 1979, Berea Coll., Bklyn. Coll., Emmanuel Coll., 1980, Colby Coll., 1981, Sienna Heights Coll., Salem State Coll., Williams Coll., 1983, Beloit Coll., 1984, Emory U., Fairfield U., Macalaster Coll., Colgate U., 1986, Dartmouth Coll., 1987. Intern U. Chgo. Clinics, 1954-55; resident in psychiatry Mass. Gen. Hosp., Boston, 1955-56, McLean Hosp., Belmont, Mass., 1956-57, Judge Baker Guidance Center-Children's Hosp., 1957-58; mem. staff children's Unit Met. State Hosp., Waltham, Mass., 1957-58; mem. staff alcoholic clinic Mass. Gen. Hosp.; teaching fellow in psychiatry, mem. psychiat. staff and clin. asst. in psychiatry Harvard Med. Sch., 1955-58; research psychiatrist Harvard U. Health Services, 1963—; lectr. gen. edn. Harvard U., 1966—, prof. psychiatry and med. humanities, 1977—; founder and editor DoubleTake Magazine, 1995—. Child psychiat. fellow Judge Baker Guidance Center, Children's Hosp., Boston, 1960-61; mem. Nat. Adv. Com. on Farm Labor, 1965—; cons. Appalachian Vols., 1965—, Rockefeller Found., 1969—, Ford Found., 1969—; mem. Inst. of Medicine, Nat. Acad. Scis., 1973-78; vis. prof. public policy Duke U., 1973—; cons. supr. dept. psychiatry Cambridge (Mass.) Hosp., 1976—; cons. Center for Study of So. Culture, U. Miss., 1979—; bd. dirs. Ctr. for Documentary Studies, Duke U.; vis. prof. psychiatry, Dartmouth Coll., 1989. Author: Children of Crisis: A Study of Courage and Fear, 1967, Dead End School, 1968, Still Hungry in America, 1969, The Grass Pipe, 1969, The Image is Yours, 1969; Wages of Neglect, 1969, Uprooted Children: The Early Lives of Migrant Farmers, 1970, Teachers and the Children of Poverty, 1970, Erik H. Erikson: The Growth of His Work, 1970, The Middle Americans, 1970, Migrants, Sharecroppers and Mountaineers, 1972, The

South Goes North, 1972, Saving Face, 1972, Farewell to the South, 1972, A Spectacle Unto the World, 1973, Riding Free, 1973, The Darkness and the Light, 1974, The Buses Roll, 1974, Irony in the Mind's Life: Essays on Novels by James Agee, Elizabeth Bowen and George Eliot, 1974, Headsparks, 1975, The Mind's Fate, 1975, Eskimos, Chicanos and Indians, 1978, Privileged Ones, Vol. V of Children in Crisis book series, 1978, (with Jane Hallowell Coles) Women of Crisis Lives of Struggle and Hope, 1978, Walker Percy: An American Search, 1978, Flannery O'Connor's South, 1980, Women of Crisis; Lives of Work and Dreams, 1980, Dorothea Lange: Photographs of a Lifetime, 1982, (with Ross Spears) Agee, 1985, The Political Life of Children, 1986, Dorothy Day: A Radical Devotion, 1987, Simone Weil: A Modern Pilgrimage, 1987, Times of Surrender: Selected Essays, 1988, Harvard Diary, 1988, That Red Wheelbarrow, 1988, The Call of Stories: Teaching and the Moral Imagination, 1989, Rumors of Separate Worlds, 1989, The Spiritual Life of Children, 1990; contbg. editor: The New Republic, 1966—, Am. Poetry Rev, 1972—, Aperture, 1974—, Lit. and Medicine, 1981—, New Oxford Rev, 1981—; mem. editorial bd.: Integrated Edn., 1967—, Child Psychiatry and Human Devel., 1969—, Rev. of Books and Religion, 1976—, Internat. Jour. Family Therapy, 1977—, Grants mag., 1977—, Learning mag., 1978—, Jour. Am. Culture, 1977—, Jour. Edn., 1979—; bd. editors: Parents' Choice, 1978—; editor: Children and Youth Services Rev., 1978— . Bd. dirs. Field Found., 1968—; trustee Robert F. Kennedy Meml., 1968—, Robert F. Kennedy Action Corps, State of Mass., 1968—, Miss. Inst. Early Childhood Edn., 1968—, Twentieth Century Fund, 1971—; bd. dirs. Reading is Fundamental, Smithsonian Inst., 1968—, Am. Freedom from Hunger Found., 1968—, Am. Parents Com., 1971—; mem. corp. Boston Children's Service, 1970; mem. adv. council Inst. for Nonviolent Social Change of Martin Luther King, Jr. Meml. Center, 1971—, Ams. for Children's Relief, 1972—; mem. nat. com. for Edn. of Young Children, 1972—; mem. nat. adv. council Rural Am., 1976—; trustee Austen Riggs Found., Stockbridge, Mass., 1976—; mem. nat. adv. com. Ala. Citizens for Responsive Public Television, 1976—; mem. adv. com. Nat. Indian Edn. Assn., 1976—; visitor's com. mem. Boston Mus. Fine Arts, 1977; bd. dirs. Boys Club Boston, 1977; vis. com. Boston Coll. Law Sch., 1977; adv. Center for So. Folklore, 1978—; mem. children's com. Edna McConnell Clark Found., 1978—; bd. dirs. Lyndhurst Found., 1978—; mem. nat. adv. bd. Foxfire Fund, Inc., 1979— . Recipient Ralph Waldo Emerson prize Phi Beta Kappa, 1967; Anisfield-Wolf award in race relations Saturday Rev., 1968; Hofheimer award Am. Psychiat. Assn., 1968; Sidney Hillman prize, 1971; Weatherford prize Berea Coll. and Council So. Mountains, 1973; Lilliam Smith Award So. Regional Council, 1973; McAlpin medal Nat. Assn. Mental Health, 1972; Pulitzer prize, 1973 (all received for Children of Crisis, Vols. II, III); disting. scholar medal Hofstra U., 1974; William A. Shonfeld award Am. Soc. Adolescent Psychiatry, 1977; MacArthur Found. award, 1981; Josepha Hale award, 1986; fellow Davenport Coll., Yale U., 1976— Fellow Am. Acad. Arts and Scis., Inst. Soc., Ethics and the Life Scis.; mem. Am. Psychiat. Assn., Am. Orthopsychiat. Assn. (past dir.), Acad. Psychoanalysis, Nat. Orgn. Migrant Children. Office: Harvard U Univ Health Svcs 75 Mount Auburn St Cambridge MA 02138-4960

COLES, ROBERT NELSON, SR., religious organization administrator; b. Aug. 1, 1929; married; 6 children. Grad., Salvation Army Officers Coll., 1956; postgrad., DePaul U., 1968. Ordained minister 1956. Field officer Salvation Army, 1960-68; with Vols. Am., 1946-55, 60-80; editor-in-chief Rescue Herald Orgn. Am. Rescue Workers, Phila., 1981-92, ordination com. chmn., dir. spl. svcs., 1988-96; nat. comm. sec. Am. Rescue Workers, 1980—, nat. info. officer, 2003—, also nat. bd. mgrs., 1956-2001. Chmn. ordination com., 2002, aid-de-camp to gen. Am. Rescue Workers, 1985-96. Editor-in-chief Rescue Herald 1988-2003. Nat. info. officer Comty. Svc. Coun.; organizer numerous youth baseball and basketball teams, and semi-profl. football team Vols. Am., Elmira, N.Y.; established 3 group homes for children from broken homes, Hagerstown, Md., 1969-81; dir. food program Am. Rescue Workers, Phila., 1981-92. Named to Elmira Sports Hall of Fame, 1990. Mem. Am. Correctional Chaplains Assn., Am. Correction Assn., Md. State Sheriff's Assn., Washington County Ministerial (treas. 1993-94), Scottish Rite Bodies, Masons (32 degree), Hagerstown Exch. Club. Office: Am Rescue Workers Nat Field Office 11116 Gehr Rd Waynesboro PA 17268 Office Phone: 717-762-2965. Personal E-mail: bigchief@comcast.net.

COLES, ROBERT TRAYNHAM, architect; b. Buffalo, Aug. 24, 1929; s. George Edward and Helena Vesta (Traynham) C.; m. Sylvia Rose Meyn, Mar. 28, 1953; children: Marion Brigette, Darcy Eliot. Student, Hampton Inst., 1947-49; BA, U. Minn., 1951, B. Arch., 1953; M.Arch., M.I.T., 1955; Litt.D. (hon.), Medaille Coll., 1977. Designer, Perry, Shaw, Hepburn and Dean (Architects), Boston, 1956-57, Shepley, Bulfinch, Richardson and Abbott (Architects), Boston, 1957-58, Carl Koch and Asso., Cambridge, Mass., 1958-59; architect, custom design mgr. Techbuilt, Inc. (housing prefabricators), Cambridge, 1959-60; coordinating architect Deleuw, Cather and Brill, Engrs., Buffalo, 1960-63; prin. Robert Traynham Coles, Architect, P.C., Buffalo, 1963—; Langston Hughes Disting. prof. architecture and urban design U. Kans., 1989. V.p. Buffalo Archtl. Guidebook Corp., 1979-82; cons. housing rsch. Union Carbide Corp., 1963; vis. prof. SUNY, Buffalo, summer 1967, U. Kans., 1969; v.p. Eastside Cmty. Orgn. Inc., 1965-68, pres., 1968-77; chmn. Com. for an Urban U., 1966-67, Goals for Met. Buffalo, 1967-68; pres. Cmty. Planning Assistance Ctr. Western N.Y., Inc., 1972-74, Archtl. Mus. and Resource Ctr., 1980-84; mem. N.Y. State Bd. for Architecture, 1984-94, vice chmn., 1990, chmn., 1991; assoc. prof. architecture Carnegie Mellon U., Pitts., 1990-95; mem. jury U.S. Post Office Nat. Design Competition, Wash., D.C., 1994, City Plaza Nat. Design Competition, Lexington, Ky., 2001; chair jury, N.Y. State Assn. Architects Design Awards, N.Y.C., 1995. Treas., v.p., editor (newsletter) Nat. Orgn. Minority Architects, 1972—80, contbr. The Urban Ecosystem: A Holistic Approach, 1974, exhibitor Design Diaspora, Black Architects and International Architecture, 1970-1990, Chgo. Athenaeum, 1993, Robert Traynham Coles: Architect, Buffalo, N.Y., 1996, Between Tradition and Memory: Constructed Shleters, Black Architects, Inst. Rsch. African Diaspora in Americas and Caribbean, N.Y.C., 1999, Robert Traynham Coles: Inner City Architect, Buffalo and Erie County Hist. Soc., Buffalo, N.Y., 2002. Mem. coun. Burchfield Art Ctr., Buffalo, 1989-92, nat. adv. com. Arts in Am., 1989, Erie County Horizons Waterfront Commn., 1988-91; bd. dirs. Build a New City, Inc., 1973-75; trustee Preservation League N.Y. State, sec., 1978; trustee Western N.Y. PBS, 1981-87, hon. trustee, 1987—. Recipient Centennial award Medaille Coll., 1975, Alumni Achievement award U. Minn. Coll. Architecture and Landscape Architecture, 1997; Edward H. Moeller scholar, 1949-53, Rotch Travelling Scholar Boston Soc. Architects, 1955; named Citizen of Distinction Mayor of Buffalo, N.Y., 1997. Fellow AIA (mem. nat. housing com. 1969-71, nat. urban design and planning com. 1971-73, chmn. social responsibility com. Buffalo-Western N.Y. chpt. 1970-71, dir. 1978-81, nat. dep. v.p. minority affairs 1974-75, sec. Coll. of Fellows 1991-93, vice-chancellor 1993-94, chancellor 1995, Whitney E. Young award 1981, James William Kideney award N.Y. State chpt. 2004); mem. Nat. Orgn. Minority Architects (treas. 1976-78, dir. 1978, v.p. 1978), Alpha Kappa Mu. Home: 321 Humboldt Pkwy Buffalo NY 14208-1023 Office: 730 Ellicott St Buffalo NY 14203-1102 Office Phone: 716-842-2280. Personal E-mail: rtcoles.arch@dservmail.com. *Because they have the ability to see things as they can be, today's architects have a special task which goes beyond simply designing the physical environment. They must be activists involved in the social and political life of the community. They must address their efforts to change in these areas as well, so that people can make the needed adjustments to an increasingly challenging and rich urban world. They must, in their works, build the demonstrative alternative to the way we live today. They must be initiators as well as implementors—leaders more than followers. They must truly be revolutionaries who see their architecture as a broad movement to enchance the quality of life of urban people.*

COLES, WILLIAM HENRY, ophthalmologist, educator; b. Rochester, N.Y. BA, Ohio Wesleyan U., 1958; MD, Emory U., 1962; MS, La. State U., 1970. Diplomate Am. Bd. Ophthalmology. Intern Grady Hosp., Atlanta, 1962-63; resident Charity-La. State U., New Orleans, 1966-70; prof. ophthalmology Emory U., Atlanta, 1980-86, dir. postgrad. edn., 1981-86; prof. ophthalmology SUNY, Buffalo, 1986—, chmn. dept., 1986—. Clin. assoc. prof. Med. Univ. S.C., Charleston, 1980-86; chief of svc. Grady Meml. Hosp., Atlanta, 1981-84; chief ophthalmology svc. VA Hosp., Atlanta, 1984-86; chmn. adv. coun. Ophthalmic Surgery, 1998. Author: Ophthalmology: A Diagnostic Text, 1989; sect. editor: Medicine for the Practicing Physician, 1984 (Med. Textbook of Yr. award). Dir. Inst. Health Assessment, 1997—2000. Nat. Eye Inst. grantee, 1975-78. Mem. AMA, ACS (chair adv. coun. 1997—99, regent 1998-2004), AAUP, Am. Acad. Ophthalmology (Disting. Svc. award 1989, sr. honor award 1998), Med. Soc. State of N.Y., Assn. Rsch. and Vision in Ophthalmology, Assn. Univ. Profs. in Ophthalmology (trustee, pres. 1996-97). Home: 120 Donegal Dr Chapel Hill NC 27517

COLE-SCHIRALDI, MARILYN BUSH, occupational therapy educator; b. N.Y.C., Jan. 29, 1945; d. George Lyman and Theis (Maurer) Bush; m. Carl E. Cole, Aug. 31, 1968 (div. June 1981); children: Charlot E. Sleeper, Bradley Eric Cole; m. Martin M. Schiraldi Sr., July 3, 1982. BA, U. Conn., 1966; grad. cert., U. Pa., 1969; MS, U. Bridgeport, 1982. Registered occupl. therapist, Conn. Staff occupational therapy Ea. Pa. Psychiat. Inst., Phila., 1968-69; dir. occupational therapy Middlesex Meml. Hosp., Middletown, Conn., 1973-76; supervising occupational therapist Lawrence & Meml. Hosps. Day Treatment Ctr., New London, Conn., 1976-79; staff occupational therapist Newington Children's Hosp., Newington, Conn., 1980-82; asst. prof. occupational therapy Quinnipiac Coll., Hamden, Conn., 1982-95, assoc. prof., tenured, 1995—. Vis. faculty fellow Yale U., 1999-2001; cons. psychiat. svcs. VA Med. Ctr., West Haven, Conn., 1983-91; cons. Fairfield Hills Hosp., Newtown, Conn., 1989-91. Author: (textbook) Group Dynamics in Occupational Therapy, 1993, 3d edit., 2005; co-author Structured Group Experiences, 1982; contbr. chpts. to books, articles to profl. jours. Grantee Quinnipiac Coll, 1986, 2004, 2005; recipient Best Seller award Slack, Inc., 1999. Fellow: Am. Occupl. Therapy Assn. (Comms. award 1976, Svc. awards 1998, cert.); mem.: AAUW (cultural chair 1972, publicity chair 1973—76, edn. chair 1989—91, nominations 1993—96, membership treas. 1998—2001), Ctr. Study Sensory Integrative Dysfunction (cert. 1979), World Fedn. Occupl. Therapists, Conn. Occupl. Therapy Assn. (sec. 1978, nominations chair 1982—89, state mental health chair spl. interest sect. 1999—2005), Nat. League Am. Pen Women, U.S. Sailing Assn., U.S. Power Squadron, Sigma Xi. Republican. Episcopalian. Office: Quinnipiac U Dept Occupl Therapy 275 Mount Carmel Ave Hamden CT 06518-1961 Office Phone: 203-582-8518. E-mail: marilyn.cole@quinnipiac.edu.

COLESCOTT, ROBERT HUTTON, artist, educator; b. Oakland, Calif., Aug. 26, 1925; s. Warrington Wickham and Lydia Kenner (Hutton) C.; m. Zdenka Falarova, 1950 (div. 1962); children: Alexander, Nicholas; m. Sally Dennett, 1962 (div. 1972); 1 son, Dennett; m. Susan Ables, 1979 (div. 1983); 1 son, Daniel. AB, U. Calif.-Berkeley, 1949, MA, 1952; postgrad., Atelier F. Leger, Paris, 1949-50. Assoc. prof. art Portland State Coll, Oreg., 1957-66; vis. prof. art Am. U., Cairo, Egypt, 1966-67; prof. art Calif. State Coll., Stanislaus, 1970-74; vis. lectr. painting and drawing U. Calif.-Berkeley, 1974-79; prof. painting and drawing San Francisco Art Inst., 1976—; vis. artist U. Ariz., Tucson, 1983-84. Exhibited numerous one-man shows, N.Y.C., 1973, 75, 77, 79-82, Albright Coll., Reading, Pa., 1983, group shows, Palm Springs Desert Mus., Calif., 1982, Orgn. Ind. Artists, N.Y.C., 1982, Indpls. Mus. Art, 1982, Corcoran Mus. Art, Washington, 1983, Whitney Mus. Am. Art, N.Y.C., 1983, Fla. Internat. U., 1983, Bucknell Coll., Pa., 1983, Hamilton Coll., N.Y., 1983, Contemporary Arts Mus., Houston, 1983, others; represented permanent collections, Seattle Art Mus., San Francisco Mus. Modern Art, Oakland Mus., Calif., Met. Mus. Art, Portland Art Mus., U. Mass., Amherst, U. S. Steel Corp., Pitts, Reed Coll., Oreg., U. Oreg., Columbia Coll., Oreg., pvt. collections; panelist painting selection, Nat. Endowment for Arts, Washington, 1982. Am. Research Center fellow, Egypt, 1965-66; grantee NEA, 1971, 80, 83. Office: care Semaphore Gallery 462 W Broadway New York NY 10012-3141 *Over the years I have tried most diligently not to censor myself.**

COLESCOTT, WARRINGTON WICKHAM, artist, printmaker, educator; b. Oakland, Calif., Mar. 7, 1921; s. Warrington W. and Lydia (Hutton) C.; m. Frances Myers, Mar. 15, 1971; children by previous marriage: Louis Moore, Julian Hutton, Lydia Alice. AB, U. Calif. at Berkeley, 1942, MA, 1947; postgrad., Acad. de la Grand Chaumiere, Paris, France, 1950, 53, Slade Sch. Art, U. London (Eng.), 1957. Mem. faculty U. Wis., Madison, 1949-86, prof. art, 1957-86, Leo Steppat chair, prof., 1979-85, Leo Steppat chair (emeritus prof.), 1986—. Printmaker emeritus So. Graphics Coun., 1991; academician Nat. Acad. Design. One-man shows include Perimeter Gallery, Chgo., 1985, 87, 88, 91, 93, 95, 99, 2002, 05, Milw. Mus. Art, 1996, Bradley U., Peoria, Ill., Peltz Gallery, Milw., Wis., 2001, 04; print retrospective Elvehjem Mus., Madison, Wis., 1989, Nelson-Atkins Mus., Kansas City, 1990, New Orleans Mus. Art, 2003, Milw. Art Mus. Retrospective, 2005; represented in permanent collections Mus. Modern Art, Victoria and Albert Mus., London, Bibliotechque Nat., Paris, Met. Mus., Chgo. Art Inst., Bklyn. Mus., Phila. Mus. Art, Milw. Art Mus., Elvehjem Art Mus., Whitney Mus. Am. Art, Corcoran Gallery Art, Fogg Mus., Harvard U. Nat. Acad., N.Y.; co-author (with Arthur Hove) Progressive Printmakers, 1999; etchings commd. Milw. Art Mus., N.Y. Print Club, 2002, Corcoran Gallery of Art, Washington DC, 2005. Recipient Print award NAD, 1991, 92, 95, 97, NSAL Award of Excellence, 1993, 99, award Internat. Triennial of Print, Cracow, Poland, 1997, award Boston Printmakers, 2003; Fulbright fellow, 1957, Guggenheim fellow, 1965, Nat. Endowment Arts Printmaking fellow, 1975, Artist fellow, 1979, 83-84, 93-94. Fellow Wis. Acad. Sci. Arts and Letters. Office: 8788 County Hwy A Hollandale WI 53544-9801

COLETTA, CHERYL NANCY, psychologist, researcher; b. Ridgewood, N.J., Aug. 1, 1975; d. Michael and Ann Marie Coletta. BS in Psychology, U. Miami, 1997; MA in Psychology, Calif. State U., 2003. Rsch. asst. U. Miami, Coral Gables, Fla., 1996, rsch. asst. Jackson Meml. Med. Ctr., Mailman Ctr. Child Devel. Miami, 1996; child care worker The Erik and Joan Erikson Ctr. Adolescent Advancement, Van Nuys, Calif., 1998—98; substitute tchr. L.A. (Calif.) Unified Sch. Dist., 2001—02; rsch. asst. Sch. of Medicine, Child Study Ctr. NYU, 2003—04. Grantee, U. Miami, 1993—97; Henry King Stanford Half-Tuition Academic scholarship, 1993. Mem.: APA (assoc.), U. Miami Alumni Assn. (mem. exec. bd. 2004—05), N.Y. State Psychol. Assn., N.Y. Acad. Scis., Am. Psychol. Soc. Roman Catholic.

COLEY, LINDA MARIE, retired secondary school educator; b. Albany, Ga., Apr. 19, 1945; d. Leonard Earl and Hazel (Brady) C. BS in Math., Piedmont Coll., 1966; MS in Math., U. Ga., 1972, postgrad. Cert. tchr., Ga.; certed gifted tchr. Tchr. Toccoa (Ga.) Pub. Schs., 1966-67, Hall County Sch. Dist., Gainesville, Ga., 1967-68, Clarke County Sch. Dist., Athens, Ga., 1968—2001. Sec., 1st v.p. Clarke County Dem. Com., Athens, 1981—, Gov.'s Club. Mem. NEA, Ga. Edn. Assn., Clarke County Assn. Educators (treas., sec.), Alpha Delta Kappa (treas., sec., pres., dist. treas.), Phi Delta Kappa. Democrat. Baptist. Home: 135 Ravenwood Pl Athens GA 30605-3344

COLEY, RANDOLPH C., lawyer; b. Atlanta, Feb. 20, 1947; BA, Vanderbilt U., 1969, JD, 1978. Bar: Ga. 1978, Tenn. 1997, Tex. 1999. Ptnr. King & Spalding LLP, Atlanta, 1978—96; exec. dir. Morgan Keegan & Co., Memphis, 1996—99; mng. ptnr. Houston office & mem. Oper. Com. King & Spalding LLP, Houston, 1999—. Exec. student writing editor: Vanderbilt Law Review 1977-78. Bd. dir. Greater Houston Partnership, The Alley Theatre. Mem. ABA, Order of the Coif., State Bar Tex. Office: King & Spalding LLP 1100 Louisiana Houston TX 77002 Office Phone: 713-751-3256. Office Fax: 713-751-3290. Business E-Mail: rcoley@kslaw.com.

COLGAN, GEORGE PHILLIPS, real estate developer, real estate analyst; b. Tokyo, June 3, 1947; s. Jack Phillips and Kimiko (Furukawa) C.; m. Ann Elizabeth Dickerson, Sept. 1, 1968; 1 child, Matthew Seth. Student, Ga. Tech. U., 1965-66; BS in Biology, Ga. State U., 1970. Credit mgr. C&S Nat. Bank, Atlanta, 1969-74; statewide credit mgr. GE Credit Corp., Atlanta, 1974-76; regional v.p. A.L. Williams & Assocs., Atlanta and Houston, 1977-81; dir. sales and mktg. Hooker Barnes Homes, Inc., Atlanta, 1982-84, Brayson/Am. Homes, Atlanta, 1984-87; real estate markets analyst, pres. Whitehall Homes, Inc., Atlanta, 1987-95, residential developer, cons., 1995—. Contbr. articles to profl. jours. Asst. scoutmaster, unit commr. Troop 525 Boy Scouts Am., Norcross, Ga., 1989-94; del. So. Bapt. Conv., Atlanta, 1985; precinct del. Rep. Nat. Party, 1986, 88; pres. Norcross H.S. Wrestling Boosters Club, 1994-96. Mem. Nat. Assn. Home Builders (Cert. of Appreciation 1986). Republican. Presbyterian. Avocations: angling, paleontology, antique automobiles. Home: 1590 Keylake Dr Suwanee GA 30024-4263 Office: Suite 203 790 PEchtree Industrial Blvd Suwanee GA 30024-1097 Personal E-mail: geocolgan@juno.com.

COLGAN, RICHARD, medical educator; b. NYC, July 30, 1955; s. John J. and Anna Patricia (Burke) Colgan; m. Deborah Ann Rooney; children: Kathleen, Michael, Conor c. BA, Cath. U. Am., Washington, 1977; MD, Aut. U. Guadalajara, Mex., 1982; postgrad., Johns Hopkins U., 1978. Diplomate Am. Bd. Family Physicians. With Fifth Pathway, Prince Georges Med. r., Cheverly, Md., 1982—83; intern Prince Georges Med. Ctr., Cheverly, 1983—84, resident in family medicine, 1984—86; chief resident dept. family medicine U. Md., 1985—86, med. dir. dept. family medicine, dir. student health, dir. employee health Balt., 1999—2005, dir. clin. ops., 2004—05, assoc. prof., dir. undergrad. edn., 2005—; family medicine physician Annapolis Family Practice, Md., 1986—99. Editor-in-chief Md. Family Dr., 2001—; contbr. articles to profl. jours.; reviewer in field. Founding mem. ALERT, 2000; med. dir. Outreach Med. Clinic, Annapolis, Md., 1998—99. Co-recipient 1st Place Resident's Rsch. award, N.Am. Primary Care, 1986; recipient Cert. of Excellence, Anne Arundel Med. Ctr., 2001, Chief Resident's award Dept. Family Medicine, 1986, Faculty Tchg. award, Dept. Family Medicine, 2004. Mem.: Infectious Disease Soc. Am. (complicated UTI guidelines com.), Am. Acad. Family Physicians (alt. del. 2002), Md. Acad. Family Physicians (pres.). Avocations: reading, running, skiing. Office: Univ Maryland Sch Med Dept Family Medicine 29 S Paca St Baltimore MD 21201 Office Phone: 410-328-2686. Business E-Mail: rcolgan@som.umaryland.edu.

COLGAN, SUMNER, manufacturing engineer, chemical engineer; b. Framingham, Mass., Sept. 11, 1934; s. Joseph and Leora C.; student Boston Coll., 1957-61, Boston U., 1961, Banff Climbing Sch.; married; 1 son, Scott Paul. Chem. engr. Beam Tube Corp., Western, Mass., 1962-63; reliability engr. Gen. Motors Corp., Framingham, 1963-86, mfg. engr., 1986-91; chemist Envirotech Operating Systems, North Haven, Conn., 1991-92; lab. mgr. New England Fertilizer, 1992—. Served in USAF, 1953-57. Mem. Hunting Ravine Avalanche Patrol, 1970-78. Mem. Matterhorn Climbers Assn. Zermatt, Pvt. Pilot Assn., Mt. Rainier Summit Climbers Assn. Clubs: Appalachian Mountain, Sea Urchins. Office: 97 E Howard St Quincy MA 02169-8711

COLGATE, CATHARINE PAMELLA, secondary school educator; b. Cedar Rapids, Iowa, Dec. 17, 1939; d. Fred Joseph and Emma H. Petrick; children: Shannon Colgate, Stephen Colgate, Stewart Colgate, Stanley Colgate. BS, Ariz. State U., 1973, MA, 1977, postgrad., 1977—94. Cert. tchr., jr. coll. educator, Ariz. Tchr. English Mesa Pub. Schs., Ariz., 1975—99; instr. English Mesa C.C., 1982—2004; prof. English Chandler/Gilbert Jr. Coll., Mesa, 2005—. Writing specialist Associacao Escola Graduada, São Paulo, Brazil, 1990; vis. prof. edn. U. São Paulo, 1988; mem. med. mission, Chiappas, Mexico, 2004; mem. ea. Iowa Presbytery mission, Forteleza, Brazil, 05; vis. English tchr. Secondary Fed. Sch., Chiappas, Mexico, 2004. Patentee sch. lecterns. Mem.: AAUP, NEA, Ariz. Sch. Bd. Assn., Mesa Edn. Assn., Nat. Coun. Tchrs. English, Nat. Sch. Bds. Assn., USAF Acad. Alumni Parents' Orgn. and Assn., Phi Lambda Theta, Phi Delta Kappa. Home: PO Box 27626 Tempe AZ 85285-7626 E-mail: Cpcolgate@aol.com.

COLGATE, DORIS ELEANOR, sailing school owner, administrator; b. Washington, May 12, 1941; d. Bernard Leonard and Frances Lillian (Goldstein) Horecker; m. Richard G. Buchanan, Sept. 6, 1959 (div. Aug. 1967); m. Stephen Colgate, Dec. 17, 1969. Student, Antioch Coll., 1958-60, NYU, 1960-62. Rsch. supr. Geyer Moyer Ballard, N.Y.C., 1962-64; administrv. asst. Yachting Mag., N.Y.C., 1964-68; v.p. Offshore Sailing Sch. Ltd., Inc., N.Y.C., 1968-78, pres. Ft. Myers, Fla., 1978—2001; pres., CEO On and Offshore, Inc., Ft. Myers, 1984-2001; v.p. Offshore Travel, Inc., City Island, 1978-88; pres., CEO Offshore Sailing Sch. Ltd., Inc., Ft. Myers, 2001—. Pres. bd. dirs. Women's Sailing Found., 1998-2000, chmn. 2000-02, adv. coun., 2002—. Author: The Bareboat Gourmet, 1983, Sailing: A Woman's Guide, 1999; co-author: Fast Track to Cruising, 2004; contbr. articles to profl. jours. Bd. dirs. Fla. Repertory Theatre. Recipient Betty Cook Meml. Lifetime Achievement award, 1994, Sail Industry Leadership award, 1996, Timothea Larr award, U.S. Sailing, 2003. Mem. Royal Ocean Racing Club (London chpt.), Nat. Women's Sailing Assn. (founder, chair nat. women's adv. bd. 1990-94, pres. 1994-2000, chair 2000-02, Leadership in Women's Sailing award, 2004), Am. Women's Econ. Devel. Corp. (adv. bd. 1980-86), Boat U.S. (nat. adv. coun. 1995—), Sail Am. (bd. dirs. 2000—), Internat. Sailing Summit (exec. com. 2000-). Avocations: piano, sailing, photography, writing, cooking. Home: 15400 Catalpa Cove Ln Fort Myers FL 33908 Office: Offshore Inc 16731 McGregor Blvd Fort Myers FL 33908-3843 Office Phone: 239-985-7511. Business E-Mail: doris@offshore-sailing.com.

COLGATE, J. EDWARD, mechanical engineering educator; b. Sept. 30, 1962; SB, MIT, 1983, SM, 1986, PhD in mech. engring., 1988. Asst. prof. Northwestern U., Evanston, Ill., 1988—94, assoc. prof., 1994—2002, prof. dept. mech. engring., 2002—; co-founder, dir., tech. adv. Stanley Cobotics Inc., pres., 1999—2000. Co-editor: Advances in Robotics, Mechatronics & Haptic Interfaces, 1993; editor (assoc.): IEEE Transactions on Robotics & Automation, 1998—, Jour. of Dynamic Systems, Measurement & Control, 1995—98; editor: (U.S.) Robotics & Computer Integrated Mfg., 1995—99; contbr. chapters to books, articles to profl. jours. Recipient Henry Hess award ASME, 1995. Mem.: ASEE, IEEE, ASME. Office: Northwestern U Dept Mech Engring 2145 Sheridan Rd Dept Mech Evanston IL 60208-0834*

COLGATE, STEPHEN, small business owner; b. N.Y.C., June 25, 1935; s. Gilbert Colgate and Nina (King) Heiner; m. Doris Eleanor Horecker, Dec. 17, 1969. BA, Yale U., 1957. CEO, owner Offshore Sailing Sch., Ltd., Ft. Myers, Fla., 1964—, Offshore Travel, Inc., N.Y.C., 1978-88, On and Offshore, Inc., Captiva Island, Fla., 1975—, Cafe Offshore Inc., City Island, Fla., 1981-84. Author: (book) Colgate's Basic Sailing Theory, 1973, Fundamentals of Sailing, Cruising and Racing, 1978, The Yachtsman's Guide to Racing Tactics, 1981, Steve Colgate on Sailing, 1991, Steve Colgate on Cruising, 1991, Steve Colgate on Racing Rules, 1991, Fast Track to Cruising, 2005. Served to capt. USAF, 1958—60. Mem.: Nat. Marine Mfrs. Assn., U.S. Olympians (Fla. chpt.), Internat. Sailing Schs. Assn. (pres.), Internat. Sailing Fedn., U.S. Sailing Assn., St. Charles Yacht Club, Cruising Club Am., Royal Ocean Racing Club (London), N.Y. Yacht Club (N.Y.C.). Republican. Episcopalian. Avocations: bicycling, sailing. Office Phone: 239-454-1700. E-mail: steve@offshore-sailing.com.

COLGLAZIER, E. WILLIAM, science academy administrator, physicist; BS in Theoretical Physics, Calif. Inst. Tech., 1966, PhD in Theoretical Physics, 1971. Rschr. theoretical physics various instns.; congl. sci. fellow U.S. Rep. George Brown, 1976-77; rsch. fellow Ctr. Sci. and Internat. Affairs, Kennedy Sch. Govt. Harvard U.; prof. physics U. Tenn., Knoxville, 1983—91, dir. numerous sci. and tech. policy ctrs.; internat. affairs exec. dir. NRC, 1991—94, exec. dir. Office of Internat. Affairs, 1994; acting exec. officer NAS, NRC, 1994, exec. officer, 1994—. Bd. dirs. Fermilab High-Energy Physics Accelerator, Oak Ridge Associated U. Author numerous publs. in field. Bd. dirs. Oak Ridge Associated Univs. Recipient Lifetime Contbn. award, sect. environ. and nat. resources adminstrn. ASPA, Commendation, State Planning Coun. on Radioactive Waste Mgmt. Office: NAS & NRC 2101 Constitution Ave NW Washington DC 20418-0007

COLGRASS, MICHAEL CHARLES, composer; b. Chgo., Apr. 22, 1932; s. Michael Clement and Ann (H) C.; m. Ulla Damgaard, Nov. 25, 1966; 1 child, Neal. MusB, U. Ill., 1956; studied with Paul Price, studied with Eugene Weigle, studied with Darius Milhand, studied with Lukas Foss, studied with Wallingford Riegger, studied with Ben Weber. Author: Tuning the Human

Instrument, 1993-94, My Lessons with Kumi-How I Learned to Perform with Confidence in Life and Work, 2000; freelance solo percussionist maj. N.Y. mus. orgns., 1956—, Narrator, Boston Symphony, 1969, Phila. Orch, 1970; dir.: Virgil's Dream, Brighton Festival; Soloist, Danish Radio Orch., 1965; dir. opera Nightingale Inc, U. Ill. Contemporary Music Festival, 1975; author, poet own theatre works, 1966—; composer: Divertimento, 1961, Fantasy Variations, 1961, Wind Quintet, 1962, Light Spirit, 1963, Rhapsody, 1963, Rhapsodic Fantasy, 1965, Sea Shadow, 1966, As Quiet As, 1966, Virgil's Dream, 1967, Three Brothers, 1951, Percussion Music, 1953, Chamber Music for Four Drums and String Quintet, 1954, Chamber Music for Percussion Quintet, 1955, Variations for Four Drums and Viola, 1957, The Earth's a Baked Apple, 1968-69, New People for mezzosoprano, viola, piano, 1969, Nightingale, Inc, Auras for Harp and Orch, 1973, Image of Man, 1974, Concertmasters for 3 violins and orch, 1975, Best Wishes U.S.A. for black and white choruses, folk instruments, jazz band and orch, 1976, Theatre of the Universe for soloists, chorus and orch, 1976, Wolf for solo cello, 1976, Letter from Mozart for orch, 1976, Dèjà Vu, 1977 (Pulitzer prize 1978), Mystery Flowers of Spring for soprano and piano, 1978, Something's Gonna Happen, children's musical theatre, 1978; Flashbacks, musical play for 5 brass, 1979; Night of the Raccoon, 5 songs for soprano and 4 players, 1979, Ghosts of Pangea-A Fantasy of Cultures Meeting for full orchestra, 2000; Delta, for violin, clarinet, percussion and orch, 1979; Tales of Power, a mus. drama for solo piano on the writings of Carlos Castaneda 1980; Metamusic for solo piano, 1981; Memento for 2 pianos and orch., 1982; Demon for amplified piano, tape, radios and orch., 1983; Chaconne for viola and orch., 1984, Winds of Nagual, for wind ensemble, 1985; Strangers: Irreconcilable Variations for clarinet, viola and piano, 1986, (Jules Legèr Chamber Music Prize 1988), Dèjà Vu for percusssion quartet and wind ensemble, 1987; Folklines: A Counterpoint of Musics for string quartet and wind ensemble, 1988, The Schubert Birds, 1989, Snow Walker for organ and orch., 1990, arctic Dreams for symphonic band, 1991, Wild Riot of the Shaman's Dreams for solo flute, 1991, Arias for clarinet and orchestra, 1992, Te Tuma Te Papa for solo percussionist, 1994, a Flute in the Kingdom of Drums and Bells, 1994, Urban Requiem for four saxophones and wind ensemble, 1995, "Hammer & Bow" for violin and marimba, 1997, 98, Dream State for solo piano, 1998, Baroque Blues for solo piano, 1998, Drummers for solo piano, 1998, "Chameleon" for solo saxophone, 1999, Memento Trio for flute, cello and piano, 1999, "Old Churches" for young band, 1999, Crossworlds for flute, piano and orch., 2002 "The Beethoven Machine" for young band, 2003, "Apache Lullaby" for young band, 2003, "Bach-Goldberg Variations" for chamber orchestra, 2003, "Gotta Make Noise" for percussion ensemble and young band; works commd. N.Y. Philharm., CBC, U. Ill. Symphonic and Concert Bands, Boston Symphony, Toronto Symphony Orch., Lincoln Center Chamber Mus. Soc., New Eng. Conservatory Wind Ensemble, Fromm Found., Corp. for Pub. Broadcasting, Ford Found., Spokane, Detroit, Springfield, Minn. symphony orchs., Musica Aeterna Orch. N.Y., Young Concert Artists N.Y., Nat. Arts Centsre Orch. of Can., Calgary Internat. Organ Festival, New World Festival Arts, Delos, Manhattan and Muir string quartets, U. Miami, Nexus percussion ensemble: works recorded various cos.: contbr. articles to publs.; columnist Music Mag.; author: My Lessons with Kumi- How I Learned to Perform with Confidence in Life and Work, 2000, Ghosts of Pangea (for orchestra), 2000, Dream Dancer (for saxophone and wind ensemble), 2001, Bali (for wind ensemble), 2005. With AUS, 1954-56. Scholar Tanglewood, Mass., 1952, 54, Aspen, Colo., 1953; Guggenheim fellow, 1964-65, 68-69; recipient Fromm award, 1966, Chem. Bank award, 1971, Emmy award for Sta. WGBH-TV film Soundings: The Music of Michael Colgrass for best documentary Nat. Acad. TV Arts and Scis., 1982; Rockefeller grantee, 1967-69; Ford Found. grantee, 1972; recipient Pulitzer prize, 1978; Winds of Nagual winner Louis B. Sudler Internat. Wind Band Composition Competition, 1985, De Moulin prize Nat. Band Assn., 1985, Barlow Internat. prize, 1986. Office: 55 Harbor Sq #2011 Toronto ON Canada MSJ 2L1 E-mail: colgrass@interlog.com. *I see the composer as a person not separate from life and community but indigenous to it. How to bridge the gap that has developed between the artist and people is the biggest challenge I know, but I find the more I reach out to people the less indifferent they are to the artistic experience.*

COLHOUN, HOWARD POST, financial executive; b. West Point, N.Y., Nov. 13, 1935; s. Daniel W. and Ella (Speer) C.; m. Patricia Reynolds, June 23, 1962; children: Elizabeth B.P. Colhoun Conner, Nina R. Colhoun Wilson, Alexander H.P., Robin R. BSE, Princeton U., 1957; MBA, Harvard U., 1961. Engr. Bethlehem Steel Corp., Sparrows Point, Md., 1958-59; staff cons. Arthur D. Little Inc., Cambridge, Mass., 1961-66; v.p. T. Rowe Price Assocs. Inc., Balt., 1966-82; chmn. bd., dir. Rowe Price New Era Fund Inc., Balt., 1971-82; founder, mng. ptnr. Emerging Growth Ptnrs., L.P., Balt., 1982—97. V.p. T. Price Growth Stock Fund, Rowe Price New Income Fund, Rowe Price Res. Fund, Rowe Price Tax Free Income Fund, Rowe Price Tax Exempt Fund, T. Rowe Price Internat. Fund; dir. Harbor Money Market Fund, Harbor Internat. Growth Fund, Harbor Internat. Fund, Harbor Bond Fund, Harbor Capital Appreciation Fund, Harbor Short Duration Fund, Storage U.S.A., OEA, Inc.; trustee Investment Mgmt. Workshop at Princeton, chmn., 1976-82, trustee Fulbright Assn., 1995-2003, treas. 1996—; mem. investment com. Md. State Pension Fund, 1982-2000; chmn. Manchester Capital Mgmt., 1997—. Author: Investing in Brooder Technology, 1969, A Fundamentalist's Approach to Growth Stock Investing, 1971; regular panelist nat. TV program Wall $treet Week, 1970-98. Pres. United Fund North Shore, Boston, 1965; trustee, treas. Bryn Mawr Sch., 1975-85, chmn. endowment com., 1992-98; trustee Balt. County Revenue Authority, 1972-82; trustee, mem. adv. bd. Nat. Aquarium Balt., 1980—, chmn. investment com., 1991—; trustee Balt. County Rev. Authority, 1972-82; bd. dris. Valleys Planning Coun., 1983—; mem. bd. Nat. Outdoor Leadership Sch., 1996-2005, vice chmn., 2004; mem. adv. bd. Outward Bound, Hurrican Island, Maine. Fulbright scholar U. Trondheim, Norway, 1957-58. Mem. Fin. Analysts Fedn., Balt. Soc. Security Analysts (trustee, bd. dirs., v.p. 1970-75), Green Spring Valley Hunt Club, Bachelor's Cotillion Club, Harvard Bus. Sch. Club Md. (trustee 1970-71, 92-95), Sigma Xi, Tau Beta Pi. Home: 14114 Mantua Mill Rd Glyndon MD 21136-4836 Office: 401 E Pratt St Ste 211 Baltimore MD 21202-3003

COLI, GUIDO JOHN, chemical company executive; b. Richmond, Va., Sept. 12, 1921; s. Guido and Rena (Pacini) C.; m. Vonda L. Coli; children: Pamela, Patricia, Deborah, Rebecca Smith. BS, Va. Poly. Inst., 1941, MS, 1942, PhD, 1949. Registered profl. engr., N.Y., Va. Asst. engr. Va. Health Dept. bur. indsl. hygiene, 1941; assoc. chemist Naval Research Lab., 1942-43; instr. chem. engring. Va. Poly. Inst., 1947-48; chem. engr. Mobil Oil Co., Paulsboro, N.J., 1949-50; with Allied Chem. Corp., N.Y.C., 1950-72, group v.p. corp., 1968-72, dir., 1970-72; pres. Am. Enka Co., Enka, N.C., 1979-82; dir. Akzo Am. Inc., 1979-86, pres., chief exec. officer, 1982-86; chmn., chief exec. officer Armira, Inc., Asheville, N.C., 1986—; pres., CEO Sisters of Mercy Svcs. Corp., Asheville, 1999—. Mem. Gov. Va. Commn. to Establish Urban Univ. in Richmond Area, 1966-67; mem. adv. council Coll. of Engring., Va. Poly. Inst. Lt. USN, 1943-46. Fellow Am. Inst. Chemists; mem. Am. Chem. Soc. (chmn. Va. 1957), Am. Inst. Chem. Engrs., Sigma Xi, Phi Lambda Upsilon, Tau Beta Pi, Phi Kappa Phi, Alpha Kappa Psi. Clubs: University (N.Y.C.); Country of Asheville. Home: 314 Town Mountain Rd Asheville NC 28804-3821 Office: Sisters of Mercy Svcs Corp 445 Biltmore Ave Asheville NC 28801-4119 Personal E-mail: v.coli@home.com.

COLIHAN, JAMES CHARLES, lawyer; b. Bridgeport, Conn., Sept. 7, 1953; s. John Charles and Eileen (Walsh) C.; m. Jane Richards, Sept. 28, 1985; children: Katherine, Leigh, John. BA magna cum laude, Holy Cross Coll., 1975; M. Internat. Affairs, Columbia U., 1977; JD, U. Va., 1979. Bar: N.Y. 1980, Conn. 1980. Assoc. Coudert Bros., NYC, 1979-82, 85-87, London, 1983-85, ptnr. NYC, 1988—, head Global Mergers & Acquisitions practice. Counsel Coun. for the U.S. and Italy, N.Y.C., 1986—; hiring ptnr. Coudert Bros., 1990—. Fundraiser New Eng. chpt. Cystic Fibrosis Found., Maine, 1987—. Internat. fellow Columbia U., 1975-76. Mem. ABA, NY State Bar Assn., Conn. State Bar Assn., Phi Beta Kappa. Avocations: golf, music, travel. Office: Coudert Bros 1114 Avenue Of The Americas Fl 4 New York NY 10036-7710 Office Phone: 212-880-4680. Office Fax: 212-626-4120. Business E-Mail: colihanj@coudert.com.

COLIJN, GEERT JAN, dean, political scientist; b. Naarden, The Netherlands, Sept. 23, 1946; came to US, 1969; s. Izak and Aaltje Cornelia (Rozeboom) C.; m. Sarah Ellen Griffith, Jan. 4, 1986; 1 child, Cornelia Alice. Kandidaat, U. van Amsterdam, 1969; MA, Temple U., 1971, PhD, 1977. From asst. prof. to assoc. prof. polit. sci. Richard Stockton Coll. NJ, Pomona, NJ, 1978-91, prof., 1991—, chmn. social and behavioral sci., 1982-85, dean of gen. studies, 1988—. Trustee Internat. House, Phila., 1990-2002; steering com. Visions of Higher Edn. Conf., Zurich, Switzerland, 1988-94; vis. fellow U. Warwick, 1987-88 Co-editor: Confronting the Holocaust, 1997, From Prejudice to Destruction, 1995, Hearing the Voices, 1999; mem. editl. bd. Jour. Genocide Studies; contbr. articles to profl. jour. Mem. exec. com. Holocaust Resource Ctr., Pomona, 1988—; trustee Community Justice Inst., Atlantic City, NJ, 1982-85; mem. nat. adv. coun. Anne Frank Ctr., 1992-94. Avocations: classical music, speedskating, travel. Home: 135 Old New York Rd Port Republic NJ 08241-9739 Office: Richard Stockton Coll NJ Jimmie Leeds Rd Pomona NJ 08240 Office Phone: 609-652-4542. E-mail: jan.colijn@stockton.edu.

COLINO, RICHARD RALPH, communications consultant; b. N.Y.C., Feb. 10, 1936; s. Victor and Caroline (Pauline) C.; m. Wilma Jane Rubinstein, June 10, 1962 (div. Oct. 1991); children: Stacey Anne, Geoffrey William; m. Charmaine Mallory Kelly, 1997. BA, Amherst Coll., 1957; JD, Columbia U., 1960. Assoc. Sargoy & Stein, N.Y.C., 1960-61; atty. FCC, Washington, 1962-64, U.S. Info. Agy., Washington, 1964-65; dir. internat. affairs Comm. Satellite Corp., Washington, 1965-68, dir. Europe/Middle East Geneva, 1968-69, asst. v.p. Washington, 1969-75, v.p. and gen. mgr. internat. ops., 1975-79; pres., CEO Continental Home Theatre, Burlingame, Calif., 1979-80, DynaCom Enterprises Ltd., Chevy Chase, Md., 1980-83; dir. gen., CEO Internat. Telecomm. Satellite Orgn., Washington, 1983-86; v.p. W. L. Pritchard & Co., Inc., Cons. Engrs., Bethesda, Md., 1990-92, Jackson-Richards Cons. Ltd. Telecom. Cons., Irvine, Calif., 1992-97; artist Oro Valley, Ariz., 1997-2000; ind. bus. cons., 1997—. Contbr. to more than 30 books and articles; group shows include Ariz. Art Gallery, Arte-Spazio, Tucson, 2000. Bd. dirs. Washington Opera, 1986-87, Overseas Devel. Coun., 1986-87, Internat. Inst. Communication, London, 1985-86, Big Bros., Washington, 1975-77; co-chmn., chmn. various fundraisers, Washington, 1983-89, AFCEA, Washington, 1975-79; docent The Irvine Mus., 1994-98. With U.S. Army, 1961-62. Named one of top 15 people in U.S. comms. Comms. Week, 1986; recipient Adam Thompson award Amherst Coll., 1982. Avocations: tennis, skiing. Home: 2 Pheasant Ln South Hadley MA 01075 Personal E-mail: rccolino@aol.com.

COLISH, MARCIA LILLIAN, history professor; b. Bklyn., July 27, 1937; d. Samuel and Daisy (Kartch) C. BA magna cum laude, Smith Coll., 1958; MA, Yale U., 1959, PhD, 1965; DHL (hon.), Grinnell Coll., 1999. Instr. history Skidmore Coll., Saratoga Springs, NY, 1962-63; instr. Oberlin (Ohio) Coll., 1963-65, asst. prof., 1965-69, assoc. prof., 1969-75, prof. history, 1975-2001, Frederick B. Artz prof. history, 1985-2001, chmn. dept. history, 1973-74, 78-81, 85-86; vis. fellow Yale U., 2001—, lectr. in history, 2004—05. Vis. prof. history and religious studies Yale U., 2002-03, vis. scholar Am. Acad. Rome, 1968-69; lectr. history Case Western Res. U., Cleve., 1966-67; editl. cons. W.W. Norton & Co., 1973, John Wiley & Sons, Inc., 1981, SUNY Press, 1983, 85, U. Chgo. Press, 1988, U. Calif. Press, 1988, Princeton U. Press, 1988, 96, 98, U. Notre Dame Press, 1991, 92, 94, 2005, U. Ill. Press, 1995, U. Pa. Press, 1995, 97, 99, Yale U. Press, 1997, 98, Oxford U. Press, 1998, 2001, 05, Blackwell's, 1998, Liturgical Press, 1999, Cambridge U. Press, 2002, 05, E.J. Brill, 2003, 04; cons. dept. history Grinnell Coll., 1974, Knox Coll., 1981, St. John's U., 1981, Whitman Coll., 1982, Hope Coll., 1995, Kenyon Coll., 1996; mem. exec. bd. Ohio Program Humanities, 1976-81, exec. bd., 1978-81, vice chmn., 1979-81; writing residency, Villa Serbelloni, Bellagio, 1995; mem. Sch. Hist. Studies, Inst. for Advanced Study, Princeton, 1986-87 Author: The Mirror of Language: A Study in the Medieval Theory of Knowledge, 2d rev. edit., 1983, The Stoic Tradition from Antiquity to the Early Middle Ages, 1985, enlarged paperback edit., 1990, Peter Lombard, 1994, Medieval Foundations of the Western Intellectual Tradition, 400-1400, 1997, 2d printing, 1998, paperback edit., 1999, (Italian transl.) La Cultura del Medioevo, 2001, Ambrose's Patriarchs: Ethics for the Common Man, 2005. Mem. exec. bd. Oberlin ACLU, 1970-74, chmn., 1972-74, rec. sec., 1976-77, vice chmn., 1979-80; mem. exec. bd. Oberlin YWCA, 1966-70. Recipient Wilbur Cross medal Yale Grad. Sch. Alumni Assn., 1993, Marianist award U. Dayton, 2000; Etienne Gilson lectr. Pontifical Inst. of Mediaeval Studies, Toronto, 2000; Samuel S. Fels fellow Yale U., 1961-62, Younger Scholar fellow Inst. for Rsch. in Humanities, U. Wis., 1974-75, Nat. Humanities Ctr. fellow, 1981-82, Guggenheim fellow, 1989-90, Woodrow Wilson Ctr. fellow, 1994-95, NEH fellow, 1968-69, 81-82; NEH summer grantee U. Calif., 1993. Fellow Medieval Acad. Am. (coun. 1987-89, 2d v.p. 1989-90, 1st v.p. 1990-91, pres. 1991-92, Haskins medal 1998); mem. Am. Hist. Assn., Medieval Assn. Midwest (coun. 1978-81), Midwest Medieval Conf. (pres. 1978-79), Renaissance Soc. Am., Ctrl. Renaissance Conf., Soc. Internat. pour Etude Philosophie Medievale, Internat. Soc. for Classical Tradition, Internat. Soc. Intellectual History, Phi Beta Kappa. Home: 80 Seaview Terr #29 Guilford CT 06437 E-mail: marcia.colish@yale.edu.

COLITTI, MARC CLAUDE-CHARLES, counselor, educator, researcher; b. Lansing, Mich., July 10, 1956; s. E. A. Colitti and Sheila Nugent; m. Joan Denny, Aug. 10, 1991. AA, Kellogg C.C., Battle Creek, Mich., 1978; BA in Music, Olivet Coll., 1991; MA in Counseling, Seina Heights U., 1991. Cert. tchr. Mich. Cons. Deloitte Touche, L.A., 1986—88, BSO Siedman, Long Beach, Calif., 1988—90; instr. Davenport U., Kalamazoo, 1993—2003; tchr., rschr. Mich. State U., East Lansing, 2003—. Author conf. papers in field. Treas. Battle Creek Youth Orch., 1995—2000. Named to, Wall of Tolerance, 2002; recipient Excellence in Edn. award, Kellogg Found., 2003. Mem.: Am. Ednl. Rsch. Assn. Roman Catholic. Avocations: classic car collecting, travel, hunting, fishing, camping. Office: Battle Creek Central HS 100 W VanBuren St Battle Creek MI 49017 Office Phone: 269-965-9500. Personal E-mail: marc_colitti@yahoo.com. E-mail: colittim@msu.edu.

COLIZZA, WAYNE ANTHONY, orthopaedic surgeon; b. Hamilton, Ont., Can., Sept. 12, 1958; came to the U.S., 1992; s. Vincent Patrick and Velma Louise C.; m. Marlene Catherine Morin, Aug. 13, 1983; children: Wayne Jr., Christina, Michael. BSc in Biochemistry with honors, McGill U., Montreal, 1982, MD, 1987. Diplomate Am. Bd. Orthopaedic Surgery. Fellow Insall Scott Kelly Inst. for Orthopedics and Sports Medicine, N.Y., 1992-93; attending surgeon St. Clares Med. Ctr., Denville, N.J., 1993—, Beth Israel Med. Ctr., N.Y., 1995-99, Morristown (N.J.) Meml. Hosp., 1996—; pvt. practice Newton, Cedar Knolls, N.J., 1996—. Contbr. articles to profl. jours. Pres. Canadian Orthopaedic Residents Assn., 1992. Recipient Zimmer Travelling Fellows award Am. Orthopaedic Assn., 1994. Fellow ACS, Internat. Coll. Surgeons, Royal Coll. Surgeons Can. (cert.), Am. Acad. Orthopaedic Surgeons; mem. Can. Orthopaedic Assn., Can. Med. Assn., N.J. Med. Soc., N.J. Orthopedic Soc. (bd. dirs.). Office: 63 Newton Sparta Rd Newton NJ 07860-2745 also: 218 Ridgedale Ave Ste 104 Cedar Knolls NJ 07927-2109 Office Phone: 973-300-5960.

COLKER, DAVID, stock exchange executive; JD, U.Va., 1982. Gen. counsel Cin. Stock Exch., 1984—90, exec. v.p., 1991—95, COO, 1995—98, pres., COO, 1998—2001, pres., CEO, 2001—. Office: Cincinnati Stock Exch 440 S LaSalle St 26th fl Chicago IL 60605*

COLKER, EDWARD, artist, educator; b. Phila., Jan. 5, 1927; Grad., Phila. Coll. Art, 1949; BS, NYU, 1965, MA, 1985. Instr., critic Phila. Coll. Art, Cooper Union, N.Y.C., 1949-66; assoc. prof. Grad. Sch. Fine Arts, U. Pa., 1968-70; dir. Sch. Art and Design, U. Ill., Chgo., 1972-78, research prof. art, 1977-80; dean of visual arts SUNY, Purchase, 1980-85; chmn. dept. art Cornell U., 1985-86; provost Univ. of the Arts, 1986-91, Cooper Union for the Advancement of Sci. and Art, N.Y.C., 1991—95, Pratt Inst., Bklyn., 1995—98, 2003. Cons. Nat. Endowment Arts, USIA; cons. in field One-person shows, Print Club, Phila., 1961, 89, Amel Gallery, N.Y.C., 1965, East Hampton Gallery, N.Y.C., 1969, Douglas Kenyon Gallery, Chgo., 1975, Ctr. Book Arts, N.Y.C., Neuberger Mus., Purchase, U. Ill., Chgo., 1985, 86, SUNY, Albany, 1990, Cooper Union, 1993, U. of Ariz. Mus. of Art, Bates Coll. Mus. of Art, 1998, Neuberger Mus. of Art, 1999, Poets House, 2002-03, others; represented in permanent collections, Mus. Art, Phila., Library of Congress, Washington, Mus. Modern Art, N.Y.C., Nat. Mus., Stockholm, Rosenwald Collection, NYU, U. Ariz., others. Guggenheim Found. fellow, 1961-62; Ill. Arts Council grantee, 1973, 80; Graham Found. grantee, 1977, R. Florsheim Art Fund grantee, 1997. Mem. Coll. Art Assn. Am., Caxton Club, Grolier Club.

COLL, EDWARD GIRARD, JR., university president; b. Pitts., Aug. 9, 1934; s. Edward G. and Alive V. (Ebeling) C.; m. Carole Hulse, Feb. 3, 1958; children— Thomas, Jean Coll Mendenhall, Peter, Karen, Kelly. BA, Duquesne U., 1960, LHD (hon.), 1983, Alfred U., 2000. Div. dir. United Fund Allegheny County, Pitts., 1959-61; asst. to exec. v.p. United Fund Dade County, 1961-63; asst. to v.p. for devel. affairs U. Miami, Fla., 1963-66, dir. corp. and found. relations, 1966-67, dir. devel., 1967-72, sec. univ. corp., 1972-73, v.p. for devel. affairs, 1973-82; pres. Alfred U., N.Y., 1982-2000; ret., 2000. Bd. dirs. Steuben Trust Co.; lectr. in field. Contbr. articles to profl. jours. Chmn. zoning bd. appeals Dade County, 1973-82; bd. dirs. Nat. Ctr. Child Abuse and Neglect, 1985-90; pres. com. NCAA, 1988-92, coun. mem. 1993-97, vice-chair divsn. III, 1990, v.p., 1994-96; trustee Coun. for Support and Advancement Edn., Washington, 1981-82, 87-89, chair, 1991-92. With U.S. Army, 1953-56. Univ. Adminstr. Fulbright fellow U. Warwick, Coventry, Eng., 1985. Mem. Ind. Colls. and Univs. N.Y. (bd. dirs. 1982-86), Duquesne Univ. Alumni Assn., Am. Mktg. Assn. (hon.), Miami Club, University Club, Genesee Valley Club, Wellsville Country Club, Delta Mu Delta, Phi Kappa Phi, Beta Gamma Sigma. Roman Catholic. Home: 4202 Dunham Pk Flowery Branch GA 30542 Office: PO Box 121 Alfred Sta Alfred NY 14803

COLL, JOHN PETER, JR., lawyer; b. Pitts., Oct. 5, 1943; s. John Peter and Lelia (Nicolussi) C.; m. Nancy Kaye Swan; children: John Peter, Alexis S. AB in Polit. Sci., Duke U., 1965; JD, Georgetown U., 1968. Bar: N.Y. 1969, U.S. Dist. Ct. (so. dist.) N.Y. 1970, U.S. Dist. Ct. (ea. dist.) N.Y. 1974, U.S. Ct. Appeals (2d cir.) 1972, U.S. Supreme Ct. 1974, U.S. Ct. Appeals (5th cir.) 1981, U.S. Ct. Appeals (11th cir.) 1981, U.S. Ct. Appeals (8th cir.) 1980, U.S. Ct. Appeals (6th cir.) 1991, U.S. Ct. Appeals (1st cir.) 1993, U.S. Ct. Appeals (3d cir.) 1994, U.S. Ct. Appeals (9th cir.) 1994, U.S. Dist. Ct. (no. dist.) Calif. 1983, U.S. Dist. Ct. (no. dist.) N.Y. 1984, U.S. Dist. Ct. (we. dist.) N.Y. 1988, U.S. Tax Ct. 1990, U.S. Ct. Appeals (fed. cir.) 1999. Assoc. Donovan Leisure Newton & Irvine LLP, N.Y.C., 1968-76, ptnr., 1976-98, chmn. exec. com., 1989-98; ptnr. Orrick, Herrington & Sutcliffe, LLP, N.Y.C., 1998—; mem. exec. com. Orrick, Herington & Sutcliffe, LLP, N.Y.C., 2000—, office leader-N.Y.C. Bd. advisors product safety and liability rep. BNA, 1991—; mem. litigation steering com. Def. Rsch. Inst., 1991—97. Contbg. author: Products Liability in New York, Strategy and Practice, 1997, 2d. edit., 2004, Commercial Litigation in New York State Courts, 2d edit., 2004. Named one of top ten litigators in N.Y.C., Nat. Law Jour., 1999. Mem. ABA (litigation sect. 1983—), Fed. Bar Coun., N.Y. State Bar Assn., Assn. of Bar of City of N.Y., N.Y. Coun. Law Assn., Legal Aid Soc. N.Y. (bd. dirs. 2003—), Lawrence Beach Club (bd. govs. 1991-2000), Cherry Valley Club, Univ. Club. Democrat. Roman Catholic. Office: Orrick Herrington and Sutcliffe LLP 666 5th Ave New York NY 10103-1798 Office Phone: 212-506-3790. Office Fax: 212-506-5151. Business E-Mail: pcoll@orrick.com.

COLL, MARIO M, engineering company executive; b. 1962; BSc in petroleum engring., Tex. A&M U. Various positions Mobil Oil, 1987—96; v.p., planning and info. tech. Ocean Energy, 1996—2003; CIO Devon Energy, 2003—. Mem.: Ind. Petroleum Assn. of Am., Soc. of Petroleum Engineers. Office: Devon Energy Corp 20 North Broadway Oklahoma City OK 73102-8260

COLL, NORMAN ALAN, lawyer; b. East Grand Rapids, Mich., Sept. 24, 1940; s. Harry H. and Elizabeth (Kelley) Coll; m. Mona Fondren, July 23, 1977; children: Kevin M., Kelley S., Patrick P. BSME, U. Mich., 1962; LLB, U. Fla., 1965. Bar: Fla. 1965, U.S. Dist. Ct. (so. dist.) Fla. 1965, U.S. Supreme Ct. 1970, D.C. 1979, U.S. Ct. Appeals (D.C. cir.) 1979, U.S. Ct. Appeals (11th cir.) 1981. Assoc. Scott McCarthy Preston & Steel, Miami, Fla., 1965-69; ptnr. Steel Hector & Davis, Miami, 1969-87; officer, shareholder Coll Davidson et al., Miami, 1987-00; ptnr. Shook, Hardy & Bacon L.L.P., Miami, 2000—. Mem.: Miami City Club, Blowing Rock Country Club, Riviera Country Club, Coral Reef Yacht Club, Sigma Alpha Epsilon. Office: Shook Hardy & Bacon LLP 2400 Miami Ctr 201 S Biscayne Blvd Miami FL 33131-4332 Office Phone: 305-358-5171. E-mail: ncoll@shb.com.

COLL, STEPHEN WILSON, journalist; b. Washington, Oct. 8, 1958; s. Robert Wilson and Shirley Lee (Baldwin) Coll; m. Susan Keselenko, May 17, 1984; children: Alexandra, Emma, Maxwell. BA cum laude, Occidental Coll., 1980. Contbg. editor Calif. mag., LA, 1983—85; staff writer The Washington Post, 1985—87, Wall St. corr., 1987—89, New Delhi bur. chief, 1989—93, investigative journalist, London bur., 1993—95, mng. editor, 1998—2004, assoc. editor, 2005; editor & pub. The Washington Post Mag., 1995—98; staff writer The New Yorker Mag., Washington, 2005—. Author: (books) The Deal of the Century: The Breakup of AT&T, 1986, The Taking of Getty Oil: From the Oil Patch to Wall Street - The Full Story of the Most Spectacular and Catastrophic Takeover of All Time, 1987, On the Grand Trunk Road: A Journey into South Asia, 1993, Ghost Wars: The Secret History of the CIA, Afghanistan, and Bin Laden, from the Soviet Invasion to September 10, 2001, 2004 (Pulitzer Prize for gen. non-fiction, 2005); co-author (with David A. Vise): Eagle on the Street: Based on the Pulitzer Prize-Winning Account of the SEC's Battle with Wall Street, 1991. Recipient Pulitzer Prize for explanatory journalism, 1990, Gerald Loeb Award, UCLA, 1990, Livingston Award, Molly Parnell Livingston Found., 1992, Ed Cunningham Award, Overseas Press, 2000, Robert F. Kennedy Internat. Print Award, 2001, Journalism Leader Award, South Asian Journalists Assn., 2002. Mem.: Phi Beta Kappa. Office: The Washington Post 1150 15th St NW Washington DC 20071-0002*

COLLAMORE, THOMAS JONES, corporate financial executive; b. Hartford, Conn., Jan. 29, 1959; s. H. Bacon Jr. and Elizabeth Caldwell (Jones) C.; m. Jacqueline Ann Kelly, Nov. 21, 1992; children: Thomas Jones Jr., Pauline Elizabeth, Sallie Ann, Katherine Muse. BA magna cum laude, Drew U., 1981. Personal aide Rome for Gov., Bloomfield, Conn., 1978, dep. dir., 1982; staff asst. George Bush for Pres., Hartford, 1979-80; confidential asst. to sec. commerce Malcolm Baldrige Washington, 1981-82; spl. asst. to sec. commerce, 1982-85; dep. asst. to V.p. of U.S. The White House, Washington, 1985-87, asst. to V.p. of U.S., 1987-89; dir. secretariat Office of Pres.-elect of U.S., Washington, 1988-89; asst. sec. for adminstrn. U.S. Dept. Commerce, Washington, 1989-91, chief of staff, asst. sec. commerce, 1991-92; v.p. corp. affairs policy and adminstrn. Philip Morris Cos. Inc., N.Y.C., 1992-95, v.p. corp. pub. affairs, 1995—. Chmn. govt. ops. com. Pres.'s Coun. on Mgmt. Improvement, Washington, 1989-91; mem. bd. advisors George Bush Presdl. Libr., 1996—. Bd. dirs. Malcolm Baldrige Scholarship Fund, Hartford, 1988—, City Meals-on-Wheels of N.Y.; trustee Kingswood-Oxford Sch., West Hartford, 1991—, Drew U., Madison, N.J., 1992—; alt. del. Rep. Nat. Conv., Detroit, 1980, del., Houston, 1992. Mem. Pi Sigma Alpha. Episcopalian. Home: 5206 Norway Dr Chevy Chase MD 20815-6672 Office: Atria Group Inc 101 Constitution Ave NW 4th Fl Washington DC 20001

COLLAR, EMILIO, JR., information systems consultant; b. Astoria, Queens, NY, Jan. 7, 1969; s. Emilio and Luisa Collar. *Parents immigrated to the United States from Cuba in 1961. Grandparents, and remaining lineage, are from the province of Asturias in northern Spain. The "Collar" name can be traced as far back as the 13th century. Records show that members of this lineage served as Knights during the regime of Carlos III during the late 1700s and early 1800s.* BBA in Mgmt. Info. Sys., Pace U., 1993, MS in Info. Sys., 1998; PhD in Info. Sys., U. Colo., Boulder, 2005. Claims analyst Gen. Reins., Stamford, Conn., 1993—95; cons. worldwide olympic games tech. IBM, Somers, NY, 1996—98; ind. cons. Danbury, Conn., 2005; asst. prof. mgmt. info. sys. Ancell Sch. Bus., Western Conn. State U. *Research interests* *include theory and methodological development for investigating the readability of programming code, breaking down code into conceptual structures for statistical analysis, the development of readability indices, and the comparisons of code conceptual structures with econometric techniques.* Recipient Outstanding Student of Yr. award, Pace U., 1998; fellow, U. Colo. at Boulder, 1998—2000; scholar, KPMG, 1998—2003. Mem.: IEEE, Assn. Info. Sys., Assn. Computing and Machinery. Republican. Home: 11 Aunt Hack Rd Danbury CT 06811 Office: Western Connecticut State Univ Ancell Sch Business 181 White St Danbury CT 06810 Office Phone: 203-837-8903. Personal E-mail: emilio.collar@colorado.edu. Business E-Mail: collare@wcsu.edu.

COLLAROS, PANDEL LEE, music educator; b. Steubenville, Ohio, Mar. 3, 1954; s. Jack Peter and Frankie Zanetos Collaros; 1 child, Zachariah Tobias. BA cum laude with honors, Ohio State U., 1989, MA, 1993. Gen. mgr. John Lotas Productions, Inc., NYC, 1984—86; lectr. in music theory U. of Kans., 1996—98; lectr. in fine arts Bethany Coll., W.Va., 1999—. Composer: Three Short Pieces for Oboe, Kyrie, Fantasy for Flute and Piano; author: (short stories) Mannequin Man (winner of lit. contest for short fiction sponsored by Mosaic, the Ohio State U. undergraduate arts and lit. mag., 1989). Judge for Ohio state sci. day Ohio Wesleyan U., 1989; faculty sponsor Kans. Composers Project at the U. of Kans., 1997—98; mem. of the Anthony B. Cius composition award com. U. of Kans. Recipient Cert. of appreciation, Ohio State U. Office for Disability Services, 1989; scholar Grad. Tchg. Assoc., Ohio State U., 1990—96; scholarship, Pan Icarian Found., 1989. Mem.: Soc. for Music Theory, Coll. Music Soc., The Biol. Sciences Honor Soc., Golden Key Nat. Honor Soc., Internat. Premedical Honor Soc., Pi Kappa Lambda Musical Honor Soc., Sigma Tau Epsilon, Bethany Coll. Music Honor Soc. (hon.), Phi Kappa Phi (Ohio State U. chpt. initiation, and mem. com. 1994—95). Home: 623 Lovers Lane A1 Steubenville OH 43953 Office: Bethany College 210 Steinman Hall Bethany WV 26032 E-mail: collaros@1st.net.

COLLAS, JUAN GARDUÑO, JR., lawyer; b. Manila, Apr. 25, 1932; s. Juan D. and Soledad (Garduño) C.; m. Maria L. Moreira, Aug. 1, 1959; children: Juan Jose, Elias Lopes, Cristina Maria, Daniel Benjamin. LLB, U. of Philippines, Quezon City, 1955; LLM, Yale U., 1958, JSD, 1959. Bar: Philippines 1956, Ill. 1960, Calif. 1971, U.S. Supreme Ct. 1967. Assoc., Sy Cip, Salazar & Assocs., Manila, 1956-57; atty. N.Y., N.H. & H. R.R., New Haven, 1959-60; assoc. Baker & McKenzie, Chgo., 1960-63, ptnr., Manila, 1963-70, San Francisco, 1970-95, Manila, 1995—. Contbr. articles to profl. jours. Trustee, sec. Friends of U. of Philippines Found. in Am., San Francisco, 1982—; co-chmn. San Francisco Lawyers for Better Govt., 1982—; chmn. San Francisco-Manila Sister City Com., 1986-92. Recipient Outstanding Filipino Overseas in Law award, Philippine Ministry Tourism Philippines Jaycees, 1979. Mem. ABA, Am. Arbitration Assn. (panelist), Ill. State Bar Assn., State Bar Calif., Integrated Bar of Philippines, Filipino-Am. C. of C. (bd. dirs. 1974-91, 94-96, pres. 1985-87, chmn. bd. dirs. 1987-89, 95-96). Republican. Roman Catholic. Clubs: Green Hills Country Club, Villa Taverna (San Francisco). Office: Baker & McKenzie 2 Embarcadero Ctr Ste 2400 San Francisco CA 94111-3909

COLLAS-DEAN, ANGELA G., former state commissioner, small business owner; b. Manila, Oct. 20, 1933; arrived in U.S., 1960; d. Juan Damocles Collas and Soledad Martinez Garduño; m. Bruce Goring Dean, Aug. 8, 1961; children: Heather Frances Dean, Jennifer Ashton Dean. BA in English Lit. and Humanities, U. of the Philippines, Diliman, Quezon City, 1955; MA in Drama, Baylor U., 1962. Owner Philippine Party Foods, Eugene, Oreg., 1984-96; dir., pres. Philippine Am. C. of C., Oreg., 1996-97. Instr. U. Philippines, Quezon City, 1963—65, Baylor U., Waco, 1965—68. Mem. Lane County Arts Adv. Com., Oreg., 1972—76, Affirmative Action Adv. Com., Lane County, Oreg., 1980—81; bd. dirs. Sign Code Bd. Appeals, Eugene, 1985—87; city commr. Human Rights Commn., Eugene, 1985—87, Cultural Arts Commn., Eugene, 1989—93; com. mem. Joint Soc. Svc. Fund, Lane County, Eugene, Springfield, 1986—88; bd. advisors U. Oreg. Ctr. Asian Pacific Studies, 1998—2000. Fulbright/Smith-Mundt grantee, U.S. Dept. Edn., Manila, 1959, Fulbright grantee, 1960. Mem.: Coun. Filipino Am. Assns. Oreg. (incorporator, trustee 2000—), Asian Am. Found. (founding mem., officer Eugene 1993—), Asian Coun. (founding mem., officer Eugene and Springfield 1985—), Philippine Am. Assn. (founding mem., officer Eugene 1983—). Office: Philippine Trading Co Inc 2092 Roland Way Eugene OR 97401-2061 E-mail: deancollas@aol.com.

COLLATOS, WILLIAM PETER, venture capitalist; b. Boston, May 7, 1954; s. Peter Nicholas and Jacqueline (Archese) C.; m. Linda C. Wisnewski, Oct. 10, 1984; children: Alexis, Adrianne, Caroline. AB in Econs., Harvard Coll. V.p. Fleet Bank, Providence, R.I., 1976-80; gen. ptnr. T A Assocs., Boston, 1980-90, Media Comm. Ptnrs., Boston, 1990—93; co-founder, gen. ptnr. Spectrum Equity Investors, Boston, 1993—. Bd. dirs. Access Television Network, Inc, CBSI, Egenera, Inc., Surebridge, Inc. Bd. dirs. Roxbury Latin and Winsor Schools. Office: Spectrum Equity Investors 1 International Pl Fl 29 Boston MA 02110-2602*

COLLEA, JOSEPH VINCENT, perinatologist, educator; b. Utica, N.Y., Sept. 10, 1940; s. Anthony and Jennie Collea; m. Margaret Elizabeth Collea, Mar. 4, 1974; children: Amy Elizabeth, Lisa Anne, Jennie Louise. AB, Hamilton Coll., 1962; MD, SUNY, Syracuse, 1966. Bd. cert. in maternal-fetal medicine Am. Bd. Ob-Gyn. Instr., resident Johns Hopkins Hosp., Balt., 1966-72; asst. prof. L.A. County-U. So. Calif. Med. Ctr., 1974-79; assoc. prof. Georgetown U., Washington, 1979-91, prof., 1991—. Cons. Matria, Inc., Atlanta, 1998—, Am. Jour. Ob-Gyn., 1978—. Contbr. articles to jours. and textbooks. Maj. U.S. Army, 1972-74. Named Outstanding Citizen of Yr., Health Babies Project, Inc., 1999, one of Best Drs. in Washington, Washington Mag., 1998; N.Y. State Regents scholar, 1958-62. Fellow ACOG; mem. Maternal-Fetal Medicine Soc., Washington Ob-Gyn. Soc., Bethesda Country Club. Office: Georgetown U Dept Ob-Gyn 3800 Reservoir Rd NW Washington DC 20007-2196

COLLEN, JOHN, lawyer, educator; b. Chgo., Dec. 26, 1954; s. Sheldon and Ann Collen; m. Lauren Kay Smulyan, Sept. 20, 1986; children: Joshua, Benjamin, Sarah, Joel. AB summa cum laude, Dartmouth Coll., 1977; JD, Georgetown U., 1980. Bar: Ill. 1980, U.S. Dist. Ct. (no. dist.) Ill. 1980, Trial 1982, U.S. Ct. Appeals (7th cir.) 1984, U.S. Supreme Ct. 1990. Ptnr. Duane Morris, LLP, Chgo. Mem. editl. adv. bd. Jour. Bankruptcy Law and Practice; adj. prof. law St. John's U. Author: Buying and Selling Real Estate in Bankruptcy, 1997; contbr. articles to profl. jours.; lectr. in field. Fellow Am. Coll. Bankruptcy; mem. ABA, Chgo. Bar Assn., Am. Bankruptcy Inst. (co-chmn. com. real estate bankruptcy), Phi Beta Kappa. Avocations: water sports, magic. Office: Duane Morris LLP 227 W Monroe St Chicago IL 60606-5016 Fax: 312-499-6701. Office Phone: 312-499-6700. Business E-Mail: jcollen@duanemorris.com.

COLLEN, MORRIS FRANK, medical association administrator, physician, researcher; b. St. Paul, Nov. 12, 1913; s. Frank Morris and Rose (Finkelstein) Collen; m. Frances B. Diner, Sept. 24, 1937; children: Arnold Roy, Barry Joel, Roberta Joy, Randal Harry. BEE, U. Minn., 1934, MB with distinction, 1938, MD, 1939; DSc (hon.), U. Victoria, B.C., Can., 2004. Diplomate Am. Bd. Internal Medicine. Intern Michael Reese Hosp., Chgo., 1939—40; resident L.A. County Hosp., 1940—42; chief med. service Kaiser Found. Hosp., Oakland, Calif., 1942—52, chief of staff, 1952—53; med. dir. West Bay divsn. Permanente Med. Group, Oakland, 1953—79, dir. med. methods rsch., 1962—79, dir. tech. assessment, 1979—83, cons. divsn. rsch., 1983—. Chmn. exec. com. Permanente Med. Group, Oakland, 1953—73; dir. Permanente Svcs., Inc., Oakland, 1958—73; adj. asst. prof. biomed. informatics Uniformed Svcs. U. Health Scis., 2000—; chmn. health care sys. study sect. USPHS, 1968—72, mem. adv. com. demonstration grants, 1967, advisor VA, 68; mem. adv. com. Automated Multiphasic Health Testing, 1971; discussant Nat. Conf. Preventive Medicine, Bethesda, Md., 1975; mem. com. on tech. in health care NAS, 1976; mem. adv. group Nat. Commn. on Digestive Diseases, U.S. Congress, 1978; mem. adv. panel to U.S. Congress Office of Tech. Assessment, 1980—85; mem. peer rev. adv. group TRIMIS program Dept. Def., 1978—90; program chmn. 3rd Internat. Conf. Med. Informatics, Tokyo, 1980; chmn. bd. sci. counselors Nat. Libr. Medicine, 1985—87, mem. lit. selection tech. rev. com., 1997—2002, chmn., 2000—02; chmn. tech. evaluation group Application of Advanced Network Infrastructure in Health and Disaster Mgmt., 2002, chmn. tech. group, 02; program chmn. Internat. Conf. Health Promotion, Atlanta, 2003; lectr. in field; cons. in field. Author: Treatment of Pneumococcic Pneumonia, 1948, Hospital Computer Systems, 1974, Multiphasic Health Testing Services, 1978, History of Medical Informatics, 1995; editor: Permanente Med. Bull., 1943—53; mem. editl. bd.: Preventive Medicine, 1970—80, Jour. Med. Sys., Methods Info. Medicine, 1980—97, Diagnostic Medicine, 1980—84, Computers in Biomed. Rsch., 1987—94; contbr. articles to profl. jours., chpts. to books. Fellow Ctr. Advanced Studies in Behavioral Scis., Stanford U., 1985—86; scholar Johns Hopkins Centennial scholar, 1976, scholar-in-residence, Nat. Libr. Medicine, 1987—2002. Fellow: ACP, Am. Inst. Med. and Biol. Engring., Am. Coll. Chest Physicians, Am. Coll. Cardiology; mem.: AMA, Salutis Unitas (v.p. 1972), Internat. Health Evaluation Assn. (pres. 1995—96, Morris F. Collen Permanente Rsch. award named in his honor 2003, Lifetime Achievement award 1992, Computers in Health Care Pioneer award 1992, David E. Morgan award for achievement in health care info. 1998, Japan Shigeaki Hinohara award for preventive medicine 2001, Cummings Psyche award for behavioral medical rsch. 2001), Am. Med. Informatics Assn. (bd. dirs. 1985—96), Nat. Acad. Practice in Medicine (chmn. 1982—88, co-chmn. 1989—91), Soc. Adv. Med. Sys. (pres. 1973), Am. Coll. Med. Informatics (pres. 1987—88, Morris F. Collen medal named in his honor 1993), Am. Fedn. Clin. Rsch., Inst. Medicine of NAS (chmn. tech. subcom. for improving patient records 1990, chmn. workshop on informatics in clin. preventive medicine 1991), Internat. Med. Informatics Assn. Sr. Officers Club, Tau Beta Pi, Alpha Omega Alpha. Home: 4155 Walnut Blvd Walnut Creek CA 94596-5834 Office: 2000 Broadway Oakland CA 94612-2304 Personal E-mail: mfcollen@aol.com.

COLLENS, LEWIS MORTON, academic administrator, law educator; b. Chgo., Feb. 10, 1938; m. Marge Collens; 1 child, Steven. BS, U. Ill., Urbana, 1960, MA, 1963; JD, U. Chgo., 1966. Bar: Ill. 1966. Assoc. Ross, Hardies, Chgo., 1966-67; spl. asst. to gen. counsel EEOC, Washington, 1967-68; asst. prof. Ill. Inst. Tech., Chgo. Kent Coll. Law, 1970-72, assoc. prof., 1972-74, prof., 1975—90; dean Coll. Law, Ill. Inst. Tech., 1974-90, pres., 1990—. Bd. dirs. Amsted Industries, Inc., Dean Foods Co., Inc.; trustee Latin Sch. Chgo. Dir. Ill. Coalition; bd. dirs. Alion Sci. and Tech. Mem. ABA, Ill. Bar Assn., Chgo. Bar Assn., Am. Law Inst., Mayors Coun. Tech. Advs., Econ. Club of Chgo. Office: Ill Inst Tech 3300 South Fed St Chicago IL 60616-3793 Office Phone: 312-567-5198.*

COLLET, VICKI S., literature educator; d. Thell James and Kathleen Peck Stewart; m. Dallas M. Collet; children: Chad, Adam, Matt, Sara, Erin. BA in Eng., U. Utah, 1983; MA in Reading, U. No. Colo., 1997. Cert. tchr. Colo., Tex., Utah. Eng. tchr. Galen Park Sch. Dist., Houston, 1983—85; pvt. lit. tchr., 1985—98; kindergarten tchr. Poudre Sch. Dist., Ft. Collins, Colo., 1996—99, lit. tchr., coach, 1999—. Author: Teaching Reading Comprehension, 2002. Pres. Young Women's Org. Ch. Jesus Christ of Latter-Day Saints, Ft. Collins, 2000—. Mem.: Internat. Reading Assn. (pres. Ft. Collins coun. 2003—), Phi Kappa Phi, Phi Eta Sigma. Mem. Lds. Avocations: gardening, reading, writing. Office: Tavelli Elem Sch 1118 Miramont Dr Fort Collins CO 80524 Office Phone: 970-484-8600.

COLLETTE, TONI, actress; b. Sydney, Australia, Nov. 1, 1972; Appeared in films: Efficiency Expert, 1991, Spotswood, 1992, This Marching Girl Thing, 1994, Muriel's Wedding, 1994, Lilian's Story, 1995, Arabian Knight, 1995 (as voice of nurse/good witch), Cosi, 1996, The Pallbearer, 1996, Emma, 1996, The Boys, 1997, Clockwatchers, 1997, The James Gang, 1997, Diana & Me, 1997, Velvet Goldmine, 1998, Hotel Sordide, 1999, Dead by Monday, 1999, 8 1/2 Women, 1999, The Sixth Sense, 1999, Shaft Returns, 2000, Changing Lanes, 2002, About a Boy, 2002, Hotel Splendide, 2000, Dirty Deeds, 2002, The Hours, 2002, Japanese Story, 2003, The Last Shot, 2004; TV appearances include The panel, 1998, Frontline, 1994, Dinner With Friends, 2001. Office: United Talent Agy care Adam Isaacs 9560 Wilshire Blvd Ste 500 Beverly Hills CA 90212-2427

COLLETTI, TERESA ANN, polymer chemist; b. Balt., Aug. 26, 1967; d. John Bruce and Elizabeth Grace (Schmidt) Schott; m. Ronald Francis Colletti, Sept. 23, 1989; children: Christopher Robert, Catherine Anne, Michael Patrick. BS, U. So. Miss., 1989. Chemist, microscopist Monsanto, Pensacola, Fla., 1990-92, process engr., 1992-93, new product engr., 1993-94, process tech. team leader Greenwood, S.C., 1994-96; sr. mktg. tech. svc. specialist Solutia, St. Louis, 1996-99, sr. credit mgr., 1999—2002; practice adminstr. St. Gerard Obstectrics & Gynecology LLC, 2002—. Presenter in field. Contbr. articles to sci. jours. Mem. Am. Chem. Soc. (mem. women chemist com. 1993-94, 95-01, treas. Pensacola sect. 1991-93), Soc. of Plastics Engrs. Home: 257 Harbour Pointe Dr Wildwood MO 63040-1956

COLLEY, DEBRA A., academic administrator; BS summa cum laude, SUNY, Buffalo, 1979, MEd, 1982, PhD, 1987. ESL tchr. Adult Edn. Programs, Nogales, Ariz., 1979, Buffalo, 1979—80; bilingual spl. edn. resource room tchr. Herman Badillo Cmty. Sch., Buffalo, 1979—82; asst. prof., bilingual spl. edn. D'Youville Coll., Buffalo, 1982—86; asst. prof., exceptional edn. dept. N.Y. State Edn. Dept., Buffalo, 1986—88, assoc. in higher edn., 1988—90, coord., program devel. and support svcs., office of vocational and ednl. svcs., 1990—97, adminstr., statewide adminstrn. tchg., office of vocational and ednl. svcs., 1997—. Mem., new student orientation com. D'Youville Coll., Buffalo, 1983, mem., judiciary com., 83, mem., faculty com., 1984—86, mem., discretionary rev. com., 1984, mem., divsnl. personnel com., 1984—86. Contbr. articles to profl. jours. Mem.: Nat. Assn. for Bilingual Edn., Coun. for Exceptional Children, N.Y. State Assn. for Bilingual Edn. (pres. 1987—88, sec. 1983—84, treas. 1984—85, 2d v.p. 1985—86, 1st v.p. 1986—87), Nat. Assn. for Adults with Spl. Learning Needs (sec. 1994—96), Performing and Visual Arts Soc. (hon.), Pi Lambda Theta.

COLLEY, KAREN J., medical educator, researcher; b. Nov. 3, 1958; BS in Chemistry, Duke U., 1981; PhD in Molecular Biology, Washington U., St. Louis, 1987. Postdoctoral fellow dept. biol. chemistry UCLA, 1987—91; postdoctoral fellow NIH, 1990; asst. prof. dept. biochemistry U. Ill., Chgo., 1991—97, assoc. prof., 1997—. Mem. med. adv. bd. Leukemia Rsch. Found., 1994—, reviewer study sect., 1994—; outside reviewer NSF Grants, 1995—, VA Rsch. Grants, 1995—; mem. pathiobiochemistry study sect. NIH, 1998—. Reviewer: Jour. Biol. Chemistry, Jour. Cell Biology, Molecular and Chem. Neuropathology, Jour. Cell Sci., Devel. Biology; contbr. articles to profl. jours.; patentee in field. Recipient Established Investigator award, Am. Heart Assn., 1996; fellow (sr.), Am. Cancer Soc., 1991; grantee, 1992, U. Ill., 1992, 1996, Leukemia Rsch. Found., Inc., 1993. Mem.: AAAS, Soc. Glycobiology, Am. Soc. Biochemistry and Molecular Biology, Am. Soc. Cell Biology, Sigma Xi. Office: U Ill Dept Biochemistry and Molecular Biology 1819 W Polk St Chicago IL 60612-7331

COLLI, BART JOSEPH, lawyer; b. Englewood, NJ, Feb. 13, 1948; s. Bart Joseph and Marie (Burns) C.; m. Mary Ellen Diemer, May 20, 1972; 1 son, Michael John. BA summa cum laude, Fordham Coll., 1968; JD cum laude, Harvard U., 1971. Bar: N.Y. 1972, Tex. 1975, N.J., 1988, Pa. 2002. Assoc. White & Case, N.Y.C., 1971-75; ptnr. Hughes & Luce, Dallas, 1976-85, McCarter & English, L.L.P., Newark, 1985—2000; exec. v.p., gen. counsel, sec. ARAMARK Corp., Phila., 2000—. Judge Entrepreneur of the Yr. awards program, 1993, 95, 96, North Jersey Venture Fairs, 1993, 94, N.J. Family Bus. of Yr. awards program, 1997, 99; lectr. in field; mem. resources com. Edison Partnership Tech.; chmn. 1st annual Mergers and Acquisitions Conf., 1999, spkr. 2d annual Conf.; lectr. in field. Contbr. numerous articles to legal publs. Trustee Tri-County Scholarship Fund, No. N.J. chpt. Leukemia Soc. Am., Inc.; coun. Lincoln Ctr. Bus. Coun. of the Consol. Fund. Capt. M.I., USAR, 1968-76. Mem. ABA (fed. regulation of securities com., sect. on corp.), N.J. State Bar Assn. (securities law com., bus. orgn. com. of the corp. and bus. law sect.), Phi Beta Kappa. Office: ARAMARK Corp ARAMARK Tower 1101 Market St Philadelphia PA 19107-2934 Office Phone: 215-238-6846. Business E-Mail: colli-bart@aramark.com.

COLLIER, ALBERT M., pediatrician, educator, director; b. Elba, Ala., May 3, 1937; s. Milford William and Ida Ruth C.; m. Mary Gaynell Wehler, July 17, 1960; children: Albert Mark, Dennis Murray, Jonathan Lee. BS, U. Miami, 1959, MD, 1963. Pediatric resident U. Miami, Coral Gables, Fla., 1963-66; fellow infectious diseases U. N.C., Chapel Hill, 1968-70, from asst. prof. to assoc. prof., 1971-80, prof., 1980—; chief U. N.C., Divsn. Infectious Disease, Chapel Hill, 1980—2004; assoc. dir. Ctr. Environ. Med. Lung Bio U. N.C., Chapel Hill, 1980—, acting dir. Frank Porter Graham Child Devel. Ctr., 1990-92, assoc. chmn. pediatrics for rsch., 1997—2003, med. sch. sci. integrity officer, 2000—. Contbr. over 100 articles to profl. jours. Recipient Louis Dienes award Internat. Orgn. Mycoplasmology, Vienna, Austria, 1988. Mem. Gideons (zone leader 1990-93). Baptist. Office: U NC Chapel Hill Dept Pediatrics 5135 Bioinformatics Cb 7220 Chapel Hill NC 27599-0001 E-mail: uncacl@med.unc.edu.

COLLIER, ALICE ELIZABETH BECKER, retired social services administrator; b. Akron, Ohio, June 09; d. Christian and Virginia (Schulmeister) Becker; m. John Robert Fenwick, Aug. 28, 1954 (dec. 1980); 1 child, Beth Alice; m. Thomas Collier, Mar. 8, 1980. BA in Edn., Heidelberg Coll., Tiffin, Ohio, 1949; MA in Ednl. Adminstrn., U. Akron, 1968. Cert. tchr., ednl. adminstr., Ohio. Tchr. Air Force Dependent Schs., Fed. Republic Germany and Eng., 1960-64, Akron Pub. Schs., 1964-68, adminstr., 1968-80; dep. mayor City of Akron, 1980-84; pres. Collier Pub. Rels./Mktg., Akron, 1984-86; gen. mgr., broker Coldwell Banker Real Estate, Akron, 1986-90; dir. comms. Area Agy. on Aging, Akron, 1990-94; v.p. Mktg. and Creative Solutions, 1994-97; ret., 1997. Author, editor: (Manual) Visual-Motor Training for the Developmentally Disabled Child, 1972, Different Strokes for Little Folks, 1974. Chmn. adv. coun. U. Akron, 1977-88; mem. Akron Health Commn., 1978-80, Akron Sr. Citizens Commn., 1980—94, Nat. Adv. Coun. on Aging, Bethesda, Md., 1982-84; pres. Tri-County Employee Assistance Program, Summit, Medina and Portage, 1985-97; charter rev. commn. Summit County, 1991; mem. women's adv. coun. Summa Health Sys., 1994—2003; v.p. Women's Network, Akron, 1987-88; trustee Comty. Health Rsch. Group, Inc., 1980—2002, Cuyahoga Falls Gen. Hosp. Found., 1992-2005; pub. rels. chmn. State of Ohio Atty. Gen. Health Info. Com.; trustee No. Ohio Golf Charities Found., Firestone Country Club, 1999—2004, World Series of Golf, Firestone Country Club, 1983—2000; vol. World Golf Championships, 2001—04. Recipient Svc. to Elderly award Am. Gerontol. Soc., 1982, Excellence in Comm. award Nat. Assn. Area Agys. on Aging, 1991. Mem.: AAUW, Akron Bd. Realtors (Salesperson of Yr. award 1988, Hall of Fame award 1988), Ohio Assn. Realtors (trustee 1988—90), Am. Mktg. Assn. (pres. Akron-Canton chpt. 1988—89, Spl. Merit award 1990), Woman's Golf Assn. (treas. 2002—04, pres. 2005—), Akron Women's City Club, Heidelberg Coll. Alumni Assn., Medina Country Club, Mission Valley Country Club (Venice, Fla.), Phi Lambda Theta (founding, charter). Republican. Avocations: church organist, golf, tennis, collecting hummel figurines. Mailing: Beechwood # 11 333 N Portage Path Akron OH 44303-1218 Home (Summer): 255 The Esplanade N Apt 204 Venice FL 34285-1518 Personal E-mail: atcollier4@comcast.net.

COLLIER, BOYD DEAN, finance educator, management consultant; b. Waco, Tex., Jan. 16, 1938; s. Denis Lee and Anne Alice (Berry) C.; m. Barbara Nell Joseph, June 20, 1966; children: Diedra Michelle, Christopher Boyd. BBA, Baylor U., 1963, MS, 1965; PhD, U. Tex., 1970. Diplomate Am. Bd. Forensic Acctg.; CPA, Tex. Asst. prof. U. N.C., Greensboro, 1969—72, asst. dean, 1970—72; assoc. prof. U. Houston, 1972—73; chief ops. auditor Glastron Boat Co., Austin, Tex., 1979; prof. bus. econs., dean Ctr. for Bus. Adminstrn. St. Edward's U., Austin, 1974—83; prof. fin., head dept. acctg. and fin. Tarleton State U., Stephenville, Tex., 1983—96, exec. dir. office planning, evaluation and instrnl. rsch., accreditation liaison officer, 1996—2003. Co-owner Vranich, Collier Co., CPA's, Austin, 1974-83; v.p. fin. Execucom Sys., Austin, 1979; sr. lectr. U. Tex., Austin, 1980-83; compliance officer Tex. A&M U.; bd. dirs. Acctg. Info. Sys., Houston, 1974-78; advisor Office of Atty. Gen., State of Tex., Austin, 1986, Office of Comptr., State of Tex., Austin, 1986. Author: Measurement and Environmental Deterioration, 1971; editl. advisor Jour. Accountancy, NYC, 1982—; contbr. articles to profl. jours. Faculty advisor Coll. Reps. of Tex., Stephenville, 1984-1988. With USN, 1955-59. Fellow Earhart Found., Ann Arbor, Mich., 1963, 68, NSF, Washington, 1966; commd. hon. Surgeon Gen. State Tex., 2004. Mem. AICPA, Nat. Acctg. Assn. (v.p. 1978-83, Outstanding Svc. award 1983, Sargent Americanism award 1989), Am. Acctg. Assn., Tex. Soc. CPA, Southwestern Fin. Assn., U. Tex. Austin Ex-Students Assn. (life), Sigma Xi (pres. Tarleton chpt. 2005—). Liberterian. Avocations: tennis, hiking, collecting coins and walking canes. Home: 930 N Charlotte Ave Stephenville TX 76401-2004 Office: Tarleton State U 1603 W Washington PO Box 505T Stephenville TX 76401-0505 Office Phone: 254-968-9908. Business E-Mail: collier@tarleton.edu.

COLLIER, BRIAN LAMAR, elementary school educator; b. Detroit, Oct. 17, 1976; s. Otto and Linda Ruth Collier; m. Jessielyn Dilla Collier, June 16, 1972. BS in Elem. Edn., U. Dayton, 1999. 2nd grade tchr. Mt. Carmel Sch., Saipan, 1999—2000; grad. level rep. Peralta Elem. Sch., Phoenix, 2003—. Active Big Bros./Big Sisters Ariz.; cmty. svc. Compass Cmty. Ch., Goodyear, Ariz., 2004—05. Scholar, U. Dayton, 1995—99. Avocations: soccer, travel, reading, bicycling, weightlifting, accordion. Office: Cartwright School District 7125 W Encanto Blvd Phoenix AZ 85035 Personal E-mail: bcollier1017@cox.net.

COLLIER, CHARLES ARTHUR, JR., lawyer; b. Columbus, Ohio, Apr. 18, 1930; s. Charles Arthur and Gertrude Clara (Roe) C.; m. Linda Louise Biggs, Aug. 5, 1961; children: Sheila Collier Rogers, Laura Collier Prescott. AB magna cum laude, Harvard U., 1952, LLB, 1955. Law clk. U.S. Dist. Ct. (cen. dist.) Calif., L.A., 1959-60; assoc. Freston & Files, L.A., 1960-66; assoc., ptnr. Mitchell, Silberberg & Knupp, L.A., 1967-82; ptnr. Irell & Manella, L.A., 1982-95, of counsel, 1995—2003; ret., 2003. Lectr. Calif. Continuing Edn. of Bar, 1976-89; advisor Restatement of Property, Donative Transfers, 1990—; speaker numerous local bar assns. Contbr. articles to profl. jours Recipient Arthur K. Marshall award Probate and Trust sect. L.A. County Bar Assn. Fellow Am. Coll. Trust and Estate Counsel (chmn. state laws com. 1986-89, regent 1989-98, joint editl. bd. uniform trust and estate acts, 1988—, chmn. expanded practice com. 1989-92, chmn. nominating com. 1998-99, spkr. 1988, exec. com. 1989-98, treas. 1992-93, sec. 1993-94, v.p. 1994-95, pres.-elect 1995-96, pres. 1996-97, immediate past pres. 1997-98), ABA Found.; mem. ABA (mem. real property, trust and probate law sect. spkr. 1985, 89, moderator teleconf. 1998, coun. 1989-93, chmn. com. trust adminstrn. 1982-85, chmn. task force on fiduciary litigation 1986-89, sr. lawyers divsn., vice chair wills, probate and trusts com. 1999-2000, chair 2000-2001, vice chair book pub. com. 2000-2002, chair editl. bd. 2001—, sec. 2005—, others), Estate Planning, Trust and Probate Law Sect. of State Bar Calif. (chmn. 1980-81, vice chmn. 1979-80, mem. exec. com. 1977-82, advisor 1982-85, chmn. probate com. 1977-78, mem. legislation com. 1977-80, sect. liaison to Calif. Law Revision Commn. 1982-88), Harvard Alumni Assn. (dir. 1975-77, v.p. 1979-82), Harvard Club So. Calif. (pres. 1970-72) Republican. Office: Irell & Manella LLP 1800 Ave Of Stars Ste 900 Los Angeles CA 90067-4276 Business E-Mail: ccollier@irell.com.

COLLIER, CINDY EDDINS, management consultant; b. Galax, Va. d. William George and Tommye Eddins; m. David Alan Collier, June 5, 1983. BA in Psychology, U. Va., 1979, MS in Acctg., 1986; M in Health Adminstrn., Duke U., 1981. CPA, Ohio; cert. valuation analyst. Planner U. Va. Med. Ctr., Charlottesville, 1981-84; tax acct. Salley, Weissinger and Co., Charlottesville, 1985-86; healthcare fin. mgmt. cons. Coopers & Lybrand, Columbus, Ohio, 1986-88; CEO Quality Mgmt. Solutions, Columbus, 1988—. V.p. physician svcs. Ctr. Healthcare Industry Performance Studies, 1996; adj. prof. Ohio State U., 1997-99, Franklin U., Columbus, 1997-99, Duke U. Fuqua Sch. Bus., Durham, N.C., 1999—; lectr. Duke U. Med. Sch., 2000-01; mem. adv.

bd. dirs. Ibbotson Assocs; vis. scholar Ohio State U. Fisher Coll. Bus., Columbus, 1997—. Contbr. articles to profl. jours. Adv. bd. dirs. Price Waterhouse Coopers Alumni, 1996—. Named Outstanding Young Career Woman, Charlottesville Bus. and Profl. Women's Club, 1981; Sam Walton fellow Ohio State U., 1999-2001. Mem. AICPA (nat. faculty, bd. dirs. 1997—), Nat. Assn. Cert. Valuation Analysts (cert.; mem. faculty 1997, bd. dirs. 1997—), U. Va. Alumni Assn. Ctrl. Ohio (pres.), Duke U. Alumni Coun. Avocations: travel, participating in community activities. Office: 1354 Hickory Ridge Ln Columbus OH 43235-1131

COLLIER, DAVID, political science professor; b. Chgo., Feb. 17, 1942; s. Donald and Malcolm (Carr) C.; m. Ruth Berins, Mar. 10, 1968; children: Stephen, Jennifer. BA, Harvard U., 1965; MA, U. Chgo., 1967, PhD, 1971. From instr. to assoc. prof. Ind. U., Bloomington, 1970-78; from assoc. prof. to prof. U. Calif., Berkeley, 1978—, chmn. dept. polit. sci., 1990-93. Faculty fellow U. Notre Dame, 1986, 87; vis. prof. U. Chgo., 1989; chmn. Ctr. for Latin Am. Studies U. Calif., Berkeley, 1980-83; co-dir., co-founder Stanford-Berkeley Joint Ctr. for Latin Am. Studies, 1981-83, founding transitional pres. qualitative methods sect., 2002-03 Author: Squatters and Oligarchs: Authoritarian Rule and Policy Change in Peru, 1976; co-author: Shaping the Political Arena, 1991 (Prize, Best Book on Comparative Politics Am. Polit. Scis. Assn. 1993—), Rethinking Social Inquiry, 2004 (Best Book award Am. Polit. Sci. Assn.); co-author, editor: The New Authoritariansim in Latin America, 1979; contbr. articles to profl. jours. Fellow Social Sci. Rsch. Coun. and Am. Coun. Learned Socs., 1974-75, 79-80, 88-89, Guggenheim Found., 1988-89, Ctr. for Advanced Studies in Behavioral Scis., Stanford, 1994-95; grantee NSF 1975-77, 80-83 Fellow: Am. Acad. Arts and Sci.; mem.: Latin Am. Studies Assn., Am. Polit. Sci. Assn. (pres. comparative politics sect. 1997, founding transitional pres. qualitative methods sect. 2002—03, Best Book Qualitative Methods prize). Office: Univ Calif Dept Polit Sci 210 Barrows Hall Berkeley CA 94720-1950

COLLIER, DAVID ALAN, management educator; b. Lexington, Ky., Aug. 3, 1947; s. J. Hamlet Jr. and Dorothy (Gifford) C.; m. Cindy Eddins, June 5, 1983; children: Christopher David, Thomas Andrew. BSME, U. Ky., 1970, MBA, 1972; PhD, Ohio State U., 1978. Materials mgr. Babcock & Wilcox Co., Barberton, Ohio, 1972-74; asst. prof. mgmt. Duke U., Durham, N.C., 1978-81; assoc. prof. U. Va., Charlottesville, 1981-86; prof. Ohio State U., Columbus, 1986—. Cons. numerous corp. exec. programs, 1980—; mem. bd. examiners Malcolm Baldrige Nat. Quality Award, 1991, 92. Author: Service Management: Automation of Services, 1985 (Freedom Found. for Econ. Excellence award, 1985), Service Management: Operating Decisions, 1987, The Service/Quality Solution, 1994, Operations Management: Goods, Services and Value Chains, 2005; contbr. over 50 articles to profl. jours. (numerous awards). Ameritech Faculty fellow, 1989, U. Warwick Vis. Faculty fellow, 1995. Mem. Am. Soc. Quality Control, Decision Scis. Inst., Sigma Alpha Epsilon. Home: 1354 Hickory Ridge Ln Columbus OH 43235-1131 Office: Ohio State U 2100 Neil Ave Columbus OH 43210-1144 Office Phone: 614-292-8305. Business E-Mail: collier.4@osu.edu.

COLLIER, DUAINE ALDEN, manufacturing and distribution company executive; b. Chambersburg, Pa., Aug. 19, 1950; s. Clyde Alden and Etta Jean (Browell) C.; m. Trudy Jean Shoap, Aug. 22, 1970; children: Patrick, Crystal. BS in Math., Shippensburg U., 1972. Product specialist ITT Domestic Pump, Shippensburg, 1972-77; pres., CEO College Town, Inc., Shippensburg, 1971—; gen. mgr. Shippensburg Pump Co., Inc., 1985—. Bd. dirs., sec.-treas. Beidel Printing House, Inc., Shippensburg, 1975—, White Mane Pub. Co., Inc., Shippensburg, 1987—. Committeeman Franklin County Rep. Party, 1989-92; pres. Shippensburg Area Devel. Corp., 1983-84, bd. dirs., 1982-84; bd. dirs. Shippensburg Midget Football Assn., Inc., coach, 1984-94, head coach, 1991-94; pres. Maroon & Grey Football Club, 1991-94; bd. dirs. Shippensburg U. Found., 1995—; bd. dirs., pres. Shippen Place, Inc., 1996-99; mem. adv. bd. Orrstown Bank, 1998—; v.p. Main St. Nonprofit Redevel. Corp. Mem. Harrisburg Regional C. of C. (bd. dirs. 2000—), The Wednesday Club, Masons (master Orrstown lodge 1979), Shippensburg Lions Club (pres. 1989-90), Sons of the Am. Legion. Methodist. Avocations: hunting, fishing, skiing, photography, painting. Office: College Town Inc PO Box 337 17 W Burd St Shippensburg PA 17257-1223

COLLIER, HERMAN EDWARD, JR., retired college president; b. St. Louis, Aug. 8, 1927; s. Herman E. and Evelyn (Saville) C.; m. Jerline L. Weston, Mar. 25, 1948; children: Herman Edward III, Michael F., Thomas W. BS, Randolph-Macon Coll., 1950, Sc.D., 1977; MS, Lehigh U., 1952, PhD, 1955, LL.D., 1971; Litt.D., Coll. of Charleston, 1976; LHD, Muhlenberg Coll., 1986, Moravian Coll., 1987. Chmn. dept. chemistry Moravian Coll., 1955-57; research chemist E. I. duPont de Nemours Co., Wilmington, Del., 1957-63; prof. chemistry, chmn. div. natural scis. Moravian Coll., 1963-69, pres., 1969-86; pres., dir. I&I Planning Assocs., 1987—89; interim pres. Salem Acad. and Coll., 1991, N.C., Wesleyan Coll., 1994-95, Chowan Coll., 1995-96, Lees-McRae Coll., 1997-98. Sr. cons. Acad. Search Consultation Svc., 1998—; bd. dirs. Horizon Health Sys. Inc., First Health Found., 2003-; cons. sci. adv. bd. EPA, 1979-85; chmn. Commn. Ind. Colls. and Univs. Pa.; bd. dirs. Bethlehem Steel Corp., 1987-95. Patentee mfg. tech. and product quality organo-lead compounds; sodium tetraphenyl boron for potassium detection; periodic table for lecture room, 1953; flame spectra Metallic ions from the H-F Flame, 1957. Mem. Com. to Employ the Handicapped, 1970-75; mem. Northampton County Citizens for Regional Progress; bd. dirs. United Fund Bethlehem, Hist. Bethlhem, Inc., Moravian Music Found., 1992-94, Roanoke Island Hist. Assn., Inc., 1996—98; trustee St. Luke's Hosp., R.K. Laros Found., Moravian Acad., Salem Acad. & Coll., 1995—. With USN, 1945-46. Mem. Lehigh Valley Assn. Ind. Colls. (dir.), Am. Chem. Soc., AAUP, Lehigh Valley Automobile Assn. (dir. 1981-86), Bethlehem C. of C. (dir.), Phi Beta Kappa, Sigma Xi, Omicron Delta Kappa, Kappa Alpha. Personal E-mail: hcollier2@earthlink.net.

COLLIER, JAMES WARREN, lawyer; b. Dallas, July 31, 1940; s. J.W. and Mary Gertrude (Roberts) C.; m. Judith Lane, Dec. 27, 1964; children: Anne Elizabeth, Jennifer Susan. BA, U. Mich., 1962, JD, 1965. Bar: N.Y. 1966, Mich. 1968. Assoc. Simpson Thacher & Bartlett, N.Y.C., 1965-66; tax atty. office gen. counsel Ford Motor Co., 1966-67; assoc. Dykema Gossett, Detroit, 1967-73, ptnr., 1973—. Mem. Dykema Gossett. Mem. Mich. Bar Assn., Econ. Club Detroit, Lochmoor Club. Office: Dykema Gossett 400 Renaissance Ctr # 3500 Detroit MI 48243-1603 E-mail: jcollier@dykema.com.

COLLIER, NATHAN MORRIS, musician, educator; b. Clinton, Okla., July 23, 1924; s. Lotan Morris and Annie Carlletta (Willsey) C.; m. Frances Aleta Snell, June 24, 1955; children: Susan Aleta Kowalski, Ray Morris. MusB, U. Okla., 1949; MusM, U. Rochester, 1951. String music cons. Lincoln (Nebr.) Pub. Schs., 1951-68; asst. concertmaster Lincoln Symphony Orch., 1953-2001; 1st violinist Lincoln String Quartet, Nebr., 1955—; first violin Omaha (Nebr.) Symphony, The Nebr. Sinfonia, 1956-79; asst. prof. violin, theory Nebr. Wesleyan U., Lincoln, 1968-84; asst. concertmaster Nebr. Chamber Orch., 1973-91; assoc. concertmaster Omaha (Nebr.) Symphony, The Nebr. Sinfonia, 1977-78; concertmaster Lincoln Symphony, Lincoln Little Symphony, 1977-78; acting concertmaster Omaha (Nebr.) Symphony, The Nebr. Sinfonia, 1978; prin. second violinist Des Moines Symphony, 1979—; asst prof. music, condr. symphony orch. Kans. State U., Manhattan, 1980-81, pvt. tchr., 1st violinist Resident String Quartet, 1980-81; string tchr. St. John Luth. Sch., Seward, Nebr., 1983-89; acting concertmaster on occasion Nebr. Chamber Orch.; concertmaster Omaha Pops Orch., 1988-90; 1st violinist Avanti String Quartet, 1990; sect. I violinist Nebr. Symphony Chamber Orch., 1995—. Vis. instr. music Concordia U., Seward, 1985, 90; 1st violinist Lincoln String Quartet, 1951—; guest prin. violinist Des Moines Symphony, 1979, 87; guest violinist, violist Myron Cohen Met. and the Midlands String Quartets, Omaha, 1988—, Hastings (Nebr.) Symphony, 1990—; concertmaster and solo violinist with Collegium Musicum Concordia, 1999—; viola instr. chamber music coach summer course U. Nebr., Lincoln, 1991; concertmaster, soloist Nebr. Camerata-Orch. Berlin tour, 1992; mem. adv. bd. Rocky Ridge Music Ctr., 1972; cons., lectr. in field. Composer various mus. pieces; arranger numerous compositions for string quartet, 1980. Tchr., co-organizer Brownville (Nebr.) Summer Music Festival, 1972-77. With USN, 1943-46. Grantee U.S. Govt., 1966; inducted into Nebr. Music Educators Hall of Fame, 2002. Mem. NEA, Am. String Tchrs. assn. (Nebr. Pvt. Studio Tchr. of Yr. 1994), Music Tchrs. Nat. Assn. (nationally cert. 1994—), Music Educators Nat. Conf., Violin Soc. Am., Chamber Music Am., Lincoln Music Tchrs. Assn., Nat. Sch. Orch. Assn., Nebr. Music Tchrs. Assn. (Music Tchr. of Yr. 2003), Nebr. State Edn. Assn., Lincoln Musicians Assn., Omaha Musicians Assn., Lincoln Arts Coun. (co-recipient Lincoln Mayor's Arts award 1995), Pi Kappa Lambda. Democrat. Methodist. Home: 4544 Mohawk St Lincoln NE 68510-4838 Office Phone: 402-488-4721. E-mail: acorelli@aol.com.

COLLIER, R(OBERT) JOHN, biomedical researcher, dean; b. Wichita Falls, Tex., Aug. 6, 1938; s. Eric Knox and Julia (Spearman) C.; m. Joan McCarthy, June 23, 1962; children: Andree, Erin, Brittany. BA in Biology, Rice U., 1959; PhD in Biology, Harvard U., 1964. Postdoctoral fellow Molecular Biology Inst., Geneva, 1964-66; asst. prof. bacteriology UCLA, 1966-70, assoc. prof. bacteriology, 1970-74, prof. microbiology, 1974-84; prof. microbiology and molecular genetics Harvard Med. Sch., Boston, 1984-88, faculty dean for grad. edn., 1988-94, Maude and Lillian Presley prof. microbiology and molecular genetics, 1989—. DuPont lectr. Harvard U., 1981; chmn. Gordon Conf., Microbial Toxins and Pathogenicity, 1982; cons. Cetus Corp., Berkeley, 1989-93, Virus Rsch. Inst., 1992—. Mem. editl. bd. Infection and Immunity, Molecular Microbiology, Microbiol. Revs.; assoc. editor Protein Sci., 1995—. Guggenheim fellow, 1973-74; recipient Eli Lilly award, 1972, co-recipient Pierce Immunotoxin award, 1988, Paul Ehrlich prize, 1990. Mem. NAS (Selman A. Waksman award in microbiology 1999), Am. Acad. Arts & Scis., Am. Field Svcs. (treas. local chpt. 1986-90), Norwegian Acad. Scis. and Letters, Phi Beta Kappa. Office: Harvard Med Sch Dept Microbiol/Molec Genet 200 Longwood Ave Boston MA 02115-5701 E-mail: jcollier@hms.harvard.edu.

COLLIER, SIMON, history educator; b. Harpenden, Eng., June 6, 1938; came to U.S., 1991; s. Daniel Henry and Margery Kate (Winter) C. BA, Cambridge (Eng.) U., 1961, PhD, 1965. Prof. history U. Essex, Colchester, Eng., 1965-91, Vanderbilt U., Nashville, 1991—. Author: Ideas and Politics of Chilean Independence, 1967, From Cortes to Castro, 1974, The Life, Music and Times of Carlos Gardel, 1985; co-editor: Cambridge Encyclopedia of Latin America, 1985, Mining in Chile's Norte Chico, 1998; co-author: Tango, 1995, A History of Chile, 1808-1994, 1996, Le Grand Tango, The Life and Music of Astor Piazzolla, 2000. Decorated comendador Order of Bernardo O'Higgins (Chile). Mem. Chilean Acad. History (corr. academician), Buenos Aires Lunfardo Acad. (corr. academician), Nat. Acad. of Tango (corr. academician), Chilean Soc. for History and Geography (corr.). Avocations: music, literature. Office: Vanderbilt U VU Sta B 350002 Nashville TN 37235-0002 Home: VU Station B-351802 Nashville TN 37235

COLLIER, TOM WARD, musician, educator; b. Puyallup, Wash., June 30, 1948; s. Ward L. and Ethel M. (Turner) Collier; m. Cheryl Anne Zilbert, May 31, 1970; children: Cara, Nina. BA, MusB, U. Wash., 1971. Freelance musician Seattle Symphony/N.W. Chamber Orch., 1967-74; drummer, vibraphonist Northwest Jazz Quintet, Seattle, 1972-80; studio musician various artists and shows including Barbra Streisand, Ry Cooder, American Music Awards, Harry O., LA, 1975-78; timpanist LA Repertoire Orch., 1976-77; jazz drummer Howard Roberts Quartet/Bill Smith Trio, LA, Seattle, 1975-82; freelance percussionist various artists including Johnny Mathis, Paul Williams, Jermaine Jackson, Sammy Davis Jr., Bob Hope, Barbra Streisand, Ry Cooder, Olivia Newton-John, The Beach Boys, Bud Shank, Earl "Fatha" Hines, Diane Schurr, LA, Seattle, 1976-91; jazz vibraphonist Collier/Dean Duo, Seattle, 1977—; rec. artist, leader band Tom Collier, Seattle, 1987—; faculty, dir. percussion studies U. Wash., Seattle, 1980—, dir. Jazz Inst., 1989—, sound prodn. evening degree adv. bd. dirs., 1994-2000, dir. jazz studies, 2001—04, adv. bd. dirs. Songwriting Cert. program, 2004—. Leader Tom Collier Duo/Trio Wash. State Arts Commn. Cultural Enrichment Program, 1980—95, Arts Edn. Program, 1996—2001; owner Mallet Head Music, 1979—, T.C. Records, 1987—91; dir. N.W. Percussion Inst., Seattle; acad. cons. Experience Music Project Mus., Seattle, 1990—2000; music amb. tour of Western Japan, 2005. Musician: (albums) Whistling Midgets, 1981, Illusion, 1987, Pacific Aire, 1991, Mallet Jazz, 2004, Duets, 2005; author: Jazz Improvisation and Ear Training, 1983, rev. edit., 2003, Studio Call Simulated Recording Sessions, 1984, History of Jazz, Lecture Notes, Overheads and Listening Examples, 1997; composer: Quintet for Percussion Ensemble, 1972, Xenolith for Jazz Quartet and String Quartet, 1973, Piece for Electric Bass, Vibraphone and Orch., 1979, Nina's Joy, Busy Body, Tightwad, Subito Sox, 1991; musician: with Larry Coryell, Buddy DeFranco, Eddie Daniels, Emil Richards, 1975—2000, (film soundtrack) with John Williams, Oliver Nelson, Kim Richmond, Henry Mancini; world premier performance of own composition: Three Movements for Solo Marimba, 2000, pub.: Bar Code, Springtide, Day In, Day Out, Studio 4 Music Pub. Bd. dirs. S. Ctrl. Sch. Dist., Seattle, 1987—91; mem. arts adv. bd. Fed. Way Sch. Dist., 1992—94. Rockefeller Rsch. grantee, U. Wash., 1967—71, Royalty Rsch. Fund grantee, 2003. Mem.: ASCAP (Spl. award 1981—97), Music Educators Nat. Conf. (faculty advisor 1986—88), Nat. Assn. Jazz Educators (Outstanding Svc. award 1980), Percussive Arts Soc., Musicians Union. Office: U Wash Sch Music 353450 Seattle WA 98195-0001 Business E-Mail: tomcollier@tomcolliervibes.com.

COLLIER, WILLIAM GAYLE, psychology professor, researcher; b. Albuquerque, July 31, 1970; s. William Robert and Judith Church Collier. BS in Psychology, Okla. Christian U., 1992; MA in Exptl. Psychology, U. Ctrl. Okla., 1994; MS in Exptl. Psychology, Tex. Christian U., 1997, PhD in Gen. Exptl. Psychology, 1998. Grad. asst. Multimedia Ctr., Coll. Edn., U. Ctrl. Okla., Edmond, 1994; dep. asst. dept. psychology Tex. Christian U., Ft. Worth, 1995-96, acad. tutor athletic dept., 1997-98, dep. asst. dept. psychology, 1998; lectr. psychology U. Tex., Tyler, 1998-99, vis. asst. prof., 1999—2002; asst. prof cognitive psychology U. N.C., Pembroke, 2002—, undergrad. student advisor dept. psychology, 2003—. Undergrad. student advisor dept. psychology U. Tex., Tyler, 1999-2002. Author poetry; contbr. articles to profl. jours. Mem.: Soc. Edn., Music and Psychology Rsch., Southwestern Psychol. Assn., Am. Psychol. Soc., European Soc. Cognitive Scis. Music (assoc.; affiliate mem.), Psi Chi, Alpha Chi. Avocations: science fiction, history, poetry, music, theater. Office Phone: 910-521-6458. E-mail: william.collier@uncp.edu.

COLLIER-EVANS, DEMETRA FRANCES, veterans benefits counselor; b. Nashville, Dec. 18, 1937; d. Oscar Collier and Earlee Elizabeth (Williams) Collier-Sheffield; m. George Perry Evans, Dec. 21, 1966; 1 child, Richard Edward. AA in Social Sci., Solano C.C., Suisun City, Calif., 1974; BA in Social Sci., Chapman Coll., Orange, Calif., 1981. Cert. tchr., Calif. Specialist placement, case responsible person employment devel. dept. City of San Diego, 1975-82; vocat. tchr. San Diego Community Coll., 1982-83; specialist placement N.J. Job Service, Camden, 1984-86, mgr. job bank, 1985; specialist placement Abilities Ctr., Westville, N.J., 1987-88; veteran's benifits counselor VA, Phila. 1988-2000, ret., 2000; mem. bd. dirs. Welfare Rights; cons. Bumble Bee Canning Co., San Diego, 1982; developer women's seminar Women's Opportunity Week, City of San Diego, 1982, network seminar Fed. Women's Week, City of Phila., 1986. Bd. dirs. Welfare Rights Orgn., San Diego, 1982; mem. Internat. YWCA. Served with USAF, 1956-59. Recipient Excellence cert. San Diego Employer Adv. Bd., 1981, Leadership cert. Nat. U., San Diego, 1981. Mem. AAUW, NAACP (life, rec. sec. San Diego 1982), Black Advs. State Svc. (charter, corr. sec. San Diego Chpt. 1981-82), Nat. Assn. Female Execs., Am. Fedn. Govt. Employees (officer of yr. award 1999), Bonton Club (svc. award 1998), Chapman Coll. Alumni Assn., Alpha Gamma Sigma. Democrat. Avocation: calligraphy. Office: PO Box 5015 Cherry Hill NJ 08034-0391

COLLIER-HORN, MARY ELIZA, literature and language educator; b. Binghamton, N.Y., May 6, 1952; d. Glenn Edgar Richardson Jr. and Virginia Margaret Weller; m. William Leon Horn, Aug. 3, 2002; m. Johnny (Jake) Clifford Collier, Jr., Feb. 14, 1981 (div. June 9, 1999); children: Carrie Ann Stevens, Johnny Clifford Collier III, James Leonard Harvey Collier, Jacob William Collier. BA cum laude, Alderson-Broaddus Coll., Philippi, W.Va., 1974; MA summa cum laude, Western Mich. U., Kalamazoo, 1991. Cert. in Choice Theory/Reality therapy William Glasser Inst., 1992. Math tchr. Comstock NE Mid. Sch., Mich., 1974—80; Tupperware sales mgr. Gay-La Sales Distributorship, Jackson, Mich., 1979—83; day care provider Delton, Mich., 1985—89; English tchr. Delton Kellogg HS, 1989—; chairperson English dept. Delton Kellogg Schs., driver's training instr., 1998—2000. Actor: (plays) The Taming of the Shrew, The Oldest Profession, The Ladies of the Corridor, Elizabeth Rex. Back stage crew Kalamazoo Civic Theatre, 2003—05; campaign worker McGovern Presdl. Campaign, Washington, 1971—72, Howard Wolpe campaign, Kalamazoo, 1991—93. Mem.: NEA. Independent. Protestant. Avocations: Shakespeare, acting, travel, reading. Home: 13153 Gurd Rd Delton MI 49046-9670 Office: Delton Kellogg HS 327 N Grove St Delton MI 49046 Office Phone: 269-623-9200. Office Fax: 269-623-9292. Personal E-mail: mec5652@aol.com. E-mail: mcollier@dkschools.org.

COLLIGAN, ED, computer company executive, communications executive; Bachelor Degree, U. Oreg. V.p., strategic and product marketing Radius Corp.; v.p. marketing Palm. Inc.; former pres., COO Handspring, Inc. (acquired by palmOne, Inc. in 2003), 1998—2003; sr. v.p., gen. mgr., Wireless Bus. Unit palmOne, Inc., 2003—04, pres. Milpitas, Calif., 2004—, interim CEO, 2005, CEO, 2005—. Office: palmOne Inc 400 N McCarthy Blvd Milpitas CA 95035 Office Phone: 408-503-7000.*

COLLIGAN, JOHN ALOYSIUS, music director, composer; b. Scranton, Pa., Mar. 24, 1955; s. John Aloysius and Mary Clare (Mullaney) Colligan. AB, Notre Dame U., 1978; MusM, U. Cin., 1983. Cert. in montessori Coll. New Rochelle, 1984, in Kodaly method NYU, 1996. Asst. tchr. Whitby Sch., Greenwich, Conn., 1981—85; music dir. St. Theresa Parish, South Ozone Park, NY, 1985—89, Holy Family Parish, Flushing, NY, 1989—92, Holy Cross Parish, NYC, 1992—96; music tchr. Hunter Coll. Elem. Sch., NYC, 1996—98; chmn. music dept. St. Hilda's and St. Hugh's Sch., NYC, 1998—. Bd. dirs. Storytelling Ctr., NYC. Composer: Now I Walk in Beauty, 1997; composer: (with others) (CD) A Pocketful of Music, 2003. Mem.: Am. Composer's Forum. Democrat. Roman Catholic. Avocations: swimming, poetry. Home: 130 W 71 St Apt 1 New York NY 10023 Office: St Hilda's and St Hugh's Sch 619 W 114 St New York NY 10025 Office Phone: 212-932-1980 ext 138. Personal E-mail: colliganjohn@hotmail.com.

COLLIN, THOMAS JAMES, lawyer; b. Windom, Minn., Jan. 6, 1949; s. Everett Earl and Genevieve May (Wilson) C.; m. Victoria Gatov, Oct. 11, 1985; children: Arielle, Elise, Sarah. BA, U. Minn., 1970; AM, Harvard U., 1972; JD, Georgetown U., 1974. Bar: Ohio 1975, U.S. Dist. Ct. (no. dist.) Ohio 1975, U.S. Ct. Appeals (10th cir.) 1977, U.S. Supreme Ct. 1980, U.S. Ct. Appeals (6th cir.) 1981, U.S. Ct. Appeals (8th cir.) 1982, U.S. Ct. Appeals (7th cir.) 1997, U.S. Ct. Appeals (11th cir.) 1999. Law clk. to Judge Myron Bright U.S. Ct. Appeals, 8th Cir., St. Louis, 1974-75; assoc. Thompson, Hine LLP, Cleve., 1975-82, ptnr., 1982—. Author: Ohio Business Competition Law, 1994, (with others) Criminal Antitrust Litigation Manual, 1983; editor: Punitive Damages and Business Torts: A Practitioner's Handbook, 1998; contbr. articles to profl. jours. Active Citizens League, Cleve., bd. trustees, 1994-99, v.p., 1995-97, pres. 1997-99; bd. trustees Citizens League Rsch. Inst., Cleve., 1999-2002. Mem. ABA (chair bus. torts and unfair competition com. antitrust sect. 1995-98, chair annual mtg. com. 2001-02, chmn. distbn. and franchising com. 2002-), Ohio State Bar Assn. (bd. govs. antitrust sect. 1988-98). Republican. Avocations: book collecting, music. Home: 7879 Oakhurst Dr Cleveland OH 44141-1123 Office: Thompson Hine LLP 127 Public Sq Cleveland OH 44114-1216

COLLINGS, ROBERT BIDDLECOMBE, judge; b. Aug. 31, 1942; s. Harry Biddlecombe and Juanita Beatrice (Huber) C.; m. Mary Clare Flintoft, Sept. 14, 1968; children: John Richard Biddlecombe, Christopher James More, Clare Yung Hee. AB, Hamilton Coll., 1964; JD, Harvard U., 1967. Bar: Mass. 1968, N.H. 1970, U.S. Ct. Mil. Appeals 1970, U.S. Dist. Ct. Mass. 1971, U.S. Ct. Appeals (1st cir.) 1971, U.S. Ct. Appeals (5th cir.) 1979, Temporary Emergency Ct. Appeals 1980. Asst. U.S. atty. Dept. Justice, Boston, 1971-82, chief criminal divsn., 1976-82, 1st asst. U.S. atty., 1978-81; U.S. magistrate judge U.S. Dist. Ct., Boston, 1982—, chief magistrate judge, 1999—2001. Lectr. law Harvard Law Sch., 1988—92, Northeastern U. Sch. Law, 1989—90; guest lectr. Stanford Law Sch., 2000—; mem. Magistrate Judge Ednl. Com. of Fed. Jud. Ctr., 1990—96, Def. Svcs. Com. Jud. Conf. U.S., 1991—97; mem. joint adv. group Adminstrv. Office of U.S. Cts., 1998—2000; mem. Fed. Jud. Ctr. Bd., 2001—05. Co-editor: Federal Court Civil Litigation in the First Circuit, 1994. Lt. USNR, 1967-71. Mem. ABA (chair magistrate judges' com. nat. conf. fed. trial judges 1999-2000, exec. com. 2000-02, sec. 2002-03, vice-chmn. 2003-04, chair elect 2004-05, chair 2005—), Nat. Coun. U.S. Magistrates (treas. 1990-91), Fed. Magistrate Judges Assn. (2d v.p. 1991-92, 1st v.p. 1992-93, pres.-elect 1993-94, pres. 1994-95, past pres. 1995-96, legis. chmn. 1995—, Founders award 1998), Mass. Bar Assn., Boston Bar Assn. Office: US Courthouse 1 Courthouse Way Ste 7420 Boston MA 02210-3002 Office Phone: 617-748-9228. Business E-Mail: honorable_robert_collings@mad.uscourts.gov.

COLLINGS, ROBERT L., lawyer; b. May 22, 1950; AB, Harvard U., 1972; JD, Boston Coll., 1977. Bar: Pa. 1977, U.S. Ct. Appeals (D.C. cir.) 1981, U.S. Dist. Ct. (ea. dist.) Pa. 1985, U.S. Ct. Appeals (3d cir.) 1984, U.S. Dist. Ct. (mid. dist.) 1992. Atty. U.S. EPA, 1977-84, sect. chief, 1979—81, br. chief, 1981-84; ptnr. Morgan, Lewis & Bockius LLP, 1984—98, Schnader, Harrison, Segal & Lewis LLP, Phila., 1998—, mem. exec. com., 2003—. Editor: Environmental Spill Reporting Handbook; contbr. Municipal Solicitors Handbook, 1994, 1999, 2003, Brownfields: A Comprehensive Guide, 1997, 2d edit., 2002. Bd. dirs. Pa. Environ. Coun., 2003. Mem. ABA (vice chair enforcement com. sect. environment, energy and resources 2003), Phila. Bar Assn. (chair environ. law com. 1986), Water Resources Assn. (sec. exec. com. 1990—). Office: Schnader Harrison Segal & Lewis LLP 1600 Market St Ste 3600 Philadelphia PA 19103-7287 Office Phone: 215-751-2074. E-mail: rcollings@schnader.com.

COLLINS, ADRIANA DELIA, banker; b. 1953; 1 child, Domenique Mara. BA in Social Sci., Fordham U., 1974; MPA in Internat. Devel., NYU, 1980. Mgmt. cons. FR Schwab & Assoc., N.Y.C., 1980-82; dir. econ. and rsch. N.Y. State Bankers Assn., N.Y.C., 1982-86; fin. acctg. officer Chem. Bank, N.Y.C., 1986-88; v.p. structured and corp. fin. Bank Austria, N.Y.C., 1988-92; sr. asst. mgr. loans/bus. devel. PT Bank Bumi Daya Indonesia, N.Y.C., 1992-95; v.p. HSBC Bank USA, N.Y.C., 1995—. Mem. NYU Mentor Program, 1993; cons. Jr. Achievement. Contbr. articles to profl. jours. Lifetime mem. Girl Scouts U.S. Mem. Fordham Alumni Student Team, Beach Club Brands. Avocations: running, skiing, travel, kayaking. Office: 452 5th Ave Fl 4 New York NY 10018-2333 Office Phone: 212-525-2536. E-mail: tanahlot96@aol.com.

COLLINS, ALLAN MEAKIN, education educator; b. Orange, N.J., Aug. 7, 1937; s. Clinton and Sarah Amy (Meakin) C.; m. Anne Marjorie Linstead, Aug. 24, 1963; children: Antony, Elizabeth. MA in Comm. Scis., U. Mich., 1962, PhD in Psychology, 1970. Sr. scientist Bolt, Beranek & Newman Inc., Cambridge, 1967-82, prin. scientist, 1982-2000; prof edn. and social policy Northwestern U., Evanston, Ill., 1989—2005; vis. sr. lectr. Harvard Grad. Sch. Edn., 2005—; co-dir. Ctr. for Tech. in Edn., Bank St. Coll. of Edn., N.Y.C., 1991-94; rsch. prof. of edn. Boston Coll., 1998—2002. Lectr. various colls. and univs. Editor: Representation and Understanding, 1975, Cognitive Science, 1976-80, Readings in Cognitive Science, 1988; author: The Cognitive Structure of Emotions, 1988. Guggenheim fellow, 1974, Sloan fellow, 1980. Fellow AAAS; mem. Nat. Acad. Edn., Cognitive Sci. Soc. (chmn. 1979-80, goving. bd. 1979-87), Am. Assn. for Artificial Intelligence (fellow 1990), Am. Ednl. Rsch. Assn. Achievements include launched research on human semantic memory (with R. Quillian); development of first intelligent tutoring system (with J.R. Carbonell); development of cognitive apprenticeship (with J.S. Brown). Home: 135 Cedar St Lexington MA 02421-6516 Business E-Mail: collins@bbn.com.

COLLINS, ALMA JONES, language educator, writer; d. Walter Melville Jones and Anne Teresa Harrington; m. Daniel Francis Collins, Apr. 9, 1994. BA, Conn. Coll., 1943; MA, Trinity Coll., 1952, U. Conn., 1962. Tchr., counselor West Hartford (Conn.) Bd. Edn., 1947-72; pres. Arts Universal Rsch. Assocs., 1978—. Interviewed Salvador Dali (CD located in archives Wadsworth Atheneum Mus. Art), 1978, 79; cons. for corp. product devel.; rep. for artists. *Since 1978 Arts Universal Research Associates has focused on concept development and publications by Alma Jones Collins with research associate Audrey Jones Burton. Art-related articles for national and international publications include Japanese woodblock prints, Oriental rugs, third world embassies, commemorative art objects, art collections and interior design. Concept development for corporations includes articles and monographs for Royal Doulton, Hallmark International and U.S. Historical Society. Presentations include Salvador Dali, Chaim Gross, Kamil Kubik, Dominic Mingolla, Eric Sloane, John Stobart, Carlos Paez-Vilaro and Bjorn Wiinblad.* Author: Danielle at the Wadsworth, 2004; contbr. articles to profl. jours. Mem. Phi Beta Kappa, Delta Kappa Gamma Internat. Avocation: writing poetry and fiction. Home and Office: 275 Steele Rd A318 West Hartford CT 06117-2763

COLLINS, ANITA MARGUERITE, research geneticist; b. Allentown, Pa., Nov. 8, 1947; d. Edmund III and Virginia (Hunsicker) C. BSc in Zoology, Pa. State U., 1969; MSc in Genetics, Ohio State U., 1972, PhD in Genetics, 1976. Instr. biology Mercyhurst Coll., Erie, Pa., 1975-76; rsch. geneticist Honey Bee Breeding Lab. Agrl. Rsch. Svc., USDA, Baton Rouge, 1976-88, rsch. leader Honey Bee Rsch. Lab. Weslaco, Tex., 1988-95, rsch. geneticist Bee Rsch. Lab. Beltsville, Md., 1995—. Co-author: Bee Genetics & Breeding, 1986; contbr. articles to profl. jours. Mem.: Soc. for Cryobiology, Internat. Union for Study of Social Insects (congress sec. 2002—), Am. Genetics Assn., Am. Beekeeping Fedn. (rsch. com. 1990, 1992—94), Assn. for Women in Sci. (pres. Baton Rouge chpt. 1982), Entomol. Soc. Am. (chair sect. C 1997), Internat. Embryo Transfer Soc., Sigma Xi. Office: USDA ARS Bee Rsch Bldg 476 BARC-East Beltsville MD 20705 Office Phone: 301-504-8570. Business E-Mail: collinsa@ba.ars.usda.gov.

COLLINS, ANNAZETTE R., state representative; b. Chgo., Apr. 28, 1962; m. Keith Langston; children: Angelique, Taylor. BS in Sociology, Chgo. State U., MS in Criminal Justice, 1983. Social worker Ada S. McKinley Interventions, 1982—83; correctional officer Fed. Bur. Prisons, 1983—86; social worker Cook County Social Svcs., 1986—90; adminstr. Dept. Children Family Svcs., 1990—2000, Chgo. Pub. Schs., 2000; mem. Ill. Ho. of Reps., 2000—. Mem. St. Joseph Sch. Bd., 1992—95; v.p. pres.'s club Cosmopolitan Cmty. Ch., 2001. Democrat. Baptist. Office: 252-W Stratton Office Bldg Springfield IL 62706 also: 259 N Pulaski Rd Chicago IL 60624 Office Phone: 773-533-0010. Personal E-mail: annazette@sbcglobal.net.

COLLINS, ANTHONY G., academic administrator; b. Australia; m. Karen Collins; 4 children. B in Civil Engring., Monash U., Melbourne, Australia, 1971; Master's Degree, Lehigh U., 1973, PhD, 1982. With environ. engring. consulting firm, Australia, Utah Devel. Co.; from asst. prof. to prof. civil and environ. engring. Clarkson U., Potsdam, NY, provost, 2001—03, pres., 2003—. Office: Clarkson Univ Office of the Pres PO Box 5500 Potsdam NY 13699-5500

COLLINS, ARISTIDE J., JR., academic administrator; s. Aristide J. Collins, Sr. and Barbara Ann Collins. MPA, Calif. State U., Long Beach, 1995—98; BA in Polit. Sci., Calif. State U., Hayward, 1993. Cert. Specialist in Planned Giving Am. Inst. for Philanthropic Studies, Ednl. Mgmt. Calif. State U., Hayward. Exec. dir. of corp. rels. Calif. State U., Long Beach, 1993—99, assoc. v.p., 2000—04, v.p., 2004—; dir. of devel. for u. projects George Wash. U., 1999—2000; assoc. v.p. Pepperdine U., 2002—04. Mem. Coun. for Advancement and Support of Edn., Washington, Pi Alpha Alpha Nat. Honor Soc. for Pub. Adminstrn., Phi Delta Gamma Nat. Grad. Honor Soc., Nat. Soc. of Fund-raising Executives, Los Angeles, Calif. Bd. of trustees Goodwill Industries of Long Beach, 2001—; bd. dirs. Long Beach Cmty. Improvement League; field organizer and office mgr. Clinton/Gore '92, Calif. Dem. Party, Oakland, 1992—92. Mem.: Nat. Soc. of Fund-raising Executives, Coun. for Advancement and Support of Edn., Calif. Faculty Assn., AAUP, Phi Delta Gamma, Pi Alpha Alpha. Roman Catholic. Avocations: sports collectibles, music, writing, sports. Office: Calif State U Long Beach 1250 Bellflower Blvd BH387 Long Beach CA 90840-0116 E-mail: acollins@csulb.edu.

COLLINS, ARLENE, secondary school educator; b. Mandan, ND, Sept. 7, 1940; d. John Marcellus and Cecelia Magdalena (Schaaf) Weber; m. Abdul Rahman Rana (dec.); children: Fazale Rahman, Habeeb Rahman; m. Freddie L. Collins. BS in math., N.D. State U., 1962; postgrad., W.Va. Inst. Tech., 1974; M in Edn. Adminstrn., WVCOGS, 1988. Cert. mid. sch. tchr., W.Va. Tchr. physics, math. Montgomery (W.Va.) H.S., 1970; tchr. math., sci. Spencer (W.Va.) Jr. H.S., 1974-80; sci. tchr. Poca (W.Va.) Mid. Sch., 1980—, team leader, 1983-96. W.Va. textbook adoption com., W.Va. Bd. Edn., 1984-90. Leader Girl Scouts U.S.A., Montgomery, 1966-70, 99—, Boy Scouts Am., Montgomery, 1966; bd. dirs. Violet Twp. Womens League, 2002-. Fellow: African Am. Law Enforcement Agts. Assn., Inc.; mem.: NOW (bd. dirs. 1986), Am. Fedn. Tchrs., Laurel Soc., Am. Legion Aux. (sec. 2002—), Buckeye Sertoma, Soroptimists Internat. Home: 7292 Fox Den Ct Pickerington OH 43147-9019 Office Phone: 614-419-4602. Personal E-mail: ac0907@aol.com.

COLLINS, ARTHUR D., JR., medical products executive; b. Lakewood, Ohio, Dec. 10, 1947; BS, Miami U., Oxford, Ohio, 1969; MBA, U. Pa., 1973. Div. v.p. Abbott Laboratories, 1984—89, corp. v.p. diagnostic products, 1989—92; pres. Medtronic Internat., 1992—94; exec. v.p. Medtronic Inc., Mpls., 1992—94, COO, 1994—96, pres., COO, 1996—2001, pres., CEO, 2001—02, chmn., CEO, 2002—. Bd. dir. U.S. Bancorp, Cargill Inc.; chmn. Advanced Med. Tech. Ind. Assn. Mem. bd. overseers Wharton Sch., Univ. Pa. Office: Medtronic Inc 710 Medtronic Pkwy Minneapolis MN 55432-5604*

COLLINS, AUDREY B., judge; b. 1945; BA, Howard U., 1967; MA, Am. U., 1969; JD, UCLA, 1977. Asst. atty. Legal Aid Found. L.A., 1977-78; with Office L.A. County Dist. Atty., 1978-94, dept. dist. atty., 1978-94, asst. dir. burs. ctrl. ops. and spl. ops., 1988-92, asst. dir. atty., 1992-94; judge. U.S. Dist. Ct. (Ctrl. Dist.) Calif., 1994—. Dep. gen. counsel Office Spl. Acad. scholar Howard U.; named Lawyer of Yr., Langston Bar Assn., 1988; honoree Howard U. Alumni Club So. Calif., 1989; recipient Profl. Achievement award UCLA Alumni Assn., 1997, Ernestine Stahlhut award, Women Lawyers Assn., 1999. Mem. FBA, Nat. Assn. Women Judges, Nat. Bar Assn. (life), Assn. Bus. Trial Lawyers (bd. dirs. 2004—), State Bar Calif. (com. bar examiners, chmn. subcom. on moral character 1992-93, co-chmn. 1993-94), Los Angeles County Bar Assn. (exec. com. litig. sect. 1999-2002, task force on criminal justice sys. 2002-03), Assn. Los Angeles County Dist. Attys. (pres. 1983), Black Women Lawyers Los Angeles County, Women Lawyers L.A. (life, Ernestine Stahlhut award 1999, bd. dirs. 2005-), Calif. Women Lawyers (life), Order of Coif, Phi Beta Kappa. Office: US Dist Ct Edward R Roybal Fed Bldg 255 E Temple St Ste 670 Los Angeles CA 90012-3334

COLLINS, BOBBY MCMANUS, II, dental educator; s. Bobby McManus Collins, Sr and Gail Patrick Collins; m. Lisa Joye Dixon, Oct. 14, 1978. BA, U. N.C., 1978, DDS, 1983; MS, U. Pitts., 2004. Diplomate Am. Bd. of Oral and Maxillofacial Pathology, 1998. With U.S. Army Dental Corps, 1984, advanced through grades to maj., 1989, dental officer, 1984—92; resident in oral pathology U. Fla., Gainesville, 1992—95; fellow in head and neck pathology U. Pitts. Med. Ctr., 1995—96; asst. prof. U. Pitts. Sch. of Dental Medicine, 1996—. Guest lectr. U.S.-Saudi Aramco, Dhahran, Saudi Arabia, 1997—97; cons. U.S. Army Dental Corps, 1999—, USN Dental Corps, Bethesda, Md., 2000—. Contbr. articles to profl. jours. Decorated 2 Army Commendation medals, Expert Field Med. badge U.S. Army 18th Airborne Corps, 5 Army Achievement medals, Meritorious Svc. medal; recipient Faculty Award of Excellence, Am. Student Dental Assn., 2000, 2003, 2004, 2005. Fellow: Acad. of Gen. Dentistry (Master 2004); mem.: Student Clinicians of the ADA, Am. Acad. of Oral and Maxillofacial Pathology (chmn., profl. and pub. rels. 2004—), Omicron Kappa Upsilon. Avocations: guitar, travel, volksmarching. Office: Univ Pitts Sch of Dental Med G-135 Salk 3501 Ter Pittsburgh PA 15261 Business E-Mail: bcollins@dental.pitt.edu.

COLLINS, BRENDAN KENNEDY, lawyer; b. Berwyn, Pa., Apr. 10, 1964; s. Donald Michael and Madeleine Mary (Murray) C.; m. Annmarie Godlewski, Jan. 12, 1985; children: Aileen Morgan, Xavier Michael, Anastasia Marie, Cecelia Anne, Peter Emmanuel. BS in Math., St. Joseph's U., 1985; JD magna cum laude, Villanova (Pa.) U., 1988. Bar: Pa. 1988, U.S. Dist. Ct. (ea. dist.) Pa. 1989, U.S. Supreme Ct. 1993. Assoc. Ballard, Spahr, Andrews & Ingersoll, Phila., 1988-97, ptnr., 1997—. Bd. editors Villanova U. Law Rev.; contbr. articles to profl. jours. Mem. West Norriton Twp. Planning Commn., Pa., 1992—; mem. adv. bd. Environ. Sci. Program, St. Joseph's Univ., Phila. Named one of Pa. Super Lawyers, Law & Politics Mag. Mem. ABA (chmn. Environ. Litigation & Toxic Tort com. 2004-05), Pa. Bar Assn., Phila. Bar Assn. (co-chmn. Environ. Law com. 1996); St. Thomas More Soc. Phila. (pres. 2000-01, mem. bd. gov.); Order of Coif. Republican. Roman Catholic. Avocations: sailing, golf. Office: Ballard Spahr Andrews & Ingersoll 1735 Market St Fl 51 Philadelphia PA 19103-7599 Business E-Mail: collins@ballardspahr.com.

COLLINS, CARDISS, retired congresswoman; b. St. Louis, Sept. 24, 1931; m. George W. Collins (dec.); 1 child, Kevin. Ed., Northwestern U.; LLD (hon.), John Marshall Law Sch., 1969, Winston-Salem State U., 1980, Spelman Coll., 1981, BarberScotia Coll., 1986; DHL (hon.), Rosary Coll., 1996; DrPsychology (hon.), Forest Inst. Profl. Psychology, 1993. Barber Scotia Coll.; mem. 93d-104th Congresses from 7th Ill. Dist., 1973-97; ret., 1997. Ranking minority mem. govt. reform & oversight com.; former chair. govt. activity and transp. subcom.; former chair commerce, consumer protection and competition subcom.; former majority whip-at-large; former asst. regional whip; former chair Congl. Black Caucus, sec.; dir. emeritus, former chair Congl. Black Caucus Found.; former chair Mems. Congress for Peace through Law. Recipient award Roosevelt U., Loyola U. Mem. NAACP, Nat. Coun. Negro Women (past v.p.), Chgo. Urban League, Black Women's Agenda, The Chgo. Network, The Links, Dem. Nat. Com., Alpha Kappa Alpha. Democrat. Baptist. Home: 1110 Roundhouse Ln Alexandria VA 22314-5934

COLLINS, CARL RUSSELL, JR., industrial engineer; b. Williamsport, Pa., Dec. 29, 1926; s. Carl Russell, Sr. and Annis (Kilmer) C.; m. Rita Thomas, Oct. 3, 1959; children— James, Michael, Nancy BS in Indsl. Engring., Pa. State U., 1953. Div. sales mgr. Fla. Power Corp., St. Petersburg, 1961-64, asst. div. mgr., 1964-65, dist. mgr., 1965-67, div. mgr., 1967-79, v.p., 1979-85, George F. Young Inc., Architects and Engrs., St. Petersburg, 1986-91. Bd. dirs. Abilities, Inc. Bd. dirs. United Way, St. Petersburg, 1978, Com. of 100, 1981; v.p. Suncoasters, Inc., St. Petersburg, 1982; mem. adv. bd. Salvation Army, 1964—; active Meth. Ch., pres. Meth. Men, chmn. adminstrv. bd., lay leader, chmn. fin. com. With USN, 1944-46, as lt., 1953-56. Mem. Pa. State U. Alumni Club (life), Tau Beta Pi. Lodges: Kiwanis (pres. 1984). Republican. Avocations: photography, fishing, boating. Home: 5937 Tangerine Ave S Saint Petersburg FL 33707-4059

COLLINS, CARON LEE, music educator; d. James and Evelyn Fitch; m. Philip Collins, Oct. 15, 1978; children: Richard, Daniel. BA in Music Edn., Ind. U. Sch. of Music, 1978; MA, Marygrove Coll., 2002. Cert. profl. tchg. Dept. of Edn./Ohio, 2002. Dir. bands Diocese of Columbus, Ohio, 1980—2005. Coord. instrumental music Diocese of Columbus, Ohio, 1983—2005. Dir.: (music) Columbus Diocese Summer Music Program, Hartley Area Jr. High Jazz-Rock Group, Columbus Diocese Music Marathon, Columbus Diocese Honor Band Program, Columbus Diocese Solo and Ensemble Contest. Vol. Meals on Wheels, Columbus, 2002—04; leader, merit badge counselor, vol. Boy Scouts Am., Columbus, 1995—2000; vol. Dem. Party, Columbus, 1992—2004; musician Redeemer Luth. Ch., Columbus, 1990—2005. Mem.: Ctrl. Ohio Assn. Cath. Educators (assoc.; negotiation com. mem. 2002—03), Music Educators Nat. Conf. (assoc.), Ctrl. Ohio Dachshund Club (assoc.), Buckeye Trail Assn. (assoc.). Avocations: hiking, camping, environment advocate. Office: Ohio State U Sch Music 1899 College Rd Columbus OH 43210 Personal E-mail: bandtchr1@hotmail.com.

COLLINS, CHRISTOPHER CARL, manufacturing executive; b. Schenectady, N.Y., May 20, 1950; s. Gerald Edward and Constance (Messier) Collins; m. Margaret Elizabeth Busby Cox, May 20, 1972 (div. Apr. 1978); 1 child, Carly Elizabeth; m. Mary Sue Kuhn, Jan. 9, 1988; children: Caitlin Christine, Cameron Christopher. BSME, N.C. State U., 1972; MBA, U. Ala., 1975. Sales engr. Westinghouse Elec. Corp., Birmingham, Ala., 1972-76, market rsch. analyst Buffalo, 1976-77, mgr. market planning, 1978-79, mgr. gearing divsn., 1980-82; pres., chmn., CEO Nuttall Gear Corp., Niagara Falls, N.Y., 1983-97; pres. Nuttall Gear, LLC, Niagara Falls, 1997-98; v.p. corp. devel. Wilson Greatbatch Ltd., Clarence, N.Y., 1999; chmn. bd., CEO, Bloch Industries LLC, Rochester, N.Y., 1999—; chmn. bd. Zepto Metrix Corp., Buffalo, 1999—; treas. Volland Electric Equipment Corp., Buffalo, 2001—; v.p. Easom Automation Sys., Detroit, 2003—. Mem. small bus. adv. coun. Fed. Res. Bank, NY, 1992—95; treas. Frontier Indsl. Supply, Buffalo, 2001—, Mead Supply, Buffalo, 2002—; chmn. Niagara Machinery Corp., Wilson, NY, 2003—; chmn. and CEO Audubon Machinery Corp., Buffalo, 2004—; treas. Niagara Ceramics Corp., Buffalo, 2004—; chmn. Bio Clin. Partners, Boston, 2004—; chmn., CEO Oxygen Generating Sys. Internat., Buffalo, 2004—; treas. Lang & Washburn Electric, Buffalo, 2004—. Bd. dirs. Kenmore Mercy Hosp., 1986-93; mem. ho. of dels. United Way, Buffalo, 1986-2003; mem. Buffalo Fin. Planning Com., 1994; exec. bd. dirs. Greater Niagara Frontier coun. Boy Scouts Am., 1998—; Rep. and Conservative candidate for U.S. Congress, 1998; mentor Ctr. for Entrepreneurial Leadership, SUNY, 1999— Mem. Chief Execs. Orgn., World Pres.'s Orgn., Young Pres. Orgn. (chmn. edn. com. 1988-89, chpt. chmn. 1989-90, chmn. membership 1990-91, chmn. exec. com. 1991-96), Brookfield Country Club, Holimont Ski Club. Republican. Roman Catholic. Avocations: golf, skiing, aviation. Home: 9660 Cobblestone Dr Clarence NY 14031-1576 Office: Bloch Industries LLC 140 Commerce Dr Rochester NY 14623-3592 Office Phone: 716-656-9900. Personal E-mail: ccc9660@prodigy.net.

COLLINS, CONNIE SUE, secondary school educator; b. Maryville, Mo. d. Clyde Lowrance and Remma (Kenny); m. Campbell Collins, Feb. 23, 1968; children: Cami, Clint. BS in Edn., Northwest Mo. State U., Maryville, 1969; MA in Tchg., Webster U:., 1998. English tchr. Cameron High Sch., Cameron, Mo.; English tchr., jour. adv. Plattsburg High Sch., Plattsburg, Mo. Student coun. adv. Recipient Tchr. of Month, Golden Apple award, 1990, 93, 97, 2004, Advisor of Yr., Mo. Student Coun., 2001, Mem. of Yr., Booster Club, 1994. Mem. PCTA, MSTA, NCTE, Mo. Assn. Student Coun. (bd. dirs. 1994-2000), Kappa Delta Gamma, Delta Zeta.

COLLINS, DANIEL FRANCIS, lawyer; b. N.Y.C., Mar. 5, 1942; s. Daniel Joseph and Madeline Elizabeth (Berger) C.; m. Margaret Mary Heyden, Jan. 15, 1966; children: Matthew C., Elizabeth C. BA in History and Polit. Sci., Hofstra U., 1964; JD, Am. U., 1967. Bar: D.C. 1968. Law clk. to E. Barrett Prettyman U.S. Ct. Appeals, Washington, 1967-68; assoc. Ross, Marsh & Foster, Washington, 1970-74, mem., 1974-78; ptnr. Brackett & Collins, P.C., Washington, 1978-87; v.p. regulatory law The Coastal Corp., Washington, 1987-2001; sr. v.p., dep. gen. counsel El Paso Corp., Washington, 2001—03; of counsel Fulbright & Jaworski, L.L.P., Washington, 2004—. Office: Fulbright & Jaworski LLP 801 Pennsylvania Ave NW Washington DC 20004 Office Phone: 202-662-4586. Personal E-mail: dfcollins@fulbright.com.

COLLINS, DANIEL W., accountant, educator; b. Marshalltown, Iowa, Sept. 1, 1946; s. Donald E. and Lorine R. (Metge) C.; children: Melissa, Theresa BBA with honors, U. Iowa, 1968, PhD, 1973. Asst. prof. acctg. Mich. State U., East Lansing, 1973-76, assoc. prof., 1976-77; vis. assoc. prof. U. Iowa, Iowa City, 1977-78, assoc. prof., 1978-81, prof., 1981-83, Murray chaired prof. acctg., 1983-88, Henry B. Tippie prof. of acctg., 1989—; vis. IBM prof. bus. Fuqua Sch. Bus., Duke U., 1988-89, chmn. dept. acctg., 1995—2003; vis. full prof. Kellogg Sch. Mgmt., Northwestern U., 2005. Mem. Fin. Acctg. Stds. Adv. Coun., acad. adv. bd. Deloitte & Touche; mem. Arthur Andersen doctoral dissertation awards com., 1996—; bd. dirs. Ira B. McGladrey Inst., U.S. Bank, Iowa City, Christian Ret. Svcs., Iowa City. Assoc. editor Acctg. Rev., 1980-86; mem. editl. bd. Jour. Acctg. and Econs., 1978—, Jour. Acctg. Rsch., 2001—; contbr. articles to profl. jours. 2d lt. U.S. Army, 1972. Recipient All Univ. Tchr. scholar award Mich. State U., 1976, Gilbert Maynard Excellence in Tchg. award U. Iowa, 1985, Collegiate Tchg. award, 1998; Univ. Faculty scholar U. Iowa, 1980-82, Faculty Excellence award Iowa Bd. Regents, 2000, Outstanding Acctg. Alumnus award, U. Iowa, 2003. Mem. Am. Acctg. Assn. (disting. vis. faculty mem. Doctoral Consortium 1980, 89, dir. Doctoral Consortium 1987, program dir. ann. conv. 1988, dir. publs. 1989-91, exec. com. 1989-91, Outstanding Acctg. Educator award 2001), Acctg. Rschrs. Internat. Avocations: jogging, gardening. Home: 11 Wildberry Ct NE Iowa City IA 52240-9173 Office: U Iowa Coll Bus W252 PBAB Iowa City IA 52242-1000

COLLINS, DAVID BROWNING, religious institution administrator; b. Hot Springs, Ark., Dec. 18, 1922; s. Charles Frederick and Agnes Elizabeth (George) C.; m. Maryon Virginia Moise, Oct. 14, 1945; children: Melissa, Christopher, Matthew, Geoffrey. BA, U. of the South, 1943, BD, 1948, STM, 1962, DD, 1974. Ordained to ministry Episcopal Ch. as deacon, 1948, as priest, 1949. Rector St. Andrew's Episc. Ch., Marianna, Ark., 1948-53; priest-in-charge Holy Cross Episc. Ch., West Memphis, Ark., 1949-53; chaplain and assoc. prof. of religion U. of the South, Sewanee, Tenn., 1953-66; dean Cathedral of St. Philip, Atlanta, 1966-84; exec. dir. Windsong Ministries, Inc., 1984—; pres. House of Deps. Episcopal Ch., 1985-91. Trustee Ch. Pension Fund, N.Y.C., 1976-88; mem. Bd. of Clergy Deployment, N.Y.C., 1971-76. Contbr. articles to profl. jours. Pres. Christian Council of Met. Atlanta, 1977-78; chaplain Atlanta Braves Booster Club, 1966-84. Served to lt. (j.g.) USNR, 1943-46. Episcopalian. Avocation: baseball. Home and Office: 132 Hearthstone Dr Woodstock GA 30189-5298

COLLINS, DELORIS WILLIAMS, secondary school educator; b. Jackson, Miss., Oct. 24, 1959; d. Eddie (Stepfather) and Mary Louise Lewis; m. Bobby Collins, July 18, 1981; children: Garrian V., Bryan L. AA, Hinds Jr. Coll., Jackson, Miss., 1987; BBA in Office Adminstrn., Jackson State U., 2000. Circulation clk. Eudora Welty Libr., Jackson, Miss., 1989—91; tech. specialist/libr. circulation clk. H.T. Sampson Libr. Jackson State U., 1991—93; libr. media tech. specialist Canton Pub. Schs. Dist., 1993—96; with U.S. Postal Svc., Jackson, 1999—2000; substitute tchr. Jackson Pub. Schs. Dist., Jackson, 2000—. Cert. facilitator Family Connections, Jackson, 1999; seminar and workshop condr. Author: They Are Throwing Rocks, 1997, Chasing After the Wind, 1998, Anointed Hyms-Poems, 1999, Treasured Recipes, 1999, Marriage in Yesterday and Today Society: There is Hope, Its All in the Lord, 2000, The Talking Partridge, 2003, of poems. Nominee Poet of the Yr., 2003, 2004; named to Wall of Tolerance, Civil Rights Meml. Ctr., 2003; recipient Editors Choice award, 2003. Mem.: Internat. Soc. of Poets (hon.). Achievements include patents for The Life's Gadgets Learning Tool; The Prayer Doll Learning Tool. Avocations: reading, cooking. Home: 403 Stillwood Dr Jackson MS 39206

COLLINS, DENNIS ARTHUR, retired foundation administrator; b. Yakima, Wash., June 9, 1940; s. Martin Douglas and Louise Constance (Caccia) C.; m. Mary Veronica Paul, June 11, 1966; children: Jenifer Ann, Lindsey Kathleen. BA, Stanford U., 1962, MA, 1963; LHD, Mills Coll., 1994, U. San Diego, 2002. Assoc. dean admissions Occidental Coll., Los Angeles, 1964-66, dean admissions, 1966-68, dean of students, 1968-70; headmaster Emma Willard Sch., Troy, N.Y., 1970-74; founding headmaster San Francisco U. High Sch., 1974-86; pres. James Irvine Found., San Francisco, 1986—2002; ret. Trustee Coll. Bd., N.Y.C., 1981-85, Ind. Ednl. Svcs., Princeton, N.J., 1981-85, Calif. Assn. Ind. Schs., L.A., 1982-86, Branson Sch., 1987-89, Aspen Inst. Nonprofit Sector rsch. Fund, 1992—; chmn. bd. So. Calif. Assn. Philanthropy, L.A., 1989-91, No. Calif. Grantmakers, 1987-90; dir. Rebuild L.A., 1992-93. Trustee Cathedral Sch. for Boys, San Francisco, 1976-82, Marin Country Day Sch., Corte Madera, Calif., 1978-84, San Francisco Exploratorium, 1984-86, Ind. Sector, Washington, 1987-95, Am. Farmland Trust, Washington, 1992—, Occidental Coll, Nat. Ctr. for Pub. Policy and Higher Edn., Ctr. for Philanthropy and Pub. Policy; bd. dirs., vice chmn. Children's Hosp. Found., San Francisco, 1984-86; chmn. bd. dirs. Coun. for Cmty. Based Devel., Washington, 1989-92. Mem. Council on Founds., World Trade Club, Univ. Club, Calif. Club (LA). Democrat. Episcopalian. Home: 432 Golden Gate Ave Belvedere Tiburon CA 94920-2447

COLLINS, DENNIS GLENN, mathematics professor; b. Gary, Ind., June 26, 1944; s. Glenn and Irene Martha (Richman) C.; m. Barbara Jean Hamilton, July 14, 1979; 1 child, Glenn H. BA, Valparaiso U., 1966; MS, Ill. Inst. Tech., 1970, PhD, 1975. Temp. instr. Mich. State U., East Lansing, 1975-76; instr. U. New Orleans, 1976-79; asst. prof. Valparaiso (Ind.) U., 1979-82; from asst. prof. to prof. math. U. P.R., Mayaguez, 1982—, chmn. math. dept. pers. com., 1994-95. Vis. scholar, U. P.R., Mayaguez, 2003-2004; vis. assoc. prof. dept. math. Mich. State U., 1988-89; judge computer sci. 38th Internat. Sci. and Engring. Fair, San Juan, P.R., 1987; presenter in field. Created copyrighted set postcards of 120 mathematicians and physicists, 1983-2001; composed short Columbus Cantata and short Spaceship Cantata, Short Cosmic Cantata, One Size Fits All, 2001; contbr. articles to conf. proceedings. NSF fellow, 1966—67, vis. scholar, Mich. State U., 1988—89, 1996—97. Mem.: N.Y. Acad. Scis., U.S. Patents, 2003, Soc. Indsl. and Applied Mathematicians (presenter), Am. Math. Soc. (informatics and cybernetics 1990, Detroit meeting 1997, dialog com. to rector 1997—2003, poster session 10th internat. math. conf. Chgo. 1998, presenter various confs.), Internat. Soc. for Optical Engring., Soc. Photo-optical Instrumentation Engrs., Internat. Soc. for Sys. Sci. (presenter), Sigma Xi (treas. local chpt. 2000—03, pres. 2003—04, del. annual mtgs., treas. local chpt. 2004—). Lutheran. Home: 7108 Grand Blvd Hobart IN 46342-6628 Office: U PR Dept Math Mayaguez PR 00681 E-mail: d-collins-pr@hotmail.com.

COLLINS, DOROTHY CRAIG, retired educational administrator; b. Evansville, Ind., Oct. 11, 1912; d. Edmund Lawrence and Mable Irene (Ross) Craig; m. Ralph Leonard Collins, June 13, 1940; 1 child, David Harrington. BA cum laude, Western Coll. for Women, 1934; MA, U. Chgo., 1937. Rsch. asst. Kinsey Inst., Ind. U., Bloomington, 1951-56; asst. dir. Instnl. Rsch., Ind. U., Bloomington, 1963-64; rsch. asst. Office of Pres., Ind. U., Bloomington, 1965-69; rsch. and editl. assoc. Office of Univ. Chancellor, Ind. U., Bloomington, 1969-92; ret., 1992. Co-author: Pictorial History of Indiana University, 1992. V.p. United Way of Monroe County, Bloomington, 1974; pres. bd. dirs. Bloomington Hosp., 1963; pres. Monroe County Comprehensive Health Planning, Bloomington, 1971-73. Mem. Univ. Women's Club (pres.), Consumers Health Task Force, Theatre Circle (pres.), Friends of Lilly Libr. (bd.), Office of Women's Affairs (adv. bd.), Collins Living-Learning Ctr. (adv. bd.). Democrat. Avocations: reading, travel, theatre attendance, art appreciation. Home: 2455 Tamarack Trl 021 Bloomington IN 47408-1286

COLLINS, DOUGLAS C., hotel executive; Pres., chair, CEO, treas. Buckhead Am. Corp., Atlanta, 1999—.

COLLINS, DOUGLAS PATRICK, JR., communications company executive, television producer; b. East Orange, N.J., May 3, 1961; s. Douglas Patrick and Julia Linda (Murphy) C.; m. Nancy Jean Moser, Sept. 21, 1985. BA, Temple U., 1983. Prodn. asst. Sta. HPERD-TV, Temple U., Phila., 1979-83, prodn. mgr., 1983-85, Medstar Communications, Allentown, Pa., 1985-88; prodr. USA Today: The TV Show, N.Y.C., 1988; pres., exec. producer Broadcast News Assocs., Inc., N.Y.C., 1988—. Producer, dir. (film) Losing You, 1983, (videos) Breakfast at the Deluxe, 1984, PRIME-MD, 1994, Direct-Mail Advertising, 1995, It's Your Business, 1996, Jumping Levels, 1997, Discussing E.D., 1998, Twenty-Four Hours, 1998, Oxyglobin, 1998,

Health Matters, 1986, (TV spls.) Cocaine: The End of the Line, 1988, Beating Heart Attacks, 1987, Immunization: Protection for Life, 1995, The Jewelry Buyer's Guide, 1996, Heart Failure, 1997, (plays) I Killed Your Dog, 1989, Echoes and Postcards, 1989, Windowspeak, 1989, How Far to Bethlehem, 1989, (commls.) Advances, Media Source, Volunteer PSA, Inside Corporate America-Fin. News Network, 1989—, (TV series) Inside Corporate America The Financial News Network, 1989-90, The Premium Dollar The Financial News Network, 1990, The Premium Dollar Today The Learning Channel, 1991—. Mem. Internat. TV Assn., Soc. Motion Picture TV Engrs., Nat. Acad. TV Arts and Scis.

COLLINS, DUANE E., manufacturing executive; BSME, U. Wis.; postgrad., Harvard U. Sales engr. Parker Hannifin Corp., Cleve., 1961, gen. sales mgr., ops. mgr. hose products divsn., gen. mgr., 1973-76, v.p. ops. fluid connectors group, 1976-80, pres. fluid connectors group, 1980-83, corp. v.p., 1983-87, pres. internat., 1987-88, corp. exec. v.p., pres. internat., 1988-92, vice chmn., 1992-93, CEO, 1993—2001, chmn., 2001—04. Bd. dirs. Parker Hannifin Corp., Sherwin-Williams Co., MeadWestvaco, MTD Holdings. Office: Parker Hannifin Corp 6035 Parkland Blvd Cleveland OH 44124-4141

COLLINS, EILEEN MARIE, astronaut; b. Elmira, NY, Nov. 19, 1956; d. James Edward and Rose Marie (O'Hara) C.; m. James Patrick Youngs, Aug. 1, 1987. AS in Math., Sci., Corning C.C., 1976; BA in Math., Econs., Syracuse U., 1978; grad., USAF Undergrad. Pilot Tng., Vance AFB, Okla., 1979, USAF Test Pilot Sch., Edwards AFB, Calif., 1990; MS in Ops. Rsch., Stanford U., 1986; MA in Space Systems Mgmt., Webster U., 1989; student, Air Force Inst. Techology, 1986; grad., Air Force Test Pilot Sch., Edwards AFB, Calif., 1990. Commd. 2d lt. USAF, 1978, advanced through grades to col., 1993, T-38 instr. pilot 71st flight tng. wing Vance AFB, 1979-82, C-141 aircraft comdr. and instructor pilot, 86th mil. airlift squadron Travis AFB, Calif., 1983-85, ret., 2005; asst. prof. math., T-41 instr. pilot USAF Acad., Colorado Springs, Colo., 1986-89; astronaut Johnson Space Ctr. NASA, Houston, 1991—. Served on astronaut support team responsible for Orbiter prelaunch check-out, final launch configuration, crew ingress/egress, landing/recovery; spacecraft communicator, CAPCOM, also served as the astronaut office spacecraft systems branch chief, chief information officer, shuttle branch chief, astronaut safety branch chief; pilot, space shuttle Discovery (STS-63), 1995 (first women pilot of space shuttle), space shuttle Atlantis (STS-84), 1997; comdr. space shuttle, Columbia (STS-93), 1999 (first women shuttle comdr.); crew comdr. space shuttle, (STS-114) Discovery; during this Return To Flight mission, the crew tested and evaluated new procedures for flight safety, shuttle inspections and repair techniques, 2005. Col. USAF. Decorated Air Force Commendation medal with one oak leaf cluster, Air Force Meritorious svc. medal with one oak leaf cluster, Armed Forces Expeditionary medal for svc. in Grenada (Operation Urgent Fury, 1983), Def. Superior Svc. medal, Def. Meritorious Svc. medal, Disting. Flying Cross, French Legion Honor, Disting. Flying Cross, NASA Outstanding Leadership medal, NASA Space Flight medals. Mem.: Am. Inst. Aeronautics and Astronautics, US Space Found., Order of Daedalians, Air Force Assn., The Ninety-Nines, Women Military Avaitors. Avocations: running, golf, hiking, camping, reading, photography, astronomy.*

COLLINS, ELWOOD F., lawyer; BA, Fordham Univ., 1968; JD, NYU, 1971. Bar: N.Y. 1972, Fla. 1979. Adminstrv. ptnr. & mem. mgmt. com. Kirkpatrick & Lockhart Nicholson Graham LLP, N.Y.C. Office: Kirkpatrick & Lockhart Nicholson Graham LLP 599 Lexington Ave New York NY 10022-6030 Office Phone: 212-536-4005. Office Fax: 212-536-3901. Business E-Mail: ecollins@klng.com.

COLLINS, ERICA HARRIET, communications executive, media consultant, model, actress, journalist; b. Camden, NJ, Mar. 19, 1975; d. Irene D. and Edward N. Collins. BA in Sociology, George Wash. U., 1996. Cert. multimedia Technologies N.Y. U., 2000; skin care and image cons. BeautiControl, Inc., Dallas, 2003, plus size fashion modeling Barbizon N.Y.C., 2001. Comm. devel. and broadcast prodn. assoc. U.S. C. of C. Broadcast Studios, Washington, 1996—97; press organizer U.S. Ho. and Senate Radio/TV Press Galleries, Washington, 1997; prodn. freelancer MSNBC, Secaucus, NJ, 1997—98; assignment desk assoc. Fox News Channel, N.Y.C., 1999—2000; media/mktg. cons. Desktop News Corp., N.Y.C., 2000—01; pres. E.C. and Assoc., L.L.C, Cherry Hill, NJ, 2002—. Model Macy's, Bloomingdale's, Fashion Bug, Boscov's, Liz Claiborne, Washington, N.J., N.Y., 1992—; media/mktg. cons. Jackie Robinson Project, George Wash. U., Washington, 1997—; entertainment media freelancer Home Box Office, Inc., N.Y.C., 1998—; adv. bd. dirs. Image and Attitude, Inc, Pennsauken, NJ, 2004—. Actor(featured extra): (acting) Stepford Wives (SAG Waiver award, 2004); author: (book) Plus Size Model's Little Instruction Book Volume I Getting Started, (poem) The Culture Exchange (Editor's Choice award, 1998), The Burn Baby (Editor's Choice award, 1997), Dare (Editor's Choice award, 1995). Platform-miss plus Am. Women's Alliance Orgn., Miami, Fla., 2003—; mentor and motivational spkr. Boys and Girls Club, Newark, 2004—; fundraiser, appearance Am. Cancer Soc.-Breast Cancer Walk, Newark, 2004; adv. bd. Image and Attitude, Inc, Pennsauken, NJ, 2004—; motivational spkr. N.Y.C. Mission Soc. and the Lady Roc/Team Roc, 2003—04. Recipient Plaque award, Camden County Coll. Essay Contest, 1989, N.J. Forenscis Tournament, 1991, KYW-News Radio Phila., 1991—92, Model of the Month photo pub. award, Venus Imaging, Inc., 2002, Semi Finalist- photo/interview pub. awards, BBW Mag.-Plus Size Model Contest, 2003; Merit scholar, Cherry Hill Minorities Civic Assn., 1992. Mem.: Internat. Soc. Poets, Nat. Assn. Black Journalist (assoc.), Princeton Club (assoc.), Cherry Hill Minorities Civic Assn. (assoc.). Achievements include Miss Plus Am. 2004-2005; Miss Plus Am. Spokes Model 2004-2005; Miss N.Y. Plus Am. 2003-2004; Miss Black Teenage World, N.J. 1992; Erica Collins Day Cherry Hill Twp., N.J. 2004; State of N.J. Resolution 1997; State of N.J. Resolution 1992. Office: EC and Assoc LLC 100 Springdale Rd A3-#112 Cherry Hill NJ 08003 Office Phone: 973-484-1346. E-mail: erica@ecandassociates.com.

COLLINS, FRANCIS S., federal agency administrator, geneticist, physician; b. Apr. 14, 1950; BS in Chemistry, U. Va., 1970; PhD in Physical Chemistry, Yale U., 1974; MD, U. N.C., Chapel Hill, 1977. Residency and chief residency in internal medicine N.C. Memorial Hospital, Chapel Hill, 1978—81; fellow in human genetics Yale U., 1981—84; prof. internal med. and human genetics, chief med. genetics U. Michigan, Howard Hughes Med. Inst, 1984—93; dir. Human Genome Project, 1992—2003; chief, genetic and molecular biology NIH, 1993; dir. Nat. Ctr. for Human Genome Rsch. (became Nat. Human Genome Rsch. Inst. in 1997), NIH, Bethesda, Md., 1993—; sr. investigator, Genome Technology Br. Nat. Human Genome Rsch. Inst., NIH, Bethesda, Md. Overseer Internat. Human Genome Sequencing Consortium; lectr. in field. Contbr. articles to profl. jours.; contbd. foreward Coming to Peace with Science: Bridging the Worlds Between Faith and Science, 2004. Vol. physician rural missionary hosp., Nigeria. Co-recipient Gairdner Found. Internat. award for work on cystic fibrosis, 1990; recipient Mendel medal, Biotechnology Heritage award, Chemical Heritage Found. and Biotechnology Industry Orgn., 2001, Gairdner Found. Internat. award for merit, 2002; named Va. Outstanding Scientist of Yr., Sci. Mus. of Va., 2001 Mem.: IOM, NAS, AMA (Scientific Achievement award 2001). Achievements include working on methods of crossing large stretches of DNA to identify disease genes, which was named "positional cloning"; identifying the gene for cystic fibrosis with Lap-Chee Tsui and Jack Riordan in 1989; identifying the neurofibromatosis gene with colleagues in 1990; identifying the defective gene that causes Huntington's Disease with colleagues in 1993; identifying the gene for multiple endocrine neoplasia type 1 and the M4 type of adult acute leukemia with colleagues; overseeing a complex multidisciplinary project, Human Genome Project, aimed at mapping and sequencing the entire human DNA, and determining aspects of its function. A working draft of the human genome sequence was announced in June, 2000, an initial analysis was published in February, 2001, and the completed sequence was announced in April, 2003; founding of the National Human Genome Research Institute Division of Intramural Research (DIR) in 1994, which has developed into one of the nation's premier research centers in human genetics; serving as strong advocate for protecting privacy of genetic information and as a national leader in efforts to prohibit gene-based insurance discrimination. Office: Nat Human Genome Rsch Inst NIH Bldg 31/4B09 31 Center Dr 9000 Rockville Pike Bethesda MD 20892 Office Phone: 301-496-0844. Fax: 301-402-2218. E-mail: fc23a@nih.gov.

COLLINS, FRANK, JR., dentist, educator; b. Jackson, Miss., Mar. 1, 1965; s. Frank Collins, Sr. and Emma H. Collins. BS in Biology, U. So. Miss., 1988; DDS, Howard U., 1996; cert. in gen. dentistry, Luth. Med. Ctr., Bklyn., 2002. Instr. Hinds C.C., Raymond, Miss., 1997—2000; gen. practice resident St. Mary's Hosp., Waterbury, Conn., 2001. Mem.: ADA (Am. Dental Assn.), Acad. Gen. Dentistry. Avocations: music, jogging.

COLLINS, FRANK EDWIN, lawyer; b. Jackson, Mo., Apr. 10, 1954; s. Arthur Black and Margaret Collins; m. Barbara Jo Justice, Oct. 26, 1974; children: Justin, Eric, Keith, Garrett. BA, U. Mo., Kansas City, 1976, JD, 1979. Bar: Mo. 1979. Counsel Mo. Divsn. Ins., Jefferson City, 1979-81; assoc. gen. counsel Blue Cross/Blue Shield, Kansas City, Mo., 1981—86; gen. counsel, sec. Prime Health, Inc., 1986—97; exec. v.p., gen. counsel, sec. Sierra Health Svcs., Las Vegas, Nev., 1997—. Pres. Sierra Health Holdings, Inc.; sec. S.W. Realty, Inc., Sierra Acquisition Corp., Prime Holdings, Inc., others; bd. dirs. numerous subsidiaries of Sierra Health Svc. Bd. dirs. United Way, Las Vegas. Mem. Mo. Bar Assn. Office: Sierra Health Svcs 2724 N Tenaya St PO Box 15645 Las Vegas NV 89128 Office Phone: 702-242-7189. Office Fax: 702-242-1532. E-mail: leg104@sierrahealth.com.

COLLINS, GAIL, editor; BA in Journalism, Marquette U., 1967; MA in Govt., U. Mass., 1971. Founder Conn. State News Bur., 1972—77; freelance writer, 1977—79; sr. editor Conn. Mag.; columnist Conn. Bus. Jour., 1977—79; host pub. affairs program Conn. Pub. TV, 1977—79; instr. journalism So. Conn. State Coll., 1977—79; fin. reporter UPI, N.Y.C., 1982—85; columnist N.Y. Daily News, N.Y.C., 1985—91, N.Y. Newsday, N.Y.C., 1991—95; mem. editl. bd. The N.Y. Times, N.Y.C., 1995—, host This Week Close-Up cable news program, 1997—, columnist op-ed page, 2000—01, editl. page editor, 2001—. Author (with Dan Collins): The Millennium Book, 1991; author: Scorpion Tongues, 1998, America's Women: Four Hundred Years of Dolls, Drudges, Helpmates and Heroines, 2003. Recipient Meyer Berger award, Columbia U., 1987, Matrix award, Women in Comm, 1989, award for commentary, AP, 1994; Bagehot fellow, Columbia U., 1981—82. Office: The NY Times 229 W 43d St New York NY 10036*

COLLINS, GALEN ROBERT, technology educator; b. Elkhart, Ind., Oct. 2, 1957; s. Galen Franklin and Ann Elizabeth C.; 1 child, Robert Jay. BBA, Fla. Internat. U., 1978, MS in Hotel Food Svc. Mgmt., 1980; PhD in Ednl. Tech., Nova Southeastern U., 2002, EdS in Ednl. Tech., 2000. Summer mgmt. trainee Walt Disney World, Orlando, Fla., 1979; asst. restaurant mgr. Tony Roma's, Miami, Fla., 1980-81; controller Indian Trail Country Club, Royal Palm Beach, Fla., 1981-82; asst. exec. mgr. Palm Beach (Fla.) Hilton, 1982-83; product tng. specialist Auditel Lodging Mgmt. Sys., Vienna, Va., 1983-84; program mgr. Robert Barrie & Ptnrs., Washington, 1984-85; asst. prof. Johnson & Wales U., Providence, 1985-87; from asst. prof. to prof. No. Ariz. U., Flagstaff, 1987—2003, assoc. dean, Sch. Hotel and Restaurant Mgmt., 1999—2004, prof., 2003—, exec. dir., Sch. Hotel and Restaurant Mgmt., 2004—. Chairperson Abacus Internet Svcs., Phoenix, 1996—. Author: Hospitality Information Technology, 1992, 5th edit., 2003, Overcoming the Customer Service Syndrome, 2003; founding pub. Internat. Jour. Hospitality Info. Technology, 1998-2003; contbr. articles to profl. jours. Bd. dirs. Epiphany Episcopal Ch., Flagstaff, 1993-96; invited mem. Ariz. Town Hall, Phoenix, 1997—. Recipient Most Prolific Author award Hospitality Rsch. Jour., 1992. Fellow Hospitality Internat. Tech. Assn. (founding, pres. 1992-97); mem. Assn. Computing Machinery, Hospitality Fin. Tech. Profls., Coun. Hotel Restaurant Instl. Edn., Lions (charter, pres. 1996, Lion of Yr. 1999), Continental Country Club (bd. dirs. 1995-99), Phi Theta Kappa, Phi Kappa Phi. Avocations: golf, racquetball. Home: 4015 N Goodwin Cir Flagstaff AZ 86004 Office: No Ariz U NAU Box 5638 Flagstaff AZ 86011 Office Phone: 928-523-7333. E-mail: galen.collins@nau.edu.

COLLINS, GEORGE J., JR., surgeon; b. Nov. 19, 1939; BS, Tex. A&M U., 1961, MS, 1963; MD, U. Tex. Med. Br., 1966. Chief vascular surgery svc. Brooke Army Med. Ctr., 1982-83, Walter Reed Army Med. Ctr., 1983-86, chief dept. of surgery, 1984-86; chief cardiovascular/thoracic surgery Madigan Army Med. Ctr., 1997—. Home: PO Box 217 La Grange TX 78945-0217

COLLINS, GORDON DENT, recording industry executive; b. Berkeley, Calif., Mar. 27, 1924; s. Edward Everett and Dorothy Janet C.; m. Louise Norma Krivicich, July 23, 1960; children: Daniel Edward, Patrick Doyle, Christine Anne, Gordon Jr. Student, U. Maine, 1943-44; BSEE magna cum laude, U. Wash., 1948; postgrad., Stanford U., 1960-63. Registered profl. engr., N.Y. Founder, chief executive officer Collins Rec. Co., Los Altos, Calif., 1962—. Assigned to Comissariat à l'energie Atomique, Ctr. Nuclear Studies, France. Served to lt. U.S. Army Signal Corps, 1943-52. Named Sr. of Yr. Elfun Soc., San Jose, Calif., 1980. Mem Soc. Engrs. and Scientists of France, Phi Beta Kappa, Tau Beta Pi, Phi Kappa Psi, Sigma Xi. Clubs: No. Calif. Golf Assn. (Pebble Beach). Achievements include patents in field of nuclear power, sodium technology, fast breeder reactors; development of atomic power. Avocations: golf, travel, photography, genealogy. Office: PO Box 934 Los Altos CA 94023-0934

COLLINS, HARKER, retired economist, retired manufacturing executive, retired publishing executive; b. Denver, Nov. 24, 1924; s. Clem Wetzel and Marie (Harker) C.; m. Emily Harvey, Aug. 23, 1957; children: Catherine Emily, Cynthia Lee, Constance Marie. BS, U.S. Naval Acad., 1945. Asst. buyer Montgomery Ward & Co., N.Y.C., 1947-51; prodn. mgr. Diamond Hosiery Mills, High Point, N.C., 1953-55; v.p. Vanette Hosiery Mills, Dallas, 1955-59; v.p., dir. Grote Mfg. Co., Madison, Ind., 1959-71; group v.p., gen. mgr. Bendix Corp., South Bend, Ind., 1971-73; pres., dir. Bandag, Inc., Muscatine, Iowa, 1973-78, chief exec. officer, 1974-78; pres., chief exec. officer, bd. dirs. Harker Collins & Co., Lubbock, Tex., 1978-98; pub. newsletters The Economy and You, Update, 1978-96; econ. counsel Automotive Svc. Industry Assn., 1978-91; exec. v.p., bd. dirs. Indsl. Molding Corp., Lubbock, 1993-97; pres., bd. dirs. Indl. Molding Corp., Lubbock, 1997; ret., 1997. Instr. U. Denver, 1948; chmn. automotive industry liaison com. with Dept. Transp., 1968-86, automotive industry excise tax com., 1964-70, automotive industry tariff com., 1964-70, joint operating com. for automotive trade shows, 1969-77 Mem. Pres.'s Com. Hwy. Safety, 1966-68; Bd. dirs. Iowa Ind. Coll. Found., 1976-86; bd. fellows Northwood Inst., 1974—; alderman City of Rancho Viejo, Tex., 1980-87. Served to ensign USN, 1945-47; to lt. USNR, 1951-53. Recipient Automotive Industry Leadership award, 1965, 74; Fin. World award as chief exec. of yr., 1975, 77 Mem. Automotive Svc. Industry Assn. (vice chmn. 1966-67, chmn. 1968-69, chmn. heavy duty exec. com. 1969-71, chmn. safety and environ. protection com. 1962-67, 70-78), Automotive Sales Coun. (bd. dirs. 1966-67, sec. 1971-72, v.p. 1972-73, pres. 1973-74), Am. Nat. Standards Inst. (chmn. task force on used vehicle standards 1966-74), Home Products Safety Coun. (pres. 1960-63), Medicine Cabinet Mfg. Coun. (pres. 1960-63, bd. dirs. 1960-68), Truck Safety Equipment Inst. (pres. 1960-63, dir. 1960-68).

COLLINS, HARRY DAVID, forensic engineer, mechanical engineer, nuclear engineer, claims consultant; b. Brownsville, Pa., Nov. 18, 1931; s. Harry Alonzo and Cecilia Victoria (Morris) Collins; m. Suzanne DyLong, May 11, 1956; children: Cynthia L., Gerard P. BSME, Carnegie Mellon U., 1954; MS in Physics, U.S. Naval Postgrad. Sch., 1961; postgrad., U.S. Army Command and Gen. Staff Coll., 1970, George Washington U., 1971—72. Registered profl. engr., Miss., La. Commd. 2nd lt. C.E. US Army, 1954, advanced through grades to lt. col., 1969; sr. advisor Vietnam Engr. Sch., 1968—69; comdr. 802d Heavy Engr. Constrn. Bn., Republic of Korea, 1972—73; dep. dist. engr. and acting dist. engr. Army Engr. Dist., New Orleans, 1973—75; v.p. deLaureal Engrs., Inc., New Orleans, 1975-78; v.p. Near East mktg. and project mgmt. Kidde Cons., Inc., 1978—82; dir. new bus. devel. and project mgmt. North Africa, Mid. East Am. Mid. East Co., Inc., 1982—84; sr. cons. Wagner, Hohns, Inglis, Inc., 1984—91; chief engr. bd. commrs. Orleans Levee Dist. State of La., 1981—82; pres. Harry D. Collins and Assoc., New Orleans, 1992—. Pres. La. Security Products & QuTech, 1994—97. Contbr. articles to profl. jours. Decorated Legion of Merit, Bronze Star, Meritorious Svc. medal with oak leaf cluster, Vietnam Nat. Commendation medal. Mem.: NSPE, ASME, N.Y. Acad. Sci., Assn. Profl. Genealogists, Nat. Acad. Forensic Engrs. (diplomate, cert.), Am. Arbitration Assn. (mem. panel arbitrators), Am. Nuc. Soc., La. Engring. Soc., Am. Soc. Mil. Engrs., Sigma Xi. Home: 2024 Audubon St New Orleans LA 70118-5518 Office Phone: 504-861-4792. Personal E-mail: hdc1@cox.net.

COLLINS, HUBERT, real estate broker, state representative; b. Riceville, Ky., Aug. 19, 1936; s. Johnnie W. and Nola (Spradlin) C.; m. Beatrice J. Madden-Daniel, May 6, 1959. BA, Morehead State U., 1969, MA, 1971. Cert. tchr., Ky. Tchr. Johnson County Bd. Edn., Paintsville, Ky., 1955-59, 69-78, 1991—; state rep. 97th Dist. Commonwealth of Ky., Frankfort, 1991—; used auto dealer Wittensville, 1972—; real estate broker, 1977—. Basketball ofcl. Ky. H.S. Athletic Assn., Lexington, 1956—. With U.S. Army, 1959-61. Mem. NRA, Odd Fellows. Democrat. Baptist. Home: 72 Collins Dr Wittensville KY 41274-9021 Office: Commonwealth of Ky Capital Annex Frankfort KY 40601

COLLINS, IRMA HELEN, music educator, consultant; b. Horatio, Ark., May 15, 1930; d. Roy DeWitt Hopkins and Irma Virginia Morgan; m. Walter Ray Collins, Aug. 27, 1960 (div. Feb. 15, 1976). BA, Ouachita Coll., 1952; BS in Music, Southwestern Sem., 1954; MusM, George Peabody Coll., 1958; D in Musical Arts, Temple U., 1979. Instr. Mars Hill (N.C.) Coll., 1954—57; assoc. prof. W.Va. Wesleyan Coll., Buckhannon, 1958—65; tchr., adminstr. Bd. Edn., Pitts., 1965—68; chair dept. music Ea. Coll., St. Davids, Pa., 1968—72; prof. music Murray (Ky.) State U., 1976—93; adj. prof. music Shenandoah U. Conservatory, Winchester, W.Va., 1998—. Arts cons.; founder Jour. Music Tchr. Edn.; rschr., writer stds. of learning in music Commonwealth Va., 2001; tchr./curriculum com. Shenandoah U. Coll. of Lifelong Learning. Contbr. articles to profl. jours.; author: (songs) I Call to Thee, In the Eyes of a Child; reviewer (jours.) including Southeastern Music Edn. Jour. Violinist Ark. State Symphony, Carnegie-Mellon Symphony, Nashville Symphony, Paducah Symphony; soloist Temple Sinai Synagogue, Pitts. Mem.: Ky. Music Educators Assn. (Tchr. of Yr. award), Soc. Music Tchr. Edn. (nat. chairperson), Sigma Alpha Iota (Outstanding Mem. award).

COLLINS, J. BARCLAY, II, lawyer, oil industry executive; b. Gettysburg, Pa., Oct. 21, 1944; s. Jennings Barclay and Golda Olevia (Hook) C.; m. Janna Claire Fall, June 25, 1966; children: J. Barclay III, L. Christian. AB magna cum laude, Harvard U., 1966; JD magna cum laude, Columbia U., 1969. Bar: N.Y. 1969. Law clk. to presiding judge U.S. Ct. Appeals (2d cir.), N.Y.C., 1969-70; assoc. Cravath, Swaine and Moore, N.Y.C., 1970-78; v.p., asst. gen. counsel City Investing Co., N.Y.C., 1978-84; exec. v.p., gen. counsel Amerada Hess Corp., N.Y.C., 1984—, also bd. dirs. Bd. dirs. Premier Oil plc, Nuvera Fuel Cells Inc. Trustee Bklyn. Hosp., Bklyn.; bd. dirs. United Hosp. Fund N.Y., past gov. Bklyn. Heights Assn. Mem. ABA, N.Y. Bar Assn., N.Y.C. Yacht Club. Clubs: Heights Casino (Bklyn.); Harvard N.Y.C. Office: Amerada Hess Corp Ste 810 1185 Avenue Of The Americas New York NY 10036-2601

COLLINS, J. MICHAEL, retired public broadcasting executive; b. Buffalo, Feb. 17, 1935; s. John Lloyd and Celestine (Buhrle) C.; m. Marilyn Anne Mercer, Aug. 5, 1961; children: Kevin Michael, Timothy David, Sheila Anne, Jeanne Mary, Julie Lynn. BS in Social Scis., Canisius Coll., 1957, LHD (hon.), 1978; postgrad., Mich. State U., 1957-58. Promotion mgr. Western N.Y. Pub. Broadcasting Assn. (Stas. WNED-TV-AM-FM, WNEQ-TV, WNJA-FM), Buffalo, 1959-60, dir. devel., 1961-62, asst. sta. mgr., 1963-65, gen. mgr., 1966-69, pres., 1970-98; sr. cons., 1998-99; ret., 1999. Co-author: ETV: The Farther Vision, 1967. Mem. ho. of dels. United Way of Buffalo and Erie County, 1967-98; trustee Ea. Ednl. Network, 1965-95, treas., 1967-70, exec. com., 1967-74, 78-81, 84-85, 88-90, 92-94, chmn. budget and fin. com., 1967-70, pres., 1971-72, chmn., 1973-74, v.p., 1980-81, 88-90, 92-93, adv. bd. interregional progam svc., 1984-90; trustee Am. Program Svc., 1993-96, exec. com., 1993-96, fin. com., 1994-96; mem. CATV com., devel. adv. com. NAEB; exec. bd. Niagara Frontier coun. Boy Scouts Am., 1971-76; exec. com. Cantalician Ctr., 1978-85; trustee St. Joseph's Collegiate Inst., 1978-85 (mem. steering com. capital campaign, 1998-2000); chmn. PBS Border Sta.Consortium, 1986-88; bd. dirs. PBS, 1972-78, 80-86, vice-chmn., 1975, nat. program policy com., 1990-95; mem. Governance Task Force, 1996; bd. dirs. PBS Enterprises, 1985-90, Nat. Data Cast, Inc., 1989-90; trustee Assn. Am. Pub. TV Stas., 1987-93, exec. com., 1989-93, chmn. nominating com., 1989; mem. Kenmore-Tonawanda Pub. Schs. Bd. Edn., 1974-81, v.p., 1977, pres., 1978; trustee Chautauqua Instn., 1988-96, devel. com., 1989, program com., 1986-95, exec. com., 1989-95, personnel com., 1990-95, mktg. com., 1994-95, fin. com., 1995-96, bldg. and grounds com., 1995-96, edn./youth/recreation com., 1989-93, 96-97, chmn., 1989-93, mission policy com., 1997-98; bd. dirs. Buffalo Coun. World Affairs, 1994-95, Blue Shield West N.Y., 1990-92; mem. fin. com. St. Amelia Ch., 1990—, mem. stewardship com., 1993—, chmn., 1993-2001, trustee, 2001—; chmn. bd. dirs. John Lodge McHugh Endowment, 2000—. Recipient Focus award Buffalo Courier Express, 1978, Signum Fidei award St. Joseph's Collegiate Inst., 1984, Man of Yr. award Nat. Columbus Day Com., 1985, 92, Matrix award Women in Comm., 1985; named one of 100 Most Influential People in Western N.Y., Bus. First, 1996; inducted into Buffalo Broadcast Pioneers Hall of Fame, 1999. Mem. N.Y. State Ednl. Radio and TV Assn. (trustee, pres. 1964-65, treas. 1963, editor newsletter 1962), Pub. Rels. Assn. Western N.Y. (pres. 1966), Nat. Assn. Ednl. Broadcasters, Buffalo Broadcasters Assn. (bd. dirs. 2005-), Canisius Coll. Alumni Assn. (bd. govs. 1960-62, 70-73). Avocations: reading, collecting and tasting wine, photography.

COLLINS, JACK ADAM, mechanical engineer; b. Columbus, Ohio, Nov. 23, 1929; married, 1958; 4 children. BSME, Ohio State U., 1952, MSc, 1954, PhD in Mech. Engring., 1963. From rsch. asst. to rsch. assoc. mech. engring. Ohio State U., 1952-63, assoc. prof. mech. engring., 1972-74; assoc. prof. Ariz. State U., 1963-72, chmn. mech. design sect. dept. mech. engring., 1975-92, prof., 1974-92; ret. Cons. Babcock & Wilcox Rsch. Ctr., GE Co., AiRsch. Mfg. Co., Worthington Industries, Owens/Corning Fiberglass. Author: Failure of Material in Mechanical Design: Analysis Prediction Prevention, 1981, rev., 1993, Mechanical Design of Machine Elements and Machines: A Failure Prevention Perspective, 2003. Mem. ASME (Machine Design award 1997), Am. Soc. Engring. Edn., Am. Soc. Testing and Materials. Achievements include experimental and analytical stress and deflection analysis; experimental and analytical failure analysis, including fatigue, creep, wear and fretting. Home: 4447 E Via Dona Rd Cave Creek AZ 85331 Business E-Mail: collins.13@osu.edu.

COLLINS, JACKIE, writer; b. London, Oct. 4, 1941; m. Oscar Lerman. Author: The World Is Full of Married Men, 1968, The Stud, 1969, Sunday Simmons and Charlie Brick, 1971 (pub. as The Hollywood Zoo, 1975), Lovehead, 1974 (pub. as The Love Killers, 1977), The World Is Full of Divorced Women, 1975, Lovers and Gamblers, 1977, The Bitch, 1979, Chances, 1981, Hollywood Wives, 1983, Sinners, 1984, Lucky, 1985, Hollywood Husbands, 1986, Rock Star, 1987, Lady Boss, 1989, American Star, 1993, Hollywood Kids, 1994, Vendetta: Lucky's Revenge, 1997, Thrill, 1998, L.A. Connections, 1998, Dangerous Kiss, 1999, Lethal Seduction, 2000, Hollywood Wives: The New Generation, 2001, Deadly Embrace, 2002. Office: c/o Simon & Schuster 1230 Ave of Amer New York NY 10020

COLLINS, JACQUELINE Y, state senator; b. McComb, Miss., Dec. 10; Grad. journalism, Northwestern Univ.; MA, Harvard's John F. Kennedy Sch. of Gov.; MA Human Svc. Admin., Spertus Coll.; MA Theol. Studies, Harvard Divinity Sch., 2003. State Senator 11 Senate, Dist. 16Ill., 2003—; min. of Comm. St. Sabina Cath. Ch., Chgo.; journalist in print, radio and TV; press sec. Congressman Gus Savage. Mem. Appropriations I, Environ. and Energy, Revenue (VC), Revenue Subcommittee on Spl. Issues. Recipient Emmy

Award - nominated news editor, CBS-TV/ Chgo.; Legislative fellow with US Senator Hillary Rodham Clinton. Democrat. Catholic. Office: Capitol Bldg M-118 Springfield IL 62706 also: 1155 W 79th St Chicago IL 60620

COLLINS, JAMES FRANKLIN, retired ambassador; b. Aurora, Ill., June 4, 1939; AB cum laude, Harvard Coll., 1961; MA, Ind. U., 1964, postgrad., 1964-67, Moscow State U., 1965-66. Asst. prof. history U.S. Naval Acad., 1967-69; vice consul Am. Consulate Gen., Izmir, Turkey, 1969-71; polit. officer European Affairs Bur., U.S. Dept. State, Washington, 1971-73; polit. officer Am. Embassy, Moscow, 1973-75; polit. analyst Bur Intelligence and Rsch. U.S. Dept. State, 1975-78, staff asst., polit. officer Near East Affairs Bur., 1978-82; polit. counselor Am. Embassy, Amman, Jordan, 1982-84; dir. ops. ctr. Dept. State, 1984-87; dir. for intelligence policy Nat. Security Coun., Washington, 1987-88; dep. exec. sec. for Europe and L.Am. U.S. Dept. State, 1988-90; dep. chief of mission Am. Embassy, Moscow, 1990-93; coord. for regional affairs for New Ind. States U.S. Dept. State, 1993-94, sr. coord. Office Amb.-at-Large for New Ind. State, 1994-95, amb.-at-large, spl. advisor to sec. state New Ind. States, 1995-97; U.S. amb. to Russian Fedn., Am. Embassy, Moscow, 1997-2001, ret., 2001; sr. internat. advisor Akin, Gump, Strauss, Hauer & Feld LLP, 2001—. Writer cons., 2001— Address: 1333 New Hampshire Ave NW Washington DC 20036 Business E-Mail: jcollins@akingump.com. E-mail: jfcollins@aol.com.

COLLINS, JAMES H., JR., architectural firm executive; BArch, MBA with distinction, Rensselaer Poly. Inst. Joined Payette Assocs. Inc., Boston, 1979, pres., 1998—. Lectr. in field. Author: Design Process for the Human Workplace, in The Architecture of Science. Recipient Fellows award, Rensselaer Alumni Assn., 2003. Office: Payette Assocs Inc 285 Summer St Boston MA 02210-1522*

COLLINS, JAMES J., biomedical engineer, educator; AB in Physics, Coll. of the Holy Cross, 1987; PhD in Med. Engring., U. Oxford, 1990. Founder, acting chief scientific officer Cellicon Biotechnologies, 2000—; prof. of biomedical engring. Boston U., Coll. Engring., 1990—. Co- dir Ctr. for Biodynamics, Boston U., Ctr. for Advanced Biotechnology, Boston U.; dir. Applied Biodynamics Lab., Boston U. Contbr. articles to profl. jours. Fellow MacArthur Found., 2003. Achievements include being pioneer in systems biology, the study of the cell as a system of biological components; being world leader in use of nonlinear dynamical techniques to reverse-engineer gene regulatory networks. Address: Boston Univ ENG Bio-Med Engineering 44 Cummington St Boston MA 02215 Office: c/o Puretech Ventures LLC 222 Berkeley St Ste 1040 Boston MA 02116 Office Phone: 617-353-0390. Office Fax: 617-353-5462. Business E-Mail: jcollins@bu.edu.

COLLINS, JAMES WILLIAM, health science association administrator, epidemiologist, mechanical engineer; b. Atlanta, Oct. 19, 1962; s. Thomas Allen and Mary Frank Collins; m. Maria Joao Ponte, Oct. 25, 1992; children: Karina Maria, James Seth. B of Mech. Engring., Ga. Inst. Tech., 1984; MSME, W.Va. U., 1989; PhD in Health Policy and Mgmt., Johns Hopkins U., 1998. Rsch. mech. engr. Ctrs. Disease Control and Prevention, Nat. Inst. Occupl. Safety and Health, Morgantown, W.Va., 1984—90, rsch. epidemiologist, 1992—2004; assoc. dir. sci. Ctrs. Disease Control and Prevention, Nat. Inst. Occupl. Safety and Health, Divsn. Safety Rsch., 2004—. Bd. editors Jour. Injury Control and Safety Promotion, Amsterdam, 2004—; guest lectr. occupational epidemiology Johns Hopkins U; guest lectr. occupational safety and health W.Va. U. Pres. Exch. Club, Fairchance, Pa., 2000—05; chmn. bd. deacons Mt. Moriah Bapt. Ch., Smithfield, 2004—05, mem., 2005—05. Capt. USPHS, 1984—2005. Recipient Spl. Assignment award, USPHS, 1991, Surgeon Gen Exemplary Svc. medal, 1992, Achievement medal, 1996, Pub. Health Svc. citation, 1996, Crisis Response Ribbon, 2002, Outstanding Unit citation, 2002, U. S. Pub. Health Svc. Engring. Lit. award, Chief Engr. USPHS, 2000, Partnering award Worker Safety and Health, Nat. Inst. Occupl. Safety and Health, 2003. Mem.: Commd. Officers Assn. USPHS (pres., v.p., treas. 1984—2005, Mem. of Yr. 1988), Soc. Am. Mil. Engrs. Conservative. Baptist. Achievements include research in Conducted intervention trials demonstrating highly effective programs to prevent back and other musculoskeletal injuries among health care workers due to patient lifting and slips and falls. Avocations: travel, hunting, fishing, softball, coaching. Home: 70 South Morgantown St Fairchance PA 15436 Office: Ctrs Disease Control & Prevention 1095 Willowdale Rd Mail stop 1900 Morgantown WV 26505 Office Phone: 304-285-5998. Business E-Mail: jcollins1@cdc.gov.

COLLINS, JEAN KATHERINE, language educator; b. Norfolk, Va., June 14, 1928; d. Elwood Brantley and Katherine Belle (Lambertson) C. BA in Liberal Arts, James Madison U., Harrisonburg, Va., 1945-49; MA in English, U. Richmond, 1950-51; edn. credits, U. Va., Eastern Shore of Va., 1950, 60; art edn. credits, Millersville State Tchrs. Coll, summer 1970. Continuity writer Radio Station WLEE, Richmond, Va., 1949; English, critic tchr. Farmville H.S., Longwood Coll., Va., 1951-53; English tchr., art tchr. Hermitage H.S., Richmond, Va., 1953-55; prin., art tchr. Cape Charles (Va.) H.S., 1957-59; head English dept., tchr. Northampton H.S., Eastville, Va., 1960-63; art tchr. Pvt. Studio, Cape Charles, Va., 1964-90. Pres. Lambda chpt. Delta Kappa Gamma Soc., Eastern Shore of Va., 1966-68; recording sec. Iota State Delta Kappa Gamma Soc., Headqtrs., Richmond, Va., 1967-69; adv. bd. Eastern Shore Pub. Libr., Accomac, Va., 1981-89; bd. dirs. Eastern Shore of Va. Hist. Soc., Onancock, Va., 1957-60. Author: (poetry) Madison Quarterly, 1948, 49; author, illustrator: An Eastern Shore Sampler, 1975; author: History of Trinity United Methodist Church, 1993. Named Woman of Yr. Young WOmen's Club of Cape Charles, Va., 1958. Mem. Eastern Shore of Va. Hist. Soc., Cape Charles Hist. Soc., Trinity United Meth. Ch., Delta Kappa Gamma Soc. Republican. Methodist. Avocations: painting, needlecrafts, history, theater, dance, writing.

COLLINS, JEFFREY G., lawyer, former prosecutor; b. Detroit, Mar. 16, 1959; m. Lois Collins; 2 children. BA in Psychology, Northwestern U., 1981; JD, Howard U. Sch. Law, 1984. Pvt. practice, 1984—94; appointed judge Detroit Recorder's Ct., 1994—96; cir. judge Wayne County Cir. Ct., 1997—98; judge Mich. Supreme Ct., 1998—2000, Mich. Ct. Appeals, 2000—01; U.S. atty. (ea. dist.) Mich. US Dept. Justice, 2001—04; atty., ptnr. litigation dept. Foley & Lardner LLP, 2004—. Mentor Man to Man program Paul Robeson Acad.; mem. Plymouth United Ch. of Christ, Detroit. Mem.: Mich. Assn. for Leadership Devel. (founder, dir. Wayne County chpt.). Office: Foley & Lardner Ste 1000 150 W Jefferson Ave Detroit MI 48226 Office Phone: 313-234-7100. E-mail: jcollins@foley.com.

COLLINS, JO MARSTON, retired elementary educator; b. Ottawa, Ont., Can., Feb. 11, 1928; d. Russell and Lillian (Stevenson) Marston; m. Charles Collins, Aug. 4, 1951; children: Steven, Beth Ann. BA, Mich. State U., 1950, U. South Fla., 1979, MA, 1982. Cert. elem. tchr. Classroom tchr. North Port Elem., Sarasota County, Fla., to 1990. Adj. prof. U. South Fla. Mem. Sarasota RC (past pres.), Fla. RA (dist. dir.), Delta Kappa Gamma, Phi Kappa Phi, Kappa Alpha Theta.

COLLINS, JODA LEE, minister; b. Modesto, Calif., May 3, 1949; s. Joda William and Retha Mae Collins; m. Laura Carmela Collins. DD, Universal Bible Inst., 1976; BA, Golden State U., 1980, PhD, 1982; BA in Psychology, Calif. State U., 1988. So. Baptist pastor various chs., Calif., Fla., Tenn., 1974—. Author: (book) Dynamic Discipleship, 1996, The Biblical Role of Woman in the Church, 1998, How to Successfully Pastor a Difficult Church, 1998, The Chronology of Revelation, 1999, Every Word Spoken by Jesus on How to do Church, 2000, A Kingdom Based Church, 2002, Introduction to New Testament Greek, 2003. With USAF, 1968—72, Vietnam. Republican. Baptist. Avocations: Karate, water-skiing, bowling, fishing. Home: 4033 Buttonbush Dr Milton FL 32583-5020 E-mail: drjlcollins@aol.com.

COLLINS, JOE LENA, retired secondary school educator; b. Mt. Pleasant, Tenn., Nov. 18, 1922; d. Morton Daniel and Rosetta Francis C. BS in English, Tenn. Tech., 1949; MA in English, George Peabody, 1968, EdS in English, 1975. Cert. tchr. Sec. to Dr. G.C. English and Dr. C.D. Walton, Mt. Pleasant, Tenn., 1942-46; tchr. Maury Co. Schs., Mt. Pleasant, Tenn., 1949-51, Tenn. Tech., Cookeville, Tenn., 1951; acct. Cookeville Prodn. Credit, Tenn., 1951-52; tchr. Metro Nashville Schs., 1952-88. Lectr. Ret. Learning Vanderbilt U., 2000—. Mem. Shepherd's Ctr. West End Book Club, 1989—2002, Metro Retired Tchrs. Assn., 1988—; chmn. Shepherd's Ctr. West Book Club; com. work Dem. Party, 1980—2003. Mem. AAUW (pres.), Tenn. Art League, Tenn. Writers Alliance, Tenn. Hist. Soc., Women in the Arts, United Meth. Women (Woman of Purpose award). Avocations: reading, writing, painting, sports. Home: 6212 Henry Ford Dr Nashville TN 37209-1738

COLLINS, JOHN ALFRED, retired obstetrician, gynecologist, educator; s. John Bandel and Vera Collins; m. Carole Joanne Sedwick West; children: John Bruce, Blayne Linda, Anne Catherine. MD, U. West Ont., 1960. Intern Victoria Hosp., London; resident ob-gyn. U. West Ont., 1961-65; McLaughlin Found. fellow Univ. Coll. Hosp., London; with clin. endocrinology rsch. unit U. Edinburgh, U.K., Middlesex Hosp., London, 1965-67; clin. rsch. fellow Ont. Cancer Found. London Clinic, 1967-76; with dept. ob-gyn. U. West Ont., 1967-77, asst. dean undergrad. edn. faculty medicine, 1975-77; prof., head dept. ob-gyn. Dalhousie U., 1977-83; prof., chmn. dept. ob-gyn. McMaster U., Hamilton, 1983—93; vis. chair internat. Francqui Found. Brussels Free U., 2000—01. Mem. editl. bd. New Eng. Jour. Medicine, 1991-96, Fertility and Sterility, 1991-96, Obstetrics and Gynecology, 2004—; assoc. editor Human Reprodn., 2003—; contbr. articles to profl. jours. Mem. Royal Coll. Physicians and Surgeons Can., Royal Coll. Obstetricians and Gynecologists U.K., Am. Coll. Obstetricians and Gynecologists, Am. Soc. Reproductive Medicine, Can. Fertility Soc., Soc. Obstetricians and Gynecologists Can. Home: 400 Maders Cove Rd RR 1 Mahone Bay NS Canada B0J 2EO Personal E-mail: collinsj@auracom.com.

COLLINS, JOHN F., lawyer; b. N.Y.C., Dec. 15, 1948; AB, Fordham U., 1970; JD, U. Chgo., 1973. Bar: N.Y. 1974, US Dist. Ct. (no. dist. Calif., NJ, ea., so., no. dist. NY), US Ct. Appeals (2d, 3d, 9th, Fed. cir.), US Ct. Fed. Claims, US Supreme Ct. Ptnr., antitrust & trade regulation practices Dewey Ballantine LLP, NYC. Editor (asst.): Antitrust Law Jour., Annual Rev. of Antitrust Law Developments. Mem. ABA, N.Y. State Bar Assn., Assn. Bar of City of N.Y., Phi Beta Kappa. Office: Dewey Ballantine 1301 Avenue Of The Americas New York NY 10019-6022 Office Phone: 212-259-7080. Office Fax: 212-259-8201. Business E-Mail: jcollins@dbllp.com.

COLLINS, JOHN PETER, lawyer; b. New Rochelle, N.Y., Mar. 3, 1944; s. William Thomas and Diane G. Collins; m. Martha Ann Gorman; children: Patrick Michael, Matthew Peter, Kathryn Corby, John Peter Jr., Meighan O'Connor. BS, Xavier U., 1966; JD, U. Cin., 1969. Bar: N.Y. 1969, U.S. Ct. Mil. Appeals 1970, U.S. Dist. Ct. (so. dist.) N.Y. 1978, U.S. Supreme Ct. 1988, U.S. Dist. Ct. (ea. dist.) N.Y. 2002. Asst. dist. atty. Westchester County Dist. Atty., White Plains, NY, 1969—70; assoc. King Edwards O'Connor, White Plains, 1977—79; ptnr. O'Connor, McGuinness Conte Doyle Oleson & Collins, White Plains, 1980—99, Burchetta Collins and Hanley, Carmel, NY, 1999—2002, Collins, Hanley & LaFrance, Carmel, NY, 2003—. Justice Town of Kent, NY, 2000—; mem. Million Dollar Advs. Forum, 2001. Maj. U.S. Army, 1970—77. Mem.: ATLA, Strathmore's (life), Putnam County Bar Assn., N.Y. State Bar Assn., Million Dollar Advocates Forum. Office: Collins Hanley & LaFrance LLP 9 Fair St Carmel NY 10512-1301 Office Phone: 845-225-5544.

COLLINS, JOHN W., JR., retired military officer, technologist, educator; b. Lackawanna, NY, Jan. 27, 1958; m. Simona E Aschenbrenner, Apr. 12, 1980; children: Mary, John III. Basic Cert. in Mgmt., City Colls. Chgo., 1975—76; Assoc. in Sci., N.Y. Regents (now Excelsior) Coll., Albany, 1977—79; BA, Columbia College, Columbia, Mo., 1981—82; M in Pub. Adminstrn., U.Okla., Norman, 1984; Command and Gen. Staff Officer Diploma, U.S. Army Command and Gen. Staff Coll., Ft. Leavenworth, Kans., 1986; Logistics Exec. Devel.Diploma, U.S. Army Logistics Mgmt. Coll., Ft. Lee, VA, 1991; Air War Coll. Diploma, Air War Coll. Air U., Maxwell AFB, Ala., 1996; EdD, Seton Hall U., South Orange, NJ, 1999. Cert. K-12 Chief Sch. Administr. cert. eligibility 1999, K-12 Prin.and Supr. cert. eligibility 1999, K-12 Sch. Bus. Administr. cert. eligibility 1999, JROTC Mil. Tchr. standard cert. 1998. Enlisted U.S. Army, 1975, rose through ranks to sgt., 1978, commd. 2d lt., 1978, advanced through grades to lt. col., retired, 1998; assoc. acad. dir. SetonWorldWide, Seton Hall U., South Orange, NJ, 1998—2001; faculty assoc. Seton Hall U., South Orange, NJ, 1998—2004; asst. prof. SetonHall U., South Orange, NJ, 2005—. Edn. tech. cons. Seton Hall U., South Orange, NJ, 1998—. Author: (National Essay Contest) Proud to Serve, 1991 (George Washington Freedom Foundation Medal, 1991), Ordnance Magazine (Bulletin), 1989 (Crimson Pen Award, 1989); contbr. articles to edn. and mil. logistics jours. Vol. Am. Overseas Schs., Germany, 1992—94. Recipient Legion of Merit, President U. S., 1988-1998, Cert. of Appreciation, President U.S., 1998, N. Y. State Conspicuous Svc. Cross (12 awards), Gov. of New York, 1999, N. Y. State Conspicuous Svc. Star (3 awards), Gov. N.Y., 2000, N.J. Meritorious Svc. medal, Gov. of N.J., 2003, Meritorious Svc. medal (4 awards), Pres. of U.S., 1987-1996. Mem.: VFW, Internat. Soc. for Tech. in Edn., Am. Ednl. Rsch. Assn., Am. Assn. Adult and Continuing Edn., Am. Legion, Disabled Am. Vets. (life). Avocations: fishing, travel. Home: 12 Hunterdon Road West Orange NJ 07052-1604 Office: Seton Hall University 421 Kozlowski Hall 400 S Orange Ave South Orange NJ 07079 Office Phone: 973-275-2823. Personal E-mail: john.collins6@us.army.mil. Business E-Mail: collinjo@shu.edu.

COLLINS, JOSEPH BERNARD, lawyer; b. Bennington, Vt., Feb. 11, 1953; s. James Bernard and Mary Agnes (O'Neil) C.; m. Denise Claire Banville, June 11, 1977. AA, Holyoke Community Coll., Mass., 1973; AB, Boston Coll., 1975; JD, Suffolk U., Boston, 1978. Bar: Mass. 1978. Assoc. Kamberg, Berman & Hendel, P.C., Springfield, Mass., 1978-82; ptnr. Hendel & Collins P.C., Springfield, 1982—. Adj. prof. law Western New Eng. Coll., Springfield, 1982-93. Fin. com. Town of Wilbraham, Mass., 1982-84. Mem. Comml. League Am. (New Eng. regional chmn. 1989-90, vice chmn. 1988-89), Hampden County Bar Assn. (chmn. young lawyers div. 1982-83). Roman Catholic. Avocations: scuba diving, skiing. Office: Hendel & Collins PC 101 State St Ste 525 Springfield MA 01103-2020

COLLINS, JOY, nurse, consultant, writer; b. NYC, Mar. 1, 1948; d. Pasquale Joseph and Millie Rita Palastro; m. John Collins, Aug. 28, 1981. BSBA, St. Joseph's Coll., 1997. Legal nurse cons. Collins Med. Legal Cons., Inc., Fountain Hills, Ariz., 2002—. Contbr. articles in field. Mem.: Am. Assn. Legal Nurse Cons. (ednl. chair Phoenix chpt. 2005). Personal E-mail: jcollins@cox.net. Business E-Mail: legalnurses@cox.net.

COLLINS, JOYCE A.P., minister, librarian, educator, realtor; b. Memphis, June 12, 1948; d. Joe Harry (Stepfather) and Lelia Mae (Strickand Powell) Armstrong; m. Warren Eugene Collins, Sept. 4, 1971 (div. 1994); adopted children: Evangeline, Warren Gabriel. BA cum laude, LeMoyne-Owen U., Memphis, 1970; MLS, Western Mich. U., Kalamazoo, 1971. Cert. tchr. Tenn., 1970, lifetime tchr. cert. La., cert. realtor La. Circulation libr. Tenn. State U., Nashville, 1971—72; catalog libr. La. State U., Baton Rouge, 1972; dir. info. and rsch. ARIC, Nashville, 1973—74; asst. prof., head libr. media svcs. Fisk U., Nashville, 1974—75; libr., lectr. Pub. Schs. Davidson Co., Nashville, 1975—77; libr., head circulation dept. Southern U., Baton Rouge, 1977—78, social sci. libr., 1978—80; realtor Baton Rouge, 1980—; dir. JACPO Ministries, Nashville, 1997—. Faculty sen. La. State U., Baton Rouge, 1970—80; reader svcs. coord. Fisk U., Nashville, 1975. Mem.: AAUW, Nat. Assn. U. Women, La. Libr. Assn. Baptist. Office: JAPCO Ministries 308 Port Dr Nashville TN 37115

COLLINS, JUDITH ANN, librarian; b. San Francisco, Aug. 12, 1941; d. Walter George and Dorothy Louise (Eisenhut) Petersen; m. Curtis Allan Collins, Dec. 22, 1962; children: Nathaniel Christopher, Hillary Victoria Collins Edwards. AA, Modesto Jr. Coll., 1962; BS, Oreg. State U., 1967; MS, Cath. U. Am., 1983. Libr. cons. World Bank, Washington, 1983—84; reference libr. Am. Bankers Assn., Washington, 1984—87; libr. cons. Monterey (Calif.) County Libr., 1987—; circulation libr. Nat. Rural Electric Coop. Assn., Washington, 1984—87; tech. svcs. libr. Zimmerman Assocs., Inc., Washington, 1986—87; substitute sch. libr. Fairfax County Schs., Va., 1986—87; media libr. Hartnell CC, Salinas, Calif., 1987—, instr., 1988—. Cons. AID, 1984—85. Election ofcl. Fairfax Electoral Bd. (Va.), 1980—87, Monterey County Electoral Bd., 1987—; ruling elder Presbyn. Ch., Springfield, Va., 1981—83. Mem.: ALA, Calif. Library Assn., Order Ea. Star. Home: 24010 Ranchito Del Rio Ct Salinas CA 93908-9652

COLLINS, KATHLEEN, writer, retired educator; b. Seattle, Jan. 30, 1931; d. Edward Donnan and Ada Myrtle (Munson) Collins; m. Thomas Kranidas, Oct. 5, 1951 (div. 1973); children: Stephen, Thomas T., Anne and Mary Caroline Kranidas. BA, Barnard Coll., 1952; MA, SUNY, Stony Brook, 1974. Cert. secondary tchr., N.Y. Tchr. high sch., Northport, N.Y., 1972-92. Advisor Identity Workshop, 1990-92; tchr. ind. writing workshops. Author: (novels) Lovers in the Present Afternoon, 1984, One Year in Autumn, 1964, (short stories) The Mountain, the Stone, 1975. Named Suffolk County Tchr. of Yr., 1991. Democrat. Avocations: feminist and political activities, swimming, walking. Address: PO Box 305 Miller Place NY 11764

COLLINS, KATHLEEN, academic administrator, art educator; b. Chgo., . BA in psychology, minor in fine arts, Stanford U.; MFA in photography. Chmn. applied photography dept. Sch. Photographic Arts & Sci., Rochester Inst. Tech., coord. summer workshops; dean Sch. Art & Design, NY State Coll. Ceramics, Alfred U., prof.; pres. Kans. City Art Inst., 1996—. Represented in permanent collections, Art Inst. Chgo., Cleve. Art Mus., Centro Cultural/Arte Contemporaneo, Mex. City, Mex., Chrysler Mus., Norfolk Va. Office: Office of President Kansas City Art Inst 4415 Warwick Blvd Kansas City MO 64111*

COLLINS, KATHLEEN ANNE, artistic director; b. Elmira, N.Y., Dec. 20, 1951; d. James G. and Joyce (Balmer) C.; m. Andrew Stephon Elston, May 28, 1977; children: Megan, Kate. BA, SUNY, Albany, 1974; MA in Theatre, U. Wash., 1976, MFA in Theatre, 1979. Dir. edn. Seattle Children's Theatre, 1975-78; instr. drama Lakeside Sch., Seattle, 1978-79; artistic dir. Honolulu Theatre for Youth, 1979-83, Fulton Opera House, Lancaster, Pa., 1983-98; prof. Cornish Coll. of Arts, Seattle, 1999—. Guest lectr. U. Hawaii, Honolulu, 1981, U. Wash., Seattle, 2002—04; guest dir. Seattle Children's Theatre, 2002—03; adj. faculty Lesley U., 2000—; guest dir. Six Minutes, Seattle Rep. Woman's Playwriting Festival, Seattle, 2004. Contbg. author: Drama With Children, 1979. Bd. dirs. PTO, Lancaster, 1990-98; pres. Winifred Ward Found. Mem. Am. Assn. Theatre Educators, Assn. and Soc. for Theatre and Children. Democrat. Roman Catholic. Personal E-mail: kalcollins@comcast.net.

COLLINS, KEITH, federal executive; BS in Math., Villanova U., 1969; MS in Econs., U. Conn., 1973; PhD in Econs. and Stats., N.C. State U., 1977. With USDA, Washington, 1978—, dir., econ. analysis staff, 1986-92, acting asst. sec. econs., 1993-95, chief economist, 1996—. Mem. Sr. Exec. Svc. Recipient Presdl. Rank award, 1990, 92, 96, 2002. Office: USDA Office Chief Economist Whitten Bldg Rm 112A Washington DC 20250-0001 E-mail: keith.collins@usda.gov.

COLLINS, KERRY, professional football player; b. Lebanon, Pa., Dec. 30, 1972; Student, Pa. State U. Quarterback Carolina Panthers, 1995-98, New Orleans Saints, 1998-99, N.Y. Giants, 1999—2004, Oakland Raiders, 2004—. Named to NFL Pro-Bowl, 1996. Office: c/o Oakland Raiders 1220 Harbor Bay Pkwy Alameda CA 94502

COLLINS, KEVIN HEATH, lawyer; b. Cedar Rapids, Iowa, May 7, 1955; s. Thomas Martin and Joanne (Heath) C.; m. Sally A. Stephenson, June 11, 1985. BA, Creighton U., 1978; JD, U. Iowa, 1980. Bar: Iowa 1981, Hawaii 1982, U.S. Dist. Ct. (no. and so. dist.) Iowa 1981, U.S. Dist. Ct. Hawaii, 1982, U.S. Ct. Appeals (8th cir.) 1981, U.S. Ct. Appeals (9th cir.) 1982, U.S. Supreme Ct. 1984. Sr. v.p. Shuttleworth & Ingersoll, P.C., Cedar Rapids, 1980-82, 84—; assoc. Dinman & Yokoyama, P.C., Honolulu, 1982-84. Exec. com. United Way of East Cen. Iowa, Cedar Rapids, 1986-87, Retired Sr. Vol. Program, Cedar Rapids, 1986-89. Fellow Iowa Acad. Trial Lawyers, Assn. Am. Bd. Trial Advocates, Fedn. of Insurance & Corp. Counsel; mem. ABA, Am. Arbitration Assn. (panel mem.), Iowa State Bar Assn. (co-chair com. on delivery of legal svcs. to the elderly 1989-90, mem. law practice mgmt. sect. 1991-98, bd. govs. 1998-2001, v.p. 2001-02, pres.-elect 2002-03, pres. 2003-04), Hawaii State Bar Assn. Office: Shuttleworth Ingersoll PLC PO Box 2107 Cedar Rapids IA 52406-2107

COLLINS, KEVIN T., lawyer; b. 1954; BA in Comm., Fordham Univ., 1976; JD, Seton Hall Univ., 1980. Bar: NY 1981. Ptnr., corp. group Dorsey & Whitney LLP, NYC, chmn., life sci. and health care group, and mem., policy com. Office: Dorsey & Whitney LLP 250 Park Ave New York NY 10177-1500 Office Phone: 212-415-9319. Office Fax: 212-953-7201. Business E-Mail: collins.kevin@dorsey.com.

COLLINS, LARRY RICHARD, artist, educator, art gallery director; b. Spokane, Wash., July 15, 1945; s. Richard Thurman and Glorious Blossom (Kingbay) C. BFA, U. Okla., 1967; postgrad., Ind. U., 1970; MFA, Mass. Coll. Art, 1980. Instr. anatomy, design, figure drawing, drawing Vesper George Sch. Art, Boston, 1980-81; instr. anatomy, figure drawing Brockton (Mass.) Art Mus. Sch., 1980-81; instr. anatomy, drawing, figure drawing Mass. Coll. Art, Boston, 1980-82, 86-95, U. N.H., Durham, 1987-88; dir. Driskel Gallery, Schoolhouse Ctr., Provincetown, 1998—2004, Larry Collins Fine Art, Provincetown, Mass., 2004—. Combat artist U.S. Army, Vietnam, 1968-69; guest lectr. in anatomy, Boston U., 1986. One-man shows include Bazza Gallery, Oklahoma City, 1962, Northeastern State Coll., Talequah, Okla., 1962, U. Okla., Norman, 1963, 1967, Mass. Coll. Art, Boston, 1979, Mabee-Gerrer Mus. Art, Shawnee, Okla., 1984, First St. Gallery, N.Y.C., 1986, N.Y. Pub. Libr., 1987, Michael Allen Gallery, Brookline, Mass., 1995, East End Gallery, Provincetown, 1996, Tiffany & Co., N.Y.C., 1996, Wohlfarth Galleries, Washington, 1997, Schoolhouse Ctr., Provincetown, 1998, 1999, Carrie Haddad Gallery, Hudson, N.Y., 1998, Amherst (Mass.) Coll., 2004, exhibited in group shows at Mus. Art, U. Okla., Norman, 1961, 1962, 1963 (Purchase awards in painting, 1962, 1963), Springfield (Mo.) Art Mus., 1962, Okla. Art Ctr., Oklahoma City, 1962, 1963, 1965, 1966, Philbrook Art Ctr., Tulsa, 1963, 1966, Joslyn Art Mus., Omaha, 1966, Brockton Art Mus., Mass., 1980, Wistariahurst Mus., Holyoke, Mass., 1980, Mass. Coll. Art, Boston, 1981, El Paso (Tex.) Mus. Art, 1982, 1993, Fairleigh Dickinson U., Teaneck, N.J., 1982, Pa. State U., University Park, 1983, Sheldon Meml. Art Gallery, Lincoln, Nebr., 1983, Gump's Gallery, San Francisco, 1983, 1984, 1985, Camera di Commercio, Lucca, Italy, 1984, Boston Visual Artists' Union, 1984, Provincetown Art Mus., 1984, 1986, Butler Inst. Am. Art, Youngstown, Ohio, 1984, Nat. Acad. Design, N.Y.C., 1984, 1986, First St. Gallery, 1984, 1985, 1986, 1987, 1988, Indiana U. Pa., 1985, NYU, 1985, Amos Eno Gallery, N.Y.C., 1986, 1987 (1st prize, 1986), John Pence Gallery, San Francisco, 1987, St. Louis Artists Guild, 1987, Grand Ctrl. Galleries, N.Y.C., 1987, Mass. Coll. Art, Boston, 1993, Provincetown Art Assn. & Mus., 1996—99, Schoolhouse Ctr., 1998—2001, Represented in permanent collections Mus. Art U. Okla., Norman, Sheldon Meml. Art Gallery, Lincoln, Nebr., Mabee-Gerrer Mus. Art, Shawnee, Print Collection, Boston Pub. Libr., Photographs Collection, Berg Collection, N.Y. Pub. Libr., Worcester (Mass.) Art Mus., Spl. Collection Libr., U. N.C., Chapel Hill, reprodns. of paintings appear in, Human Anatomy and Figure Drawing (Jack N.Kramer), 1984, Old Love Story (Allen Ginsberg), 1986, The Am. Painting Collection Sheldon Meml. Art Gallery (Norman A. Geske), The Hopper House at Truro (Lawrence Ferlinghetti). Served with U.S. Army, 1967-69, Vietnam. Decorated Bronze Star; grantee Individual Artists' Painting N.H. State Coun., 1987-88, Artists' Opportunity, 1989-90; travel fellow Creative Art Studios, Rome, Florence, Pisa, Arezzo, Italy, 1984. Mem. Provincetown Art Assn. Home: PO Box 2 Provincetown MA 02657-0002 Office Phone: 508-487-6600. E-mail: larry@larrycollinsfineart.com.

COLLINS, LAURA JANE, music educator, singer, accompanist; b. Mauston, Wis., Mar. 25, 1957; d. Horace Rexford and Mary Jean Collins; m. Thomas Henry Buchholz, Dec. 30, 1977 (div. Dec. 19, 1982); 1 child, Erik. Student, Viterbo Coll., LaCrosse, Wis., 1977; BA, Cameron U., Lawton, Okla., 1979. Cert. music educator K-12 Okla., 1979, Yamaha Music Sch. Tchr. Yamaha Internat. Corp., 1980. Yamaha music sch. tchr. Keynote Music Co., Tulsa, Okla., 1980—82; vocal, gen. music educator Tulsa (Okla.) Pub. Schs., 1981—. Instr. Tulsa Opera Childrens Workshop, 1986—87; chapel accompanist All Souls Unitarian Ch., 1993—96, choir accompanist, 1995—96; chapel organist Hillcrest Hosp., Tulsa, 2000—; jazz ensemble vocalist R.F. Singers, 2003—04; chorus mem. Gilbert and Sullivan Opereta Soc. of Tulsa, 1988—89. Cast mem. Tulsa, Gilbert and Sullivan Operetta Soc., 1988—89. Vol. Tulsa Boy Singers; co-mgr. office Anderson for Pres., Tulsa, 1980; vol. Jones for U.S. Senate, 1980; vol. Orza for Gov., Tulsa, 2002; liason Dem.Tulsa Pub. Sch. Tchrs.; mem. Children's Advocacy Team of All Souls Unitarian Ch., Tulsa, 1993. Mem.: AAUW, NEA (del. 2003—05), Okla. Choral Dir. Assn., Am. Choral Dir. Assn., Music Edn. Nat. Assn., Okla. Music Edn. Assn., Music Tchr. Nat. Assn. (accredited voice and piano 1982), Okla. Edn. Assn. (del. 2003—05), Tulsa Classroom Tchrs. Assn. (bd. dir. 2003—05). Democrat. Unitarian. Avocations: gardening, reading, walking, composing, politics. Home: 3903 S Rockford Ave Tulsa OK 74105 Office: Hoover Elementary Sch 2327 S Darlington Tulsa OK 74114 E-mail: collila@tulsaschools.org.

COLLINS, LEWIS, JR., music educator; b. Memphis, Nov. 16, 1942; s. Louis Collins and Susie Rhodes; m. Barbara Latham, July 1985; children: Teri, Christopher, Alicia, Ansul. BS in Music Edn., Miss. Valley State Coll., 1965; M in Spl. Edn., Chgo. State U., 1991; M in Edn. Adminstrn., Nat. Louis U., Chgo., 1995. Tchr., band dir. Holtzclaw HS, Crystal Springs, Mo., 1965—66, Riverton Jr. HS, Clarksdale, Mo., 1966—70, Georgian Hills Jr. HS, Memphis, 1970—71, Fenger Acad. HS, Chgo., 1993—; musician Memphis, 1971—85; security LA Zoo, 1985—87; spl. edn. tchr. Cook County Jail Sch., Chgo., 1987—93. Mem.: ASCD, Inter-Collegiate Athletic Dirs. Assn., Music Educators Nat. Conf. Democrat. Baptist. Home: 7447 S Shore Dr Apt 16G Chicago IL 60649

COLLINS, MARGARET HELEN, pathologist; b. Bronx, NY, July 5, 1950; d. Michael Robert and Catherine (Murray) C. BS cumma cum laude, Fordham U., 1972; MD, Georgetown U., 1977. Diplomate Am. Bd. Pathology. Intern in pathology Cornell U.-N.Y. Hosp., N.Y.C., 1977-78, resident in pathology, 1978-80; chief resident in pediatric pathology Columbia-Presbyn. Med. Ctr., N.Y.C., 1980-82, rsch. resident in pediatric pathology, 1982-83, asst. prof. clin. pathology, 1983-91; assoc. prof. pathology Ind. U., Indpls., 1991-95; pathologist Children's Hosp. Phila., Phila., 1995-98, Children's Hosp. Med. Ctr., Cin., 1999—; prof. pathology and pediats. U. Cin., 2000—. Contbr. rsch. articles to med. jours. Rsch. fellow N.Y. Lung Assn., 1983-85, Am. Lung Assn., 1985-87. Mem. AMA, AAAS, U.S.-Can. Acad. Pathology, Soc. Pediatric Pathology, Phi Beta Kappa. Democrat. Roman Catholic. Office: Children's Hosp Med Ctr 3333 Burnet Ave Cincinnati OH 45229-3026 Office Phone: 513-636-4261. Personal E-mail: mhcollins@hotmail.com. Business E-Mail: margaret.collins@uc.edu.

COLLINS, MARIBETH WILSON, foundation president; b. Portland, Oreg., Oct. 27, 1918; d. Clarence True and Maude (Akin) Wilson; m. Truman Wesley Collins, Mar. 12, 1943; children: Timothy Wilson and Terry Stanton (twins), Cherida Smith, Truman Wesley Jr. BA, U. Oreg., 1940. Pres. Collins Found., Portland, 1964—. Dir. Collins Pine Co., Collins Holding Co. Life trustee Willamette U., Salem, Oreg., also mem. campus religious life. Mem. Univ. Club, Gamma Phi Beta. Republican. Methodist. Home: 2275 SW Mayfield Ave Portland OR 97225-4400 Office: Collins Found 1618 SW 1st Ave Ste 505 Portland OR 97201-5708 Personal E-mail: maribeth@teleport.com.

COLLINS, MARTHA, English language educator, writer; b. Omaha, Nov. 25, 1940; d. William E. and Katheryn (Essick) C.; m. Theodore M. Space, Apr. 1991. AB, Stanford U., 1962; MA, U. Iowa, 1965, PhD, 1971. Asst. prof. N.E. Mo. U., Kirksville, 1965-66; from instr. to prof. English U. Mass., Boston, 1966—2002, co-dir. creative writing, 1979—2000; Pauline Delaney prof., co-dir. creative writing Oberlin (Ohio) Coll., 1997—. Author (poetry): The Catastrophe of Rainbows, 1985, The Arrangement of Space, 1991, A History of Small Life on a Windy Planet, 1993, Some Things Words Can Do, 1998; translator: The Women Carry River Water, 1997. Fellow Bunting Inst., 1982-83, Ingram Merrill Found., 1988, NEA, 1990; grantee Witter Bynner/Santa Fe Art Inst., 2001, Lannon Found. Residency, 2003; recipient Pushcart prize, 1985, 96, 98, Di Castagnola award, 1990, Lannan residency, 2003. Mem. Poetry Soc. Am., Assoc. Writing Programs. Democrat. Office: Oberlin Coll Rice Hall Oberlin OH 44074

COLLINS, MARTHA TRAUDT See ROLLE, MARTHA

COLLINS, MARY, health science association administrator, retired legislator; b. Vancouver, B.C., Can., Sept. 26, 1940; d. Fredrick Claude and Isabel Margaret (Copp) Wilkins; children: David, Robert, Sarah. Student, U. B.C., Queen's U., Kingston, Ont., Can.; LLD (hon.), Royal Rds. Mil. Coll., 1994. Mem. Can. Ho. of Commons, 1984-93; pres., CEO B.C. Health Assn., 1994-97; pres. Amarok Holdings, Ltd.; health care policy advisor WHO, Moscow. Mem. fed. cabinet Can., assoc. min. nat. def., 1989-92, min. Western econ. diversification, 1993, min. state environ., 1993, min. responsible for status of women, 1990-93, min. of health, 1993. Mem. Internat. Womens Forum. Office: WHO Russia 28 Ostozhenka 119034 Moscow Russia E-mail: mcollins@who.org.ru.

COLLINS, MARY ALICE, psychiatric social worker, educator; b. Everett, Wash., Apr. 20, 1937; d. Harry Edward and Mary (Yates) Caton; BA in Sociology, Seattle Pacific Coll., 1959; MSW, U. Mich., 1966; PhD, Mich. State U., 1974; m. Gerald C. Brocker, Mar. 24, 1980. Diplomate Am. Bd. Social Workers. Dir. teenage, adult and counseling depts. YWCA, Flint, Mich., 1959-64, 66-68; social worker Catholic Social Services, Flint, 1969-71, Ingham Med. Mental Health Center, Lansing, Mich., 1971-73; clin. social worker Genesee Psychiat. Center, Flint, 1974-82, Psychol. Evaluation and Treatment Ctr., East Lansing, Mich., 1982-84; pvt. practice, East Lansing, 1984—; instr. social work Lansing C.C.; lectr. Mich. State U., 1974, 87-93, part-time adj. asst. prof., 1993—; vis. prof. Hurley Med. Center, 1979-84; v.p. Brief Psychotherapy Coalition, 1994; cons. Ingham County Dept. Social Services, 1971-73. Advisor human relations Youth League, Flint Council Chs., 1964-65; sec. Genesee County Young Democrats, 1960-61, pres. Round Lake Improvement Assn., 1984-87. Mem. NASW, Acad. Cert. Social Workers, Phi Kappa Phi, Alpha Kappa Sigma. Contbr. articles to profl. jours. Home: 5945 Round Lake Rd Laingsburg MI 48848-9454

COLLINS, MARY ANN, lawyer; b. Aurora, Colo., May 12, 1953; d. Harold Ernest and Gertrude Elizabeth (Shannon) C.; m. Ronald Jay Sklar, Jan. 20, 1984; 1 child, Jacob Michael. BA, Western Ill. U., 1974; MA in Polit. Sci., U. Ill., 1976; JD, Loyola U., 1980. Bar: Ill. 1980, Calif. 1984. Assoc. Chapman and Cutler, Chgo., 1980-83, Orrick, Herrington & Sutcliffe, San Francisco, 1983-88, ptnr., 1988—. Chair transp. fin. group. Orrick, Herrington & Sutcliffe, San Francisco, co-chair health care, higher edn., and 501(c) revenue transactions group. Contbr. articles to profl. jours. Mem. ABA, Calif. Bar Assn., San Francisco Mcpl. Forum. Office: Orrick Herrington & Sutcliffe 405 Howard St San Francisco CA 94105 Office Phone: 415-773-5998. E-mail: marycollins@orrick.com.*

COLLINS, MERLE, English and comparative literature educator; b. Oranjestaad, Aruba, Sept. 29, 1950; d. John and Dorothy Helena Collins Grenada. BA, U. West Indies, 1972; MA, Georgetown U., 1981; PhD, U. London, 1990. Cert. in translation. Sr. lectr. Caribbean Studies U. North London, Eng., 1990-94; prof. English and Comparative Lit. U. Md., College Park, 1995—. Dir. U. Md. Study in Mexico City, 1997; vis. prof. St. George's U., Grenada, 1998; cons. editor Jour. of Caribbean Women Writers, Miami, 1998—. Author: Angel, 1987, Rain Darling, 1990, Rotten Pomerack, 1992; co-editor: Watchers and Seekers, 1987 Grantee U. Md., 1996. Mem. Assn. of Caribbean Women Writers and Scholars, Caribbean Studies Assn. Office: U Md Dept English 3101 Susquehanna Hall College Park MD 20742-8800 E-mail: merle_collins@umail.umd.edu.

COLLINS, MICHAEL, aerospace consultant, former astronaut; b. Rome, Oct. 31, 1930; s. James L. and Virginia (Stewart) C. (parents Am. citizens); m. Patricia M. Finnegan, Apr. 28, 1957; children: Kathleen, Ann Stewart, Michael L. BS, U.S. Mil. Acad., 1952; grad., Advanced Mgmt. Program, Harvard U., 1974; DSc, Northeastern U., 1970, Stonehill Coll., 1970; LLD, St. Michael's Coll., 1970, Southeastern U., 1975. Commd. officer U.S. Air Force, advanced through grades to maj. gen., 1969; fighter pilot, flight comdr. U.S., Europe; exptl. flight test officer Edwards AFB, Calif.; astronaut NASA, 1963-69, Gemini 10, 1966; astronaut, space walker, comdr., Command Module pilot Apollo 11, 1969; apptd. asst. sec. state for pub. affairs Washington, 1970-71; dir. Nat. Air and Space Mus., Smithsonian Instn., Washington, 1971-78; undersec. Smithsonian Instn., 1978-80; v.p. LTV Aerospace & Def. Co., 1980-85; pres. Michael Collins Assocs., Washington, 1985—. Bd. dirs. Avemco Corp. Author: Carrying the Fire, 1974, Flying to the Moon and Other Strange Places, 1976, Liftoff, 1988, Mission to Mars, 1990. Trustee Nat. Geog. Soc. Decorated D.S.M., D.F.C.; recipient Presdl. Medal of Freedom, NASA Distinguished Service and Exceptional Service medals, Hubbard medal, Collier trophy, Goddard Meml. trophy, Harmon trophy, Gen. Thomas D. White USAF Space trophy, gold space medal Fedn. Aeronautique Internat. Mem. Soc. Exptl. Test Pilots. Clubs: Alfalfa, Alibi.

COLLINS, MICHAEL A. (MAC COLLINS), former congressman; b. Flovilla, Ga., Oct. 15, 1944; m. Julie Watkins; 4 children. Owner Collins Trucking Co., 1962—; former chmn. Butts County Commn., 1977—81; mem. 2 terms Ga. State Senate, 1989—93; mem. Congress from 8th Ga. dist., 1993—2005; mem. House com. ways and means; mem. House com. on the budget; dep. majority whip Rep. leadership. Mem. House Com. on Ways and Means; dep. majority whip. Republican.

COLLINS, NANCY LEE, mathematician, educator; b. St. Louis, May 17, 1925; d. Charles Alonzo and Leno Rosie (Squires) Roberts; m. Major Charles Brown Sr., Dec. 23, 1946 (dec. Feb. 1984); children: Major Charles Brown Jr., Victor Ivy Brown; m. James Pickett Collins, Nov. 29, 1986. BA, Harris Stowe State Coll., 1947; MEd, St. Louis U., 1955; MA in Counseling, Washington U., St. Louis, 1968. Cert. elem. and secondary counselor, Mo. Elem. tchr. St. Louis Bd. Edn., 1947-87, adult basic edn. tchr., 1967-72, secondary counselor, 1967-87; supr. computer math. lab. Meramec C.C., St. Louis, 1989—90. Counselor seven up program Villa Duschesne, Ladue, Mo., summer, 1970; tutor continuing edn. program. Univ. City, Mo., 1972-74. Author: Potpourri and Remembrances, 2003; co-editor: Profiles and Silhouettes: The Contribution of Black Women in Missouri, 1979; contbr. poetry to publ. Nat. Libr. of Poetry, 1997; artist compact disc For God and Country, 2004. Spl. advocate vol. Juvenile Ct., St. Louis, 1989-95; mem. exec. bd. Women's Missionary Soc., St. James A.M.E. Ch.; vol peer counselor Older Adult Svcs. Info. Sys. Parsons Blewett scholar St. Louis Bd. Edn., 1977; NSF fellow, 1963; recipient Top Teens Thrust award Top Ladies of Distinction, Inc., St. Louis, 1993, Black History in Mo. Appreciation award AAUW, 1994, Cert. Appreciation Ct. Appointed Spl. Advocates, 1994, Editor's Choice award Outstanding Achievement in Poetry, 2001, Internat. Libr. Poetry, 2003; honoree St. James Ch., 1997. Mem. Mo. Conf. Womens Missionary Soc. (membership, recruitment chair 1995), Mo. Conf. Lay Orgn. (local pres. 1993-95, now 3d v.p.), Internat. Soc. Poets (life), Order Eastern Star (worthy matron), Delta Sigma Theta (chor mem. 1986-95, 50 Yr. Mem. award 1995, Cert. Appreciation award 1993), Am. Assn. U. Women, Nat. Assn. U. Women, Mo. State Tchrs. Assn., Retired Sch. Employees of St. Louis. Democrat. African Methodist Episcopalian. Avocations: mathematics, reading, piano, aerobics, Scrabble. Home: 955 Jeanerette Dr University City MO 63130-2719

COLLINS, NANCY WHISNANT, foundation administrator; b. Dec. 20, 1933; d. Ward William and Marjorie Adele (Blackburn) Whisnant; m. James Quincy Collins, Jr., Apr. 25, 1959 (div. 1974); children: James Quincy III, Charles Lowell, William Robey; m. Richard F. Chapman, May 29, 1982. Student, Queens Coll., Charlotte, 1951—53; AB in Journalism, U. N.C., 1955, MS in Pers. Adminstrn., 1967; postgrad., Cornell U., 1955—56. Pers. asst. R.H. Macy & Co., Inc., N.Y.C., 1955; jr. exec. placement dir. Scofield Placement Agy., San Francisco, 1956—57; freelance journalist London, Paris, and Frankfurt, Germany, 1957—59; program dir. Girl Scouts U.S., Hampton, Va., 1959—61; dir. tour Tokyo, Hong Kong, Singapore, 1965—66; asst. dir. Sloan Exec. Program Stanford (Calif.) U., 1968—78; asst. dir. Hoover Instn., 1979—81; asst. to pres. Palo Alto (Calif.) Med. Found., 1981—2000; asst. to chmn. Novo Ventures, 2000—. Bd. dirs. Am. Healthway Sys.; fund raising cons. Stanford U. Equestrian Ctr., 1994—2004. Author: Professional Women and Their Mentors, 1988, Women Leading: Making Tough Choices on the Fast Track, 1988, Love at Second Sight, 2003, Playing the MidLife Dating Game, 2003; editor: Have a Great Day: Today and Every Day of Your Life; contbr. articles short stories, and poems to mags. and newspapers. Fundraiser Cornell U., N.Y.C., 1975—81; fundraising consultant Stanford Univ., Equestrian Cender, 1994—2004; mem. coun. Trinity Episcopal Ch., Menlo Park, Calif., 1975—80; mem. leadership team Menlo Park Presbyn. Ch.; bd. dirs. Santa Clara County coun. Girl Scouts U.S.; mem. exec. coun. Stanford area coun. Boy Scouts Am., 1980—81; mem. San Mateo County Charter Rev. Com.; mem. pers. bd. City of Menlo Park, 1979—; mem. women's program bd. Coro Found.; trustee Pacific Grad. Sch. Psychology; sec.-treas. Chapman Rsch. Fund. Fellow, Cornell U.; grantee, Richardson Found., 1967. Mem.: AAUW, Catalyst, Peninsula Profl. Women's Network, Am. Mgmt. Assn., Menlo Circus Club, Overseas Press Club, Commonwealth Club, Mayflower Soc. Club, Kappa Delta. Home: 1850 Oak Ave Menlo Park CA 94025-5842

COLLINS, PAUL JOHN, banker; b. West Bend, Wis., Oct. 26, 1936; s. Curtis Alvin and Adele (Stopenbach) C.; m. Carol Lee Hoffmann, May 8, 1965; children: Ronald Alvin, Julia Downing. BBA, U. Wis., 1958; MBA, Harvard U., 1961. With Citibank, N.Y.C., 1961-2000, investment analyst, portfolio mgmt., 1961-70, sr. v.p., chmn. investment policy com., 1970-75, sr. v.p., head corp. planning, 1976-77, sr. v.p., head fin. div., 1977-79, exec. v.p. acctg. and control, 1980-81, group exec. investment br., 1982-85, sr. corp. officer N.Am., 1985-88, vice chmn., 1988-98, also bd. dirs., Citigroup vice chmn., 1998-2000. Bd. dirs. Nokia Corp., BG Group, Enster Group, Actis Capital LLP. Bd. dirs. Glyndebourne Arts Trust, U. Wis. Found. Republican. Congregationalist. Home: 29 Wilton Crescent London SW1 X8SA England E-mail: pcollins@pjcpartners.com.

COLLINS, PAUL STEVEN, vascular surgeon; b. Portsmouth, Ohio, July 24, 1954; s. Paul Whitney and Geralda Pearl (Hoskins) C.; m. Cathy Ann McWicker, Jan. 17, 1981; children: Lauren Elizabeth, Paul McWicker, Andrew Steven. BS, Davidson Coll., 1976; MD, U. South Fla., 1979. Diplomate Am. Bd. Surgery, spl. qualifications in gen. vascular surgery and surg. critical care; diplomate Nat. Bd. Med. Examiners; lic. surgeon, Fla., Va. Commd. 2d lt. U.S. Army, 1979, advanced through grades to lt. col., 1990, resident in gen. surgery Walter Reed Army Med. Ctr. Washington, 1979-84, chief gen. surg. Würzburg, West Germany, 1984-86, fellow peripheral vasc. surgery Walter Reed Army Med. Ctr. Washington, 1986-87, chief vascular surgery Letterman Army Med. Ctr. San Francisco, resigned, 1992; pvt. practice St. Petersburg, Fla., 1990—; asst. clin. prof. surgery U. S. Fla., Tampa, 1995—. Asst. clin. prof. surgery Uniformed Svcs. U. Health Scis., Bethesda, Md., 1984—; chief of surgery St. Anthony's Hosp., St. Petersburg, 1998—2000, dir. vascular lab., 1994—97, chmn. dept. surgery, 1998—2000; profl. mem. Keystone, Tampa, Fla., 1993—97; pres. Bay Plaza Outpatient Surgery, 1994—2001; bd. dirs., trustee St. Anthony's Found.; team surgeon Tampa Bay Devil Rays Baseball Team, 1996—. Contbr. chpts. to books, articles to med. jours. Bd. dirs. St. Anthony's Found. Recipient Physicians Recognition award AMA, 1992, Sigvaris award Camp Internat., 1987. Fellow ACS (Regional Trauma award 1984), Internat. Soc. for Cardiovascular Surgeons; mem. So. Assn. for Vascular Surgery (Pres.'s award 1992), Fla. Vascular Soc., (sec., treas. 2002-04, pres. elect 2004).Fla. Med. Assn., Pinellas County Med. Soc. (bd. govs.). Avocations: golf, tennis, snow and water skiing, gardening. Office: 1201 5th Ave N Ste 200 Saint Petersburg FL 33705-1410 Personal E-mail: sclpac@aol.com.

COLLINS, PHILIP A., management consultant; Regional dir. third-party eligibility Medstandard, Inc., 1992—2000, exec. dir. billing svcs., 1998—2000; sr. bus. cons. Medcath, Inc., 2001—02, ctrl. bus. office dir., 2002—03; sr. healthcare cons. Unicare Corp., 2003—04; dir. quality assurance Medstandard, Inc., 2004—05. Mem. Gerson Lehrman Group Healthcare Coun. Mem.: Soc. Industry Leaders. Address: 9117 Windy Crest Dr Dallas TX 75243 E-mail: philipacollins@aol.com.

COLLINS, RICHARD DAVID, lawyer, writer; b. Manhasset, NY, Apr. 8, 1959; LLB, Hofstra U., 1981; JD, Hofstra U. Sch. Law, 1984. Bar: NY 1985, Mass. 2004, Pa. 2004, U.S. Dist. Ct. (ea. dist.) NY 1987, U.S. Dist. Ct. (we. dist.) Tex. 2000, U.S. Dist. Ct. (so. dist.) NY 2004, U.S. Ct. Appeals for Armed Forces 1993, U.S. Supreme Ct. 1993. Asst. dist. atty. Nassau County Dist. Atty's. Office, Mineola, NY, 1984—89; ptnr., prin. Collins, McDonald & Gann, P.C., Carle Place, 1990—. Legal counsel United Supplement Freedom Assn., Inc., 2002—, Internat. Fedn. BodyBuilders, Montreal, Que., Canada, 2004—, Internat. Soc. Sports Nutrition, Woodland Park, Colo., 2004—. Author: (book) Legal Muscle: Anabolics in America. Mem.: Criminal Courts Bar Assn. Nassau County (pres. 2001—02), Nassau County Bar Assn. (dir. 2003—05), NY State Bar Assn. (exec. com. dist. rep. 1998—2005, criminal justice sect.), Nat. Assn. Criminal Def. Lawyers (life). Office: Collins McDonald & Gann PC One Old Country Rd Carle Place NY 11514 Office Phone: 516-294-0300. Office Fax: 516-294-0477. E-mail: info@cmgesq.com.

COLLINS, RICHARD LAWRENCE, editor; b. Little Rock, Nov. 28, 1933; s. Leighton Holden Collins and Sarah Aloysia (Banks) Polk; m. Ann Terry Slocomb, Feb. 14, 1958; children— Charlotte, Sarah, Richard Jr. Chief pilot Ben M. Hogan Co., Little Rock, 1957-58; mng. editor Air Facts mag., Princeton, N.J., 1958-68; sr. editor Flying mag., N.Y.C., 1968-77, editor in chief, 1977-88; editor in chief, pub. Pilot, sr. v.p. Aircraft Owners and Pilots Assn., Frederick, Md., 1988-89; aviation cons., 1989—. Author numerous aviation books including: Flying Safely, 1977, Tips to Fly By, 1980, Thunderstorms and Airplanes, 1982, Flight Level Flying, 1985, Air Crashes, 1986, The Perfect Flight, 1988, Pilot Upgrade, 1989, Mastering the Systems, 1991; contbr. articles to mags. Chmn. Ark. Aero. Commn., Little Rock, 1976. Served with U.S. Army, 1955-57 Recipient Earl D. Osborn award Aviation Writers, 1978, Sherman Fairchild award Flight Safety Found., 1965, platinum wing award NBAA, 2000; named to Ark. Aviation Hall of Fame, 1988 Mem. Flying Physicians Assn. (hon.), Lawyer Pilots Bar Assn. (hon.), Civil Aeromed. Assn. (hon.) Clubs: Quiet Birdmen. Avocation: sailing. Office: 1633 Broadway 45th Fl New York NY 10019

COLLINS, RICHARD STRATTON (DICK COLLINS), retired public relations executive; b. Smith Center, Kans., Dec. 11, 1929; s. Edgar Wesley and Rosina Ann (Allbert) C.; children: Ann Michelle, Jennifer Lee, Logan Reed. BA, U. Tex., 1952. Editor of Lookout Look Mag., N.Y.C., 1952-53, asst. circulation promotion mgr., 1953-57, circulation promotion mgr., 1957-64, pub. rels. mgr., 1964-67; v.p., dir. corp. pub. rels. Cowles Comm., N.Y.C., 1967-74; assoc. The Jonathan Rinehart Group, N.Y.C., 1974-76; dir. pub. rels. ABA, Chgo., 1976-80, dir. comms., 1980-89, dir. comms./pub. affairs, 1989-94, ret., 1994. Writer mag. advts. (award of Excellence Communication Arts Mag. 1971); contbr. articles to profl. jours.; newspaper columnist. Bd. dirs., pres. Family Counseling Svcs., Bergen County, N.J., 1968-76. Recipient Silver Screen award U.S. Indsl. Film Festival, 1979, The Chris Plaque, Columbus Film Festival, 1979. Mem. Pub. Rels. Soc. of Am. (Silver Anvil award 1964). Avocations: golf, gardening, reading history, civil liberties organizations, recording for the blind.

COLLINS, ROBERT ARNOLD, literature and language professor; b. Miami, Fla., Apr. 25, 1929; s. John William and Edna (Arnold) C.; m. Laura Virginia Roberts, June 3, 1960; 1 child, Judith. BA in English, U. Miami, Coral Gables, Fla., 1951; MA in English, U. Ky., 1960, PhD in English, 1968. Chair English Midway (Ky.) Jr. Coll., 1960-64; assoc. prof. English No. Ill. U., DeKalb, 1964-68, Morehead (Ky.) State U., 1968-69; from assoc. prof. to prof. English Fla. Atlantic U., Boca Raton, 1970—2005, prof. emeritus, 2005—. Founder, dir. Internat. Conf. on the Fantastic in the Arts, Ft. Lauderdale, Fla., 1980—. Author: Thomas Burnett Swann: A Critical Biography, 1980, Science Fiction and Fantasy Book Review Annual, 1987-91; editor: Scope of the Fantastic, 1985, Modes of the Fantastic, 1995; editor Fantasy Rev., 1981-87; mng. editor Jour. of the Fantastic in the Arts, 1995—2003; contbr. articles to profl. jours. Recipient World Fantasy award World Fantasy Conv., New Haven, 1982, Balrog award Sword and Shield, 1982, 83. Home: 1320 SW 5th St Boca Raton FL 33486-4404 Office: Prof Emeritus Fla Atlantic U English Dept 777 Glades Rd Boca Raton FL 33431-6424 Business E-Mail: collins@fau.edu.

COLLINS, ROBERT JOHN, music educator; b. Elk Grove, Ill., May 24, 1970; s. Daniel Charles and Diane Lyn Collins. BA, Millikin U., 1992. Cert. tchr. Ill. Educator Harvard Sch. Dist. #50, Ill., 1992—. Vocalist Throughout Chgo., Chgo.; dir. choral activites Buffalo Grove Park Dist., Ill., 1982—. Composer: (vocal compositions) Ave Maria, 1994. Pres. Harvard Edn. Found., Harvard, Ill., 2000; sec. Trinity Luth. Ch., Harvard, Ill., 1997—99. Recipient Scholarship and Leadership award, Kappa Sigma, Millikin U., 1992, Leadership award, Ill. Parks and Recreation, 2000. Mem.: Am. Choral Dir. Assn., Ill. Music Educators Assn. (chmn. 2000), Music Educator's Nat. Conf. Republican. Lutheran. Avocations: travel, golf, music. Home: 1167 S Wells St #3 Lake Geneva WI 53147-2495 Office: Harvard High Sch 1103 N Jefferson St Harvard IL 60033 E-mail: rcollins@d50.mchenry.il.us.

COLLINS, ROBERT OAKLEY, history professor; b. Waukegan, Ill., Apr. 1, 1933; s. William George and Louise Van Horsen (Jack) C.; m. Janyce Hutchins Monroe, Oct. 6, 1974; children by previous marriage: Catharine Louise, Randolph Ware, Robert William. BA, Dartmouth Coll., 1954; AB (Marshall scholar 1954-55), Balliol Coll., Oxford U., 1956, MA, 1960; MA (Ford fellow), Yale U., 1958, PhD, 1959. Instr. history Williams Coll., Williamstown, Mass., 1959-61; lectr. U. Mass. Extension, Pittsfield, 1960-61; vis. asst. prof. history Columbia U., N.Y.C., 1962-63; asst. prof. history Williams Coll., 1963-65; mem. faculty U. Calif., Santa Barbara, 1965—, prof. history, 1969-94, dir. Ctr. for Study Developing Nations, 1967-69, acting vice chancellor for research and grad. affairs, 1970-71, dean grad. div., 1971-80; prof. emeritus, 1994—; vis. sr. assoc. fellow St. Antony's Coll., Oxford U., Eng., 1980-81; Trevelyan fellow Durham U., 1986—. Dir. Washington Ctr. U. Calif., Santa Barbara, 1992-94; mem. Internat. Adv. Group for the Nile Basin, World Bank, 1997. Author: The Southern Sudan, 1883-1898, 1962, King Leopold, England and the Upper Nile, 1968, Problems in African History, 1968, The Partition of Africa, 1979, Land Beyond the Rivers: The Southern Sudan, 1898-1918, 1971, Europeans in Africa, 1971, An Arabian Diary, 1969, The Southern Sudan in Historical Perspective, 1975, Shadows in the Grass: Britain in the Southern Sudan, 1983, The British in the Sudan, 1898-56, 84, The Waters of the Nile: Hydropolitics and the Jonglei Canal, 1900-1988, 1990, Western African History, Eastern African History, Central and Southern African History, 1990, The Nile Waters: An Annotated Bibliography, 1991, Problems In African History, The Pre-Colonial Centuries, 1993, Requiem for the Sudan, 1994, Historical Problems of Imperial Africa, 1994, Problems in the History of Modern Africa, 1996, Africa's Thirty Years' War: Chad, Libya and the Sudan, 1963-1993, 1999, Historical Dictionary of Pre-Colonial Africa, 2001, Documents from the African Past, 2001, The Nile, 2002, Revolutionary Sudan: Hasan al-Turabi and the Islamist State, 1989-2000, 2003, Civil Wars and Revolution in the Sudan: Essays on the Sudan, Southern Sudan, and Darfur, 1962-2004, 2005, The World of Islamic Charities, 2005, Africa: A Short History of the Sub-Saharan Continent, 2005. Recipient Gold class award Order Scis. and Arts Dem. Republic of Sudan, 1980; John Ben Snow Found. prize, 1984; NDEA lang. fellow, 1960-61, Social Sci. Rsch. Coun. fellow, 1962-63; Rockefeller Found. scholar-in-residence Bellagio, Italy, 1979, 87; Ford Found. fellow, 1979-81; Fulbright sr. rsch. fellow, 1982, 90; Woodrow Wilson fellow, 1983; vis. fellow Trevelyan Coll. mem. Soc.

Fellows Durham U., 1986, fellow Balliol Coll., Oxford U., 1986-87; fellow Am. Coun. Learned Soc. 1990. Fellow Am. Philos. Soc.; mem. Am. Hist. Assn., African Studies Assn., Western River Guides Assn., Sudan Studies Assn., Explorers Club, Phi Beta Kappa. Home: 735 Calle De Los Amigos Santa Barbara CA 93105-4438 Office: U Calif Dept History Santa Barbara CA 93106-9410 Office Phone: 805-893-2248. Business E-Mail: rcollins@history.ucsb.edu.

COLLINS, RONALD LESLIE LEOPOLD, neurosurgeon; b. Nov. 19, 1944; Came to U.S., 1979; MB BS, U. W.I., Kingston, Jamaica, 1968. Diplomate Am. Bd. Neurological Surgery, Am. Bd. Minimally Invasive Spinal Surgery. Intern Harlem Hosp. Ctr., 1979-80, resident, 1980-81, King/Drew Med. Ctr., 1985-88; fellow Cook County Hosp., 1984-85, Robert Wood Johnson U. Hosp., 1988-89; neurosurgeon N.Y.C., 1989—. Contbr. articles to profl. jours.; inventor in field. Fellow Royal Coll. Surgery (Edinburgh), Internat. Coll Surgeons, Masons. Home: 681 E 78th St Brooklyn NY 11236-3307 Office Phone: 732-613-7272. E-mail: rllcolins@aol.com.

COLLINS, RONALD WILLIAM, psychologist, educator; b. NYC, Jan. 6, 1947; s. Edward H. Collins Jr. and Estelle Lott. BA, Rutgers U., 1969; MS, Nova U., 1987; EdD, Fla. Internat. U., 1990; PhD, Saybrook Inst., 1996. Diplomate Am. Bd. Psychol. Spltys.; lic. profl. counselor, Mont., mental health counselor, Fla., psychologist, Colo. Spl. agt., ret. U.S. Secret Svc., Miami, Fla., 1971-91; adj. prof. St. Thomas U., Miami, 1990-91; asst. prof. Ea. Mont. Coll., Billings, 1991-94, Mont. State U., Billings, 1994-95; psychol. intern Inst. for Psychol. Growth, Ft. Lauderdale, Fla., 1994-95; adj. prof. instrnl. analysis/design Fla. Internat. U., Ft. Lauderdale, 1995-96; psychologist Dept. Corrections, Canon City, Colo., 1998-99, in pvt. practice, Miami, 1999-2000; dept. chair gen. studies U. Phoenix, Ft. Lauderdale, Fla., 2000—00; prof. Am. Inter Continental U., 2001—. Pvt. cons., adj. prof. U. Phoenix, Nova Southeastern U., Ft. Lauderdale, Keiser Coll., 2001—. Author: Kabiroff Papers, 1988, Transfer of Learning, 1990, Psychological Perspectives on Security Issues, 2000; contbr. articles to profl. jours. Mem. Billings Family Violence Task Force, 1992. Mem. APA, Am. Coll. Forensic Examiners, Am. Ednl. Rsch. Assn., Mental Health Assn. Broward County. Episcopalian. Avocations: skiing, horseback riding, flying, fiction writing, jogging. Office: PO Box 2053 Fort Lauderdale FL 33303-2053 Fax: 954-446-6392. Business E-Mail: rcollins@aiufl.edu.

COLLINS, SAMUEL W., JR., judge; b. Caribou, Maine, Sept. 17, 1923; s. Samuel Wilson Collins & Elizabeth Black C; m. Dorothy Small, 1952; children: Edward, Elizabeth, Diane. BA, U. Maine; JD, Harvard U. Lawyer, Rockland, Maine, 1947—; justice Supreme Jud. Ct., Portland, Maine. Trustee Rockland Sch. Dist, 1949-61; Maine State Senate Dist. 21, 1975-84, majority leader, 1981-82, minority leader, 1983-84. Recipient Disting. Svc. award Jaycees, 1978. Mem. Maine Bar Assn., Rotary, Phi Beta Kappa, Phi Kappa Phi, Delta Tau Delta. Unitarian Universalist. Republican. Office: Knox County Courthouse 62 Union St Rockland ME 04841-2836

COLLINS, SARAH JANE, secondary school educator; b. Paterson, N.J., Aug. 28, 1965; d. Charles Lewis and Phyllis Mae (Garner) D. Student, Ocean County Coll., Toms River, N.J., 1988—89, Georgian Ct. Coll., 1989—92; postgrad., Georgian Ct. U., 2003—; BS in Biology, Richard Stockton Coll. N.J., 1995. Teller First Nat. Bank of Toms River, 1985-87; legal and exec. sec. Shackleton, Hazeltine & Bishop, Ship Bottom, N.J., 1987-91; tchr. Blessed Sacrament Regional Sch., 1997-99; biology tchr. So. Regional High Sch., 1999—. Avocations: swimming, aerobics, softball. Home: 264 Forge Rd West Creek NJ 08092 Office: So Regional High Sch 600 N Main St Manahawkin NJ 08050-3093

COLLINS, STEVEN M., lawyer; b. Atlanta, Oct. 22, 1952; s. E.B. and Judith (Morse) C.; divorced; 1 child, Erin M.; m. Anne Frances Garland, Oct. 31, 1987; 1 child, Timothy G. AB, Harvard U., 1974, JD, 1977. Bar: Ga. 1977, U.S. Dist. Ct. (no. dist.) Ga. 1977, U.S. Ct. Appeals (11th cir.) 1981, U.S. Dist. Ct. (mid. dist.) Ga. 1982, U.S. Tax Ct. 1984, U.S. Ct. Appeals (4th cir.) 1986, U.S. Ct. Appeals (6th cir.) 2001, U.S. Supreme Ct. 1994. Assoc. Alston & Bird, Atlanta, 1977-83, ptnr., litig., trial practice group, 1983—. Editor-in-chief Ga. State Bar Journal, Atlanta, 1982-84. Mem. ABA, State Bar Ga., Atlanta Bar Assn. Office: Alston & Bird One Atlantic Ctr 1201 W Peachtree St NW Atlanta GA 30309-3424 E-mail: scollins@alston.com.

COLLINS, SUSAN MARGARET, senator; b. Caribou, Maine, Dec. 7, 1952; BA in Govt. magna cum laude, St. Lawrence U., 1975. Prin. advisor bus. affairs to Senator William S. Cohen US Senate, 1975—78; commr. Maine Dept. Profl. and Fin. Regulation, 1987—92; dir. New England ops. U.S. Small Bus. Adminstrn., 1992—93; exec. dir. Ctr. Family Bus., Husson Coll., Bangor, Maine, 1993—96; U.S. senator from Maine, 1997—. Staff dir. Senate Subcom. on Oversight Govt. Mgmt., 1981-87; chair Cabinet Coun. on Health Care Policy, State of Maine; mem. U.S. Senate com. health, edn., labor and pensions, 1997—, subcom. on children and families, 1997—, subcom. on pub. health and safety, 1997—, com. on govtl. affairs, 1997—; chmn. permanent subcom. on investigations, 1997—; mem. spl. com. on aging. Author (with Catherine Whitney): (Books) Nine and Counting: The Women of the Senate, 2000. Rep. candidate for Gov., State of Maine, 1994. Recipient Outstanding Alumni award St. Lawrence U., 1992. Mem. Bangor Rotary Club, Phi Beta Kappa. Republican. Roman Catholic. Office: 461 Dirksen Sen Office Bldg Washington DC 20510*

COLLINS, THEODORE JOHN, lawyer; b. Walla Walla, Wash., Oct. 2, 1936; s. Robert Bonfield and Catherine Roselle (Snyder) C.; m. Patricia Spengler Pasieka, May 11, 1968; children: Jonathan, Caitlin, Matthew, Patrick, Flannary. BA, U. Notre Dame, 1958; postgrad., U. Bonn, Fed. Republic Germany, 1959; LLB, Harvard U., 1962. Bar: Wash. 1962, U.S. Supreme Ct. 1982, U.S. Ct. Appeals (fed. cir.) 1982, U.S. Dist. Ct. (ea. dist.) Wash. 1965, U.S. Dist. Ct. (we. dist.) Wash. 1962. Ptnr. Perkins Coie Law Firm, Seattle, 1962-86; v.p., gen. counsel The Boeing Co., Seattle, 1986-98, sr. v.p., gen. counsel, 1998-2000; of counsel Perkins Coie Law Firm, 2001—. Adj. prof. Seattle U. Law Sch. Mem. ABA, Wash. State Bar Assn., King County Bar Assn., Wash. Athletic Club. E-mail: tcoll10236@aol.com, collt@perkinscoie.com.

COLLINS, THOMAS HANSEN, US Coast Guard Commandant; b. Quincy, Mass., June 25, 1946; s. Harley Hartford and Inger Dagmar (Hansen) C.; m. Constance Ann Monahan, June 7, 1968; children: Christine Ann, Kathryn. BS, USCG Acad., New London, Conn., 1968; MA in Liberal Studies, Wesleyan U., 1972; MBA, U. New Haven, 1976. Commd. 1st lt. USCG, 1968, advanced through grades to rear adm., 1994; comdg. officer USCG Cutter, Cape Morgan, Charleston, S.C., 1969-71; instr., prof. USCG Acad., 1972-76; mem. planning program, budget staff Office of R&D USCG Hdqs., Washington, 1976-80; dep. group comdr. USCG Group, St. Petersburg, Fla., 1980-83; mem. program rev. staff USCG Hdqs., Washington, 1983-87; group comdr. USCG Group L.I. Sound, New Haven, 1987-90; chief adminstrn. divsn. USCG Dist. 14, Honolulu, 1990-92; chief program divsn. USCG Hdqs., Washington, 1992-94, dep. chief of staff, 1994—98, chief office of acquisition, 1994—; comdr, Pac. area and 11th Coast Guard dist. U.S. Coast Guard, 1998—2000, vice-commandant, 2000—02, commandant, 2002—. Decorated Legion of Merit, Meritorious Svc. medal (2), Coast Guard Commendation medal (3), Coast Guard Distinguished Service medal Mem. Am. Soc. Naval Engrs. (hon.). Avocations: golf, gardening, reading. Office: Comdt US Coast Guard 2100 2nd St SW Washington DC 20593

COLLINS, THOMAS WILLIAM, caterer, consultant; b. Lewiston, Idaho, Nov. 4, 1926; s. William James and Mary (Egan) C.; m. Mary Charlene Tracy, Aug. 1, 1947 (dec. Apr. 1984); children: Kathleen, William, Charles. Grad. high sch., Staples, Minn., 1944. Owner Collins Cafe, Park Rapids, Minn., 1947-63, Tom Collins Restaurant, Walker, Minn., 1963-83, Tom Collins Catering, Walker, 1983—. Author: Collins Cooking Secrets, 1981. Fundraiser DFL, 1976-83; adv. bd. Lake Country Food Bank, Mpls., 1981-86, bd. dirs., 1987-98. Served with USN, 1945-46, 51-52. Recipient Recognition award Mont. Gov., 1978, cert. of Spl. Congl. Recognition, 1995; Tom Collins Day proclaimed by Minn. Gov., 1977. Mem. Assn. Great Lakes Outdoor Writers, Am. Legion. Lodges: Masons (sr. warden 1958), Shriners. Avocations: hunting, fishing, photography. Home and Office: PO Box 33 Walker MN 56484-0033

COLLINS, WALTER LLOYD GEORGE, editor; b. Broken Arrow, Okla., Dec. 6, 1917; s. Dow Otho and Myrtle Hester (Campbell) C.; m. Ruth Leona Hamilton, Sept. 3, 1935; children: Mary, Walter, Alvin, Shirley. BA, Pan Am. U., 1966; MA, U. Tulsa, 1975. Aviation cadet USAAF, 1942; advanced through grades to maj. USAF, 1962; exec. in charge C-E Installation Project NATO, Europe, North Africa, Mid. East, 1956-57; sr. editor radar and missiles project USAFE, 1957-58; ops. officer C-E divsn. Def. Atomic Support Agy., Albuquerque, 1959-63; dir. comm.-elec., spacetrack NORAD, Colorado Springs, 1963-64; ret., 1964; gen. mgr. Desert Lodge, Moab, Utah, 1967-68; design engr. planner Beech Aircraft Corp., Wichita, Kans., 1968-72; dir. internat. student affairs Spartan Sch. Aeronautics, Tulsa, 1979-83; pres. R&W Internat., Tulsa, 1984-88, Alpha-Omega Press, Tulsa, Ponca City, Okla., 1990—. Adv. bd. edn. com. Okla. Acad. State Goals, 1977—95. Author: On the Razor's Edge, 1990, Manner of Man, 2001, Into Fields of Fire, 2004. Mem. Kay County (Okla.) Rep. Com., 1993—; mem. Ponca City Traffic Commn., 1997-2000. Mem. Acad. Am. Poets, Nat. Author's Registry, Nat. Order Battlefield Commns., Am. Air Mus. in Great Britain, Air Force Assn., Mil. Officers Assn. Am. Avocations: writing, editing, photography. Office: Alpha-Omega Press PO Box 2163 Ponca City OK 74602-2163 E-mail: gcollins@poncacity.net, alphaopress@poncacity.net.

COLLINS, WAYNE DALE, lawyer; b. Portsmouth, Va., Dec. 23, 1951; s. Wayne D. Sr. and Mary. L. (Higdon) C.; m. Mary Ann Bradshaw, Aug. 9, 1981; children: Laura, Melissa, Christopher. BS with honors, Calif. Inst. Tech., 1973, MS, 1974; JD, U. Chgo., 1978; postgrad., U. Minn., 1979. Bar: N.Y. 1979, U.S. Supreme Ct. 1983, D.C., 1991. Assoc. Shearman & Sterling, N.Y.C., 1978-81, 83-86, ptnr., 1987—; spl. asst. to V.P. George Bush, Washington, 1981-82; dep. asst. atty. gen. antitrust div. U.S. Dept. Justice, Washington, 1983. Vis. lectr. Yale Law Sch., 1991-95; vis. com. U. Chgo. Law Sch., 2003—. Co-author: Horizontal Mergers: Law and Policy, 1986, Non-Horizontal Mergers: Law and Policy, 1988, State Antitrust Practice and Statutes, 1991. White House fellow, 1981-82. Fellow Am. Bar Found.; mem. ABA (chmn. antitrust sect. subcom. on fin. markets and instns. 1983-87, chmn. pub. com. 1987-91, coun. mem. antitrust sect. 1991-94, officer antitrust sect. 1994-1999), Am. Law Inst., Assn. of Bar of City of N.Y., Am. Econ. Assn., Econometric Soc., Soc. for Advancement of Econ. Theory, Am. Coun. Nationalities Svc. (bd. dirs. 1988-1999). Republican. Roman Catholic. Office: 599 Lexington Ave New York NY 10022-6030 also: 801 Pennsylvania Ave NW Washington DC 20004-2615

COLLINS, WILLIAM EDWARD, aeromedical administrator, researcher, psychologist; b. Bklyn., May 16, 1932; s. William Edward and Loretta Agnes (Brasier) C.; m. Corliss Jean Barnes, June 20, 1970; 1 child, Corliss Adora. BS, St. Peter's Coll., 1954; MA, Fordham U., 1956, PhD, 1959. Lic. psychologist, Okla. Psychol. rsch. asst. Fordham U., 1954-56, tchg. fellow, 1958, grad. instr., 1958-59, rsch. asst., 1958-59; rsch. psychologist U.S. Army Med. Rsch. Lab., Ft. Knox, Ky., 1959-61; rsch. psychologist Aviation Psychology Lab. FAA Civil Aeromed. Inst., Oklahoma City, 1961-63, chief sensory integration sect., 1963-65, lab. supr., 1965-86, human resources rsch. br. mgr., 1986-88, dep. dir., 1988-89, dir., 1989-2001; adj. assoc. prof. psychology U. Okla., Norman, 1963-70, adj. prof., 1970-89; adj. assoc. prof. rsch. psychology dept. psychiatry and behavioral scis. U. Okla. Health Scis. Ctr., Oklahoma City, 1965-71, adj. prof., 1971—. Mem. Nat. Acad. Sci.-NRC Com. on Vision, 1963-82, mem. exec. coun., 1973-81; mem. Nat. Acad. Sci.-NRC Com. on Hearing, Bioacoustics and Biomechanics, 1963-87; appearances before House Sub-Com. on Pub. Health and Environ., 1971, House Sub-Com. on Investigations and Oversight, 1983, House Sub-Com. on Transp., Aviation and Materials, 1987, 88; judge Okla. State Sci. and Engring. Fair, Ada, 1980, 81, 82; mem. Okla. Bd. Examiners Psychologists, 1981-84, chmn., 1982-84; evaluator proposals NSF, 1968-82, HEW, 1971-80; lectr. in field. Contbr. chpts., numerous articles to profl. publs.; numerous rsch. presentations in field. Served to res. capt. Med. Services Corps, U.S. Army, 1959-61. Recipient citation for svc. to aviation medicine Okla. State Legislature, 1999, Disting. Career Svc. award FAA, 2001; named to Okla. Aviation and Space Hall of Fame, 2004. Fellow AAAS, APA (abstractor Psychol. Abstracts 1962-2002, citation 1973), N.Y. Acad. Scis., Aerospace Med. Assn. (Raymond F. Longacre award 1971, presdl. exec. com. 1982-84, exec. coun. 1982-85, editl. bd. Aviation, Space and Environ. Medicine 1974-2000, assoc. editor 1980-2000, Pres.'s Citation 1993, Harry G. Moseley award 1998, Life Scis. and Biomed. Engring. Profl. Excellence award 1989, Pres.'s award 1999), Am. Psychol. Soc. (charter), Aerospace Human Factors Assn. (charter, Paul T. Hansen award 1998, William E. Collins ann. award for excellence in human factors established 2002); mem. Assn. Aviation Psychologists (pres. 1974-75), Okla. Psychol. Assn. (Disting. Psychologist award 1984), South African Soc. Aerospace and Environ. Medicine (Silver Medal award 1998), Nat. Mus. Am. Indian (charter mem. 1992-, cert. of appreciation 1995), So. Poverty Law Ctr., Nat. Campaign Tolerance (founding mem.). Achievements include William E. Collins Ann. award for Outstanding FAA Publs. in Aerospace Medicine named in his honor, 2003. Home: 8900 Sheringham Dr Oklahoma City OK 73132-4764 Office: Dept Psychiat Behavior Sci Okla U Health Sci Ctr Room ORI-332 PO Box 26901 Research Building Oklahoma City OK 73190-3048

COLLINS, WILLIAM F., JR., neurosurgery educator; b. New Haven, Conn., Jan. 20, 1924; MD, Yale U., 1947. Diplomate Am. Bd. Neurol. Surgery. Intern Barnes Hosp., St. Louis, 1947-49, asst. resident in neurosurgery, 1951-52, resident, 1952-53; fellow neurophysiology Washington U., 1953-54; instr. neurosurgery Western Res. U., Cleve., 1954-55, sr. instr., 1955-57, asst. prof., 1957-60, assoc. prof., 1960-63; prof., chmn. divsn. neurosurgery Med. Coll. Va., 1963-67; prof. Yale U., New Haven, chief sect. neurosurgery, 1963—86, chmn. dept. surgery, 1986-93, prof. neurosurgery emeritus, 1994—; clin. prof. neurosurgery U. Calif. Sch. Medicine, San Diego, 1997—. With M.C., U.S. Army, 1949-51. Office: Yale Sch Medicine Dept Neurosurgery PO Box 208082 New Haven CT 06520-8082 Office Phone: 203-785-2806. Personal E-mail: wfcollin@aol.com.

COLLINS, WILLIAM J. (BILLY COLLINS), poet, educator; b. N.Y.C., Mar. 1941; Prof. English Lehman Coll., CUNY. Author: (books of poetry) Pokerface, 1977, Video Poems, 1980, The Apple That Astonished Paris, 1988, Questions About Angels, 1991 (Selected by Edward Hirsch for Nat. Poetry Series), The Art of Drowning, 1995 (finalist for Lenore Marshall Poetry Prize), Picnic, Lightning, 1998, Taking Off Emily Dickinson's Clothes, 2000, Sailing Alone Around the Room: New and Selected Poems, 2001, Nine Horses, 2002; contbr. poetry to profl. jours. and publs.; editor: Poetry 180: A Turning Back to Poetry, 2003; reader (recording) The Best Cigarette, 1997. Named a Literary Lion, N.Y. Pub. Libr., 1992; named U.S. Poet Laureate, 2001; recipient Oscar Blumenthal Prize, Bess Hokin Prize, Frederick Bock Prize, Levinson Prize; fellow, N.Y. Found. for the Arts, NEA, Guggenheim Found. Office Phone: 718-960-8550.

COLLINS, WILLIAM LEROY, retired telecommunications engineer; b. Laurel, Miss., June 17, 1942; s. Henry L. and Christene E. (Finnegan) C. Student, La Salle U., 1969; BS in Computer Sci., U. Beverly Hills, 1984. Sr. computer operator Dept. Pub. Safety, Phoenix, 1975-78, data communications specialist, 1978-79, supr. computer ops., 1981-82; mgr. network control Valley Nat. Bank, Phoenix, 1979-81; mgr. data communications Ariz. Lottery, Phoenix, 1982-85; mgr. telecommunications Calif. Lottery, Sacramento, 1985—2004. Mem. Telecomm. Study Mission to Russia, Oct. 1991. Contbr. to profl. publs. Served as sgt. USAF, 1964-68. Mem. IEEE, Nat. Sys. Programmers Assn., Centrex Users Group, DMS Centrex User Group, Accunet Digital Svcs. User Group, Telecomms. Assn. (v.p. edn. Sacramento Valley chpt. 1990-94, pres. 1995, chpt. assn. dir. 1996-97, chpt. past pres. 1996, Prestigious Svc. award 1997), Telecom. Assn. (chmn. corp. edn. com. 1994-95, conf. com. 1994-95, co-chair conf. program com. 1996, program dir. edn. 1996, corp. dir. edn. 1996-97, pres.-elect 1998, pres. and ceo, 1999), SynOptics User Group, Timeplex User Group, Assn. Data Comm. Users, Soc. Mfg. Engrs., Data Processing Mgmt. Assn., Am. Mgmt. Assn., Assn. Computing Machinery, Am. Soc. for Quality Control, Bldg. Industry Cons. Svc. Internat., Assn. for Quality and Participation, KC, Calif. Integrated Svcs. Digital Network User Group, Computer Security Inst., Assn. Pub. Comms. Officials, Armed Forces Comms. and Electronics Assn., Assn. Info. Tech. Profls., H.P. Open View Forum. Roman Catholic. Home: 503 Mointain Shadow Dr Bayfield CO 81122 E-mail: wlc0617@wmconnect.com.

COLLINS-ADLER, CATHERINE KAY, social services professional; b. Aurora, Colo., May 3, 1964; d. Carroll Gail and Mary Kay Collins; m. John Thomas Adler, June 22, 1985. Student, S.D. State U., 1982-85. Tech. support specialist Gary Snow & Assocs., Pierre, S.D., 1988-91; co-owner Whistlestop, Pierre, 1992-93; program asst. S.D. Bankers Assn., Pierre, 1993-95; owner Simply Office Support, Pierre, 1989—; arts coord. Short Grass Arts Coun., Pierre, 1993—; exec. dir. Capital Area United Way, 1991—. Mem. Healthy Starts Com. Healthy Communities/Healthy Youth Com., Pierre Area Charitable Orgns., Am. Red Cross Disaster Team, Pierre Econ. Devel. Corp., Ctrl. South Dakota Leadership Alumni Group; past mem. Nat. Historic Preservation Com., S.D. Archives Registered Rschr., Youth at Risk Big Sister, Pierre Fire Dept. Auxiliary and S.D. Arts. Coun., Hughes/Stanley Counties Families First Partnership, River Hills Vol. Ctr. Bd., South Dakota Planned Giving Coun., Adolescent Health Coalition, Retired Sr. Vol. Program Adv. Bd., I-3 Work Group for Free Immunization Clinics for Youths 0-6, Central Edn. Network for Tech. Tng., Youth Power Task Force, Gifts-in-Kind Am. Pres.'s Coun., Project Care Coalition, Pierre Assn. Vol. Leaders, Nat. Soc. Fundraising Execs., Pierre City Commn. Traffic Safety Bd., Pierre Postal Adv. Com., Mayor's Non-profit Task Force. Recipient Dottie Rosso scholarship, 1994, Gus Shea Meml. scholarship, 1996, Outstanding Young Woman award, 1997. Office: Capital Area United Way 221 S Central Ave Pierre SD 57501-2428 Office Phone: 605-224-9229. Business E-Mail: pfpuw@iw.net.

COLLINS-MARTIN, PATRICIA A., psychologist; d. William Joseph Collins, Sr. and Doris M. Collins; m. Lawrence A. Martin, Aug. 19, 1978; children: Brett Lawrence Martin, Allison Marie Martin. AA, Broome C.C., 1974; BS, Pa. State U., 1975; MA, Marywood U., 1979, cert., 1990. Cert. elem. tchr. N.Y., 1976, tchr. spl. edn. N.Y., 1976, lic. sch. psychologist N.Y., 1990. Tchr. spl. edn. Cortland (N.Y.) Madison BOCES, 1976—78, Binghamton (N.Y.) U., 1978—79, Maine-Endwell (N.Y.) Sch. Dist., 1979—91, sch. psychologist, 1991—. Chmn. subcom. CSE, Endwell, 2004—; adv. ski club Mid. Sch. Maine-Endwell (N.Y.) Sch. Dist. Named Tchr. of Yr., Nat. Assn. of PTA, 1995. Mem.: Nat. Assn. Sch. Psychologist (assoc.), N.Y. Assn. Sch. Pschologist (assoc.; archivist 2000—05, lobbyist 2004—05). Democrat. Roman Catholic. Avocations: skiing, reading. Office: Maine-Endwell Central School District 1119 Farm to Market Road Endwell NY 13760 Office Phone: 607-786-8212.

COLLINSON, DALE STANLEY, lawyer; b. Tulsa, Okla., Sept. 1, 1938; s. Harold Everett and Charlotte Elizabeth (Bonds) C.; m. Susan Waring Smith, June 7, 1969; children: Stuart, Eleanor. AB in Politics and Econs. summa cum laude, Yale U., 1960; LLB, Columbia U., 1963. Bar: N.Y. 1963, U.S. Tax Ct. 1977. Law clk. U.S. Ct. Appeals (2d cir.), N.Y.C., 1963-64; law clk. to Justice Byron R. White U.S. Supreme Ct., Washington, 1964-66; asst. prof. Stanford (Calif.) Law Sch., 1966-68, assoc. prof., 1968-72; atty.-advisor Office of Tax Policy, U.S. Dept. Treasury, Washington, 1972-73, assoc. tax legis. counsel, 1973-74, dep. tax legis. counsel, 1974-75, tax legis. counsel, 1975-76; tax ptnr. Willkie Farr & Gallagher, N.Y.C., 1976-2000; spl. counsel fin. instns. and products IRS, Washington, 2000—. Panel mem. Practising Law Inst. programs, 1981, 82, 84, 86, 88, Am. Law Inst.-ABA program, 1984, Investment Co. Inst. programs, 1992, 94, 97, 2003, others. Contbr. articles to legal jours Fellow Am. Coll. Tax Counsel; mem. ABA, N.Y. State Bar (chmn. tax sect. 1985), Assn. of Bar of City of N.Y. (tax coun. 1990-93, vice chmn. taxation of corps. com. 1990-93). Republican. Home: 5480 Wisconsin Ave Apt 920 Chevy Chase MD 20815 Office: IRS 1111 Constitution Ave Washington DC 20224 Office Phone: 202-622-3900. Business E-Mail: dale.collinson.td.60@aya.yale.edu.

COLLIS, CHARLES, aircraft company executive; b. Bklyn., Aug. 6, 1920; s. Charles and Marie (Barnaby) C.; m. Margaret Howell, July 11, 1942; children: Jane, Joy. BSMechE, Brown U., 1942. V.p. Stratos div. Fairchild Hiller Corp., 1946-65, sr. v.p. Republic Aviation div., 1965-67, exec. v.p. corp., 1967-81; pres. Fairchild Hiller-F.R.G. Corp., 1966-69, Fairchild Republic Co., 1973-75, ret., 1981; mgmt. cons. Babylon, N.Y., 1982—. Mem. grad. mgmt. engring. adv. council C.W. Post Coll., L.I., 1965-66. Served as lt. USNR, 1942-45. Mem. AIAA, L.I. Assn. Commerce and Industry (bd. dirs. 1964-66), Babylon Yacht Club, Southward Ho Country Club. Home and Office: 116 Peninsula Dr Babylon NY 11702-3336

COLLIS, JOHN STANLEY, neurosurgeon; b. Lexington, Ky., Apr. 6, 1931; s. John Stanley and Elizabeth (Stefanis) C.; m. Helen Levas; children: Maribeth, John. BS, U. Ky., 1950; MD, U. Louisville, 1955. Program dir. Good Samaritan Hosp., Lexington, 1956; resident in gen. surgery Cleve. Clinic, 1957, resident in neurol. surgery, 1958-61, head spinal surgery, 1968-74, neuro anatomy instr., 1964-69, mem. neurosurgery dept., 1963-74; assoc. prof. neurosurgery Case Western Res. U., Cleve., 1976-82; neurosurg. adv. coun. Alcon Surg., 1983; dir. neurosurgery St. Luke's Hosp., Cleve., 1974-83, St. Vincent Charity Hosp., Cleve., 1984—, Luth. Med. Ctr., Cleve., 1988—. Founder Cleve. Spine and Arthritis Ctr., 1988, co-dir.; lectr. in field. Inventor surg. hood, surg. instruments for total disc replacement, laminectomy retractor, surg. see-0thru-barrier drape; contbr. articles to profl. jours.; editl. bd. Principle and Technic of Spinal Surgery, 1989. Chmn. sect. ch. and soc. Archdiocese Coun., Orthodox Ch., N.Y., 1983-84, co-chmn. fin. com. for Pitts.-Cleve. Diocese, mem. coun., 1984—; chmn. expansion com. St. Constantine & Helen, Cleve., 1985-87, co-chmn. expansion fund, tchr. adult edn., 1988-96; pres. Hawken Sch. Swimming Booster Club, 1979-80; mem. Hellenic Univ. Club, 1984; me., trustee Leadership 100, N.Y.C., 1986-97; exec. com. bd. trustees Hellenic Coll., Boston, 1997-98. Recipient St. Paul award Orthodox Ch., 1992. Mem. AMA, AAAS, Am. Assn. Neurol. Surgeons, Ohio State Neurosurg. Soc., Congress of Neurol. Surgeons, N.E. Ohio Neurosurg. Soc., Fellowship of Acad. Neurosurgeons, Cleve. Surg. Soc., Ohio State Med. Assn., N.Am. Lumbar Spine Assn., Order of St. Paul, Order of St. Andrew. Republican. Greek Orthodox. Avocations: bible study, philosophy. Office: Cleveland Spine and Arthritis Ctr 2709 Franklin Blvd Cleveland OH 44113-2993

COLLIS, SIDNEY ROBERT, retired telephone company executive; b. Oak Park, Ill., Mar. 24, 1924; s. Sidney John and Celia (Steele) C.; m. Lois E. Harding, Feb. 23, 1946 (dec.); children— Robert H., Elizabeth A., Gail M., April L. Student, Ill. Inst. Tech., 1941-43, U. Santa Clara, 1943-44; BS in Elec. Engring, Northwestern U., 1947. Registered profl. engr., Ill. With Ill. Bell Telephone Co., 1947-54, 60-61; with Am. Tel. & Tel. Co., 1954-60, 61-62, asst. v.p., 1968-83; v.p. Am. Tel. & Tel. Communications, 1984. Asst. v.p. N.Y. Telephone Co., 1962-63, v.p., 1963-68. Home: 70 Fieldstone Dr Basking Ridge NJ 07920-1607

COLLISCHAN, JUDY KAY, art gallery and museum director, critic, artist; b. Red Wing, Minn., Oct. 19, 1940; d. Michael J. and Olive Amanda (Sundberg) Collischan; m. Robert Grey Van Wagner, Oct. 4, 1969; 1 son, Brien Grey Collischan Van Wagner. BA, Hamline U., 1962; postgrad. Nat. U. Mex., summer 1963; MFA, Ohio U., 1964; PhD, U. Iowa, 1972. Asst. prof. art history U. No. Iowa, Cedar Falls, 1970-71, U. Nebr.-Omaha, 1971-75; assoc. prof. SUNY-Plattsburgh, 1975-82; dir. Hillwood Art Gallery, LI U., C.W. Post Campus Greenvale, N.Y., 1982—94; assoc. dir. Neuberger Mus. Art, SUNY, Purchase, N.Y., 1995-2000; pvt. practice cons., 2001—; art critic Arts, Art Express, NYC, 1982-; field rep. N.Y. State Council on Arts, NYC, 1983, mem. visual arts panel, 1986—; cons. Gen. Motors art collections, NYC 1983. Author: Women Shaping Art, 1984, Lines of Vision: Drawings by

Contemporary Women, 1989, Welded Sculpture of The 20th Century, 2000; contbr. articles to profl. jours. Fellow Kress Found., 1970; recipient award SUNY, 1981. Mem. Am. Assn. Mus. Office Phone: 212-505-9657. Personal E-mail: jcollischan@nyc.rr.com.

COLLISON, JIM, publishing executive; b. Blue Earth, Minn., May 24, 1933; s. Elliott Eugene and Rosa Theresa (Whitcomb) C.; m. Valerie Ann Thul, Oct. 28, 1954; children: Judith, Michelle, Daniel, Michael, Rebecca, David. BA, St. John's Univ., 1955. Sports editor Blue Earth Post and Faribault County Register, 1953; staff writer St. Cloud Daily Times, Minn., 1953-55, Waterloo Courier, Iowa, 1955-57, Mason City Globe Gazette, Iowa, 1958-63; bus. and edn. cons. Jim Collison Assoc., Mason City, Iowa, 1963-77; exec. dir. Employers of Am., Mason City, Iowa, 1978-81, pres., 1981—; pres., pub. Sunburst Publ., Mason City, Iowa, 1990—. Co-founder Employers of Am., 1978; chmn. bd. ISBE Ins. Alliance, Mason City, 1986—, Select Advantage, Inc., ISBE Bus. Ins. Assn., ISBE Employer Benefits Assn.; pres. Am. Corp. Advisors, Inc.; workshop presenter. Author: Skill Building in Advanced Reading, 1968, Mental Power in Reading, 1970, Complete Employee Handbook Made Easy, 1994, 97, 2001, The Employer Protection Workshop, 1996, No-How Coaching, 2001, Complete Suggestion Program Make Easy, 2001; pub., sr. editor (e-newletter) HRmadeEasy. Asst. min. Orchard (Iowa) Congreg. Ch., 1985—; designer Adult Literacy and Employment Reading Training Program. Democrat. Avocations: flower gardening, hiking. Home: 310 Meadow Ln Mason City IA 50401-1717 Office: Employers of Am PO Box 1874 Mason City IA 50402-1874

COLLMAN, JAMES PADDOCK, chemistry professor; b. Beatrice, Nebr., Oct. 31, 1932; married. B.Sc., U. Nebr., 1954, MS, 1956; PhD (NSF fellow), U. Ill., 1958; Docteur Honoris Causa, U. Dijon, France, 1988, U. Borgogne, 1988; D (hon.), U. Nebr., 1988. Instr. chemistry U. N.C., Chapel Hill, 1958-59, asst. prof., 1959-62, asso. prof., 1962-67; prof. chemistry Stanford U., 1967—; George A. and Hilda M. Daubert prof. chemistry Stanford U., 1980—. Frontiers in Chemistry lectr., 1964, Nebr. lectureship, 1968; Venable lectr. U. N.C., 1971; Edward Clark Lee lectr. U. Chgo., 1972; vis. Erskine fellow U. Canterbury, 1972; Plenary lectr. French Chem. Soc., 1974; Dreyfus lectr. U. Kans., 1974; Disting. inorganic lectr. U. Rochester, 1974; Reilley lectr. U. Notre Dame, 1975; William Pyle Philips lectr. Haverford Coll., 1975; Merck lectr. Rutgers U., 1976; FMC lectr. Princeton, 1977; Julius Steiglitz lectr. Chgo. sect. Am. Chem. Soc., 1977; Pres.'s Seminar Series lectr. U. Ariz., 1980; Frank C. Whitmore lectr. Pa. State U., 1980; Plenary lectr. 3d IUPAC Symposium on Organic Synthesis, 1980, 2d Internat. Kyoto Conf. on New Aspects Inorganic Chemistry, 1982, Internat. Symposium on Models of Enzyme Action, Brighton, Eng., 1983, Internat. Symposium, Italy, 1984; Brockman lectr. U. Ga., 1981; Samuel C. Lind lectr. U. Tenn., 1981, Syntex Disting. lectr. Colo. State U., 1983; Disting. vis. lectr. U. Fla., 1983; vis. prof. U. Auckland, New Zealand, 1985; Nelson J. Leonard lectr. U. Ill., 1987; plenary lectr. Internat. Symposium on Activation of Dioxygen and Homogeneous Catalytic Oxygenations, Tsukuba, Japan, 1987; plenary lectr. 12th Internat. Symposium on Macrocyclic Chem., Hiroshima, Japan, 1987; lectr. Texas A&M, 1988; J. Clarence Karcher lectr. U. Okla., 1989; Musselman lectr. Gettysburg Coll., 1990; Davis lectr. U. New Orleans, 1991; PLU lectr. Okla. State U., 1991; lectr. 5th Internat. Fischer Symposium, Karlsruhe, Ger., 1991; lectr. Euchem Conf., 1991; Pratt lectr. U. Va., 1992, others; lectr. series Harvard/MIT, 1992, Yale U., 1993; invited speaker symposia, univs., confs. Recipient Disting. Teaching award Stanford U., 1981, Calif. Scientist of Year award, 1983, Allan V. Cox medal for excellence in fostering undergrad. rsch., 1988, LAS Alumni Achievement award Coll. Liberal Arts and Scis. U. Ill., 1994, John C. Bailar Jr. medal, 1995, Joseph Chatt medal Royal Soc., 1998; named George A. and Hilda M. Daubert Prof. Chemistry (endowed chair, Stanford U.), 1980; Guggenheim fellow, 1977-78, 85-86, Churchill fellow, Cambridge, 1977—, Bing fellow, 1996. Fellow AAAS, Calif. Acad. Sci. (hon.); mem. Am. Chem. Soc. (Calif. sect. award 1972, soc. award in inorganic chemistry 1975, Arthur C. Cope scholar 1986, Pauling award Puget Sound and Oreg. sect. 1990, Disting. Svc. award in inorganic chemistry 1991, Alfred Bader award in bioinorganic or bioorganic chemistry 1997, Joseph Chatt lectr. 1998, Marker lectr. medal 1999), N.Y. Acad. Sci. (Basolo medal 2000), Chem. Soc. (London), Nat. Acad. Sci., Am. Acad. Arts and Scis., Phi Beta Kappa, Sigma Xi, Phi Lambda Upsilon, Alpha Chi Epsilon (Hans Fischer award 2002). Office: Stanford U Dept Chemistry Stanford CA 94305 Office Phone: 650-493-1378.

COLLMER, ROBERT GEORGE, language educator; b. Guatemala, Central Am., Nov. 28, 1926; (parents Am. citizens); s. G. Russell and Constance Ethel (Cravener) C.; m. Linnie Maffett Burney, Jan. 5, 1948 (dec. 1979); children: Carol Linda Collmer McLaren, Mark Wesley; m. Alys Edney, July 4, 1981. BA, Baylor U., 1948, MA, 1949; PhD, U. Pa., 1953. Asst. instr. U. Pa., Phila., 1949—52; instr. Phila. Bibl. U., 1952—54; from assoc. prof. to prof., chmn. dept. English Hardin-Simmons U., Abilene, Tex., 1954-58, 61; Smith-Mundt vis. prof. Inst. Technologico, Monterrey, Mexico, 1958—60; independent rschr. U. Leiden, Netherlands, 1960; acad. dean, prof. Wayland Bapt. U., Plainview, Tex., 1961—66; Fulbright vis. prof. Universidad Nacional, Asuncion, Paraguay, 1966—67; prof. English Tex. Tech U., Lubbock, 1967—73; prof., chmn. dept. English Baylor U., Waco, 1973—80, dean grad. studies and rsch., 1979—92, disting. English prof., 1992—97, emeritus disting. English prof., 1997—. Vis. English prof. U. of Jordan, fall, 1997. Editor: (with others) American Bypaths, 1980, The English Journals of Lodewijck Huygens, 1982, Bunyan in Our Time, 1989; contbr. articles to profl. jours. Served to cpl. U.S. Army, 1945-46. Fellow Rockefeller Found., 1958, Smith-Mundt, 1958-60, Fulbright-Hays, 1966-76, Hon. Rsch. fellow U. Glasgow, 1994; grantee Dutch Ministry Edn. Scis., 1981, Fulbright-Hays sr. rsch. grantee, 1982, Am. Philosophical Soc. grantee, 1976. Mem. Deans Conf. So. Assn. Bapt. Schs. (pres. 1963-64), S. Central Renaissance Conf. (pres. 1970-71), Assn. Tex. Grad. Schs. (pres. 1982-83), Conf. Christianity and Lit. (pres. 1982-85), Conf. Coll. Tchrs. of English (pres. 1983-84). Democrat. Avocations: traveling to Latin America and Europe, book collecting. E-mail: rcol1017@aol.com.

COLLOMB, BERTRAND PIERRE, cement company executive; b. Lyon, France, Aug. 14, 1942; came to U.S., 1985; s. Charles and Helene (Traon) C.; m. Marie Caroline Wirth, July 1, 1967; children: Cedric, Alex, Stephanie. Engring. student, Ecole Poly., Paris, 1960—62; engring. degree, Ecole des Mines, Paris, 1966; law degree, U. Nancy, France, 1968; PhD in Mgmt., U. Tex., 1972. Mining engr. Ministry of Industry, France, 1967-74; spl. asst. to Minister of Edn. Paris, 1974-75; with Lafarge, 1975—; regional v.p. Ciments Lafarge, Paris, 1976-77, pres., 1978-82; pres., CEO Orsan, Paris, 1982-85; CEO Gen. Portland, Inc., Dallas, 1985-87, Lafarge Corp., Reston, 1987-88, chmn. bd., 1989—; sr. v.p. Lafarge, Paris, 1988-89, CEO, 1989—2002, chmn., 2003—. Bd. dirs. Total, Unilever; chmn. French Inst. Internat. Rels. Chmn. World Bus. Coun. for Sustainable Devel., French Inst. Internat. Rels. Home: 4 rue de Lota 75116 Paris France also: Oakwood Farm 7433 Oakwood Dr Warrenton VA 20186 Office: Lafarge 61 rue des Belles Feuilles 75116 Paris France also: Lafarge NAm 12950 Worldgate Dr Ste 400 Herndon VA 20170

COLLOREDO-MANSFELD, FERDINAND, real estate company executive; Founder, ptnr. Cabot Partners Ltd., Boston; CEO Cabot, Cabot & Forbes. Bd. dir. Raytheon Co. Hon. trustee, past chmn. Mass. Gen. Hosp. Office: Cabot Partners LP 60 State St Boston MA 02109-1800

COLLOTON, STEVEN M., federal judge; b. Iowa City, Jan. 9, 1963; m. Deborah Colloton. AB, Princeton U., 1985; JD, Yale Law Sch., 1988. Law clk to Hon. Laurence H. Silberman U.S. Ct. Appeals, DC cir., Washington, 1988—89; law clk. to Hon. William H. Rehnquist U.S. Supreme Ct., Washington, 1989—90; special asst. to Asst. Atty. Gen. Dept. Justice Office Legal Counsel, 1990—91; asst. U.S. Atty. No. Dist. Iowa, 1991—99; assoc. counsel Office Ind. Counsel Kenneth W. Starr, 1995—96; ptnr. Belin Lamson McCormick Zumbach Flynn, Des Moines, 1999—2001; U.S. Atty. so. dist. Iowa, 2001—03; judge U.S. Ct. Appeals, 8th cir., 2003—. Office: US Courthouse Annex 110 E Court Ave Ste 429 Des Moines IA 50309-2053*

COLLUM, RICK DANIEL, lawyer; b. Atlanta, Sept. 25, 1969; s. Wesley Daniel and Mary Elizabeth Collum; m. Donna Lee Rogers, Sept. 12, 1992; children: Danielle Elizabeth, Jared Lee. BS in Criminal Justice, BA in Sociology, Valdosta State U., 1992; JD, Cleve. State U., 1999. Bar: Ga. 2000, U.S. Dist. Ct. (no., mid. and so. dists.) Ga. 2001, U.S. Tax Ct. 2001, U.S. Ct. Appeals (11th cir.) 2001, U.S. Surpeme Ct. 2004. Dep. U.S. marshal U.S. Marshals Svc., Cleve., 1992—99; legal instr. Fed. Law Enforcement Tng. Ctr., Brunswick, Ga., 1999—2000; jud. law clk. Hon. W. Louis Sands, Mid. Dist. Ga., Albany, 2000—02; lawyer Hall, Booth, Smith & Slover, Albany, 2002—04, The Collum Law Frim, Moultrie, 2004—. Tchr. Sunday Sch. Autryville (Ga.) Bapt. Ch., 2001—. Baptist. Avocations: golf, fishing, hunting, weightlifting. Office: The Collum Lawfirm PO Box 1867 Moultrie GA 31776 Office Phone: 229-891-3000.

COLLUMB, PETER JOHN, communications company executive; b. Newark, July 29, 1942; s. Peter A. and Rose M. (Coffey) C.; 1 child, Alexandra Christine. BS in Indsl. Psychology, East Tex. State U. (now Tex. A&M U.), Commerce, 1967. Registered lobbyist. Dir. pers./labor rels. Roper Corp., Chattanooga, 1969-71; v.p. human resources Nat. Sharedata Corp., Dallas, 1971-74; dir. pers./labor Dallas Times Herald, 1975-78; dir. econ. devel. divsn. Tex. Dept. Community Affairs, Austin, 1978-80; dep. exec. dir. Tex. Dept. Cmty. Affairs, 1978-81; legis./adminstrv. dir. U.S. Senator John G. Tower, Washington and Dallas, 1980-83; member U.S. Senate Armed Services Com., Washington, U.S. Senate Banking, Finance and Labor Com.; personal envoy Pres. Ronald W. Reagan, 1981—82; pres. N.Am. Sys., Inc., Dallas, 1981—; v.p. fin., sec.-treas. Diversified Packaging Co., Inc., 1983-85; chmn., pres. Collumb Communications Co., 1983—; chmn. of bd. and pres. Collumb, Hess, Navarro Pub. Rels., Dallas, Austin, Washington, Sacramento, 1991—; chmn. Komatsu, Ashcraft and Collumb Inc. Adj. prof. Bishop Coll., Dallas; bd. dirs. Tex. Housing Agy., Govs. Coms. on Aging and Migrant Affairs; guest lectr. So. Meth. U., Dallas, 1988—; chmn. bd. D.S.P. Corp., Dallas, 1985-98, C.H.N. Internat., Washington, Geneva, London and Tokyo; advisor to U.S. Sec. of Labor, Houston Econ. Summit, 1990; labor cons. Kullman, Lange, Inman & Bee, New Orleans; dir. Drug Prevention and Treatment Divsn., Tex. Dept. Cmty. Affairs; city adminstr., City of Westminster, Tex. Author: Political Process, 1982. Bd. dir. Plano Child Guidance Ctr., Collin County Mental Health-Mental Retardation Coun., Edna Gladney Ctr., Ft. Worth, 1979—, Free Shakespeare Festival, Dallas, 1978-85, v.p. finance; Outstanding Young Men Am., Atlanta, 1982—, Nat. Com. Adoption, 1986—, Ark. State Vocat./Tech. Schs., Ft. Worth State Sch. for the Retarded, Beautify Tex. Coun., 1980-85, Westminster Ind. Sch. Dist. Bd.; lobbyist, City of Fairview, Tex.; dir. advance staff Reagan/Bush Presdl. Campaign, Washington, 1978-85, Sam Johnson for Congress Campaign, 1991, Bush-Quayle 1992 Presdl. Campaign, Elizabeth Dole Senate Campaign, 2002, Lamar Alexander Senate Campaign, 2002; vice-chmn., dir. fin. Fair Housing Coun., 1988—; mem. community adv. coun. Coord. Bd. Tex. Colls. and Univs.; mem. Rep. Presdl. Task Force, 1984—; co-chair, parents counc., Mary Baldwin Coll., chmn. Fourth Border Conf. on Drug Abuse; candidate U.S. Ho. Reps., Dallas, 1982-84; del. White House Confs. on Aging, Small Bus. and the Family, Tex. Rep. Party Convs., 1984, 88, 92; pvt. advisor to Pres. U.S.: Ronald Reagan; exec. dir., receiver Dallas County Community Action Com.; cons. U.S. Can. Free Trade Commn., Washington, 1986-87, Plano Sister Cities, Inc., Big Brothers & Sisters, others; chmn., v.p. fin., v.p. devel. Tex. World of Children; chmn. Pres.'s Adv. Coun., HUD Tech. Adv. Coun., Hillcrest Acad. Found., 1986-91, George W. Bush Re-Election Campaign, 1994, George Bush Presidential Campaign, Jim Talent for Senate Campaign, 2002, nat. fin. com., Marshall Program, Bush-Cheney Presdl. Campaign, Bush-Cheney Inaugural Com., 1999-2000, Bush-Cheney Re-Election Campaign, 2004, Hutchinson for U.S. Senate, 1994, Ralph Hall for Congress Re-Election Campaign, 2004; Welfare to Work Pilot Project, State of Tex., office of Gov. George W. Bush. Named to Outstanding Young Men Am., Jaycees, 1981, Amigo Extradonaire, Govt. of Mexico, 1984. Mem. Centros de Juv Mexico (chmn. 1980-84), North Dallas C. of C. (bus. resource, internat. affairs, govt. affairs com.), Dallas Coun. on World Affairs, Tex. Sheriffs Assn. (charter), Tex. A&M Commerce Alumni Assn., Stallion Club (pres.), Lions (v.p. Mena, Ark. 1976-77), Rotary, Lambda Chi Alpha (pres. 1967-69, chmn. alumni control bd., pres. alumni assn.). Republican. Presbyn. Avocations: tennis, golf, reading, politics. Office: Collumb Communication Co 3404 Mission Ridge Rd Ste 100 Plano TX 75023-8115 Office Phone: 469-241-1290. Personal E-mail: collumb2@aol.com.

COLLYER, ROBERT B., trade association administrator; b. Decatur, Ill., Oct. 16, 1932; s. Murray Gordon and Frances Mary (Evans) C.; m. Margaret Mary Hebel, Feb. 27, 1960; 1 son, Bryan. BA, Humboldt Coll., 1956. Cons. DeLeuw Cather & Co., 1957-59; claims and mgr. govt. relations Indsl. Indemnity Co. Calif., San Francisco, San Jose, Sacramento, 1960-73; exec. asst. UBA Inc., Washington, 1974-81; dep. under sec. Employment Standards Adminstrn. U.S. Dept. Labor, Washington, 1981-84; pres. The Collyer Co., 1984—; exec. dir. Internat. Assn. Indsl. Accident Bds. and Commns., 1990-96; exec. dir., sec.-treas. Internat. Workers' Compensation Found., 1990—; dean Internat. Workers' Compensation Coll., 1990-96. Co-founder, dir. Nat. Symposium Workers Compensation U. Maine, 1976-80; dir. Western States Self-Ins. Colloquim, Inc., Nat. Employers' Adv. Council on Workers Compensation; cons. Nat. Indsl. Council; mem. Nat. Adv. Commn. on State Workers Compensation Law Compliance U.S. Dept. Labor; mem. Nat. Adv. Commn. on Indsl. Rehab. Research and Tng. Program U. N.C.; mem. steering com. Nat. Workers Compensation Info. Exchange Group; mem. steering com. Permanent Disability Study Adv. Commn. NSF; mem. steering com. U.S. Longshoremen and Harbor Workers' Reform Group Pres. Marin county Republican Council, (Calif.), 1973; mem. Calif. Rep. Central Com., 1970-73; asst. county chmn. Com. to Re-elect Pres., 1972. Named Republican of Yr. Marin County, 1972 Home and Office: Spruce Creek Fly In 25 Lazy Eight Dr Port Orange FL 32128 Office Phone: 386-304-1993. E-mail: tobobcollyer@aol.com.

COLMAN, CHARLES KINGSBURY, academic administrator, criminologist; b. Nashua, N.H., May 14, 1929; s. Charles David Colman and Lela (Bessey) Sproul; m. Marjorie Gertrude Bahe, Aug. 19, 1950 (dec. May 2003); children: Charles David, Cathleen Ann. Diploma, Yale U., 1961; BA, U. Md., 1963; MEd, Stetson U., 1972; EdD, Fla. Atlantic U., 1978. Spl. agt. USAF, U.S. Army, 1947-67; asst. prin. Satellite High Sch., Satellite Beach, Fla., 1969-81, dean acad. edn., 1981-85; ctr. dir. Brevard C.C., Patrick AFB, Fla., 1985-92, provost Palm Bay, Fla., 1992-94; pres. emeritus, 1994—. Mem. Fla. State Adv. Com. on Mil. Edn., Patrick AFB, 1985—; edn. rep. Semiconductor Mfg. Tech., Dallas, 1985—. Author: Formative Years, 1970; author computer software. Co-founder Boys Club Am., Melbourne, Fla, 1968. Grantee Fla. Dept. Edn., 1987, 89, 90, 91, U.S. Dept. Edn., 1991-92; recipient Ace award Fla. Dept. Edn., 1991. Mem. ASCD, Ret. Officers' Assn., Assn. Former Intelligence Officers (v.p. 1998-2000, pres. 2001-02, Fla. chpt.), Assn. Former OSI Spl. Agts. (sec. 1998—, Space Coast chpt.), Phi Delta Kappa (chpt. pres. 1983-84). Avocations: golf, computer programming. Home: 1717 Timberline Ln SE Salem OR 97306 Office: Brevard Community Coll Palm Bay Campus 250 Community College Pky Palm Bay FL 32909-2206

COLMAN, JAMES PETER, academic administrator; b. Gainesville, Fla., June 30, 1960; m. Rebecca Sue Colman. B in Music Edn., Grace Coll., Winona Lake, Ind., 1982; MusM, Mich. State U., 1986, PhD, 1990. Prof. music Cedarville (Ohio) U., 1989—2003, chair dept. music, 1997—2003; sr. v.p. for acad. affairs Okla. Bapt. Univ., 2003—. Dir. strategic planning, Cedarville U., 1996—. Office: Okla Bapt Univ 500 W Univ Shawnee OK 74804 Fax: 405-878-2046. Office Phone: 405-878-2022.

COLMAN, ROBERT WOLF, hematologist, educator; b. NYC, June 7, 1935; s. Jack K. and Miriam (Greenblatt) C.; m. Roberta Fishman, June 16, 1957; children: Sharon, David. AB summa cum laude, Harvard U., 1956, MD cum laude, 1960. Cert. Internal Medicine, Hematology. Intern Boston City Hosp., 1960-61; resident Beth Israel, Brookline, Mass., 1961-62; clin. assoc. USPHS, NIH, 1962-64; resident Barnes Hosp., St. Louis, 1964-65, fellow in hematology, 1965-67; assoc. in medicine Harvard Med. Sch., Cambridge, Mass., 1967-69, asst. prof., 1969-73, assoc. prof., 1973, U. Pa., Phila., 1973-77, prof. medicine, 1977-78, Temple U. Sch. Medicine, Phila., 1978—, prof. thrombosis rsch., 1981—, prof. physiology, 1992—, dir. Sol Sherry Thrombosis Rsch. Ctr., 1979—, Sol Sherry prof. of medicine, 1989—. Hematology study sect. NIH, Bethesda, Md., 1977-81; parent com. to review SCORs in Ischemic Heart Disease; chemistry spl. emphasis panel to review SBIR, STTR grants, NIH, study sect. rev. therapeutic modulation angiogensis disease, study sect. to rev. tng. grants and careeer devel. awards; invited lectr. Gordon confs., Internat. Congress Hemostasis and Thrombosis, Fedn. Am. Socs. Exptl. Biology; plenary lectr. and chair Gordon Conf. Internat. Soc. Kallikreins and Kinins, others. Editor: Hemostasis and Thrombosis, 5th edit., 2005; editor Platelet Jour.; mem. editorial bd. Jour. Clin. Investigation, Blood, Procs. Soc. Exptl. Biology, Thrombosis Rsch. Platelets, Thrombosis Hemostasis; contbr. numerous articles to profl. jours. Surgeon USPHS, 1962—64. Recipient Leon Resnick prize Harvard U., Career Devel. award NIH, Sr. Investigator award S.E. Pa. chpt. Am. Heart Assn., Disting. Career award Internat. Soc. Thrombosis and Hemostasis. Fellow ACP; mem. Assn. Am. Physicians. Am. Soc. Clin. Investigation, Am. Soc. Biochemistry and Molecular Biology, Internat. Soc. Hemostasis and Thrombosis (councillor 1989-95), Peripatetic Club, Interurban Clin. Club, Phi Beta Kappa, Sigma Xi, Alpha Omega Alpha. Achievements include 8 patents in field. Avocation: travel. Office: Temple U Sch Medicine Sol Sherry Thrombosis Rsch Ctr 3400 N Broad St Philadelphia PA 19140-5104 Office Phone: 215-707-4665. Business E-Mail: colmanr@temple.edu.

COLMAN, STEPHANIE G., music educator; b. N.Y.C., Dec. 9, 1952; d. Henry S. and Florence C. Colman; 1 adopted child, Jonathan Leonard. BA, MA magna cum laude, Queens Coll., 1975. Freelance musician and tchr., N.Y. and Fla., 1974-84; tax preparer H&R Block, NY and Fla., 1975—2004; tchr. music and gifted Broward County Schs., Ft. Lauderdale, Fla. Mem. Music Educators Nat. Conf. Composer: (vocal composition) The City Child, 1975 (Edna Mills award). Mem. Humane Soc. Ft. Lauderdale, 1981—. Recipient Tchr. of Yr. award 1989, 2000. Mem. Music Educators Nat. Conf., Broward Elem. Music Tchrs. Assn. (pres.), Fla. Music Educators Assn., Fla. Elem. Music Educators Assn., Mensa (Am. chpt.). Democrat. Jewish. Avocations: piano, video production, swimming. E-mail: suncom@aol.com.

COLMANT, ANDREW ROBERT, lawyer; b. Bklyn., Oct. 10, 1931; s. Edward J. and Mary Elizabeth (Byrne) C.; children: Elizabeth, Carolyn, David (dec.), Stephen, Robert. BBA, St. Johns U., Jamaica, N.Y., 1957, LLB, 1959. Bar: N.Y. 1959, U.S. Dist Ct. (so. and ea. dists.) N.Y. 1961, U.S. Ct. Appeals (2nd cir.) 1969, U.S. Ct. Appeals (4th cir.) 1977, U.S. Supreme Ct. 1991. Assoc. Hill, Rivkins, Carey, Loesberg O'Brien & Mulroy and predecessor firms, 1959-73, ptnr., 1973-87; of counsel Jerrold E. Hyams, 1988—91, Peter F. Broderick, 1992. Proctor in admiralty; active USMC amphibious reconnaissance; Amtrac Driver, Army Gen. Intelligence Sch. Author: Outline of General Average. Interpretive vol. Sandy Hook Lighthouse and History House, Fort Hancock, NJ, Navesink Light Sta., Highland, NJ; active Conservation Coun. for Hawaii, Honolulu, St. Stephans Indian Sch., Am. Indian Mus. Natural History, Deep Cut Gardens, Middleton, NJ; vol. Twin Lighthouse, NJ, Highlands Hist. Soc., Highlands, NJ; VIP Nat. Park Svc.; vol. Sandy Hook Lighthouse, History House, Hancock, NJ, 2002—, Cmty. St. Benedict, Holmdel, NJ; rep., leader Bayshore Comty. Hosp., Holmdel, NJ, 1978—; min. of eucharist St. Benedict Parish, Holmdel, NJ; extraordinary min. Holy Eucharist Asssigned; Sunday contingent; mem., track chmn. Parish Coun., Fin. Funding, Constl. Lance cpl. USMC, 1952—54. Recipient Social Min. award, Diocese Trenton Bishop Riess, VIP award, Dept. Interior. Mem.: ACLU, ABA (torts and ins. and admiralty com., sr. com.), St. John's Sch. Law Admiralty Soc., Social Security Com., Assn. Internationale de Droit des Assurances, Pacific Rim Maritime Law Assn., Asia Pacific Lawyers Assn., NY State Bar Assn. (admiralty), Maritime Law Assn. U.S. (life; proctor in admiralty 1960, carriage goods com.), NY County Lawyers Assn. (life; admiralty com. 1963.), Nat. Trust for Hist. Preservation, Nat. Maritime Hist. Soc., Navy League U.S., Amnesty Internat., Anti-defamation League, Nat. Park Conservation Assn., Twin Light Hist. Soc., Nat. Wildlife Fedn., ATLA (admiralty com. 1995), Sierra Club. Home: Bethany Manor 500 Broad St Apt 11Y Keyport NJ 07735-1640

COLMES, ALAN, political commentator, radio personality; Overnight host Sta. WABC, NYC, 1982—84, morning host, 1984; with Sta. WNBC, NYC, Sta. WMCA, NYC; morning host Sta. WZLX, Boston; ptnr, on-air host Daynet radio network, 1990—94; worked in develop. of radio divsn. United Stations, 1996; co-host Hannity & Colmes FOX News Channel, NYC, 1996—, host FOX News Live with Alan Colmes, 2003—; host Sta. WEVD, NYC, 1998—2001. Author: Red, White & Liberal: How Left Is Right & Right Is Wrong, 2003. Office: FOX News Channel 1211 Avenue of the Americas New York NY 10036*

COLMES, DORIS HARRIETT, writer; b. Meiningen, Germany, June 29, 1929; d. Max Lang Goldsmith and Isabelle Sicklick; m. Eugene Mitchell Colmes (div. 1976); children: Victoria, Scott, Andrea. BS, Concordia Coll., Portland, Oreg., 1992; MSW, Portland State U., 1996. MCSE mediation specialist; cert. EMT 1972; credentialed minister Oreg., 1982; cert. reality therapy counselor Inst. for Reality Therapy, La., Calif., 1988, sexual abuse practitioner 1986. Mediation specialist City of Portland, 1977—79; program mgr. Janus Youth Programs, Portland, 1979—96; case mgr. drug/alcohol offenders INACT, Inc., Portland, 1996—97; program dir. DePaul Youth Svcs., Portland, 1997—98; counselor in pvt. practice Portland, 1990—2000. Drug/alcohol counselor Our House of Portland, 2000—02, mem. patient care team. Author: The Iron Butterfly, 2002; contbr. essays to profl. pubs. Hospice vol. Legacy Vis. Nurses Assn. Hospice, Portland; AIDS vol. Our House of Portland; activist Sch. of the Ams. Watch, Moveon.org, Portland; minister Ch. of Movement of Spiritual Awareness, 1981—. Recipient Kay Snow Lit. award for nonfiction, Willamette Writers, Portland, 2003, Award for Sustained Dedication and Commitment to Human Diversity, Janus Youth, 1994, Award for Sustained Excellence, 1991. Avocations: playing flute, jogging, Scrabble, dance, swimming.

COLODNY, EDWIN IRVING, lawyer, retired air transportation executive; b. Burlington, Vt., June 7, 1926; s. Myer and Lena (Yett) Colodny; m. Nancy Dessoff, Dec. 11, 1965; children: Elizabeth, Mark, David. AB with distinction, U. Rochester, 1948; LLB, Harvard U., 1951; D in Comml. Sci. (hon.), Robert Morris Coll., 1985; LLD (hon.), Middlebury Coll., 1986; HHD (hon.), Kings Coll., 1988; LLD (hon.), U. Vt., 2004. Bar: N.Y. 1951, DC 1958. With CAB, 1954-57, USAirways Inc. (formerly Allegheny Airlines Inc.), 1957-91; exec. v.p. mktg. and legal affairs USAirways, Inc. (formerly Allegheny Airlines Inc.), 1969-75, pres., 1975-90, CEO, 1975-91, chmn. bd. dirs., 1978-92; also chmn. USAirways Group, Inc., 1978-92; ret., 1992; of counsel Paul, Hastings, Janofsky and Walker, Washington, 1991—2002; chmn. Comsat Corp., 1997-2000; of counsel Dinse, Knapp & McAndrew, Burlington, Vt., 2004—. Interim pres. U. Vt., 2001—02; interim pres., CEO Fletcher Allen Health Care, Burlington, 2002—03. Lt. U.S. Army, 1952—54. Recipient James D. McGill Meml. award, U. Rochester, Wright Bros. Meml. award, 1990, Tony Jannus award, 1990. Mem.: ABA, U. Rochester (bd. trustees). Personal E-mail: eic8225@aol.com.

COLOMA, ROLAND SINTOS, education educator; b. Quezon City, Philippines, Nov. 19, 1972; arrived in U.S., 1985; s. Jesus C. and Aida S. Coloma. BA in Liberal Studies, U. Calif., Riverside, 1995, MA in Ednl. Adminstrn., 1998; MA in Cultural Studies in Edn., Ohio State U., 2002, PhD in Cultural Studies in Edn., 2004. Coord. student affairs U. Calif., Riverside, 1993—96; English tchr. Ramona H.S., Riverside, 1997, Baldwin Park (Calif.) H.S., 1997—99, L.A. H.S., 1999—2000; fellow, instr. Ohio State U., Columbus, 2000—04; asst. prof. Otterbein Coll., Westerville, Ohio, 2004—. Fellow, Wash. State U., 2003. Mem.: History Edn. Soc., Filipino Am. Nat. Hist. Soc., Am. Ednl. Rsch. Assn. (Spencer fellow 2002—03). Office: Otterbein Coll Dept Edn 1 Otterbein Coll Westerville OH 43081

COLOMBIK, RICHARD M., lawyer; b. Chgo., July 16, 1953; s. Robert and Rose (Ziegler) C.; m. Colleen S. Bennett, May 17, 1989; children: Jeremy, Justin, Samantha. BS, U. Colo., 1977; JD cum laude, John Marshall Law

Sch., 1980. Bar: Ill., U.S. Dist. Ct. (no. dist.) Ill., U.S. Tax Ct., U.S. Supreme Ct.; CPA, Ill. Tax acct. Henry Crown Co., Chgo., 1980-82; sr. ptnr. Colombik & Bell, P.C., Palatine, Ill., 1982-86, Colombik & Assoc., P.C., Schaumburg, Ill., 1987—. Liason to dist. dir. IRS-ISBA, 1990-97. Author: Business Entities Within Illinois, 1996, Offshore Trusts that Really Work, 1997; contbr. articles to profl. publs. Mem. ABA (vice chmn. taxation sect. gen. practice com. 1995-97), N.W. Suburban Bar Assn. (chmn. estate planning probate and tax com. 1989-90, gov. 1990-94, treas. 1995-96, sec. 1994, v.p. 1994-97, chmn. budget com. 1995-96, Ill. State Bar Assn. (sec. coun. fed. taxation 1990-94, bus. advice and fin. planning 1990), North Shore Estate Planning Counsel, Gavel Soc. (hon. legal soc. for leadership), Am. Assn. of Attys. CPAs (v.p. 1992-97), North Suburban Bar Assn. (gov. 1991-94), Offshore Inst., Beta Alpha Psi (v.p.). Republican. Office: 540 W Frontage RD STE 2255 Northfield IL 60093-1229 E-mail: rcolombik@colombik.com.

COLOMBI-MONGUIO, ALICIA DE, language educator, humanities educator; b. Buenos Aires; came to the U.S., 1967; d. Carlos and Rosa de Colombí; m. Luis Monguió, Aug. 8, 1979. BA in History, U. Santa Clara, 1969; MA in Spanish and Portuguese, Stanford U., 1971, PhD in Spanish and Humanities, 1973. Asst. prof. Spanish Mills Coll., Oakland, Calif., 1973-79; faculty Bennington (Vt.) Coll., 1979-82; prof. Spanish SUNY, Albany, 1982-84, 86-98, chair dept. Hispanic and Italian studies, 1986-90, rsch. prof. Hispanic and humanistic studies, 1998—; prof. Spanish U. Ariz., 1984-86. Chair divsn. letters Mills Coll., Oakland, 1975-79; chair fgn. langs. and lits. Bennington Coll., 1979-82; head dept. Spanish and Portuguese U. Ariz., Tucson, 1984-86; chair dept. Hispanic and Italian studies SUNY, Albany, 1986-90, rsch. prof. Hispanic and humanistic studies, 1998—. Author: De amor y poesia en la Espana Medieval, 1976, Petrarquismo Peruano, 1985, Del exe antiguo a nuestro nuevo polo, 2003, 3 books poetry; contbr. more than 90 articles to profl. jours. Recipient Diploma de Honor, U. P.R., Mayagüez, 1981; Guggenheim fellow, 1978-79. Mem. MLA, Assn. Internat. Hispanistas, Renaissance Soc. Am. Avocations: gardening, travel. Office: Office VP Acad Affairs Ad Bldg 203 State U Albany Albany NY 12222 E-mail: amonguio@aol.com.

COLOMBO, CHARLES A., artist; b. Wilmington, Del., Nov. 3, 1927; s. Anthony P. and Rose (DeFeo) Colombo; divorced; 1 child, Charles. Student, Pa. Acad. Fine Arts. Owner Charles Colombo Studio, Wilmington, 1969—. Represented in permanent collections Vatican, Rome, White House, Prince Ranier and Princess Grace Kelly, Monaco. Sgt. USAR, 1951—59. Mem.: Am. Watercolor Soc. (award 1966), Nat. Arts Club. Roman Catholic. Home: 1410 Delaware Ave B-1 Wilmington DE 19806 Office Phone: 302-654-9105.

COLOMBO, JOHN ROBERT, poet; b. Kitchener, Ont., Can., Mar. 24, 1936; s. John Anthony and Irene (Nicholson) C.; m. Ruth Florence Brown, May 11, 1959. BA, U. Toronto, 1959, postgrad., 1959-60, DLitt (hon.), 1998. Editorial asst. U. Toronto Press, 1957-59; asst. editor Ryerson Press, Toronto, 1960-63; sr. adv. editor McClelland & Stewart, Toronto, 1964-70; publ. cons. Toronto, 1971—; editor Tamarack Rev., Toronto, 1960-82. Spl. instr. Atkinson Coll., York U., Toronto, 1965-68; mem. adv. arts panel Can. Council, 1968-70; advisor Ont. Council Arts, 1965-68 Author (over 180 books, including); author: Colombo's Canadian Quotations, 1974; author: (with Nikola Roussanoff) The Balkan Range: A Bulgarian Reader, 1976; author: Colombo's Canadian References, 1976, (anthology) The Poets of Canada, 1978, Other Canadas: An Anthology of Science Fiction and Fantasy, 1979, Colombo's Hollywood, 1979, 222 Canadian Jokes, 1981, Friendly Aliens, 1981, Selected Poems, 1982, Selected Translations, 1982, Songs of the Indians, 1983; author: (with George Faludy) Learn This Poem of Mine by Heart, 1983; author: Canadian Literary Landmarks, 1984, 1001 Questions about Canada, 1986, Colombo's New Canadian Quotations, 1987, (poetry) Off Earth, 1987, Mysterious Canada, 1988, Extraordinary Experiences, 1989, 999 Questions About Canada, 1989, Songs of the Great Land, 1989, Mysterious Encounters, 1990, Mackenzie King's Ghost, 1991, UFOs Over Canada, 1991, The Dictionary of Canadian Quotations, 1991, Worlds in Small, 1992, Dark Visions, 1992, The Little Blue Book of UFOs, 1992, Walt Whitman's Canada, 1992, The Mystery of the Shaking Tent, 1993, Colombo's All-Time Great Canadian Quotations, 1994, Ghost Stories of Ontario, 1995, Voices of Rama, 1995, Strange Stories, 1995, Shapely Places, 1996, Haunted Toronto, 1996, Ether, 1997, What is What, 1998, All about Us, 1998, Marvellous Stories, 1998, More Iron Curtains, 1998, Closer than You Think, 1998, Quotable Canada, 1998, Interspaces, 1999, Self-Schrift, 1999, Mysteries of Ontario, 1999, Ghosts in our Past, 2000, The UFO Quote Book, 2000; gen. editor: The Canadian Global Almanac, 1992—2000, Colombo's Famous Lasting Words, 2000, The Penguin Book of Canadian Jokes, 2001, Ghost Stories of Canada, 2001, Half Life, 2002, Only in Canada, 2002, Making Light, 2002, Say It Again, Sam, 2003, More or Less, 2003, True Canadian Ghost Stories, 2003, One Hundred Poems, 2003, O Rare Denis Saurat, 2003, The Denis Saurat Reader, 2004, The Native Series, 2004, The Monster Book of Canadian Monsters, 2004; gen. editor A Algernon Blackwoods Canadian Talnoy Terror, 2004, The Stephen Leacock Qupte Style Book, 2004, To Take from Life, 2004. Recipient Can. Centennial medal, 1967, Order Cyril and Methodius 1st class, Esteemed Knight of Mark Twain, lit. prize Harbourfront's Internat. Festival Authors, 1985; mem. Order of Can., 2004. Mem. P.E.N., League Can. Poets (provisional coordinator 1966-67), Assn. Can. TV and Radio Artists. Home and Office: 42 Dell Park Ave Toronto ON Canada M6B 2T6 Fax: 1 (416) 782-0285. Office Phone: 416-782-0285. E-mail: jrc@ca.inter.net.

COLOMBO, MICHAEL A., lawyer; b. Lumberton, NC, Sept. 2, 1948; BS, NC State Univ., 1970; JD, Univ. SC, 1979. Bar: NC, SC, US Ct. of Appeals, US Dist. Ct., US Tax Ct. Ptnr. Colombo Kitchin Attys., Greenville, NC. Capt. fighter pilot USAF, 1970—75. Mem.: ABA, Am. Coll. of Trust and Estate Counsel, Pitt County Bar Assn. (pres. 1988—89), NC Bar Assn. (bd. gov. 1998—2001, pres. 2005—). Office: Colombo Kitchin Attys 1698 E Arlington Blvd Greenville NC 27858 Office Phone: 252-321-2020.

COLOMER, VERONICA, medical educator, researcher; b. Mexico City, Mex., Nov. 9, 1957; married. BS, U. Mexico City, Mex., 1983; PhD, NYU, 1990. Postdoctoral fellow in lab. dept. cell biology NYU Med. Ctr., 1990-94; instr. lab. dept. cell biology Cornell Med. Coll., 1995; instr. in lab. dept. psychiatry Johns Hopkins U. Sch. Medicine, 1996—. Guest investigator in lab. dept. cellular physiology and immunology Rockefeller U., 1982-84. Contbr. articles to profl. jours. Recipient Minority Scientist Devel. award Am. Heart Assn., 1996, Career award MSDA Am. Heart Assn., 1996—; Undergrad. Student fellowship Consejo Nacional de Ciencia y Tecnologia, 1981-82, Grad. Student fellowship, 1984-87, Ella Fitzgerald fellow Am. Heart Assn., 1991, Postdoctoral Participating Lab. award fellowship Am. Heart Assn., 1991-94. Mem. Am. Soc. Cell Biology, Royal Soc. Tropical Medicine and Hygiene, N.Y. Acad. Scis., Mex. Soc. Biochemistry, Mex. Soc. Immunology. Office: Johns Hopkins U Sch Medicine Dept Psychology 720 Rutland Ave # 618 Baltimore MD 21205-2109

COLON, CARLOS WILDO, librarian; b. Shreveport, La., Apr. 23, 1953; s. Wildo Domingo and Mercedes (Alejandro) C.; m. Alma Maria Mutzi, June 17, 1979; 1 child, Gina Marie. BA in English, La. State U., Shreveport, 1975; MLS, La. State U., 1977. Ref. libr. Memphis-Shelby County Pub. Libr. and Info. Ctr., 1978-81; ref./reader's adv. supr. Shreve Meml. Libr., Shreveport, 1981—. Libr. practicum instr. La. State U., Shreveport, 1982—. Author: The Worst of Almira Gulch, 1984, Almira Gulch: Confessions of a Social Wallflower, 1987, Jiminy Limericks, 1991, 94, Blue Jay on a Bowling Pin, 1991, Mountain Climbing, 1993, Clocking Out, 1996; (with Alexis K. Rotella) Nothing Inside, 1996, (with Alexis K. Rotella) Sassy, 1998; editor: Shreve Memorial Library Public Service Statistics 1922-89, 1990, Voices and Echoes: Haiku Soc. of America Members' Anthology, 2001; sr. editor A Selective Index to the Shreveport Journal, 1985-91, A Selective Index to the Shreveport Times, 1985-96, The Best of the Electronic Poetry Network, 2000, (with Raffael de Gruttola) Circling Bats, 2001; co-editor: Area Agencies and Organizations Directory, 1985—, Between Quiet and Confrontation, 2003; contbr. articles to profl. jours. Vol. disk jockey Sta. WEVL, Memphis, 1981; lit. panel chmn. Shreveport Regional Arts Coun., 1990—, bd. dirs., 1991—. Named Outstanding Young Man of Am., Outstanding Young Men of Am., 1986; recipient Pushcart Prize nomination, 1994; Shreveport Regional Arts Coun. lit. fellow, 2002. Mem. ALA, Acad. Am. Poets, La. Libr. Assn., Am. Contract Bridge League, Shreveport Bridge Assn., Poets & Writers, Haiku Soc. Am., Shreveport Writers Club, Yellow Bus Tour, LogJam. Roman Catholic. Home: 185 Lynn Ave Shreveport LA 71105-3523 Office: Shreve Meml Libr 424 Texas St Shreveport LA 71101-5452 Office Phone: 318-226-5894. Business E-Mail: ccolon@shreve.net.

COLON, JOSÉ MARIANO, obstetrician, gynecologist, educator; s. Rafael Alberto Colon and Susana Margarita Pesquera. BA, Brown U., 1975; MD, NYU, 1980. Diplomate Am. Bd. Ob-gyn., Am. Bd. Reproductive Endocrinology and Infertility. Tchg. asst. dept. ob-gyn. Sch. Medicine NYU, N.Y.C., 1981—83, clin. instr. dept. ob-gyn. Sch. Medicine, 1983—86; instr. dept. ob-gyn. N.J. Med. Sch. U. Medicine and Dentistry, Newark, 1986—88, asst. prof. dept. ob-gyn. N.J. Med. Sch., 1988—95, assoc. prof. dept. ob-gyn. N.J. Med. Sch., 1995—. Fellow: ACOG, Am. Soc. Reproductive Medicine; mem.: Soc. Assisted Reproductive Endocrinology and Infertility. Office: Univ Reproductive Assocs 214 Terrace Ave Hasbrouck Heights NJ 07604 Office Phone: 201-288-6330.

COLON, SUZANNE MARY, religious organization administrator, musician; d. Warren Anthony and Geraldine Martin; m. Ralph Colon, Aug. 19, 1978; children: Teresa Carolyn, Rachel Amanda. BA in music edn., Wagner Coll., 1971—75; MS in edn., State U. of NY at New Paltz, k, 1979—80; Cert. in Ch. Music & Liturgy, St. Joseph Coll., 2001—03. Public School Teacher Certificate U. of the State of NY, 1981. Organist/choir dir. Plattekill Ref. Ch., Saugerties, NY, 1980—84; music min. St. Mary of the Snow Cath. Ch., Saugerties, NY, 1984—96, St. Anthony Cath. Ch., Brooksville, Fla., 1996—. Chmn. Liturgy Com. of St. Anthony Ch., Brooksville, Fla., 1999—2005; vol. organist Notre Dame Interparochial Sch., Spring Hill, Fla., 1996—99; dir. of music Vacation Bible Sch., Brooksville, Fla., 2004—05; accompaniest Various Sch. Choruses, Spring Hill, Fla., 1996—2005. Recipient Named to Outstanding Young Women of Am., 1987, Named to Student Bd., St. Joseph Coll., 2002. Mem.: Am. Guild of Organists, Nat. Pastoral Musicians, Columbiettes, Alpha Tau Mu. Avocations: birdwatching, reading. Office Phone: 352-796-2096.

COLONEY, WAYNE HERNDON, civil engineer; b. Bradenton, Fla., Mar. 15, 1925; s. Herndon Percival and Mary Adore (Cramer) C.; m. Anne Elizabeth Benedict, June 21, 1950; 1 child, Mary Adore. B.C.E. summa cum laude, Ga. Inst. Tech., 1950. Registered profl. engr. and surveyor, Fla., Ga., Ala., N.C. Project engr. Constructora Gen. S.A., Venezuela, 1948-49, Fla. Rd. Dept., 1950-55; hwy. engr. Gibbs & Hill, Inc., Guatemala, 1955-57, project mgr. Tampa, Fla., 1957-59; project engr., then assoc. J.E. Greiner Co., Tampa, 1959-63; ptnr. Barrett, Daffin & Coloney, Tallahassee, 1963-70; pres. Wayne H. Coloney Co., Inc., Tallahassee, 1970-78, chmn., bd. chief exec. officer, 1978-85; pres., sec. Tesseract Corp., 1975-85; dep. chmn. Howden Airdynamics Am., Tallahassee, 1985-90; pres. Coloney Co. Cons. Engrs., Inc., 1978—; v.p., dir. Howden Coloney Inc., Tallahassee, 1985-90; prin. Coloney-Von Soosten & Assocs. Inc., Tallahassee, 1990—2002, Coloney Bell Engring., 1996—, Aurora Mgmt. Ptnrs., Tallahassee, 2002—03; prin. engr. Coloney Bell Engring., 1996—. Chmn. adv. com. Area Vocat. Tech. Sch., 1965-78; pres. Retro Tech. Corp., 1983-93, Profl. Mgmt. Con. Group, 1983-87; pres., bd. dirs. Internat. Enterprises Inc., 1967-73; bd. dirs., exec. com. GTO, Inc., 1990—. Patentee roof framing system, dense packing external aircraft fuel tank, tile mounting structure, curler rotating device, bracket system for roof framing; contbr. articles to profl. jours. Pres. United Fund Leon County, 1971-72; bd. dirs. Springtime Tallahassee, 1970-72, pres., 1981-82; bd. dirs. Heritage Found., 1965-71, pres., 1967; mem. Pres.'s Adv. Council on Indsl. Innovation, 1978-79; bd. dirs. LeMoyne Art Found., 1973, v.p., 1974-75; bd. dirs. Goodwill Industries, 1972-73, Tallahassee-Popoyan Friendship Commn., 1968-73; mem. Adv. Com. for Hist. and Cultural Preservation, 1969-71; vice chmn. Govs. Commn. for Purchase from the Blind, 1980-2002. Served with AUS, 1943-46. Fellow ASCE, Nat. Acad. Forensic Engrs. (pres.); mem. NSPE, Am. Def. Industries Assn., Fla. Engring. Soc. (sr.), Fla. Inst. Cons. Engrs., Fla. Surveying and Mapping Soc., ANAK, Koseme Soc., Fla. Small Bus. Assn. (pres. 1981), Gov.'s Club, Phi Kappa Phi, Omicron Delta Kappa, Sigma Alpha Epsilon, Tau Beta Pi. Episcopalian. Home: 1304 Hollow Oak Cir Tallahassee FL 32308 Office: Coloney Bell Engring Ste 200 1520 Killearn Center Blvd Tallahassee FL 32309 Office Phone: 850-222-8193. E-mail: whc@coloneybell.com.

COLONNIER, MARC LEOPOLD, retired anatomist; b. Quebec, Can., May 12, 1930; s. Jean and Enilda (Bourguignon) C.; m. Lise De Gagne, Oct. 24, 1959; 1 son, Jean. BA, B.Ph., U. Ottawa, 1951, MD, 1959, MS, 1960; PhD, U. Coll. London, 1963. Asst. prof. anatomy U. Ottawa, 1963-65; asst. prof. dept. physiology U. Montreal, Que., Can., 1965-67; assoc. prof., assoc. fellow neurol. scis. group Med. Research Council Can., 1967-69; prof., head dept. anatomy U. Ottawa, 1969-76; prof. dept. anatomy Laval U., Quebec City, Que., 1976-91; ret., 1991. Recipient Lederle Med. Faculty award, 1966, Charles Judson Herrick award Am. Assn. Anatomists, 1967 Fellow Royal Soc. Can.; mem. Am. Assn. Anatomists; Mem. Soc. Neurosci.; mem. Can. Assn. Anatomists (pres. 1973-75) Clubs: Cajal. Personal E-mail: marc@colonnior.net.

COLOSI, GIOVANNA R., director; b. Syracuse, N.Y., May 25, 1975; d. Nick Colosi and Fiorina Nave-Colosi. BA in Psychology, SUNY, Oswego, 1997, MS in Counseling, 2004. Dir. residence life Bryant & Stratton Coll., Syracuse, 1997—99; asst. dir. admissions Cayuga CC, Fulton, NY, 2000—04; dir. student life Coll. So. Md., La Plata, 2004—. Mem.: ACUI, ACPA, Kappa Delta Pi. Democrat. Roman Catholic. Avocations: dance, reading, animal welfare. Office: Coll So Md 8730 Mitchell Rd La Plata MD 20646 Office Phone: 301-934-7508.

COLOSIMO, ANTONIO, architect; b. Dayton, Ohio, Apr. 3, 1949; s. Joseph Antonio and Maria Antonietta Colosimo; divorced; 1 child, Marcus Antonio. BS in Architecture, Ohio State U., 1974. Registered architect, Ohio, Ill., Ga., Va., N.Y., N.J., Pa., Mass., Ariz., Colo., Fla., Ind., Kans., Ky., Md., Mich., Minn., Mo., N.C., S.C., Tenn., Tex., Utah. Founder, pres. 3D/Group, Inc., Columbus, 1978—. Panel speaker on Adaptive Re-Use of Bldgs. for Elderly Housing, U.S. Conf. Mayors, Washington, 1987, Nat. Conv. of County Officials, 1989. Recipient several awards for various hist. renovation projects including HUD Chief Architect Award for Design and Constrn. Mgmt. Mem. Nat. Cert. Archtl. Registration Bds. (cert.), Urban Land Inst. Roman Catholic. Office: 3D/Group Inc 266 N 4th St Columbus OH 43215-2511 E-mail: 3dinfo@3dgroup.com.

COLOSO, VICTOR FRANCISCO, pediatrician; b. Manila, Nov. 2, 1960; came to U.S., 1986; s. Ernesto Cruz Coloso and Ramona De Guzman Francisco; m. Regina Sanson Sitchon, Jan. 12, 1992; children: Nina Therese, Patrick Angelo, Regine Victoria. BS in Zoology cum laude, U. of The Philippines, Quezon City, 1982; MD, U. of The Philippines, Manila, 1986. Bd. cert. Am. Bd. Pediats., Am. Bd. Neonatology. Resident in pediats. Monmouth Med. Ctr., Long Branch, N.J., 1991-94; neonatal fellow U. Miami-Jackson Meml. Hosp., Miami, Fla., 1994-97; asst. prof. pediat. U. Miami Sch. Medicine, 1997-98, Pediatrix med. Group, 1999—. Mem. Am. Acad. Pediats. Home: 11610 Stonehaven Way West Palm Beach FL 33412 Office: St Mary's HOsp NICU 901 45th St West Palm Beach FL 33407 Office Phone: 561-881-2980.

COLP, NORMAN BARRY, artist, curator; b. Bronx, N.Y., Sept. 3, 1944; s. Joseph Johnny Colp and Martha (Berman) Colp Levine; m. Marsha Stern, July 18, 1981. BA in Art, CUNY, 1967; postgrad., Pratt Inst., 1967, Parsons Sch. Design, 1971. Archtl. modelmaker Milton Glaser Inc., N.Y.C., 1978—80; assoc. curator Alternative Mus., N.Y.C., 1979—80; curator exhibits Ctr. Book Arts, N.Y.C., 1980—83, exhbn. coord., 1983; instr. Pratt Graphics Ctr., N.Y.C., 1983—84, Sch. Visual Arts, N.Y.C., 1982—86, acad. advisor, 1984—87; photog. artist, curator N.Y.C., 1978—. Cons. curator Anchorage Mus. History and Art, 1990, Golden & Dresnin Design, Phila., 1990, Islip Art Mus., East Islip, N.Y., 1990, Boca Raton (Fla.) Mus. Art, 1991; cons. on book Exploring Color Photography, 1991, 97, The Girls' Guide to Hunting and Fishing, 1999-2000; artist-in-residence Pub. Sch. 1, Long Island City, N.Y., 1977-78, Cabin Creek Ctr. for Work and Environ. Studies, N.Y.C., 1979; workshop presenter-in-residence Mus. Holography, N.Y.C., 1985; cons. Artists Found., Inc., Boston, 1986, juror, 1989; lectr. in field. Author: Freud's Recipe, Crazy Hair, A Primer on Art Criticism, 1983; one-man shows include Victoria and Albert Mus., London, 1991, Islip Art Mus., 1993, UCLA, 1994, Coll. of Charleston, 1997, Hugo de Pagano Gallery, NYC, 1998, The Tiny Cinema, Red Mills, Claverack, NY, 2001, exhibited in group shows at Mus. Modern Art Libr., Mus. Fine Arts, St. Petersburg, Fla., Boca Raton Mus., Corcoran Gallery of Art, Washington, U. Art Mus., U. Calif., Berkeley, Wadsworth Atheneum, Hartford, Conn., The Ralls Collection, Washington, FotoFest 2002, Houston, 2002, Art in Embassies Program, U.S. Dept. State, Havana, Cuba, 2003, Lima, Peru, 2003, Fine Print Auction FotoFest Internat., Houston, 2004, Martha Stewart Incarcerated Living Eyewear Promotional Mailing, 2005, at The Flipbook Show, Kunsthalle, Düsseldorf, Germany, 2005, Represented in permanent collections Nat. Libr., Paris, Victoria and Albert Mus., Corcoran Gallery, Libr. Congress, Mus. Modern Art Libr., NYC, NY Pub. Libr., Queens Mus. of Art, Flushing, NY, Islip Art Mus., East Islip, NY, Bklyn. Mus. of Art, Archives of Am. Art, Smithsonian Instn., Washington, Whitney Mus. Am. Art, Internat. Ctr. Photography, NYC. Grantee, Com. for Visual Arts, 1980, Met. Transit Authority, 1991, Fieldcrest Cannon Inc., 1991, The Merchant and Ivory Found., 2002, FotoFest, 2002. Avocation: collecting american art and japanese redware pottery and gutta-purcha frames. Home: 180 W End Ave Apt 3R New York NY 10023-4913

COLPETZER, KEITH EDWARD, entomologist, consultant; b. Lewistown, Pa., June 4, 1970; s. Richard William and Gloria Kay Colpetzer; m. Laurel Lynn Smith, Oct. 21, 1995; 1 child, Ryan William. BS in Biology and Ecology, West Chester U. of Pa., 2000; MS in Entomology and Ecology, U. of Del., Newark, 2003; postgrad., Spring Garden Coll., Phila., 1984—88. Contract cons. James McCulley, IV - Environ. Cons., Inc., Glasgow, Del., 1999—2000; survey technician Del. Dept. of Agr., Dover, Del., 2000—01; rsch. asst. U. of Del., Newark, 2001—03; USDA-APHISs contract entomologist USDA Plant Epidemiology and Risk Analysis Lab., Raleigh, NC, 2003—. Aquatic macroinvertebrate cons. Aquatic Invertebrate Identification Svcs., Raleigh, NC, 2003—. Contbr. articles to profl. jours. Mem.: N.C. Entomol. Soc., Am. Entomol. Soc. (Phila. chpt.), Entomol. Soc. of Am. (Asa Fitch Meml. award of ea. br. 2004). Achievements include research in Biological control of mile-a-minute weed, Polygonum perfoliatum L.: Host specificity, feeding and oviposition preferences of the Asian weevil, Rhinoncomimus latipes Korotyaev; Methods for estimating the risk of invasion and establishment of quarantine-significant plant pests on imported fruits, vegetables and ornamental plants. Avocations: rock climbing, kayaking, hiking, mountain biking. Home: 1507 Pinewinds Dr Apartment 202 Raleigh NC 27606 Office: USDA APHIS PPQ CPHST PERAL 1730 Varsity Dr Ste 300 Raleigh NC 27603 Personal E-mail: kcolpetzer@hotmail.com. E-mail: kecolpet@aphis.usda.gov.

COLSON, EARL MORTON, lawyer, educator; b. Bklyn., Mar. 8, 1930; s. Abraham and Rebecca (Hecker) C.; m. Helen Theresa Austern, Apr. 24, 1960; children: Adam Thomas, Amy Esther, Deborah Austern. BS magna cum laude, Syracuse U., 1950; LLB magna cum laude, Harvard U., 1957. Bar: N.Y. 1958, D.C. 1960. Assoc. Chadbourne, Parke, Whiteside & Wolff, N.Y.C., 1957-60, Arent, Fox, Kintner, Plotkin & Kahn, Washington, 1960-68, ptnr., 1968—91, of counsel, 1992—. Adj. prof. law Georgetown U., 1970—2003; lectr on tax subjects. Author: Capital Gains and Losses, 1975; co-author: Federal Taxation of Estates, Gifts and Trusts, 1975. Bd. dirs. Washington Hebrew Congregation, 1979—, v.p., 1984-90, pres., 1990-92; trustee Kingsbury Ctr., 1978-81; mem. N.Y. bd. overseers Hebrew Union Coll., 1995-97; bd. dirs. D.C. chpt. Am. Jewish Com., 1995-98. Mem. ABA (chmn. estate and gift tax com. sect. taxation 1972-73), D.C. Bar Assn. (chmn. tax com. 1971-72, treas., bd. govs. 1974-76), Am. Law Inst., Assn. of Bar of City of N.Y., Cosmos Club Washington. Office: 1050 Connecticut Ave NW Washington DC 20036-5303

COLSON, JOHN R., electric power industry executive; With PAR Elec. Contractors Inc. (subs. of Quanta Svcs.), 1971—97, pres., 1997—97; CEO Quanta Svcs., Houston, 1997—, chmn., 2002—. Bd. dir. Quanta Svcs., 1998—, US Concrete Inc., 1999—. Mem.: Mo. Valley Chpt. Nat. Elec. Contractors Assn. (bd. dir.). Office: Quanta Svcs 1360 Post Oak Blvd Houston TX 77056 Office Phone: 713-629-7600.*

COLSON, ROSEMARY, music educator; b. Madison, Ind., July 15, 1937; d. Howard Paul and Mary Wilder Colson. Student, Georgetown Coll., 1955—56; MusB, George Peabody Coll., 1960; MusM, Yale U., 1965. Tchr. piano Wilmington Music Sch., Del., 1965—66, Settlement Music Sch., Phila., 1966—77, Chestnut Hill Acad., Phila., 1969—78; piano tchr. Acad. Cmty. Music, Ft. Washington, Pa., 1993—; tchr. pvt. piano Phila., 1967—; organist, choir master Grace Epiphany Episcopal Ch., Phila., 1987—2000. Contbr. articles to profl. jours. Treas. West Ctrl. Germantown Neighbors, Phila., 1981—83; bd. dirs. YWCA Germantown, Phila., 1990—94; mem. Music Tchr.'s Nat. Assn., 1999—2004; bd. dirs. Women's Sacred Music Project, 2003—05. Mem.: Am. Guild Organists, Delta Omicron (advisor to U. Pa. chpt. 1963—64). Democrat. Presbyterian. Avocations: gardening, reading, travel. Home: 6021 McCallum St Philadelphia PA 19144 Personal E-mail: rsmrclsn@aol.com.

COLSTON, FREDDIE CHARLES, political science educator; b. Gretna, Fla., Mar. 28, 1936; s. Henry Bill and Willie Mae (Taylor) C.; m. Doris Marie Suggs, Mar. 13, 1976; 1 child, Deirdre Colston Graddick BA, Morehouse Coll., 1959; MA, Atlanta U., 1966; PhD, Ohio State U., 1972. Chmn. dept. social studies Attucks H.S., Hollywood, Fla., 1960—64; instr. social sci. Ft. Valley (Ga.) State Coll., 1966-68; assoc. prof. polit. sci. So. U., Baton Rouge, 1972-73, U. Detroit, 1973-76; assoc. prof., chmn. div. social sci. Dillard U., New Orleans, 1976-78; asst. prof. polit. sci. Delta Coll., University Center, Mich., 1978-79; assoc. dir. Exec. Seminar Ctr. U.S. Office Pers. Mgmt., Oak Ridge, 1980-87; prof. Inst. of Govt. Tenn. State U., Nashville, 1987-88; prof., dir. pub. adminstrn. program N.C. Ctrl. U., Durham, 1988-91; prof. dept. history and polit. sci. Ga. Southwestern State U., Americus, 1992-97. Pres. Broward County (Fla.) Social Studies Coun., 1961-62; mem. constn. com. Fla. State Tchrs. Assn., 1963-64; chmn. human rels. coun. Ga. Southwestern State U., 1997. Author: Dr. Benjamin E. Mays Speaks. Representative Speeches of a Great American Orator, 2002; contbr. articles to profl. jours. Mem. bd. mgmt. Northwestern Br. YMCA, Detroit, 1976; mem. govt. subcom. Task Force 2000, City of Midland, Mich., 1979. Scholar Morehouse Coll., 1955, Atlanta U., 1965, Nat. Def. Edn. Act, 1964; fellow Ford Found., 1967, So. Fellowships Fund, 1968-71; grantee C-Span, 1994, 95, 96; recipient Mr. Psi award Omegi Psi Phi, 1959, Outstanding Faculty award Kappa Delta Sorority, Ga. Southwestern State U., 1995, Outstanding Faculty award Ga Southwestern State U., 1997 Mem. Am. Polit. Sci. Assn. (com. on the status of blacks in the profession 1977-80), Nat. Conf. Black Polit. Scientists, Ctr. for Study of Presidency, Assn. for Study of Afro-Am. Life, Am. Soc. Pub. Adminstrn., Pi Sigma Alpha, Alpha Phi Gamma. Avocations: reading biographies, photography, spectator sports. Home: 126 Hazleton Ln Oak Ridge TN 37830-7929 Personal E-mail: freedie12@comcast.net.

COLTEN, HARVEY RADIN, pediatrician, educator; b. Houston, Jan. 11, 1939; s. Oscar Aaron and Zina Mae (Radin) Colten; m. Susan J. Kaplowitz, July 29, 1959; children: Jennifer J., Lora, Charles Thomas. BA, Cornell U., 1959; MD, Western Res. U., 1963; MA (hon.), Harvard U., 1978. Diplomate Am. Bd. Allergy and Clin. Immunology, Am. Bd. Pediats. Intern Univ. Hosps., Cleve., 1963, resident in pediat., 1964—65, Children's Hosp. of D.C., Washington, 1968—69; rsch. assoc. Nat. Inst. Child and Human Devel., NIH, Bethesda, Md., 1965—67; asst. prof. pediat. George Washington U., 1969—70; from asst. prof. pediat. to prof. Harvard U., 1970—97; chief divsn. cell biology, dir. cystic fibrosis program Children's Hosp. Med. Ctr., Boston, 1976—86; pediatrician-in-chief Jewish Hosp., 1986—89; Harriet B. Spoehrer prof. pediat. Washington U. Med. Sch., St. Louis, 1986—97, chmn. dept. pediat., 1986—95; pediatrician-in-chief Children's and Barnes Hosps., 1986—95; dean, v.p. med. affairs Northwestern U. Sch. Medicine, Chgo., 1997—99; chief med. officer iMetrikus, Inc., Carlsbad, Calif., 2000—. Prof. pediat. and microbiology/immunology Northwestern U. Sch. Medicine, 1999—2000; clin. prof. pediat. U. Calif., San Francisco, 2001—02; pres., v.p. and sr. assoc. dean for acad. affairs Columbia U. Med. Ctr., 2002—; prof. pediat. Columbia U., 2003—; past chmn. pediat. allergy Nat. Inst. Allergy and Infectious Disease Task Force on Asthma and Allergy; past mem. Nat. Inst. Child and Human Devel. Task Force on Cystic Fibrosis; past rsch. rev. com. Nat. Cystic Fibrosis Found.; past mem. pulmonary diseases adv. com. NIH. Assoc. editor Jour. Immunology, 1971—74, Immunochemistry, 1972—75, Jour. Allergy and Clin. Immunology, 1977—80, New Eng. Jour. Medicine, 1978—81, Jour. Clin. Investigation, 1982—85, Am. Jour. Respiratory Cell and Molecular Biology, 1988—91, New Insights into CF, 1993—94, editl. bd. Molecular and Cellular Biochemistry, 1983—87, Jour. Pediat., 1981—88, Jour. Clin. Immunology, 1985—89, Ann. Rev. Immunology, 1986—90, Clin. Immunology and Immunopathology, 1987—91, Blood, 1987—92, New Eng. Jour. Medicine, 1990—98, Jour. Biomed. Sci., 1992—, Proc. Assn. Am. Physicians, 1995—99, Ency. of Life Scis., 1997—; contbr. articles to profl. jours. Vice chmn. bd. dirs. Parents As Tchrs. Nat. Ctr.; bd. dirs. The Oasis Inst., Immtech Internat. Inc.; past mem. pediat. scientist program selection com. AMSPDC; sci. adv. coun. March of Dimes; mem. Nat. Heart, Lung, Blood Adv. Coun. NIH; past bd. mgrs. Ctrl. Inst. for Deaf. Lt. comdr. USPHS, 1964—68, hon. discharge. Recipient Spl. Faculty Rsch. award, Western Reserve U., 1963, E. Mead Johnson award, 1979. Fellow: AAAS, Am. Acad. Pediat., Am. Acad. Allergy and Immunology; mem.: NAS (vice-chmn. coun. Inst. Medicine 1997—), Inst. of Medicine, Am. Soc. Biochem. and Molecular Biology, Am. Thoracic Soc., Am. Pediatric Soc., Soc. Pediatric Rsch., Hungarian Soc. Immunology (hon.), Assn. Am. Physicians, Am. Soc. Clin. Investigation, Am. Assn. Immunologists (past sec.-treas., Disting. Svc. award), E. Mead Johnson Award Program Com. (past chmn.), Fedn. Am. Socs. for Exptl. Biology. Address: 299 Hollow Hill Rd Tamworth NH 03886 Office: Columbia Univ Med Ctr 2-401 630 W 168 St New York NY 10032

COLTHUP, NORMAN BERTRAM, retired spectroscopist; b. Paris, July 6, 1924; BS, Antioch Coll., 1949; DS (hon.), Fisk U., 1974. Co-author: Introduction to Infrared and Raman Spectroscopy, 3d edit., 1990, The Handbook of Infrared and Raman Characteric Frequencies of Organic Molecules, 1991. Recipient Williams-Wright award, Coblentz Soc., 1979, Maurice Hasler award, 1999. Address: 71 Strawberry Hill Ave Apt 704 Stamford CT 06902-2723

COLTMAN, JOHN WESLEY, physicist; b. Cleve., July 19, 1915; s. Robert White and Louise (Tyroler) C.; m. Charlotte Waters Beard, June 10, 1941; children: Sally Louise Condit, Nancy Jean Horner. BS in Physics, Case Inst. Tech., 1937; MS, U. Ill., 1939, PhD in Physics, 1941. Rsch. scientist Rsch. Labs. Westinghouse Electric Corp., Pitts., 1941—49, mgr. electronics and nuc. physics dept., 1949—60, assoc. dir. rsch. labs., 1960—64, dir. rsch. mth. and radiation, 1964—69, dir. rsch. industry, def. and pub. sys., 1969—74, dir. rsch. and devel. planning, 1974—80. Mem. adv. group on electron devices Dept. Def., 1958-62; mem. Naval Intelligence Sci. Adv. Com., 1971-73, NRC Commn. on Human Resources, 1977-80; privately sponsored rschs. on acoustics of the flute. Contbr. articles to profl. jours. Recipient Longstreth medal Franklin Inst., 1960; Roentgen medal Remscheid, W. Ger., 1970; Gold medal Radiol. Soc. N.Am., 1982 Fellow Am. Phys. Soc., IEEE; mem. Nat. Acad. Engring., Am. Musical Instrument Soc. Presbyterian. Achievements include inventing x-ray image amplifier, scintillation counter. Home: 3319 Scathelocke Rd Pittsburgh PA 15235-5122 E-mail: coltmanjw@att.net.

COLTON, CLARK KENNETH, chemical engineering professor; b. NYC, July 20, 1941; s. Sidney and Goldie (Chases) C.; m. Ellen Ruth Brandner, June 20, 1965; children: Jill Erin, Jason Adam, Michael Ross, Brian Scott. B of Chem. Engring., Cornell U., 1964; PhD, MIT, 1969. Asst. prof. chem. engring. MIT, Cambridge, 1969-73, assoc. prof., 1973-76, prof., 1976—, Bayer prof. chem. engring., 1980-85, dep. head dept. chem. engring., 1977-78, chmn. centennial chem. engring. edn., 1988. Cons. to NIH, FDA, various indsl. orgns.; mem. adv. bd. mil. personnel supplies NRC, 1971-75 Mem. editl. bd. Jour. Membrane Sci., 1975-81, 97, Jour. Bioengring., 1976-79, Preparative Chromatography, 1988-94, Isolation and Purification, 1994—, ASAIO Jour., 1985-94; mem. editl. bd. Cell Transplantation, 1991-94, 97, assoc. editor, 1997—; contbr. articles to sci. jours. Ford found. fellow, 1969-70; recipient Tchr./Scholar award Camille and Henry Dreyfus Found., 1972, Lifetime Contbn. award in bioartificial organs Engring. Found., 1998. Fellow AAAS; mem. AIChE (dir. food, pharm. and bioengring. div. 1978-81 (food, Pharm. and Bioengring. div. award, 1999, Allan P. Colburn award 1977), N.Y. Acad. Scis., Am. Soc. Artificial Internal Organs (editorial bd. 1978-84), Am. Diabetes Assn., Am. Soc. for Apheresis, Am. Soc. for Engring. Edn. (Curtis W. McGraw rsch. award 1980), North Am. Membrane Soc., Am. Heart Assn., Cell Transplantation Soc. (sec. 1994-2001, treas. 2001—), Transplantation Soc., Internat. Pancreas and Islet Transplant Assn., Internat. Soc. on Oxygen Transport to Tissue, Am. Chem. Soc., Am. Inst. Med. and Biol. Engring. (founding mem.), Internat. Soc. Articificial Organs, Internat. Soc. Blood Purification (Gambro award 1986), Biomed. Engring. Soc., Cornell Club, Sigma Xi, Tau Beta Pi, Phi Lambda Upsilon. Home: 279 Commonwealth Ave Chestnut Hill MA 02467-1012 Office: MIT Dept Chem Engring Cambridge MA 02139 Office Phone: 617-253-4585. Business E-Mail: ckcolton@mit.edu.

COLTON, DAVID See COLTON, STERLING

COLTON, DAVID LEM, mathematician, educator; b. San Francisco, Mar. 14, 1943; s. Ellis and Myrl (Crowder) C.; m. Renate, Dec. 20, 1968; children— Claire, Natasha. BS, Calif. Inst. Tech., 1964; MS, U. Wis., 1965; PhD, U. Edinburgh, Scotland, 1967, DSc, 1977. Asst. prof. math. Ind. U., 1967-71, assoc. prof., 1972-74; prof. U. Strathclyde, Glasgow, Scotland, 1975-78, U. Del., Newark, 1978—, Unidel prof., 1996—. Vis. prof. McGill U., 1968-69, U. Glasgow, 1971-72, U. Konstanz, 1974-75 Author various rsch. monographs; rschr. numerous publs. in field. Mem. Soc. Indsl. and Applied Math. (mem. editl. bd. Inverse Problems). Office: U Del Dept Math Newark DE 19716 Business E-Mail: colton@math.udel.edu.

COLTON, ELIZABETH WISHART, government agency administrator; b. Rockville Centre, N.Y., June 25, 1929; d. Ronald Sinclair Wishart and Elizabeth Lathrop Phillips. BA cum laude, We. Coll. for Women, 1951; postgrad., Am. U., 1951—52, Bowie State Coll., 1989—90. Jr. mgmt. asst. U.S. C.S.C., Washington, 1954, test developer, 1954—55, civil svc. insp., 1955—58, stds. developer and writer of qualification and classification stds., 1958—59, developer and implementer nationwide evauation plans of maj. fed. depts., 1958—62; developed and implemented bureauwide pers. mgmt. improvement programs Bur. of Reclamation Dept. of Interior, Washington, 1962—65, asst. dir. of pers. for nat. pk. svc., 1965—70, staff specialist dir. equal opportunity Office of Equal Employment Opportunity Programs, 1970; dep. dir. of pers. for pers. mgmt. evaluation and asst. to dep. dir. for classification and pay Dept. of Treasury, Washington, 1970—78; dir. divsn. pers. sys. imrprovement Office Asst. Sec. Health and Human Svcs., Washington, 1978—85. Real estate broker, Annapolis, Md., 1985—2003; antique dealer, Annapolis, 1985—2003. Job counselor displaced homemakers YWCA, Annapolis, 1985—92, active, 1985—92; ct. -apptd. spl. advocate for a foster child; developer and leader inner-city boys cooking class N.Y. Ave. Presbyn. Ch., Washington, 1960—69. Mem.: We. Coll. Alumnae Assn. Miami U. (bd. trustees 2004—), Victoria Walk Unit Owners Assn. (sec. treas. 2003—). Presbyterian. Avocations: ancient history, gardening, travel, genealogy. Home: 402-B Goldsborough St Easton MD 21601 E-mail: bcolton@goeaston.net.

COLTON, JAMES PATRICK, academic administrator; m. Margaret Hill; children: Rebecca, Barbara, William. AA, Weatherford (Tex.) Coll., 1976; BS cum laude, Tex A&M U., 1978, MEd, 1979. Grad. asst. Tex. A&M U., College Station, 1978, grad. fellow, 1978-79; agr. instr. Poolville (Tex.) H.S., 1979-80, Weatherford Coll., 1980-87, instnl. rsch. dir., 1987-93, dir. student devel., 1993-98, dean student devel., 1998—. Chmn. occupl. adv. bd. Aledo (Tex.) Ind. Sch. Dist., 1983-85; mem. rsch. com. North Tex. C.C. Consortium, 1988-92; presenter programs. Bd. dirs. Palo Pinto County Hosp. Dist., Mineral Wells, Tex., 1999—; del. Tex. Dem. State Conv., Austin, 1985; Pan Am. Exposition beef supt. State Fair Tex., Dallas, 1981-88; mem. Parker County Youth Com., chmn., 1981-83. Named Faculty Mem. of Yr., Weatherford Coll., 1984, Staff Mem. of Yr., 1991; named to Outstanding Young Men of Am., 1988. Mem. Weatherford Bus. and Profl. Men's Club (publicity chmn.), Phi Theta Kappa, Gamma Sigma Delta. Alpha Zeta. Avocations: computers, history, youth development, bassets. Office: Weatherford Coll 225 College Park Dr Weatherford TX 76086-6265 E-mail: colton@wc.edu.

COLTON, JOEL, historian, educator; b. N.Y.C., Aug. 23, 1918; s. Philip and Theresa (Cotler); m. Shirley Baron, May 8, 1942 (dec. Dec. 2003); children— Valerie Beth, Kenneth Richard. BA magna cum laude, CCNY, 1937, MS, 1938; MA, Columbia U., 1940; PhD, 1950. Lectr. history Columbia U., 1946-47; successively instr., asst. prof., assoc. prof., prof. history Duke U., 1947-89, prof. emeritus, 1989—, chmn. dept. history, 1967-74, chmn. acad. council, 1971-73; dir. for humanities Rockefeller Found., 1974-81. U.S. mem. Internat. Commn. on History of Social Movements and Social Structures, 1975—, v.p., 1980-85, co-pres., 1985-90, hon. pres., 1990—; vis. prof. U. Wis., Makerere U., Uganda; lectr. Cadi-Ayyad U., Morocco. Author: Compulsory Labor Arbitration in France, 1936-39, 1951, (Japanese transl. 1999), Léon Blum: Humanist in Politics, 1966 (French transl. 1968), rev. edit., 1987, Twentieth Century: Time-Life Great Ages of Man Series, 1968, rev. edit., 1980; co-author: (with R.R. Palmer) A History of the Modern World, 2d - 8th edits., 1956-95 (transl. into Arabic, Persian, Swedish, Finnish, Spanish, Italian and Chinese), (with R.R. Palmer and L. Kramer), 9th edit., 2002, Study Guide for A History of the Modern World, 9th edit., 2002; editor: The Humanities in an International Context, 1976, The Search for a Value Consensus, 1978, Toward the Restoration of the Liberal Arts Curriculum, 1979; co-editor: Technology, The Economy and Society, 1987; bd. editors: Jour. Modern History, 1967-70, Third Republic/Troisième République, 1975-85, French Hist. Studies, 1985-88; mem. adv. bd. Hist. Abstracts, 1981--; contbr. articles to profl. jours., encys., internat. conf. procs. and yearbooks. Mem. adv. bd. Duke U. Press, 1982-88; trustee Triangle Univs. Ctr. for Advanced Studies, N.C., 1982-85. U.S. Army, 1942-46, 1st lt. M.I., 1944-46, ETO. Recipient book award Mayflower Soc., 1967, Townsend Harris medal CCNY Alumni Assn., 1980, Disting. Tchg. award Duke U., 1986, award for contbns. to study and tchg. French history Western Soc. for French History, 1994; Guggenheim fellow, 1957-58, fellow Rockefeller Found., 1961-62, sr. fellow NEH, 1970-71. Fellow Am. Acad. Arts and Scis. elected 1979, Phi Beta Kappa (vis. scholar 1983-84), Phi Beta Kappa Soc.; mem. Am. Hist. Assn. (com. on internat. hist. activities 1980-85), So. Hist. Assn. (chmn. European sect. 1975-76), Soc. French Hist. Studies (v.p. 1972-73), PEN Am. Ctr. Home: 2701 Pickett Rd # 3044 Durham NC 27705 Office: Duke U Dept History Box 90719 Durham NC 27708-0719 E-mail: jcolton2@earthlink.net.

COLTON, STERLING DAVID (DAVID COLTON), lawyer; b. 1955; s. Sterling Don and Ellie Colton. BA in economics, Brigham Young U., 1979, JD, 1982. Bar: Utah 1982. Ptnr. VanCott, Bagley, Cornwall & McCarthy, Salt Lake City; sr. counsel for exploration and devel. group Phelps Dodge Mining Co., 1988-95; v.p., counsel Phelps Dodge Exploration Corp., 1995-98; v.p., gen. counsel Phelps Dodge Corp., Phoenix, 1998-99, sr. v.p., gen. counsel, 1999—. Mem. ABA, Utah Bar Assn. Office: Phelps Dodge Corp 1 N Ctrl Ave Phoenix AZ 85004-2306

COLTON, STERLING DON, lawyer, hotel executive; b. Vernal, Utah, Apr. 28, 1929; s. Hugh Wilkins and Marguerite (Maughan) C.; m. Eleanor Ricks, Aug. 6, 1954; children: Sterling David, Carolyn, Bradley Hugh, Steven Ricks. BS in Banking and Fin., U. Utah, 1951; JD, Stanford U., 1953. Bar: Calif. 1954, Utah 1954, D.C. 1967. Ptnr. Van Cott, Bagley, Cornwall & McCarthy, Salt Lake City, 1957-66; vice chair, sr. v.p., gen. counsel, bd. dirs. Marriott Corp. and Marriott Internat., 1966—95. Pres. Can. Vancouver Mission Ch. of Jesus Christ of Latter Day Saints, 1995-98, Washington DC Temple, Ch. of Jesus Christ of Latter Day Saints, 1999-2002; v.p. Colton Ranch Corp., Vernal, 1987—; former bd. dirs. Megaherz Corp. and Dyncorp; former chmn. bd. dirs. Nat. Chamber Litigation Ctr. Former bd. dirs. Polynesian Cultural Ctr.; former chmn. nat. adv. coun. U. Utah, Ballet West, nat. adv. counsel; mem. adv. coun. The Nat. Conservancy; bd. trustees So. Va. U., 2003—. Maj. JAG, U.S. Army, 1954-57. Mem. ABA, Calif. Bar Assn., Utah Bar Assn., D.C. Bar Assn., Washington Met. Corp. Counsel Assn. (former pres., dir.), Sigma Chi. Republican. Mem. Lds Ch. Personal E-mail: sdercolton@yahoo.com.

COLUMBUS, CHRIS, film director, screenwriter; b. Spangler, Pa., Sept. 10, 1958; s. Alex Michael and Mary Irene (Puskar) C., m. Monica Devereux, 1983. BFA, NYU, 1980. Writer: (films) Reckless, 1983, Gremlins, 1984, Goonies, 1985, Young Sherlock Holmes, 1985, Little Nemo, 1992, Daredevil, 2002; dir.: (films) Adventures in Babysitting, 1987, Home Alone, 1990, Home Alone 2: Lost in New York, 1992, Mrs. Doubtfire, 1993,; dir., writer: (films) Heartbreak Hotel, 1988, Only the Lonely, 1991; dir., writer, prodr.: (films) Nine Months, 1995; dir., prodr.: Stepmom, 1998, Bicentennial Man, 1999; dir. exec. prodr: Harry Potter and the Sorcerer's Stone, 2001 (Las Vegas Film Critics Award, 2001, Broadcast Film Critics Award, 2001), Harry Potter and the Chamber of Secrets, 2002; (films) prodr.: Jingle All the Way, 1996, Harry Potter and the Prisoner of Azkaban, 2004. Democrat. Office: Creative Artists Agy c/o Beth Swofford 9830 Wilshire Blvd Beverly Hills CA 90212-1804

COLUSSY, DAN ALFRED, aviation executive; b. Pitts., June 3, 1931; s. Dan and Viola E. (Andreis) C.; m. Helene Graham, June 6, 1953; children: Deborah, Jennifer. BS U.S. Coast Guard Acad., 1953; MBA, Harvard U., 1965. Applications engr. Jet Propulsion div. Gen. Electric Co., 1956-63; dir. ops. Am. Airlines, N.Y.C., 1965-66; v.p. mktg. N.E. Airlines, Boston, 1966-69; v.p. Wells, Rich, Green Advt. Agy., N.Y.C., 1969-70; v.p. mktg. devel. Pan Am. World Airways, N.Y.C., 1970-72, v.p. passenger mktg., 1972-74, sr. v.p. passenger mktg., 1974, sr. v.p. field ops., 1974-75, sr. v.p. mktg. and services, 1975-76, exec. v.p. mktg. and services, dir., 1976-78, pres., chief operating officer, mem. exec. com., 1978-80; chmn., chief exec. officer Columbia Air, Balt., 1981-82; pres., CEO Can. Airlines Internat., Vancouver, B.C., 1982-84, chmn., 1985-86; bd. dirs., mem. exec. com. Can. Pacific Hotels, 1983-84; pres., chief exec. officer UNC Inc., Annapolis, Md., 1985-97, chmn. bd., chmn. exec. com., 1989-97; chmn. Gemini Capital, Palm Beach Gardens, Fla., 1997—. Mem. bd. visitors Coll. Bus. and Mgmt. U. Md.; pres. adv. bd. St. John's Coll.; mem. Johns Hopkins Medicine Bd. Visitors.; bd. dirs. Balt. Gas and Electric o., Hist. Annapolis Found.; chmn. Care First Inc. Mem. Campaign Cabinet, U.S. Naval Ist., Chesapeake Bay Found. (pres.' coun.), Larchmont Yacht, Annapolis Yacht, Harvard (N.Y.C.) Club, Old South Country Club, Wings Club (N.Y.C.), Econ. Club Washington, Met. Club Washington, Order of St. John (Can.), Chartwell Country Club, Ballen Isles Country Club. Office: 20 Saint Thomas Dr Palm Beach Gardens FL 33418-4598

COLVARD, DEAN WALLACE, emeritus university chancellor; b. Ashe County, N.C., July 10, 1913; s. W. P. and Mary (Shepherd) C.; m. Martha Lampkin, July 7, 1939; children: Carol Lampkin, Mary Lynda, Dean Wallace. BS, Berea Coll., 1935; MA, U. Mo., 1938; PhD, Purdue U., 1950, DAgr (hon.), 1961; LHD (hon.), Belmont Abbey Coll., 1978; D of Pub. Svc. (hon.), U. N.C., Charlotte, 1979; LHD, Berea Coll., 2003. Instr. agr., farm mgr. Brevard Coll., 1935-37; supt. N.C. Mountain Expt. Sta., 1938-46; prof. animal sci. N.C. State Coll., 1947-48, head dept. animal sci., 1948-53; dean agr., 1953-60; pres. Miss. State U., 1960-66; chancellor U. N.C., Charlotte, 1966-78, chancellor emeritus, 1978—. Mng. cons. Sci. Mus. of Charlotte, 1980-81; dir. Fed. Res. Bank of Richmond, 1955-60, dep. chmn., 1959-60; dir. Mut. Savs. & Loan, 1975-91; Spl. cons. ICA, Bangkok, Thailand, 1960; mem. Gov.'s Rsch. Triangle Devel. Coun., 1957-59; co-ordinator Agr. Rsch. Mission in Peru, S. Am., 1954-60; mem. agr. adv. com. W. K. Kellogg Found., 1954-60; chmn. Miss. Gov.'s Com. on Latin Am. Edn., 1961. Author: Mixed Emotions, A University President Remembers, 1985, Knowledge is Power, 1987, University Research Park, The First Twenty Years, 1988; contbr. to publs. in animal sci., agrl. econs., ednl. adminstrn. Chmn. Miss. Rhodes Scholar Com., 1965-66; chmn. N.C. Rhodes Scholar Com., 1967, 78; mem. Miss. Jr. Coll. Commn., 1960-66; vice chmn. Dimensions for Charlotte-Mecklenburg, 1973-76; mem. N.C. Council on State Goals and Policy, 1972-76, So. Growth Policies Bd., 1977-85, Mecklenburg and Union Counties Health and Hosp. Council, 1967-76; chmn., 1974-76; bd. dirs., exec. com. U. Research Park, Charlotte, 1967-87, vice chmn., 1974-79; trustee Berea Coll., 1956-76, St. Andrews Coll., 1969-76, Cordell Hull Found. for Internat. Edn., 1961-67; chmn. bd. trustees N.C. Sch. Sci. and Math., 1978-83. Recipient Disting. Svc. award N.C. Farm Bur., 1956, Disting. Svc. award Miss. Farm Bur., 1965, Disting. Svc. award N.C. Grange, 1958, Outstanding Civilian award U.S. Dept. Army, 1966, Charlotte News Man of Yr. award, 1977, Disting. Alumnus award Berea Coll., 1980, U. N.C. Disting. Svc. award, 1989, N.C. Disting. Pub. Svc. award, 1990, Lifetime Achievement award Nat. 4H CLub Found., 1998, award Echo Found., 2004; named Man of Yr. in Agr. in N.C., 1954. Mem. Nat. Assn. State Univs. and Land Grant Colls. (co-chmn. joint com. edn. for govt. svc. 1961-65, chmn. president's coun. 1966), Am. Coun. Edn. (commn. internt. edn. 1966-68, chmn. com. higher adult edn. 1966-68), Am. Assn. State Colls. and Univs. (bd. dirs. 1978), Charlotte C. of C. (bd. dirs. 1968-70), Charlotte Country Club, Blue Key, Sigma Xi, Omicron Delta Kappa, Phi Kappa Phi, Gamma Alpha, Alpha Gamma Rho, Gamma Sigma Delta, Alpha Zeta. Clubs: Charlotte Country, Charlotte Rotary (pres. 1978, hon. 1984—). Home: 3600 Cypress Club Dr Apt B403 Charlotte NC 28210-2478

COLVIN, GRETA WILMOTH, entrepreneur; b. Odessa, Tex., Mar. 24, 1962; d. Charles Hayden and Sherry Beth (Browning) Wilmoth; m. Michael Anthony Colvin, Aug. 16, 1986; 1 child, Michael Anthony Jr. AA in Radio-TV-Film, San Antonio Coll.; BS, U. Tex.; grad., Dale Carnegie, 1993; postgrad., St. Mary's U., San Antonio, 1997—. Lic. broadcaster, paralegal, pvt. investigator. Various media positions W.M. Entertainment, San Antonio, 1978-86; co-owner Image Nightclubs, San Antonio, 1986-88; owner W.C. Advt., San Antonio, 1980-88; retail mgr. Hastings, San Antonio, 1989-94; pres. Paradigm Enterprises, Flagstaff, Ariz., 1994—. Democrat. Avocations: motorcycle racing, skiing, reading, rock scaleing, going to drag races. Address: 2800 Cerrillos Rd Santa Fe NM 87507-2313 also: 11623 Whisper Valley St San Antonio TX 78230-3737

COLVIN, HARRY WALTER, JR., physiology educator; b. Schellsburg, Pa., Dec. 5, 1921; s. Harry Walter and Maude Elizabeth (Girven) C.; m. Marie Catherine McNinch, Apr. 8, 1950; children: Sarah Lee, William McNinch. BS, Pa. State U., 1950; PhD, U. Calif., Davis, 1957. Instr. Okla. State U., Stillwater, 1955-57; assoc. prof. physiology U. Ark., Fayetteville, 1957-65; prof. U. Calif., Davis, 1965—. Cons. Pel-Freez Biologicals, Inc., Rogers, Ark., 1960-65. Assoc. editor Hilgardia, 1981-92; contbr. articles to profl. jours. Served with U.S. Army, 1942-45, ETO. Recipient Fulbright award CIES, Washington, 1972, 86. Mem. Am. Dairy Sci. Assn., Am. Soc. Animal Sci., Sigma Xi, Phi Kappa Phi, Alpha Zeta, Gamma Sigma Delta, Phi Sigma, Phi Eta Sigma. Clubs: El Macero (Calif.) Country. Republican. Avocations: golf, flying. Home: 1515 Shasta Dr Apt 3326 Davis CA 95616 Office: U Calif Davis Dept Neurobiology Physiol & Behavior Davis CA 95616 Business E-Mail: hwcolvin@ucdavis.edu.

COLVIN, O. MICHAEL, medical association administrator, medical educator; b. Princeton, Ind., June 15, 1936; s. Jack Gene and Evelyn Mae (Satkamp) C.; m. Arline Mae Lockerbie, Aug. 23, 1959; children: Michael Eric, Jennifer Susan, Kimberly Anne, Christopher Andrew. BA in Chemistry, Ind. U., 1957; MD, Washington U., St. Louis, 1961. Intern, resident Johns Hopkins Hosp., Balt., 1961-64; clin. assoc. Nat. Cancer Inst., Bethesda, Md., 1964-66; fellow in pharmacology Johns Hopkins U., Balt., 1966-68, physician, 1968-95, from asst. prof. to prof. medicine, 1968-95; dir. Duke Comprehensive Cancer Ctr. Duke U. Med. Ctr., Durham, NC, 1995—2002; Wm. Shingleton prof. cancer rsch. Duke U. Sch. Medicine, Durham, 2002—. Grant rev. study sect. Nat. Cancer Inst., Bethesda, 1968—. Recipient Career Devel. award Nat. Cancer Inst., 1975-80. Mem. AAAS, Am. Soc. Clin. Oncology, Am. Soc. Bone Marrow Transplantation, Am. Assn. Cancer Rsch. Home: 208 Arcadia Ln Chapel Hill NC 27514-1472 Office: Duke U Med Ctr 419 Jones Bldg PO Box 3843 Durham NC 27702-3843 Business E-Mail: colvi003@mc.duke.edu.

COLVIN, SHERRILL WILLIAM, lawyer; b. Jeffersonville, Ind., Sept. 13, 1938; s. Hewitt L. and Mary (Sutton) C.; m. Sarah Albin, Aug. 12, 1962; children: John, Betsy. AB, Wabash Coll., 1960; LLB, Ind. U., 1965. Bar: Ind. 1965, U.S. Supreme Ct. 1968. Pres. Ind. Trial Lawyers Assn., 1991—; ptnr. Haller & Colvin PC, Fort Wayne, Ind., 1965—. Mem. disciplinary commn. Ind. Supreme Ct.; mem. faculty Nat. Inst. Trial Advocacy Fellow Am. Coll. Trial Lawyers; mem. Ind. State Bar Assn. (pres. 2003-2004), disciplinary commn. Supreme Ct. (chair 1995-96). Methodist. Home: 5700 Old Mill Rd Fort Wayne IN 46807-3043 Office: Haller & Colvin 444 E Main St Fort Wayne IN 46802-1910 Office Phone: 219-426-0444.

COLVIN, THOMAS STUART, agricultural engineer, farmer; b. Columbia, Mo., July 17, 1947; s. Charles Darwin and Miriam Elizabeth (Kimball) C.; m. Sonya Marie Peterson, Sept. 11, 1982; children: Christopher, Kristel. BS, Iowa State U., 1970, MS, 1974, PhD, 1977. Registered profl. engr., Iowa. Farmer, Hawkeye and Cambridge, Iowa, 1970—; rsch. assoc. Iowa State U., Ames, 1972-77; agrl. engr. USDA/Agrl. Rsch. Svc., Ames, 1977—. Cons. WillowCreek Cons., Manning, Iowa, 1978-85. Sgt. USAF, 1970-72, Vietnam. Recipient Air Force Commendation medal USAF, 1971. Mem. Am. Soc. Agrl. Engrs. (power machinery stds. com. St. Joseph, Mich. 1989—, Iowa sec., Young Engr. of Yr. 1986, Engr. of Yr. 2004), Soil and Water Conservation Soc., Iowa Acad. Sci. (chair agrl. scis. sect. 1991-92), Sigma Xi, Alpha Epsilon (pres. 1978), Gamma Sigma Delta, Phi Mu Alpha. Achievements include design and development of first computer program to help farmers manage tillage and residue cover for erosion control. Office: Nat Soil Tilth Lab USDA ARS 2150 Pammel Dr Ames IA 50011-3120

COLVIS, JOHN PARIS, aerospace engineer, mathematician, research scientist; b. St. Louis, June 30, 1946; s. Louis Jack and Jacqueline Betty (Beers) C.; m. Nancy Ellen Fritz, Mar. 15, 1969 (div. Sept. 16, 1974); 1 child, Michael Scott; m. Barbara Carol Davis, Sept. 3, 1976; 1 child, Rebecca Jo; stepchildren: Bruce William John Zimmerly, Belinda Jo Zimmerly Little. Student, Meramec Community Coll., St. Louis, 1964-65, U. Mo., 1966, 72-75, Palomar Coll., San Marcos, Calif., 1968, U. Mo., Rolla, 1968-69; BS in Math., Washington U., 1977. Assoc. system safety engr. McDonnell Douglas Astronautics Co., St. Louis, 1978-81; sr. system safety engr. Martin Marietta Astronautics Group-Strategic Systems Co., Denver, 1981-87; sr. engr. Martin Marietta Astronautics Group-Space Launch Systems Co., Denver, 1987-95, Lockheed Martin Astronautics Co.-Space Launch Sys., Denver, 1995—. Rschr. in field. Lance cpl. USMC, 1966-68, Vietnam. Mem. VFW (post 4171), Colo. Home Educators' Assn. (pres. 1989), Khe Sanh Vet Incorp., Math. Assn. Am. Evangelical. Achievements include research in the quantum postulate; the quantum philosophy of science and mathematics. Avocations: camping, hiking, swimming. Home: 4978 S Hoyt St Littleton CO 80123-1988 Office: Lockheed Martin Space Sys Co PO Box 179 Denver CO 80201-0179 Business E-Mail: john.p.colvis@lmco.com.

COLWELL, BRYAN YORK, private investor, philanthropist; b. Atlanta, Feb. 10, 1964; BA magna cum laude, Harvard U., 1983; postgrad., U. Pa. Wharton Sch., 1985; MBA with distinction, Columbia U., 1986. Strategic planner SmithKline Beckman Corp., Phila., 1983-85; v.p. Goldman, Sachs and Co., NYC, 1986—2000; mng. dir., head of global power and utilities Corp. Fin. Group, ABN Amro Inc., NYC, 2000—02; pres. Colwell Found., 2002—. Mem. bd. Archtl. Rev. and Planning for Tuxedo Pk., NYC. Author: The Public-Private Partnership (Harvard University), 1983. Mem. dirs. coun. Mus. of City of NY; bd. dirs., chmn. assocs. com. Lenox Hill Neighborhood House, 1994—; bd. dirs. Tuxedo Park Archtl. Rev. Bd., Nat. Hypertension Assn. Named Outstanding Young Am., WSB-Radio-TV Network, Atlanta,

1979; recipient Young Scholar award Harvard Club of Atlanta, 1979, Outstanding Student cup Atlanta Jour., 1979. Mem. Am. Fin. Assn. (v.p. 1985-86), Columbia Bus. Sch. Alumni Assn., Harvard U. Inst. Politics, World Affairs Coun., Harvard Architecture Soc. (pres. 1980), Brook Club, Links Club, Owl Club, Hasty Pudding Club (v.p. 1981-83, Cambridge chpt.), Harvard Club of NY, Racquet and Tennis Club, Tuxedo Club, Sea Island Club, Southampton Club, Corviglia Club of St. Moritz.

COLWELL, GENE THOMAS, engineering educator; b. Chattanooga, Aug. 3, 1937; s. William Clarence and Mary Virginia (Smith) C.; m. Peggy Ann Fletcher, June 1, 1973. BSME, U. Tenn., 1959, MSME, 1962, PhD, 1966. Rsch. engr. Oak Ridge (Tenn.) Nat. Lab., 1959-62; instr. U. Tenn., Knoxville, 1962-65; rsch. engr. Oak Ridge Nat. Lab., 1965-66; asst. prof. Ga. Inst. Tech., Atlanta, 1966-71, assoc. prof., 1971-77, prof., 1977-95; prof. emeritus, 1995—; assoc. dir. Ga. Inst. Tech., Atlanta, 1984-87. Vis. prof. U. Carabobo, Venezuela, 1971; cons. in field. Patentee in field; contbr. articles to profl. jours. Recipient numerous Rsch. grants. Fellow ASME (life); mem. Sigma Xi, Pi Tau Sigma. Avocations: tennis, golf, hiking. Home: 9145 Prestwick Club Dr Duluth GA 30097-2442

COLWELL, HOWARD OTIS, advertising executive; b. New Rochelle, N.Y., Sept. 16, 1929; s. Robert Talcott and Louise (Otis) C.; m. Barbara Elaine Hrosenchik, Aug. 14, 1954 (dec. Feb. 27, 2001; children: John Robert, Christian, Mary Louise; m. Lydia Macdonald, April 6, 2002. *Father, Robert T. Colwell, was a pioneer in the early "boom days" of radio, having been a script writer for Edgar Bergen, Eddie Cantor and Burns and Allen. He also authored a Broadway play titled "Strictly Dynamite." In 1947 he became a founding partner of the ad agency Sullivan Stauffer, Colwell and Bayles.* AB, Colgate U., 1953. Copy group head Batten, Barton, Durstine & Osborn, N.Y.C., 1953-59; v.p., creative dir. Tatham-Laird & Kudner, N.Y.C., 1959-68; sr. v.p., creative dir. William Esty Advt., N.Y.C., 1968-87; v.p., corp. creative dir. Combe, Inc., White Plains, NY, 1987-98, sr. creative cons., 1998—. Guest lectr. NYU, 1979-81, Pace U., 1980-84, adj. prof., 1982-83 *Key contributor to many successful TV advertising Campaigns. One example was starring Robert Conrad, who dared viewers to, "knock this Eveready Energizer off my shoulder." This was the introduction of Irish Spring soap for Colgate-Palmolive.* Chmn. YMCA Indian Guides Norwalk-Wilton, 1966; chmn. Wilton Voice on Edn., 1972-75, Wilton Arts Council, 1980-83; v.p. bd. dirs. Wilton Orch., 1985—, pres., 1986-87. Mem. Phi Beta Kappa. Congregationalist. Office: 1101 Westchester Ave White Plains NY 10604-3503

COLWELL, JOHN AMORY, physician; b. Boston, Nov. 4, 1928; s. Arthur Ralph and Jeane (Haskins) C.; m. Jane Kuebler, June 19, 1954; children: John Clayton, Ann Kimbell, Karen Elizabeth, James Lewis. AB, Princeton U., 1950; MD, Northwestern U., 1954, MS in Medicine, 1957, PhD in Physiology, 1968. Intern Univ. Hosps., Cleve., 1954-55; resident in internal medicine Passavant Meml. Hosp., Chgo., 1955-57, VA Research Hosp., Chgo., 1959-60; from instr. to assoc. prof. medicine Northwestern U. Med. Sch., 1960-71; fellow in endocrinology and diabetes Northwestern U. Med. Ctr., Chgo., 1960-63; clin. investigator, then chief metabolic sect. VA Research Hosp., 1961-71; prof. medicine Med. U. S.C., Charleston, 1971—, dir. endocrinology-metabolism-diabetes div., dept. medicine, 1972-94, dir. diabetes ctr. Charleston, 1994—, rsch. coord., 1973-79; assoc. chief staff rsch. and devel. VA Med. Center, Charleston, 1971-93. Bd. dirs. Am. Diabetes Assn., 1982-88, v.p. 1985, pres. elect 1986, pres., 1987; bd. dirs. S.C. Dabetes Assn., 1971-80/ Author: Clinical Recognition and Treatment of Diabetic Vascular Disease, 1975; co-author: Diabetes and Metabolic Disorders, 1975, 82, Diabetes, Endocrinology and Metabolic Disorders, 1981; contbr. articles med. jours. Served to capt. M.C. USAF, 1957-59. Grantee: NiH, VA, 1962-94. Fellow ACP; mem. AAAS, Am. Diabetes Assn., Am. Fedn. Clin. Rsch., Am. Physiol. Soc., Ctrl. Soc. Clin. Rsch., Endocrine Soc., So. Soc. Clin. Investigation. Clubs: Skokie Country (Glencoe, Ill.), Carolina Yacht (Charleston), Yeamans Hall (Charleston), Cloister Inn (Princeton U.). Republican. Episcopalian. Home: 182 Broad St Charleston SC 29401-2429

COLWELL, RITA ROSSI, microbiologist, former federal agency administrator, medical educator; b. Nov. 23, 1934; BS in Bacteriology with distinction, Purdue U., 1956, MS in Genetics, 1958; PhD, U. Wash., 1961; DSc, Heriot-Watt U., Edinburgh, Scotland, 1987; DSc (hon.), Hood Coll., 1991; DSc, Purdue U., 1993; DSc (hon.), U. Surrey, Eng., 1995, U. Bergen, Norway, 1999, Coastal Carolina U., 1999, U. Md. Balt. County, 1999, St. Mary's Coll., 1999, Mich. State U., 2000, Washington Coll., 2000, U. Conn., 2000, Williams Coll., 2000, SUNY, Albany, 2000, U. Ancona, Italy, 2001, George Washington U., 2001, Mount Holyoke, 2001, Washington U., St. Louis, 2001, Calif. Poly. Inst., San Luis Obispo, 2001, Renssalaer Poly. Inst., 2001, U. Newcastle, U.K., 2001, Mercy Coll., 2002, U. Queensland, Australia, 2002; DSc, U. Glasgow, 2002, Weizmann Inst. Sci., Israel, 2002, Tuskegee Inst., 2003, U. Ill., 2003, Dartmouth Coll., 2003; LLD, U. Nebr., 2003, Notre Dame Coll., 1994; DHL (hon.), U. Ala., 2001. Rsch. asst. genetics lab. Purdue U., West Lafayette, Ind., 1956—57; rsch. asst. U. Wash., Seattle, 1957—58, predoctoral assoc., 1959—60, asst. rsch. prof., 1961—64; asst. prof. biology Georgetown U., Washington, 1964—66, assoc. prof. biology, 1966—72; prof. microbiology U. Md., 1972—98, v.p. for acad. affairs, 1983—87; dir. Ctr. Marine Biotech., 1987—91; founder, pres. Biotech. Inst. U. Md., 1991—98; dir. NSF, Arlington, Va., 1998—2004; chmn. Canon US Life Scis., Inc., 2004—; Disting. Univ. prof. U. Md., College Park, 2004—, Johns Hopkins Bloomberg Sch. Pub. Health, 2004—. Hon. prof. U. Queensland, Brisbane, Australia, 1988; mem. ocean scis. bd. NAS, 1977—80; hon. prof. Quindao U., China, 1995; cons. Washington area comms. media, congressman, legislators, 1978—; external examiner various univs. abroad, 1964—; vice chmn. polar rsch. bd. NAS, 1990—94; mem. Nat. Sci. Bd., 1984—90; mem. sci. adv. bd. Oak Ridge Nat. Labs., 1988—90, 1993—96; adv. com. FDA, 1991—92, food adv. com., 1993—96, sci. bd., 1996—; Koch lectr., Berlin, 2000. Author (manual numerical taxonomy): Collecting the Data, 1970; author: (with M. Zambruski) Rodina-Methods in Aquatic Microbiology, 1972; author: (with L.H. Stevenson) Estuarine Microbial Ecology, 1973; author: (with R.Y. Morita) Effect of the Ocean Environment on Microbial Ecology, 1973; author: (with A. Sinsky and N. Pariser) Marine Biotechnology, 1983; author: Vibrios in the Environment, 1985, Nucleic Acid Sequence Data, 1988; author: (with others) Marine Biotechnology, 1995; Microbial Diversity, 1996; author: Viable But Nonculturable Microorganisms in the Environment, 2000, others; mem. editl. bd.: Microbial Ecology, 1972—91, Applied and Environ. Microbiology, 1969—81, Oil and Petrochemical Pollution, 1980—91, Jour. Washington Acad. Scis., 1981—87, Johns Hopkins U. Oceanographic Series, 1981—84, Revue de la Fondation Oceanographique Ricard, 1981—, Estuaries, 1983—89, Zentralblatt fur Bacteriologie, 1985—, Jour. Aquatic Living Resources, 1987—, Sys. Applied Microbiology, 1985—2000, World Jour. Microbiology and Biotech., 1988—95, Environ. Microbiology, 2001—; contbr. articles to profl. jours.; (Koch lecture) Anatomy Lesson, Amsterdam, 2002. Named Prof. Extraordinairo, U. Catolica Valparaiso, Chile, 1976, Scholar of Yr., Phi Kappa Phi, 1992; recipient Gold medal, Internat. Biotech. Inst., 1990, Purkinje Gold medal for achievment in sci., Czechoslavakian Acad. Sci., 1991, Civic award, Gov. Md., 1990, Woman of the Yr. award, Women Legis. of Md., 1996, Cert. of Recognition, NASA, 1984, Alice Evans award, Am. Soc. Microbiol., 1988, Andrew White medal, Loyola Coll., 1994, medal of distinction, Barnard Coll./Columbia U., 1996, Gold medal, Charles U., Prague, 2000, Gold medals, UCLA, 2000, Alumna Summa Laude Dignata award, U. Wash., 2000, Achievement award, AAUW, 2001, Carey award, Am. Assn. Adv. Sci., 2001, Thomas award, Explorer's Club Lowell, 2000. Fellow: AAAS (chmn. sect. biol. scis. 1993—94, pres. 1995, chmn. bd. 1996, Carey award 2001), Marine Tech. Soc. (exec. com. 1982—88), Washington Acad. Scis. (bd. mgrs. 1976—79, pres. 1996—98), Am. Acad. Microbiology (chmn. bd. govs. 1989—99), Grad. Women. Sci., Can. Coll. Microbiologists; mem.: NAS, Royal Swedish Acad. Sci., Soc. Gen. Microbiology, Internat. Coun. Sci. Unions, Am. Soc. Limnology and Oceanography, World Fedn. Culture Collections, Classification Rsch. Group Eng. (charter), Am. Soc. Microbiology (hon.; various sci. coms. 1961—, pres. 1985, chmn. program com. REGEM-1 1988, Fisher award 1985), U.K. Soc. Applied Microbiology (hon.), Bangladesh Soc. Microbiology (hon.; fgn.), French Soc. Microbiology (hon.), Israeli Soc. Microbiology (hon.), Australian Soc. Microbiology (hon.), Soc. Indsl Microbiology (bd. govs. 1976—79, Charles Thom award 1998), U.S. Fedn. Culture Collections (governing bd. 1978—88), Internat. Coun. Sci. Unions (exec. bd. 1993—96, gen. com.), Am. Inst. Biol. Scis. (bd. govs. 1976—82), Internat. Union Microbiol. Soc. (v.p. 1986—90, pres. 1990—94), World Fedn. Culture Collections, Royal Soc. Can., Explorers Club (Lowell Thomas award 2000), Omicron Delta Kappa, Phi Beta Kappa, Sigma Delta Epsilon, Sigma Xi (nat. pres. 1991, Ann. Achievement award 1981, Rsch. award 1984), Delta Gamma (Delta Gamma Rose award 1989). Achievements include research in marine biotechnology; marine and estuarine microbial ecology; survival of pathogens in aquatic environments; ecology of Vibrio cholerae and related organisms; microbial systematics; marine microbiology; antibiotic resistance; environmental aspects of Vibrio cholerae in transmission of cholera; in global climate and cholera transmission.*

COLWILL, JACK MARSHALL, physician, educator; b. Cleve., June 15, 1932; s. Clifford V. and Olive A. (Marshall) Colwill; m. Winifred Stedman, 1954; children: James F., Elizabeth Ann, Carolyn. BA, Oberlin Coll., 1953; MD (George Whipple scholar), U. Rochester, 1957. Diplomate Am. Bd. Med. Examiners, Am. Bd. Internal Medicine, Am. Bd. Family Practice. Intern Barnes Hosp., Washington U. Sch. Medicine, St. Louis, 1957—58; resident in medicine U. Washington Affiliated Hosps., Seattle, 1958—60; chief resident U. Hosp., 1960—61; instr. medicine, dir. med. outpatient dept. U. Rochester (N.Y.) Sch. Medicine and Dentistry, 1961—62, sr. instr. medicine, dir. med. outpatient dept., 1962—64; asst. dean, asst. prof. medicine, asst. prof. cmty. health and med. practice U. Mo. Sch. Medicine, Columbia, 1964—67, assoc. dean, asst. prof., 1967—69, assoc. dean for acad. affairs, asst. prof., 1969—70, assoc. dean, assoc. prof., 1970—76, interim chmn. dept. family and cmty. medicine, 1976—77, prof., 1976—97, prof. emeritus, 1999—, chmn. dept., 1977—97, interim dean, 2000. Cons. Bur. Health Manpower, NIH, 1969—75, Office Divsn. Dir. USPHS, 1977—; mem. Coun. on Grad. Med. Edn. Health Resources and Svcs. Adminstrn., 1990—96. Contbr. articles to profl. jours. Chair commn. on Gulf War and Health Inst. of Medicine, NAS, 1999—2003; dir. Robert Wood Johnson Found. Generalist Physician Initiative, 1991—2000; bd. dirs. Am. Bd. Family Medicine, 1998—2003. Mem.: AMA, Inst. Medicine NAS, Am. Acad. Family Physicians (commn. on govtl. legis. affairs 1984—87), Soc. Tchrs. Family Medicine (bd. dirs. 1978—82, 1983—87, pres.-elect 1987—88, pres. 1988—89), Assn. Med. Am. Colls. (chmn. Midwest-Gt. Plains Group on Student Affairs 1971—73, nat. vice chmn. group 1973—74, chmn. working group on non-cognitive assessment 1974—77, adv. to com. on admissions assessment 1974—77), Alpha Omega Alpha. Office: U Mo-Columbia Sch Medicine Dept Family And Medicine Columbia MO 65212-0001

COLYER, KIRK KLEIN, insurance executive, real estate investment executive; b. Fayetteville, N.C., Jan. 30, 1956; s. Joe Bill and Charlotte (Klein) C. Assoc. in Bus., SUNY, Albany, 1977; BBA in Polit. Sci., U. Incarnate Word, 1980; student, Leonard's Tng. Sch., 1985, Tex. Crime Prevention Inst., 1985. Lic. recording agt.; lic. mortgage loan officer Tex. Councilman City of Balcones Heights, San Antonio, 1977-82, mayor, 1982-86, mayor emeritus, 1986; pres. Colyer Real Estate Investments, San Antonio, 1980—; pres., founder Colyer Ins. Agy., San Antonio, 1982—; pres. Colyer Oil Co., San Antonio, 1982—; loan officer Spinner Mortgage, 2002; founder, pres. Healthysa.com, 2003—. Pres. Dominion Village, San Antonio, Tex., 1991—, ABC Colyer Nursery, 1999; adv. coun. U.S. Postal Svc., 1994, Nat. Consumers, 1998-99; campaign dir. Congl. Rep. nominee Carl Bill Colyer, San Antonio; campaign treas. Gerry Richkoff County Clk., Bexar County, 1994, Leon M. Hernandez; mem. dinner com. U.S. Congress Dist. 20 Charlie Gonzalez, 1998—; founder, pres Healthysa.com, 2005 Featured extra (films) Miss Congeniality, 2000, speaking role Reason to Believe, 2001, appeared in TV comml., 2004. V.p. Balcones C. of C., San Antonio, 1978, San Antonio Young Reps., 1991; bd. mem. Beautify San Antonio, 1982; bd. dirs. South Tex. Charities, 1998, chmn. Tex. largest Halloween party benefiting kids; mem. exec. bd. Alamo Area Coun. Govts., 1979-84; pres. Tex. Mcpl. League Region 7, San Antonio, 1985; founder Bexar County Young Reps., 1995; bd. dirs. San Antonio March of Dimes, 1985; grad. Leadership San Antonio, 1985; pres. Lulac Coun. 602, 1998-2000; host. Com. for Nat. Rep. Conv. 2000 Bid for San Antonio, Tex.; campaign treas. Leon Hernandez Dem. Precinct, 2000—; campaign worker Mayor Clint Eastwood, Carmel, Calif., 1986, Campaign for George Gervin for Mud King, San Antonio, 1997; treas. Hunters Creek North Homeowners Assn., 1995, bd. dirs., 2004-05; bd. dirs. U.S. Postal Adv. Com., San Antonio, 1994; mem. raffle com. corp. donations San Antonio Stock Show Rodeo, 2001, life mem. raffle com., 2004—; judge Miss San Antonio U.S. Galaxy, 2004; chmn. Tex. Largest Halloween Party Benefit, Kids South Tex. Charities, 2004; bd. dirs. San Antonio Martini Found., 1992—; hon. deputy constable Bexar County, Tex., 2003; campaign exec. mgr. Miss Tex. Kristin Howsley, 2004; campaign exec. mgr. Kristin Howsley Miss Galaxy, 2004, Miss San Antonio Galaxy, 2005; mem. fin. com., silent auction chmn. Bexar County Rep. Party, 2005; mem. nat. panel Home Testing Inst. Am., 2005. Named one of Outstanding Mems. of Am., U.S. Jaycees, 1977-91; USANA Health Scis. Dist. Achiever, 2003; Rey Feo XLIX, 1996-97. Mem. IHIO Corridor (founder, pres. 1984-86), San Antonio Ind. Car Dealers Assn. (founder, pres. 1993—), Tex. Auto Dealers Assn. (bd. dirs. 1994—), San Antonio City Club, San Antonio Plaza Club (life), Rey Feo '97, Distributive Edn. Clubs of Am. (life), Lions (bd. dirs. Balcones chpt. 1976-78), Tex. Jaycees (dist. bd. dirs. 1978, pres. Balcones Hts. chpt. 1977, Top Recruiter 1980), San Antonio Crime Stoppers (bd. dirs. 1984—), San Antonio Martini Found. (bd. dirs. 1988—), San Antonio Parrot Head Club, San Antonio P.A.R.T.I. Found. (bd. dirs. 1998—), South Tex. Charities., Shoppers Voice Consumer Product Survey Am. Avocations: fishing, hunting, hiking, jogging, roller blading. Home: 13290 Hunters View St San Antonio TX 78230-2032 Office: Colyer Ins Agy 4311 Ih 10 W San Antonio TX 78201 Office Phone: 210-735-1499. Personal E-mail: kirkkcolyer@aol.com.

COMANOR, WILLIAM S., economist, educator; b. Phila., May 11, 1937; s. Leroy and Sylvia (Bershad) C.; m. Joan Thall; children: Christine, Katherine, Lauren, Gregory. Student, Williams Coll., 1955—57; BA, Haverford Coll., 1959; MA, PhD, Harvard U., 1963; postgrad., London Sch. Econs., 1963—64. Spl. econ. asst. to asst. atty. gen. Antitrust divsn. U.S. Dept. Justice, Washington, 1965-66; asst. prof. econs. Harvard U., Cambridge, Mass., 1966-68; assoc. prof. Stanford (Calif.) U., 1968-73; dir. bur. econs. FTC, Washington, 1978-80; prof. econs. U. Calif., Santa Barbara, 1975—, dept. chmn., 1984-87; prof. Sch. Pub. Health UCLA, 1990—. Author: National Health Insurance in Ontario, 1980, Advertising and Market Power, 1974, Competition Policy in Europe and North America, 1990, Competition Policy in the Global Economy, 1997, Law and Economics of Child Support Payments, 2004; contbr. articles to profl. jours. Recipient Dist. fellow award, Indsl. Orgn. Soc., 2003. Mem.: Indsl. Orgn. Soc. (pres. 1991, Disting. Fellow award 2003), Am. Econ. Assn. Home: 519 S Arden Blvd Los Angeles CA 90020-4737 Office: U Calif Dept Econs Santa Barbara CA 93106 E-mail: comanor@ucla.edu.

COMAR, MARY ALICE, retired art educator, farmer; b. Adrian, Mich., Mar. 2, 1945; d. Rae Jack and Pauline Isabelle Comar; children: Jack Michael Findley, J. Brent Findley. MA in Humanities, Ctrl. Mich. U., 1993; BS, Siena Heights U., 1967. Teaching Cert. State of Mich., 1967. K-12 art tchr. Benton County Cmty. Schools, Oxford, Ind., 1967—68; sr. high art instr. Lafayette Diocese, Lafayette, Ind., 1968—71; instr. speech comm. Alpena C.C., Oscoda, Mich., 1979; instr. secondary art and English Alpena Pub. Schools, Mich., 1974—2005; ret., 2005. Set dir./play dir. sch. musicals Lafayette Diocese, Lafayette, Ind., 1969—70; practicing artist, photographer, videographer, Ossineke, Mich.; yearbook advisor/drama club advisor/play dir. Alpena H.S., 1985—99; secondary curriculum revision com. mem.; designed course Film as Lit. Alpena Pub. Schools; mem. sch. improvement team Alpena H.S. Exhibited in group shows at Greater Lafayette Art Festival, 1968 (Grand prize), Indpls. 500 Festival of Arts, 1968 (2d Most Meritorious Work amateur divsn.), Detroit Inst. of Arts Rental Gallery; author: numerous poems. Mem., sec. and vice chairperson Alpena Twp. Planning and Zoning Commn., 1980—88; vol. prop artist Alpena Civic Theatre and Thunder Bay Theatre, 1972—84; program com. Very Spl. Arts Festival Mich. Coun. for Very Spl. Arts, Alpena, 1980—80; vol. docent Jesse Besser Mus., Alpena, 1978; 4-H youth leader Mich. State County Ext. 4H Program, Alpena, 1978; vol. demonstrator artist Mich. Art Train Mich. Coun. for Arts, Alpena, 1978; vol. art work contbr. Jesse Besser Mus. Art Auction Fund Raiser, Alpena, 1980; adv. for those too young, old, sick, or unborn toward clean air and a healthy environment Citizen and registered voter of Mich. and the USA, Alpena, Mich., 1972—2003; bd. mem., sec., spkrs. bur., com. co-chairperson toxic and hazardous waste study com., chairperson ERA study com. Alpena County LWV, 1977—80; religious edn. tchr. St. John the Bapt. Cath. Parish, Alpena, 1999; lectr. and eucharistic min. St. Bernards Cath. Ch., Alpena, 1983—85; initiated a ch. youth group St. Bernard's Parish, Alpena, 1983—85. Recipient Classrooms of Tomorrow Tchr., Mich. Gov. Blanchard, 1990. Mem.: So. Poverty Law Ctr. (charter mem., leadership coun.), Siena Heights U. Alumni Assn., Nat. Mus. of Women in Arts (corr.). Democrat. Roman Catholic. Avocations: horse training, swimming, dance, golf.

COMBE, JOHN CLIFFORD, JR., lawyer; b. New Orleans, Jan. 5, 1939; s. John Clifford and Gladys Ann (Reine) C.; m. Lynne Wendel Watson, July 11, 1964; children: John, Wendy, Holly. BBA, Tulane U., 1960, LLB, 1965. Bar: La. 1965, U.S. Dist. Ct. (ea. and mid. dists.) La. 1965, U.S. Ct. Appeals (5th cir.) 1965, U.S. Supreme Ct. 1971, U.S. Ct. Appeals (11th cir.) 1981, U.S. Dist. Ct. (we. dist.) La. 1986. Assoc. Jones, Walker, Waechter, Poitevent, Carrere & Denegre, New Orleans, 1965—, ptnr., 1970—, sr. ptnr., 1989—. Editor: La. Bar Jour., 1975-77; contbr. articles to legal jours. Organizer, mem. Crestmont Pk. Improvement Assn.; organizer Greater New Orleans Law Explorer program Boy Scouts Am., 1974; mem. St. Catherine of Siena Parish Sch. Bd., 1976-89; trustee Acad. of Sacred Heart, 1993-96. Lt. (j.g.) USN, 1960-62. Fellow: ABA (mem. ho. of dels. 1982—88), La. State Bar Found., Am. Bar Found., Am. Coll. Trial Lawyers (state chair 1999—2000); mem.: La. Bar Assn. (mem. bd. govs. 1973—74, sec.-treas. 1975, mem. bd. govs. 1975—76, 1977—78, 1978—80, pres. 1979—80), So. Regional Conf. Bar Pres., Nat. Conf. Bar Pres., Def. Rsch. Inst., Am. Judicature Soc. (mem. bd. govs. 1982—86), La. Assn. Def. Counsel (bd. dirs. 1969—75, faculty trial acad. 2000—02), Internat. Assn. Def. Counsel (speaker 1989, mem. faculty trial acad. 1991), Stratford Club (pres. 1993—95), Boston Club, Metairie Country Club. Republican. Roman Catholic. Office: Jones Walker Waechter Poitevent Carrere & Denegre 201 Saint Charles Ave Ste 50 New Orleans LA 70170-5100 Office Phone: 504-582-8144. Business E-Mail: jcombe@joneswalker.com.

COMBS, CHARLES DONALD, academic administrator; b. Levelland, Tex., Mar. 28, 1952; s. Harold Bloyd and Emma Laura (Cole) C.; m. Pamela Quattlebaum, Mar. 31, 1983. BA with high honors, Tex. Tech U., 1972, MA, 1974; PhD, U. N.C., 1980; PhD (hon.), State Univ. Medicine and Dentistry, Moldova, 2003. Instr. polit. sci. Tex. Tech U., Lubbock, 1973-76, Elon (N.C.) Coll., 1975-76; instr. pub. adminstrn. N.C. Cen. U., Durham, 1976-77; sr. program assoc. Robert Wood Johnson Found., Chapel Hill, N.C., 1977-79; adminstr. Surry (Va.) Family Health Group, 1978-81; program dir. Ea. Va. Med. Sch., Old Dominion U., Norfolk, 1980-85; asst. v.p. adminstrn. and svcs. Ea. Va. Med. Sch., Norfolk, 1985-87; assoc. v.p. instl. advancement Med. Coll. Hampton Rds., Norfolk, 1987-88, v.p. instl. advancement, 1988-92, v.p. planning and program devel., 1992—2000, co-dir. Nat. Ctr. Collaboration Med. Modelling and Simulation, 2000—. Cons. numerous health and human svc. orgns., Va., N.C., Tex., Kans., Eastern and Ctrl. Europe, Africa, Asia and C.Am.; chmn. exec. com. Va. Statewide Health Edn. Adv. Com., 1992-2000; chmn. Regional Perinatal Coordinating Coun., 1989—; treas. Women's Health Va., 1998-2000. Contbr. articles to profl. jours. Grantee City of Durham, 1976, Kresge Found., 1979, Dept. Health and Human Svcs., 1981-85, 90—, Champus Mental Health Demonstration Program, 1986-89; sr. fellow Naval Postgrad. Sch., 1996-2003; recipient Disting. Alumni award South Plains Coll., 1998. Mem. APHA, Am. Assn. Univ. Adminstrs., Am. Hosp. Assn., Am. Soc. Pub. Adminstrs., Hampton Rds. C. of C. (mem. regional legis. affairs com. and health care task force 1985-96), Assn. of Acad. Health Ctrs. (nat. program chair 1996). Methodist. Home: 7800 N Shore Rd Norfolk VA 23505-1735 Office: Ea Va Med Sch PO Box 1980 Norfolk VA 23501-1980 E-mail: combscd@evms.edu.

COMBS, HOLLY MARIE, actress; b. San Diego, Dec. 3, 1973; m. Bryan Smith, 1993 (div. 1997); m. David W. Donoho, 2004. Actor: (films) Walls of Glass, 1985, Sweet Hearts Dance, 1988, New York Stories, 1989, Born on the Fourth of July, 1989, Simple Men, 1992, Dr. Giggles, 1992, Chain of Desire, 1993, A Reason to Believe, 1995; (TV films) A Perfect Stranger, 1994, Sins of Silence, 1996, Love's Deadly Triangle: The Texas Cadet Murder, 1997, Daughters, 1997, See Jane Date, 2003; (TV series) Picket Fences, 1992—96 (best young actress in a new TV series Young Artist award, 1993), Charmed, 1998—; prodr.:, 2000—. Office: c/o SFM 1122 S Robertson Blvd #15 Los Angeles CA 90035

COMBS, JANET LOUISE, sales and advertising company executive; b. Houston, Jan. 13, 1959; d. James Lee and Mary Lynn (Woolley) Combs. BSBA, U. Ark., 1981. With Exxon Chem. Co., Houston, 1981-82; account exec. Promotional Products Co., Houston, from 1982, asst. v.p., 1982-86, v.p., 1986—. Adminstrv. bd. mem., leisure ministries core team mem. Chapelwood Meth. Ch. Mem. Houston Downtown Rotary, Houston Young Profl. Reps., Girls' Cotillion, Mortar Bd., Blue Key, Houston C. of C., Kappa Alpha Theta (Founder's Meml. scholar 1980-81), Beta Gamma Sigma, Alpha Mu Alpha, Omicron Delta Kappa, Arkansas Alumni Assn. (Houston chpt. bd. mem.). Republican. Methodist. Home: 12611 Trail Hollow Dr Houston TX 77024-4010 Office: Promotional Products Co Inc 1700 W Sam Houston Pkwy N Houston TX 77043-2797

COMBS, LINDA MORRISON, federal official; b. Lenoir, N.C., June 29, 1946; d. Robert Hugh and Vera Ludema (Bryant) Morrison; m. David Michael Combs, June 20, 1970. AA, Gardner Webb Coll., 1966, PhD (hon.), 1985; BS, Appalachian State U., 1968, MA, 1978; EdD, Va. Poly. Inst. and State U., 1985. Tchr., adminstr. Winston-Salem (N.C.)/Forsyth County Schs., 1968-79, sch. bd. mem., 1980-82; exec. sec., dep. U.S. Dept. Edn., Washington, 1982-84, dep. under-sec. mgmt., 1984-86; pub. edn. advisor State of N.C., Raleigh, 1986-87; owner Combs Group Cons., Winston-Salem, 1987; acting asst. dir. for mgmt. U.S. Dept. Vet. Affairs, Washington, 1987-89; asst. sec. mgmt. U.S. Dept. Treasury, Washington, 1989—91; CFO EPA, Washington, 2002—04; asst. sec., budget & fin. mgmt., CFO U.S. Dept. Transport., Washington, 2004—05; contr., Office Fed. Fin. Mgmt. Office Mgmt. & Budget, Washington, 2005—. Pres., founder Combs Music Internat., Winston-Salem, NC, 1991—2001. Gov.'s advocate Com. for Children and Youth, Winston-Salem, 1974-75; treas. Michael Britt for N.C. Senate, Forsyth County, 1976; v.p. Forsyth County Young Reps. Club, 1980-81. Recipient Honor and Outstanding Svc. award Combined Fed. Campaign, Washington, 1983, Alumnus of Yr. award Gardner Webb Coll., Boiling Springs, N.C., 1987, Disting. Alumnus of Yr. Appalachian State U., Boone, N.C., 1986. Mem. Forysth County Rep. Womens Club, Pres.'s Coun. on Mgmt. Improvement (vice chair, Outstanding Leadership award 1989), Phi Delta Kappa, Delta Kappa Gamma. Republican. Baptist. Avocations: running, cooking, tennis. Office: Office Mgmt & Budget 1650 Pennsylvania Ave NW Rm 263 Washington DC 20503*

COMBS, MERRITTA A., family and consumer science educator; b. Kans. BS in Vocat. and Home Econ., Kans. State U., Manhattan, 1973; M in Ednl. Counseling, Emporia State U., Kans., 1993. Cert. vocat. instr. Kans. Dept. Edn., 1973. Family and consumer sci. educator, psychology tchr. Pomona HS, Pomona, Kans., 1974—, advisor Family, Career, and Cmty. Leaders Am. Dist. advisor Kans. Leadership Coun., 1995—98. Prin. works include City Pk. Mural, 1985. Named Dist. Outstanding Tchr., Tchr. Cmty. Svc. Work, Kans., 2004; Health Grant, Kans. Health Fedn., Health Dept. for Ponoma City Children, 1985. Mem.: Kans. Assn. Tchrs. of Family and Consumer Sci., Beta Sigma Phi. Avocations: gardening, crafts.

COMBS, ROBERTA, religious organization administrator; m. Andy Combs (dec.); children: Karen, Michele. SC state chmn. Christian Coalition of Am., exec. v.p., 1999—2001, chmn., pres., 2001—. Office: Christian Coalition of America PO Box 37030 Washington DC 20013*

COMBS, SEAN (DIDDY), record company executive, producer; b. Harlem, NY, Nov. 4, 1969; s. Melvin and Janice Combs; 1 child. Attended, Howard U., Washington, DC. Various pos. including intern, head A&R dept. Uptown Records, 1988—93; CEO, founder Bad Boy Entertainment, 1993—; launched clothing line Sean John, 1998—. Prodr.: Forever My Lady (Jodeci), 1991, Diary of a Mad Band (Jodeci), 1993, What's the 411? (Mary J. Blige), 1993, My Life (Mary J. Blige), 1994, Project: Funk Da World (Craig Mack), 1994, Ready to Die (The Notorious B.I.G.), 1994, Think of You (Raymond Usher), 1994, Faith (Faith Evans), 1995; also prodr. records by Supercat, 1996, Keith Sweat, Caron Wheeler, Mix Tape Volume 2, 1997, Money Talks, 1997, Diana, Princess of Wales: Tribute, 1997, Chef Aid: The South Park Album, 1998; performer (appeared on): (albums) In Tha Beginning...There Was Rap, 1997; performer: No Way Out, 1997 (Grammy Award, Best Rap Album); prodr., performer: (albums) Forever, 1999, The Saga Continues, 2001 exec. prodr.: (TV series) Making the Band II, 2002; actor: (films) Made, 2000, Monster's Ball, 2001, Death of a Dynasty, 2003; exec. soundtrack prodr.: Bad Boys II, 2003; actor: (Broadway plays) A Raisin in the Sun, 2004. Named one of 50 Most Influential African-Americans, Ebony Mag., 2004; recipient ASCAP, Songwriter of the Year, 1996.

COMBS, STEPHEN PAUL, pediatrician, health facility administrator; b. Bristol, Tenn., Feb. 11, 1966; s. Paul Willis and Janis Rose C. BS, East Tenn. State U., 1988, MD, 1992. Diplomate Nat. Bd. Med. Examiners, Am. Bd. Pediat. (fellow), Am. Bd. Forensic Examiners (fellow), Am. Bd. Forensic Medicine. Resident pediat. Duke U., Durham, NC, 1992—95, asst. chief pediat. residents Duke Children's Hosp., 1994—95; ptnr. Mountain Region Pediats., Kingsport, Tenn., 1995—98, sec., 1998—; pediatrician Gray Sta. Pediat., Tenn., 1999—. Dir. pediat. intensive care Wellmont Health Sys., 1998—, chmn. pediat. critical care, 1996—; quality oversight com. Holston Valley Med. Ctr., Kingsport, Tenn., 1998—99, sec., treas. med. staff, 2004, pres. elect med. staff, chief of staff, 05; chmn. dept. pediat. Indian Path Med. Ctr., 1999—2003; mem. med. adv. bd. Am. Homepatient, Nashville, 1995—98; regional faculty PALS Tenn. chpt. AHA, 1995—; mem. child fatality rev. bd. jud. Dist. II State of Tenn., 1995—; bd. dirs. Wellmont Holston Valley Med. Ctr., 2000—04, sec.-treas. med. staff, 2004—05; med. dir. clin. trials program Highlands Physicans Inc., 2001—04, bd. dirs., mem. various coms.; assoc. clin. prof. pediatrics East Tenn. State U., 2002—05, clin. prof. pediatrics, 2005—; bd. dirs. Highlands Wellmont Health Network. Contbr. articles to profl. jours. Recipient Forty Under 40 award, Bus. Jour., Health Care Hero award, 2003. Fellow Am. Acad. Pediat. (resident rep. 1993-95, program chmn. Tenn. chpt. 2000, nominating chair Tenn. chpt. 2001, fellow at large 2005—, Am. Soc. Clin. Pediat.; mem. AMA, Tenn. Med. Assn., N.C. Med. Assn., Duke Med. Alumni Assn., East Tenn. State U. Med. Alumni Assn. (rep. 1992—), History of Appalachia Soc., Alpha Omega Alpha. Republican. Baptist. Avocations: civil war, revolutionary war, gardening, skiing, golf. Home: 405 Westfield Pl Kingsport TN 37664-6410 Office: Gray Sta Pediat 2103 Forest Dr Ste 5 Gray TN 37615-8423 Personal E-mail: spcombs1@juno.com.

COMBS, STEVEN PAUL, orthopedic surgeon; b. Ft. Dodge, Iowa, Apr. 9, 1944; s. Eugene Charles and Marie Wilhelmina (Mack) C.; m. Penelope Ann Calvey, July 6, 1974; children: Patrick, Mary Katherine, Meaghan, Bridget. BS, U. Iowa, 1966, MD, 1970; MBA, Lake Erie Coll., 1991. Diplomate Am. Bd. Orthopedic Surgery; cert. physician exec. Intern Robert Packer Hosp., Sayre, Pa., 1970-71; resident in orthopedics Cleve. Clinic, 1971-75; orthopedic surgeon Drs. DeMarco & Irwin, Willoughby, Ohio, 1979—. Pres. med. staff Lake Hosp. Sys., 1998-02. Served to maj. USAF, 1975-79. Fellow ACS; mem. AMA, Am. Acad. Orthopedic Surgeons, Orthopedic Rsch. Soc., Coll. Physician Execs., Lake County Med. Soc. (pres. 1991), Lake Hosp. Found. (chmn. 1993-96), Ohio State Med. Assn. (alt. del. AMA 1997-2002, chmn. legis. com. 1997-2000, 5th dist. coun. 2000-03, pres.-elect, 2003—). Republican. Roman Catholic. Home: 8685 King Memorial Rd Mentor OH 44060-7960 Office: Lake Orthopaedic Assn 36100 Euclid Ave Ste 170 Willoughby OH 44094-4475 E-mail: stevencombs@hotmail.com.

COMBS, SUSAN, state agency administrator; married; 3 children. Grad., Vassar Coll.; JD, U. Tex. Formerly asst. dist. atty., Dallas; mem. Tex. Legislature, 1993-96; owner, operator ranch in West Tex.; commr. of agr. State of Tex., 1999—. Named Outstanding Legis. Crimefighter, Greater Dallas Crime Commn., 1993. Mem. Tex. Wildlife Assn. (bd. dirs., Tex. and Southwestern Cattle Raisers Assn. (bd. dirs.). Office: Tex Dept Agr PO Box 12847 Austin TX 78711-2847 Business E-Mail: commissioner@agr.state.tx.us.

COMEAU, LUDOVIC, JR., economist, educator; b. Port-au-Prince, Haiti, Sept. 9, 1960; arrived in U.S., 2000; s. Ludovic and Marie Thérèse (Martelly) Comeau; life ptnr. Bernadette Desruisseaux; m. Clairemirène Dieujuste, Dec. 21, 1991 (div.); children: Dominique, Claire Thérèse, Anne Estelle, Niabelle Luce; m. Maude Toussaint, Jan. 7, 1999. BS in Bus. Adminstrn., State U. Haiti, 1983; degree in Law, State U. Haiti, Port-au-Prince, Haiti, 1989; MA in Economics, MBA, U. Ill., 1994, PhD in Economics, 1997; MA in French Lit., U. Chgo., 2005. Tchr. French and Haitian lit. and Haitian history St. Martial Prep. Sem. and Primary-Secondary Sch., Port-au-Prince, Haiti, 1979—91, dir. studies, 1984—88; asst. dir. cultural affairs, head transl. svcs. Ministry Fgn. Affairs and Worships, Port-au-Prince, 1980—88; dir. personnel Ministry Edn., Youth and Sports, Port-au-Prince, 1988—90, cons. Nat. Bur. Alphabetization, 1990—91; econ. cons. Money and Econ. Analysis Divsn, Bank of Republic Haiti, Port-au-Prince, 1997—99, dir. Money and Econ. Analysis Divsn., 1999—2001; asst. prof. DePaul U., Chgo., 2001—. Author: Il pleut des larmes (It's raining tears). Treas. Haiti's Opportunity for Primary Edn., Chgo., 2005; mem. Fortify Haitians to Fortify Haiti, Chgo., 2005; mem. exec. com. DuSable Heritage Assn., Chgo., 2004. Recipient Oscar Miller Tchg. Excellence award, Economics Dept., U. Ill., 1997, Winifred Geldard Meml. award, 1996, Outstanding Devotion to Humanitarian Svc. award, Lions Club Port-au-Prince, Ctrl., Haiti, 1988, 1989, 1990, 1991, Appreciation award for enriching the cmty. and serving as example for all, Midwest Assn. Haitian Am. Women, Chgo., 2005; grantee, Pew Hispanic Ctr., 2004; scholar, Fulbright Found., 1991. Mem.: Haitian Studies Assn., Midwest Econs. Assn., We. Econ. Assn. Internat., Am. Econ. Assn. Office Phone: 312-362-8484. Personal E-mail: lcomeaujr@hotmail.com.

COMELLA, PHILLIP L., lawyer; b. 1955; BA cum laude, Beloit Coll., 1978; JD with honors, George Washington U., 1983. Bar: Ill. 1983, US Ct. Appeals DC cir., US Dist. Ct. (no. dist.) Ill. Ptnr. Seyfarth Shaw LLP, Chgo., chmn., Environ. Safety & Toxic Tort Practice Group. Spkr. in field; contbr. articles to profl. jour. Mem.: Ill. State Bar Assn., ABA. Office: Seyfarth Shaw LLP 55 East Monroe St Ste 4200 Chicago IL 60603 Office Phone: 312-269-8501. Office Fax: 312-269-8869. Business E-Mail: pcomella@seyfarth.com.

COMER, CLARENCE C., gas industry executive; b. 1948; married. BBA, Lamar U, 1971. Auditor Arthur Andersen & Co., 1971-75; controller Stratford of Tex., Inc., 1975-77; v.p. fin. Southdown Sugars Inc., 1977-79; treas. Southdown Inc., Houston, 1979-80, controller, then v.p., 1980-85, exec. v.p., 1985-86, pres., 1986—, chief oper. officer, from 1986, chief exec. officer, 1987—, pres., CEO, 1989—. Office: CEMEX 840 Gessner Rd #1400 Houston TX 77024-4152

COMER, DONALD, III, investment company executive; b. N.Y.C., June 23, 1938; s. Donald and Isabel (Anderson) C.; m. Jane Stephens, May 4, 1962; children: Jason Legare, Luke McDonald, Carrie St. George. BS, U. Ala., 1962. With Cowikee Mills, Eufaula, Ala., 1962-82, plant mgr., 1965-66, v.p., 1966-68, pres., treas., dir., 1968-82; pres., dir. Aurizon Inc., 1982—; past pres., treas., dir. Avondale Mills., Sylacauga, Ala. Past chmn. Ala. Ethics Commn. Served with USAF, 1961-64. Mem.: Mountain Brook Country (Birmingham). Home: 3905 Hillock Dr Birmingham AL 35213-3223

COMER, EVAN PHILIP, manufacturing executive; b. Cumberland Gap, Tenn., May 29, 1927; s. Evan Mitchell and Margaret Nola (Estep) C.; m. Mary Blanc, Aug. 28, 1948; children: Vivian, Jane. BA, Carson-Newman Coll., Jefferson City, Tenn., 1948; MA, Columbia U., 1949. Asst. prof. psychology, dir. student personnel and placement Furman U., Greensville, S.C., 1949-52; self-employed writer, 1952-53; supervisory conf. leader Union Carbide Nuclear Co., Oak Ridge, 1953-55; instr. in-plant tng. U. Tenn., Knoxville, 1955-56; with Foote Mineral Co., 1956-67, 69-84, v.p., gen. mgr. chems. and minerals div., 1970-80, pres., chief exec. officer Exton, Pa., 1980-84, also bd. dirs.; pres., chief exec. officer, chmn. bd. Ashram Farm, Inc., Rutledge, Tenn., 1984-98. Mem. Pa. adv. bd. Liberty Mut. Ins. Co.; chmn. exec. com., dir. Phila. Mfrs. Mut. Ins. Co. Pres. Southeastern C.C., Whiteville, N.C., 1967-69; mem. adv. bd. Carson-Newman Coll.; bd. dirs. Pa. Sci. and Engring. Found.; mem. Pa. Gov's Sci. Adv. Com.; mem. adv. coun. Pa. Tech. Assistance Program, Pa. State U.; chmn. bd. Chester County Pvt. Industry Coun., 1983-84; mem. Jefferson County (Tenn.) Planning Commn., 1998—, Jefferson County Zoning Appeals Bd., 1998—; mem. regional resource stewardship coun. TVA, 2000—; pres. Jefferson County Hist. Soc., 2003—. With USNR, 1945-46. Mem.: AIME, Am. Mining Congress, Ferroalloys Assn. (chmn. bd. dirs. 1983—84), Mining Club (N.Y.C.). Republican. Baptist. Home: 1548 Smoky View Dr Dandridge TN 37725-6328 Personal E-mail: PhilMary@att.net.

COMER, JAMES PIERPONT, psychiatrist, educator; b. East Chicago, Ind., Sept. 25, 1934; s. Hugh and Maggie (Nichols) C.; m. Shirley Ann Arnold, June 20, 1959 (dec. Apr. 1994), Bettye Fletcher Comer, July 11, 2004; children: Brian Jay, Dawn Renee. AB, Ind. U., 1956; MD, Howard U., 1960; MPH, U. Mich., 1964; DSc (hon.), U. New Haven, 1977; LittD (hon.), Calumet Coll., 1978; LHD (hon.), Bank St. Coll., N.Y.C., 1987, Albertus Magnus Coll., 1989, Quinnipiac Coll., 1990, DePauw U., 1990; DSc (hon.), Ind U., 1991, Wabash Coll., 1991; EdD (hon.), Wheelock Coll., 1991; LLD (hon.), U. Conn., 1991; LHD (hon.), SUNY Buffalo, 1991, New Sch. for Social Rsch., 1991; DPed (hon.), R.I. Coll., 1991; DSc (hon.), Amherst Coll., 1991; LHD (hon.), John Jay Coll. Criminal Justice, 1991, Wesleyan U., 1991; DH (hon.), Princeton U., 1991; DSc (hon.), Northwestern U., 1991, Worcester Poly. Inst., 1991; LHD (hon.), U. Pa., 1992; DPed (hon.) (hon.), Niagara U., 1992; LHD (hon.), Hamilton Coll., 1992; DSc (hon.), Brown U., 1992; LHD (hon.), U. Mass. Lowell, 1992; DSc (hon.), Med. Coll. Ohio, 1992, Howard U., 1993, W.Va. U., 1993; LLD (hon.), Lawrence U., 1993; DSc (hon.), Morehouse Sch. Medicine, 1993; LLD (hon.), Columbia U., 1994, Boston Coll., 1994; LHD (hon.), Briarwood Coll., 1994, Cleve. State U., 1996; DSc (hon.), St. Mary's Coll., Md., 1996, Albion Coll., 1997, Conn. Coll., 1997, So. Conn. State Coll., 1998; DPed (hon.), Long Island U., 1999; LHD (hon.), Ea. Mich. U., 2000; LHD (hon.), N.C.State Univ., Rosemont Coll., 2002. Served with USPHS, Washington and Chevy Chase, Md., 1961-68; intern St. Catherine's Hosp., East Chicago, 1960-61; resident Yale Sch. Medicine, 1964-67; asst. prof. psychiatry Yale Child Study Center and dept. psychiatry, 1968-70, assoc. prof., 1970-75, prof., 1975-76, Maurice Falk prof. child psychiatry, 1976—; assoc. dean Yale Med. Sch., New Haven, 1969—. Dir. pupil svcs. Baldwin-King Sch. Project, New Haven, 1968-73; dir. sch. devel. program Yale Child Study Ctr., 1973-97, founder sch. devel. program adv. bd., 1997—; dir. Conn. Energy Corp., 1976-2000, Nat. Acad. Found. N.Y., N.Y.C., 1993-98; co-dir. Black Family Roundtable Greater New Haven, 1986-90; cons. Joint Commn. on Mental Health of Children, 1967-68, Nat. Commn. on Causes and Prevention of Violence, NIMH; 1976-77. Author: Beyond Black and White, 1972, Black Child Care, 1975, 2d edit., 1992, School Power, 1980, 2d. edit., 1993, Maggie's American Dream, 1988, Rallying the Whole Village: The Comer Process for Reforming Education, 1996, Waiting For a Miracle: Why Schools Can't Solve Our Problems-And How We Can, 1997, Child by Child: The Comer Process for Change in Education, 1999, The field guide to Corner Schools in Action, 2004, Leave No Child Behind: Preparing Today's Youth for Tomorrow's World, 2004; mem. editl. bd. Am. Jour. Orthopsychiatry, 1969-76, Youth and Adolescence, 1971-87, Jour. Negro Edn., 1973-83, rev. Africal Am. Edn., 2003-; guest editor Jour. Am. Acad. Child Psychiatry, 1985; columnist Parents mag.; contbr. articles to profl. jours. Bd. dirs. Yale Afro-Am. House, 1970-72, trustee Hazen Found., 1974-78 Field Found., 1981-88, Nellie Mae, Mass., 2002-, Wesleyan U., 1978-84, Nat. Coun. for Effective Schs., 1985-90, Albertus Magnus Coll., 1989-2000, Carnegie Corp., 1990-98, Milton S. Eisenhower Found., Washington, 1991—, Conn. State U., 1991-94, Tchrs. Coll, Columbia U., 1999-; profl. adv. bd. Children's TV Workshop, 1970-86; mem. adv. coun. Nat. Assn. Mental Health, Nat. Com. for Citizens in Edn., Hogg Found. for Mental Health, 1983-86, Nat. Com. for Citizens in Edn., 1983—; mem. Nat. Bd. for Profl. Teaching Standards, Carnegie Forum on Edn. and the Economy, 1987-1991; mem. Nat. Commn. on Teaching and America's Future, Teachers College, Columbia U., 1994; mem. edn. adv. bd., bd. dirs. (hon.) Kids Voting USA, 1997—; mem. nat. evaluation adv. coun. Kellogg Youth Initiative Partnerships W.K. Kellogg Found., 1997—; adv. bd., Energy East, Bridgeport, Conn., 2000-04; mem. Com. Nat. Rsch. Coun., Institute of Med. of the Nat. Academies, 2001-2003; mem. Chair's Exec. Com., Yale U. Child Study Center, 2002-; mem. Blue Ribbon Panel Carroll and Milton Petrie New York City Teacher Fellowship Program, Teachers Coll., Columbia U., 2004-. Recipient Child Study Assn.-Wel-Met Family Life book award, 1975, Howard U. Disting. Alumni award, 1976, Rockefeller Public Svc. award, 1980, Media award NCCJ, 1981, Cmty. Leadership award Greater New Haven C. of C., 1983, Disting. Fellow award Conn. chpt. Phi Delta Kappa, 1984, Elm and Ivy award New Haven Found., 1985, Disting. Svc. award Conn. Assn. Psychologists, 1985, Outstanding Leadership award Children's Def. Fund, 1987, Whitney M. Young Jr. Svc. award Boy Scouts Am., 1989, Prudential Leadership award Prudential Found., 1990, Harold W. McGraw Jr. prize in Edn., 1990, James Bryant Conant award Edn. Commn. States, 1991, Disting. Svc. award Coun. Chief State Sch. Officers, 1991, Family Focus Nat. award, 1991, Charles A. Dana award for pioneering achievement in edn., 1991, Ind. U. Disting. Alumni Svc. award, 1992, Burger King Disting. Svc. to Edn. award, 1992, Conn. Assn. for Human Svcs. Pres. award, 1992, Golden Acorn award Bronx C.C., 1994, Presdl. citation Am. Ednl. Rsch. Assn., 1995, Health Trac Found. prize, 1996, Heinz Family award, 1996, Lehigh U. Outstanding Svc. to Coll. Edn. award, 1996, Ann Vanderbilt Achievement award for ednl. leadership, 1997, Great Friend to Kids award Assn. Youth Mus., 1997, Disting. Svc. medal Tchrs. Coll., 1997, Friends of the Family citation, Working Mother Mag., 1997, World of Children award Judge Baker Children's Ctr., 1997, Michael Bolton Lifetime Achievement award, 1997, Edn. award Inst. Student Achievement, 1999, Disting. Pub. Svc. award Conn. Bar Assn., 1999, Martin Luther Freedom award New Haven Chpt. NAACP, 2000; John and Mary Markle Found. scholar, 1969-74; James Comer NIMH Minority Fellowship established in his honor, 1991.; Disting. Svc. Award, Covenant Care, Inc., 2001, Disting. Life award, Am. Psychiatric Assn., 2003, Assn. Yale Alumni Med., Appreciation award, 2003, John P. McGovern Behavioral Science award, Smithsonian, 2004, Disting. Citizen award, West Haven Black Coalition, 2004, First Annual Tapestry award, New Haven Family Alliance, 2004, Conn. Black Nurses Assn. award, 2004, Friend of Public Edn. award, Conn. Assn. of Bds. of Edn., 2004. Mem. APA (Disting. Svc. award 1993), Am. Acad. Child Adolescent Psychiatry, Nat. Med. Assn., Nat. Mental Health Assn. (Lela Rowland Prevention award 1989), Am. Psychiat. Assn. (Agnes Purcell McGavin award 1990, Solomon Carter Fuller award 1990, Spl. Presdl. Commendation 1990, Disting. Svc. award 1993), Am. Orthopsychiat. Assn. (Vera S. Paster award 1990), Am. Acad. Child Psychiatry, Black Psychiatrists of Am., NAACP, Black Coalition of New Haven, Greater New Haven Black Family Roundtable (co-dir. 1986—), Alpha Omega Alpha, Alpha Phi Alpha. Avocations: photography, travel, sports fan. Office: Yale U Child Study Ctr PO Box 207900 New Haven CT 06520-7900 E-mail: james.comer@yale.edu. *As a black child, I sometimes had doubts about my future opportunities for success in our predominantly white country. My parents counselled me never to let the issue of race stand in my way; that the time of greater opportunity for blacks would come. They advised me to work hard, prepare myself, to strive to be the best or among the best in every undertaking, and at the same time be respectful of all people, regardless of their abilities, race, beliefs, or station in life. I have lived by this advice and it has served me well. I have learned not to strive for top position but to let my work take me where it will in line with my interests.*

COMER, NATHAN LAWRENCE, psychiatrist, educator; b. Phila., Nov. 10, 1923; s. Rubin L. and Fannie (Cassover) C.; m. Rita Ellis, June 19, 1949 (dec. Mar. 1978); children: Robert, Susan Comer Kitei, Debra R., Marc J. BA, U. Pa., 1944; MD, Hahnemann Med. Coll., 1949; postgrad., U. Pa. Diplomate Am. Bd. Psychiatry and Neurology, Am. Bd. Profl. Disability Cons., Sr. Disability Analyst of Am. Bd. Disability Analysts, Am. Bd. Forensic Examiners, Am. Bd. Forensic Medicine. Intern Hahnemann Med. Coll., Phila., 1949-50; resident, NIMH fellow Inst. of Pa. Hosp., Phila., 1951-53, sr. attending psychiatrist, 1968—, resident in psychiatry, 1951-53; chief of psychiatry Ford Rd. campus Thomas Jefferson U. Hosp., Phila., 1978-94; clin. assoc. prof. psychiatry and human behavior Jefferson Med. Coll., Thomas Jefferson U., Phila., 1994—; clin. assoc. prof. psychiatry Drexel U. Coll. Medicine, Phila., 1978—; emeritus attending psychiatrist Hosp. Med. Coll. Pa., 2000—. Pres. med. staff Belmont Ctr. Comprehensive Treatment (formerly Phila. Psychiat. Ctr.), 1975—77, emeritus sr. attending physician, 1988—; pres. med. staff Inst. of Pa. Hosp., 1983—85. Contbr. articles to profl. jours. Bd. dirs. Temple Adath Israel of Main Linc, Merion, Pa., 1958-78. Fellow Coll. Physicians Phila., Am. Psychiat. Assn. (disting. life); mem. AMA, Am. Soc. for Adolescent Psychiatry, Hahnemann Med. Coll. Alumni Assn. (pres. 1973-74), B'nai B'rith. Republican. Jewish. Home and Office: 1100 Hillcrest Rd Narberth PA 19072-1224 Office Phone: 610-667-1111. Office Fax: 610-668-7417. *Do things to the best of your ability and be willing to go that extra mile. Alsobe willing to express your opinion if you think you're right even if you seem to be in the minority. Being respected is more important than being liked.*

COMERFORD, CRISTETA, chef; b. Phillipines; naturalized, US; m. John Comerford; 1 child. B in Food Tech., Univ. Phillipines; studied classic French cooking, Vienna. Chef La Ciel Restaurant, Vienna, Westin Restaurant, Washington, ANA Restaurant, Washington; asst. to exec. chef The White House, Washington, 1995—2005, exec. chef, 2005—. Achievements include being first woman appointed head chef of The White House. Office: The White House 1600 Pennsylvania Ave Washington DC 20500*

COMEROTA, ANTHONY JAMES, vascular surgeon, biomedical researcher; b. Newark, Aug. 4, 1948; s.Louis Anthony and Eleanor Dorothy (Dombroski) C.; m. Elsa Benavides, Aug. 18, 1973; children: Anthony James, Maya Christine, Mark Anthony. BA, Millikin U., 1970; MD, Temple U., 1974. Diplomate Am. Bd. Surgery. Surg. resident Temple U. Hosp., Phila., 1974-78; vascular surgery fellow Good Samaritan Hosp., Cin., 1979-81; from asst. prof. to prof. surgery Temple U. Hosp, Temple U. Sch. Medicine, Phila., 1981-88, prof. surgery, chief vascular surgery, 1988—2002; dir. Ctr. for Vascular Diseases Temple U. Hosp., Temple U. Sch. Medicine, Phila., 1995—2002; dir. Jobst Vascular Ctr., Toledo; clin. prof. U. Mich., Ann Arbor, 2002—. Editor: Thrombolytic Therapy for Peripheral Vascular Disease, 1995; co-editor: Prevention of Venous Thromboembolism, 1994. Fellow ACS, Royal Australian Coll. Surgeons; mem. Am. Surg. Assn., Soc. Vascular Surgery, Peripheral Vascular Soc. (pres. 1988-89), Am. Venous Forum (pres. 2000-01), Phila. Acad. Surgery (pres. 1996-97), Temple U. Sch. Medicine Alumni Assn. (pres. 1993-95), Alpha Omega Alpha. Office: Jobst Vascular Ctr 2109 Hughes Dr # 400 Toledo OH 43606 Office Phone: 419-291-2088. Business E-Mail: acomerota@jvc.org.

COMETTO-MUNIZ, J. ENRIQUE, research scientist; b. Buenos Aires, May 31, 1954; arrived in U.S., 1988; s. Teresa Muniz Saaavedra and Jorge Raul Cometto; m. Adriana Nora Merlo, Nov. 5, 1979; children: Carolina Sofia Cometto, Lucas Marcelo Cometto, Tomas Pablo Cometto. PhD in BioChemistry, U. Buenos Aires. Tchg. asst. to adj. prof. U. Buenos Aires, 1976—93; fellow to adj. investigator Nat. Coun. for Sci. and Tech., Buenos Aires, 1978—93; asst. fellow John B. Pierce Lab., New Haven, 1988—94; assoc. rsch. scientist Yale U. Sch. Medicine, New Haven, 1988—94; assoc. project scientist U. Calif., San Diego, 1994—95, assoc. rsch. scientist, 1996—2001, rsch. scientist, 2001—. Contbr. articles to profl. jours. Grantee, NIH, Ctr. for Indoor Air Rsch., Rsch. Mgmt. Group, 1994—. Mem.: Soc. Toxicology (corr.), Internat. Soc. Indoor Air Quality and Climate (corr.), European Chemoreception Rsch. Orgn. (corr.), Assn. for Chemoreception Scis. (corr.). Office: Univ Calif 9500 Gilman Dr Mail Code 0957 La Jolla CA 92093-0957 Office Phone: 858-622-5832. E-mail: ecometto@ucsd.edu.

COMEY, JAMES B., JR., former federal agency administrator; b. Yonkers, N.Y., Dec. 14, 1960; m. Patrice Comey; 5 children. BS in Chemistry & Religion, Coll. William and Mary, 1982; JD, U. Chgo., 1985. Law clk. to Hon. John M. Walker US Dist. Ct., Manhattan, 1985—85; assoc. Gibson, Dunn & Crutcher, 1986—87; asst. U.S. atty. (So. dist.) N.Y. US Dept. Justice, Manhattan, 1987—93; ptnr. McGuire Woods, LLP, Richmond, Va., 1993—96; mng. asst. U.S. Atty. Office (Ea. dist) Va. US Dept. Justice, 1996—2002, U.S. atty. (So. dist.) N.Y., 2002—03, dep. atty. gen. Washington, 2003—05. Former adj. prof. law U. Richmond. Recipient Henry L. Stimson Medal, NYC Bar Assn., 1993. Avocations: squash, bicycling, New York Giants and Knicks, teaching Sunday school.

COMFORT, JEFFERY JOSEPH, music educator; b. Niles, Mich., Nov. 10, 1974; s. Dennis Joseph and Nancy Marie Comfort. MusB Edn., VanderCook Coll. Music, Chgo., 1997. Lic. for ednl. pers. Nev., 2004. Band dir. Dowagiac (Mich.) Union H.S., 1997—2004, Arbor View H.S., Las Vegas, 2004—. Contbr. articles to band mags. Methodist. Office: Arbor View High School 7500 Whispering Sands Drive Las Vegas NV 89131 Office Phone: (702) 799-6660.

COMFORT, WILLIAM TWYMAN, JR., banker; b. Ellsworth, Kans., Aug. 3, 1937; s. William Twyman and Leoti Dora (Shackleford) C.; m. Nathalie Pierrepont, June 6, 1964; children: Nathalie Pierrepont, William Twyman III, James Theodore, Stuyvesant Pierrepont. BA, Okla. U., 1959, LLB, 1961; LLM, NYU, 1964. With W.E. Hutton & Co., N.Y.C., 1962-73, ptnr., 1969-73, sr. v.p., 1973-74, Citibank, N.Y.C., 1974—; exec. dir. Citicorp Internat. Bank Ltd., London, 1976-78; chmn. bd. dirs. 399 Venture Ptnrs. Inc., Citigroup Venture Capital, Ltd. Chmn. bd. dirs. CourtSquare Capital Ltd.; adj. prof. Columbia Bus. Sch., N.Y.C.; bd. dirs. I-Flex (India), Flender AG (Germany); trustee The John A. Hartford Found., Inc. Trustee NYU Law Ctr. Found.; former trustee Pine Mano Coll., Chestnut Hill, Mass.; advisor to bd. dirs. Old Westbury (L.I.) Gardens. With U.S. Army, 1961. Mem. N.Y. Bar Assn., Okla. Bar Assn., Piping Rock Club (Locust Valley, N.Y.), Jupiter Island Club (Hobe Sound, Fla.). Home: 340 Duck Pond Rd Box 507 Locust Valley NY 11560-2404

COMFORT, WILLIAM WISTAR, mathematics professor; b. Bryn Mawr, Pa., Apr. 19, 1933; s. Howard and Elizabeth (Webb) Comfort; m. Mary Constance Lyon, Mar. 30, 1957; children: Martha Wistar, Howard III. BA, Haverford Coll., 1954; MS, U. Wash., 1957, PhD, 1958; MA ad eundem gradum, Wesleyan U., Middletown, Conn., 1969. Tchg. asst., rsch. asst. U. Wash., Seattle, 1954-58; B. Peirce instr. Harvard U., Cambridge, Mass., 1958-61; asst. prof. U. Rochester, N.Y., 1961-65; assoc. prof. U. Mass., Amherst, 1965-67; prof. math. Wesleyan U., 1967—, Edward Burr Van Vleck prof. math., 1982—, chmn. dept., 1969-70, 80-82, 96-97. Vis prof Univ Ark, 1965, McGill Univ, Montreal, Canada, 1970—71, Univ Heidelberg, 1974, Istituto Matematico Leonida Tonelli, Pisa, Italy, 1974, Athens Univ, Greece, 1978, Univ Nacional Autonoma de Mex, 1983, Univ São Paolo, 1983, 99, Vrije Univ, Amsterdam, The Netherlands, 1984, 95, Technische Hochschule Darmstadt, Germany, 1991, Univ Jaume I Castellon, Spain, 1995. Author (with S Negrepontis): The Theory of Ultrafilters, 1974, Continuous Pseudometrics, 1975, Chain Conditions in Topology, 1982; mem. editl. bd.: Procs Am Math Soc, 1972—75; editor (managing ed), 1974—75; mem. editl. bd.: Topology Procs, 1976—, Am Math Monthly, 1983—86, Karachi Jour Math, 1984—, Scientiae Mathematicae, 1992—, Topology and Its Applications,

1993—, Jour. Kerala Math. Assoc., 2004—; contbr. articles to profl. jours. Bd mgrs Haverford Col, 1971—74; trustee Ind Day Sch, Middlefield, Conn., 1972—75. Recipient Excellence-in-Teaching Award, Univ Rochester, 1966. Mem.: AAUP, Asn Concerned Scientists, Conn Acad Sci and Eng, Am Math Soc (coun 1972—75, 1982—93, assoc secy eastern region 1982—93), Math Asn Am, Phi Beta Kappa. Mem. Soc. Of Friends. Office: Wesleyan U Math Dept Middletown CT 06459-0001 Home: 3 Ball Ln Old Lyme CT 06371 Office Phone: 860-685-2632. Business E-Mail: wcomfort@wesleyan.edu.

COMINGS, DAVID EDWARD, medical geneticist; b. Beacon, N.Y., Mar. 8, 1935; s. Edward Walter and Jean (Rice) C.; m. Shirley Nelson, Aug. 9, 1958; children: Mark David, Scott Edward, Karen Jean; m. Brenda Gursey, Mar. 20, 1982. Student, U. Ill., 1951—54; BS, Northwestern U., 1955, MD, 1958. Intern Cook County Hosp., Chgo., 1958-59, resident in internal medicine, 1959-62; fellow in med. genetics U. Wash., Seattle, 1964-66; dir. dept. med. genetics City of Hope Med. Ctr., Duarte, Calif., 1966—2003, dir. emeritus, 2003—; dir. Carlsbad Sci. Found., Monrovia, Calif., 2004—. Mem. genetics study sect. NIH, 1974-78; mem. sci. adv. bd. Hereditary Disease Found., 1975-, Nat. Found. March of Dimes, 1978-92. Author: Tourette Syndrome and Human Behavior, 1990, Search for the Tourette Syndrome and Human Behavior Genes, 1996, The Gene Bomb, 1996; editor: (with others) Molecular Human Cytogenetics, 1977; mem. editl. bd.: (with others) Cytogenetics and Cell genetics, 1979—; editor-in-chief Am. Jour. Human Genetics, 1978-86. Served with U.S. Army, 1962-64. NIH grantee, 1967-. Mem. Assn. Am. Physicians, Am. Soc. Clin. Investigation, AAAS, Am. Soc. Human Genetics (dir. 1974-78, pres. 1988), Am. Soc. Cell Biology, Am. Fedn. Clin. Rsch., Western Soc. Clin. Rsch., Coun. Biology Editors. Office: Carlsbad Sci Found 605 E Huntington Dr Monrovia CA 91016

COMINI, ALESSANDRA, art historian, educator; b. Winona, Minn., Nov. 24, 1934; d. Raiberto and Megan (Laird) C. BA, Barnard Coll., 1956; MA, U. Calif., Berkeley, 1964; PhD with distinction, Columbia U., 1969. Tchg. asst. U. Calif., Berkeley, 1964, vis. instr., 1967; preceptor Columbia U., 1965-66, 67-68, instr., 1968-69, asst. prof., 1969-74; vis. asst. prof. So. Methodist U., summers 1970, 72, assoc. prof. art history, 1974-75, prof., 1975—, univ. disting. prof., 1983—. Alfred Hodder resident humanist Princeton U., 1972-73; disting. vis. lectr. Oxford U., 1996; vis. asst. prof. Yale U., 1973; vis. humanist various univs.; lectr. in English, German and Italian; keynote spkr. Gewandhaus Symposia, Leipzig, Germany, 1983, 85, 87, 89, Mahler Internat Congress, Amsterdam, 1988, 95, Hamburg, 1989, Oxford, 1996, Montpellier, 1996, Internat. Mahler Fest, Boulder, Colo., 1998; featured spkr. Purchase, N.Y., 1989, Leningrad, 1990, Stockholm, 1991, Berlin, 1993, Bethoven Extravaganza, Milw., 1994, Schiele Symposium, Indpls., 1994, Helsinki, 1996, Schubertiads at Curtis Inst., Phila., Reed Coll., Oreg. and So. Meth. U., 1997, Santa Fe Opera, 1997, 98, 99, 2000, 01, 02, Dallas Symphony Orch., 1998, 99, 2000, 01, 03, 04, 05, Mozart Internat. Symposium U. Dublin, Ireland, 1999, San Diego Mus., 1999, 2000, 01, 02, 03, 05; panelist NEH Mus. and Pub. Programs, 1978—; vis. scholar Kalamazoo Coll., 1999. Author: Schiele in Prison, 1973, Egon Schiele's Portraits, 1974 (Nat. Book award nominee 1975, reissued 1990, Charles Rufus Morey Book award 1975), Gustav Klimt, 1975, reissued 1986, 90, 93, also German, French and Dutch edit., Egon Schiele, 1976, reissued 1986, 94, also German, French and Dutch edits., The Fantastic Art of Vienna, 1978, The Changing Image of Beethoven, 1987, Egon Schiele: Nudes, 1995, In Passionate Pursuit: A Memoir, 2004; contbg. author: World Impressionism, 1990, Käthe Kollwitz, 1992, Egon Schiele, 1994, Violetta and her Sisters, 1994, Salome, 1996, By a Finnish Fireside: An Evening with Akseli Gallen-Kallela and Gustav Mahler, 1997, The Visual Wagner, 1997, Irony and Gustav Mahler, 2000, Toys in Friend's Attic, 2001, Beethoven and His World, 2000, Pilgrimage to Schiele, 2005; contbr. numerous articles to Stagebill, Arts Mag., English Nat. Opera, Chgo. Lyric Opera; also author various catalogue and book introductions, also book revs. for N.Y. Times, Women's Art Jour. Awarded Grand Decoration of Honor for svcs. to Republic of Austria, 1990; recipient Charles Rufus Morey Book award Coll. Art Assn. Am., 1976, Laural award AAUW, 1979; named Outstanding Prof., 1977, 79, 83, 85, 86, 87, 88, 90, 98, 99, 2000, 01, 02, 03, 04, Laurence Perrine prize Phi Beta Kappa Gamma of Tex., 2003; AAUW travel fellow, 1966-87; NEH grantee, 1975; named Meadows Disting. Tchg. Prof., 1986-87, Tchr./Scholar of Yr., United Meth. Ch., 1996. Mem. ASCAP, Nat. Mus. for Women in the Arts (nat. bd. 1997—), Coll. Art Assn. Am. (bd. dirs. 1980-84), Women's Caucus for Art (bd. dirs. 1974-78, Life Achievement award 1995, Tex. Women's Hall of Fame 2002), Tex. Inst. Letters. Democrat. Home: 2900 McFarlin Blvd Dallas TX 75205-1920 Office: So Meth U Divsn Art History Dallas TX 75275 Business E-Mail: acomini@smu.edu.

COMINSKY, LYNN RUTH, physics and astronomy educator; b. Buffalo, Nov. 19, 1953; d. Martyn Francis Cominsky and Lois Mona (Joseph) Klein; m. Jesse Garrett Jernigan, Jr., June 1, 1980. BA, Brandeis U., 1975; PhD, MIT, 1981. Sci. ops. and data analysis adminstr. U. Calif. Space Scis. Lab., Berkeley, 1984-85, systems devel. mgr., 1985-86; assoc. prof. Sonoma State U., Rohnert Park, Calif., 1986-91, prof., 1991—, chmn., 2004—. Vis. prof. Stanford Linear Accelerator Ctr., 1993—. Author numerous rsch. papers. Named CASE Calif. Prof. of Yr., 1993. Mem. Am. Astron. Soc., Am. Phys. Soc., Am. Assn. Physics Tchrs., Assn. Women in Sci., Nat. Sci. Tchrs. Assn., Sigma Xi. Office: Sonoma State U Dept Physics and Astronomy Rohnert Park CA 94928 E-mail: lynnc@universe.sonoma.edu.

COMISKY, HOPE A., lawyer; b. Phila., Apr. 23, 1953; married; three children. BA with distinction, Cornell U., 1974; JD, U. Pa., 1977. Bar: Pa. 1977, U.S. Dist. Ct. (ea. dist.) Pa. 1978, D.C. 1979, U.S. Ct. Appeals (3d cir.) 1979, U.S. Supreme Ct. 1987, U.S. Dist. Ct. (mid. dist.) Pa. 1991, N.Y. 1993, U.S. Ct. Appeals (6th cir.) 1996, U.S. Ct. Appeals (7th cir.) 2005. Law clerk ea dist. U.S. Dist. Ct., Pa., 1977-78; assoc. Dilworth, Paxson, Kalish & Kauffman, Phila., 1978-84, ptnr., 1985-91, Anderson Kill & Olick, P.C., Phila., 1992-98, mng. ptnr. Phila. office, 1995-98; ptnr. labor and employment law group Pepper Hamilton LLP, Phila., 1998—, co-chair ERISA and employment litigation practice group, 2005—. Spkr. in field. Author: Decamus Maximus The life and The Life of Medical School Dean; contbr. articles pub. to articles to profl. jours. Bd. dirs. Phila. Sch., 1989-2003, pres. 2001-03, hon. bd. dirs., 2004—; bd. dirs. Fedn. Day Care Svcs., 1991-97, mem. exec. com., chmn. pers. practices com., 1985-91; bd. dirs. Ctr. for Literacy, 1996-, v.p., 2004-, chmn. pers. com. 2000-; bd. dirs. Women's Law Project, 1998-2004, Fedn. Early Learning Svcs., 2003-. Mem. Am. Arbitration Assn. (comml. and employment arbitrator), elected to Coll. Labor and Employment Attys., Phi Beta Kappa, Mortar Bd. Office: Pepper Hamilton LLP 3000 Two Logan Sq 18th & Arch Sts Philadelphia PA 19103-2799

COMISKY, IAN MICHAEL, lawyer; b. Phila., Feb. 5, 1950; s. Marvin and Goldye (Elving) C. BS magna cum laude, U. Pa., 1971, JD, 1974; LLM in Taxation, U. Miami, 1984. Bar: Pa. 1974, Fla. 1976, D.C. 1976, U.S. Ct. Appeals (3rd and 11th cirs.), U.S. Ct. Claims, U.S. Tax Ct., U.S. Supreme Ct., U.S. Dist. Ct. (ea. dist.) Pa., U.S. Dist. Ct. (so. dist.) Fla., U.S. Dist. Ct. (mid. dist.) Fla. Law clk. to Hon. Alfred Luongo Jr. U.S. Dist. Ct. Pa., Phila., 1974-75; asst. dist. atty. Office of Dist. Atty., Philadelphia County, Phila., 1975-78; asst. U.S. atty. So. Dist. Fla., 1978-80; spl. asst. Office of Dist. Atty., So. Dist. Fla., 1980; ptnr., comml. litigation and white collar crime Blank Rome LLP, Phila., 1980—. Presenter various profl. confs. seminars, 1981—; guest TV and radio programs, 1990. Co-author: Tax Fraud and Evasion (2 vols.); contbr. articles to profl. pubs. Sec. Mann Music Ctr. Mem. ABA (chmn. special projects com., past chmn. civil and criminal tax penalties com. tax sect., mem. CLE com. tax sect., vice chmn. COGS spl. projects, mem. various coms. criminal justice and litig. sect.), ATLA, Am. Law Inst., Am. Coll. Tax Counsel, Fed. Bar Assn., Pa. Bar Assn., Fla. Bar Assn. (bd. govs. 1998), D.C. Bar Assn., Phila. Bar Assn., Assn. Fellows and Legal Scholars or Ctr. for Internat. Legal Studies (hon.). Avocations: sailing, gardening, jogging. Office Phone: 315-369-5646. Business E-Mail: icomisky@blamerome.com.

COMISO, JOSEFINO CACAS, research scientist; b. Narvacan, Philippines, Sept. 21, 1940; arrived in U.S., 1964; s. Severino Cacho and Silvestra (Cacas) C.; m. Diana Parreñas Jimenez, June 27, 1970; children: Glen Arnold, David Arnel, Melissa Jane. BS in Physics, U. Philippines, Quezon City, 1962; MS in Physics, Fla. State U., 1966; PhD in Physics, UCLA, 1972. Scientist Philippine Atomic Rsch. Ctr., Quezon City, 1962-63; instr. U. The Philippines, Quezon City, 1963-64; asst. rsch. physicist UCLA, 1972-73; rsch. assoc. U. Va., Charlottesville, 1973-77; sr. mem. tech. staff Computer Scis. Corp., Greenbelt, Md., 1977-79; phys. scientist Goddard Space Flight Ctr. NASA, Greenbelt, 1979—. Co-author: Arctic & Antarctic Sea Ice, 1992; contbr. articles to profl. jours. Pres. Philippine-Am. Acad. Sci. and Engrs., Washington, 1987. Mem. Am. Geophys. Union, Am. Phys. Soc., Internat. Glaciol. Soc., Com. on Polar Meteorology and Oceanography, Electromagnetics Acad. Achievements include space based assessments and studies of surface temperatures, sea ice distributions, heat and salinity fluxes in polynyas, and phytoplankton blooms in the polar regions and the development of satellite sensor algorithms. Home: 11013 Elon Dr Bowie MD 20720-3509 Office: NASA/GSFC Lab for Hydrospheric Processes Code 971 Greenbelt MD 20771-0001 Office Phone: 301-614-5708. Business E-Mail: josefino.c.comiso@nasa.gov.

COMITAS, LAMBROS, anthropologist, educator; b. N.Y.C., Sept. 29, 1927; s. Dennis and Magdaline (Livanis) C.; m. Irene Mousouris. AB, Columbia U., 1948, PhD in Anthropology, 1962. Instr. anthropology Columbia U., N.Y.C., 1958-61, asst. prof., 1962-64, assoc. prof. anthropology and edn. Tchrs. Coll., 1965-67, prof., 1967-87, Gardner Cowles prof. anthropology and edn., 1988—, dir. div. philosophy, social scis. and edn., 1979-96, dir. Inst. Latin Am. and Iberian studies, 1977-84; dir. Rsch. Inst. study of man, 1985-2001; adminstr. Ruth Landes Meml. Rsch. Fund, 1991—; pres. Comitas Inst. Anthrop. Study, 2003—. Mem. drug abuse, clin., behavioral and psychosocial rsch. rev. com. Nat. Inst. Drug Abuse, 1977-81. Author books and articles in field. With U.S. Army, 1946-47. Office Edn. fellow, 1968-69, Guggenheim fellow, 1971-72; Fulbright grantee, 1957-58, Nat. Inst. Drug Abuse grantee, 1975-79. Mem. Soc. Applied Anthropology (pres. 1970-71), Am. Anthrop. Assn., Am. Ethnol. Soc., Nat. Acad. Edn. (chmn. com. anthropology and edn.), N.Y. Acad. Scis. Home: 1107 5th Ave New York NY 10128-0145 Office: Teachers Coll Columbia U New York NY 10027 Office Phone: 212-678-4040. Business E-Mail: lc137@columbia.edu.

COMMANDER, CHARLES EDWARD, lawyer, real estate consultant; b. Jacksonville, Fla., Aug. 17, 1940; s. Charles Edward Jr. and Eleanor (Wood) C.; m. Victoria Coxe, Aug. 10, 1963; children: Eleanor, Charles IV, Christopher. BS in Commerce, Washington & Lee U., 1962; JD, U. Fla., 1965. Bar: Fla. 1966. Atty., assoc. ptnr. Mahoney, Hadlow, Chambers and Adams, Jacksonville, 1966-73; pres. Barnett Winston Properties, Jacksonville, 1973-74; founding ptnr. Commander, Legler, Werber, Dawes, Sadler & Howell, Jacksonville, 1974-91; ptnr., mgmt. com. Foley & Lardner, 1991—2003. Cons. First Union Nat. Bank Fla., Jacksonville, 1990-95; chmn. bd. dirs. First Nat. Bank, Jacksonville, 1979-84; chmn. Property Investment Svcs., Inc., Jacksonville, 1974—; bd. Everbank Fin. Corp., 1994-, Everbank FSB, 2002-; trustee Builders Investment Group, King of Prussia, Pa. and Fullerton, Calif., 1977-80; dir. Koger Equity Inc., 1993-95, Computer Power, 1974-79, 86-92; bd. dirs. U. Fla. Law Ctr. Assn., 2002-, Patient Transp. Holding Co., 2004-. Editor Law Review U. Fla., 1964-65; reporter Fla. Law Revision Coun., 1975-76. Trustee The Bolles Sch., Jacksonville, 1980-90; pres. U. No. Fla. Found., 1994-97, Cummer Gallery of Art, 1993—2002; bd. dirs. Jacksonville Housing Authority, 1995—2003; vice chmn. Mus. Sci. and History, Jacksonville, 1968-73, Jacksonville Zool. Soc., 1972-76; pres. bd. dirs. The River Club, Jacksonville, 1977-84. Episcopalian. Avocations: fishing, hunting, boating, farming. Office: Foley & Lardner Ste 1300 One Independent Dr Jacksonville FL 32202-5017 E-mail: ccommander@foley.com.

COMMER, JOHN ANDREW, video director; b. Pine Bluff, Ark., July 16, 1964; s. Jake Baggarly and Ann Laverne Commer; m. Amy Elizabeth Rogers, June 28, 1997; children: Jacob Andrew, William Ramsey. BS, Ark. State U., 1987; MS, Miss. State U., 1995. Asst. video coord. Atlanta Falcons, 1987—89; video coord. Miss. State U., 1989—95, U. Miss., Oxford, 1995—97, U. Ark., 1997—. Coord. Am. Cancer Soc. Promotional Video, 1999. Vol. St. Paul's Episcopal Ch., Fayetteville, Ark., 1997—2004; motivator Athletic Dept. Highlights Promos, 1997—2004. Mem.: Trout Unlimited, Coll. Sports Video Assn. Avocations: fly fishing, running. Home: 711 Calvin St Fayetteville AR 72703 Office: Univ Ark Athletic Dept Broyles Complex Fayetteville AR 72703 E-mail: acommer@uark.edu.

COMMIRE, ANNE, playwright, writer, editor; b. Wyandotte, Mich., Aug. 11, 1939; BS, Eastern Mich. U., 1961; postgrad., Wayne State U., NYU. Author: (plays) Shay, 1973, Transatlantic Bridge, 1977, Put Them All Together, 1978, Sunday's Red, 1982, Melody Sisters, 1983, Starting Monday, 1988; author: (with Mariette Hartley) (book) Breaking the Silence, 1990; editor: Something About the Author, 1970—90, Yesterday's Authors of Books for Children, 1977—78, Historic World Leaders, 1994, Women in World History: A Biographical Encyclopedia, 1999—2002 (Dartmouth medal, 2002). Recipient Eugene O'Neill Theatre award, 1973, 1978, 1983, 1988; grantee, Creative Artists Program, 1975; playwriting grant, Rockefeller Found., 1979. Mem.: PEN, Writers Guild Am., Dramatists Guild, Authors Guild. Home: 11 Stanton St Waterford CT 06385-1400

COMMONER, BARRY, biologist, educator; b. Bklyn., May 28, 1917; s. Isidore and Goldie (Yarmolinsky) C.; m. Lisa Feiner, 1980; children by previous marriage: Lucy Alison, Frederic Gordon. AB with honors, Columbia U., 1937; MA, Harvard U., 1938, PhD, 1941; DSc (hon.), Hahnemann Med. Coll., 1963; D.Sc. (hon.), Clark U., 1967, Grinnell Coll., 1968, Lehigh U., 1969, Williams Coll., 1970, Ripon Coll., 1971, Colgate U., 1972, Cleve. State U., 1980; LL.D. (hon.), U. Calif., 1974, Grinnell Coll., 1981; D.Sc. (hon.), St. Lawrence U., 1988; D.H.L. (hon.), Lowell U., 1990; DSc (hon.), Conn. Coll., 1992, Queens Coll., 2001. Asst. biology Harvard, 1938-40; instr. biology Queens Coll., 1940-42; asso. editor Sci. Illus., 1946-47; asso. prof. plant physiology Washington U., St. Louis, 1947-53, prof., 1953-76, chmn. dept. botany, 1965-69; dir. Washington U. (Center for the Biology of Natural Systems), 1965-81, Univ. prof. environ. sci., 1976-81; prof. dept. geology Queens Coll., Flushing, N.Y., 1981-87, prof. emeritus, 1987—, dir. Center for the Biology of Natural Systems, 1981-2000, sr. scientist, 2000—. Vis. prof. cmty. health Albert Einstein Coll. of Medicine, N.Y.C., 1981-87; disting. univ. prof. indsl. policy U. Mass., Lowell, 1992-95; pres. St. Louis Com. for Nuclear Info., 1965-66, bd. dirs., 1966; mem. Nat. Tb Commn. on Air Conservation, 1966-68; bd. dirs. Scientists Inst. Pub. Info., 1963—, co-chmn., 1967-69, chmn., 1969-78, chmn. exec. com., 1978—; chmn. spl. cons. group sonic boom Dept. Interior, 1967-68; mem. adv. coun. on environ. edn. Office Edn., HEW, 1971; mem. internat. sponsoring com. Chaim Weizmann Centenary Celebration, 1974-75; mem. adv. com. Coalition Health Communities, 1975; mem. sec.'s adv. coun. Dept. Commerce, 1976; mem. sci. adv. coun. on dioxin Vietnam Vets. Am. Found., 1985—; mem. sci. adv. N.Y. State Com. on Sci. and Tech., 1981—; mem. adv. bd. Com. for Responsible Genetics, 1983—. Author: Science and Survival, 1966, The Closing Circle, 1971 (Phi Beta Kappa award), (Internat. prize City of Cervia, Italy), La Technologia del Profitto, 1973, The Poverty of Power, 1976 (Premio Iglesias award, Sardinia, Italy 1978), Ecologia e Lotte Sociali, 1976, l'energia alternativa, 1978, The Politics of Energy, 1979 (Premio Iglesias award 1982), Se Scoppia La Bomba, 1984, Il Cerchio Da Chiudere, 1986, Making Peace With the Planet, 1990; editorial bd. World Book Ency., 1968-73, Environment mag., 1977; mem. adv. bd. Science Year, 1967-72; editorial adv. bd. Hon. Chemosphere, from 1972; bd. sponsors In These Times, 1976— . Bd. cons. experts Rachel Carson Trust for Living Environment, 1967—; adv. com. Center for Devel. Policy, 1978; mem. bd. Univs. Nat. Anti-War Fund; adv. bd. Fund for Peace, 1978, Citizens Party candidate for pres. of U.S., 1980. Served to lt. USNR, 1942-46. Recipient Newcomb Cleveland prize AAAS, 1953; 1st Humanist award Internat. Humanist and Ethical Union, 1970; medal AIA, 1979; decorated comdr. Order of Merit Italy, 1977 Fellow AAAS (chmn. com. sci. in promotion of human welfare 1958-65, dir. 1967-74, chmn. com. on environ. alterations 1969-72), Am. Sch. Health Assn. (hon.); mem. Soc. Biol. Chemists, Soc. Gen. Physiologists, Am. Soc. Plant Physiologists, Sierra Club, Nat. Parks Assn. (trustee 1968-70), Soil Assn. Eng. (hon. life v.p.), Am. Chem. Soc., Am. Soc. Biol. Chemists, Fedn. Am. Scientists, Ecol. Soc. Am., Inst. Environmental Edn. (trustee), Phi Beta Kappa, Sigma Xi. Office: Queens Coll Ctr for Biol Natural Systems Flushing NY 11367 E-mail: commoner@cbns.qc.edu.

COMMONS, RICHARD B., headmaster; m. Lindsay Commons. BA, U. Va.; MA, Stanford U., Breadloaf Sch. of English, Middlebury Coll. Former staff mem. Camp Dudley, YMCA, Woodberry Forest Sch., Va., McDonough Sch., Md.; headmaster Groton Sch., Groton, Mass., 2002—. Bd. trustees Groton Sch., 2004—05. Office: Groton Sch Box 991 Farmers Row Groton MA 01450-0991*

COMP, PHILIP CINNAMON, medical researcher; b. Kewanee, Ill., Feb. 28, 1945; s. Franklin Howard and Alberta (Cinnamon) C.; m. Carol Lee Winter, May 11, 1974; children: Vanessa Cinnamon, Justin Philip, Aubrie Elizabeth. BA, Reed Coll., 1967; MD, U. Wash., 1971; PhD, U. Okla., 1978. Intern, then resident U. Pa. Hosp., Phila., 1971-74; fellow allergy sect. U. Okla. Health Sci. Ctr., Oklahoma City, 1974-76, asst. prof. medicine, 1976-82, assoc. prof. medicine, 1982-88, prof. medicine, 1988—, dir. thrombosis/coagulant lab., 1979—99, dir. gen. clin. rsch. ctr., 2000—04; attending physician med. svc. VA Med. Ctr., Oklahoma City, 1976—, assoc. chief of staff rsch., 1992—; dir. adult sect. Okla. Comprehensive Hemophilia Treatment Ctr., Oklahoma City, 1980—. Affiliated mem. cardiovasc. biology rsch. program Okla. Med. Resident Found., Oklahoma City, 1988—; program dir. Gen. Clin. Rsch. Ctr., 2000—04. Avocations: amateur mycology, breadmaking. Office: VA Med Ctr 921 NE 13th St (151) Oklahoma City OK 73104 Office Phone: 405-271-6466.

COMPAGNON, ANTOINE MARCEL, French language educator; b. Brussels, July 20, 1950; came to U.S., 1985; s. Jean and Jacqueline (Terlinden) C. Ecole, Nat. des Ponts et Chaussees, Paris, 1975; D es Lettres, U. Paris VII, 1985. Rsch. attache Centre Nat. de la Recherche Scientifique, Paris, 1975-78; lectr. Ecole Poly., Paris, 1978-85, French Inst., London, 1980-81, U. Rouen, France, 1981-85; prof. Columbia U., N.Y.C., 1985—, Blanche W. Knopf prof., 1991—; prof. U. Le Mans, France, 1989-90, U. Paris, Sorbonne, 1994—. Vis. prof. U. Pa., Phila., 1986, Phila., 90. Author: La Seconde Main, 1979, Ferragosto, 1985, Proust entre deux Siecles, 1989; editor: Marcel Proust, Sodome et Gomorrhe, 1988. Fellowship Found. Thiers, 1975-78, Guggenheim Found., 1988, All Souls Coll., Oxford U., 1994. Mem. Am. Acad. Arts and Scis. Office: Columbia U 517 Philosophy Hall New York NY 10027 E-mail: amc6@columbia.edu.

COMPAIN, RITA, librarian; b. N.Y.C., Dec. 4, 1926; d. Benjamin and Sara (Modell) Romer; m. Ernest A. Compain, Apr. 17, 1948 (div. 1987); children: Michael, Daniel, Andrew. BS, CUNY, 1947; MLS, L.I. U., 1963; Profl. Dipl., St. John's U., N.Y.C., 1975; postgrad., Columbia U., 1969-70, Lang. & Lit. Inst. Genosee, 1985. Children's librarian Bklyn. Pub. Library, 1947-49; library coordinator Oceanside (N.Y.) pub. schs., 1959-61; librarian Franklin Sq. (N.Y.) pub. schs., 1961-71; staff developer BOCES Nassau, Jericho, N.Y., 1974-76, BOCES Ulster County, N.Y., 1992-93; serials librarian Am. Mus. Natural History, N.Y.C., 1977-79; library cons. Rita Compain Agy., N.Y.C., 1980-85; project dir. "Open Sesame" Am. Reading Council, N.Y.C., 1985-88; staff developer library media Kingston (N.Y.) pub. schs., 1988-93. Asst. prof. L.I. U., Greenvale, 1969-75; libr. cons. Great Neck Pub. Schs., 1975-76; adj. prof. SUNY, New Paltz, 1988-94, U. South Fla., Sarasota, 1996-99; ednl. cons.; lectr. in field; mem. com. nassau County Jail Libr. Pilot Program, East Meadow, 1979. Contbg. author: Open Sesame Guide to Implementation, 1987; contbg. author, dir. video: Teacher Training Film, 1986; author: New Connections: An Integrated Approach to Literacy, 1994, Giants a Thematic Guide, 1992. Recipient Educator award, Young Playwrights Festival, 2001, 2002. Mem. Nassau-Suffolk Sch. Libr. Assn. (pres. 1969-70), Amnesty Internat., Delta Kappa Gamma. Avocations: tennis, golf, travel. Home: 7742 Whitebridge Gln University Park FL 34201-2244 Personal E-mail: bechev@comcast.net.

COMPANS, RICHARD W., microbiology educator; b. Syracuse, N.Y., Sept. 15, 1940; m. Marian Merly Compans. BA magna cum laude, Kalamazoo Coll., 1963; PhD, Rockefeller U., 1968. Asst. prof. The Rockefeller U., 1969-73, assoc. prof., 1973-75; prof. dept. microbiology The U. Ala., Birmingham, 1975-92, prof. dept. biochemistry, 1985-92; prof., chmn. dept. microbiology and immunology Emory U., 1992—. Guest investigator Inst. Cancer Rsch., Villejuif, France, 1968; hon. fellow John Curtin Sch. Med. Rsch., Canberra, Australia, 1968-69; vis. scientist Nat. Inst. Med. Rsch., Mill Hill, U.K., 1998-99; vis. investigator Scripps Clinic and Rsch. Found., 1982; vis. prof. U. Geneva, 1988-89, U. Marburg, Germany, 1999; numerous univ. appointments including sr. scientist Cancer Ctr., U. Ala., 1975-92; dir. Electron Microscope Core Facility, 1975-92dir. Molecular Cell Biology Grad. Program, 1982-92, others; mem. various virology task forces. Editor: Virus Research, 1983—2002; mem. editl. bd. Jour. Gen. Virology, 1972—77, Jour. Virology, 1974—82, 1991—94, Intervirology, 1974—90, Virology, 1974—76, 1992—, CRC Handbook Series in Clin. Lab. Sci., Archives of Virology, 1980—83, Jour. Biol. Chemistry, 1983—88, Current Topics Microbiology and Immunology, 1985—; contbr. numerous articles to profl. jours. Recipient Wright A. Gardner award Ala. Acad. Scis., 1988, Alexander von Humboldt Rsch. award, 1999; grantee NIH, 1972—, others. Mem. Am. Acad. Microbiology, Am. Soc. Virology, Am. Soc. Biol. Chemists, Am. Soc. Cell Biology, Am. Assn. Immunologists, Soc. Gen. Microbiology, Am. Soc. Microbiology, Soc. Mucosal Immunology, Phi Beta Kappa. Office: Emory U Sch Med Dept Micro & Immunology Rm 3001 1510 Clifton Rd NE Atlanta GA 30322-4218 Office Phone: 404-727-8230. E-mail: rcompan@emory.edu.

COMPER, TONY (F. ANTHONY COMPER), bank executive; b. Toronto, Ont., Can., Apr. 24, 1945; m. Elizabeth Comper. BA in English, U. Toronto, 1966; DHL (hon.), Mt. St. Vincent U. With Bank of Montreal, 1967—, with ops. and sys. group, 1971-82, sr. v.p. personal banking, 1982, sr. v.p., sr. ops. officer treasury group, 1982-84, sr. v.p., mgr. London br., 1984-86, sr. v.p., sr. mktg. officer corp. and govt. banking, 1986-87, exec. v.p. ops., 1987-89, pres., chief gen. mgr., COO, 1989-90, pres., COO, 1990-99, pres., CEO, 1999, chmn., CEO, 1999—2004, pres., CEO, 2004—, also bd. dirs. Bd. dirs. Bank of Montreal and subs., Harris Fin. Corp., BMO Nesbitt Burns Corp. Ltd., Internat. Monetary Conf. Vice chair, C.D. Howe Inst.; bd. dirs. C.D. Howe Meml. Found., Catalyst, NY; chmn. Catalyst's Can. Bd. Adv.; chmn. corp. adv. bd. Learning Partnership; N.Am. policy com. Can. Coun. Chief Execs.; Forging our Futures campaign com. U. New Brunswick; hon. chair bd. govs. Yee Hong Ctr Geriatric Care; chair Capital Campaign U. Toronto; past chair capital campaign, past chair governing coun. U. Toronto; past vice-chair St. Michael's Hosp.; active Women in Capital Markets Adv. Coun., Internat. Bus. Leaders Adv. Coun. of Mayor of Beijing, Internat. Bus. Coun. World Econ. Forum Can. Club, Toronto. Recipient Human Rels. award Can. Coun. Christians and Jews, 1998, Award of Merit B'Nai Brith, Canada, 2003. Avocations: golf, classical music, theater, art. Office: Bank Montréal First Canadian Pl 100 W King West Toronto ON Canada M5X 1A1

COMPOLY, ALBERT WILLIAM, JR., human services administrator; b. Irvington, N.J., July 13, 1950; s. Albert William Compoly Sr. and Grace Janet Compoly; m. Alice Elaine Stinson, Mar. 9, 1957; children: Albert William III, Paul Edward. BA, Coll. N.J., 1979. Cert. Am. Art Therapy Assn., 1981. Program coord. spl. treatment unit Woodbridge Child Diagnostic & Treatment Ctr., Woodbridge, NJ, 2001—04, ceo, 2004—. Organizer Neighborhood Watch Response Orgn., Asbury Park, NJ, 1980—2004. Staff sgt. USAF, 1971—72. R-Consevative. Roman Catholic. Avocations: model railroads, country music, woodworking, guitar. Home: 319 Lower Lakeview Dr East Stroudsburg PA 18301 Office: Woodbridge Child Diagnostic & Treatment 15 Paddock St Avenel NJ 07701 Office Phone: 732-499-5010. Personal E-mail: lowerlakeview@yahoo.com. Business E-mail: eagle55@ptd.net.

COMPTE, MARIA EMILIA, physician, educator, administrator; b. Buenos Aires, Jan. 17, 1958; arrived in U.S., 1989, naturalized, 2002; d. Alberto J. Compte and Hilda M. Hostansky. MD, U. Buenos Aires, 1984; MPH, TM,

Tulane U., 1992. Cert. Ednl. Commn. for Fgn. Med. Grads., 1995, in tropical medicine and travel health Am. Soc. Tropical Medicine and Hygiene, 2000, lic. Ministry of Health, Argentina, 1984, physician U.S. Med. Licensing Exam. Bd., 1997. Pvt. med. practice, Buenos Aires, 1985—87; med. dir. & program adminstr. Dooley Found. -Intermed, Honduras, 1988—91; dep. med. dir. Item Home-Hosp. Corp., Buenos Aires, 1993—94; vol. program dir. Dooley Found.-Intermed Internat., NYC, 1994—2003, v.p. for programs, 2004—; dir. cmty. medicine Mercy Coll., Dobbs Ferry, NY, 1998—2004, asst. prof., 1998—2004; v.p. programs Intermed Internat., 2004—. Bd. dirs. Intermed Internat., NYC; adj. assoc. prof. St. John's U., NYC, 1998—2000, CUNY, NYC, 1998—2001, Adelphi U., Garden City, NY, 1999. Recipient Excellence in Vol. Med. Work award, Friends of the Americas, 1991; fellow, NY Acad. Medicine, 2002. Mem.: AAUP, APHA, Argentine-Am. Med. Soc., The Global Health Coun., Am. Com. on Clin. Tropical Medicine & Traveler's Health, Am. Soc. Tropical Medicine & Hygiene, Soc. Tchrs. of Family Medicine (assoc.), Infectious Disease Soc. Am. (assoc.), Tulane Med. Alumni Assn., The Cornell Club, Tulane Club NY. Independent. Roman Catholic. Achievements include design, development, implementation, and evaluation of comprehensive rural health and emergency programs for refugees in Central America. Avocations: anthropology, tennis, trekking. Office: Dooley Found Intermed Internat 420 Lexington Ave Rm 2331 New York NY 10170 Office Phone: 212-687-3620. E-mail: compte@dooleyintermed.org.

COMPTON, ALLEN T., retired state supreme court justice; b. Kansas City, Mo., Feb. 25, 1938; 3 children. BA, U. Kans., 1960; LL.B., U. Colo., 1963. Pvt. practice, Colorado Springs, 1963-68; staff atty. Legal Svcs. Office, Colorado Springs, 1968-69, dir., 1969-71; supervising atty. Alaska Legal Svcs., Juneau, Alaska, 1971-73; pvt. practice Juneau, 1973-76; judge Superior Ct., Alaska, 1976-80; justice Alaska Supreme Ct., Anchorage, 1980-98, state supreme ct. chief justice, 1995-97, ret., 1998. Office Phone: 907-783-3189. E-mail: atcusa@earthlink.net.

COMPTON, ASBURY CHRISTIAN, state supreme court justice; b. Portsmouth, Va., Oct. 24, 1929; BA, Washington and Lee U., 1950, LLB, 1953, LLD, 1975. Bar: Va. 1957. Mem. firm May, Garrett, Miller, Newman & Compton, Richmond, 1957-66; judge Law and Equity Ct., City of Richmond, 1966-74; justice Supreme Ct. Va., Richmond, 1974-2000, sr. justice, 2000—. Trustee Collegiate Schs., Richmond, 1972-89, chmn. bd., 1978-80; former chmn. adminstrv. bd. Ginter Park United Meth. Ch., Richmond; former mem. adminstrv. bd. Trinity United Meth. Ch., Richmond; trustee Washington and Lee U., 1978-90. With USN, 1953-56, USNR, 1956-62. Decorated Letter of Commendation. Mem. Va. Bar Assn., Va. State Bar, Bar Assn. City Richmond, Washington and Lee U. Alumni Assn. (past pres., dir.), Omicron Delta Kappa, Phi Kappa Sigma, Phi Alpha Delta. Clubs: Country of Va. Office: Va Supreme Ct 100 N 9th St Richmond VA 23219-2335

COMPTON, CHARLES DANIEL, chemistry professor; b. Elizabeth, NJ, Jan. 8, 1915; s. Charles Daniel and Janie (Little) C.; m. Ida Lightman, Dec. 19, 1953. AB cum laude, Princeton U., 1940; PhD in Chemistry, Yale U., 1943. Rsch. chemist Calco Chem. Co., 1943; instr. Princeton, 1944-46; rsch. assoc. Manhattan Dist. Project, Princeton, 1943-45; faculty Williams Coll., 1946—, prof., 1957—, chmn. chemistry dept., 1964-74, Halford R. Clark prof. natural sci., 1966-72, Ebenezer Fitch prof. chemistry, 1972-77, Ebenezer Fitch prof. chemistry emeritus, 1977—. Lectr. chemistry New Coll., U. South Fla., 1979-81. Author: Introduction to Chemistry, 1958, Inside Chemistry, 1979, Japanese transl., 1982; contbr. articles to profl. jours. Allied Chem. and Dye Co. fellow, Yale U., 1942—43. Fellow AAAS; mem. Am. Chem. Soc., Phi Beta Kappa, Sigma Xi. Address: 3409 26th St W Apt 113 Bradenton FL 34205

COMPTON, CLYDE D., lawyer; BA in Polit. sci., DePauw Univ.; JD, Ind. Univ. Sch. of Law, Bloomington. Atty. Portage City Coun. and Portage Twp. Trustee, Hodges & Davis, Merrillville, Ind. Bd. dir. (past pres.) Vis. Nurse Assn.; bd. dir. Salvation Army, Goodwill Industries; mem. (past pres.), Ind. Univ. Law Sch. Alumni Assn.; master Calumet Am. Inn of Ct. Mem.: Am. Trial Lawyers Assn., Ind. Bar Found. (dir., treas., sec., pres.), Lake County Bar Assn., Am. Bar Assn., Indiana State Bar Assn. (pres.-elect 2004, bd. mgrs., mem., Ho. of Del., treas.). Presbyn. Office: Hodges & Davis 8700 Broadway Merrillville IN 46410

COMPTON, DORIS MARTHA, lay worker; b. Eudora, Kans., July 9, 1927; d. Roscoe John and Mabel Ann Robinson; 1 child, Christine Lee Compton-Smith. BA, Ft. Hays State U., Hays, Kans., 1949; MA, U. Ark., Fayetteville, 1951; Cert. Lay Pastor, Sterling (Kans.) Coll., 2000. Commissioned Lay Pastor Presbytery of No. Kans./Kans., 2000; life credential tchr. Dept. of Edn./Kans., 1951. Tchr. of English, speech, journalism, drama, and Latin Kans. Pub. Schs., Winfield, Ashland, Marysville, Washington, 1951—71; English instr. Am. U. Cairo, 1972—74; founder and dir. Colegio Internacional Miguel Otero Silva, Ciudad Guayana, Venezuela, 1975—80; speech and linguistics U. P.R./Interamerican U., Rio Piedras, PR, 1982—84; temp. English instr. Kans. State U., Manhattan, 1987—89; chmn. English dept. Ramses Coll. for Girls, Cairo, 1989—93; stated supply pastor Little Blue River Parish, Narka, Kans., 1993—97; commd. lay pastor Faith United Ch. Presbyn., Clifton, Kans., 2000—. English instr. for an immersion sch. for ESL Fordham U., San Juan, PR, 1982; completed evaluation for Commonwealth HS, Rio Pedro, P.R. Mid. States Assn., Phila., 1981—82, mem. evaluation team for St. Dunstan's Sch., St. Croix, U.S. Virgin Islands, 1982. Author: (book of poetry) Whisper In The Pines (awards for individual poems); contbr. poems to lit. jours. ($1000 by Am. Poetry Assn., San Francisco, 1985, $200 by Internat. Soc. Poets, Washington, D.C., 1996, First Pl. by Kans. Author's Club, 2000); singer: (solo vocal concerts) Egypt, Venezuela, Am.; performer: (47 dramatic prodns.) Egypt, Venezuela, P.R., Am. Spkr. Presbyn. Ch., 81 cities in Kans., Nebr., Iowa, Mo., Ill.; author of VBS curriculum Presbyn. Ch., Clifton, Kans., 2001—03; display of art and antiquities for schools pub. schs., 5 cities in Kans., 1996—2003. Recipient numerous scholarships for internat. peacemaking, Presbyn. Ch., 1994—. Mem.: Synod of Mid Am. (assoc.; commr. of higher edn. 2001—03), Presbytery of No. Kans. (assoc.), Clifton (Kans.) C. of C. (assoc.). Presbyn. Avocations: music, collecting art and antiquities, poetry, travel, caring for two grandchildren. Home: 207 East Bartlett Clifton KS 66937 Office: Faith United Ch Presbyterian 200 West Hwy Clifton KS 66937

COMPTON, JOHN CARROLL, accountant; b. Woodruff, SC, July 3, 1941; s. Ligon Grant and Thelma (Blythe) C.; m. Monnie Digh, Jan. 7, 1967; children: Gillian Nicole, Jeanne Christen. BSBA in Acctg., U. N.C., 1963. CPA, N.C., Fla., S.C. Sr. acct. Peat, Marwick, Mitchell & Co., Greenville, S.C., 1963-64, supervising sr. acct., 1967-69; treas. Henderson Advt. Agy., Inc., Greenville, 1969-70; audit mgr. Cherry, Bekaert & Holland, Charlotte, N.C., 1970-71, ptnr., 1971-75, resident mng. ptnr., 1975-76, 1976-78, asst. dir. acctg. and auditing, 1978-80, resident mng. ptnr., 1980-85, dir. acctg. and auditing Greensboro, NC, 1985—99, dir. quality and compliance, 1999—. Treas., exec. com., chmn. fin. com. of bd. trustees All Children's Hosp.; vice-chmn., bd. dirs. All Children's Found.; past pres., exec. com., bd. dirs. Suncoast Ronald McDonald House, Inc.; sr. warden St. Thomas' Episc. Ch. Lt. (j.g.) USNR, 1963-67. Mem. AICPA (past com. on banking, auditing stds. bd., ethics divsn. spl. taks force on firms performing govtl. grant audits, adv. bd. Nat. Sch. Banking), Fla. Inst. CPAs (practice rev. com., chmn. com. legis. policy, quality control com., pvt. cos., practice sect. com.), Nat. Assn. Corp. Dirs., Assn. Govt. Accts., NC Assn. CPAs, Inst. Mgmt. Accts., Greensboro City Club, Greensboro Country Club. Independent. Office: 100 S Elm St Ste 500 Greensboro NC 27401-2639 Business E-Mail: jcompton@cbh.com.

COMPTON, JOHN JOSEPH, philosophy educator; b. Chgo., May 17, 1928; s. Arthur Holly and Betty Charity (McCloskey) C.; m. Marjorie Ann Yaple, July 8, 1950; children: Elizabeth Holly, Catherine Marchus, John Arthur. BA, Coll. of Wooster, 1949; MA, Yale U., 1951, PhD, 1953. Asst. prof. philosophy Vanderbilt U., Nashville, 1952-55, assoc. prof., 1955-68, prof., 1968-98, prof. emeritus, 1998—, chmn. or acting chmn. dept., 1966-73, 84-85, 88-89, 93-95. Vis. prof. Colo. Coll., Colorado Springs, 1977, Wesleyan U., Middletown, Conn., 1984. Contbr. articles to profl. jours. and chpts. in books. Mem. bd. advisers Matchette Found., 1968—; trustee Coll. of Wooster, Ohio, 1975—. Recipient Harbison award for disting. teaching Danforth Found., 1966; fellow Belgian-Am. Edn. Found., 1956-57, sr. fellow NEH, 1974-75, fellow Ctr. for Humanities, Wesleyan U., 1974-75. Mem. AAAS, AAUP, Am. Philos. Assn. (sec. ea. div. 1970-73, v.p. 1974), Metaphys. Soc. Am. (pres. 1979), Soc. for Phenomenology and Existential Philosophy, So. Soc. for Philosophy and Psychology, Philosophy of Sci. Assn., Soc. for Values in Higher Edn. (Kent fellow 1951), Phi Beta Kappa. Democrat. Avocations: hiking, camping, gardening, choral singing, cooking. Home: 3708 Whitland Ave Nashville TN 37205-2430 E-mail: jjcompton@aol.com.

COMPTON, MICHAEL, music educator; s. Mary Jane Chaffee; m. Andrea Arnold, June 25, 1988; children: Ian, Nathan. MA, Calif. State U., Sacramento, 1993. Dir. music Galt (Calif.) H.S., 1990—95; dir. bands Barton County C.C., Great Bend, Kans., 1995—.

COMPTON, NORMA HAYNES, retired dean, artist; b. Washington, Nov. 16, 1924; d. Thomas N. and Lillian (Laffin) Haynes; m. William Randall Compton, Mar. 27, 1946; children: William Randall, Anne Elizabeth. AB, George Washington U., 1950; MS, U. Md., 1957, PhD, 1962; D of Letters, Purdue U., 1996. Rschr. Julius Garfinckel & Co., Washington, 1955; tchr. Montgomery Blair High Sch., Silver Spring, Md., 1955-57; instr. U. Md., 1957-60, teaching and rsch. fellow Inst. Child Study, 1960-61, assoc. prof., 1962-63; psychology extern St. Elizabeths Hosp., Washington, 1962-63; assoc. prof. Utah State U., 1963-64, prof., 1964-68, head dept. clothing and textiles, 1963-68, dir. Inst. for Rsch. on Man and His Personal Environment, 1967-68; dean Sch. Home Econs. Auburn (Ala.) U., 1968-73; dean Sch. Consumer and Family Scis. Purdue U., 1973-87, prof. family studies, 1987-90; faculty The Edn. Ctr., Longboat Key, Fla., 1991-2000, mem. ednl. adv. bd., 1995-98. Cons. Burgess Pub. Co., Mpls., 1975-81, Nat. Advt. Rev. Bd., N.Y.C., 1978-82; bd. dirs. Armour & Co., Phoenix, 1976-82, Home Hosp., Lafayette, Ind., 1983-89; adv. com. Women's Resource Ctr. of Sarasota, Fla., 1992-96; chair Adv. Commn. Status Women, Sarasota, 1993-96; mem. advocates coun. Family Law Network Sarasota, 1994-2000; exec. bd. Sarasota-Manatee Phi Beta Kappa Assn., 1996-99. Author: (with Olive Hall) Foundations of Home Economics Research, 1972, (with John Touliatos) Approaches to Child Study, 1983, Research Methods in Human Ecology/Home Economics, 1988; contbr. articles to profl. jours. Trustee Plymouth Harbor Inc., Sarasota, 2003—; pres. Plymouth Harbor Residents Assn., Sarasota, 2005—. Recipient Woman of Impact Lifetime Achievement award, 1997. Mem.: PEO, APA, Nat. League Am. Pen Women (v.p. Sarasota br. 2000—04), Am. Assn. Family and Consumer Sci., Bird Key Yacht Club, Sigma Xi, Phi Beta Kappa, Psi Chi, Omicron Nu, Phi Kappa Phi. Congregational United Ch. Christ. E-mail: normahc@aol.com.

COMPTON, OLIN RANDALL, consulting electrical engineer, researcher; b. Parsons, W.Va., Apr. 12, 1925; s. Troy William and Strauda Belle (Robinson) C.; m. Patricia Ruth Osborne, June 3, 1947; children: Patricia Randall, Olin Bryan, Lisa Adrienne, Barry Christopher. BSEE, W.Va. U., 1949; Cert., Advanced Sch. Electric Utility Engring., Pitts., 1961. Registered profl. engr., Va. Jr. engr. Va. Electric & Power Co., Richmond, 1949-56, asst. supt elec. equipment, 1956-59, supt. elect. equipment, 1959-64, asst. substa. engr., 1965-79, elec. systems coord., 1979-83, corp. engring. advisor, 1983-85, prin. engr., 1985-91; pvt. practice cons., elec. rsch. Richmond, 1991—. Chmn. C76 Am. Nat. Standards Inst., Washington, 1968-72, C29, 1983-86; U.S. expert on transformers Internat. Electrochem. Commn., Geneva, Switzerland, 1982-86, on insulators, 1986-89. Contbr. 60 articles to profl. jours. Dir. Ctrl. Va. Ednl. TV Group, Richmond, 1972-79; commr. Tuckahoe Little League, Richmond, 1972-80; dir. United Meth. Lay Tng. Sch., Richmond, 1973-79; Native Am. Ministries coord. Va. Conf. United Meth. Ch., 1995—; chmn. State Spl. Edn. Adv. Com., Richmond, 1976-79; constrn. chmn., 1995-97, bd. dirs. Richmond Metro Habitat for Humanity, Inc., 1995—. 2d lt. USAAF, 1943-47. Fellow IEEE (chmn. substa. com. 1976-78, chmn. transformer com. 1985-88, Disting Svc. awards, best paper prizes 1948, 89). Republican. Avocation: bible study. Home and Office: 8423 Kalb Rd Richmond VA 23229-4133 Office Phone: 804-270-3732. Personal E-mail: orcompton@aol.com.

COMPTON, R. BRIAN, finance company executive; s. Ralph Lewis and Marilynn Ruth Compton; m. Theresa Ann Bardwil, Feb. 11, 1984; children: Andrew Brian, Jack Henry. BA in Econs., UCLA, 1982. CPA Calif., 1986. CPA KPMG, L.A., 1982—88; mgr. planning analysis PepsiCola Co. East, Phila., 1988—92; contr. Villeroy & Boch, Princeton, NJ, 1992—94; dir. ops. fin. Coach, N.Y.C., 1994—99; sr. v.p. fin., CFO, CIO Universal Studies Hollywood, Universal City, 1999—2004; pres. Tax Resolution Svcs. Co., Encino, Calif., 2004—. Bd. mem. Discover A Star Found., L.A., 2002—04; scout leader Boy Scouts Am., L.A., 2002—. Mem.: AICPA, Calif. Soc. CPAs.

COMPTON, RALPH THEODORE, JR., electrical engineering educator; b. St. Louis, July 26, 1935; s. Ralph Theodore and Ethel (Evans) C.; m. Lorraine Fielding, Nov. 9, 1957; children: Diane Marie, Ralph Theodore III, Richard Thomas. S.B., MIT, 1958; M.Sc., Ohio State U., 1961, PhD, 1964. Jr. engr. DECO Electronics, Leesburg, Va., 1958-59; sr. engr. Battelle Meml. Inst., Columbus, Ohio, 1959-62; asst. supr. Antenna Lab., Columbus, 1962-65; asst. prof. Case Inst. Tech., Cleve., 1965-67; guest prof. Tech. Hochschule, Munich, 1967-68; assoc. prof. Ohio State U., Columbus, 1968-78, prof. elec. engring., 1978-91; pres. Compton Rsch., Inc., Columbus, 1992—. Cons. to various orgns., U.S., Europe, Israel, 1969— Author: Adaptive Antennas-Concepts and Performance, 1988; contbr. chpts. to books, articles to profl. jours. Fellow Battelle Meml. Inst., 1961; NSF fellow, 1967; recipient Outstanding Paper awards Ohio State Electro-Sci. Lab., 1978, 80, 82, M. Barry Carlton award IEEE Aerospace and Electric Systems Soc., 1983, Sr. Research award Ohio State U. Engring. Coll., 1983 Fellow IEEE (assoc. editor Jour. Trans. on Antennas Propagation 1970); mem. Antenna and Propagation Soc. (chmn. Columbus chpt. 1971-72), Sigma Xi (sec.-treas. Case Inst. Tech. chpt. 1965-67), Pi Mu Epsilon Home and Office: 477 Poe Ave Worthington OH 43085-3036 Office Phone: 614-885-0907. Business E-Mail: compton@ieee.org.

COMPTON, ROBERT H., lawyer; Adminstrv. v.p., gen. counsel Ashland (Ky.) Petroleum Co., until 1988; adminstrv. v.p. Ashland Oil, Inc., Russell, (Ky.), 1988-92; bus. cons., atty pvt. practice, Ashland, 1992—. Chmn. West Penn/W.Va. AAA, 1999—; magistrate Juvenile Ct., Lawrence County, Ohio. Office: HO-7th Fl 1401 Winchester Ave Ashland KY 41101-7555

COMPTON, ROGER H., dean, engineering educator; BS in Naval Arch. and Marine Engring., MS in Naval Arch., Webb Inst.; DEng. in Ocean Engring., Cath. U. Prof., chmn. dept. naval arch., ocean, and marine engring. U.S. Naval Acad.; dean, prof. engring. Webb Inst. Naval Arch., Glen Cove, NY; prof. emeritus U.S. Naval Acad., 2000. Bd. dir. Hydromechanics Lab. USNA. Recipient E.L. Cochrane prize, W.S. Owen award, Webb Inst., 2005. Fellow: Am. Soc. Naval Engrs. (nat. coun., Solberg award 1995); mem.: Soc. Naval Architects and Maine Engrs. (pres. 2005—, fellow, Disting. Svc. award). Office: Webb Inst 298 Crescent Beach Rd Glen Cove NY 11542-1398 Office Phone: 516-671-2215.

COMPTON, TONIA MICHELLE, historian, educator; b. Iowa City, Iowa, July 11, 1977; d. Ancel Eugene and Karen Sue Compton. BA, Columbia (Mo.) Coll., 1999; MA, Tex. A&M U., 2001. Compliance reviewer Mo. Dept. Higher Edn., Jefferson City, Mo., 2001—03; grad. tchg. asst. U. Nebr., Lincoln, Nebr., 2003—. Scholar in-residence Gt. Plains Chautauqua Soc., Bismarck, ND, 2004—. H.Y. Benedict fellowship, Alpha Chi, 1999. Mem.: We. Assn. Women Historians, Am. Hist. Assn., Orgn. Am. Historians. Office: University of Nebraska-Lincoln 612 Oldfather Hall Lincoln NE 68588 Office Phone: 402-472-3269. Personal E-mail: tcompton@hotmail.com.

COMPTON, W. DALE, physicist, researcher, engineer; b. Chrisman, Ill., Jan. 7, 1929; s. Roy L. and Marcia (Wood) D.; m. Jeanne C. Parker, Oct. 14, 1951; children: Gayle Corinne, Donald Leonard, Duane Arthur. BA, Wabash Coll., 1949; MS, U. Okla., 1951; PhD, U. Ill., 1955; D.Eng. (hon.), Mich. Technol. U., 1976. Physicist U.S. Naval Ordnance Test Sta., China Lake, Calif., 1951-52, U.S. Naval Research Lab., Washington, 1955-61; prof. physics U. Ill. at Urbana, 1961-70, dir. coordinated sci. lab., 1965-70; dir. chem. and phys. scis., exec. dir. sci. research staff, v.p. research Ford Motor Co., Dearborn, Mich., 1970-86; sr. fellow Nat. Acad. Engring., 1986-88; disting. prof. indsl. engring. Purdue U., West Lafayette, Ind., 1988—2004, disting. prof. indsl. engring. emeritus, 2004—, interim head Sch. Indsl. Engring., 1998-2001. Mem. Presdl. Commn. for Award of Medal of Sci., 1978—80; mem. vis. com. Nat. Bur. Stds., 1975—79, chmn. vis. com., 1979; mem. coun. Nat. Acad. Engrs., 1990—96, 2000—, home sec., 2000—; bd. govs. NRC, 1991—95, 2000—, mem. com. engring. and tech. sys., 1996—97, chmn., 1997—99. Author: (with J.H. Schulman) Color Centers in Solids, 1962; editor: Interaction of Science and Technology, 1969, Design and Analysis of Integrated Manufacturing Systems, 1988; co-editor (with J. Heim): Manufacturing Systems, Foundations of World Class Practice, 1992, Engineering Management: Creating and Managing World Class Operations, 1997. Mem. energy rsch. adv. bd. Dept. Energy, 1979—80; bd. dirs. Mich. Cancer Found., 1975—86; Coordinating Rsch. Coun., 1983—85; adv. com. Combustion Rsch. Facility Sandia Nat. Lab., 1983—86; bd. govs. Argonne Nat. Lab., 1983—86; mem. Coun. Energy Engring. Rsch., 1983—2001. Recipient M. Eugene Merchant Mfg. medal ASME/SME, 1999, Disting. Svc. award U. Ill. Coll. Engring. Alumni, 2002. Fellow AAAS, Am. Phys. Soc., Soc. Automotive Engrs., Engring. Soc. Detroit, IC2 Inst. U. Tex.; mem. NAE, Rsch. Soc. Am.

COMPTON, WILLIAM F., retired air transportation executive; b. Apr. 1947; m. Dreana Compton. A in Aeronautical Sci., Miami-Dade Coll. Flight instr., 1966; pilot TWA, 1968; exec. v.p. ops. Trans World Airlines, Inc., St. Louis, 1996—97, pres., COO, 1997—99, pres., CEO, 1999—2001, TWA LLC (subsidiary Am. Airlines), 2001; ret. Chmn. TWA br. Air Lines Pilots Assn., 1991-95, mem. exec. bd.; dir., gen. mgr., exec. v.p. Opa Locka Flight Ctr.; pilot Iran Air and Nigeria Airways; chief pilot Make Believe Farm/Arabian Horse World mag.; guest lectr. Stanford U. Grad. Sch. Bus./Law Sch., Midwest Acad. Mgmt.

COMPTON, WILLIAM HENRY, JR., mental health services professional; b. Rockford, Ill., Oct. 6, 1945; s. William Henry and Rosella Louise Compton; 1 child, Edward Errol Ellis-Compton. *Named for father, grandfather and great grandfather. Great grandfather was in the United States Secret Service. Grandfather was an artist who designed for Buffalo Lithograph the Ringling Brothers Circus posters. Father is an engraver and inventor and was listed in Who's Who in the Midwest in 1952.* BA, U. Akron, 1969, MA, 1986. Dir. Project Return: the Next Step, L.A., 1994—. Chmn. bd. Pacific Clinics, Arcadia, Calif., 2003—; bd. mem. Nat. Mental Health Assn., Alexandria, Va., 2002—. Protection and Advocacy Inc., Sacramento, 2002—. Exec. com. mem. Southland Theatre Artists Goodwell Event, L.A., 2000—03. Recipient Clifford Beers award, Nat. Mental Health Assn., 2001, Consumer Adv. award, Internationa Assn. Psychosocial Rehab. Svcs., 2002, The Howie Harp award, Calif. Network Mental Health Clients, 2002, Helping Move Lives Forward Reintegration award (2nd Pl.), Eli Lilly, 2003. Office: Project Return: The Next Step 1138 Wilshire Suite 100 Los Angeles CA 90017 Personal E-mail: bilbelvoir@aol.com.

COMPTON, WILLIAM THOMAS, real estate investor; b. Bedford, Ind., Dec. 1, 1945; s. Thomas Franklin and Dorothy Jane (Smith) C.; m. Nancy Marie Radocchia, Sept. 13, 1969 (div. Aug. 1994); children: Kimberly Dawn, Lindsay Ann. BS in Mgmt., MIT, 1968, Postgrad., 1968-70. Cert. data processor. Sr. systems analyst First Nat. Bank Boston, 1970-73; systems analyst Gen. Computer Systems, Wellesley, Mass., 1973-76; bus. systems analyst Fram Corp., East Providence, R.I., 1976-78; v.p. Span Mgmt. Systems, East Providence, 1978; project leader Prime Computer Inc., Natick, Mass., 1979-81; owner Compton Software Solutions, Tiverton, R.I., 1981-88; prodn. foreman Tillotson Rubber Co., Inc., Fall River, Mass., 1988-89. Author several computer software programs, 1982-85. Loaned officer United Fund Boston, 1970. Mem. Data Processing Mgmt. Assn. (cert. data processing instr. 1985-86). Lodges: Kiwanis (local v.p. 1985, pres. 1985-86). Democrat. Methodist. Avocations: stained glass, model railroading. Home and Office: 250 Ash St Brockton MA 02301-4140

COMSTOCK, AMY L., social services administrator; BA, Bard Coll.; JD, U. Michigan. Attorney U.S. Dept. of Education, 1988—93; asst. gen. counsel for ethics Dept. of Education, 1993—98; assoc. counsel to the Pres. White House, 1998—2000; dir. U.S. Office of Govt. Ethics, 2000—03; exec. dir. Parkinson's Action Network, Washington, 2003—. Office: Parkinsons Action Network Ste 1120 1025 Vermont Ave NW Washington DC 20005 Office Phone: 202-638-4101. Business E-Mail: acomstock@parkinsonaction.org.

COMSTOCK, BETH (ELIZABETH J. COMSTOCK), marketing executive; married; 2 children. BA, Coll. of William and Mary. Program dir. Nat. Cable TV Assn., Washington, Arlington Cmty. TV, Va.; publicist, media mgr. NBC, Washington, 1986, corp. comm. mgr. NYC; publicity dir. media rels. Turner Broadcasting, NYC, 1990-92; dir. entertainment publicity CBS/Broadcast Group, NYC, 1992-93; v.p. news media rels. NBC, NYC, 1993-96, sr. v.p. corp. comm. and media rels., 1996—98; v.p., corp. communications GE Co., NYC, 1998—2003, corp v.p. mktg., chief mktg. officer, 2003—. Dir. Genworth Financial, 2004—. Named Mktg. Executive of the Year, BtoB mag., 2003, PR Professional of the Year, PR Week mag., 2004; named one of Magnificent Seven Gurus of Innovation, BusinessWeek, 2005; recipient Clarion award Women in Comm., 1995. Mem.: Assn. of Nat. Advertisers, Inc. (bd. dir.). Office: GE Co 3135 Easton Turnpike Fairfield CT 06828-0001*

COMSTOCK, DALE ROBERT, mathematics professor; b. Frederic, Wis., Jan. 18, 1934; s. Walter and Frances (Lindroth) C.; m. Mary Jo Lien, Aug. 18, 1956; children— Mitchell Scott, Bryan Paul. BA, Ctrl. Wash. State Coll., 1955; MS, Oreg. State U., 1962, PhD, 1966. Tchr. math. Kennewick (Wash.) High Sch., 1955-57, 59-60; instr. Columbia Basin Coll., Pasco, Wash., 1956-57, 59-60; programmer analyst Gen. Electric Co., Hanford Atomic Works, Richland, Wash., 1963; prof. math. Cen. Wash. U., Ellensburg, 1964—, dean Grad. Sch. and Research, 1970-90; on leave as sr. program mgr. U.S. ERDA, also Presdl. interchange exec., 1976-77; mem. Pres.'s Commn. on Exec. Devel., 1976-77; bd. dirs. Council Grad. Schs. in U.S., 1981-84, dean in residence, 1984-85. Cons. Indian program NSF, 1968, 69, USIA, India, 1985, NSF, Saudi Arabia, 1986; mem. grant proposal rev. panels NSF, 1970, 71, 76, 77, 89, 90; pres. Western Assn. Grad. Schs., 1979-80, sec.-treas. 1984-90; pres. N.W. Assn. Colls. and Univs. for Sci., 1988-89; Russian exch. prof., St. Petersburg, 1993; vis. prof. U. Wash., 1990-91. With U.S. Army, 1957-59. NSF fellow, 1960-61; grantee, summer 1964 Mem. Am. Math Soc., Math. Assn. Am., Assn. Computing Machinery (exec. com.), Soc. Indsl. and Applied Math., Northwest Coll. and Univ. Assn. for Sci. (pres. 1980-83) Methodist. Office: Cen Wash U Dept Math Ellensburg WA 98926

COMSTOCK, ROBERT DONALD, JR., real estate executive; b. Miami, Fla., Sept. 28, 1921; s. Robert Donald Sr. and Gertrude C.; m. Mary Evans, Oct. 12, 1949; children: Carol Frances, Robert Donald III (dec.). BS in Commerce, U. Miss., 1943. Lic. real estate broker. Acct. New Orleans Pub. Service Co., 1946-47; salesman, br. mgr. Capitol Records, Inc., New Orleans and Charlotte, N.C., 1948-51; regional v.p. Atlanta, 1952-57; owner, pres. Comstock Distbg. Co., Atlanta, 1957-74, Comstock and Assocs., Atlanta, 1968-74, Cartridge Control Corp., Atlanta, 1968-80, Comstock Properties, Atlanta, 1980—. Pres. Ctr. for Rehab. Tech., Ga. Tech. U., Atlanta, 1987-91, chmn. bd., 1991—. Mem. Atlanta Arts Alliance, 1970—, Atlanta Symphony, 1970—; bd. dirs. Christian Council Met. Atlanta, 1975-77; trustee So. Ctr. for Internat. Studies; mem. Atlanta Hist. Soc. Served to exec. officer U.S.S. Pollux, 1943-46, PTO. Named #1 Distbr. CBS Records, Columbia Broadcasting, N.Y.C., 1965, 69, Outstanding Distbr. Columbia Phonographs, Columbia Broadcasting, 1968, 70-72. Mem. Atlanta Bd. Realtors, Capital City Club, Commerce Club, Breakfast Club (pres. 1970-71), Trinity Presbyn.

Ch. Men's Club (pres. 1977, Rotary (pres. Atlanta Midtown 1978-79), Omicron Delta Kappa. Avocations: golf, swimming, foreign affairs. Home: 3400 Ridgewood Rd NW Atlanta GA 30327-2418 Office: 3400 Ridgewood Rd Atlanta GA 30327-3029

COMSTOCK, ROBERT FRANCIS, lawyer; b. Lincoln, Ill., June 4, 1936; s. William Bryan and Mary Euceba (Durham) C.; m. Jean Joyce Herring, May 9, 1970; children: James, Michael, Kelly, Jennifer, Margaret. AB, Cath. U., 1958, LLB, 1964. Bar: U.S. Dist. Ct. 1965, U.S. Ct. Appeals (DC cir.) 1965, U.S. Tax Ct. 1971. Ptnr. Comstock & Reilly LLP, Washington, 1965—. Chmn. bd. dirs. Balt. Bancorp, 1991, Met. Fed. Savs. & Loan, Bethesda, Md., 1986-87, Met Holding Co., Bethesda, 1985-87, First Continental Bank, Silver Spring, Md., 1983-86; dir. Nat. Capital Bank Washington, 1999—. Trustee, vice chmn. bd. trustees Cath. U. Am., Washington, 1987—; bd. dirs. Cath. Cemeteries Washington, 1986—, Cath. Youth Orgn. Capt. USAF, 1958-61. Named Knight of St. Gregory, Knight of Holy Sepulchre, Papal Award of Holy See, named to Athletic Hall of Fame, Cath. U., 1985. Mem. ABA, DC Bar Assn., Cath. U. Alumni Assn. (bd. govs.), Columbia Country Club (Chevy Chase, Md.), Univ. Md. M. Club. Roman Catholic. Avocation: sports. Home: 7707 Brookville Rd Chevy Chase MD 20815-3933 Office: Comstock & Reilly LLP Ste 300 5225 Wisconsin Ave NW Washington DC 20015-2014

COMSTOCK, STEVEN MARK, accountant, educator; b. Colorado Springs, Colo. s. J.A. and Jeanne D. Comstock; m. Angela C. Comstock, May 23, 1981; children: Lonigan Print, David Anthony. BSBA, Mo. So. State Coll., 1980; PhD, U. Okla., 1991. CPA, Mo. Sales rep. Armour-Dial Corp., Phoenix, 1980-82; investment broker Merrill Lynch, N.Y.C., 1984-86; acctg. prof. N.C. State U., Raleigh, 1991-93, Mo. So. State U., Joplin, 1993—, chair dept. of acctg. Cons. USN, Norfolk, Va., 1991-93. Contbr. articles to profl. jours. Mem. AICPA, Am. Acctg. Assn., Mo. State Soc. CPA's, Inst. of Mgmt. Acctg. Republican. Office: Mo So State Univ 3950 Newman Rd Joplin MO 64801

COMUS, LOUIS FRANCIS, JR., lawyer; b. St. Marys, Ohio, Feb. 26, 1942; BA, Antioch Coll., 1965; JD, Vanderbilt U., 1968. Bar: N.Y. 1969, Ariz. 1973. Dir. Fennemore Craig P.C., Phoenix, 1975—. Notes editor Vanderbilt Law Rev., 1967-68. Fellow Am. Coll. Trust and Estate Counsel; mem. ABA, State Bar Ariz., Maricopa County Bar Assn. Office: Fennemore Craig PC 3003 N Central Ave Ste 2600 Phoenix AZ 85012-2913 Office Phone: 602-916-5314. E-mail: lcomus@fclaw.com.

CONA, LOUIS, publishing executive; married; 3 children. Grad., NYU. Advt. sales positions USA Today, Scholastic Inc.; sales rep. to advt. divsn. mgr. People mag., 1989—94; pub. In Style, 1996—2001, Vanity Fair, 2001—02, v.p., pub., 2002—05, The New Yorker mag., 2005—. Office: The New Yorker Conde Nast Publs 4 Times Sq New York NY 10036*

CONABOY, RICHARD PAUL, federal judge; b. Scranton, Pa., June 12, 1925; m. Marion Hartnett; children: Mary Ann, Richard, Judith, Conan, Michele, Kathryn, Patrick, William, Margaret, Janet, John, Nancy. BA, U. Scranton, 1945; LLB, Cath. U. Am., 1950. Bar: Pa. 1951. Ptnr. firm Powell & Conaboy, Scranton, 1951-54; dep. atty. gen., 1953-62; assoc. firm Kennedy O'Brien & O'Brien, 1954-62; judge Pa. Ct. Common Pleas, 1962-79, pres. judge, 1978-79; judge U.S. Dist. Ct. (mid. dist.) Pa., Scranton, 1980—, chief judge, 1989-93, now sr. judge. Pres. Pa. Joint Council on Criminal Justice System, 1971-79; mem. Nat. Conf. Juvenile Justice, Nat. Conf. Corrections. Contbr. articles to legal jours. Bd. dirs. Marywood Coll., U. Scranton; apptd. chmn. U.S. States Sentencing Commn., 1994. Mem. Pa. Conf. State Trial Judges (pres. 1976-77, v.p. 1973-76, sec. 1968-73), ABA, Pa. Bar Assn., Am. Judicature Soc. Office: US Dist Courthouse & Post Office Bldg PO Box 189 Scranton PA 18501-0189

CONANT, ALLAH B., JR., lawyer; b. Waco, Tex., July 24, 1939; s. Allah B. and Frances Louise (James) C.; m. Sheila Conant; children: Heather Lee Arsham, Lisa Lynn, Leslie Marie Thorne; stepchild, Thomas R. Bone II. BA, N. Tex. State Coll., Denton, 1961; JD cum laude, Baylor U., 1963. Bar: Tex. 1963, U.S. Tax Ct. 1963, U.S. Dist. Ct. (no. dist.) Tex. 1964, U.S. Dist. Ct. (so. dist.) Tex. 1969, U.S. Ct. Appeals (5th cir.) 1970, U.S. Supreme Ct. 1971, U.S. Ct. Appeals (8th cir.) 1975, U.S. Ct. Appeals (4th and 7th cirs.) 1978, U.S. Ct. Appeals (3d and 11th cirs.) 1981, U.S. Dist. Ct. (ea. dist.) Tex. 1986, U.S. Dist. Ct. (we. dist.) Tex. 1986, U.S. Ct. Appeals (10th cir.) 1987, U.S. Ct. Appeals (2d cir.), 2004. Since practiced in, Dallas; ptnr. Shank, Irwin, Conant, Lipshy & Casterline, 1964-90; owner ABC Ranch, 1981-89; of counsel Whittenburg Whittenburg and Schachter, 1990; mem. Conant Whittenburg French & Schachter, Dallas, 1991-99; ptner. Conant French & Chaney, LLP, Dallas, 1999—. Contbr. to legal jours. Trustee St. John's Episcopal Sch., 1987-90. Fellow Am. Bar Found. (life), Tex. Bar Found. (life), Dallas Bar Found. (life); mem. ABA (coun. gen. practice sect. 1977-80, chmn. 1982-83, del. 1983-86), Dallas Bar Assn., State Bar Tex., Trial Attys. Am., Baylor Law Sch. Counsellors, Baylor Law Alumni Assn. (dir. 1979-82), Baylor Law Rev. Ex-Editors Assn., N.Tex. State U. Alumni Assn. (dir., v.p.), Sigma Phi Epsilon, Omicron Delta Kappa, Phi Delta Phi (historian 1962). Clubs: Petroleum (Dallas). Avocations: swimming, reading, travel, boating. Home: 98 Tanda Trail Trinidad TX 75163 Office: Conant French & Chaney LLP 1601 Elm St Ste 4150 Dallas TX 75201 Office Phone: 214-915-0620. Business E-Mail: abconant@cfc-law.com.

CONANT, DOUGLAS R., food products executive; BA, MBA, Northwestern U. With mktg. dept. Gen. Mills, 1976—86; mgmt. Kraft, 1986—92; with Nabisco, 1992—95; pres. Nabisco Food Co., 1995—2000; pres., CEO Campbell Soup Co., 2001—. Bd. dirs. Applebee's Internat. Inc., NJ Network. Bd. dirs. Safe Am. Found., Students in Free Enterprise; vice chmn. Conference Bd.; trustee Seeing Eye NJ, Intern. Tennis Hall Fame, Newport, RI. Mem.: NJ C. of C. (bd. dirs.). Office: Campbell Place Camden NJ 08103-3878*

CONANT, HOWARD SOMERS, artist, educator; b. Beloit, Wis., May 5, 1921; s. Rufus P. and Edith B. (Somers) C.; m. Florence C. Craft, June 18, 1943; children: Judith Lynne Steinbach, Jeffrey Scott; m. Virginia E. Lusk, June 7, 1999. Student, Art Students League of N.Y., 1944-45; BS, U. Wis.-Milw., 1946; MS, U. Wis.-Madison, 1947; Ed.D., U. Buffalo, 1950. Instr. art, asst. head housefellow U. Wis., 1946-47; asst. prof. art SUNY, Buffalo, 1947-50, prof. art, 1950-55; chmn. dept. art and art edn. also chmn. art collection NYU, 1955-76; head dept. art U. Ariz., Tucson, 1976-86, prof. art, 1986-87; profl. artist, 1987—. Art edn. cons. NBC-TV, also Girl Scouts Am. TV series, 1958-60; field reader, also Title III program cons. U.S. Office of Edn.; adviser N.Y. State Council on Arts, 1962-63, Conn. Commn. on Arts, 1967-68; cons. Ford Found., 1973, Children's Theatre Assn., 1973, Getty Trust, 1985; examiner Internat. Baccalaureate Orgn., 1998. Moderator: weekly TV program Fun to Learn About Art, WBEN-TV, Buffalo, 1951-55; numerous one man shows; represented maj. group exhbns. pub. art mus. and coll. art collections; represented by Sol Del Rio Gallery, San Antonio, Art Source Inc., Tulsa, Ideas and Products, Tucson; executed mural Sperry High Sch., Henrietta, N.Y., 1971, Good Samaritan Med. Ctr., Phoenix, 1982, Valley Nat. Bank, Tucson, 1983; one-man retrospectives, Amarillo (Tex.) Art Mus., 1989, Tucson Jewish Cmty. Ctr., 1995, Sun City (Ariz.) Art Mus., Prescott (Ariz.) Fine Arts Assoc., 1996; author: (with Arne Randall) Art in Education, 1959, 63; author, editor: Art Workshop Leaders Planning Guide, 1958, Masterpieces of the Arts, New Wonder World Cultural Library, Vol. 4, 1963, Art Education, 1964, Seminar on Elementary and Secondary School Education in the Visual Arts, 1965, Lincoln Library of the Arts (2 vols.), 1973; art editor: Intellect, 1975-78, USA Today, 1978-85; assoc. editor Arts mag., 1973-75; contbr. articles profl. publs. Dept. State lectr., India, 1964; Dir. Waukesha County (Wis.) YMCA Art Program, 1946-48; pres., dir. Children's Creative Art Found., 1959-60; mem. adv. com. Coll. of Potomac, 1966; mem. cultural exchange mission to Mex., Ptnrs. of the Ams., 1988, 90; Lt. USAAF, 1943-46. Recipient 25th Ann. medal Nat. Gallery Art, 1966, Disting. Alumnus award U. Wis.-Milw., 1968, Purchase award Richard Florsheim Art Fund, 1992; Disting. fellow Nat. Art Edn. Assn., 1985, Nat. Endowment Arts sr. fellow in painting, 1985. Mem. Coll. Art Assn., Nat. Art Edn. Assn., Internat. Art Critics Assn., Alliance for Arts in Edn., Nat. Assn. Schs. Art and Design, AAUP, Nat. Com. Art Edn. (council, chmn. 1962-63), Inst. Study of Art in Edn. (bd. govs. 1965-72, pres. 1965-68) Clubs: Torch (N.Y.C.) (pres. 1965-66). Studio: 6954 E Cicada Ct Tucson AZ 85750-1395 *I have learned to freely follow my interests from one area of concern or involvement to another without feeling guilty about "putting off until tomorrow what one can do today." I have learned to be an innovator and an enjoyer, rather than a solemn plodder. I have learned how to do two or three things more or less at once, much like an organist handling contrapuntal melodies. As a result, I am a happy artist, author, lecturer and private human being whose multiple interests seem highly compatible and, indeed, essential to one another.*

CONANT, KIM UNTIEDT, retired elementary school educator; b. Del Norte, Colo., July 26, 1944; d. Warren Malvern and Annine (Gredig) Untiedt; m. Spicer Van Allen Conant, July 9, 1966 (div. Mar. 1983); children: Spicer V., Reid F., Lee G. BA in Am. Studies, Scripps Coll., 1966; MA in Secondary Reading, San Diego State U., 1996. Cert. elem. tchr., Calif. Tchr. asst. Greenwich (Conn.) Country Day Sch., 1966-67; tchr. Katherine Delmar Burke Sch., San Francisco, 1969-70, Cupertino (Calif.) Schs., 1968-69, Kachina Country Day Sch., Phoenix, 1980-83, Paterson (N.J.) Schs., 1985, Black Mountain Mid. Sch., San Diego, 1985-89, Bernardo Heights Mid. Sch., San Diego, 1989—2004, ELD coord., 2000—04; ret., 2004. Tchr. trainer Poway (Calif.) Unified Schs., 1996—2004. Fulbright Exch. tchr. Exeter, Eng., 1998-99. Avocations: swimming, reading, gardening. Home: 14735 Poway Mesa Dr Poway CA 92064-2961

CONANT, PATRICIA CAROL, printmaker, educator; b. Boston, Oct. 8, 1939; d. George Bernard and Bernice Jessica (Smith) Madsen; BFA, Mass. Coll. Art, 1961; MFA, Tufts U./Boston Mus. Sch., 1962; m. Ronald Conant, Sept. 2, 1962 (div. 1969); 1 dau., Tara. Art tchr. Boston Pub. Schs., 1962-64, Woburn (Mass.) H.S., 1968-69; mem. faculty Westfield (Mass.) State Coll., 1969—, prof. printmaking, 1977—; group shows include: Mass. Coun. Arts and Humanities, Boston, 1967, 12th-22d Ann. Boston Printmakers Exhbns., 1962-70, 23d Ann. Exhbn., DeCordova Mus., Lincoln, Mass. (Purchase award), 1971, N.Y. Pub. Libr., 1972, Boston Ctr. for Arts, 1972, 76, Conn. Acad. Fine Arts, Hartford, 1976, SUNY, Potsdam, 1976, Silvermine (Conn.) Guild Artists, 1976, Berkshire Art Mus., Pittsfield, Mass. (Graphics award; Cain, Hibbard and Myers Purchase award), 1976, Worcester (Mass.) Art Mus., 1977, Conn. Acad. Fine Arts (prize for Graphics), 1978, Phila. Print Club, 1979, 32d Boston Printmakers Nat. Exhbn., 1980, 4th Miami Internat. Print Exhbn., Coral Gables, Fla., 1980, Silvermine Guild Artists, 1980, Walkey Gallery, Lincoln, Mass., 1982, Wenniger Gallery, Boston, 1982, New Eng. Print and Pot exhbn. Newport Art Mus., 1985, Beth El 63d Exhbn., 1987, Printworks Exhbn., Greenfield, Mass., 1988, Soc. Am. Graphic Artists 63d Nat. Print Exhbn., 1989, U. Mass., Worcester, 1990, Acad. Artist Assn., 1990, G.W.V.S. Mus., Springfield, Mass., 1990, Slater Meml. Mus., Norwich, Conn., 1990, U. Hartford, 1991, Mus. Fine Arts, Springfield, 1991, Springfield Art League, 1992, Schenectady (N.Y.) Mus., 1992, Assoc. Artists Gallery, Winston Salem, N.C., 1992, Conn. Acad. Fine Arts (painting award 1992), Allied Artists of Am., Inc., N.Y.C., 1992, Holyoke (Mass.) Heritage State Park Mus., 1992, Somerstown Gallery, Somers, N.Y., 1992, Acad. Artists Assn., Springfield, 1993, Albany Mus., 1993, Arts Alive Galleries, Springfield, 1993, Chadron State Coll., Ctrl. Coll., Pella, Iowa, 1994, Albany Print Club, 1995, Westfield State Coll., 1995, Art Inst. Permian Basin, 1996, Day Six Gallery, North Adams, Mass., 1997/98; one-woman shows include Westfield Atheneum, 1997; Atlantic Ctr. for the Arts (assoc. artist), 1994, Finalist 1% Arts Wash., DC and Phila., PA, Am. Print Survey, Plainview, TX, 1999, The Boston Printmakers Black and White Exhbn., Boston, Mass., 1999, "Consanguinity", mother/daughter Exhbn. (Tara Conant), Springfield, Mass., 2000, "Small Works", Attleboro Mus., Mass., 2000, "Women Printmakers", Univ. Ctrl. Ark., 2001, New England Watercolor Soc. Exhbn., Marblehead, Mass., 2001, N.E. Juried Exhbn., Springfield Art League, Mass., 2000-02, Mass. Mutual Fin., Springfield, 2004, Westfield State Coll. Faculty Exhbn., Mass., 2004; mural commd. for Charles A. Gallagher Terminal, Lowell, Mass., 1983; mural Westfield Dist. Courthouse, Mass., 1985; mural Baystate Med. Complex, Springfield, 1987, Bench Design "ButtStop ART" SBID & PVTA, Springfield, Mass., 2003; represented in permanent collections: N.Y. Public Library, DeCordova Mus., Library of Congress, U. Pitts., Pine Manor Jr. Coll., Newton, Mass., State St. Bank, Boston. Author (book): Broadsides; (poems) by Robert D'Amato, 1966, Shawmut Bank Baystate Med. Complex. Mem. Boston Printmakers, Springfield Art League, Atlantic Ctr. for the Arts (assoc. 1990), Albany Print Club, Phila. Print Club, Berkshire Art Assn. Home: 13 Heritage Ln Westfield MA 01085-3404 Office: Westfield State Coll Westfield MA 01086 Office Phone: 413-572-5301. Business E-Mail: pconant@wsc.ma.edu.

CONANT, RALPH WENDELL, retired academic administrator, writer, educator; b. South Hope, Maine, Sept. 7, 1926; s. Earle Raymond Conant and Margaret Verrill (Long) Young; m. Audrey Florence Karl, Aug. 27, 1950 (dec. Feb., 2001); children: Beverlie Elaine, Lisa Audrey, Jonathan Arnold (dec.). BA, U. Vermont, 1949; MA, U. Chgo., 1954, PhD, 1959. Asst. prof. Mich. State U., E. Lansing, Mich., 1955-57; rsch. assoc. Nat. Mcpl. League, N.Y.C., 1957-59; asst. prof. U. Denver, 1960-62; asst. dir. Joint Ctr. for Urban Studies, Harvard U. and MIT, Cambridge, Mass., 1962-67; assoc. dir. Ctr. for Study of Violence, Brandeis U., Waltham, Mass., 1967-69; pres. S.W. Ctr. for Urban Rsch., Houston, 1969-75, Shimer Coll., Mt. Carroll, Ill., 1975-78, Unity (Maine) Coll., 1978-80, Conant Assocs., Winslow, Maine, 1980-87; dean Mercy Coll., Dobbs Ferry, N.Y., 1987-89; sr. fellow Phelps Stokes Fund, N.Y.C., 1989—. Author 15 books, including The Prospects for Revolution, 1971, The Conant Report, A Study of the Education of Librarians, 1980, Public Ends, Private Means, 1987, Toward a More Perfect Union: The Governance of Metropolitan America, 2002, (with Daniel J. Myers and Chandler E. Sharp) The Future of Poverty in American Cities, 2003; contbr. articles to profl. jours. Exec. dir. Citizens for Mich., 1959-60; trustee Shimer Coll., 1978—; chmn. Shimer Coll. Found., 1982—; candidate U.S. Congress, 1st Dist., Maine, 1982, 86; mem. Dem. State Com., 1984-92, Maine State Bd. Edn., 1985-90. Named Disting. Alumnus, U. Vt., Burlington, 1978. Office: Asgard Found 1326 Stagecoach Rd Trinidad CA 95570-9705

CONANT, RICHARD PAUL, retired music educator, vocalist; b. N.Y.C., Mar. 16, 1941; s. Russell George and Dorothy Halse Conant; m. Kim Elizabeth Peters, Apr. 15, 1957. AB in Music, UCLA, 1963; MusM in Choral Conducting, U. Md., 1970; DMA in Choral Conducting, U. Tex., 1977. Prof. music U. S.C., Columbia, 1973—2002; choir dir. Trinity United Meth. Ch., Blythewood, SC, 1992—. Opera/concert singer. Mem. disaster action team, pub. affairs officer ARC, Columbia, 2004—05; vol. police officer State of S.C., 1977—2005. Served with U.S. Army, 1966—70. Named to Order of the Palmetto, Gov. S.C., 2002. Mem.: Am. Choral Dirs. Assn. (life). Avocations: scuba diving, reading, travel. Home: 137 Woodlands W Columbia SC 29229 Office: U SC Sch Music Columbia SC 29208 Office Phone: 803-777-4280. Personal E-mail: rconant@sc.rr.com.

CONANT, SALLY LORENSEN, textile conservator, art historian; b. Santa Monica, Calif. d. John Burton Wykoff and Margaret Delene Roth; m. Rogers Leonard Conant, Nov. 26, 1991; children: Kurt Oeler, Rolf Oeler, Paula Oeler, Peter Malcolm Joseph Gross. BA, Wellesley Coll., 1960; MA, Bryn Mawr Coll., 1982, PhD, 1987. From mus. vol. to mus. prof. Allentown (Pa.) Art Mus., 1970—87; tchr. Pa. State U., Media, 1983—84, Reading, 1985—87, Allentown, 1987, Main Line Sch. Night Assn., Radnor, Pa., 1985; asst. to curator of collections Bryn Mawr (Pa.) Coll., 1987; instr. Beaver Coll., Glenside, Pa., 1988; Nat. Endowment for the Arts intern dept. prints, drawings and photographs Yale U. Art Gallery, New Haven, 1988; mem. staff slide and photograph collections Art and Architecture Libr. Yale U., 1989—90; v.p. mktg. MARSARS/Gt. Ea. Marine, Inc., Shelton, Conn., 1991—94; co-owner Orange Derby (Conn.) Fabric Care Ctr., 1991—2004; pres. Orange (Conn.) Restoration Labs., 1991—. Contbr. articles to profl. jours. Originator, coord. Halloween attraction Lehigh Valley Conservancy, 1974; active United Way Lehigh County, Pa., 1977—87; v.p. YWCA, Allentown; mem. exec. com. YM/YWCA Joint Coun., 1981—86, chair membership com., 1983—85, 1st v.p., 1984—86, mem. devel. fund com., 1984—87, v.p., 1985—86; mem. corp. com. Muhlenberg Coll., Allentown, 1984—86, chair annual corp. dinner-theater party, 1984—86; area chair art and antiques night Gt. On-Air Auction WLVT-TV39, Lehigh Valley, guest auctioneer, 1980—86; active troop newsletter Boy Scouts Am., Allentown, 1978—83, chair troop com. New Haven, 1990—91, active troop newsletter, 1989—90. Named Master Bridal Vendor, Assn. Bridal Consultants, 2002; recipient Internat. Dry Cleaners Congress award, 2005; grantee Samuel H. Kress Found., 1984, 1986. Mem.: Assn. Wedding Gown Specialists (exec. dir. 1994—). Office: Assn Wedding Gown Specialists 454 Old Cellar Rd Orange CT 06477 Office Phone: 203-501-5005.

CONARD, ALFRED FLETCHER, legal educator; b. Grinnell, Iowa, Nov. 30, 1911; s. Henry S. and Laetitia (Moon) C.; m. Georgia Murray, Aug. 7, 1939; children— Joy L., Deborah J. AB, Grinnell Coll., 1932, LL.D., 1971; postgrad., U. Iowa, 1932-34; LL.B., U. Pa., 1936; LL.M., Columbia, 1939, J.S.D., 1942. Bar: Pa. 1937, Mich. 1967. Practice in Phila., 1937-38; asst. prof. U. Kansas City (Mo.) Law Sch., 1939-42, acting dean, 1941-42; atty. OPA, 1942-43, Office Alien Property Custodian, 1945-46; asso. prof., then prof. law U. Ill. Law Sch., 1946-54; prof. law U. Mich. Law Sch., 1954-81, prof. emeritus, 1981—. Vis. prof. U. Tex., 1952, U. Colo., 1957, 84, U. Ariz., 1982, U. Calif., Berkeley, 1983, Pepperdine U., 1985-86, U. San Diego, 1989; vis. prof. Stetson U., 1990, vis. scholar, 1991-93; lectr. U. Istanbul, 1958-59, Luxembourg, 1959, Mex., 1963, Brussels, 1965, Salzburg, 1971, Saarbrucken U., 1988, 90; chmn. editorial adv. bd. Bobbs-Merrill Co., 1962-78; exec. com. Am. Assn. Law Schs., 1964-65, chmn. rsch. com., 1968-70, pres. 1971, chmn. bus. assns. sect., 1979. Author: Studies in Easements and Licenses, 1942, Cases on Business Organization, 3d edit., 1965, Automobile Accident Costs and Payments: Studies in the Economics of Injury Reparation, 1964, Corporations in Perspective, 1976, Enterprise Organization, 4th edit., 1987; editor-in-chief Am. Jour. Comparative Law, 1968-71; chief editor bus. and pvt. orgns.: Internat. Ency. Comparative Law, 1965-82; editorial adv. bd. Am. Bar Found. Rsch. Jour., 1976-86. Served OSS AUS, 1943-45. Decorated Purple Heart; Ordre des Chevaliers de la Couronne Belgium; recipient Kulp Meml. award Am. Risk & Ins. Assn., 1965; Guggenheim fellow, 1975 Mem. AAUP (chpt. pres. 1963-64), NRC, Am. Bar Assn. (exec. com. corp. law sect. 1967-71, com. on corp. laws 1974-80, com. on clin. legal edn. 1981-84), Internat. Acad. Comparative Law, State Bar Mich., Am. Law Inst., Law and Soc. Assn. (trustee 1968-75), Council on Law-Related Studies (trustee 1969-74), Phi Beta Kappa, Order of the Coif. Clubs: Rotarian (club pres. 1976-77). Mem. Soc. Of Friends. Address: 80 Kendal Dr Kennett Square PA 19348-2326

CONARD, JANE REISTER, lawyer; b. Eldora, Iowa, Apr. 10, 1947; d. Eugene Lowell and Lois Sylvia (Reed) Reister; m. William Jarrett Conard, June 12, 1971 (div. 1980); 1 child, Tacy Jane; m. Richard A. Maneval, Apr. 8, 1985. BA, Macalester Coll., 1969; MA, U. Iowa, 1971; JD, U. Calif., Davis, 1976. Bar: Calif. 1976, Utah 1983. Legal counsel Calif. State Dept. Health, 1976—78; staff counsel Calif. Dept. Mental Health, Sacramento, 1978—82; counsel Intermountain H ealth Care, Inc., Salt Lake City, 1982—. Chair Utah Dept. Workforce Svcs. Ctrl. Region Coun., 2002—03; mem. State of Utah Health Adv. Coun., 2002—. Trustee Wasatch Canyons Hosp., Utah Disability Law Ctr., 2001—. Mem.: Utah Women Lawyers (exec. bd. 1984—86), Am. Health Lawyers Assn. (exec. bd. 2002—), Salt Lake County Bar Assn. (pres. 1992—93). Democrat. Unitarian. Home: 829 Grandridge Dr Salt Lake City UT 84103-3306 Office: Intermountain Health Care Inc 36 S State St 22d Fl Salt Lake City UT 84111 E-mail: cojconar@ihc.com.

CONARD, JOHN JOSEPH, finance company executive; b. Coolidge, Kans., June 30, 1921; s. Joseph Harvey and Jessie May (Shanstrom) C.; m. Virginia Louise Powell, Sept. 13, 1947; children— Joseph Harvey II (dec.), James Powell, Spencer Dean, John Joseph. BA, U. Kans., 1943, MA, 1947; D. Internat. Law, U. Paris, 1951. Instr. polit. sci. U. Kans., 1946-49, asst. to chancellor, 1970-75; spl. asst. U.S. Mut. Security Agy., Paris, France, 1951-54; editor, pub. Kiowa County Signal, Greensburg, Kans., 1955-70; exec. officer bd. regents State of Kans., Topeka, 1976-82; pres. Higher Edn. Loan Program of Kans., Inc., Overland Park, Kans., 1982-86; v.p. Higher Edn. Assistance Found., 1982-86; legis. liaison Gov. of Kansas, 1987-88. Dir. Haviland (Kans.) State Bank. Mem. Kans. Ho. of Reps., 1959-69; mem. State Fin. Council, 1961-69; speaker of House, 1967-69; exec. asst. to Gov. Kans., 1975-76; trustee William Allen White Found., 1959— . Served to ensign USNR, 1943-45. Summerfield scholar, 1939-42; Rotary Found. fellow, 1949-50 Mem. VFW, Rotary, Am. Legion, Phi Beta Kappa, Sigma Delta Chi, Pi Sigma Alpha, Tau Kappa Epsilon. Republican. Methodist. Home: 904 Joseph Dr Lawrence KS 66049-3255 Personal E-mail: jnvaparis@sunflower.com.

CONARROE, JOEL OSBORNE, foundation administrator, educator, editor; b. West Orange, NJ., Oct. 23, 1934; s. Elvin Hamn and Elizabeth (Lofland) C. BS, Davidson Coll., 1956, LHD (hon.), 1987; MA, Cornell U., 1957; PhD, NYU, 1966; LHD (hon.), Rhodes Coll., 1983; PhD (hon.), U. Md., 1989, Tulane U., 1996. Asst. prof. English U. Pa., 1966-71, assoc. prof., 1971-77, prof., 1977—, ombudsman, 1971-73, chmn. dept. English, 1973-77, master Van Pelt Coll. House, 1974-77, dean faculty arts and scis., 1983-85; pres. John Simon Guggenheim Meml. Found., 1985—2003, pres. emeritus, 2003—. Exec. dir. MLA, NYC, 1978-83; selection com. Commonwealth Award in Lit., 1980-83; v.p. Nat. Book Critics Circle, 1981-85; chmn. Nat. Book Award Fiction Jury, 1988, Pulitzer Prize Fiction Jury, 1989, 94, 97, 2000, 02, Nat. Book Found., 1991-94; bd. dirs. PEN, pres. PEN Am. Ctr., 2002-04, Am. Acad. Poets, Yaddo. Author: William Carlos Williams' Paterson: Language and Landscape, 1970, John Berryman: An Introduction to the Poetry, 1977, Six American Poets, 1992, Eight American Poets, 1994, essays and revs.; editor PMLA, 1978-83. With U.S. Army, 1957-58. Recipient Founders Day award NYU, 1966, Lindback Tchg. award U. Pa., 1970, Disting. Alumni award NYU, 1995; Yaddo fellow, 1973, 76, Guggenheim fellow, 1977-78. Mem. MLA, Am. Acad. Arts Sci., Century Assn., Phi Beta Kappa. Home: 126 W 11th St New York NY 10011-8330 Personal E-mail: jc@gf.org.

CONATON, MICHAEL JOSEPH, diversified financial services company executive; b. Detroit, Aug. 3, 1933; s. John Martin and Margaret Alice (Cleary) C.; m. Nancy D. Kelley, June 13; children: Catherine, Macaira (dec.), Michael, Margaret, Elizabeth. BS, Xavier U., 1955. Public accountant Stanley A. Hitter, C.P.A., Cin., 1956-58; controller The Moloney Co., Albia, Iowa, 1958-61; v.p. fin. The Midland Co., Cin., 1961-80, sr. v.p., chief fin. officer, 1980-83, exec. v.p., chief fin. officer, 1983-88, pres., chief operating officer, 1988—, also dir., vice-chmn., 1998—. Interim pres. Xavier U., 1990-91. City councilman, Albia, 1959-61; trustee, chmn. bd. Xavier U., 1972. Served to lt. USMC, 1955-56. Mem. Fin. Execs. Inst., New Ohio Inst. (chmn.), Cin. Soc. Fin. Analysts, Athenaeum of Ohio (trustee), Met. Club (chmn. bd.). Home: 736 Elsinboro Dr Cincinnati OH 45226-1706 Office: The Midland Company PO Box 1256 Cincinnati OH 45201-1256 Office Phone: 513-947-5211.

CONATY, WILLIAM J., electric power industry executive; b. Johnson City, N.Y., Dec. 30, 1945; m. Sue Wonsettler; children: Kim, Kelly. BSBA, Bryant Coll., 1967. With corp. mfg. mgmt. program GE, 1967-71, various transp. divsn. Erie, Grove City, Pa., 1971-78, plant mgr. diesel engine plant Grove City, 1978-79, with aerospace human resources, 1979-81, mgr. plant rels., 1981-84; mgr. human resources GE Aircraft Engines, Lynn, Mass., 1984-87, head human resources, 1987-90, officer, v.p. human resources Evendale, Ohio, 1990-93; sr. v.p. corp. human resources GE, 1993—. Named HR Exec. of Yr., Human Resource mag., 2004. Office: GE 3135 Easton Tpke Fairfield CT 06828-0001 Office Phone: 203-373-2211. Office Fax: 203-373-3131. E-mail: bill.conaty@corporate.ge.com.*

CONAWAY, CHARLES C., former retail company executive; b. Saginaw, Mich., June 9, 1960; s. Corinne Conaway; m. Lisa deBeaubien; 2 children. BS in acctg., Mich. State U., 1982; MBA in fin., U. Mich., 1984. Co-founder, exec. v.p., COO Reliable Drug Stores, Inc., Indpls., 1989-92; sr. v.p. pharmacy CVS Corp., Woonsocket, RI, 1992-95, exec. v.p., CFO, 1995-99, pres., COO, 1999-2000; chmn., CEO Kmart Corp., Troy, Mich., 2000—02.

CONAWAY, JANE ELLEN, elementary school educator; b. Fostoria, Ohio, July 9, 1941; d. Robert and Virginia C. BA in Elem. Edn., Mary Manse Coll., Toledo, Ohio, 1966—67; MEd in Elem. Edn., U. Ariz., 1969; postgrad. in reading, U. Toledo, 1975—77; postgrad., U. Wis., 1987—. Cert. reading specialist in diagnostic and remedial reading Wis. Tchr. Sandusky pub. schs., Ohio, 1969—70; coord. 1st grade small group instrn. program St. Mary's Grade Sch., Sandusky, 1970—71; tchr. Title I remedial reading Eastwood Local schs., Pemberville, Ohio, 1971—87; dist. dir. Right to Read program; reading specialist Middleton-Cross Plains (Wis.) Area Sch. Dist., 1987—. Mem.: NEA, Wis. State Reading Assn., Madison Area Reading Coun., Middleton Edn. Assn., Wis. Edn. Assn., Delta Kappa Gamma. Home: 1302 Wexford Dr Waunakee WI 53597-1842 Office: Middleton Cross Plains Sch Dist Sauk Trail Sch 2205 Branch St Middleton WI 53562-2840 Office Phone: 608-829-9190.

CONAWAY, JOAN WELIKY, biochemist; d. Irving and Virginia Weliky; m. Ronald C. Conaway, Dec. 4, 1982. AB in Chemistry, Biology with honors, Bryn Mawr Coll., 1978; PhD in Cell Biology, Stanford U., 1987. Rsch. fellow DNAX Inst. Molecular and Cellular Biology, Palo Alto, Calif., 1987—88; from asst. prof. to prof. Okla. Med. Rsch. Found., Oklahoma City, 1989—2001; adj. prof. U. Okla. Health Sci. Ctr., Oklahoma City, 1991—; assoc. investigator Howard Hughes Med. Inst., 1997—2001; prof. U. Kans. Med. Ctr., Kansas City, 2001—; investigator Stowers Inst. for Med. Rsch., Kansas City, 2001—. Mem. molecular biology study sect. NIH, 1994—98; presenter, spkr. in field. Mem. editl. bd.: Jour. Biol. Chemistry, 1993—98, assoc. editor:, 1999; contbr. articles to profl. jours. Fellow: Am. Acad. Arts and Scis.; mem.: Am. Soc. for Biochemistry and Molecular Biology (councilor 2004—). Office: Stowers Inst for Med Rsch 1000 E 50th St Kansas City MO 64110 Office Phone: 816-926-4091. E-mail: jlc@stowers-institute.org.

CONAWAY, MARGARET GRIMES (PEGGY CONAWAY), library administrator; b. Minot, N.D., June 6, 1944; d. John Francis and Veronica Ann (McCarthy) Grimes; m. Steven L. Conaway, July 15, 1967 (div. July 1991); 1 child, Anne Marie. BS in Edn., Minot State Coll., 1966; MA in English, San Jose State U., 1978, MLS, 1988. Cert. secondary tchr., Calif.; cert. c.c. tchr., Calif. Instr. Boise (Idaho) Ind. H.S., 1966-67, Santa Maria (Calif.) Joint Union H.S. Dist., 1967-72; libr. asst. San Jose (Calif.) Pub. Libr., 1984-86, libr., 1986-89, sr. libr., 1989-97, divsn. mgr., 1997—2000; libr. dir. Los Gatos (Calif.) Pub. Libr., 2000—. Oper. design project mgr. San Jose Pub. Libr./San Jose State U. Joint Libr., 1998—2000; vice chmn. adminstrv. coun. Silicon Valley Libr. Sys., 2001—02, chmn. adminstrv. coun., 2002—03. Author: (Ency. of Lib.and Info.Sci.) Shared Libraries, 2003, (libr. jour.) One Reference Service for Everyone?, 2000, (book) Images of America: Los Gatos, 2004. Recipient Helen Putnam award for excellence League of Calif. Cities, 1997. Mem. ALA, Calif. Libr. Assn., Pub. Libr. Assn., Libr. Adminstrn. and Mgmt. Assn. Avocations: writing, antiques, history, travel. Office: Los Gatos Pub Libr 110 E Main St Los Gatos CA 95030 Office Phone: 408-354-6895. Business E-Mail: pconaway@losgatosca.gov.

CONAWAY, MATTHEW R, music educator, composer; b. Dearborn, Mich., May 13, 1979; s. Edward Ray and Debra Ann Conaway. MusB, Ind. U., 1997—2001. Teaching Certificate Ind., 2001. Dir. of bands West Lafayette Cmty. Sch. Corp., Ind., 2002—. Staff music arranger Purdue U. Bands, West Lafayette, Ind., 2001—. Dir.: Fiddler on the Roof, Music Man, Joseph and the Amazing Technicolor Dreamcoat. Bd. mem. Ind. U. Alumni Band, 2003—. Mem.: Music Educators Nat. Conf., Ind. Music Educators Assn., Ind. Bandmasters Assn. Personal E-mail: matconaway@insightbb.com.

CONAWAY, MIKE, congressman; b. Borger, Tex., June 11, 1948; m. Suzanne Conaway; 4 children. BBA, Tex. A&M Univ., 1970. CPA. Acct. Price Waterhouse, Midland, Tex.; CFO Bush Exploration, Midland, Tex.; mem. U.S. Ho. Reps., 109th Congress, 11th Dist. Tex., 2005—. Mem. Tex. State Bd. Public Accountancy, 1995—2002. Served U.S. Army, 1970—72. Named Volunteer of the Decade, Midland, Tex., YMCA, 1990. Republican. Baptist. Office: 511 Cannon House Office Bldg Washington DC 20515-4311 Office Phone: 202-225-3605.*

CONBOY, KENNETH, lawyer, retired federal judge; b. 1938; AB, Fordham Coll., 1961; JD, U. Va., 1964; MA in History, Columbia U., 1980. Asst. dist. atty., exec. asst. dist. atty. Manhattan Dist. Atty.'s Office, 1966-77; dep. commr., gen. counsel N.Y. Police, 1978-83; criminal justice dir. N.Y.C., 1984-86; N.Y.C. commr. of investigation, 1986-87; judge U.S. Dist. Ct. (so. dist.) N.Y, 1987-93; sr. litigation ptnr. Mudge, Rose, Guthrie, Alexander & Ferdon, N.Y.C., 1994-95; ptnr. Latham & Watkins, N.Y.C., 1995—. Summer faculty Cornell Law Sch.; adj. prof. of law Fordham Law Sch. Author: Grand Jury Examination of the Recalcitrant Witness, 1977; contbr. articles to profl. jours. Mem. N.Y. State Crime Control Planning Bd., N.Y. Sovern Commn. Capt. U.S. Army, 1964-66. Mem. Am. Soc. Legal History, N.Y. State Bar Assn., Assn. of Bar of City of N.Y., Fed. Bar Coun. Office: Latham & Watkins 885 3rd Ave Ste 1000 New York NY 10022-4834

CONBOY, KEVIN, lawyer; b. Amityville, N.Y., Feb. 23, 1952; BA, Le Moyne Coll., 1974; JD cum laude, U. Ga., 1979. Bar: Ga. 1979. Law clk. to Hon. Marvin H. Shoob U.S. Dist. Ct. (no. dist.) Ga., 1979-82; mem. Powell, Goldstein, Frazer & Murphy, Atlanta; mng. ptnr. Paul, Hastings, Janofsky& Walker LLP, Atlanta. Contbr. articles to profl. jours. Mem. ABA, State Bar Ga., Atlanta Bar Assn. Office: Paul Hastings Janofsky & Walker LLP 600 Peachtree St NE Ste 2400 Atlanta GA 30308-2222 Office Phone: 404-815-2211. Office Fax: 404-815-2424. Business E-Mail: kevinconboy@paulhastings.com.

CONCANNON, GEORGE ROBERT, business educator; b. Berkeley, Calif., June 2, 1919; s. Robert Lawrence and Hilda (Morgan) C. AB, postgrad., Stanford U.; MBA, Harvard U.; postgrad., U. Calif., Berkeley, Hudson Inst., U.S. Fgn. Svc. Inst., U.S. Nat. War Coll., U.S. Indsl. Coll. Armed Forces. Sales exec. Marchant Calculators, Inc.; U.S. govt. v.p. Holiday Airlines; corp. v.p. Kaiser Industries; pres., CEO Concannon Wine Co., Concannon Co.; prof. bus. U. Calif., Berkeley; ret. Mem. Dun's Rev. Indsl. Roundtable; vis. prof. Webster U., Austria, Ecole Superieure Commerce de Tours, France, U. Wollongong, Australia, Urals Electromech. Inst., Russia, Estonian Bus. Sch., Estonia, Concordia Internat. U., Estonia. Contbr. articles to profl. jours. Tech. advisor State of Calif. Econ. Devel. Agy.; bd. dirs. Stanford Camp Assn.; mem. Am. Indsl. Devel. Coun., World Affairs Coun.; vol. chaplain damage unit and ICU Palo Alta VA Hosp. Lt. comdr. USN. Recipient Service to Country award Internat. Exec. S.C. Mem. Urban Land Inst. Home: 2995 Woodside Rd Ste 400 Woodside CA 94062-2448

CONCANNON, JAMES M., lawyer, educator, dean; b. Columbus, Ga., Oct. 2, 1947; s. James M. Jr. and Mary Jane (Crow) C.; m. Melissa P. Masoner, June 9, 1988. BS, U. Kans., 1968, JD, 1971. Law clk. Kans. Ins. Commn., Topeka, 1971; rsch. atty. Kans. Supreme Ct., Topeka, 1971-73; asst. prof. law Washburn U., Topeka, 1973-75, assoc. prof. law, 1976-81, prof., 1981—, dean, 1988-2001. Vis. prof. law Washington U., St. Louis, 1979; active Kans. Commn. on Pub. Understanding of Law, 1983-89, Task Force on Law Enforcement Consolidation, Topeka, 1991-92; mem. Nat. Conf. Commrs. on Uniform State Laws, 1998—, Pattern Instrns. for Kans.-Civil and Criminal Com., Kans. Jud. Coun., 2001—. Co-author: Kans. Appellate Practice Manual, 1978, Kansas Statutes of Limitations, 1988; sr. contbn. editor: Evidence in America-Federal Rules in the States, 1987. Coord. Citizens to Keep Politics Out of Our Courts, Topeka, 1984; mem. bd. dirs. Kans. Legal Svcs. for Prisoners, 2003—; co-reporter Citizens Justice Initiative, 1997-99; chmn. legal com. Concerned Citizens Topeka, 1995-99; bd. dirs. Mut. Funds Waddell and Reed, Inc., 1997—. Master: Topeka Am. Inn. of Ct. (pres. 2001—02); fellow: Kans. Bar Found., Am. Bar Found. (state chair 2002—); mem.: Assn. Am. Law Schs. (com. on bar admission, lawyer performance 1994—97), Kans. Bar Assn. (CLE com. 1976—2001, Outstanding Svc. award 1982, 2003), Washburn Law Sch. Alumni Assn. (life), Order of Coif. Office: Washburn U Law Sch 1700 SW College Ave Topeka KS 66621-0001

CONCHA, MARIO, chemicals executive; b. Bogota, Columbia; BSc in chem. engring., Cornell U.; sr. exec. program, U. Va. Grad. Sch. Bus. With Union Carbide Corp.; internat. v.p. Occidental Chem., 1985—92; pres.-internat. GS Industries, 1992—98; with Ga. Pacific, 1998—, pres. chem. divsn., 2000—. Fin. com. mem. Atlanta Opera, bd. mem. Mem.: Founders Club Chem. Industry, Am. Chem. Soc., Am. Inst. Chem. Engr. Office: 1201 W Peachtree St NE Ste 1200 Atlanta GA 30309

CONCIALDI, MICHAEL F., secondary school educator, speech educator; b. Park Ridge, Ill., Sept. 23, 1972; s. Barbara A. Concialdi. MA in math edn., DePaul U., 2001—03. Partnership acct. First Capital Fin. Corp., Chgo., 1994—95; math. tchr. Rolling Meadows (Ill.) H.S., 1995—. Chairperson - profl. expense reimbursement com. Rolling Meadows H.S., Ill., head coach speech team, graduation coord. Teen counselor St. Marcelline Ch., Schaumburg, Ill., 1992—98. Mem.: Ill. Speech and Theatre Assn., Ill. Coun. Tchrs. Math., Nat. Coun. Tchrs. Math., Internat. Thespian Soc. (v.p. 1989—90), Nat. Honor Soc. Office Phone: 847-718-5725. E-mail: mconcial@dist214.k12.il.us.

CONDAYAN, JOHN, foreign service officer; b. Addis Ababa, Ethiopia, Sept. 1, 1933; s. Vahram Hagop and Sirvart (Parthog) C.; m. Eileen Mary Ferguson, Nov. 6, 1965; children: Christopher Charles, Alicia Elizabeth BS, Bucknell U., 1955; MPA, Syracuse U., 1974; postgrad., Nat. Def. U., 1978. Mng. dir. V.H. Condayan & Co., N.Y.C., 1955-63; joined Fgn. Service, Dept. State, 1965; adminstrv. officer Am. embassy, Niamey, Niger, 1965-67, gen. services officer Manila, 1967-69; spl. asst. to dep. asst. sec. Dept. State, Washington, 1969-71; adminstrv. officer Am. embassy, Copenhagen, 1971-73, exec. dir. Office Fgn. Bldgs., 1974-75, spl. exec. dir. to asst. sec. of state for adminstrn., 1975-77, counselor of embassy Moscow, 1978-80, Bangkok, 1980-82; exec. dir. Bur. E. Asian and Pacific Affairs, 1982-83; dep. asst. sec. for ops. bur. adminstrn. U.S. Dept. State, Washington, 1983-87, dir. office fgn. missions, 1987-89; minister-counsellor Am. Embassy, London, 1989-91; assoc. dir. for mgmt. USIA, Washington, 1991-94, acting dir., 1994; pvt. cons., 1994—. Bd. dirs. Internat. Sch., Copenhagen, 1970-71, Anglo-Am. Sch., Moscow, 1978-80, Am. Employee Assn., Moscow, 1978-80, Am. Employee Support Orgn., Bangkok, 1980-82; mem. assets and liability com. State Dept. Fed. Credit Union, 1985, 92-93, bd. dirs., 1993-98, treas., 1994-95. Recipient Presdl. Humanitarian award (The Philippines), 1968, Meritorious Honor award Dept. State, 1975, Superior Honor award, 1985, 92, Presdl. Meritorious award, 1987, Dir.'s award for Superior Achievement, 1993. Mem. Armenian Orthodox Ch. Avocations: photography, reading, sports.

CONDE, CRISTOBAL I., computer company executive; b. Santiago, Chile; BS in Astronomy and Physics, Yale U. Co-founder Devon Sys. Internat., Inc., 1987—90; head trading sys. divsn. SunGard Data Sys., Inc., Wayne, Pa., 1990—99, COO, 1999—2002, pres., CEO, 2002—; also bd. dirs. Office: Sungard Data Sys Inc 680 E Swedesford Rd Wayne PA 19087

CONDE, JUAN-CARLOS, literature and language educator; b. Madrid, July 7, 1962; s. Antonio Conde and Francisca Lopez; m. Margarita Garzon, Oct. 4, 1991; children: Ignacio, Carlos. PhD in Spanish Philology, U. Autonoma, Madrid, 1994. Rschr. Real Acad. Española, Madrid, 1985—2001; assoc. prof. U. Complutense, Madrid, 1996—2001, Ind., Bloomington, 2001—. Recipient Menéndez Prize, 1994.

CONDE, YVONNE M., freelance journalist; b. Havana, Cuba, Oct. 28, 1950; came to the U.S., 1961; d. Pedro M. and Maria L. Conde; m. B. Loret de Mola, Apr. 10, 1989. BA in Communication, SUNY, N.Y.C., 1989; MA in Journalism, NYU, 1991. Freelance journalist, N.Y.C., 1991—. Author: Operation Pedro Pan, 1999. Recipient award for best news and pub. affairs work Nat. Assn. Coll. Broadcasters, 1991. Mem.: Nat. Assn. Hispanic Journalists. Roman Catholic. Avocation: sporting clays. Home: 340 E 64 St Apt 23B New York NY 10021-7510 E-mail: nytropical@aol.com.

CONDER, DEAN JOSESPH, state agency administrator; b. Walsenburg, Colo., Oct. 31, 1965; s. James Lee and Charolette Rose Conder; m. Kelly Ann McCormack, May 15, 1993; 1 child, Hazel Rae. BS, U. So. Colo., Pueblo, 1989; MS, U. Denver, 1997. Dep. state social security adminstr. State of Colo., Denver, 2001—; mem. Colo. Juvenile Parole Bd., Denver, 2003—. 1st v.p. Nat. Conf. of State Social Security Adminstrs., 2004—; pres. Nat. Conf. State Social Security Adminstrs., 2005. Contbr. articles to profl. jours. Republican. Roman Catholic. Avocations: fly fishing, camping. Home: 1955 Union Dr Lakewood CO 80215 Office: State of Colo 1515 Arapahoe St Denver CO 80202 Office Phone: 303-318-8060. Office Fax: 303-318-8069. Personal E-mail: dean.conder@state.co.us.

CONDIC, KRISTINE SALOMON, librarian, educator; b. Battle Creek, Mich., Dec. 18, 1955; d. John and Helen Salomon; m. Eric Condic, Oct. 6, 1990; 2 children. BA, Western Mich. U., 1979, MSL, 1980. Reference libr. Univ. Nebr., Omaha, 1981-84; coord. computer search svcs. Kresge Libr. Oakland U., Rochester, Mich., 1984-93, assoc. prof., 1993—, coord. electronic resources, 1993—. Contbr. articles to libr. sci. jours. Mem. ALA, Mich. Libr. Assn. Office: Oakland U Kresge Libr Rochester MI 48309-4401

CONDICT, EDGAR RHODES, manufacturing executive, minister; b. Boston, Apr. 27, 1940; s. Clinton Adams and Elizabeth May (Lane) C.; m. Judith Pond, June 9, 1962; children: Edgar Rhodes Jr., Robert Adams, Carolyn Helen. Student, Bucknell U., 1962, U. Pa., NYU. Cert. lic. min., clin. pastoral edn.; ordained min. ABC-USA, 2003. Chmn. bd., pres., founder Bio-Tronics Rsch., Inc., 1962—, Kearsarge Healthcare, Inc., 1978—, Condict Instruments, Inc., 1985—; cons. U. Tex. Med. Sch., 1968-70; pres. Medel Corp., patent devel. investment, 1965—; pres., chmn. bd. Erin Eye Clinics, 1998—. Cons. in med. electronics, electronics, biophysics, biofeedback, telecomm., environ. health and welfare; pastor 1st Bapt. Ch. Lyme (NH), 2002—. Author: A Theory of Anesthesia, 1962, Feedback Anesthesia, 1968, Electronic Pain-Killing Devices, 1970, Healing in 1993, 1993, How Your Brain Works, 1993, Your Temperament, 1993, Mediation and the Law, 1993, Healing in the '90's, 1992, We Need Religion-Now!, 1994, others. Patentee in med. electronics, telecommunications fields. Vol., bereavement coord. Lake Sunapee Hospice, 2001; tchr. ch. sch. Bapt. ch., 1962—97; supt., 1995—97; Am. Bapt. Ch. Cert. Lay Minister program, 1996; trustee Am. Bapt. Chs., Vt. and N.H., 2002; bd. dirs. Lake Sunapee Area Mediation Program, 1988—90, pres., 1990; chmn. bd. World Mediators, 1990—. Recipient various grants in neuro-brain scis.; numerous med. awards from fgn. countries. Mem. Sigma Chi. Avocations: flying, (W1EU), computers. Address: PO Box 1110 New London NH 03257-1110 Office Phone: 603-526-2222. E-mail: ed@condict.com.

CONDIE, CAROL JOY, anthropologist, science administrator; b. Provo, Utah, Dec. 28, 1931; d. LeRoy and Thelma (Graff) Condie; children: Carle Ann, Erik Roy, Paula Jane. BA in Anthropology, U. Utah, 1953; MEd in Elem. Edn., Cornell U., 1954; PhD in Anthropology, U. N.Mex., 1973. Edn. coord. Maxwell Mus. Anthropology, U. N.Mex., Albuquerque, 1973, interpretation dir., 1974-77; asst. prof. anthropology U. N.Mex., 1975-77; cons. anthropologist, 1977-78; pres. Quivira Rsch. Ctr., Albuquerque, 1978—. Cons. anthropologist U.S. Congl. Office Tech. Assessment, chair Archeol. Resources Planning Adv. Com., Albuquerque, 1985-86; leader field seminars Crow Canyon Archeol. Ctr., 1986-97; appointee Albuquerque dist. adv. coun., bur. land mgmt. U.S. Dept. Interior, 1989; study leader Smithsonian Instn. Tours, 1991; mem. Albuquerque Heritage Conservation Adv. Com., 1992. Author: The Nighthawk Site: A Pithouse Site on Sandia Pueblo Land, Bernalillo County, New Mexico, 1982, Five Sites on the Pecos River Road, 1985, Data Recovery at Eight Archaeological Sites on the Rio Nutritas, 1992, Data Recovery at Eight Archaeological Sites on Cabresto Road Near Questa, 1992, Archaeological Survey in the Rough and Ready Hills/Picacho Mountain Area, Dona Ana County, New Mexico, 1993, Archaeological Survey on the Canadian River, Quay County, New Mexico, 1994, Archaeological Testing at LA 103387, Nizhoni Extension, Gallup, McKinley County, New Mexico, 1995, Two Archaeological Sites on San Felipe Pueblo Land, New Mexico, 1996, Four Archaeological Sites at La Cienega, Santa Fe County, New Mexico, 1996, A Brief History of Berino, Berino Siding, and Early Mesilla Valley Agriculture, Dona Ana County, New Mexico, 1997; author: (with M. Kent Stout) Historical and Architectural Study of the Old Peralta Elementary School, Valencia County, New Mexico, 1997, Archaeological Survey of 720 Acres on Ball Ranch, Sandoval County, New Mexico, 1998; author: (with H.H. Franklin and P.J. McKenna) Results of Testing at Three Sites on Tesuque Pueblo Land, Santa Fe County, New Mexico, 1999, Cultural Resources Investigations at the Old Roswell Airport for the Proposed Cielo Grande Recreation Area, Chaves County, New Mexico, 2000, Archaeological Survey in Las Lomas de la Bolsa, Santa Fe County, New Mexico, 2001, A Plethora of Walls...the Vigil Properties, Old Town Albuquerque, 2002; author: (with P.W. Bauer, R.P. Lozinsky and L.G. Price) Albuquerque: A Guide to Its Geology and Culture, 2003; author: (with Carol Raish) Indigenous and Traditional Use of Fire in Southwestern Grassland, Woodland, and Forest Ecosystems, 2003; author: (with Susan Dewitt) Doves Along the Ditchbank: La Orilla de la Acequia Historic District, 2003; author: Main Street Project, Aztec, New Mexico, 2004, Testing Data Recovery at Seven Sites Cabezon Subdivision Sandoval Co., 2005; co-editor: Anthropology in the Desert West, 1986. Mem. Downtown Core Area Schs. Com., Albuquerque, 1982. Ford Found. fellow, 1953-54; recipient Am. Planning Assn. award, 1985-86, Gov.'s award, 1986. Fellow: Am. Anthrop. Assn.; mem.: Albuquerque Archaeol. Soc. (pres. 1992), N.Mex. Archaeol. Coun. (pres. 1982—83, Hist. Preservation award 1988), Archaeol. Soc. N.Mex. (trustee 2001—), Soc. Am. Archaeology (chmn. Native Am. rels. com. 1983—85), Hist. Albuquerque Inc., The Archaeol. Conservancy (bd. dirs. 2003—), N.Mex. Heritage Preservation Alliance, Maxwell Mus. Assn. (bd. dirs. 1980—83), Las Arañas Spinners and Weavers Guild (pres. 1972). Democrat. Avocations: spinning, weaving, gardening. Home and Office: Quivira Research Ctr 1809 Notre Dame Dr NE Albuquerque NM 87106-1011 Office Phone: 505-255-9264. E-mail: cjc1453@gbronline.com.

CONDIT, GARY ADRIAN, former congressman; b. Salina, Okla., Apr. 21, 1948; AA, Modesto Jr. Coll., 1970; BA, Calif. State Coll., 1972. Councilman City of Ceres, Calif., 1972-74, mayor, 1974-76; supr. Stanislaus County, Calif., 1976-82; assemblyman State of Calif., 1982-89; mem. U.S. Congress from 18th Calif. dist., 1989—2002; mem. agr. com. Democrat.

CONDIT, LINDA FAULKNER, retired economist; b. Denver, May 30, 1947; d. Claude Winston and Nancy Isobel (McCallum) Faulkner; m. John Michael Condit, Dec. 20, 1970; 1 child, David Devin. BA, U. Ark., 1969; MA, U. Wis., 1970; postgrad., U. Minn., 1974-77. Rsch. asst. U. Wis., Madison, 1969—70; economist St. Louis Fed. Res. Bank, 1971—73; ops. analyst No. States Power co., Mpls., 1973-76; energy economist, 1976—78; from ecoomist to v.p. Pennzoil Co., Houston, 1978—95, v.p., 1995—98; v.p., corp. sec. Pennzoil-Quaker State Co., Houston, 1998—2002. Econ. cons. Jr. Achievement, 1983. Recipient Alumni award, U. Ark., 1969. Mem. Internat. Assn. Energy Economists (pres., v.p., treas.), Nat. Assn. Bus. Economists, Internat. Bus. Coun. (v.p.), Am. Econ. Assn., N.Am. Soc. Corp. Planners, Am. Soc. Corp. Secs. (membership chmn.), Hits Theatre (bd. dirs.), Corp. Alliance To Eliminate Ptnr. Violence (bd. dirs.), Leadership Am., Harvard Discussion Group Indsl. Economists, Forst Club, River Oaks Women's Breakfast Club (v.p., pres.), Mortar Bd., Phi Beta Kappa, Kappa Alpha Theta. Home: 11822 Village Park Cir Houston TX 77024-4418

CONDO, JAMES ROBERT, lawyer; b. Somerville, NJ, Mar. 2, 1952; s. Ralph Vincent and Betty Louise (MacQuaide) C. BS in Bus. and Econs., Lehigh U., 1974; JD, Boston Coll., 1979. Bar: Ariz. 1979, Colo. 2001, U.S. Dist. Ct. Ariz. 1979, U.S. Ct. Appeals (9th cir.) 1982, U.S. Supreme Ct. 1983, U.S. Ct. Appeals (D.C. cir.) 1989, U.S. Ct. Appeals (10th cir.) 1989, U.S. Ct. Appeals (6th cir.) 1991, U.S. Ct. Appeals (4th cir.) 1994. Assoc. Snell & Wilmer, Phoenix, 1979-84, ptnr., 1985—. Judge pro tem Ariz. Ct. Appeals. Active Ariz. Town Hall, 1985—. Fellow Ariz. Bar Found.; mem. ABA, State Bar Ariz., Maricopa County Bar Found., Defense Rsch. Inst. Office: Snell & Wilmer One Arizona Ctr Phoenix AZ 85004-2202 Office Phone: 602-382-6353. Business E-Mail: jcondo@swlaw.com.

CONDO, PATRICK C., information technology executive; BSBA, Suffolk Univ. Pres., CEO Excalibur Technologies, Vienna, Va., 1995—2001, Convera Corp., Vienna, Va., 2001—. Office: Convera Corp 1921 Gallows Rd Ste 200 Vienna VA 22182*

CONDON, ANN BLUNT, psychotherapist; b. Brockton, Mass., Sept. 25, 1938; d. Hugh Francis and Ann Collins Blunt; m. John Weston Condon, Jan. 2, 1965 (div. Feb. 1966); 1 child, Pamela Condon Porter. BA, Newton Coll. Sacred Heart, 1960; MSW, Boston U., 1981. LCSW Mass.; cert. profl. coach. Pvt. practice psychotherapy, Centerville, Mass., 1982—; pvt. career coach, 1998—; pvt. writing coach, 2000—. Seminar leader Landmark Edn., Quincy, Mass., 1986—92; workshop leader Greening Prodns., Centerville, 1988—. V.p. Svc. Employees Internat. Union, Boston, 1965—69; town meeting mem. Town of Barnstable, 1973—75; trustee Cape Cod C.C., 1975—82. Mem.: NASW (ACSW, diplomate), Altrusa Club Cape Cod (founding mem., 1st pres.). Democrat. Roman Catholic. Avocations: gardening, writing, cooking, baseball. Office: PO Box 58 7 Woodvale Ln Centerville MA 02632 Office Phone: 508-775-2059. E-mail: acondoncapecod@comcast.net.

CONDON, BRODY KIEL, computer graphics designer; b. Nayarit, Mex., 1974; BFA in Sculpture, U. Fla., 1997; MFA in Visual Arts, U. Calif. San Diego, 2002; attended, Skowhegan Sch. Painting & Sculpture, 2001. Visiting prof. Central Nationalities U., Beijing, 2002, ICAM, U. Calif, San Diego, 2003; adj. prof. studio arts U. Calif. Irvine, 2004—. One-man shows include Staring Contest, Sushi Visual Art, San Diego, 2000, Half Life, Marcuse Gallery, San Diego, 2001, Chinatown, C-Level, LA, 2002, Adam Killer, Electronic Orphanage, LA, 2002, EndGames, The Kitchen, NY, 2003, Untitled War, Machine, LA, 2004, exhibited in group shows at Flauma: Series for Non-Architecture, Space Untitled, NY, 2001, Glitch, Oslo Art Acad., Norway, 2001, New Fangle, Herbst Exhbn. Hall, San Francisco, 2002, Provocations, Next Art Festival, Orlando, Fla., 2003, While You Were Playing, Flux Factory, NY, 2003, Digital Media, Am. Mus. Moving Image, NY, 2003, Electrofringe, New Castle, New South Wales, 2003, Whitney Biennial, Whitney Mus. Am. Art, 2004. Geraldine R. Dodge Found. Fellowship, Coll. Art Assn., 2001, Future of the Present Grant, Franklin Furnace, 2002. Office: University California Irvine Irvine CA 92697 Office Phone: 213-413-5625. E-mail: bcondon@uci.edu.*

CONDON, FRANCIS EDWARD, retired chemistry professor; b. Abington, Mass., Oct. 12, 1919; s. Maurice Francis and Eva Isabel (Cole) C.; m. Mary Anna Medvetz, Jan. 9, 1943; children: Francis E., Mary Ellen Condon Laessig, John M., Arthur T., Dorothy A. Condon Waldt, James M., Rita C. Condon McCarthy. AB, Harvard, 1941, PhD, 1944. Research chemist Phillips Petroleum Co., Bartlesville, Okla., 1944-52; asst. prof. chemistry CCNY, 1952-61, assoc. prof., 1962-66, prof., 1967-82, ret., 1982, Louis J. Curtman prof., 1976-78; founder, chmn. Seven Siblings Found., Ltd., 1977-94. Vis. prof. Purdue U., 1960 Author: (with H. Meislich) Introduction to Organic Chemistry, 1960, Study Projects in Physical Chemistry, 1963, Chess monographs, 1992—, also articles; contbr. chpt. to Catalysis, 1958. Mem. planning bd. Borough of Bogota, N.J., 1963; Trustee, pres. Bogota Swim Club, Inc., 1967-71. Petroleum Research Fund grantee, 1967-70; NSF Sci. Faculty fellow U. So. Calif., 1964-65 Mem. Am. Chem. Soc. (dir. N.Y. sect. 1967-68), U.S. Chess Fedn. (life), Glen Rock (N.J.) Chess Club (pres. 1975-79, Washington Twp. (N.J.) Chess Club (pres. 1990-92), Dumont (N.J.) Chess Mates (sec. 1992-99), St. Joseph's Holy Name Soc. (pres. 1974-75, sec. 1992—), Alpha Chi Sigma, Sigma Xi. Home: 471 Larch Ave Bogota NJ 07603-1058

CONDON, FRANK, theater director, playwright; b. Matlock, Derbyshire, England, Dec. 24, 1943; arrived in U.S., 1952; s. Louis and Nettie Condon; m. Kim Simons Condon, July 4, 1983 (dec.); 1 child, Chloe. BA in History and Lit. of Art History, U. Calif., Santa Barbara, 1967, MA in Dramatic History and Lit., 1970; MFA in Directing, U. Calif., San Diego, 1976. Master apprenticeship Dell'Arte Sch. of Comedy, Blue Lake, Calif., 1977; Commedia Dell'Arte cons. Mark Taper Forum, L.A., 1977—79; guest artist Am. Acad. of Dramatic Arts, Pasadena, 1978; assoc. dir. Odyssey Theatre Ensemble, West Los Angeles, 1978—83; guest artist/dir. South Coast Repertory, Costa Mesa, 1978—80; dir. improvisational theatre project Mark Taper Forum, L.A., 1980—81; guest dir. El Teatro Campesino, San Juan Bautista, 1981; assoc. artistic dir. Odyssey Theatre, West Los Angeles, 1983—90; artistic dir. River Stage, Sacramento, 1994—. Vis. assoc. prof. UCLA, 1988—90, U. Calif., Santa Barbara, 1990—93; prof. Cosumnes River Coll., Sacramento, 1994—; dir. numerous original contemporary and classical plays throughout the U.S.; vis. Calif. Arts Coun. Playwright: The Chgo. Conspiracy Trial, 1978; Ghost Dance, 2003; dir.: (plays) The Chgo. Conspiracy Trial, 1978—80, 1991, 1994, 2001, Rap Master Ronnie, 1985—88, McCarthy, 1988—90, Gunfighter: A Gulf War Chronicle, 2001. Recipient L.A. Drama Critics' Cir. Directing and Playwriting award, 1980, Lifetime Achievement award, Sacramento Metro. Arts Commn., 1999, numerous others; Dir.'s fellow, NEA, 1983. Mem.: Nat. Orgn. of Am. Theatre (Theatre Comm. Group), Dramatists Guild, Soc. Stage Dirs. and Choreographers. Office: River Stage 8401 Ctr Pkwy Sacramento CA 95823

CONDON, GEORGE EDWARD, journalist; b. Fall River, Mass., Nov. 6, 1916; s. John Joseph and Mary Agnes (O'Malley) C.; m. Marjorie Philona Smith, May 9, 1942; children— Theresa, John, George, Katherine, Mary, Susan. BSc in Journalism, Ohio State U., 1940. Publicity dir. Mt. Union Coll., Alliance, Ohio, 1941; info. dir. Agrl. Adjustment Adminstrn. for Ohio, 1941-42; mem. staff Cleve. Plain Dealer, 1943-84; TV critic, 1948—62; gen. columnist Cleve. Plain Dealer, 1962-84; pres. George Condon & Assocs., Inc., 1985—. Author: Cleveland-The Best-Kept Secret, 1967, Laughter from the Rafters, 1968, Stars in the Water, 1972, Yesterday's Cleveland, 1976, Yesterday's Columbus, 1977, Cleveland: Prodigy of the Western Reserve, 1979, History of Ohio Farmers Insurance Company, 1985, Gaels of Laughter and Tears, 1995, The Man in the Arena, 1995, West of the Cuyahoga, 2005. Recipient Ohioana Library Assn. Lit. award, 1975, Cleve. Women's City Club Lit. award, 1975, Emily Gray Burke Meml. award lit., 1979; award Cleve. Newspaper Guild; awards for public service, copy editing and column writing Press Club Cleve.; Disting. Service award Nat. Soc. Profl. Journalists, 1980; named to Cleve. Journalism Hall of Fame, Press Club Cleve., 1990. Mem. Sigma Delta Chi, Pi Sigma Alpha. Home: The Waterford 12500 Edgewater Dr Lakewood OH 44107 E-mail: georgec@apk.com.

CONDON, ROBERT EDWARD, surgeon, educator, consultant; b. Albany, N.Y., Aug. 13, 1929; s. Edward A. and Catherine (Kilmartin) C.; m. Marcia Jane Pagano, June 16, 1951; children: Sean Edward, Brian Robert. AB, U. Rochester, 1951, MD, 1957; MS, U. Wash., 1965. Diplomate Am. Bd. Surgery, Nat. Bd. Med. Examiners. N.Y. Bd. Regents scholar U. Rochester, 1957; intern King County Hosp., Seattle, 1957-58; resident dept. surgery U. Wash. Sch. Medicine (and affiliated hosps.), 1958-65; postdoctoral rsch. fellow Nat. Heart Inst., 1961-63; asst. prof. surgery Baylor Coll. Medicine, Houston, 1965-67; assoc. prof. surgery U. Ill. Coll. Medicine, Chgo., 1967-69, prof., 1969-70; prof., head dept. surgery U. Iowa Coll. Medicine, Iowa City, 1971-72; prof. surgery Med. Coll. Wis., Milw., 1972—98, prof. emeritus, 1998, chmn. dept. surgery, 1979-95; chief surg. svcs. Wood VA Hosp., Milw., 1972-81. Attending surgeon Froedtert Meml. Luth. Hosp., 1982-98; cons. Columbia Hosp., Milw., St. Joseph Hosp., Milw.; clin. prof. surgery U. Wash., 2000—. Author: (with others) Abdominal Pain: A Guide to Rapid Diagnosis, 2d edit., 1995, Manual of Surgical Therapeutics, 9th edit., 1996, Hernia, 4th edit., 1995, Surgical Care, 1980. Recipient sr. class award as Outstanding Faculty Mem. Baylor U. Coll. Medicine, 1966, Excellence in Tchg. award Phi Chi, 1967, Cert. Appreciation U. Iowa Coll. Medicine, 1971, Tchr. of Yr. award U. Iowa Coll. Medicine, 1972, Tchr. of Yr. award Med. Coll. Wis., 1983, 95, Disting. Svc. award Med. Coll. Wis., 1993, Disting. Alumnus award U. Wash., 1998; rsch. fellow Guggenheim Found., 1963-64. Mem. ACS (bd. govs.), Am. Surg. Assn. (v.p.), Surg. Infection Soc. (pres.), Am. Assn. Surgery of Trauma, Internat. Soc. Surgery, Collegium Internationale Chirurgiae Digestivae (pres.), Assn. for Acad. Surgery, Ctrl. Surg. Assn. (pres.), So. Surg. Assn., We. Surg. Assn., Wis. Surg. Soc. (pres.), Milw. Surg. Soc. (pres.), Chgo. Surg. Soc., Soc. Univ. Surgeons, Soc. Clin. Surgery, Milw. Acad. Medicine, Soc. Surgery Alimentary Tract (v.p.), Milw. Acad. Surgery (pres.). Home and Office: 2722 86th Ave NE Clyde Hill WA 98004-1653 Office Phone: 425-453-7860. E-mail: rec@wolfenet.com.

CONDON, STANLEY CHARLES, gastroenterologist; b. Glendale, Calif., Feb. 1, 1931; s. Charles Max and Alma Mae (Chinn) C.; m. Vaneta Marilyn Mabley, May 19, 1963; children: Lori, Brian, David. BA, La Sierra Coll., 1952; MD, Loma Linda (Calif.) U., 1956. Diplomate Nat. Bd. Med. Examiners, Am. Bd. Internal Medicine, Am. Bd. Gastroenterology; recertified Nutritional Support Physician 2002. Intern LA County Gen. Hosp., 1956-57, resident gen. pathology, 1959-61, active jr. attending staff, 1964-65; resident in internal medicine White Meml. Med. Ctr., LA, 1961-63, attending staff out-patient clinic, 1963-64; dir. intern-resident tng. program Manila Sanitarium and Hosp., 1966-71, med. dir., 1971-72; chief resident internal medicine out-patient clinic Loma Linda U. Med. Ctr., 1972-74, attending staff, asst. prof. medicine, 1976-91, assoc. prof. medicine, 1991—, med. dir. nutritional support team, 1984—; fellow in gastroenterology Barnes Hosp./Wash. U., 1974-76. Contbr. articles to profl. jours. Capt. U.S. Army, 1957-59. Fellow: ACP; mem.: AMA, San Bernardino County Med. Soc., So. Calif. Soc. Gastroenterology, Calif. Med. Assn., Am. Gastroent. Assn., Am. Soc. for Parenteral and Enteral Nutrition. Republican. Seventh-day Adventist. Avocations: trombone, choral singing, camping, hiking, gardening. Home: 11524 Ray Ct Loma Linda CA 92354-3630 Office: Loma Linda U Med Ctr 11370 Anderson St Loma Linda CA 92354-3450

CONDON, THOMAS BRIAN, retired hospital executive; b. Beverly, Mass., June 1, 1942; s. Thomas William and Marguerite Mary (Welch) C.; m. Carol Therese Sicilliano, Apr. 29, 1969; children: Therese Beth, Tara Bridget, Colleen Marguerite, Caroline Susan. BA in English, Boston Coll., 1964; MPA, U. New Haven, 1973, MA in Community Psychology, 1975, MA in Indsl. and Organizational Psychology, 1977. Dir. unit mgmt. Yale New Haven Hosp., 1971—, asst. adminstr., 1975, v.p., 1980-94, v.p. clin. adminstrn., 1994-99, sr. v.p. clin. adminstrn., 1999—2005; ret., 2005. Assoc. prof. Quinnipiac Coll., Hamden, 1982-2003; bd. dirs. Nat. Inst. Cmty. Health Edn., Hamden, Conn., Spectronics, Phila.; bd. dirs. New Eng. Organ Bank, 1996-2004; chmn. bd. dirs. Gateway Tech. and C.C. Found., New Haven, 1988-96. Elected mem. Cheshire (Conn.) Planning and Zoning Commn., 1976—87; chmn. bd. dirs. Conn. Student Loan Found., Rocky Hill, 1976—; mem. Gov.'s Task Force on Student Aid, Hartford, Conn., 1986—87; mem. bd. advisors Clelian Ctr. Adult Day Care Ctr., Hamden, 1990; v.p. Conn. chpt. Nat. Kidney Found., 1999—2000, pres., 2000—02; bd. dirs. So. Conn. Jr. Achievement, 1994—2000, Conn. Sports Found., 2001, pres., 2003—. Recipient Community Svc. award Bd. Trustees Conn. State Coll., 1991, Disting. Alumni award U. New Haven, 1997. Mem. Grad. Club Assn. New Haven (bd. dirs. 1993-99), Lyman Orchards Golf Club. Roman Catholic. Avocations: golf, antiques, netsuke, film collector, golf. Home: 150 Hotchkiss Rdg Cheshire CT 06410-3041 E-mail: Brian@BrianCondon.com.

CONDON, THOMAS JOSEPH, university historian; b. New Haven, July 27, 1930; m. Ann Kathleen Gorman, 1962 (dec. June 2001); children: Katherine, Caroline, Gregory. BA, Yale U., 1952; MA, Boston Coll., 1953; PhD, Harvard U., 1962. Teaching fellow history Harvard U., 1959-62; asst. prof. history U. N.B. (Can.), Fredericton, 1962-66; exec. asso. Am. Council Learned Socs., N.Y.C., 1966-70; vis. asso. prof. history Ind. U., 1967-68, City U. N.Y., 1968-69; prof. history, dean of Arts U. N.B., 1970-77; prof. history, dean and v.p. U. N.B. (St. John Campus), 1977-79, acting pres., 1979-80, v.p., 1980-87, prof. history, 1977-96, v.p. emeritus, gov. emeritus, 1996—, acting v.p., 2001—03. Hon. rsch. fellow Inst. U.S. Studies, U. London, 1975-76; mem. Humanities Rsch. Coun. Can., 1972-73, Commn. on Fgn. Students Policy, Can. Bur. Internat. Edn., Ottawa, 1980-83, Maritime Provinces Higher Edn. Commn., 1982-85; chmn. adv. com. on arts in N.B. Min. of Youth, 1973-75; bd. govs. Rothesay Collegiate Sch., 1977-88, U. N.B., 1977-87, 90-96; chmn. engring. task force Maritime Provinces Higher Edn. Commn., 1977-78; chmn., pres. Bi-Capitol Project, Inc., 1982-91; chmn. Festival by the Sea, Sur Mer, 1985, Bi-Capitol Found., 1984—; bd. govs., exec. com. Can. Conf. Arts, 1988-94; bd. dirs. Writers Devel. Trust; bd. govs. Internat. Scholarship Found., 1996—. Author: New York Beginnings: The Commercial Origins of New Netherland, 1968; Mem. editorial bd.: Computers and the Humanities, 1969-70, Acadiensis, 1970—; contbr. articles to profl. jours. V.p. St. John Can. Games, 1977—87; pres. Symphony New Brunswick, 2003—. With USNR, 1953—57. Recipient Lescarbot award Can. govt., 1991, Commemorative medal for 125th anniversary of Confedn. of Can., 1992, Queen's Golden Jubilee medal, 2002; Can. Coun. grantee, 1964, 65. Mem. Am. Hist. Assn., Can. Assn. Am. Studies, Can. Hist. Assn., Order of Can Home: 268 Princess St Saint John NB Canada E2L 1L3 Office: Box 5050 Saint John NB Canada E2L 4L5 Office Phone: 506-648-5694. Business E-Mail: tjc@unbsj.ca.

CONDON, WILLIAM (BILL), director, writer, producer; b. NYC, Oct. 22, 1955; Degree in philosophy, Columbia Coll. T.V. and motion picture dir., writer, prodr. Writer, dir. Gods and Monsters, 1998 (Best Writing Oscar award 1999, Flanders Internat. Film Festival award 1998, Golden Satellite award 1999, Ind. Spirit award 1999, others), Kinsey, 2004; dir. films Candyman: Farewell to the Flesh, 1995; T.V. films include Murder 101, 1991, White Lie, 1991, Dead in the Water, 1991, Deadly Relations, 1993, The Man Who Wouldn't Die, 1995; dir. TV series The Others, 2000; actor: Now You See Him: The Invisible Man Revealed, 2000; actor, writer, prodr. Strange Behavior, 1981; actor, writer, Strange Invaders, 1983; actor, writer, dir. Sister, Sister, 1987; writer F/X2, 1991, The Devil & Daniel Webster, 2002, Chicago: The Musical, 2002, Chicago, 2002. Office: c/o Adam Shulman The Firm 9465 Wilshire Blvd Ste 600 Beverly Hills CA 90212

CONDOR, JACQUES LEVIERGNE, writer, educator; b. St. Jean, Que., Can., Nov. 5, 1928; (parents Am. citizens); s. Leo Vaughn Condor and Laura Alberta Hampshire; m. Diana Seno Condor; 1 child, Michelle Michiko; m. Rosella M. Albertson (div.); children: Morgan, Mark, Joel. M in TV Prodn., Philippine U. Fine Arts, 1957; MFA, Colo. State U., 1967. Tchr. numerous schs., Alaska, 1957—62; gallery mgr. Kailua Art Ctr., Kona, Hawaii, 1978—82; prof. Anchorage C.C., 1967—76, U. Redlands, Calif., 1984—87; instr. Native Am. edn., 1984—95; ret. writer Vivisphere Pub., Poughkeepsie, NY, 1999—; cons. Southwestn Mus., Pasadena, Calif., 1989—99, Hara Maqua's Friends, L.A., 1994—2005. Author: Condor Tales, 2001, Children of the Turtle, 2003, Raven's Children, 2003. Pres. Alaska Club Ariz., Phoenix, 2003—05; dir. Hoop of Many Colors, San Bernardino, Calif., 1990—94. With USAF, 1951—57. Grantee, Calif. Arts Coun., Sacramento, 1989—94. Mem.: Writers Roundtable, Ariz. Authors. Independent. Avocations: painting, theater, acting, Native American Abenaki. Personal E-mail: makataimeb@earthlink.net.

CONDOS, BARBARA SEALE, real estate broker, real estate developer, investor; b. Kenedy, Tex., Feb. 24, 1925; d. John Edgar and Bess Rochelle (Ainsworth) Seale; m. George James Condos, Dec. 24, 1955 (dec.); 1 child, James Alexander. MusB magna cum laude, U. Incarnate Word, San Antonio, 1946. Lic. real estate broker, Tex. Ptnr., CEO Mountain Top-V.I. Devel. Properties, V.I., 1977-85; pres. Investment Realty Co., L.C., San Antonio, 1978—. Choreographer, dancer San Antonio Symphony's Youth Concerts and Opera Festival; actress San Antonio Little Theatre-Patio-Players 1948—. Trustee San Antonio Little Theatre, 1953-76; mem. coun. McNay Mus., 1986—, chmn. coun., 1987—, chair coun., 1988—, trustee, 1989-97, trustee emerita, 1997—; bd. dirs. San Antonio Performing Arts Assn., 1978—; mng. trustee Russell Hill Rogers Fund for Arts. Mem. Internat. Real Estate Fedn., Internat. Real Estate Inst., Nat. Assn. Realtors, Tex. Assn. Realtors, San Antonio Bd. Realtors, Tex. Watercolor Soc. (signature mem.), The Argyle Club. Avocation: painting. Home: 217 Geneseo Rd San Antonio TX 78209-5913 Office: Investment Realty Co 1635 NE Loop 410 San Antonio TX 78209-1625 Business E-Mail: bsc@investmentrealty.com.

CONDOS, J. ALEXANDER, mortgage company executive; b. San Antonio, Nov. 19, 1959; s. George James and Barbara Seale Condos; m. Linda Sue Warner, Aug. 18, 1990 (div. Dec. 12, 2001); children: Elliot Warner, Alexa Nicole. BA with honors, U. Tex., 1981; MBA, U. Chgo., 1984. Lic. real estate broker Tex. and Ill. Sr. investment officer Lomas Fin. Corp., Chgo., 1984—88; owner Alexander Condos Real Estate, San Antonio, 1989—92; prin. Investment Realty Co., L.C., San Antonio, 1993—. Bd. dirs. N.E. YMCA/San Antonio & the Hill Country, 2002; confidence index panelist Tex. Bus. Leaders; corp. campaign com. McNay Art Mus. Mem.: San Antonio Bd. Realtors (comml. investment div.), Internat. Coun. Shopping Ctrs., Chgo. Real Estate Coun., Tex. Assn. Realtors (comml. investment divsn. 1993—), Nat. Assn. Realtors, Real Estate Coun. of Austin, Real Estate Coun. of San Antonio (govt. affairs com. 1996—), Mortgage Bankers Assn. of Am. (capital markets com. 2000—), Rotary. Methodist. Avocation: running. Office: Investment Realty Co LC 1635 NE Loop 410 Ste 910 San Antonio TX 78209-1622 Office Phone: 210-828-9261 20.

CONDRA, ALLEN LEE, retired lawyer, state official; b. Middlesboro, Ky., Apr. 11, 1950; s. Allen and Dorothy Dell (Douglas) C. BA, We. Ky. U., 1972; JD, No. Ky. U., 1978. Bar: Ky. 1979, U.S. Dist. Ct. (we. dist.) Ky. 1980. Staff atty. West Ky. Legal Svcs., Madisonville, 1979—81; dist. atty. dept. transp. Commonwealth of Ky., Madisonville, 1981—2003; ret., 2003. Mem. Ky. Bar Assn., Elks, Masons, K.T., Phi Alpha Delta. Democrat. Methodist.

CONDRAN, CYNTHIA MARIE, gospel musician; b. Avon Park, Fla., Apr. 29, 1953; d. Kenneth Dale and Ruth Mae (Garber) Grubb; m. Lee Light Condran, July 3, 1971. Student, Lebanon Valley Coll., 1970—72. Piano tchr., Sebring, Fla., 1968-70, Annville, Pa., 1971—; gospel musician, writer, arranger Condran Music Co., Annville, Pa., 1972—, also recording engr. Sang by spl. invitation at Elipse of The White House, 1982; composer The Only Thing Holding You Back, 1977, Just A Few More Rivers, 1975, The Patchwork Quilt, 1978, Freedom, 1976, The Little Things, 1980, We're America, Heavens Fiesta, He's the Lord of Everyday, 1989, I've Never Known Such Love, 1990, I Just Want To Talk To You, 1990, Sweep Our Sins, 1990, Eternal Friends, 1991, The Precious Jewels At Christmas Time, 1992, Lost On My Way Back Home, 1993, I Believe in the Power of Love, 1993, To Speak Your Name, 1994, Forever, 1994, We Praise You Lord, 1994, R.D. #11, Heaven, 1996, Surprise, 1997, Patience, 1998, His Healing Blood, 1999, Back Door Blessings, 2000; writer comml. jingles. Recipient Contemporary Country Artists of Yr. award Internat. Country Gospel Music Assn., 1995, Internat. Star Music award, 1997, Contemporary Country Duo of Yr. award, 1999, Entertainer of Yr. Silver Heart award, 1999, Female Vocalist of Yr. northeast region, 1999, Golden Heart award for the Nat. Female Vocalist of Yr., 1999; named Female Vocalist of the Yr., Country Gospel Music Assn., 1999, Reciter of the Yr., Country Gospel Music Assn., 2000, 2002. Mem. Gospel Music Assn., Broadcast Music Inc., Christian Bus. and Prof. Women (music chmn.), So. Gospel Music Guild. Republican. Avocations: skiing, golf, swimming, tennis, racquetball. Home: 935 N Route 934 Annville PA 17003-9803 Office Phone: 717-867-4137. Personal E-mail: leecindyco@aol.com.

CONDRELL, WILLIAM KENNETH, lawyer; b. Buffalo, N.Y., Sept. 19, 1926; s. Paul Kenneth and Celia Olga (Schinas) C.; m. Stacie J. Oliver, June 9, 1991; children: Paul, William, Alexander. BS, Yale U., 1946; S.M., MIT, 1947; JD, Harvard U., 1950. Bar: N.Y. 1951, D.C. 1964, U.S. Ct. Appeals (4th cir.) 1974, U.S. Ct. Appeals (Fed. cir.) 1982, U.S. Ct. Appeals (D.C. cir.) 1984, U.S. Supreme Ct. 1965. Assoc. econ. adv. Exec. Office Pres., Washington, 1951—54; mgmt. cons. McKinsey and Co., Chgo., 1954-55; mgr. budgets Hotpoint div. GE, Chgo., 1955—59; sole practice, 1959-68; ptnr. Steptoe & Johnson, Washington, 1968—90, of counsel, 1990—. Adj. prof. Duke U., Durham, NC, 1975—95, chmn. Ctr. for Forestry Investment, 1980—93; chmn. Ctr. for Continuing Edn., Washington, 1980—. Bd. trustees Hope Housing, 1992—96, Kingsbury Ctr., 1994—98; dir. mediation D.C. Pub. Schs., 1998—99. Lt (j.g.) USNR, 1944—46. Mem.: ABA, Congl. Country Club (Bethesda, Md.). Home: 2510 Virginia Ave NW # 502 Washington DC 20037-1904 Office: 1330 Connecticut Ave NW Washington DC 20036-1704

CONDRILL, JO ELLARESA, freelance/self-employed small business owner, writer, consultant; b. Hull, Tex., Oct. 25, 1935; d. Freddie (dec.) and Ida (Donatto) Founteno; m. Edwin Leon Ellis, Jan. 9, 1955 (div. 1979); children: Michael Edwin, James Alcia, Resa Ann, Thomas Matthew; m. Donald Richard Condrill, Sept. 21, 1980 (div. 1985). BSBA, Our Lady of the Lake U., 1982; MS in Pub. Adminstrn., Ctrl. Mich. U., 1987; grad., U.S. Army War Coll., 1993. Editorial asst. Airman Mag., San Antonio, 1978; mgmt. analyst San Antonio Air Logistics Ctr., San Antonio, 1979-82; inventory mgr. ground fuels Detachment 29, Alexandria, Va., 1982-83; logistics plans officer Mil. Dist. Washington, 1983-85, chief logistics plans ops. and mgmt., 1985-88; chief integration br. Office of the Dep. Chief of Staff for Logistics, 1990-95; deputy chief logistics plans and ops. div. Hdqs. U.S. Army, The Pentagon, 1995-97; owner Seminars by Jo, Alexandria, Va., 1984-86, GoalMinds, Beverly Hills, Calif., 1997—. Author: Leadership: From Vision to Victory in Six Powerful Steps, 1996, 101 Ways to Improve Your Communication Skills Instantly, 1998, A Millennium Primer: Take Charge of Your Life, 1999, From Book Signing to Best Seller: An Insider's Guide to a Successful Low-Cost Booksigning Tour, 2001 (Best Writer's Ref. Guide, Bay Area Ind. Pubs. Assn. 2001-2002), Take Charge of Your Life: Dare to Pursue Your Dreams, 2003. Civilian v.p. student coun. Army War Coll., Carlisle, Pa. Recipient decoration for Exceptional Civilian Svc., U.S. Army, 1997; Best Speaker award Def. Logistics Agy. Mem. NAFE, Nat. Spkrs. Assn., Rotary Internat., Toastmasters Internat. (dist. 27 gov. 1991-92, internat. dir. 1994-96, top ranking dist. gov. in internat. orgn. 1991-92, Internat. Pres. Disting. Dist. award 1991-92). Roman Catholic. Avocations: travel, dance, reading. Office: Goal Minds Inc 6300 Rue Marielyne #308 San Antonio TX 78238 Office Phone: 310-993-7553. Business E-Mail: condrill@goalminds.com.

CONDRIN, J. PAUL, insurance company executive; Exec. v.p., personal market mgr. Liberty Mut. Ins. Group, Boston. Office: Liberty Mutual Group 175 Berkeley St Boston MA 02116-5066

CONDRON, BARBARA O'GUINN, philosopher, educator, academic administrator, writer; b. New Orleans, May 1, 1953; d. Bill Gene O'Guinn and Marie Gladys (Newbill) Jackson; m. Daniel Ralph Condron, Feb. 29, 1992; 1 child, Hezekiah Daniel. BJ, U. Mo., 1973; MA, Coll. Metaphysics, Springfield, Mo., 1977, DD, D in Metaphysics, 1979. Cert. counselor; ordained min. Interfaith Ch. Metaphysics. Field rep. Sch. Metaphysics, New Orleans, 1978-80; dir. Interfaith Ch. Metaphysics, 1884-89; pres. Nat. Hdqs., Sch. Metaphysics, Windyville, Mo., 1980-84, prof., 1989—, chmn. bd. dirs., 1991-98, mem. coun. elders, bd. govs. internat. edn., 1998—; CEO SOM Pub., Windyville, 1989-98. Guest lectr., instr. Wichita (Kans.) State U., 1977, U. New Orleans, 1979, La. State U., 1981, Am. Bus. Womens Assn., 1982, U. Mo., Kansas City, 1984, Unity Village, 1985, Kans. Dept. Social Svcs. Conf., Topeka, 1986, U. Mo., Columbia and St. Louis, 1986, Mo. Tchrs. Conf., St. Louis, 1991, U. Okla., Norman, 1988—89, Parliament of World's Religions, Chgo., 1993, Mo. Writers Guild Conf., 2001, many others; creator Sch. Metaphysics Assocs., 1992; initiator Universal Hour Peace, 1995; initiator, internat. coord. Nat. Dream Hotline, 1988—; radio and TV guest, 1977—; creator Maker's Dozen-Visionary Schs. Recognition, 1999, Taraka Yoga Psi Counseling Program; initiator Spiritual Focus Sessions, 1997—; internat. coord. Peace Dome dedication and One Voice Initiative, 2003, Soc. for Intuitive Rsch., 2003—. Author: What will I do Tomorrow?, Probing Depression, 1977, Search for a Satisfying Relationship, 1980, Strangers in My Dreams, 1987, Total Recall: An Introduction to Past Life & Health Readings, 1991, Kundalini Rising, 1992, Dreamers Dictionary, 1994, The Work of the Soul: Past Life Recall & Spiritual Enlightenment, 1996, Uncommon Knowledge, 1996, First Opinion: 21st Century Wholistic Health Care, 1997, Spiritual Renaissance Elevating Your Conciousness for the Common Good, 1999, The Bible Interpreted in Dream Symbols, 2000, Remembering Atlantis: The History of the World Vol. 1, 2002, How to Raise an Indigo Child, 2002, Peacemaking: 9 Lessons for Changing Yourself, Your Relationships and Your World, 2003, The Wisdom of Solomon, 2004, The Invitation: A Play and Film in Four Acts, Satyagraha: A Play Based on the Life of Mohandas K. Gandhi, Every Dream is About the Dreamer, 2004; author series When All Else Fails; editor-in-chief Thresholds Jour., 1990-2001; editor Wholistic Health and Healing Guide, 1992-2000; dir. film Making Peace, 2003; prodr., dir. films The Silver Cord, 2004, Vision Quest, 2005, The Invitation-8 Nobel Peace Laureates Meet in the Peace Rome, 2005; dir. Documentary Vision Quest; numerous poems Mem. Internat. Platform Assn., Am. Bus. Women's Assn., Interfaith Ministries, Kundalini Rsch. Network, Planetary Soc., Heritage Found., Mo. Writers Guild, Sigma Delta Chi. Office: Sch Metaphysics World Hdqs Windyville MO 65783 Office Phone: 417-345-8411. Business E-Mail: bgc@dreamschool.org. E-mail: som@som.org.

CONDRON, CHRISTOPHER M. (KIP CONDRON), investment company executive; b. Scranton, Pa. m. Margaret Condron; 3 children. B in bus., U. Scranton, 1970. Sr. v.p. C.S. McKee & Co., Pitts., 1972—78; founder Condron Assoc., 1978—85; co-pres. AYCO Corp., 1985—89; head priv. client group Boston Co., 1989; pres. Boston Safe Deposit and Trust Co., 1989—99; exec. v.p. Mellon Bank Corp. (Mellon acquires Boston Co.), 1993—94; vice chmn. Boston Co., 1994—95, chmn., CEO, 1995—99; vice chmn. Mellon Bank Corp., 1994—98; chmn., CEO The Dreyfus Corp., 1995—99; pres., COO Mellon Fin. Corp. (formerly Mellon Bank Corp.), 1999—2001; pres., CEO, mem. Group Mgmt. Bd. AXA Fin. Inc., 2001—; chmn., CEO AXA Equitable Life Ins. Co. Bd. govs. Investment Co. Inst., 1997—, exec. com., 1998—2000; bd. dirs. Fin. Svcs. Roundtable. Former trustee U. Scranton, head Pres.'s Coun.; trustee St. Sebastian's Country Day Sch., Needham, Mass, University Pitts.; dir., treas. Am. Ireland Fund, 1999-. Office: AXA Financial 1290 Avenue of the Americas New York NY 10104

CONDRON, DANIEL RALPH, academic administrator, metaphysics educator; b. Chillicothe, Mo., Jan. 30, 1953; s. Ralph Wesley and Rosa Irene (Garber) C.; m. Barbara Gail O'Guinn, Feb. 29, 1992; 1 child, Hezekiah Daniel. BS, U. Mo., 1975, MS, 1978; DDiv, Coll. Metaphysics, Springfield, Mo., 1982, D in Metaphysics, 1985. Cert. counselor; ordained to ministry Interfaith Ch. of Metaphysics. Dir. Sch. Metaphysics, Des Moines, 1980, Kansas City, Mo., 1981, regional dir. Colo., 1982-85, Chgo. and Detroit, 1985-90, pres. bd. nat. hdqs. Windyville, Mo., 1988—; chancellor, prof. Coll. Metaphysics, Windyville, Mo., 1990—97, chmn bd., 1997—. Tchg. asst. U. Mo., Columbia, 1977; sales and mgmt. cons. Am. Media, Des Moines, 1980-83; spkr. in field. Author: Dreams of the Soul, 1991, Permanent Healing, 1992, Universal Language of Mind, 1994, Understanding Your Dreams, 1994, Seven Secret Keys to Prosperity and Abundance, 1996, Superconscious Meditation, 1997, The Four Stages of Growth, 2001, Atlantis: The History of the World, Vol. 1, 2002, Tao Te Ching, Interpreted and Explained, 2003, The Purpose of Life, 2004; pub. jour. Thresholds Quar., 1988-; internat. radio and TV guest including BBC, Radio Hong Kong, Voice of Am., 1979-. Mem. Sch. Metaphysics Assocs. (pres.), Nat. Space Soc., Planetary Soc., Alpha Gamma Rho, Alpha Zeta. Achievements include implementer and designer of organic and bio-dynamic farming and agriculture at the 1500 acre College of Metaphysics campus, landscape designer and creator of energetic campus using sacred geometry, including octahedrons, cosehedrons and dodecahedrons placed along ley lines for 1500 acre college of metaphysics campus, discoverer and developer of the Universal language of mind as it applies to dreams, to the Bible and other holy works; discoverer of specific attitudes that cause specific disease and disorders in the body. Home: 163 Moon Valley Rd Windyville MO 65783 Office: Sch Metaphysics Nat Headquarters Windyville MO 65783 Office Phone: 417-345-8411.

CONDRY, ROBERT STEWART, retired hospital administrator; b. Charleston, W.Va., Aug. 16, 1941; s. John Charles and Mary Louise (Jester) C.; m. Mary Purcell Heinzer, May 21, 1966; children: Mary-Lynch, John Stewart. BA, U. Charleston, 1963; MBA, George Washington U., 1970. Asst. hosp. dir. Med. Coll. of Va., Richmond, 1970-73, assoc. adminstr., 1973-75; assoc. hosp. dir. McGaw Hosp., Loyola U., Maywood, Ill., 1975-84, hosp. dir., 1984-93, ret., 1993. Pres. Inter-Hosp. Planning Assn. of Western Suburbs, Maywood, 1983-93; bd. dirs. PentaMed, Inc., San Antonio. Bd. dirs. Met. Chgo. Healthcare Coun., 1985-93, mem. exec. com., 1989-93; bd. dirs. Cath. Hosp. Alliance, 1992, chmn. bd. dirs., 1992, mem. exec. com. 1988-94; mem. Ill. Gov.'s Adv. Bd. on Infant Mortality Reduction, 1988-93, Rev. Bd. on Emergency Medicine Svcs., 1989-93. With U.S. Army, 1964-66. Recipient preceptorship George Washington U., 1985, U. Chgo., 1984, St. Louis U., 1984, Tulane U., 1984, Yale U., 1991. Fellow Am. Coll. Healthcare Execs., Am. Acad. Med. Adminstrs.; mem. Am. Hosp. Assn., Cath. Hosp. Assn., Am. Mgmt. Assn. Republican. Roman Catholic. Avocations: golf, tennis, camping, travel. E-mail: carmelcondry@comcast.net.

CONE, GEORGE WALLIS, lawyer; b. Augusta, Ga., Aug. 20, 1945; s. William Harry and Agnes M. (Hill) Cone; children: Jennifer Lee, Laura Katherine, David Willis. Student, Clemson Coll., 1963—64; BS in PHarmacy, U. Ga., 1967, JD, 1973. Bar: Ga. 73, SC 74. Pharmacist-in-charge Walterboro (SC) Drug, Inc., 1967—76; atty. firm McLeod, Fraser & Unger, Walterboro, 1976—84, McLeod, Fraser & Cone, Walterboro, 1985—; city atty. City of Walterboro, 1995—. Bd. dirs. Found. for Human Svcs., 1986—90, Bank of Walterboro, sec. corp., vice chmn.; sec. corp., vice chmn., bd. dirs. Communitycorp, 1995—. Notes editor: Ga. Jour. Internat. and Comparative Law, 1971—72, revs. and comments editor:, 1972—73. Mem. SC Bd. Pharmacy, 1981—87; chmn. SC Bd. PHarmacy, 1986—87; bd. dirs. SC Humane Assn., 1978—85, treas., 1979—84, PRES., 1984—85; bd. dirs. Colleton County SPCA, 1975—85, pres., 1975—77; mem. Colleton County Alcohol and Drug Abuse Com., 1979—81, chmn., 1980—81; bd. dirs. Pub. Defender Corp. Colleton County, 1978—, sec., 1979—; mem. Colleton County Bd. Voter Registration, 1982—84; bd. dirs. Nat. Assn. Bds. Pharm. Found./Bur. Voluntary Compliance, 1983—85, Low Country Cmty. Action Agy., Inc., 1980—85, sec., 1983—85; chmn. Colleton County Old Jail Restoration and Preservation Com., 1984—95; mem. City of Walterboro Downtown Rev. Bd. With SC Army NG, 1970—76. Mem.: ABA, Omar Temple A.A.O.N.M.S., 14th Dist. Pharm. Assn. (pres. 1980—82), SC Pharm. Assn., SC Bar Assn. (ho. of dels. 1975—76, 1977—78, 1979—85), State Bar Ga. (ho. of dels. 1985—89), Am. Soc. Pharm. Law, Colleton County Hist. Soc. (past pres.), Sertoma, Lowcountry Sertoma Club, Dogwood Hills Country Club (pres. 1979—81), Unity Lodge, A & A Scottish Rite Freemasonry, Coastal Shrine Club, Grand Lodge Masons, Phi Alpha Delta, Delta Chi. Democrat. Baptist. Office: PO Box 230 Walterboro SC 29488 Mailing: PO Box 233 Walterboro SC 29488 Personal E-mail: george@coneonline.com. Business E-Mail: gcone@lowcountry.com.

CONE, JAMES HAL, theologian, educator, author; b. Fordyce, Ark., Aug. 5, 1938; s. Charlie M. and Lucy (Frost) Cone. BA, Philander Smith Coll., 1958; BD, Garrett Theol. Sem., 1961; MA, Northwestern U., 1963, PhD, 1965; DD (hon.), Garrett Evang. Theol. Sem., 2000. Asst. prof. religion and philosophy Philander Smith Coll., Little Rock, 1964-66; asst. prof. religion Adrian (Mich.) Coll., 1966-69; asst. prof. theology Union Theol. Sem., N.Y.C., 1969-70, asso. prof., 1970-73, prof., 1973-77, Charles A. Briggs prof. systematic theology, 1977-87, Briggs disting. prof., 1987—. Vis. prof. Afro-Am. history U. Pacific, Stockton, Calif., 1969; vis. assoc. prof. religion Barnard Coll., N.Y.C., 1969-71, 74; vis. prof. theology Drew U., Madison, N.J., 1973; lectr. systematic theology Woodstock Coll., N.Y.C., 1971-73; vis. prof. theology Princeton (N.J.) Theol. Sem., 1976, Notre Dame Sch. Theology, New Orleans, 1977, Candler Sch. Theology, Emory U., Atlanta, Howard U. Sch. Religion, Washington, 1980, Pacific Luth. Theol. Sem., Berkeley, Calif., Maryknoll (N.Y.) Sch. Theology, 1983, Inst. Justice and Peace; vis. prof., Diana Blabon Holt fellow Rollins Coll., Winter Park, Fla., 1989. Author: Black Theology and Black Power, 1969 (transl. into Dutch, 1970, German, 1971, Japanese, 1971, Korean, 1979), A Black Theology of Liberation, 1970 (transl. into Spanish, 1973, Italian, 1973, Japanese, 1974), The Spirituals and the Blues: An Interpretation, 1972 (transl. into German, 1973, Japanese, 1975, Korean, 1987), God of the Oppressed, 1975 (transl. into Japanese, 1976, Italian, 1978, Korean, 1979, German, 1982, Portuguese, 1985, French, 1989, Malayalam, 1993), My Soul Looks Back, 1982 (transl. into Japanese, 1987), For My People, 1984 (transl. into German, 1987), Speaking the Truth, 1986, Martin and Malcom and America: A Dream or a Nightmare, 1991, Risks of Faith: The Emergence of a Black Theology of Liberation, 1968-98, 1999, Black Faith and Public Talk: Critical Essays on James H. Cone's Black Theology and Black Power, 1999; contbr. articles to profl. publs.; mem. editorial bd.: Jour. Religious Thought, 1975—, Jour. Interdenominational Theological Ctr.; co-editor: Black Theology: A Documentary History, 1966-79, 1979, Black Theology: A Documentary History Vol. II, 1980-92, 1993; assoc. editor Henry McNeal/Sojourner Truth Series in Black Religion; mem. editl. bd. Sojourners mag. Recipient Am. Black Achievement award in Religion, Ebony Mag., 1992, theol. Scholarship and Rsch. award Assn. Theol. Schs., 1994; Rockefeller Found. grantee, 1973-74 Mem. Black Theology Project Theology in Ams., Am. Acad. Religion (Fund for Theol. Edn. award 1999), Soc. Study Black Religion, Ecumenical Assn. Third World Theologians. Mem. African Methodist Episcopal Ch. Office: Union Theol Sem 3041 Broadway New York NY 10027-5710

CONE, LAWRENCE ARTHUR, medical educator; b. N.Y.C., Mar. 23, 1928; s. Max N. and Ruth (Weber) C.; m. Julia Haldy, June 6, 1947 (dec. 1956); m. Mary Elisabeth Osborne, Aug. 20, 1960; children: Lionel Alfred. AB, NYU, 1948; MD, U. Berne, Switzerland, 1954; DSc (hon.), Rocky Mountain Coll., 1993. Diplomate Am. Bd. Internal Medicine, Am. Bd. Infectious Diseases, Am. Bd. Allergy and Immunology, Am. Bd. Med. Oncology. Intern Dallas Meth. Hosp., 1954-55, resident internal medicine, 1955; resident Flower 5th Hosp., N.Y.C., 1957-59, Met. Hosp., N.Y.C., 1959-60; rsch. fellow infectious diseases and immunology NYU Med. Sch., N.Y.C., 1960-62; from asst. prof. to assoc. prof. N.Y. Med. Coll., N.Y.C., 1962-72, chief sect immunology and infectious diseases, 1962-72; assoc. clin. prof. medicine Harbor UCLA Med. Sch., 1984—; clin. prof. internal medicine U. Calif., Riverside, 1997-98, clin. prof. medicine. Career scientist Health Rsch. Coun. N.Y.C., 1962-68; chief sect. immunology and infectious diseases Eisenhower Med. Ctr., Rancho Mirage, Calif., 1973-2002, chmn. dept. medicine, 1976-78, pres. elect, pres., past pres. med. staff, 1984-90; cons. infectious disease Desert Hosp., Palm Springs, Calif., 1980-85; lectr. basic sci. U. Calif., Riverside Biomed. Scis.; mem. mycosis study group NIAID, 1993—, co-investigator Coccidiodemtcosis study group, 1993—, eastern coop. oncology group affil. Stanford U., 1994, 2003-. Contbr. articles to profl. jours. Bd. dirs., bd. trustees Desert Bighorn Rsch. Inst., Palm Desert, Calif., pres., bd. dirs., 1995-99; nat. adv. coun., mem., bd. trustees Rocky Mountain Coll., Billings, Mont.; mem. med. adv. staff Coll. of Desert, Palm Desert; Pres. Cir. Desert Mus., Palm Springs, Calif., Idaho Conservation League, Gilcrease Mus., Tulsa, Sun Valley Ctr. for Arts and Humanities. L.A. County Mus., Smithsonian Inst., Buffalo Bill Historic Mus., Cody, Wyo.; mem. Nat. Mus. Wildlife Art; life mem. The Living Desert, Palm Desert, L.A. County Mus.; mem. cmty. adv. coun. Jr. League; CEO Genetic Rsch. Inst. of Desert. Recipient Outstanding Contbn. to Medicine award Riverside County Med. Assn., 1998, Disting. Achievement award AMC Cancer Rsch. Ctr., 1998, Stone Chase award, 2000. Fellow ACP, Royal Soc. Medicine, Interam. Soc. Chemotherapy, Am. Coll. Allergy, Am. Acad. Allergy and Immunology, Am. Soc. Infectious Diseases, Am. Geriatric Soc. (founding fellow we. divsn.); mem. AAAS, Internat. AIDS Soc., Am. Soc. Microbiology, Reticulocudothelial Soc., Am. Fedn. for Clin. Rsch., Faculty Soc. UCLA, Surg. Soc. N.Y. Med. Coll. (hon.), Woodstock Artists Assn., Harvey Soc., N.Y. Acad. Scis., European Soc. Clinical Microbiology and Infectious Disease, Internat. Soc. Infectious Disease, NYU Alumni Assn., Berne Alumni Assn., Lotos Club, Tamarisk Country Club, Coachella Valley Gun and Wildlife Club, Faculty Soc. UCLA Harbor Med. Ctr., O'Donnell Golf Club, Sigma Xi. Republican. Avocations: golf, fishing, hunting, skiing. Home: 765 Via Vadera Palm Springs CA 92262-4170 Office: Probst Profl Bldg #308 39000 Bob Hope Dr Rancho Mirage CA 92270-3221 also: Larkspur Condominiums PO Box 1503 Sun Valley ID 83353-1503 Personal E-mail: lacmedicine@aol.com.

CONE, MICHAEL MCKAY, venture capitalist; b. Washington, Oct. 14, 1947; s. Montie Fowler and Eleanor Newcomb (Faulk) C.; m. Constance Anne Hennessy, July 21, 1971. AB, Princeton U., 1969; MPhil, Yale U., 1973, PhD, 1976. Chemist E.I. DuPont de Nemours, Wilmington, Del., 1977-81, area supt. LaPlace, La., 1981-84, bus. analyst Wilmington, 1984-85, tech. svc. specialist, 1985-86, devel. mgr. Parlin, N.J., 1986-89, cons. Wilmington, 1989-94, mgr. new bus. devel. Deepwater, N.J., 1994-98; ptnr. Crossway Ventures, Toms River, N.J., 1998—. Bd. dirs. Wayn-Tex Inc., Waynesboro, Va., F.T. Industries, LLC, Franklinville, N.J., Gen. Econopak, Inc., Phila. Patentee in field. Mem. AAAS, Am. Chem. Soc., Product Devel. & Mgmt. Assn. (dir. sponsor devel. 1994-97), Sigma Xi, Princeton Club N.Y., Corinthian Yacht Club Phila. Avocations: sailing, skiing, music. Home: 1910 Spruce St Philadelphia PA 19103-6613 Office: Crossway Ventures 1826 Route 35 N Seaside Heights NJ 08751-1535

CONELLI, MARIA ANN, art educator, dean, architect; b. Bklyn., Nov. 1, 1957; d. Carmine S. and Mary Conelli; m. Kim J. Hartswick, May 11, 1990. BA in Art History, Bklyn. Coll., 1980; MA, NYU, 1983; MPhil, Columbia U., PhD in Archtl. History, 1992. Educator Met. Mus. Art, NYC, 1981—84; instr. Parsons Sch. Design, NYC, 1983—2001; chair Parsons/Smithsonian Inst., NYC, Washington, 1992—2001; dean Fashion Inst. Tech., NYC, 2001—05; dir. Am. Folk Art Mus., NYC, 2005—. Contbr. articles to profl. jours., books; co-editor: Newsletter Decorative Art Soc., 1995—. Trustee Skyscraper Mus., N.Y.C., 1999—; mem. mus. com. Coll. Art Assocs., N.Y.C., 2003—. Pub. Works Challenge grantee, Nat. Endowment for the Arts, Washington, 2002—03, J. Paul Getty Postdoctoral fellow, 1997. Fellow: Am. Acad. in Rome (fellow 1987—88); mem.: Coll. Art Assn. Roman Catholic. Office: Am Folk Art Mus 45 W 53d St New York NY 10019-5401 Office Phone: 212-265-1040 ext. 114. Office Fax: 212-265-2350. Business E-Mail: mconelli@folkartmuseum.org.

CONERLY, RICHARD PUGH, retired manufacturing executive; b. Jackson, Ala., May 6, 1924; s. William L. and Eunice (Pugh) C.; m. Iva Jean Brightwell, Aug. 12, 1956; children: William Edward, Robert Andrew, Christopher Brightwell, Elizabeth Anne. Student, Howard Coll., Birmingham, Ala., 1942; B.J., U. Mo., 1948; LL.B., Harvard U., 1952. Bar: Mo. 1952. Practice in, St. Louis, 1952-65; assoc., partner Thompson & Mitchell, 1952-65; v.p., gen. counsel, exec. v.p. Peabody Coal Co., St. Louis, 1965-69; pres. Pott Industries Inc., St. Louis, 1969-87; vice-chmn. Houston Natural Gas Corp., 1979-85; chmn. Orion Capital Inc., St. Louis, 1988-94. Served with USAAF, 1943—. Home: 22 Webster Oaks Dr Webster Groves MO 63119 E-mail: rconerly@earthlink.net.

CONEWAY, NELLY TZENKOVA, journalist, television producer; b. Sofia, Bulgaria, Sept. 16, 1968; d. Nadka Simeonova Nikolova and Tzenko Nikolov Kamenov; 1 child, David. Law degree, Sofia U., 1991—94; degree, Hollywood Film Inst., 1998. Prodr. and author Bulgarian Nat. TV, Bulgaria, 1991—97; host and author Bulgaria TV, Los Angeles, 1997—2004; publicity adviser, book covers designer Kurt Lehovec, PhD, 1997—2004; talent mgr., owner and prodr. Hollywood Dream Enterprise, Sherman Oaks, 1997—2003; Calif. area corr. and rep. Nedelnik Press, N.Y.C., 1997—; Hollywood corr. TRUD (Bulgarian newspaper), 2005—. Owner and prodr. Hollywood Dream Entertainment, Sherman Oaks, Calif., 1999—2002; mem., corr. internat. fgn. press. Editor: (newspaper) Black Belt; author: Revelations, My Interviews with the Enlightened, 2005, Revelations in Hollywood, 2005; prodr. (and host): (TV series) Fire Mystery Show, 2000—02; ticket mktg./celebrity booking (radio show) Love Calls, KMPC 1540, 2005—. Mem.: Internat. Orgn. Journalists. Avocations: kundalini yoga, martial arts, kabbalah, art, esoteric literature. Personal E-mail: nellyk1@yahoo.com. E-mail: firemystery@yahoo.com.

CONEY, AIMS C., JR., lawyer, labor-management negotiator; b. Cleve., Sept. 22, 1929; s. Aims Chamberlain and Elizabeth (Lee) C.; m. Rita Newbold Platt, Feb. 20, 1954; children: Aims C. III, Sylvia L., Anne F. BA, Yale U., 1951; JD, U. Pa., 1954. Bar: Pa. Assoc. Kirkpatrick, Lockhart, Johnson & Hutchison, Pitts., 1956-69; ptnr. Kirkpatrick & Lockhart, Pitts., 1969-89, of counsel, 1990—. Contbr. articles in field of union-management relations and legal ethics to profl. jours. Bd. dirs. Arthritis Found., Pitts., 1967—, pres., 1972-75; bd. dirs. Ellis Sch., Pitts., 1974-91, Freedom House Amb. Svc., 1968-75, Indian Lake (N.Y.) Zoning Commn., 1993-95, Transitional Svcs. Inc., 1992-98; bd. dirs. Pace Sch., Pitts., 1980-94, pres., 1990-91. With U.S. Army, 1954-56. Mem. Pa. Bar Assn. (co-chmn. ethics com. 1999-2001), Allegheny County Bar Assn. Republican. Home: 516 Glen Arden Dr Pittsburgh PA 15208-2809 Office: Kirkpatrick & Lockhart Nicholson Graham LLP 535 Smithfield St Pittsburgh PA 15222-2312 Office Phone: 412-355-6406. Business E-Mail: aconey@klng.com.

CONEY, ELAINE MARIE, language educator; b. Magnolia, Miss., Aug. 9, 1952; d. Allen Leroy and Katie Jane (McLeod) C. BA in Spanish, Millsaps Coll., 1974; MA in Spanish, U. Interam. Saltillo Coahuila, Mex., 1975, PhD, 1977; MEd, U. So. Miss., 1979, EdS in Higher Edn. Adminstrn., 1997. Tchr. fgn. langs. South Pike High Sch., Magnolia, Miss., 1977-91; tchr. English Amite County Schs., Liberty, Miss.; instr. Jackson (Miss.) State U.; GED instr. South Pike Schs., Magnolia, Miss.; instr. Spanish and English composition S.W. Miss. Community Coll., Summit, 1989—. Mem. NEA (del. conv. 1986, 88), MLA, Am. Coun. Tchrs. Fgn. Langs., Am. Assn. Tchrs. French, Am. Assn. Tchrs. Spanish and Portuguese, Miss. Assn. Educators (instructional profl. devel. com.), Nat. Coun. Tchrs. English, Miss. Fgn. Lang. Assn. (pres. 1991-93, Disting. Svc. award 1998), SPAE (treas.). Home: PO Box 208 Magnolia MS 39652-0208 Office Phone: 601-276-3871.

CONFER, ANTHONY WAYNE, veterinary pathologist, educator; b. Hot Springs, Ark., July 29, 1947; s. Edwin M. and Gloria V. (Parker) C.; m. Carolyn Gay Pope, Aug. 15, 1970; children: Andrew W., Aaron J., Michael E., Christina A. DVM, Okla. State U., 1972; MS, Ohio State U., 1974; PhD, U. Mo., 1978. Diplomate Am. Coll. Vet. Pathologists. Assoc. prof. La. State U., Baton Rouge, 1978-81, Okla. State U., Stillwater, 1981-85, prof., 1985—, dept. head, 1986-99, 2004—, assoc. dean for rsch. Coll. Vet. Medicine, 1999-2001, Sitlington endowed chair food animal rsch., 1995—, regents prof., 2003—. Vis. prof. U. B.C., Vancouver, 1990-91; cons. Ft. Dodge (Iowa) Lab., 1987-92, 2003—, Baxter Healthcare Corp., Round Lake, Ill., 1988-89, Vet. Reference Lab., Dallas, 1988-89, Smith Kline Beechan Ltd., Lincoln, Nebr., 1990; mem. Conf. Rsch. Workers-Animal Diseases, 1981—; cons. Diamond Animal Health, Des Moines, 1994-98, Pfizer Animal Health, Lincoln, Nebr., 1997—. Mem. editl. bd. Am. Jour. Vet. Rsch., 1993-2004, Vet. Pathology, 1995-97, 2005—; contrib. over 140 sci. publs. in field. V.p. Stillwater Soccer Assn., 1987-91, pres., 1992-93; pub. rels. specialist Stillwater H.S. Soccer Club, 1990-96; cub master Cub Scout pack 22, Stillwater, 1987-89. Capt. USAF, 69-77. Recipient Beecham award for rsch., SmithKline Beecham Lab., 1985, Norden Disting. Tchr. award, Pfizer, Inc., 1987, 2002, Eminent Faculty award, Okla. State U., 2003. Mem. AVMA (Vet. Rsch. award 1992), Am. Coll. Vet. Pathologists (chair standing edn. com. 1994-96, program chair 1995), Morris Animal Found. (sci. advisor 1991-95), Sigma Xi (chpt. lectr. 1993). Mem. Lds Ch. Avocations: physical fitness, guitar, cooking. Home: 2817 W 28th Ave Stillwater OK 74074-2212 Office: Okla State U Dept Vet Pathobiology Stillwater OK 74078-2007 Office Phone: 405-744-4542. Business E-Mail: aconfer@cvm.okstate.edu.

CONFORTI, MICHAEL PETER, museum director, art historian; b. Bradford, Mass., Apr. 3, 1945; s. Sven and Cecile Conforti; m. Licia Peterson; children: Peter, Julia. BA, Trinity Coll., Hartford, Conn., 1968; MA, Harvard U., 1973, PhD, 1977. Cataloguer Sotheby & Co., London, 1968-69, dir. tng. program N.Y.C., 1969-71; curator sculpture and decorative arts Fine Arts Mus., San Francisco, 1977-80; chief curator, Bell curator decorative arts and sculpture Mpls. Inst. Arts, 1980-94; dir. Sterling and Francine Clark Art Inst., Wiliamstown, Mass., 1994—. Curated (exhibitions) Sweden: A Royal Treasury, 1988, The American Craftsman and the European Tradition, 1620-1820, 1989, Art and Life on the Upper Mississippi, 1890-1915, 1994, A Grand Design--The History of London's Victoria and Albert Museum, 1997, organizer Uncanny Spectacle: The Public Career of John Singer Sargent, 1997, Impression: Painting Quickly in France 1820-1890, 2001, Gustav Klimt: Landscapes, 2002, Turner: The Late Seascapes, 2003, Jacques-Louis David: Empire to Exile, 2005; contbr. articles on sculpture, decorative arts, collecting and mus. history. Trustee Am. Acad. Rome, 2000—, mem. exec. com., 2003—; vice chmn. Nat. Com. for the History of Art, 2000—; chair Art Mus. Image Consortium, 2003—05. Decorated Order of Polar Star (Sweden); recipient Robert Smith award, 1987, Charles Montgomery award, 1990; Nat. Endowment Arts Mus. fellow, 1974, Am. Acad. in Rome fellow, 1975-77; Bush fellow, 1985; Getty guest scholar, 1988; Andrew Mellon fellow Ctr. for Advanced Study in the Visual Arts, Nat. Gallery of Art, 1993. Mem.: Assn. Art Mus. Dirs. (trustee 2001—04). Office: Sterling & Francine Clark Art Inst 225 South St Williamstown MA 01267-2878 Office Phone: 413-458-9545.

CONGALTON, CHRISTOPHER WILLIAM, lawyer; b. N.Y.C., Apr. 8, 1946; s. William Alexander and Jacqueline Rose (Ryan) C.; m. Susan Tichenor, May 29, 1971. AB, Fairfield (Conn.) U., 1968; JD, Georgetown U., 1971. Bar: N.Y. 1972, U.S. Dist. Ct. (so. dist.) N.Y. 1974, U.S. Ct. Appeals (2d cir.) 1974, U.S. Supreme Ct. 1976, Ill. 1988, Colo. 1990. Assoc. Dunnington, Bartholow & Miller, N.Y.C., 1971-78; asst. gen. counsel Diamond Internat. Corp., N.Y.C., 1978-82; gen. counsel, v.p. Children's TV Workshop, N.Y.C., 1987-88; chmn. and ceo Moffitt Co., Schiller Park, Ill., 1988—. Mem. ABA, (corp. banking & bus. sect.), Am. Corp. Counsel Assn., N.Y. State Bar Assn., Assn. of Bar of City of N.Y., Chgo. Bar Assn., Eagle Springs Golf Club. Home: 1500 N Lake Shore Dr Chicago IL 60610-6657 Office: Moffitt Co 9347 Seymour Ave Schiller Park IL 60176-2206

CONGALTON, SUSAN TICHENOR, lawyer; b. Mt. Vernon, N.Y., July 12, 1946; d. Arthur George and M. Marjorie Tichenor; m. Christopher William Congalton, May 29, 1971. BA summa cum laude, Loretto Heights Coll., 1968; JD, Georgetown U., 1971. Bar: N.Y. 1972, Ill. 1986, Colo. 1990. Assoc. Reavis & McGrath (now Fulbright & Jaworski), N.Y.C., 1971-78, ptnr., 1978-85; v.p., gen. counsel, sec. Carson Pirie Scott & Co., Chgo., 1985-87, sr. v.p. fin. and law, 1987-89; mng. dir. Lupine LLC (formerly known as Lupine Ptnrs.), Chgo., 1989—; chmn., CEO Calif. Amforge Corp., 2002—. Bd. dirs. Harris Fin. Corp., Harris Bankcorp, Inc.; chmn. Cmty. Reinvestment Act Com., 1990-97, chmn. audit com., 1997—; chmn. bd., CEO, Calif. Amforge Corp., 2002—. Mem. editorial staff Georgetown U. Law Jour., 1969-70, editor, 1970-71. Mem. bd. overseers Ill. Inst. Tech., Chgo., Chgo. Kent Coll. Law, 1985-89; mem. bus. adv. coun. Bus. Sch., U. Ill., Chgo., 1987-90; mem. planning com. Ann. Corp. Counsel Inst., 1986-89; bd. dirs. Ill. Inst. Continuing Legal Edn., 1992-95; mem. Chgo. Workforce Bd., 1995-98; chmn. Strategic Planning Task force, 1995-96, chmn. Performance Rev. Com., 1996-98. Mem. ABA, Nat. Assn. Corp. Dirs. (bd. dirs. Chgo. chpt. 2001—), Econ. Club Chgo., Chgo. Club (bd. dirs. 1996—2004, treas. 1999-02, sec. 2002—04). Office: Lupine LLC 1520 Kensington Rd Ste 112 Oak Brook IL 60523-2140

CONGDON, CHARLES B., lawyer; b. Phila., 1957; BA, Univ. Pa., 1979; JD, Villanova Univ., 1984. Bar: Pa. 1984. Joined Drinker Biddle & Reath LLP, Phila., 1984, now ptnr., bus., fin. dept. Mem.: Pa. Assn. Bond Lawyers, Nat. Assn. Bond Lawyers. Office: Drinker Biddle & Reath LLP One Logan Sq 18th & Cherry Sts Philadelphia PA 19103-6996 Office Phone: 215-988-2659. Office Fax: 215-988-2757. Business E-Mail: charles.congdon@dbr.com.

CONGDON, JOHN RHODES, transportation executive; b. Balt., Feb. 17, 1933; s. Earl Everett and Lillian Francis (Herbert) C.; m. Barbara Natalie Neblett, June 17, 1952; children: Susan Lee, John Rhodes, Jeffrey Whitefield. Student, U. Richmond, 1952-53. Driver Old Dominion Freight Line, 1951; founder, chmn. Old Dominion Truck Leasing, 1963—; vice chmn. Old Dominion Freight Line. Deacon River Rd. Ch., 1981; pres. Dorset Woods Civic Assn., 1973-74. With U.S. Army, 1953-55. Mem. Va. Hwy. Users Assn. (pres. 1976-78), River Rd. Citizens, Country Club of Va., Masons, Shriners. Home: Randolph Sq 112 W Square Dr Richmond VA 23238 Office: 7511 White Pine Rd Chesterfield VA 23832 Office Phone: 804-275-7832.

CONGDON, JON HARVEY, music educator; b. Decatur, Ga., May 11, 1969; s. Frederick Voorhees Congdon and Katherine Elizabeth Bray, Rebecca Ann Congdon (Stepmother) and Roy Bray (Stepfather); m. Lesley Susan Day, Aug. 14, 1999; children: Kaitley Alexis, Ellie Margaret. Assoc. Fine Arts in Music, Brevard Coll., 1989; BS Music Edn., Ga. State U., 1995. Cert. K-12 music tchr. Ga. Beginning band dir. DeKalb County Bd. Edn., Decatur, Ga., 1996—98, mid. sch. band dir., 1998—2000, H.S. band dir., 2000—02, Hall County Bd. Of Edn., Gainesville, Ga., 2002—. Dist. elem. honor band coord. DeKalb County Bd. Edn., 1997—98, dist. mid. sch. large ensemble band festival coord., 1999—2000, dist. all-state audition coord., 2001—02, dist. chair, 2001—02. Mem.: Ga. Music Educator's Assn., Music Educators Nat. Conf. Avocations: golf, tennis, baseball. Home: 5188 Migration Point Gainesville GA 30506 Office: Flowery Branch HS 4950 Hog Mountain Rd Flowery Branch GA 30542 Personal E-mail: jlc814@yahoo.com.

CONGDON, JULIE CARA, entomologist, researcher; b. St. Petersburg, Fla., Oct. 25, 1970; d. Susan Thompson and Philip Congdon; life ptnr. Ricardo Jose Vazquez. AA, Santa Fe C.C., Gainesville, Florida, 1998; BS, U. Fla., 2001, MS, 2004. Rsch. asst. USDA, Gainesville, Fla., 2000—01; grad. rsch. asst. U. Fla., 2001—. Grantee, Fla. Entomol. Soc., 2003—04, U. Fla. Grad. Student Coun., 2003, Travel Grant, Inst. Food and Agrl. Sciences, 2003; scholar Excellence in Urban Entomology, Bayer Corp., 2002, Agrl. Women's Club Scholarship, U. Fla., 2004, Outstanding Student Scholarship, Cert. Pest Control Operators Fla., 1999, John A. Mulrennan, Sr. Scholarship, U. Fla., 2000, Cert. Operators of SW Fla., 2000, Carolyn D. Richardson Urban Pest Mgmt. Scholarship, U. of Fla., 1999. Mem.: Cert. Pest Control Operators of Fla., Entomol. Soc. Am., Fla. Entomol. Soc., Fla. Turfgrass Assn., Urban Entomol. Soc. (sec 1998—2000, tchg. collections com. chairperson 2000—02, historian 2004), Entomology & Nematology Student Orgn. (sec. 2002—03). Office: University of Florida Bldg 970 Natural Area Drive Gainesville FL 32611 Office Phone: 352-392-1901 164. Personal E-mail: c1squirrel@aol.com. E-mail: congdon@ufl.edu.

CONGDON, KIRBY, artist; b. West Chester, Pa., Nov. 13, 1924; s. William Ellsworth Congdon and Ragna Jorgensen; m. Ralph Simmons Jr. Student, Biarritz Am. U., France, 1945; BA, Columbia U., 1950, postgrad., 1951—52. Editor, pub. Interim Books and Cycle Press, Key West, Fla., 1962—. Address: 715 Bakers Ln Key West FL 33040-6819 E-mail: simmonsralphjr@aol.com.

CONGDON, ROGER DOUGLASS, theology studies educator, minister; b. Ft. Collins, Colo., Apr. 6, 1918; s. John Solon and Ellen Avery (Kellogg); m. Rhoda Gwendolyn Britt, Jan. 2, 1948; children: Rachel Congdon Lidbeck, James R., R. Steven, Jon B., Philip F., Robert N., Bradford B., Ruth A. Mahner, Rebecca York Brooks, Rhoda J. Miller, Marianne C. Potter, Mark Alexander. BA, Wheaton Coll., 1940; postgrad, Eastern Bapt. Sem., 1940-41; ThM, Dallas Theol. Sem., 1945; ThD, Dallas Theology Sem., 1949. Ordained to ministry Bapt. Ch., 1945. Exec. sec., dean Altanta Bible Inst., 1945-49; prof. theology Carver Bible Inst., Atlanta, 1945-49; prof. Multnomah Bible Coll., Portland, Oreg., 1950-87; pastor Emmanuel Bapt. Ch., Vancouver, Wash., 1985—. Past dean of faculty, dean of edn., v.p., chmn. libr. com., chmn. achievement-award com., chmn. lectureship com., advisor grad. div. and mem. pres.'s cabinet Multnomah Bible Co.; chmn. Chil Evang. Fellowship of Greater Portland, 1978-97; founder, pres. Preaching Print Inc., Portland, 1953—. Founder, speaker semi-weekly radio broadcast Bible Truth Forum, KPDQ, Portland, Oreg., 1989—, DZAM, Manila, Philippines, 1996—, Radio Africa 2, 1998—, Radio E. Africa, 2003—; author: The Doctrine of Conscience, 1945. Chmn. Citizen's Com. Info. on Communism, Portland, 1968-75. Recipient Outstanding Educators of Am. award, 1972, Loraine Chafer award in Systematic Theology, Dallas Theol. Sem., 1949.

Mem. Am. Assn. Bible Colls. (chmn. testing com. 1953-78), N.Am. Assn. Bible Colls. (N.W. rep. 1960-63), Near East Archaeol. Soc., Evang. Theol. Soc. Republican. Home: 16539 NE Halsey St Portland OR 97230-5607 Office: Emmanuel Bapt Ch 14810 NE 28th St Vancouver WA 98682-8357 *A base person's problems usually consist in selecting between overt evils. The average person chooses between the shady and the good. But the truly noble person, who follows Jesus Christ, never bothers with evils or shady acts; he ever seeks to discern the transcendent, to choose the best of all good choices.*

CONGER, CYNTHIA LYNNE, financial planner; b. Omaha, Dec. 8, 1948; d. Bob Bruce Ashton and Cleo (Artz) Ashton Taplin; m. Terry H. Conger, Dec. 21, 1969 (div. June 1989); children: Cynthia T., Scott A. BA in Acctg., U. Ark., Little Rock, 1980, MBA in Fin. and Econ., 1983. CPA, Ark.; cert. fin. planner. Staff acct. Leaseway Ark., Inc., Little Rock, 1981-83; agt. Conn. Mutual Life, Little Rock, 1983-84; v.p., fin. planner Ark. Fin. Group, Inc., Little Rock, 1984-94, pres., 1995—, Cynthia L. Conger, CPA, PA, Little Rock, 1989—. Mem. found. bd. U. Ark., 2002—. Mem.: LWV (adv. bd. 1997—), Registry Fin. Planning Practitioners, Internat. Assn. Fin. Planning (Ark. chpt., v.p. 1986—87, pres. 1987—89, nat. bd. dirs. 1994—98). Methodist. Avocations: reading, travel, cooking. Office: Ark Fin Group Inc 1001 N University #200 Little Rock AR 72207 Office Phone: 501-376-9051. Business E-Mail: cindyc@arfinancial.com.

CONGER, HARRY MILTON, mining company executive; b. Seattle, July 22, 1930; s. Harry Milton Jr. and Caroline (Gunnell) C.; m. Phyllis Nadine Shepherd, Aug. 14, 1949 (dec.); children: Harry Milton IV, Preston George; m. Rosemary L. Scholz, Feb. 22, 1991. D in Bus. Adminstrn. (hon.), S.D. Sch. Mines and Tech., 1983; D. in Engring. (hon.), Colo. Sch. Mines, 1988, hon. degrees. Registered profl. engr., Ariz., Colo. Shift foreman Asarco, Inc., Silver Bell, Ariz., 1955-64; mgr. Kaiser Steel Corp. Eagle Mountain Mine, 1964-70; v.p., gen. mgr. Kaiser Resources, Ltd., Fernie, B.C., Can., 1970-73, Consolidation Coal Co. (Midwestern div.), Carbondale, Ill., 1973-75; v.p. Homestake Mining Co., San Francisco, 1975-77, pres., 1977-78, pres., chief exec. officer, 1978-82, chmn., pres., chief exec. officer, 1982-86, chmn., chief exec. officer, 1986-96, chmn., 1996-98, chmn., CEO emeritus, also bd. dirs., 1998, ret., 1998, PG& E Corp., 1982—2001, Baker Hughes Inc., 1987—97, Calmat Inc., 1986—97. Bd. dir., ASA Ltd., Apex Silver Mines; chmn. Am. Mining Congress, 1986—89, World Gold Coun., 1995—97. Trustee Calif. Inst. Tech. With C.E. U.S. Army, 1956. Recipient Disting. Achievement medal Colo. Sch. Mines, 1978, Am. Mining Hall of Fame, 1990, Disting. Svc. award Am. Mining Congress, 1995. Mem. NAE, Nat. Mining Assn. (hon. bd. dirs.), Am. Inst. Mining Engrs. (disting., Charles F. Rand gold medal 1990), Mining and Metallurgy Soc. Am., Mining Club, Bohemian Club, Commonwealth Club, Pacific Union Club. Republican. Episcopalian. Personal E-mail: hmconger111@aol.com.

CONGER, JOHN JANEWAY, psychologist, educator; b. New Brunswick, NJ, Feb. 27, 1921; s. John C. and Katharine (Janeway) Conger; m. Mayo Trist Kline, Jan. 1, 1944; children: Steven Janeway, David Trist. BA magna cum laude, Amherst Coll., 1943; MS, Yale U., 1947, PhD, 1949; DSc (hon.), Ohio U., 1981, Amherst Coll., 1983; DS (hon.), U. Colo., 1989. Asst. prof. psychology Ind. U., 1949—53; chief staff psychologist U.S. Naval Acad., 1951—52; mem. faculty U. Colo. Sch. Medicine, prof. psychology, 1957—88, assoc. dean, 1961—63, v.p. for med. affairs, 1963—70, dean, 1963—68, acting chmn. dept. psychiatry, 1983—84, acting chancellor, 1985—86, prof. emeritus, 1988—. V.p., dir. health program John D. and Catherine T. MacArthur Found., 1980—83, cons., 1983—85, NIH, VA, USPHS; vice chmn. Colo. Bd. Psychology Examiners, 1961—64; mem. Gov. Colo. Com. Mental Health, 1957; chmn. mental health adv. coun. Colo. Dept. Pub. Health, 1957—61; mem. tng. com. Nat. Inst. Mental Health, 1959—62; mem. Western coun. mental health rsch. & tng. Western Interstate Commn. Higher Edn., 1959—66; chmn. rsch. com. Pres.'s Com. Traffic Safety, 1960—63; vice chmn. nat. motor vehicle safety adv. coun. Dept. Transp., 1967—70; mem. inter-coun. com. constrn. univ.-affiliated facilities for mentally retarded Dept. Health, Edn. and Welfare, 1967—70, mem. sec.'s adv. com. traffic safety, 1966—69; coun. rsch. and planning Am. Hosp. Assn., 1965—68; nat. adv. mental health coun. USPHS, 1965—69; nat. adv. com. John F. Kennedy Ctr. Rsch. on Edn. and Human Devel., 1965—76, chmn., 1970—74; mem. adv. com. on undergrad. med. edn. AMA, 1969—70; adv. com. on casualty ins. Dept. Transp., 1970; mem. Pres.'s Task Force on Hwy. Safety, 1970, Pres.'s Commn. on Mental Health, 1977—78; mem. com. study nat. needs for biomed. and behavioral sci. rsch. personnel Nat. Acad. Scis., 1976—80; mem. Inst. Medicine/Nat. Acad. Scis., 1983—; bd. mental health and behavioral medicine, 1986—92; vis. scholar Inst. Human Devel. U. Calif., Berkeley, 1978. Author: Child Development and Personality, 7th edit., 1990, Readings in Child Development, 3d edit., 1984, Personality, Social Class and Delinquency, 1965, Adolescence and Youth: Psychological Development in a Changing World, 5th edit., 1997, The Shape of the Tree: Selected Poems, 1993, Basic and Contemporary Issues in Developmental Psychology, 1975, Contemporary Issues in Adolescent Development, 1975, Psychological Development: A Life-Span Approach, 1979, Essentials of Child Development and Personality, 1980; contbr. articles to profl. jours.; Applied and Preventive Psychology, 1991—. Lt. USNR, 1944—46, lt. USNR, 1951—52. Recipient Stearns Alumni medal for extraordinary svc., U. Colo., 1970, U. Colo. medal, 1986, disting. profl. achievement award, Am. Bd. Profl. Psychology, 1979; fellow, Ctr. Advanced Study in Behavioral Scis., Stanford, Calif., 1970—71; vis. scholar, Inst. Human Devel., U. Calif., Berkeley, 1978. Fellow: AAAS, APA (mem. policy and planning bd. 1967—70, rec. sec., dir. 1974—79, pres. 1980—82, award for disting. contbns. psychology in pub. interest 1986), Soc. Rsch. in Child Devel. (program chmn. 1975, fin. com. 1989—93, Disting. Contbns. to Pub. Policy for Children award 1995); mem.: Colo. Med. Soc. (Disting. Svc. award 1970), Colo. Psychol. Assn. (pres. 1959), Denver Med. Soc. (hon.), Am. Psychol. Found. (bd. dirs. 1982—86, pres. 1985—86), Sigma Xi, Phi Beta Kappa, Alpha Omega Alpha (hon.). Home: 130 S Birch St Denver CO 80246-1017

CONGER, LUCINDA, retired librarian; b. Ft. Bragg, NC, June 11, 1941; d. Meredith Moore and Ann Oliver (Mumford) Dickinson; m. Bruce C. Conger, June 25, 1966. BA, Radcliffe Coll., 1963; MLS, Rutgers U., 1964; student, Wesley Sem., Washington, 1990. Reference libr. U. Calif., Davis, 1964-65; cataloger Libr. of Congress, Washington, 1965, reference libr., 1966; compact storage libr. Princeton (N.J.) U., 1966-70; dir. reclassification Albion (Mich.) Coll., 1970-71, serials libr., 1971-73; reference libr. Yale U., New Haven, 1973-75, U.S. Dept. State, Washington, 1976—2000; chief Reader Svcs. Br., 1994—2000; ret., 2000. Author: Online Command Chart, 1977, 81; columnist Database Mag., 1980-90; contbr. articles to profl. jours. Vol., Washington Cathedral, 1976—. Recipient Govt. Computer News award, 1992, Sec. Career Achievement award, 2000. Mem.: DAR, Archology Inst. of Am., Harvard Club of Washington, Nat. Soc. of Colonel Dames. Democrat. Episcopalian. Avocations: classical greek, archaeology, genealogy, travel. Home: 4906 Jamestown Rd Bethesda MD 20816-2709 Office: State Dept Libr 2201 C St NW Washington DC 20520-0001

CONGER, SUE ANN, computer information systems educator; b. Akron, Ohio, Nov. 6, 1947; d. Scott Stanley and Norma Marie (Bauknecht) Summerville; m. David Boyd Conger, July 3, 1971 (dec. June 1997); 1 child, Kathryn Summerville. BS, Ohio State U., 1970; MBA, Rutgers U., 1977; PhD, NYU, 1988. Programmer, analyst USDA, Washington, 1970-72; project leader Ednl. Testing Svc., Princeton, N.J., 1972-73; 2d v.p. Chase Manhattan Bank, N.Y.C., 1973-77; tech. dir. Lambda Technology, Inc., N.Y.C., 1977-80; sr. cons. Mobil Corp., N.Y.C., 1980-83; asst. prof. computer info. systems Ga. State U., Atlanta, 1988-90; asst. prof. Baruch Coll. CUNY, 1990-94; assoc. prof. So. Meth. U., Dallas, 1994-99; dir. electronic commerce Sewell Automotive Cos., Dallas, 1999—2001; assoc. prof., dir. and project mgr. IT programs U. Dallas, Irving, 2001—. Freelance cons., educator, 1970—. Author: The New Software Engineering, 1994, Planning and Designing Effective Web Sites, 1998; contbr. articles to profl. jours. Grantee, U.S. Army Info. Systems Engring. Command, 1989, The CMI Group, 2002. Mem. IEEE, AIS, Assn. for Computing Machinery, Acad. of Mgmt. Avocations: reading, sports, cooking. Office: Univ of Dallas 1845 W Northgate Dr Irving TX 75062

CONGER, WILLIAM FRAME, artist, educator; b. Dixon, Ill., May 29, 1937; s. Robert Allen and Catherine Florence (Kelly) C.; m. Kathleen Marie Onderak, May 23, 1964; children: Sarah Elizabeth, Clarisa Lynn. Student, Art Inst. Chgo., 1954, 56-57, 60, 62; BFA, U. N.Mex., 1960; MFA, U. Chgo., 1966. Asst. prof. Rock Valley Coll., Rockford, 1966-71; vis. lectr. Beloit Coll., 1969; prof., chmn. dept. art DePaul U., Chgo., 1971-85; vis. artist U. Chgo., 1976, 83, Cornell U., 1980; Sch. Art Inst. Chgo., 1985, Univ. Iowa; adj. prof. So. Ill. U., 1984; chmn. dept. art theory and practice Northwestern U., Evanston, Ill., 1985-99, prof., 1985—; numerous lectures. One man shows Burpee Mus., Rockford, Ill., 1971, Douglas Kenyon Gallery, Chgo., 1974, 75, Krannert Ctr. for Arts, Urbana, Ill., 1976, Zaks Gallery, Chgo., 1978, 80, 83, Roy Boyd Gallery, Chgo., 1985, 87, 90, 92, 94, 96, 97, 98, 99, 2000, 01, 02, 04, Janus Gallery, Santa Fe, 1992, Tarbel Mus., Ill., 1993, Univ. Club Chgo., 1998, Jonson Mus., Albuquerque, 1998, Walters Art Ctr., Tulsa, 2000, 01, Tadu Contemporary Santa Fe, 2003, 04, 05; group shows include Art Inst. Chgo., 1963, 71, 73, 78, 80, 84-85, Mus. Contemporary Art, Chgo., 1976, 96-97, Krannert Mus., Urbana, 1976, Ill. State Mus., 1978, 88-89, E.B. Crocker Gallery, Sacramento, 1977, Phoenix Mus., 1977, Mitchell Mus., 1980, Notre Dame U., 1981, Sonoma State U., 1983, Cowles Mus., 1983, Arts Club Chgo., 1983-97, Sheldon Meml. Gallery, U. Nebr., 1984, Anchorage Fine Arts Mus., 1985, Ark Art Ctr., 1985, Block Gallery, Northwestern U., 1986, 90, 96-97, 2005, Smart Mus., 1996; represented in permanent collections Art Inst. Chgo., Mus. Contemporary Art, Chgo., Smart Mus., U. Chgo., Ill. State Mus., Chgo., No. Ill. U., DePaul U., Jonson Mus., U. N.Mex., Block Gallery, City of Chgo. Public Art Collection, others; also pvt. collections U.S. and worldwide; numerous catalogs, revs. and commentary in Arts mag., Art Forum, Art in Am., Ciamese, Art News, Art Criticism, Art & Antiques; others; author essays in Whitewalls, Chicago/Art/Write, Psychoanalytic Perspectives on Art, Psychoanalytic Studies of Biography, Critical Inquiry, other jours. Bd. dirs. Ox Bow Art Sch., 1982-86; adv. bd. Renaissance Soc., 1988-99; bd. trustees St. Benedict H.S., Chgo., 1994—; referee NEH, 1989; interviewee TV and radio programs including Am. Art Forum. Recipient Bartels award Art Inst. Chgo., 1971; Clusmann award, 1973; Friedman awards U. Chgo., 1965, 66. Mem. Coll. Art Assn. Am., Phi Sigma Tau. Office: Northwestern U Dept Art Theory & Practice Rm 244 Kresge Hall Evanston IL 60201 Home: 3500 N Lake Shore Dr 15A Chicago IL 60657-1815 Studio: 3711 N Ravenswood Chicago IL 60613 Office Phone: 773-296-4595. Personal E-mail: w-conger@sbcglobal.net. Business E-Mail: w-conger@northwestern.edu.

CONGLETON, JOSEPH PATRICK, lawyer, preservationist; b. Barbourville, Ky., June 8, 1947; s. Isaac and B. (Johnson) C.; m. Rose Willingham Stewart; children: Isaac Tyler, Rosalie Mallary. Grad., McCallie Sch., Chattanooga; MA, Centre Coll., 1969; JD, U. Va., 1972. Bar: Tenn. 1972. Ptnr. Fowler & Rowntree, Knoxville, Tenn., 1972-83; ptnr., capital fin. and real estate Hunton & Williams, Knoxville, Tenn., 1983—. Adv. editor Jour. Mineral Law and Policy, 1985—. Chmn. atty. divsn. United Way, Knoxville, 1985-87; bd. dirs. Tenn. Nature Conservancy, 1980-88, Knoxville Symphony, 1985—, pres., 1988-91; bd. dirs. Thompson Cancer Survival Ctr., 1987—, Gt. Smoky Mountain Conservation Assn., Knoxville, 1985—, pres., 1992—; sec. Webb Sch., Knoxville, 1986-2000; pres. Knoxville Watersports Festival, 1986-87; mem. Leadership Knoxville, 1986-87. Fellow Tenn. Bar Found.; mem. ABA, Tenn. Bar Assn., Knoxville Bar Assn. (bd. govs.), Nat. Assn. Bond Lawyers, Ea. Mineral Law Found. (trustee, exec. com. 1980—, pres. 1991-92), Trout Unltd. (nat. bd. dirs.), Knoxville Racquet Club (bd. dirs. 1980-82), Cherokee Country Club, Rotary (v.p. Knoxville 1985-87), Appalachian Club (Elkmont, Tenn.), Omicron Delta Kappa, Delta Kappa Epsilon. Avocations: upland and waterfowl hunting, fly fishing, appalchian ecology. Office: Hunton & Williams 2000 Riverview Twr 900 S Gay St Knoxville TN 37902-1810 Office Phone: 865-549-7777. Office Fax: 865-549-7704. Business E-Mail: jcongleton@hunton.com.*

CONGLETON, ROBERT J., librarian, educator, archivist; b. Newton, N.J., June 3, 1956; m. Ming-Ying Liu, Jan. 28, 1993. BA, Rider U., Lawrenceville, N.J., 1978; MA, U. of Conn., 1980; MLS, Rutgers U., 1988. Serials librn. Temple U., Phila., 1988—2001; prof., serials librn., archivist Rider U., Lawrenceville, 2002—. Co-author: (book) Critical Thinking: An Annotated Bibliography; contbr. articles to profl. jours. Mem.: ALA, Mid-Atlantic Endeavor Users Group, N.J. Libr. Assn., Mid-Atlantic Regional Archives Conf. (pres. 2002—03), N.Am. Serials Interest Group. Office: Rider Univ 2083 Lawrenceville Rd Lawrenceville NJ 08648 Office Phone: 609-896-5248. Personal E-mail: congliu1@comcast.net. E-mail: rcongleton@rider.edu.

CONINE, ERNEST, columnist; b. Dallas, Dec. 31, 1925; s. Ernest and Myrtle Conine; m. Phyllis Joan Hoyland, Nov. 28, 1953 (dec.); m. Ulla Fisher, Jan. 10, 1981. BS, So. Methodist U., 1948. Staff writer UPI, Dallas, 1948-51; Washington corr. Dallas Times Herald, 1952-55; successively Washington corr., Moscow corr., New Eng. mgr. Bus. Week mag., 1955-63; fgn. corr. L.A. Times, Vienna, 1963-64, public affairs columnist, mem. editorial bd., 1964-87, contbr., 1988-92. Mem. Ctr. Internat. and Strategic Affairs, UCLA, 1975-90, Internat. Inst. for Strategic Studies, 1984-98; mem. Calif. Seminar Internat. Security and Fgn. Affairs, 1970-93, L.A. Com. Fgn. Affairs, 1973-93. Contbr. articles to popular mags. Served with Army Air Corps, 1944-46, AUS, 1951-52. Mem. Soc. Profl. Journalists. Home and Office: 205 Dasher Dr Austin TX 78734-5040

CONISON, JAY, lawyer; b. Cin., Oct. 21, 1953; s. Allan Abraham and Theresa (Yudofsky) C.; m. Nancy Jo Kelber, Sept. 7, 1980; children: Alexander, David. BA, Yale U., 1975; MA, U. Minn., 1978, JD, 1981. Bar: Ill. 1981, U.S. Dist. Ct. (no. dist.) Ill. 1980, U.S. Dist. Ct. (ea. dist.) Wis. 1984, U.S. Dist. Ct. (no. dist. trial) Ill. 1985, U.S. Ct. Appeals (7th cir.) 1986, U.S. Dist. Ct. (we. dist.) Okla. 1990, U.S. Supreme Ct. 1990. Atty. Sonnenschein, Carlin, Nath & Rosenthal, Chgo., 1981-90; asst. prof. Oklahoma City U. Sch. Law, 1990-92, assoc. prof., 1992-94, prof., assoc. dean, 1994-97, interim dean, 1997-98; dean, prof. Valparaiso (Ind.) U. Sch. Law, 1998—. Chair employee benefits com. Assn. Am. Law Schs., 2002; mem. employee benefits adv. bd. John Marshall Law Sch., 2003—. Author: Employee Benefit Plans in a Nutshell, 1993, 3d edit., 2003. Bd. dirs. Jewish Fedn. of N.W. Ind., 2002—. Fellow Ind. Bar Found. (trustee 1998—); mem. ABA (sect. on legal edn. and admission to the bar, co-chair sect. on legal edn. and admission to the bar, clin. skills edn. com. 2001-2004), Ill. Bar Assn., Ind. Bar Assn. (chair profl. legal edn. admission and devel. com. 2001-02, vice chair legal edn. conclave com. 2001-03, chair 2003-2004). Home: 2103 Chandana Trl Valparaiso IN 46383-2295 Office: Valparaiso U Sch Law Wesemann Hall Valparaiso IN 46383 E-mail: jay.conison@valpo.edu.

CONKEL, ROBERT DALE, lawyer, consultant; b. Oct. 13, 1936; s. Chester William and Marian Matilda (Ashton) Conkel; m. Elizabeth A. Cargill, June 15, 1958; children: Debra Lynn, Dale William, Douglas Alan; m. Brenda Jo Myers, Aug. 2, 1980; 1 child, Chelsea Ashton. BA, Mt. Union Coll., 1958; JD cum laude, Cleve. Marshall Law Sch., 1965; LLM, Case Western Res. U., 1972. Bar: Ohio 1965, U.S. Ct. Appeals (5th cir.) 1979, U.S. Tax Ct. 1974, U.S. Supreme Ct. 1974, Tex. 1978. Supr. Social Security Adminstrn., Cleve., 1958—65; trust officer Harter Bank & Trust Co., Canton, Ohio, 1965—70; exec. v.p. Am. Actuaries, Inc., Grand Rapids, Mich., 1970—73; mgr. plans and rsch. A.S. Hansen, Inc., Dallas, 1973—74; pvt. practice Dallas, 1973—; pension cons., southwest regional dir. Am. Actuaries, Inc., Dallas, 1974—88. Sr. cons. Coopers & Lybrand, Dallas, 1989; pres. Robert D. Conkel, Inc., 1989—; mem. devel. bd. Met. Nat. Bank, Richardson, Tex.; instr. Am. Mgmt. Assn., 1975, Am. Coll. Advanced Pension Planning, 1975—76; enrolled actuary Joint Bd. Enrollment U.S. Depts. Labor and Treasury. Contbr. articles to legal publs.; mem. editl. adv. bd.: jour. Jour. Pension Planning and Compliance, 1974—83. Chmn. Zoning Bd. Adjustments, Richardson, Tex.; sustaining mem. Rep. Nat. Com., 1980—2004. Mem.: ABA (employee benefit com. sect. taxation), Am. Acad. Actuaries, Am. Soc. Pension Actuaries (dir. 1973—81), Dallas Bar Assn., Tex. Bar Assn., Ohio State Bar Assn. Office: 100 N Central Expy # 519 Richardson TX 75080-5332 Office Phone: 972-997-8211.

CONKIN, PAUL KEITH, history professor; b. Chuckey, Tenn., Oct. 25, 1929; s. Harry Thomas and Dorothy (Staten) C.; m. Dorothy L. Tharp, 1954; 3 children. BA, Milligan Coll., 1951; MA, Vanderbilt U., 1953, PhD, 1957. Asst. prof. history U. Southwestern La., 1957-59; asst. prof., assoc. prof., prof. U. Md., 1959-67; prof. U. Wis., Madison, 1967-76, Merle Curti prof., 1976-79; disting. prof. history Vanderbilt U., Nashville, 1979—2000, emeritus, 2000—, chmn. dept. history, 1984-87. Author: The New Deal, 1967, F.D.R. and the Origins of the Welfare State, 1967, Puritans and Pragmatists, 1968, Self-Evident Truths, 1974, Prophets of Prosperity, 1980, Gone with the Ivy: A Biography of Vanderbilt U., 1985, Big Daddy from the Pedernales: Lyndon Baines Johnson, 1986, The Southern Agrarians, 1988, Cane Ridge: America's Pentecost, 1991, Four Foundations of American Government, 1994, The Uneasy Center: Reformed Christianity in Antebellum America, 1995, American Originals: Homemade Varieties of Christianity, 1997, When All the Gods Trembled: Darwinism, Scopes, and American Intellectuals, 1998, Requiem for the American Village, 2000, Peabody College: From a Frontier Academy to the Frontiers of Teaching and Learning, 2002; co-author: The Heritage and Challenge of History, 1971; author: (with others) A History of Recent America, 1974; co-editor: New Directions in American Intellectual History, 1979. Guggenheim fellow, 1965-66; sr. fellow Nat. Endowment for Humanities, 1972-73, 90. Mem. Am. Hist. Assn. (Beveridge award 1958), Orgn. Am. Historians, So. Hist. Assn. (pres. 1996-97). Home: 1003 Tyne Blvd Nashville TN 37220-1026 Office Phone: 615-322-1088. Business E-Mail: paul.k.conkin@vanderbilt.edu.

CONKLIN, DONALD DAVID, academic administrator; b. Waynesburg, Pa., Oct. 29, 1944; s. Donald David and Esther Louise (McCracken) C.; children: Donald David III, Elizabeth Ann. BA, Pa. State U., 1966, MEd, 1967; EdD, NYU, 1975. Asst. dean. instrn. SUNY, Farmingdale, 1970-72, exec. asst. to pres., 1972-78; spl. asst. N.J. Dept. Higher Edn., Trenton, 1978-80; dean for planning and devel. Mercer County Community Coll., Trenton, 1980-83, dean for adminstrn., 1983-86, dean for acad. affairs, 1986-92; pres. Dutchess Community Coll., Poughkeepsie, N.Y., 1992—. Cons. AAA of No. N.J., Morristown, 1984, Harrisburg Area C.C., 1983, Ednl. Testing Svc., Princeton, N.J., 1990, Educom Cons. Svcs., Princeton, 1985-90, Md. Higher Edn. Commn., 1992-95. Contbr. articles to profl. jours., chpts. to books. Chair Dutchess County Empire Zone Bd.; chmn. bd. dirs. United Way of Dutchess County; vice chmn., bd. dirs. St. Francis Hosp., Cmty. Fund of Dutchess County, Hudson Valley Philharm., Hudson Valley coun. Boy Scouts Am., Dutchess County Econ. Devel. Corp.; mem. SUNY Coun. of Pres.; chmn. Coll. Bd. CC Adv. Com.; bd. trustees Poughkeepsie Day Sch. Recipient Adminstrs. award for excellence in aviation edn. FAA, 1989. Mem. Poughkeepsie C. of C., Rotary, Phi Theta Kappa, Alpha Mu Gamma, Phi Delta Kappa, The Club. Presbyterian. Avocations: tennis, golf, reading. Home: 57 Pendell Rd Poughkeepsie NY 12601-1512 Office: Dutchess CC Pendell Rd Poughkeepsie NY 12601 Office Phone: 845-431-8980. Business E-Mail: conklin@sunydutchess.edu.

CONKLIN, DONALD RANSFORD, retired pharmaceutical company executive; b. Bound Brook, N.J., Sept. 10, 1936; s. Walter Ransford and Dorothy Ann (Haase) C.; m. Louise Sealey, July 13, 1960; children: Elizabeth, Edward. BA, Williams Coll., 1958; MBA, Rutgers U., 1961; grad. program for mgmt. devel., Harvard U., 1970. Dir. mktg. Schering Corp. U.S.A. (name changed to Schering-Plough 1971), Kenilworth, N.J., 1970-74; dir. mktg. Europe div. Schering-Plough, Lucerne, Switzerland, 1975-76, v.p. internat. mktg. Kenilworth, 1977-79, regional dir., sr. v.p. Latin Am. div. Miami, Fla., 1980-83, sr. v.p. internat. hdqrs. Kenilworth, 1984—, pres., 1985, group v.p. pharm. ops., 1986, exec. v.p. pharm. ops., 1987-89, pres. pharm. ops., 1989-94, pres. healthcare products, 1994-96; ret., 1996. Bd. dirs. Ventiv Inc., Alfacell Inc. Home: 66 Youngs Rd Basking Ridge NJ 07920

CONKLIN, ERIC LINWOOD, artist; b. Balt., Apr. 20, 1950; s. Vernon Linwood Conklin and Thelma Mae Helgoe; m. Victoria Lynn Davis, Apr. 21, 1984. Exhibited in group shows at Marr Gallery, Santa Fe, 2002, McBride Gallery, Annapolis, Md., 2002, Eleanor Ettinger Gallery, N.Y.C., 2002, Phoenix Art Mus., 2003, Leigh Yawkey Woodson Art Mus., Wausau, Wis., 2003. Master: Trompe l' Oeil Soc. Artists (rsch. historian 2001); mem.: Allied Artists Am., Md. Fedn. Art (artist mem. 1998), Delaplaine Visual Arts Ctr. (artist mem. 1999, Hon. Mention 2000), Md. Hall Sch. for Art's (artist mem. 2000).

CONKLIN, GAYLE F., retired elementary school educator; b. Rochester, N.Y., July 21, 1935; d. Newton Ayers and Emily Frances (Kingston) C. BS, Geneseo and Brockport Coll., 1957, MS in Edn., 1964. Cert. elem. and secondary tchr., N.Y. Elem. tchr. Rochester City Sch. Dist.; ret., 1995. Mentor; presenter in field. Mem. Nat. Tchrs. Assn., Rochester Tchrs. Assn., Ctr. for Ednl. Devel., Rochester Ednl. Assn. for Children and Tchrs.

CONKLIN, GEORGE HENRY, sociologist, educator; b. Dumont, N.J., Apr. 9, 1941; s. Richard Brown and Heloise Sealey Conklin; m. Verna Gibble, Aug. 21, 1966; children: Heather, Wendy, Dawn. AB, Colgate U., 1963; PhD, U. Pa., 1971. Asst. prof. Syracuse (N.Y.) U., 1969—74; assoc. prof. Sweet Briar (Va.) Coll., 1974—78; prof. sociology N.C. Ctrl. U., Durham, 1978—, chair faculty senate, 1999—2000. Vice chmn. faculty assembly U. N.C., 2002—03. Contbr. articles to profl. jours., chapters to books and ednl. software; editor: Sociation Today, 2003—. Airport commr. Raleigh-Durham Airport Authority, 1990—99; chair bd. of adjustment Durham County Planning Dept., 1984—90; planning commr. Durham City/ County Planning Dept., 2000—05. Grantee Fulbright grantee, U.S. Ednl. Found. in India, 1963—64, rsch. grantee, Am. Inst. Indian Studies, 1968, Coll. Tchg. Improvement grantee, Fund for Improvment of Postsecondary Edn. (FIPSE), 1982—86, Computer-Based Instrnl. Materials grantee, NSF, Lilly Endowment, 1982—93. Mem.: Internat. Sociol. Assn., So. Sociol. Assn., N.C. Sociol. Assn. (pres. 1998—99, webmaster, editor Sociation Today, Contbns. to Sociology award 1998). Liberal. Presbyterian. Avocation: collecting antique phonographs. Home: 2905 Scuppernong Ln Durham NC 27703-9264 Office: NC Ctrl U Fayetteville St Durham NC Office Phone: 919-530-7327. Business E-Mail: gconkin@nccu.edu.

CONKLIN, GEORGE MELVILLE, retired food products executive; b. Roselle Park, N.J., Dec. 29, 1921; s. Melville Guy and Anna Elizabeth (McMahon) Conklin; m. Jean Austin Wiley, Feb. 19, 1944; children: Andrea(dec.), Blair. BS, Clarkson Coll. Tech., 1947; MS, Newark Coll. Engring., 1951; DSc (hon.), Clarkson U., 1987. Draftsman Babcock & Wilcox, N.Y.C., 1939-42; indsl. engr. Johns-Manville Co., Manville, NJ, 1947-48, Western Electric Co., Kearny, NJ, 1948-50, Gen. Ceramics, Keasby, NJ, 1950-51; indsl. engring. supr. Gen Electric Co., Bloomfield, NJ, 1951-52; with M & M/Mars, Hackettstown, NJ, 1952—, pres., 1968-78, chmn., 1980-82; group pres. Mars, Inc., 1979-80; ret., 1982. Trustee Clarkson U., 1976—86. With inf. AUS, 1943—45. Decorated Combat Inf. badge; named Hon. Commodore, Lake Waco, Tex.; recipient Key to City of Cleveland, Tenn. Mem.: Tex. Rangers (hon.), Evergreen Club (Palm City, Fla.), Tau Beta Pi. Home: Apt 2227 1221 SW Shoreline Dr Palm City FL 34990-4555 *Be a leader that most people do not notice so that when a job is done well, the people believe that they did it themselves.*

CONKLIN, HAROLD COLYER, anthropologist, educator; b. Easton, Pa., Apr. 27, 1926; s. Howard S. and May W. (Colyer) C.; m. Jean M. Morisuye, June 11, 1954; children: Bruce Robert, Mark William. AB, U. Calif.-Berkeley, 1950; PhD, Yale U., 1955. From instr. to assoc. prof. anthropology Columbia U., 1954-62; lectr. anthropology Rockefeller Inst., 1961-62; prof. anthropology Yale U., 1962-96, chmn. dept., 1964-68, Crosby prof. anthropology, 1990-96; curator of anthropology Yale Peabody Mus. Natural History, 1974-96, dir. divsn. anthropology, 1994-96, Crosby prof. emeritus, curator emeritus, 1996—. Mem. Inst. for Advanced Study, Princeton, N.J., 1972; fellow Ctr. for Advanced Study in Behavioral Scis., Stanford, Calif., 1978-79; field rsch. in Philippines, 1945-48, 52-54, 55, 57-58, 61, 62-63, 64, 65, 68-69, 70, 73, 80-81, 82-85, 90-91, 95, 2000-01, 04, Malaya, Malaysia and Indonesia, 1948, 57, 83, Melanesia, 1987, N.Y., 1942, 48, 52, Calif., 1943, 48, 51, Guatemala, 1959, Peru, 1987; dir., com. problems and policy Social Sci. Rsch. Coun., 1963-70; bd. dirs. Survival Internat. USA, 1985-90; spl. cons. Internat. Rice Rsch. Inst., Los Baños, Philippines, 1962—; book rev. editor Am. Anthropologist, 1960-62; mem. Pacific sci. bd. Nat. Acad. Scis.-NRC, 1962-66. Author: Hanunóo Agriculture, 1957, Folk Classification, 1972, Ethnographic Atlas of Ifugao, 1980; other publs. on ethnol., linguistic and ecol. topics. Served with AUS, 1944-46. Guggenheim fellow, 1973; recipient Internat. Sci. prize Fyssen Found., 1983. Mem. NAS; Fellow Am. Acad. Arts and Scis., Am. Anthrop. Assn. (exec. bd. 1965-68), Royal Anthrop. Inst., N.Y. Acad. Scis. (sec. sect. anthropology 1956); mem. Am. Ethnol. Soc. (councilor 1960-62, pres. 1978-79), Koninklijk Inst. voor Taal- Land- en Volkenkunde, Conn. Acad. Arts and Scis., Linguistic Soc. Am., Kroeber Anthrop. Soc., Phila. Anthrop. Soc., Am. Geog. Soc., Am. Oriental Soc., Assn. Asian Studies, Classification Soc., Linguistic Soc. Philippines, Indo-Pacific Prehistory Assn., Soc. Econ. Botany (Disting. Econ. Botanist award 2005), Internat. Assn. Plant Taxonomy, AAAS, Phi Beta Kappa, Sigma Xi. Home: 106 York Sq New Haven CT 06511-3625 Address: Yale U Dept of Anthropology PO Box 208277 New Haven CT 06520-8277

CONKLIN, HOWARD LAWRENCE, lawyer; b. N.Y.C., Apr. 16, 1943; s. Weldon F. and Gladys (Meyer) C. BS, Fairleigh Dickinson U., 1961; MBA, Syracuse U., 1969; JD, Fordham U., 1974. Bar: Fla. 1974, U.S. Dist. Ct. (so. dist.) 1976, U.S. Supreme Ct. 1978, U.S. Dist. Ct. (mid. dist.) Fla. 1980; lic. pilot FAA; lic. capt. USCG. Mktg. planning specialist Trans World Airlines, N.Y.C., 1969-71; sr. transp. analyst Paine Webber, N.Y.C., 1971-74; ptnr. Tripp, Scott, Conklin & Smith, Ft. Lauderdale, Fla., 1974-97; v.p. govt. and airport rels. Alamo Rent-a-Car, Inc., Ft. Lauderdale, 1997; v.p. govt. rels. AutoNation, Inc., Ft. Lauderdale, 1997—. Chmn. Ft. Pierce Area Coun. C. of C.; chmn. investment advisory com. St. Lucie County; vice chair Ft. Pierce Port Advisory Com.; bd. dirs. ARC; elected del. Dem. Party Nat. Conv., 2004. Col. USAF, 1964—68, Vietnam. Decorated Bronze Star, Legion of Merit. Mem. ABA, Air Force Assn., Res. Officers Assn., St. Lucie County Bar Assn., Indian River County Bar Assn., Mil. Officers Assn. (life), Army Navy Club (Washington), Pelican Yacht Club, Sons of Norway. Avocations: flying, sailing. Office: Howard L Conklin Atty 2030 Harbortown Dr Ste A Fort Pierce FL 34946-1438

CONKLIN, JACK L., education educator; b. Pt. Jefferson, N.Y., Dec. 9, 1942; s. John A. and Jeanne C.; m. Susan J. Kuceluk, July 25, 1981; children: Susanne, Danielle, Genevieve, Michelle. BA, Dowling Coll., 1967; MA, Adelphi U., 1970; PhD, U. So. Calif., L.A., 1972. Tchr. Comsewogue Sch. Dist., Pt. Jefferson Sta., N.Y., 1967-70; asst. prin. intern Toll Jr. H.S., Glendale, Calif., 1971-72; prof. edn. Mass. Coll. Liberal Arts, 1972—2002; chmn. edn. dept. North Adams (Mass.) State Coll., 1982-92, cert. officer, 1988-93; prin. Chester Brook Acad., NJ, 2002—04; prof. edn. Georgian Ct. U., Lakewood, NJ, 2004—. Chmn. Commonwealth Tchr. Edn. Consortium, 1981-83; cons. U.S. Dept. Edn. Drug Free Schs. and Communities, 1989-94; field reader safe and drug-free schs. program U.S. Dept. Edn., 1990—; bd. regents Joint Commn. on Tchg. Preparation in Mass., 1999-2002. Bd. dirs. Berkshire Ctr. for Families and Children, Pittsfield, Mass., 1977, South Forty Alternatives, North Adams, 1978, Old Castle Theatre Co., Bennington, Vt., 1994-98; vestry mem. St. John's Episcopal Ch., Williamstown, Mass., 1983-84, St. John's Episcopal Ch., N. Adams, Mass., 1996-98, Pumpkin Hollow Farm Conf. Ctr. Retreat, 1998-2002; cons. N.E. Regional Ctr. for Drug Free Schs., 1988-94; mem. sch. coun. Mt. Greylock Regional Sch. Dist., Williamstown, 1996-99. Mem. Am. Assn. Colls. for Tchr. Edn. (adv. coun. state reps.), Mass. Assn. Colls. for Tchr. Edn. (pres. 1988-89), North Adams State Faculty Assn. (pres. 1980-83), Cmty. Edn. Legis. Task Force, Mass. State Senate, 1998—Joint Task force on Tchr. Preparation, Phi Delta Kappa, Pi Lambda Theta (nat. officers nominating com., Outstanding Faculty Advisor award 1998-99). Democrat. Avocations: jazz-cocktail piano, sailing. Office: Georgian Ct Univ Raymond Hall Rm 210 900 Lakewood Rd Lakewood NJ 08701 Home: 5 Fallingwater Dr Linwood NJ 08221

CONKLIN, JOHN EVAN, sociology educator; b. Oswego, NY, Oct. 2, 1943; s. Evan Nelson and Susan Estelle (Brenner) C.; m. Ruth Tiffany Edmonds, July 10, 1965 (div. Oct. 1974); children: Christopher Perry, Anne Tiffany; m. Sarah Hubbard Belcher, Jan .2, 1982; children: Lydia Catherine, Gillian Jane. AB, Cornell U., 1965; PhD, Harvard U., 1969. Research assoc. Harvard U. Law Sch., Cambridge, Mass., 1969-70; asst. prof. sociology Tufts U., Medford, Mass., 1970-76, assoc. prof. sociology, 1976-81, prof. sociology, 1981—, chmn. dept. sociology, 1981-86, 90-91. Author: Robbery and the Criminal Justice System, 1972, The Impact of Crime, 1975, Illegal But Not Criminal, 1977, Criminology, 1981, 8th edit., 2004, Sociology: An Introduction, 1984, 2d edit., 1987, Art Crime, 1994, Why Crime Rates Fell, 2003; editor: The Crime Establishment, 1973, New Perspectives in Criminology, 1996. Mem. Am. Soc. Criminology, Acad. Criminal Justice Scis. Avocations: collecting books, movie memorabilia. Office: Tufts U Dept of Sociology Eaton Hall Medford MA 02155 Business E-Mail: john.conklin@tufts.edu.

CONKLIN, KENNETH EDWARD, lawyer, utilities executive; b. Keota, Iowa, Aug. 21, 1939; s. Cleo W. and Viola C.; children: David S., Steven J. Student, St. Ambrose Coll., 1957-59, Ariz. State U., 1960-61; BS, N.E. Mo. State U., 1966; JD, Washington Coll. Law Am. U., 1969. Bar: Md., D.C., U.S. Supreme Ct., U.S. Ct. Appeals, U.S. Ct. Claims. Atty. Pub. Defender Office, 1969-70; partner firm Conklin & Noble, Chevy Chase, Md., 1970-76, Leighton, Conklin, Lemov, Jacobs and Buckley, Washington, 1977-83; pres. CEO. Noramco Internat., Inc., Noramex Trading Corp. Bd. dirs. Ea. Pines Devel. Corp., Personal Protection Internat. Inc., Topos Holding Corp., Falls Church Profl. Ctr. Adviser, atty. Legal Aid, 1969-75; mem. Montgomery County (Md.) Rep. Club, v.p., 1972-73. Served with spl. forces AUS, 1962-65, Vietnam. Mem. Am., Montgomery County, Md. State, D.C. bar assns., Assn. Trial Lawyers Am. Home: 1510 12th St N Apt 603 Arlington VA 22209-3634 Office: Noramco Intenat Inc 200 Little Falls St Ste 508 Falls Church VA 22046-4302

CONKLIN, ROBERT EUGENE, electronics engineer; b. Loveland, Ohio, Apr. 21, 1925; s. Charles and Alberta (Reynolds) Conklin; m. Virginia E. McCann, June 14, 1952; children: Carl Lynn, Jill Elaine Conklin Bradford. BSEd, BS in Sci., Wilmington Coll., 1949. Electronic scientist Electronic Technol. Lab. Wright-Patterson AFB, Ohio, 1951—55, electronic engr. AF Avionics Lab., 1956—60, supr. elec. engr., 1960—72; cons. electronic engr., 1972—78; supervisory electronic engr., 1978—82; electronic engr. VHSIC, 1982—84; cons. engr. REC Electronics, Fairborn, Ohio, 1984—. Mem. Inst. Navigation, 1968—72. With USAAC, 1943—46. Mem.: IEEE (H. V. Noble award for Achievements in Electronic Devices 1998), Lions (Fairborn). Republican. Mem. Soc. Friends. Home and Office: 114 Wayne Dr Fairborn OH 45324-5228 E-mail: recelect@earthlink.net.

CONKLIN, THOMAS WILLIAM, lawyer; b. Chgo., Mar. 1, 1938; s. Clarence Robert and Ellen Pauline (Gleason) C.; children: Thomas William, Sarah Adrienne. BA, Yale U., 1960; JD, U. Chgo., 1963. Bar: Ill. 1964, Mich. 1997. Ptnr. Upton, Conklin & Leahy, Chgo., 1969-72, Conklin, Leahy & Eisenberg, Chgo., 1972-79, Conklin & Adler, Ltd., Chgo., 1979-87, Conklin & Roadhouse, Chgo., 1988-95; Rivkin, Radler & Kremer, Chgo., 1995-97; ptnr. Conklin, Murphy, Conklin & Snyder, Chgo., 1997—2004, Conklin & Snyder LLC, Chgo., 2004—05, Conklin & Conklin LLC, Chgo., 2005—. Contbr. numerous articles to legal jours. With USAF, 1963-64. Mem. ABA, Fed. Bar Assn., Am. Arbitration Assn., Internat. Assn. Ins. Counsel, Chgo. Bar Assn., Maritime Law Assn., Mich. Bar Assn., Chgo. Bar Assn., Union League Club Chgo. Home: PO Box 189 Bangor MI 49013-0189 Office: Conklin & Conklin LLC 53 W Jackson Blvd Ste 1150 Chicago IL 60604-3790 Office Phone: 312-341-9500. E-mail: tconk@msn.com.

CONKLIN, WILLIAM FRANK, writer; b. Cambridge, Mass., Apr. 8, 1926; s. Frank Alvin and Helen Pearl (Harvison) Conklin; m. Cecia Bass, Aug. 13, 1948. Student, Bucknell U., U. Colo., U. Va. Lic. comml. pilot FAA; master U.S. Mcht. Marine. Enlisted USN, 1944, naval aviator, combat missions in Korea and Vietnam, 1947—68, exch. officer Fleet Air Arm, Royal Navy, 1956—58, ret. comdr., 1968; sys. analyst Ctr. Naval Analyses, Rosslyn, Va., 1968-71; freelance writer various publs., 1971-80; capt. Am. Cruise Lines, Haddam, Conn., 1981; founder Conklin Marine Ctr. and Chesapeake Area Profl. Capts. Assn., Annapolis, Md., 1982-91; owner, writer BBC Comm., Naples, Fla., 1991—. Decorated 2 Disting. Flying Cross, Bronze Star, 17 Air medals. E-mail: bbccomm@earthlink.net.

CONKLING, ROGER LINTON, management consultant, business administration educator, retired utilities executive; b. Bloomington, Ill., July 12, 1917; s. Robert Edwin and Helen (Ricketts) C.; m. Meta Baskerville, Apr. 4, 1941; children: Mary Beth, Jane Linton, Roger Marc. BBA, Northwestern U., 1941; MA, U. Oreg., 1948; LLD, U. Portland, 1972. With Pub. Svc. Co. No. Ill., Chgo. and Joliet, 1936-42; economist Bonneville Power Adminstrn., Portland, Oreg., 1945-47, asst. to power mgr., 1948-51, chief system devel., 1952-53, chief customer svc., 1954, dir. budget and mgmt., 1955-56, asst. to adminstr., 1957; v.p., assoc. H. Zinder & Assocs., Inc., Washington, 1958-61; pres., cons. Conkling, Inc., Portland, 1962-67; v.p. N.W. Natural Gas Co., Portland, 1967-76, sr. v.p., CFO, 1976-82; ret., 1982. Adj. prof. bus. adminstrn. U. Portland, 1988—; former pres., dir. Pacific Western Pipeline Corp., Portland; mem. grad. faculty Oreg. System Higher Edn., Portland, 1946-56; cons. in field. Author: Marginal Cost in the New Economy, 2004. Past pres., chmn. Oreg. United Appeal; pres. Delauney Inst. Mental Health, 1964; mem. Gov.'s Com. Child Care, 1964; bd. dirs. Cath. Charities, Inc., Portland, 1957-58, 61-64; pres. Oreg. State Soc., Washington, 1960; chmn. exec. com. Nat. Found., 1958-60; chmn. March of Dimes campaign, Portland, 1957; bd. dirs. Mental Health Assn., 1957-58, Cath. Services for Children, 1954-57, Oreg. Symphony Assn., NCCJ, 1980-82, Found. Oreg. Research and Edn., 1967-80; chmn. bd. regents U. Portland; trustee Providence Children's Center; chmn. ann. fund dr. Oreg. Symphony, 1981; mem. fin. council Archdiocese of Portland, 1988-98. With USNR, 1942-45. Recipient Distinguished Service award Dept. Interior, Arthur S. Fleming award Jr. C. of C., Papal honor, Benemerenti medal. Mem. Am. Econ. Assn., Western Econ. Assn., Fed. Govt. Accts. Assn., Am. Gas Assn., Pacific Coast Gas Assn., Assn. Wash. Gas Utilities (trustee, past pres.), Beta Gamma Sigma, Delta Mu Delta. Clubs: Multnomah Athletic (Portland). Home and Office: 2539 SW Hill Crest Dr Portland OR 97201-1749 Office Phone: 503-223-4304. Business E-Mail: conkling@up.edu.

CONLEY, BRUCE W., management consultant; b. Milw., Dec. 10, 1951; s. Jay W. and Joyce M. (Woythal) C.; m. Sandra A. Francis. BS in Computer Sci., U. Pitts., 1986. Systems analyst H.B. Maynard, O'Hara, Pa., 1981-83; cons. Computer Task Group, Pitts., 1983-85, Software Cons., Inc., Pitts., 1985-86; sr. systems engr. Davy-McKee Corp., Pitts., 1986-88; cons. QCI, Carnegie, Pa., 1988-90; systems architect ESA, Inc., Cranberry Twp., Pa., 1990-2000, Affiliated Computer Svcs. Inc., Pitts., 2000—02; computer/networking cons., pres. SMC Info Tech Solutions, 2004—; founder TAG Team USA Tech. Alliance Group, 2004—. Owner, cons. B.C. Computer Tng. and Cons. Svcs., Wexford, Pa., 1990—. Pres. Cloverdale Estates Civic Assn., Wexford, 1994-96, pub. editor, 1992-98. Mem. IEEE, Assn. Computing Machines, DEC User Group, Cranberry C. of C. (pres. bus. devel. group, 2004—). Office: SMC Info Tech Solutions 467 Cloverdale Dr Wexford PA 15090 Office Phone: 724-316-9737. Business E-Mail: bruce.conley@smcinfotechsolutions.com.

CONLEY, CHARLES SWINGER, lawyer; b. Montgomery, Ala., Dec. 8, 1921; s. Prince E. and Fannie (Thompson) C.; m. Ellen Johnson. BS, Ala. State U., 1942; AM in Edn., U. Mich., 1947, AM in History, 1948; JD, NYU, 1955. Assoc. prof. law Fla. A&M U., Tallahassee, 1956-60; judge Ala. Dist. Ct., Tuskegee, 1975; atty. So. Leadership Conf., 1976-85; county lawyer Macon County, Tuskegee, 1988-89; pvt. practice Montgomery, 1989—. Counsel Ala. S.W. Farmer's Coop., 1967-79, Ala. Legal Def. Com., Montgomery, 1968-80; juvenile ct. judge, 1970-74. Cpl. USAF, 1943-46. Mem. ABA, Nat. Bar Assn. (regional dir.). Democrat. Home: 3321 Rosa Parks Ave Montgomery AL 36104 Office: 315 S Bainbridge St Montgomery AL 36104-4315

CONLEY, HELEN DONOVAN, artist, poet; b. N.Y.C., Apr. 9, 1959; d. Robert A.M. and Mary Jane (Samborski) C. AA in Fine Art magna cum laude, No. Va. C.C., 1992. Dir. Escape, Fredericksburg, Va., 1993—. Author: Musical Shadows, 1996, Nightlights, 2001, Transitions, 2000; songwriter (album/cassette) The Train, 1996, (CD) The Songs of Helen Conley; songwriter (songs) The Train, Kings, Another Land, Christmas; artist (mag. cover) Fredericksburg Times, 1994. Named to Wall of Tolerance Meml., Nat. Campaign for Tolerance, Montgomery, Ala. Mem. Nat. Pks. and Conservation Assn. (assoc.), Nat. Com. to Preserve Social Security and Medicare, Phi Theta Kappa (v.p. 1991-92). Democrat. Roman Catholic. Avocations: photography, sketching, writing.

CONLEY, JOHN WALLACE, academic administrator; b. Portsmouth, Ohio, Feb. 15, 1932; s. Hollie Conley and Dora Lee COnley; m. Dolores Holton Conley, July 13, 1954; 1 child, Konni Lee Gargour. AB, Asbury Coll., 1956; MTH, St. Thomas U., 1974; DD (hon.), Asbury Coll., 1974. Pastor First Ch. God, Morehead, Ky., 1960—66, 1991—94, 5th Ave. Ch. God, South Charleston, W.Va., 1966—73; pres. Gulf Coast Bible Coll., Houston, 1973—84, Mid-Am. Bible Coll., Oklahoma City, 1984—90, Circlesville Bible Coll., Ohio, 1994—2004. With U.S. Army, 1951—52. Home: 592 Sycamore Dr Circleville OH 43113

CONLEY, MARK A., lawyer; b. Phila., Nov. 22, 1951; BA magna cum laude, U. Pa., 1973; JD, Columbia U., 1977. Bar: NY 1978, Calif. 1989. With Debevoise & Plimpton, Will and Emery; ptnr. corp. law Katten Muchin Zavis Rosenman, LA. Mem.: U. So. Calif. Inst. for Corp. Counsel, LA Venture Assn., LA County Bar Assn., Calif. State Bar Assn. Office: Ste 2600 2029 Century Park E Los Angeles CA 90067 Office Phone: 310-788-4690. Office Fax: 310-712-8225. E-mail: mark.conley@kmzr.com.

CONLEY, NED LEROY, lawyer; b. Lovelady, Tex., Dec. 7, 1925; s. Robert Preston and Myrtle Ida (Snell) C.; m. Betty Jean Bailey, June 20, 1948; children: Robert Eugene, Richard Owen. BSME, Tex. A&M U., College Station, 1947; LLB, So. Tex. Coll. Law, Houston, 1955. Bar: Tex. 1955. Engr. Mission Mfg. Co., Houston, 1948-55; engr. Hudson Engring. Co., Houston, 1955-56; examiner U.S. Patent Office, 1957; atty. Sun Oil Co., Phila., 1957-59; ptnr. Butler & Binion, Houston, 1959-91, adminstrv. ptnr. patent law sect., 1978-90; sr. ptnr. Conley, Rose & Tayon, P.C., Houston, 1991-97. Past pres. Lamar Terrace Civic Club, Bayou Woods Civic Assn.; mem. Harris County Heritage Soc.; founder, 1st chmn. bd. Meml. Dr. Christian Ch., 1968, chmn. bd., Bethany Christian Ch., 1997. With U.S. Naval Res., 1944-68, ret. lt. comdr. Recipient Layman of Yr. award Disciples of Christ in Tex., 1971 Mem. ABA, Am. Intellectual Property Law Assn., Houston Bar Assn., State Bar Tex. (chmn. intellectual property law sect. 1980-81), Houston Intellectual Property Assn. (pres. 1972), Alumni Assn. South Tex. Coll. Law, Tex. Bar Found., Houston Club, Century Club of Tex. A&M U.

CONLEY, OLGA L., retail executive; CPA. Audit staff Coopers & Lybrand; corp. contr. Project Software and Devel. Inc.; with J. Jill Group, Quincy, Mass., 1991—, various sr. fin. positions, 1991—96, treas., 1993—, CFO, 1997—2003, v.p. fin., 1996—98, sr. v.p. fin., 1998—2001, pres. corp. svc., 2001—03, exec. v.p., CFO, 2003—, chief adminstrv. officer, 2005—. Office: J Jill Group 4 Batterymarch Park Quincy MA 02169

CONLEY, PATRICK T., lawyer, writer, historian, educator, real estate developer; b. Branford, Conn., June 22, 1938; s. William Lincoln Conley and Edith Mae De Stasio; m. Gail C. Cahalan-Conley, Dec. 30, 1994; m. Virginia M. Anderson (div.); children: Patrick Jr., Kathleen, Carolyn, Sharon; m. Donna L. Arruda (div.); m. Ruth E. Trainor (div.); children: Thomas, Colleen. AB, Providence Coll., 1959; JD, Suffolk U., 1973; MA, U. Notre Dame, 1963, PhD, 1970. Bar: R.I.; lic. real estate broker. Prof. history and constitutional law Providence Coll., 1963—88, dir. grad. rsch. Am. history, 1964—94, spl. lectr. history, 1988—94; spl. lectr. constitutional law Salve Regina Coll., 1972—81; tchr. LaSalle Acad., Providence, 1961—62; teaching asst. U. Notre Dame, 1962—63; mem. corp., law sch. adv. com., chmn. libr. adv. com. Roger Williams Coll.; proproetor P.T. Conley Books, 1963—97; ptnr. Foreseeable Devel., Providence. Pres. Phoenix Realty, Four Seas Realty, Hardscrabble Land Co., Sedona Assocs., Options Realty, Phoenix Gambino, Zeus Realty Co.; spkr. in field; developer Conley's Wharf. Author: Democracy in Decline: Rhode Island's Constitutional Development, 1776-1841, 1977, Rhode Island Profile, 1982, An Album of Rhode Island History, 1986, First in War: Last in Peace: Rhode Island and the Constitution, 1786-1970, 1987, Liberty and Justice: A History of Law and Lawyers in Rhode Island, 1636-1998, 1998, Neither Seperate Nor Equal: Legislature and Executive in Rhode ISland Constitutional History, 1999, Rhode Island in Rhetoric and Reflection, 2002; co-author (with Matthew Smith): Catholicism in Rhode ISland: The Formative Era, 1976; co-author: (with Paul Campbell) Providence: A Pictorial History, 1982, Firefighters and Fires in Providence, 1954-1984, 1985; co-author: (with William MacKenzie Woodward and Robert Jones) The Statehouses of Rhode Island: An Architectural and Historical Survey, 1988; editor: Proceedings of Rhode Island Constitutional Convention of 1973, 1973; co-editor: The Constitution and the States, 1988, The Bill of Rights and rhe States, 1992; mem. editl. bd.: Rhode Island Bar Jour., 1980—81, 1985—88, 1990—93, 1998—; editor: R.I. Ethnic Heritage Pamphlet series (13 vols.). Bd. trustees Bicentennial Coun. Thirteen Original States, 1970—92, vice chmn., 1986—87; chmn. U.S. Constitution Coun., 1988—90; pres. Cath. Assn. Coll. Alumni, 1976; chmn. Cranston Historic Dist. Commn., 1970—72; mem. Gov.'s Justice Commn., 1967—69; chmn. Cranston Charter Rev. Commn., 1972—73; policy advisor Gov. Frank Licht, Gov. Philip Noel, Lt. Gov. J. Joseph Garrahy, Atty. Gen. Herbert F. DeSimone, 1966—76; chmn. R.I. Bicentennial Commn. and Found., 1974—77; dir. Provicence Crime Commn., 1977—84; v.p. Human Rels. Commn. Diocese Providence, 1968—69; bd. trustees R.I. Hist. Soc.; chmn. libr. adv. com. Roger Williams Coll., 1990—93, mem. law sch. adv. bd., 1991—97; pres. R.I. Heritage Hall Fame, 2003—; chmn. R.I. Sr. Olympics, 2004—; spl. asst., chmn. adv. coun. U.S. Congressman Robert O. Tiernan, 1967—74; sec., del. R.I. Constitutional Convention, 1973; gen. counsel to pres. R.I. Constitutional Conv., 1986; bd. dirs. Heritage Harbor Mus., 1999—. Named Historian Laureate of RI, 2005. Mem.: Bristol Train Artillery Found. (bd. dirs. 2001—), Providence Maritime Heritage Found. (v.p., dir. 1998—), Bristol Statehouse Found. (founder, pres. 1995—99), R.I. Pubs. Soc. (chmn. 1981—), Bristol Hist. and Preservation Soc. (life), R.I. Hist. Soc. (life), Am. Hist. Assn. (life), Orgn. Am. Historians (life), R.I. Heritage Hall of Fame (pres. 2003—, inducted 1995), R.I. Sr. Olympics (chmn. 2004—), Brahmin Soc. Bristol County, Rotary, Eagles, Elks, KC, The Squatum Assn., Delta Epsilon Sigma. Roman Catholic. Avocations: track and field, travel, interior decorating. Home: 1 Bristol Point Rd Bristol RI 02809 Office: 1445 Wampanoag Trail Providence RI 02918 also: Conley's Wharf State Pier No 1 200 Allens Ave Providence RI 02905 Office Phone: 401-273-1787.

CONLEY, PHILIP JAMES, JR., retired air force officer; b. Providence, May 22, 1927; s. Philip James and Lillian Loretta (Burns) C.; m. Shirley Jean Andrews, Jan. 26, 1956; children: Sharon, Kathleen, Anne, James. BS, U.S. Naval Acad., 1950; MS, U. Mich., 1956, Rensselaer Poly. Inst., 1963. Commd. 2d lt. USAF, 1950, advanced through grades to maj. gen., 1979; dep. chief staff, ops. Air Force Systems Command, Andrews AFB, Washington, 1974-75, chief staff, 1975-78; comdr. Air Force Flight Test Center, Edwards AFB, Calif., 1978-82; vice-comdr. Electronic Systems Divn. Hanscom AFB, Mass., 1983; ret., 1983. Decorated Disting. Svc. medal (2), Legion of Merit (2), Disting. Flying Cross, Bronze Star, Air medal (3). Mem. Air Force Assn., Order of Daedalians, U.S. Naval Acad. Alumni Assn., Am. Legion, Vikings Club (L.A.), Santa Barbara Yacht Club, Monticeto Country Club. Roman Catholic. Home: 930 Camino Viejo Santa Barbara CA 93108-1920

CONLEY, RICHARD SCOTT, orthodontist, educator; m. Janet Lynn Esbiornson, June 28, 1997. BA, Hamilton Coll., Clinton, NY, 1992; DMD, U. Pa., Phila., 1996; cert. in Orthodontics, Vanderbilt U., Nashville, 1999. Instr. Oral and Maxillofacial Surgery dept. Orthodontics divsn. Vanderbilt U. Med. Ctr., Nashville, 1999—2001, asst. prof. Oral and Maxillofacial Surgery dept. Orthodontics divsn., 2001—. Manuscript reviewer Angle Orthodontist Jour., Edina, Minn., 2003—. Deacon, Sunday sch. tchr. Covenant Presbyn. Ch., Nashville, 2002—03. Recipient Tarbell prize, Hamilton Coll., 1990, Philip I. Bowman award, 1991. Mem.: ADA, Am. Cleft Lip and Craniofacial Assn., Nashville Dental Soc., Tenn. Dental Assn. (ACE award 2000, 2002), Edward H. Angle Soc. of Orthodontists (lectr. in field), Tenn. Assn. of Orthodontists, So. Assn. of Orthodontists (lectr. in field), Am. Assn. of Orthodontists (Robert M. Ricketts Sunflower Orthodontic fellowship 2001—02), Omicron Kappa Upsilon, Psi Omega. Achievements include Carnegie Hall Performance (Hamilton College Jazz Ensemble, Mid-America Production: Youth in Music); 1990. Avocations: model trains, reading, music. Office: Vanderbilt Orthodontic Ctr 1500 21st Ave S Ste #3400 Nashville TN 37212 Office Phone: 615-343-0633. E-mail: scott.conley@vanderbilt.edu.

CONLEY, TERENCE P., human resources specialist; BA, NYU, 1985. Various positions in human resources RH Macy & Co.; with PepsiCo, Inc., 1990—99; human resources mgr. to dir. Kentucky Fried Chicken, 1990—92; v.p. human resources PepsiCo, Inc., 1994—96; regional dir. Frito-Lay, 1996—98; exec. v.p. human resources and corporate svcs. Cendant Corp., NYC, 1999—. Dir. Cendant Charitable Found. Office: Cendant Corp 9 W 57th St New York NY 10019*

CONLEY, THOMAS PATRICK, lawyer; b. Nov. 1, 1955; BA, Carleton Coll., 1977; JD, DePaul U., 1980. Bar: Ill. 1980, U.S. Dist. Ct. (no. dist.) Ill. 1980. Ptnr. Arnstein & Lehr LLP, Chgo., 1980—. Exec. dir., gen. counsel Ill. Edn. Facilities Authority; mem. bus. org. acts adv. com. Ill. Sec. of State; lectr. in field. Editor: Survey of Illinois Law: Health Care jour., 1996. Mem.: ABA, Health Care Compliance Assn., Am. health Lawyers Assn., Chgo. Bar Assn. (former chair health care and hosp. law com.), Ill. State Bar Assn. (former chmn. health care sect. coun.). Business E-Mail: tpconley@arnstein.com.

CONLEY, TOM CLARK, literature educator; b. New Haven, Dec. 7, 1943; s. Walter Frederick and Hazel Mason (Hatch) C.; m. Verena Andermatt; children: David, Francine. BA, Lawrence U., 1965; MA, Columbia U., 1966; PhD, U. Wis., 1971. Prof. U. Minn., Mpls., 1971-95; prof. renaissance lit., cinema Harvard U., Cambridge, Mass., 1995—, dir. grad. studies in French. Vis. prof. U. Calif., Berkeley, 1978-79, CUNY Grad. Ctr., 1985-87, Miami U., Ohio, 1989, UCLA, 1995; instr. Folger Inst., 1998; summer seminar leader NEH, 1998; seminar leader Sch. Critical Theory, 2003. Author: Lectura de Bunuel, 1988, Film Hieroglyphs, 1991, Graphic Unconscious, 1992, Self-Made Map, 1995; translator 5 books, editor 2 books; editor jour. Lendemains, 1985—, Diacritics, 2000—; corr. jour. Litterature, 1988—; contbr. articles to profl. jours. Woodrow Wilson fellow, 1965-66, Fulbright fellow, 1968-69, study fellow Am. Coun. Learned Socs., 1975-76, summer fellow NEH, 1974, 89, Inst. for Rsch. in Humanities fellow, 1990, Newberry Libr. fellow, 1992, Soc. Humanities fellow, 1998, Harvard Cabot fellow, 2002, Guggenheim fellow, 2003—. Mem. MLA, Renaissance Soc. Am., Assn. Study Dada/Surrealism, Midwest MLA (mem. exec. com. 1977-80), Sixteenth Century Studies Soc. (exec. com. 1994—), Alpha Omega Alpha. Avocations: handball, fishing, mycology. Office: Harvard U Romance Langs 201 Boylston Hall Cambridge MA 02138 Office Phone: 617-495-2546. Business E-Mail: tconley@fas.harvard.edu.

CONLEY, WILLIAM CLELAND, statistician, educator; b. Lansing, Mich., June 19, 1948; s. William Cleland Conley Sr. and Joan Joyce Conley. BA in Math. cum laude, Albion Coll., 1970; MA in Math., Western Mich. U., 1971; MSc in Math., U. Windsor, Can., 1973; PhD, U. Windsor, 1976. From lectr. to asst. prof. U. Windsor, 1973—77; from asst. prof. to assoc. prof. U. Wis., Green Bay, 1977—99, prof., 1999—. Cons., presenter in field. Author:

Computer Optimization Techniques, 1980, Optimization: A Simplified Approach, 1981, Basic II Advanced, 1983; contbr. articles to profl. jours. Named to Albion Coll. Athletic Hall of Fame, 1995; recipient Faculty award, Founders Assn., 2001. Fellow: Instn. Electronic and Telecomm. Engrs.; mem.: Soc. for Computer Simulation Internat. (sr.), Phi Beta Kappa, Phi Kappa Phi. Achievements include discovery of multi stage monte carlo optimization, TSP statis. for multivariate work. Avocations: jogging, golf, tennis, music. Office: Univ Wis 2420 Nicolet Dr Green Bay WI 54311 Office Phone: 920-465-2051, 920-435-2499. Office Fax: 920-465-2660. Business E-Mail: conleyw@uwgb.edu.

CONLIN, JUDITH, retired director; b. Sun Prairie, Wis., Aug. 25, 1949; d. Harold and Evelyn Quamme; m. Joseph Conlin, May 29, 1971; children: Anthony, Erin. MS in Edn., U. Wis.-Whitewater, 1976. Cert. dir. of instrn. Marian Coll., Wis., 1999, dir. pupil svcs. Marian Coll., Wis., 2003. Tchr. elem. spl. edn. Tomorrow River Sch. Dist., Amherst, Wis., 1971—73; tchr. mid. sch. spl. edn. Sch. Dist. of Tomahawk, Wis., 1973—74; tchr. early childhood spl. edn. and learning disabilities Sch. Dist. of Rhinelander, Wis., 1975—91, elem. tchr., 1991—97; dir. of profl. devel. Coop. Ednl. Svc. Agy. #9, Tomahawk, Wis., 1997—99; dir. of instrn. and pupil svcs. Sch. Dist. of Tomahawk, Wis., 1999—2005; ret., 2005. Presenter Internat. Coun. for Exceptional Children. Mem. early childhood spl. edn. delegation Citizen Amb. Program of People to People; pastoral coun. Nativity of Our Lord Parish, Rhinelander, Wis., 2002—05. Recipient Outstanding Svc. award, Wis. divsn. for early childhood, Coun. for Exceptional Children, 1997 and 1977. Mem.: Wis. Assessment Consortium, Assn. of Wis. Sch. Administrs. Avocations: travel, hiking and biking, reading. Home: 5619 Riverview Dr Rhinelander WI 54501 Personal E-mail: cenlinj@charter.net.

CONLIN, KELLY P., communications executive; BA magna cum laude, Carleton Coll., 1982; MBA, Harvard U., 1987. Mem. Phi Beta Kappa. Chief assignment editor CNN, N.Y.C.; reporter, strategic planning mgr. for mag. divsn. The N.Y. Times; dir., bus. devel. Internat. Data Group, Boston, 1989—91, pres., marketing services div., 1991—95, pres., 1995—2002, CEO, 1999—2002; pres., CEO PRIMEDIA Inc., New York, 2003—. Named One of the Top Five Execs. in Bus. Pub. Field by Media Industry Mag., One of 40 under 40 Most Influential Execs. in Boston by Boston Bus. Jour. Office: PRIMEDIA Inc 745 Fifth Ave New York NY 10151*

CONLIN, LINDA MYSLIWY, bank executive, former federal agency administrator; b. Springfield, Mass. m. Joseph F. Conlin Jr. Pres. Park-Main Travel Agy.; protocol visits officer U.S. Dept. State; from corp. liaison officer for US/USSR intiatives to assoc. dir. Office of Pvt. Sector Coms. U.S. Info. Agy.; asst. sec. commerce for mktg. U.S. Travel and Tourism Adminstrn., 1989—93; dir. Office Travel and Tourism N.J. Commerce Dept., 1994—98; exec. dir. Office Travel and Tourism N.J. Commerce and Econ. Growth Commn., 1998—99; dep. to program chmn. 2000 Rep. Nat. Conv.; sr. campaign coord. Bush/Cheney 2000-Southeastern Pa. Region; asst. sec. trade devel. US Dept. Commerce, Washington, 2001—04. Bd. dir. Export-Import Bank of the US, 2004—. Republican. Office: Export Import Bank of the US 811 Vermont Ave NW Washington DC 20571

CONLIN, ROXANNE BARTON, lawyer; b. Huron, SD, June 30, 1944; d. Marion William and Alyce Muraine (Madden) Barton; m. James Clyde Conlin, Mar. 21, 1964; children: Jacalyn Rae, James Barton, Deborah Ann, Douglas Benton BA, Drake U., 1964, JD, 1966, MPA, 1979; LLD (hon.), U. Dubuque, 1975. Bar: Iowa 1966. Assoc. Davis, Huebner, Johnson & Burt, Des Moines, 1966-67; dep. indsl. commr. State of Iowa, 1967-68, asst. atty. gen., 1969-76; U.S. atty. So. Dist. Iowa, 1977-81; ptnr. Conlin, P.C., Des Moines, 1983—. Adj. prof. law U. Iowa, 1977-79; chmn. Iowa Women's Polit. Caucus, 1973-75, del. nat. steering com., 1973-77; cons. U.S. Commn. on Internat. Women's Year, 1976-77; gen. counsel NOW Legal Def. and Edn. Fund, 1985-88, pres., 1986-88; lectr. in field. Co-editor: ATLAs Litigating Tort Cases, 6 vols., 2003; contbr. articles to profl. jours. Nat. committeewoman Iowa Young Dems.; pres. Polk County Young Dems., 1965-66; del. Iowa Presdl. Conv., 1972; Dem. candidate for gov. of Iowa, 1982; bd. dirs. Riverhills Day Care Ctr., YWCA; chmn. Drake U. Law Sch. Endowment Trust, 1985-86; bd. counselors Drake U., 1982-86; pres. founder Civil Justice Found., 1986-88; pres. Roscoe Pound Found., 1994-97; chair Iowa Dem. Party, 1998-99; chair Edwards For Pres. Iowa, 2004. Named scholarship in her honor, Kansas City Women Lawyers; named one of Top Ten Litigators, Nat. Law Jour., 1989, 100 Most Influential Attys., 1991, 50 Most Powerful Women Attys., Nat. Law Jour., 1998, 10 Most Influential Women Attys., 2002; recipient award, Iowa ACLU, 1974, Alumnus of Yr. award, Drake U. Law Sch., 1989, ann. award, Young Women's Resource Ctr., 1989, Verne Lawyer award as Outstanding Mem., Iowa Trial Lawyers Assn., 1994, Rosalie Wahl award, Minn. Women Lawyers, 1998, Marie Lambert award, 2000, Mary Louise Smith award, YWCA, 2001, Lifetime Achievement award, Des Moines Human Rights Commn., 2003, Ruth Bader Ginsberg award, 2004; scholar Reader's Digest scholar, 1963—64, Fishcher Found., 1965—66. Mem.: ATLA (chmn. consumer and victims coalition com. 1985—87, chmn. edn. dept 1987—88, parliamentarian 1988—89, sec. 1989—90, v.p. 1990—91, pres.-elect 1991—92, pres. 1992—93, Lifetime Achievement award 2003), ABA, NOW, Nat. Ctr. State Ct. Lawyers Com. (com. mem. 2003—), Nat. Inst. Trial Advocacy (bd. trustees 2003—), Trial Lawyers Care (bd. dirs.), Inner Circle of Advocates, Higher Edn. Commn. Iowa (co-chmn. 1988—90), Iowa Acad. Trial Lawyers, Internat. Acad. Trial Lawyers, Assn. Trial Lawyers Iowa (bd. dirs.), Iowa Bar Assn., Chi Omega, Alpha Lambda Delta, Phi Beta Kappa. Office: Griffin Bldg 319 7th St Ste 600 Des Moines IA 50309-3826 Office Phone: 515-283-1111. E-mail: rconlin@roxanneconlinlaw.com.

CONLIN, THOMAS, conductor; b. Arlington, Va., Jan. 29, 1944; BMus, Peabody Conservatory Music, 1966, MMus, 1967; studied with Leonard Bernstein, Erich Leinsdorf, Sir Adrian Boult. Artistic dir. Chamber Opera Soc., Balt., 1966-72; assoc. condr. N.C. Symphony Orch., 1972-74; music dir. Queens (N.Y.) Orchestral Soc., 1974-76; condr. Amarillo (Tex.) Symphony Orch., 1976-84, W.Va. Symphony Orch., 1983-2001, condr. laureate, 2001—; prin. condr. Toledo Opera, 2002—. Asst. prof. mus. CUNY, 1974-76. Composer: Naxos and Bridge. Recipient Grammy award for Contemporary Classical Composition, 2001, Indie award nomination for Best Orch. Rec., 2002. Mem. Am. Symphony Orch. League, Nat. Opera Assn., Condrs. Guild, Opera America. Studio: 8440 Augusta Ln Holland OH 43528 Office Phone: 419-867-6977. E-mail: thconmusic@aol.com.

CONLIN, THOMAS JAMES, lawyer; b. Willison, N.D., June 9, 1957; s. Clement William and Patricia (Scofield) C.; m. Kathleen Anne Marron, May 8, 1985; children: Riley, Erin. BA, U. Notre Dame, 1979; JD, U. Minn., 1982. Bar: Minn. 1982, U.S. Dist. Ct. Minn. 1982, U.S. Ct. Appeals (8th cir.) 1985, U.S. Supreme Ct. 1995. Assoc. Robins, Kaplan, Miller & Ciresi, Mpls., 1982-88, ptnr., 1988—. Bar: Minn. 1982, U.S. Dist. Ct. (Minn.) 1982, U.S. Ct. Appeals (8th cir.) 1985, U.S. Supreme Ct. 1995. Mem. Vol. Lawyers Network, Mpls. Mem. ABA, ATLA, Minn. State Bar Assn., Minn. Trial Lawyers Assn., Trial Lawyers for Pub. Justice, India Assn., Hennepin County Bar Assn. Home: 1305 Spring Valley Rd Golden Valley MN 55422-4747 Office: Robins Kaplan Miller & Ciresi LLP 800 Lasalle Ave Ste 2800 Minneapolis MN 55402-2015 E-mail: tjconlin@rkmc.com.

CONLON, EDWARD, police officer, writer; b. Bronx, NY, 1965; s. John Conlon. BA in English, Harvard U., 1987. Freelance writer; social worker Bklyn.; with NYC Police Dept., 1995—, now detective 44th precinct. Columnist (under byline Marcus Laffey) The New Yorker. Author: Blue Blood, 2004. Office: NYPD 44th Precinct 2 E 169th St Bronx NY 10452*

CONLON, MICHAEL WILLIAM, lawyer; b. Wilkes Barre, Pa., Nov. 9, 1946; s. William Peter and Dorothy Conlon; m. Alice Cario, June 14, 1969; children: Michele, Stacia. AB magna cum laude, Cath. U., 1968; JD, Duke U., 1971. Bar: Tex. 1971, D.C. 1993. Ptnr. Fulbright & Jaworski, Houston, 1978-93, 98—, ptnr. in charge Washington, 1993-98, co-head corp., banking and bus. practice dept., 1999—, co-ptnr. in charge Houston Office, 2001—. Office: Fulbright & Jaworski LLP 1301 McKinney St Houston TX 77010-3031 Office Phone: 713-651-5427. Office Fax: 713-651-5246. E-mail: mconlon@fulbright.com.

CONLON, PEGGY EILEEN, publisher; b. Santa Monica, Calif., Mar. 2, 1951; d. Daniel Francis and Mary Eileen (Garrity) C.; m. Robert J. Reale, May 21, 1993. AA, Victor Valley Jr. Coll., Apple Valley, Calif.; BA, Calif. State U., Fullerton; MA, U. So. Calif.-Annenberg, L.A. Account exec. Dozier Eastman, Santa Ana, Calif., 1973-75; advt. and pub. rels. mgr. ITT Marine Divsn., Costa Mesa, Calif., 1975-80, EECO, Santa Ana, 1980-82; group pub. CMP Publs., Manhasset, N.Y., 1982-92; pub. Broadcasting & Cable, N.Y.C., 1992—; pres. The Advt. Coun., 1999—. Lt. USNR, 1974-81. Mem. Internat. Radio and TV Soc. (bd. dirs. 1993-96), exec. coun. The Quills. Office: Broadcasting & Cable 245 W 17th St New York NY 10011-5300 also: Advertising Council Fl 11 261 Madison Ave New York NY 10016*

CONLON, SUZANNE B., federal judge; b. 1939; AB, Mundelein Coll., 1963; JD, Loyola U., Chgo., 1968; postgrad., U. London, 1971. Law clk. to judge U.S. Dist. Ct. (no. dist.) Ill., 1968-71; assoc. Pattishall, McAuliffe & Hostetter, 1972-73, Schiff Hardin & Waite, 1973-75; asst. U.S. atty. U.S. Dist. Ct. (no. dist.) Ill., 1976-77, 82-86, U.S. Dist. Ct. (cen. dist.) Calif., 1978-82; exec. dir. U.S. Sentencing Commn., 1986-88; spl. counsel to assoc. atty. gen., 1988; judge U.S. Dist. Ct. (no. dist.) Ill., 1988—. Asst. prof. law De Paul U., Chgo., 1972-73, lectr., 1973-75; adj. prof. Northwestern U. Sch. Law, 1991-95; vice chmn. Chgo. Bar Assn. Internat. Inst., 1993—; vis. com. U. Chgo. Harris Grad. Sch. Pub. Policy, 1997—; bd. mem. DePaul U. Coll. Law, Internat. Human Rights Law Inst. Bd. mem. Ill. St. Andrew Soc. Mem. ABA, FBA, Am. Judicature Soc., Internat. Bar Assn. Judges Forum, Lawyers Club Chgo. (pres. 1996-97). Office: US Dist Ct No Dist Everett McKinley Dirksen Bldg 219 S Dearborn St Ste 2356 Chicago IL 60604-1878

CONLON, THOMAS JAMES, marketing executive; b. NYC, July 30, 1935; s. Kenneth Charles and Catherine (Gavaghan) C.; m. Joan Anna Erickson, Jan. 19, 1957; children: Brian T., Michael K., Keith J.K. Ed., Art Students' League, N.Y.C., 1951-53, St. Peter's Coll., Jersey City, 1953-56. Staff artist N.Y. News, N.Y.C., 1953-57, spl. features writer-reporter, 1957-59; mktg. mgr. Tricolator Inc., Wantagh, N.Y., 1959-64; assoc. dir. promotion Benton & Bowles, N.Y.C., 1964-68; chmn. D.L. Blair Inc., Garden City, NY, 1968—, PMI, Inc., Atlanta, 1986—, DLB/W, Beverly Hills, Calif., 1987—; mng. dir./gerant Blair Europe, Paris, 1991-98; mng. ptnr. Conlon Holdings Inc., 1999—; pres. Conlon Assocs., LP, 1999—. Illustrator for various mags., 1952-53. Home: Wolver Hollow Rd Oyster Bay NY 11771-4301 Office: DL Blair Inc 1051 Franklin Ave Garden City NY 11530-2931

CONLON, WILLIAM F., lawyer; b. Chgo., Jan. 14, 1945; AB, Ind. U., 1967; JD, U. Ill., 1970. Bar Ill. 1970, Iowa 1970, U.S. Supreme Ct. 1975. Asst. U.S. Atty. U.S. Attys. Office (no. dist.) Ill., 1974-79, chief civil divsn., 1977-79; ptnr. corp. criminal def. and internal investigations Sidley Austin Brown & Wood, Chgo., gen. counsel and mem. exec. com. Chmn. Ill. State Bd. Ethics, 1986-88, active, 1982-88, Jud. Inquiry Bd., 1992—97; adj. prof. law Northwestern U., 1991—. Pres. Glencoe (Ill.) Sch. Bd., 1987-88, active, 1981-89. 1st lt. US Army, 1970-72. Fellow Am. Coll. Trial Lawyers. Office: Sidley Austin Brown & Wood LLP Bank One Plz 10 S Dearborn St Chicago IL 60603 Office Phone: 312-853-7384. Office Fax: 312-853-7036. Business E-Mail: wconlon@sidley.com.

CONLY, JOHN FRANKLIN, retired engineering educator; b. Ridley Park, Pa., Sept. 11, 1933; s. Harlan and Mary Jane (Roberts) Conly; m. Jeannine Therese McDonough, Apr. 14, 1967; children: J. Paul, Mary Ann. BS, U. Pa., 1956, MS, 1958; PhD, Columbia U., 1962. Instr. U. Pa., Phila., 1956-58; rsch. asst. Columbia U., N.Y.C., 1959-62; asst. prof. engring. San Diego State U., 1962-65, assoc. prof., 1965-69, prof., 1969—2003, prof. emeritus, 2003—, chmn. dept., 1971-74, 77-85, wind tunnel dir., 1978—2001. D. and F. Guggenheim fellow, 1958. Fellow: AIAA (assoc.; sect. chmn. 1970, best U.S. sect.). Republican. Episcopalian. Office: San Diego State U Dept Aerospace Engring San Diego CA 92182

CONN, ERIC EDWARD, plant biochemist; b. Berthoud, Colo., Jan. 6, 1923; s. William Elmer and Mary Anna (Smith) C.; m. Louise Carolyn Kachel, Oct. 17, 1959; children: Michael E., Kevin E. BA in Chemistry, U. Colo., 1944; PhD in Biochemistry, U. Chgo., 1950. Instr. biochemistry U. Chgo., 1950-52; instr. U. Calif., Berkeley, 1952-53, asst. prof., 1953-58, assoc. prof. Davis, 1958-63, prof., 1964—. Author: (with P.K. Stumpf) Outlines of Biochemistry, 1963, 5th edit., 1987; editor: (with P.K. Stumpf) (book series) Biochemistry of Plants, 1980-90. With U.S. Army, 1944-46. Recipient Pergamon Phytochemistry prize and cert., 1994;, USPHS, 1960, Fulbright Rsch. grantee, 1965, Australian acacia "Acacia conniana" named in his honor, 1984. Mem. NAS, Phytochem. Soc. N.Am. (hon. life mem., pres. 1971-72, editor in chief 1984-89), Am. Soc. Plant Biology (pres. 1986-87, Charles Reid Barnes life mem.), Am. Soc. Biol. Chemistry, Phytochemistry Soc. Europe, Am. Soc. Pharmacognasy. Democrat. Avocations: gardening, stamp collecting/philately. Office: U Calif Sect Molecular & Cellular Biol Davis CA 95616 Office Phone: 530-753-4174.

CONN, GORDON BRAINARD, JR., lawyer; b. St. Louis, Dec. 20, 1944; BA, Macalester Coll., 1967; JD, U. Mich., 1970. Bar: Minn. 1970, U.S. Supreme Ct. 1986; cert. in bus. bankruptcy law Am. Bd. Certification. Law clk. to Chief Justice Minn. Supreme Ct., St. Paul, 1970-71; ptnr. Faegre & Benson, Mpls., 1971-99, Kalina, Wills, Gisvold & Clark, P.L.L.P., Mpls., 1999—. Mem. ABA, Am. Bankruptcy Inst., Minn. State Bar Assn., Comml. Law League Am., Nat. Assn. Bankruptcy Trustees. Office: # 560 6160 Summit Dr N Minneapolis MN 55430-2100 Office Phone: 612-789-9000.

CONN, REX BOLAND, JR., pathologist, educator; b. Marengo, Iowa, Aug. 3, 1927; s. Rex Boland and Helena Dorothea (Schoenfelder) C.; m. Victoria Grace Sellens, Dec. 28, 1950; children: Elizabeth Marian, Victoria Anne, Mary Catherine. BS, Iowa State U., 1949; MD, Yale U., 1953; BSc, U. Oxford, Eng., 1955; MS, U. Minn., 1960. Prof. pathology, dir. clin. labs. W.Va. Med. Center, Morgantown, 1960-68; prof. lab. medicine, dir. dept. Johns Hopkins Med. Instns., Balt., 1968-77; prof. pathology and lab. medicine, dir. clin labs. Emory U., Atlanta, 1977-87; prof. and vice chmn. dept. pathology and cell biology, dir. clin. labs. Thomas Jefferson U., Phila., 1987-97; prof. emeritus Jefferson Med. Coll., Phila., 1997—. Mem. pathology tng. com. NIH, 1972-73, mem. pathology A study sect., 1968-72; cons. Walter Reed Army Med. Center, 1972-77; cons. Armed Forces Inst. of Pathology, 1984-88. Editor: Current Diagnosis, 1997, Yearbook of Pathology and Clinical Pathology, 1980, Applied Laboratory Medicine, 1992. Served with USNR, 1945-46. Mem. Coll. Am. Pathologists, Am. Soc. Clin. Pathologists (dir. 1975-81, pres. 1993-94), Acad. Clin. Lab. Physicians and Scientists (pres. 1972). Office: Thomas Jefferson Univ Jefferson Alumni Hall 212 Philadelphia PA 19107 Office Phone: 215-238-1977. Business E-Mail: rex.conn@mail.tju.edu.

CONN, RICHARD LEE, computer scientist, educator; b. Logansport, Ind., Apr. 11, 1954; s. Harry Richard and Forest Geneva Conn. BS in Computer Sci., Rose-Hulman Inst. Tech., 1976; MS in Computer Sci., U. Ill., 1978. Cert. instr., GE Aircraft Engines. Tech. cons. U.S. Army Satellite Comm. Agy., Ft. Monmouth, N.J., 1978-80; instr. Air Force Inst. Tech., Wright-Patterson AFB, Ohio, 1980-82; computer scientist U.S. Army Software Devel. and Support Ctr., Ft. Monmouth, 1982-84; software design engr. Tex. Instruments, Dallas, 1984-85; mgr. Ada Software Repository Project, White Sands, N.Mex., 1984-93; pvt. practice Plano, Tex., 1986; software engr. advanced engring. tech. dept. software engring. section GE Aircraft Engines, Cin., 1986-92; mgr. Mgmt. Assistance Corp. Am., White Sands Missile Range, 1987-91; with Defense Advanced Rsch. Projects Agy./Ada Joint Program Office, Washington, 1991-92; mem. fed. adv. bd. Ada Joint Program Office The Pentagon, Washington, 1992-93; mgr. Pub. Ada Libr. Monmouth Coll., West Long Branch, N.J., 1993-97; prof. software engring. dept. Monmouth U., 1995-97; sr. software process engr. Lockheed Martin Aeronautics, Marietta, Ga., 1997—2003; rsch. prof. info. sci. and tech. Monmouth Coll., West Long Branch, N.J., 1993-95; mem. tech. staff MITRE Corp., Eatontown, N.J., 1992-95; acad. liaison Micrsocft, Atlanta, 2003—. Adj. prof. dept. elec. and computer engring. U. Cin., 1990-92; adj. prof. computer sci. and info. sys. Kennesaw (Ga.) State U., 1998—; adj. prof. computing and software engring. So. Polytech. State U., 2002—; instr. dept. elec. engring. Air Force Inst. Tech., Wright-Patterson AFB, 1980-82, human resources dept. GE Aircraft Engines, Cin., 1987-92; co-chair Assn. Computing Machinery/Spl. Interest Group Ada Edn. Working Group; mem. DoD Ada Awareness Group; working group on Ada as design lang. IEEE; mem. Ada quality and style guide team Software Productivity Consortium. Author: ZCPR3: The Manual, 1985, The Ada Software Repository and the Defense Data Network: A Resouce Handbook, 1987; editor Walnut Creek Ada CDRom; editor, lead Ada and Software Engring. Libr. and CDRom. Lead Software Devel. and Engring. SIG, Atlanta PC User's Group, Atlanta, Ga., 2001—03. Capt. US Army Signal Corps, 1976—82, Wright-Patterson AFB, OH. Recipient 2 Army Commendation medals. Master: Software Devel. and Engring. SIG, Atlanta PC User's Group (lead 2001—02); mem.: IEEE, Am. Legion, Assn. Computing Machinery (edn. co-chair Spl. Interest Group in Ada 1984—95), Masons, Tau Beta Pi. Achievements include development of Created the ZCPR series of Operating and Software Development Systems; research in Performed funded research in software reuse; developed the ZCPR3, CSPARTS, SCATC, and DCS3 Domain Specific Software Development Kits; first to Played a role in the development of the Ada programming language; served on Federal Advisory Board for Ada; Reviewer for DoD Software Reuse Initiative; Awarded Outstanding Contributions to the Ada C; development of Wrote numerous courses distributed world-wide in the Public Ada Library, the Ada and Software Engineering Library, and the ACM Journal for Educational Resources in Computing. Avocations: chess, swimming.

CONN, RUTH HELEN, music educator; b. Laurel, Miss., Jan. 25, 1947; d. Baker Frank NcNair and Mary Magdalene McNair; m. Thomas C. Conn, Dec. 24, 1965 (dec. Jan. 2003); 1 child, Tommy Jr. B of Music Edn, Miss. State U., 1999. Tchr. choral music Leake County Schs., Carthage, Miss., 1999—2000, Scott County Sch. Dist., Forest, 2000—. Ch. painist, organist. Mem.: Music Educators Nat. Conf., Am. Choral Dirs. Assn. Avocations: music, gardening. Home: 102 Jackson Ave Carthage MS 39051 Office: Scott County Sch Dist 2415 Old Jackson Rd Forest MS 39074

CONNAIR, STEPHEN MICHAEL, financial analyst; b. Fredericksburg, Va., Sept. 10, 1950; s. Thomas Joseph Jr. and Wilma Melvina (McCarty) C.; m. Karen Lee Matusoff, Feb. 15, 1986. BA in Philosophy, Duns Scotus Coll., 1973; MA in Religious Studies, U. Dayton, 1976; PhL in Philosophy, Cath. U. Am., 1983; MPA, Va. Tech., 1992; grad., grad., Columbia Grad. Sch. Bus., 2004. Tchr. Cath. Sch. Sys., Cin., 1973-83; fin. analyst USAF The Pentagon, Washington, 1985—. Mem. Smithsonian resident assoc. program, Washington, 1987—; sec., bd. dirs. Arlington Run Homeowners Assn., 1990-92; v.p. Sleepy Hollow Woods Civic Assn., 1996-97, pres., 1997-98. Mem. Am. Soc. Mil. Comptrs. (Profl. award 1990, Outstanding Analysis and Evaluation award 1992), Soc. Cost Estimating and Analysis, Am. Cath. Philos. Assn., Air Force History Found., Air Force Assn., Naval War Coll. Found., Nat. Air and Space Soc., Wilson Ctr. Assn., Nat. Trust for Hist. Preservation, Am. Acad. Polit. Sci., Am. Soc. Pub. Adminstrn., Am. Econ. Assn., George C. Marshall Found., James Madison Inst., Nat. Hist. Soc., Va. Hist. Soc., Arlington County Hist. Soc., Fairfax County Hist. Soc., Soc. for Mil. History, Nat. Assn. Scholars, Libr. of Congress Assn., Civil War Round Table, Hon. Order of Ky. Cols., Pi Alpha Alpha. Roman Catholic. Avocations: civil war buff, american history, movies, reading. Home: 3808 Moss Dr Annandale VA 22003-1917

CONNALLY, SANDRA JANE OPPY, retired art educator, artist; b. Crawfordsville, Ind., Feb. 10, 1941; d. Thomas Jay and Helen Louise (Lane) Oppy; m. Thomas Maurice Connally, Nov. 9, 1962 (dec. May 2004); children: Leslie Erin Connally Hosier Dakins, Tyler Maurice. BS, Ball State U., 1963, MA, 1981. Freelance writer, Muncie, Ind., 1971-76; art/freelance, 1964-81; substitute tchr. Muncie (Ind.) Cmty. Schs., 1980—81, art tchr., 1981—2003; ret., 2003. Two women shows include Emens Auditorium, Ball State U., 1983; exhibited in group shows at Ball State U., 1964, Alford House/Anderson (Ind.) Fine Arts Ctr., 1979-81, Historic 8th St. Exhbn., 1981, Patrons Watercolor Gala, Oklahoma City, 1983, Whitewater Valley Annual Drawing, Painting and Printmaking Competition, Richmond, Ind., 1983; represented in pvt. collections; contbr. short stories to profl. publs. Grantee Container Corp. Am., 1981, Ball State U. Mus. Art/Margaret Ball Meml. Fund, 1992, Robert B. Bell, 1993-95; recipient Achievement award Ind. Dept. Edn., 1992-94, Nat. Gallery Videodisc Competition, 1993; named disting. UniverCitizen Ball State U., 1992, Tchr. Intergalactic Art First Place Ind. State winner, 1998. Mem. NEA, Ind. State Tchr. Assn., Muncie Tchrs. Assn., Nat. Art Edn. Assn. (del. nat. convention 1998, 2000-03), Art Edn. Assn. Ind. Republican. Methodist. Avocations: computer art, watercolor, handmade paper and glass fusing, arts, travel. Home: 1932 Bay Pointe Dr E Bloomington IN 47401-8136

CONNAUGHTON, JAMES L., federal official; m. Susanna Connaughton; children: Spencer, Grace. Grad., Yale U.; JD magna cum laude, Northwestern U. Law clk. U.S. Dist. Judge Marvin Aspen No. Dist. Ill.; U.S. negotiator ISO 14000, 1993—2001; ptnr. environ. practice group Sidley Austin Brown & Wood; chmn. Coun. on Environ. Quality Exec. Office of the Pres., Washington, 2001—. Lectr. in field. Coordinating articles editor: Northwestern U. Law Rev. Scholar Austin scholar, Northwestern U. Mem.: Order of the Coif. Avocations: sailing, singing, beach combing. Office: Exec Office of the Pres Coun on Environ Quality 730 Jackson Pl NW Washington DC 20503

CONNELL, ALASTAIR MCCRAE, physician; b. Glasgow, Scotland, Dec. 21, 1929; came to U.S., 1970; s. Alex McCrae and Maud (Crawford) C.; m. Joyce Dethlefs, 1983; children: Stewart, Fiona, Alison, Iain, Andrew. BS, U. Glasgow, 1951, MB, ChB, 1954, MD, 1969. Intern Western Infirmary, Glasgow, 1954-55; resident in gastroenterology Cen. Middlesex and St. Mark's Hosp., London, 1957-60; practice medicine specializing in gastroenterology, 1960—; mem. med. staff Med. Rsch. Coun., 1960-64; sr. lectr. clin. sci. Queen's U., Belfast, No. Ireland, 1964-70; Mark Brown prof. medicine Med. Ctr., U. Cin., 1970-79, dir. div. digestive diseases, 1970-79, prof. physiology, 1972-79, assoc. dean, 1975-77; dir. Office Clin. Affairs, 1975-77; dean Coll. Medicine, U. Nebr. Med. Ctr., 1979-84, prof. internal medicine, 1979-84; v.p. health scis. Va. Commonwealth U., Richmond, 1984-88; scholar-in-residence Inst. Medicine, 1988-89; vice chancellor health scis. Ea. Carolina U., 1989-90; dir. Office Healthcare Inspections, Dept. Vets. Affairs, Washington, 1991-96; adj. prof. med. George Washington U., 1992-97; prof. kinesiology Coll. William and Mary, 2005—. Vis. prof. dept. moral philosophy U. St. Andrews, Scotland, 1984-86; mem. sci. adv. bd. Nat. Found. for Ileitis and Colitis, 1974-80, chmn. rsch. devel. com., 1974-78; mem. Personal Health Com. Ohio, 1974-76; trustee Medco Peer Rev., 1974-79; adj. prof. health adminstrn. Va. Commonwealth U., 1996-2000; med. dir. Williamsburg Landing, 1999-2002; chair Sr. Svcs. Coalition, Williamsburg, Va., 2005—. Author: Clinical Tests of Gastric Function, 1973; author: (with T. Wan) Monitoring the Quality of Health Care, 2002; assoc. editor Am. Jour. Digestive Diseases; contbr. articles to profl. jours. Served with M.C. Royal Army, 1955-57. Fellow Royal Coll. Physicians (Edinburgh), ACP; mem. Am. Assn. Home Care Physicians, Brit. Soc. Gastroenterology, Internat. Group for Study Intestinal Motility (past pres.). Address: 3523 Hollingsworth Dr Williamsburg VA 23188 E-mail: alastaird@verizon.net.

CONNELL, CAROL MATHESON, corporate communications specialist, consultant; d. David Matheson and Marion Elizabeth Frances Connell. MBA in Mktg., Columbia U., 1992; PhD, U. Glasgow, Scotland, 2001. Dir. corp. comms. and rsch. Seagram Co. Ltd., N.Y.C., 1980-96; dir. mktg. and rsch. Juvenile Diabetes Found., N.Y.C., 1996-98; sr. strategy cons. IBM, Armonk, NY, 1998—2004; asst. prof. Econs. Bklyn. (N.Y.) Coll. CUNY, 2004—. Peer coach prof. tchg. act, 2001—. NDEA and Columbia U. fellow Columbia

U. Grad. Faculties, 1971, 72. Mem. IEEE, AAAS, Airplane Owner and Pilot Assn. (assoc.). Roman Catholic. Avocation: aviation (private pilot). Office Fax: 973-484-8598. Personal E-mail: templetuttle@aol.com.

CONNELL, GEORGE EDWARD, retired academic administrator, research scientist; b. Saskatoon, Sask., Can., June 20, 1930; s. James Lorne and Mabel Gertrude (Killins) C.; m. Sheila Harriet Horan, Dec. 27, 1955; children: James, Caroline, Thomas, Margaret. BA, U. Toronto, Ont., Can., 1951, PhD in Biochemistry, 1955; DSc, U. Toronto, 1993; LLD (hon.), McGill U., 1987. NSF postdoctoral fellow, 1956-57; asst. prof. biochemistry U. Toronto, 1957-62, assoc. prof., 1962-65, prof., chmn. dept. biochemistry, 1965-70, assoc. dean faculty of medicine, 1972-74, v.p. rsch. and planning, 1974-77, pres., 1984-90, U. Western Ont., London, 1977-84; chair Nat. Round Table on Economy and Environ., 1990-95; vice chair Environ. Assessment Bd., Ont., 1990-93. Bd. dirs. So. Time, 1985-95; chmn. TC207, Internat. Stds. Orgn., 1993-96; prin. adviser Commn. Inquiry on Blood Sys. Can., 1993-95; chmn. bd. protein engring. Nat. Ctr. Excellence, 1995-97; chmn. Task Force on Funding and Delivery Med. Care in Ont., 1995-96; sr. policy advisor Can. Found. for Innovation, 1997; bd. dirs. Allelix Biopharms., Inc., 1994-99; mem. Ont. Press Coun., 1996-2002; trustee McLaughlin Found., 1996-2002; vice-chair Premier's Rsch. Excellence Awards, Ont., 1999-02; chair mgmt. com. Can. Prostate Cancer Rsch. Initiative, 2000-02; mem. rsch. adv. panel Walkerton Inquiry; bd. dirs. Lake Simcoe Region Conservation Found., 2001-, Energy Probe Found., 2002-. Recipient Order of Can., 1987. Fellow Chem. Inst. Can., Royal Soc. Can.; mem. Am. Soc. Biol. Chemists, Can. Biochem. Soc. (pres. 1973-74). E-mail: george.connell@sympatico.ca.

CONNELL, JOHN GIBBS, JR., former government official; b. Atlanta, Sept. 26, 1914; s. John Gibbs and Vena Estelle (Turner) C.; m. Bernice E. Siewerdsen, Oct. 2, 1941 (dec. June 2001); children: Sharon Elaine, Candace Anne. AA, George Washington U., 1948, AB, 1952. With U.S. Civil Service Commn., 1935-38, U.S. Housing Authority, 1938-40; with War Dept. and Army Dept., 1940-79; personnel mgr. Office of Sec. Army, 1942-54, asst. for security and personnel, 1954-62, dep. adminstrv. asst. to sec. army, 1962-66, adminstv. asst. to sec. army, 1966-79. Chmn. Army Security Screening Bd., 1953-66; prin. adminstrv. officer Army Loyalty-Security Program, 1950-79; mem. Army Bd. Correction Mil. Records, 1947-62; Army Dept. rep. interdepartmental com. to study govt. employee security programs for Pres. Truman, 1951-52; Army rep. Exec. Officers Group, 1968-79; mem. Dept. Def. Concessions Com., 1966-79; Army rep. Fed. Exec. Bd., 1969-79; mem. adv. com. Nat. Archives and Records Service, 1973 Bd. dirs. Army-Air Force Civilian Welfare Fund, Youth Devel. Inst. Served to 2d lt. USAAF, 1943-45; 1st lt. OSS, 1945-46; maj. M.I. Army Res. Recipient Army Exceptional Civilian Svc. medal, 1973, 75, 79, 40-Yr. cert. of svc. award, 1975, Meritorious Civilian Svc. award, 1977, sculpture award Faculty-Student Show, Art League, Alexandria, Va., 1982, 89; hon. mention for sculpture Young at Art Exhbn., 1991, hon. mention, 1992, 93. Mem.: OSS Soc., Sculptor, Coun. Former Fed. Execs., Nat. Assn. Ret. Fed. Employees, Fed. Sr. Exec. Svc. (charter), Art League of Alexandria, Sigma Nu. Presbyterian (elder). Home: 302 Cloverway Dr Alexandria VA 22314-4818 *I try to govern my life so as to serve others as I would have them serve me. I believe in the inherent dignity of man as an individual.*

CONNELL, JOSEPH F., academic administrator; b. Johnstown, Pa., Mar. 13, 1980; s. Louis and Patricia Connell. BA in Bus. Adminstrn., Lycoming Coll., 2002; MS, MS in Coll. Student Pers., Miami U., 2004. Admission counselor, grad. asst. Miami U., Oxford, Ohio, 2002—04; adminstr., commuter coord. Marist Coll., Poughkeepsie, NY, 2004—. Leadership cons. Marist Coll., Poughkeepsie, 2005—, adj. instr., 2005—; tchr. Kaplan, White Plains, 2005—. Youth min. Young Life, Williamsport, Pa., 1998—2000. Recipient Pax Christi medal, Lycoming Coll., 2002; scholar, 1998—2002. Mem.: Am. Coll. Pers. Assn., Sigma Tau Delta, Phi Kappa Phi, Delta Mu Delta. Roman Catholic. Avocations: tennis, travel, basketball, community service. Home: 15 Summer Set Dr Montgomery NY 12549 Office: Marist Coll 3399 North Rd Poughkeepsie NY 12589 Office Phone: 845-575-3787. Personal E-mail: joseph_f_connell@hotmail.com. E-mail: joseph.connell@marist.edu.

CONNELL, JUDSON T., dentist; b. Covington, Ga. m. Elaine Connell; children: Lauren, Logan. BS, Mars Hill Coll.; DMD, Med. Coll. Augusta, 1991; grad, Las Vegas Inst. Advanced Dental Studies. Lic. Ga. Bd. Dentistry, Nat. Dental Bd., 1991. Founder Premier Dental Designs, Rincon, Ga., 1992—. Mem.: Acad. Gen. Dentistry, Am. Dental Assn. Baptist. Avocations: fishing, hunting, woodworking. Office: 5871 Highway 21, S Rincon GA 31326 Office Phone: 912-826-4037. E-mail: info@PremierDentalDesigns.com.*

CONNELL, MARY ELLEN, diplomat; b. Laconia, N.H., Jan. 20, 1943; d. Howard Benjamin and Jessie Louise Smith Naylor; m. O. J. Connell III, Nov. 4, 1969 (div. Aug. 1988); 1 child, Piers Andrew. BA, Smith Coll., Northampton, Mass., 1964; MPhil, U. Kans., 1969; MS, Nat. War Coll., 1992. Info. ctr. dir. U.S. Fgn. Svc., Nairobi, Kenya, 1978-80, pub. affairs officer Bujumbura, Burundi, 1980-82; officer African affairs USIA, Washington, 1982-85, exec. asst. to assoc. dir. for policy, 1985-86; counselor pub. affairs U.S. Fgn. Svc., Copenhagen, 1986-90; vis. scholar St. Deiniol's Wales, 1991; exec. sec. USIA, Washington, 1992-95; pub. affairs advisor U.S. Mission to NATO, Brussels, 1995-97; spl. asst. to asst. sec. defense for pub. affairs Washington, 1997-99; mem. policy planning staff Dept. of State, Washington, 1999—; sr. policy analyst Ctr. for Naval Analyses, 2001—. Mem. Internat. Inst. Strategic Studies, Am. Fgn. Svc. Assn., Atlantic Coun., Army and Navy Club. Episcopalian. Office: CNA 4825 Mark Ctr Dr Alexandria VA 22311-1850 Office Phone: 703-824-2281. E-mail: connellme@aol.com.

CONNELL, PAUL J., lawyer; s. James E. and Geraldine M. Connell; m. Kathryn W. Sparks, June 16, 2001. BS in Engring., Cornell U., 1973, MBA, 1974; JD, Emory U., 1980. Bar: Ga. 1980. Cons. Kurt Salmon Assocs., Atlanta, 1974—80, dir. fin., 1980—83; assoc. Kilpatrick & Cody, London, 1983—87, ptnr., 1987—92, Paul Hastings Janofsky Walker, Atlanta, 1992—. Named Super Lawyer, Ga., 2004—05; named one of Best Lawyers in Am., 2003—05; named to Ga.'s Legal Elite, 2004. Mem.: TAPPI, ASME, ABA, Internat. Bar Assn., Law Soc. Eng. and Wales, Atlanta Bar Assn. Office: Paul Hastings Janofsky & Walker 600 Peachtree St NE Ste 2400 Atlanta GA 30308 Office Phone: 404-815-2200. Business E-Mail: paulconnell@paulhastings.com.

CONNELL, PHILIP FRANCIS, food industry executive; b. Hamilton, Ont., Can., Jan. 20, 1924; s. Maurice W. and Kathleen (Richardson) C. BA, McMaster U., Can., 1946. Chartered acct. With Clarkson Gordon & Co. (Ernst & Young), Hamilton and Toronto, 1946-57; comptroller Canadian Westinghouse Co. Ltd., Hamilton, 1957-67; controller Domtar Ltd., Montreal, 1967-68; v.p. fin. George Weston Ltd., Toronto, Ont., 1968-75, Loblaw Cos., Ltd., Toronto, Ont., 1972-75; exec. v.p. Oshawa Group Ltd., Toronto, Ont., 1976-92, dir., 1976-97. Fellow Inst. Chartered Accts.; mem. Fin. Execs. Inst. (pres. Hamilton chpt. 1966-67), Ont. Inst. Chartered Accts., Hamilton Club, Nat. Club. Home: 400 Walmer Rd Apt 2510 Toronto ON Canada M5P 2X7 Fax: 416-920-3638.

CONNELL, SHIRLEY HUDGINS, public relations professional; b. Washington, Oct. 5, 1946; d. Orville Thomas and Mary (Beran) H.; m. David Day Connell, Dec. 13, 1980 (div. 1985). BA, U. R.I., 1968, MA, 1970. Lic. property, casualty broker, N.Y. Clk., editor MGM Studios, Culver City, Calif., 1970-72; scriptor, talent Monarch Records, Studio City, 1972-73; communications specialist U. So. Calif., L.A., 1973-81; dir. pub. rels. Six Flags Movieland, Buena Park, Calif., 1981-82, Donald J. Fager & Assocs., N.Y.C., 1982-93, dir. policy holder/pub. rels., 1993-99, asst. v.p., 1999—. Cons. Children's TV Workshop, N.Y.C., 1978; ind. beauty cons. Mary Kay Cosmetics, 1991—; instr. Princeton Rev., 1990-91. Editor: Coastal Ocean Space Utilization III, 1995; contbr. articles to profl. jours.; contbg. editor Greater N.Y. Doctor's Shopper mag., 1987—. Pres. bd. trustees Oaks at North Brunswick Condominium Assn., 1987-2000; founding mem. Mcpl. Svcs. Com., North Brunswick; mgr. Animal Rescue Force, 1988—; chair environ. com. Twp. of North Brunswick, 1990-2001, vice chair, 2001—; snuggler pediat. and neonatal units St. Peter's Hosp.; Blue Belt Tiger Schulmann's Karate, 1997; founding mem., trustee, bd. dirs. Lawrence Brook Watershed Partnership, 1998—. Mem. NAFE, Marine Tech. Soc. (vice chmn. 1980-81), Mensa (pub. rels. adv. com. 1989—, pub. rels. coord. Ctrl. N.J. chpt. 1992—, bd. dirs. 1992—), Oceanic Soc. (bd. dirs. 1979-81), Stony Brook Millstone Watershed Assn. (water qualification monitor 1994—), Ctrl. N.J. Mensa (trustee, chair pub. rels. 1990—). Avocations: photography, reading, swimming, wood finishing, writing. E-mail: sconnell@mlmic.com.

CONNELL, WILLIAM D., lawyer; b. Palo Alto, Calif., Apr. 1, 1955; s. Robert Charles and Audrey Elizabeth (Steele) C.; m. Kathy Lynn Mleko, Aug. 13, 1977; children: Hilary Anne, Andrew James. BA in Polit Sci. with honors, Stanford U., 1976; JD cum laude, Harvard U., 1979. Bar: Calif. 1979, U.S. Dist. Ct. (cen., no. and ea. dists.) Calif. 1979, U.S. Ct. Appeals (9th cir.) 1979. Assoc. Gibson, Dunn & Crutcher, L.A., 1979-80, San Jose, Calif., 1980-87, ptnr., 1988-97, GCA Law Ptnrs. LLP, 1997—. Mem. Christian Legal Soc. Mem. Stanford Alumni Assn. (life), Commonwealth Club Calif., U.S. Golf Assn., The Federalist Soc., Phi Beta Kappa. Republican. Avocations: photography, golf. Business E-Mail: bconnell@gcalaw.com.

CONNELL, WILLIAM TERRENCE, lawyer, judge; b. Montclair, N.J., July 29, 1949; s. Raymond Charles and Kathryn (Hanley) C.; m. Honor Marilyn McMahon, July 19, 1975; children: Sean William, Heather Erin, Lauren Blythe. AB, Providence Coll., 1971; JD, Seton Hall U., 1976. Bar: N.J. 1977, D.C. 1979, U.S. Dist. Ct. N.J. 1977, U.S. Ct. Appeals (3d cir.) 1984; cert. trial atty. Investigator Comml. Union Ins. Co., West Orange, N.J., 1971, Essex County Prosecutors Office, Newark, 1971-77; mem. Dwyer, Connell & Lisbona, Montclair, NJ, 1977—, Fairfield, N.J., 1997—. Arbitrator Middlesex County Superior Ct., New Brunswick, N.J., 1984—; judge Mcpl. ct. Borough of Roseland, N.J., 1988—. Mem.: Def. Rsch. Inst., Trucking Ind. Def. Assn., Middlesex County Trial Lawyers Assn., Middlesex County Bar Assn., Essex County Bar Assn., N.J. Bar Assn., Am. Bd. Trial Attys. (adv.), Assn. Trial Lawyers Am., ABA, Bear Lakes Country Club (Fla.), Essex Fells Country Club (N.J.). Roman Catholic. Home: 18 Ford Ln Roseland NJ 07068-1456 also: 3360 S Ocean Blvd Palm Beach FL 33480 Office: Dwyer Connell & Lisbona Greenbrook Corp Ctr 100 Passaic Ave Fairfield NJ 07004-3508 Office Phone: 973-276-1800. Business E-Mail: wconnell@dcllaw.com.

CONNELL-ALLEN, ELIZABETH ANN, elementary school educator; b. Portsmouth, Va., Sept. 21, 1949; d. Robert Joseph and Juanita Georgia (Harrill) C.; m. Larry Allen. BS in Edn., Old Dominion U., Norfolk, Va., 1971; MA in Reading Edn., U. No. Colo., Greeley, 1975; PhD in Edn., Lit. and Curriculum, U. Colo., Boulder, 1991. Cert. elem. edn. K-6, reading edn. K-12, K-12 adminstrn. Tchr. 6th grade Norfolk Pub. Schs., 1971-74; tchr. Littleton (Colo.) Pub. Schs., 1975—2004, Peoria Unified Sch. Dist., Ariz., 2004—. Tchg. assoc. U. Colo., Boulder, 1988-90; instr. U. Colo., Denver, 1994; lit. com. When Author Meets Author, Colo. Coun. of Internat. Reading Assn., Denver; judge children's writing contest Friends of the Libr., Littleton, 1992-96. Author: A Community of Learners Selecting and Developing Writing Topics, 1991, Eternal Portraits, 2003. Recipient Outstanding Tchr. award Assn. for Childhood Edn. Internat., Denver, 1992; multicultural grantee Summit CHART: Pub. Edn. Coalition, Denver, 1994. Mem. ASCD, NEA, Internat. Reading Assn., Colo. Edn. Assn., Littleton Edn. Assn., Phi Delta Kappa. Avocations: reading, singing, playing piano. Office: Peoria Unified Schs Marshall Ranch Glendale AZ 85308

CONNELLAN, WILLIAM WESLEY, adult education educator; b. Detroit, Apr. 25, 1945; s. Thomas Kennedy and Florence Irene Connellan; m. Mary Emma Solonika Simms, Aug. 17, 1969 (div. Jan. 1979); 1 child, Brian Patrick; m. Catherine Joanne Marine, Oct. 12, 1985 (div. Dec. 2000). BA, Oakland U., Rochester, Mich., 1967; MA, U. Mich., 1971, PhD, 1981. Reporter Detroit News, 1965-70; acting v.p., assoc. provost, dir. pub. rels., vice provost, prof. Oakland U., 1970—; sr. v.p. Detroit Metro. Convention Vis. Bur., 2002—04. Vis. scholar U. Mich., Ann Arbor, 1987, Harvard U., 1999-2000; participant Inst. for Edn. Mgmt., Harvard U., Cambridge, Mass., 1993. Mem. exec. com. Met. Detroit Conv. and Visitors Bur., 1979-2001, chair, 1999-2000; mem. Rochester Hills (Mich.) Bldg. Authority, 1981-97; mem. Avon Twp. Charter Commn., Rochester Hills, 1982-84; active Habitat for Humanity, Rochester Downtown Develop. Authority, 2003-; bd. dirs. Rochester Regional Chamber, 2004—. Sigma Xi. Presbyterian. Avocations: international research projects, recreational sports. Home: 1267 Putnam Cir Rochester MI 48307-6045 Office: Oakland Univ 508 Wilson Rochester MI 48309 Business E-Mail: connella@oakland.edu. E-mail: connellan@comcast.net.

CONNELLY, DAVID O'BRIEN, museum administrator, journalist; b. Canton, Ohio, Apr. 25, 1952; s. Harold O'Brien and Mary Louise (Wells) C. BA in English with honors, summa cum laude, Mt. Union Coll., 1974; MA in Coll. Student Pers., Bowling Green State U., 1975; MA in Latin Am. Studies, U. Tex., Austin, 1995, postgrad., 1977-78. Dir. men's housing Southwestern U., Georgetown, Tex., 1975-76; cmty. educator, publicist Planned Parenthood Assn. Summit County, Akron, Ohio, 1976-77; arts/entertainment editor Shreveport (La.) Jour., 1978-90; asst. grants dir. Mus. Fine Arts, Houston, 1991-93; pub. rels. dir. Mus. of Fine Arts, St. Petersburg, Fla., 1996—. Staff writer The Archer M. Huntington Art Gallery, U. Tex., Austin, 1993-95; staff rep. long-range plan and devel./mktg. coms. bd. trustees Mus. Fine Arts, St. Petersburg. Editor, chief writer Mosaic; arts critic The Daily Texan, 1977-78; contbr. articles to profl. jours. Organizing com. Inner City Soup Kitchen, Shreveport, 1986-87; organizing com., first sec. exec. com., grants writer N.W. La. AIDS Task Force, Shreveport, 1988-91. Harmon O. DeGraff Meml. scholar Akron YMCA, 1977; Emmett Walter fellow U. Tex., 1977-78, Music Critics Inst. fellow, 1980, Aspen Summer Music Festival; named one of Outstanding Young Men of Am., 1989; grantee Tinker Found., 1994. Mem. Am. Assn. Mus., St. Petersburg Mus. Consortium, Fla. Assn. of Mus., Blue Key, Phi Kappa Phi, Psi Kappa Omega. Democrat. Jewish. Avocations: reading, travel, swimming, film, the arts. Home: 5190 Salmon Dr SE Apt B Saint Petersburg FL 33705-6351 Office: Mus Fine Arts 255 Beach Dr NE Saint Petersburg FL 33701-3498 Office Phone: 727-896-2667 224. E-mail: david@fine-arts.org.

CONNELLY, DONALD PRESTON, retired electric and gas utility company executive; b. Newark, Del., Nov. 27, 1939; s. Walton Theodore and Edna Rocelia (Lee) C.; m. Margaret Burnetta Boylan, Oct. 29, 1940; children: Donald Preston Jr., Pamela Margaret. AS, U. Del., 1970, BS, 1980. Clk. Delmarva Power, Wilmington, Del., 1961-66, supr., 1966-67, spl. acct., 1967-72, sr. acct., 1972-73, gen. supr., 1973-76, coordinator customer info. system, 1976-79, mgr., 1979-85, mgr., asst. sec., 1985, corp. sec., 1985-88; corp. sec., ethics officer Delmarva Power Subs. Cos., Wilmington, Del., 1988-98, ret., 1998. 1st v.p. Civic League for New Castle County, Wilmington, 1985-86, treas., 1987-91; mem. Metroform Coun. Civic Assns., 1993-96, Churchman's Crossing Civic Assn., 1996—. With USN, 1957-60. Mem. Am. Soc. Corp. Secs. (nat. bd. dirs. 1994-97, exec. steering com. 1995-97, v.p. Mid Atlantic chpt. 1989-91, pres. 1991-92, adv. com. 1988-97), Ethics Officer Assn. Methodist. Avocations: hiking, coin collecting/numismatics, photography. Home: 7 Greenridge Rd Newark DE 19711-6704

CONNELLY, ELIZABETH ANN, retired state legislator; b. N.Y.C. d. John Walter and Alice Marie (Mallon) Keresey; m. Robert Vincent Connelly; children: Alice, Robert, Margaret, Therese. Grad. H.S., Bronx; LLD (hon.), Wagner Coll., 1996. Telephone sales Pan Am. World Airways, N.Y.C., 1946-54; mem. N.Y. State Assembly, Albany, 1973-2000, chair com. on mental health, retardation/devel. disabilities, 1977-92, chair com. on standing coms., 1993-95, speaker pro tem, 1995-2000, chair intern com., 1995-2000; ret., 2000. Chair Legis. Women's Caucus, N.Y. State, 1993-95. Recipient over 350 awards and honors including S.I. Hosp. Vol. of Yr. award, 1972-73, Cert. Appreciation Willowbrook chpt. Benevolent Soc. Retarded Children, 1978, Legislator of Yr. award N.Y. State Coun. on Alcoholism, 1983, Woman of Yr. award Epilepsy Ctr., 1984, Disting. Humanitarian of Yr. award S.I. Ctr. Ind. Living, 1987, Alliance for Mentally Ill of N.Y. State award, 1988, Thomas G. Gilbert Meml. award N.Y. State Mental Health Soc., 1989, Nat. Barrier Awareness Found., 1990, Irish Am. Heritage Mus., 1991, N.Y. State Head Injury Assn. Pub. Policy award, 1994, N.Y. State Cath. Conf. Pub. Policy award 1996, St. John's U. Pres.' medal, 1998, Pres.' medal CUNY Coll. of S.I. Mem. Am.-Irish Legislators' Soc. (pres. 1999—). Democrat.

CONNELLY, JENNIFER, actress; b. Catskill Mountains, NY, Dec. 12, 1970; d. Gerard and Eileen Connelly; m. Paul Bettany, Jan. 1, 2003; children: Stellan Bettany, Kai Dugan. Actress: appeared in Italian, Canadian, British, Argentinian, and U.S. films: Once Upon a Time in America, 1984, Phenomena, 1985, The Valley, 1985, Labyrinth, 1986, Seven Minutes in Heaven, 1986, Some Girls, 1988, Etoile, 1988, The Hot Spot, 1990, Career Opportunities, 1991, The Rocketeer, 1991, Higher Learning, 1994, Far Harbor, 1996, Mulholland Falls, 1996, Of Love and Shadows, 1996, Dark City, 1997, Inventing the Abbots, 1997, Waking the Dead, 2000, Requiem for a Dream, 2000, Pollock, 2000, A Beautiful Mind, 2001 (Best Supporting Actress Acad. award 2001, Golden Globe, 2001, Am. Film Inst. award, Brit. Acad. award, Golden Satellite award, KCFCC award, OFCS award, SEFCA award and BFCA award 2001-2002, nominee Best Actress SAG award 2001, Featured Actor of Yr. Female Movies AFI Film award 2002), The Hulk, 2003, House of Sand and Fog, 2003, Dark Water, 2005; TV movies: The Heart of Justice, 1993; TV series: The $treet, 2000. Office: Internat Creative Mgmt 8942 Wilshire Blvd Beverly Hills CA 90211-1934*

CONNELLY, JOAN BRETON, archaeologist; BA, Princeton U., 1976, MA, 1979; PhD, Bryn Mawr Coll., 1984. Asst. dean undergrad. coll., lectr. in classical and Near Eastern archaeology Bryn Mawr Coll., 1984—86; assoc. prof. fine arts NYU, 1986—, Lillian Vernon chair for tchg. excellence, 2002—, dir. Yeronisos Island Excavations, 1990—. Mem. French Archaeol. Mission to Failaka, Kuwait U. de Lyon, 1985—; mem. Pres.'s Cultural Property Adv. Com. U.S. Dept. State, 2003—. Author: Votive Sculpture of Hellenistic Cyprus, 1988. Named hon. citizen, Republic of Cyprus, Municipality of Peyia, 2000; recipient MacArthur Genius award, 1996; Classical fellow and Norbert Schimmel fellow, Met. Mus. Art, 1982—84, Oxford U. vis. fellow, All Souls Coll., 1994—95, New Coll., 1997, Magdalen Coll., 1998, John D. and Catherine T. MacArthur Found. fellow, 1996—2001, Radcliffe Inst. for Advanced Study, Harvard U., 2000, vis. scholar, Phi Beta Kappa Soc., 2000—01. Fellow: Explorers Club, Royal Geog. Soc., Soc. Antiquaries of London; mem.: Soc. for Preservation of the Greek Heritage (trustee), Soc. Women Geographers. Office: NYU Dept Fine Arts 303 Main Bldg 100 Washington Sq E New York NY 10003-6688 E-mail: joan.connelly@nyu.edu.

CONNELLY, MARK, writer, educator; b. Phila., July 8, 1951; s. Edward James and Hilda Virginia (Pfleger) C. BA in English and History, Carroll Coll., 1973; MA in Creative Writing, U. Wis., Milw., 1974, PhD in English, 1984. Instr. English Milw. Area Tech. Coll., 1986—. Cons. Great Lakes Precision Products. Author: The Diminished Self: Orwell and the Loss of Freedom, 1987, The Sundance Reader, 1997, Orwell and Gissing, 1997, The Sundance Writer, 1999, Deadly Closets, 2000, Get Writing, 2005, Sundance Choice, 2005, Fifteen Minites, 2005. V.p. Irish Cultural and Heritage Ctr. of Wis., 2000—. Recipient Ann. Fiction award Milw. Mag., 1982, 1st Place Fiction award Ind. Mag., 1982. Presbyterian. Avocations: reading, travel, Irish studies. Office: Milw Area Tech Coll 700 W State St Milwaukee WI 53233-1419 E-mail: markconn@earthlink.net.

CONNELLY, MICHAEL, writer; Crime reporter L.A. Times. Author: (novels) The Black Echo, 1992 (Edgar award, 1992), The Black Ice, 1993, The Concrete Blonde, 1994, The Last Coyote, 1995, The Poet, 1996, Trunk Music, 1997, Blood Work, 1998, Angels Flight, 1999, Void Moon, 2000, A Darkness More Than Night, 2001, City of Bones, 2002 (Notable Book of Yr., NY Times, 2002), Chasing The Dime, 2002, Lost Light, 2003, The Narrows, 2003, The Closers, 2005 (Publishers Weekly Bestseller list, 2005, NY Times Bestseller list, 2005); writer, creator (TV series) Level 9, 2000. Mem.: Mystery Writers Am. (pres.). Office: c/o Author Mail Little Brown & Co 1271 Ave of the Americas New York NY 10020*

CONNELLY, SHARON RUDOLPH, lawyer; b. Kingwood, W.Va. d. John E. and Lorene E. Rudolph; 1 child, John. BS, W.Va. State Coll., 1966; MBA, Ind. U., 1968; JD, Cath. Univ., 1976; LLM in Taxation, Georgetown U., 1995. Bar: Va. 1977. Mgr. IRS, Washington, 1969-76; asst. contr. Mfrs. Hanover, N.Y.C., 1976-77; compliance chief D.C. Dept. Labor, Washington, 1977-79; dir. compliance U.S. Dept. Commerce, Washington, 1979-82; asst. insp. gen. NASA, Washington, 1982-84; dir. insp. office Nuc. Regulatory Commn., Washington, 1984-89, spl. asst. internal controls, 1989-98. Financier, 1998—. Contbr. articles to profl. jours.

CONNELLY, TERRENCE JOHN, SR., television and cable station executive; b. Chgo., Aug. 23, 1947; s. Charles Bernard, Jr. and Margaret Agnes (Gilmore) C.; m. Andrea Susan Hahn, Feb. 12, 1972; children: Terrence John, Jr., Bridget Colleen. BS in Comms., U. Ill., 1970. Reporter WITI-TV, Milw., 1970-73, WRGB-TV, Schenectady, N.Y., 1973-74; news dir. WNYT-TV, Albany, N.Y., 1974-76, WDAF-TV, Kansas City, Mo., 1976-78; exec. news producer WMAQ-TV, Chgo., 1978-80; v.p. TV news Taft Broadcasting, Cin., 1980-86; v.p., gen. mgr. WCPO-TV, Cin., 1986-88, WKRC-TV, Cin., 1988-92, WSYX-TV, Columbus, Ohio, 1992-95; pres., gen. mgr. WJLA-TV, Washington, 1995-98; sr. v.p., gen. mgr. The Weather Channel, Atlanta, 1999—. Dir. teletext, Taft Broadcasting, Cin., 1981-86; mem. broadcast adv. bd. UPI, N.Y.C., 1983-85. Editor/gen. mgr.: WCPO TV news, 1987 (Peabody award for investigative report 1987). Bd. dirs. United Way, Washington, 1995-99, Easter Seals Bd., Washington, 1995-97, Muscular Distrophy Assn., Columbus, 1992-95; chmn. Neediest Kids, Inc., Washington, 1995-99. With U.S. Army, 1970-76. Mem. Soc. Profl. Journalists, Radio-TV News Dirs. Assn., Nat. Assn. TV Program Execs., Rotary. Roman Catholic. Office: The Weather Channel 300 Interstate North Pkwy SE Atlanta GA 30339-2403

CONNELLY, THOMAS M., JR., pharmaceutical executive; b. Toledo, Ohio, 1952; m. Patricia Connelly; 2 children. Grad. with highest honors, Princeton U.; PhD in Chem. Engring., U. Cambridge, 1977. Global product mgr. Permasep, Del., 1985—87; mgr. Polymer Products; dir. European Tech. Ctr., Geneva; bus. dir. Delrin, Kevlar, Richmond, Va.; v.p., gen. mgr. DuPont Fluoroproducts, 1999—2000, sr. v.p. & chief sci. and technology officer, 2000—.

CONNELLY, WARREN E., lawyer; b. Mt. Vernon, NY, Nov. 18, 1946; BA cum laude, Dartmouth Coll., 1968; JD, Georgetown U., 1973. Bar: DC 1973. Atty. Cost of Living Coun., 1973-74; mem. Akin, Gump, Strauss, Hauer & Feld LLP, Washington, 1975—, now ptnr. internat. trade. Active NAFTA Binat. Panel. 1st lt. U.S. Army, 1968-70. Mem. DC Bar. Office: Akin Gump Strauss Hauer & Feld LLP 1333 New Hampshire Ave NW Washington DC 20036-1564 Office Phone: 202-887-4046. Office Fax: 202-887-4288. Business E-Mail: wconnelly@akingump.com.

CONNER, ANN LOUISE, artist, educator; b. Wilmington, N.C., Aug. 11, 1948; d. Robert Walter Conner and Martha Louise (Robeson) Long; m. W. Rex Fountain, May 20, 1980. BFA, Salem Coll., 1970; MA, U. N.C., 1972, MFA, 1975. Mem. faculty U. N.C., Wilmington, 1972—, prof., 1990—. One-woman shows include Waterworks Visual Arts Ctr., Salisbury, N.C., 1987, Southeastern C.C., Whiteville, N.C., 1988, Whiteville, N.C., Chapel Hill, 1991, Lilly Libr., Duke U., Durham, 1992, Flatbed Press Gallery., Austin, Tex., 1998, Greenville (N.C.) Mus., 1998, New Elements Gallery, Wilmington, N.C., 1998, Rutledge Gallery, Winthrop U., Rock Hill, S.C., 2000, Trish Higgins Fine Arts, Wichita, Kans., 2002, NC Mus. Forestry, Whiteville, NC, 2003, exhibited in group shows at numerous group shows including most recently, Internat. Print Ctr. N.Y., 2000, 2001, 2003, 2004, 2005, Arlington (Tex.) Mus. Art, 2001, Trish Higgins Fine Art, Wichita,

Kans., 2000, 2002, US Embassy, Riyadh, Saudi Arabia, 2002, Somerhill Gallery, Chapel Hill, N.C., 2004, commd., N.C. Gov.'s Bus. award for Arts and Humanities Print Edition, 1991, Phillip Morris USA, 1992, Represented in permanent collections Mus. Fine Arts, Boston, Libr. of Congress, Achenbach Found. for Graphic Arts, State Dept. Art in Embassies Program, Phillip Morris USA, IBM, N.Y. Pub. Libr., Chem. Bank, N.Y., numerous others. Trustee Cape Fear Mus., Wilmington, 1990-97. Grantee, fellow Arts Coun. N.C., U. N.C.-Wilmington, 1970—. Presbyterian.

CONNER, CHARLES F., federal agency administrator; b. Lafayette, Ind., Dec. 30, 1957; m. Druscilla Conner; 4 children. BS in Agriculture, Purdue U., 1980. Agrl. aide to Sen. Richard Lugar US Senate, 1980—87; minority staff dir. Com. on Agrl., Nutrition & Forestry, US Senate, 1987—95, majority staff dir., 1995—97; pres. Corn Refiners Assn., 1997—2001; spl. asst. to the Pres. for Agrl., Trade, & Food Assistance Nat. Econ. Coun., 2001—05; dep. sec. USDA, Washington, 2005—. Office: USDA 12th & Jefferson Dr SW Rm 202-B Washington DC 20250

CONNER, DAVID LEE, secondary school educator; b. Hattiesburg, Miss., Mar. 16, 1934; s. Charlie Conner and Ernestine Blanks; m. Vilene Hundley, July 10, 1959 (dec. July 1977); children: Valoree Conner-Dye, Doreese Conner, Darin Van, David Lee Jr., Richard Vaughn. BS in Math., Alcorn State U., 1957. Tchr., coach Hattiesburg Pub. Schs., 1959-69, Milw. Pub. Sch., 1969-97; life jeep operator Pabst Brewery, Milw., 1975-81; mentor, coach U. Wis., Milw., 1975 summer, h.s. math. tchr., 1984 summer; shelter care counselor St. Charles Boys Homes, Milw., 1984-87. Grantee NSF, 1960-61, 63, 64, 65 summer; named Miss. Coach of Yr. for football and track Southeastern Athletic Conf. for Jr. H.S., 1964-68; named to Alcorn State U. Hall of Fame, 1999. Mem. Milw. Spartans Track Club (founder, Coach of Yr. 1998), Kappa Alpha Psi (vice polemarch Hattiesburg chpt. 1961-69). Avocations: bowling, flag football, tennis (city of hattiesburg recreational mens singles champion 1967), basketball. Home: 6641 N 75TH St Apt 7 Milwaukee WI 53223-5655

CONNER, ERNEST LEE, JR., lawyer; b. Jasper, Ala., Dec. 17, 1955; s. Ernest Lee and Sara Lynette (Maroney) C.; m. Lisa Ann Doig, Dec. 14, 1980; children: Melissa Ann, Jessica Lee. BS in Polit. Sci., E. Carolina U., 1984; JD, U. N.C., 1987. Bar: N.C. 1987, U.S. Dist. Ct. (ea. dist.) N.C. 1991. Ptnr. Dixon, Doub & Conner, Greenville, N.C., 1987—. Editor Hawaii Army Weekly newspaper, 1977. Bd. dirs. New Directions Family Violence Ctr., Greenville, 1989-91. Staff sgt. U.S. Army, 1974-81. Mem. N.C. Bar Assn. (chair criminal justice sect. 1997-98), N.C. Acad. Trial Lawyers, Pitt County Bar Assn. (treas. 1992—), Kiwanis. Democrat. Episcopalian. Avocations: jogging, water-skiing, chess. Office: Dixon Doub & Conner 110 Arlington Blvd Greenville NC 27835 Office Phone: 252-355-8100. Personal E-mail: ernestcon@aol.com.

CONNER, FRANK M. (RUSTY), III, lawyer; b. Richmond, Va., Sept. 30, 1956; BA, Univ. Va., 1978, JD, 1981. Bar: Va. 1981, Ga. 1981, DC 1990. Ptnr., head, fin. svcs. and products group, ptnr. in charge Alston & Bird LLP, Washington. Mem.: ABA, DC Bar Assn., Raven Soc., Omicron Delta Kappa, Phi Beta Kappa. Office: Alston & Bird LLP North Bldg 10th Fl 600 Pennsylvania Ave NW Washington DC 20004-2601 Office Phone: 202-756-3303. Office Fax: 202-756-3333. Business E-Mail: fconner@alston.com.

CONNER, JAMES LEON, II, lawyer, arbitrator, mediator; b. Roanoke, Va., June 29, 1956; s. James Leon and Avis Christine (Craig) C.; m. Lorraine Joyce McNamara, Aug. 11, 1979 (div. 1987); children: Patrick James, Daniel Silas; m. Kathy Lynelle Watson, July 28, 1996; children: Benjamin Micah, Caleb Thomas. AB, Duke U., 1978; JD, U. N.C. Bar: N.C. 1983, U.S. Dist. Ct. (mid. dist.) N.C. 1984; U.S. Ct. Appeals (4th cir.). Vis. law instr. U. Ill. Coll. Law, Champaign, 1983-84; assoc. editor Environ. Law Inst., Washington, 1984-85; ptnr. Abernathy, Roberson & Conner, Graham, N.C., 1985-88; recycling dir. Alamance County, Burlington, N.C., 1988-89; assoc. atty. Brooks Pierce Mclendon Humphrey & Leonard, Greensboro, N.C., 1989-93; lead environ. atty. Kennedy Covington Lobdell & Hickman, Charlotte, N.C., 1993-95; prin. atty. J. Conner & Assocs., Durham, N.C., 1995—. Mem. coun. environ. and natural resources law sect. N.C. Bar Assn., 1987-91. Contbr. articles to profl. jours. Mem. Durham (N.C.) City and County Environ. Affairs Bd., 1995—, vice chair 1997-98, chmn. 1998—; bd. dirs. Piedmont Land Conservancy, Greensboro, 1992-93; elder Presbyn. Ch.; founder U. N.C. chpt. Equal Justice Found., 1982; bd. dirs. North State Legal Svcs., 1986-89. Recipient Chpt. Svc. award N.C. Sierra Club, 1990, Am. Jurisprudence award Avocations: hiking, canoeing, golf.

CONNER, JOHN SHULL, lawyer; b. Sioux City, Iowa, Jan. 9, 1954; s. Raymond Dudley and Sally Elizabeth (Shull) C.; m. Mary Ziemba, Aug. 16, 1980; children: Courtney, John, Margaret. BSBA, U. Nebr., 1976; JD, Drake U., 1979. Bar: Mo. 1979, U.S. Dist. Ct. (we. dist.) Mo. 1979,U.S. Dist. Ct. (no. dist.) Calif. 1984, U.S. Supreme Ct. 1988, U.S. Dist. Ct. Ariz. 1992, U.S. Ct. Appeals (10th cir.) 1992, U.S. Dist. Ct. Kans. 1998. Assoc. Shughart Thomson & Kilroy, P.C., Kansas City, Mo., 1979-83, dir., 1984—. Co-author: Kansas and Missouri Law for Design Professionals, 1997, Missouri Civil Actions, Vol. 1, 1989; contbr. articles to various publs. Coord. United Way, Kansas City, 1984—, loaned exec., 1998—; bd. dirs., pres. Pinehurst Estate, Overland Park, Kans., 1992-94; bd. dirs. Gillis Ctr., Kansas City, 1996—; com. mem. Valley View United Meth. Ch., Overland Park, 1998. Mem. ABA (constrn. forum), Mo. Bar Assn., Kansas City Bar Assn., Kansas City Club. Office: Shughart Thomson & Kilroy 120 W 12th St Ste 1500 Kansas City MO 64105-1929

CONNER, LINDSAY ANDREW, investment banker; b. NYC, Feb. 19, 1956; s. Michael and Miriam Conner. BA summa cum laude, UCLA, 1976; MA, Occidental Coll., 1978; JD magna cum laude, Harvard U., 1980. Bar: Calif. 1980, U.S. Dist. Ct. (cen. dist.) Calif. 1983. Assoc. Kaplan, Livingston, Goodwin, Berkowitz & Selvin, Beverly Hills, Calif., 1980—81; Fulop & Hardee, Beverly Hills, 1982—83, Wyman, Bautzer, Kuchel & Silbert, L.A., 1983—86; ptnr., entertainment dept. head Hill Wynne Troop & Meisinger, L.A., 1986—93; screenwriter and prodr. 54 St. Prodns., L.A., 1994—99; COO, I-Drop, Inc., L.A., Calif., 1999—2001; investment banker, cons. Beverly Hills, Calif., 2001—. Author: (with others) The Courts and Education, 1977; editor: Harvard Law Rev., 1978-80. Trustee L.A. Community Coll., 1981-97, bd. pres., 1989-90; pres. Calif. Community Coll. Trustees, 1992-93. Mem. ABA, UCLA Alumni Assn. (life), Harvard-Radcliffe Club, Phi Beta Kappa.

CONNER, STEWART EDMUND, lawyer; b. Louisville, Oct. 7, 1941; s. James Pleasant and Lucille (Winter) C.; m. Joan E. Fish, May 20, 1989; children: Shannon Lynn, Erin Eileen, Margaret Eisele; stepchildren: Hunt Rounsavall, Gibbs Rounsavall, Christine Rounsavall. BS, U. Louisville, 1963, JD cum laude, 1966. Bar: Ky. 1966, U.S. Dist. Ct. (ea. and we. dists.) Ky. 1966, U.S. Tax Ct. 1967. Assoc. Wyatt, Tarrant & Combs, Louisville, 1966-72, ptnr., 1972—, chmn. gen. corp. sect., 1980-90, mng. ptnr., 1988-2001, chmn. exec. com., 1988—2004. Bd. dirs. DNP Select Income Fund, 2004—, Louisville Water Co., 1990—, chmn., 2004—. Author, editor: Kentucky Business Practice Handbook, 1988; editor Kentucky Legal Forms, 1988; contbr. to U. Ky. Law Rev. Bd. dirs. Coun. on Higher Edn., 1992-95, Lincoln Heritage coun. Boy Scouts Am., 1989—, chair, 2005-, dePaul Sch., 1996-2004. With U.S. Army, 1968-69, Vietnam. Fellow Am. Bar Found., Ky. Bar Found.; mem. ABA (banking com. 1983), Ky. Bar Assn., Louisville Bar Assn. (chmn. ethics com. 1980), Ky. C. of C. (bd. dirs. 1992-96), Greater Louisville Inc. (bd. dirs. 1996-2001), Law Club, Lawyers Club, Harmony Landing Country Club. Republican. Office: Wyatt Tarrant & Combs 2800 PNC Plz Louisville KY 40202 Office Phone: 502-562-7223. Business E-Mail: sconner@wyattfirm.com.

CONNER, SUSAN, music educator; b. Amarillo, Tex., June 8, 1949; d. James Walter Patrick and Mary Jean Ross; m. Randall Conner, Jan. 15, 1972; children: Kevin, Dennis, Craig. MusB, Tex. Tech. U., 1971. Nat. cert. tchr. music. Piano tchr., 1974—; ch. pianist First Bapt., Winters, Tex., 1975—; substitute tchr. Winters H.S., 1997—. Officer Boy Scouts, Winters, 1985-92, Winters Athletic Boosters, Winters, 1992-99. Named Woman of the Yr., Winter C. of C., 1999. Mem.: Abilene Music Tchrs. Assn. (Tchr. of Yr. 1981, 1995), Tex. Music Tchrs. Assn. (rec. sec. 1976—99, chmn. 1989—91, bd. dirs. 1992—95, editor 1996—99), Nat. Guild Piano Tchrs. (adjudicator), Music Tchrs. Nat. Assn., Pi Kappa Lambda. Baptist. Avocations: crocheting, reading. Home: 216 Circle Dr Winters TX 79567-3504

CONNER, TERRY W., lawyer; b. Houston, Feb. 27, 1951; BA, U. Tex., 1972, JD with honors, 1975. Bar: Tex. 1975. Ptnr., Fin. Haynes and Boone LLP, Dallas. Adj. prof. So. Meth. U. Sch. Law, 1987-92, also co-dir. ann. comml. lending inst. Note and comment editor Tex. Law Rev., 1974-75; spl. contbg. editor: Comml. Loan Documentation Guide, 1988. Mem. ABA (mem. corporation, banking and bus. law sect.), State Bar Tex. (mem. fin. instns. com. 1981—), Tex. Assn. Bank Counsel (bd. dirs. 1987-91), Dallas Bar Assn. Office: Haynes & Boone LLP 3100 Nationsbank Plz 901 Main St Ste 3100 Dallas TX 75202-3789 Office Phone: 214-651-5604. Office Fax: 214-200-0408. Business E-Mail: terry.conner@haynesboone.com.

CONNER, WILLIAM CURTIS, federal judge; b. Wichita Falls, Tex., Mar. 27, 1920; s. D.H. and Mae (Weeks) C.; m. Janice Files, Mar. 22, 1944; children: William Curtis, Stephen, Christopher, Molly. BBA, U. Tex., 1941, LLB, 1942; student, Harvard, 1942-43, MIT, 1943. Bar: Tex. bar 1942, N.Y. State bar 1949. Asso., mem. firm Curtis, Morris & Safford (and predecessor firm), N.Y.C., 1946-73; judge U.S. Dist. Ct. (so. dist.) N.Y., White Plains, 1973—, now sr. judge. Editor Tex. Law Rev. Served to lt. USNR, 1942-45, PTO. Recipient Jefferson medal N.J. Patent Law Assn., Outstanding Pub. Svc. award N.Y Intellectual Property Law Assn. Mem. NY Patent Law Assn. (pres. 1972-73), St. Andrews Golf Club. Presbyterian (elder). Office: US Dist Ct US Courthouse 300 Quarropas St White Plains NY 10601-4140

CONNER, WILLIAM EDWARD, lawyer; b. Omaha; s. Clifford Eugene and Sharon Jeanette Conner; 1 child, Darby Virginia Mullis. BA, U. Ariz., Tucson, 1993; JD, John Marshall Law Sch., Atlanta, 1998; LLM, Case Western Reserve U., Cleve., 2003. Bar: Ga.; cert. gen. mediator State of Ga., 1998. Prin. cons. Conner Consulting, Ariz., 1991—96; paralegal, investigator Law Office of Tim McEwing, Atlanta, 1996—98; atty. Law Office of William Conner, Atlanta, 1998—2004. Adminstrv. intern Pima County Bd. Suprs., Tucson, 1992—93; at-large del. Gov.'s NAFTA Task Force, Tucson, 1993; bd. mem. City Adv. Com., El Mirage, Ariz., 2004. Recipient Hdqs. Vol. Award, Pima County Republican Party, 1992, Achievement Award, Republican Nat. Com., 1992, Cmty. Svc. Award, Metro Atlanta Police Emerald Soc., 2000. Mem.: Scottish Rite Century Club, Omaha Tangier Shrine, Omaha Valley Scottish Rite Lodge, Covert Masonic Lodge. Republican. Avocations: hunting, history, farming. Home: 13019 W Desert Cove Rd El Mirage AZ 85335 Office: Law Office of William E Conner 13019 W Desert Cove Rd El Mirage AZ 85335

CONNER, WILLIAM HERBERT, lawyer; b. Columbus, Ohio, Jan. 29, 1940; s. Herbert Lee and Beulah Doris C.; m. Julie Ann Katzan, Aug. 13, 1966; children: W. David, Kristen Ann. Student, Purdue U., 1960-61; AB magna cum laude, Miami U., Oxford, Ohio, 1964; JD cum laude, U. Mich. Law Sch., 1967. Bar: Ohio 1967, U.S. Dist. Ct. (no. dist.) Ohio 1967. Assoc. Squire, Sanders & Dempsey L.L.P., Cleve., 1967-77, ptnr., 1977—. Contbr. articles to profl. jours. Mem. ABA (tax exempt financing com. 1981--), Ohio Bar Assn. (chmn. taxation com. 1981-84), Cleve. Bar Assn. (chmn. gen. tax com. 1983-84), Nat. Assn. Bond Lawyers (bd. dirs. 1991, 94-99, treas. 1995-96, pres. elect 1996-97, pres. 1997-98, immediate past pres. 1998-99). Republican. Methodist. Home: 3139 Falmouth Rd Shaker Heights OH 44122-2844 Office: Squire Sanders & Dempsey LLP 4900 Key Tower 127 Public Sq Ste 4900 Cleveland OH 44114-1304

CONNERY, MICHAEL M., lawyer; b. Providence, 1943; Student, U. Fribourg, Switzerland; BSFS, Georgetown U., 1968; JD with high honors, U. Conn., 1975. Bar: Conn. 1975, NY 1976. Ptnr., practice leader labor and employment law Skadden, Arps, Slate, Meagher & Flom LLP, NYC. Office: Skadden Arps Slate Meagher & Flom LLP 4 Times Sq New York NY 10036 Office Phone: 212-735-2920. Office Fax: 917-777-2920. Business E-Mail: mconnery@skadden.com.

CONNERY, SIR SEAN (THOMAS SEAN CONNERY), actor; b. Edinburgh, Scotland, Aug. 25, 1930; s. Joseph and Euphamia C.; m. Diane Cilento, Dec. 6, 1962 (div. Sept. 6, 1973); 1 son, Jason; m. Micheline Roquebrune, 1975; 1 stepdaughter. D.Litt. (hon.), Heriot-Watt U., 1981, St. Andrews U., 1988. Founder Fountainbridge Films, Los Angeles, 1992—2002. First theater appearance in road show co. of South Pacific, Eng., 1953, also in Macbeth, Judith; films include: Let's Make Up, 1955, No Road Back, 1956, Action of the Tiger, 1957, Hell Drivers, 1957, Time Lock, 1957, Another Time, Another Place, 1958, Tarzan's Greatest Adventure, 1959, Darby O'Gill and the Little People, 1959, The Frightened City, 1961, Operation Snafu, 1961, The Longest Day, 1962, Dr. No., 1962, From Russis With Love, 1963, Marnie, 1964, Woman of Straw, 1964, Goldfinger, 1964, The Hill, 1965, Thunderball, 1965, A Fine Madness, 1966, You Only Live Twice, 1967, Shalako, 1968, The Molly Maguires, 1970, The Red Tent, 1971, The Anderson Tapes, 1971, Diaonds are Forever, 1971, The Offence, 1973, Zardoz, 1974, The Terrorists, 1974, Murder on the Orient Express, 1974, The Wind and the Lion, 1975, The Man Who Would be King, 1975, Robin and Marian, 1976, The Next Man, 1976, A Bridge Too Far, 1977, The Great Train Robbery, 1979, Cuba, 1979, Meteor, 1979, Outland, 1981, Time Bandits, 1981, Sword of the Valiant, 1982, Wrong is Right, 1982, Five Days One Summer, 1982, Never Say Never Again, 1983, Highlander, 1986, The Name of the Rose, 1986, The Untouchables, 1987 (Acad. award for best supporting actor), The Presidio, 1988, Indiana Jones and the Last Crusade, 1989, Family Business, 1989, The Hunt for Red October, 1990, The Russia House, 1990, Highlander 2: The Quickening, 1991, Robin Hood: Prince of Thieves, 1991, Rising Sun, 1993, A Good Man in Africa, 1994, Just Cause, 1995, First Knight, 1995, The Rock, 1996, (voice) Dragon Heart, 1996, Playing By Heart, 1998; actor, prodr., Entrapment, 1999, Finding Forrester, 2000; actor, exec. prodr. The Avengers, 1998, The League of Extraordinary Gentlemen, 2003; actor, co-exec. prodr.: Medicine Man, 1992; TV movies include Requiem For a Heavyweight, 1957, Women in Love, 1957, The Square Ring, 1959, The Crucible, 1959, Colombe, 1960, Without the Grail, 1961, MacBeth, 1961, Anna Karenina, 1961, Male of the Species, 1969,; prodr., dir.: The Bowler and the Bonnet (film documentary), I've Seen You Cut Lemons (London stage); prodr.: Something Like the Truth, Playing by Heart, 1998, (narrator) Macbeth, 1999. Served with Brit. Royal Navy. Named Star of the Yr., Nat. Assn. Theater Owners, 1987, Commander of Arts, France; recipient Tribute award Brit. Acad. Film and Television Arts, 1990, Career Achievement award Nat. Bd. Rev., 1993, Cecil B. DeMille Golden Globe award Hollywood Fgn. Press Assn., 1996, Lifetime Achievement award ShoWest Conv., 1999. Office: Creative Artists Agy 9830 Wilshire Blvd Beverly Hills CA 90212-1804

CONNICK, HARRY, JR., musician, actor, vocalist, composer, lyricist; b. New Orleans, Sept. 11, 1967; s. Harry Connick, Sr. and Anita Connick; m. Jill Goodacre, Apr. 16, 1994. Student, New Orleans Ctr. Creative Arts; studied with, Ellis Marsalis; student with, James Booker; student, Hunter Coll., Manhattan Sch. Music. Musician: (albums) Harry Connick, Jr., 1987, 20, 1988, We Are in Love, 1990 (Grammy award for Best Jazz Vocal Performace, 1991), Lofty's Roach Souffle, 1990, Blue Light, Red Light, 1991, Eleven, 1992, 25, 1992, When My Heart Finds Christmas, 1993, She, 1994, Star Turtle, 1996, To See You, 1997, Come By Me, 1999, 30, 2001, Songs I Heard, 2001 (Grammy Award for Best Traditional Pop Vocal Album, 2002), Harry for the Holidays, 2003, Other Hours, 2003, Only You, 2004; musician: (with Branford Marsalis) Occasion, 2005; contributed music to soundtrack When Harry Met Sally, 1989 (Grammy award for Best Jazz Vocal Male, 1990), The Godfather Part III, 1991 (nom. for Golden Globe award, 1991), Sleepless in Seattle, 1993, The Mask, 1994; contributed music to album/video: Simply Mad About the Mouse, 1991; actor: (films) Memphis Belle, 1990, Little Man Tate, 1991, Copycat, 1995, Independence Day, 1996, Excess Baggage, 1997, Hope Floats, 1998 (nom. Favorite Actor-Drama/Romance Blockbuster Awards, 199), The Iron Giant, 1999, My Dog Skip, 2000; (TV series) Cheers, 1991, Will & Grace, 2002—; (TV films) South Pacific, 2001; appeared on (TV spl.) PBS' Great Performances (nom. for Emmy award Best Performance Variety Special, 1991), PBS presents Harry Connick, Jr.: Romance In Paris, 1998, The Worlds of Harry Connick, Jr., 1999; performer: (TV spl.) The Harry Connick, Jr. Christmas Special, 1993; guest performer (TV spl.) PBS Evening Pops, 2001, band leader Harry Connick's Big Band; musician: (videos) Singin' & Swingin', 1990, Swingin' Out Live, 1991, The New York Big Band Concert, 1993, The Harry Connick, Jr. Christmas Special, 1994; writer/arranged music: (Broadway plays) Thou Shalt Not, 2000; co-prodr.(with Tracey Freeman): (soundtrack), 2002 (Tony nom. Best Original Score (Music & Lyrics) Written for the Theatre, 2002). Office: Wilkins Mgmt Inc 323 Broadway Cambridge MA 02139

CONNICK, ROBERT ELWELL, retired chemistry professor; b. Eureka, Calif., July 29, 1917; s. Arthur Elwell and Florence (Robertson) C.; m. Frances Spieth, Dec. 19, 1952; children: Mary Catherine, Elizabeth, Arthur, Megan, Sarah, William Beach. BS, U. Calif. at Berkeley, 1939, PhD, 1942. Mem. faculty U. Calif., Berkeley, 1942-88, researcher Manhattan project, 1942—46, asst. prof. then assoc. prof. chemistry, 1945-52, prof., 1952-88, chmn. dept. chemistry, 1958-60, dean Coll. Chemistry, 1960-65, vice chancellor acad. affairs, 1965-67, vice chancellor, 1969-71, acting dean Coll. Chemistry, 1987-88. Contbr. articles profl. jours. Guggenheim fellow, 1949, 59 Mem. Am. Chem. Soc., Nat. Acad. Scis., Phi Beta Kappa, Sigma Xi, Pi Mu Epsilon. Home: 50 Marguerita Rd Kensington CA 94707-1020 E-mail: connick@berkeley.edu.

CONNOLA, DONALD PASCAL, JR., management consultant; b. New Brunswick, NJ, Sept. 25, 1948; s. Donald Pascal and Josephine (Montalbano) C. AB, Rutgers U., 1970, MBA, 1973; JD, Bklyn. Law Sch., 1977. Mktg. control analyst Gen. Foods Corp., White Plains, NY, 1973—74, product analyst, 1974, sr. fin. analyst, 1974—75, fin. assoc., 1975—79, fin. specialist, 1979, internal mgmt. cons., 1979—82, mgmt. cons., 1983—. Prof. mgmt. Fairleigh Dickinson U., Rutherford, N.J., 1983-86, dir. MBA program, dir. undergrad. student svcs., 1986-94; prof. bus. adminstrn. Concordia Coll., Bronxville, N.Y., 1995-97; team leader Verizon Comm., 2000—. Mem. ASTD, NJ State Bar Assn., Assn. MBA Execs., Soc. for Human Resource Mgmt. Home: 1220 Cellar Ave Apt 12 Clark NJ 07066-2044 Office: 1500 Teaneck Rd Teaneck NJ 07666

CONNOLLY, COLM F., prosecutor; BA, U. of Notre Dame; MSc, London Sch. Econs.; JD, Duke U. Asst. U.S. atty. dist. Del. US Dept. Justice, 1992—99, U.S. Atty. dist. Del., 2001—; ptnr. Morris, Nichols, Arsht and Tunnel, Wilmington, Del., 1999—2001. Recipient Director's award for Superior Performance as Asst. U.S. Atty., U.S. Atty. Gen., 1996. Office: US Atty PO Box 2046 Wilmington DE 19899-2046

CONNOLLY, ELMA TROUTMAN, artist, muralist, art gallery owner; b. Middleburg, Pa., May 10, 1931; d. Benjamin F. and Eva Ellen (DeLong) Hollenback; m. Kenneth R. Troutman, Aug. 15, 1950; children: Kenneth, Linda, Robert, Terri; m. Jerome P. Connolly, Apr. 15, 1973. Student, Lock Haven State Tchrs. Coll., 1949. Profl. dancer, 1949—51; instr. Sunbury, Pa.; cons. for exceptions unit Pa. Tax Bur., Harrisburg; owner, founder, pres. Arts ETC Co., Sunbury, Pa.; owner Art Gallery, 1976-93. Bus. cons. Cohen, Danville, 1970-72; art restoration work, 1955-2004; art instr., Pa., Fla. and Idaho, 1959-2004. Murals (with Jerome Connolly): Nature Ctr., Winston Salem, N.C., 1974, South Am. Hall-Smithsonian Nat. History Mus., Washington, 1975, George Page Mus. La Brea Discoveries, LA, 1976, Makah Mus., Neah Bay, Wash., 1978, Woolly Mammoth Background, Frazer Delta Diorama Provincial Mus. B.C., Can., 1979, African Hall Springfield (Mass.) Sci. Mus., 1980, Big Cypress Nature Ctr., Naples, Fla., 1982, Indian Hall Ill. State Mus., 1984, Edn. Ctr. Taipei, Taiwan, 1987, African Water Hole, American Kudu, Carnagie Mus. Natural History, Pa., 1992, Elk Diorama, 1974, Alaskan Brown Bear, Carnagie Mus. Natural History, Pitts., 1994; sculpture, murals George Page Mus., Provincial Mus., Springfield Sci. Mus., Big Cypress Nature Ctr. Fla., Pa. State U., 2000, Pa. Messiah Coll. Oak Mus., 2001-02, Messiah Coll., Jordan Sci. Ctr., African Water Hole, Muskox Backyard Sheep of the World, 2000-2001, entire Page Mus.; sculpture Foregrounds for Mass. Mus., Nature Ctr. Fla.; restoration of painting, design jewelry and costume La Brea Women. Pres. Susquehanna Art League, 1999. Named Woman of Yr., ABI, 1991; recipient Am. Women's award. Mem. NAFE, Sunbury Mchts. Coun. (pres.), C. of C. (govt. affairs com.), Susquehanna Art Soc. (pres.), Internat. Platform Assn. Republican. Avocations: writing, art, politics. Home: RR 2 Box 1763 Selinsgrove PA 17870-9657 Office Phone: 570-734-7008. Personal E-mail: murals051031@aol.com.

CONNOLLY, GERALD EDWARD, lawyer; b. Boston, Oct. 13, 1943; s. Thomas E. and Grace J. (Fitzgerald) C.; m. Elizabeth Heidi Eckert, Jan. 6, 1968; children: Matthew F., Dennis F., David D., Edward F. BS, Coll. of Holy Cross, 1965; JD, U. Va., 1972. Bar: Wis. 1972, U.S. Tax Ct. 1973. From assoc. to ptnr. Whyte & Hirschboeck S.C., Milw., 1972-78; ptnr. Minahan & Peterson S.C., Milw., 1978-91, Quarles & Brady, 1991—. Bd. dirs., sec. Reinhart Real Estate Group, Inc., Reinhart Retail Group; sec. Hometown Inc.; bd. dirs. Viterbo U., LaCrosse, Wis., Hatco Corp., Milw., Adaptive Engring. Lab., Inc., Diversatek, Inc., Medovations Inc., Sunlite Plastics, Inc., Milw.; sec. The Medalcraft Mint, Inc., Radisson LaCrosse Hotel, Water Blasting Inc. Trustee Emory T. Clark Family Charitable Found., D.B. Reinhart Family Found.; mem. Circle of Care Children's Hosp. Wis.; vice chmn., bd. dirs. Children's Hosp. Wis. Found. Lt. USN, 1966-69. Mem. ABA, Kiawah Island Club, Milw. Club, Milw. Athletic Club, North Shore Country Club, Order of Coif. Home: 10134 N Range Line Rd # 27W Mequon WI 53092-5435 Office: Quarles & Brady LLP 411 E Wisconsin Ave Ste 2040 Milwaukee WI 53202-4497 Office Phone: 414-277-5373. Business E-Mail: gec@quarles.com.

CONNOLLY, JANET ELIZABETH, retired sociologist and criminal justice educator; b. New Rochelle, N.Y., June 28, 1929; d. Michael A. and Vincentia (Bonitatibus) Dandry; m. Edward C. Connolly, June 7, 1952; children: Michael, Matthew, Christopher, Benedict, Andrew. BA, Chestnut Hill Coll., Phila., 1951; MA, Temple U., Phila., 1970, PHD, 1975; hon. degree, Rilski Neofit U., Blagoevgrad, Bulgaria, 1992. Intelligence clk. CIA, Washington, 1951-52; tchr. Prince George's County Bd. Edn., Hyattsville, Md., 1952-53; rsch. assoc. Pa. Prison Soc., Phila., 1974-76; field dir. rsch. Georgetown U. Law Sch., Washington, 1976-77; rsch. dir. Phila. Commn. for Effective Criminal Justice, 1977-78; mem. faculty dept. criminal justice Temple U., Phila., 1980-91; mem. faculty dept. sociology Am. U. in Bulgaria, Blagoevgrad, 1991-96; guest lectr. Sch. Law Kiril E Metodi Univerzitet, Skopje, Macedonia, 1993. Cons. Bucks County Correctional Facility, Doylestown, Pa., 1987-91; evaluator Phila. Prison System, 1973. Campaign chairperson, Doylestown, Pa., 1980, 82, 84, 86, 90; pres. Bucks County Assn. for Corrections and Rehab., Doylestown, 1988-91; trustee Bucks County Community Coll., Newtown, Pa., 1989-91; bd. dirs. ARC, Bucks County chpt., Doylestown, 1980-82; mem. New Hope (Pa.) Civil Svc. Commn., 1986-91; bd. dirs. Planned Parenthood, 1986-88. U.S. Justice Dept. dissertation grantee, Washington, 1972. Mem. ACLU, LWV, Law and Soc. Assn., Am. Correctional Assn., Balkan Ednl. and Sci. Assn. (mem. sci. senate). Democrat. Avocations: gardening, embroidery, painting. Home: 762 Fairview Ave Apt C Annapolis MD 21403-2962

CONNOLLY, JEFFREY JAMES, biologist; b. Chgo., Dec. 13, 1972; s. James Paul Connolly and Judith Gail Novacek; m. Elizabeth Ann Cools, July 26, 1997; children: James, Ryan, Liam. BS in Biology, U. Ill., 1994. Cert. quality mgr. Assoc. biochemist Abbott Labs., Abbott Park, Ill., 1996—98, assoc. scientist, 1998—99, compliance coord, 1999—2000, quality assurance profl., 2000—02; program mgr. TAP Pharm. Products, Inc., Lake Forest,

2002—05; project mgr. Abbott Labs., 2005—. Mem.: U. Ill. Alumni Assn., Am. Soc. Quality (cert.), World Wildlife Fund, The Nature Conservancy, Phi Kappa Phi, Phi Beta Kappa. Avocations: hiking, metal detecting, snorkeling, travel, photography.

CONNOLLY, JOHN EARLE, surgeon, educator; b. Omaha, May 21, 1923; s. Earl A. and Gertrude (Eckerman) C.; m. Virginia Hartman, Aug. 12, 1967; children: Peter Hart. John Earle, Sarah. AB, Harvard U., 1945, MD, 1948. Diplomate: Am. Bd. Surgery (bd. dirs. 1976-82), Am. Bd. Thoracic and Cardiovascular Surgery, Am. Bd. Vascular Surgery. Intern. in surgery Stanford U. Hosps., San Francisco, 1948-49, surg. research fellow, 1949-50, asst. resident surgeon, 1950-52, chief resident surgeon, 1953-54, surg. pathology fellow, 1954-55, 1957-60, John and Mary Markle Scholar in med. scis., 1957-62; surg. registrar professional unit St. Bartholomew's Hosp., London, 1952-53; resident in thoracic surgery Bellevue Hosp., N.Y.C., 1955; resident in thoracic and cardiovascular surgery Columbia-Presbyn. Med. Ctr., N.Y.C., 1956; from instr. to assoc. prof. surgery Stanford U., 1957-65; prof. U. Calif., Irvine, 1965—, chmn. dept. surgery, 1965-78; attending surgeon Stanford Med. Ctr., Palo Alto, Calif., 1959-65; chmn. cardiovascular and thoracic surgery Irvine Med. Ctr. U. Calif., 1968—; attending surgeon Children's Hosp., Orange, Calif., 1968—, Anaheim (Calif.) Meml. Hosp., 1970—. Vis. prof. Beijing Heart, Lung, Blood Vessel Inst., 1990, A.H. Duncan vis. prof. U. Edinburgh, 1984; Hunterian prof. Royal Coll. Surgeons Eng., 1985-86, Kinmonth lectr., 1987, Hume Lectr. Soc. for Clin. Vascular Surgery, 1998; King James IV lectr. Royal Coll. Surgeons Edinburgh, 2003; Dist. Prof. Lectr. Uniformed Svcs. U. Health Scis., Bethesda, 1998; adv. coun. Nat. Heart, Lung, and Blood Inst.-NIH, 1981-85; Emile F. Holman lectr. Stanford U. Sch. Medicine, 2005; cons. Long Beach VA Hosp., Calif., 1965—. Contbr. articles to profl. jours.; mem. editl. bd.: Jour. Cardiovascular Surgery, 1974-03, chief editor, 1985-96; mem. editl. bd. Western Jour. Medicine, 1975—, Jour. Stroke, 1979—, Jour. Vascular Surgery, 1983-95. Bd. dirs. Audio-Digest Found., 1974—, Franklin Martin Found., 1975-80; regent Uniformed Svcs. U. Health Scis., Bethesda, 1992-03. Served with AUS, 1943-44. Recipient Cert. of Merit, Japanese Surg. Soc., 1979, 90. Fellow ACS (gov. 1964-70, regent 1973-82, vice chmn. bd. regents 1980-82, v.p. 1984-85), Royal Coll. Surgeons Eng., 1982 (hon.), Royal Coll. Surgeons Ireland, 1988 (hon.), Royal Coll. Surgeons Edinburgh, 1983 (hon.); mem. Japanese Surg. Soc. (hon.), Vascular Soc. of Great Britian & Ireland (hon.), Am. Surg. Assn., Soc. U. Surgeons, Am. Assn. Thoracic Surgery (coun. 1974-78), Pacific Coast Surg. Assn. (pres. 1985-86), San Francisco Surg. Soc., L.A. Surg. Soc., Soc. Vascular Surgery, Western Surg. Assn., Internat. Cardiovascular Soc. (pres. 1977), Soc. Internat. Chirurgie, Soc. Thoracic Surgeons, Western Thoracic Surg. Soc. (pres. 1978), Orange County Surg. Soc. (pres. 1984-85), James IV Assn. Surgeons (councillor 1983—), San Francisco Golf Club, Pacific Union Club, Bohemian Club (San Francisco), Harvard Club (N.Y.C.), Big Canyon Club (Newport Beach, Calif.), Cypress Point Club (Pebble Beach), Pacific Union Club. Home: 7 Deerwood Ln Newport Beach CA 92660-5108 Office Phone: 714-456-5756. E-mail: jeconnol@uci.edu.

CONNOLLY, JOHN JOSEPH, publishing executive; b. Worcester, Mass., Feb. 4, 1940; s. Nicholas John and Margaret Anne (Flynn) C.; m. Ingrid Schlemminger, Apr. 11, 1964; children: Sean Timothy, Cheryl Lea. BS, Worcester State Coll., 1962; MA., U. Conn., 1963; EdD, Columbia U., 1972; LLD, Mercy Coll., 1980. Pres. Dutchess C.C., Poughkeepsie, N.Y., 1972-81; pres., CEO N.Y. Med. Coll., Valhalla, N.Y., 1981-92, Castle Connolly Med. Ltd., N.Y.C., 1992—. Bd. dirs. Mortons Restaurant Group, Inc.; chmn. Alpha Gene Inc Chmn. Dutchess County Indsl. Devel. Agy., 1978—81; hon. chmn. Dutchess/Columbia br. Am. Lung Assn., 1993—; pres. Westchester Hist. Soc., 1985—88; pres.'s adv. coun. United Hosp. Fund; bd. advisors Whitehead Inst. for Biomed. Rsch.; adv. com. Funding First, Inc.; bd. dirs., vice-chmn. Profl. Exam. Svc., 1998—; bd. dirs. United Way of Dutchess County, pres., 1978; chmn. bd. trustees St. Francis Hosp., Poughkeepsie, 1976—80; trustee, chmn. acad. affairs Com. N.Y. Med. Coll.; trustee Culinary Inst. Am., 1976—2002, chair, 1996—98; trustee Poughkeepsie Area Fund, 1973—78, St. Agnes Hosp, White Plains, 1988—99; bd. dirs. Econ. Devel. Corp. Dutchess County, Westchester County Mental Health Assn., Lupus Found., Am. Lyme Disease Found., 1993—2001, founder, chair, 1994—99. Recipient Disting. Svc. award Poughkeepsie Jaycees, 1974, Marie Y. Martin award Assn. Community Coll. Trustees, 1978; named Man of Yr. Dutchess County Legislature, 1980, One of 100 Outstanding Young Leaders in Higher Edn. Change Mag., 1979. Fellow N.Y. Acad. Medicine, N.Y. Acad. Sci., Assn. Colls. Mid-Hudson Area (pres. 1976-79), Friends of the Nat. Libr. Medicine (dir. 1994-96), Friends of Hudson Valley (chmn. 1990), Westchester County Assn. (bd. dirs. 1991-2001), Phi Delta Kappa. Roman Catholic. Office: Castle Connolly Med Ltd 42 W 24th 2nd Floor New York NY 10010 Office Phone: 212-367-8400.

CONNOLLY, JOSEPH FRANCIS, II, academic administrator, government agency administrator; b. Quincy, Mass., Feb. 15, 1944; s. Joseph Francis and Flora Frances C.; m. Donna M. Cameron, May 4, 1968; children: Jennifer S., Joseph F. III. BA magna cum laude, Park Coll., Parkville, Mo., 1971; LLB, Blackstone Sch. Law, Chgo., 1972, JD, 1977; postgrad., U. South Fla., 1977-79, Fla. Inst. Tech., Melbourne, Liberty U., Lynchburg, Va., Am. Mil. U., Manassas, Va.; MEd, Nat. Coll. Edn., 2000; MMA, Coll. of Higher Edn. for, Martial Arts, U.K., 2001; MS, Knightsbridge U., 2002. Cert. EMT, firefighter and law enforcement officer, Fla.; cert. in homeland security Level V, Am. Bd. for Cert. in Homeland Security; diplomate Homeland Security, Am. Bd. Cert., 2005. Former coord. emergency med. svcs. City of Quincy, 1971-73; former EMT Boston Ambulance Squad, 1973-74; former coord. 14-community emergency med. svcs. program, 1974; formerly safety tng. coord., lead instr. Fire Tng. Acad. Orange County Pub. Schs., Fla., 1979-82; former dir. pub. safety Poinciana, Fla., 1985-86; sr. cons. Resource, Studies, and Devel. Internat., Inc., 1988-91; CEO Connolly, Hudson, Taylor & Assocs., Orlando, Fla., 1988-91; pres. Joseph F. Connolly II, P.A., Fla., 1982-95; internat. radio show host Internet Radio Network, 2004—. Adj. faculty mem. Pikes Peak C.C., Valencia C.C., Fla. Inst. Tech., Nat. Fire Acad., So. Coll.; tng. counselor emeritus NRA; med. cons. State of Bahrain Def. Force; former mem. Health Planning Coun. Greater Boston; dir. Royal Nat. Lifeboat Instn., Ireland, U.K.; dir. U.S. Jujitsu Fedn. Mem. Orange County subcom. Health Systems Agy. of East Ctrl. Fla.; fire commr. Conway Fire control Dist. of Orange County, 1980-84; former combat lt., staff capt. res. program Orange County Fire Dept.; com. chmn. Orange County Rep. Exec. Com., 1985-93; former Safety Tng. Coord. Orange County Pub. Schs., Fla., pres. Coun. of Vol. Coords., Orange County, 1987; mem. Rep. Presdl. Task Force, Nat. Rep. Senatorial Commn.; active Boy Scouts Am., 1954—; life mem. Nat. Eagle Scout Assn.; chmn. bd. trustees Inst. of Mil. Arts, 1999—. Master sgt. Spl. Forces U.S. Army, 1961—96, col. Fla. Guard, 2003—, lt. col. CAP, 1989, ret., ret. USCG Aux., 1999. Decorated Purple Heart with two oak leaf clusters, 24 other U.S. and fgn. mil. decorations or citations, Knight Sovereign Mil. Order St. John of Jerusalem (Austria); recipient Gill Robb Wilson award CAP, Aerospace Edn. Achievement award, 1987, Resolution of Tribute award Orange County Sch. Bd., 1989, Presdl. Sports award for martial arts, 1999, Pres.'s Leadership award and gold medal U.S. Ju-Jitsu Fedn., 2003, cert. of commendation Nat. Mus. of U.S. Army; named Vietnam Vet. of the Yr., Vietnam Vets. Ctrl. Fla., Inc., 1988; named to Order Knights Templar, 1985; inducted into state, nat. and internat. martial art halls of fame. Fellow Soc. Martial Arts U.K.; mem. Aircraft Owners and Pilots Assn., Boat/US, Sons of the Union Vets. of the Civil War, Ducks Unltd., VFW (life), DAV (life), Nat. Fire Acad. Alumni Assn. (pres. 1984-92), Internat. Assn. Counselors and Therapists, Nat. Eagle Scout Assn. (life), Am. Coll. of Forensic Examiners Inst., Legion of Frontiersmen of the British Commonwealth, Third Order St. Francis, Mil. Order of Purple Heart, Mensa, Masons, U.S. Judo Assn. (life, 8th degree black belt in jujitsu, 9th degree black belt in judo, inducted into World Martial Arts Hall of Fame, 1996), Asahi Internat. Dojo (pres.), Midori Yama Budokai, U.S. Yudo Assn. (founder 1998, chmn. bd. trustees 1998—), Internat. Yudo Fedn. (founder 2000, chmn. bd. trustees 2000—). Celtic Ch. Office: 4409 Hoffner Ave Ste 327 Orlando FL 32812-2331

CONNOLLY, JUDITH, financial consultant; b. N.Y.C., Nov. 29, 1939; d. Alfred and Gladys Newman; m. Arthur Kessler (div. Apr. 1971); children: Scott, Todd; m. Gerald Connolly, May 25, 1971 (dec. Nov. 1982). BS, Cornell U., 1964. Tchr. N.Y.C. Pub. Schs., 1964-66, Linden Hill Sch., Hawthorne, N.Y., 1966-69, Lynbrook Pub. Schs., N.Y.C., 1969-79; v.p., sr. fin. cons. Merrill Lynch, N.Y.C., 1979—. Adv. mem. Senator Roy Goodman, N.Y. Avocations: reading, travel. Office: Merrill Lynch 717 Fifth Ave 8th Fl New York NY 10022 E-mail: Judith_Connolly@ml.com.

CONNOLLY, KEVIN JUDE, lawyer; b. NYC, May 25, 1954; s. John William and Beatrice Joan (Fallon) C.; m. Audrey Mason, May 25, 1995; children: Shea Alexander, Ciaran Jude. BA cum laude, Fordham Coll., 1976; JD, Fordham U., 1985. Bar: NY 1990. Assoc. Stroock & Stroock & Lavan, NYC, 1985-89; pres. Imagetronics, Inc., Mineola, NY, 1989-92; counsel Schreiber, Simmons, MacKnight & Tweedy, NYC, 1992-94, Eaton & Van Winkle, NYC, 1994-97; assoc. Robinson, Silverman, Pearce, Aronsohn & Berman LLP, NYC, 1998—2001; ptnr. Duval & Stachenfeld LLP, NYC, 2001—. Vis. lectr. Sch. Visual Arts, NYC, 1996—2000; dir. Internet Soc., NYC chpt., 1997—2000; outside counsel Internet Policy Adv. Body, Geneva, 1997—99, Internet Coun. Registrars, Geneva, Hatewatch, Inc., 1998—2002; faculty mem. Practising Law Inst., 2003—. Author: Law of Internet Security and Privacy, 2003; contbr. Handling Constrn. Risks, 2003. Avocations: antiques, paintball. Home: 205 Blackheath Rd Lido Beach NY 11561-4838 Office: Duval & Stachenfeld LLP 300 E 42nd St New York NY 10017 Business E-Mail: kconnolly@dsllp.com.

CONNOLLY, MELISSA KANE, public relations executive; b. Wilmington, Del., Aug. 8, 1967; BA, Hofstra U., 1989. Bus. mgr. Fairchild Pub., N.Y.C., 1990—93; VISTA vol. Project Challenge, Long Beach, NY, 1993—94; dir. circulation and mktg. Richner Pub., Lawrence, NY, 1994—97; dir. mktg. Farrell Fritz P.C., Uniondale, NY, 1997—2001; dir. comm. Senator Kemp Hannon, Albany, NY, 2001—03; v.p. u. rels. Hofstra U., Hempstead, NY, 2003—. Mem. govt. affairs team. Commn. Indep. Coll. and U., Albany, NY, 2003—; adv. bd. Inst. Devel. and Advancement of Edn. in Sci., Hempstead, 2004—. Adv. bd. PULSE, NY, 2003—; v.p. legis. affairs Long Island Women's Agenda, Plainview, NY, 2004—. Mem.: Internat. Assn. Bus. Comm. (L.I.) (com. chair, Pres. Achievement award 2001, Achievement in Comm. award 1998, 1999), Pub. Rels. Soc. Am. Office: Hofstra Univ 202 A Hofstra Hall Hempstead NY 11549

CONNOLLY, ROBERT, retail executive; BSBA, Rochester Inst. Tech. With Sibleys, 1970—84, gen. merchandise mgr., 1979—84; head corp. level splty. div. Carson Pirie Scott, 1984—85, gen. merchandise mgr. for accessories, shoes, intimate apparel, cosmetics, children's, furs, and all leased depts., 1985—87; v.p. and gen. merchandise mgr. women's apparel Montgomery Ward, 1987—89, exec. v.p., 1994—96; v.p. and merchandise mgr. apparel Wal-Mart Stores, Inc., v.p. shoes and jewelry merchandising, v.p. women's apparel, sr. v.p. and gen. merchandise mgr., 1996—98, exec. v.p. merchandise Wal-Mart Stores div., 1998—2001, exec. v.p. mktg. and consumer comm., 2001—. Mem. adv. bd. Walton Coll. Bus. U. Ark. Office: Wal-Mart Stores Inc 702 SW Eighth St Bentonville AR 72716

CONNOLLY, THOMAS EDWARD, judge; b. Boston, Nov. 7, 1942; s. Thomas Francis and Catherine Elizabeth (Skehill) Connolly. AB, St. John's Coll., Brighton, Mass., 1964; JD, Boston Coll., 1969. Bar: Mass. 1969. Assoc. Schneider & Reilly, Boston, 1969-73; ptnr. Schneider, Reilly, Zabin, Connolly & Costello, P.C., Boston, 1973-85, Connolly Leavis & Rest, Boston, 1986-90; judge Mass. Superior Ct., Boston, 1990—. Instr. law Northeastern Law Sch., Boston, 1975—76. Mem. governing coun. Boston Coll. Law Sch. Alumni Coun., 1980—82, 2001—03. Fellow Am. Coll. Trial Lawyers; mem. ABA (vice chmn. products liability sect. 1978-80), Trial Lawyers Assn. Am. (nat. gov. 1977-80), Mass. Acad. Trial Lawyers (gov. 1976-90), Univ. Club (Boston). Roman Catholic. Home: 253 Marlborough St # 4 Boston MA 02116-1731 Office: The Superior Ct Boston MA 02109 Office Phone: 617-788-8130. Personal E-mail: tommyc57@aol.com.

CONNOLLY, THOMAS P., marketing professional; BA, U. Toledo, 1974. V.p., gen. mgr. Toledo to regional v.p. North Cen. Region Amerisource Health Corp., Toledo, 1983-99, corp. v.p., sales and mktg. Malvern, Pa., 1999—, sr. corp. v.p., sales and mktg., 2001—; sr. v.p. Amerisource Bergen Corp., Malvern. Office: Amerisource Bergen Corp 1300 Morris Dr Wayne PA 19087 Business E-Mail: tconnolly@amerisourcebergen.com.

CONNOLLY, VIOLETTE M., small business owner; b. N.Y.C., Nov. 25, 1918; d. Gysbert Martens and Marie Therese dePont; m. Joseph Vincent Connolly Jr., Feb. 27, 1957 (dec.). BA, Hunter Coll., 1940; MS, Columbia U., 1941. Accredited Pub. Rels. Soc. Am. Analyst The Payne Fund, N.Y.C., 1941-53; ptnr. Elser & Assocs., N.Y.C., 1954-56, The J.V. Connolly Co., N.Y.C., 1957-64; cons. on pub. rels., radio and TV Assn. of the Jr. Leagues of Am., N.Y.C., 1964-72; asst. dir. N.Y. Assn. for Brain Injured Children, N.Y.C., 1973-74; circulation mgr. Plants and Gardens Bklyn. Botanic Garden, N.Y.C., 1974-82; adminstr. Nat. Broadcasting Co., N.Y.C., 1983-86; owner, mgr. The White House, Block Island, R.I., 1986—; clk. Town of New Shoreham, Block Island, 1986—. Bd. mem., publicist The Village Art Ctr., N.Y.C., 1944-54; pres. Washington Sq. Bus. and Profl. Women's Club, N.Y.C., 1953-55; founder, chair House and Garden Tours Com., Block Island Hist. Soc., 1971-96; pres. Block Island Gardeners, 1986-97. Capt. First Assembly Dist., Rep. Club, N.Y.C., 1945-57; mem. Bishop's com. St. Ann's Ch., 1995—. Republican. Avocations: oriental gardens, antique collecting, travel. Home: The White House PO Box 447 Block Island RI 02807-0447

CONNOLLY, WILLIAM M., state supreme court justice; b. 1938; Undergrad., Creighton U., 1956—59, JD, 1963. Dep. atty. Adams County, 1964—66, atty., 1967—72; pvt. law practice Hastings, 1972—91; former judge Nebr. Ct. of Appeals, Lincoln, 1992—94; assoc. justice Nebr. Supreme Ct., Lincoln, justice, 1994—. Mem.: Nebr. State Bar Assn. Office: Nebr Supreme Ct Room 2210 State Capital Bldg Lincoln NE 68509

CONNOR, BERNADETTE YVONNE, retired writer; d. Richard Oscar Smith and Inez Patterson; m. Edsel Louis Connor, Jan. 16, 1971 (div. Mar. 23, 1983); children: Edsel Louis, Eros Lamaas, Erica Latice. Author: (novels) Damaged!, The Parcel Express Murders, Damaged!, 1998, The Parcel Express Murders, 2002, Inherited, 2005. Achievements include first psychological thriller written and published by an African American in the fiction genre. Office: Bee-Con Books Po Box 27708 Philadelphia PA 19118 Office Phone: 215-381-0768. Personal E-mail: beeconbooks@aol.com.

CONNOR, CATHERINE BROOKS, educational media specialist; b. Dothan, Ala., Oct. 29, 1955; d. James Bolling and Margaret Elizabeth (Jones) Brooks; m. Joseph Yauger Whealdon, Jr., June 12, 1983 (div. Aug. 1990); 1 child, Joseph Yauger III; m. William Christopher Connor, Dec. 28, 1991. BS, Fla. State U., 1980, MS in Libr. Sci., 1990. Cert. profl. media specialist, Fla., nat. bd. cert. libr. media specialist. 2002. Asst. br. mgr. City Fed. Savs. and Loan, Birmingham, Ala., 1976-77; elem. tchr. Louise S. McGehee Sch., New Orleans, 1981-85; kindergarten tchr. Lafayette Elem. Sch., New Orleans, 1986; grad. asst. Fla. State U. Sch. Libr. Sci., Tallahassee, 1990; media specialist Lely H.S., Naples, Fla., 1990-91, Frank M. Golson Elem. Sch., Marianna, Fla., 1991—, chmn. sch. adv. coun., 1995-98, leadership team, 1994—. Bd. dirs. Jackson County Pub. Libr.-Friends of Libr., Marianna, 1992-94, mem. adv. bd. 1998—, sec. 1998—; bd. dirs. Jackson County unit Am. Cancer Soc., 1998-2000, chair nominating com., 1998-99; charter mem. Libr. of Congress, Washington, 1994—; mem. Panhandle Pub. Libr. Coop. Sys. Bd., 1998—, mem. pers. com., 2000—. Mem. DAR (libr. 2000—), Colonial Dames, Descs. of Knights of the Garter. Democrat. Episcopalian. Avocations: geneology, travel. Home: PO Box 507 Marianna FL 32447-0507 Office: Frank M Golson Elem Sch 4258 2d Ave Marianna FL 32446-1905

CONNOR, FRANCES PARTRIDGE, retired education educator; b. Bklyn., May 4, 1919; d. Horace K. and Sybil V. (Rafters) P.; m. Leo E. Connor, June 7, 1952. BA, St. Joseph's Coll., 1940; MA, Columbia U., 1948, EdD, 1953; LLD (hon.), Coll. New Rochelle, 1976. Cert. history, social studies tchr., spl. edn. tchr., N.Y. Tchr. history/econs. Haverstraw (N.Y.) Schs., 1940-42; tchr. N.Y. State Rehab. Hosp., West Haverstraw, 1942-49; lectr. Hunter Coll., CCNY, N.Y.C., 1946-54; tchr. spl. edn. Ramapo Ctrl. Schs., Suffern, N.Y., 1949-53; coord. spl. edn. U. Ga., Athens, summers 1952-53; rsch. assoc. U.S. Office of Edn., Washington, 1954-58; survey assoc. Tchrs. Coll., Columbia U., N.Y.C., 1953-54, prof., dir. Rsch. and Demonstration Ctr./Inst. for LD, 1955-87, dept. chair, 1962-85, Richard March Hoe prof. emeritus, 1989—. Mem. profl. adv. bd. Willowbrook Consent Decree, N.Y. State Dept. of Mental Retardation/Devel. Disabilities, Albany, 1977—; mem. bd. dirs. Family Resource Assocs., Shrewsbury, N.J. Author: Education of Homebound and Hospitalized Children, 1964, Experimental Curriculum for Young Mentally Retard Children, 1964; editor: Critical Issues for Low Incidence Populations, 1987. Mem. bd. trustees Mt. Saint Mary Coll., Newburgh, N.Y., 1970—, Human Resources Schs., Albertson, N.Y., 1984—; mem. Pres.'s Com. on Employment of Handicapped, Washington, 1972-89; del., mem. steering com. White House Conf. on the Handicapped, Washington, 1975-78; mem. Coalition of Disabled Women and Their Advocates, Ocean County, N.J., 1990—; bd. trustees Leikemia & Lymphoma Soc. So. Fla., 2003—. Recipient Behavioral Sci. award Nat. Hemophilia Found., 1968, Pioneer in Spl. Edn. award Hofstra U., 1986. Fellow Am. Assn. on Mental Retardation; mem. Coun. for Exceptional Children (pres. 1964-65, Wallin award 1982, Outstanding Contbr. award 1992, R.P. MacKie award 1998), Com. Rehab. Internat. Roman Catholic. Avocations: choral/choir singing, swimming, writing. Home: 23343 Blue Water Cir Apt B113 Boca Raton FL 33433-7074 also: 200 4th Ave Spring Lake NJ 07762 E-mail: franleo@att.net.

CONNOR, GEOFFREY MICHAEL, lawyer; b. Washington, Oct. 2, 1946; s. John Thomas and Mary (O'Boyle) C.; m. Maud Holly Pyne, July 24, 1976; children: Taylor Pyne, Michael Buck, Grafton Wright. BA, Williams Coll., 1968; JD, Harvard U., 1973. Bar: N.Y. 1974, N.J. 1975. Clk. to presiding judge U.S. Ct. Appeals (2d cir.), N.Y.C., 1973; assoc. Cleary, Gottlieb, Steen & Hamilton, N.Y.C. and London, 1974-79, Shanley & Fisher, N.J., 1979-83; v.p. Carteret Savs. Bank, FA, N.J., 1984-86, sr. v.p. Morristown, N.J., 1987-90; commr. N.J. Dept. Banking, Trenton, 1990-94; pntr. Reed Smith LLP, Princeton, N.J., 1994—. Lt. (j.g.) USN, 1968-70. Mem. N.J. State Bar Assn. Home: 52 Potterstown Rd PO Box 355 Oldwick NJ 08858-0355 Office: 136 Main St Princeton Forrestal Village Princeton NJ 08543-7839 Office Phone: 609-520-6002. E-mail: gconnor@reedsmith.com.

CONNOR, GEOFFREY SCOTT, state official, lawyer; b. Ballinger, Tex., July 24, 1963; s. Michael Lynn Connor and Pamela Sue Underwood Hodges. BA, S.W. Tex. State U., San Marcos, 1985; student, U. London, England, 1985; JD, U. Tex., 1988. Asst. gen. counsel office of the gov., Austin, Tex., 1988-90, dep. gen. counsel, 1990-91; asst. commr. legal affairs dept. agriculture, Austin, Tex., 1991-95; gen. counsel Tex. Natural Resource Conservation Commn., 1995-99; atty. Akin, Gump, Strauss, Hauer and Feld, 1999—2000; asst. sec. state State of Tex., 2000—03, sec. of state, 2003—. Com. mem. standing com. agr. law, Austin, 1991-96, bar hist. com., Austin, 1994—, Coun. of Govt. lawyers, 1991-97, com. on the arts, Austin, 1994—; mem. Austin Coun. Foreign Affairs, 1989—. Rep. del., Austin, 1982-96, nat. Rep. alt. del., Houston, 1992, nat. Rep. del., San Diego, 1996; bd. dirs. Helping Our Brothers Out, Inc., 1995—. Mem. ABA, State Bar of Tex. (bd. cert. in adminstrv. law by Tex. Bd. of Legal Specialization), Tex. Young Lawyers Assn. Episcopalian. Avocations: travel, reading, hunting, gardening. Office: Sec of State PO Box 12887 Austin TX 78711 Office Phone: 512-463-5770. Office Fax: 512-475-2761. Business E-Mail: gconnor@sos.state.tx.us.

CONNOR, JAMES RICHARD, retired foundation administrator; b. Indpls., Oct. 31, 1928; s. Frank Elliott and Edna (Felt) C.; m. Zoe Ezopov, July 7, 1954; children: Janet K., Paul A. BA with highest distinction, U. Iowa, 1951; MS, U. Wis., 1954, PhD, 1961. Asst. prof. history Washington and Lee U., 1956-57, Va. Mil. Inst., 1958-61; asst. dir. Salzburg Seminar in Am. Studies, 1961-62; joint staff mem. Wis. Coordinating Com. Higher Edn., 1962-63; dir. Inst. Analysis; asst. prof. history U. Va., 1963-66; assoc. prof. history, assoc. provost No. Ill. U., 1966-69; provost, acad. v.p., prof. history Western Ill. U., 1969-74; chancellor, prof. history U. Wis., Whitewater, 1974-91, chancellor, prof. emeritus, 1991. Exec. dir. James S. Kemper Found., Long Grove, Ill., 1991-99; assoc. dir. Va. Higher Edn. Study Com., 1964-65; intern acad. adminstrn. Am. Coun. Edn., Stanford U., 1965-66; staff dir. Study of Governance of Acad. Med. Ctr., Josiah Macy Jr. Found., 1968-70; mem. commn. on higher edn. North Ctrl. Assn. 1970-75, 79-84, cons.-examiner, 1972-91; chair adv. com. on alcohol and drug use U. Wis. System, 1984-85; mem. nat. adv. com. Woodrow Wilson Nat. Fellowship Found., 1990-96, trustee, 1996-2005, trustee emeritus, 2005; dir. Fairhaven Retirement Corp., 1994—. Author: Studies in Higher Education, 1965; contbr., Ency. Brit. Served with AUS, 1946-47, 51-53. Woodrow Wilson fellow, 1953-54; So. fellow, 1957-58 Mem. AAUP, Orgn. Am. Historians, Blue Key, Golden Key, Order of Omega, Phi Beta Kappa, Phi Eta Sigma, Phi Kappa Phi, Phi Delta Kappa, Beta Gamma Sigma, Phi Alpha Theta, Delta Sigma Pi. Home: N7447 Linden Dr Whitewater WI 53190-4357 E-mail: j31z29connor@webtv.net.

CONNOR, JOHN MURRAY, agricultural studies educator; b. Attleboro, Mass., July 7, 1943; s. John Murray Sr. and Victoria Rose (Moro) C.; m. Ulla Maija Niemelä, Apr. 3, 1972; 1 child, Timo. BA cum laude, Boston Coll., 1965; MA, U. Fla., 1974; MS, U. Wis., 1974, PhD, 1976. Vol. U.S. Peace Corps, 1966—68; agrl. economist Econ. Rsch. Svc.1979 USDA, Madison, 1976, head food mfg. rsch. Econ. Rsch. Svc. Washington, 1979—83; assoc. prof. agrl. econs. Purdue U., West Lafayette, Ind., 1983—89, prof., 1989—, asst. dept. head, 1985—88. Adj. prof. Cath. U. Sacred Heart, Piacenza, Italy, 1991—; vis. prof. Åbo (Finland) Akademi U., 1994; cons. subcom. on multinats. U.S. Senate, Washington, 1974-76, select com. on nutrition, 1977-78, UN Ctr. on Transnats., 1981-82, U.S. Dept. Justice, 1999, Nat. Assn. Attys. Gen., 2000-03; chair Orgn. and Performance World Food Systems, 1988-93. Author: Market Power of Multinationals, 1977, Food Frocessing: An Industrial Powerhouse in Transition, 1988, 2d edit., 1997, Global Price Fixing, 2001; (with others) Food Manufacturing Industries, 1985; contbr. articles to profl. jours., chpts. to books. Grantee US Office Tech. Assessment, 1984-85, Inst. Food Technologists, 1986-88, 94-95, Ind. Dept. Commerce, 1987-91, Econ. Rsch. Svc., USDA, 1988-89, Coop. State Rsch. Svc., USDA, 1989—; recipient Antitrust Writing award Jerry S. Cohen Meml. Trust, 2003. Mem. AAUP (pres. Purdue U. chpt. 1988-90, exec. bd. ind. conf. 1990-94, nat. coun. 1991-92), Am. Agrl. Econs. Assn. (Policy award 1980, Quality of Comm. award 1985, 2002, Disting. Extension Program award 1993), Indsl. Orgn. Soc., Am. Econs. Assn., ACLU. Home: 4355 Creekside Pass Zionsville IN 46077-9292 Office: Purdue U 403 W State St West Lafayette IN 47907-2056 Office Phone: 765-494-4260.

CONNOR, JOHN THOMAS, JR., portfolio manager; b. N.Y.C., June 16, 1941; s. John Thomas and Mary (O'Boyle) Connor; m. Susan Scholle, Dec. 18, 1965; children: Seanna, Marin, John. BA cum laude, Williams Coll., 1963; JD, Harvard U., 1967. Bar: N.Y. 1968, DC 1980. Assoc. Cravath, Swaine & Moore, N.Y.C., 1967-71; dep. dir. Office Econ. Policy and Case Analysis, Pay Bd., Washington, 1971-72, Bur. East-West Trade, U.S. Dept. Commerce, Washington, 1972-73; sr. v.p. U.S.-USSR Trade and Econ. Coun., Moscow, 1973-76; assoc. Milbank, Tweed, Hadley & McCloy, N.Y.C., 1976-79; ptnr. Curtis, Mallet-Prevost, Colt and Mosle, Washington, 1980-82; v.p., gen. counsel, sec. PHH Corp., 1982-88; v.p., asst. gen. counsel Prudential Ins. Co. Am., Newark, 1988-90; ptnr. Sills Cummis, Newark, 1990-94; counsel Chadbourne & Parke, N.Y.C., 1994-96, Patterson, Belknap, Webb & Tyler, LLP, 1996-98; portfolio mgr. Third Millennium Russia Fund, 1998—. Bd. dirs., chmn. audit com. Teton Energy, 2003—. Pres., trustee Newark Boys Chorus Sch.; Fulbright tutor Ferguson Coll., Poona, India, 1963—64; chmn. Coun. Econ. Priorities; exec. dir. N.J. Dems., 1969—70. Mem.: Am. Law Inst., Coun. Fgn. Rels., DC Bar Assn., N.Y. State Bar Assn., Mountain Lake

Club (Fla.), Baltusrol Golf Club N.J., Union Club (N.Y.C.), Wianno Club (Cape Cod), Chevy Chase Club (Md.), Phi Beta Kappa. Home: PO Box 832 Lake Wales FL 33859-0832 Office Phone: 863-676-6301. E-mail: jtconnor@tampabay.rr.com.

CONNOR, JOSEPH PATRICK, III, lawyer; b. Phila., Apr. 15, 1953; s. Joseph Patrick Jr. and Wanda Delores (Filipkowski) C.; m. Mary Margaret Kazanicka, Aug. 13, 1977; children: Cathleen Marie, Christopher Joseph, Christine Anne. BA in Polit. Sci., Villanova U., 1974; JD, St. Mary's U., San Antonio, 1974. Bar: Pa. 1977, U.S. Dist. Ct. (ea. dist.) Pa. 1977, U.S. Dist. Ct. (mid. dist.) Pa. 1997, U.S. Ct. Appeals (3d cir.) 1977, U.S Supreme Ct. 1982. Assoc. ptnr. Gibbons, Buckley, Smith, Palmer & Proud, Media, Pa., 1977-82; pres. Connor & Weber, P.C., Phila., Paoli, 1982—. Mem. ABA (tort & litigation sects.), Pa. Bar Assn., Pa. Def. Inst., Def. Research Inst., Pa. Trial Lawyers Assn., Chester County Bar Assn. Clubs: Overbrook County (Bryn Mawr). Republican. Roman Catholic. Avocations: flying, golf, swimming, travel. Office: Connor & Weber PC 2401 Pennsylvania Ave Philadelphia PA 19130-3010 Address: 171 W Lancaster Ave Paoli PA 19301

CONNOR, JOSEPH ROBERT, editor; b. N.Y.C., Jan. 31, 1927; s. Joseph M. and Ethel May (Ball) Connor; m. Marie Louise Zolezzi, Sept. 6, 1952; children: Jeanne Marie, Robert Brian, Ellen Louise. BA, Hunter Coll., 1951. Copy editor sports desk N.Y. Mirror, N.Y.C., 1950-52; mng. editor Mechanix Illustrated Mag. div. Fawcett Publs., N.Y.C., 1953-70; editor in chief CBS Publs., N.Y.C., spl. interest publs., 1970-72; editor in chief Motor Mag. div. Hearst Corp., N.Y.C., 1972-77; editor Construction Contracting, 1978-79; editor in chief Graduating Engr. McGraw-Hill, Inc., 1979-81, 88-90; editor Bus. Week New Product Devel., 1981—, Bus. Week Almanac, 1981—; editor in chief Bus. Week Careers, 1982-87; editor-in-chief Graduating Engr., 1988-90; exec. editor Graduating Engr. Peterson's-Cog Publs., 1990-91; freelance writer, editorial cons., 1991—; editor MOTORScoop Mag., GRG Pubs. Inc., 1995-96. Author: A Job With a Future in Automative Mechanics, 1969; author: (with Heinz Ulrich) The National Job-Finding Guide, 1981; author: Cracking the Over-50 Job Market, 1992, Living with Your Bulldog, 2001; contbr. articles to popular mags. With AUS, 1945—46. Mem.: Am. Soc. Mag. Editors, Internat. Motor Press Assn. (pres. 1966—67). Home: 8 Woodvale Ln Huntington NY 11743-2324 Office Phone: 631-271-5537. Personal E-mail: scoop09@aol.com.

CONNOR, KEVIN M., lawyer; b. 1962; BA, Vanderbilt U.; JD, U. Kans. Bar: 1988. Shareholder Seigfreid, Bingham, Levy, Selzer, and Gee, 1994, ptnr., 1995—2002; sr. v.p. legal AMC Entertainment, Kans. City, Mo., 2002—03, sr. v.p., gen. counsel, sec., 2003—. Office: AMC Entertainment Inc 920 Main St Kansas City MO 64105-2017 Office Phone: 816-221-4000. Office Fax: 816-480-4700.

CONNOR, LAURENCE DAVIS, lawyer, director; b. Columbus, Ohio, May 14, 1938; s. Laurence R. and Gladys C. (Davis) C.; m. Clare Elizabeth Hartwick, Aug. 8, 1964; children: Jeffrey H., Lynne D. Scoville. BA, Miami U., Oxford, Ohio, 1960; JD, U. Mich., 1965. Bar: Mich. 1966, U.S. Dist. Ct. (ea. dist.) Mich. 1966, U.S. Ct. Appeals (6th cir.) 1973, U.S. Supreme Ct. 1979. Assoc. Dykema Gossett, Detroit, 1965-73, ptnr., 1973—2002, mem. exec. com., 1984-90, dir. litigation sect., 1987-91. Mem. coun. sect. on alternative dispute resolution State Bar of Mich., 1992—, chairperson, 1996-97; pres. Vis. Nurse Assn. Met. Detroit, 1980-81, Vist. Nurse Corp., Detroit, 1986-88; asst. clin. prof. law U. Mich., 2002-05. Mem. ABA, Am. Judicature Soc., Country Club Detroit, Detroit Athletic Club, Yondotega Club. Office: Dykema Gossett 400 Renaissance Ctr Ste 3500 Detroit MI 48243-1602 Office Phone: 313-568-6573. E-mail: lconnor@dykema.com.

CONNOR, MICHAEL S., lawyer; b. Gastonia, NC, Sept. 13, 1962; Student, US Naval Acad.; BSME cum laude, Clemson Univ., 1984; JD, Univ. NC, 1987. Bar: NC 1988. Ptnr., co-leader, intellectual property litig. group Alston & Bird LLP, Charlotte, NC. Frequent speaker and author in field. Bd. dir. Metrolina Entrepreneurial Coun. Named one of Legal Elite, Bus. NC Mag., 2003. Mem.: Fed. Circuit Bar Assn., Am. Intellectual Property Law Assn., NC Bar Assn. Office: Alston & Bird LLP Ste 4000 Bank of Am Plz 101 S Tryon St Charlotte NC 28280-4000 Office Phone: 704-444-1022. Office Fax: 704-277-8588. Business E-Mail: mconnor@alston.com.

CONNOR, NANCY L., small business owner; b. Chgo., Sept. 7, 1960; d. Edward Joseph and Bernadette Marie Cider; m. Martin David Connor, June 16, 1984 (div. Nov. 1987). BS, Towson State U., 1982. Sys. adminstr. Ballistics Rsch. Lab., Aberdeen, Md., 1982-84; programmer, documentation specialist Symbolics, Inc., Boston, 1984-86; pres., chmn. FTP Software, Inc., Boston, 1986-93; pres. Ringing Rocks Found., Sedona, Ariz., 1995—2004, chmn., 2004—; owner S.A.G.E. Crafts, Sedona, 2005—. Co-chmn. discretionary fund Women's Way, Phila., 1995-2001. Mem. Internat. Soc. Study Subtle Energy and Energy Mgmt., Inst. Noetic Scis., James Smithson Soc. of Smithsonian Instn. Avocations: gardening, crafts. Office: S.A.G.E Crafts 1590 W Hwy 89A Sedona AZ 86336 E-mail: nconnor@sage-crafts.com.

CONNOR, PAULA MAEDER, clergy; b. Cleve., Sept. 3, 1949; d. Edgar Samuel and Betty Jane (Moore) Maeder; m. David Alan Connor, Sept. 1, 1979; children: Brenna Maeder, Greer Margaret. BA, Capital U., 1971; MDiv, Trinity Luth. Sem., Columbus, Ohio, 1978, M of Sacred Theology, 1996. Ordained to ministry Luth. Ch., 1978. Vol. U.S. Peace Corps, Thailand, 1972-74; pastor St. Matthew Luth. Ch., Sugar Grove, Ohio, 1978-83; assoc. pastor Capital U. Law Sch., Columbus, 1986-88; chaplain Franklin Pre-Release Ctr., Columbus, 1989-90; interim dean religious life Denison U., Granville, Ohio, 1988-89; pastor Trinity Luth. Ch., Lakewood, Ohio, 1990—. Bd. dirs. Ohio Luth. Campus Ministry, 1986-89; mem. Ch. in Society Com., Cleve., 1990-95; mem. steering com. Commn. for Women, Chgo., 1996—; founder Peace Camp at Trinity, 1991. Mem. Music Boosters, Lakewood; key spkr. Lakewood Pub. Schs.; pres. Lakewood Ministerial Assn., 1993—98. Recipient Ctr. for Ednl. Ministry in the Parish ann. award, Trinity Luth. Sem., 1997, Lilly Endowment Clergy Renewal Program grant, 2002. Mem.: Lakewood Ministerial Assn. Avocations: art shows, depression glass, camping, music, volunteering. Home: 1485 Marlowe Ave Lakewood OH 44107-4318 Office: Trinity Luth Ch 16400 Detroit Ave Lakewood OH 44107-3626

CONNOR, TERENCE GREGORY, lawyer; b. Chelsea, Mass., Dec. 28, 1942; s. Joseph Gerard Sr. and Rosalie Cecilia (Ryan) C.; m. Julie Kaye Berry, Dec. 18, 1971; children: Cormac, Kristin, Etain, Brendan. AB, Georgetown U., 1964; LLB, Seton Hall U., 1967; LLM, Georgetown U., 1975. Bar: D.C. 1968, U.S. Supreme Ct. 1976, Fla. 1980. Trial atty. U.S. Dept. Justice, Washington, 1973-76; labor counsel Nat. Airlines Inc., Miami, Fla., 1976-79; practicing atty. Morgan, Lewis & Bockius, Miami, 1979-96, mng. ptnr., 1996—2002. Mem. firm wide governing bd., 1996-2000. Chmn. Miami: Dade citizen com. for Observance Bicentennial of U.S. Constitution, 1986. Served to capt. JAG, USAF, 1968-73. Mem. Fla. Bar Assn. (chair labor and employment law sect. 1994-95, mem. exec. coun. 1986-93), Miami C. of C. (co-chair pers. and Labor mgmt. com. 1993-94) Home: 1517 San Rafael Ave Miami FL 33134-6241 Office: Morgan Lewis & Bockius Wachovia Fin Ctr 200 S Biscayne Blvd Ste 5300 Miami FL 33131-2339 Office Phone: 305-415-3316. Business E-Mail: tconnor@morganlewis.com.

CONNOR, ULLA M., linguistics educator, writer, researcher; m. John M. Connor; 1 child, Timo. BA in English Philology, U. Helsinki, 1970, MA in English Philology magna cum laude, 1974; MA in English Lit., U. Fla., 1971; MA in Comparative Lit., U. Wis., 1973, PhD in Edn., English Linguistics, 1978. Asst. prof. Georgetown U., DC, 1980—83, Ind. U.-Purdue U. Indpls., 1984—87, assoc. prof., 1987—93, prof., 1993—, founder, dir. ESL program, 1985—94, 1997—98, dir. Ind. Ctr. Intercultural Comm., 1997—, Barbara E. and Karl R. Zimmer chair in intercultural communication, 2003—. Asst. dean grad. sch. Purdue U., West Lafayette, Ind., 1988—90; donner guest prof. Abo Akademi U., Finland, 1994, 2000; vis. prof. Temple U. Japan, 1995; vis. rschr. U. Jyvaskyla, Finland, 1995; guest prof. Lund U., Sweden, 1998; academic advisor dept. of fgn. langs. Poly. U. Hong Kong, China, 1999—2001. Author: Contrastive Rhetoric: Cross-cultural Aspects of Second Language Writing, 1996; co-author (with others): Successful Grant Proposals. A Guide for Researchers in the European Union; co-editor (with R.B. Kaplan): Writing Across Languages: Analysis of L2 Text, 1987; co-editor: (with A.M. Johns) Coherence in Writing: Research and Pedagogical Perspectives, 1990; co-editor: (with D. Belcher) Reflections on Multiliterate Lives, 2001; co-editor: (with T.A. Upton) Applied Corpus Linguistics: A Multidimensional Perspective, 2004, Discourse in the Professions: Perspectives from Corpus Linguistics; guest editor: Multilingua: Jour. Cross-Cultural and Interlanguage Communication, 2004, Jour. English Academic Purposes Spl. Issue, guest editor with T. Seiler: jour. New Directions for Philanthropic Fundraising. Understanding and Improving Lang. Fundraising. Recipient Glenn Irwin Experience Excellence Recognition award, Ind. U. -Purdue U. Indpls., 1992; Internat. Peace scholarship, U. Fla., 1970-1971, grant, Exxon Edn. Found., 1985-1987, Finland's Acad. Scis. and Tech. (TEKES), 1995, Philanthropy grant, Ind. U., 1999. Mem.: Finnish Soc. Scis. and Letters (elected fgn. mem. 2000), Tchrs. English to Spkrs. of Other Langs., Nat. Coun. Tchrs. English, Am. Assn. Applied Linguistics. Office: Indiana Ctr Intercultural Comm 620 Union Dr Rm 411 Indianapolis IN 46202 Office Fax: 317-274-5616. Business E-Mail: uconnor@iupui.edu.

CONNOR, W. ROBERT (WALTER ROBERT CONNOR), foundation administrator, classicist, educator; b. Worcester, Mass., Aug. 30, 1934; m. Carolyn Loessel; children: Christopher, Stephan. BA, Hamilton Coll., 1956, LHD, 1991; PhD in Classics, Princeton U., 1961; LHD, Knox Coll., 1993. Instr. U. Michigan, Ann Arbor, 1960-63; jr. fellow Ctr. Hellenic Studies, 1963-64; asst. prof. Princeton U., Princeton, N.J., 1964-70, assoc. prof., 1970-72, prof., 1972-89, Andrew Fleming West prof. classics, 1978-89, chmn. dept. classics, 1972-77, chmn. com. Hellenic studies, 1979-85, chmn. coun. humanities, 1982-89; pres., dir. Nat. Humanities Ctr., Rsch. Triangle Pk., NC, 1989—2002; prof. classics Duke U., Durham, NC, 1989-99; pres., CEO The Teagle Found. Inc., NYC, 2003—. Vis. prof. U. Mich., U. Colo., Breadloaf Sch. of English, Inst. Advanced Study, 1985-86; mem. ad hoc com. Radcliffe Inst. Advanced Study, Harvard U., 2000; mem. univ. coun. com. on lit. Yale U., 1979-83; mem. mng. com. Am. Sch. Classical Studies in Athens, 1973-89, exec. com., 1976-80, 85-89; trustee William Alexander Procter Found., 1980-89, Princeton U. Press, 1989, The Glaxo Wellcome Found., 1995—, Athens Coll., 1995-98, Inst. for Advanced Study, 2002-; pres. com. on the Arts and Humanities, 2000—; mem. adv. bd. U. N.C., Asheville, 1990-94, Athens (Greece) Coll., 1996-2000. Author: Greek Orations, 1966, Theopompus and Fifth Century Athens, 1968, The New Politicians of Fifth Century Athens, 1971, Thucydides, 1984; (with C.L. Connor) Life of St. Luke of Steiris, 1994. Alumni trustee Princeton U., 1993-97. Fulbright fellow U. Coll., Oxford, 1956-57, U. Melbourne; Woodrow Wilson fellow, Danforth Fellow, Am. Coun. Learned Socs. fellow, NEH fellow; recipient Howard Behrman award, 1986. Fellow Am. Acad. of Arts and Scis.; mem. Am. Philos. Soc., Princeton Club, Am. Philol. Assn. (pres. 1987-88), Phi Beta Kappa. Office: The Teagle Found Ten Rockefeller Plz Rm 920 New York NY 10020 E-mail: wrconnor@teaglefoundation.org.*

CONNOR, WALTER DOWNING, political scientist, educator, researcher; b. Bay Shore, NY, Apr. 20, 1942; s. Edward Joseph and Mary Margaret (Downing) Connor; m. Eileen Mary Donohue, Oct. 22, 1966; children: Christine Marie, Elizabeth Catherine. AB, Holy Cross Coll., Worcester MA, 1963; MA, Princeton U., 1966, PhD, 1969. Asst. prof., assoc. chair dept. of sociology U. Mich., Ann Arbor, 1968—76; dir. Soviet and East European studies Fgn. Svc. Inst., US Dept. of State, Washington, 1976—84; prof. polit. sci., sociology and internat. rels. Boston U., 1983—, chair, dept. of polit. sci., 1987—92. Cons. fgn. area fellowship program Ford Found., 1969—71; cons. Internat. Rsch. Exchanges Bd., 1973—76, mem., program com., 1980—89; dep. coord. nat. targets project Nat. Coun. Fgn. Lang. Internat. Studies, 1980—81; vis. prof. sociology U. Va., Charlottesville, 1981—84; profl. lectr. govt. Georgetown U., Washington, 1982; vis. prof. polit. sci. Columbia U., NYC, 1989. Author: Deviance in Soviet Soc.: Crime, Delinquency and Alcoholism, 1972, Socialism, Politics and Equality: Hierarchy and Change in Ea. Europe and the USSR, 1979, Socialism's Dilemmas: State and Soc. in the Soviet Bloc, 1988, The Accidental Proletariat: Workers, Politics and Crisis in Gorbachev's Russia, 1991, Tattered Banners: Labor, Conflict and Corporatism in Post-Communist Russia, 1996; co-author: Pub. Opinion in European Socialist Systems, 1977; co-editor: Soviet Social Problems, 1991, The Polish Rd. from Socialism, 1992; mem. editl. bd.: Studies Comparative Communism, 1980—89, Ea. European Politics Socs., 1986—88; mem. editl. bd. Am. Sociol. Rvw., 1987—90; contbr. articles to profl. jours. Recipient Meritorious Honor award, U.S. Dept. of State, 1984; fellow Davis Ctr. Russian and Eurasian Studies, Harvard U., 1984—, Sr. fellow, Sociology, U. Pa., 1981—84, John Simon Guggenheim Found., 1986—87; grantee, Am. Coun. Learned Socs., 1973, 1975—76, Nat. Coun. Soviet and East European Rsch., 1986—87, 1992—93. Mem.: Boston World Affairs Coun. (bd. dirs. 1990—96), Am. Assn. Advancement Slavic Studies (treas., bd. dir. 2001—04). Republican. Roman Catholic. Home: 26 Downing Rd Brookline MA 02445-2153 Office: Boston Univ Dept of Political Science 232 Bay State Rd Boston MA 02215 Business E-Mail: wdconnor@bu.edu.

CONNORS, ALFRED FRANCIS, internist, researcher; b. Bklyn., Ny, May 14, 1950; s. Alfred Francis and Mary Elizabeth Connors; m. Mimi Lam, June 10, 1978; children: Lisa Marie, Christopher Hin-Laam. BA, St. Louis U., 1971; MD, Med. Coll. of Ohio, 1974. Diplomate Am. Bd. Internal Medicine, Am. Bd. Pulmonary Diseases, Am. Bd. Critical Care Medicine. Prof. of health evaluation sciences and internal medicine U. of Va. Sch. of Medicine, Charlottesville, Va., 1996—2002; Charles H. Rammelkamp Jr. prof. of medicine Case Western Res. U., Cleve., 2002—. Chmn., dept. of medicine Case Western Res. U., MetroHealth campus, Cleve., 2002—; dir., divsn. of health svcs. rsch. and outcomes evaluation U. of Va. Sch. of Medicine, Charlottesville, Va., 1996—2002; dir., pulmonary and critical care medicine Metrohealth Med. Ctr. / Case Western Res. U., Cleve., 1995—96. Contbr. articles to profl. jours. Office: MetroHealth Med Ctr / CWRU 2500 Metro-Health Dr Cleveland OH 44120 E-mail: aconnors@case.edu.

CONNORS, EUGENE KENNETH, lawyer, educator; b. Dobbs Ferry, NY, Oct. 3, 1946; s. Edward Micheal and Eileen (Burke) C.; children: Kevin Patrick, Kathryn Margaret. BA in English, Holy Cross Coll., Worcester, Mass., 1968; JD, Columbia U., 1971. Bar: Pa. 1971. Assoc. Reed Smith Shaw & McClay, Pitts., 1971-76; ptnr. Reed Smith LLP (formerly Reed Smith Shaw & McClay), Pitts., 1977—. Adj. prof. St. Francis U. Grad. Sch., Loretto, Pa., 1975—; ski instr. Holiday Valley Ski Area, Ellicottville, N.Y., 1987—; bd. dirs. Green Garden Inc., 1985—, arbitrator, Am. Arbitration Assn.; spkr. in field. Contbr. articles to profl. jours. Bd. dirs. Sch. Vol. Assn. Pitts., 1973-78, Pitts. Human Resources Assn., 1988-95, TEC/Pa. Smallers Mfrs. Coun., 1993-94, Pitts. Pub. Theater, 1999—, exec. com., 2000—. Mem. ABA, Pa. Bar Assn., Allegheny County Bar Assn., Pitts. Human Resources Assn. (bd. dirs. 1988-95, treas. 1987-95), Tri-State Employers Assn. (bd. dirs. 1992-93), Profl. Ski Instrs. Am. Avocations: alpine (downhill) skiing, scuba diving, golf. Office: Reed Smith LLP PO Box 2009 435 6th Ave Pittsburgh PA 15219-1886 Office Phone: 412-288-3375. Business E-Mail: econnors@reedsmith.com.

CONNORS, JACK, JR., advertising executive; m. Eileen Connors; 4 children. Grad., Boston Coll. Founding ptnr., chmn. Hill, Holliday, Connors, Cosmopulos, Inc., Boston, 1968, CEO. Bd. dirs. Navic Networks, 2000—. Chmn. bd. dir. Partners HealthCare Sys.; chmn. bd. trustees Boston Coll.; bd. dir. Nativity Preparatory Sch., Greater Boston C of C, Newton Country Day Sch., Belmont Hill Sch.; trustee, past chmn. Wang Ctr. for Performing Arts. Recipient Heritage Soc. award, Brigham & Women's Hosp., 2003, John Joseph Moakley Pub. Svc. award, 2004, Eternal Light honoree, Jewish Theol. Sem., 2004. Office: Hill Holliday 200 Clarendon St Boston MA 02116*

CONNORS, JAMES PATRICK, lawyer; b. N.Y.C., May 28, 1952; s. Joseph Patrick Connors and Edna Theresa Fitzgerald; m. Gloria Ann Ciccarelli, Jan. 12, 1974; children: Nicholas, Patrick, Jamie Cathleen. BA, Herbert H. Lehman Coll., 1974; JD, N.Y. Law Sch., 1977; LLM, NYU, 1985. Bar: N.Y. 1978, U.S. Dist. Ct. (so. and ea. dists.) N.Y. 1978. Assoc. Bower & Gardner, N.Y.C., 1978-80, Joseph W. Conklin, N.Y.C., 1980-82; ptnr. Jones, Hirsch, Connors & Bull, N.Y.C., 1982—. Lectr. NYU Sch. Medicine, 1983, N.Y. Law Jour., 1984, Bellevue Hosp., 1984, Hillcrest Gen. Hosp., 1984, Mt. Sinai Hosp., 1985, Am. Coll. Ophthalmologists, 1986—88. Contbr. Recipient Am. Jurisprudence award, Lawyers Pub. Coop., 1977. Mem.: ABA, Lawyer Pilot Bar Assn., Def. Assn. of N.Y., N.Y. County Bar Assn., N.Y. State Bar Assn. Home: 85 Mayflower Dr Yonkers NY 10710-3801 Office Phone: 212-527-1000. E-mail: jconnors@jhcb.com.

CONNORS, JOHN G., former computer software company executive; m. Kathy Connors. BA in Acctg., U. Mont., 1984. CPA. Corp. contr. PIP Printing, Inc.; with fin. dept. Safeco Corp., Deloitte, Haskins and Sells; mgmt. Microsoft Corp., 1989, gen. mgr. worldwide fin. ops., corp. controller, 1994-96, v.p. worldwide enterprise group, sr. v.p. fin., CFO, 1999—2005; ptnr. Ignition Partners LLC, Bellevue, Wash., 2005—. Recipient Disting. Alumni award, U. Mont., 1997. Office: Ignition Partners LLC 11400 SE 6th St Ste 100 Bellevue WA 98004

CONNORS, JOSEPH ALOYSIUS, III, lawyer; b. Washington, June 24, 1946; s. Joseph Aloysius Jr. and Charlotte Rita (Fox) C.; m. Mary Louise Bucklin, June 14, 1969. BBA, U. Southwestern La., 1970; JD, U. Tex., 1973. Bar: Tex. 1973, U.S. Dist. Ct. (so. dist.) Tex. 1975, U.S. Supreme Ct. 1976, U.S. Ct. Appeals (5th cir.) 1976, U.S. Dist. Ct. (ea., we. and no. dists.) Tex. 1981, U.S. Ct. Appeals (11th cir.) 1981, U.S. Ct. Appeals (3d, 4th, 6th, 7th, 8th, 9th, 10th and D.C. cirs.) 1986. Law clk. to assoc. justice Tex. Ct. Civil Appeals, Amarillo, 1973-74; assoc. Rankin & Kern, McAllen, Tex., 1974-76; asst. criminal dist. atty. Hidalgo County, Tex., 1976-78; pvt. practice, McAllen, 1978—. Faculty Criminal Trial Advocacy Inst., Huntsville, Tex., 1981-84; spkr. seminars State Bar Tex., 1980-81, 84; adj. prof. Reynaldo G. Garza Sch. Law, Edinburg, Tex., 1988-89. Contbg. editor Criminal Trial Manual, Tex., 1984-95; contbr. articles to profl. jours. Bd. dir. Tex. RioGrande Legal Aid, 1991—, pres. bd. dir., 1994-96. With USMCR, 1966-71. Mem. NACDL, State Bar Tex. (grievance com. 12B 1984-91, chmn. com. 1989-90, profl. enhancement program 1997-2000), Tex. Assn. Criminal Def. Lawyers (bd. dir. 1982-89, Excellence award 1983, medal of honor 1987), Hidalgo County Bar Assn. (bd. dir. 1981-83), Am. Soc. Writers on Legal Subjects, Hidalgo County Criminal Def. Lawyers Assn. (bd. dir. 1991-98). Democrat. Roman Catholic. Home: 605 E Violet Ave Ste 3 Mcallen TX 78504-2469 Office: Law Offices Joseph A Connors III 605 E Violet Ave Ste 3 Mcallen TX 78504 Office Phone: 956-687-8217. E-mail: joeconnors@gmail.com.

CONNORS, JOSEPH CONLIN, lawyer, pharmaceutical executive; b. Mineola, N.Y., Sept. 9, 1948; s. Gerard Edward and Mary Helen (Conlin) C.; m. Mary Napolitano, May 29, 1971; children: J.C., Ryan. BA, SUNY-Oneonta, 1970; JD, Fordham U., 1973. Bar: N.Y. 1974, Tenn. 1985. Confidential law sec. to judge N.Y. Supreme Ct., Cortland, 1973-75; atty. Chevron Corp., Perth Amboy, N.J., 1975-76, Schering-Plough Corp., Kenilworth, N.J., 1976-82, assoc. gen. counsel Memphis, 1982-87, staff v.p., planning and bus. devel. Kenilworth, NJ, 1987, dep. gen. counsel Madison, NJ, 1987-91, v.p., gen. counsel, 1991-92, sr. v.p., gen. counsel, 1992-96, exec. v.p. and gen. counsel, 1996—. Mem. adv. com. Met. Corp. Counsel; sr. advisor N.J. Corp. Counsel Assn. Mem. ABA (com. of corp. gen. counsel), N.Y. Bar Assn., Tenn. Bar Assn. (former chmn. corp. sect.), Assn. Nat. Advertisers (bd. dirs. 1987-90), N.J. Legal Aid and Defender Assn. (corp. adv. com.), N.J. Corp. Counsel Assn. (sr. advisor), N.J. Panel of the CPR Inst. for Dispute Resolution (bd. dirs.), Food and Drug Inst. (trustee, editl. adv. bd.), Pharm. Rsch. and Mfrs. Am. (exec. com. law sect. 1998). Roman Catholic. Avocations: travel, golf. Office: Schering Plough Corp 2000 Galloping Hill Rd Kenilworth NJ 07033-0530

CONNORS, KENNETH ANTONIO, retired chemistry professor; b. Torrington, Conn., Feb. 19, 1932; s. Peter Francis and Adeline (Gioia) C.; m. Patricia R. Smart, Dec. 30, 1972. BS, U. Conn., 1954; MS, U. Wis., 1957, PhD, 1959. Rsch. assoc. dept. chemistry Ill. Inst. Tech., Chgo., 1959-60, Northwestern U., Evanston, Ill., 1960-61; asst. prof. U. Wis. Sch. Pharmacy, Madison, 1962-65, assoc. prof., 1965-72, prof., 1972-97, prof. emeritus, 1997—, acting dean, 1991-93. Author: A Textbook of Pharmaceutical Analysis, 3d edit., 1982, Reaction Mechanisms in Organic Analytical Chemistry, 1973, Chemical Stability of Pharmaceuticals, 2d edit., 1986, Binding Constants, 1987, Chemical Kinetics, 1990, Thermodynamics of Pharmaceutical Systems, 2002. Served with U.S. Army, 1961. Fellow AAAS, Acad. Pharm. Scis., Am. Assn. Pharm. Scis.; mem. Am. Chem. Soc., N.Y. Acad. Scis. Office: U Wis Sch Pharmacy 777 Highland Ave Madison WI 53705-2222

CONNORS, MARY JEAN, communications executive; V.p. human resources Phila. Newspapers, Inc., 1989—95; asst. to sr. v.p. news and ops. Knight Ridder, Inc., San Jose, Calif., 1988—89, sr. v.p. human resources, 1996—2003, sr. v.p., 2003—. Chmn. bd. Bd. Calif. Strategic Human Resources Partnership. Office: Knight Ridder Inc 50 W San Fernando St Ste 1500 San Jose CA 95113-2429 Office Phone: 408-938-7700. Office Fax: 408-938-7766.*

CONNORS, PETER J., lawyer; b. Huntington, N.Y., June 25, 1951; s. John Anthony and Jeanne (Labate) Connors; m. Claudine Minieri, Nov. 13, 1979; children: Priscilla, Grayson. BA, Cath. U., 1973; JD, U. Richmond, 1976; LLM, NYU, 1979. CPA N.Y., 1979, Va., 1979; bar: N.Y. 1977. Mgr. JC Penney & Co., N.Y.C., 1983—87; sr. mgr. KPMG, N.Y.C., 1987—90; prin., dir. Ernst & Young LLP, N.Y.C., 1990—95; ptnr. Baker & McKenzie, N.Y.C., 1995—2001, Orrick, Herrington & Sutcliffe LLP, N.Y.C., 2001—. Fellow: Am. Coll. Tax Counsel; mem.: ABA (tax sect. 2005). Avocation: squash. Office: Orrick Herrington & Sutcliffe LLP 666 5th Ave New York NY 10103 Office Phone: 212-506-5120. Business E-Mail: pconnors@orrick.com.

CONNORS, ROBERT, computer programmer; b. Phila. s. John and Grace (Morrissey) Connors; m. Claire Fuller, Sept. 24, 1988; 1 child, Neil. BSW, St. Francis Coll., 1973—74; MSW, U. Louisville, 1974—75. Social worker Salvation Army, Phila., 1975—76, Middlesex Gen. Hosp., New Brunswick, NJ, 1977—78; computer programmer U.S. Dept. Agriculture, 1988—. Mem.: Nat. Cath. Honor Soc. Democrat. Cath.

CONOBY, JOSEPH FRANCIS, chemist; b. Albany, June 12, 1930; s. Joseph Francis and Helen Emma (Brucker) C.; m. Mary Joan A. Ryan, June 21, 1958; children: James Francis, Mark Joseph. BS, Union Coll., 1952. Sr. tech. svc. engr. Allied Chem. Corp., Syracuse, N.Y., 1956-66; rsch. chemist Conversion Chem. Corp., Rockville, Conn., 1966-69; environ. engr., indsl. hygienist Honeywell Bull, Billerica, Mass., 1969-87, mgr. environ. and health engring., 1969-87; mgr. environ. engring. Bull HN Worldwide Info. Sys., 1987-95; sr. scientist Concorp, Inc., Acton, Mass., 1996—. Adv. bd. Mass. Water Resources Authority Sewer Use (rules and regulations, policy and procedures, and facilities planning task forces); cons. exptl. project course Mass. Inst. Tech., 1977-78. Contbr. articles to profl. jours.; patentee in field. Lt. USN, 1952-56. Mem. Am. Indsl. Hygiene Assn., Nat. Assn. Environ. Mgmt. Home: 5 Samuel Parlin Dr Acton MA 01720-3206 Office: Concorp Inc PO Box 2766 Acton MA 01720-6766 Office Phone: 978-263-8530. E-mail: jfconoby@concorp.com.

CONOM, TOM PETER, lawyer; b. Seattle, Jan. 2, 1949; s. Peter T. and Madeline (Barbas) C.; m. Ann H. Earsley, Jan. 28, 1978; children: Lisa, Tracy, Derek. BA in Journalism, U. Wash., 1971, JD, 1974. Bar: Wash. 1974, U.S. Dist. Ct. (we. dist.) Wash. 1974, U.S. Ct. Appeals (9th cir.) 1984, U.S. Supreme Ct. 1984. Pvt. practice, Seattle, Lynnwood, Edmonds, Wash., 1974—. Mem. adv. bd. nat. jour. The Champion. Contbr. articles to profl. jours. Dem. state del. King, Snohomish County, 1972—. Mem. Wash. Assn. Criminal Def. Attys. (founder, bd. dirs. 1987-89, columnist jour. 1987—), Wash. State Trial Lawyers Assn. (bd. dirs. 1982-86, chmn. criminal law sect. 1986-88, contbr. articles to jour.), Nat. Assn. Criminal Def. Lawyers (life), Assn. Trial Lawyers Am. Snohomish County Bar Assn., Seattle-King County Bar Assn. Office: 51 W Dayton St Ste 206 Edmonds WA 98020-4111

CONOMY, JOHN PAUL, neurologist, educator, lawyer; b. Cleve., July 31, 1938; s. John and Marie Conomy; m. Sharon Sopata; children: John, Lisa, Christopher, Francesca Maria. BS cum laude, John Carroll U., 1960; MD, St. Louis U., 1964; JD, Case Western Res. U., 1992. Diplomate Am. Bd. Psychiatry and Neurology (examiner 1975—). Student rsch. fellow in neurology St. Louis U., 1963-64; intern in straight medicine St. Louis U. Hosps., 1964; resident in neurology U. Hosps. of Cleve., 1965-68; fellow in neuropathology Cleve. Met. Gen. Hosp. and Case Western Res. U., Cleve., 1968; career teaching fellow U. Pa., 1970; asst. prof. neurology Case Western Res. U. Med. Sch., Cleve., 1972-77, assoc. clin. prof., 1979, prof. clin. neurology, 1992—; chmn. dept. neurology Cleve. Clinic Found., 1975-92, chmn. clin. rsch. projects and instl. rev. com., 1978-82, founder, dir. Mellen Ctr. Multiple Sclerosis Treatment and Research, 1984-92, exec. dir., 1987—, also exec. dir. consortium of multiple sclerosis ctrs.; assoc. prof. neurology Pa. State U., 1989—; prof. clin. neurology, adj. prof. law Case Western Res. U., 1992—; dir. clin. neuroscis., dir. Office of Profl. Affairs Innova Med. Svcs., Cleve., 1994—. Attending physician U. Hosps. Cleve., 1968, attending neurologist, 1972-78, mem. bd. govs. dept. medicine, 1974-75; attending physician Highland View Hosp., Cleve., 1968; assoc. neurologist Hosp. U. Pa., 1970; sr. staff neurologist Scott and White Clinic and Hosp., Temple, Tex., 1971; cons. in neurology VA Ctr., Temple, 1971; clins. attending neurologist Parkland Hosp., Dallas, 1971-72; clin. instr. neurology U. Tex. Southwestern Med. Sch., Dallas, 1971-72; vis. lectr. neuroscis. U. Tex. Med. Sch., San Antonio, 1971-72; cons. physician evaluation bd. Whittaker Internat. Services for Saudi Arabia and United Arab Emirates, 1980; mem. physician evaluation bd. Whittaker Corp., 1980-85, sci. adv. bd. Communicative Disorders Found., 1980—; med. advisor Huntington's Disease Found., Cleve., 1984-87; mem. biotech. adv. bd. State of Ohio, 1983-85; cons. HHS, SSA, 1990—; participant Manpower in Neurology Conf., San Diego, 1985; numerous vis. professorships and consultantships throughout U.S., Can., Cen. Am., Europe, Asia and Mid. East; vis. prof. London Hosp. Med. Sch., 1982-83, U. Louvain, Belgium, 1983, Oxford (Eng.) U., 1983, Nat. Ctr. Nervous, Mental and Muscular Disorders, Tokyo, 1984, Kyoto (Japan) U., 1984, Kyushu U., Fukuoka, Japan, 1984, U. Bursa, Turkey, 1985, U. Istanbul, 1985, 86, 88, vis. neurologist Christian Med. Coll., Vellore, India, 1986, vis. export Ministry of Health, Singapore, 1988; vis. neurologist numerous univs. and colls.; hon. cons. The London Hosp. and Tower Hamlets Health Dist., 1982-83; co-investigator neurogenic factors in the pathogenesis of arterial hypertension NIH, 1978; sr. investigator Quantitation of Cutaneous Sensation VA Hosp., Cleve., 1974, neuroscis. rsch. program Cleve. Clinic Found., 1975—; adj. prof. law Case Western Res. U., 1992—; pres. Health Systems Design Inc., 1992—, CompEval Corp., True North Med. Svcs.; cons. Atty. Gen. State of Ohio, 1992—, FTC, 1994—, U.S. Dept. Justice, U.S. Dept. Social Security. Contbr. numerous articles to profl. jours.; mem. editorial bd. Postgrad. Medicine, 1985—, Jour. Neurologic Rehab., 1987—, Surg. Neurology, 1986—, Health Matrix, 1990; reviewer Neurology, 1977—, Cleve. Clin. Quar., 1977—, Neurosurgery, 1979—Am. Jour. Physiology, 1980-81, Archives of Neurology, 1982—, Residency Rev. Com. in Psychiatry and Neurology, 1983—. Served as capt. USAF, 1968-70. Recipient Francis M. Grogan prize St. Louis U. Med. Sch., 1964, Clin. Tchr. of Yr. award U. Hosps. Cleve., 1973; grantee Mary B. Lee Fund, 1973, Reinberger Found., 1976-82, Mellen Fund, 1976, 84, Hostetler Found., 1989, NIH, 1970—. Fellow ACP (invited speaker 1979, 85, reviewer health care delivery programs 1984), Royal Soc. Medicine (London), Am. Acad. Neurology, Am. Heart Assn. (stroke coun.); mem. AAAS, AMA (sect. coun. on neurology 1977-81, vice chmn.-sec. 1979-81; del. Health Policy agenda for the Am. People, 1983), Soc. Neurosci. (pres. Cleve. chpt. 1975-79), ABA, Am. Assn. History Medicine, Ohio State Med. Assn., Cleve. Acad. Medicine, No. Ohio Neurologic Soc., Assn. Rsch. in Nervous and Mental Disease, Internat. Soc. Tech. Assessment in Health Care, Am. Neurol. Assn. (chmn. pub. rels. com. 1981-85), Soc. Clin. Neurologists (councillor 1976-79, program chmn. 1982), Assn. U. Profs. Neurology, Am. Electroencephalographic Soc., Internat. Assn. Study Pain, Am. Acad. Neurology, Cleve. Med. Libr. Assn. (trustee 1980—, chmn. pubs. com. 1984), Clin. Neurosci. Soc. (pres. elect 1992), Cleve. Health Scis. Libr. (exec. com. 1984-86), Behavioral Neurology Soc., Nat. Multiple Sclerosis Soc., Worshipful Soc. Apothecaries London, Coun. Med. Specialty Socs., 1985—), Nat. Multiple Sclerosis Soc. (med. adv. bd. 1987-92), Internat. Fedn. Multiple Sclerosis Socs. (med. adv. bd. 1989—), Health Svcs. Rsch. Com. (chmn. 1986), Am. Assn. Neurol. Surgeons (assoc. membership bd. 1982—), Inst. Clin. Neuroscis. London, Internat. Med. Scholar's Program, European Neurol. Soc. (pres. 1991), Can. Neurol. Assn. (hon.), Am. Soc. Law and Medicine, Am. Coll. Legal Medicine, ABA, Ohio State Bar Assn., World Assn. for Med. Law, Alpha Omega Alpha. Avocations: travel, biking, racquetball, photography, music. Office Phone: 216-292-1875. Personal E-mail: 2br026@msn.com.

CONOSCENTI, CRAIG STEPHEN, physician; b. Jersey City, Jan. 11, 1955; s. Gerald Raoul and Constance Theresa (Niosi) C.; m. Rosanne Denise Scarpa, June 27, 1982; 1 child, Stephen Joseph. BS, Fordham U., 1977; MD, St. Georges U., 1981. Diplomate Am. Bd. Internal Medicine. Resident in internal medicine Meth. Hosp., Bklyn., 1981—82, Hackensack U. Med. Ctr., 1982—84, chief resident, 1984—85; fellow in pulmonary critical care medicine Norwalk (Conn.) Hosp., Yale U. Sch. Medicine, 1985—87, chief diving and hyperbaric medicine, 1991—, med. dir. comprehensive wound care, sr. attending physician pulmonary and critical care medicine; pvt. practice Norwalk, 1987—. Med. dir. Norwalk Hosp. Sch. Respiratory Therapy, 1987-90, med. dir. advanced cardiac life support program, 1986-90. Contbr. articles to profl. jours.; co-inventor Bronchoscopy Catheter; Probal Bronchoscopic Catheter. Orator Norwalk Sons of Italy, 1990-92, v.p., 1992-93, pres., 1993-97. Norman Brady Internat. fellow Brompton Chest Hosp., London, and Norwalk Hosp., 1986. Fellow: Am. Coll. Chest Physicians; mem.: ACP, Fairfield County Lung Assn. (bd. dirs. 1987—94), Conn. Thoracic Soc. (bd. dirs. 1994—, pres. 1997—), Undersea and Hyperbaric Med. Soc., Am. Lung Assn. (bd. dirs. Conn. chpt. 1994—), Am. Thoracic Soc. Avocation: boating. Office: Norwalk Hosp Dept Pulmonary and Critical Care Medicine Maple St Norwalk CT 06856

CONOUR, WILLIAM FREDERICK, lawyer; b. Indpls., June 21, 1947; s. William E. and Marian L. (Smith) C.; m. Jennifer Conour; children: Tonja, Andrea, Erin, Rachel, Tyler, Elise. BA History, Ind. U., 1970, JD cum laude, 1974. Bar: Ind. 1974, U.S. Dist. Ct. (so. dist.) Ind. 1974, U.S. Dist. Ct. (no. dist.) Ind. 1996, U.S. Ct. Appeals (7th cir.) 1975, U.S. Supreme Ct., 1982; cert. mediator Ind. Supreme Ct., 1992—. Dir. training Ind. Pros. Attys. Council, Indpls., 1974-82; ptnr. Conour & Davis, Indpls., 1974-86; assoc. prof., adj. faculty Ind. U., 1975—89; pvt. practice Indpls., 1986-88; spl. dep. prosecutor State of Ind. v. Ford Motor Co. (Ford Pinto Prosecution); ptnr. Conour Doehrman, Indpls., 1988—2003; ptnr., owner Conour Law Firm, Indpls., 2003—. Assoc. prof., adj. faculty Ind. U. Purdue U. Indpls., 1976-86; lectr. Ind. Law Enforcement Acad., otehr lectrs. in field; rsch. analyst Ind. Criminal Law Study Commn., 1973-74. Contbg. author Indiana Criminal Procedure Sourcebook, 1974, Indiana Penal Code, 1974, Indiana Prosecuting Attorney's Deskbook, New Indiana Penal Code, 1976, Lawyers Cooperative Publishing, 1996, The Indiana Lawyer, 2000; editor profl. bulletins; editor, contbg. author: Indiana Prosecuting Attorney's Deskbook, 1978; contbr. articles to profl. jours.; author: Indiana Penal Code, 1977, Res Gestae Mag., 1977-90, The Prosecutor, 1980, Verdict mag., 1992, The Indiana Lawyer, 1996, 99. Guarantor Butler U. Clowes Hall; patron Ind. Repertory Theatre, Indpls. Symphony Orch.; mem. Gov.'s club Ind. Dems., Conner Prairie Pioneer Settlement, Nat. Safety Coun., Hoosier Safety Coun.; mem., co-chmn. task force cmty. based missions second Presbyn. ch.; mem. bd. dirs. U. HS; chess coach U. HS Chess Team; life mem.U.S. Chess Fedn.; life mem. Ind. U. Alumi Assn.; life mem. Woodburn Guild Ind. U.; life mem., mem. bd dirs. Hoosier Salon, U.S. Centenial Olympic Com., Ind., 1996; mem. Five Seasons Country Club; life mem. Ind. Dressage Soc., U.S. Dressage Fedn., NA/WPN, Am. Horse Show Assn.; mem. gold club U.S. Equestrian Team. Recipient commendation Drug Enforcement Adminstrn. U.S. Dept. Justice, 1977, Commendation award Hoosier Safety Coun., 1989, Commendation award Ind. State Bar Assn. Criminal Justice Sect., 1990. Fellow Roscoe Pound Found. (life), Found. Am. Bd. Trial Advocates (sr. life), Indpls. Bar Found. (life); mem. ABA (litigation sect.), Am. Bd. Trial Advocates (pres. Ind. chpt., honoree, charter sr. life fellow 1996), Am. Soc. Safety, Ind. Bar Assn. (sec. litigation 1981-82, ad hoc com. on legal cert., mem. litigation sect., criminal justice sect., sec. 1977-78, treas. 1981-82), Am. Coll. Legal Medicine (assoc.), Indpls. Bar Assn. (grievance com. 1983-91, litigation sect.), Assn. Trial Lawyers Am. (cert. Nat. Coll. Advocacy 1979, Advanced Coll. Advocacy 1981, cons. site litigation group, M Club, lectr., cert. civil trial advocate), Ind. Bar Assn. (grievance com. 1984-91), Coll. of Legal Medicine, Am. Coll. of Legal Medicine, Ind. Trial Lawyers Assn. (sustaining mem., bd. dirs., lectr., amicus curie com., rule of evidence com.), Ind. Lawyers Commn. (ad hoc com. on criminal justice standards and goals 1976-80), Am. Bd. Trial Advs., Ind. U. Alumni Assn. (life), Ind. State Bar Assn. (litig. sect. 1983-, appellate law sect. 1996-, ad hoc com. legal cert., chmn. lawyers adv. com. 1996-98, commendation criminal justice sect. 1990), Trial Lawyers Pub. Justice (sustaining founder), Indpls. Law Club, Indpls. Athletic Club, US Equestrian Team (contbg. mem.), Nat. and Hoosier Safety Coun. (commendation 1989), US Dressage Fedn. Ind. Dressage Soc. (dir.), Indpls. Mus. Art, Sagamore Am. Inn of Ct. (pres. 1999-2001, pres.-elect 1997-99, counselor 2001-), Nat. Am. Inns Ct. Found. (trustee 2001-), Am. Coll. Barristers (sr.counsel), Phi Delta Phi (hon.). Clubs: Inpls. Athletic; Ind. Soc. Chgo., Atla "M". Democrat. Home: 10858 Sedgemoor Cir Carmel IN 46032-9189 Office: Conour Law Firm LLC Ste 150 500 E 96th Street Indianapolis IN 46240-3765 Office Phone: 317-846-5550. Business E-Mail: wfc@tortsurfer.com.

CONOVER, DALE E., geological engineer; b. Boise, Idaho, Sept. 13, 1957; s. Dale Everette and Alice Christina Conover; m. Karen D Conover, Sept. 11, 1999; children: Kelly Lynn Jones, Matthew Everette, Dale Everette Chase. BS in geol. engring., BS in geology, U. of Idaho, 1975—80; MS in engring. geology, Tex. A&M U., 1982—85. Professional Engineer, Ariz., 2004, State Bd. of Registration for Profl. Engineers, N.Mex No., 1996, Bd. of Registration of Profl. Engineers, Idaho, 1991; Professional Geologist State Bd. of Tech. Registration, Ariz., 2004, State Bd. of Registration for Geologists, Calif., 1990, Bd. of Registration for Prof Geol, Idaho, 1988, Bd. of Geologist Examiners, Oreg., 1988, Water Systems Operator Level 4 State of N.Mex Water Quality Control Commn., 1999, Grade 4 Water Treatment Plant Operator Ariz. Dept. of Environ. Quality, 2004. Geol. engr./hydrogeologist Reidel Environ. Services, Inc., Portland, Oreg., 1985—89; sr. geol. engr. Morrison Knudsen Environ., Inc., Boise, Idaho, 1989—94; geol. engr./hydrogeologist ERM Program Mgmt., Inc., Los Alamos, N.Mex., 1994—95; sr. environ. engr. State of N.Mex, Bur. of Hazardous Materials, 1996; ops. supt. New Mex. Am. Water Co., 1996—2003; sr. ops. engr. Ariz. Am. Water Co., 2003—. Cons. hydrogeologist/geol. engr. Ground Water Solutions, Santa Fe, 1994—96. Pres. and past pres. Noon Day Lions Club, Clovis, N.Mex., 1997—2002. Office: Ariz Am Water Co 19820 N 7th St Ste 201 Phoenix AZ 85024-1694 Office Phone: 623-445-2405. Office Fax: 623-445-2454. E-mail: dconover@amwater.com.

CONOVER, JERRY NEIL, finance educator; b. Terre Haute, Ind., Oct. 30, 1950; s. James August and Jane C.; m. Carey Lea Lumpkin, June 2, 1979; children: Michael David, Robert Steven. AB in Psychology, U. Mich., 1972; MA in Psychology, U. Mo., 1975; PhD in Psychology, U. MO., 1979; PhD in Bus. Adminstrn., U. Mo., 1982. Instr. grad. U. Mo., Columbia, 1979—81; asst. prof. U. Ariz., Tucson, 1981—85, No. Ariz. U., Flagstaff, 1985—88, assoc. prof., 1988—97, dir. MBA program, 1990—94, prof., 1997—. Pres. Assn. Univ. Bus. and Econ. Rsch., 2005-06; dir. Bur. Bus. and Econ. Rsch., 1994-2003; exec. dir. Ind. Bus. Rsch. Ctr., 2003—; adj. prof. Ind. U., 2003—. Contbr. articles to profl. jours. Mem. Am. Mktg. Assn. Address: 3159 Mattatha Dr Bloomington IN 47401 E-mail: jerry.conover@nau.edu.

CONOVER, LLOYD HILLYARD, retired research scientist; b. Orange, N.J., June 13, 1923; s. John Howard and Marguerite Anna (Cameron) C.; m. Virginia Rogers Kirk, Aug. 24, 1944 (dec. Dec. 1988); children: Kirk Howard, Roger Lloyd, Heather Cameron, Craig Scott; m. Marie Strauss Solomons, Oct. 18, 1990 (dec. May 2003). BA, Amherst Coll., 1947; PhD, U. Rochester, 1950. Rsch. chemist, mgr. Chas. Pfizer & Co., Bklyn. and Groton, Conn., 1950—68; dir. chem. rsch. and chemotherapy Pfizer Cen. Rsch., Groton, 1968-71, rsch. dir. Europe, Sandwich, Eng., 1971-74, v.p. agrl. R & D Groton and Sandwich, 1975-84. Contbr. articles on antibiotics, anthelmintics and animal health drugs to sci. jours.; patentee tetracycline and pyrantel Chmn. Waterford Planning, 1961-63. Lt. (j.g.) USNR, 1943-46, PTO. Recipient Eli Whitney award Conn. Patent Law Assn., 1983, Third Century award Found. Creative Am., 1990; inductee Nat. Inventors Hall of Fame, 1992. Fellow Royal Soc. Chemistry, Royal Soc. Arts; mem. Am. Chem. Soc., Phi Beta Kappa, Sigma Xi. Republican. Avocations: travel, gardening, genealogical research.

CONOVER, PAMELA C., cruise line executive; married. Cashier Wells Fargo Bank, London, with NYC, 1979—81; asst. treas. US Line, 1981—85; various positions to mng. dir. N. Am. ship financing divsn. Citicorp, 1985—94; pres. Epirotiki Cruises, Carnival Corp., 1994; v.p. strategic planning Carnival Corp., 1994—98; COO Cunard Line Ltd., Carnival Corp., 1998—, pres., 2001—. Achievements include only female pres. major cruise line; Cunard Line Ltd. launched Queen Mary II in 2004, largest transatlantic cruise ship to date. Office: Cunard Line Ltd 6100 Blue Lagoon Dr Ste 400 Miami FL 33126

CONOVER, ROBERT WARREN, retired librarian; b. Manhattan, Kans., Oct. 6, 1937; s. Robert Warren and Grace Darline (Grinstead) C. BA, Kans. State U., 1959; MA, U. Denver, 1961. Libr., supervising libr. County of Fresno, Calif., 1961-66; county libr. County of Yolo, Woodland, Calif., 1967-68; dir. City of Fullerton (Calif.) Pub. Libr., 1968-73, City of Pasadena (Calif.) Pub. Libr., 1973-80, Palos Verdes Libr. Dist., Palos Verdes Peninsula, Calif., 1980-85, City of Commerce (Calif.) Pub. Libr., 1985-97; ret., 1997. Retired librarian; b. Manhattan, Kans., Oct. 6, 1937; s. Robert Warren and Grace Darline (Grinstead) C.; BA, Kans. State U., 1959; MA, U. Denver, 1961. Librarian, supervising librarian County of Fresno, Calif., 1961-66; county librarian County of Yolo, Woodland, Calif., 1967-68; dir. City of Fullerton (Calif.) Pub. Library, 1968-73, City of Pasadena (Calif.) Pub. Library, 1973-80, Palos Verdes Library Dist., Palos Verdes Peninsula, Calif., 1980-85, City of Commerce (Calif.) Pub. Library, 1985-97, ret. Pres. Kapalua Bay (Hawaii) Villas, Inc. Recipient Pres.'s award Fresno Jaycees, 1963. Mem. ALA, Orange County Libr. Assn. (pres. 1971), Spl. Librs. Assn., Calif. Libr. Assn. (pres. Yosemite chpt. 1965, mem. coun. 1981), Santiago Libr. System Coun. (pres. 1972), Met. Coop. Libr. System (exec. com. mem., 1994, vice chair 1995, chair 1996), Univ. Club, Pi Kappa Alpha. Episcopalian. E-mail: rconover@maui.net. Recipient Pres. award Jaycees, Frenso, 1963. Mem. ALA, Orange County Libr. Assn. (pres. 1971), Spl. Librs. Assn., Calif. Libr. Assn. (pres. Yosemite chpt. 1965, coun. mem. 1981), Santiago Libr. Sys. Coun. (pres. 1972), Met. Coop. Libr. Sys. (exec. com. 1994, vice-chmn. 1995, chmn. 1996), Univ. Club, Pi Kappa Alpha. Episcopalian. Home: Kapalua Bay Villas 500 Bay Dr Lahaina HI 96761-9034 E-mail: rconover@maui.net.

CONOVER, WILLIAM JAY, statistics educator; b. Hays, Kans., Dec. 6, 1936; s. William Joseph Conover and Viola Marie (Herman) Beishline; m. Patricia Louise Solomon, June 11, 1960 (div. Apr. 1994); children: Christopher Michael, Robert Andrew, Judith Ann, Therese Marie, William Joseph; m. Susan Theresa Mole, Dec. 27, 1996. BS, Iowa State U., 1958; MA, Cath. U., 1962, PhD, 1964. Asst. prof. stats. Kans. State U., Manhattan, 1964-67, assoc. prof. stats., 1967-73; vis. prof. stats. U. Zürich, Switzerland, 1970-71; prof. stats. Tex. Tech U., Lubbock, 1973-81, Horn prof., 1981—, area coord. of info. systems/quantitative scis., assoc. dean, 1978-88. Vis. prof. U. Calif., Davis, 1976-77; vis. staff mem. Los Alamos (N.Mex.) Sci. Lab., 1976—; cons. Sandia Lab., Albuquerque, 1979—. Author: Practical Nonparametric Statistics, 1971, 3rd edit., 1999, Modern Bus. Stat., 1983, 2d edit., 1989; co-author 9 textbooks on statistics; contbr. articles to profl. jours. Lt. (j.g.) USN, 1958-61. Recipient Rushing Faculty Rsch. award Tex. Tech Dad's Assn., 1983, Samuel Wilks award US Army, 1997. Fellow Am. Statis. Assn. (Don Owen award San Antonio chpt. 1986); mem. Inst. Math. Stats., Biometric Soc., Inst. Decision Scis. Roman Catholic. Avocations: chess, basketball. Office: Tex Tech U Coll Bus Adminstrn Lubbock TX 79409 Office Phone: 806-742-1546. Business E-Mail: conover@ba.ttu.edu.

CONQUEST, (GEORGE) ROBERT (ACWORTH), writer, political scientist; b. Malvern, Worcestershire, Eng., July 15, 1917; s. Robert Folger Westcott and Rosamund Alys (Acworth) C.; m. Joan Watkins, 1942 (div. 1948); children: John, Richard; m. Elizabeth Neece, Dec. 1, 1979. Student, Winchester Coll., Eng., 1931-35, U. Grenoble, France, 1935-36, U. Oxford, 1936-39; MA, U. Oxford, Eng., 1972; DLitt, U. Oxford, 1975. First sec. H.M. Fgn. Svc., Sofia, Bulgaria, U.N., London, 1946-56; rsch. fellow London Sch. Econs., 1956-58; vis. poet U. Buffalo, N.Y., 1959-60; lit. editor The Spectator, London, 1962-63; sr. fellow Russian Inst. Columbia U., N.Y.C., 1964-65; fellow Woodrow Wilson Internat. Ctr., Washington, 1976-77; sr. rsch. fellow Hoover Inst., Stanford (Calif.) U., 1977-79, 81—. Disting. vis. scholar Heritage Found., Washington, 1980-81; adv. bd. Freedom House, N.Y.C., 1980—; rsch. assoc. Ukrainian Rsch. Inst. Harvard U., Cambridge, Mass., 1983—; adj. fellow Washington Ctr. Strategic Studies., 1984—. Author: Poems, 1955, A World of Difference, 1955, Common Sense About Russia, 1960, Power and Policy in the USSR, 1961, The Pasternak Affair, 1962, Between Mars and Venus, 1962, (with Kingsley Amis) The Egyptologists, 1965, Russia after Khrushchev, 1965, The Great Terror, 1968, Arias from a Love Opera, 1969, The Nation Killers, 1970, Where Marx Went Wrong, 1970, V I Lenin, 1972, Kolyma: The Arctic Death Camps, 1978, Coming Across, 1978, The Abomination of Moab, 1979, Forays, 1979, Present Danger: Towards a Foreign Policy, 1979, We and They: Civic and Despotic Cultures, 1980, (with Jon. M. White) What to do When the Russians Come, 1984, Inside Stalin's Secret Police: NKVD Politics 1936-39, 1985, The Harvest of Sorrow: Soviet Collectivization and the Terror-Famine, 1986, New and Collected Poems, 1988, Stalin and the Kirov Murder, 1988, Tyrants and Typewriters, 1989, The Great Terror: A Reassessment, 1990, Stalin: Breaker of Nations, 1991, Demons Don't, 1999, Reflections on a Ravaged Century, 1999, The Dragons of Expectation, 2005 Capt. inf. Brit. Army, 1939-46, ETO. Decorated Officer Order of the Brit. Empire, London, 1955, Companion Order St. Michael and St. George, London, 1996; recipient Alexis de Tocqueville award, 1992, Light Verse award Acad. Arts and Letters, 1997; Jefferson lectr. humanities, Washington, 1993, Richard M. Weaver prize for scholarly letters, 1999; Royal Soc. Lit. fellow, 1972. Fellow Brit. Acad., Brit. Interplanetary Soc., AAAL-Michael Braude Award Light Verse, Royal Soc. Literature, British Acad, Am. Acad. Arts & Sci., Soc. Promotion Roman Studies; Mem. Literary Soc.; Clubs: Travellers (London). Home: 52 Peter Coutts Cir Stanford CA 94305-2506 Office: Stanford U Hoover Inst Stanford CA 94305-6010

CONRAD, BETTE ANNE KESTER, lawyer, writer, minister; b. Chester, Pa., Oct. 27, 1944; d. Robert Howard Kester, Sr. and Grace Elizabeth Kester; m. Michael Allan Conrad; children: James David, Kristine Marie Conrad Connors. BBA, Columbia Coll., 1978; JD magna cum laude, U. Miami, 1987; DD, Am. Inst. Holistic Theology, 1999. SFC / Recruiter / Chief Data Analyst US Army & Army Reserve, 1975—93; spkr., cons. West Palm Beach, Fla., 1970—; author, 1975—; atty., shareholder Gunster, Yoakley & Stewart, P.A., West Palm Beach, 1988—; min., spiritual counselor, life coach United Christian Fellowship Ch., West Palm Beach, 2001—. Career and personal transition cons., 1981—. Author: The Tao of Legal Ethics, 2003, The Golden Fishing Pole, 1997 (Internat. Soc. Poets Editor's Choice award, 1997); contbr. articles to profl. jours.; author: numerous poems. Vol. VISTA, Pompano Beach, Fla., 1974—75. Sgt. 1st class U.S. Army, 1975—91, Fla., Ind., Va., Pa. Decorated Achievement medal with 2 oak-leaf clusters U.S. Army; recipient Acad. Achievement in Adminstrv. Law award, Am. Jurisprudence, 1987, Acad. Achievement for Bankruptcy, 1987, Acad. Achievement for Profl. Mgmt., 1987. Mem.: Order of Coif. Office: Gunster Yoakley & Stewart PA 777 N Flagler Dr Ste 500-E West Palm Beach FL 33401 Office Phone: 561-650-0549. Personal E-mail: kitkanpro@aol.com. Business E-Mail: bconrad@gunster.com.

CONRAD, DAVID PAUL, portfolio manager, retired food service executive; b. Greensboro, NC, Jan. 11, 1946; s. Lucas Lee and Elizabeth Gertrude (Kincaid) Conrad; 1 child, Lucas Wilfong. BSBA, East Carolina U., 1970; cert. in Real Estate, Forsyth Tech. Coll., 1979. From cashier to cook Libby Hill Seafood, Greensboro, 1962—64; plant mgr. Libby Hill Seafood Restaurants, Inc., Greensboro, 1970—76, mgr. Winston-Salem, NC, 1976—85, v.p., dir. ops. Greensboro, 1985—93, also bd. dirs., 1985—93; comml. real estate broker Allied Comml. Real Estate, Kernersville, NC, 1993; franchise owner Swisher Maids of West Greensboro, NC, 1994—99, regional dir., 1996—98; broker-in-charge VR Bus. Brokers, 1998—2000; founder, former owner Triad Bus. Brokerage, Greensboro, 2002—04, Star Video Games, Greensboro, High Point and Wilkesboro, NC, 2002—05; founder, owner CedarMountain Log Homes, Beech Mountain, NC, 2005—, Blue Ridge Bus. Brokerage Co., Boone, NC, 2005—. Pvt. pilot. Mem. Greensboro Jaycees, 1973—81; vol. Wesley Long Hosp. Staff sgt. NC N.G., 1968—74. Mem.: Inst. Cert. Bus. Counselors, Masons. Republican. Methodist. Avocation: music. E-mail: davidconrad@skybest.com.

CONRAD, DAVID WILLIAMS, lawyer; b. St. Louis, Jan. 10, 1930; s. Lawrence Henry and Roberta (Williams) C.; m. Marilyn Russo, Sept. 26, 1959; children: Roberta Lucy, Philip Lloyd, Angela Beth. AB, Colgate U., 1951; JD, Harvard U., 1954. Bar: N.J. 1954, U.S. Supreme Ct. 1973. Assoc. McCarter & English, Newark, 1956-59; ptnr. Conrad & Jones, Montclair, N.J., 1964-71; pvt. practice Montclair, 1959-64, 71-93; ptnr. Conrad & Boutillier, Montclair, 1993—. Counsel Montclair State U. Found., 1959—, Homes of Montclair Ecumenical Corp., 1988—. Legis. candidate N.J. State Assembly, 1971; pres. N.J. Chamber Music Soc., 1984-86, Union Congl. Ch., Montclair, 1988-91. With U.S. Army, 1954-56. Mem.: Essex County Bar Assn., N.J. State Bar Assn. Democrat. Congregationalist. Avocations: piano, music composition, travel. Home: 23 Hyde Rd Bloomfield NJ 07003-3018 Office: 31 S Fullerton Ave Montclair NJ 07042-3358 Office Phone: 973-783-6060.

CONRAD, DONALD GLOVER, insurance executive; b. St. Louis, Apr. 23, 1930; s. Harold Armin and Velma Glover (Morris) C.; m. Stephania Shimkus, Feb. 8, 1980; 1 child, Christina; 1 stepchild, Alexa Sanzone Paolella; children by previous marriage: Marcy Conrad Tramont, Suzanne Conrad, Mark. Student, Wesleyan U., 1948-49; BS, Northwestern U., 1952; MBA, U. Mich., 1957. With Exxon Co., 1957-70; fin. adv. Exxon Co. (Esso Natural Gas), The Hague, Netherlands, 1965-66; treas. Exxon Co. (Esso Europe), London, 1966-70; sr. v.p. Aetna Life & Casualty Co., Hartford, Conn., 1970-72, exec. v.p., dir., 1972-88, ret., 1988; prin. owner, chmn. Hartford Whalers Hockey Club, 1988-92; sr. advisor to the pres. World Bank, Washington, 1995—2003. Bd. dirs. Chevy Chase (Md.) F.S.B.; founder Greater Hartford Arts Coun.; chief governance officer Sci. Ptnrs., LLC; adv. bd. Kanturk Ptnrs., Washington; chmn. adv. bd. Apollo Resources Internat., Dallas. Chmn. emeritus Am. Coun. for Arts N.Y., Greater Hartford Arts Coun. Lt. USNR, 1952-55. Mem. Watch Hill Yacht Club, The Club at Windermere, Bath and Tennis Club (Palm Beach), Teton Pines Country Club (Jackson Hole), Chevy Chase Club (Washington).

CONRAD, GEOFFREY WENTWORTH, archaeologist, educator; b. Boston, Dec. 24, 1947; s. Albert Austin and Ruth Wentworth (Cadieux) C.; m. Karen Ann Hildebrant, June 12, 1971; children: Matthew, Peter, Marc. AB, Harvard U., 1969, PhD, 1974. Curatorial asst. Smithsonian Inst., Washington, 1974-75; asst. prof. and asst. curator Harvard U., Cambridge, Mass., 1976-81, assoc. prof. and assoc. curator, 1981-83; dir. William Hammond Mathers Mus. Ind. U., Bloomington, 1983—, assoc. prof. anthropology, 1983-91, prof., 1991—, chair, 1991-95, assoc. dean faculties, 2003—05, spl. advisor for arts and humanities, office v.p. for rsch., 2004—. Cons. Nat. Geog. Soc., Washington, 1982-83. Co-author: Religion and Empire, 1984, The Andean Heritage, 1982; co-editor: Ideology and Precolumbian Civilizations, 1992; contbr. articles to profl. jours.; mem. editl. bd. Jour. of Field Archaeology, 1986-96. Bd. dirs. Monroe County Hist. Soc., Bloomington, 1989-92. Grantee NSF, 1978, 85, Ind. Humanities Coun., 1983, 86, 88, 95, Wenner-Gren Found., 1987, Inst. Mus. and Libr. Svcs., 2000, 04, Howard Heinz Endowment, 2004. Fellow AAAS; mem. Archaeol. Inst. Am. (pres. Ctrl. Ind. chpt. 1989-91, acad. trustee 1994-97), Soc. Am. Archaeology, Assn. for Field Archaeology, Am. Assn. Mus., Internat. Assn. of Caribbean Archaeologists,

Assn. Midwest Mus., Assn. Coll. and Univ. Mus. and Galleries (Midwest rep. 1990-91). Home: 3130 Saint James Ct Bloomington IN 47401-7105 Office: Mathers Mus Ind U 601 E 8th St Bloomington IN 47408-3812 also: Ind U Dept Anthropology Student Bldg Bloomington IN 47405 Address: Ind U Office VP Rsch Bryan Hall 104 Bloomington IN 47405 Office Phone: 812-865-5340. Business E-Mail: conrad@indiana.edu.

CONRAD, HANS, materials science and engineering educator; b. Konradstahl, Germany, Apr. 19, 1922; came to U.S., 1926, naturalized, 1944; s. Henry K. and Martha Ann (Bader) C.; m. Emma Ann Bort, June 10, 1944; children— Sandra Joy, Roberta Lee, Gary Richard. Student, Washington and Jefferson Coll., 1940-42; BS in Metall. Engring, Carnegie Inst. Tech., 1943; M.Eng., Yale, 1951, D.Eng., 1956. Research metallurgist Chase Copper & Brass Co., Waterbury, Conn., 1953-55; supervisory engr. Westinghouse Research Labs., Churchill Boro, Pa., 1955-59; sr. research specialist Atomics Internat., Canoga Park, Calif., 1959-61; head dept. physics Aerospace Corp., El Segundo, Calif., 1961-64; tech. dir. Franklin Inst. Research Labs., Phila., 1964-67; prof., chmn. dept. metall. engring. and materials sci., assoc. dir. Inst. Mining and Minerals Research, U. Ky., Lexington, 1967-80; prof., head dept. materials engring., dir. minerals and materials research programs N.C. State U., 1981-85, prof., 1985—. Japan Soc. Promotion Sci. vis. prof. 1976; Disting. vis. prof. Am. U., Cairo, 1983, Soviet Acad. Scis, 1984; Ministry Metall. Industry, PRC, 1986. Contbr. articles to profl. jours. and books. Recipient Rsch. award U. Ky., 1971, U.S. Sr. Scientist award Alexander von Humboldt-Stiftung, 1974; Alcoa Rsch. award N.C. State U., 1985, Alumni Rsch. award, 1991. Fellow: Am. Soc. Materials, The Minerals, Metals and Materials Soc. (Structural Materials Disting. Sci. award 2000); mem.: Tau Beta Pi, Sigma Xi. Home: 205 Glasgow Rd Cary NC 27511-6517 Personal E-mail: hans_conrad@ncsu.edu.

CONRAD, HAROLD AUGUST, retired religious pension board executive; b. Cleve., Dec. 18, 1928; s. August and Olga (Heise) C.; m. Anne Chernosky, July 10, 1948 (dec. Mar. 1956); children: Deborah Anne Hamer, Loren Harold, Rebecca Faith Towle; m. Naomi Ruth Sweeny, Dec. 31, 1960; 1 child, Paul Alan. BA, Anderson U., Ind., 1952; MDiv, Christian Theol. Sem., Indpls., 1970; DD, Mid-Am. Christian U., Oklahoma City, 1975. Pastor Akron Ch. of God, Akron, Ind., 1952-63, First Ch. of God, Winchester, Ky., 1963-66, Glendale Ch. of God, Indpls., 1966-74; exec. sec. treas. Bd. of Pensions of Ch. of God, Anderson, Ind., 1974-93; ret., 1993. State chmn. Ind. Ministerial Assembly, Indpls., 1961-62; vice chmn. Ky. Ministerial Assembly, Winchester, 1965-66; mem. Bd. of Pensions of Ch. of God, Anderson, Ind., 1964-74; bd. dirs. Exec. Coun. of Ch. of God, Anderson, Ind., 1976-84, 87-90. Mem. Nat. Ch. Pensions Conv. (pres. 1985). Republican. Mem. Ch. Of God. Avocations: stamp collecting/philately, gardening, walking, reading, travel. Home: 810 Northwood Dr Anderson IN 46011-1072 E-mail: conradhn@cs.com.

CONRAD, HAROLD THEODORE, psychiatrist; b. Milw., Jan. 25, 1934; s. Theodore Herman and Alyce Barbara Conrad; m. Elaine Marie Blaine, Sept. 1, 1962 (dec.); children: Blaine, Carl, David, Erich, Rachel. AB, U. Chgo., 1954, BS, 1955, MD, 1958. Diplomate Am. Bd. Psychiatry. Intern USPHS Hosp., San Francisco, 1958-59, commd. sr. asst. surgeon, 1958, advanced through grades to med. dir., 1967, resident psychiatry Lexington, Ky., 1959-61, Charity Hosp., New Orleans, 1961-62; chief of psychiatry USPHS Hosp., New Orleans, 1962-67, clin. dir., 1967; dep. dir. divsn. field investigation NIMH, Chevy Chase, Md., 1968; chief NIMH Clin. Rsch. Ctr., Lexington, 1969-73; cons. psychiatry region IX USPHS, HEW, San Francisco, 1973-79; dir. adolescent unit Alaska Psychiat. Inst., Anchorage, 1979-81, supt., 1981-85; clin. assoc. prof. psychiatry U. Wash. Med. Sch., 1981-85; psychiatrist pvt. practice, Houma, La., 1985—2004; ret., 2005. Contbr. articles to profl. jours. Recipient cmty. awards for contbns. in field of drug abuse and equal employment opportunity for minorities. Fellow: Am. Psychiat. Assn. (Disting. life), Royal Soc. Medicine; mem.: AMA, Alpha Delta Phi, Alpha Omega Alpha. Address: 3504 Jackson Ave Gulfport MS 39507

CONRAD, JARIK E., management consultant; b. St. Louis, July 18, 1972; s. Rita R. Conrad; m. Adrienne L. Jennings, June 3, 2000. BA, U. Ill., 1994; MBA, M in Indsl. and Labor Rels., Cornell U., 1998; postgrad., U. North Fla., 2001. Cert. sr. prof. in human resources HRCI, 2001. Asst. v.p. human resources Citibank, Jacksonville, Fla., 1998—2001; dir. human resources CSX Corp., Jacksonville, 2001—04; founder, pres. The Conrad Consulting Group, LLC, Jacksonville, 2004—; exec. dir. Bleuprint for Prosperity, 2005—. Participant Leadership Jacksonville, 2004—05; adv. com. Blueprint for Leadership, Jacksonville, 2003—04; fin. com. Nat. Conf. for Cmty. Justice (NCCJ), Jacksonville, 2004; advocacy com. Cmty. Connections, Jacksonville, 2004; bd. mem. 100 Black Men of Jacksonville, Inc, 2003. Recipient Black Achiever award, YMCA, 2002, Jackson Up and Comer, 2005. Mem.: ASCD, Soc. for Human Rsources Mgmt. (bd. dirs. Jacksonville chpt. 2003—), Am. Ednl. Rsch. Assn., Acad. Mgmt., Deerwood Country Club (membership com. 2003—04), The Lodge & Club at Ponte Vedra, Phi Lambda Theta, Kappa Alpha Psi (membership chmn. 2001—03). Avocations: drawing, public speaking, golf, travel. Office: The Conrad Consulting Group LLC 9838 Old Bayeadows Rd #325 Jacksonville FL 32256 Office Phone: 904-565-1080. Office Fax: 904-565-1080. Business E-Mail: jconrad@consultinggroup.net.

CONRAD, JOHN R., retired electric power industry executive; b. Chgo., Dec. 3, 1915; s. Nicholas John and Irene Edna (Billups) Conrad; m. Ruth Osborne Good, July 14, 1940 (div. 1957); children: Lynn, Joanne, Catherine; m. Arlys Mafra Streitmatter, Apr. 11, 1958. Student, Yale U., 1934-36; BS in Econs., U. Chgo., 1937; postgrad., Boeing Sch. Aeros., 1938; LHD (hon.), Ill. Inst. Tech., 1991. Mem. staff engring. and mfg. Douglas Aircraft, Santa Monica, Calif., 1938-44, mgr. properties Long Beach, Calif., 1944-45; v.p. S&C Electric Co., Chgo., 1945-52, pres., 1952-88, CEO, chmn. bd. dirs., 1988-97, chmn. bd. dirs., 1997—2000, chmn. emeritus, 2001—. Bd. dirs. S&C Electric Can. Ltd., Toronto, Ont. Mem. Mid-Am. Com., Chgo., 1983—; mem. Chgo. com. Coun. Fgn. Rels., 1980—; life mem. Ill. Coalition; gov. mem. John G. Shedd Aquarium Soc.; mem. St. Francis Hosp. Evanston Founders Soc.; mem. adv. bd. Northwestern U. J. L. Kellogg Grad. Sch. Mgmt.; pres. coun. U. Ill.; mem. adv. bd. Exec. Club Chgo. Recipient Progress award, Soc. Mfg. Engrs., 1972, Bus. in the Arts award, Esquire/Bus. Com. Arts, 1975, Founders' Day award, St. Francis Hosp. Evanston Founders Soc., 1983, Spl. award for support and contbns. to switchgear industry, IEEE Power Engring. Soc. Switchgear Com., 1990, Citizen's Coun. Cmty. Svc. award, Gateway Found., 1991, 25th Anniversary Cmty. Svc. award, 1992, Civic award, Loyola U., 1993, award for excellence in power distbn. engring., IEEE, Inc. Power Engring. Soc., 1994. Mem.: IEEE (life), Ill. Bus. Roundtable, Conf. Internat. Grandes Reseaux Electriques (mem. U.S. nat. com., U.S. v.p. 1971—72), Mid-Am. Club. Achievements include patents for terminal construction. Avocation: charitable and civic activities. Office: S&C Electric Co 6601 N Ridge Blvd Chicago IL 60626-3925

CONRAD, JOHN REGIS, lawyer, engineering executive, consultant; b. Bloomington, Ind., Feb. 23, 1955; s. John Francis and Patricia Ann (English) C.; m. Paula Jane Vessels, July 4, 1980; children: William Celestine Vessels, John Paul Vessels, Zander Mathew Alekanekela Vessels, David Thomas Kelamalamalamanokeakua Vessels, Rachel Elizabeth Ho'ouluolaikealoha Vessels. AB cum laude, Harvard U., 1977; MBA, JD, Ind. U., 1981. Bar: Hawaii 1981, Fla. 1994, Tex. 1994, N.C. 1995, U.S. Dist. Ct. Hawaii 1981, U.S. Ct. Appeals (9th cir.) 1981, U.S. Ct. Claims 1981, U.S. Tax Ct. 1981. Assoc. Cades, Schutte, Fleming & Wright, Honolulu, 1981-85, 89-90, Thompson & Chan, Honolulu, 1985-89; ptnr. Cades Schutte Fleming & Wright, Honolulu, 1991-94; regional bus. mgr. Kimley-Horn and Assocs., Inc., West Palm Beach, Fla., 1994-96, regional prodn. mgr., 1996-98, regional bus. mgr., sr. assoc., sr. v.p. Phoenix, 1999—. Lectr. law Kapiolani C.C., Honolulu, 1984-86; adj. prof. Richardson Sch. Law, U. Hawaii, 1989-90; webmaster Conrad-Vessels Genealogy. Author: A Conrad Genealogy, 1979, Hawaii Probate Sourcebook, 1985, rev. 1986, rev. 1992; co-author: Beyond the Basics: Hawaii Estate Planning & Probate, 1985, Hawaii Wills & Trusts Sourcebook, 1986, Hawaii Guardianship Sourcebook, 1988; editor HICLE Fin. and Estate Planning Manual, vol. II, 1989, vol. I, 1990. Planned giving com. Hawaii Heart Assn., Honolulu, 1983-86; arbitrator Hawaii Ct. Annexed Arbitration Program, 1989-94; sch. bd. Star of the Sea Sch., Honolulu, 1992-94, pres., 1993-94, chair Carnival, 1992; chair Cub Scout Pack Aloha Coun. Boy Scouts Am., den leader Cub Scout Pack, Gulf Stream Coun., Grand Canyon Coun.; lector Good Shepherd of the Hills Ch., Cave Creek, Ariz.; trustee St. Paul's Prep. Acad. (vice chair 2003-05, chair 2005—, strategic planning com. chair 2002-03), Phoenix, 2002—; mem. contracts task force ACEC-Ariz., 2003-05; mem. profl. liaison com. CELSOC, 2003-05. Fellow Am. Coll. Trust and Estate Coun.; mem. ABA, Am. Arbitration Assn., Hawaii Bar Assn. (chmn. estate and gift tax com. 1984-85, CFO probate and estate planning sect. 1989-90), Hawaii Bar Found. (bd. dirs. 1985-92, v.p. 1989, pres. 1989-91), Ancestral Trails Hist. Soc., Sons of Am. Legion, John T. Reilly Hist. Soc., Hawaii Estate Planning Coun. (bd. dirs. 1991-94, sec. 1993), Filson Club Hist. Soc., Sons Union Vets. Civil War (Eagle Scout coord. 2004-). Roman Catholic. Avocations: genealogy, coin collecting/numismatics. Office: Kimley-Horn and Assocs Inc 7878 N 16th St Ste 300 Phoenix AZ 85020-4335 Home: 33214 N 61st St Scottsdale AZ 85262-8206 Office Phone: 602-944-5500. Business E-Mail: jrconrad@post.harvard.edu, john.conrad@kimley-horn.com.

CONRAD, KENT, senator; b. Bismarck, ND, Mar. 12, 1948; m. Lucy Calautti, Feb. 1987; 1 child, Jessamyn Abigail. Student, U. Mo., 1967; BA, Stanford U., 1972; MBA, George Washington U., 1975. Asst. to tax commr. State of N.D. Tax Dept., Bismarck, 1974-80, tax commr., 1981-87; U.S. senator from N.D. Washington, 1987—. Mem. agr. nutrition and forestry com., mem. budget com. and fin. coms., ethics com., Indian affairs com., senate Dem. steering and coord. com., forestry com. Democrat. Office: US Senate 530 Hart Senate Office Bldg Washington DC 20510-0001*

CONRAD, MARCEL EDWARD, hematologist, educator; b. N.Y.C., Aug. 15, 1928; s. Marcel Edward and Lulu Marie (Geraghty) C.; m. Marcia Louise Grove; children: Marcel Edward, III, Mark E., Carol J., Erin E., Julia P. BS, Georgetown U., 1949, MD cum laude, 1953. Diplomate Am. Bd. Internal Medicine, Am. Bd. Hematology. Commd. 1st lt. M.C. U.S. Army, 1953, advanced through grades to col., 1968; intern Walter Reed Gen. Hosp., Washington, 1953-54, resident, then chief resident in internal medicine, 1955-60; mem. staff Walter Reed Army Inst. Rsch., 1961-74, chief dept. hematology, 1965-74; chief clin. investigation svc. Walter Reed Army Med. Ctr., 1971-74; clin. asst. prof., then clin. assoc. prof. medicine Georgetown U. Med. Sch., 1964-74; prof. medicine U. Ala. Med. Sch., Birmingham, 1974-83, also dir. div. hematology and oncology, 1974-83; prof. medicine, pathology, dir. divsn. hematology, oncology U. South Ala., Mobile, 1983-2001, dir. USA Cancer Ctr., 1985-2001, disting. prof. medicine, 2001. Prin. investigator Minority Based Cmty. Cancer Oncology Program, 1990—2004. Contbr. numerous articles to med. publs. Decorated Legion of Merit with oak leaf cluster; recipient Skinner medal U.S. Army, 1955, Hoff medal, 1962, John Shaw Billings award, 1967, William Beaumont award, 1972, Walter Reed award, 1974, Harry Hines award Nat. Cancer Inst., 2003, Eagle Scout. Fellow Internat. Soc. Hematology, ACP (Laureate award 1989, named Disting. Prof. Medicine, 2001); mem. AAAS, Assn. Am. Physicians, Internat. Soc. Hematology, Am. Soc. Clin. Investigation, Am. Physiol. Soc., Internat. Soc. Blood Transfusion, Am. Soc. Hematology, Am. Soc. Clin. Oncology, Am. Chem. Soc., Soc. Exptl. Biology and Medicine, So. Soc. Clin. Investigation, Am. Fedn. Clin. Rsch., Alpha Omega Alpha. Roman Catholic. Home: 28451 Perdido Pass Dr Orange Beach AL 36561-3602 Personal E-mail: mconrad2@comcast.net.

CONRAD, PAUL ERNEST, transportation consultant; b. Hartford, Conn., June 11, 1927; s. Ernest and Agnes Anita (Eis) C.; m. Audrey Grace Lindner, June 17, 1947; children: Cynthia Dale, Robin Sue, Kristen Diane. BS, U. Conn., 1949. Hwy. engr. Fed. Hwy. Adminstrn., Southeast U.S., Conn. and N.Y., 1949-55; prin. assoc. Wilbur Smith & Assocs., Columbia, S.C., 1955-69, sr. v.p., 1969-72, exec. v.p., 1972-91, also bd. dirs. Bd. dirs. Spring Valley Homeowners Assn., 1976-77, 97-98, Enclave Cmty. Assn., 1999-2004. With USN, 1945-46. Mem. NSPE, ASCE, Inst. Transp. Engrs., Am. Cons. Engrs. Coun., Spring Valley Country Club (bd. govs. 1993-96, v.p. house). Lutheran. Home: 103 Enclave Loop Columbia SC 29223-3260 E-mail: pauleconrad@aol.com.

CONRAD, PAUL FRANCIS, cartoonist; b. Cedar Rapids, Iowa, June 27, 1924; s. Robert H. and Florence G. (Lawler) C.; m. Barbara Kay King, Feb. 27, 1954; children: James, David, Carol, Elizabeth. BA, U. Iowa, 1950. Editorial cartoonist Denver Post, 1950-64, L.A. Times, 1964-93; cartoonist L.A. Times Syndicate, 1973-2000, Tribune Media Svcs., 2000—. Richard M. Nixon chair Whittier Coll., 1977-78 Exhibited sculpture and cartoons, Los Angeles County Mus. Art, 1979, Libr. of Congress, 1999; author: The King and Us, 1974, Pro and Conrad, 1979, Drawn and Quartered, 1985, CONArtist: Thirty Years With The Los Angeles Times, 1993, Drawing The Line, 1999. Served with C.E. AUS, 1942-46, PTO. Recipient Editl. Cartoon award, Sigma Delta Chi, 1963, 1969, 1971, 1981—82, 1988, 1997, Pulitzer prize editl. cartooning, 1964, 1971, 1984, Overseas Press Club award, 1970, 1981, Journalism award, U. So. Calif., 1972, Robert F. Kennedy Journalism award 1st prize, 1985, 1990, 1992, 1993, Hugh M. Hefner 1st Amendment award, 1990, Lifetime Achievement award, Am. Assn. Editl. Cartoonists, 1998, Lifetime Pub. Svc. award, Edmund G. Brown Inst. Pub. Affairs, 2000; fellow sr. fellow, Sch. Pub. Policy and Social Rsch., UCLA, 2001—03. Fellow Soc. Profl. Journalists; mem. Phi Delta Theta. Democrat. Roman Catholic. Office: 904 Silver Spur Rd 358 Rolling Hills Estates CA 90274 Office Phone: 310-544-0497.

CONRAD, ROBERT DAVID, broadcast executive, educator; b. Kankakee, Ill., July 17, 1933; s. Clarence P. and Geneva (Beatty) C.; m. Jean Smith, July 11, 1959; children: Caroline, Allison, Christopher (dec.), Susan, Andrea. BS, Northwestern U., 1955; DFA (hon.), Baldwin Wallce Coll., 1983; MusD (hon.), Cleve. Inst. Music, 1998; DHum (hon.), Oberlin Coll., 2002. Announcer KULA, KAIM, Honolulu, 1956-57, WKAN, Kankakee, 1947-51; announcer, program dir. WEAW AM/FM, Evanston, Ill., 1951-54; announcer WFMT, Chgo., 1954-55, announcer, ops. mgr., 1957-60; program dir. WDTM, Detroit, 1960-62; v.p., program mgr. WCLV, Cleve., 1962-92, pres., broadcast mgr., 1992—. Prodr., commentator Cleve. Orch., 1965—; broadcasting instr. Cuyahoga C.C., Cleve., 1984-91; adj. prof. broadcasting Case We. Res. U./Cleve. Inst. Music, 1991—. Bd. dirs., trustee Cleve. Music Sch. Settlement, 1995—; bd. dirs. Rainey Inst., Cleve. Sch. Arts, 1998—; bd. trustees Cleve. Orch., 2002—. Named Program Dir. of Yr., Billboard Mag., N.Y., 1982, Excellence in Broadcasting award Cleve. Assn. Broadcasters, 2001; named to No. Ohio Radio Hall of Fame, 1993, City Club Hall of Fame, 2000; recipient award of achievement Cleve. Radio Broadcasters Assn., 2000, Lifetime Achievement award Cleve. Achievement in Radio Awards, 2002. Mem. Concert Music Broadcasters Assn. (bd. dirs., pres. 1980-83), City Club Cleve. (past bd. dirs., v.p. 1975-78). Office: WCLV 26501 Renaissance Pkwy Cleveland OH 44128-5798 Office Phone: 216-464-0900. E-mail: rconrad@wclv.com.

CONRAD, ROBERT J., federal judge, former prosecutor; b. Chgo., May 17, 1958; BA Clemson U., 1980, JD U. Va., 1983. Law clk. Michie, Hamlett, Donato and Lowry, 1981—83, assoc., 1983—86; ptnr. Horn and Conrad, 1986—87; sole practice Robert J. Conrad Jr., PA, 1987—88; ptnr. Bush, Thurman and Conrad, 1988—89; asst. U.S. atty. (we. dist.) N.C. U.S. Dept. Justice, 1989—2001, U.S. atty. (we. dist. N.C.), 2001—04; ptnr. Mayer, Brown, Rowe & Maw LLP, Charlotte, NC, 2004—05; judge US Dist. Ct. (we. dist.) NC, 2005—. Office: US Dist Ct 210 Fed Bldg 401 W Trade St Charlotte NC 28202 Office Phone: 704-350-7460. Business E-Mail: robert_conrad@ncwd.uscourts.gov.

CONRAD, SARAH NICHOLE, medical technician; b. Greenfield, Ind., Dec. 15, 1977; d. Junior B. and Sarah Dalrymple, Pamela J. Kinman; m. Charles Mason Conrad, Mar. 8, 2003; 1 child, Carson Mason. AS, Ind. U., 2000. Registered radiologist Am. Registry Radiologic Technologists, 2000, mammographer Am. Registry Radiologic Technologists, 2004. Radiol. technologist Ind. U., Indpls., 2000, St. Francis Hosp., Indpls., 2000, Ind. Orthopedic Ctr., Indpls., 2000—03; radiol. technologist, mammographer Irvington Radiologists, Indpls., 2003—. Named Harness Horse Youth of Yr., Harness Horse Youth Found., 1997. Mem.: Ind. Standard Assn., Am. Soc. Radiol. Technologist. Home: 7080 N Stubbington Ave Mc Cordsville IN 46055

CONRAD, SHERRY K. LYNCH, counselor; b. Nov. 20, 1957; d. Robert Emmett and Norma Lea Lynch; married Nov 20, 2004. BA, Randolph-Macon Woman's Coll., 1979; MS, Emporia State U., 1980; PhD, Kans. State U., 1987. Vocat. rehab. counselor Rehab. Svcs., Topeka, 1980-81, cmty. program cons., 1981-86; counseling intern Winthrop Coll., Rock Hill, SC, 1986-87; counselor Ripon (Wis.) Coll., 1987-90, Va. Poly. Inst. and State U., 1991—. Mem. exec. com. Sexual Assault Counseling Program, Topeka, 1983-86, recruitment coord., 1983-86, counselor, 1981-86, Nat. Singles Conf. Planning Com., Green Lake, Wis., 1987-90; area admissions rep. Randolph-Macon Woman's Coll., Lynchburg, Va., 1981-87; mem. Student Outreach Schs. coun. Northbrooke Hosp., 1988-90; mem. Student Affairs Devel. Com., 1991-94, chairperson, 1992-94, mem. Sexual Assault Victim Edn. and Support Com., 1991-95, Wellness Com., 1993-2000, Leadership Resource Team, 1994-96; bd. dirs., sec. Ripon Chem. Abuse and Awareness Program, 1987-90; bd. dirs. New River Family Shelter, sec., 1993-98, chair pers. com., 1999-2000; pro bono counselor Mental Health Assn. of New River Valley, 2002—; clin. mental health counselor certification exam com. Nat. Bd. Cert. Counselors, 1996—. Bd. dirs. Haymarket Sq. Homeowners Assn., 1992-2004, treas., 1993-2004; chair ch. and soc. com. Blacksburg United Meth. Ch., 1992-94, mem. coun. ministries, 1992-94; asst. class agt. Class of 1979, Randolph-Macon Woman's Coll., 2000-04, mem. reunion com., 2005—. Recipient Kans. 4-H Key award Ext. Svc. of Kans. State U., 1974; named Internat. 4-H Youth Exch. Amb. to France, 1977. Mem. ACA, Nat. Rehab. Counseling Assn. (bd. dirs. 1982-88, chair br. devel. subcoun. 1982-87, chair policy and program coun. 1987-88), Gt. Plains Rehab. Counseling Assn. (newsletter editor 1982-85, bd. dirs. 1983-87, pres. 1984-85, sec. 1986-87), Gt. Plains Rehab. Assn. (bd. dirs. 1983-85, awards chairperson 1984-85), Kans. Rehab. Counseling Assn. (bd. dirs. 1983-86, pres. 1984-85), Kans. Rehab. Assn. (bd. dirs. 1982-85, advt. chair 1983-85), Topeka Rehab. Assn. (bd. dirs. 1982-85, sec. 1982-83, pres. 1983-84), Am. Coll. Pers. Assn. (chair commn. VII counseling and psychol. svcs. 1996-98, directorate body 1989-93, 95-99, 2004—, membership commn. 1990-93, planning com. 1997-99, sec. 2000-02, exec. coun. 2000-02, archivist 2004—, continuing edn. com. 2004—, Outreach and Advocacy Core Coun., sec. 1999-2000), Wis. Coll. Pers. Assn. (bd. dirs. 1988-90), Assn. for Specialists in Group Work, Va. Coll. Pers. Assn. Methodist. Avocation: tennis. Home: 6317 Old Ferry Rd Hiwassee VA 24347 Office: Va Tech Counseling Ctr 240 McComas Hall Blacksburg VA 24061 Office Phone: 540-231-6557. Business E-Mail: sklynch@vt.edu.

CONRAD, STEVEN ALLEN, critical care and emergency physician, biomedical engineer, educator; b. St. Martinville, La., Aug. 23, 1953; s. Karl Donovan and Dolores Beatrice (Bienvenu) C.; m. Mona Theresa Hollier, Aug. 9, 1974; children: David, Lesley, Taylor. BS, U. S.W. La., 1974; MD, La. State U., Shreveport, 1978; MS, Case Western Reserve U., Cleve., 1980, PhD, 1985; MS in Engring., La. Tech. U., 1981; MBA, La. State U., 2001, MS in Info. Sys. Tech., 2003. Diplomate Am. Bd. Internal Medicine, Critical Care Medicine, Am. Bd. Emergency Medicine; cert. nutritional support physician; cert. clin. rsch. investigator Assn. Clin. Rsch. Investigators, 2004. Postdoctoral trainee in biomed. computing Case Western Res. U., 1979—80; resident internal medicine La. State U., Shreveport, 1981-84; fellow in critical care medicine Mayo Grad. Sch. Medicine, Rochester, Minn., 1984-86; from asst. prof. medicine to prof. bioinformatics and computational biology La. State U. Med. Ctr., Shreveport, La., 1986—2003, prof. medicine, emergency medicine, pediatrics, anesthesiology, bioinformatics and computational biology, 2003—, dir. critical care medicine tng. program, 1987—; instr. computer sci. Winona State U., 1985—86. Cons. physician critical care VA Med. Ctr., 1986—2003, dir. extracorporeal life support program, 1993—, co-dir. nutritional support svc., 1994—, transplant intensivist Willis Knighton Regional Heart Transplant Program, 1994—2004, attending physician in pediat. ICU, 1994—; mem. emergency med. svcs. task force Shreveport Fire Dept., 1992—; prin. investigator in multiple device and drug trials. Editor: Pulmonary Function Testing: Principles and Practice, 1984; mem. editl. bd. Internat. Jour. Electronic Healthcare, 2003—, ASAIO Jour., 2004—; manuscript reviewer ASAIO Jour., 2004-, Artificial Organs, Intensive Care Medicine, Critical Care Chest Medicine, Chest; abstract reviewer Critical Care Medicine; contbr. chpts. to books and articles to profl. jours. Grantee, Am. Heart Assn., NHLBI. Fellow ACP, Am. Coll. Critical Care Med., Am. Coll. Chest Physicians, Am. Coll. Emergency Physicians, Am. Acad. Emergency Physicians; mem. IEEE (sr.), Biomed. Engring. Soc., Shock Soc., Am. Soc. Artificial Internal Organs, Internat. Soc. for Artificial Organs, Soc. for Acad. Emergency Medicine, Am. Soc. for Parenteral and Enteral Nutrition, Internat. Soc. for Computational Biology, Assn. Clin. Rsch. Profls., Alpha Omega Alpha, Sigma Xi, Phi Kappa Phi, Beta Gamma Sigma, Sigma Iota Epsilon. Office: La State U Health Scis Ctr 1501 Kings Hwy Shreveport LA 71103-4228 Office Phone: 318-675-6885. Business E-Mail: sconrad@lsuhsc.edu.

CONRAD, WILLIAM MERRILL, architect; b. Sapulpa, Okla., Sept. 5, 1926; s. William Samuel and Lillian Lorraine (Strain) C.; m. Esther Marian Lenz, Nov. 8, 1952. BS in Architecture, U. Kans., 1950, BSBA, 1951. Lic. architect. Prin., architect William M. Conrad, F.A.I.A., Kansas City, Mo., 1956—; asst. prof., Sch. of Architecture and Urban Design U. Kans., Lawrence, 1956-59. Mem. adv. com. U. Kans. Sch. of Architecture and Urban Design, 1974-86; vis. Fulbright prof., U. Helsinki, 1958-59. Mem. Kans. City-St. Joseph Bldg. Commn., 1970-82; leader People to People Internat. Peace Mission Overseas Tours, 1994—. Recipient Patriotic Svc. award Dept. Army, 1974, 84, Nat. Friend of Park and Recreation award Nat. Assn. Park and Recreation Ofcls., 1982, Urban Design award Mcpl. Art Com., Kansas City, 1976, Disting. Alumnus award U. Kans. Sch. Arch. and Urban Design, 1993, Achievement award PTP Philippines, 1999, PTP Taiwan, 1999. Mem. AIA (treas. nat. conv. 1979, Kansas City chpt. pres. 1968, past sec., other offices, mem. numerous coms., Fellow, 1986, Cmty. Svc. award 1990, numerous other awards), SAR (Good Citizenship award 1997), Mo. Coun. Architects (past dir. and treas.), People to People Internat. (pres. Greater Kansas City chpt. 1972-74, chmn. Gt. Plains regional coun. 1974-77, chmn. bd. dirs., trustee 1985-89, internat. pres. 1988-91, Disting. Mem. award 1986, Eisenhower Lifetime Achievement award 1996), Optimists (past pres. Honor Club), Masons, Shriners (pres. 1990), Sertoma Kans. dist. gov. 1984-86, pres. Honor Club 1982-84, Sertoman of Yr. 1987, Outstanding Regional Sec. award 1995), Christian the Fourth Guild (hon. Denmark, 2000), Tau Beta Pi (life), Tau Sigma Delta. Methodist. Home: 6120 W 69th St Overland Park KS 66204-1411

CONRAD, WINTHROP BROWN, JR., lawyer; b. Detroit, May 26, 1945; s. Winthrop Brown and Dolores (Millard) C.; m. Ellen Rouse, May 12, 1973; children: Parker Rouse, Louisa Katherine, Frances Winthrop. AB, Yale U., 1967; JD, Harvard U., 1971. Bar: N.Y. 1972, U.S. Dist. Ct. (so. dist.) N.Y. 1975, U.S. Ct. Appeals (2d cir.) 1975. Ptnr. Davis, Polk & Wardwell, N.Y.C., 1979—, Paris Office, 1985-88. Bd. dirs. Found. for Joffrey Ballet, N.Y.C., 1985-86, British-Am. Ednl. Found.; former trustee Estate and Property of the Conv. of the Diocese of N.Y., Episcopal Diocese of N.Y., Ch. Pension Fund; trustee, chair Vt. Studio Ctr.; dir., BAR Vermont Inc. Mem. ABA, Assn. of Bar of City of N.Y. Home: 1120 5th Ave New York NY 10128-0144 Office: Davis Polk & Wardwell 450 Lexington Ave Fl 31 New York NY 10017-3982 also: 856 Old Post Rd Bedford NY 10506-1215

CONRAD-ENGLAND, ROBERTA LEE, pathologist; b. Meriden, Conn., Aug. 25, 1950; d. Hans and Emma Ann (Bort) Conrad; m. Gary Thomas England, June 6, 1976; children: Eric Bryan, Christopher Ryan. BS in Microbiology, U. Ky., 1972, MD, 1976. Diplomate Nat. Bd. Med. Examiners, Bd. Am. Pathologists. Resident anatomic and clin. pathology Emory U. Affiliated Hosps., Atlanta, 1976-80; pathologist Western Bapt. Hosp., Paducah, Ky., 1980—. Cons. Marshall County Hosp., Benton, Ky., 1985—, chair infection control com., 1985—. Mem., com. chairperson PTA, Poducah, Ky., 1993-94; mother's asst. Boy Scouts Am., Poducah, 1991-94. Fellow Coll. Am. Pathologists, Am. Soc. Clin. Pathologists; mem. Ky. Med. Assn., Ky. Soc. Pathologists, Ky. Women Mentors in Sci., Alpha Omega Alpha, Phi Beta Kappa. Avocations: swimming, snorkeling, interior decorating.

CONRADER, CONSTANCE RUTH, artist, writer; b. Vandalia, Mo., Apr. 13, 1919; d. Gilbert Fordyce and Elizabeth Florence (Cleghorn) Stone; m. Jay Merten Conrader, Nov. 29, 1941 (dec. 1996). Student, Carroll Coll., 1938-40, North Park Coll., 1940-41. Cert. pub. libr. Artist, author, Oconomowoc, Wis., 1940—. Libr. Oconomowoc Pub. Libr., 1947-82, vol. 1982—; illustrator Turtox classroom charts Gen. Biol. Supply House, Chgo., 1940-60; manuscript critique Baha'i Pub. Trust, Wilmette, Ill., 1970-89, editor, 1988. Author, illustrator: Blue Wampum, 1958; co-editor: Tokens From the Writings of Baha'u'llah, 1973, Baha'i newsletter, 1997—; illustrator: Northwoods Wildlife Region, 1983; co-author, illustrator articles to profl. jours.; co-editor regional Baha'i Newsletter, 1997—. Chair UN Day, Oconomowoc, 1976-86. Avocations: gardening, music, reading, cooking. Home: 738 E Washington St Oconomowoc WI 53066-3110

CONRAD-SMITH, DIANE LOUISE, elementary school educator; b. Allentown, Pa., Dec. 4, 1951; d. Norman P. and Eleanor H. (Lentz) C. BS summa cum laude, West Chester U., 1973; MEd, Lehigh U., 1977. Tchr. 2d grade Parkland Sch. Dist., Allentown, Pa. Nat. Writing Project fellow, 1990. Mem. Pa. Edn. Assn., Parkland Edn. Assn., Kappa Delta Pi, Alpha Lambda Delta. Home: 1593 Country Club Rd Allentown PA 18106-9534

CONRADT, JODY, basketball coach; b. Goldthwaite, Tex., May 13, 1941; BS in Phys. Edn., Baylor U., 1963, MS in Phys. Edn., 1969. Women's basketball, volleyball and track head coach Sam Houston State U., Huntsville, Tex., 1969—73; women's basketball, volleyball and softball head coach U. Tex., Arlington, 1973—76, head women's basketball coach Austin, 1976—, women's athletic dir., 1992—2001. Mem. Coaches vs. Cancer/Am. Cancer Soc.; hon. chair Susan B. Komen Race for the Cure fundraising walk/run, Austin, 2003; vol. annual walk Austin's SafePlace. Named one of Top 50 Women's Sports Execs. in the nation, Street & Smith's Sports Bus. Jour., 1998; named to Internat. Women's Sports Hall of Fame, N.Y.C., 1995, Naismith Meml. Basketball Hall of Fame, 1998, Women's Basketball Hall of Fame, 1999, Internat. Scholar-Athlete Hall of Fame, 2003, Tex. Women's Hall of Fame, 1986, Tex. Sports Hall of Fame, 1998, U. Tex. Women's Athletics Hall of Honor, 2000; recipient John and Nellie Wooden Nat. Coach of the Yr. award, 1996—97, Nat. Coach of the Yr. award, ESPN.com, 2002—03, Harvey Penick award for Excellence in the Game of Life, Caritas, Austin, 2003, Carol Eckman award, Women's Basketball Coach's Assn., 1987, Nat. Award for outstanding commitment to women's athletics, Nat. Assn. for Girls and Women in Sports, 1991, award for contbn. to sports, NCAA, 1992. Office: Univ of Texas Athletics Office PO Box 7399 Austin TX 78713

CONRAN, JOSEPH PALMER, lawyer; b. St. Louis, Oct. 4, 1945; s. Palmer and Theresa (Bussmann) C.; m. Daria D. Conran, June 8, 1968; children: Andrew, Lisabeth, Theresa. BA, St. Louis U., 1967, JD with honors, 1970. Bar: Mo. 1970, U.S. Ct. Mil. Appeals 1971, U.S. Ct. Appeals (8th cir.) 1974. Assoc. Husch and Eppenberger, St. Louis, 1974-78, ptnr., 1978—, chmn. litigation dept., 1980-95, chmn. mgmt. com., 1995—. Mem. faculty Trial Practice Inst. Capt., JAGC, USAF, 1970-74. Mem. Bar Assn. Met. St. Louis (Merit award 1976, 77), Mo. Bar Assn. (bd. govs. 1987-92), Mo. Athletic Club (pres. 1986-87), Norwood Hills Country Club, St. Louis Club. Roman Catholic. Home: 53 Hawthorne Est Saint Louis MO 63131-3035 Office: Husch & Eppenberger 100 N Broadway Ste 1300 Saint Louis MO 63102-2789 Office Phone: 314-480-1900. E-mail: joe.conran@husch.com.

CONRAN, MICHAEL ARTEMUS, voice educator, director; b. Chgo., Ill., June 22, 1960; s. Robert Wilson and Kathleen Conran; married, Aug. 17, 1985. B in Vocal Performance and Music Edn., New England Conservatory, Boston, 1983; M in Vocal Performance, San Franicsco Conservatory, 1987; D in Choral Conducting, U. Ariz., 2003. With Tanglewood Festival Chorus, Boston Symphony, 1982; choir mem. San Francisco Symphony, 1985; with Carmel Bach Festival, 1987, 1988; vocal instr. Santa Clara U., Calif., 1986, 1987, 1988; music dir. Our Lady of Mercy Sch., Daly City, Calif., 1986—94; choir dir. Stuart Country Day Sch., Princeton, NJ, 1994—2000; choral dir. U. Ala., Huntsville, 2003—. Opera singer Pippin's Pocket Opera, San Francisco, 1985—94; freelance singer, San Francisco, 1985—94; singer Phila. Symphony, 1998, Phila. Singers, 1999; chorale dir. Camp Encore, Sweden, Maine, 2001—03, chorale sir., 2003. Founder Greater Huntsville Youth Chorale. Scholar, Blossom Sch. Music, 1986, Calif. Summer Arts, 1984; Wolf scholar, U. Ariz., 2000. Mem.: Am. Choral Dirs. Assn., Am. Guild of Musical Artists. Avocation: travel. Home: 266 Pine Ridge Rd Madison AL 35758 Office: Roberts Hall Univeristy Alabama Huntsville AL 35899 Office Phone: 256-824-2581. Business E-Mail: conranm@uah.edu.

CONRATH, BARNEY JAY, astrophysicist; b. Quincy, Ill., June 23, 1935; s. Frederick Barney and Jayme Wilson (Cason) C.; m. Marjorie Ann Hilder, Sept. 3, 1962; children: Ann, Frederick, Susan. BA, Culver-Stockton Coll., Canton, Mo., 1957; MA, U. Iowa, 1959; PhD, U. N.H., 1966. Astrophysicist Goddard Space Flight Ctr., NASA, Greenbelt, Md., 1960-90, sr. fellow, 1990-95; vis. sr. scientist Ctr. Radiophysics Space Rsch., Cornell U., Ithaca, N.Y., 1995—. Co-author: Exploration of the Solar System by Infrared Remote Sensing, 1991, Exploration of the Solar System by Infrared Remote Sensing, 2d edit., 2003. Recipient Exceptional Sci. Achievement medal NASA, 1982, 90. Mem. Am. Astron. Soc. (Gerard P. Kuiper prize 1996), Am. Geophys. Union, Sigma Xi. Achievements include serving as principal investigator of Voyager infrared spectroscopy experiment which determined helium abundance, thermal structure, energy balance, and atmospheric composition of Jupiter, Saturn, Uranus and Neptune. Business E-Mail: Barney.J.Conrath@gsfc.nasa.gov.

CONROE, HENRY GERALD, psychiatrist; b. Newark, Nov. 22, 1946; s. William Randolph and Sylvia (Wolt) C.; m. Harriet Gonzer, Aug. 17, 1969; children: Andrew, Gabriel, Daniel. BS, Rutgers U., 1968; MD, Hahnemann U., 1972. Diplomate Am. Bd. Psychiatry and Neurology. Intern Phila. Gen. Hosp., 1972-73; resident in psychiatry Michael Reese Hosp., Chgo., 1973-76; pvt. practice Chgo., 1976—. Cons. Social Security Adminstrn., Chgo., 1980—, Jewish Vocat. Svc., Chgo., 1986; clin. asst. prof. Rush Med. Coll., 1989—. Mem. Am. Psychiatry Assn. Democrat. Jewish. Avocations: reading, jazz, exercise. Home: 2811 Garrison Ave Evanston IL 60201-1775 Office: 55 E Washington St Ste 3105 Chicago IL 60602-2206 Office Phone: 312-782-2335.

CONRON, MICHAEL WILLIAM, lawyer; b. Teaneck, NJ, Apr. 22, 1964; s. Michael John and Madelyn Mary (Higgins) C. BS in Econs., U. Pa., 1986; JD cum laude, U. Md., 1993. Bar: Md. 1993, DC 1999, admitted to practice: US Dist. Ct. (Dist. Md.) 1994. Assoc. Venable, Baetjer and Howard, LLP, Balt., 1993—; ptnr., Bus. Trans. Dept. & Mergers and Acquisitions Dept. Venable LLP, Balt. Adj. prof., Securities Regulation U. Md. Sch. Law. Articles editor & exec. bd. mem. The Business Lawyer. Mem. festival com. Fed. Hill-Fells Point Preservation Soc., Balt., 1994—; bd. dir. USS Constellation Mus.; chmn., Basic Securities Law Program Md. Inst. for Continuing Prof. Edn. of Lawyers. Lt. USN, 1986—90, comdr. USN. Recipient Navy Commendation medal, Navy Achievement medal, Navy Expeditionary medal. Mem.: DC Bar, Am. Law Inst., Balt. Jr. Assn. Commerce, Bar Assn. Balt. City (fee arbitration com.), Md. Bar Assn., ABA, Order of Coif. Roman Catholic. Office: Venable LLP 575 7th St NW Washington DC 20004 Office Phone: 202-344-4752. Office Fax: 202-344-8300. Business E-Mail: mwconron@venable.com.

CONRON, RICHARD WELLS, JR., surgeon; b. Boston, May 24, 1966; s. Richard Wells and Marilyn Frances (Coughlan) C.; m. Kristin Abbruzzi, Sept. 5, 1998. BA, Holy Cross Coll., 1988; DO, U. New Eng., 1994. Rotating intern Allentown (Pa.) Osteo. Med. Ctr., 1994-95; gen. surg. resident St. Luke's Hosp., Bethlehem, Pa., 1995-99, chief surg. resident, 1999—. Contbr. rsch. articles to profl. jours. Recipient Nat. Cert. Merit, ARC, 1984. Mem. AMA, Am. Osteo. Assn., Sigma Sigma Phi (pres. 1992-94), Psi Sigma Alpha. Roman Catholic. Home: 4509 Susan Dr Bethlehem PA 18017-8405 Office: 5325 Northgate Dr Ste 204 Bethlehem PA 18017 Office Phone: 610-865-5535.

CONROY, DANIEL FREDERICK, writer, playwright, poet, painter; b. Chgo., Apr. 8, 1946; s. Martin James and Helen Dolores Conroy; m. Marilyn K. O'Brien, Apr. 9, 1976; children: Kelly, Daniel, Shannon, Katie, Sara, Colleen. BA cum laude, Regis U., 1968. Exec. v.p. Bally Mfg., Chgo., 1968—76; pres. Danmar Enterprises, Boulder, Colo., 1976—84. Author: Over 40 mph, 1989, 2d edit., 1995, (plays) My Mother's Son, 1995, Quack, 1990, numerous poems; one-man shows include Anne Peck Gallery, Chgo., 2004; author: (novels) Into the Black Sun, 2005. Playwright grant, Boulder Art Commn., 1992. Mem.: Mensa. Democrat. Avocations: hiking, bicycling. Home: 1061 9th St Boulder CO 80302

CONROY, FRANCES, actress; b. Monroe, Ga., Nov. 13, 1953; m. Jan Munroe, 1992. Student, The Neighborhood Playhouse Sch. of the Theatre, New York, Dickinson Coll., Carlisle, Penn.; degree in Drama, Juilliard Sch., New York. Actor: (films) Manhattan, 1979, Othello, 1979, Falling in Love, 1984, Amazing Grace and Chuck, 1987, In the Hands of the Enemy, 1987, Rocket Gibraltor, 1988, Another Woman, 1988, Dirty Rotten Scoundrels, 1988, Hostile Witness, 1988, Crimes and Misdemeanors, 1989, Billy Bathgate, 1991, Scent of a Woman, 1992, Sleepless in Seattle, 1993, The Adventures of Huck Finn, 1993, Angela, 1995, The Neon Bible, 1995, Developing, 1995, The Crucible, 1996, Maid in Manhattan, 2002, Die, Mommie, Die, 2003, Catwoman, 2004, The Aviator, 2004, Broken Flowers, 2005, Shopgirl, 2005; (plays, stage debut) Measure for Measure, 1978; (Broadway plays) The Lady from Dubuque, 1980, The Secret Rapture, 1990 (Drama Desk Award, 1990), The Ride Down Mt. Morgan, 2000 (Tony Award nom., Outer Critics Circle Award, 2000); (TV series) Six Feet Under, 2001—05 (Emmy Award nom., 2002, Golden Globe award for best actress in a dramatic series, 2004, Screen Actors Guild Award for best actress in a drama series, 2004); (TV films) Carl Sandburg: Echoes and Silences, 1982, The Royal Romance of Charles and Diana, 1982, Kennedy, 1983, LBJ: The Early Years, 1987, Terrorist on Trial: The United States vs. Salim Ajami, 1988, Our Town, 1989, One More Mountain, 1994, Journey, 1995, Innocent Victims, 1996, Thicker Than Blood, 1998, Murder in a Small Town, 1999; (TV miniseries) Queen, 1993.*

CONROY, J. MICHAEL, lawyer; b. 1945; BA, Univ. of Notre Dame, 1967; JD, Georgetown Univ. Law Ctr., 1971, LLM in Taxation, 1986. Ptnr. Conroy & Williams, 1972—80; public defender State of Md., Montgomery County, 1976—79; ptnr. Conroy, FitzGerald & Ballman, 1980—87; Conroy, Ballman & Dameron, 1987—2004; prin. Pasternak & Fidis PC, Bethesda, Md., 2004—. Mem. Assn. of Trial Lawyers of Am., 1973—2000. Vol. Ronald McDonald House, Cath. Youth Orgn. Mem.: Montgomery County Bar Found. (dir. 1985—98, treas. 1989—90, pres. 1995—96), Montgomery County Bar Assn. (pres. 1994—95), Md. State Bar Assn. (pres.-elect 2004). Office: Pasternak & Fidis PC Ste 1100 7735 Old Georgetown Rd Bethesda MD 20814-6183

CONROY, JOHN J., JR., lawyer; 7 children. BA summa cum laude, U. Notre Dame, 1975; grad., U. Strasbourg, U. Catholique de L'Ouest; JD, Northwestern U., 1979. Bar: Ill. 1979, U.S. Dist. Ct. (No. dist. Ill.) 1981. Law clk. Ill. Supreme Ct.; with Baker & McKenzie, Chgo., 1980—, ptnr., 1987—, N.Am. mng. ptnr., 1998—2004, chmn. exec. com., 2004—, chmn. global banking and fin. steering com., chmn. N.Am. regional coun. Fellow, Rotary Found. Mem.: ABA, Ill. State Bar Assn., Chgo. Bar Assn. Office: Baker & McKenzie One Prudential Plaza Ste 2500 Chicago IL 60601 Office Phone: 312-861-8171. E-mail: john.j.conroy@bakernet.com.

CONROY, MARY ELIZABETH, history professor; b. Hammond, Ind., Sept. 2, 1937; d. Edward Michael and Branche Gisela (Schellenbauer) Schaeffer; m. Thomas Francis Conroy, June 19, 1965; children: Alexandra Blanche, Margaret Eleanor. BA, St. Mary's Coll., South Bend, Ind., 1959; MA, Ind. U., Bloomington, 1962, PhD, 1964. Asst. prof. Kans. State U., Manhattan, Kans., 1964—65, U. Ill., Chgo., 1965—68, U. Colo., Denver, 1975—78, assoc. prof., 1978—85, prof. Russian and Soviet hist., 1985—2005, prof. emerita, 2005. Author: (book) P.A. Stolypin: Practical Politics in late Tsarist Russia, 1977 (George Urdang award, 1997), In Health and In Sickness: Pharmacy Pharmacists and the Pharmaceutical Industry in late Imperial Russia, 1994, The Soviet Pharmaceutical Business During the First Two Decades 1917-1937, 2005; editor: (book) Emerging Democracy in Late Imperial Russia, 1998. Grantee, Ford Found., 1960—64; Internat. Rsch. and Exchanges grants, 1990. Mem.: Assn. Study of Health Democracy in Former Soviet Union, Am. Inst. Hist. Pharmacy, Am. Hist. Assn., Am. Assn. Advancement Slavic Studies. Republican. Roman Catholic. Avocations: art, music, architecture, travel. Home: 3825 Colorado Blvd Cherry Hills Village CO 80113-4202 Fax: 303-761-6273. E-mail: maryesconroy@earthlink.net.

CONROY, PAT (DONALD PATRICK CONROY), writer; b. Atlanta, Oct. 26, 1945; s. Donald and Frances Dorothy (Peek) C.; m. Barbara Bolling, 1969 (div. 1977); children: Jessica, Melissa, Megan; m. Lenore Gurewitz, 1981 (div. 1995); children: Gregory, Emily, Susannah. BA in English, The Citadel, 1967. Author: The Boo, 1970, The Water Is Wide, 1972 (Anisfield-Wolf award Cleve. Found. 1972), The Great Santini, 1976, The Lords of Discipline, 1980 (Lillian Smith award for fiction So. Regional Council 1981), The Prince of Tides, 1986, Beach Music, 1995, The Losing Season, 2002, The Pat Conroy Cookbook: Recipes of My Life, 2004; screenwriter: (TV movie) Invictus, 1988, (with Becky Johnson) The Prince of Tides, 1991 (Academy Award nomination best adapted screenplay 1991). Ford Found. Leadership Devel. grantee, 1971; recipient NEA award for achievement in education, 1974, Ga. Gov.'s award for Arts, 1978, Golden Plate award Am. Acad. Achievement, 1992, Thomas Cooper Libr. Soc. Literary award U. S.C., 1995, S.C. Gov.'s award in the Humanities for disting. achievement, 1996, Humanitarian award Ga. Commn. on the Holocaust, 1996, Lotos medal of Merit for outstanding literary achievement, 1996. Mem. Authors Guild Am., Writers Guild, PEN. Democrat. Office: care Doubleday 1540 Broadway New York NY 10036-4039

CONROY, TAMARA BOKS, artist, special education educator, retired nurse; b. Most, Bohemia, Czechoslovakia; came to U.S., 1947; d. Alois and Tatiana (Shapilova) Boks; m. John P. Conroy, Aug. 19, 1950 (dec. Oct. 1973); 1 child, Michael Thomas (dec.). Student, U. Graz, Austria, 1945-47; RN, New Rochelle (N.Y.) Med. Ctr., 1950; student, Coll. of William & Mary, 1958, 59, Cath. U. Am., 1960; BS in Nursing Edn., Columbia U., 1963, MA in Spl. Edn., 1965. RN, N.Y.; cert. spl. edn. tchr., N.Y. Nurse accident rm. New Rochelle Hosp./Med. Ctr., 1950-51; pub. health nurse Va. Dept. of Health, Richmond, 1958-59; tchr. spl. edn. Southern Westchester Bd. Coop. Edn. Svcs., Portchester, N.Y., 1965-83; freelance artist and painter N.Y.C. and Pelham, N.Y., 1969—. Asst. to chmn. math. dept. Columbia U., N.Y.C., 1975-76. Author math. program Learning Numbers-Step by Step, 1977. Pres., founder Classical Music Lovers' Exch., Pelham, N.Y., 1980-98. Mem. Am. Fedn. Tchrs., N.Y. State United Tchrs., BOCES Tchrs. Assn. (profl.), Women's Mus. Group, Mamaroneck Artists Guild, Silvermine Artists Guild, Westchester Musicians Guild (assoc.), Kappa Delta Pi. Avocations: flying, reading, music, fashion designing, painting and drawing.

CONROY, THOMAS FRANCIS, insurance company consultant; b. Chgo., Sept. 26, 1938; s. Thomas Francis and Eleanor Althea (Heatherly) C.; m. Mary Elizabeth Schaeffer, June 19, 1965; children: Alexandra B., Margaret E. BSc, De Paul U., 1959; MBA, U. Chgo., 1969. CPA, CDP. Mgr. Ernst & Whinney, Chgo., 1959-74; exec. v.p. fin., treas., contr. Security Life of Denver, 1974-93; prin. Ea. Hemisphere Trading Corp., Denver, 1990—2003; pres. Security Life Reins., 1993-99, ING Re Internat., 2000-01; mng. prin. Strategic Reins. Cons. Internat., Englewood, Colo., 2001—; mng. ptnr. Mann Conroy Eisenberg & Assoc., LLC, Greensboro, 2002—; dir. Teton Petroleum Co., 2002—. Bd. dirs. Buffalo Mountain Met. Dist. Trustee Denver Chamber Orch., 1988-93; bd. dirs. Denver Affiliate Susan G. Fonen Found. Capt. U.S. Army, 1960-62. Fellow Life Mgmt. Inst. Roman Catholic. Office Phone: 303-762-8812. Business E-Mail: tom-conroy@strategicre.com.

CONRY, RUTH P, language educator; d. Harold W and Elizabeth (Betty) Ruth Schmid; m. Neal Conry (div.); m. F. Walters (div.); children: John Walters, Will Walters, Michael Walters, Dietra Walters. MA in English, Ctrl. State U., Edmond, Okla., 1985; AA Bibl. Studies, Christian Practice Ctr., 1997. Instr. Rose State Coll., Midwest City, Okla., 1986—88; assoc. prof. of English Walters State CC, Morristown, Tenn., 1988—; instr. Okla. CC, Okla. City; grad. asst. Ctrl. State U., Edmond, Okla. Tutor/work study supr. Walters State CC, online tchg. Author poetry, journals, and short stories. Lay min.- lic. and ordained. Mem.: Nat. Coun. ot Teachers of English, Two-Year Coll. English Assn.- SE, Alpha Delta Kappa-International Hon. Sorority for Women Educators. Office: Walters State Community College 500 S Davy Crockett Morristown TN 37814 Business E-Mail: ruth.conry@ws.edu.

CONRY, THOMAS FRANCIS, mechanical engineering educator; b. West Hempstead, N.Y., Mar. 7, 1942; s. Thomas and Bridget Anne (Walsh) C.; m. Sharon Ann Silverwood, June 10, 1967; children: Christine Elizabeth, Carolyn Danielle, Anne Marie. BS, Pa. State U., 1963; MS, U. Wis.-Madison, 1967, PhD, 1970. Registered profl. engr., Wis., Ill. Engr. Gen. Motors Corp., Milw., 1963-66, sr. research engr. Indpls., 1969-71; asst. prof. gen. engring. U. Ill., Urbana, 1971-75, assoc. prof. gen. and mech. engring., 1975-81, prof. gen. and mech. engring., 1981—; co-dir. mng. engring. program Coll. Engring., Urbana, 1986-89, head dept. gen. engring., 1987-98, founding coord. program in tech. and mgmt., 1995—98. Sr. visitor U. Cambridge (Eng.), 1978; cons. Zurn Industries, 1974-83; staff cons. Sargent & Lundy, Engrs., 1977, 79; cons.-evaluator commn. on instns. of higher edn. North Ctl. Assn., 1983—; cons. indsl. firm on machine dynamics, optimization and tribology. NSF trainee, 1968-69; NASA/ASEE summer faculty fellow, 1974-75. Contbr. articles to profl. jours. Mem. Bd. Edn. St. Matthews Parish Roman Catholic Ch., Champaign, 1981-84. Fellow ASME (chmn. design engring. divsn. 1979-80, tech. editor Jour. Vibration, Acoustics, Stress and Reliability in Design, 1984-89, mem. bd. on comm. 1989-93, 96-00, mem. com. on fin. and investment 1999-04); mem. Am. Soc. Engring. Edn., Rotary, Sigma Xi, Lambda Chi Alpha, Phi Kappa Phi. Home: 3301 Lakeshore Dr Champaign IL 61822-5205 Office: 104 S Mathews Ave Urbana IL 61801-2925

CONSAGRA, SOPHIE CHANDLER, academic administrator; b. Radnor, Pa., Apr. 28, 1927; d. Alfred D. and Carol (Ramsay) Chandler; children: Maria, Pierluigi, Francesca, George. BA, Smith Coll., 1949; MA, Cambridge (Eng.) U., 1952. Exec. dir. Del. Arts Council, 1972-78; dir. visual arts and architecture N.Y. State Council Arts, 1978-80; dir. Am. Acad. in Rome, 1980-84, pres., 1984-88, pres. emerita, vice chmn./spl. projects, 1988-90. Cons. Nat. Endowment Arts. Recipient Smith Coll. award, 1986, Centennial medal Am. Acad. in Rome, 1995. Address: 955 Lexington Ave New York NY 10021-5128

CONSEY, KEVIN EDWARD, museum administrator; b. N.Y.C., Jan. 15, 1952; s. Edward and Dorothy (Kemmann) C.; m. Susan Mary Kirsch, Aug. 26, 1972. BA, Hofstra U., 1974; M in Mus. Practice, MA, U. Mich., 1977; MBA, Northwestern U., 1999. Dir. Emily Lowe Gallery, Hofstra U., Hempstead, N.Y., 1977-80, San Antonio Mus. Art., 1980-83; dir., chief exec. officer Newport Harbor Art Mus., Newport Beach, Calif., 1983-89, Mus. Contemporary Art, Chgo., 1989-2000; dir. art mus. and pacific film archive U. Calif., Berkeley, 2000—. Panelist profl. devel. Nat. Endowment for Arts, Washington, 1987-88, John D. and Catherine T. MacArthur Found., Nat. Arts Journalism Fellowship program, 45th Venice Biennale Sch. of Curators, Mus. Studies Program at the Art Inst. of Chgo., Ill. Arts Alliance, Calif. Arts Coun., Tex. Commn. on the Arts, NY State Coun. on the Arts, panelist challenge grant, 1988, panelist mus. program, 1989-90, panelist F.A.C.I.E., 1991-94; bd. dir. Com. Internat. Mus. Modern Art. Bd. dir. Nat. Audubon Soc., Chgo. Latin Sch., Golden Gate Chpt., Berkeley Cmty. Found.; advisory com. Girls Inc., Oakland, Calif. Hofstra U. scholar, 1970-74, Guggenheim Mus. intern, 1976; grantee Nat. Mus. Act, 1976-77; teaching fellowships U. Va., Toledo Mus. Art, Ohio, U. Mich. Mus. Art, Nat. Gallery Art, Wash., DC, Solomon R. Guggenheim Mus., NYC. Mem. Assn. Art Mus. Dirs., Coll. Art Assn., Internat. Assn. Art Critics Office: BAM/FFA U Calif Berkeley 2625 Durant Ave Berkeley CA 94720-2250 Office Phone: 510-642-1295. Business E-Mail: kconsey@berkeley.edu.

CONSIDINE, JOHN, pharmaceutical company executive; Attended, Villanova Univ., Pace Univ. With Arthur Andersen, 1973—83; mgmt. positions through sr. v.p., CFO Am. Home Products Corp., Madison, NJ, 1983—2000; exec. v.p., CFO Becton, Dickinson & Co., Franklin Lakes, NJ, 2000—. Bd. mem. St. Vincent's Svc., Animal Cancer Found. Office: Becton Dickinson & Co 1 Becton Dr Franklin Lakes NJ 07417-1880*

CONSIDINE, RUSSEL A., publishing executive, real estate company officer; b. New Hyde Park, N.Y., July 14, 1950; s. Howard and Dorothy M. Considine; m. Margaret A. Waters, May 28, 1983; children: Blake, Noelle. BA, Hofstra U., 1974. Investment officer TIAA-CREF, N.Y.C., 1977-88; pres., founder BMR Corp., Hastings-on-Hudson, N.Y., 1988-2000, NOELLeBooks.com Corp., Hastings-on-Hudson, N.Y., 2000—. Founder, CEO Considine Real Estate Adv. Group Inc., Hastings-on-Hudson, N.Y., 2001—; co-founder www.globalcalm.com., 2000—. Author, illustrator: Moonlight's Sleepy-Time Story, 2000 (Children's e-book cert. distinction, Writer's Digest, 2001); author: Armu-The King's Favorite Horse, 2000, Woofy & Noelle's Pocantico Hills Adventure, 1999. Coach Colts Youth Club, Yonkers, NY, 1996—99. Recipient Investor of Yr. award Interstate Mortgage Co., 1987. Avocations: golf, skiing, writing, hiking, reading. Home: 83 Rosedale Ave Hastings On Hudson NY 10706 Office: NOELLeBooks dot com Corp 83 Rosedale Ave Hastings On Hudson NY 10706 E-mail: russconsidine@considinerealestate.com, pax@globalcalm.com.

CONSIDINE, TERRY, real estate company executive; m. Betsy Considine. BA, Harvard College, 1968; JD, Harvard Law Sch., 1971. State senator, Colo., 1987—92; founder, CEO Considine Co. (now AIMCO), Denver, 1975—. Office: AIMCO Ste 1100 4582 S Ulster St Pkwy Denver CO 80237 Office Phone: 303-757-9101.*

CONSIGLIO-RUNK, JACQUELINE RENEE, psychologist; b. Altoona, Pa., Dec. 14, 1968; d. Richard Anthony and Sally Ann Consiglio; m. Robert Paul Runk, Sept. 30, 1995; children: Damian Robert Runk, Julia Frances Runk. Bachelor's degree in Elem. Edn., St. Francis U., 1991; Master's degree in Counseling, Ind. U. Pa. Cert. Ednl. Specialist in Sch. Psychology Pa. Dept. Edn., 1997. Early intervention svc. coord. Home Nursing Agy., Altoona, Pa., 1995—96; sch. psychologist Philipsburg-Osceola Sch. Dist., Philipsburg, Pa., 1997—98, Glendale Sch. Dist., Flinton, Pa., 1998—. Mem.: Nationally Cert. Sch. Psychologist, Nat. Orgn. Sch. Psychologists. Republican. Roman Catholic. Avocations: reading, travel. Home: 620 Beaumont Dr Altoona PA 16602

CONSOLI, MARC-ANTONIO, composer; b. Catania, Italy, May 19, 1941; came to U.S., 1956, naturalized, 1967; s. Francesco Gabriele Settimio and Rosa (Puglisi) C. B.Mus., N.Y. Coll. Music, 1966; M.Mus., Peabody Conservatory, 1967; M.Mus. Arts, Yale U., 1971, D.Mus. Arts, 1977. Lectr. Bridgeport U.; vis. prof. U. Western Ont., 1975 Composer, works performed by Balt. Symphony Orch., N.Y. Philharm., Los Angeles Philharm., Louisville Orch., Ensemble Kontrapunkte, Vienna, Austria, Monday Evening Concerts, Los Angeles, Berkshire Music Center, Yale Players for New Music, Gaudeamus Festival, Netherlands, Royan Festival, France; commns. for Graz

(Austria) radio sta., Royan Festival, others; performer, dir.-mem., Yale Players for New Music, 1969-71, The Experiment, 1974, Equinox I, 1967, Equinox II, 1968, Isonic, 1970, Interactions I-V, 1970-71, Profiles, 1972-73, Music for Chambers, 1974, Canti Trinacriani, 1975, Sciuri Novi I, 1974, Sciuri Novi II, 1975, Tre Canzoni, 1976, Odefonia, 1976, Vuci Siculani, 1979, Tre Fiori Musicali, 1979, Naked Masks, 1980, The Last Unicorn, 1981, Orpheus' Meditation, 1981, Saxlodie, 1981, Afterimages, 1982; String Quartet, 1983, Fantasia Celeste, 1983, Ancient Greek Lyrics, 1984, Musiculi II (summer), 1985, Reflections, 1986, Eyes of the Peacock, 1987, Sans Parole I and II, 1988, Cello Concerto, 1988, String Quartet II, 1989, Arie Mutate, 1990, Musiculi IV (winter), 1990/92, Musiculi III (autumn), 1992/94, Games for 2 and 3, 1994/95, Cinque Canti, 1995, Varie Azioni, Di-ver-ti-mento (Games for 4), 1995, Sciuri Novi III, 1997, Pensieri Sospesi, 1997, Rounds & Relays, 1997, Varie Azioni II, 1998, Varie Azioni III, 1999, Four Shades of Tango, 1999, Rounds' Separation, 1999, Passaggi Obbligati, 2000, Estratti Obbligati I, II and III, 2001, Night Whispers, 2002, Sciuri Novi IV, 2004, Varie Azioni IV, 2004, Collected Moments II, 2005. Recipient award Nat. Inst.-Am. Acad. Arts and Letters, 1975; Guggenheim Found. fellow, 1971-72, 79-80; Fulbright fellow Poland, 1972-74; Creative Artists Pub. Service grantee, 1975; Nat. Endowment for Arts grantee, 1979, 81, 85. Mem. Broadcast Music Inc., Am. Composers Alliance, Am. Music Center.

CONSOLO, FAITH HOPE, real estate broker; b. Ohio; BFA, NYU; MFA, Parsons Sch. Design; AA in Real Estate Studies, NYU. Owner internat. promotional modeling agy.; owner interior design studio; small stores real estate broker; joined Garret-Aug Assocs. Store Leasing Inc., N.Y.C., 1985, sr. mng. dir., vice chmn., 1999—; founder, vice chmn. Garrick-Aug Worldwide. Apptd. cons. The 42nd St. Redevel. Corp., N.Y.C., Penn Sta. Redevel., N.Y.C., The Downtown Alliance, N.Y.C.; lectr. Assn. Women on Econ. Devel., Nat. Assn. Women Bus. Owners, The Women's Econ. Roundtable, Inst. Internat. Rsch., Nat. Assn. Appraisers & Planners, Women Inc.; bd. dirs. The Real Estate Bd. N.Y., Internat. Coun. Shopping Ctrs., Nat. Broker's Network; advisor Mayor's Coun. on the Aging Related Issues; instr. NYU Parsons Sch. Design, The Wharton Bus. Sch.; lectr. in field. Author: (internet newsletter) The Faith Report; contbr. N.Y. Post, The N.Y. Times, Crain's N.Y. Bus., Real Estate Weekly, N.Y. Real Estate Jour., Real Estate N.Y., others. Named Woman of Yr., Associated Builders and Owners of Greater N.Y., 1999, Woman of Outstanding Achievement, Assn. Real Estate Women, 2003, Woman of Valor, Capuchin Food Pantries of St. John the Bapt. Friary, 2003; named one of N.Y. Most Influential Women in Bus., Crain's N.Y. Bus., 1996, 1999. Mem.: Young Men's/Women's Real Estate Assn., Assn. Real Estate Women (past pres., creator The Founder's award). Office: Garrick-Aug 360 Lexington Ave 4th Fl New York NY 10017

CONSTABLE, STEVEN, geophysics educator, researcher; b. Nottingham, Eng., May 23, 1957; s. Phil and Wendy Constable; m. Catherine Lindsay, Sept. 9, 1958; children: Ian, Claire. BSc with honors, U. Western Australia, Perth, 1979; PhD, Australian Nat. U., Canberra, 1983. Postdoctoral rsch. geophysicist Scripps Instn. Oceanography, La Jolla, Calif., 1983—98, prof.-in-residence, 1998—. Contbr. over 50 articles to profl. jours. Recipient Rex T. Prider medal, U. Western Australia, 1979, G.W. Hohmann award, Hohmann Soc., 2003. Mem.: European Assn. Geoscientists and Engrs., Royal Astron. Soc., Am. Geophys. Union (life; sec. gp sect. 2000—02). Achievements include patents for seafloor electromagnetic recorder. Office: Scripps Instn Oceanography Igpp 0225 La Jolla CA 92093-0225 Office Fax: 858-534-8090. Personal E-mail: sconstable@ucsd.edu.

CONSTANCE, BARBARA ANN, financial planner, small business owner, consultant; b. Springfield, Mass., Dec. 24, 1945; d. Edward F. and Margaret E. (Price) Corcoran; m. Thomas F. Tiedgen, Apr. 27, 1968 (div. 1975); m. G. Lawrence Gadsby Jr., May 5, 1978 (div. 1991); m. F. David Constance, Dec. 6, 1991. AA, Vt. Coll., Montpelier, 1965. CLU; chartered fin. cons. Adminstrv. asst. Mass. Mut. Life Co., Springfield and Hartford, Conn., 1965-75; office mgr. Am. Nat. Life Ins. Co., Springfield, 1976; traveling trainee Conn. Gen. Life Ins. Co., Bloomfield, 1976, sales rep. Springfield, 1976-77; dir. mktg. NN Life Ins. Services, Johnston, R.I., 1978-80; sales rep. New Eng. Mut. Life Co., Providence, 1980-82; pvt. practice fin. planner Tiverton, R.I., 1982-97. Pres., founder Heritage Prodns., Ltd., Tiverton, R.I., 1988-91; cons. Northwestern Mutual Life Ins. Co., Providence, 1986-87; co-founder, bd. dirs. Career Connections, Inc.; co-capt. SV/Nootka, 1997-2005 Bd. dirs. YWCA of Greater R.I., Big Sister Assn. of R.I., Friends Brooks Libr. Mem. Am. Soc. CLUs and ChFC (past pres. R.I. chpt.), Nat. Assn. Life Underwriters, R.I. Life Underwriters, Assn. Health Ins. Agts., Newport County Women's Network (co-founder), R.I. Woman's Career Network, R.I. Bus. Esch., R.I. Estate Planning Coun. Republican. Episcopalian. Home: 11 Kent Rd PO Box 637 South Harwich MA 02661 Personal E-mail: svnootka@verizon.net.

CONSTANDA, CHRISTIAN, mathematics professor; m. Lia Constanda, Apr. 26, 1969; 1 child, Dan. MSc, U. Iasi, Romania, 1966; PhD, Romanian Acad. Scis., 1972; DSc, U. Strathclyde, Glasgow, Scotland, 1997. Rschr. Romanian Acad. Scis., Iasi, 1967—73; lectr. U. Strathclyde, Glasgow, 1976—89, sr. lectr., 1989—93, reader, 1993—2000, prof. math., 2000—02, prof. emeritus, 2002—; Oliphant prof. math. scis. U. Tulsa, Okla., 2002—. Chmn. Internat. Consortium for Integral Methods in Sci. and Engring., 1990—; bd. dirs. Internat. Soc. for Analysis, its Applications, and Computation, 1997—2002. Author: (books) A Mathematical Analysis of Bending of Plates with Transverse Shear Deformation, 1990, Direct and Indirect Boundary Integral Equation Methods, 1999; author: (with Igor Chudinovich) Variational and Potential Methods in the Theory of Bending of Plates with Transverse Shear Deformation, 2000; author: Solution Techniques for Elementary Partial Differential Equations, 2002 (Outstanding Academic Title by Choice Mag.); editor: Integral Methods in Science and Engineering, 2002. Mem.: Edinburgh Math. Soc., London Math. Soc., Am. Math. Soc. Avocations: travel, reading, music, creative writing. Office: U Tulsa Dept Math and Computer Scis 600 S College Ave Tulsa OK 74104

CONSTANT, ANITA AURELIA, publisher; b. Youngstown, Ohio, Jan. 5, 1945; d. Sandu Nicholas and Erie Marie (Tecau) C. BA, Ind. U., 1967; postgrad., Northwestern U., Evanston, Ill., 1991. Sales rep. Economy Fin. Inc., St. Louis, 1967-69; recruiter Case Western U. Hosp., Cleve., 1969-70; sales rep. Internat. Playtex Inc., Chgo., 1970-71, John Wiley & Sons, Inc., Chgo., 1971-77; sr. product mgr. CBS Pub. Inc., The Dryden Press, Chgo., 1977-80; exec. editor Dearborn Fin. Pub., Inc., Chgo., 1980-81, v.p., 1981-89, sr. v.p., prin., 1989-97; cons. to pub. industry, 1997-98; prin. Ea. European investment venture EUROTEC, 1997-99; sr. v.p., editor-in-chief Southwestern Coll. Pub. divsn. ITP Inc., 1988-94; sr. v.p. new bus. devel. South-Western/Thomson Learning, 2000—; v.p. devel. and contract mgmt. Riverside Pub. Divsn. Houghton Mifflin, 1995—. Bd. dirs. Romanian Heritage Ctr., Detroit, 1988—, Orthodox Brotherhood of Am., Detroit, 1985—. Mem.: Nat. Assn. Women Bus. Owners, Chgo. Book Clinic (bd. dirs. 1987—88, v.p. 1988—90, pres. 1990—91, past pres. 1991—92, Mary Alexander award 1995), Internat. Assn. Fin. Planners, Real Estate Educators Assn., Chgo. Women in Pub. Eastern Orthodox. Avocations: property development and renovation, hiking, bicycling. Office: 425 Springlake Dr Itasca IL 60143

CONSTANT, TERRY LYNN, lawyer; b. Decatur, Ill., Dec. 16, 1942; s. Mathew Jacob and Virginia Florence C.; div.; children: Nicole L., Brett A., Amber K. BS, U. Wis., 1965; JD, Marquette U., 1968. Bar: 1968, U.S. Dist. Ct. (ea. dist.) Wis. 1968. Asst. city atty. City of Kenosha, Wis., 1970-75; atty. Baumgartner & Anderson, Kenosha, 1976-77; pvt. practice Kenosha, 1975-76, 77—. Tchr. law Gateway Tech. Inst., Kenosha, 1975-80. Bd. dirs. United Way of Kenosha Inc., Salvation Army, Kenosha, 1982; svc. mem. Kenosha Family Counseling, 1975-81. Mem. ATLA, Wis. Assn. Trial Lawyers, Kenosha County Bar Assn., Kenosha Golf Assn. (treas. 1987—). Avocations: golf, travel, reading. Office: 5712 6th Ave Kenosha WI 53140-4104 Office Fax: 262-654-8696. Personal E-mail: tlconstant@sbcglobal.net.

CONSTANTELOS, DEMETRIOS JOHN, priest, educator; b. Spilia, Messinia, Greece, July 27, 1927; came to U.S., 1955; naturalized, 1958; s. John and Christine (Psilopoulos) C.; m. Stella Croussouloudis, Aug. 15, 1954; children: Christine, John, Eleni, Maria. BTh, Holy Cross Sch. Theology, 1958; ThM, Princeton Theol. Sem., 1959; MA, Rutgers U., 1963, PhD, 1965; DD, Hellenic C/Holy Cross, 1991. Ordained priest Greek Orthodox Ch., 1955. Pastor St. Demetrios, Perth Amboy, NJ, 1955—64, St. Nicholas Ch., Lexington, Mass., 1965—67; interim pastor St. Barbara Ch., Toms River, NJ, 1972—74, St. Anthony Ch., Vineland, NJ, 1975—82, Holy Trinity Ch., Egg Harbor Twp., NJ, 1982—89; prof. Hellenic Coll., Brookline, Mass., 1965—71; prof. history Richard Stockton Coll. of N.J., Pomona, 1971—86, Charles Cooper Townsend Disting. prof., 1986—97, prof. emeritus, 1997—, disting. rsch. scholar in residence, 2001—. Mem. Orthodox-Cath. Theol. Consultation, 1965-84, New Rev. Standard Version Bible Com., 1974—, Anglican-Orthodox Theol. Consultation; vis. lectr. Boston Coll., 1967-68; vis. prof. religion, Onassis vis. prof. Hellenic studies NYU, spring 1991. Author: Byzantine Philanthropy, 1968, 2d edit., 1991, Understanding the Greek Orthodox Church, 1982, 4th edit., 2005, Poverty, Society and Philanthropy in the Late Mediaeval Greek World, 1992, Christian Hellenism, 1998, Christian Faith and Cultural Heritage, 2005, Interrelationship Between Christianity and Hellenism in Greek, 2005; editor: Encyclicals, 1976, Orthodox Theology, 1981, Archbishop Iakovos, Visions and Expectations for a Living Church, 1998, Archbishop Iakovos: The Torch Bearer, vol. 1 1999, vol. II, 2001, Archbishop Iakovos, Paideia, 2002; editor Greek Theol. Rev., 1965-71, assoc. editor Jour. Ecumenical Studies, 1976—. Lane Cooper fellow Rutgers U., 1962, Jr. fellow Dumbarton Oaks, 1964. Mem. Orthodox Theol. Soc. (pres. 1968-71), Modern Greek Studies Assn., Parnasos Philol. Soc. (corr.), Medieval Acad. Am., U.S. Nat. Com. for Byzantine Studies. Home: 304 Forest Dr Linwood NJ 08221-1511 Office: Richard Stockton Coll NJ Dept History Pomona NJ 08240 Office Phone: 609-652-4433. Office Fax: 609-652-4433. Business E-Mail: constand@stockton.edu. E-mail: djconstantelos@aol.com.

CONSTANTINE, ANDREW, conductor; b. England; Studied, with John Carewe; studied with Norman Del Mar, Royal Coll. Music Conducting Class; studied with Ilya Musin, Leningrad State Conservatory. Condr., London Philharmonic; asst. condr. Stats Oper, Munich, 1993. Recipient Donatella Flick/Academia Italiana Conducting Competition. Office: Baltimore Symphony Orchestra 1212 Cathedral St Baltimore MD 21201-5545*

CONSTANTINE, JAN FRIEDMAN, lawyer; b. N.Y.C., Jan. 22, 1948; d. Howard J. and Elayne (Sercus) Friedman; m. Lawrence Levien, Oct. 11, 1970 (div. Sept. 1974); m. Lloyd E. Constantine, June 22, 1975; children: Isaac, Sarah, Elizabeth. BA, Smith Coll., Northampton, Mass., 1970; JD, George Washington U., 1973. Bar: N.Y. 1974, U.S. Dist. Ct. (so. and ea. dists.) N.Y. 1975, U.S. Ct. Appeals (2d cir.) 1975. Staff atty. div. spl. projects FTC, Washington, 1973-75, staff atty. N.Y. office N.Y.C., 1975-77; asst. atty. U.S. Dist. Ct. (ea. dist.) N.Y., Bklyn., 1977-82; litigation counsel Macmillan, Inc., N.Y.C., 1982-84, assoc. gen. counsel, 1985-90, dep. gen. counsel, 1990-91; exec. v.p. and dep. gen. counsel News Am. Inc., N.Y.C., 1992—; sr. gen. counsel News Am. Mktg. and Pub. Groups, N.Y.C.; sr. v.p. The News Corp. Ltd., N.Y.C., 1996—. Vis. asst. prof. George Washington U. Law Sch., Washington, 1974; bd. mem. The Feminist Press. Mem. Assn. of Bar of City of N.Y. (mem. consumer protection com. 1981-84, corp. law com. 1987-90, media law com. 1991-94, women in the law com. 1994-96, comm. and media law com. 1996—, chair 1999-2001). Avocations: tennis, singing. Home: 10 W 66th St New York NY 10023-6206 Office: The News Corp Ltd Ste 300 1211 Avenue Of The Americas New York NY 10036-8795

CONSTANTINE, KATHERINE A., lawyer; b. 1955; BS magna cum laude in Fgn. Svc., Georgetown Univ., 1977, JD, 1980. Bar: Minn. 1980. Assoc., gen. litig. Nichols, Kruger, Starks and Carruthers, 1980—83; assoc. Fabyanske Svoboda & Westra PA, 1983—85, Dorsey & Whitney LLP, Mpls., 1986—88, ptnr., banking comml. dept., 1989—, and co-chair, bus. restructuring and bankruptcy. Assoc. editor Georgetown's The Tax Lawyer, 1979—80. Named a Leading Atty. in bankruptcy law, Minn. Bus. Guidebook to Law and Leading Attorneys, 1994—96, Guide to Leading Am. Attorneys, 1998, Minn. Super Lawyer, 2000—03. Mem.: ABA, Am. Bankruptcy Inst., Minn. Women Lawyers, Hennepin Co. Bar Assn., Minn. State Bar Assn., Phi Beta Kappa. Office: Dorsey & Whitney LLP Ste 1500 50 S Sixth St Minneapolis MN 55402-1498 Office Phone: 612-340-8792. Office Fax: 612-340-2868. Business E-Mail: constantine.katherine@dorsey.com.

CONSTANTINE, KEVIN, professional hockey coach; b. International Falls, Minn., Dec. 27, 1958; 2 children. Head coach Rochester (Minn.) USHL, 1987-88, Kansas City IHL, 1991-92, San Jose Sharks, 1993-94, 95-96; asst. coach Calgary Flames, 1996-97; head coach Pitts. Penguins, 1997—2000, NJ Devils, 2001—02, Pitts. Forge, 2001—03, Everett Silvertips, 2003—. Runner-up for Jack Adams award as NHL Coach of Yr., 1993-94, IHL Coach of Yr., 1991-92; career NHL coaching record (all with the Sharks) is 55-78-24; coached USHL championship team in 1987-88, and IHL championship team in 1991-92. Office: Everett Silvertips 2000 Hewitt Ave Ste 100 Everett WA 98201

CONSTANTINE, LYNNE MARY, writer, photographer, consultant; b. Queens, N.Y., July 29, 1953; d. Arthur Anthony and Anne Jasmine (D'Angelo) C.; partner Suzanne Scott, Nov. 15, 1980; stepchildren: Elizabeth, William, Stephanie, David. BA summa cum laude, Canisius Coll., 1973; MA, Yale U., 1975, MPhil, 1976; postgrad., George Mason U., 1998—. Asst. prof. English James Madison U., Harrisonburg, Va., 1977-80; mng. dir. Health Edn. Found., Washington, 1981-83; exec. dir. Energy Conservation Coalition, Washington, 1983-85; ptnr., creative dir. Cmty. Scribes, Arlington, Va., 1985-97; CEO Intellectual Capital, Inc., Arlington, 1997—. Cons. APA Pres.'s Commn. on Violence in the Family, Washington, 1994-95, Commn. on Violence and Youth, 1992-93, Carnegie Coun. on Adolescence, Washington, 1994-95, D.C. Area Rape Crisis Ctr., 1985—. Co-author: Migraine: The Complete Guide, 1994; mng. editor: Woman's Monthly, 1992-97, Passages award, 1995. Mem. Washington Ind. Writers, No. Va. Photog. Soc. Home: 4600 S Four Mile Run Dr Apt 636 Arlington VA 22204-3514 Office: PO Box 6674 Arlington VA 22206-0674

CONSTANTINESCU, ALEX R., pediatrician, nephrologist; MD, Med. Inst. Timisoara, Romania, 1985. Diplomate Am. Bd. Pediat. Intern Flushing (N.Y.) Hosp., 1989—90; resident in pediat. Westchester County Med. Ctr., Valhalla, NY, 1990—92; fellow in pediat. nephrology Montefiore Med. Ctr., Bronx, NY, 1992—95; physician Robert Wood Johnson U. Med. Group, New Brunswick, NJ, 1995—2002; dir. pediat. nephrology Joe DiMaggio Children's Hosp., Hollywood, Fla., 2003—. Office: Docs-4-Kidneys 1861 N Federal Hwy # 129 Hollywood FL 33020 Office Phone: 954-894-9344. Business E-Mail: docs4kidneys@yahoo.com.

CONSTANTINIDES, MINAS SPIROS, otolaryngologist, plastic surgeon; b. Thessaloniki, Greece, Jan. 17, 1961; BA in biochemistry magna cum laude, Brown U.; MD, Coll. Physicians and Surgeongs, Columbia U., 1987. Bd. cert. facial plastic surgery and otolaryngology. Intern and resident in gen. surgery Harvard U. Surgical Svc., New England Deaconess Hosp., Boston, 1987—89; resident in otolaryngology- head and neck surgery NYU Sch. Medicine, 1989—93; fellow U. Toronto, 1993—94; dir. facial plastic and reconstructive surgery Dept. Otolaryngology, NYU Med. Ctr., 1994—; asst. prof. otolaryngology NYU Sch. Medicine, 1994—. Named one of Top Cosmetic Surgeons in US, Town and Country Mag., 1999, Top Drs. NY, Converse and Connolly, 2000. Fellow: ACS, Am. Acad. Otolaryngology - Head and Neck Surgery, Am. Acad. Facial Plastic and Reconstructive Surgery (mem. nat. task force domestic violence 1999); mem.: AMA, Hellenic Med. Soc. NY, Facial Plastic Surgery Soc. NY. Office: NYU Med Ctr 530 First Ave Ste 7U New York NY 10016 Office Phone: 212-263-5882, 212-263-8490.

CONSTANTINO, JOHN NICHOLAS, medical educator, researcher; b. St. Louis, Aug. 30, 1962; s. Henry Franklin and Julia Shamia Constantino; m. Michele Ann McDermott; children: Anna Marie, Benedict John, Celia Terese. BA, Cornell U., 1984; MD, Wash. U., 1988. Diplomate bd cert. pediatrics Am. Bd. Pediat., 1993, gen. psychiatry Am. Bd. Psychiatry and Neurology, 1999, subsplty. child and adolescent psychiatry Am. Bd. Psychiatry and Neurology, 2000. Asst. prof. psychiatry and pediat. Wash. U. Sch. Medicine, St. Louis, 1996—. Author: A Poor Man's Proof for the Existence of God; contbr. articles to profl. jours. Grantee, Nat. Inst. Child Health and Human Devel. Pub. Health Svc. Rsch., 2003; scholar, Cornell U., 1980. Office: Washington U Sch Medicine 660 South Euclid Ave Campus Box 8134 Saint Louis MO 63110 E-mail: constantino@psychiatry.wustl.edu.

CONSTANTINOPLE, ALEXANDRA, communications executive; d. Nicholas and Donna Constantinople; m. Jordan Hoffner, Oct. 2, 1999; 1 child, Nicholas. BA in English lit., Dennison U. Sr. publicist Larry King Live, CNN, Wash., DC, 1991—93; sr. publicist news info. Today Show and Meet the Press, NBC, NYC, 1993; dir. corp. media rels. NBC, NYC, 1997—98, v.p. news comm., 1998—2002; gen. mgr. corp. and mktg. comm. Gen. Electric, 2002—. Mem.: NY Women in Comm. Office: Gen Electric 3135 Easton Turnpike Easton CT 06431

CONSTANTINOU, PHOEBE A.E., education educator, researcher; d. Achilleas Constantinou and Eugenia Panagy. EdD, Columbia U., 2003. Adj. prof. Hofstra U., LI, NY, 2000; asst. prof. Ithaca Coll., 2003—. Phys. educator The Grammar Sch., Nicosia, Cyprus, 1992—97. Mem.: Am. Alliance for Health, Phys. Edn., Recreation, and Dance. Office: Ithaca Coll 953 Danby Rd Ithaca NY 14850 Office Phone: 607-274-5791. Business E-Mail: pconstantinou@ithaca.edu.

CONSTON, HENRY SIEGISMUND, lawyer; b. Dresden, Germany, Dec. 18, 1928; arrived in U.S., 1947, naturalized, 1952; BSBA, NYU, 1955, JD, 1958, LLM, 1961. Bar: N.Y. 1959. With Calif. Tex. Oil Corp., NYC, 1947-61; sr. ptnr. Walter, Conston, Alexander & Green PC, NYC, 1961—95; sr. counsel, corp. tax, estate law Alston & Bird, NYC, 2001—. Contbr. articles to profl. jours. Bd. dirs. Margaret Tietz Ctr. for Nursing Care. Office: 90 Park Ave New York NY 10016-1301 Office Phone: 212-210-9420.

CONSUL, VINCENT A., lawyer; b. Alameda, Calif., June 7, 1953; BA, Univ. Calif., Berkeley, 1975; JD, Univ. Pacific, 1980. Dep. dist. atty. Clark County, Nev., 1980—83; asst. US atty. Dist. of Nev., 1983—85; ptnr. Dickerson, Dickerson, Consul & Pocker. Recipient Am. Jurisprudence award for family law. Mem.: ABA, Eighth Judicial Dist. Pro Bono Found. (mem, bd. dir. 1997—), State Bar of Calif., State Bar of Nev. (bd. gov. 1997—, pres. 2005—06). Office: Dickerson Dickerson Consul & Pocker Rainbow Corp Ctr Ste 350 777 N Rainbow Blvd Las Vegas NV 89107

CONTA, RICHARD VINCENT, actuary; b. N.Y.C., Sept. 4, 1946; s. Antonio and Eugenia Theresa (Cavally) C.; m. Joanne Shultis, July 14, 1979 (div. 1990); children: Kerry, Gregory; m. Maureen Fitzgerald, June 8, 1991; 1 child, Tracy. BA, Fordham U., 1968. Pension clk. Tchrs. Retirement Sys., City of N.Y., 1968-69; actuarial student U.S. Life Ins. Co., N.Y.C., 1969-74; pension actuary Laiken, Siegel & Co., N.Y.C., 1974-75; enrolled actuary Guardian Life Ins. Co., N.Y.C., 1975-99; ptnr. Fitzgerald & Conta Pension Svcs., Bloomfield, N.J., 1990—. Mem.: Am. Acad. Actuaries, Am. Soc. Pension Actuaries. Roman Catholic. Office: Fitzgerald & Conta Pension Svcs 104 Davis Ave Bloomfield NJ 07003-4140 Fax: 973-338-7834. Office Phone: 973-338-7757. Personal E-mail: Fitzconta@aol.com.

CONTE, GREGORY MICHAEL, lawyer; b. Bridgeport, Conn., May 8, 1947; s. Patsy Anthony and Lora Mary (Caselli) C.; m. Ellen Ciotti, Apr. 17, 1970 (div. Mar. 1980); children: Mark, Nicole, Sean, Michael; m. Bertha Marie Paris, May 11, 1986; children: Jessica, Justin. BA, Sacred Heart U., Bridgeport, Conn., 1969; MA, Fairfield (Conn.) U., 1974; JD, U. Bridgeport, 1980. Bar: Conn. 1980, U.S. Dist. Ct. Conn. 1981. Tchr. Bridgeport Bd. Edn., 1969-80; assoc. Law Offices Joseph Mirsky, Bridgeport, 1980-83; ptnr. Conte & Paoletti, Bridgeport, 1984-89, Conte, Paoletti & Lonergan, Bridgeport, 1990-91, Conte & Longergan, Bridgeport, 1992-96; pvt. practice Bridgeport, 1997—; dep. chief of staff City of Bridgeport Mayor's Office, 2001—; asst. city atty. City of Bridgeport City Atty.'s Office, 2002—. Spl. counsel to selectman Town of Monroe, Conn., 1995—; dep. chief of staff Mayors Office, Bridgeport, Conn., 2001—02; asst. city atty. City of Bridgeport, 2002—. Chmn. Dem. Town Com., Monroe, 1992-96; mem., sec. Parks and Recreation Commn., Monroe, 1988-92; mem. city coun. City of Bridgeport, 1976-80. Recipient Cert. of Merit, Parks and Recreation Commn., Monroe, 1992, Disting. Svc. award Dem. Town Com., Monroe, 1996. Mem. ATLA, Conn. Trial Lawyers Am., Conn. Bar Assn., Bridgeport Bar Assn., Monroe Italian Am. Soc. (counsel 1993-96), Nat. Italian Am. Bar Assn., Conn. Italian Am. Bar Assn., Miamoque Yacht Club (judge advocate), KC. Roman Catholic. Avocations: fishing, gardening, boating. Home: 136 Wheeler Rd Monroe CT 06468-2428 Office: 4270 Main St Ste 206 Bridgeport CT 06606-2347 E-mail: gbjj@aol.com, gmjc136@cs.com.

CONTE, JULIE VILLA, nurse, administrator; b. Manila, July 4, 1951; came to U.S., 1970; d. Gregorio Cortes and Lourdes (Villa) Dirige. BSN, Calif. State U., L.A., 1974; MBA, U. Phoenix, San Diego, 1993. RN, Calif. Staff nurse Santa Monica (Calif.) Hosp., 1976-78; pub. health nurse Kaiser Found. Hosp., Panorama City, Calif., 1978-85; nursing supr. Nat. Med. Homecare, L.A., 1985-86; dir. home health Holy Cross Hosp., Mission Hills, 1986-88; dir. profl. svcs. Care Home Health, San Diego, 1988; dir. nursing Health Prime Home Health Svcs. of San Diego, Inc., 1988-92; dir. home health svcs. Alvarado Home Health Agy., San Diego, 1993-94; expert consulting Home Health and Bus. Cons., San Diego, 1994—; dir. patient care svcs. Unlimited Care, Inc., 1995-96; CEO, pres., adminstr. We Care Home Health Svc., Inc., 1996—. Cons. in field. Mem. Bapt. Nursing Fellowship (pres. Calif. chpt. 1997-2004, nat. pres., pres.-elect 1999-2003), Alpha Delta Chi Republican. Avocations: travel, foreign language, collecting, piano, organ. Office Phone: 619-229-3800. Personal E-mail: juliecare1@aol.com.

CONTESCU, CRISTIAN ION, chemist, researcher; b. Galati, Romania, Apr. 17, 1948; s. Nelu Marcel and Aurora C.; m. Adriana Ghitulescu, Aug. 22, 1971; 1 child, Corneliu Daniel. MS, Bucharest U., Romania, 1971; PhD, Bucharest Poly. Inst., 1979. Chemist Ctr. Phys. Chem., Bucharest, Romania, 1971-76; rsch. scientist Inst. Phys. Chem, Bucharest, Romania, 1976-82, sr. rsch. scientist, 1982-92; rsch. assoc. Syracuse U., Syracuse, NY, 1992-96, rsch. scientist, 1996-97; sr. scientist Hitco Carbon Composites, Inc., Gardena, Calif., 1999-2001, Material Methods LLC, Newport Beach, Calif., 2001—04; sr. rsch. staff mem. Oak Ridge Nat. Lab., 2004—. Adj. assoc. prof. Syracuse U., 1997; cons. in field. Editor: Surfaces of Nanoparticles and Porous Materials, 1999, Dekker Encyc. Nanoscience and Nanotechnology, 2004; contbr. articles to profl. jours. Recipient Romanian Acad. Gheorghe Spacu award, 1991. Mem. Am. Chem. Soc. (co-chmn. symposia, 2001, 02, 04), Am. Carbon Soc. Home: 2577 Brighton Farms Blvd Knoxville TN 37932 E-mail: ccontescu@juno.com.

CONTI, INDALICIO PALOMAR, finance educator; b. Dinas, Philippines, Dec. 22, 1953; s. Ismael Hernandez Conti and Irenea Demit Palomar. BS in Mgmt., Philippine Coll. of Commerce, Manila, 1976, BSc in Acctg., 1977; LLB, U. of the East, Manila, 1985; MBA, Polytechnic U. of Philippines. CPA. Jr. acct. Gen. Textile Mills Inc., Libis, Quezon City, Philippines, 1978; dir., acct. Supreme Traders, Inc., Manila, 1978-79; auditor PUP Credit Union, Manila, 1978-83; legal rschr. Polytechnic U. Philippines, Manila, 1992; prof. Coll. Accountancy, Polytechnic U. Philippines, Manila, 1993—; mgng. ptnr. Conti & Assoc. CPA's, Quezon City, Philippines. Fin. cons., bd. trustees Fieldridge Learning Ctr., Brgy. San Felipe, Batangas, 11999; tax cons., legal rschr. V.C. Ramirez Law Office, Quezon City, 1997—; external auditor N.F.K. Constrn., Merto Manila, 1998—, Vincent Mark Security Agy., Quezon City, 1998—, Psychol. Ext. Evaluation Rsch. Svcs., Quezon City, 1999—; assoc. prof. CBIBE Philippine Women's U., Manila, 1999; mem. faculty Colegio San Lorenzo Project 6, Quezon City, 2000—; CPA, tax practitioner, chief legal rschr., Fabella & Assocs. Law Office, Quezon City, 2002; profl. lectr., Trinity Grad. Sch. (Cmty. Outreach), 2000; prof. Polytechnic U. Philippines

Coll. Accountancy, Manila, 2003—. Author: (textbooks) Income Taxation Law, 1984, Transfer and Business Taxes, 1986, Fundamentals of Transfer and Business Taxes, 1987, Fundamentals of Income Tax, 1988. Mem. PICPA, GACPA, CALFCI. Roman Catholic. Avocations: martial arts, dance, playing chess, bowling, reading. E-mail: ipc-cpa@yahoo.com.

CONTI, JAMES JOSEPH, retired chemical engineer, educator; b. Coraopolis, Pa., Nov. 2, 1930; s. James Joseph and Mary (Smrekar) Conti; m. Concetta Razziano, May 13, 1961; children: Lori Ann, James Robert. B.Chem. Engring. summa cum laude, Poly. Inst. Bklyn., 1954, M.Chem. Engring., 1956, D. Chem. Engring., 1959. Sr. engr. Bettis atomic power divsn. Westinghouse Electric Corp., 1958—59; mem. faculty Polytech. U. N.Y., 1959—90, prof. chem. engring., 1965—90, chmn. dept., 1964—70, provost, 1970—78, v.p. ednl. devel., 1978—90; pres. Webb Inst. Naval Architecture, Glen Cove, NY, 1990—99, ret., 1999. Cons. in field. Contbr. articles to profl. jours.; patentee in field. Trustee Webb Inst. Naval Architecture, 1974—99. Fellow: AAAS, Am. Inst. Chemists; mem.: AIChE, Am. Soc. Engring. Edn., Omega Chi Epsilon, Phi Lambda Upsilon, Tau Beta Pi, Sigma Xi. Home: 26 Miami Rd Bethpage NY 11714-2229 Office Phone: 516-931-5568.

CONTI, JOY FLOWERS, judge; b. Kane, Pa., Dec. 7, 1948; d. Bernard A. Flowers and Elizabeth (Tingley) Rodgers; m. Anthony T. Conti, Jan. 16, 1971; children: Andrew, Michael, Gregory. BA, Duquesne U., 1970, JD summa cum laude, 1973. Bar: Pa. 1973, U.S. Dist. Ct. (we. dist.) Pa. 1973, U.S. Ct. Appeals (3d cir.) 1976, U.S. Supreme Ct. 1993. Law clk. Supreme Ct. Pa., Monessen, 1973-74; assoc. Kirkpatrick & Lockhart, Pitts., 1974-76, 82-83, ptnr., 1983-96; shareholder Buchanan, Ingersoll, P.C., Pitts., 1996—2002; dist. judge U.S. Dist. Ct.(we. dist.) Pa., Pitts., 2002—. Prof. law Duquesne U., Pitts., 1976-82; hearing examiner Pa. Dept. State, Bur. Profl. Occupation and Affairs, 1978-82; chairperson search com. for judge U.S. Bankruptcy Ct. (we. dist.) Pa., 1987, 95; active Pa. Futures Commn. on Justice in 21st Century, 1995-97. Contbr. articles to profl. jours. Mem. disciplinary hearing com. Supreme Ct. Pa., 1982-88; v.p. Com. for Justice Edn., Pitts., 1983-84; mem. Leadership Pitts., 1987-88. Named one of Ten Outstanding Young Women in Am., 1981. Fellow Am. Bar Found. (Pa. state chair 1991-97); mem. ABA (ho. of dels. 1980-86, 91-97), Am. Law Inst., Am. Coll. Bankruptcy, Pa. Bar Assn. (gov. 1993-95, ho. of dels. 1978—, corp. banking and bus. law sect. coun. 1983-89, treas. 1991-93, v.p. 1993-95, chair-elect 1995-97, chmn. 1997-99, chmn. commn. comml. law 1990-93, co-chair 1995-2002, chair civil rights and responsibilities com. 1986-89, Achievement award 1982, 87, 99, Anne X. Alpern award 1995), Nat. Conf. Bar Pres. (exec. coun. 1993-96), Am. Inns Ct. (Pitts. chpt., counselor 2004—), Nat. Assn. Women Judges, Fed. Judges Assn., Allegheny County Bar Assn. (adminstrv. v.p. 1984-86, 90, chairperson corp. banking and bus. law sect. 1987-89, treas. 1988-90, gov. 1991, pres.-elect 1992, pres. 1993), Internat. Women's Insolvency and Restructuring Confedn. (chair Tri-State Network 1996), Pa. Bar Inst. (dir. 1991-97), Duquesne Club. Roman Catholic. Office: US Dist Judge 5250 US Courthouse and Post Office 700 Grant St Pittsburgh PA 15219 Office Phone: 412-208-7330.

CONTI, KAREN, lawyer, educator; b. Berwyn, Ill., Feb. 3, 1962; d. Joseph and Marilyn (Derrick) C. BA in Polit. Sci., No. Ill. U., 1983; JD, U. Ill., 1986. Bar: Ill. 1986, U.S. Dist. Ct. Ill. 1986, Calif. 1994, U.S. Supreme Ct. Assoc. Peterson & Ross, Chgo., 1986-88, Tressler, Soderstrom, Maloney & Pries, Chgo., 1989-90; ptnr. Adamski & Conti, Chgo., 1990—. Adj. prof. U. Ill. Coll. Law, 1997—; spkr., legal commentator for local and nat. TV and radio programs; mem. faculty Inst. Law and Advocacy program Stanford U., Am. U. Talk show host finalist best radio talk show, best interview and best new talent in Chgo. market for radio show "Chicago Law", 1986, 87. Mem. alumni adv. bd. U. Ill. Coll. Law, Champaign, 1995-97; tutor Chgo. Literacy Coun., 1986-90; mentor Women for Achievement Mentor Program. Named One of 40 Attys. Under 40 to Watch, Law. Bull. Pub. Co. Mem. Chgo. Bar Assn., Chgo. Inn of Ct. Avocations: running, body building, handwriting analysis. Office: Adamski & Conti 100 N La Salle St Ste 1520 Chicago IL 60602-2407

CONTI, LOUIS THOMAS MOORE, lawyer; b. Phila., Aug. 31, 1949; s. Alexander and Yolanda (DiLorenzo) Conti; m. Christina M.S. Moore, May 1, 1982; children: Charles Alexander, Whitney Caroline. BS, LaSalle Coll., 1971; MBA, Drexel U., 1972; JD, Creighton U., 1975; LLM, Temple U., 1981. Bar: Pa. 1975, U.S. Claims Ct. 1975, U.S. Tax Ct. 1975, U.S. Dist. Ct. (ea. dist.) Pa. 1978, U.S. Ct. Appeals (3d cir.) 1979, U.S. Supreme Ct. 1981, Fla. 1982, U.S. Dist. Ct. (mid. dist.) Fla. 1988. Tax atty. Office Chief Counsel IRS, Washington and Phila., 1975-81; tax mgr. Touche Ross & Co., Phila., 1981-84; assoc. Saul, Ewing, Remick & Saul, Phila., 1984-87; shareholder Swann & Haddock, P.A., Orlando, Fla., 1987-89; ptnr., chmn. corp. tax and securities dept. Holland & Knight, Orlando, 1989—. Mem. fin. com. S.E. Pa. chpt. ARC, Phila., 1984—87; advisor Vol. Lawyers for Arts, Phila., 1984—87; bd. dirs. Fla. Hosp. Found., Ctrl. Fla. Planned Giving Coun., 1989—97, Cmty. Found. Ctrl. Fla. Inc., World Trade Ctr., Orlando, 1992—95; mem. internat. bus. adv. bd. Metro Orlando; grad. Leadership Orlando, 1994, Leadership Fla., 1996; chair recruiting com. East Ctrl. Region of Leadership Fla., 1997; bd. dirs. Orlando Performing Arts and Edn. Ctr., Inc., 1998—2001. Mem.: ABA (chmn. task force on drafting prototype ltd. liability co. operating ag 1998—, chmn. Fla. Bar drafting com. 1999, tax and bus. law sect.), Orange County Bar Assn. (chmn. tax sect. 1990—91), Fla. Bar Assn. (chmn. drafting com. ltd. liability co. statutes 1998—, bus. law sect. 1999—2001, chair tax sect. 2001—02, tax and bus. law sect., chair corps. and securities com.), Seminole County C. of C. (bd. dirs. 1994—97). Republican. Avocation: travel, skiing, golf, tennis, theatre. Home: 603 Genius Drive Winter Park FL 32779 Office: Holland & Knight PO Box 1526 Orlando FL 32802-1526 Office Phone: 407-244-5118. E-mail: louis.conti@hklaw.com.

CONTI, PAUL LOUIS, management consulting company executive; b. Utica, N.Y., Sept. 3, 1945; s. Louis Joseph and Dorothy Mae (Kellogg) C.; m. Lee Ann Scheuerman, Apr. 18, 1970; children: Meghan Elizabeth, Dawn Michelle. BA, So. Ill. U., 1972, MBA, 1974. Sr. cons. Lester B. Knight & Assocs., Chgo., 1974-76; dir. pers. Applied Info. Devel., Oak Brook, Ill., 1976-80; v.p. Comsi, Inc., Oak Brook, 1980-82; CEO Prestige Mgmt. Sys., Inc., Glen Ellyn, Ill., 1982-86; v.p. human resources Rand McNally & Co., Skokie, Ill., 1986-87; assoc. dir. Ernst & Young (formerly Ernst & Whinney), Chgo., 1987-93; regional v.p. Alexandria Alexander, Inc., Chgo., 1993-97; COO, sr. v.p. AON Corp., 1997-99; sr. v.p. Apropos Tech., Inc., Oak Brook, Ill., 1999—; pres., chief assets officer Vericlaim, Inc., Chgo., 1999—. Bd. dirs. So. Ill. U. Coll. Bus. Adminstrn. Lobbyist Invest in the Future, Invest in Edn., State of Ill., 1988; bd. dirs., exec. com. So. Ill. U.-Carbondale Found., 1991—, pres., 1994-97. Named to So. Ill. U. COBA Hall of Fame, 1988; named Cmty. Ambassador So. Ill. U., 1980. Mem. Soc. Human Resource Profls., Soc. Human Resources Mgmt., Human Resources Mgmt. Assn. of Chgo., Employment Mgmt. Assn., Pontikes Ctr. for Mgmt. Info. (bd. dirs. 1989—), So. Ill. U. Alumni Assn. (pres. 1986-88, bd. dirs. 1986—, exec. com. 1991—), Ideal Club (pres. 1986-88), McCullom Lake Club. Republican. Roman Catholic. Avocations: hunting waterfowl and upland game, golf, various participative sports, coaching women's fast pitch softball. Home: 635 S Park Blvd Glen Ellyn IL 60137-6977 Office Phone: 312-559-4829. Business E-Mail: pconti@vericlaiminc.com. E-mail: contip@msn.com.

CONTI, PETER SELBY, astronomy educator; b. N.Y.C., Sept. 5, 1934; s. Attilio Carlo and Marie (Selby) C.; m. Carolyn Safford, Aug. 26, 1961; children: Michael, Karen, Kathe BS, Rensselaer Poly. Inst., 1956; PhD, U. Calif-Berkeley, 1963; Honoris Causa degree, U. Utrecht, 1993. Rsch. fellow Calif. Inst. Tech., Pasadena, 1963-66; asst. prof. astronomy U. Calif./Santa Cruz, 1966-71; astronomer Lick Obs., Santa Cruz, 1966-71; prof., fellow Joint Inst. Lab. Astrophysics U. Colo., Boulder, 1971-99, chmn., 1989-90, chmn. dept. astrophys., planetary scis., 1980-86, prof. emeritus, 1999—. Chmn. bd. dirs. Assoc. Univs. for Rsch. in Astronomy Inc., Tuscon, 1983-86; vis. prof. U. Utrecht, The Netherlands, 1969-70, minnaert prof. U. Utrecht, 1995. Editor: Mass Loss and Evolution of O-type Stars, 1979, O Stars and Wolf Rayet Stars, 1988; contbr. over 200 articles to profl. jours. Served to lt. (j.g.) USNR, 1956-59 Recipient Gold medal U. Liege, Belgium, 1975; Fulbright fellow, 1969-70 Fellow AAAS (chmn. sect. D in astronomy 1980); mem. Am. Astron. Soc. (councillor 1983-86), Astron. Soc. of Pacific, Internat. Astron. Union (organizing com. 1983-85, v.p. 1985-88, pres. 1988-91, commn. 29 stellar spectra). Home: 3225 Mariner Ln Longmont CO 80503 Office: U Colo-Boulder Joint Inst Lab Astrophysics Campus Box 440 Boulder CO 80309-0440

CONTI, TOM, actor, theater director, writer; b. Paisley, Scotland, Nov. 22, 1941; s. Alfonso and Mary (McGoldrick) C.; m. Kara Drummond Wilson, July 2, 1967; 1 child, Nina. Appeared in plays on London's West End, Jesus My Boy, 1998, Chapter Two, The Ride Down Mount Morgan, Savages, Other People, The Black and White Minstrels, Don Juan, The Devil's Disciple, Romantic Comedy, Chapter Two, Jesus My Boy Last of the Red Hot Covers Barrymore Broadway debut in Whose Life Is It Anyway, 1979 (Tony award), Jeffrey Bernard is Unwell, 1990; appeared in They're Playing Our Song, 1980; dir. Before the Party, 1980; dir., star Present Laughter, 1993; film appearances include Galileo, Eclipse, Merry Christmas Mr. Lawrence, Reuben, Reuben (Acad. Award nomination), 1983, American Dreamer, 1984, Saving Grace, Miracles, Heavenly Pursuits, Beyond Therapy, The Dumb Waiter, White Roses, Shirley Valentine, Someone Else's America, 1995, Sub Down, Something To Believe In, 1996, Don't Go Breaking My Heart, 1998, Out of Control, 1997, The Enemy, 2000; appeared in TV plays including the Beaux Strategem; appeared in American TV prodns. Princess and the Pea, Faerie Tale Theatre, the Beate Klarsfeld Story, The Quick and the Dead, Fatal Dosage, When Rabbit Howls, Wright Verdicts, The Inheritance, Friends, Deadline, Cinderella and Me, 2001, (miniseries) Donovan, 2004, 05, (Miramax film) Derailed, 2005, Beyond Friendship, 2005, Paid, 2005; author (novel): The Doctor, 2004; appeared in Brit. TV prodns. The Glittering Prizes, Norman Conquests, Madame Bovary. Named Most Popular Actor for Last 20 Yrs., Theatre Goers of U.K., 2000. Mem.: Garrick Club (London). Address: Finch and Ptnrs 4-8 Heddar St London WIP4BS England Office Phone: 411 20 7851 7144. E-mail: abi@inchandpartners.com.

CONTINETTI, ROBERT E., chemistry professor; Prof. dept. chemistry U. Calif. San Diego, La Jolla, Calif., 1992—. Recipient Packard Found. fellow, 1994. Fellow: Am. Phys. Soc. Office: U Calif San Diego Dept Chem & Biochem Dept 332 MC-0340 9500 Gilman Dr La Jolla CA 92093-0340 Office Phone: 858-534-5559. E-mail: rcontinetti@ucsd.edu.

CONTINO, FRANCIS A., food products executive; Exec. v.p. strategy & planning, CFO McCormick & Co., Inc., Sparks, Md., 1998—. Bd. dir. Mettler Toledo. Bd. mem. B&O Railroad Mus. Office: McCormick & Company Inc 18 Loveton Cir Sparks Glencoe MD 21152

CONTIS, GEORGE, medical products executive; MD, MPH. Pres. Med. Svc. Corp. Internat. Address: 1716 Wilson Blvd Arlington VA 22209-2504

CONTORNO, MICHAEL, lawyer; b. Birmingham, Ala., Feb. 27, 1956; s. Paul Anthony and Virginia C BSc, Spring Hill Coll., Mobile, Ala., 1978; JD, Loyola U., New Orleans, 1981; LLM in Tax, Boston U., 1987. Bar: Ala. 1981, La. 1982, Tex. 2002. Petroleum landman Amoco Prodn. Co., New Orleans, 1981-86; assoc. Lange, Simpson, Robinson & Somerville, Birmingham, 1987-88; tax atty. Amoco Corp., Chgo., 1989-92; atty. Prudential, Houston, 1992-94; with Brit. Airways, Houston, 1995-97; assoc. gen. counsel ICO, Inc., Houston, 1997-2000; corp./tax atty. Stanford Fin. Group, 2000—. Home: 2609 Hopkins St Houston TX 77006 Office: Stanford Fin Group 5050 Westheimer Rd Houston TX 77056 Office Phone: 713-964-5134.

CONTRACTOR, FAROK, business and management educator; b. Bombay, Dec. 24, 1946; arrived in US, 1967; s. Jamshed Phirozshaw and Hilla C. Contractor; children: Cyrus, Sahm, Eric. BSME, U. Bombay, 1967; MS in Indsl. Engring., U. Mich., 1968; MBA, U. Pa., 1977, PhD in Managerial Sci. and Applied Econs., 1980. Staff indsl. engr. Max Factor, Inc., L.A., 1969; rsch. fellow U. Mich., Ann Arbor, 1969-70; exec. officer, asst. to mng. dir. TATA Group subs. TATA Adminstrv. Svcs., India, 1970-74; asst. instr. bus. and mgmt. Wharton Sch. Bus., U. Pa., Phila., 1975-77, instr., 1977-80; assoc. prof. Grad. Sch. Mgmt., Rutgers U., Newark and Piscataway, N.J., 1980-90, prof. internat. bus., 1991—, chmn. internat. bus. dept., 1986-88, 90-93. Lectr. Wharton Sch. Bus., U. Pa., 1985-86; vis. scholar UN Ctr. on Transnat. Corps., N.Y., fall 1988; mem. Internat. Bus. Inst., Rutgers U., 1986—, rsch. dir. CIBER, 1997-99, com. mem., 1980-90; NSF reviewer, 1980, 84, 94; organizer, co-chmn. joint conf. on coop. ventures in internat. bus. Rutgers U. and Wharton Sch. Bus., U. Pa., 1986, co-chmn. conf. on coop. strategies and alliances, Lausanne, Switzerland, 2001; licensing and tech. transfer agreements cons.; Unilever Group vis. fellow, vis. prof. Indian Inst. Fgn. Trade, New Delhi, spring 1994; vis. prof. Copenhagen Bus. Sch., 1995, Lubin Sch. Pace U., 1997, Fletcher Sch. Law and Diplomacy, Tufts U., 2000; presenter in field. Author: International Technology Licensing: Compensation, Costs and Negotiation, 1981, Licensing In International Strategy: A Guide for Planning and Negotiation, 1985, Government Policies And Foreign Direct Investment, 1991, Cooperative Strategies in International Business, 1988, Economic Transformation in Emerging Countries: The Role of Investment, Trade and Finance, 1998, the Valuation of Intangible Assets in Global Operations, 2001, Cooperative Strategies and Alliances, 2003, others; co-author: Introduction to International Business, 1986. Grantee, The German Marshall Fund of U.S., 1986, Carnegie Bosch Found., 1996—98; Esmee Fairbairn fellow, U. Reading, Eng., 1982, Fulbright fellow, 1991—92. Fellow Acad. Internat. Bus. (bd. dirs., sec.-treas. 1992-94); mem. Licensing Execs. Soc., Acad. Mgmt. (exec. bd. 1997—2002, pre-conf. workshop chair San Diego meeting 1998, program chmn. Chgo. meeting 1999, pres. internat. mgmt. divsn. 2000—), European Internat. Bus. Assn., Zoroastrian Assn. Greater N.Y., Internat. Trade and Fin. Assn. (bd. dirs. 1995-97). Avocations: antique restoration, skiing, trekking, canoeing, interior design. Office: Rutgers Univ Sch Mgmt 81 New St Newark NJ 07102 Office Phone: 973-353-8348.

CONTRENI, JOHN JOSEPH, JR., humanities educator; b. Savannah, Ga., Aug. 31, 1944; s. John Joseph Sr. and Elfriede Johanna (Hille) C.; m. Margarita Lee Partridge, July 3, 1986; children: Judith, Rachel, Daniel, Maureen, Jennifer Rogers, Paul Rogers. BA, St. Vincent Coll., 1966, HHD (hon.), 1996; PhD, Mich. State U., 1971. From asst. prof. to prof. history Purdue U., West Lafayette, Ind., 1971—, head dept. history, 1985-97, asst. dean Sch. Humanities, Social Sci. and Edn., 1981-85, interim head dept. fgn. langs. and lits., 1983—85; interim dean Grad. Sch., 2002—04, dean, 2004—. Pres. Midwest Medieval Conf., 1980-81. Author: The Cathedral School of Laon from 850 to 930: Its Manuscripts and Masters, 1978, (John Nicholas Brown prize 1982), Codex Laudunensis 468: A Ninth-Century Guide to Virgil, Sedulius, and the Liberal Arts, 1984; co-author: Glossae Divinae Historiae: The Biblical Glosses of John Scottus Eriugena, 1997: translator: Education and Culture in the Barbarian West, Sixth Through Eighth Centuries (Pierre Riché), 1976, Carolingian Learning, Masters, and Manuscripts, 1992; co-editor: Religion, Culture, and Society in the Early Middle Ages: Studies in Honor of Richard E. Sullivan, 1987, French Historical Studies, 1991-2000, Word, Image, Number: Communication in the Middle Ages, 2002; mem. editl. bd. Internat. History Rev., 2001-03; contbr. articles to profl. jours. and chpts. to books. Pres., bd. trustees Brookston-Prairie Twp. Pub. Libr., 1995-01. Grantee Am. Philos. Soc., 1973, 76, 82, 86, NEH, 1973, 86, Am. Coun. Learned Socs., 1975, 77-79, 83, 89, Purdue U., 1973, 75-76, 81, 83, 89, 99. Mem. Soc. for Promotion Eriugenian Studies, Medieval Acad. of Am. (councillor 1987-90, grantee 1973, fellow, 2003), Phi Beta Kappa. Home: 504 W 5th St Brookston IN 47923-8100 Office: Purdue Univ Grad Sch Young Hall 302 Wood St West Lafayette IN 47907-2108 E-mail: contreni@purdue.edu.

CONTRERAS, CARLOS ARTURO, history professor; b. Morazon, Honduras, Feb. 16, 1922; s. Jose Del Carmen Contreras and Guillermina Zuniga; m. Hada Margot Lopez, Aug. 26, 1989. BA, Brigham Young U., Provo, Utah, 1955; MA, UCLA, 1964, PhD, 1972. History prof. Calif. State U., L.A., 1967—68, Fresno, 1968—92. Mem. editl. adv. bd. Collegiate Press, San Diego. Author: Entre El Marasmo: Crisis Del Partio Liberal, 1970; contbr. articles to profl. jours. Recipient Loyalty in Action award, Paralyzed Veterans Am., 1981. Mem.: Medieval Acad. Am., Am. Hist. Assn., Commanders' Club, Disable Am. Veterans. Avocations: piano, gardening, carpentry. Home: 9 W Norwich Clovis CA 93612

CONTRERAS, FRANK R., musician; s. Francisco Javier Contreras and Arquelina Rodríquez Elorriaga. MusB, Millikin U., 1965; MusM, E. Carolina U., 1966; D in Musical Arts (fellow 1970-73), W.Va. U., 1977. Instr. piano Millikin U., Decatur, Ill., 1966—67, Alderson Broaddus Coll., Phillippi, W.Va., 1973—76, U. Ala., Huntsville, 1977—94, Oakwood Coll., Huntsville, 2000—. Tchr. Colors Fine Arts Ctr. Musician (pianist): Huntsville Symphony, Pitts. Symphony, E. Carolina U. Symphony, W.Va. Symphony, W. N.Mex U. Symphony. Organist 1st Presbyn. Ch., Huntsville, 1988—, Temple B'Nai Shalom, Huntsville, 1994—. With U.S. Army, 1968—69, Vietnam. Recipient Anne M. Gannett award, Nat. Fed. Music Clubs, 1970. Mem.: Am. Guild Organists, Am. Fedn. Musicians, Nat. Guild Piano Tchrs. (adjudicator). Democrat. Episcopalian. Avocations: history, literature, travel. Home: 4312 Chalet Cir Huntsville AL 35810 Office: 1st Presbyn Ch 307 Gates Ave Huntsville AL 35801

CONVERSE, ELIZABETH, artist, writer; b. Springfield, Ill., Jan. 17, 1946; d. Frank Thomas and Frances Converse (Deal) Sheets; m. Daniel B. A. Richter, Apr. 12, 1979 (div. Mar. 1996); children: William, Joan Clair; m. Eddie Truman, June 2002. BA in Anthropology, Lake Forest Coll., 1964-67; student Writing Ctr., Sarah Lawrence Coll., N.Y.C., 1991; MA in Human Devel., Pacific Oaks Coll., 1999. Cert. multiple-subject tchr., Calif. Tchr., enrichment program Washington Accelerated Sch. Anthropol. field worker, interviewer NIMH, Chgo., 1967-70; v.p., creative dir. Prodn. Sys., Inc., N.Y.C., 1984-89; with The Light/Bright Project at youth activity ctrs.; exec. dir. Calif. Living Histories, 1999-2002; mem. We 7 Collaborative. Performer Absolute Reality Theatre, N.Y.C., The Bridge Collective, N.Y.C., The Performance Group, N.Y.C., 1971-78; dir. Whitney Counterweight, N.Y.C., 1971-78; dir. Uto Theatrical Experiment, N.Y.C., 1971-78; writer, dir., actor: (short film) Mercy, 1971-78; prodr., writer, actor: (ind. film) Alexyx, 1978-83; works included in publs. Artweek, Visions, Pasadena Weekly, L.A. Reader, mus. and galleries; author: (fiction) The Pursuit of Happiness, The Clearing, Imbroglio, Wild Thing, Dust and Gold, The Citadel, Stories for Our Times, Our Dream; exhibited in group shows Pierce Coll., Sierra Madre Libr., SouthBay Contemporary Mus., Restaurant Lozano, The Armory, Pasadena; commns. include Susan Chen, Above the Rest, Jim Grancich, Carol Tannenbaum, Judy Webb-Martin, Little Stuga, Eddie Truman, City of Sierra Madre, Dopkins Chapel, Lozano Restaurant; mural project for Mayor Riordan's Office, L.A., 2000. Chair Gooden Sch. Silent Auction, Sierra Madre, Calif., 1992, Harvest Ball Silent Auction, Greenwich, Conn., 1987. Avocations: bicycling, gardening, horse racing, travel. Home: 851 Woodland Dr Sierra Madre CA 91024-1449

CONVERSE, PHILIP ERNEST, social sciences educator; b. Concord, N.H., Nov. 17, 1928; s. Ernest Luther and Evelyn (Eaton) C.; m. Jean Gilmore McDonnell, Aug. 25, 1951; children: Peter Everett, Timothy McDonnell. BA, Denison U., 1949, DHL (hon.), 1974; MA, State U. Iowa, 1950; cert., U. Paris, 1954; MA, U. Mich., 1956, PhD, 1958; DHL (hon.), U. Chgo., 1979. Asst. prof. sociology U. Mich., 1960-65, prof. sociology and polit. sci., 1965-89, Robert C. Angell Disting. prof., 1975-89. Asst. study dir. Inst. Social Rsch. U. Mich., 1956-58, study dir., 1958-65, program dir., 1965-82, dir. Ctr. for Polit. Studies, 1982-86, dir. Inst. Social Rsch., 1986-89; dir. Ctr. Advanced Study in Behavioral Scis., 1989-94; trustee Ctr. Advanced Study in Behavioral Scis., 1980-86, 94-2000, Russell Sage Found., 1982-92. Co-author: The American Voter, 1960, Elections and the Political Order, 1966, The Human Meaning of Social Change, 1972, The Quality of American Life, 1976, Political Representation in France, 1986; contbr. articles to profl. jours. Served with U.S. Army, 1950-52. Recipient Disting. Faculty Achievement award U. Mich., 1973; Fulbright fellow, 1959-60; NSF fellow, 1967-68; Guggenheim fellow, 1975-76; Ctr. Advanced Study in Behavioral Scis. fellow, 1979-80 Mem. AAAS, Am. Sociol. Assn., Am. Polit. Sci. Assn. (pres. 1983-84), Internat. Soc. Polit. Psychology (pres. 1980-81), Nat. Acad. Scis., Am. Acad. Arts and Scis., Am. Philos. Soc. Home: 9 Haverhill Ct Ann Arbor MI 48105-1406

CONVERSE, SANDRA, city finance director, financial planner; b. Galion, Ohio, July 23, 1949; d. Mervin E. Harper and Phyllis R. Bowden (dec.); m. Robert W. Marsh, June 19, 2001; children: Kimberly Spencer, Kelly Converse. Payroll clk. Neighborhood Youth Corps., Mansfield, Ohio, 1977-78; asst. fin. dir. Mansfield City, 1978-93, fin. dir., 1993—. Charter commn. mem. City of Mansfield, 1988. Mem. NAFE, La. Edn. Assn., Govt. Fin. Officers Assn. U.S. and Can., Mcpl. Treas. Assn. U.S. and Can., Nat. Assn. Tax Preparers, Ohio Govt. Fin. Officers Assn., Mcpl. Fin. Officers Assn. Ohio (at-large bd. mem.). Democrat. Pentecostal. Avocations: reading, learning, sewing, painting. Office: City of Mansfield 30 N Diamond St Mansfield OH 44902-1738 Home: 155 W Prospect St Mansfield OH 44907-1305 Office Phone: 419-755-9775. E-mail: sconverse@CI.mansfield.oh.us.

CONVERY, ROBERT, composer, educator; b. Wichita, Kans., Oct. 4, 1954; AA, Franklin Coll., Lugane, Switzerland, 1976; MusB in Music Edn., Westminster Choir Coll., Princeton, NJ, 1980; MusB in Composition, Curtis Inst. Music, Phila., 1983; MusM in Composition, Juilliard Sch., NYC, 1985, D in Musical Arts in Composition, 1992. Music faculty Dickinson Coll., Carlisle, Pa., 1989—90, composer resident; artistic adminstr. Spoleto Festival USA, Charleston, 1994—95; music faculty Coll. Charleston, SC, 1996—97; artist resident YADDO, Rockefeller Found. Study Ctr., Bellagio, Italy; composer resident Phillips Exeter Acad., NY Concert Singers. Adj. instr. Juilliard Sch., Columbia U. Composer: I Have a Dream, 1986, Songs of Children, 1991, Clara, 2004, Variations and Fugue, Elegy for Strings, Organ Concerto, Mass, Pyramus and Thisbe, The Nativity of Our Lord, The Passion of Lizzie. Recipient Charles Ives award, Am. Acad. and Inst. Arts and Letters, NYC, 1983, Meet the Composer award, ASCAP award, Samuel Barber award. Home: 37-27 Crescent St #51 Long Island City NY 11101

CONVEY, JOHN J., academic administrator; Provost Cath. U. Am., Washington. Author: Catholic Schools Make a Difference: Twenty-Five Years of Research, 1992, Catholic Schools Still Make a Difference: Ten Years of Research, 1991-2000, 2002; co-author: Catholic Schools and Society, 1991, Strategic Planning for Catholic Schools: A Diocesan Model of Consultation, 1996, Benchmarks of Excellence: Effective Boards of Catholic Education, 1997, Assessment of Catholic Religious Education Weaving Christ's Seamless Garment, 1999, Catholic Schools at the Crossroads: Survival and Transformation, 2000; co-editor: Catholic Character of Catholic Schools, 2000. Office: Provost 103 McMahon Hall The Cath Univ Am Washington DC 20064

CONVEY, KEVIN R., editor; b. Medford, Mass. m. Kathleen Convey; children: Eamon, Mairead. Grad., Colby Coll., 1977. Reporter Times Record, Brunswick, Maine, Std. Times, New Bedford, Mass.; bus. reporter Boston Herald Am. (predecessor of Boston Herald), 1981; reporter State House bur. Boston Herald, city editor, asst. mng. editor, 1984, Sunday editor, exec. city editor, 1990—94, mng. editor, 2004—; articles editor Boston Mag., 1987—90; editor-in-chief Herald Media, Needham, Mass., 2001—04. Office: Boston Herald One Herald Sq PO Box 2096 Boston MA 02106

CONWAY, CONNIE ANNE See HELLYER, CONSTANCE

CONWAY, CRAIG A., former computer software company executive; b. Ft. Wayne, Ind., Oct. 17, 1954; m. Tina Conway; 2 children. BS in Math. & Computer Sci., SUNY, Brockton, 1976. Applications cons. Tymeshare, 1976—79; with Atari, 1979—83; dir. worldwide distbn. Digital Research, 1983—85; exec. v.p. mktg., sales & ops. Oracle Corp., 1985—93; pres., CEO TGV Software, Inc., 1993—96, OneTouch Systems., 1996—99; pres., COO

PeopleSoft Inc., Pleasanton, Calif., 1999, pres., CEO, 1999—2004. Bd. dirs. Aspect Telecomm. Corp., SalesLogix Corp. Recipient Cap Gemini Ernst & Young Leadership award for Global Integration, 2002.

CONWAY, DANIEL EDWARD, management consultant; b. L.A., Nov. 5, 1940; s. Daniel Edward and Kathryn Lenora C.; m. Lise Lapointe Conway, Nov. 12, 2004; children: Daniel E. III, Patrick A., Charlotte J. BA, U. Md., 1962, MA, 1964, postgrad., 1969; cert., U. Geneva, 1964; diploma, Ctrl. Am. Inst. Trade Union Studies, San Pedro Sula, Honduras, 1966. Spl. asst. to dep. dir. gen. adminstrn. Internat. Labor Orgn., Geneva, 1974-78; divsn. chief office of personnel Orgn. of Am. States, Washington, 1978-79; chief personnel Internat. Civil Aviation Orgn., Montreal, Can., 1979-83; head personnel svcs., spl. advisor to high commr. UN High Commr. for Refugees, Geneva, 1984-89, rep. Ankara, Turkey, 1989-91, Bangkok, Thailand, 1991-93, dir. human resources mgmt. Geneva, 1993-95; dir. ctrl. adminstrn. MIGA/World Bank Group, Washington, 1995-99; internat. cons. Conway Group Internat., Carlsbad, Calif., 1999—. Asst. inspector San Diego County Bd. Elections, Carlsbad, Calif., 1999. Grantee J. Frederick Brown Found., 1963, 65. Mem. Internat. Who's Who of Profl. Mgmt., Inst. for Internat. Human Resources, Assn. for Human Resources Mgmt. in Internat. Orgns., Acad. of Polit. Sci. Avocations: historical studies, model railroads, travel. Home: 3211 Celinda Dr Carlsbad CA 92008 E-mail: conwaycgi@aol.com.

CONWAY, DAVID ANTONY, marketing professional; b. N.Y.C., Dec. 31, 1941; s. David A. and Elizabeth (Reidy) C.; m. Rosanne Kearney, July 30, 1966; children: Jennifer Stanton, Caroline Sloane. BS in Econs., Fordham Coll., 1963, MS in Econs., 1965. With Allied Chem. Corp., N.Y.C., 1967-68, CBS, Inc., N.Y.C., 1968-75, Goldman Sachs & Co., N.Y.C., 1975-76; v.p. adminstrn. Keene Corp., N.Y.C., 1976-86; v.p. adminstrn., bd. dirs. KDI Corp., Cin., 1986-93; pres. Modern Edn. Svcs., N.Y.C., 1994-97; pres., CEO WaterChef, Inc., Glen Head, NY, 1998—, also chmn. bd. dirs. 1st lt. U.S. Army, 1965-67. Mem. Manhasset Bay Yacht Club (Port Washington, N.Y.). Republican. Roman Catholic. Office: WaterChef Inc 1007 Glen Cove Ave Glen Head NY 11545-1589 Personal E-mail: conway@waterchef.net.

CONWAY, DWIGHT COLBUR, chemistry professor; b. Long Beach, Calif., Nov. 14, 1930; s. Dee A. and Ruth (Mills) Conway; m. Diane Faye Coulter, Aug. 25, 1962; children: Kathleen Conway Jurell, Karyn Conway Hasselbrinck, Michael Dwight, Patrick Hugh. BS, U. Calif. at Berkeley, 1952; MS, U. Chgo., 1953, PhD, 1956. Postdoctoral student Purdue U., West Lafayette, Ind., 1956-57, asst. prof., 1957-63; assoc. prof. chemistry Tex. A.&M. U., College Station, 1963-67, prof., 1967—. Recipient Excellence in Tchg. award, Std. Oil Co. of Ind., 1969, Disting. Achievement award, Assn. of Former Students, 2003; fellow, U.S. Rubber Co., 1953—54; DuPont tchg. fellow, 1954—55. Mem. Am. Chem. Soc. (chmn. local chpt.), Am. Phys. Soc., Am. Soc. Mass Spectrometry, Phi Beta Kappa, Sigma Xi (pres. local chpt.), Alpha Chi Sigma. Home: 1909 Bee Creek Dr College Station TX 77840-4871 Office: Tex A&M U Dept Chemistry College Station TX 77843-3255 Business E-Mail: conway@mail.chem.tamu.edu.

CONWAY, E. VIRGIL, financial consultant, lawyer; b. Southhampton, N.Y., Aug. 2, 1929; m. Elaine Wingate, June 28, 1969; children: Allison, Sarah, William, John. BA in Philosophy and Religion magna cum laude, Colgate U., 1951; LLB cum laude, Yale U., 1956; LLD (hon.), Pace U., 1990; LHD (hon.), SUNY, Stony Brook, 1998; LLD (hon.), Colgate U., 2002. Bar: N.Y. 1956. Assoc. firm Debevoise & Plimpton, N.Y.C., 1956-64; 1st dept. supt. Banks of State N.Y., 1964-67; sec. N.Y. State Banking Bd., 1964-67; exec. v.p. Manhattan Savs. Bank, N.Y.C., 1967-68; vice chmn., bd. dirs. Seamen's Corp., 1986-89; pres., chmn. The Seamen's Bank for Savs., 1969-88; chmn. Rittenhouse Advisors LLC, 2001—. Bd. dirs. Union Pacific Corp., chmn. exec. compensation com., mem. exec. com. 1978-2002; bd. dirs. J.P. Stevens & Co., Inc., 1974-88; trustee, mem. exec. com., chmn. audit com. mut. funds managed by Phoenix Funds, 1990-; dir., mem. audit com. of mut. funds managed by Phoenix Duff & Phelps Funds, 1990-; trustee, mem. exec. com., chmn. exec. devel. & comp. Atlantic Mut. Ins. Co., 1974-2002; trustee, mem. exec., chmn. exec. pers. and pension coms. Consol. Edison Co. of N.Y., 1970-2002; trustee, chmn. compensation com., mem. exec. com. Urstadt Biddle Property Co., 1989—; adv. dir. Blackrock BFM, Freddie Mac Securities Mortgage Fund, 1968-2001; N.Y. rep. Conf. of State Bank Suprs., 1970-77, mem. adv. coun., 1973-74, mem. adv. com. to N.Y. State Supt. Banks, 1967-70; chmn. Fin. Acct. Standards Adv. Coun., 1992-1995; adv. dir. Fund Directions; dir. chmn. comp. com. Trism, Inc., 1995-2001; dir., mem. exec. com., audit com., chmn. stock option com. Accuhealth, Inc., 1995-2002. Editor: Yale Law Jour. Mem. Met. Transp. Authority, chmn. audit and real estate coms., mem. Metro North L.I. R.R. and N.Y.C. Transit coms., 1992-95; chmn. Met. Transp. Authority, L.I. R.R., Metro North, Transit Authority of City of N.Y., Triborough Bridge and Tunnel Authority, 1995-2001; chmn. Temporary State Commn. on Water Supply Needs of Southeastern N.Y., 1970-75; mem. Audit Com. N.Y.C., 1981-1996, chmn., 1990-1996, Mayor's Mgmt. Adv. Bd., N.Y.C., 1975-77; mem., chmn. meml. design com. N.Y.C. Korean Vets. Meml. Commn.; del. Rep. State Conv. N.Y., 1962, 66; pres. N.Y. Young Rep. Club, 1962-63; mem. adv. bd. N.Y. U. Real Estate Inst.; bd. dirs. Realty Found. N.Y.; bd. dirs., chmn. audit, fin., exec. coms. Josiah Macy, Jr. Found.; trustee, former vice chmn., mem. exec. com. Citizens Budget Commn.; life trustee N.Y.C. Police Found., Pace U., N.Y.C., Colgate U.; trustee N.Y. coun. Boy Scouts Am.; hon. life trustee South Street Seaport Mus.; bd. govs., pres. Fed. Hall Meml. Assos., Inc., 1981-84; bd. dirs., vice chmn, treas., mem. audit and fin., compensation, project planning and pub. policy com., N.Y.C. Partnership, Inc., 1980-91, hon. ptnr., 1991—; elder Reformed Ch. of Bronxville. Recipient Humanitarian award Jewish Hosp. and Rsch. Ctr., Denver, 1977, Good Scout award Greater N.Y. couns. Boy Scouts Am., 1980, Spl. Recognition award NAACP, 1980, Disting. Svc. to Higher Edn. medal Brandeis U., 1976, Urban Leadership award NYU, 1981, Hundred Yr. Assn. Gold Medal award, 1986, Eagle Scout award, 1988, Silver Beaver award Boy Scouts Am., 1989, Alexander Hamilton award Bowling Green Assn., Disting. Svc. award Bklyn. Bur. Cmty. Svc., 1995, Family of Yr. award Family Svc. Westchester, Inc., 1996, Norman Vincent Peale award, Insts. Religion and Health, 1998, Ellis Island medal of honor, Nat. Ethnic Coalition, 1998; Gov.'s Parks and Preservation award, 1999, March of Dimes Svc. to Humanity award, 2000, Urban Visionaries award, Cooper Union, 2002, Hudson Valley Hero's award, Historic Hudson Valley, 1998.; named Man of Yr. Realty Found. N.Y., 1978. Mem. ABA, N.Y. State Bar Assn., Assn. of Bar of City of N.Y., Nat. Assn. Mut. Savs. Banks (past dir.), Savs. Banks Assn. N.Y. State (pres. 1978-79, past dir. and chmn. legis.), N.Y. C. of C. and Industry (bd. dirs., exec. com., sec.-treas. 1974-91, chmn. mission rev. com. 1985), Real Estate Bd. N.Y. (bd. govs. 1976-79), Econ. Club N.Y., Knights of St. Patrick (bd. dirs., co-chmn.), Union League Club, Links Club, Siwanoy Country Club, Phi Beta Kappa. Office: 101 Park Ave Rm 2500 New York NY 10178-3099 Office Phone: 212-808-7155.

CONWAY, EARL CRANSTON, business educator, retired manufacturing company executive, educator; b. Asbury Park, N.J., Nov. 14, 1931; s. Earl Cranston and Alda Evelyn (Hendrickson) C.; m. Nancy Lou Schucker, Oct. 23, 1954; children: Karen Marie, Anne Margaret, Earl Edward, Nancy Maureen. BA in Polit. Sci. and Internat. Rels., U. Pa., Phila., 1954. Sales-mktg. rep. Procter & Gamble, Phila., 1957-59, unit mgr. Balt. and Chgo., 1960-64, dist. mgr. Minn., Pa., 1964-69, divsn. mgr., nat. sales mgr. Cin., 1970-81, gen. sales mgr. Europe Brussels, 1981-85, corp. dir. worldwide quality Cin., 1985-92; pres., COO Innovative Food Technology, Inc., 1998-99. Co-chmn. U.S. Quality Coun. of Conf. Bd., N.Y.C., 1989-92; adj. prof. U. Cin., 1990-2005; adj. faculty Indian River C.C., Indian River County, Fla., 1996-99; lectr. quality and strategic planning Ministry of Light Industry, Hong Kong, Shanghai, Guangzhou and Wuxi, Peoples Republic of China, 1992—, Moscow and Kirov, Russia, 1994—; vis. lectr. bus. and engring. schs.; advisor quality mgmt. V.P. Gore, U.S. and Gov. Jim Hunt, N.C., 1992-93, 93-94. Vice chmn. nat. bd. dirs. Vols. of Am., New Orleans, 1991-96; mem., bd. trustees Ursuline Acad., Cin., 1992-93; mem. planning and zoning bd. City of Vero Beach, Fla., 1995-99; bd. dirs. Civic Assn., Indian River County, Fla., Vero Beach, Fla., 1995—; vice chmn., bd. dirs. Indian River Meml. Hosp., Indian River County, 1999-2004. 1st lt., inf. U.S. Army, 1955-56. Recipient Taguchi Quality Engring. award Am. Supplier Inst., 1989, Recognition by Ministry of Light Industry, People's Republic of China, Guangzhou and Wuxi, 1992-93. Mem. Am. Soc. Quality. Republican. Roman Catholic. Home: 1020 Olde Doubloon Dr Vero Beach FL 32963-2449

CONWAY, EVELYN ATKINSON, accountant, financial analyst; b. Goose Creek, Tex., Aug. 14, 1922; d. George Henry and Sadie Ray (Bouldin) Atkinson; m. Lucian Gideon Conway, Nov. 2, 1945; children: Lucian Gideon Conway Jr., Karen Elizabeth Conway, Rebecca Annette Conway, Terri Ruth Conway, Jerry Andrew Conway, Priscilla Janice Conway. BS in Acctg., La. Tech. U., 1943; postgrad., New Orleans Bapt. Theol. Sem., 1949—51. Sr. acct. McGuire & Mazur CPAs, Houston, 1943—45; math. tchr. Enterprise Sch., Summit, Miss., 1953—54; sr. ptnr. Conley & Conway, Coushatta, La., 1955—56; office mgr. Annuity Bd. Rep. SBC, Alexandria, La., 1959—83; regional mgr., pers. fin. analyst Primerica Life & PFS Investments, Inc., Alexandria, La., 1984—. Auditor The Bapt. Message, Alexandria, 1962—64. Emergency evacuation officer Civil Def., Coushatta, 1955—57; treas. Dist. 8 La. Bapt. Missions, Coushatta, 1955—56. Named Hometown All Am., Alexandria Daily Town Talk, 1995. Republican. Baptist. Avocations: sewing, music. Home: 118 Pearce Rd Pineville LA 71360

CONWAY, FRENCH HOGE, lawyer; b. Danville, Va., June 11, 1918; s. Lysander Broadus and Mildred (Hoge) C.; BS, U. Va., 1942, JD, 1946; m. Louise Throckmorton, Feb. 3, 1961; children: French Hoge Jr., William Chenery, Helen (Mrs. Carlton Bedsole), Donna F. LeFevers. Bar: Va. 1942. Sole practice, Danville, 1942—; mem. firm Clement, Conway & Winston, 1950-60. Sec., Danville City Bd. Rev., 1985—; v.p. Va. Election Bd. Assn., 1974. Served with USNR, 1942-46. Mem. ABA, Va. Bar Assn., Danville Bar Assn. (pres. 1985-86), Am. Trial Lawyers Assn., Va. Trial Lawyers Assn., Soc. Cincinnati in State of Va., Ret. Officers Assn., Boat Owners Assn. U.S. Lodges: Kiwanis, Masons. Office: 105 S Union St Danville VA 24541-1113 Home: 410 Maple Ln Danville VA 24541-3532

CONWAY, GEORGE A., medical epidemiologist, physician; MD, U. N.Mex., 1985; MPH, U. S.C., 1988. Bd. cert. pub. health and gen. preventive medicine Am. Bd. Preventive Medicine, 1990, cert. aviation med. examiner FAA (USA), 2000. Chief Alaska field sta. Centers for Disease Control/Nat. Inst. for Occupl. Safety and Health, Anchorage. Contbr. articles to profl. jours. Office: CDC/NIOSH Alaska Field Station Ste 310 4230 University Dr Anchorage AK 99508 Office Phone: 1-907-271-5249. Office Fax: 1-907-271-2390. E-mail: gconway@cdc.gov.

CONWAY, HOBART MCKINLEY, JR., futurist; b. Hackleburg, Ala., Nov. 1, 1920; s. Hobart McKinley and Eva (Kelly) C.; m. Rebecca Warner Kellam, Sept. 17, 1942; children: Linda, Laura. BS, Ga. Inst. Tech., 1940, BA in Engring., 1941. Rsch. engr. NASA, 1941-44, 46-47; dir. So. Assn. Sci. and Industry, Atlanta, 1948-53; pres. Conway Rsch., Inc., Atlanta, 1954—; dir. Sitenet, 1983—. Mem. U.S. Devel. Mission to S.E. Asia, 1962; cons. AID, 1963-68; chmn. Ga. Sci. and Tech. Commn., 1965-66, Caracas Interam. Devel. Seminar; indsl. devel. cons., 15 countries. Editor: Indsl. Devel. mag, 1954-64, Site Selection Handbook, 1954-64, Weather Handbook, 1974, Industrial Facility Planning, 1976, Industrial Park Growth, 1979, Site Net World Guide, 1988—; editor Site World, 1990, 92; author: The Airport City, 1977, 93, Pitfalls in Development, 1978, Marketing Industrial Buildings and Sites, 1980, Disaster Survival, 1981, The Good Life Index, 1981, Facility Planning Technology, 1987, A Glimpse of the Future, 1992, Geo-Economics, The New Science, 1994, The Telcom Coup, 1994, Development Highlights of the Twentieth Century, 1997, Three Tomorrows, 2002; also rsch. reports on facilities planning. Mem. Ga. Senate from 41st Dist., 1963-64, 67-68; sponsor The Safe Skies award, 1989—. With USNR, 1944-46. Recipient medal Time mag., 1953 Fellow AAAS; mem. World Devel. Fedn. (chmn.), Internat. Devel. Rsch. Coun. (founder, dir., recipient award 1979), Aircraft Owners and Pilots Assn. Methodist. Office: Conway Data Inc 6625 The Corners Pky Ste 200 Norcross GA 30092 Home: 10952 Country Road 320 #3 Micanopy FL 32667

CONWAY, JAMES CLAUDE, periodontist; b. Raven Run, Pa., June 24, 1920; s. Patrick Joseph and Maude (Hoats) C.; m. Elizabeth Jane Davenport, June 7, 1947; children: Timothy Patrick, Deborah Ann. BS in Edn., Kutztown (Pa.) U., 1943; DDS, Georgetown U., 1950; BS, Baylor U., 1957; MS in Edn., U. Pitts., 1977. Diplomate Am. Bd. Periodontology. Asst. assoc. prof. dept. periodontics U. Pitts., 1967-76, chmn. dept. periodontics, 1976-87, assoc. chmn. dept. periodontics, 1987-90, vol. faculty dept. periodontics, 1990—, prof. emeritus, 1991—. Cons. Coun. on Dental Edn., 1975-81, VA Hosp., Butler, Pitts., 1975-90, Commn. on Accreditation, Pitts., 1975-80. Contbr. articles to profl. jours. Lt. col. U.S. Army, 1942-45, 49-67. Fellow Am. Coll. Dentistry, Internat. Coll. Dentistry; mem. ADA, Am. Acad. Periodontology. Republican. Roman Catholic. Avocation: model building. Home: 4051 Tall Timber Dr Allison Park PA 15101-3043

CONWAY, JAMES HYDE, pediatrician, educator; s. James A. and Linda Hyde Conway; m. Katherine Elizabeth Trace, June 2, 1990. MD, Cornell U., 1990. Diplomate Am. Bd. Pediat., Am. Bd. Pediat. Infectious Disease 1997. Resident pediat. Northwestern U., Chgo., 1990—93; fellow pediat. infectious disease U. Colo. Health Scis. Ctr., Denver, 1994—97; assoc. prof. clin. pediat. Ind. U. Sch. Medicine, Indpls., 1997—. Recipient Trustees Tchg. award, Ind. U., 2001. Fellow: Am. Acad. Pediat. Office: 600 Highland Ave H4/4 CSC Madison WI 53792-4108

CONWAY, JAMES JOSEPH, radiologist, educator; b. Chgo., July 1, 1933; s. Frank and Mary (Tuohy) Conway; m. Dolores Mazer, June 30, 1956; children: Laurie, John, Cheryl. BS, DePaul U., 1959; MD, Northwestern U., 1963. Asst. instr. U. Pa., 1964—68; assoc. in radiology McGaw Med. Ctr. Northwestern U., Chgo., 1968—71, asst. prof. to assoc. prof. radiology, 1974—80; attendant radiology Children's Meml. Hosp., Chgo., 1968—98, prof. radiology, 1980—. Contbr. articles over 110 to profl. jours. With U.S. Army, 1953—55. Recipient Gold medal, Chgo. Radiol. Soc., 1993, Scroll of Appreciation award, Radiol. Soc. N.Am., 1983. Fellow: Am. Coll. Radiology, Am. Coll. Nuc. Physicians, P.R. Soc. Nuc. Medicine (hon.); mem.: Soc. Nuclear Medicine (pres. 1994—95). Avocation: collector of Chicago memorabilia. Office: Childrens Meml Hosp 2300 N Childrens Plz Chicago IL 60614-3394 Personal E-mail: nukedr@comcast.net.

CONWAY, JOHN E., federal judge; b. 1934; BS, U.S. Naval Acad., 1956; LLB magna cum laude, Washburn U., 1963. Assoc. Matias A Zamora, Santa Fe, 1963-64; ptnr. Wilkinson, Durrett & Conway, Alamogordo, N.Mex., 1964-67, Durrett, Conway & Jordon, Alamogordo, 1967-80, Montgomery & Andrews, P.A., Albuquerque, 1980-86; city atty. Alamogordo, 1966-72; mem. N.Mex. State Senate, 1970-80, minority leader, 1972-80; chief fed. judge U.S. Dist. Ct. N.Mex., Albuquerque, 1994—2000, sr. fed. judge, 2000—. Mem. Jud. Resources Com., 1995—98. 1st lt. USAF, 1956-60. Mem. 10th Cir. Dist. Judges Assn. (pres. 1995-98), Fed. Judges Assn. (bd. dirs. 1996-2001), Nat. Commrs. on Uniform State Laws, N.Mex. Bar Assn., N.Mex. Jud. Coun. (vice chmn. 1973, chmn. 1973-75, disciplinary bd. of Supreme Ct. of N.Mex. vice chmn. 1980, chmn. 1981-84.). Office: US Dist Ct Chambers #740 333 Lomas Blvd NW Albuquerque NM 87102-2272 Office Phone: 505-348-2200. Business E-Mail: jconway@nmcourt.fed.us.

CONWAY, JOHN K., lawyer; Gen. counsel Kemper Ins. Co., Long Grove, Ill. Office: Lumbermens Mutual Casualty Co 1 Kemper Dr Long Grove IL 60049-0001

CONWAY, JOHN S., history professor; b. London, Dec. 31, 1929; s. Geoffrey S. and Elsie (Philips) C.; m. Ann P. Jefferies, Aug. 10, 1957; children— David, Jane, Alison BA, Cambridge U., Eng., 1952; MA, Cambridge U., 1955, PhD, 1956. Asst. prof. U. Man., Can., 1955-57; asst. prof., assoc. prof., then prof. history U. B.C., Vancouver, 1957-94, prof. emeritus, 1995—. Mem. editl. bd. dirs. Holocaust and Genocide Studies, Kirchliche Zeitgeschichte; Smallman Disting. vis. prof. history U. Western On., 1998. Author: The Nazi Persecution of the Churches, 1968, 2d edit., 1997. Contbr. numerous articles on churches and the holocaust to topical publs. Pres. Tibetan Refugee Aid Soc., Can., 1971-81; chmn. Vancouver Coalition with World Refugees, 1982-84. Recipient Queen's Silver Jubilee medal, 1977. Mem. Can. Inst. Internat. Affairs, German Studies Assn., Can. Hist. Assn. Anglican. Home: 4345 Locarno Crescent Vancouver BC Canada V6R 1G2 Office: U BC Dept History East Mall Vancouver BC Canada V6T 1Z1 E-mail: jconway@interchange.ubc.ca.

CONWAY, JOHN THOMAS, federal agency administrator, lawyer, engineer; b. NYC, May 10, 1924; s. John Joseph and Johannah (Stanley) C.; m. Priscilla Harris, Sept. 13, 1947 (div. 1978); children: John, Daniel, Sean, Thomas, Christopher, Johannah; m. Virginia McLaughlin, Mar. 17, 1989. BNS, Tufts U., 1945, BS in Engring., 1947; JD, Columbia U., 1949. Bar: N.Y. 1949, U.S. Supreme Ct. 1952. Spl. agt. FBI, Washington, 1950-56; asst. dir. U.S. Congress Joint Com. on Atomic Energy, Washington, 1956-62, exec. dir., 1962-68; exec. asst. to chmn. Consol. Edison, N.Y.C., 1968-78, exec. v.p., 1982-89; chmn. Def. Nuc. Facilities Safety Bd., Washington, 1989—. Pres. Am. Nuc. Energy Coun., Washington, 1978-82, chmn. bd., 1983-89; bd. dirs. Empire State Energy Rsch. Com., N.Y., 1970-76, Atomic Indsl. Forum, 1976-78; mem. oversight com. U.S. Com. Energy Awareness, Washington, 1982-89. Bd. dirs. Americans for Energy Independence, Washington, 1982-89, Youth for Energy Independence, Washington, 1982-89, Assn. For A Better N.Y., 1982-89, N.Y. Fire Safety Found., 1984-89; mem. N.Y.C. Mayor's Com. for Sci., 1969-76. Lt. (j.g.) USNR, 1943—52. Mem. Am. Legion (life), U.S. Army Ft. Meyer Officer Club, Dem. Club (Washington). Democrat. Roman Catholic. Office: Def Nuc Facilities Safety Bd 625 Indiana Ave NW Ste 700 Washington DC 20004-2909

CONWAY, JOHN W., manufacturing executive; BA in econ., U. Va., 1967; JD, Columbia Law Sch., 1970. Pres. Continental Can Internat. Corp., 1988; sr. v.p. Crown Cork & Seal (acquired Continental Can Internat. Corp.), Phila., 1991-93; exec. v.p., pres. internat. divsn. Crown Cork & Seal, Phila., 1993-96, pres., exec. v.p. Am. divsn., 1997-2001; chmn. bd., pres., CEO Crown Holdings Inc., Phila., 2001—. Bd. dirs. Crown Cork & Seal, Nat. Food Processors Assn., The West Co.; chmn. Can Mfrs. Inst. Office: Crown Cork & Seal 1 Crown Way Philadelphia PA 19154-4599*

CONWAY, KERRY LYNN, retired pilot; b. Laconia, N.H., Dec. 4, 1971; d. James Lester and Donna Lynn Conway. Assoc. Sc. Flight Ops., BA Flight Operation, Daniel Webster Coll., Nashua, N.H., 1999. Food svc. employee USAF, Laconia, NH, 1990—92, missile ops. tech., 1990—92, flight ops., 1992—93, sgt. recreation, 1993—95; airport ops. Houston Airport, Tex., 1999—2002; 2d lt., pilot USAF, Houston, 2002, med. retirement; head fin. Tex. Air Nat. Guard, Houston, 1999—2002. Contbr. poems to Internat. Poetry. Vol. Big Sisters, Big Brothers, Grand Forks, ND, 1992—95. 2d lt. USAF, 1990—2002. Lds. Avocations: hockey, poetry, writing, competitively. Home: 100 Dome Rd Center Tuftonboro NH 03816

CONWAY, KEVIN, actor, performing company executive; b. NYC, May 29, 1942; s. James John C. and Margaret O'Brien; m. Mila Quiros, Apr. 5, 1966. Broadway and Off-Broadway appearances include: Dinner at Eight, Elephant Man, Of Mice and Men, Moonchildren, Red Ryder, One Flew Over the Cuckoo's Nest, Life Class, Other Places, King John, Other People's Money, 1988 (Outer Critics Circle award for best actor, 1989), On the Waterfront, Lawyers; films include: Slaughterhouse Five, Portnoy's Complaint, FIST, Paradise Alley, The Funhouse, Flashpoint, Homeboy, Jesse, One Good Cop, Ramblin Rose, Jennifer 8, Gettysburg, Lawnmower Man II, Whipping Boy, The Quick and the Dead, Rage of Angels, The Scarlet Letter, The Deadliest Season, The Lathe of Heaven, Elephant Man, Something About Amelia, When Will I Be Loved, Breaking the Silence, (miniseries) Mark Twain, Gettysburg, Streets of Laredo, Flamingo Rising, Calm at Sunset, Sally Hemmings, Oz; (films) Black Knight, Gods and Generals, 13 Days, Looking for Richard, Mercury Rising, The Confession, Mystic River, Invincible; (TV) Miami Vice, Law and Order, Jag, Equalizer, Law and Order/Criminal Intent; voice of Mark Twain in Ken Burns Documentary; dir.: (plays) Off-Broadway and Lincoln Ctr. Mecca, Old Flames, Milk Train Doesn't Stop Here, Chgo. and L.A. prodn. Other Peoples Money, 1990; star, dir.: (feature film) The Sun and the Moon, 1985. Bd. dirs. Second Stage Co. Served with USN, 1960-62. Recipient Village Voice Obie award, 1973; recipient Drama Desk award, 1973-74. Mem. Screen Actors Guild (bd. dirs. 1979-81), Nat. Acad. TV Arts and Scis. Home and Office: 25 Central Park W New York NY 10023-7253 Office Phone: 212-582-9235. E-mail: gemicon@aol.com.

CONWAY, LYNN, computer scientist, electrical engineer, educator; b. Mt. Vernon, N.Y., Jan. 2, 1938; BS, Columbia U., 1962, MSEE, 1963; D (hon.), Trinity Coll., 1997. Rsch. staff IBM Corp., Yorktown Heights, N.Y., 1964-68; sr. staff engr. Memorex Corp., Santa Clara, Calif., 1969-73; rsch. staff Xerox Corp., Palo Alto, Calif., 1973-78, rsch. fellow, mgr. VLSI systems area, 1978-82, rsch. fellow, mgr. knowledge systems area, 1982-83; asst. dir. for strategic computing Def. Advanced Research Projects Agy., Arlington, Va., 1983-85; prof. elec. engring. and computer sci., assoc. dean U. Mich. Coll. Engring., Ann Arbor, Mich., 1985—. Vis. assoc. prof. elec. engring. and computer sci. MIT, Cambridge, Mass., 1978-79; sci. adv. bd. USAF, 1987-90. Co-author: textbook Introduction to VLSI Systems, 1980; contbr. articles to profl. jours.; patentee in field. Mem. coun. Govt.-Univ.-Industry Rsch. Roundtable, 1993-98; mem. corp. Charles Stark Draper Lab., 1993—; mem. bd. visitors USAF Acad., 1996-2000, presdl. appt.; mem. Air Force Sci. and Tech. Bd., Nat. Acads., 2000—. Recipient Ann. Achievement award Electronics mag., 1981, Harold Pender award U. Pa., 1984, Wetherill Medal Franklin Inst., 1985, Sec. of Def. Meritorious Civilian Svc. award, 1985. Fellow IEEE; mem. NAE, AAAS, Soc. Women Engrs. (Ann. Achievement award 1990), Assn. Computing Machinery. Avocations: canoeing, natural landscaping, travel. Office: U Mich 152 ATL Bldg Ann Arbor MI 48109-2110 Business E-Mail: conway@umich.edu.

CONWAY, FATHER MICHAEL JAMES, priest; b. Boston; s. John Thomas and Elizabeth Lucille Conway. BA in Philosophy, Don Bosco Coll., Newton, N.J., 1985; MDiv, Pontifical Coll. Josephinum, Columbus, Ohio, 1992; postgrad., U. San Francisco, 2001—. Tchr. Mary Help of Christians Sch., Tampa, Fla., 1985—87, Archbishop Shaw H.S., Marrero, La., 1987—88, coord. youth ministry, 1992—97, prin., 2003—; exec. dir. Salesian Boys and Girls Club, East Boston, Mass., 1997—99; coord. youth ministry St. Petersburg (Fla.) Cath. H.S., 1999—2001; prin. Don Bosco Tech. H.S., Paterson, NJ, 2001—02; coord. youth ministry Salesian H.S., New Rochelle, NY, 2002—03. Mem.: ASCD, Nat. Cath. Edn. Assn.

CONWAY, MICHAEL MAURICE, lawyer; b. St. Joseph, Mo., Mar. 11, 1946; s. Michael Maurice and Genevieve (Hepburn) C.; m. Kathleen Stevens; children: Michael, Cara, Mary. BS in Journalism, Northwestern U., 1968; JD, Yale U., 1973. Bar: Ill. 1973, U.S. Dist. Ct. (no. dist.) Ill. 1973, U.S. Tax Ct. 1975, U.S. Ct. Claims 1976, U.S. Ct. Appeals (7th cir.) 1976, U.S. Ct. Appeals (1st cir.) 1979, U.S. Supreme Ct. 1980, U.S. Ct. Appeals (5th and 11th cirs.) 1981, U.S. Ct. Appeals (fed. cir. 1982). Ptnr. Hopkins & Sutter now Foley & Lardner, Chgo., 1979—, chmn. Chgo. litigation dept. Counsel U.S. Ho. Reps. com. on judiciary impeachment inquiry Richard M. Nixon, 1974. Chmn. Ill. Lawyers Com. Clinton/Gore, Chgo., 1992; alt. del. Dem. Nat. Conv., 1992, del., 1996. Mem. Am. Coll. Trial Lawyers, Union League Club. Roman Catholic. Avocation: baseball coaching. Office: Foley & Larndner 321 N Clark St Chicago IL 60610 Office Phone: 312-832-4351. E-mail: mconway@foley.com.

CONWAY, NANCY ANN, newspaper editor; b. Foxboro, Mass., Oct. 15, 1941; d. Leo T. and Alma (Goodwin) C.; children: Ana Lucia DaSilva, Kara Ann Martin. Cert. in med. tech., Carnegie Inst., 1962; BA in English, U. Mass., 1976, cert. in secondary edn., 1978. Tchr. Brazil-Am. Inst., Rio de Janeiro, 1963-68; freelance writer, editor Amherst, Mass., 1972-76; staff writer Daily Hampshire Gazette, North Hampton, Mass., 1976-77; editor Amherst Bull., 1977-80, Amherst Record, 1980-83; features editor Holyoke

(Mass.) Transcript/Telegram, 1983-84; gen. mgr. Monday-Thursday Newspapers, Boca Raton, Fla., 1984-87; dir. editorial South Fla. Newspaper Network, Deerfield Beach, 1987-90; pub., editor York (Pa.) Newspapers, Inc., 1990-95; metro editor Denver Post, 1995-96; exec. editor, v.p. Alameda Newspaper Group Oakland (Calif.) Tribune, 1996—2003; editor The Salt Lake (Utah) Tribune, 2003—. Bd. dirs. Math.: Opportunities in Engring., Sci. and Tech.-Pa. State, York, 1991-95. Recipient writing awards, state newspaper assns. Mem. Am. Soc. Newspaper Editors, Soc. Profl. Journalists. Avocations: literature, photography, communication, gardening. Office: Editor Salt Lake Tribune 143 S Main St Salt Lake City UT 84111 Business E-Mail: nconway@angnewspapers.com.

CONWAY, RICHARD ASHLEY, environmental engineer; BS, U. Mass., 1953; MS, MIT, 1957. Registered profl engr., W.Va. Sr. corp. fellow Union Carbide Corp., South Charleston, W.Va., 1957-97; pvt. cons., 1997—. Cons. sci. adv. bd. EPA, chmn. environ. engring. com., 1988-93; sci. adv. bd. DOD Strategic Environ. R&D Program, 1992-98; mem. report rev. com. NAS. Author: Industrial Waste Disposal, 1980; editor: Hazardous Solid Waste Testing, 5 vols., 1981-87, Enivronmental Risk Analysis, 1982; patentee in field. Served to 1st lt. U.S. Army, 1954-56. Recipient Personal Achievement award in Chem. Engring., Chem. Engring. mag., N.Y.C., 1986. Fellow ASCE (chmn. environ. engring. divsn. 1975, Hering medal 1974), Am. Acad. Environ. Engrs. (diplomate, trustee 1994-97, Kappe award 1999, Fair award 2004), Internat. Water Quality Assn. (governing bd. 1978-88), Soc. Environ. Chemistry and Toxicology (bd. dirs. 1983-86, Rachel Carson award 1997); mem. NAE, ASTM (Dudley medal 1984), Water Environ. Fedn. (Gascoigne medal 1967, Rudolfs medal 1974, 83). Avocations: tennis, history. Personal E-mail: conwayenv@aol.com.

CONWAY, RICHARD FRANCIS, investment company executive; b. Greenwich, Conn., Jan. 4, 1954; s. Francis Xavier and Marie (Bohan) C.; m. Greta Weil, Oct. 29, 1988; children: Signe Charlotte Weil, Anna Augusta Weil. BA, Harvard Coll., 1976; MBA, Yale U., 1981. Mgmt. trainee Citibank, N.Y.C., 1976-79; assoc. L.F. Rothschild, Unterberg, Towbin Inc., N.Y.C., 1981-83, v.p., 1983-86, prin., 1986-88; v.p. Salomon Bros. Inc., N.Y.C., 1988-90, Security Pacific Mcht. Bank, N.Y.C., 1990-91; sr. v.p. Needham and Co. Inc., N.Y.C., 1992-94; v.p. Smith Mgmt. Co., N.Y.C., 1994-97, Lone Star Securities Mgmt., Inc., N.Y.C., 1998-99; ptnr. Lampe, Conway & Co., LLC, N.Y.C., 1999—. Trustee Choate Rosemary Hall Sch., Wallingford, Conn., 1974-78; class com. Harvard Coll. Fund, Cambridge, Mass., 1991, 2001. Mem. Harvard Club (N.Y.C.), Knickerbocker Club (N.Y.C.), Georgica Assn. (Wainscott, N.Y.). Roman Catholic. Home: 1361 Madison Ave New York NY 10128-0713 Office: 680 5th Ave Ste 1202 New York NY 10019 Office Phone: 212-581-8989. E-mail: richardconway@nyc.rr.com, conway@lampeconway.com.

CONWAY, ROBERT GEORGE, JR., lawyer; b. Albany, NY, Apr. 26, 1951; s. Robert George Sr. and Kathryn Ann (Kelly) C.; m. Lynda Rae Christenson, Dec. 15, 1979; 1 child, Phillip Christopher. AB, Dartmouth Coll., 1973; JD, Albany Law Sch., 1976; diploma, U.S. Army JAGC Sch., 1986. Bar: Pa. 1978, U.S. Ct. Mil. Appeals 1978, N.C. 1983, U.S. Dist. Ct. (ea. dist.) N.C. 1983, U.S. Dist. Ct. (no. dist.) N.Y. 1998, U.S. Army Ct. Mil. Rev. 1986, U.S. Supreme Ct. 1986, U.S. Ct. Appeals (4th and fed. cirs.) 1987, N.Y. 1998; cert. USMC judge advocate. Commd. 2d lt. USMC, 1975, advanced through grades to maj., 1983, gen. staff sec. Camp Lejeune, N.C., 1982-83, chief rev. officer, 1983-84, spl. asst. U.S. atty., 1984-85, dir. joint law ctr. air sta. Cherry Point, N.C., 1986-88, chief rsch. officer air sta., 1988, dep. asst. staff judge adv. to comdt. Washington, 1989; mil. justice officer Marine Corps Base, Quantico, Va., 1990-91; assoc. counsel for land use law Ea. Area Counsel Office USMC Dept. of Navy Office of Gen. Counsel, Camp Lejeune, N.C., 1991-96; ret. USMC, 1996; counsel N.Y. State Divsn. Mil. and Naval Affairs, Latham, 1996—. Adj. faculty mem. Ga. Inst. Tech., 1993, Webster U., 1994-96; spkr. in field. Trustee Cath. student ctr. Aquinas House, Dartmouth Coll., Hanover, N.H., 1973-89, sec. Dartmouth class of 1973, 1994-2003. Decorated Legion of Merit. Mem.: ABA, Marine Corps Assn., U.S. Naval Inst., Dartmouth Lawyers Assn., Fed. Bar Assn. (contbg. author assn. news and jour. 1990), N.Y. Bar Assn., N.C. Bar Assn., Pa. Bar Assn., Dartmouth Club Ea. N.Y. (v.p. 1998—2001, pres. 2001—), KC (adv. 1984—85), Am. Legion. Roman Catholic. Home: 27 Manor Dr Glenmont NY 12077-3326 Office: NY State Divsn Mil and Naval Affairs Attn MNLA 330 Old Niskayuna Rd Latham NY 12110-3514 Office Phone: 518-786-4541.

CONWAY, SAMUEL ANTHONY, retired chiropractor; b. Dallastown, Pa., Jan. 19, 1917; s. Clarence C. and Coletta Elizabeth (Smith) C.; m. Irene May Runkle, Feb. 6, 1944; 1 son, Samuel A. Student, Lebanon Valley Coll., 1947-48; DC, Nat. Coll. Chiropractic, 1951. Lic. nursing home adminstr., Pa. Gen. practice chiropractic medicine, Hanover, Pa., 1951-83. Chmn. bd., pres. Golden Age Nursing Home, Inc., Hanover, 1961-82; trustee Nat. Coll. Chiropractic, 1960-80, mem. exec. bd. dirs., 1969-80, ret., 1982, chmn. bldg. fund com. 1961-64; participant internat. profl. confs. With Signal Corps, U.S. Army, 1942-46. Recipient Disting. Svc. award Nat. Coll. Chiropractic, 1972. Mem. VFW, DAV, Nat. Coll. Alumni Assn., Am. Chiropractic Assn., Pa. Chiropractic Assn., Pa. Assn. Drugless Therapists (pres. 1968-69, bd. dirs., Disting. Svc. award 1969), Health Care Facilities of Pa., Am. Nursing Home Assn., York County (Pa.) Hist. Soc., Hanover Area Hist. Soc., Antique Automobile Club, Am. Legion, Hanover Area C. of C., Masons, Shriners, Elks. Democrat. Mem. United Ch. of Christ (trustee). Address: 434 Deerfield Dr Hanover PA 17331-5203

CONWAY, WILLIAM E., JR., telecommunications industry executive, venture capitalist; BA, Dartmouth Coll.; MBA, Univ. Chgo., 1974. Various positions The Nat. Bank of Chgo., 1974—84; pres., treas. MCI Commn. Corp., 1981—84, sr. v.p. CFO, 1984—87; founding ptnr., mng. dir. The Carlyle Group, Washington, 1987—; chmn. Nextel Comm., Inc., Reston, Va., 2001—. Chmn. bd. United Defense Inst.; bd. dirs. several pvt. co. Office: Nextel Commn Inc 2001 Edmund Halley Dr Reston VA 20191*

CONWAY, WILLIAM GAYLORD, zoologist, zoo director, conservationist; b. St. Louis, Nov. 20, 1929; s. Frederick Eldridge and Alice Harriet (Gaylord) C. AB, Washington U., 1951; ScD (hon.), St. Lawrence U., 1979, Fordham U., 1981, Trinity Coll., 1984. Curator birds St. Louis Zoo, 1951-56, N.Y. Zool. Soc. (now The Wildlife Conservation Soc.), N.Y.C., 1956-72, assoc. dir., 1960-61, zoo dir., 1962-99, gen. dir., 1966-99, pres., 1992-99; sr. conservationist, 1999—. Mem. expdns. to Trinidad, Argentina, Chile, Bolivia, China; advisor Fundación Patagonia Natural, Argentina; mem. advisory bd. Internat. Zoo Yearbook, 2004; bd. dirs. Caribbean Conservation Corp. Contbr. articles to profl. jours. Decorated comdr. Order of the Golden Ark (The Netherlands); recipient Mayor's award of honor for arts and culture, 1979, Marlin Perkins award AAZPA, 1986, Disting. Achievement award Soc. for Conservation Biology, Disting. Svc. medal Am. Assn. Mus., 1998, Heini Hediger award World Zoo Orgn., 1999, Peter Scott medal IUCN-Survival Svc. Commn., 2001, Henry Shaw medal Mo. Botanical Gardedn, 2002; hon. fellow Zool. Soc. London, 2002. Fellow: N.Y. Zool. Soc.; mem.: Wildlife Conservation Soc. (bd. dirs., Gold medal 2000), Internat. Crane Found. (bd. dirs.), Nat. Audubon Soc. (Audubon medal 1999), Am. Zoo and Aquarium Assn., Am. Assn. Zool. Pks. and Aquariums (past pres.), Am. Assn. Museums (medal 1998), Am. Conservation Assn. (bd. dirs.), Cultural Instns. Group (past pres.), Internat. Survival Svc. Commn. (Peter Scott medal 2000), Wilson Ornithol. Club, Brit. Avicultural Soc., Cooper Ornithol. Soc., Am. Ornithologists Union. E-mail: w.conway@wcs.org, wgcwcs@optonline.net.

CONWAY DE MACARIO, EVERLY, immunologist, molecular biologist; b. Buenos Aires, Apr. 20, 1939; d. Delfín E. and Maria Gloria (Benatuil) Conway; m. Alberto J. L. Macario, Mar. 16, 1963; children: Alex, Everly. PhD in Pharmacy, Nat. U. Buenos Aires, 1960, PhD in Biochemistry, 1962. Rsch. fellow Nat. Acad. Medicine Argentina, Buenos Aires, 1962-63; head lab. oncology and immunology Argentinian Assn. against Cancer, Buenos Aires, 1966-67; chief of immunology Sch. Medicine, Buenos Aires, 1967-68; rsch. fellow dept. tumor-biology Karolinska Inst., Stockholm, 1969-71; sr. rsch. scientist Lab. Cell Biology, NRC Italy, Rome, 1971-73; vis. scientist Internat. Agy. Rsch. on Cancer, WHO, Lyon, France, 1973-74, Brown U., Providence, 1974-76; rsch. scientist Wadsworth Ctr. NY State Dept. Health, Albany, 1976—; prof. dept. biomed. scis. Sch. Pub. Health, Albany, 1986—2002, mem. admission com., 1986-89. Grant referee in field. Co-editor: Monoclonal Antibodies against Bacteria, 1985-86, vols. I-III, Gene Probes for Bacteria, 1990; assoc. editor profl. jour. 1986—; mng. editor Frontiers on Biosci.; contbr. articles to profl. jours.; contbr. chpts. to books and encyclopedias. Recipient Prof. J.M. Mezzadra award Nat. U. Buenos Aires, 1969, Travel award to Eng., 2nd Internat. Immunology Congress, 1974, Gold medal Argentinian Soc. Biochemistry, 1980, Hans Osterman Found. grantee, Sweden, 1969, Sir Samuel Scott of Yews Trust grantee, Sweden, 1970, Winifred Cullis grantee Internat. Fedn. Univ. Women, 1972, NATO rsch. grantee, 1975, 81, U.S. Dept. Energy grantee, 1981, 84; Travel award to China, 1985, Spain, 1993, South Africa, 1994. Mem. Scandinavian Soc. Immunology, Italian Assn. Immunologists, French Soc. Immunology (travel award 1974), Am. Assn. Immunologists (chmn. com. on status of women 1980-86, edn. com. 1982-87, awards com. 1991-92, travel award to Australia 1977), Am. Soc. Microbiology (sr. editor Manual Clin. Lab. Immunology 4th-5th edits.), Internat. Soc. Microbial Ecology, Cell Stress Soc. Internat., Nat. Acad. Microbiology (chmn. Morrison Rogosa awards com. 2002—, chmn. internat. subcom. on taxonomy of methanogens). Achievements include patents for microcircle system, microsample holder and carrier; invention of ultrasensitive micro-immunoenzyamtic assay and multipurpose modular system for use in lab and field settings, of the antigenic fingerprinting method; creation of immuntechnology for rapid identification of microbes directly in samples of complex microbial mixtures; first to establish the antigenic cohesiveness of methanogenic and halophilic archaea and demonstrate clusters overlapping phylogenetic branches; sequenced for the first time archaeal transportes and chaperone genes; found new morphotype of methanosarcina; created an integration vector for transformation of methanogens; participated in the sequencing of the genomes of two methanogens; discovered an archaeon with the four main chaperoning systems. Home: 18 Carriage Rd Delmar NY 12054-3704 Office: Wadsworth Ctr Empire State Plz Albany NY 12201 Business E-Mail: everlym@wadsworth.org.

CONWAY-GERVAIS, KATHLEEN MARIE, reading specialist, educational consultant; b. Bklyn., Apr. 18, 1942; d. John Joseph and Mary Josephine Conway; m. Stephen Paul Gervais, July 10, 1976; 1 child, John Joseph. BA, Coll. Mt. St. Vincent, 1970; MS, Hunter Coll. of N.Y.C., 1973, Reading Specialization, 1974. Cert. reading and social studies tchr., nursery and elem. ecuator, N.Y., N.J. Elem. tchr. Archdiocese of N.Y., N.Y.C., 1963-74; reading specialist Malverne (N.Y.) Union Free Sch. Dist., 1974-86, dist. reading, testing coord., 1986-91, reading specialist, 1992-95, East Meadow (N.Y.) Union Free Sch. Dist., 1995-96; reading cons., tchr. trainer, staff devel. team Uniondale (N.Y.) Union Free Sch. Dist., 1996—2003. Adv. bd. mem. Newsday in Edn., Melville, 1982—; adj. prof. Nassau C.C., Garden City, N.Y., 1995—, L.I. U. Grad. Sch., 2003—, Touro Coll. Grad Sch., 2005—. Active Getting Out the vote presdl. election, N.Y., 1992. Recipient Ambassador in Edn. award Newsday, Melville, 1982, Congruence Model Project award N.Y. State Dept. Edn., Albany, 1988, Elizabeth Ann Seton award Office of Cathechesis and Worship, Long Island, 1991. Mem. ASCD, Internat. Reading Assn., N.Y. State Reading Assn. (del. L.I., regional dir. 2004—), Orton Dyslexia Soc. (del.), Nassau Reading Coun. (bd. dirs., pres., exec. bd.). Democrat. Roman Catholic. Avocations: travel, reading, theater, swimming, computer. Home and Office: 174 Nassau Blvd West Hempstead NY 11552-2218 Office Phone: 516-483-3784. E-mail: watcher@optonline.net.

CONWELL, ESTHER MARLY, physicist, researcher; b. N.Y.C., May 23, 1922; d. Charles and Ida (Korn) C.; m. Abraham A. Rothberg, Sept. 30, 1945; 1 son, Lewis J. BA, Bklyn. Coll., 1942, DSc, 1992; MS, U. Rochester, N.Y., 1945; PhD, U. Chgo., 1948. Lectr. Bklyn. Coll., 1946-51; mem. tech. staff Bell Tel. Labs., 1951-52; physicist GTE Labs., Bayside, NY, 1952-61, mgr. physics dept., 1961-72; vis. prof. U. Paris, 1962-63; Abby Rockefeller Mauze prof. MIT, Cambridge, 1972; prin. scientist Xerox Corp., Webster, NY, 1972-80, rsch. fellow, 1981-98. Adj. prof. U. Rochester, 1990—2001, prof., 2001—; cons., mem. adv. com. engring. NSF, 1978—81. Author: High Field Transport in Semiconductors, 1967, also rsch. papers; mem. editl. bd. Jour. Applied Physics, Proc. of IEEE, patentee in field. Fellow IEEE (Edison medal 1997), Am. Phys. Soc. (sec.-treas. divsn. condensed matter physics 1977-82); mem. AAAS, NAS, NAE, Soc. Women Engrs. (Achievement award 1960). Office: U Rochester Dept Chemistry and Physics Rochester NY 14627 Business E-Mail: conwell@chem.rochester.edu.

CONWELL, HALFORD ROGER, physician; b. Cin., Jan. 28, 1924; s. Halford Fredrick and Erma Pearl (Cornelius) C.; m. Margaret Ann King, Dec. 15, 1965; children: Mark A., Sherri L., John H. BA, U. Wooster, 1948; MA, U. Louisville, 1950; MD, U. Cin., 1955. ATP; diplomate crew coordination tng. Continental Airlines. Practice in aviation medicine, Huntsville, Tex., 1959—; mem. staff Huntsville (Tex.) Meml. Hosp., chief of staff, 1974-75, chief medicine, 1976-80, bd. trustees, 1991—2005. Sr. U.S. med. officer Brit. Caledonian Airways, 1977-89; cons. Aeromexico; chief flight surgeon Continental Airlines, 1996—; mem. Walker County Hosp. Dist., 1975-79, chmn., 1976-79; asst. dean of men, instr. psychology Heidelberg U., Tiffin, Ohio, 1950-51; instr. psychology Cin. Coll.; sr. med. examiner FAA; sr. examiner C.A.A. (U.K.), C.A.A. (Australia); newspaper columnist, 1992—. Trustee Biol. Analysis and Rsch. Found.; capt. (hon.) Tex. Internat. Airline; founder Bomber Command Mus. (R.A.F.) Lt. USNR, 1942-46. Recipient safe pilot award Nat. Pilots Assn., Pilot Proficiency award FAA, Profl. Svc. Citation. Fellow Aerospace Med. Assn. (John A. Tamisiea award 2000); mem. Brit. Assn. Aerospace Medicine, Latin Am. Aviation Med. Assn., Scottish Assn. Aviation Med. Examiners, Airline Med. Dirs. Assn., Civil Aviation Med. Assn. (v.p. 1968-80, dir. 1968—, pres. 1980-81, Award of merit 1994, 97), Mitchell Pediatric Soc., Academie Internationale de Medicine Aeronatque et Spatiale, Aircraft Owners and Pilots Assn. (med. adv. panel), Confederate Air Force (founding mem.), Air Transp. Assn. (med. com.), Order Ky. Cols., Quiet Birdmen, Masons, Psi Chi, Alpha Psi Omega (hon.). Office: 2800 Lake Rd Huntsville TX 77340-5632 Office Phone: 936-295-5222. E-mail: saxet@lcc.net.

CONWELL, YEATES, psychiatrist, educator; b. Wilmington, Del., Feb. 21, 1953; s. Yeates and Mary Atwood Conwell; m. Evelyn Gay Mills, June 30, 1979; children: William, Claire, August. AB, Princeton U., 1976; MD, U. Cin., 1980. Diplomate Am. Bd. Psychiatry and Neurology. Resident in psychiatry Yale U., New Haven, 1980—85; asst. prof. psychiatry U. Rochester Sch. Medicine, NY, 1985—92, assoc. prof., 1992—2000, prof., 2000—, assoc. chair acad. affairs dept. psychiatry, 2000—, co-dir. Ctr. Study and Prevention Suicide, 2000—. Grantee Rsch. Career Devel., NIMH, 1987—92, 1999—, Investigator Initiated Rsch., 1994-2002, Instl. Nat. Rsch. Svc., 2001—. Office: U Rochester Med Ctr 300 Crittenden Blvd Rochester NY 14642 Business E-Mail: yeates_conwell@urmc.rochester.edu.

CONYERS, CLAUDE BRUNSON, publishing consultant, editor, dance historian; b. Cartersville, Ga., June 19, 1934; s. Claude Brunson and Rachel Keith (Stephens) C. BA, Vanderbilt U., 1956; MA, Columbia U., 1962; dance tng., New Dance Group, N.Y.C., 1959, Sch. of Am. Ballet, 1960, Ballet Russe Sch., 1961-64. Sr. editor Prentice-Hall, Inc., Englewood Cliffs, NJ, 1960-64; dancer PACT Ballet, Johannesburg, 1965-66, Les Grands Ballets Canadiens, Montreal, 1967; editl. dir. Greystone Press, N.Y.C., 1968-70; editl. cons. N.Y.C., 1970-74; spl. projects editor Praeger Pubs., N.Y.C., 1975; sr. projects editor Macmillan Pub. Co., N.Y.C., 1975-87; editl. dir., scholarly and profl. reference Oxford U. Press, N.Y.C., 1988-98, v.p., 1995-99. Mem. publs. com. N.Y. Acad. Scis., 1990-95. Bd. dirs. George Balachine Found., 1999—, Hillbrow Pub. Svcs., 2001—; project dir. Popular Balanchine, 2000-04. Lt. (j.g.) USNR, 1956-58. Recipient R.R. Hawkins award Profl. and Scholarly Pub./Assn. Am. Pubs., 1991, 93, 96, 98, Dartmouth medal ALA, 1987, 99. Mem. ASPCA, People for the Ethical Treatment of Animals, Internat. Assn. History Religions, Am. Acad. Religion, Am. Soc. for Theatre Rsch., Congress on Rsch. in Dance, Popular Culture Assn., Soc. Dance History Scholars (editl. bd. 1989-94, 2000—), Clan Keith Soc., World Dance Alliance, Soc. for Scholarly Pub., Alley Cat Allies, Humane Soc. U.S., Humane Farming Assn., Pawling Garden Club, Kappa Alpha Order. Democrat. Episcopalian. Home and Office: 116 S White Rock Rd Holmes NY 12531-5409 Office Phone: 845-878-9451. E-mail: cconyers@rcn.com, cconyers@suscom.net.

CONYERS, JEAN LOUISE, chamber of commerce executive; b. Memphis, Nov. 10, 1932; d. Marshall Daniel and Jeffie (Ledbetter) Farris; m. James E. Conyers, June 4, 1956 (div.); children: Judith, James Jr., Jennifer. BA, LeMoyne Coll., 1956; MBA, Atlanta U., 1967. Exec. sec. Dept. Zoology, Wash. State U., Pullman, 1958-62, Sch. Bus., Atlanta U., 1965-68; dep. dir., planner Community Action Agy, Terre Haute, Ind., 1968-78, exec. dir., 1978-79; sr. assoc. exec. United Way of Genesee/Lapeer, Flint, Mich., 1980-82; pres., chief exec. officer Conyers & Assocs., Flint, 1982-86, Met. C. of C., Flint, 1986—, Ultimate Learning Systems, Inc., Flint, 1990—. Program coord. Greater Flint OIC, 1983-85. Bd. dirs. Urban Coalition, Flint, 1988—, Dort-Oak-Pk. Neighborhood Ho., Flint, 1982—. Recipient Cmty. Svc. award Negro Bus. and Profl. Women, Terre Haute, 1977, Supportive Svcs. award Top Ladies of Distinction, Flint, 1989, Black Caucus Found. of Mich.'s Cmty. Svc. award, 1994, Nat. Negro Bus. and Profl. Women's Club Sojourner Truth award, 1994; named Woman of Distinction for contbns. to minority bus. U. Mich., Flint, Mott Coll., Mayor of Flint, Mich. legis., Mich. Dept. of Labor, 1992; enshrined Zeta Phi Beta Hall of Fame, Flint, 1988. Mem. Kiwanis, Zonta Club of Flint II, Alpha Kappa Alpha (Outstanding Grad. Soror of Great Lakes Region 1992). Avocations: reading, travel. Office: 400 N Saginaw St Ste 101A Flint MI 48502-2045 E-mail: metro@tir.com.

CONYERS, JOHN, JR., congressman; b. Detroit, May 16, 1929; s. John and Lucille (Simpson) C.; m. Monia Estes; children: John Jr., Carl Edward. BA, Wayne State U., 1957, JD, 1958; LLD, Wilberforce U., 1969. Bar: Mich. 1959. Legis. asst. to Congressman John Dingell, 1959-61; sr. ptnr. firm Conyers, Bell & Townsend, 1959-61; referee Mich. Workmen's Compensation Dept., 1961-64; mem. U.S. Congress from 14th Mich. dist., 1964—; former chmn. Govt. Ops. Com., former chmn. subcom. on legis. and nat. security; ranking mem. Judiciary Com. Past dir. edn. Local 900, United Auto Workers; mem. adv. council Mich. Liberties Union; gen. counsel Detroit Trade Union Leadership Council; vice chmn. nat. bd. Ams. for Democratic Action; vice chmn. adv. council ACLU; an organizer Mems. Congress for Peace through Law; bd. dirs. numerous other orgns. including African-Am. Inst., Commn. Racial Justice, Detroit Inst. Arts, Nat. Alliance Against Racist and Polit. Repression, Nat. League Cities. Sponsor, contbg. author: Am. Militarism, 1970, War Crimes and the American Conscience, 1970, Anatomy of an Undeclared War, 1972; contbr. articles to profl. jours. Trustee Martin Luther King Jr. Ctr. for Non-Violent Social Change. Served to 2d lt. U.S. Army, 1950-54, Korea. Recipient Rosa Parks award SCLC. Mem. NAACP (exec. bd. Detroit), Kappa Alpha Psi. Democrat. Baptist. Office: 2426 Rayburn Bldg Washington DC 20515-2214 also: District Office 669 Federal Building 231 W Lafayette Detroit MI 48226*

COOGAN, MELINDA ANN STRANK, chemistry and biology educator; b. Davenport, Iowa, Mar. 29, 1955; d. Gale Benjamin and Margie Delene (Admire) Strank; children: James Benjamin, Jessica Ann. AA, Stephens Coll., Columbia, Mo., 1975; BS, E. Carolina U., Greenville, N.C., 1978; MS, Western Ill. U., 2004. Biology and phys. sci. educator York (Pa.) Catholic H.S., 1989-90; sci. advisor Bettendorf (Iowa) Children's Mus., 1993; gifted, chemistry and physics educator St. Katherine' Coll. Prep. Sch., Bettendorf, 1994; biology educator Lewisville (Tex.) H.S., 1996-99, chemistry educator, 1996-99; ALS rsch. asst. U. Tex. Southwestern Med. Ctr., Dallas, 1998; chemistry, biology and human anatomy educator Milford HS, Ill., 2000—04; rsch. asst., PhD candidate U. No. Tex., Dept. Environ. Scis., Tex., 2004—. Violinist Augustana Symphony Orch., Rock Island, Ill., 1993-94; pres. bd. dirs. Flower Mound (Tex.) Cmty. Orch., 1994-95; founder, instr. Northlakes Violin Acad., Flower Mound, 1994-99; violinist Waterforde Women's String Ensemble, Lewisville, 1995-98, Clinton Symphony, 1999-2001, Country Theater, Cissna Park, Ill., 2002-2004; bd. dirs. Family Mus. Art and Sci., Bettendorf, 2000-01. student mentor, Earthwatch Prog., We. Ill. U. 2003-2004. Student mentor Earthwatch, 2003. Mem. Roanoke Art Mus. (docent 1983-86), Jr. Bd. of Quad City Symphony (chair promotion 1987-88), Jr. Svc. League Moline (Ill.) (chair Riverfest 1987-88), Jr. League of York (Pa.) (chair thrift shop spl. sales 1989-92), Jr. League of Quad Cities (nom./placement 1993-94), Jr. League of Dallas (sustaining 1995-96), Gamma Beta Phi, Chi Beta Phi, Phi Kappa Phi. Democrat. Roman Catholic. Home: 2100 Preston Pl Denton TX 76209 E-mail: mcoogan@verizon.net.

COOGAN, PHILIP SHIELDS, pathologist; b. Peoria, Ill., Feb. 13, 1938; s. Paul Mathew and Elizabeth Ann (Shields) C.; m. Carol Jean Gerlach, June 18, 1960 (div. 1985); children: Mary Brighid, Philip Gerlach, Joseph Baker, Clare Ann; m. Joan C. Storozynski, Dec. 24, 1987. Student, U. Notre Dame, 1955-58; MD, St. Louis U., 1962. Diplomate: Am. Bd. Pathology. USPHS summer research trainee pathology St. Louis U. Med. Sch., 1959-61; intern Presbyn.-St. Luke's Hosp., Chgo., 1962-63, resident, 1963-67; research pathologist, chief histopathology U.S. Air Force Sch. Aerospace Medicine, 1967-69; asst. prof. pathology Rush Med. Coll., Chgo., 1971-73, assoc. prof., 1972-75; assoc. prof. pathology Northwestern U., Chgo., 1974-78; dir. anatomic pathology Northwestern Meml. Hosp., Chgo., 1974-78; prof. pathology James H. Quillen Coll. Medicine, East Tenn. State U., Johnson City, 1978—2004. Cons. FDA, 1972-81, USPHS, 1962-67 Assoc. editor: Year Book Pathology and Clinical Pathology, 1978-80. Served with USAF, 1967-69. Recipient Hektoen award Chgo. Path. Soc., 1969; named Outstanding Tchr. East Tenn. State U. Coll. Medicine, 1980, 81, 83, 84, 85 Mem. AMA, AAAS, U.S. and Can. Acad. Pathology, Am. Soc. Exptl. Pathology, Am. Soc. Clin. Pathology, Coll. Am. Pathology, Am. Soc. Investigative Pathology, Alpha Omega Alpha. Roman Catholic. Home: 3409 Stoneridge Dr Johnson City TN 37604-2182 Office: East Tenn State U Dept Pathology Johnson City TN 37614 Office Phone: 423-439-6789. E-mail: coogan@etsu-tn.edu. *"Don't shoot the wounded." As a teacher of medical students and residents, it is advisable to treat those struggling under adversity with special care. They often become the most empathetic physicians.*

COOGAN, TIMOTHY CHRISTOPHER, II, history professor, researcher; b. Oakland, Calif., June 17, 1947; s. Emmons Wellington and Margaret Slocumb Coogan; m. Alice Pendleton Poor, Oct. 26, 1979. BS, Lewis and Clark Coll., 1969; MA in Tchg., San Francisco State U., 1974, MA, 1976; PhD, NYU, 1992. Cert. K-9 tchr. Calif. Pvt. instr. Salisbury Prep. Sch., Salisbury, Conn., 1970; tchr. ESL and cmty. orgn. Peace Corps, Asor, Ulithi, 1970—72, Calif. state elem. tchr. Calif., 1972; history instr., alternative sch. for disruptive students Dept. of Edn., San Francisco, 1973—74; adj. lectr. history and social sci. dept. Fiorello H. LaGuardia CC, N.Y.C., 1979—2004, asst. prof. history LI City, NY, 1992—2002, assoc. prof. history N.Y.C., 2004—; adj. assoc. prof. history, dept. social sci. Pace U., Pleasantville and White Plains, NY, 1985—87; student tchr. supr. Rutgers U., Newark, 1990—92, co-adjutant asst. prof. history, 1992—2004, asst. prof. history, 2004—05; adj. lectr. history, dept. polit. sci., history and philosophy Kingsborough CC, N.Y.C., 1989—90; adj. asst. prof. history Cooper Union for Advancement of Sci. and Art, N.Y.C., 1992—2003, adj. lectr. history, humanities and social sci. dept., 1987—92; supr. tchg. assts., history dept. NYU, 1992—94, adj. asst. prof. history, grad. program of liberal studies, 1993—94; asst. prof. history CUNY, 2004—05. Tutor San Francisco State U., 1973—75; dir. sr. seminar paper, history dept. Rutgers U., 1987—2005, instr. cultural awareness for state police troopers of NJ, Inst. for Ethnicity, Culture &Modern Experience, 2003. Co-dir.: Holocaust Remembrance, 2005; contbr. articles, revs., essays to profl. publs. Guest spkr., panelist Amnesty Internat., N.Y.C., 2002. Scholar, NYU, 1977—80, Tchg. Assistantship, 1978—79, Rsch. Assistantship, 1977; univ. scholar, San Francisco State U., 1974—76. Fellow: Phi Theta Kappa (hon.; keynote spkr. 1997). Avocations: travel, reading, walking, hiking, basketball. Home: 19 Grove St Apt 2 D New York NY 10014-5349 Office: Fiorello H LaGuardia CC 31-10 Thomson Ave Long Island City NY 11101 Office Phone: 718-482-5785. Office Fax: 718-482-6049. Personal E-mail: tpc4cats@aol.com. Business E-mail: tcoogan@lagcc.cuny.edu.

COOK, ADDISON GILBERT, chemistry educator; b. Caracas, Venezuela, Apr. 1, 1933; s. Harold Reed and Florence (Sloan) C.; m. Nancy Lois Spriggs, Aug. 18, 1956; children— Virginia Lynn, Shirley June, Diane Joyce. BS, Wheaton Coll., 1955; PhD, U. Ill., 1959. Research assoc. Cornell U., 1959-60; from asst. prof. to prof. chemistry Valparaiso U., 1960—, chmn. dept., 1970-93. Cons. chemistry divsn. Argonne (Ill.) Nat. Lab., 1961-69; rsch. assoc. Amoco, Whting, Ind., 1960. Editor, contbr.: Enamines: Synthesis, Structure, and Reactions, 1969, 2d edit., 1988; Contbr. articles profl. jours. Recipient Research Corp. grant, 1960-61; Petroleum Research Fund grant, 1963-69. Mem. Am. Chem. Sco., Chem. Soc. (London), Ind. Acad. Sci., Sigma Xi, Phi Lambda Upsilon, Pi Mu Epsilon. Mem. Evangel. Free Ch. Am. Home: 2308 Shannon Dr Valparaiso IN 46383-2427 Office: Valparaiso U Dept Chemistry 210 Neils Sci Ctr Valparaiso IN 46383 Office Phone: 219-464-5389. Business E-Mail: Gil.Cook@valpo.edu.

COOK, ALBERT THOMAS THORNTON, JR., financial advisor; b. Cleve., Apr. 24, 1940; s. Albert Thomas Thornton and Tyra Esther (Morehouse) C.; m. Mary Jane Blackburn, June 1, 1963; children: Lara Keller, Thomas, Timothy. BA, Dartmouth Coll., 1962; MA, U. Chgo., 1966. Asst. sec. Dartmouth Coll., Hanover, NH, 1972-77; exec. dir. Big Bros., Inc., NYC, 1977-78; underwriter Boettcher & Co., Denver, 1978-81; asst. v.p. Dain Bosworth Inc., Denver, 1981-82, Colo. Nat. Bank, Denver, 1982-84; pres. The Albert T.T. Cook Co., Denver, 1984—. Arbitrator Nat. Assn. Securities Dealers, NYC, 1985—, Mcpl. Securities Rulemaking Bd., Washington, 1987-98. Pres. Etna-Hanover Ctr. Cmty. Assn., Hanover, NH, 1974-76; active Mayor's Task Force, Denver, 1984; bd. dir. Rude Park Cmty. Nursery, Denver, 1985-87, Willows Water Dist., Colo., 1990-2004, pres., 1998-99, 2003-04; trustee The Iliff Sch. Theol., Denver, 1986-92; com. on trustees Dartmouth Coll., 1990-93. Mem.: Dartmouth Alumni Coun. (chmn. nominating and trustee search coms. 1987—89, exec. com.), Yale Club, Dartmouth Club of NYC, University Club (chmn. admissions com. 1997—98), Cactus Club, Lions (bd. dir. Denver chpt. 1983—85, treas. 1986—87, pres. Denver Found. 1987—88, 2d v.p. 2001—02, 1st v.p. 2002—03, pres. 2003—04), Delta Upsilon. Congregationalist. Avocations: fly fishing, furniture making, running, skiing, backpacking. Home: 7099 E Hinsdale Pl Centennial CO 80112-1610 Office: One Tabor Ctr 1200 17th St Ste 960 Denver CO 80202-5835

COOK, ALEXANDER BURNS, curator, artist, educator; b. Grand Rapids, Mich., Apr. 16, 1924; s. Gorell Alexander and Harriette Florence (Hinze) C.; m. Marilyn Bierschwal Coffey, Aug. 11, 1992. BA, Ohio Wesleyan U., 1949; MS, Case Western Res. U., 1967. Editl. cartoonist, artist Cleve. Plain Dealer, 1949-55; account exec. Edward Howard & Co., Cleve., 1955-61; spl. art tchr. Cleve. Pub. Schs., 1964-88; curator exhibits Inland Seas Maritime Mus. (formerly Gt. Lakes Mus.), Vermilion, Ohio, 1970-78, curator, 1978—, chmn. mus. oper. com., 1977—. Contbr. editl. cartoons to Reid Cartoon Collection, U. Kans. Jour. Hist. Ctr., The Critique, 1975-88; editl. advisor, columnist Inland Seas Quar. Jour., 1957—, The Chadburn, 1976—; cover illustrations for Ohioana Quar., 1979—; book cover illustrations Dodd, Mead & Co., 1984; paintings represented in pvt. collections, 1960—; executed murals depicting Gt. Lakes shipping Gt. Lakes Mus., 1969, Great Lakes shipwreck Inland Seas Maritime Mus., 2001. Trustee Berkshire Condominium Owners Assn., 1981-83, pres., 1982-83; trustee Shaker Hist. Soc., 1999—. With AUS, 1943-45. Recipient award of honor Ohio Wesleyan U., 1955, Disting. Achievement award Gt. Lakes Hist. Soc., 1973, 1st pl. award for editl. cartoons Union Tchr. Comm. Assn., 1980, 81, 82, 87, Vermilion C. of C. Svc. Award, 2000, Disting. Mus. Profl. award Ohio Museums Assn., 2001. Mem. Gt. Lakes Hist. Soc. (exec. v.p. 1959-64, v.p. 1964-95, trustee, mem. exec. com. 1959—), Ohioana Libr. Assn., Art Inst. Chgo., Akron Art Mus., Cleve. Mus. Art, Am. Soc. Marine Artists (artist mem.), Assn. for Great Lakes Maritime History, Chgo. Maritime Soc., English Speaking Union, Ohio Acad. History, Northeastern Ohio Inter-Mus. Coun., Vermilion Boat Club, The Union Club,Delta Tau Delta, Pi Delta Epsilon, Pi Sigma Alpha. Republican. Episcopalian. Avocations: gardening, sailing, model railroading. Home: 2449 Saybrook Rd University Heights OH 44118

COOK, ANN JENNALIE, literature educator, cultural organization administrator; b. Wewoka, Okla., Oct. 19, 1934; d. Arthur Holly and Bertha Mable (Stafford) C.; children: Lee Ann Merrick, Amy Ceil Leonard; m. Gerald George Calhoun, Apr. 1994. BA, U. Okla., 1956, MA, 1959; PhD, Vanderbilt U., 1972. Instr. English U. Okla., 1956-57; tchr. English N.C. and Conn., 1958-61; instr. So. Conn. State Coll., 1962-64; asst. prof. U. S.C., 1972-74; adj. asst. prof. Vanderbilt U., Nashville, 1977-82, assoc. prof., 1982-89, prof., 1990-98, prof. emerita, 1999—. Exec. sec. Shakespeare Assn. Am., 1975-87; chmn. Internat. Shakespeare Assn., 1988-96, v.p. 1996—. Author: Privileged Playgoers of Shakespeare's London, 1981, Making a Match: Courtship in Shakespeare and His Society, 1991; assoc. editor Shakespeare Studies, 1973-80; contbr. articles to profl. jours. Trustee Folger Shakespeare Libr., 1985—90, Shakespeare Birthplace Trust (life), Friends of the Shakespeare Birthplace Trust, Nashville Symphony, 2000—, Univ. Sch. Nashvillle, 2000—04, Nashville Opera Guild, 2000—03, Nashville Shakespeare Festival, 2002—, Shakespeare on the Cumberland; pres. English-Speaking Union, 2003—, nat. bd. dirs., 2004—. Recipient Letseizer award, 1956, Nat. Leadership award Delta Delta Delta, 1956; Danforth fellow, 1968-72, Folger summer fellow, 1973, Donelson fellow, 1974-75, fellow Rockefeller Found., 1984, Guggenheim Found., 1984-85; grantee Folger seminar NEH, 1992-93. Mem. MLA, AAUP, Shakespeare Assn. Am., Shakespeare Inst., Deutsche Shakespeare Gesellschaft, Renaissance Soc. Am. (bd. dirs.), Vanderbilt Libr. Heard Soc. (pres. 2004—), Phi Beta Kappa. Episcopalian. Home: 114 Prospect Hl Nashville TN 37205-4721 Office: Vanderbilt U Dept English Nashville TN 37235 Office Phone: 615-322-2541. Personal E-mail: gercalhoun@aol.com.

COOK, ANNE WELSH, lumber company executive; b. Hilo, Hawaii, July 9, 1948; d. Charles Edward and Charlotte Annabelle (Redfield) Welsh; m. Thomas Rollin Kramer, Sept. 12, 1970 (div. Dec. 1981); 1 child, Jeanne Elizabeth; m. Jeffrey Dean Cook, June 22, 1985; children: Julia Charlotte, Andrea Michelle, Daniel James Welsh. BS in Math., Duke U., 1970, MA in Math., Computer Sci., 1971; PhD in Stats., Am. U., 1983. Programmer, researcher Duke U. Hosp., Durham, N.C., 1969-71; math. statistician Bur. Census, Suitland, Md., 1971-73; sr. programmer, mgr. EG&G Mason REsearch, Rockville, Md., 1973-74, 75-78; project mgr. Price, Williams & Assocs., Silver Spring, Md., 1974-75; instr. Am. U., Washington, 1981-82; asst. prof. math. Pacific Luth. U., Tacoma, 1983-87; statis. cons. Donald Murtha, Washington, 1981-83, EPA, Washington, 1982-83. Cons. Fairchild, Puyallup, Wash.; elected mem. rank and tenure com. Pacific Luth U., 1984-86; majority stockholder, treas. Cook Lumber Co., Tacoma, 1991—. Newsletter editor St. Joseph/St. John's Episcopal Ch., Tacoma, 1989-91; treas. Northwest Investors Club, 1993-95, St. Frances Cabrini Parent's Assn., 2000-2002; mem. fin. com. Greater Lakes Mental Health, 2003—. Home: 7308 North St SW Lakewood WA 98498-5212 Office: 7308 North St SW Lakewood WA 98498-5212

COOK, AUGUST JOSEPH, lawyer, accountant; b. Devine, Tex., Sept. 25, 1926; s. August E. and Mary H. (Schmidt) C.; m. Matie M. Brangan, July 12, 1952; children: Lisa Ann, Mary Beth, John J. BS, Trinity U., 1949; BBA, U. Tex., 1954; JD, St. Mary's U., 1960. Bar: Tex. 1960, Tenn. 1975. Bus. mgr., corp. sec. Life Enterprises, Inc. and affil. cos., San Antonio, 1950-58, also bd. dirs.; mgr. Ernst & Young, San Antonio, 1960-69, ptnr., Memphis, 1970-84; ptnr. McDonnel Boyd, Memphis, 1984-91; of counsel Harris, Shelton, Dunlap and Cobb, Memphis, 1991-97, Pietrangelo Cook, Memphis, 1997—. Author: A.J. $ Tax Court, 1987; author newspaper column A.J.'s Tax Fables, 1983—; contbr. articles to profl. jours. Alderman City of Castle Hills, Tex., 1961-63, mayor, 1963-69; chmn. Bexar County Coun. Mayors, 1967-69; v.p. Tex. Mcpl. League, 1968-69; bd. dirs. San Antonio Met. YMCA. With U.S. Army, 1945-46, PTO. Mem. AICPA, Tex. Soc. CPAs, Tex. Bar Assn., Estate Planning Coun. San Antonio (pres. 1967), Tenn. Soc. CPAs, Tenn. Bar Assn. (chmn. tax, probate and trust sect., 1993-95), Estate Planning Coun. Memphis (pres. 1983-84), Toastmasters (pres. 1963), Delta Theta Phi, Kappa Pi Sigma, University Club (Memphis), Canyon Creek Country Club (San Antonio, bd. dirs.), Chicksaw Country Club, Optimists (bd. dirs.), Rotary (treas. 1978, 99, bd. dirs. 1986-87, 96-97). Home: 6785 Slash Pine Cv Memphis TN 38119-5617 Office: Pietrangelo Cook PLC 6410 Poplar Ave Ste 190 Memphis TN 38119-4841

COOK, B. THOMAS, lawyer; b. Dallas, July 15, 1946; s. Bryan Jennings and Winifred Texana (Tipps) C.; m. Nancy Illback, Nov. 8, 1969; children: Rachel Lynn, David Thomas, Hayden Paul. AB, Wheaton Coll., 1968; JD, U. Tex., 1974. Bar: Tex. 1974, U.S. Ct. Appeals (5th cir.) 1975, U.S. Dist. Ct. (so. dist.) Tex. 1975, U.S. Dist. Ct. (ea. dist.) Tex. 1981, U.S. Dist. Ct. (no. dist.) Tex. 1985, U.S. Dist. Ct. (we. dist.) Tex. 1990. Atty., ptnr. Bracewell & Patterson L.L.P., Houston, 1974—. Capt. U.S. Army, 1968-71. Named Disting. Military Grad. U.S. Army, 1968. Fellow: Tex. Bar Found., Houston Bar Found.; mem.: Tex. Bar Assn., Houston Club. Avocation: skiing. Office: Bracewell & Patterson LLP 711 Louisiana St Ste 2900 Houston TX 77002-2781

COOK, BENJAMIN C., music educator; b. Pitts., July 16, 1976; s. Daniel Anderson and Patricia Lee Cook. BS in Music Edn., Ind. U. Pa., 1999. Music educator Elizabeth (Pa.) Forward Mid. Sch., 2000—; elem. band dir. Cath. Diocese of Pitts., 1999—2000. Recipient Eagle Scout, Boy Scout of Am., 1993. Mem.: Pa. Music Educators Assn. (assoc.). Office: Elizabeth Forward Middle School 401 Rock Run Road McKeesport PA 15037 Office Phone: 412-896-2300 7740. Office Fax: 412-751-6669. E-mail: bcook@efsd.net.

COOK, BERNARD ANTHONY, historian, educator; b. Meridian, Miss., July 11, 1941; s. Bernard Aloysius and Mirian Theresa (Stroble) Cook; m. Rosemary Frances Petralle, Dec. 28, 1966; children: Bernard Joseph, Jennifer Rose. BA, Notre Dame Seminary, 1963; attended, Gregorian U., 1964; MA, St. Louis U., 1966, PhD, 1970; prof. (hon.), U. Banat, Romania, 2002. Instr. No. Mich. U., Marquette, 1968; instr. to prof. Loyola U., New Orleans, 1968—2004, provost dist. prof., hist., 2004—. Co-dir. Loyola Summer Study Program, Leuven, Belgium, 1993—; mem. Nat. Faculty, Atlanta, 1997—2003; dir. Inst. for the Study of Cath. Culture and Tradition, Loyola U., New Orleans, 2001—. Author: Belgium: A history, 2002; editor: Europe Since 1945: An Encyclopedia, 2001. Recipient Fulbright fellowship, U. Marburg, Germany, 1967. Mem.: US Comm. on Mil. Hist., Assn. Internat. D'Histoire Contemporaing De L' Europe, Assn. for Study of Ethnicity and Nationalism, Consortium on Revolutionary Europe, Ctrl. European Acad. Sci. and Art (hon.). Roman Catholic. Office: Loyola U Dept Hist 6363 St Charles Ave New Orleans LA 70118 Office Phone: 504-865-2564. Business E-Mail: cook@loyno.edu.

COOK, BLANCHE WIESEN, historian, educator, journalist; b. N.Y.C., Apr. 20, 1941; d. David Theodore and Sadonia (Ecker) Wiesen. BA, Hunter Coll., 1962; MA, Johns Hopkins U., 1964, PhD, 1970; DHL (hon.), Russell Sage Coll., 1998. Instr. Hampton Inst., Va., 1963; instr. Stern Coll. for Women, Yeshiva U., N.Y.C., 1964-67; prof. history John Jay Coll., Grad. Faculty CUNY, 1968—, disting. prof., 1995—. Prodr., broadcaster program stas. WBAI and WKPFK Radio Pacifica, N.Y.C. and L.A., 1978—; prodr.-host Jewish Women in Am., CUNY-TV, 2004-05; vis. prof. UCLA, 1982-83; syndicated journalist; bd. dirs. Women's Fgn. Policy Adv. Coun., v.p., co-chair Fund for Open Info. and Accountability; mem. freedom to write com. PEN; elected univ.-wide union officer PSC-CUNY, 2000. Author: Crystal Eastman on Women and Revolution, 1978, Declassified Eisenhower, 1981 (N.Y. Times Notable Book), Biography of Eleanor Roosevelt, vol. 1, 1992 (L.A. Times Book award, N.Y. Times Notable Book), vol. 2, 1999, ER I, ER II (Best Books), Christian Sci. Monitor, 1999 (Notable Book award 1999); sr. editor: The Garland Library of War and Peace, 360 vols., 1970-80, Bella Abzug in Jewish Women's Encyclopedia, 1997; contbr. articles to various publs. Appointed to com. on documents for fgn. rels. U.S. Dept. State, 1986-90. Named Scholar of the Yr. N.Y. Coun. Humanities, 1996, Alumna of Yr. Hunter Coll. Hall of Fame, 1999; recipient Breakthrough award Women, Men and Media, 1992, Feminist of Yr. award Feminist Majority Found., 1992, Lambda Lit. Prize, 1992; faculty fellow CUNY, 1978, 84, 91. Mem. Orgn. Am. Historians (co-chair freedom of info. com.), Am. Hist. Assn. (v.p. for rsch. 1991-94), Coordinating Com., Women in Hist. Profession (pres. N.Y.C. chpt. 1969-71), Berkshire Women Historians, Soc. Historians Am. Fgn. Rels., Conf. on Peace Rsch. in History (bd. dirs., v.p.), Peace History Soc. Women's Internat. League for Peace and Freedom, Pi Sigma Alpha, Phi Alpha Theta. Office: CUNY John Jay Coll Dept History 445 W 59th St New York NY 10019-1104 Office Phone: 212-237-8827.

COOK, BRUCE LAWRENCE, editor; b. Chgo., Dec. 12, 1942; s. David Charles, III and Anna Mae (Lawrence) Cook; m. Carolyn Winslow Smith Hammock (div. Dec. 1972); 1 child, Steven Winslow; m. Eileen Clare McPeak, Jan. 3, 1973; children: Christopher David, Helen Clare, Bruce Michael. BA in Radio-TV, Ohio Wesleyan U., 1965; MA in Speech Arts, San Diego State U., 1967; PhD in Comm., Temple U., 1979. Trustee comm. rsch. David C. Cook Found., Elgin, Ill., 1972-83; dir. Ill. Mcpl. Inst., Dundee, 1983-88; mng. editor Sr. Am. Newspapers, Dundee, 1988-90; dir. Cook Comm., Dundee, 1990—; rsch. analyst Copley Chgo. Newspapers, Plainfield, 1995-2000; sr. rsch. analyst Reach Chgo., Hollinger Inc. Chgo. (Ill.) Sun-Times, 2000—04, sr. rsch. analyst, 2004—. Instr. Columbia Coll., Chgo., 1989—, DeVry U./Keller Grad. Sch. Mgmt., Oak Brook, Ill., 1991—. Author: (monograph) Understanding Pictures in Papua, 1981, (booklet) Serving Mentally Impaired People, 1983; founder, editor (website) author-me.com. Trustee Village of Sleepy Hollow, Ill., 1983—87; alt. bd. rev. Kane County, Batavia, Ill., 1993—95; v.p. gen. edn. adv. bd. DeVry Inst. Tech., 1997—. Capt. USAF, 1967—72. Mem.: IEEE, Am. Legion. Republican. Home: 1211 Carol Crest Dr Sleepy Hollow IL 60118-2643 Office: Chgo Sun Times 350 N Orleans St Chicago IL 60654 Personal E-mail: cookcomm@gte.net.

COOK, BRUCE W., music educator; s. Jesse Wooden and Lucille Dalton Cook. BMus, Greensboro Coll., 1982; MusM, U. NC, Greensboro, 1985; DMA, U. Colo., 1996; postgrad., U. Calif., Davis, 2003—. Holotropic breathwork practitioner Grof Transpersonal Tng., 1996. Music tchr. (Ariz.) H.S., 1986—89; instr. U. Colo. Continuing Edn., Boulder, 1993—96; prof. music Diablo Valley Coll., Pleasant Hill, Calif., 1996—. Guest lectr. Contra Costa Music Tchrs. Assn. Calif., 1997; guest adjudicator local, regional and state piano competitions, Calif., 1997—2005. Contbr. articles to profl. jours.; mem. internat. adv. bd. Internat. Jour. Humanities and Peace. Named 1st Runner Up Tchr. of Yr. for Ariz. award, U.S. West, 1989, Best of Boulder: Chamber Music Category, Wes Blomster, Boulder Daily Camera, 1993; fellow, U. Colo., 1994—96; grantee, 1994, 1995; scholar Children of WWII Vets., State of NC, 1980—84; fellow dept. music, U. Calif., Davis, 2004, George and Dorothy Zalls fellow, 2005—, Grad. Sch. Rsch. grant., U. Calif., Davis, 2005—. Mem.: Soc. for Ethnomusicology, Music Tchrs. Assn. Calif. (assoc.), Mu Phi Epsilon (hon.). Office: Diablo Valley Coll 321 Golf Club Rd Pleasant Hill CA 94523 Office Phone: 925-685-1230 ext. 2809. Personal E-mail: soundscape3@earthlink.net. E-mail: bcook@dvc.edu.

COOK, BRYSON LEITCH, lawyer; b. Balt., Apr. 17, 1948; s. A. Samuel Cook. BA magna cum laude, Princeton U., 1970; JD cum laude, MBA, U. Pa., 1973. Bar: Md. 1974, U.S. Dist. Ct. Md. 1976, U.S. Tax Ct. 1977. Assoc. Alex Brown & Sons, Balt., 1973-75, Venable, Baetjer & Howard, Balt., 1975-81, ptnr., 1981—; ptnr., Bus. Trans. Dept. and Taxation Dept. Venable LLP, Balt. Adj. prof. U. Md. Law Sch., Balt., 1981, Loyola U. Bus. Sch., Balt., 1980-82. Contbr. articles to legal jours.; author tax mgmt. portfolios. Trustee Balt. Ballet, 1980-83, Keswick Home for the Incurables, Balt., 1983—; bd. dirs. Balt. City Jail, 1980-82; counsel Md. Hist. Soc., Balt., 1981—. Recipient Gordon A. Block award U. Pa. Law Sch., 1973. Mem. ABA, Bar Assn. Balt. City, Md. State Bar Assn., Internat. Fiscal Assn., Order of Coif, Elkridge Club (Balt.). Republican. Methodist. Office: Venable LLP Mercantile Bank & Trust Bldg 2 Hopkins Plz Ste 1800 Baltimore MD 21201-2971 also: Venable LLP 575 7th St NW Washington DC 20004 E-mail: blcook@venable.com.

COOK, CAMILLE WRIGHT, retired law educator; b. Tuscaloosa, Ala. d. Reuben Hall and Camille Tunstall (Searcy) Wright; children: Sydney, Reuben, Cade, Camille. AB, U. Ala., 1945, JD, 1948. Bar: Ala. 1948. Asst. prof. law, Law Sch. Auburn (Ala.) U., 1968; mem. faculty Sch. Law U. Ala., 1968-93, assoc. dean, dir. continuing legal edn., prof. law, Law Sch., 1975-93, asst. acad. v.p., 1984-85; prof. emeritus, 1993—. Bd. dirs. U. Ala. Law Sch. Found., Am/South. Mem. Smithsonian Coun., Washington, 1972-78, Ala. Air Pollution Commn., 1971-81; vestry Christ Episcopal Ch. Recipient outstanding commitment to tchg. award U. Ala., 1990, disting. alumni award, 1996, Algernon Sydney Sullivan award, 1999. Fellow Am. Bar Found., Ala. Bar Assn. (award merit 1973); mem. ABA (Rawles Spl. Merit award 1983), Farrah Law Soc. (trustee 1972—, disting. alumnae award 1992), Am. law Inst. (coun., Rawles Spl. Merit award 1983). Episcopalian. Home: 32 Ridgeland Tuscaloosa AL 35406-1607 Personal E-mail: camillewcook1@comcast.net.

COOK, CHARLES WILKERSON, JR., retired bank executive, retired municipal official; b. Nashville, Sept. 10, 1934; s. Charles Wilkerson and Virginia (Jones) C.; m. Sally Randolph Frierson, June 24, 1961 (dec. May 2001); children: Charles Wilkerson III, John Stephenson Frierson; m. Mary Hawkins, Jan. 18, 2003. BS, Yale U., 1956; postgrad., Stonier Grad. Sch. Banking, Rutgers U., 1964-66. With Third Nat. Bank, Nashville, 1959-85, pres., 1979-83, chmn., 1983-85, also dir.; with Third Nat. Corp., Nashville, 1985-89, pres., chief exec. officer, 1985-87, chmn. bd. dirs., chief exec. officer, 1987-89, dir., 1983-90; exec. v.p. Sun Trust Banks, Inc., 1989-90; dir. fin. Met. Govt. of Nashville-Davidson County (Tenn.), Nashville, 1991-93; pres., CEO, dir. Union Planters Bank of Mid. Tenn., N.A., Nashville, 1993-99, chmn., bd. dirs., 2000—01; ret., 2001; vice chmn. Nashville Bank and Trust Co., 2004—, dir., 2004—; mem. Met. Govt. Bd. Equalization, 2004—. Bd. dirs. Nashville Electric Power, chmn. bd. dirs., 1997-2003; bd. dirs. Quality Industries, Inc., Centennial Med. Ctr, 1993-99, Richland Place, Inc. Author: History of a Bank Merger, 1969. Mem. Nashville-Davidson County Govt. Social Svcs. Commn., 1970-85; sr. warden Christ Episcopal Ch., Nashville, 1970-71; pres. Episc. Churchmen of Tenn., 1974; mem. bishop and coun. Episc. Diocese of Tenn., 1979-81; chmn., bd. dirs. United Way Nashville, 1984-85, 1993-97; chmn. Project PENCIL, 1988-89, Jr. Achievement of Nashville, Bill Wilkerson Hearing and Speech Ctr., Nashville, 1970-80, Ensworth Sch., 1978-81, Better Bus. Bur. Nashville, 1980-83, Nashville Meml. Hosp., 1974-89, Tenn. Performing Arts Mgmt. Corp., 1985-89, vice-chmn., 1987-89, Tenn. State Mus. Found., 1986-89; mem. adv. bd. Salvation Army, Nashville, 1976-79; bd. dirs. Episcopal Ch. Found., 1991-92, St. Luke's Cmty. House, 1999-2004, chmn., 2002-03; bd. dirs. Nashville Pub. TV Corp., 1998—, Nashville Cmty. Found., 2000—, Tenn. Hist. Soc., 2000—; campaign chmn. United Way Mid. Tenn., 1994. With USN, 1956-59; capt. Res., 1977-84. Mem. Nashville C. of C. (bd. govs. 1982-84, 95-2000), Belle Meade Country Club (bd. dirs. 1996-2000, pres. 1999-2000), Army-Navy Club (Washington), Yale Club NYC, Univ. Club (Nashville).

COOK, CHARLES WILLIAM, aerospace engineer, consultant, educator; b. Yankton, SD, Sept. 27, 1927; s. William O. and Kathryn S. (Eymer) C.; m. Virginia M. Fosness, May 30, 1950; children: Jennifer Cook Clark, William O. II, Amy Cook Lewandowski. AB summa cum laude, U. S.D., Dean Akeley fellow, 1951; MS, Calif. Inst. Tech., 1954, PhD, 1957. Head nuclear physics Convair Corp., San Diego, 1957-60; chief Ballistic Missile Def. br. Advanced Rsch. Project Agy., Washington, 1961; corp. dir. elec. rsch. and devel. No. Am. Aviation Inc., El Segundo, Calif., 1961-67; dep. div. chief. CIA, Washington, 1961-71; asst. dir. def. rsch. and engring. Dept. Def., Washington, 1971-74; dep. under sec. for space systems, acting dir. NRO Air Force, 1974-79, dep. asst. sec. for space plans and policy, 1979-88. Adj. prof. George Mason U., Fairfax, Va., 1988-90; cons. aerospace engring., plans and policy Inst. Def. Analyses, Alexandria, Va., Sys. Planning Corp., Arlington, Def. Sci. Bd., Pentagon, Global Outpost Inc., Alexandria, ANSER, Arlington, George Washington U., VEDA, Alexandria, Kistler Aerospace, Kirkland, Wash., McGraw-Hill Inc., 1988—. Contbr. articles to profl. jours., chpts. to books. With A.C. AUS, 1944-47. Decorated Air Force Exceptional Civilian Svc. award with three oak leaf clusters; named to Coyote Hall of Fame, U. SD, 1976; recipient Meritorious Civil Svc. award, Sec. Def., 1974, Disting. Svc. award, 1976, Disting. Alumni award, U. S.D., 1982, cert. of appreciation, Intelligence R&D Coun., 1987, Disting. Svc. medal, NASA, 1988, Nat. Intelligence medal of achievement, 1988, Disting. Svc. award, Nat. Reconnaissance Office, 1998; fellow Dean Akeley, U. SD, 1951, Dobbins, Calif. Inst. Tech., 1953, 1954—56. Fellow AIAA; mem. IEEE (sr.), Am. Phys. Soc., Am. Inst. Physics, Sigma Xi, Phi Beta Kappa, Sigma Pi Sigma. Achievements include determination of astrophysical significance of B12 with respect to element synthesis in stellar interiors. Home: 1180 Daleview Dr Mc Lean VA 22102-1540 Office: Inst for Def Analyses 4850 Mark Center Dr Alexandria VA 22311-1882 Office Phone: 703-845-2312. Personal E-mail: cwcook22102@aol.com. Business E-Mail: ccook@ida.org.

COOK, CHRISTINE, elementary school educator; b. Phila., Jan. 24, 1964; d. James Joseph and Ann (Kolankiewicz) B.; m. Kenneth Mark Cook, June 9, 1990; children: Jennifer Lynn, Megan. B in Elem. Edn., West Chester U., 1985; M in Elem. Edn., Millersville U., 1992; MEd Instructional, M in Instrnl. Tech., Duquesne U., 2004. Nat. bd. cert. tchr. Kindergarten tchr. Somerton Nursery Sch. and Kindergarten, Phila., 1985-86, Milton Hershey Sch., Hershey, Pa., 1986—. Field hockey coach Milton Hershey Sch., 1986-92, softball coach, 1986-92, driver edn. instr., 1989-91. Mem. Assn. for Edn. of Young Children, Assn. for Childhood Edn. Internat. Democrat. Roman Catholic. Office: Milton Hershey Sch PO Box 830 Hershey PA 17033-0830 Business E-Mail: cookc@mhs-pa.org.

COOK, CHRISTOPHER L., accountant; b. San Bernardino, Calif., Dec. 6, 1974; s. Lee and Gayle Cook. AA in Bus. Adminstrn., San Antonio Coll., 1994; BBA in Acctg. and Mgmt., U. Tex., San Antonio, 1996, MBA in Mgmt. Acctg., 2002. Contr. Boys and Girls Clubs of San Antonio, 1996-97; MIS product support specialist Columbia Industries, San Antonio, 1997-98; acctg. mgr. GW Plastics, San Antonio, 1998-99; acct. Columbia Industries, San Antonio, 1999—2005; sr. acct. Taco Cabana, San Antonio, 2005—. Cons., contr. Boys and Girls Club of San Antonio, 1997—2001. E-mail: valla@worldnet.att.net.

COOK, CLARENCE EDGAR, science administrator, consultant; b. Jefferson City, Tenn., Apr. 27, 1936; s. Edgar Marion and Lillie Grey (Hodge) C.; m. Gail O'Connor McKee, June 1, 1957; children— David Grey, Lisa O'Connor Priebe, Kevin McKee. BS, Carson-Newman Coll., 1957; PhD, U. N.C., 1961; postdoctoral, U. Cambridge, Eng., 1961. Chemist, sr. chemist Rsch. Triangle Inst., Research Triangle Park, N.C., 1962-68, group leader, 1968-71, asst. dir. chem. life sci., 1971-75, dir. life sci. bioorganic chemistry, 1975-80, dir. bioorganic chemistry, 1980-85, research v.p., 1983-96, chief scientist, 1996—2004; ret., 2004. Adj. prof. Sch. Pharmacy, U. N.C., Chapel Hill, 1985-96. Mem. editorial adv. bd. Drug Metabolism and Disposition, 1977-93; mem. editl. bd. Emerging Drugs: The Prospect for Improved Medicines, 1999-2003; contbr. articles to profl. jours., chpts. to books; patentee in field. Recipient Margaret Elliott Knox Excellence award, 2003. Fellow N.Y. Acad. Scis.; mem. AAAS, Am. Chem. Soc., Am. Soc. Pharmacology and Exptl. Therapeutics, Coll. on Problems of Drug Dependence, Nat. Inst. on Drug Abuse (biomed. rsch. rev. com. 1985-89). Avocation: gardening. Office Phone: 540-885-2945. Business E-Mail: cec@rti.org.

COOK, COLIN BURFORD, psychiatrist; b. London, Jan. 20, 1927; arrived in U.S., 1952, naturalized, 1975; s. Bertram William and Anna Marie (Forster-Jones) C. MD, London U., 1951. Diplomate Am. Bd. Psychiatry and Neurology. Rotating intern Bridgeport (Conn.) Hosp., 1952-53; resident Goodmayes Hosp., Warlingham Park Hosp., London, 1955-57; gen. med. practitioner London, 1960-66; resident in psychiatry Marquette (Wis.) Sch. Medicine, 1968-69, Cornell U., White Plains, NY, 1969-71; fellow Nat. Hosp. Neurol. Disease, U. London, 1973; practice medicine specializing in psychiatry, Stamford, Conn., 1975—. Prof. psychiatry Columbia U., NYC, 1992-95; attending physician, psychiatrist Regional Network Programs, Inc., Conn.,

1995-96. Author: (as Alan Phillips) Jazz Improvisation and Harmony, 1965, 4th edit., 1998. Served with Brit. Navy, 1953-55, 57-59. Fellow: Am. Soc. Psychoanalytical Physicians; mem.: AMA, Authors League, Masons (32d degree). Address: 373 Strawberry Hill Ave Stamford CT 06902-2512 Office Phone: 203-348-9091. Personal E-mail: ccookie3210@aol.com.

COOK, DAVID, editor; b. Boston, Dec. 28, 1946; s. Theodore N. and Charlotte M. (Stachelhaus) Cook; m. Linda Markarian, Dec. 19, 1981; children: Matthew D., Christopher E., Timothy T. BA, Principia Coll., 1969; postgrad., Columbia U., 1977, Mich. State U., 1979-81. Staff writer Christian Sci. Monitor, Boston and Washington, 1971-77, bus. corr. Boston, 1981-82, Washington corr., 1982-88; chief bur. McGraw Hill World News, Detroit, 1977-79, dep. chief Chgo., 1980-81; corr. Bus. Week Mag., Detroit, 1979-80; mng. editor Monitor TV, Boston, 1988-92; editor Monitor Radio, Boston, 1992-94, The Christian Sci. Monitor, Boston, 1994—2001, Washington bur. chief, sr. editor, 2001—. With U.S. Army, 1969—71. Christian Scientist. Avocation: reading. Office: Christian Sci Monitor Washington Bur 910 16th St Washington DC 20006 Business E-Mail: cookd@csmonitor.com.

COOK, DAVID MARSDEN, physics professor; b. Troy, N.Y., Apr. 3, 1938; s. Marsden Alfred and Ethel Margaret (Minkwitz) C.; m. Cynthia Ann Gray, July 10, 1965; children: Brian David, Nathan James. BS in Physics, Rensselaer Poly. Inst., 1959; AM in Physics, Harvard U., 1960, PhD in Physics, 1965. Asst. prof. physics Lawrence U., Appleton, Wis., 1965-71, assoc. prof. physics, 1971-79, prof. physics, 1979—, Philetus E. Sawyer prof. sci., 1989—. Manuscript reviewer Am. Jour. Physics, 1974-94, 97—. Author: Theory of the Electromagnetic Field, 1975, reprint, 2003, Computation and Problem Solving in Undergraduate Physics, 2004; editor conf. procs., assoc. editor Computers in Physics, 1994—98. Grantee NSF, 1988, 93, 97, 2000, Keck Found., 1988, 93, 2002. Mem. Am. Assn. Physics Tchrs., Am. Phys. Soc., Sigma Xi. Avocations: church organist, gardening. Office: Lawrence U PO Box 599 Appleton WI 54912-0599 Business E-Mail: david.m.cook@lawrence.edu.

COOK, DEANNA DWORAKOWSKI, lawyer; b. Dayton, Ohio, June 22, 1966; m. Richard D. Cook, Sept. 3, 1993; children: Spencer Lane, Brett Alexander. BA, U. Richmond, 1988, JD, 1991. Bar: Va. 1991. Ptnr. Bremner, Janus Cook & Marcus, Richmond, Va., 1991—. Fellow Am. Acad. Matrimonial Lawyers; mem. Va. Trial Lawyer Assn., Metro Women's Bar Assn., Metro Family Law Bar Assn., Richmond Bar Assn. Office: Bremner Janus Cook & Marcus 701 E Franklin St Ste 1500 Richmond VA 23219-2510

COOK, DEBORAH L., federal judge, former state supreme court justice; b. Pittsburgh, Feb. 8, 1952; BA in English, U. Akron, 1974, JD, 1978, LLD (hon.), 1996. Ptnr. Roderick & Linton, Akron, 1976-91; judge 9th dist. Ohio Ct. Appeals, 1991-94; justice Ohio Supreme Ct., 1995—2003; judge U.S. Court of Appeals, 6th cir., Cincinnati, Ohio, 2003—. Bd. trustees Summit County United Way, Vol. Ctr., Stan Hywet Hall and Gardens, Akron Sch. Law, Coll. Scholars, Inc.; bd. dirs. Women's Network; vol. Mobile Meals, Safe Landing Shelter. Named Woman of Yr., Women's Network, 1991. Fellow Am. Bar Found.; mem. Omicron Delta Kappa, Delta Gamma (pres., Nat. Shield award). Office: 532 Potter Stewart US Courthouse 100 E Fifth St Cincinnati OH 45202-3988*

COOK, DEENA WHITE, music educator; b. San Antonio, Texas, Aug. 3, 1932; d. Robert Luther and Ora (Haggard) White; m. Gilbert William Muegge, Oct. 2, 1950 (div. Apr. 1976); children: Steven William, Gilbert William, Melissa Kay. Grad., High Sch., San Antonio, Tex., 1949. Sales Alamo Music Ctr., San Antonio, 1964—71; sales Alamo Windshield, San Antonio, 1971—75, Alamo Music Ctr., San Antonio, 1979—99; Owner, pres. Brook Hollow Sch. of Music, Inc., San Antonio, 1995—. Asst. to Dr. Peter Petroff, composer, recording artist.: albums. Mem. pastoral coun. St. Mark The Evangelist Ch., San Antonio, 1995—96; bd. dirs. Miller Child Devel. Ctr., 1974—79. Mem.: San Antonio Music Tchrs. Assn., Tex. Music Tchrs. Assn, Nat. Music Tchrs. Assn., San Antonio Coun. of Presidents, Pan Am. Round Table (pres. 2001—03). Roman Catholic. Home: 14910 Heimer Rd San Antonio TX 78232

COOK, DON LLOYD, lawyer, consultant, marketing educator; b. Sacramento, July 7, 1962; s. Don Lloyd and Bonnie Mae Cook; m. Elizabeth Bampfield Jacoby, Aug. 21, 1992. D, U. Ark., 1988, MBA, 1994; PhD, Va. Poly. Inst. and State U., 2003. Bar: Ark. 1989. Assoc. Lisle Law Firm, Springdale, Ark., 1992-93; asst. prof. La. Tech U., Ruston, 1999-2000; asst. prof. mktg. Ga. State U., Atlanta, 2000—. Am. Mktg. Assn.-Sheth fellow Va. Poly. Inst. and State U., 1998. Mem. ABA, Am. Mktg. Assn. (pres. doctoral spl. interest group 1997-98), Assn. for Consumer Rsch., Acad. Mktg. Sci., Decision Scis. Inst., Soc. for Consumer Psychology, Tech. Alliance Ga., Ga. Electronic Commerce Assn. Home: 110 Paisades Rd NE Atlanta GA 30309 Office: Ga State U Ste 1300 RCB University Plz Atlanta GA 30303-3083 Fax: 404-65104198. E-mail: doncook@gsu.edu, donlc@bellsouth.net.

COOK, DORIS MARIE, retired accountant, educator; b. Fayetteville, Ark., June 11, 1924; d. Ira and Mettie Jewel (Dorman) Cook. BSBA, U. Ark., 1946, MS, 1949; PhD, U. Tex., 1968. CPA Okla., Ark. Jr. acct. Haskins & Sells, Tulsa, 1946-47; instr. acctg. U. Ark., Fayetteville, 1947-52, asst. prof., 1952-62, assoc. prof., 1962-69, prof., 1969-88, Univ. prof. and Nolan E. Williams lectr. in acctg., 1988-97, emeritus disting. prof., 1997—. Mem. Ark. State Bd. Pub. Accountancy, 1987-92, treas., 1989-91, vice chmn. 1991-92; mem. Nat. Assn. State Bds. of Accountancy, 1987-92; appointed Nolan E. Williams lectureship in acctg., 1988-97; Doris M. Cook chair in acctg. U. Ark., Fayetteville, 2000. Mem. rev. bd. Ark. Bus. Rev., Jour. Managerial Issues; contbr. articles to profl. jours. Recipient Bus. Faculty of Month award Alpha Kappa Psi, 1997, Outstanding Faculty award Ark. Tchg. Acad., 1997, Charles and Nadine Baum Outstanding Tchr. award, 1997, Outstanding Leadership and Svc. award for Women's History Month, 1999, AAUW, others. Mem. AICPA, Ark. Bus. Assn. (editor newsletter 1982-85), Am. Acctg. Assn. (chmn. nat. membership 1982-83, Arthur Carter scholarship com. 1984-85, membership Ark. 1985-87), Am. Women's Soc. CPAs., Ark. Soc. CPA's (life, v.p. 1975-76, pres. N.W. Ark. chpt. 1980-81, sec. Student Loan Found. 1981-84, treas. 1984-92, pres. 1992-97, chmn. pub. rels. 1984-88, 93-95, Outstanding Acctg. Educator award 1991, Outstanding Com. Svc. award 1995, Student Loan Found. Bd. award 2001, 21 Yrs. Outstanding Svc. award 2001), Acad. Acctg. Historians (life, trustee 1985-87, rev. bd. of Working Papers Series 1984-92, sec. 1992-95, pres.-elect 1995, pres. 1996), Ark. Fedn. Bus. and Profl. Women's Clubs (treas. 1979-80), Fayetteville Bus. and Profl. Women's Clubs (pres. 1973-74, 75-76, Woman of Yr. award 1977) Mortar Bd., Beta Gamma Sigma, Beta Alpha Psi (editor nat. newsletter 1973-77, nat. pres. 1977-78, Outstanding Alumni in Edn. Iota chpt. 1999, Outstanding Svc. award Iota chpt. 1997), Phi Gamma Nu, Alpha Lambda Delta, Delta Kappa Gamma (sec. 1976-78, pres. 1978-80, treas. 1989-2000), Phi Kappa Phi. Home: 1655 Amy Ave Glendale Heights IL 60139

COOK, DOUGLAS NEILSON, theater educator, producer, artistic director; b. Phoenix, Sept. 22, 1929; s. Neil Estes and Louise Y. (Wood) C.; m. Joan Stafford Buechner, Aug. 11, 1956; children: John Richard, Peter Neilson, Stephen Barton. Student, LA Art Inst., 1948, Phoenix Coll., 1948—49, U. Chgo., 1949—50, UCLA, 1950—51; BFA, U. Ariz., 1953; MA, Stanford U., 1955; postgrad., Lester Polakov Studio Stage Design, 1966—67. Instr. San Mateo (Calif.) Coll., 1955-57, Nat. Music Camp, Interlochen, Mich., 1961; asst. prof. drama U. Calif., Riverside, 1957-66, assoc. prof., chair theatre dept., 1967-70; head dept. Pa. State U., University Park, 1970-88, sr. prof. theatre arts, 1970—92, disting. prof. emeritus, 1992—; prodr., artistic dir. Utah Shakespearean Festival, Cedar City. Actor Corral Theatre, Tucson, 1952-53, Orleans (Mass.) Arena Theatre, 1953; dir., designer Palo Alto (Calif.) Cmty. Theatre, 1954, Peninsula Children's Theatre, 1956-57; assoc. prodr. Utah Shakespearean Festival, Cedar City, 1964-90, producing artistic dir., 1990-2002, dir. emeritus, 2003—; prodr. Pa. State Festival Theatre, State College, 1970-85, The Nat. Wagon Train Show, 1975-76. Instl. rep. Juniata Valley coun. Boy Scouts Am., 1973-77; bd. dirs. Ctrl. Pa. Festival Arts, 1970-75, 84-87, v.p., 1984-86; bd. dirs. Nat. theatre Conf., 1980-90, v.p. 1983-85, pres. 1987-88. Recipient Disting. Alumni award U. Ariz., 1990; named to Coll. of Fellows Am. Theatre, 1994. Mem. AAUP, Shakespeare Theatre Assn. Am. (v.p. 1990-92, pres. 1993-94), Nat. Assn. Schs. Theatre, Am. Theatre Assn. (bd. dirs. 1977-86, exec. com. 1979-80, pres. 1984-85), U.S. Inst. Theatre Tech., Am. Soc. Theatre Rsch., Univ. Resident Theatre Assn. (bd. dirs. 1970-88, v.p. 1975-79, pres. 1979-83), Theatre Assn. Pa. (bd. dirs. 1972-76). Home: PO Box 10194 Phoenix AZ 85064-0194

COOK, EDWARD JOSEPH, college president; b. N.Y.C., July 8, 1925; s. Clinton J. and Catherine A. (Cullen) C.; m. Dorothy A. Collins, July 21, 1951; children: Barbara A., Thomas E., Patricia M. BS summa cum laude, Fordham U., 1949, PhD, 1958; MA, Columbia U., 1950. Assoc. prof., chmn. dept. econs. Sch. Bus., Fordham U., N.Y.C., 1950-62; asst. dean Sch. Bus., chmn. econs. dept. St. John's U., N.Y.C., 1962-64; prof. econs., dir. div. bus. C.W. Post Coll., Greenvale, N.Y., 1964-69, exec. dean Sch. Bus. Adminstrn., 1969-73; pres. C. W. Post Center, L.I. U., Greenvale, 1973-86. Mgmt. cons. to U.S. Navy and pvt. industry, 1969-73 Author: Causes of Commercial Bank Failures in New York State, 1958, (with R. Vizza) The Marketing Concept, 1968, (with A.F. Chapman) Peter Drucker, Contributions to Business Enterprises, 1970, (with J.N. Macri) Maternal Serum Alpha-Fetoprotein Patient-Specific Risk Reporting: Its Use and Misuse, 1990, (with J.N. Macri) Maternal Serum Down Syndrome Screening: Free Beta Protein, 1990. Chmn., L.I. Regional Planning Bd. Served with U.S. Army, 1942-45. Decorated Purple Heart. Mem. Am. Econ. Assn. Roman Catholic.

COOK, EUGENE AUGUSTUS, lawyer; b. Houston, May 2, 1938; s. Eugene A. and Estelle Mary (Stiner) C.; m. Sondra Attaway, Aug. 27, 1968; children: Laurie Ann, Eugene A. BBA, U. Houston, 1961, JD, 1966; LLM, U. Va., 1992. Bar: Tex. 1966, U.S. Dist. Ct. (so. dist.) Tex. 1967, U.S. Ct. Appeals (5th cir.) 1969, U.S. Supreme Ct. 1971, U.S. Ct. Claims 1972, U.S. Tax Ct. 1974, U.S. Ct. Appeals (11th cir.) 1982, U.S. Dist. Ct. (no., we. and ea. dists.) Tex. 1983. Ptnr. Butler & Binion, Houston, 1966-85; founding ptnr. Cook, Davis & McFall, 1985-88; justice Tex. Supreme Ct., Austin, 1988-93, chmn. jud. edn. exec. com., chmn. professionalism com., 1988-92; sr. ptnr. Bracewell & Patterson, Houston, 1993—. Adj. asst. prof. law U. Houston, 1971-72, 74. Editor in chief, contbg. author: Creditors Rights in Texas, 2d edit., 1981; bd. dirs. U. Houston Law Rev., 1978-79; contbr. articles to profl. jours. Vice-chmn. bd. YMCA, 1977; bd. dirs. Spl. Olympics, Tex., 1989-95, chmn. bd. dirs., 1994. Recipient Disting. Alumnus award U. Houston Law Ctr., 1990, Am. Inns of Ct.-Lewis F. Powell Jr. award, 1992. Fellow Am. Coll. Trial Lawyers, Am. Acad. Matrimonial Lawyers, Internat. Acad. Matrimonial Lawyers, Am. Bar Found., Tex. Bar Found. (Outstanding Pub. Svc. award 1990); mem. ABA, Am. Inns of Ct. (pres. Austin Inn 1990-91), Tex. Bar Assn. (chmn. grievance com. 1971-72, vice chmn. consumer law sect. 1976-77, chmn. consumer law sect. 1979-80, Presdl. Citation 1979, dir. family law sect. 1984-88, Presdl. Cert. Merit, 1983, 84, 86, Pres.'s award as most outstanding lawyer in Tex., 1989, chmn. pubs. com. 1981-82, Achievement award 1982, chmn. litigation sect. 1982-84, chmn. CLE, 1988-89), Houston Bar Assn. (seminar com. 1976-77, Chmn. of Yr. award, 1976-77, chmn. insts. com. 1977-78, Outstanding Svc. award 1977-78, chmn. CLE com. 1978-79, Pres.'s award, 1978-79, 96-97; chmn. consumer law sect. 1978-79, vice-chmn. family law sect. 1981-82, chmn. family law sect. 1982-83, Officers award 1983, chmn. staff and staffing com. 1985-86, chmn. Spl. Olympics Com. 1987-88, chmn. long range planning and devel. com. 1988-89, dir. 1984-86, 2d v.p. 1986-87, 1st v.p. 1987-88, pres. elect 1988-89, pres. 1989-90, chmn. profl. com. 1996-97), Texas Bd. Legal Specialization (cert.), Civil Trial and Family Law, Nat. Bd. Trial Advocacy (bd. cert. civil trial law), Tex. Assn. Cert. Civil Trial Law Lawyers, Gulf Coast Family Law Specialists Assn., Tex. Acad. Family Law Specialists, ABA, State Bar Tex., Phi Kappa Phi, Phi Theta Kappa (chmn. bd. dirs. 1966-71, 87-88, Most Disting. Alumnus in Nat. award, 1988), Omicron Chi Epsilon, Omicron Delta Kappa, Phi Rho Pi, U. Houston Alumni Assn. (bd. dirs. 1996—). Office: Bracewell & Patterson LLP S Tower Pennzoil Pl 711 Louisiana St Ste 2900 Houston TX 77002-2781

COOK, FRANCES D., management consultant; b. Charleston, W.Va., Sept. 7, 1945; d. Nash and Vivian Cook. BA, Mary Washington Coll. of U. Va., 1967; MPA, Harvard U., 1978; LLD, Shenandoah U., 1998. Certificats d'Etudes, Université d'Aix-Marseille (France), 1966. Commd. fgn. svc. officer Dept. State, 1967; spl. asst. to R.S. Shriver amb. to France, Paris, 1968-69; mem. U.S. Del. Paris Peace Talks on Viet-Nam, 1970-71; cultural affairs officer, consul Am. Consul Gen., Sydney, Australia, 1971-73; cultural affairs officer, first sec. Am. Embassy, Dakar, Senegal, 1973-75; personnel officer for Africa USIA, Washington, 1975-77; dir. office public affairs African Bur. Dept. State, Washington, 1978-80, amb. to Republic of Burundi at Bujumbura, 1980—83, consul gen. Alexandria, Egypt, 1983-86, dep. asst. sec. of state for refugees Washington, 1986-87, dir. Office of West African Affairs, 1987-89, amb. to Cameroon Yaoundé, 1989-93, U.S. coord. for Sudan, 1993; dep. asst. sec. of state for political-military affairs Dept. of State, Washington, 1993-95, amb. to Oman Muscat, 1996-99; founder The Ballard Group, LLC, 2002. Bd. dirs. ATK, Pegasus Energy Ltd.; chmn. bd. dirs. Gulf Environment, 2005—. Recipient various honor awards Dept. State and Def. Mem. Am. Fgn. Svc. Assn., Coun. of Fgn. Rels., Harvard Club of N.Y.C., Washington Inst. Fgn. Affairs, Phi Beta Kappa (alumni). Home: PO Box 40882 Washington DC 20016-0882 Office Phone: 202-237-7446. Business E-Mail: francesdcook@ballardgroupllc.com.

COOK, GARETH, reporter; b. Ann Arbor, Mich. m. Amanda Cook; 1 child. BA in Internat. Rels., BA in Math. Physics, Brown Univ., 1991. Asst. editor Fgn. Policy Mag., 1991—93; reporter US News & World Report, 1993—94; editor position Washington Monthly, 1995; news editor Boston Phoenix; New England editor, city desk Boston Globe, 1999, Sunday metro editor, 1999—2000, sci. writer, 2000—. Recipient Pulitzer Prize for explanatory reporting, 2005. Mem.: Sigma Xi, Phi Beta Kappa. Office: Boston Globe 135 Morissey Blvd PO Box 55819 Boston MA 02205-5819 Office Phone: 617-929-2000.

COOK, GARY RAYMOND, academic administrator, minister; b. Little Rock, Ark., Sept. 27, 1950; s. Raymond C. and Vada (James) C.; m. Sheila Gayle Raymer, Dec. 28, 1974; children: David Daniel, Mark Andrew. BA, Baylor U., 1972; MDiv, So. Sem., Louisville, 1975; MA, U. North Tex., 1977; D in Ministry, Southwestern Sem., 1977. Pastor 1st Bapt. Ch., McGregor, Tex., 1976-78; dir. denomination and community rels. Baylor U., Waco, Tex., 1978-88; pres. Dallas Bapt. U., 1988—. Author: Retirees in Mission, 1977; co-editor: Abner McCall: One Man's Journey, 1981. Mayor pro tem City of Waco, 1983-84, mem. city coun., 1981-84; past bd. dirs. Tex. Dept. on Aging; past internat. bd. dirs. Habitat for Humanity. Recipient Humanitarian award Waco Conf. Christians and Jews, 1986, Disting. Alumnus award Southwestern Sem., 2000, Baylor U., 2003. Mem. Rotary (sustaining). Home and Office: 3000 Mountain Creek Pkwy Dallas TX 75211-6700

COOK, GEORGE VALENTINE, lawyer, consultant; b. Glendale, N.Y., Feb. 14, 1927; s. Walter Preston and Ida Ruth (Smith) C.; m. Edith Wengler, Sept. 4, 1948 (dec. Dec. 2002); children: George V., James, Robert, Laura, Barbara, Mary, Walter, Elizabeth. BA, Columbia U., 1949, LL.B., 1952. Bar: N.Y. 1953, U.S. Dist. Ct. (so. dist.) N.Y. 1955, U.S. Dist. Ct. (ea. dist.) N.Y. 1955, U.S. Ct. Appeals (2d cir.) 1955, U.S. Ct. Appeals (3d cir.) 1982, US. Dist. Ct. (no. dist.) N.Y. 1987. Assoc. Dewey, Ballantine, Bushby, Palmer & Wood, N.Y.C., 1952-56; mem. legal staff N.Y. Telephone Co., N.Y.C., 1956-59, 60-61; atty. AT&T, N.Y.C., 1959-60, 61-65, v.p., 1972—76; v.p. regulatory matters Western Electric Co., Inc., N.Y.C., 1966-72, v.p. gen. counsel, 1976-83, also dir.; exec. v.p., gen. counsel AT&T Technologies, Inc., N.Y.C., 1984-85; counsel Hunton & Williams, 1985-90; cons., 1990—. Contbr. articles to profl. jours. Active alumni activities Columbia U. Served to 2d lt. U.S. Army, 1945-47. Fellow Am. Bar Found.; mem. ABA, N.Y. State Bar Assn., Assn. Gen. Counsel, Assn. of Bar of City of N.Y. Home: 127 Somerset Ave Garden City NY 11530-1348

COOK, GERALD, electrical engineering educator; b. Hazard, Ky., Oct. 31, 1937; s. Rudolph H. and Rose I. (Boyer) C.; m. Nancy Anne Gillespie, June 9, 1962; children: Gerald Boyer, Allan Binford. BS, Va. Poly. Inst., 1961; MS, MIT, 1962, ScD, 1965. Registered profl. engr., Va. Lectr. U. Colo., Colorado Springs, 1966—68; asst. prof. U.S. Air Force Acd., Colorado Springs, 1966—68; assoc. prof. U. Va., Charlottesville, 1968—73, prof., 1973—81; prof., chmn. dept. Vanerbilt U., Nashville, 1981—85; Earle C. Williams prof. elec. engring. George Mason U., Fairfax, Va., 1985—, chmn. dept. elec. and computer engring., 1990—98. Vis. prof. Tech. U. Denmark, 1979-80; vis. rschr. Night Vision Lab., Ft. Belvoir, 1998-99. Editor-in-chief IEEE Trans. on Indsl. Electronics, 1984-91. Recipient Outstanding Rsch. award USAF Office Aerospace Rsch., 1968, Cert. of Achievement, U.S. Army, 1981; NSF fellow, 1961-64. Fellow IEEE (life, pres. Indsl. Electronics Soc. 1981-83, Centennial medal 1984, Eugene Mittelmann Achievement award 1989), Am. Soc. Engring. Edn. (Outstanding Rsch. awrd S.E. sect. 1971), Sigma Xi, Eta Kappa Nu, Phi Kappa Phi, Tau Beta Pi. Home: 4821 Fox Chapel Rd Fairfax VA 22030-4508 Office: George Mason U Dept Elec Engring Fairfax VA 22030 Office Phone: 703-993-1699. Business E-Mail: gcook@gmu.edu.

COOK, GLORIA HOUSTON, civic leader; b. Portland, Maine, Aug. 22, 1933; d. Ellwyn Kenelm and May Elvera (Delay) Houston; m. James Thomas Cook Jr., Jan. 28, 1952; children: Victoria Cook Leonhardt, Sheryl Ann. Student, U. Fla., 1950-52. Invitee, White House Conf. on Food, Nutrition and Health, 1969, cons. to Fla. conf., 1970; Gen. Synod del. from Fla., United Ch. of Christ, 1975-77; dir. pub. rels., trustee, chmn. nominating com., mem. pulpit com., tchr. Sunday sch., mem. stewardship bd., Seabreeze United Ch.; legis. appointee, sec. exec. bd., Volusia County Charter Rev. Commn., 1975-77; mem. Volusia County Pers. and Merit Bd., 1974-85, chmn., 1980-83; bd. counselors, Bethune-Cookman Coll., 1977-84; bd. dirs., Atlantic Ctr. for Arts, New Smyrna Beach, Fla.; pres., bd. dirs., exec. com. Meml. Health Care Systems, Ormond Beach, Fla., 1980-2000, mem. hosp. estate planning com., chmn., treas. pers. com., chmn. fin. com., v.p., CEO search, evaluation and compensation com.; hon. life dir. Volusia/Flagler Easter Seals, 1955—, fundraising capital campaign chmn., 1999-2004; past pres., v.p., sec. Fla. Easter Seals; past pres., v.p., chair, vice chmn. Ho. of Dels. Nat. Easter Seals; mem. nat. adv. child health and human devel. Coun. Nat. Insts. Health, 1990-94; past pres., sustaining mem. Jr. League Daytona Beach, Civic League Halifax Area. Recipient Meritorious Service and Outstanding Vol. Service awards Nat. Easter Seals, Humane Carer of Yr. Meml. Health Sys., 1991, Easter Seal Lily award, 2004; named Layman of Yr., Fla. Med. Soc., 1985, one of 100 Outstanding Jr. League Mems. Internat. Jr. Leagues, named Vol. of Distinciton, Centennial Yr., 1995. Mem. Nat. League Am. Pen Women (patron), Highlands Country Club (N.C.), Hammock Dunes Country Club (Fla.). Republican. Avocations: collecting perfume bottles, photography, gardening. Home: 15 Madeira Ct Palm Coast FL 32137-2103 also: 78 S Sassafras Ct Highlands NC 28741-6635

COOK, HARRY CLAYTON, JR., lawyer; b. Washington, Mar. 25, 1935; s. Harry Clayton and Lillian June (A'harrah) Cook; m. Jane Clare Mellius, 1963 (div. 1974); children: Christianne Pier, Nicole, Harry Clayton III; m. Judith Ann Taber, 1994; children: Rebecca Lyeth Kelsey, Parker Burr Kelsey. BSChemE, Princeton U., 1956; LLB, U. Va., 1960. Bar: Colo. 1960, N.Y. 1961, Pa. 1966, D.C. 1973. Assoc. Sullivan & Cromwell, N.Y.C., 1960-63, Holme Roberts & Owen, Denver, 1964, Pepper Hamilton & Scheetz, Phila., 1965-69, ptnr., 1969-70, 73; on assignment as sr. tax counsel Sun Oil Co., Phila., 1970; ptnr. Cadwalader Wickersham & Taft, Washington, 1974-87, Bishop, Cook, Purcell & Reynolds, Washington, 1988-90; pvt. practice H.C. Cook Law Offices, Langley, Va., 1991; of counsel Bastianelli, Brown & Touhey, Washington, 1992—2002; ptnr. Mgmt. & Transp. Assoc., Inc., Essex, Conn., 2001—05; sr. counsel Fulbright & Jaworski LLP, Washington, 2002—04; counsel, maritime law Seward & Kissel LLP, Washington, 2004—. Page to U.S. Sen. E. D. Millikin, Colo., 1950—52; gen. counsel Maritime Adminstrn.; mem. Maritime Subs. Bd., U.S. Dept. Commerce, Washington, 1970—73; U.S. del. to Soviet Union Maritime Agreement between U.S. and USSR, 1971—73; mem. Adminstrv. Conf. U.S., 1980—90, chmn. com. jud. rev., 1982—88, sr. fellow, 1988—90; mem. Nat. Def. Exec. Res., U.S. Mil. Sealift Command, 1983—91, U.S. Office Tech. Assessment; mem. citizens adv. panel U.S. Maritime Ind., 1982—85, cargo policy workshop particpant, 1984—85. Mem. editl. bd.: Va. Law Rev., 1958—60, exec. editor:, 1959—60; contbr. articles to profl. jours. Bd. dirs. Com. on the Present Danger, 1978—87; bd. govs. United Svc. Orgns., 1998—2002; bd. dirs. New World Inst., 2000—, Inst. Fgn. Policy Analysis, 1975—87. Mem.: ABA, Maritime Law Assn. U.S. (marine fin. com., proctor in admiralty), D.C. Bar Assn., Am. Law Inst. (life), Raven Soc., Univ. Club (N.Y.C.), Fishers Island Club (N.Y.), Chevy Chase (Md.) Club, Cosmos Club (Washington), Hay Harbor Club (N.Y.), Met. Club (Washington), Order of Coif, Phi Delta Phi. Office: Seward & Kissel LLP Ste 350 1200 G Ste NW Washington DC 20005 Office Phone: 202-737-8833. Personal E-mail: plimsolldc@aol.com.

COOK, HARVEY CARLISLE, law enforcement official; b. Cambridge, Md., June 19, 1936; s. John Morrison and Lula Arbelia (Warfield) C.; m. Shirley Marie Cox, Aug. 4, 1973; children: Brenda, Claudine, John, Anne. AA in Police Sci., Charles Ct. C.C., 1973; BBA, U. Md., 1979, cert. in paralegal, 1980; cert. in criminal justice, FBI Nat. Acad., 1983. lic. USCG Masters, 1988. Insp. Tidewater Fisheries Dept., Hughesville, Md., 1958—61, dist. insp., 1962—64; lt. Md. State Marine Police, Hughesville, 1965—69, capt. LaPlata, 1970—72, Md. Natural Resources Police, LaPlata, 1973—75, maj. Annapolis, 1976—86, dep. supt., 1986—88; dir. Hovercraft tng. and ops. Hover Sys., Inc., 1988—93; dir. health & indsl. safety Mech. Constrn. Inc., 1994—; dir. marine & indsl. safety & security Cook & Assocs., 1995—. Liaison officer Emergency Mgmt. Agy., Pikesville, Md., 1974-86. Bd. dirs. Charles County Fair, LaPlata, 1985. Recipient Instr. Svc. award, 2001, Pa. Fish and Boat Commn. Instr. award, 2003; Disting. Svc. award Gov. of Md., 1987, Sustained Aux. Svc. award USCG Aux., 2000; named Best Engring. Soldier Md. Nat. Guard 121st Engr. Bn., 1967, Disting. Citizen, Mass. Gov.'s Office, 1983; Ky. Col., 1983. Mem. Fraternal Order Police, NRA (life), Nat. Police Officers Assn. Am. (charter), Hoverclub Am., U.S. Hovercraft Soc. Inc. (bd. dirs. 1987, v.p. 1990-92, pres. 1993), U.S. Coast Guard Aux. (Ann. Safe Boating award 1975, Pub. Educator award 1999, Instr. Svc. award 2004, state liaison officer 1982-86, vice Flotilla comdr. 1996, comdr. 1997-98, Flotilla staff officer 1998-2005), Chesapeake Bay Profl. Capts. Assn., Potomac River Pilots Assn., FBI Nat. Acad. Assocs., Dr. Samuel A. Mudd Soc. Inc. (treas. 1987), So. Md. Bd. Realtors, Md. Chiefs Police Assn., Charles County C.C. Alumni Assn. (pres. 1984). Republican. Methodist. Avocations: hunting, fishing, power boating, antiques. Office: Cook & Assocs 408 Briarwood Rd Wallingford PA 19086-6503 Office Phone: 610-999-4286. Personal E-mail: hscook1@comcast.net.

COOK, IAN AINSWORTH, psychiatrist, researcher, educator; b. N.Y.C., May 1, 1960; s. Charles David and Bobette Cook; m. Hallie Houck; 1 child, Natalie. BS in Engring. magna cum laude, Princeton U., 1982; MD, Yale U., 1987. Diplomate Nat. Bd. Med. Examiners, Am. Bd. Psychiatry and Neurology. Resident in surgery U. Colo., Denver, 1987-88; resident in psychiatry Neuropsychiat. Inst. UCLA, 1991-94, chief resident in liaison psychiatry, 1993-94, instr. dept. psychiatry, 1995-96, assoc. dir. residency edn. dept. psychiatry, 1995-96, asst. prof psychiatry, 1996—2003, assoc. prof. psychiatry, 2003—; registrar Neuropsychiat. Inst., 1999—2001; dir. NPI Acad. Info. Tech. Core, 1999—; assoc. dir. Office of Profl. and Cmty. Edn., 1998—. Examiner Am. Bd. Psychiatry and Neurology, 1998—. Mem. editl. bd. Jefferson Jour. Psychiatry, 1992-94; contbr. articles to profl. jours. Rsch. fellow Nat. Inst. Mental Health, 1993-96; recipient Young Investigator award Nat. Alliance Rsch. Schizophrenia and Depression, 1995, 97. Mem. Am. Psychiat. Assn. (Burroughs-Wellcome fellow 1992, mem. com. of resident and fellows 1992-94, mem. steering com./practice guidelines 1994—, mem. exec. com. 2002—), Nat. Eagle Scout Assn., Sigma Xi, Tau Beta Pi. Achievements include four patents in biomed. devices and methods. Office: UCLA Neuropsychiat Inst & Hosp 760 Westwood Plz Los Angeles CA 90095-8353

COOK, IAN M., consumer products company executive; With Colgate, United Kingdom, 1976, mktg. dir., gen. mgr., Colgate's Nordic Group, Copenhagen; exec. v.p. mktg., Colgate N. Am. Colgate-Palmolive Co., N.Y.C., 1994—97, pres. Colgate-N. Am., 1997—2002, exec. v.p., 2000—04, COO, 2004—. Office: Colgate-Palmolive Co 300 Park Ave New York NY 10022

COOK, IRIS M., science educator; b. Harrison, NY, July 7, 1934; children: Christine Grenell, Marjorie Kenney. AAB, Rochester C.C., 1954; BA, U. Bridgeport, 1970, MS, 1971; PhD, Fordham U., 1982. Cert. Med. Tech. Am. Med. Tech. Prof. SUNY, Valhalla, NY, 1971—. Dir. Va. Med. Ctr. Rsch. Found., Bronx, NY, 1990—, UCC Found., Valhalla, NY, 1994—, NY State Soc. of Med. Tech., 1974—; book reviewer Microbiology, 2004. Commnr. Conservation Commn., Ridgefield, Conn., 1978—87. Named Dist. Chmn. Biology, UCC Found., 1992; recipient Excellence in Tchg., SUNY, 1974, Excellence in Faculty Svc., 2004. Mem.: AAAS, NY Acad. of Sci., Sigma Xi. Avocation: travel. Office: SUNY Westchester C C 75 Grasslands Rd Valhalla NY 10595 Office Phone: 914-606-6769. Office Fax: 914-606-6889. E-mail: iris.cook@sunywcc.edu.

COOK, JAMES IVAN, clergyman, educator; b. Grand Rapids, Mich., Mar. 8, 1925; s. Cornelius Peter and Cornelia (Dornbos) C.; m. Jean Rivenburgh, July 8, 1950; children: Mark James, Carol Jean, Timothy Scott, Paul Brian (dec.). BA, Hope Coll., 1948; MA, Mich. State U., 1949; BD, Western Theol. Sem., 1952; ThD, Princeton Theol. Sem., 1964. Ordained to ministry Reformed Ch. America, 1953. Pastor Blawenburg Reformed Ch., N.J., 1953-63; from instr. to asst. prof. bibl. langs. Western Theol. Sem., Holland, Mich., 1963-67, prof. bibl. langs. and lit., 1967-77, Anton Biemont prof. New Testament, 1977-95, prof. emeritus, 1995—; chmn. Theol. Commn., Reformed Ch. Am. N.Y.C., 1980-85; pres. Gen. Synod-Reformed Ch. Am., N.Y.C., 1982-83. Author: Edgar Johnson Goodspeed, 1981, Shared Pain and Sorrow: Reflections of a Secondary Sufferer, 1991, One Lord/One Body, 1991; editor Reformed Rev., 1987-2002; contbg. editor: Grace Upon Grace, 1975, Saved by Hope, 1978, The Church Speaks, 1985; founding editor Perspectives: A Jour. of Reformed Thought, 1986-90, The Church Speaker, vol. 2, 2002. Served with U.S. Army, 1943-45, ETO. Recipient Disting. Alumni award, Hope Coll., 1985, Western Theol. Sem., 2004. Home: 1004 S Shore Dr Holland MI 49423-4539 Office: Western Theol Sem 101 E 13th St Holland MI 49423-3622

COOK, JAMES JUNIOR, academic administrator; b. Pryor, Okla., Oct. 25, 1946; s. Paul Amos and Gladys Blanche (Davis) C.; m. Stephanie Karlene Schneidewent, May 6, 1967; children: Adrian Leigh, Shaun Michael. BA in Edn., Northeastern State U., 1970; MA in History, S.W. Tex. State U., 1973; EdD in Higher Edn., Tex. Tech. U., 1977. Asst. prof. history Schreiner Coll., Kerrville, Tex., 1972-76; dir. student activities Midland (Tex.) Coll., 1977-78; asst. campus dir. N.Mex. State U., Alamogordo, 1978-81; dir. acad. and student svcs. East Tex. State U., Texarkana, 1981-82; v.p. student affairs Seminole (Okla.) Jr. Coll., 1982-84, v.p. acad. affairs, 1984-89, pres., 1987-96; exec. v.p. Rose State Coll., Midwest City, Okla., 1996-2000, pres., 2000—. Chmn. East Cen. Okla. Edn. Consortium, 1989-91; pres. Bi-State Athletic Conf., 1989-90. Contbr. articles to profl. jours. Alumni v.p. Leadership Okla., Oklahoma City, 1990; active Seminole Spl. Edn. Found., 1989-96; mem. troop com. Boy Scouts Am., Seminole, 1989-95, chmn. Big Teepee dist., 1998-2000; v.p. Jasmine Moran Children's Mus., Seminole, 1989-96; grad. Leadership Midwest City, 1997; chmn. Studio Mid-Del, 2002-04; v.p. Defenders of Dreams Heritage Ctr., 2002—; mem. Govs. Coun. on Workforce and Econ. Devel., 2003—. Named Citizen of Yr., Seminole C. of C., 1989; recipient Silver Beaver award, Boy Scouts Am., 2001, Dist. award of merit, 2001. Mem. Coun. Pres. Okla. (chmn. 1995-96, 2003-04), Seminole Hall of Fame, Phi Theta Kappa (Shirley Gordon award of distinction 2005). Avocations: tennis, reading. Home: 10201 SE 55th St Oklahoma City OK 73150-4532 Office: Rose State Coll 6420 SE 15th St Midwest City OK 73110-2704

COOK, JANE HAMPTON, communications consultant; b. Nurnberg, Bavaria, Germany, June 8, 1970; (parents Am. citizens); d. Larry Wayne and Judith Travis Hampton; m. John Kim Cook, Apr. 23, 1994. BA in Music, Baylor U., 1992; MS in Ednl. Adminstrn., Tex. A&M U., 1995. Spl. events coord. Tex. A&M U., Coll. Sta., Tex., 1995—98; internet comm. dir. and writer Office of the Gov. of Tex., Austin, Tex., 1998—2001; dep. dir. for internet news svcs. The White House, Washington, 2001—03; cons., spkr., writer Alexandria, Va., 2003—. Author: Maggie Houston: My Father's Honor, 2002. Spkr. Tex. Book Festival, Austin, 2002—02; vol. Rep. Nat. Conv., Phila., 2000—00; worship group leader McLean (Va.) Bible Ch., 2001—. Fellow: Orgn. Am. Historians, White House Hist. Assn.; mem.: Soc. Children's Book Writers and Illustrators (corr.), Nashville Spkrs. Bur. Achievements include design of White House web site for President George W. Bush, 2001-2003. Avocations: singing, writing, reading, crafts, walking. Personal E-mail: jane.cook@juno.com.

COOK, JANICE ELEANOR NOLAN, retired elementary school educator; b. Middletown, Ohio, Nov. 22, 1936; d. Lloyd and Eleanor Lee (Caudill) Nolan; m. Kenneth J. Cook, May 16, 1980 (dec.); children: Gerald W. Fultz Jr., Jana Linn Perkins, Jennylee Heard. BSEd, Miami U., 1971; MEd, reading specialist cert., Xavier U., 1982, rank 1 cert., 1987, spl. edn. cert., 1988. Tchr. pre-sch. and elem. Middletown (Ohio) Pub. Schs., 1957-58, 71-80; tchr. Boone County Schs., Florence, Ky., 1980-99; ret., 1999. Resource tchr. Ky. Internship Program, 1985—95; substitute tchr. Lebanon City Schs. Fellow: ABI Rsch. Assn. (life); mem.: NEA, Nat. Coun. Tchrs. Math., Assn. Childhood Edn. Internat., Boone County Edn. Assn., Ky. Edn. Assn., Nat. Coun. Tchrs. English, Internat. Reading Assn., Nat. Assn. Edn. Young Children. Home: 926 Pineneedle Pl Maineville OH 45039-7019

COOK, JANICE MCDONALD, art educator; b. Dothan, Ala., Apr. 17, 1950; d. Archie and Mary Evelyn McDonald; m. James F. Cook, Mar. 18, 1972; children: Julie, Jeremy, Jordan, Jarrod. B, Troy State U., 1972. Art tchr. Huffman HS, Birmingham, Ala., 1972—77; art tchr., fine arts dept. chmn. E.B. Erwin HS, Birmingham, 1984—. Visual art chairperson Nat. Edn. Assn. Fine Arts Caucus, 2002—03; cultural arts chmn. Ala. PTA, Birmingham, Ala., 1985—; workshop instr. Ala. Edn. Assn., 1990—2001. Friendship Angel, 2002, Ripped Out My Heart, 2002 (People's Choice award). Mem. Civitans Internat. Ctr. Point, 2002. Named Secondary Art Tchr. of Yr., Ala. Art Edn. Assn., 2000; recipient Parental Involvement award of Merit, Ala. Edn. Assn., 2003, Jefferson County Tchr. of Yr., Jefferson County Parent Tchr. Assn., 1993. Mem.: Carrollton Art Guild, Birmingham Art Assn., Birmingham Art Educators Assn. (pres. 2000—02). Avocations: gardening, spl. olympics, art camps.

COOK, JAY MICHAEL, accounting company executive; b. N.Y.C., Sept. 16, 1942; m. Mary Anne Griffith, July 11, 1964; children: Jennifer Lynn, Angela Marie, Jeffrey Thomas. BS in Bus. Adminstrn. cum laude, U. Fla., 1964. C.P.A., N.Y., Fla. Ptnr. Deloitte, Haskins & Sells, N.Y.C., 1974-81, ptnr.-in-charge Miami, 1981-83, mng. ptnr. N.Y.C., 1983-86, chmn., CEO, 1986-89, Deloitte & Touche, 1989-99; ret. Adv. com. Securities Regulation Inst.; chmn. GAO Accountability Adv. Panel; bd. dirs., chmn. nominating and governing coms. The Dow Chem. Co.; bd. dirs., Internat. Flavors and Fragrances, Comcast Corp., Northrop Grumman Corp.; ind. trustee, bd. dirs. The Fidelity Group Mut. Funds. Bd. govs., past chmn. United Way Am.; chmn. emeritus Catalyst; mem. adv. com. Sch. Bus., U. Fla., Gainesville; past chmn. bd. trustees Fin. Acctg. Found. Recipient Disting. Alumnus award U. Fla., John McCloy award, 2001; named to Acctg. Hall of Fame, 1999. Mem. AICPA (mem. coun. 1983—, vice-chmn. 1985-86, chmn. 1986-87, John J. McCloy award 2001), Greenwich (Conn.) Country Club, Blind Brook Club. Republican. Presbyterian. Avocations: tennis, golf.

COOK, JEANNINE SALVO, librarian, consultant; b. N.Y.C., Apr. 11, 1929; d. Ernest August and Edith Agatha (Lombardo) Salvo; m. Donald Carter Cook, June 9, 1962; 1 child, Carter Steven. BA, Hunter Coll., 1951; MLS, Columbia U., 1958, postgrad., 1973. Chemist Charles Pfizer and Co., Inc., Bklyn., 1951-56, lit. chemist, 1956-58; cen. med. librarian Am. Cyanamid, N.Y.C., 1958-60; sr. profl. adminstr. Engring. and phys. scis. library Columbia U., N.Y.C., 1960-62; assoc. librarian SUNY, Stony Brook, 1962-63; dir. Emma S. Clark Meml. Library, Setauket, N.Y., 1966-93; cons. Bro Dart, Williamsport, Pa., 1990—. Mem. adv. bd. Gale, Rsch. Pub., Detroit, 1986—88, mem. editl. bd., 1989; mem. design com. Gaylord Bros., Syracuse, NY, 1987. Pres. bd. dirs. 3 Village Cmty. Youth Coun., Stony Brook, 1978—88; bd. dirs. Ministries Coun., Setauket, 1978—85, 3 V Schs.-Cmty. Youth at Risk, Stony Brook, 1989—; c0chmn. edn. com. Assn. Cmty. Univ. Cooperative, Stony Brook, 1973—80; v.p. Health House, 1991—93; bd. dirs. 3 Village Civic Assn., 1991—95; aux. mem. Mather Meml. Hosp., 1991—, rec. sec., 2000—. Recipient Pub. Rels. award, Libr. Pub. Rels. Coun., 1978, Recognition for voluntarism, Brookhaven Youth Bur., 1984, Recognition for Outstanding Svc., Cmty. Youth Svcs., Stony Brook, 1988. Mem.: ALA (Pub. Rels. award 1987), Med. Libr. Assn., Spl. Libr. Assn., Pub. Libr. Dirs. Assn. (exec. bd. 1976—), Brookhaven Libr. Dirs. (pres. 1976—80). Home and Office: 40 Seabrook Ln Stony Brook NY 11790-3328 Personal E-mail: jpcook40@yahoo.com.

COOK, JEFFERY BLANE, history professor, consultant; b. New Martinsville, W.Va., Jan. 21, 1960; s. Russell Jerry and Betty Lee Cook; m. Laura J. Willis, July 7, 2001; children: Margaret Anne, Adam Winston. BA, Fairmont State Coll., 1986; MA, W.Va. U., 1989, PhD in History, 1998. Assoc. prof. history, chmn. dept. history and polit. sci. Nyack (N.Y.) Coll., 1999—2003, North Greenville Coll., Tigerville, SC, 2003—. Cons. Hist. Assocs., Taylors, SC, 2003—; adj. faculty U. Md. Univ. Colls., Adelphi, 2004—; adj. in history Limestone Coll., Gaffney, SC, 2003—; adj. DeVry U., Chgo., 2005—. Mem.: Churchill Ctr., Am. Assn. History and Computing, Am. Hist. Assn. Republican. Avocation: fighting arts. Home: 145 Brooke Lee Cir Taylors SC 29687 Office: North Greenville Coll PO Box 1892 Tigerville SC 29688 Office Phone: 864-895-8943.

COOK, JOHN, mayor; b. Bklyn., Feb. 27, 1946; m. Tram Cook, 1970; 6 children. ABA Bus. Arts, El Paso Community Coll.; BA Bus. Conferred Mgmt., Univ. Texas El Paso, 1973—77; Alternative Cert Spl Edn, Univ. Tex. El Paso, 1992—93. Ctrl. office installer Western Electric Co., 1965—72; mgr. network options Southwestern Bell Telephone Co., 1983—91; v.p. and marketing plant mgr. Hoang Food Products Inc., 1993—95; pres. mktg. mng. and fundraising consultants Cook and Assoc., 1994—; quality assurance coord. and v.p. mktg. Cooks Catering, 1998—; city rep. Dist. IV, 1999—. Vol. exec. dir. El Paso Charities Comm. Chest, 1994—; quality assurance coord. and grant writer Bienvivir Sr. Health Svc., 1996—97; pres. El Paso Housing Fin. Corp., 1999—, El Paso Health Care Facilities Financing Corp. M.d. counterintelligence U.S. Army, 1971, Vietnam. Recipient Gen. Mgr. award for comm. svc., SW Bell Tel. Co., 1989, Golden Hammer award, Habitat for Humanity, 2002. Mem.: United Way El Paso, El Paso Transp. Collaborative (pro-bono cons. 1996—), Am. Legion, LULAC Project Amistad (chmn. 2000—). Office: Office of the Mayor 10th Fl 2 Civic Ctr Plz El Paso TX 79901*

COOK, JOHN M., finance company executive; Former CFO Caldor Stores and Kaufmann's Dept. Stores divsn. May Dept. Stores Co.; pres., CEO Roy Greene Assocs., 1989-90; founder, CEO, chmn. The Profit Recovery Group Internat. Inc., Atlanta, 1991—. Office: The Profit Recovery Group Schultz Intl Inc 600 Galleria Pkwy SE #100 Atlanta GA 30339-5991

COOK, JOHN ROSCOE, JR., communications executive, marketing professional; b. Houston, Apr. 17, 1943; s. John Roscoe and Ruth Mildred (Spargo) C.; m. Loxi June Gumienny, Aug. 28, 1964 (dec. 1993); children: John T., Andrew J., Wesley A.; m. Crystal R.E. Grennan, May 6, 2000. BA, U. Houston, 1968. With Allstate Ins. Co., Northbrook, Pa., Tex, Va., various states, 1968-80; v.p. pub. affairs Am. Ins. Assn., Washington, 1980-85; sr. v.p. Ins. Inst. Hwy. Safety, 1985-87, exec. v.p., 1987-89; sr. v.p., chief comm. officer USAA, San Antonio, 1989-97, Nationwide Ins. Enterprise, Columbus, Ohio, 1997—2003. Chmn. Walkamerica March of Dimes, Franklin County, Ins. Edn. Foun., Columbus Jazz Arts, Riverwalk, Live at the Landing, Buckeye Ranch Found. Fellow Pub. Rels. Soc. Am.; mem. Nat. Press Club, Capitol Hill Club, The Lakes C.C., The Capitol Club, Club Giraud, Gainey Ranch Golf Club. Home: 5854 Via Los Caballos Paradise Valley AZ 85253 E-mail: cook57@cox.net.

COOK, J(OHN) ROWLAND, lawyer; b. Dallas, July 20, 1942; s. John Hubbard and Nancy Eva Cook; m. April Beall, Dec. 24, 1966 (div. 1984); children: Matthew Rowland, Samantha, Joshua Malcolm, Abigail; m. Diane E. Ireson, Aug. 10, 1990; stepchildren: Eric Perlmutter, Lindsay Perlmutter. Student, Tex. A&M U., 1960, So. Meth. U., 1961; BBA, U. Tex., 1964, LLB, 1965. Tax law specialist IRS, Washington, 1965-66; adminstrv./legis. asst. U.S. congressman J. J. Pickle, Washington, 1966-69; spl. counsel, staff atty. div. corp. fin. SEC, Washington, 1969-76, chief, asst. dir. Office of Disclosure Policy and Proceedings div. corp. fin., 1976-79; asst. atty. gen. ins., banking and securities dept. State of Tex., Austin, 1979-80; from assoc. to ptnr. Salmanson, Smith & Mouer, Austin, 1980-81; ptnr., mem. Johnson & Wortley, P.C., Austin, 1981-95; shareholder Jenkens & Gilchrist, P.C., Austin, 1995—, mng. shareholder Austin office, 2003—. Bd. dirs., pres. Travis County Dispute Resolution Ctr., 1990-95. Contbr. articles to profl. jours. Bd. dirs. Peoples' Cmty. Clinic. Office: Jenkens & Gilchrist PC Ste 2500 401 Congress Ave Austin TX 78701-3238 Office Phone: 512-499-3800.

COOK, KATHRYN ANNE, secondary school educator; b. Coral Gables, Fla., Dec. 5, 1951; d. Raymond Clarence Cook and Dorothea Pauline Glühr-Cook; 1 child, Kimberley Spinney. BA, Marquette U., 1973; diploma in German lang., Goethe Inst., Germany, 1973; EdM, Cambridge Coll., 1998. English tchr. Goethe Inst., Germany, 1973; liason office Royal Embassy Saudi Arabia, London, 1973—76; adminstrv. asst. Dr. Kenneth G. Robbins, DDS, Springfield, Mass., 1988—96; computer tchr. Mount Carmel Sch., Springfield, 1989—95; telemarketer Media One, Springfield, 1991—98; tchr. City of Springfield Dept. Edn., 1996—. Tutor Mass. Comprehensive Assessment Sys. Dept. Edn., Springfield, 2000—; tchrs. tutor City of Springfield, 2000—; athletes tutor Play It Smart, Springfield, 2001—, sr. class advisor, 2003—04. Author: Journey Through the Abyss, 2000. Co-chairperson Resources Team Accreditation Coord., 2000—03; Mass. state advisor Rep. Nat. Com., Springfield, 2001. Mem.: Alumni Assn. Marquette, Phi Mu, Alpha Delta Kappa (historian elect 2000—). Republican. Lutheran. Avocations: writing, horseback riding, rowing, travel, cooking. Home: 151 White St Springfield MA 01108

COOK, KENNETH RAY, radiologist; b. Sublette, Kans., Sept. 16, 1953; s. Curtis Carl and Carmen Madonna (Countryman) Cook; m. Paula Rose Petryszyn, July 22, 1978; children: Erin Michelle, Leah Nicole, Tara Rachelle. AA, Hutchinson (Kans.) C.C., 1976; BA, U. Kans., 1979, MD, 1983. Diplomate Am. Coll. Radiology; lic. pvt. pilot. Resident in diagnostic radiology U. Kans. Med. Ctr., 1983-87; pvt. practice, Corpus Christi, Tex., 1987—; chmn. mgmt. com. Radiology Assocs., Corpus Christi, 1997—2002. Staff radiologist Spohn Meml. Med. Ctr., Columbia N.W., Corpus Christi, 1987-99; chief radiology Bay Area Med. Ctr., 1993-99, vice chmn., trustee, 1993-94, chmn., 1994-96, bd. dirs., 1993-98; chief radiology Rehab. Hosp. South Tex., 1989-91; asst. clin. prof. family practice U. Tex., San Antonio; med. dir. Del Mar Coll. Ultrasound Technol. Sch.; chief Corpus Christi Med. Ctr., 1998-99. Recipient Resident Tchg. award, Dept. Radiology, U. Kans., Kansas City, 1985-86, Resident Tchg. award, Med. Ctr. Kans. U., 1986-87. Mem. AMA, Am. Coll. Radiology, Radiologic Soc. N. Am., Tex. Med. Soc., Tex. Radiologic Soc., Am. Inst. Ultrasound in Medicine, Nueces County Med. Soc. Republican. Roman Catholic. Avocations: fishing, hunting, camping, flying. Office: Radiology Assocs PO Box 5608 Corpus Christi TX 78465-5608 Office Phone: 361-561-3100. E-mail: kcook@xraydocs.com, kcook963@msn.com.

COOK, KEVIN FRANCIS, lawyer; b. Mt. Vernon, NY, Oct. 7, 1948; s. Charles Francis and Alice Theresa Cook; m. Christine Mary Shelf, Dec. 8, 1972; children: Ariel, Matthew. AB, Fairfield U., 1970; MA, Univ. Coll., Dublin, Ireland, 1972; JD, Suffolk U., 1975. Bar: N.Y. 1976, U.S. Dist. Ct. (so. and ea. dists.) N.Y. 1978, U.S. Ct. Appeals (2d cir.) 1978, Supreme Ct. U.S. 1980, Conn. 1997. With Mendes & Mount LLP, N.Y.C., 1979—. Contbr. articles to profl. jours. Mem.: ATLA, Am. Judicature Soc., Conn. Bar Assn. (litigation sect. 1997—), NY State Bar Assn. (trial lawyers sect. 1976—). Office: Mendes & Mount LLP 750 7th Ave New York NY 10019-6829 Business E-Mail: kevin.cook@mendes.com.

COOK, LARRY NORMAN, pediatrician, neonatologist, educator; b. Erie, Pa., Dec. 8, 1943; s. Charles Fremonst and Virginia June (Weinheimer) C.; m. Christine Louise DuBois, June 17, 1973; children: Kirk, Brian, Amelia. BS with honors, U. Louisville, 1964, MD with highest honors, 1968. Diplomate Am. Bd. Pediat., Am. Bd. Neonatal-Perinatal Medicine; cert. in neonatal advanced life support; cert. in controlled substances Drug Enforcement Adminstrn.; cert. in aspects of AIDS, Ky. Straight pediatric intern U. Colo. Med. Ctr., Denver, 1968, resident in pediat., 1969; fellow in neonatology U. Louisville Sch. Medicine, 1970-72, asst. clin. prof. pediat., 1972-74, asst. clin. prof. ob.-gyn., 1972-79, assoc. prof. pediat. and ob-gyn., 1979-84, prof. pediat., 1984—, billy F. Andrews prof., chmn. dept., 1994—, co-dir. divsn. neonatology, 1974-94; pvt. practice, Louisville, 1984—. Cons. on neonatology Ireland Army Hosp., Ft. Knox, Ky., 1974—, St. Joseph's Informary, Louisville, 1974-76; chief staff Kosair Children's Hosp., Louisvlle, 1994—; pres. Med. Sch. Fund, Louisville, 1994—; numerous presentations in field. Contbg. author: Fetal and Maternal Medicine, 1980, Management of High Risk Pregnancy, 1980, 85; contbr. over 200 articles and abstracts to med. jours., including Pediat., Am. Jour. Ob-Gyn., Am. Jour. Diseases of Children, Jour. Ky. Med. Assn., Archives Perinatal Medicine. Mem. med. adv. ad hoc com. Louisville area region ARC Blood Svcs., 1982-84; bd. dirs., mem. exec. com. Univ. Pediat. Found., Inc., Louisville, 1983—, acting pres., 1992-94, pres., 1995—; trustee Children's Hosp. Found., Alliant Health Sys., Louisville, 1991—; pres. Louisville Pediatric Found., Inc., 1993—. Maj. M.C., U.S. Army, 1972-74. Named Outstanding Young Man of Ky., Ky. Jaycees, 1977; recipient Lawrence Grever award Nat. Assn. Residents and Interns, 1993, Order of Merit award U. Louisville Alumni Assn., 1996, Roger J. Fox award Kosair Charities, 1998; alumni scholar U. Ky., 1964, summer rsch. scholar, 1965-67, Pfizer med. scholar, 1966, John Walker Moore scholar, 1967; Norman Joliffe med. student fellow, 1967; numerous grants, 1974—, including Burroughs Wellcome Co., WHAS Crusade for Children, Humana Inc., Univ. Health Care, Inc. Mem. AMA, Am. Acad. Pediat. (manuscript reviewer Pediat. 1991—), Assn. Am. Med. Colls., Assn. Med. Sch. Pediatric Dept. Chairmen (exec. com. 1993—), Extracorporeal Lif Support Orgn. (treas. 1989—), Am. Pediatric Soc., So. Perinatal Assn., So. Soc. for Pediatric Rsch., Ky. Pediatric Soc. (exec. com. 1993—), Ky. Med. Assn. (maternal and child health adv. bd. 1974—), Calif. Perinatal Assn., Jefferson County Med. Soc., Louisville Pediatric Soc., Med. Sch. Practice Assn. (pres. 1993—), Alpha Omega Alpha. Avocations: fly fishing, hiking, interior design. Office: U Louisville Dept Pediat 571 S Floyd St Ste 300 Louisville KY 40202-3829

COOK, LEWIS ANDERSON, physician, anthropologist; b. Beckley, W.Va., June 22, 1942; s. Wilson and Anne (Legato) C.; m. Vicki Miles, May 23, 1966; children: Wilson, Tiffany Anne. BA, W.Va. U., 1968, MD, 1973; MS, U. Coll. London, 1999. Diplomate Am. Bd. Family Practice, Nat. Bd. Med. Examiners. Intern, resident in family practice Med. Coll. Va./Va. Commonwealth U., Richmond, 1973-76; family practice physician Fayetteville, W.Va., 1976-97, 2000—; clin. asst. prof. W.Va. Sch. Medicine, 1990-2000. Cons., reviewer W.Va. Med. Inst., 1980-86, bd. dirs., pres. bd. dirs., 2005—; chmn. dept. family practice Raleigh Gen. Hosp., 1984-97, pres. bd. trustees, 1988, chief of staff, 1985, 91. Author: History of Fayetteville, 1983; contbr. articles to profl. jours. Chmn. pk. bd. City of Fayetteville, W.Va., 1981-84; pres. Keep Am. Beautiful, Fayette County, 1900-98; chmn. Fayetteville Hist. Bd.; chmn. Fayette County Litter Control, 1992-97; physician Fayetteville Sports, 1976-97; mem. W.Va. Gov.'s Adv. Bd. for State Health Policy, 1996; mem. Regional Health Adv. Com. for State of W.Va., 1990-95; mem. Fayette Fine Arts Coun., 1990-97. With U.S. Army, 1962-65. Fellow Am. Acad. Family Practice; mem. W.Va. State Med. Assn., Raleigh County Med. Soc., Fayette County Med. Soc. (pres. 1980), Am. Anthrop. Assn., W.Va. Archaeol. Soc., Soc. Primitive Tech., Early Am. Industries Assn. (bd. dirs. 1995-98), Sci. Instrument Soc. (Eng.), Surveyors Hist. Soc., Med. Collectors Assn., Mid-West Tool Collectors Assn. (v.p. 1994-97), Oughtred Soc., Ohio Tool Collectors Assn., Astron. Soc. of Pacific, Kanawha Valley Astron. Soc., Astron. League, Rotary (pres. W.Va. chpt. 1984, Fayetteville chpt. 1984-2002). Avocations: woodworking, astronomy, architecture, tennis, golf. Home: RR 3 Box 4-a Fayetteville WV 25840-9502 Office: RR 3 Box 458E Fayetteville WV 25840 Office Phone: 304-574-1888. E-mail: miles2@earthlink.net.

COOK, MANDY LEE HILL, education educator; b. Durham, NC, July 5, 1977; d. Ronald Charles and Lenora Jane Hill; m. Ted Edwin Cook, Aug. 2, 2003. BS, U. NC at Wilmington, 1995—99, MS, 1999—2002. Boat capt. UNCW Ctr. for Marine Sci., Wilmington, NC, 1997—2002; marine mammal mitigator USN, Italy, 2000; marine mammal aerial observer US Army Corp. of Engineers, Wilmington, NC, 2000—01; rsch. asst. U. NC at Wilmington, 2001—02, tchg. asst., 1999—2002, U. South Fla., 2003, rsch. asst., 2002—. Sunday sch. asst. Northside Bapt. Ch., Wilmington, NC, 1999—2002; adminstrv. bd. mem. Suncrest United Meth. Ch., Morgantown, W.Va., 1994—95; sci. judge and moderator Nat. Sci. Bowl, Washington, 2001. Recipient Chancellor's Achievement award, U. NC at Wilmington, 1995—98, New Scholar award, 1999—2000, Disting. Grad. award, 1999; scholar Charles and Kay Bolles scholarship, 1997—98; Protect Wild Dolphin Program rsch. grant, Harbor Br. Oceanog. Instn., 2003—, UNCW Undergraduate Rsch. fellowship, U. NC at Wilmington, 1998—99, Dovie P. Bowden scholarship, 1998—99, Jack Lake Endowed fellowship, USF Coll. of Marine Sci., 2004—, P.E.O. Scholar award, P. E. O. Internat., 2004—, Paul L. Getting Meml. Endowed fellowship, USF Coll. of Marine Sci., 2003—04, Von Rosenstiel Endowed fellowship, 2002—03, Grad. Assistantship, 2002—, Frances Peter Fensel Meml. fellowship, U. NC at Wilmington, 2001—02. Mem.: Acoustical Soc. Of Am. (best student paper 2004), Soc. for Marine Mammalogy, Sigma Xi (assoc.), UNCW Biology Club (sec. 1998—98), USF Marine Sci. Adv. Com., Phi Kappa Phi (life), Phi Eta Sigma (life), Beta Beta Beta (life). Office: USF Coll of Marine Science 140 Seventh Ave South Saint Petersburg FL 33701-5016 Office Phone: 727-553-1193.

COOK, MARCELLA KAY, retired theater educator; b. Albuquerque, Dec. 22, 1949; d. Joseph Raymond and Vivian Francis (Mullinax) Murdick; m. James Rogers Cook, Mar. 25, 1975 (dec. Aug. 1991); 1 child, Amanda Kay. BA, U. Albuquerque, 1971; MA, Eastern N.Mex. U., 1973. Prof. theatre, speech Vernon (Tex.) Coll., 1973—2002; co-owner, publicity dir. Umpire Entertainment and Enterprise Records, 1998—2001; dir. 112 plays Vernon Regional Coll., 1973—2002. Fine arts chair Vernon Regional Jr. Coll., 1982—87, 1997—2001; stage mgr. Columbia Cmty. Concert Series, 1976—91; actress, dir. Bill Fegan Attractions, Raton, N.Mex., 1974; costume designer Ea. N.Mex. U., Portales, 1972—73; head wardrobe mistress Cinegai Films, Rome, 1971, Paramount Studios, 1971. Writer, dir.: (plays) Waggoner Ranch's Entry Tex. Ranch Roundup, 1987, 1988, 1989. Named Outstanding Young Women Am., 1978; recipient Humanitarian Svc. award, Tex. Army N.G., 1979, Am. Coll. Theater Festival awards Excellence in Directing, 1987, 1997, Friends of Arts award, 2002; grantee, Stokes Found., Tex. Commn. Arts. Mem.: S.W. Theatre Assn., Tex. Ednl. Theatre Assn., Delta Psi Omega, Alpha Psi Omega, Phi Theta Kappa. Avocations: sculpting, travel, collecting classic cars, collecting classic rock and roll music. Home: 4302 Mt Scott Dr Wichita Falls TX 76310

COOK, MARY MARGARET, steamfitter, educator; b. Royal Oak, Mich., Apr. 28, 1944; d. John Patrick and Agnes Hannah (Anderson) McMahon; m. Barney Albert Cahill, Aug. 19, 1967 (div. Apr. 1971); m. Frank Melvin Cook, Jan. 26, 1974. BA in Elem. Edn., Ariz. State U., 1971; cert. United Assn. instr., Mich. State U., 1990; Cert., Ariz. C.C. Cert. elem. tchr., Ohio, Ariz.;

mech. lic. journeyman and steamfitter. Tchr. St. Agnes Elem. Sch., Phoenix, 1967-71, Bevis Elem. Sch., Cin., 1971-73; GED instr. Scottsdale, Ariz., 1975-78; steamfitter United Assn. Local 469, Phoenix, 1978—. Instr. apprentices Rio Salado C.C., Phoenix, 1984-90; math. cons. Ariz. Dept. Edn., 1988-90; state dir. AFL-CIO Apprenticeship Awareness Program, 1990-92. Chair State Con. Emerging Careers for Women, 1992—98; mem. Apprenticeship Adv. Coun., 1990—97, chair, 1995—97; staff dept. commerce Workforce Devel. Coun., 1997—; mem. Gov.'s Commn. on Nontraditional Employment for Women; state dir. Project Nontraditional Assistance and Info. Link, 1992—99; extended staff Gov.'s Workforce Devel. Policy, 1997—2004; cons. Pro Max, 1999—; apprenticeship and tng. rep. Ariz. Dept. Commerce, 2000—04; project specialist Ariz. Dept Transp., 2004—. Mem.: Ariz. State U. Alumni Assn. (life), Toastmasters Internat. (Advanced Toastmaster silver). Avocations: computers, reading, weightlifting. Home: 22452 N 80th Ln Peoria AZ 85383-2149 Office Phone: 602-712-4074. Business E-Mail: mcook@azdot.gov.

COOK, SISTER MARY MERCEDES, school system administrator, director; b. Hagerstown, Md., Dec. 18, 1939; d. Garland and Anita Rideoutt (Willis) C. Student, Fordham U.; BA, Ea. Conn. State U., 1974, MS, 1983; grad., Norwich Dicocesan Prins. Acad., Conn., 1991; postgrad., U. Dayton, 1999. Joined Sistes of Charity of Our Lady of Mother of the Ch., Roman Cath. Ch.; cert. tchr., Conn. Tchr., prin. St. Joseph Sch., Baltic, Conn., 1959-61; tchr. Sacred Heart Sch., Byram, Conn., 1961-63, Bloomfield, Conn., 1963-66, Taftville, Conn., 1966-67, Acad. of Holy Family, Baltic, 1967-84; tchr., vice prin. Assumption Sch., Manchester, 1984—; vice-prin., tchr., chair dept. English, guide counselor Acad. of the Holy Family, Baltic, Conn., 1990—2003; dir. Sacred Heart Ednl. Ctr., Baltic, 2003—. Mem.: Nat. Cath. Ednl. Assn., Math. Assn. Am., Nat. Coun. Tchrs. English. Republican. Avocations: reading, writing, painting, cooking, interior decorating.

COOK, MAURICE GAYLE, soil science educator, consultant; b. Frankfort, Ky., Dec. 26, 1931; s. Price Cash and Evelyn (Moore) C.; m. Eva Nancy Blalock, Aug. 27, 1966; 1 child, Stephen Price. BS, U. Ky., 1957, MS, 1959; PhD, Va. Poly. Inst., 1961. From asst. prof. to prof. N.C. State U., Raleigh, 1961-92, Alumni Disting. prof., 1975; ret., 1992. Spl. advisor Gov. N.C., 1999-2000. Author: Concepts in Soil Science, 1973; contbr. numerous articles to profl. jours. With U.S. Army, 1957; col. USAR, 1962-90. Named to Hall of Disting. Alumni, U. Ky., 2000. Fellow Soil Sci. Soc. Am., Am. Soc. Agronomy, Soil and Water Conservation Soc. (bd. dirs. 1979-88, pres. 1986-87), Nat. Assn. Colls. and Tchrs. Agr.; mem. Soil Sci. Soc. N.C. (Achievement award 1991), N.C. Divsn. Soil and Water Conservation (exec. dir. 1982-84), Am. Water Resources Assn., Internat. Erosion Control Assn., Gamma Sigma Delta (Merit award 1986), Epsilon Sigma Phi, Alpha Zeta (pres. 1976-85). Democrat. Baptist. Home: 3458 Leonard St Raleigh NC 27607-6827 Office: NC State U Dept Soil Science Raleigh NC 27695-0001 E-mail: mgcook@mindspring.com.

COOK, MELANIE K., lawyer; b. Salt Lake City, June 3, 1953; BS, UCLA, 1974, JD, 1978. Assoc. Bloom Hergott Cook Diemer & Klein, Beverly Hills, Calif., 1987—92, ptnr., 1992—2002; of counsel Ziffren, Brittenham, Branca, Fischer, Gilbert-Lurie, Stiffelman, LLP, L.A., 2002—03, ptnr., 2003—. Office: 1801 Century Park W Los Angeles CA 90067-6406 Office Phone: 310-552-6535.

COOK, MICHAEL ALLAN, social sciences educator; b. Newark, Eng., Dec. 24, 1940; s. John Manuel and Enid May (Robertson) Cook. BA, Cambridge (Eng.) U., 1963. Lectr. Sch. Oriental and African Studies U. London, 1966—84, reader, 1984—86; Cleveland E. Dodge prof. Near Ea. studies Princeton (N.J.) U., 1986—. Author: Early Muslim Dogma, 1981, Muhammad, 1983, The Koran, 2000, others. Fellow: Am. Acad. Arts and Scis., Royal Asiatic Soc.; mem.: Am. Philos. Soc., Am. Oriental Soc. Office: Princeton Univ Dept Near Eastern Studies Princeton NJ 08544 Office Phone: 609-258-5360. Business E-Mail: mcook@princeton.edu.

COOK, MICHAEL BLANCHARD, government executive; b. Buffalo, May 8, 1942; s. Gerhard Albert and Lura (Lincoln) C.; m. Le Thi Kim Oanh, Feb. 10, 1942; children: Arthur, Benjamin. BA, Swarthmore Coll., 1963; postgrad., Princeton U.; B in Philosophy, Oxford U., 1966. Field advisor Agy. for Internat. Devel., Saigon, Vietnam, 1966-68; model cities rep. HUD, Phila., 1968-70; consular officer Dept. of State, Udorn, Thailand, 1971-73; exec., Water Programs EPA, Washington, 1973-80, superfund dir., 1980-81, dep. dir. hazardous waste, 1981-85, dir. drinking water, 1985-91, dir. wastewater enforcement and compliance, 1991-94, dir. wastewater mgmt., 1994—2002, dir. superfund remediation and technology innovation, 2002—. Author numerous articles on sewage treatment, hazardous waste and drinking water. Rhodes scholar Rhodes Trust, Oxford U., Eng., 1964; recipient Meritorious Honor awards U.S. Dept. of State, 1967, 72, Gold, Silver, Bronze medals EPA, 1975-87, Disting. Exec. award, Pres. Ronald Reagan, 1987. Avocations: running marathons, triathlete. Home: 3406 Rose Ln Falls Church VA 22042-4015 Office: EPA Superfund Remediation 5201G 1200 Pennsylvania Ave NW Washington DC 20460-4201 Office Phone: 703-603-8960. Business E-Mail: cook.mike@epa.gov.

COOK, MICHAEL HARRY, lawyer; b. June 9, 1947; s. Leonard James and Ethel (Shapiro) C.; m. Michele Anne Reday, Apr. 21, 1979; children: Noah Reday, Megan Rose. Student, U. Wis., Madison, 1965-66; BA with honors cum laude, Temple U., 1969; JD, Villanova U., 1973. Bar: Pa. 1973, D.C. 1979, U.S. Dist. Ct. (no. dist.) Ill. 1977, U.S. Dist. Ct. D.C. 1981, U.S. Ct. Claims 1982, U.S. Ct. Appeals (3d cir.) 1982, U.S. Ct. Appeals (5th cir.) 1981, U.S. Ct. Appeals (9th cir.) 1979, U.S. Ct. Appeals (11th cir.) 1981, U.S. Ct. Appeals (7th cir.) 1984, U.S. Ct. Appeals (10th cir.) 1984, U.S. Ct. Appeals (fed. cir.) 1984, U.S. Ct. Appeals (D.C. cir.) 1981, U.S. Supreme Ct. 1976. Atty. Gen. Counsel's Office U.S. Dept. Health and Human Svcs., Washington, 1973-80; assoc. Wood, Lucksinger & Epstein, Washington, 1981-85, ptnr., 1985-90, Katten, Muchin & Zavis, Washington, 1991-97; mem. Mintz, Levin, Cohn, Ferris, Glovsky and Popeo, P.C., Washington, 1997-98; shareholder Jenkens & Gilchrist, P.C., Washington, 1998—2003; ptnr. Baker & McKenzie, Washington, 2003—. Lectr. Am. Health Lawyers Assn., Aspen Sys., Inc., various state and nat. hosps. and long-term care assns. Contbg. author: book Handbook of Subacute Health Care, 1994, Subacute Care: A Guide to Devel., Implementation and Mgmt., 1995, Health Law and Compliance Update, 2005, The Long Term Care Handbook: Regulatory, Operational, and Fin. Guideposts, 2000; mem. editl. bd. McKnight's Long Term Care News; contbr. articles to profl. health care jours. V.p. Taylor Run Citizens Assn., Alexandria, Va., 1982-84, pres., 1984-85, bd. dirs., 1985—. Named one of 100 Most Influential People in Long Term Care, McKnight's Long Term Care News, 1996; Pres.'s scholar, Temple U., Phila., 1969. Mem.: ABA, No. Va. Dem. Bus. Coun., Nat. Assn. for Support of Long Term Care, Assisted Living Fedn. Am. (former mem. task force on managed care, former mem. public policy force, leadership coun., mem. pres.'s coun., mem. legal task force), Sword Soc., Tau Epsilon Phi, Phi Eta Sigma. Democrat. Jewish. Home: 2724 King St Alexandria VA 22302-4009 Office: Baker & McKenzie LLP 815 Connecticut Ave NW Washington DC 20006-4078 Office Phone: 202-452-7013. E-mail: michael.h.cook@bakernet.com.

COOK, MICHAEL L., lawyer; b. De Leon, Tex., May 13, 1940; BBA, Tex. Tech U., 1962; JD, U. Tex., 1968. CPA Tex., 1965; bar: Tex. 1968. Shareholder Jenkens & Gilchrist, P.C., Austin, firm leader tax practice group. Co-author: Federal Tax Aspects of Cancellation of Indebtedness and Foreclosures, 1993. Fellow: Tex. Bar Found.; mem.: ABA, Am. Coll. Tax Counsel (bd. regents), State Bar Tex. Office: Jenkens & Gilchrist PC Ste 2500 401 Congress Ave Austin TX 78701 Office Phone: 512-499-3849. Office Fax: 512-499-3810. Business E-Mail: mcook@jenkens.com.

COOK, MICHAEL LEWIS, lawyer; b. Rochester, NH, Mar. 5, 1944; s. Israel J. and Molly L. Cook; m. Roberta Tross, Feb. 25, 1995; children: Jonathan, Alexander. AB, Columbia U., 1965; JD, NYU, 1968. Bar: NY 1969, registered: US Dist. Ct. (So. Dist.) NY 1970, US Dist. Ct. (Ea. Dist.) NY 1970, US Ct. Appeals (2nd Cir.) 1972, US Supreme Ct. 1973, US Ct. Appeals (7th Cir.) 1984, US Ct. Appeals (4th Cir.) 1986, US Dist. Ct. (No. Dist.) NY 1996, US Ct. Appeals (3rd Cir.) 2001. Assoc. Weil, Gotshal & Manges, NYC, 1970-75, ptnr., chair corp. restructuring group, 1975-80; ptnr. Skadden, Arps, Slate, Meagher & Flom, LLP, NYC, 1980-2000, Schulte Roth & Zabel LLP, NYC, 2000—, head Dept. Bus. Reorganization. Lectr. bus. law Herbert H. Lehman Coll., CUNY, 1968—70; adj. prof. law NYU Law Sch., 1975—2001. Co-author: A Practical Guide to the Bankruptcy Reform Act, 1979, Creditors' Rights, Debtors' Protection and Bankruptcy, 1985, rev. edit., 1997; contbr.: Collier on Bankruptcy, 1979, rev. edit., 2003, Collier Bankruptcy Practice Guide, 2003; editor and contbg. author: Bankruptcy Litigation Manual, rev. edit., 2004-05. Bd. dirs. Goddard Riverside Cmty. Ctr.; bd. dirs., former chair Lawyers Alliance for NY. Fellow: Am. Bar Found., Am. Coll. Bankruptcy; mem.: Practicing Law Inst. (bankruptcy law adv. com.), Assn. Bar City NY, ABA (Litig. Sect. 1976—81, chmn., creditors' rights litig. com.), Bankruptcy Litig. Inst. (chmn. 1980—96), Columbia Coll. Alumni Assn. (v.p., bd. dir.). Office: Schulte Roth & Zabel LLP 919 Third Ave New York NY 10022 Office Phone: 212-756-2150. Office Fax: 212-593-5955. Business E-Mail: michael.cook@srz.com.

COOK, MICHELLE WESTERMAN, special education educator; b. Ft. Stockton, Tex., Feb. 17, 1959; d. Carl Anthony and Jacquelyn Cecil (Smith) Westerman; m. Bruce Duncan Cook, Aug. 11, 1984; children: Carl Gary, Ashley Rose. Student, St. Gregory's Jr. Coll., Shawnee, Okla., 1977-78; BSEd, Okla. U., 1985; postgrad., Tex. Tech. U., 1993—. Cert. tchr. lang. arts, spl. edn./secondary edn., visual impairments. Spl. edn. tchr. Springhill Jr. High, Longview, Tex., 1991—. Owner WCR, Inc., Longview, 1993. Author: (newsletter) The Ascension, 1994—; co-author: What America's Teachers Wish Parents Knew, 1993. Mem. United We Stand, Dallas, 1992. Tutition scholar Tex. Tech., Lubbock, 1993-95. Mem. Coun. Exceptional Children, Assn. Tex. Profl. Educators,Assn. for Edn. and Rehab. of Blind and Visually Impaired. Avocations: music, sailing, painting, yoga. E-mail: shellcook@aol.com.

COOK, MOLLY MALONE, literary agent; b. San Francisco, Jan. 5, 1925; d. Fred Joseph Cook and Ruth Margaret Allen. Student, U. Calif. Pres. Molly Malone Cook Lit. Agy., Provincetown, Mass., 1976—. Author short stories. With USMC. Avocation: genealogy. Office: Molly Malone Cook Lit Agy PO Box 619 Provincetown MA 02657

COOK, NENA, lawyer; b. Salt Lake City, Jan. 25, 1966; BA, Gonzaga U., 1988; JD, Willamette U., 1991. Bar: Oreg. 1991, U.S. Dist. Ct. Oreg. 1992, U.S. Dist. Ct. Ea. and We. Dist. Wash. 2000. Ptnr. Sussman Shank LLP, Portland, Oreg. Chair employment law group Sussman Shank LLP; spkr. in field. Prodn. editor: Willamette Law Rev., 1990—91; contbr. articles to profl. jours. Named one of Forty under 40 Outstanding Leadership in Bus. and Civic Affairs, Portland Bus. Jour., 2002. Mem.: ABA, Soc. Human Resource Mgmt., Portland Human Resource Mgmt. Assn., Fed. Bar Assn., Oreg. Women Lawyers, Oreg. State Bar Assn. (mem. fed. practice procedure com. 1997—99, chmn. 1998—99, ninth cir. jud. conf. rep. 2000—03, mem. bd. govs. 2002—, pres.-elect 2004, mem. jud. screening com.), Wash. State Bar Assn. Office: Sussman Shank LLP 1000 SW Broadway Ste 1400 Portland OR 97205 Office Phone: 503-227-1111. Office Fax: 503-248-0130. E-mail: nena@sussmanshank.com.

COOK, NOEL ROBERT, manufacturing executive; b. Houston, Mar. 19, 1937; s. Horace Berwick and Leda Estelle (Houghton) C.; children: Laurel Jane, David Robert. Student, Iowa State U., 1955-57; BS in Indsl. Engring., U. Mich., 1960. Registered profl. engr., Mich.; cert. Fluid Power Engr. Engr. in tng. Eaton Mfg., Saginaw, Mich., 1960-61; mgr. mfg. and contracting J.N. Fauver Co., Madison Heights, Mich., 1961-65; pres. Newton Mfg., Royal Oak, Mich., 1965—; sec. Indsl. Piping Contractors, Birmingham, Mich., 1969-75; pres. RNR Metal Fabricators, Inc., Royal Oak, 1974-78; chmn. bd. dirs. Kim Internat. Sales Co., 1978-88; pres. Newton Sales Co., Royal Oak, 1978-90, Power Package Windsor Ltd., Windsor, Ont., Can., 1981—. Patentee in field. With U.S. Army, arty. officer, 1960-61. Mem. ASME, Fluid Power Soc., Nat. Fluid Power Assn., Birmingham Jr. C. of C. (past bd. dirs.), Delta Tau Delta. Home: 4481 Cherry Hill Dr Orchard Lake MI 48323-1615 Office: Newton Mfg Co 4249 Delemere Blvd Royal Oak MI 48073-1897 Office Phone: 248-549-9600. Personal E-mail: ncook@mindspring.com.

COOK, PAMELA MARGARET, French educator; b. Gateshead, Eng., Apr. 11, 1955; came to U.S., 1983; d. John Andrew and Doreen Cook; m. Philip Edward Mirowski, June 14, 1986; 1 child, Alexander John Daniel Mirowski. BA with honors, U. Nottingham, Eng., 1977; MA, MPhil, PhD, Yale U., 1991. Tchr. Sawston Coll., Cambridge, Eng., 1978-83; asst. head dept. Hitchin Sch., Herts, Eng., 1983-85; part-time asst. prof. French St. Mary's Coll., Notre Dame, ind., 1990—. Mem. Hoosier Environ. Coun., Indpls., 1997—; mem. Ind. Opera North. Christine Jankowski fellow, 1984. Mem. MLA. Avocations: singing, flute, piano, theater. Home: 3015 Hilltop Dr South Bend IN 46614-2213

COOK, PAUL CHRISTOPHER, intelligence officer; b. Corpus Christi, Tex., Mar. 24, 1953; s. William Eckford and Nelle (Gladney)C. AA, Ocean City Coll., Md., 1973; BA, U. Ariz., Tucson, 1978; MA, U. Ariz., 1981, PhD, 1987. Oceanographer Dept. Natural Resources State of Md., Annapolis, 1973—75; rschr. Child Psychology Lab., Tucson, 1977—78; behavioral and video cons. Intermt. Ctrs. for Human Devel., Tucson, 1978—79; rsch. assoc. Family & Community Medicine Ariz. Health Sci. Ctr., Tucson, 1982—84, rsch. cons., 1989—98; rsch. and analysis assoc. U. Ariz., Tucson, 1980—87, rsch. cons. Coll. Medicine, 1989—98; sr. human factors engr. U.S. Army Electronic Proving Ground, Ft. Huachuca, Ariz., 1986—87; engring. psychologist U.S. Army Yuma Proving Ground, Ariz., 1988; cons. engr. Cook Enterprises, Tucson, 1989—91; pres. World Trade Assocs. Ltd. Sterling, Inc., Tucson, Lake Havasu, Ariz., 1991—97; pres., ptnr. Unicus Imports, Inc., 1997—2000; candidate, sr. exec. svcs., sr. rsch. scientist U.S. Navy Space and Naval Warfare Sys. Ctr., San Diego, 1999; ops. specialist, intelligence warfare test directorate commd. Ft. Huachuca (Az.), Ft Hood (Tex.), 2000—01; ops. rsch. analyst intelligence electronic warfare Theatre Missle Def., Fort Huachuca, 2000—00; ops. analyst U.S.A. Intelligence Electronic Warfare Reconnaissance, Spl. Projects, Ft. Huachuca, 2001—02; intelligence officer U.S. Army Intelligence Ctr., Ft. Huachuca, 2002—. Rsch. cons. Coll. Medicine Ariz. Health Scis. Ctr., U. Ariz., Tucson, 1989—; pres. World Trade Assocs. Ltd. of Sterling, Inc., Tucson, Sterling, Va. and Lake Havasu, Ariz., 1990-98. Scuba diver Pima County Sheriff's Dept., 1985-90; plank owner USN Meml., Washington. Mem. Navy League (life), U.S. Naval Inst., Human Factors Soc., Internat. Platform Assn., Profl. Assn. Diving Instrs., U.S. C. of C. Republican. Methodist. Home: 6537 E Santa Elena Tucson AZ 85715-3132 Office: Trail Dust Town #10 PO Box 10 6541 E Tanque Verde Rd Tucson AZ 85715-3813 Business E-Mail: cookp@hua.army.mil.

COOK, PAUL MAXWELL, technology company executive; b. Ridgewood, N.J. BSChemE, MIT, 1947. With Stanford Rsch. Inst., Menlo Park, Calif., 1948-53, Sequoia Process Corp., 1953-56, Raychem Corp., Menlo Park, Calif., 1957-95, founder, former pres., CEO, until 1990, chmn., bd. dirs., until 1995; chmn., CEO CellNet Data Sys., San Carlos, Calif., 1990-94; chmn., bd. dirs. SRI Internat., 1993-98; chmn. DIVA Sys. Corp., Menlo Park, Calif., 1995—, CEO, 1995-99; founder, CEO, Agile TV Corp., 2000—. Mem. exec. com. San Francisco Bay Area Coun., 1988-94, chmn., 1990-91. Recipient Nat. Medal Tech., 1988; named to San Francisco Bay Area Bus. Hall of Fame, 1999. Mem. NAE, Am. Acad. Sci., Environ. Careers Orgn. (past chmn., bd. trustees), MIT Corp. (life, emeritus). Office: Diva Sys Corp 15233 Ventura Blvd 9th Fl Sherman Oaks CA 91403-2201 E-mail: pcook@agile.tv.

COOK, PHILIP CARTER, lawyer; b. Atlanta, Nov. 4, 1946; BS, Ga. Inst. Tech., 1968; JD cum laude, Harvard U., 1971. Bar: Ga. 1972. Law clk. to Hon. Lewis R. Morgan U.S. Ct. Appeals (5th cir.), 1971-72; mem. Alston & Bird, Atlanta, dep. mng. ptnr. Atlanta & Washington. Pres. Harvard Journal of Legislation 1970-71. Fellow Am. Coll. Tax Counsel; mem. ABA (chmn. sect. taxation, com. on banking and savs. instns. 1995), D.C. Bar, State Bar Ga. (chmn. taxation sect.), Am. Law Inst., Atlanta Tax Forum (trustee 1986-91, pres. 1991), Phi Kappa Phi, Omicron Delta Kappa. Office: Alston & Bird 1 Atlantic Ctr 1201 W Peachtree St NW Atlanta GA 30309-3424 Office Phone: 404-881-7491. Office Fax: 404-881-7777. Business E-Mail: pcook@alston.com.

COOK, PHILIP JACKSON, economist, educator; b. Buffalo, Oct. 15, 1946; s. Gerhard Albert and Lura (Lincoln) C.; m. Judith Walmsley, June 27, 1966; children; Elizabeth Camden, Brian Lincoln. BA, U. Mich., 1968; PhD, U. Calif., Berkeley, 1973. Prof. Duke U., Durham, NC, 1973—, dir. Inst. Policy Scis., 1985-89, dir. Sanford Inst. Pub. Policy, 1997-99. Vis. scholar Inst. Rsch. in Social Sci. U. NC, Chapel Hill, 1980; expert Office Poly. and Mgmt. Analysis, criminal divsn. U.S. Dept. Justice, 1982; mem. rsch. adv. com. U.S. Sentencing Commn., 1986—91, chair rsch. adv. com., 1986; mem. adv. bd. Injury Prevention Rsch. Ctr. U. NC, 1990—; mem. adv. bd. H. John Heinz III Sch. Pub. Policy and Mgmt. Carnegie Mellon U., 1992—; mem. Ctr. Gun Policy Rsch. Johns Hopkins U., 1995—2003; cons. enforcement divsn. U.S. Dept. Treasury, 1999—2000; rsch. assoc. Nat. Bur. Econ. Rsch., 1996—; mem. adv. com. Harvard Injury Control Ctr. Author: Selling Hope, 1989, The Winner-Take All Society, 1995, Gun Violence, 2000, Evaluating Gun Policy, 2003. Recipient Kenneth J. Arrow award for best paper published in health econ., 1993, Vernon Prize in Pub. Policy, 1997; grantee, US Dept. Justice, Robert Wood Johnson Found.; Spl. Career fellow, Ford Found., 1968—72. Fellow: Am. Soc. Criminology; mem.: Inst. Medicine of NAS, Am. Econ. Assn., Assn. Pub. Policy and Mgmt. (treas. 1985—93). Office: Duke Univ Inst Pub Policy PO Box 90245 Durham NC 27708-0245 Business E-Mail: pcook@duke.edu.

COOK, QUENTIN LAMAR, lawyer, health products executive, church administrator; b. Sept. 8, 1940; s. J. Vernon and Bernice (Kimball) C.; m. Mary Gaddie, Nov. 30, 1962; children: Kathryn Cook Knight, Quentin Laurance, Joseph Vernon III. BS, Utah State U., 1963; JD, Stanford U., 1966. Bar: Calif. 1966. Assoc. Carr, McClellan, Ingersoll, Thompson & Horn, Burlingame, Calif., 1966-69, ptnr., 1969-93; interim pres., CEO Calif. Healthcare Sys., San Francisco, 1993-94, pres., CEO, 1994-95; vice chmn. Sutter Health/Calif. Healthcare Sys., San Francisco, 1996; gen. authority LDS Ch., 1996—. City atty. Town of Hillsborough, Calif., 1982-93; mem. adv. bd. Utah State U., Logan, 1985-95; mem. bd. visitors Brigham Young U. Law Sch., Provo, 1994-96.

COOK, RICHARD KELSEY, aerospace transportation executive; b. White Plains, NY, Nov. 14, 1931; s. Albert James and Frances Elizabeth (Butler) C.; m. Marjorie S. Schellabarger, Sept. 10, 1959 (div.); children: Geoffrey, Patrick, Sarah, Catherine; m. Fleur Wales-Baillie, Oct. 14, 1987. BA, George Washington U., 1958; postgrad., Stanford U., 1979. Legis staff Am. Trucking Assn., 1959-61; adminstrv. asst. Rep. Edwin B. Dooley, 1961; legis. asst. Rep. Oliver P. Bolton, 1963-65; profl. minority staff mem. Banking and Currency Com., U.S. Ho. of Reps., Washington, 1965-69; spl. asst. to Pres. of U.S., Washington, 1969-71, dep. asst., 1971-73; v.p. Lockheed Corp., Washington, 1973-94, sr. v.p., 1994-95; pres. RKC Ltd., 1995—. Spl. adv. O'Connor & Hannan, Washington, 1995-98; cons. to major U.S. and South African Companies, with offices in Johannesburg and Washington, 1995-99; cons. telecom. cos. Thorlock Corp. Ltd., Perth, Australia, 1999-2001; registered lobbyist; pioneered internet lobbying with PanAmSat Corp., 1998-2000; internet cons. European Aerospace Def. Space Co.-N.Am., 2004-2005; v.p., dir. Grove Tactical Tng. Ctr., 2005—; adv. Congressman Lewis, Calif.; chmn. com. appropriations, Ho. Reps., 2005— Served with USAF, 1949-53. Mem. Aero. Club (pres. 1979), Met. Club, 116 Club (D.C.), Burning Tree Club (Bethesda, Md.), Captiva Island Yacht Club (Fla.), Inanda Club (Johannesburg, South Africa), Tau Kappa Epsilon.

COOK, RICHARD KENT, music educator, musician; b. Big Spring, Tex., July 31, 1962; s. Rebecca Ann and Julian Oakey Hagood (Stepfather); life ptnr. Roger Allen Roe. MusB, Baylor U., Waco, TX, 1985; MusM, Ind. U., Bloomington, 1987, MusD, 1994. Asst. prof. of music DePauw U., Greencastle, Ind., 1995—99; assoc. prof. of music Ill. Wesleyan U., Bloomington, Ill., 1999—. Musician (concert pianist): (soloist and chamber musician) Active Performing Schedule; Over 100 Professional, Public Performances Since 1995. Grantee Artistic and Scholarly Devel., Ill. Wesleyan U., 2000, Presdl. Grant, DePauw U., 1997; scholar Fulbright Scholarship for study in Germany, Fulbright Assn., 1992—93. Mem.: Music Teachers Nat. Assn., Pi Kappa Lambda (pres. 2002—04), Phi Mu Alpha Sinfonia (faculty advisor 2001—05). Avocations: travel, hiking, jogging. Office: Illinois Wesleyan Univ 303 East University Bloomington IL 61702-2900 Office Phone: 309-556-3124.

COOK, RICHARD W., motion picture company executive; b. Bakersfield, Calif., Aug. 20, 1950; Ed., U. So. Calif. Saels rep. Disneyland, 1971-74, sales mgr., 1974-77; mgr. pay TV and non-theatrical releases Disney Studios, 1977-80; asst. domestic sales mgr. Buena Vista, 1980-81, v.p., asst. gen. sales mgr., 1981-84, v.p., gen. sales mgr., 1985-88, sr. v.p. domestic distbn., 1988-94; pres. Buena Vista Pictures Distbn., 1994; pres. worldwide mktg. Buena Vista Pictures Mktg., 1994-97; chmn. Walt Disney Motion Pictures Group, Burbank, Calif., 1997—2002, Walt Disney Studios, 2002—. Office: Walt Disney Studios 500 S Buena Vista St Burbank CA 91521-0006

COOK, ROBERT S., JR., lawyer; b. Syracuse, N.Y., 1940; m. Sally Williams. BA, Amherst Coll., 1962; LLB, Yale U., 1965. Bar: N.Y. 1966. Assoc. Hancock, Ryan, Shove & Hust, Syracuse, N.Y., 1965-68; urban renewal rep. HUD, N.Y.C., 1968-71; exec. dir. The Parks Coun., Inc., N.Y.C., 1972-73; v.p., co-founder Project for Pub. Spaces, Inc., N.Y.C., 1974-77; cons. N.Y.C., 1978-80; assoc. Tufo & Zuccotti, N.Y.C., 1981-86; assoc., then ptnr. Brown and Wood, N.Y.C., 1986-94; ptnr. DeForest & Duer, N.Y.C., 1995—2001, Anderson, Kill & Olick, P.C., NYC, 2002—. Author: Zoning for Downtown urban Design, 1980. V.p., bd. dirs. Citizens Housing and Planning Coun., 1985; cons. The Denver Partnership, 1981; mem. N.Y. State Freshwater Wetlands Appeals Bd., 1991-94. Design project fellow Nat. Endowment for Arts, Washington, 1978-79; Graham Found. for Advanced Studies in the Fine Arts fellow, Chgo., 1979. Mem. N.Y. State Bar Assn., Assn. Bar City N.Y. (com. environ. law 1979-82, com. land use planning and zoning, 1994-2000, chmn. 1997-2000, com. N.Y.C. affairs 2000-01). Office: Anderson Kill & Olick PC 1251 Ave of the Americas New York NY 10020-1182 E-mail: rcook@andersonkill.com.

COOK, ROBIN, writer; b. N.Y.C., May 4, 1940; s. Edgar Lee and Audrey (Koons) C.; m. Barbara Ellen Mougin, July 18, 1979. BA, Weslyan U., 1962; MD, Columbia U., 1966. Resident in gen. surgery Queen's Hosp., Honolulu, 1966-68; resident in ophthalmology Mass. Eye and Ear Infirmary, Boston, 1971-75, mem. staff, from 1975; clin. instr. Harvard U. Med. Sch., 1972. Author: The Year of the Intern, 1972, Coma, 1977, Sphinx, 1979, Brain, 1981, Fever, 1982, Godplayer, 1983, Mindbend, 1986, Outbreak, 1987, Mortal Fear, 1988, Mutation, 1989, Harmful Intent, 1990, Vital Signs, 1990, Blindsight, 1991, Terminal, 1992, Fatal Cure, 1994, Acceptable Risk, 1995, Invasion, 1997, Chromosome 6, 1997, Toxin, 1998, Vector, 1999, Shock, 2001, Abduction, 2002, Seizure, 2003, Marker, 2005 (Publishers Weekly Bestseller list, 2005). Lt. comdr. USN, 1969-71. Avocations: skiing, surfing, painting, cooking.*

COOK, ROBIN NATHANIEL, organizational development consultant; b. N.Y.C., Nov. 22, 1952; s. Meyer and Flora Cook. BA in Philosophy, U. Okla., 1972, MA in Human Rels., 1974. Supr. program compliance monitoring unit Chgo. Dept. Human Svcs., 1974—81; mgmt. cons./prin. R. Cook & Assocs., Consultants, Chgo., 1981—92; dir. local planning YMCA of Met. Chgo., 1992—2000; orgnl. devel. cons. JigZaw, Inc., Chgo., 2000; freelance orgnl. devel. profl. Chgo., 2001—. Spkr., presenter in field. Mem. Alderman's com. to structure cmty. policing pilot project; chmn., nat. platform conv. del. Chgo. chpt. New Jewish Agenda; bd. dirs., mem. exec. com. Shalom Project. Recipient Key to City, San Diego, George Land World Class Innovator award,

1998, Innovation Univ. fellowship, 1998—99. Jewish. Achievements include design of organizational molecular model diagnostic tool. Home: 1227 W North Shore Chicago IL 60626 Office Phone: 773-262-7018. Personal E-mail: rnc@interaccess.com.

COOK, RUDOLPH EMANUEL, psychologist; b. Chgo., May 30, 1928; m. Shirley Thrower, Aug. 3, 1973. PhB, Northwestern U., 1949; MA, Loyola U., Chgo., 1956; PhD, U. Oreg., 1965. Lic. psychologist, Calif. Boys counselor Cook County Juv. Home, Chgo., 1952-56; psychologist Elgin (Ill.) State Hosp., 1956-62; tchg. asst. U. Oreg., Eugene, 1962-65; poverty worker Portland (Oreg.) Urban League, 1965-66; psychol. counselor San Jose (Calif.) State U., 1966-90; ret. Forensic evaluator Santa Clara County (Calif.) Superior Ct.; psychologist Calif. Disability Evaluation Div. Recipient Service award Continental Socs., 1982-83. Mem. Kappa Alpha Psi (Svc. award 1975, 76). Democrat. Home: 1094 Pomeroy Ave Santa Clara CA 95051-4427 Office: 95 S Market St Ste 300 San Jose CA 95113-2350

COOK, SANDY, dean; d. Madge Rua and Frank McFadden (Stepfather); children: Siobhan Lowe, Sean Lowe. PhD, Cornell U., 1987. Ednl. specialist U. Chgo., 1989—2001, assoc. dean for curriculum, 2001—. Chmn. Chgo. Asthma Consortium, 2001. Office: U Chgo 924 E 57th St Ste 104 Chicago IL 60637 Business E-Mail: scook@uchicago.edu.

COOK, SCOTT, communications executive; BA in Economics and Math., U. So. Calif.; MBA, Harvard U. Various mktg. positions to brand mgr. Procter & Gamble; cons. Bain Co.; founder, pres., CEO Intuit Inc., Menlo Park, Calif., 1984-94, dir., 1984—, chmn. bd. dirs., 1993—. Bd. dirs. eBay, Procter & Gamble. Bd. dirs. Asia Found.; bd. visitors Harvard Bus. Sch. Mem.: Phi Beta Kappa. Office: Intuit Inc 2632 Marine Way Mountain View CA 94043 Office Phone: 650-944-6000.*

COOK, SCOTT, literature educator; b. Shelbyville, Tenn., May 28, 1980; s. Ronnie Lynn Cook and Sheree Lynn Hester; m. Meghan Leah Delaney, Aug. 11, 2001. AS in Polit. Sci., Psychology and History summa cum laude, Motlow State C.C., Lynchburg, Tenn., 2001; BS summa cum laude in Polit. Sci., Mid. Tenn. State U., 2001; M in Liberal Studies in English, Ft. Hays State U., 2004. Adj. instr. history and devel. studies Motlow State C.C., Smyrna, Tenn., 2001—04; asst. prof. English and remedial edn. Ga. Mil. Coll., Columbus, 2004—. Coord. learning support svcs. Ga. Mil. Coll., Columbus, 2004—, coord. testing, 2004—, creator Learning Ctr., 2004—, bulldog bark advisor, 2005—. Mem.: MLA, Am. Polit. Sci. Assn., Am. Hist. Assn., Nat. Coun. Tchrs. English, Pi Sigma Alpha, Phi Kappa Phi, Golden Key, Phi Alpha Theta. Office Phone: 706-568-5191.

COOK, SHARLA J., career officer; BS in Edn. with honors, Brigham Young U., 1971; disting. grad., Officer Tng. Sch., 1972; aircraft maintenance officer course, Chanute AFB, Ill., 1973; M in Logistics Mgmt., Air Force Inst. of Tech., 1977; grad., Air Command and Staff Coll., 1985; disting. grad., Indsl. Coll. of Armed Forces, 1993. Commd. 2d lt. USAF, 1972, advanced through grades to brigadier gen., 1998; wing job control officer U-Tapao Air Base, Thailand, 1975-76; aide-de-camp air logistics ctr. comdr. Sacramento Air Logistics Ctr., McClellan AFB, Calif., 1981-82, dep. br. chief inventory and scheduling br., 1982-84; comdr. 374th Orgnl. Maintenance Squadron, Clark Air Base, The Philippines, 1985-87; maintenance ops. officer 58th Tactical Tng. Wing, Luke AFB, Ariz., 1988-90, asst. dep. comdr. for maintenance, 1990-91; dep. comdr. 58th Support Group, Luke AFB, 1991-92; comdr. 8th Logistics Group, Kunsan Air Base, South Korea, 1993-94; chief maintenance engring. Hdqs. Pacific Air Forces, Hickam AFB, Hawaii, 1994-95, asst. dir. logistics, 1995-96; dir. aircraft directorate Ogden Air Logistics Ctr., Hill AFB, Utah, 1996-97; dir. logistics Hdqs. Air Edn. and Tng. Command, Randolph AFB, Tex., 1997—; comdr. 82d tng. wing Air Edn. and Tng. Command, Sheppards AFB, Tex., 1999—. Decorated Legion of Merit, Meritorious Svc. medal with 4 oak leaf clusters. Address: 82 TRW/CC Sheppard Afb TX 76311

COOK, SHIRLEY GRACE, secondary school educator; b. Vidalia, Ga., Nov. 6, 1946; d. Pierce Arnold and Bobbie Nell (Stanley) Grace; m. Harry Mercer Cook, Jan. 11, 1969; children: Pamela Grace, Harry Bert. BSc, Berry Coll., 1968; MEd, Troy U., 2004. Cert. Am. Assn. Family and Consumer Scis. Pres., treas. Cook Farms, Talbotton, Ga., 1969—89; case mgr. Muscogee Dept. Family and Consumer Scis., Columbus, Ga., 1989—96, Talbolton (Ga.) County Dept. Family and Consumer Scis., 1996—98; tchr. Muscogee County Sch. Dist., Columbus, 1998—. Named Ga. New Family and Consumer Sci. Tchr. of Yr., Ga. Assn. Tech. Career Educators, 1992. Mem.: Ga. Assn. Family and Consumer Scis. (pres. dist. 2004—05). Home: 210 Cook Rd Talbotton GA 31827 Office: Shaw High School 7601 Schomburg Rd Columbus GA 31909

COOK, STANTON R., media company executive; b. Chgo., July 3, 1925; s. Rufus Merrill and Thelma Marie (Borgerson) C.; m. Barbara Wilson, Sept. 23, 1950 (dec. Nov. 1994). BS in Mech. Engring., Northwestern U., 1949. With Shell Oil Co., 1949-51, Chgo. Tribune Co., 1951-81, v.p., 1967-70, exec. v.p. and gen. mgr., 1970-72, pres., 1972-74, pub., 1973-90, CEO, 1974-76, chmn., 1974-81; dir. Tribune Co., 1972-96, v.p., 1972-74, pres., 1974-88, chmn., 1989-92, CEO, 1974-90; chmn. Chgo. Nat. League Ball Club, Inc., 1990-94. Bd. dirs. AP, 1975-84, 2d vice chmn., 1979-84; bd. dirs. Newspaper Adv. Bur., 1973-92, Am. Newspaper Pubs. Assn., 1974-82; dep. chmn., bd. dirs. Fed. Res. Bank Chgo., 1980-83, chmn., 1984-85; bd. dirs. Robert R. McCormick Tribune Found., 1990-2001. Trustee Robert R. McCormick Trust, 1972-90, Savs. and Profit Sharing Fund of Sears Employees, 1991-94, U. Chgo., 1973-87, Mus. Sci. and Industry, Chgo., 1973—, Field Mus. Natural History, Chgo., 1973—, Gen. Douglas MacArthur Found., 1979—, Northwestern U., 1987—, Shedd Aquarium Soc., 1987—. Am. Newspaper Pubs. Assn. Found., 1973-82. Mem. Newspaper Assn. Am. (bd. govs. 1992), Chgo. Coun. Fgn. Rels. (bd. dirs. 1973-93), Comml. Club (past pres.), Econ. Club (life, past pres.), Glen Lake Assn. (pres. 2001-04). Home: 224 Raleigh Rd Kenilworth IL 60043-1209

COOK, STEPHEN ARTHUR, mathematics and computer science educator; b. Buffalo, Dec. 14, 1939; s. Gerhard Albert and Lura C.; m. Linda Marie Craddock, May 4, 1968; children— Gordon, James. BS in math., U. Mich., 1961; S.M. in math., Harvard U., 1962, PhD in math., 1966. Asst. prof. U. Calif.-Berkeley, 1966-70; assoc. prof. U. Toronto, 1970-75, prof., 1975—, univ. prof., 1985—. Contbr. articles to profl. jours. E.W.R. Staecie Meml. fellow, 1977-78; Killam research fellow Can. Council, 1982-83; recipient ACM Turing award Assn. Computing Machinery, 1982, Killam prize Can. Coun., 1997. Fellow Royal Soc. Can., Royal Soc. London; mem. Nat. Acad. Scis., Am. Acad. Arts and Scis. Office: Dept Computer Sci U Toronto Toronto ON Canada M5S 3G4 Office Phone: 416-978-5183. E-mail: sacook@cs.toronto.edu.

COOK, STEPHEN CHAMPLIN, shipping company executive; b. Portland, Oreg., Sept. 20, 1915; s. Frederick Stephen and Mary Louise (Boardman) C.; m. Dorothy White, Oct. 27, 1945 (dec. Sept. 1998); children: Mary H. Cook Goodson, John B., Samuel D., Robert B. (dec.). Student, U. Oreg., 1935-36. Surveyor U.S. Engrs. Corp., Portland, Oreg., 1934-35; dispatcher Pacific Motor Trucking Co., Oakland, Calif., 1937-38; manifest clk. Pacific Truck Express, Portland, 1939; exec. asst. Coastwise Line, San Francisco, 1940-41, mgr. K-Line svc., 1945-56; chartering mgr. Ocean Svc. Inc. subs. Marcona Corp., San Francisco, 1956-75, 1975—. Author 1 charter party, 1957. Steering com. Dogwood Festival, Lewiston, Idaho, 1985-92; sec. Asotin County Reps., Clarkston, Wash., 1986-88; adv. bd. Clarkston Pt. Commrs., 1989-92. Lt. USN, 1941-45, PTO; grand marshall Asotin Christmas Parade, 2000. Recipient Pres.'s award Marin (Calif.) coun. Boy Scouts Am., 1977, Order of Merit, 1971, 84, Skillern award Lewis Clark coun., 1982, Silver Beaver award 1987; Lewis-Clark Valley Vol. award, 1987, Youth Corps award Nat. Assn. Svc. and Conservation Corps, 1990, Pres.'s Spl. award Clarkston C. of C., 1983, Asotin Citizen of Yr. award, 1999. Mem. VFW, Asotin County Hist. Soc. (hon. life pres. 1982-83, bd. dirs.), Asotin C. of C. (v.p. 1994-95). Republican. Mem. Stand for United Ch. of Christ. Avocations: hiking, camping, stamp collecting/philately.

COOK, STEPHEN DAY, art educator; b. Jackson, Miss., Sept. 10, 1951; s. Alfred G. and Lottye Greenlee Cook; m. Jeanne Elizabeth Wells, May 19, 1984. BA, Miss. Coll., 1973; MFA, U. Miss., 1975; cert. in Printmaking, Royal Coll. Art, London, Eng., 1976. Prin., owner New Leaf Graphics, Jackson, Miss., 1976—2005; chmn. Dept. Printmaking Miss. Mus. Art Sch., Jackson, Miss., 1977—78; instr. art Academic and Performing Arts Complex Jackson (Miss.) Pub. Schs., 1980—82; assoc. prof. art Miss. Coll., Clinton, Miss., 1983—. Instr. art Hinds C.C., Raymond, Miss., 1978; instr. printmaking U. Miss., Oxford, Miss., 1978. Exhibitions include Milhouse (France) Biennale, 1977, 1979, exhibited in group shows at So. Graphics Coun., 1979, Represented in permanent collections Victoria and Albert Mus., London, one-man shows include Meridian Mus. Art, 1979. Deacon Northminster Bapt. Ch., Jackson, 1989—91. Recipient Ann. award, Henry Bellamann Meml. Found., 1975, Merit award, Miss. Artists Competition, 1977; fellow, Internat. Telephone and Telegraph Corp., 1975—76, U. Miss., 1973—75; grantee, NEA, 1977—78. Mem.: Father Waters Pipes and Drums (pipe major 2005). Baptist. Avocations: music, woodworking. Home: 3924 Oakridge Dr Jackson MS 39216 Office: Mississippi Coll Clinton MS 39058 Office Phone: 601-925-3452.

COOK, STUART DONALD, neurologist, educator; b. Boston, Oct. 23, 1936; s. Martius and Nina (Schwartzman) C.; m. Josepha Emdin, June 26, 1960; children— Andrew, Peter, Jonathan. AB, Brandeis U., 1957; MS, U. Vt., 1959, MD, 1962. Diplomate: Am. Bd. Psychiatry and Neurology. Intern Upstate Med. Center, Syracuse, N.Y., 1962-63; resident in neurology Albert Einstein Coll. Medicine, Bronx, N.Y., 1965-67, chief resident, 1967-68, instr. dept. neurology, 1968-69; asst. prof. neurology Coll. Physician and Surgeons, Columbia U., N.Y.C., 1969-71; prof. medicine NJ Med. Sch., Newark, 1971, chmn. dept. neuroscis., 1972-98, prof. neurology, neurosciences, 1972—; chief neurology svc. VA Med. Ctr., East Orange, N.J., 1971-86; acting dean NJ Med. Sch., 1987-89; pres. U. Medicine and Dentistry N.J., 1998—2004. Vis. scientist div. virology Nat. Inst. Med. Research, London, 1977-78; vis. scientist Swiss Inst. for Cancer Research, 1985. Contbr. articles to profl. jours. Served with USN, 1963-65. Mem. Am. Acad. Neurology (S. Weir Mitchell award 1968), AAUP, Harvey Soc., Am. Neurol. Assn., Sigma Xi, Alpha Omega Alpha. Home: 26 Dogwood Dr Morristown NJ 07960-3310 Office: U Medicine and Dentistry Rm 1435 65 Bergen St Newark NJ 07107-3001 Office Phone: 973-972-9181. Business E-Mail: cooksd@umdnj.edu.

COOK, SUSAN FARWELL, associate director planned giving; b. Boston, Apr. 28, 1953; d. Benjamin and Beverly (Brooks) Conant; m. James Samuel Cook Jr., Aug. 17, 1985; children: Emily Farwell, David McKendree. AB, Colby Coll., 1975; MBA, Thomas Coll., 2002. Bank teller Boston 5 Cent Savs. Bank, 1975-76; asst. technician plan cost John Hancock Mut. Life Ins. Co., Boston, 1976-77, technician plan cost, 1977-78, sr. technician plan cost, 1978-79, asst. mgr. group pension plan cost, 1979-81; assoc. dir. alumni rels. Colby Coll., Waterville, Maine, 1981-86, dir. alumni rels., 1986-97, assoc. dir. planned giving, 1997—2005, asst. dir. campaign, 2005—. Co-dir. adv. bd. women's studies Colby Coll., 1987-89, adv. women's group, 1987-89; bd. dirs. Maine Planned Giving Coun., 2001-2004, treas., 2002-04 Bd. dirs., newsletter sec. Literacy Vols. Am., Waterville, 1986—89, 1991—92, v.p., 1995—97, pres., 1997—99; treas. Pitcher Pond Improvement Assn., 1988—95, Gagnon/100 Campaign, 1996, 1998; coach Waterville Area Youth Hockey Assn., 1997—2001; bd. dirs. Youth Hockey Assn., 2001—05; treas. Gagnon for Senate, 2000, 2002; trustee Universalist-Unitarian Ch., Waterville, 2001—, v.p., 2003—05, pres., 2005—; bd. dirs. Congress Lake Assns., Yarmouth, Maine, 1988—92, Waterville Youth Soccer Assn., 2001—, pres., 2002—05; bd. dirs. Kennebec Montessori Sch., 1999—2001, Soccer Maine, 2005—, sec., 2005—. Mem. AAUW (sec. Waterville br. 1989-91, pres. 1991-93, co-pres. 1993-95, treas. 2003-), Coun. Advancement and Support of Edn., CASE Dist. I (exec. bd. dirs. 1994-97, sec. 1996-97, nominating com. 1997-99). Avocations: skiing, sewing, golf. Home: 6 Pray Ave Waterville ME 04901-5339 Office: Colby Coll 4372 Mayflower Hl Waterville ME 04901-8843

COOK, SYBILLA AVERY, school library consultant; b. Buffalo, Aug. 20, 1930; d. Edward Carrington and Elizabeth (Boorum) Avery; m. John D. Cook, June 12, 1951; children: Harold John, Robert Sherman, Raymond Avery. BS, Northwestern U., 1951; MLS, Rosary Coll., River Forest, Ill., 1968; MA, U. Oreg., 1982. Cert. ednl. media tchr. and supr., Oreg., Ill. Tchr. Glenview (Ill.) Pub. Schs., 1951; librarian Deerfield (Ill.) Pub. Schs., 1968-69; media specialist Des Plaines (Ill.) Pub. Schs., 1969-76; librarian Dillard (Oreg.) Pub. Schs., 1976-78; libr. media specialist Glide (Oreg.) Pub. Schs., 1978-90; sch. libr. cons., Roseburg, Oreg., 1986—. Adj. instr. Western Oreg. State Coll., Monmouth, 1988-93; mem. libr. info. skills com. Oreg. Dept. Edn., 1987. Author: Instructional Design for Libraries, 1986, Walking Portland, 1998; author: (with Cheryl Page) Battles, and Bees, 1994; author: (with B. Fonnesbeck and F. Corcoran) Battle of the Books and More, 2001, 2004; author: (with F. Corcoran, B. Fonnesbeck, R. Goodman) Elementary Battle of the Books, 2005; contbr. articles to profl. jours. Recipient Gandalf award Douglas County Libr. System, 1994. Mem. ALA, AAUW (v.p. 1999-2003), Am. Assn. Sch. Librs., Author's Guild, Lane Douglas Regional Libr. Assn. (chmn. 1982-84), Oreg. Ednl. Media Assn. (exec. bd. 1987—, Tchr. of Yr. 1984), Soc. Children's Book Writers, Friends of the Libr. (pres. 2002—), Willamette Writers, Beta Phi Mu. Home and Office: 19 N River Dr Roseburg OR 97470-9473 E-mail: sybilla@rosenet.net.

COOK, TRACI, sports association executive; BA in History, English and Polit. Sci., U. Miss., 1987. With Nat. Dem. Inst., Malawi, Central African Republic; staff mem. Sr. Christopher Dodd (Conn.), 1992; mktg., bus. devel. exec. Physicians' Online; v.p. mktg. comm. Shepardson, Stern and Kaminsky; sr. dir. strategic and corp. rels. Women's Nat. Basketball Assn., N.Y.C., 2001—. Office: Women's Nat Basketball Assn Olympic Tower 645 Fifth Ave New York NY 10022

COOK, VICTOR JOSEPH, JR., marketing educator, consultant; b. Durant, Okla., June 25, 1938; s. Victor Joseph and Athelene Ann (Arduser) C.; m. Linda Lee Potter, June 6, 1960 (div. 1971); children: Victor Joseph III, William Randall, Christopher Phelps; m. barbara Brainard, Dec. 29, 1989 (div. 1997). BA, Fla. State U., 1960; MS, La. State U., 1962; PhD, U. Mich., 1965. Rsch. assoc. Mktg. Sci. Inst., Phila., 1965-68; assoc. rsch. dir. Boston, 1968-69; asst. prof. U. Chgo., 1969-75; pres., dir. Mgmt. & Design, New Orleans, 1975-78; prof. Freeman Sch. Bus. Tulane U., 1978—. Pres. The Styjl Furniture, 1998—; cons. Ford Motor Co., Dearborn, Mich., 1964-67, IBM, N.Y.C., 1968-72, Sears, Roebuck & Co., Chgo., 1975-77, Internat. Computers Ltd., ICL, London, 1982-91, The DuPont Co., Wilmington, 1986—, The Bases Group, Cin., 1986-89. Author: Brand Policy Determination, 1967, Readings in Marketing Strategy, 1989 Mem. Am. Mktg. Assn., Am. Econ. Assn., Inst. for Ops. Rsch. and The Mgmt. Scis., Beta Gamma Sigma, Phi Beta Kappa. Republican. Achievements include patents for furniture The Style. Office: Tulane U AB Freeman Sch Bus New Orleans LA 70118 Personal E-mail: vcook@thestyle.com. Business E-Mail: victor.cook@tulane.edu.

COOK, WILLIAM E., JR., lawyer; AB, Duke Univ., 1984; JD, Harvard Univ., 1987. Bar: D.C. Law clk. Chief Judge Richard C. Erwin, US Dist. Ct., Middle Dist. N.C.; ptnr., Diversity Affairs Arnold & Porter, Washington. Office: Arnold & Porter 555 Twelfth St NW Washington DC 20004-1206 Office Phone: 202-942-5996. Office Fax: 202-942-5999. Business E-Mail: william.cook@aporter.com.

COOK, WILLIAM HOWARD, architect; b. Evanston, Ill., Dec. 19, 1924; s. Clare Cyril and Matilda Hermine (Schuldt) C.; m. Nancy Ann Dean, Feb. 1, 1949; children: Robert, Cynthia, James. BA, UCLA, 1947; BArch, U. Mich., 1952. Chief designer Fabrica de Muebles Camacho-Roldan, Bogota, Colombia, S.Am., 1949-52; assoc. architect Orus Eash, Traverse City, Mich., Ft. Wayne, Ind., 1952-60; ptnr. Cook & Swaim (architects), Tucson, 1961-68; project specialist in urban devel. Banco Interamericano de Desarrollo, Buenos Aires, Argentina, 1968-69; pres. Cain, Nelson, Wares, Cook and Assocs., architects, Tucson, 1969-82. Vis. lectr. architecture U. Ariz., 1980-89; coord. archtl. exch. with U. LaSalle, Mexico City, 1983, 85, 87, 89, 93. Served to lt. (j.g.) USNR, 1943-46. Fellow AIA (pres. So. Ariz. 1967); mem. Ariz. Soc. Architects (pres. 1970), Ariz. Soc. of AIA (Architect's medal 1981) Presbyterian. Home and Office: PO Box 347 Sonoita AZ 85637-0347

COOK, WILLIAM M., manufacturing executive; b. Aug. 1954; BSBA, MBA, Va. Tech. Univ. Sr. v.p., comml. & indsl. Donaldson Co., Mpls., 1996—2000, sr. v.p. internat., CFO, 2001—04, pres., CEO, 2004—05, chmn., pres., CEO, 2005—. Office: Donaldson Co 1400 W 94th St Minneapolis MN 55431*

COOK, WILLIAM WILBERT, literature and language professor, department chairman; b. Trenton, N.J., Aug. 4, 1933; s. Cleve and Frances (Carter) C. BA, Coll. of N.J., 1954; MA, U. Chgo., 1976; PhD, Rivier Coll., Manchester, N.H., 1994. Tchr. William G. Cook Sch., Trenton, 1954-56, Jr. H.S. 1, Trenton, 1956-61; tchr., chmn. English dept. Princeton (N.J.) H.W., 1961-73; prof. English, Dartmouth Coll., Hanover, N.H., 1973—, chmn. dept., 1994—, Israel Evans prof. oratory and belles lettres, 1993. Workshop leader, cons., in-svc. tchr. trainer various sch. sys., 1973—, Nat. Faculty Arts and Scis., Atlanta, 1976—. Author: Hudson Hornet and Other Poems, 1989, Spiritual and Other Poems, 1999, (play) Flight to Canada, 1982; editor: Tapping Potential, 1985; contbr. essays and poems to various jours. Selection panel mem., workshop leader Nat. Endowment for the Humanities Nat. Endowment for the Arts; founder, v.p. African Grove Inst. for Arts, 1996—. With U.S. Army, 1957-59. Recipient Disting. Alumni citation Coll. of N.J., 1977; named N.H. Prof. of Yr., Coun. for Advancement and Support Edn., 1993. Mem. MLA, Nat. Coun. Tchrs. English (exec. com. 1971-73), Conf. on Coll. Composition and Comm. (asst., assoc. chmn. 1990-92). Democrat. Baptist. Avocations: acting, painting, reading. Office: Dartmouth Coll Box 6032 Hanover NH 03755

COOK-BENNETT, GAIL, pension fund administrator; BA in Econ., Carleton U., 1962; MA in Econ., U. Mich.; PhD in Econ., U. Mich.i; LLD honoris causa, Carleton U. Former acad. positions U. Toronto; former sr. exec. position C.D. Howe Inst.; vice-chair Bennecon Ltd., 1982—98; chairperson Can. Pension Plan Investment Bd., Toronto, 1998—. Bd. dirs. Manulife Fin. Corp., Petro-Can, Emera Inc. Recipient Honour for Contbn. to Working Women, Montreal YWCA, 1977. Fellow: Can. Inst. Corp. Dirs. Office: Can Pension Plan Investment Bd Ste 2700 PO Box 101 1 Queen St E Toronto ON M5C 2W5 Canada Business E-Mail: gcook-bennett@cppib.ca. E-mail: gcook-bennett@sympatico.ca.

COOK-DEEGAN, ROBERT MULLAN, physician, educator; s. William Raymond Cook and Merry (Mullan) Low. BA in Chemistry, Harvard Coll., 1975; MD, U. Colo., 1979. Intern U. Colo., Denver, 1979-80, postdoctoral fellow, rsch. pathologist, 1980-82; sr. assoc. Office Tech. Assessment, U.S. Congress, Washington, 1982-88; acting exec. dir. biomed. ethics adv. com. U.S. Congress, Washington, 1988-89; expert Nat. Ctr. Human Genome Rsch., Bethesda, Md., 1989-90; dir. div. bio-behavioral scis. and mental disorders Inst. Medicine, NAS, Washington, 1991-94; sr. program officer NAS, 1994-96; Cecil and Ida Green fellow U. Tex., Dallas, 1996; dir. Nat. Cancer Policy Bd., 1996-2000, Robert Wood Johnson Health Policy Fellowship Program, 2001—02, Ctr. Genome Ethics Law and Policy, Duke U., 2002—. Author: The Gene Wars: Science, Politics, and the Human Genome, 1994; contbr. articles and chpts. in field. Bd. dirs. Physicians for Human Rights, Boston, 1987-96; dir. ctr. excellence Ethical, Legal & Social Implications Rsch., NIH, 2004—. Recipient Robert Johnson Health Policy Rsch. Investigator award, 1999—2002; grantee Alfred P. Sloan Found., Georgetown U., 1988—91, NSF, 1990—91, Nat. Cancer Inst. and Robert Wood Johnson, 1992—2000, Burroughs Wellcome Fund, 2000—01. Fellow AAAS. Achievements include research in history of human genome project, public policy in cancer, health policy, tobacco control, neurology, psychiatry, behavioral medicine, neuroscience and addiction; U.S. federal policy on Alzheimer's disease and other dementing disorders, public policy on human gene therapy and bioethics. Office: Duke Univ Box 90141 Durham NC 27708-0141 Office Phone: 919-668-0793.

COOKE, CARLTON LEE, JR., mayor; b. Marion, Ala., July 12, 1944; s. Carlton Lee and Willie (Rinehart) Cooke; married; 1 child, Kimberly Ann. Student, U. Hawaii, 1962-65; BA, La. Tech. U., 1966; postgrad., U. Tex., 1970-72. Mfg. engr. Tex. Instruments, Austin, 1972-75, site personnel mgr., 1975-81, mktg. mgr., 1981-83; pres., CEO Greater Austin C. of C., 1983-87; mayor City of Austin, Austin, 1988—91. CEO, pres. good2CU.com, Inc., 1999—2000; chmn., CEO Habitek Internat., Inc., 1991—, Tanisys Tech. Corp., 2002—03; pres., CEO U.S. Med. Sys., Inc., 1992—, The Life Store Med. Group, LLC, 2004—; bd. dirs. New Century Equity Holdings Corp., Bill Concepts Corp., U.S. Long Distance Corp., Sharps Compliance Corp., Med. Polymers Tech., Inc., ProActive Med. Techs., Inc., CUville.com, Inc., FIData.com, Inc., Staubach Co., Tanisys Tech. Corp., Stewart Title, Reliability, Inc., CTLLC; participant U.S. Conf. Mayors, Washington, 1991; mem. Anthony Commn., U.S. Congress. Contbg. editor: to mags. Co-chmn. Jerry Lewis Telethon, Austin, 1986—87; chmn. United Negro Telethon, 1991, Tex. Housing Fin. Corp., 1992—94, Austin Charter Com., 1993—94, Tex. Walk of Stars, 1991—2003; mem. Austin City Coun., 1977—91, mayor pro tem, 1979; mem. adv. bd. U. Miami Rosenstiel Sch. Ctr. Sustainable Fisheries, 2001—02. Capt. USAF, 1966—72, Vietnam. Decorated Bronze Star; named Jaycee of the Yr., Austin Jaycees, 1976; named one of Five Outstanding Young Texans, Tex. Jaycees, 1979; recipient Carl Burnett Cmty. award, 1981, Disting. Austin Citizen's award, 1992, Excellence award, Real Estate Coun. Austin, 1992. Mem.: VFW, Austin-San Antonio Corridor Coun. (pres. 1988, 1991), Tex. Mcpl. League (pres. 1991), Nat. League Cities (chair fin. steering com.). Baptist. Avocations: travel, reading, civic work, movie history, art. Home: PO Box 50442 Austin TX 78763-0442 Office: Office of Mayor 2705 Bee Cave Rd Ste 160 Austin TX 78746 Office Phone: 512-347-8800 1125. Business E-Mail: usmedsys@austin.rr.com.

COOKE, CAROLYN ELIZABETH, writer; b. Bar Harbor, Maine, Feb. 6, 1959; d. John Eliot and Dorothy Elaine (Peterson) Cooke; m. Randall Leigh Babtkis, June 1, 1987; children: Zachary Cooke Batkis, Callie Lana Cooke Babtkis. BA in English, Smith Coll., Northampton, Mass., 1980; MFA, Columbia U., N.Y.C., 1986. Author: (short stories) The Bostons, 2001 (Notable Book of Yr., N.Y. Times, 2001, LA Times selection for Best Books, 2001), 1 in Prize Stories: The O'Henry awards, 1 in Best Am. Short Stories. Founder (with others) Pacific Comty. Charter Sch., Point Arena, Calif., 1999. Fellow, Corp. of Yadoo, Saratoga Springs, N.Y., 1987, Breadloaf, Middlebury, Vt., 2001; grantee, NEA, 1999—2000. Mem.: PEN, Authors' Guild. Home and Office: 35534 Ten Mile Cutoff PO Box 462 Point Arena CA 95468 E-mail: redtag@mcn.org.

COOKE, CHRISTOPHER ROBERT, lawyer, retired judge; b. Springfield, Ohio, Dec. 23, 1943; s. Warren and Margaret Louise (Martin) Cooke; m. Margaret Nick, July 1, 1970 (dec. 1996); children: Karen, Anastasia, Nicholas. BA, Yale U., 1965; JD, U. Mich., 1968. Bar: Ohio 1968, Alaska 1970, U.S. Dist. Ct. Alaska 1970. Atty. Alaska Legal Svcs. Corp., Anchorage, 1968—71, supervising atty. Bethel, 1971—73; mem. firm Rice, Hoppner & Hedland, Bethel, 1973—76; superior ct. judge State of Alaska, Bethel, 1976—86; ptnr. Hedland, Fleischer, Friedman, Brennan & Cooke, Bethel, Anchorage, 1986—2003, Cooke, Recca & Valearee, Anchorage, 2004—. Composer, singer: Chris Cooke's Tundra Music, 1981. Mem. com. Alaska Humanities Forum, Anchorage, 1979—86; adv. bd. Bethel Sch. Bd., 1982—88; chmn. Alaska Dems., 1999—2001; bd. regents U. Alaska, Fairbanks, 1975—77. Mem.: ABA, Alaska Bar Assn. Office: 3700 Jewel Lake Rd Anchorage AK 99502

COOKE, EDMUND, lawyer; BA, Kent State U., 1965; JD, U. Mich. Law Sch., 1973. Bar: Mich. 1973, DC 1979. Atty., Appellate Ct. Divsn. Nat. Labor Relations Bd.; spl. asst. to vice-chair EEOC, dep. dir., Field Svc. Office; staff counsel US Ho. of Reps.; ptnr., Labor & Employment Dept. Venable LLP, Washington. Contbr.; co-editor: Disability Law Reporter Svc. Capt. USAF, 1966—70. Office: Venable LLP 575 7th St NW Washington DC 20004 Office Phone: 202-344-4983. Office Fax: 202-344-8300. Business E-Mail: edcooke@venable.com.

COOKE, KENNETH LLOYD, mathematician, educator; b. Kansas City, Mo., Aug. 13, 1925; s. Sidney Kenneth and Mildred Blanche (Brown) C.; m. Margaret Sarah Burgess, Aug. 18, 1950; children: Catherine Sarah, Robert K., Susan E. BA, Pomona Coll., 1947; MS, Stanford, 1949, PhD, 1952. Instr., then asst. prof. math. State Coll. Wash., Pullman, 1950-57; mem. faculty Pomona Coll., 1957-93, Joseph N. Fiske prof. math., 1963—, chmn. dept., 1961-71, W.B. Keck disting. service prof., 1985-93. Cons. RAND Corp., 1956-65; mathematician Rsch. Inst. Advanced Studies, Balt., 1963-64; NSF sci. faculty fellow Stanford, 1966-67; Fulbright rsch. scholar U. Florence, Italy, 1971-72; vis. prof. Brown U., 1978-79, Inst. Math. Applications, U. Minn., 1983, Cornell U., 1987; Fulbright lectr. U. São Paulo, Sao Carlos, Brazil, 1987. Author: (with Richard Bellman) Differential-Difference Equations, 1963, Modern Elementary Differential Equations, 2d edit., 1971, (with Richard Bellman and J.A. Lockett) Algorithms, Graphs and Computers, 1970, (with Donald Bentley) Linear Algebra with Differential Equations, 1973, (with Colin Renfrew) Transformations: Mathematical Approaches to Culture Change, 1979, (with Stavros Busenberg) Vertically Transmitted Diseases, 1993; co-editor: Differential Equations and Applications in Ecology, Epidemics, and Population Problems, 1981, Differential Equations and Applications to Biology and to Industry, 1995. Served with USNR, 1944-46. Mem.: AAAS, Soc. Math. Biology, Soc. Indsl. and Applied Math., Math. Assn. Am., Am. Math. Soc., Sigma Xi, Phi Beta Kappa. Mem. United Ch. Christ.

COOKE, MICHAEL, editor-in-chief; b. England; m. Barbara Cooke; 3 children. BA, Auckland U., 1969. Joined Toronto Star, 1974, copy editor, city editor; co-mng. editor Montreal Gazette; mng. editor Edmonton Jour., 1992—95; editor-in-chief The Vancouver Province, 1995—2000, The Fin. Post, Canada, 1998; founding editor The Nat. Post, 1998; editor-in-chief Chgo. Sun Times, 2000—05, NY Daily News, NYC, 2005—. Office: Editor-in-Chief NY Daily News 450 W 33rd St New York NY 10001-2681*

COOKE, MIRIAM, Arabic educator; b. Denver, Aug. 30, 1948; d. Hedley Vicars and Edit (Meyersohn) Cooke; m. Bruce B. Lawrence, Apr. 24, 1983. MA with honors, Edinburgh U., Scotland, 1971; PhD, Oxford U., Eng., 1980. Prof. Arabic Duke U., Durham, N.C., 1980—, chair Asian and African langs. and lit., 1987-99. Author: Anatomy of an Egyptian/Intellectual, 1984, Choice Oustanding, 1985, War's Other Voices, 1988, Women and the War Story, 1997; co-editor: (with M. Badran) Opening the Gates, 100 Years of Arab Feminist Writing, 1990, (with Angela Woollacott) Gendering War Talk, 1993, (with Roshni Rustomji-Kerns) Blood Into Ink, 1994, Hayati, My Life, 2000, Women Claim Islam, 2000. Fulbright scholar, 1982, 95-96; grantee Social Sci. Rsch. Coun., 1985, AAUW, 1986, Dartmouth 1990 Humanities Inst. Home: 5717 Buck Quarter Rd Hillsborough NC 27278-7866 Office: Duke U 2101 Campus Dr Durham NC 27708-0414

COOKE, PAUL LEWIS, state fire marshal; b. Rochester, N.Y., Oct. 4, 1957; s. Percy Charles and June Mary (Oswold) Cooke; m. Linda Gail Hinds, July 6, 1978 (div. Oct. 1986); 1 child, Jennifer; m. Sherry Elaine Webster, Oct. 14, 1986; children: Stephanie, Paul Jr., Jessica. AAS in Fire Suppression, AAS in Fire Prevention, Red Rocks C.C., 1985; BS in Fire Svcs. Adminstrn., Met. State Coll., 1989. Fire protection specialist Buckley ANG Base Fire Dept., Aurora, Colo., 1981-82; fire chief Cunningham Fire Protection Dist., Denver, 1982-91; dep. dir. Colo. Divsn. of Fire Safety, Denver, 1991-93, dir., state fire marhsal, 1993—. V.p. Nat. Fire Info. Coun., dir. v.p. 1991-99. Adult leader Boy Scouts Am., Aurora, Colo., 1994—. With U.S. Army, 1975-81. Mem. Colo. State Fire Chiefs Assn. (legis. liaison 1989-91), Nat. Assn. of State Fire Marshals (com. chair 1992—), Nat. Fire Protection Assn., Internat. Assn. of Fire Chiefs. Protestant. Avocations: hiking, camping. Office: Colo Divsn Fire Safety 700 Kipling St Ste 1000 Denver CO 80215-5897 Fax: 303-239-4405. E-mail: plcooke@worldnet.att.net.

COOKE, ROBERT WILLIAM, science journalist; b. Alhambra, Calif., Mar. 26, 1935; s. Loren Elvin and Edith (Mason) C.; m. Sue B. Cato, Sept. 10, 1960; children: Gregory, Karen, Emily. BS in English, Calif. State Poly. Coll., 1961; MS in Journalism, UCLA, 1962; postgrad. in advanced sci. writing (Univ. fellow), Columbia U., 1969-70. Reporter-photographer Pomona (Calif.) Progress-Bull., 1962-63; newsman AP, Los Angeles, 1963-67; sci. writer Calif. Inst. Tech., 1967-69, Pasadena (Calif.) Star-News, 1970-73; sci. editor Boston Globe, 1973-84; sci./medicine writer Atlanta Jour. and Constn., 1984-86; sci. writer Newsday, L.I., NY, 1986—2003; ret., 2003. Author: Improving on Nature, The Brave New World of Genetic Engineering, 1977, Earthfire; the Eruption of Mt. St. Helens, 1982, Dr. Folkman's War, 2001. With USCG, 1954—58. Recipient James T. Grady award Am. Chem. Soc., 1981, Lewis Thomas award for communicating life scis. Woods Hole Marine Biology Lab., 1991, Sci. Writing award AAAS/Westinghouse, 1991. Mem. Nat. Assn. Sci. Writers, Kappa Tau Alpha. Democrat. Methodist.

COOKE, STEVEN JOHN, chemical engineer, consultant, scientist; b. Grand Rapids, Mich., Oct. 1, 1954; s. Edward G. and Annette M. (Minnema) C.; m. Marguerite K. Oldenburger, June 18, 1977; children: Allison, Jonathan. BS in Chemistry, Calvin Coll., 1977; M in Chem. Engring., Ill. Inst. Tech., 1987; postgrad. in Engring., Calif. Coast U. Registered profl. engr., Ill.; cert. profl. chemist, quality engr., quality auditor. Chemist, lab. supr. Matheson Gas Products, Joliet, Ill., 1977-80; chief chemist Cardox, Countryside, Ill., 1980-85; scientist Am. Air Liquide, Countryside, 1985-92; asst. quality mgr. Alphagaz Divsn. of Liquid Air, Countryside, 1992-93; quality assurance/quality control mgr. Am. Air Liquide, Countryside, 1993-95; quality mgr. Carbonic Industries Corp., 1995-98, Airgas Carbonic, Duluth, Ga., 1998—2000; pres. Process Systems Consulting, 2000—. Online faculty U. Phoenix, 2003—. Contbr. chpt. to book, articles on quality systems to profl. jours. Group leader Hazardous Materials Emergency Response Team; treas. Christian Reformed Ch. Mission, Western Springs, Ill., 1982-93, Chicagoland Diaconal Task Force Bd., Palos Heights, Ill., 1989-92. Fellow Am. Inst. Chemists; mem. Am. Soc. Quality Control, Am. Chem. Soc. (publicity chair I&EC divsn. 1989-95, chair I&EC divsn. 1999-2001, chair small chem. bus. divsn. 2004-05), Compressed Gas Assn. (CO2 task force, gas specifications com.) Achievements include patent for portable gas analyzer. Address: 1117 Mineral Springs Rd Charlotte NC 28262 Office Phone: 704-598-4819. E-mail: scooke@sprynet.com.

COOKE, TERRI L., director; d. Paul and Barbara Andary; m. Bruce Cooke Nathan, June 3, 2000. BA, Ohio Wesleyan U., 1998; MA in Higher Edn., Geneva Coll., 2001. Campus min., residence dir. York Coll. Pa., 1998—2001; asst. dean students, dir. greek life and student leadership Franklin and Marshall Coll., Lancaster, Pa., 2001—, asst. dir. residential programs, 2001—03, Franklin & Marshall Coll., Lancaster, Pa., 2003—04. Mem.: Assn. Frat. Advisors (assoc.), Nat. Assn. Student Pers. (assoc.), Am. Coll. Pers. Assn. (assoc.), Delta Zeta (life; collegiate chpt. dir. 2004—05). Office: Franklin & Marshall Coll PO Box 3003 Lancaster PA 17604 Office Fax: 717-358-7156.

COOKE, WILLIAM NELSON, labor management professor, consultant; b. Alton, Ill., Feb. 14, 1948; m. Julie Dee VanDyke, July 5, 1968; children: Jayna K., Keegan G., Connor W., Colton W. children: Benjamin Conant. BS in Econs., Ea. Ill. U., 1970; MA, U. Ill., 1973, PhD, 1977. Vis. scholar U. of Calif., Berkeley, Calif., 1979—80; vis. fellow Cornell U., Ithaca, NY, 1980—81; assoc. prof. Purdue U., West Lafayette, Ind., 1981—83, Sch. of Bus., U. of Mich., Ann Arbor, Mich., 1983—90; instr. Exec. Edn. Ctr., U. of Mich., 1984—; sr. rsch. prof. Coll. of Urban, Labor & Met. Affairs, Wayne State U., Detroit, 1990—. Dir. Fraser Ctr. for Workplace Issues, Detroit, 1998—2005, Labor-Mgmt. Rels. Ctr., Ann Arbor, Mich., 2003—; co-director Joint Labor-Mgmt. Rels. Ctr., 1987—90. Editor: (book) Multinational Companies and Global Human Resource Strategies; author: Labor-Management Cooperation: New Partnerships or Going in Circles, Union Organizing and Public Policy: Failure to Secure First Contracts; contbr. articles to profl. jours. Grantee, Russel Sage Found., 2001-2003, Rockefeller Found., 2001-2003, NSF. Office: Fraser Ctr for Workplace Issue 255 Reuther Library 5401 Cass Avenue Detroit MI 48202 Office Phone: 313-577-2100. Home Fax: 734-429-1295; Office Fax: 313-577-7599. Personal E-mail: wmncooke@comcast.net. E-mail: w.cooke@wayne.edu.

COOKER, MATTHEW ALAN, musician; b. Midland, Mich., Feb. 17, 1954; s. Clarence David and Ramona (Bialik) Cooker; m. Veronica Nancy Stensby, June 21, 1985. MusB in Performance, U. Mich., 1976, MusM in Performance, 1984. Cellist Orch. del Teatro alla Scala, Milan, 1976—77, Toledo (Ohio) Symphony, 1977—80; asst. prin. cellist Sacramento (Calif.) Symphony, 1981—83; cellist Hollywood Bowl Orch., L.A., 1996—. Instr. cello Henry Mancini Inst., L.A., 2000—. Composer (musician): (songs) Thanks Eddie, 2004; musician: (films) Freaky Friday, 2003, others. Avocation: yoga. Home: 4678 Cerro Verde Pl Tarzana CA 91356

COOKS, PAMALA ANIECE, insurance agent; b. Harvey, Ill., Dec. 31, 1973; d. Anthony T. Washington and Deloris Townsend; m. Paul Anthony Cooks, Dec. 8, 2002; 1 child, Olivia Janai Washington. BA, Govenors State U., 2001. Lic. prodr. Ill., 2000. Sales assoc. Aetna Inc., Chgo., 1996—. Evangelism ministry St. Mark Missionary Bapt. Ch., Harvey, 2002—03. Mem.: Nat. Campaign for Tolerance (assoc. Wall of Tolerance award 2002, 2003). Office Phone: 847-619-5590, 708-880-0436. Office Fax: 847-619-4936. Personal E-mail: pamalawashington@msn.com.

COOKS, R(OBERT) GRAHAM, chemist, educator; b. Benoni, South Africa, July 2, 1941; came to U.S., 1968; s. Audrey Owen Eva Mitchie; m. Maria-Luisa Raduan Ripoll, Aug. 19, 1967; children: Owen, Barry, Jude. BSc, U. Natal, 1961, PhD, 1965, Cambridge U., 1967. Asst. prof. Kansas State U., Manhattan, 1968-71; from assoc. dir. to disting. prof. Purdue U., Lafayette, Ind., 1971—. Author: Metastable Ions, 1973; contbr. articles to profl. jours.; patentee in field. Recipient ACS award in analytical chemistry Am. Chem. Soc., 1997. Mem. Am. Soc. Mass Spectrometry (pres. 1984-86), Internat. Mass Spectrometry Soc. (pres. 1997-2000). Home: 177 Prophet Dr West Lafayette IN 47906-1235 Office: Purdue U Dept Chemistry West Lafayette IN 47907 Business E-Mail: cooks@purdue.edu.

COOKSEY, JOHN CHARLES, congressman, ophthalmologist; b. Aug. 20, 1941; s. Henry Oscar and Ruth (Lee) C.; m. Dorothy Ann Grabill, Dec. 30, 1969; children: Karen, Carol Ann, Catherine. MD, La. State U., New Orleans, 1966; MBA, U. Tex., Austin, 1994. Mem. Congress from 5th La. Dist., 1996—2002, mem. agr. and internat. rels. coms.; practice medicine specializing in ophthalmology Monroe, La., 1972—. Mem. teaching staff E.A. Conway Hosp., Monroe, 1972—; vis. lectr. Alton Ochsner Med. Found., New Orleans, 1978—; asst. clin. prof. La. State U. Med. Sch., New Orleans, 1979—. Republican. Address: 1310 N 19th St Monroe LA 71201 E-mail: jcook20@aol.com.

COOKSEY, KAREN, conductor; b. Sewickley, Pa., Aug. 29, 1978; d. Kennon and Kim Cooksey. BA in Music Philosophy summa cum laude, Butler U., 2000; MusM in Choral Conducting, Ind. U., 2002. Dir. music Unitarian Universalist Ch., Indpls., 2002—05; dir. women's chorus, asst. choral dir. Earlham Coll., Richmond, 2002—04; asst. dir. Richmond Symphony Orch., 2003—05. Conductor, participant Oreg. Bach Festival, Eugene, Oreg., 2003. Dir.: (annual music festival) Heartland Choral Festival. Recipient 2d pl., 3rd Internat. Competition for Young Choir Dirs., Vienna, 2004. Mem.: Coll. Music Soc., Internat. Fedn. Choral Musicians, Am. Symphony Orch. League, Chorus Am., Conductors Guild, Am. Choral Dirs. Assn. (pres. student chpt. 1997—2000), Pi Kappa Lambda. Avocations: hiking, reading, travel. Personal E-mail: karen_cooksey@yahoo.com.

COOKSON, ALAN HOWARD, electrical engineer, researcher; b. London, July 3, 1939; arrived in U.S., 1968; s. Joseph and Rachel Cookson; m. Elizabeth Rosamond Ritblat, Oct. 24, 1965; children: Richard Jonathan, Simon Charles. BSc in Engring. with 1st class honors, Queen Mary Coll., London U., 1961, PhD of Elec. Engring., 1965. Chartered engr., Gt. Brit. Rsch. fellow Queen Mary Coll., London, 1964—65; rsch. officer Ctrl. Elec. Rsch. Labs., Leatherhead, England, 1965—69; sr. engr. Westinghouse R & D Ctr., Pitts., 1968—75; mgr. gas cable rsch. Westinghouse Power Circuit Breaker, Westborough, Mass., 1975—80; mgr. polymers, dielectrics and advanced batteries Westinghouse Sci. & Tech. Ctr., Pitts., 1980—92; dep. dir. Electronics and Elec. Engring. Lab. divsn. Nat. Inst. Stds. and Tech., Gaithersburg, Md., 1992—. U.S. rep. advanced materials for electro tech. com. Internat. Conf. Large Elec. Systems, 1996—; mem. US nat. com. Internat. Electrotech. Commn.; convener Working Group on Gas Insulated Cables, Internat. Conf. Large Elec. Systems, 1980-90. Editor: Digest of Literature on Dielectrics, 1970; contbr. articles to profl. jours.; patentee in field. Mem. adv. com. Miss. State U., 1983. Fellow IEEE (pres. Dielectrics and Elec. Insulation Soc. 1993-94), Inst. Elec. Engrs. London; mem. Phys. Soc., Inst. Physics London. Home: 15717 Bondy Ln Darnestown MD 20878-2114 Office: Nat Inst Standards/Tech Rm B358 Bldg 220 Gaithersburg MD 20899-8100 Business E-Mail: alan.cookson@nist.gov.

COOKSON, PETER WILLIS, JR., sociologist, writer; b. N.Y.C., Nov. 17, 1942; s. Peter Willis and Maureen (Grey) C.; m. Susan Stern, Sept. 16, 1968; children: Alexandra Genvieve, Aram Nathaniel. BA, NYU, 1966, MA, 1968, PhD, 1981; cert. advanced study, Harvard U., 1991. Prof. Dean, Lewis & Clark Grad. Sch. Edn. Columbia U.; pres. Cookson and Assocs. Author: School Choice and the Struggle for the Soul of American Education, 1994, Preparing for Power: America's Elite Boarding Schools, 1985, The International Handbook for Educational Reform, 1992, Making Sense of Society, 1993, Exploring Education, 1994, Choosing Schools, 1996, Autonomy and Choice in Context, 1997, A Parent's Guide to Standardized Tests in School, 1998; contbr. articles to profl. jours. With USAR, 1963-69. Rsch. grantee found., govt. and pvt. sector. Mem. N.Y. Acad. Scis., Am. Sociol. Assn. (Congrl. fellow 1993), Am. Ednl. Rsch. Assn. Democrat. Roman Catholic. Home: 1728 NW Hoyt St Portland OR 97209 Office: Lewis & Clark Coll Grad Sch Edn 0615 SW Palatine Hill Rd Portland OR 97219 Office Phone: 503-768-6002.

COOL, KIM PATMORE, retail executive, needlework consultant; b. Cleve., Feb. 1, 1940; d. Herman Chester Earl and Eva (Geneau) Patmore; m. Kenneth Adams Cool Jr., Mar. 12, 1963; 1 child, Heidi Adams. BA in Econs., Sweet Briar Coll., 1962; postgrad., Case Western Reserve U., 1962-63. Test adminstr. Pradco, Cleve., 1962-63; pvt. needlework cons. Cleve., 1970-72; retail v.p., treas., custom designer And Sew On, Inc., Cleve., 1973-92, exec. v.p., treas., 1982-92; v.p. Shure Stiches Inc., 1991-92; owner Shure Stitches, Inc., Cleve., 1992-93, The Hare Necessities, Venice, Fla., Germany, 1994—, Hare Necessities Craft & Needlework Mfg., Venice, Fla. Lectr. bus. seminars Nat. Needlework Assn.; tchr. Wellesley Coll. Continuing Edn. Program, 1986; pub. Fredericktown Press, Md.; designer and mktg. assoc. Kappie OriginalsLtd., 1988-93. Co-author: How to Market Needlepoint-The Definitive Manual, 1988, Easy Macrame, 1990, Basic Macrame, 1990, Wearable Macrame, 1990, Playmate Dolls to Stitch, 1991, Pillows and Purses to Stitch, 1991, Needlepoint from Start to Finish, 1992, Pathway to Profit in the Needlework Industry, 1995, Ghost Stories of Venice, 2002, Ghost Stories of Sarasota, 2003, Circus Days in Sarasota & Venice, 2004, Ghost Stories of Clearwater and St. Petersburg, 2004, Cool Road Trips in SW Florida, 2005; homes corr.: Venice (Fla.) Gondolier, 1995—, bus. editor:, 1998—, features editor: Venice Gondolier Sun. Rep. committeeman Cuyahoga County, Shaker Heights, Ohio, 1964-72. Recipient 1st pl. environ. writing, 3d pl. headline, Fla. Press Assn., 2002, 1st pl. spl. sect. and newspaper promotion, 2003, 1st pl. environ. writing, Fla. Press Club, 2004, 1st Pl. Environ. Writing award, Fla. Press Assn., 2004. Mem.: Sweet Briar Coll. Alumnae Assn. (nat. bd. dirs., upper Midwest region 1965—66, class sec. 1988—92), S.E. Yarncrafters Guild (condr. merchandising seminars 1989—), Embroiderers Guild of Cleve. (bd. dirs. 1980—82), Am. Profl. Needlework Retailers, Nat. Needlework Assn. (lectr. seminar on mktg. needlepoint, seminars on buying and merchandising 1988—, charter assoc. retail), U.S. Figure Skating Assn. (gold test judge 1967—, competitions com., ea. vice chair precision, judges edn. tng. com., nat. vice chair for precision, nat. precision judge, sr. competiton judge), Fla. Curling Club (charter), Mayfield Country Club, Cleve. Skating Club. Mem. United Ch. of Christ. Avocations: skating, curling (attended 1st Women's Olympic Tng. Camp for Curlers, Regional champion 1987-88). Home and Office: Hist Venice Press 312 Shore Rd Venice FL 34285-3725 Office Phone: 941-468-6556.

COOL, LINDA LOU, retired elementary school educator; b. Frankfort, Ind., Aug. 28, 1940; d. Charles Edward and Olive Mae (Wyatt) Shaffer; m. Joseph Howard Cool, Aug. 31, 1963; children: Anita Kay, Susan Marie. BS, Ball State U., Muncie, Ind., 1961, MS in Edn., 1968. Cert. tchr. Tchr. grade 4 Lincoln Sch. Community Schs. Frankfort (Ind.), 1961-65, tchr. grade 4 Kyger Sch., 1966-76, tchr. grade 5 Kyge Sch., 1976-86, tchr. grade 3 Kyger Sch., 1986-95, 2nd grade tchr., 1995—2001. Mem. State Textbook Adoption Com., Ind., 1983, North Cen. Evaluating Team, Ind., 1987, 89. Avocations: needlecrafts, reading, travel. Home: 255 N East St Rossville IN 46065-0196 Office: Kyger Elem Sch 300 S 3rd St Frankfort IN 46041-2313

COOLEDGE, RICHARD CALVIN, lawyer; b. Charleston, SC, Apr. 20, 1943; s. Russell Clarence and Lorena Ann (Weymuth) C.; m. Nancy Jean Western, June 15, 1965 (div. Dec. 1986); children: Dean Richard, Mark Alan, Jocelyn Joy; m. Jeanine Diana Smith, Apr. 12, 1989 (div. Nov. 1993). BA in Econs. with honors, U. Mo., Columbia, 1965; JD, U. Mich., 1968. Bar: Ariz. 1969, U.S. Dist. Ct. Ariz. 1969, U.S. Ct. Appeals (9th cir.) 1973, U.S. Supreme Ct. 1973. Mem. Brown & Bain P.A., Phoenix, 1968—2004, Perkins Coie Brown & Bain, Phoenix, 2004—. Contbg. editor: Banking and Lending Institutions Forms, Business Workouts Manual; contbr. articles to profl. jours. Fellow Ariz. Bar Found.; mem. Motorcycle Safety Found. (instr. 1994-2003), BMW Owners Assn. Avocations: motorcycling, golf, music, aviculture. Office: Perkins Coie Brown & Bain PA 2901 N Central Ave Fl 20 Phoenix AZ 85012-2700 Office Phone: 602-351-8425. Business E-Mail: rcooledge@perkinscoie.com.

COOLEY, ANDREW LYMAN, computer company executive; b. St. Louis, Oct. 14, 1934; s. Andrew L. and Algretta R. (Carr) C.; m. Joan Lynn Wheatley, Jan. 9, 1958; children: Cathleen Wheatley, Caroline Carr. BA, George Washington U., 1964, MA, 1967; MS, U.S. Army Command and Gen. Staff Coll., 1966; postgrad., U.S. Army War Coll., 1972-73. Commd. 2d lt. U.S. Army, 1955, advanced through grades to maj. gen., 1955-64; bn. adv. Vietnam, 1964-65; aide to chief of staff SHAPE, Belgium, 1967-69; tank bn. comdr. Germany, 1969-70; mem. staff Dept. of Army Pentagon, 1970-72; brigade comdr. and div. chief of staff Korea, 1975-77; exec. to comdr. in chief Pacific, 1978-79; asst. div. comdr. 101st Airborne Div., 1979-81; asst. dep. dir. for politico-mil. affairs, plans and policy directorate Joint Chiefs of Staff, Washington, 1981-83; mil. adviser Habib-Draper Mission, Lebanon, 1982-83; dir. strategy, plans and policy Dept. Army, Washington, 1983-85; comdg. gen. 24th Inf. Div. (Mech.) and Fort Stewart, Hunter Army Air Field, Fort Stewart, Ga., 1985-87; chief Office Military Cooperation, Cairo, 1987-89; ret., 1989; program mgr. Vinnell Brown Root, Turkey Base Maintenance Agreement, 1989-91; project mgr. ops. and maintenance Brown and Root Svcs. Corp., Houston, 1991-94; program mgr. Project Restore Hope Somalia, 1993. Ind. cons. with expertise in Africa, Croatia, Bosnia and Haiti, 1994-97; dir. ops. Dyncorp Internat. LLD Svcs., 1998—. Author: Diplomatic Significances of the Great White Fleet, 1966, Realistic Deterrence in NATO, 1973. Decorated Def. D.S.M. with oak leaf cluster, Legion of Merit with oak leaf cluster, Bronze Star, Air medal, others; Fed. Exec. fellow Brookings Instn., 1977-78; named to Officer Candidate Sch. Hall of Fame, 1979. Mem. Assn. U.S. Army, Armor Assn. Episcopalian. Home: 13235 W Pine Creek Sedalia CO 80135 Office Phone: 972-871-6754. E-mail: andrew.cooley@dyu-nett.com.

COOLEY, CHARLES P., chemicals executive; married; 3 children. BA in Philosophy, Yale Coll.; MBA, Dartmouth Coll. With nat. banking div. Mfrs. Hanover Trust Co., N.Y.C.; various positions Atlantic Richfield; controller and v.p. fin. and adminstrn. ARCO Products Co.; asst. treas. corp. fin. Atlantic Richfield Co., L.A.; v.p., treas., CFO The Lubrizol Corp., Wickliffe, Ohio, 1998—. Office: The Lubrizol Corp 29400 Lakeland Blvd Wickliffe OH 44092

COOLEY, CYNTHIA FURBER, artist; b. Mpls., July 17, 1931; d. John Roscoe and Jessie Anna (Vilendrer) Furber; m. William Warren Cooley; children: Warren, Robin. BA, Lawrence U., 1953; postgrad., Mpls. Coll. Art & Design, 1954, Boston Mus. Fine Arts Sch., 1957. Artist-in-residence Am. Wind Symphony, summer European tour, 1989. Watercolors and acrylics shown in numerous exhbns.; 43 one-woman shows include Bird in Hand Gallery, Pitts., 1972-04, Pitts. Ctr. for the Arts, 1996, Nat Acad. Scis., Washington, 1994; represented in permanent collections State Mus. Pa., Pa. State U. Mineral Scis. Mus., U. Pitts., Pitts. Regional History Ctr., Duquesne Club, U. Pitts., Consol. Energy, Highmark Blue Cross. Named Pitts. Artist of Yr. Pitts. Ctr. for the Arts, 1989, Pitts. Master Artist, 1998; Distng. Career Achievement award Lawrence U., 1997. Mem. Nat. Assn. Women Artists (Elizabeth Morse Genius Found. award), Associated Artists of Pitts. (bd. dirs. 1979-85, life mem.), Pitts. Soc. Artists (founding mem.), Pitts. Watercolor Soc. (bd. dirs., pres. 1976-85). Avocations: tennis, swimming, photography. Home: 1609 Powers Run Rd Pittsburgh PA 15238-2411 Office Phone: 412-963-8729. Personal E-mail: moll@cynthiacooley.com.

COOLEY, DENTON ARTHUR, surgeon, educator; b. Houston, Aug. 22, 1920; s. Ralph C. and Mary (Fraley) C.; m. Louise Goldsborough Thomas, Jan. 15, 1949; children: Mary, Susan, Louise, Florence, Helen. BA, U. Tex., 1941; MD, Johns Hopkins U., 1944; Doctorem Medicinae (hon.), U. Turin, Italy, 1969; H.H.D. (hon.), Hellenic Coll., 1984, Holy Cross Greek Orthodox Sch. of Theology, 1984; DSc honoris causa, Coll. of William and Mary, 1987. Diplomate: Am. Bd. Surgery, Am. Bd. Thoracic Surgery. Intern Johns Hopkins Sch. Medicine, Balt., 1944-45, resident surgery, 1945-50; sr. surg. registrar thoracic surgery Brompton Hosp. for Chest Diseases, London, Eng., 1950-51; assoc. prof. surgery Baylor U. Coll. Medicine, Houston, 1954-62, prof. surgery, 1962-69; clin. prof. surgery U. Tex. Med. Sch., Houston, 1975—; founder, surgeon-in-chief Tex. Heart Inst., 1962—. Served as capt., M.C., 1946-48. Named one of ten Outstanding Young Men in U.S., U.S. C. of C., 1955, Man of the Yr. award Kappa Sigma, 1964; recipient Rene Leriche prize Internat. Surg. Soc., 1967, Billings Gold medal Am. Surg. Soc., 1967, Vishnevsky medal Vishnevsky Inst., USSR, 1971, Theodore Roosevelt Award, 1980, Presdl. Medal of Freedom, presented by Pres. Reagan, 1984, Gifted Tchr. award Am. Coll. Cardiology, 1987, Disting. Svc. award AMA, 1997, Nat. Medal of Tech., U.S. Dept Commerce, 1998 Hon. fellow Royal Coll. Physicians and Surgeons of Glasgow, Royal Coll. Surgeons of Ireland, Royal Australasian Coll. Surgeons, Royal Coll. Surgeons of Eng.; mem. ACS, Am. Surg. Assn., Internat. Cardiovascular Soc., Am. Assn. Thoracic Surgery, Soc. Thoracic Surgery, Soc. Univ. Surgeons, Am. Coll. Cardiology, Am. Coll. Chest Physicians, Soc. Clin. Surgery, Soc. Vascular Surgery, Western Surg. Assn., Tex. Surg. Soc., Halsted Soc. Achievements include performance of numerous heart transplants; implanted 1st artificial heart, 1969. Office: Tex Heart Inst PO Box 20345 Houston TX 77225-0345 Business E-Mail: dcooley@heart.thi.tmc.edu. *As a person progresses along the path of life, he may achieve certain goals he set for himself as a youth. But to be more completely fulfilled, he must forever extend hid goals to utilize his talents ans accomplishments more fully. Too often, a man receives recognition for his deeds early in life and contents himself prematurely with living in peace and self-satisfaction.*

COOLEY, JAMES WILLIAM, retired executive researcher; b. N.Y.C., Sept. 18, 1926; s. William F. and Anna (Fanning) C.; m. Ingrid Uddholm, May 1, 1957; children: William, Anna-Carin, Lars. BA, Manhattan Coll., Riverdale, N.Y., 1949; MA, Columbia U., 1951, PhD, 1961. Programmer Inst. Advanced Study, Princeton, N.J., 1953-56; research staff Courant Inst., NYU,

1956-62; research staff mem. IBM Watson Research Ctr., Yorktown Heights, N.Y., 1962-91; with dept. elec. engring. U. R.I., Kingston, 1991-93; ret., 1993. Inventor fast fourier transform. Served with USAAF, 1945-46. Fellow IEEE (life, Third Millennium medal, Jack Kilby medal 2002); mem. NAE.

COOLEY, KRISTA GRACE, academic administrator; b. Harvey, Ill., Dec. 21, 1970; d. Stanley Wayne and Pauline (Lipsky) Deress; m. Thomas V. Cooley, Aug. 28, 1993. BS in Environ. Health with honors, Ill. State U., 1992, MS in Environ. Health and Safety, 2003. Indsl. hygienist intern U. Chgo. Hosps., 1992; indsl. hygienist U. Chgo., 1992-94, sr. indsl. hygienist, 1994—2003, assoc. dir. safety and environ. affairs, 2003—. Mem.: Am. Soc. Safety Engrs., Am. Indsl. Hygiene Assn., Am. Conf. Govtl. Indsl. Hygienists, Golden Key Nat. Honor Soc., Phi Eta Sigma, Omicron Delta Kappa, Eta Sigma Gamma. Office: U Chgo 5555 S Ellis Ave Fl 2D Chicago IL 60637-1401

COOLEY, SETH VAN DEN HOEK, lawyer; b. Flemington, N.J., Apr. 30, 1957; s. Richard S. and Nancy (van den Hoek) Cooley; m. Kathy Joan Trevorrow, May 9, 1981; children: Ian D., Hannah C., Benjamin T. BA, Rutgers U., 1980; JD, U. NC, Chapel Hill, 1984. Bar: Pa. 1984, US Dist. Ct. Ea. Dist. Pa. 1984, US Ct. Appeals 3rd Cir. 1984, US Dist. Ct. Mid. Dist. Pa. 1990, NJ 1988, US Dist. Ct. Dist. NJ, Supreme Ct. Pa., Supreme Ct. NJ. Assoc. Duane Morris LLP, Phila., 1984-93, ptnr., 1994—, chair firm environ. law practice group. Mem. ABA (sect. environment, energy & resources), Pa. Bar Assn. (environ., mineral & natural resources sect.), Phila. Bar Assn. (sec. environ. law com. 1997, co-chair 1998), Del. Valley Environ. Am. Inn Ct. (barrister), Pa. Environ. Coun. (bd.dirs.) Office: Duane Morris LLP One Liberty Pl Philadelphia PA 19103-7396 Office Phone: 215-979-1838. Office Fax: 215-979-1020. Business E-Mail: scooley@duanemorris.com.

COOLEY, STACY RAELYN, administrative assistant; b. Turlock, Calif., June 25, 1979; d. Kenneth Rae Cooley and Linda Gail Maines. Grad., Turlock H.S., 1997. Cashier McDonald's, Turlock, 1997—98; asst. road crew dir. Shake the Nations, Sacramento, 1998—2001; account rep. Wittman Enterprises, Sacramento, 2001—02; customer svc. mgr. Bed, Bath & Beyond, Elk Grove, Calif., 2001—02; adminstrv. asst. Book of Hope, Internat., Pomano, Fla., 2002—03, Century 21 M & M, Oakdale, Calif., 2003—. Mem.: Am. Family Assn., Phi Theta Kappa, Alpha Gamma Sigma. Republican. Mem. Assembly Of God. Home: 6449 Estelle Ave Riverbank CA 95367

COOLEY, STEVE, prosecutor; b. L.A., May 1, 1947; m. Jana Cooley; 2 children. BA, Calif. State U., L.A., 1970; JD, U. So. Calif., 1973. Joined Dist. Attys. Office, 1973; dist. atty. L.A. County, 2000—. Named Alumnus of Yr., Calif. State U., L.A., 1998, Pros. of the Yr., Century City Bar Assn., 2001, L.A. County Bar Assn., 2005, Champion of the People, Nat. Black Pros. Assn., Crime Victims Star of the Yr., Justice for Homicide Victims; recipient Leaders in Pub. Svc. award, Encino C. of C., Cmty. Justice award, Calif. NAACP. Mem.: Phi Kappa Phi. Office: County of Los Angeles Foltz Justice Ctr 210 W Temple St Ste 18000 Los Angeles CA 90012-3210 Business E-Mail: scooley@lacountyda.org.

COOLEY, THOMAS F., dean, economist, educator; b. Rutland, Vt., Jan. 3, 1943; s. Thomas J. and Marjorie (Batcheldor) C.; m. Patricia Bower; children: Noah, Joshua, Aaron, Frederika Prott. BS, Rensselaer Polytech., 1965; MA, U. Pa., 1969, PhD, 1971; doctorate (hon.), Stockholm Sch. Econs., 1987. Systems engr. IBM Corp., 1965—66; asst. prof. econs. Tufts U., Medford, Mass., 1970—76; rsch. assoc. Nat. Bur. Econ. Rsch., 1973—77; vis. asst. prof. Carnegie-Mellon U., 1973—74; vis. prof. U. Western Australia, 1974; faculty assoc. Joint Ctr. for Urban Studies, MIT and Harvard, 1976—80; assoc. prof. econs. U. Calif., Santa Barbara, 1976—79, prof. econs., 1980-87; vis. prof. Birbeck Coll., U. London, 1979—80, Stockholm Sch. Econs., 1984, 1985; prof. econs and applied stats. Simon Sch. Bus. and prof. econs. Dept. Econs. U. Rochester, 1987—92; prof. econs. U. Pa., 1995—97; Fred H. Gowan Prof. Econs. Simon Sch. Bus. and prof. econs. Dept. Econs. U. Rochester, 1992—2000, dir. Bradley Policy Rsch. Ctr., 1995—2000; Paganelli-Bull Prof. Econs. Stern Sch. Bus. and prof. econs. Faculty Arts and Scis. NYU, 1999—, Richard R. West Dean Stern Sch. Bus., 2002—. Mem. editl. bd. Jour. Monetary Econs., 1988—; coordinating editor Review of Econ. Dynamics. Author: Frontiers of Business Cycle Research, 1995. Recipient Superior Teaching Award, Rochester-Erasmuc Exec. MBA program, 1990, 1992, MBA Class of 1993, Simon Sch. Bus., 1992, MBA class of 1996, Simon Sch. Bus., 1995; fellow NSF, 1967—70, Econometric Soc., 1998; grantee, US Dept. Labor, 1970—72, 1974—76, 1978—79, Nat. C. of C. Found., 1976—77, NSF, 1976—78, 1990—93, 1993—95, 1997—2000, 2001—03, US Dept. Housing and Urban Devel., 1978—79, 1981—82, Nat. Inst. Justice, 1984—86; Irving Scholar, 1963—65. Mem. Am. Econ. Assn., Econometric Soc., Soc. for Econ. Dynamics (pres. 2000-03). Office: Dept Econs Leonard N Stern Sch Bus NYU 44 W 4th St New York NY 10012-1126

COOLEY, WILLIAM CROCKETT, mechanical engineer, retired educator; b. Lakeland, Fla., Dec. 19, 1924; s. Sumner Dewey Cooley and Kate Lilah Crockett; m. Anne Waterman, June 4, 1949 (div.); children: Jean, Brian, Stuart, Laura. ME, MIT, 1944, ScD, 1951; MS in Aeronautics, Calif. Inst. Tech., 1947. Student engr. on nuclear propulsion Fairchild project Nuclear Energy for Propulsion of Aircraft, Oak Ridge, Tenn., summer 1947; staff engr. Lexington project MIT, summer 1948; rsch. engr. N.Am. Aviation, L.A., 1951-53, 58-61; nuc. propulsion engr. GE, ANPD, Cin., 1953-58; chief space propulsion and aux. power program NASA, Washington, 1961-63; v.p., tech. dir. Exotech, Inc., Alexandria, Va., 1963-68; pres. Terraspace Inc., Rockville, Md., 1968-84; assoc. prof. engring. George Mason U., Fairfax, Va., 1985-91, ret., 1991. Patentee water jet tech.; contbr. articles to rsch. publs. Lt. USNR, 1952-61. Recipient Pioneer award U.S. Nat. Water Jet Conf., Pitts., 1985. Mem. ASME (life), Water Jet Tech. Assn. (opening lectr. 5th Pacific Rim Internat. conf. 1998). Democrat. Unitarian Universalist. Avocations: swimming, skiing, ballroom dancing, poetry. Home: 5480 Wisconsin Ave Apt 1101 Chevy Chase MD 20815-3519

COOLEY, WILLIAM EDWARD, research scientist, consultant; b. St. Louis, Mar. 7, 1930; s. Charles Frederic and Lillian Marie (Williams) C.; m. Marion Grace Sherman, June 5, 1952; children: Charles, Marilyn, Harold, Noele. AB, Cen. Coll., 1951; PhD, U. Ill., 1954. Rsch. chemist Procter & Gamble Co., Cin., 1954-61, product devel. chemist, 1961-65, product devel. group leader, 1965-75, product devel. regulatory sect. mgr., 1975-90, regulatory affairs sect. mgr., 1990-91; worldwide regulatory coordination sect. mgr., 1991-94; pres. Cooley Cons., Inc., 1994—. Contbr. articles to profl. jours. Mem. Am. Assn. Dental Rsch., Internat. Assn. Dental Rsch., Drug Info. Assn., Assn. Food Drug Ofcls., Regulatory Affairs Profl. Soc. (bd. editors 1990), Consumer Healthcare Products Assn. (bd. dirs. 1987-91), Food and Drug Law Inst. Republican. Achievements include patents in field. Avocations: music, motorcycling, railroading, flying, astronomy. Home and Office: Cooley Cons Inc 531 Chisholm Trail Wyoming OH 45215-2517 Office Phone: 513-522-3797.

COOLEY, WILLIAM EMORY, JR., radiologist; b. Charlottesville, Va., Jan. 28, 1941; s. William Emory Sr. and Madelle Elizabeth (Fullen) C.; m. Janella Mahoney Haney, Dec. 26, 1966; children: Angela Janette, William Emory, James Haney. BA, Emory U., 1963; MD, U. Va., 1967. Diplomate Am. Bd. Radiology. Rotating intern. U.S. Naval Hosp., Phila., 1967-68; resident radiology U.S. Naval Regional Med. Ctr., Phila., 1972-75, radiologist Portsmouth, Va., 1975-76, asst. chief radiology, 1976-77; radiologist Bloomington (Ill.) Radiology S.C., 1977-79, pres., 1979—. Chief radiologist Brokaw Hosp., Normal, Ill., 1979-85, St. Joseph Hosp., Bloomington, Ill., pres. med. staff, 1981, med. dir. radiology, 2000—; med. dir. radiology Bromenn Health Care System, Bloomington, 1985—, pres. med. staff, 1990; founding mem. bd. Ft. Jesse Imaging Ctr., Normal, Ill., 2002—; bd. dirs. Bloomington-Normal Healthcare. Mem. citizens adv. coun. Sch. Dist. 87, Bloomington, 1981-84; v.p. McLean County unit Am. Cancer Soc., 1989-90, pres., 1990-94. Comdr. USN, 1966-77. Fellow Am. Coll. Radiology (alt. councillor 1987-92, councillor 1993-99, mem. commn. on small and rural practices 2000); mem. AMA, Radiol. Soc. N.Am., Am. Roentgen Ray Soc., Am. Inst. Ultrasound Medicine, Ill. Radiol. Soc. (exec. com. 1986-99, pres. 1994-95), Ctrl. Ill. Radiol. Soc. (pres. 1990-91), Clin. Magnetic Resonance Soc., Soc. Nuc. Medicine, Bloomington Country Club, Masons. Republican. Presbyterian. Avocations: book collecting, tennis, personal computers. Office: Bloomington Radiology SC 2200 Fort Jesse Rd Ste 280 Normal IL 61761-2155

COOLIDGE, ARCHIBALD CARY, JR., English language educator, literature researcher; b. Oxford, Eng., June 9, 1928; s. Archibald Cary and Susan Thistle (Jennings) C.; m. Lillian Dobbel Merrill, June 29, 1951; children: Lillian, Emily, Sarah, Archibald, Anne, John, Alexander. BA, Harvard U., 1951; MA, Brown U., 1954, PhD, 1956. Instr. English, U. Iowa, Iowa City, 1956-59, asst. prof., 1959-65, assoc. prof., 1965-74, prof., 1974—2001, prof. emeritus, 2001—. Author: Charles Dickens as Serial Novelist, 1967, Beyond the Fatal Flaw: A Study of the Neglected Forms of Greek Drama, 1980, A Theory of Story, 1989, English Laws and American Problems, 1995, Political Metaphors, 2000, Hollywood Looks at Women, 2001. With USMC, 1945-46, CBI. Mem. U. Iowa Rsch. Club, Phi Beta Kappa. Avocations: fishing, movies. Home: 304 Brown St Iowa City IA 52245-5802 Office: U Iowa Dept English Iowa City IA 52242 Business E-Mail: archibald-coolidge@uiowa.edu.

COOLIDGE, DANIEL SCOTT, lawyer; b. Portland, Maine, Sept. 20, 1948; s. John Walter and Mary Louise (Arnold) C.; m. Carolyn Stiles, Nov. 23, 1984; children: Lillian Mae, Lydia Stiles. BS summa cum laude, U. Bridgeport, 1976; JD, Harvard U., 1980. Bar: Conn. 1980, N.H. 1982, Mass. 2001, U.S. Patent Office 1999, U.S. Ct. Appeals (1st cir.) 1983, U.S. Supreme Ct. 1985. Assoc. Cummings & Lockwood, Stamford, Conn., 1980-82, Sheehan, Phinney, Bass & Green PA, Manchester, N.H., 1982-87, ptnr., 1987—. Chmn. juvenile diversion com. Pittsfield (N.H.) Dist. Ct., 1982-85. Author: Survival Guide for Road Warriors, 1996; mem. editl. bd. Law Tech. News; columnist Law Office Computing, 1997—; patentee tel. test equipment. Chmn. Bradford Constitution Bicentennial Com.; mem. Pittsfield Planning Bd., 1984-85; treas., trustee First Congl. Ch., Pittsfield, 1984-85, First Bapt. Ch. Bradford; pres. Pittsfield Arts Coun., 1985; del. N.H. Constl. Conv., Concord, 1984-94; moderator Town of Bradford, N.H., 1999-, Kearsarge Reg. Sch. Dist, 2002-; founding bd. dirs., officer U.S. Found. for Inspiration and Recognition of Sci. and Tech. Mem. ABA (environ. law sect., intellectual property law sect., acting chmn., chmn. computer and tech. divsn., vice-chmn. sys. and tools law practice mgmt. sect. 1994—, governing coun. 1996—, advisor UCC article 2B drafting com. 1995-99), N.H. Bar Assn. (vice-chmn. tech. sect. 1993-96, chmn. lex mundi intellectual property sect. 1992-93), Manchester Bar Assn. Avocations: computers, physics, fly fishing, hiking, machining. Home: 106 Bible Hill Ln Warner NH 03278-3701 Office: Coolidge and Graves 108 Bible Hill Warner NH 03278 Office Phone: 603-456-2532. Personal E-mail: dancoolidge@yahoo.com. Business E-Mail: dancoolidge@ipbizlaw.com.

COOLIDGE, EDWIN CHANNING, chemistry educator; b. Mt. Vernon, Ohio, Jan. 30, 1925; s. Walter Hatheral and Sarah Helen (Fay) C.; m. Bonita Mae Warner, May 1, 1953; 1 son, Edwin Channing. AB in Chemistry, Kenyon Coll., 1944; PhD, Johns Hopkins, 1949. Research chemist Procter & Gamble Co., Cin., 1949-54; asst. prof. chemistry Hamilton Coll., Clinton, N.Y., 1954-58; asst. prof. N.Mex. Inst. Mining and Tech., Socorro, 1958-61; asso. prof. Stetson U., Deland, Fla., 1961-64, prof. chemistry, 1965-95, prof. emeritus, 1995—; dir. NSF Undergrad. Research Program, Stetson U., 1964-67. Dir. Mid-Fla. Colls. Year Abroad Program, Inc., 1968-69, German dir., 1969-70; Fulbright lectr. Paedagogische Hochschule, Freiburg, Germany, 1982-83 Contbr. articles to profl. jours. Served with AUS, 1950-52. Mem. Am. Chem. Soc., Royal Soc. Chemistry, Phi Beta Kappa, Sigma Xi, Gamma Sigma Epsilon, Omicron Delta Kappa. Episcopalian. Home: 2446 E New York Ave Deland FL 32724-6330 E-mail: ecoolidg@stetson.edu.

COOLIDGE, MARTHA, film director; b. New Haven, Aug. 17, 1946; MFA, RISD, 1968; ed., Columbia U.; MA, NYU, 1971. Dir.: (films) David: Off and On, 1972, Old-Fashioned Woman, 1974, More Than a School, 1974, (also prodr.) Not a Pretty Picture, 1975, Employment Discrimination: The Troubleshooters, 1976, Bimbo, 1978, Valley Girl, 1983, City Girl, 1984, Joy of Sex, 1984, Real Genius, 1985, Plain Clothes, 1988, Rambling Rose, 1991, Lost in Yonkers, 1992, Angie, 1994, Three Wishes, 1995, Out to Sea, 1997, Introducing Dorothy Dandridge, 1999, If These Walls Could Talk II, 2000, The Prince & Me, 2004; (TV films) Trenchcoat in Paradise, 1989, Bare Essentials, 1991, Crazy in Love, 1992, Flaming Rising, 2001, The Ponder Heart, 2001; (documentaries) David; On and Off, 1972 (Am. Film Festival award), More Than A School, 1973 (Am. Film Festival award), Old Fashioned Woman, 1974 (Am. Film Festival award), Not A Pretty Picture, 1975 (Am. Film Festival award); (TV series) Winners, 1978, The Twilight Zone, 1985, Sledge Hammer, 1986, Sex and the City, 1998, Leap Years, 2001; exec. prodr.: (TV films) Rip Girls, 2000. Recipient Best Dir. and Picture Rambling Rose, Independent Spriit Awards, nomination for If These Walls Could Talk II, Emmy awards. Mem.: Dir. Guild of Am. (pres. 2002—03).

COOLIDGE, ROBERT TYTUS, deacon, historian, educator; b. Boston, Mar. 30, 1933; s. Lawrence and Victoria Stuart (Tytus) C.; m. Ellen Osborne, Sept. 10, 1960 (div.); children: Christopher, Miles, Matthew. Grad., Groton (Mass.) Sch., 1951; AB, Harvard U., 1955; MA, U. Calif. at Berkeley, 1957; BLitt, U. Oxford, Eng., 1966. Ordained deacon Episcopal Ch., 1967. Non-stipendiary min. Christ Ch. Cathedral, Montreal, Que., Can., 1967-69, 71—, dir. Montreal Fund for the Diaconate, 1984—; non-stipendiary min. St. Marylebone Ch., London Clin., 1969-71; mem. faculty Loyola Coll. (now Concordia U.), Montreal, 1963—, assoc. prof. history, 1968-88, adj. assoc. prof., 1988—2000, assoc. prof. emeritus, 2000—. Historian Monticello Assn., 1975—. Contbr. to hist. vols. Fellow Royal Hist. Soc.; mem. Am. Soc. Ch. History, Ecclesiastical History Soc., Medieval Acad. Am., Am. Hist. Assn., Soc. d'Histoire de l'Eglise de France, Oxford and Cambridge Club (London), Univ. Club (Montreal), Royal St. Lawrence Yacht Club. Home: POB 4070 Westmount PQ Canada H3Z 2X3 *If you really want to help your fellow humans, don't think it is their fault if they refuse or reject your help. Look instead at how you react to help offered to you.*

COOLIO, (ARTIS IVEY JR.), rap artist; b. Compton, Calif., Aug. 1, 1963; m. Josefa Salinas, 1997. Album (with MC and the MADD Circle) Ain't a Damn Thang Changed, 1991, albums It Takes a Thief, 1994, Gangsta's Paradise, 1995, C U When U Get There, 1997, Straight Butta, 2000, El Cool Magnifico, 2002; composer: (films) Dangerous Minds, 1995. Recipient World Wide Music award, 1995, Favorite Rap Artist Am. Music award, 1995, Billboard Music award, 1995, Grammy award Best Rap Solo Performance, 1996. Office: Crowbar Management PO Box 5147 Culver City CA 90231-5147*

COOMANSINGH, JOHNNY, geographer, educator; b. Sangre Grande, Trinidad and Tobago, Aug. 9, 1954; arrived in U.S., 1996; s. Rolland Coomansingh and Adolphine Carmino; children from previous marriage: Josh Randall, Jessel Reuen. Diploma in agr., Eastern Caribbean Inst. Agr. and Forestry, Centeno, Trinidad, 1978; B in Tech., Andrews U., Berrien Springs, Mich., 1996; MS, Ft. Hays State U., 1998; MA, Kans State U., 2002, PhD, 2005. Tchr. Bates Meml. HS, Sangre Grande, 1972—80; agrl. asst. Ministry Agr., Port of Spain, Trinidad and Tobago, 1981—90; asst. pub. rels. officer Trinidad and Tobago Petroleum Co., Santa Flora, 1990—93; pub. rels. practitioner Petroleum Co. Trinidad and Tobago, Pointe-a-Pierre, 1993—96; lectr. geography S.W. Mo. State U., Springfield, 2003—. Exec. mem. Monitoring & Implementation Com., Sangre Grande, 1986; student advisor Nazarene Students Assn., Springfield, 2004—05. Author: (poems) Show Me Equality, 1998; mem. editl. bd. Perrotrin, 1993. Sec., program dir. Trintopec/Palo Seco (Trinidad and Tobago) Games, 1994; mem. Nature Conservancy, 2003—. Recipient 1st pl. Agrl. Ext. award, Ministry Agr., 1986; grantee, S. Caribbean Conf., 1976—78; Bessie West scholar, Kans. State U., 1999, 2000. Mem.: Assn. Am. Geographers, Gamma Theta Upsilon (pres. Beta Psi chpt. 2001—02). Avocations: woodworking, camping, travel. Office: SW Mo State U 901 S National Ave Springfield MO 65806

COOMBE, BOB, academic administrator; BA in Chemistry, Williams Coll., 1970; PhD in Phys. Chemistry, U. Calif., Berkeley, 1973. Postdoctoral rsch. assoc. U. Toronto, Canada, 1973—74; tech. staff Rockwell Internat. Sci. Ctr., 1974—81; asst. prof. U. Denver, 1981—85, assoc. prof., 1985—89, prof., 1989—, dean grad. studies, 1985—87, chair dept. chemistry and biochemistry, 1988—95, dean natural scis., math. and engring., 1995—2001, provost, 2001—. Office: Univ Denver Office of the Provost Mary Reed Bldg Rm 203 Denver CO 80208

COOMBE, GEORGE WILLIAM, JR., lawyer, retired bank executive; b. Kearny, NJ, Oct. 1, 1925; s. George William and Laura (Montgomery) Coombe; m. Marilyn V. Ross, June 4, 1949; children: Susan, Donald William, Nancy. BA, Rutgers U., 1946; LLB, Harvard U., 1949; MLA, Stanford U., 2005. Bar: NY 1950, Mich. 1953, Calif. 1976. Practice US Supreme Ct., NYC, 1949—53, Detroit, 1953—69; atty., mem. legal staff Gen. Motors Corp., Detroit, 1953—69, asst. gen. counsel, sec., 1969—75; exec. v.p., gen. counsel Bank of Am., San Francisco, 1975—90; ptnr. Graham and James, San Francisco, 1991—95; sr. fellow Stanford Law Sch., 1995—. Lt. USNR, 1942—46. Mem.: NYC Bar Assn., Los Angeles Bar Assn., San Francisco Bar Assn., Calif. Bar Assn., Mich. Bar Assn., Am. Bar Assn., Phi Gamma Delta, Phi Beta Kappa. Presbyn. Home: 2190 Broadway St Apt 2E San Francisco CA 94115-1312 E-mail: gwcoombe@aol.com.

COOMBE, V. ANDERSON, retired valve manufacturing company executive; b. Cin., Mar. 5, 1926; s. Harry Elijah and Mary (Anderson) C.; m. Eva Jane Romaine, Sept. 26, 1957; children— James, Michael, Peter. B.E., Yale, 1948. Asst. to pres. Wm. Powell Co., Cin., 1953-57, v.p., 1957-63, exec. v.p., 1963-69, pres., treas., 1969-91, chmn. bd., 1991—. Mem.: Cin. Country Club, Queen City Club (Cin.), Camargo Club (Cin.). Home: 6 Corbin Dr Cincinnati OH 45208-3302 Office: 2503 Spring Grove Ave Cincinnati OH 45214-1729

COOMBES, DAVID HARRISON, health facility administrator; b. Washington, Apr. 14, 1939; s. David Russell and Christine (Spignul) C.; m. Mary Gaasterland, June 9, 1962; children: Karen Marie, David Harrison. BA, Duke U., 1962; MHA, U. Minn., 1969. Diplomate Am. Coll. Healthcare Execs. Exec. dir. Health Facilities Commn. State of Tenn., Nashville, 1973-75; exec. dir. Hosps. and Clinics U. Tenn., Memphis, 1975-80, vice chancellor, 1980-82; pres., CEO Diagnosticorp, Inc., Nashville, 1982-85, U. Minn. Clin. Assocs., Mpls., 1985-88; founder, co-ptnr. Medicant, Inc., Oklahoma City, 1988-96; pres., CEO Nat. Assn. Integrated Health Orgns., Fredericksburg, Va., 1996—2001; CEO Clin. Focus, Inc., Mt. Vernon, NY, 2001—. Asst. prof. U. Tenn., Memphis, 1975-80. Chmn. planning commn. Town Colonial Beach, Va., 1996-2002, councilman, 1992-2002. 1st lt. USAF, 1964-67. Mem. Am. Hosp. Assn., Am. Soc. Assn. Execs. Home: 1313 Irving Ave Colonial Beach VA 22443 Office: Clin Focus Inc 825 Gramatan Ave Mount Vernon NY 10552 E-mail: dcoombes@3n.net.

COOMER, KEVIN D., insurance company executive, underwriter; BA in Econ., Washington Coll., Chestertown, Md., 1976. Trainee to loan officer APG Fed. Credit Union, Md., 1976—78; field claims rep. Liberty Mutual Ins. Co., Balt., 1979—81; regional Claims mgr. Crum & Forster Ins., Morristown, NJ, 1992—99, regional bus. mgr., 1999—2000, mgr. spl. projects, 2000—. Mem.: Mensa. Address: 3312 Cherrywood Ct Bethlehem PA 18020

COOMER, STEVEN ROBERT, music educator, musician; b. Muncie, Ind., Dec. 23, 1946; s. Robert and Thelma Geneva Coomer; m. Jeannette Oyler, June 19, 1993; m. Pamela Ann Shaver, Aug. 12, 1978 (div. Apr. 23, 1993); m. Sharon Lynn Zimmerman, Nov. 26, 1969 (div. June 18, 1976); children: Stefanie Lynne Shultz, Stacie Roberta Dixon, Stephanie Lynne Brown. BS, Ball State U., Muncie, In., 1964—68. Band dir. Del. Cmty. Schs., Muncie, Ind., 1968—69, East Chgo. Pub. Schs., East Chicago, Ind., 1969—70; music dir. Crown Point Cmty. Schs., Crown Point, Ind., 1970—71; band & choral dir. Wash. Twp. Sch., Valparaiso, Ind., 1971—72; band dir. Franklin County Schs., Brookville, Ind., 1972—73; orch. dir. Anderson Cmty. Schools, Anderson, Ind., 1973—74; band dir. Brebeuf Prep. Sch., Indpls., 1975—76; freelance musician & educator Cary, Ill., 1976—88; band dir. Randolph Ea. Sch. Corp., Union City, Ind., 1988—89, Indpls. Pub. Schs., 1989—; fre lance musician Anderson, Ind., 1974—75. Coord. of all-city h.s. bands Indpls. Pub. Schs., 1992—, mgr. marching band tournament, 2002—; dir. bands Murat Shrine Temple, Indpls., 1996—2002; prin. trumpet Athenaeum Pops Orch., Indpls., 2000—, Scottish Rite Orch., Indpls., 1998—; founder Ind. All Star Masonic Band, Franklin, 1997—2001; pres. Shrine Band Assoc. N.Am., Tampa, Fla., 2000—04; dir. bands Sahara Grotto, Indpls., 1995—98; assoc. band condr. Greenwood Cmty. Band, Ind., 1992—95; adjudicator band, orch., solo and ensemble Ind. State Sch. Music Assn.; pvt. trumpet tchr., Indpls., 2000—; 2nd trumpet Ft. Wayne Philharm., 1968—69; 3rd trumpet Muncie Symphony Orch., 1966—68; prin. trumpet Anderson Symphony Orch., 1973—75. Mem. Indpls. 500 Festival Band Com., Indianapolis, Ind., 2001—, York Rite, Cary, Ill., 1988—; jr. deacon & mem. Cary Grove Masonic Lodge, Cary, Ill., 1987—; mem. Scottish Rite, Indianapolis, Ind., 1996—; dir. of bands & mem. Murat Shrine Temple, Indianapolis, Ind., 1995—. Mem.: NEA, Nat. Band Assn., Am. Fedn. Musicians, Ind. State Tchr.'s Assn., Ind. Music Educator's Assn., Music Educator's Nat. Conf., Ind. Band Assn., Murat Shrine Band Bd. Dirs., Scottish Rite Valley of Indpls. (32nd degree trumpeter 1996—), York Rite, Dunkirk Masonic Lodge #275. Avocation: woodworking. Home: 1333 Shawnee Rd Indianapolis IN 46260

COONERTY, MARY ELIZABETH, special education educator; b. Mineola, N.Y., Oct. 24, 1954; d. Thomas Bartholomew and Vivian Irene Coonerty; m. John Charles Coppola, Aug. 7, 2004; children: Patrick David Hait, Meaghan Elizabeth Hait. BS in Spl. Edn. summa cum laude, Dowling Coll., 1995; MA in Liberal Studies, SUNY, Stony Brook, 1999. Cert. sch. dist. adminstr. Queens Coll., N.Y., 2004. Spl. educator Ea. Suffolk Bd. Cooperative Ednl. Svcs., West Hampton Beach, NY, 1998—99, curriculum tchr. Bellport, NY, 1999—. Bd. mem. Mid East Suffolk Tchr. Ctr., Riverhead, NY, 2003—. Tchr. Our Lady of Snow RC, Blue Point, NY, 2004—04. Mem.: ASCD, Nat. Staff Devel. Coun. Roman Catholic. Avocations: travel, reading, embroidery, knitting, gardening. Home: 90 Corey Ave Blue Point NY 11715 Office: Eastern Suffolk BOCES 350 Martha Ave Bellport NY 11713 Office Phone: 631-286-6535. Personal E-mail: marysail5@att.net. Business E-Mail: mcoonert@esboces.org.

COONEY, JOAN GANZ, broadcast executive, director; b. Phoenix, Nov. 30, 1929; d. Sylvan C. and Pauline (Reardan) Ganz; m. Timothy J. Cooney, 1964 (div. 1975); m. Peter G. Peterson, 1980. BA, U. Ariz., 1951; degrees (hon.), Boston Coll., 1970, Hofstra U., Oberlin Coll., Ohio Wesleyan U., 1971, Princeton U., 1973, Russell Sage Coll., 1974, Harvard U., 1975, Allegheny Coll., 1976, Georgetown U., 1978, U. Notre Dame, 1982, Smith Coll., 1986, Brown U., 1987, Columbia U., 1991, NYU, 1991. Reporter Ariz. Republic, Phoenix, 1953—54; publicist NBC, 1954—55, U.S. Steel Hour, 1955—62; prodr. Sta. WNET, Channel 13, pub. affairs documentaries N.Y.C., 1962—67; TV cons. Carnegie Corp. N.Y., N.Y.C., 1967—68; exec. dir. Children's TV Workshop (producers Sesame Street, Electric Company, others) (name changed to Sesame Workshop 2000), N.Y.C., 1968—70, pres., trustee, CEO, 1970—88, chmn., CEO, 1988—90, chmn. exec. com., 1990—. Bd. dirs. Johnson & Johnson; bd. dirs. Met. Life Ins. Co. Mem. Pres.'s Commn. on Marijuana and Drug Abuse, 1971—73, Nat. News Coun., 1973—81, Pres.'s Commn. for Agenda for 80's, 1980—81, Adv. Com. for Trade Negotiations, 1978—80, Carnegie Found. Nat. Panel on High Sch., 1980—82, Gov.'s Commn. on Internat. Yr. of the Child, 1979; Mus. TV and Radio; bd. dirs. Edison Schs.; trustee N.Y. Presbyn. Med. Ctr. Named to Hall of Fame, Acad. TV Arts and Scis., 1990; recipient numerous awards for Sesame Street and other TV programs including Nat. Sch. Pub. Rels. Assn. Gold Key, 1971, Disting. Svc. medal, Columbia Tchrs. Coll., 1971, Soc. Family Man award, 1971, Nat. Inst. Social Scis. Gold medal, 1971, Frederick Douglass award, N.Y. Urban League, 1972, Silver Satellite award, Am. Women in Radio and TV, Woman of Yr. in Edn. award, Ladies Home Jour., 1975, NAEB Disting. Svc. award, NEA Friends of Edn. award, Kiwanis Decency award, 5th Women's Achiever award, Girl Scouts U.S.A., Stephen S. Wise award, 1981, Harris Found. award, 1982, Ednl. Achievement award,

AAUW, 1984, Disting. Svc. to Children award, Nat. Assn. Elem. Sch. Prins., 1985, DeWitt Carter Reddick award, Coll. Comm., U. Tex.-Austin, 1986, Emmy Lifetime Achievement award, Acad. TV Arts and Scis., 1989, Presdl. medal of Freedom, 1995, Nat. Humanities Medal, 2003. Mem.: NATAS, Am. Women in Radio and TV, Internat. Radio and TV Soc., Nat. Inst. Social Scis. Office: Children's TV Workshop 1 Lincoln Plz New York NY 10023-7129

COONEY, JOHN FONTANA, lawyer; b. Worcester, Mass., Jan. 1, 1949; s. John Joseph and Ida (Fontana) Cooney. AB magna cum laude, Brown U., 1970; JD, U. Chgo., 1973. Bar: Mass. 1973, DC 1977, admitted to practice: US Supreme Ct. 1978, US Dist. Ct. (DC) 1978, US Dist. Ct. (Dist. Mass.) 1977, US Ct. Appeals (DC Cir.) 1977, US Ct. Appeals (1st Cir.), US Ct. Appeals (3rd Cir.), US Ct. Appeals (4th Cir.), US Ct. Appeals (9th Cir.), US Ct. Appeals (Fed. Cir.). Atty. Gaston Snow & Ely Bartlett, Boston, 1973-75; asst. to solicitor gen. Dept. Justice, Washington, 1975-76; atty. Wilmer, Cutler & Pickering, Washington, 1977-82; dep. gen. counsel Office Mgmt. & Budget, Washington, 1982-87; atty. Dickstein, Shapiro & Morin, Washington, 1987-88, Venable, Baetjer, Howard & Civiletti, Washington, 1988—; ptnr., Econ. Regulatory Litig. Dept. and Adminstrv. Regulation Dept. Venable LLP, Washington. Co-author: Environmental Crimes Deskbook, 1995; assoc. editor U. Chgo. Law Rev., bd. editors Adminstrv. Law Rev. Mem.: ABA (Counsel Sect., Adminstrv. Law & Regulatory Policy 2000—03), DC Bar, Order of Coif, Phi Beta Kappa. Fluent in French. Office: Venable LLP 575 7th St NW Washington DC 20004 Office Phone: 202-344-4812. Office Fax: 202-344-8300. Business E-Mail: jfcooney@venable.com.

COONEY, J(OHN) GORDON, JR., lawyer; b. Alexandria, Va., Mar. 22, 1959; s. John Gordon Sr. and Patricia Ruth (McEwen) C.; m. Gretchen Smith Millspaugh, July 17, 1999. BA, Wesleyan U., 1981; JD magna cum laude, Villanova U., 1984. Bar: Pa. 1984, U.S. Dist. Ct. (ea. dist.) Pa. 1986, U.S. Ct. Appeals (5th cir.) 1997, U.S. Ct. Appeals (3d cir.) 1988, U.S. Supreme Ct. 2002. Law clk. to hon. judge J. William Ditter Jr. U.S. Dist. Ct. (ea. dist.) Pa., Phila., 1984-86; assoc. Morgan, Lewis & Bockius, LLP, Phila., 1986-92, ptnr., 1992—. Adj. lectr. Villanova U. Sch. Law, 1993-2004, The Acad. Advocacy, 2004—; master Villanova U. Inn of Ct., 1999—; barrister U. Pa. Law Sch. Inn of Ct., 1994-96. Editor-in-chief Villanova U. Law Rev., 1983-84; mem. editl. bd. The Legal Intelligencer, 1997-2001. Trustee Rosemont Sch. of the Holy Child, 1997-, chmn., 2001—; alumni bd. mgrs. Episcopal Acad., 1996-2002; trustee Gesu Sch., 2002—, World Affairs Coun. Phila., 2005—. Mem. ABA (com. on class actions and derivative suits), Pa. Bar Assn., Phila. Bar Assn. (profl. guidance com., fed. cts. com.), Union League Phila., Merion Cricket Club, Pyramid Club, Wesleyan U. Alumni Assn. (pres. Phila. area 1993-96), Arthritis Found. (bd. dirs Ea. Pa. chpt. 1993-96), Order of Coif. Republican. Roman Catholic. Office: Morgan Lewis & Bockius LLP 1701 Market St Philadelphia PA 19103-2903 Office Phone: 215-963-4806. Business E-Mail: jgcooney@morganlewis.com.

COONEY, JOHN THOMAS, retired banker; b. Warren, Pa., Jan. 20, 1927; s. Willis Edward and Elaine Cooney; m. Clara Jean Ellberg, Dec. 22, 1950; children: John B., Michael T., Lisa J. BS in Bus., Gannon U., 1951. Asst. personnel mgr. Nat. Biscuit Co., Houston, 1951-52; v.p. Bank of Southwest, Houston, 1956-80, exec. v.p., and sr. trust officer, 1980-85; vice chmn. M Trust Corp., 1985-90, Ameritrust Tex. N.A., Houston, 1990-92. Adv. dir. Legacy Trust Co., 1993—; bd. dirs. Marine Safety Systems, Inc., 1996—; mem. SEI II Bd. of Trustees, 1994—. Pres. Mental Health Assn., Houston; bd. dirs. Am. Heart Assn., state treas., Tex.; established TBA Tex. Sch. of Trust Banking (chmn. 1978). Served as cpl. U.S. Army, 1945-46. Recipient Medal of Honor Gannon U., 1951. Mem. Tex. Bankers Assn. (trust divsn. chmn. 1982-83), Lakeside Country Club, The Houstonian Club. Republican. Roman Catholic.

COONEY, MIKE, former secretary of state; b. Washington, Sept. 3, 1954; s. Gage Rodman and Ruth (Brodie) C.; m. Dee Ann Marie Gribble; children: Ryan Patrick, Adan Cecelia, Colin Thomas. BA in Polit. Sci., U. Mont., 1979. State rep. Mont. Legislature, Helena, 1976-80; exec. asst. U.S. Sen. Max Baucus, Butte, Mont., 1979-82, Washington, 1982-85, Helena, Mont., 1985-89; sec. of state State of Mont., Helena, 1988—2001; coord. Lewis & Clark Bicentennial Public Safety Project, 2001; ex. dir. Healthy Mothers/ Healthy Babies: The Montana Coalition, 2001—. Bd. dirs. YMCA; mem. adv. panel Fed. Clearinghouse. Mem. Nat. Secs. of State (pres.), Nat. Assns. Secs. of State (pres. 1997) Democrat. Office: 1235 Birch St, Ste 1 Helena MT 59601

COONEY, PATRICIA RUTH, civic worker; b. Englewood, N.J. d. Charles Aloysius and Ruth Jeannette (Foster) McEwen; m. J. Gordon Cooney, June 8, 1957; 1 child, J. Gordon, Jr. Student, Fordham U., 1950-51; DHL honoris causa, Phila. Theol. Sem. St. Charles Boromeo, 1991. Blood bank chmn. Strafford Village Civic Assn., 1968-69, sec., 1970-71; vice chmn. Spl. Gifts Com. Cath. Charities Appeal of Archdiocese of Phila., 1980—, chmn., 1985. Mem. Coun. of Mgrs. Archdiocese of Phila., 1982-88, sec., exec. com., 1983-88; bd. dirs. Cath. Charities of Archdiocese of Phila., sec., exec. com., 1988-90, v.p., exec. com., 1991—; bd. dirs. Village of Divine Providence, Phila., sec., 1983-85, v.p. exec. com., 1990—; bd. dirs. St. Edmond's Home for Crippled Children, Phila., v.p. exec. com., 1990—; bd. dirs. Don Guanella Village of Archdiocese of Phila., v.p. exec. com., 1990—; v.p. exec. com. St. Francis Homes for Boys, 2000—, St. Joseph House for Boys, 2000--, St. Vincent Svcs. for Women and Children, 2000—, St. Joseph Cath. Home for Children, 2000—, St. Gabriel's Sys., 2000—, St. Vincent's Home, Tacony, 2003; mem. Archdiocesan Adv. Com. on Renewal, 1991-2000; Women's Com. Wills Eye Hosp., 1973—, mem.-at-large, 1st v.p.; mem. Women's Aux. St. Francis Country House, Darby, Pa., 1976—, treas., 1978-82; exec. com. United Way of Southeastern Pa., 1984-90, sec., 1986-88; bd. dirs. Chapel of Four Chaplains, 1984-89, Phila. Criminal Justice Task Force, 1989-90. Decorated Cross Pro Ecclesia et Pontifice, 1982, Lady Order St. Gregory the Gt., 1998. Republican. Avocations: reading, tennis, sailing. Home: 320 Gatcombe Ln Bryn Mawr PA 19010-3628

COONEY, PATRICK LOUIS, writer; b. Bellflower, Calif., Apr. 7, 1947; s. Jack William and Lauretta (Jenkins) C.; m. Rosemary Santana Cooney, Sept. 10, 1967; 1 child, Carl. BA in Sociology, Fla. State U., 1969; MA, PhD, U. Tex., 1976; MBA, Fordham U., 1979; cert. in Field Botany, N.Y. Bot. Garden, Bronx, 1993. Asst. prof. sociology Coll. Mount St. Vincent, Bronx, 1975-77; mktg. exec. pub. firms, 1980-89; Cert. in Field Botany. Spkr. Martin Luther King Jr. Inst. for Non-Violence, Westchester County, N.Y., 1994. Author: Discovering the Mid-Atlantic: Historical Tours, 1991, Seeing the United States as the South and the World Community of the North: Using the Approach of Martin Luther King Jr. to Invigorate the Next Civil Rights Movement, 1994, The Role of Multiculturalism in Establishing A New Period of Separate but Equal Segregation in the United States: A Comparison of the Periods After and First and Second Civil Wars, 1997, (with Henry W. Powell) The Life and Times of the Prophet Vernon Johns: Father of the Civil Rights Movement, 1998; editor: Witness to Civil Rights History: The Essays and Autobiography of Henry W. Powell, 2001. Civil rights activist. With Army Nat. Guard, 1966-73. Dissertation fellow Sweden-Am. Inst., N.Y.C., 1973-74. Mem. Torrey Bot. Club (chairperson field com.). Democrat. Mem. Soc. Of Friends. Home: 221 Mount Hope Blvd Hastings On Hudson NY 10706

COONEY, PATRICK RONALD, bishop; b. Detroit, Mar. 10, 1934; s. Michael and Elizabeth (Dowdall) C. BA, Sacred Heart Sem., 1956; STB, Gregorian U., Rome, 1958, STL, 1960; MA, Notre Dame U., 1973. Ordained priest Roman Cath. Ch., 1959, ordained bishop Roman Cath. Ch., 1983. Assoc. pastor St. Catherine Ch., Detroit, 1960—62; asst. chancellor Archdiocese of Detroit, 1962—69, dir. dept. worship, 1969—83; rector Blessed Sacrament Cathedral, 1977—83; regional bishop Roman Cath. Ch., Detroit, 1983—89; apptd. bishop Diocese of Gaylord, Mich., 1989—. Office: Diocese of Gaylord Pastoral Ctr 611 W North St Gaylord MI 49735-8349*

COONEY, RORY PATRICK, musician, director, composer; b. Delaware, Ohio, May 29, 1952; s. Patrick Francis Cooney and Martha Ann Dunlap; m. Theresa Mary Donohoo, Nov. 23, 1994; m. Therese Marie Riedel, June 7, 1974 (div. Oct. 12, 1994); children: Desmond James, Joel Vincent, Claire Suzanne, Aidan Isaac, Jeremy Nathan, Declan Sean. BA, St. Mary's Sem., 1973. Cert. liturgy Corpus Christi Ctr. Advance Liturgical Study, 1986. Dir. liturgy and music St. Jerome Cath. Cmty., Phoenix, 1983—94, St. Anne Cath. Cmty., Barrington, Ill., 1994—. Mem. team N.Am. Forum Catechumenate, Washington, 1985—. Composer (lyricist): (albums) You Alone, 1984, Do Not Fear to Hope, 1986, Safety Harbor, 1989, Vision, 1992, Change Our Hearts, 1994, Stony Landscapes, 1994, This Very Morning, 1998, Keep Awake, 2001. Mem.: N.Am. Acad. Liturgy (assoc.). Roman Catholic. Office: St Anne Catholic Community 120 North Ela Street Barrington IL 60010 Office Phone: 847-620-3064. Personal E-mail: rory@rorycooney.com. E-mail: rcooney@stannebarrington.org.

COONING, CRAIG R., career officer; BSc in Engring., Auburn U., 1973; grad. student, U. Ala., 1976—77, MBA, 1977; student, Squadron Officer Sch., 1979, Air Command and Staff Coll., 1982, Armed Forces Staff Coll., 1986; course, Nat. Security Mgmt. course, 1986; student, Indsl. Coll. Armed Forces, 1993—94; sr. acquisition course, Nat. Def. U., 1994. Vice comdr. Space and Missile Sys. Ctr., L.A. Air Force Base, 1973; sys. program officer dir., warranted contract officer, plant rep. office comdr., comd. ROTC program Auburn U., 1973—; procurement contracting officer San Antonio Air Logistics Ctr., Kelly AFB, Tex., 1973—76; contracting and mfg. career mgmt. assignment officer Air Force Mil. Personnel Ctr., Randolph AFB, Tex., 1982—86; dep. comdr. Detachment 48 Air Force Contract Mgmt. divsn. Air Force Plant Rep. Office Hughes Missile Sys. Group, Tucson, 1986—88; comdr. Detachment 43 Air Force Contratc Mgmt. divsn. Air Force Plant Rep. Office Morton Thiokol Inc., Brigham City, Utah, 1988—90; chief Commodities Contracting divsn. Contracting Directorate, Hill AFB, Utah, 1990—91; dir. Directorate Specialized Mgmt., Hill AFB, Utah, 1991—93, Space Acquisition, Office Undersec. Air Force, Wash., 1993—. Decorated Legion of Merit, Meritorious Svc. medal with five oak leaf clusters.

COONROD, DELBERTA HOLLAWAY (DEBBIE COONROD), retired elementary school educator, consultant; b. Eldon, Mo., Oct. 21, 1937; d. Delbert Leland and Zealoth (Stevens) Hollaway; m. Charles Ralph Coonrod, Aug. 26, 1961; children: Charles Leland, Marcia Renee. BS in Edn., U. Kans., 1961; MS in Edn., Ind. U., 1972, EdD in Edn., 1977; postgrad., U. Tex., Tex. Women's U. Cert. elem. tchr., Kans. Classroom tchr. Hood Sch. & Heizer Elem., Barton County, Kans., 1957-60, Emporia (Kans.) Pub. Schs., 1961-62, Lincoln (Nebr.) Pub. Schs., 1964-66, South Bend (Ind.) Sch. Corp., 1967-72; assoc. instr., vis. asst. prof. Ind. U., Bloomington, 1972-79; asst. prof. Ind. State U., Terre Haute, 1975-76; pres. Debcon, Inc., Bloomington, 1979-81; pvt. practice cons. Bloomington, 1981-85; classroom tchr. Ft. Worth Ind. Sch. Dist., 1985—2001; assoc. prof., dir. tchr. edn. Culver-Stockton Coll., Canton, Mo., 2001—02; ret., 2002. Cons. Ft. Hays State U., Kans., 1990, Edison C.C., Piqua, Ohio, 1994; instr. Tarrant County (Tex.) Jr. Coll., 1992-94; adj. asst. prof. Tex. Woman's U., Denton, 1987-2000; adj. prof. Tex. Christian U., Ft. Worth, 1991-92; adminstrv. project dir. Monroe County Sch. Corp., Bloomington, 1983-85; instr. Weatherford (Tex.) Coll., 1996-97; kindergarten cons. Penn-Harris-Madison Sch. Corp., Mishawaka, Ind., 1970-71; head adminstr. Hoosier Cts. Nursery Sch., Ind. U., 1978-79; nat. approved trainer Head Start, 1982-85; chair emeritus Who's Who in Am. Edn. adv. bd.; mem. FWISD Dist. adv. com., 1996-98. Reporter Shelby County Herald, Shelbyville, Mo., 2003—; contbr. articles to profl. jours. Bd. dirs. 4C's of Monroe County, 1979—85; mem. Greater Ft. Worth Lit. Coun., 1990—99; mem. Hist. Commn. City of Bedford, Tex., 1993—97; chmn. early literacy com. Tex. State Reading Assn., 1993—96; com. co-chair Campaign for Children, 1st Tex. coun. Camp Fire, 1992—94; educator Ft. Worth Sister Cities, 1991—2001; Harashin Educator scholar Nagaoka, Japan, 1992; bd. dirs. Ft. Worth Assn. Edn. Young Children, 1986—87; chmn. spkrs. bur. Ind. Gov.'s Com. for Internat. Yr. of the Child, 1979—80; mem. Shelby County Outreach and Ext. Coun. U. Mo., 2003—; host parent Am. Field Svc., 2003—; others. Recipient Excellence in English Edn. award Tex. Joint Coun. Tchrs. English, 1990, Ethel M. Leach award Tex. Woman's U., 1990, Outstanding Tchr. award Fort Worth Bus. Cmty./Adopt-A-Sch. Adv. Com., 1991; named Woman of Yr., Monroe County (Ind.) Girls Club, 1985, Yellow Rose of Tex., 1989, Dillard Tchr. of Week, 1992-93; named to Hon. Order Ky. Cols., 1987; Joe E. Mitchell Disting. Educator honoree Tex. Wesleyan U., 1991; honored Tex. Edn. Agy. Early Childhood Promising Practices (inclusion model), 1993-94, NYL Care Health Plans Chair for Tchg. Excellence in Early Childhood Edn., 1997-98, Extension Leaders Honor Roll, U. Mo.-Columbia, 2004. Mem. Ind. Assn. Edn. Young Children (bd. dirs. 1974-80, pres. 1979-80), Pi Lambda Theta (nat. v.p. 1985-89, pres. 1982-84, pres. Great Lakes Region II 1993-97, internat. 1st v.p. 2003, Greater Ft. Worth area chpt. Internat. Recognition award region VII Outstanding Pi Lambda Thetan 1992, pub. adv. bd. 1995-97, Edn. Endowment bd. 1996-2002), PEO (M chpt.), Delta Theta Tau, Delta Kappa Gamma; Am. Field Svc. Host parent, 2003-04. Republican. Baptist. Avocations: poetry, piano, photography, public speaking, journalism. Home: 1362 J Spur Bethel MO 63434-2312 Personal E-mail: coonrod@marktwain.net.

COONS, BARBARA LYNN, public relations executive, librarian; b. Peoria, Ill., June 1, 1948; d. Harold Leroy and Norma (Brauer) C. BA, Stephens Coll., Columbia, Mo., 1970; MA, U. N.C., 1972; MLS, Cath. U., 1982. Rsch. asst. Am. Revolution Bicentennical Office Libr. of Congress, Washington, 1974-76, editl. asst., office of the Asst. Librarian, 1976-78; ednl. liaison specialist Libr. of Congress, Washington, 1978-82; dir. rsch. svc. Gray and Co., Washington, 1982-85, v.p., 1985-86; from v.p., dir. rsch. svcs. to sr. mng. dir. Hill and Knowlton Pub. Affairs Worldwide, Washington, 1986—96; U.S. dir. rsch. svcs. Hill and Knowlton USA, 1996—2004; sr. v.p., dir. media analysis and competitive intelligence Strategy One, Washington, 2004—. Pres. Library of Congress Profl. Assn., 1982. Mem. Spl. Libraries Assn., Stephens Coll. Alumnae Club of Greater Washington (pres. 1987). Lutheran. Home: 709 Arch Hall Ln Alexandria VA 22314-6208 Office: Strategy One Ste 900 1925 Eye St NW Washington DC 20006 Office Phone: 202-326-1733. E-mail: barbara.coons@strategyone.net.

COONS, ELDO JESS, JR., manufacturing executive; b. Corsicana, Tex., July 5, 1924; s. Eldo Jess and Ruby (Allison) Coons; m. Beverly K. Robbins, Feb. 6, 1985; children from previous marriage: Roberta Ann, Valerie, Cheryl. Student Engring., U. Calif., 1949—50. Owner C & C Constrn. Co., Pomona, Calif., 1946—48; sgt. traffic divsn. Pomona Police Dept., 1948—54; nat. field dir. Nat. Hot Rod Assn., L.A., 1954—57; pres. Coons Custom Mfg., Inc., Oswego, Kans., 1957—68; chmn. bd. Borg-Warner Corp., 1968—71; pres. Coons Mfg., Inc., Oswego, 1971—84, E.B.C. Mgmt. Cons., Lake Havasu City, Ariz., 1984—. Mem. Kans. Gov.'s Adv. Com. State Archichitects Assn. With C.E. U.S. Army, 1943—46. Named to Exec. and Profl. Hall of Fame, Recreational Vehicle/Mobile Homes Hall of Fame, Hot Rod Hall of Fame, 1961, Internat. Drag Racing Hall of Fame, 1991; recipient Paul Abel award, Recreational Vehicle Industry Assn., 1978, 1st Ann. New Product award, Kans. Gov.'s Office and Kans. Engring. Soc., 1982—83. Mem.: AIM (fellow pres.'s coun.), Mcpl. Officers Assn., Nat. Juvenile Officers Assn., Oswego C. of C. (dir.), Rotary (pres. Oswego club 1962—63), Shriners, Young Pres. Orgn., Am. Legion, KT, Masons. Achievements include originator first city sponsored police supervised drag strip. Home and Office: EBC Mgmt Cons 2634 Diablo Dr Lake Havasu City AZ 86406-8450

COONS, RONALD EDWARD, historian, educator; b. Elmhurst, Ill., July 24, 1936; s. William A. and Madeline Louise (Theisen) C. BA, DePauw U., Greencastle, Ind., 1958; A.M., Harvard U., 1959, PhD, 1966. Teaching fellow history Harvard U., 1961-62, 63-66; research fellow Inst. Europäische Geschichte, Mainz, Germany, 1962-63; mem. faculty U. Conn., Storrs, 1966—2002, prof. history, 1979—2002, prof. emeritus, 2002—, dir. grad. studies, dept. history, 1983-87, 90-98, assoc. chmn., 1993—94, 2000—02, interim chmn., summer 1994. Author: Steamships, Statesmen and Bureaucrats: Austrian Policy Towards the Steam Navigation Company of the Austrian Lloyd, 1836-1848, 1975, I primi anni del Lloyd Austriaco, 1983; editor: Over Land and Sea. Memoir of an Austrian Rear Admiral's Life in Europe and Africa, 1857-1909 (Ludwig Ritter von Höhnel), 2000; mem. editl. bd. Austrian History Yearbook, 1992-94, 96-97, mem. adv. bd., 1994-96, also articles and revs. Mem. exec. com. St. Mark's Episcopal Ch., Storrs, 1976-82, 83-85, asst. organist, 1980-87; mem. exec. com. U. Conn. Friends of Soccer, 1989-98, v.p., 1993-95, pres. 1995-97; mem. exec. com. New Eng. Hosta Soc., 1989-92; co-chair interim com. St. Paul's Episcopal Ch., Willimantic, 1998-2001, mem. vestry, 2001-04, archivist, 2003—, sr. warden, 2005—. Nat. Endowment Humanities summer fellow, 1969; Am. Council Learned Socs. grantee, 1974, Am. Philos. Soc. grantee, 1974; NIH grantee, 1979; Gladys K. Delmas Found. grantee, 1983-84; Am. Council Learned Socs. grantee, 1985 Mem. AAUP, Am. Hist. Assn., Conf. Group Cen. European History, German Studies Assn., Soc. for Austrian and Habsburg History (exec. com. 1992-97, exec. sec. 1994-96), New Eng. Hist. Assn., Vienna Hist. Soc., Conn. Acad. Arts and Scis., Conn. Hort. Soc., Phi Beta Kappa (chpt. sec. 1976-86, v.p. 1987-88, 99-2000, pres. 1988-89, 2000-2001), Phi Alpha Theta, Phi Mu Alpha. Democrat. Office: U Conn Dept History 241 Glenbrook Rd Storrs Mansfield CT 06269-2103 Home: 1 Gin Still Ln West Hartford CT 06107-2647 Office Phone: 860-486-3722. Personal E-mail: recoons@hotmail.com.

COONS, THOMAS WAYNE, lawyer; b. Wash., DC, Mar. 26, 1947; s. Richard Laurence and Elizabeth Madison Coons; m. Donna Marie Clarke, Aug. 30, 1969. BS, U. Tenn., 1969; JD, Georgetown U. Law Ctr., 1972. Bar: Va. 1972, MD 1973, DC 1977. Law clerk Honorable Alexander Harvey, II, Judge U.S. Dist. Ct. for the Dist. of MD, Balt., 1972—73; assoc. Ober, Kaler, Grimes and Shriver, Balt., 1973—79; atty. Office of Gen. Counsel, health Care Financing Divsn., Dept. of Health and Human Svcs., Balt., 1980—98; shareholder Ober, Kaler, Grimes and Shriver, Balt., 1998—. Mem.: DC Bar, Health Law Section, Am. Bar Assn., Am. Health Lawyers Assn. Office: Ober Kaler Grimes and Shriver 120 E Balt St Baltimore MD 21202 Office Phone: 410-947-7389. Office Fax: 410-547-0699. E-mail: twcoons@ober.com.

COONTZ, STEPHANIE JEAN, history professor, writer; b. Seattle, Aug. 31, 1944; d. Sidney Coontz and Patricia (McIntosh) Waddington; 1 child, Kristopher. BA with honors, U. Calif., Berkeley, 1966; MA, U. Wash., Seattle, 1970. Mem. faculty Evergreen State Coll., Olympia, Wash., 1975—. Dir. rsch. and pub. edn. Coun. Contemporary Families, 1993—. Author: The Way We Never Were: American Families and the Nostalgia Trap, 1992, The Social Origins of Private Life: A History of American Families, 1988, The Way We Really Are: Coming to Terms With America's Changing Families, 1997, Marriage, A History: From Obedience to Intimacy, or How Love Conquered Marriage, 2005; (with others) Women's Work, Men's Property: On the Origins of Gender and Class, 1986, History and Family Theory, vol. II, 1989; contbr. numerous articles to profl. jours. Woodrow Wilson Found. fellow, 1968-69; recipient Washington Gov's. Writer's award, 1989, Dale Richmond award Am. Acad. Pediatrics, 1995. Mem. Am. Studies Assn., Am. Hist. Assn., Orgn. Am. Historians. Office: Evergreen State Coll 2700 Evergreen Pwy NW Olympia WA 98505-0001 Address: c/o Viking Publicity 375 Hudson St New York NY 10014 Office Phone: 360-867-6703. E-mail: coontz@evergreen.edu.

COOP, FREDERICK ROBERT, retired city manager; b. San Diego, Mar. 1, 1914; s. Ernest Frederick and Hazel (Angier) C.; m. Jean Haven, Feb. 11, 1939; children: Susan, Robert, Thomas, Elizabeth. AB, U. Calif., Berkeley, 1935; MS in Pub. Adminstrn, U. So. Calif., 1937. Pers. technician Calif. State Pers. Bd., 1937-41; pers. dir. Pasadena, Calif., 1941-49; pers. cons. UN, 1947; city mgr. Inglewood, Calif., 1949-56, Fremont, Calif., 1956-58; chief pub. svcs. divsn. U.S. Ops. Mission to Yugoslavia, 1958-61; city mgr. Newport Beach, Calif., 1961-64, Phoenix, 1964-69; regional dir. HEW, San Francisco, 1969-71; dir. pub. adminstrn. svcs. Arthur D. Little, Inc., San Francisco, 1972-78; pres. Coop Mgmt. Svcs. Inc., 1978—91. Pres., bd. dirs. Pub. Svc. Skills Inc. Served to lt. comdr. USNR, WW II. Named Young Man of Yr. Pasadena Jr. C. of C., 1947. Mem. Internat. City Mgmt. Assn. (regional v.p. 1965-67, Disting. Svc. award 2000), Am. Soc. Pub. Adminstrn. (bd. dirs.), Nat. Acad. Pub. Adminstrn., League Calif. Cities (hon. life, city mgrs. dept.).

COOPER, ALAN SAMUEL, lawyer, educator; b. June 13, 1942; s. Rudey and Rosalie (Schwartz) C.; m. Maxine Jacobs, Aug. 13, 1966 (dec.); children: Lauren K., Jennifer D.; m. Linda Morguelan Klein, April 18, 1999. BA, Vanderbilt U., 1964, JD, 1968. Bar: Tenn. 1968, D.C. 1969, U.S. Dist. Ct. D.C. 1969, U.S. Supreme Ct. Appeals (Fed. cir.) 1975, U.S. Supremem Ct. 1980. Law clk. U.S. Dist. Ct. (mid. dist.), Tenn., 1967-68; assoc. Browne, Schuyler & Beveridge and Browne, Beveridge & DeGrandi, Washington, 1968—72, Schyler, Birch, Swindler, McKie & Beckett, Washington, 1972-74; ptnr. Schyler, Banner, Birch, McKie & Beckett, Washington, 1974-94; mem. bd. dirs., shareholder Banner & Witcoff, Ltd., Washington, Chgo., Boston, 1995-97; ptnr. Shaw Pittman Potts & Trowbridge, Washington, N.Y.C., L.A., London, 1997—2005, Howrey LLP, 2005—. Adj. prof. Georgetown U. Law Ctr., 1985-1997; adviser on trademark law to U.S. del. to Diplomatic Conf. on Revision of Paris Conv. for Protection of Indsl. Property, Nairobi, Kenya, 1981. Mem. ABA (faculty Nat. Insts. on Trademark Litigation 1978-79), Internat. Trademark Assn., D.C. Bar, Bar Assn. D.C., Tenn. Bar Assn., Bethesda Country Club. Jewish. Office: 1299 Pennsylvania Ave NW Washington DC 20004 Personal E-mail: cooper.alan@comcast.net. Business E-Mail: coopera@howrey.com.

COOPER, ANDERSON HAYS, news correspondent, cable news anchor; b. NYC, June 3, 1967; s. Wyatt Cooper and Gloria Vanderbilt. BA in Polit. Sci., Yale U., 1989; attended, U. Hanoi. Producer & chief internat. correspondent Channel One News; correspondent ABC News, ABC's World News Saturday/Sunday, ABC's World News Tonight; anchor ABC's World News Now, 2000—01; host The Mole, ABC, 2001; weekend anchor CNN, 2001—03, weekday anchor, 2003—; anchor, host Anderson Cooper 360, CNN, 2003—. Contr. editor Details mag. Recipient Emmy award, Silver Plaque, Chicago Internat. Film Festival, Bronze Telly, Bronze award, Nat. Ed. Film and Video Festival, GLAAD Media award for outstanding TV journalism. Office: CNN 10 Columbus Cir New York NY 10019*

COOPER, APRIL HELEN, family practice nurse practitioner; b. Evergreen Park, Ill., Dec. 24, 1951; d. Frank and Anne (Mirocha) Stevens; m. Michael Dennis, June 20, 1970; children: Christine Michelle, Brian Michael, Jeannette Michelle. AAS, Ohio U., 1981, BSN, 1996; MS, Wright State U., 2000. RN Ohio; cert. family nurse practitioner, ANCC. Supr. home health care Med. Pers. Pool, Cambridge, Ohio, 1989-91; primary nurse pediat. home care Primary Care Nursing Svcs., Dublin, Ohio, 1989-91; case mgr. Buckeye Home Health Svc., Zanesville, Ohio, 1990-91; with home health svcs. Genesis Home Care, Zanesville, 1981-98; family practice nurse practitioner Bucyrus Cmty. Hosp., 2001—. Mem. ANA, Golden Key. Phi Kappa Phi, Sigma Theta Tau, Gamma Pi Delta. Republican. Methodist. Avocations: reading professional journals, travel. Home: 3172 Oak Dr Bucyrus OH 44820-9654

COOPER, ARNOLD COOK, management educator, researcher; b. Chgo., Mar. 9, 1933; s. Millard and Sarah Ellen C.; m. Jean Phillips Lord, Sept. 12, 1959; children: Katherine Lord, David Andrew. BS in Chem. Engring., Purdue U., 1955, MS in Mgmt., 1957, PhD (hon.), 2005; D in Bus. Adminstrn., Harvard U., 1962. Engr. Proctor & Gamble, Cin., 1957-58; asst. prof. Harvard U., Cambridge, Mass., 1961-63; assoc. prof. Purdue U., West Lafayette, Ind., 1963-70, prof., 1970-84, Weil prof. mgmt., 1984—2005, emeritus, 2005—. Vis. assoc. prof. Stanford Univ., Palo Alto, Calif., 1967-68; vis. prof. Manchester (Eng.) Bus. Sch., 1972, IMEDE Mgmt. Devel. Inst., Lausanne, Switzerland, 1977-78; past dir. Grad. Profl. Programs, chmn. Mgmt. Policy Com., Purdue U., West Lafayette; mem. Ind. Employment Devel. Commn., 1982-89, Fed. Adv. Com. on Indsl. Innovation, 1978-79. Author: The Founding of Technologically Based Firms, 1971; co-author: Small Business Management, 1966, Technical Entrepreneurship: A Symposium, 1972, The Entrepreneurial Function, 1977, New Business in America, 1990; contbr. numerous articles to profl. jours. and bus. publs.; mem. editorial bd. Stategic Mgmt. Jour., 1979—, Jour. of Bus. Venturing, 1985—. Acad. of Mgmt. Jour., 1978-84, Jour. High Tech. Mktg., 1986-87. 2nd lt. U.S. Army, 1956. Recipient Honeywell Master Tchr. award, 1990, Disting. Scholar award, Internat. Coun. on Small Bus., 1987, Ten Year Author award, Babson Entrepreneurship Conf., 1990, John S. Day Disting. Alumni Acad. Svc. award, 2001. Mem. Acad. Mgmt. (chmn. bus. policy and strategy divsn.

1978-79, Outstanding Paper award Entrepreneurship Divsn. 1991, 92, Coleman Entrepreneurship Mentor award, 1993), Soc. Fellows (Richard D. Irwin outstanding educator award, 1999, Internat. award for entrepreneurship and small bus. rsch. 1997), Internat. Coun. Small Bus., Strategic Mgmt. Soc. (bd. govs. 1984-86). Home: 616 Ridgewood Dr West Lafayette IN 47906-2367 Office: Purdue Univ Krannert Sch of Mgmt 1310 Krannert West Lafayette IN 47907-1310 Business E-Mail: coopera@mgmt.purdue.edu.

COOPER, ARTHUR WELLS, ecologist, educator; b. Washington, Aug. 15, 1931; s. Gustav Arthur and Josephine (Wells) C.; m. Jean Farnsworth, Aug. 30, 1953; children: Paul Arthur, Roy Alan. BA, Colgate U., 1953, MA, 1955; PhD, U. Mich., 1958. Asst. prof. botany N.C. State U., Raleigh, 1958-63, assoc. prof., 1963-68, prof., 1968-71, prof. forestry, 1976—2001, prof. emeritus, 2001—, head dept. forestry, 1980-94, faculty athletics rep., 1990-2001. Asst. sec. N.C. Dept. Natural and Econ. Resources, Raleigh, 1971-76; mem. N.C. Coastal Resources Commn., Raleigh, 1976-89, N.C. Environ. Mgmt. Commn., Raleigh, 1989-91; chmn. Com. Scientists for Nat. Forest Mgmt. Act, Washington, 1977-79, 82, Govs. Task Force on Forest Sustainability, 1995-96; bd. dirs. N.C. Environ. Def. Fund, 1987-90, So. Environ. Law Ctr., 1987-90. Trustee N.C. Nature Conservancy, Chapel Hill, 1977-87; mem. coun. NCAA, 1995-96, mem. Divsn. 1 mgmt. coun., 1996-2001. Recipient Am. Motors Conservation award, 1972, Sol Feinstone award SUNY Coll. Environ. Sci. and Forestry, Syracuse, 1982, Outstanding Svc. to Forestry award N.C. Forestry Assn., 2002; named Conservationist of Yr., N.C. Wildlife Fedn., 1982. Fellow AAAS, Soc. Am. Foresters (chmn. N.C. chpt. 1984, Appalachian Soc. 1990, Gifford Pinchot medal 1999); mem. Ecol. Soc. Am. (cert. sr. ecologist 1982-2005, v.p. 1974, pres. 1981, Disting. Svc. award 1984), N.C. Acad. Sci. (pres. 1979), Assn. Southeastern Biologists. Democrat. Home: 719 Runnymede Rd Raleigh NC 27607-3103 Office: NC State U Dept Forestry Raleigh NC 27695-8008 E-mail: awcooper@earthlink.net, arthur_cooper@ncsu.edu.

COOPER, AUSTIN MORRIS, chemist, consultant, chemical engineer, researcher; b. Long Beach, Calif., Feb. 1, 1959; s. Merril Morris and Charlotte Madeline (Wittmer) C. BS in Chemistry with honors, Baylor U., 1981; BSChemE with honors, Tex. Tech U., 1983, MSChemE with honors, 1985. Solar energy researcher U.S. Dept. Energy, Lubbock, Tex., 1983-85; advanced mfg. and process engring. mgr. McDonnell Douglas Space Systems Co., Huntington Beach, Calif., 1986-87, chem.-process line mgr., 1987-89, prin. material and process engr., 1999—. Contbr. articles to profl. jours. Mem. AIChE, Am. Chem. Soc., Soc. Advancement of Materials and Process Engrs., SCV, SAR, Sigma Xi, Omega Chi Epsilon, Kappa Mu Epsilon, Beta Beta Beta.

COOPER, BILLY J., lawyer; b. Great Lakes, Ill., July 21, 1956; BA with high honors, Ohio No. Univ., 1978; JD, Univ. Okla., 1981. Bar: Okla. 1981, Va. 1989, Colo. 1992. Gen. counsel & mem. exec. com. Foster Wheeler Environ. Corp.; ptnr., Public Policy, Bus. Transactions practices, mem. mgmt. com., mng. ptnr. Denver office Patton Boggs LLP, Denver. Chmn. & legal liaison Product Stewardship Code Legal Adv. Group, 1992. Served to lt. comdr. JAGC USN, 1981—88. Decorated Commendation medal USN, Achievement medal (2), Sea Svc. Deployment medal, Meritorious Unit medal. Mem.: Colo. Bar Assn., ABA (vice chmn. Law of the Sea com. 1991). Office: Patton Boggs LLP Suite 1900 1660 Lincoln St Denver CO 80264-1901 Office Phone: 303-894-6326. Office Fax: 303-894-9239. Business E-Mail: bcooper@pattonboggs.com.

COOPER, BYRON STANLEY, internist, educator; b. Washington, May 21, 1947; s. Joseph David and Ruth (Zeidner) C.; m. Jane Ann Kanter, Feb. 5, 1978; children: Joseph, Allison. BA, Johns Hopkins U., 1969; MD, Washington U., St. Louis, 1973. Diplomate in internal medicine and pulmonary medicine Am. Bd. Internal Medicine. Clin. prof. George Washington U., Washington, 1981—. Fellow Am. Coll. Chest Physicians; mem. AMA (alt. del. 2000--), ACP, D.C. Thoracic Soc. (pres. 1994), Med. Soc. D.C. (pres. 1998-99). Avocations: photography, computers, running. Office: Capital Pumonary Internists 2440 M St NW Washington DC 20037-1404 Personal E-mail: bscooper547@hotmail.com.

COOPER, CECILIA MARIE, lawyer, prosecutor; b. Erie, Pa., Apr. 22, 1966; d. Ronald C. and Mary Anne Cooper. BA, Washington & Jefferson Coll., 1988; JD, Emory U., 1991. Bar: Ga. 1992, U.S. Dist. Ct. (mid. dist.) Ga. 1996. Law clk. Southwestern Jud. Cir., Americus, Ga., 1991-93; pvt. practice law Americus, 1993—; dist. atty. Southwestern Jud. Cir. Mediator 3rd Adminstrv. Jud. Dist., Columbus, Ga., 1996—. Coach mock trial team Sumter County H.S., Americus, 1997-2000. Mem. Exch. Club Americus (pres. 1997), Kiwanis. Democrat. Roman Catholic. Avocations: guitar, reading.

COOPER, CHARLES DONALD, military association executive, editor, retired military officer; b. Exeter, N.H., Dec. 19, 1932; s. Herbert Almon and Mildred (Pitcher) C.; m. Beverly Lorraine Hummel, May 18, 1957; children: Liane, Dale, Kristin. BS, Northwestern U., 1954; grad., Indsl. Coll. Armed Forces, Washington, 1975. Commd. 2d lt. USAF, 1954, advanced through grades to col., 1977, mem. ops. staff various AF bases, 1955-76; dep. chief pub. affairs USAF Fifth AF, Yokota Air Base, Japan, 1975-77; dep. chief community rels. USAF, Washington, 1977-78, dep. chief media rels., 1978-80, chief media rels., 1980-82, dir. internal info., 1982-83; vol. community svc. Springfield, Va., 1984-86; exec. editor The Ret. Officer Assn., Alexandria, Va., 1986-88, dir. publs., 1988-96. Contbr. articles to mags. and newspapers in field. Trustee Messiah United Meth. Ch., Springfield, 1985-96, mem. adminstrv. bd., 1998—2002, asst. treas., 1999—, mem. fin. com., 1999—, alt. del. Va. United Meth. Ch. Conf., 2003—. Decorated Meritorious Svc. Medal, D.F.C., Air medal with five oak leaf clusters, Legion of Merit. Mem. Mil. Officers Assn. Am., Am. Legion, Daedalians, Masons, Shriners. Avocations: gardening, skiing. E-mail: flyboyfifty6@netscape.net.

COOPER, CHARLES FISHER, chemist, researcher; b. Rusk, Tex., Jan. 12, 1952; s. Charles Marion Cooper and Serena Carlin Fisher; m. Connie Jeanne MacDonald, Dec. 13, 1975; 1 child, David Michael. BS in Chemistry, U. Okla., Norman, 1970—74; PhD, U. Mo., Rolla, 1974—80; postgrad., U. Minn., 1978—80. Rsch. chemist ARCO Chem. Co., Newtown Sqaure, Pa., 1980—98, Lyondell Chem. Co., Newtown Square, Pa., 1998—. Mem.: Am. Chem. Soc. Independent. Office: Lyondell Chemical Co 3801 West Chester Pike Newtown Square PA 19073 Office Phone: 610-359-2302. E-mail: charles.cooper@lyondell.com.

COOPER, CHARLES GILBERT, toiletries and cosmetics company executive; b. Chgo., Apr. 4, 1928; s. Benjamin and Gertrude Cooper; m. Miriam Meyer, Feb. 11, 1951 (dec. Oct. 17, 1983); children: Debra, Ruth, Janet, Benjamin; m. Nancy Cooper BS in Journalism, U. Ill., 1949. With sales promotion dept. Maidenform Co., N.Y.C., 1949-51; with circulation promotion dept. Esquire mag., Chgo., 1951-52; with Helene Curtis Industries Inc., Chgo., 1953-96, pres. salon div., 1971-75, pres. consumer products div., 1975-82, corp. exec. v.p., 1982-85, exec. v.p., COO, 1985-93, sr. v.p., 1993-96; sr. ptnr. GCG Ptnrs. Adj. prof. Loyola U. With AUS, 1952-53. Office: 200 S Wacker Dr Ste 4000 Chicago IL 60606 Personal E-mail: coop333@aol.com.

COOPER, CHARLES GORDON, retired insurance company executive; b. Providence, May 31, 1927; s. Irving and Helen Christina (Skog) C.; m. Barbara Caroline Termohlen, June 17, 1950; 1 dau., Marie Suzanne. BA, Ohio Wesleyan U., 1949. C.L.U. Group rep. Washington Nat. Ins. Co., 1949-53, asst. mgr., 1953-58, mgr., 1958-63, dir. assn. field services, 1963-65, asst. sec., 1965-67, 3d v.p., 1967-72, 2d v.p., 1972-77, v.p., 1977-79, sr. v.p., 1979-83, exec. v.p. Evanston, Ill., 1983-85, dir., mem. exec. com., 1979-85; sr. v.p.-mktg. Washington Nat. Corp., parent co. Washington Nat. Ins. Co., Evanston, 1983-85, cons., 1985—; pres. Charles G. Cooper & Assocs., Inc., 1985—95. Dir. Washington Nat. Trust Co., 1974-85, chmn. exec. com., 1979-85; chmn., dir. Washington Nat. Fin. Services, Inc., 1979-85; pres., dir. Washington Nat. Equity Co., 1973-85, chmn. bd., 1983-85 Bd. dirs. North Shore Assn. for Retarded, Evanston, 1983— . Served with USNR, 1945-46, PTO. Mem. Am. Coll. Life Underwriters, Chartered Life Underwriters, Nat. Assn. Life Underwriters, Chgo. Life Underwriters Assn., Nat. Assn. Health Underwriters, Chgo. Health Underwriters Clubs: Ivanhoe (Ill.). Lodges: Masons, Shriners. Republican.

COOPER, CHARLES HOWARD, retired photojournalist, retired publishing executive; b. Clinton, N.C., July 17, 1920; s. John Howard and Ella Jane (Bass) C.; m. Nell Elizabeth Slaughter, Jan. 2, 1943; children: Charles Howard II, John Phillip. Grad., U.S. Air Force Sch. Photography, 1943. Chief photographer, mgr. photo dept. Durham Herald Co. (N.C.), 1945-85; pub. Durham Morning Herald, 1945, Durham Sun, 1945-85. Chmn. Miss Nat. Press Photographer Pageant, 1952, 53, 55 Mem. Citizens Safety Com., Durham, 1961-71. Served with USAAF, 1942-45, ETO. Mem. Nat. Press Photographers Assn. (life, exec. dir. 1963-2000, exec. dir. emeritus 2001—, Fellowship award, Joseph A. Sprague award 1961, Pres.'s medal 1964, 67, 2001, Merit award 1965, Joseph Costa award 1977, exec. dir. emeritus 1998, interim exec. dir. 2001), Carolinas Press Photographers Assn. (life, pres. 1952-54) Democrat. Baptist. Personal E-mail: chcscoop@aol.com.

COOPER, CORINNE, communications consultant, lawyer; b. Albuquerque, N.Mex., July 12, 1952; d. David D. and Martha Lucille (Rosenblum) C. BA magna cum laude, U. Ariz., 1975, JD summa cum laude, 1978. Bar: Ariz. 1978, U.S. Dist. Ct. Ariz. 1978, Mo. 1985. Assoc. Streich, Lang, Weeks & Cardon, Phoenix, 1978-82; asst. prof. U. Mo., Kansas City, 1982-86, assoc. prof., 1986-94, prof., 1994-2000, prof. emerita, 2000—; pres. Profl. Presence, Comm. Cons., Tucson and Kansas City, Mo., 2001—. Vis. prof. U. Wis., Madison, 1985, 91, U. Pa., Phila., 1988, U. Ariz., 1993, U. Colo., 1994. Author: (with Bruce Meyerson) A Drafter's Guide to Alternative Dispute Resolution, 1991; editor: The Portable UCC, 1993, 3d edit., 2001, 4th edit., 2004, Getting Graphic I and II, 1993, 94, The New Article 9, 1999, 2d edit., 2000; editor in chief Bus. Law Today, 1995-97; mem. editl. bd. ABA Jour., 1999-; contbr. articles to profl. jours., chpts. to books. Legal counsel Mo. for Hart campaign, 1984; dir. issues Goddard for Gov. campaign, 1990; bd. dirs. Com. for County Progress, Kansas City, 1985-95. Mem. ABA (mem. coun. bus. sect. 1992-96, uniform comml. code com., chmn. bus. sect. membership com. 1992-94, editl. bd. Bus. Law Today, 1991-97, sect. of bus. law pubs. 1998-2002, standing com. on strategic comm. 2001—, coun. gen. practice sect. 2003—), Am. Law Inst., Am. Assn. Law Schs. (comml. law 1982-2000), Ariz. Bar Assn., Mo. Bar Assn. (comml. law com.), Order of Coif, Phi Beta Kappa, Phi Kappa Phi. Democrat. Jewish. Office: Profl Presence 4558 N 1st Ave Tucson AZ 85718 Office Phone: 520-795-0522. Business E-Mail: c2@professionalpresence.com.

COOPER, CYNTHIA, professional basketball player; b. Chgo., Apr. 14, 1963; Degree in phys. edn., U. So. Calif., 1986. Basketball player Segovia, Spain, 1986—87, Parma, Italy, 1987—94, 1996—97, Alcamo, Italy, 1994—96, Houston Comets, 1997—2000, 2003—; head coach Phoenix Mercury, 2001—02. Mem. U.S. Goodwill Games, 1986, 90, World Championships, 1986, 90, Pan Am. Games, 1987. Named MVP, Women's NBA Championship, 1997, 1998; recipient Gold medal, Pan Am Games, 1987, U.S. Olympic Basketball, 1988, Bronze medal, 1992; mem. WNBA champion, Houston Comets, 1997, 1998, 1999. Achievements include Won two NCAA championships with USC, 1983-1984.

COOPER, DAVID EARL KALEOIKAIKA, foundation executive; b. Honolulu, Aug. 12, 1941; s. Robert Lewis and Lucy Kapuakela (Kamaka_ C.; m. Katherine S. Arakaki, June 16, 1962; children: Troy A.K., Bradley H.K., Ethan Scott K.K. BA in English, U. Hawaii Manoa, Honolulu, 1963; MA in English Lit., U. Mo., Kansas City, 1974; MS in Counseling Psychology, L.I. U., 1976; postgrad., Harvard U., 1992. Cert. fin. planner. Commd. 2d lt. U.S. Army, 1963, advanced through grades to brig. gen., 1993, ret., 1993; pres. Pacific Am. Found., Washington, 1993—; CEO Hana Engring., Inc., Honolulu, 1994—, Pacific Nations Internat., Washington, 1997—. Contbr. articles to army mags. Chmn. Fed. Adv. Com. on Minority Vets., Washington, 1995—; bd. govs. Japanese Am. Nat. Mus., L.A., 1996—. Decorated Silver Star with oak leaf cluster, Combat Inf. badge; Coun. on Fgn. Rrels. fellow, 1985. Mem. U Hawaii Alumni Assn. (pres. Nat. Capital Region chpt. 1997—), Kamehameha Alumni Assn. (dir. East Coast chpt. 1994—), Inst. for Cert. Fin. Planners, 173rd Soc., 25th Inf. Divsn. Soc., Phi Kappa Phi. Avocations: tennis, running, biking. Home: 1106 W Abingdon Dr Alexandria VA 22314-1201

COOPER, DAVIS A., city official; b. South Fort Mitchell, Ky., Mar. 8, 1956; s. Davis A. and Geneva A. (Rudd) C.; children: Clinton C., Stephanie L. BS in Acctg., Western Ky. U., 1980. Cert. govt. fin. officer, Ky. Treas. City of Bowling Green, Ky., 1980—2001, CFO, 2002—. Bd. dirs. United Way of So. Ky., Bowling Green, 1994-99, treas., 1996-97. Mem. Govt. Fin. Officers U.S.A., Ky. Govt. Fin. Officers (bd. dirs. 1982-90, treas. 1983-84, pres. 1985-86). Avocations: basketball, soccer, football, hockey, family. Office: City of Bowling Green PO Box 430 Bowling Green KY 42102-0430 Office Phone: 270-393-3000. E-mail: davis.cooper@bgky.org.

COOPER, DONALD LEE, physician; b. Columbus, Kans., Aug. 11, 1928; s. Calvin M. and J. Pearl (Mullen) C.; m. Dona Faye Maddux, June 4, 1950; children— Donald Lee, Catherine Susan, Cheryl Lyn, Tad Houston. AB, Pittsburg State U., 1949; MD, U. Kans., 1953. Intern St. Mary's and Childrens Mercy hosps., Kansas City, Mo., 1953-54; pvt. practice medicine Manhattan, Kans., 1956-57; team physician, asst. dir. Health Center Kans. State U., 1957-60; dir. health service, team physician Okla. State U. Hosp. and Clinic, Stillwater, 1960-90, dir. athletic medicine, 1990-98, emeritus dir., 1998—. Vis. lectr. div. sportsmedicine, dept. orthopedic surgery Coll. Medicine U. Okla. Health Scis. Center, 1974—; liaison officer Am. Coll. Health Assn. to Nat. Athletic Trainers Assn., 1963—; Am. chmn. 1st Am.-Soviet Conf. on Student Health, Moscow, Russia, 1967; team physician U.S. Olympic Team, 1967-68; mem. Pres.'s Coun. Phys. Fitness and Sports, 1981-92, del. to Moscow to rev. phys. culture and olympic tng. sites in Russia, 1989; team physician U.S. Deaf Olympic Team, Los Angeles, 1985; elected chmn. Joint Commn. on Competitive Safeguards and Med. Aspects of Sports, 1986. Author: (with others) Standard Nomenclature of Athletic Injuries, 1966; Contbr. (with others) articles med. jours. Served to capt. USAF, 1954-56. Recipient Pres.'s Challenge Sportsmedicine award Nat. Athletic Trainers Assn., 1974, Bill Coltrin Meml. award Western Athletic Conf. Sports Writers Assn., 1974, Edward Hitchcock award Am. Coll. Health Assn., 1975; named among 10 healthy American fitness leaders Nat. Jaycees, Pres.'s Coun. on Physical Fitness and Sports, Allstate Ins. Co., 1995; inductee Okla. Hall of Fame, 1998. Mem. AMA (chmn. com. med. aspects sports 1971-76, chmn. 1976-77, mem. coun. sci. affairs 1976-79), Nat. Collegiate Athletic Assn. (med. cons. to football rules com. 1969-75), Am. Coll. Health Assn. (past pres., exec. com.), Southwestern Coll. Health Assn. (past pres.), Nat. Athletic Trainers Assn., Alpha Omega Alpha, Nu Sigma Nu. Presbyterian (elder 1971—). Club: Lion. Home: 1001 W Liberty Ln Stillwater OK 74075-2113 Office: Okla State U Hosp & Clinic 1202 Farm Rd Stillwater OK 74078-0001 Office Phone: 405-744-7031. *We must realize and accept that life is neither fair nor unfair; one must accept it as a unique journey composed of all types of experiences. It is not so much what happens to us as we go along in life, it is how we react to what happens that is so very important.*

COOPER, DORIS JEAN, market research executive; b. N.Y.C., Dec. 17, 1934; d. James N. and Georgina N. (Cassidy) Breslin; m. S. James Cooper, June 17, 1956; 1 son, David Austin. Student, Sch. of Commerce, NYU, 1953-55, Hunter Coll., 1956-57. Asst. coding supr. Crossley S-D Surveys, N.Y.C., 1955-57; asst. field supr. Trendex, Inc., N.Y.C., 1957-59; coding dir. J. Walter Thompson Co., N.Y.C., 1960-63, Audits & Surveys, N.Y.C., 1964-65; pvt. practice cons. N.Y.C., 1965-73; pres. Cooper Svcs., Hastings-on-Hudson, N.Y., 1973—; pres., CEO computer tabulation and lang. manipulation Doris J. Cooper Assocs., Hastings-on-Hudson, 1989—. Cons. market rsch. Mem. Am. Mktg. Assn. (N.Y. chpt.), nat. Bus. Women Owners Assn., Am. Assn. Pub. Opinion Researchers (N.Y. chpt.), Acad. Health Svcs. Mktg., Hastings C. of C. Republican. Episcopalian. Office: Doris J Cooper Assocs Ltd 447 Warburton Ave Hastings On Hudson NY 10706-1542 Personal E-mail: doris.cooper@verizon.net.

COOPER, EDWARD HAYES, lawyer, educator; b. Highland Park, Mich., Oct. 13, 1941; s. Frank Edward and Margaret Ellen (Hayes) C.; m. Nancy Carol Wybo, June 29, 1963; children: Lisa, Chandra. AB, Dartmouth Coll., 1961; LL.B., Harvard U., 1964. Bar: Mich. 1965. Law clk. Hon. Clifford O'Sullivan, U.S. Ct. of Appeals, 1964-65; practice law, Detroit, 1965-67; adj. prof. Wayne State U. Law Sch., 1965-67; assoc. prof. U. Minn. Law Sch., 1967-72; prof. law U. Mich. Law Sch., Ann Arbor, 1972-88, assoc. dean for acad. affairs, 1981-94, Thomas M. Cooley prof. of law, 1988—. Advisor Restatement of the Law, 2d Judgments, 1976-80, Complex Litigation Project, Restatement of the Law, 3d Torts-Apportionment, Fed. Jud. Code Project, Transnational Procedure Project, Internat. Jurisdiction Judgment, Aggregation; reporter fed. state jurisdiction com. Jud. Conf. U.S., 1985-91; mem. civil rules adv. com., 1991-92, reporter, 1992—; reporter Uniform Transfer of Litigation Act, 1989-91. Author: (with C.A. Wright and A.R. Miller) Federal Practice and Procedure: Jurisdiction, Vols. 13-19, 1975-81, 2d edit., 1984-2002, 3d edit., 1999—; contbr. articles to law revs. Mem. ABA, Mich. Bar Assn., Am. Law Inst. (council). Office: U Mich 330 Hutchins Law Sch Ann Arbor MI 48109-1215 Office Phone: 734-764-4347. Business E-Mail: coopere@umich.edu.

COOPER, EDWARD SAWYER, cardiologist, internist, educator; b. Columbia, S.C., Dec. 11, 1926; s. Henry Howard and Ada Crosland (Sawyer) Cooper; m. Jean Marie Wilder, Dec. 2, 1951; children: Lisa Marie Cooper Hudgins, Edward Sawyer Jr.(dec.), Jan Ada, Charles Wilder. AB, Lincoln U., Pa., 1946; MD, Meharry Med. Coll., Nashville, 1949; MS (hon.), U. Pa., 1972. Diplomate Nat. Bd. Med. Examiners, Am. Bd. Internal Medicine. Intern Phila. Gen. Hosp., 1949—51, resident in medicine, 1951—54, NIH fellow in cardiology, 1956—57, pres. med. staff, 1969—71, co-dir. Stroke Rsch. Ctr., 1968—74, chief med. svc., 1973—76; prof. Sch. Medicine U. Pa., 1976—96, prof. emeritus medicine Phila., 1996—. Bd. dirs. Independence Blue Cross. Bd. trustees Am. Heart Assn., pres.-elect, pres., chmn. Stroke Coun.; adv. com. NIH; trustee Am. Found. Negro Affairs, 1969—, Rockefeller U., 1992—, Hosp. of the U. of Pa., 2002—. Served to capt. USAF, 1954—56. Master: ACP; fellow: Phila. Coll. Physicians (coun.); mem.: Am. Heart Assn. (chmn., bd. dirs., past nat. pres.), Alpha Omega Alpha. Democrat. Methodist. Achievements include research in stroke and hypertension. Home: 6710 Lincoln Dr Philadelphia PA 19119-3155 Office: Univ Penn Hosp 3400 Spruce St Philadelphia PA 19104-4206 Personal E-mail: ecoopmdphila@aol.com.

COOPER, ELVA JUNE, artist; b. Wilmore, Ky., Mar. 18, 1933; d. Scott Combs and Rhoda Mae (Hundley) Bishop; m. Lowell Howard Cooper, Nov. 29, 1952; children: Lowell Scott, Linda Janet, Candace Lea, Connie Lynn, June Roxanne. Student, Georgetown Coll., 1952-53, Southwestern Jr. Coll., 1961, U. West Fla., 1994, Pensacola Jr. Coll., 1998. Owner June Bug Art and Gifts, Pensacola, Fla., 1973—2003, The Studio, Pensacola, Fla., 1986—. Cons. editor Church Recreation, 1993-95; contbr. articles to mags. Drama writer, dir. Myrtle Grove Bapt. Ch., Pensacola, Fla., 1977-96, artist in residence, 1973-96, discipleship tng. dir., 1973-79, 88-97; sec. Lillian (Ala.) First Bapt. Ch., 1984-95; writer Bapt. Sunday Sch. Bd., Nashville, Tenn., 1987-98; state recreation counselor Fla. Bapt. Conv., Jacksonville, 1994—; discipleship tng. dir. Pensacola Bay Bapt. Assn., 1994-96. Three time winner of Peggy award Popular Ceramics Mag., 1970; numerous other awards in art shows; inducted into Internat. Soc. Poetry as Disting. Mem. Mem. Quayside Art Gallery (asst. publicity 1984, pub. rels. dir. 2005—, bd. dirs. 2005—), Art Study Club. Baptist. Avocations: porcelain doll making, sewing, flower arranging, stained glass artist. Office Phone: 850-455-2379. E-mail: junepens@aol.com.

COOPER, EUGENE BRUCE, speech pathology/audiology services professional, educator; b. Utica, N.Y., Dec. 20, 1933; s. Clements Everett and Beulah (Wetzel) C.; m. Crystal Silverman, Sept. 12, 1965; children: Philip Adam, Ivan Bruce. BS, SUNY, Geneseo, 1955; MEd, Pa. State U., 1957, DEd, 1962. Pathologist speech and lang. Franklin County Schs., Chambersburg, Pa., 1957-59; asst. prof. Ohio U., 1962-64, Pa. State U., 1964-66; program specialist U.S. Office Edn., 1966; exec. sec. sensory study sect., rsch. and demonstrations Rehab. Services Adminstrn., HEW, Washington, 1966-67; faculty U. Ala., Tuscaloosa, 1967-96, prof. speech-lang. pathology, 1969-96, chmn. dept. communicative disorders, dir. Speech and Hearing Ctr., 1967-96, prof., chair emeritus, 1996—; Disting. prof. comm. scis. and disorders Nova Southeastern U., 1997—. Chmn. Ala. Bd. Examiners Speech Pathology and Audiology, 1979; cons.-at-large Nat. Student Speech-Lang.-Hearing Assn., 1983-88. Author: Personalized Fluency Control Therapy, 1976, Understanding Stuttering: Information for Parents, 1979, revised edit., 1990; (with Crystal Cooper) The Cooper Personalized Fluency Control Therapy Program, 1985, 2d edit., 2003, Cooper Assessment for Stuttering Syndromes, 1995; contbr. articles to profl. jours. Fellow Am. Speech, Lang. and Hearing Assn. (legis. coun. 1971-72, 85-97), Divsn. Fluency and Fluency Disorders (steering com. 1993-99, divsn. coord. 1994-99), Am. Speech, Lang. and Hearing Found. (chmn. adv. and devel. bd. 1988-89, trustee 1989-94); mem. Coun. Exceptional Children (pres. divsn. children comm. disorders 1975-76), Nat. Coun. Grad. Programs in Speech, Lang. Pathology and Audiology (pres. 1978-80), Nat. Coun. State Bds. Examiners Speech-Lang. Pathology and Audiology (pres. 1980, 91, mem. exec. bd. 1988-91), Nat. Coun. Comm. Disorders (chmn. 1982), Nat. Alliance Prevention and Treatment on Stuttering (pres. 1985-86), Internat. Fluency Assn. (bd. dirs. 1991-96, pres. 2d world congress on fluency disorders 1997, chmn. specialty commn. on fluency disorders 1997-99). Office Phone: 954-385-1422.

COOPER, FRANK G., lawyer; b. Boston, Oct. 21, 1946; AB, George Washington U., 1968; JD, U. Pa., 1971. Bar: Pa. 1971, US Ct. Appeals 3rd Cir., US Dist. Ct. Ea. Dist. Pa., US Tax Ct., Supreme Ct. Pa. Assoc. Duane Morris LLP, Phila., 1971—78, ptnr., 1978—, chair firm estates and asset planning group, 1994—, mem. partners bd. Bd. mem. William B. Dietrich Found. Mem.: ABA, Phila. Bar Assn., Pa. Bar Assn. Office: Duane Morris LLP One Liberty Pl Philadelphia PA 19103-7396 Office Phone: 215-979-1906. Office Fax: 215-979-1020. Business E-Mail: fgcooper@duanemorris.com.

COOPER, G. DAVID, psychologist; b. Hagerstown, Md., July 7, 1935; s. George Emmanuel and Mary Elva (Longanecker) C. BA, Shepherd Coll., 1957; PhD, Duke U., 1962. Lic. psychologist, Va., W.Va., Md. Clin. psychologist Newton Baker Vets. Ctr., Martinsburg, W.Va., 1964—73; assoc. prof. psychology George Mason U., Fairfax, Va., 1975—79; clin. dir. Glaydin Sch., Leesburg, Va., 1979—83; chief psychologist MCTC, Hagerstown, 1984—. Vis. assoc. prof. W.Va. U., Morgantown, 1968-69. Mem. APA, Kiwanis. Republican. Methodist. Avocations: music, photography. Home: PO Box 27 Shepherdstown WV 25443 Office: MCTC 18800 Roxbury Rd Hagerstown MD 21746 Business E-Mail: gdcooper@citlink.net.

COOPER, GEORGE, writer, consultant; b. Balt., May 31, 1937; s. Harry and Hilda C.; m. Jill Zimmerman, June 19, 1960 (div. 1972); 1 child, Amanda; m. Judy Blume, 1987. BS, U. Pa., 1958; LLB, Harvard U., 1961; cert. in celestial nav. Hayden Planetarium, 1972. Bar: D.C. 1961, N.Y. 1975, U.S. Supreme Ct. 1966. Assoc. Covington & Burling, Washington, 1963-66; faculty Columbia Law Sch., 1966-85, prof. law, 1969-85; writer, consultant, 1985—; vis. prof. Harvard U. Law Sch., 1975, U. Witwatersrand, Johannesburg, Republic South Africa, 1979. Author: A Voluntary Tax, 1979; (with Rabb and Rubin) Equal Employment Opportunity, 1975; editor: Law and Poverty, 1972.

COOPER, GERALD RICE, clinical pathologist; b. Scranton, S.C., Nov. 19, 1914; s. Robert McFadden and Viola Lavender Cooper; m. Lois Corrina Painter, Mar. 9, 1946; children: Annetta, Gerald Jr., Rodney. AB, Duke U., 1936, MA, 1938, PhD, 1939, MD, 1950. Cert. Am. Bd. Clin. Chemistry.

Intern Atlanta VA Hosp., 1950-51, resident, 1951-52; rsch. assoc. Duke U. Sch. Medicine, Durham, N.C., 1939-46; chief chemistry, hematology and pathology Ctrs. for Disease Control, Atlanta, 1952-72; rsch. med. officer Ctrs. for Disease Control, Nat. Ctr. Environ. Health, Atlanta, 1973—. Author (with others) books; contbr. articles to profl. jours. Col. USPHS. Decorated commendation medal, Superior Svc. award, Disting. Svc. medal, Asst. Sec. for Health award for exceptional achievement; recipient Hektoen Silver medal AMA, 1954, Fulton County Med. Achievement award, 1954, Billings Silver medal, 1956, Sigma Xi rsch. award, 1997, Lifetime Sci. Achievement award CDC, 2002. Mem. Am. Assn. for Clin. Chemistry (pres. 1984, bd. dirs. 1975-77, chmn. bd. editors of selected methods 1967-80, bd. editors Clin. Chemistry jour. 1970-76, Fischer award 1975, Dade Internat. award 1975, N.J. Gerulat award 1979, SE Sect. Meritorious Svc. award 1989, Outstanding Contbn. Clin. Chemistry award 1992), Internat. Fedn. Clin. Chemistry (apolipoprotein expert panel 1985), Am. Soc. Clin. Pathologists (chmn. clin. chemistry coun. 1974, Continuing Edn. award 1967, 77). Methodist. Home: 2165 Bonnevit Ct NE Atlanta GA 30345-4126 Office: Ctrs for Disease Control Chamblee 102/2319 F25 4770 Buford Hwy Atlanta GA 30341-3724 Office Phone: 770-488-7952. Business E-Mail: grcl@cdc.gov.

COOPER, GLORIA, editor, press critic; b. Oak Park, Ill., Jan. 8, 1931; c. Sam and Madelyn (Brandt) Glaser; m. Wallace J. Cooper, June 3, 1950; children— Alison, Julie BA summa cum laude, Briarcliff Coll., 1970; MA, Columbia U., 1974. From asst. editor to mng. editor to dep. exec. editor Columbia Journalism Rev., N.Y.C., 1974—. Editor: Squad Helps Dog Bite Victim, 1980, Red Tape Holds Up New Bridge, 1987; contbr. articles, revs., editorials to Columbia Journalism Rev., 1974— Mem. Soc. Prof. Journalists, Princeton Club (N.Y.C.). Home: 91 Long Hill Rd E Briarcliff Manor NY 10510-2611 Office: Columbia U Columbia Journalism Rev 207 Journalism Bldg New York NY 10027 Office Phone: 212-854-1887. Business E-Mail: gc15@columbia.edu.

COOPER, GREGORY SCOTT, epidemiologist, gastroenterologist, educator; b. Newark, July 14, 1960; s. Murray and Frances Cooper; m. Cathy Lynne Cooper, Feb. 3, 1991; children: Marissa, Ryan, Nicole. BA, MA, U. Pa., 1982, MD, 1986. Diplomate Am. Bd. Internal Medicine. Intern, resident in internal medicine Univ. Hosps., Cleve., 1986-89, chief resident, 1991-92, fellow in gastroenterology, 1989-91, 92-93; instr. medicine Case Western Res. U., Cleve., 1991-93, asst. prof. medicine, 1993-96, asst. prof. medicine and epidemiology, 1996-98, assoc. prof. medicine and epidemiology, 1998—, dir. cancer epidemiology-health rsch., staff investigator, 2000—. Tng. program dir. Case Western Res. U., 1997—; dir. disease mgmt. U. Hosps. Cleve., 1997-99. Contbr. chpts. to books, more than 90 articles to profl. jours. Grantee Nat. Cancer Inst., 1996—. Fellow ACP (med. sch. rep.), Am. Coll. Gastroenterology; mem. Am. Fedn. Med. Rsch. (midwest coun.), Am. Cancer Soc. (rsch. project grants 1997—). Avocation: long distance running. Office: Univ Hosps Cleveland 11100 Euclid Ave Cleveland OH 44106-5066 Office Phone: 216-844-5386. Business E-Mail: greg.cooper@case.edu.

COOPER, HAL, television director; b. N.Y.C., Feb. 23, 1923; s. Benjamin and Adeline (Raichman) C.; m. Mary Patricia Meikle, Dec. 21, 1944 (div. 1971); children: Bethami, Pamela; m. Marta Lucille Salcido, June 26, 1971; 1 child, James Benjamin. BA, U. Mich., 1946. Ind. TV dir., writer, producer various prodn. cos., 1948—. Performer Big Bro.'s Rainbow House, Mut. Network, 1936-41, asst. dir. Dock Street Theatre, Charleston, S.C., 1946-48; writer, prodr. TV Babysitter, DuMont TV Network, 1948-52, The Magic Cottage, 1950-56; dir., prodr. various daytime TV shows including Search For Tomorrow, others, 1950-57; prodr. stage play The Troublemakers, London, 1952; dir. numerous TV shows (various episodes) including Death Valley Days, 1965-67, Dick Van Dyke Show, 1962, Gilligan's Island, 1966, I Dream of Jeannie, 1965-69, I Spy, 1966, That Girl, 1967-69, Courtship of Eddie's Father, 1968-71, The Odd Couple, 1970-72, Mary Tyler Moore, 1972, All in the Family, 1972, (pilots) Hot L Baltimore, 1974, One Day At a Time, 1975, All's Fair, 1976, Nancy Walker Show, 1976, The Time of Their Lives, 1987; dir., exec. prodr.: TV shows including Maude, 1972-78, Phyl and Mikky, 1980, Love, Sydney, 1982-83, Gimme a Break, 1983-87, Empty Nest, 1988-89, Dear John, 1989-92, The Powers That Be, 1992-93. Served to lt. (j.g.) USNR, 1943-46, PTO. Mem. Writers Guild Am., ASCAP, Screen Actors Guild, AFTRA, Actors Equity Assn., Dirs. Guild Am. (mem. dirs. council, nat. bd. dirs.). E-mail: halcoop@aol.com.

COOPER, HAL DEAN, lawyer; b. Marshall County, Iowa, Dec. 8, 1934; s. Truman Braton and Golda Frances (Chadwick) C.; m. Constance Bellinger Simms, Dec. 31, 1960; children: Shannon, Charles, Ellen. Student, Neb. U., 1952-54; BS in Mech. Engring., Iowa State U., 1957; JD with honors, George Washington U., 1963. Bar: Iowa 1963, Ohio 1963, U.S. Supreme Ct. 1971. Assoc., ptnr. Fay & Fay, Cleve., 1962-67; ptnr. Meyer, Tilberry & Body, Cleve., 1967-69, Yount, Tarolli, Weinshenker & Cooper, Cleve, 1969-72; trial judge U.S. Ct. Claims, Washington, 1972-75; ptnr. Jones, Day, Reavis & Pogue, Cleve., 1975-95; owner Halco Enterprises, Ltd., Austinburg, Ohio, 1995—; pvt. arbitrator, mediator, 1996—. Bd. trustees Ashtubula County Dist. Lib., 2004—, pres., 2005—. With AUS, 1957—59. Mem. Cleve. Intellectual Property Law Assn., Rowfant Club, Clifton Club, Rotary. Episcopalian. Personal E-mail: halco@apk.net.

COOPER, HARRY EDWIN, historian; b. Oak Park, Ill., Sept. 2, 1939; s. William Cortland Jr. and Adelaide Elizabeth (Beggs) C.; m. Kathleen Mary Lewandowski, Oct. 30, 1985; children: Sean Patrick, Meaghan Mary Kathleen. BS in Bus. Adminstrn., U. Wis., 1965. Cert. scuba diver. Customer svc. mgr. Motorola, Elk Grove Village, Ill., 1965-69; inventory control mgr. No. Petrochem., Des Plaines, Ill., 1969-76; dir. pers. Consumer Periodical, Schaumburg, Ill., 1983-85; v.p. NPC Co., Marion, Iowa, 1985-87; pres. Sharkhunters, Hernando, Fla., 1983—. Organizer, leader various hist. trips, 1987—; leading expert on history, activities and pers. of German U-Boats during World War II; founder, exec. dir. Eaglehunters. Guest Today in Chgo., 1969; sportscaster Motorsports Internat, 1969; substitute news anchor U.S. Cable 6:00 News, 1980; asst. hist. data for documentaries; contbr. articles to profl. jours.; author: Sponsorship, 1978, 1001 Things to do in Florida for Free, 1984, U-Boat, 1997. Sgt. USAF, 1957-61. Class Champion major drag racing event, 1964, set 2 nat. records, 1964, nat. class champion, 1965. Avocation: drag racing. Home: 6885 N Beechnut Loop Hernando FL 34442-3806 Office: Sharkhunters PO Box 1539 Hernando FL 34442-1539

COOPER, ILENE LINDA, magazine editor, author; b. Chgo., Mar. 10, 1948; d. Morris and Lillian (Friedman) C.; m. Robert Seid, May 28, 1972 (div. 1995). BJ, U. Mo., 1969; MLS, Rosary Coll., 1973. Head of children's svcs. Winnetka (Ill.) Libr. Dist., 1974-80; editor children's books Booklist Mag., ALA, Chgo., 1981—. Author: Susan B. Anthony, 1983, Choosing Sides, 1990 (Internat. Reading Assn.-Children's Book Coun. choice 1990), Mean Streak, 1991, Jewish Holidays All Year Round, 2002, Sam I Am, 2004, (series) Frances in the Fourth Grade, 1991, The Dead Sea Scrolls, 1997, numerous others. Mem. Soc. Midland Authors, Soc. Children's Book Writers, Children's Reading Roundtable. Jewish. Office: Booklist Mag 50 E Huron St Chicago IL 60611-5295*

COOPER, J. MICHAEL, lawyer; BA, Swarthmore Coll., 1970; JD, Harvard U., 1973. Ptnr., mem. exec. com. Bryan Cave LLP, Washington, DC. Office: Bryan Cave LLP 700 Thirteenth Street NW Washington DC 20005 Office Phone: 202-508-6070. E-mail: wfbavinger@bryancave.com.

COOPER, JACK ROSS, pharmacology educator, researcher; b. Ottawa, Ont., Can., July 26, 1924; came to U.S., 1948; s. Harry and Jean (Levine) C.; m. Helen Achbar, Aug. 14, 1951; children: Marilyn, Sheila, Nancy. BA, Queen's U. Kingston, Ont., 1948; MA, George Washington U., 1952, PhD, 1954; MA (hon.), Yale U., 1971. Instr. Yale U., New Haven, 1956—58, asst. prof. pharmacology, 1958—63, assoc. prof., 1963-71, prof., 1971—. Author: The Biochemical Basis of Neuropharmacology, 8th edit., 2003. Served with RCAF, 1944. Smith, Kline and French rsch. fellow, 1950-52; USPHS predoctoral fellow, 1952-54; postdoctoral fellow USPHS, 1954-56; spl. fellow USPHS, London, 1965-66. Mem. Am. Soc. Neurochemistry, Internat. Soc. Neurochemistry, Am. Soc. Pharmacology and Exptl. Therapeutics, Soc. Neurosci. Democrat. Jewish. Home: 11 Jenick Ln Woodbridge CT 06525-1935 Office: Yale U Sch Medicine 333 Cedar St New Haven CT 06510-3289

COOPER, JACQUELINE, director; d. Thomas James and Mary Ruth Cooper. BS, Jackson State U., 1983, MS in Edn., 1986; PhD, U. Mo., 2004. Coord. summer programs U. Mo. Columbia Sch. of Medicine, 1995—96; sr. recruiter/amb. U. Mo. Columbia Grad. Sch., 1995—2000; program coord. Show-Me State Games U. Mo. Columbia, 1996—2000, grad. tchg. instr., 1999—2000; asst. dir. admission/coord. orientation Tex. State U., San Marcos, 2000—. Exhibition, Jackson (Miss.) State U., 1992. Thurgood Marshall fellow, U. of Mo. Columbia, 1994-1998. Mem.: Assn. for the Study of Higher Edn., Tex. Assn. of Coll. Admission Counselors, Nat. Orientation Dirs. Assn., Delta Sigma Theta Sorority, Inc. (life; custodian/properties 1997—99). Avocations: travel, pottery, photography. Office: Tex State Univ 429 N Guadalupe St San Marcos TX 78666 Office Phone: 512-245-2340.

COOPER, JACQUELYN BARBER, librarian; b. Harrisburg, Pa., Jan. 7, 1940; d. John and Belinda (Weakley) Barber; m. Stephen T. Toy, Aug. 11, 1962 (div. 1972); 1 child, Deborah Lynne; m. Arthur Raymond Cooper, Jan. 10, 1987. BS magna cum laude, Susquehanna U., 1961; MLS, Kent. State U., 1969. Tchr. music Tredyffrin-Eastern Schs., Berwyn, Pa., 1961-62; supr. music Alachua County Schs., Gainesville, Fla., 1962-66; reference libr. Providence (R.I.) Pub. Libr., 1969-73, br. libr., 1973-87, br. head, 1987-95, regional libr., 1995—2000, collection devel. mgr., 2000—03; ret. Sec. Mt. Hope Day Care Ctr. Inc., Providence, 1985-1998; substitute organist Providence Presbyn. Ch., 1989—, trustee, 1994—. Pa. State Edn. Assn. scholar, 1957; recipient SAT scholar award Sigma Alpha Iota, 1961. Mem. ALA, New Eng. Libr. Assn. (exec. bd. 1982-92), R.I. Libr. Assn. (chmn. intellectual freedom com. 1980-82, Libr. of Yr. award 1992), Providence Pub. Libr. Staff Assn. (pres. 1971-72, 86-87, treas. 1987-89), Coalition Libr. Advs. (treas. 1994—), Beta Phi Mu, Sigma Alpha Iota. Democrat. Presbyterian. Avocations: French horn, organ, natural history, sewing. E-mail: jackicr@hotmail.com.

COOPER, JAMES D., lawyer; b. Whittier, Calif., Oct. 19, 1954; AB summa cum laude, Univ. Chgo., 1976; JD, Yale Univ., 1976. Bar: NY 1981. Assoc. Cravath, Swaine & Moore LLP, NYC, 1979—86, ptnr., corp., 1986—. Mem.: Phi Beta Kappa. Office: Cravath Swaine & Moore LLP Worldwide Plz 825 Eighth Ave New York NY 10019-7475 Office Phone: 212-474-1326. Office Fax: 212-474-3700. Business E-Mail: jcooper@cravath.com.

COOPER, JAMES HAYES SHOFNER (JIM COOPER), congressman, lawyer; b. Nashville, Tenn., June 19, 1954; s. William Prentice Jr. and Hortense (Powell) C.; m. Martha Hays; children: Mary Argentine Adams, John James Audubon, Hayes Hightower. BA, U. N.C., 1975, Oxford U., 1977; JD, Harvard U., 1980. Atty. Waller, Lansden, Dortch & Davis, Nashville, 1980-82; mem. 98th-103rd Congresses from 4th Tenn. dist., Washington, 1983—95, mem. budget com., mem. energy and commerce com.; mng. dir. Equitable Securities, 1995-99; founder, ptnr. & chmn. bd. Brentwood Capital Adv. LLC, 1999—; mem. 108th Congress from 5th dist., Washington, DC, 2003—. Bd. dirs. Resources for the Future, 1997—. Rhodes scholar, 1975, Morehead scholar, 1972. Mem.: Phi Beta Kappa. Democrat. Episcopalian. Mailing: Wash Office Office Bldg 1536 Longworth Ho Office Bldg Washington DC 20515-1535 also: District Office 706 Church St Ste 101 Nashville TN 37203 E-mail: jim.cooper@brentwoodcap.com.*

COOPER, JAMES MICHAEL, education educator; b. Steubenville, Ohio, July 29, 1939; s. James Stanley and Regina Marie (Coen) C.; m. Susan Callaway, Sept. 1, 1962 (div. June 1978); children: Jeffrey, Craig, Cynthia; m. Shamim Sisson, June 13, 1987. AB in History with distinction, Stanford U., 1961, AM in Edn., 1962, AM in History, 1966, PhD in Edn., 1967. Tchr. Jordan Jr. High Sch. of Palo Alto (Calif.) Unified Sch. Sys., 1961-63, Palo Alto High Sch., 1963-65; lectr. Stanford U. Sch. Edn., 1967; asst. prof. edn. U. Mass., Amherst, 1968-71; assoc. prof. U. Houston, 1971-74, prof., 1974-84; Commonwealth prof. U. Va. Curry Sch. Edn., Charlottesville, 1984—2004, dean, 1984-94, prof. emeritus, 2004—. Chmn. U. Houston faculty senate, 1982; mem. exec. bd. dirs. Holmes Group, East Lansing, Mich., 1985-94; mem. unit accreditation bd. Nat. Coun. Accreditation of Tchr. Edn., Washington, 1986-90. Co-author: Those Who Can, Teach, 10th edit., 2004; editor: Developing Skills for Instructional Supervision, 1984, Classroom Teaching Skills; co-editor: Kaleidoscope: Readings in Education, 10th edit., 2004. Recipient Florence B. Stratemeyer award Assn. for Student Teaching, Washington, 1967, Fulbright-Hays award Portugal Coun. Internat. Exch. Scholars, Washington, 1980, Outstanding Leader in Tchr. Edn. award Assn. Tchr. Educators, 1990. Mem.: ASCD, Raven Soc. (The Raven award 2001), Am. Assn. Colls. for Tchr. Edn. (bd. dirs. 1990—93), Am. Ednl. Rsch. Assn., Omicron Delta Kappa, Phi Delta Kappa. Democrat. Roman Catholic. Avocations: golf, travel. Office Phone: 434-977-5216. Business E-Mail: jimcooper@virginia.edu.

COOPER, JAMES NELSON, medical educator; b. Staten Island, N.Y., Aug. 6, 1938; s. Charles Sylvester and Ella (Sabine) C.; m. Carolyn Olverson; children: John Emerson, Charles Key, James Ashley, Catherine Quesenberry. BA, Columbia U., 1959; MD, NYU, 1963. Diplomate Am. Bd. Internal Medicine and Gastroenterology. Intern Georgetown U., 1963-65; resident Boston City Hosp., 1965-66; fellow gastroenterology U. Chgo., 1966-68; clin. assoc. prof. medicine Georgetown U., Washington, 1977-83, prof. medicine, 1983—, asst. dean Sch. Medicine, 1985—, dir. transitional residency program, 1985—2001; pres. med. staff Fairfax Hosp., Falls Church, Va., 1975-77, chief gastroenterology, 1971-82, chmn. dept. medicine, 1982—; dir. Inova Inst. Rsch. & Edn., 1991—. Cons. State Dept., Washington, 1970—74; affiliate prof. George Mason U., 2001—; prof. medicine Va. Commonwealth Univ., Sch. of Medicine, 2003—. Editor: Gastrointestinal and Hepatic Complications In Pregnancy, 1986. Served to maj. USAR, 1964-71. Fellow ACP (Laureate award 1997), ACG; mem. Am. Gastroent. Assn., Am. Assn. Study Liver Diseases, No. Va. Acad. Internal Medicine (pres. 1975), Cosmos Club, Sigma Xi. Office: Fairfax Hosp 3300 Gallows Rd Falls Church VA 22042-3300 Office Phone: 703-776-3582. Business E-Mail: james.cooper@inova.com.

COOPER, JAMES RUSSELL, retired law educator; b. New Kensington, Pa., July 21, 1928; s. John Edward and Isabella Bird (Bowen) C.; m. Carolyn Hocker, Sept. 21, 1953 (div. Dec. 1975); children: L. Rachel, Julia Anderoni, Evan Lloyd, Jennifer Meyer; m. Leigh Ann Brian, Feb. 25, 1995 (div. Nov. 1999). BS Econs., U. Pa., 1952, JD, 1955. Bar: D.C., 1955, U.S. Supreme Ct., 1964; ordained to ministry Universal Brotherhood Movement, Inc., Meeting House for Aspiring Spirits. Pres., chmn. Radio WKPA-AM, WYDD-FM, New Kensington, 1959-64; urban renewal dir. Redevelopment Authority, New Kensington, 1964-68; assoc. prof. U. Ill., Champaign-Urbana, 1968-74; prof. legal studies Ga. State U., Atlanta, 1974-94, emeritus prof., 1994—. Author: Twilights Last Gleaming, 1992, Real Estate Investments, 3d edit. 1992. Sgt. U.S. Army, 1946-48. Mem. Fed. Bar Assn., D.C. Bar Assn., Am. Real Estate Soc. (founder, dir.). Home: 2822 Peavine Trail Lakeland FL 33810-2332 Office Phone: 863-838-5682, 863-859-7909. Personal E-mail: jrcooper1@verizon.net.

COOPER, JAMIE LEE, writer; d. Ralph Francis Cooper and Esther Allene Kellner, Lee Frederick Kellner (Stepfather). Grad., Fairfax Hall, Waynesboro, Va., 1947. Radio comml. writer Sta. WKBV, Richmond, Ind., 1947—49; profl. writer, novelist, short stories, essays, libretti various pubs., N.Y.C., Paris, 1955—; creative writing tchr. Ind. U., Bloomington, 1964—88, Ball State U., Muncie, Ind., 1964—88, Evansville (Ind.) U., 1964—88. Liaison, mentoring, judging novel scholarships, nat. competitions Ind. U., Ball State U., Evansville U., judging competitions for several out of state univs., Ind., 1963—88. Author: The Horn in the Forest, 1963 (Most Disting. Fiction of Midwest, 1964), Shadow of a Star, 1965 (Most Disting. Fiction of Midwest, 1966), Rapaho, 1967 (Most Disting. Fiction of Midwest, 1968), The Castaways, 1970 (Most Disting. Fiction of Midwest, 1971), The Great Dandelion, 1972 (Most Disting. Fiction of Midwest, 1973), Grasshopper Summer, 1974 (Most Disting. Fiction of Midwest, 1975); librettist: chorale Song of Mankind, 1970 (Friends of Am. Writers award, 1971), We, the Dreamers, 1975 (Friends of Am. Writers award, 1976), Bad That Woman, 1976 (Friends of Am. Writers award, 1977). Grantee, NEA, 1976. Mem.: PEN, Nat. Writers' Union, Authors Guild. Avocations: playing the sitar, cooking, gardening. Personal E-mail: jleighcooper@aol.com.

COOPER, JANE TODD (J. C. TODD), poet, writer, educator; b. Bklyn., Dec. 24, 1943; d. John Curtis and Margaret E. (Johnston) C.; m. William Hudson Shoff; children: Donald Charles Taylor, Eamon Robert Shoff, Savannah Elizabeth Cooper-Ramsey. BA in Liberal Arts, Duquesne U., 1965; MFA in Creative Writing, Warren Wilson Coll., 1990. Instr. H.S., Pitts., 1967-73; ednl. dir. drug and alcohol treatment facility Pa. Dept. Corrections, Camp Hill, 1974-78; project mgr. domiciliary care, boarding home provider tng. Pa. State Coll. Medicine, Hershey, 1979-80, 82; dir. primary health care project Elizabethtown Hosp., Pa., 1980-81; instr. creative writing Coll. N.J., 1993-94; instr. writing Bryn Mawr Coll., 1999—; instr. creative writing Kutztown (Pa.) U., 2003—. Cons. Pa. Coun. on Arts, 1979-91; bd. dirs. Poetry Ctr., Phila., 1990-97, dir., 1994-97; artist in residence N.J. State Arts Coun., Pa. Coun. on the Arts, 1982—. Author: Entering Pisces, 1985, Nightshade, 1995; contbg. editor: The Drunken Boat. Recipient Pa. Coun. on Arts Fellowship in Poetry award, 1998, Disting. Tchg. Artist award, N.J. State Arts Coun., 1999—2001, N.J. Gov.'s award for arts edn., 1999, Disting. Artist award, NEA, 1999—2000, Leeway Found. Poetry award, 2001, Leeway Found. award, 2004; lit. fellow, Geraldine R. Dodge Found., 1987—, Carroll scholar, 1964—65, Warner Lambert/Nat. Merit scholar, 1961—65, fellow poetry, Hambidge Ctr., 1991—93, Va. Ctr. Creative Arts, 1997, VCCA Internat. exch. fellow, Schloss Wiepersdorf, Germany, 2002, Pa. Coun. on Arts Profl. Devel. grantee, 1999, 2000, 2002—03, 2004. Mem. Acad. Am. Poets, Poetry Soc. Am., Friends of Writers.

COOPER, JANELLE LUNETTE, neurologist, educator; b. Ann Arbor, Mich., Dec. 11, 1955; d. Robert Marion and Madelyn (Leonard) C.; children: Lena Christine, Nicholas Dominic. BA in Chemistry, Reed Coll., 1978; MD, Vanderbilt U., 1986. Diplomate Nat. Bd. Med. Examiners; diplomate in neurology Am. Bd. Psychiatry and Neurology; registered med. technologist Am. Soc. Clin. Pathologists. Med. technologist Swedish Hosp. Med. Ctr., Seattle, 1978-80, U. Wash. Clin. Chemistry, Seattle, 1980-82, Vanderbilt U. Hosp., Nashville, 1983-84; intern medicine Vanderbilt U. Med. Ctr., Nashville, 1986-87, resident neurology, 1987-90; instr. neurology Med. Coll. Pa., Phila., 1990-91, asst. prof., clerkship dir., 1991—, mem. curriculum com., 1990-91, vis. asst. prof., 1991-95; neurologist Greater Ann Arbor Neurology Assocs., 1991-93; dir. neurol. svcs., med. dir. Indsl. Rehab. Program St. Francis Hosp., Escanaba, Mich., 1993-98; founder, dir. No. Neuroscis., Escanaba, 1993-98; pres. HolderLady, Ltd., 1996—; chmn. dept. medicine St. Francis Hosp., Escanaba, Mich., 1998-99; dir. Affinity Health Sys., Oshkosh, Wis., 1998—; med. dir. Memory Clinic of the Upper Peninsula, Escanaba, Mich., 1998—. Neurologist Affinity Med. Group, Oshkosh, Wis., 1998—; physician MCP Neurology Assocs., Phila., 1990-91; emergency rm. physician Tenn. Christian Med. Ctr., 1989-90. Contbr. articles to Annals of Ophthalmology, Ophthalmic Surgery. Vol. Rape and Sexual Abuse Ctr., Nashville, 1988-90; mem. adminstrv. bd. Edgehill United Meth. Ch., Nashville, 1989-90; mem. editorial bd. Nashville Women's Alliance, 1989-90; bd. dirs. Upper Peninsula Physicians Network, 1995-98; mem. adv. bd. Perspective Adult Daycare Ctr., 1996-99; founding dir. Memory Clinic of Upper Peninsula, 1998-00; profl. adv. com. NE Wis. Alzheimer's Assn., 1999—. Recipient Svc. award for outstanding contbns. Rape and Sexual Abuse Ctr., 1990; epilepsy minifellow Bowman Gray U., 1995. Mem. AMA (physician's Recognition award 1989—), AAAS, Am. Med. Women's Assn., Am. Acad. Neurology, Am. Psychol. Soc., Wis. State Med. Soc., N.Y. Acad. Scis., Upper Peninsula Neuro Assn. (v.p. 1998-99, trustee 1998-99), Upper Peninsula Physician Network (bd. dirs. 1995-98), Aircraft Owners and Pilots Assn., Women in Aviation Internat. (charter), Air Force Assn. (life patron). Methodist. Achievements include first synthesis of Difluoromethanedisulfonic Acid; research on neurobehavioral disorders; on neuroendocrinology of sexual development, identity and orientation; on the history of women in medicine on effects of dietary lipids on the etiology of Alzheimer's disease; clinical investigation trials for new medications for dementias and epilepsy. Office: Affinity Med Group Dept Neurology 2725 Jackson St Oshkosh WI 54901-1513 Home: 2819 Hughes St Oshkosh WI 54902-7158 E-mail: jcooper@affinityhealth.org.

COOPER, JASON P., lawyer; b. Chipping Norton, Eng., May 30, 1966; BS in Mech. Engring., Purdue Univ., 1988; JD cum laude, Ind. Univ., 1992. Bar: NC 1992, registered: US Patent and Trademark Off. 1994. Product engr. Rexnord Corp.; ptnr., chmn., intellectual property mech. group Alston & Bird LLP, Charlotte, NC. Co-author: The Art and Science of Patent Law, 2004; frequent lectr., writer on patent law. Intellectual Property Adv. Bd. Ind. Univ. Law Sch. Mem.: Fed. Circuit Bar Assn., FICPI Commn. d'Étude et de Travail for Internat. Patents, US Sect., Fédération Internationale des Conseils en Propriété Industrielle (FICPI) (councilor). Office: Alston & Bird LLP Ste 4000 Bank of Am Plz 101 S Tryon St Charlotte NC 28280-4000 Office Phone: 704-444-1031. Office Fax: 704-578-1234. Business E-Mail: jcooper@alston.com.

COOPER, JAY LESLIE, lawyer; b. Chgo., Jan. 15, 1929; s. Julius Jerome and Grayce (Wolkenheim) Cooper; m. Darice Richman, July 30, 1970; children: Todd, Leslie, Keith. JD, De Paul U., 1951. Bar: Ill. 1951, Calif. 1953, U.S. Supreme Ct. 1965, N.Y. 1987. Ptnr. Cooper, Epstein & Hurewitz (and predecessors), Beverly Hills, Calif., 1955-93, Manatt, Phelps & Phillips, L.A., 1993—2001; shareholder Greenberg Traurig, LLP, 2002—. Guest lectr. Advanced Profl. Program Legal Aspects of Music and Rec. Industry, U. So. Calif., 1968, 70, 75, Entertainment Industry Conf., 1971, Harvard Law Sch., 1985, Calif. Copyright Conf., 1967, 71, 73, 75, 77, 97, v.p., 1975, pres., 1976-77; co-chmn. annual program The Rec. Contract, UCLA, 1977—; lectr. Midem, 1977-95, 96-97; adj. prof. entertainment law Loyola U. Law Sch., LA, 1978-80; moderator UCLA Seminar, 1994. Profl. musician with, Les Brown, Charlie Barnet, Frank Sinatra, Los Angeles Philharm. others, 1945-55; editor: (with Irwin O. Spiegel) Record and Music Publishing Forms of Agreement in Current Use, 1971, Annual Program on Legal Aspects of Entertainment Industry, Syllabus, 1966-70; co-author: Talent in the New Millennium, 2001, The Work Made For Hire Conundrum, 2001. Named Entertainment Lawyer of Yr. Billboard mag., 1975, Best of the Best, 2000, Beverly Hills Bar Assn. Entertainment Atty of Yr., 2003, So. Calif. Super Lawyers for 2004 LA Magazine, Chambers and Partners US Guide as Leading Business Lawyer, listed in Best Lawyers in Am., 1987—. Mem.: NARAS (chpt. pres. 1973—75, nat. pres. 1975—77), ABA (chmn. forum on entertainment and sports industries 1983—86), Internat. Assn. Entertainment Lawyers (exec. com.), LA Copyright Soc., Ill. Bar Assn., Calif. Bar Assn., LA County Bar Assn., Calif. Copyright Soc. (pres. 1976), Beverly Hills Bar Assn. (co-chmn. entertainment law com. 1972—75). Office: Greenberg Traurig LLP 2450 Colorado Ave #400 E Santa Monica CA 90404 Office Phone: 310-586-7888. Business E-Mail: cooper@gtlaw.com.

COOPER, JEAN SARALEE, judge; b. Huntington, N.Y., Mar. 7, 1946; d. Ralph and Henrietta (Halbreich) Cooper; stepchildren: Mitzi Concklin Prochnow, John Todd Concklin. BA, Sophie Newcomb Coll. of Tulane U., 1968; JD, Emory U., 1970. Bar: La. 1970, Ga. 1970, U.S. Dist. Ct. (ea. dist.) La. 1970, U.S. Ct. Appeals (5th cir.) 1972, U.S. Ct. Appeals (2d cir.) 1976, U.S. Ct. Appeals (4th cir.) 1977, U.S. Ct. Appeals (fed. cir.), U.S. Supreme Ct. 1974. Trial atty. Office of Solicitor, U.S. Dept. Labor, Washington, 1970-73, spl. projects asst., 1973, sr. trial atty., 1973-77; adminstrv. judge Bd. Contract Appeals, HUD, Washington, 1977—2003, acting chmn. and chief judge, 1980-81, vice chmn., 1983—2003; bd. mem. Coalition for Free Trade, 2003—. Cons.; lectr. Contbr. articles to profl. jours. Recipient Moot Ct. award, Tulane Law Sch., 1968. Fellow: Am. Bar Found. (vice chair debarment and suspension com. pub. contracts sect. 1992—97, sr. vice chair alcohol beverage com., adjudication com., adminstrv. law sect.); mem.: ABA (sec. jud. conf. 1979—, standing com. on jud. selection, tenure and compensation. 1992—95, sec. jud. divsn. Nat. Conf. Adminstrv. Law Judges 1979—, chair 1999—2000, standing com. on fed. jud. improvements 2000—01, adminstrn. law sect), Nat. Conf. Bd. Contract Appeals Mems., Nat. Assn. Women Judges (founder), Prettyman-Leventhal Am. Inn of Ct. (past pres., master of bench), Am. Law Inst. (life), Am. Inns of Ct. Found. (trustee 1992—98, leadership com. 1998—), La. Bar Assn. Republican. Home: 2800 Flagmaker Dr Falls Church VA 22042-2200 Personal E-mail: jeansaralee@cs.com. *My approach to life has been "anything is possible." That removed the boundaries in my mind, so that I could move past the boundaries that might hold me back. I firmly believe in mentoring young people so that they, too, will see past boundaries real and imagined.*

COOPER, JEROME MAURICE, architect; b. Memphis, Jan. 24, 1930; s. Samuel and Bessie (Phillips) C.; m. Jean Kanter, Dec. 29, 1957; children: David Franklin, Samuel Randolph, Beth Lauren. BS, Ga. Inst. Tech., 1952, BArch, 1955; postgrad., U. Rome, Italy, 1956-57. Fulbright fellow, Rome, 1956-57; pres. Cooper, Carry & Assocs., Inc., Atlanta, 1960—, chmn. Vis. artist Am. Acad. Rome. Prin. works include Coll. of Architecture bldg. Ga. Inst. Tech., Siemens Corp. Hdqrs., Nat. Svc. Industries Corp. Hdqrs., Adtraw Corp. Hdqrs., Huntsville, Ala., Sci. Atlanta Corp. Hdqrs, Lazarus Dept. Store, Pitts., Clin. Info. Mgmt. Ctr., Drake U. Med. Ctr., Sch. of Theology, Mercer U., Green Hill Mall (AIA design award), Heritage Village at Sea Pines, Underground Atlanta, C&P Hdqrs., No. Va., Rich's Dept. Store, Northpoint Mall, Atlanta, Jordan Marsh Dept. Store, Natick Mall, Boston. Trustee Nat. Bldg. Mus. Served to lt. (j.g.) USN, 1952-54. Recipient Rothschild medal, 1985, Silver medal Atlanta chpt. AIA, 1987. Fellow AIA (pres. chpt., nat. dir., task force on ethics, task force on certification, task force on long span buildings, Silver medal firm award Atlanta chpt. 1987), Nat. Jud. Coun. Home: 1070 Judith Way NE Atlanta GA 30324-2905 Office: Cooper Carry & Assocs Inc 3520 Piedmont Rd NE Ste 200 Atlanta GA 30305-1595

COOPER, JERROLD STEPHEN, historian, educator; b. Chgo., Nov. 24, 1942; s. Emanuel Cooper and Adele (Faberson) Smith; m. Elaine Abrams, Dec. 22, 1962 (div. 1969); children: Nina Lynn, Sari Jean; m. Carol Manson Bier, Nov. 18, 1982; 1 child, Jenny Alexandra. AB, U. Calif., Berkeley, 1963, MA, 1964; PhD, U. Chgo., 1969. Asst. prof. Johns Hopkins U., Balt., 1968-74, assoc. prof., 1974-79, prof., 1979—2003, W.W. Spence prof. semitic lang., 2003—, chmn. dept. Near Eastern Studies Balt., 1983-91; acting chmn. Near Eastern Studies, 1992-93; acting chmn. classics Johns Hopkins U., Balt., 1988-91. Vis. prof. UCLA, 1975, U. Calif., Berkeley, 1981, U. Padua, Italy, 1992, U. Rome, 1998. Author: The Return of Ninurta, 1979, The Curse of Agade, 1983, Sumerian and Akkadian Royal Inscriptions, 1985; assoc. editor Jour. of Cuneiform Studies, 1972-89. NEH grantee, 1980-86, NSF grantee, 2002-2005. Mem. Am. Oriental Soc. (dir. 1982-85), Am. Schs. of Oriental Rsch. (trustee 1987-97), Internat. Assn. Assyriology (founding bd. mem. 2003—). Avocation: early music. Office: Johns Hopkins U Dept Near East Studies Baltimore MD 21218 Office Phone: 410-516-7498. E-mail: anzu@jhu.edu.

COOPER, JOEL, psychologist, educator; b. N.Y.C., Dec. 3, 1943; s. Samuel Cooper and Sarah Tobias; m. Barbara Orenstein, Dec. 17, 1966; children: Jason, Aaron, Grant. BS, CCNY, 1965; PhD in Social Psychology, Duke U., 1969. Asst. prof. psychology Princeton (N.J.) U., 1969-73, assoc. prof., 1973-78, prof., 1978—, chmn. psychology dept., 1985-92, dir. grad. studies dept. psychology, 1976-83. Chmn. Inst. Rev. Bd. Princeton U., 1974-81, 84-87, 96-99, com. appointments and advancements, com. on grad. sch.; sr. fellow East-West Population Inst., 1975. Author: Understanding Social Psychology, 1976, 5th edit., 1991, Social Psychology, 1999, Gender and the Computer: Understanding the Digital Divide, 2003; editor: Attribution Processes, Person, Perception, and Social Interaction: The Legacy of Edward E. Jones, 1998, Sage Handbook of Social Psychology, 2003; editorial bd. Jour. Personality, Jour. Exptl. Social Psychology, Social Psychology Quar.; contbr. chpts. to books in field, articles to profl. jours. Office: Princeton U Dept Psychology Green Hall Princeton NJ 08544

COOPER, JOHN, university football coach; b. Powell, Tenn., July 2, 1937; m. Helen Cooper; children: John Jr., Cindy. BS, Iowa State U., 1962. Freshman football coach Iowa State U., 1962-63; asst. football coach Oreg. State U., 1963-67; defensive coord. U. Kans., 1967-72; asst. coach U. Ky., 1972-77; coach U. Tulsa, 1977-84, Ariz. State U., 1985-87; head football coach Ohio State U., Columbus, 1987—. Coach East-West Shrine Bowl Game, Hula Bowl, Japan All-State games. Active civic orgns., Columbus, including Big Bros./Big Sisters, Alzheimer's Found., Arthur James Cancer Hosp., Children's Hosp. With US Army. Named Nat. Coach of Yr., 1986; winner Rose Ball games with Pac-10 and Big Ten conf. teams. Mem. Am. Football Coaches Assn. (past pres.). Achievements include Finalist, Paul (Bear) Bryant Coach of Year award, 1998.

COOPER, JOHN ALFRED, JR., community development company executive; b. Memphis, Sept. 13, 1938; s. John Alfred and Mildred (Borum) C.; m. Pat McInnis, Oct. 23, 1965; children: Mary Virginia, John Alfred III, Borum. Student, U. Ark., 1961. With Cherokee Village Devel. Co., Inc., 1962—, exec. v.p., 1967-68; pres. John A. Cooper Co., 1968-90, Cooper Communities Inc., 1972-90, vice chmn., 1990-91; chmn. Cooper Communities, Inc., 1991-97, pres., CEO, 1997—. Bd. dirs. 1st Nat. Bank of Sharp County, J.B. Hunt Transport Svcs., Inc. Mem.: Memphis Country, Little Rock Country. Office: Cooper Communities 903 N 47th St Rogers AR 72756-9615

COOPER, JOHN AMBROSE, management consultant, marketing professional; b. Freetown, Sierra Leone, Mar. 5, 1948; s. Daniel Philip and Nancy Etta Cooper; children: John Ambrose, Daniel Kalen. AA in Humanities, Onondaga C.C., SUNY, Syracuse, 1979; AA in Bus., Columbia (Mo.) Coll., 1984, BA in Individual Studies, 1986; MSc in Internat. Mktg., Syracuse U., 1988; BS in Indsl. Mgmt., Empire State Coll., SUNY, 1992; MBA, Syracuse U., 1996. Acct. gen. dept. City of Freetown, Sierra Leone, 1969-71; quality assurance insp., inventory control coord. Joseph Schlitz Brewing Co., Baldwinsville, N.Y., 1976-80; prin. clk. J.A. Jones Constrn. Co., Baldwinsville, 1980-82; mgmt. coord. Anheuser-Busch, Inc., Baldwinsville, 1982—. Mem. editing staff Baldwinsville (N.Y.) Eagle Newsletter. Tng. participant Resolve: A Ctr. for Dispute Settlement, Inc., Syracuse, 1982, Muscular Dystrophy Assn., Baldwinsville, N.Y. (lock-up fundraiser participant for children summer camp, 1996). Mem. Am. Mktg. Assn., Indsl. Rels. Rsch. Assn., West Indian Cultural Assn. (exec. com. 1990), Internat. Stars Soccer Orgn. (gen. sec., coach), Internat. Exhibitors Assn., Anheuser-Busch Employee Assn. (exec. bd. 1983), Hon Appointment to the rsch. bd Advisors, Am. Biographical Inst., Internat. Platform Assn., Soc. Competitive Intelligence Profls., Am. Mgmt. Assn., Eagle Club Crystal Cathedral Ministries. Roman Catholic. Avocations: competitive sports (soccer), debate, travel. Home: 111 Lafayette Rd Apt 625 Syracuse NY 13205-2936 also: One Busch Pl Saint Louis MO 63118

COOPER, JOHN ARNOLD, financial analyst; b. Detroit, Oct. 27, 1917; s. Gage Whitman and Helen Dorothy (Danger) Cooper; m. Sylvia Grace, Sept. 6, 1941 (div. 1977); 1 child, Maud Cooper Plumer; m. Virginia Bailey Svagr, Mar. 11, 1977 (dec. 1981); m. Anny Marion Van Dyke, Apr. 9, 1983. BA, Williams Coll., Williamstown, Mass., 1939; MBA, Mich. State U., 1968. CFA Inst. Chartered Fin. Analysts. Treas. Cooper Supply Co., Detroit, 1941-44, sec., 1944-56, pres., 1956-67; v.p. Texas Industries, Inc., Dallas, 1963-67; pres. Cooper, Van Dyke Assocs. Inc., Birmingham, Mich., 1970—2000; mem. Cooper, Van Dyke LLC, 2000—. Pres. Transit Mixed Concrete Inst. Met. Detroit, 1952—53, 1955—77, Constrn. Assn. Mich., 1967—68; assoc. prof. fin. Faculty Bus. Adminstrn. U. Windsor, Ont., Canada, 1977—83. Vice chair Oakland County Planning Commn., 1968—70; trustee Fin. Analysts Seminar, 1980—82; class agt. Williams Coll., 1989—94; chmn. preservation fund drive Cmty. House, Birmingham, Mich., 1995—98, fin. com. mem., 1988—2001, bd. dirs., 1996—2000. Mem.: Investment Analysts Soc. Detroit (pres. 1980—81, chmn. profl. conduct/ethics com. 1988—99), Inst. Chartered Fin. Analysts, Am. Trucking Assn. (bd. dirs. 1961—63), Mich. Trucking Assn. (bd. govs. 1958—63), Williams Club N.Y., Beta Gamma Sigma. Republican. Episcopalian. Avocations: photography, hiking, gardening, travel.

COOPER, JOHN BYRNE, JR., airline pilot; b. Balt., May 13, 1942; s. John Bryne and Mary Louise (Shaffer) C.; m. Virginia Johnson, Oct. 30, 1964 (div. 1974); children: John Byrne, Tracy Diane; m. Jane Marian Simpson, Apr. 1, 1977; children: Julie Allison, Scott David. B in Indsl. Engring., Ga. Inst. Tech., 1964. Pilot Delta Air Lines, Inc., Atlanta, 1970—2002, capt. B727, B767, L-1011 Internat., B777, 1986—, B727 line check pilot, 1988-92, lead B727 line check pilot, 1991-93, lead B767ER line check pilot, 1994—, B777 line check pilot, 1999—2002. Mem. exec. com. Homeowners Assn., Marietta, Ga., 1988, v.p. bd. dirs., 1995-96; soccer coach Metro North/East Cobb Soccer, Marietta, 1985-92. Decorated DFC, Air medals (23), Navy Commendation medal. Mem. U.S. Naval Inst., Assn. Naval Aviation, Naval Res. Assn., Tailhook Assn., Barefoot Sailing Club (fleet capt.), So. Sailing Club, Coronado 15 Nat. Assn. (bd. dirs. 1976), Beta Theta Pi. Lutheran. Avocations: tennis, sailing, skiing, golf. Personal E-mail: jbcooper2@mindspring.com.

COOPER, JOHN JOSEPH, lawyer; b. Vincennes, Ind., Oct. 20, 1924; s. Homer O. and Ruth (House) C.; m. Nathalie Brooke, 1945. AB, Stanford, 1950, LLB, 1951; LLM, U. So. Calif., 1964. Bar: Calif. 1952. Pvt. practice, San Francisco, 1951-54; counsel Shell Oil Co., L.A., 1954-61; gen. counsel, v.p. Varian Assocs., Palo Alto, 1961—90, sr. v.p., 1990, also bd. dirs. Speaker, lectr. Am. Law Inst., ABA, other legal orgns. Contbr. articles to law revs. and profl. jours. Aviator USNR, 1942-45. Mem. ABA, Calif. Bar Assn. Home: 191 Ramoso Rd Portola Valley CA 94028

COOPER, JOHN MADISON, philosophy educator; b. Memphis, Nov. 29, 1939; s. Marion Armon and Bernardine (Sheehan) C.; m. Marcia Louise Coleman, Aug. 21, 1965; children: Stephanie Coleman, Katherine Alexander. AB magna cum laude, Harvard U., 1961, PhD, 1967; BPhil, Corpus Christi Coll., Oxford, Eng., 1963. Asst. prof. philosophy and the classics Harvard U., Cambridge, Mass., 1966-71; assoc. prof. U. Pitts., 1971-76, prof., 1976-81, chmn. philosophy dept., 1977-81; prof. Princeton U., N.J., 1981—, chmn. philosophy dept., 1984-92, Stuart prof., 1998—. Author: Reason and Human Good in Aristotle, Seneca: Moral and Political Essays, Plato: Complete Works, Reason and Emotion, Knowledge, Nature, and the Good; mem. editl. bd. Am. Philos. Quar., 1977-80, History of Philosophy Quar., 1983-86, The Monist, 1987—, Ratio, 1988, Archiv für Ges. d. Phil., 1994—; contbr. articles to profl. jours. Recipient Ctr. for Advanced Studies fellow U. Ill., 1969-70, NEH fellow, 1982-83, John Simon Guggenheim fellow, 1987-88, Ctr. for Advanced Study in the Behavioral Scis. fellow, 1992-93, Am. Coun. Learned Socs. fellow, 2002-03. Fellow Am. Acad. Arts and Scis.; mem. Am. Philos. Assn. (ea. divsn. exec. com. 1984-87, chmn. com. def. profl. rights 1983-88, ea. divsn. nominating com. 1991-94, chmn. ea. divsn. program com. 1980, v.p. 1998-99, pres. 1999-2000). Home: 182 Western Way Princeton NJ 08540-7208 Office: Princeton Univ Dept of Philosophy 1879 Hall Princeton NJ 08544-1006 E-mail: johncoop@princeton.edu.

COOPER, JOHN MILTON, JR., history educator, author; b. Washington, Mar. 16, 1940; s. John Milton and Mary Louise (Porter) C.; m. Judith Karin Widerkrantz, June 9, 1962; children: John Milton III, Elizabeth Karin Doyle. AB summa cum laude, Princeton U., 1961; MA, Columbia U., 1962, PhD, 1968. Instr. history Wellesley (Mass.) Coll., 1965-67, asst. prof., 1967-70; asst. prof. history U. Wis., Madison, 1970-71, assoc. prof., 1971-76, prof., 1976-87, William Francis Allen prof. history, 1987-99, E. Gofdon Fox prof. Am. instns., 1999—, chmn. dept., 1988-91. Fulbright prof. Coun. Internat. Exch. Scholars, Moscow, 1987. Author: Vanity of Power, 1969, Walter Hines Page, 1977, Warrior and Priest, 1983, Pivotal Decades, 1990, Breaking the Heart of the World: Woodrow Wilson and the Fight for the League of Nations, 2001; editor: Causes and Consequences of World War I, 1971, The Wilson Era, 1991. Woodrow Wilson Found. fellow, 1961, NEH fellow, 1969, 91, Guggenheim Found. fellow, 1979. Mem.: Ctr. for Nat. Policy, State Hist. Soc. Wis. (bd. curators), Woodrow Wilson Birthplace Found. (hon. pres.), Coun. Fgn. Rels., So. Hist. Assn., Orgn. Am. Historians, Am. Hist. Assn., Rotary, Phi Beta Kappa. Democrat. Congregationalist. E-mail: jmcooper@facstaff.wisc.edu.

COOPER, JOSEPH, political scientist, educator; b. Boston, Sept. 10, 1933; s. Charles and Esther (Balder) Cooper; m. Frances Lorna Wollin, Aug. 24, 1965; children: Samuel Wollin, Meryl Charlotte. AB summa cum laude, Harvard U., 1955, AM, 1959, PhD, 1961. Asst. prof. govt. Harvard U., 1963-67; mem. faculty Rice U., Houston, 1967-91, prof. polit. sci., 1970-91, chmn. dept., 1967-72, Lena Gohlman Fox prof., 1978-89, dean Sch. Social Scis., 1979-88, Herbert S. Autrey prof. social scis., 1989-91, pres. Rice Inst. for Policy Analysis Sch. Social Scis., 1989-91; provost, v.p. for acad. affairs Johns Hopkins U., Balt., 1991-96, prof. dept. polit. sci., 1991—. Vis. Olin prof. polit. sci. Stanford U., 1988—89; staff dir. commn. adminstrv. rev. U.S. Ho. Reps., 1976—78; vis. prof. govt. Harvard U., 1984—85; mem. acad. adv. coun. Ctr. Congress Ind. U.; mem. editl. adv. bd. Ctr. Legis. Archives; bd. dirs. Dirksen Congl. Ctr., 1994—2000, 2002—, Consortium Social Sci. Orgns., 1994—97, Pub. Campaign, 1997—. Author: (book) The Origins of the Standing Committes and the Development of the Modern House, 1970, Congress and Its Committees, 1988; contbr. articles to profl. jours.; co-editor: (book) Sage Yearbook on Electoral Studies, 1975—82; mem. bd. editors: Congress and the Presidency, Ency. of U.S. Congress, Legis. Studies Quar., 1987—90, 2001—03, assoc. editor: Ency. of Am. Legis. Sys., Congress of U.S. 1789-1989. Mem. adv. com. Records of Congress U.S. Congress and Nat. Archives, 1995—; bd. dirs. Balt. Hebrew U., 1994—2001. Recipient Press award, Congl. Quar., 1989; fellow Brookings Rsch., Harvard U., 1959—60, Sr., NEH, 1973. Mem.: D.C. Area Polit Sci. Assn. (mem. coun. 1993—94, v.p. 1994, pres. 1996), Midwest Polit. Sci. Assn., So. Polit. Sci. Assn., Southwestern Polit. Sci. Assn. (pres. 1977), Am. Polit. Sci. Assn. (sec. 1979, program chmn. 1985, nominations chmn. 1992, exec. com. legis. studies sect. 1999—2001, chair Rosenthal prize com. 2004—05), Asia Soc. (bd. dirs. 1990—92), Jefferson Davis Assn. (dir. 1980—91), Phi Beta Kappa, Sigma Xi. Office: Dept Polit Sci Johns Hopkins Univ Baltimore MD 21218-2685 Office Phone: 410-516-4879. Business E-Mail: jcooper@jhu.edu.

COOPER, JOSEPHINE SMITH, trade association and public affairs executive; b. Raleigh, N.C., Aug. 2, 1945; d. Joseph W. and Marie (Peele) S. BA in Bus. and Econs., Meredith Coll., Raleigh, 1967; MS in Mgmt., Duke U., 1977. Program analyst Office of Air & Quality Planning and Stds. EPA, Rsch., Triangle Park, NC, 1968-78; environ. protection specialist Office of Rsch. and Devel., Washington, 1978-80; mem. profl. staff majority leader Howard H. Baker, Jr., U.S. Senate Com. on Environ. and Pub. Works, Washington, 1980-83; asst. adminstr. for external affairs EPA, Washington, 1983-85; asst. v.p. for environ. and health program Am. Paper Inst., Washington, 1985-86; sr. v.p. for policy Synthetic Organic Chem. Mfrs. Assn., Washington, 1986-88; sr. v.p., dir. environ. policy Hill & Knowlton, Inc., Washington, 1988-91; founder, dir. Capitoline Internat. Group, Ltd., Washington, 1991-92; v.p. environ. and regulatory affairs Am. Forest & Paper Assn., 1992-99; pres., CEO Alliance of Automobile Mfrs., Washington, 1999—2004; group v.p. for govt. and industry affairs Toyota Motor N.Am., 2004—. Treas. RTP Fed. Credit Union, 1969—72, pres., CEO, 1975; pres. Women's Coun. on Energy and Environment, 1986—88, Nat. Coun. on Clean Indoor Air, 1988—96; mem. nat. adv. environ. health scis. coun. NIH, 1990—94; mem. adv. com. EPA Clean Air Act, 1994—2005; liaison mem. trade and environ. policy adv. com. USTR, 1994—2002; chmn. bd. Nat. Urban Air Toxic Rsch. Ctr., 2003—; bd. dirs. Washington First Bank. Bd. visitors Duke U. Nicholas Sch. Environment, 1994—2002, Duke U. Fuqua Sch. Bus., 2004—; bd. dirs. Washington Performing Arts Soc., 2005—. Congl. fellow, 1979-80. Mem.: NAM (coun. bd. dirs. 2000—04), Orgn. of Internat. Auto Assn. (pres.), Orgn. d'Internationale Constructeurs d'Automobiles (chmn. 2003—04), Am. Soc. Assn. Execs. (bd. dirs. 2000—03), U.S. C. of C. (Com. of 100 2000—04), Women in Govt. Rels., Federally Employed Women (pres. 1972—77, treas.). Mem. Christian Ch. (Disciples Of Christ). Office Phone: 202-463-6830. Business E-Mail: jo_cooper@tma.toyota.com.

COOPER, JUDITH KASE, retired theater educator, playwright; b. Wilmington, Del., Dec. 13, 1932; d. Charles Robert and Elizabeth Edna (Baker) Kase; stepchildren: James, Elizabeth, John, Katherine, Ann, Patty, Doreen, Jeff. BA, U. Del., 1955; MA, Case Western Res. U., 1956. Tchr., dir. children's theatre Agnes Scott Coll., 1956, U. Tenn., 1957, U. Md., Germany, 1958-60, Denver Civic Theatre, Denver U., Kent Sch., 1960-61; dir. children's theatre U. N.H., Durham, 1962-69; dir. theatre resources for youth Somersworth, N.H., 1966-69; assoc. prof. theatre U. South Fla., Tampa, 1969-74, assoc. prof. edn., 1975-83, prof., 1984—99, artistic dir. ednl. theatre, 1976—99, ret., 1999. Project dir. Hillsborough County Artists-in-Schs. Evaluation and Inservice Project, 1980—82; dir. Internat. Ctr. for Studies in Theatre Edn.; mem. Nat. Theatre Conf., Coll. Fellows Am. Theatre. Author: The Creative Drama Book: Three Approaches, other books; editor: Creative Drama in a Developmental Context; Children's Theatre, Creative Drama and Learning, Drama as a Meaning Maker, Introduction to Drama Teacher Resource Guide, Interconnecting Pathways to Human Experience, Teaching the Arts Across the Disciplines; contbr. articles to profl. jours.; pub. (plays) Snow White and The Seven Dwarfs, 1960, The Emperor's New Clothes, 1966, Southern Fried Cracker Tales, 1995. Bd. dirs. Fla. Alliance for Arts Edn., sec., 1976-77, vice-chmn., 1979-82, chmn., 1982-84; chmn. Wingspread Conf. on Theatre Edn., 1977; drama adjudicator Nat. Arts Festival, Ministry of Edn., Bahamas, 1975, 76, 79, 80; regional chmn. Alliance for Arts Edn., chmn. nat. adv. coun., mem. edn. adv. com., 1986—; trustee Children's Theatre Found.; bd. dirs. Coll. Fellows Am. Theatre of J.F. Kennedy Ctr. for Performing Arts, 1991-93, Fla. Assoc. Theatre Ed., exec. dir. 1995-99, Coll. Bus., 1993—; cons. S.E. Ctr. for Edn. in Theatre, 1995, Fla. Dept. Edn., 1994-96; cons. theatre edn. and prodn.; steering com. Arts for a Complete Edn., 1991-92; mem. curriculum writing com. Fla. Dept. Edn., 1994-96. Recipient Disting. Book of Yr. award, 1989, Arts Recognition award, Arts Coun. Hillsborough County, 1995. Mem. Children's Theatre Assn. Am. (pres.-elect 1975-77, pres. 1977-79, chmn. symposia 1981-85, spl. recognition citation 1984), Am. Theatre Assn. (chief divsn. pres.'s coordinating coun. 1977-78, commn. on theatre edn. 1982—, elected), Am. Alliance for Theatre and Edn. (dir. & project dir. theatre literacy collaborative study Internat. Ctr. for Studies in Theatre Edn., Presdl. award 1992), Speech Comm. Assn. (membership dir. 1961), Southeastern Theatre Confs. (Sara Spencer award 1980), Fla. Theatre Confs. (Disting. Career award), Nat. Theatre Conf., Internat. Assn. Theatres for Children and Youth, Internat. Amateur Theatre Assn. (N.Am. bd. dirs.), Fla. Assn. for Theater Edn. (Theatre Edn. of Yr. award 1986, exec. dir. 1994-99), Arts Coun. Hillsborough County (Arts Recognition award), Children's Theatre Found. Am.(bd. trustees 1977-), Tampa Mus. Republican. Episcopalian.

COOPER, KATHLEEN BELL, federal agency administrator; b. Dallas, Feb. 3, 1945; d. Patrick Joseph and Ferne Elizabeth (McDougle) Bell; m. Ronald James Cooper, Feb. 6, 1965; children: Michael, Christopher. BA in Math. with honors, U. Tex., Arlington, 1970, MA in Econs, 1971; PhD in Econs, U. Colo., 1980. Research asst. econs. dept. U. Tex., Arlington, 1970-71; corp. economist United Banks of Colo., Denver, 1971-79, chief economist, 1980-81; v.p., sr. fin. economist Security Pacific Nat. Bank, Los Angeles, 1981-83, 1st v.p., sr. economist, 1983-85, sr. v.p., economist, 1985-86, sr. v.p., chief economist, 1986-87, exec. v.p., chief economist, 1988-90; chief economist Exxon Corp., Irving, Tex., 1990-99; chief economist, mgr. econs. & energy divsn. corp. planning Exxon Mobil Corp., 1999-2001; under sec. for econ. affairs U.S. Dept. Commerce, Washington, 2001—. Trustee Scripps Coll., 1987-2001, Com. for Econ. Devel.1993-2001; mem. Coun. on Fgn. Rels., Internat. Women's Forum. Mem. Nat. Assn. Bus. Economists (past pres. Denver and L.A. chpts.; bd. dirs. 1975-78, pres. 1985-86), Nat. Bur. Econ. Rsch. (bd. dirs. 1987-2001, exec. com., vice-chair 1999-2001), Am. Bankers Assn. (econ. adv. com. 1979-81, 86-90, chmn. 1989-90), U.S. Assn. Energy Econs. (pres. 1996), Am. Econ. Assn., Conf. Bus. Economists (tech. cons. to bus. coun. 1993-94). Office: US Dept Commerce Rm 4848 14th and Constitution NW Washington DC 20230

COOPER, KEN ERROL, retired management educator; b. Bryan, Ohio, Mar. 10, 1939; s. George Wayne and Agnes Anibel (Fisher) C.; m. Karen Cremean, June 17, 1961; children: Kristin, Andrew. BS, Bowling Green State U., 1961; MBA, Miami U., Oxford, Ohio, 1962; PhD, U. Minn., 1984. Chartered fin. cons. Instr. Miami U., 1962-63; lectr. U. Minn., 1965-67, 84-86; group v.p. Land O'Lakes, Inc., Mpls., 1967-82; v.p. fin. and adminstrn. Hamline U., 1982-84; dean Coll. Bus., Ohio No. U., Ada, 1986-90, prof., 1990-2000; prof., post chair for ethics and professions Am. Coll., Bryn Mawr, Pa., 1994-95, ret., 1995; lectr. Ohio No. U., 2003—; now lectr. in philosophy. Vis. prof. (on leave) Coll. of St. Thomas, St. Paul, 1981-82, vis. prof. mgmt. U. San Diego, 2001-02, U. Evansville, 2002—03. Trustee Westmar Coll., 1980-86; bd. dirs., sec.-treas. Acad. Mgmt., 1989-95; mem. Iowa Supreme Ct. Adv. Coun., 1972-75, North Ctrl. Devel. Found. Republican. Methodist. Office: Ohio No U Coll Bus Adminstrn Ada OH 45810

COOPER, KIM, publishing executive, writer; b. L.A. d. Barbara Cooper; children: Evel Watson, Talullah Belle. BA, U. Calif., Santa Cruz, Calif., 1988; MA, U. Calif., Santa Barbara, Calif., 1990. Exhbn. coord., archivist Mus. Contemporary Art, L.A., 1995—2000; press officer Cacophony Soc., L.A., 2000—. Editor: Lost in the Grooves: Scram's Capricious Guide to the Music You Missed, Bubblegum Music is the Naked Truth: The Dark History of Prepubescent Pop from the Banana Splits to Britney Spears (nominee Firecracker award, 2001), Scram (Factsheet 5 Editor's Choice awards, named Best of L.A., L.A. (Calif.) Weekly, 1994); actor: (plays) Institute of Mental Decay; dir.: Bubblegum Achievement Awards (The Gummys); editor: Lost in the Grooves blog, http:/blog.lostinthegrooves.com, The Catalog of Cool website, Filmnik website; author: Neutral Milk Hotel: In the Aeroplane Over the Sea; contributed: timeline to catalogue Out of Actions, Living the Good Life: The Arts & Crafts Movement in California. Bd. dir. Friends of Palace Theatre, L.A., 2001—02. Recipient Hon. Gummy award, Bubblegum Achievement Awards, 2003. Mem.: L.A. (Calif.) Cacophony Soc. (life; press officer 2000—05, Silver Lance award 2002). Avocations: thrift shopping, archaeology, spelunking, adventure dining, confectionary. Office: Scram Magazine PO Box 461626 Hollywood CA 90046 Office Phone: 323-223-2767. E-mail: scram@scrammagazine.com.

COOPER, LANGDON MCILROY, lawyer; b. Chgo., Ill., Apr. 27, 1941; s. George Langdon and Lois McIlroy Cooper; m. Mary H. Cooper, June 1964 (div.); children: Marya Ladd, Abigail Harrill. BA, Duke U., 1964; JD, U. N.C., 1969. Bar: U.S. Dist. Ct. (we., mid. and ea. dists.) N.C. 1980, U.S. Ct. Appeals (4th and 3rd cirs.), U.S. Supreme Ct. 1992, cert.: N.C. State Bar (bd. cert. bankruptcy law), Am. Bd. Cert. (bd. cert. bus. and consumer bankruptcy). Mng. dir. Alala Mullen Holland & Cooper P.A., Gastonia, NC, 1985—. Mem. panel of chpt. 7 trustees U.S. Bankruptcy Ct. (we. dist.) N.C., 1978—; lectr. in field. Contbr. articles to profl. jours. Initial dir. Jobquest program City of Gastonia, NC. Mem.: ABA, Nat. Assn. Bankruptcy Trustees, Am. Bankruptcy Inst., Gaston County Bar Assn., N.C. Bar Assn. (bd. govs. 1985—88). Office: Alala Mullen Holland & Cooper PA 301 S York St Gastonia NC 28052

COOPER, LEON N., physicist, researcher; b. NYC, Feb. 28, 1930; s. Irving and Anna (Zola) Cooper; m. Kay Anne Allard, May 18, 1969; children: Kathleen Ann, Coralie Lauren. AB, Columbia U., 1951, AM, 1953, PhD, 1954, DSc (hon.), 1973, U. Sussex, Eng., 1973, U. Ill., 1974, Brown U., 1974, Gustavus Adolphus Coll., 1975, Ohio State U., 1976, U. Pierre et Marie Curie, Paris, 1977. NSF postdoctoral fellow, mem. Inst. for Advanced Study, 1954—55; rsch. assoc. U. Ill., 1955—57; asst. prof. Ohio State U., 1957—58; assoc. prof. Brown U., Providence, 1958—62, prof., 1962—66, Henry Ledyard Goddard U. prof., 1966—74, Thomas J. Watson Sr. prof. sci., 1974—; dir. brain sci. program Inst. for Brain and Neural Sys., Providence, 1978—91; dir. Inst. for Brain and Neural Systems Brown U., Providence,

1991—. Lectr. pub. lectrs., internat. confs. and symposia; vis. prof. various univs. and summer schs.; cons. indsl., ednl. orgns.; sponsor Fedn. Am Scientists; mem. Def. Sci. Bd., 1989—93; co-chair Nester Inc.; assoc. Neurosci. Rsch. Program. Author: Introduction to the Meaning and Structure of Physics, 1968, Structure and Meaning, 1992, How We Learn, How We Remember: Toward an Understanding of Brain and Neural Systems, 1995, Memories and Memory: A Physicist's Approach to the Brain, 2000; contbr. articles to profl. jours. Recipient Nobel prize (with J. Bardeen and J.R. Schrieffer), 1972, award of Excellence, Grad. Faculties Alumni of Columbia U., 1974, Descartes medal, Acad. de Paris, U. Rene Descartes, 1976, John Jay award, Columbia Coll., 1985, award for Disting. Achievement, Columbia U., 1990, Alexander Hamilton award, Columbia Coll., 1995; fellow Alfred P. Sloan Found. rsch., 1959—66, John Simon Guggenheim Meml., 1965—66. Fellow: AAAS, Am. Acad. Arts and Scis., Am. Phys. Soc.; mem.: NAS (Comstock prize with J.R. Schrieffer 1968), Internat. Neural Network Soc., Soc. Neurosci., Am. Philos. Soc., Sigma Xi, Phi Beta Kappa. Office: Dept Physics and Neurosci Brown U Box 1843 Providence RI 02912-1843 E-mail: leon_cooper@brown.edu.*

COOPER, LYNN DALE, retired minister, retired navy chaplain; b. Aberdeen, Wash., Aug. 11, 1932; s. Lindsay Monroe and Mattie Ann (Cattron) Cooper; m. Doris Marlene Aydelott, June 2, 1956; children: Kevin Dale, Kathy Cooper O'Briant, Karen Cooper Holton. Student, Gray's Harbor Coll., 1950—51; BTh, Northwest Christian Coll., 1955; MDiv, Phillips U., 1961, D Ministry, 1977. Ordained to ministry Christian Ch., 1954. Commd lt. (j.g.) USN, 1965, advanced through grades to comdr., 1988, ret., 1988; assoc. pastor First Christian Ch., Olympia, Wash., 1955-57, min. Aline, Okla., 1957-61, Sumner, Wash., 1961-66; chaplain U.S. Navy, 1966-88; min. Cen. Christian Ch., Prosser, Wash., 1988-97. Bd. dirs. Jubilee Ministries, Prosser, Wash., 1988-96. Recipient many Navy and Marine Corps awards and medals; decorated Bronze Star medal. Mem. Mil. Chaplains Assn. U.S.A. (life), Disciples of Christ Hist. Soc. (life), Navy League of U.S. (life), Mil. Officers Assn. (life), Kiwanis (past pres. Prosser, Wash. chpt.), De Molay (past master councillor 1950—). Avocations: hiking, snowshoeing, kayaking. Home: 1818 Benson Ave Prosser WA 99350-1547

COOPER, MARGARET J., cultural organization administrator; Pres. Nat. Assn. Colored Women's Clubs, Inc. Named one of 100 Most Influential Black Americans, Ebony Mag., 2004. Office: Nat Assn Colored Womens Clubs 5808 16th St NW Washington DC 20011*

COOPER, MARGARET LESLIE, lawyer; b. Geneva, N.Y., Apr. 13, 1950; d. Jack Frederick and Barbara Ann (Hitchings) C. BA in Math., Rollins Coll., 1972; JD, Mercer U., 1976. Bar: Fla. 1976, U.S. Dist. Ct. (so. dist.) Fla. 1977, U.S. Dist. Ct. (mid. dist.) Fla. 2001, U.S. Ct. Appeals (5th cir.) 1977, U.S. Ct. Appeals (11th cir.) 1981, U.S. Supreme Ct. 03, bd. cert. civil trial advocacy: Nat. Bd. Trial Advocacy 2002; bd. cert. civil litigation and bus. litigation Fla. Bar Assn. Assoc. Jones, Foster, Johnston & Stubbs, PA, West Palm Beach, Fla., 1976-81, ptnr., 1981—. Assoc. prof. Palm Beach Jr. Coll., West Palm Beach, 1985-86. Pres. Young People's Pres.'s Coun., Norton Gallery Art, West Palm Beach, 1982—84; bd. trustees Norton Sculpture Gardens; chmn. campaign Lou Frey for Gov., Palm Beach County, 1986; bd. dirs. Planned Parenthood of Palm Beach. Named to Sports Hall Fame, Rollins Coll., 1986, Winter Park H.S. Sports Hall of Fame, 1998. Fellow: Am. Bar Found. (Best Lawyers in Am. 2003); mem.: Fla. Bar (chmn. grievance com. 15th Jud. Cir., mem. client security fund com.), Fla. Tennis Assn. (treas. 1992—98, pres.-elect. 1999), U.S. Tennis Assn. (vice chair grievance com., capt. Maria Bueno Cup Team, fin. com., adult sn. competitive com.), Women's Internat. Tennis Assn. (disciplinary rev. bd. 1985), Palm Beach Jr. League, Exec. Women Palm Beach, Palm Beach County Bar Assn., The Beach Club. Republican. Avocations: tennis, skiing. Home: 2121 S Flagler Dr West Palm Beach FL 33401-8005 Office: Jones Foster Johnston & Stubbs PA PO Box 3475 West Palm Beach FL 33402-3475

COOPER, MARVIN D., paper company executive; BS in Engineering, Virginia Polytechnical Institution and University. Prodn. mgr. Kentucky Medium Mill, Hawesville, Ky., 1980; resident mgr. Red River Mill, Campti, La.; regional mgr., paper mills Willamette Industry, Fort Mill, 1988—91, div. v.p., Fine Paper Mills, 1991—96, group v.p., Pulp and Paper Mills, 1996-97, sr. v.p., pulp and paper mills, 1997—2002; sr. v.p., Pulp, Paper, Containerboard Manufacturing and Engineering Weyerhaeuser Co., 2002—. Chmn. Northern Technical College Foundation. Office: Williamette Industries Inc 100 Kingsley Park Dr Fort Mill SC 29715-6476

COOPER, MARY LITTLE, federal judge, retired bank commission official; b. Fond du Lac, Wis., Aug. 13, 1946; AB in Polit. Sci. cum laude, Bryn Mawr Coll., 1968; JD, Villanova U., 1972; LLD (hon.), Georgian Ct. Coll., 1987. Bar. N.J. 1972. Assoc. McCarter & English, Newark, 1972-80, ptnr., 1980-84; commr. N.J. Dept. Banking, Trenton, 1984-90; assoc. gen. counsel Prudential Property & Casualty Ins. Co., Holmdel, N.J., 1991-92; judge U.S. Dist. Ct. N.J., 1992—. Chmn. bd. Pinelands Devel. Credt Bank. Bd. trustees Exec. Commn. Ethical Standards, Trenton, 1984-90, Corp. Bus. Assistance, Trenton, 1984-91, N.J. Housing & Mortgage Fin. Agy., Trenton, 1984-90, N.J. Cemetery Bd. Assn., 1984-90, N.J. Hist. Soc., 1976-79., YMCA of Greater Newark, 1973-76; mem. Supreme Ct. N.J. Civil Practice Com., 1982-84, Supreme Ct. N.J. Dist. Ethics Com., 1982-84. Fellow Am. Bar Found.; mem. ABA, N.J. Bar Assn., Princeton Bar Assn., John C. Lifland Am. Inn of Ct. Office: US Courthouse 402 E State St Ste 5000 Trenton NJ 08608-1507 Office Phone: 609-989-2105.

COOPER, MATTHEW, journalist; b. NJ; m. Madeleine Grunwald, Nov. 29, 1997; 1 child, Benjamin. B, Columbia U., 1984. Writer & rschr. US Commn. Civil Rights, 1984—86; Washington corr. Thompson Newspapers, 1986—87; editor Washington Monthly; sr. editor US News & World Report, 1989—95, Atlanta bur. chief, 1989—93, White House corr. Washington, 1993—95; sr. editor & columnist, White House Watch The New Republic, Washington, 1995—96; dep. Washington bur. chief & nat. corr. Newsweek, Washington, 1996—99; dep. Washington bur. chief Time mag., Washington, 1999—2003, White House corr., 2003—. Stand-up comedian, 1984—. Named Washington's Funniest Celebrity, DC Improv, 1998. Avocations: cooking, running, travel. Office: Time Mag 555 12th St NW Ste 600 Washington DC 20004*

COOPER, MAX DALE, pediatrician, researcher; b. Hazlehurst, Miss., Aug. 31, 1933; s. Ottis Noah and Lily (Carpenter) Cooper; m. Rosalie Lazzara, Feb. 6, 1960; children: Owen Bernard, Melinda Lee Cooper Holladay, Michael Kane, Christopher Byron. Student, Holmes Jr. Coll., 1951—52, U. Miss., 1952—54; postgrad., U. Miss. Med. Sch., 1954—55; MD, Tulane U., 1957. Diplomate Am. Bd. Pediat. Intern Saginaw (Mich.) Gen. Hosp., 1957—58; resident dept. pediat. Tulane Med. Sch., New Orleans, 1958—60; house officer Hosp. for Sick Children, London, 1960, rsch. asst. dept. neurophysiology, 1961; allergy fellow dept. pediat. U. Calif. Med. Ctr., San Francisco, 1961—62; instr. Tulane Med. Sch., New Orleans, 1962—63; med. fellow specialist U. Minn., Mpls., 1963—64, instr., 1964—66; asst. prof. dept. pediat. U. Ala., Birmingham, 1967—71, assoc. prof. dept. microbiology, 1967—71, dir. rsch. Rehab. Rsch. and Tng. Ctr., 1968—70, prof. dept. microbiology, 1971—, dir. Cell. Identification Lab., 1987—90, dir. Ctr. Interdisciplinary Rsch. in Immunological Diseases, 1987—95, dir. Divsn. Devel./Clin. Immunology, 1987—, prof. dept. medicine, 1987—, investigator Howard Hughes Med. Inst., 1988—. Sr. scientist Comprehensive Cancer Ctr., U. Ala., Birmingham, 1971—, Multipurpose Arthritis Ctr., Birmingham, 1979—, Cystic Fibrosis Rsch. Ctr., Birmingham, 1981—; dir. Cellular Immunobiology Unit of Tumor Inst. U. Ala., Birmingham, 1976—87; vis. scientist, tumor immunology unit, dept. zoology U. Coll. London, 1973—74, Inst. D'Embryologie Nogent-Sur-Marne and Inst. Pasteur, Paris, 1984—85. Co-author: Acute Hemiplegia in Childhood, 1962, Ontogeny of Immunity, 1967, Immunologic Incompetence, 1971, Immunodeficiency in Man and Animals, 1975, numerous others; editl. bd. Immunology Today, 1986, Immunodeficiency Revs., 1987—94, Clin. Immunology and Immunopathology, 1987—90, Internat. Immunology, 1988—, assoc. editor Jour. Immunology, 1972—76, 1977—79, Arthritis and Rheumatism, 1985—90, Jour. Clin. Immunology, 1979—83, co-editor Seminars in Immunopathology, 1988—91, editor Current Topics in Microbiology and Immunology, 1981—; contbr. over 450 articles to profl. jours. Trustee Leukemia Soc. Am., 1983—88; faculty rsch. assoc. Am. Cancer Soc., 1966—71; bd. sci. advisors St. Jude Hosp., Memphis, 1981—84, 1991—, Becton-Dickinson Monoclonal Antibody Ctr., 1980—90; mem. med. adv. com. Immune Deficiency Found., 1981—99; bd. sci. counselors Nat. Cancer Inst., Bethesda, Md., 1982—86, Nat. Inst. Allergy and Infectious Diseases, 1978—82, 1990—95, Inst. Merieux, Lyons, France, 1985—90, Med. Biology Inst., La Jolla, Calif., 1986; mem. internat. sci. adv. bd. Basel (Switzerland) Inst. Immunology, 1987—91; mem NIH Immunobiology Study Sect., 1974—78. Recipient tchg. trainee award, Nat. TB Assn., 1962—63, Samuel J. Meltzer Founder's award, Soc. Exptl. Biology and Medicine, 1966, Life Scis. award, 3M, 1990, Sandoz prize for immunology, 1990, award for sci. leadership in immunology, Irvington Inst., 1999; fellow postdoctoral rsch., USPHS, 1964—66. Mem.: AAUP, AAAS, NAS, Ala. Healthcare (Hall of Fame 2002), Soc. Mucosal Immunology, Am. Acad. Arts and Scis., Inst. Medicine of NAS, Am. Acad. Scis., Clin. Immunology Soc. (Achieve. award 2004), Jefferson County Med. Assn., Ctrl. Soc. Clin. Rsch., So. Soc. Pediatric Rsch. (pres. 1975), Soc. Pediatric Rsch. (v.p. 1978), Soc. Francaise d'Immunologie (life Membre d'Honneur), Internat. Soc. Devel. and Comparative Immunology, Med. Assn. State Ala., Fedn. Am. Scientists, Am. Pediatric Soc., Am. Acad. Pediat., Am. Assn. Cancer Rsch., Am. Soc. Clin. Investigation, Am. Soc. Exptl. Pathology, Am. Assn. Microbiology (named one of Best Drs. in Am. 1992, Abbot Labs. award in Clin. and Diagnostic Immunology 2001), Am. Assn. Immunologists (chmn. membership com. 1974—77, councilor 1983—86, pres. 1988—89, Lifetime Achievement award 2000), Sigma Xi, Alpha Omega Alpha. Achievements include research in developmental immunobiology with emphasis on B cell and T cell differentiation; clinical immunology with emphasis on immunodeficiency diseases and lyhmphoid malignancies. Office: Howard Hughes Med Inst U Ala Birmingham Birmingham AL 35294-0001 Office Phone: 205-934-3370. Business E-Mail: max.cooper@ccc.uab.edu.

COOPER, MICHAEL ANTHONY, lawyer; b. Passaic, New Jersey, Mar. 29, 1936; BA, Harvard U., 1957, LLB, 1960. Bar: N.Y., 1961, U.S. Supreme Ct., 1969. With Sullivan and Cromwell, N.Y.C., 1960, ptnr., 1968—2003, of counsel, 2004—. Pres. Legal Aid Soc., 1981-83, chair, pro bono net, 2000-. Co-chair Lawyers Com. for Civil Rights Under Law, 1993-95; bd. dir. Fund for Modern Ct., Vol. of Legal Svc. Fellow: Am. Coll. Trial Lawyers (bd. regents 2000—, pres.-elect 2004—05, pres. 2005—, sec. 2002—03, treas. 2003—04); mem.: ABA, Supreme Ct. Hist. Soc. (trustee 2004—), Am. Judicature Soc., Am. Law Inst., Fed. Bar Coun. (trustee 1994—2000), Assn. Bar City N.Y. (chair exec. com. 1996—97, v.p. 1997—98, pres. 1998—2000), N.Y. State Bar Assn. Office: Sullivan & Cromwell 125 Broad St Fl 28 New York NY 10004-2489 Office Phone: 212-558-3712. Business E-Mail: cooperm@sullcrom.com.

COOPER, MICHAEL R., dean; b. Bklyn., Mar. 8, 1946; s. Sam and Shirley (Boris) C.; m. Ruth Mines, Sept. 7, 1969; children: Carolyn S., Jordan D. BA, Hofstra U, 1968; PhD, Ohio State U., 1972; grad. Owners and Pres. Mgmt. Program, Harvard U., 1999. Lic. psychologist, Mass.; diplomate Am. Bd. Adminstrv. Psychology. Sr. ptnr. The Hay Group, Phila., Washington, 1980-89; pres. Hay Rsch. for Mgmt., 1985-89, Hay Strategic Mgmt. Assocs., 1987-89; chmn., CEO Opinion Rsch. Corp., Princeton, 1989—2000, also dir.; prin. Cooper Interests LLC, Princeton, 1998—; pres., CEO Tempest Software, Inc., N.Y.C., 2000; CEO Optimization Scis., San Francisco, 2001; dean Exec. Leadership Inst., Stevens Inst. Tech., Hoboken, NJ, 2002—. Bd. dirs. Xlibis, Patient Passport, Trade Web Srs., N.Y. Pvt. Placement Exch. Bd. trustees Mktg. Sci. Inst.; bd. dirs. European Info. Centre, Gordon Simmons Rsch. Group, Strategic Rsch. and Cons., Opinion Rsch. Corp.; mem. exec. bd. Sen. Evan Bayh, 1999-2000. Finalist, Entrepreneur of the Year, 1992; Eisenhower Commission: Consigned Full and Honorable Commission by President G. Ford, President R. Reagan and President G. Bush,1995. Mem. Am. Psychol. Soc., Psychologists in Mgmt. (bd. dirs. 1996-99). Office: Cooper Interests LLC 44 Coppervail Ct Princeton NJ 08540-7714 Office Phone: 609-466-9505.

COOPER, N. LEE, lawyer; m. Joy Clark; children: Clark, Catherine. BS, U. Ala., 1963, LLB, 1964. Pvt. practice, Birmingham, Ala., 1966—; founder Maynard, Cooper & Gale, P.C., Birmingham. Vice chair U.S. Congl. Commn. on Structural Alternatives for the Fed. Cts. of Appeals; dir. Lawyers Com. for Civil Rights. Articles and Notes editor Ala. Law Rev., 1962-64. Nat. bd. dirs. U. Ala.; trustee Ala. Law Sch. Found.; bd. overseers Rand Inst. for Civil Jusice. 1st lt. U.S. Army, 1964-66, capt. USAR. Fellow Am. Bar Found.; mem. ABA (chair, litig. sect. 1985-86, sec. litig. sect. 1976-78, Birmingham bar del. to ho. of deps. 1979-80, Ala. del. to ho. of dels. 1980-89, mem. drafting com. on model rules of profl. conduct 1982-84, mem. commn. on professionalism 1985-87, chair select com. on ho. of dels. 1989-90, chair ho. of dels. 1990-92, pres.-elect 1995-96, pres. 1996-97), Am. Judicature Soc. (dir.), Am. Bar Endowment (dir.), Am. Law Inst. (coun., advisor project on restatement of law governing lawyers), Ala. Bar Assn. (pres. young lawyers sect. 1974-75, Merit award 1976), Birmingham Bar Assn. (sec.-treas. 1972). Office: AmSouth Harbert Plz 1901 6th Ave N Ste 2400 Birmingham AL 35203-4604 Office Phone: 205-254-1000.

COOPER, NEAL ANDREW, lawyer; b. Chgo., Oct. 12, 1966; s. Arnold F. Sr. and Jeanne K. Cooper; m. Christine Weber, Oct. 29, 2003; 1 child, John C. BS in Acctg., James Millikin U., 1988; JD, John Marshall Law Sch., 1998. CPA Ill.; bar: Ill. 1998, Ind. 2003, Mich. 2003. Medicare audit supr. HCSC, Blue Cross Blue Shield, Chgo., 1988—98; assoc. Jenner & Block, Chgo., 1998—2001, Hall, Render, Killian, Heath & Lyman, Indpls., 2002—; ptnr. Weber & Cooper, Chgo., 2001—02. Office: Hall Render Killian Heath & Lyman 1 American Sq Ste 2000 Indianapolis IN 46282 Office Phone: 317-977-1455. Business E-Mail: ncooper@hallrender.com.

COOPER, NORTON J. (SKY COOPER), liquor, wine and food company executive; b. Phila., Aug. 16, 1931; s. Maurice J. and Elsie (Goldstein) C.; m. Kim Muller, July 7, 2001; children from previous marriage: John Amos, Rob. BA, Cornell U., 1953. With Charles Jacquin et Cie Inc., Phila., 1955—, pres., CEO, prin. owner, 1979—, Chambord et Cie, France, Doumen Canton Liquer Co. Ltd., Guandong, People's Republic of China, St Dalfour et Cie, Marmande, France; pres. Lost Horizons Wines Pty, Capetown, South Africa, Pravda Vodka Factory, Bielsko-Biala, Poland. Author: off-Broadway prodn. Ballad of Jazz Street, 1959. Served to 1st lt. AUS, 1953-55. Decorated Ordre de Chevalier de Provence. Mem. Confrerie des Chevalier, du Tastevin

COOPER, PATRICIA ANN, historian, educator; b. Blacksburg, Va., Aug. 29, 1949; d. Byron Nelson and Elizabeth (Doyne) C. BA, Wittenberg U., 1971; MA, U. Md., 1973, PhD, 1981. Post-doctoral fellow Smithsonian Inst., Washington, 1982; historian Service Employees Internat. Union, Washington, 1983; asst. prof. of history Drexel U., Phila., 1984-88, assoc. prof., 1988-93, bd. dirs. Women's Studies com., 1988-93; assoc. prof. history and women's studies U. Ky., Lexington, 1993—, dir. women's studies program, 1994-98. Vis. sr. lectr. Centre for Study Social History, U. Warwick, Coventry, England, 1991, assoc. prof. U. Iowa, Iowa City, 1991. Author: Once a Cigar Maker: Men, Women and Work Culture in American Cigar Factories 1900-1919, 1987. Bd. dirs. U. City Arts League, Phila., 1987-88, Women Against Abuse, Phila., 1992-93. U.S. Dept. Labor grantee, 1979-80; recipient Drexel U. Research Scholar award 1987; NEH/Mellon fellow, 1989. Mem. Orgn. Am. Historians, Am. Hist. Assn., Pa. Hist. Soc., Oral History in the Mid-Atlantic Region (pres., 1983), Oral History Assn., Labor and Working Class History Assn. (bd. dirs. 2000—). Office: Univ Ky Dept History and Politics Dept History Lexington KY 40506-0001 E-mail: pacoop@pop.uky.edu.

COOPER, PAUL, retired mechanical engineer, science association director, researcher; b. Mt. Holly, N.J., May 21, 1934; s. Frederick and Katherine Lena (Sixt) C.; m. Therese Adams, Apr. 11, 1959; children: Margaret Mary, Gregory, Timothy Richard, Peter Dunstan. BSME, Drexel U., 1957; MSME, MIT, 1959; PhD in Engring., Case Western Res. U., 1972. Registered profl. engr., Ohio. Rsch. asst. MIT, Cambridge, 1957-59; instr. Case Western Res. U., Cleve., 1968, 72; fluids engring. specialist TRW Inc., Cleve., 1959-77; rschr., sr. staff Ingersoll-Rand Rsch., Inc., Princeton, N.J., 1977-85; dir. hydraulic tech. Ingersoll-Rand Co., Phillipsburg, N.J., 1986-87, dir. R & D Pump Group, 1987-92; dir. advanced tech. Ingersoll-Dresser Pump Co., Phillipsburg, N.J., 1992-99. Mem. adv. bd. Internat. Pump Symposium, Tex. A&M U., 1983-99; bd. dirs. R&D Coun. N.J., 1987-92. Co-editor: Pump Handbook, 3d edit., 2001; contbr. articles to profl. jours. Recipient George Stephenson Rsch. prize Instn. of Mech. Engrs., London, 1984. Fellow ASME (exec. com. fluids engring. divsn. 1982-87, fluid machinery design award 1992, Henry R. Worthington medal 1993, Robert Henry Thurston lectr. 1995, Fluids Engring. award 2002); mem. Soc. Petroleum Engrs., Sigma Xi, Pi Tau Sigma, Tau Beta Pi. Episcopalian. Achievements include patents relating to aircraft fuel pumps and commerical industrial pumps. Home: 415 Pennington Titusville Rd Titusville NJ 08560-2012 E-mail: paul.cooper1@att.net.

COOPER, PAUL DOUGLAS, lawyer; b. Kansas City, Mo., July 22, 1941; s. W.W. and Emma Marie (Ringo) C.; m. Elsa B. Shaw, June 15, 1963 (div. 1991); children: Richard, Dean; m. Kay J. Rice, Aug. 30, 1992 (div. 2004); 1 child, Natanya BA in English, U. Mich., 1963; LLB, U. Calif., 1966. Bar: Colo. 1966, U.S. Dist. Ct. Colo. 1966, U.S. Ct. Appeals (10th cir.) 1967, U.S. Supreme Ct. 1979. Dep. dist. atty., Denver, 1969-71; asst. U.S. atty. Dist. of Colo., 1971-73; ptnr. Yegge, Hall & Evans, Denver, 1973-80; pres., dir. Cooper & Kelley PC, Denver, 1980-94, Cooper & Clough PC, Denver, 1994—. Faculty trial practice seminar Denver U. Law Sch., 1982; spl. asst. U.S. atty. Dist. of Colo., 1973-75; spl. prosecutor Mar. 1977 term, Garfield County Grand Jury; pres. Bow Mar Owners, Inc., 1976-77; mem. English adv. bd. U. Mich., 2000—. Mem. English adv. bd. Univ. Mich., 2000—. Recipient Spl. Commendation award for outstanding svc., 1972. Mem. ABA, Am. Bd. Trial Advocates, Colo. Bar Assn. (interprofl. com., bd. govs.), Denver Bar Assn. (trustee, 1st v.p. 1982-83), Colo. Med. Soc. (chmn. interprofl. com., Denver bar liaison com), Internat. Assn. Def. Counsel (exec. com. 1989-92). Republican. Home: 11571 Eliot Ct Westminster CO 80234-1665 Office: 1512 Larimer St Ste 600 Denver CO 80202-1610 Office Phone: 303-607-0077. Business E-Mail: pcooper@cooper-clough.com.

COOPER, PAULA, art dealer; b. Mass., Mar. 14, 1938; Student, Pierce Coll., Athens, Greece, Sorbonne, Paris, Goucher Coll., Inst. Fine Arts, NYU; DFA (hon.), R.I. Sch. Design, 1995. Asst. World House Galleries, N.Y.C., 1959-61; pvt. dealer, 1962-63; with Paula Johnson Gallery, N.Y.C., 1964-65; dir. Park Place Gallery, N.Y.C., 1965-67, Paula Cooper Gallery, N.Y.C., 1968—. Chmn. bd. dirs. Kitchen Ctr., N.Y.C., 1985-95. Named honoree, N.Y. Studio Sch., 2001; recipient Art Table award for disting. svc. to the visual arts, 2001. Mem.: Art Dealers Assn. Am. (bd. dirs. 1982—86, 1988—90, 1997—2000, v.p. bd. dirs. 1997—2000), Art Students League. Office: Paula Cooper Gallery 534 W 21st St New York NY 10011-2812 Office Phone: 212-255-1105. Office Fax: 212-255-5156.*

COOPER, PEGGY (MARY MARGARET), artist, educator, poet, composer, choreographer; b. Huntington, W.Va., Sept. 30, 1941; d. James Edwin and Lois Lucille (Sweeney) Hedger; m. Ralph Harold Gebhard, June 9, 1962 (div. July 1981); children: Stephan Marc, Timothy Michael, Peter Thomas, Christopher Todd; m. Earl Lee Cooper, Apr. 1, 1983. Student, Hamline U., St. Paul, 1960-63; BA cum laude, Drew U., Madison, N.J., 1965; MA, Pacific Oaks Coll., Pasadena, 1991; Waldorf Tchr. Cert., Antioch New Eng. Grad. Sch., 1996. Founding tchr. Creative Arts Workshop, Ill., 1968-75; artistic dir. Comedia Dance Co., 1968—84; artist-in-residence Colo. Coun. on Arts and Humanities, 1976-77; founding tchr. Holly/Lamar Sch. of the Arts, Colo., 1978-81; arts dir. Tom Sawyer, Pasadena, 1988-90; tutor Pasadena City Coll., 1984-90; founding tchr. Children's Garden, Madison, Wis., 1991—. Area coord. Joseph Chilton Pearce, So. Calif., 1986-91 Artist paintings: Goddess series, 1987 (gallery award), Eternal Madonna, 1988; composer children's opera: singer Luminous Pearl, 2000; composer, poet: Singing the Spiral, 2001; poet, illustrator: Colors are Children of the Sun, 2002; poet, illustrator, composer The Story of Mother Turtle, 2005. Audition com. Colo. Coun. on Arts and Humanities, Denver, 1978-80; vol. asst. Richards Inst. Ednl. Rsch., 1985-90; adv. bd. Chgo. Indian Village, 1972-75; gray lady ARC, 1958-70; vol. Children's Theater of Madison, 1993—, Elvhjem Mus. Art, 2000—; singer Madison Symphony Chorus, 1994—, Winds of So. Wis., 1998—; presenter Children's Mus. Peace Day, 1996-99; spkr., writer Waldorf Without Walls, 1996—; bd. dirs., singer Madison Chamber Choir, 1992—; singer, dancer Madison Early Music Festival, 2000—, Isthmus Vocal Ensemble, 2003—; mentor Oak Song Sch., Madison, Three Rivers Sch., La Cross, 2001-. Richards Inst. scholar, 1986, Pasadena Art Club scholar, 1988, Pasadena City Coll. scholar, 1988, recipient choral arts award, 1989; named Outstanding Young Woman, Colo., 1979. Democrat. Methodist. Avocations: gourmet cooking, gardening, felting, marionette craft, storytelling. Home and Office: 405 Stang St Madison WI 53704 Office Phone: 608-242-1471. Personal E-mail: ecooper@uwc.edu.

COOPER, R. JOHN, III, lawyer; b. East Orange, NJ, Mar. 2, 1942; s. Russell John and Cynthia Rhe (Runser) C.; m. Unni Irene Langaanes, June 20, 1964; children: Kirsten Elizabeth, R. John IV. AB, Amherst Coll., 1964; postgrad., U. Oslo, 1965; JD, Harvard U., 1968. Chief law clk. Supreme Jud. Ct. Mass., Boston, 1968-69; assoc. Cravath, Swaine & Moore, N.Y.C., 1969-77; ptnr. Casey Lane & Mittendorf, N.Y.C., 1977-82; gen. counsel video group Time Inc., N.Y.C., 1982-84; exec. v.p., gen. counsel, sec. Young & Rubicam, Inc., N.Y.C., 1984-94, also bd. dirs.; of counsel Hogan & Hartson, LLC, N.Y.C., 1995-2000, 2004—; exec. v.p., gen. counsel, mng. dir. N.Am. hdqrs. Havas S.A., Paris, 2000—03. Bd. dirs. Dentsu Young & Rubicam Partnerships, N.Y.C., Tokyo, DWD, Tokyo, Y&R Sovero, Moscow; pres. Interweave, 2003—. Editor: Cablespeech, 1983 Vestry Christ Ch., Short Hills, N.J., 1978-82, 99-02, lay min., 1980—; trustee N.J. Shakespeare Fest, 1986; chmn. Millburn-Short Hills Cable TV Com., 1986-94; prof. Salzburg Seminars, Austria, 1986; pres. Juniper Point Village Improvement Soc., Boothbay Harbor, Maine, 1997-99, Interweave, 2004—. Amherst Coll. fellow, Oslo, Norway, 1964-65 Mem. ABA (governing com., forum com. on sports and entertainment industries 1983-86), Assn. Bar City N.Y. (mem. antitrust and trade regulation com. 1982-84, corp. law depts. com. 1986-92), Am. Assn. Advt. Agys. (govt. rels. com. 1986-94), Short Hills (N.J.) Club, Boothbay Harbor Yacht Club (Maine), Harvard Club. Republican. Episcopalian. Home: 9 East Ln Short Hills NJ 07078-3202 E-mail: john.cooper@havas.com.

COOPER, REGINA CAROL, history educator; b. Calico Rock, Ark., Nov. 24, 1965; d. William Jefferson Cooper and Lovella Cooper (Gillihan) Landsrud. BS in Edn., Ark. State U., 1988, MA in Polit. sci., 1992; postgrad., So. Ill. U., 1997. Cert. tchr. Ark. Social sci. tchr. Ozarka Coll., Melbourne, Ark., 1993—96; reporter, staff writer White River Current, Calico Rock, 1997—2001; history tchr. Festus (Mo.) R-6 Pub. Schs., 2001—. Mem. Stratford Hall-Monticello Summer Seminar for Tchrs., 2005. Sec., bd. dirs. Calico Rock C. of C., 1998—99. Recipient Merit award, Ark. Press Assn., 2001, Tchr. Appreciation award, Mo. Scholars Acad., 2002, Summer Tchr. Inst. award, NEH, 2002. Mem.: NEA, Am. Hist. Assn. (presenter ann. conf. 2002), Nat. Coun. Social Studies. Democrat. Avocations: travel, fly fishing, photography. Office: Festus Sr HS 501 Westwind Dr Festus MO 63028 Office Phone: 636-937-5410.

COOPER, REGINA GREER, librarian; b. New Albany, Miss., May 24, 1953; d. James Norris Greer and Billie Margaret (Lokey) Benefield; m. William Henry Cooper, Jr., Nov. 12, 1977; children: William Greer, Benjamin Edward. BA, U. Miss., 1975; MLS, Vanderbilt U., 1976. Asst. catalager Ref. Theol. Sem., Jackson, Miss., 1976-77; catalog and reference libr. Miss. Coll., Clinton, 1977-78; reference libr. Wheeler Basin Regional Libr., Decatur, Ala., 1978-80, Huntsville (Ala.)-Madison County Pub. Libr., 1981-83, head collection dept., 1983—2001, assoc. dir., 2001—. Cons. to libr. com. Westminster Christian Acad., Huntsville, 1986-88. Assoc. editor Ala. Libr., 1983-84. Co-chmn. music performance Panoply of Arts, Huntsville, 1988. Mem. ALA, Southeastern Libr. Assn., Ala. Libr. Assn. (co-chmn. conv. 1986-87, v.p. 1988-89, pres. 1989-90, sec. pub. libr. adminstrn. div. 1987-88), Alpha

Lambda Delta, Kappa Delta Pi, Phi Kappa Phi, Beta Phi Mu. Presbyterian. Avocations: music, reading, tennis, sewing, cooking. Office: Huntsville-Madison County Pub Libr 915 Monroe St SW Huntsville AL 35801-5007 Office Phone: 205-532-5954.

COOPER, REGINALD RUDYARD, orthopedic surgeon, educator; b. Elkins, W.Va., Jan. 6, 1932; s. Eston H. and Kathryn (Wyatt) C.; m. Jacqueline Smith, Aug. 22, 1954; children: Pamela Ann, Douglas Mark, Christopher Scott, Jeffrey Michael. BA with honors, W.Va. U., 1952, BS, 1953; MD, Med. Coll. Va., 1955; MS, U. Iowa, 1960. Diplomate Am. Bd. Orthopedic Surgeons (examiner 1968-70). Orthopedic surgeon U.S. Naval Hosp., Pensacola, Fla., 1960-62; assoc. in orthopedics U. Iowa Coll. Medicine, Iowa City, 1962-65, asst. prof. orthopedics, 1965-68, assoc. prof. orthopedics, 1968-71, prof. orthopedics, 1971—, chmn. orthopedics, 1973-99, prof. emeritus orthopaedics, 2003—. Rsch. fellow orthopedic surgery Johns Hopkins Hosp., Balt., 1964-65; exch. fellow to Britain for Am. Orthopedic Assn., 1969. Trustee Jour. Bone and Joint Surgeons, 1989-94, chmn. 1993-94. Trustee Nat. Easter Seals Rsch. Found., 1977-81, chmn., 1979-81. Served to lt. comdr. USN, 1960—62. Mem. Iowa, Johnson County Med. Socs., Orthopedic Rsch. Soc. (sec.-treas. 1970-73, pres. 1974-75), Am. Acad. Orthopedic Surgeons (Kappa Delta award for outstanding rsch. in orthopedics 1971), Can. Orthopedic Assn., Am. Orthopedic Assn., N.Y. Acad. Sci., Assn. Bone and Joint Surgeons, AMA, Am. Rheumatism Assn., Am. Acad. Cerebral Palsy, Am. Acad. Orthopedic Surgeons (chmn. exams. com. 1978-82, sec. 1982, 2d v.p. 1985-86, 1st v.p. 1986-87, pres. 1987-88, ortho residency rev. com. 1989-95, chmn. 1993-95). Avocations: travel, photography, anthropology, history. Home: 201 Ridgeview Ave Iowa City IA 52246-1625 Office: U Iowa Hosps & Clinics 450 Newton Rd Iowa City IA 52242

COOPER, RICHARD ALAN, lawyer; b. Hattiesburg, Miss., July 19, 1953; s. H. Douglas and Elaine (Reece) C. BA, BS, U. Ark., Little Rock, 1976; JD, Washington U., St. Louis, 1979. Bar: Mo. 1979, Ill. 1980, U.S. Dist. Ct. (ea. dist.) Mo. 1980, U.S. Dist. Ct. (so. dist.) Ill. 1988. Law clk. U.S. Dist. Ct., St. Louis, 1979-80; assoc. William R. Gartenberg, St. Louis, 1980-81, Davis, Reid, Murphy, Tobben & Cooper, St. Louis, 1983-87, ptnr., 1987-88, Law Office Terry Sharp, P.C., 1988-89; pvt. practice, 1989-90; ptnr. Danis & Boyce, 1990—93, Danis, Cooper, Cavanagh & Hartweger, LC, 1994—98; CFO MedCard Am., Inc., 1997-99; pvt. practice, 1999—. Liaison to Washington U. Sch. Law, Mo. Assn. Trial Attys., St. Louis, 1983-85; presenter in field. Bus. mgr. Urban Law Jour., 1978-79; editor Bankruptcy Law Reporter, 1983-88, co-mgr., editor, 1984-88; author: supplement to Missouri Desk Book Civil Procedure, 2000, 04; co-author numerous seminars; contbg. author: Missouri CLE Deskbook Civil Procedure on Rule 76, Executions; spkr. in field Recipient Milton F. Napier trial award Lawyers Assn. St. Louis, 1979, Outstanding Sr. Bus. Major award Wall St. Jour., 1976. Mem. Mo. Bar Assn., Boulder Yacht Club (commodore 1998-99), Commonwealth Yacht Club. Avocation: sailing. Office: Law Offices Richard Alan Cooper 2379 Cedar Dale Ct Maryland Heights MO 63043 Office Phone: 314-579-2422. Business E-Mail: richard@richardalancooperattorney.com.

COOPER, RICHARD ALAN, hematologist, benefits compensation analyst; b. Milw., Sept. 23, 1936; s. Peter and Annabelle (Schlomovitz) C.; m. Jaclyn Koppel, June 22, 1958 (dec.); children: Stephanie, Jonathan; m. Andrea Pastor, Aug. 20, 1988. BS, U. Wis., 1958; MD, Washington U., St. Louis, 1961. Intern Harvard U. med. svcs. Boston City Hosp., 1961-63, resident in medicine, 1965-66, fellow in hematology Thorndike Meml. Lab., 1966-69; asst. prof. medicine Harvard U. Med. Sch., 1969-71; chief hematology divsn. Thorndike Meml. Lab. and Harvard Med. Svcs., Boston City Hosp., 1969-71; prof. medicine, dir. Cancer Ctr., chief hematology-oncology sect. U. Pa., Phila., 1971-85; prof. medicine, exec. v.p., dean Med. Coll. Wis., Milw., 1985-94, dir. health policy inst., 1992—2005; prof. medicine Leonard Davis Inst., U. Pa., Phila., 2005—. Mem. editl. bd. Blood, 1979-84, Lipid Research, 1983-84. Served with USPHS, 1963-65. NIH grantee. Mem. Am. Soc. Hematology, Am. Fedn. Clin. Rsch., Am. Soc. Clin. Investigation, Assn. Am. Physicians, Am. Clin. Climatol. Assn., Phi Beta Kappa, Alpha Omega Alpha. Office: 3641 Locust Wake Philadelphia PA 19104-6218 Office Phone: 215-746-3173. Business E-Mail: cooperra@wharton.upenn.edu.

COOPER, RICHARD CASEY, lawyer; b. Tulsa, Jan. 20, 1942; s. Winston Churchill and Frances Margaret (Coppinger) Cooper; m. Ireen Lysbeth Evans, Nov. 24, 1965; children: Christopher Casey, Kimberly Ireen. BSBA, U. Tulsa, 1965, JD, 1967. Bar: Okla. 1967, U.S. Dist. Ct. (no., ea. and we. dists.) Okla. 1967, U.S. Ct. Mil. Appeals 1967, U.S. Ct. Appeals (10th cir.) 1972. Assoc. Boesche, McDermott & Eskridge, Tulsa, 1972-76, ptnr., 1977-92, mng. ptnr., 1990—2001, Cooper, McKinsey & Woosley, Tulsa, 2001—. Editor-in-chief: Tulsa Law Jour., 1967. Counsel Tulsa Philharm. Orch., 1990—92; trustee Mervin Bovaird Found., Tulsa, 1991—, pres., 1995—; trustee Philbrook Mus. Art, 1997—. Tulsa Opera, 2000—, Bacone Coll., 2001—. Lt. USNR, 1967—71, mil. judge JAGC USNR, 1970—71. Recipient Order of Curule Chair, 1967; Villard Martin scholar, U. Tulsa, 1967. Mem.: ABA, Tulsa County Bar Assn., Okla. Bar Assn., So. Hills Country Club. Republican. Avocations: fly fishing, travel. Home: 2923 E 58th St Tulsa OK 74105-7453 Office: Cooper McKinney and Woosley 401 S Boston Ave Tulsa OK 74103

COOPER, RICHARD CRAIG, lawyer; b. Pittsfield, Mass., July 9, 1941; s. John Bradley and Agnes Hall (Thomson) C.; divorced; children— Jeffrey, Scott, Ethan. B.E., Yale U., 1963, LL.B., 1966. Bar: N.J. 1967. Assoc. McCarter & English, Newark, 1966-72, mem. firm, 1972— . Founding mem. bd. dirs. Craig Sch., Rockaway, N.J.; panel of arbitrators Am. Arbitration Assn. Mem. ABA, Am. Judicature Soc., Supreme Ct. Hist. Soc., Essex County Bar Assn., Morris County Bar Assn., N.J. Bar Assn., Soc. Mayflower Descendants, Essex. Club (Newark), Yale of Cen. N.J. Club, Salmagund Club. Presbyterian. Home: 39 North Ter Maplewood NJ 07040-1378 Office: McCarter & English 4 Gateway Ctr 100 Mulberry St Newark NJ 07102-4004

COOPER, RICHARD F., lawyer; b. Jacksonville, Tex., 1951; BA, U. Ark., 1974, JD, 1977. Bar: Ark. 1977. Gen. counsel Ark. Best Corp., Ft. Smith, Ark., 1986—, sec., 1987—, v.p. risk mgmt., 1991—95, v.p. adminstrn., 1995—2004, sr. v.p. adminstrn., 2004—. Office: Ark Best Corp 3801 Old Greenwood Rd PO Box 10048 Fort Smith AR 72917-0048 Office Phone: 479-785-6130. Office Fax: 479-785-6124. E-mail: rcooper@arkbest.com.*

COOPER, RICHARD LEE, newspaper editor, journalist; b. Grand Rapids, Mich., Dec. 8, 1946; s. Harold Ralph and Elizabeth (DeSchipper) C.; m. Carol Jean Bonjernoor, Sept. 5, 1968; children— Jason Adam, Jessica Lynne. Student, Grand Rapids Jr. Coll., 1965-67; BA, Mich. State U., 1969. Reporter Rochester (N.Y.) Times-Union, 1969-77; reporter Phila. Inquirer, 1977—, Neighbors editor, 1983—, asst. city editor, 1988-91, Main Line editor, 1991—; editor Main Line & Del. County Neighbors, 1993—, Main Line, Del. County and Chester County Neighbors, 1995—, asst. regional editor, 1997-99; editor News Innovations, 1999—; rsch. svcs. dir. Phila. Newspapers, Inc., 2001. Instr. journalism Temple U., 1980— Recipient N.Y. State Asso. Press Spot News First Place award, 1972, 76; Pulitzer prize for gen. local reporting, 1972; Distinguished Alumni award Grand Rapids Jr. Coll., 1974; Outstanding Contbn. in Pub. Info. award N.Y. State Bar Assn., 1977; 1st prize for investigative reporting Gannett News, 1977; Mich. Journalism fellow, 1990—. Mem. Pen and Pencil Club, Swan Creek Sailing Assn., Chesapeake Bay Triton Fleet, Rock Hall Sailing Club, Sigma Delta Chi. Presbyterian. Office: Phila Inquirer 400 N Broad St Philadelphia PA 19130-4099 Office Phone: 215-854-4824.

COOPER, RICHARD MELVYN, lawyer; b. Phila., Nov. 13, 1942; s. Arthur Martin and Sophia Phyllis (Gottlieb) C.; m. Sabina Abbe Karp, June 12, 1965 (div. 1978); children: Alexander, Stephanie; m. Judith Carole Areen, Feb. 17, 1979; children: Benjamin, Jonathan. BA summa cum laude, Haverford Coll., 1964; BA 1st class, Oxford U., 1966, MA, 1970; JD summa cum laude, Harvard U., 1969. Bar: D.C. 1970, U.S. Ct. Appeals (5th, 6th and 9th cirs.) 1988, U.S. Ct. Appeals (10th cir.) 1982, U.S. Ct. Appeals (11th cir.) 1984, U.S. Ct. Appeals (fed. cir.) 1985, U.S. Ct. Appeals (4th cir.) 1997, U.S. Supreme Ct. 1973. Law clk. to Justice William J. Brennan, Jr. U.S. Supreme Ct., Washington, 1969-70; sr. lectr. Law Devel. Ctr., Kampala, Uganda, 1970-71; assoc. Williams, Connolly & Califano, Washington, 1971-77; chief counsel FDA, Rockville, Md., 1977-79; ptnr. Williams & Connolly, LLP, Washington, 1980—; mem. exec. com. Williams & Connolly, Washington, 1983-84, 89-92. Sr. mem. Office Energy Policy and Planning, Exec. Office of Pres., Washington, 1977; adj. prof. Georgetown U. Law Ctr., Washington, 1987-92, 96; mem. Adminstrv. Conf. U.S., 1978-79, Jud. Conf. D.C., Washington, 1979; mem. Adv. Panel on Strategies for Med. Tech. Assessment, Washington, 1980-81; mem. coms. NAS, 1980-83, 87-90. Editor: Food and Drug Law, 1991; co-editor: Fundamentals of Law and Regulation, 1997; contbr. articles to profl. jours. Chief counsel credentials com. Dem. Nat. Conv., Washington and N.Y.C., 1976; adv. bd., Jelleff Boys and Girls Club, Washington, DC, 1993-2003; bd. mgrs. Haverford Coll., 1997—; Georgetown Univ. Law Ctr. Supreme Ct. Inst.; co-chmn. Finance Com., 2000-; bd. dir., Good Shepherd Ministries, Inc., Washington, DC, and member, Exec. Com., 2001-; Washington Shakespeare Co., 2004- Rhodes Trust scholar 1964; recipient FDA Award of Merit, 1979. Jewish. Office: Williams & Connolly 725 12th St NW Washington DC 20005-5901 E-mail: rcooper@wc.com.

COOPER, RICHARD NEWELL, economist, educator; b. Seattle, June 14, 1934; s. Richard Warren and Lucile (Newell) C.; m. Carolyn Jane Cahalan, June 5, 1956 (div. 1980); children: Laura Katherine, Mark Daniel; m. Ann Lorraine Hollick, Jan. 1, 1982 (div. 1994); m. Jin Chen, Oct. 13, 2000; children: William Chen, Jennifer. AB, Oberlin Coll., 1956, LLD (hon.), 1978; MSc, London Sch. Econs., 1958; PhD, Harvard U., 1962; MA (hon.), Yale U., 1966; D (hon.), U. Paris II, 2000. Sr. staff economist Coun. Econ. Advisers, 1961-63; asst. prof. econs. Yale U., 1963-65, prof., 1966-77, provost, 1972-74; dep. asst. sec. state internat. monetary affairs Dept. State, 1965-66, undersec. for econ. affairs, 1977-81; prof. econs. Harvard U., Cambridge, Mass., 1981—. Chmn. Fed. Res. Bank Boston, 1990-92; chmn. Nat. Intelligence Coun., 1995-97; bd. dirs. Inst. Internat. Econs., CNA Corp., Global Devel. Network; mem. Trilateral Commn. Author: Economics of Interdependence, 1968, Currency Devaluation in Developing Countries, 1971, Economic Policy in an Interdependent World, 1986, The International Monetary System, 1987, Economic Stabilization and Debt in Developing Countries, 1992; author: (with others) Boom, Crisis and Adjustment, 1993; author: Environmental and Resource Policies for the World Economy, 1994; editor, contbr.: A Reordered World, 1973, The International Monetary System under Flexible Exchange Rates, 1982, Can Nations Agree?, 1989, Trade Growth in Transition Economies, 1997, What the Future Holds, 2002; contbr. articles to profl. jours. Trustee Oberlin Coll., 1993-98. Fellow Am. Acad. Arts and Scis.; mem. Am. Econ. Assn., Coun. Fgn. Rels. Office: Harvard U Weatherhead Ctr Internat Affairs 1737 Cambridge St Cambridge MA 02138-3016 E-mail: rcooper@fas.harvard.edu.

COOPER, RICHARD S., lawyer; BA cum laude, Syracuse U.; JD cum laude, Georgetown U., 1981. Bar: Ohio 1981. Bd. dirs. Habitat for Humanity, Cleve., The Cleve. Food Bank, Am. Heart Assn., Cleve. Named Ohio Super Lawyer, Cin. Mag., 2004—05; named one of Best Lawyers in Am., 1994—2005. Mem.: ABA, Cleve. Bar Assn., Ohio Bar Assn. Office: McDonald Hopkins Co LPA 600 Superior Ave E Cleveland OH 44114

COOPER, RICKEY EUGENE, writer, educator; b. Stockton, Calif., May 27, 1946; s. Robert Evertt and Barbara Louise Cooper. AA in Physics, San Joaquin Delta Jr. Coll., 1970; student, Calif. State U., Fresno, 1973. File and unit clk. Stockton (Calif.) State Hosp., 1974-75; billing unit supr. Divsn. Substance Abuse, Sacramento, 1976-78; bus. mgr. Nat. Socialist White People's Party, Arlington, Va., 1978-80; med. transcriptionist Georgetown U. Hosp., Washington, 1980-82, Silas B. Hays Army Cmty. Hosp., Ft. Ord, Calif., 1983-85, Hood River (Oreg.) Meml. Hosp., 1985-87, Columbia Gorge Orthopedics, Hood River, Oreg., 1986-88, Emanuel Hosp., Portland, Oreg., 1988-98, Webb & Assocs., Portland, Oreg., 98-99, Rodeer Sys., Portland, Oreg., 1999-2000, N.W. Mediscript, Kennewick, Wash., 2000—01. Spokesperson Nat. Socialist Vanguard. Sgt. USAF, 1964-68. Office: Nat Socialist Vanguard PO Box 328 The Dalles OR 97058 E-mail: rcooper@gorge.net.

COOPER, ROBERT E., lawyer; b. Sept. 6, 1939; AB, Northwestern Univ., 1961; LLB, Yale Univ., 1964. Bar: Calif. 1965. Joined Gibson Dunn & Crutcher LLP, 1964—, now ptnr. litig. dept. LA. Bd. dir. Nat. Inst. of Transplantation Found., 1989; sec. Citizens Rsch. Found., 1980—90; mem. Calif. Law Revision Commn., 1996—99. Mem. Yale Law Jour., 1963—64, contbg. author Antitrust Advisor, 1971. Fellow: Am. Coll. Trial Lawyers; mem.: ABA, Los Angeles County Bar Assn. (vice-chmn., criminal practice and procedure com., antitrust law sect. 1984—86), US Courts for Ninth Cir., Phi Beta Kappa, Order of Coif. Office: Gibson Dunn & Crutcher LLP 333 S Grand Ave Los Angeles CA 90071-3197 Office Phone: 213-229-7179. Office Fax: 213-229-6179. Business E-Mail: rcooper@gibsondunn.com.

COOPER, ROBERT ELBERT, state supreme court justice; b. Chattanooga, Oct. 14, 1920; s. John Thurman and Susie Inez (Hollingsworth) C.; m. Catherine Pauline Kelly, Nov. 24, 1949; children: Susan Florence Cooper Hodges, Bobbie Cooper Martin, Kelly Ann Smith, Robert Elbert Jr. BA, U. N.C., 1946; JD, Vanderbilt U., 1949. Bar: Tenn. 1948. Assoc. Kolwyck and Clark, 1949-51; ptnr. Cooper and Barger, 1951-53; asst. atty. gen. 6th Jud. Ct. Tenn., 1951-53; judge 6th Jud. Circuit Tenn., 1953-60, Tenn. Ct. Appeals, 1960-70, presiding judge Eastern divsn., 1970-74; justice Tenn. Supreme Ct., 1974-90, chief justice, 1976-77, 84-85. Chmn. Tenn. Jud. Coun., 1967-90; chmn. Tenn. Code Commn., 1976-77, 84-85; mem. Tenn. Jud. Standards Commn., 1971-77. Mem. exec. bd. Cherokee coun. Boy Scouts Am., 1960-64; bd. dirs. Met. YMCA, 1956-65, St. Barnabas Nursing Home and Apts. for Aged, 1966-69. With USNR, 1941-46. Recipient Nat. Heritage award Downtown Sertoma Club, Chattanooga, 1989. Mem. Am., Tenn., Chattanooga bar assns., Conf. Chief Justices, Phi Beta Kappa, Order of Coif, Kappa Sigma, Phi Alpha Delta. Clubs: Signal Mountain Golf and Country, Masons (33 deg.), Shriners. Democrat. Presbyterian. Home and Office: 196 Woodcliff Cir Signal Mountain TN 37377-3147

COOPER, ROBERT MICHAEL, consultant, retired nuclear energy industry specialist; b. Little Rock, Nov. 27, 1948; s. John William and Rachel Lou Ann (Merritt) C.; m. Beverly Jean Wiles, Aug. 25, 1972; 1 child, Kristen Amanda. AA in Gen. Studies, Ark. Tech. U., 1984; BS in Indsl. Tech., So. Ill. U., 1990; MS in Ops. Mgmt., U. Ark., 1994. Electrician helper Ark. Power and Light Co., Pine Bluff, 1971-75, journeyman electrician Ark. Nuclear One, 1975-77, relay engr. Ark. Nuclear One, 1977-79; sr. quality assurance engr. Ark. Nuclear One, Russellville, 1979-90, nuclear safety and licensing specialist, 1990—2003; pres. RMC Cons., Inc., 2003—. Mem. fire protection issues task force Nuc. Energy Inst., 2002—. Author: Quality Surveillance Handbook, 1991; contbr. articles to Am. Nuclear Soc., Am. Soc. Quality Control. Lt. London (Ark.) Rural Vol. Fire Dept., 1985-95. Mem. Am. Nuclear Soc., Am. Soc. Quality Control (cert. quality engr. 1982, vice chair quality verification subcom., 1988-90, chair bylaws com. 1990). Baptist. Home: 780 Bowen Estates Rd Russellville AR 72802-1969 E-mail: mcooper48@yahoo.com.

COOPER, ROGER MERLIN, information technology executive, school system administrator, federal agency administrator; b. Scottsbluff, Nebr., Feb. 25, 1943; s. Dean P. and Bette Jane (Ward) C.; children: Gregory Joseph, Lisa Jane. BS, U. Utah, 1964; MSA, George Washington U., 1970; MBA, U. So. Calif., 1970; grad., Fed. Execs. Inst. U. Utah, 1980, Harvard U. Kennedy Sch. Govt., 1984. Masters's lic. USCG. Mgr. sys. programming Larwin Group, Beverly Hills, Calif., 1973-74; chief teleprocessing sect. U.S. CSC, Washington, 1974-76, chief info. tech. divsn., 1976-77; dir. Office Automated Sys. Devel., Macon, Ga., 1977-78; asst. dir. U.S. Office Pers. Mgmt., Washington, 1979-82; dir. med. info. resources mgmt. office VA, Washington, 1982-85; dep. asst. sec. for info. sys. U.S. Dept. Treasury, Washington, 1985-88; dep. adminstr. Farmers Home Adminstrn., Washington, 1988-91; dep. asst. atty. gen. info. mgmt. U.S. Dept. Justice, Washington, 1991-95; v.p. I-NET Inc., Bethesda, Md., 1995-96; dir. info. tech. Fairfax County Pub. Sch. Sys., Alexandria, Va., 1996—. CEO The Cooper Group, Ltd.; mem. Coun. of Prins., Nat. Comms. Systems, Coun. Sch. Networks; mem. adv. bd. FTS2000; chmn. Nat. Computer Security and Privacy Bd.; exec. bd. Inter-agy. Coun. on Info. Resources Mgmt., Fed. Micro Adv. Bd.; active Fed. Info. Ctr. Adv. Coun., Fed. Info. Rsch. Policy Coun., Fed. Data Ctrs. Dirs. Conf.; bd. dirs. Naval Liaison Office; mem. Consortium for Sch. Networking; mem. Dell Edn. Coun. Lt. USN, 1964-69; capt. USNR. Recipient Dept. Def. Joint Svc. achievment medal, 1988. Mem.: Armed Forces Comms. and Electronics Assn. (bd. dirs.). Home: 175 Moonlight Dr Melbourne Beach FL 32951 Office Phone: 703-927-9649. Business E-Mail: cooper_roger@alumni.ksg.harvard.edu.

COOPER, RONALD, broadcast executive; Grad., Wesleyan U. Various sr. exec. positions Continental Cablevision; exec. v.p., mktg. and new bus. devel., 1996; exec. v.p. mktg., tech. and new product and svc. devel. MediaOne, 1996—97, exec. v.p. ops., 1997—2000; COO AT&T Broadband, 2000—03; pres., COO Adelphia, Greenwood Village, Colo., 2003—. Office: Adelphia 5619 DTC Pkwy Greenwood Village CO 80111

COOPER, ROY ASBERRY, III, state attorney general; b. Rocky Mount, N.C., June 13, 1957; s. Roy Asberry Jr. and Beverly (Batchelor) C.; m. Kristin Bernhardt, Mar. 28, 1992; children: Hilary Godette, Natalie Rose, Claire Kristin. BA, U. N.C., 1979, JD, 1982. Bar: N.C. 1982. Ptnr. Fields and Cooper, Rocky Mount, 1982—2001; atty. gen. State of N.C., 2001—. Mem. N.C. Ho. of Reps., 1987-91, chmn. jud. com., 1989-91; mem. N.C. Senate, 1991-2001, chmn. jud. com., 1991-2000. Morehead scholar U. N.C., 1975-79. Democrat. Presbyterian. Office: c/o NC Attorney Generals Office 9001 Mail Service Center Raleigh NC 27699-9001

COOPER, SHARON KAY, school librarian, multi-media specialist; b. Junction City, Kans., Jan. 9, 1952; d. Duane Harvey and Helen Lucille Gugler; m. Stevan Frank Cooper, Aug. 3, 1974; children: Susan Kay, Shelley Kay. BS in Home Econs., Ft. Hays State U., 1974; postgrad., Wichita State U., 1979, Kans. State U., 1983, Emporia State U., 1988; MS in Edn. Adminstrn., Ft. Hays State U., 1996. Home econs. tchr., libr. Brewster (Kans.) H.S., 1974—75; lang. arts tchr., libr. West Smith County Jr. and Sr. H.S., Kensington, Kans., 1975-77; home econs., vocational tchr. Little River (Kans.)-Windom H.S., 1977-80; home econs. tchr. Chase-Raymond (Kans.) Schs., 1980-88; library media specialist Quivira Heights H.S., Bushton, Kans., 1988-95, Quivira Heights K-12 Schs., Holyrood and Bushton, Kans., 1995—2003; dist. libr. media specialistl USD # 328, Bushton, Holyrood and Wilson, Kans., 2003—. Sch. libr. rep., vice chair Kans. Interlibrary Loan Bd. Dirs., Topeka, 1999-2003; chmn. Reading Is Fun, Quivira Hts. Elem./Jr. High, 1995—; chmn. Red Ribbon Week Quivira Hts. Pre K-12, 1995—. Troop leader Wheatbelt coun. Girl Scouts U.S., Chase, 1989-96, svc. unit mgr., 1995-97. Mem. NEA, Kans. Assn. Sch. Librs., Kans. Edn. Assn. (pres. local chpt. 1999-2000, v.p. 2005—) Methodist. Avocations: reading, cooking, sewing, skiing, travel. Home: 213 Cedar Chase KS 67524 Office: USD # 328 500 S Main St Bushton KS 67427-9749 Office Phone: 620-562-3596.

COOPER, SHELDON MARK, medical educator, immunologist, researcher, rheumatologist; b. N.Y.C., Dec. 5, 1942; s. Alex and Sylvia (Silverman) Cooper; m. Amy Diane Freedman, Nov. 23, 1966; 1 child, Jonas Eric. BS cum laude, Hobart Coll., 1963; MD, NYU, 1967. Diplomate Am. Bd. Internal Medicine, Am. Bd. Rheumatology. Intern, asst. resident in internal medicine King's County Hosp. Ctr., Bklyn., 1967-69; fellow rheumatic disease study unit NYU Med. Ctr., N.Y.C., 1970-72; asst. prof. medicine U. So. Calif. Sch. Medicine, L.A., 1974-80, assoc. prof., rsch. coord., 1980-82; assoc. prof. medicine, dir. rheumatology and clin. U. Vt. Coll. Medicine, Burlington, 1982-86, prof. medicine, dir. rheumatology and clin. immunology unit, 1986—. Mem. staff Los Angeles County U. So. Calif. Med. Ctr., 1974—82, Med. Ctr. Hosp. Vt., Burlington, 1982—. Contbr. articles to profl. jours. Mem. exec. com. Vt. chpt. Arthritis Found., Burlington, 1982—, chmn., trustee, 1990—; mem. panel gen. and plastic surgery devices FDA. Maj. USAF, 1972—73. Grantee, Nat. Cancer Inst., 1976, Nat. Inst. Arthritis Musculoskeletal and Skin Diseases, 1984—, NIH, 1984—; NIH fellow, 1971. Mem.: Union Concerned Scientists, Physicians Social Responsibility, Reticuloendothelial Soc., Am. Assn. Immunologists, Am. Fedn. Clin. Rsch., Am. Coll. Rheumatology. Democrat. Jewish. Avocations: jogging, swimming, travel, cinema. Home: Barstow Rd Shelburne VT 05482 Office: U Vt Given Bldg D301 Burlington VT 05405-0001 Office Phone: 802-656-2285. Business E-Mail: sheldon.cooper@uvm.edu.

COOPER, STEPHEN HERBERT, retired lawyer; b. NYC, Mar. 29, 1939; s. Walter S. and Selma (Herbert) C.; m. Linda Cohen, Aug. 29, 1965 (dec.); m. Karen Gross, Sept. 6, 1981; 1 child, Zachary Noel. AB, Columbia U., 1960, JD cum laude, 1965. Bar: N.Y. 1965. Assoc. Weil, Gotshal & Manges, LLC, NYC, 1966-73, ptnr., 1973—2005, ret., 2005. Bd. dirs. Hurco Cos. Inc, Advisen Ltd.; lectr. Nat. Inst. Securities Regulation U. Colo., Boulder, 1985, Practicing Law Inst. 25th Annual Nat. Inst. Securities Regulation, N.Y.C., 1993, Law Jours. Seminars, 1997, 98; adj. prof. law, N.Y. Law Sch., N.Y.C., 2002-. Served to lt. USNR, 1960-62. Fellow Am. Bar Found.; mem. ABA (com. fed. regulation securities, subcom. internat. securities matters, co-chmn. 1990—22004). Office: Weil Gotshal & Manges LLC 767 5th Ave New York NY 10153-0119 Business E-Mail: stephen.cooper@weil.com.

COOPER, STEVEN HAROLD, education educator; s. Harold Cooper. and Rose Ann Denman. BS in Criminal Justice, Calif. State U., Sacramento, 1994—96; MS in Criminology, Fla. State U., 1997—98. Mil. Customs Inspector U.S. Customs, 2001, Phys. Security Specialist U.S. Army, 2001, Mil. Police Instr. U.S. Army Mil. Police Sch., 2002. Mil. police officer/instr. U.S. Army, Irvine, Calif., 1989—; prof. Chapman U., Orange, Calif., 1999—. Cons. to law enforcement organizations. Editor Stand!: Crime and Criminology, Perspectives: Criminology. Nat. v.p. Nat. Criminal Justice Honor Soc., Miami, 1996—97. Staff sgt. U.S. Army, 1989. Mem.: Am. Soc. of Criminology, Acad. of Criminal Justice Sciences (life). Office: Chapman U One University Dr Orange CA 92866 E-mail: stcooper@chapman.edu.

COOPER, SUZANE, physician; b. Phila., Oct. 12, 1954; d. Entriken E. Ruth. BS in Med. Tech., BA in Biology, U. Pa., 1976; MD, Temple U., 1980. Diplomate Am. Bd. Anesthesiology. Asst. prof. anesthesia Temple U. Hosp., Phila., 1986—91, assoc. prof. anesthesia, 1991—93; dir. anesthesia Citizens Bapt. Med. Ctr., Talladega, Ala., 1993—. V.p. med. staff Citizens Bapt. Med., 1995, chief staff, 1996. Named Outstanding New Med. Dir. Premier Anesthesiology, 1994, Woodbridge Tchg. award Temple U., 1988. Mem. Talladega County Med. Soc. (pres. 1996). Avocations: piano, organ, flying, wind surfing. Office: Citizens Bapt Med Ctr Anesthesiology Dept 604 Stone Ave Talladega AL 35160-2217 Office Phone: 256-761-4047. E-mail: suzanecoop@aol.com.

COOPER, THOMAS ASTLEY, bank executive; b. Phila., July 19, 1936; s. Thomas Astley and Elmira (Betts) C.; m. Anita June Danenberger, Sept. 7, 1957; children: Aleta Cooper Bossert, Anita Cooper Barbato, Alane Cooper Inacker, Allison Cooper Cardona, Anne Cooper Fleming, Thomas Astley III. BA, Haverford Coll., 1957; BD, Drew U., 1960; postgrad., Pa. U., Wharton, 1972; Program for Mgmt. Devel., Harvard U., 1976. Pres. Girard Bank, Phila., 1978; vice chmn. Mellon Bank, Mellon Nat. Corp., Pitts., 1982; pres. Bank of Am., Bank Am. Corp., San Francisco, 1984; chmn. Investment Svcs. for America, Tampa, Fla., 1986-90; pres., CEO Goldome, Buffalo, 1986-90; prin. TAC Assocs., Buffalo, 1992-95; CEO Chase Fed. Bank, Miami, Fla., 1993-96; chmn. Flatiron Credit, Denver, 1997—2003. Dir. Dela. No. Cos., Buffalo, Rennaisance Reins., Bermuda, Wheeling Island Gaming, Inc., BISYS, N.Y.C.; CEO, TAC Assocs. Inc. Mem. Island Country Club, Brant Beach Yacht Club (N.J.). Office: 1291 Laurel Ct Marco Island FL 34145-2351

COOPER, THOMAS J., lawyer; b. Cambridge, Mass., Dec. 8, 1943; BA, George Washington U., 1966, MA in Internat. Affairs, 1971; JD, Tulane U., 1974. Bar: DC 1975, admitted to practice: US Ct. Appeals (DC Cir.). Minority counsel US House Adminstrn. Com., 1976—77; adminstrv. asst. to Congressman Matthew J. Rinaldo, 1979—82; exec. asst. to asst. sec. commerce Trade

Adminstrn., 1983; asst. to dep. asst. sec. commerce Export Adminstrn., 1983—86; ptnr., Internat. Trade Dept. Venable LLP, Washington. Lectr. in field. Mem.: Phi Delta Phi. Office: Venable LLP 575 7th St NW Washington DC 20004 Office Phone: 202-344-4857. Office Fax: 202-344-8300. Business E-Mail: tjcooper@venable.com.

COOPER, THOMAS LOUIS, lawyer; b. Pitts., Mar. 16, 1938; s. Louis D. and Gertrude V. (Edmonds) C.; m. Leah Mary Meyers, Aug. 5, 1961; children: Marcia, Jeffrey, Daniel. BA, Dartmouth Coll., 1959; LLB, U. Pitts., 1962. Bar: Pa. 1962, U.S. Dist. Ct. (we. dist.) Pa. 1962, U.S. Ct. Appeals (3d cir.) 1962, U.S. Supreme Ct., 1962. Assoc. McArdle & McLaughlin, Pitts., 1962-69; ptnr. Gilardi & Cooper, Pitts., 1969—. Mem. civil procedural rules com. Pa. Supreme Ct., 1985-92, continuing legal edn. bd., 1992—, common pleas automation implementation team, 1990-92; adj. prof. U. Pitts. Sch. Law, 1986—. Contbr. articles to profl. jours. Fellow Am. Coll. Trial Lawyers; mem. Pa. Bar Assn. (v.p. 1989, pres.-elect 1990-91, pres. 1991-92, bd. govs., ho. of dels.), Allegheny County Bar Assn. (pres. 1984), Allegheny County Acad. Trial Lawyers (pres. 1982), Pa. Trial Lawyers Assn. (bd. govs.), Western Pa. Trial Lawyers Assn. (bd. govs.). Office: Gilardi Cooper & Lomupo 223 4th Ave Pittsburgh PA 15222-1717

COOPER, THOMAS LUTHER, retired printing company executive; b. Statham, Ga., Sept. 30, 1917; s. William Henry and Ovelia Jane (Arnold) C.; m. Helen Brown, Aug. 30, 1941; 1 son, Thomas Luther. Student, Ga. State U., 1938-39, High Mus. Art, Atlanta, 1946. With Constn. Pub. Co., Atlanta, 1936-50, head photoengraving and art dept., 1947-50; pres. So. Engraving Co., Atlanta, 1950-75, Photo Process Engraving Co., Atlanta, 1954-75; pres., gen. mgr. So. Photo Process Engraving Co., Atlanta, 1955-75; v.p., bd. dir. Perry Comms., 1976-90, Beck Engraving Co., Inc., Phila., 1968-75. Bd. dirs. J.M. Tull Metals Co., Inc. *Thomas Cooper served as Captain in the USAF. He served as photo-intelligence officer in the 8th Air Force in England 1943-45. He was awarded 6 battle stars. At wars end, he served as target intelligence briefing officer on the staff of a Commanding General.* Mem. exec. bd. Atlanta Area coun. Boy Scouts Am., Silver Beaver award, 1972; trustee Shorter Coll., Rome, Ga.; mem. adv. coun. Ga. State U.; chmn. bd. Ga. State U. Found. Served as capt. USAAF, 1942-45. Recipient Craftsman of Year award Inland Printer and Am. Lithographer mag., 1961 Mem. Internat. Assn. Printing House Craftsmen (pres. 1959-60), Am. Photoengravers Assn. (exec. com. 1952-54), Southeastern Photoengravers Assn. (pres. 1951-52), Nat. Soc. Art Dirs., Printing Industry Assn. Ga., Advt. Club Atlanta, Mil. Order World Wars, Am. Legion, Capital City Club, Masons, Shriners, Rotary (pres. Atlanta 1975, dist. gov. Ga. dist. 6900 1981-82). Baptist. Home: 1002 Dunwoody Chace NE Atlanta GA 30328-6012

COOPER, TIMOTHY J., music producer; b. Ind. BA, SUNY, Oswego, 1973; MusM, U. Colo., 1977. Cert. rec. engr., Conservatory Rec. Arts and Scis., 2000. Musical dir./composer Starworld Corp., Kansas City, Mo., 1986—87, Aladdin Hotel, Las Vegas, 1987—90, Excalibur Hotel, Las Vegas, 1990—2000; pres. Cooper Assocs., Las Vegas, 2000—. Composer: (soundtrack) King Arthur's Tournament, Winds of the Gods, Mass For A New Millenium. Recipient Class Achievement award, SUNY, 1998. Mem.: Am. Guild Organists. Personal E-mail: gonewest@earthlink.net.

COOPER, VALERIE GAIL, minister; b. Houston, May 30, 1962; d. Rev. M.C. and Mildred Chappel Cooper. BS in Pre-Medicine, Paul Quinn Coll., 1985; D in Theology and Ministry, Interdenominational Theol. Ctr. Sem., 1998; D in Theology, Immauel Sch. Bible, 2005. Elder Full Gospel Bapt. Ch., 2001. Pastor Vistors Chapel African Meth. Episc. Ch., El Paso, Tex., 1998—2000; asst. pastor Morning Star Full Gospel Bapt. Ch., Houston, 2001—05; pastor Faithful Anointed Victorious Always with God Ministries, Houston, 2005—. Mem.: Sigma Gamma Rho. Home: 3805 Brill St Houston TX 77026 Personal E-mail: vallevonettecooper@yahoo.com. E-mail: morninstarfgbc@aol.com.

COOPER, VIVIAN M., minister, writer; b. Benton Harbor, Mich., July 22, 1923; d. Jacob Edwin and Sylvia Ellen Green; m. Ed N. Cooper, Nov. 23, 1978; children: Shirley, Barbara, Joey. Diploma in art, Washington Art, Tucson, 1961. LPN, Ariz., 1970; ordained minister Western Bible Coll., Tucson, 1988. Farmer, Barnettsville, Ind.; nurse TMC Hosp., Tucson; min. Assembly of God, Tucson; ret. Author: (novel) Those Outrageous Buckaroos, 2004, Jumpin' Jehoshaphat! Hot Tamales at Happy Jack!, 2004. Mem. Assembly Of God. Avocations: crafts, writing, art, cooking, sewing. Home: 14022 N Palm Ridge Dr Sun City AZ 85351 E-mail: vcdeerlope@earthlink.com.

COOPER, WAYNE, conceptual artist; b. Depewq, Okla., May 7, 1942; s. Orville and Mary Ellen Cooper; m. Clara Marie Beck, Mar. 26, 1962. One-man shows include various U.S. cities, exhibitions include Circle Gallery, N.Y.C., Rennes, France, Gilcrease Mus., Am. Indian Mus., Heritage Mus., Will Rogers Mus., Ky. U., Ind. Captial Bldg., N. Mex. U., Gov. Mansion, Idpls., Okla. State Capital Bldg., Represented in permanent collections Will Rogers Mu., Okla. State Capital, Okla. Heritage Mus., Am. Indian Mus., Okla. Home: PO Box 106 Depew OK 74028 also: PO Box 361 Hebron IN 46341 Office: 126 W 1025 S Kouts IN 46347 Office Phone: 219-766-3807.

COOPER, WILLIAM ALLEN, bank executive; b. Detroit, July 3, 1943; BS in Acctg., Wayne State U., 1967. CPA, Mich. With Touche, Ross & Co., Detroit, 1967-71; chm. Minn. Rep Party. Sr. v.p. Mich. Nat. Bank of Detroit, 1971-72; sr. v.p. Mich. Nat. Corp., 1971-78; exec. v.p. Huntington Nat. Bank, Columbus, Ohio, 1978-83, pres., 1983-84; pres., Am. Savs. & Loan Assn. of Fla., Miami, 1984-85, also dir.; chmn. bd., chief exec. officer TCF Bank, FSB, Mpls., 1985—; chmn., TCF Fin. Corp., Mpls., from 1987, now chmn. bd., past chief exec. officer, bd. dirs. Mem. AICPA. Office: TCF Bank Office of Chmn Bd 801 Marquette Ave Minneapolis MN 55402-3475 also: Minn Rep Party 480 Ceder Street Ste 560 Castle Rock MN 55010

COOPER, WILLIAM COPELAND, public library director; b. Laurens, S.C., Aug. 3, 1946; s. James Lafayette Jr. and Dorothy (Copeland) C. Ba in History, Presbyn. Coll., 1968; MA in History, Wake Forest U., 1969; MS in Libr. Sci., U. N.C., 1971. Tchr. Wade Hampton H.S., Greenville, S.C., 1969-70; reference asst. U. N.C. Libr., Chapel Hill, 1970-71, reference libr., 1971-72; head reference dept. Greenville County Libr., 1972-74; dir. Laurens County Libr., 1974—. Contbr. articles to profl. jours. Treas. Laurens Hist. Soc., 1990-2003, Laurens County Arts Coun., 1994-97; preas. Cmty. Concert Assn., Clinton, 1980-82. Mem. ALA, Southeastern Libr. Assn., S.C. Libr. Assn., Piedmont Libr. Assn. (pres. 1998-99), Pub. Libr. Adminstrs. (pres. 1982, treas. 1997-2005), Laurens County C. of C., Kiwanis (preas. 1998). Avocations: piano and organ, running, swimming, historical houses. Home: PO Box 42 Laurens SC 29360-0042 Office: Laurens County Libr 1017 W Main St Laurens SC 29360-2663 E-mail: BCooper@LCPL.Org.

COOPER, WILLIAM EDWIN, academic administrator, psychologist, linguist, educator; b. Balt., Md., Mar. 20, 1951; s. William Daniel and Mildred (Hively) C.; m. Clarissa Holmes, July 5, 1984; children: Ashley, Courtney. AB magna cum laude, AM, Brown U., 1973; PhD, MIT, 1976. NIH postdoctoral fellow speech comm. group MIT Rsch. Lab. Electronics, Cambridge, 1976—78, rsch. affiliate, 1978—83; asst. prof. psychology Harvard U., Cambridge, 1978—81, assoc. prof. psychology, 1981—83; prof. psychology U. Iowa, Iowa City, 1983—89, assoc. dean R&D Coll. Liberal Arts, 1987—89; prof. psychology Tulane U., New Orleans, 1989—96, dean Coll. Arts and Scis., 1989—91, dean faculty liberal arts and sci., 1991—96; prof. linguistics and psychology Georgetown U., Washington, 1996—98, exec. v.p. main campus, 1996—98; pres. U. Richmond, Va., 1998—. Fellow Newcomb Coll., 1989-96. Author: Speech Perception and Production: Studies in Selective Adaptation, 1979; co-author: Syntax and Speech, 1980, Fundamental Frequency in Sentence Production, 1981; editor: Cognitive Aspects of Skilled Typewriting, 1983; co-editor: Sentence Processing: Psycholinguistic Studies Presented to Merrill Garrett, 1979; contbr. articles to profl. jours. Recipient Harold Schlosberg Meml. award in psychology, 1973, Acoustical Soc. Am. Biennial award, 1986; NSF grad. fellow, 1973, John Simon Guggenheim fellow, 1983; Fulbright Sr. scholar U. Fed. de Minas Gerais, Belo Horizonte, Brazil, 1984. Mem. Phi Beta Kappa, Sigma Xi. Office: U Richmond Office of Pres Richmond VA 23173 Office Phone: 804-289-8100. E-mail: bcooper@richmond.edu.

COOPER, WILLIAM EWING, JR., retired army officer; b. Birmingham, Ala., June 19, 1929; s. William Ewing and Margaret (Tate) C.; m. Mary Jane Beers, Feb. 16, 1952; children: William Ewing III, Leslie Beers. BA in History, Citadel, 1951; MA in History, U. Miami, 1961; postgrad., Georgetown U., 1970-72, U.S. Army Command and Gen. Staff Coll., 1961-62, Armed Forces Staff Coll., 1966-67, Army War Coll., 1970-71. Commd. 2d lt. U.S. Army, 1951, advanced through grades to maj. gen., 1979, comdr. arty. group Darmstadt, Germany, 1972-73, sr. liaison officer to Brit. Army Germany, 1973-75, comdg. gen. arty. brigade Homestead AFB, Fla., 1976-79, chief of staff NORAD Peterson AFB, Colo., 1979-81, comdg. gen. 32d Army Air Def. Command Darmstadt, Fed. Republic Germany, 1981-83, dep. dir. Def. Intelligence Agy. Washington, 1983-85; ret., 1985; assoc. Burdeshaw Assocs. Ltd., Bethesda, Md., 1986-93; ret., 1993. Decorated D.S.M., Def. Superior Service medal with oak cluster, Legion of Merit, Bronze Star with V and 2 oak leaf clusters, Air medal with 3 oak leaf clusters, Army Meritorious Service medal; knights cross (Germany), Honor medal (Vietnam). Mem. Phi Alpha Theta, Phi Sigma Alpha Clubs: Fla. Citadel (v.p. 1976-78); Colo. Citadel (pres. 1980-81). Democrat. Presbyterian. Avocations: golf, skiing, hunting. Home: 4925 Old Creek Dr Sarasota FL 34233-3942

COOPER, WILLIAM JAMES, JR., history professor; b. Kingstree, S.C., Oct. 22, 1940; s. William James and Mamie (Mayes) C.; m. Patricia Holmes, Sept. 1, 1962; children: William James III, Michael Holmes. AB, Princeton U., 1962; PhD, Johns Hopkins U., 1966. Asst. prof. history La. State U., Baton Rouge, 1968-70, assoc. prof., 1970-78, prof., 1978—, dean Grad. Sch., 1982-89, Boyd prof., 1989—. Douglas Southall Freeman prof. U. Richmond, 2000. Author: The Conservative Regime: South Carolina 1877-1890, 1968, The South and the Politics of Slavery 1828-1856, 1978, Liberty and Slavery: Southern Politics to 1860, 1983, Jefferson Davis, American, 2000; co-author: The American South: A History, 1990, 3d edit., 2001; editor: Jefferson Davis, The Essential Writings, 2003, co-editor: A Master's Due: Essays in Honor of David Herbert Donald, 1985, Writing the Civil War: The Quest to Understand, 1998; editor: Social Relations in Our Southern States (Daniel Hundley), 1979, So. Biography Series, 1979-93; also articles. Served to capt. U.S. Army, 1966-68. Recipient Prize for Biography L.A. Times, 2001, Jefferson Davis award Mus. of Confederacy, 2001; sr. fellow Inst. So. History, Johns Hopkins U., 1971-72, rsch. fellow Charles Warren Ctr. Studies in Am. History, Harvard U., 1975-76, Guggenheim fellow, 1980-81, NEH fellow, 1988-89; named Disting. Rsch. Master La. State U., 1980. Fellow Soc. Am. Historians; mem. Am. Hist. Assn., Orgn. Am. Historians, So. Hist. Assn. Presbyterian. Home: 250 Amherst Ave Baton Rouge LA 70808-4603 Office: La State U Dept History Baton Rouge LA 70803-0001 Office Phone: 225-578-4495. Business E-Mail: wcooper@lsu.edu.

COOPER, WILLIAM LEWIS, research librarian, lawyer, consultant; b. Highland Park, Mich., Sept. 11, 1944; s. Frank Edward and Margaret Ellen (Hayes) C.; m. Bonnie McIntyre Devine, June 7, 2002. AB, Dartmouth Coll., 1966; JD, U. Mich., 1972, AM in Library Sci., 1974. Bar: Mich. 1972, D.C. 1976. Assoc. Miller-Canfield, Detroit, 1972-74; reference libr. U. Pa., 1974-75; libr. Hogan & Hartson, Washington, 1975-77; dir. legal rsch. Dykema Gossett, Detroit, 1977-91, Williamsbury Assocs., Birmingham, Mich., 1991-95; rsch. libr. Coll. William and Mary, Williamsburg, Va., 1995-99; legal practice prof. U. Mich., 1999-2002; assoc. prof. John Marshall Law Sch., Atlanta, 2002-04; cons. Mitford Legal Info. Assocs., 2004—. Contbr. articles to profl. jours. With US Army, 1967-69. Mem. Mich. State Bar Assn. (legal econs. sect.), Detroit Bar Found. (treas. 1980-82, trustee 1979-85). Episcopalian. Office: 8031 Langhorne Rd Scottsville VA 24590-4024 Home: 8031 Langhorne Rd Scottsville VA 24590-4024 Office Phone: 434-989-0407. E-mail: wlcoop@earthlink.net.

COOPER, WILLIAM MARION, physician; b. Pitts., Jan. 12, 1919; s. Lardin Monroe and Sophia Antoinette (Swartz) C.; m. Sara Georgia Thomas, Jan. 19, 1942; children: Mikell Lee Cooper Schenck, William Marion, Thomas L., George Robert. BS, Pa. State U., 1939; MD, Hahnemann Med. Coll., 1943; JD, U. Pitts., 1987. Diplomate Am. Bd. Internal Medicine, Am. Bd. Hematology; cert. in Geriatrics. Intern Shadyside Hosp., Pitts., 1943; resident U. Pitts. Sch. Medicine, 1946-48, Cleve. Clin. Found., 1948; practice medicine specializing in internal medicine and hematology Pitts., 1948—; mem. staff Presbyn.-Univ., Shadyside; chief dept. medicine Shadyside Hosp., 1980-91; mem. med. faculty U. Pitts., 1948—, clin. prof. medicine, 1958—, dir. div. continuing edn., 1970-80, assoc. dean continuing edn., 1974-80; dir. continuing edn. Univ. Health Center, Pitts., 1975-80; sr. asst. vice-chancellor Univ. Health Ctr. Pitts., 1979-80. Med. dir. Ctrl. Blood Bank, Pitts., 1951-60, Pitts. Skin and Cancer Found., 1958-65. Contbr. articles to med. jours. Served with M.C. U.S. Army, 1944-45. Mem. AMA, AAAS, ACP (master; bd. govs. 1965-71), Pa. Med. Soc., Allegheny County Med. Soc., Am., Internat. Socs. Hematology, Am. Soc. Internal Medicine, Am. Coll. Legal Medicine, Oakmont (Pa.) Country Club. Home: The Mews 302 Fox Chapel Rd Pittsburgh PA 15238-2335 Office: Shadyside Hosp Hallman Cancer Ctr 5230 Centre Ave Pittsburgh PA 15232-1381

COOPER, WILLIAM S., state supreme court justice; b. Sept. 15, 1941; BA, U. Ky., 1963, JD with high distinction, 1970; attended, Nat. Jud. Coll., 1980—93. Law clerk Faurest, Collier, Arnett, Hensley & Coleman, 1968; ptnr. Collier, Arnett, Coleman & Cooper, 1970—79; judge Ky. 9th Judicial Cir., Div. 1, 1979—96; vice-regional judge Ky. Central Region, 1981—83, Ky. Green River Region, 1983—92, chief regional judge, 1992—96; justice Ky. Supreme Ct., Frankfort, 1996—. Mem. Council for Higher Education Subcom. for Legal Education, 1983—85, U. Ky. Coll. of Law Visiting Com., 1986—, Ky. Evidence Rules Review Commn., 1995—, chair., 2000—; mem. Ky. Supreme Ct. Criminal Rules Com., 1997—, Am. Law Inst., 2003—; lecturer U. Ky., 1983—, U. Louisville, 1977—85, Murray State U., 1978, Northern Ky. U., 1986, Circuit Judges Jud. Coll., 1981—93, Dist. Judges Jud. Coll., 1992. Captain USAF, 1963—67. Recipient Community Service award, Knights of Columbus, 1991, Hall of Fame award, Elizabethtown-Hardin County Chamber of Commerce, 1997. Fellow: Ky. Bar Foundation (bd. directors 1992—96); mem.: Circuit Judges Assn. (continuing education com. 1980—84, chair 1982—84), Ky. Bar Assn. (evidence rules com. 1987—92, chair. 1991—93, com. on jury instructions 1991—97, Ky. Bar Center award 1992). Office: Ky Supreme Ct 700 Capital Ave Frankfort KY 40601 also: Ky Supreme Ct Hardin Co Justice Ctr 120 E Dixie Ave Elizabethtown KY 42701-1469*

COOPER, WILLIAM SECORD, information science educator; b. Winnipeg, Man., Can., Nov. 7, 1935; m. Helen Clare Dunlap, July 22, 1964. BA, Principia Coll., 1956; MSc, MIT, 1959; PhD, U. Calif., Berkeley, 1964. Alexander von Humboldt scholar U. Erlangen, Germany, 1964-65; asst. prof. info. sci. U. Chgo., 1966-70; assoc. prof. info. sci. U. Calif., Berkeley, 1971-76, prof., 1976-94, prof. Grad. Sch., 1994-96, prof. emeritus, 1996—. Miller prof. Miller Inst., Berkeley, 1975-76. Hon. rsch. fellow Univ. Coll., London, 1977-78; ACM/SIGIR Triennial Rsch. award, 1994. Office: Univ Calif Sch Info Mgmt & Sys Berkeley CA 94720-0001 Office Phone: 510-642-4690. Business E-Mail: wcooper@calmail.berkeley.edu.

COOPER, WILLIAM THOMAS, natural history artist; b. Adamstown, NSW, Australia, Apr. 6, 1934; s. William and Coral (Bird) C.; m. Wendy Elizabeth Price, June 25, 1979. One-man shows include Artarmon Galleries, Sydney, 1973, 1980, City of Newcastle Art Gallery, 1973, Represented in permanent collections, Woodhall Art Found., Australian Nat. Libr., Papua New Guinea Govt., Newcastle Art Gallery, Rockhampton City Art Gallery; work represented in A Portfolio of Australian Birds, 1968, Parrots of the World, 1973, The Birds of Paradise and Bowerbirds, 1977, Australian Parrots, 1980, Kingfishers and Related Birds vol. I, 1983, vol. II, 1985, vol. III, 1987, vol. IV, 1993, vols. V & VI, 1995, Fruits of the Rainforest, 1995, The Turacos, 1997, The Cockatoos, 2001, illustrator Fierce Encounter, 1970, The Birds of Paradise, 1998, Cockatoos: A Portfolio of All Species, 2001, Fruits of the Australian Tropical Rainforest, 2004, designer (stamps), Papua, New Guinea, 1973; co-dir.:. Decorated Order of Australia, Australian Govt., 1994; recipient Gold medal Distinction, Natural History Art Acad. Natural Scis., Phila., 1992. Office: PO Box 314 Malanda 4885 Australia Fax: 07 40968 333.

COOPER, WILLIAM WAGER, economics professor, accounting and finance professor, dean; b. Birmingham, Ala., July 23, 1914; s. William Wager and Rae (Rossman) C.; m. Ruth Fay West, Sept. 11, 1944. AB, U. Chgo., 1938; postgrad., Columbia U., 1940-42; DSc (hon.), Ohio State U., 1969; MA (hon.), Harvard U., 1976; DSc (hon.), Carnegie Mellon U., 1982; D (hon.), U. Alicante, Spain, 1995. Asst. to comptroller TVA, 1938-40; prin. economist Bur. Budget, 1942-44; asst. prof. econs. U. Chgo., 1944-46; asst. prof. to prof. Carnegie-Mellon U., 1946-68; dean Carnegie-Mellon U. (Sch. Urban and Pub. Affairs), 1968-75, univ. prof. mgmt. sci. and pub. affairs, 1975-76, research prof. mgmt. sci. and pub. policy, 1976—; Arthur Lowes Dickinson prof. accounting Grad. Sch. Bus. Adminstrn., Harvard U., 1976-80; prof. mgmt. and acctg., mgmt. scis. and info. systems, Grad. Sch. Bus. Adminstrn. U. Tex., Austin, 1980-94; Foster Parker prof. fin. and mgmt. emeritus Grad. Sch. Bus. Adminstrn. U. Tex., Austin, 1994—; chmn. mgmt. sci. and info. systems dept. U. Tex., 1986-88. Vis. disting. internat. lectr. acctg. Am. Acctg. Assn., 1986, dir. pubs., chmn., pubs. com., exec. com., 1987-89; disting. IBM vis. prof. Aoyama Gakuin U., Tokyo, 1993. Author (with A. Charnes): Management Models and Industrial Applications of Linear Programming; author: (with H. Leavitt, M.W. Shelly) New Perspectives in Organization Research; author: (with others) Studies in Budgeting; author: (with A. Charnes and R. Niehaus) Studies in Manpower Planning; author: (with Y. Ijiri) Eric Louis Kohler: Accounting's Man of Principles; author: (with A. Charnes, A. Lewin and L. Seiford) Data Envelopment Analysis: Theory, Methodology, Applications; author: (with A. Whinston) New Directions in Computational Economics; author: (with R.G. Thompson and R.M. Thrall) Extensions and New Developments in DEA: The Annals of Operations Research; author: (with L.M. Seiford and Kaoru Tone) Data Envelopment Analysis: A Comprehensive Text, 2000; author: (with L.M. Seiford and J. Zhu) Handbook of Data Envelopment Analysis, 2004; author: (with L.M. Seiford and Kaoru Tone) Introduction to Data Envelopment Analysis, 2005; editor: Auditing: A Jour. Practice and Theory, 1978—81; co-editor (with Y. Ijiri): Kohler's Dictionary for Accountants, 6th edit.; mem. editl. bd. Mgmt. Sci., 1954—74, Naval Rsch. Logistics Quar., 1957—74; contbr. articles to profl. jours. Co-recipient John Von Neumann theory prize, 1982; recipient award Am. Inst. Accts., 1945, Profl. Achievement citation U. Chgo. Alumni Assn., 1986, Outstanding Contbr. to Auditing award Am. Acctg. Assn., 1988, Outstanding Acctg. Educator award, 1990, Notable Contbns. to Lit. award in govtl. and non-profit acctg., 1991; named to U. Tex. Coll. Bus. Adminstrn. Hall of Fame, 1990, Acctg. Hall of Fame, 1996, Lifetime Contbns. to Mgmt. Acct. award, 2002, Gold medal award Soc. Multi-Criteria Decision Making, 2004; Erskine fellow, U. Canterbury, New Zealand, 1991, fellow Inst. Ops. Rsch. and Mgmt. Sci., 2002. Fellow Econometric Soc., AAAS, INFORMS; mem. Inst. Mgmt. Sci. (1st pres.), Ops. Research Soc. Am. (editorial bd. 1957-68), Inst. of Operational Rsch. and Mgmt. Scis. Office: U Tex Dept Mgmt Sci & Info Sys B6500 1 University Station Austin TX 78712-0212 Home: Apt 304 1034 Liberty Park Dr Austin TX 78746-6853 Business E-Mail: cooperw@mail.utexas.edu.

COOPERMAN, ALVIN, television and theatrical producer; b. Bklyn. s. Nathan and Marietta (Steinman) C.; m. Marilyn Frances Fisher; Children: Karen Lynn, Audrey Joan, Margot Jane. Exec. dir. booking Shubert Theatre Enterprises, N.Y.C., 1963-68; v.p. spl. programs NBC, N.Y.C., 1967-68; exec. v.p. Madison Sq. Garden Ctr., Inc., N.Y.C., 1968-72; pres. Madison Sq. Garden Prodns., N.Y.C., 1968-72; CEO Athena Comms. Corp., N.Y.C., 1972—. Developed and produced spl. program Wide Wide World, 1955; exec. prodr. Producer's Showcase, 1955-56, Big Event, 1976-77, Screen Gems, 1957-58; prodns. include Dodsworth, Rosalinda, Jack and the Beanstalk, Shirley Temple Storybook, 1956-57, The Untouchables, 1962-63, Bolshoi Ballet Romeo and Juliet (Emmy award nomination 1976), Pele's Last Game, Amahl and the Night Visitors, A Tribute to Toscanini (Emmy award 1980), An Evening with Jerome Robbins (Emmy award 1981), The Life of Pope John Paul II, Ain't Misbehavin, 1985 (Emmy award, Best Musical of the Year award NAACP), My Two Loves, 1986, Safe Passage, 1987, Family Album, 1987, Witness to Survival, 1988-90; prodr./writer animated spl. NBC-TV Fourth King, 1984; prodr./dir./writer TV spl. Mobs and Mobster, 1993; prodr. cable TV show The Higgins Boys and Gruber Show, 1993 (Ace award nominee), ABC movie: Follow the River, 1994; writer: (stage musical) Honky Tonk Heaven, 1995, (ABC spl.) Susan B. Anthony Slept Here, 1995 (Am. Women in Radio and TV Best Documentary award), (feature film) Charity Royall, 1997-98; (play) Thrall, 1999; creator, writer: (websites) The Stork Club, Platinum, 1996; writer, lyricist (musical) The Life and Adventures of Santa Claus, 1998, weathertainment.com, 1999; established Infotainment Internat., Inc., 1999; website developer (with Herman Rush) Weathertainment.com, 1999. Creative cons. Rep. Nat. Conv., 1972; mem., trustee Judy Holliday Meml. Com. for Am. Med. Ctr., Denver; chmn. N.Y. chpt. Arthritis Found.; pres. Broadway Walk Stars Found., 2000. Recipient Peabody award, 1957, Christopher award, 1957, Judy Holliday Humanitarian award, 1972. Mem. Newcomen Soc. N.Am., Am. Theatre Planning Bd., Players Club. Home: 146 Central Park W 4F New York NY 10023-2005

COOPERMAN, BARRY S., academic administrator, chemist, educator; b. N.Y.C., Dec. 11, 1941; married, 1963; 2 children. BA, Columbia U., 1962; PhD in Chemistry, Harvard U., 1968. NATO fellow biochemistry Pasteur Inst., 1967-68; from asst. prof. to assoc. prof. dept. chemistry U. Pa., 1968-72, prof. bioorganic chemistry, 1977—, vice provost for rsch., 1982-95. Dir. French Inst., 1993-2001. Trustee Assoc. Univs., Inc., 1983—, chmn. bd., 1989-91; mem. policy governing bd. Advanced Tech. Ctr. S.E. Pa., 1984-88; bd. mgrs. Morris Arboretum, 1985-91; bd. dirs. Wistar Inst., 1987-2001; internat. sci. adv. bd. Max-Planck Inst. for Molecular Genetics, 2001—. Mem. Am. Soc. Biol. Chemists, Am. Chem. Soc. Achievements include research in mechanism of phosphoryl transfer enzymes; ribosomes; serum serine protease inhibitors; ribonucleotide reductase. Office: Univ Pa Dept Chemistry 358 Chemistry Philadelphia PA 19104 Office Phone: 215-898-6330.

COOPERMAN, DANIEL, computer software company executive, lawyer; b. Perth Amboy, N.J., Nov. 27, 1950; s. Eli Louis and Dorothy (Salinger) C.; m. Linda Louise Schmidt, June 10, 1979; children: Jeffrey Eli, Justin Andrew. AB summa cum laude, Dartmouth Coll., 1972; JD, MBA, Stanford U., 1976. Bar: Calif. 1976. Cons. McKinsey & Co., San Francisco, 1976-77; atty. McCutchen Doyle Brown & Enersen, San Francisco, 1977-83, ptnr., 1983-97; sr. v.p., gen. counsel Oracle Corp., Redwood Shores, Calif., 1997—, PeopleSoft Corp., 2004—. Sec., bd. dirs. Children's Discovery Mus., San Jose, Calif., 1993—; bd. advisors Cmty. Found. Santa Clara County, San Jose, 1994—. Mem. Santa Clara County Bar Assn. (chair bus. law sect. 1992-93), NASDAQ's Listing and Hearing Review Counsil, ABA's Com. Corp. Gen. Counsel, Adv. Coun. for Law, Science & Tech. Program Stanford Law Sch. Avocation: squash. Office: Oracle Corp 500 Oracle Pkwy Redwood City CA 94065-1675

COOPERMAN, GENE DAVID, computer information scientist, researcher; b. Union, N.J., May 14, 1952; s. Philip and Elsie (Blumen) C.; m. Celeste Kostopulos, Apr. 1983; children: Adam, Sarah. BS, U. Mich., 1974; PhD, Brown U., 1978. Postdoctoral fellow Mich. State U., East Lansing, 1978-80; prin. mem. tech. staff GTE Labs., Waltham, Mass., 1980-86; assoc. prof. computer sci., Northeastern U., Boston, 1986-92, prof. 1992—. Mem. editorial bd. CRC series, 1990—; contbr. chpt., articles to profl. publs. Co-patentee optical pulse generator. NSF grantee, 1989—. Mem. Soc. Indsl. and Applied Math., Assn. Computing Machinery (sec. pl. interest group on symbolic and algebraic manipulation 1991-93, treas. 1993—), Sigma Xi (br. treas. 1985-86). Office: Northeastern U Computer Sci 360 Huntington Ave Boston MA 02115-5005

COOPERMAN, LEON G., investment company executive; b. N.Y.C., Apr. 25, 1943; s. Harry and Martha (Rothenstein) C.; m. Toby F.; children: Wayne M., Michael S. BA, CUNY-Hunter Coll., 1964; MBA, Columbia U., 1967. Cert. fin. analyst. Quality control engr. Xerox Corp., Webster, NY, 1965-67; ptnr. Goldman, Sachs & Co., NYC, 1967-90, of counsel, 1990—; ltd. ptnr. Goldman Sachs Group, L.P., 1992—; chmn., chief exec. officer Goldman, Sachs Asset Mgmt., NYC, 1989-90, cons., chmn. profit-sharing and pension coms., 1992—; founder, chmn., CEO Omega Advisors, Inc., NYC, 1992—. Trustee United Jewish Appeal, N.J., 1980, St. Barnabas Hosp., Livingston, N.J.; bd. overseers Grad. Sch. Bus. Columbia U., bd. dirs., vice-chmn. finance and treasurer, Damon Runyon Cancer Rsch. Found. Mem. Fin. Analyst Fedn. (dir. 1980-), N.Y. Soc. Security Analysts (pres. 1980) Clubs: Atlantis Yacht (Monmouth Beach, N.J.). Office: Omega Advisors Inc 88 Pine St #31 New York NY 10005-1801 Office Phone: 212-495-5200. Office Fax: 212-495-5236.

COOPERMAN, SAUL, retired educational association administrator; b. Newark, Dec. 18, 1934; s. Louis Frank and Lucille (Swarthberg) C.; m. Paulette Beth Koch, Aug. 17, 1958; children: Suzanne, Deborah, David. BS, Lafayette Coll., 1956; MEd, Rutgers U., 1964, EdD, 1969; DHL (hon.), Drew U., 1984. Tchr. North Plainfield H.S., N.J., 1960-64; prin. Belvidere H.S., N.J., 1964-68; rsch. asst. Rutgers U., New Brunswick, N.J., 1968-69; supt. schs. Montgomery Twp., N.J., 1969-74, City of Madison, N.J., 1974-82; commr. N.J. State Dept. Edn., Trenton, 1982-90; ret., 1990. Pres. Educate Am., 1990—2000; chmn. edn. adv. panel New Am. Sch. Devel. Corp., 1990—97; sec., treas. New Am. Schs., 2000—05; founder, chmn. bd. dirs. Acad. for Tchg. and Leadership, 2004—. Author: How Schools Really Work: Practical Advice to Parents from an Insider; contbr. articles; columnist (newspaper) Star Ledger, 1998—2003. Pres. 10,000 Mentors, Newark, 1996-2000. Served to rank of comdr. USNR, 1956—82. Avocations: reading, athletics, travel. Address: 181 Roundtop Rd Bernardsville NJ 07924-2106 Office Phone: 908-630-9900.

COOPERRIDER, TOM S., botanist, educator; b. Newark, Ohio, Apr. 15, 1927; s. Oscar Harold and Ruth Evelyn Cooperrider; m. Miwako Kunimura, June 13, 1953; children: Julie Ann, John Andrew. BA, Denison U., 1950; MS, U. Iowa, 1955, PhD, 1958. Instr. biol. scis. Kent State U., Ohio, 1958—61, asst. prof., 1961—65, assoc. prof., 1965—69, curator herbarium, 1968—93, prof., 1969—93, dir. bot. gardens, 1972—93, emeritus prof., 1993—. NSF rschr. Mountain Lake Biol. Sta. U. Va., 1958; faculty mem. Iowa Lakeside Lab. U. Iowa, 1965; cons. endangered and threatened species U.S. Fish and Wildlife Svc. Dept. Interior, 1976—83; cons. Ohio Natural Areas Coun., 1983, Davey Tree Expert Co., 1979—85; asst. prof. Botany dept. U. Hawaii, 1962—63. Author: (book) Ferns and Other Pteridophytes of Iowa, 1959, Vascular Plants of Clinton, Jackson and Jones Counties, Iowa, 1962, The Dicotyledoneae of Ohio, Part 2, 1995; editor (co-author): Endangered and Threatened Plants of Ohio, 1983, Seventh Catalog of the Vascular Plants of Ohio, 2001. Personnel placement U.S. Census Bur., Washington, 1950—51; orderly VA Hosp., Iowa City, 1952—53; active YMCA-YWCA Students in Govt., Washington, 1950; Quaker Internat. vol. Germany, 1951. With U.S. Army, 1945—46. Named dedicatee Kent Bog State Nature Preserve, Ohio Dept. Natural Resources, 1995, dedicatee Tom S. and Miwako K. Cooperrider Herbarium, Kent State U., 2005; recipient Osborn award, Ohio Biol. Survey, 1994, Alumni Citation award, Denison U., 2000; fellow NSF predoctoral, 1957—58. Fellow: AAAS, Ohio Acad. Scis. (chair Ohio flora com. 1969—97), Explorers Club; mem.: So. Appalachian Bot. Soc., Bot. Soc. Am., Internat. Assn. Plant Taxonomists, Wilderness Soc., Nature Conservancy, Blue Key, Sigma Xi. Home: 548 Bowman Dr Kent OH 44240-4512

COOR, CAREN BARBARA, art educator; d. Chauncey Bryan and Cleo Barbara Coor. BSc, No. Ariz. U., Flagstaff, 1968; MA, Ariz. State U., Tempe, 1970. Cert. Ariz. Std. Secondary Tchg. Cert. Ariz. Dept. Edn., Phoenix, 1968. Art tchr. Phoenix Union HS Dist., Ariz., 1968—70; art history guest lectr. Phoenix Coll., 1970—71; graphic arts tchr. Scottsdale Sch. Dist., Ariz., 1971—72, Chinle Unified Sch. Dist., Ariz., 1973; artist, designer Tucson, 1973—80; art tchr., curriculum developer, dir. fed. programs, counselor Hopi Tribe Edn. Dept., Kykotsmovi, Ariz., 1980—88; tchr., counselor, missionary Watchtower Soc., Guayaquil, Ecuador, 1988—94; comm. specialist Raychem Corp., Menlo Park, Calif., 1994—99; art tchr., drawing and ceramics Chinle Unified Sch. Dist. 24, 1999—2005; mem. curriculum devel. bd. Phoenix Union HS Dist., 1968—70, Chinle Unified Sch. Dist., 2004—05, mem. fine arts and acad. showcase, 1999—2005. Mem.: NEA, Chinle Edn. Assn., Nat. Art Edn. Assn. Jehovah'S Witness. Avocations: reading, drawing, painting, flute, hiking. Office: Chinle Unified School District PO Box 587 Chinle AZ 86503 Office Phone: 928-674-9387.

COOR, LATTIE FINCH, university president; b. Phoenix, Ariz., Sept. 26, 1936; s. Lattie F. and Elnora (Witten) C.; m. Ina Fitzhenry, Jan. 18, 1964 (div. 1988); children: William Kendall, Colin Fitzhenry, Farryl MacKenna Witten; m. Elva Wingfield, Dec. 27, 1994. AB with high honors (Phelps Dodge scholar), No. Ariz. U., 1958; MA with honors (Univ. scholar, Universal Match Found. fellow, Carnegie Corp. fellow), Washington U., St. Louis, 1960, PhD, 1964; LLD (hon.), Marlboro Coll., 1977, Am. Coll. Greece, 1982, U. Vt., 1991, No. Ariz. U., 2002. Adminstrv. asst. to Gov. Mich., 1961-62; asst. to chancellor Washington U., St. Louis, 1963-67, asst. dean Grad. Sch. Arts and Scis., 1967-69, dir. internat. studies, 1967-69, asst. prof. polit. sci., 1967-76, vice chancellor, 1969-74, univ. vice chancellor, 1974-76; pres. U. Vt., Burlington, 1976-89, Ariz. State U., Tempe, Ariz., 1990—2002, prof. pub. affairs, Ernest W. McFarland Ariz. Heritage chair in leadership and pub. policy, pres. emeritus, 2002—, chmn. leadership and pub. policy. Cons. HEW; spl. cons. to commr. U.S. Commn. on Edn., 1971-74; chmn. Commn. on Govtl. Rels., Am. Coun. on Edn., 1976-80; dir. New Eng. Bd. Higher Edn., 1976-89; co-chmn. joint com. on health policy Assn. Am. Univs. and Nat. Assn. State Univs. and Land Grant Colls., 1976-89; mem. pres. commn. NCAA, 1984-90, chmn. div. I, 1989; mem. Ariz. State Bd. Edn., 1993-98; chmn. Pacific 10 Conf., 1995-96; chmn., CEO Ctr. Future Ariz., 2002—. Trustee emeritus Am. Coll. Greece. Mem. Nat. Assn. State Univs. and Land Grant Colls. (chmn. bd. dirs. 1991-92), New Eng. Assn. Schs. and Colls. (pres. 1981-82), Am. Coun. on Edn. (bd. dirs. 1991-93, 2000-02), Kellogg Commn. on Future of State and Land-Grant Univs. Office: Ctr for Future of Ariz 541 E Van Buren Ave Ste B-5 Phoenix AZ 85004 Office Phone: 480-727-5005. Business E-Mail: Lattie.Coor@asu.edu.

COORS, JEFFREY H., technology manufacturing executive; b. Denver, Feb. 10, 1945; s. Joseph. B.Chem. Engring., Cornell U., 1967, M.Chem. Engring., 1968. With Coors Porcelain Co., 1968-70; with Adolph Coors Co., Golden, Colo., 1970-92, pres., 1985-89; chmn., chief exec. officer Coors Techs. Cos., Golden, 1989-92; pres. ACX Techs., Golden, 1992—2000; chmn., pres., CEO Graphic Packaging Corp., 2000—03; exec. chmn. bd. Graphic Packaging Internat., Inc., Golden, Colo., 2003—. Office: Graphic Packaging Internat Inc 4455 Table Mountain Dr Golden CO 80403

COORS, PETER HANSON, brewery company executive; b. Denver, Sept. 20, 1946; s. Joseph and Holly (Hanson) C.; m. Marilyn Gross, Aug. 23, 1969; children: Melissa, Christien, Carrie Ann, Ashley, Peter, David. BS in Idsl. Engring., Cornell U., 1969; MBA, U. Denver, 1970; PhD (hon.), Regis U., 1991; PhD, Wilberforce U., 1991, Johnson & Wales U., 1997. Prodn. trainee, specialist Adolph Coors Co., Golden, Colo., 1970-71, dir. fin. planning, 1971-75, asst. sec.-treas., 1974-76, dir. market research, 1975-76, v.p. self distbn., 1976-77, v.p. sales and mktg., 1977-78, sr. v.p. sales and mktg., 1978-82, div. pres. sales, mktg. and adminstrn., 1982-85, exec. v.p., 1991—93, chmn., 2002—; pres. Coors Brewing Co. (formerly brewing div.), Golden, Colo., 1985—92; vice-chmn., CEO Coors Brewing Co., Golden, Colo., 1993—2002, chmn., 2002—; dir. Adolph Coors Co., 1973—. Bd. dirs. U.S. Bancorp, Inc., H. J. Heinz Co., Energy Corp. of Am. Bd. dirs. Nat. Wildlife Fedn., 1978-81, Wildlife Legis. Fund, 1987—, Colo. Hosp., 2004-; hon. bd. dirs. Colo. Spl. Olympics Inc., 1978—; trustee Colo. Outward Bound Sch., 1978—, Adolph Coors Found., Pres.'s Leadership Com., U. Colo., 1978—; chmn. Nat. Commn. on the Future of Regis Coll., 1981-82, chmn. devel. com., 1983—, now trustee. Mem. Nat. Indls. Adv. Council, Opportunities Ctrs. of Am., Young Pres.' Orgn., Ducks Unlimited (nat. trustee 1979, sr. v.p., mem. mgmt. com., exec. com. 1982—, dir. Can. 1982—, pres. 1984-85, chmn. bd. 1986—) Clubs: Met. Denver Exec. (dir 1979, pres. 1981—). Office: Adolph Coors Co & Coors Brewing 311 Tenth St Golden CO 80401

COOVER, CHRISTOPHER R., art appraiser; Asst. bookseller Albert J. Phiebig; cataloger, rare book dept. Sotheby's; head, rare book dept. Strand Bookstore, NYC; sr. cataloger, books & manuscripts dept. Christie's, NYC, 1980—85, sr. specialist, manuscripts, v.p., 1985—. Appraiser Antiques Roadshow, WGBH-PBS. Editor: New Grove Dictionary of Music; lectr. on rare manuscripts. Recipient rsch. grant, Bibliographical Soc. Am, 1986. Mem.: Manuscript Soc. (trustee 1989, past pres.). Office: Christie's 20 Rockefeller Plz New York NY 10020 Office Phone: 212-636-2665. Office Fax: 212-636-4928. Business E-Mail: ccoover@christies.com.

COOVER, HARRY WESLEY, manufacturing executive; b. Newark, Del., Mar. 6, 1919; s. Harry Wesley and Anna (Rohm) C.; m. Muriel Zumbach, Sept. 17, 1941; children: Harry Wesley, Stephen R., Melinda Coover Paul. BS in Chemistry (Southerland prize), Hobart Coll., Geneva, N.Y., 1941; MS, Cornell U., 1942, PhD, 1944. Rsch. chemist Eastman Kodak Co., Rochester, N.Y., 1944-49; sr. rsch. chemist Tenn. Eastman Co., Kingsport, 1949-54, rsch. assoc., 1954-63, head polymers div., 1963-65, dir. rsch., 1965-73, v.p., 1970-73, exec. v.p., 1973-81; v.p. Eastman Kodak Co., Kingsport, 1981-84; internat. mgmt. cons. Kingsport, 1984-85; pres. New Bus. Devel. Loctite Corp., Newington, Conn., 1985-88, Mgmt. Cons., Kingsport, Tenn., 1988—. Bd. dirs. Reilly Industries Inc. Author; patentee in field. Named to, Nat. Inventors Hall of Fame, 2004. Mem. AAAS, Internat. Union Pure and Applied Chemistry, Am. Chem. Soc. (So. Chemist award 1960, Speaker of Yr. award N.E. Tenn. sect. 1962, Earle B. Barnes award 1985, Chem. Pioneers award 1986), Am. Inst. Chemists, Indsl. Rsch. Inst. (pres. 1981-82, medal award 1984, Holland award 1987, Achievement award 1999, Soc. Chem. Industry), Nat. Acad. Engrs.; over 460 patents in field. Presbyterian. Achievements include discovery of cyanoacrylate adhesives. Office: PO Box 3866 Kingsport TN 37664-0866 Office Phone: 423-378-3733. Business E-Mail: drhw@coover.com.

COOVER, ROBERT, writer, scriptwriter, educator; b. Charles City, Iowa, 1932; BA, Ind. U., 1953; MA, U. Chgo., 1965. Disting. prof. Brown U., Providence, 1981—. Author: The Origin of the Brunists, 1966, The Universal Baseball Association, Inc., J. Henry Waugh, Prop., 1968, Pricksongs and Descants (short stories), 1969, On a Confrontation in Iowa City (film), 1969, A Theological Position (plays), 1972, The Public Burning, 1977, Hair o' the Chine, 1979, Charlie in the House of Rue, 1980, A Political Fable, 1980, Spanking the Maid, 1982, In Bed One Night and Other Brief Encounters, 1983, Gerald's Party, 1986, A Night at the Movies (short stories), 1987, Whatever Happened to Gloomy Gus of the Chicago Bears?, 1987, Pinocchio in Venice, 1991, John's Wife, 1996, Briar Rose, 1997, Ghost Town, 1998. Mem. Am. Acad. Arts and Letters (dept. lit.). Office: Brown U PO Box 1852 Providence RI 02912-1852 E-mail: robert_coover@brown.edu.

COPE, JAMES DUDLEY, retired trade association executive; b. Nelsonville, Ohio, Apr. 22, 1932; s. James Wesley Cope; m. Katherine Clark (Bealle), July 9, 1994. BA, Denison U., 1954; student, Inst. Orgn. Mgmt., Yale U., 1959. Exec. dir. Ohio State Pharm. Assn., Columbus, 1957—61; corp. sec. Nonprescription Drug Mfr. Assn., Washington, 1961—66, v.p., sec., 1966—67, exec. v.p., 1967—73, pres., 1973—99, name changed to Consumer Healthcare Products Assn., Washington, 1999; ret., 1999. Pres. Nat. Conf. Pharm. Orgn., Washington, 1975, 83, 88, 98; bd. overseers U. Calif. Sch. Pharmacy, San Francisco, 1997-2000; exec. v.p. adv. com. Am. Assn. Colls. Pharmacy; lectr. govt. and legis. process; lectr. in crisis mgmt. Stage actor Fine Arts Guild of the Rockies, 2000-; appeared in shows: Forty Carats, 2000, The Music Man, 2001, The Mikado, 2002, Arsenic and Old Lace, 2003, Into the Woods, 2004, My Fair Lady, 2005; quartet mem. The Music Men of Estes Pk, 2001-; contbr. articles to profl. jours. Pres. Glen Mar Pk. Civic Assn., Bethesda, Md., 1963; pres. bd. trustees Faith United Meth. Ch., Rockville, Md., 1978; bd. dirs. Coun. on Family Health, N.Y.C., 1967-99, Children's Hosp., 1968-76, Fine Arts Cuild of the Rockies, 2002—; vol. Rocky Mountain Park, 2003—; pres. Stanley Views Homeowners Assn., Estes Park, Colo., 2004—. Cpl., U.S. Army, 1954-56. Recipient Achievement medal Alpha Zeta Omega, 1960, Alumni citation Denison U., 1979, FDA Commr. spl. citation, 1987, 99; named Man of Yr., Am. Druggist, 1959. Mem.: Nat. Assn. Execs. (pres. 1984), World Self-Medication Industry (vice chmn. 1979—86, 1989—99), Greater Washington Soc. Assn. Execs., Am. Soc. Assn. Execs (bd. dirs. 1979—82), Denison U. Alumni Assn., Met. Club (N.Y.C.), Sky Club (N.Y.C.), Congl. Country Club (Potomac, Md.), Met. Club (Washington). Republican. Home: 631 Findley Ct Estes Park CO 80517-9038

COPE, JAMIE H., music educator; d. Robert j. and Nancy H. Harris; m. Dennis E. Cope, Nov. 19, 1988. MusB, Susquehanna U., Selinsgrove, Pa., 1984; MusM, West Chester U., Pa., 1989; Tech. Degree Level II, U. Arts, 2001. Cert. tchr. Pa. Dept. Edn., 1984. Tchr. music Upper Adams Sch. Dist., Biglerville, Pa., 1984—. Mem. Adams County Hist. Soc., 1993—, Adams County Land Conservancy, 1995—. Named Outstanding Young Educator, Pa. Jaycees, 1997, Tchr. of Excellence, Upper Adams Sch. Dist., 1998, Tchr. of Yr., Wal-Mart, 2003. Mem.: NEA, Adams County Music Educators Assn., Music Educators Nat. Conf., Sigma Alpha Iota. Avocations: golf, running, baseball. Mailing: PO Box 514 Arendtsville PA 17303-0514

COPE, JEANNETTE NAYLOR, executive search consultant; b. Corpus Christi, Tex., Feb. 9, 1956; d. Glen R. and Jeannine (Withington) N.; m. John R. Cope, May 22, 1993. BA in Psychology and Sociology, Trinity U., 1978. Asst. fin. dir. Jim Baker for Atty. Gen. Campaign, Houston, 1978; fin. dir. Rep. Party of Tex., Austin, 1979-81; regional Eagle rep. Rep. Nat. Com., Washington, 1981-83; devel. officer Nat. Endowment for the Arts, Washington, 1983-87; sr. project mgr. Internat. Skye Assocs., Washington, 1988; spl. asst. to Pres. of U.S. The White House, 1989-90, dep. asst. to Pres. of U.S., dep. dir. of presdl. pers., 1990-93; pres. J. Naylor Cope Co., Washington, 1994—. NEA liaison Pres.' Com. on Arts and Humanites, Washington, 1985-87; dir. Internat. Skye Advisor, Washington, 1988; bd. dirs. Bush/Quayle Alumni Assn., TransTech. Corp.; mem. Officer Pers. Mgmt.'s Task Force on Exec. and Mgmt. Devel., Washington, 1990; bd. dirs. Washington First Bank. Mem. Pres.'s Com. on the Arts and Humanities, 2001—; chmn. alumni admissions coun. Trinity U., Washington, 1986—87; mem. Bush Cheney Transition Team, 2001; vestrywoman St. John's Episcopal Ch., Washington, 1990—94, co-chmn. outreach com., 1991—94, chmn. search com. for 14th rector, jr. warden, 1994—97, sr. warden, 1998—2001; bd. dirs. The Compass Rose Soc. of the Anglican Communion, 1999—, exec. com., 2000—04; trustee Protestant Episcopal Cathedral Found., 2004—; bd. dirs. Coop. Urban Ministry Ctr., Washington, 1987—89, Pennsylvania Ave. Devel. Corp., 1993—96, Decatur House, Washington, 1998—, exec. com., 2000—, vice-chmn., bd. dirs., 2001—03, chmn. bd. dirs., 2004—; bd. visitors Kanuga Confs., 2001—. Scholar, Tex. Coun. of Ch. Related Colls., 1974. Mem. Am. Soc. Assn. Execs. (exec. recruiter), Tex. State Soc. (chmn. membership com. 1981), Nat. Trust for Hist. Preservation, Smithsonian Instn., Am. Film Inst., Mcpl. Art Soc. (N.Y.C.), 1925 F Street Club (chmn. mems. com.), Pres.'s Club, Columbia Country Club (Chevy Chase, Md.), Tex. Breakfast Club, Blue Key (sec. 1976-78), City Tavern Club, Chi Beta Epsilon (v.p. San Antonio coun. 1976). Republican. Episcopalian. Office: J Naylor Cope Co PO Box 40069 Washington DC 20016-0069 Business E-Mail: jnc@jnaylorcopecompany.com.

COPE, JOHN R(OBERT), lawyer; b. San Angelo, Tex., May 30, 1942; s. Robert Lloyd and Meta (Young) C.; m. Jeannette L. Naylor; 1 child, Lloyd Chapman. BBA, U. Tex., 1964, JD, 1966; MTS summa cum laude, Wesley Theol. Sem., Washington, 2001; DMin, Seabury-Western Theol. Sem., 2005. Bar: Tex. 1966, D.C. 1976. Ptnr. Bracewell & Patterson, Attys., Houston, 1966-76, Washington, 1976—, mem. adv. mgmt. com., 1987-90; sr. ptnr., 1994—. Vice chmn. bd. dirs., gen. counsel Century Nat. Bank, Washington, 1982-2001; bd. dirs., gen. counsel Columbia Nat. Bank, Washington, 1987-90; bd. dirs., v.p., gen. counsel Century Bancshares, Washington, 1985-2001; mem. fed. savs. and loan adv. coun. Fed. Home Loan Bank Bd., Washington, 1980-81; chmn., lectr. Practicing Law Inst. Seminars on Energy Litigation, Washington, 1980, 81; chief judge Wake Island Ct., Wake Island, North Pacific Ocean, 1989. Mem. exec. com., chmn. personnel and acad. affairs com. Wesley Theol. Sem., Washington, 1997—2003, bd.govs., 1997-2004; mem. devel. bd. Lon Morris Coll., Lake Jackson, Tex., 1974-76; mem. Southwest U. Spl. Edn. Found., San Marcos, Tex., 1973-76; v.p., dir. Harris County Easter Seal Soc., Houston, 1972-76; bd. dirs., sec. Nemours Wildlife Found., Yemassee, S.C., 1993—; treas. Dem. Party Harris County, Houston, 1976-77; mem. nat. fin. coun. Dem. Nat. Com., Washington, 1976-80; cert. lay spkr. United Meth. Ch., former dist. dir. lay speaking dist. Washington-Columbia; mem. bd. visitors and program com. Kanuga Episcopal Conf. Ctr., Hendersonville, NC, Seabury Inst. adv. bd. Seabury-Western Theol. Sem., Evanston, Ill.; mem. legal com. Episcopal Diocese Washington. Mem. ABA (mem. litigation sect.), D.C. Bar Assn. (mem. litigation and govt. contracts sect.), Tex. Bar Assn. (mem. litigation sect.), Houston Bar Assn. (mem. gen. litigation sect.), Orton Soc. Republican. Office: Bracewell & Patterson 2000 K St NW Ste 500 Washington DC 20006-1872 E-mail: jcope@bracepatt.com.

COPE, KENNETH WAYNE, retail executive; b. Rifle, Colo., May 31, 1924; s. William Grant and Mary (Park) C.; m. Patricia Miller, Feb. 1, 1946; children: Kimberly Ann, Bradley Mark. BA, La Sierra Coll., Arlington, Calif., 1948; postgrad., U. Wash., 1948-50. CPA, Calif. From staff acct. to mgr. Price Waterhouse & Co., CPAs, L.A., 1950-58, resident mgr. Phoenix, 1959-63; regional contr. Lucky Stores, Inc., San Leandro, Calif., 1963-68, v.p., corp. contr., 1968-83, sr. v.p. adminstrn., 1984-86, v.p. corp. affairs, 1986-87, ret., 1987. Served with AUS, 1943-46. Mem. AICPA, Calif. Soc. CPAs, Fin. Execs. Inst. Republican. Episcopalian.

COPE, LAURENCE BRIAN, utilities executive, economist, consultant; b. White Plains, New York, May 28, 1951; s. Lawrence Lyndon and Dorothea Anne (Herrick) C.; m. Ana Virginia (Ambrosini), June 7, 1986. BS in Bus., Fla. So. Coll., 1974; MS in Govt. and Pub. Adminstrn., So. Ill. U., Edwardsville, 1980; postgrad. in Econ., George Washington U., 1982. Mgr. cost estimating Potomac Electric Power Co., Washington, 1974—77, systems and tng. specialist, 1977—82, project mgr., 1982—84, mem. spkr. bur., 1978—84; project mgr., cons. Nat. Rural Utilities Coop. Fin. Corp., Herndon, Va., 1984—. Cons. Cope Assoc., Washington, 1978-84; trustee Cope Family Trusts; chmn. budget com. Oakton Condominium Assn., 1986-88. Contbr. articles to profl. jours. Co-chmn. Christian Young Adults Group, Washington, 1983. Mem. ASTD (reporter chpt. orgn. The Torch 1977, 78); Am. Soc. Pub. Adminstrn. (budget and fin. divsn.); Nat. Economists Club (rapporteur 1985—); CFC Investment Club (pres. 1995). Roman Catholic. Home: 5407 Newington Rd Bethesda MD 20816-3317 Office: Nat Rural Utilities Coop Fin Corp Woodland Pk 2201 Cooperative Way Herndon VA 20171-4583 Office Phone: 703-709-6700. Business E-Mail: copel@nrucfc.org.

COPE, LEWIS, journalist; b. Sweetwater, Tex., June 24, 1934; s. Millard L. and Margaret Wallace (Kilgore) C.; m. Betty Joan Ball, June 28, 1958; children— Margaret, Elizabeth, Mary Amelia. BA, Washington and Lee U., 1955. Reporter Greenville (Tex.) Herald-Banner, 1957-60; copy editor Richmond (Va.) Times Dispatch, 1960-62; copy editor, news editor San Antonio Express, 1962-66; sci. reporter Mpls. Star and Tribune, 1966-95; freelance science writer, newspaper cons., 1995—. Bd. dirs. Coun. Advancement of Sci. Writing, 1996—; writer-in-residence Nat. Cancer Inst., 1976. Author: Save Your Life, 1979, (with Victor Cohn) News and Numbers, 2001. Served as officer AUS, 1955-57. Recipient Merit award Am. Assn. Blood Banks, 1974, Journalism award Am. Acad. Family Physicians, 1976, 79, Penney award lifestyle reporting U. Mo., 1977, Nat. Media award Am. Cancer Soc., 1977, Blakeslee award Am. Heart Assn., 1979, Cecil award Arthritis Found., 1982, Harvey award Am. Med. Writers Assn., 1993; Sci. Writing fellow Columbia U. Grad. Sch. Journalism, 1963-64. Mem. Nat. Assn. Sci. Writers (exec. com. 1982-93, treas. 1985-88, v.p. 1989-90, pres. 1991-92), Sigma Delta Chi (pres. Minn. chpt. 1973-74, dep. regional dir. 1974-86). Episcopalian. Home: 5217 W 91st St Minneapolis MN 55437-1819 E-mail: lcope@mn.rr.com.

COPE, MELBA DARLENE, volunteer, photographer; b. Des Moines, Iowa, Feb. 16, 1944; d. Murray J. and Mary Lorena Van Hemert; m. Harvey J. Helgeland, 1964 (dissolved 1971); 1 child, Ingrid; m. Thom K. Cope, Nov. 8, 1980. Student, Nebr. Wesleyan U., Lincoln, 1975—76; BA in Women's Studies, U. Nebr., 1996. Bus. mgr. Williamson Olds/Honda, Lincoln, 1982—88; Granny Smith Washington Apple Commn., Wenatchee, Wash., 1999—2000; photographer Images by Melba, Tucson, 2002—. Photographer Habitat for Humanity Bldg. Project, Lincoln, Nebr., 1998. Contbr. chapters to books. Bd. dirs., sec., v.p. Rape Spouse Abuse Crisis Ctr., 1993—2002; mem. Older Women's League, 1998—2002; mentor Women in Trades program YWCA, Lincoln, 1999; big sister Heartland Big Bros./Big Sisters Orgn., 2001—02; com. mem. Girls and Women in Sports and Fitness, 2001—02; bd. dirs. YWCA, 2001; bd. dirs., v.p. Women's Studies Adv. Coun., Tucson, 2004—; co-chair Am. Cancer Soc. Annual Climb to Conquer Cancer, Tucson, 2005; commr., mem. exec. bd., v.p. Lincoln Lancaster Women's Commn., 1997—2001; bd. dirs. Coll. Arts and Scis. Alumni Assn. U. Nebr., 1997—2000; mem. com. Women in Transition, 1999; mem. Bd. Friends Commn., 2000—01; mem. comms. com. Sunflower Cmty. Assn., Tucson, 2002—04; bd. mem., v.p. Women's Studies Adv. Coun., Tucson, 2004—. Recipient Elizabeth Kurtz Vol. award, Rape Spouse Abuse Crisis Ctr., Lincoln, Nebr., 2000, Outstanding Vol. award, United Way, Lincoln, 2000, Alice Paul award, Lincoln/Lancaster Women's Commn., Lincoln, 2001. Mem.: Sigma Alpha Iota (Sword of Honor award 1994), Phi Beta Kappa. Avocations: photography, hiking, reading, music, travel.

COPE, RHIAN BRIANNA, toxicologist, educator; b. Brisbane, Australia, Oct. 1, 1965; B in Vet. Sci., U. Queensland, 1989; BSc with 1st class honors, Murdoch U., 1991; PhD, U. Sydney, 1996. Clinician dept. companion animal medicine and surgery U. Queensland, 1990; rsch. asst. Sch. Vet. Sci. Murdoch U., 1991—92; lectr. lab. animal medicine and animal genetics TAFE, Perth, Australia, 1991—92; clinician emergency medicine Ku-Ring-Gai Vet. Hosp., Sydney, 1997—98; postdoctoral rsch. asst. Australian Photobiology Testing Facility, 1997; hon. postdoctoral rsch. fellow dept. animal sci. U. Sydney, 1997; postdoctoral rsch. fellow Commonwealth Sci. and Indsl. Rsch. Orgn., 1998; postdoctoral rsch. assoc. dept. vet. bioscis. U. Ill., Urbana, 1999, asst. prof. morphology dept. vet. bioscis., 1999—2002; asst. prof. toxicology dept. biomed. scis. Oreg. State U., Corvallis, 2002—. Contbr. articles to profl. jours., chpt. to book. Del. People to People Amb. Program, Internat. Union Toxicology, China, 2003. Recipient award for outstanding presentation, Am. Coll. Vet. Microbiologists, 2002; grantee, U. Ill., 2000—01, USDA, 2000—01, Ill. Dept. Agr., 2001, Am. Cancer Soc., 2001—02, Oreg. State U., 2003. Fellow: Am. Acad. Toxicology, Am. Acad. Vet. and Comparitive Toxicology; mem.: Am. Soc. Photobiology, Soc. Toxicology. Home: PO Box 2478 Corvallis OR 97339 Office: Oreg State U Coll Vet Medicine Corvallis OR 97331 Office Phone: 541-737-6946. Business E-Mail: rhian.cope@oregonstate.edu.

COPE, THOMAS FIELD, lawyer; b. Oak Park, Ill., Feb. 29, 1948; s. Benjamin Thomas and Myra Norma (Lees) C.; m. Ann Watts, Mar. 21, 1970; children: Elizabeth Ann, Philip Thomas. BA, U. Denver, 1970, JD, 1974, MA, 1976; PhD, U. Chgo., 2001. Bar: Colo. 1974, Ill. 1978, Wyo. 1996, D.C. 2001, U.S. Ct. Appeals (9th cir.) 2005. Assoc. Holme Roberts & Owen, Denver, 1974-78, 81-83, ptnr., 1984—2003, of counsel, 2003—. Instr. IIT/Chgo.-Kent Coll. Law, 1980, Loyola U. Sch. Law, Chgo., 1980-81, adj. prof. U. Denver Coll. Law, 2003-04; chief of party ABA Ctrl. European and Eurasian Law Initiative, Republic Moldova, 2002-03. Co-editor: Colorado Environmental Law Handbook, 1989, 4th rev. edit., 1996, Colorado Environmental Compliance Update, 1993-96; contbg. editor Oil & Gas Law and Taxation Rev., Oxford, Eng., 1987-93; mng. editor Shepard's Environ. Liability in Comml. Transactions Reporter, 1990-92; mem. bd. editors Denver Law Jour., 1972-74; contbr. articles to profl. jours. Bd. dirs. Colo. Fourteeners Initiative, 1996-2002. Mem. Am. Law Inst., Am. Soc. Legal History, Irish

Legal History Soc., Selden Soc. (state corr. Colo. 1997—), Rocky Mountain Mineral Law Found. (mem. grants com. 1983-95, chmn. 1995-2002), Order St. Ives, Am. Alpine Club, Colo. Mountain Club (chair high altitude mountaineering sect. 2001-02). Democrat. Mem. Orthodox Ch. in Am. Avocations: mountain climbing, history. Home: 2800 S University Blvd Unit 108 Denver CO 80210-6072 Office: Holme Roberts & Owen LLP 1700 Lincoln St Ste 4100 Denver CO 80203-4541 Office Phone: 303-866-0295. E-mail: thomas.cope@hro.com.

COPE, WENDY, poet; b. 1945; Tchr. Portway Jr. Sch., London, 1967-69, Keyworth Jr. Sch., London, 1969-73, Cobourg Primary Sch., 1973-81, Brindishe Primary Sch., 1984-86; writer, TV columnist The Spectator, London, 1986-90. Arts editor ILEA Contact Tchrs. Newspaper, 1982-84. Author: Across the City, 1980, Hope and the 42, 1984, Making Cocoa for Kingsley Amis, 1986, Poem from a Colour Chart of Housepaints, 1986, Men and Their Boring Arguments, 1988, Does She Like Word-Games?, 1988, Twiddling Your Thumbs, 1988, The River Girl, 1991, Serious Concerns, 1992, If I Don't Know, 2001; editor: Is That the New Moon?, Poems By Women Poets, 1989, The Orchard Book of Funny Poems, 1993, The Funny Side, 1998, The Faber Book of Bedtime Stories, 2000, Heaven on Earth: 101 Happy Poems, 2001; George Herbert: Verse and Prose (a selection), 2002. Recipient Cholmondeley award for poetry, 1987, Michael Braude award AAAL, 1995. Fellow Royal Soc. Lit. Office: Faber & Faber 3 Queen Sq London WC1N 3AU England

COPELAND, ANN See FURTWANGLER, VIRGINIA WALSH

COPELAND, ANN (VIRGINIA W. FURTWANGLER), writer, educator; b. Hartford, Conn., Dec. 16, 1932; d. William Michael and Agnes (Bresnahan) Walsh; m. Albert J. Furtwangler, Aug. 17, 1968; children: Thomas Gavin, Andrew Edward. BA, Coll. New Rochelle, 1954; MA, Cath. U. Am., 1959; PhD, Cornell U., 1970; D of Letters (hon.), U. N.B., 1997. Asst. prof. Mt. Allison U., Sackville, Canada, 1976—77; vis. prof. Linfield Coll., McMinnville, Oreg., 1980—81; vis. fiction writer U. Idaho, Moscow, 1986—87, Bemidgi State U., Idaho, 1987, Wichita State U., 1988; writer in residence Mt. Allison U., Sackville, Canada, 1990—91; prof. english, vis. fiction writer Willamette U., Salem, Oreg., 1996—99. Workshop condr. Haystack, Portland State, Linfield Coll., New Brunswick, Nova Scotia, Oreg., Idaho. Author: At Peace, 1978, The Back Room, 1979, Earthen Vessels, 1984, The Golden Thread, 1989, Strange Bodies on Strange Shore, 1994, The ABC's of Writing Fiction, 1996, Season of Apples, 1996; contbr. articles to newspapers. Recipient Ingram Merrill award Ingram Merrill Found., N.Y.C., 1990; grantee Can. Coun., 1977, 80, 82, 88; writing fellow Nat. Endowment for Arts, 1978, 94. Mem. Internat. Women's Writing Guild, Author's Guild Avocation: piano. Home: 235 Oak Way NE Salem OR 97301-4333

COPELAND, CORI STUDEBAKER, music educator; b. Waukegan, Ill., Sept. 17, 1955; d. Wendell Gordan and Virginia Joy Studebaker; m. Michael R. Copeland, Nov. 19, 1977; children: Reece Michael, Heath Alexander. MusB, Ea. Ill. U., Charleston, 1977. Music tchr. Dist. 348 Schs., Mt. Carmel, Ill., 1978—. Elected bd. mem. Edwards County Sch. Bd., 1995—2002; church choir dir. 1st United Methodist Church, Albion, 2000—. Mem. Women's Club of Albion, 2000—, Angel of hope, 2002—. Mem.: Ill. Music Educators Assn. Republican. Methodist.

COPELAND, DOUGLAS ALLEN, lawyer; b. St. Louis, Mar. 22, 1956; s. William H. and Margaret J. (Wilson) C.; m. Amy Elizabeth Miles, May 18, 1985; children: Gregory Miles, Margaret Jane. BA, U. Mo., 1977; JD, St. Louis U., 1980. Bar: Mo. 1980, Ill. 1981, U.S. Dist. Ct. (ea. dist.) Mo. 1981, U.S. Ct. Appeals (8th cir.) 1987, U.S. Supreme Ct. 1988. Assoc. Brackman, Copeland, Oetting, Copeland, Walther & Schmidt, St. Louis, 1980-84, ptnr., 1985-86, Copeland, Gartner, Thompson & Jeep, St. Louis, 1987-88, Copeland, Gartner & Thompson, St. Louis, 1988-92, Copeland, Gartner, Thompson & Farris, St. Louis, 1993, Copeland Thompson Farris PC, St. Louis. Mem. ABA, NSBA (coun. sch. attys.), Mo. Bar Assn. (young lawyers sect., chmn. 1990-91, coun. mem. 1982-92, coun. sch. attys., pres.-elect 2004), St. Louis County Bar Assn. (pres. 1988-89, exec. com. 1983-90, Outstanding Young Lawyer 1987), Bar Assn. of Met. St. Louis, Estate Planning Coun. of St. Louis, Nat. Health Lawyers Assn. Republican. Baptist. Avocations: tennis, softball, hunting. Office: Copeland Thompson Farris PC Ste 1220 231 S Bemiston Ave Saint Louis MO 63105

COPELAND, DOUGLAS WALLACE, JR., publishing executive; b. Greensboro, N.C., Sept. 9, 1952; s. Douglas Wallace and Mary Lee (Wood) C.; m. Jean Cortright, June 16, 1990; children: Douglas W. III, Scott W., William C. BA in English, U. N.C., 1978. Chief of staff U.S. Congressman Richardson Preyer, Washington, 1974-81; dir. pub. and govt. affairs Brick Assn. of N.C., Greensboro, 1981; dir. pub. affairs The Moses H. Cone Meml. Hosp., Greensboro, 1981-86, v.p. mktg., 1986-99; pub. the Bus. Jour., Greensboro, 2000—. Chmn. 6th Congl. Dist. Dem. Party, Greensboro, 1982-91; bd. dirs. N.C. Agy. for Pub. Telecommunications, Raleigh, 1985-89, Gen. Greene coun. Boy Scouts Am., 1987-88, Leadership Greensboro; pres. Mental Health Assn., Greensboro, 1987-89; bd. dirs. Vol. Ctr., 1996—; bd. visitors U. N.C., Greensboro, 1998—. N.C. Inst. Polit. Leadership fellow. Mem. Am. Coun. Young Polit. Leaders, Greensboro C. of C. (co-chmn. govtl. liaison coun.). Episcopalian. Home: 2310 Lafayette Ave Greensboro NC 27408-5512 Office: The Bus Jour 100 S Elm St Ste 400 Greensboro NC 27401-2641

COPELAND, EDWARD JEROME, lawyer; b. Chgo., Oct. 29, 1933; s. Harvey and Lilyan (Rubin) C.; m. Ruth Caminer, Sept. 2, 1962; children: Ellyn, Bradley. BA, Carleton Coll., 1955; JD, Northwestern U., 1958. Bar: Ill. 1959, N.Y. 1981. Mem. Ill. Ho. of Reps., Springfield, 1967-71; ptnr. Foss, Schuman, Drake & Barnard, Chgo., 1971-86, Wood, Lucksinger & Epstein, Chgo., 1986-88, Shefsky & Froelich, Ltd., Chgo., 1988-89, Schuyler, Roche & Zwirner, Chgo., 1989—. Chmn. Bank of North Shore, Northbrook, Ill., 1976-81. Mem. Ill. Bd. Edn., 1975-83, chmn., 1981-83. Mem. ABA, Ill. Bar Assn., Chgo. Bar Assn. Republican. Office: One Prudential Plaza Ste 3800 Schuyler Roche & Zwirner 130 E Randolph St Chicago IL 60601-6312 Office Phone: 312-565-8327. Business E-Mail: ecopeland@srzlaw.com.

COPELAND, EDWARD MEADORS, III, surgeon, educator; b. Augusta, Ga, Oct. 6, 1937; s. Edward Meadors Jr. and Louise (Leggitt) C.; m. Martha Patterson, Ar. 24, 1964; children: Edward Meadors IV, Catherine Leggitt. BA, Duke U., 1959; MD, Cornell U., 1963. Diplomate Am. Bd. Surgery (bd. dir. 1983-91, chmn. 1990-91). Intern in surgery U. Pa. Hosp., Phila., 1963-64, resident in gen. surgery, 1964-69; resident surg. oncology Anderson Hosp., Houston, 1971-72; asst. prof. to prof. U. Tex. Med. Sch., Houston, 1972-82, U. Tex. M.D. Anderson Hosp. and Tumor Inst., Houston, 1972-82; prof. U. Fla. Coll. Medicine, Gainesville, 1982—, chmn. dept., 1982—2003, disting. prof., 2004—. Project dir. Nat. Large Bowel Cancer Project, Nat. Cancer Inst., Houston, 1981-82. Bd. dir. Sun Bank No. Ctrl. Fla., Ocala, 1987—. Maj. US Army, 1969-71, Vietnam. Decorated Bronze Star Rep. Vietnam; recipient Seale Harris award So. Med. Assn., 1984, Disting. Alumnus award M.D. Anderson Hosp. and Tumor Inst., 1987. Fellow Am. Surg. Assn., So. Surg. Assn. (pres. 1998-99); mem. ACS (chmn. bd. govs. 1995-96, bd. regents 1997—, vice chmn. 2002-2003, chmn. 2004—), Assn. for Acad. Surgery (pres. 1978-79), Soc. Surg. Oncology (pres. 1998-99), Soc. Surg. Chmn. (pres. 1996-98), Halsted Soc. (pres. 1993), Southeastern Surg. Congress (pres. 2000-2001), Soc. Univ. Surgeons, Gainesville Country Club. Avocations: fishing, golf, tennis. Home: 2605 NW 7th Rd Gainesville FL 32607-2600 Office: Univ Fla Coll Medicine Dept Surgery PO Box 100286 Gainesville FL 32610-0286

COPELAND, ERIC, venture capital company executive; BS, MS in elec. engrng. and computer sci., U. Calif., Berkeley; MBA, Stanford U. Grad. Sch. Bus. Various elec. engr. positions Hewlett-Packard, E-ON, Orbital Sci. Corp., Aloha Networks; dir., gen. ptnr. Venrock Assoc., Calif., 1998—. Bd. mem. 2Wire, Gen. Bandwidth, SteelEye Tech., Arcwave Networks, MaXXan Sys., Kineto Wireless, Hellosoft, Kenet, Keynotes, Anchor Bay Tech., Teranetics; former bd. mem. Kendin Comm. (acquired by Micrel), Cadant (acquried by Arris), TalkingNets. Achievements include co-led Venrock's Investments in AccessLine Comm., AcceLight Networks, Polaris Networks, ZettaCom. Office: Venrock Assoc 2494 Sand Hill Rd Ste 200 Menlo Park CA 94025 Office Phone: 650-561-9580. Office Fax: 650-561-9180.

COPELAND, EUGENE LEROY, lawyer, writer; b. Fairfield, Iowa, Mar. 5, 1939; BA, Parsons Coll., 1961; JD with distinction, U. Iowa, 1965. Admitted to Colo. bar, 1965, Iowa bar, 1965, U.S. Supreme Ct. bar, 1966. Individual practice law, Denver, 1965-66; sr. v.p., gen. counsel, sec. Security Life of Denver, Denver, 1966—; gen. counsel Nationale Nederlanden N.Am. Corp., Denver, 1986—. Lectr., speaker at legal and industry convs., seminars, meetings; participant contemporary issue program Today show NBC, 1980. Author: Preventive Law for Medical Directors and Underwriters, 1973; Underwriting in a New Age of Legal Accountability, 1978; Insurance Law, 1982; bd. editors Iowa Law Rev., 1965. Bd. dirs. Colo. Pub. Expenditures Coun., 1988—, Buffalo Mountain Met. Dist., Summit County, Colo., Friends Found. of Denver Pub. Libr., Denver Pub. Libr. Commn. Served with U.S. Army. Fulbright scholar (alt.). Mem. ABA, Colo. Bar Assn., Denver Bar Assn., Iowa Bar Assn., Assn. Life Ins. Council, Am. Council Life Ins. (state v.p. 1973-83, legis. com., reins. com., policyholder tax com., litigation com.), Colo. Life Conv. (pres. 1988-90, v.p. 1987-88, legis. chmn. 1973-86), Colo. Assn. Corp. Counsel, Denver Estate Planning Council, Colo. Assn. Life Underwriters (co-author learning guide 1978), Law Club Denver, Phi Kappa Phi. Unitarian Universalist. Office: Security Life Ctr 1290 Broadway Fl 6 Denver CO 80203-2122

COPELAND, FLOYD DEAN, insurance company executive, lawyer; b. Jackson, Miss., Apr. 11, 1939; s. Clyde Xenephon and Dorothy Russell (Dean) C.; m. Linda Gail Langston, Dec. 22, 1965; children: Albion Ehlers, Russell Braden. BA in history, U. Miss., 1961; BA in jurisprudence, U. Oxford, Eng., 1963; LLB, Yale U., 1965. Bar: Ga. 1967, Tenn. 1998. Assoc. Alston, Miller & Gaines, Atlanta, 1967-71; ptnr. Alston & Bird, Atlanta, 1972-97; exec. v.p., gen. counsel Provident Companies, Inc., Chattanooga, 1997-99; exec. v.p. legal and adminstrv. affairs, gen. counsel UnumProvident Corp., Chattanooga, 1999—2002, sr. exec. v.p., gen. counsel, 2002—, chief adminstrv. officer, 2003—. Bd. dirs. Atlanta Metro Boys and Girls Clubs, 1986-97; sec. State and Dist. Rhodes Scholarship Selection Committees, Atlanta, 1976-97. Capt. U.S. Army, 1965—67. Rhodes scholar, 1961, Carrier scholar, 1957. Mem. Am. Law Inst. Presbyterian. Avocations: bicycling, reading, travel. Office: UnumProvident Corp One Fountain Sq Chattanooga TN 37402

COPELAND, HENRY JEFFERSON, JR., former college president; b. Griffin, Ga., June 13, 1936; s. Henry Jefferson and Emory (Drake) C.; m. Laura Harper, Dec. 21, 1958; children: Henry Drake, Eleanor Harper. BA, Baylor U., 1958; PhD, Cornell U., 1966. Instr. Cornell U., Ithaca, N.Y., 1965-66; asst. prof. history Coll. Wooster, Ohio, 1966-69, assoc. dean, 1969-74, dean, 1974-77, pres., 1977-95, prof. history, 1995-98. Woodrow Wilson fellow, 1960 Presbyterian.

COPELAND, HUNTER ARMSTRONG, retired real estate executive; b. Birmingham, Ala., Oct. 22, 1918; s. Miles Axe and Leonora (Armstrong) C.; m. Suzanne Curl, 1942 (div. 1954); children: Susan Diane, Hunter Armstrong; m. Patricia Ann McGregor, 1956 (div. 1976); children: John McGregor, Miles, Ann; m. Courteney Bass, May 27, 1978. Student, U. Ala., 1936-37; grad. advanced mgmt. course, Harvard U., 1952. Mortgage appraiser Prudential Ins. Co. Am., Birmingham, 1946-54; mortgage broker Huntoon-Paige, N.Y.C., 1954-57; pres. Huntoon Copeland & Hedin, N.Y.C., 1958-70; exec. dir. Hunter Copeland and Assocs., N.Y.C., 1970-75; v.p. Colwell Co., N.Y.C., 1970-75; pres. Copeland-Tresnan & Hornblower Inc., N.Y.C., 1975-78, Hunter Copeland and Assocs., Birmingham, Ala., 1978—2002. Trustee Md. Realty Trust, Balt.; organizer, dir. New Canaan Bank & Trust Co., Conn.; mem. Ala. Cert. Bd. Alcoholism and Drug Counselors Mem. Am. Coun. on Alcoholism; exec. dir. Alcohol and Drug Abuse Coun. With inf. AUS, 1941-45; maj. USAF, 1952-54. Decorated Legion of Merit, Silver Star, Bronze Star with 4 oak leaf clusters, Purple Heart with oak leaf cluster, Legion of Merit, Croix du Combattant Voluntaire (France), War Cross Royal Yugoslav Army Peter II King of Yugoslavia, Medaille Commemorative Francaise, Medaille de France Liberee; named to Inf. Officers Hall of Fame, Ft. Benning, Ga., 1982. Mem. Mortgage Bankers Assn. Am., Mortgage Bankers Assn. N.Y. (pres. 1974-76, gov.), Am. Pub. Health Assn., Nat. Assn. Alcoholism and Drug Abuse Counselors, ASCD, Internat. Coun. Alcohol and Addictions, Vets. of Battle of the Bulge, Newcomen Soc., Commerce Exec. Soc. U. Ala., Chi Phi. Clubs: Kiwanis; Union League (N.Y.C.), Met. (N.Y.C.); Country of Birmingham. Address: PO Box 55912 Birmingham AL 35255

COPELAND, JACQUELINE TURNER, music educator; b. Birmingham, Ala., Mar. 22, 1939; d. Charles Smith and Julia (Northrop) Turner; m. William Edward Copeland, Apr. 20, 1962; children: Denise Arlene, Dawn Alane. B in Music Edn., Birmingham-So. Coll., 1960; M in Music Edn., Wichita State U., 1977. Cert. music tchr. grades K-12, Ala., Ga., Kans., La., Va. Music tchr. Jefferson County Bd. Edn., Birmingham, 1960-62, 63-64, DeKalb County Bd. Edn., Decatur, Ga., 1965-68; choral music tchr. Fairfax (Va.) County Bd. Edn., 1968-69, Derby (Kans.) Unified Sch. Dist. #260, 1977-80, Maize (Kans.) Unified Sch. Dist. #266, 1980-84; music tchr. Montgomery (Ala.) County Pub. Schs., 1984-85; instr. voice and piano Acad. Performing Arts, Montgomery, 1985-95, Studio of Jacqueline T. Copeland, Montgomery, 1995—. Accompanist County-Wide Music Festivals, Birmingham, 1960-65; sect. leader Dekalb Cmty. Chorus, Decatur, Ga., 1965-68; sect. leader, exec. bd. New Orleans Concert Choir, 1970-74; asst. dir., dir. chorale Wichita Choral Soc., 1974-84; dir. opening ceremony Bicentennial Fair, Wichita, 1976; mem. Montgomery (Ala.) Civic Chorale, 1984-87; musical dir. for theatre depts. Performing Arts Jr. High, Performing Arts H.S., Faulkner U., 1986—. Author: Music Teacher Handbook, 1967; editor, contbg. author: Teacher Advisement Handbook, 1980. Secret svc. wife White House Wives, Washington, 1968-70; leader, trainer, area chmn. Camp Fire Girls, New Orleans, 1970-74; leader, membership com., exec. bd. Camp Fire Girls, Wichita, 1974-82; elected ofcl. Citizens Participation Orgn., Wichita, 1984; area chmn. Am. Heart Assn., Montgomery, 1988-94; vol. DA Election, Montgomery, 1994. Recipient Groovey Tchr. award WQXI Radio, Atlanta, 1967, Gov.'s commendation Revolutionary Bicentennial Com., Wichita, 1976; named Outstanding Young Women of Am., New Orleans, 1971. Mem. NOW, AAUW, Music Tchrs. Nat. Assn., Ala. Music Tchrs. Assn., Montgomery Music Tchrs. Forum, Alpha Chi Omega (Montgomery chpt. treas. 1995-99, pres. 1999—), Alpha Chi Omega Alumnae (del. to 4 nat. convs., pres., v.p.). Democrat. Baptist. Avocation: searching for collectibles for country decor. Home: 6121 Bell Road Mnr Montgomery AL 36117-4362

COPELAND, KARIN A., training director; b. New Britain, Conn., Dec. 5, 1961; d. Ovide Joseph and Emilie Albert; m. James Philip Copeland, Sept. 27, 1991; children: Taylor Jacqueline, Garrett Ovide. AS in Retail Mktg., Lasell Coll., 1982; BSBA, Cen. Conn. State U., 1984. Acctg. clk., pub. rels. asst. Constructive Workshops, Inc., New Britain, 1985-88; account mgr. Beekley Corp., Bristol, Conn., 1988-91, sales supr., 1991-92, asst. product mgr., 1992-94, acting sales mgr., 1994-95, continuous learning mgr., 1995-97, dir. continuous learning, 1997—. Mem. ASTD, Am. Teleservices Assn. Avocations: painting, writing. Office: Beekley Corp Prestige Ln Bristol CT 06010

COPELAND, LOIS JACQUELINE, physician; b. Malden, Mass., Sept. 16, 1943; d. Arnold Alan and Ann Copeland; m. Richard A. Sperling, June 7, 1970; children: Mark Edward, Larissa Lynn, Lauren Anne, Lorraine Elizabeth. BA magna cum laude with distinction, Cornell U., 1964, MD, 1968. Intern N.Y. Hosp., N.Y.C., 1968-69, resident, 1969-70, Bellevue Hosp., NYU Med. Ctr., 1970-72; tchg. asst. internal medicine NYU Med. Ctr., 1971—; attending physician Pascack Valley Hosp., Westwood, N.J., 1974—. Mem. courtesy staff Valley Hosp., Ridgewood, N.J., 1980—. Mem. secondary schs. com. Cornell U., 1978—; bd. dirs. Found. for Free Enterprise, 1994—; steering com. physicians coun. Heritage Found., 1993—; pres. Coun. Cornell Women, 1993-95 Mem. Assn. Am. Physicians and Surgeons (bd. dirs. 1991-99, pres. 1994), Assn. Liberty Choice and Self-Autonomy (pres. 1998—), Phi Beta Kappa, Phi Kappa Phi, Alpha Lambda Delta. Achievements include being originator and physician-plaintiff of landmark constitutional lawsuit Stewart v. Sullivan, which reaffirmed the right of senior citizens to contract privately with physicians, and Amicus in United Seniors v. Shalala for the right to pay privately for medical services. Home: 25 Sparrowbush Rd Upper Saddle River NJ 07458-1400 Office: 47 Central Ave Hillsdale NJ 07642-2118 Office Phone: 201-664-1212. E-mail: loisjcope@aol.com.

COPELAND, MICHELLE, plastic surgeon; b. NYC, July 15, 1948; DMD magna cum laude, Harvard Dental Sch., 1977; MD, Harvard Med. Sch., 1980. Cert. Am. Bd. Plastic & Reconstructive Surgery. Oral maxillofacial surgery residency Mass. General Hospital, Boston, 1977—79; fellowship NY Hosp. Cornell Med. Ctr., NYC, 1980—82, Mt. Sinai Hospital, NYC, 1982—83, SUNY Downstate Med. Ctr., NYC, 1983—85; staff mem., div. plastic surgery Mount Sinai Med. Ctr.; former chief, div. plastic surgery City Hosp. Ctr., Elmhurst, NY; pvt. practice plastic surgery NYC; assist. prof. surgery Mount Sinai Sch. of Medicine, NYC; attending surgeon Mount Sinai Med. Ctr. & Manhattan Eye, Ear and Throat Hospital, NYC. Mem. med. advisory bd. Soc. for Advancement of Women's Health Rsch. Co-author: Change Your Looks, Change Your Life, 2002; commentator NBC Today Show, ABC Good Morning America; contbr. articles to newspapers & magazines; author: numerous articles for scientific publications. Fellow: Am. Coll. of Surgeons; mem.: Lipoplasty Soc., Am. Soc. for Laser Medicine & Surgery, Am. Med. Women's Assn., Am. Coll. of Maxillofacial Surgeons, Am. Soc. of Plastic & Reconstructive Surgeons, Am. Soc. for Aesthetic Plastic Surgery. Achievements include development of line of skin care products. Office: Cosmetic Plastic & Reconstructive Surgery 1001 Fifth Ave New York NY 10028 Business E-Mail: mcopeland@covact.net.

COPELAND, PETER, editor; b. Sept. 19, 1957; m. Maru Montero, 1987; children: Isabella, Lucas. Degree in govt., Lawrence U., Appleton, Wis., 1979. Staff mem. City News Bur., Chgo.; joined staff El Paso Herald Post, Tex., 1982; L.Am. corr. Scripps Howard News Svc., Mexico City, Pentagon and Justice Dept. reporter, asst. mng. editor news, mng. editor, 1998—99, editor, gen. mgr. Washington, 1999—. Co-author (with Rhonda Cornum): She Went to War: The Rhonda Cornum Story, 1992; co-author: (with Dean Hamer) The Science of Desire: The Gay Gene and the Biology of Behavior, 1994; co-author: (with Heidi von Beltz) My Soul Purpose: Living, Learning, and Healing, 1996; co-author: (with Dean Hamer) Living With Our Genes: Why They Matter More than You Think, 1998. Recipient Nathan R. Pusey Award, Lawrence U., 1995. Office: Scripps Howard Media Ctr 1090 Vermont Ave NW Ste 1000 Washington DC 20005

COPELAND, PHILLIPS JEROME, retired academic administrator, retired military officer; b. Oxnard, Calif., Mar. 22, 1921; s. John Charles and Marion (Moffatt) C.; m. Alice Janette Lusby, Apr. 26, 1942 (dec. April 1998); children: Janette Ann Copeland Bosserman (dec. Aug. 2000), Nancy Jo Copeland Briner; m. Joanne Barra Lankenau, July 9, 1999. Student, U. So. Calif., 1947-49; BA, U. Denver, 1956, MA, 1958; grad., Air Command and Staff Coll., 1959, Indsl. Coll. Armed Forces, 1964. Commd. 2d lt. USAF, 1943, advanced through grades to col., 1964; pilot 8th Air Force, Eng., 1944-45; various flying and staff assignments, 1945-51; chief joint tng. sect. Hdqrs. Airsouth (NATO), Italy, 1952-54; asst. dir. plans and programs USAF Acad., 1955-58; assigned to joint intelligence Washington, 1959-61; plans officer Cincpac Joint Staff, Hawaii, 1961-63; staff officer, ops. directorate, then team chief Nat. Mil. command Ctr., Joint Chiefs of Staff, Washington, 1964-67; dir. plans and programs USAF Adv. Group, 1967-68; prof. aerospace studies U. So. Calif., L.A., 1968-72, exec. asst. to pres., 1972-73, assoc. dir. office internat. programs, 1973-75, dir. adminstrv. svcs. Coll. Continuing Edn., 1975-82, dir. employee rels. L.A., 1982-84. Advisor Vietnamese Air Force, Vietnam, 1967-68. Decorated D.F.C., Bronze Star, Air medal with 3 clusters, Medal of Honor (Vietnam). Mem. Air Force Assn., Order of Daedalians.

COPELAND, POPPY CARLSON, psychotherapist; b. Evanston, Ill., Dec. 18, 1939; d. Frederick Winsor and Polly (Packard) C.; m. Marshall S. Johnson (div. 1979), children: Erica Winsor, Lara Siree; m. Lawrence E. Carlson, June 15, 1985. BA, U. Calif., Berkeley, 1962; MA, U. Denver, 1975; ABD (hon.) in Internat. Studies, U. Colo., 1980; M in Psychology, Counseling Inst. Transpersonal, Palo Alto, Calif., 1992. Lic. profl. counselor, Colo.; lifetime tchg. credential, Calif. Tchr. Temple City (Calif.) Sch. Dist., 1965-67; chmn. sch. assistance Mitrapah Found., Bangkok, Thailand, 1969-73; rsch. assoc. edn. Commn. of States, Denver, 1976-78; rsch. assoc. Boulder County Bd. Developmental Disabilities, Boulder, Colo., 1978-79; social policy writer Boulder Camera, Denver Post, 1981-84; sr. trainer Tucker Internat., Boulder, 1984—; psychotherapist in pvt. practice Boulder, 1990—. Dir. Internat. Women's Week, U. Colo., 1981-83, Internat. Pedestrian Conf., City of Boulder, 1981-83; cons. Colo. Civil Rights Commn., 1987-89; bd. dirs. Rocky Mountain Survivors Ctr. Bd. dir. Boulder Peace Consortium, 1983-86, Friendship City Nicaragua, Boulder, 1984-86, Burma Lifeline; series chair Conf. on World Affairs, U. Colo., 1999. Mem. ACA. Avocations: skiing, bicycling, hiking, gardening. Home: 2541 Bluff St Boulder CO 80304-3721 Office: 711 Walnut St Ste 200 Boulder CO 80302-5032 E-mail: copelandco@aol.com.

COPELAND, ROBERT BODINE, internist, cardiologist; b. Arab, Ala., Jan. 24, 1938; s. Haden Paul and Jimmie Alice (Bodine) Copeland; m. Virginia (Jenny) Ruth Trammell, June 26, 1960; children: Robert Theodore, Haden McTieyre. BS, Auburn U., 1960; MD, U. Ala., Birmingham, 1963. Diplomate Am. Bd. Internal Medicine, cert. internal medicine, cardiovasc. diseases and geriatrics. Intern then resident, clin. rsch. fellow in cardiology Mass. Gen. Hosp., Harvard Med. Sch., Boston, 1963-67; physician Clark Holder Clinic, LaGrange, Ga., 1967-77; founder, dir. Ga. Heart Clinic, LaGrange, 1972—; founder, pres. So. Cardiopulmonary Assocs., LaGrange, 1977—2003; clin. prof. med. U. Ala., Birmingham, 1980—, Emory U., Atlanta, 1980—. Bd. govs. Am. Bd. Internal Medicine, Phila., 1980—86, Joint Commn. on Accreditation of Healthcare Orgns., Chgo., 1991—97; chair bd. trustees ACP Found., Phila., 1999—2002; bd. dirs. Gaston Laughlin Inc., Atlanta; trustee West Ga. Med. Sys., LaGrange. Contbr. Trustee LaGrange Coll.; chmn. bd. trustees ACP-ASIM Found., 1999—2002. Recipient Disting. Alumni award, U. Ala., Birmingham, 1985. Fellow: ACP (gov. Ga. chpt. 1987—91, Master 1993, regent 1993, chair bd. regents 1998—99), Am. Coll. Cardiology, Royal Coll. Physicians; mem.: NAS, Am. Clin. and Climatological Assn. (mem. exec. com.), Inst. of Medicine, Am. Heart Assn. (pres. Ga. affiliate 1985—86). Office: 1551 Doctors Dr Lagrange GA 30240-4139 Personal E-mail: rbcopelandmd@yahoo.com.

COPELAND, ROBERT GLENN, lawyer; b. San Diego, Mar. 15, 1941; s. Glenn Howard and Luella Louise (Schmid) C.; m. Harriet S. Smith, June 27, 1964 (div. Jan. 1977); children: Katherine Louise, Matthew Robert; m. Lynne Newman, Oct. 10, 1993; 1 child, Zachary Newman. AB, Occidental Coll., 1963; JD, U. So. Calif., 1966. Bar: Calif. 1966, U.S. Dist. Ct. Calif. (so. dist.), 1967. Ptnr. Gray, Cary, Ware & Freidenrich, San Diego, 1966-95, Luce, Forward Hamilton & Scripps, LLP, 1995—2004, Duane Morris LLP, 2004—. Mem. ABA, Calif. Bar Assn. Republican. Avocations: shooting, fly fishing, hiking, racquetball. Office: Duane Morris LLP 101 W Broadway Ste 900 San Diego CA 92101-3311 Office Phone: 619-744-2228. Business E-Mail: rcopeland@duanemorris.com.

COPELAND, ROBERT MARSHALL, music educator, department chairman; b. Douglas, Wyo., Jan. 30, 1945; s. Wilbur Clyde and Arvilla Estella (Walkinshaw) C.; m. Louise Margaret Edgar, June 10, 1966; children: Thomas Edgar, Anne Louise, Kathryn Elizabeth. BS, Geneva Coll., 1966; MM, U. Cin., 1970, PhD, 1974; postgrad., Westminster Choir Coll., 1981-82, Emory U., 1988. Asst. prof. to prof. music Mid-Am. Nazarene Coll., Olathe, Kans., 1971-81; prof. music, dir. choral activities Geneva Coll., Beaver Falls, Pa., 1981—, chmn. dept. music, 1981-99. Vis. lectr. U. Kans., Lawrence, 1977; trustee, sec. Ref. Presbyn. Theol. Sem., Pitts., 1981-93, vis. lectr.,

1983-84; mem. Presbyn. and Ref. Joint Commn. on Chaplains and Mil. Pers., 1988-2002, sec., 1995-2002. Author: Spare No Exertions, 1986, Isaac Baker Woodbury: The Life and Works of an American Musical Populist, 1995; co-editor: The Book of Psalms for Singing, 1973; contbr. articles to profl. jours. Dir. music Internat. Covenanter Conf., Northfield, Minn., 1970, 76, 80, 84; ruling elder Ref. Presbyn. Ch., 1973—; moderator, Synod of the Ref. Presbyn. Ch. of N.Am., 1995-97; mem. Rep. County Com., 1992-2005. With AUS, 1966-68. NDEA fellow, 1968-71. Mem. AAUP (v.p. Kans. Conf. 1980-81), Am. Musicological Soc. (v.p. Allegheny chpt. 1987-89, 97-99, pres. 1989-91, 99-2001, coun. mem. 1992-95, 2001-04), Sonneck Soc. for Am. Music (founding mem., program com. 1982), Am. Choral Dirs. Assn. (co-editor Pa. Newsletter 1983-85, editor 1985-90), Soc. for Ethnomusicology, Huguenot Fellowship (bd. dirs. 1987—), Presbyn. and Ref. Joint Commn. on Chaplains and Mil. Pers. (sec. 1995-2002). Republican. Office: Geneva Coll 3200 College Ave Beaver Falls PA 15010-3557 Home: 116 Breezewood ct Beaver Falls PA 15010 Office Phone: 724-847-6665. Business E-Mail: rmc@geneva.edu.

COPELAND, SUZANNE JOHNSON, real estate executive; b. Chgo., Aug. 01; d. John Berger and Eleanor (Dreger) Johnson; m. John Robert Copeland, Aug. 1, 1971 (div. June 1976). Assoc. French Lang. and Culture, Richland Coll., Dallas, 1974; BFA, Ill. Wesleyan U., Bloomington, 1965. Commercial artist Barney Donley Studio, Inc., Chgo., 1966-69; art dir. Levines Dept. Store, Dallas, 1970-74; creative dir. Titche-Goettinger, Inc., Dallas, 1974-78; catering mgr. Dunfey Hotel, Dallas, 1978-82; regional dir. corp. sales Rayburn Country Resort, Austin, Tex., 1982-84; real estate sales assoc. Henry S. Miller, Dallas, 1984-86; v.p. Exclusive Properties Internat., Inc., Dallas, 1986—. Cons. North Tex. Commn., Dallas, 1988. Acquisitions editor: Unser, An American Family Portrait, 1988. Mem. The Rep. Forum, Dallas, 1983-94; vol. Stars for Children, Dallas, 1988, Soc. for Prevention of Cruelty to Animals, Dallas, 1973-92, Preservation of Animal World Soc., 1986-92, Sedona Acad., 1996—, Sedona Humane Soc., 1996—, Sedona Women, 2001—; charter mem. P.M. League Dallas Mus. Art.; mem. Keep Sedona Beautiful, 1999—, Sedona Art Ctr., 2001—. Mem. Nat. Assn. Realtors, Tex. Assn. Realtors, Greater Dallas Assn. Realtors (com. chmn., Summit award 1984, 85), North Tex. Arabian Horse Club (bd. dirs. 1975-76, Pres.'s award 1978), Dallas Zool. Soc., Humane Soc. Dallas County (v.p. 1973-74), Humane Soc. U.S./Gulf States Humane Edn. Assn. (bd. dirs. 1990-91), Am. Montessori Soc., VASA Order of Am. (bd. dirs. Nordic Red Rocks Lodge 2004—), Delta Phi Delta, Phi Theta Kappa. Lutheran. Avocations: arabian and thoroughbred horses, scuba diving, equitation instr. Office: Exclusive Properties PO Box 1973 Sedona AZ 86339 Personal E-mail: azmtnlion@aol.com.

COPELAND, TATIANA BRANDT, accountant; b. Dresden, Germany; came to U.S., 1959, naturalized, 1967; d. Cyril Alexander and Maria (von Satin) Brandt; m. Gerret van Sweringen Copeland, May 12, 1979. BS summa cum laude, UCLA, 1964; MBA, U. Calif., Berkeley, 1966. Sr. tax cons. Price Waterhouse & Co., L.A., 1966-72; asst. tax mgr. Whittaker Corp., L.A., 1972-75; mgr. internat. dept. E.I. Du Pont de Nemours, Wilmington, Del., 1975-80; pres. Tebec Assocs., Ltd., Wilmington, 1980—. Co-owner, CFO, Bouchaine Vineyards, Inc., Napa, Calif.; owner The Wine & Spirit Co., Greenville, Del.; co-owner, v.p. Rokeby Realty Co., Wilmington. Bd. dirs. Del. Symphony, Grand Opera House, Nat. Symphony Orch., Washington; mem. President's Adv. Com. for Trade Negotiations, 1982-87. Mem. AICPA, Am. Woman's Soc. CPA's, Am. Soc. Women Accts., Internat. Fiscal Assn., Del. Soc. CPA's, Rodney Square Club (bd. dirs.) Phi Kepa Kappa. Home: 175 Brecks Ln Wilmington DE 19807-3008 Office: PO Box 3662 Wilmington DE 19807-0662

COPELAND, TRENT BREHON, lawyer; b. 1962; BA, Dartmouth Coll.; JD, George Washington U. Bar: Calif. 1988. Atty. pvt. practice, LA. Legal analyst CBS News, CNN, Fox News, Ct. TV, The O'Reilly Factor, US mag.; temporary judge LA Superior Cts. Office: Ste 500 1925 Century Park E Los Angeles CA 90067 Office Phone: 310-789-1050. Office Fax: 310-479-8696. E-mail: trentcopeland@earthlink.net.

COPELAND, W(ILLIAM) JOEL, JR., clergyman; b. Pitts., June 1, 1946; BS, United Wesleyan Coll., 1967; MDiv, Asbury Sem., 1970; STM, Luth. Theol. Semin., 1976; D of Ministry, Asbury Sem., 1980. Ordained to ministry Wesleyan Ch., 1968; bd. cert. chaplain NAVAC, 2004. Student pastor Red Lion United Meth. Ch., Franklin, Ohio, 1967—70; pastor Parkway Wesleyan Ch., Wilmington, Del., 1970—83, First Wesleyan Ch., Batavia, NY, 1983—88; chaplain Coatesville VA Med. Ctr., Batavia, 1985—88; pastor Zion Evang. Congl. Ch., Myerstown, Pa., 1988—95, Rexmont Evang. Congl. Ch., Pa., 1995—98; chaplain Coatesville VA Med. Ctr., Pa., 1996—. Advisor Salvation Army, Wilmington, 1979-83, City Youth Bur., Batavia, 1984-88, Children's Chapel, Wilmington, 1973-83, Youth for Christ, Batavia, 1985-88; dist. sec. West N.Y. dist. The Wesleyan Ch., 1984-88. Co-editor E.C. Doors and Windows, 1991-95. Mem. Wesleyan Theol. Soc. Republican. Avocations: collecting stamps, coins, sports cards, reading. Home: PO Box 113 Myerstown PA 17067-0113 Office: VA Med Ctr 1400 Blackhorse Hill Rd Coatesville PA 19320-2040 E-mail: ecparson@hotmail.com.

COPELIN, SHAUN PATEN, military officer; b. Scottsbluff, Nebr., Aug. 24, 1962; s. John Paten Copelin and Katherine Sue Wilkson; m. Lucianne Gambino, July 21, 1990; 1 child, Gage Paten. BA in Pub. Affairs and Adminstrn., U. Okla., 1985; MA in Mil. History, Am. Mil. U., 1996. Senior Navigator USAF, 1997. Commd. 2d lt. USAF, 1985, advanced through grades to lt. col.; squadron comdr. 12th Combat Tng. Squadron, Ft Irwin, Calif., 2001—03; dep. divsn. chief info. ops. divsn. Air Combat Command HQ, Hampton, Va., 2003—. Amb. Promise Keepers, Williamsburg, Va., 2004—05. Lt col USAF, 1985, Langley AFB, Va. Decorated Def. Meritous Svc. medal USAF, Air Force Commendation medal, Humanitarian Svc. medal, Kuwait Liberation medal Kingdom of Saudi Arabia, Govt. of Kuwait, Global War on Terrorism Svc. medal USAF, Air medal (4), Aerial Achievement medal, Outstanding Unit award with Valor, Def. Meritorious Svc. medal USAF, Army Commendation medal US Army. Mem.: Am. Legion, Air Force Assn. (life). Republican. Baptist. Avocations: scuba diving, motorcycling, photography. Office: Air Combat Command Headquarters 202 Dodd Ave Hampton VA 23665 Office Phone: 757-764-2734.

COPENHAVER, DAVID CHARLES, real estate developer; b. Portland, Oreg., Nov. 18, 1962; s. Robert Charles and Joyce Hancock Copenhaver; m. Caryl Ann Copenhaver, Sept. 7, 1963; children: Chelsea, Paige, Faith. BSc, Portland (Oreg.) State U., 1986. Ptnr. Gramor Devel., Inc., Tualatin, Oreg., 1989—. Bd. dirs. Whipple Creek Ch., Responsive Growth Forum. Mem.: Internat. Coun. Shopping Ctrs. Republican. Office: Gramor Devel Inc 19767 SW 72d Ave Ste 100 Tualatin OR 97062-8354

COPENHAVER, MARION LAMSON, retired state legislator; b. Andover, Vt., Sept. 26, 1925; d. Joseph Fenwick and Christine (Forbes) Lamson; m. John H. Copenhaver, June 30, 1946; children: John III, Margaret, Christine, Eric, Lisa. Student, U. Vt., 1945-46. Mem. N.H. Ho. of Reps., Concord, ranking Dem. health and human svcs. com., 1973-2000, mem. adminstrv. rules com., 1982-2000, mem. health and human svcs. oversight, 1990-2000; ret., 2000. Chair Grafton County Dems., 1986-91; assoc. supr. Grafton County Soil Conservation Dist., 1980-2002, supr., 2002—; supr. Hanover (N.H.) Dem. Town Com., 1992; mem.-at-large Dem. State Com., Concord, 1992; bd. dirs. Dartmouth Hitchcock Found., Hanover, 1991—; bd. incorporators Dartmouth Hitchcock Med. Ctr., Lebanon, N.H., 1984—; bd. dirs. Grafton County Sr. Citizens Coun., Inc., 1995-96, 2001, vice chair, Outreach House, an Assisted Living Facility, 2001—, Hanover, Friends of Norris Cotton Cancer Ctr., Women's Policy Inst. N.H. Named N.H. Legislator of Yr. N.H. Nurses Assn., 1989; recipient Meritorious award N.H. Women's Lobby, 1996, James A. Hamilton award N.H. Hosp. Assn., 1997. Mem. NOW, Bus. and Profl. Women's Club (Outstanding Mem. award 1990). Democrat. Unitarian Universalist. Avocations: golf, skiing. Home: 80 Lyme Rd 158 Hanover NH 03755

COPENHAVER, W. ANDREW, lawyer; b. Roanoke, Va., Nov. 10, 1946; s. William Pierce and Jane Foote (Farrier) C.; m. Anne Phillips, July 7, 1973; children: William, Catherine, Andrew. BA, Duke U., 1969; cert. in internat. law, U. London, 1971; JD, U. N.C., 1972. Bar: N.C. 1972, U.S. Supreme Ct. 1981. Rsch. and teaching asst. Inst. Govt., 1970-72; assoc. Womble Carlyle Sandridge & Rice, Winston-Salem, N.C., 1972-77; ptnr. Womble, Carlyle, Sandridge & Rice, Winston-Salem, N.C., 1978-98, Washington, 1999—; head anti-trust and trade regulations sect. Womble Carlyle Sandridge & Rice, Winston-Salem, NC, 1992—2000. Mem. Fed. Bar Adv. Coun., N.C., 1992-98, chmn., 1994-95; permanent mem. Fourth Cir. Judicial Conf., 2000—. Bd. dirs. Winston-Salem Arts Coun., 1992-97, vice chmn., 1995-97; bd. dirs. U. N.C. Law Alumni Assn./Law Found., Inc., 1994—, The Creel Found., 1998—, The Summit Sch., 1984-91, chmn., 1988-90; trustee Centenary United Meth. Ch., 1992-94. Mem. Winston-Salem Rotary Club (bd. dirs. 1993-96), Old Town Club, Piedmont Club. Home: 2540 Warwick Rd Winston Salem NC 27104-1944 Office: Womble Carlyle Sandridge & Rice 1120 19th St NW Washington DC 20036-3605 Address: 3306 R St NW Washington DC 20007-2309

COPES, MARVIN LEE, academic administrator; b. Connersville, Ind., Sept. 19, 1938; s. Kenneth Edward and Frances Gertrude (Bean) C.; m. Luretta Ann Grenard, Aug. 26, 1961; children: Bradley Alan, Brian Keith, Brent Lee. BS, Purdue U., 1961, MS, 1962, PhD, 1975; postgrad., Ind. State U., 1967—68, Ind. U.Southeast, 1967—68. Cert. pub. mgr., Ky. Grad. asst. agrl. edn. Purdue U., West Lafayette, Ind., 1961—62, grad. instr., 1968—69; tchr. vocat. agriculture Tri-County Sch. Corp., Walcott, Ind., 1964—65; vocat. dir. Met. Sch. Dist. Vernon Twp., Crothersville, Ind., 1965—68; also dir. Ind. Vocat. Agr. Demonstration Ctr., 1965—68; asst. exec. sec. Kappa Delta Pi Hdqrs., West Lafayette, 1969—70; dir. Blue River Vocat.-Tech. Ctr., Shelbyville, Ind., 1970—79; nat. curriculum devel. coord. ITT Ednl. Svcs., Indpls., 1979—80, nat. dir. edn., 1980—82; dir. ITT Tech. Inst., Ft. Wayne, Ind., 1982—83, Indpls., 1983—86, Am. Coll., Mobile, Ala., 1986—89; nat. dir. edn. Am. Career Educators, Charlotte, NC, 1989, v.p. ednl. resources, 1989—91; pres. Treasure Wheel, Inc., Mobile, 1991—93; dean acad. affairs Phillips Jr. Coll., Mobile, 1992—96; v.p. acad. affairs Am. Inst. Commerce, Davenport, Iowa, 1993—96; dir. Ky. Tech. Jefferson State Campus, Louisville, 1996—98; pres. Jefferson Cmty. & Tech. Coll., 1998—2000, exec. dir. of occupl., tech. and apprenticeship programs, 2000—02, CEO Spl. Programs, 2001—02; dir. Heritage Inst., Falls Church, Va., 2002—03; edn., cmty. svc. AARP, Maylene, Ala., 2004—; ctr. mgr. Jefferson County WIA Career Ctr., Maylene, 2004—. Chmn. profl. devel. com. Ky. Postsecondary Tchr. Credentialing Adv. Bd.; mem. Welfare Reform Task Force, Ky.; bd. dirs. Pvt. Ind. Coun., Future Connections Sch. to Work; organizer Advanced Tech. Skills Acad., Advanced Welding Tech. Ctr.; pres. CopeSkills Cons., Power Ptnrs. cons.; ombudsman Employer Support of Guard and Res., 2004—; columnist, Shelby County Reporter Newspaper, Sr. Living Newspaper Author: A Curriculum Guide for Training in Agricultural Supply, 1968, Student Handbook for Cooperative Progress in Agricultural Occupations, 1968, A Predictability of Career Choices of High School Seniors, 1975, Personal Awareness Handbook, 1989, Retention Handbook, 1989, Placement Handbook, 1990, Vocational Adjustment Handbook, 1990, Train The Trainer Handbook, 1990, Instructor Certification Handbook, 1990, Administrative Certification Handbook, 1990, Master Teacher, 1990, Wheel of Fortune Enterprise Training Manual, 1991, Instructor Training Manual, 1993, Faculty Inservice Training Manual, 1993, Disaster Plan, 1993, Contract Training, 1994, School-to-Work Training, 1994, Assessment Planning, 1995, Welfare Reform, 1996, Guidelines for Apprenticeship Training, 2002, Guidelines for Corporate College, 2002. Mem. ops. coun. Met. Coll.; pres. Loper PTO, 1974-76; leader 4-H, 1964-68; advisor Future Farmers Am., 1964-70; cubmaster Boy Scouts Am., 1976-80, commr., bd. dirs. Shelbyville coun., 1978-92; mem. vocat. gng. com. Futuring Project, N.Y. State Dept. Edn.; bd. dirs. N.E. India Christian Mission, 1974, Kentuckiana Works; chmn. Shelby County Youth for Christ; mem. Nat. Curriculum Focus Group, 1993-96; bd. dirs., treas. Accrediting Coun. for Ind. Colls. and Schs., 1994; deacon area So. Bapt. Ch., 1995; mem. Kentukiana Edn. and Workforce Inst., Louisville Area Workforce Devel. Coun., School-to-Work Partnership Coun., Louisville/Jefferson County Redevel. Authority; bd. dirs. Career Resources One Stop Shop/Job Link, Pvt. Ind. Coun.; Louisville/Jefferson County Workforce investment bd., North Ctrl. Ky. Workforce Investment Bd.; mem. Louisville/Jefferson County Youth Coun., North Ctrl. Ky. Youth Coun., chmn.; mem. Immigrant/Refugee Task Force, Kentuckiana Works Skilled Trades Roundtable; mem. Leadership Louisville, 2000, Leadership Shelby County, 2005. 1st lt. U.S. Army, 1962-64. Recipient U.S. Congrl. award, Dist. 6 Ala. Mem. ASCD, Am. Vocat. Assn., Ind. Vocat. Assn., Nat. Coun. Local Adminstrs., Ind. Coun. Local Adminstrs., Bus. Profls. Am., Nat. Bus. Edn. Assn., Soc. Mfg. Engrs., Ky. Vocat. Assn. (pres. region 13), Robotics Internat., Network Iowa Svc. Learning, Ind. Assn. Pvt. Career Schs. (bd. dirs.), Future Farmers Am. Alumni Assn., Shelby County C. of C., Prichard C. of C. (bd. dirs.), Pershing Rifles, Gideons Internat., Metro Scholars, Davenport C. of C., Masons, Kiwanis, Order Ea. Star, Alpha Tau Alpha, Kappa Delta Pi, Phi Delta Kappa, Delta Pi Epsilon. Home: 108 Grande Club Dr Maylene AL 35114 Personal E-mail: mlcopes@charter.net. *Be a bridge for the life of others that they may cross on their life's journey. Education, motivation, goal setting and training are those bridges.*

COPES, PARZIVAL, economist, researcher; b. Nakusp, B.C., Can., Jan. 22, 1924; s. Jan Coops and Elisabeth Catharina Coops-van Olst; m. Dina Gussekloo, May 1, 1946; children: Raymond Alden, Michael Ian, Terence Franklin. BA in Econs. & Polit. Sci., U. B.C., 1949, MA in Econs., 1950; PhD in Econs., London Sch. Econs., 1956; D in Mil. Sci. (hon.), Royal Roads Mil. Coll., 1991; D in Philosophy (hon.), U. Tromsö, 1993; DLitt (hon.), Meml. U. Newfoundland, 2004. Economist, statistician Dominion Bur. of Stats., Ottawa, Canada, 1953—57; from assoc. prof. to prof., head econs. dept. Meml. U. Nfld., St. John's, Canada, 1957—64; founding dir. econ. rsch. Inst. Social and Econ. Rsch. Meml. U. Nfld., St. John's, 1961-64; prof. Simon Fraser U., Burnaby, Canada, 1964—91, founding head dept. econs. and commerce, 1964-69, chmn. dept. econs. and commerce, 1972—75, founding dir. Ctr. for Can. Studies, 1978—85, founding dir. Inst. of Fisheries Analysis, 1980—94, prof. emeritus, 1991—. Gov. Inst. Can. Bankers, Montreal, Que., 1967-71; dir. Can.-Fgn. Arrangements Project, Can. Govt. Dept. Environment, 1976; pres., chmn. Pacific Regional Sci. Conf. Orgn., 1977-85; spl. advisor to Minister of Fisheries, B.C., 1998; initiator, dir. collaborative rsch. and tng. agreement with Asian Fisheries Social Sci. Rsch. Network, 1989-94. Author: The Statistical Measurement of Morbidity Frequency, 1957, St. John's and Newfoundland: An Economic Survey, 1961, The Backward-Bending Supply Curve of the Fishing Industry, 1970, The Resettlement of Fishing Communities in Newfoundland, 1972, Factor Rents, Sole Ownership and the Optimum Level of Fisheries Exploitation, 1972, A Critical Review of the Individual Quota as a Device in Fisheries Management, 1986, The Extended Economics of an Innate Common Use Resource: The Fishery, 1998, Equity and the Rights Basis of Fishing in Iceland and Canada: Reflections on the Icelandic Supreme Court Decision, 1999, Sharing the Fishery Resources of the North Pacific for Mutual Advantage: Toward an International Management Regime, 1999, Aboriginal Fishing Rights and Salmon Management in British Columbia: Matching Historical Justice with the Public Interest, 2000, (with G Palsson) Challenging ITQs: Legal and Political Action in Iceland, Canada and Latin America, 2001, Fisheries Management Options: The Case for Limited Entry over ITQs, 2001, An Exploration of Fishery Access Rights and Community-Based Fishery Management for the Central and North Coast of British Columbia, 2003, A Vision for Community-Based Development of the Fisheries Sector on the Central and North Coast of British Columbia, 2003.(with A. Charles) Socio-Economics of Individual Transferable Quotas and Community-Based Fishery Management, 2004. With Netherlands Resistance Army, 1942—45, attached Can. Army, 1945—46, with Can. Officers Trng. Corp., 1946—49, lt. Can. Army, 1950—51, capt. 113 Manning Depot Can. Army Militia, 1953—57, capt. to maj. CO122 Manning Depot Can. Army Militia, 1957—63. Can. Forces Decoration, Can. Army, 1963, Fgn. fellow Acad. Natural Scis. of Russian Fedn., Moscow, 1992, Disting. Svc. award Internat. Inst. Fisheries Econs. & Trade, 1996. Mem. Internat. Inst. Fisheries Econs. and Trade (exec. com. 1982-86, Disting. Svc. award 1996), Internat. Assn. for Study of Common Property, Can. Regional Sci. Assn. (pres. 1983-85), Can. Econs. Assn. (v.p. 1972-73), Assn. for Can. Studies, Western Regional Sci. Assn. (pres. 1977-78), Social Sci. Fedn. Can. (dir., v.p. 1979-83), Can. Assn. Univ. Tchrs., Internat. Arctic Sci. Com., Simon Fraser U. Faculty Assn. (life). Achievements include some of earliest research contributions to establish sub-discipline of fisheries economics; writing, speaking, research and international consulting in fisheries policy and resource management. Home and Office: 2341 Lawson Ave Vancouver BC Canada V7V 2E5 Business E-Mail: copes@sfu.ca.

COPITHORNE, DAVID A., public relations executive; BS, Harvard U., 1975. CEO, co-founder Copithorne & Bellows (now Porter Novelli Convergence Group), Boston, 1988—2002; principal Aquarius Advisers, Newton Ctr., Mass., 2002—. Chief mktg. officer Outside the Classroom. Office: Aquarius Advisers 152 Homer St Newton Center MA 02459*

COPLE, WILLIAM JAMES, III, lawyer; b. Glen Cove, N.Y., May 13, 1955; s. William James Jr. and Harriet Frances (Anderson) C.; m. Bethanne Katherine Kinsella, May 29, 1982; children: Alexandra Catherine, Sydney Lee. BA, Washington and Lee U., 1977; JD, St. John's U., 1980; LLM, Georgetown U., 1986. Bar: N.Y. 1981, Va. 1990, D.C. 1985, U.S. Dist. Ct. D.c. 1985, U.S. Dist. Ct. (ea. dist.) Va. 1993, U.S. Ct. Appeals (4th cir.) 1983, U.S. Ct. Appeals (D.C. cir.) 1985, U.S. Ct. Claims 1984, U.S. Supreme Ct. 1984. With Office of the Sec. Def., Office of Gen. Counsel, Va., 1980-83; spl. asst. U.S. Atty's. office Ea. Dist. Va., Alexandria, 1984-85; atty. King & Spalding, Washington, 1986-92; ptnr. Spriggs & Hollingsworth, Washington, 1993—. Editor jour. St. John's Law Review, 1979; contbr. articles to profl. jours. Gen. counsel Nat. Capital Area Coun., Boy Scouts Am., 1993—. Capt. U.S. Army, 1980-85. Mem. ABA, Rep. Nat. Lawyers Assn., Assn. U.S. Army, Nat. Contract Mgmt. Assn., Nat. Def. Indsl. Assn., Phi Gamma Delta. Republican. Roman Catholic. Avocations: skiing, lacrosse, scuba diving. Office: Spriggs & Hollingsworth 1350 I St NW Ste 900 Washington DC 20005-3399 Office Phone: 202-898-5859.

COPLEY, CYNTHIA SUE LOVE, insurance adjuster; b. Defiance, Ohio, Oct. 26, 1957; d. Thomas Lee and Pauline Ann (Brandt) Love, Jr.; m. James Earl Copley, Jr., Oct. 19, 1985. B in Criminal Justice, Ohio U., 1981, A in Law Enforcement, 1979, A in Fire and Safety Tech., 1982. Cert. profl. ins. woman. With Spangler Candy Co., Bryan, Ohio, 1976-77; guard Juvenile Detention Ctr., Chillicothe, Ohio, 1978; security officer J.C. Penney Corp., Inc., Chillicothe, Ohio, 1979, Rink's Bargain City, Chillicothe, Ohio, 1979; with Rubbermaid Sales Corp., Chillicothe, Ohio, 1980; asst. dept. sec. and computer lab asst. Ohio U., Chillicothe, 1977-81; supr. collections and investigation Bur. of Support, Ross County, Chillicothe, 1981-82; asst. mgr. Tecumseh Claims Svc., Chillicothe, 1982—; owner Copley Adjusting, Chillicothe, 1982—. Part-time employee Ross County Bd. Elections, 1998-2003. Poll worker Rep. Party, Chillicothe, 1983-98; mem. Rep. Women Ross County, sec., 2000-2004. Mem. So. Ohio Claims Assn., Ohio Assn. Ind. Ins. Adjusters (sec.-treas. 1994, v.p. 1995, pres. 1996), Ohio Assn. Mut. Ins. Cos., Nat. Soc. Profl. Ins. Investigators. Lutheran. Avocations: golf, cooking, weekend trips. Home and Office: Tecumseh Claims Svc PO Box 15 Chillicothe OH 45601-0015

COPLEY, DAVID C., newspaper publishing company executive; s. Mrs. James S. Copley. BSBA, Menlo Coll., 1975. Pres., CEO, chmn. Copley Press, Inc., La Jolla, Calif., 1988—; chair, exec. com., chmn. sr. mgmt. bd. and bd. dir. The Copley Press, Inc., La Jolla, Calif.; pub. The San Diego Union-Tribune, 2001—, The Borrego Sun. Chair, pres. Copley N.W., Inc., Puller Paper Co.; pres. Copley News Svc.; trustee Copley Ohio Newspapers, The Peoria Jour. Star, Inc., The Gales. Print. and Publ. Co.; pres. Copley Northwest, Inc. and puller paper Co., others. Mem. editl. bd. San Diego Union-Tribune. Pres., trustee & pres. James S. Copley Found.; trustee Canterbury Sch., San Diego Crew Classic Found.; trustee emeritus La Jolla Playhouse, Am. Craft Coun., Mus. Photog. Arts; pres. assoc., pres. adv. com., exhibits com. Zool. Soc. San Diego; adv. bd. San Diego Automotive Mus.; pres. coun. Scripps Clinic and Rsch. Found., San Diego Kind Corp.; active Pres. Club U. San Diego, San Diego Aerospace Mus., San Diego Hall Sci., San Diego Maritime Mus., San Diego Coun. on Literacy. Mem. Nat. Newspaper Assn., U.S. Humane Soc., San Diego Hist. Soc., San Diego Humane Soc., Bachelor Club San Diego. Office: The Copley Press Inc PO Box 1530 La Jolla CA 92038-1530 Office Phone: 858-454-0411.

COPLEY, EDWARD ALVIN, lawyer; b. Memphis, Jan. 17, 1936; m. Connie James Patterson, Nov. 17, 1990; children: Julie, Ward, Drew, Kelly, Zeke. BA, So. Meth. U., 1957, JD, 1960. Bar: U.S. Dist. Ct. (no. dist.) Tex., U.S. Ct. Claims 1962, U.S. Supreme Ct. 1963, U.S. Tax Ct. 1966, U.S. Ct. Appeals (5th cir.) 1968. Atty. U.S. Dept. Justice, Washington, 1960-64, Ft. Worth, 1964-66; assoc. Akin, Gump, Strauss, Hauer & Feld, Dallas, 1966-67, ptnr., 1968—. Fellow Am. Coll. Probate Counsel; mem. Internat. Acad. Estate Trust Law, Dallas Bar Assn. (tax sect.), Dallas Estate Coun. (pres. 1975-76), So. Meth. U. Law Sch. Alumni Assn. (pres. 1978-79), Salesmanship Club, Order of Woolsac, Barristers, Dallas Petroleum Club, Dallas Country Club, Phi Alpha Delta. Avocations: racquetball, photography, hunting, fishing, reading. Home: 3711 Shenandoah St Dallas TX 75205-2120 Office: Akin Gump Strauss Hauer & Feld Ste 4100 1700 Pacific Ave Dallas TX 75201-4675 E-mail: ecopley@akingump.com.

COPLEY, R. EVAN, music educator; b. Liberal, Kans., Mar. 22, 1930; s. Claude Elmer and Elizabeth (Blackburn) Copley; children: Shelley, Mark, Delynne, Vaughn, Forrest. B in music, U. Denver, 1952; M in music, Mich. State U., 1955, PhD, 1958. Prof. music theory and organ Iowa Wesleyan Coll., Mt. Pleasant, Iowa, 1958—64, Okla. State U., Stillwater, Okla., 1964—68; prof. music theory and composition U. N. Colo., Creeley, Colo., 1968—. Author: Harmony-Baroque to Contemporary, 1980, composer various sonatas, trios, quartets, preludes and fugues, various works for orch. and band, symphonies and concertos. With U.S. Army, 1952—54. Recipient Dist. Scholar of Yr., U. No. Colo., 1988, Composer in Residence, Breckenridge Music Fest., 1991. Home: 1803 45th Ave Greeley CO 80634 Office Phone: 970-351-2484.

COPLEY, STEPHEN MICHAEL, retired materials engineer, manufacturing executive, consultant; b. Urbana, Ill., Apr. 29, 1936; s. Michael Joseph and Marion Elizabeth (Partlow) C.; m. Marcia Elizabeth Thornton, Nov. 28, 1957 (div. Nov. 1983); children: Michael Thornton, Sara Marie, Philip Stephen, Paul Ellis, Peter Leland, Susan Elizabeth, Stephen Joseph; m. Judith Ann Todd, Aug. 3, 1984; 1 child, Amy Elizabeth. BA, U. Calif. at Berkeley, 1959, MS, 1961, PhD, 1964. Research assoc., sr. research assoc., group leader, sect. supr. Advanced Materials Research and Devel. Lab., Pratt & Whitney Aircraft Co., Middletown, Conn., 1964-70; assoc. prof. materials sci. and mech. engrng. U. So. Calif., Los Angeles, 1970-76, Kenneth T. Norris prof., 1972-90, chmn. dept. materials sci. and engrng., 1975-81, 83-88, founder, dir. mfg. engrng. program, 1976, prof. materials sci. and mech. engrng., 1976-90; prof. metall. and materials engrng. dept. Armour Coll., Ill. Inst. Tech., Chgo., 1990-95; chmn. metall. and materials engrng. dept. Ill. Inst. Tech., Chgo., 1990-91, vice provost for acad. planning and budgeting, 1991-92, dean Armour Coll. Engrng. and Scis., 1992-95; dir. Mfg. Inst., prof. mech., materials and aerospace engrng dept., 1995-96; pres., CEO STE, Inc., Naperville, Ill., 1996; CEO Packer Engrng. Inc., 1997-98; pres., CEO The Packer Group, Inc., Naperville, Ill., 1997-2000. Bd. dirs. The Packer Group, Inc., 1997—, Packer Engrng., Inc., K&P Agile, Inc., Smart Signal Corp. Subject editor Ency. of Materials Sci.; contbr. articles to profl. jours.; patentee in field. Recipient Edn. Achievement award Soc. Mfg. Engrs., 1978, Vanadium award Inst. of Metals, Eng., 1990. Fellow Am. Soc. Metals (mem.); mem. ASM Internat. (truse 1986-92, pres. 1990-91), ASME, SME, Am. Foundrymen's Soc., Sigma Xi.

COPLIN, MARK DAVID, lawyer; b. Balt., Dec. 1, 1928; m. Judith Charlotte Levinson, Jan. 27, 1991. BA, U. Md., 1949, LLB, 1952. Bar: Md. 1952. Law clk. presiding justice U.S. Ct. Appeals (4th cir.), 1952-53; assoc. Weinberg and Green, LLC, Balt., 1953-60, mem., 1960-98; sr. ptnr. Saul

Ewing, Balt., 1998-2001, of counsel, 2001—. Pres. Md. chpt., Am. Jewish Congress, 1971-74, Balt. Jewish Coun., 1976-78; pres. HIAS of Balt., Inc., 1972-74; mem. adv. com. Md. Blue Sky, 1968-92; bd. dirs. Jewish Family Svc., 1992-98; chmn. bd. trustees Balt. Hebrew U., 1987-89; mem. bd. visitors Balt. City Coll., 1990-97, sec., 1992-97. Mem. ABA, Md. Bar Assn., Balt. City Bar Assn., Balt. Bar Found. (pres. 1991-93), Order of Coif, Omicron Delta Kappa, Jewish. Office Phone: 410-332-8720. E-mail: mcoplin@saul.com, mdc12128@aol.com.

COPMAN, LOUIS, radiologist; b. Phila., Jan. 17, 1934; s. Jacob and Eve (Snyder) C.; m. Avera Schuster, June 8, 1958; children: Mark, Linda. BA, U. Pa., 1955, MD, 1959. Diplomate Am. Bd. Radiology; Nat. Bd. Med. Examiners. Commd. ensign Med. Corps USN, 1958; advanced through grades to capt. M.C. USN, 1975; ret., 1975; asst. chief radiology dept. Naval Hosp., Pensacola, Fla., 1966—69; chief radiology dept. Doctors Hosp., Phila., 1969—73; radiologist Mercer Hosp. Ctr., Trenton, NJ, 1973—75; chmn. radiology dept. Naval Hosp., Phila., 1975—84; chief. radiology dept. Naval Med. Clinic, Pearl Harbor, Hawaii, 1984—89; pvt. practice radiologist Honolulu, 1989—92. Cons. Radiology Svcs., Wilmington, Del., 1978-84, Yardley (Pa.) Radiology, 1979-84. Author: The Cuckold, 1974. Capt. med. corps USN, 1958—89, ret., 1989. Recipient Albert Einstein award in Medicine, U. Pa., 1959. Mem. AMA, Assn. Mil. Surgeons U.S., Royal Soc. Medicine, Radiol. Soc. N.Am., Am. Coll. Radiology, Photographic Soc. Am., Sherlock Holmes Soc., Phi Beta Kappa, Alpha Omega Alpha. Avocations: photography, hang-gliding, scuba diving. Home: PO Box 384767 Waikoloa HI 96738-4767 Office: 68-1771 Makanahele Pl Waikoloa HI 96738-5128 Office Phone: 808-883-0059. Personal E-mail: louiscopman@earthlink.net. *Throughout one's life, one should choose his companions wisely.*

COPPA, FRANK JOHN, historian, educator; b. N.Y.C., July 18, 1937; s. Peter Paul and Rafaella Coppa; m. Rosina Genovese, Aug. 7, 1965; children: Francesca, Melina. BA in History, Bklyn. Coll., 1960; MA in History, Cath. U. Am., Washington, 1962, PhD in History, 1966. Tchg. fellow Cath. U. Am., Washington, 1963—64; lectr. Bklyn. Coll., 1964; from instr. to assoc. prof. St. John's U., N.Y.C., 1965—79, prof., 1979—. Guest spkr. Sta. WNBC-AM, N.Y.C., 1972—73, Sta. WPAT-FM, N.Y.C., 1972—73. Author: Economics and Politics in the Giolittian Age, 1971, Camillo di Cavour, 1973, Pope Pius IX, 1979, Cardinal Giacomo Antonelli and Papal Politics in European Affairs, 1990, The Origins of the Italian Wars of Independence, 1992, The Modern Papacy since 1789, 1998, The Papacy Confronts the Modern World, 2003; editor (with B. Bast and W. Griffin): From Vienna to Vietnam: War and Peace in the Modern World, 1969; editor: (with P. Dolce) Cities in Transition: From the Ancient World to Urban America, 1974; editor: Religion in the Making of Western Man, 1974, Screen and Society: The Impact of Television upon Aspects of Contemporary Civilization, 1979, Dictionary of Modern Italian History, 1985, Studies in Modern Italian History: From the Risorgimento to the Republic, 1986, Italian History: An Annotated Bibliography, 1990, Controversial Concordats: The Vatican's Relations with Napoleon, Mussolini, and Hitler, 1999, Encyclopedia of the Vatican and Papcy, 1999, Great Popes Through History: An Encyclopedia, 2002; editor: (with T. Curran) The Immigration Experience in America, 1976; editor: (with R. Hammond) Technology in the Twentieth Century, 1983; contbr. articles to profl. jours.; lectr. (TV series) The Evolution of Cities: From the Village to Megalopolis and Beyond, 1972, acad. coord., participant (TV miniseries) The Immigrant in American Life, 1973, The Italian American-Experience: Past and Present, 1979. Fellow, KC, 1960—64; grantee, NEH, 1977, Banca Commerciate Italiana; Genoroso Pope scholar, 1956, Fulbright grantee, Italy, 1964—65, U.S. Ednl. Program Found. grantee, Belgium, 1965, Italian Ministry of Fgn. Affairs grantee, Columbia U., 1989. Mem.: Italian Hist. Soc. Am. (bd. dirs. 1991—), Interuniversity Ctr. European Studies, Instituto per la storia del Risorgimento, N.Y. State Assn. European Historians, Am. Cath. Hist. Soc. (mem. exec. coun. 1991—), Soc. Italian Hist. Studies, Am. Hist. Assn. Office: Saint Johns U Dept History Jamaica NY 11439 Office Phone: 718-990-6090. Business E-Mail: coppaf@stjohns.edu.

COPPEL, LAWRENCE DAVID, lawyer; b. Washington, July 3, 1944; s. Albert and Anne (Gold) C.; m. Arlene Cohen, Aug. 10, 1968; children: Jennifer, Allison. BA, U. Md., 1966, JD, 1969. Bar: Md. 1969, U.S. Dist. Ct. Md. 1971, U.S. Ct. Appeals (4th cir.) 1976, U.S. Ct. Appeals (3d cir.) 1983. Law clk. Md. Ct. Appeals, Annapolis, 1969-70; assoc. Gordon, Feinblatt, Rothman, Hoffberger & Hollander, LLC, Balt., 1970-77, mem., 1977—. Fellow Am. Coll. Bankruptcy; mem. ABA, Md. State Bar Assn., Bankruptcy Bar Assn. Dist. Md. (pres. 1988-89), Balt. City Bar Assn. Office: Gordon Feinblatt Rothman Hoffberger & Hollander LLC 233 E Redwood St Baltimore MD 21202-3332 Office Phone: 410-576-4000. E-mail: lcoppel@gfrlaw.com.

COPPENBARGER, KERRY BRENT, music educator; b. Olathe, Kans., Oct. 22, 1959; s. Roger Dean and Eva Lavonne Coppenbarger; m. Sonja Condit Coppenbarger, July 18, 1999; children: Ethan, Rebecca. MusB in Performance, U. Wis., 1982; MusM in Performance, Roosevelt U., 1983; MusD, U. Wis., 1988. Assoc. prof. music Clarion (Pa.) U., 1990—91; freelance musician Virginia, Wis., 1992—94; adj. woodwing instr. North Greenville Coll., Tigerville, SC, 1995—2000, assoc. prof. music, 2001—. Editor: Crusell Clarinet Concerto No. 1, 1990. Grantee, Greenville Met. Arts Coun., 1998, 2002. Republican. Presbyn. Home: 1415 Winding Way Taylors SC 29687 Office: North Greenville Coll PO Box 1892 Tigerville SC 29688

COPPER, JAMES ROBERT, manufacturing executive; b. St. Louis, Aug. 19, 1939; s. Charles Alva and Cora Imogene (Shifley) Copper; m. Patricia Leeper, Aug. 12, 1961; children: Susan, Robin, Julie. AB, Culver-Stockton Coll., 1961; MS, U. Tenn.-Knoxville, 1969. Tchr. Mo. Mil. Acad., Mexico, 1961-63; mgr. applications analysis Nuclear div. Union Carbide, Oak Ridge, Tenn., 1963-69; mgr. corp. mgmt. scis. Coca-Cola Co., Atlanta, 1969-76; v.p. strategic planning and analysis Pillsbury Co., Mpls., 1976-80; v.p. strategic planning IC Industries, Inc., Chgo., 1980-86, sr. v.p. corp. planning and devel., 1986-88; pres., COO Pet, Inc., St. Louis, 1988, pres., CEO, 1989—. Mem. Civic Progress; bd. dirs. YMCA Greater St. Louis area counc. Boy Scouts Am., United Way St. Louis, Boatmen's Nat. Bank of St. Louis, Christmas in St. Louis, St. Louis Variety Club, Culver-Stockton Coll. Mem. Mo. Athletic Club, St. Louis Club, Old Warson Country Club. Home: 5777 Gene Sarazen Dr Braselton GA 30517-4057

COPPERFIELD, DAVID (DAVID KOTKIN), illusionist, director, producer; b. Metuchen, N.J., 1956; Student, Fordham U., LHD (hon.), 1999. Prof. magic NYU, 1974. Levitated across Grand Canyon, 1984; walked through Great Wall of China, 1986; escaped from Alcatraz prison, 1987, vanished Statue of Liberty, 1989, survived bldg. implosion challenge, 1989; went over Niagara Falls, 1990; vanished Orient Express, 1991, introduced flying illusion, 1992; escaped from burning ropes 13 stories above ground before 15,000 people, 1993; survived inside core of 2000 degree tornado of fire, 2001; performer, dir., producer, writer (TV spls.) The Magic of David Copperfield annually since 1978; presdl. command performance, 1981, 82, 85, 87, 92; performer (musical) Magic Man, 1974; appeared in film Terror Train, 1980; author: Tales of the Impossible, 1995, Beyond Imagination, 1996. Creator, founder Project Magic, 1982; nat. spokesperson at Olympics U.S. Orgn. Disabled Athletes, Seoul, Republic of Korea, 1988; founder Internat. Mus. Library of the Conjuring Arts, 1992. Decorated chevalier Arts and Letters (France); recipient Emmy awards and/or nominations, 1979, 80, 81, 83, 84, 85, 86, 88, 89, 90, 91, 92, 2001, Golden Rose award Montreux Film Festival, 1987, Bambi award-European equivalent of Oscars, 1993; named Magician of Yr. Acad. Magical Arts, 1980, 87; named Entertainer of Yr. Am. Guild Variety Artists, 1981, City of Atlantic City, 1986, Nat. Assn. Campus Activities, 1987; named one of Ten Outstanding Young Men in Am. U.S. Jaycees, 1985; named one of Top Ten Entrepreneurs (age 30 or under) Young Entrepreneur Orgn., 1987; named America's Fastest Rising Star by Forbes Mag., 1993, Mardi Gras King, 1996, Magician of Millennium, Fedn. Internat. des Soc. Magiques, 2000, Magician of Century, Internat. Magician's Soc.; named a living legend Libr. of Congress, 2000; recipient Bambi award, 1993, Golden Rose award, Montreux Film Festival; named to Forbes Highest Paid Celebrity List. Achievements include being youngest magician to be inducted into the Soc. Am. Magicians at age 14, most awarded magician in history, Guinness Book of World Records, 2005, most amount of money earned by a magician, 2005, created world's largest magic collection/museum, 2005, highest total internat. TV audience for a magician, 2005, largest amount of shows per year, 2005, Am. producer to premiere Am. TV spl. in Peoples Republic of China, 1986; Broke box office attendance records Miami Knight Ctr., 1984, Warner Theater, Washington, 1985, Caesars Palace, Las Vegas, Nev., 1985, Taipei Sports and Cultural Stadium, 1987, Premier Theater, Mexico City, 1987, Coliseum, Hong Kong, 1988, World Trade Ctr., Singapore, 1988, Putra World Trade Ctr., Kuala Lumpur, 1988, Giganto Arena, Porto Allegre, Brazil, 1988, Fox Theatre, Detroit, 1989, 92; broke European attendance record Dortmond, Germany, 1993; Broadway record holder, Dreams and Nightmares with Francis Ford Coppola, 1997; Madame Tussaud's Waxworks, London, 1995; inducted Hollywood Walk of Fame, 1995; featured on postage stamps for 4 countries, 2000, record for largest total tickets sold worldwide for a solo entertainer, 2005.*

COPPERMAN, STUART MORTON, pediatrician, educator; b. Bklyn., June 5, 1935; s. Irving and Anne (Reisfield) C.; m. Renee Stein, Aug. 17, 1958; children: Beth, Alan, Cara. BA cum laude, Bklyn. Coll., 1956; MD, SUNY-Bklyn., 1960. Diplomate Am. Bd. Pediatrics. Rotating intern. L.I. Jewish Hosp., New Hyde Park, N.Y., 1960-61, resident in pediat., 1961-63; practice medicine specializing in pediat. Merrick, N.Y., 1965-2000; sr. med. cons. Med. Advisers, P.C., 2001—02; mem. staff L.I. Jewish Hillside Med. Ctr., Schneider Children's Hosp., New Hyde Park, Nassau County Med. Ctr., East Meadow, Winthrop U. Hosp., Mineola, North Shore Univ. Hosp., Manhasset; clin. assoc. prof. pediat. SUNY Med. Sch., Stony Brook, 1972-2000; asst. prof. clin. health studies SUNY Sch. Allied Health, Stony Brook, 1977-2000; clin. instr. physicians asst. program Stony Brook Med. Ctr., 1972-2000; prof. pediat. St. George's Med. Coll., St. Vincent, W.I., acting chmn. pediat., 1979-80; healthcare security analyst, healthcare cons., 2000—; medico-legal expert, 2000—; physician exec. Health and Info. Svcs., 2001—02; pres. SMCMD, Ltd., 2003—; dir. Professional.PracticeBroker-s.com, 2003—. Med. advisor Assn. Children with Downs Syndrome, 1971-98; mem. com. for handicapped Bellmore Sch. Dist., 1976-86; mem. ad hoc com. on cmty. as sch. Merrick-Bellmore Schs., 1976-90; bd. dirs. North Shore-L.I. Jewish I.P.O., L.I. Sch. Health Edn. Coalition, North Shore Physicians Orgn., North Shore - L.I. Jewish PHO; mem. Nassau County Sch. Health Edn. Commn., 1990-93; mem. ad hoc com. on prevention of birth defects March of Dimes; preceptor in pediat. Physicians Asst. Program, Cath. Med. Ctr.; mem. doctor's adv. com. Shaare Zedek Hosp., Jerusalem, 1974-98; med. cons. Matchbox Toys, 1985-88, Proctor & Gamble, 1988, Carnation Co., 1989-90, Disney Ednl. Svcs., 1990-95, vaccine divsn. Merck Corp., 1997—, Sepracor, 1999—; cons., mem. spkrs. bur. N.Y. State Med. Soc., N.Y. State Senate Com. Mental Hygiene, 1988—, Lederle Labs., 1989-95, Merck Labs., 1996—, Wallace Labs., 1996—, ucb Pharma, 1999—, Connaught, 1999—, Abbott Labs., 1996—, Pfizer, 1998—, Sepracor, 1999—; author, co-founder, pres., bd. dirs. Child Health Imagery Prodns.; founder, dir. brokerage website, 2002—. Appearance TV shows on Downs Syndrome, learning disabilities, CPR, first aid, infant exercise programs, TV's effects on children, infectious disease, parent-infant bonding, immunizations, enuresis, toilet training, prevention of cigarette smoking among children, 1972—, also on HealthLinks (Life Time TV), 1990-93; mem. editl. adv. bd. Jour. Assn. for Physician Assts., 1987—; editl. cons. Jour. Pediat. Mgmt., 1991—; contbr. chpt. to Textbook Pediat. Sports Medicine; developer Babycise (infant parent interactive program in video tape and book form), 1985; rschr. on hetacillin, 1966, pyridoxine effect on serotonin level and performance in children with Down's Syndrome, 1970-75, Alice in Wonderland syndrome as presenting sympton of infectious mononucleosis, 1966-77, on transmission of group A Beta hemolytic strep infection from pet reservoirs to children, 1963-81; med. editor Air Fair Mag., 1991-93, L.I. Parent Mag., 1985-93, L.I. Family Mag., 1994-95; contbr. articles to profl. jours. Mem. sch. bd. Temple Beth Am., Merrick, 1972-78, mem. exec. com., 1973-74, chmn. com. Israel and World Affairs, 1976-78, mem. sch. com., 1976-78, mem. ritual com., 1976-93; mem. N.Y. State Senate com. on mental hygiene, 1990—; mem. profl. adv. bd. So. Shore divsn. YM-YWHA; benefactor Merrick Libr., 1992—. With U.S. Army, 1963-65. Recipient Physician Recognition award AMA, 1966—, testimonial dinner and plaque Assn. Children with Down Syndrome, 1972, Best Clin. Tchrs. of Pediat. award Nassau County Med. Ctr., 1981-82; named Merrick Profl. of Yr., 1994. Fellow Am. Acad. Pediat. (chmn. com. TV effects on children 1976—, mem. nat. com. comm. and pub. info. 1984-85, mem. nat. com. on substance abuse 1998-2001, media spokesperson 1988—, tobacco, alcohol and drug-free generation coord. 1988-98, chmn. substance abuse com. 1992—, N.Y. state chmn. substance abuse com. 1992-94, managed care com. chpt. 2 1993-95), Internat. Coll. Pediat.; mem. AMA, N.Y. State Med. Soc. (com. on alcohol 1997—), Nassau County Med. Soc. (com. on mental health 1980—, project assist 1992—, Nassau Acad. Medicine Pub. Health com. 1991—, libr. com. 1993—, chmn. pediat. sect. 1995—), Nassau Pediat. Soc. (mem. exec. bd. 1972—, chmn. com. on mental health 1972-88, v.p. 1994-95, pres. 1996-97). A Non-Smoking Generation Internat. (organizer, med. dir. Am. divsn.), Am. Lung Assn., Nassau-Suffolk Lung Assn. (life mem., dir. 1982-84), Am. Physicians Fellowship for Israel Med. Assn., Assn. Children with Learning Disabilities (mem. profl. adv. bd.), La Leche League, Latin Am. Parents Assn., L.I. Sch. Health Edn. Coun. (bd. dirs. 1989-92), Alpha Epsilon Pi (chancellor Phi Theta chpt. 1955-56), Phi Delta Epsilon (consul Zeta chpt. 1960), B'nai Brith. Office: 676 Balfour Pl Melville NY 11747 Office Phone: 516-520-1000. Personal E-mail: smcmd@aol.com. *No one person can do everything - but every person can do something. If you want something done, give it to a busy person. We must live for today with an eye toward tomorrow. I'd like my epitaph to read "While alive, he lived".*

COPPERSMITH, SAM, lawyer; b. Johnstown, Pa., May 22, 1955; m. Beth Schermer, Aug. 28, 1983; children: Sarah, Benjamin, Louis. AB in Econs. magna cum laude, Harvard U., 1976; JD, Yale Law Sch., 1982. Bar: Calif. 1982, Ariz. 1983. Fgn. svc. officer U.S. Dept. State, Port of Spain, Trinidad and Tobago, 1977—79; law clk. to Judge William C. Canby Jr. U.S. Ct. Appeals (9th cir.), Phoenix, 1982—83; atty. Sacks, Tierney & Kasen, P.A., Phoenix, 1983—86; asst. to Mayor Terry Goddard City of Phoenix, 1984; atty. Jones, Jury, Short & Mast P.C., Phoenix, 1986—88, Bonnett, Fairbourn & Friedman P.C., Phoenix, 1988—92; mem. 103d Congress from 1st Ariz. Dist., 1993—95; atty. Coppersmith Gordon Schermer Owens & Nelson PLC, 1995—. Former dir., pres. Planned Parenthood Ctrl. and No. Ariz.; former chair City of Phoenix Bd. Adjustment; former dir. Ariz. Cmty. Svc. Legal Assistance Found., 1986—89; trustee Devereux Found., 1997—; chair Ariz. Dem. Party, 1995—97. Mem. ABA, Maricopa County Bar Assn. Democrat. Office: Coppersmith Gordon Schermer Owens & Nelson PLC 2800 N Central Ave Ste 1000 Phoenix AZ 85004-1007 E-mail: sam@cgson.com.

COPPERSMITH FREDMAN, MARIAN UNGAR, magazine publisher; b. Wilkes-Barre, Pa., June 11, 1933; d. Max H. and Tillie (Landau) Ungar; m. Sy Barash, Jan. 31, 1954 (dec. Feb. 1975); children: Carol Lynn, Nan Ruth; m. W. Louis Coppersmith, Apr. 29, 1978 (dec. Jan. 1989); m. Samuel G. Fredman, Feb. 24, 1990. BA in Journalism with honors, Pa. State U., 1953; postgrad., 1953-55. Tech. writer Kling Studios, Chgo., 1951; editl. dir. Daily Collegian, State College, Pa., 1953; grad. asst., instr. dept. speech Pa. State U., State College, 1953-55, 61; instr. mktg., 1974-75, 78; writer, salesman Friedman & Barash, State College, 1956-59; ptnr. Barash Advtsg., 1959-60, Morgan Signs, Inc., 1960-75; pub. State College Town-Gown, Where & When, 1959—; pres. The Barash Group, 1975—2000, chmn., 2000—. Bd. dir. Milton S. Hershey Med. Sch.; cons. mktg. and pub. rels. to various fin. instns.; guest lectr. speech, journalism, mktg. Pa. State U., 1965—; v.p Palmer Mus Adv. Bd., 1998-99, pres., 1999-2001 Contbr. articles to profl. jours. Chmn. Art Alliance Fund Campaign, 1971; mem.pub. rels. com. Ctrl. Pa. Heart Assn., 1973; chmn. Cancer Crusade, State College, 1973-74; mem. Pa. Commn. for Women, 1980-87; bd. govs. Pa. Free Enterprise Week, 1981-85; chmn. bd. govs. Ctr. County Cmty. Found., 1987-89; pres. Nittany Coun. Rep. Women, 1960-61; bd. dirs. United Fund, 1965-70, asst. chmn., 1969; alumni trustee Pa. State U., 1976-97, vice-chmn., 1988-91, chmn., 1991-93; bd. dirs. Pennsylvanians for Effective Govt., 1978, United Way Pa., 1977-82, treas., 1978; bd. dirs. Capital Blue Cross, 1978-84, Women's Campaign Fund., 1982-85, Pa. Ben Franklin Partnership, 1983-87, Mercy Hosp., Johnstown, Pa., 1983-89, Ctrl. Pa. Festival of the Arts, 1995—2000, Allegheny Highlands Regional Theatre, Pa. Ctr. Stage, Pa. Humanities Coun., Pa. Women's Campaign Fund., Renaissance Scholarship Fund Pa. State U., 1976—; bd. advs. Palmer Mus. Art, 1994—; mem. leadership coun. Ctr. Performing Arts SUNY, Purchase, 1994—96; mem. adv. coun. subcom. small bus. and commerce com. Pa. Ho. of Reps., 1983-86; mem. B'nai B'rith; chair Women's Resource Ctr, Hemlock Girl Scout Council; bd. adv., Palmer Museum Art, 1994-; trustee emerita, Penn State U.; capital campaign coord. Alpha Com. Ambulance, 2001-04 Alumni fellow Pa. State U., 1997; recipient Kiwanis award, 1976, Small buisnesperson of Yr., 1981, Svc. to Soc. award Coll. Liberal Arts Pa. State U., 1984; named Disting. Pennsylvanian, Pa. Gov., 1981, Phila. C. of C. (Disting. Dau. Pa. 1990), One of Pa.'s Best 50 Women in Bus., Pa. Commn. Women, 1996, Crl. Pa. Entrepreneur of Yr., Ctrl. Pa. Bus. Jour., 1996, Disting. Alumna, Pa. State U., 1998; Paul Harris fellow, Rotary, 2004. AAUW, LWV, Mem. Eight-sheet Outdoor Adv. Assn., Nat. Cable TV Assn. (pub. rels. com. 1972-73), Outdoor Adv. Assn., Outdoor Adv. Inc., Pa. Cable TV Assn. (pub. rels. counsel 1967-75), Pa. Outdoor Adv. Assn., Eight-sheet Outdoor Adv. Assn., Specialties Adv. Assn., Inc., Women in Comms., Friends of Palmer Mus. Art, Pa. State U., Friends of Schlow Libr., Clearwater Conservancy, Mt. Nittany Conservancy, Delta Sigma Rho, Omicron Delta Kappa, Nittany Lion Club. Office: Morgan Signs Inc 403 S Allen St Ste 77 State College PA 16801-5252 Office Phone: 814-238-5051. E-mail: mimi@barashgroup.com.

COPPIE, COMER SWIFT, retired state official; b. Washington, Oct. 19, 1932; s. John Lee and Marion (Peck) C.; m. Judith Ann Wright, Apr. 29, 1961; children: Cynthia, Sean, Scott. AB, Hamilton Coll., 1955; M in Pub. Adminstrn., Syracuse U., 1959. Budget analyst Bur. of Budget, State of Md., Balt., 1958—62; exec. dir., trustee Md. State Colls., Balt., 1963—68; dep. budget dir. Govt. of D.C., Washington, 1968—69; dir. Office of Budget and Mgmt. Systems, Washington, 1969—78; exec. dir. N.Y. State Fin. Control Bd., N.Y.C., 1978—86; CFO U.S. Postal Svc., Washington, 1986—92; 1st dep. compt. Office of State Compt., Albany, NY, 1993—99; ret., 1999. Bd. dirs., past pres. Homeless and Travelers Aid Agy., Albany. Served with USN, 1955-57. Recipient Gold medal Fin. Officers Assn. of U.S. and Can., 1978. Mem. Cosmos Club (Washington). Episcopalian. Avocation: swimming. Personal E-mail: csc@aol.com.

COPPLESTONE, DAVID WESLEY, artist, small business owner; b. Newton, Mass., Feb. 29, 1952; s. Wesley and Elizabeth (Winchell) C.; m. Margaret Carroll, Dec. 1996; children: Hannah E., Sarah E. Diploma, Art Inst. of Boston, 1975. Owner Landscape Design, Wellesley, Mass., 1967-73, Home Improvement Contractor, Wellesley, 1973—, Copplestone Artworks: Fine Art, Gifts, Games, Wellesley, 1975—. Product design, graphic artist Fun-N-Safe Inc., Natick, Mass., 1991; owner gourmetgames.com, 1998—. Inventor of games: Lots, C.A. Hoopster, Copplestone's Putting Rail, Pandemonium, Tick Tack Toes, Geronimo, Stackm, Meltdown, Peggotty, Jumbling, Dots. Mem. Mus. of Fine Art, Boston. Mem. Cambridge Art Assn., Coply Soc., Italo Am. Ednl. Club. Avocations: golf, tennis, windsurfing, classic films, billiards. Home and Office: 6 Shadow Ln Wellesley MA 02482-4311

COPPOCK, BRUCE, orchestra executive; m. Linda Marder. Cellist Boston Symphony Orch.; ops. & orch. mgr. St. Louis Symphony Orch., exec. dir., 1992-97; dep. dir. Carnegie Hall, N.Y.C., 1997-98; v.p. Am. Symphony Orch. League, Washington, 1998-99; dir. Orch. Leadership Acad., Washington, 1998-99; pres., mng. dir. St. Paul Chamber Orch., 1999—. Mem. Boston Chamber Music Soc. (founder). Office: St Paul Chamber Orch 408 Saint Peter St Flr 3 Saint Paul MN 55102-1130

COPPOCK, JANET ELAINE, mental health nurse; b. Tipton, Ind., June 2, 1954; d. Jack Donavon and Bonnie Ruth (Luse) Weismiller; divorced; children: Jonathan Andrew, Daniel Jason. Student, Ball State U., 1972—73; ASN, Ind. U. Kokomo, 1977. RN, Ind., Mich.; cert. psychiat./mental health nurse ANCC. RN charge staff and med.-surg. Tipton County Meml. Hosp., Ind., 1977—79; RN psychiat. staff Howard Cmty. Hosp., Kokomo, 1987—89; pvt. nurse Kokomo, 1989—95; RN psychiat. and addiction treatment, instr. Koala Hosp. & Counseling Ctr. Behavioral Healthcare Corp., Kokomo, 1995—98; RN psychiat. and addiction treatment Lafayette Behavioral Health System, Ind., 1998—99; RN psychiat. staff, patient care coord. Home Hosp. of Greater Lafayette Health Svcs., Inc., Lafayette, 1999—. Instr. parenting edn. Kinsey Youth Ctr., Kokomo, 1995-96; co-developer Koala Halfway House, Behavioral Healthcare Corp., Kokomo, 1996, house mgr., 1996-98. Author: Poetic Reflections, Expressions and Inspirations, 1986, Faithful Resolutions, 1993, Coming to Terms, 1998. Recipient Golden Poet award World Poetry Orgn., 1987, 88. Mem.: Nurses Svc. Orgn., Internat. Platform Assn, Ind. U. Alumni Assn. (life). Avocations: musical instruments, art, movies, basketball. Home: 2711 President Ln Kokomo IN 46902-3066 Office Phone: 765-449-5034.

COPPOCK, MARK STEPHEN, not-for-profit executive; b. Atlanta, July 9, 1948; s. Ernest Rozar and Sandra Elizabeth Coppock; 1 child, Jennifer Anne Campbell. MBA, Alemeda Coll., Phoenix, 2003. Chair, CEO MRT Distbn., Inc., Powells Point, NC, 1990—94; chief profl. officer New Hope Charities, Inc., West Palm Beach, Fla., 1994—. Author: (book on taxation) How to Estimate Federal Estate Taxes. Sec., treas. Glades Acad., Pahokee, Fla., 2001—03, Everglades Prep. Acad., Pahokee, Fla., 2002—03, The Imagine Sch., West Palm Beach, Fla., 2002—03; co-founder Qual Internat., Inc. Recipient The Jefferson award, U.S. Congress, 2002. Conservative. Baptist. Home: 333 Kelsey Park Cir Palm Beach Gardens FL 33410 Office: New Hope Charities Inc 626 N Dixie Hwy West Palm Beach FL 33401 Personal E-mail: copp2070@bellsouth.net. E-mail: mark_coppock@floridacrystals.com.

COPPOCK, RICHARD MILES, retired not-for-profit administrator; b. Salem, Ohio, Mar. 17, 1938; s. Guy Lamar and Helen Angeline (Johnston) Coppock; m. Rita Mae McArtor, June 20, 1961 (div. 1973); 1 child, Carole; m. Trelma Anne Kubacak, Nov. 21, 1973; children: James, Lori. BS, USAF Acad., 1961; MSME, U. Colo., 1969. Commd. 2d lt. USAF, 1961, advanced through grades to lt. col., 1983, ret., 1983; pres., CEO Assn. Grads. USAF Acad., Colo., 1983-99, ret., 1999. Decorated DFC (4), Air medal (29); named Outstanding Alumnus, Salem HS, 1980. Mem.: VFW (life), Ret. Officers Assn., Colorado Springs C. of C. (mem. mil. affairs coun. 1985—90), Elks, Am. Legion. Republican. Methodist. Avocations: music, history. Home: 2513 Mirror Lake Ct Colorado Springs CO 80919-3515

COPPOLA, ANDREW JOSEPH (LIBERO), JR., sculptor, educator; b. Copiage, N.Y., Jan. 6, 1941; s. Andrew Joseph L. and Mary (Feri-Coppola) C. BFA, U. Hartford, 1963; postgrad., Academ di Belle Arti, Florence, Italy, 1964. Freelance sculptor, Hartford, Conn., 1964—. Adj. faculty sculpture dept. U. Hartford, West Hartford, Conn., 1970-71, 84; instr. sculpture Greater Hartford Jewish Cmty. Ctr., West Hartford, 1973-83, 85, West Hartford Art League, 1983—; curator Beth El Temple Sisterhood Ann. Juried Exhbn., West Hartford, 1983. Prin. works include bronze plaque Conn. State Seal, Hartford, 1964, limestone bldg. sculpture reliefs U.S. Mil. Acad., West Point, N.Y., 1968, cast aluminum courtyard sculpture Town Hall, Berlin, Conn., 1975, 7 bronze sculptures Nat. Jewish Fedn., Boston, 1976, bronze head Amistad Resource Ctr., Hartford, 1977, granite fountain, Winsted, conn., 1979, copper hanging light sculpture, Avon, Conn., 1984, inlay glass top copper table with neon, Avon, 1985. Mem. nat. screening com. sculpture Fulbright and Overseas Grants, Inst. Internat. Edn., N.Y.C., 1983, 84, 85. Recipient Dessie Greer award Nat. Acad. Art, 1971, Sculpture award Ellsworth Gallery, 1980; Fulbright-Hays fellow Inst. Internat. Edn., 1964-65; Italian Govt. grantee, 1964-65, Conn. Commn. on Arts grantee, 1977, 78. Mem. Internat. Sculpture Ctr. Home: 262 Hudson St Hartford CT 06106-1777

COPPOLA, CLAIRE, art educator, artist; d. Charles and Lois Coppola; m. David H. Blair; children: Andrew Blair, Lauren Blair. BS in Edn., Ark. State U., Jonesboro, 1976, MA, 2003. Art and French instr. Montessori Sch.,

Jonesboro, 1984—86; art educator Jonesboro Pub Schs., 1986—. Adj. prof. Ark. State U., Jonesboro, 2003; ESL instr. Jonesboro Pub. Schs., 2004; textbook cons. Rainbow Publ., Jonesboro, 2003—05. Named Outstanding Educator, Ark. Govs. Sch., 2003. Mem.: Ark. Art Edn. Assn., Nat. Art Edn. Assn., C. of C. (edn. com. 2003—05). Avocations: glass fusing, photography, calligraphy, sculpting. Business E-Mail: coppola@aghs.jps.k12.ar.us.

COPPOLA, ELAINE MARIE, librarian; b. Dunkirk, N.Y., Aug. 5, 1947; d. Henry Stanley and Althea May Hruby. BA, St. Bonaventure U., 1969; MLS, Syracuse U., 1979, MS Sc, 1989. Asst. mgr. manpower planning and devel. Oneida (N.Y.) Ltd., 1972-74, asst. mgr. pub. rels., 1974-78; libr. SUNY Inst. Tech., Utica, 1979; from catalog libr. E.S. Bird Libr. to ref. libr. Syracuse U., 1979—2005, ref. libr. ref. and documents E.S. Bird Libr., 2005—. Author: Political Science Annotations within the Supplement to the Guide to Reference Books, 1992, Political Science Annotations in Guide to Reference Books, 11th edit., 1996. Mem. Dem. com. Town of Manlius, town councilor, 1998-2001. Mem. ALA, N.Y. Libr. Assn., Assn. of Coll. and Rsch. Librs. (ea. N.Y. chpt. pres. 1992-93, v.p. 1991-92, sec. 1989-91, Libr. of the Yr. 1996), Manlius Hist. Soc. (bd. trustees 1999--, sec. 2002--), Beta Phi Mu. Home: 103 Kenny St Fayetteville NY 13066-1230 Office: ES Bird Libr Syracuse Univ Syracuse NY 13244-0001 E-mail: emcoppol@syr.edu.

COPPOLA, FRANCIS FORD, film director, producer, writer; b. Detroit, Apr. 7, 1939; s. Carmine Coppola; m. Eleanor Neil; children: Gian-Carlo(dec.), Roman, Sofia. BA, Hofstra U., 1958; Master of Cinema, UCLA, 1968. Pub. mag., San Francisco, 1975-76. Artistic dir. Zoetrope Studios.; dir. films including Dementia 13, 1964, You're a Big Boy Now, 1967, Finian's Rainbow, 1968, The Rain People, 1969, One from the Heart, 1981, Peggy Sue Got Married, 1986, Gardens of Stone, 1987, Tucker: The Man and His Dream, 1988, Bram Stoker's Dracula, 1992, The Rainmaker, 1997; writer films This Property Is Condemned, 1966, Reflections In a Golden Eye, 1967, The Rain People, 1969, Is Paris Burning, 1966, Patton, 1970, The Great Gatsby, 1974; co-writer, dir. The Cotton Club, 1984, Life Without Zoe (segment in New York Film Stories), 1990, writer, prodr., dir. The Godfather (Acad. awards for Best Screenplay and Best Picture, nominee for Best Dir., Film Dir.'s award Dirs. Guild Am. 1972), The Godfather, Part II, 1974 (Acad. awards for Best Screenplay, Best Dir. and Best Picture), The Conversation, 1974 (Golden Palm award Cannes Film Festival 1974), Apocalypse Now, 1979 (Golden Palm award Cannes Film Festival 1979), Rumble Fish, 1983, writer, dir. The Godfather: Part III, 1990, The Rainmaker, 1997, prodr., dir. (films) The Outsiders, 1983, Jack, 1996, The Rainmaker, 1997; prodr.(films): THX 1138, 1971, The Escape Artist, 1982, The Black Stallion Returns, 1983, Lanai-Loa, 1998, The Florentine, 1999, The Virgin Suicides, 1999, Grapefruit Moon, 2000; exec. prodr.(films): Black Stallion, 1979, Hammett, 1983, Lionhart, 1987, The Secret Garden, 1993, Mary Shelley's Frankenstein, 1994, My Family/Mi Familia, 1995, Don Juan DeMarco, 1995, Buddy, 1997, The Third Miracle, 1999, Goosed, 1999, Sleepy Hollow, 1999; co-exec. prodr. Mishima, 1985; dir. TV Movie The People; prodr. (TV series) White Dwarf, 1995, First Wave, 1998; exec. prodr. TV movie Dark Angel, 1996, Outrage, 1998; exec. prodr.: (TV mini-series) The Odyssey, 1997, Moby Dick, 1998; dir. (play) Private Lives, opera The Visit; appeared in TV movie Marlon Brando: The Wild One, 1996. Mem.: Dirs. Guild Am. Inc.*

COPPOLA, MICHAEL N., automotive parts executive; m. Dawn Coppola. BS in mktg., mgmt., Canisius Coll., Buffalo, 1970. Previously with Tops Friendly Markets, Buffalo, exec. v.p. mktg., 1991—97; sr. v.p. mdse. Advance Auto Parts Inc., Roanoke, Va., 2001—03, exec. v.p., COO, 2003—05, pres., CEO, 2005—. Office: Advance Auto Parts Inc 5673 Airport Rd Roanoke VA 24012

COPPOLA, NICOLAS See CAGE, NICOLAS

COPPOLA, PATRICIA FINEGAN, biology professor, small business owner; AA, North Country C.C., 1986; BSc, SUNY Brockport, 1988; MSc, Springfield (Mass.) Coll., 2003. Cert. tchr. phys. edn. Tchg. fellow Springfield Coll., 1996—98; instr. biology C.C. So. Nev., 1998—. Author: P.F. Flier Newsletter, 2004—. Mem.: Am. Coll. Sports Medicine. Avocations: cross country skiing, hiking, reading, camping. Office: Community College Southern Nevada 3200 E Cheyenne Ave North Las Vegas NV 89030

COPPOLA, SOFIA CARMINA, film director, scriptwriter, actress; b. N.Y.C., May 1971; d. Francis Ford and Eleanor Coppola; m. Spike Jonze, 1999. Intern with Karl Lagerfield Chanel; designer Milk Fed. Actor: (films) The Godfather, 1972, The Godfather: Part II, 1974, The Outsiders, 1983, Rumble Fish, 1983, The Cotton Club, 1984, Frankenweenie, 1984, Peggy Sue Got Married, 1986, Anna, 1987, The Godfather: Part III, 1990, Inside Monkey Zetterland, 1992, Star Wars: Episode I-The Phantom Menace, 1999, CQ, 2001; dir., prodr., screenwriter (films) Lick the Star, 1998, Lost in Translation, 2003 (Golden Athena, Athens Intl. Film Festival, 2003, Boston Soc. of Film Critics award for best dir., 2003, Nat. Bd. of Review award for special achievement, 2003, NY Film Critics Circle award for best dir., 2003, Toronto Film Critics Assoc. award for best screenplay, 2003, Golden Globe for best screenplay, 2004, Academy award for best screenplay, 2004), dir., screenwriter The Virgin Suicides, 1999, host (TV series) Hi-Octane, 1994, segment writer N.Y. Stories, 1989, costume designer, 1989, series creator Platinum, 2003, writer, 2003; exec. prodr.: (TV series) Platinum, 2003; costume designer (plays) The Spirit of '76, 1990.

COPPOLA-BETTUA, MARIA SOFIA, educational association administrator; arrived in U.S., 1960; d. Anthony Coppola and Eleanor Conte-Coppola; m. Peter Jerry Bettua; children: Michael Jerry Bettua, Thomas Jeffrey Bettua, Gerald Anthony Bettua. BA in English Textual Studies, Syracuse U., 1992; MA in Pub. Adminstrn., Syracuse (N.Y.) U., 2000. Asst. dir. Global Affairs Inst. Syracuse U., 1993—2001; dep. dir. Internat. Divsn. Zogby Internat., Utica, NY, 2001—02; exec. dir. Zogby Worldwide, Utica, 2003—04; asst. dir. Europe and Eurasia Coun. Internat. Exch. of Scholars, Washington, 2004—. Grantee, Coun. for Internat. Exch. of Scholars, 1994—2000; Edmund S. Muskie/Freedom Support Act Grad. fellowship, Internat. Rsch. and Exchanges Bd., 1997—2001, Russian-U.S. Leadership fellows program, 1998—2001, Ron Brown fellows program, Dept. Commerce, 1998—2001. Office Phone: 202-686-6245. E-mail: mbettua@cies.iie.org.

COPPRIDGE, ALTON JAMES, urological surgeon; b. Roanoke, Va., Dec. 8, 1926; s. William Maurice Coppridge and Ferrie (Patterson) Choate; m. Helen Allen Burnett, June 24, 1950; children: William Allen, Virginia Choate. BA, U. N.C., 1949; MD, U. Va., 1953. Diplomate Am. Bd. Urology. Intern N.C. Meml. Hosp., Chapel Hill, 1953-54; surg. resident State U. of Iowa, Iowa City, 1954-56; urology resident U. Mich., Ann Arbor, 1956-59; mem. Coppridge Urologic Group, P.A., Durham, N.C., 1959-89; dept. chmn. Durham County Gen. Hosp., 1978-84; asst. clin. prof. Duke Med Ctr., Durham, N.C., 1970-89; clin. instr. U. N.C. Med. Sch., Chapel Hill, 1960-75. Contbr. articles to urologic lit. Served with U.S. Army, 1944-46; Japan. Mem.: ACS, NRA, Carolina Urol. Soc. (pres. 1985), N.C. Med. Soc. (pres. sect. urology 1978), Am. Urol. Assn. (exec. com. S.E. sect. 1983—86), Safari Internat. Club (Tucson) (pres. N.C. chpt. 1979—80), Durham Pistol and Rifle Club. Democrat. Presbyterian. Avocations: hunting, shooting, farm work. Home: A213 - 2600 Croasdaile Farm Pky Durham NC 27705 Office Phone: 919-384-2783.

COPPS, MICHAEL JOSEPH, federal agency administrator; b. Milw., Apr. 23, 1940; s. Edmund J. and Ruth E. (Klemm) C.; m. Elizabeth Miller, Sept. 5, 1970; children: Robert, Mary, Michael, William, Claire. BA, Wofford Coll., 1963; PhD, U. N.C., 1967. Asst. prof. history Loyola U., New Orleans, 1967-70; adminstrv. asst. to U.S. Sen. Ernest F. Hollings U.S. Senate, Washington, 1970-85; dir. govt. affairs Collins & Aikman Corp., Washington, 1985-89; sr. v.p. Am. Meat Inst., Washington, 1989-93; dep. asst. sec. Dept. Commerce, Washington, 1993-98, asst. sec. for trade devel., 1998-2001; commr. FCC, Washington, 2001—. Mem. Phi Beta Kappa, Pi Gamma Mu. Democrat. Avocations: reading, automobiles. Office: FCC Off of Comn 445 12th St SW Washington DC 20554 E-mail: mcopps@FCC.gov.

COPPS, SHEILA, former Canadian government official; b. Hamilton, Ont., Can., Nov. 27, 1952; d. Victor Kennedy and Geraldine (Guthro) C.; m. Austin Thorne; 1 child, Danelle. BA in French, English with hons., U. Western Ont., London; postgrad., U. Rouen, France, McMaster U., Hamilton. Reporter Ottawa Citizen, 1974-76, Hamilton Spectator, 1977; asst. to Ont. Liberal leader Stuart Smith, Hamilton, 1977-81; mem. Legis. Assembly Ont., Toronto, 1981-84, House of Commons, Ottawa, 1984-97; apptd. dep. leader Liberal Party Can., Ottawa, Ont., 1990—; dep. prime min. Govt. of Can., Ottawa, 1993-97, min. environ., 1993-96, min. of Can. heritage, 1996—2003. Author: Nobody's Baby, 1986. Mem. Liberal Party. Office: House of Commons Rm 509-S Ottawa ON Canada K1A 0A6 also: 275 Queenston Rd L8K 1G9 Hamilton ON Canada

COPSETTA, NORMAN GEORGE, real estate executive; b. Pennsauken, NJ, Mar. 11, 1932; s. Joseph J. and Mary P. (DeMello) C.; m. Patricia Fitzpatrick, Mar. 5, 1971 (dec.); children: Gregory, Margaret, Andrew, Norman G. Jr.; stepchildren: Samuel Sassano, James Sassano. Cert. real estate, Rutgers U. Extension, Camden, N.J., 1952; AA, Internat. Accts. Soc. Schl. Acctg., Chgo., 1968. Lic. title insurance agent, N.J. Settlement clk. Market Street Title Abstract Co., Camden, 1949-53; settlement administrator West Jersey Title & Guaranty Co., Camden, 1953; title examiner, abstract adminstr. Realty Abstract Co., Cherry Hill, N.J., 1954-64; mcpl. treas., tax collector Borough of Somerdale, N.J., 1961-65; title examiner, legal adminstr. Davis, Reberkenny & Abramowitz, Cherry Hill, 1974-97; pres., title officer Cooper Abstract Co., Cherry Hill, 1974-99, chmn. bd., 1997—. N.J. fgn. commr. of deeds in and for Pa., 1959—2000; mem. faculty Title Acad. N.J., The Title Ins. Sch. Custodian of funds Somerdale Bd. Edn., 1960-64. Mem. N.J. Title Ins. Agts. Assn., Haddonfield (N.J.) Hist. Soc., Camden County Hist. Soc. Avocation: local history. Office: Cooper Abstract Co 401 Cooper Landing Rd Ste C6 Cherry Hill NJ 08002-2598 Office Phone: 856-667-4800.

COQUILLETTE, DANIEL ROBERT, lawyer, educator; b. Boston, May 23, 1944; s. Robert McTavish and Dagmar Alvida (Bistrup) C.; m. Judith Courtney Rogers, July 5, 1969; children: Anna, Sophia, Julia. AB, Williams Coll., 1966; MA Juris., U. Coll., Oxford U., Eng., 1969; JD, Harvard U., 1971. Bar: Mass. 1974, U.S. Dist. Ct. Mass. 1974, U.S. Ct. Appeals (1st cir.) 1974. Law clk. Mass. Supreme Ct., 1971-72; to chief justice Warren E. Burger U.S. Supreme Ct., 1972-73; assoc. Palmer & Dodge, Boston, 1973-75, ptnr., 1980-85; assoc. prof. law Boston U., 1975-78; dean, prof. Boston Coll. Law, 1985-93, prof., 1993-96, J. Donald Monan prof. law, 1996—. Vis. assoc. prof. law Cornell U., Ithaca, N.Y., 1977-78, 84; vis. prof. law Harvard U., 1978-79, 84-85, 94-2001, overseers com., Lester Kissel vis. prof., 2001—; reporter com. rules and procedures Jud. Conf. U.S.; mem. task force on rules of atty. conduct Supreme Jud. Ct. of Mass., 1996-97. Author: The Civilian Writers of Doctors Commons, London, 1988, Francis Bacon, 1993, Lawyers and Fundamental Moral Responsibility, 1995, Working Papers on Rules Governing Attorney Conduct, 1997, (with Basile, Beston, Donahue) Lex Mercatoria and Legal Pluralism, 1999, The Anglo-American Legal Heritage, 1999, 2d edit., 2004, (with McMorrow) Federal Law of Attorney Conduct, 2001; editor: Law in Colonial Massachusetts, 1985, Moore's Federal Practice, 3d edit., 1997; bd. dirs. New Eng. Quar., 1986—; contbr. articles to profl. jours. Trustee, sec.-treas. Ames Found; bd. overseers vis. com. Harvard Law Sch., 1993-2003; propr., trustee emeritus Boston (Mass.) Athenaeum. Recipient Kaufman prize in English Williams Coll., 1966, Sentinel of the Republic prize in polit. sci. Williams Coll., 1965; Hutchins scholar, 1966-67, Fulbright scholar, 1966-68 Mem. ABA (com. on profl. ethics 1990-93), Am. Law Inst., Mass. Bar Assn. (task force on model rules of profl. conduct), Boston Bar Assn., Am. Soc. Legal History (bd. dirs. 1985-89), Mass. Soc. Continuing Legal Edn. (bd. dirs. 1985-89), Selden Soc. (state corr.), Colonial Soc. Mass. (v.p., mem. coun.), Anglo-Am. Cathedral Soc. (bd. dirs.), Mass. Hist. Soc., Am. Antiquarian Soc., Phi Beta Kappa. Democrat. Mem. Soc. Of Friends. Home: 12 Rutland St Cambridge MA 02138-2503 Office: Boston Coll Sch Law 885 Centre St Newton MA 02459-1148 Office Phone: 617-552-8650. E-mail: coquill@bc.edu.

COQUILLETTE, WILLIAM HOLLIS, lawyer; b. Boston, Oct. 7, 1949; s. Robert McTavish and Dagmar (Bistrup) C.; m. Mary Katherine Templeton, June 19, 1971 (div. Oct. 1984); 1 child, Carolyn Patricia; m. Janet Marie Weiland, Dec. 8, 1984; children: Benjamin Weiland, Madeline Marie, Elizabeth Charlotte. BA, Yale U., 1971, Oxford U., 1973; JD, Harvard U., 1975. Bar: Ohio 1976, Mass. 1976. Law clk. to presiding justice Mass. Supreme Ct., Boston, 1975-76; assoc. Jones Day, Cleve., 1976-83, ptnr., 1984—. Trustee Cleve. Foodbank, Playhouse Sq. Found. Mem. Kirtland Club, Yale Club (N.Y.C.), Union Club (Cleve.), Cleve. Skating Club, Rowfant Club, N.Y. Yacht Club. Office: Jones Day 901 Lakeside Ave E Cleveland OH 44114-1190 Office Phone: 216-586-7137. Business E-Mail: whcoquillette@jonesday.com.

CORA, SPIRO PETE, retired secondary education educator; b. Greenville, Miss., Jan. 7, 1935; s. Pete George and Nina (Papaspiridon) C.; m. Virginia Lee Brothers, July 9, 1961; children: Michael S., Cathrine Ann, Christopher S. BA in History, Miss. Coll., Clinton, 1963, MA in History, 1969. Cert. tchr. social studies, Miss. Restaurant mgr. Shamrock Drive Inn, Jackson, Miss., 1958-61; tchr. social studies Collier County Schs., Immokalee, Fla., 1963-66; tchr. social studies Enochs Jr. H.S. Jackson Pub. Schs., 1966-69, tchr. social studies Wingfield H.S., 1969-96, ret., 1996. Mem. social studies Miss. Textbook Selection Com., Jackson, 1979-80; mem. Miss. evaluation team Close Up Found., Washington, 1981-82; chmn. dist. social studies dept. Jackson Pub. Schs., 1975-77, 79-80, 91-92. Reviewer of textbooks. Apptd. mem. Miss. Commn. for Nat. and Cmty. Svc., Jackson, 1994—. Mem. Nat. Coun. for Social Studies, Miss. Coun. for the Social Studies (dir. 1982-84), Nat. Coun. for History Edn., World History Assn. Greek Orthodox. Avocations: reading, camping, boating, birding (eagle watching). Home: 230 Swan Lake Dr Jackson MS 39212-5336

CORACE, JOSEPH RUSSELL, automotive executive; b. Mt. Clemens, Mich., July 22, 1953; s. Joseph Anthony and Josephine (Coniglario) C.; m. Judith Agnes Cynowa, June 24, 1977; children: Christina Marie, Joseph R., Anthony Casmier. AA, Macomb Coll., 1973; BSME, Wayne State U., 1976; MBA, Mich. State U., 1980. Staff engr. GM Corp., Warren, Mich., 1976-81; mgr. Volvo Cars N. Am., Rockleigh, N.J., 1981-85; dir. Volvo Automated Sys., Sterling Heights, Mich., 1985-88; pres., CEO Inalfa Roof Sys., Auburn Hills, Mich., 1988-98; pres., CEO, owner Forum Motors Group, 1999—2003; COO, Cornerstone Schs., 2004—. Mem. Rockleigh Sch. Bd., 1986, Holy Name Ch., 1987; lector St. Fabian Ch. Recipient Disting. Engring. Alumnus award Wayne State U.; named to Wayne State U. Hall of Fame; Sloan fellow Volvo Cars N.Am., 1981. Mem. Soc. Automotive Engrs. (jour. contbr.), Soc. Mfg. Engrs., Young Pres. Orgn. (pres. East Mich. chpt. 1997, bd. dirs., officer), Legatus (bd. dirs., pres. Detroit chpt. 1998—), Oakland Hills Country Club, Engring. Soc. Detroit, Detroit Econ. Club, Am. Mgmt. Assn. (pres.'s coun.), Walnut Creek Country Club (bd. dirs., pres.), Rochester Racquet Club, Detroit Athletic Club, KC (officer Detroit 1979). Roman Catholic. Avocations: racquetball, golf, squash, harley davidson motorcycles, hunting. Home: 5658 Springbrook Dr Troy MI 48098-5351

CORAGGIO, LINUS, sculptor, consultant; b. Bennington, Vt., Feb. 15, 1962; s. Henry Dreyfuss Brant and Patricia Elizabeth Gorman. BFA, SUNY, Purchase, 1984; postgrad., Skowhegan Sch. Painting & Sculpture, 1987; postgrad, Whitney Mus. Studio Program, 1987. Founder Rivington Sch., NYC, 1984—91, Space 2B, NYC, 1986—95; cons. Landair, NYC, 1994—. Sculptor (permanent collections) including Storm King ATCT Ctr., N.Y. Resident welder 100 St. Block Assn., NYC, 1999—2003. Mem.: Anit-Bush Sculptors Group, Burning Man Festival Welded Art Comdrs., Am. Motorcyclist Assn. Avocations: martial arts, skateboarding, surfing, snowboarding, recycling. Home: 314 W 100 St New York NY 10025 E-mail: linus@nyc.rr.com.

CORALLO, N. RALPH, retired health care products design engineer; b. Paterson, N.J., Apr. 14, 1937; s. Ralph John and Sylvia (DeStefano) C.; m. Mary Ann Katherin Glasstetter, Sept. 7, 1959; children: Ralph Charles, Charles Joseph, Mary Ann Catherine. Assoc. Engring., N.J. Inst. Tech., Newark, 1958; BSME, Fairleigh Dickinson U., 1968, MBA in Mgmt. cum laude, 1972. Engring. asst. Curtiss Wright Co., Inc., Woodridge, NJ, 1956; mgr. sensor engring. Thermo Electric Co., Inc., Saddle Brook, 1958-68; dir. rsch. and devel. Becton Dickinson & Co., Inc., Franklin Lakes, 1968-94; pres. Corco Sys., Elmwood Park, 1994—2004; ret., 2004. Session editor Human Comfort and Biological Thermometry, Sixth Symposium on Temperature, 1982. Mem. ASTM (vice chmn. E20 1980-83, Robert D. Thompson award 1981), Internat. Soc. Pharm. Engrs., Instrument Soc. Am., Parenteral Drug Assn. (com. mem. 1989—). Roman Catholic. Achievements include patent for spring loaded thermocouple.

CORA-LOCATELLI, GABRIELA, psychiatrist; d. Ettore Corá and Rose Falasconi; m. Eduardo Raúl Locatelli; children: Natalia Locatelli, Marcos Locatelli. B in Langs., Barker Coll., Argentina; MD, U. Buenos Aires, 1989. Intern, resident St. Elizabeth's Hosp.; clin. rschr. NIH, Nat. Inst. Neurol. Disorders and Stroke, Bethesda, Md., 1991—92; resident in psychiatry St. Elizabeth's Hosp., DC Commn. Mental Health Systems, Washington, 1992—95; clin. rschr. NIH, NIMH, Bethesda, 1995—99; dir., regional med. rsch. specialist Pfizer Pharm., Southeast US, 1999—2002; pres. Exec. Health & Wealth Inst., Miami, Fla., 2002—. Exec. MBA and health care adminstrn. U. Miami, 2004—. Contbr. articles. Lt. cmdr. USPHS, 1997—99, Bethesda. Recipient Hannah Cashman Meml. award, NIMH/NIH, 1997; grantee, Pfizer Pharm., 1998-1999. Mem.: Assn. for Conflict Resolution (trustee at large, internat. sec. 2003—), Greater Miami C. of C. (co-chair com. internat. svcs., rsch. and edn. 2002—03, dir. 2003), South Fla. Psychiatry Soc. (v.p., pres. elect 2003—), Anxiety Disorders Assn. Am., Am. Psychiat. Assn. (chair com. residents and fellows, bd. trustees 1995—97, psychiatry in workplace com. 2002—, APA rels. 2004—). Avocations: travel, exercise, reading, writing. Office: Executive Health & Wealth Inst 9999 NE 2nd Ave Ste #213 Miami Shores FL 33138 Office Phone: 305-762-7632. E-mail: gcl@coralg.com, gcl@ExecutiveHealthWealth.com.

CORAN, ARNOLD GERALD, pediatrician, surgeon; b. Boston, Apr. 16, 1938; s. Charles and Ann (Cohen) C.; m. Susan Myra Williams, Nov. 17, 1960; children: Michael, David, Randi Beth. AB, Harvard U., 1959, MD, 1963. Diplomate Am. Bd. Surgery, Am. Bd. Thoracic Surgery, Am. Bd. Pediat. Surgery. Intern in surgery Peter Bent Brigham Hosp., Boston, 1963-64, resident in general and thoracic surgery, 1964-69; resident in pediatric surgery Children's Hosp., Boston, 1966-68; chief pediat. surgery, assoc. prof. surgery U. South Calif. Med. Sch., L.A., 1972-74; chief pediat. surgery, prof. surgery U. Mich., Ann Arbor, 1974—; surgeon in chief C.S. Mott Childrens Hosp., Ann Arbor, 1981—. Contbr. articles to profl. jours. Lt. comdr. USN, 1970-72. Mem.: Am. Pediat. Surg. Assn. (pres. 2001—02). Avocations: skiing, golf, running. Home: 505 E Huron St Apt 802 Ann Arbor MI 48104-1553 Office: CS Mott Childrens Hosp Rm F3970 Ann Arbor MI 48109-0245 Office Phone: 734-764-6482. Business E-Mail: acoran@umich.edu.

CORASH, MICHÈLE B., lawyer; b. May 6, 1945; BA, Mt. Holyoke Coll., 1967; JD cum laude, NYU, 1970. Legal advisor to chmn. FTC, 1970-72; dep. gen. counsel U.S. Dept. Energy, 1979; gen. counsel EPA, 1979-81; ptnr. Morrison & Foerster, San Francisco and L.A. Bd. editors Toxics Law Reporter; bd. advisors Jour. Environ. Law and Corporate Practice, Ecology Law Quarterly; mem. nat. editl. adv. bd. Prop 65 Clearingho. Bd. dirs. Calif. Counsel on Environ. and Econ. Balance, 1991—; mem. blue ribbon commn. Calif. Environ. Protection Agy. Unified Environ. Statute; mem. V.P. Bush Regulatory Task Force, 1981, mem. adv. council Environ. Curriculum Stanford Law Sch., bd. adv. Hastings WEst-Northwest Jour. Environmental Law & Practice. Named one of Best Lawyers in Am., Environ. Law, Corp. Counsel, Am. Lawyer, 2003, Top 50 Women Litigators in Calif., Daily Journal Extra, 2003, 100 Most Influential Lawyers in Calif., L.A. & S.F. Daily Jour., 2002, Top 30 Women Litigators in Calif., 2002. Mem. ABA (mem. standing com. on environ. 1988-91, chair com. environ. crimes 1990), Inter-Pacific Bar Assn. (chair environ. law com.). Office: Morrison & Foerster 425 Market St San Francisco CA 94105-2482 E-mail: mcorash@mofo.com.

CORBANI, CANDACE BEDFORD, antiques broker, political campaign consultant, researcher; b. Sellersville, Pa., Sept. 1, 1944; d. Harry Clay and Gwendolyn Murdoch Bedford; m. John Francis Corbani, July 3, 1963; children: Kim, Donna. BA in Sociology, U. Calif., Santa Barbara, 1968; AS in Hotel Restaurant Mgmt., Santa Barbara City Coll., 1977. Orgnl. cons. Party Makers, Santa Barbara, 1977-84; owner C&G Collection, Santa Barbara, 1981-90; owner, appraiser, cons. Candi Corbani & Collector's Resource Network, Santa Barbara, 1989—; owner EstatesaleSB.com, Santa Barbara, 1999—. Events coord. Brinkerhoff Mchts. Assn., Santa Barbara, 1985-90; cons. Wood Glen Hall, Santa Barbara, 2001. Author: Bright Ideas I, 1980, II, 1984; contbr. articles to jours.; prodr. (talk radio show) Collector's News Hour, 1989-91. Chair affirmative action com. Santa Barbara Sch. Dist., 1986-89; pres. Bus. Women Environment, Santa Barbara, 1995-2001; mem. Santa Barbara County Rep. Ctrl. Com., 1998-2001; pres. G.A.L.S. Federated Rep. Women, 1999; founding pres. Moderate Rep. Majority, Santa Barbara; del. Calif. Reps., Santa Barbara County. Recipient Women of Achievement award Calif. State Senate, Assembly & Santa Barbara County, 1987. Mem. Am. Soc. Appraisers, Assn. Online Appraisers, Santa Barbara Bus. & Profl. Women (v.p. 1988). Deist. Home and Office: 4760 Calle Camarada Santa Barbara CA 93110 E-mail: condicorbani@aol.com.

CORBATO, CHARLES EDWARD, geology educator; b. L.A., July 12, 1932; s. Hermenegildo and Charlotte Carella (Jensen) C.; m. Patricia Jeanne Ferg, May 18, 1957; children: Steven, Barbara, Susan. BA, UCLA, 1954, PhD, 1960. Instr. geology U. Calif., Riverside, 1959, Los Angeles, 1959-60, asst. prof., 1960-66; assoc. prof. Ohio State U., Columbus, 1966-69, prof., 1969-92, chmn. dept. geology and mineralogy, 1972-80, assoc. provost office of acad. affairs, 1987-92, prof., assoc. provost emeritus, 1992—. Geophysicist U.S. Geol. Survey, 1966-74; dir. State Postsecondary Rev. Entity, Ohio Bd. Regents, 1994-95, dir. info. svcs., 1995-99. Fellow: Geol. Soc. Am.; mem.: Am. Geophys. Union, Delta Tau Delta. Home: 2400 Buckley Rd Columbus OH 43220-4616 Office: Ohio State U 125 S Oval Mall Columbus OH 43210-1308 E-mail: ccorbato@columbus.rr.com.

CORBET, KATHLEEN A., financial information company executive; b. Feb. 22, 1960; BS in mktg. and computer sci., Boston Coll.; MBA in fin., NYU. Chief investment opers. and global trading Alliance Capital, 1997—99, chmn., 1998—2000, 1998—2000; CEO Alliance Capital Ltd., London, 1998—2000; CEO fixed income divsn. Alliance Capital Mgmt., 2000—04; pres. Standard & Poor's, 2004—. Mem. bd. trustees Boston Coll. Mem.: Coun. Fgn. Rels. Office: Standard & Poor's 55 Water St New York NY 10041

CORBET, RICHARD HUGH, trade policy specialist, writer; b. Perth, Australia, Nov. 18, 1936; arrived in U.S., 1990; s. John Arthur and Freda Marian (Sherwood) Corbet; m. Rosalind Mary Willett Bevan, June 10, 1961 (div. Oct. 1978). BA, U. Adelaide, Australia, 1960; postgrad., U. Keele, Eng., 1990-93. Cert. journalist Brit. Inst. Journalists. Rsch. asst. Cazenove & Co., stockbrokers, London, 1961-62; rsch. asst. conservative backbench com. on European cmty. Brit. Ho. of Commons, London, 1962-63; econs. corr. Thomson Newspapers, London, 1963-65; specialist writer The Times, London, 1965-68; dir. Trade Policy Rsch. Ctr., London, 1968-89; mng. editor The World Economy, Boston and Oxford, England, 1977-89; guest scholar Woodrow Wilson Internat. Ctr. for Scholars and the Brookings Inst., Washington, 1990-92; sr. fellow Manhattan Inst., N.Y. and Washington, 1992-93; dir. trade policy program Sigur Ctr. for Asian Studies George Washington U., Washington, 1993-97; pres. Cordell Hull Inst., Washington, 1998—. Spl. advisor Opposition Spokesmen on Trade Brit. Ho. Commons, London, 1978—79; cons. on trade policy Internat. C. of C., Paris, 1979—83; mem. adv. com. on studies internat. trade policy U. Mich. Press, Ann Arbor, 1989—; mem. adv. bd. The World Economy., Oxford and Boston, 1990—2001; cons.

European Inst. Japanese Studies, Stockholm, 1994—97, Swiss-Asia Found., Lausanne, Switzerland, 1996—99. Author: Beyond the Rhetoric of Commodity Power, 1974; co-author: Trade Strategy for the Asia-Pacific Region, 1970, Opportunity of a Century to Liberalise Farm Trade, 2002; co-editor: Europe's Free Trade Area Experiment, 1970, Commonwealth Policy in a Global Context, 1971, In Search of a New World Economic Order, 1974, Reason vs. Emotion: Requirements for a Successful WTO Round, 1999; contbr. articles to profl. jours. Office: Ste 960 1701 Pennsylvania Ave NW Washington DC 20006 Office Phone: 202-496-9199. Business E-Mail: hugh.corbet@cordellhullinstitute.org.

CORBETT, ALICE CATHERINE, investor; d. Marshal Richard and Coralyn Estelle Reckard; BS, U. Oreg., 1943. Tchr. Portland (Oreg.) Dept. Edn., 1944—47; mem. Oreg. Senate, Salem, 1950—58; commr. Multnomah County, Portland, 1964—68; investor Portland, 1964—. Mem.: Multnomah Club. Home: 2947 SW Plum Ct Portland OR 97219

CORBETT, GORDON LEROY, minister; b. Melrose, Mass., Dec. 11, 1920; s. Winfield Leroy and Lalia Estey (Fiske) C.; m. Winifred Pickett, Sept. 7, 1946; children: Douglas Leroy, Christine, Patricia, Carolyn. AB, Bates Coll., 1943; MDiv, Yale U., 1948. Ordained to ministry Bapt. Ch., 1948. Pastor Montowese Bapt. Ch., North Haven, Conn., 1948-52; assoc. pastor First Presbyn. Ch., Glen Falls, N.Y., 1952-59; synod exec. Synod of Ky., Lexington, 1959-71; assoc. synod exec. for Alaska, 1971-84; interim synod exec. Synod of Lincoln Trails, Indpls., 1987-88; interim Presbyn. exec. Santa Barbara (Calif.) Presbytery, 1991-92. Trustee Appalachian Regional Hosps., Lexington, 1969-72, Sheldon Jackson Coll., Sitka, Alaska, 1972-84; chmn. chaplaincy com. Alaska Christian Conf., 1975-78, Alaska Pipeline Chaplaincy. Author: Thirteen Generations of Descendants of Robert Corbett, who died in Woodstock, Conn., 1695, 1995. Mem. Santa Barbara Presbytery; chmn., bd. dirs. Encina Royale, Inc., 1997-98. Dist. chmn. Rep. Party, Anchorage, 1974-78. 1st lt. USAAF, 1944-45, China. Recipient Christian Citizenship award Sheldon Jackson Coll., 1984. *"Since we are surrounded by so great a cloud of witnesses... let us run with perserverance the race that is set before us". (Hebrews 12:1).*

CORBETT, JOHN DUDLEY, chemistry professor; b. Yakima, Wash., Mar. 23, 1926; s. Alexander Hazen and Elizabeth (Dudley) C.; m. Irene Lienkaemper, Aug. 7, 1948(wid. Nov. 1996); children: John Scott, Julia Barton, James Dudley. BS cum laude, U. Wash., 1948, PhD (duPont research fellow), 1952. Asst. prof., asso. chemist Iowa State U. dept. chemistry and Ames Lab. AEC (now Dept. of Energy), 1952-58; assoc. prof., chemist Iowa State U. and Ames Lab. AEC, 1958-63, prof., sr. chemist, 1963—, disting. prof. scis. and humanities, 1983—, chmn., div. chief, 1968-73, program dir., materials chemistry, 1974-78. Chmn. molten salts Gordon Research Confs., 1963, mem. council, 1964-67; cons. E.I. duPont de Nemours & Co., 1956-63, 73-79, Oak Ridge Nat. Lab., 1969-72, Monsanto, 1977-78 Contbr. articles to profl. jours. Served with USNR, 1944-46. Recipient A. von Humboldt Sr. U.S. scientist award, 1985, Outstanding Sci. Accomplishments award U.S. Dept. Energy, 1987, Sustained Outstanding Rsch. in Materials Chemistry award, 1995, J.C. Bailar Jr. medal U. Ill., 1988, F.H. Spedding award Rare Earth Rsch., 2005. Mem. Nat. Acad. Scis., Am. Chem. Soc. (councilor, past chmn. Ames sect., Iowa award 1984, Midwest award 1985, award in inorganic Chemistry 1986, Disting. Svc. Inorganic Chemistry award 2000), AAUP, Sigma Xi, Phi Lambda Upsilon, Phi Kappa Phi, Pi Mu Epsilon, Delta Tau Delta. Episcopalian. Home: 2337 Woodview Dr Ames IA 50014-8259

CORBETT, LUKE R., energy executive; m. Becky Corbett; 1 child, Carrie. Grad., U. Ga., 1969. Geophysicist Amoco Prodn. Co., Mitchell Energy, Aminoil; with Kerr-McGee Corp., 1985—, pres., COO, 1995—97, chmn., 1997—99, CEO, 1999. Mem. Nat. Petroleum Coun.; bd. dirs. Domestic Petroleum Coun., OGE Energy Corp., BOK Fin. Corp., Noble Corp., Integris Health, Inc. Trustee Okla. United Meth. Ch.; bd. dirs. Allied Arts Found., United Way. Mem.: Okla. Bus. Roundtable, Soc. Exploration Geologists, Am. Assn. Petroleum Geologists, Oklahoma City C. of C. (bd. dirs.). Office: Kerr-McGee Corp 123 Robert S Kerr Ave Oklahoma City OK 73102

CORBETT, LUKE ROBINSON, lawyer; b. Pinehurst, N.C., May 21, 1930; s. Paschal Butler and Delia Jane (McKenzie) C.; m. Joan Cole (div.); children: Steven, Rebecca, Laurie, Charles, Carolyn. AB in Polit. Sci., U. N.C., 1956, JD, 1959. Bar: Calif. 1959, U.S. Dist. Ct. (so. dist.) Calif. 1960. Assoc. Lindley, Scales & Patton, San Diego; ptnr. Scales, Patton, Ellsworth & Corbett, San Diego; shareholder, dir., pres. Lindley, Scales & Corbett and predecessor firm, San Diego. 1st lt. USAF, 1951-55. Mem. ABA, San Diego County Bar Assn. (bd. dirs., treas., v.p. 1971-74), Am. Bar Found., San Diego County Bar Found. (bd. dirs.), State Bar Calif. (del., chmn. exec. com. conf. of dels. 1975-78), Am. Inns. of Ct. (master Louis F. Welch chpt. 1984), Assn. of Bus. Trial Lawyers (bd. dirs.). Office: Lindley Scales & Corbett 550 W C St Ste 1800 San Diego CA 92101-3545 Office Phone: 619-234-9181. Business E-Mail: lrc@lsc-law.net.

CORBETT, SIOBHAN AIDEN, surgeon; b. Aug. 11, 1959; BA, Princeton Univ., 1981; MD, UMDNJ Robert Wood Johnson Med. Sch., 1987. Diplomate Am. Bd. Surgery. Postdoctoral fellow Princeton (N.J.) U.; asst. prof. surg. scis. Robert Wood Johnson Med. Sch., New Brunswick, NJ, 1997—2004, assoc. prof. surg. sci. Recipient Clin. Sci. award Am. Heart Assn., 1995-96, Chmns. Fac. Rsch. award, Dept. Surgery UMDNJ, 1998. Mem.: Assn. Academic Surgery. Address: Clin Acad Bldg 125 Paterson St New Brunswick NJ 08901-1962 Office: 1 Robert Wood Johnson Pl New Brunswick NJ 08901-1928*

CORBETT, THOMAS WINGETT, JR., state attorney general, lawyer; b. Phila., June 17, 1949; s. Thomas Wingett and Mary Bernadine (Diskin) C.; m. Susan Jean Manbeck, Dec. 16, 1972; children: Thomas Wingett III, Katherine. BA, Lebanon Valley Coll., 1971; JD, St. Mary's U., 1975. Bar: Pa., 1976, US Dist. Ct. (we. dist.) Pa., 1976, US Ct. Mil. Appeals, 1979, US Supreme Ct., 1984. Asst. dist. atty. Allegheny County, Pitts., 1976—80; asst. US atty. (we. dist.) Pa US Dept. Justice, Pitts., 1980—83, US atty., 1989—93; assoc. Rose, Schmidt, Hasley & DiSalle, Pitts., 1983—86, ptnr., 1986—89; mem. US atty. gen.'s adv. com. We. Dist. Pa., Pitts., 1991—93, chmn., 1992—93; ptnr. Thorp, Reed & Armstrong, Pitts., 1993—95, 1997—98; atty. gen. State of Pa., Harrisburg, 1995—97; asst. gen. counsel for govt. affairs Waste Mgmt. Inc., Pitts., 1998—2002; ptnr. Thomas Corbett & Assocs., 2002—05; atty. gen. State of Pa., Harrisburg, 2005—. Mem. Shaler Twp. Rep. Com., 1984-89, Allegheny County Rep. Com., 1985-89, 2002—, Gov. Tom Ridge's Partnership for Safe Children, 1995-2003, Pa. Weed and Seed Program, 1995-2003; chmn. Pa. Commn. on Crime and Delinquency, 1995—2003, del. Rep. Nat. Conv., 2000. Pres. St. Mary's Parent-Tchr. Guild, Glenshaw, Pa., 1983-85. Served in Pa Army Nat. Guard, 1971—84. Mem. ABA, Pa. Bar Assn., Allegheny County Bar Assn. (judiciary com.), NRA, Ancient Order Hibernians. Roman Catholic. Avocations: skiing, golf, reading. Office: Office Atty Gen 1600 Strawberry Sq Harrisburg PA 17120

CORBETT, WILLIAM JOHN, prosecutor, public relations executive, consultant; b. Bklyn., Mar. 15, 1937; s. John Joseph and Mildred (Bauer) Corbett; m. Ann Virginia Teplitz, June 25, 1966; children: William John, Spencer Thomas, Sally Ann. BA, Hobart Coll., 1959; JD, Fordham U., 1965. Bar: N.Y. 1966, U.S. Dist. Ct. (fed. dist.) 1968, Customs Ct. 1968, U.S. Supreme Ct. 1990. Info. officer USAF, Greenville, S.C., 1959-62; trial lawyer Nassau County Legal Aid Soc., Mineola, N.Y., 1966-67; asst. dist. atty. County of Nassau, 1967-68; corp. dir. pub. rels. Avon Products, Inc., N.Y.C., 1968-84; v.p. comm. AICPA, N.Y.C., 1984-90; chmn. Corbett Assocs., Inc., 1990—. Pros. atty. Inc. Village of Floral Park, NY, 1975—84, acting village justice, 1984—98; cons. status UN Office Info. and ECOSOC, N.Y.C., 1979—84, N.Y.C., 1990—93; pub. rels. advisor USIA, Washington, 1981—93; adj. asst. prof. Iona Coll. Grad. Sch. Comm., 1990—2000. Mem. adv. bd. Pub. Rels. News (Leadership award, 1984). Participant White House Conf. Indsl. World Ahead, 1972, White House Conf. Consumer Elderly, 1979, White House Conf. Small Bus., 1986, 1995, White House Conf. Librs. and Info. Svcs., 1991; staff mem. N.Y. State Senate, Albany, 1962—63. Capt. USAF, 1959—62. Named to Hall of Fame, U.S. Dept. Def. Info. Sch., 1990; recipient N.Y. State Conspicuous Svc. medal, 1970, Legion of Honor, Internat. Coun. Order DeMolay, 1982, Alumni award, Hobart Coll., 1984, Pinnacle award, 1990. Fellow: Internat. Pub. Rels. Assn. (bd. dirs. 1984—90, pres. 1990); mem.: Nat. Commn. Pub. Rels. Edn., Nat. Assn. Corp. Dirs. N.Y. (v.p. 1993—94), Pub. Affairs Coun., Ctr. Study Presidency (adv. bd.), Corp. Forum N.Y., Pub. Rels. Soc. N.Y. (past pres.), Pub. Rels. Soc. Am. (accredited, Fellow Pres. award 1985, 1988), Am. Legion (commdr. Floral Park chpt. 2001—02). Home: 102 Chestnut Ave Floral Park NY 11001-2421 Office: 111 S Tyson Ave Floral Park NY 11001-1822 Office Phone: 516-775-6849. E-mail: wjcorbett@corbettpr.com.

CORBI, LANA, communications executive; Sr. v.p. network distbn. Fox Broadcasting Co., 1994—95, exec. v.p. network distbn., 1996—97, pres. network distbn., 1997—99; pres., COO Blackstar, L.L.C., 1995—96; COO Odyssey Holdings, 1999—2000; exec. v.p., COO Crown Media Holdings, 2000—01; CEO Hallmark Channel, Coral Gables, Fla., 2001—.

CORBIN, DAVID P., counselor; b. Ripley, W.Va., Jan. 23, 1943; s. Oliver Paige and Catherine Elaine Corbin; m. Shirley Mae Francis, July 3, 1968; children: Max David, Beth Ann. AA in Speech, Potomac State Coll., 1962; BA in Speech, W.Va. U., 1965; MEd in Counseling, Ohio U., 1991. Lic. counselor Ohio. Contbr. articles to profl. jours. Pres. Sugar Lane Improvement Assn., Rivesville, W.Va., 1972, Neighborhood Watch, Little Hocking, Ohio, 1986. Corr. U.S. Army, 1966—67, Vietnam. Mem.: Ohio Counselors Assn., Mensa (winner fiction Region III 1994). Avocations: piano, writing, acting, walking, harmonica. Home: PO Box 68 Little Hocking OH 45742

CORBIN, DONALD L., state supreme court justice; b. Hot Springs, Ark., Mar. 29, 1938; BA, U. Ark., 1964, JD, 1966. Bar: Ark. 1966, U.S. Dist. Ct. (we. dist.) Ark. 1966. Atty. pvt. practice, DeQueen, Ark., 1966—67; lawyer Lewisville and Stamps, 1967-80; judge Ark. Ct. Appeals, 1981-87, chief judge, 1987-90; assoc. justice Ark. Supreme Ct., Little Rock, 1991—. State rep. Ark. Gen. Assembly, 1971-80. Served with USMC, 1955-59. Mem. ABA, Ark. Bar Assn., SW Ark. Bar Assn., Sigma Alpha Epsilon. Democrat. Avocation: duck hunting. Office: Supreme Ct Justice Bldg 625 Marshall St, 120 Justice Buiilding Little Rock AR 72201-1054*

CORBIN, FRANK WAYNE, music educator; b. Springfield, Tenn., Jan. 28, 1959; s. Martha Jean and William Albert Corbin. MusB, Oberlin Coll., 1980; diploma in advanced Music performance studies, Concordia U., Montreal, Que., Can., 1981; MusM, U. Cin., 1983; D of Musical Arts, Eastman Sch. of Music, 1988. Dir. of chapel music, lectr. in music Assumption Coll., Worcester, Mass., 1989—, dir., human arts, 2000—. Founder/dir. The Young Organists Coop., Worcester, Mass., 1991—. Musician: (recording) Frank Corbin plays Franck. Sub-dean Am. Guild of Organists, Worcester, Mass., 1992—94. Recipient 2nd prize, Arthur Poister Competition, 1987. Mem.: Am. Guild of Organists (sub-dean 1992—94, finalist Nat. Young Artists Competition). Democrat. Avocations: literature, murder mysteries, history, biographies. Office: Assumption Coll 500 Salisbury St Worcester MA 01609 Personal E-mail: frank.corbin@verizon.net. Business E-Mail: fcorbin@assumption.edu.

CORBIN, HERBERT LEONARD, public relations executive, director; b. Bklyn., Mar. 30, 1940; s. H. Dan and Lillian Corbin; m. Carol Heller, June 2, 1963; children: Jeffrey, Leslie Faith. BA, Rutgers U., 1961. Staff corr. Newark News, 1961-63; asst. dir. pub. rels. Rutgers U. News Svc., New Brunswick, N.J., 1963-65; account exec. A.A. Schechter Assocs., N.Y.C., 1965-66; sr. account exec. Daniel J. Edelman, Inc., N.Y.C., 1967-69; founder, chmn., mng. ptnr. KCSA Pub. Rels. Worldwide, N.Y.C., 1969—. Chmn. pub. rels. com. AJC; bd. dirs. Vision Fund Am. Mem. nat. bd. govs., chmn. pub. rels. com. Am. Jewish Com., White Plains Pub. Access Cable TV Commn.; mem. mktg. adv. com. United Jewish Appeal-Fedn. N.Y. Mem.: Vision Fund (bd. dirs.), Soc. Profl. Journalists, Pub. Rels. Soc. Assn. (counsellors Acad.), Old Oaks Country Club (bd. dirs., sec., sec.). Home: 31 Hathaway Ln White Plains NY 10605-3610 Office: KCSA Pub Rels Worldwide 800 2nd Ave New York NY 10017-4709 Business E-Mail: hcorbin@kcsa.com.

CORBIN, JAMES H., engineering executive, meteorologist, oceanographer; BSEE, U. Nebr., 1971; MS in Oceanography and Meteorology, Naval Postgrad. Sch., Monterey, Calif., 1977. Commd. USN, 1962, advanced through grades to, various sea and shore commands, 1962-77; spl. projects officer Naval Oceanography Command Ctr., Guam, 1977-80; meteorol. and oceanographic officer Aircraft Carrier John F. Kennedy, 1980-82; officer in charge Naval Oceanography Command Detachment, Monterey, Calif., 1982-86; dir. operational oceanography ctr. U.S. Naval Oceanographic Office, 1986-90; mgr. exptl. ctr. for mesoscale ocean prediction Inst. for Naval Oceanography, 1990-92; dir. Ctr. for Air Sea Tech. (now Engring. Rsch. Ctr.), Miss. State U., Stennis Space Center, 1992—. Office: Miss State U Engring Rsch Ctr Engring Rsch Ctr Bldg 1103 Bay Saint Louis MS 39529-0001

CORBIN, LYNN S., vocational school educator; b. Booneville, Miss., Sept. 8, 1960; d. Ruby G. and Henry Clifford Smart; m. Freddie G. Corbin, Nov. 14, 1980; children: Holly S., Annie R. BS in Edn., Blue Mountain Coll., 1992; MS, Miss. State U., 1995. Cert. career and tech. edn. tchr. Miss., 2001. Sec./adult edn. instr. Prentiss County Vo-Tech, Booneville, Miss., 1981—90; bus. edn. instr. Prentiss County Schs., Booneville, Miss., 1993—96; tech. discovery tchr. Booneville H.S., Miss., 1996—99; coop. edn. instr. Prentiss County Vo-Tech, Booneville, Miss., 1999—. Nat. bd. mentor World Class Tchg., Tupelo, Miss., 2004—05. Baptist. Office: Prentiss County Vo-Tech Sch 302 W George Allen Dr Booneville MS 38829 Office Phone: 662-728-3915. Personal E-mail: lscorbin@hotmail.com.

CORBIN, MICHAEL, diplomat; b. NYC; m. Mary Ellen Hickey; 2 children. BA, Swarthmore Coll. Staff asst. Bur. Near Eastern and South Asian Afafirs US Dept. State, staff asst. UN Polit. Affairs Bur. Internat. Orgn. Affairs, with US Embassy in Tunis, 1985—87, polit.-military affairs officer US Embassy in Kuwait, 1987—89, polit.-military affairs officer US Embassy in Cairo, 1994—97, dir. Counter-Narcotics Sect., US Embassy in Caracas, 1997—2001, dep. dir. Office of Arabian Peninsula Affairs, 2001—03, minister counselor Economic and Polit. Affairs, US Embassy in Cairo, 2003—, chargé d'affaires in Cairo, 2005. Volunteer, agricultural extension officer Peace Corps, Mauritania, 1982—84. Fluent in French, Spanish and Arabic. Office: 7700 Cairo Pl Washington DC 20521-7700*

CORBIN, ROSEMARY MACGOWAN, former mayor; b. Santa Cruz, Calif., Apr. 3, 1940; d. Frederick Patrick and Lorena Maude (Parr) MacGowan; m. Douglas Tenny Corbin, Apr. 6, 1968; children: Jeffrey, Diana. BA, San Francisco State U., 1961; MLS, U. Calif., Berkeley, 1966. Libr. Stanford (Calif.) U., 1966-68, Richmond (Calif.) Pub. Libr., 1968-69, Kaiser Found. Health Plan, Oakland, Calif., 1976-81, San Francisco Pub. Libr., 1981-82, U. Calif., Berkeley, 1982-83; mem. coun. City of Richmond, 1985-93, vice mayor, 1986-87, mayor, 1993—2001. Mem. Solid Waste Mgmt. Authority, 1985-2001, Contra Costa Hazardous Materials Commn., Martinez, Calif., 1987-2001, San Francisco Bay Conservation and Devel. Commn., 1987-2001; mem. League of Calif. Cities Environ. Affairs Com., 1994-2001; mem. energy and environ. com. U.S. Conf. Mayors and Nat. League of Cities, 1993-2001. Contbr. articles to profl. publs. Pres. Ujima Family Svcs.; mem. Rosie the Riveter Trust Bd., San Francisco Bay Trail Bd. Mem. LWV, NOW, Nat. Women's Polit. Caucus, Calif. Libr. Assn., Sierra Club, Inst. for Local Govt. (pres.), Ujima Family Svcs. (pres.). Democrat. Avocations: reading, hiking, golf, quilting, gardening. Home: 114 Crest Ave Richmond CA 94801-4031

CORBIN, SOL NEIL, lawyer; b. N.Y.C., Apr. 16, 1927; s. Nathan I. and Sarah (Kaiser) Corbin; m. Tanya Jacobs, Aug. 7, 1953; 1 child, David J. BS, Columbia U., 1948; JD cum laude, Harvard U., 1951. Bar: N.Y. 1952. Pvt. practice, N.Y.C., 1952—; law clk. Judge Charles D. Breitel, 1954-56; counsel Gov. of N.Y., 1962-65; ptnr. Corbin, Silverman & Sanseverino LLP, N.Y.C., 1970—96, sr. counsel, 1997—2001, Taylor, Colicchio & Silverman, LLP, N.Y.C., 2001—. Chmn. N.Y. State Commn. Constl. Conv., 1966—67, N.Y. State Crime Control Planning Bd., 1974—75; mem. N.Y. State Banking Bd., 1969—76, N.Y. State Commn. Local Govt. Powers, 1971—73; mem. chief judge's com. to recruit state ct. adminstr., 1973; trustee bankruptcy Franklin N.Y. Corp., 1974—90; spl. counsel to v.p. U.S., 1975; apptd. counsel to trustee BCCI, 1990—97. Trustee N.Y. Pub. Libr., 1977—; mem. chief judge's com. availability legal svcs., 1988—90. With USNR, 1945—46. Mem.: ABA, Am. Law Inst., New York County Bar Assn., Assn. Br. City of N.Y., Lotos Club. Home: 1100 Park Ave New York NY 10128-1202 Office: 99 Park Ave Ste 1703 New York NY 10016

CORBIN, WILLIAM R., wood products executive; BS in Forest Products, U. Wash., 1964; MS in Forestry, Yale U., 1956. Cons. forest products, Seattle, 1970's; v.p. ops. Vancouver Plywood Co., Inc.; v.p. So. timber and wood products Zellerbach Corp., 1974; sr. v.p. timber and wood products, group pres.; exec. v.p. wood products Weyerhaeuser Co., 1992-95, 98—, exec. v.p. timberlands and distbn., 1995-98. Bd. dirs. Weyerhaeuser Can. Ltd.; mem. mgmt. bd. World TimerFund. Trustee, mem. exec. com. Weyerhaeuser Co. Found., mem. policy com.; mem. adv. bd. U. Wash. Sch. Bus. Adminstrn. and Coll. Forest Resources, charter mem. internat. adv. bd. Inst. Environment and Natural Resoruce Rsch. and Policy; v.p., mem. exec. com. The Mountains to Sound Greenway Trust. Office: Weyerhaeuser PO Box 9777 Federal Way WA 98063-9777

CORBIN WALKER, KAROL, lawyer; b. Jersey City, Oct. 11, 1958; BA cum laude, N.J. City U., 1980; JD, Seton Hall U., 1986. Bar: N.J. 1986, N.Y. 1991, U.S. Dist. Ct. N.J. 1986, U.S. Dist. Ct. (so. and ea. dists.) N.Y. 1987, U.S. Dist. Ct. (no. dist.) N.Y. 1994, U.S. Ct. Appeals (3d cir.) 1991, U.S. Supreme Ct. 1993. Jud. law clk. to Hon. Davis S. Baime, Superior Ct. N.J., Appellate Divsn., 1986—87; adj. prof. law Seton Hall U. Sch. Law, 1988—90; atty. St. John & Wayne, LLC, Newark. Mem. adv. bd. Salvation Army Morristown Corps; active United Way of Essex and West Hudson. Mem.: ABA, Assn. Fed. Bar of State of N.J., Nat. Bar Assn. (treas. 1994—96, sec. 1998—99, sec. divsn. ptnrs. in majority law firms 1999—2002, 2d vice chair 1999—2002, comml. law sect. 1st vice chair 2002—), Garden State Bar Assn. (trustee 1989—91, pres. 1991—93), Essex County Bar Assn. (Young Lawyers divsn. exec. bd. 1990—92, chair minorities in profession com. 1991—93, chair continuing legal edn. com. 1993—97, trustee 1994—97), Morris County Bar Assn., N.J. State Bar Assn. (Young Lawyers divsn. exec. bd. 1990—93, chair minorities in profession com. 1991—93, trustee 1995—99, chair diversity com. 1997—98, chair jud. and prosecutorial appointments com. 1998—99, sec. 1999—2000, treas. 2000—01, 2d v.p. 2001—02, 1st v.p. 2002, pres.-elect 2002—03, pres. 2003—04), Phi Alpha Delta. Office: St John and Wayne LLC 2 Penn Plz E Newark NJ 07105-2249

CORBITT, EUMILLER MATTIE, special education educator; b. Detroit, Jan. 07; d. Harrison and Arnetha (Tatum) Jones; m. Luther Corbitt (div. Dec. 1976); children: Tonya, Stephen. BS, Wayne State U., 1969, MEd, 1976, EdS, 1995. Cert. elem. and secondary sch. tchr., cert. tchr. spl. edn. emotionally and mentally impaired, grades K-12, elem. secondary sch. and central office administration. Tchr. mentally impaired Detroit Pub. Schs., 1969-72, tchr. emotionally impaired, 1972-75, spl. edn. tchr. cons., 1975—, Title I tchr. math. and sci., summers 1993-96; mediator Spl. Edn. Mediation Svcs., Lansing, Mich., 1986-96, Spl. Edn. Mediation Svcs. State Project PL 94-142, Lansing, Mich., 1985—; spl. edn. hearing officer Mich. Dept. Edn., Lansing, 1985—. Developer at-risk program for emotionally impaired, socially maladjusted and ADHD students 12-17 yrs. Wolverine Human Svcs., Detroit, Mich. 1998—; mem. U.S. del. educators and attys. to South Africa for evaluation of schs. and govtl. agys. under leadership of Nelson Mandella Citizen Amb. program People to People, Spokane, Wash., 1996; mem. citizens alliance to uphold spl. edn. study adv. com. Emotionally Impaired Children in Mich./Lansing, 1986; mem. North Ctrl. Assn. accreditation com. Grand Rapids (Mich.) Pub. Schs., 1981; presenter profl. devel. conf. Detroit Fedn. Tchrs. and Det. Pub. Sch. Adminstrs., 1996. Chairperson Met. Detroit chpt. March of Dimes, 1987; chairperson Women Who Dare to Care com. United Negro Coll. Fund, Detroit, 1987-89; gen. coord. Mus. African Am. History, Detroit, 1987; tutor, usher, chairperson Hartford Meml. Bapt. Ch., Detroit, 1979—. Recipient Mayor's award of merit for Cmty. Svc., City of Detroit, 1987, plaque and cert. March of Dimes, 1987; recognized as outstanding educator Detroit Tchr., Detroit Fedn. Tchrs., 1987, 94. Mem. Coun. for Exceptional Children (presenter nat. conv. 1983, cert. 1983), Soc. Profls. in Dispute Resolution, Wayne State U. Alumni Assn., Delta Sigma Theta (chairperson 1965—), Phi Delta Kappa (chairperson). Avocations: golf, poetry, racquetball, painting, reading. Office: Martin Luther King Jr Sr HS 3200 E Lafayette Detroit MI 48207 Home: 1249 Navarre Pl Detroit MI 48207 E-mail: eumillercorbitt@aol.com.

CORBUSIER, DRUE, apparel and home furnishings executive; Corp. exec. v.p., dir. Dillard's, Inc., Little Rock, 1998—; pres. Ft. Worth divsn. Office: Dillards Inc 4501 N Beach Fort Worth TX 76137

CORBY, FRANCIS MICHAEL, JR., finance company executive; b. Chgo., Feb. 2, 1944; s. Francis M. and Jean (Wolf) C.; m. Diane S. Orselli, Aug. 5, 1972; children: Francis Michael III, Brian A., Christopher S. BA, St. Mary of the Lake, 1966; MBA, Columbia U., 1969. With Chrysler Corp., 1969-80; treasury mgr. Chrysler Peru S.A., Lima, 1973-74; fin. dir. Chrysler Wholesale Ltd., London, 1974-76; mng. dir. Chrysler Comml. S.A. de C.V., Mexico City, 1976-77; v.p., treas. Chrysler Fin. Corp., Troy, Mich., 1977-80; treas. Joy Mfg. Co., Pitts., 1980-83, contr., 1983-86, v.p., 1984-86; sr. v.p. fin., CFO Harnischfeger Industries, Inc., Milw., 1986-94, exec. v.p. fin. and adminstrn., 1994-99; exec. v.p. Frederick & Co., 2000-2001; exec. v.p., CFO Guide Corp., Pendleton, Ind., 2001—04; sr. v.p., CFO GST Autoleather Inc., Hagerstown, Md., 2004—. Bd. dirs. Magnasphere Corp. Mem.: Country Club of Naples. Office: 13712 Crayton Blvd Hagerstown MD 21742 Business E-Mail: francis.corby@gstautoleather.com.

CORCORAN, ANDREW PATRICK, JR., lawyer; b. Fredrrick, Md., Nov. 20, 1948; s. Andrew Patrick and Beatrice Josephine (Poletti) C.; m. Margaret Cecila Boyle, July 3, 1971; children: Maureen Meredith, Andrew Patrick III. BA, Villanova U., 1970; JD, Seton Hall U., 1973. Bar: Pa. 1973, U.S Dist. Ct. (ea. dist.) Pa. 1974, U.S. Ct. Appeals (7th cir.) 1976, U.S. Ct. Appeals (3d cir.) 1977, U.S. Supreme Ct. 1982, Va. (corp. counsel) 2004. Atty. Pa. Cen. Transp. Co., Phila., 1973-75, sr. atty., 1975-79; asst. gen. atty. Consol. Rail Corp., Phila., 1979-82, gen. atty., 1982-85, sr. gen. atty., 1985-92, assoc. gen. counsel, 1992-99; gen. atty. Norfolk (Va.) So. Corp., 1999—. Mem.: Assn. of Am. R.R.'s (legal affairs com.). Republican. Roman Catholic. Home: 2433 Haversham Close Virginia Beach VA 23454-1157 Office: Norfolk So Corp Three Commercial Pl Norfolk VA 23510-9241 Business E-Mail: andy.corcoran@nscorp.com.

CORCORAN, BARBARA, real estate company executive; b. Edgewater, N.J. m. Dale Barlow, 1979 (div.); m. Bill Higgins, 1988; 1 child, Thomas. BA in English and Theology, St. Thomas Aquinas Coll.; Doctorate (hon.), Marymount Coll. Founder Corcoran Group, NYC, 1973—80, founder, chmn., 1980—, Barbara Corcoran Prodn., NYC, 2005—. Author: If You Don't Have Big Breasts, Put Ribbons in Your Pigtails, 2003, Use What You've Got: And Other Business Lessons I Learned From Mom, 2003, (newsletter) Corcoran Report, 1981—. Former chair N.Y. chpt. Young Pres. Orgn.; former bd. govs. Real Estate Bd. N.Y. Office: Corcoran Prodn. Fl 11 660 Madison Ave New York NY 10021 Office Phone: 212-848-0450.

CORCORAN, CLEMENT TIMOTHY, III, lawyer, retired judge; b. Kansas City, Mo., Dec. 18, 1945; s. Clement T. and Bette Lou (Hohl) C. BA, U. N.C., 1967; JD, U. Va., 1973. Bar: Fla. 1973, U.S. Dist. Ct. (mid. dist.) Fla. 1973, D.C. 1974, U.S. Dist. Ct. (no. and so. dists.) Fla. 1975, U.S. Supreme Ct. 1979, U.S. Ct. Appeals (11th cir.) 1981; cert. cir. mediator Fla. Supreme Ct. Law clk. U.S. Dist. Ct., Tampa, Fla., 1973-75; assoc. Carlton, Fields,

Ward, Emmanuel, Smith & Cutler, P.A., Tampa, 1975-78, ptnr., 1978-89; judge Bankruptcy Ct. (mid. dist.) Fla., Orlando, 1989-93, Tampa, 1993—2003. Dir. Bay Area Legal Svcs., Inc., Tampa, 1983-89, v.p., 1987, pres., 1988; bd. dirs. Fla. Coun. Bar Pres., 1982-88, pres., 1986-87; arbitrator Ct. Annexed Arbitration Program, U.S. Dist. Ct. (mid. dist.) Fla., 1984-89; counselor U. Tampa, 1981-86, fellow, 1986-89. Co-author: Conflicts of Interest, 1984; contbr. articles to legal jours. Lt. USNR, 1967-70. Mem. ABA (litigation sect., coun. mem. 1999-2002, co-chair comm. com. 1990-92, chair book pub. bd. 1992-98, assoc. editor Litigation News 1982-87, mng. editor 1987, editor-in-chief 1988-90, 2002-04, co-dir. pubs. divsn. 2004—05, Nat. Conf. of Lawyers and Reps. of Media 1992-95, mem. adv. com. on nominations 1994-95, chair media-law roundtable 1994, chair sect. officers conf. com. on non-dues revenue 1995-96, mem. working group on ABA bus. plan for pub. 1995-96, standing com. on pub. oversight 1996-2002, ho. of dels. 2003-2005), Fla. Bar (chmn. voluntary bar liaison com. 1985-04, chmn. grievance com. 13-D 1986-88, chmn. legal edn. com. 1981-82, Most Productive Young Lawyer award 1981), Am. Judicature Soc., Hillsborough County Bar Assn. (Robert W. Patton Outstanding Jurist award 2002, Red McEwen award 1980, pres. 1982-83), Am. Inns of Ct. (Master of the Bench 1990-93, 96—). Roman Catholic. Office: 400 N Ashley Dr Ste 2540 Tampa FL 33602 Office Phone: 813-769-5020. Personal E-mail: ctcorcoran@mindspring.com.

CORCORAN, DAVID, newspaper editor; b. N.Y.C., July 22, 1947; s. William and Ruth (Brody) Diebold; m. Karrie Olick; children: Thomas, Daniel, Katie. BA, Amherst Coll., 1969; fellow journalism, Stanford U., 1976-77. Tchr. Rockland Country Day Sch., Congers, N.Y., 1969-70; reporter Hackensack (N.J.) Record, 1969-73, from editl. writer to asst. editor, 1973-77, editor editl. page, 1977-87, chief news editor, 1987-88; staff editor N.Y. Times, 1988—2001, asst. sci. editor, 2001—. Trustee Ctr. Analysis of Pub. Issues, 1983-91. Mem. Am. Soc. Newspaper Editors, Nat. Conf. Editorial Writers, Soc. Profl. Journalists (dir. N.J. chpt. 1980—, pres. N.J. chpt. 1983-84). Home: 437 Wildwood Rd Northvale NJ 07647-1221 Office: NY Times 229 W 43rd St New York NY 10036-3959 E-mail: corcoran@nytimes.com.

CORCORAN, JOSEPH P., health facility administrator; Pres., CEO The NY Eye and Ear Infirmary, NYC, 2000—. Bd. trustees Healthcare Assn. NY State; immediate past chmn. Am. Assn. Eye and Ear Hosps. Office: The NY Eye and Ear Infirmary 310 E 14th St New York NY 10003

CORCORAN, PAUL JOHN, physician; b. Washburn, Wis., June 8, 1934; s. Thomas F. and Mary Rose (McCauley) C., m. Patricia Ann Bounds, Nov. 10, 1956; children: Mary Colbourne, Ann Campbell, Clare Bounds, Thomas Bounds, Peter Campbell, David Pusey. BS, Georgetown U., 1955, MD, 1959; MS in Phys. Medicine and Rehab., U. Wash., 1968. Diplomate Am. Bd. Phys. Medicine and Rehab. Intern U. Oreg. Hosps., 1959-60; resident in rehab. medicine NYU, 1963-66; postdoctoral fellow dept. rehab. medicine HEW-Social and Rehab. Services; Acad. Career trainee dept. rehab. medicine U. Wash. Med. Center, 1966-68; asst. attending physiatrist Presbyn. Hosp. City N.Y.; asst. prof. rehab. medicine Columbia U., 1968-72; dir. residency tng. in rehab. medicine Columbia-Presbyn. Med. Center, N.Y.C., 1969-72; assoc. prof. rehab. medicine Boston U., 1972-76; chief rehab. medicine Boston City Hosp., 1975-77; from assoc. prof. to prof. Tufts U., 1976-85, clin. prof., 1985—, acting chmn. dept. rehab. medicine, 1976-77, 89-90, chmn. dept., 1977-81; physiatrist-in-chief Rehab. Inst., New England Med. Ctr. Hosp., Boston, 1976-81, 89-90; chief rehab. medicine service Boston VA Med. Center, 1980-85; med. dir. Easter Seal Soc./N.H., Manchester, 1985-91; chief phys. medicine and rehab. New England Sinai Hosp. and Rehab. Ctr., Stoughton, Mass., 1989-90, Newton-Wellesley (Mass.) Hosp., 1991-93; dir. rehab. medicine Spaulding Rehab. Hosp., Boston, 1992-96; interim dir. divsn. phys. medicine and rehab. Harvard Med. Sch., Boston, 1993-96; assoc. in neurology Mass. Gen. Hosp., Boston, 1993-96. Lectr. phys. medicine and rehab. Harvard Med. Sch., 1997—; instr. NYU Grad. Sch. Prosthetics and Orthotics, 1970-77; vis. physician rehab. medicine U. Hosp., Boston, 1972-76; project dir. New England Regional Rehab. Rsch. and Tng. Ctr., 1977-81; chief med. cons. Mass. Rehab. Commn., 1991-96; vis. prof. Harvard Med. Sch., Boston, 1993-96. Contbr. chpts. to books, articles to profl. publs.; editorial bd. Archives Phys. Med. and Rehab., 1971-77. Trustee Easter Seal Rsch. Found., 1975-78, 88-90, Carroll Rehab. Ctr. for Blind, 1975-78; mem. rehab. svcs. nat. adv. com. HEW, 1976-77; chmn. Mass. Interagy. Coun. on Ind. Living, 1977-79. Lt. M.C., USN, 1960-63. Recipient Licht award Am. Congress Rehab. Medicine, 1985, Physician of Yr. award Pres.'s Com. on Employment of Handicapped, 1986, Disting. Clinician award Am. Acad. Phys. Medicine and Rehab., 1995. Mem. Am. Assn. Acad. Physiatrists (pres. 1981-83, Outstanding Svc. award 1996). Home: 37 Main St Hancock NH 03449-5321 Office: Spaulding Rehabilitation Hosp 125 Nashua St Boston MA 02114

CORCORAN, ROBERT THOMAS, lawyer; b. Jersey City, N.J., July 3, 1951; m. Susan Corcoran; children: Sara, Chelsea. BS cum laude, Fairleigh Dickinson U., 1974; JD, Ohio No. U., 1977. Bar: N.J. 1977, U.S. Dist. Ct. N.J. 1977, N.Y. 1986, U.S. Dist. Ct. N.Y. (so. dist.) 1988, U.S. Ct. Appeals (3d cir.) 1988, U.S. Supreme Ct. 1991; cert. mediator Am. Acad. Matrimonial Lawyers, 1997. Prof. bus. law Fairleigh Dickinson U., 1978-83; lectr. Law Edn. Inst. Bur. Nat. Affairs, Bergen County Bar Assn., N.J. Inst. for Continuing Legal Edn., Assn. Trial Lawyers (fam. law sect.), Am. Acad. Matrimonial Lawyers (N.J. chpt.), orientation seminar for newly-apptd. judges, 1998. T.V. appearances: NBC News, CBS News, MSNBC News, TCI Cable, Justice Jour., ABC Radio with Mitch Albom; contbr. articles to profl. jours. Bus. adv. coun. Nat. Rep. Congrl. Com., 2003. Fellow Am. Acad. of Matrimonial Lawyers (econ. law com. 1996-97, bd. mgrs. N.J. chpt. 1996—, parliamentarian 1999-2000, continuing legal edn. com. 1998-99, treas. 2002-2003) mem. ABA (family law sect.), Assn. Trial Lawyers Am. (family law sect.), Assn. Trial Attys. Am. (N.J. affiliate), Trial Attys. N.J. (chpt. chmn. 2001), Bergen County Bar Assn. (co-chmn. fam. law com. 1995-97, 99-2001, chmn. 1998-99, matrimonial early settlement panel, bench bar liason com.), N.J. State Bar Assn. (exec. com. family law sect. 1995-2004, mem. com., subcom. mem: Keeping Child Support in Family Ct., early settlement panel study), Supreme Ct. N.J. (bd. atty. cert., matrimonial law com. 1996-2004), Matrimonial Lawyers Alliance. Office: 401 Hackensack Ave Hackensack NJ 07601-6411 Office Phone: 201-342-5151. Business E-Mail: law@robertcorcoran.com.

CORDARO, MATTHEW CHARLES, energy and utility executive, educator; b. N.Y.C., July 25, 1943; s. Matteo C. and Josephine (Picone) C.; m. Janet Chick, June 24, 1967; children: Anne-Marie, Allison; m. Martha Warnock, July 18, 1987; 1 child, Marie Elena. BS, C.W. Post Coll., 1965; MS in Nuclear Engring., NYU, 1967; PhD in Engring. and Physics, Cooper Union, 1970. Asst. engr. L.I. Lighting Co., Hicksville, NY, from 1966, successively assoc. engr., nuclear physicist, sr. environ. engr., mgr. environ. engring., v.p. engring., 1978-84, v.p. engring. and adminstrn., 1984-85, sr. v.p. ops. and engring., 1985-88; pres. Long Lake Cogeneration Corp., Melville, NY, 1988-93; sr. v.p. Long Lake Energy Corp., N.Y.C., 1988-93; pres. and CEO Nashville Electric Svc., 1993-99, Midwest Ind. Transmission Sys. Operator, 1999-2001; assoc. dean Coll. Mgmt., dir. Ctr. for Mgmt. Analysis Long Island U., Brookville, NY, 2001—. Cons. Bechtel, CMS, GE, Panhandle, Shoreham Project, 1992-93, R.J. Rudden Assocs., Hauppauge, N.Y.; guest rsch. assoc. Brookhaven Nat. Lab., 1968-71; adj. assoc. prof. nuclear engring. Poly. Inst. N.Y., 1979-80; adj. asst. prof. engring. C.W. Post Coll., 1968-72; former bd. dirs. ctr. for energy studies Adelphi U. Edtl. advisory bd. L.I. Business News, 2005-; contbr. articles to profl. jours. Mem. Coun. overseers C.W. Post Coll., 1968-72; former mem. campaign coun. L.I. U., cmty. adv. bd. Sta. WLIW Pub. TV, Garden City, N.Y., Nashville C. of C., bd. dirs., Nashville Urban League, Nashville BBB, Nashville Jr. Achievement, Nashville Heart Assn., Tenn. Mcpl. Elec. Power Assn., Tenn. Valley Pub. Power Assn., Nature Conservancy of Tenn., corp. bd. Nashville Bapt. Hosp., adv. com. Nashville Girl Scouts; chmn. Mid. Tenn. U.S. Savs. Bond campaign, 1995-97; trustee Elec. Power Rsch. Inst. 1997-2001. AEC fellow, 1965-66 Mem. Am. Pub. Power Assn. (bd. dirs. 1994-00). Office: Post Campus Long Island University Greenvale NY 11548-1300 Personal E-mail: mcsqd22@aol.com. *One must try with all their heart to achieve anything of value on this earth. The tragedy of life is not giving your full effort for fear of failure. Never give up, never give in.*

CORDDRY, ROB, comedian, actor; b. Weymouth, Mass., Feb. 4, 1971; m. Sandra Corddry. Grad., U. Mass. Appeared with Third Rail Comedies, N.Y.C., Naked Babies, N.Y.C.; performer, tchr. Uprights Citizen's Brigade Theater, N.Y.C. Actor: (films) Old School, 2003, Blackballed: The Bobby Dukes Story, 2004; (TV series) Lake Night with Conan O'Brien, 1998—2002, The Daily Show with Jon Stewart, 2002, Upright Citizens Brigade, 1998—2002. Office: The Daily Show 513 W 54th St New York NY 10019

CORDEIRO, CARLOS DE MORAIS, computer scientist, researcher; b. Recife, Brazil; s. Carlos Alberto Coutinho and Marlene de Morais Cordeiro; m. Wilma Ramos; 1 child, Matheus. BS in computer sci., Fed. U. of Pernambuco, 1994—98, MS in computer sci., 1999—2000; PhD in computer sic. and engring., U. of Cin., 2001—04. Rsch. asst. Fed. U. of Pernambuco, Recife, Brazil, 1995—2000; software engr. IBM Corp., San Jose, Calif., 2001; rsch. asst. U. of Cin., 2001—03; sr. rsch. engr. Nokia Rsch., Tampere, Finland, 2004; sr. mem. rsch. staff Philips Rsch., Briarcliff Manor, NY, 2004—; rsch. assoc. U. of Cin., 2004. Mem.: IEEE (assoc.; chmn. Mac subcom.). Achievements include patents for protocols for wireless networks; invention of novel protocols for wireless networks. Office: Philips Rsch 345 Scarborough Rd Briarcliff Manor NY 10510 E-mail: carlos.cordeiro@philips.com.

CORDELL, BEULAH FAYE, special education educator; b. Clifty, Ark., Mar. 5, 1939; m. Jack Cordell; children: Dennis, Kevin. B in English and Social Studies, U. Ark., 1987, M in Spl. Edn. and Reading, 1994. Cert. tchr. K-12, Ark. Tchr. Benton County Alternative Sch., Rogers, Ark., 1988-90, Job Tng. Partnership Act at Fayetteville, Ark., 1990-91; reading and study skills tchr. N.W. Ark. C.C., Rogers, 1991-94; dir. spl. edn. tutoring The One-Room Sch., Springdale, 1993—; kindergarten tchr. Springdale, 1994-96; tchr. ESL and GED N.W. Tech. Inst., 1996—. Contbg. writer The Mailbox Mag., 1999—; author, illus.: Pinky's Family, 2001, The Christmas Coloring Book, Pinky's Coloring Book, The Artist's Coloring Book, 2001. Bd. dirs. Ozark Literacy, Inc., Fayetteville, 1984-90; contbg. mem. Beaver Lake Lit., Inc., Rogers, 1994—. Recipient Tchg. Excellence award Gamma Beta Phi, 1993, Outstanding Achievement cert. Internat. Biog. Inst., Cambridge, Eng., 1998. Mem. Coun. for Exceptional Children, Am. Assn. Mentally Retarded, Poets and Writers Assn., Am. Biog. Inst. (rsch. bd. of advisors 1999). Avocations: painting, writing poetry and children's fiction. Home: 1100 N Monitor Rd Springdale AR 72764-9024 Office: 807 C Bailey St Springdale AR 72764-4247

CORDELL, BOBBIE B., music educator; b. Greenville, S.C., June 1, 1937; d. James Marvin Bishop and Allie Mae Moody; m. Ralph D. Cordell, Mar. 16, 1957 (dec. Oct. 1967); children: Ralph D. Jr., J. Gregory, Elizabeth G. Cottle. Student, Shorter Coll., 1955—57; BS, U. N.C., Greensboro, 1970, EdM, 1976. Min. music St. Martins Episcopal Ch., San Francisco, 1958—60; choir master, organist Army Chapels, Ansbach, Germany, 1961—63; min. music Sharpe Rd. Bapt. Ch., Greensboro, 1967—80, South East Bapt. Ch., Greensboro, 1981—88, organist, 1988—; pvt. piano and voice tchr. Greensboro, 1968—. Mem.: Nat. Fedn. Music Club, Nat. Assn. Music Tchrs., N.C. Assn. Music Tchrs., Greensboro Music Tchrs. (pres. 1983—85), Mil. Officers Assn. Am. (Piedmont chpt.), Greensboro Enterpe Club (first v.p. 1993—95). Avocations: bridge, travel.

CORDELL, CYNDY BINDER, entrepreneur, technical writer; b. St. Louis, May 23, 1954; d. George Farrell and Mary Virginia (Loewe) Binder; m. John Stewart Cordell, Dec. 30, 1976; children: Jonathon, Christopher, Allison. BS cum laude, Western Mich. U., 1976; MBA, DePaul U., 1983. Med. technologist Boulder (Colo.) Meml. Hosp., 1977-78, Skokie (Ill.) Valley Hosp., 1978-79; tech. svcs. specialist, assoc. product mgr., product mgr. Travenol Labs., Deerfield, Ill., 1979-82; product mgr., internat. specialist Abbott Labs., Abbott Park, Ill., 1982-86; exec. v.p. Ledell, Inc., Vernon Hills, Ill., 1987—2000; pres. Remedica Comm., Inc., 2002—03; dir. Condell Health Network, 2003—05, cons., 2005—. Adj. instr. W.R. Harper Coll., Palatine, Ill., 1986-88, mem. mktg. adv. bd., 1986-88. Comms. chair Assn. Parents and Tchrs., Lake Forest, Ill., 1988; mem. sch. bd. Dist. 67, Lake Forest, 1993-2000; pres. sch. bd. Dist. 67, 1998-2000; v.p. Physicians Interactive All Scripts Healthcare, 2000-2001. Mem. Am. Soc. Clin. Pathologists, Lake Forest Caucus. Republican. Roman Catholic. Avocations: swimming, skiing, walking, boating, reading. Home: 60 E Woodland Rd Lake Forest IL 60045-1727 Office Phone: 847-234-1748.

CORDELL, JOANN MEREDITH, music educator; b. Memphis, Tenn., Jan. 16, 1952; d. Lena Clark Hurd; m. Ronald Eugene Cordell, Sept. 24, 1976; children: David Chadwick, Andrea Kristin. BS, U. Memphis, 1975; BA in Vocal Performance, U. Charleston, 1998. Cert. Orff Music Level 1 U. Memphis, 1998, Kodaly Level 1 Colorada Coll., 1997, Kindermusik Kindermusik Internat., 1996, tchr.spl. edn. Nat. Tchr. Assn. Spl. edn. tchr. Memphis City Sch. Sys., Memphis, 1975—81; children's music dir. St. Matthew's Episcopal Ch., Charleston, W.Va., 1993—96, St. Anthony Cath. Sch., Charleston, W.Va., 1997—2001, Christ Ch. United Meth., Charleston, W.Va., 1997—2000; Kindermusik instr. Bapt. Temple Ch., Charleston, W.Va., 1999—; founder/artistic dir. WomanSong Chorale, Charleston, W.Va., 1997—; assoc. dir. Appalachian Children's Chorus, Charleston, W.Va., 2000—; music instr. leap program Kanawha County Schs., Charleston, W.Va., 2000—02; coord. of soothing sounds music program for pregnant women and high risk teens Charleston Area Med. Ctr., Charleston, W.Va., 2001—. Creator Cantus Early Childhood Music Edn. Program Appalachian Children's Chorus, Charleston, W.Va., 2000—; music clinician arts camp Charleston Stage Co., Charleston, W.Va., 1999—; music clinician for Camp William U. of Charleston, Charleston, W.Va., 2003—; founder of childsong music edn. program, 2004—. Dir.(artistic director): (choral performance) Kennedy Ctr. Performing Arts (womanSong Chorale chosen by jury to represent W.Va. at the nation's capitol for WV day, 2001). Campaign mgr. Com. to elect Nancy Kessel, Charleston, W.Va., 1993—97; state legis. chairperson W.Va. State Med. Alliance, W.Va., 1993—95; dir. of program to fundraise for W.Va. chpt. Susan G. Komen Assn. WomanSong, Charleston, W.Va., 2002; dir. of choral program to raise funds for Ronald McDonald Ho. of So. W.Va. WomanSong and Ronald McDonald Charities of So. W.Va., Charleston, W.Va., 2003; creator of children's early childhood music program Christ Ch. United Meth., Charleston, W.Va., 1990—2000; v.p. Jr. League of Charleston, Charleston, W.Va., 1990—91; mem. Cantori Montani Choral Ensemble, Charleston, W.Va., 1993—98. Grantee, W.Va. Humanities Found. and W.Va. Fund for the Arts, 2003. Mem.: Am. Guild Organists (bd. dirs. 2002—03), Music Educators Nat. Coun., Am. Orgn. Kodaly Educators, Am. Choral Dirs. Assn. (stds. and repertoir chmn. for women's choirs, W.Va. divsn. 2003—), W.Va. Orff Schulwerk Assn. (assoc.; none). Democrat. United Meth. Achievements include development of pilot music education for kindergarten, 1st and 2d graders. Avocations: creating English gardens, reading, playing piano/autoharp, cooking, scuba diving.

CORDELL, MARTIN LEWIS, lawyer; b. N.Y.C., Apr. 21, 1950; BA cum laude, City Coll. N.Y., 1971; JD, Stetson U., 1975. Bar: Fla. 1975, U.S. Dist. Ct. (mid. dist.) Fla. 1976, U.S. Ct. Appeals (5th cir.) 1977, U.S. Ct. Appeals (11th cir.) 1981. Assoc. Gurney & Handley P.A., Orlando, Fla., 1976-78; sole practice Orlando, 1978—. Mem. ABA, Fla. Bar Assn., Orange County Bar Assn., Assn. Trial Lawyers Am., Acad. Fla. Trial Lawyers, Phi Delta Phi. Avocation: fishing.

CORDELL, PHILIP GRANVILE, music educator, musician; b. Urbana, Ohio, Sept. 12, 1959; s. Granville Ogden and Pauline Davis Cordell; life ptnr. Don W Roush, Jan. 1, 2003; 1 child, Athena Gambrina Doe. BMus in Piano Performance with Organ and Harpsichord Studies, Wittenberg U., 1981; MMus in Composition, Ohio U., 1982, MMus in Piano Performance/Pedagogy, 1984. Nat. cert. tchr. of music in piano. Instr. The Ctr. for Musical Devel., Springfield, Ohio, 1977—86; accompanist dance dept. The Ohio State U., Columbus, 1987—89; lectr. Capital U., Bexley, Ohio, 1988—2001, instr., 2001—, orchestral pianist, theatre dept., 2003. Freelance musician, 1976—; pianist Ballet Met, Columbus, 1988—91; profl. accompanist Opera Columbus, 2001—. Composer: (piano solos) Theme and Variation, 1979, Five Piano Preludes, 1980, Three Sketches, 1996, A Search for Peace, 2003, The Wonder of Love, 1999, Sacred Arrangements for Solo Piano and Solo Organ, (work for two violins) Dances for Two Violins; musician: (faculty rec.) Cmty. Music Sch. Faculty Concert, 1998, Conservatory of Music Faculty Concert, 1999; musician: (producer) (conservatory faculty concert) Conservatory Faculty Concert Rec., 2000. Super swimmer Ctrl. Ohio Diabetes Assn., Columbus, 1989—2003; organist/musician New Life United Meth. Ch., Columbus, 1987—2003; organist/pianist St. Paul's Luth. Ch., Westerville, Ohio, 2003—. Mem.: Midwestern Keyboard Hist. Soc. (life), Coll. Music Soc. (life), Nat. Fedn. of Music Clubs (life; profl. adjudicator 1979—), Music Tchrs. Nat. Assn. (life; profl. adjudicator 1981—, dist. festival co-chmn. 1991, condr. for pianorama 1991—, dist. festival judge com. 2000—01, time keeper 2001, graves piano competition door monitor 2003), Ctrl. Ohio Diabetes Assn. (life). Avocations: swimming, walking, playing electronic keyboard instruments.

CORDER, DONNA NELL, elementary school educator; b. Brownfield, Tex., Nov. 27, 1965; d. Lonnie Max Horn and Wanda Nell Cockerham; m. Elven Odell Corder, June 1, 1985; children: Jennifer Michelle, Jessica Mallory. BS in Family Consumer Scis. Edn. magna cum laude, Tex. Tech. U., 1988. Sec. asst. Tex. Tech. U. Facility Planning & Constrn., Lubbock, 1984—87; asst. mgr. Victoria's Secret, 1988; substitute tchr. Lubbock Ind. Sch. Dist., 1989; tchr. kindergarten Bushland Ind. Sch. Dist., 1989—94, tchr. 5th grade, 1994—96, tchr. family consumer sci., speech, 1996—. Advisor Family, Career Cmty. Leaders Am., Bushland, 2004—05, Teen Leadership Coun., 1998—2005, Nat. Honor Soc., 1994—99. Advisor United Way, Amarillo, Tex., 2004—05; chair Applejack Ranch, 1998—2000, 2002—04; leader Girl Scouts Am., 1999—2004. Mem.: Career & Tech. Adminstrn. Tex., Family & Consumer Tchrs. Assn. Tex., Am. Assn. Family & Consumer Scis. Avocations: sewing, scrapbooks, walking, reading. Home: 812 Kachina Dr Amarillo TX 79124

CORDERO, JOSE FERNANDO, pediatrician, federal agency administrator, USPHS officer; b. Camuy, P.R., July 25, 1948; s. Fernando and Ana T. Cordero; m. Milagros J. Garcia, June 18, 1970; children: Jose F., Ana M., Joann M., Maria M. BS in Biology, U. P.R., Rio Piedras, 1969; MD, U. P.R., San Juan, 1973; MPH, Harvard U., 1979. Diplomate Nat. Bd. Med. Examiners, Am. Bd. Med. Genetics, Am. Bd. Pediatrics; lic. physician, Ga. Intern Boston City Hosp., 1973-74, jr. asst. resident dept. pediatrics, 1974-75; clin. and rsch. fellow pediatrics Mass. Gen. Hosp., 1975-77; pediatrican South End Cmty. Health Ctr., Boston, 1977-79; epidemiology intelligence svc. officer Bur. Epidemiology Ctrs. for Disease Control & Prevention, Atlanta, 1979-81, dep. chief birth defects and genetic diseases br., 1985-88, acting chief birth defects and genetic diseases bd., 1988-89, asst. dir. sci. divsn. birth defects and devel. disabilities, 1989-94, dep. dir. nat. immunization program, 1994—2001, dir. Nat. Ctr. on Birth Defects and Devel. Disabilities, 2001—; asst. surgeon gen. USPHS. Clin. instr. pediatrics Children's Hosp., Boston, 1978-79; clin. asst. prof. pediatrics Emory U., 1982—. Co-editor jour. Teratology, 1983-86; mem. editl. bd. Birth Defects Ency., 1988; reviewer jours.; contbr. numerous articles and abstracts to publs. Mem. working group cancer chemotherapy Internat. Agy. Cancer Rsch., 1980; mem. task force on child health and related issues FDA, 1980-83; mem. rev. coms. NIH; coord. U.S. Govt. Task Force Premature Thelarche in P.R., 1982-85; trustee Calif. Birth Defects Monitoring Program, 1983-89; mem. adv. bd. TERIS, Seattle, 1986—, Fla. Teratogen Info. System, 1986-90; cons. WHO, Guatemala, 1990, 91, 92, Copenhagen, 1991; founding mem. Emmaus Community, 1992—; mem. troop 547 com. Boy Scouts Am., 1983-94. Recipient Arthur S. Flemming award, 1988, Physician's Recognition award AMA, 1980, 84, 88. Mem. APHA, Am. Soc. Human Genetics, Am. Bd. Med. Genetics, Am. Acad. Pediatrics (nutrition com. 1980, com. on drugs 1988-93, genetic com. 1985), Am. Epidemiology Soc., Mass. Med. Soc., Genetics Soc. Ga., Coalition of Spanish Speaking Mental Health and Human Svcs. Orgn., Teratology Soc., Soc. Pediatric Rsch. Roman Catholic. Avocations: bird watching, flying, painting, travel. Office: Ctrs for Disease Control & Prevention 1600 Clifton Rd E87 Atlanta GA 30333 E-mail: jcordero@cdc.gov.

CORDES, EUGENE HAROLD, pharmacy and chemistry educator; b. York, Nebr., Apr. 7, 1936; s. Elmer Henry and Ruby Mae (Hofeldt) C.; m. Shirley Ann Morton, Nov. 9, 1957; children: Jennifer Eve, Matthew Henry James. BS, Calif. Inst. Tech., 1958; PhD, Brandeis U., 1962. Instr. chemistry Ind. U., Bloomington, 1962-64, asst. prof., 1964-66, assoc. prof., 1966-68, prof., 1968-79, chmn., 1972-78; exec. dir. biochemistry Merck, Sharp and Dohme Research Labs., Rahway, N.J., 1979-84, v.p. biochemistry, 1984-87; v.p. R & D Eastman Pharms., Malvern, Pa., 1987-88; pres. Sterling Winthrop Pharms. Rsch. divsn. Sterling Winthrop Inc., Collegeville, Pa., 1988-94; prof. U. Mich., Ann Arbor, 1995—2002; chmn. bd. dirs. Vitae Pharma (formerly known as Concurrent Pharms.), 2002—. Author: (with Henry Mahler) Biological Chemistry, 1966, 2d. edit., 1971, Basic Biological Chemistry, 1969, (with Riley Schaeffer) Chemistry, 1973; also articles. Recipient NIH Career Devel. award, 1966; Alfred P. Sloan Found. fellow, 1968. Mem.: AAAS, Am. Soc. Biol. Chemists. Home: 3603 Saint Davids Rd Newtown Square PA 19073-1410 Office Phone: 215-461-2027. Personal E-mail: cordeseh@aol.com.

CORDESMAN, MICHAEL J., waste management administrator; Formerly with Wast Mgmt., Inc., Superior Waste Svcs., Inc.; regional v.p. Ea. Region Republic Svcs., Inc., Ft. Lauderdale, Fla., 2001—02, COO, 2002—, pres., 2003—. Office: Republic Svcs Inc 110 SE 6th St 28th Fl Fort Lauderdale FL 33301

CORDOBA, MIKE, food products executive; b. Vancouver, Canada, Dec. 2, 1963; BBA, Simon Fraser U., 1988. Contr. Boston Pizza Internat., Richmond, Canada, 1993, v.p. fin., 1994—97, exec. v.p., 1997—2000, pres., COO, 2000—04, CEO, 2004—. Office: Boston Pizza Internat 5500 Parkwood Way Richmond BC Canada V6V 2M4 Office Phone: 604-270-1108.

CORDOVA, FRANCE ANNE-DOMINIC, academic administrator, astrophysicist; b. Paris, Aug. 5, 1947; came to U.S., 1953; d. Frederick Ben Jr. and Joan Francis (McGuinness) C.; m. Christian John Foster, Jan. 4, 1985; children: Anne-Catherine Cordova Foster, Stephen Cordova Foster. BA in English with distinction, Stanford U., 1969; PhD in Physics, Calif. Inst. Tech., 1979. Staff scientist earth and space sci. div. Los Alamos Nat. Lab., 1979-89, dep. group leader space astronomy and astrophysics group, 1989; prof., head dept. astronomy and astrophysics Pa. State U., University Park, 1989-93; chief scientist NASA, Washington, 1993-96; vice chancellor for rsch. U. Calif., Santa Barbara, 1996—2002, chancellor Riverside, 2002—. Mem. Nat. Com. on Medal of Sci., 1991-94; mem. adv. com. for astron. scis. NSF, 1990-93, external adv. com. Particle Astrophysics Ctr., 1989-93; bd. dirs. Assn. Univs. for Rsch. in Astronomy, 1989-93; mem. Space Telescope Inst. Coun., 1990-93; mem. com. space astronomy and astrophysics Space Sci. Bd., 1987-90, internat. users com. Roentgen X-ray Obs., 1985-90, extreme ultraviolet explorer guest observer working group NASA, 1988-92, com. Space Sci. and Applications Group, NASA, 1991-93; mem. Hubble Telescope Adv. Camera Team, 1993; chair Hubble Fellow Selection Com., 1992. Guest editor Mademoiselle mag., 1969; editor: Multiwavelength Astrophysics, 1988, The Spectroscopic Survey Telescope, 1990; contbr. over 150 articles, abstracts and revs. to Astrophysics Jour., Nature, Astrophysics and Space Scis., Advanced Space Rsch., Astron. Astrophysics, Mon. Nat. Royal Astron. Soc., chpts. to books. Named One of Am.'s 100 Brightest Scientists under 40, Sci. Digest, 1986; numerous grants NASA, 1979—, recipient group achievement award, NASA, 1991, Distinguished Svc. medal, NASA, Kilby Laureate, 2000. Mem. Internat. Astron. Union (U.S. nat. com. 1990-93), Am. Astron. Soc. (v.p. 1993-96, chair high energy astrophysics divsn. 1990, vice chair 1989), Sigma Xi. Achievements include analysis of ultra-soft x-ray emission from active galactic nuclei; observations and modeling of the winds from accretion disks; studies of the interstellar medium using ultraviolet spectroscopy of nearby hot binary stars; observations and modeling of extended x-ray emitting regions in close binary systems; understanding the accretion geometry of magnetic binaries with accreting white dwarfs; coordinating radio and x-ray observations of x-ray binaries in an effort to find a unified model for correlated behavior; search for evidence of galactic magnetic monopoles by identifying a class of ultrasoft x-ray emitters; studying the multispectial emission from neutron stars; making observations of x-ray emitting pulsars and their associated supernova remnants in the radio and infrared; conceiving space instruments and data systems for imaging detectors (U.S. principal investigator for optical/UV Telescope launched 1999 on ESA's X-Ray Multi-Mirror mission); making multifrequency observations of high-energy sources. Office: U Calif Riverside Office of Chancellor 900 University Ave Riverside CA 92521

CORDOVA, MARIA ASUNCION, dentist; b. Punta Arenas, Magallanes, Chile, May 14, 1941; came to U.S., 1972; d. Miguel Cordova and Maria Asuncion Requena; m. Carlos F. Salinas, July 27, 1963; children: Carlos M., Claudio A., Lola. DDS, U. Chile, Santiago, 1965; DMD, Med. U. S.C., 1986. From instr. to assoc. prof. physiology U. Chile, Valparaiso, 1965—72; postdoctoral fellow Johns Hopkins U., Balt., 1972-75; from instr. to asst. prof. dept. physiology Med. U. S.C., Charleston, 1975—86; pvt. practice Charleston, 1986—. Vis. scientist N.Y. Med. Coll., 1975. Contbr. articles to profl. jours. V.p. Circulo Hispanic Charleston; country specialist Amnesty Internat. U.S.A., Spoleto, Charleston, mem. outreach com.; bd. dirs. YWCA, Trident Urban League, Robert Ivey Ballet, S.C. Humanities Coun., 1996—2002. Mem. Charleston Women's Network (pres. 1989-90). Roman Catholic. Office: 159 Wentworth St Charleston SC 29401-1731 Office Phone: 843-577-2898.

CORDY, ROBERT J., state supreme court justice; b. Manchester, Conn., May 18, 1949; married; 4 children. AB cum laude, Dartmouth Coll., 1971; JD, Harvard U., 1974. Def. atty. Mass. Defenders Com., 1974—78; spl. asst. atty. gen. Mass. Dept. Revenue, 1978—79; assoc. gen. counsel in charge of enforcement Mass. State Ethics Commn., 1979—82; asst. U.S. atty., 1982—87; ptnr. Burns & Levinson, Boston, 1987—91; chief legal counsel to Gov. William F. Weld, Boston, 1991—93; mng. ptnr. McDermott, Will & Emery, Boston, 1993—2001; assoc. justice Mass. Supreme Jud. Ct., 2001—. Lectr. Harvard Law Sch., 1987—96. Office: 1 Beacon St 3rd Fl Boston MA 02108*

CORE, ORVILLE BEN, retired lawyer; b. Aug. 23, 1924; s. Opal Arch and Elizabeth (Ming) C.; m. Polly Anna Williams, Apr. 8, 1951; children: Michelle Eileen, Grady Bruce, Patrick Keith, Kathleen. BS in Pub. Adminstrn. with honors, U. Ark., 1949, LLB with honors, 1951. Bar: Ark. 1951, U.S. Dist. Ct. Ark. 1951, U.S. Supreme Ct. 1971. City atty. City of DeQueen, Ark., 1956-60; pros. atty. 9th Jud. Cir. Ark., 1961—63; city atty. City of Ft. Smith, Ark., 1966-70; ptnr. Daily & Woods, Ft. Smith, 1964—2001, Daily & Woods P.L.L.C. (and predecessor firm), Ft. Smith, 1970—, mng. ptnr., 1992—2001, ret., 2001, of counsel, 2002—. Bd. dirs., sec. Ark. Inst. for Continuing Legal Edn., 1990-92. Contbr. articles to profl. jours. Mem. Ark. Bar Assn. (ho. of dels.), Ark. Assn. Def. Coun. (pres. 1982-83), Def. Rsch. Inst. (state chmn. 1979-92), Rotary (pres. Ft. Smith 1968-69). Office: Daily & Woods PLLC PO Box 1446 623 Garrison Ave Fort Smith AR 72901-2531 Office Phone: 479-782-0361.

COREIL, RAYMOND CLYDE, language educator; b. Ville Platte, La., Nov. 29, 1939; s. Armand Bernard and Thelma (Perrodin) C.; m. Vivian Jr Yi Tsao, June 5, 1976. BA in English, U. S.W. La., 1961; MFA in Theatre, Carnegie-Mellon U., 1976; PhD in Linguistics, CUNY, 1992. Writer--journalist Daily Advertiser Newspaper, Lafayette, La., 1961-62, La. State U., Baton Rouge, 1963-67; tchr. English U. Hue, Vietnam, 1967-68, U. Abdulaziz, Jeddah, Saudi Arabia, 1968-69, 77-80, U. Saigon, Vietnam, 1970-74, New Jersey City Univ., 1981—. Founder Ctr. for Imagination in Lang. Learning, 1997, dept. chair, 1999—2005, founder certificates in Am. English Lang. and Am. Culture, 2000; keynote spkr. confs. on lang. and imagination Richmond (Va.) U., 2001, Simon Fraser U., Vancouver, B.C., 2003; founder, co-chmn. Ann. Conf. on Imagination and Lang. Learning, 1991—. Playwright numerous stageplays and screenplays; songwriter: (musical plays) Remembering Hue, 1998, Homelands, 1999; editor, founder Jour. Imagination, 1993—; editor anthology: Multiple Intelligences Howard Gardner and New Methods in Coll. Tchg., Articles by Howard Gardner and 41 Educators. Recipient Edward Sapir award N.Y. Acad. Scis., 1992; Fulbright grant U.S. Govt., 1972; grantee Nat. Endowment Arts, 1976. Roman Catholic. Avocations: photography, music, painting, linguistics. Home: 17 Fuller Pl Brooklyn NY 11215-6006 Office: New Jersey City Univ 2039 Kennedy Blvd Jersey City NJ 07305-1527 Fax: (201) 200-2202. Office Phone: 201-200-3237. Business E-Mail: ccoreil@njcu.edu. E-mail: coreil@erols.com.

CORELL, ROBERT WALDEN, science administrator, educator; b. Detroit, Nov. 4, 1934; s. George W. and Grace (Hagland) C.; m. Billie Jo Proctor, June 16, 1956; children: Robert Walden, David Proctor, Beth Anne. BSME, Case Inst. Tech., 1956; MS, MIT, 1959, PhD, 1964. Engr. GE, Cleve., 1955, program engr., Lynn, Mass., 1956-57; instr. U. N.H., 1957-58, asst. prof., 1959-60, assoc. prof., 1964-66, prof., 1966-90, chmn. dept. mech. engring., 1964-72, dir. marine program, 1975-87; asst. dir. geoscis. NSF, Arlington, Va., 1987-2000; sr. rsch. fellow Belfer Ctr. Sci. for Science and Internat. Affairs, 2000; sr. rsch. fellow Kennedy Sch. Govt. Harvard U., 2000—; sr. fellow Am. Meterol. Soc., Wash., 2000—. Rsch. engr. Huggins Hosp., Wolfeboro, N.H., 1957-60, Highland View Hosp., Cleve., 1960-64; vis. investigator Woods Hole Oceanographic Inst., 1965; rsch. assoc., vis. prof. Scripps Instn. Oceanography, 1971-72; vis. prof. U. Wash., 1985; chair U.S. Global Change Rsch. Com. of U.S. Govt., 1987-2000; sr. rsch. fellownumerous positions as chair of interagy. sci. coms. and internat. bodies. Contbr. articles to profl. jours. Founding chair Internat. Group of Funding Agencies for Global Change Rsch., 1988-90; chair Implementation Com. for Inter-Am. Inst. for Global Change Rsch., 1992-95; dir. White House Conf. on Sci. and Econs. to Global Change Rsch., 1990. Fellow Sr. Rsch. fellow, Harvard U., 2000—04. Mem. AAAS, IEEE, Am. Meterology Soc. (chair Arctic Climate Impact Assessment 2000-), Am. Soc. Engring. Edn., Marine Tech. Soc., Adv. Group Sci. and Tech. Sustainable Devel. (ad hoc 2003-), Sigma Xi, Tau Beta Pi, Sigma Alpha Epsilon. Achievements include research in global change, climate and environmental research, medicine, medical engineering, ocean science and technology. Office: Am Meteorol Soc 1120 G St N W Ste 800 Washington DC 20005-737 E-mail: global@dmv.com.

CORELLI, JOHN CHARLES, physicist, researcher; b. Providence, Aug. 6, 1930; s. John Dominic Corelli and Immacolata (Caldarelli) C.; separated; children: Carolyn Margaret, John Joseph. BS in Physics, Providence Coll., 1952; MS in Physics, Brown U., 1954; PhD in Physics, Purdue U., 1958. Physicist Knolls Atomic Power Lab. GE, Schenectady, N.Y., 1958-61, cons., 1979-81; prof. nuclear engring. and engring. physics Rensselaer Poly. Inst., Troy, N.Y., 1962-96, prof. emeritus, 1997—. Contbr. more than 100 articles to Jour. Applied Physics, Jour. Nuclear Materials, Phys. Rev., Jour. Vacuum Sci. and Tech. Spl. fellow NIH, Rochester Univ., N.Y., 1971., 1971. Mem. Am. Phys. Soc., Am. Nuclear Soc. Home: 11A Salem Ct Albany NY 12203-5932 Business E-Mail: corelj@rpi.edu.

COREN, LANCE SCOTT, automotive executive, consultant; b. Inglewood, Calif., Dec. 19, 1949; s. Melville and Shirley Ann (Ehrlich) C.; m. Susan Hodges; 1 child, Amy Elizabeth. BSBL, Van Norman U., L.A., 1973; cert. ins. law, UCLA, 1975; cert. comparative psychology, The Calif. Grad. Inst., 1975; MBA, Cal-Western U., 1976; cert. automotive impact nalysis, UCLA/SAE Traffic Inst., 1976. Cert. automotive expert, Calif., Nat. Inst. Automotive Svc. Elegance; cert. master appraiser Internat. Auto Appraisers Assn. Kelley Blue Book Offcl. Guide. Auto claims adjustor Gulf & Western Cos., L.A., 1974-77; western regional mgr., field ops. Guaranty Nat. Ins. Group, L.A., 1977-80; pres., chief exec. officer L.S.C. Enterprizes, Inc., Torrance, Calif., 1980—. Pres., CEO L.S.C. Ent., Inc./Corenco Corp., N.Y.C./Torrance, Calif., 1980—; ptnr. C&H Racing Team U.S.A., 1989—; bd. dirs. Capital Investment Trust, N.Y., L.S.C. Investment Co., L.A., N.Y.C., Palm Springs Ann. Rd. Races-Concours D'Elegance, Newport Invitiational Concours D'Elegance, Palos Verdes Concours D'Elegance; cons. Auto Assn. Am., L.A., 1984-88, State Farm Inst. Co., L.A., 1984-92, Guaranty Nat. Cos., 1993-96, U.S.A.A. Ins. Co. L.A., 1986-92, Inst. Inst. Hwy. Safety, 1987-92; mem. Internat. Orgn. of Experts to UN, 1992-1999; adv. bd. dirs. Nat. Automobile Dealers Assn., 2000-05, Cars of Particular Interest, 2001-2005, Kelley Blue Book, El Camino C.C., 2000-2003, Nat. Inst. Automotive Svc. Excellence; chief mng. dir. L.S.C. Ins. Svcs., 2005 Author: The International Firm, 1976, Exotic Automotive Investments, 1985; mem. adv. bd.: Vehicle Values, 1999—2005, Vintage Racecar Jour., 2000—; editor: Exotic Car Values; value guide editor Rolls-Royce Owners Club, 2003—. Fund raiser Children's Hosp., Orange County, 1987, Soroptimist Internat., Newport Beach, 1983, Children's Hosp. Soc. of Calif., Fresno, 1985; mem. govs. coun. Ins. Practices, 1987-91, Carroll Shelby Heart Fund, L.A., 1990; vice chmn. The Coren Found., Fresno, Calif., 1998-2005, Marconi Children's Charities, 2000-05, Chldren's Charities of Am., 1985-2000. Named One of Outstanding Young Men in Am., U.S. Jaycees, 1986; recipient Presdl. Sports award (skiing), Washington, 1973, Internat. Man of Yr. Automotive Internat. Fedn. of Automotive Analysts, London, 1992. Mem. Internat. Automotive Appraisers Assn.(master appraiser, advisory bd. mem. 2003-05), Internat. Soc. Automotive Appraisers (pres. 1983-84), Am. Assn. Auto Appraisers (pres. 1984-85, co-exec. dir. all-auto-appraisal-industry conf., 2002-05), Soc. Automotive Engrs., Internat. Soc. Automotive Analysis, All Auto Appraisal Industry Conf. (bd. dirs. 2004-2005) Democrat. Jewish. Avocations: tennis, skiing, vintage auto racing. Office: L S C Enterprizes Group Inc PO Box 429 Prather CA 93651-0429 Office Phone: 559-299-0429. E-mail: LSCENT@hotmail.com.

COREY, DARRYL LYNN, mathematics and computer science professor, researcher, consultant; s. Dallas Corey Sr. and Diane Corey. PhD, Fla. State U., 2000. Asst. prof. Valdosta State U., Ga., 2003—. Vis. asst. prof. Fla. State U., Tallahassee, 2000—; pres. Darryl L. Corey Edn. Cons., Tallahassee, 2004—, CEO, 2004—. Grad. Rsch. assistantships, Ctr. Nonlinear Analysis, Hampton U. Math. Dept., 1990 - 1992. Mem.: Soc. Indsl. and Applied Math., Internat. Group for Psychology of Math. Edn., Assn. for Advancement of Computing in Edn., Ga. Coun. Tchrs. of Math., Math. Assn. Am., Nat. Coun. Tchrs. of Math. D-Liberal. Office: Valdosta State Univ Dept Math Computer Sci Valdosta GA 31698 Office Fax: 229-219-1257. Business E-Mail: dlcorey@valdosta.edu.

COREY, DONALD EDWARD, elementary school educator; b. Terre Haute, Ind., Nov. 5, 1950; s. Paul Edward and Norma Ruth (Stufflebean) C.; m. Carole Elaine Lee Hos, July 10, 1977 (div. July 1981); 1 child, Andrew Joseph. BS, Ind. State U., 1980, MS, 1986. 6th grade tchr. North Vermillion Elem., Cayuga, Ind., 1981-97; tchr. English North Vermillion H.S./Jr. H.S., 1997—. Sgt. U.S. Army, 1973-75. Baptist. Home: 410 S 34th St Terre Haute IN 47803-2352 Office: North Vermillion Elem RR # 191 Cayuga IN 47928 Office Phone: 765-492-3364. E-mail: dcorey@nvc.k12.in.us.

COREY, ELIAS JAMES, chemistry professor; b. Methuen, Mass., July 12, 1928; s. Elias and Tina (Hashem) Corey; m. Claire Higham, Sept. 14, 1961; children: David, John, Susan. BS, MIT, 1948, PhD, 1951; AM (hon.), Harvard U., 1959; DSc (hon.), U. Chgo., 1968, Hofstra U., 1974, Colby Coll., 1976, Oxford U., 1982, U. Liege, 1985, U. Ill., 1985, Kenyon Coll., 1989, Helsinki Coll., 1990, Ariz. U., 1990, Merrimac Coll., 1990, Hokkaido U., 1991, Rennselaer Polytechnic Inst., 1991, Boston Coll., 1992, Tex. A&M U., 1997, Nat. Chung Cheng U., 1999, U. Alicante, 1999, Cambridge U., 2000. From instr. to asst. prof. U. Ill., Champaign-Urbana, 1951—55, prof., 1955—59; prof. chemistry Harvard U., Cambridge, Mass., 1959—68, Sheldon Emory prof. of Chemistry, 1968—98, prof. emeritus, 1998—. Adv. bd. Microbia Scientific, 2002. Edtl. bd. mem. Jour. Organic Chemistry, 1962—65; contbr. articles to profl. jours. Recipient Intrasci. Found. award, 1968, Ernest Guenther award in chemistry, 1968, Centenary Medal, Chem. Soc. London, 1971, Harrison Howe award, 1971, Ciba Found. medal, 1972, Evans award, Ohio State U., 1972, Linus Pauling award, 1973, Dickson prize in sci., Carnegie Mellon U., 1973, George Ledlie prize in sci., Harvard U., 1973, Nichols medal, 1977, Buchman award, Calif. Inst. Tech., 1978, Franklin medal in sci., Franklin Inst., 1978, Sci. Achievement award, CCNY, 1979, J.G. Kirkwood award, Yale U., 1980, C.S. Hamilton award, U. Nebr., 1980, Chem. Pioneer award, Am. Inst. Chemists, 1981, Lewis S. Rosenstiel Award, Brandeis U., 1981, Medal of Excellence, U. Helsinki, 1982, Paul Karrer Award, U. Zurich, 1982, Tetrahedron Prize, 1983, Paracelsus Award, Swiss Chem. Soc., 1984, V.D. Mattia award, Roche Inst. Molecular Biology, 1985, Wolf prize in chemistry, Wolf Found., 1986, Silliman award, 1986, Japan prize, 1989, Nat. Med. Sci. award, 1988, Order of Rising Sun, Gold and Silver Star, Govt. Japan, 1989, Nobel prize in chemistry, 1990, Gold medal, AIC, 1990, Janot Medal, U. Paris, 1990, Messel Medallist, Soc. for Chem. Industry, 1994, Gold medal, AIC, 2003, Priestly medal, 2004; fellow, Swiss-Am. Exch., 1957, Guggenheim Found., 1957—58, 1968—69, Alfred P. Sloan Found., 1956—59, AAAS, 2000. Mem.: AAAS, Royal Soc. of London (foreign mem.), Inst. Medicine, Robert A. Welch Found. (mem. sci. adv. bd. 1968—), Franklin Inst., NAS (Award in Chem. Scis. 2002), Am. Acad. Arts and Scis., Soc. Synthetic Organic Chemistry (hon.), Pharm. Soc. Japan (hon.), Chem. Soc. Finland (hon.), Royal Soc. Chemistry (hon. Robert Robinson Medal 1988), Chem. Soc. Japan (hon.), Am. Chem. Soc. (hon. Pure Chemistry award 1960, Fritzche award 1968, award in synthetic chemistry 1971, Remsen award 1974, Arthur C. Cope award 1976, Willard Gibbs Award 1984, Madison Marshall award 1985, Roger Adams award organic chemistry 1993), Sigma Xi. Office: Harvard U Dept Chemistry Rm 319 12 Oxford St Dept Cambridge MA 02138-2902*

COREY, ELIZABETH B., poet, writer; b. Orlando, Fla., Oct. 26, 1962; d. Arthur E. and Margaret Fannie (Dinsfelder) Corey. Student, Loyola U., New Orleans, 1980—82, Tulane U., 1982—84, Hofstra U., 1985, NY Inst. Tech., 1986—87, Yeshiva U.; BA in Art History, Adelphi U., 1984—86. Cert. diabetes educator. Patient rels. Tulane U. S.E. Regional Renal Transplant Unit, 1980—81; med. asst. Charity Hosp., New Orleans, 1981—83; customer svc. rels. Publisher's Clearinghouse, 1986—89, BP Gas & Oil, 1991—92; social worker Albert Einstein Coll. Med., 1989—90, Salvation Army, 1990—91; mus. asst. Cleveland Mus. Art, 1993. English dept. cons. Trinity Prep. H.S., Winterfield, Fla.; activities coord. Creedmoor State Hosp., Queens, 1986—90; vol. Vienna State Opera Ball, 1998—2002. Pres. Tulane U. Hillel, Adelphi U. Fine Arts Club. Fellow: Mensa; mem.: SAG, Alexandre Dumas Soc., Victor Hugo Soc., Nat. Writers Union, Acad. Am. Poets. Democrat. Jewish. Avocations: fencing, surfing, diving, swimming, weight-lifting.

COREY, GORDON RICHARD, financial advisor, former utilities executive; b. Osceola, Wis., Sept. 27, 1914; s. Ralph Watson and Bessie Mabel (Simpson) C.; m. Margarete Moeller Grenn, 1967; children by previous marriage: Eleanor Corey Tatge, Margaret Corey Amundson, Gordon Ralph, Martha Elizabeth. BA, U. Wis., 1936; MBA, Northwestern U., 1940. CPA, Ill. V.p. Commonwealth Edison Co., 1952-62, exec. v.p., 1962-64, chmn. fin. com., 1964-73, vice chmn., from 1973; now ret.; now pvt. fin. adv. Mem.: Wayfarers, Ridge and Valley Tennis. Home: Two Arbor Ln Apt 411 Evanston IL 60201-1970

COREY, JAMES WILLIAM, political scientist, educator; b. North Charleroi, Pa., Dec. 17, 1937; s. James William Corey and Elizabeth Marie Munch; m. Daria Ann Slentz, July 16, 1960; children: Kathleen Elizabeth Rhodes, Margaret Ann Buckwald, James Matthew, David Anthony. BS, Villanova U., 1959; PhD, Fla. State U., 1999. Commnd. ensign USN, Washington, 1959, advanced through grades to comdr., with, 1959—84; asst. prof. polit. sci. High Point U., NC, 1999—. Dir. Credit for Prior Learning Program High Point U., 2003—; participant Oxford Roundtable, 2005; bd. dirs. Hispanic Ctr., Piedmont Internat. Visitors Program. Author: Annotated U.S. Constitution, 2003; contbr. articles to profl. jours. Participant Cmty. Chorus, High Point, 2000—04; organizer candidate forums High Point U.; choir mem., lector Immaculate Heart Of Mary, High Point, 1999—2004. Mem.: Am. Polit. Sci. Assn. (assoc.), Phi Theta Kappa. Republican. Roman Catholic. Avocations: physical exercise, walking. Office: High Point U Montelieu Ave High Point NC 27262-3598 Office Phone: 336-841-4583. Business E-Mail: jcorey@highpoint.edu.

COREY, JUDITH ANN, retired elementary school educator; b. Peoria, Ill., Dec. 1, 1937; d. Lyle William and Eileen A. (Zigrang) Springston; m. Thomas W. Corey, Aug. 12, 1961; children: John William, Jeffrey Michael, Gregory Lyle, Mark Andrew. BA in Bus., English, Marycrest Coll., 1960; MA in Counseling, Bradley U., 1972. Lic. tchr. K-12, Ill.; lic. clin. profl. counselor. Tchr. Riverview Sch., Spring Bay, Ill., 1960-61, Lincoln Sch., East Peoria, Ill., 1963-64; counselor Bradley U., Peoria, 1972-73; clin. psychologist intern Zeller Zone Ctr., Peoria, 1973; dean students Morton (Ill.) High Sch., 1974-85; tchr. Jefferson Sch., Morton, 1985—2002; ret., 2002. Contbr. poem to Worlds Greatest Contemporary Poems, 1981 (Hon. Mention). Campaign work Grace Bunn Lievens Ill. Rep., 89th Dist. Ill., Morton, 1994; mem. exec. bd. Ill. State Deans' Assn., 1980-84, historian, 1980-82, membership com., 1982-84. Named to Outstanding Young Women in Am., 1973. Mem. NEA, Ill. Edn. Assn., Morton Edn. Assn. (newsletter editor 1987-90, mem. exec. com. and maj. negotiator, 1987-2000, v.p. 1993-95), Assn. Play Therapy, Phi Kappa Phi (life), Kappa Gamma Pi, Pi Lambda Theta. Roman Catholic. Avocations: reading, writing, photography, music, nature. Home: 20432 Tennessee Ave Morton IL 61550-9777

COREY, KAY JANIS, business owner, designer, nurse; b. Detroit, Aug. 22, 1942; d. Alexander Michael Corey and Lillian Emiline (Stanley) Kilborn; divorced; children: Tonya Kay, William James, Jason Ronald. Student, C.S. Mott Community Coll., 1960-62, Mich. State U., 1962-64; AA, AS in Nursing, St. Petersburg Jr. Coll., 1978; student, U. South Fla., 1985-86. RN; cert. perioperative nurse; cert. varityypist. Mgr. display Lerner Shops, Flint, Mich., 1960-62; layout artist Abdulla Advt., Flint, 1966-67; varitypist, artist City Hall Print Shop, Flint, 1967-70; nurse Suncoast Hosp., Largo, Fla., 1976-78; nurse, coord. plastic surgery svc., perioperative staff nurse Largo Med. Ctr. Hosp., 1978-81, 84-90; assoc. dir. nursing Roberts Home Health Svc., Pinellas Park, Fla., 1982-84; co-owner Sand Castle Resort, White Bay, Jost Van Dyke, Brit. Virgin Island, 1990-95; perioperative nurse HCA Gulf Coast Surgery Ctr., 1995-99; perioperative nurse, surg. nurse Blake Med. Ctr. Hosp., 2000—. Designer, artist K.J. Originals clothing line, 1990-95, The Magic Needle clothing line, 1998; insvc. edn. instr., dir. video edn., team leader oncology dept. Largo Med. Ctr. Hosp., 1980-81; designer, mfr. Haelan Jewelers--Fine Custom Jewelry, 1999. Editor, illustrator: (book) Some Questions and Answers About Chemotherapy, 1981, Thoughts for Today, 1981; illustrator (cookbooks) Spices and Spoons, 1982, Yom Tov Essen n' Fressen, 1983; various brochures and catalogues; art work in permanent collection of C.S. Mott Jr. Coll., Flint, 1962; artist, designer of casual and hand painted clothing for children and adults. Historian Am. Businesswomen's Assn., Flint, 1968-73 (scholarship 1976); outreach chmn. Temple B'nai Israel, Clearwater, Fla., 1981-85; regional outreach coord. Union of Am. Hebrew Congregations, N.Y.C., 1983-85. Mem. Assn. of Oper. Rm. Nurses, Phi Theta Kappa. Republican. Jewish. Avocations: sailing, scuba diving, tennis, original teddy bear making, golf. Address: 4080 Kingsfield Dr Parrish FL 34219 Personal E-mail: bubbekay@msn.com.

COREY, KENNETH EDWARD, urban planning and geography educator, researcher; b. Cin., Nov. 11, 1938; s. Kenneth and Helen Ann (Beckman) C.; m. Marie Joann Fye, Aug. 26, 1961; children: Jeffrey Allen, Jennifer Marie. BA with honors, U. Cin., 1961, MA, 1962, M of Cmty. Planning, 1964, PhD, 1969. Instr. U. Cin., 1962-65, asst. prof. cmty. planning, 1965-69, assoc. prof., 1969-74, prof., 1974-79, head grad. comty. planning and geography, 1969-78; assoc. prof. cmty. planning and geography U. R.I., 1966-67; prof. geography, planning, chmn. dept. geography, dir. urban studies U. Md., 1979-89; prof. geography and urban and regional planning Mich. State U., East Lansing, 1989—, dean Coll. Social Sci., 1989—99, sr. rsch. advisor to v.p. for rsch. and grad. studies, 1999—2004. Vis. prof. geography Univ. Wales, Aberystwyth, 1974-75, Peking U., 1986; chmn. Cin. Model Cities Bd., 1974; Fulbright rsch. scholar Inst. S.E. Asian Studies, Singapore, 1986, Fulbright group study abroad, Sri Lanka, 1983; trustee Met. Washington Housing Planning Assn., 1980-82. Author: The Local Community, 1968, Community Internships for Undergraduate Geography Students, 1973, The Planning of Change, 3d edit., 1976, Information Tectonics, 2000. Bd. dirs. Potomac River Basin Consortium, Washington, 1982-85. Recipient Svc. award Cmty. Chest and Coun. Cin., 1979; recipient Svc. award Planning Divsn., 1979, Svc. award Coalition of Neighborhoods, Cin., 1979, 83, medal of city Mayor of Seoul, South Korea, 1980. Fellow Royal Geog. Soc.; mem. Am. Inst. Cert. Planners, Am. Planning Assn., Assn. Am. Geographers (award spl. group on planning and regional devel. 1985), Assn. Asian Studies, Asia Soc., Pacific Rim Coun. on Urban Devel., World Future Soc. Democrat.

COREY, MARK, historic site director; b. DeKalb, Ill., Aug. 3, 1950; BA, U. Miss., Oxford, 1972. Supt. Ocmulgee Nat. Park, Macon, Ga., 1988-92, Andrew Johnson Nat. Hist. Site, Greenville, Tenn., 1992—. Office: Andrew Johnson Nat Hist Site College and Depot Sts Greeneville TN 37743 also: PO Box 1088 Greeneville TN 37744-1088

COREY, ORLIN RUSSELL, publishing executive; b. Nowata, Okla., May 4, 1926; s. Lue A. and Nada Gladys (Patton) C.; m. Irene Lockridge, Aug. 25, 1949 (div. 1974); m. Shirley Trusty, Nov. 27, 1975. BA, Baylor U., 1950, MA, 1952; cert. of directing and acting, Ctrl. Sch. Speech and Drama, London, 1956. Drama dir., asst. prof. Georgetown (Ky.) Coll., 1952-59; drama dir., assoc. prof. Centenary Coll., Shreveport, La., 1960-68; dir. touring repertory theatre of classics Everyman Players, Pineville, Ky., 1958-80; pub., editor Anchorage Press, Inc., New Orleans, 1977-2000, editl. advisor, 2000—. Guest dir. U. N.H., Durham, 1968; lectr. Ohio State U., also other univs., 1968—75; prodr. John F. Kennedy Ctr., Washington, 1973—75; pres. Children's Theatre Found., Inc., Greensboro, NC, 1977—2001; mem. exec. com. Nat. Theater Conf., 1985. Author: Theatre for Children, 1973, Towers of the Brazos, Theatre for Children—Kid-Stuff or Theatre?, 1974, An Odyssey of Masquers: The Everyman Plwyers, 1990, Religious Drama: A Classic Quartet, 1999; adapter, dir. drama of book of Job, 1960; prodr. La. World Expo, World Theatre Festival, New Orleans, 1984. Bd. dirs. New Orleans Ctr. Creative Arts, 1975—, Nat. Theatre Conf. With USN, 1944-46, PTO. Recipient religious drama award Nat. Cath. Theater Assn., 1968, Radius, London, 1974. Fellow Am. Theatre (dean Coll. Fellows 1994-96, Jennie Heiden award 1970); mem. Children's Theater Assn. Am. (pres. 1971-73), Am. Alliance for Theatre and Edn. Avocations: photography, cooking, reading. Office: Childrens Theatre Found Am PO Box 8067 New Orleans LA 70182-8067

COREY, RAYMOND CANFIELD, organist; b. Poughkeepsie, N.Y., Mar. 10, 1918; s. Herbert Edgar and Alida Matilda Corey; m. Heather Alicia Harrison, May 19, 1957; children: Cheryl Corey Hoffman, Raymond Kier. BS, Juilliard Sch. Music, 1955, MS, 1957. Ch. organist St. Margaret's Episc. Ch., Staatsburg, 1938—42; chaplain's asst. Baton Rouge, 1942—45, Malden, Mo., 1942—45; organist various local chs., 1946—54; organist St. James Meth. Ch., Kingston, NY, 1954—, 1st Luth. Ch., Poughkeepsie, 1970—94, Ch. of Messiah, Rhinebeck, NY, 1994—. Organ cons. for redesign instruments St. James Meth. Ch., Kingston, Washington St. Meth. Ch., Poughkeepsie, 1st Luth. Ch., Poughkeepsie, 1983—84. Sgt. USAF, 1943—45. Mem.: Am. Guild Organists (life; sgt.-at-arms local 238/291).

COREY, SCOTT D., music educator; b. Chateau, Mont., Mar. 8, 1959; s. Herbert R. and Helen B. (Kelsh) Corey; m. Ruth Ann Robbins, June 11, 1994; children: Thomas Lowell, Robbin Elizabeth, Matthew Aaron, Ellise Ruthann. BS in Bus. Mgmt., Mont. State U., Bozeman, 1981, BMusE, 1990. Music dir. Simms (Mont.) H.S., 1990—93; choral dir. Colstrip H.S., 1993—95, Billings H.S., Billings, Mont., 1995—. Performer Intermountain Opera, Bozeman, Mont., 1990, Montana Chorale, Grant Falls, 1994—98; chair music dept. Billings H.S., 1999—; music festival adjudicator Mont., Wyo., 1993—; guest clinician honors choir festivals, Mont., 1996—. Named Tchr. in Cmty.,

Clearwater Comm, 2004. Mem.: Mont. Music Edicators Assn., Mont. Choral Dir. Assn. (treas. 1999—). Mem. Ch. Lds. Home: 1944 Phoebe Dr Billings MT 59105 Office: Billings Sr HS 425 Grand Ave Billings MT 59101

CORIA, GUILLERMO, professional tennis player; b. Rufino, Argentina, Jan. 13, 1982; s. Oscar and Graciela Coria. Profl. tennis player ATP Tour, 2000—. Achievements include Winner of 8 singles titles: Vina del Mar, 2001, Basel, 2003, Hamburg TMS, 2003, Kitzbuhel, 2003, Sopot, 2003, Stuttgart, 2003, Buenos Aires, 2004, Monte Carlo TMS, 2004. Office: c/o ATP Tour Internat Hdqs 201 ATP Tour Blvd Ponte Vedra Beach FL 32082

CORIC, VLADIMIR, psychiatrist; s. Vladimir and Ljerka Coric; m. Elizabeth Ann Feely, July 10, 1999; children: Christina, Julia. BS in Neurobiology and Physiology, U. Conn., 1992; MD, Wakeforest Sch. Medicine, 1996; postgrad., Yale U., 1996—2001. Asst. clin. prof. psychiatry Yale U., New Haven, 2001—. Chief inpatient svcs. Yale Clin. Neurosci. Rsch. Unit, New Haven, 2001—; bd. dirs. Yale Rsch. Clinic, New Haven. Co-author: Appleton & Lange's Reason of Psychology, 2003; contbr. chapters to books. Recipient Nat. Endowment Merit award, Laughlin Found., 2000, Young Investigator award, Nat. Alliance for Rsch. on Schizophrenia and Depression, 2003, 2005; Glaxowellcome fellow, APA, 1998—2000. Mem.: AMA, Conn. Psychiat. Soc. (sec. 2004—05), Am. Psychiatric Assn., Phi Beta Kappa. Office: Yale Univ Sch Medicine Dept Psychiatry 34 Park St New Haven CT 06519

CORIDEN, MICHAEL WARNER, lawyer; b. Sioux City, Iowa, June 3, 1948; s. Thomas Lou and Patricia (Warner) C.; m. Karen Baldrige, Oct. 12, 1974; children: Courtney Anne, Torrey Erin, Shannon Marielle. B of Gen. Studies, U. Iowa, 1971; postgrad., Inst. Internat. & Compar. Law, Paris, 1973; JD, Creighton U., 1974; MBA, U. Denver, 1983. Bar: Iowa 1974, Nebr. 1974, U.S. Tax Ct. 1974, U.S. Ct. Claims 1976, U.S. Internat. Trade 1976, Colo. 1980, U.S. Supreme Ct. 1980. Atty. Land of Lincoln Legal Assistance Found., Champaign, Ill., 1974-75; asst. atty. gen. State of Iowa, Des Moines, 1975-77; atty. Peter Kiewit Sons' Inc., Omaha, 1977-79; counsel La. Land and Exploration Co., Lakewood, Colo., 1979-83; gen. counsel Tenneco Minerals Co., Lakewood, 1983-85; pvt. practice Denver, 1985-88; gen. counsel, sec. CF&I Steel Corp., Pueblo, Colo., 1988-93; gen. counsel CF&I Steel, L.P., Pueblo, 1993—; of counsel LeBouef, Lamb, Greene & MacRae, Denver, 1993-95; pvt. practice Denver, 1995—. Bd. dirs. Pueblo Diversified Industries, Inc., Aspen Lane Ltd., Ctr. Hearing, Speech & Lang.; instr. Denver Paralegal Inst., 1988. Mem. Colo. Bar Assn., Colo. Assn. Corp. Counsel. Office: 2289 S Hiwan Dr Evergreen CO 80439-8927

CORIGLIANO, JOHN PAUL, composer; b. N.Y.C., Feb. 16, 1938; s. John and Rose (Buzen) C. BA cum laude, Columbia U., 1959. Disting. prof. music Lehman Coll., N.Y.C.; mem. faculty Juilliard Sch. of Music, N.Y.C., 1991—. Composer: Violin Sonata, 1963, Tournaments Overture, 1965, The Cloisters for Voice and Orch., 1965, Concerto for Piano and Orch., 1988, A Dylan Thomas Trilogy: A Choral Symphony, 1961-76, Concerto for Oboe and Orch., 1975, Etude Fantasy for Piano, 1976, Concerto for Clarinet and Orch., 1977, Promenade Overture, 1981, Summer Fanfare, 1982, Pied Piper Fantasy: Concerto for Flute and Orch., 1982, Fantasia on an Ostinato for Orch., 1985, The Ghosts of Versailles, 1987, Symphony # 1, 1991 (Grawemeyer award 1991), Troubadours (Variations for Guitar and Chamber Orch.), 1993, Fanfares to Music, 1993, Phantasmagoria for Cello and Piano, 1993, String Quartet, 1996, The Red Violin (chaconne for violin and orch., Acad. award for best original score 1999), 1997 (Genie award Best Original Score 1998), A Dylan Thomas Trilogy, rev. edit., 1998, Vocalise for Soprano, Orchestra and Electronics, 1999, Phantasmagoria for Orchestra, 2000, Mr. Tambourine Man: Seven Poems by Bob Dylan, 2000; film scores Altered States, 1981, Revolution, 1985, The Red Violin, 1998; commns. from N.Y. Philharm., Boston Symphony Orch., James Galway, Van Cliburn Found., Inc., Met. Opera Assn. Guggenheim fellow, 1968; nominee Acad. award and Grammy award for film score Altered States, 1981; recipient Anthony Asquith award for Best Film Score, Brit. Film Inst., 1985, Acad. Inst. Arts and Letters award, 1989, Grawemeyer award for Symphony Number 1, 1991, 2 Grammy awards for Symphony No. 1, 1992, Internat. Classical Music award Composition of Yr. The Ghosts of Versailles (opera), 1992; named Composer of Yr., Musical America, 1992, 2 Grammy awards for string quartet, 1996, Grammy for Symphony No. 1, 1996 (Classical CD of Yr.). Fellow: Am. Acad. Arts. and Scis.; mem.: ASCAP, Bohemian, Acad. Inst. Arts and Letters, Assn. Classical Music. Home: 365 W End Ave New York NY 10024-6511 Office: care G Schirmer Inc 257 Park Ave S 20th Fl New York NY 10010-7304*

CORK, LINDA KATHERINE, veterinary pathologist, educator; b. Texarkana, Tex., Dec. 14, 1936; d. Albert James and Martine Sessions (Buntyn) Collins; m. P.S. Cork Jr., Mar. 1955 (div. 1965); children: Robin E., Jerald W. BS, Tex. A&M U., 1969, DVM, 1970; PhD, Wash. State U., 1974. Diplomate Am. Coll. Vet. Pathologists. Fellow Wash. State U., Pullman, 1970-74; asst. prof. U. Ga., Athens, 1974-76, Johns Hopkins U., Balt., 1976-82, assoc. prof., 1982-88, assoc. dir. rsch. Alzheimer's Disease Rsch. Ctr., 1985-93, prof., 1988-93; prof., chmn. Dept. Comparative Medicine Stanford U., 1994—. Coun. mem. NIH div. Rsch. Resources, Bethesda, Md., 1985-89; adv. bd. Registry Comparative Pathology, Bethesda. Grantee Nat. Inst. on Aging, 1985-89, Nat. Inst. Health, 1986-91, 86-93, 87-92. Mem. Inst. Medicine, Am. Assn. Neuropathologists (chmn. June 1988), Am. Assn. Pathology, U.S.-Can. Acad. Pathology. Methodist. Avocation: music. Office: Stanford Univ Dept Comparative Medicine MSOB Bldg Stanford CA 94305-5415 Home: 1788 Oak Creek Dr Apt 206 Palo Alto CA 94304-2127

CORKER, FRANK THOMAS, physician, retired military officer; b. Atlanta, Dec. 12, 1935; s. Newman and Thayer Davenport (Hopper) C.; m. Diane Blankenship, Sept. 22, 1955; children: Thayer Diane Corker, Frank Thomas Jr., Thomas Angel. BA, Emory U., 1957, MD, 1961; MPH, Johns Hopkins U., 1969. Diplomate Am. Bd. Preventive Medicine. Commd. 1st lt. USAF, 1960, advanced through ranks to col., 1976, ret., 1981; intern USAF Hosp. Lackand AFB, San Antonio, Tex., 1961-62; jr. asst. resident ob-gyn Grady Meml. Hosp., Atlanta, 1964-65; resident in aerospace medicine Sch. Aerospace Medicine, Brooks AFB, San Antonio, 1969-70; flight surgeon 832 TAC Hosp., Cannon AFB, N.M., 1962-64; asst. chief aerospace med. div. USAFE Hdqrs., Wiesbaden, Fed. Republic Germany, 1965-68; dispensary cmmdr., dir. med. svcs. 56th USAF Dispensary, Thailand, 1970-71; cons. preventive medicine USAF Hdqrs., Washington, 1971-76, chief of preventive medicine, 1976-77; hosp. commdr., dir. med. svcs. USAF Hosp., Moody AFB, Ga., 1977-81; pvt. practice in occupational and aerospace medicine Valdosta, Ga., 1981-96; retired, 1996. Cons. in aerospace medicine USAF Surgeon Gen., 1977-81; bd. dirs. Drs. Lab., Inc., Valdosta, Ga. Contbr. articles to profl. jours. Active Cub Scouts, Potomac, Md., 1973-75 (past chmn.); team leader United Way of Valdosta and Lowndes County, 1982-86. Decorated Legion of Merit, D.F.C., Air medal with silver oak leaf cluster, Meritorious Svc. medal. Fellow Aerospace Med. Assn., Am. Coll. Preventive Medicine; mem. AMA, Am. Coll. Occupational and Environ. Medicine, Norfolk So. Assn. Physicians, Valdosta C. of C. (past dir.), Rotary (past dir.), Alpha Tau Omega (chpt. sec. 1954-55, v.p. 1955-56) Episcopalian. Avocations: hunting, fishing, boating, gardening, travel, photography.

CORKERY, JAMES CALDWELL, retired Canadian government executive, mechanical engineer; b. East Orange, N.J., June 23, 1925; S. Kirk James and Helen May (Caldwell) C.; m. Jane Woodruff, Sept. 19, 1953; children—Kirk, Candace BA Sc., U. Toronto, Ont., Can., 1948, MA Sc., 1950. Registered profl. engr., Ont. Plant mgr. Can. Gen. Electric, Montreal, Que., 1956-61, plant mgr. Oakville, Ont., 1961-68, mng. mfg. Toronto, 1968-70; regional gen. mgr. Can. Post, Toronto, 1970-77, dep. postmaster gen. Ottawa, Ont., 1977-82. Pres. Royal Can. Mint., Ottawa, 1982-86, chmn. bd., 1986-95; pres. Gold. Inst., 1986-88 Chmn. bd. Oakville Trafalgar Hosp., 1968-72; chmn. Easter Seal Campaign, Ottawa, 1985; chmn. bd. Ottawa Children Treatment Hosp., 1986-89. With RCAF, 1943-45. Mem. Profl. Engrs. Ont., Mint Dirs. Conf. (sec. 1984-86). Lodges: Rotary. Anglican. Avocations: furniture refinishing, antiques, gardening.

CORKERY, TIMOTHY JAMES, painter, educator; b. Washington, Oct. 30, 1931; s. Michael Joseph and Frances Cecilia (Hamman) Corkery; m. Judith S. O'Donnell Corkery, Nov. 24, 1990; 1 child, Laura Ann. BFA, Art Inst. Chgo., 1960; MFA, Inst. Allende, Guanajuato, Mexico, 1964. Instr. drawing, painting Inst. Allende, Guanajuato, 1964—65; instr. painting, design Corcoran Sch. Art, Washington, 1965—67; instr. painting Md. Inst. Coll. Art, Balt., 1967—77; vis. artist U. Oreg., Eugene, 1977—78, Sch. Art Inst. Chgo., Chgo., 1978—79; instr. painting, design RI Coll., Providence, 1989—97. One-man shows include Max Hutchinson Gallery, NYC, 1973—74, U. Md., Balt., 1975, U. Oreg., Eugene, 1978, exhibited in group shows at Max Hutchinson Gallery, NYC, 1972—73, Royal Marks Gallery, 1970, Albright Knox Gallery, Buffalo, 1970, MIT hayden Gallery, 1971, Balt. Mus., 1972 (Mcpl. Arts Soc. award), Represented in permanent collections U. Balt., Balt. Art Tower, Dept. Housing and Cmty. Devel., Balt., Alcoa Aluminum, Idaho First Nat. Bank, Johnson and Johnson, Newark, Chgo. Sun Times, 1963—64, Chgo. Daily News, 1958—60, NY Post, 1980—88, NY Daily News, 1964—65, 1980—84. With USN, 1951—55. Recipient M.S. Mach Found. award, 1970, F.C. Marino Found. award, 1970, David Lloyd Kreeger Purchase award, Balt. Mus., 1970. Home: 3 Theresa Ct Providence RI 02909

CORKILL, JOHN FRANKLIN, JR., architect, real estate developer, consultant; b. Springfield, Mass., Aug. 31, 1938; s. John Franklin Sr. and Catherine Gladys (Kieffer) C.; m. Mary Elizabeth Newlon, Feb. 1, 1964; children: John F. III, Steven Earl. BA, U. Md., 1962; B Arch., Ohio State U., 1967. Registered architect, Md., Pa., Va., Del. Sr. assoc. Edwin F. Ball Assocs., 1973-77; prin. Corkill Cusk Reeves Architects P.A., Lanham, Md., 1977—. Sec. standing com. on architecture Mo. Synod Luth. Ch., 1982—, cons. on architecture of Southeastern dist., Mo., 1974—; developer office bldgs., Lanham. Author slide lecture narrative Energy in Church Buildings, 1981. Sec. Laborers for Christ Ch. Bldg. Program, Luth. Ch.-Mo. Synod, St. Louis, 1984—; pres. ch. coun. Assension Luth. Ch., Landover Hills, Md., 1974-78, 90—. Mem. AIA (Potomac Valley chpt., pres.-v.p. 1989-93, nat. bd. dirs. 1997-2000), Md. Soc. Architects (pres., v.p., 1993-97), Organ hist. soc., Ohio Railway Mus. Club. Home: 10000 Worrell Ave Glenn Dale MD 20769-9263 Office: Corkill Cush Reeves Architects PA 10111 George Palmer Hwy Lanham Seabrook MD 20706-4316

CORKRAN, VIRGINIA B., retired real estate agent; b. N.Y.C., Feb. 13, 1924; d. Stuart H. and Bessie (Moses) Bowman; m. Sewell H. Corkran, Jr., June 15, 1946; children: Sewell H. III, Leslie C. Price. BA, Conn. Coll., 1945. Tchr. Low-Heywood Sch., Stamford, Conn., 1946—47; editor North Shore Calendar, Winnetka, Ill., 1955—59; real estate assoc. Lodge McKee Realty Inc., Naples, Fla., 1963—2001; ret., 2001. Mem. Naples City Coun., 1974-78; pres. Old Naples Assn., 1995-97; past bd. dirs. Big Cypress Nature Ctr., Naples, The Conservancy, Inc., Collier County LWV, Naples Garden Club, Collier Co. Audubon; past bd. dirs. S.W. Heritage, Inc., Naples, hon. bd. dirs., 2002 Recipient Guy Bradley award Collier County Audubon, ONA award Old Naples Assn., 1998.

CORLE, FREDERIC WILLIAM, II, marketing professional; b. Phila., June 20, 1945; s. Frederic William and Marjorie (Dudley) Corle; m. Pamela Gaus White, Apr. 16, 1983 (div. May 1987); children: Alison Gaus, Louise Armour; m. Morrell T. Taggart, Dec. 9, 1995. BA, Marietta Coll., 1967; MBA, U. Denver, 1973. Supply mgmt. officer Fed. Deposit Ins. Corp., Washington, 1970—72; program analyst Exec. Office of Pres., Washington, 1973—77; dir. Commn. on Budget U.S. Ho. of Reps., Washington, 1977—78; v.p. City Sports Mgmt., Inc., Washington, 1978—82; asst. to adminstr. White House, Washington, 1983—84; dir. mktg. Interand Corp., Washington, 1984—85; spl. asst. Dept. of Interior, Washington, 1985—86; regional dir. fed. mktg. Datapoint Corp., Washington, 1987—89; CEO Mktg. Solutions Internat., Inc., Washington, 1989—; bd. dirs., dir. fed. mktg. Sun Microsystems Fed. Inc., Washington, 1991—96; ptnr. Potomac Rsch. Group, Washington, 1996—98; pres. Spatial Techs. Industry Assn., Washington, 1996—. Lt. (j.g.) USN, 1967—70. Mem.: Army Navy Country Club. Republican. Episcopalian. Office Phone: 703-508-9773. E-mail: fred_corle@aftonvillagardens.com.

CORLE, JAMES THOMAS, lawyer; b. Jay County, Ind., Dec. 28, 1927; s. Herbert R. and Mary M. (Reitenour) Corle; m. Jean Polhemus, July 16, 1950; children: James Thomas, Sarah Corle Thomas, Kenneth D. BS Engring. Law, Purdue U., 1955; JD, Ind. U., Bloomington, 1955. Bar: Ind. 1955, DC 1964. With E.I. DuPont de Nemours & Co., Wilmington, Del., 1955; patent counsel Washington, 1967—70; sr. supervising patent counsel, legal dept., 1970—85; corp. counsel, legal dept., 1986—92; intellectual property cons., 1993—. Lt. col. USAR, 1946—52. Mem.: Del. bar Assn., Phila. Patent Law Assn., Am. Patent Law Assn., ABA. Republican. Meth. E-mail: jimcorle@comcast.net.

CORLESS, DOROTHY ALICE, nursing educator; b. Reno, Nev., May 28, 1943; d. John Ludwig and Vera Leach (Wilson) Adams; children: James Lawrence Jr., Dorothy Adele Carroll. RN, St. Luke's Sch. Nursing, 1964. Clinician, cons., educator, grant author, adminstr. Fresno County Mental Health Dept., 1991—94; instr. police sci. State Ctr. Tng. Facility, 1991-94; pvt. practice, mental health cons., educator, 1970—; sr. assoc. guidance distbn. disaster svcs. ARC, 2003—04. Res. asst. officer ARC, Disaster Mental Health Svcs., 1993-2003. Maj. USAFR, 1972-94. Mem. USAF Acad. Assn. Grads. (assoc. life), Forensic Mental Health Assn. Calif., Calif. Peace Officers Assn., Critical Incident Stress Found. Office: 1849 E Everglade Fresno CA 93720 Office Phone: 559-325-9599. E-mail: dorothydmh@aol.com.

CORLEY, FLORENCE FLEMING, retired history educator; b. Augusta, Ga., Jan. 6, 1933; d. William Cornelius and Sarah Virginia (Sibley) Fleming; m. James Weaver Corley, Jr., Dec. 29, 1955; children: Florence Hart Corley Johnson, James Weaver Corley III, Mary Anne Corley Herbert, Sarah Virginia Corley, William Thomas Corley. BA, Agnes Scott Coll., 1954; MA, Emory U., 1955; PhD, Ga. State U., 1985. Cert. tchr., T-5, Ga. Alumnae rep. Agnes Scott Coll., Decatur, Ga., 1955; history tchr. The Westminster Schs., Atlanta, 1968-88, The Walker Sch., Marietta, Ga., 1989; history instr. Kennesaw State U., Marietta, Ga., 1989-91, asst. prof. history, 1991-98, ret., 1998. U.S. history cons. The Coll. Bd., N.Y.C., 1978—; reader, table leader Ednl. Testing Svc., Princeton, N.J., 1975—. Assoc. editor: American Presbyterians, Phila., 1984—, Ga. Jour. of So. Legal History, Atlanta, 1989; editor: The Landmarker, 1978-79; author: Confederate City: Augusta, Georgia 1860-65, 1960, 74, 95; contbr. articles to hist. jours.; compiler (slides/tape) Where Were the Women? 1979. Sixth grade and adult tchr. First Presbyn. Ch., Marietta, 1960—, elder, 1990—; active U.S. history contest DAR, Marietta, 1991—; cons. Girls club of Cobb/Marietta 1981; mem. Ga. Nat. Registry Rev. Bd., 1994—, chmn. 1996-97; mem. Marietta Town Com. Nat. Soc. Colonial Dames Am. in Ga. Woodrow Wilson fellow Emory U., 1954-55; recipient fellowship in women's history NEH, Stanford U., Palo Alto, Calif., 1978-79, scholarship in classical studies, Vergilian Soc., Cumae, Italy, 1982, scholarships in medieval Eng. and Eng. today, English Speaking Union, U.K., 1979, 80. Mem. Nat. Soc. Colonial Dames of Am., Cobb Landmarks and Hist. Soc. (charter bd. dirs., co-pres. 1985-86, 87-88), Atlanta Hist. Soc., Atlanta Civil War Round Table, Soc. Civil War Historians, Ga. Assn. Historians, Ga. Hist. Soc., So. Assn. Women Historians, So. Hist. Assn., So. Garden History Soc., Richmond County Hist. Assn., Presbyn. Hist. Soc., Phi Beta Kappa, Phi Alpha Theta. Democrat. Avocations: researching family and local history, oral history taping/interviewing, world travel, lecturing. Home: 285 Kennesaw Ave Marietta GA 30060-1671 E-mail: jwcorley2@mindspring.com.

CORLEY, JENNY LYND WERTHEIM, elementary school educator; b. Lincoln, Ill., June 18, 1937; d. Robert Glenn and Nancy Lynd (Hoblit) Wertheim; m. William Gene Corley, Aug. 9, 1959; children: Anne Lynd Corley Baum, Robert William, Scott Elson. BS in Music Edn., U. Ill., 1959, MS in Music Edn., 1961; postgrad., U. Ill., Loyola U., 1985—2003. Tchr. choral music Mahomet (Ill.)/Seymour K-12, 1959-61; supr. music Fairfax County (Va.), 1961-63; tchr. music Highland Park (Ill.) 107, 1969, dir. gifted edn., 1969-70; tchr. music Glenview (Ill.) 34, 1981—2003, Corley Studio, 1959—. V.p. Corley Agroleum Properties, 1993—; water safety instr./trainer ARC; lifeguard instr./trainer Cmty. First Aid & Safety, 1995. Dir. mid-Am. bd. ARC, Chgo., 1980-86; mem. Chgo. Symhony Orch. Chorus, 1965-75. Recipient Heart of Gold United Way, 1992, Cmty. Svc. award Ill. Park & Recreation Assn./Ill. Assn. Park Dists., 1994, Disting. Svc. award Boys and Girls Swimming Ofcl., Ill. HS Assn., 1994, 25 yr. recognitiuon as swimming ofcl. Mem. Music Edn. Nat. Conf., North Shore Music Tchrs. Assn. (treas. 1987-90, pres. 2004—), Jr. League Chgo. (treas. 1978-81), Sigma Alpha Iota, Phi Delta Kappa (found. chmn. 1994—), U. Ill. Music Alumnae (pres. bd. dirs. 1995-97). Presbyterian. Home: 744 Glenayre Dr Glenview IL 60025-4411 E-mail: corley@corleywg.com.

CORLEY, JOHN D. W., career military officer; BS in Engring., USAF Acad., 1973; grad., Squadron Officer's Sch., 1978; MBA, U. of The Philippines, Manila, 1984; grad., Air Command and Staff Coll., 1985, Naval Command and Staff Coll., 1986; M in Nat. Security and Strategic Studies, 1986; grad., Army War Coll., 1993; grad. Russian & US Gen. Officer Exec. Program, Harvard U., 1999; grad. Program for Sr. Exec. in Nat. & Internat. Security, Harvard U., 2002. Commd. 2d lt. USAF, 1973, advanced through grades to gen., 2005; instr. pilot, flight examiner 64th Flying Tng. Wing, Reese AFB, Tex., 1974-78, 49th Tactical Fighter Wing, Holloman AFB, N.Mex., 1979-82; flight comdr. 26th Aggressor Squadron, chief Aggressor Ops., Clark Air Base, Philippines, 1982-85; analyst advanced tactical fighter Air Force Ctr. for Studies and Analyses, Washington, 1986-88; analyst comdr.'s action group Tactical Air Command, Langley AFB, Va., 1988-90; ops. officer 7th Fighter Squadron, comdr. 8th Fighter Squadron, 49th Fighter Wing, Holloman AFB, N.Mex., 1990-92; comdr. 33d Ops. Group, 33d Fighter Wing, Eglin AFB, Fla., 1993-95; chief Western Hemisphere divsn. Directorate of Strategic Plans and Policy, J-5 Joint Staff, 1995-97; comdr. 355th Wing, Davis-Monthan aFB, Ariz., 1997—; dir. studies and analysis USAF Europe, Ramstein AFB, Germany, 1999—2000; dir. global power programs USAF, Washington, 2000—03, prin. dep. asst. sec. for acquisition, 2003—05, vice chief of staff, 2005—; mil. dir. USAF Scientific Advisory Bd., 2003—05. Decorated Def. Superior Svc. medal, Legion of Merit, Bronze Star medal, Def. Meritorious Svc. medal, Meritorious Svc. medal with 4 oak leaf clusters, Aerial Achievement medal with oak leaf cluster, Joint Svc. Commendation medal, Air Force Commendation medal, Joint Meritorious Unit award with oak leaf cluster, Combat Readiness medal, Southwest Asia Svc. medal with bronze star, Kosovo Campaign medal with bronze star, Global War on Terrorism Expeditionary medal, Kuwait Liberation medal (Govt. of Kuwait) Office: USAF 1670 Air Force Pentagon Washington DC 20330*

CORLEY, LARRY STEVEN, chemist; b. Johnson City, Tenn., June 17, 1954; s. Grady VanBuren and Kathleen Selma (Carmack) C.; m. Stephanie Renee Johnson, June 23, 1996; children: Kendall Ann, Kelsey Renee. BS in Chemistry, King Coll., 1974; MS in Polymer Sci. and Engring., U. Mass., 1976, PhD in Polymer Sci. and Engring., 1979. Rsch. chemist Shell Devel. Co., Houston, 1978-83, sr. rsch. chemist, 1983-87; staff rsch. chemist Shell Devel. Co./Shell Chem. Co., Houston, 1987-99, sr. staff rsch. chemist, 1999-2000; sr. staff rsch. chemist Resolution Performance Products Hexion Specialty Chemicals, Houston, 2000—. Assoc. editor Progress in Polymer Sci., 1987-93, editl. bd. mem., 1994-98; contbr. chpt. to book and articles to profl. jours. Mem. Am. Chem. Soc. Achievements include over 55 U.S. patents in epoxy, bismaleimide, bisbenzocyclobutene and other thermosetting resins chemistry; first discovery of optical activity (based on helicity only) in a solid polymer (polytrichloroacetaldehyde); developer of high-toughness, high-processability thermoset resin systems with very high heat resistance, others. Home: 8718 Chelsworth Dr Houston TX 77083-5656 Office: Hexion-Specialty Chemicals WTC C-2150 3333 Highway 6 S Houston TX 77082-3101 Office Phone: 832-486-6624. Business E-Mail: steve.corley@hexionchem.com.

CORLEY, ROSE ANN MCAFEE, government official; b. Lawton, Okla., Aug. 21, 1952; d. Claude James and Mary Margaret (Holman) McAfee; m. Gary Michael Griffin, Feb. 14, 1973 (div. Oct. 1984); m. Terry Joe Corley, July 31, 1988 (div. Oct. 2002); stepson Troy Justin Corley. BS, Cameron U., Lawton, Okla., 1970; diploma, Army Command and Staff Coll., Ft. Leavenworth, Kans., 1989; MCJA, Oklahoma City U., 1990; cert., Army Mgmt. Staff Coll., Ft. Belvoir, Va., 1991. Cert. in Distbn. Mgt. Supply clk. Dept. of Army, Ft. Sill, Okla., 1972-80, supply mgmt. asst., 1980-82, supply systems analyst Ft. Lee, Va., 1982, supply tech. Ft. Sill, Okla., 1982-83, supr. inventory mgmt. specialist, 1983-86, manprint program mgr., 1986-91; weapon system advisor Def. Logistics Agy., San Antonio, 1991-96, customer svc. rep. Robins AFB, Ga., 1996-98; dir. supply mgmt. NIH, Rockville, Md., 1998—2002, dir. divsn. logistics svcs., 2002—05; deputy assoc. commr., publications and logistics Social Security Adminstrn., 2005—. Equal employment counselor USA Field Artillery Sch., Ft. Sill, Okla., 1976-82; mentor Fed. Women's Program, Kelly AFB, Tex., 1991-96. Active Md. Citizen Foster Care Rev. Bd., 1999-2001. Decorated Order of St. Barbara U.S. Army Arty. Sch., Ft. Sill; recipient cert. Appreciation, U.S. Sec. of Def., 1984, Directorate of Engring. and Housing, Ft. Sill, 1986; Excellence in Govt. Sr. fellow, Council for Excellence in Govt., 2001—. Mem. Fed. Women's Program, Soc. Logistics Engrs., Fed. Mgrs. Assn., Kelly Mgmt. Assn., World Affairs Coun. of San Antonio, Internat. City Mgmt. Assn., Tex. Corvette Assn. Avocations: autocrossing, reading, golf, crafts. Office: NIH Office Logistics and Acquisitions 6011 Executive Blvd Rockville MD 20852-3804 Home: 930 Mosby Dr Frederick MD 21701-3264 Office Phone: 301-451-8177. Business E-Mail: corleyr@mail.nih.gov. E-mail: ra.corley@verizon.net.

CORLEY, WILLIAM EDWARD, hospital administrator; b. Pittsburgh, Sept. 2, 1942; s. Robert Ray and Helen (Wise) C.; m. Angela Irvine Blose, Mar. 22, 1969; children: Laura, Matt BA in Bus. and Econs., Coll. of William and Mary, 1964; MHA in Hosp. Adminstrn., Duke U., Durham, 1966. Adminstrv. asst. Duke U., Durham, N.C., 1965-66; mgmt. cons. Booz, Allen & Hamilton, Chicago, 1968-71; assoc. hosp. dir. U. Ky., Lexington, 1971-75; hosp. dir. Milton S. Hershey Med. Ctr. of Pa. State U., Hershey, 1975-78; pres. Akron Gen. Med. Ctr., Ohio, 1978-84; pres., CEO Cmty. Health Network, 1984—. Bd. dirs. Vol. Hosps. Am. Tri-State, Indpls., Indpls. C. of C., Nat. City Bank, Indpls., Ind. Pro Health; tri-state chmn.; chmn. United Hosp. Svcs., Indpls., 1986-88; lectr. Ind. U.-Purdue U. at Indpls., 1984-98; high sch. basketball referee. Co-author: Ray E. Brown-A Manager's Manager: Lectures, Messages, Memoirs, 1990; contbr. articles to profl. jours. Chmn. United Hosp. Svc., 1986-88, Vol. Hosp. Am. Tri-State, 1989-91; bd. dirs. United Way. Named Sagamore of the Wabash, Gov. of Ind. Presbyterian. Avocations: photography, basketball, coaching, running. Home: 13570 N Gray Rd Carmel IN 46033-9708 Office: Cmty Health Network 1500 N Ritter Ave Indianapolis IN 46219-3095

CORLEY, WILLIAM GENE, engineering research executive; b. Shelbyville, Ill., Dec. 19, 1935; s. Clarence William and Mary Winifred (Douthit) C.; m. Jenny Lynd Wertheim, Aug. 9, 1959; children: Anne Lynd, Robert William, Scott Elson. BS, U. Ill., 1958, MS, 1960, PhD, 1961. Lic. profl. engr., Ill., Va., Wash., Calif., Miss., Fla., La., Pa., Ala., Hawaii, Tenn., Tex., Utah, Mich., Mo., S.D., S.C., Kans., Ohio, NJ, NY; lic. structural engr., Ill.; chartered structural engr., U.K. Devel. engr. Portland Cement Assn., Skokie, Ill., 1964-66, mgr. structural devel. sect., 1966-74, dir. engring. devel. divsn., 1974-86; sr. v.p. Constrn. Tech. Labs., Inc. (formerly Portland Cement Assn.), Skokie, 1986—. Adv. panels NSF.; prin. investigator, Bldg. Performance Study Okla. City Bombing; team leader, WTC Bldg. Performance Study. Contbr. articles to profl. jours. Pres. caucus Glenview (Ill.) Sch. Bd., 1971-72; elder United Presbyn. Ch., 1975-79; sec. bd. dirs. Assn. Ho., Chgo., 1976, treas., 1977, pres., 1978-79; chmn. bd. dirs. North Cook dist. ARC, bd. dirs. Mid-Am. chpt., chmn. North Region Coun., 1988-92; mem. Gov.'s (Ill.) Earthquake Preparedness Task Force. Recipient Wason medal, 1970, Martin Korn award Prestressed Concrete Inst., 1978, Authur J. Boase award Reinforced Concrete Rsch. Coun., 1986; named Tchr. of Yr., U. Ill., Chgo., Ill., 2004. Fellow: Inst. Structural Engrs., Am. Concrete Inst. (hon.; bd. dirs. 1994—97, Bloem award 1978, Reese Structural Rsch. award 1986, Henry C. Turner award 1988, Ferguson lectr. 1991, Henry Crown award 1997, Lindau award 1999, Alfred E. Lindau award 2000); mem.: NAE (award 2000), ASCE (hon. T.Y. Lin award 1979, lifetime achievement award 1994, Pres.'s award 2003, Chgo. Civil Engr. of Yr.), NSPE (Pres.'s award 2003), Nat. Coun.

Structural Engrs. Assns. (pres. 1996—97, Best Paper award 1999, Disting. Svc. award 1999), Post-Tensioning Inst., Nat. Coun. Examiners Engring. and Surveying (v.p., bd. dirs. 2002—04, Disting. Svc. award 2000), Structural Engrs. Assn. Ill. (pres. 1986—87, meritorious publ. award 1993, 1997, John Parmer award 1997, meritorious publ. award 2003), Internat. Assn. Bridge and Structural Engring., Earthquake Engring. Rsch. Inst. (chpt. sec., treas. 1980—82, chmn. 1984—86), Reunion Internat. des Laboratoires d'Essais et Rsch. sur Materiaux Constrn., U. Ill. Alumni Assn. (Chicago Illini of Yr. 2004), Bldg. Seismic Safety Coun. (vice-chmn. 1983—85, sec. 1985—87), Chgo. Com. High-Rise Bldgs. (vice-chmn. 1978—82, chmn. 1982—84). Presbyterian. Home: 744 Glenayre Dr Glenview IL 60025-4411 Office: Construction Tech Labs Inc 5400 Old Orchard Rd Skokie IL 60077-1053 Office Phone: 847-965-7500. E-mail: gcorley@ctlgroup.com.

CORLISS, JOHN OZRO, zoology educator; b. Coats, Kans., Feb. 23, 1922; s. Clark L. and Catharine (Smith) C.; children: Susan Elizabeth, Joan Alison, Kimberley Ann, Jennifer Sara, Catharine Megan Corliss; m. Yuemei Geng, June, 1992. BS, U. Chgo., 1944; BA, U. Vt., 1947; PhD, NYU, 1951; DSc (hon.), Universite de Clermont, France, 1973. Postdoctoral fellow AEC, Coll. de France, Paris, 1951-52; instr. zoology Yale, 1952-54; asst. prof. to prof. zoology U. Ill., Urbana, 1954-64, prof., head dept. biol. scis. Chgo. Circle, 1964-69; dir. systematic zoology NSF, 1969-70; prof., chmn. dept. zoology U. Md., College Park, 1970-87, prof., 1987-89, emeritus prof., 1989—. Adj. prof. U. N.Mex., Albuquerque, 1988-96; hon. rsch. assoc. zoology Univ. Coll., London, 1960-61; vis. prof. zoology U. Exeter, Eng., 1961-62; vis. prof. protozoology, Shanghai, China, 1980, 86, Geneva, 1980; mem. panel systematic biology NSF, 1966-69; active Nat. Com. Internat. Biol. program, 1966-68; mem. Internat. Commn. on Zool. Nomenclature, 1972-96; mem. corp. Marine Biol. Lab., Woods Hole, Mass. Author: The Ciliate Protozoa, 1961, 2d edit., 1979; joint editor 5 books on protistology, 1984-91; contbr. articles on protozoology/protistology to profl. jours. Served to capt. USAAF, 1943-46. Fellow AAAS, Am. Inst. Biol. Scis., Am. Acad. Microbiology; mem. Soc. Protozoologists (past pres, mem. editl. bd., past editor), Am. Micros. Soc. (past editor, past pres.), Am. Zool. Soc. (hon.), French Zool. Soc. (hon.), Spanish Zool. Soc. (hon.), Mexican Zool. Soc. (hon.), Italian Zool. Soc. (hon.), Coun. Biology Editors (past chmn., CBE Meritorious award 1982), Am. Soc. Zoologists (past pres.), Soc. Systematic Zoology (past pres.), Am. Soc. Parasitologists, Am. Soc. Microbiology (U.S. Fedn. Culture Collections/J. Roger Porter award 1994), Internat. Congress Systematic and Evolutionary Biology (convenor 1970-74, 76-80), Internat. Union Biol. Scis. (chmn. U.S. nat. com. 1971-73), numerous others. Home: 730 Yale Rd Bala Cynwyd PA 19004-2116 Address: PO Box 2729 Bala Cynwyd PA 19004-6729 E-mail: jocchezmoi@aol.com.

CORMAN, MARVIN LEONARD, surgeon, educator; b. Phila., Dec. 17, 1939; s. Joseph Mayer and Dorothy Frances (Stern) C.; children: John Mayer, Alexander Stern. BA, U. Pa., 1961, MD, 1965. Diplomate Nat. Bd. Med. Examiners, Am. Bd. Surgery, Am. Bd. Colon and Rectal Surgery; lic. surgeon, Calif., N.Y. Sr. registrar, vis. lectr. gen. infirmary, profl. surg. unit U. Leeds, Eng., 1968-69; surg. intern Boston City Hosp.-Fifth (Harvard) Surg. Svc., 1965, surg. resident, 1966-68, surg. resident, chief surg. resident, 1969-71; staff surgeon divsn. colon and rectal surgery, dept. surgery Lahey Clinic Med. Ctr., Boston, 1971-81, Sansum Med. Clinic, Santa Barbara, Calif., 1981-95; surgeon divsn. colon and rectal surgery UCLA, 1996-98; prof. surgery U. So. Calif. Sch. Medicine, 1998—2001; vice chmn. dept. surgery, assoc. surgeon-in-chief L.I. Jewish Med. Ctr., New Hyde Park, NY, 2001—04; prof. surgery Albert Einstein Coll. Medicine, 2001—05, SUNY, Stony Brook, 2004—. Instr. surgery Sch. Medicine Harvard U., Boston, 1972-77, clin. asst. prof. surgery, 1977-82, prof. surgery UCLA, 1996-98; co-dir. tng. program colon and rectal surgery Sansum Med. clinic, 1981-95, chmn. divsn. edn., 1983-90; credentials com. Santa Barbara Cottage Hosp., 1984-95, mem. libr. com., 1985-95, mem. com. on grad. med. edn., 1989-94, vice-chmn. dept. surgery, 1994-95; pres. alumni assn. Harvard Surg. Svc., Boston City Hosp., 1983-84; vis. prof. U. Tex. Health Sci. Ctr., San Antonio, 1982, Throckmorton Surg. Soc., Des Moines, 1985, Ogden (Utah) Surg. Soc., 1985, 20th ann. Surg. Congress Orange County Surg. Soc., Newport Beach, Calif., 1988, Royal Australasian Coll. Surgeons, Adelaide, Australia, 1989, Northwest Permanente Dept. Surgery, Portland, Oreg., 1990, Hahnemann U., Phila., 1991, El Colegio de Cirujanos Generales de Mexicali, Mexico, 1991, Cleve. Clinic Fla., Ft. Lauderdale, Fla., 1992, Univ. Hosp. de Clinicas do Parana, Curitiba, Brazil, 1993; Ralph Coffey vis. prof. Sch. Medicine, U. Mo., Kansas City, 1988; Ralph B. Samson Meml. lectr. Grant Med. Ctr., Columbus, Ohio, 1991; Louis A. Buie vis. lectr. Mayo Med. Sch., Rochester, Minn., 1992; ann. vis. surgeon Queen Elizabeth Hosp. Ctr. of Montreal, Que., 1993; vis. prof. U. So. Calif. Sch. Medicine, L.A., 1995, U. Zurich., 2004, others; Neil Swinton vis. prof. Lahey Clinic, Burlington, Mass., 1997; del. leader Citizen Amb. Program Colon and Rectal Surgery Del. to Russia, Hungary and Czechoslovakia, 1992. Author: (textbook) Colon and Rectal Surgery, 1984, 89, 93, 99, 2005; assoc. editor: Diseases of the Colon and Rectum, 1977-92, Lahey Clinic Bull., 1972-81; contbr. numerous articles to profl. jours. Recipient Hoffman-LaRoche award, 1965, Piedmont Proctologic Soc. award, 1973, 1st prize of Med. Book award, 1985, John C. Goligher Meml. medal Assn. Coloproctology of Gt. Britain and Ireland, 1999, 25th Ann. award Crohn's and Colitis Found. Am., 2000. Fellow ACP; mem. ACS (So. Calif. chpt.), AMA (chmn. residency rev. com. for colon and rectal surgery 1985-86), Internat. Soc. Univ. Colon and Rectal Surgeons, Am. Soc. Colon and Rectal Surgeons (v.p. 1995-96), Am. Surg. Assn., Am. Med. Writers Assn. (hon.), Am. Coll. Gastroenterology, Assn. for Program Dirs. in Colon and Rectal Surgery, We. Surg. Assn., Pan Am. Med. Assn. (coun. sect. on colon and rectal surgery 1989—), Royal Australasian Coll. Surgeons (hon., sect. colon and rectal surgery 1989), New Eng. Surg. Soc., New Eng. Soc. Colon and Rectal Surgeons (sec.-treas. 1977-81), Boston Surg. Soc., Northeastern Soc. Colon and Rectal Surgeons, Soc. Surgery Alimentary Tract, N.Y. Surg. Soc., N.Y. Soc. Colon and Rectal Surgeons,Piedmont Proctologic Soc. (hon.), Argentine Soc. Coloproctology (hon.). Office: Dept Surgery SUNY Stony Brook HSC T 18-060 Stony Brook NY 11794-8191 Office Phone: 631-444-1793. Business E-Mail: mcorman@lij.edu.

CORMAN, RANDY, lawyer; b. El Paso, Tex., Sept. 24, 1960; s. Theodore Howard and Joan (Golaszewski) C.; m. Kathleen Glynn, July 27, 1996; children: William Joseph, Justin Ryan, Bridget Alexandra, Maura Elizabeth. BA, Rutgers U., 1982; JD, Rutgers U., Newark, 1985. Bar: N.J. 1985. Assoc. counsel State Senate Rep. Staff, Trenton, N.J., 1986-92; state senator N.J. Senate, Trenton, 1992-94; of counsel Donington, Karcher, Salmond, Ronan and Rainone, Edison, N.J., 1994-95, Karcher and Rainone, Sayreville, 1996-97; dir. law N.J. Turnpike Authority, New Brunswick, 1997—2002; exec. dir. Sayreville Econ. and Redevelopment Agency, 2002—. Counsel Perth Amboy City Coun., 1995-96; borough atty. Borough of Spotswood, 1996-97; vice chmn. Senate Environment Com., 1992-94; spl. counsel Howell Twp., 2002-; adj. prof. Berkeley (N.J.) Coll., 2002. Mem. Bd. of Edn., Sayreville, N.J., 1980-84; councilman Borough of Sayreville, 1985-92; chmn. Sayreville Rep. Com., 1986-87, 94-98; trustee St. Stanislaus Kostka Roman Cath. parish, 1998—. Decorated knight comdr. Order of Merit of St. Angilbert, knight comdr. Order of Noble Companions of the Swan, knight Order of Merit of the Bear of Alabona. Mem. Phi Beta Kappa. Republican. Roman Catholic. Office: Sayreville Econ & Redevelopment Agency 167 Main St Sayreville NJ 08872

CORMAN, ROGER WILLIAM, motion picture producer, director; b. Detroit, Apr. 5, 1926; s. William and Anne C.; m. Julie Ann Halloran, Dec. 26, 1970; children: Catherine Ann, Roger Martin, Brian William, Mary Tessa AB, Stanford, 1947; postgrad., Oxford (Eng.) U., 1950; D in Fine Arts (hon.), Am. Film Inst., 1998. Founder, pres. New World Pictures, 1970-83, Concorde-New Horizons Corp., 1983—. Prodr.: Carnosaur, The Fantastic Four, I Never Promised You a Rose Garden, St. Jack, Battle Beyond the Stars, Deathrace 2000, Piranha, Avalanche, Munchies, Crime Zone, The Terror Within, Black Scorpion, others; dir.: Five Guns West, 1955; prodr., dir.: The Intruder, Fall of the House of Usher, Masque of the Red Death, Machine Gun Kelly, Little Shop of Horrors, The Trip, The Man with X Ray Eyes, Von Richthofen and Brown, Frankenstein Unbound, 1989, others; distbr.: Cries and Whispers, Autumn Sonata, Amarcord, Small Change, The Tin Drum, Cabeza de Vaca, others; films shown at numerous film festivals; prodr., dir., screenwriter: Roger Corman's Frankenstein Unbound; exec. prodr.: Hollywood Boulevard, Rock and Roll High School, Avalanche Alley, Firefight, Fire OVer Afghanistan; actor Silence of the Lambs, The Godfather, Part II, Philadelphia, Apollo 13, Looney Tunes-Back in Action, The Manchurian Candidate. Recipient Grand prize Venice Film Festival, 1979, Lifetime Achievement award L.A. Film Critics, 1997, 1st Prodrs. of Century award Cannes Film Festival, 1998, Lifetime Achievement award Am. Film Market, 2001, Empire award U.K., 2004. Mem. Producers Guild Am., Dirs. Guild Am. Office: Concorde-New Horizons Corp 11600 San Vicente Blvd Los Angeles CA 90049-5102

CORMIE, DONALD MERCER, investment company executive; b. Edmonton, Alta., Can., July 24, 1922; s. George Mills and Mildred (Mercer) C.; m. Eivor Elisabeth Ekstrom, June 8, 1946; children: John Mills, Donald Robert, Allison Barbara, James Mercer, Neil Brian, Buce George, Eivor, Robert. BA, U. Alta., 1944, LLB, 1945; LLM, Harvard U., 1946. Bar: Alta. 1947. Queens counsel, 1964; sessional instr. faculty law U. Alta., 1947-53; sr. ptnr. Cormie, Kennedy, Edmonton, Barristers, 1954-87; instr. real estate law Dept. of Extension, U. Alta., 1958-64; pres., bd. dirs. Collective Securities, Ltd., Cormie Ranch, Inc., Sea Investors Corp.; With Can. Mcht. Marine, 1943-44. Recipient Judge Green Silver medal in law. Mem. Dean's Coun. of 100 Ariz. State U., World Pres.'s Orgn., Chief Execs. Orgn. (bd. dirs. 1976-79), Can. Bar Assn. (mem. coun. 1961-76, chmn. adminstrv. law 1963-66, chmn. taxation 1972-82, v.p. Alta. 1968-69), Found. Legal Rsch. Can. (hon. life). Home and Office: 5101 N Casa Blanca Dr Unit 314 Scottsdale AZ 85253-6989 Office Phone: 486-947-2817. E-mail: anchorsea@qwest.net.

CORMIER, ELIZABETH FERGUSON, piano educator; b. Hutchinson, Kans., July 14, 1925; d. Oliver Wendell and Lura Olive (Tackwell) F. AB, Smith Coll., Northampton, Mass., 1947; BMus, New Eng. Conservatory Music, Boston, 1950; MA, Columbia U., 1955. Tchr. piano Conservatory of Music of Univ. Kansas City (Mo.), 1956-63, Charlotte, N.C., 1963-67, Blair Sch. Music Vanderbilt U., Nashville, 1967—2001, emerita, 2001—. Clinician Nat. Piano Found., 1964-77; cons. Internat. Piano Teaching Found., 1977—. Mem. Tenn. Music Tchrs. Assn. (bd. dirs. 1981—), Nashville Area Music Tchrs. Assn. Episcopalian. Office: Blair Sch Music 2400 Blakemore Ave Nashville TN 37212-3499

CORMIER, PATRICIA PICARD, academic executive; AS, Univ. Bridgeport, 1958; BS, Boston Univ., 1964; MEd, Univ. Va., 1969, EdD, 1975. Pvt. practive, 1958-64; instr. Northeastern Univ., Boston, 1964-68; instr. social dentistry Tufts Univ., Boston, 1964-68; instr. pediatrics Univ. Va., Charlottesville, 1968-72, rsch. assoc., 1969-72; asst. dean. dental auxiliary Univ. Pa., Phila., 1975-79, assoc. dean acad. affairs, assoc. prof. dental care, 1979-82; spl. asst. to pres. Wilson Coll., Chambersburg, Pa., 1982-83, acting dean, 1983-84, v.p., dean of coll., 1984-88; v.p. devel. and alumnae rels. Medical Coll. Pa., Phila., 1989-93; v.p. acad. affairs, prof. ednl. leadership Winthrop Univ., Rock Hill, S.C., 1993-96; pres., prof. edn. Longwood Coll., Historic Farmville, Va., 1996—. Regional v.p. devel. Allegheny Health, Edn. and Rsch. Found., 1991-93; exec. dir. Am. Diabetes Assn., Phila., 1988-89. Named Outstanding Young Women of Am., 1969. Fellow Coll. Physicians of Phila., Am. Coun. on Edn.; mem. Sigma Phi Alpha, Phi Delta Kappa. Home: 1403 Johnston Dr Farmville VA 23901-2807 Office: Longwood Coll 201 High St Farmville VA 23909-1800

CORN, DAVID, editor, political correspondent; Washington editor The Nation; contbr. FOX News Channel, Washington. Contbr. polit. satire and book reviews to the Washington Post, NY Times, LA Times, Philadelphia Inquirer, Boston Globe, Newsday, Harper's, The New Republic, Mother Jones, Washington Monthly, and Village Voice, to online magazines such as Slate, HotWired and Salon, to weekly column, "Loyal Opposition", NY Press; author: (novels) Deep Background, 1999. Office: The Nation 33 Irving Pl New York NY 10036 Address: FOX News Channel 1211 Avenue of the Americas New York NY 10036*

CORN, MILTON, dean, physician, consultant; b. Berlin, Jan. 17, 1928; came to U.S., 1934; m. Gilan Akbar Tocco; children: Stephanie, Sarah, Paul, Rhoya Tocco. BS with highest honors, Yale U., 1952, MD with highest honors, 1955. Diplomate Nat. Bd. Med. Examiners, Am. Bd. Internal Medicine, Am. Bd. Hematology. Intern then resident Peter Bent Brigham Hosp., Boston, 1955-58; fellow in hematology Johns Hospkins Sch. Med., Balt., 1958-60; asst. prof. medicine Seton Hall Coll. Medicine, 1960-63; from asst. to assoc. prof. medicine George Washington U., 1963-72, prof. medicine, 1972-73; chief of hematology D.C. Gen. Hosp. div. George Washington U., 1963-73, chief of medicine, 1970-73; dir. blood bank and emergency dept. Georgetown U., Washington, 1973-78; dir. clerkship jr. medicine, dir. med. residency tng. program Georgetown U., Washington, 1978-84, also vice chmn. medicine, 1978-84, assoc. dean hosp. liaison, 1984, med. dir. hosp., 1984-85; dean Sch. Medicine, Georgetown U., Washington, 1985-89; dir. Office of Clin. Informatics Georgetown U. Med. Ctr., Washington, 1989-90; spl. cons. to dir. Nat. Libr. Medicine, 1990—, assoc. dir. extramural programs, 1990—. Dir. med. edn., hematologist St. Michael's Hosp., Newark, 1960-63; cons. hematology FDA, 1978—; chief physician Cath. Relief Svcs. Refugee Cqpt, Thailand, 1981, 83; regional dir. rev. courses CX ACP, 1981-87; mem. UN Relief and Works Agy. Inspection Team for Palestinian Refugee Camps, 1984; guest lectr. U. Southampton, Eng., 1981; keynote speaker India Med. Soc., New Delhi, 1985. Co-editor Hematology Revs., 1984—; contbr. articles to profl. publs. Recipient Golden Apple award Georgetown U. Student Med. Assn., 1971, 83, Teaching award Kaiser Permanente, 1983, Maimonides award Anti Defamation League, 1989. Home: 6404 Goldleaf Dr Bethesda MD 20817-5830 Office: Nat Libr Medicine NIH Biomed Comms Bethesda MD 20894-0001 Office Phone: 301-594-4928. Personal E-mail: miltoncorn@comcast.net. Business E-Mail: cornm@mail.nih.com.

CORN, MORTON, environmental engineer, educator; b. N.Y.C., Oct. 18, 1933; s. Julius and Sophie (Haber) C.; m. Jacqueline Karnell, Aug. 21, 1955; children: Matthew Irwin, Frederick Eliot. BS in Chem. Engring., Cooper Union, 1955; MS, Harvard U., 1956, PhD, 1961. Asst. san. engr. USPHS, Cin., 1956-58; rsch. assoc. Harvard, 1960-61; asst. prof. U. Pitts., 1962-65, assoc. prof., 1965-66, prof. Grad. Sch. Pub. Health and Sch. Engring., 1967-79; prof. and divsn. head environ. health engring. Sch. Hygiene and Public Health, Johns Hopkins U., Balt., 1980-97; prof. emeritus Johns Hopkins U., Balt., 1997—; pres. Morton Corn; Assocs., Cons. Engrs., 1977—. Cons. divsn. biology and medicine AEC, 1965—74; chmn. air pollution rsch. grants com. EPA, 1968—71, mem. sci. adv. bd., 1978—84; mem. com. no biol. effects air pollution NAS, 1971, mem. com. risk assessment, 1982—83; mem. expert panel occupl. health WHO, 1973—98; asst. sec. labor for occupl. safety and health U.S. Dept. Labor, 1975—77; mem. Allegheny County Air Pollution Adv. Com., 1967—72; mem. nat. adv. com. health vital stats. Dept. HHS, 1979—81; mine health rsch. adv. com. Nat. Inst. Occupl. Safety and Health, 1986—89, GM/UAW joint health and safety adv. com., 1988—92; chmn. OTA Commn. Preventing Injury and Illness in the Workplace, 1982—84; chmn. tech. adv. bd. Clean Sites, Inc., Alexandria, Va., 1984—87; trustee Assoc. Univ., Inc., 1991—93; mem. Hanford tank adv. panel DOE, 1993—99; cons. Health, Safety and Environment, 1993. Chmn. Gov. of Md.'s Toxic Coun., 1986-89. NSF postdoctoral fellow U. London, 1961-62; WHO fellow, 1970; Guggenheim fellow, 1972 Fellow APHA; mem. Am. Soc. Safety Engrs., Am. Indsl. Hygiene Assn. (bd. dirs. 2000-03), Am. Conf. Govt. Indsl. Hygienists (chmn. 1983-84). Home and Office: Morton Corn Assocs Inc 3208 Bennett Point Rd Queenstown MD 21658-1126 Office Phone: 410-827-3205. Personal E-mail: mjcorn@friend.ly.net.

CORN, ROBERT W., management consultant; Tech. program mgr. Burroughs Corp-Unisys Corp., Atlanta, 1976—94; project exec., core team mgr. jt. project mgmt. office Bellsouth, Atlanta, 1994—95; from sr. bus. devel. mgr. profl. svcs. to exec. client mgr. Hewlett Packard Co., Atlanta, 1996—2002; pres., gen. mgr. corp. devel. and sales Info. Tech. Devel., Miami, Fla., 2002—03; exec. dir. sales info. tech. cons. Mahindra British Telecom Internat., Atlanta, 2003—04; bus. devel. exec. info. tech. outsourcing Software Paradigms Internat., Atlanta, 2005—. Bd. adv. Smart Video; bd. dirs. Info. Tech. Devel. Founding bd. dirs. Commerce Net SE. With USAF, 1971—75. Mem.: Global Outsourcing Soc., Tech. Assn. Ga. Home: 3337 Shadyside Rd Marietta GA 30008

CORN, STEPHEN LESLIE, lawyer; b. Danville, Ill., June 12, 1944; s. Clyde C. and Minnie Kathryn (Collins) C.; m. Judith Rae Petkas, June 11, 1966; children: Stephanie Lynn, Suzanne Michelle. BA, U. Ill., 1966, JD, 1969. Bar: Ill. 1969, U.S. Dist. Ct. (so. and cen. dists.) Ill. 1971, U.S. Ct. Appeals (7th cir.) 1976, U.S. Supreme Ct. 1976. Ptnr. Craig & Craig, Mattoon, Ill., 1969—. Bd. dirs. Mattoon Area YMCA, 1981-88, pres., 1987-88; bd. dirs. Harlan E. Moore Heart Rsch. Found., Champaign, Ill., 1982—, Lawyers Trust Fund of Ill., 1991-97. Mem. Ill. Bar Assn., Coles Cumberland Bar Assn. (pres. 1987-88), Ill. Assn. Def. Trial Counsel (pres. 1991-92), Ill. Bar Found., Am. Coll. Trial Lawyers. Episcopalian. Office: Craig & Craig 1807 Broadway Ave Mattoon IL 61938-3800 Business E-Mail: slc@craiglaw.net.

CORN, WANDA MARIE, fine arts educator; b. New Haven, Nov. 13, 1940; d. Keith M. and Lydia M. (Fox) Jones; m. Joseph J. Corn, July 27, 1963. BA, NYU, 1963, MA, 1965, PhD, 1974. Instr. art history Washington Sq. Coll., NYU, 1965-66; lectr. U. Calif.-Berkeley, 1970, vis. asst. prof., 1976; lectr. Mills Coll., Oakland, Calif., 1970, vis. asst. prof., 1971, asst. prof., 1972-77, assoc. prof., 1977-80; assoc. prof. Stanford U., Calif., 1980-89, prof., 1989—, chair dept. of art, 1989-91; acting dir. Stanford Mus., 1989-91; dir. Stanford Humanities Ctr., 1992-95; vis. curator Fine Arts Mus., San Francisco, 1972, 73, 76; vis. curator Mpls. Inst. Arts, 1983-84, Grant Wood travelling exhbn. to Whitney Mus. Am. Art, N.Y.C., Art Inst. Chgo., Fine Arts Mus. San Francisco. Author: The Color of Mood, American Tonalism, 1880-1910, 1972; The Art of Andrew Wyeth, 1973; Grant Wood: The Regionalist Vision, 1983, The Great American Thing: Modern Art and National Identity 1915-35, 1999; contbr. articles to profl. jours. Commr. Nat. Mus. Am. Art, 1988—. Ford Found. fellow, 1966-70; recipient Graves award 1974-75; Smithsonian fellow, 1978-79; Woodrow Wilson fellow, 1979-80; Stanford Humanities Ctr. fellow, 1982-83, Regents fellow Smithsonian Instn., 1987; Am. Coun. Learned Socs. grantee, 1982, 86; rsch. assoc. Smithsonian Instn., 1983—; Phi Beta Kappa scholar, 1984-85. Mem. Coll. Art Assn. (bd. dirs. 1970-73, 1980-84, program chmn. ann. meeting, 1981, mem. numerous coms.), Women's Caucus for Art, Am. Studies Assn. (nat. coun. 1986-89), Assn. Historians of Am. Art. Office: Stanford U Dept Art and Art History Stanford CA 94305-2018 Office Phone: 650-723-6282. Business E-Mail: wcorn@stanford.edu.

CORNABY, KAY STERLING, lawyer, retired state senator; b. Spanish Fork, Utah, Jan. 14, 1936; s. Sterling A. and Hilda G. Cornaby; m. Linda Rasmussen, July 23, 1965; children: Alyse, Derek, Tara, Heather, Brandon. AB, Brigham Young U., 1960; postgrad. law, Heidelberg, Germany, 1961-63; JD, Harvard U., 1966. Bar: NY 1967, Utah 1969, U.S. Patent and Trademark Office 1967. Assoc. Brumbaugh, Graves, Donahue & Raymond, N.Y.C., 1966-69; ptnr. Mallinckrodt & Cornaby, Salt Lake City, 1969-72; sole practice Salt Lake City, 1972-85; mem. Utah State Senate, 1977-91, majority leader, 1983-84; shareholder Jones, Waldo, Holbrook & McDonough, Salt Lake City, 1985—. Mem. Nat. Commn. on Uniform State Laws, 1988-93; mem. adv. bd. U. Mich. Ctr. for Study of Youth Policy,1990-93; mem. Utah State Jud. Conduct Commn., 1983-91, chmn., 1984-85; bd. dirs. KUED-KUER Pub. TV and Radio, 1982-88; adv. bd. KUED, 1990—; bd. dirs. Salt Lake Conv. and Visitors Bur., 1985—. Mem. N.Y. Bar Assn., Utah Bar Assn., Utah Harvard Alumni Assn. (pres. 1977-79), Harvard U. Law Sch. Alumni Assn. (pres. 1995—). Office: Jones Waldo Holbrook & McDonough Ste 1500 170 S Main St Salt Lake City UT 84101-1644

CORNEAL, SETH DAVID, lawyer; s. David Barton and Sandra Yeager Corneal. BA, Wash. & Lee U., Lexington, VA, 1996; JD, Stetson U. Coll. Law, 1999. Bar: US Dist. Ct. So. Dist. Fla. 2001, US Dist. Ct. Mid. Dist. Fla. 2001. Ind. contractor The Salvador Dali Mus., St. Petersburg, Fla., 1998—99; atty. Horan, Horan & Wallace, LLP, 2000—02, The Smith Law Firm, 2002—. Exec. dir. of sales,mktg. Old Island Hotels, Inc., 2000—. Mem.: Unlicensed Practice of Law Com. Avocations: scuba diving, volleyball, investments, exercise, snorkeling. Office: Smith Law Firm 333 Fleming St Key West FL 33040 Office Phone: 305-296-0029. Office Fax: 305-296-9172. Personal E-mail: scorneal@thesmithlawfirm.com.

CORNELISON, ALBERT OTTO, JR., (BERT CORNELISON), lawyer; b. NYC, Apr. 22, 1949; s. Albert O. and Margaret E. (Adams) C.; m. Diane Snow, Jan. 26, 1980; children: Adam Snow, Brendan Stover. BS cum laude, U. Santa Clara, 1971; JD, U. Calif., Davis, 1974. Bar: Calif. 1975, DC 1975, US Dist. Ct. DC 1975, US Ct. Appeals DC cir. 1976, Md. 1989, Tex. 1992. Assoc. Howrey & Simon, Washington, 1974—82, ptnr., 1983—84; sr. assoc. counsel litigation Ogden Corp., NYC, 1984—86; v.p. and gen. counsel Ogden Fin. Services, NYC, 1987; dep. gen. counsel Electronic Data Systems (EDS); staff v.p., assoc. gen. counsel litig. Dresser Industries, 1994—98; v.p., assoc. gen. counsel Halliburton Co., Houston, 1998—2002, v.p., gen. counsel, 2002, exec. v.p., gen. counsel, 2002—. Mem.: ABA, Assn. Gen. Counsels, State Bar of NY. Office: Halliburton 5 Houston Ctr 1401 McKinney Ste 2400 Houston TX 77010

CORNELISON, FLOYD SHOVINGTON, JR., retired psychiatrist, former educator; b. San Angelo, Tex., Apr. 30, 1918; s. Floyd Shovington and Nannie Lee (Brewer) C.; m. Erwina Ladelle Bode, Aug. 30, 1940 (div. 1966); 1 child, Ann Brewer; m. Ruth Reeder Williams, Sept. 17, 1966. BA, Baylor U., 1939; postgrad., Northwestern U., 1939-40, Columbia U., 1943-45; MD, Cornell U., 1950; MS, Boston U., 1958. Diplomate Am. Bd. Psychiatry and Neurology. Intern Grasslands Hosp., Valhalla, N.Y., 1950-51; resident in psychiatry Mass. Meml. Hosp., Boston U. Sch. Medicine, also Boston State Hosp., 1951-54; from asst. in psychiatry to instr. Boston U. Sch. Medicine, 1951-58; lectr. psychology Tufts Coll., 1954-56; successively asst. prof., assoc. prof., cons. prof. psychiatry U. Okla. Sch. Medicine, 1958-64; prof. psychiatry Jefferson Med. Coll., Thomas Jefferson U., Phila., 1962-83, hon. prof., 1983—, chmn. dept., 1962-74; past mem. staff numerous hosps.; med. staff Wilmington Med Center; cons. area hosps., 1962—. Med. dir. Freedom From Fear, Inc., 1980-83; dir. Marka T. du Pont Inst. Human Behavior, Wilmington, Del., 1971-75; initiated self-image experience, photog. confrontation technique in psychiat. rsch. Author articles; prodr. films in field. Fellow psychiat. films Med. Audio-Visual Inst., Assn. Am. Med. Colls., 1951-53; candidate Boston Psychoanalytic Inst., 1954-58 Fellow Am. Coll. Psychiatrists (emeritus), Am. Psychiat. Assn. (life), Royal Australian and New Zealand Coll. Psychiatrists (hon.); mem. AMA, Del. Psychiat. Soc., Del. County Med. Soc., New Castle County Med. Soc., Sigma Xi. Home and Office: 16 Stone Hill Rd Wilmington DE 19803-4411 Office Phone: 302-655-9021.

CORNELIUS, JACQUELYN H., high school principal, educator; b. Jacksonville, Fla., Feb. 26, 1948; d. Jack Allen and Dorothy Mae Henson; m. Carey Michael Cornelius, May 21, 1982; children: Amber, Heather. BA, U. Fla., 1970; MEd, U. No. Fla., 1984. Eng. tchr. Forrest High Sch., Jacksonville, 1970-84, asst. prin., 1984-87; arts dir. Douglas Anderson Sch. of the Arts, Jacksonville, 1988-95, prin., 1996—. Vis. evaluation team mem. So. Accreditation of Colls. and Schs., 1989—; dir. Fla. Edn. Found., 1991-95; spkr. in field; bd. dirs. Fla. Women's Consortium, Duval County Assn. Secondary Sch. Adminstrs., Fla. Fedn. Bus. and Profl. Women, Inc., The Fla. Women's Alliance. Choreographer, host pub. TV. programs Inside Your Schs., The Hearing Impaired: The Creative Tchr., Testing: Pros and Cons. Active Jacksonville Symphony Edn. com., 1999—, Theatre Jacksonville, 1991—; mem. Mayor's Insight com., 1993-94, Mayor's Task Force on Domestic Violence, 1997-98; bd. dirs. Gateway Girl Scout Coun., 1991-94, Youth Leadership Jacksonville, 1992-94, Cultural Coun. Greater Jacksonville, 1998—. Recipient Excellence award Fla. Commr. of Edn., 1988, Arts Educator award Jacksonville Arts Assembly, 1995. Mem. Nat. Network of Performing and Visual Arts Schs. (treas., nominating chair arts advocacy com., arts achievement chair, southeast regional publicity chair), Nat. Assn. Secondary Sch. Prins. (Fla. chpt.), Jacksonville Women's Network, Bus. and Profl. Women's Club (First Coast, River City chpts., pres. 1995, vol. chair, jr. civitan com., mem. chair, program chair, ace com.), Jacksonville Rotary (internat. edn. chair, publicity com., charity com.). Avocations: travel, reading. Home: 4103 Cedar Rd Orange Park FL 32065-6903 Office: Douglas Anderson Sch of Arts 2445 San Diego Rd Jacksonville FL 32207-3699 E-mail: cornelius@educationcentral.org.

CORNELIUS, JAMES MILTON, pharmaceutical company financial executive; b. Oct. 28, 1943, Kalamazoo; s. Charles D. and Eleanor F. (Short) C.; m. Kathleen McGovern; children: Andrew, Lindsay. BA in Acctg., Mich. State U., 1965, MBA in Fin., 1967. Assoc. accountant Eli Lilly & Co., Indpls., 1967, fin. planning analyst, 1969-73, adminstr. corporate finance, 1973-75, mgr. econ. studies, 1975-78, dir. health care bus. planning, 1978-80, corp. treas., 1982-83, v.p. fin., CFO, 1983—1995, also bd. dirs.; exec. chmn. Guidant, 1995-2000, non-exec. chmn., 2000-; pres. IVAC Corp. subs. Eli Lilly & Co., San Diego, 1980-82; dir. Chubb Corp., Given Imaging Ltd., Hughes Electronic Corp., Nat. Bank Indpls. Corp. Contbg. author: The CFO's Handbook, 1986. Treas. Noyes Found., Indpls., 1983—; treas. bd. governors Indpls. Mus. Art.; mem. adv. bd. bus. corp. Mich. State U., 1983—; bd. dirs. Mcpl. Recreation, Inc., 1982—, Cmty. Hosp. Found., 1991—, Walker Rsch., 1991—; trustee U. Indpls. Zool. Soc. Served to 1st lt. U.S. Army, 1967-69. Mem. Fin. Execs. Inst., Pharm. Mfg. Assn. (past chmn. fin. sect.), Ind. C. of C. (bd. dirs. 1982—, exec. com. 1983—). Republican. Roman Catholic. Avocations: tennis, reading, jogging. Office: Eli Lilly & Co Lilly Corporate Ctr Indianapolis IN 46285-0001*

CORNELIUS, LARRY, band director; s. Adrian and Betty Cornelius; m. Jeanna Cornelius. MusB in Edn., U. of Montevallo, Ala., 1992; MEd in Music, Auburn (Ala.) U., 1996. Band dir. Auburn Jr. H.S., 1992—. Orch. dir. Lakeview Bapt. Ch., Auburn, 1998—2005. Named Tchr. of Yr., Auburn Jr. H.S., 2000. Mem.: Nat. Band Assn. (assoc.), Internat. Assn. for Jazz Edn. (assoc.), Ala. Bandmasters Assn. (assoc.), Phi Beta Mu (assoc.). Home: 1251 S Gay St Auburn AL 36830 Office: Auburn Junior HS 332 E Samford Ave Auburn AL 36830 Office Phone: 334-887-1969. Personal E-mail: lcornelius@auburnschools.org.

CORNELIUS, RICHARD MEREDITH, literature and language professor; b. Phila., May 18, 1934; s. Frederick Meredith Cornelius and Elizabeth Marie Yahraes; m. Donna Jean Black, Aug. 15, 1959; children: Craig Alan, Crista Lynn. BA, William Jennings Bryan Coll., 1955; MA, U. Tenn., 1961, PhD, 1971. Tchr. Beulah Beal Elem. Sch., Jacksonville, Fla., 1957-58; prof. English William Jennings Bryan Coll., Dayton, Tenn., 1961-99, W.J. Bryan/Scopes trial liaison, archivist, 1978—, prof. English emeritus, 1999—. Adj. prof. Chattanooga State Tech. C.C., 2000-01; chmn. English dept. William Jennings Bryan Coll., Dayton, 1962-76, 91-99, chair divsn. lit. and modern langs., 1974-76, 90-91, faculty chmn., 1979-80, co-chmn. 75th ann. planning com., 2003—; co-chmn. Bryan Coll. 75th Ann. Plan Com., 2003—; guest lectr. U. Tenn., Knoxville, 1991, The Citadel, Charleston, S.C., 1991, Natchez (Miss.) Nat. Lit. Celebration, 2000, Maryville (Tenn.) Coll., 1998, Conf. Am. Coll. Family Trial Lawyers, New Orleans, 1998, Cedarville (Ohio) U., 2002, Jilin U., Changchun, China, 2002; exhibit designer U. Tenn. Theater, Knoxville, 2001, Cedarville Univ. Theater, 2002, Bryan Coll., 1986—; presenter and cons. in field. Author: Christopher Marlowe's Use of the Bible, 1984, (booklet) Understanding William Jennings Bryan and the Scopes Trial: A Study Guide, 1998, (hist. supplement) Bryant Coll. 75th Anniversary Supplement of New American Standard Bible, 2004; editor: (books) Dandilines, 1971-87, Legacy of Faith: The Story of Bryan College, 1995, Selected Orations of William Jennings Bryan, 1996, 2000; editor, author: (book) Impact: The Scopes Trial, 2000, (booklet) Selected, Annotated Bibliography of William Jennings Bryan, the Scopes Trial, Creation, and Evolution, 1993, 4th edit., 2001; TV appearances include The History Channel, 1998, Sta. WTCI-TV 45 (PBS), 2001, Coral Ridge Ministries, 1988; contbr. articles to profl. publs. and chpts. to books. Co-founder, mem. Scopes Trial Festival Com., Dayton, 1988—; co-chmn. Scopes Trial Festival Symposia, Dayton, 1995-98, 2000, 02; dir. Scopes Trial Trail Markers Project, Dayton, 1995—; mem. bd. elders Grace Bible Ch., Dayton, 1962-99, 2000-03; mem. Southeastern Conf. on Christianity and Lit., 1979—, chmn., 1979-80; mem. Rhea County Hist. and Geneal. Soc., 2001—, bd. dirs. 2003—; chmn. Scopes Trial Mus. Com., 2003—, mem., vice chmn. planning com. Rhea County Heritage Mus., 2001—. Summer workshop grantee Christian Coll. Coalition/NEH, 1983, 88, 89, Tenn. Assn. Museums/Humanities Tenn., 2003. Mem. MLA, Nat. Coun. Tchrs. English, South Atlantic MLA, Tenn. Assn. Museums. Republican. Evangelical Christian. Avocations: creative writing, photography. Home: 311 Cedar Ln Dayton TN 37321-6234 Office: Bryan Coll Box 7591 721 Bryan Dr Dayton TN 37321-7000 Office Phone: 423-775-7247. Business E-mail: cornelri@bryan.edu.

CORNELIUS, WAYNE ANDERSON, electrical and computer engineering consultant; b. Russellville, Ky., Nov. 8, 1923; s. Eldon and Mabel Ruth (Gentle) C.; m. Elizabeth Grider (dec. Sept. 1946); children: Johanna Vastola, Keith, John(dec.); m. Linda Brady, Apr. 27, 1985; stepchildren: Pam Gondzur, Mark Smith, Todd Smith, Allison Stines. BS, U. Ky., 1953, EE, 1966; MS, U. Louisville, 1962; DEd, U. Cin., 1972. Elec. engr. U.S. Naval Ordnance Sta., Louisville, 1953-66, dir. engring. electronics lab., 1973-85; rsch. assoc. Pa. State U., State College, 1966-67; prof. engring. tech. Miami U., Oxford, Ohio, 1967-72; elec. engr. System Devel. Corp., Dayton, Ohio, 1972-73; chmn. dept. electronics tech. Ivy Tech. Coll., Sellersburg, Ind., 1985-90. Adj. prof. elec. engring. tech. Purdue U., New Albany, 1992-95, U. Louisville, 1976-84; adj. prof. math. Bellarmine Coll., Louisville, 1964-66, Ind. U., New Albany, 1990-91. With USN, 1942-45. Named to Honorable Order of Ky. Cols., 1963. Mem. NSPE, Am. Soc. for Engring. Edn., Phi Delta Kappa. Democrat. Presbyterian. Office: 9005 Lethborough Dr Louisville KY 40299-1437 Personal E-mail: lbcwac@prodigy.net.

CORNELL, ANNIE AIKO, nurse, administrator, retired military officer; b. L.A., Sept. 23, 1954; d. George and Fumiko (Iwai) Okubo; m. Max A. Cornell, Dec. 10, 1990. BSN, U. Md., 1976. RN, Calif. Enlisted U.S. Army, 1972, advanced through grades to maj., clin. staff nurse surg. ICU Presidio of San Francisco, clin. head nurse ICU Seoul, Korea, clin. head nurse gen. medicine ward Ft. Ord, Calif., chief nursing adminstrn., ret., 1992; nursing supr. Home Health Plus; dir. patient svcs. Hollister Vis. Nurses Assn., Calif.; asst. dir. patient svcs. Monterey Vis. Nurses Assn., Calif.; case mgr. supr. Cmty. Hosp. Home Health Svcs., Monterey, asst. mgr. Recipient Walter Reed Army Inst. nursing scholarship. Mem. Sigma Theta Tau. Home: 11725 Fir Dr Reno NV 89506

CORNELL, CHRISTOPHER J., musician; b. Seattle, Wash, July 20, 1964; m. Susan Silver, 1990. Musician Jones St. Band, Shemps, 1982-84; drummer, singer Soundgarden, 1984—97; singer Audioslave, 2001—. Singer, musician: (albums) (with Soundgarden) Ultramega OK, 1988, Louder Than Love, 1990, Badmotorfinger, 1991, Superunknown, 1994, Songs from the Superunknown, 1995, Down on the Upside, 1996; singer: (albums) Temple of the Dog, 1990, (solo albums) Euphoria Morning, 1999, (albums) Audioslave, 2002; prodr.: (albums) (with Screaming Trees) Uncle Anesthesia, 1991. Office: Sony Music 550 Madison Ave New York NY 10022

CORNELL, DEWEY GENE, psychologist; b. Louisville, June 22, 1956; m. Nancy Emily Trinka, Aug. 19, 1978; children: Cristina, Allison, Erin. AB, Transylvania U., 1977; MA, U. Mich., 1979, PhD, 1981. Lic. clinical psychologist. Intern U. Mich. Psychol. Clinic, Ann Arbor, 1979-81; postdoctoral scholar dept. psychiatry U. Mich., Ann Arbor, 1981-83; clin. psychologist Ctr. Forensic Psychiatry, Ann Arbor, 1983-86; asst. prof. Sch. Edn., U. Va., Charlottesville, 1986-91, assoc. prof., 1991-99, prof., 1999—, faculty assoc. Inst. Law, Psychiatry and Pub. Policy, 1986—. Dir. Va. Youth Violence Project, 1996—; asst. prof. psychology Mich. State U., East Lansing, 1985-86; pvt. practice, Charlottesville, 1986—. Author: Families of Gifted Children, 1984, Designing Safer Schools for Virginia, 1998; co-editor: Juvenile Homicide, 1989, Issues in School Violence Research, 2004; co-author: Recommended Practices in Gifted Education, 1991, Guidelines for Responding to Student Threats of Violence, 2005; contbr. articles to profl. jours. Fellow Internat. Soc. Rsch. Aggression; mem. APA, Am. Psychology Law Soc., Am. Ednl. Rsch. Assn., Va. Psychol. Assn. Avocations: Go, basketball, tennis. Office: U Va Sch Edn 405 Emmet St Charlottesville VA 22903 Office Phone: 434-924-0793. Business E-Mail: dcornell@virginia.edu.

CORNELL, ERIC ALLIN, physics professor; b. Palo Alto, Calif., 1961; s. Allin and Elizabeth (Greenberg) Cornell; 2 children. BS in Physics with honors, Stanford U., 1985; PhD in Physics, MIT, 1990. Tchr. English as Fgn. Lang. Taichung YMCA, Taiwan, 1982; rsch. asst. Stanford (Calif.) U., 1982—85; tchg. fellow Harvard Ext. Sch., 1989; postdoctoral Rowland Inst., Cambridge, Mass., 1990; postdoctorate Joint Inst. Lab. Astrophysics, Boulder, Colo., 1990—92; asst. prof. adj. dept. physics U. Colo., Boulder, 1992—95; staff scientist Nat. Inst. Stds. and Tech., Boulder, 1992—; fellow JILA U. Colo and Nat. Inst. Stds. and Tech., Boulder, 1994—; prof. adj. dept. physics U. Colo., Boulder, 1995—. Contbr. over 30 articles to profl. jours.; patentee in field. Recipient Grad. fellowship, NSF, 1985—88, Undergrad. Rsch. award for Excellence, Firestone, 1985, Samuel Wesley Stratton award, 1995, Newcomb-Cleveland prize, 1995—96, Carl Zeiss award, 1996, Fritz London prize in low temperature physics, 1996, Gold medal, Dept. Commerce, 1996, Presdl. Early Career award in sci. and engring., 1996, I.I. Rabi prize in atomic, molecular and optical physics, Am. Phys. Soc., 1997, King Faisal Internat. prize in sci., 1997, Alan T. Waterman award, NSF, 1997, Benjamin Franklin Medal in Physics, 1999, The Nobel Prize in Physics, 2001. Fellow: Optical Soc. of Am., 2000 (R.W. Wood Prize, 1999); mem.: Am. Phys. Soc., 1997 (fellow), Royal Netherlands Acad. of Arts & Sci. (Lorentz Medal, 1998), NAS, 2000. Achievements include first to successfully complete Bose-Einstein condensation, 1995. Office: Univ Colo JILA Campus Box 440 Boulder CO 80309-0440

CORNELL, HENRY, lawyer; BA, Grinnell Coll., 1976; JD, New York Law Sch., 1981. Assoc. Davis Polk & Wardwell, NYC, 1981—84, Goldman Sachs & Co., NYC, 1984—94, ptnr., mng dir., 1994—. Trustee Asian Art Mus., San Francisco, Citizens Com. for NY, Whitney Mus. Am. Art; bd. dir. The Ping Ins. Co. of China, The Kookmin Bank of Korea, The Dusit Thani Group, Rajadamri Pub. Co. Ltd. Mailing: Whitney Mus Am Art 945 Madison Ave New York NY 10021*

CORNELL, JOHN ROBERT, lawyer; b. Boston, Nov. 7, 1943; s. Robert Cole Cornell and Thelma Marjorie (Bassett) Strout; m. Susan Lindsay Jordan, June 11, 1966; children: Jared, Joshua, Alexandra, Margaret. AB, Colby Coll., 1965, MA, 1997; JD, Georgetown U., 1968; LLM in Taxation, NYU, 1972. Bar: N.Y. 1969, Maine 1972, U.S. Dist. Ct. Maine 1972, U.S. Tax Ct. 1990. Assoc. Dewey Ballantine, N.Y.C., 1968-72; from assoc. to ptnr. Drummond, Woodsum & MacMahon, Portland, Maine, 1972-81; ptnr. Jones Day, Cleve., 1981-98, Atlanta, 1998-2000, former tax group coord. for S.E., ptnr. N.Y.C., 2001—. Former chmn. tax group's employee benefits sect. Jones Day; lectr. in field. Overseer Colby Coll., 1992-97, trustee, 1997-2003; trustee Cleve. San Jose Ballet, 1994-98, treas., 1995-98. Mem. ABA, Maine Bar Assn. (chmn. tax sect. 1980-81), Colby Coll. Alumni Assn. (chmn. 1979-82), Cleve. Yachting Club (Rocky River, Ohio), Anglers Club (N.Y.C.), Megantic Club (Eustis, Maine), DKE Club (N.Y.C.). Republican. Avocations: sailing, bicycling, skiing, fly fishing. Office: 222 E 41st St New York NY 10017 Office Phone: 212-326-8332. Business E-Mail: jrcornell@jonesday.com.

CORNELL, ROBERT ARTHUR, federal official; b. Mineola, N.Y., Sept. 8, 1936; s. Herbert and Clara (Lange) C.; m. Nadine E. Dittmer, May 4, 1962 (div. June 1993); children: Robert Arthur Jr., James E., Suzanne N.; m. Catherine Rescoussie, Aug. 29, 1995. AB, Columbia U., 1958, postgrad., 1965-66, Pacific Luth. U., 1960-61, Am. U., 1964-65; MBA, NYU, 1963. With Grace Nat. Bank, N.Y.C., 1961-63, U.S. Govt., Washington, 1963-69, IBM World Trade Corp., 1970, S.J. Rundt & Assocs., N.Y.C., 1970-71; dep. dir. Office Econ. Research U.S. Internat. Trade Commn., Washington, 1971-76, dir. Office Trade and Industry, 1976-77, dep. dir. ops., 1977-79; asst. dir. for stockpile trans. GSA, Washington, 1979-80; dep. asst. sec. for internat. trade and investment policy U.S. Treasury Dept., Washington, 1980-88; dep. sec.-gen. OECD, Paris, 1988-95; cons., writer, editor France, 1995—. Mem. faculty U. Md., 1968; pvt. cons. in econs. and fin. With USN, 1958-61. Recipient Arthur S. Flemming award, 1974. Mem. Am. Econ. Assn., Western Econ. Assn., Nat. Economists Club, Nat. Assn. Bus. Econs. Lutheran. E-mail: 106035.1767@compuserve.com.

CORNELL, ROBERT WITHERSPOON, engineering consultant; b. Orange, N.J., Aug. 16, 1925; s. Edward Shelton and Helen Lauretta (Lawrence) C.; m. Patricia Delight Plummer, June 24, 1950; children: Richard W., Delight W. Cornell Dobby, Elizabeth Cornell Wilkin, Roberta Shelton Wolfe. BSME, Yale U., 1945, MSME, 1947, D in Engring., 1950. Registered profl. engr., Conn., N.Y. Instr. math. New Haven Jr. Coll., 1947-48; analytical engr. Pratt & Whitney Aircraft, East Hartford, Conn., 1947; with Hamilton Standard, Windsor Locks, Conn., 1948-87, chief applied mechanics and aerodynamics, 1961-87; instr. engring. Hillyer Coll., Hartford, 1955; pres. Cornell Cons., 1973—2000, Cornell Enterprises, West Hartford, 1984—2000. Adj. prof. Yale U., 1985, 90. Contbr. articles to profl. jours.; patentee in field. Bd. dirs., treas. Yale Sci. and Engring. Assn., 1969-2001, Conn. State Taxpayers Assn., Stratford, 1984-86; past pres., bd. dirs. West Hartford Taxpayers Assn., 1972-97, 2002-03; Rep. state senatorial candidate 5th dist. State of Conn., 1988, 94, state Rep. candidate 18th dist., 1990; mem. Svc. Corps Ret. Execs., 1989-2002, chmn., 1998-2000; dir. Agawam Coun., 1993-99. With USN, 1943-46. Fellow ASME; mem. Yale Club of Hartford, Hartford Golf Club, Sigma Xi, Tau Beta Pi. Avocations: tennis, squash, jogging, swimming, gardening. Home: 80 Loeffler Rd Apt G404C Bloomfield CT 06002-4314 Personal E-mail: cornellrp@aol.com.

CORNELL, SYLVIA RYCE, business development consultant, librarian; b. Cordele, Ga., Apr. 13, 1941; d. Amos and Emmal Lallage (Burton) R.; m. Elluin Clifford Cornell, Apr. 25, 1970; children: Elanore Crystal, Elluin Christopher. BA, Paine Coll., 1962; MLS, Atlanta U., 1969; MS in Occupational Edn., U. Houston, 1990. Libr. U. Mo., St. Louis, 1973-74, St. Louis Community Coll., 1974-75, Houston Pub. Libr., 1983-85; libr. indsl. edn. Houston Community Coll., 1985-90; libr. bus. industry Wharton County Jr. Coll., Sugar Land, Tex., 1990-92; prin. Creative Concepts Unltd. Mem. adv. bd. Small Bus. Devel. Ctr., Houston, 1986-91; presenter papers to confs. Candidate Fort Bend Ind. Sch. Bd., Sugar Land, 1990; sec. Briargate Civic Assn. Bd., Missouri City, 1982-84; mem. Fort Bend County Libr. Bd., 1992—; mem. Houston Bus. Coun., 1992—. Named Women of Achievement, Fedn. of Houston Profl. Women, 1995. Mem. ASTD (Trainer of Yr. 1989, 91), Am. Vocat. Assn., Rotary, Phi Kappa Phi. Baptist. Avocations: reading, writing, horticulture. Home and Office: 6310 W Ridgecreek Dr Missouri City TX 77489-2822

CORNELL, THOMAS BROWNE, artist, educator; b. Cleve., Mar. 1, 1937; s. Norman Monrod and Betty (Browne) C.; m. Christa Vaughan Kinkel, May 1, 1976; children: Anna Olivia, Nicolas Browne, Diana Camille BA, Amherst Coll., 1959; postgrad. art and architecture, Yale U., 1959-60. Faculty U. Calif., Santa Barbara, 1960-62; prof. art Bowdoin Coll., Brunswick, Maine, 1962—. Mem. visual arts program Princeton U., 1969-70 Author: The Monkey with 11 etchings, 1959, The Defense of Gracchus Babeuf with 21 etchings, 1964, Voiceprints with 5 etchings, 1988; one-man shows, Yale U. Art Gallery, Williams Coll. Art Mus., Santa Barbara Mus. Art, 1965, Wesleyan U., Conn., 1967, Bowdoin Coll., Maine, Princeton U., 1971, Muhlenberg Coll., 1976, Barridoff Galleries, Maine, U. Bridgeport, Conn., 1977, U. Redlands, Calif., 1979, A. M. Sachs Gallery, N.Y.C., 1979, 81, Santa Barbara (Calif.) Mus. Art, 1980, Morehead State U., Ky., 1986, G.W. Einstein Co., N.Y.C., 1986, 89, 97, Bowdoin Coll. Mus. Art, Maine, 1990; group shows include, DeCordova Mus., Lincoln, Mass., 1963, Mus. Modern Art, N.Y.C., 1966, Pa. State U., 1974, Maine State Mus., Bklyn. Mus., 1976, Cleve. Mus. Art, 1976, USIA, 1977, U. Va. Art Mus., 1978, Tatistcheff & Co., N.Y.C., 1979, Nat. Portrait Gallery, Washington, Artists Choice Mus., N.Y.C., Weatherspoon Art Gallery, N.C., Pratt Graphic Center, N.Y.C., 1980, Brit. Internat. Print Biennele, West Yorkshire, 1982, Robert Schoelkopf Gallery Ltd., N.Y.C., 1982, 84, 89, Twentieth Century Am., travelling exhbn., 1984-85, G.W. Einstein Co., N.Y.C., 1985, 86, 87, 88, 91, 92, 93, 94, 95, 96, Bayly Art Mus., U. Va., 1987, Bank of Boston, Plein Air-an Exhibition, 1986, So. Alleghenies Mus. Art, 1988, Robert Schoelkopf Gallery, N.Y.C., 1989, Kuznutsky Most Exhbn. Hall, Moscow, 1989, The Baxter Gallery, Portland, Maine, 1989, The Ark. Arts Ctr., Little Rock, 1989; The Mus. of Modern Art, art adv. svc. exhbn. at Am. Express Co., 1987, 88, 94, Md. Inst. Coll. Art, 1989, Douglas F. Cooley Meml. Art Gallery, Portland, Oreg., 1990, Noyes Mus., Oceanville, N.J., 1990, Ark. Arts Ctr., Little Rock, 1990, 94, U. Maine, Augusta, 1990, So. Alleghenies Mus. Art, 1991, Barn Gallery, Ogunquit, Maine, 1991, Nat. Acad. Design, N.Y.C., 1991, 93, 94, 96, 97, Webster U., St. Louis, 1992, The Monmouth Mus., Lincroft, N.J., 1992, Portland Mus. of Art, Portland, Maine, 1993, Ark. Arts Ctr., 1994, Icon Gallery, Brunswick, Maine, 1994, J.S. Ames Fine Art, Belfast, Maine, 1995, Bowdoin Coll. Mus., Brunswick, 1996. Recipient Louis Comfort Tiffany award, 1961, Nat. Inst. Arts and Letters award, 1964; Nat. Found. on Arts and Humanities fellow, 1966-67; Fulbright grantee Inst. for Internat. Edn., 1966; grantee Ford Found., 1969-70, Pollock-Krasner Found., 1993. Mem. Coll. Art Assn., Figurative Alliance N.Y., NAD, Union Maine Visual Artists (pres. 1990-91).*

CORNELL, WILLIAM DANIEL, mechanical engineer; b. Valley Falls, Kans., Apr. 17, 1919; s. Noah P. and Mabel (Hennessy) C.; m. Barbara L. Ferguson, Aug. 30, 1942; children: Alice Margaret, Randolph William. BS in Mech. Engring., U. Ill., 1942. Registered profl. engr., NY. Rsch. engr. Linde Air Products Co., Buffalo, 1942-48, cons. to Manhattan Dist. project, 1944-46; project engr. devel. of automatic bowling machine Am. Machine and Foundry, Buffalo, 1948-55; cons. Gen. Electric Co., Hanford, Wash., 1949-50; project engr. devel. of automatic bowling machine Brunswick Corp., Muskegon, Mich., 1955-59, mgr. advanced engring., 1959-72; mgr. advanced concepts and tech. Sherwood Med. Industries divsn. Am. Home Products Corp., St. Louis, 1972-85; mem. faculty Coll. Engring., U. Buffalo, 1946-47; cons. Cornell Engring., St. Louis, 1985—; mem. faculty Coll. Engring. Washington U., St. Louis, 1993-94. Patentee numerous inventions, including automatic golf and bowling game apparatus, med. instruments; developer new method of measuring hemoglobin and new method of counting platelets in whole blood. Recipient Navy E award, 1945, Manhattan Project Recognition award, 1945, Merit award Maritime Commn., 1945. Republican. Presbyterian. Achievements include development of copensating i.v. flow controller; string guided golf bag cart that follows the golfer without his attention; a rotary sensor for remote applications that requires no power supply. Home and Office: 907 Camargo Dr Ballwin MO 63011-1506

CORNELL, WILLIAM HARVEY, clergyman; b. Pitts., May 27, 1934; s. Floyd Anderson and Audrey Fern (Wasson) C.; m. Betty Jean Yates, July 24, 1954; children: Deborah Jean, William Mark, Darla Ruth. AA, Central (S.C.) Wesleyan Coll., 1953; AB in Religion, Ind. Wesleyan U., 1956. Ordained to ministry Wesleyan Meth. Ch., 1958. Clergyman Wilgus Wesleyan Meth. Ch., Gypsy, Pa., 1956-59, Wolf Summit (W.Va.) Wesleyan Meth. Ch., 1959-63, Canal Wesleyan Meth. Ch., Utica, Pa., 1968-73, Greenville (Pa.) Wesleyan Meth. Ch., 1973-76, Salem (Ohio) Wesleyan Meth. Ch., 1976-78, Sagamore (Pa.) Wesleyan Meth. Ch., 1963-68, 78-95, Niles (Ohio) Wesleyan Meth. Ch., 1995-2000, ret., 2000—. Mem. mission bd. Allegheny Wesleyan Meth. Connection, 1965—2003, sec., 1973-98, editor ann. jour., 1973-98, mem. adv. bd., 1978-98; sec. N.W. Indian Bible Sch., Alberton, Mont., 1969—. Republican. Avocations: hunting, travel. Home and Office: PO Box 115 7695 Rte 85 Beyer PA 16211

CORNELSEN, PAUL FREDERICK, manufacturing and engineering company executive; b. Wellington, Kans., Dec. 23, 1923; s. John S. and Theresa Albertine (von Klatt) C.; m. Floy Lila Brown, Dec. 11, 1943; 1 son, John Floyd. Student, U. Wichita, 1939-41, 45-46; BS in Mech. Engring., U. Denver, 1949. With Boeing Airplane Co., 1940-41, Ralston Purina Co., St. Louis, 1946—, v.p. internat. divsn., 1961-63, adminstrv. v.p., gen. mgr. internat. divsn., 1963-64, v.p., 1964-68, dir., 1966—, exec. v.p., 1968-78, vice-chmn. bd., COO, 1978-81, pres. internat. group, 1964-77; pres., CEO Moehlenpah Industries Inc., St. Louis, 1981-82; chmn., CEO Mitek Inc. (formerly Moehlenpah), St. Louis, 1982-93; prin. Conifer Investments LLC, Town and Country, Mo., 1993—. Founding mem. L.Am. Agribus. Investment Corp., 1970—; founding mem. industry coop. program UN Agys., Rome; chmn. Point Of Purchase Corp., St. Louis. 1st lt. AUS, World War II, AUS, Korea. Decorated Silver Star. Office: 1129 Jo Carr Dr Town And Country MO 63017-8401 Office Phone: 636-207-1641. E-mail: plcornelsen@earthlink.net.

CORNELSON, GEORGE HENRY, IV, retired textile company executive; b. Spartanburg, S.C., July 12, 1931; s. George Henry Cornelson III and Elizabeth Marshall (Woodward) Cornelson; m. Ann Martin Shaw, Oct. 6, 1956; children: George Henry Cornelson V, Martin Shaw, Scott Montgomery, Elizabeth Woodward. Student, Davidson Coll., 1949-51; BS in Textiles, N.C. State U., 1953; postgrad. in Bus. Adminstrn., Harvard U., 1953—54; DHL (hon.), Presbyn. Coll., 2003. With indsl. engring. dept. Clinton (S.C.) Mills, Inc., 1954-55, 57-58, from v.p. to pres., 1958—86, CEO, 1985—86; v.p. Clinton Mills Sales Corp., N.Y.C., 1958—86. Bd. dirs. Elastic Fabrics of Am., N.C. Textile Found., exec. com.; mem. S.C. Gov.'s Trade Mission to Far East, Hong Kong; pres. Clinton Investment Co., 1985—86; bd. dirs. Clinton Mills of Geneva, past pres., dir.; vice chmn. bd. dirs. Bailey Fin. Corp., 1996—99; bd. dirs. Anchor Bank, Myrtle Beach, SC, 1999—2000, Carolina First Bank, Greenville, SC, 2000—03; mem. S.C. Gov.'s Trade Mission to Far East, Singapore, 1979, Kuala Lumpur, 79, Taiwan, 79, Malaysia, 79. *While serving as organizing Chairman of the Greater Clinton Planning Commission, planning was initiated to remove the Columbia, Newberry and Laurens Railroad Tracks in downtown Clinton in order to improve auto traffic. Also planning was initiated with the So. Car. Hwy. Dept. to construct the ring road by-pass for hwy. 72 and hwy. 56. Planning was also commenced for the construction of the Clinton City Hall in 1967-68.* Trustee Presbyn. Coll., Clinton, 1959—68, 1994—2005, Davidson (N.C.) Coll., 1992—95, bd. visitors, 1986—91; trustee Ind. Coll. and Univs. S.C., 1971—92, life trustee, 1993—; trustee Thornwell Home for Children, Clinton, 1968—76, exec. com., 1973—74, sec. bd. trustees, 1974; organizing chmn. Greater Clinton Planning Commn., 1967—68; pres. Cmty. Chest and United Fund, 1963—64; chmn. Laurens County dist. Boy Scouts Am., 1973, exec. bd. Blue Ridge coun., 1974; chair adv. com. Bailey Found., 1969—; dir. S.C. State Mus. Found., 1986—89; expansion com. mem. Carolina's NFL, 1988—92; bd. dirs. Columbia Theol. Sem., Decatur, Ga., 1990—93; trustee Laurens County Health Care Sys., 1996—2000, chmn., 1997—99; deacon 1st Presbyn. Ch., Clinton, 1959—67, elder, 1967—73, 1976—81, 1983—87, 1988—93. Officer USAF, 1955—57. Recipient Disting. Svc. award, Clinton Jr. C. of C., 1962, Outstanding Young Alumnus award, N.C. State U., 1965, Disting. Alumnus award, McCallie Sch., 1989, N.C. State U., 1999. Mem.: S.C. Textile Mfrs. Assn. (bd. dirs. 1973—82, pres. 1979—80), Am. Textile Mfrs. Inst. (rsch. and tech. svcs. com. 1964—71, vice chmn. Crafted With Pride in USA com. 1985—87, vice chmn. edn. com. 1975—76, cotton com. 1981—82, safety and health com. 1981—82), Clinton C. of C. (bd. dirs. 1959—61, 1966, v.p. 1968, pres. 1969), S.C. C. of C. (bd. dirs., exec. com. 1975—79), Musgrove Mill Golf Club (founder, bd. dirs.), Lions Club, Kappa Alpha, Phi Psi. Home: Merrie Oaks 1644 Hwy 56 S Clinton SC 29325

CORNETT, GREGG, publishing executive, editor, computer company executive; b. Dayton, Ohio, May 12, 1954; BA, U. Ark., 1985, MA, 1988; PhD in Computer Sci., Berkeley U., 1995. Pres. Computer Commuter, Batesville, Ark., 1982—87, Gregg Cornett Assocs., Batesville, Bald Knob, Searcy, Ark., 1984—; pub., editor Bald Knob Banner, 1987—; CEO G.C.A. Computer Svcs., 1993—; v.p. Wood Nursery, Inc., 1995—96; systems analyst Arkansas Pub., 1996—. Police photographer Bald Knob Police Dept., 1988—; computer cons. Gregg Cornett Assocs., 1984—, freelance journalist, Bald Knob, 1987—. Author (booklet) Neighborhood Crime Prevention, 1989; contbr. articles to newspapers. Area coord. City Crime Prevention, Bald Knob, 1988—; assoc. KARK-TV Community Network, Little Rock, 1990—; acting city clk. City of Bald Knob, 1991; rural community cons. City of Bald Knob, 1988—; founding bd. dirs. Rsch. Internat., Aruba; scoutmaster cub scout troop Boy Scouts Am., 2001—. Recipient Better Newspaper Advt. award Ark. Press Assn., 1988; Gregg Cornett Day proclaimed by City of Bald Knob, 1990. Fellow Rotary; mem. C. of C. (bd. dirs. 1988—). Avocations: writing, photography, electronics. E-mail: gcornett@bscn.com.

CORNETT, LLOYD HARVEY, JR., retired historian; b. Seminole, Okla., Aug. 29, 1930; s. Lloyd Harvey and Edna Lee (Walker) C.; children from previous marriage: Lloyd Harvey III, Rosemary Lynne, Carlton Wayne, Curtis Lee; m. Sarah Frances Missildine, Apr. 15, 1992. BA, U. Okla., 1951, MA, 1954; postgrad., U. N.Mex., 1965, Auburn U., 1977. Asst. dir. command history 2d Air Force, U.S. Air Force, 1955-57; historian Air Def. Command, 1957-58; asst. dir. command history Continental Air Def. Command, 1958-59; asst. dir. command history N.Am. Air Def. Command, 1959-61; ctr. historian Air Force Missile Devel. Ctr., 1961-70; historian Air Force Spl. Weapons Ctr., 1970-72; command historian Aerospace Def. Command, 1972-73; command historian Air Tng. Command, 1973-74; dir. U.S. Air Force Hist. Rschr. Ctr., Maxwell AFB, Ala., 1974-89; prin. Ind. Hist. Rsch./Adv. Svc., Montgomery, Ala., 1989—. Mem. Gov.'s Com. for Ala. Conf. on Libr. and Info. Svcs.; bd. advisors Ala. Hist. Commn. Co-editor: Alabama History: An Annotated Bibliography, Vol. of Am. Astronautical Soc. Hist. and (sch. text) Hist. of Ala., 1998; contbr. to hist. jours. Committeeman Boy Scouts Am., 1963-70, 75-79; mem. at large adminstrv. bd. Meth. Ch., 1978-81. Served with USMCR, 1951-53. Mem. AIAA (chmn. tech. com. on history 1983-96), Am. Astronautical Soc. Hist. Com., Western History Assn., Soc. for History in Fed. Govt. Democrat. Home and Office: 3751 Marie Cook Dr Montgomery AL 36109-1509

CORNETT, MICK, mayor; b. Oklahoma City, Oklahoma, 1958; m. Lisa Cornett; 3 children. Degree in journalism television news, Univ. of Oklahoma. Sportscaster and news anchor KOCO-5, 1981—97, city hall news anchor, 1997—99; pres. Mick Cornett Video Productions Inc., 1999—; ward 1 council mem. Oklahoma City Council, 2001—04; mayor Oklahoma City, 2004—. Office: 200 N Walker 3rd Floor Oklahoma City OK 73102 Business E-Mail: mayor@okc.gov.

CORNETT, ROBERT ARNOLD, philosophy educator; b. Jackson County, Ky., Apr. 9, 1920; s. Marion Hall Cornett and Eva Gabbard; m. Barbara Ann Schamberger, Aug. 17, 1946; children: Robert Jr., Kathryn, Donald, Virginia. BA, Butler U., 1944; BDiv, Princeton (N.J.) Theol. Sem., 1946; PhD, U. Ill., 1953. Prof. philosophy Berea (Ky.) Coll., 1953—58, Randolph-Macon Womans Coll., Lynchburg, Va., 1958—90, prof. philosophy emeritus, 1990—. Contbr. articles to profl. jours. Fulbright grantee. Mem. Am. Philos. Assn. Democrat. Avocations: old books, minerals, rivers and mountains activities, writing. Home: 1542 Club Dr Lynchburg VA 24503 Personal E-mail: cornett25@msn.com.

CORNETT, STANLEY ORIN, music educator; b. Shawnee, Okla., Feb. 14, 1949; s. Richard Orin and Lorene Huston Cornett; m. Eileen Therese Condon, May 19, 1964; children: Lydia Elizabeth, Emily Joan. MusB, Eastman Sch. Music, 1973, MusM, cert. in Voice and Opera, Eastman Sch. Music, 1975; DMA in Musical Arts, U. Md., 1982. Asst. prof. U. Mich., Ann Arbor, Mich., 1983—87; voice fac., Peabody Conservatory Music Johns Hopkins U., Balt., 1987—. Co-dir. Seagle Colony Music Festival, Schroon Lake, NY, 1989—94; mem. faculty ARIA Internat. Music Acad., Ont., Canada, 2002. Singer (tenor) over 30 opera roles; singer: Carnegie Hall, Avery Fisher Hall, Kennedy Ctr., N.Y.C. Opera, Washington Opera, Balt. Opera, solo and maj. symphony orchs., (broadcast) Pub. Broadcasting Station, Nat. Pub Radio. With U.S. Army, 1970—73. Mem.: Nat. Assn. Tchrs. Singing. Democrat. Home: 508 N Chapelgate Lane Baltimore MD 21229 Office: Peabody Inst of Johns Hopkins Univ 1 E Mt Vernon Place Baltimore MD 21202

CORNFELD, DAVE LOUIS, lawyer; b. St. Louis, Dec. 24, 1921; s. Abraham and Rebecca (David) C.; m. Martha Herrmann, May 30, 1943; children: Richard Steven, James Allen, Lawrence Joseph. AB, Washington U., St. Louis, 1942, LLB, 1943. Bar: Mo. 1943. Practice law, St. Louis; ptnr. Husch & Eppenberger, 1954—2001, of counsel, 2001—. Adj. prof. Washington U., 1966-87. Co-author: Missouri Estate Planning, Will Drafting and Estate Administration, 2 vol., 1988, supplement, 2004; editor Law Quar. 1943. Bd. dirs. Jewish Fedn., St. Louis, 1977-80, 83-88, Jewish Ctr. for Aged, 1981-88; mem. adv. com. U. Miami Inst. Estate Planning, 1979—. Served with AUS, 1945-46. Mem. ABA (past chmn. com. taxation income estates and trusts, vice chmn. sect. taxation 1977-80, editor-in-chief Tax Lawyer 1977-80, sr. assoc. editor Probate and Property), St. Louis Bar Assn. (past chmn. taxation com), Am. Law Inst., Am. Coll. Trust and Estate Counsel (regent 1984-90), Am. Coll. Tax Counsel (regent 1980-88), Internat. Acad. Estate and Trust Law, Order of Coif. Jewish (trustee temple 1967-91). Club: Masons. Home: 834 Oakbrook Ln Saint Louis MO 63132-4812 Office: Husch & Eppenberger LLC 190 Carondelet Plz Ste 600 Saint Louis MO 63105-3441 Office Phone: 314-480-1616. E-mail: dcornfeld@charter.net, dave.cornfeld@husch.com.

CORNFELD, RICHARD STEVEN, lawyer; b. St. Louis, Aug. 21, 1950; s. Dave Louis and Martha (Herrmann) C.; m. Marcia Jackoway, Aug., 1, 1982; children: Lisa Sydney, Sarah Reva. AB, U. Mich., 1972; JD, Northwestern U., Chgo., 1975. Bar: Ill. 1975, U.S. Dist. Ct. (no. dist.) Ill. 1975, U.S. Dist. Ct. D.C. 1977, D.C. 1977, Mo. 1981. Assoc. Schwartz & Freeman, Chgo., 1975; law clk. to presiding justice U.S. Dist. Ct. (no. dist.) Ill., Chgo., 1976; assoc. Bergson, Borkland, Margolis & Adler, Washington, 1976-80, Coburn, Croft & Putzell, St. Louis, 1980-83; ptnr. Thompson Coburn LLP and prececessor firms, St. Louis, 1983—, co-chair toxic tort practice group. Contbr. articles to profl. jours. Mem. ABA, Bar Assn. of Met. St. Louis, Mo. Bar, D.C Bar, Order of the Coif. Home: 21 Ladue Estates Dr Creve Coeur MO 63141-8321 Office: Thompson Coburn LLP One US Bank Plaza Saint Louis MO 63101-1693

CORNFIELD, DANIEL BENJAMIN, sociology educator; b. Washington, Nov. 5, 1952; s. Melvin and Edith (Haas) C.; m. Hedy Merrill Weinberg, June 30, 1985. A.B., U. Chgo., 1974, A.M., 1977, Ph.D., 1980. Assoc. prof. sociology Vanderbilt U., Nashville, 1980— . Appearances on various TV and radio programs. Contbr. articles to profl. jours. Grantee Russell Sage Found., 1985. Nat. Council Employment Policy, 1980. Mem. Am. Sociol. Assn., So. Sociol. Soc., Indsl. Relations Research Assn. Democrat. Jewish. Avocations: guitar; clarinet; saxophone; piano; labor union organizing. Office: Dept Sociology Vanderbilt U Nashville TN 37203

CORNFIELD, MELVIN, lawyer, director; b. Chgo., June 5, 1927; s. Harry and Annabelle (Maltz) C.; m. Edith Pauline Haas, June 24, 1951; children: Daniel Benjamin, Deborah S. Cornfield Alexander. AB, U. Chgo., 1948, JD, 1951. Bar: D.C. 1951, N.Y. 1958. Atty. durable goods divsn. Office Price Stblzn., Washington, 1951-53; atty., advisor Chief Counsel's Office IRS, Washington, 1953-58; assoc. Willkie, Farr, Gallagher, Walton & FitzGibbon, N.Y.C., 1958-63; dir. taxes NBC, Inc., 1963-66; staff v.p. tax affairs RCA Corp., N.Y.C., 1966-76, v.p., treas., 1976-82, v.p. tax affairs, 1982-85; dir. NYU Tax Inst., 1985-94. With USAAF, 1946-47. Home: 4703 Iselin Ave Bronx NY 10471-3323

CORNFORTH, SIR JOHN WARCUP, chemist; b. Sydney, Australia, Sept. 7, 1917; s. John William and Hilda (Eipper) Cornforth; m. Rita H. Harradence, Sept. 27, 1941; children: Brenda Osborne, John, Philippa Horder. BSc, U. Sydney, 1937, MSc, 1938; DPhil, Oxford U., 1941, DSc (hon.), 1976; DSc (hon.), E.T.H. Zurich, 1975, Trinity Coll., Dublin, Univs. Liverpool, Warwick, Aberdeen, Hull, Sussex, Kent and Sydney. Mem. sci. staff Med. Rsch. Coun., London, 1946—62; dir. Milstead Lab. Chem. Enzymology, Shell Rsch. Ltd., Sittingbourne, England, 1962—75; Royal Soc. rsch. prof. U. Sussex Sch. Chemistry and Molecular Scis., Brighton, England, 1975—82, prof. emeritus. Contbr. articles to profl. jours. Decorated comdr. Brit. Empire, knight, Companion of the Order of Australia; recipient Stouffer prize, 1967, Prix Roussel, 1972, Nobel prize in chemistry, 1975, Companion of the Order of Australia, 1991, Centenary of Federation medal, 2003. Fellow: Am. Chem. Soc. (Ernest Guenther award 1969), Royal Soc. Chemistry (Corday-Morgan medal 1953, Flintoff medal 1966), Royal Soc. (Davy medal 1968, Royal medal 1976, Copley medal 1982); mem.: NAS (assoc.), Netherlands Acad. Sci., Biochem. Soc. (CIBA medal 1966), Australian Acad. Sci. (corr.), Am. Soc. Biol. Chemists (hon.), Am. Acad. (hon.). Achievements include research in chemistry of penicillin, synthesis of steroids and other biologically active natural products, chemistry of heterocyclic compounds, biosynthesis of steroids, enzyme chemistry. Home: Saxon Down Cuilfail Lewes BN7 2BE England Office: U Sussex Sch Life Sci Falmer Brighton BN1 9QJ England

CORNGOLD, STANLEY ALAN, language educator, writer; b. Bklyn., June 11, 1934; s. Herman and Estelle (Bramson) C.; m. Marie Josephine Brettle, July 29, 1961 (div. May 1969); 1 child, Isabel Anna; m. Regine Schmidt-Üllner, Feb. 18, 1995. AB, Columbia U., 1957; postgrad., Sch. Oriental and African Studies-U. London, 1957-58; MA, Cornell U., 1963, PhD, 1969; postgrad., U. Basel (Switzerland), 1965-66. Instr. English U. Md. European div., 1959-62; teaching asst. English Cornell U., 1963-64; teaching asst. French Cornell U, 1964-65; asst. prof. German Princeton U., 1966-72, assoc. prof., 1972-79, assoc. prof. German and comparative lit., 1979-81, prof., 1981—, dir. grad. studies dept. German, 1979-82, 85, 93-95, 96-97. Vis. prof. Inst. Advanced Study, Princeton, 2003—04; disting. vis. scholar McMaster U., 2003. Author: The Commentators' Despair, 1973, The Fate of the Self, 1986, 2d edit., 1994, Franz Kafka: The Necessity of Form, 1988, Complex Pleasure: Forms of Feeling in German Literature, 1998, Literary Paternity, Literary Friendship: Essays in Honor of Stanley Corngold, 2002, Lambent Traces: Franz Kafka, 2004; co-author: Borrowed Lives, 1991; editor: Ausgewählte Prosa by Max Frisch, 1968, Aspekte der Goethezeit, 1975, Thomas Mann, 1875-1955, 1976, Norton Critical Edition of The Metamorphosis (Franz Kafka), 1996; translator (editor): The Metamorphosis (Franz Kafka), 1972; translator: (essays) Walter Benjamin, Selected Writings, 1996. Served with U.S. Army, 1955-57. Fellow Am. Coun. Learned Soc., 1965—66, NEH, 1973—74, Guggenheim Found., 1977—78; Fulbright fellow, 1986, Hölderlin Residence fellow, 1990, 1998, Literarisches Colloquium Berlin fellow, 1990, Princeton Honorific fellow, 2003, Internat. Forschungszentrum Kulturwissenschaften, Vienna, 2004. Mem. PEN, MLA (exec. com. divsn. on philos. approaches to lit. 1993-97, past chair, pub. com. 1993-95), Acad. Lit. Studies, N.Am. Nietzsche Soc., Kafka Soc. Am. (past pres.), Heidelberg Club Internat. Home: 51 Ridgeview Cir Princeton NJ 08540-7603 Office: Princeton U Dept German 219 E Pyne Bldg Princeton NJ 08544 Office Phone: 609-258-4137. Business E-Mail: corngold@princeton.edu.

CORNICK, MICHAEL F(REDERICK), accounting educator; b. Evansville, Ind., Apr. 15, 1940; s. Isadore John and Belle (Wigdor) C.; m. Charlotte Bozovich, Mar. 2, 1985; children: Elizabeth Ann, Ann Elliott. BS in Indsl. Mgmt., Purdue U., 1963; MBA, U.N.C., Chapel Hill, 1970, PhD, 1980. CPA, N.C. Stockbro. Thomson and McKinnon, Winston-Salem, N.C., 1965-68; bank officer 1 st. Nat. Atlanta, 1970-72; assoc. prof. acctg. U. N.C., Charlotte, 1985—2002, Winthrop U., 2002—. Adv. Internat. Bus. Club, Charlotte, 1987—; leader Internat. Acctg. Overseas, Fed. Rep. Germany, London, 1988—. Author: Bank Accounting, 1984; contbr. articles to profl. jours. Mem. British Am. Bus. Coun. 1st lt. U.S. Army, 1963-65. Recipient cert. appreciation, Retarted Citizens Greensboro, 1983. Mem. AICPA, Inst. Mgmt. Accts. (dir. 1985-88), Am. Acctg. Assn., N.C. Soc. CPAs, Charlotte World Trade Assn. Avocations: reading, tennis, basketball. Home: 1409 Biltmore Dr Charlotte NC 28207-2556 Office: Winthrop Univ Rock Hill SC 29733 Office Phone: 803-323-4624. E-mail: cornickm@winthrop.edu.

CORNIES, LARRY ALAN, journalist, educator; b. Leamington, Ont., Can., Apr. 4, 1953; s. William Walter and Helen Louise (Rempel) C.; m. Jacquelyn Ann Brown, Aug. 17, 1974; children: Darryl, Graeme, Andrew, Natalie. BA in Religious Studies, U. Waterloo, 1975; postgrad., Wichita State U., 1981-84; MA in Journalism, U. Western Ontario, 1986. Comm. officer Conrad Grebel Coll., Waterloo, Ont., 1974-75; secondary sch. tchr. United Mennonite Ednl. Inst., Leamington, 1975-80; assoc. editor The Mennonite, Newton, Kans., 1980-84; comm. dir. Mennonite Ch. Hdqs., Newton, 1984-85; mng. editor London (Ont.) Mag., 1986-88; arts and entertainment editor The London Free Press, 1989-93, cluster editor, 1993-97, asst. city editor, 1997-98, Forum editor, 1998-2000, assoc. editor, 2000, editor, 2000—. Adj. prof. faculty info. and media studies U. Western Ont., 1987-97, 2004—; corr. World Report, Washington, 1983-85, Ecumedia News, N.Y.C., 1982-85; bd. govs. Conrad Grebel Coll., U. Waterloo, Ont., 1994-97; bd. dirs. Mennonite Pub. Svc., 2004—. Author: Essays in Journalism, 1986. Bd. dirs. divsn. gen. svcs. Gen. Conf. Mennonite Ch., Newton, Kans., 1995-2002. Recipient Derose-Hinkhouse award Religious Pub. Rels. Coun., 1985, Western Ont. Newspaper awards, 1997, 2002; fellow Knight Ctr. for Specialized Journalism, U. Md., 2001, 2003. Mem. Coun. Ch. and Media (chmn. 1991-93). Avocations: music, baseball. Home: 759 Barclay Rd London ON Canada N6K 1K4 Office: London Free Press 369 York St London ON Canada N6A 4G1 Office Phone: 519-667-4549. E-mail: lcornies@lfpress.com.

CORNING, CAITLIN, historian, educator; d. Robert and Corlee Corning. BA, Seattle Pacific U., 1990; MA, U. of Leeds, Leeds, Eng., 1992; PhD, U. of Leeds, 1996. Vis. prof. Northwestern Coll., Orange City, Iowa, 1995—96; chair, assoc. prof. George Fox U., Newberg, Oreg., 1996—. Assoc. editor Religion in Ea. Europe, 2003—; lectr. in field. Author: (book) The Celtic and Roman Traditions, 1996-2006; contbr. articles to profl. jours. Bd. dirs. Conf. Faith and History. Grantee Tech. in the Classroom, Oreg. Tech. in Edn., 2002, Palm Prof. grantee, 2001—02. Mem.: Cmty. of Christ Tchr., Late Antique, Medieval and Renaissance Soc. of Greater Portland, Am. Hist. Assn. (bd. mem.), Conf. on Faith and History, Medieval Acad. of Am. Episcopal. Office: George Fox University 414 N Meridian St #6207 Newberg OR 97132 Office Phone: 503-554-2673. E-mail: ccorning@georgefox.edu.

CORNING, JOY COLE, retired state official; b. Bridgewater, Iowa, Sept. 7, 1932; d. Perry Aaron and Ethel Marie (Sullivan) Cole; m. Burton Eugene Corning, June 19, 1955; children: Carol, Claudia, Ann. BA, U. No. Iowa, 1954; hon. degree, Allen Coll. Nursing. Cert. elem. tchr., Iowa. Tchr. elem. sch. Greenfield (Iowa) Sch. Dist., 1951-53, Waterloo (Iowa) Cmty. Sch. Dist., 1954-55; mem. Iowa Senate, Des Moines, 1984-90, asst. Rep. leader, 1989-90; lt. gov. State of Iowa, Des Moines, 1991-99. Past chmn. Nat. Conf. Lt. Govs. Bd. dirs. Inst. for Character Devel.; mem. policy bd. Performing Arts Ctr., U. No. Iowa, also trustee UNI Found.; bd. dirs. Nat. Conf. Cmty. and Justice, Des Moines Symphony, Planned Parenthood of Greater Iowa. Named Citizen of Yr., Cedar Falls C. of C., 1984; recipient ITAG Disting. Svc. to Iowa's Gifted and Talented Students award, 1991, Pub. Svc. award Iowa Home Econs. Assn., 1994, Friend of Math. award Iowa Coun. Tchrs. of Math., 1995, Iowa State Edn. Assn. Human Rights award, 1996, Govs. Affirmative Action award, Spl. Recognition award Nat. Foster Parent Assoc., Des Moines Human Rights Commn. award, Pub. Svc. award Coalition for Family and Children's Svcs in Iowa, Friends of Iowa Civil Rights, Inc. award, Martin Luther King Jr. Lifetime Svc. award, 1999, Svc. award Des Moines Area Religious Coun., 2002, NCCJ Brotherhood-Sisterhood award, 2003, Senator Barry Goldwater award Planned Parenthood Fedn. Am., 2003; recognized for Extraordinary Advocacy for Children of Iowa chpt. Nat. Com. for Child Abuse, award for leadership Early Care and Edn. Congress, Alumni Achievement award U. No. Iowa; named among YWCA Women of Achievement, 2000, Woman of Influence, Bus. Record, 2003; Nat. Conf. for Cmty. and Justice honoree, 2003; named to Iowa Women's Hall Fame, 2004. Mem. AAUW, LWV, PEO, Nat. Assn. for Gifted Children (mem. adv. bd. 1991-99), Rotary Club, Delta Kappa Gamma, Alpha Delta Kappa. Republican. Mem. United Ch. Of Christ. Home: 4323 Grand Ave No 324 Des Moines IA 50312-2443 Personal E-mail: corningj@aol.com.

CORNISH, BONITA CLARK, retired secondary school educator; b. Live Oak, Calif., Feb. 18, 1911; d. Cyrus Benito Clark and Anna Margretha Carstenbrook; m. Edwin Robert Cornish, July 23, 1935 (dec. Mar. 31, 1970); children: William Robert, Susan Margretha. AB, U. Calif., Berkeley, 1932, MA, 1933; postgrad., Fresno State U., 1944—2001, Coll. Pacific, 1956; EdD, Calif. Coast U., 2001. Life tchg. cert. Calif. Phys. edn., music and math. tchr., dean of girls Dunsmuir (Calif.) Internat. Union, 1934—38; pvt. music tchr. Yosemite Valley, Calif., 1943; asst. to prin. Fresno (Calif.) County Sys., 1944; spl. edn. tchr. Fresno City Sys., 1946—72; tchr. Bullard HS, Fresno, 1972, Roosevelt HS, Fresno, 1973—76; ret., 1976. Dramatics Calif. Ret. Tchrs. Assn., Fresno, 1976—2001; lectr. gerontology classes Fresno State U., 1990—2001; tchr. Elderhostel-Wonder Valley, Fresno, 1990—95. PTA pres. Coll. Elem., Alan Houdlin Jr. High, 1940—60; city coun. Assembley Woman elected, Calif., 1980—93; bd. mem. YWCA, Fresno, 1985—90. Mem.: AARP, Fresno County Dem. Women's Club (pres. 1990), Order of Ea. Star (life; conductress 1937), Alpha Delta Kappa (Ca Xi cptr. charter pres. 1945). Avocations: camping, gardening, reading, folk art, cooking. Home: Apt 320E 9525 N Ft Washington Rd Fresno CA 93720-0681

CORNISH, EDWARD SEYMOUR, magazine editor; b. NYC, Aug. 31, 1927; s. George Anthony and Elizabeth Furniss (McLeod) C.; m. Sally Woodhull, Oct. 12, 1957 (dec. Mar. 1992); children: George Anthony, Jefferson Richard Woodhull, Blake McLeod. Diplome d'etudes, U. Paris, France, 1948; AB, Harvard U., 1950. Copy boy, cub reporter Evening Star, Washington, 1950-51; staff corr. U.P. Assn., Richmond, Va., 1951-52, Raleigh, N.C., 1952-53, London, 1953-54, Paris, 1954-55, Rome, 1956; staff writer Nat. Geog. Soc., 1957-69; founder, pres. World Future Soc., Washington, 1966—2004; creator, editor The Futurist Mag., 1966—; editor World Future Soc. Bull., 1968-77. Cons. to govt., bus. and ednl. orgns. Author: The Study of the Future, 1977; editor: Resources Directory for America's Third Century, 1977, The Future: A Guide to Information Sources, 1977, 1979: The World of Tomorrow, 1978, Communications Tomorrow, 1982, Global Solutions, 1984, The Computerized Society, 1985, Careers Tomorrow, 1988, The 1990s and Beyond, 1989, Exploring Your Future: Living, Learning and Working in the Information Age, 1996, The Opportunity Society, 2000, Futuring: The Exploration of the Future, 2003; editl. cons. Nat. Goals Rsch. Staff, 1970, White House Report Toward Balanced Growth, 1970, Russian Acad. Forecasting, 1999—, UNESCO Coun. on the Future, 1999—. Bd. dirs. World Watch Inst., 1974-2000; adv. bd. Inst. for Alternative Futures. Mem. Russian Future Studies Acad. (hon.). Home: 5501 Lincoln St Bethesda MD 20817-3723 Office: World Future Soc 7910 Woodmont Ave Bethesda MD 20814-3002 Office Phone: 301-656-8274. Business E-Mail: ecornish@wfs.org.

CORNISH, GEOFFREY ST. JOHN, golf course architect; b. Winnipeg, Man., Can., Aug. 6, 1914; came to U.S., 1947, naturalized, 1955; m. Carol Burr Gawthrop, Mar. 31, 1951 BSA., U. B.C., Can., 1935; MS, U. Mass., 1952, Dr. Sci. (hon.), 1987. Golf course architect Thompson-Jones & Co., Toronto, Ont., Can., 1935-47; instr. U. Mass., 1947-52; pvt. practice golf course architecture Amherst, Mass., 1952—. Vis. lectr. U. Mass. Co-author: The Golf Course, 1981, rev. edit., 1987, The Architects of Golf, 1993, Golf Course Design, 1998, Eighteen Stakes on a Sunday Afternoon, 2002, Classic Golf Hole Design, 2002; subject of Interview mag., Apr. 1987; contbr. articles to profl. jours. Served to maj. Can. Army, 1940-45 Recipient Disting. Svc. award Golf Course Supts. Am., 1981; named Can. Golf Hall of Fame, 1996. Mem. Am. Soc. Golf Course Architects (pres. 1975, Donald Ross award 1982), Brit. Assn. Golf Course Architects (hon.), Soil Sci. Soc. Am., Sigma Xi, Phi Kappa Phi Episcopalian Home and Office: Fiddlers Grn 1030 S East St Amherst MA 01002-3078

CORNISH, RICHARD JOSEPH, international affairs consultant, retired diplomat; b. Omaha, Nov. 7, 1925; s. Lebbeus Morrison and Lydia Christine (Hermann) Cornish; m. Beverly Anne Cormier, July 28, 1958; children: Pamela Anne, Allyson Juillette, Carolyn Lydia. BA, Yale U., 1949; MA, Am. U., 1965; diploma, U.S. War Coll., 1976. Commd. fgn. svc. officer Dept. State, 1959; 2d sec., vice consul U.S. Embassy, Rangoon, Burma, 1959—62, 2d sec., consul Lome, Togo, 1964—66; regional dir. AID, Savannakhet and Vietiane, Laos, 1967—71; polit. advisor Dept. Def., Frankfurt, Germany, 1973—75, dir. mil. assistance Addis Ababa, Ethiopia, 1975—77; 1st sec. for polit. and econ. affairs U.S. Embassy, Yaounde, Cameroon, 1979—81, 1st sec. polit. affairs London, 1981—85; ret., 1985. Cons. London Diplomatic Assn., 1985—87, The Parvus Co., 1985—90, Trefoil Partnership, Ltd., London, 1987—90, CIA, 1991—98; chmn. bd. dirs. Cornish Assocs., 1987—. Author: The Development of Nationalism in Burma, 1966, The National Decision Making Process, 1975, Deployment of Military Forces, 1975. With USAAF, 1944—46, PTO, lt. col. USAFR, 1949—77. Mem.: Royal Commonwealth Soc., Assn. Asian Studies, Am. Fgn. Svc. Assn., Diplomatic and Consular Officers Ret., RAF Club, Kipling Soc., Rotary (bd. dirs. 1976—77), Yale Club, Univ. Club, Travellers Club, Chevy Chase Club, Masons.

CORNISH, RICHARD POOL, lawyer; b. Evanston, Ill., Sept. 9, 1942; s. William A. and Rita (Pool) C.; children: William Darby, Richard Gordon. BS, Okla. State U., 1964; LLB, U. Okla., 1966. Bar: Okla. 1966, U.S. Dist. Ct. (ea. dist.) Okla. 1969, U.S. Supreme Ct. 1979. Ptnr. Baumert & Cornish, McAlester, Okla., 1967-71, Cornish & Cornish, Inc., McAlester, 1971-77; magistrate U.S. Dist. Ct. for Ea. Dist. Okla., McAlester, 1976—2000; prin. Richard P. Cornish, Inc., McAlester, 1977—. Bd. dirs. McAlester Boys Club, 1970-80, pres., 1974. Capt. JAGC, USAR, 1966-78. Mem. Okla. Bar Assn. (legal aid to servicemen com., legal specialization com.), Pittsburg County Bar Assn., McAlester C. of C. (bd. dirs. 1973-75). Roman Catholic. Home: 611 E Creek Ave Mcalester OK 74501-6929 Office: PO Box 1106 Mcalester OK 74502-1106 Office Phone: 918-423-5070. Business E-Mail: cornish@cwis.net.

CORNISH, THELBERT BERNARD, JR., Internet company executive; b. Atlanta, Nov. 1, 1974; s. Thelberg Bernard Cornish and Kathleen Ross Henderson; stepfather, William L. Fentress; m. Marta Marie Rush, Apr. 22, 1996; children: Thelberg B. III, Solomon R., Jade B., Ashani L. Degree in multidisciplinary studies, N.C. State U., 1995. Cert. Apple server engr., svc. tech., solutions expert. Pres., CEO Eternal Computing, Inc., Raleigh, N.C., 1997-2000, chmn., 2000—; pres., CEO Subspace Wave Corp., Raleigh, 2000—. Musician, disc jockey radio broadcasting Underground 88, WKNC-FMN, 1995. USAF scholar, 1991; N.C. leadership fellow N.C. State U., 1992. Mem. Greater Raleigh C. of C., Coun. for Entrepreneurial Devel. Avocations: reading, design, inventing, wrestling, computers.

CORN-REVERE, ROBERT, lawyer; m. Sigrid Fry-Revere, 1984; children: Nathan Revere, Ian Revere, Jackson Revere, Lauren Revere. BA, Eastern Ill. U., 1977; MA, U. Mass., Amherst, 1980; JD, Catholic U. of Am., 1983. Bar: DC 1983, US Supreme Ct., US Ct. Appeals 2nd, 3rd, 4th & 10th Circuits. Assoc. Steptoe & Johnson, 1983—85, Hogan & Hartson LLP, 1985—90, ptnr., 1994—2003, Davis Wright Tremaine LLP, Washington, 2003—; legal advisor to commr. James H. Quello FCC, 1990—94. Adj. prof. Columbus Sch. Law, Cath. U. of Am., 1987—2001. Bd. trustees Media Inst., 1997—2003; bd. mem. Freedom to Read Found., 2000—02. Office: Davis Wright Tremaine LLP Ste 450 1500 K St NW Washington DC 20005-1272 Office Phone: 202-508-6625. E-mail: bobcornrevere@dwt.com.

CORNSTUBLE, HERMAN LOGAN, retired industrial engineer; b. Wayne City, Aug. 20, 1921; s. Logan Stephen and Mary Cathern (Feeny) C. A in Indsl. Engring. Mgmt., Washington U., St. Louis, 1966, BS in Indsl. Mgmt., 1988. Mfg. indsl. engr. Boring Mfg. Corp., St. Louis, 1956-91. Cons. to univ. students Boring Mfg. Corp., St. Louis. Cpl. U.S. Army, 1943-45, WWII, China, Burma, India; USN, 1952, Korea. Mem. Assembly of God Ch. Achievements include the manufacturing of the first Mercury Space Capsule used in the first American orbital space flight piloted by Lt. Col. John Glenn who completed three orbits around the world which was considered the forerunner of current Moon flight. Home: 699 Covered Bridge Dr Delaware OH 43015-3192

CORNWALL, JOHN MICHAEL, physics professor, consultant; b. Denver, Aug. 19, 1934; s. Paul Bakewell and Dorothy (Zitkowski) C.; m. Ingrid Linderos, Oct. 16, 1965. AB, Harvard U., 1956; MS, U. Denver, 1959; PhD, U. Calif., 1962. NSF postdoctoral fellow Calif. Inst. Tech., Pasadena, 1962-63; mem. Inst. Advanced Study, Princeton, N.J., 1963-65; prof. physics UCLA, 1965—. Vis. prof. Niels Bohr Inst., Copenhagen, 1968—69, Inst. Physique Nucleaire, Paris, 1973—74, MIT, 1974, 87, Rockefeller U., N.Y.C.,

1988; cons. Inst. Theoretical Physics, Santa Barbara, Calif., 1979—80; assoc. Ctr. Internat./Strategic Affairs UCLA, 1987—; dir.'s adv. com. Lawrence Livermore Labs., 1991—, chmn., 2002—; mem. Def. Sci. Bd., 1992—93, mem. task force, 1996; chmn. external rev. com. accelerator oper. and technol. divsn. Los Alamos Nat. Labs., 1995—97, rev. com. advanced hydrodynamics facility, 2001—; adv. bd. Los Alamos Neutron Scattering Ctr., 2000—01; chmn. external rev. com. Ctr. Internat. Security and Arms Control Stanford U., 1996; adv. commn. Accelerator Prodn. Tritium Project, 1997—2000; prof. sci. and policy analysis RAND Grad. Sch., 1998—; sci. and tech. panel Def. Threat Reduction Agy., 2000—02; rev. com. Advanced Accelerator Applications, 2001—02; mem. Missile Def. Agy. Countermeasures White Team, 2001—; tech. adv. group Integrative Grad. Edn. Rsch. and Tng. program in pub. policy and nuc. threat U. Calif., 2003—; chmn. advanced simulations and computing predictive sci. com. Dept. Energy, 2004—; program rev. panel Nat. Ignition Facility Lawrence Livermore Labs., 2005; cons. in field. Author: (with others) Academic Press Ency. of Science and Technology, Union of Concerned Scientists Report on Nat. Missile Def., other encys. and books; contbr. numerous articles to profl. jours. With U.S. Army, 1956—58. Grantee Dept. Energy, NSF, NASA, Dept. Edn.; pre and postdoctoral fellow NSF, 1960-63, A.P. Sloan fellow, 1967-71. Fellow AAAS; mem. Am. Phys. Soc., Am. Geophys. Union, N.Y. Acad. Sci. Avocations: jogging, bicycling, golf, bridge. Office: UCLA Dept Physics & Astronomy Los Angeles CA 90095-0001 Business E-Mail: cornwall@physics.ucla.edu.

CORNWELL, DAVID GEORGE, biochemist, educator; b. San Rafael, Calif., Oct. 8, 1927; s. John Nevius and Nora (Jonasen) C.; m. Normagene Coon, Mar. 14, 1959; children: Karen Sue, David Andrew. BA (hon.), Coll. Wooster, 1950; MA, Ohio State U., 1952; PhD, Stanford U., 1955. NRC fellow Harvard U., 1954-56; faculty Ohio State U., 1956-92, prof. molecular and cellular biochemistry, 1963-92; part-time prof., 1993—; chmn. dept. medical biochemistry Ohio State U., 1965-80, assoc. dean acad. affairs Coll. Medicine, 1979-92, prof. and assoc. dean emeritus, 1992—; mem. nutrition study sect. NIH, 1966-70, nutrition sci. tng. rev. sect., 1970-73; hon. prof. Tongji Med. U., Wuhan, China, 1993—. Mem. editl. bd. Jour. Lipid Rsch., 1962-66, 88-95, Jour. Nutrition, 1969-72; mem. adv. bd. Jour Lipid Rsch., 1974-78, Chem. Abstracts, 1979-84; contbr. articles to profl. jour. Trustee Children's Hosp. Rsch. Found., Columbus, 1982-93. With AUS, 1946-47. Co-recipient hon. mention for rsch. 6th Internat. Congress Hematology, 1956. Mem. Am. Chem. Soc., Am. Soc. Biol. Chemists, Am. Oil Chemists Soc., Am. Inst. Nutrition, Alpha Omega Alpha, Sigma Xi. Presbyterian (elder). Home: 2290 Middlesex Rd Columbus OH 43220-4646 Office Phone: 614-292-7411. E-mail: cornwell.1@osu.edu.

CORNWELL, DAVID JOHN MOORE See LE CARRÉ, JOHN

CORNWELL, EDWARD E., III, surgeon; b. Washington, Nov. 30, 1956; s. Edward E. Cornwell, II and Shirley Cornwell; m. Maggie Burdette Covington, June 24, 1989; 1 child, Michael Elijah. BA, Brown U., 1978; MD, Howard U., 1982. Asst. prof. surgery Howard U., Washington, 1989—93, U. So. Calif., L.A., 1993—97, assoc. prof. surgery, 1998, Johns Hopkins U., Balt., 1998—, assoc. prof. surgery and critical care medicine, 1999—. Chief editor: Multi-Disciplinary Critical Care Knowledge Assessment Program, 1996—98. Pres. Hopkins Injury Prevention and Cmty. Outreach Collaboration, 2000—; Bd. dirs. Police Athletic League, Balt., 1998—; bd. dirs. New Song Cmty. Learning Ctr., Balt., 2001—. Grantee Am. Trauma Soc., 2001, Ctr. for Disease Control and Prevention, 1996, Agy. for Healthcare Policy Rsch., 1993. Mem.: ACS, Soc. Univ. Surgeons, Am. Assn. for Surgery of Trauma, Nat. Med. Assn. (invited William H. Sinkler lectr. 1995, invited William E. Matory lectr. 1997, pres. surg. sect. 2002—), Soc. Black Acad. Surgeons (pres. 2001—), Alpha Omega Alpha. Office: Johns Hopkins Hosp CSIER 625 600 N Wolfe St Baltimore MD 21287

CORNWELL, GIBBONS GRAY, III, retired internist, educator; b. West Chester, Pa., Jan. 17, 1933; s. Gibbons Gray and Eva Chambers (Parke) C.; m. Mary Helen Fortmiller, Sept. 13, 1958; children: Gibbons Gray IV, Heidi Cornwell Trout, Holly Fortmiller. BS, Yale U., 1954; MD, U. Pa., 1963; MA (hon.), Dartmouth Coll., 1993. Diplomate Am. Bd. Internal Medicine, Am. Bd. Hematology. Resident in medicine Hosp. U. Pa., Phila., 1963-64, 65-66; research fellow Cambridge U., Eng., 1964-65; hematology fellow Hosp. U. Pa., Phila., 1966-68; biochemistry fellow Dartmouth Med. Sch., Hanover, N.H., 1968-70, asst. prof. medicine, 1971-74, assoc. prof., 1974-80, prof., 1980-95, prof. pathology, 1990-95, prof. emeritus medicine and pathology, 1995—, assoc. dean student and acad. affairs, 1973-76, chmn. sect. hematology-oncology, 1977-84. Vis. prof. Inst. Immunology, Oslo, 1976-77; dir. clin. rsch. Norris Cotton Cancer Ctr., Hanover, 1978-91; bd. dirs. Cancer and Leukemia Group B, Boston, 1978-91; trustee, chmn. Hitchcock Found., Hanover, 1978-90; staff bd. govs. Mary Hitchcock Meml. Hosp., Hanover, 1981-88; vis. scientist Inst. Pathology/Swedish Med. Rsch. Coun., Uppsala, Sweden, 1987. Contbr. articles to profl. jours. Bd. dirs. Upper Valley Hospice, Lebanon, N.H., 1980; mem. sch. bd. Town of Lyme, N.H., 1973-76, health officer, 1970-74, mem. conservation com., 1970-74, budget com., 1996—; trustee Lyme Found., 1998—, chmn., 2000—. Lt., jet fighter pilot USAF, 1955-59. Clin. rsch. grantee NIH, 1978-91. Fellow ACP; mem. Am. Fedn. Clin. Rsch. (emeritus), Am. Soc. Hematology, N.H. Med. Soc. Republican. Episcopalian. Avocations: bicycling, stamp collecting/philately, whale watching, computer animation, scuba. Home: 1 Orfordville Rd Lyme NH 03768-3305

CORNWELL, JIMMY LEE, not-for-profit developer, consultant, retired military officer; b. Willitts, Calif., Jan. 11, 1933; s. Virgil Lee and Millicent Mae C.; m. Margaret Jane, Jan. 14, 1967; m. Peggy Joyce Tanner, July 27, 1956 (dec. Jan. 26, 1966); children: Cindy Lee, James Nolan. AA, Modesto Jr. Coll., 1952; BS, Ball State U., 1972, MBA, 1974; grad. with honors, Indsl. Coll. Armed Forces, 1974-75. Cert. fundraising exec. Flight comdr., chief trng. USAF, Vietnam, 1969—70, squadron comdr., wing dir. opers. Grissom AFB, Ind., 1971—73; chief nuc. policy Office Joint Chiefs of Staff, Pentagon, Washington, 1975—78; ret. USAF, 1978; sr. v.p., 2d chief tng. Kennedy Sinclaire, Inc., North Haledon, NJ, 1979—89; pres. Cornwell and Assoc., Granite Bay, Calif., 1989—; chief devel. officer U. Calif. Davis Med. Ctr., Sacramento, 1994—98, chief devel. officer, donor asset planning, 1999—2001; ret., 2001. Pres. Planned Giving Forum, Sacramento, 1987-89; mem. planned giving com. McGeorge Sch. Law, Sacramento, 1989-94, Sutter Hosp. Found., Sacramento, 1987-92; presentation spkr. Sons in Retirement (SIRS), 1995-2000, Rotary Club, 1995-2000, Kiwanis Club, 1995-2000, Non-Profit Resource Ctr., Sacramento, 1990-2000. Author: The Planned Giving Guide, 1991; contbr. to newsletter. Mem. adv. bd. Logstar, McClellan AFB, Sacramento, 1997-99. Recipient Outstanding Fundraising Exec. Yr., Nat. Soc. Fundraising Exec., 1997. Mem. Nat. Soc. Fundraising Execs. (trustee, Outstanding Fundraising Exec. of Yr. 1997), Nat. Com. Planned Giving, Air Force Assn., Aircraft Owners and Pilot Assn., Ret. Officers Assn. Republican. Protestant. Avocations: flying, boating, public speaking, bowling, fishing. E-mail: jimcornwell1@earthlink.net.

CORNWELL, LINDA LEE, media specialist; b. Milw., Sept. 4, 1944; d. Charles Robert and Leona Dorothy (Bennett) C. BS in secondary edn., Butler U., 1967, MS in edn., 1975. Cert. Sch. Libr. Media Specialist Endorsement Butler U., 1975. Tchr. Westfield Wash. Sch. Corp., Ind., 1973—76, M.S.D of Wash. Twp., Indpls., 1975—85; cons. Ind. Dept. Edn., Indpls., 1985—99, program mgr., 1987—95, dir., 1998—99; coord. Ind. State Tchrs. Assn., office sch. quality, profl. improvement, 1999—2000, Ind. Dept. Edn., Fed. Goals 2000, 1999—2001; assoc. dir. Scholastic, Inc., N.Y.C., 2001—. Staff developer Devel. Studies Ctr., 1990—2000; mem. to facilitator Ind. Profl. Standards Bd. Early Adolescent Generalist Adv. Group, 1994—96; reading cons. Children's Press and Franklin Watts, 1995—; co-pres. Ind. Staff Devel. Coun., 2001—03; bd. advisors Coll. Edn. Marian Coll., 2004—. Mem. NEA Reading Task Force, 2000, Am. Assn. of Sch. Librs., Task Force, 1994—96, Am. Assn. of Sch. Librs., Tchg. Learning Com., 2001, Am. Assn. of Sch. Librs., Reading for Understanding Com., 2002—03, Young Hoosier Book Award Com., 1988—2000, Am. Assn. of Sch. Librs., Seventh Nat. Conf. Com., 1992—94; chair Am. Assn. of Sch. Librs., Spl. Literacy Task Force, 1992—94, Ind. Staff Devel. Leadership Coun., 1999—2001; bd. mem. Butler U. Bd of Dist. Visitors, Coll. of Edn., 2001—, Ball State U. Bd. of Dist. Visitors, Coll. of Edn., 1999—2001; mem. Newbery Com., 1998; editl. bd. mem. Am. Libr. Assn., 1998—2002; mem. Grolier Pubs. Classroom Adv. Bd., Libr. Adv. Bd., 1995—2001; chair Am. Assn. of Sch. Librs., Sixth Nat. Conf. Com., 1989—92; bd. mem. Mid. Grades Reading Network's Adv. Bd., 1994—98; adv. bd. Coll. Edn., Marion Coll., Indpls., 2003—. Mem. AASL (conf. chmn. Balt. chpt. 1990—), Delta Kappa Gamma. Avocations: travel, reading, theater. Office Phone: 317-566-0634.

CORNWELL, LLOYD D., art educator; s. Lloyd D. Cornwell and Arlene E. Cornwell-Justice; m. Maria L. Cornwell, July 10, 1993; children: Sabrena B., Brett D. AA in Gen. Edn., Chabot C.C., Livermore, Calif., 1989; BA in Art/Design, San Jose (Calif.) State U., 1993; art credential, Calif. State U., Hayward, 1995. Art tchr. Liberty H.S., Brentwood, Calif., 1995—. Mem.: Calif. Art Educators. Republican. Avocation: travel.

CORNWELL, PATRICIA DANIELS, writer; b. Miami, Florida, June 9, 1956; d. Sam and Marilyn Daniels; m. Charles Cornwell, 1980 (div. 1989). BA in English, Davidson Coll., 1979. Police reporter Charlotte Observer, NC, 1979-81; tech writer to computer analyst Office Chief Med. Examiner, Richmond, Va., 1984—90. Author: A Time for Remembering: The Story of Ruth Bell Graham, 1983 (Medallion award), Life's Little Fable, 1999, Food to Die For, 2001, Portrait of a Killer: Jack the Ripper, Case Closed, 2002, (novels) Postmortem, 1990 (only novel ever to simultaneously win Edgar, Creasey, Anthony and Macavity awards), Body of Evidence, 1991, All That Remains, 1992, Cruel and Unusual, 1993, The Body Farm, 1994, From Potter's Field, 1995, Cause of Death, 1996, Hornet's Nest, 1997, Unnatural Exposure, 1997, Point of Origin, 1998, Southern Cross, 1998, Scarpetta's Winter Table, 1998, Black Notice, 1999, The Last Precinct, 2000, Isle of Dogs, 2001, Blow Fly, 2003, Trace, 2004. Vol. police officer. Address: ICM 40 W 57th St Fl 16 New York NY 10019-4001 also: Cornwell Enterprises PO Box 5235 Greenwich CT 06831-0504*

CORNYN, JOHN, senator; b. Houston, Feb. 2, 1952; s. John and Gale Cornyn; m. Sandy Cornyn; children: Danley, Haley. BA in Journalism, Trinity U., 1973; JD, St. Mary's U., 1977; LLM, U. Va., 1995. Cert.: Tex. Bd. Legal Specialization (personal injury trial law). Assoc., ptnr. Groce, Locke & Hebdon, San Antonio, 1977—84; judge 37th Dist. Ct., Bexer County, 1985—90; presiding judge 4th Adminstrv. Jud. Region, 1989—92; justice Supreme Ct. Tex., Austin, 1991—97; atty. Thompson & Knight; atty. gen. State of Tex., Austin, 1999—2002; U.S. senator from Tex., 2002—; mem. Senate Judiciary com. Bd. vis. Trinity U., Pepperdine U. Sch. Law; Tex. Supreme Ct. liaison Bd. Law Examiners, 1991—, Gender Bias Task Force, 1993—95; lectr. CLE programs. Fellow: San Antonio Bar Found., Tex. Bar Found.; mem.: Robert W. Calvent Inn of Ct. (pres. 1994—95), William Sessions Inn of Ct. (master bencher 1988—90, pres. 1989—90), Am. Law Inst. Republican. Ch. Christ. Office: US Senate 517 Hart Senate Office Bldg Washington DC 20510 Office Phone: 202-224-2934. Office Fax: 202-228-2856.*

CORONA, JOSEPH ANTHONY, operations research analyst, mathematician, educator; b. North Miami, Fla., Apr. 28, 1973; s. John Victor and Elizabeth Vance Corona. AA, Broward C.C., 1997; BS with hons. in Math., Fla. Atlantic U., 2000; MS in Ops. Rsch., Fla. Inst. Tech., 2003. Math tutor Broward C.C., Davie, Fla., 1996—98; tchg. asst. Fla. Atlantic U., Boca Raton, Fla., 1998—99; math tutor Palm Beach C.C., Boca Raton, 1999—2000; ops. rsch. analyst TRADOC Analysis Ctr., Fort Lee, Va., 2001—. Mem. math. team Broward C.C., Davie, Fla., 1997. With U.S. Army, 1992—94. Decorated Achievement medal U.S. Army. Mem.: Math. Assn. Am. (assoc.), Golden Key Nat. Honor Soc. (assoc.), Phi Kappa Phi (assoc.). Independent. Avocations: travel, concerts, reading, stained glass art. Home: 231 Crater Woods Court Petersburg VA 23805 Office: TRADOC Analysis Center - Fort Lee 401 First Street Ste 401 Fort Lee VA 23801 Office Phone: 804-765-1814. Personal E-mail: coolio1729@hotmail.com. E-mail: joseph.corona@us.army.mil.

CORONITI, FERDINAND VINCENT, physics professor, astronomy educator; b. Boston, June 14, 1943; s. Samuel Charles and Ethel Marie (Havlik) C.; m. Patricia Ann Smith, Aug. 30, 1969; children: Evelyn Marie, Samuel Thomas. AB, Harvard U., 1965; PhD, U. Calif.-Berkeley, 1969. Rsch. physicist UCLA, 1967-70, asst. prof. physics, 1970-74, assoc. prof., 1974-78, prof. physics and astronomy, 1978—. Cons. TRW Systems Contbr. articles to sci. jours. NASA grantee, 1974, NSF grantee, 1974—. Fellow Am. Geophys. Union, Am. Phys. Soc.; mem. Am. Astron. Soc., Internat. Union Radiol. Sci. Home: 10475 Almayo Ave Los Angeles CA 90064-2301 Office: UCLA Dept Physics & Astronomy 405 Hilgard Ave Los Angeles CA 90095-1547 Office Phone: 310-825-3923. E-mail: coroniti@astro.ucla.edu.

COROTIS, ROSS BARRY, civil engineer, educator, academic administrator; b. Woodbury, N.J., Jan. 15, 1945; s. A. Charles and Hazel Laura (McCloskey) C.; m. Stephanie Michal Fuchs, Mar. 19, 1972; children: Benjamin Randall, Lindsay Sarah. SB, MIT, Cambridge, 1967, SM, 1968, PhD, 1971. Lic. profl. engr., Ill., Md., Colo., structural engr., Ill. Asst. prof. dept. civil engring. Northwestern U., Evanston, Ill., 1971-74, assoc. prof. dept. civil engring., 1975-79, prof. dept. civil engring., 1979-81, Johns Hopkins U., Balt., 1981-82, Hackerman prof., 1982-83, Hackerman prof., chmn. dept. civil engring., 1983-90, Hackerman prof., assoc. dean engring., 1990-94; dean Coll. Engring. and Applied Sci. U. Colo., Boulder, 1994-2001, Denver Bus. Challenge prof., 2001—. Mem. bldg. rsch. bd. Nat. Rsch. Coun., Washington, 1985-88; mem. steering com. Natural Disasters Roundtable, NRC, 2002—; lectr. profl. confs. Editor in chief Internat. Jour. Structural Safety, 1991-2000; contbr. articles to profl. jours. Mem. Mayor's task force City of Balt. Constrn. Mgmt., 1985. Recipient Engring. Tchg. award Northwestern U., 1977, Disting. Engring. Alumnus award U. Colo. Coll. Engring. and Applied Scis., 2000; named Md. Engr. of Yr., Balt. Engrs. Week Coun., 1989; rsch. grantee NSF, Nat. Bur. Stds., U.S. Dept. Energy, 1973-96. Fellow: ASCE (chmn. safety bldgs. com. 1985—89, chmn. tech. adminstrv. com. structural safety and reliability 1988—92, chmn. probabilistic methods com. 1996—98, v.p. Md. chpt. 1987—88, pres. 1988—89, editor Jour. Engring. Mechanics 2004—, Walter L. Huber rsch. prize 1984, Civil Engr. of Yr. award Md. chpt. 1987, Outstanding Educator award Md. chpt 1992); mem.: NAE, Nat. Inst. Bldg. Scis. (mem. multihazard mitigation coun. 2002—, affiliate), Nat. Inst. Stds. and Tech. (panel on assessment 1999, chair panel on bldg. and fire rsch. lab. 2002—), Am. Nat. Stds. Inst. (chmn. live loads com. 1978—84), Am. Concrete Inst. (chmn. structural safety com. 1986—88), Am. Soc. Engring. Edn. (mem. pub. policy com. 1998—2001, mem. deans exec. bd. 1998—2001), Internat. Assn. Structural Safety and Reliability (chair exec. bd. 1998—2001). Office: U Colo Coll Engring & Applied Sci PO Box 428 Boulder CO 80309-0428 Office Phone: 303-735-0539.

CORPORON, JOHN ROBERT, broadcast executive; b. Arcadia, Kans., Mar. 1, 1929; s. George William and Portteus (Stephens) C.; m. Harriett Sloan; children: John Robert Jr., David Sloan. BS in Journalism, U. Kans., 1951, MA in Polit. Sci., 1953. Reporter Pitts. Sun, 1950, UP, New Orleans, 1955, bur. chief Baton Rouge, 1956, New Orleans, 1956-58; correspondent Sta. WDSU-TV, New Orleans, Washington, 1958-60, La. and Miss., 1960-62; news dir. Sta. WDSU-TV-AM, New Orleans, 1962-66; v.p., news dir. Sta. WNEW-TV, Metromedia, N.Y.C., 1967; v.p. news Metromedia TV, N.Y.C., Los Angeles, Washington and Kansas City, 1967-68; v.p., gen. mgr. Sta. WTOP-TV, Washington, 1968-71; exec. prodr. Newsweek Broadcast Svc., 1971-72; v.p., news dir. Sta. WPIX, N.Y.C., 1972-83, sr. v.p., 1983-96. Founding pres. Ind. TV News Assn., 1980; co-founder Ind. Network News, 1980. Spl. reporter London Economist, Washington Post, 1960's. Mem. Park Slope Civic Assn.; trustee William Allen White Found., U. Kans., 1994—; mem. adv. bd. Pew Charitable Trust Project, 1997—; v.p. Overseas Press Club Found., 2000—. Served with U.S. Army, 1953-55. Recipient Nat. Emmy award Acad. Arts and Scis., 1965. Mem. N.Y. State Associated Press Broadcasters (bd. dirs. 1984-96, pres. 1986-87), Radio TV News Dirs. Assn. (bd. dirs. 1988-91), Nat. AP Broadcasters (bd. dirs. 1989-2000, pres. 1995-97), Deadline Club, Overseas Press Club (pres. 1996-98). Democrat. Avocations: jogging, swimming, reading. Home: 671 10th St Brooklyn NY 11215-4501 Office: Overseas Press Club 40 W 45th St New York NY 10036-4202 E-mail: jhcorpny@aol.com.

CORPPETTS, HEZEKIAH, minister, educator; b. Walls, Miss., May 21, 1948; s. Cornelia Corppetts; m. Yvonne Dolores Corppetts, Feb. 1, 1990; children: Hezekiah, Montsho, Shawn, Brittany. BA in Psychology, Park U., 1975; MA in Human Rels., Webster U., 1989; MDiv, Memphis Theol. Sem., 1994, D in Ministry, 2000. Cert. chaplain, clin. pastoral edn. Commd. officer USAF, 1969, advanced through grades to capt., 1981, chief edn. and tng., 1969—89, chief logistics, 1969—89; pastor, moderator St. Andrew Presbytery, Oxford, Miss., 1992—2001; chief of chaplains Northern Ind. Health Care Sys., Marion, Ind., 2001—, Ft. Wayne, Ind., 2001—. Mem. doctoral degree curriculum adv. bd. Memphis Theol. Seminary, Memphis, 1998—2000; mem. Evangelism and ch. devel. com. St. Andrew Presbytery, Oxford, 1998—2001. Author: A Church in Transition, 2000. Decorated Air Force commendation USAF, Chief of Chaplains Meritorious Svc. award; grantee Teen Parent Program grantee, Eli Lilly Corp., Kokomo, Ind., 1990—92. Avocation: basketball. Home: 1700 E 38th St 38 Marion IN 46953 Office: Corppetts Ministries Southaven MS 38671

CORPREW, JAMES CROSBY, management consultant; b. Norfolk, Va., Sept. 8, 1942; s. John Elmer Sr. and Dorothy Ruth (Outlaw) C. BSBA, Old Dominion U., 1969, MBA, 1970; DBA, Miss. State U., 1973; Master in Decision Scis., Ga. State U., 1974. Rsch. asst., teaching asst. Miss. State U., 1970-73; instr.quantitative methods and postdoctoral studies Ga. State U., Atlanta, 1973-74; asst. prof. mgmt. Va. Commonwealth U., Richmond, 1974-75; asst. prof. gen. adminstrn. Cleve. State U., 1975-77; mgr., prin. Cass & Co., Stamford, Conn., 1977-83; mgmt. cons., mgr. Fenvessy & Scwab, Inc., N.Y.C., 1983-84, KPMG, Peat Marwick, N.Y.C., 1984-87; prin. Fairfield Assocs., Bethel, Conn., 1987—. Home: PO Box 6929 Chesapeake VA 23323-0929 Office: Fairfield Assocs 211 Greenwood Ave # 190 Bethel CT 06801-2113

CORPUS, CHRISTINE ANN, voice educator, director; b. St. Louis, Apr. 1, 1968; d. Joseph Leo and Elizaeth Mary Malon; m. Anthony Steven Corpus. BSc in Music Edn., U. Ill., 1989, MSc in Music Edn., 1996. Cert. in Profl. Tchg. Stds. for Early Adolescent and Young Adult Music, Master Music Tchr. (kindergarten through sixth grades) Ill., Master Music Tchr. (sixth through twelfth grades) Ill. Choral dir. Eureka C.U.S.D. 140, Ill., 1989—91, Hillsboro HS, Ill., 1991—98, U. HS, Normal, Ill., 1998—. Finalist 2004 Tchr. of Yr., Ill. State Bd. Edn., Springfield; recipient Those Who Excel award of Excellence, 2004. Mem.: Am. Guild Dirs. Assn., Music Educators Nat. Conf. Avocation: marathons. Office: Univ HS 7100 Ill State Univ Normal IL 61790

CORPUZ, MARCELO NAVARRO, III, lawyer; b. Quezon City, The Philippines, May 22, 1968; came to U.S., 1969; s. Marcelo Barrios and Amy (Navarro) C. BA, Georgetown U., 1990; MPH, JD, George Washington U., 1995. Bar: Ohio 1995, D.C. 1997, Ill. 1998. Rsch. asst. Ctr. Health Policy Rsch., Washington, 1993; law clk. Horty, Springer, & Mattern, Pitts., 1994; assoc. Bricker & Eckler, LLP, Columbus, Ohio, 1995-97, Ross & Hardies, Chgo., 1998-2000, Latham & Watkins, Washington, 2000—. Prof. health law Ill. Inst. Tech., Chgo.-Kent Coll. Law, 2001—. Editl. bd. ABA Health Lawyer; co-author: Ambulatory Surgery Centers: Legal and Regulatory Considerations. Bd. dirs. Asian Am. Profls. Columbus, Asian Am. Cmty. Svcs. Columbus; logistics com. mem. Christmas in April, Columbus, 1996-97. Mem. ABA (Young Lawyers divsn. health law com. planning bd. mem.), Am. Health Lawyers Assn., Asian Am. Bar Assn., Columbus Bar Assn. (immersion com.), Chgo. Bar Assn. Roman Catholic. Avocations: golf, skiing. Office: Latham & Watkins 555 11th St NW Ste 1000 Washington DC 20004-1304 Fax: 312-920-7230. E-mail: marcelo.corpuz@lw.com.

CORR, EDWIN GHARST, ambassador; b. Edmond, Okla., Aug. 6, 1934; s. E.L. and Rowena C.; m. Susanne Springer, Nov. 24, 1957; children: Michelle Ruth, Jennifer Jean, Phoebe Rowena. BS, U. Okla., 1957, MA, 1961, U. Tex., 1969. Fgn. svc. officer Dept. State, Washington, 1961-62; assigned to Mex., 1962-66; Peace Corps dir. Cali, Colombia, 1966-68; Panama desk officer Dept. State, 1969-71; program officer Inter Am. Found., 1971; exec. asst. to amb. Am. Embassy, Bangkok, 1972-75, counselor polit. affairs Quito, Ecuador, 1976, dep. chief of mission, 1977-78; dep. asst. sec. internat. narcotics matters Dept. State, 1978-80; U.S. Amb. to Peru Lima, 1980-81; U.S. Amb. to Bolivia La Paz, 1981-85; U.S. Amb. to El Salvador San Salvador, 1985-88; Dept. State diplomat-in-residence U. Okla., 1988-90, prof. polit. sci., 1990-96; dir. Energy Inst. Ams., 1996—2002; assoc. dir. Internat. Programs Ctr., 1996—. Author: The Political Process in Colombia, 1971; co-editor: Low-Intensity Conflict: Old Threats in a New World, 1992, The Middle East Peace Process: Vision vs. Reality, 2002; co-author: The Search for Security: The U.S. Grand Strategy in the 21st Century, 2003; contbr. to books and profl. jours. Mem. bd. dirs., chair Meml. Inst. for Prevention of Terrorism, Bd. Med. Assistance Programs Internat. Served to capt. USMC, 1957-60. Mem. Am. Fgn. Service Assn. Home: 1617 Jenkins Ave Norman OK 73072-6508 E-mail: ecorr@ou.edu.

CORR, JAMES VANIS, furniture manufacturing executive, accountant; b. Selma, Ala., June 28, 1922; s. Mark Stroud and Julia (Dozier) C.; m. Judith Ann Hackney, Feb. 3, 1971; children by previous marriage: James Jr., William V., Emily S., Julia D. BS, U. Ala., 1948, LLB, 1951. CPA, Ala., Ga. Ptnr. Dent & Corr, CPA's, Birmingham, Ala., 1954-61; exec. v.p. Buck Creek Industries, Inc., Atlanta, 1961-70, pres., 1970-77, also bd. dirs.; v.p. Sperry & Hutchinson Co., N.Y.C., 1976-78, group v.p. furnishings divsn. Atlanta, 1976-78. Pres. JVC Enterprises, Inc., Atlanta, 1978—; speaker tax clinic U. Ala., 1954—. Bd. dirs. Met. YMCA, Birmingham. With AC, USMCR, 1944-46 Decorated D.F.C., Air medal with 2 oak leaf clusters. Mem. Ala. Soc. CPAs (past chmn. Birmingham chpt.), Ga. Soc. CPAs, ABA, Ala. Bar Assn., Am. Inst. CPAs, Ala. Textile Assn., Ga. Textile Assn., Exch. Club (Birmingham), Mountain Brook (Ala., past pres.). Home: 545 River Chase Pt NW Atlanta GA 30328-3555

CORR, PETER B., pharmaceutical executive; B, Union U.; D, Georgetown U. Asst. prof. medicine and pharm. Wash. U., 1977—83, assoc. prof., 1983—88, prof. cardiology and molecular biology, 1988; pres. Discovery Rsch. Monsanto/Searle; pres. pharm. rsch. & devel. Warner-Lambert Co., corp. v.p.; sr. v.p., exec. v.p. global rsch. & devel., pres. worldwide devel. Pfizer, Inc., N.Y.C., 2000—02, sr. v.p. sci. and tech., 2002—. Mem. editl. bd.: Am. Jour. Physiology, Jour. Cardiovascular Electrophysiology, assoc. editor: Circulation, Cardiology in Rev.; contbr. articles to profl. jours. Recipient Brit. Cardiac award, Gordon Moe award, 1994. Mem.: Alpha Omega Alpha. Office: Pfizer Inc 235 E 42d St New York NY 10017

CORRADA DEL RIO, BALTASAR, lawyer, former state supreme court justice; b. Morovis, PR, Apr. 10, 1935; s. Romulo and Ana Maria (del Rio) Corrada del R.; m. Beatrice Betances, Dec. 24, 1959; children: Ana Isabel, Francisco Javier, Juan Carlos, Jose Baltasar. BA in Social Scis., U. PR, 1956, JD, 1959. Bar: PR, 1959. Ptnr. McConnell Valdes Sifre & Ruiz Suria, San Juan, PR, 1959-75; atty., chmn. Civil Right Commn., PR, 1970-72; mem., resident commr. from PR 95th-98th Congress; mayor City of San Juan, 1985-89; atty. Baltasar Corrada Law Office, 1989-92; sec. of state Govt. of PR, 1993-95; assoc. justice PR Supreme Ct., 1995—2005; prin. McConnell Valdés law, San Juan, PR, 2005—. Pres. New Progressive Party, 1986-89. Pres. editl. bd. PR Human Rights Rev., 1971-72. Bd. dirs. PR Teleradial Inst. Ethics. Recipient Great Cross of Civil Merit of Spain King Juan Carlos I, 1987. Mem. ABA, Fed. Bar Assn., PR Bar Assn., Exch. Club, San Juan Rotary. Roman Catholic. Office: McConnell Valdés 270 Muñoz Rivera Avenue San Juan PR 00918 Office Phone: 787-759-9292.

CORRADINI, DEEDEE, real estate company executive, former mayor; Student, Drew U., 1961—63; BS, U. Utah, 1965, MS, 1967. Adminstrv. asst. for pub. info. Utah State Office Rehab. Svcs., 1967-69; cons. Utah State Dept.

Cmty. Affairs, 1971-72; media dir., press sec. Wayne Owens for Congress Campaign, 1972; press sec. Rep. Wayne Owens, 1973-74; spl. asst. to N.Y. Congl. Rep. Richard Ottinger, 1975; asst. to pres., dir. cmty. rels. Snowbird Corp., 1975-77; exec. v.p. Bonneville Assocs., Inc., Salt Lake City, 1977-80, pres., 1980-89, chmn., CEO, 1989-91; mayor Salt Lake City, 1992—2000; prin. Corradini & Co., Salt Lake City, 2000—; sr. v.p. Prudential Utah Real Estate, 2004—. Pres. U.S. Conf. of Mayors, 1998—, mem. unfunded fed. mandates task force, mem. crime and violence task force; chair Mayor's Gang Task Force; mem. intergovtl. policy adv. com. U.S. Trade Rep., 1993-94, 99—; mem. transp. and comm. com. Nat. League of Cities, 1993-94. Bd. trustees Intermountain Health Care, 1980-92; bd. dirs., exec. com. Utah Symphony, 1983-92, vice chmn., 1985-88, chmn., 1988-92; dir. Utah chpt. Nat. Conf. Christians and Jews, Inc., 1988; bd. dirs. Salt Lake Olympic Bid Com., 1989—; chmn. image com. Utah Partnership for Edn. and Econ. Devel., 1989-92; co-chair United Way Success by 6 Program; pres. Shelter of the Homeless Com.; active Sundance Inst. Utah Com., 1990-92; disting. bd. fellow So. Utah U., 1991; v.p. Internat. Women's Forum, co-chair program com.; trustee Am. Comm. Sch., Beirut; vice-chair 2012 Bid Selection Com., U.S. Olympic Com.; active numerous other civic orgns. and coms. Fellow Disting. sr. fellow in Urban Studies, Richard Riley Inst. Govt., Politics and Pub. Adminstrn., Furman U., 2000—. Mem. Salt Lake Area C. of C. (bd. govs. 1979-81, chmn. City/County/Govt. com. 1976-86). Democrat.

CORRAL, CELESTINO, electrical engineer, researcher; b. Havana, Cuba, Apr. 28, 1962; s. Celestino and Lydia Corral; m. Dunia Hernandez, July 26, 1992; children: Daniel, Lydia. PhD, U. Miami, 1993. Mem. tech. staff Sandia Nat. Laboratories, Albuquerque, 1988—90; assoc. staff engr. Scientific-Atlanta, 1994—97; sr. staff engr. Origin Data Systems, Boca Raton, Fla., 1997—98; sr. mem. tech. staff Motorola, Plantation, Fla., 1998—2003; disting. mem. tech. staff Freescale Semiconductor, Inc., Boca Raton, 2003—. Cons. Sociocybernetics, Inc., Miami, 1992—97. Mem.: Alpha Epsilon Lambda (pres. 1992—93), Eta Kappa Nu, Tau Beta Pi. Conservative. Achievements include patents pending in the field of wireless communications. Avocations: bicycling, classical music, reading. Office Phone: 561-434-9530.

CORREA, NEREIDA, women's health physician; b. P.R., 1946; married. AAS, Bronx C.C., 1966; BS, L.I. U., 1977; MA in Nursing Edn., NYU, 1979; MD in Psychopharmacology, Albert Einstein Sch. Medicine, 1985. Numerous positions as staff nurse, nurse educator and adminstr.; nurse educator Manpower and Career Devel. Agy., N.Y.C., 1968—71; instr., counselor L.I. Physician's Asst. Program, 1971—78; asst. prof. maternal-child health nursing Medgar Evers Coll., 1978—82; resident in family practice Montefiore Med. Ctr., 1985—88, resident in ob-gyn., 1990—93. Nurse Internat. Health Outreach, Kosovo, HIV/AIDS care and women's health problems, N.Y.C.; mem. women's, infants' and children's nat. adv. com. Dept. Agr. and Women's Health Steering Com., Health Resources and Svcs. Adminstr., U.S. Dept. Health and Human Svcs. Selected as part of, NIH's "Changing the Face of Medicine" exhbn., 2003. Fellow: Am. Coll. Ob-Gyn.; mem.: Nat. Hispanic Med. Assn. (adv. com.), N.Y. State Acad. Family Practice (chairperson leadership commn.). Office: Lincoln Hosp 234 E 149th St Bronx NY 10451 Office Phone: 718-549-5830.

CORREALE, ROBERT D., lawyer; b. Morristown, N.J., Jan. 30, 1955; s. Salvatore Gerald and Edith Jean Correale; m. Margaret Alice Correale, Nov. 16, 1985; children: Catherine, Mary. BS, Trenton State Coll., 1977; JD, Ohio No. U., 1982. Bar: N.J. 1982, U.S. Dist. Ct. N.J. 1981, U.S. Ct. Appeals (3d cir.) 1989. Asst. pros. Somerset County Pros.'s Office, Somerville, N.J., 1981-84; assoc. Cohen & Kron, Succasunna, N.J., 1984-88; ptnr. Kron & Correale, Succasunna, N.J., 1988-2001, Maynard and Truland LLC, Morristown, N.J., 2001—. Mem. ABA, ATLA, Morris County BAr Assn., Nat. Dist. Atty.'s Assn., Morris County Mcpl. Pros.'s Assn., KC. Republican. Roman Catholic. Avocations: tennis, travel, history. Office: Maynard and Truland LLC 6 Dumont Pl Morristown NJ 07960

CORREA-PEREZ, JUAN RAMON, embryologist, researcher; b. San Juan, Pr, May 3, 1968; s. Juan Antonio Correa-Matos and Isabel Perez-Marquez; m. Nirma Aixa Corchado-Pastor, Dec. 19, 1998; 1 child, Fernando Juan Antonio Correa-Corchado. BS cum laude, U. Puerto Rico-Mayaguez Campus, 1991; MS, U. Ky., 1991, PhD, 1997. Cert. Lab. Dir. Am. Assn. Bioanalysts, 2004. Rsch. asst., reproductive physiology U. Ky., Lexington, Ky., 1991—96, post-doctoral fellow, reproductive physiology-medicinal chemistry pharm., 1994—97; andrology lab. dir. Centro de Fertilidad del Caribe, Rio Piedras, PR, 1998—99, sci. dir., 1999—; assoc. prof. physiology/pathology San Juan Bautista Sch. Med, Caguas, PR, 2004—; pres., co-founder Andrology Consultants, Inc., Caguas, 2004—. Ad hoc rev. Theriogenology, Gainesville, Fla., 1997—, Mid. East Fertility Soc., Cairo, Fertility and Sterility, 2005; assoc. mem., instl. animal care and use com. (IACUC) San Juan Bautista Sch. Med., 2004—; columnist-male reproductive health Bus. PR Mag., San Juan, PR, 2004—, El Vocero Newspaper, San Juan, PR, 2004—; develop. support groups-male issues Andrology Consultants, Inc., Caguas, PR, 2004—; lect. PR Urol. Assn., San Juan, PR, 2005—; lectr. Endometriosis Support Group-Ponce Sch. Medicine, 2005—, Coll. Med. Technologists-Puerto Rico, Guaynabo, 2005—. Founder Andrology Consultants, Inc., Caguas, PR, 2004—05. Mem.: Am. Assn. Bioanalysts (life), Am. Assn. Bioanalysts' Coll. Reproductive Biology (life), Reproductive Lab. Technologists Profl. Group-American Soc. for Reproductive Medicine (life), Soc. Assisted Reproductive Tech. (life), Am. Soc. Reproductive Medicine (life), NY Acad. Sciences (life), Am. Soc. Andrology (life), Golden Key Nat. Honor Soc. (life), Gamma Sigma Delta (life). Catholic. Achievements include research in Development and adaptation of a physiological test for frozen-thawed sperm membrane based on swelling of the sperm tail; Development of vaginal contraceptives based on spermicides consisting of nonoxynol-9 and iodine with anti-HIV properties; Development of tablet/capsule delivery systems for vaginal contaceptives consisting of spemicides with anti-HIV properties; Development of standardized methods for sperm processing based on the swim-up effect; Methods for increasing the quantity and quality of human semen for purposes of infertility therapy; Incorporation of the colloid osmotic pressure effect to improve the selection of healthy spermatozoa for use in invitro fertilization; Assessment of factors contributing to the occurrence of epididymal necrospermia-a condition characterized by high levels of dead sperm in semen. Avocations: basketball, astronomy, reading, movies, history. Home: PO Box 30810 San Juan PR 00929-1810 Office: Andrology Consultants Inc PO Box 30810 San Juan PR 00929-1810 Office Phone: 787-453-0909. Home Fax: 787-750-0888; Office Fax: 787-750-0888. Personal E-mail: dr_andologo@yahoo.com. E-mail: dr_andrologo@yahoo.com.

CORREDOR, MARY B., director, language educator; b. Fairbury, Ill. d. Agnes K. Runyon; 1 child, Erik. MA, Ill. State U., 1976; MA TESOL, Am. U., Washington, 1996. Lectr. Spanish, ESL, and pedagogy Sul Ross State U., Alpine, Tex., 1996-98; dept. chair ESL Austin (Tex.) C.C., 1998—. Freelance translator, Austin, 1999—. Mem. TESOL, Austin Translators and Interpreters Assn., Am. Assn. Tchrs. of Spanish and Portuguese. Office: Austin CC-Rio Grande Campus 1212 Rio Grande Austin TX 78701 Home: 2702 Deeringhill Dr Austin TX 78745-5112 E-mail: mcorredo@austin.cc.tx.

CORREIA, JOAQUIM JOSE, physician; b. Portugal, July 29, 1960; MD, NYU, 1986. Resident Columbia-Presbyn. Med. Ctr., N.Y.C., 1986-89, with, 1993—; dir. cardiac care unit St. James Hosp., Newark. Asst. prof. medicine N.J. Med. Sch., Newark, 1995—. Cardiology fellow Columbia-Presbyn. Med. Ctr., 1989—. Mem. Am. Coll. Physicians. Office: 243 Chestnut St 2L Newark NJ 07105 also: Cardiac Care Unit St James Hosp Newark NJ 07105 Office Phone: 973-589-8668. Personal E-mail: jcdccorreia@comcast.net.

CORRELL, ALSTON DAYTON, JR., (PETE CORRELL), forest products company executive; b. Brunswick, Ga., Apr. 28, 1941; s. Alston Dayton and Elizabeth (Flippo) Correll; m. Ada Lee Fulford, June 23, 1963; children: Alston Dayton, Elizabeth Lee. BSBA, U. Ga., 1963; MS in Pulp and Paper Tech., U. Maine, 1966, MS in Chem. Engring., 1967. Tech. svc. engr. Westvaco, 1963—64; instr. U. Maine, Orono, 1964—67; various pulp and paper mgmt. positions Weyerhaeuser Co., 1967—77; pres. paperboard divsn. Mead Corp., Dayton, Ohio, 1977—80, group v.p. paperboard, 1980, group v.p. paper, 1981, group v.p. forest products, 1981—83, sr. v.p. forest products, 1983—88; sr. v.p. pulp and printing paper Ga.-Pacific Corp., Atlanta, 1988—89, exec. v.p. pulp and paper, 1989—91, pres., COO, 1991—93, pres., CEO, 1993, CEO, chmn. bd. and pres., 1993—. Bd. dirs. SunTrust Banks, Atlanta, SunTrust Banks, Inc., SunTrust Banks Ga., Inc., Mirant Corp., Norfolk Southern Corp.; chmn. Inst. Paper Sci. and Tech., Inc.; bd. councilors The Carter Coun. Trustee U. Ga. Found., Robert W. Woodruff Arts Ctr.; mem. Atlanta coun. Boy Scouts Am.; mem. Atlanta Action Forum; mem. exec. com. Nat. Coun. Paper Industry for Air and Stream Improvement, Inc., past chmn. bd.; bd. dirs. Miami Valley (Ohio) Boy Scouts, Nature Conservancy, Keep Am. Beautiful Inc.; Ga. Rsch. Alliance; chmn. United Negro Coll. Fund, vice chmn. Atlanta Campaign; bd. dirs. Ctrl. Atlanta Progress, chmn., 1995—97. Named CEO of Yr., Atlanta Bus. League, 1998, Exec. Papermaker of Yr., PaperAge, 1999; named one of 100 Most Influential Georgians, Ga. Trend Mag., 1994, 1995, 25 Most Influential Georgians, 1996, 1997, 1998; recipient Nat. Brotherhood award, 1991, Disting. Alumnus award, U. Ga., Terry Coll. Bus., 1994, Salute to Greatness award, The King Ctr., 1999. Mem.: Am. Forest and Paper Assn. (bd. dirs., forest resource product group exec. com.), Atlanta C. of C. (bd. dirs., Forward Atlanta Policy Group, chmn. 1997—98), Ga. C. of C. (bd. dirs.), Commerce Club (bd. dirs. Atlanta chpt.). Republican. Presbyterian. Office: Ga-Pacific Corp PO Box 105605 133 Peachtree St NE Fl 51 Atlanta GA 30303-1808*

CORRELL, CHRISTOPH U., psychiatrist, researcher; b. Hamburg, Germany, June 9, 1966; MD, Free U.-Berlin, 1993. Cert. gen. psychiatry Am. Bd. Psychiatry and Neurology, 2002, child and adolescent psychiatry Am. Bd. Psychiatry and Neurology, 2003. Neurology resident Neurologische Klinik, Bad Neustadt, Germany, 1995—97; psychiatry intern Beth Israel Med. Ctr., N.Y.C., 1997—98; psychiatry resident: pgy-2, pgy-3, pgy-4 (chief and rsch. residency) Hillside Hosp., Glen Oaks, N.Y., 1998—2001; child and adolescent psychiatry fellow Schneider Children's Hosp., New Hyde Park, N.Y., 2001—03; rsch. psychiatrist The Zucker Hillside Hosp., Glen Oaks, 2003—. Co-dir. advanced ctr. for intervention and svcs. rsch. knowledge transfer unit The Zucker Hillside Hosp., Glen Oaks, 2004. Author: (presentation) NIMH-sponsored New Clinical Drug Evaluation Unit Meeting (New Investigator award for Outstanding Rsch. Submission, 2001), scientific article, numerous sci. articles (Charlotte Marker Zitrin, MD Paper award for Best Rsch. Paper, 2001, Am. Assn. of Directors of Psychiat. Residency Tng. Peter Henderson, M.D., Meml. Paper award for Best Paper, 2002), research study. Recipient Outstanding Resident award, Hillside Hosp. Dept. Psychiatry, 2001, First Prize for Outstanding Achievement in Med. Writing, L.I. Jewish Med. Ctr., 2001, Rsch. Colloquium for Jr. Investigators award, Am. Psychiat. Assn., 2002, John and Maxine Bendheim Fellowship award for Rsch., Schneider Children's Hosp., 2003, Pfizer Psychiatry Resident of Yr., Tng. Internat. Medical Grad. Mentorship Program award in Psychiatry, Am. Assn. Dirs. Psychiatric Residency, Young Scientist award for Excellence in Sci. Rsch., 11th Biennial Winter Workshop on Schizophrenia, Presdl. Scholar award for Outstanding Rsch. Achievements, Am. Assn. Child and Adolescent Psychiatry; fellow Clin. Rsch. Methodology Workshop Fellowship award, Am. Soc. Clin. Psychopharmacology, 2002. Mem.: Am. Assn. Dirs. of Psychiat. Residency Tng., Am. Acad. Child and Adolescent Psychiatry (Presdl. Scholar award 2003, Pilot Rsch. award 2004, George Ginsberg Fellowship award for Outstanding Achievement in Edn. and Tchg. 2003), Am. Psychiat. Assn. (Resident Rsch. award for exceptional unpublished manuscript 2002). Achievements include listing in the Guide to America's Top Psychiatrists by the Consumers Rsch. Coun. Am. Office: The Zucker Hillside Hospital 75-59 263rd St Glen Oaks NY 11004 Office Phone: 718-470-4812. Business E-Mail: ccorrell@lij.edu.

CORRELL, LARRY GORDON, music educator; b. Borger, Tex., July 18, 1949; s. Claude Larry Gilchrist and Lois Estelle Reuss, Lewis Allen Correll (Stepfather); m. Sue Ellen Christian, Aug. 6, 1994. B in Pub. Sch. Music, Concordia Coll., 1971; M in Music Edn., SW Tex. State U., 1979; M in Ch. Music, Shenandoah U., 1998. Band dir. Staples H.S., Minn., 1971—77, Canyon H.S., New Braunfels, Tex., 1977—85, Comal ISD, New Braunfels, Tex., 1984—87, Sequin High Sch., 1987—89, Mexia High Sch., Mexia, 1989—91, Floresville High Sch., 1991—93, Augusta County Schools, Fort Defiance, Va., 1993—2000, Loudoun County Sch., Leesburg, Va., 2001—. Organist Sacred Heart Cath. Ch., Staples, Minn., 1971—77; min. of music St. Paul's Luth. Ch., New Braunfels, Tex., 1977—85; percussion instr. Tex. Luth. Coll. Band Camp, Seguin, Tex., 1983—85; dir. Lions of Tex. All State Band, San Antonio, 1983—90; asst. dir. Tex. Luth. Coll. Band Camp, Seguin, 1986—89; min. of music St. Andrews Luth. Ch., Canyon Lake, Tex., 1993—98; organist St. Paul's United Meth. Ch., Staunton, Va., 1993—2000; organ cons. Massnetta Worship Conf., Harrisonburg, Va., 1995—95; cons. Ch. Music Inst., Winchester, 1998—2000; min. of music St. Mark's Luth. Ch., Hagertown, Md., 2001. Composer: (hymns and music for organ) Joi for Two Trumpets, Servants of the Lord, 1994. Mem. Lions Club, Floresville, Tex., 1988—90. Recipient Grad. Assistantship, SW Tex. State U., 1977—79. Mem.: Va. Educators Assn., Tex. Music Educators Assn., Tex. Band Masters Assn., Percussive Arts Soc., Va. Band and Orch. Dir. Assn., Va. Music Educators Assn., Am. Guild Organists, Am. Luth. Ch. Musicians, Music Educators Nat. Conf. Lutheran. Avocations: theater, travel. Home: 111 Settlers Cir Winchester VA 22602 Office: Loudoun County Sch JL Simpson MS 490 Evergreen Mill Rd SE Leesburg VA 20175 Personal E-mail: correll@visawalllink.com. E-mail: lcorrell@loudoun.k12.va.us.

CORRENTE, ROBERT CLARK, prosecutor; BA, Dartmouth Coll., 1978; JD, NYU, 1981. Mng. ptnr. Corrente, Brill & Kusinitz, Providence, 1985—98; ptnr. Hinckley, Allen & Snyder, Providence, 1998—2004; US atty. dist. RI US Dept. Justice, 2004—. Chair RI Judicial Nom. Commn., 1998—2000; ethics adv. bd. RI Supreme Ct., 1997, chair, 2000. Office: US Atty Fleet Ctr 50 Kennedy Plz 8th Fl Providence RI 02903

CORRERO, ANTHONY JAMES, III, lawyer; b. Monroe, La., Dec. 15, 1941; s. Anthony James Jr. and Robbie Lee (Pace) C.; m. Margaret Aline O'Meara, May 30, 1966; children: Margaret Hollis, Edward Thomas Eliot, Marshall Alan. BA, N.E. La. U., 1962; LLB, La. State U., 1965. Bar: La. 1965, U.S. Supreme Ct. 1968. Spl. asst. atty. gen. State of La., Baton Rouge, 1965-68; assoc. Jones, Walker, Waechter, Poitevent, Carrere & Denegre, New Orleans, 1968-72, ptnr., 1972-94, Correro, Fishman & Casteix, LLP, New Orleans, 1994-96, Correro Fishman Haygood Phelps Walmsley & Casteix, LLP, New Orleans, 1996—. Adj. prof. law La. State U., Tulane U., Loyola U.; bd. dirs. T.L. James & Co., Inc., Ruston, La., La. Partnership for Tech. 1st lt. USAR, 1965-71. Mem. ABA, La. Bar Assn. (chmn. sect. corp. and bus. law 1978-79), Am. Law Inst. Democrat. Roman Catholic. Office: Correro Fishman et al 201 Saint Charles Ave New Orleans LA 70170-4600 Office Phone: 504-586-5252. Business E-Mail: acorrero@cfhlaw.com.

CORRIERE, JULES, playwright, theater director; b. Opelousas, La., Jan. 6, 1968; d. John James and Catherine Julianne Curry; m. John Martin Corriere, Oct. 31, 1992; children: Cassidy Johanna, Ian Joshua. Student, Christopher Newport U., 1993—96. Asst. dir. Yoder Barn Theater, Newport News, Va., 1997—99; assoc. artist Cmty. Performance, Inc., Chgo., 1998—. Ptnr. Cmty. Performance, Inc., Chgo., 2001—. Editor: Long Ago Gone; author: (plays) Let My People Go (Performed At Kennedy Ctr., 2003), Guns, Knives, Wives, and Miscellaneous, Turn the Washpot Down (Named by Legislature as South Carolina's Ofcl. Folk Life Play, 2003), The Lost Ranch, Nuthin' But A Will, 2005, Deep Enough to Swallow Me Whole, A Night at the Barn, Talking Trash, American Voices, Little Victories, Old Time Radio Christmas, Storylines, Between The Arrows; co-author Swamp Gravy: Brothers and Sisters; author: (monthly radio show) Whatcha Know Good?; dir.: (plays) Standing Like Angels, Plowing Outback, Hand Me Down Shoes, Pieced Together, Whistle Stop: Etowah, Grit and Grace, Slew Water Stories, Moffat Memories. Asst. leader Girl Scouts of Colonial Coast, Newport News, 2002—04. Recipient Presdl. award, Points of Light Found., 2002. Avocations: writing, listening to a community's stories, travel. Home: 1245 Patrick Lane Newport News VA 23608 Office: Community Performance Inc 5611 North Winthrop 1-A Chicago IL 60660 Office Phone: 773-728-3999. Personal E-mail: jcorriere@aol.com.

CORRIGAN, E(DWARD) GERALD, investment banker; b. Waterbury, Conn., 1941; BS, Fairfield U.; MA, PhD, Fordham U. Group v.p. mgmt. and planning Fed. Res. Bank of N.Y., 1976-80; spl. assignment to chmn. bd. govs. Fed. Res. Sys., 1979-80; pres. Fed. Res. Bank of Mpls., 1981-84, Fed. Res. Bank of N.Y., N.Y.C., 1985-93; chmn. internat. advisors Goldman, Sachs & Co., N.Y.C., 1994-96, mng. dir., 1997—. Co-chair The Bretton Woods Com., The Per Jacobsson Found., The Group of Thirty, The Inst. for Fin. Stability, Bank for Internat. Settlements, The Trilateral Commn., Aspen Inst. Program on the World Economy, Internat. Adv. Panel of Monetary Authority of Singapore. Mem. Aspen Inst. (co-chmn.), Econ. Club of N.Y. Office: Goldman Sachs and Co 85 Broad St New York NY 10004-2456

CORRIGAN, HELEN GONZALEZ, retired cytologist; b. San Diego, Tex., Sept. 30, 1922; d. Rodrigo Simon and Eva Ruby (Corrigan) Gonzalez. BS, Our Lady of Lake, San Antonio, 1943. Registered cytologist Internat. Acad. Cytology. Tchr. San Diego HS, 1943-45; microbiologist Nix Hosp. Profl. Lab., San Antonio, 1952-59; med. technologist Tucson Med. Ctr., 1959-60; cytologist in charge Jackson-Todd Cancer Detection Ctr., San Antonio, 1961-64; cytologist in charge cytology sect. Pathology Lab. 4th and 5th U.S. Army Ref. Area Lab., Ft. Sam Houston, Tex., 1964-78; instr. trouble shooters, quality control analyst cytology sect. Brooks Med. Ctr., Fort Sam Houston, 1978-81; owner Corrigan Enterprises, San Diego, 1981-91; ret., 1997. Cytologist Waco (Tex.) Med. Lab. Svc., Waco, 1988—89, Nat. Health Lab., San Antonio, 1989—90, Internat. Cancer Screening Lab., San Antonio, 1990—91; head cytologist Dr. R. Garza & Assocs., Weslaco, Tex., 1992—. Adv. bd. mem. EEO, Ft. Sam Houston, 1972—74. Mem.: NAFE, Am. Soc. Clin. Pathologists (assoc. registered cytologist, registered med. technologist), Greater San Antonio Women's C. of C. Republican. Roman Catholic. Avocations: fishing, hunting, tennis, skiing, dance. Home: 149 Perry Ct San Antonio TX 78209-6211

CORRIGAN, JAMES JOHN, JR., pediatrician, educator, dean; b. Pitts., Aug. 28, 1935; BS, Juniata Coll., Huntingdon, Pa., 1957; MD, U. Pitts., 1961. Diplomate Am. Bd. Pediats. (hematology-oncology). Intern, then resident in pediat. U. Colo. Med. Ctr., 1961-64; trainee in pediat. hematology-oncology U. Ill. Med. Center, 1964-66; assoc. in pediat. Emory U. Med. Sch., 1966-67, asst. prof. Atlanta, 1967-71; mem. faculty U. Ariz. Coll. Medicine, Tucson, 1971-90, prof. pediat., 1974-90; chief sect. pediat. hematology-ongology, also dir. Mountain States Regional Hemophilia Ctr., U. Ariz., Tucson, 1978-90; chief of staff U. Med. Ctr. U. Ariz., Tucson, 1984-86; prof. pediat., vice dean for acad. affairs Tulane U. Sch. Medicine, New Orleans, 1990-93, interim dean, 1993-94, dean, 1994-2000, v.p., 2000—02, prof. emeritus pediat., 2002—; clin. prof. pediat. U. Ariz. Coll. Medicine, Ariz., 2003—. Assoc. editor Am. Jour. Diseases of Children, 1981-89, 90-93, interim editor, 1993; contbr. numerous papers to med. jours. Grantee NIH, Mountain States Regional Hemophilia Ctr., Ga. Heart Assn., GE, Am. Cancer Soc. Mem. Am. Acad. Pediatrics, Am. Soc. Hematology, Soc. Pediatric Rsch., Western Soc. Pediatric Rsch., Am. Heart Assn. (coun. thrombosis), Internat. Soc. Thrombosis and Haemostasis, Am. Pediatric Soc., World Fedn. Hemophilia, Pima County Med. Soc. (v.p., 1986—, pres. 1988—), Alpha Omega Alpha. Republican. Roman Catholic. Office: Univ Ariz Health Scis Ctr Dept Pediatrics 1501 N Campbell Ave Tucson AZ 85724 Business E-Mail: jcorrig@tulane.edu.

CORRIGAN, JANET M., health science association administrator; MBA, M in Cmty. Health, U. Rochester; M in Indsl. Engring., U. M in Indsl. Engring., PhD in Health Svcs. Orgn. and Policy, U. Mich. V.p. planning and devel. Nat. Com. for Quality Assurance, 1991-95; prin. rschr. Ctr. for Studying Health Sys. Change Robert Wood Johnson Found., 1995—98; exec. dir. consumer protection and quality in health care industry Pres.'s Advisory Commn., 1998; dir. Health Care Svcs. Bd. Inst. Medicine of Nat. Academies, 1998—. Office: Inst Medicine Nat Acad Scis Health Care Svcs 500 5th St, NW, Rm 760 Washington DC 20418-0007 Fax: 202-334-1463. E-mail: jcorriga@nas.edu.

CORRIGAN, JOHN EDWARD, JR., retired banker, lawyer; b. Chgo., Sept. 26, 1922; s. John Edward and Veronica (Mulvey) C.; m. Eileen Williams, Nov. 4, 1950 (div. 1979); m. Sylvia Dennison McElin, Sept. 24, 1983. BA, Harvard U., 1943, JD, 1949. Bar: Ill. 1950. With First Nat. Bank Chgo., 1949-79, asst. v.p., 1960-61, v.p., 1961-72, sr. v.p., 1972-79; prin. Hedberg, Tobin, Flaherty & Whalen P.C., Chgo., 1980-87; of counsel Hedberg, Tobin, Flaherty & Whalen Inc., Chgo., 1988-92. Asst. atty., 1954—59. With AUS, 1943-46, 51-52. Home: 560 Greenwood Ave Kenilworth IL 60043-1024 Personal E-mail: jscorrigan@comcast.net.

CORRIGAN, MAURA DENISE, state supreme court justice; b. Cleve., June 14, 1948; d. Peter James and Mae Ardell (McCrone) Corrigan; m. Joseph Dante Grano, July 11, 1976 (dec.). BA with hon., Marygrove Coll., 1969; JD with hon., U. Detroit, 1973; LLD (hon.), No. Mich. U., 1999, Mich. State U., 2003; JD (hon.), Mercy Law Sch., 2002, Ea. Mich. U., 2004, Schoolcraft Coll., 2005. Bar: Mich. 1974. Jud. clk. Mich. Ct. Appeals, Detroit, 1973—74; asst. prosecutor Wayne County, Detroit, 1974—79, asst. U.S. atty., 1979—89, chief appellate divsn., 1979—86, chief asst. U.S. Atty., 1986—89; ptnr. Plunkett & Cooney PC, Detroit, 1989—92; judge Mich. Ct. Appeals, 1992—98, chief judge, 1997—98; justice Mich. Supreme Ct., Detroit, 1999—, chief justice, 2001—04. Vice chmn. Mich. Com. to formulate Rules of Criminal Procedure, Mich. Supreme Ct., 1982-89; mem. Mich. Law Revision Commn., 1991-98; mem. com. on standard jury instrns., State Bar Mich., 1978-82; lectr. Mich. Jud. Inst., Sixth cir. Jud. Workshop, Inst. CLE, ABA-Cin. Bar Litigation Sects., Dept. Justice Advocacy Inst.; v.p. Conf. Chief Justices, 2003-04; bd. dirs. Vista Maria, Internat. Ctr. Healing and Law. Co-author book on civil procedure; contbr. chpt. to book, articles to legal revs. Vice chmn. Project Transition, Detroit, 1976-92; mem. citizens Adv. Coun. Lafayette Clinic, Detroit, 1979-87; bd. dirs. Detroit Wayne County Criminal Advocacy Program, 1983-86; pres., bd. dirs. Rep. Women's Bus. and Profl. Forum, 1991; mem. Pew Commn. on Children in Foster Care, 2003-05. Named disting. Alumna, Marygrove Coll., 2003, U. Detroit Mercy Law Sch., 2004, Detroit News Michiganian of Yr., 2005; recipient award of merit, Detroit Commn. on Human Rels., 1974, Dir.'s award, Dept. Justice, 1985, Outstanding Practitioner of Criminal Law award, Fed. Bar Assn., 1989, award, Mich. Women's Commn., 1998, Grano award, 2001, Disting. Svc. award, HHS, 2002, disting. Alumna, St. Joseph Acad., 2004. Mem. Mich. Bar Assn., Detroit Bar Assn., Fed. Bar Assn. (pres. Detroit chpt. 1990-91), Inc. Soc. Irish Am. Lawyers (pres. 1991-92, Achievement award 2001), Federalist Soc. Office: Mich Supreme Ct 8-500 3034 W Grand Blvd Detroit MI 48202 Office Phone: 313-972-3232.

CORRIGAN, ROBERT ANTHONY, academic administrator; b. New London, Conn., Apr. 21, 1935; s. Anthony John and Rose Mary (Jengo) C.; m. Joyce D. Mobley, Jan. 12, 1975; children by previous marriage: Kathleen Marie, Anthony John, Robert Anthony; 1 stepdau., Erika Mobley. AB, Brown U., 1957; MA, U. Pa., 1959, PhD, 1967; LHD (hon.), 1995. Researcher Phila. Hist. Commn., 1957-59; lectr. Am. civilization U. Gothenburg, Sweden, 1959-62, Bryn Mawr Coll., 1962-63, U. Pa., 1963-64; prof. U. Iowa, 1964-73; dean U. Mo., Kansas City, 1973-74; provost U. Md., 1974-79; chancellor U. Mass., Boston, 1979-88; pres. San Francisco State U., 1988—. Author: American Fiction and Verse, 1962, 2d edit., 1970, also articles, revs.; editor: Uncle Tom's Cabin, 1968. Vice chmn. Iowa City Human Rels. Commn., 1970-72, Gov.'s Commn. on Water Quality, 1983-84; mem. Iowa City Charter Commn., 1972-73; chmn. Md. Com. Humanities, 1976-78, Assn. Urban Univs., 1988-92; mem. Howard County Commn. Arts, Md., 1976-79; bd. dirs. John F. Kennedy Libr.; trustee San Francisco Econ. Devel. Corp., 1989-92, Adv. Coun. of Calif. Acad. Scis., Calif. Hist. Soc., 1989-92; chmn., bd. dirs. Calif. Compact, 1990—; mem. exec. com. Campus Compact, 1991—, chmn., 1995-2004; Mayor's Blue Ribbon Commn. on Fiscal Stability, 1994-95;

chmn. Pres. Clinton's Steering Com. of Coll. Pres. for Am. Reads and Am. Counts, 1996-2000. Smith-Mundt prof., 1959-60; Fulbright lectr., 1960-62; grantee Std. Oil Co. Found., 1968, NEH, 1969-74, Ford Found., 1969, Rockefeller Found., 72-75, Dept. State, 1977; recipient Clarkson Able Collins Jr. Maritime History award, 1956, Pa. Colonial Soc. Essay award, 1958, 59, William Lloyd Garrison award Mass. Ednl. Opportunity Assn., 1987; Disting. Urban Fellow Assn. Urban U., 1992. Mem. San Francisco C. of C. (bd. dirs.), San Francisco World Affairs Coun. (bd. dirs.), Pvt. Industry Coun. (bd. dirs.), Boston World Affairs Coun. (1983-88), Greater Boston C. of C. (v.p. 1987-89), Fulbright Alumni Assn. (bd. dirs. 1978-80), Univ. Club, World Trade Club, St. Francis Yacht Club, Commonwealth Club (bd. dirs. 1995-99), Phi Beta Kappa. Democrat. Office: San Francisco State U 1600 Holloway Ave San Francisco CA 94132-1722

CORRIGAN, WILFRED J., computer company executive; b. 1938; Divsn. dir. Motorola, Phoenix, 1962-68; pres. Fairchild Camera & Instrument, Sunnyvale, Calif., 1968-80; CEO LSI Logic Corp., Milpitas, Calif., 1980—2005, chmn., 1980—2005, non-exec chmn., 2005—. Bd. dir. Silicon Power Corp., FEI Co., Lucas Film Entertainment Co. Recipient Robert N. Noyce award, Semiconductor Industry Am., 1998. Fellow: London's City and Guild Inst., Imperial Coll., Royal Acad. Engring. Office: LSI Logic Corp 1621 Barber Ln Milpitas CA 95035*

CORRIGAN, WILLIAM M., lawyer; b. St. Louis, Dec. 3, 1958; BBA, U. Notre Dame, 1981; JD, U. Mo., Columbia, 1985. Bar: Mo. 1985, Ill. 1986. Contbr. articles to profl. jours. Mem.: ABA, St. Louis County Bar Assn. (Outstanding Young Lawyer award 1992), Bar Assn. Met. St. Louis, Ill. State Bar Assn., Mo. Bar (chair Young Lawyers sect. 1992—93, bd. govs. 1995—, pres.-elect 2003, Pres.'s award 1993). Office: Armstrong Teasdale LLP One Metropolitan Sq Ste 2600 Saint Louis MO 63102-2740

CORRIGAN, WILLIAM THOMAS, retired broadcast news executive; b. Bridgeport, Conn., Sept. 18, 1921; s. Thomas F. and Anna M. (Callan) C.; m. Harriett Bell, Sept. 1, 1951; children: Kevin, Brian. BS, Am. U., 1948. Reporter Bridgeport Herald, sports broadcaster sta. WUST, Washington, 1947; writer, reporter, prodr. NBC News, 1948-51; prodr., editor NBC-TV (newsreel), 1951-52; assignment editor NBC-TV News, 1952-53; Washington mgr. CBS Newsfilm, Washington bur. chief, 1953-59; dir. news and pub. affairs Sta. KNXT-TV, West Coast bur. chief CBS TV News, 1959-61; Am. Networks prodr./editor Eichmann Trial, Jerusalem, Israel, 1961; mgr. Washington bur. NBC News, 1962; prodr. Huntley Brinkley Report, Wash., 1963-65; dir. news ops. NBC, N.Y.C., 1965-68; gen. mgr. ops. NBC News, N.Y.C., 1968-73, gen. mgr., 1973-79, dir. broadcast svc., 1979-81. Staff sgt. USAAF, 1943—45, WWII. Decorated D.F.C., Air medal. Mem.: Soc. Profl. Journalists, Nat. Press Club, Radio-TV Corrs. Assn., White House Photographers Assn., Radio-TV News Dirs. Assn., Bath Club (Nokomis), Phi Sigma Kappa. Home: 710 Bird Bay Dr W Venice FL 34285 Personal E-mail: harbil4@juno.com.

CORRIN, LISA G., museum director; BA in Art History, with honors, Mary Washington Coll.; grad. studies, SUNY, Stony Brook, Johns Hopkins U. Co-founder & chief curator The Contemporary Mus. of Balt., 1989—97; chief curator The Serpentine Gallery, London, 1997—2001; dep. dir. art & Jon and Mary Shirley curator of modern and contemporary art Seattle Art Museum, 2001—05; dir. Williams Coll. Mus. Art, Williamstown, Mass., 2005—. Curator (exhibitions) Mining the Museum: An Installation by Fred Wilson, 1992 (Named Exhbn. of Yr., Am. Assn. Museums, 1992, Wittenborn Prize for book on exhbn., North Am. Assn. Art Librarians). Rockefeller Fellow for Multicultural Scholarship in Visual Arts, Coll. Art Assn., 1993. Office: Williams Coll Mus Art Ste 2 15 Lawrence Hall Dr Williamstown MA 01267*

CORRIPIO, ARMANDO BENITO, chemical engineering professor; b. Mantua, Cuba, Mar. 6, 1941; came to U.S., 1961; s. Bernardo Manuel and Maria Teresa (Pedraja) C.; m. Consuelo Lucia Careaga, June 9, 1962; children: Consuelo T., Bernardo M., Mary A., Michael G. B of Chem. Engring, La. State U., 1963, M of Chem. Engring., 1967, PhD, 1970. Registered profl. engr., La. Systems engr. Dow Chem. Co., Plaquemine, La., 1963-68; instr. La. State U., Baton Rouge, 1968-70, asst. prof., 1970-74, Disting. Faculty fellow, 1974, assoc. prof., 1974-81, prof. dept. chem. engring., 1981-98, Jay Affolter prof., 1998—. Pvt. cons., 1968—; vis. engr. MIT, Cambridge, 1978-79. Author: Tuning of Industrial Control Systems, 1990, 2d edit., 2000, Design and Application of Industrial Control System, 1998; co-author: Automatic Process Control, 1985, 2d edit., 1997; contbr. numerous articles to profl. jours. Chmn. St. George Bd. Edn., Baton Rouge, 1975-77; lector St. Aloysius Cath. Ch., Baton Rouge, 1989—. Recipient Excellence in Instrn. award Exxon Co., 1986, Excellence in Tchg. award Dow Chem. Co., 1989, Faculty Professionalism award La. Engring. Found., 1997. Fellow Am. Inst. Chem. Engrs. (instr. 1977-87, chmn. Baton Rouge sect. 1990, Charles E. Coates Meml. award with Am. Chem. Soc. 1990); mem. Instrument Soc. Am. (sr., instr. 1977—), Tau Beta Pi, Phi Lambda Upsilon, Phi Kappa Phi. Avocations: sailing, swimming, reading, duplicate bridge. Home: 9344 Bermuda Ave Baton Rouge LA 70810-1121 Office: La State Univ Dept Chem Engring Baton Rouge LA 70803-7303 Personal E-mail: conniecorripio@aol.com. Business E-Mail: corripio@lsu.edu.

CORRITORE, CYNTHIA L., information scientist, educator; b. Mpls., May 22, 1956; d. Michael J. and Charlotte L. Stella; m. Paul J Stella, Mar. 21, 1951; children: Samantha L, Josephine J, Dominic P. MSN, U. Nebr., 1981, MS, 1991, PhD, 1995. Asst. prof. of nursing Med. Ctr. Coll. Nursing U. Nebr., Omaha, 1981—90, instr. Computer Sci. Dept., 1990—95; asst. prof. info. sys. & tech. Coll. of Bus. Adminstrn. Creighton U., Omaha, 1995—2001, assoc. prof. info. sys. & tech. Coll. of Bus. Adminstrn., 2001—. Presenter in field. Contbr. articles to profl. jours. Recipient Mary E. and Elmer H. Dohrmann Fellowship, U. of Nebr. - Lincoln, 1995-6, Best Paper award, Internat. Symposium Info. Sys. and Engring., 2001; Selected Professions Engring. fellowship, AAUW Ednl. Found., 1995—96. Mem.: AAUW (assoc.), Women in Info. Tech. (assoc.), ACM (assoc.; mem. spl. interest group computer human interaction), Assn. Computing Machnery ACM (assoc.), NonProfit Assn. of the Midlands (co-chmn. tech. com. 2001—). Democrat. Office: Creighton University College of Business Administration Omaha NE 68178 Office Phone: 402-280-5512. Business E-Mail: cindy@creighton.edu.

CORROW, JOHN HUBERT, secondary school educator; b. Lynnwood, Calif., Aug. 3, 1970; s. Albert Bernard and Linda Jane Corrow; m. Gina Kaye Fano, Aug. 20, 1994; 1 child, Brooke Alison. MA, U. of Calif., Riverside, 1999. Single subject tchg. credential social studies Calif. Tchr. Montclair (Calif.) H.S., 1995—, chairperson social studies dept., 1999—. Adj. prof. Cal Bapt. U., Riverside, Calif., 2003—. Mem.: ASCD (assoc.), Am. Ednl. Rsch. Assn. (assoc.), Phi Delta Kappa (assoc.). Republican. Roman Catholic. Achievements include research in Impact of student tracking in schools; Impact of teacher tracking on student performance; High school responses to accountability systems. Avocations: martial arts, running, reading science and history.

CORRY, CHARLES ELMO, geophysicist, not-for-profit developer; b. Salt Lake City, May 15, 1938; s. Elmo Leigh Corry and Sylvia Birch; children: Christopher Charles, Matthew Lee. BS in Geology, Utah State U., 1970; MS in Geophysics, U. Utah, 1972; PhD in Geophysics, Tex. A&M U., 1976. Electronic missile checkout GD Convair-Astronautics, San Diego, 1960-64; rsch. assoc. Scripps Inst. Oceanography, La Jolla, Calif., 1965-68, Woods Hole (Mass.) Oceanographic Inst., 1968; mgr. geophys. rsch. AMAX, Golden, Colo., 1977-82; v.p. Nonlinear Analysis, Inc., Bryan, Tex., 1982-84; vis., adj., assoc. prof. geophysics Tex. A&M U., College Station, 1983-87; assoc. prof. geophysics U. Mo., Rolla, 1984-89; coord. world ocean circulation experiment Woods Hole Oceanographic Inst., 1990—95; database cons. Denver and Colorado Springs, 1995—2001; pres. Equal Justice Found., 2001—. Author: Laccoliths, Mechanics of Emplacement and Growth, 1988, Geology of the Solitario, Trans-Pecos Texas, 1990, Domestic Violence Against Men, 1999, (award); contbr. articles to profl. jours. and conf. procs., including Trans. Am. Geophys. Union, Jour. Applied Geophysics, others. Cpl., USMC, 1956-59, Calif. Fellow Geol. Soc. Am.; mem. IEEE, ACLU, Am. Geophys. Union, Soc. Exploration Geophysicists, Marine Corps League. Republican. Buddhist. Achievements include overturning of paradigm that had existed for over 150 years regarding galvanic current flow in ore bodies; discovery that ore minerals are commonly ferroelectrics and that ore bodies behave as a polarized dielectric medium, or solid plasma, in electrical surveys; development of the controlled source audiomagnetotelluric method for electrical exploration; field and theoretical studies of magmatic intrusions; terrestrial heat flow studies in the North Pacific; coordination of hydrographic program of World Ocean Circulation Experiment; relational database design and data modeling; civil liberties, voting rights and prevention of election fraud. Home: 455 Bear Creek Rd Colorado Springs CO 80906-5820 Business E-Mail: ccorry@ejfi.org.

CORRY, DALILA BOUDJELLAL, internist, educator; b. El-Arrouch, Algeria, July 7, 1943; came to U.S., 1981; MD, U. Algiers, 1974. Diplomate in internal medicine and nephrology Am. Bd. Internal Medicine. Intern Hosp. Mustapha Algiers, 1972-73; resident Hosp. Tenon, Paris, 1975-79; fellow in nephrology UCLA, 1981-83; chief renal divsn. Olive View-UCLA Med. Ctr., Sylmar, Calif., 1983—; from asst. prof. to prof. clin. medicine UCLA, 1993, prof. clin. medicine, 2001—. Fellow Am. Heart Assn. Office: Olive View-UCLA Med Ctr Dept Medicine 2B182 14445 Olive View Dr Sylmar CA 91342-1437 Office Phone: 818-364-3205. Business E-Mail: dbcorry@ucla.edu.

CORRY, EMMETT BROTHER, librarian, educator, archivist; b. NYC; s. Patrick Joseph and Bridget Corry. BA, St. Francis Coll., N.Y.C., 1960; MS, Columbia U., 1962; PhD, NYU, 1977. Tchr. Franciscan Bros. Schs., Bklyn., 1960-69; libr. St. Francis Coll., Bklyn., 1970-71, St. Anthony's H.S., Smithtown, N.Y., 1971-77; prof. divsn. libr. and info. sci. St. John's U., Jamaica, N.Y., 1977-94; archivist Franciscan Bros., 1994—; dir. St. John's U., Jamaica, N.Y., 1988-93. Cons. N.Y.C. Bd. Edn., 1984-88, St. Francis Coll., 1996—. Author: Grants for Libraries, 1982, 2d edit., 1986, History of the Franciscan Brothers of Brooklyn in Ireland and America, 2003. Pres. N.Y. Irish History Roundtable, 1994-96. Mem. Cath. Libr. Assn. (pres. 1989-91, Libr. of Yr. 1991), N.Y. Irish History Roundtable (pres. 1994-96). Avocations: classical music, N.Y.C. Irish history. Home: Our Lady of Angels Friary 344 73rd St Brooklyn NY 11209 Office: St Francis Monastery 135 Remsen St Brooklyn NY 11201-4212 Office Phone: 718-858-8217 x17. Personal E-mail: franciscan135@aol.com.

CORRY, JENNIFER MARIE, language educator; b. Cleve., Nov. 7, 1966; d. Joseph James and Barbara Elsie Corry. BA, U. Wis., Eau Claire, 1988; MA, No. Ill. U., 1994; PhD, U. Wis., 2000. Tchg. asst. dept. fgn. lang. No. Ill. U., Dekalb, 1991—94; tchg. asst. dept. Spanish, U. Wis., Madison, 1994—2000; asst. prof. Spanish, Berry Coll., Rome, Ga., 2000—. Vol. tutor Armurchee Elem. Sch., 2001. Dir., actress Spanish Play Troupe, Rome, 2001. Mem.: AAUW, MLA, Rocky Mt. MLA. Avocations: Tae Kwon Do, Hapkido. Home: 1349 Redmond Cir J11 Rome GA 30165 Office: Berry Coll Box 5044 Rome GA 30149 Business E-Mail: jcorry@berry.edu.

CORSARO, FRANK ANDREW, theater director; b. N.Y.C., Dec. 22, 1924; s. Joseph and Marie (Quarino) C.; m. Mary Cross Bonnie Lueders, May 30, 1971; 1 child, Andrew. Grad. in Drama, Yale, 1947. Tchr. pvt. acting class for singers and actors; artistic dir. Actors' Studio and Julliard Opera Ctr., Julliard Sch. Head music drama div. opera/music theatre Inst. N.J.; trustee Nat. Opera Inst. Dir.: Broadway prodn. A Hatful of Rain, 1955-56, The Night of the Iguana, 1961-62, Treemonisha, 1975, Cold Storage, 1978, Whoopee, 1979, Knockout, 1979, It's So Good to be Civilized, 1987; off-Broadway prodn. Master Class, 1986; dir.: N.Y.C. Opera, 1958—, Washington Opera Soc., 1970-74, St. Paul Opera, 1971, Houston Grand Opera, 1973-77, assoc. artistic dir., 1977—, Glyndebourne Festival, 1982-85, Deutsches Oper, Berlin, 1983, Chgo. Lyric Opera, 1984, 96, Covent Garden, 1984, Met. Opera, 1984, Spitalfields Festival, London, 1985, Den Norske Opera, Oslo, 1985, Australian Opera, 1986. appeared in: Broadway prodn. Mrs. McThing, 1951; film Rachel, Rachel, 1967; author: adaptation L'Histoire du Soldat, 1974, Memoir Maverik, 1978, Love for Three Oranges Glyndebourne Version, 1985, (novel) Kunma, 2003; dir. (double bill) Where the Wild Things Are, Higgeldy Piggelby Pop, 1985, Los Angeles Opera, 1986, Amsterdam Netherlanders Opera, 1986, Montreal Opera, 1986 Ravel: L'enfant et les Sortileges, L'heure Espagnol, Glyndebourne Festival, 1987, Hansel and Gretel, Houston Can. Opera Co., Rigoletto, 2001, Traviata, 2003; (libretto) Heloise and Abelard. Mem. Dirs. Guild Am., Soc. Stage Dirs., Choreographers, Am. Guild Mus. Artists. Home: 33 Riverside Dr New York NY 10023-8012 Office Phone: 212-799-5000 Ext. 261.

CORSE, JOHN DOGGETT, academic administrator, lawyer; b. Jacksonville, Fla., Mar. 16, 1924; s. Herbert Montgomery and Carita Ann (Doggett) C.; m. Margaret Murchison, Aug. 4, 1951; children: Carita Doggett, Cameron Murchison, John Doggett, Margaret Murchison. BS, U.S. Naval Acad., 1946; LLB, U. Va., 1957. Bar: Fla. 1957, Ga. 1974. Commd. ensign U.S. Navy, 1946, advanced through grades; resigned, 1954; ptnr. Ulmer, Murchison, Ashby & Ball, Jacksonville, 1957-75, Powell, Goldstein, Frazer & Murphy, Atlanta, 1975-92; sr. dir. devel. U. Va. Law Sch. Found., Charlottesville, 1992—. Pres. Gt. Am. Mgmt. Corp., Atlanta, 1972-75, chmn. bd., 1975; sr. v.p., dir. UniCapital Corp., Atlanta, 1972-75; mng. trustee Gt. Am. Mortgage Investors, 1972-75 Editor-in-chief: Va. Law Rev, 1956-57. Mem.: ABA, Ga. Bar Assn., Va. Bar Assn., D.C. Bar Assn., Fla. Bar Assn., The River Club Jacksonville, Timuquana Country Club, Farmington Country Club (Charlottesville). Office: 3588 Richmond St Jacksonville FL 32205 Office Phone: 434-924-6883. E-mail: jdc8a@virginia.edu.

CORSIGLIA, ROBERT JOSEPH, electrical construction company executive; b. Chgo., Jan. 22, 1935; s. John Robert and Marie Virgina Corsiglia; m. Patricia Ann Ryan, Jan. 26, 1960 (div. Jan. 1984); children: Nancee, Thomas, Karen; m. Emilie Clementz, Sept. 10, 1989. BSEE, Ill. Inst. Tech., Chgo., 1963. Registered profl. engr., Ill., Ind., Calif., Tex., Fla. CEO, pres. Hyre Electric Co. Ind., Highland, 1970-90, JWP/Hyre Electric Co. Ind., Highland, 1990—; CEO Midwestern region JWP Mech./Elec. Svcs. Inc., Oak Brook, Ill., 1991-93; chmn. C & H Engring. Co., Inc., Highland, 1984-90; sec.-treas. Adventures in Travel, Highland, 1984-95. Bd. dirs. Bank One, Highland. Bd. dirs. No. Ind. Arts Assn., Munster, 1989-93, v.p. devel., 1990; bd. dirs. N.W. Ind. United Way, Highland, 1985, Chgo. Engring. Found., 1991-97; bd. dirs. IIT Alumni Bd., Chgo., 1985, v.p. adminstrn., 1986; mem. IIT Pres.' Coun., 1985—; mem. Legacy Found. Inc. Lake County, Griffith, Ind., 1993—; mem. exec. bd. Boy Scouts of Am. Calumet Coun., 1993—; pres. Nat. Elec. Contractors Assn., 1975, 76, 77. Served with U.S. Army, 1964-70. Mem. Internat. Brotherhood of Elec. Workers (hon.), Chgo. Pres. Orgn., Young Pres. Orgn., World Pres. Orgn., Union League Club. Republican. Roman Catholic. Avocations: collecting, golf. Home: 8701 Northcote Ave Munster IN 46321-2726 Office Phone: 219-923-6100. Business E-Mail: rjcorsig@sbcglobal.net.

CORSO, JASON JOSEPH, computer scientist; b. N.Y.C., Aug. 6, 1978; s. Joseph Michael and Lois Corso; m. Aileen Marie Cuddy, Apr. 30, 2005. BS, Loyola Coll. in Md., Balt., 2000; MS in Computer Sci., Johns Hopkins U., Balt., 2002; PhD in Computer Sci., Johns Hopkins U., 2005. Rsch. asst. Computational Interaction and Robotics Lab, The Johns Hopkins U., Balt., 2001—; temp. rsch. scientist Siemens Corp. Rsch., Princeton, NJ, 2003. Contbr. articles to profl. jours. Recipient James D. Rozics Computer Sci. medal, Loyola Coll. in Md., 2000; fellow, Link Found., 2004; scholar, Upsilon Pi Epsilon, 1998; Presdl. scholar, Loyola Coll. in Md., 1996—2000, Bell Atlantic scholar, 1996—2000. Mem.: Assn. of Computing Machinery, IEEE Computer Soc., Alpha Sigma Nu., Upsilon Pi Epsilon. Achievements include invention of The 4D-Touchpad: An interactive platform for video-based human-computer interaction. Office: The Johns Hopkins University 3400 N Charles St New Eng Bld 224 Baltimore MD 21218 Office Phone: 410-516-6089.

CORSO, JOHN ANTHONY, management consultant, educator; s. Vero R. and Rita Jane Corso; m. Maria Lourdes Cano, Sept. 8, 1990; children: Sara Susan children: Mary Bridget, Bernadette Jane. BS, U. Md., 1980; MS in Adminstrn., Ctrl. Mich. U., 1991; MPA, DPA, U. So. Calif., L.A., 2001. Cert. charter cert. Myers-Briggs type indicator profl. Consulting Psychologists Press, 2001, profl. contracts mgr. Nat. Contract Mgmt. Assn., 1995. Mgmt. cons. Booz, Allen, & Hamilton, McLean, Va., 1992—92; contract specialist U.S. Dept. Vet. Affairs, Washington, 1992—97, 1993—99, sr. procurement analyst, 1997—99, mgmt. and program analyst, 1999—. Program dir./adj. prof. Georgetown U. Ctr. for Profl. Devel., Washington, 2001—. Contbr. articles to profl. jours. Extraordinary min. holy communion St. Raphael's Cath. Parish, Rockville, Md., 1996—2002. Lt. USN, 1983—92, Various, ret. comdr. USNR, 2002. Decorated Navy Expeditionary Medal USN, Navy Commendation Medal. Mem.: ASPA, Nat. Career Devel. Assn., Leadership VA Alumni Assn., Soc. Cath. Social Scientists, Acad. Mgmt., KC (outside guard 1976—76). Roman Catholic. Home: 12601 Orchard Brook Terr Potomac MD 20854 Office: US Dept Vets Affairs 810 Vermont Ave NW Washington DC 20420 Personal E-mail: corsojohn@aol.com.

CORSON, J. JAY, IV, lawyer; b. Richmond, Va., May 19, 1935; s. John Jay III and Mary Turner (Tilman) C.; children: John Jay V, Catherine Anne, Clare Tilman, Jennifer Page. BA, U. Va., 1957, LLB, 1960. Bar: Va. 1960. Assoc. Davis, Polk, Wardwell, Sunderland & Kiendl, N.Y.C., 1960, Boothe, Dudley, Koontz & Blankenship, Fairfax, Va., 1963-68; ptnr. McGuire, Woods, Battle & Boothe & predecessor firms, McLean, Va., 1968-2000. Capt. USAF, 1960-63. Fellow Am. Coll. Trial Lawyers, Am. Bar Found., Va. Law Found.; mem. Va. Assn. Def. Attys. (pres. 1981-82), Va. State Bar (pres. 1988-89, del. ABA 1989-96). Episcopalian. Avocations: golf, skiing, fishing, gardening. Home: 3137 Trenholm Dr Oakton VA 22124-1329 Office: McGuire Woods LLP 1750 Tysons Blvd Ste 1800 Mc Lean VA 22102-4231 Office Phone: 703-712-5409. Business E-Mail: jcorson@mcguirewoods.com.

CORSON, JOSEPH MARTIN, multimedia designer; b. Paineville, Ohio, June 13, 1953; s. Joseph Fredrick Corson and Judith Ann Powell. AA in Specialized Tech. and Photographic Sci., Art Inst. Pitts., 1983; cert. in med. photography, U. Pitts., 1987. Prodn. artist Artcrafts Unltd. Inc., Pitts., 1984—86; asst. dir. photographic rsch. lab. U. Pitts., 1986—89; freelance tech. illustrator Invention Submission Corp., Pitts., 1988—94; art dir. Maguire Group Inc., Pitts., 1989—94; art and antique conservator, owner Vestige Restorations, Warren, Ohio, 1994—; govt. inspector Parker Hannifin Aerospace, Andover, Ohio, 2000—02; technician/engring. Sport Masters Inc., Newton Falls, Ohio, 2003—. Guest lectr. Edinboro (Pa.) U., 1995—2000, U. Pitts., 1995—2000, C.C. Allegheny County, Pitts., 1995—2000. (med. textbook) Differential Diagnosis of the Head and Neck, 1987, New Eng. Jour. Medicine, 1986—89, exhibitions include NYU, Represented in permanent collections P.P.G. Contemporary Art Collection, exhibitions include A.M. Pitts. TV Show;, author of poems. Avocations: astronomy, geology, stamp collecting/philately, creative writing. Home: 968 Buckeye St # 1 Warren OH 44485-2918

CORSON, MARK LAWRENCE, human resources specialist; s. John Roberts and Patricia Leonard C.; m. Talana Mei Erasmus; children: Zoe, Amy BA, Case Western Res., 1970; MBA, U. Cape Town, 1977. With Olivetti Africa Ltd., Johannesburg, 1970-71, NCR Corp., Johannesburg, 1972—75; sr. mgr. Andersen Cons., Chgo., 1976-90; ptnr. Ernst & Young LLP, Cleve., 1990-2000; v.p. Intellinex LLC, Cleve., 2000—05. Chmn. Pepper Pike Civic League. Mem.: ASTD, Internat. Soc. for Performance Improvement. Avocations: world travel, sailing, skin diving. Home: 3005 Lander Rd Pepper Pike OH 44124 Office Phone: 216-570-0833. E-mail: marklcorson@aol.com.

CORSON, THOMAS HAROLD, retired manufacturing executive; b. Elkhart, Ind., Oct. 15, 1927; s. Carl W. and Charlotte (Keyser) C.; m. Dorthy Claire Scheide, July 11, 1948; children: Benjamin Thomas, Claire Elaine. Student, Purdue U., 1945-46, Rennsselaer Poly. Inst., 1946-47, So. Meth. U., 1948-49. Chmn. bd. dirs. Coachmen Industries, Inc., Elkhart, 1965-97, chmn. emeritus, dir., 1997—2005, ret., 2005. Bd. dirs. R.C.R. Sci. Inc., Goshen, Ind., Micrology Labs., Inc., Goshen, Elkhart County Econ. Devel. Corp., Elkhart, Ind.; chmn., sec. Greenfield Corp., Middlebury. Adv. coun. U. Notre Dame; past trustee Ball State U.; dir., past trustee, past vice chmn. Interlochen (Mich.) Arts Acad. and Nat. Music Camp. With U.S. Naval Air Force, 1945-47. Mem. Ind. Mfrs. Assn. (past dir.), Elkhart C. of C. (past bd. dirs.), Ind. C. of C. (past bd. dirs.), Ind. Hist. Soc. (past dir.), Royal Poinciana Golf Club, Elcona Club (past bd. dirs.), 33 Degrees, Mason, Shriners. Methodist. Home: PO Box 340 Middlebury IN 46540-0340

CORTADA, JAMES WILLIAM, management consultant, business historian; b. Havana, Cuba, Sept. 7, 1946; s. James Nicholas and Shirley (Barlow) C.; m. Dora Jane Tappy, July 2, 1947; children: Elizabeth, Julia. BA, Randolph-Macon Coll., 1969; MA, Fla. State U., 1970, PhD, 1973. With IBM Corp., various locations, 1974—, br. mgr. Madison, Wis., 1987-89, mgr. market driven quality, 1989-91, mgmt. cons., 1992—. Author 22 books including Strategic Data Processing, 1984, Historical Dictionary of Data Processing (3 vols.), 1987, Before the Computer, 1993, TQM for Sales and Marketing Management, 1993, The Computer in the United States, 1993; contbr. numerous articles to refereed and other profl. publs. Mem. fundraising coun. United Way, Madison, 1988; bd. dirs. Madison Urban League, 1989, 92—. Mem. Am. Hist. Assn., Charles Babbage Inst., Am. Soc. Quality Control, Soc. Spanish and Portuguese Studies, Va. Hist. Soc., Orange County Hist. Soc., Kiwanis. Roman Catholic. Avocations: writing, hiking. Home: 2917 Irvington Way Madison WI 53713-3411 Office: IBM Corp 3113 W Beltline Hwy Madison WI 53713-2897

CORTELYOU, CYNTHIA ANN, elementary school educator; d. James Arthur and LaMona Maryann Hennigar; m. David Wayne Cortelyou; children: Toby Wayne, Leisa Marie Breitfelder. MSEd, Western Ill. U., 2004. Elem. tchr. Bushnell-Prairie City Sch. Dist., Bushnell, Ill., 1981—. Office: Bushnell-Prairie City Elem Sch 345 East Hess St Bushnell IL 61422 Office Phone: 309-772-9464.

CORTES, ENRIC, marine biologist; b. Barcelona, Aug. 2, 1958; arrived in U.S., 1991; s. Enrique Cortes and Consuelo Perez; m. Kristen Edwards, Mar. 2, 1991; 1 child, Ariane. BSc, U. Barcelona, 1981; MSc, U. Miami, 1987; PhD, U. Barcelona, 1991. Post-doctoral rschr. Mote Marine Lab., Sarasota, Fla., 1992—97; rsch. assoc. Fla. State U., Panama City, Fla., 1997—98; rsch. fishery biologist Nat. Oceanographic and Atmospheric Adminstrn., Nat. Marine Fisheries Svc., Panama City, 1998—. Spanish astronaut candidate European Space Agy., Ministry Industry and Energy; cons. in field; presenter in field; shark specialist Internat. Union for the Conservation of Nature, 1998—. Co-author 4 book chpts.; contbr. over 50 articles to profl. jours. Recipient Employee of Yr. award, Nat. Marine Fisheries Svc., 2002; fellow, Ministry Edn. and Sci., Spain, 1992—94, Govt. Catalonia, Spain, 1994—95; scholar, Fulbright-La Caixa, 1984—86, U.S. Joint Com. for Cultural and Ednl. Cooperation, 1986—87; Reitmeister fellowship, U. Miami, 1986. Mem.: Fisheries Soc. Brit. Isles, Deutsche Elasmobranchier Gesellschaft, Soc. Brasileira Estudio de Elasmobranquios, Ecol. Soc. Am., Soc. Conservation Biology, Am. Fisheries Soc., Am. Elasmobranch Soc. (bd. dirs. 1996—2005). Office: NOAA NMFS 3500 Delwood Beach Road Panama City FL 32408 Office Phone: 850-234-6541.

CORTÉS, PEDRO, secretary to commonwealth; m. Lissette Lizardi-Cortés; 1 child, Gabriela Paola. BS in Hotel, Restaurant and Travel Adminstrn., Univ. Mass.; M in Pub. Adminstrn., Penn State Univ.; Law Degree, Penn State Dickinson Sch. of Law. Cert. in Pub. Sector Human Resources Mgmt. Penn State Univ. Exec. dir. PA Govs. Adv. Commn. on Latino Affairs; served with PA State Civil Service Commn., PA Dept. of Pub. Welfare; sec. to commonwealth State of Pa, 2003—. Actively involved Latino Luncheon, Inter-Agency Taskforce on Civil Tension, PA Commn. on Crime and Delinquency's Disproportionate Minority Confinement Subcommittee, PA Minority Bus. Devel. Authority, PA Small Bus. Coalition, PA Statewide Latino Coalition, PA

Supreme Ct. Com. on Racial and Gender Bias in the Judicial Sys. and State Sys. of Higher Education's Diversity Plan, Neighborhood Dispute Settlement, Coun. for Utility Choice, Kutztown Univ. Small Bus. Devel. Ctr. Democrat. Office: Office of Sec of Commonwealth 302 N Capitol Bldg Harrisburg PA 17120

CORTESE, ALFRED WILLIAM, JR., lawyer, consultant; b. Phila., Apr. 2, 1937; s. Alfred William and Marie Ann (Coccio) C.; m. Rosanna S. Zimmerman, Aug. 18, 1962 (div. Aug. 1981); children: Aline Elizabeth, Alfred William III, Christina Nicole; m. Diana P. Nowezki, May 16, 2003. BA cum laude, Temple U., 1959; JD, U. Pa., 1962. Bar: Pa. 1963, U.S. Supreme Ct. 1972, D.C. 1977. Assoc., ptnr. Pepper, Hamilton & Scheetz, Phila., 1962-71; asst. exec. dir. FTC, Washington, 1972-73; assoc. Dechert, Price & Rhoads, Phila., 1974-76; ptnr. Clifford & Warnke, Washington, 1977-81; chmn., CEO Cortese & Loughran Inc., Washington, 1982-84; ptnr. Kirkland & Ellis, Washington, 1985-94, Pepper Hamilton, LLP, Washington, 1994-98; mng. mem. Cortese PLCC, Washington, 1999—. Cons. Gen. Motors Corp., Detroit, 1985—2003. Lt. U.S. Army, 1959-60. Mem.: ABA, Pa. Bar Assn., Lawyers for Civil Justice, D.C. Bar Assn., Am. Law Inst. Avocations: vintage automobile racing and restoration, art & antique collecting, cooking. Office: 113 3rd St NE Washington DC 20002-7313 Office Phone: 202-637-9696. Business E-Mail: awc@corteseplle.com.

CORTESE, DENIS A., medical educator, healthcare executive; b. Phila., Feb. 27, 1944; MD, Temple U., 1970. Cert. Nat. Bd. Med. Examiners, diplomate Am. Bd. Internal Medicine, in pulmonary disease Am. Bd. Internal Medicine, cert. Am. Bd. Laser Surgery. Intern Mayo Clinic, Rochester, 1970—71; resident in internal medicine Mayo Grad. Sch. Medicine, Mayo Clinic, Rochester, 1970—72, resident in thoracic medicine, 1972—74; fellow in thoracic diseases and bronchoscopy Mayo Clinic, 1976, pulmonary medicine specialist, 1976; prof. medicine Mayo Med. Sch.; pres., CEO Mayo Found., Rochester, Minn., 2003—. Mem. Ctr. Corp. Innovation. Mem. Healthcare Leadership Coun., Harvard/Kennedy Sch. Healthcare Policy Group; bd. govs. Mayo Clinic, Rochester, 1987—92, trustee, 1990—94, 1997—, chair bd. govs. Jacksonville, 1999—2002; bd. dirs. St. Luke's Hosp., Jacksonville, 1999—2002, chair exec. com., 2002. Office: 200 1st St SW Rochester MN 55905 Office Phone: 507-284-2663.

CORTESE, EDWARD, marketing and public relations executive; Grad., Fordham U. Tchr. English Tulane U.; mktg., advt. exec. Loew's-MGM; sr. v.p. mktg. Levitt and Sons; sr. v.p. mktg. and pub. rels. Lefrak Orgn Inc, N.Y., NY. With USN. Office: Lefrak Orgn Inc 40 West 57th St New York NY 10019

CORTESE, JOSEPH SAMUEL, II, lawyer; b. Des Moines, Aug. 17, 1955; s. Joseph Anthony and Kathryn Mary (Marasco) C.; m. Diane Caniglia, Aug. 5, 1978; children: Joseph III, James David, Kathryn Elizabeth. BA, Ind. U., 1977; JD with honors, Drake U., 1980. Bar: Iowa 1981, U.S. Dist. Ct. (no. and so. dists.) Iowa 1981, U.S. Ct. Appeals (8th cir.) 1984. Assoc. Jones, Hoffman & Huber, Des Moines, 1981-85; ptnr. Huber, Book, Cortese, Happe & Lanz, P.L.C., Des Moines, 1985—. Ordained permanent deacon Diocese Des Moines Roman Cath. Ch., Iowa, 1997. Mem. ABA, ATLA, Iowa State Bar Assn., Polk County Bar Assn., Def. Rsch. Inst., Iowa Trial Lawyers Assn. Roman Catholic. Home: 2915 Sherry Ln Urbandale IA 50322-6813 Office: Huber Book Cortese Happe & Lanz PLC 317 6th Ave Ste 200 Des Moines IA 50309-4127 Fax: 515-243-5481. E-mail: jcortese@desmoineslaw.com.

CORTESE, RICHARD ANTHONY, computer company executive; b. New London, Conn., Dec. 4, 1942; s. Anthony John and Winifred Silvia (Beebe) Cortese; m. Cindy Sue Folsom, Feb. 9, 1983; children: Cynthia Ann, Jennifer Lynn; m. Susan Louise Turner, Feb. 13, 1965 (div. 1973). BS, U. So. Calif., 1965, MBA, 1967. Fin. dir. Nat. Semiconductor Corp., Santa Clara, Calif., 1973-78; fin. control dir. TRW Corp., L.A., 1978-79; v.p. fin. No. Telecom Sys. Corp., Minn. and Calif., 1979-80; v.p., gen. mgr. Gen. Automation Inc., Anaheim, Calif., 1980-82; pres., CEO Alpha Microsystems, Santa Ana, Calif., 1982-87, also bd. dirs.; pres., CEO Hugin Sweda, Pine Brook, N.J., 1987-89; pres., CEO, vice-chmn. BOD, 1990-96; pres., CEO Racotek, Burnsville, Minn., 1990-96; pres. RMB Assocs., Durango, Colo., 1996—. Active Young Pres.'s Orgn., N.J. Named All-Am. in track and field NCAA, 1964, All-Am. in track and field AAU, 1964. Mem. Computer Communication Industry Assn. (mem. exec. com. 1983—), SoCal 10 (founding mem., bd. dirs. 1983—). Clubs: Chancellor's. Avocation: reading.

CORTEZ, JOSIE DANINI, science educator; b. Laredo, Tex., Oct. 23, 1955; d. Geuriel and Josefina Flores Danini; m. Albert Cortez; children: Carisa, Celena, Adam, Kristen Supik. BA, U. Notre Dame, 1977; MA, Case Western Res. U., 1980. Dir. Intercultural Devel. Rsch. Assn., San Antonio, 1986—, rsch. and evaluation dir., 1992—99. Res. and eval. dir. Intercultural Devel. Rsch. Assn., San Antonio, 1992—99; adj. clin. asst. prof. U. Tex. Health Sci. Ctr., San Antonio, 1993—; presenter in field. Contbr. articles to profl. jours. Scholar, U. Notre Dame, 1973—75; Merit scholar, 1973—75. Mem.: Am. Ednl. Rsch. Assn. Achievements include research in Dropout Research; development of Exemplary Dropout Prevention Program; research in Cross-Cultural Medical Ethics and Health Care Access for Minority and Low-Income Patients; Increasing Minority Student Access to Colleges and Universities; design of National Research Study on Bilingual Education. Avocation: travel. Home: 7537 Steeple Dr San Antonio TX 78256 Office: Intercultural Development Research Assoc Ste 3500 5835 Callaghan Rd San Antonio TX 78228 Office Phone: 210-444-1710. Office Fax: 210-444-1714. Business E-Mail: josie.cortez@idra.org.

CORTEZ, MILES COGLEY, JR., lawyer; b. Chgo., Dec. 7, 1943; s. Miles and Carol (Sandstrom) C.; m. Janice Lynn Gillespie; children: Miles III, Amy, Jeff Salzenstein, Drew. BA in Econs., Trinity U., San Antonio, 1964; JD, Northwestern U., 1967. Bar: Ill. 1967, Colo. 1970, U.S. Dist. Ct. Colo. 1970, U.S. Ct. Appeals (10th cir.) 1970, U.S. Ct. Appeals (3d cir.) 1974. Ptnr. Welborn, Dufford & Brown, Denver, 1970-84; pres. Cortez Friedman & Coombe, P.C., Denver; sr. ptnr. Cortez, Macaulay, Bernhardt & Schuetze LLC, Denver; exec. v.p., gen. counsel, sec. AIMCO Properties, Denver, 2001—. Lectr. Continuing Legal Edn. Seminars, Colo., 1978—. Contbr. articles to profl. jours. Bd. dirs. Colo. Youth Tennis Found., Denver, 1982-84, '88-90. Capt. U.S. Army, 1967-69. Fellow Colo. Bar Found., Am. Bar Found.; mem. ABA (ho. of dels. 1990—95), Denver Bar Assn. (pres. 1982-83), Colo. Bar Assn. (bd. dirs. 1976-78, exec. com. 1981-83), Nat. Conf. Bar Pres., Colo. Hispanic Bar Assn. Avocation: tennis. Home: 44 Sedgwick Dr Englewood CO 80110-4110 Office: AIMCO 4582 S Ulster St Pky Ste 1100 Denver CO 80237 Office Phone: 303-757-8101. Office Fax: 303-757-8735.

CORTEZ, RICARDO LEE, investment management executive; b. NYC, Mar. 9, 1950; s. Eddie Adam and Marian Ruth (Lee) C.; children: Vanessa, Natalie, Rebecca; m. Harriet Anne Howard, Jan. 16, 1993. BA cum laude, CUNY, 1971; postgrad., Columbia U., 1971—73. Sr. stock market analyst Merrill Lynch, NYC, 1971-76; exec. v.p. Trident Investment-Grace Capital, NYC, 1976-78; pres. Liberty Capital Mgmt., NYC, 1978-84, Cortez Capital Mgmt., NYC, 1984-89; v.p., dir. fixed income Summit (NJ) Trust Co., 1985-86; 1st v.p., dir. programs and comm. Prudential Securities, NYC, 1989-96, nat. sales dir. investment mgmt. svcs., 1996—; No. divsn. dir. Prudential Investments, 1998—, nat. dir. investment mgmt. svcs. divsn.; v.p. global multi-mgr. strategies, mgr. Goldman Sachs, NYC, 2000, program mgr., v.p., 2000—01; pres. pvt. client group Torrey Assocs., NYC, 2001—. Lectr. stock market analysis NY Inst. Fin., NYC, 1973—75; bd. advisors Investment Mgmt. Cons. Assn., 1998—; guest lectr. Harvard U., 2004—, U. Pa., 2004—. Author: (with Edson Gould) Industry and Stock Forecast, 1976. Named Spkr. of Yr., Mcpl. Treas.'s Assn. Calif., 1981. Avocations: former lead guitar for mitch ryder, jay and the americans, coasters, other musical rock groups. Office: Torrey Assocs 505 Park Ave New York NY 10022 Office Phone: 212-644-7800. Business E-Mail: rcortez@thetorreyfunds.com.

CORTEZ, ROBERT V., secondary school educator, music educator; s. Vincent and Minda Cortez; m. Mikelle J. Van Dusen, Mar. 28, 1999; children: Alexander, Ryan, Nicholas. MusB in Music Edn., U. Nev., 1995; MA in Edn., U. Phoenix, 2000. Lic. ednl. personnel Nev., 1995, cert. tchr. Mo., 2005, lic. prin. Mo., 2005. Tchr., coord. dept. Clark County Sch. Dist., Las Vegas, 1995—2003; dir. bands, coord. dept. Boulder City (Nev.) H.S., 2003—05; dir. bands Dixie Gray Marching Band Mex. (Mo.) H.S., 2005—.

CORTINA, BETTY, magazine editor; B in journalism, U. Fla., 1992. City hall reporter Miami Herald; LA staff corr. People Weekly, 1995—96; assoc. editor People En Espanol, 1996—99; sr. writer Entertainment Weekly, 1999; founding news editor O, the Oprah mag., 1999—2001; editl. dir. Latina mag., 2001—. Adv. coun. Journalism Dept., U. Fla. Office: Latina Mag 1500 Broadway Ste 700 New York NY 10036 E-mail: betty@latina.com.

CORTINA, MARTHA C., music educator; b. Florida, Cuba, Apr. 11, 1950; arrived in U.S.A., 1962; d. Pedro J. Abreu and Mria Consuelo Perez; m. Juan Gonzalo Cortina, June 25, 1966; children: Zabrina A., Juan Carlos, Veronique M. MusB magna cum laude, U. Miami, 1979, MusM, 1980. Cert. Tchr. Fla. Piano prof. Broward C.C., Davie, Fla., 1981—83; music tchr. Dade County Pub. Sch., Miami Springs, Fla., 1984—. Piano tchr. Miami Springs Sr. H.S., Coral Gables, Fla., 1993—. Performer: U. Miami Gusman Hall, 1979, 1980. Mem.: Miami Music Tchr. Assn., Pi Kappa Lambda. Office: Miami Springs Senior High 751 Dove Ave Miami FL 33166

CORTNER, HANNA JOAN, retired research scientist, political scientist; b. Tacoma, May 9, 1945; d. Val and E. Irene Otteson; m. Richard Carroll Cortner, Nov. 14, 1970. BA in Polit. Sci. magna cum laude with distinction, U. Wash., 1967; MA in Govt., U. Ariz., 1969, PhD in Govt., 1973. Grad. tchg. and rsch. asst. dept. govt. U. Ariz., Tucson, 1967-70, rsch. assoc. Inst. Govt. Rsch., 1974-76, rsch. assoc. forest-watershed and landscape resources divsns. Sch. Renewable Natural Resources, 1975-82, adj. assoc. prof. Sch. Renewable Natural Resources, 1983-89; exec. asst. Pima County Bd. Suprs., 1985-86; adj. assoc. prof. renewable natural resources, assoc. rsch. scientist Water Resources Rsch. Ctr. U. Ariz., Tucson, 1988-89, prof., rsch. scientist Water Resources Rsch. Ctr., 1989-90, prof., rsch. scientist, dir. Water Resources Rsch. Ctr., 1990-96, prof., rsch. scientist Sch. Renewable Resources, 1997-2000; rsch. prof., assoc. dir. Ecol. Restoration Inst. No. Ariz. U., Flagstaff, 2001—04; ret. Program analyst USDA Forest Svc., Washington, 1979-80; vis. scholar Inst. Water Resources, Corps of Engrs., Ft. Belvoir, Va., 1986-87; com. arid lands AAAS, 1986-89; com. natural disasters NAS/NRC, 1988-91, com. on planning and remediation of irrigation-induced water quality impacts, 1994-95; rev. com. nat. forest planning Conservation Found., Washington, 1987-90; chair adv. com. renewable resources planning techs. for pub. lands Office of Tech. Assessment U.S. Congress, 1989-91; policy coun. Pinchot Inst. Conservation Studies, 1991-93, bd. dirs. 2005-; co-chair working party on evaluation of forest policies Internat. Union Forestry Rsch. Orgns., 1990-95, chair working party on forest instns. and forestry adminstrn., 1996; vice-chair Man and the Biosphere Program, Temperate Directorate, US Dept. State, 1991-96; cmtys. com. steering com., Am. Forest Congress, 1996-2004, rsch. com., 1996-97; sci. adv. com. Consortium for Environ. Risk Evaluation, 1996-97; cons. Greeley and Hansen, Cons. Engrs., US Army Corps Engrs., Ft. Belvoir, US Forest Svc., Washington, Portland, Oreg., Ogden, Utah. Assoc. editor Society and Natural Resources, 1992-94; book reviewer Western Polit. Sci. Quar., Am. Polit. Quar., Perspectives, Natural Resources Jour., Climatic Change, Society and Natural Resources, Jour. of Forestry, Environment; mem. editl. bd. Jour. Forest Planning, 1995—, Forest Policy and Econs., 1999-2002; co-author: The Politics of Ecosystem Management, 1999; co-editor: The State and Nature, 2002; contbr. articles to profl. jours. Bd. dirs. Planned Parenthood So. Ariz., 1992-94, planning com., 1992, bd. devel. and evaluation com., 1994; bd. dirs. N.W. Homeowners Assn., 1982-83, v.p., 1983-84, pres., 1984; vice chmn., chmn. Pima County Bd. Adjustment Dist. 3, 1984; active Tucson Tomorrow, 1984-88; water quality subcom. Pima Assn. Govts., 1983-84, environ. planning adv. com., 1989-90, chmn., 1984, mem. Avra Valley task force, 1988-90; bd. dirs. So. Ariz. Water Resources Assn., 1984-86, 87-95, sec., 1987-89, mem. com. alignment and terminal storage, 1990-94, CAP com., 1988-92, chair, 1989-90, basinwide mgmt. com., 1983-86, chair, 1992-93; active Ariz. Interagy. Task Force on Fire and the Urban/Wildland Interface, 1990-92; wastewater mgmt. adv. com. Pima County, 1988-92, subcom. on effluent reuse Joint CWAC-WWAC, 1989-91, citizens water adv. com. Water Resources Plan Update Subcom., 1990-91; bd. dirs. Ctrl. Ariz. Water Conservation Dist., 1985-90, fin. com., 1987-88, spl. studies com., 1987-88, nominating com., 1987; mem. Colo. River Salinity Control, 1989-90; chair adv. com. Tucson Long Range Master Water Plan, 1988-89; water adv. com. City of Tucson, 1984. Travel grantee NSF/Soc. Am. Foresters; Rsch. grantee US Geol. Survey, US Army Corps of Engrs., USDA Forest Svc., Soil Conservation Svc., Utah State U., Four Corners Regional Commn., Office of Water Rsch. & Tech.; Sci. & Engring. fellow AAAS, 1986-87; recipient Copper Letter Appreciation cert. City of Tucson, 1985, 89, SAWARA award, 1989. Mem. Am. Water Resources Assn. (nat. award com. 1987-90, statues and bylaws com. 1989-90, tech. co-chair ann. meeting 1993), Am. Forests Assn. (forest policy ctr. adv. coun. 1991-95), Soc. Am. Foresters (task force on sustaining long-term forest health and productivity 1991-92, com. on forest policy 1994-96, sci. and tech. bd. 2001-04), Am. Polit. Sci. Assn., Western Polit. Sci. Assn. (com. on constrn. and bylaws 1976-80, chair 1977-79, exec. coun. 1980-83, com. on profl. devel. 1984-85, com. on status of women 1984-85), Nat. Fire Protection Assn. (tech. com. on forest and rural fire protection 1990-94), Phi Beta Kappa. Democrat. Achievements include research in political and socioeconomic aspects of natural resources policy, administration, and planning, water resources management, ecosystem management, wildland fire policy and management. Home: 6064 E Mountain Oaks Flagstaff AZ 86004-7222 Personal E-mail: hannacortner@aol.com.

CORTNEY, MICHAEL C., construction executive, civil engineer; BS in Civil Engring., U. N.Mex., 1971. Project engr., project mgr. Irvine (Calif.) Co.; project mgr. Akins Co.; from head project mgmt. and land acquisition to pres. Std. Pacific Corp., Irvine, 1982—2001, pres., 2001—, bd. dirs. Mem. Home Ownership Advancement Found. With civil engring. corps. USNR. Named to Bldg. Industry Hall Fame, Calif., 2000. Mem.: Home Builders Assn. No. Calif. Office: Standard Pacific Corp 15326 Alton Pkwy Irvine CA 92618

CORTO, DIANA MARIA, coloratura soprano; b. N.Y. d. Samuel and Margaret C.; 1 child, Christian Miles Stomsvik. BA, CUNY, 1977, MA, 1984; studied drama, Am. Place Theatre; studied voice with Maria Kurenko, studied ballet with Maria Nevelska, Bolshoi Theatre, Moscow. Founder, dir. Am. Opera Musical Theatre Co., Inc., 1995—. Prof. drama for musical theatre Pace U., N.Y.C.; mem. voice faculty Calif. State U., L.A., also stage dir. opera program; founder, dir. Am. Opera/Mus. Theatre Co.; appearance with Nat. Symphony Orch. of Cuba, 2004. Starred as Maria in West Side Story in numerous opera houses in Spain, Germany, Switzerland, Austria, 1984; appeared on Broadway in Her First Roman, Status Quo Vadis, Thirteen Daughters, West Side Story Revival, Stop the World, I Want To Get Off; concert tours in U.S., S.Am., Moscow, 1989-91; lead singer City of Angels Opera, Met. Studio; lyric-coloraturist in operas in U.S. and Europe; road tours include King and I, Man of La Mancha, Kismet; prodr. (N.Y. debut performance) The Jewel Box by Mozart/Griffiths; co-prodr. The Jewel Box with N.J. State Opera, Dmitiri Shostakovich concert with Fedn. of Russia, La Bohéme, and others; prodr., dir. Am. premiere of La Molinara by Paisiello at Town Hall, La Boheme; prodr.: Iolanta by Tchaikowski at Town Hall, Embassy of Russian Fedn., La Boheme, Rigoletto, Nat. Performing Arts Ctr. Taiwan. E-mail: corto@mindspring.com.

CORTOR, ELDZIER, artist, printmaker; b. Richmond, Va., Jan. 10, 1916; s. John and Ophelia (Twisdale) C.; m. Sophia Schmidt, Aug. 20, 1951; children: Michael, Mercedes, Stephen, Miriam. Student, Art Inst. Chgo., 1936-41, Inst. Design, 1942, 43, 47, Columbia U., 1946. Painting instr. Centre D'Art, Port au Prince, Haiti, 1949-51; printmaker Pratt Inst., Bklyn., 1972-74. One-man shows include Le Museè de Peuple Haitien, Port-au-Prince, Haiti, 1950, Ctr. d'Art, Port-au-Prince, 1950, Elizabeth Nelson Gallery, Chgo., 1951, James Whyte Gallery, Washington, 1953, exhibited in group shows at Met. Mus. Art, N.Y.C., 1950, Studio Mus. Harlem, 1973, 1982, Boston Mus. Fine Arts, 1975, Museo de Arte Moderno La Pertulia, Cali, Colombia, 1976, Columbia Mus. Art, S.C., 1980, Kenkeleba Gallery, N.Y.C., 1988, Taipei Fine Arts Mus., 1988, San Antonio Mus. Art, 1994, Michael Rosenfeld Gallery, N.Y.C., 1995, 1996, 1997, 1998, 1999, Mus. Contemporary Art, Chgo., 1996—97, M. Rosenfeld Gallery, 1998—2003, Schomburg Ctr., N.Y.C., 1998, Flint (Mich.) Inst. Arts, 1999, Kenkeleba Gallery, N.Y.C., 2000, Represented in permanent collections Smithsonian Inst., Washington, Am. Fedn. Art, N.Y.C., Mus. Modern Art, IBM Corp., Portland (Oreg.) Art Mus., Art Inst. Chgo., Mus. Fine Arts, Boston. Recipient Bertha A. Florsheim award Art Inst. Chgo., 1945; recipient William H. Bartels award, 1946, Carnegie Inst. award, 1947; Julius Rosenwald fellow, Chgo., 1945-47; John Simon Guggenheim fellow, N.Y.C., 1949-50. Home: 35 Montgomery St Apt 19E New York NY 10002-6531

CORTRIGHT, BARBARA JEAN, writer; b. Oxford, Miss., Dec. 29, 1927; d. Lewis Stephen and Lucile (Chevalier) Grandy; m. Lem R. Cortright, Aug. 19, 1946 (dec. Oct. 2002); children: Lewis Stephen, Clyde Kenneth, Eric Allen, Barbara Edith. BFA with honors, Ariz. State U., 1949, MA in Humanities, 1977, MA in German Lang., 1979; PhD in Art History, U. N.Mex., Albuquerque, 1993. Instr. in art history Scottsdale (Ariz.) Coll., 1974-78; newsletter editor Heard Mus., Phoenix, 1978-79; lectr. in non-fiction Ariz. State U., Tempe, 1979-80; publicist O.K. Harris West Gallery, Scottsdale, 1981-84. Author: The Reach of Solitude, 1984; contbr. articles to profl. jours. NEA fellow, 1976. Mem. Phi Kappa Phi, Alpha Mu Gamma. Democrat. Episcopalian. Home: 516 E Erie Dr Tempe AZ 85282-3713 Personal E-mail: GreenPer@aol.com.

CORTRIGHT, LOUISE VERA, medical technician, small business owner; b. Buffalo, Apr. 22, 1938; d. Asa Lawrence and Mary Lois (Ward) C. BS (hon.), Fairleigh Dickson U., 1960; postgrad., Rutgers U., 1965-67. Nationally registered med. technologist. Bacteriology supr. Middlesex Gen. Hosp., New Brunswick, N.J., 1963-64; hematology supr. Princeton Hosp., Princeton, N.J., 1964-65; tchg. supr. Somerset Med. Ctr., Somerville, N.J., 1965-67, chief technologist, 1966-79; owner, operator Aurora Kennel, Bridgewater, N.J., 1973-92. Cons. N.J. State Dept. of Health, Trenton, 1979-80. Treas., v.p. Bridgewater Twp. Bd. of Health, 1974, 1975; chmn. Regional Animal Shelter, 1978-81. Mem. Morris Hills Dog Training Club (founding mem. 1961), North Jersey Shetland Sheepdog Club (founding mem. 1965). Avocations: organic gardening, cross country skiing, sewing, reading, participating in earth watch and habitat for humanity projects.

CORTS, PAUL RICHARD, federal agency administrator; b. Terre Haute, Ind., Sept. 15, 1943; s. Charles H. and Hazel Corts; m. Diane Stevens, May 29, 1965; children: Kenneth Stevens, Daniel Paul, Susan Diane. BA, Georgetown Coll., 1965; MA, Ind. U., 1967, PhD, 1971. Assoc. prof. speech communication Western Ky. U., Bowling Green, 1968-78, dir. internat. edn., 1973-76, dir. univ. honors program, 1972-78, asst. dean for instrn., 1973-78, assoc. v.p. for instrn., 1978; exec. v.p., chief adminstrv. officer Okla. Bapt. U., Shawnee, 1978-83; pres. The Corts Co., Shawnee, 1983, Wingate (N.C.) Coll., 1983-91, Palm Beach Atlantic U., West Palm Beach, Fla., 1991—2002; asst. atty. gen. justice mgmt. divsn. Dept. Justice, 2002—. Cons. bd. govs. U. N.C., Chapel Hill, 1987-88; mem. president's mgmt. coun., coun. chief fin. officers, enduring constl. govt. coordinating coun., exec. bd. internat. cooperative adminstrv. support svcs. Dept. of State, strategic mgmt. coun., sr. exec. rev. bd.; bd. dirs. Fed. Prisons Industries; designated agency ethics ofcl., chief procurement officer, chmn. exec. coun. justice prisoner and alien transp. sys. Co-author: Fundamentals of Effective Group Communication, 1979, Let's Talk Business, 1983. Pres. coun. pres.' Carolinas Intercollegiate Athletic Conf., 1986-88; mem. edn. com. Bapt. World Alliance, McLean, Va., 1990—; bd. dirs. United Way Cen. Carolinas, Monore and Charlotte, 1984-91. Mem. Am. Assn. Pres. Ind. Colls. and Univs. (bd. dirs., pres. 2000-01), Charlotte Area Ednl. Consortium (pres. 1987-88), Am. Coun. Edn., Ind. Colls. and Univs. Fla. (chmn. 2000—), Williamsburg Pres. Colloquy (chmn. 1990), Palm Beach Lit. Soc. (pres. 1992-2000), Coun. Christian Colls. and Univs. (bd. dirs. 1999—), Fla. Coun. 100, Gov.'s Club (bd. dirs. 2000-), Good Samaritan Med. Ctr. (gov. bd. 2002-), Rotary. Office: Dept Justice Justice Mgmt Divsn 950 Pennsylvania Ave NW Washington DC 20530-0001

CORTS, THOMAS EDWARD, university president; b. Terre Haute, Ind., Oct. 7, 1941; s. Charles Harold and Hazel Louise (Vernon) C.; m. Marla Ruth Haas, Feb. 15, 1964; children: Jennifer Ruth Corts Fuller, Rachel Anne Corts Wachter, Christian Haas BA, Georgetown (Ky.) Coll., 1963; MA, Ind. U., 1968, PhD, 1972; DLitt (hon.), Georgetown Coll., 1991; DHL (hon.), Campbell U., 1995, U. Ala., 2002. Asst. to pres. Georgetown Coll., 1963-64, 67-69, asst. prof., 1967-69, exec. dean, 1969-73, exec. v.p., 1973; coord. Higher Edn. Consortium, Lexington, Ky., 1973-74; pres. Wingate (N.C.) Coll., 1974-83, Samford U., Birmingham, Ala., 1983—. Bd. dirs. Samford U. Found., 1990—, Found. Ind. Higher Edn., 1988-92; chmn. Ala. Commn. on Sch. Performance and Accountability, 1993-94. Contbr. articles to profl. jours. Bd. dirs. Birmingham chpt. ARC, 1983-89, Ala. Citizens for Constl. Reform, 2000-05; mem. adv. bd. Salvation Army, 1987-97; mem. exec. coun. Boy Scouts Am., Birmingham, 1984-2005; bd. dirs. Leadership Birmingham, 1984-95, Exec. Com. Birmingham Better Bus. Bur., 1996—, Birmingham Summerfest, 1984-95, Birmingham Area Consortium on Higher Edn., Ala. Poverty Project, Inc., gen. coun. mem. Baptist World Alliance, 1996-; mem. Pub. Affairs Rsch. Coun. Ala. Recipient Outstanding Alumnus award Georgetown Coll., 1987, Jefferson award Downtown Action Com., Birmingham, 1988, Outstanding Educator award Ala. Assn. Coll. and Univs.-Ala. Assn. Women, Birmingham, 1989, Good Shepherd award Assn. Bapt. for Scouting, 1990, Citizen of Yr., 1990, Most Supportive Pres. award Am. Assn. of Colls. for Tchr. Edn., 1991. Mem. Am. Assn. Pres. of Ind. Colls. and Univs. (v.p. 1990-92, pres. 1992-95, bd. dirs. 1989-2002, 2004), Coun. for Advancement of Pvt. Colls. in Ala. (past pres.), Ala. Assn. Ind. Colls., Nat. Fellowship Bapt. Educators (pres. 1988-89), Assn. So. Bapt. Colls. and Schs. (v.p. 1988-89, pres. 1990-91, bd. dirs. 2002-), So. Assn. Colls. and Schs. (trustee 1991-98, mem. commn. on colls., vice chmn. 1991, chmn. exec. coun. 1992-94, pres. 1996, Disting. Leadership award 2001), Coun. Higher Edn. Accreditation (bd. dirs. 1995-97), Assn. Governing Bds. (pres.'s commn., chmn. 2003-04), Birmingham Area C. of C. (bd. dirs. 2000-04), Ala. Acad. Honor, Country Club Birmingham, The Club, The Summit Club, Rotary. Democrat. Office: Samford U 800 Lakeshore Dr Birmingham AL 35229-0002

CORTY, ANDREW P., publishing executive; b. Wilmington, Del., June 16, 1952; s. Claude and Susanne Corty; m. Betty L. Wallace, Apr. 30, 1983; children: Robert Wallace, Edward Wallace. AB, Harvard U., 1974; MBA, Stanford U., 1978. Copy editor The Morning News, Wilmington, 1974—75; reporter The Record, Havre de Grace, Md., 1975—76; asst. to pub. The St. Petersburg (Fla.) Times, 1978—80; pub. Fla. Trend mag., St. Petersburg, 1981—85; gen. mgr. Washington Post mag., 1985—89; mktg. dir. St. Petersburg Times, 1989—91; v.p., sec., bd. dirs. Times Pub. Co., St. Petersburg, 1991—; vice chmn. Congrl. Quar., Inc., Washington, 1991—; pres. Fla. Trend, St. Petersburg, 1991—. Trustee Salvador Dali Mus., St. Petersburg, Fla. Office: St Petersburg Times PO Box 1121 Saint Petersburg FL 33731-1121

CORVETTO, ESTUARDO ALEXANDER, auditor, financial analyst; s. Estuardo Alejandro Ayasta and Yesary Nancy Corvetto; m. Stephanie Michelle Sheffield, Nov. 11, 2003; children: Bailey Michelle, Niccolo Alexander James. BA in Econs., George Mason U., 2000; PhD in Internat. Bus. Adminstrn., Kennedy Western U., 2005. Fin. analyst WHO, UN, DC, 2000—04, supervisory com. mem., 2000—04; sr. grants specialist U. Fla., Gainesville, 2004—05; auditor, buyer analyst Gainesville Regional Utilities, 2005—. Mem.: Ctr. for Internat. Rels., Nat. Soc. Hispanic Profls., Downtown Athletic Club.

CORVINO, BETH BYSTER, lawyer; b. Dec. 8, 1956; m. John Corvino. BA, Ind. U.; JD with honors, DePaul U. Assoc. Katten Muchin Zavis Rosenman, 1982; various positions Am. Hospital Supply Corp., Staley Continental Inc.; gen. counsel Whitman Corp., 1989—92, Gen. Instrument Corp., 1992—98; v.p., gen. counsel, corp. sec. Chas. Levy LLC, 1999—2004; exec. v.p., gen. counsel, corp. sec. Laidlaw Internat. Inc., 2004—. Office: Laidlaw Internat Inc 55 Shuman Blvd Ste 400 Naperville IL 60563 Office Fax: 630-848-3167. Business E-Mail: bcorvino@laidlaw.com.

CORWELL, ANN ELIZABETH, public relations executive; b. Battle Creek, Mich. d. James Albert Corwell and Marion Elizabeth (Petersen) Shertzer. BA, Mich. State U., 1971, MBA, 1981; cert. fin., Wharton Sch., 1986. Sr. publicist City of Dearborn, Mich., 1972-76; sr. assoc. GM, Detroit, 1976-77, media coord. N.Y.C., 1977, mgr. cmty. rels. Pontiac, Mich., 1977-81, mgr. internal comm., 1981-82; dir. pub. rels. Pillsbury Co., Mpls., 1982-85, Avon Products Inc., N.Y.C., 1985-87; exec. v.p. MECA Internat., Flat Rock, Mich., 1987-95; v.p. coll. rels. William Tyndale Coll., Farmington Hills, Mich., 1995—. Dir. Mich. State U. Nat. Alumni Bd. Mem. Pub. Rels. Soc. Am., Women In Comm., Oakland County C. of C. (dir. 1988-91), Dearborn C. of C. (dir. 1989-91). E-mail: acorwell@williamtyndale.edu.

CORWIN, BERT CLARK, optometrist; b. Rapid City, SD, Oct. 4, 1930; s. Meade and Adeline (Clark) C.; m. Lydia M. Forehand; children: B. Clark II, Kelley Linette Fromm. AS, S.D. State U., 1952; BS, Ill. Coll. Optometry, Chgo., 1956, OD, 1957. Pvt. practice, Rapid City, 1957—. Projects chmn. S.D. Lions Sight and Svc. Found., 1964; chmn. med. adv. com. to S.D. Dept. Pub. Welfare, 1968-76; mem. S.D. Adv. Coun. for Regional Med. and Health Planning, 1971; cons. S.D. Dept. Human Svcs., 1989—; adv. bd. S.D. Dept. of Svc. to Visual Impaired; bd. dirs. Super 8 Motel Developers, Rapid City Regional Airport, v.p., 1999-2000, pres., 2000—; chmn. bd. dirs. Transaction Network, Inc., 1997—; mng. ptnr. Tight Line Lake, 1999-2002. Contbr. articles to profl. jours. Pres. Cleghorn PTA, Rapid City, 1968-70; bd. dirs. Am. Optometric Found., 1989-90, v.p., 1990-94, pres., 1994-96; chmn. bd. dirs. Terry Peak Condominiums, 2001—. Recipient Presdl. medal of honor Pres. of Ill. Coll. of Optometry, 1999, 2002, Spl. honor Am. Optometric Found. Fellow Am. Acad. Optometry (diplomate contact lens sect., sec.-treas. 1985-86, pres.-elect 1987-88, pres. 1988-90, chmn. 1st internat. meeting 1992, nom. com. 2000-02); mem. Am. Optometric Assn. (exec. com. 1974-76, Am. Optometrist of the Yr. 1993), S.D. Optometric Soc. (pres. 1970-71), North Ctrl. State Optometric Conf. (bd. dirs. 1970-71), Black Hills Optometric Soc. (sec.-treas. 1958-69), S.D. State Bd. Examiners (pres. 1982-85), Nat. Acad. Practice Optometry (sec.-treas. 1990-94, Disting. Practitioners award, co-chmn. 1994-96). Clubs: Black Hills Water Ski (pres. 1963). Lodges: Masons, Elks, Lions (pres. Rushmore chpt. 1961-62, Robert Tyler award 1998). Republican. Methodist. Avocations: skiing, water-skiing, hunting, piloting, public speaking. Home: 5048 Carriage Hills Dr Rapid City SD 57702 Office: 2800 3rd St Rapid City SD 57702-2520 Office Phone: 605-718-2303. Personal E-mail: bc.corwin@juno.com.

CORWIN, JEFF, biologist, anthropologist, television host; BS in Biology, BS in Anthropology, Bridgewater State Coll., degree (hon.) in pub. edn., 1999; grad., U. Mass. Co-founder Emerald Canopy Rainforest Found.; mem. environ. program UN. Co-creator, prodr., host: (TV series) Going Wild With Jeff Corwin, Disney Channel, 1997—99; exec. prodr. The Jeff Corwin Experience, 2000—. Mailing: 1 Discovery Pl Silver Spring MD 20910

CORWIN, JOYCE ELIZABETH STEDMAN, construction company executive; b. Chgo. d. Cresswell Edward and Elizabeth Josephine (Kimbell) Stedman; m. William Corwin, May 1, 1965; children: Robert Edmund Newman, Jillanne Elizabeth McInnis. Pres. Am. Properties, Inc., Miami, Fla., 1966-72; v.p. Stedman Constrn. Co., Miami, 1971—. Owner Joy-Win Horses, Gray lady ARC, 1969-70. Guidance worker Youth Hall, 1969-70; sponsor Para Med. Group of Coral Park H.S., 1969-70; hostess, Rep. presdl. campaign, 1968; aide Rep. Nat. Conv., 1972. Mem. Dade County Med. Aux. (chmn. directory com. 1970), Marion County Med. Aux., Fla. Psychiat. Soc. Aux., Fla. Morgan Horse Assn., Fla. Thoroughbred Breeders Assn., Coral Gables Jr. Women's Club (chmn. casework com.), Royal Dames of Ocala. Home: Windrift Farm 8500 NW 120th St Reddick FL 32686-4513

CORWIN, NORMAN, scriptwriter, film producer, film director; b. Boston, May 3, 1910; s. Samuel H. and Rose (Ober) C.; m. Katherine Locke, Mar. 1947; children: Anthony, Diane. Student, Boston, also Winthrop, Mass.; LittD, Columbia Coll., 1967, LHD, 1978; D in Lit. Arts, Lincoln Coll., 1990; LHD (hon.), Calif. Luth. U., 1996. Writer, producer, dir. CBS; vis. prof. U. So. Calif., 1981—; Patten Meml. lectr. Ind. U., 1981. Dir. creative writing Idyllwild (Calif.) Sch. Music and Art, 1970—; mem. LaGuardia One World Meml. Commn. to Europe, 1948; trustee L.A. Internat. Film Expn.; film adv. bd. L.A. County Mus. Art; adv. bd. Inst. for Readers Theatre, Poetry Therapy Inst.; lectr. in field. Wrote, produced radio broadcasts; commemorative broadcasts: We Hold These Truths, on 150th anniversary of Am. Bill of Rights, 1941, Bill of Rights: 200, 1991; chief spl. projects, UN Radio; wrote films for, RKO, MGM, 20th-Century Fox, UN; writer, dir., prod.: 26 By Corwin, 1941, This is War, 1942, An American in England, 1942, Columbia Presents Corwin, 1944-45; writer, dir.: (stage plays) The Hyphen, The Rivalry, The World of Carl Sandburg, Together Tonight--Jefferson, Hamilton and Burr; writer for: films Scandal at Scourie, Lust for Life (Oscar nominee), The Blue Veil, The Story of Ruth; producer, host: TV series Norman Corwin Presents for Westinghouse Group W, 1972; author: TV spl. The Ct. Martial of the Tiger of Malaya, 1974; writer, host: TV series Academy Leaders, 1979, radio series More by Corwin, 1996-97. Author: They Fly Through the Air With the Greatest of Ease, 1939, Thirteen by Corwin, 1942, More by Corwin, 1944, On a Note of Triumph, 1945, Untitled and Other Dramas, 1945, Dog in the Sky, 1952, The Plot to Overthrow Christmas, 1952, The World of Carl Sandburg, 1961, Overkill and Megalove, 1963, Prayer For the 70s, 1969, Jerusalem Printout, 1978, Holes in a Stained Glass Window, 1978, Greater than the Bomb, 1981, A Date with Sandburg, 1981, Trivializing America, 1988, Years of the Electric Ear, 1994, Norman Corwin's Letters, 1994; plays Cervantes, 1973; stage play The Rivalry (produced as Hallmark TV spl.); contbr. articles to mags.; writer: text of Human Rights Cantata, Yes Speak Out Yes (commd. by UN), text CONartist (cartoons of Paul Conrad), 1993; Norman Corwin's Letters, 1993, Years of the Electric Ear, 1994. Recipient Page One award Am. Newspaper Guild, 1944-45, award UCLA Ctr. Aging, 2001, Ray Bradbury award, 2001, Distinguished Merit award NCCJ, 1945, UCLA Icon award, 2001, Calif. Hist. Soc. Cmty. Enrichment award, 2003, Human Nuturance award, Ashley Montague Inst., 2005; Unity award Interracial Film and Radio Guild, 1945; citation Nat. Council Tchrs. English, 1945; citation Assn. Tchrs. Social Studies of N.Y., 1945; award Am. Schs. and Colls. Assn., 1946; first place in nat. poll radio editors Billboard mag., for On a Note of Triumph, 1946; co-winner 1st prize Met. Opera awards for new Am. opera, The Warrior, produced Jan. 1947; Freedom award telecast Between Americans, 1951; hon. grant Am. Acad. Arts and Letters; Valentine Davies award Writers Guild Am., 1972; Artists award U. Judaism, 1972; Pacific Pioneer Broadcasters' Carbon Mike award, 1974; Preceptor's award San Francisco State U., 1979; PEN award for body of work, 1986, Friends of Old Time Radio award, 1990, Byron Kane medal SPERDVAC, 1990, Gold medal Internat. Radio Festival, 1992, Lifetime Achievement award N.Y. Festival, 1992, Lifetime Achievement award League of Women Voters, 1993, Alfred I. duPont-Columbia U. award for 50 Yrs. after 14th Aug. commemorating surrender of Japan, 1997. Fellow Radio Hall of Fame; mem. Acad. of Motion Picture Arts and Scis. (chmn. documentary awards com. 1967-82, 85-92, co-chmn. scholarship com., bd. govs. 1979-86, 1st v.p. acad. 1988, sec. Acad. Found. 1983-88), Aspen Film Conf. (steering com.), Authors League Am., Dramatists Guild, Writers Guild Am. (dir.), Dirs. Guild Am., ASCAP, Internat. Documentary Assn. (bd. dirs.), Soc. Preservation of Radio Drama, Variety and Comedy. Wendell Willkie One World Flight award (flew around world, recording speeches leaders of state, artists and scientists, June-Oct. 1946), first award Inst. for Edn. by Radio, 1946; prod. and narrated One World Flight, 1947; being the subject of two film documentaries. Home: 1840 Fairburn Ave Los Angeles CA 90025-4958 Personal E-mail: corwin@usc.edu.

CORWIN, PHILLIP, writer, educator, political organization worker; children: Meghan Corwin Moore, Charles, Daniel, Gregory. BA, Wesleyan U., 1967; MA, Cornell U., 1972. Assoc. editor Barron's Weekly, Dow Jones & Co., N.Y.C., 1964—69; info. officer, polit. ofcl. UN, 1969—96; adj. lectr. CUNY, 2003—. Author: Doomed in Afghanistan, Dubious Mandate, (short stories) Skeletons, Bittersweet, The Way Things Are. Mem.: Poetry Soc. Am., Author's Guild, Mensa. Personal E-mail: philcor2000@yahoo.com.

CORWIN, STANLEY JOEL, book publisher; b. N.Y.C., Nov. 6, 1938; s. Seymour and Faye (Agress) C.; m. Donna Gelgur; children: Alexandra, Donna, Ellen. AB, Syracuse U., 1960. Dir. subsidiary rights, v.p. mktg. Prentice-Hall, Inc., Englewood Cliffs, N.J., 1960-68; v.p. internat. Grosset & Dunlap, Inc., N.Y.C., 1968-75; founder, pres. Corwin Books, N.Y.C., 1975; pres., pub. Pinnacle Books, Inc., L.A., 1976-79; pres. Stan Corwin Prodns. Ltd., 1980—; pres., CEO Tudor Pub. Co., N.Y.C. and L.A., 1987-90. Lectr. Conf. World Affairs U. Colo., 1976, U. Denver, 1978, Calif. State U., Northridge, 1980, The Learning Annex; participant Pubmart Seminar, N.Y.C., 1977, UCLA, 1985, 93, 98; guest lectr. U. So. Calif., 1987—, iVillage Internet Chat Room, 1999—2001; expert witness nat. media trials; columnist Buddhascape Internet Network. Author: Where Words Were Born, 1977, How to Become a Best Selling Author, 1984, 3rd edit., 1999, The Creative Writer's Companion, 2001; contbr. articles L.A. Times, N.Y. Times, short stories to Signature mag.; prodr.: (films) Remo Williams-The Adventure Begins, 1986, (video) How to Golf with Jan Stephenson, 1987; exec. prodr.: The Elvis Files TV Show, 1991, The Marilyn Files, 1993; pub.: The Movie Script Libr., 1994. Mem. Pres. Carter's U.S. Com. on the UN, 1977. Served with AUS, 1960. Nat. prize winner short story contest Writers' Digest, 1966 Mem. Assn. Am. Pubs., PEN. Home and Office: 9309 Burton Way Beverly Hills CA 90210

CORWIN, STEVEN, hospital administrator; BS, Northwestern U., 1977; MD summa cum laude, Northwestern U. Sch. Medicine, 1979. Bd. cert. in internal medicine and cardiology. Intern and resident Columbia-Presbyn. Med. Ctr., N.Y.C., 1979—82, chief med. resident, dept. medicine, 1982—83; asst. prof. clin. medicine Coll. Physicians and Surgeons, Columbia U., N.Y.C., 1986—98, assoc. prof. clin. medicine, 1998—; med. dir. Milstein Hosp. Columbia-Presbyn. Med. Ctr., N.Y.C., 1997—98, dir. critical care svcs., 1991—97, dir. cardiac intensive care unit, 1986—91; chief med. officer N.Y. Presbyn. Hosp., N.Y.C., 1998—, sr. v.p., 1999—. Office: 161 Fort Washington Ave New York NY 10032

CORWIN, TIMON J., coach; b. Washington, June 10, 1964; s. Stanley Charles Corwin and Karen Nowak Bachman; m. Rachel Grenier Corwin, June 13, 1992; children: Timothy Raymond, Felix Jon, Emma Lucienne. BA, Kalamazoo Coll., 1986; JD, Marquette U., 1992. Tournament dir. USTA Boy's 18 & 16 Nat. Tennis Championships, Kalamazoo, 1993—; coach men's tennis Kalamazoo Coll., 1993—, athletic dir., 2003—. Bd. dirs. Intercollegiate Tennis Assn., Princeton, NJ; com. mem. U.S. Tennis Assn., White Plains, NY, 2001—02, 2005—. Bd. dirs. YMCA, Kalamazoo, 2002—. Recipient ITA Coach of Yr., NCAA Divsn. III, 1997, Nat. Cmty. Svc. award, U.S. Tennis Assn., 1997, Regional Coach of Yr., ITA, 1999. Mem.: Rotary. Avocations: sports, reading, movies. Home: 1417 Acad St Kalamazoo MI 49006 Office: Kalamazoo Coll 1200 Acad St Kalamazoo MI 49006

CORY, WALLACE NEWELL, retired civil engineer; b. Olympia, Wash., Mar. 10, 1937; s. Henry Newell and Gladys Evelyn (Nixon) C.; m. Roberta Ruth Matthews, July 4, 1959; children: Steven Newell, Susan Evelyn Cory Carbon. BS in Forestry, Oreg. State U., 1958, BSCE, 1964; MSCE, Stanford U., 1965. Registered profl. engr., Idaho, Oreg. Asst. projects mgr. CH2 M/Hill, Boise, Idaho, 1965-70; environ. mgr. Boise Cascade Corp., 1970-78, dir. state govt. affairs, 1978-82; dir. indsl. group JUB Engrs., Boise, 1982-84; chief engr. Anchorage Water & Wastewater, 1984-90; dir. pub. works City of Caldwell, Idaho, 1990-92; prin. engr. Montgomery Watson, Pasadena, Calif., 1992-95; adminstr. Idaho Divsn. Environ. Quality, Boise, 1995-98; planning and assessment leader Alexandria Wastewater Project Chemonics Internta., 1998-99. Precinct committeeman Idaho Rep. Com., Boise, 1968-72, region chmn., 1973-77. Capt. USAF, 1958-62. Fellow ASCE; mem. NSPE, Idaho Soc. Profl. Engrs. (pres. 1976-77, Young Engr. of Yr. award 1971), Air Pollution Control Assn. (chmn. Pacific N.W. sect. 1977-78), Idaho Assn. Commerce and Industry (chmn. environ. com. 1974-75). Avocations: hunting, fishing, shooting. Home: 7247 Cascade Dr Boise ID 83704-8635

CORYELL, GLYNN HEATH, financial services executive; b. Lexington, Ky., May 8, 1929; s. Glynn Lawrence Coryell and Allie May (Heath) C.; m. Diane Garnett Dobyns, Dec. 27, 1955 (div. Aug. 1981); children: Heather Diane, Holly. Grad., Culver (Ind.) Summer Cavalry Sch., 1947; AB, Harvard U., 1951; student, Harvard Law Sch., 1951-52, 54-55; MBA, Northwestern U., 1957. Supr. cost acctg. Procter & Gamble Co., Cin., 1957-60; sr. fin. analyst Socony Mobil Oil Corp., N.Y.C., 1961-62; dir. corp. profit planning, corp. economist Libby, McNeill & Libby, Chgo., 1962-67; treas. Lyntex Corp., N.Y.C., 1968-69; asst. treas. Std. Brands, Inc., N.Y.C., 1969-71; v.p. adminstr. and ops. Std. Brands Foods Co., N.Y.C., 1971-73; fin. v.p. Grand Union Co., Elmwood Park, NJ, 1973-76; exec. v.p., CFO, dir. Cramer Electronics, Inc., Newton, Mass., 1976-79; sr. v.p., CFO, dir. Kuhn's-Big K Stores Corp., Nashville, 1979-81; v.p. fin. and adminstrn., sec. Sunmark, Inc., St. Louis, 1981-83; corp. fin. cons. Lemoyne, Pa., 1984-88; pres. Glynn H. Coryell & Assocs. Inc. doing bus. as Travel Agts. Internat., Falls Church, Va., 1988-94; corp. fin. cons. Alexandria, Va., 1994—2004. Mem. Rep. Nat. Com., John Harvard Soc. With Intelligence U.S. Army, 1953—54. Mem.: Indiana Soc. of Washington, Ky. Soc. of Washington, Culver Edn. Found., Civil War Preservation Trust, Ky. Hist. Soc., Ind. Hist. Soc., Korean War Vets. Assn., Alumni Assn. Kellogg Grad. Sch. Mgmt. Northwestern U. Republican. Baptist. Home and Office: Garnett Hall 200 Masonic Home Dr Apt 110 Masonic Home KY 40041 Office Phone: 502-259-5392.

CORY-JONES, SARA ANN, art educator; b. Columbus, Ohio, Apr. 21, 1976; d. Robert Corwin Cory Jr. and Joetta Ann Cory; m. Philip Aaron Jones, June 8, 2002; children: Sadira, Zoey. BFA, Ohio U., 2000; M in Classroom, U. Rio Grande, 2005. Cert. art educator Ohio. Art educator Adena Sch., Frankfort, Ohio, 2000—01, Smith and Mt. Logan Mid. Sch., Chillicothe, Ohio, 2001—02, So. Hills Acad., Chillicothe, 2002—03, Chillicothe H.S., 2002—. Author: (lesson plan) The Multiple Intelligences of the Arts, 2004. Mem.: NEA, Nat. Art Edn. Assn., Ohin Edn. Assn. Democrat. Methodist. Avocations: art, gardening.

CORZINE, JON STEVENS, senator, former investment banker; b. Taylorville, Ill., Jan. 1, 1947; s. Roy Allen and Nancy June (Hedrick) C.; m. Joanne Dougherty, Sept. 8, 1968 (div.); children: Jennifer, Joshua, Jeffrey. BA, U. Ill., 1969; MBA, U. Chgo., 1973. Bond officer Continental Ill. Nat. Bank, Chgo., 1970-73; asst. v.p. BancOhio Corp., Columbus, 1974-75; with Goldman, Sachs & Co., N.Y.C., 1975—99, v.p., 1977, pntr., 1980, mem. mgmt. com., 1985-94, co-head fixed income divsn., ptnr., 1985-94, chmn., CEO, 1994-99; senator NJ, 2001—; mem, fgn. rels. com. US Senate. Bd. dirs. NJ Performing Arts Ctr., 1993-94, chmn. coun. trustees, 1995-, NY Philharmonic, 1996, Overlook Hosp., Summit, NJ; dir. Family Services, Summit, NJ; co-chaired the Summit area YMCA's Second Century Campaign; trustee Kennedy Ctr. for the Performing Arts in Washington, DC, U. Chgo., NY Univ. Child Study Ctr. Reserve USMC, 1969—75. Mem. Pub. Securities Assn. (vice chmn. 1985, chmn. 1986) Democrat. Office: 502 Hart Senate Office Building Washington DC 20510 also: One Gateway Center, 11th Floor Newark NJ 07102 also: 208 White Horse Pike, Suite 18 Barrington NJ 08007*

CORZO, MIGUEL ANGEL, academic administrator; b. Mexico City, Mar. 2, 1942; came to U.S., 1985; s. Miguel A. and Josefina (Melgar) C.; m. Liliane Maunier, June 13, 1964; children: Liliane, Alexandre, Xavier Edward. BS, UCLA, 1967; MS, Nat. U. Mexico, Mexico City, 1970; DSc, Tech. U. Munich, Germany, 1974. Prof. Nat. U., Mexico City, 1967-74; dean acad. affairs Met. U., Mexico City, 1974-77; spl. adviser Mexican Ministry Urban Devel., Mexico City, 1977-80; sec. tourism Mexican Ministry Tourism, Mexico City, 1980-82; pres. Friends Arts of Mex., LA, 1988-91; dir. spl. projects Getty Conservation Inst., LA, 1986-88, dir., 1991—2000; pres. Univ. of Arts, Phila., 2000—. Mem. Cultural Property Adv. Com., 1995. Author: Engineering Design, 1971, Human Settlements, 1979 (gold award 1979); editor over 20 books. Fulbright fellow Harvard U., 1979. Office: Univ Arts 320 S Broad St Philadelphia PA 19102*

COSAR, EDIZ FERGÜN, pathologist, researcher; b. Igdir, Turkey, July 16, 1964; s. Ergün and Sevgi (Cölkesen) C.; m. Elifce Özlem (Koca) Cosar, July 27, 1990. MD, Cukurova U., Adana, Turkey, 1988. Cert. anatomic and clin. pathologist 2002. Pathologist, clin. prof. Cukurova U., Adana, Turkey, 1995—97; resident Cukurova U. Sch. Med., Adana, Turkey, 1989—95, Ill. Masonic Med. Ctr., Chgo., 1998—99, Loyola U. Med. Ctr., Maywood, Ill., 1999—2002, fellow in molecular genetic pathology, 2002—03, U. Mass. Meml. Med. Ctr., 2003—04. Editor (book): Cancer Incidence in Turkey, 1994; contbr. articles to profl. jours. Mem. European Soc. Pathology, Friends and Alumni of Armed Forces Inst. Pathology, U.S., Turkish Assn. Cancer Rsch. and Control, Cukurova Pathology Soc., US and Can. Acad. Pathology, Am. Assn. Cancer Rsch., Assn. Molecular Pathology, Coll. Am. Pathologists. Avocations: tennis, swimming. Office: U Mass Meml Med Ctr Dept Pathology 55 Lake Ave North Worcester MA 01655-0002

COSBY, BILL, actor, television producer; b. Phila., July 12, 1937; s. William Henry and Anna C.; m. Camille Hanks, Jan. 25, 1964; children: Erika Ranee, Erinn Chalene, Ennis William (dec.), Ensa Camille, Evin Harrah. Student, Temple U.; MA, U. Mass., 1972, EdD, 1976; MusD (hon.), Berklee Coll. Music, 2004. Pres. Rhythm and Blues Hall of Fame, 1968—. Appeared in numerous night clubs, including The Gaslight, N.Y.C., Hungry I, San Francisco, Shoreham Hotel, Washington, Basin St. East, N.Y.C., Hilton, Las Vegas, Nev., Harrah's Lake Tahoe; guest appearances on numerous TV shows, including The Electric Co., 1971-72, Capt. Kangaroo, Touched by an Angel, 1997, 99, King of Queens, 1999, Everybody Loves Raymond, 1999, Becker, 1999; co-star: TV show I Spy, 1965-68; star (TV series) The Bill Cosby Show, 1969-71, The New Bill Cosby Show, 1972-73, (host, voices) Fat Albert and the Cosby Kids, 1972-79, Cos, 1976, (host, voices) The New Fat Albert Show, 1979-82, The Cosby Show, 1984-92, The Cosby Mysteries, 1994-95, Cosby, 1996-2000; host, TV game show You Bet Your Life, 1992-93, Kids Say the Darndest Things, 1998-2000, Jack Paar "As I Was Saying...", 1997; interviewee 4 Little Girls (TV), 1997; exec. prodr. TV show A Different World, 1987-93, Here and Now, 1992-93; TV movies include I Spy Returns, 1994, The Bill Cosby Mystery Movies, 1994; recs. include: Revenge (Grammy award Nat. Acad. Performing Arts and Scis. 1967), To Russell, My Brother, With Whom I Slept, 1968 (Grammy award), Why Is There Air, 1965 (Grammy award), Wonderfulness, 1966 (Grammy award), It's True, It's True, Bill Cosby is a Very Funny Fellow...Right, 1963, I Started Out as a Child, 1964 (Grammy award), Reunion, 1982, Bill Cosby...Himself, 1983 (dir., prodr.), Those of You With or Without Children, You'll Understand, (jazz albums) Where You Lay Your Head, 1990, My Appreciation, 1991, Hello Friend: To Ennis With Love, 1997; films include Hickey and Boggs, 1972, Man and Boy, 1972, Uptown Saturday Night, 1974, Let's Do It Again, 1975, Mother, Jugs and Speed, 1976, A Piece of the Action, 1977, California Suite, 1978, (voice) Aesop's Fable, 1978, Devil and Max Devlin, 1979, Bill Cosby...Himself, 1985, Leonard: Part VI, 1987, Ghost Dad, 1990, The Meteor Man, 1993, Jack, 1996; exec. prodr., writer Fat Alber, 2004; co-exec. prodr., writer (TV series) Fatherhood, 2004; recipient 4 Emmy awards 1966, 67, 68, 69, 8 Grammy awards, named number 1 in comedy field Top Artists on Campus Poll (album sales) 1968; author: The Wit and Wisdom of Fat Albert, 1973, Bill Cosby's Personal Guide to Power Tennis, Fatherhood, 1986, Time Flies, 1988, Love and Marriage, 1989, Childhood, 1991. Served with USNR, 1956-60. Named to Hall of Fame, Acad. TV Arts and Scis., 1994; recipient Bob Hope Humanitarian award, Academy of Television Arts & Sciences, 2003. Achievements include setting concert attendance record Radio City Music Hall, 1986.*

COSBY, MARK S, retail executive; BBA, MBA, U. Wis. Sr. fin. analyst, cost acctg. supr., fin. analyst Gen. Food Corp., 1982—85; mgr., bus. planning Hayes Micro Computer Products, 1985—87; mgr. bus. planning, so. divsn. Taco Bell/PepsiCo, 1988—89; mgr. corp. strategic planning PepsiCo, 1989—90; various positions KFC/PepsiCo, 1991—97; chief develop. officer Tricon, 1997—2000; COO KFC/Tricon(now Yum! Brands, Inc.), 2000—02; pres., full line stores Sears, Roebuck and Co., 2002—; exec. v.p. Sears Roebuck and Co., 2002—. Office: Sears Roebuck and Co 3333 Beverly Rd Hoffman Estates IL 60179

COSBY, STEPHANIE BENNETT, health services professional; b. Boynton Beach, Fla., Apr. 26, 1967; d. David Hendrie Cosby and Carolyn Clem Fant; m. Gary Merrill Brown, Aug. 21, 1956. BS, U. of Fla., 1987—89; BSN, Emory U., 1994—96. RN Ga., 1996, S.C., 1999. Staff nurse Emory U. Hosp., 1996—97; travel nurse Travcorps, LA, 1997—98, Mission St. Joseph's Hosp., Asheville, NC, 1998—99; sch. nurse Haywood Co. Health Dept., Waynesville, NC, 1999—2001; regional svc. coord. for the best chance network Am. Cancer Soc., Charleston, SC. Prodr., co-director, co-editor Haywood Active Youth Unlimited, Waynesville, NC, 2000—01; cons. Haywood County Domestic Task Force Resource Video, Waynesville, SC, 2001—01. Prodr.(co-director, co-editor): (video) H.A.Y.U. Health Promotion Video Project (Aegis Award, 2001); editor (consultant): (video) Fear Factor-Orientation Video for Waynesville M.S. (Aegis Award, 2001); editor: (director) You Are Not Alone-Resource Video for the Haywood Co. Domestic Task Force; author: (manual) Operation V.Y.D.E.O.-Health Promotion Video Projects; singer: (compact disc) Music of the Baha'i World Congress, 1992; singer: (soloist) (choir) Voices of Baha; singer: (concert at carnegie hall). Mem.: Womens Cancer Coalition. Independent. Baha'I Faith. Avocations: sailing, singing, travel. Home: 2174 Saint James Dr Charleston SC 29412-2036 Personal E-mail: sailaway2k@earthlink.net.

COSELL, BERNARD, retired computer systems architect; b. N.Y.C., Aug. 28, 1946; s. Bernard Delfy and Julia Cocozziello; m. Lynn Karyl Marquardt, Sept. 7, 1968. MS in Math., Northeastern U., 1977. Sr. systems arch. Bolt Beranek and Newman, Cambridge, Mass., 1965—92. Mem. adj. faculty Va. Western C.C. Treas., bd. dirs. Triangle Ruritan, Pearisburg, Va., 1996—2005. Achievements include development of the modern notion of network management and implementation of the first network management system; participation on the team that implemented the original switching software for the ARPAnet network node; help in development and operational deployment of the first dialup terminal access system for the ARPAnet; design of the will/wont, do/dont machinery for the ARPAnet telnet protocol. Avocation: shepherding. Personal E-mail: bernie@fantasyfarm.com.

COSENS, KIM JAY, investment advisor; b. San Francisco, Calif., Sept. 28, 1959; s. Robert John and Lois Jean Cosens; m. Shelly Marie Cosens. MusB, U. SD, 1983. Dir. instrumental music Mitchell HS, Mitchell, SD, 1983—87, Spirit Lake (Iowa) HS, 1987—93, North HS, Sioux City, Iowa, 1993—94, Waseca HS, Waseca, Minn., 1994—2002; investment rep. Edward Jones, Owatonna, Minn., 2002—. Jazz edn. chair Minn. Music Educators, Minn., 2000—02; fin. bd. Wellness Ptnrs., Owatonna, Minn., 2004—. Accompanist, bd. mem. Rotary, Owatonna, Minn., 2004—, pres-elect, 2005, pres., 2006. Named one of Outstanding Young Men of Am. Republican. Bapt. Avocations: piano, golf, music consulting, saxophone. Home: 780 18th St NE Owatonna MN 55060 Office: Edward Jones 685 W Bridge St Ste 1A Owatonna MN 55060 Office Phone: 507-451-1324. Office Fax: 877-266-9397. E-mail: kjcosens@charter.net.

COSENZA, ARTHUR GEORGE, opera director; b. Phila., Oct. 16, 1924; s. Luigi and Maria (Piccolo) C.; m. Marietta Muhs, Sept. 16, 1950; children: Louis John, Arthur William, Maria. Student, Ornstein Sch. Music, Phila., 1946-48, Berkshire Music Festival, 1947, Am. Theater Wing, N.Y.C., 1948-50. Asso. prof. Coll. Music, Loyola U. of South, 1954-84, dir. opera workshop, 1954-84; dir. Opera Program for City of New Orleans, 1955-73 Appeared in maj. opera houses throughout U.S., Can.; baritone New Orleans Opera, 1954-70, prodr., 1960-74, dir., 1965-98, dir. emeritus, 1998- Served with AUS, 1943-45. Decorated Purple Heart medal; cavaliere Order Star Italian Solidarity; cavaliere Ufficiale dell' Ordine al Merito Italy; officier Ordre des Arts et des Lettres. Mem. Am. Guild Mus. Artists (hon. life), Blue Key.

COSGRIFF, JAMES ARTHUR, physician; b. Lamberton, Minn., Mar. 18, 1924; s. James Arthur and Elsie Ann (Forster) C. BS summa cum laude, Coll. St. Thomas, 1944; MD, U. Minn., 1946. Intern St. Mary's Hosp., Duluth, Minn.; pvt. practice Olivia, Minn., 1949—. With USN, 1947-49. Fellow Am. Acad. Family Physicians; mem. Minn. Acad. Family Physicians (pres. 1963, Merit award 1964), Alpha Omega Alpha. Roman Catholic. Avocations: travel, photography, reading, music. Home: 802 E Park Ave Olivia MN 56277-1361 Office: Olivia Clinic 619 E Lincoln Ave Olivia MN 56277-1349 Office Phone: 320-523-2131.

COSGRIFF, STUART WORCESTER, internist, consultant, medical educator; b. Pittsfield, Mass., May 8, 1917; s. Thomas F. and Frances Deford (Worcester) C.; m. Mary Shaw, Jan. 23, 1943; children: Mary, Thomas, Stuart, Richard, Robert. BA cum laude, Holy Cross Coll., 1938; MD, Columbia U., 1942, D Med. Sci., 1948. Diplomate Am. Bd. Internal Medicine. Intern Presbyterian Hosp., N.Y.C., 1942-43; asst. resident in medicine, 1943, 46-47; chief resident, 1947-48; instr. in medicine Columbia U., N.Y.C., 1948-50, clin. asst. prof. medicine, 1951-63, clin. assoc. prof., 1963-73, clin. prof. medicine, 1973-83, clin. prof. emeritus, 1983—; attending physician Presbyn. Hosp., N.Y.C., 1948-83, cons. emeritus, 1984—; individual practice medicine, specializing in internal medicine and vascular diseases, 1948—. Cons. in medicine to dir. Selective Svc., N.Y.C., 1957-73, N.Y. Giants Baseball Club, 1951-57, San Francisco Baseball Club, 1958-61; dir. thrombo-embolic clinic Vanderbilt Clinic, N.Y.C., 1948-83. Contbr. articles to med. jours. Served to capt. M.C., U.S. Army, 1943-45, ETO. Fellow ACP, Pan Am. Med. Assn.; mem. Am. Heart Assn., N.Y. Heart Assn., Alpha Omega Alpha Clubs: Knickerbocker Country (Tenafly, N.J.). Roman Catholic. Home and Office: 11 Park St Tenafly NJ 07670-2217 Office: 161 Ft Washington Ave New York NY 10032-3713

COSGROVE, DELOS M., health facility administrator, surgeon; b. Watertown, N.Y., July 28, 1940; s. Delos M. and Margaret C.; m. Anita Desiderio, May 8, 1976; children: Nicole Ashley, Britt Lindsey. BA, Williams Coll., Williamstown, Mass., 1962; MD, U. Va., 1966. Diplomate Am. Bd. Surgery, Am. Bd. Thoracic Surgery. Intern Strong Meml. Hosp., Rochester, N.Y., 1966-67, resident in surgery, 1967-68, Mass. Gen. Hosp., Boston, 1970-72, sr. resident in cardiac surgery, 1973-74; registrar in cardiac surgery Brook Gen. Hosp., London, 1972-73; chief resident Boston Children's Hosp., 1974; assoc. staff dept. thoracic and cardiovascular surgery The Cleve. Clinic, 1975-76, profl. staff, 1976—, chmn. dept. thoracic and cardiovascular surgery, 1990—, CEO, 2004—, chmn., bd. governors, 2004—. Contbr. articles to profl. jours. Mem. Am. Assn. Thoracic Surgery (pres. 2000), Internat. Soc. Cardiovascular Surgery, Am. Coll. Cardiology, Am. Coll. Chest Physicians, ACS, Am. Heart Assn., AMA, Am. Surg. Assn., Cleve. Surg. Soc., Ohio State Med. Assn., Ohio Thoracic Soc., Cleve. Acad. Medicine, Soc. Thoracic Surgeons, Soc. for Thoracic Surg. Edn. (chmn. membership com. 1985-87), Peruvian Coll. Angiology (hon.), Chilean Soc. Cardiology (hon.), Dominican Republic Soc. Cardiology (hon.), Argentine Coll. Cardiology (hon., mem. editorial bd. The Annals of Thorace Surgery). Avocation: sailing. Office: Cleve Clinic Surgery 9500 Euclid Ave Cleveland OH 44195-0001

COSGROVE, GARTH REES, neurosurgeon; b. Montreal, Canada, Sept. 22, 1956; s. James Bert Cosgrove and Alison Mabel Chown; m. Karen Ann Roche, Apr. 13, 1954; children: Kathryn, Priscilla. MD, Queen's U., Kingston, Ontario, 1980. Fellow Royal Coll. of Surgeons Can., 1989. Instr. Harvard Med. Sch., Boston, 1986—90; asst. prof. U. Va., Charlottesville, 1990—92; chmn., dept. of neurosurgery Lahey Clinic, Burlington, Vt., 2005—. Office: Lahey Clinic 41 Mall Rd Burlington MA 01805 Office Phone: 781-744-1990. E-mail: g.rees.cosgrove@lahey.

COSGROVE, HOWARD EDWARD, JR., utilities executive; b. Phila., Apr. 12, 1943; s. Howard Edward and Margaret C. (May); m. Roberta Joyce Olewine, Apr. 19, 1965; children: Pamela Joyce, Susan Ann. BS in Mech. Engring., U. Va., 1966; MBA, U. Del., 1970. Registered profl. engr., Del. With Delmarva Power Co., Wilmington, Del., 1966—, mgr. fin., 1979, v.p., chief fin. officer, 1979—, exec. v.p., 1984-92, chmn., CEO, 1992—2002; now chmn., pres. & CEO Conectiv, Wilmington, Del.; chmn. NRG Energy, 2003—. Mem.: Fin. Execs. Inst., Nat. Soc. Profl. Engrs. Home: PO Box 197 Rockland DE 19732-0197 Office: Delmarva Power & Light Co 800 N King St Wilmington DE 19801-3518

COSGROVE, JOHN FRANCIS, lawyer, state legislator; b. Coral Gables, Fla., July 1, 1949; s. Francis Freheil and Vivian Adair (Rafferty) C.; m. Bernardine Elizabeth Cosgrove, Dec. 19, 1981; children: Michael, Tiffany, Colleen. AA, U. Fla., 1969, BS in Journalism, 1971; JD, Cumberland Sch. Law, 1975. Bar: Fla., U.S. Dist. Ct. (so. dist.) Fla., U.S. Ct. Appeals (5th cir.), U.S. Supreme Ct. Assoc. Hall & Hedrick, Miami, Fla., 1975-80; sole practice Miami, 1980—. Mem. Fla. Ho. of Reps., 1981-84, 1986—; gen. counsel Biscayne Coll.; columnist Miami Rev.: Juris Conspectus, 1975—; chair Nat. Conf. State Legislatures Com. on Commerce and Comm.; chair property and casualty com., mem. exec. com. Nat. Conf. Ins. Legislatures. Chmn. Coral Gables Code Enforcement Bd.; mem. Coral Gables Econ. Devel. Bd.; mem. Jr. Orange Bowl Com.; chmn. Metro-Dade Econ. Devel. Bd., Miami Budget Rev. Com.; mem. South Miami Hosp. Assocs. Mem. ABA, Fla. Bar Assn. (Jud. Selection, Adminstrn. and Tenure Com., vice chmn. jud. nominating com.), Dade County Bar Assn. (3d v.p.), Am. Judicature Soc., ATLA, Pvt. Industry Coun. Dade County, Emerald Soc. South Fla., Miami Springs-Hialeah C. of C., Coral Gables C. of C., Grtr. Miami C. of C., Blue Key, Serra Club, Viscayans Civic Club, Le Lega Civic Club, Grtr. Miami Leadership Prayer Breakfast Club, KC (grand knight Coral Gables; pres. Dade County chpt.), Kiwanis, Knight of Malta, Phi Kappa Tau. Democrat. Roman Catholic (chmn. Cath. Svc. Bur.-50th anniversary). Home: 8230 SW 192nd St Miami FL 33157-8013 Office: 18320 SW 97th Ave Miami FL 33157 Office Phone: 305-373-5313. E-mail: jfc7149esq@aol.com.

COSGROVE, JOHN PATRICK, editor; b. Pittston, Pa., Sept. 25, 1918; s. Raymond Patrick and Alice (Gilroy) C.; m. Patricia Ellen O'Hara, Mar. 26, 1951. Ed. pub. schs., Pa. Reporter, Wilkes-Barre (Pa.) Record, 1936-37, AP, Washington, 1938-40; writer, research Nat. Republican Congl. Com., Washington, 1940; exec. asst. U.S. Senator Hiram W. Johnson, 1941-42; free lance writer, 1946-48; dir. publs. Broadcasting Publs., Inc. (pubs. Broadcasting Businessweekly, Television monthly, Broadcasting Yearbook), Washington, 1948-68. Author: The Gendreau Story: War History of DE 639; editor: SHRDLU-An Affectionate Chronicle of the first fifty years of the Nat. Press Club, 1959. Publicity dir. Honor Am. Day Celebration, 1970; exec. dir. Am. Hist. and Cultural Soc., Inc., 1970-88; sec. Nat. Christmas Pageant of Peace, 1974—, v.p., 1985—, mem. com. to light nat. Christmas tree; Washington rep. Nat. Com. Neurol. Disorders and Stroke, 1972-78, R.R. Task Force for Northeast Region, 1973-75; bd. dirs. Am. Irish Found., 1967-87, pres., 1971-73; bd. dirs. Washington chpt. Nat. Multiple Sclerosis Soc., 1962-70, Am. Ireland Fund, 1987—2001; mem. bd. dirs. USN Meml. Found., Washington, 1986—, sec. and chmn. dedication com., 1987-; bd. dirs. Ellis Island Restoration Commn., N.Y., 1989—, Destroyer-Escort Hist. Mus., 1993—; vice chmn. Am. Fedn. Irish Heritage, 1988—; bd. dirs. Internat. Svc. Agys., 1992-99, mem. bd. govs. Internat. Grad. U., 2003-. Served with USNR, 1942-46; assigned Office Censorship, Washington 1942; U.S.S. Gendreau 1944-46. Named Gael of Yr., Washington D.C. St. Patrick's Parade, 1999. Mem. VFW (life), White House Corrs. Assn. (hon.), Soc. Profl. Journalists, Destroyer-Escort Sailors Assn. (life, bd. dirs. 1981-96), Am. Legion (life), Nat. Press Club (Post no. 20, comdr. 1999—), Soc. Friendly Sons of St. Patrick (life, bd. dirs. 1976-82), Nat. Headliners Club (Atlantic City), Circus Saints and Sinners Club (exec. v.p., dir. P.T. Barnum tent 1973-89, pres. 1989-91), Nat. Press Club (Washington) (bd. govs. 1956-59, v.p. 1960, pres. 1961, chmn. awards com. 1974, chmn. election com. 1978). Roman Catholic. Home: 7906 Jensen Pl Bethesda MD 20817-4671 Office: 1124 National Press Building Washington DC 20045-2101 Office Phone: 202-628-3400.

COSIER, RICHARD A., dean, finance educator; b. Jackson, Mich., May 18, 1947; s. Roy A. and Wilma M. (Braund) C.; m. Rae L. Pettelle, June 14, 1969 (div. Feb. 1985); children: Jeffrey R., Nathan R.; m. Lynn M. Hays, Aug. 30, 1986; children: Courtney M., Kelsey L. BS, Mich. State U., 1969; MBA, Loyola U., 1972; PhD, U. Iowa, 1976. From asst. to assoc. prof. mgmt. Ind. U., Bloomington, 1976-86, prof. mgmt., 1986-92, chairperson, prof. mgmt., 1983-90, assoc. dean for acads., prof. mgmt., 1990-92; dean, Fred E. Brown chair U. Okla., Norman, 1993-99; dean and Leeds prof. mgmt. Purdue U., 1999—, dir. Burton D. Morgan Ctr. Entrepreneurship, 2002—05; with faculty U. Notre Dame. Bd. dirs. Kite Realty Group Trust, Roll Coater, Inc.; cons. in field. Contbr. over 75 articles and book chpts. to profl. jours.; co-author mgmt. textbook; contbr. book chpts.; inventor patented packaging technique. Active with United Way Am.; mem. exec. com. Greater Lafayette Comty. Devel. Corp., 2001; chmn. United Way campaign Purdue U., 2003—. Fellow Richard D. Irwin . Mem.: Acad. Mgmt. Republican. Office: Krannert Sch Mgmt Rm 122 Purdue U West Lafayette IN 47907-1310 Office Phone: 765-494-4366. E-mail: rcosier@purdue.edu.

COSIMI, A. BENEDICT, surgeon; MD, U. Colo., 1964. Diplomate Am. Bd. Surgery. Resident in transplantation Mass. Gen. Hosp., Boston, 1968-69, fellow, 1969, resident in surgery, 1970, divsn. chief transplant unit, dir. liver surgery and liver-small bowel transplantation. Office: Mass Gen Hosp White 5-15 Boston MA 02114 Office Phone: 617-726-8256. Business E-Mail: cpadyk@partners.org.

COSING, ARTHUR PAUL, JR., writer, artist; b. Miami, Fla., May 11, 1926; s. Arthur Paul Cosing Sr. and Ruby Myrtledean Ogorek; m. Shirley Mae Baumann, Oct. 16, 1954 (dec. June 7, 1997); 1 child, Arthur Paul III. BS, U. Md., 1950. Artist Washington Post, Washington, 1950—52; visual info. specialist NIH, Bethesda, Md., 1952—55, pub. info. specialist, 1955—60; speech writer Office Surgeon Gen. USPHS, Washington, 1960—63; pub. info. officer Bur. Family Svcs. HEW, Washington, 1963—67; asst. chief Office Comm. NIMH, Rockville, Md., 1967—78, chief tech. svcs., 1978—88; ret. Contbr. articles to profl. jours. and lit. publs.;, co-author paperback book of humor. With U.S. Army, 1944—45, ETO. Decorated Combat Badge, Purple Heart, Bronze Star; recipient award, NIH, 1958, HHS, 1985. Mem.: Omicron Delta Kappa, Pi Delta Epsilon, Theta Chi. Avocations: sketching, writing, travel, golf. Home: 3693 Persimmon Cir Fairfax VA 22031 E-mail: apc1@erols.com.

COSLER, STEVEN DOUGLAS, managed care company executive; b. Indpls., July 17, 1955; s. Robert Douglas Cosler and Ruth (Beasley) Pape; m. Lynne Ulbrich, Jan. 14, 1978; children: Stephanie Lynne, Robert Louis. BS in Indsl. Mgmt., Purdue U., 1977. Sales engr. Ross Gear div. TRW, Lafayette, Ind., 1977-78; mktg. rep. IBM Corp., Louisville, 1978-83, regional mktg. staff Cin., 1983-84, mktg. mgr. Indpls., 1984-87, bus planning mgr. Chgo., 1987-88, br. mgr. Indpls., 1989—; v.p. 1st Benefit Corp., Anderson, Ind., 1992—96; sr. v.p., gen. mgr. Priority Healthcare Svcs. (subs. Bindley We. Industries), 1996—97; exec. v.p., pharmacy svcs. Priority Healthcare, Lake Mary, Fla., 1997—2000, exec. v.p., 2000—01, COO, 2000—02, pres., 2001—, CEO, 2002—. Mem. bd. advisors 1st Benefit Corp., 1990-92. Mem. state bd. dirs. Fellowship of Christian Athletes, Indpls., 1985—, nat. bd. dirs., Orlando, Fla., 1989—; chmn. sub. com. NCAA Championships, Indpsl., 1991, PGA Championship, 1993, U.S. Women's Open, 1993; deacon E 91st St. Christian Ch., Indpls., 1989-90. Mem. Highland Golf and Country Club, Gold Coats of Purdue U., Rotary. Avocations: golf, travel, sports, reading. Office: Priority Healthcare 250 Technology Pk Lake Mary FL 32746*

COSLETT, HARRY BRANCH, neurologist, behavioral neurologist; b. Phila., Mar. 14, 1950; s. Edward Worthington and Judith (Connelly) C.; m. Janet Goldwater, Aug. 25, 1982; children: Caitlin, Addavail. BA, Princeton U., 1972; MD, U. Pa., 1977. Diplomate Am. Bd. Psychiatry and Neurology. Resident in neurology U. Va., Charlottesville, 1978-81, asst. prof. neurology, 1981-82; fellow in behavioral neurology U. Fla., Gainesville, 1982-83; asst. prof. neurology Temple U., Phila., 1983-86, assoc. prof., 1986-91, prof., 1992—. Examiner, question writer Am. Bd. Psychiatry and Neurology, 1990—. Editor Neurocase, 1994—; contbr. articles to Brain, Brain and Brain Lang., Neuropsychologia, others. NIH grantee, 1984—, McDonnell-Pew Founds. grantee, 1994-95. Fellow Am. Acad. Neurology; mem. Acad. of Aphasia, Internat. Neuropsychology Soc. Democrat. Avocations: basketball, tennis, archery. Home: 2003 Wallace St Philadelphia PA 19130-3221 Office: Hosp U Penn 3400 Spruce St Philadelphia PA 19104

COSMAN, FRANCENE JEN, former government official; b. Windsor, Ont., Can., Jan. 14, 1941; d. John Douglas and Dorothy Mae (Machel) McCarthy; m. David Killam Cosman, July 25, 1964 (div.); children: Lara Machel, Andrea Leigh; m. Aza Avramovitch, June 27, 1998 (dec.). Diploma in Nursing, St. John Gen. Hosp., N.B., 1962; postgrad. diploma, Margaret Hague Hosp., Jersey City, 1963. RN Can. Various nursing positions, 1963-68; county councillor County of Halifax, N.S., 1976-79; mayor Town of Bedford, N.S., 1979-82; pres. Adv. Coun. on Status of Women, N.S., 1982-86; exec. dir. N.S. Liberal Party, 1989-93; mem. Legis. Assembly, House of Assembly of N.S., Halifax, 1993-99, dep. spkr., min. comty. svcs., 1995-99; ret. Chair Sr. Citizens Secretariat, 1997-99; min. responsible adminstrn. Adv. Coun. Status Women Act, 1997-99; min. Cmty. Svcs., 1997-99; min. responsible Disabled Persons Commn. Act, 1997-99; mem. Healing Touch Ministry, 2000—. Contbr. numerous reports, brief, documents to provincial and fed. levels of govt.; opinion col. writer Chronicle Herald Newspaper, 1987-88. Liberal. Mem. United Ch. Avocations: artist, poetry, swimming, healing touch practitioner. E-mail: fjc@eastlink.ca.

COSMANO, VINCENT JAMES, retired music educator; b. Chgo., Ill., Nov. 10, 1941; s. James Joseph and Genevieve Henriette Cosmano; m. Sue Ellen Hopkins, July 23, 2001; m. Sheila Joy Smith, June 19, 1965 (div. June 1985); children: Timothy, Jeffrey, Patrick. AA, Wilson Jr. Coll., 1962; BSc in edn., Ill. State U., 1965, MSc in music edn., 1971. Band instr. Wyo. H.S., Wyoming, Ill., 1965, Piper City Cmty. Schools, Piper City, Ill., 1965—68, Ill. Valley Ctrl. H.S., Chillicothe, 1968—76, O'Fallon Twp. H.S., 1976—2001; ret., 2001. Recipient Outstanding Music Educator, Ill. H.S. Assn., 2000, Excellence in Tchg., Emerson Elec., St. Louis, Mo., 1997, Award of Excellence, C. of C., Ill., 1988. Home: 25895 Bass Lake Lane Spooner WI 54801

COSPOLICH, JAMES DONALD, electronics executive, consultant; b. New Orleans, Dec. 19, 1944; s. Clarence James and Olga Marie C.; m. Shirley Patricia Knipper, Feb. 4, 1967; children: Brian James, Jeffery Donald, Stephen William. BEE, La. State U., 1967, MEE, 1972. Registered profl. engr., La., Calif., Tex. Geophysicist Pan Am. Petroleum Corp. subs. AMOCO, New Orleans, 1967; elec. engr. Waldemar S. Nelson & Co., New Orleans, 1967-74, asst. v.p., mgr. elec. engring., 1974-83, v.p., mgr. elec. engring., 1983-85, sr. v.p. ops., 1985-91, exec. v.p., 1991—. Mem. Nat. Elec. Code Panel 14. Mem. Rep. Nat. Com., Washington, 1988; v.p. Ormond Civic Assn., Destrehan, La., 1985, pres., 1986; mem. representing St. Charles Parish, New Orleans Internat. Airport Noise Abatement Com. With USCGR, 1964-72. Mem. NFPA (nat. elec. code com.), IEEE, NSPE, Instrument Soc. Am. (sr., mem. various coms. 1975—), Am. Petroleum Inst. (com. recommended practice stds.), Gas Processors Assn., La. Engring. Soc., Ormond Country Club, The Am. Legion. Republican. Roman Catholic. Avocations: fishing, tennis, golf, skiing, boating, woodworking. Home: 61 Rosedown Dr Destrehan LA 70047-2529 Office: Waldemar S Nelson & Co Inc 1200 Saint Charles Ave New Orleans LA 70130-4334 Office Phone: 504-593-5293. Personal E-mail: jimcospolich@wsnelson.com.

COSS, STEPHEN K., lawyer; b. 1969; BA, Duke U.; JD, U. Va. Gen. counsel Sonic Automotive Inc., Charlotte, NC, 2000—04, sr. v.p., gen. counsel, 2004—. Mem.: ABA, 1994. Office: Sonic Automotive 6415 Idlewild Rd Ste 109 Charlotte NC 28212 Office Phone: 704-566-2420.

COSSÉ, STEVEN A., lawyer; b. Dec. 2, 1947; m. Andree D. Cossé. BA, Southeastern La. U.; JD, Loyola U. Gen. counsel Murphy Oil Corp., El Dorado, Ariz., 1991—, v.p., 1993—94, sr. v.p., 1994—. Office: Murphy Oil Corp 200 Peach St El Dorado AR 71731 Home: 2406 Pathway El Dorado AR 71730-5263 Office Phone: 870-862-6411. Office Fax: 870-864-6373. Business E-Mail: steve_cosse@murphyoilcorp.com.

COSSINS, EDWIN ALBERT, biology professor, academic administrator; b. Havering, Eng., Feb. 28, 1937; came to Can., 1962; s. Albert Joseph and Elizabeth H. (Brown) C.; m. Lucille Jeannette Salt, Sept. 1, 1962; children: Diane Elizabeth (dec. 1995), Carolyn Jane. BSc, U. London, 1958, PhD, 1961, DSc, 1981. Rsch. assoc. Purdue U., Lafayette, Ind., 1961-62; from asst. prof. to prof. U. Alta., Edmonton, Can., 1962-96, acting head dept. botany, 1965-66, assoc. dean of sci., 1983-88, prof. biol. scis. emeritus, 1996—. Mem. grant selection panel Natural Scis. and Engring. Research Council, Ottawa, Ont., Can., 1974-77, 78-81 Author: (with others) Plant Biochemistry; 1980, 1988, Folates and Pterins, 1984. Assoc. editor Can. Jour. Botany, 1969-78. Contbr. numerous articles to profl. jours. Recipient Centennial medal Govt. of Can., 1967 Fellow Royal Soc. Can. (life); mem. Can. Soc. Plant Physiologists (western dir. 1968-70, pres. 1976-77, Gold medal 1998), Faculty Club (U. Alta.), Derrick Golf and Winter Club. Avocations: gardening, golf, curling, cross country skiing. Home: 99 Fairway Dr Edmonton AB Canada T6J 2C2 Business E-Mail: ecossins@ualberta.ca.

COSTA, DANIEL LAWRENCE, architect; b. Providence, Feb. 16, 1953; s. Dimas and Laurinda (Diogo) C.; m. Shepley Patterson Metcalf, May 31, 1980 (div. Mar. 1988); 1 child, Hilary Metcalf. AB, Brown U., 1974; MArch, Harvard U., 1980. Architect Archtl. Resources Cambridge (Mass.), Inc., 1980-87, Shepard/Quraeshi Assocs., Watertown, Mass., 1987-88; prin. Costa/Flenniken Assocs., Boston, 1988-90, Dan Costa AIA, Boston, 1990—. Mem. Somerville (Mass.) Design Rev. Bd., 1988; bd. dirs. Somerville Hist. Preservation Commn., 1991-96. Recipient Home of Yr. award Met. Home Mag., 1997, Best in Am. Living award Profl. Builder Mag., 1995, Southern Home award So. Living Mag., 1995. Mem. AIA, Boston Soc. Architects. Office: 368 Congress St Fl 4 Boston MA 02210-1864 Office Phone: 617-451-5898. E-mail: dancosta@earthlink.net.

COSTA, GUSTAVO, Italian studies scholar; b. Rome, Mar. 21, 1930; came to U.S., 1961; s. Paolo and Ida (Antonangelo) C.; m. Natalia Zalessow, June 8, 1963; 1 child, Dora L. Maturità Classica, Liceo Virgilio, Rome, 1948; PhD cum laude, U. Rome, 1954. Asst. Istituto di Filosofia, Rome, 1957-60; instr. Italian Univ. de Lyon, Lyons, France, 1960-61, U. Calif., Berkeley, 1961-63, asst. prof., 1963-68, assoc. prof., 1968-72, prof., 1972-91, prof. emeritus, 1991—, chmn. dept. Italian, 1973-76, 88-91. Vis. prof. Scuola di Studi Superiori, Naples, 1984, Inst. Philosophy, U. Rome La Sapienza, 1992, Scuola Europea di Studi Avanzati, Naples, 2003, Inst. Italiano per Gli Studi Filosofici, Naples, 2004; reviewer RAI Corp., Rome, 1982-89 Author: La leggenda dei secoli d'oro nella lett. ital., 1972, Le antichità germaniche nella cultura italiana, 1977, Il sublime e la magia da Dante a Tasso, 1994, Vico e l'Europa: Contro la boria delle nazioni, 1996, Malebranche e Vico, 1998, Vico e l' Inquisizione, 1999, Malebranche e Roma, 2003, La Santa Sede Di Froute a Locke, 2003, La Congregarious dell'Judice e Jonathan Swift, 2004; mem. editl. bd. Nouvelles de la République des Lettres, New Vico Studies, Cuadernos sobre Vico Inst. Italiano Studi Storici fellow, Naples, Italy, 1954-57, Guggenheim Meml. Found. fellow, N.Y.C., 1977; grantee French Govt., Paris, 1956, Belgian Govt., Brussels, 1956, Targa d'oro Apulia, Italy, 1990. Mem. Am. Assn. Tchrs. Italian, Am. Soc. for Eighteenth-Century Studies, Renaissance Soc. Am., Am. Soc. for Aesthetics, Dante Soc. Am., Faculty Club (Berkeley). Avocations: gardening, stamp collecting/philately. Office: U Calif MC 2620 Dept Italian Studies Berkeley CA 94720-2620 Office Phone: 510-642-2704.

COSTA, JIM, congressman; b. Fresno, Calif., Apr. 13, 1952; BA Polit. Sci., Calif. State U., Fresno, 1974. Spl. asst. to Congressman John Krebs, 1975-76; adminstrv. asst. Assembly Mem. Richard Lehman, 1976-78; mem. Calif. Assembly, 1978-94, Calif. State Senate, 1994—2004, chmn. agr. and water resources com., housing and land use com., mem. fin., investment and internat. trade com., transp. com.; mem. U.S. Congress, 20th Calif. dist., 2005—; mem. Agriculture com., Resources com. and Sci. com. Senate rep. Calif. World Trade Commn., 1995-2004; pres. Nat. Conf. State Legislatures, 2000-01. Mem. Fresno County Farm Bur., I.D.E.S. Men's Lodge, Fresno Cabrillo Club. Democrat. Roman Catholic. Office: 1004 Longworth House Office Bldg Washington DC 20515-0520 Office Phone: 202-225-3341.*

COSTA, MARY, soprano; b. Knoxville, Tenn. Student, Los Angeles Conservatory of Music; PhD (hon.), Hardin-Simmons U., 1973. Film voice of Sleeping Beauty by Walt Disney; appeared TV commls., 1955—57; debut Los Angeles Opera, 1958; in La Boheme, San Francisco Opera, 1959; as Violetta in La Traviata Met. Opera, N.Y.C., 1964; soloist John F. Kennedy Meml. Svc. at Sports Arena, LA, 1963; appeared Glyndebourne Opera House, 1958, Royal Opera House Covent Garden, Teatro Nacional de San Carlos, Grand Theatre de Geneve, Vancouver, Lisbon, Kiev, Leningrad, Tbilisi, Boston, Cin., Hartford, Newark, Phila., San Antonio, Seattle; toured U.S. with Bernstein's Candide; appeared English prodn. Candide; revival Bernstein's Candide at John F. Kennedy Center for Performing Arts, 1971; tour Soviet Union, 1970; Bolshoi debut in La Traviatta, 1970; starring role motion picture The Great Waltz, 1972; command performance White House, 1974; Met. Opera tour of Japan as Musetta in La Boheme, 1975; appeared internat. recitals, orchs. V.p. Hawaiian Fragrances, Honolulu, 1972, Calif. Inst. Arts. Featured artist Hollywood Bowl Tribute to Walt Disney: 75 Years of Music, 2004. Apptd. to Nat. Coun. on the Arts, 2003. Named Woman of Yr., Los Angeles, 1959, Tenn. Woman of Distinction, Am. Lung Assn., 2000; recipient DAR Honor medal, 1974, Tenn. Hall of Fame award, 1987, Women of Achievement award, Northwood Inst., Palm Beach, Fla., 1991, Woman of Achievement award, So. Birmingham Coll., 1993, Women in Performing Arts, 1993, Puccini award, 1999, Disney Legends award, 1999, Distinguished Verdi performances of the 20th Century, Metropolitan Opera Guild, 2001; Mary Costa Scholarship established at U. Tenn., 1979. Mem.: Nat. Endowment for the Arts. Address: 3340 Kingston Pike Unit 1 Knoxville TN 37919-4674

COSTA, PAUL JOSEPH, psychologist; b. Allison Park, Pa., Mar. 9, 1968; s. Ralph Felix and Therese Marie Costa; m. Rashida Stacy-Ann Campbell, Apr. 16, 2004. BS cum laude in Biology, Wofford Coll., 1990; MS summa cum laude in Gen. Psychology, Carlos Albizu U., 1996, PsyD summa cum laude in Clin. Psychology, 2001. Lic. Dept. of Health, Fla., 2002. Staff psychologist Ctr. Clin. and Forensic Psychology, Inc., Plantation, Fla., 2002—04; designated mental health authority Eckerd Youth Devel. Ctr., Okeechobee, Fla., 2004—. Lab. and tchg. asst. Wofford Coll., Spartanburg, SC, 1987—90, Spartanburg, 1987—90; psychotherapist Goodman Psychol. Svcs. Ctr., Miami, Fla., 1996—97; psychol. evaluator PsychSolutions, Coral Gables, Fla., 1998; clin. psychology intern Atlantic Shores Hosp., Fort Lauderdale, Fla., 1999—2000; neuropsychological resident Cognitive Rehabilitative Assoc. of South Fla., Inc., Miami, 2001—02; clin. neuropsychologist Ctrs. Psychol. Growth, Inc., Miami, 2002—03; spkr. in field. Musician: The Invertebrates; author: (short stories) Waiting for the Furnace to Kick On (Nat. Honors, Scholastic Writing Awards, 1986), Visions of Terror (Nat. Honors, Scholastic Writing Awards, 1986); composer (musician): (film soundtrack) Frustration; musician: (musical) Grease: The Musical. Benjamin Wofford scholar, Wofford Coll., 1986—90. Mem.: APA, Fla. Psychol. Assn. R-Consevative. Roman Catholic. Avocations: singing, naturalist, music, writing. Home: 6765 NE 72nd Cir W Okeechobee FL 34972-8649 Office: Eckerd Youth Devel Ctr 7200 Hwy 441 N Okeechobee FL 34972 Office Phone: 863-763-2174 ext. 306.

COSTA, WALTER HENRY, architect; b. Oakland, Calif., July 2, 1924; s. Walter H.F. and Mamie R. (Dunkle) C.; m. Jane Elisabeth Ledwich, Aug. 28, 1948; 1 dau., Laura. BA, U. Calif., Berkeley, 1948, MA, 1949. Designer Mario Corbett (architect), San Francisco, 1947-48, Ernst Born (architect), San Francisco, 1949; draftsman Milton Pflueger, San Francisco, 1950-51; designer Skidmore, Owings & Merrill, San Francisco, 1951-57, participating assoc., then assoc. prtnr., 1957-69, gen. prtnr., 1969-89, ret., 1990. Bd. dirs. East Bay Regional Park Dist., 1977-87, pres., 1984-85; mem. city council, Lafayette, Calif., 1972-76, mayor, 1973. Served with USSNR, 1943-46. Mem.: AIA. Home: 2130 Cactus Ct #2 Walnut Creek CA 94595

COSTA-GAVRAS, (CONSTANTIN GAVRAS), film director, writer; b. Athens, Greece, Feb. 13, 1933; naturalized French citizen; m. Michele Ray, Sept. 12, 1968; children: Alexandre, Helene, Romain. Student, U. Sorbonne, Paris. Diplomate Inst. Higher Cinematic Studies. Ballet dancer, Greece; asst. to film dirs. Yves Allegret, Jacques Demy, Rene Clair, Rene Clement, Jean Giorno. Pres. Cinematheque francaise, 1982—, Festival Paris-Cinema, 2003—. Dir., screenwriter films: The Sleeping Car Murders, 1964; Z, 1969 (Acad. awaard for best fgn. lang. film, 70, Jury prize, Cannes Film Festival, 69, Raoul-Levy prize, 69, Golden Globe award, 70); Missing, 1982 (Golden Palm award Cannes, 82, Acad. Award for best screenplay, 82); dir.: (films) Un Homme de Trop, 1966 (Moscow Film Festival prize), L'Aveu, 1970 (The Confession), State of Siege, 1973 (Cannes Film Festival award, 75), Special Section, 1975, Madame Rosa (also actor), 1978, Clair de Femme, 1979, Hanna K, 1983, Conseil de Femme, 1986, Betrayed, 1988, Music Box, 1990 (Golden Bear award Berlin film festival, 90), Little Apocalypse, 1992, Mad City, 1996, The Parthenon, 2004; prodr, dir., writer: The Ax, 2004; dir.: (Operas) Il Mondo Dela Luna (Joseph Haydn), 1994, Mad City, 1997; co-dir.: A Propos de Nice, 1995; Lumiere and Compagnie, 1995; Amen, 2001 (named Best European movie, 2002, Globo D'oro Assn. Fgn. Press, 2002); dir.: (theater musical show) All Around is Light, 2003. Named Best Dir., Cannes Film Festival 1975, Officier Ordre National du Merite; decorated Comdr. Arts and Letters, France, Chevalier Legion d'Honneur; recipient Life Achievement award De l'Academie Francaise, 1998, Gold medal of Bellas Artes King of Spain. Personal E-mail: kyprod@wanadoo.fr.

COSTAGLIOLA, FRANCESCO, retired government official; b. Cranston, R.I., Aug. 24, 1917; s. Luigi and Rose (Lubrano) C.; m. Agnes Mary Ross, June 14, 1952 (dec.); children: Francesca Danieli, Marisa Costagliola, Antonia Burns, Roseanne Rubin. Student, U. R.I., 1935-37; BSEE, U.S. Naval Acad., 1941; postgrad., Naval Postgrad. Sch., 1946-47, MIT, 1947-49, Cath. U. Am., 1967-71; MBA, Am. U., Washington, 1974. Commd. ensign USN, 1941, advanced through grades to capt., 1960, served in U.S.S. Phoenix in 24 ops. PTO, 1941-46; comdg. officer U.S.S. Halsey Powell, Republic of Korea, 1951-52; various positions naval sea and shore assignments involving atomic energy USN, 1952-64; mil. asst. to asst. to Sec. Def. for atomic energy, 1964-67; ret., 1968; commr. AEC, 1968-69; engr. RCA, 1974-76; staff mem. Joint Congl. Com. on Atomic Energy, Washington, 1967-68, 69-71, 76-77, Office of Sec. of Senate, Washington, 1977-86. Mem. Md. Radiation Control Adv. Bd., 1973-81. Contbr. articles to profl. jours. Treas. Class of '41 U.S. Naval Acad., 1997—. Decorated Bronze Star with Combat V (2). Mem. AAAS, Inst. Ops. Rsch. and Mgmt. Scis., Am. Nuc. Soc., U.S. Naval Inst., Pearl Harbor Survivors Assn. (rep. Vets. Day nat. com. 1990—, pres. No. Va. chpt. 1991-1993, 2003-04), Naval Acad. Alumni Assn., Mil. Order World Wars, Mil. Order Carabao, Army and Navy Club (Washington). Roman Catholic. Home: 307 Gibbon St Alexandria VA 22314-4129 Personal E-mail: costagliola@comcast.net.

COSTANDI, WISAM EMILE, application developer, biomedical researcher, consultant; b. Aley, Lebanon, May 24, 1975; arrived in US, 1992; s. Emile Costandi and Afaf Maasri Costandi; m. Elodie Mancel, Sept. 29, 1997. BSc in Biomedical Engring., Northwestern U., 1996; MS in Biomedical Engring., MBA in Tech. Mgmt., U. Calif., Davis, Calif., 2001. Dir., tech. support GDI, Orlando, Fla., 1996—98; sr. cons. Deloitte and Touche LLP, San Francisco, 2001—03; ptnr. Cil LLC, Berkeley, Calif., 2003—. Contbr. articles to profl. jours. Recipient The Duke of Edinburgh award, HRH The Duke of Edinburgh KG, KT, 1992; fellow, NIH, 1998. Mem.: Healthcare Info. and Mgmt. Sys. Soc., Northwestern U. Alumni Admissions Coun., Math. Assn. Am., Mensa. Achievements include research in optical detection of particles within microdroplets using immunoassay methodologies. Office: CA 94705 Office Phone: +1-510-868-1044. E-mail: wcostandi@ciloi.com.

COSTANTINIDIS, TERESA ANN, academic administrator; d. Henry Alvy and Betty May Sparks; m. Peter Costantinidis, Feb. 1, 1986; 1 child, Katherine Marie. BSc, U.C. Davis, 1981—85; MBA, U.C. Berkeley, 2000—03. COO, sr. asst. dean Walter A. Haas Sch. of Bus., U.C. Berkeley, 1999—. Office: Univ of Calif Berkeley Walter A Haas Sch of Bus Berkeley CA 94720-1900 Office Phone: 510-643-0341.

COSTANTINO, FILOMENA CATHERINE, mathematics educator, director; b. Wilkes-Barre, Pa., Dec. 10, 1966; d. Suaerio and Eugenia Costantino. BA in Math., Bloomsburg U., BS in Math Edn., 1988, M in Curriculum and Instrn., 2001; postgrad., Temple U., 2001—. Tchr. cert., math. supervisory cert. Tchr., math coord. Wilkes-Barre Area Sch. Dist., 1988—. Mem.: Nat. Coun. Tchrs. Math., Math. Supervisory Assn., Pa. State Educators Assn. Roman Catholic. Avocations: flute, singing. Office: Coughlin HS 80 N Washington St Wilkes Barre PA 18701 Office Phone: 570-826-7201. E-mail: fcostantino@verizon.net.

COSTANZO, GREGG MICHAEL, director; b. Ridgeway, Pa., Nov. 30, 1974; s. Carlos Costanzo and Mary Abplanalp. BA, Gannon U., 1997, MA, 2004. Chair theology dept. Elyria Cath. High Sch., Ohio, 1999—2003; dir. campus ministry Ea. Mich. U., Ypsilanti, 2003—. Mem. grad. adv. bd. Gannon U., Erie, Pa., 1997—98. Moderator study higher edn. and common good U. Mich., 2004; facilitator alochol summit N.Am. Inter-Fraternity, 2004; vol. Vision, Ea. Mich. U. Mem.: Cath. Campus Ministry Assn., Sigma Phi Epsilon (chpt. counselor 2004—). Independent. Roman Catholic. Office: Ea Mich U 511 W Forest Ypsilanti MI 48197

COSTAS, BOB (ROBERT QUINLAN COSTAS), sportscaster; b. Queens, NY, Mar. 22, 1952; s. John George and Jayne (Quinlan) C.; m. Carole Randall Krummenacher, June 24, 1983; children: Keith Michael, Taylor. Student, Syracuse U., 1970-74. Sportscaster Sta. KMOX-AM, St. Louis, 1974-81; sportscaster, host sports programs NBC Sports, N.Y.C., 1980—; substitute anchor Larry King Live, 2005—. Announcer: (TV series) Game of the Week, 1982—89; host Later with Bob Costas, 1988—94; TV and film appearances include: Diamonds on the Silver Screen, 1992; Cheers: Last Call, 1992; The Drew Carey Show, 1999; NewsRadio, 1996; ESPN Sports Century, 2000—04; host: (TV series) On the Record with Bob Costas, 2001; TV and film appearances include: Coach Carter, 2005; others. Recipient 12 Emmy awards, 8 for outstanding sports broadcaster, 2 Emmy awards for writing, 1 Emmy award for interview show, 1996, one for play-by-play braodcast of 1997 World Series; named Nat. Sportscaster of Yr., Nat. Sportscasters and Sportwriters Assn., 1985, 87, 88, 91, 92, 95, 97. Office: 7730 Carondelet Ave Ste 304 Clayton MO 63105-3328

COSTA-ZALESSOW, NATALIA, foreign language educator; b. Kumanovo, Macedonia, Dec. 5, 1936; arrived in US, 1951; d. Alexander P. and Katarina (Duric) Z.; m. Gustavo Costa, June 8, 1963; 1 child, Dora. BA in Italian, U. Calif., Berkeley, 1959, MA in Italian, 1961, PhD in Romance Langs. and Lits., 1967. Tchg. asst. U. Calif., Berkeley, 1959-63; instr. Mills Coll., Oakland, Calif., 1963; asst. prof. San Francisco State U., 1968-74, assoc. prof., 1974-79, prof., 1979-98, coord. Italian program, 1992-98, prof. emerita, 1998—. Author: Scrittrici italiane dal XIII al XX secolo, Testi e critica, 1982; editor: Anima, 1997; transl.: Her Soul, 1996; contbr. articles to profl. jours. Sidney M. Ehrman scholar U. Calif., Berkeley, 1957-58, Gamma Phi Beta scholar U. Calif., Berkeley, 1958, Herbert H. Vaughan scholar U. Calif., Berkeley, 1959-60, Advanced Grad. Traveling fellow in romance lang. and lit. U. Calif., Berkeley, 1964-65. Mem. MLA, Am. Assn. Tchrs. Italian, Renaissance Soc. Am., Dante Soc. Am., Croatian Acad. Am. Roman Catholic. Avocations: swimming, hiking, opera, symphony, gastronomy. Office: San Francisco State U Dept Fgn Lang and Lit San Francisco CA 94132

COSTELLO, DANIEL WALTER, retired bank executive; b. MIch., June 17, 1930; s. Walter William and Rose Angela (Dimond) Costello; m. Sylvia Michael; children: MIchael Joseph, Colleen Marie. BS in Engring. sci., Purdue U., 1952. Varoius sales, mktg. and real estae positions Shell Oil Co., 1955—63; dir. real estate devel. and constrn. Ford Land Devel. Corp., Dearborn, Mich., 1971—75; chmn. Am. Express Realty Mgmt. Co., N.Y.C., 1975—82; exec. v.p. corp. real estate divsn. Bank of Am., San Francisco, 1982—95; ret., 1995. Comdr. U.S. Army, 1952—55, Korea. Mem.: Bldg. Owners and Mgrs. Assn., Nat. Assn. Corp. Real Estate Execs. (cert. master corp. real estate), Internat. Real Estate Inst. (bd. govs.), Nat. Assn. Rev. Appraisers (bd. dirs.), San Francisco Bankers Club, Country Club, Meadow Club, Theta Xi.

COSTELLO, ELVIS (DECLAN PATRICK MCMANUS), musician, songwriter; b. London, 1954; s. Ross McManus; m. Cait O'Riordan, 1986; 1 child from previous marriage. Composer: (songs) Alison, 1977, Watching the Detectives, 1977, (I Don't Want To Go To) Chelsea, 1979, Radio Radio, 1978, 1978;: (songs) Crawling to the USA, 1978, Radio Radio, 1978, Stranger in the House, 1978, Girls Talk, 1979, Oliver's Army, 1979, Boy With a Problem, 1982, Every Day I Write the Book, 1983; (albums) My Aim is True, 1977, This Year's Model, 1978, Armed Forces, 1979, Get Happy!!, 1980, Trust, 1980, Almost Blue, 1981, Taking Liberties, Imperial Bedroom, 1982, Goodbye Cruel World, Punch the Clock, 1984, The Best Of, 1985, Blood and Chocolate, King of America, 1986, Spike, 1989, Girls, Girls, Girls, 1990, Mighty Like a Rose, 1991, (with Steve Nieve, Pete Thomas, Bruce Thomas and Nick Lowe albums) Brutal Youth, 1994, (with the Brodsky Quartet albums) The Juliet Letters, 1993, (albums) The Very Best of Elvis Costello and the Attractions, 1994, Kojak Variety, 1995, All This Useless Beauty, 1996, Extreme Honey, 1997, Painted From Memory, 1998 (Grammy, 1999); When I Was Cruel, 2002 (nominated for 3 Grammy awards); albums Cruel Smile, 2002, North, 2003, Il Sogno, 2004, The Delivery Man, 2004, appears in concert U.S. and Eng., 1978—, appeared in film Americathon, 1979—; actor(appeared in): Austin Powers 2: The Spy Who Shagged Me, 1999; recorded (with Burt Bacharach): I'll Never Fall in Love Again. Inducted into Rock and Roll Hall of Fame, 2003.*

COSTELLO, FRANCIS WILLIAM, lawyer; b. Cambridge, Mass., Apr. 16, 1946; s. Frank George and Anna M. (Sinnott) C. BA, Columbia U., 1968, JD, 1973. Bar: N.Y. 1974, Calif. 1977. Assoc. Whitman & Ransom, N.Y.C., 1973-74, Anderson, Mori & Rabinowitz, Tokyo, 1974—76, Whitman & Ransom, L.A., 1976-82, ptnr., 1982-93, Whitman, Breed, Abbott & Morgan, L.A., 1993-2000, Holland & Knight, LLP, L.A., 2000—. Bd. dirs. Hamazawa Corp., L.A., Japan Travel Bur. Internat., L.A.; dir. com. Holland & Knight, LLP., L.A., Calif., 2001-04. Served with U.S. Army, 1968-70, Vietnam. Mem. ABA, State Bar Calif., State Bar N.Y., L.A. County Bar Assn., Pumpkin Ridge Golf Club (Oreg.), Wilshire Country Club (L.A.), Calif. Club (L.A.). Home: 415 Knight Way La Canada Flintridge CA 91011-2725 Office Phone: 213-896-2452. Business E-Mail: fcostell@hklaw.com.

COSTELLO, JERRY F., JR., congressman, former county official; b. Sept. 25, 1949; m. Georgia Jean Cockrum; children: Jerry, Gina, John. AA, Bayeville Area Coll., 1971; BA, Maryville Coll. of Sacred Heart, 1973. County bd. chmn. St. Clair County, Ill.; dir. ct. svcs. and probation 20th Jud. Cir. Campaign; chmn. Heart Assn., Belleville, Ill., 1983; vice chmn. Ill. div. United Way, 1984, chmn., 1985; mem. U.S. Congress from 21st (now 12th) Ill. Dist., 1988—; former mem. budget com.; mem. transp., infrastructure and sci. coms. Bd. dirs. Ill. Ctr. for Autism; active St. Clair County Big Bros./Big Sisters, Belleville Women's Crisis Ctr., Children's Ctr. for Behavioral Devel.; helped establish St. Clair County chpt. Vets. Outreach Info. Ctr.; mem. East St. Louis Econ. Opportunity Commn., Ill.; vice chmn. Southwestern Ill. Bus. Devel. Fin. Corp., 1985—; bd. dirs. So. Ill. Leadershp Council; pres. Urban Counties Council of Ill. Recipient cert. of Appreciation, Bus. and Profl. Women's Assn., 1985; honored Citizens League for Adequate Social Services; 1985 AAHMES Court #84, Daus. ISIS Ann. Humanitarian award, Gene Hughes award Ill. Ct. Services and Probation Assn. Democrat. Office: US Ho of Reps 2454 Rayburn House Off Bldg Washington DC 20515-1312*

COSTELLO, JOHN H., III, business and marketing executive; b. Akron, Ohio, June 2, 1947; s. John H. Jr. and Lia Costello; children from previous marriage, Michael, Jeffrey, Matthew. BS in Indsl. Mgmt., Akron U., 1968; MBA, Mich. State U., 1970. Mktg. dir. Procter & Gamble Co., Cin., 1971—84; sr. v.p. Pepsi-Cola USA, Purchase, NY, 1984—86; exec. v.p. Wells, Rich, Greene, Inc., N.Y.C., 1986—88; pres., chief oper. officer Nielsen Mktg. Rsch. U.S.A., Chgo., 1988—93; sr. exec. v.p. Sears, Roebuck & Co., Hoffman Estates, Ill., 1993—98; pres. Auto Nation, Inc., Ft. Lauderdale, Fla., 1999—; CEO MVP.com, 1999—2001; chief global mktg. officer Yahoo!, 2001—02; exec. v.p. Home Depot, 2002—. Sr. mktg. execs. panel Conf. Bd., N.Y.C., 1985-87; industry speaker on bus. trends and issues, 1985—; bd. dirs. The Quaker Oats Co, Sears Can., Bombay Co. Mem. exec. bd. N.E. Ill. coun. Boy Scouts Am., 1993-97; trustee Multiple Sclerosis Soc., Chgo., 1990—, vice chmn., 1995—; bd. dirs. Nat. Multiple Sclerosis Soc., 1989—, chair fundraising, 1990-94, mem. exec. com., 1990—, chair nominating com., 1996—. Mem. Assn. Nat. Advertisers (bd. dirs. 1995—, vice chmn. 1998, chmn. 1999), Direct Ad Coun. (bd. dirs. 1996—, vice chmn. 1998), Direct Retail Advt. and Mktg. Assn. (bd. dirs. 1995—, Retail Mktg. Hall of Fame 1997), Econ. Club Chgo., Conway Farms Golf Club. Episcopalian. Avocations: skiing, golf, travel. Office: Home Depot 2455 Paces Ferry Rd Atlanta GA 30339-5000 Home: 4716 Northside Dr NW Atlanta GA 30327-4552 Business E-Mail: john_costello@homedepot.com.

COSTELLO, KENNETH R., lawyer; b. Teaneck, NJ, July 12, 1953; m. Janet Costello: children: Quinn, Ian. BA, Loyola Marymount U., LA, 1975; JD magna cum laude, U. Santa Clara, 1978. Bar: Calif. 1978. Ptnr. Thelen, Marrin, Johnson & Bridges, LA, 1986-92, Loeb & Loeb LLP, LA, 1992-98; shareholder Jenkens & Gilchrist, P.C., LA, 1998—, firm co-leader franchise & distribution practice group. Spkr. in field. Co-author: Franchising Law: Practice and Forms, 1996, Franchising: Legal Compliance Check-Ups: Business Clients, 1985; contbr. articles to bus. and profl. jours.; mem. bd. editors Law Rev., U. Santa Clara, 1978. Office: Jenkens & Gilchrist PC 12100 Wilshire Blvd 15th Fl Los Angeles CA 90025-7120 Office Phone: 310-442-8844. Office Fax: 310-820-8859. E-mail: kcostello@jenkens.com.

COSTELLO, SHERI ANN, primary school educator; b. Grand Rapids, Mich., Nov. 14, 1967; d. Gary Allen and Ellen Hedderman Robbins; m. James Cloyd Costello, June 29, 1991. AA, Grand Rapids Jr. Coll., Mich., 1987; BA, Mich. State U.; BS in Edn., Athens State U., Ala., 1999; MEd, Ala. A&M U., 2002. Social worker Dept. Human Resources, Camden, Ark., 1992—94; counselor/supr. Three Springs, Courtland, Ala., 1995—2000; tchr. kindergarten Decatur City Schs., Ala., 2002—. Mem.: Internat. Reading Assn. Lutheran. Home: 1070 W Sternberg Rd Norton Shores MI 49441 Office: Decatur City Schs Somerville Rd Elem Sch 910 Somerville Rd Decatur AL 35601

COSTELLO, THOMAS, JR., lawyer, computer company executive; BA cum laude, Ohio U.; JD cum laude, Thomas M. Cooley Law Sch. Sr. v.p. human resources, gen. counsel, sec. Compuware Corp., 1995—. Asst. coach, asst. gen. mgr. Windsor Compuware Spitfires, Ontario Hockey League; fac. mem. Wayne State U. Mem.: State Bar Mich. (chairperson Computer Law Sec.), Generation of Promise Prog. (past pres., mem. bd. trustees, Bridge Builder Award 2004), Detroit Golf Club. Avocation: NASCAR. Office: Compuware Corp One Campus Martius Detroit MI 48226

COSTELLO, THOMAS JOSEPH, retired bishop; b. Camden, N.Y., Feb. 23, 1929; s. James G. and Ethel A. (Dupont) C. Lic. in Sacred Theology, Cath. U. Am., 1954, JCB, 1960. Ordained priest Roman Cath. Ch., 1954. Sec. Diocesan Tribunal, Diocese of Syracuse, 1958; supt. schs. Cath. Diocese of Syracuse, 1960—75; pastor Our Lady Lourdes Ch., Syracuse, NY, 1975—78; aux. bishop Syracuse, 1978—2004. Roman Catholic. Home: 1515 Midland Ave Syracuse NY 13205-1447 Office: PO Box 511 240 E Onondaga St Syracuse NY 13201 Office Phone: 315-470-1460. E-mail: costello@syracusediocese.org.

COSTES, NICHOLAS CONSTANTINE, aerospace scientist, educator, retired government agency administrator; b. Athens, Greece, Sept. 20, 1926; came to U.S., 1948, naturalized, 1959; s. Constantine Nicholas and Anna (Papadopoulou) C.; m. Polytime Andros, Nov. 22, 1958; children: Constantine Nicholas, Anna Amalia, Christina Smaragtha. Diploma, Sci. Sch., Athens Coll., 1945; student, Athens Nat. Tech. U, 1945-48; AB, Darthmouth Coll., 1950, MSC.E. (George W. Davis scholar), 1951; A.M., M.E.N., Harvard U., 1962; MS, N.C. State U., 1955, PhD (Ford Found. fellow), 1965. Registered profl. engr., N.C., Ill. Teaching fellow dept. civil engring. N.C. State U., Raleigh, 1951-53, instr., 1962-63; materials engr. N.C. State Hwy. and Pub. Works Commn., Raleigh, 1953-56; research civil engr. U.S. Army Cold Regions Research and Engring. Lab., Hanover, N.H., 1956-62; sr. research scientist space sci. lab Marshall Space Flight Center, NASA, Huntsville, Ala., 1965-98, team leader Apollo II Soil Mechanics Investigation Sci. Team, co-prin. investigator Apollo 12, 13 Lunar Geology Experiment, Apollo 14-17 Soil Mechanics Expt., 1991—, prin. investigator, co-investigator, project scientist Mechanics of Granular Materials Microgravity Expt., 1991—. Cons. geotech. engring., 1965—; adj. prof. U. Colo., Boulder, 1998. Contbr. articles and tech. reports to profl. jours. Recipient Dartmouth Soc. Engrs. prize, 1951; recipient NASA awards including cert. of appreciation, 1970, Group Achievement award Lunar Roving Vehicle Team, 1971, invention award, 1971, Astronauts' Silver Snoopy award, 1972, dirs. commendation achievement, 1973, Group Achievemnt award Flow Process Modeling Space Shuttle Main Engine, 1985, Group Achievement awards Environs Definition of Space Shuttle Solid Rocket Motor Team, Challenger Incident, 1986, Mechanics of Granular Materials (MGM) Microgravity Expt. Fellow ASCE (life, Norman medal 1972, chmn. program com. aerospace council 1973-75, exec. com. aerospace div. 1976-82, chmn. 1980-81, profl. coordination com. 1982—), AIAA (assoc. fellow, dir. Ala./Miss. sect. 1976-79, Outstanding Aerospace Engr. award 1976, Martin Schilling award 1979, Herman Oberth award 1998); mem. NSPE, AAAS, Am. Geophys. Union, Dartmouth Soc. Engrs., Soc. Harvard Engrs. and Scientists, Assn. Civil Engrs. Greece (hon.), N.Y. Acad. Scis., Am. Men and Women of Sci., Sigma Xi, Phi Kappa Phi, Chi Epsilon Greek Orthodox. Office: PMB 190 Ste 30 4800 Whitesburg Dr S Huntsville AL 35802-1600 E-mail: nccostes@hotmail.com.

COSTIGAN, CONSTANCE FRANCES, artist, educator; b. Hoboken, N.J., July 3, 1935; d. Charles Francis and Joan Aletta (Visser) C.; m. John Francis Christian, June 6, 1959 (div. 1972); m. Michael Krausz, May 14, 1976. BS, Simmons Coll. and Boston Mus. Sch. Fine Arts, 1957; MA, Am. U., 1965; postgrad., U. Calif.-Berkeley, 1971, U. Va.-Fairfax, 1968-69, U. D.C., 1972-73. Cert. tchr. Va. Designer Smithsonian Instn., Washington, 1957-59, mus. svcs. staff mem., 1962-68, drawing and design instr., 1971-76; art and crafts instr. Arlington County (Va.) Pub. Schs., 1970-75; prof. fine arts George Washington U., Washington, 1976—2002, prof. fine arts emeritus, 2003—; curator Arlington Art Ctr., Va., 1980; disting. vis. prof. Am. U. in Cairo, 1980-81; vis. prof. in drawing Haystack Mt. Sch. Crafts, Deer Isle, Maine, 1990. Jurist and judge art show D.C. area, 1975, 76, 90, 82, area show Del. Ctr. for Contemporary Arts, 1985; judge art show Sussex County Arts Coun. Mems. Show, 1991; mem. adv. bd. So. Del. Ctr. for the Arts and Humanities, 2003—; panelist Del. Divsn. of the Arts, 2004— Author: Leonardo, 1982, Elements of Art: Line, 1980; one-woman shows Hodson Gallery, Hood Coll. Frederick, Md., 2005, Visual Arts Gallery, Habitat Ctr. for the Arts, Dehli India, 2003, Lavinia Ctr., Milton, Del., 2003, Soho 20 Gallery, N.Y.C., 1997, Hampshire Coll. Gallery Hampshire Coll., Amherst, Mass., 1996, Dimock Gallery, George Washington U., 1987, Franz Bader Gallery, Washington, 1985, 90, No. Va. C.C., Alexandria, 1983, Barbara Fiedler Gallery, Washington, 1979, 82, Phillips Collection, Washington, 1977, Gulbenkian Gallery, U. Kent, Canterbury, Eng., 1975, Talbot Rice Arts Ctr., Edinburgh, Scotland, 1974, Design Ctr. Gallery, Cleve., 1974, Annenburg Arts Ctr., Phila., 1973; represented pub. collections Hirschhorn Mus. and Sculpture Garden, Washington, Phillips Collection, Washington, U. Iowa Mus., Iowa City, Dimock Gallery, George Washington U., Del. Mus. Art, others; included in numerous pvt. collections USA and abroad Sec. steering com. Del. chpt. Nat. Mus. for Women in the Arts, Newark, 1997—01. Named to Nat. Mus. for Women in Arts to represent Del., 1998; fellow, Macdowell Colony, 1977, Ossabaw Island project, 1980; grantee, Lester Hereward Cooke Found., 1978—79, GSAS Facilitating Fund, 1990. Fellow Royal Soc. Arts. Home: 210 NE Market St Lewes DE 19958-1574 Office: 210 NE Market ST Lewes DE 19958-1574

COSTIGAN, EDWARD JOHN, retired investment banker; b. St. Louis, Oct. 31, 1914; s. Edward J. and Elizabeth Keane; m. Sara Louise Guth, Mar. 30, 1940 (dec. Nov. 1988); children: Sally, Edward John, James (dec.), Betsy, Robert, David, Louise; m. Mildred F. Fabick, Dec. 27, 1995. AB, St. Louis U., 1935; MBA, Stanford U., 1937. Analyst, v.p. Whitaker & Co., St. Louis, 1937-43; ptnr. Edward D. Jones & Co., 1943-72; sr. v.p. Stifel Nicolaus & Co. Inc., St. Louis, 1972-74, pres., 1974-79, vice chmn., 1979-83, emeritus, 1983, ret., 2001. Gov. Nat. Assn. Securities Dealers, 1967-70, Investment Bankers Assn., 1968-69, Midwest Stock Exch., Chgo., 1962-64; bd. dirs. 12 cos. Trustee Cath. Cemeteries Arch Diocese St. Louis, 1956—. Mem. St. Louis Soc. Fin. Analysts (pres. 1956), Harvard Club St. Louis (pres. 1955), Bellerive Country Club, Mo. Athletic Club, Old Warson Country Club, Noonday Club, Univ. Club, Moorings Country Club (Naples, Fla.). Republican. Roman Catholic. Office: 501 N Broadway Fl 8 Saint Louis MO 63102-2102

COSTIGAN-KERNS, LOUISE E., musician; arrived in U.S., 1971; d. Thomas John Costigan and Beatrice Mary Trono; m. John S. Breen, Aug. 20, 1983 (div. Nov. 1991); m. Ralph Charles Kerns, Sept. 4, 1994; children: Stephen James, Jacqueline Victoria. MusB in Piano Performance, New Eng. Conservatory Music, 1975, MusM in Piano Performance, 1977. Cert. Music Tchr.'s Nat. Assn. Piano faculty preparatory divsn. New Eng. Conservatory, Boston, 1975—94, chairperson, musical dir. opera studio ext. divsn., 1978—94; opera coach Opera San Jose, 1995—96; part-time chorus accompanist San Francisco Symphony, 2000—. Opera coach/coord. opera dept. Boston U., 1983—84; piano prof. Phillips Exeter (N.H.) Acad., 1988—93; mem. long range planning com. New Eng. Conservatory Music, 1988—90; artist in residence Brandeis U., Waltham, Mass., 1990—94; freelance concert pianist and accompanist, San Francisco, 1994—; opera coach San Francisco Internat. Summer Music Festival, San Francisco Conservatory Music, 2000—. Grantee, Boston Arts Lottery, 1985, 1986. Mem.: New Eng. Piano Tchrs. Assn. (bd. mem. 1989—92), Nat. Opera Assn. (gov. New Eng. 1990—94, gov. Calif. 1995—98), Pi Kappa Lambda. Home: 890 Regent Ct San Carlos CA 94070 Office: Music Tchr's Nat Assn Carew Tower 441 vine St Ste 505 Cincinnati OH 45202-2811 Office Phone: 650-592-3140.

COSTIKYAN, EDWARD N., lawyer; b. Weehawken, N.J., Sept. 14, 1924; s. Mihran Nazar and Berthe (Muller) C.; m. Frances Holmgren, 1950 (div. 1975); chldren: Gregory, Emilie; m. Barbara Heine, Mar. 6, 1977. AB, Columbia U., 1947, LLB, 1949. Bar: N.Y. 1949, U.S. Dist. Ct. (so. dist.) N.Y. 1950, U.S. Ct. Appeals (2d cir.) 1950, U.S. Supreme Ct. 1964. Law sec. to judge Harold R. Medina U.S. Dist. Ct., N.Y.C., 1949-51; ptnr. Paul, Weiss, Rifkind, Wharton & Garrison, N.Y.C., 1960-93, of counsel, 1994—. Spl. advisor to mayor on sch. and borough governance City of N.Y., 1994-96, chairperson mayor's investigative commn. on sch. safety, 1995-96; mem. Commn. on Integrity in Govt., N.Y.C., 1986, mem. joint com. on jud. adminstrn., 1985-92; adj. fellow Ctr. for Edn. Innovation, 1997—. Author: Behind Closed Doors: Politics in the Public Interest, 1966, How to Win Votes: The Politics of 1980, 1980; co-author: Re-Structuring the Government of New York City, 1972, New Strategies for Regional Cooperation, 1973; rsch. editor Columbia Law Rev.; mem. editl. bd. City Jour., 1992—; mem. bd. editors N.Y. Law Jour., 1976—; contbr. articles on legal and polit. subjects to profl. publs. Chmn. N.Y. State Task Force on N.Y.C. Juristiction and Structure, 1971-72; vice chmn. State Charter Revision for N.Y.C., 1972-77; county leader New York County Dem. Com., 1962-64; Dem. presdl. elector, 1964, 88; trustee, mem. exec. com., chmn. alumni adv. bd. Columbia U., 1981-93, trustee emeritus, 1993—; bd. dirs., mem. coun. Mcpl. Art Soc., 1993-98; chmn. bd. dirs. N.Y. Found. for Sr. Citizens, 1993—. 1st lt. inf. U.S. Army, 1943-46. Recipient William J. Brennan Jr. award for Outstanding Cont. to Pub. Discourse, 1997. Fellow Am. Coll. Trial Lawyers; mem. Assn. of Bar of City of N.Y. (mem. exec. com. 1986-90), Century Club. Unitarian Universalist. Home: 50 Sutton Pl S New York NY 10022-4167 Office: Paul Weiss Rifkind Wharton & Garrison Ste 12J 1285 Avenue Of The Americas Fl 21 New York NY 10019-6028 Office Phone: 212-688-0829.

COSTILOW, VIRGINIA KATHERINE, artist, sculptor, poet; b. Soddy, Tenn., Mar. 28, 1942; d. Youldon Chauncy and Frances (Schumann) Howell; children: Christopher, Timothy, Mathew. Student, Pasadena City Coll., UCLA, Mesa Jr. Coll. Graphic designer, San Diego. Exhibited in group shows at Bullock's Pasadena Students Exhibit, Escondido Municipal Gallery, J.Rod Lowell and Assocs., Annette Reinker; one-woman shows include Church of the Resurrection, Escondido, Calif., St. James By the Sea, La Jolla, Calif.; pvt. collections Tana Cleaves, Karen Backman, Vets. Mus. Balboa Park, San Diego, Calloway Winery, Timicula, Calif. Home: Apt R 427 W 4th Ave Apt R Escondido CA 92025-5048

COSTIN, JOSEPH LAURENCE, JR., information services executive; b. Chgo., Mar. 14, 1941; s. Joseph Laurence and Maribel (Cummings) Costin; m. Joan Gayley, June 20, 1964 (dec. June 1998); children: Jennifer, Michael. BA, U. Chgo., 1966. Divsn. mgr. Marshall Field and Co., Chgo., 1967—81; sr. v.p. Seligman and Latz, Inc., NYC, 1981—83; exec. v.p. CCC Info. Svcs., Inc., Chgo., 1983—93, vice-chmn., 1993—. Lifetime trustee emeritus ICAR Edn. Found.; mem. vis. com. on the coll. U. Chgo.; trustee Omega chpt. Psi Upsilon Fraternity; immediate past pres. bd. dirs. Westmoreland Country Club Scholarship Found. With Ill. Army N.G., 1963—69. Mem.: Am. Ins. Svcs. Group (com. automobile phys. damage), Contemporary Arts Coun., East Bank Club, Chgo. Curling Club, Westmoreland Country Club. Roman Catholic. Avocations: golf, curling, contemporary art, urban history. Office: World Trade Ctr Chgo 444 Merchandise Mart Plz Chicago IL 60654-1005

COSTIN, REA-SILVIA, civil engineer; b. Salonika, Greece, Oct. 24, 1946; arrived in US, 1981, naturalized, 1986; d. Stefan and Steliana Costin. MS in Civil Engring., Faculty of Hydrotech. Constrn., Bucharest, 1969; postgrad., U. Fla., 1985. Registered profl. engr., Fla. Design engr. Inst. of Mining, Bucharest, Romania, 1969—75; project engr. Machine Constrn., Bucharest, 1975—80; engr. III Fla. Dept. Environ. Regulation, Jacksonville, 1981—83; design engr. Aikenhead Engring., Jacksonville, 1983—88; project engr. Smith & Gilespie Engrs., Jacksonville, 1988—90; project mgr. City of Jacksonville, 1990—, engr. mgr., 2004—. Author: Short Stories: The Story of a Refugee, 1997, Thiana-A Macedonian Village, 2003, Athens, 2004. Named Poet Laureate, The Internat. Libr. Poetry, 2002; recipient Editors Choice award, Poetry.com, 2001, 2002, Pres'. award for Lit. Excellence, Nat. Authors Registry, 2003. Mem.: NSPE, Am. Pub. Works Assn., Fla. Engring. Soc., Toastmasters Internat. Greek Orthodox. Avocations: reading, writing, running, weightlifting, skiing. Home: 1645 Flagler Ave Jacksonville FL 32207-3119 Office Phone: 904-630-1345. E-mail: rsc500@comcast.net.

COSTLEY, GARY EDWARD, food company executive; b. Caldwell, Idaho, Oct. 26, 1943; s. Donald Clifford and Verna C.; m. Cheryl J. Zesiger, Dec. 21, 1963; children: Angela I., Chad D. BS, MS, PhD in Nutrition-Biochemistry, Oreg. State U. Formerly dir. nutrition, dir. public affairs, v.p. public affairs, v.p. and asst. to pres. Kellogg Co., sr. v.p. corp. devel., sr. v.p. sci. and quality, exec. v.p. sci. and tech., exec. v.p.; pres. Kellogg USA Inc.; area dir. Kellogg N.Am., to 1994; chmn., pres., CEO Internat. Multifoods, Mpls., 1997—; dean Grad Sch. Mgmt. Wake Forest U., 1995-97. Bd. dirs. Candlewood Inc., Pharmacopeia, Inc., ecFood.com. Trustee Miller Found, Battle Creek, Youth for Understanding Internat. Exch., Am. Health Found., Sarah W. Stedman Ctr.-Duke U. Med. Sch. Mem. Am. Inst. Nutrition. Lutheran. Home: 257 Barefoot Beach Blvd 404-202 Bonita Springs FL 34134-8594

COSTNER, KEVIN, actor; b. Lynwood, Calif., Jan. 18, 1955; s. Bill and Sharon Costner; m. Cindy Silva Mar. 5, 1978 (div. Dec. 12, 1994); children: Annie, Lily, Joe., Liam; m. Christine Baumgartner Sept. 25, 2004. Degree in mktg., Calif. State U., Fullerton, 1978. Owner prodn. co. TIG Prodns. Film appearances include Sizzle Beach U.S.A., 1974, Shadows Run Black, 1981, Chasing Dreams, 1981, Frances, 1982, Night Shift, 1982, Testament, 1983, Table for Five, 1983, Stacy's Knights 1983, The Gunrunner, 1983, The Big Chill, 1983, American Flyers, 1985, Fandango, 1985, Silverado, 1985, The Untouchables, 1987, No Way Out, 1987, Bull Durham, 1988, Field of Dreams, 1989, Revenge (also exec. prodr.), 1990, Dances with Wolves (also co-prodr., dir.) 1990 (Acad. award for best dir. 1991, Star of Tomorrow award Nat. Assn. Theatre Owners 1987, Hasty Pudding Man of Yr., Harvard U. 1990, Acad. award for best picture, 1991, Acad. award nominee best actor 1991, Dir's. Guild Am. award Best Dir. Feature Film 1991), Robin Hood: Prince of Thieves, 1991, JFK, 1991, Truth or Dare, 1991, The Bodyguard (also co-prodr.) 1992, A Perfect World, 1993, Wyatt Earp, 1994, The War, 1994, Waterworld (also co-prodr.), 1995, Tin Cup, 1996, The Postman (also prodr., dir.) 1997, Message in a Bottle (also prodr.), 1999, For Love of the Game, 1999, Play It to the Bone, 1999, Thirteen Days, 2000 (also prodr.), 3000 Miles to Graceland, 2001, Dragonfly, 2002, Open Range, 2003 (also prodr., dir.), The Upside of Anger, 2005; host, exec. prodr. (TV series) 500 Nations; co-prodr. China Moon, 1993; exec. prodr. Rapa Nui, 1994.*

COSTON, SUZANNE, television producer; m. Harold Coston; 2 children. Pres. de Passe Entertainment, L.A., 1992—. Co-prodr.: (TV specials) Motown Returns to the Apollo, 1985 (Emmy award for outstanding variety, music or comedy program, 1985); prodr.: (TV films) Buffalo Girls, 1995; exec. prodr.: (TV specials) Motown 40: The Music is Forever, 1998; (TV films) Someone Else's Child, 1994, Zenon: Girl of the 21st Century, 1999, The Loretta Claiborne Story, 2000, Cheaters, 2000, Zenon: The Zequel, 2001; (TV miniseries) The Temptations, 1998; (TV series) Sister, Sister, 1994—99, Smart Guy, 1997—99; music supervisor (TV films) Happy Endings, 1983, Bridesmaids, 1989, (films) The Last Dragon, 1985. Office: care DePasse Entertainment 5750 Wilshire Blvd Ste 640 Los Angeles CA 90036-3685

COSTON, WILLIAM DEAN, lawyer; b. Ann Arbor, Mich., Oct. 9, 1950; s. Dean Walter and Kathryn (Moran) C.; m. Barbara Ellen Carney, Aug. 18, 1973; children: Elizabeth, Nicholas. BA with highest honors, U. Mich., 1972; JD cum laude, Harvard U., 1975. Bar: Mass. 1976, DC 1979, admitted to practice: US Supreme Ct. 1979, DC Ct. Appeals, US Ct. Appeals (Fed. Cir.) 1997, US Dist. Ct. (Dist. Mich.), US Dist. Ct. (Dist. Ariz.), US Dist. Ct. (Dist. Md.), US Dist. Ct. (DC), US Ct. Appeals (2nd Cir.) 1997, US Ct. Appeals (3rd Cir.), US Ct. Appeals (4th Cir.), US Ct. Appeals (5th Cir.), US Ct. Appeals (6th Cir.), US Ct. Appeals (8th Cir.), US Ct. Appeals (9th Cir.), US Ct. Appeals (10th Cir.). Law clk. Ct. Appeals MIch., Detroit, 1975-76; atty. U.S. Dept. Justice Antitrust div., Washington, 1976-79; spl. asst. U.S. atty. U.S. Atty's Office, Alexandria, Va., 1979; assoc. and ptnr. Peabody, Rivlin, Lambert & Meyers, Washington, 1979-84; ptnr. Bishop Cook Purcell & Reynolds, Washington, 1984-90, Venable, Baetjer, Howard & Civiletti, Washington, 1990—; ptnr., Copyright & Unfair Trade Dept. Venable LLP, Washington. Recipient Atty. Gen. Spl. Achievement Awards, 1977—78. Fellow: Am. Coll. Trial Lawyers; mem.: ABA (Antitrust Sect., Litig. Sect., Intellectual Property Sect.), Phi Beta Kappa. Avocations: swimming, gardening, mayan culture. Office: Venable ILP 575 7th St NW Washington DC 20004 Office Phone: 202-344-4813. Office Fax: 202-344-8300. Business E-Mail: wdcoston@venable.com.

COSTRELL, ROBERT MICHAEL, economist; b. Washington, Apr. 10, 1950; s. Louis and Esther (Klaiman) C.; m. Rochelle Myrna Ryman, Dec. 17, 1983; children: Sarah Anne, Benjamin David. BA, U. Mich., 1972; PhD, Harvard U., 1978. Asst. prof. U. Mass., Amherst, 1978—85, assoc. prof., 1985—92, prof., 1992—. Vis. asst. prof. U. Toronto, 1982-84; adj. assoc. prof. Brandeis U., Waltham, Mass., 1986; cons. panel on tech. and employment NAS, Washington, 1986, joint econ. com. U.S. Congress, 1987-88; vis. scholar Boston U., 1993-94; dir. R&D Mass. Exec. Office for Adminstrn. and Fin., 1999-2002, chief economist, 2003—; steering com. NAEP Econ. Framework and Specifications, 2001-02, Mass. Sch. Bldg. Authority, 2005— *Professor Costrell's academic career has featured seminal publications on the incentive logic of educational standards and standard-setting. During his tour of service in the administrations of Massachusetts Governors Romney, Swift, and Cellucci, he has conducted or directed policy development research in school finance, standards-based education reform, public sector unionism, taxes, long-term budget trends, housing supply, pension funding, and other topics. His extensive expert testimony in the landmark Hancock school finance case proved critical to the state's successful defense. His publications on school finance have been quite influential in Massachusetts and nationally.* Contbr. articles to profl. jours. Pres. Brookline Com. for Quality Edn., 1990-95; gov. appointee Mass. Tax Alternatives Commn., 1997-98; adv. coun. on edn. stats. US Dept. Edn., 2001-02; gov.'s designee Pub. Employee Retirement Adminstrn. Commn. 2001-2003 Mem. Am. Econ. Assn., Phi Beta Kappa. Home: 311 Russett Rd Chestnut Hill MA 02467-3609 Office: Exec Office for Adminstrn and Fin State House Rm 373 Boston MA 02133 E-mail: bob.costrell@state.ma.us.

COTCHETT, JOSEPH WINTERS, lawyer, writer; b. Chgo., Jan. 6, 1939; s. Joseph Winters and Jean (Renaud) C.; children— Leslie F., Charles P., Rachael E., Quinn Carlyle, Camilla E. BS in Engring., Calif. Poly. Coll., 1960; LLB, U. Calif. Hastings Coll. Law, 1964. Bar: Calif. 1965, DC 1980. Ptnr. Cotchett, Pitre, Simon & McCarthy, Burlingame, Calif., 1965—. Mem. Calif. Jud. Coun., 1975-77, Calif. Commn. on Jud. Performance, 1985-89, Commn. 2020 Jud. Coun., 1991-94; select com. on jud. retirement, 1992—. Author: (with R. Cartwright) California Products Liability Actions, 1970, (with F. Haight) California Courtroom Evidence, 1972, (with A. Elkind) Federal Courtroom Evidence, 1976, (with Frank Rothman) Persuasive Opening Statements and Closing Arguments, 1988, (with Stephen Pizzo) The Ethics Gap, 1991, (with Gerald Uelmen) California Courtroom Evidence Foundations, 1993; contbr. articles to profl. jours. Chmn. San Mateo County Heart Assn., 1967; pres. San Mateo Boys and Girls Club, 1971; bd. dirs. U. Calif. Hastings Law Sch., 1981-93. With Intelligence Corps, U.S. Army, 1960-61; col. JAGC, USAR, ret. Named one of Top Ten Lawyers in Bay Area, San Francisco Chronicle, 2003. Fellow Am. Bar Found., Am. Bd. Trial Advs., Am. Coll. Trial Lawyers, Internat. Acad. Trial Lawyers, Internat. Soc. of Barristers, Nat. Bd. Trial Advs. (diplomate civil trial adv.), State Bar Calif. (gov. 1972-75). Clubs: Commonwealth, Press (San Francisco). Office: 840 Malcolm Rd Burlingame CA 94010-1401 also: 9454 Wilshire Blvd Ste 907 Beverly Hills CA 90202

COTE, DAVID EDWARD, state legislator; b. Nashua, N.H., Oct. 28, 1960; s. Edward David and Dorothy Eliza (Soucy) C. Mem. N.H. Ho. of Reps., Concord, 1982-88, 89—, asst. Dem. whip, 1991-92, dep. Dem. whip, 1992-96; mem. House Dem. Leadership, 1996—2003. Del. N.H. Constl. Conv., 1984, N.H. Dem. Convs., 1982—; mem. platform com. N.H. Dem. Com., 1984; vice chmn. Nashua City Dem. Com., 1985-86; active various Dem. campaigns. Home: 96 W Hollis St Nashua NH 03060-3146 Office: NH Ho of Reps N State St Rm 306 Concord NH 03301-3229 Business E-Mail: david.cote@leg.state.nh.us.

COTE, DAVID M., diversified technology and manufacturing company executive; BS in Bus. Adminstrn., 1976, LLD (hon.) Pepperdine U., 2001. With GE, 1974—99, corp. sr. v.p., and pres., CEO appliances divsn., 1996—99; chmn., pres., CEO TRW, Cleve., 1999—2002; pres., CEO, chmn. Honeywell Internat. Inc., 2002—. Appointed mem. Nat. Security Telecommunications Adv. Com. Office: 101 Columbia Rd Morristown NJ 07962

COTE, DENISE LOUISE, federal judge; b. St. Cloud, Minn., Oct. 13, 1946; d. Donald Edward and Dorothy (Garberson) C.; m. Howard F. Maltby, Dec. 24, 1987. BA, St. Mary's Coll., 1968; MA, Columbia U., 1969, JD, 1975. Bar: N.Y. 1976, U.S. Dist. Ct. (so. and ea. dist.) N.Y. 1976, U.S. Ct. Appeals (2d cir.) 1984. Law clk. to Hon. Jack B. Weinstein U.S. Dist. Ct. (ea. dist.) N.Y., 1975-76; assoc. Curtis Mallet-Prevost, N.Y.C., 1976-77; asst. U.S. Attys. Office (so. dist.), N.Y.C., 1977-85; dep. chief criminal divsn. so. dist. U.S. Attys. Office, N.Y.C., 1983-85, chief criminal divsn. so. dist., 1991-94; atty. Kaye Scholer Fierman Hays & Handler, N.Y.C., 1985-88, ptnr., 1988-91; judge U.S. Dist. Ct. (so. dist.) N.Y., 1994—. Mem. Assn. of Bar of City of N.Y. Office: US District Court 500 Pearl St Room 1040 New York NY 10007-1316*

COTE, MICHAEL RICHARD, bishop; b. Sanford, Maine, June 19, 1949; Student, Our Lady of Lourdes Sem., Cassadaga, N.Y., St. Mary's Sem. Coll., Balt., Gregorian U. Rome, Cath. U. Washington; JCL, Cath. U., 1981. Ordained priest Roman Cath. Ch. 1975. Asst. SS Athanasius & John, Rumford, Maine, 1975—78; assoc. Holy Rosary, Caribou, 1978—79; notary Vice-Officialis Diocesan Tribunal, Portland, 1980—89; sec. Apostolic Nunciature, Washington, 1989—94; pastor Sacred Heart, Auburn, Maine, 1994—95; titular bishop Diocese of Cebarades, 1995—; aux. bishop Diocese of Portland, 1995—2003; bishop Diocese of Norwich, Conn., 2003—. Office: 274 Broadway Norwich CT 06360-4353*

COTE, RICHARD JAMES, pathologist, researcher; b. L.A., May 10, 1954; s. Richard Patrick and Kathrine C.; m. Anne Louise Foxen, Feb. 8, 1992; children: Nicholas Foxen, Juliet Anne, Grace Elizabeth. BS in Biology, BA in Chemistry, U. Calif., Irvine, 1976; MD, U. Chgo., 1980. Diplomate Am. Coll. Pathologists. Intern in surgery U. Mich. Hosp., Ann Arbor, 1980-81; rsch. fellow, immunology Meml. Sloan-Kettering Cancer Ctr., N.Y.C., 1981-83; rsch. assoc., immunology Meml. Sloan-Kettering Hosp., N.Y.C., 1983-85, fellow, pathology, 1987-88, chief fellow, pathology, 1988-90; resident, pathology Cornell U. Med. Ctr., N.Y.C., 1985-87; asst. prof., pathology Keck Sch. Medicine, U. So. Calif., L.A., 1990-95, assoc. prof., 1995-99, prof., 1999—; dir. genitourinary program Keck Sch. Medicine, U. So. Calif./Norris Cancer Ctr., 1997—; attending pathologist Kenneth Norris Cancer Ctr., 1990—, dir. lab. immuno and molecular pathology, 1991—. Founder, dir. IMPATH, Inc., N.Y.C., 1987—2003; chief med. officer Chromavision Med. Sys. (now Clarient Inc.), 2004—05; mem. numerous nat. and internat. adv. bds.; sci. cons. MD Anderson Cancer Ctr., Houston, 2001—, Sidney Kimmel Cancer Ctr., San Diego, 2001—, U. Calif., L.A., 2002—, San Francisco, 2002—, Roche Molecular Sys., 2002—. Author: Immunomicroscopy, 1994, 2005; editor Modern Surg. Pathology; assoc. editor Applied Immunohistochemistry; contbr. articles to profl. jours., book chpts. Patentee in field. Am. Cancer Soc. fellow, 1988; recipient rsch. grants, awards NIH, ACS, others, 1981—. Mem.: Am. Assn. Cancer Rsch., Phi Beta Kappa. Office: U So Calif Keck Sch Medicine 1441 Eastlake Ave Los Angeles CA 90089-0112 E-mail: cote_r@ccnt.usc.edu.

COTE ROBBINS, RHEA JEANNINE, writer, educator; b. Waterville, Maine, May 26, 1953; d. G. Raymond and Rita Lucille (St. Germain) Cote; m. David Maurice Robbins, July 3, 1971; children: Bridget, Benjamin, Jesse. AA in Liberal Arts, U. Maine, Presque Isle, 1982; BS in Edn. with honors, U. Maine, Orono, 1985, MA in Liberal Studies, 1997; LHD (hon.), U. Maine, Farmington, 2004. Cert. tchr., Maine. Comm. coord. Franco-Am. Ctr., Orono, 1986-96; founder, exec. dir. Franco-Am. Women's Inst., Brewer, Maine, 1996—; adj. asst. prof. U. Maine, Orono, 1999—. Co-editor, designer: I Am Franco-American and Proud of It, 1995; editor Initiative, 1996; co-author: Old Women's Wisdom, 1996; author: Wednesday's Child, 1997, 2d edit., 1999 (Maine Writers Chapbook award 1997). Mem. sys. diversity com. U. Maine, 1998—; mem. grants rev. com. Susan G. Komen Race for the Cure, 1999—; mem. adv. bd. edn. and cultural Franco-Am. Heritage Ctr., Lewiston. Recipient Terry Plunkett Maine Writers Collection, U. Maine, Augusta, 1998, Maine Women Writers Collection, Abplanalp Libr., 1999, Yale Collection Am. Lit. award Yale U., 1999. Mem.: Franco-Am. Studies Com., Maine Franco-Am. Studies Alliance, Maine Women's Studies Consortium. Avocations: quilting, web page authoring, boating, walking. Home and Office: 641 S Main St Brewer ME 04412-2516 Fax: 207-989-7059.

COTHORN, JOHN ARTHUR, lawyer; b. Des Moines, Dec. 12, 1939; s. John L. and Marguerite (Esters) C.; m. Connie Cason, Aug. 6, 1996; children: Jeffrey, Judith. BS in Math., BS in Aero. Engring., U. Mich., 1961, JD, 1980. Bar: Mich. 1981, U.S. Dist. Ct. (ea. dist.) Mich. 1981, U.S. Ct. Appeals (6th cir.) 1981, U.S. Dist. Ct. (we. dist.) Mich. 1986, U.S. Supreme Ct. Exec. U.S Govt., 1965-78; asst. prosecutor Washtenaw County, Ann Arbor, Mich., 1981-82; ptnr. Kitch, Saurbier, Drutchas, Wagner & Kenney P.C., Detroit, 1982-94, Meganck & Cothorn P.C., Detroit, 1994-97, Meganck, Cothorn & Stanczyk P.C., Detroit, 1997-98, Cothorn & Stanczyk, P.C., Detroit, 1998-2000, Cothorn & Braceful, Detroit, 2000—02, Cothorn & Assocs., P.C., Detroit, 2002—04, Cothorn & Mackley, P.C., 2004—. Served to capt. U.S. Army, 1961-65. Mem. ABA, Nat. Bar Assn. (numerous fed. and state coms.), Soc. Automotive Engrs., Assn. Def. Trial Counsel, Phi Alpha Delta. Republican. Avocations: bridge, golf. Office: 535 Griswold St Ste 530 Detroit MI 48226-3696 Office Phone: 313-964-7600. Business E-Mail: jcothorn@comcast.net.

COTHRAN, ANNE JENNETTE, educational administrator; b. Buffalo, Nov. 28, 1952; d. Raymond John and Thelma Lorraine C. BA in English, Gordon Coll., 1975; MBA in Specialization Mktg., U. Chgo., 1989; MEd, Loyola U., Chgo., 2000, EdD, 2004. Mgr. 1776 House, Salem, Mass., 1974-75; dept. mgr. Goldblatt's Dept. Store, Chgo., 1975-77; sales rep. Sta. WWMM, Arlington Heights, Ill., 1977-79, Sta. WYEN, Des Plaines, Ill., 1979-81; coop. mgr. Southtown Economist Newspapers, Chgo., 1981-83, div. sales mgr., 1983-88; retail advt. mgr. Lansing (Mich.) State Jour., 1988-90; advt. & mktg. dir. Herald-Bulletin Newspapers, Anderson, Ind., 1990-92; mgr. Dealer Network Advt. Sys. Newspaper Assn. of Am., Chgo., 1993-94; pub. dir. Standard Rate and Data Svc., Chgo., 1994—95; exec. dir. Sylvan Learning Systems, Contract Svcs. Divsn., Balt., 1996-98; tchr. Chgo. Pub. Schs., 1998-2000; dean J. Sterling Morton H.S. Dist. 201, 2000—02; sys. dir. Sch. Dist. 201, 2002—. Bd. dirs. Cabrini Green Legal Aid Clinic, Chgo., 1981-83. Mem. ASCD, U. Chgo. Women's Bus. Group (bd. dirs. chpt. devel., chair 1987), Am. Ednl. Rsch. Assn., Rotary (v.p. Anderson suburban chpt. 1992-93), Ikebana Internat., Nat. Mid. Sch. Assn., Internat. Reading Assn. Avocations: theater, ikebana, gardening.

COTHRUN, THOMAS KEITH, secondary school educator; b. Miami, Ariz., Mar. 9, 1959; s. Milton James and Nadine L. (Thomas) Cothrun. BA in Edn., U. Ariz., 1982; MA in German Studies, U. N.Mex., 1993. Tchr. German, Alamogordo (N.Mex.) H.S., 1983-86, Las Cruces (N.Mex.) H.S., 1986—. Dir. German Weekend, N.Mex., 1985-89, 99-01; mem. task force Nat. Stds. in Fgn. Lang., Yonkers, N.Y., 1993-96; cons. Coll. Bd., Princeton, N.J., 1993—. Co-author: German-American Partnership Program Handbook, 1993; also articles. Named Tchr. of Yr., Las Cruces Pub. Schs., 1995, Walt Disney Am. Tchr. award honoree, 1995; recipient fellowship U.S. Holocaust Meml. Mus. Mandel, 1999-2000, award for excellence in tchg., Am. Couns. for Internat. Edn., 1999. Mem. ASCD, NEA, Am. Assn. Tchrs. German (v.p., pres.-elect 1994-95, pres. 1996-97, cert. of merit 1993, Outstanding German Educator 2001), Am. Coun. on Tchg. Fgn. Langs. (pres.-elect 2003, pres. 2004), S.W. Conf. on Lang. Tchg., N.Mex. Orgn. Lang. Educators (Creativity in Tchg. award 1993, Tchr. of Yr. 2002), Nat. Bd. for Profl. Tchg. Stds. (fgn. lang. stds. chair 1998-01, bd. dirs. 2002—). Office: Las Cruces Pub Schs 1755 El Paseo St Las Cruces NM 88001-6011

COTLEUR, MARK A., hospital administrator; b. Cleve., July 31, 1964; s. Neil Edward and Ruth L. (Cordiak) C.; m. Laurie J. Liss, Oct. 22, 1994 (div. June 1997). BA in History and Philosophy, Borromeo Sem. Coll., 1986; MA in Theology, Marquette U., 1993. Theology tchr. St. Peter Chanel H.S., Bedford, Ohio, 1986-90; prospect rsch. mgr. Children's Hosp. Wis., Milw., 1993-97, Children's Hosp., Boston, 1997-2000; asst. dir. devel. Univ. Hosps. Cleve., 2001—. Rsch. cons. Abbey Group Ltd., Milw., Northeast Health Found., Beverly, Mass., 2002—. Asst. editor Foundation Directory, Foundations in Wisconsin, 1992. Mem. planning com. No. Ohio Planned Giving Coun.; mem. edn. comm. St. Peter Chanel High Sch. Mem. Assn. Profl. Rschrs. for Advancement (bd. dirs. 2000-02, mem. nominating com. 2003--, media rels. advisor 2003--, v.p. Wis. chpt. 1995-96, pres. 1996-97), New Eng. Devel. Rsch. Assn. Avocations: golf, cooking, reading, computers. Office: 11100 Euclid Ave Cleveland OH 44106-1736

COTON, CARLOS DAVID, finance manager; b. Havana, Cuba, Dec. 29, 1950; arrived in US, 1960; s. Jose Manuel Coton and Guillermina (Guitian) Coton Lopez; m. Susana M. Muriel, May 18, 1997; children: Alexandra Beatriz, David Alexander, Sean Stephen. AA, Miami Dade C.C., 1971; BA, Fla. Internat. U., 1973, MS, 1983; PhD in Internat. Bus., Kennedy Western U., 1992. Supr. trainee Richards Dept. Store, Miami, Fla., 1967-68, supr., 1968-73, mgr. distbn., 1973-76; dir. ops. Bassett Furniture Mfg., 1976-79; asst. dir. Fla. Internat. U., Miami, 1979-82; dir. Luth. Ministries Projects, Miami, 1982-84; fin. mgr. Emery Worldwide, Miami, 1984-90; v.p. fin. Transworld Computers, Miami, 1989—; v.p. Carinter Miami, 1991-95; v.p. ops. Internat. Sys. and Electronics, Miami, 1995—. Substitute tchr. Dade County Pub. Schs., Miami, 1973—; adj. prof. Fla. Internat. U., 1980—; pres. CDC Cons.; cons. in field. Author: (poetry book) ... And Other Poems, 1973; contbr. articles to profl. jours. Mem. Council on Laraza, Calif., 1980; mem. Dade County United Way. Mem.: Nat. Soc. Tax Profls., Am. Inst. Profl. Bookkeepers, Ecuadorian Inter-Am. C. of C., Nat. Coun. Tchrs. English, Acad. Internat. Bus., Am. Mgmt. Assn., Miami=Santiago Sister Cities Program, Am. C. of C., Cuban-Am. Orgn., Fla. HS Activities Assn. (ofcl.), Greater Miami Football Ofcls. Assn., Greater Miami C. of C. (mentor STAR/HOPE, hispanic com. mem., S.Am. com. mem.W. Dade com. mem.), Greater Miami Basketbal Ofcls.Assn., Miami Ofcls. club, Phi Delta Kappa. Democrat. Roman Catholic. Avocations: football referee, basketball referee. Home: 1320 SW 91st Ave Miami FL 33174-3130 E-mail: cdc@ise-corp.com, cdc1229@concentric.net.

COTRELL, CHARLES L., academic administrator; m. Abbie Massey; 4 children. B in Polit. Sci., St. Mary's U., 1962, M in Polit. Sci., 1964; PhD in Polit. Sci., U. Ariz., 1970. Instr. Tex. A&M, Kingsville, 1965—66; tchr. St. Mary's U., San Antonio, 1966—71, chmn. dept. polit. sci., 1971, dir. grad. program polit. sci. and pub. adminstrn., dean arts and sci., dean sch. humanities social sci., 1983—86, asst. to pres., 1983, acad. v.p., 1986—99, pres., 2000—. Vice chmn. Mayor's com. Integrity Trust in Local Govt.; coord. subcom. campaign fin. Recipient Marianist Heritage award, 1985, Disting. Alumnus award, St. Mary's U., 1992, Gonzalez Hispanic Achievement award, St. Mary's Law Alumni Assn., 1994, Career Achievement award, Am. Polit. Sci. Assn., 1995; fellow Ctr. Behavioral Social Rsch., Wesleyan U., 1969—70. Office: One Camino Santa Maria San Antonio TX 78228-8503

COTROS, CHARLES H., food products company executive; b. 1937; Grad. Christian Brothers Coll., 1960. Exec. v.p, pres. food svc. ops. Sysco Corp., Houston, 1988—95, COO, 1995—2000, pres., 1999—2000, chmn., CEO, 2000—02; ret., 2002. Bd. dirs. AmerisourceBergen Corp. Office: Sysco Corp 1390 Enclave Pkwy Houston TX 77077-2099

COTRUBAS, ILEANA, opera singer, retired lyric soprano; b. Galati, Romania; d. Vasile C. and Maria C. m. Manfred Ramin, 1972. Student, Scoala speciala de Musica, Bucharest, Ciprian Porumbescu Conservatory, Musikakademie, Vienna, Austria. Tchr. master-classes, interpretation and operatic roles. Debut as Yniold in Pelleas et Melisande, Bucharest Opera, 1964; appeared with Frankfurt (Fed. Republic Germany) Opera, 1968-71, Staatsoper, Vienna, 1970—, Covent Garden, London, 1971—, Staatsoper, Munich, 1973—, Lyric Opera Chgo., 1973-75, 83—, Opera Paris, 1974—, La Scala, Milan, 1975—, Met. Opera, N.Y.C., 1977—, San Francisco Opera, 1978, Ehrenmitglied Vienna Staatsoper, 1991; major roles include: Zerlina, Susanna, Pamina, Norina, Gilda, Violetta, Elisabetta (Don Carlos), Mimi, Tatyana, Micaela, Manon, Antonia, Melisande; ret., 1990; author: Truth

About Opera, 1998. Recipient 1st prize Internat. Singing Competition, Hertogenbusch, Netherlands, 1965; 1st prize Munich Radio Competition, 1966; Kammersängerin Vienna Staatsoper, 1981; Great Officer of the Order Sant' Iago da Espada, Portugal, 1990, Great Officer of Star of Romania, 2000.

COTRUVO, JOSEPH ALFRED, environmental sciences administrator; b. Toledo, Aug. 3, 1942; s. Nicholas and Angela (Campanale) C.; m. Karen Shrum, June 18, 1983; 1 child, Joseph Alfred Jr. BS in Chemistry, U. Toledo, 1963; PhD, Ohio State U., 1968; postgrad., U. Bologna, Italy, 1969. Mgr. R & D ChemSampCo, Columbus, Ohio, 1970-72; programs analyst EPA, Washington, 1973-76, dir. drinking water criteria and stds. divsn., 1976-90, dir. health and environ. rev. divsn., 1990-92; dir. risk assessment divsn., 1992-96; sr. regulatory exec. NSF Internat., Washington, 1996-98. V.p. environ. health scis. NSF Internat., 1998—2000; coun. pub. health cons. Nat. Sanitation Found., Ann Arbor, Mich., 1980—96; dir. NSF Internat./WHO Collaborating Ctr. for Water Safety and Tech., 1996—2005; adj. prof. environ. scis. Am. U., 1997; mem. rsch. adv. bd. Nat. Water Rsch. Inst.; mem. sci. adv. bd. Santa Ana River Water Quality and Health; ind. adv. bd. Tampa Water Resource Reuse Panel, 1997—98; pres. J. Cotruvo & Assocs. LLC; mem. sci. adv. bd. Cal-Fed Delta Water Quality Project; rsch. adv. bd. Water Reuse Found.; sci. panel on water sys. security rsch. NAS, 2003, Heterotrophic Plate Counts, 2003, Emerging Pathogen, 2004; mem. San Diego Water Reuse Adv. Com., 2004—; vis. prof. environ. sci. Tech. U. Bari, 2005. Co-editor: Ozone/Chlorine Dioxide, 1978, Water Chlorination, 1983, Procs. Safe Drinking Water in Small Sys.: Tech., Ops. and Econs., 1999; chmn., editor book series NATO/CCMS Drinking Water Pilot, 1980; co-editor WHO series on Emerging Pathogens in Drinking Water; contbr. articles to jours. in field. Recipient Environ. Leadership award Nat. Sanitation Found., Ann Arbor, 1988, Donald R. Boyd award Assn. Met. Water Agys., 1990; named Meritorious Exec., Pres. U.S., 1983. Mem. Am. Chem Soc., Am. Water Works Assn. (hon. life, mem. editl. adv. bd. Jour., 1987-90), InterAm. Assn. Sanitary and Environ. Engring. (dir. at large 2000-2002, v.p. 2003—). Roman Catholic. Avocations: woodworking, light construction. Office Phone: 202-362-3076. Personal E-mail: joseph.cotruvo@verizon.net.

COTSAKOS, CHRISTOS MICHAEL, former internet financial services company executive; b. Paterson, N.J., July 29, 1948; s. Michael John and Lillian (Scoulikas) C.; m. Hannah Batami Fogel, July 1, 1973; 1 child, Suzanne Renee. BA in Communications and Polit. Sci., William Paterson Coll., 1972; MBA, Pepperdine U., 1984. Tour guide Universal Studios, Burbank, Calif., 1973; courier Fed. Express Corp., Burbank, 1973-74, sales rep. Long Beach, Calif., 1974, sta. mgr. San Jose, Calif., 1974, we. dist. mgr., 1974, region engring. mgr. Denver, 1975, mng. dir. Chgo., 1975-80, v.p. Sacramento, 1980-92; pres., COO Nielsen, Europe, Middle East, Africa, 1992-93; pres., CEO Nielsen Internat., 1993-95; pres., co-CEO, COO, dir. A.C. Nielsen, Inc., 1995-96; CEO, chmn. E*TRADE Group, Inc., Palo Alto, Calif., 1996—2003. Instr. Consumers River Coll., Placerville, Calif., 1985-86; bd. dirs. Airlifeline, Sacramento, Nat. Processing, Inc., Louisville, Forté Software, Inc., Oakland, 4th Comms. Network, San Jose, Datacard, Mpls. Author: (book) It's Your Money: The E*Trade Step by Step Guide to Online Investing, 2000. Served as sgt. U.S. Army, 1967-70, Vietnam. Decorated Bronze Star, 1967, Purple Heart, 1967. Mem. World Econ Forum (Davos, Switzerland), Sutter Club, Comstock Club.

COTSEN, LLOYD E., retired consumer products company executive; b. Feb. 25, 1929; m. Margit Cotsen. Grad., Princeton U., 1950; MBA, Harvard U., 1957. With Neutrogena Corp. (formerly Natone), 1957—95; pres. Neutrogena Corp., 1967—95, CEO, 1982—95, chmn., 1991—95; pres. Cotsen Mgmt. Corp., LA, 1994—. Mem. bd. trustees J. Paul Getty Trust, 2002—. Avocation: Collector of worldwide folk art. Office: J Paul Getty Trust 1200 Getty Ctr Dr Los Angeles CA 90049

COTTAM, KEITH M., librarian, educator, administrator; b. St. George, Utah, Feb. 13, 1941; s. Von Bunker and Adrene (McArthur) Cottam; m. Laurel Springer, June 16, 1961 (div. Feb. 4, 2000); children: Mark Patrick, Lisa Diane, Andrea Jill, Brian Lowell, Heather Dawn; m. Mary Bultena Albertson, Oct. 5, 2001. BS, Utah State U., 1963; MLS, Pratt Inst., 1965. Trainee Bklyn. Pub. Libr., 1963—65, asst. instr. reading improvement program, 1964—65, adult services libr., 1965; asst. social scis. libr., instr. So. Ill. U., Edwardsville, 1965—67; head, social sci. libr., instr. asst. prof. Social Scis. Libr., Brigham Young U., Provo, Utah, 1967—72; supr., inst. Libr. Technician Program Brigham Young U., Provo, Utah, 1969—72; head undergrad. libr., assoc. prof. U. Tenn., Knoxville, 1972—75, asst. dir. librs., assoc. prof., 1975—77; asst. dir. for pub. svcs. and employee rels. Vanderbilt U. Libr. (formerly Joint Univ. Librs.), Nashville, 1977—80, assoc. dir., 1980—82, acting dir., 1982—83; dir. libraries, prof. U. Wyo., Laramie, 1983—2000, dean univ. librs., 2001; assoc. dean outreach sch., dir. U. Wyo./Casper Coll. Ctr., Casper, 2001—05, emeritus prof., 2005—. Cons. tng. program Assn. Rsch. Librs., 1979—80; mem. Leadership Wyo. Tng. Program, 2002—03; bd. dirs. Casper Area C. of C., 2004—, Platte River Pkwy. Trust, 2004—, Wyo. Commn. for Nat. and Cmty. Svc. Author: Writer's Research handbook, 1977, 2d edit., 1978; editor Utah Libraries jour., 1971-72; mem. editl. bd. RQ jour., 1980-84; contbr. articles to profl. jours. Fellow Coun. Libr. Resources, 1975-76; sr. fellow UCLA Grad. Sch. Libr. Info. Sci., 1985-86. Mem.: ALA, Wyo. Libr. Assn. (pres. 1998—99), Phi Kappa Phi, Beta Phi Mu. Republican. Mem. Ch. of Jesus Christ of Latter-day Saints. Avocations: bicycling, racing and touring, free-lance writer, gardening. Home: 1751 W Coffman Ave Casper WY 82604-3453 E-mail: kcottam@uwyo.edu.

COTTEN, SAMUEL RICHARD, former state legislator, consultant; b. Juneau, Alaska, July 16, 1947; s. Samuel L. Cotten and Kathryn Russell; m. Martha Tillion, June 16, 1984; children: Samuel Tillion, Augustus O'Dwyer Russell. AA, U. Alaska, 1971. Rep. Alaskan Ho. of Reps., Juneau, 1975-82, 85-91, speaker, 1989-91; senator Alaska State Senate, Juneau, 1991-93; chmn. Alaska Pub. Utilities Commn., 1995—99; fisheries cons., 1999—. Spl. advisor Intergovtl. Consultative Com. to North Pacific Fisheries Adv. Bd., 1989-92; advisor Internat. North Pacific Fisheries Commn., 1984-90; bd. dir. Fire Lake Recreational Ctr., Eagle River, Alaska. Co-chmn. Alaska Criminal Code Revision Commn., Juneau, 1976; mem. Anchorage Planning and Zoning Commn., 1983-84; candidate for Gov. Alaska, 1994—. Recipient Nat. Def. award Vietnam Svc. (2); named Outstanding Vietnam Vet. No Greater Love Found., 1976. Mem. Cook Inlet Seiners Assn., Navy League, Elks, VFW (life), Anchorage Ski Club. Democrat. Avocations: fishing, skiing, bowling. Home: PO Box 770296 Eagle River AK 99577-0296 Office Phone: 907-274-7573. E-mail: samc.er@gci.net.

COTTER, JOSEPH FRANCIS, retired bank executive, hotel executive; b. Brockton, Mass., May 18, 1927; s. Joseph and Sarah (Thornell) C.; m. Catherine Florence Sullivan, 1950 (dec.); m. Barbara Tribou Salter, 1986. BS cum laude, Boston Coll., 1949. CPA, Mass., N.Y. Accountant Price Waterhouse & Co., N.Y.C., 1949-67; v.p., contr. Howard Johnson Co., Braintree, Mass., 1967-70; exec. v.p., comptr., dir. Sheraton Corp., Boston, 1970-85, exec. v.p. planning and devel., 1985-87; ret., 1987-89; exec. Bank of Boston, 1989-95; ret., 1995. Former vice chmn. bd. trustees Boston Coll.; former chmn. bd. dirs. Greater Boston YMCA.; former v.p., bd. dirs. Greater Boston C. of C.; trustee for life Dana-Farber Cancer Rsch. Inst.; former bd. dirs. United Way of Mass. Bay. Mem. AICPA, N.Y. Soc. CPAs, Mass. Soc. CPAs, Boston Coll. Alumni Assn. (past pres.), Purpoodock Club. Home: 11 Running Tide Rd Cape Elizabeth ME 04107-2933

COTTER, KA, real estate company executive; Founding mem. The Staubach Co., Addison, Tex., 1979, exec. v.p., S.W. regional mgr., 1987—92, vice chmn., mem. exec. com. and bd. dirs. Office: The Staubach Co Ste 400 15601 Dallas Pkwy Addison TX 75001

COTTER, MICHAEL WILLIAM, retired ambassador, management consultant; b. Madison, Wis., Aug. 1, 1943; s. Patrick William and Lois Katherine (Schaus) Cotter; m. Joanne Marie Miller, Aug. 30, 1974. BSFS, Georgetown U., 1965; JD, U. Mich., 1968; MS, Stanford U., 1976. Polit.-mil. affairs officer Am. Embassy, Ankara, Turkey, 1980-82; sr. Turkish desk officer U.S. Dept. State, Washington, 1982-84; polit. officer Am. Embassy, Kinshasa, Zaire, 1984-86, polit. counselor, 1986-88; mgmt. analyst sec. of mgmt. U.S. Dept. State, 1988-90, office dir. politico-military affairs, 1990-92; dep. chief of mission Am. Embassy, Santiago, Chile, 1992-95; U.S. amb. to Turkmenistan, 1995-98; internat. bus. cons. Washington, 1999-2001; internat. bus. cons., lectr. Chapel Hill, NC, 2001—. V.p., assoc. publ. Am. Diplomacy Publs., Chapel Hill, NC, 2001—. Mem.: Am. Fgn. Svc. Assn. (secy 1989—91, bd govs 1988—89). Home and Office: 685 Fearrington Post Pittsboro NC 27312-8523 E-mail: mwcotter@hotmail.com.

COTTER, PATRICIA O'BRIEN, state supreme court justice; b. South Bend, Ind., 1950; m. Michael W. Cotter, 1979; 2 children. BS in Polit. Sci. and History with honors, We. Mich. U, 1972; JD, Notre Dame, 1977. Pvt. practice, South Bend, 1977—83, Great Falls, Mont., 1984; ptnr. Cotter & Cotter, Great Falls, 1985—2000; justice Mont. Supreme Ct., 2001—. Mem.: Mont. Trial Lawyers Assn. (Public Service award 1999). Office: Rm 323 PO Box 203003 Helena MT 59620

COTTER, PHILIP DAVID, molecular biologist, geneticist; arrived in U.S., 1990; BSc, U. Canterbury, 1983; MSc with hons. in Applied Sci., Lincoln (New Zealand) U., 1986; PhD, CUNY, 1994. Cert. clin. cytogeneticist Am. Bd. Med. Genetics, 1996, clin. molecular geneticist Am. Bd. Med. Genetics, 1996. Dir. cytogenetics and molecular genetics Children's Hosp. and Rsch. Ctr., Oakland, Calif., 1996—; dir. advanced molecular diagnostics U.S. Labs., Irvine, Calif., 2002—04; v.p., clin. labs. Biocept Labs., San Diego, 2004—. Pres., CEO Pheidon Software Corp., Oakland, 2000—; adj. assoc. prof. U. Calif., San Francisco, 2003—. Fellow: Am. Coll. Med. Geneticists. Office: Biocept Laboratories 5810 Nancy Ridge Drive San Diego CA 92121 Office Phone: 858-320-8206.

COTTER, ROBERT F., hotel executive; b. Brockton, Mass. married; 3 children. BA in Philosophy, Boston Coll., 1973. With, 1973—; various sales and mktg. positions Sheraton Hotels, L.A., Honolulu, area dir. mktg. Hawaii, 1980-82, v.p. dir. advt. Hawaii, Japan & Far East divsn., 1983-85, sr. v.p., dir. mktg. Hawaii-Japan divsn., 1985-88, dir., hotel mktg., 1988—89, v.p., hotel mktg., 1989—91, sr. v.p., mktg. & product mgmt., 1991—93, exec. v.p., mktg. & product mgmt., 1993—94, pres., COO Europe Brussels, 1994-99; pres. internat. ops. Starwood Hotels & Resorts Worldwide, Inc., COO White Plains, N.Y., 1999—, pres., 2003—. Named One of the 25 most influential execs. in the travel industry. Fellow Inst. of Cert. Travel Agts., Am. Hotel and Motel Assn. (mktg. com.) Office: Starwood Hotels & Resorts Worldwide Inc 1111 Westchester Ave White Plains NY 10604*

COTTER, WILLIAM DONALD, retired commissioner, retired editor; b. Hartford, Conn., June 5, 1921; s. William Joseph and Alice I. (Murphy) C.; m. Alice K. Liller, Jan. 22, 1944; children: Carol A., Mary L., Alice E., William J., James D., Donald W. BA, Fordham U., 1943; postgrad. Polit. Sci., St. John U., 1956-57, Syracuse U., 1958. Reporter L.I. Star-Jour., Long Island City, 1947-51; night city editor Nassau Rev., Rockville Centre, N.Y., 1952-53; night editor Jersey Jour., Jersey City, 1954; mag., Sunday editor L.I. Press, Jamaica, N.Y., 1955-58; city editor Syracuse Herald-Jour./Am., 1958-66, editor, 1966-83; chmn. N.Y. State Energy R & D Authority, 1983-92; commr. N.Y. State Energy Office, 1983-92, N.Y. State Pub. Svc. Commn., 1992-96. Trustee N.Y. Power Authority, 1989-92; instr. journalism Syracuse U., 1960-66. Former bd. dirs. Cmty. Gen. Hosp., Boys Town of Italy, Erie Canal Mus.; past chmn. communications com. LeMoyne Coll.; chmn. Onondaga County Energy Com., 1975-83. Served with USNR, 1943-46. Mem. N.Y. State Soc. Newspaper Editors (pres.), Auburn Golf and Country Club (dir.). Roman Catholic. Home: 8238 Penstock Way Manlius NY 13104

COTTER, WILLIAM RECKLING, foundation administrator; b. Detroit, Mar. 9, 1936; s. Fred Joseph and Esther Jean (Reckling) C.; m. Linda Jane Kester, June 14, 1959; children: David Andrew, Deborah Anne, Elizabeth Anne. BA in Polit. Sci. magna cum laude, Harvard U., 1958, JD cum laude, 1961; LHD (hon.), Bowdoin Coll., 1987, West Brook Coll., 1995, U. New Eng., 2000, Colby Coll., 2000, Thomas Coll., 2003. Bar: N.Y. 1962, U.S. Supreme Ct. 1965. Law clk. to U.S. Fed. Judge, N.Y.C., 1961-62; MIT fellow in Africa Nigeria, 1962-63; assoc. firm Cahill, Gordon, Sonnett, Reindell & Ohl, N.Y.C., 1963-65; White House fellow Washington, 1965-66; Ford Found. rep. to Colombia and Venezuela, 1966-70; pres. African-Am. Inst., N.Y.C., 1970-79, Colby Coll., 1979-2000, Oak Found., Boston and Geneva, Switzerland, 2000—, chair adv. com., 1997—. Contbr. articles on fgn. policy and edn. to profl. jours. Bd. dirs. Pvt. Agys. Collaborating Together, 1975-81, Waterville ARC, 1980-87, Kennebec Valley Regional Health Agy., 1982-88, Mid-Maine Econ. Devel. Corp.; chmn. bd. trustees Oyster Bay-East Norwich (N.Y.) Pub. Libr., 1975-79; trustee African-Am. Inst., 1970-2001; bd. dirs. Maine Pub. Broadcasting, 1979-2000; chair bd. dirs. Waterville Regional Arts and Cmty. Ctr., 1996-2000; chmn. bd. visitors Baxter Sch. for the Deaf, 1982-87; chmn. com. for study ct. structure, probate and family law matters, 1985; bd. advisors Carrabassett Valley Acad., 1981-91; chair com. on pub. disclosure New Eng. Assn. Schs. and Colls., 1987; trustee Westbrook Coll., 1986-92; past mem. exec. com. South African Edn. Program; past mem. commn. on govt. rels. Am. Coun. on Edn.; commr. State of Maine Edn. Commn.; mem. Nat. Commn. on Responsibilities for Financing Postsecondary Edn., 1991-93; bd. visitors U. Maine Sch. Law; past chair and dir. Nat. Assn. Ind. Colls. and Univs.; trustee Colby Coll., 1979-; trustee Olin Coll., 2002-; chmn. Robertson Scholans Program, Duke U., U. NC, 2004-. Named Educator of Yr. The Washington Ctr., 1993, Leader of Yr. Equity Inst. Maine, 1996, Disting. Citizen Waterville C. of C., 1998. Mem. Nat. Assn. Ind. Colls. and Univs. (past chair and dir.), Coun. Fgn. Rels., Harvard Club (NYC), Harvard Club (Boston); trustee Mass. Hist. Soc. Office: 47 Winter St Boston MA 02108-4706

COTTER-SMITH, CATHLEEN MARIE, art educator, artist; b. Dallas, 1950; d. Robert Jay and Betty Ann Cotter; 1 child, Ryan Patrick Holt; m. Jack Glendon Smith, Jr., 1991. BS, East Tex. State U., 1974; MS, Tex. A&M U., Commerce, 1977. Freelance artist, Garland and Plano, Tex., 1976—; assoc. prof. art Grayson County Coll., Dennison, Tex., 1981-85; prof. art Collin County C.C., Plano, Tex., 1986—, coord. art dept., 1986-97. Cons. on book Equine Images, 1992. One-woman shows include Cultural Art Ctr., Plano, 1990, Collin County C. C. Gallery, Plano, 1994, Biblical Arts Ctr.; exhibited in group show S.W. Watercolor Soc., Dallas, 1990, juried show Southwestern Watercolor Soc. (signature status), 2000, Invitational Water Media Show, 2001, Western Fedn. Watercolor Exhbn., 2003, Rotunda of Russell Senate Bldg, The Mall at the Lincoln Meml., Hillcrest Gallery, Dallas, 2004, Hillcrest Gallery, Dallas; represented in permanent collection Farmerville C. of C., 2004, Webb Chapel Ch. of Christ; illustrator for nat. card line, 1997-2000. Mentor Boles Children's Home, Quinlan, Tex., 1996—2003. Recipient award S.W. Watercolor Soc. Mem.: Southwestern Watercolor Soc. (signature mem., award in group 1999). Republican. Mem. Ch. of Christ. Avocation: nature lover. Office: Collin County CC 2800 E Spring Creek Pkwy Plano TX 75074-3300 Office Phone: 972-881-5817.

COTTING, JAMES CHARLES, manufacturing executive, director; b. Winchester, Mass., Oct. 15, 1933; s. Edward L. and Mary Ellen (Worrell) C.; m. Marjorie A. Kirsch, Feb. 8, 1963; children: James Charles, Steven Robert, Brenda Ann-Marie. BA cum laude, Ohio State U., 1955. Acctg. supr. U.S. Steel Corp., Pitts., 1959-61; mgr. profit analysis Ford Motor Co., Dearborn, Mich., 1961-63; mgr. devel. planning A.O. Smith Corp., Milw., 1963-66; asst. contr. Gen. Foods Corp., White Plains, N.Y., 1966-71; v.p. planning Internat. Paper Co., N.Y.C., 1971-76, v.p., contr., 1976-79; sr. v.p. fin. and planning, CFO Navistar Internat. Corp., Chgo., 1979-82, exec. v.p. fin., 1982-83, vice chmn., CFO, 1983-87, chmn., CEO, 1987-95, chmn. bd., 1995-96. Mem. Pres. Reagan's Task Force on Mkt. Mechanisms; bd. dirs. USG Corp.; former dir. Asarco Inc., Interlake Corp., Chgo. Stock Exchange. Dir. Jr. Achievement of Chgo.; trustee Adler Planetarium. Lt. USN, 1955-58. Mem. Chgo. Coun. on Fgn. Rels., Comml. Club Chgo., Econ. Club Chgo., Montclair Golf Club, Barrington Hills Country Club, Chgo. Club, Phi Beta Kappa, Alpha Tau Omega.

COTTINGHAM, JENNIFER JANE, city official; b. Salt Lake City, July 10, 1961; d. Miles Dixon and Ruth Eugenia (Skeen) Cottingham; m. Richard Frame Cavenaugh, July 23, 1983 (div. Apr. 1989); 1 child, John Douglas. BS in Civil Engring., So. Meth. U., 1984; MBA, U. Dallas, 2001. Lic. profl. engr., Tex. Estimator Avery Mays Constrn., Dallas, 1981-83, project engr., 1984; owner, gen. contr. Dallas, 1985-89; asst. project mgr. Austin Comml., Dallas, 1989; ct. appointed receiver 14th Dist. Ct., State of Tex., Dallas, 1990-91; mgr. project Dallas Water Utilities, 1990—91, project mgr., program mgr. capital improvements, 1991—2004; adv. bd. environ. & civil engring. program Southern Meth. Univ., 2004—. Dir. CBC Investors, L.P., Dallas. Goodwill ambassador City of Dallas Water Utilities, 1990-92, 95-96, fin. strength com., 1991. Mem. CBC Investments (founding pres.), DAR (pres. jr. group 1989-92), Cotillion Book Club (founding mem.). Republican. Episcopalian. Avocations: creative writing, reading, travel. Office: City of Dallas Water Utilities 2121 Main St Ste 300 Dallas TX 75201-4336

COTTINGHAM, RICHARD SUMNER, paper company executive; b. Columbus, Ohio, May 7, 1941; s. Robert E. and Lee Alice (Gasaway) C.; m. Sheila L. Robertson, Dec. 20, 1980. BA in History, Ohio State U., 1964. Pres. Cottingham Paper Co., Columbus, 1968—. Bd. dirs. Network Svcs. Co., 1984-90, chmn., 1986-88. Served as lt. (j.g.) USN, 1964-67, Vietnam. Recipient Ernst & Young Master Entrepreneur of Yr. award for Columbus and Ctrl. Ohio, Bus. First Newspaper, 1998, Bus. First Fast Fifty award, 2001, 02; named among Columbus Bus. First Fast Fifty Cos., 2001, 02; named Family Firm of Distinction, Weatherhead Sch. Mgmt., 2001. Mem. Nat. Paper Trade Assn. (young exec. com. 1976), Am. Mgmt. Assn., Nat. Assn. Wholesale Distbrs., Internat. Sanitary Supply Assn., Chief Exec. Bds. Columbus, Econ. Club Columbus, Columbus C. of C., Worthington Country Club. Republican. Address: Cottingham Paper Co 324 E 2d Ave PO Box 163579 Columbus OH 43216-3579 E-mail: rcottingham@cottinghampaper.com.

COTTINGHAM, ROBERT, artist; b. Bklyn., Sept. 26, 1935; s. James G. and Aurelia Ann C.; m. Jane Marie Weismann, Dec. 23, 1967; children: Reid Ann, Molly Jane, Kyle Annie Bliss. Student, Pratt Inst., Bklyn., 1959-64; AA, Pratt Inst., 1962. Art dir. Young & Rubicam Advt., Inc., N.Y.C., 1959-64, L.A., 1964-68; tchr. Art Ctr. Coll. Design, L.A., 1969-70. One man shows include Molly Barnes Gallery, Los Angeles, 1968, 69, 70, O.K. Harris Gallery, N.Y.C., 1971, 74, 76, 78, Aldrich Mus., Ridgefield Conn., 1979, Galerie de Gestlo, Cologne, Fed. Republic Germany, 1979, Delta Gallery, Rotterdam, Netherlands, 1979, Getler-Pall Gallery, N.Y.C., 1979, Thomas Segal Gallery, Boston, 1980, Ball State U., 1980, U. Bridgeport (Conn.), 1980, Fendrick Gallery, Washington, 1981, 84, Mattatuck Mus., Waterbury, Conn., 1981, Swain Sch. Design, New Bedford, Mass., 1981, Coe Kerr Gallery, N.Y.C., 1982, 84, Signet Arts, St. Louis, 1983, 86, Wichita Art Mus., Kans., 1983, Springfield Art Mus., Mo., 1984, retrospective exhbn., 1986-88; numerous group shows including Abilene Christian U., Roger Ramsay Gallery, Chgo., Reynolds House Mus. Am. Art, Winston-Salem, N.C., Ark. Arts Ctr., Little Rock, Fendrick Gallery; represented in numerous permanent collections including Whitney Mus. Am. Art, N.Y.C., Cleve. Art Mus., Detroit Mus. Art, Phila. Mus. Art, Harvard, Honolulu Acad. Art, Carnegie Inst., Pitts., U. Iowa, Long Beach (Calif.) Mus. Art, Indpls. Mus. Art, Dartmouth Coll., Mus. Modern Art, N.Y.C., Guggenheim Mus., N.Y.C., Detroit Inst. Arts, Hirshhorn Mus. and Sculpture Garden, Washington, Library of Congress, Washington, Nat. Mus. Am. Art, Washington, Princeton U., Yale U., Met. Mus. Art, N.Y.C., Mus. City of N.Y., Art Inst. Chgo., others, including numerous European museums; commns. include 12 enamel panels One Union Pl., Hartford, Conn. With U.S. Army, 1955-58. Nat. Endowment Arts grantee, 1974-75; named Artist of Yr., Fairfield C. of C., 1988. Address: Blackman Rd PO Box 604 Newtown CT 06470-0604 Office Phone: 203-426-4072.*

COTTINGHAM, TRACY THOMAS, III, lawyer; b. Fayetteville, N.C., July 17, 1947; s. Tracy Thomas and Frances (Godwin) C.; m. Gloria Jean Schmidt; children: Tracy Thomas, Christopher Todd. BA, Davidson (N.C.) Coll, 1969; JD, Cornell U., 1976. Bar: Ala. 1976, U.S. Dist. Ct. (no. dist.) Ala. 1976, U.S. Dist. Ct. (mid. dist.) Ala. 1987, U.S. Dist. Ct. (so. dist.) Ala. 1988, U.S. Ct. Appeals (5th cir.) 1976, U.S. Ct. Appeals (11th cir. 1981), N.C. 1989. Assoc., then ptnr. Burr & Forman, Birmingham, Ala., 1976—98; ptnr., litig., intellectual property, antitrust Hunton & Williams LLP, Charlotte, NC. Served to capt. U.S. Army, 1969-73, Vietnam. Decorated Bronze Star. Mem. ABA (litigation sect.), N.C. Bar Assn., Birmingham Bar Assn., Ala. Def. Lawyers Assn., Def. Research Inst. Avocations: running, history, wildlife. Office: Hunton & Williams LLP Bank of Am Plz Ste 3500 101 S Tryon St Charlotte NC 28280 Office Phone: 704-378-4714. Office Fax: 704-378-4890. Business E-Mail: tcottingham@hunton.com.

COTTLE, HAROLD RANSON, pathologist, laboratory executive; b. Bklyn., Dec. 7, 1925; s. Kenneth Raymond and Katharine Habershon (Blelloch) C.; m. Betty Lowell, July 15, 1950; children: David Lowell, Andrew Geoffrey, Susan Elizabeth. Student, Bard Coll., 1942-43, Dartmouth Coll., 1943-44; MD, N.Y. Med. Coll., 1948. Diplomate Nat. Bd. Med. Examiners; cert. Am. Bd. Pathology. Intern Meth. Hosp., Bklyn., 1948-49, resident in pathology, 1949-50, Kings County Hosp., Bklyn., 1952-54; asst. pathologist Kings County Hosp., SUNY, 1954-55, asst. to dir. of labs., 1955-56, chief autopsy svc., 1956-60, chief surg. pathology, 1960-62, vis. pathologist, 1962-70; clin. assoc. prof. SUNY, Downstate Med. Ctr., Bklyn., 1970-85; dir. Harold R. Cottle, M.D. Lab., 1975—. Asst. instr. SUNY, 1953-54, instr., 1954-56, asst. prof., 1956-62, prof., 1956-62, clin. asst. prof., 1962-70; assoc. dir. labs. Maimonides Hosp., Bklyn., 1962-66; dir. anatomic pathology Bklyn.-Cumberland Med. Ctr., 1966-70; pathologist Altoona (Pa.) Hosp., 1970-72, dir. lab. svcs., 1972-74, mem. exec. com., 1972-74; dir. lab. medicine Indiana (Pa.) Hosp., 1974-84; cons. pathologist VA Hosp., Altoona, 1973-89; coroner's pathologist various counties, Pa.; cons. staff Mercy Hosp., Altoona; mem. staff Conemaugh Valley Meml. Hosp. Contbr. articles to profl. jours. Chair Bklyn. chpt., bd. N.Y. State ACLU, 1956-70; various offices Sheepshead Bay Meth. Ch., 1950-70, 1st United Meth. Ch., Altoona, 1971-80; mem. Human Rights Commn., 1971-74. Lt. USNR, 1944-45, 50-52. Fellow Coll. Am. Pathologists, Am. Soc. Clin. Pathologists; mem. AMA, AAAS, AAUP, Pa. Med. Soc., Blair County Med. Soc., N.Y. Path. Soc., N.Y. State Soc. Pathologists, N.Y. State Assn. Pub. Health Labs., Pitts. Pathology Soc., Pitts. Comparative Pathology Soc., Ctrl. Pa. Regional Soc. Pathologists, Pa. Assn. Pathologists, Internat. Assn. Coroners and Med. Examiners, Pa. Assn. Coroners and Med. Examiners. Avocations: outdoor sports, firearms, books. Home and Office: 25 Sylvan Dr Hollidaysburg PA 16648-2718 Office Phone: 814-695-0659. E-mail: bcottlemd@aol.com.

COTTLE, KAREN OLSON, lawyer; b. Aug. 14, 1949; m. Robert Cottle. BA, Pomona Coll., Claremont, Calif., 1971; JD, U. Calif., Berkeley, 1976. Bar: Calif., Utah. Law clk. to Judge Spencer Williams U.S. Dist. Ct. (no. dist.) Calif., San Francisco, 1976-78; assoc., ptnr. Farella, Braun & Martel, San Francisco, 1978-86; corp. counsel Raychem Corp., Menlo Park, Calif., 1986-96, gen. counsel, 1996—99; v.p., gen. counsel Vitria Technology Inc., 2000—02; sr. v.p., gen. counsel, corp. sec. Adobe Systems Inc., San Jose, 2002—. Office: Adobe Systems Inc 345 Park Ave San Jose CA 95110-2704

COTTNER, DONALD, pathologist; b. Wichita, Mar. 26, 1937; s. Edward Floyd and Augusta Mae Cottner; m. Joreen Smith, Sept. 6, 1974 (div. June 1994); children: Dereck, Regina, John; m. Karolynne Kelly Cottner, June 12, 1996; stepchildren: Greg, Michael, Laquinta, Clifford. BA, Wichita State U., 1961; M of Religious Edn., Midwestern Sem., 1966; PhD, Southeastern U., 1982; D of Min., Evangel. Bible Sem.; DDiv, U. Ctrl. Am., 1984. Janitor Dunbar Elem. Sch., Wichita, 1958—61; lawn cutter Ctrl. Bapt. Theol. Sem., 1961—62; agt. Western So. Life Ins., 1962—63; ins. cons. MEt. Life Ins., 1964—66; counselor Todd Phillips Home for Boys, Detroit, 1967; instr. Wolverine Bapt. Assn., 1967—68; counselor Neighborhood Youth Corps, Kansas City, 1968—69, exec. dir., 1969—70; with Operation Mainstream,

1970—72; tng. officer, counselor Neighborhood Youth Corp.s, 1972—73; dir. bus. inst. Black Econ. Union, 1973—78; psychotherapist pvt. practice, Kansas City, 1978—85; ret. Grant writer Eastside Ctr., St. Joseph, Mo., 1973—74; adj. prof. Penn Valley C.C., Kansas City, 1974. Mem.: Charles F. Menninger Soc. Republican. Baptist. Avocations: reading, writing. Home: 3201 McKinley Ave Fort Worth TX 76106

COTTON, FRANK ALBERT, chemist, educator; b. Phila., Apr. 9, 1930; s. Albert and Helen (Taylor) Cotton; m. Diane Dornacher, June 13, 1959; children: Jennifer Helen, Jane Myrna. Attended, Drexel Inst. Tech., 1947—49; BA, Temple U., 1951; PhD, Harvard U., 1955; DSc (hon.), Temple U., 1963; Dr. (hon.), Bielefeld U., 1979; DSc (hon.), Columbia U., 1980, Northwestern U., 1981, U. Bordeaux, 1981, St. Joseph's U., 1982, U. Louis Pasteur, 1982, U. Valencia, 1983, Kenyon Coll., 1983, Technion Israel Inst. Tech., 1983, U. Cambridge, 1986, Johann Wolfgang Goethe U., 1989, U. S.C., 1989, U. Rennes, 1992, Lomonosov U., 1992, Fujian Inst. Rsch., Chinese Acad. Sci., 1993, U. Pisa, Italy, 1994, U. Zaragoza, 1994, Cleve. State U., 1995, U. Crete, 1996, Mich. State U., 1996, U. Pierre and Marie Curie, 1997, U. Palermo, 1997, U. Jaume I, 2000, N.C. State U., 2000, Ohio State U., 2001, Hebrew U., Jerusalem, 2002, Drexel U., 2002. Instr. chemistry Mass. Inst. Tech., 1955—57, asst. prof., 1957—60, assoc. prof., 1960—61, prof., 1961—71; Robert A. Welch disting. prof. chemistry Tex. A and M U., 1971—, dir. lab. for molecular structure and bonding, 1983—. Cons. Am. Cyanamid, Stamford, Conn., 1958—67, Union Carbide, N.Y.C., 1957—94; Todd prof. Cambridge U., 1985—86. Editor: Progress in Inorganic Chemistry, volumes 1-10, 1959—68; co-author (with L. Lynch and C. Darlington): Chemistry, An Investigative Approach, 1969; editor: Inorganic Syntheses, vol. 13, 1971; editor: (with L.M. Jackman) Dynamic Nuc. Magnetic Resonance Spectroscopy, 1975; author: Chem. Applications of Group Theory, 3d edit., 1990; co-author (with R.A. Walton and C.A. Murillo): Multiple Bonds Between Metal Atoms, 3rd edit., 2005; co-author: (with G. Wilkinson and P.L. Gaus) Basic Inorganic Chemistry, 3d edit., 1995; editor (with R.D. Adams): Catalysis by Di and Poly Nuc. Metal Atom Clusters, 1998; author (with G. Wilkinson, C.A. Murillo, and M. Bochmann): Advanced Inorganic Chemistry, 6th edit., 1999. Recipient Michelson, Morley Award, Case Western Res. U., 1980, Nat. Medal of Sci., 1982, King Faisal Prize, 1990, Paracelsus Medal, Swiss Chem. Soc., 1994, prize, Welch Found., 1994, Polyhedron Medal, 1995, John Scott Medal, City of Phila., 1997, Gold Medal, Am. Inst. Chemists, 1998, Lavoisier Medal, French Chem. Soc., 2000, Wolf Found. Prize, State of Israel, 2000, hon. fellow, Robinson Coll., Cambridg U., Eng. Mem.: NAS (chmn. phys. sci. 1985—88, coun. 1991—94, gov. bd. NRC 1992—94, Cosepup 1992—94), Chinese Acad. Sci., Inst. de France Acad. Sci., Royal Soc. London, Am. Philos. Soc., Göttingen Acad. Sci. (Gaus Prof. 2002), Am. Acad. Arts and Sci., Am. Chem. Soc. (Award 1962, Baekeland medal N.J. sect. 1963, Aaward 1974, Nichols Medal N.Y. sect. 1975, Pauling Medal, Oreg. and Puget Sound sect. 1976, Kirkwood Medal, N.Y. sect. 1978, Gibbs Medal, Chgo. sect. 1980, Richards Medal, N.E. sect. 1986, F.A. Cotton Medal, Tex. A and M sect. 1995, Priestley Medal 1998), European Acad. Scis. (hon.), Indian Nat. Sci. Acad. (hon.), Acad. Europe (hon.), Royal Soc. Edinburgh (hon.), Indian Acad. Sci. (hon.), Italian Chem. Soc. (hon.), Royal Danish Acad. Sci. and Letters (hon.), Royal Soc. Chemistry (hon.), N.Y. Acad. Sci. (life). Home: 4101 Sand Creek Rd Bryan TX 77808-8337 Office: Tex A and M Univ Dept Chemistry College Station TX 77843-0001

COTTON, JOHN G., career military officer; m. Cindy Cotton; children: Jennifer, Charles, Christine. Grad., US Naval Acad., 1973. Commd. 2d lt. USN, 1973, advanced through ranks to vice adm., 2003; comdr. Light attack Wing, US Pacific Fleet, Lemoore, Calif., 1978—80, VFA-204 "River Rattlers", 1993—94; commdg. officer NAS Keflavik 1066, 1994-96; commanding officer Navy Command Ctr. 106, 1996—97; dep./vice comdr. Naval Air Force, U.S. Atlantic Fleet, Norfolk, Va., 1997—99; dep. dir. Naval Reserve N095B USNR, 1999—2000; mem. Reserve Forces Policy Bd., 2000—03; asst. dep. chief of naval ops. (warfare requirements & programs N6/N7R) USNR, 2000—03, chief, 2003—; comdr. USNR Force, 2003—. Decorated Meritorious Svc. awards (2 times), Navy Commendation medals (2 times), Navy Achievement medals; Adm. Stanley David Griggs Excellence in Leadership Mem. award, 1995. Office: 4400 Dauphine St New Orleans LA 70146-5000

COTTON, JOHN WHEALDON, psychology professor; b. McMinnville, Oreg., Oct. 8, 1925; s. Earl Bogart and Ruth Whealdon Cotton; m. Corliss Ailene Clark (dec. Mar. 2004); children: Carolyn Ruth, Keith Allen; m. Anne Gree Cushing, Apr. 9, 2005. BA in Psychology, Williamette U., 1947; MA in Psychology, Ind. U., 1951, PhD in Psychology, 1952. From instr. to asst. to assoc. prof. Northwestern U., Evanston, Ill., 1951—60; from assoc. prof. to prof. U. Calif., Santa Barbara, 1960—93, chair dept. psychology, 1861—1963, assoc. dean Grad. divsn., 1963—64, prof. emeritus, 1993. Author: Analyzing Within Subjects Experiments, 1998; co-author: Elementary Statistics, 1990; contbr. articles various profl. jours. Bd. dirs. First United Meth. Ch., Santa Barbara, 1963—2005; bd. dirs, treas. Santa Barbara chpt. NAACP, 1980; bd. chair Drop-In Tutorial Ctr., 2003—04. With USN, 1943—46. Recipient Postdoc. award, Com. on Stats., U. Chgo., 1957—58; Rsch. grants, NSF, 1959—61, 1963—64, 1966—70. Mem.: Psychometric Soc., Am. Statis. Assn., Am. Ednl. Rsch. Assn. Democrat. Meth. Avocations: reading, table tennis. Office: U Calif Santa Barbara Dept Edn Santa Barbara CA 93106 Office Phone: 805-893-3101. Office Fax: 805-687-5540. E-mail: jwcotton@education.ucsb.edu.

COTTON, PAUL, nutritionist; m. Phyllia Ann Cotton, July 4, 1992; 1 child, Phylicia Andre. BS, MS, Howard U., PhD, 1999. Head wrestling coach, lectr. Howard U., Washington, 1983—2000; rsch. nutritionist USDA, Beltsville, Md., 2000—. Mem.: APHA, Am. Dietetic Assn. (registered dietician), Alpha Phi Alpha (life; chpt. pres.). Office: USDA Bldg 005 Rm 117 10300 Baltimore Ave Beltsville MD 20705 Office Phone: 301-504-0637. Office Fax: 301-504-0698. E-mail: paulcotton@alumni.howard.edu.

COTTON, W(ILLIAM) PHILIP, JR., architect; b. Columbia, Mo., July 11, 1932; s. William Philip and Frances Barbara (Harrington) C. AB, Princeton U., 1954; MArch, Harvard U., 1960. Registered architect, Mo., Ill. Pvt. practice architecture, St. Louis, 1964—. Author: 100 Historic Buildings in St. Louis County, 1970. Treas. New Music Circle, St. Louis, 1968-96, Pub. Revenue Edn. Coun., St. Louis, 1977—; v.p. Music Diversions Soc., St. Louis, 1993—2005; pres. Collegium Vocale, 1999—. Recipient St. Louis AIA/CPC Urban Design Merit award, 2002, Pres.'s award, Landmarks Assn. St. Louis. Fellow AIA (Ctrl. States Spl. Honor award 1981, Rozier award for Hist. Preservation 1991); mem. Valley Sailing Club (commodore 1985). Roman Catholic. Home: 5145 Lindell Blvd Saint Louis MO 63108-1221 Office: W Philip Cotton Jr Architect 1221 Locust St Ste 1410 Saint Louis MO 63103-2364

COTTON, WILLIAM ROBERT, retired dentist; b. Miami, Fla., Nov. 29, 1931; s. Robert Lee and Mamie Bell (Daniel) Cotton; m. Marye Ruth Hartz; children: Caroline Ruth, William Robert Jr., David Michael, Lynn Cathryn Tavel. DDS, U. Md., 1955; MS, Northwestern U., Chgo., 1963; MA, Roosevelt U., 1973; EdS, George Washington U., 1980. With USN, 1955-81, commd. capt., 1973, ret., 1981; asst. dental officer Marine Corps Schs. and USS F.D. Roosevelt CVA 42, Quantico, Va. and Mayport, Fla., 1957-61; head exptl. pathology div. Naval Med. Rsch. Inst., Bethesda, Md., 1963-67; dental officer USS Fulton AS-11, New London, Conn., 1967-69; chief histopathology div. Naval Dental Rsch. Inst., Great Lakes, Ill., 1969-72, exec. officer, 1972-73, dep. comdg. officer, 1973-76; chmn. dental scis. dept. Naval Med. Rsch. Inst., Bethesda, Md., 1976-79; dir. Casualty Care Rsch. Program Ctr., Naval Med. Rsch. Inst., Bethesda, Md., 1979-81; assoc. prof. dept. operative dentistry Temple U., Phila., 1981-83; prof., chmn. dept. operative dentistry Georgetown U., Washington, 1983-90; pvt. practice Rockville, Md.; ret., 1999; dentist Mission of Mercy, Fairfield, Pa., 2001—. Adv. com. dental tech. program So. Ill. U., Carbondale, 1976—85; cons. Naval Dental Rsch. Inst., Great Lakes, 1981—85, Dentsply Internat., York, Pa., 1984—88; mem. spl. study sect. NIH, Washington, 1984, Washington, 87; clin. dentist Mission of Mercy, Brunswick, Md., 2001—; adj. clin. prof. dept. restorative dentistry U. Md. Dental Sch., Balt., 2004—. Contbg. author: book Biology Dental Caires, 1968, Dental Clinics of North America, 1986, editl. bd.: Jour. Dental Rsch., 1976—86, 1988, Jour. Operative Dentistry, 1986—92. Elder Presbyn. Ch. Fellow: Internat. Coll. Dentists (life), Am. Coll. Dentists (life); mem.: ADA (life), D.C. Dental Soc. (life; bd. dirs. 1986—89). Democrat. Home: 11816 Winterset Ter Potomac MD 20854-2846 Personal E-mail: wmrc@comcast.net.

COTTRELL, DAVID MILTON, sound recording engineer; b. Ft. Dodge, Iowa, Mar. 27, 1961; s. Milton and Evelyn Cottrell. AA in Counseling, Iowa Ctrl. Coll.; BS in Counseling, Almeda Coll. Music pub. My Friend Music, Hollywood, Calif., 1975—76; recording engr., prin. Super Sound, Ft. Dodge, 1986—97, Soul Survivor Sound, Lemars, Iowa, 2000—. Singer: (albums) Mr. Fingers, 1971, I Want You I Need You, 1981, Can You Rock Me, 1989, Good Gosh, 2002. Independent. Episcopalian. Home: 414 First St SE Le Mars IA 51031 Office Phone: 712-546-6500. E-mail: davecottrell@frontiernet.net.

COTTRELL, DUANE COLES, music educator, minister; b. Birmingham, Ala., July 12, 1973; s. Ted Barnette and Ellen Coles Cottrell; m. Elisa Ann Leidenheimer, Sept. 2, 1995; children: Cason Taite, Jackson Thomas. MusB in Edn., La. State U., 1995; MA in Christian Edn., Southwestern Bapt. Theol. Sem., Ft. Worth, 1998. Ordained min. Bapt. Ch., 1998; cert. tchr. K-12 music Tex., La. Student ministry assoc. Trinity Bapt. Ch., San Antonio, 1995—98; assoc. staff, h.s. ministry Saddleback Ch., Lake Forest, Calif., 1998—99; lead pastor, ch. planter The Village, Raleigh-Durham, NC, 1999—2003; vocal music dir. John Jay H.S., San Antonio, 2003—. Scholar, La. State U., 1991—95. Mem.: Tex. Choral Dirs. Assn., Tex. Music Educators Assn., Am. Choral Dirs. Assn. Personal E-mail: duaneco@mac.com.

COTTRELL, G. WALTON, manufacturing executive; b. Auburn, N.Y., Sept. 26, 1939; s. George H. and Eleanor H. (Day) C.; m. Jean H. Springer, June 15, 1963; children: Lisa, Lori. BSME, Cornell U., 1962, MBA, 1963. Various positions Owens-Ill., Inc., Toledo, 1965-85, treas., 1980-83, v.p. corp. planning, 1984-85; dir. fin. Europe Owens-Ill. Internat., Geneva, 1976-80; v.p. fin. The Allen Group, Inc., Melville, NY, 1986; v.p., treas. Squibb Corp., Princeton, N.J., 1987-88; sr. v.p. fin., CFO Carpenter Tech. Corp., Reading, Pa., 1989-2001, sr. v.p. strategic planning, 2001; ret., 2001. Dir. Andersen Labs., Inc., Bloomfield, Conn., 1992-98. Bd. dirs. Jr. Achievement N.W. Ohio, Toledo, 1980-86, Planned Parenthood N.W. Ohio, Toledo, 1982-86, United Way Berks County, 1990-97, Berks County Cmty. Found., 1999-03, Sciencenter Discovery Mus., 2004-; mem. coun. Cornell U., 1985-95. Lt. USNR, 1963-65. Mem. Fin. Execs. Inst. (bd. dirs. 1982-85), Nat. Assn. Corp. Treas. (pres. 1997-98, chair bd. dirs. 1998-99). Republican. United Ch. of Christ. Home: 15 Windjammers Way Ithaca NY 14850 Personal E-mail: cottrellgw@aol.com.

COTTRELL, JAMES E., anesthesiologist, medical educator; b. Charleston, W.Va., Nov. 9, 1942; m. Geraldine Kincaid. BS, Morris Harvey Coll., 1961; MD, W.Va. U., 1968. Diplomate Am. Bd. Anesthesiologists. Asst. prof. NYU Sch. of Medicine, 1974-78, assoc. prof., 1978-79; prof., chmn. SUNY Downstate Med. Ctr., Bklyn., 1979—. Editor books; contbr. articles to profl. jours. Mem. Am. Soc. of Anesthesiologists (v.p. 2001, pres. 2003), N.Y. State Soc. of Anesthesiologists, Assn. of Univ. Anesthesiologists, Soc. of Acad. Anesthesia Chmn., World Congress in Anesthesiology. Office: SUNY Downstate Med Ctr 450 Clarkson Ave Brooklyn NY 11203-2056 E-mail: jcottrell@downstate.edu.

COTTRELL, JEANNETTE ELIZABETH, retired librarian; b. Buffalo, Dec. 10, 1923; d. Benjamin Birch and Mary Jeannette (Ashdown) Milnes; m. William Barber Cottrell, Jan. 21, 1944 (dec.); children: Karen Jean, Susan Marie, William Milnes, Scott Barber, Stephen Ashdown. BA in Sociology, U. Tenn., 1970, MS, 1976; student, Alfred U., 1940-43. Cert. tchr. libr., Tenn. Nursery sch. tchr. Concord Meth. Ch., Knoxville, Tenn., 1964-65; libr. City Sch. Sys., Knoxville, Tenn., 1971-84, ret., 1984. Author: (with husband) An American Family in the 20th Century, 1987; recorder textbooks for the blind, 1983—. Libr. Concord United Meth. Ch., Knoxville, 1975—, reading chair Suzanna Wesley Circle. Mem. DAR, Phi Kappa Phi, Beta Phi Mu. Republican. Methodist. Avocations: singing, bridge, cooking, travel, reading. Home: 308 Camelot Ct Knoxville TN 37922-2076

COTTRELL, MICHELLE LEIGH, management analyst; b. Smithtown, N.Y., 1976; d. Lee and Evelyn Wansor; m. Jeffrey Lawrence Cottrell. B in Design (hon.), U. Fla., 2000. Jr. designer IA, Washington, 2000—01; mgmt. analyst McKissack & McKissack, Washington, 2001—. Recipient People's Choice award, AIA CANstruction, 2001, 1st Place, GingerBuild Com., 2000. Mem.: Internat. Interior Design Assn. (assoc.). Avocation: travel. Office: McKissack & McKissack 1401 New York Ave NW Ste 900 Washington DC 20005 Business E-Mail: michellew@mckissackdc.com.

COTTRELL, TERRANCE LUTHER, library director, educator, entrepreneur, consultant; b. Joliet, Ill., Sept. 17, 1977; s. Sylvester Cottrell Jr. and Deborah Rae Cottrell; m. Michelle Louise Taylor, Aug. 6, 2005. BA in English, U. St. Francis, Joliet, Ill., 1999; MS in Libr. and Info. Sci., U. Ill., 2001; MBA in Mgmt., U. St. Francis, Joliet, Ill., 2003. Web developer, info. tech. support U. St. Francis, Joliet, Ill., 1995—2000; grad. rsch. asst. U. Ill., Urbana-Champaign, 2000—01; libr. systems coord. U. St. Francis, Joliet, Ill., 2002—03, asst. dir. libr. svcs., 2003—. Mng. ptnr. Computer Tech. Solutions, Inc., Joliet, Ill., 1998—99; info. tech. cons. Ind. Forms Svcs., Inc., Joliet, Ill., 2002—03; mng. cons. Agile Med. Systems, Inc., Joliet, Ill., 2004—; ptnr. Filmore Group, LLC, Aurora, Ill., 2005—; adj. faculty U. of St. Francis, Joliet, Ill., 2004—. Recipient Loquitur prize in art, U. St. Francis, Joliet, Ill., 1998; SBC Excelerator grant, SBC Comm., Inc., 2003. Mem.: ALA, South Met. Higher Edn. Consortium, Am. Soc. for Info. Sci. and Tech., Sigma Tau Delta (life), Delta Mu Delta (life). Achievements include development of AgileEMR, Electronic Medical Records Software. Home: 3743 Buck Ave Joliet IL 60431 Office: Univ St Francis 600 Taylor St Joliet IL 60435 Office Phone: 815-740-3476. Home Fax: 815-740-3364; Office Fax: 815-740-3364. Personal E-mail: cottreter@yahoo.com. Business E-Mail: tcottrell@stfrancis.edu.

COTTY, WILLIAM FRANK (BILL COTTY), lawyer, state legislator; b. Aug. 9, 1946; s. William O. and Marie (Frank) C.; m. Amelia Dunlap, Dec. 26, 1969; children: William D., Mary K., Anne Marie. BA, Erskine Coll., Due West, S.C., 1969; JD, U. S.C., 1974. Bar: S.C. 1974. Adminstrv. asst. Congressman Tom Gettys, Washington, 1969-71; atty., legis. liaison S.C. Wildlife Dept., Columbia, 1974-77; assoc. atty. Ratchford & Eleazer, Columbia, 1977-81; sole practitioner Columbia, 1981-95; with Cotty & Jonas, 1995—; mem. S.C. Ho. of Reps., 1994—. Trustee Richland County Sch. Dist. Two, Columbia, 1986-94. Lt. col. S.C. Army NG. ret. Recipient Legis. Conservationist of the Yr. award S.C. Wildlife Fedn., 1971. Republican. Presbyterian. Home: 324 Valley Springs Rd Columbia SC 29223-6934 Office: 1328 Blanding St Columbia SC 29201-2903

COUCH, DANIEL MICHAEL, healthcare executive; b. Chgo., July 1, 1937; s. Arthur Daniel and Helen Margret (Kreamer) C.; m. Marilee Hermon, Sept. 12, 1958; children: Laura Ann, Mark Allen, Kristina Lynn, Michelle Louise, Daniel Michael Jr. BS in Bus., Ind. U., 1958; MBA, Butler U., 1977. Field examiner Ind. State Bd. Accounts, Indpls., 1959-61; controller Community Hosp., Anderson, Ind., 1961-67; field rep. Am. Hosp. Assn., Chgo., 1967-68; treas./controller Health & Hosp. Corp. of Marion County, Indpls., 1968-71; assoc. adminstr. Winona Meml. Hosp., Indpls., 1971-78; pres. Huntington (Ind.) Meml. Hosp., 1978-80; dep. exec. dir. Truman Med. Ctr., Kansas City, Mo., 1980-99; CFO Health Care Found. Greater Kansas City, 2005—. Bd. dirs. Nat. Pub. Health and Hosp. Inst., Washington, 1987-90, chmn., 1989. Bd. dirs, mem. exec. com. Labor-Mgmt. Coun., Kansas City, Mo., 1982—, co-chmn, 1991—97; bd. dirs. Greater Kans.City Mental Health Found., 1984—93, pres., 1992—93; bd. dirs. Kans. City Care Ctr., 1990—, treas., 1999—; bd. dirs. Resource Devel. Inst., Kans. City, 1998—; pres., 2002—04; bd. dirs. Vis. Nurse Home Care Svcs, Kans. City, 1991—98; chmn., 1993—98; bd. dirs. A Rising Tide-The Greater Kansas City Healthcare Found., 2003—05. 1st lt. USAR, 1958—67. Fellow Am. Coll. Healthcare Execs. (life fellow, nominating com. 1995-99); mem. Am. Hosp. Assn. (ho. of dels. and Regional Policy Bd. 7 1989-92, governing coun. sect. met. hosps. 1990-93, chmn. 1993), Nat. Assn. Pub. Hosps. (bd. dirs. 1981-99, chmn. 1989), Kansas City Area Hosp. Assn. (bd. dirs. 1990-96), Greater Kansas City C. of C. (various coms. 1985-99), Healthcare Fin. Mgmt. Assn. (advanced), Kansas City Care Network (bd. dirs. 1995-99, pres. 1995-99), Family Health Ptnrs. (bd. dirs. 1995-99), Found. Fin. Officers Group, Masons, Rotary. Episcopalian. Avocations: golf, bowling, reading. Office Phone: 816-241-7006. E-mail: dcouch@healthcare4kc.org. *While into life a little rain must fall, I like to dwell on the fact that into every life a little joy must come.*

COUCH, GEORGIA KAYE WISNER, lawyer, musician, educator; b. Oakland, Calif., Feb. 17, 1939; d. George Thomas and Kathryn Billie (Adamson) Wisner; m. Roy Edward Couch, May 2, 1959; children: Thomas Edward, Tracey Elinor Johnson. Student, Calif. State U., San Francisco, 1957—58; AA, Diablo Valley Coll., Pleasant Hill, Calif., 1979; JD, John F. Kennedy U. Law Sch., Walnut Creek, Calif., 1987. Bar: Calif. 1989. Law clk. Centra Costa County DA's Office, Martinez, Calif., 1986; assoc. Law Office Phyllis Loya, Martinez, Calif., 1990—99; atty. sole practice Law Office Georgia K.W. Couch, Lafayette, Calif., 1989—. Pvt. piano tchr., performer, Lafayette, Calif., 1970—; owner Wisner Vineyards, Livermore, Calif. Editor: John F. Kennedy Law Rev., 1987. Atty. pro bono Battered Women's Alternatives, Martinez, Calif., 1991—99, Contra Costa Legal Assistance / Elderly, Martinez, 1991—99; vol Rep. Nat. Com., Walnut Creek, Calif., 2004—05; vol. various local theaters, Walnut Creek, Calif., 1990—. Named Outstanding Law Student, Commencement Speaker, JFK U., Walnut Creek, 1989. Mem.: Music Tchrs. Assn. (Hons. Recital Chair 2001—), Performing Arts Soc., Contra Costa County Bar Assn. Avocation: winemaking. Office: PO Box 1533 Martinez CA 94553

COUCH, JESSE WADSWORTH, retired insurance company executive; b. Atlanta, Mar. 2, 1921; s. Jesse Newton and Laura (Day) W.; m. Charlotte Lucretia Collins, Jan. 13, 1945 (dec.); children: Robert Collins (dec.), Laura W.; m. Charlotte H. Gran, Oct. 17, 1997. AB, Princeton, 1947. With 1st Nat. Bank Houston, 1947-51; assoc. Wray Assocs., Houston, 1951-60; ptnr. Wray, Couch & Elder, Houston, 1960-69; v.p. Marsh & McLennan, Inc., 1969-83; pvt. cons., 1983-95. Mem. exec. bd. Episcopal Diocese of Tex., 1965-67, 68-71; trustee St. Luke's Episcopal Hosp., 1971-76; bd. dirs. Houston-Harris County YMCA, 1969-74, Houston Soc. Prevention Cruelty to Animals, 1974—2004; Bd. dirs. Tex. divsn. Am. Cancer Soc., mem. exec. com., 1982-91; chmn. Am. Cancer Soc. Greater Houston, 1981-83; trustee Mus. Fine Arts, Houston, 1970-74. Served to capt. USAAF, 1943-46. Mem.: Houston C. of C. (aviation com. 1965—75), Allegro Club, Bayou Club, Houston Country Club, Rod & Gun Club, Eagle Lake. Home: 6015 Pine Forest Rd Houston TX 77057-1431 Office: 800 Bering Dr Ste 125 Houston TX 77057-2130 Personal E-mail: jcouch@pdq.net.

COUCH, JOHN D., health products executive; BSI in Computer Sci., MS in Elec. Engring. and Computer Sci., U. Calif., Berkeley. With Hewlett-Packard, section mgr. gen. systems divsn.; with Apple Computers, dir. new products, v.p. software and pubs., v.p., gen. mgr. personal office systems divsn.; exec.-in-residence Mayfield Fund; chmn. Double Twist Inc., Oakland, Calif., 1997—.

COUCH, ROBERT BARNARD, physician, medical researcher, educator, microbiologist, immunologist; b. Guntersville, Ala., Sept. 25, 1930; s. Ezekiel Harvey and Frances Jane (Barnard) C.; m. Katherine Frances Klein, Apr. 23, 1955; children: Robert Steven, Leslie Ann, Colleen Frances, Elizabeth Lee. BA, Vanderbilt U., 1952, MD, 1956. Diplomate Am. Bd. Internal Medicine. Intern Vanderbilt U. Hosp., Nashville, 1956—57, resident in medicine, 1959—60, chief resident in medicine, 1960—61; clin. assoc. NIH, Washington, 1957—59, sr. investigator, 1961—65, head clin. virology sect., 1965—66; assoc. prof. Baylor Coll. Medicine, Houston, 1966—71, dir. influenza rsch. ctr., 1974—91, prof. microbiology, immunology and medicine, 1971—2000, Disting. prof., 1995—, head infectious diseases sect. medicine, 1987—92, chmn. dept. microbiology and immunology, 1989—2000, dir. acute viral respiratory diseases unit, 1991—96, dir. respiratory pathogens rsch. unit, 1996—, dir. Ctr. for Infection and Immunity Rsch., 1999—, prof. molecular virology, microbiology and medicine, 2000—. Mem. rsch. rev. panels infectious diseases; cons. NIH, Dept. Def., FDA. Contbr. articles to profl. jours. Served to sr. surgeon USPHS, 1957-66. Mem. ACP, AAAS, Soc. Exptl. Biology and Medicine, Am. Soc. Microbiology, Infectious Diseases Soc. Am., Am. Assn. Immunologists, Am. Fedn. Clin. Rsch., Am. Soc. Clin. Investigation, So. Soc. Clin. Investigation, Am. Assn. Physicians, Am. Soc. Epidemiology, Am. Soc. Virology, Alpha Omega Alpha. Office: Baylor Coll Medicine 1 Baylor Plz Houston TX 77030-3411 Office Phone: 713-798-4474. E-mail: rcouch@bcm.tmc.edu.

COUCH, TIM, professional football player; b. July 31, 1977; s. Elbert and Janice. Quarterback Cleve. Browns, 1999—2004, Green Bay Packers, 2004—. Participant DARA prog., Leslie County; guest spkr. two youth football leagues, 1996-97; guest Chldn's Miracle Network t.v. show. Office: c/o Green Bay Packers 1265 Lombardi Ave Green Bay WI 54304

COUCHMAN, ROBERT GEORGE JAMES, foundation executive; b. Toronto, Ont., Can., Feb. 21, 1937; s. Robert George and Mary (Bigelow) C.; m. Jane Barker (div. 1985); children: Barbara, Stephen, Michael. BA, Queen's U., Kingston, Ont., 1965; MEd, U. Toronto, 1969. Tchr. Scarborough (Ont.) Bd. Edn., 1957-63; dir. student svcs. Etobicoke (Ont.) Bd. Edn., 1963-74; exec. dir. Family Svc. Assn. Met. Toronto, 1974-89; pres. Donner Can. Found., Toronto, 1989-93; assoc. Re Think Group, 1993; dir. Terra Nova, 1995-97; chmn. Outward Bound Can., 1990—94. Co-chmn. UN Can. Com. Internat. Yr. of Family, 1993-94; patron Outward Bound Can., 1995-99; mem. nat. adv. com. Fed. Minister of Health on Rural Health. Author: Reflections on Canadian Character, 2003; contbr. 40 articles to profl. jours Chmn. Outward Bound Wilderness Sch., 1987-88, Outward Bound Can., 1990-94; pres. Can. Mental Health Assn., Ont., 1971-73; dir. White Ribbon Found. of Can.; bd. dirs. Addiction Rsch. Found., Ont., 1980-86, Metro Toronto Housing Co., 1982-88, United Way Metro Toronto, 1994-96; vice chmn. Vanier Inst. of the Family, 1988-90; chmn. Atlin Big Water Soc.; gov., Grey Owl Nature Trust, 1997-2000, advisor Can. Arctic Resources Com.; exec. dir. PQR Found., 1993— Mem.: Yukon Family Svcs. Assn. (exec. dir. 1999—2001), Ont. Assn. Profl. Social Workers (hon.), Rotary (com. chmn.). United Church. Office: 137 Wilson Dr Whitehorse YT Canada Y1A 5Rd Office Phone: 867-393-2398. Personal E-mail: bcouchman@yknet.ca.

COUDERT, DALE HOKIN, real estate executive, marketing consultant; b. Chgo., Nov. 29, 1941; d. Sidney and Ruth (Brower) Manowitz; m. Frederic R. Coudert (div.); children Dana, Alexandra. BA, Northwester U., 1964. V.p. Cross & Brown, N.Y.C., 1975-86; dir., sec. First Women's Bank, N.Y.C., 1980-87; head bus. devel., office of pres. 1st N.Y. Bank for Bus., 1988-91; mktg. dir. Lafer Mgmt., N.Y.C., 1993-94; pres., CEO Coudert Assocs. Ltd., N.Y.C., 1991—; broker Brown Harris Stevens Palm Beach Real Estate, Pal, 1999—; founder, pres. Coudert Inst., 2001—. Dir. Hosp. Tak Co., L.I., NY, 1979—98; creator, chmn., CEO Coudert Inst. at Villa Dei Fiori, Palm Beach, Fla., 2001—. Pub., editor: (book) Business and Pleasure, 1986-87. Bd. dirs. Women's Rep. Club, N.Y.C., 1994, N.Y. Drama League, N.Y.C., 1975—; mem. nat. bd. dirs. Aspen Art Mus., Kennedy Ctr., 1996-98; trustee, treas. Zoo of the Palm Beaches at Dreker Park, 1996-98, bd. dirs., 1996—; regent St. John the Divine, N.Y.C., 1988. Fellow Aspen Inst. (life); mem. Internat. Womens Forum, Met. Opera Club, Women's Forum Fla. Avocations: piano, voice, dance, golf, tennis. Home: 485 Park Ave New York NY 10022-1228 also: 163 Seminole Ave Palm Beach FL 33480-3732 also: Brown Harris Stevens Palm Beach Real Estate Ste 329 340 Royal Poinciana Plz Palm Beach FL 33480-4048 Office: 163 Seminole Ave Palm Beach FL 33480-3732 E-mail: dal1129@aol.com.

COUGAR, JOHN See MELLENCAMP, JOHN

COUGHENOUR, JOHN CLARE, federal judge; b. Pittsburg, Kans., July 27, 1941; s. Owren M. and Margaret E. (Widner) C.; m. Gwendolyn A. Kieffaber, June 1, 1963; children: Jeffrey, Douglas, Marta. BS, Kans. State Coll., 1963; JD, U. Iowa, 1966. Bar: Iowa 1963, D.C. 1963, U.S. Dist. Ct. (we. dist.) Wash. 1966. Ptnr. Bogle & Gates, Seattle, 1966-81; vis. asst. prof. law U. Washington, Seattle, 1970-73; judge U.S. Dist. Ct. (we. dist.) Wash., Seattle, 1981—, chief judge, 1997—2005. Recipient William L. Dwyer Outstanding Jurist award, King County Bar Assn. Mem. Iowa State Bar Assn., Wash. State Bar Assn., Ninth Cir. Dist. Judges' Assn. (past pres.). Office: US Dist Ct US Courthouse 1010 5th Ave Ste 609 Seattle WA 98104-1130 also: Dist Judge Ste 16229 700 Stewart St Seattle WA 98101-1271*

COUGHENOUR, KAVIN LUTHER, career officer, military historian; b. New Kensington, Pa., Mar. 1, 1947; s. Roy Edgar and Anna Louise (Coleman) C.; m. Kathryn Mary Domurat, May 17, 1969; 1 child, Stacey Anne. BA in Social Scis., Ind. U. of Pa., 1969; MA in Pers. Mgmt., Ctrl. Mich. U., 1979; diploma, U.S. Army War Coll., 1990. Commd. 2d lt. U.S. Army, 1969, advanced through grades to col., 1991, adj. Ft. Meade, Md., 1973-75, adj. gen. 79th Res. Command Willow Grove, Pa., 1976-79, adj. 5th Spl. Forces Group Ft. Bragg, N.C., 1979-82, adj. gen. 3d Armored Divsn. Frankfurt, Germany, 1985-86, commdg. officer U.S. Mil. Entrance Processing Sta., Dept. Defense Chgo., 1986-88, tng. officer Spl. Forces Sch. Ft. Bragg, 1988-89, spl. forces br. chief Pers. Command Alexandria, Va., 1990-92, dep. comdr. Ctr. Mil. History Washington, 1992-95; lic. battlefield guide Gettysburg (Pa.) Nat. Mil. Park, 1995—. Decorated Legion of Merit; recipient Gold medal, Nat. Hon. Soc. Pershing Rifles, 1968, Supts. award of Excellence, Gettysburg Nat. Mil. Park, 2001, Eagle Scout. Mem. Spl. Forces Assn., Soc. Mil. History, U.S.A. War Coll. Assn., Philmont Staff Assn., Assn. Lic. Battlefield Guides. Republican. Methodist. Avocation: civil war history. Home: Lake Heritage 964 Johnson Dr Gettysburg PA 17325-8970 Office Phone: 717-476-1015. Personal E-mail: kavinc@aol.com.

COUGHLAN, GARY PATRICK, pharmaceutical company executive; b. Fresno, Calif., Feb. 14, 1944; s. Edward Patrick and Elizabeth Claire (Ryan) C.; m. Mary Cary Kelley, Dec. 21, 1967; children: Christopher, Sarah, Laura, Claire, Moira. BA, St. Mary's Coll., 1966; MA in Econs., UCLA, 1967; MBA, Wayne State U., 1971. Sr. fin. analyst Burroughs Corp., Detroit, 1969-72; with Dart Industries, L.A., 1972-81, group v.p. field services, 1978-81, v.p. ops. services, 1981, Dart & Kraft Inc., Northbrook, Ill., 1981-82, v.p. fin., contr., 1984-85, sr. v.p. fin. affairs, 1985-86, sr. v.p., CFO, 1986; v.p. fin. retail food group Kraft Inc., Glenview, Ill., 1982-84, sr. v.p., CFO, 1986-88; sr. v.p. fin. Kraft Gen. Foods, Glenview, 1989-90; sr. v.p. fin., CFO Abbott Labs., Abbott Park, Ill., 1990-2001, ret., 2001. Instr. prof. fin. ext. program UCLA, 1974—80; bd. dirs. Arthur J. Gallagher, Itasca, Ill., Hershey (Pa.) Corp., Chgo. Hort. Soc., Glencoe, Ill.; mem. adv. coun. Coun. Fgn. Rels., Chgo. Com. Mem. Fin. Execs. Inst. Republican. Roman Catholic. Home: 1135 Central Rd Glenview IL 60025-4432 Office: Ste 306 1200 Central Ave Wilmette IL 60091 Office Phone: 847-920-1677. Personal E-mail: gcoughlan@earthlink.com.

COUGHLAN, KENNETH L., lawyer; b. Chgo., July 8, 1940; s. Edward and Mary C.; m. Therese Koziol; 1 child. BA, U. Notre Dame, 1962; JD, Northwestern U., Chgo., 1966. Bar: Ill. 1967. Trust officer Am. Nat. Bank & Trust Co., Chgo., 1969-72; sec. bd., sr. v.p., gen. counsel, cashier Ctrl. Nat. Bank., Chgo., 1972-82; sec., gen. counsel Ctrl. Nat. Chgo. Corp., 1976-82; sr. v.p., gen. counsel Exch. Nat. Bank, Chgo., 1982-83; gen. counsel Exch. Internat. Corp., Chgo., 1982-83; chmn. bd., pres. Union Realty Mortgage Co., Inc., Chgo., 1981-83; shareholder DeHaan & Richter P.C., 1983-2000; mem. Kelly, Olson, Michod, DeHaan & Richter, L.L.C. Capt. U.S. Army, 1966-68. Fellow Ill. Bar Found.; mem. ABA, Ill. State Bar Assn. (chmn. sect. on comml., banking and bankruptcy law 1981-82), Chgo. Bar Assn. (chmn. fin. instns. com. 1980-81, chmn. comml. fin. com. 1979-80), Lawyers Club (Chgo.).

COUGHLAN, PATRICK CAMPBELL, lawyer, mediator; b. Orange, N.J., May 28, 1940; s. Gerald Noel and Carter (Van Schaick) C.; m. Joyce Miskuf; children: Kimberly Campbell,Devon Gerald, Carter Turner. BA, Duke U., 1962, JD, 1965. Bar: Fla. 1965, U.S. Supreme Ct. 1968, Calif. 1974, Maine 1985. Assoc. Alley, Maass, Rogers & Lindsay, Palm Beach, Fla., 1969-72, ptnr., 1972-74; judge Mcpl. Ct., Ocean Ridge, Fla., 1970-72; assoc. firm Richards, Watson & Gershon, Los Angeles, 1974-75, ptnr., 1975-84; city atty. City of Rancho Palos Verdes, Calif., 1975-82, City of San Fernando, Calif., 1977-82, City of Seal Beach, Calif., 1978-84, City of La Habra Heights, Calif., 1979-84, Avalon, Calif., 1981-84, Rolling Hills, Calif., 1981-84, Westlake Village, Calif., 1981-84; chair bd. appeals Raymond, Maine, 1985-98; pres. Kingsley Pines, Inc.; prin. Coughlan Assoc., 1987-88; pres. Resolve Disputes, Inc. N.Am., Portland, Maine, 1989-92, Conflict Solutions, Portland, Maine, 1992—, Naples, Fla., 1992—. Ptnr. Atlanean Ptnrs. LLC. Pres. No. Pines, Inc., 1980-86; trustee, sec. Gulf Stream Sch. Found., Inc., 1970-85; bd. dirs. Mountains Restoration Trust, 1981-82; trustee North Yarmouth Acad., 1984-93, pres., 1985-89; treas., trustee Natural Resources Coun. Maine, 1989-93; pres. parish coun. Our Lady of Perpetual Help, 1983-85; pres. World Affairs Coun. of Maine, 1986-89, trustee, 1985-93; trustee Portland Stage Co., 1989-93, sec., 1990-91, v.p., 1991-92; trustee Maine Youth Camps Assn., 1989-96, sec., 1990, v.p., 1990-93, pres., 1993-95; trustee Susan Curtis Found., 1991-96; dir. Pvt. Adjudication Ctr. Duke U., 1994-2002, mediator 1998-2002; dir. The Club at La Peninsula, 1997-98, Adms. Watch at Windstar, 2004-2005. Capt. USAF, 1965-68. Fellow Internat. Acad. Mediators (bd. dirs. 1999—, v.p. 2001-2005); mem. ABA, State Bar Calif., Fla. Bar, Maine State Bar, Soc. Profls. in Dispute Resolution, Am. Acad. Civil Trial Mediators, Maine Assn. Dispute Resolution Profls. (pres. 1990-92), Windstar Country Club (Naples, Fla.). Roman Catholic. Home: 1540 Star Pointe Lane Naples FL 34112 Office: 112 Plains Rd Raymond ME 04071 Personal E-mail: coglan@aol.com. Business E-Mail: pat@conflictsolutionsinc.com.

COUGHLIN, ANNE M., law educator; b. NJ, 1956; BA, Tufts U., 1978; MA, Columbia U., 1979; JD, NYU, 1984. Bar: NY 1987. Law clk. to Hon. Jon O. Newman US Ct. Appeals 2nd Cir., Hartford, Conn., 1984—85; law clk. to Hon. Lewis F. Powell, Jr. US Supreme Ct., Washington, 1985—86; assoc. Cravath, Swaine & Moore, NYC, 1986—88, Miller, Cassidy, Larroca & Lewin, Washington, 1988—91; asst. prof. Vanderbilt U. Law Sch., 1991—94, assoc. prof., 1994—96; prof. U. Va. Sch. Law, 1996—, now O.M. Vicars prof. law, Barron F. Black rsch. prof. Vis. assoc. prof. U. Va. Sch. Law, 1995—96. Office: U Va Sch Law 580 Massie Rd Charlottesville VA 22903-1789 Office Phone: 434-924-3520. E-mail: amc6z@virginia.edu.

COUGHLIN, CHRISTOPHER J., financial executive; With Ernst & Young (formerly Arthur Young), Sterling Winthrop, Inc., 1982-96, CFO, bd. dirs., 1993-96; exec. v.p., CFO Nabisco Internat., 1996—98, Pharmacia & Upjohn, Inc., Peapack, NJ, 1998—2003; COO Interpub. Group Cos., Inc., N.Y.C., 2003—; exec. vice-pres., CFO Tyco Internat. Ltd. Office: Interpub Group Cos Inc 1271 Ave of Americas New York NY 10020*

COUGHLIN, FRANCIS RAYMOND, JR., surgeon, educator, lawyer; b. N.Y.C., Feb. 22, 1927; s. Francis Raymond and Isabel (Archibald) C.; m. Barbara Ann Blunt, June 9, 1951; children: Hilary, Mary, Patricia, Christopher Francis, Geoffrey Blunt, Daniel Taylor, Isabel, David Carleton. BS, Fordham U., 1948; MD, Yale U., 1952; MS, McGill U., Montreal, Que., Can., 1955, diploma in surgery, 1959; JD, U. Bridgeport, 1988. Bar: N.Y., Conn., D.C., U.S. Supreme Ct.; diplomate Am. Bd. Surgery, Am. Bd. Thoracic Surgery. Intern N.Y. Hosp., N.Y.C., 1952-53; resident McGill U. Teaching Hosp., Montreal, 1953-57, Overholt Thoracic Clin., Boston, 1958-60; mem. staff Stamford (Conn.) Hosp., 1960—; practice medicine specializing in thoracic surgery Stamford, 1960—88; medico-legal cons., 1988—. Dir. thoracic and vascular surgery St. Josephs Hosp., Stamford, 1970-73, 80-85, assoc. chief surgery, 1971-73, chief surgery, 1973-77; assoc. prof. clin. surgery N.Y. Med. Coll., 1981-2002; mem. staff Norwalk Hosp., 1965-89; vice chair Conn. State Commn. Medicolegal Investigations, 1990-2002. With U.S. Maritime Svc., 1945-46. Recipient Encaenia award Fordham U., N.Y.C., 1958; Teaching fellow Harvard U., 1958. Fellow ACS (sec.-treas. Conn. chpt. 1966-70), Royal Coll. Surgeons (Can.), Am. Coll. Cardiology, Am. Coll. Chest Physicians, Royal Soc. Medicine; mem. Soc. Thoracic Surgeons (founding mem.), N.Y. Acad. Medicine, Conn. Heart Assn. (dir. 1961-64), Conn. Lung Assn. (dir. and exec. com. 1963-69, v.p. 1967-69), Lung Assn. So. Fairfield County (pres. 1963-68, dir. 1960-70), Soc. Med. Jursiprudence (v.p. 1992-93, pres. 1995-97), English-Speaking Union, Scottish-Am. Found., Can. Soc. N.Y., Yale Club N.Y., Army Navy Club (Washington), Yale Med. Sch. Alumni Assn. (v.p. 1999-2001, pres. 2001-03). Republican. Office: 20 Mead St New Canaan CT 06840-5701 Office Phone: 203-966-2197. E-mail: fcoughlinmd@att.net.

COUGHLIN, JACK, printmaker, sculptor, art educator; b. Greenwich, Conn., Feb. 19, 1932; s. John J. and Gabrielle S. (Jones) Coughlin; m. Joan M. Hopkins, July 5, 1958; children: Maura, Molly. Student, Art Students League, N.Y.C., 1950-52; BFA, R.I. Sch. Design, 1954, MS, 1961. Asst. prof. art U. Mass., Amherst, 1964-68, assoc. prof., 1968-73, prof., 1973-94, prof. emeritus, 1994—. Hendriks Gallery, Dublin, Ireland, 1971, one-man shows include, 1974, 1976, 1978, 1980, 1983, 1987, Harvard U., 1974, Associated Am. Artists, N.Y.C., 1977, Dublin Writers Mus., 1993, Brandeis U., 1995, Springfield Coll., 2004, exhibited in group shows at 17th Biennial Am. Printmaking, Bklyn., 1970, Davidson Nat. Print Show, 1973, NAD, 1974—2003, Represented in permanent collections Met. Mus. Art, N.Y.C., Mus. Modern Art, Nat. Collection Arts, Washington, commd. regularly, The New Republic. With U.S. Army, 1954—56. Recipient numerous awards, prizes for work, Nat. Inst. Arts and Letters, 1969, prize for drawing 158th Nat. Exhbn., NAD, 1983, 33d N.D. Print and Drawing Ann., 1991, 34th Nat. Pring Exhbn., Hunterdon Art Ctr. Mem.: NAD (academician), Soc. Am. Graphic Artists.

COUGHLIN, JAMES PATRICK, mathematician, educator; s. Patrick and Mary Ellen (Duffy) Coughlin. BS, Fordham Coll., 1960; MA, Columbia U., 1961; PhD, U. Colo., 1973. Instr. Arlington (Tex.) State Coll., 1962, Rockhurst Coll., Kans. City, Mo., 1962—63, Regis Coll., Denver, 1963—65; prof. math. Towson (Md.) U., 1979—. Physicist U.S. Naval Surface Weapons Lab., Dahlgren, Va., 1960—83. Co-author: Neural Computation From The Hopfield Net To The Boltzmann Machine, 1995. Mem.: Math. Assn. Am., Sigma Xi. Avocations: history, cryptography, bridge. Office: Mathematics Dept Towson 8000 York Road Towson MD 21252 Business E-Mail: coughlin@towson.edu.

COUGHLIN, JEANNINE M., music educator; b. Midland, Mich., May 30, 1969; d. Jeremiah Thomas and Marciann Coughlin. BA in Music Edn., Saginaw Valley State U., 1992, postgrad., 1996, postgrad., 2003. Instrumental music tchr. Saginaw (Mich.) Pub. Schs., 1993—. Tennis coach Saginaw H.S., 1998—2000, softball coach, 2001—; dir. Herter Band Camp, 1995—, Mich. H.S. All Star Band, 2001—; cons., presenter Reading and Writing in the Arts, Bay City, Mich., 2001, Success of Baldridge in the Classroom, Saginaw, Bay City, 2001—03. Co-author: (anthology) Reflections: Threads-Words that Bind Us, 2001. Leader Arenac County 4-H Club, Standish, Mich., 1999—. Named Saginaw Valley Tchr. of the Yr., Mich. H.S. Athletic Assn., 2000; recipient Excellence in Edn. award, Mich. Edn. Assn., 1996. Democrat. Roman Catholic. Avocations: reading, writing, sports, music. Home: 2640 Midland Rd Saginaw MI 48603 Office: Saginaw High Sch 3100 Webber St Saginaw MI 48601

COUGHLIN, KIMBERLY ANN, music educator; b. Libertyville, Ill., May 25, 1958; m. Daniel Francis Coughlin, May 27, 1995; 1 child, Kerrie Lynn. B of Music Edn., No. Ill. U., 1980; M of Music Edn., Vander Cook Coll. Music, 2002. Band dir. Summit Hill Dist. 161, Frankfort, Ill., 1981—. Jazz band, percussion ensemble, cologuard, concert & symphonic bands Summit Hill Dist. 161, 1981—. Mem. Jaycees, Ill., 1983—. Mem.: Ill. Music Educators Assn. (festival chair 2002—03), Music Educators Nat. Conf. Avocations: scrapbooks, horseback riding. Office: Summit Hill Dist 161 20130 S Rosewood Dr Frankfort IL 60423

COUGHLIN, NATALIE, Olympic athlete; b. Vallejo, Calif., Aug. 23, 1982; d. Jim and Zennie Coughlin. Student, U. Calif., Berkley. Swimmer U.S. Olympic Team, Athens Olympic games, 2004. Named Nat. High School Swimmer of the Yr., 1998, NCAA Swimmer of the Yr., 2001, 2002, 2003; recipient Female Swimmer of the Yr., Swimming World Mag., 2002. Achievements include world record-holder in 100m back (first woman under one minute - 59.58); world record-holder in the 100m and 200m back (short course); first U.S. woman to break 54 seconds in 100m free (long course) - 53.99; gold medal, 100m back, 800m free relay, World Championships, 2001; Am. record-holder in over 10 events, including the 50m, 100m and 200m back (long course); won 9 NCAA Titles, Univ. of California-Berkley, 2001-03; gold medal, 100m backstroke, 4x200m free relay, Silver medal, 4x100m free relay, 4x100m MR, Bronze medal, 100m free, Athens Olympic games, 2004. Office: c/o USA Swimming One Olympic Plaza Colorado Springs CO 80909

COUGHLIN, SHAUN R., research scientist; BS, MS, MIT, 1976, PhD, 1981; MD, Harvard Med. Sch., 1982. Intern, resident Mass. Gen. Hosp., 1982—84; postdoctoral asst. rsch. cardiologist, clin. fellow Cardiovascular Rsch. Inst., U. Calif., San Francisco, 1984—86, dir., 1997—; asst. prof. U. Calif., San Francisco, 1986—91, assoc. prof., 1991—96, prof. medicine, 1996—, prof. cellular and molecular pharmacology, 1997—. Dir. Millennium Pharm., Inc. Recipient Jeffrey M. Hoeg award, Am. Heart Assn., 2000, Freedom to Discover award for Disting. Achievement in Cardiovascular Rsch., Bristol-Myers Squibb, 2004. Mem.: Inst. Medicine, NAS. Office: UCSF Cardiovascular Rsch Inst 505 Parnassus Ave Box 0130 San Francisco CA 94143-0130 Business E-Mail: coughlin@cvrimail.ucsf.edu.

COUGHLIN, TOM, professional football coach; b. Waterloo, N.Y., Aug. 31, 1946; m. Judy Coughlin; children: Keli, Katie, Tim, Brian. BA Educ., Syracuse U.; MA Educ. Grad. asst. Syracuse U., 1969; head coach Rochester Inst. Tech., 1970-73; offensive backfield coach Syracuse U., 1974-76, offensive coord., 1977-80, Boston Coll., 1981-83; wide receivers coach Philadelphia Eagles, 1984-85; receivers coach Green Bay Packers, 1986-87, N.Y. Giants, 1988-90; head coach Boston Coll., 1991-93, Jacksonville Jaguars, 1994—2002, N.Y. Giants, 2004—; founder The Jay Fund Found. Named AFC Coach of the Year, 1996. Avocations: reading, running, golf. Office: c/o New York Football Giants Stadium East Rutherford NJ 07073

COUGHRAN, WILLIAM M., JR., management consultant, researcher; s. William M. Coughran, Sr. and Marianne Coughran; m. Bridget A. McGuire, Sept. 2, 1972; children: Megan J., Brendan W. BS, MS, Calif. Inst. Tech., 1975, Stanford U., 1977, PhD, 1980. V.p. Computing Scis. Rsch. Ctr., Bell Labs, Murray Hill, NJ, 1996—99; sr. v.p. Bell Labs Rsch. Silicon Valley, Palo Alto, Calif., 1998—2000; CEO, founder Entrisphere, Inc., Santa Clara, Calif., 2000—02; prin. Coughran Consulting, Palo Alto, 2003—. Bd. dirs. nSolutions, Inc., Santa Clara, Calif.; mem. tech. adv. bd. Hammerhead Systems, Inc., Mountain View, Calif., 2002—. Home: 820 Arroyo Ct Palo Alto CA 94306 Personal E-mail: bill@coughran.net.

COUGILL, ROSCOE MCDANIEL, retired military officer; b. Charleston, Ill., Oct. 24, 1941; s. Oral Wilson and Malora Emaline (Vaughn) C.; m. Sallie Anne Carrow, Feb. 15, 1969; children: Christopher McDaniel, Andrew Ashby. BS in Edn., Ea. Ill. U., 1963; MS in Guidance and Counseling, Troy (Ala.) State U., 1976; postgrad., Air Command and Staff Coll., Maxwell AFB, Ala., 1976, Army War Coll., Carlisle, Pa., 1981. Commd. 2d lt. USAF, 1964, advanced through grades to brig. gen., 1989, ret., 1992; staff and exec. officer Hdqrs. USAF, Washington, 1976-80, dir., 1985-86, dep. asst. chief staff, 1988-89; comdr. 2179th Command Group, Patrick AFB, Fla., 1981-83; exec. officer internat. mil. staff NATO, Brussels, 1983-85; chief staff Air Force Comm. Command, Scott AFB, Ill., 1986-88; dir. command and control, comm. and computer sys. Hdqrs. U.S. Cen. Command, MacDill AFB, Fla., 1989-92; mayor City of Charleston, Ill., 1993—2005. Decorated DSM, Legion of Merit, Def. Superior Svc. medal.

COUKIS, PETER GEORGE, musician, composer; b. Waterbury, Conn., Jan. 15, 1955; s. George Peter and Antoinette (Kachulis) C.; m. Lucrecia Monje, Aug. 20, 1998; 1 child: George Joshua. BA, Western Conn. State U., 1978; AS, Mattatuck C.C., Waterbury, 1987. Musical arranger, composer Waterbury Children's Found., 1977-78; arranger, songwriter Youth Theatre Ensemble, Watertown, Conn., 1985-87; prodr., performer Laurel Cablevision, Litchfield, Conn., 1988-91; solo recording artist Waterbury, Wallingford, Conn., 1990—; founder Blue Plum Records, 1993—, Weird Garden Records. Composer, keyboardist The Nutmeg Ballet, Torrington, Conn., 1988; songwriter World Star Prodns., New Haven, 1988; keyboardist South Mich. Ave, Wolcott, Conn., 1980-86; synthesizer player Angels and Co. (Nunsense), N.Y.C. and Waterbury, 1989; artist, prodr. cable In Performance, 1988, Repertoire, 1989 (Laurel award 1989), Kaleidoscope, 1991, 13-week cable series, 1991, cable spl., 1992; released cassette single Girl, 1992; rec. artist Stick Bride, 1994, Strange Beauty, 1995, Believe in Me, 1995, Midgetmajority, 1997, Tournament, 1997, Stephania in Orange, 1997, Blossoms of Beauty, 1999, (15 CD set) Archive of Tracks, 2000, The Orchard, 2001, Harp, 2001, Curtains of Autummn, Organ Symphony No.1, 2002, Songs for Eluthera, 2003, Orchestral Suit for John Paul II, 2005, Mystery Disc; Daughter of Cacophony, 2005; several instrumental suites and sets of piano music, 2004. Talk show guest Barbara Davitt's Coffee Break, Sta. WATR, Waterbury, 1990; feature guest Lifestyles with Dr. Kotler, Sta. WCAT-13, Waterbury, 1990. Mem. NARAS, Am. Composers Forum, Conn. Songwriters Assn. (3-yr. award 1985, 5-yr. award 1987). Democrat. Avocations: reading, travel, outdoors, environmental awareness. Office Phone: 203-597-8163. E-mail: weirdgardenracords@juno.com.

COULOMBE, CHARLES AQUILA, writer, educator; b. NYC, Nov. 8, 1960; s. Guy Joseph Coulombe and Patricia Jaye Collins. Student, N.Mex. Mil. Inst., 1978-80, Calif. State U., 1980-82. Reviewer West Coast Rev. of Books, Hollywood, Calif., 1982-85; contbg. editor Nat. Cath. Register, L.A., 1989-96; reporter L.A. Lay Mission, 1995—; mem. rsch. bd. Almanach De Gotha, London, 1998—. Cons. Cath. Treasures, Monrovia, Calif., 1985—; L.A. corr. Fidelity of Australia, Melbourne, 1989-94, Creole mag., LaFayette, La., 1991-97, Bourbons mag., Paris, 1996—; adv. bd. Almanach de Bruxelles, Brussels, 1996—; bd. dirs. Can. Royal Heritage Trust, Toronto. Author: Everyman Today Call Rome, 1987, The White Cockade, 1990, Puritans Progress, 1996, The Muse in the Bottle, 2002, Vicars of Christ: A History of the Popes, 2003, Classic Horror Tales, 2003, Rum: The Epic Story of the Liquor that Conquered the World!, 2004, America's Haunted Places, 2004, Haunted Castles of the World, 2005; contbg. author: Tolkein: A Celebration, 1999 Mem. Monarchist League Can., Toronto, 1989—; West Coast del. Monarchist League, London, 1993—. Decorated knight comdr. Order of St. Sylvester; recipient Christ the King Journalism award Cath. Lay Inst., El Paso, Tex., 1992. Mem.Cath. Writers Guild, Authors Guild, Drones Club, Weisse Rose (Vienna), Royal Stuart Soc. (London), Acad. Am. Poets, Nat. Trust for Historic Preservation, Irish Georgian Soc. (Dublin), Assn. Can.-Ams., The Green Rm. Club, City Tavern Club, Order St. Sylvester, Delta Phi Epsilon Roman Catholic. Avocations: poetry, ballroom dancing, drinking. Home: PO Box 660771 Arcadia CA 91066-0771

COULSON, CHARLENE ANNE, elementary school educator; d. C. E. and Lola M. Overlease; m. Rick Coulson; children: Melanie, Jim, Stacy, Kala. BA in Edn., U. N.C., Greeley, 1969; MA in Art and Sci and Curriculum, Lesley Coll., 1989. Tchr., Bethune, Colo., 1969—70, Wray, Colo., 1970—80, Florence, Colo., 1981—2005. Lutheran. Office: Re-2 500 W 5th St Florence CO 81226

COULSON, ELIZABETH ANNE, physical therapist, educator, state representative; b. Hastings, Nebr., Sept. 8, 1954; d. Alexander and Marilyn (Marvel) Shafernich; m. William Coulson, Feb. 14, 1986. Student, Wellesley Coll., 1972-73; BS in Edn., U. Kans., 1976; cert. in phys. therapy, Northwestern U., Chgo., 1977; MBA, Keller Grad. Sch. Mgmt., 1985; postgrad., U. Ill., 1991. Lic. phys. therapist, Ill. Assoc. prof. dept. phys. therapy Chgo. Med. Sch., North Chicago, Ill., chmn. dept. phys. therapy, 1993-96. Contbr. articles to profl. jours. Trustee Northfield Twp., Ill., 1993-97; Ill. state rep. 17th dist., 1997—. Mem. APHA, Am. Phys. Therapy Assn. (Ill. del. 1986-93, chief del. 1991-93), Ill. Phys. Therapy Assn. (chmn. jud. com. 1989-91). Home: 1701 Sequoia Trl Glenview IL 60025-2022 Office Phone: 847-724-3233.

COULSON, ROBERT, arbitrator, writer, retired association executive; b. New Rochelle, N.Y., July 24, 1924; s. Robert Earl and Abby (Stewart) C.; m. Cynthia Cunningham, Oct. 16, 1961; children: Cotton Richard, Dierdre, Crocker, Robert Cromwell, Christopher. BA, Yale U., 1949; LLB, Harvard U., 1953; DSc in Bus. Adminstrn. (hon.), Bryant U., 1985; LLD (hon.), Hofstra U., 1987. Bar: N.Y. 1954, Mass. 1954. Assoc. Whitman, Ransom & Coulson, N.Y.C., 1954-61; ptnr. Littlefield, Miller & Cleaves, N.Y.C., 1961-63; exec. v.p. Am. Arbitration Assn., N.Y.C., 1963-71, pres., 1971-94; ret., 1994. Cons. N.Y. State Div. Youth, 1961-63; pres. Youth Consultation Service of N.Y., 1970 Author: How to Stay Out of Court, 1968, Labor Arbitration: What You Need to Know, 1973, Business Arbitration: What You Need to Know, 1980, The Termination Handbook, 1981, Fighting Fair, 1983, Arbitration in Schools, 1985, Business Mediation, 1987, Alcohol and Drugs in Arbitration, 1988, Empowered at Forty, 1990, Police Under Pressure, 1993, ADR in America, 1994, Family Mediation, 1996; editor: Racing at Sea, 1958; contbr. articles to profl. jours. Bd. dirs. Fedn. Protestant Welfare Agys., pres., 1982-84, chmn. 1985-87; adv. com. Internat. Coun. for Comml. Arbitration. Mem. N.Y. Yacht Club, Cruising Club Am., Riverside Yacht Club. Avocations: sailing, travel, writing. Home: 9 Reginald St Riverside CT 06878-2522 Personal E-mail: coulfamily@aol.com.

COULTER, ANN, lawyer, writer; b. New Caanan, Conn., Dec. 8, 1961; d. John and Nell Martin Coulter. Grad. with honors, Cornell U. Sch. Arts & Scis., 1985; JD, U. Mich. Law Sch. Law clk. to Hon. Pasco Bowman II US Ct. Appeals (8th cir.), Kansas City, 1989; atty. US Dept. Justice Honors Program for outstanding law sch. grads.; corp. lawyer, pvt. practice NYC; handled crime and immigration issues for Senator Spencer Abraham Senate Judiciary Com., Mich., 1994—96; polit. commentator MSNBC, 1996; litigator Ctr. Individual Rights, Wash., DC; legal affairs corr. Human Events. Writer syndicated column, Universal Press Syndicate; guest appearances Politically Incorrect, Larry King Live, Hannity and Colmes, The O'Reilly Factor, Am. Morning with Paula Zahn, Crossfire, "This Week", ABC, Good Morning Am., The Leeza Show. Author: High Crimes and Misdemeanors: The Case Against Bill Clinton, 1998, Slander: Liberal Lies About the American Right, 2002, Treason: Liberal Treachery From the Cold War to the War on Terrorism, 2003, How to Talk to a Liberal (If You Must), 2004; editor: The Mich. Law Review. Named one of Time Mag. 100 Most Influential People, 2005. Office: Human Events One Mass Ave NW Washington DC 20001*

COULTER, BEVERLY NORTON, singer, pianist, opera director; b. Dallas, Feb. 27, 1953; d. George Melville Norton and Dorothy May Morrison; m. Fred P. Coulter, Apr. 24, 1981. BFA, Fla. Atlantic U., 1975; MusM, U. Miami, 1977, D of Mus. Arts, 1985. Grad. asst. U. Miami, Coral Gables, Fla., 1976—80; founder, artistic dir. Riuniti Opera, Inc., Miami, 1999—; prof. music. Miami-Dade C.C., 1981—2002, prodr. cmty. outreach program, 1992—; Stanley Sutnick endowed tchg. chair Miami-Dde C.C., 1994—97; prof. music, dir. opera and musical theatre Barry U., Miami Shores, Fla., 2002—. Adjudicator Silver Knight award Miami Herald, 2000, 01. Prodr., dir. numerous operas, musical and shows. Musician Ctrl. Presbyn. Ch., Miami, 1992—2001, Christ the King Luth. Ch., Miami, 2002—, Temple Judea, Miami, 2002—. Mem.: Miami Music Tchrs. Assn. (rec. sec. 2000—01), Music Tchrs. Nat. Assn., Nat. Assn. Tchrs. of Singing. Democrat. Avocations:

running, caring for homeless animals, collecting ethnic sculptures, collecting historical manuscripts. Home: 7345 SW 108 Ter Miami FL 33156 Office: Barry U 11300 NE 2d Ave Miami FL 33161-6695

COULTER, CHAD W., lawyer, insurance company executive; b. 1962; BA, Haverford Coll.; JD, U. Pa. Bar: Pa. 1987. V.p., gen. counsel Delphi Capital Mgmt., Inc., Wilmington, Del. Office: 1105 N Market St Ste 1230 Wilmington DE 19801-1216

COULTER, CHARLES ROY, lawyer; b. Webster City, Iowa, June 10, 1940; s. Harold L. Coulter and Eloise (Wheeler) Harrison; m. Elizabeth Bean, Dec. 16, 1961; 1 child, Anne Elizabeth. BA in Journalism, U. Iowa, 1962, JD, 1965. Bar: Iowa 1965. Assoc. Stanley, Bloom, Mealy & Lande, Muscatine, Iowa, 1965-68; v.p. Stanley, Lande & Hunter, Muscatine, 1969—, also bd. dirs. County fin. chmn. Leach for Congress, 1980-96; county coord. George Bush for Pres., 1980, 88, Reagan-Bush Campaign, 1984. Fellow Coll. of Law Practice Mgmt. (dir. 1994-2004, pres. 2001-04), Am. Bar Found., Iowa State Bar Found., Am. Coll. Trust and Estate Counsel; mem. ABA (mem. coun. law practice mgmt. sect. 1984-88, sec. 1988-89, vice chair 1989-90, chair 1991-92, chair coord. commn. legal tech. 1994-97, mem. standing com. on tech. and info. sys. 1997-98), Iowa Bar Assn., Muscatine County Bar Assn., Thirty-Three Club (pres. 1981), Rotary, Order of Coif. Episcopalian. Avocation: tennis. Office: Stanley Lande & Hunter 2201 E Grantview Dr Ste 220 Coralville IA 52241 Office Phone: 319-248-9000. Business E-Mail: chuckcoulter@slhlaw.com.

COULTER, DAVID A., investment banker; b. Pitts. BA in Math., MA in Indsl. Adminstrn., Carnegie-Mellon U. Chmn., CEO BankAmerica, 1996—98; CEO Bank of Am. NT&SA, 1996—98; ptnr. Beacon Group LP, 2000; pres. Chase Fin. Svcs., 2000—01; vice chmn. investment bank, private equity, asset & wealth mgmt. JP Morgan & Chase Co., NYC, 2001—04, chmn. West Coast Ops., 2005—. Bd. dirs. PG&E, 1996—, Pub. Policy Inst. Calif., 1997—, Coors Tek, Internat. Inst. Fin., Joint Venture Silicon Valley Network; mem. adv. coun. Fed. Res. Bank N.Y. Bd. trustees U. So. Calif., Carnegie-Mellon U., U. Calif., San Francisco, 1997—2000. Recipient Global Bus. Leader award, Com. of 100, 2003. Office: JP Morgan & Chase Co 1999 Ave Stars Fl 26 Los Angeles CA 90067*

COULTER, ELIZABETH JACKSON, biostatistician, educator; b. Balt., Nov. 2, 1919; d. Waddie Pennington and Bessie (Gills) Jackson; m. Norman Arthur Coulter Jr., June 23, 1951; 1 child, Robert Jackson. AB, Swarthmore Coll., 1941; A.M., Radcliffe Coll., 1946, PhD, 1948. Asst. dir. health study Bur. Labor Stats., San Juan, P.R., 1946; research asst. Milbank Meml. Fund, N.Y.C., 1948-51; economist Office Def. Prodn., 1951-52; research analyst Children's Bur.-HEW, 1952-53; from statistician to chief statistician Ohio Dept. Health, 1954-65; lectr. econs., then clin. asst. prof. preventive medicine Ohio State U., 1954-65; asst. clin. prof. biostats. U. Pitts. Sch. Pub. Health, 1958-62; assoc. prof. biostats. U. N.C., Chapel Hill, 1965-72, assoc. prof. econs., 1965-78, biostats. prof., 1972-90; adj. assoc. prof., hosp. adminstr. Duke U., 1972-79; assoc. dean undergrad. pub. health studies U. N.C., Chapel Hill, 1979-86, prof. biostats. emerita, 1990—. Contbr. articles to profl. jours. Mem. AAAS, AAUP, APHA (governing coun. 1970-72), Am. Econ. Assn., Am. Statis. Assn., Am. Acad. Polit. and Social Sci., Biometric Soc., Am. Evaluation Assn., Assn. for Health Svcs. Rsch., Sigma Xi, Delta Omega. Methodist. Home: 1825 N Lakeshore Dr Chapel Hill NC 27514-6734

COULTER, JACK BENSON, JR., financial planner; b. Louisville, Jan. 30, 1947; s. Jack Benson and Mary Belle (Roby) C.; m. Mary Llew Browne, July, 1977. BS, Fla. State U., 1967, MBA, 1969. CPA, Fla. Staff acct. Arthur Andersen & Co., Miami, Fla., 1971-73; sales rep. Commerce Clearing House, Inc., Miami, 1973-80; pres. First Fin. Planners, North Palm Beach, Fla., 1980-92, Coulter Fin. Advisors, Inc., Juno Beach, 1992—. Capt. U.S. Army, 1969-71. Mem. Inst. CFPs (nat. bd. dirs. 1986-89), Fla. Assn. CFPs (chmn. 1989-91), Fin. Planning Assn., Fla. Inst. CPAs. Republican. Office Phone: 561-627-6992. E-mail: ben@coulterfinancial.com.

COULTER, JAMES BENNETT, state official; b. Vinita, Okla., Aug. 2, 1920; s. Robert Leslie and Louise (Robinson) C.; m. Norma R. Brink, June 1, 1942; children: Linda Coulter Prandoni, James Bennett. BS in Civil Engring, U. Kans., 1950; MS, Harvard U., 1954; DSc (hon.), Washington Coll., 1979. Registered profl. engr., Md., Kans. Commd. officer USPHS, 1950-66; asst. commr. environ. health Md. Dept. Health, Balt., 1966-69; sec. Md. Dept. Natural Resources, Annapolis, 1969-82. Mem. vis. com. Sch. Engring. and Applied Physics, Harvard U.; mem. adv. com. Sch. Engring., U. Kan., Civitan. Bd. dirs. Blue Shield Md.; trustee Chesapeake Research Consortium; mem. exec. bd. Md. Save Our Streams. Served with C.E. AUS, 1940-45. Decorated Bronze Star Mem. APHA, NAE, Am. Acad. Environ. Engrs. (Gordon M. Fair award 1971, pres. 1978), Am. Water Works Assn. (Fuller award 1987), Water Pollution Control Fedn., Tau Beta Pi, Sigma Tau. Home: 778 Eastern Point Rd Annapolis MD 21401-6945

COULTER, MYRON LEE, retired academic administrator; b. Albany, Ind., Mar. 21, 1929; s. Mark Earl and Thelma Violet (Marks) C.; m. Barbara Bolinger, July 21, 1951; children: Nan and Benjamin (twins). BS, Ind. State Tchrs. Coll., 1951; MS, Ind. U., 1956, EdD, 1959; HLD (hon.), Coll. Idaho, 1982. Tchr. English Reading (Mich.) Pub. Schs., 1951-52; tchr. elem. grades Bloomington (Ind.) Pub. Schs., 1954-56; instr. edn. Ind. U., Bloomington, 1958-59; asst. prof. Pa. State U., 1959-64, asso. prof., 1964-66; vis. prof. U. Alaska, Fairbanks, 1965; asso. dean edn., prof. edn. Western Mich. U., Kalamazoo, 1966-68, v.p. for adminstrn., prof. edn., 1968-76, interim pres., 1974; pres. Idaho State U., Pocatello, 1976-84; chancellor Western Carolina U., Cullowhee, N.C., 1984-94, chancellor emeritus, 1994—. Del. Israeli Univs., 1976, Am. Assn. State Colls. and Univs. to People's Republic of China, 1981, Swaziland Coll. Tech., 1985, People's Republic China, 1985, 87, 88, 90, Jamaica, 1986, 89, 91, 94, Thailand, 1987, 90, The Netherlands, 1991; mem. U.S. Panama Canal Treaty Com., 1977-79 Author school textbooks. Bd. dirs. Kalamazoo C. of C., 1975-76, Pocatello Jr. Achievement; bd. dirs., chair N.C. Arboretum, 1994-98; bd. dirs. WNC Pub. Radio, WNC Devel. Assn., WNC Tomorrow, Joint PVO/Univ. Rural Devel. Ctr., WNC Commn. Found., Friends of Great Smoky Mountain Nat. Park, 1994—, Inter-Regional Ctr., 2001—; lay leader Kalamazoo Meth. Ch., 1971-74; mem. Gov.'s Task Force on Aquaculture, 1988, N.C. Bd. Sci. and Tech., 1993—, Commn. for Competitive N.C., 1993—; chair N.C. Indian Gaming Cert. Commn., 1994—98; trustee Bronson Hosp., Kalamazoo, 1975-76, N.C. Ctr. Advancement Tchg., C.J. Harris Cmty. Hosp.; chmn. Cherokee Preservation Found., 2001-05; chair devel. com. Givens Estates, CCRD, 2005—. With U.S. Army, 1952-54. Named Disting. Alumnus, Ind. State U., 1975, Ind. U., 1994; recipient award Western Mich. U. Alumni Assn., 1974, resolution of tribute Mich. State Legislature, 1976, N.C. Order of the Long Leaf Pine, 1994. Mem. Internat. Reading Assn., Am. Assn. State Colls. and Univs. (bd. dirs. 1981-84, exec. com. 1981-84, sec.-treas. 1984-87, found. bd. dirs. 1987—, chmn. 1988-89), Nat. Soc. Study of Edn., N.C. Assn. Colls. and Univs. (bd. dirs.), Western Coll. Assn., Pocatello C. of C. (bd. dirs. 1977-80), Asheville C. of C. (bd. dirs. 1985-86), Cherokee Hist. Assn., Ind. U. Coll. Edn. Alumni Assn. (Disting. Alumnus award 1994), Phi Delta Kappa, Omicron Delta Kappa, Phi Kappa Phi, Beta Gamma Sigma. Office: Western Carolina Univ Office Chancellor Emeritus 61 Hunter Cullowhee NC 28723 Business E-Mail: coulter@email.wcu.edu.

COULTER, NORMAN ARTHUR, JR., biomedical engineering educator emeritus; b. Atlanta, Jan. 9, 1920; s. Norman Arthur and Carabelle (Clark) C.; m. Elizabeth Harwell Jackson, June 23, 1951; 1 child, Robert Jackson. BS, Va. Poly. Inst., 1941; MD, Harvard U., 1950; postdoctoral fellow, Johns Hopkins U., 1950-52. Instr. math. dept. Va. Poly. Inst., 1946; asst. to assoc. prof. physiology dept. Ohio State U., 1952-65; dir. biophysics div., physiology dept., 1962-65; assoc. prof. depts. surgery and physiology U. N.C., Chapel Hill, 1965-67, prof., 1967-90, prof. emeritus, 1990—, chmn. bioengring.-biomath. program, 1969-82, dir. grad. studies, 1982-90. Author: Synergetics: An Adventure in Human Development, 1976; also articles in profl. jours. Served to maj. Anti-Aircraft Art. AUS, 1941-46. Mem. AMA, IEEE, Internat. Soc. Biorheol, Biophys. Soc., Am. Physiol. Soc., Biomed. Engring. Soc., Soc. Gen. Sys. Rsch., Physicians for Social Responsibililty, Sigma Xi. Home: 1825 N Lakeshore Dr Chapel Hill NC 27514-6734

COULTER, WILLIAM KIRK, lawyer; b. Wilmington, Del., May 31, 1946; s. George R. and Jane (Jernee) C.; m. Mary Susan Pearson, Feb. 14, 1972; children: Michael William, Kathryn Amanda BA cum laude, Franklin & Marshall Coll., 1968; JD with honors, U. Pitts., 1971; cert. Internat. bus., Univ. Va.; cert. Govt. Contracting, William & Mary Univ. Bar: Pa. 1972, D.C. 1972. Deputy atty. gen. Del. Atty. Gen. Office, Wilmington, 1970; assoc. Richards, Layton & Finger, Wilmington, 1971—; v.p., gen. counsel, dir. COMSAT Internat. Corp., Washington, 1988-94; ptnr. Baker, Donelson, Bearman & Caldwell, Washington, 1994-95; sr. v.p., internat. trade & new ventures COMSAT, Washington, 1995—98; ptnr. Coudert Bros. LLP, Washington, 1998—, head Tech., Media & Telecom. practice, 2005—. Com. counsel to U.S. Sen. Howard Baker, Washington, 1993—98; mem. legal adv. com. U.S. State Dept., Washington; rep. Nat. Security Comm. Working Group, U.S. Dept. Def., Washington; founding mem. Internat. Telecom. Union Legal Symposium; gen. counsel Global Mobile Satellite Users Assn., World Teleport Assn., Worldwide Internet Forum. Author: Earth Station Ownership Worldwide. Mem. Fed. Comm. Bar Assn. (internat. chmn. 1988-92), sust. mem. Pac. Telecom. Council. Office: Coudert Bros LLP 11th Fl 1627 I St NW Washington DC 20006 Office Phone: 202-775-5100. Office Fax: 202-775-1168. Business E-Mail: coulterw@coudert.com.

COULTRIP, MARSHA LOUISE, secondary school educator; d. Charles Joseph and Bertha Rita Coultrip. AS, Lorain C.C.; BS, Ohio U.; M of Sports Sci., postgrad, Ashland U. Tchr. health, physical edn. Wellington Schs., Ohio. Head coach volleyball Wellington Schs., asst. coach softball, head coach track. Avocations: travel, reading, golf, baseball.

COUNCIL, PAULINE CARTER, lawyer; b. Camilla, Ga., Apr. 26, 1950; d. Willie Frank D. and Bernice (Brown) Carter; m. James F. Jr., Jan. 26, 1980; children: Dawn Nichole, Kimberly Michelle, Ashley Monique, James F. III. BA, Morris Brown Coll., 1972; JD, U. Fla., 1994. Asst. planner S.W. Ga. Area Planning and Devel. Commn., Camilla, 1972—73, rev. coord., 1973—74, sr. planner, 1974—75; area agy. on aging coord. South Ga. Area Planning and Devel. Commn., Valdosta, 1975—77, area agy. on aging dir., 1977—85; dir. Quitman/Brooks CDC, 1987—89, worker adjustment specialist, 1989—91; pvt. practice law, 1995—; spl. asst. atty. gen., 2000—. Chmn. Foster Grandparents, Valdosta, 1982—85, Dist. 8 social Svcs. Adv. Coun. Valdosta/Albany Area, 1985; mem. Ga. Coalition of black Women; mem. minority affairs com. Moody AFB, Valdosta, 1975—78; mem. Nat. Congress Cmty. Econ. Devel., Citizens for Better Valdosta/Lowndes County, Lowndes County Cmty. Ptnrs. in Edn.; local rep. Martin Luther King Jr. Ctr. for Non-Violent Social Change, Atlanta, 1984—85; Brownie troop leader Flint River coun. Girls Scouts U.S.A., Valdosta, 1982; asst. leader Girl Scouts U.S.A., 1996—; chmn. workforce devel. bd. South Ga. Area Agy. on Aging, 2000—; mem., asst. dir. youth dept. Macedonia First Bapt. Ch.; chmn. Westside Neighborhood Assn., 1994—96, LMS Adv. Com., 1994—95; bd. dirs. Area Agy. on Aging, 1996—. Com. for Humanities grantee, 1977, 1979, Ga. Dept. Human Resources grantee, 1977—85. Mem.: Ga. Assn. AAAs, Nat. Assn. AAAs, Nat. Coun. on Aging, Lowndes County Bar Assn., Ga. Bar Assn. Democrat. Pentecostal Ch. Home: 2410 Patrick Pl Valdosta GA 31601-7936 Office: PO Box 5774 124 McKey St Valdosta GA 31603 Personal E-mail: pccouncil@hotmail.com.

COUNSIL, WILLIAM GLENN, electric utility executive; b. Detroit, Dec. 13, 1937; s. Glenn Dempsey and Jean Beverly (Rzepecki) C.; m. Donna Elizabeth Robinson, Sept. 10, 1960; children: Glenn, Craig. Student, U. Mich., 1955-56; BS, U.S. Naval Acad., 1960; Advanced Mgmt. Program, Harvard U., 1991. Ops. supr., asst. plant supt. sta. supt. N.E. Nuclear Energy Co., Waterford, Conn., 1967-76; project mgr., v.p. nuclear engring. and ops. N.E. Utilities, Hartford, Conn., 1976-80, sr. v.p. nuclear engring. and ops., 1980-85; exec. v.p. nuclear engring. and ops., electric-generating div. Tex. Utilities Generating Co., 1985-88; vice chmn. Tex. Utilities Electric Co., 1989-93; mng. dir. Wash. Pub. Power Supply System, Richland, 1993-96. With USN, 1956-67. Recipient Outstanding Leadership award ASME, 1986. Republican. Presbyterian. E-mail: wcounsil@aol.com. *My goal has been to improve our quality of life first through service in the United States Navy and second by ensuring an adequate and safe energy supply for our country.*

COUNTRYMAN, DAYTON WENDELL, lawyer; b. Sioux City, Iowa, Mar. 31, 1918; s. Cleve and Susie (Schaeffer) Countryman; m. Ruth Hazen, Feb. 2, 1941 (dec.); children: Karen, Joan, James, Kay. BS, Iowa State Coll., 1940; LLB, State U. Iowa, 1948, JD, 1969. Bar: Iowa 1948. Practiced in, Nevada; ptnr. Hadley & Countryman, Nevada, Iowa, 1949-64; mem. Countryman & Zaffarano P.C., 1984-87, Dayton Countryman Law Offices, P.C., 1987—; county atty. Story County, Iowa, 1950-54; atty. gen. State of Iowa, 1954-56. Candidate for U.S. Senate, 1956, 1960, 68. Air Force Res. pilot USAAF, 1941—46. Mem. ABA, Iowa Bar Assn., Story County Bar Assn., VFW, Am. Legion, Iowa State U. Alumni Assn. (pres. 1970-71), Iowa 2B Jud. Dist. Assn., Masons, Lions (pres. 1975-76). Methodist. Office: PO Box 28 Nevada IA 50201-0028 Office Phone: 515-382-2605.

COUNTRYMAN, EDWARD FRANCIS, historian, educator; b. Glens Falls, N.Y., July 31, 1944; s. Edward Francis and Agnes (Alford) C.; m. Evonne von Heussen, 1987; children: Karon Samantha, Kirstein Dawn; 1 son from previous marriage, Samuel Robert. BA, Manhattan Coll., 1966; MA, Cornell U., Ithaca, N.Y., 1969; PhD, Cornell U., 1971; LHD, Manhattan Coll., 1999. Lectr. in history U. Canterbury, N.Z., 1970-74; lectr. U. Warwick, Eng., 1975-83, sr. lectr., 1983-88, reader, 1988-91; prof. So. Meth. U., Dallas, 1991-99, disting. prof., 1999—. Vis. lectr. U. Cambridge, Eng., 1979-80, Mellon vis. sr. scholar, 1999; vis. scholar NYU, N.Y.C., 1980-81; Cardozo vis. prof. Yale U., spring 1989; coun. mem. Omohundro Inst. Early Am. History and Culture, 1999—. Cons. editor Radical History Rev., 1982—; author: A People in Revolution, 1981 (Bancroft prize 1982), The American Revolution, 1985, rev. edit. 2003; (video) American Independence 1776, 1989, Americans: A Collision of Histories, 1996; co-author: Who Built America, 1990, Shane, 1999; editor: How Did American Slavery Begin?, 1998, What Did the Constitution Mean to Early Americans?, 1998; co-author: The Empire State, 2001. Active civil rights movement, U.S., 1965-68; spokesperson Anti-War Movement, N.Z., 1970-73; active Campaign for Nuclear Disarmament, Eng., 1981—. Woodrow Wilson fellow, 1966-67, Danforth fellow, 1966-71, Samuel Foster Haven fellow, 1983; Mellon vis. sr. scholar U. Cambridge, 1998. Home: 5454 Anita St Dallas TX 75206-5336 Office: So Meth U Dept History Dallas TX 75275-0001 E-mail: ecountry@mail.smu.edu.

COUNTRYMAN, GARY LEE, retired insurance company executive; b. South Bend, Wash., July 30, 1939; s. William T. and Vernela K. (Stewart) C.; m. Sally Ann Mathews, Aug. 16, 1958; children: Christopher John, Susan Michelle, Sherry LeeAnn, Stefanie May. BS, U. Oreg., 1961, MS, 1963. With Liberty Mut. Ins. Co., Boston, 1963—, pres., 1981-86, pres., chief exec. officer, 1986-91, chmn., pres., CEO, 1991-92, chmn., 1992-99, CEO, 1998; pres. Liberty Fin. Co., Inc., Boston, 1999-2000, chmn., pres., CEO, 2000—01, chmn emeritus, 2001—. Bd. dirs. Liberty Mut. Ins. Group, Bank of Boston Corp., 1st Nat. Bank Boston, Boston Edison Co., Harcourt Gen., Inc., Alliance Am. Insurers; chmn. bd. dirs. Boston Mgmt. Consortium, Inc. Bd. dirs. Inst. Civil Justice, Jobs for Mass., Inc., Com. for Econ. Devel.; trustee Northeastern U., U. New Eng., Mus. Sci., Sudbury Valley Trustees; chmn. bd. Dana-Farber Cancer Inst.; bd. overseers Mass. Gen. Hosp. H.T. Miner fellow, 1962-63 Mem. NAM, Am. Inst. Property and Liability Underwriters (bd. dirs.), Algonquin Club.

COUNTS, STANLEY THOMAS, retired military officer, retired electronics executive; b. Okfuskee County, Okla., July 3, 1926; s. Claud Curtley and Thelma (Thomas) C.; m. Bettejan Heft, Nov. 18, 1949; children:Ashlie Heft Jenkins. BS, U.S. Naval Acad., 1949; BS in Elec. Engring, U.S. Naval Postgrad. Sch., 1954, MS in Elec. Engring, 1955. Commd. ensign U.S. Navy, 1949, advanced through grades to rear adm., 1972; comdg. officer USS Bronstein, 1963-64; comdg. officer USS Towers, 1966-68; project mgr. NATO Seasparrow Surface Missile System, 1968-70; comdg. officer USS Chgo., 1970-71; dir. ships, weapons, electronics and asso. systems Office Asst. Sec. Def. for Installations and Logistics Washington, 1971-73; dep. comdr. Naval Ordnance Systems Command, 1973-74; designated Naval ordnance engr., 1974; comdr. (Naval Ordnance Systems Command), 1974; vice comdr. Naval Sea Systems Command, 1974-76; comdr. Cruiser-Destroyer Group 5 San Diego, 1976-78; ret., 1978; exec. Hughes Aircraft Co., Fullerton, Calif., 1979-89; ret., 1989; aerospace cons., chief exec. officer Bjan Enterprises, La Jolla, Calif., 1989-99. Chmn. Seasparrow steering com. NATO, 1973-76. Bd. dirs. San Diego chpt. Freedoms Found. at Valley Forge, 1992-94, 97-98; bd. dirs. Greater La Jolla Meals on Wheels, Inc., 1998—, pres., 2000—01. Decorated Legion of Merit with three oak leaf clusters, Bronze Star with combat distinguishing device. Mem. VFW, Surface Navy Assn. (life, bd. dirs. 1985-93), U.S. Naval Inst. (life), DAV (life), Ret. Officers Assn. (life), Navy League, USNA Alumni Assn. (life), Am. Legion, Rest and Aspiration Club San Diego. Home: 856 La Jolla Rancho Rd La Jolla CA 92037-7408 Personal E-mail: radmstc1949@msn.com.

COUPE, JAMES WARNICK, lawyer; b. Utica, N.Y., Mar. 3, 1949; s. J. Leo and Helen Carbery (Brennan) C.; m. Andrea Jean Schaaf, Nov. 26, 1983; children: Helen Shriver, Benjamin Warnick, Charlotte Fitzgerald. AB, Hamilton Coll., 1971; JD, Vanderbilt U., 1974. Bar: N.Y. 1975, Calif. 1981, Tenn. 1995, U.S. Dist. Ct. (so. and ea. dists.) N.Y. 1975, U.S. Ct. Appeals (2d cir.) 1975. Law clk. to judge U.S. Dist. Ct. (so. dist.) N.Y., N.Y.C., 1974-75; assoc. Donovan, Leisure, Newton & Irvine, N.Y.C., 1975-79, Phillips, Nizer, Benjamin, Krim & Ballon, N.Y.C., 1979-81; sr. atty. Atlantic Richfield Co., L.A., 1981-86; chief counsel Beverly Enterprises, Inc., Pasadena, Calif., 1986-88; gen. counsel Completion Bond Co., Inc., Century City, Calif., 1988-93; exec. Sullivan Curtis Monroe Ins. Brokers, Pasadena, Calif., 1993-95; v.p. bus. & legal affairs Cinema Completions Internat. Inc., L.A., 1995-97; sr. v.p. bus. and legal affairs Cinema Completions Internat., 1997—2002; atty. pvt. practice, 2002—. Mem. L.A. County Bar Assn., State Bar Calif. Republican. Roman Catholic. Office: Law Offices of James W Coupe Esq 444 S Flower St 31st Fl Los Angeles CA 90071-2932 Office Phone: 213-236-1604. E-mail: barrister74@msn.com.

COUPER, JAMES MAXWELL, painter, educator; b. Atlanta, Nov. 21, 1937; s. J. Maxwell and Frances (Ellis) C.; m. Carol Elaine Whitelaw, Apr. 1, 1960 (div. 1972); children: Sarah K., J. Maxwell. AB in English, Ga. State U., 1959, AB in Art, 1961; MA in Art, Fla. State U., Tallahassee, 1963. Instr. U. Miami, Fla., 1963-64, Miami-Dade C.C., Miami, 1964-67; artist-in-residence Miami Art Ctr., 1967-69; prof. Fla. Internat. U., Miami, 1972—, chair dept., 1976—77, founding dir. Art Mus., 1977—80, founding dir. grad. program, 1998. Exhibitor numerous solo and group nat. and regional exhbns; founding dir. Fla. Internat. U. Art Mus., 1977-1980, Grad. Program Fla. Internat. U., 1997-2000. Hand Hollow Found. fellow, 1982; State of Fla. Individual Artists' grantee, 1983, Fla. Internat. U. grantee, 1983, Yaddo fellow, 1987, Hambridge fellow, 1990, 1991, 2000, 2003.

COUPER, WILLIAM, bank executive; b. N.Y.C., May 3, 1947; s. John Lee and Margery (Beemer) Couper; m. Elise Marie Palma, Oct. 4, 1969; children: Elise, Margery, Dorothy. BS in Commerce, U.Va., 1968; cert., Coll. Fin. Planning, 1986. Trainee Am. Security Bank, N.A., Washington, 1972, asst. treas., asst. br. mgr., 1972-76, asst. v.p., mgr. main office, 1976-77, v.p., regional mgr., 1977-80, v.p. strategic planning, 1981-83, v.p. retail banking devel., 1983-84, sr. v.p. retail banking, 1984-89; sr. v.p. Md. Nat. Bank, Greenbelt, 1989-92; vice chmn. Va. Fed. Savs. Bank, 1991-93; exec. v.p. Am. Security Bank, Md. Nat. Bank, Washington, 1993-94; pres. Bank Am., Balt., 1994-2000, Washington, 2000—. Chmn. United Way Nat. Capital Area, Washington; bd. dirs. Greater Washington Bd. Trade, Fed. City Coun. Greater Washington Initiative. Mem.: Md. C. of C., Chartwell Golf and Country Club, Ctr. Club Balt. Republican. Episcopalian. Home: 1114 Bellevista Ct Severna Park MD 21146-4846 Office: Bank of Am 730 15th St NW Washington DC 20005 Office Phone: 202-624-1066. E-mail: william.couper@bankofamerica.com.

COUPEY, SUSAN MCGUIRE, pediatrician, educator; b. Montreal, Que., Can., June 29, 1942; came to U.S., 1978; d. Clarence Herbert and Paulette (Lefevre) McGuire; m. Pierre M.L. Coupey, July 1964 (div. 1981); children: Marc M.R., Ariane S.; m. James R. English III, Nov. 23, 1988. BA, Queen's U., Kingston, Ont., Can., 1962; postgrad., McGill U., Montreal, 1962-63; MD, U. B.C., Vancouver, Can., 1975. Diplomate Am. Bd. Pediatrics, subboard in adolescent medicine. Devel. chemist Merck, Sharp & Dohme, Ltd., Montreal, 1963-64; rotating intern Montreal Gen. Hosp., 1975-76; resident in pediatrics Montreal Children's Hosp., 1976-78; fellow in adolescent medicine Montefiore Med. Ctr., Bronx, N.Y., 1978-79, attending pediatrician, 1980—; rsch. asst. Cancer Rsch. Ctr., U. B.C., 1967-72; instr., asst. prof. pediatrics Albert Einstein Coll. Medicine, Bronx, 1979-85, assoc. prof., 1985-93, prof., 1993—, assoc. dir. div. adolescent medicine, 1984—2001, course dir. introduction to clin. medicine, 1989—, mem. faculty senate, 1983-84, 88-90, co-chair divsn. edn., 2000—, chief adolescent medicine, 2002—. Attending pediatrician North Ctrl. Bronx Hosp., 1979-97; cons. in adolescent medicine Flushing (N.Y.) Hosp. and Med. Ctr., 1982-96; Maricopa-Pima vis. prof. U. Ariz., 1989; vis. prof. Children's Hosp. Ea. Ont., U. Ottawa and Ea. Can. chpt. Soc. for Adolescent Medicine, 1990; vis. prof. Philippine Children's Med. Ctr., U. Philippines Coll. of Medicine, 1997; chmn. health svcs. adv. com. Children's Aid Soc., 1985—, bd. trustees, 1993—; mem. adv. bd. Office Substance Abuse Ministry, Archdiocese of N.Y., 1983-85; spkr. Hosp. Italiano, Buenos Aires, Argentina, 1999, Israeli Soc. Adolescent Medicine, Jeruseleum, Israel, 2000, Greek Soc. Adolescent Med., Athens, Greece, 2000. Editor: Primary Care of Adolescent Girls, 2000; assoc. editor Adolescent Medicine Clinics, 1990—; assoc. editor Jour. Devel. & Behavioral Pediatrics, 1992-96, editl. bd., 1996-00; assoc. editor Jour. Pediat. & Adolescent Gynecology, 1992-98, editl. bd. 1998—; editl. bd. Jour. of Youth and Adolescence, 1998—; contbr. articles to med. jours., also chpts. to books and monographs. Fellow Am. Acad. Pediatrics (exec. com. sect. on adolescent health 1993-96); mem. Soc. for Adolescent Medicine (nominations com. 1984-85, chmn. jour. adv. com. 1987-97, program com. 1991-93, awards com. 1992-95, bd. dirs. 1997-2000), Am. Pediat. Soc. (abstract review com. 1999—2001), Soc. for Behavioral Pediatrics, N.Am. Soc. Pediat. and Adolescent Gynecology (bd. dirs. 1993-96, sec. 1996-2001, chair publs. com. 1996—, pres.-elect 2001-2002, pres. 2002-03), Sex Info. and Edn. Coun. U.S., Am. Acad. Physicians and Patients, Albert Einstein Coll. Medicine Alumni Assn. (v.p. pediatrics 1983-84, pres. 1984-85), Alpha Omega Alpha (Kappa chpt. councilor). Office: Albert Einstein Coll Medicine Montefiore Med Ctr 111 E 210th St Bronx NY 10467-2401 Office Phone: 718-920-6781. E-mail: scoupey@montefiore.org.

COUPLAND, DOUGLAS CAMPBELL, writer; b. Baden Söllingen, Germany, Dec. 30, 1961; s. Douglas Charles Thomas and C. Janet (Campbell) C. Student, Emily Carr Coll. Art and Design, Vancouver, Can., 1984. Author: Generation X: Tales for an Accelerated Culture, 1991, Shampoo Planet, 1992, Life After God, 1994, Microserfs, 1995, Hey Nostradamus, 2003, Eleanor Rigby, 2005; contbr. articles to periodicals including The New Republic, The New York Times, Saturday Night, Artforum. Office: c/o Harper Collins 10 E 53rd St New York NY 10022-5244

COUPLES, FREDERICK STEVEN, professional golfer; b. Seattle, Oct. 3, 1959; m. Thais; 2 children: Gigi, Oliver. Student, U. Houston. Mem. U.S. Ryder Cup golf team, 1989, 91, 93, 95, 97; mem. nat. teams USA vs. Japan, 1984, Asahi Glass Four Tours World Championship of Golf, 1990, 91, Dunhill Cup, 1991, 92, 93, 94, World Cup, 1992, 93, 94, 95, Pres.'s Cup, 1994, 96, 98. Named All-Am., 1978, 79; winner numerous golf tournaments including Kemper Open, 1983, Tournament Players Championship, 1984, Byron Nelson Golf Classic, 1987, French PGA, 1988, Nissan L.A. Open, 1990, 92, Tournoi Perrier de Paris, 1991, B.C. Open, 1991, Federal Express

St. Jude Classic, 1991, Johnnie Walker World Championship, 1991, Nestle Invitational, 1992, The Masters, 1992, (with Jan Stephenson) J.C. Penney Classic, 1983, (with Mike Donald) Sazale Classic, 1990, (with Raymond Floyd) RMCC Invitational, 1990, Buick Open, 1994, World Cup, 1994, Dubai Desert Classic, 1995, Johnnie Walker Classic, 1995, The Player's Championship, 1996, Bob Hope chrysler Classic, 1998, Memorial Tournament, 1998; Shell Houston Open, 2003; recipient Vardon trophy, 1991, 92; named PGA Player of Yr. Golf World Mag., 1991, 92, Golf Writers Assn., 1991, 92, PGA Tour Player of Yr, 1993, 94. Achievements include being the leading money winner PGA, 1992. Address: c/o PGA Tour 100 Ave of The Champions PO Box 109601 Palm Beach Gardens FL 33410

COURANT, ERNEST DAVID, physicist, educator; b. Goettingen, Germany, Mar. 26, 1920; came to U.S., 1934, naturalized, 1940; s. Richard and Nina (Runge) C.; m. Sara Paul, Dec. 9, 1944; children: Paul N., Carl R. BA, Swarthmore Coll., 1940; MS, U. Rochester, 1942, PhD, 1943; MA (hon.), Yale U., 1962; DSc (hon.), Swarthmore Coll., 1988. Scientist Atomic Energy Project, Montreal, Que., Can., 1943-46; rsch. assoc. physics Cornell U., 1946-48; staff Brookhaven Nat. Lab., 1947—, sr. physicist, 1960-89, disting. scientist emeritus, 1990—; Brookhaven prof. physics Yale U., 1962-67, vis. prof., 1961-62; prof. physics and engring. SUNY, Stony Brook, 1967-85. Vis. asst. prof. Princeton, 1950-51; cons. Gen. Atomic divsn. Gen. Dynamics Corp., 1958-59; vis. physicist Nat. Accelerator Lab., 1968-69; vis. prof. U. Mich., 1989—; cons. Superconducting Supercollider Lab., Dallas, 1990-93; hon. prof. U. Sci. and Tech. of China, Hefei, 1994. Co-originator strong-focusing particle accelerators Fulbright Rsch. fellow Cambridge (Eng.) U., 1956; recipient Fermi award U.S. Dept. of Energy, 1986. Fellow Am. Phys. Soc. (R.R. Wilson prize 1987), AAAS; mem. Nat. Acad. Scis., N.Y. Acad. Scis. (Boris Pregel prize 1979). Home: 40 W 72nd St Apt 41 New York NY 10023-4192 E-mail: ecourant@msn.com.

COURANT, PAUL NOAH, economist, educator, academic administrator; b. Ithaca, N.Y., Jan. 5, 1948; s. Ernest David and Sara (Paul) Courant; m. Katherine Olive Johnson, Sept. 21, 1969 (dissolved 1984); children: Ernest Mendel, Noah Albert; m. Marta Anne Manildi, Jan. 30, 1988; 1 child, Samuel Robinson Manildi. BA, Swarthmore Coll., 1968; MA, Princeton U., 1972, PhD, 1973. Jr. economist Coun. Econ. Advisers, Washington, 1969—70, sr. economist, 1979—80; asst. prof. econs., pub. policy U. Mich., Ann Arbor, 1973—78, assoc. prof., 1978—84, prof. econs. and pub. policy, 1984—, dir. Inst. Pub. Policy Studies, 1983—87, 1989—90, chmn. econs. dept., 1995—97, assoc. provost, 1997—2001, provost, exec. v.p. acad. affairs, 2002—05. Mem. task force long-term econ. growth State of Mich., 1983—84; cons. Mich. Dept. Commerce, Lansing, 1984—85, Congl. Budget Office, Washington, 1988—89; bd. dirs. Mich. Future. Author: (book) America's Great Consumption Binge, 1986; co-author: Economics, 12th edit., 1999; contbr. articles to profl. jours. Bd. dirs. Ctr. Watershed and Cmty. Health, Eugene, Oreg., 1997—. Grantee, NSF, 1976—77, 1979—81, 1994—97, Rockefeller Found., 1985—87, Nat. Cancer Inst., 1992—95. Mem.: Nat. Tax Assn., Assn. Pub. Policy Analysis and Mgmt. (mem. policy coun. 1994—98), Am. Econ. Assn. Avocations: sailing, skiing, tennis, hiking, clarinet. Office: U Mich 3074 Fleming Bldg Ann Arbor MI 48109-1340 Office Phone: 734-764-9292. E-mail: pnc@umich.edu.

COUREY, EDWARD GEORGE, retired insurance agent; b. Lennox, SD, Jan. 23, 1919; s. Samuel T. and Mabel Barbara Courey; m. Jean Mary Corbett, Feb. 14, 1946; children: Edward G., Taylor D., Cinderita Marie, Melinda J. Attended, Md. U. Staff intelligence U.S. Air Force, Montgomery, Ala.; insurance broker various companies, Silver Springs, 1954—84; ret., 1984. Founder One Kidney Clubs of Am., 1960; chmn. Jimmy Jabara Meml. Found., 1996—. Chmn. Lincoln Day Dinner, 1966; precinct ctrl. command Rep. Party, Md., 1958—80. Home: 14919 Pennfield Cir Silver Spring MD 20906 Office Phone: 301-717-7840. Office Fax: 301-717-7840.

COURIC, KATIE (KATHERINE ANNE COURIC), newscaster, journalist; b. Arlington, Va., Jan. 7, 1957; d. John and Elinor; m. John Paul (Jay) Monahan III, 1989 (dec. 1998); children: Elinor Tully Monahan, Caroline Couric Monahan. Grad. in Am. Studies, U. Va., 1979. Desk asst. ABC News, Wash., 1979; prodr. news show CNN, Atlanta, 1980; reporter, WTVJ NBC, Miami, 1984—86, reporter, WRC-TV Washington, 1987—89, Pentagon reporter, 1989, nat. corr., Today, Washington, 1990—91, co-anchor, Today, 1991—. Contbg. anchor Dateline NBC; co-host Macy's Thanksgiving Day Parade, 1991—, Summer Olympics, Barcelona, 1992. Anchor: (documentaries) Everybody's Business: America's Children, 1995; author: The Brand New Kid, 2000, The Blue Ribbon Day, 2004; actor: (films) Austin Powers in Goldmember, 2002, Shark Tale (voice only), 2004. Co-founder Nat. Colorectal Cancer Rsch. Alliance (NCCRA), 1999. Named News Person Yr., TV Guide, 2001; named one of 25 Most Intriguing People, People mag., 2001, Most Powerful Women, Forbes mag., 2005; recipient six Emmys, Associated Press award, Nat. Headliner award, Sigma Delta Chi award, Nat. Soc. Profl. Journalists, Matrix award, Gracie Allen award, Peabody award, 2001, Julius B. Richmond award, Harvard Sch. Pub. Health, 2003. Address: NBC TV Today Show 30 Rockefeller Plz Fl 2 New York NY 10112-0002

COURSON, JOHN EDWARD, state legislator, insurance company executive; b. Aug. 21, 1944; s. James W. and Mary C. (Harris) C.; m. Elizabeth Poinsett Exum, Apr. 1973; children: James Poinsett, Elizabeth Boykin, Harris Russell. BA, U. S.C., 1968. Sr. v.p. Keenan & Suggs. Field dir. S.C. Republican Party, 1969—75, sec., 1976—80; nat. committeeman for S.C. Rep. Nat. Committee, 1980—88; chmn. campaign '80 for S.C.; Presdl. elector Rep., 1980, 1984; chmn. edn. com. SC Senate; co-chmn., treas. Re-elect Thurmond Com., 1990—95. With USMCR, 1968—74. Named Young Agt. of Yr., Ind. Ins. Agts. S.C., 1981; recipient Mounted Gold Elephant, S.C. Republican Party, 1975, 1980, 1982, Order of Palmetto. Mem.: Am. Legion, Marine Corps League, Palmetto Club, Columbia Ball Club, Forest Lake Club, Tarantella Club, Sigma Chi. Episcopalian. Avocations: tennis, politics. Office: 402 Gressette Senate Office Bldg PO Box 142 Columbia SC 29202 E-mail: siv@scsenate.org.

COURSON, MARNA B.P., public relations executive; b. Waynesboro, Pa., Feb. 22, 1951; d. Eugene Perry and Charlotte Mae (Sherman) Roschli; m. Sydney E. Courson, May 24, 1982 (dec. 1999); 1 child, Sydney Alexandra; m. David W. Bowen, Oct. 14, 2001. BA, Franklin and Marshall Coll., 1973; postgrad., U. Kans., Kansas City. Reporter Beach Haven Times/The Beacon, Manahawkin, N.J., 1973-74, Dailey Observer Newspaper, Toms River, N.J., 1974-76; comm. mgr. Frick India Ltd., New Delhi, 1976-77; reporter, dictationist UPI, Washington, 1978-80, reporter Richmond, Va.; reporter, editor AP, Balt., 1980-84; comm. coord. St. Luke's Hosp. Found., Kansas City, Mo., 1986-88; exec. v.p. pub. rels. Spaw and Assocs., Inc., Overland Park, Kans., 1988-89; exec. v.p. CCI Pub. Rels. & Mktg. Comm., Inc., Shawnee Mission, Kans., 1990-92, pres. Kansas City, Mo., 1992—. Former bd. dirs. Wonderscope Children's Mus., Ctr. Mgmt. Assistance; active Kansas City Downtown Coun.; bd. mem. Notre Dame de Sion; bd. dirs. Platte county Citizens Coalition, mem. exec. com.; former bd. dirs., former exec. com. Mid Am. Youth Aviation Assn. Recipient Prism award for Fund Raising, numerous awards and honors for reporting, 1973—80, pub. rels. awards, 1988—2005. Mem.: Nat. Assn. Women Bus. Owners, Pub. Rels. Soc. Am. (Pres.'s award with GKC), Internat. Assn. Bus. Communicators, World Futurists Soc., Greater Kansas City C. of C., Northland Sertoma Club, Northland Regional Chamber (bd. exec. com.mem. Platte county Citizens Coalition). Office: CCI Public Rels and Mkgt Comms 934 Wyandotte Ste 800 Kansas City MO 64105 Office Phone: 816-471-2900. Business E-Mail: marna@cci-pr.com. *Every step in my career has been building on my accumulated experience skill and knowledge, providing the basis for creativity and learning for the next stage. In every case, I've found that for me the process is as important as achieving the goal.*

COURT, LEONARD, lawyer, educator; b. Ardmore, Okla., Jan. 11, 1947; s. Leonard and Margaret Janet (Harvey) C.; m. JoAnn Dilleshaw, Sept. 2, 1967; children: Chris, Todd, Brooke. BA, Okla. State U., 1969; JD, Harvard U., 1972. Bar: Okla. 1973, U.S. Dist. Ct. (we. dist.) Okla. 1973, U.S. Dist. Ct. (no. dist.) Okla., 1978, U.S. Dist. Ct. (ea. dist.) Okla. 1983, U.S. Ct. Appeals (10th cir.) 1980, U.S. Ct. Mil. Appeals 1973. Assoc. Crowe & Dunlevy, Oklahoma City, Okla., 1977-81, shareholder, dir., 1981—. Adj. prof. Okla. U. Law Sch., Norman, 1984-85, 88-89, 99—, Okla. City U. Law Sch., 1998—; planning com. Ann. Inst. Labor Law, S.W. Legal Found., Dallas, 1984—. Contbg. author: (supplement book) The Developing Labor Law, 1978, Corporate Counsel's Annual, 1974, Labor Law Developments, 1993, Employment Discrimination Law, Supplement, 1998, 2000. Chmn. bd. elders Meml. Christian Ch., Oklahoma City, 1980, 98-2000; cubmaster Last Frontier coun. Boy Scouts Am., 1984, co-chmn. sustaining fund raising drive Oklahoma City Downtown YMCA, 1989, mem. bd. mgmt., 1994-96; participant Leadership Oklahoma City, 1987-88, bd. govs. Okla. State U. Found., 1990-2002; Oklahoma City Ronald McDonald House, 1990-93, mem. exec. com. 1991-93; co-chmn. ann. teleparty fundraising drive Am. Heart Assn., Okla. City, 1996-98, bd. dirs., 1996-98. Capt. USAF, 1973-77. Fellow Am. Coll. Labor and Employment Lawyer; mem. Am. Employment Law Coun., U.S. C. of C. (mem. labor rels. com. 1997—, chmn. fair labor stds. act subcom. 1999—, mem. steering com. 1999—), Oklahoma City C. of C. (mem. sports and recreation com. 1982-85, indsl. devel. com. 1986), Okla. State U. Alumni Assn. (nat. bd. dirs. 1989—, nat. exec. com., 1992-97, pres. 1995-96, chmn. alumni ctr. task force 1998—, Disting. Alumni award 1998), Okla. County Alumni Assn. (bd. sec. 1987-88, treas. 1988-89, v.p. 1989-90, pres. 1990-91), Harvard Law Sch. Assn., ABA (labor and employment law sect. com. on devel. of law under Nat. Labor Rels. Act, com. on EEO law, litigation sect./employment and labor rels. law com.), Okla. Bar Assn. (labor and employment law sect. coun. 1978-83, 85-87, chmn. 1986), Okla. County Bar Assn., Fed. Bar Assn., U.S. Tennis Assn. (life). Office: Crowe & Dunlevy Mid America Tower 20 N Broadway Ave Ste 1800 Oklahoma City OK 73102-8273 Office Phone: 405-235-7700. E-mail: courtl@crowedunlevy.com.

COURT, STACIE LORRAINE, musician, tax specialist; b. Kittery, Maine, Aug. 7, 1964; d. Donald Arnold Downie and Lorraine Lucille Downie (neé Dion); m. David James Court, Mar. 22, 2003; m. Joseph Michael O'Connor, Dec. 28, 1985 (div. Mar. 14, 2002); children: Joseph Patrick O'Connor, Rachel Marie O'Connor. BA in German Lit., U. Va., 1985; BA in Music Vocal Performance, Armstrong Atlantic State U., 1997. Professional Tax Preparer IRS, 2003. Long-term substitute tchr. fgn. langs. Dozier and Reservoir Mid. Schs., Newport News, Va., 1986—86; chorus intern Va. Opera Assn., Norfolk, 1986—87; soloist various organizations, Savannah, Ga., 1989—; dir. youth choir Wilmington Island Presbyn. Ch., 1996—97; instr. voice Pvt. Studio, 1996—; tchr. music St. James Cath. Sch., 1997—99; dir. music Sacred Heart Cath. Ch., 1998—2002; tax preparer Jackson Hewitt Tax Svc., 2003—. Asst. and soloist Savannah Deanery Choir, 1999—2002; singer I Cantori, 1993—98, Savannah Symphony Chorus, 1997—2001; co-founder, treas. Nat. Assn. Pastoral Musicians, 1998—2002; dir. and founder Espíritu: The Voices of Hospice, 2003—05; dir., founder, and singer A Una Voz, 2004—; soloist St. Frances Cabrini Cath. Ch., 1989—99, el Coro Hispano, 2002—. PTA rep. Largo-Tibet Elem. Sch., Savannah, 1992—94; treas. St. James Home and Sch. Assn., 1999—2001; tax advisor Youth Cleaner Environment, 2003—05; cub scout leader Boy Scouts Am., 1993—94; parish coun. rep. St. Frances Cabrini Cath. Ch., 1991—92, youth group coord., 1989—91, mothers' morning out coord., 1991—92; music vol. Hospice Savannah, 2003—05. Named Outstanding Young Layperson, Savannah Jaycees, 1992; recipient Outstanding Jr. award, The Presser Found., 1996; J. Harry Persse scholar Excellence Music Theory, Armstrong Atlantic State U., 1995. Mem.: Am. Choral Dirs. Assn. (assoc.), Nat. Assn. Tchrs. Singing (assoc.), Am. Taekwondo Assn. (assoc.), Armstrong Atlantic State U. Alumni Assn. (assoc.), U. Va. Alumni Assn. (life). Roman Catholic. Achievements include Soloist, Cathedral Rededication Mass: Savannah, GA 2000; Member, National Honor Choir, National Association of Pastoral Musicians, Washington, DC, 2001. Avocations: music composition & arranging, First Degree Black Belt, reading, needlecrafts, sewing, gardening. Home: 2335 E 37th St Savannah GA 31404 Office Phone: 912-236-4503. Personal E-mail: Nachtigall179@aol.com.

COURTAUD, BERNARD JEAN-JACQUES, human resource consulting executive; b. Massy, France, June 22, 1945; s. Paul and Simone (Mustel) C.; children: Sebastien, Alexandre, Stanilas, Paul. Engring. degree, Ecole Centrale, Paris, 1968; MBA, Insead, Fontainebleau, France, 1972. Cons. Commissariat a l'energie Atomique, 1968—72; cons. Port N.Y. Authority, N.Y.C., 1970-71, Peat Marwick Mitchell & Co., 1972-74; chmn. Groupe Courtaud, Paris, 1974-98; founder H.R. Cons. Network, 1998—2005; with Hestia Ptnrs., Paris, 2005—. Chmn. Insead Alumni Assn., France, 1983-88. Office: Hestia Ptnrs 17 Av Victor Hugo 75016 Paris France Office Phone: 33 0 607011617. E-mail: courtaud@hestiapartner.com.

COURTEAU, GIRARD ROBERT, retired prosecutor; b. St. Paul, Minn., Aug. 21, 1942; s. Robert William and Laura Gertrude Courteau; m. Mary Linda Lucas, Apr. 3, 1964 (div. May 1997); m. Susan Frances DeBaca, Aug. 8, 1997; children: Steven, Girard, Devin, Heather. AA, Coll. Marin, 1965; BA, U. Calif., Berkeley, 1967; JD, U. Calif., 1970. Bar: Calif. 1971, U.S. Dist. Ct. (ctrl. dist.) Calif. 1971, U.S. Dist. Ct. (no. dist.) Calif. 1983. Dep. dist. atty. Monterey County, Calif., 1971, Marin County, San Rafael, Calif., 1972-2001; ret., 2001. Mem. editl. bd. Hasting's Law Jour., 1970; editor Marin Law Enforcement Newsletter, 1974-89. Named Prosecutor of the Yr., Marin County Dist. Attys. Office, San Rafael, Calif., 1987. Mem. Order of the Coif, Thurston Soc., Corvettes of Sonoma County, Palm Springs Corvettes Team ZR-1. Roman Catholic. Avocations: gardening, reading, corvettes. Home: 1307 Park St Santa Rosa CA 95404-3542 Personal E-mail: courvettes@sbcglobal.net.

COURTENAY, LISA A., paralegal, foundation administrator; b. Melrose, Mass., Oct. 17, 1962; d. Joseph C. and Angelé S. Surette; m. Michael F. Courtenay, Sept. 20, 1992; children: Andrea Keene, Michael Keene, Ryan. BA, Newbury Coll., 2000. Paralegal Nigro, Pettepit & Lucas, Wakefield, Mass., 1995—; adminstr. Angel Fund Inc., Wakefield, 1999—. Roman Cath. Avocations: camping, travel, writing. Office: Nigro Pettepit & Lucas 649 Main Street Wakefield MA 01880

COURTENAY, WILLIAM JAMES, historian, educator; b. Neenah, Wis., Nov. 5, 1935; s. Walter Rowe and Emily (Simpson) C.; children: Elizabeth Spire, William Todd. AB, Vanderbilt U., 1957; STB, Harvard U., 1960, PhD, 1967. Instr. history Stanford (Calif.) U., 1965-66; asst. prof. U. Wis., Madison, 1966-69, assoc. prof., 1969-71, prof., 1971—, C.H. Haskins prof., 1988—, Hilldale prof., 1998. Vis. scholar Am. Acad. in Rome, 1995, 97, 98. Author: Adam Wodeham, 1978, Covenant and Causality, 1984, Schools and Scholars in 14th Century England, 1987, Capacity and Volition. A History of the Distinction of Absolute and Ordained Power, 1990, Parisian Scholars in the Early Fourteenth Century: A Social Portrait, 1999; editor: Rotuli Parisienses. Supplications to the Pope from the University of Paris, vol. I: 1316-1349, 2002, vol. II: 1352-1378, 2003; also over 100 scholarly articles; co-editor (4 vols.) Gabriel Biel, Canonis Misse Expositio, 1963-67; mem. editl. bd. Jour. the History Ideas, 1976—, Vivarium, 1990—, Medieval Acad. Am., 1978-82; sr. editor series: Education and Society in the Middle Ages and Renaissance, 1990- Recipient Younger Scholar award NEH, Washington, 1968-69, 83; fellow Alexander von Humboldt Stiftung, Germany, 1975-76, 79-80, Guggenheim Found, 1980, NEH, Newberry Libr., Chgo., 1983, Humboldt Preis, 1988, Inst. for Advanced Study, Princeton, N.J., 1989, Herzog August Bibliothek fellow, 1997, 2002, 2003, Am. Coun. Learned Socs. fellow, 1995-96. Fellow Medieval Acad. Am. (mem. coun. 1974-77, 2001-04), Am. Acad. Arts and Scis., Royal Hist. Soc. (London); mem. Am. Soc. Ch. History (councillor 1982-85, pres. 1988), Internat. Soc. for the Study of Medieval Philosophy (assesseur de bureau), Univ. Club. Avocation: sailing.

COURTER, JAMES A., communications executive, retired congressman; b. Montclair, N.J., Oct. 14, 1941; s. Joseph A. and Madeleine C.; m. Carmen McCalmen, Dec. 5, 1970; children: Donica, Katrina. BA, Colgate U., 1963; JD, Duke U., 1966. Vol. U.S. Peace Corps, Venezuela, 1967-69; asst. corp. counsel City of Washington, 1969-70; atty. Union County Legal Services, Plainfield, N.J., 1970-71; 1st asst. prosecutor Warren County, 1973-77; mem. 96th-101st Congresses from 12th N.J. Dist., 1979—91; chmn. President's Defense Base Closure and Realignment Commission, 1991—94; ptnr. Verner, Liipfert, Bernhard, McPherson & Hand, 1994—96; CEO IDT Corp, 1996—, vice chmn., 1999—. Adjunct professor NJIT. Mem. civic adv. council Hackettstown Community Hosp.; bd. dirs. Warren County Legal Services; Rep. candidate for Gov. of N.J., 1989 Mem. Nat. Dist. Atty.'s Assn., County Prosecutors N.J. Assn., N.J. Fedn. Planning Ofcls., N.J. Inst. Mcpl. Attys., N.J. Trial Attys. Assn., N.J. Bar Assn., Am. Bar Assn., Warren County Bar Assn., Washington Bar Assn. Clubs: Hackettstown Rotary (past pres.). Office: c/o IDT Corp 520 Broad St Newark NJ 07102*

COURTÉS, JOSEPH JEAN-MARIE, humanities educator, writer; b. Hérault, France, Feb. 6, 1936; s. Jean and Marthe (Carles) C.; m. Annie Joullié, June 22, 1974; children: Sophie, Jean-Noël, Benoît. Lic., Paris U., 1964, doctorate, 1965, doctorate, 1971, doctorate, 1983. Dir. Internat. Ctr. Semiotics and Linguistics, Urbino, Italy, 1971-73; asst. prof. Ecole de Hautes Études en Scis. Soc., Paris, 1973-84; prof. semiotics Toulouse (France) U., 1985—2005. Pres. of commn. of semiotics and linguistics Toulouse U., 1986-92, 98-2005; emeritus prof. of French U., internat. cons. EHESS, 1985—; mem. Sci. Coms. of Revs., France, 1986—; emeritus prof. Univs. Author: Lévi-Strauss et les contraintes de la pensée mythique, 1973, Introduction à la sémiotique narrative et discursive, 1976, Sémiotique, dictionnaire raisonné de la théorie du langage, vol. I, 1979, vol. II, 1986, Le conte Populaire: poétique et mythologie, 1986, Sémantique de l'énoncé, 1989, Sémiotique du discours: de l'énoncé à l'énonciation, 1991, Du signifié au signifiant, 1992, Sémiotique narrative et discursive, 1993, Du lisible au visible: analyse sémiotique d'une nouvelle de Maupassant, d'une bande dessinée de B. Rabier, 1995, Éthnolittérature, rhétorique et sémiotique, 1995, Stratégies d'écriture et instabilité du sens, 1996, Des motifs ethno-litleraines aux topoi, 1997, L'énonciation comme acte sémiotique, 1998, Sémiotique du langage, 2003. Mem. Assn. for Devel. Semiotics (pres. 1988—), Semio-Linguistics Soc. Ctr. (pres. 1991-93). Office: Toulouse II Univ 31058 Toulouse France Personal E-mail: joseph.courtes@wanadoo.fr.

COURTICE, THOMAS BARR, academic administrator; b. Dayton, Ohio, Oct. 31, 1943; s. Allyn J. and Mary Louise (Barr) C.; children: Heather, Ryan, Lindsey; m. Lisa Schweitzer. BS, U. Pitts, 1965; MBA, Ind. U., 1967; PhD, U. Minn., 1974; cert. Inst. Edn. Mgmt., Harvard U., 1977. Dir. placement, instr. Econs. Hamline U., St. Paul, 1967-69, asst. to pres., 1969-75, v.p. for univ. affairs, 1975-77; pres. Westbrook Coll., Portland, Maine, 1977-86, W.Va. Wesleyan Coll., Buckhannon, 1986-94, Ohio Wesleyan U., Delaware, 1994—. Accreditation evaluator North Ctrl. and New Eng. Assn. Schs. and colls., 1980—; mem. exec. com. Found. for Ind. Higher Edn., 1994—, NCAA Pres. Commn. Divsn. III, 1998-2002; bd. dirs. Ednl. and Instnl. Ins. Adminstrs., Inc. Trustee Wayneflete Sch., Portland, 1980-86, Portland Symphony Orch, 1982-86, Delaware Cmty. Found., 1996— Bush Found. summer fellow, St. Paul, 1977. Mem. Nat. Assn. Ind. Colls. and Univs. (bd. dirs. and exec. com. 1993), Nat. Assn. Schs. and Colls. of the United Meth. Ch. (bd. dirs., pres. 1996-97), Appalachian Coll. Assn. (pres. 1992-94). Home: 135 Oak Hill Ave Delaware OH 43015-2519 Office: Office of Pres Ohio Wesleyan Univ Delaware OH 43015 E-mail: tbcourti@cc.owu.edu.

COURTNEY, ANDREW, artist; b. N.Y.C., Oct. 17, 1936; s. Harry and Jane Courtney. BFA, Syracuse U., 1958; MFA, Columbia Tchrs. Coll., 1971. Tchr. fine arts Woodlands H.S., Hartsdale, NY, 1961—91; prof. photography Manhattanville Coll., Purchase, NY, 1999—2003; tchr. photography Evening Star Photography, Peekskill, NY, 1991—2004; film maker, dir. Red Hill Films. Regional presenter Mid. East Peace Solutions. Still photography, Success: Welfare Women Return to Work, 2000 (WAC award, 2000), Salaam: Arab Americans, 2004 (WAC award, 2004); filmmaker: (documentaries) The Word on the Street, 2004 (Croton Film Festival 1st prize, 2004). Activist Palestine Right of Return, N.Y. and N.J., 1999—; organizer Nicaragua Constrn. Brigade, 1984—87, Palestine Med. Relief, 1991; sec. bd. W.I.S.E. Sch. Reform, White Plains, NY, 1991—; bd. dirs. Wise Individualized Sr. Experience, 1991—2005; organizer Wespac Found., White Plains, 1982—. Recipient 1st prize, Westchester Arts Coun., 2000, 2004, Justice and Peace award, Wespac, 1992. Avocations: kayaking, birdwatching, dogs. Home: 12 Mountain Trail Croton On Hudson NY 10520

COURTNEY, BARBARA WOOD, artist, educator; b. Pratt, Kans., Nov. 12, 1929; d. James Vernon and Bessie Ann (Stover) Wood; m. Howard Conway Courtney Jr., Aug. 1, 1947; children: Christine Gulley, Mark James, Jeffrey Wood. Student, Okla. State U., 1947-50. Demonstrator, instr. workshops in field, Tex., Okla., Ark., N.Mex. Exhibited works at Gallery at Kingspointe, Tulsa, Molly Gerkin Interior Designer, Tulsa, Gables Gallery, Joplin, Okla.; represented in permanent collections at CCI, Tulsa, Phillips Petroleum, Bartlesville, Okla., Utica Bank, Tulsa, Franks Trucking, Big Cabin, Okla., Salina (Kans.) Pub. Bldg., Bank IV, Witchita, Kans.; executed mural for cmty. ctr. City of Grove, Okla. Judge art competitions Nowata (Okla.) County Fair, 1975, Hosman's Annual, Joplin., 1990, Spring River Gallery, Neosho, Mo., 1991. Recipient Best of Show award Okla. Mus. of Art, 1980, 1st Pl. award Arts Crafts & Design, 1982, Okla. Arts Workshops, 1984, Premium award, 1985, Sager Creek awards, Siloam Springs, Mo., 1994, 98, 99, 2002, 2003. Mem. Bartlesville Art Assn. (pres. 1971-72), Brush & Palette Club (show chmn. 1990-91, co-chmn. 1989-90), Art Central, Brush & Palette Club. Republican. Avocations: reading, boating. Home: 2300 Hendryx Point Dr Eucha OK 74342-9755 Office: Fox Hollow Studio 2300 Hendryx Point Dr Eucha OK 74342-9755

COURTNEY, CAROLYN ANN, school librarian; b. Plainview, Tex., Aug. 1, 1937; d. John Blanton and Geneva Louise (Stovall) Ross; m. Moyland Henry Courtney, Aug. 17, 1957; 1 child, Constance Elaine. BA summa cum laude, Wayland Bapt. Coll., 1969; MEd, W. Tex. State Coll., 1976; MLS, U. North Tex., 1990. Cert. elem., secondary, libr. tchr. 5th grade tchr. Hale Ctr. (Tex.) Ind. Sch. Dist., 1970-77, libr., 1977—. Bd. dirs. Plainview Cmty. Concerts, 2000—. Mem. LWV (bd. dir. 1970-75), DAR (Good Citizen chair 1981-85), Tex. State Tchs. Assn. (life), Tex. Classroom Tchrs. Assn. (sec. 1983-85), Tex. Libr. Assn., Delta Kappa Gamma (rsch. chair 1975-77, publs. chair 1984-86, pres. 2002--, scholarship 1975), Plainview Country Club. Methodist. Avocations: genealogy, travel. Home: 209 S Floydada St Plainview TX 79072-6665 Office: Hale Center Ind Sch Dist PO Box 1210 Hale Center TX 79041 E-mail: ccourtlibr@hotmail.com.

COURTNEY, DIANE TROSSELLO, library director, consultant; b. N.Y.C., June 29, 1951; d. Frank and Louise Trossello; m. Patrick K. Courtney, Sept. 2, 1972; 1 child, Heather. BA, NYU, 1972; MLS, Rutgers U., 1973; MPA, CUNY, 1995. Cert. profl. libr., N.Y. Outreach libr. Yonkers Pub. Libr., NY, 1972—75, youth svcs. libr., 1975—77, reference libr., 1977—82, head libr. info. svcs., 1983—87; cons. adult/young adult/media Westchester Libr. Sys., NY, 1987—95; dir. Larchmont Pub. Libr., NY, 1995—. Author (jour.) Bookmark, 1988, Nat. Video Resource Report #12, 1993. Founder, chair N.Y. State Pub. Libr. Sys. Video Consortium, 1989-96. Mem. ALA, N.Y. Libr. Assn. (chmn. ref. and adult svcs. sect. consumer health com. 1988-91, dir. membership 1993—, v.p. 1995, pres. 2002-03), Westchester Libr. Assn. (pres. 1991, v.p. 1990), Pi Alpha Alpha. Office: Larchmont Pub Libr 121 Larchmont Ave Larchmont NY 10538-3793 Office Phone: 914-834-1977. Business E-Mail: courtney@wlsmail.org.

COURTNEY, EDWARD, retired classics educator; b. Belfast, Northern Ireland, Mar. 22, 1932; came to U.S., 1982; s. George and Kathleen (Nicholson) C.; m. Brenda Virginia Meek, Dec. 18, 1962; children: Richard Marcus, Adam Matthew. BA, Trinity Coll., Dublin, Ireland, 1954; MA, Oxford U., 1957. Research lectr. Christ Ch., Oxford, 1955-59; lectr. in classics King's Coll., London, 1959-70, reader in classics, 1970-77, prof. Latin, 1977-82; prof. classics Stanford U., Calif., 1982-93, Ely prof. humanities, 1986-93; Gildersleeve prof. classics U. Va., Charlottesville, Va., 1993—2002, prof. emeritus, 2002—. Author: Commentary on the Satires of Juvenal, 1980, The Poems of Petronius, 1991, The Fragmentary Latin Poets, 1993, 2d edit., 2003, Musa Lapidaria, A Selection of Latin Verse Inscriptions,

1995, Archaic Latin Prose, 1999, A Companion to Petronius, 2002; editor: Valerius Flaccus, Argonautica, 1970, Juvenal, The Satires, A Critical Text, 1985, Statius, Silvae, 1990; joint editor: Ovid, Fasti, 1978, 4th edit., 1997. Mem. Am. Philol. Assn. Avocation: chess. E-mail: Edcourt2@cs.com.

COURTNEY, EUGENE WHITMAL, computer company executive; b. East St. Louis, Ill., Jan. 3, 1936; s. Eugene and Goldie Genell (Mitchell) C.; m. Barbara Ann Beckwith, Aug. 1, 1959; children: Kevin Eugene, Kyle Patrick. BSEE, Princeton U. with honors, 1957. Exec. v.p., gen. mgr., dir. Digital Sci. Corp., San Diego, 1970-75, pres., CEO, 1975-79; dir. Digital Sci./Europe, 1975-79; v.p. corp. devel. Topaz, Inc., San Diego, 1979, Nat. Computer Sys., Mpls., 1980-81, v.p., gen. mgr. scanning divsn., 1981-83, group v.p., 1983-88; exec. v.p., COO, dir. HEI Inc., Victoria, Minn., 1988-90, pres., CEO, 1990-99; dir., 1989-2000; prin. and dir. Triangle Industries, Inc., 1988—; pres., CEO RSI Sys., Edina, Minn., 1999-2001; prin. E.W. Courtney & Assocs., 2001—. Dir., chmn. Datakey, Inc., Mpls., 1995-2005; mem. Minn. Software Tech. Com., 1985-86; dir. Waters Instruments, Inc., Mpls., 2003—. Contbr. articles to profl. jours. Trustee, v.p. engrng. San Diego Hall of Sci., 1974-79; mem. State of Calif. gov.'s task force on edn. and industry, 1977-78; mem. Rancho Santa Fe (Calif.) Park and Recreation Bd., 1978; mem. tech. adv. bd. Minn. Dept. Corrections, Shakopee, 1985-86. Am. Electronics Assn. (nat. bd. dirs., chmn. San Diego coun. 1976-79, chmn. Minn. coun. 1993-96), Princeton Club (N.Y.C.). Avocation: print collecting. Home and Office: 7312 Claredon Dr Minneapolis MN 55439-1722

COURTNEY, WILLIAM HARRISON, marketing professional; b. Balt., July 18, 1944; s. Wilbur Harry Courtney and Mary Lee (Mitchell) Fleming; m. Laryssa Lapychak; children: William Jr., Mary Alison. BA in Econs., W.Va. U., 1966; PhD in Econs., Brown U., 1980. Fgn. svc. officer Dept. State, Washington, 1972-99; dep. exec. sec. NSC, The White House, Washington, 1987-88; dep. U.S. negotiator U.S.-Soviet Def. and Space Talks, Geneva, 1988-91; amb. Nuc. Testing and Nuc. Weapons Safety, Security, and Dismantlement, ACDA, Washington, 1991-92, Kazakhstan, 1992-95, 1995-97; spl. asst. to Pres. for Russia, Ukraine and Eurasia, White House, Washington, 1997-98; sr. advisor Fgn. Affairs Reorgn. U.S. Dept. State, Washington, 1998-99; sr. advisor U.S. Commn. Security & Coop. Europe, 1999; sr. v.p. nat. security programs DynCorp, Alexandria, Va., 2000—04; sr. mktg. exec. Computer Scis. Corp., Falls Church, Va., 2004—. Mem.: Coun. Fgn. Rels. Home: 3722 48th St NW Washington DC 20016-3213 Office: 3160 Fairview Park Dr Falls Church VA 22042-3160 Office Phone: 202-215-4243. Personal E-mail: courtneywmh@earthlink.net.

COURTOIS, BERNARD ANDRE, communications executive; BA, U. Mont., 1965, LLB, 1968. Bar: Que. 1969, Ont. 1984. Various regulatory, legal and exec. roles Bell Can., Ottawa, Canada, 1991—2003; pres., CEO, Info. Tech. Assn. Can., Ottawa, 2004—. Bd. dirs. Info. Tech Assn. Can., Ottawa, 1999—. Dir., treas. Nat. Gallery of Can. Found. Mem.: Internat. Inst. Communications (pres.). Office: Info Tech Assn Can 130 Albert St Ste 500 Ottawa ON Canada K1P 5G4 Office Phone: 613-238-4822. Business E-Mail: bcourtois@itac.ca.

COURTOIS, JEAN-PHILIPPE, information technology executive; DECS, The Ecole Superieure de Commerce, Nice, France. Product mgr. Memsoft; chanel sales rep. Microsoft France, 1984—86, So. Europe sales mgr., head mktg. dept., 1986—89, dep. gen. mgr., 1989—91, gen. mgr. sales and mktg., 1991—94, gen. mgr., 1994—98; v.p. Worldwide Customer Mktg., Microsoft, Redmond, Wash., 1998—2000; sr. v.p. Microsoft Corp., 2000—; pres., Europe, Mid. East & Africa Microsoft, Redmond, Wash., 2000—03, CEO, Microsoft Europe, Mid. East & Africa, 2003—. Office: Coeur Defense Tour B La Defense 4 100 Esplanade du Gen de Gau 92932 Paris France

COURVILLE, ARTHUR F., lawyer; b. Jan. 5, 1959; BA, Stanford U., 1981; MBA, JD, U. Calif., 1987. Bar: Calif. 1987. Atty. Gibson, Dunn & Crutcher, 1987—92; with Symantec Corp., Cupertino, Calif., 1993—, dir. legal dept., 1994—97, dir. product mgmt. Internet tools bus. unit, 1997, dir. legal dept., 1998, v.p., gen. counsel, 1999—. Bd. dirs. Bus. Software Alliance; trustee Software Patent Inst. Office: Symantic Corp 20330 Stevens Creek Blvd Cupertino CA 95014-2132 Office Phone: 408-517-8000. Office Fax: 408-517-8186. E-mail: artcourv@symantec.com.

COURY, ROBERT J., pharmaceutical executive; BS in indsl. engrng., U. Pitts., 1984. Founder, CEO, prin. owner Coury Cons., L.P., Pitts., 1989—2002; dir., vice-chmn. of bd., CEO Mylan Labs. Inc., Canonsburg, 2002—. Office: Mylan Labs Inc 1500 Corp Dr Ste 400 Canonsburg PA 15317 Office Phone: 724-514-1800.

COUSER, WILLIAM GRIFFITH, medical educator, academic administrator, nephrologist; b. Lebanon, N.H., July 11, 1939; s. Thomas Clifford and Winifred Priscilla (Ham) C. BA, Harvard U., 1961, MD, 1965; BMS, Dartmouth Med. Sch., 1963. Diplomate Am. Bd. Internal Medicine. Intern Moffitt Hosp./U. Calif. Med. Ctr., San Francisco, 1965-66, 66-67; resident Boston City Hosp., 1969-70; asst. prof. medicine U. Chgo., 1972-73; asst. prof. Boston U., 1972-77, assoc. prof., 1977-82; prof., head divsn. nephrology U. Wash., Seattle, 1982—2002, Belding Scribner prof. medicine, 1995—2004, affiliate prof. medicine, 2004—. Mem. sci. adv. bd. Kidney Found. Mass., Boston, 1974—82; mem. rsch. grant com. Nat. Kidney Found., N.Y.C., 1981—86; mem. rev. bd. for nephrology VA, Washington, 1981—84; mem. exec. com. Coun. on Kidney in Cardiovasc. Disease, Am. Heart Assn., Dallas, 1982—85; mem. pathology A study sect. NIH, chmn., 1988—89; subsplty. bd. in nephrology Am. Bd. Internal Medicine, 1988—92; dir. George M. O'Brien Kidney Rsch. Ctr. U. Wash., 1993—2003. Co-editor: Immunologic Renal Diseases, 1997, 2d edit. 2001; contbr. numerous articles, chpts., abstracts to profl. publs.; mem. editl. bd. Kidney Internat., 1982-96, Am. Jour. Kidney Diseases, Am. Jour. Nephrology, Jour. Am. Soc. Nephrology, editor-in-chief, 2001—. Served to capt. U.S. Army, 1967-69, Vietnam. Recipient Rsch. Career Devel. award NIH, 1975-80, Method to Extend Rsch. in Time award, 1991-97; fellow Nat. Kidney Found., 1971, NIH, 1973; grantee, 1974-2004. Fellow: ACP, AAAS, Western Assn. Physicians (coun.), Am. Assn. Exptl. Nephrology, Internat. Soc. Nephrology (coun. 1999, v.p. 2001—03, pres.-elect 2003—05, pres. 2005—), Am. Soc. Nephrology (coun. 1991—94, pres. 1996), Am. Assn. Physicians, Am. Soc. Clin. Investigation (v.p. 1983—84). Avocation: boating. Mailing: 16050 169th Ave NE Woodinville WA 98072 Office Phone: 425-990-4542. Business E-Mail: wgc@u.washington.edu.

COUSINEAU, KELLEY CUNNINGHAM, writer, artist; b. Milw., Nov. 5, 1963; d. Donald Robert Cunningham and Carol Ann Sulewsky; m. Edward Michael Cousineau, May 5, 1990; children: Samuel, Noah, Nathaniel. Student, Syracuse U., 1981—82, Parsons Sch. of Design, 1983—84; BA, Montclair State U., 1986. Art dir. McCann Erickson Direct, N.Y.C., 1990—92, Hakuhodo Advt., N.Y.C., 1992—94; sr. art dir. J. Walter Thompson Direct, N.Y.C., 1994—95; freelance writer, illustrator Maplewood, NJ, 2003—; prin., owner Kelley Cunningham Illustration. Contbr. articles to popular mags.; illustrator: Connecting Dots, 2004; illustrator others. Vol. Maplewood Schs. and Libr. Recipient Hon. Mention, NJ chpt. Am. Artists Profl. League, art show at Paper Mill Playhouse Gallery, 2004. Avocations: travel, running, poetry, reading. Home and Office: 1 Kensington Terr Maplewood NJ 07040 Personal E-mail: kelleycc@comcast.net.

COUSINO, JOE ANN, sculptor; b. Toledo, Nov. 17, 1925; d. George Carl and Lucille Caroline (Kocher) Bux; m. (div.); children: Paula Rene, Richard Nils. BA in Art, U. Toledo, 1947; stud., U. of Mex., 1948, U. So. Ill., 1953; attended, Internatl. Wkshp., Pietra Santa, Italy, 1980. Art tchr. Ctrl. YMCA & YWCA, Toledo, 1945-47; sculpture tchr. U. Tex. Jr. Coll., Gainesville, 1965, Defiance (Ohio) Coll., 1970, Bowling Green (Ohio) State Univ., 1971; instr. sculpture Sch. Art and Design Toledo Mus. Art, 2003—. Founder, pres. Toledo Potters Guild, 1951—55; Ohio rep. Am. Craft Coun., N.Y.C., 1960—62; pres. Fed. Art Socs. North Ohio, 1965—67, trustee, 1963—; co-chair midwest Kefauver com. Art in the Embassies Program, Dept. State, Washington, 1966; guest sculptor U. So. Calif., Berkley, 1981; sculptor instr. Toledo Botanical Gardens, 2005. One-woman shows include Toledo Mus. Art, Frank Ryan Gallery, Chgo., Forsythe Gallery, Mich., Mount St. Joseph Gallery, Cin., Arndt Mus. Art, Elmira, N.Y., Button Gallery Ltd., Saugatuck, Mich., Bowling Green State U. Grad. Ctr. Gallery, Ohio State Gallery, Kent State U. Gallery, Toledo Mus. Westgate Gallery, 2003, Exhbn. Bangkok, 1990, Sculpture In the Garden, Toledo Bot. Garden (sculpture honorarium), 2000; prin. sculptures include Ency. Britannica Hdqs., Rome, 1960, Scerbo Assocs., Cairo, 1960, Rio de Janeiro Brazil Dept. of Commerce, 1963, the John Leslie Stevens Meml., Oak Harbor, Ohio, Mame Gordon Meml., United Ch., Sylvania, Ohio, Greek Orthodox Holy Cathedral, Christ the King Ch., Toledo Hosp., Riverside Hosp., Toledo, U. Toledo, Med. Coll. Ohio, Toledo Botanical Gardens, U. Toledo Student Union Bldg., 1994, Way Libr., Perrysburg, Ohio, 1986, U. Toledo McMaster Astronom Bldg., 1989, Sister of St. Francis, Mother House Commons, Tiffon, Ohio, 1999, Toledo Opera Sculpture Honor Opera Condrs. Presentation, 1999, Schedel Arboretum and Gardens, Elmore, Ohio, 2001, Eagle Pitcher Bearing divsn. Bunting Brass of U.S.A., Engrng. Soc. Ohio, (in film) Folks, 20th Century Fox, Push Point: Sculpture, 1982 (Bronze medal); works featured in mags. and jours. including The Blade Newspaper, Toledo, 2000, Chgo. Tribune Newspaper, Ceramics Monthly Internat., 1965, U. Toledo Alumnai Mag., 2002. Featured spkr. UNICEF, Madras, India, 1984; bd. dirs. Toledo Arts Commn., 1978-84, Rare Books Ctr., U. Toledo, 1965-66; pres. Toledo Women's Art League, 1950-51. Recipient Outstanding Svc. in Field of Art award Fedn. of Arts, Toledo, 1967, Woman of Toledo Civic award, 1987, Touchstone nomination award Press Club of Toledo, 2000, Lifetime Achiever award, 2000; named Outstanding Intellectual of 21st Century, Internat. Biog. Ctr., London, 2001. Mem. Internat. Sculpture Ctr., Pan Pacific S.E. Asia Women's Assn., Scandinavian Club of Toledo. Episcopalian. Avocations: travel, folk dancing, jazz, photography. Home and Studio: 3717 Indian Rd Toledo OH 43606-2408

COUSINS, ROBERT JOHN, nutritional biochemist, educator; b. N.Y.C., Apr. 5, 1941; s. Charles Robert and Doris Elizabeth (Sifferlen) C.; m. Elizabeth Anne Ward, Jan. 25, 1969; children: Sarah, Jonathan, Allison. BA, U. Vt., 1963; PhD, U. Conn., 1968. NIH postdoctoral fellow biochemistry U. Wis., 1968-70; asst. prof. nutrition Rutgers U., 1971-74, assoc. prof., 1974-77, prof. nutritional biochemistry, 1977-79, prof. II (disting. Prof.), 1979-82, dir. grad. program in nutrition, 1976-82, mem. grad. programs in biochemistry, nutrition and toxicology; Boston family prof. human nutrition and biochemistry U. Fla., Gainesville, 1982—, eminent scholar chair, 1982—; dir. Nutritional Sci. Ctr., U. Fla., 1987—, grad. coun., 1990-93. Mem. nutrition study sect. NIH, 1980-84; mem. USDA Expt. Sta., dir. subcom. on human nutrition, 1987-2001; J.L. Pratt vis. prof. Va. Poly. Inst. and State U., 1980; Wellcome vis. prof. Auburn U., 1986; C. Malcolm Trout vis. scholar Mich. State U., 2003; mem. NAS, Inst. of Med. Commn. on opportunites in nutrition and food scis., 1991-93, Food & Nutrition Bd., 1997-2002, Dietary Reference Intakes Sci. Evaluation Commn., 1999—2001, Ad Hoc Bionutrition Commn., NIH, 1993; lectr. in field. Assoc. editor Jour. Nutrition, 1990-96; mem. editl. com. Ann. Revs. Nutrition, 1985-90, 96-99, assoc. editor, 1999-2004, editor, 2005-; contbg. editor Nutrition Revs., 1980-88; mem. editl. bd. FASEB Jour., 1994-99, Biol. Trace Element Rsch. 1982-2003; contbr. articles in nutritional biochemistry to profl. jours., chpts. to books Recipient Mead Johnson award in nutrition, 1979, Osborne and Mendel award for basic rsch. in nutrition, 1989, U. Conn. Disting. Alumnus award, 1991, Merit award NIH, 1992, USDA Sec.'s Honor award, 2000, Am. Coll. Nutrition Rsch. award, 2003, Bristol-Myers Squibb/Mead Johnson award for disting. achievement in nutrition rsch., 2003; Future Leader grantee Nutrition Found., Inc., 1973, NIH grantee, 1972—, Am. Coll. Nutrition Rsch. award, 2003. Mem. AAAS, NAS (elected mem. 2000), Am. Soc. Biochem. and Molecular Biology, Am. Soc. Nutrition Sci. (chmn. nominating com. elected officers 1983, coun. 1986-89, pres.-elect 1995-96, pres. 1996-97), Biochem. Soc. U.K., Soc. Exptl. Biology and Medicine (edit. bd. Proc. 1980-86), Am. Chem. Soc., Soc. Toxicology, Fedn. Am. Socs. Exptl. Biology (vice chmn. summer conf. 1985, chmn. summer conf. 1989, bd. dirs. 1989—, v.p. 1990-92, pres., chmn. bd. 1991-92, chmn. subcom. consensus conf. biomed. funding 1991-94, chmn. pub. affairs exec. com. 1992-93), Sigma Xi, Phi Kappa Phi, Gamma Sigma Delta (U. Conn. Disting. Alumni). Home: 4510 NW 20th Pl Gainesville FL 32605-3441 Office: U Fla Ctr for Nutritional Sciences 201 Food Sci & Human Nutr Bldg Gainesville FL 32611 Business E-Mail: cousins@ufl.edu.

COUSINS, SCOTT DAVID, lawyer; b. Pt. Pleasant, N.J., Dec. 15, 1961; s. David Neil and Margaret (Jones) C.; m. Dawn Lee Rieb, Mar. 10, 1990; children: Ryan Lee, Bradley Scott. BA, Stockton State Coll., 1989; MBA, JD, Widener U., 1992. Bar: Del. 1993, U.S. Dist. Ct. Del. 1993, U.S. Ct. Appeals (3d cir.) 2001. Sr. atty. Columbia Gas Sys., Wilmington, Del., 1992-95; atty. Young Conaway Stargatt & Taylor, Wilmington, 1996-97, The Bayard Firm, Wilmington, 1997-99, Greenberg Traurig LLP, Wilmington, 1999—. Office: Greenberg Traurig LLP The Brandywine Bldg 100 West St Ste 1540 Wilmington DE 19801 Office Phone: 302-661-7373. Office Fax: 302-661-7360. Business E-Mail: cousinss@gtlaw.com.

COUSINS, STEVEN, lawyer; b. St. Louis, Mo., Feb. 15, 1954; BA, Yale U., 1977; JD, U. Pa., 1980. Bar: Mo. 1981. Ptnr. Armstrong Teasdale LLP, St. Louis. Mem. bd. editors Am. Bankruptcy Law Jour., 1997—2000. Co-author: Basic Bankruptcy in Missouri, 1989. Bd. trustees St. Louis Art Mus.; co-chair Inner-City HS Summer Internship Program, St. Louis Pub. Schs. Found.; gen. counsel/exec. com. St. Louis Regional Chamber & Growth Assn.; vice chmn. bd. trustees St. Louis Children's Hosp.; mem. property and facilities com. BJC Health Sys. Named one of Am. Top Black Lawyers, Black Enterprise Mag., 2003. Fellow: Am. Coll. Bankruptcy; mem.: ABA, Bar Assn. Met. St. Louis, Mo. Bar, Am. Bankruptcy Inst., The Pvt. Bank. Office: Armstrong Teasdale LLP One Metropolitan Sq Ste 2600 Saint Louis MO 63102-2740 Business E-Mail: scousins@armstrongteasdale.com.

COUTANT, MARY MCELWEE, retired editor; b. Charleston, Ill., Oct. 14, 1919; d. William Willard Merritt and Mary Emma Turman; m. Laurence Allen McElwee (dec.); m. Albert Syze Coutant. Cert., Utterback's Bus. Coll., 1943. Catalog editor Ea. Ill. U., Charleston, 1967—86. Mem. Coles County Farm Bureau. Named to Wall of Tolerance, Nat. Campaign for Tolerance, 2002, Legion of Honor., NRA. Mem.: Kaskaskia Archeol. Soc., Ea. Ill. U. Found., Ea. Ill. U. Annuitants Assn., Coles County Hist. Assn. (v.p. 1992—98), Nat. Assn. Ednl. Office Personnel (life), Ill. Assn. Ednl. Office Personnel (life). Republican. Methodist. Home: 9228 N County Rd #1840 Charleston IL 61920

COUTERMARSH, EVA MARINA, personnel executive; b. Salisbury, Md., Oct. 29, 1967; d. Ernest Richard Jr. and Marina (Hernandez) C. BA in English and Comms., Mass. Coll. Liberal Arts, 1997. Cert. personnel cons. Nat. Assn. Personnel Svcs. Area coord. Experiment in Internat. Living, Brattleboro, Vt., 1992; adminstrv. asst. Nathan & Co., Pittsfield, Mass., 1992-93; personnel asst. Assoc. Staffing, Inc., Phoenix, 1993-94, staffing coord., 1994-95, sr. staffing coord., 1995-97, staffing mgr. Mesa, Ariz., 1997-98; sr. pers. cons. KNF&T, Boston, 1998-01, sales mgr., 2001—; dir. Hollister Assocs., Boston, 2002—04; divisional v.p. UBS Fin. Svcs., Houston, 2004—. Mem. Ariz. dist. 28 Republican Com., Scottsdale, 1997-98. Mem. NAFE, New Eng. Human Resources Assn., Mass. Assn. Pers. Cons., Houston Young Reps. Republican. Roman Catholic. Avocations: reading, travel, entertaining, outdoors. Office: UBS Fin Svcs 5065 Westheimer #1000 Houston TX 77056 Home: 2214 Melanie Park Dr Spring TX 77388-4186 Office Phone: 713-965-8122. Office Fax: 713-965-8199. Business E-Mail: eva.coutermarsh@ubs.com.

COUTSOFTIDES, THEODORE, surgeon; b. Cairo, Jan. 12, 1944; came to U.S., 1971; s. Nicolas Coutsoftides and Electra Lyras Butcher; m. Ilana Sklarz, Mar. 24, 1971; children: Michael, Lela. MS with distinction, Hebrew U., Jerusalem, 1967; MD with distinction, Hebrew U., 1970. Rsch. fellow Hebrew U., Jerusalem, 1970-71; fellow in gen. surgery Cleve. Clinic Found., 1971-73, Royal Victoria Hosp., Montreal, Que., Can., 1973-76; fellow in colon and rectal surgery Cleve. Clinic Found., 1976-77; chief colon and rectal surgery VA Hosp., Long Beach, Calif., 1977-79, U.Calif.-Irvine Med. Ctr., Orange, 1994—; attending surgeon St. Joseph's Hosp., Orange, 1979—, chief of staff, 1998—; pvt. practice Orange, 1979—. Asst. prof. surgery U. Calif.-Irvine, 1977-94, assoc. prof., 1994—; sec. med. staff St. Joseph's Hosp., 1994-96, vice chmn. med. staff, 1996-98. Contbr. articles to profl. jours. Bd. trustees Golden West Coll., Huntington Beach, Calif., 1995—, St. Joseph's Hosp., Orange, 1996—. WHO fellow, 1962-71. Fellow ACS, Am. Soc. Colon and Rectal Surgeons, Royal Coll. Surgeons Can., Royal Soc. Medicine, So. Calif. Soc. Colon and Rectal Surgeons; mem. Calif. Med. Assn., Orange County Med. Soc., Orange County Surg. Soc. (pres.-elect 1996). Avocations: fishing, skiing. Office: 1310 W Stewart Dr Ste 605 Orange CA 92868-3857 Office Phone: 714-532-2544. E-mail: coutsoftides@msn.com.

COUTTS, LAWRENCE ROBERT, publisher; b. La Crosse, Wis., Oct. 9, 1948; s. Robert Samuel and Margaret Yvonne (Hougen) C.; m. Linda Lee Florio, May 23, 1970; children: Melissa, Marcia, Michelle, Michael. BS in political science, Carroll Coll., Waukesha, Wis., 1970; MBA, U. Wis., Milw., 1976. Advt. mgr. The Ansul Co., Marinette, Wis., 1970; mgr. comm. and advt. Will Ross Inc., Milw., 1970—74; advt. specialist GE Med. Sys. divsn., Waukesha, Wis., 1974—77; mgr. advt. and promotion Pfizer Med. Sys. Inc., Columbia, Md., 1977—78; mktg. svcs. dir. Extrocorporeal Med. Spec., King of Prussia, Pa., 1978—80; pres. Coutts Enterprises LLC, Scottsdale, Ariz., 1980—; pub. Nephrology News and Issues and Hematology Oncology News and Issues, Scottsdale, Ariz., 1986—; co-founder, pres. Med. News & Issues, Inc., Medicalnews.com., Inc., HON&I, Inc. and NN&I, Inc., 2001—. Chmn. dialysis mktg. subcom. Health Industry Mfrs. Assn., Washington, 1979-80; patient advocacy task force, Am. Kidney Fund, 2000-03; pubs. adv. com., BPA Internat., Inc., 2001—. Recipient Bell Ringer award with direct mail campaign Bus./Profl. Advt. Assn. Milw., 1978, NKF Pub. Svc. award, 1988, 90. Republican. Lutheran. Avocations: golf, tennis, bridge, gardening, horseback riding. Home: 7335 East Quail Track Rd Scottsdale AZ 85262 Office: Medical News & Issues 13880 N Northsight Blvd Ste 101 Scottsdale AZ 85260-3666 Office Phone: 480-443-4635. E-mail: larry@medicalnews.com.

COUTTS, ROBERT B., electronics corporation executive; b. Westbury, N.Y. BSME, Tufts U.; advanced management courses, Harvard Univ. With General Electric Corp. (merged w/ Martin Marietta), 1972—93; v.p., Material Acquisition and Subcontract Management Martin Marietta (merged w/ Lockheed Martin), 1993—94, pres., Aero & Naval Systems, 1994—95; pres., Gov. Electronic Systems Lockheed Martin Corp., 1995—98, pres., COO electronics sectr, 1998—99, exec. v.p., Systems Integration, 1999—. Bd. dirs. Lockheed Martin. Former bd. dirs. local YMCAs, County United Way; bol. Greater Cin. and No. Ky. Area Boy Scout Coun.; bd. dirs. Balt. Symphony Orchestra; trustee Maryvale Prep. Sch.; bd. govs. Wesley Theol. Seminary. Mem. ASME, Tau Beta Pi. Office: Lockheed Martin Corp 6801 Rockledge Dr Bethesda MD 20817-1836

COUTURE, SISTER DIANE RHEA, sister, artist, educator; b. Hartford, Conn., Jan. 8, 1952; d. Rheal Paul Couture and Mary O'Shea. BA, Flagler Coll., 1979; student, U. North Fla., 1979—80; student in Pastoral Studies, Baptist Hosp., 1981—82; student in Spiritual Direction, San Pedro Ctr., 1989—92; student in Painted Glass, Klopfenstein Studios, 1995—98; student in Glass Painting, Millard Studio, 2002—03. Sister St. Joseph of St. Augustine, Fla., 1973. With Pine Hills Bike & Mower Shop, Orlando, Fla., 1968—72, Senco of Fla., Orlando, Fla., 1972—73; psych. counselor Flagler Hosp., St. Augustine, Fla., 1975—76; pastoral asst. St. Catherine Labouere Manor, Jacksonville, Fla., 1979—83; counselor Oncology Unit Mercy Hosp., Miami, Fla., 1983—87; youth minister St. Agnes Cath. Ch., Key Biscayne, Fla., 1987—89; dir. social svcs. Fla. Manor Nursing Home, Orlando, 1989—94; dir. Sisters of St. Joseph Archl. Stained Glass Studio, Orlando, 1992—99, Sisters of St. Joseph Stained Glass Studio, Orlando, 2000—. Adj. art prof. Flagler Coll., St. Augustine, Fla., 2000—05; spkr. in field. Prin. works include Meml. Window for 9/11 Victims, N.Y., Meml. Window, St. Francis of Assisi Nat. Shrine. Recipient Nat. Leadership award, Pres. U.S., 2003. Mem.: Stained Glass Assn. Am. Roman Catholic. Avocations: fishing, hiking. Office: SSJ Stained Glass 2745 Industry Ctr Rd 6 Saint Augustine FL 32084 Office Phone: 904-823-1918.

COUTURE, JEAN GUY, bishop; b. Quebec, Can., May 6, 1929; s. Odilon and Eva (Drolet) C. BA, PhB, Laval U., Quebec, 1949, L.Theol., 1953, L.Sc.Phys., 1959. Ordained priest Roman Cath. Ch., 1953. Prof. math. and scis. St. Georges H.S. and Coll., Beauce, Que., 1953-65, adminstr. coll., 1961-68; mem. adminstrn. Roman Cath. Diocese Quebec, 1968-75; bishop of Hauterive, 1975-79; bishop of Chicoutimi, 1979—2004; bishop emeritus of Chicoutimi, 2004—. Mem. Order of Can., Order of Red Cross (officer). Roman Catholic. Home: 4864 050 Ch St Éloi Jonquière PQ Canada G7X 7V4 E-mail: jeanguyc@sympatico.ca.

COUTURE, RONALD DAVID, art association administrator, web site designer, consultant; b. Ware, Mass., Dec. 1, 1944; s. Roy and Thelma Mary (Ledger) C.; m. Sandra Elaine Sharpe, Sept. 28, 1968; children: David, Meredith. Diploma, Butera Sch. Art, Boston, 1966. Graphic designer Sta. WGBH-TV Ednl. Found., Cambridge, Mass., 1970-73; promotion art dir. The Boston Globe, 1973-74, editl. design dir., 1974-77; asst. mng. art dir. N.Y. Times, 1977-78, assoc. mng. art dir., 1978-79, mng. art dir., 1979-84, dep. dir./editl. art, 1984-86, mng. dir./editl. art, 1986-88; owner, pres. Newsvision Inc., Mt. Kisco, N.Y., 1988-95. Owner Riverbend Design, 1996-2002, Riverbend Gallery and Workshop, 2003—; design cons. for Web and corp. pub.; design cons. Met. Cultural Alliance, Boston, 1972-77, IBM Corp. Pubs., 1991-93; guest lectr. Boston U. Sch. Comm., 1977; judge 62d and 64th Ann Exhibit, The Art Dirs. Club of N.Y., 1983; internat. editl. design Internat. Editl. Design Forum, N.Y.C., 1983. Contbr. articles in field to profl. jours. Mem. Westborough Planning Bd., Mass., 1977; apptd. regional rep. Ctrl. Mass. Regional Planning Bd., Westborough, 1977; apptd. chmn. Archtl. Rev. Bd., Mount Kisco, N.Y., 1978, 81, 84, 86, 89, 92, 95; mem. task force Labor Market Info. Network of N.Y. Labor Dept. and N.Y.C. Dept. Employment, 1979; bd. dirs. Blanchard Means Found., 1997—; mem. Brookfield Hist. Commn., 1999—. Recipient Gold medal set design New England Theater Conf., 1974, Gold medal newspaper design Soc. Newspaper Design, 1980; Lucy Stone Cmty. Svc. award, 2005. Mem. Soc. Newspaper Design (Gold medal chart design 1981, bd. dirs., nat. conf. dir. 1987-90), Art Dirs. Club N.Y., Am. Inst. Graphic Artist, Art Dirs. Club Boston, Nat. Computer Graphics Assn., Soc. Publ. Design Roman Catholic. Home: 44 Lake Rd Brookfield MA 01506-0537 Office: PO Box 537 9 S Maple St Brookfield MA 01506-0537

COUVILLION, DAVID IRVIN, federal judge; b. Simmesport, La., Oct. 27, 1934; s. J. Forest Couvillion and Leontine Rabalais. BS, La. State U., 1956, JD, 1959; LLM, Georgetown U., 1973. Bar: La. 1959. Pvt. practice, Marksville, La., 1959-67; adminstrv. asst. U.S. Congressman Speedy O. Long, Washington, 1967-72; assoc. McCollister, McCleary, Fazio and Holliday, Baton Rouge, 1974-85; spl. trial judge U.S. Tax Ct., Washington, 1985—. Mem. ABA, La. State Bar Assn. Office: US Tax Ct 400 2nd St NW Washington DC 20217-0002 Office Phone: 202-874-6097.

COVALIN - SHARFMAN, ALEJANDRO, biomedical engineer, consultant; b. Mexico, D.F., Mexico, July 9, 1969; s. Jorge Covalin and Guita Sharfman; m. Tanya Mizrahi, Dec. 16, 2000; children: Daniel Kai Covalin, Gabriel Soli Covalin. BS, Universidad Iberoamericana, Mexico City, 1994; MS, UCLA, 2005. New projects engr. MTF, Mexico City, 1994—96, new project dir., 1996—99. Recipient Academic excellence award, Universidad Iberoamericana, 1999; grad. fellow, U. Calif. Inst. for Mex. and the US, 2003—05, Internat. scholar, Consejo Nacional de Ciencia y Tecnologia, 2000—04. Mem.: IEEE (Exellence in Neural Engrng. 2005), Soc. for Neurosci., Biomed. Engrng. Soc., IEEE Engrng. in Medicine and Biology. Achievements include patents pending for techniques for modulating energy expenditure using deep brain stimulation. Office: UCLA Rm 7523 Boelter Hall 420 Westwood Plz Los Angeles CA 90095 Personal E-mail: acovalin@ucla.edu.

COVALT, ROBERT BYRON, chemicals executive; b. Chgo., Nov. 8, 1931; s. Byron L. and Thelma A. (Adams) C.; m. Virginia, Aug. 17, 1952; children: Karen Elizabeth Ryberg, David Byron. BSChemE, Purdue U., 1953, DEng (hon.), 1992; MBA, U. Chgo., 1967. Devel. engr. B.F. Goodrich Chem. Co., Avon Lake, Ohio, 1953-54; with Morton Chem. div. Morton Thiokol, Inc., 1956—, v.p. engring. and mfg. Chgo., 1973-78, group v.p., 1978-79, pres., 1979-87; pres. specialty chems. group, group v.p. Morton Thiokol, Inc., 1987-89; pres. splty. chems. group, group v.p. Morton Internat. Inc., 1989-90, exec. v.p., 1990-94; chmn., pres. and CEO Sovereign Specialty Chems., Inc., 1994—2002, dir., 1994—2004; pres. RBC Assocs., Inc., 2004—. Bd. dirs. CFC Internat. Served as 1st lt. USAF, 1954-56. Recipient Disting. Engring. Alumnus award Purdue U. Mem. AIChE, Am. Chem. Soc. Office: RBC Associates Inc 10 S Riverside Plz Ste 1800 Chicago IL 60606 *Success in business is truly based upon teamwork and the accomplishment of all members working in concert toward a common goal. In the end, it is the result of what you do with your people, not what you do to your people.*

COVAULT, CRAIG, editor; b. Dayton, Ohio, 1949; BS in Journalism, Bowling Green State U., 1971. Writer Urbana Citizen, 1971—72; sr. space editor Aviation Week & Space Tech., Washington, 1972—92, chief Paris bur., 1992—96, sr. editor, 1996—. Mailing: Aviation Week & Space Technology 1200 G St Washington DC 20005

COVENEY, RAYMOND MARTIN, JR., geology educator; b. Marlboro, Mass., Oct. 15, 1942; s. Raymond Martin and Rita Marie (Brani) C.; m. Anne Marie Keating, Feb. 22, 1965; children: Christine, Maureen, David. BS in Geology, Tufts U., 1964; MS in Geology, U. Mich., 1968, PhD in Geology, 1972. Asst. geologist N.J. Zinc Co., Hanover, N.Mex., 1968; geologist Dickey Exploration Co., Alleghany, Calif., 1969-70; grad. tchg. asst. U. Mich., Ann Arbor, 1966-70; from asst. prof. to prof. dept. geosci. U. Mo., Kansas City, 1971—, interim dean Coll. Arts and Scis., 1992-93, chair dept. geoscis., 1996—2005, dir. environ. studies, 1998—2004. Cons. ProSoCo., Inc., Kansas City, 1986-92, Midwest Rsch. Inst., Kansas City, 1986-91, Woodward Clyde, Kansas City, 1981, Hunt Midwest, 1997; review panel Earth and Environ. Sci. Finish Acad., 2004 Contbr. articles to profl. jours. Lt. (j.g.) USNR, 1964-66. Rackham Predoctoral Rsch. fellow, U. Mich., 1970-71; NSF Rsch. grantee, 1981-85, 90-93, 95-98; recipient N.T. Veatch award, 1988. Fellow Geology Soc. Am., Soc. Econ. Geologists (councilor 1993-96, trustee 1992-96, chair pubs. com. 1995-2001); mem. AAAS, Geol. Soc., Am. Geophys. Union. Roman Catholic. Achievements include research in metal-rich black shales and related deposits of molybdenum, zinc, platinum. Home: 5405 Locust St Kansas City MO 64110-2443 Office: U Mo 5100 Rockhill Rd Kansas City MO 64110-2481 Office Phone: 816-235-2980. E-mail: coveneyr@umkc.edu.

COVENSKY, EDITH, language educator, poet; b. Bucharest, Romania, Apr. 14, 1945; arrived in U.S., 1965, naturalized; d. Moshe Friedrich Michaeli and Gizy Heinish Michaeli Bizaoui; m. Harvey Covensky, June 26, 1969; children: Jeffrey, Laurice. BA, MA, Wayne State U., 1971, PhD qualifications, 1980. Tchr. Congregation Shaarey-Zedek, Southfield, Mich., 1968—75; instr. Hebrew Wayne State U., Detroit, 1987, lectr. Hebrew, 1998—. Author: Other Words, 1985, Syncopations, 1987, Night Poems, 1992, An Anatomy of Love, 1992, Partial Autobiography, 1993, Origins, 1994, Synesis, 1995, Jerusalem Poems, 1996, Poetics, 1997, After Auschwitz, 1998, Metamorphosis and Other Poems, 1999, Steps, 2000, Electrifying Love, 2000, Collage, 2002, Zohar, 2002, Anatomy of Love: Selected Poems, 1992-2002, 2005; contbr. poetry to numerous publs. Scholarship chair Hillel Found. of Met. Detroit, 2000—, bd. dirs., 1991—. Sgt. comm. corps Israeli Army, 1963—65. Finalist, Nat. Libr. Poetry, 1995; recipient Editor's Choice award, 1995, Internat. Poet of Merit award, 1996. Mem.: Internat. Soc. Poets (disting., nominee Poet of Yr. 1996). Avocations: reading, running, music, tennis. Home: 3816 Columbia Bloomfield Hills MI 48302 Office: Wayne State U 455 Manoogian Hall Detroit MI 48202 Office Phone: 313-577-6267. Home Fax: 248-865-9242. E-mail: edithpoet@aol.com.

COVENTRY, DEBRA ANN, mathematician, educator; b. Little Rock, Sept. 3, 1968; d. JC and Imogene Bryant; m. Jeffrey Raymond Coventry, Aug. 18, 1990; children: Kelsey Mae children: Samuel Armistead. BS in Edn., Henderson State U., 1989, MS in Edn., 1991; PhD, Okla. State U., 1998. Grad. asst. Henderson State U., Arkadelphia, Ark., 1990—91; tchr. Arkadelphia H.S., 1991—92; instr. Henderson State U., Arkadelphia, Ark., 1991—98, asst. prof., 1998—2002, assoc. prof., 2002—05; tchg. asst. Okla. State U., Stillwater, 1992—96, assessment of math. placement, 1994—94, corr. instr., 1996—98, calculus tutor evaluator, 1997—97, rsch. assoc., 1996—98, Tex. A&M, Texarkana, 2005—. Author: (multimedia education materials) Maple Picture Book; dir.(author): (high school course development) Functional Mathematics. Fin. officer Mothers of Preschoolers, Arkadelphia, 2000. Grantee Multimedia OSU, NSF, 1996—99. Mem.: Math. Assn. Am. (2nd vice chair 2000—00, 1st vice chair 2001—01, Okla.-Ark. sect. chair 2002—02). Office: Henderson State Univ 1100 Henderson St Arkadelphia AR 71999-0001 also: Tex A&M Texarkana Texarkana TX Business E-Mail: coventd@hsu.edu.

COVERT, EUGENE EDZARDS, aerospace engineer, aeronautics professor; b. Rapid City, SD, Feb. 6, 1926; s. Perry and Eda (Edzards) C.; m. Mary Solveig Rutford, Feb. 23, 1946; children: David H., Christine J., Pamela M., Steven P. BS, U. Minn., 1946, MS, 1948; ScD, MIT, 1958. Registered profl. engr., Mass.; chartered engr., U.K. Preliminary design group USNADC, Johnsville, Pa., 1948-52; mem. staff MIT Aerophysics Lab., 1952-63, assoc. dir., 1963-75, assoc. prof. aeronautics and astronautics, 1963-68, prof., 1968—97, T. Wilson prof. aeronautics, 1993-96, head dept. aeronautics and astronaut., 1985-90; T. Wilson prof. of aeronautics emeritus, 1997—. Cons. Bolt, Beranek & Newman, Inc., Boeing Co., CACI, Inc., Govt. Israel, Pratt and Whitney Aircraft divsn. United Tech., Hercules, Inc., MIT Lincoln Lab., Sverdrup Tech., U.S. Army Rsch. Office, Rand Corp.; chief scientist USAF, 1972—73; mem. panel Naval Aeroballistic Adv. Com., 1965—75; mem. NASA Aeronautical Adv. Com., 1985—89, Aeronautics and Space Engring. Bd., 1986—92, chmn., 1992; mem., chmn. USAF Sci. Adv. Bd., 1975—86, 1990—94; chmn. Power, Energet. and Propulsion panel Adv. Group for Aerospace R&D NATO, 1982—86; aero. policy com. Office Sci. and Tech. Policy, 1976—92; mem. Pres. Commn. for Investigation of Space Shuttle Accident. Mem. Blue Ribbon Com. on the Osprey, 2001; mem. nonadvocate rev. NASA Aeronautics Program, 2004. Served with USNR, 1943—47. Recipient Exceptional Civilian Sci. award USAF, 1973, 86, 94, Univ. Educator of Yr. award, Am. Soc. Aerospace Edn., 1980, Tech. Leadership award U. Minn. Alumni Assocs., 1993, Pub. Svc. award NASA, 1991, von Karman medal Adv. Group for Aerospace R & D, 1980, Wright Brothers Lectureship Aeronautics AIAA, 1997. Fellow AAAS, Royal Aero. Soc., AIAA (hon.; bd. dirs., Ground Testing award 1990, W.F. Durand lectr. for pub. svc. 1992, Wright Bros. lectr. 1997); mem. NAE, N.Y. Acad. Scis., Sigma Xi. Office: MIT 77 Massachusetts Ave Rm 9-335 Cambridge MA 02139-4307

COVEY, JAMES EDWARD, state representative; b. LA, Feb. 1, 1949; s. Edward M. and Joyce Elaine (Logan) Covey; m. Yvonne Debord; children: Justin Zane, Burke Wayne, Jill Vonn. BBA, U. Okla., 1973. Farmer, rancher, 1974—; mem. Okla. Ho. of Reps., 1997—, chmn. agr. and rural devel. com., asst. majority fl. leader; pres. J and Y Investments. With Okla. Army N.G., 1970—76. Mem.: Masons. Democrat. Office: State Capitol 2300 N Lincoln Blvd Rm 435 Oklahoma City OK 73105 Office Phone: 405-557-7325. E-mail: jamescorey@okhouse.gov.

COVEY, STEPHEN MERRILL RICHARDS, business consultant, speaker, author; b. Provo, Utah, Apr. 25, 1962; s. Stephen Richards and Sandra Renee (Merrill) C.; m. Jerolyn Shae Hutchings, Apr. 26, 1985; children: Stephen Hutchings, McKinlee Louise. BA magna cum laude, Brigham Young U., Provo, Utah, 1985; MBA, Harvard U., 1989. Leasing agt. Trammell Crow Co., Dallas, 1985-87; summer assoc. First Boston Corp., N.Y.C., 1988; pres., CEO Covey Leadership Ctr. (now FranklinCovey Co.), Provo, 1989, also bd. dirs.; now co-chairman FranklinCovey Co. Author: Seven Habits of Highly Effective People, 1990, Principle-Centered Leadership, 1991, First Things First, 1994, Seven Habits of Highly Effective Families, 1997, Living the Seven Habits, 1999, Seven Habits of Highly Effective Teens, 1998, Beyond the Seven Habits, 2003, The Eighth Habit, 2004, translations into multiple languages, numerous audio books. Recipient Mc-Feely award for significant contributions to mgmt. and edn., Internat. Mgmt. Coun., Thomas More Coll. Medallion for svc. to humanity. Mem. Lds Ch. Avocations: travel, reading, sports. Office: FranklinCovey Co 2200 W Parkway Blvd Salt Lake City UT 84119 Office Phone: 801-975-1776. Office Fax: 801-817-8313.*

COVEY, STEVEN K., lawyer; b. Chgo., Aug. 5, 1951; Bachelors, U. Ill., 1973; JD, DePaul U., 1977. Corp. sec. Navistar Internat. Corp., Warrenville, Ill., 1990—2000, dep. gen. counsel, 2000—04, sr. v.p., gen. counsel, 2004—. Office: Navistar Internat Corp 4201 Winfield Rd Warrenville IL 60555

COVIELLO, ROBERT FRANK, retail executive; b. Hartford, Conn., Dec. 20, 1941; s. James Joseph Coviello and Ann Frances (Links) Leary; m. Anne Elizabeth Lomasney, Oct. 22, 1966; 1 child, Michael James. Student, U. Conn., 1960-61, U. Madrid, 1961-62; grad., Machine Accts. Tng., 1963; student, Northeastern U., Boston, 1969. Data processing mgr. Chadwick-Miller, Inc., Boston, 1964-66; systems design analyst nat. accts. KeyData Corp., Watertown, Mass., 1969-70, systems designs mgr. N.Y.C., 1970-72, western regional mgr. Chgo., 1972-73; pres. Gallery of Gifts Shoppes, Inc. (doing bus. as Kitchen Etc.), Hampton, N.H., 1973-93; co-founder, exec. v.p. merchandising Kitchen Etc., N.H., Vt., Mass., Conn., 1993-95; pres., founder Housewares Tabletop Internat., 1995—; founder, pres. HTI Buying Group, Inc., N.H., 1998—. Chmn. Downtown Bd. of Trade, Dover, N.H., 1975-77, 82-83; pres. Merchants Assn. of Lilac Mall, Rochester, N.H., 1982-83. Dir. C. of C., Dover, 1983-86. With U.S. Army, 1966-68. Recipient Buyer's award of recognition Housewares Club New Eng., 1986, Potter's Club award Pfaltzgraff Co., 1986, 89. Mem. Retail Mchts. Assn. N.H. (past pres. 1985-87, dir. 1980-96, named Retailer of Yr. 1988), Am. Mgmt. Assn. (pres.'s Assn divsn. club), Gift Assn. Am. (dir. 1981-95), World Cup (St. Paul). Avocations: cooking, travel, flying, railroads, deep sea sports fishing. Office: HTI 47 Charles St Rochester NH 03867-2927 Office Phone: 888-484-3380. Personal E-mail: htibuying@verizon.net. E-mail: rfcoviello@yahoo.com.

COVILLE, ANDREA, public relations executive; BA in English Lit. and Journalism, U. N.H. With Franson & Assocs.; joined Infocom, 1984, Brodeur Worldwide, Boston, 1987, mng. ptnr., gen. mgr., pres., C.E.O., founding ptnr. Began career in New England Newspapers and magazines. Mem. Brodeur Worldwide Global Bd. Avocations: family activities, outdoor activities. Office: Brodeur Worldwide 855 Boylston St Boston MA 02116-2622

COVIN, DAVID L., retired political science professor; b. Chgo., Oct. 3, 1940; s. Odell Jerry and Lela Jane (Clements) Johnson; m. Judy Bentinck Smith, May 7, 1965; children: Wendy, Holly. BA, U. Ill., 1962; MA, Colo. U., 1966; PhD, Wash. State U., 1970. From asst. prof. to assoc. prof. govt. and Pan African studies Calif. State U., Sacramento, 1970—79, prof., 1979—, assoc. dean gen. studies, 1972-74, acting dir. Pan African studies, 1979-81, dir. Pan African studies, 1986—. Commr. Edn. Mgmt. and Evaluation Commn., 1977—81; trustee Congl. Black Caucus, Washington, 1977—92; adj. prof. Union Grad. Sch., 1979—82; mem. Criminal Justice Brain Trust; co-dir. Race and Democracy in Ams. Project, 1999—. Author: (novels) Brown Sky, 1987 (Best New Novel 1987 Calif. Black Faculty and Staff Assn. News), (book) Axe: The Unified Black Movement in Brazil and the Search for Political Power (1978-2002), 2005; contbr. articles to profl. jours.; mem. bd. editors Jour. Pan African Studies. Active Sacramento Black Area Caucus, 1972—, Com. Fair Adminstrn. Justice, Sacramento, 1985—; edn. co-chmn. Sacramento Black Cmty. Activist Com., 1985—90; founder, bd. dirs. Black Sci. Resource Ctr.; bd. dirs. Women's Civic Improvement Ctr.; co-chmn. Nat. Black Ind. Polit. Party, Sacramento, 1981—85. Recipient Cmty. Svc. award, Sacramento Area Black Caucus, 1976, Omega Psi Phi, 1982, All African People's Revolutionary Party, 1986, John L. Livingston Disting. Faculty Lecture award, 1992, medal of honor, Cooper Woodson Coll., 1998, Walter R. Bremond Cmty. Svc. award, Sacramento Black United Fund, 1998, Sacramento Observer medallion for edn., 2003, Cmty. Svc. award, Coll. Social Scis. and Interdisciplinary Studies, 2004. Mem.: Assn. Caribbean Studies, Western Polit. Sci. Assn. (mem. com. status blacks), Nat. Conf. Black Polit. Scientists (pres. 2003—05), Nat. Coun. Black Studies. Avocations: fishing, skiing, reading. Home: 4131 44th St Sacramento CA 95820-2829 Office: Calif State U 6000 J St Sacramento CA 95819-2605 Business E-Mail: covindl@csus.edu.

COVINGTON, ANN K., lawyer, former state supreme court justice; b. Fairmont, W.Va., Mar. 5, 1942; d. James R. and Elizabeth Ann (Hornor) Kettering; m. James E. Waddell, Aug. 17, 1963 (div. Aug. 1976); children: Mary Elizabeth Waddell, Paul Kettering Waddell; m. Joe E. Covington, May 14, 1977. BA, Duke U., 1963; JD, U. Mo., 1977. Bar: Mo. 1977, U.S. Dist. Ct. (we. dist.) Mo. 1977. Asst. atty. gen. State of Mo., Jefferson City, 1977-79; ptnr. Covington & Maier, Columbia, Mo., 1979-81, Butcher, Cline, Mallory & Covington, Columbia, Mo., 1981-87; justice Mo. Ct. Appeals (we. dist.), Kansas City, 1987-89, Mo. Supreme Ct., 1989—2001, chief justice, 1993-95; ptnr. Bryan Cave, St. Louis, 2001—. Bd. dirs. Mid Mo. Legal Services Corp., Columbia, 1983-87; chmn. Juvenile Justice Adv. Bd., Columbia, 1984-87. Bd. dirs. Ellis Fischel State Cancer Hosp., Columbia, 1982-83, Nat. Ctr. for State Cts., 1998—; chmn. Columbia Indsl. Revenue Bond Authority, 1984-87; trustee United Meth. Ch., Columbia, 1983-86, Am. Law Inst., 1998—. Recipient Citation of Merit, U. Mo. Law Sch., 1993, Faculty-Alumni award U. Mo., 1993; Coun. of State Govt. Toll fellow, 1988. Fellow Am. Bar Found.; mem. ABA (jud. adminstrv. divsn., mem. adv. com. on Evidence Rules, U.S. Cts.), Mo. Bar Assn., Boone County Bar Assn. (sec. 1981-82), Am. Law Inst., Acad. Mo. Squires, Order of Coif (hon.), Mortar Bd. (hon.), Phi Alpha Delta, Kappa Kappa Gamma. Office: Bryan Cave One Metropolitan Sq 211 N Broadway Ste 3600 Saint Louis MO 63102-2750

COVINGTON, DONALD KINGSLEY, JR., plywood sales executive; b. Newport News, Va., May 28, 1920; s. Donald Kingsley and Jessie Alexandria (MacNeill) C.; m. Minnie Virginia Seay, Mar. 13, 1943; children: Donald Kingsley III, Duncan Seay. BS in Aero. Engring., Parks Coll. St. Louis U., 1941; postgrad., U. Md., 1942. Lic. aircraft mechanic, pvt. pilot; cert. sales exec. Sales exec., engring. draftsman to project flight test engr. Glenn L. Martin Co., Balt., 1942-48; with Harbor Sales Co., Inc., Balt., 1948—, successively asst. sales mgr., sales mgr., gen. sales mgr., dir. and sec., pres., chmn. bd., chmn. emeritus, 2002—. Bd. dirs. YMCA Greater Balt. Area, 1963-78; trustee Md. Masonic Homes, 1982-85, 88-93; pres. Sales Exec. Coun. of Balt. Assn. Commerce, 1958; trustee Sales and Mktg. Execs. Accredition Inst., 1988—, SMEI Acad. Achievement. Mem. AIAA, Sales and Mktg. Execs. Internat. (cert. sales exec. Accreditation Inst., v.p., dir., trustee, Outstanding Svc. award 1981, 86, dir. emeritus 1991), Sash and Door Jobbers Assn. (dir.), Forest Products Rsch. Soc., Exptl. Aircraft Assn., Sales and Mktg. Execs. Balt. (hon.), Sales Execs. Coun. Balt. (past pres.), Rsch. Inst. Am. (charter), So. Sash and Door Jobber Assn. (past dir.), Ponderosa Pine Woodwork Assn., Plywood Pioneers Assn., Inst. Aero. Scis. (past sec. Balt. sect.), Balt.-Washington Lumber Sales Club, York Rite K.T., Shriners, Masons (past master, past pres. Knights of Mecca, sr. grand warden Grand Lodge of Md., 33 degree, grand rep. to Australia), Salmagundi Club. Office: 1000 Harbor Ct Sudlersville MD 21668-1818

COVINGTON, EILEEN QUEEN, secondary school educator; b. Washington, May 25, 1946; d. Louis Edward and Evelyn (Travers) Q.; m. Norman Francis Covington; children: Norman, Marina, Deanna, Trena. BS, D.C. Tchrs. Coll., 1971; postgrad., George Washington U., 1978-81. Tchr., coach Evan Jr. High Sch., D.C. Pub. Schs., Washington, 1971, Woodrow Wilson H.S., Washington, 1971-95, chmn. phys. edn. dept., 1971-75, 77-81, 1984-87, athletic dir., 1988-95, Anacostia Sr. H.S., Washington, 1995—, chmn. dept. health and phys. edn., tchr. health/phys. edn., 1995—, swim coach, 1996, softball coach, 1996—, student activities dir., 1995. Cons. Coaches Assn., Washington, 1973-76; athletic dir. Woodrow Wilson H.S., 1988-95; pres. DCAA Athletic Dir. Assn., 1997—; sports chmn. in field. Named Coach of Yr., Ea. Bd. Ofcls., 1977, Nat. Coaches Assn. 2d Region, 1982, 86, Nat. Fedn. State H.S. Assns., 2000, Winningest Coach Washington Coaches Assn., 1982, Coach of Yr. U.S., 1986, Coach of Yr. Washington Post, 1987, Athletic Dir. of Yr., 1989, Volleyball All-Interhigh Coach, 1989; recipient Billie Jean King award Women Sports and Am. Fedn. Coaches, 1980-81, Disting. Women award D.C. Polit. Women Com., 1996, D.C. Women's Bd. Affiliated Chs., 1996; inducted into Nat. High Sch. Athletic Coaches Assn. Hall of Fame, 2000. Mem. NAFE, Nat. High Sch. Athletic Coaches Assn. (bd. dirs., named to Hall of Fame 2000, regional dir. region II), D.C. Coaches Assn. (3rd v.p., v.p. volleyball 1981-83, softball coach 1990, Athletic Dir. of Yr. 1992, pres. 1993-96, chmn. crew coun. 1994, Regional Softball Coach of the Yr. 1993, Coach of the Yr. in Volleyball and Softball 1993, Softball Coach of Yr. 1994, 95, Coach/Athletic Dir. of Yr. 1988), NIAAA and D.C. Coaches Assn. (named Athletic Dir. of Yr. 1998, mem. dir.), Assn. Health, Phys. Edn. Athletics, D.C. High Sch. Coaches Club, Women's Sports Found., DCIAA (pres. athletic dir. 1997—). Home: 7601 Ingrid Pl Landover MD 20785-4624 Office: Anacostia Sr HS 16 & R Sts SE Washington DC 20020 Office Phone: 202-698-2173. Personal E-mail: ecovin@hotmail.com.

COVINGTON, GEORGE MORSE, retired lawyer; b. Lake Forest, Ill., Oct. 4, 1942; s. William Slaughter and Elizabeth (Morse) C.; m. Shelagh Tait Hickey, Dec.28, 1966 (div. May 1995); children: Karen Morse, Jean Tait, Sarah Ingersoll Covington; m. Barbara Schilling Trentham, Dec. 19, 1998. AB, Yale U., 1964; JD, U. Chgo., 1967. Assoc. Gardner, Carton & Douglas, Chgo., 1970-75, ptnr., 1976-95; atty. pvt. practice, Lake Forest, Ill., 1995—2005. Lectr. in field. Contbr. articles to profl. jours. Active Grant Hosp. of Chgo., 1974-95, chmn. of bd. 1990-95; bd. dirs. Grant Healthcare Found., 1995—, chmn. 1999—2001; trustee Chgo. Acad. Sci., 1974-85, pres., 1980-82; trustee, chmn. Ill. chpt. Nature Conservancy, Chgo., 1974-88; bd. dirs. Latin Sch Chgo., 1979-80, Open Lands Project, Chgo., 1972-86, Chgo. Farmers, 1994-96; bd. dirs., sec. Lake Forest Open Lands Assn., 1984—; bd. dirs., sec., treas. Les Cheneaux Found., 1978—; bd. dirs. Student Conservation Assn., 1996—, vice chmn., 1999-2002, chmn., 2002-04; bd. dirs. Little Traverse Conservancy, 1998—; mem. Bd. Fire and Police Commrs., Village of Lake Bluff, Ill., 1991—. With U.S. Army, 1967-69. Mem. ABA, Ill. Bar Assn., Lake County Bar Assn., Chgo. Bar Assn., Univ. Club (bd. dirs. 1985-88), Commonwealth Club, Lawyers Club, Shoreacres (Lake Bluff, Ill.), Les Cheneaux Club (Cedarville, Mich.), Lambda Alpha. Office: 500 N Western Ave Ste 204 Lake Forest IL 60045-1955 Office Phone: 847-735-8764. Personal E-mail: gcovington@sbcglobal.net.

COVINGTON, GERMAINE WARD, municipal agency administrator; BS in Social Work, Ind. State U., 1966; MA in Urban Studies, Occidental Coll., 1972; postgrad., Harvard U., 1998. Budget analyst City of Seattle, Office Mgmt. and Budget, 1978-87; cmty. affairs mgr. City of Seattle, Engring. Dept., 1987-90, property and ct. svcs. mgr., 1990-91, dir. exec. mgmt., 1993-94, acting dir. drainage and wastewater utility, 1993-94; dep. chief staff City of Seattle, Mayor's Office, 1991-93; dir. office for civil rights City of Seattle, 1994—. Office: Seattle Office for Civil Rights 700 3rd Ave Ste 250 Seattle WA 98104-1827 Office Phone: 206-684-4500. E-mail: germaine.covington@seattle.gov.

COVINGTON, JAMES EDWIN, government agency administrator, psychologist; b. Wadesboro, NC, June 26, 1943; s. James Edwin and Louise (Memory) C.; m. Linda Doreen Davis, May 31, 1971 (div. Feb. 1982); children: James Edwin III, Bradley Davis; m. Lisa Marie Ryglewicz, June 26, 2004. BA, Duke U., 1965; MSc, N.C. State U., 1977, PhD, 1981. Lic. psychologist, N.C. Commd. 2d lt. U.S. Army, 1967, advanced through grades to col., 1989, ret., 1992, spl. advisor for arms control and chem. demilitarization Dept. of Def. Washington, 1993—2001, chief Chem. Biol. Def. Divsn. Army Acquisition Office, 2001—. Psychol. cons., Alexandria, Va., 1992—; first prof. mil. sci. Duke U., Durham, N.C., 1983; primary planner for retrograde U.S. Chem. Weapons from Germany, 1989; del. 1st U.S. visit to former Soviet Chem. Weapons Sites in Russia, 1990; mem. U.S. delegation for negotiation of worldwide Chem. Weapons Conv., Geneva, 1992; advisor U.S. Delegation to Chem. Weapons Preparatory Commn., The Hague, 1993; mem. oversees prog. to destroy all U.S. chem. weapons as mandated by the worlwide Chem. Weapons Conv. Decorated Def. Superior Svc. medal, Purple Heart with oak leaf cluster, Bronze Star, Air Medal with 7 oak leaf clusters, Army Commendation Medal with valor device, 5 oak leaf clusters, others; decorated for heroism at Hamburger Hill, Vietnam, 1969. Mem. APA, Va. Psychol. Assn. Methodist. Avocations: military history, music, physical fitness. Home: 5909 Dawes Ave Alexandria VA 22311-1116 Office: Office of Asst Sec of the Army 2511 Jefferson Davis Hwy Arlington VA 22202-3926 Office Phone: 703-604-7270. Personal E-mail: nedcovington@aol.com. Business E-Mail: james.e.covington@us.army.mil.

COVINGTON, ROBERT NEWMAN, law educator; b. Evansville, Ind., Sept. 9, 1936; s. George Milburn and Roberta (Newman) C.; m. Paula Anne Hattox, July 29, 1972. BA, Yale U., 1958; JD, Vanderbilt U., 1961. Bar: Tenn. 1961. Asst. prof. law Vanderbilt U., Nashville, 1961-64, assoc. prof., 1964-69, prof., 1969—. Chair faculty senate Vanderbilt U., 1988-89; vis. prof. U. Mich., 1971, U. Calif., Davis, 1975-76, U. Tex., 1983; adminstrv. law officer Calif. Agrl. Labor Rels. Bd., 1975-76; cons. Tenn. Dept. Labor, 1972, Tenn. Law Libr. Commn., 1965-75. Author works in field. Mem. ABA, Tenn. Bar Assn., Am. Arbitration Assn., Tenn. Employment Rels. Rsch. Assn. (pres.-elect 2000-01, pres. 2001-02), Order of Coif, Univ. Club (Nashville), Phi Beta Kappa. Democrat. Episcopalian. Home: 907 Estes Rd Nashville TN 37215-1008 Office: Vanderbilt U Sch Law 21st Ave S Nashville TN 37203 Office Phone: 615-322-0036. Business E-Mail: robert.covington@law.vanderbilt.edu.

COVINGTON, VONDA RUSSELL, lawyer; b. Kenosha, Wis., Feb. 7, 1958; d. Kenneth Kirk Marshall and Wanda Ann Belmont; m. Ronald L. Russell, Aug. 18, 1990; 1 child, Samantha. BA in Psychology, U. Calif., San Diego, 1980; MA in Psychology, Rice U., 1984; JD, U. Houston, 1992. Bar: Oreg. 1992, 1993 (Tex.). Law clk. Martin, Herring & Fjeldal, Houston, 1990—91; office mgr. Challenger Drywall, Inc., 1991—92; law clk. Fjeldal & Assocs., Houston, 1993, atty., 1993—95; pvt. practice Houston, 1995—. Mem.: Coll. State Bar Tex., Houston Bar Assn. (mem. family law sect.), Internat. Assn. Collaborative Profls., Alliance Collaborative Family Law Attys. (founder, bd. mem.), Assn. Women Attys. Unitarian-Universalist. Avocations: rock climbing, camping, weightlifting. Office: Ste 1515 1314 Texas Houston TX 77002 E-mail: vonda@pdq.net.

COVINO, CHARLES PETER, chemicals executive; b. West New York, N.J., Dec. 9, 1923; s. Isaac L. and Rose (Luongo) C.; m. Sylvia A Covino, Dec. 27, 1947; 1 child, Candida. Student, U. Ala., 1941-43; BBA, Manhattan Coll., 1951; MBA, NYU; Dr honoris causa, Philathea U., Can., 1963; DrSc (hon.), Manhattan Coll., 1995. Chmn. bd., CEO Gen. Magnaplate Corp., Linden, N.J. Mem. Hoover Inst./UN Coun. for Global Polit. and Econ. Transition, 1994; lectr. in field. Contbr. over 28 articles to profl. jours. Recipient Air Force Assn. N.J. Wing award for space contbns., 1960, Royal Cross Austria Prince Rudolph, 1964, Eloy Alfaro Found. of Panama award, 1965, Manhattan Coll. Outstanding Alumni award, 1972, Vaaler award Chem. Engring. Inst., 1976, Indsl. Rsch. 100 award for Material Devels. of Yr., 1964, 68, 78, ASM award for Disting. Svc. and Contbns. to Metals Industry, 1967, Cookware Design of Yr. award Housewares Mfr.'s Assn., 1967, award of yr. Packaging Inst., 1967-68, Outstanding New Product award Popular Sci. mag., 1967, Packaging Design award Design Inst., 1968, Outstanding USA Design award U.S. Info. Agy., 1968, Italian-Am. Man of Sci. award 1978, Churchill Medal of Wisdom award, 1995, Heros of Chemistry award Am. Chem. Soc., 1996, Am. Chem. Soc. award, 1996, Thomas Alva Edison award for best N.J. invention of Yr., 1999; named to N.J. Inventors Hall of Fame, 1994-95, Manhattan Coll. Athletics Hall of Fame, 1998, N.J. Corp. Inventors Hall of Fame, 1999. Achievements include over 101 patents and trademarks; invention of non-destructive testing method for thick lead shielding in nuclear reactors, ultrasonic test method for nuclear tubing used for condensors, various metal surface enhancement processes, low-cost (permanent composite) mold form by plasma spray method; featured in Guinness World Book of Records for world's slipperiest solid lubricant. Office: Gen Magnaplate Corp 1331 Route 1 & 9 N Linden NJ 07036 E-mail: cpcovino@aol.com.

COVINTREE, GEORGE E., retired anesthesiologist; b. Camden, NJ, Apr. 18, 1913; s. Clarence C. and Jessie E. (Snyder) C.; m. Laura Claye Fraley, July 11, 1942 (dec.); children: George Edward Jr., David Elwood, Ruth Ann. AB, Temple U., 1935; MD, Hahnemann U., 1941. Diplomate Am. Bd. Anesthesiology. Intern Deaconess Hosp., Cin., 1941-42; resident West Jersey Hosp., Camden, Berlin, Voorhees, 1947-49, mem. staff, 1956—, chief dept. anesthesiology, 1957-78, emeritus chief dept. anesthesiology, 1979—; fellow in anesthesiology Hahnemann Med. Coll., Phila., 1949-50; mem. staff Hahnemann Hosp., Phila., 1950-56; cons. anesthesiology Vets. Hosp., Phila., 1953-58; instr. anesthesiology Hahnemann Med. Coll., 1950-52, asst. prof. anesthesiology, 1952-56. Founder Annual NJ Postgrad. Anesthesia Seminar, 1959. With U.S. Army M.C., 1942-46. Fellow Am. Coll. Anesthesiologists; mem. AAAS, AMA, Am. Soc. Anesthesiologists, Internat. Anesthesia Rsch. Soc., Med. Soc. NJ, NJ State Soc. Anesthesiologists (Disting. Svc. award 1981), NY Acad. Scis. E-mail: doccovintree@att.net.

COVITZ, CARL D., state official, real estate company officer; b. Boston, Mar. 31, 1939; s. Edward E. and Barbara (Matthews) C.; m. Aviva Habert, May 15, 1970; children: Philip, Marc. BS, Wharton Sch., U. Pa., 1960; MBA, Columbia U., 1962. Product mgr. Bristol-Myers Co., N.Y.C., 1962-66; dir. mktg. Rheingold Breweries, N.Y.C., 1966-68; nat. mktg. mgr. Can. Dry Corp., N.Y.C., 1968-70; v.p. mktg., dir. corp. devel. ITT/Levitt & Sons, Lake Success, N.Y., 1970-73; owner, pres. Landmark Communities, Inc., Beverly Hills, Calif., 1973-87, pres., 1989-91; dep. sec. HUD, Washington, 1987-89; sec. bus., transp. and housing State of Calif., Sacramento, 1991-93; pres. Landmark Capital, Inc. (formerly Landmark Communities, Inc.), 1993—; chmn. bd. Century Housing Corp., 1995-2000. Bd. dirs. Arden Realty Group, chmn. acquisition com., Molina Healthcare, Inc., 2002-03; chmn. bd. Fed. Home Loan Bank, San Francisco, 1989-91, Century Housing Corp., 1995-2003; trustee SunAmerica Annuities Funds, 2000—, Phoenix Kane Anderson Mut. Funds, 2000—. Exec. com. Presl. Commn. Cost Control and Efficiency (Grace Commn.); co-chmn. Dept. Def. Task Force; past chmn. ops. com. Mus. Contemporary Art Los Angeles; chmn. L.A. County Delinquency and Crime Commn.; dir. Columbia U. Grad. Bus. Sch. Alumni Assn. Mem. Young Pres. Orgn.; chmn. L.A. Housing Authority Commn., 1989-91. Office: 9595 Wilshire Blvd Beverly Hills CA 90212-2512 Office Phone: 310-273-7320. Business E-Mail: cdc@landmarkcapital.com.

COVUCCI, GEORGE E., lawyer; b. Aug. 15, 1951; BA, CCNY, 1972; JD, Georgetown Univ., 1976. Bar: Va. 1976, D.C. 1977. Ptnr., Real Estate Practice Group Arnold & Porter, Washington. Contbr. articles to profl. jours. Mem.: ABA, Va. State Bar, D.C. Bar. Office: Arnold & Porter 555 Twelfth St NW Washington DC 20004-1206 Office Phone: 202-942-5026. Office Fax: 202-942-5999. Business E-Mail: george.covucci@aporter.com.

COWAN, ANDREW GLENN, television writer, producer, performer; b. Phila., Dec. 24, 1951; s. Raymond Harold and Audrey Rene (Federman) C. BA in Psychology, The Am. U., 1973; MS in Broadcasting, Boston U., 1975. News reporter, writer Sta. WLYH-TV, Lancaster, Pa., 1975; announcer, news reporter Sta. WHUM, Reading, Pa., 1975; comedy performer various clubs, nationwide, 1976-81; talent coordinator, writer, performer, segment producer The Merv Griffin Show, Paris, L.A., N.Y.C., Atlantic City, and Las Vegas, 1981-86; freelance writer TV series Cheers Paramount, L.A., 1985-87; host, writer L.A. Singles, Group W Cable, L.A., 1985-86; freelance writer TV series Throb Taft Entertainment, L.A., 1986; story editor TV series Take Five Imagine Entertainment, CBS, L.A., 1987; freelance writer TV series Family Ties Paramount, L.A., 1988; staff writer, performer The Pat Sajak Show, CBS, L.A., 1988-90; staff writer Into the Night ABC, 1990; staff writer My Talk Show Second City Entertainment, 1990; freelance writer for Jay Leno The Tonight Show, NBC, L.A., 1990; Walt Disney Prodns., 1991; creator, writer TV pilot Howie Republic Pictures, L.A., 1991; staff writer TV pilot Only Human CBS Entertainment, 1991-92; freelance writer TV series Seinfeld Castle Rock Entertainment, L.A., 1994, then program cons., 1994-95; story editor TV series Double Rush Shukovsky-English Entertainment, L.A., 1994; exec. cons. TV series 3rd Rock from the Sun Carsey-Werner Co., L.A., 1995-96; exec. prodr., co-creator, writer, host tv pilot Evening Stew, 1996-97; writer, tv pilot Barely Fitz, 1999, Outer Child, 2000, Howie, 2001. Vocalist various clubs and venues, L.A., 1987—; vocalist pilot theme song Life As We Know It, Second City Entertainment, 1990; voice-over announcer Aerospace Ednl. Svcs., L.A., 1985-89, Cutler Prodns., CBS Morning Zoo, L.A., 1990; host, writer, prodr., co-dir. video short Six Minutes, Showtime, The Movie Channel, Bravo, PBS, 1989-91. Voice-over actor Seinfeld, 1994, 3rd Rock from the Sun, 1995, Best Damn Sports show Period, 2002, Time-Warner Audio Books, Lucas Films, Star Wars-Dark Empire, The Audio Drama, 1994, Star Wars-Dark Empire 2, 1995; writer, co-host (on internet) Up & Down Guys, 2000; contbr. articles to profl. jours Recipient CableAce award for best short-form programming spl., 1991; named one of 50 Creatives to Watch, Variety, 1996. Mem. AFTRA, Writers Guild Am. West. Avocations: cartooning, playing keyboards. *You're better off creating your own opportunities, rather than waiting for someone to create them for you. Ignore the naysayers. And if you listen to conventional wisdom, develop a serious case of amnesia afterwards.*

COWAN, BARTON ZALMAN, lawyer; b. Cleveland, Mar. 3, 1934; s. Milton Jerome and Clara (Umans) Cowan; m. Teri Anne Thomas, June 25, 1961; children: Pamela B., Cynthia R. Stewart, Susan L. Kraft. BA (hon.), U. Mich., 1955; JD cum laude (hon.), Harvard U., 1958. Bar: Ohio 1958, Pa. 1962, U.S. Dist. Ct. (we. dist.) Pa., U.S. Ct. Appeals (3d, 4th, and DC cir.), U.S. Supreme Ct. Assoc. Eckert, Seamans, Cherin, and Mellott, Pitts., 1961—67; mem. Eckert, Seamans, Cherin, and Mellott, LLC, Pitts., 1968—99, sr. counsel, 2000—. Chmn. lawyers com., mem. policy com. Atomic Indsl. Forum, Washington, 1981—87; chmn. lawyers com. Nuc. Mgmt. and Resource Coun., Washington, 1988—90; vis. prof. Coll. Law W. Va. U., 2001—. Bd. dirs. Union for Reform Judaism, 2002—; life trustee Pitts. chpt. Am. Jewish Com.; life trustee, past pres. Rodef Shalom Congregation, Pitts.; mem. bd. of mgmt. Internat. Nuc. Law Assn., 2003—; mem. bd. overseers Jewish Inst. Religion, 1986—2003; mem. bd. govs. Hebrew Union Coll., Inst. of Religion, 1992—2000; bd. dirs. ARZA World Union N. Am., 1992—2000, bd. overseers, 1988—; mem. Pitts. Symphony Soc. 1st lt. USAF, 1958—61. Recipient Clyde A. Lilly Award, Atomic Indsl. Forum, Inc., 1985, Leadership Award, Hebrew Inst. Pitts., 1991, Dedication and Commitment to Jewish Edn. Award, Jewish Edn. Inst., 1992, Am. Jewish Com. Human Rels. Award, 1996, Bonds Award, State of Israel, 2002. Mem.: ABA (chmn. energy resources law com. tort and ins. practice sect. 1986—87), Internat. Nuc. Law Assn., Allegheny County Bar Assn., Pa. Bar Assn., Duquesne Club. Republican. Office: Eckert Seamans Cherin and Mellott LLC 600 Grant St Ste 44th Pittsburgh PA 15219-2702 Personal E-mail: teribart61@aol.com. Business E-Mail: bcowan@eckertseamans.com.

COWAN, DALE HARVEY, internist, lawyer; b. Cleve., Jan. 25, 1938; s. Milton Jerome and Clara (Umans) jC.; m. Deborah Wolowitz, Jan. 28, 1967; children: Rachel, Morris Benjamin, William Ezra. AB, Harvard U., 1959, MD, 1963; JD, Case Western Res. U., 1981. Diplomate Am. Bd. Internal Medicine with subspecialty cert. in hematology and med. oncology. Bar: Ohio 1981. Intern Cleve. Met. Gen. Hosp., 1963-64, resident, 1964-65, 67-70; practice medicine specializing in internal medicine, hematology and oncology; dir. hematology and oncology Marymount Hosp., Cleve., 1982-2001; asst. prof. medicine Case Western Res. U., Cleve., 1970-75, assoc. prof., 1975-84, clin. prof. environ. health scis., 1985—; assoc. Health Sys. Mgmt. Ctr., 1982-90; of counsel Burke, Haber & Berick, 1984-86; pres. med. staff Parma (Ohio) Cmty. Gen. Hosp., 1997-98; med. dir. Cmty. Oncology Group Cleve. Clinic Found., Cleve., 1999—. Spl. cons. President's Commn. on Bioethics, Washington, 1981-82; nat. adv. coun. Nat. Heart Lung and Blood Inst., Bethesda, Md., 1982-85. Author: Preferred Provider Organizations, 1984; co-editor: Human Organ Transplantation, 1987; contbr. articles to profl. jours. Bd. dirs. Bur. Jewish Edn., 1977-87, Northeast Ohio affiliate Am. Heart Assn., 1982-86; pres. Ohio/W.Va. Oncology Soc., 1990-94; trustee No. Ohio Cancer Resource Ctr., 1998-2001, chmn. 1999-2001. Lt. comdr. USPHS, 1965-67. Lt. comdr. USPHS, 1965—67. Recipient David J. Greenburg Service Award, Am. Health Lawyers Assn., 1995. Fellow ACP, Am. Coll. Legal Medicine (bd. govs. 2001—); mem. AMA, Am. Soc. Hematology, Am. Soc. Clin. Oncology, Am. Assn. for Cancer Rsch., Am. Health Lawyers Assn. (bd. dirs. 1988-94), Am. Soc. Law and Medicine, Acad. Medicine Cleve. (pres. 1997-98), Cleve. Med. Libr. Assn. (pres. 2004-05), Ohio State Bar Assn., Greater Cleve. Bar Assn. Home: 19600 Shaker Blvd Cleveland OH 44122-1830 Office: 6100 W Creek Rd Ste 15 Cleveland OH 44131-2133 Office Phone: 216-524-7979. E-mail: cowand@ccf.org.

COWAN, DOUGLAS LEO, lawyer; b. L.A., May 22, 1943; s. Douglas L. and Mildred R. (Zimmerman) C.; m. Bettina VanDeKamp, Sept. 12, 1964 (div. Jan. 1972); 1 child, Kristina; m. Corinne Ellen Crawley, July 21, 1973; children: John, Greg. BA, Wash. State U., 1965; JD, U. Wash., 1968. Bar: Wash. 1968, U.S. Dist. Ct. (we. dist.) Wash. 1969. Ptnr. Shafer, Mitchell & Cowan, Seattle, 1969-74, Kinzel, Cowan & Allen, Bellevue, Wash., 1978-87; pros. atty. City of Bellevue, 1974-78; ptnr. Cowan Hayne & Fox, Bellevue, 1988-98; founder The Cowan Law Firm, Bellevue, 1998—. Pres. Wash. Found. for Criminal Justice, Bellevue, 1987—98. Mem. Nat. Coll. for DUI Def. (founder, dean 1996-97), Wash. Assn. Criminal Def. Lawyers (bd. govs. 1987-88), East King County Bar Assn. (pres. 1979). Office: Cowan Smith Kirk Law Firm 4040 Lake Washington Blvd NE #300 Kirkland WA 98033

COWAN, EDWARD, journalist, editor; b. Bklyn., Nov. 14, 1933; s. Marcy Hamilton and Jennie (Taleisnik) C.; m. Ann Louise Wrubel, July 1, 1962; children: Jeffrey Wrubel, Emily Martha, Rachel Jennifer. BA, Columbia Coll., 1954; MA in Econs., Johns Hopkins U., 1960. With UPI, 1957-62; with N.Y. Times, 1962-86, banking reporter, 1963-65, Benelux corr. Brussels, 1965-66, corr. London bur., 1966-67, corr. Toronto (Can.) Bur., 1967-72, Washington corr., 1972-83, Washington econs. editor, 1983-86; Washington mgr. Ried, Thunberg and Co., Inc., 1986-99; assoc. editor Am. Enterprise Inst., 2000—02; pres. Editorial Svc., 2003—. Instr. econs. Johns Hopkins, 1956-57; cons. U.S. Bur. Budget, 1963, Nat. Inst. Standards and Tech. 2001, Congl. Budget Office, 2003, World Bank, 2004, Dawson Assocs., 2004; co-founder Chronicle, Barton, Vt., 1974; vol. tutor, D.C. Pub. Schs., 2000-. Author: Oil and Water: The Torrey Canyon Disaster, 1968; contbr. to The Economist, 1977-90, op-ed pages Washington Post, Washington Times, L.A. Times, New Eng. Regional Rev., Jour. Commerce, Indonesnian Daily News, Jakarta Post, Milw. Jour. Sentinel, Edn. Week, Coos County (N.H.) Democrat, Littleton (N.H.) Courier, and Barton (Vt.) Chronicle. Dir. and treas. Anne Frank Ho., 1987—90; bd. dir. Cmty. Coun. Homeless, 2005—. With U.S. Army, 1954—56. Fellow Knight Internat. Press; recipient Chanler Hist. Essay prize Columbia, 1954, Gerald R. Loeb Found. award for fin. reporting, 1971. Mem. Nat. Econs. Club (v.p. programs 1989-90, pres. 1990-91, chmn. 1991-93, bd. govs. 2003-05). Home: 3924 Harrison St NW Washington DC 20015

COWAN, ERIC WARD, lawyer; b. Boston, Nov. 26, 1957; s. Frederick S. and H. Ellen (Glazer) Cowan. BLS, Boston U., 1981; JD, Cath. U. Am., 1987. Bar: Pa. 1987, Mass. 1988, Md. 1989. Atty. State Mut. Cos., Worcester, Mass., 1987-88; assoc. Frank Bernstein Conaway & Goldman, Balt., 1988—; ptnr., bus. dept. Thelen Reid & Priest LLP, Washington. Bd. dir. Nat. Found. for Ileitis & Colitis, Boston, 1980—82. Mem.: ABA. Democrat. Jewish. Office: Thelen Reid & Priest LLP 701 Pennsylvania Ave NW Ste 800 Washington DC 20004-1608 Office Phone: 202-508-4309. Office Fax: 202-829-2284. Business E-Mail: ecowan@thelenreid.com.

COWAN, FAIRMAN CHAFFEE, lawyer; b. Wellesley Hills, Mass., Apr. 22, 1915; s. James Franklin and Hortense Victoria (Fairman) C.; m. Martha Logan Allis, Apr. 24, 1943; children: Douglas Fairman, Frederick Allis, Leonard Chaffee. AB magna cum laude, Amherst Coll., 1937; LLB, Harvard U., 1940; AMP, Harvard Bus. Sch., 1963. Bar: Mass. 1940. Assoc. Goodwin, Procter & Hoar, Boston, 1940-41, ptnr., 1952—54; gen. counsel, clk., sec., v.p., dir. Norton Co., 1955-79; counsel Bowditch & Dewey, Worcester, Mass., 1979-90. Mem. Citizen Plan E Assn. Worcester, 1957-87; vice chmn. Worcester Civic Ctr. Commn., 1977-79; chmn. Pvt. Industry Coun., Worcester Area CETA Consortium, 1979-83; bd. dirs. Legal Assistance Corp. of Ctr. Mass., 1982-86, Social Svc. Planning Corp., 1975-88, Worcester Mcpl. Rsch. Bur., Inc., 1986—, Mass. Job Tng. Inc., 1983-92, Elder Home Care Svcs. of Worcester, Inc., 1987-92, Daybreak, Inc., 1993-96; incorporator Alliance for Edn., 1986—2003, Worcester Dynamy, Inc., 1992—, Worcester YWCA, 2001—, Worcester Hist. Mus., 1995—, YOU, Inc., 1983—, ARC Ctrl. Mass., 2000—; mem. State Job Tng. Coordinating Coun., 1985-87, Worcester Housing Partnership, 1986-93; trustee Clark U., 1964-76, 79—, Meml. Hosp., Worcester, 1967-86, United Way Ctrl. Mass., 2000—; mem. bd. overseers Planned Parenthood League Mass., 1992-2001, mem. adv. bd. Mass. Coastal Resource Bd., 1992—. Lt. USNR, 1942-45.2003 Co-recipient Worcester State Coll. Cmty. Svc. award; recipient Isaiah Thomas award, 1995. Mem. Am. Antiquarian Soc., Mass. Civic League (v.p. 1947), Worcester Club, Worcester Com. on Fgn. Rels., Phi Beta Kappa, Alpha Delta Phi. Home: 48 Berwick St Worcester MA 01602-1443 Personal E-mail: fcowan1059@aol.com.

COWAN, FREDERIC JOSEPH, lawyer; b. N.Y.C., Oct. 11, 1945; s. Frederic Joseph Sr. and Mary Virginia (Wesley) C.; m. Linda Marshall Scholle, Apr. 28, 1974; children: Elizabeth, Caroline, Allison. AB, Dartmouth Coll., 1967; JD, Harvard U., 1978. Bar: Ky. 1978, U.S. Dist. Ct. (we. dist.) Ky. 1979, U.S. Ct. Appeals (6th cir.) 1984, U.S. Supreme Ct. 1989. Vol. Peace Corps, Ethiopia, 1967-69; assoc. Brown, Todd & Heyburn, Louisville, 1979-83; ptnr. Rice, Porter, Seiller & Price, Louisville, 1983-87; atty. gen. Commonwealth of Ky., 1988-92; counsel Lynch, Cox, Gilman & Manan P.S.C., 1992—. Ky. State Rep., 32d legis. dist., 1982-87; chair Ky. Child Support Enforcement Commn., 1988-91, Ky. Sexual Abuse and Exploitation Prevention Bd., 1988-91; bd. dirs. Ky. Job Tng. Coordinating Council, Frankfort, Louisville Bar Found., 1986. Vice chmn. judiciary criminal com. Ky. Ho. of Reps., 1985-87; chmn. budget com. on justice Judiciary and Corrections Ky. Ho. of Reps., 1985-87, Leadership Ky., 1985; U.S. del. election mission to Namibia Nat. Dem. Inst. for Internat. Affairs, 1989; U.S. del. dem. instns. seminar Nat. Dem. Inst. for Internat. Affairs, Slovenia, 1992; electoral supr. Orgn. for Security and Cooperation in Europe, Bosnia and Herzogovina, 1996; adv. com. Samara Oblast, Russia, 2001. Mem. ABA (adv. com. east european law initiative 2001), Ky. Bar Assn., Louisville Bar Assn., Ky. Acad. Trial Attys. Methodist. Home: 1747 Sulgrave Rd Louisville KY 40205-1643 Office: 2100 PNC Plaza Louisville KY 40202-3354

COWAN, GEORGE ARTHUR, chemist, bank executive, director; b. Worcester, Mass., Feb. 15, 1920; s. Louis Abraham and Anna (Listic) C.; m. Helen Dunham, Sept. 7, 1946. BS, Worcester Poly. Inst., 1941, DSc (hon.), 2002; DSc, Carnegie-Mellon U., 1950, DSc and Tech. (hon.), 2002; DHL (hon.), Coll. of Santa Fe, 2003. Rsch. asst. Princeton U., 1941-42, U. Chgo., 1942-45; mem. staff Columbia U., N.Y.C., 1945; mem. staff, dir. rsch., sr. fellow Los Alamos (N.Mex.) Sci. Lab., 1945-46, 49-88, sr. fellow emeritus, 1988—; tchg. fellow Carnegie Mellon U., Pitts., 1946-49. Chmn. bd. dirs. Trinity Capital Corp., Los Alamos, 1974-95; pres. Santa Fe Inst., 1984-91; mem. The White House Sci. Coun., Washington, 1982-85, cons., 1985-90, Air Force Tech. Applications Ctr., 1952-88; chmn. Los Alamos Nat. Bank, 1965-94. Contbr. sci. articles to profl. jours. Bd. dirs. Santa Fe Opera, 1964-79; treas. Santa Fe Opera Found., 1970-79; regent N.Mex. Inst. Tech. Socorro, 1972-75; pres. The Delta Found.; bd. dirs. Los Alamos Nat. Lab. Found., Adv. Bd. Ctr. for Neural Basis of Cognition, Carnegie-Mellon U. Recipient E.O. Lawrence award, 1965, Disting. Scientist award N.Mex. Acad. Sci., 1975, Robert H. Goddard award Worcester Poly. Inst., 1984, Enrico Fermi award, Presdl. Citation, Dept. Energy, 1990; disting. fellow Santa Fe Inst., 2003, Los Alamos Nat. Lab. medal, 2003. Fellow AAAS, Am. Phys. Soc., Am. Acad. Arts and Scis.; mem. Am. Chem. Soc., N.Mex. Acad. Sci., Sigma Xi. Avocations: skiing, fly-fishing. Home: 721 42nd St Los Alamos NM 87544-1804 Office: Santa Fe Inst 1399 Hyde Park Rd Santa Fe NM 87501-8943 Office Phone: 505-946-2725. Business E-Mail: gac@santafe.edu.

COWAN, JOHN ANDREW, lawyer; b. Montreal, Que., Can., Oct. 28, 1963; s. Daniel Francis and Bette Ann (Carter) C.; 1 child, Christian. BA in Philosophy, U. Houston, 1986; JD, U. Tex., 1991. Bar: Tex. 1992, U.S. Dist. Ct. (ea. dist.) Tex. 1993, U.S. Ct. Appeals (5th cir.) 1994, U.S. Supreme Ct. 1996. Law clk. to Hon. Wendell C. Radford U.S. Dist. Ct. (ea. dist.) Tex., Beaumont, 1992-93; assoc. Provost & Umphrey Law Firm LLP, Beaumont, 1993-94, 95—; law clk. to Hon. Robert M. Parker U.S. Ct. Appeals (5th cir.), Tyler, Tex., 1994-95. Mem. Am. Inns of Ct. Office: Provost & Umphrey Law Firm PO Box 4905 Beaumont TX 77704-4905

COWAN, JOHN JAMES, physicist, astronomer, educator; b. Washington, Apr. 3, 1948; s. John Robert and Anna V. Cowan; m. Linda Elaine Demetry, May 24, 1971. BA, George Washington U., 1970; MS, Case Inst. Tech., 1972; PhD, U. Md., 1976. Postdoctoral fellow Harvard U., Cambridge, Mass., 1976—79; asst. prof. U. Okla., Norman, 1979—84, assoc. prof., 1984—89, prof. physics and astronomy, 1989—, S.R. Noble Presdl. prof., 1998—2002, David Ross Boyd prof., 2002—; rsch. fellow U. Tex., 2002. Mem. rev. panel NASA, Washington, 1987; vis. rsch. assoc. Harvard U., Cambridge, 1987—88; vis. prof. Columbia U., N.Y.C., 1991—92; mem. com. visitors NSF, Washington, 2002; lectr. in field. Reviewer: Astrophys. Jour., 1976—; contbr. articles to profl. jours. Recipient Kinney-Sugg Outstanding Prof. award, Coll. Arts and Scis., U. Okla., 2004; grantee, NASA, 1994—, NSF, 1997—. Mem.: Am. Astron. Soc., Phi Beta Kappa. Achievements include co-discoverer of gold in one of the oldest stars in the universe. Avocations: racquetball, physical fitness. Office: Univ Okla 440 W Brooks St Norman OK 73019 Office Phone: 405-325-3961. Business E-Mail: cowan@nhn.ou.edu.

COWAN, JOYCE A., lawyer; BA in Polit. Sci. cum laude, U. Wash., 1983; JD with honors, George Washington U., 1986. Ptnr. Epstein Becker & Green, Washington, Sonnenschein Nath & Rosenthal LLP, Washington, 2004—. Mem.: ABA (mem. health law sect.), Am. Health Lawyers Assn. Office: Sonnenschein Nath & Rosenthal LLP Ste 600, E Tower 1301 K St NW Washington DC 20005 Office Phone: 202-408-3239. Office Fax: 202-408-6399. Business E-Mail: jcowan@sonnenschein.com.

COWAN, KEITH O., telecommunications industry executive; b. Hartford, Conn., 1956; Grad. in Econs., Polit. sci., U. N.C., 1978; JD, U. Va., 1982. Atty. Alston & Bird, 1982—90, ptnr., 1990—96; from exec. officer to pres. mktg. and product mgmt. BellSouth Corp., Atlanta, 1996—2005, pres. mktg. and product devel., 2005—. Former mem. adminstrv. com., chmn. securities practice group, chmn. continuing legal edn. com. Alston & Bird; bd. dirs. Atlanta Landmarks, Inc. Mem. bd. dirs. Metro Atlanta YMCA, VSA Arts of Ga. Mem.: Atlanta Bar Assn. (former bd. dirs., chmn. bus. and fin. law sect., chmn. continuing legal edn. com.). Office: BellSouth Corp 2180 Lake Blvd Ste 1250 Atlanta GA 30319

COWAN, MARIE JEANETTE, nurse, medical educator; b. Albuquerque, July 20, 1938; d. Adrian Joseph and Leila Bernice (Finley) Johnson; m. Samuel Joseph Cowan, Aug. 14, 1961; children: Samuel Joseph, Kathryn Anne, Michelle Dionne. Diploma, Mary's Help Coll., 1961; BS, U. Wash., 1964, MS, 1972, PhD, 1979. Charge nurse Herrick Meml. Hosp., Berkeley, Calif., 1961-62; staff nurse ICU Univ. Hosp., Seattle, 1966-68; asst. prof. Seattle U., 1972-75; from asst. prof. to prof. nursing U. Wash., Seattle, 1979-97, assoc. dean rsch., 1985-96; dean UCLA Sch. Nursing, 1997—. Rsch. grant reviewer Am. Heart Assn. Wash., Seattle, 1977-82, divsn. rsch. grants reviewer nursing study sect., 1987-90; chair CVN AHA, 1989-91. Mem. editl. bd. Ann. Rev. Nursing Rsch., Rsch. in Nursing and Health, Nursing Rsch.; contbr. articles to profl. jours. Grantee, NIH, 1977, 1981, 1984, 1985, 1991, 1996, 2000. Fellow: Am. Acad. Nursing; mem.: ANA, AACN, Wash. State Nurses Assn., Calif. State Nurses Assn. Roman Catholic. Office: UCLA Sch Nursing PO Box 951702 Los Angeles CA 90095-1702

COWAN, MARTIN B., lawyer; b. N.Y.C., June 6, 1935; s. Joseph and Yetta (Wilkes) C.; m. Dorrit A. Blech, Dec. 20, 1959; children: Alison, Jillian, David. AB, Columbia U., 1957, JD, 1959. Bar: N.Y. 1960, Fla. 1976, U.S. Supreme Ct. 1963, U.S. Tax Ct. 1961. Assoc. Casey Lane & Mittendorf, N.Y.C., 1960-62, Reavis & McGrath, N.Y.C., 1966-68; tax atty. U.S. Dept. Justice, Washington, 1962-66; ptnr. Wien Lane & Malkin, N.Y.C., 1968-84, Milbank Tween Hadley & McCloy, N.Y.C., 1984-93. Adj. assoc. prof. NYU, 1977, Miami Law Sch., 1994; mem. adv. bd. real estate Bur. Nat. Affairs Tax Mgmt., 1972—; cert. review appraiser Nat. Assn. Rev. Appraisers; v.p. Nat. Jewish Commn. Law & Pub. Affairs, 1980—; vis. prof. Fla. State U. Coll. of Law, 1995, Quinnipiac Coll. Sch. of Law, 1995-96. Bd. advisors Jour. Real Estate Taxation. Mem. ABA (tax sect., council 1993-95), Am. Coll. Tax Counsel, Am. Law Inst., N.Y. Bar Assn. (tax sect., mem. exec. com. 1985-86). E-mail: mbcowan@aol.com.

COWAN, NELSON, cognitive psychologist, researcher; b. Washington, Mar. 7, 1951; s. Arthur and Shirley B. Cowan; m. Priscilla Roth, 1982 (div. 1985); mem. Jean Mona Ispa, Aug. 16, 1987; 1 child, Alexander; stepchildren: Simone, Zachary. BS, U. Mich., 1973; PhD, U. Wis., 1980. Postdoctoral fellow NYU, N.Y.C., 1981-82; asst. prof. U. Mass., Amherst, 1982-85, U. Mo., Columbia, 1985-89, assoc. prof., 1989-94; prof., 1994-95; Middlebush prof. social scis., 1995—. Author: Attention and Memory: An Integrated Framework, 1995, Working Memory Capacity, 2005; editl. bd. Psychonomic Bull. and Rev., 1993—; mem. editl. bd. Jour. Exptl. Psychology: Learning, Memory and Cognition, 1993—, assoc. editor, 1995—; assoc. editor Quar. Jour. Exptl. Psychology, 2000-04. Achievements include observation of effects of the duration of speech output on verbal short-term memory; effects of attention on sensory memory. Office: U Mo Dept Psychology 210 Mcalester Hall Columbia MO 65211-2500 Office Phone: 573-882-4232. E-mail: CowenN@missouri.edu.

COWAN, PATRICIA LOUISE, nurse; b. Greensburg, Pa., Feb. 10, 1952; d. John Jacob and Marian Rebecca Rahl; m. Richard Keith Cowan, June 5, 1970; children: Michael, Jason. AS in Nursing, Westmoreland CC, Youngwood, Pa., 1989; BS in Nursing, Carlow U., Greensburg, Pa., 2004. LPN Westmoreland Manor, Greensburg, Pa., 1982—89, RN, 1989—, nursing supr., 1995—, dir., adult night care, 2004. Mem.: Pa. Assn. Dirs. Nursing Adminstrs., Am. Assn. Legal Nurse Cons., Sigma Theta Tau. Home: 508 Mt View Dr Scottdale PA 15683 Office: 2480 S Grande Blvd Greensburg PA 15601

COWAN, RICHARD OLSEN, religious studies educator; b. LA, Jan. 24, 1934; s. Lee Richard and Edith Olsen Cowan; m. Dawn Sandra Houghton, Aug. 14, 1958; children: Sandra, Linda, Reed, Lee, Patricia, Donna. BA, Occidental Coll., 1958; MA, Stanford U., 1959, PhD, 1961. Prof. church history & doctrine Brigham Young U., Provo, Utah, 1961—. Author: (book) Temples T. Dot the Earth, 1997, The Latter-Day Saint Century, 1999; co-editor: Encyclopedia of Latter-Day Saint History, 2000, Unto Every Nation, 2003. Mem.: Morman History Assn. (exec. coun. 1977—80). Lds Ch. Office: Brigham Young U 270L JSB Provo UT 84602

COWAN, ROBERT DUANE, physicist; b. Lincoln, Nebr., Nov. 24, 1919; s. Ralph Ellis and Florence Athey (Eller) C.; m. Dorothy Mable Martinson, July 6, 1944 (dec. Jan. 1987); children: Nancy Jean Lemons, Charles Eller, Gerald Stanley, Marjorie Sue Larson; m. Wilma Lou Thornburg, July 14, 1990. BA, Friends U., Wichita, Kans., 1942; PhD, Johns Hopkins U., 1946; PhD honoris causa, Lund (Sweden) U., 1982. Jr. instr. Johns Hopkins U., Balt., 1942-44; Nat. Rsch. fellow U. Chgo., 1946-47, rsch. assoc., 1947-48; prof. physics Friends U., 1948-51; mem. staff Los Alamos (N.Mex.) Nat. Lab., 1951-82, fellow, 1982—. Vis. prof. Purdue U., West Lafayette, Ind., 1971; vis. scientist Rutherford Appleton Lab., Culham, Eng., 1977, Zeeman Lab., U. Amsterdam, 1984, 87, Lund U., 1988, Manne Siegbahn Inst., Stockholm, 1989, 90. Author: The Theory of Atomic Structure and Spectra, 1981. Explorer leader Boy Scouts Am., Los Alamos, 1970-76. Fulbright lectr., Lima, Peru, 1958-59.

Fellow Am. Phys. Soc., Optical Soc. Am. (William F. Meggers award 1984). Avocations: hiking, mountain climbing, genealogy. Home: 2917 Nickel St Apt B Los Alamos NM 87544-2199 E-mail: rcowan@lanl.gov, rdc-wlc@juno.com.

COWAN, ROBERT RANDALL, science educator; s. Robert B. and Yoland V. Cowan; m. Donna R. McBrian, June 20, 1970; children: Jeffrey S., Christa M. BA in Biology, So. Ill. U., 1970, MS, 1976. Cert. tchr. secondary edn. Ill., 1972, athletic adminstr. Nat. Interscholastic Athletic Adminstrs. Assn., 2002, in gen. adminstrn. Ill., 2004. Sci. tchr. Madison Jr. HS, Ill., 1971—72; math tchr. Ctrl. Jr. HS, Granite City, 1972—73; baseball, football coach Granite City HS, 1972—85, sci. club sponsor, 1973—78, biology, sci. tchr., 1973—85, anatomy, physiology tchr., 1993, asst. athletic dir., 1993, sci. dept. chmn., 1996; biology, anatomy, health instr. Southwestern Ill. Coll., Belleville, GraniteCity, Ill., 1985—93. Bd. mem. Granite City Sports Hall of Fame, 2000. Mem.: Ill. Fedn. Tchrs. (assoc.; bldg. rep.), Nat. Interscholastic Athletic Adminstrs. Assn. (assoc.), Ill. Athletic Dirs. Assn. (assoc.; state conf. com. chmn., exec. bd. mem. 1999—), Nat. Assn. Biology Tchrs. (assoc.). Office: Granite City HS 3101 Madison Ave Granite City IL 62040 Office Phone: 618-451-5808 ext. 2522. Office Fax: 618-451-6296.

COWAN, STUART MARSHALL, lawyer; b. Irvington, N.J., Mar. 20, 1932; s. Bernard Howard and Blanche (Hertz) C.; m. Marilyn R.C. Toepfer, Apr., 1961 (div. 1968); m. Eleanor Schmerel, June, 1953 (dec.); m. Jane Alison Averill, Feb. 24, 1974 (div. 1989); children: Fran Lori, Michael L., Catherine R.L., Erika R.L., Bronwen P.; m. Victoria Yi, Nov. 11, 1989. BS in Econs., U. Pa., 1952; LLB, Rutgers U., 1955. Bar: N.J. 1957, Hawaii 1962, U.S. Supreme Ct. 1966. Atty. Greenstein & Cowan, Honolulu, 1961—70; counsel Cowan & Frey, Honolulu, 1970—89; pvt. practice, 1989—; of counsel Price Okamoto Himeno & Lum, 1993—. Arbitrator Fed. Mediation & Conciliation Svc., Honolulu, 1972—, Am. Arbitration Assn., Honolulu, 1968—, Hawaii Pub. Employee Rels. Bd., 1972—. Pres. Hawaii Epilepsy Soc., 1984-86, 2004—; acquisition chair Hawaii Family Support Ctr., 1995-97; bd. dirs. Hawaii Epilepsy Found. Lt. USN, 1955-61. Mem. ABA, ATLA (state committeeman for Hawaii 1965-69, bd. gov. 1972-78), Hawaii Bar Assn., Am. Judicature Soc., Consumer Lawyers Hawaii, Hawaii Trial Lawyers Assn. (v.p. 1972-78), Japan-Hawaii Lawyers Assn., Soc. Profls. in Dispute Resolution, Inter Pacific Bar Assn., Honolulu Symphony Soc. (bd. dirs. 1989-99), Royal Order of Kamehameha, Order of St. Stanislas, Sovereign Order of St. John of Jerusalem Knights Hospitallers, Mil. Order of Temple at Jerusalem, Queen's Club, Mil. Order of World Wars, Waikiki Yacht Club, St. Francis Yacht Club, Hawaii Yacht Club, Hawaii Scottish Assn. (chieftain 1983-88), St. Andrews Soc., Caledonian Soc. (vice chieftain 1983-85), Honolulu Pipes and Drums (sec. treas. 1985-90), Celtic Pipes and Drums Honolulu, New Zealand Police Pipe Band, Masons (York Rite, Scottish Rite No. and So. jurisdictions, 33d deg., Grand Lodge Hawaii, grand orator 1992, sr. grand steward 1993, jr. grand warden 1994, sr. grand warden 1995, grand master 1997), Red Cross of Constantine, Royal Order Scotland, Pearl Harbor (master 1971, 2001-04), Masonic Kilties N.J., Azure Masada (#51 N.J.), USS Missouri Meml. Assn., Nat. Sojourners (pres. 2005—), Elks, Chinese Acacia Club, Royal Hawaiian Ocean Racing Club. U.S. Coast Guard Aux., Navy League of U.S. (nat. dirs. for Honolulu coun.). Jewish. Home: 47-339 Mapumapu Rd Kaneohe HI 96744-4922 Office: Ste 728 Ocean View Ctr 707 Richards St Honolulu HI 96813-4616 also: 47-653 Kamehameha Hwy # 202 Kaneohe HI 96744-4965 Office Phone: 808-538-1113. Personal E-mail: stuartgm@juno.com.

COWAN, WALLACE EDGAR, lawyer; b. Jersey City, Jan. 28, 1924; s. Benjamin and Dorothy (Zunz) C.; m. Ruth Daitzman, June 8, 1947; children: Laurie, Paul, Judith. BS magna cum laude, NYU, 1947; JD cum laude, Harvard U., 1950. Ptnr. Stroock, Stroock & Lavan, N.Y.C., 1950-93. Dir. Ametek, Inc., Paoli, Pa., 1982-93, sec., 1969-93, sec. H.S. Stuttman, Inc., Westport, Conn., to 1996; adv. bd. Hackensack River Greenway, Teaneck, N.J. Mem. Teaneck (N.J.) Adv. Bd. on Parks, Playgrounds and Recreation, 1966—, chmn., 1974—; pres. No. Valley Commuters Assn.; past pres., life trustee Congregation Beth Sholom, Teaneck; mem. Forum adv. bd. Sch.-Based Youth Svcs. Project, 1998-2003. 1st lt. USAF, 1942-45, ETO. Decorated Air medal with silver cluster; recipient Vol. in the Parks award Bergen County, N.J., 1993, Disting. Svc. award Bergen County, N.J., 1994, Disting. Achievement award Bergen County, N.J., 2001. Mem. Beta Gamma Sigma. Home: 499 Emerson Ave Teaneck NJ 07666-1927 Office: Stroock Stroock & Lavan 180 Maiden Ln New York NY 10038-4937

COWARD, NICHOLAS F., lawyer; BA, Union Coll.; JD, George Mason U., 1981. Bar: DC 1982. Mng. ptnr. Baker & McKenzie, Washington, DC, ptnr., exec. com. mem. Mem.: ABA. Office: Baker & McKenzie LLP One Prudential Plaza Ste 2500 Chicago IL 60601 Office Phone: 202-452-7021. E-mail: nicholas.f.coward@bakernet.com.

COWARD, PAMELA KINNEY, elementary school educator; b. Asheboro, N.C., July 16, 1956; d. Harvey Ray and Nellie Jean (Stout) Kinney; m. Thomas Wellons Coward, June 18, 1983. AB in Edn., Wingate Coll., 1976; BS in Edn., High Point Coll., 1978; MEd, Elon College, 1989. Cert. tchr., N.C. Tchr. Archdale (N.C.) Elem. Sch., 1978-79, Randleman (N.C.) Mid. Sch., 1979-81, Randleman Elem. Sch., 1981-82, Coleridge (N.C.) Elem. Sch., 1982—. Mem. Nat. Assn. for Edn., N.C. Assn. for Edn., Randolph County Reading Assn, Tchrs Sorority Alpha Delta Kappa Avocations: reading, walking, cooking. Home: 890 Brady Street Ext Ramseur NC 27316-8708 Office Phone: 336-879-3348.

COWART, RICHARD G., lawyer; b. Bourne, Mass., 1954; BSBA magna cum laude, Univ. Southern Miss., 1975; JD with honors, Univ. Miss., 1978. Ptnr., chmn. health law dept. Baker Donelson Bearman Caldwell & Berkowitz PC, Nashville. Adj. faculty Univ. Miss. Med. Ctr., 1993—. Articles editor Miss. Law Jour., 1977—78, health law columnist Medical News Inc. Mem.: ABA, Miss. Bar, Tenn. Bar Assn., Am. Health Lawyers Assn. (pres. 2004, bd. dir.), Phi Delta Phi, Omicron Delta Kappa, Phi Kappa Phi. Office: Baker Donelson Bearman PC Commerce Ctr Ste 1000 211 Commerce St Nashville TN 37201 Office Fax: 615-726-5660, 615-744-0464. Business E-Mail: dcowart@bakerdonelson.com.

COWART, T(HOMAS) DAVID, lawyer; b. San Benito, Tex., June 12, 1953; s. Thomas W. Jr. and Glenda Claire (Miller) C.; children: Thomas Kevin, Lauren Michelle, Megan Leigh; m. Greta E. Gerberding, Aug. 12, 1995. BBA, U. Miss., 1975, JD, 1978; LLM in Taxation, NYU, 1979. CPA Tex., Miss.; bar: Miss. 1978, Tex. 1979. Assoc. Dossett, Magruder & Montgomery, Jackson, Miss., 1978, Strasburger & Price, Dallas, 1979-87; ptnr., assoc., shareholder Johnson & Gibbs, Dallas, 1988-90; shareholder Jenkens & Gilchrist, Dallas, 1991—. Adj. prof. law So. Meth. U. Sch. Law, 1988; mem. key dist. adv. coun. IRS, Dallas, 1989—95, chmn., 1990—93; mem. Coll. State Bar Tex.; lectr. in field. Mem. editl. bd.: Flexible Benefits, 1993—, 401k Advisor, 1994—, COBRA, 1996—. Mem. adv. com. Goals for Dallas, 1984-85; vol. Children's Med. Ctr., 1992-96. Named Tex. Super Lawyer, 2003—04; recipient Best Lawyer in Am. award, 2001—05, Best Lawyer in Dallas award, 2003—05, Best Lawyer award, Corp. Coun., 2003. Mem.: ABA (health care task force 1991—98, sect. 83 issues task force, chmn. health plan designs issues subcom. 1992—95, sect. taxation, employee benefit com., vice-chmn. 1995—97, chmn.-designate joint com. on employee benefits 1997—99, chmn. 1998—99, chmn. joint com. employee benefits 1999—2000), Dallas Bar Found., Am. Law Inst., Phi Alpha Phi, Dallas Benefits Soc. (co-moderator 1991—92, bd. dirs. 1991—93), S.W. Benefits Assn. (bd. dirs. 1994—97), Dallas Bar Assn. (lectr. 1985—, coun. mem. employee benefits sect. 1989—92, treas. 1992, sec. 1993, v.p. 1994, pres. 1995), State Bar Tex. (fed. legislation, regulations and revenue rulings subcom. 1986—87, chmn. fiduciary stds. for trustees subcom. 1987—88, sect. taxation, com. compensation and employee benefits), Am. Coll. Employee Benefits Counsel (1st chair, charter mem.), Beta Alpha Psi, Omicron Delta Kappa. Office: Jenkens & Gilchrist 1445 Ross Ave Ste 3200 Dallas TX 75202-2785 Office Phone: 214-855-4500. E-mail: dcowart@jenkens.com.

COWEE, JOHN WIDMER, retired university chancellor; b. Wausau, Wis., Aug. 1, 1918; s. Charles Arthur and Hattie L. (Widmer) C.; m. Nancy Lee Pendleton, Dec. 22, 1973; children— John Widmer, Jeffrey Deane. BA, U. Wis.-Madison, 1947, MBA, 1948, PhD, 1950, LLB, 1956. Bar: Wis. Mem. faculty U. Calif.-Berkeley, 1954-66, prof. bus. adminstrn., 1960-66, chmn. dept., 1961-66, prof. law, 1954-66; dean Sch. Bus. Adminstrn., also Grad. Sch. Bus. Adminstrn. U. Calif., 1961-66; provost Marquette U., Milw., 1967-74, v.p. bus. and fin., 1966-67, prof. law and bus. adminstrn., 1966-76, exec. v.p. Med. Sch., 1967-69; prof. bus. adminstrn., prof. law U. Colo., Boulder, from 1976; chancellor health affairs U. Colo. Med. Center, 1976-85; now ret. Trustee, asst. sec. Calif. Physicians Svc., 1959-66; mem. bd. govs. Internat. Ins. Seminars; bd. dirs. Calif.-Western States Life Ins. Co., Nordberg Mfg. Co., Milw., Marine Nat. Exch. Bank, Milw., Sta-Rite Industries, Milw.; chmn. policyowners exam. com. Northwestern Mut. Life Ins. Co., Milw., WICOR, Milw. Author studies, reports. Trustee Am. Conservatory Theatre Found., San Francisco, Univ. Sch., Milw., Davis Inst. Care and Study of Aging, Denver; bd. dirs. Marquette U. Sch. Medicine, Wis. Heart Assn.; adv. com. Lingnan Inst. Bus. Adminstrn., Chinese U., Hong Kong. Served with AUS, 1942-46. Decorated Bronze Star. Mem. ABA, Wis. Bar Assn., Internat. Assn. Ins. Law (co-founder Am. sect.), Internat. Ins. Seminars, Am. Assn. U. Adminstrs., Univl Club (Milw.), Denver Club. Clubs: University (Milw.); Denver. Home: 12464 E Wesley Ave Aurora CO 80014-1992

COWELL, SIMON, television personality, music producer; b. London, Oct. 7, 1959; s. Eric and Julie Cowell. Mail room clerk EMI Music Pub., with, 1977—82; founder, co-owner Fanfare Records, 1982—89; A&R cons. BMG records, London, 1989—; founder, co-owner S Records, 2001—03. Judge (TV series) Pop Idol, 2001—02, American Idol, 2002—; exec. prodr.: (TV series) Cupid, 2003; prodr.: (albums) Sonia, 1991, Robson & Jerome, 1995, 5ive: The Album (5ive), 1998, Invincible, (5ive), 1999, Westlife, 1999, Coast to Coast (Westlife), 2000, World of Our Own (Westlife), 2001;, prodr. many others; guest appearance (film) Scary Movie 3, 2003; author: I Don't Mean to Be Rude, But...:Backstage Gossip from American Idol & the Secrets that Can Make You A Star, 2003. Office: BMG Records UK Ltd BMG Enterprises Bedford house 69-79 Fulham High St London SW6 3JW England Office Phone: 020 7384 7520. Office Fax: 020 7371 8987.*

COWEN, EDWARD S., lawyer, consultant; b. NYC, Mar. 3, 1936; s. Michael and Edith (Cohen) C.; m. Lesley J. Hoffman, Nov. 16, 1958; children: Adrienne Zammiello, Justine Bons. BS, Syracuse U., 1957; JD, NYU, 1961. Bar: N.Y. 1962, U.S. Dist. Ct. (so. dist.) N.Y. 1965, U.S. Ct. Appeals (2d cir.) 1965, U.S. Supreme Ct. 1967, U.S. Dist. Ct. (ea. dist.) N.Y. 1979. Law clk. to judge U.S. Dist. Ct. (so. dist.) N.Y., 1961-62; ptnr. Seligson & Morris, N.Y.C., 1963-69, Robinson, Silverman, Pearce, Aronsohn & Berman, N.Y.C., 1975-90, Kirkland & Ellis, N.Y.C., 1991-96; of counsel Pillsbury Winthrop, LLP, N.Y.C., 1996—2001. Cons. Poorman-Douglas Corp., 2002—; mem. faculty Practicing Law Inst. Author: Bankruptcy in Joint Venture Partnerships, Practicing Law Institute, 1985, Enforcing Liens Post-petition, Bankruptcy Strategist, 1998. With USAF, 1958. Named Honoree of Yr. Fedn. N.Y. Lawyers Divsn. Mem. ABA, N.Y. State Bar Assn., Assn. Bar City N.Y. (chmn. bankruptcy and corp. reorgn.) Home: 1400 S Ocean Blvd Boca Raton FL 33432 Office Phone: 561-955-0016. Personal E-mail: ecowen@verizon.net.

COWEN, EDWARD WEST, dermatologist, researcher; b. Madison, Wis., Oct. 30, 1972; s. William Frank and Kathleen Ruth Cowen; m. Kelly Joyce, Nov. 2, 2002; 1 child, Katherine Elise. BS in Biology and Sociology, Cornell U., 1994; MD, Penn State Coll. Medicine. Diplomate Am. Bd. Dermatology, 2002. Internship, internal medicine Penn State Hershey Med. Ctr., Hershey, Pa., 1998—99; residency, dermatology U. of Rochester Med. Ctr., Rochester, NY, 1999—2002, chief resident, dermatology, 2001—02; clin. rsch. fellow Dermatology Br., Nat. Cancer Inst., Bethesda, Md., 2002—04; staff clinician Dermatology Br., Nat. Cancer Inst., NIH, Bethesda, Md., 2004—. Editl. bd. Jour. of the Am. Acad. of Dermatology, 2004. Fellow: Am. Acad. of Dermatology; mem.: Md. State Med. Soc., Med. Dermatology Soc., Montgomery County Med. Soc., Wash. DC Dermatol. Soc. Office: Nat Cancer Inst 10 Center Dr Bldg 10 Rm 12N238 Bethesda MD 20892 Office Phone: 301-496-4299.

COWEN, EUGENE SHERMAN, broadcast executive; b. N.Y.C., May 2, 1925; s. Jacob M. and Shirley (Sherman) C.; m. Phyllis L. Wallach, Jan. 29, 1948; children: James Sherman, Stephanie Jane. BA magna cum laude, Syracuse U., 1949, MA, 1954. Reporter Syracuse Herald-Jour., 1948-52, Newhouse News Bur., Washington, 1952-53; press sec. Rep. Frances P. Bolton, Washington, 1953-56; info. officer HEW, Washington, 1956-58; v.p. Standard Pub. Rels., Washington, 1958-59; chief staff Senator Hugh Scott, 1959-69; spl. asst., dep. asst. to pres. White House, 1969-71; v.p.-Washington Capital Cities/ABC, Inc., 1971-90; cons. in field Washington, 1990—. Author: (book) My Life, A Novel, 2003. Legis. affairs dir. Svc. Corps Ret. Execs. With USAAF, 1943-46. Decorated Air medal. Mem. Phi Beta Kappa. Home: 2700 Calvert St NW Washington DC 20008-2621

COWEN, ROBERT E., federal judge; b. Newark, Sept. 4, 1930; s. Saul and Lillie (Selzer) C.; m. Toby Cowen, Dec. 21, 1973; children: Shulie, Eve. BS, Drake U., 1952; LLB, Rutgers U., 1958. Bar: NJ. Assoc. Schreiber, Lancaster & Demos, Newark, 1959-61; asst. prosecutor Essex County, N.J., 1969-70; dep. atty. gen. organized crime Criminal Justice Dept., N.J., 1970-72, dir. Div. Ethics and Profl. Svcs., 1972-78; magistrate U.S. Dist. Ct. N.J., Newark, 1978-85, judge Trenton, 1985-87, U.S. Ct. Appeals (3d cir.), Trenton, 1987-98, sr. judge, 1998—. Pvt. practice, Newark, 1961-69. Office: Clarkson S Fisher Jud Complex Rm 207 402 E State St Trenton NJ 08608-1507*

COWEN, ROY CHADWELL, JR., language educator; b. Kansas City, Mo., Aug. 2, 1930; s. Roy Chadwell and Mildred Frances (Schuetz) Cowen; m. Hildegard Bredemeier, Oct. 6, 1956 (dec.); 1 child, Ernst Werner (dec.). BA, Yale U., 1952; PhD, U. Gottingen, Federal Republic of Germany, 1960. Instr. U. Mich., Ann Arbor, 1960-64, asst. prof., 1964-67, assoc. prof., 1967-71, prof., 1971—, chmn. dept. Germanic langs., 1979-85. Author: (book) Christian Dietrich Grabbe, 1972, Naturalismus Kommentar zu einer Epoche, 1973, Hauptmann Kommentar zum dramatischen Werk, 1981, Poetischer Realismus: Kommentar zu einer Epoche, 1985, Das deutsche Drama im 19. Jahrhundert, 1988, Christian Dietrich Grabbe-Dramatiker ungeloester Widersprueche, 1998. With USN, 1952—56. Decorated Sr. Officer's Cross Federal Republic of Germany; recipient Williams Tchg. award, U. Mich., 1967; fellow Sr., NEH, 1972—73. Mem.: MLA, Internationale Vereinigung fur Germanistik. Democrat. Methodist. Home: 2874 Baylis Dr Ann Arbor MI 48108-1764 Office: U Mich Dept Germanic Langs/Lits Ann Arbor MI 48109 Business E-Mail: rcowen@umich.edu.

COWEN, SCOTT S., academic administrator; m. Marjorie Cowen; 4 children. BS, U. Conn., 1968; MBA, George Washington U., 1972, DBA in Fin., 1975. Asst. prof. mgmt. Bucknell U., 1974—76; faculty Case Western Res. U., Cleve., 1976—98, dean, Albert J. Weatherhead III prof. mgmt., 1984—98; pres. Tulane U., New Orleans, 1998—, Seymour S Goodman Meml. prof. bus. A.B. Freeman Sch. Bus., 1998—, prof. econs. Faculty of Liberal Arts and Scis., 1998—. Eleanor F. and Philip G. Rust vis. prof. Colgate Darden Grad. Sch. Bus. Adminstrn., U. Va., 1982—83; bd. dirs. Newell Rubbermaid, Inc., Am. Greetings Corp., Jo-Ann Stores, Inc., Forest City Ent., Inc.; cons. in field. Co-author: Introduction to Business: Concepts and Applications, 1981, Information Requirements of Corporate Boards of Directors, 1983, Accounting Today: Principles and Applications, Innovation in Professional Education: Steps on a Journey From Teaching to Learning, 1995; contbr. articles to profl. jours. Bd. dirs. New Orleans Bus. Coun., Com. for a Better New Orleans, New Orleans Bldg. Corp. With U.S. Army, 1968—71. Co-recipient award of Achievement in Edn., No. Ohio Live Mag., 1991; named Disting. Alumni, George Washington U., 1998—99; named to, Sch. Bus. Adminstrn. Hall of Fame U. Conn.; recipient Torch of Learning, Hebrew U., Torch of Liberty, Anti-Defamation League, Leadership Cleve. award, Greater Cleve. Growth Assn., 1987—88; fellow, Ernst & Whitney, Cleve., 1978, 1979. Mem.: Nat. Assn. Ind. Colls. and Univs., Am. Coun. Edn. (bd. dirs.), Am. Assembly of Collegiate Schs. Bus. (pres.). Office: Tulane University 218 Gibson 6823 Saint Charles Ave New Orleans LA 70118-5698 Office Phone: 504-865-5210. Office Fax: 504-865-5202. Business E-Mail: scowen@tulane.edu.*

COWGER, GARY L., automotive executive; b. Kansas City, Ks., 1947; m. Kay Cowger; 2 children. BS in Industrial Engring., General Motors Inst., 1970; MS in Mngmnt., MIT, 1978. Plant superintendent General Motors Corp., Kansas City, variety of engring. & mfr. positions, 1965—79, general superintendent Oldsmobile Division Lansing, Mich., 1979—80, production manager GM Assembly Division St. Louis, 1981—82, plant manager GM Assembly Division Wentzville, Mo., 1982—85, complex manager Lordstown Assembly facilities, 1985—87, mfr. mgr. Cadillac Motor div., 1987—90, exec. dir. adv. mfr. engring. GM Tech. Ctr. Warren, Mich., 1990—92, exec.-in-charge NAO Mfr. Ctr., 1993, pres. & mng. dir. Mexico div., 1994—98, v.p., 1994—; v.p. mfr. General Motors Europe, 1998; chmn. & mng. dir. Adam Opel AG, 1998; v.p. & group exec. Labor Relations, N.A. Internal Comm. General Motors Corp., 1998—2001, v.p. mfr. & labor relations, 2001, pres. General Motors N. Am., 2001—05. Co-chmn. fin. com. Mo. Gov.'s Com. on Sci. Tech. Vice chmn. bd. mgrs. St. Charles YMCA. bd. dirs. Mo. C. of C.; exec. com. St. Louis Regional Commerce and Growth Assn.; Gov.'s Hawthorn Found.; bd. dirs. Career Productivity Inst. of Lindenwood Coll., Mo. Incu Tech. Found.; adv. bd. dirs. St. Charles County Council of Chambers; pub. mem. Blue Cross Corp. Assembly; bd. trustees Lindenwood Coll.; pres.'s council St. Louis U. Office: Buick Oldsmobile Cadillac Group PO Box 444 Wentzville MO 63385-0444

COWGILL, URSULA MOSER, biologist, educator, environmental consultant; b. Bern, Switzerland, Nov. 9, 1927; came to U.S., 1943, naturalized, 1945; d. John W. and Mara (Siegrist) Moser. AB, Hunter Coll., 1948; MS, Kans. State U., 1952; PhD, Iowa State U., 1956. Staff MIT, Lincoln Lab., Lexington, Mass., 1957-58; field work Doherty Found., Guatemala, 1958-60; research assoc. dept. biology Yale U., New Haven, 1960-68; prof. biology and anthropology U. Pitts., 1968-81; environ. scientist Dow Chem. Co., Midland, Mich., 1981-84, assoc. environ. cons., 1984-91; environ. cons., 1991—. Mem. environ. measurements adv. com. Sci. Adv. Bd. EPA, 1976-80; Internat. Joint Commn., 1984-89. Contbr. numerous articles on ecology, biology and minerology to sci. publs. Trustee Carnegie Mus., Pitts., 1971-75. Grantee NSF 1960-78, Wenner Gren Found., 1965-66, Penrose fund Am. Philos. Soc., 1978; Sigma Xi grant-in-aid, 1965-66 Mem. AAAS, Am. Soc. Limnology and Oceanography, Internat. Soc. Theoretical and Applied Limnology. Home and Office: PO Box 1329 Carbondale CO 81623-1329 E-mail: ucowgill@sopris.net, ucowgill@direcway.com.

COWHER, BILL, professional football coach; b. Pitts., May 8, 1957; m. Kaye Cowher; children: Meagan Lyn, Lauren Marie, Lindsay Morgan. Degree in edn., N.C. State. Football player Cleve. Browns, 1980-82, spl. teams coach, 1985-86, secondary coach, 1987-88; football player Phila. Eagles, 1983-84; def. coord. Kansas City Chiefs, 1988-91; head coach Pitts. Steelers, 1992—. Office: 3400 S Water St Pittsburgh PA 15203-2349*

COWHEY, PETER FRANCIS, international relations educator, consultant; b. Chgo., Sept. 28, 1948; s. Eugene F. and Vivien (High) C.; m. Mary Pat Williams, July 1973 (div. June 1978); m. M. Margaret McKeown, June 29, 1985; 1 child, Megan. BS in Fgn. Svc., Georgetown U., 1970; MA, PhD, U. Calif., Berkeley, 1976. Lectr. U. Calif., Berkeley, 1975-76; from asst. to assoc. prof. polit. sci. U. Calif. San Diego, La Jolla, 1976-88, prof. polit. sci. & internat. rels., 1989—, dir. Inst. Global Conflict Coop., 1999—, dean grad. sch. internat. rels. and Pacific studies, 2002—; sr. counselor internat. econ. and competition policy FCC, Washington, 1994-97, chief internat. bur., 1997. Market planner AT&T Internat., Basking Ridge, N.J., 1985-86; advisor Telemation Assocs., Washington, 1987-88; mem. telecom. adv. bd. A.T. Kearney, Chgo., 1988-91; co-dir. project on internat. and security affairs U. Calif., San Diego, 1990-94; rsch. scholar Berkeley Roundtable on the Internat. Economy, 1992-94; vis. prof. Juan March Inst., Madrid, 1992; rsch. prof. Inst. of Oriental Culture, U. Tokyo, 1993; U.S. del. G-7 Ministerial, 1995, U.S. del. Asian Pacific Econ. Cmty. Ministerial, 1995; mem. sec. gen. Internat. Telecomm. Union Expert Group on Acctg. Rates, 1997-98; internat. adv. bds. Silicon Wave, SkyFlow, UN Devel. Program, Agy. for Internat. Devel. Author: Problems of Plenty, 1985; co-author: Profit and the Pursuit of Energy, 1983, When Countries Talk, 1988, Managing the World's Economy, 1993; co-editor: Structure and Policy in Japan and the United States, 1994; mem. editl. bd. Internat. Orgn., 1989-94. Mem. adv. bd. Project Promothee, Paris, 1985-94, Ctr. on Telecom. Mgmt., Lincoln, Nebr., 1988-92; com. mem. NRC, 1992-93. Rockefeller Found. internat. affairs fellow, 1984-87. Mem. Am. Polit. Sci. Assn., Coun. Fgn. Rels. (internat. affairs fellow 1985-86), Internat. Studies Assn. Democrat. also: UC San Diego 9500 Gilman Dr La Jolla CA 92093-5004 Home: 2447 Ardath Rd La Jolla CA 92037-3501 E-mail: pcowhey@ucsd.edu.

COWHILL, WILLIAM JOSEPH, retired naval officer, consultant; b. Bklyn., May 29, 1928; s. Joseph Henry and Lucy Rose (Foppiano) C.; m. Jennifer Jackson, Apr. 16, 1955; children Robin, Joseph, Beth, Michael, Douglas. BS, Northwestern U., 1950. Commd. ensign USN, 1950, advanced through grades to vice adm., 1979, comdg. officer USS Dace and USS Will Rogers, 1965-68, PCO instr., div. Naval Reactors, AEC, 1968-70, comdg. officer USS Holland, Rota, Spain, 1970-72, nuclear power program mgr. Bur. Naval Personnel, 1972, comdr. tng. command, U.S. Atlantic Fleet, 1973-75, asst. dep. chief naval ops. for submarine warfare, Office Chief Naval Ops., Washington, 1975-77, comdr. submarine force, U.S. Pacific Fleet, 1977-79, dep. chief ops. for logistics, office chief naval ops., 1979-83, dir. logistics, joint chiefs of staff, 1983-85, ret.; pvt. cons. Washington, 1985—. Decorated Def. D.S.M., Navy D.S.M., Legion of Merit. Home and Office: 9428 Vernon Dr Great Falls VA 22066

COWIN, JUDITH ARNOLD, state supreme court judge; b. Boston, Mass., Apr. 29, 1942; m. William I. Cowin, 1965; 3 children. BA, Wellesley Coll., 1963; LLD, Harvard U., 1970. Asst. legal counsel Mass. Dept. Mental Health, 1971—72; legal counsel for chief justice Mass. Dist. Ct., 1972—79; asst. dist. atty. Norfolk County, 1979—91; judge Mass. Superior Ct., 1991—99; assoc. justice Mass. Supreme Jud. Ct., Boston, 1999—. Clinical field supervisor Harvard Law Sch., 1980. Office: Mass Supreme Judicial Ct One Pemberton Sq #2 Boston MA 02108

COWIN, STEPHEN CORTEEN, biomedical engineering educator, consultant; b. Elmira, N.Y., Oct. 26, 1934; s. William Corteen and Bernice (Reidy) C.; m. Martha Agnes Eisel, Aug. 10, 1956; children: Jennifer Marie, Thomas Burrows. BCE, Johns Hopkins U., 1956, MCE, 1958; PhD in Engring. Mechanics, Pa. State U., 1962. Registered profl. engr., La. Prof. mech. engring. Tulane U., 1969-77, prof. mechanics dept. biomed. engring., 1977-85, adj. prof. orthopedics, 1978-88, prof.-in-charge Tulane-Newcomb Jr. Yr. Abroad program, 1974-75, chmn. applied math. program, 1975-79, prof. applied stats., 1979-88, Alden J. Laborde prof. engring., 1985-88; disting. prof. CUNY, 1988—, chmn. dept. biomed. engring., 2002—03; dir. N.Y. Ctr. for Biomed. Engring., 2000—03. Sci. Rsch. Coun. Gt. Brit. sr. vis. fellow U. Strathclyde, 1974, 80; vis. research prof. Instituto de Matematica, Estatistica e Ciencia de Computaao, Universidade Estadual de Campinas, Brazil, 1978; participant U.S. Nat. Acad. Scis. interacad. exch. program with Bulgaria, 1983; fellow Japan Soc. for the Promotion Sci., 1987. Editor: (with M. Satake) Continuum Mechanical and Statistical Approaches in the Mechanics of Granular Materials, 1978, Mechanics Applied to the Transport of Granular Materials, 1979, (with M.M. Carroll) The Effects of Voids on Material Deformation, 1976, Bone Mechanics, 1988, Bone Mechanics Handbook, 2001, Cardiovascular Soft Tissue Mechanics, 2001; assoc. editor: Jour. Applied Mechanics, 1974-82, Jour. Biomech. Engring., 1982-88; editl. adv. bd. Handbook of Materials, Structures and Mechanics, 1981—, Handbook of Bioengineering, 1981, Acta Biomechanica, 1986—; editl. bd. Annals Biomed. Engring., 1985—; editl. cons. Jour. Biomechanics, 1988—. Served to capt. U.S. Army, 1957-64 Recipient Maurice A. Biot medal ASCE, 2004; grantee NSF, NIH, NASA, U.S. Army Rsch. Office, Edward G. Schlieder

Found.; fellow Fogarty Internat. Ctr., Amsterdam, 1996-97, Johns Hopkins U., 1958; Md. state scholar, Ambrose Howard Carner scholar. Fellow AAAS, ASME (Melville medal 1993, Lissner medal 1999), Am. Inst. Med. and Biol. Engring., European Soc. Biomechanics (Rsch. award 1994), Am. Acad. Mechanics; mem. Nat. Acad. Engring., Orthopedic Rsch. Soc., Soc. Rheology, Soc. Natural Philosophy (treas. 1977-79), Soc. Engring. Sci., Math. Assn. Am., N.Y. Acad. Scis., Sigma Xi. Home: 2166 Broadway Apt 12D New York NY 10024 Office Phone: 212-650-5208. Personal E-mail: scowin@earthlink.net.

COWLES, CHARLES, art dealer; b. Santa Monica, Calif., Feb. 7, 1941; s. Gardner and Jan (Streate) C. Student, Stanford, 1963. Assoc. pub. Artforum mag., San Francisco, 1964-65; pub., pres. Artforum, Inc., Los Angeles, 1965-67, pub., pres., chmn. N.Y.C., 1967-75, pres., chmn., 1975-79; chmn. Collegiate Press, N.Y.C., 1968-71; curator modern art Seattle Art Mus., 1975-79; pres. Charles Cowles Gallery, N.Y.C., 1980—. Mem. Fine Arts Council Fla., 1972-75; Trustee Studio Mus. in Harlem, N.Y.C., 1967-75, Miami Art Ctr., 1973-75, San Francisco Art Inst., 1978-80, Cowles Charitable Trust, 1983—; mem. internat. council Mus. Modern Art, N.Y.C., 1967-79. Mem. Seattle Arts Commn., 1976-79; trustee Wolfsonian F.I.U., Miami Beach, 1995—, Laueier Sculpture Pk. St. Louis, 1996—, Am. Fedn. of the Arts, N.Y., 2000—, Alliance for the Arts, 2001--; trustee N.Y. Studio Sch., 1985-2003, chmn., 1987-95; trustee com. for librs. Mus. of Modern Art, N.Y., 2000—. With USCG, 1962—63, with USCGR, 1963—70. Mem. Art Dealers Assn. Am. (bd. dirs. 1988-90, 93-96). Office: Charles Cowles Gallery 537 W 24th St New York NY 10011-1104 Fax: 212-925-3501. E-mail: charlie@cowlesgallery.com.

COWLES, DOUGLAS MOODEY, lawyer; b. Painesville, Ohio, May 28, 1947; s. Charles Moodey and Marilyn (Greentree) C.; children: Michael, Megan, Jessica, Victoria. BA, Miami U., Oxford, Ohio, 1971; JD, U. Calif., San Francisco, 1975. Bar: Calif. 1975, Ohio 1976, U.S. Supreme Ct. 1980. Referee Franklin County Probate Ct., Columbus, Ohio, 1976-80; ptnr. Douglas M Cowles, Gallipolis, Ohio, 1980—; city solicitor City of Gallipolis, 1983—; spl. counsel Ohio Atty. Gen., Gallipolis, 1983—. Author, lectr. on wills. Adv. bd. Gallipolis Devel. Ctr., 1983—. With U.S. Army, 1968-70, Vietnam. Mem. ABA, Assn. Trial Lawyers Am., Calif. Bar Assn., Ohio State Bar Assn., Ohio Trial Lawyers Assn. Avocations: flying, tennis, running. Office: Douglas M Cowles PO Box 969 435 2nd Ave Gallipolis OH 45631-0969

COWLES, FREDERICK OLIVER, lawyer; b. Steubenville, Ohio, Oct. 18, 1937; s. Oliver Howard and Cornelia Blanche (Regal) C.; m. Christina Monica Muller, Sept. 9, 1961; children: Randall, Eric, Gregory, Cornelius. AB magna cum laude, Yale U., 1959; JD, Harvard U., 1962. Bar: R.I. 1963, Mich. 1967, Ill. 1969, N.Y. 1998, Conn. 1998. Assoc. Hinckley, Allen, Salisbury & Parsons, Providence, 1962-67; internat. atty. Upjohn Co., Kalamazoo, Mich., 1967-69; chief internat. atty. Am. Hosp. Supply Crp., Evanston, Ill., 1969-71; internat. atty. Kendall Co., Boston, 1971-73; chief internat. counsel Colgate Palmolive Co., N.Y.C., 1973-86, assoc. gen. counsel, asst. sec., 1986-90, assoc. gen. counsel, asst. sec., v.p. legal ops., 1990-94, sr. assoc. gen. coun., asst. sec., v.p. legal ops., 1994-97, multinat. estate planning, 1997—. Dir. various cos. Co-founder Internat. House R.I. Inc.; group leader Operation Crossroads Africa, Gambia. Mem. ABA, Am. Corp. Coun. Assn., Internat. Bar Assn., Westchester Fairfield Corp. Csl. Assn., Yale Alumni Assn. Westchester, Internat. Lawyers Assn., Phi Beta Kappa. Home: 111 Oscaleta Rd South Salem NY 10590-1003 Office: Multinational Estate Planning PLLC 111A Oscaleta Rd South Salem NY 10590-1003

COWLES, JOE RICHARD, biology professor; b. Edmonson County, Ky., Oct. 29, 1941; s. Otis Wilson and Mamie E. (Rountree) C.; m. Barbara Sutton, June 5, 1965; children: Richard William, Daniel Morgan. BS, Western Ky. U., 1963; MS, U. Ky., 1965; PhD, Oreg. State U., 1968. Postdoctoral fellow Purdue U., West Lafayette, Ind., 1968-69, U. Ga., Athens, 1969-70; asst. prof. U. Houston, 1970-75, assoc. prof., 1976-81, chmn. biology dept., 1981-90, prof., 1982-90; head biology Va. Tech. U., Blacksburg, 1990—2002, prof., 1990—. Contbr. more than 40 articles to profl. jours. Grantee NASA, NSF, Dept. Energy, USDA. Mem. Am. Soc. Plant Physiology, Sigma Xi. Democrat. Baptist. Avocation: sports. Office: Virginia Tech U Dept Biology Blacksburg VA 24061 E-mail: cowlesjr@vt.edu.

COWLES, JOHN, JR., publishing executive, sports promoter; b. Des Moines, May 27, 1929; s. John and Elizabeth (Bates) C.; m. Jane Sage Fuller, Aug. 23, 1952; children: Tessa Sage Flores, John, Jane Sage, Charles Fuller. Grad., Phillips Exeter Acad., 1947; AB, Harvard U., 1951; LittD (hon.), Simpson Coll., 1965. With Cowles Media Co. (formerly Mpls. Star and Tribune Co.), 1953-83, v.p., 1957-68, editor, 1961-69, pres. or chmn., 1968—83, dir., 1956-84; pres. Harper's Mag., Inc., 1965-68, chmn. bd., 1968-72; dir. Harper & Row, Pubs., Inc., N.Y.C., 1965-81, chmn., 1968-79. Dir. Des Moines Register & Tribune Co., 1960-84, Farmers & Mechanics Savs. Bank, Mpls., 1960-65, Cowles Comms., Inc., N.Y.C., 1960-65, Equitable Life Ins. Co. Iowa, Des Moines, 1964-66, 1st Bank Systems, Inc., Mpls., 1964-68, A.P., N.Y.C., 1966-75, Midwest Radio-TV, Inc., Mpls., 1967-76; fitness instr. Sweatshop Fitness Ctr., St. Paul, 1989-93; guest artist Bill T. Jones/Arnie Zane & Co., 1990-92; vice chmn. Women's Pro. Softball League LLC, Denver, 1994-2002, chmn. Pro Softball Founders LLC, 2002—04; ptnr. St. Anthony Films LLC, 1998—2004, "Herman USA", 2001; investor Block E Hotel Capital LLC, 2000—. Mem. adv. bd. on Pulitzer Prizes, Columbia U., 1970-83; campaign chmn. Mpls. United Fund, 1967; bd. dirs. Guthrie Theatre Found., 1960-71, pres., 1960-63, chmn., 1964-65, arch. selection com., 2000-01, endowment campaign steering com., 1987-91; trustee Phillips Exeter Acad., 1960-65; bd. dirs. Walker Art Ctr., 1960-69, 87-92, Minn. Civil Liberties Union, 1956-61, Urban Coalition Mpls., 1968-70, Mpls. Found., 1970-75, German Marshall Fund U.S., 1975-78; bd. dirs. Am. Newspaper Pubs. Assn., 1975-77; mem. govt. affairs com., 1976-79; mem. Woodhill Country Club, 1954-84, Century Assn., 1967-92, Coun. on Foreign Rels., 1969-92, Minn. Bus. Partnership, 1977-83, Minn. Project Corp. Responsibility, 1977-83, Trilateral Commn., 1978-82. Served to 2d lt. US Army, 1951-53. Named one of Ten Outstanding Men of Yr. U.S. Jr. C. of C., 1964, 200 Rising Leaders in Am. Time Mag., 1974; recipient John Phillips award Exeter, 1977, US Bank Sally Ordway Irvine award, St. Paul, 2000, Regents award U. Minn., 2004; Hill fellow Humphrey Inst., U. Minn., 2005-. Mem. Greater Mpls. C. of C. (dir. 1978-81, chmn. stadium site task force 1977-82), Mpls. Club, Mill Reef Club (Antigua), A.D. Club at Harvard, Signet Assn. at Harvard (pres. 1950-51). Home: 700 S 2nd St Loft 91 Minneapolis MN 55401 Office: 155 Fifth Ave S Ste 1000 Minneapolis MN 55401-2550 Office Phone: 612-359-9449.

COWLES, JOHN JAY, III, investment company executive, entrepreneur; b. Mpls., Nov. 1, 1953; s. John Jr. and Jane Sage (Fuller) C.; m. Elizabeth Page Knudsen, Sept. 8, 1984; children: Lucia, Colin, Maxwell. BA in Govt. cum laude, Harvard Coll., 1981; MBA, Harvard Bus. Sch., 1983. Pres., CEO Classic Printers, Prescott, Ariz., 1975-79, chmn., 1979-96; cons. Office Cable Comm. Boston City Hall, 1980-81; dir. planning Cowles Media Co., Mpls., 1985-88, vice chmn. bd. dirs., 1991-93, chmn. bd. dirs., 1993-98; dir. fin. analysis United Satellite Comm., Inc., N.Y.C., 1983-85; v.p. Sentinel Pub. (divsn. Cowles Media Co.), Denver, 1988-91, Book Ventures, Inc., Mpls., 1992-93; pres., CEO Women's Pro Softball, Mpls., 1993-95; chmn. bd. Nat. Pro Fastpitch, Mpls., 1993—; mng. dir. Lawrence Creek, LLC, pvt. investment co., 2004—. Bd. dirs. St. Paul Riverfront Corp., chmn., 1998-2002, Open Book, Mpls., chmn., 1998-2002; vice chmn. St. Paul Found., 2004-, Unity Ave. Found. Bd. dirs. Minn. Ctr. Book Arts, Mpls., 1991-98, chmn. bd. dirs., 1995-98, acting exec. dir., 1995-97; bd. dirs. Prescott Coll., 1976-82, Mpls. Found., 1987-88, Guthrie Theater, Mpls., 1993-98. Mem. Mpls. Club. Office: Ste 804 123 N 3d St Minneapolis MN 55401 Office Phone: 612-359-9449. E-mail: jay@unityave.com.

COWLES, ROGER E., computer consultant; b. Boston, Feb. 9, 1950; s. S. Edwin C. and Irene M. Woodard. BA in Internat. Econs. with honors, Ohio Wesleyan U., 1974. Network cons. LAN Sys., Inc., N.Y.C., 1988-91, Network Alternatives, Inc., Washington, 1991-92; dir. network syss. Quad Microsystems, Inc., Southampton, Pa., 1992-93; network cons. Integrated Microcomputer Syss., Inc., Rockville, Md., 1993-95; sys. cons. Emtec, Inc., Mt. Laurel, N.J., 1995—; prin., owner DINET Corp., 1998—. Cons. World Bank, Washington, 1992, Judge Tech. Svcs., Bala Cynwyd, Pa., 1997; sr. cons. Chem. Bank, N.Y.C., 1995-96; sr. network cons. Arco Chem. Co., 1998—; founder Transcend Media Corp., 1998, Di-Net.Corp., 1998. Mem. IEEE, Assn. Sys. Mgmt. Avocations: reading, politics, economics, sports, travel. Home: 407 W Oxford St Philadelphia PA 19122-3732 E-mail: rcowles@earthlink.net.

COWLES, WILLIAM STACEY, newspaper publisher; b. Spokane, Wash., Aug. 31, 1960; s. William Hutchinson 3rd and Allison Stacey C.; m. Anne Cannon, June 24, 1989. BA in Econs., Yale Coll., 1982; MBA in Fin., Columbia U., 1986. With The Spokesman Rev., Spokane, Wash., 1989—, pres., pub., 1992—. Office: Cowles Publishing Co PO Box 2160 Spokane WA 99210-2160 Office Phone: 509-459-5217.

COWLEY, ALLEN WILSON, JR., physiologist; b. Harrisburg, Pa., Jan. 21, 1940; m. Theresa Ann Malinoski BA, Trinity Coll., Hartford, Conn., 1961; MS, Hahnemann Med. Coll., Phila., 1965, PhD, 1968. Instr. physiology and biophysics U. Miss. Med. Ctr., Jackson, 1968-69, asst. prof. physiology and biophysics, 1969-72, assoc. prof. physiology and biophysics, 1973-75, prof. physiology and biophysics, 1975-80; prof. physiology, chmn. physiology dept. Med. Coll. Wis., Milw., 1980—; chmn. dept. physiology Marquette U., Milw., 1990—. Lectr. and invited spkr. in field; organizer various confs. Mem. editl. bd. Clin. and Exptl. Hypertension, 1977—, Am. Jour. Physiology: Circulation Sect., 1979-83, Hypertension, 1980-91, 93—, Am. Jour. Physiology: Regulatory, Integrative and Comparative Physiology, 1984-88, Internat. Jour. Cardiology, 1985—, Am. Jour. Physiology: Heart and Circulatory Physiology, 1987-89, Clin. Exptl. Pharmacology Physiology, 1993-96, Jour. Hypertension, 1993-96, Physiol. Revs., 1997—, News in Physiol. Scis., 1997—, assoc. editor 1988-91; guest editor Hypertension, Ann. Supplement Procs. Coun. for High Blood Pressure Rsch., 1981-84; contbr. 30 chpts. to books and symposia, over 180 articles to profl. jours. and conf. procs. Recipient numerous NIH rsch. grants, 1971—; recipient Established Investigatorship award Am. Heart Asnsn., 1973-78, Alumnus of Yr. award Hahnemann Med. Coll., 1975, MERIT award NIH, 1996. Fellow Am. Heart Assn. Coun. High Blood Pressure Rsch. (chmn. publs. com. 1982-84, mem. various coms., Disting. Achievement award 1996, Novartis award 1997), Am. Heart Assn. Coun. on Circulation (various coms.), Am. Physiol. Soc. Cardiovasc. Sect.; mem. Am. Physiol. Soc. (various coms., pres.-elect 1996-97, pres. 1997—, Ernest H. Starling Disting. lectureship 1996, Wiggers award 1997), Internat. Soc. Hypertension, Am. Soc. Nephrology, Microcirculation Soc., Assn. Chairmen Depts. Physiology (various offices and coms., pres. 1990), Hungarian Physiol. Soc. (hon.), Brazilian Acad. Sci. (hon.), Sigma Xi. Office: Med Coll Wisconsin Dept Physiology 8701 W Watertown Plank Rd Milwaukee WI 53226-3548

COWLEY, GERALD DEAN, architect; b. Great Bend, Kans., Oct. 2, 1931; s. Stone Oden and Elizabeth (Lillich) C.; m. Lois Ester Traudt, Aug. 10, 1957 (div. 1983); children: Tara Elizabeth, Craig Stone; m. Frances Leach, Dec. 28, 1986. BArch, Kans. State U., 1960. Lic. architect, Colo. Architect James H. Johnson Architect, Lakewood, Colo., 1963-74, James H. Johnson & Assocs. Architects, Lakewood, 1963-74; architect, ptnr., prin. Johnson Hopson & Ptnrs., Denver, 1974-82, JHP Architecture Interior Design and Planning, Denver, 1982—. Prin. works include Rocky Mountain Energy Headquarters Bldg., others. Sgt. USAF, 1951-55. Mem.: AIA, Constrn. Specifications Inst. Republican. Avocations: golf, sailing, skiing, watercolor. Home and Office: 1226 Hampstead Ln Ormond Beach FL 32174

COWLEY, JOSEPH GILBERT, writer; b. Yonkers, N.Y., Oct. 9, 1923; s. Joseph Gilbert and Gertrude Hersey Cowley; m. Ruth Muriel Wilson, Feb. 28, 1948; children: Barbara, Charles, Jennifer, Joseph. BA with honors, Columbia U., 1947, MA, 1948. Ptnr. Writing-Editing Svcs., N.Y.C., 1946-47; instr. English, Cornell U., Ithaca, N.Y., 1948-49; salesman Allyn & Bacon, N.Y.C., 1949-54; sales promoter Home Life Ins. Co., N.Y.C., 1954-56; editor, then mng. editor Rsch. Inst. Am., N.Y.C., 1956-82; ret., 1982. Author: The Executive Strategist, 1969, The Chrysanthemum Garden, 1981, The Stargazers, 1991, Dust Be My Destiny, 1999, Home by Seven, 2000, The House on Huntington Hill, 2000, The Night Billy Was Born and Other Love Stories, 2002. 2nd lt. USAAF, 1943-45, ETO. Avocation: reading. Home: 630 Oriole Dr Southold NY 11971 E-mail: jgcowley@suffolk.lib.ny.us, joecowley@nyway.com.

COWLEY, ROBERT WILLIAM, editor, writer, consultant, lecturer; b. NYC, Dec. 16, 1934; s. Malcolm and Muriel (Maurer) C.; m. Blair Phillips (div.); children: Elizabeth Blair Roberts, Miranda Phillips Heller; m. Edith Pray Lorillard, June 24, 1978; children: Olivia Lorillard, Savannah Caroline Lorillard. AB, Harvard U., 1956. Assoc. editor Am. Heritage, N.Y.C., 1956-64; mng. editor Sky, N.Y.C., 1964; asst. editor The Reporter, N.Y.C., 1965-66; articles editor, mng. editor Horizon, N.Y.C., 1966-72; co-editor The Saturday Review of the Arts, N.Y.C. and San Francisco, 1972-73; sr. editor, exec. editor Houghton Mifflin, Boston, 1973-77; sr. editor Random House, N.Y.C., 1977-84, Henry Holt, N.Y.C., 1984-88; founding editor, editor-in-chief MHQ: The Quarterly Jour. of Military History, N.Y.C., 1988-98; cons., writer, 1998—2003. Author: The Rulers of Britain, 1982; editor, contbr.: Experience of War, 1992, The Great War, 2003; co-editor: (with Malcolm Cowley) Fitzgerald and the Jazz Age, 1966; (with Geoffrey Parker) The Reader's Companion to Military History, 1996; (with Thomas Guinzburg) West Point: Two Centuries of Honor and Tradition, 2002; contbg. author: A Weekend with the Great War: Proceedings of the Fourth Annual Great War Inter-Conf. Sem., 1997, To the Best of My Ability: The American Presidents, 2000, What Might Have Been, 2004, The Cold War: A Military HIstory, 2005; editor, contbr. What If?: The World's Foremost Military Historians Imagine What Might Have Been, 1999, The Collected What If?, 2004; editor: No End Save Victory, 2001, With My Face to the Enemy, 2001, What If? 2, 2001, What Ifs? of American History, 2003. Fellow Soc. Am. Historians; mem. Soc. Mil. History. Democrat. Episcopalian. Avocations: jazz collecting, military archaeology. Home: PO Box 268 Sherman CT 06784-0268 E-mail: cowleyrw219@aol.com.

COWLISHAW, MARY LOU, government educator; b. Rockford, Ill., Feb. 20, 1932; d. Donald George and Mildred Corinne (Hayes) Miller; m. Wayne Arnold Cowlishaw, July 24, 1954; children: Beth Cowlishaw McDaniel, John, Paula Cowlishaw Rader. BS in Journalism, U. Ill., 1954; DHL, North Ctrl. Coll., 1999; DHL (hon.), Benedictine U., 2000. Mem. editorial staff Naperville (Ill.) Sun newspaper, 1977-83; mem. Ill. Ho. of Reps., Springfield, 1983—2003, chmn. elem. and secondary edn. com., 1995—97, vice-chmn. pub. utilities com., 1995—2003, mem. joint Ho.-Senate edn. reform oversight com., 1985—97; assoc. Ctr. for Govtl. Studies No. Ill. U., 2003—; adj. prof. North Ctrl. Coll., Naperville, Ill., 2003—. Mem. Ill. Task Force on Sch. Fin., 1990-96; vice chmn. Ho. Rep. Campaign Com., 1990—; co-chair Ho. Rep. Policy Com., 1991-2003; chmn. edn. com. Nat. Conf. State Legislatures, 1993-97; mem. Joint Com. Adminstrv. Rules, 1992-2003; commr. Edn. Commn. of the States, 1995-2002; chair, Ill. Women's Agenda Task Force, 1994—; mem. Nat. Edn. Goals Panel, 1996—, bd. govs. Lincoln Series for Excellence in Pub. Svc., 1996—. Author: This Band's Been Here Quite a Spell, 1983; columnist Ill. Press Assn., 2003—. Mem. Naperville Dist. 203 Bd. Edn., 1972-83; co-chmn. Ill. Citizens Coun. on Sch. Problems, Springfield, 1985-2003. Recipient 1st pl. award Ill. Press Assn., 1981, commendation Naperville Jaycees, 1986, Golden Apple award Ill. Assn. Sch. Bds., 1988, 90, 92, 94, Outstanding Women Leaders of DuPage County award West Suburban YWCA, 1990, Activator award Ill. Farm Bur., 1996, 1998, Bd. of Dirs. award Little Friends, Inc., 1998, Honor award Ill. Math. and Sci. Acad., 2002, Pub. Svc. award West Suburban Higher Edn. Consortium, 2002; named Best Legislator, Ill. Citizens for Better Care, 1985, Woman of Yr., Naperville AAUW, 1987, Best Legislator, Ill. Assn. Fire Chiefs, 1994, Outstanding Edn. Adv. Indian Prairie Sch. Dist. 204, 1994, Legislator of Yr., Ill. Assn. Pk. Dists., 1995; commr. Edn. Commn. of the States, 1994-2002; Mary Lou Cowlishaw Elem. Sch. named in her honor, 1997, Legislator of Yr., Ill. Assn. Mus., 1998. Mem. Am. Legis. Exch. Coun., Conf. Women Legislators, Nat. Fedn. Rep. Women, DAR, Naperville Rep. Women's Club (pres. 1994—), Jr. League of Greater DuKane (cmty. adv. bd. 1997—). Methodist. Avocation: the violin. Home: 924 Merrimac Cir Naperville IL 60540-7107 Office: North Central Coll 30 N Brainard St Naperville IL 60540-4690

COWPERTHWAIT, LINDLEY MURRAY, lawyer; b. Abington, Pa., Mar. 13, 1933; s. Lindley Murray Cowperthwait and Ruth Bronde Nicholas; m. Suzanne Dewees, Nov. 26, 1955 (div. July 1976); children: Murray, Mary Ruth, Edward, Linda, Tom, Suzanne; m. Karin Schmid Cowperthwait, Apr. 1, 1989. BA, Calif. State U., 1957; LLB, U. Pa., 1960, JD, 1970. Bar: Pa., Md. Assoc. Wisler, Pearlstine, Talone Craig & Garrity, Norristown, Pa., 1960-68, ptnr., 1968-80; pvt. practice Norristown, 1980-96; of counsel High, Swartz, Roberts & Seidel, LLP, Norristown, 1997—2002. Prodr., author, dir. (video) Medicine for Lawyers, 1980-93; author: Damages-Delay and Punitive 1999, 2000, 01, 04, HIPPA-A Thorn in the side of the Legal Profession, 2004, Scrivener Med-Leg Code of Ethics, 1960, 75, 94, 2001, 04 Bd. dirs. ARC, Norristown, 1993-95, Big Bros./Big Sisters, Norristown, 1985-92. Recipient Citizenship award Big Bros./Big Sisters, 1992, Comm. award Montgomery County Med. Soc., 2002. Mem. Pa. Trial Lawyers Assn. (pres. 1974-75), Montgomery County Trial Lawyers (founder, sec. 1965-74, Trial Lawyer of Yr. 2003), Assn. Trial Lawyers of Am., Pa. Bar Assn., Md. Bar Assn., Am. Coll. Legal Medicine (invited mem., litigator cons., counselor), Pa. Soc., Md. State Bar Assn Republican. Episcopalian. Avocation: sailing. Office Phone: 410-639-7406.

COWSER, DANNY LEE, lawyer, mental health specialist; b. Peoria, Ill., July 7, 1948; s. Albert Paul Cowser and Shirley Mae (Donaldson) Chatten; m. Nancy Lynn Hatch, Nov. 11, 1976; children: Kimberly Catherine Hatch Cowser, Dustin Paul Hatch Cowser. BA, No. Ill. U., 1972, MS, 1975; JD, DePaul U., 1980. Bar: Ill. 1980, Wis. 1981, U.S. Dist. Ct. (no. dist.) Ill. 1981, U.S. Ct. Appeals (7th cir.) 1983, U.S. Dist. Ct. (ea. and we. dists.) Wis. 1984, U.S. Supreme Ct. 1984, Ariz. 1985, U.S. Ct. Appeals (9th cir.) 1987, U.S. Dist. Ct. Ariz. 1989, U.S. Tax Ct. 1990, U.S. Ct. Claims 1990, Colo. 2000. Adminstr. Ill. Dept. Mental Health, Elgin, 1972-76, psychotherapist, 1976-79; assoc. Slaby, Deda & Henderson, Phillips, Wis., 1982-83; ptnr. Slaby, Deda & Cowser, Phillips, 1983-86; asst. atty. City of Flagstaff, Ariz., 1986-88; pub. defender Coconino County, Flagstaff, 1988-89; pvt. practice Flagstaff, 1989-97. Atty. City Park Falls, Wis., 1982-86; spl. dep. Mohave County capital def., 1989-90; instr. speech comms. No. Ariz. U., 1992-93; adminstrv. law judge Ariz. Dept. Econ. Security, 1997—. Bd. dirs. DeKalb County (Ill.) Drug Coun., 1973-75, Counseling and Personal Devel., Phillips, 1985-86. Reginald Heber Smith fellow, 1980-81; C.J.S. legal scholar, 1979. Mem. Nat. Assn. Criminal Def. Lawyers, Ariz. Bar Assn., State Bar Ariz. (cert. specialist in criminal law 1993-98), State Bar Wis., Nat. Assn. of Criminal Def. Lawyers. Democrat. Avocations: skiing, photography, bicycling.

COWSIK, RAMANATH, physics professor; b. Nagpur, Madhya, India, Aug. 29, 1940; came to U.S., 1970; s. Ramakrishna K. and Saraswati C. (Ayyar) C.; m. Shyamala Balasubrahmanian, Aug. 20, 1979 (div. Feb. 1989); 1 child, Siddhartha. BS, Mysore U., Bangalore, India, 1958; MS in Physics, Karnatak U., India, 1960; PhD, Bombay U., 1968. Jr. rsch. assoc. Tata Inst. Fundamental Rsch., Bombay, 1961—, reader, 1975—, assoc. prof., 1977—, prof., 1984—, disting. prof.; asst. prof. U. Calif., Berkeley, 1970-73; vis. scientist Max-Planck Inst. Extension Physik, Munich, 1973-74; dir. Indian Inst. for Astrophysics. Vis. prof. Washington U., St. Louis, 1987—. Contbr. articles to Jour. Physics Rev., Astrophys. Jour. Recipient Sarabhai award Hari om Soc./Phys. Rsch. Lab., 1981, Group Achievement award NASA, 1986. Fellow Indian Acad. Scis., Indian Nat. Sci. Acad. (Bhatnagar award 1984); mem. Am. Phys. Soc. (life), Internat. Astron. Union (life), Nat. Acad. Scis. (fgn. assoc.) Achievements include development of the theory that weakly interacting particle relicts from the big bang are the constituents of dark matter and set the upper bound on the sum of their masses, in particular of neutrinos; recognized the cosmological significance of the hard x-ray background; derived the leaky box and nested leaky box models for cosmic rays; research in high energy astrophysics of nonthermal emissions from quasars and supernova remnants and in astroparticle physics and experimental gravitation; measurement of the double beta decay life-time of the tellurium-128 nucleus as 7.7x10 24 years the longest, implying the Majorana mass of the neutrino to be less than 1 eV. Home: 6351 Waterman Ave Saint Louis MO 63130-4708 Office: Washington U Box 1105 1 Brookings Dr Saint Louis MO 63130-4862

COX, ALBERT HARRINGTON, JR., economist; b. St. Louis, Oct. 13, 1932; s. Albert Harrington and Hildegarde (Raab) C.; m. Frances Marie French, Apr. 12, 1960; children: Cynthia, Bruce Harrington. BBA, U. Tex., 1954, MBA, 1956; PhD, U. Mich., 1965. Asst. prof. finance So. Meth. U., Dallas, 1959; economist First Nat. City Bank, N.Y.C., 1960-61; sec. research com. Am. Bankers Assn., N.Y.C., 1962-64; v.p., economist First Nat. Bank, Dallas, 1965-68; spl. asst. to chmn. Pres.'s Council Econ. Advs., Washington, 1969-70; exec. v.p., chief economist, dir. Lionel D. Edie & Co., N.Y.C., 1970-75; sr. econ. adv. Merrill Lynch, Pierce, Fenner & Smith, Inc., N.Y.C., 1970-75; pres. Merrill Lynch Econs., Inc., N.Y.C., 1976-81, chmn., 1982-84; chief economist Merrill Lynch & Co., 1976-81. Mng. dir. Merrill Lynch Capital Markets Group; dir. Merrill Lynch Capital Fund; mem. econ. adv. bd. Dept. Commerce, 1974-76; dir., sr. econ. adviser BIL Trainer, Wortham Inc. (Bank in Liechtenstein, A.G.), 1985-90; sr. econ. adviser Trainer Wortham, Inc., 1991; portfolio cons. The Seibels Bruce Ins. Cos., Columbia, S.C., 1993-94, dir., 1994-97; mem. Pres.'s Inflation Policy Task Force, 1980; disting. lectr. in bus. and econs. U. S.C., Hilton Head, 1988-90; dir. Nestor, Inc., 2003—. Author: Regulation of Interest Rates on Bank Deposits, 1966; contbg. economist Coast Business, 1997-99, Bankers Monthly mag., 1970-88; bus. columnist Hilton Head News, 1990-98; contbr. articles to profl. jours. Mem. Nat. Assn. Bus. Economists (past dir.), Securities Industries Assn. (chmn. econ. adv. com. 1979-80), Am. Econ. Assn., Beta Gamma Sigma, Beta Theta Pi, Phi Eta Sigma. Republican. Mem. Reformed Ch. Home: 2002 Claudette Cv Biloxi MS 39531-2426 Office Phone: 228-388-8865. Personal E-mail: ahcox@bellsouth.net.

COX, ALBERT REGINALD, retired dean, retired cardiologist; b. Victoria, B.C., Can., Apr. 18, 1928; s. Reginald Herbert and Marie Christina (Fraser) C.; m. Margaret Dobson, May, 1954; children: Susan Margaret, David John, Steven Fraser. BA, U. B.C., 1950, MD, 1954. Intern Vancouver Gen. Hosp., 1954-55, resident, 1955-59; fellow in cardiology U. Wash., 1959-61; asst. prof. medicine U. B.C., 1962-65, assoc. prof., 1966-69; prof., chmn. medicine Meml. U., St. John's, Nfld., Can., 1969-74, dean medicine, 1974-87, v.p. Health Scis. and Profl. Sch., 1988-90, v.p. acad., pro-vice chancellor, 1990-91; ret., 1991. Decorated mem. Order of Can. Fellow ACP, Royal Coll. Physicians and Surgeons Can., Am. Coll. Cardiology; mem. Nfld. Med. Assn., Can. Med. Assn., Can. Soc. Clin. Investigation, Assn. Can. Med. Colls. (pres. 1980-81), Coun. of Royal Coll. Physicians and Surgeons (v.p. medicine 1990-91), Alpha Omega Alpha. United Ch. Home: 1275 Campbell Rd Cobble Hill BC Canada V0R 1L0

COX, ALLAN JAMES, management consultant; b. Berwyn, Ill., June 13, 1937; s. Brack C. and Ruby D. C.; m. Jeanne Begalke, 1961 (div. 1966); 1 child, Heather; m. Bonnie Lynne Welden, 1966 (div. 1990); 1 child, Laura; m. Cheryl Patric, 1991. BA, No. Ill. U., 1961, MA, 1962; postgrad., McCormick Theol. Sem., Chgo., 1962-63, Alfred Adler Inst. of Chgo., 1965-67, Gestalt Inst. of Chgo., 1994-96. Instr. Wheaton (Ill.) Coll., 1963-65; assoc. Case and Co., Inc., Chgo., 1965-66, Spencer Stuart & Assos., Inc., Chgo., 1966-68; v.p. Westcott Assos., Inc., Chgo., 1968-69; founder, pres. Allan Cox & Assocs., Inc., 1969—; chmn. Berryman Comm. Co., Chgo., 1994-98; chmn. of the bd. Amateur Baseball, Inc., Chgo., 1992-96, CEO, 1996-98; chmn., CEO Assn. for Internat. Youth Sports, Inc., Chgo., 1998-99. Adj. staff Ctr. for Creative Leadership, Greensboro, NC, 1985-90; mem. vis. com. U. Chgo. Div. Sch., 1996-2005; mem. San Diego Regional Econ. Devel. Corp Author: Confessions of a Corporate Headhunter, 1973, Work, Love and Friendship, 1974, The Cox Report on the American Corporation, 1982, The Making of the

Achiever, 1985, The Achiever's Profile, 1988, Straight Talk for Monday Morning, 1990, Redefining Corporate Soul: Linking Purpose and People, 1996; columnist L.A. Times Syndicate, 1986-90; contbr. articles to profl. jours. Chmn. bd. Ctr. for Ethics and Corp. Policy, 1987-92; Elder Fourth Presbyn. Ch. of Chgo. Mem.: Corp. Dirs. Forum, Nat. Assn. Corp. Dirs., Chgo. Club, Alpha Kappa Delta. Presbyterian. Office: 45 East Bellevue Pl Chicago IL 60611-1133 Office Phone: 312-337-8010. Business E-Mail: allan@allancox.com.

COX, ANN, literature and language educator, media specialist; d. Shirley and Robert Kelly; m. Kevin Cox, Oct. 20, 2001. BS in English, Ill. State U., 1998—98. English tchr., media specialist Ctrl. Cath. H.S., Bloomington, Ill., 1998—. Tchr. cons. Ill. State Writing Project, Normal, Ill., 2004—; presenter in field. Author of poems. Mem.: ALA, Young Adult Libr. Svcs. Assn., Ill. Sch. Libr. Media Assn., Nat. Cath. Edn. Assn., Ill. Assn. of Tchrs. English, Nat. Coun. of Tchrs. English, Nat. Writing Project. Roman Catholic. Avocations: writing, reading, rubber stamping, paper crafting. Office: Central Cath High Sch 1201 Airport Rd Bloomington IL 61704 Office Phone: 309-661-7000.

COX, ARCHIBALD, JR., investment company executive; b. Wayland, Mass., July 13, 1940; s. Archibald and Phyllis (Ames) C.; children: Suzanne, Archibald III, Christopher. Pres., CEO The First Boston Corp., N.Y.C., 1990-93; chmn. Sextant Group, Inc., N.Y.C., 1993—; pres., CEO Magnequench, Inc., Indpls., 1995—. Bd. dirs. Hutchinson Tech. Inc., Builders Info. Group, Magnequench, Inc. Bd. dirs. Claremont McKenna Coll., 1992-97. Mem.: Harvard Club of Boston, Links Club N.Y.C., NY Yacht Club. Avocations: bicycling, sailing, hiking. Office: c/o Magnequench Inc 9775 Crosspoint Blvd Indianapolis IN 46256 also: Sextant Group Inc PO Box 489 Scotch Plains NJ 07076-0489 Office Phone: 765-631-2000. E-mail: acox@mqii.com, acox5005@aol.com.

COX, BARBARA MARGARETE, artist, educator; b. Wittenberg, Germany, June 24, 1937; arrived in U.S., 1963; d. Ulrich Schroth and Ursula Schroth-Pritzel; m. Donald A. Cox, Sept. 7, 1963 (div. Apr. 1973); children: Jennifer Ann, Roger Anthony. Grad., Acad. Fine Arts Sculpture, Munich, Germany, 1963; MA Humanistic Psychology, Vt. Coll. Norwich U., 1991. Cert. profl. tchr. Colo., 1974. Art instr. Cmty. Tree Sch., Boulder, Colo., 1971—72; art instr. children's classes Boulder Fine Arts Ctr., Colo., 1972—73; dir., instr., coord. U. Meml. Ctr., Boulder, Colo., 1974—85; art instr. drawing City Recreation Ctr., Boulder, Colo., 1985—; art instr. stone sculpture U. Boulder Continuing Edn., 1985—. Grantee grant for tng. mgmt. program arts and crafts, Western Art Found., 1976. Democrat. Lutheran. Avocations: hiking with dog, cross country skiing, playing recorder-flutes, puppetry, gardening. Home: 638 Pleasant St Boulder CO 80302

COX, BEULAH ELIZABETH, violinist, music educator; b. Newport News, Va., Mar. 15, 1955; d. Willis Franklin and Rosemary Christian Coates Cox. BA, Coll. of William and Mary, 1973—77. Violinist Colonial Williamsburg Found., Williamsburg, Va., 1975—78, Hudson Valley Philharm., Poughkeepsie, NY, 1984—95, The Greenwich Symphony, Conn., 1984—; violinist/founder The Ambrosia Trio, NYC, 1990—; violin soloist Allegro Chamber Ensemble, New York, NY, 1991, Virtuoso Strings, NYC, 1992, Doansburg Chamber Ensemble, Brewster, NY, 1993; violinist Nat. Chorale, NYC, 1994—; violin soloist Buglisi/Foreman Dance Co., NYC, 1996. Violinist Joseph Fuchs Chamber Music Inst., Alfred, NY, 1976—83, Grand Teton Music Festival, Teton Village, Wyo., 1984, Am. Inst. of Musical Studies, Graz, Austria, 1985, Banff Chamber Music, Banff, Canada, 1995; adj. prof. of violin Fordham U., Bronx, NY, 2000—; string tchr. Ethical Culture Sch., NYC, 1997—; violin and piano tchr. Riverdale YM-YWHA - Rhoda Grundman Sch. of Music, Bronx, 1999—; violin tchr. Bronx Arts Ensemble Sch., Bronx, 2000—. Musician: (recording) Peter and the Wolf, Baroque Sonatas and Trios, 1975, Berlioz Te Deum - Voices of Ascension, 1996, Meet The Ambrosia Trio!, 1997, The Ambrosia Trio Close Up, 2000. Mem.: Am. Fedn. of Musicians, Chamber Music Am.

COX, BOBBY (ROBERT JOE COX), professional baseball manager; b. Tulsa, Okla., May 21, 1941; m. Pamela Cox; children: Kami, Keisha, Skyla. Student, Reedley Jr. Coll., Calif. Player Calif. League, Reno, 1960, Northwest League, Salem, Oreg., 1961-62, Texas League, Albuquerque, 1963-64, Pacific Coast League, Salt Lake City, 1965, Tacoma, 1966, Internat. League, Richmond, Va., 1967, New York Yankees, N.Y.C., 1968-69, Internat. League, Syracuse, N.Y., 1970, Fla. State League, Ft. Lauderdale, 1971, mgr., 1971, Ea. League, West Haven, Conn., 1972, Internat. League, Syracuse, 1973-76; 1st base coach New York Yankees, N.Y.C., 1977; mgr. Atlanta Braves, 1978-81, Toronto (Ont., Can.) Blue Jays, 1982-85, Atlanta Braves, 1990—. Named Am. League Mgr. of Yr., 1985, Nat. League Mgr. of Yr., 1991, 2004 Achievements include coach World Series Champion Atlanta Braves, 1995; 9th manager in MLB history to win 2,000 games, 2004. Office: care Atlanta Braves PO Box 4064 Atlanta GA 30302-4064

COX, BRIAN, actor; b. Dundee, Scotland, June 1, 1946; m. Caroline Burt, 1968 (div. 1986); 2 children; m. Nicole Ansari, 2002; 2 children. Actor: (films) Nicholas and Alexandra, 1971, In Celebration, 1975, Manhunter, 1986, Hidden Agenda, 1990, Bravehart, 1995, Chain Reaction, 1996, The Long Kiss Goodnight, 1996, Kiss the Girls, 1997, Desperate Measures, 1998, Rushmore, 1998, For Love of the Game, 1999, The Invention of Dr. Morel, 2000, The Affair of the Necklace, 2001, Strictly Sinatra, 2001, The Rookie, 2002, The Bourne Identity, 2002, The Ring, 2002, Adaptation, 2002, 25th Hour, 2002, X2: X-Men United, 2003, The Reckoning, 2003, Troy, 2004, The Bourne Supremacy, 2004, Get the Picture, 2004, Match Point, 2005, Red-Eye, 2005; (TV films) Shoot for the Sun, 1986, Murder by Moonlight, 1989, Secret Weapon, 1990, The Lost Language of Cranes, 1991, The Cloning of Joanna May, 1992, Sharpe's Eagle, 1993, Sharpe's Rifles, 1993, The Negotiator, 1994, Witness Against Hitler, 1996, Food for Ravens, 1997, Poodle Springs, 1998, Longitude, 2000, The Biographer, 2002, Blue/Orange, 2005, The Strange Case of Sherlock Holmes & Arthur Conan Doyle, 2005, others; (TV miniseries) Nuremberg, 2001 (Emmy award Oustanding Supporting Actor in Miniseries, 2001); dir.: (plays) The Man with a Flower in His Mouth, 1973; stage appearances include: As You Like It, 1966—67; In Celebration, 1969; Danton' Death, 1982; Strange Interlude, 1984; Rat in the Skull, 1984 (Laurence Olivier Theatre award Best Actor in a New Play, 1985); Titus Andronicus, 1988 (Laurence Olivier Theatre award Best Actor in a Revival, 1989); Frankie and Johnnie in the Clair-de-Lune, 1989; St. Nicholas; Skylight, 1997; Art, 1998; Dublin Carol, 2000; others. Recipient London Critics Circle Theatre award, 1984, 1987, comdr., Order. Brit. Empire, 2002. Office: IFA Talent Agency 8730 Sunset Blvd Ste 490 Los Angeles CA 90069 also: Jo Gurnett Personal Mgmt Ltd No 2 New Kings Rd London SW6 4SA England*

COX, CAROLE BETH, social worker, educator; b. L.A. d. Morris and Esther Bebe Abramson; m. Colin Roy Cox; children: Amanda, Susannah. BA, U. Calif., Berkeley; Diploma Social Adminstrn., London Sch. Econs., 1967; MSW, Va. Commonwealth U., 1975; PhD, U. Md., 1980. Rsch. asst. Addiction Rsch. Found., Toronto, Canada, 1969—71; tech. officer WHO, Geneva, 1972—73; cmty. health educator Md. State Dept. Health, Balt., 1976—77; asst. prof. San Jose State U., Calif., 1980—86; asst. to assoc. prof. Cath. U. Am., Washington, 1987—97; prof. Fordham U., N.Y.C., 1997—. Cons. Alzheimers Assn., Chgo., 1995—2000, Nat. Acad. on Aging, Washington, 1995, Nat. Coun. on Aging, Washington, 1994—95, Am. Assn. Ret. Persons, Washington, 1986—90. Author: (book) Home Care: An International Perspective, 1991, The Frail Elderly: Problems, Needs, Community Resources, 1993, Ethnicity and Social Work Practice, 1998, Empowerment Training for Custodial Grandparents, 2000, Community Care for an Aging Society: Issues, Policies and Services, 2005; editor: To Grandmother's House We Go to Stay: A Perspective on Custodial Grandparents, 2000; contbr. numerous articles to profl. jours., chpts. to books. Mem. pub. policy bd. Citizens Com. on Aging, N.Y.C., 1999—2001; commr. Commn. on Aging, Howard County, Md., 1989—95; bd. dirs. KinCare Task Force, N.Y.C., 1999—; adv. bd. Coun. on Aging, Santa Clara County, 1983—84. Postdoctoral fellow, NIMH, 1984—85, Mental Health fellow, 1978—79, Resident scholar, Nat. Inst. Social Work, London, 1995. Mem.: NASW, Am. Soc. on Aging, Gerontol. Soc. Am. Avocations: theater, painting, yoga, running. Office: Fordham Univ 113 W 60th St New York NY 10023 Office Phone: 212-636-6649. E-mail: ccox@fordham.edu.

COX, CARRIE LEE, secondary school educator; b. Chgo., June 29, 1956; d. Leonard Charles and Lea Marie (Spezia) C. BS, Ill. State U., 1978; M of Health Sci., Governor's State U., 1987. Cert. K-12 tchr., Ill. Tchr., driver edn., health, phys. edn., softball coach Consol. High Sch. Dist. 230, Tinley Park, Ill., 1979—, golf coach, 1983—. Coach softball IHSA Elite Eight Softball Team, 2003; golf teams Dist. 230, Tinley Pk., Ill., 1979—89. Developer/designer newsletter in field, 1987. Mem. Ill. Polit. Action Com. for Edn., Dist. 230 Tchrs. Assn., 1987; officer Govtl. Affairs Com., 1986-88. Recipient Connections 2000 award sponsored by Ill. State Bd. Edn., 1992. Mem. Ill. Edn. Assn. (bldg. chmn. 1985-91, dist. 230 Tchr. Assn. v.p. 2002—, chief negotiator 2005), AAHPERD (N.E. dist. rep. Ill. Divsn., 1986-88) Democrat. Roman Catholic. Avocations: golf, cross country skiing, walking, swimming, travel. Office: Victor J Andrew High Sch 9001 171st St Tinley Park IL 60477-6098 Office Phone: 708-342-5800. E-mail: golfngal56@comcast.net.

COX, CATHY, state official; b. Bainbridge, Ga., July 18, 1958; d. Walter Cox; m. Mark Dehler. A.Agr., Abraham Baldwin Agrl. Coll., 1978; BJ summa cum laude, U. Ga., 1980; JD magna cum laude, Mercer U., 1986. Newspaper reporter The Gainesville Times, Gainesville, 1980-82, Post-Searchlight, Bainbridge, 1982-83; atty. Hansell & Post, Atlanta, 1986-88, Lambert, Floyd & Conger, Bainbridge, Ga., 1988-95; mem. Dist. 160 Ga. Gen. Assembly, 1993-96; asst. sec. of state State of Ga., Atlanta, 1996-98, sec. of state, 1999—. Editor Mercer U. Law Rev. Named Conservation Legislator of Yr., Ga. Wildlife Fedn., 1994, Woman of Courage award, Woman's Policy Group, 1995, Woman of Yr., Ga. Commn. on Women, 2000, named one of 11 Pub. Officials of Yr., Governing Mag., 2002. Democrat. Methodist. Office: Office of Sec of State 214 State Capitol SW Atlanta GA 30334-1600 E-mail: sosweb@sos.state.ga.us.

COX, CHAPMAN BEECHER, retired lawyer, retired charitable organization executive, retired aerospace transportation executive; b. Dayton, Ohio, July 31, 1940; s. Charles Benjamin and Jewel Lorene (Nicholson) C.; m. Jeannette Gail Korody, Aug. 28, 1964; children: Charles Benjamin, Andrew David. BA, U. So. Calif., 1962; JD, Harvard U., 1965. Bar: Calif. 1966, Colo. 1972, U.S. Ct. Mil. Appeals 1966, U.S. Supreme Ct. 1986. Assoc. Adams, Duque & Hazeltine, Los Angeles, 1968-72, Sherman & Howard, Denver, 1972-74, ptnr., 1974-80, mng. ptnr., 1980-81, ptnr., 1987-90; dep. asst. sec. U.S. Dept. Navy, Washington, 1981-83, asst. sec., 1983-84; gen. counsel Dept. Def., Washington, 1984-85, asst. sec., 1985-87; pres., CEO United Svc. Orgns., Inc., 1990-96; sr. v.p. Lockheed Martin IMS, 1996-2000; ret., 2000. Vis. lectr. U. Colo. Sch. Law, Boulder, 1977-78; def. policy bd. US Dept. Def., 1988-90; comml. space transp. adv. com. US Dept. Transp., 1989-91; chmn. Colo. Commn. Space Sci. and Industry, 1988-90. Gen. counsel Colo. Reps., Denver, 1977-81; del. U.S. Dept. State cultural exch. mission to Syria and Jordan, 1979; ruling elder Presbyn. Ch., 1976—; bd. dirs. United Svc. Orgns., 1985-96, Colorado Springs Symphony Orch., 1988-90, MicroLithics Corp., 1989-91, Presbyn. Ch. U.S.A. Found., 1990-99, Freedoms Found., 1994-99, Fund for Am. Studies, 1995-00, New Covenant Trust Co., 1996-99, Presbyn. Lay Com., 1997-2000, Alliance Def. Fund, 2002—; bd. govs. Army-Navy Club Washington, 1998-00. Col. USMCR, 1962-93, ret. Fellow: Am. Coll. Trust and Estate Counsel; mem.: ABA (standing com. law and nat. security 1988—2002), Colo. Bar Assn. (bd. govs. 1977—79, chmn. probate and trust law sect. 1978—79), Calif. Bar Assn., Army-Navy Club of Washington. Personal E-mail: chapmancox@att.net.

COX, CHARLES C., economist; b. Missoula, Mont., May 8, 1945; m. Monica Lewis, 1984. BA magna cum laude, U. Wash., 1967; AM, U. Chgo., 1970, PhD, 1975. Asst. prof. econs. Ohio State U., Columbus, 1972-80; nat. fellow Hoover Instn., 1977-78; asst. prof. mgmt. Tex. A&M U., College Station, 1980-82; chief economist SEC, Washington, 1982-83, commr., 1983-89, acting chmn., 1987; prin., sr. v.p. Lexecon, Inc., Chgo., 1989—. Nat. fellow Hoover Institution, 1977-78. Mem. Am. Econ. Assn., United Shareholders Assn. (chmn. 1990-93), Mt. Pelerin Soc., Phi Beta Kappa. Office: Lexecon Inc 332 S Michigan Ave Ste 1300 Chicago IL 60604-4397

COX, CHARLES SHIPLEY, oceanography researcher, educator; b. Paia, Hawaii, Sept. 11, 1922; s. Joel Bean and Helen Clifford (Horton) C.; m. Maryruth Louise Melander, Dec. 23, 1951; children: Susan (dec.), Caroline, Valerie, Ginger, Joel. BS, Calif. Inst. Tech., 1944; PhD, U. Calif., San Diego, 1955. From asst. rschr. to prof. U. Calif., San Diego, 1955—. Rschr. in field. Fellow AAAS, NAS (Alexander Agassiz medal 2001), Am. Geophys. Union (Maurice Ewing medal 1992), Royal Astron. Soc. Democrat. Office: U Calif San Diego Scripps Inst Oceanography La Jolla CA 92093-0213 E-mail: cscox@ucsd.edu.

COX, CHRISTOPHER (CHARLES CHRISTOPHER COX), federal agency administrator, former congressman; b. St. Paul, Minn., Oct. 16, 1952; s. Charles C. and Marilyn A. (Miller) C.; m. Rebecca Gernhardt; children: Charles, Kathryn, Kevin. BA magna cum laude, U. So. Calif., 1973; MBA with honors, Harvard Bus. Sch., 1977; JD with honors, Harvard Law Sch., 1977. Bar: Calif. 1978, D.C. 1980. Law clk. to Hon. Herbert C. Choy U.S. Ct. Appeals (9th cir.), 1977—78; assoc. Latham & Watkins, Newport Beach, Calif., 1978-82, ptnr., 1984-86; lectr. bus. adminstrn. Harvard U., 1982-83; sr. assoc. counsel to President Ronald Reagan The White House, Washington, 1986-88; mem. U.S. Congress from 48th dist. Calif. (formerly 47th), Washington, 1989—2005, mem. energy and commerce com., steering com., mem. fin. svcs. com.; chmn. house Rep. policy com., 1994—2005, house com. on homeland security, 2003—05; mem. Bipartisan Commn. on Entitlement and Tax Reform, Washington, 1994—2005; mem, leadership steering com.; chmn. SEC, Washington, 2005—. Prin., co-founder Context Corp., St. Paul, 1984-86. Editor Harvard Law Rev., 1975-77; pub. Pravda. Mem. adv. bd. U. Calif., Irvine, Brain-Imaging Ctr.; bd. trustee Chapman U. Named a Taxpayer Fighter, Nat. Limitation Com., Hero of the Taxpayer, Americans for Tax Reform, Super Friend of Seniors, 60/Plus Assn., Guardian of Small Bus., Nat. Fedn. Ind. Bus.; recipient People of the Year award, PR Computing mag., 1999, Founders Circle award, TechNet, 2002, Friend of Small Bus. award, Nat. Fedn. Ind. Bus., Friend of the Consumer award, Consumer Alert, Golden Bulldog award, Watchdogs of the Treasury, Hero to the Taxpayer award, Citizens Against Govt. Waste, Taxpayers Friend award, Nat. Taxpayers Union. Republican. Roman Catholic. Office: SEC 100 F St NE Washington DC 20549*

COX, CLAIR EDWARD, II, urologist, medical educator; b. Lawrenceville, Ill., Sept. 2, 1933; s. Clair Edward and May E. (Judy) C.; m. Clarice Wicks, Aug. 23, 1958; children— Clair Edward III, Daniel Paul, Kevin Christopher, Kenneth Harold. Student, U. Mich., 1951-54, MD, 1958. Diplomate Am. Bd. Urology. Intern U. Colo. Med. Center, Denver, 1958-59, surg. resident, 1959-60; resident urology U. Cal. Med. Center at San Francisco, 1960-63; mem. faculty Bowman Gray Sch. Medicine, Wake Forest U., Winston Salem, N.C., 1963-72, assoc. prof., 1967-70, prof. urology, 1970-72; prof., chmn. dept. urology U. Tenn. Med. Sch., Memphis, 1972—. Contbr. profl. jours. Fellow ACS; mem. AMA, Am. Assn. Genito-Urinary Surgeons, Am. Urol. Assn., Internat. Soc. Urology, N.Y. Acad. Scis., Infectious Disease Soc. Am., Soc. Univ. Urologists, Am. Assn. Med. Colls., Am. Soc. Microbiology. Achievements include research in urinary tract infectious disease. Home: 6011 Sweetbriar Cv Memphis TN 38120-2514

COX, CLIFFORD ERNEST, information systems consulting executive, former academic administrator; b. Chgo., Apr. 28, 1942; s. Clifford Ernest and Beulah May (Lynn) C.; m. Scenobia Butler, June 20, 1964; children: Clifford, Fred, Sean. BA, U. Chgo., 1964, MBA, 1966; postgrad., No. Ill. U., 1988—. Cert. in data processing. Sr. systems engr. IBM, Chgo., 1966-69; v.p. MIS Golden Fifty Pharm., Chgo., 1969-71; sr. mgr. Arthur Andersen & Co., Chgo., 1971-79; pres. Cenox Systems, Inc., Chgo., 1979-81, 97—; chief info. officer Chgo. Pub. Schs., 1981-92; deputy supt. Detroit Pub. Schs., 1992-97; pres. Cenox Sys. Am., Cleve., 1998—. Lectr. Keller Grad Sch. Mgmt., 1986-89; del. Ill. Regional White House conf., 1990. Contbr. articles to profl. jours. Bd. dirs. Assn. House, Chgo., 1991; mem. Chgo. Assembly. Office: Cenox Sys 4289 Stoddard Rd West Bloomfield MI 48323 Office Phone: 248-626-4861. E-mail: cliffcox@cenox.com.

COX, COURTLAND, minority business administrator; b. N.Y.C., Jan. 27, 1941; married; 1 child. Student, Howard U. Co-owner, mgr. Drum and Spear Bookstore, Drum and Spear Pubs.; spl. asst. to dep. mayor for econ. devel. D.C. Govt., dir. Minority Bus. Opportunity Commn., dir. Office of Internat. Bus.; spl. asst. to dep. asst. sec. for Africa, Near East and South Dept. of Commerce, Washington, 1993, dir. Office of Civil Rights, 1994, dir. Minority Bus. Devel. Agy., 1998—. Bus. con. drafting D.C. Small, Minority and Disadvantaged Bus. Legislation. Office: Dept of Commerce Minority Bus Devel Agy 14th And Constitution NW Washington DC 20230-0001

COX, CYNTHIA A., art education specialist; b. Cleve., Mar. 29, 1957; d. Jerry L. and Lynn (Hargrove) C. BFA, Kent State U., 1979; MSEd with all honors, Lake Erie Coll., 1996. Cert. visual arts K-12, edn. specialist, Ohio. Art edn. specialist East Cleveland Schs., 1980-86, Kenston Schs., Chagrin Falls, Ohio, 1987—. Instr. profl. devel. grad. program Lake Erie Coll., Painesville, Ohio, 1996, in-svc. spkr. Kenston Schs., Chagrin Falls, Ohio, 1993, East Cleveland Schs., 1981; spkr. U.S. Joint Conf. on Edn., Beijing, 1992; vis. tchr. J.F.K. Schule, Berlin; Am. spkr. 1994 Commemorative Ceremony for Tearing Down Berlin Wall, 1994; apptd. del. leader People to People, Japan, 1999. Author, designer: Building Bridges: An International Approach to the Fine Arts, 1996; author: A Social, Cultural and Political Comparison Study of Children's Art Work from China, Germany, Bosnia and the United States, 1996. Elder Lake Shore Christian Ch., 1986-93. Mem. Ohio Art Edn. Assn., Ohio Edn. Assn., Internat. Assn. Edn. Through Art, Dwight D. Eisenhower Citizen Ambassador Program, Am. Acad. Disting. Students, Internat. Assn. of Asian Studies (presenter conf. 2000). Office: Kenston Schs 9421 Bainbridge Rd Chagrin Falls OH 44023-2703

COX, DAVID JACKSON, biochemistry professor; b. NYC, Dec. 22, 1934; s. Reavis and Rachel (Dunaway) C.; m. Joan M. Narbeth, Sept. 6, 1958 (dec. Oct. 8, 1982); children: Andrew Reavis, Matthew Bruce, Thomas Jackson; m. Tamara L. Compton, Nov. 26, 1983. BA, Wesleyan U., 1956; PhD, U. Pa., 1960. Instr. biochemistry U. Wash., 1960-63; asst. prof. chemistry U. Tex., 1963-67, assoc. prof., 1967-73; prof., head dept. biochemistry Kans. State U., 1973-89; prof. chemistry Ind. U./Purdue U., Ft. Wayne, 1989-2000, prof. emeritus, 2000—. Vis. prof. U. Va., 1970-71; dean arts scis. Ind. U./Purdue U., Ft. Wayne, 1989-96. NSF predoctoral fellow, 1956-59; NSF sr. postdoctoral fellow, 1970-71 Mem. Am. Soc. Biochemistry, Molecular Biology Soc., Am. Chem. Soc., Phi Beta Kappa, Sigma Xi. Democrat. Presbyterian. Home: 309 Crown Ln Bellingham WA 98229-5929 E-mail: comcox@yahoo.com.

COX, DAVID LEON, telecommunications company executive; b. Lima, Ohio, Sept. 8, 1952; s. Leon Hamiln and Mildred Marie (Johnson) C.; m. Carolle Marie Mallette, July 17, 1978; children: Paul David, Elizabeth Christine. BS in Chemistry, Mich. State U., 1975, BS in Computer Sci., 1976; MBA in Telecomms., Parkwood U., London, 2001. Registered profl. engr., Va. 76asst. v.p. engring. KollMorgan Corp., Newburgh, NY, 1975; staff mgr. AT&T, Bedminster, N.J., 1976-79; asst. v.p. Satellite Bus. Systems, McLean, Va., 1979-83; devel. mgr. MCI, Washington, 1983-84; chief engr. Harris Corp., Melbourne, Fla., 1984-95; asst. dir. GTE, Rockville, Md., 1997-2000, dir. Irving, Tex., 1998-2000; exec. dir. engring. Parsons Brinkerhoff, Dallas, 2000; dir. Sprint PCS, Flower Mound, Tex., 2001—04; exec. engr. mgr. Rockwell-Collins Govt. Sys., Richardson, Tex., 2004—. Mem. Pres.'s Commn. on Crit. Infrastructure Protection, advisor, 1996—2002 Pres.'s Nat. Security Telecomms. adv. com., cons., 1995-2002; bd. dirs. GTE, Irving, Tex. Contbr. articles to profl. jours. Active Friends of the Palm Bay (Fla.) Libr., Space Coast Sci. Ctr., 1000 Friends of Fla., Tallahassee, Turkey Creek Homeowners Assn., Turkey Creek Santuary Bd., Palm Bay PTA; vice chmn. pub. rels. Boy Scouts of Am., 1991-95, dist. com. mem., 1991-95, unit commr., 1990-95, troop com. mem., 1992-95, park com. mem., 1987-95; mem. Comprehensive Plan Com., Palm Bay, Fla., 1986-87. Mem. IEEE, Am. Chem. Soc., Am. Inst. Plant Engrs., Mensa, Assn. for Computing Machinery, N.Y. Acad. Sci., Nat. Fire Protection Assn., Building Industry Cons. Svc. Internat., Am. Radio Relay League, Nat. Eagle Scout Assn. (life), Nat. Coun. Boy Scouts of Am., Mich. State U. Alumni Assn., Lyman Briggs Coll. Alumni Assn., Mason (3d deg.), Orlando Scottish Rite (32nd deg., Master of Royal Secret), Alpha Phi Omega (Beta Beta chpt.). Republican. Presbyterian. Achievements include 7 patents in integrated svcs. digital network tech., signaling system 7, and surveillance technologies. Home: 6000 Grand Meadow Ln Flower Mound TX 75028-4830 Office: Rockwell Collins 3200 E Renner Rd Richardson TX 45082 Office Phone: 972-705-3070. Fax: 214-513-8413. E-mail: coxdl@gte.net.

COX, DONALD CLYDE, electrical engineering educator; b. Lincoln, Nebr., Nov. 22, 1937; s. Elvin Clyde and C. Gertrude (Thomas) C.; m. Mary Dale Alexander, Aug. 27, 1961; children: Bruce Dale, Earl Clyde. BS, U. Nebr., 1959, MS, 1960, DSc (hon.), 1983; PhD, Stanford U., 1968. Registered profl. engr., Ohio, Nebr. With Bell Tel. Labs., Holmdel, N.J., 1968-84, head radio and satellite systems rsch. dept., 1983-84; mgr. radio and satellite systems rsch. divsn. Bell Comm. Rsch., Red Bank, NJ, 1984-91, exec. dir. radio rsch. dept., 1991-93; prof. elec. engring. Stanford (Calif.) U., 1993—, Harald Trap Friis Prof. Engring., 1994—, dir. telecomms., 1993-99. Em. commns. U.S. nat. com. Internat. Union of Radio Sci.; participant enbanc hearing on Personal Comm. Sys., FCC, 1991; mem. rsch. visionary bd. Motorola Labs., 2002-03. Contbr. articles to profl. jours.; patentee in field. 1st lt. USAF, 1960-63. Recipient Guglielmo Marconi prize in Electromagnetic Waves Propagation, Inst. Internat. Comm., 1983, Alumni Achievement award U. Nebr., 2002; Johnson fellow, 1959-60. Fellow IEEE (Morris E. Leeds award 1985, Alexander Graham Bell medal 1993, Millenium medal 2000), AAAS, Bellcore 1991, Radio Club Am.; mem. NAE, Comm. Soc. of IEEE (Leonard G. Abraham Prize Paper award 1992, Comms. Mag. Prize Paper award 1990), Vehicular Tech. Soc. of IEEE (Paper of Yr. award 1983), Antennas and Propagation Soc. of IEEE (elected mem. adminstrn. com. 1986-88), Sigma Xi. Achievements include rsch. in wireless communication systems, cellular radio systems, radio propagation. Home: 924 Mears Ct Stanford CA 94305-1029 Office: Stanford U Dept Elec Engring Packard 361 Stanford CA 94305-9515 Office Phone: 650-723-5443. Business E-Mail: dcox@spark.stanford.edu.

COX, DOUGLAS JAMES, agricultural studies educator; b. Jefferson City, Mo., May 8, 1979; s. James Don Cox and Deborah Lynn Gore. BS in Agrl. Edn. with honors, U. Mo., Columbia, 2001, MS in Agrl. Edn. with honors, 2003. Agrl. instr. Green Ridge (Mo.) R-8 Sch., 2001—. FFA advisor Green Ridge (Mo.) R-8 Sch., 2001—; advisor Mo. FFA State Champion Farm Bus. Mgmt. Career Devel. Event Team, 2005. Mem.: Mo. Vocat. Agrl. Tchrs. Assn. (sec. area 6 2003—04, pres. area 6 2004—05). Home: 1818 S Vermont Ave Sedalia MO 65301 Office: Green Ridge R-8 Sch 401 W Pettis St Green Ridge MO 65332 Office Phone: 660-527-3315 107. Office Fax: 660-527-3291. Personal E-mail: coxd@greenridge.k12.mo.us.

COX, DOUGLAS LYNN, financial corporation executive; b. Des Moines, Dec. 13, 1945; s. Carol Eugene and Maribelle (Harter) C.; m. Janice C. Kuchka, Nov. 15, 1969; children: David Michael, Kristen Anne. BS, U. Pa., 1968, MBA, 1973. With IU Internat. Corp., Phila., 1974-88, treas. assoc. long-term fin., 1974-76, sr. treas. assoc. internat. fin., 1976-77, mgr. internat. fin., 1977-79, dir. treas. planning, 1979-80, asst. treas., 1980-85, v.p., treas., 1985-88; sr. v.p. fin., CFO Elf Atochem N.Am., Phila., 1988-98; exec. v.p., CFO Opinion Rsch. Corp., Princeton, 1998—. Class gift chmn. U. Pa.; bd. dirs., treas. Big Bros./Big Sisters; treas. Old Pine St. Presbyn. Ch.; bd. govs. Pa. Econ. League; trustee Friends Select Sch., pres. bd. trustees; bd. dirs. Pa. Bus. Roundtable. With USCG, 1969-72. Decorated Gallantry Cross (Vietnam). Mem. Phila. Racquet Club, TPC Jasna Polana, Phi Kappa Sigma. Home: 1220 Rodman St Philadelphia PA 19147-1130 Office: Opinion Rsch Corp PO Box 183 Princeton NJ 08542-0183 E-mail: dcox@prn.opinionresearch.com.

COX, EMMETT RIPLEY, federal judge; b. Cottonwood, Ala., Feb. 13, 1935; s. Emmett M. Jr. Cox and Myra E. (Ripley) Stewart; m. Ann MacKay Haas, May 16, 1964; children: John Haas, Catherine MacKay. BA, U. Ala., 1957, JD, 1959. Bar: Ala. 1959, U.S. Ct. Appeals (5th, 8th and 11th cirs.), U.S. Supreme Ct. Assoc. Mead, Norman & Fitzpatrick, Birmingham, Ala., 1959—64; assoc. then ptnr. Gaillard, Wilkins, Smith & Cox, Mobile, Ala., 1964—69; ptnr. Nettles, Cox & Barker, 1969—81; judge U.S. Dist. Ct. (so. dist.) Ala., Mobile, 1981—88, U.S. Ct. Appeals (11th cir.), Mobile, 1988—2000, sr. judge, 2000—. Mem. def. svcs. com. Jud. Conf. U.S., 1992—98, chair, 1995—98, mem. jud. br. com., 2001—. Mem.: FBA, Maritime Law Assn. of the U.S., Mobile Bar Assn., Ala. Bar Assn., Alpha Tau Omega (past pres.), Phi Delta Phi, Omicron Delta Kappa. Office: US Courthouse 11th Circuit 113 Saint Joseph St Ste 433 Mobile AL 36602-3624 also: 56 Forsyth St NW Atlanta GA 30303

COX, FRANK D. (BUDDY COX), oil industry executive; b. Shreveport, La., Dec. 20, 1932; s. Ohmer M. and Beulah O. (Scott) Cox; m. Betty Jean Hand, June 19, 1956; children: Cynthia Cox Sanford, Carolyn Cox Patton, Frank D. Jr. BS in Bus. Adminstrn., La. Tech. U., 1956; postgrad., Centenary Coll., 1958-59. Cert. profl. landman; lic. real estate, Fla. Various positions Exxon Corp., Houston, 1955-86, chief landman, v.p. coal resources, 1980-86; pvt. practice Houston, 1986-89; sr. v.p. Energy Exploration Mgmt. Co., Houston, 1989-94; v.p., mgr. T-Bar-X Ltd. Co., Houston, 1994-2000; v.p., dir. Power Exploration Internat., Houston, 1994-2000; ptnr. East Tex. Reef Fund, Ltd., 1994—; land mgr. Thomson-Barrow Corp., 1994-2000, Tecolotita, Inc., 1994-2000; exploration cons. Houston, 2000—. Active Second Bapt. Ch., Houston. Capt. USAF, 1956-58. Named disting. mil. grad. La. Tech. U., Ruston, 1955. Mem. Am. Assn. Profl. Landmen, Houston Assn. Profl. Landmen, W. Houston Assn. Profl. Landmen, W. Houston Exxon Annuitant Club, 100 Club of Greater Houston, La. Tech. U. Found., Crimestoppers Inc., Pi Kappa Alpha Ednl. Found., Omicron Delta Kappa Found., Delta Sigma Pi. Republican. Avocations: golf, tennis, amateur radio. Home and Office: 14830 Carolcrest St Houston TX 77079-6312 Office Phone: 281-493-6906. E-mail: b2cox@swbell.net.

COX, FREDERICK MORELAND, retired dean, social worker; b. L.A., Dec. 8, 1928; s. Frederick Alfred Edward and Ethel (Moreland) C.; m. Gay Campbell, June 1951 (dec. June 1991); children: Lawrence, Elizabeth, Sherman. BA, UCLA, 1950, MSW, 1954; DSW, U. Calif., Berkeley, 1968. Caseworker child welfare L.A. Bur. Public Assistance, 1952-53; mental health counselor L.A. Superior Ct., 1953; caseworker Family Service Bur., Oakland, Calif., 1954-57; program dir. Easter Seal Soc., Oakland, 1957-60; asst. prof. to prof. social work U. Mich., Ann Arbor, 1964-76; prof., dir. Sch. Social Work, Mich. State U., East Lansing, 1976-80; prof., dean Sch. Social Welfare, U. Wis., Milw., 1980-89, ret., 1989. Author: As We See It: Men's Stories About Their Experiences with Prostate Cancer, 1999; sr. co-editor: Cmty.-Action Planning Development, A Casebook, 1974, Tactics and Techniques of Community Practice, 1977, 2d edit., 1984, Strategies of Community Organization, 4th edit, 1987; co-editor: Families in Trouble (5 vols.), 1988. Pres. Wis. Coun. Human Concerns, 1985-86. Spl. Rsch. fellow NIMH, 1960-63. Mem. NASW (v.p. Wis. chpt. 1984-86), Acad. Cert. Social Workers, Nat. Deans and Dirs. Schs. Social Work (sec.-treas. 1985-87), Coun. Social Work Edn. (bd. dirs. 1985-89). Home: 11300 First Ave NE # 221 Seattle WA 98125-6038 Personal E-mail: fredmcox@hotmail.com.

COX, GARY WALTER, political science professor; b. Patuxent River, Md., Sept. 23, 1955; s. Dale William and Patricia Broadway Cox; m. Diane Christine Lin, June 18, 1988 (dec. Jan. 1999); 1 child, Dylan Gregory; m. Karen J. Cox, Oct. 4, 2003; . BS, Calif. Inst. Tech., 1978, PhD, 1982. From asst. prof. to assoc. prof. U. Tex., Austin, 1982-86; assoc. prof. U. Calif., La Jolla, 1986-90, prof., 1990—. Author: (books) The Efficient Secret, 1987 (George Hallet prize 2002), Making Votes Count, 1997 (Woodrow Wilson Found. award 1998; co-author: (books) Legislative Leviathan, 1993 (Fenno prize 1994), Elbridge Gerry's Salamander, 2002. Guggenheim fellow, 1995, Am. Acad. Arts and Scis. fellow, 1996, NAS fellow, 2005. Business E-Mail: gcox@weber.ucsd.edu.

COX, GLENN ANDREW, JR., petroleum company executive; b. Sedalia, Mo., Aug. 6, 1929; s. Glenn Andrew and Ruth Lonsdale (Atkinson) C.; m. Veronica Cecelia Martin, Jan. 3, 1953; children: Martin Stuart, Grant Andrew, Cecelia Ruth. BBA, So. Meth. U., 1951. With Phillips Petroleum Co., Bartlesville, Okla., 1956-91, asst. to chmn. oper. com., 1973-74, v.p. mgmt. info. and control, 1974-80, exec. v.p., 1980-85, dir., 1982-91, pres., COO, 1985-91. Bd. dirs. BOK Fin. Corp., Bank of Okla., The Williams Co.'s, Inc., Helmerich and Payne, Tulsa, Union Tex. Petroleum Holdings, Houston, Thermon Industries, Inc., San Marcos, Tex., Cimarex Energy, Inc., Denver. Pres. Cherokee Area coun. Boy Scouts Am., 1977-82, South Ctrl. region, 1987-90, mem. nat. exec. bd., 1987-94; mem. bd. curators Ctrl. Meth. Coll., Fayette, Mo., 1984-88, 1997—; trustee Philbrook Mus. Art, 1987-92, So. Meth. U., Dallas, 1988-96; bd. dirs. Okla. United Meth. Found.; mem. Okla. State Regents for Higher Edn., 1990-96. Mem. Am. Petroleum Inst. (bd. dirs. 1982-91), Nat. Assn. Mfrs. (bd. dirs. 1985-91), Bartlesville Area C. of C. (pres. 1978), Hillcrest Country Club. Methodist. Office: Reda Bldg 401 S Dewey Ave Ste 318 Bartlesville OK 74003-3545

COX, HEADLEY MORRIS, JR., lawyer, educator; b. Mt. Olive, N.C., July 25, 1916; s. Headley Morris and Frank (English) C.; m. Irene Todd, June 26, 1940; children: John Morris, Deborah English, Thomas Headley; m. Elizabeth Shelton Smith, Dec. 30, 1994. AB, Duke, 1937, AM, 1939; postgrad., U. Colo., 1944-45; PhD, U. Pa., 1958; JD, U. S.C., 1984. Successively instr., asst. prof., assoc. prof., prof. English Clemson (S.C.) U., 1939-82, head dept., 1950-69, dean Coll. Liberal Arts, 1969-80; of counsel Olson, Smith, Jordan & Cox, P.A., 1984—. Sr. Fulbright lectr. in Am. lit. Universitat Graz, Austria, 1958-59 Served with USNR, 1944-46. Mem. Phi Beta Kappa. Methodist. Home: 213 Riggs Dr Clemson SC 29631-1427 Office: PO Box 1633 Clemson SC 29633-1633

COX, HENRY, electronics executive; b. Phila., Mar. 7, 1935; s. Henry Robert and Helen (Kane) C.; m. Mary Ann Shaw, Sept. 3, 1960 (dec.); children: James, Daniel, Michael, Diane. BS, Coll. Holy Cross, 1956; ScD, MIT, 1963. Analyst Office Sec. of Def., 1970-72; research assoc. Scripps Instn. Oceanography, LaJolla, Calif., 1972-73; officer in charge Naval Underwater Systems Ctr., New London, Conn., 1973-76; div. dir. Def. Advanced Research Projects Agy., 1976-78; project mgr. Naval Electronic Systems Command, Arlington, Va., 1978-81; divisional v.p. BBN Systems and Tech. Corp., Arlington, 1981-91; chief tech. officer, sr. v.p. Orincon Corp., Arlington, 1991—2003; chief tech. officer Lockheed Martin Orincon Def., Arlington, 2003—. Contbr. articles to tech. jours. Served to capt. USN, 1956-81. Decorated Legion of Merit; decorated Meritorious Service medal, Navy Commendation medal; recipient Def. Superior Service medal Dept. Def., 1978 Fellow Acoustical Soc. Am., IEEE (Disting. Tech. Achievement award Oceanic Engring. Soc. 1991); mem. Am. Soc. Naval Engrs. (hon. Gold medal), Nat. Acad. Engring., U.S. Naval Inst. Roman Catholic. Home: 6513 Waterway Dr Falls Church VA 22044-1328 Office: Lockheed MartinOrincon Def 4350 Fairfax Dr Arlington VA 22203-1695 Office Phone: 703-351-4440. Business E-Mail: harry.cox@lmco.com.

COX, HOWARD ELLIS, JR., venture capitalist; b. NYC, Feb. 1, 1944; s. Howard Ellis and Anne Delafield (Finch) C BA, Princeton U., 1964; JD, Columbia U., 1967; MBA, Harvard U., 1969. Bar: NY 1967. Ptnr. Greylock, Boston, 1971—. Bd. dir. Greylock Mgmt. Corp., Boston, Stryker, Kalamazoo, In-Q-Tel, Washington; mem. investment com. Ptnr. Healthcare. Bd. dir. Nat. Venture Capital Assn., Washington, 1997—, chmn., 2002; trustee Dana Farber Cancer Inst., 1987—; v.p., trustee Assn. Relief of the Elderly, NYC; overseer Mus. Fine Arts; mem. bd. fellow Harvard Med. Sch. Capt. US Army, 1969-71; bd. dir. Boston Pub. Libr. Found. Mem.: Coun. Fgn. Rels., Bus. Assoc. Club Boston (pres. 1979—80), New Eng. Venture Capital Assn. (pres. 1986—88), Comml. Club Boston. Episcopalian. Office: Greylock 880 Winter St Ste 300 Waltham MA 02451 Office Phone: 781-622-2244.

COX, ILO B., civic worker; b. Boone County, Ind., Nov. 22, 1911; d. Thomas W. and Golda F. (Staton) Bohannon; m. Le Roy Cox, June 27, 1930; children— Patsy Lee, Sally Elaine. Sec.-bookkeeper Hall-Neal Furnace Co., Indpls., 1929-34; officer mgr. Grand View Meml. Gardens, Grand Haven, Mich., 1957-61; sec. typist Clk. V.; Dept. Natural Resources, Lansing, Mich., 1961-71; dir. Nat. Safety Council, 1980-82, Broward chpt., Fla.; one of 15 citizens apptd. by mayor of Fort Lauderdale (Fla.) to plan Internat. Lethal Yellowing Conf. and 5 day conf.; beautification and bylaws chmn. Fort Lauderdale Hist. Soc., 1980-82, historian chmn., 1982-84; leader Girl Scouts U.S.A., 1949-55; assisted 32 orgns. of City of Fort Lauderdale plan and carry out Clean Up, Paint Up, Fix Up, 1979-81; registration chmn. Fort Lauderdale Fla. Woman's Club, 1973-75, treas., 1975-77, 2d v.p., 1978, pres., 1978-80; pres.'s aide and protocol chmn. Fla. Fedn. Women's Clubs, 1982-84, serving chmn., 1984-86, program chmn. free enterprise, 1986-88, Woman of the Yr., 1984; conservation chmn. Grand Haven Mich. Woman's Club, 1966-68. Republican. Presbyterian. Clubs: Spring Lake County (Mich.); Lehigh Country (Fla.); Toastmistress (Mich.) (pres.). Home: 3051 Walton Way EXT Augusta GA 30909-3471

COX, J. ARTHUR, minister; b. Utica, N.Y., Aug. 5, 1940; s. James F and Margaret (Craig) Cox; m. Mahaillie Tillson, Dec. 29, 1962; children: Deborah Jean, James Andrew. AAS, Mohawk Valley C.C., 1961; BTh, Concordia Sem., 1975; D Ministry, Faith Sem., Tacoma, 1991. Cert. Ordained to ministry Luth Ch-Mo Synod, 1975. Pastor Grace Luth. Ch., Bradford, Pa., 1975-2000; pres. devel. leaders for ministry Mo. Synod., 2000—. Del. Synodical Conv., Dallas, 1977; counselor Cattaraugus Ctr., Bradford, 1982; chmn. Dist Open House, Bradford, 1982, Dist. Ext. Fund, Buffalo, 1982—85; chmn. ea. dist., bd. dirs. mission svcs. Alive in Christ, 1982—88, mem. evangelism com. ea. dist., 1992—97, bd. dirs.; chmn. dist. bd. Congl. Svcs., 1997—2002; counselor Cattanaugus Ct., 2002—03. Chmn. bd. Excell Personnel Svcs., Inc., 1999—; bd dirs Evergreen Hylands, 1979, Am Cancer Soc 1980, Vis Nurse Assn., 1980—86, Bradford Hosp, 1985—; bd. dirs. Bradford Area Sch. Dist., 2004—. Mem.: Rotary (bd dirs 1978—82, pres 1982—83). Republican. Home: 465 Interstate Pky Bradford PA 16701-2733 E-mail: jacox@penn.com. *Life is a sequence of God-given opportunities to serve Him and His people. The excitement is derived from accepting His call to service and experiencing His magnificent power working through you to accomplish His purpose.*

COX, JACK RONALD, JR., finance educator; b. Houston, Aug. 29, 1964; s. Jack Ronald Sr. and Peggy Lou (Mitchell) C. BS, Park U., 1997; MS, Lesley Coll., 1998; PhD, Capella U., 2001. Spl. weapons & tactics cert. 1988; cert. law enforcement Fla. 1988; cert. advanced peace officer Tex. 1990; advanced EMT; basic EMT. Patrolman USAF, Woodbridge, UK, 1992-93, sr. patrolman, program mgr. Incirlik, Turkey, 1993-94, program mgr. personal readiness Cheyenne, Wyo., 1994-97, Songtan, South Korea, 1997-98, program mgr. Tercierra, Azores, 1999—; faculty criminal justice, bus., mgmt. U. Md., Tercierra, Portugal, 2000—. Vol. Wyo. Emergency Mgmt. Assn., 1994—97, ARC, New Philadelphia, Ohio, 1983—86, numerous fire depts., Nelsonville, Ohio, 1984—90; asst. fire chief Normagee Vol. Fire Dept., 2003; mem. coun. Leon County Govt., Tex.; bd. dirs. Jewett EMS, 2004—. E-5 SSgt USAF, 1991—2001. Mem. Acad. Mgmt., VFW. Avocations: historical research, music collection. Home: PO Box 276 Normangee TX 77871 Office Phone: 972-279-6511. Business E-Mail: jcox@cnbactn.edu. E-mail: drjcox@tconline.net.

COX, JAMES ALLAN, chemistry professor; b. Chisholm, Minn., Sept. 19, 1941; s. Robert Earl and Mary Jean (Berdey) C.; m. Kersti Suik, Aug. 21, 1965; children: Kaila Ann, Alison Jean. AA, Hibbing State Coll., 1961; BChem, U. Minn., 1963; PhD, U. Ill., 1967. Lectr., rsch. assoc. U. Wis., Madison, 1967-69; faculty, prof. chemistry So. Ill. U., Carbondale, 1969-86; prof., chair chemistry Miami U., Oxford, Ohio, 1987-94, prof. chemistry, 1994—. Cons. NIH, Washington, 1988—; environ. chem. cons. various industries, 1980—. Author book chpts. on coal chemistry; contbr. more than 150 articles to environ., chem., and electrochemistry jours. Mem.: Soc. Electroanalytical Chemists, Electrochemistry Soc., Am. Chem. Soc. (ACS) (named Cin. Chemist Yr. 2002), Internat. Soc. Electrochemistry. Achievements include discovery of catalysts for oxidation of environmental pollutants and various biological compounds including insulin and various amino acids. Office: Miami U Chemistry-Hughes Hall Oxford OH 45056

COX, JAMES D., law educator; b. 1943; JD, U. Calif. Hastings Sch. Law, 1969; LL.M., Harvard U., 1971; D in Mercature (hon.), U. South Denmark, 2001. Bar: Calif. 1970. Atty.-adv. Office Gen. Counsel FTC, Washington, 1969-70; teaching fellow Boston U., 1970-71; asst. prof. U. San Francisco, 1971-74; assoc. prof. U. Calif. Hastings Sch. Law, 1974-75; vis. assoc. prof. Stanford U., 1976-77; prof. U. Calif. Hastings Sch. Law, 1977-79; vis. prof. Duke U. Sch. Law, spring 1979, prof., 1979-2000, Brainerd Currie prof. law, 2000—. Com. on corps. State Bar Calif., N.C. bus. corp. act. draft com., NC nonprofit corp. draft com.; E.T. Bost rsch. prof., 1980, 96; legal adv. com. NY Stock Exch., 1995—; legal adv. bd. NASD, 1999—. Author: Financial Information, Accounting and the Law, 1980, Quick Review of Corporations, 4th edit., 2004, (with Hillman and Langevoort) Securities Regulation: Cases and Materials, 4th edit., 2004; (with Hazen) Corporations, 2d edit., 2003. Sr. Fulbright Rsch. fellow, Australia, 1989. Mem. Am. Law Inst., Order of Coif, Phi Kappa Phi Office: Duke U Sch Law Durham NC 27708-0360 Office Phone: 919-613-7056. Business E-Mail: cox@law.duke.edu.

COX, JAMES L., surgeon, educator; s. Jess L. and Ruby H. Cox; m. Jennifer M. Magee, Sept. 6, 1986; children: Justin Lewis, Juliana Lynn. MD, U. Tenn., Memphis, 1964—67. Cert. in thoracic surgery Am. Bd. Thoracic Surgery, 1983. Assoc. prof., surgery Duke U. Sch. Medicine, Durham, NC, 1978—83; Evarts A. Graham prof., chief, cardiothoracic surgery Wash. U. Sch. Medicine, St. Louis, 1983—97, emeritus Evarts A. Graham prof. surgery, 2003—; prof. and chmn., dept. cardiothoracic surgery Georgetown U. Sch. Medicine, Washington, 1997—2000. Founder 3f Therapeutics, Inc., Lake Forest, Calif., 1999—2005; advisor, cons. Chase Med., Inc., Richardson, Tex., 2000—05; cons. St. Jude Med., Inc., St. Paul, 2004—05. Maj. USMC, 1970—72, Ft. Knox. Grantee, NIH, 1978—2005. Fellow: ACS (life), Am. Coll. Chest Physicians (life; mem., steering com. 1990—94), Am. Coll. Cardiology (life), Am. Heart Assn. (life); mem.: So. Thoracic Surg. Assn. (life), So. Surg. Assn. (life), Am. Surg. Assn. (life), Thoracic Surgery Found. for Rsch. and Edn. (life; founding mem., bd. of directors 1992—2003), Soc. Thoracic Surgeons (life; coun. mem. 1992—95), Soc. Clin. Surgery (membership chmn. 1993—94), The Cosmos Club (life). Conservative. Avocations: boating, golf, travel. Office Phone: 314-362-6185.

COX, JAMES SIDNEY, physician; b. Homer, La., Nov. 17, 1950; s. Sidney and Rita (Haynes) C.; m. Judy Katherine Vickers, Oct. 21, 1984; children: Shannon Ruth, Sarah Anne, Megan Elizabeth. Student, La. State U., 1968-71; MD, Tulane U., 1971-75. Diplomate Am. Bd. Family Practice, Am. Bd. of Emergency Medicine. Intern, resident in family practice John Peter Smith Hosp., Ft. Worth, 1975-78; city health officer family practice City of Athens, Tex., 1978-84; pvt. practice Athens, 1978-84, Ft. Worth, 1984—; mem. staff Henderson County Meml. Hosp., Athens, vice chief med. staff, 1981-82; mem. staff Lakeland Med. Ctr., Athens, chief med. staff, dir., 1983-84; vice chief emergency medicine dept. Harris Meth. Hosp., Ft. Worth, 1988-91, dir. occupational medicine, 1989—, chief emergency dept. Ft. Worth, 1992-93, 98-2000, sec. med. staff, 1994-95, sec. emergency medicine divsn., 1996-97. Pres., chmn. bd. dirs. Occuhealth Physicians Group, P.A., Ft. Worth; mem. faculty U. Tex. Health Sci. Ctr.-Dallas Cmty. Medicine Dept., John Peter Smith Hosp., Ft. Worth, 1978-96, course dir. ACLS, 1989-1998, mem. affiliate faculty ACLS, 1991-95, med. rev. officer for urine drug testing; med. bd. Harris Meth. Hosp., 1992-95, 98-2000; team chmn. emergency dept. redesign Rochester Inst. Tech. Coll. Bus., 1996; v.p. for physician affairs Emergency Medicine Cons., 1998—; assoc. med. dir. Harris Meth., Ft. Worth, 2000—; med. dir. ACLS, Campbell Health Sys., 1997-98; exec. dir. Emergency Medicine Cons., 2005— Author: Intestinal Obstruction: A Programmed Text, 1975. Recipient Quality Cup award of Excellence, USA Today, 1996. Fellow Am. Acad. Family Physicians, Am. Coll. Emergency Physicians; mem. AMA (Physician's Recognition award), Am. Coll. Occupl. and Environ. Medicine, Tex. Med. Assn. (alt. del. 1994-96, 2003—), Tarrant County Med. Soc. (bd. dirs. 1994-96, 2003—), Rotary (bd. dirs. Athens chpt. 1983-84), Alpha Epsilon Delta. Presbyterian. Avocations: reading, skiing, bonsai, horticulture, astronomy. Home: 3458 Lantern Holw Fort Worth TX 76109-2411 Office: Emergency Medicine Cons 6451 Brentwood Stair Rd Ste 200 Fort Worth TX 76112-3200 Office Phone: 817-496-9700. Personal E-mail: jimcoxem@charter.net. Business E-Mail: jcox@emdocs.com.

COX, JAMES TALLEY, lawyer; b. Temple, Tex., Sept. 22, 1921; s. George Allan and Jane (Talley) C.; m. Alice Tarver, Jan. 12, 1945; children: Martha Cox Daniels, Louise Cox McGuire, Anne Cox, Allan. BBA, U. Tex., 1943; LL.B., 1947. Bar: Tex. 1947, U.S. Supreme Ct. 1951. Spl. atty. Justice Dept., Washington, 1947-48; staff atty. Tax Ct. U.S., Washington, 1948-50; trial atty. Treasury Dept., Phila., 1950-51; tax counsel Schlumberger Well Services, Houston, 1951-65; ptnr. Hoover, Cox & Shearer, Houston, 1965-86; sole practice Houston, 1986-90; pres. James T. Cox, P.C., Houston, 1990—, Advent Trust Co., 1991-99. V.p., bd. dirs. Westchase Travels, Inc., 1972-82; bd. dirs. Paradigm Valve Svcs. Inc., Embedded Sys. Products Inc. Contbr. articles to profl. publs. Bd. dirs. Houston Met. YMCA, 1972-78, Pin Oak Charity Horse Show Assn., 1972—, Retina Rsch. Found., 1977—. Served to lt. USNR, 1943-46. Mem. Am., Tex., Houston Bar Assns., Tax Rsch. Assn. (exec. com. 1950-67), Delta Theta Phi, Phi Kappa Psi. Republican. Presbyterian. Home: 11701 Forest Glen St Houston TX 77024-6433 Office: 908 Town and Country Blvd Ste 225 Houston TX 77024 E-mail: alicetcox@yahoo.com.

COX, JANSON L., museum administrator; MA in History Museology, Cooperstown Grad. Sch., 1967. Chief historian State of S.C., 1968-73; mgr. Charles Towne Landing 1670, Charleston, S.C., 1973-98; exec. dir. S.C. Cotton Mus., Bishopville, 1998—. Office: SC Cotton Mus 121 W Cedar Ln Bishopville SC 29010-1454 Office Phone: 803-484-4497. E-mail: sccottonmus@ftc-i.net, coxjl1@juno.com.

COX, JOHN CURTIS, health facility administrator; b. Lovington, N.Mex., July 27, 1947; s. Samuel Spurgeon and Monah LaJoyce (Perry) King; m. Mary Margaret King, May 27, 1967; children: Melissa Lynn Ewing, Melinda Leanne Field. BBA, Hardin-Simmons U., Abilene, Tex., 1969; MHA, Baylor U., 1978; PhD, Tex. A&M U., 1988. Commd. 2d lt. U.S. Army, 1969, advanced through grades to lt. col.; chief Ft. Hood Health Facility Project Office, Office Surgeon Gen., 1978-85; assoc. dir., mgr. field office, health facilities planning U.S. Army Med. Command, Stuttgart, Germany, 1988-89, dir. health facilities planning Heidelberg, Germany, 1989-90; chief programming div. Def. Med. Facilities Office, Office Asst. Sec. Def., Washington, 1990-91; ret. U.S. Army, 1991; adminstrv. asst. Garland (Tex.) Ind. Sch. Dist., 1991-93, exec. dir. sch. facilities, 1993-95; planning & cons. coord. HED Baylor Health Care Sys., 1995-98; adminstrv. dir. support svcs. Baylor Med. Ctr., Grapevine, Tex., 1997-98; project dir. Med. Cities Inc., Dallas, 1998-2001. Owner Cox Cons., 2001—. Editl. adv. bd. Facility Care; contbr. articles to profl. jours. Trustee Belton (Tex.) Ind. Sch. Dist., 1981-84; mem. pub. sch. bd. mems. adv. com. Tex. State Bd. Edn., 1982-84; fund raiser Galand br. Dallas YMCA, 1992-94. Decorated Legion of Merit, Bronze Star medal, Meritorious Svc. medal with 2 oak leaf clusters, Army Commendation medal, others; recipient Svc. Citation award Tex. Fellow Am. Coll. Healthcare Execs., Am. Soc. Healthcare Engrs., Phi Kappa Phi, Alpha Chi. Baptist. Avocations: woodworking, antiques, exercise.

COX, JOHN FRANCIS, retired cosmetic company executive; b. Chgo., Sept. 25, 1929; s. Roland Francis and Vera Pauline (Paisley) C.; m. T. Joanne Brown, Nov. 27, 1954 (dec.); children: James O., Thomas B., Paul A. BJ, U. Ill., 1951; MS in English and Edn., Western Ill. U., 1954. Reporter Galesburg (Ill.) Register Mail, 1954-56; staff writer pub. rels. United Airlines, Chgo., 1956-58; press rels. mgr. Kiekhaefer Corp., Fond du Lac, Wis., 1958-60, Internat. Minerals and Chems. Corp., Skokie, Ill., 1960-67, Heublein Inc., Hartford, Conn., 1967-69, v.p. pub. affairs Farmington, Conn., 1981-83; v.p. pub. rels. and advt. Warner Nat. Corp., Cin., 1969-72; v.p. franchising and pub. rels. Ky. Fried Chicken, Louisville, 1972-81; group dir. pub. rels. R. J. Reynolds Industries, Inc., Winston-Salem, N.C., 1983-84; sr. v.p. comm. Avon Products, Inc., N.Y.C., 1984-91. Staff sgt. U.S. Army, 1951—53. Mem.: Soc. Profl. Journalists. Personal E-mail: johnfcox@aol.com.

COX, JOHN THOMAS, JR., lawyer; b. Shreveport, La., Feb. 9, 1943; s. John Thomas and Gladys Virginia (Canterbury) C.; m. Tracey L. Tanquary, Aug. 27, 1966; children: John Thomas, III, Stephen Lewis. BS, La. State U., 1965; JD, 1968. Bar: La. 1968, U.S. Dist. Ct. (we., mid. and ea. dist.) La., U.S. Dist. Ct. (ea. dist.) Tex., U.S. Ct. Appeals (5th and 8th cir.), U.S. Tax Ct., U.S. Supreme Ct. Assoc. Sanders, Miller, Downing & Keene, Baton Rouge, 1968-70, Blanchard, Walker, O'Quin & Roberts, Shreveport, La., 1970-71; ptnr., 1971—. Tchr. bus. law Centenary Coll. La., La. State U., Shreveport. Lt. USAR, 1963—69. Recipient George Washington Honor medal Valley Forge Freedoms Found. Mem. ABA, La. Bar Assn., Caddo parish Bar Assn., Am. Assn. Def. Counsel, La. Assn. Def. Counsel, Com. of 100, Shreveport Club. Presbyterian. Address: 555 Dunmoreland Dr Shreveport LA 71106-6124 Office Phone: 318-221-6858. Business E-Mail: jcox@bwor.com.

COX, KAREN DENISE, literature and language educator; b. Stubenville, Ohio, July 24, 1957; d. Robert Jackson and Ruth Flaherty; m. Charles Walton. BS in Edn., Ohio State U., 1980, MA in Edn., 1987. Nat. bd. cert. tchr. 1999. Tchr. Big Walnut High Sch., Sunbury, Ohio, 1985—87; tchr. English Johnstown-Monroe High Sch., 1987—91; tchr. lang. arts Deer Park High Sch., Cin., 1991—. Mem.: Nat. Mid. Sch. Assn., Ohio Coun. Tchrs. English. Avocations: writing, archery, travel, languages. Home: 7423 Kennesaw Dr West Chester OH 45069 Office: Deer Park High Sch 8351 Plainfield Rd Cincinnati OH 45236

COX, KATHY, school system administrator; m. John Hamilton Cox Jr.; children: John, Alex. BA, MA in Polit. sci., Emory U., Atlanta. Tchr. social studies McIntosh H.S., Fayette County Bd. Edn., Atlanta, 1987—2002; rep. Ga. Ho. of Reps., Atlanta, 1998—2002; supt. of edn. State of Ga., Atlanta, 2002—. Supporter Boy Scouts Am. Cub Scout Pack 201, Boy Scout Troop 275. Mem.: Kiwanis, Phi Beta Kappa. Meth. Office: Ga Dept Edn 2054 Twin Towers E Atlanta GA 30334

COX, KENNETH ALLEN, lawyer, consultant, communications executive; b. Topeka, Dec. 7, 1916; s. Seth Leroy and Jean (Sears) C.; m. Nona Beth Fumerton, Jan. 1, 1943; children— Gregory Allen, Jeffrey Neal, Douglas Randall. BA, U. Wash., 1938, LL.B., 1940; LL.M., U. Mich., 1941; LL.D., Chgo. Theol. Sem., 1969. Bar: Wash. 1941. Law clk. Wash. Supreme Ct., 1941-42; asst. prof. U. Mich. Law Sch., 1946-48; with firm Little, LeSourd, Palmer, Scott & Slemmons (and predecessor), Seattle, 1948-61, chmn. bd., 1953-61; spl. counsel com. interstate and fgn. commerce charge TV inquiry U.S. Senate, 1956-57; chief broadcast bur. FCC, Washington, 1961-63, commr., 1963-70; counsel to comm. law firm Haley, Bader & Potts, 1970-99; sr. v.p., dir. MCI Comm. Corp., 1970-87; cons. MCI, 1987—2000. Lectr. U. Washington Law Sch., part-time 1954, 60; adj. prof. Georgetown U. Law Center, 1971, 72. Vice pres. Municipal League Seattle and King County, 1960, Seattle World Affairs Council, 1960; pres. Seattle chpt. Am. Assn. UN, 1957; chmn. one of five citizen subcoms. Legis. Interim Com. Edn., 1960; Bd. dirs. Nat. Pub. Radio, 1971-80; bd. dirs. Nat. Advt. Rev. Bd., 1971-74, chmn. bd., 1976-96 . Served to capt. Q.M.C. AUS, 1943-46, 51-52. Recipient Alfred I. duPont award in broadcast journalism Columbia U., 1970; Everett C. Parker award, the Minortiy Media and Telecommunications Coun., 2003. Mem. Am., Fed. Communications, Wash. State, D.C. bar assns., Order of Coif, Phi Beta

Kappa, Phi Delta Phi. Democrat. Congregationalist. Home: 5836 Marbury Rd Bethesda MD 20817-6076 Office: MCI Comm Corp 1133 19th St NW Washington DC 20036 Office Phone: 202-736-6421. Personal E-mail: coxk10@sc.com. Business E-Mail: 100-4689@mcimail.com.

COX, KENNETH LEE, medical educator; b. Klamath Falls, Oreg., Jan. 27, 1946; m. Kathleen Cox. BS, Seattle U., 1968; MD, U. Wash., 1971. Diplomate Am. Bd. Pediat., Am. Bd. Pediat. Gastroenterology, Nat. Bd. Med. Examiners. Assoc. prof. pediat. U. Calif., Davis, 1978-89; chmn. pediat. Calif. Pacific Med. Ctr., San Francisco, 1989-95, sr. assoc. dean clin. affair for obstetrics and pediats.; prof. pediat. Stanford U., Palo Alto, Calif., 1995—. Contbr. over 100 articles to profl. jours. Office: Stanford U 750 Welch Rd Ste 116 Palo Alto CA 94304-1508 Office Phone: 650-723-5070.

COX, KEVIN MONTEREY, educational association administrator; b. New London, Conn., Nov. 30, 1965; s. Carroll Monterey and Barbara Freeman Cox. BS, U. S.C., Spartanburg, 1987; MEd, Converse Coll., 1990, EdS, 1993. Tchr. Clinton (S.C.) H.S., 1990-96; asst. prin. Bell St. Middle Sch., 1996—97; adminstrv. asst. Clinton (S.C.) H.S., 1997—2001; asst. prin. Lewisville H.S., Richburg, SC, 2001—. State sponsor S.C. Beta Club, 1999—; adj. prof. Lander U., Greenwood, S.C., 1998—. Recipient S.C. Ambassador of Acad. Excellence award S.C. State Dept. Edn., 1992. Mem. ASCD, S.C. Sci. Coun., Exch. Club Clinton (pres. 1996-97), Phi Delta Kappa. Methodist. Avocations: movies, reading, music. Home: 625 Britt Ln Richburg SC 29729 Office: 1330 JA Cochran Chester SC 29706 Office Phone: 803-377-3161. E-mail: coxkm_lhs@chester.k12.sc.us.

COX, L. KEVIN, human resources specialist; With rsch. and devel. labs. Pepsi Bottling Group, 1989—92, dir. human resources Altantic Coast bus., 1992—94; dir. orgnl. capability and sales devel. Pepsi-Cola Co., 1994—96, v.p. orgnl capability, 1996; sr. v.p. human resources Pepsi-Cola Bottling Co., 1997—98, sr. v.p., chief personnel officer, 1998—2004, exec. v.p., 2004—05; exec. v.p. human resources Am. Express, 2005—, mem. global mgmt. team, 2005—, bd. dirs. compensation and benefits com., 2005—. Office: Am Express Co World Fin Ctr 200 Vesey St New York NY 10285 Office Phone: 212-640-2000.*

COX, LINDA SMOAK, real estate broker; b. Yonges Island, SC, Sept. 5, 1943; d. Ryan Lanier Smoak and Frances Lapish Bock. Grad., Kings Coll., Charlotte, N.C., 1962. Lic. real estate broker, relocation specialist, new homes specialist. Exec. sec. Charlotte Observer Transp. Co., 1963-65; various positions Eastern Airlines, Charlotte, 1965-88; real estate salesperson Allen Tate Realtors, Charlotte, 1990—. Program dir. Delta Investment, Charlotte, 1984-88; mem. bd. Realtors, Charlotte, 1990—; mem. Bd. Realtors, Rock Hill, S.C., 1993—. Troop leader Girl Scouts U.S., Charlotte, 1964; mem., vol. U.S. Humane Soc., Charlotte, 1964, 96—; co-founder, vol. Midway Meth. Ch. Libr., Kannapolis, N.C., 1958; mem. coun. River Hills Cmty. Ch., Lake Wylie, S.C., 1980-82, chair fellowship com., 1979-80, mem. edn. com., 1984-85, bd. trustees, 2002—; founding mem., vol. Stowe Bot. Gardens, Belmont, N.C., 1994—. Mem.: Charlotte Regional Realtor Assn., N.C. Assn. Realtors. Avocations: water sports, snow ski race team, sailing, gardening. Home: PO Box 240173 Charlotte NC 28224-0173 Office Phone: 704-367-7217. E-mail: linda.cox@atcmail.com.

COX, LINDA SUSAN, allergist, immunologist; b. Oakland, Calif., Aug. 17, 1955; d. James Lee Dolan and Nancy Jane (Christie) C.; m. Robert Louis Wolfgram Jr.; children: Mary Elizabeth Cox, Christopher Alexander Cox-Wolfgram. BA cum laude, Boston U., 1978; postgrad., Harvard U., 1978-79, Hahnemann Med. Coll., 1979-80; MD, Northwestern U., 1985. Diplomate Am. Bd. Internal Medicine, Am. Bd. Allergy and Immunology. Intern in internal medicine Jackson Meml. Hosp., U. Miami, Fla., 1985-88; emergency room physician North Ridge Med. Ctr., Ft. Lauderdale, Fla., 1988-89; fellow in allergy and immunology Nat. Jewish Hosp., Denver, 1989-91; pvt. practice Allergy, Asthma and Clin. Immunology Ctr., Miami, Fla., 1991-92, Adult and Pediat. Allergy and Immunology, Ft. Lauderdale, 1992—; emergency rm. physician Imperial Point Med. Ctr., 1997—. Part-time emergency room physician Fitzsimmons Med. Ctr., Aurora, Colo., 1989-91, Palmetto Gen. Hosp., 1992—; rschr. U. Miami Sch. Medicine Dept. Clin. Immunology, 1987, U. Colo. Sch. Medicine Dept. Allergy and Clin. Immunology, 1990-91; asst. clin. prof. medicine U. Miami Sch. Medicine, 1996—, also bd. dirs.; asst. clin. prof. medicine Nova Southeastern U. Ortho. Sch. Medicine. Fellow Am. Coll. Allergy and Immunology, ACP; mem. Am. Acad. Allergy and Immunology, Am. Coll. Chest Physicians, Fla. Allergy and Immunology Soc. (mem. exec. com. 1998—, sec. practice std. com., mem. edn. com.), Broward County Med. Assn. (bd. dirs. 1996—). Episcopalian. Avocations: ballet, skiing. Home: 5802 Poinsettia Ave West Palm Beach FL 33407-2536 Office: 5333 N Dixie Hwy Ste 210 Fort Lauderdale FL 33334-3454

COX, LOUIS ANTHONY, JR., telecommunications executive; b. Washington, Aug. 7, 1957; s. Louis Anthony and Frances McKee Cox; m. Christine Anne Cox, Sept. 8, 1979; 1 child, Emeline Dickinson. AB, Harvard U., 1978; SM, MIT, 1985, PhD, 1986; postgrad., Stanford U., 1993. Sr. rsch. assoc. Am. Inst. for Rsch., Washington, 1978-79; mgr. ops. rsch. Arthur D. Little, Inc., Cambridge, Mass., 1980-86; pres. Cox Assocs., Denver, 1986—; sr. dir. U.S. West Advanced Techs., Boulder, Colo., 1987-96. Hon. full prof. math. U. Colo., Denver, 2000—; clin. prof. preventive medicine and biometrics U. Colo. Health Scis. Ctr., 2000—; counselor Ops. Rsch. Soc. Am. Spl. Interest Group-Telecomm., 1992-94. Co-author: Beyond Probation: Juvenile Corrections and the Chronic Delinquent, 1979; contbr. articles to profl. jours., chpts. to books; co-editor: New Risks: Issues and Management, 1990, Jour. Heuristics, 1995; patentee in field. Fellow Soc. Risk Analysis (life, sec., co-founder New Eng. chpt. 1985-86); mem. Am. Statis. Inst., Inst. Ops. Rsch. and Mgmt. Scis., N.Y. Acad. Scis. Office: Cox Assocs 503 Franklin St Denver CO 80218 Fax: (303) 388-0609. Office Phone: 303-388-1778. E-mail: tcoxdenver@aol.com.

COX, M. CAROLYN, lawyer; b. June 10, 1949; BA, Agnes Scott Coll., 1971; JD, Yale Univ., 1974. Bar: Ala. 1975, DC 1976. Law clk. Judge Frank M. Johnson, US Dist. Ct., Middle Dist. Ala., 1974—75; ptnr., Corp. dept., chmn. Ethics com. Wilmer Cutler Pickering Hale & Dorr, Washington. Dir. Yale Barristers Union. Office: Wilmer Cutler Pickering Hale & Dorr 1801 Pennsylvania Ave NW Washington DC 20006 Mailing: Wilmer Cutler Pickering Hale & Dorr 2445 M St NW Washington DC 20037 Office Phone: 202-663-6645. Office Fax: 202-663-6363. Business E-Mail: carolyn.cox@wilmerhale.com.

COX, MALCOLM, academic administrator, medical educator; b. South Africa, Jan. 27, 1944; m. Rosalie Cox. Student, U. Witwatersrand; MD, Harvard U.; degree Wyeth-Ayerst APM Exec. Mgmt. Program, The Wharton Sch., U. Penn. Intern Hosp. U. Penn., 1970—71, resident in med., 1971—73, 1975—76, fellow in nephrology, 1973—75; vice chmn. dept. med. Hosp. U. Penn; various postions Phila. VA Med. Ctr.; assoc. dean U. Penn. Sch. Med.; dean med. edn. Harvard Med. Sch., 2003—04, Carl W. Walter prof. med. and med. edn. Office: Harvard Med Sch Gordon Hall Rm 103 25 Shattuck St Boston MA 02115

COX, MARGARET STEWART, photographer; b. Indpls., Jan. 9, 1948; d. Douglass Falconer and Margaret Geraldine (Gates) Stewart; m. Herbert Leo Cox Jr., Dec. 21, 1977 (dec. Nov. 1985); 1 child, Matthew Michael. Student, Butler U., 1965-67, Rollins Coll., 1990-93. Real estate agt. Don Asher & Assocs., Orlando, Fla., 1972-80; real estate agt., appraiser Mary P. Logvin Real Estate, Orlando, 1987-90; freelance photographer Orlando, 1990—. Exhibited photographs in group shows at Marie Selby Bot. Gardens, 1993, 94, 98 (Merit awards), 1999 Exhibit, Orlando Artists Biennial Exhbn., 1992 (Merit award), Mt. Dora Ctr. for the Arts, 1994 (Merit award), others. Bd. dirs. Adult Literacy League, Inc., Orlando, 1987-95, pres., 1994; active Fla. Literacy Coalition, 1988-96; vice chair Orange City Devel. Adv. Bd., Orlando, 1991-95; active United Way Spkrs. Bur., 1994, 95; judge Chertok Nature Photo Contest, 1993, chairperson, 1995, 96, 98; mem. Lake County Dem. Exec. Com., 1997-2001. Recipient Spl. Mission Recognition award United Meth. Women, 1985. Mem. High Country Art and Craft Guild, Nat. Audubon Soc., Fla. Audubon Soc. (bd. dirs. 1998-99), Audobon Fla. (bd. dirs. 2003-), Orange Audubon Soc. (bd. dirs. 1993-96, 97—, 98-99, rec. sec. 1996, bd. pres. 1998—2002, conservation chmn. 2002-). Democrat. Avocations: reading, travel, wildlife art, birdwatching, gardening. Office: 9410 Oak Island Ln Clermont FL 34711-7304 Office Phone: 352-429-1042.

COX, MARK STANLEY, public relations professional; b. Uvalde, Tex., May 9, 1953; s. George Washington and Ora Faye (Wilson) C.; m. Jennifer Holinsworth Tidwell, Jan. 10, 1972 (div. Feb. 1977); 1 child, Amy Melissa; m. June Lynn Long; children: George Michael, Stephen William. BA, U. Okla., 1980; MS in Mass Comm., San Diego State U., 1983. Asst. editor Communicator Mag., San Diego, 1982-83; pub. info. coord. City of Chula Vista, Calif., 1983-89; dir. pub. comms. City of Chesapeake (Va.), 1989—. Instr. pub. rels. San Diego State U., 1988-89, Old Dominion U., 1993-97, Va. Wesleyan Coll., 1997—. Bd. dirs. Chesapeake Consortium for Arts and History, 1996-2000, Chesapeake Care Free Clinic, 1996-2000. With USAF, 1972-76. Mem. Pub. Rels. Soc. Am. (pres. Hampton Roads chpt. 1995, 2005, Profl. of Yr. 2005), Tall Ship Soc. San Diego County (chmn. 1986-89), Hampton Roads C. of C. (bd. dirs. Chesapeake divsn. 1997-2001, 2003—), San Diego Club, Chesapeake Rotary Club. Roman Catholic. Avocations: personal computers, golf, writing, guitar, chess. Home: 1305 Grenadier Ct Chesapeake VA 23322-4356 Office: City of Chesapeake Pub Comm Dept 306 Cedar Rd Chesapeake VA 23322-5597

COX, MARSHALL, lawyer; b. Cleve., Nov. 17, 1932; s. Marshall H.C. and Mary (Bateman) Mills; m. Nancy Huntley, Aug. 3, 1957 (div. Oct. 1994); 1 child, Vanessa; m. Nathalie Menapace, Jan. 3, 1997. BA, Vanderbilt U., 1954; JD, Ohio State U., 1958. Bar: D.C. 1974, N.Y. 1959. Assoc. Cahill Gordon & Reindel, N.Y.C., 1959-67, ptnr., 1968-97. Served to 1st. lt. U.S. Army, 1955-57, Korea. Republican. Episcopalian.

COX, MELVIN MONROE, lawyer; b. Omaha, Jan. 31, 1947; s. Monroe M. Cox and Wilma Grace (Prickett) McPherson. BA with high honors, U. Wyo., 1969; JD, Harvard U., 1972. Bar: Pa. 1972, US Dist. Ct. (we. dist.) Pa. 1972, NJ 1987, US Dist. Ct. (NJ) 1987. Assoc. Rose, Schmidt & Dixon, Pitts., 1972-78; atty. Chgo. Pneumatic Tool Co., NY, 1978-81, asst. sec. NYC, 1981-88; asst. gen. counsel Sun Chem. Corp., Ft. Lee, NJ, 1989-93, asst. gen. counsel, asst. sec., 1993-97, v.p., gen. counsel, sec., 1997—2004, sr. v.p., gen. counsel, sec., 2004—. Adj. prof. engring. law The Cooper Union, N.Y.C., 1984—91; asst. sec. DIC Ams., Inc., Ft. Lee, NJ, 1993—97; mng. dir. Sun Chem. B.V., Soest, Netherlands, 1996—2004; bd. visitors U. Wyoming, Coll. Arts and Scis., 1997—, vice chmn., 1998—2001. Bd. dirs. Good Shepherd Cmty. Svcs., Inc., Ft. Lee, 1999-2001; trustee U. Wyoming Found., 2001-; mem. collections com. U. Wyo. Art Mus, 2004-; Chair, mem. exec. com. pub. responsibility com. 2004. Recipient Outstanding Alumnus award, U. Wyo., 2002. Mem.: ABA, Am. Corp. Counsel Assn., Phi Beta Kappa, Phi Kappa Phi. Office: Sun Chem Corp 35 Waterview Blvd Parsippany NJ 07054 Office Phone: 973-404-6500.

COX, MIKE, state attorney general; m. Laura Cox; 4 children. BA in Polit. Sci. with distinction, U. Mich., 1986, JD, 1989. Asst. pros. atty. Office Pros. Atty. Oakland County, Pontiac, Mich., 1989—90; asst. pros. atty. spl. crimes sect. Office Pros. Atty. Wayne County, Detroit, 1990—2001, dep. chief homicide unit, 2001—03; atty. gen. State of Mich., Lansing, 2003—. With USMC, 1980—83. Mem.: Inc. Soc. Irish/Am. Lawyers, State Bar Mich. (criminal law sect.), Pros. Attys. Assn. Mich. (instr. Basic Sch.). Republican. Office: G Mennen Williams Bldg 7th Fl PO Box 30212 525 W Ottawa St Lansing MI 48909

COX, MITCHEL NEAL, editor; b. Portsmouth, Ohio, Sept. 8, 1956; s. Walter Eugene and Mary Agnes (Orlett) Cox; m. Lisa Renee LaLonde, Sept. 8, 1979 (dec. May 2001); children: Harmony, Leigh Ann, Katie. BS in Journalism, Ohio State U., 1985. Mng. editor The Puller, Columbus, Ohio, 1984-87; editor Bicycles Today, Columbus, 1985-87, Fur-Fish-Game, Columbus, 1987—. Mem. Outdoor Writers Assn. Am. Office: Fur-Fish-Game 2878 E Main St Columbus OH 43209-2698 Office Phone: 614-231-9585. E-mail: ffgcox@ameritech.net.

COX, MURRAY W., mathematics professor; b. Denver, Feb. 10, 1969; s. William Murray and Dorothy Ellen Cox. AS in Engring., Union Coll., Riverside, California, 1991; BA in Math., Union Coll., Lincoln, Nebr., 1991; MS in Math. and Edn., U. Calif., Riverside, 2000. Math. tchr. h.s. Mile High Acad., Denver, 1993—98; asst. prof. math. Southwestern Adventist U., Keene, Tex., 2001—. Boxing coach J.C.B.C., Keene, Tex., 1990—. Mem.: Am. Math. Soc. Avocations: boxing, acro gymnastics. Office: Southwestern Adventist U 300 N College Dr Keene TX 76059 Office Phone: 817-202-6503. Personal E-mail: murray87@juno.com. E-mail: mcox@swau.edu.

COX, NATHAN J., art educator; b. Virginia, Ill., Feb. 11, 1975; s. Virgil A. and Marcia K. Cox; m. Amy M. Kuhl Cox, Nov. 30, 2002. MFA, Bradley U., 2000. Instr. Carl Sandburg C.C., Galesburg, Ill., 1999—2001; lectr. Western Ill. U., Macomb, 2001; instr. art Monmouth Coll., Ill., 2001—02; asst. prof. art Anderson Coll., SC, 2002—. Mem.: Foundations Art: Theory and Edn., Coll. Art Assn., Phi Kappa Phi. Home: 1420 Hilltop Dr Anderson SC 29621 Office: Anderson Coll 316 Boulevard Anderson SC 29621 Office Phone: 864-231-2047. Business E-Mail: ncox@ac.edu.

COX, PATRICK, historian, writer; s. Wilburn Ford Cox and Doris Lee Varnon; m. Brenda Gail Potts, July 25, 1981; 1 child, Lauren Anne. BA, U. Tex., 1974, PhD, 1996; MA, Tex. State U., San Marcos, 1988. Editor The Wimberley (Tex.) View, 1975—83; asst. land commr. Tex. Gen. Land Office, Austin, 1983—88; pres. Cox & Assocs., Austin, 1988—98; historian/lectr. St. Edwards U., Austin, 1996—97; asst. dir. Ctr. for Am. History U. Tex., Austin, 1998—. Mem. adv. bd. Austin Coll. Southwestern and Mex. Am. Studies, Sherman, Tex., 2004—. Author: Ralph W. Yarborough: The People's Senator (finalist Robert Kennedy Found. Ann. Book award, 2002), Profiles in Power: Twentieth Century Texans in Washington, D.C.; curator ExxonMobil Historical Archive, (historical archive) Vice President John Nance Garner, mem. editl. bd. Digital Journalist, 2003—; author: (Book) The First Texas News Barons; curator (historical archive) Speaker Sam Rayburn. Pres. Wimberley Lions Club, 1979—80, Wimberley Valley Watershed Assn., 2001—, Barton Springs Edwards Aquifer Conservation Dist., Austin, 1988—96. Finalist best nonfiction, Western Writers Am., 2002; named Featured Author, Tex. Book Festival, 2002; recipient C.K. Chamberlain award, East Tex. Hist. Assn., 2001, hon. mention Photojournalism and the Am. Presidency, Accessibility Internet Rally for Univs., 2003; John H. Jenkins fellowship in Tex. history, Tex. State Hist. Assn., 2000, Clements-DeGolyer grantee, So. Meth. U., 2001. Mem.: Am. Journalism Historians Assn. (bd. dirs. 2002—, editl. adv. bd. 2003—), Tex. State Hist. Assn., Am. Hist. Assn., Philos. Soc. Tex. Home: 570 River Mountain Rd Wimberley TX 78676 Office: Ctr for Am History U Tex at Austin Austin TX 78712

COX, PAUL ALAN, ethnobotanist, educator; b. Salt Lake City, Oct. 10, 1953; s. Leo A. and Rae (Gabbitas) C.; m. Barbara Ann Wilson, May 21, 1975; children: Emily Ann, Paul Matthew, Mary Elisabeth, Hillary Christine, Jane Margaret. BS, Brigham Young U., 1976; MSc, U. Wales, 1978; AM, Harvard U., 1978, PhD, 1981; DSc (hon.), U. Guelph, Can., 2000. Teaching fellow Harvard U., Cambridge, Mass., 1977-81; Miller research fellow Miller Inst. Basic Research in Sci., Berkeley, Calif., 1981-83; asst. prof. Brigham Young U., Provo, Utah, 1983-86, assoc. prof., 1986-91, prof., 1991—98, dean gen. edn. and honors, 1993-97; King Gustav XVI prof. environ. sci. Swedish Biodiversity Ctr., 1997—98; dir. Nat. Tropical Botanical Garden, Kalaheo, Hawaii, 1998—2004, Inst. for Ethnomedicine, Provo, 2004—. Disting. prof. Brigham Young U., Hawaii, 2000—; ecologist Utah Environ. Coun., Salt Lake City, 1976; project ecologist Utah MX Coordination Office, Salt Lake City, 1981. Mem. editorial bd. Pacific Studies. Recipient Bowdoin prize, The Goldman Environ. prize, 1997; Danforth Found. fellow, 1976-81, Fulbright fellow, 1976-77, NSF fellow, 1977-81, Linnean Soc. fellow, named NSF Presdl. Young Investigator, 1985-90, Hero of Medicine, Time Mag., 1997, Rachel Carson award, 1999. Mem. AAAS, Brit. Ecol. Soc., Internat. Soc. Ethnopharmacology (former pres.), Am. Soc. Naturalists, Assn. Tropical Biology, Soc. Econ. Botany (former pres.), Seacology Found. (founder and chmn.), AIDS Rsch. Alliance (bd.), Ctr. for Plant Conservation (bd.). Mem. Lds Ch. Office: Inst for Ethnomedicine PO Box 3464 Jackson WY 83001 Office Phone: 801-375-6214.

COX, PETER, artist; b. New York, 1942; Grad., Phoenix School of Design, Parsons School, Holy Cross Coll. V.p. Nat. Arts Club, 1986—97; instr. Arts Students League, 1984—, N.Y. Academy of Art, 1994—2000, Nat. Academy of Design Museum School, 2002—; represented Caravaggio Studios Inc. Exhibitions include, Carolyn Hill Gallery, 1989—91, Joseph Keiffer Inc., 1992, Louis Newman Galleries, 1993, CFM Galleries, 1994, Gallery Dai, 1996, M B Modem, 1998, exhibited in group shows, Artists of America, 1981—92, John Pence Gallery, 1991—92, In Collaboration Gallery, 1992, Amot Museum, 1993, Allan Stone Gallery, 1995—96, National Arts Club, 1997, M B Modem, 1997, Survey of the Am. Figure in Painting, 1820-Present Babcock Galleries, 2000, Represented in permanent collections, Arkansas Art Center, Arnot Museum, Redding Museum, Nat. Academy of Design. Named to National Acad., 2002; recipient John Gordon Mem. Award, Soc. of the Four Arts, 1986, Gold Medal, Pastel Soc. of Am., 1987, Cert. of Merit, Nat. Academy of Design, 1988, Gold Medal, Nat. Arts Club, 1988, 1997, Gary Melchers Award, Artist Fellowship, 1998. Office: c/o Caravaggio Studios Inc 315 West 39th Suite #506 New York NY 10018 Office Phone: 212-736-6635. Personal E-mail: petercox@verizonmail.com.

COX, REED ELBREDGE, lawyer; b. Lauderdale County, Ala., July 4, 1934; BA, U. No. Ala., 1956; MBA, Ga. Coll., 1970; JD, John Marshall U., 1979. Bar: Ga. 1979. Pvt. practice, Marietta, Ga., 1979—. With U.S. Army, 1956-76. Mem. Ga. Bar Assn., Cobb County Bar Assn., Officers Club, Indian Hills Country Club. Republican. Avocation: tennis. Office: 591 Lawrence St NE Marietta GA 30060-2172 Office Phone: 707-427-4441.

COX, RICHARD HORTON, civil engineering executive; b. Paia, Hawaii, Oct. 10, 1920; s. Joel B. and Helen Cliford (Horton) C.; m. Hester Virginia Smith, Dec. 12, 1942 (dec. Aug. 12, 1995); children: Millicent, Janet, Lydia, Evelyn, David, Samuel (dec.). BS, Calif. Inst. Tech., 1942, MS, 1946. Registered profl. engr., surveyor, Hawaii. Supr. rocket range Calif. Inst. Tech., Pasadena, 1942-46; civil engr. McBryde Sugar Co., Eleele, Hawaii, 1946-56; land mgr. Alexander & Baldwin, Honolulu, 1956-71, v.p., 1971-86; engring. cons. Honolulu, 1986—. Mem. State Commn. on Water Resource Mgmt., 1987-94, 95-99. Fellow: ASCE; mem.: NSPE, AAAS, Am. Geophys. Union. Mem. Soc. Of Friends. Home and Office: 1951 Kakela Dr Honolulu HI 96822-2156

COX, ROBERT HAMES, chemist, consultant; b. Toronto, Can., Mar. 23, 1923; came to U.S., 1951; s. Giffard and Lavinia Sarah (Hames) C.; m. Dora Maria Forstrom, Sept. 5, 1953; children: William H., Frederick G., Irene M. B of Pharmacy, U. Toronto, 1946; BS in Pharmacy, U. Sask., Saskatoon, Can., 1948, MSc, 1950; PhD in Medicinal Chemistry, U. Mich., 1954. Lic. pharmacist, Ont. Head dept. pharm. chemistry U. B.C., Vancouver, Canada, 1949-51; asst. to mgr. product devel. Mallinckrodt Chem. Works, St. Louis, 1954-56; tech. dir. Vick Internat. divsn. Richardson-Merrell, N.Y.C., 1956-60, assoc. dir. tech. svcs., 1960-64, v.p. rsch. and devel. Walker Labs. Mt. Vernon, NY, 1964-66; dir. new products Winthrop Labs. divsn. Sterling Drug, N.Y.C., 1966-75; co-founder, pres. New Eng. Pharms., Inc., Randolph, Mass., 1978-82; pres. Robert H. Cox & Co., Scarsdale, NY, 1975—, Cox & Fay, Inc., Scarsdale, 1991—. Cons. Drug Enforcement Adminstrn., Washington, 1976-78, Nat. Cancer Inst., Bethesda, Md., 1980-81, Indonesian Govt., Jakarta, Java, 1991—. Co-editor-in-chief: Medicinal Chemistry, Vol. III, 1956, Vol. IV, 1959. Leader Jamaica Mission, UN Adv. Svcs., 1988; mem. U.S. Exchs. del. to China, 1990. Recipient Roberts medal Ont. Coll. Pharmacy, 1955, George E. Parke medal, 1957. Fellow Am. Inst. Chemists (pres. N.Y. 1986-87, leader sci. del. to China 1986, co-leader to USSR 1989); mem. Am. Chem. Soc. (treas. medicinal chemistry divsn. 1962-63), Parenteral Drug Assn., Ctrl. Atlantic States Assn. Food and Drug Ofcls., Chemists Club (trustee). Episcopalian. Achievements include patents for drugs (sympatholytics/cycloplegics) and medical devices including hemodialysis; conducted practical synthesis of suberone precursor of early antihypertensive, guanethidine; early evaluation (1940s) of oxidized cholesterols in etiology of experimental atherosclerosis. E-mail: bcox@snet.net.

COX, ROBERT HAROLD, physiology educator; b. Phila., Sept. 10, 1937; BS, Drexel Inst. Tech., 1961, MS, 1962; PhD in Biochemical Engring., U. Pa., 1967. Assoc. physiologist U. Pa., Phila., 1967-69, asst. prof. physiology, 1969-72, assoc. prof., 1972-80, prof., 1980—, assoc. prof. biomechanics, 1973—, assoc. dir. Bockus Rsch. Inst., 1970-80, dir. Bockus Rsch. Inst., 1980—. Mem. IEEE, AAAS, Am. Physiol. Soc., Am. Heart Assn., Sigma Xi. Achievements include research in vascular smooth muscle mechanics, arterial wall physiology, hypertension, carotid sinus reflex, ion channels, patch clamp electrophysiology. Office: U Penn 93 John Morgan Bldg Philadelphia PA 19104

COX, RODY P(OWELL), internist, educator; b. New Brighton, Pa., June 24, 1926; s. Raymond James and Hazel (Powell) C.; m. Jane Beverly Birks, Sept. 5, 1953 (dec. Apr. 1995); children: Shelley Lea, Rody Powell, Sue Ellen; m. LaVaun Jeanne Sears, Mar. 1, 1997. Student, Franklin and Marshall Coll., 1946-48; MD, U. Pa., 1952. Diplomate Am. Bd. Internal Medicine. Intern U. Mich., 1952-53, resident in medicine, 1953-54, U. Pa., Phila., 1953-57, asst. prof. medicine, 1957-60; rsch. assoc. U. Glasgow, Scotland, 1960-61; prof. medicine NYU, N.Y.C., 1961-79, prof. pharmacology, 1972-79, chief div. human genetics, 1972-79; prof., vice chmn. dept. medicine Case-Western Res. U., Cleve., 1979-88; chief med. svc. VA Med. Ctr., Cleve., 1979-88; dean Med. Sch. U. Tex. Southwestern Med. Ctr., Dallas, 1988-89, prof. internal medicine, 1988—. Mem. metabolism study sect. NIH, 1970-74, chmn. genetics study sect., 1978-79, chmn. mammalian genetics study sect., 1979-81; mem. panel on clin. scis. NRC, 1976-86. Editor: Cell Communication, 1974; co-editor: Epithelial Cell Culture, 1981; contbr. articles to profl. publs. Sgt. U.S. Army, 1944-46, NATOUSA. Fellow ACP; mem. Am. Soc. Clin. Investigation (emeritus), Assn. Am. Physicians, Ctrl. Soc. Clin. Rsch., John Morgan Soc. U. Pa., Harvey Soc., Am. Clin. Climatol. Assn., Am. Soc. Human Genetics, Interurban Clin. Club, Alpha Omega Alpha (councillor NYU chpt. 1970-76). Home: 5 Connaught Ct Dallas TX 75225-2459 Office: U Tex Southwestern Med Ctr 5323 Harry Hines Blvd Dallas TX 75390-8889 Office Phone: 214-648-7805. Business E-Mail: rcox@mednet.swmed.edu.

COX, ROGER FRAZIER, lawyer; b. Phila., Sept. 11, 1939; s. Roger Newcomb and Ethel May (Frazier) Cox; m. Lucy Jakstas, June 24, 1967. BA, Amherst Coll., 1962; LLB, U. Pa., 1966. Bar: DC 1967, Pa. 1967, Calif. 1970. Law clk. to presiding judge U.S. Dist. Ct., N.Y.C., 1966-67; asst. dist. atty. Phila. Dist. Atty.'s Office, 1967-69; staff atty. Alameda County Legal Aid Soc., Oakland, Calif., 1969-71; from assoc. to ptnr. Blank Rome LLP, Phila., 1971—. Mem.: ABA, Phila. Bar Assn., Pa. Bar Assn., Am. Judicature Soc., Order of Coif. Home: 303 Delancey St Philadelphia PA 19106-4208 Office: Blank Rome LLP One Logan Sq Philadelphia PA 19103-6998 Office Phone: 215-569-5601. Business E-Mail: cox@blankrome.com.

COX, RON DEAN, non-commissioned officer, educator, retired psychologist; b. Miami, Fla., June 26, 1939; s. Fred Raymond and Wilbour Handy C.; m. Sue James, Aug. 8, 1964; 1 child, Victor. AA, Gulf Coast Cmty. Coll., 1984; BS in Psychology, Fla. State U., Panama City, 1986, MS in Applied Psychology, 1988. Enlisted USAF, 1957, advanced through grades to master sgt., 1974, ret., 1978; adj. prof. Gulf Coast Cmty. Coll., Panama City, Fla., 1988-95, ret., 1995. Chair ad-hoc com. computer selection City of Callaway, Fla., 1982. Designer of modifications for B-52 Flight Simulator, 1969, 70.

Asst. campaign mgr. Mayor, Callaway, 1984. Mem. Phi Beta Kappa. Republican. Baptist. Avocations: reading, aviation history, politics. Home: 6521 Hiwassee St Panama City FL 32404-8020

COX, RONADH, physical science educator, geologist; b. Dublin, Jan. 17, 1962; PhD, Stanford U., 1993. Assoc. prof. geoscis. Williams Coll., Williamstown, Mass., 1996—. Office: Williams Coll Dept Geoscis Williamstown MA 01267 Office Phone: 413-697-2297.

COX, TERI POLACK, public relations executive; b. Pitts., May 21, 1952; d. Meyer and Faye Helen (Tischler) Polack; m. William R. Cox, Jan. 1, 1982. BA, U. Pitts., 1974; MBA in Mktg., NYU, 1989. Info. dir. United Mental Health; prodr., host weekly PA radio program; pub. rels. dir. Atlanta Merchandise Mart; mktg. rsch., pub. rels. cons. Pfizer Inc., NYU Stern Sch. Bus.; acct. supr. Burson-Marsteller; mng. ptnr. Cox Comms. Ptnrs., Lawrenceville, N.J., 1992-98, sr. mng. ptnr., 1998—. Chair Bd. Devel. Workgroup; mem. Advocacy Leadership Team, Prevention and Detection Workgroup; legis. amb. Am. Cancer Soc. Named Pharma Voice 100 Most Inspiring and Influential Individuals Life Scis. Industry, 2005. Mem.: Nat. Am. Cancer Soc. (Capitol Dome award, NJ Gov.'s Task Force on Cancer Prevention, St. George Medal award), Women Execs. in Pub. Rels., Healthcare Businesswomen's Assn. (past pres., adv. bd.), Pub. Rels. Soc. Am. Office: Cox Comm Ptnrs 2 Roseberry Ct Lawrenceville NJ 08648-1058 Office Phone: 609-896-3250. Personal E-mail: coxcomptnr@aol.com.

COX, THOMAS, history professor; s. L. Hughes and Judith Cox. BS, BA, Birmingham So. Coll., 1994; MA, SUNY, Buffalo, 1998, PhD, 2004. Adj. instr. SUNY, Buffalo, 1999—2001; vis. asst. prof. U. Nebr., Kearney, 2003—05; assc. prof. Sam Houston State U., Tex., 2005—. Recipient Larry J. Hackman rsch. resident award, NY State; Golden Dream dissertation fellow. Mem.: Am. Hist. Assn. Home: 3802 22nd Ave Apt A3 Kearney NE 68845 Office: Univ Nebr Dept History 103 A Copeland Hall Kearney NE 68845 E-mail: thcox@lyros.com.

COX, WALTER THOMPSON, III, lawyer, law educator, retired federal judge; b. Anderson, SC, Aug. 13, 1942; s. Walter Thompson and Mary (Johnson) C.; m. Victoria Grubbs, Feb. 8, 1963; children: Lisa, Walter. BS, Clemson U., 1964; JD, U. S.C., 1967. Bar: S.C., 1967, U.S. Dist. Ct. S.C., 1967, U.S. Ct. Appeals (4th cir.), 1976, U.S. Ct. Appeals for Armed Forces, 1984, U.S. Supreme Ct., 1987. Commn. capt. U.S. Army, 1964, atty., 1964-73; ptnr. Jones, McIntosh, Threlkeld, Newman & Cox, Anderson, SC, 1973-78; trial judge 10th cir. State S.C., Anderson, 1978-84; judge US Ct. Appeals Armed Forces, Washington, 1984-95, chief judge, 1995-99, sr. judge, 1999—2000; sr. lecturing fellow Duke U. Law Sch., Durham, NC; of counsel Nelson Mullins Riley & Scarborough, LLP, Charleston, SC, 2003—. Adj. prof. Charleston Sch. Law, 2005. Mem. ABA, FBA, Judge Adv.'s Assn., S.C. Bar Assn. (del.), Wild Dune Golf and Racquet Club. Episcopalian. Office: Nelson Mullins Riley & Scarborough LLP 151 Meeting St St 600 Charleston SC 29401 Office Phone: 843-853-5200. Business E-Mail: wcox@law.duke.edu.

COX, WARREN JACOB, architect; b. N.Y.C., Aug. 28, 1935; s. Oscar Sydney and Louise Bryson (Black) C.; m. Claire Christie-Miller, July 1, 1975; children: Alexandra Louise, Samuel Oscar. BA magna cum laude, Yale U., 1957, MArch, 1961. Ptnr. Hartman-Cox Architects, Washington, 1965—. Vis. archtl. critic Yale, 1966, Cath. U. Am., 1967, U. Va., 1976; lectr. Works include master plan, dormitory and chapel, Mt. Vernon Coll., EURAM bldg. Nat. Perm. Bldg., Folger Shakespeare Libr. addition, Washington, Immanuel Presbyn. Ch. Va., Nat. Humanities Ctr., Raleigh, Am. Embassy, Malaysia, HEB corp. hdqrs., San Antonio, Chrysler Mus. remodeling, Norfolk, Dumbarton Oaks remodeling, Monroe Hall and McIntire Sch. Commerce, U. Va., Charlottesville, Sumner Sq., 1001 Pa. Ave., Market Sq., Franklin Sq., Georgetown U. Law Ctr. Libr. and Residence Hall, Washington, John Carter Brown Libr. addition, Providence, Winterthur New Exhbn. Bldg., Wilmington, Del., Tulane Law Sch., New Orleans, Law Sch. Libr. Univ. Conn., Hartford, Law Sch. Washington U., St. Louis, Libr. Case We. Res. U., Cleve., Fed. Courthouse, Corpus Christi, Tex., Concert Hall remodeling Kennedy Ctr. for Performing Arts, Washington, New Dist. and Cir. Courthouses, Lexington, Kennedy Warren Apts. addition, Lincoln and Jefferson Memls. restoration, Patent Office Bldg. renovation, Nat. Archives Bldg. renovation, Washington, Jefferson Libr., Monticello and spl. collections libr., U. of Va., Charlottesville, Div. Sch. addition Duke U., Durham, N.C. Mem. Georgetown Commn. Fine Arts, 1971-75; chmn. Friends of Folger Shakespeare Libr., 1987-88; bd. dirs. Ctr. for Palladian Studies in Am., 1982-, D.C. Preservation League, 1987-89. Recipient Henry Adams prize 1961, over 110 nat. and regional design awards including Louis Sullivan Prize (1972), six AIA Nat. Honor awards, and the AIA Archtl. Firm award, 1988. Fellow AIA. Home: 3111 N St NW Washington DC 20007-3420 also: PO Box 1 Church Hill MD 21623-0001 Office: Hartman Cox Architects 1074 Thomas Jefferson St NW Washington DC 20007-3832

COX, WILFORD DONALD, retired food company executive; b. Marion, Ill., Sept. 5, 1925; s. James Roy and Mamie (Stahlhut) C.; m. Helen Eunice Turner, Sept. 8, 1945; 1 child, James Dexter. Grad. high sch., Crab Orchard, Ill. Asst. plant mgr. Std. Brands Inc., San Antonio, 1956-60; plant mgr. Dallas, 1960-64; asst. div. mgr. Kansas City, Mo., 1964-70; div. mgr., 1972-78; v.p. procurement N.Y.C., 1978-81; v.p. Cal-Maine Foods, Jackson, Miss., 1970-72; v.p. commodities Nabisco Brands Inc., East Hanover, N.J., 1981-84; v.p. oil procurement Kraft Inc., Glenview, Ill., then Memphis, 1984-90, ret., 1990. Mem. Nat. Inst. Oilseed Processors, Nat. Soybean Processors Assn., Nat. Assn. Purchasing Mgrs., Colonial Country Club (Memphis). Republican. Avocation: golf. Office Phone: 901-682-8085. Personal E-mail: jchcmtw@aol.com.

COX, WILLIAM ANDREW, cardiovascular thoracic surgeon; b. Columbus, Ga., Aug. 3, 1925; s. Virgil Augustus and Dale Jackson C.; m. Nina Recelle Hobby, Jan. 1, 1948; children: Constance Lynn Cox Rogers, Patricia Ann Cox Brown, William Robert, Janet Elaine Cox Sidewater. Student, Presbyn. Coll., 1942, Harvard U., 1944-45, Cornell U., 1945; BS, Emory U., 1950, MD, 1954; MS in Surgery, Baylor U., 1961. Diplomate Am. Bd. Surgery, Am. Bd. Thoracic Surgery. Active duty USN, 1943-46; lt. (j.g.) USNR, 1946-54; commd. 1st lt. M.C. U.S. Army, 1954, advanced through grades to col., 1969; intern Brooke Army Med. Ctr., San Antonio, 1954-55, resident gen. surgery, 1956-60; resident cardiovasc. thoracic surgery Walter Reed Army Med. Ctr., Washington, 1960-62, staff cardiothoracic surgeon, 1962; asst chief cardiothoracic surgery Letterman Gen. Hosp., San Francisco, 1962-65; chief dept. surgery and cardiothoracic surgery 121 Evaculation Hosp, Seoul, Korea, 1965-66; cons. cardiothoracic surgery Korean Theatre, 1965-66; asst. chief cardiothoracic surgery Brooke Army Med Ctr., 1966-69, chief, 1969-73, bd. dirs. thoracic surgery residency programs, 1966-73, ret., 1973. Brooke Tower, on call for Pres. Lyndon B. Johnson when he visited his Tex. Ranch, 1967-72; clin. prof. cardio-thoracic surgery U. Tex. Sch. Medicine, San Antonio, 1971—; practice specializing in cardiovasc. thoracic surgery, Corpus Christi, Tex., 1973-93; cons. cardio-thoracic surgery Brooke Army Med. Ctr., San Antonio, 1977—; chief staff Meml. Med. Ctr., 1980; dir. disaster med. care region 3A Tex. State Dept. Health, 1973-88; mem. Coastal Bend Coun. Gov.'s Emergency Med. Svc. Commn., 1979-88; adv. bd. on congenital heart disease Tex. Dept. Health, 1980-88; participant joint confs. on cardiovasc. surgery and thoracic surgery Am. People Amb. Program, Leningrad, Moscow, Bucharest, Romania, Belgrade, Yugoslavia, Prague, Czechoslovakia, 1987; del. Vanderbilt U. Joint conf. vascular surgery Dublin, Ireland, Edinburgh, Scotland, London, 1986; participant joint confs. cardiovasc. surgery and thoracic surgery Am. Amb. People to People Program, Singapore, Kuala Lumpur, Malaysia, Hanoi, Vietnam, DaNang, Vietnam, Hue, Vietnam, Saigon, Vietnam, Hong Kong, 1992, People to People Am. Amb. Program, Eng., Scotland, Wales, 1996, 13th worldwide conf., Chester, England, 1998, 14th worldwide conf., Hong Kong, 2000, Denton A. Cooley Cardiovasc. Surgery Soc. mtg. Coeur d'Alene, Idaho, 2000; spkr. symposium Controversies in Cardiology, Dr. Willis Hurst, Holland Am. Lines Veendam, 1997; invited spkr. on open heart surgery 780 Bomb Squadron, Gainesville, 2001 Contbr. articles to profl. jours. Ruling elder Presbyn. Ch., 1960—. Decorated Legion of Merit, Army Commendation medal; recipient A Prefix award Surgeon Gen. U.S. Army, commendation Surgeon Gen. South Korea, commendation Eighth U.S. Army Commdg. Gen. for Emergency Surgery on Adm. Blackburn U.S. Negotiator for Peace, Pan mun jom, North Korea; named hon. citizen Phila. by Mayor Edward G. Rendell, 1995; recipient Tex. Med. Assn. Mem. Recognition 50 Yrs. award 1954-2004, 2004. Fellow Am. Coll. Chest Physicians (emeritus); mem. AMA, Soc. Thoracic Surgeons, Denton A. Coley Cardiovasc. Surgery Soc., Tex. Med. Assn. (del. conf. infectious diseases Bangkok, Hong Kong, Beijing, Shanghai, 1983), So. Thoracic Surgery Assn., Nueces County Med. Soc., Corpus Christi Surg. Soc., 38th Parallel Med. Soc., U.S. Power Squadron, People to People Internat., Internat. Platform, USN League (life), Ret. Officers Assn. (life), Navy Meml. Yacht Club (past commodore presidio San Francisco), T-Bar-M Racquet Club, Corpus Christi Country Club, Corpus Christi Athletic Club, Corpus Christi Town, Ft. Sam Houston Officers Club. Republican. Home: 5214 Wooldridge Rd Corpus Christi TX 78413-3833

COX, WILLIAM JACKSON, retired bishop; b. Valeria, Ky., Jan. 24, 1921; s. Robert Lee and Ora Ethel (Lawson) C.; m. Betty Drake, Dec. 20, 1941; children: Sharon Lee, William Richard, Michael Colin Student, U. Cin., 1939-40, George Washington U., Washington, 1945-46, U. Md. overseas extension, London, 1951-53, Va. Theol. Sem., Alexandria, 1957, D.Div. (hon.), 1974, Episcopal Theol. Sem. Ky., Lexington, 1980. Ordained priest Episcopal Ch., 1957. Pres., gen. mgr. McCook Broadcasting Co., McCook, Nebr., 1947-49; rector Church of the Holy Cross, Cumberland, Md., 1957-72; suffragan bishop of Md. Episcopal Ch., Frederick, Md., 1972-80, asst. bishop Okla. Tulsa, 1980—88; ret., 1988. Pres. Appalachian Peoples Service Orgn., Blacksburg, Va., 1974-80; chmn. Standing Com. on the Church in Small Communities, N.Y.C., 1976-82 Pres., Nursing Home Bd. of Allegany County, Cumberland, Md., 1965-72; pres. Episcopal Ministries to the Aging, Balt., 1973-80. Served to lt. col. U.S. Army, 1942-46, 1949-54; ETO. Episcopalian. Avocation: flying. Office: St Johns Ch 4200 S Atlanta Pl Tulsa OK 74105-4331 Home: 3701 N Cincinnati Ave #7 Tulsa OK 74106-1533

COX, WILLIAM MARTIN, lawyer, educator; b. Bernardsville, NJ, Dec. 26, 1922; s. Martin John and Nellie (Fotens) Cox; m. Julia Sebastian, June 14, 1952; children: Janice Cox Trautman, William Martin, Joann Cox Cahoon, Julieann Cox Allen. AB, Syracuse U., 1947; JD, Cornell U., 1950. Bar: NJ 1950, US Dist. Ct. 1950. Mem. Dolan & Dolan, Newton, NJ, 1950—; mem. faculty, tchr. zoning admintrn. Rutgers U., New Brunswick, NJ, 1968—98. Gen. counsel emeritus NJ Planning Ofcls.; pres. NJ Inst. Mcpl. Attys., 1982—84; mem. Land Use Law Drafting Com., 1970—, chmn., 1993—98; dir. emeritus Equip, Inc., Marion, NC; bd. dirs. Newton Cemetery Co., v.p., 2000—. Author: Zoning and Land Use Adminstrn. in New Jersey, 22nd edit., 2003, 24d edit., 2005. With U.S. Army, 1943—45. Named Citizen Yr., Town Newton, 2002; recipient Resolution Appreciation award, NJ Senate Gen. Assembly, 1994, Pres.'s Disting. Svc. award, NJ League Municipalities, 1999, Excellence Land Use Law award, NJ Inst. Mcpl. Attys., 1999, Professionalism Law award, Sussex County NJ State Bar Assn., 2003, Michael A. Pane award integrity local govt., 2003, Newton Pride Found. award, 2004. Mem.: N.J. Bar Assn., Sussex County Bar Assn., N.J. Planning Ofcls., Am. Planning Assn., Non-Commd. Officers Assn., VFW, Rotary (pres. 1978—79, Vocat. award 1996), Monarchist League, Am. Legion. Baptist. Office: 1 Legal Ln Newton NJ 07860-1827

COX, WILLIAM VAUGHAN, lawyer; b. Jersey City, Nov. 12, 1936; s. Walter Miles and Emily (McNenney); divorced; children: Millicent S., Jennifer V. BA, Princeton U., 1958; LLB, Yale U., 1964. Bar: Colo. 1965, N.Y. 1974. Law clk. Holland & Hart, Denver, 1963; atty. Conoco Inc., Denver, 1966-72, asst. to v.p., gen. counsel Stamford, Conn., 1972-73; v.p., gen. counsel Stromberg-Carlson Corp., Rochester, N.Y., 1974-78; mng. ptnr. Bader & Cox, Denver, 1979—80, 1979—88; pres. William V. Cox, P.C., Denver, 1988—, also bd. dirs.; project and planning dir. Interwest Comm. Corp., 1995-97. Pres., bd. dirs. New West Indies Trading Co., Denver, 1984—; pres. Coll. Football Ltd., Denver, 1990—. Sportswriter/editor: Colorado Springs (Colo.) Free Press, 1960-61. Football coach Cheyenne Mountain H.S., Colorado Springs, 1961; founder, bd. dir., v.p., com. chmn., editor Colo. chpt. Nat. Football Found., 1992-2001; mem. adv. bd. Downtown Denver Dist., 1991-93; bd. dir., com. chmn. Downtown Denver Residents, 1990-93; pres., bd. dir. Barclay Towers Condominiums, Denver, 1990-92, sec., bd. dir., 1998-99, pres. bd. dir., 1999-2000, 2001-2003, sec. bd. dir., 2000-2001, 2003-; dist. capt. Rep. Com., Cherry Hills, Colo., 1980-85; bd. dir. Monroe County Humane Soc., Rochester, 1975-78. With inf., intelligence USAR, 1959—65. Mem.: Am. Arbitration Assn. (arbitrator 2002—), Denver Bar Assn., Colo. Bar Assn., Law Club Denver (com. chmn. 1971), Princeton Rocky Mountain Club (com. chmn. 1972), Univ. Club Denver (bd. dirs. 1997—2000), Am. Legion, Corbey Ct., Phi Delta Phi. Roman Catholic. Avocations: running, politics, college football history, military history, animal rights. Office: 1625 Larimer St Ste 2707 Denver CO 80202-1538 Business E-Mail: wvcsq@citynetdsl.com.

COX ARQUETTE, COURTENEY, actress; b. Birmingham, Ala., June 15, 1964; d. Richard L. Lewis and Courteney Bass-Copland; m. David Arquette, June 12, 1999; 1 child, CoCo. Student, Mt. Vernon Coll. Appearances include (music video) Bruce Springsteen's Dancing in the Dark, 1984, The Rembrandts I'll Be There For You, 1995; (TV series) As The World Turns, 1984, Murder, She Wrote, 1984, Misfits of Science, 1985-86, Family Ties, 1987-88, Dream On, 1990, Seinfeld, 1990, The Larry Sanders Show, 1992, The Trouble with Larry, 1993, Friends, 1994-2004; (TV Pilots) Sylvan in Paradise, 1986; (TV Movies) If It's Tuesday, It Still Must Be Belgium, 1987, A Rockport Christmas, 1988, Roxanne: The Prize Pulitzer, 1989, Judith Krantz's Till We Meet Again, 1989, Curiosity Kills, 1990, Morton and Hays, 1991, Topper, 1992, Sketch Artist II: Hands That See, 1995; (films) Down Twisted, 1986, Masters of the Universe, 1987, Cocoon: The Return, 1988, Mr. Destiny, 1990, Blue Desert, 1990, Shaking the Tree, 1992, The Opposite Sex (and How to Live with Them), 1993, Ace Ventura, Pet Detective, 1994, Scream, 1996, Commandments, 1996, Scream 2, 1997, The Runner, 1999, Scream 3, 2000, 3000 Miles to Graceland, 2001, The Shrink Is In, 2001 (also exec. prodr.), Get Well Soon, 2001, Alien Love Triangle, 2002, November, 2004, The Longest Yard, 2005; exec. prodr. TV Series Mix It Up, 2003. Office: Brillstein Grey Entertainment 9150 Wilshire Blvd Beverly Hills CA 90212

COY, CHRISTOPHER JAMES, architect; b. Hackensack, NJ, Dec. 19, 1950; s. James Joseph and Evelyn Theresa (Popitti) Coy; m. Joann Owen, June 25, 1983; 1 child, Camille Violet. BArch, CCNY, 1986. Registered arch., NY. Prin. Barnes Coy Archs., Bridgehampton, NY, 1993—. Mem.: AIA. Business E-Mail: christopher@barnescoy.com.

COY, CRAIG P., airport terminal executive; Degree, U.S. Coast Guard Acad.; MBA, Harvard U. Various sr. level positions Fed. Govt., 20 yrs; v.p., gen. mgr. Lear Siegler Svcs. Inc., 1992-97; CEO HR Logic, Waltham, Mass., 1997—2001, Mass. Port Authority, 2001—. Past bd. dirs. White House Fellows Assn., U.S. Coast Guard Acad. Office: Mass Port Authority One Harborside Drive Ste 200S East Boston MA 02128-2909 E-mail: info@hrlogic.com.*

COYE, MOLLY JOEL, state agency administrator; b. Bennington, Vt., May 11, 1947; d. Robert Dudley Coye and Janet (Loper) Coye Nelson; m. Daniel Noah Lindheim, Sept. 22, 1974 (div. 1980); m. Mark Douglas Smith, Feb. 22, 1980; 1 child, Langston Matthew Coye. BA, U. Calif., Berkeley, 1968; MA, Stanford U., 1972; MPH, MD, Johns Hopkins U., 1977. Diplomate Am. Bd. Preventive Medicine. Chief of occupational health clinic U. San Francisco, 1979-84; med. officer Nat. Inst. for Occupational Safety & Health, 1980-85; advisor health and environment Gov.'s Office of Policy & Planning, Trenton, N.J., 1985-86; dep. commr. N.J. Dept. Health, Trenton, 1986-87; v.p. strategic devel. Health Desk Corp., Berkely, Calif., 1988-98; sr. v.p. The Lewin Group, San Francisco, 1998—. Chair adv. com. graduate program in pub. health U. Medicine and Dentistry of N.J., Newark, 1986—; mem. tech. bd. Milbank Meml. Fund, N.Y.C., 1986-88; mem. com. role of primary care physician in occupational/environ. medicine Nat. Acad. Scis, Inst. Medicine, Washington, 1986-88; mem. adv. com. AIDS U.S. Pub. Health Svc., Washington, 1989; mem. adv. coun. Nat. Inst. for Environ. Health Scis., Betheseda, Md., 1989. Co-author, editor: China: Inside the People's Republic, 1972, co-editor: China Yesterday and Today. Contbr. peer review articles to profl. jours. Founding bd. dirs. The Calif. Endowment. Recipient Virginia Apgar award March of Dimes, Plainsboro, N.J., 1988, Woman of the Yr. award Jersey Woman mag., 1989. Mem. AMA, Am. Coll. Preventive Medicine, Am. Pub. Health Assn. (chair exec. bd. 1988), Assn. for Health Svcs. Rsch., Assn. State and Territorial Health Officers (chair exec. bd. 1988—, mem. AIDS com. 1988—), Soc. for Occupational and Environ. Health (mem. governing coun. 1988—). Avocations: murder mysteries, cooking.

COYLE, AMY D., medical technician; b. N.J., Aug. 14, 1964; d. Julian Allen and Patricia B Dickinson; m. Paul F Coyle, June 1, 1962; children: Ailish Eileen, Fiona Patricia. AS, Bergen C.C., Paramus, N.J., 1990. Registered vascular technologist ARDMS, 1995. Sr. vascular technologist Englewood Hosp. and Med. Ctr., Englewood, NJ, 1991—. Ink painting, Highland Mist. R-Consevative. Roman Catholic. Avocations: painting, Kung Fu, travel, photography.

COYLE, DENNIS PATRICK, lawyer, retired utilities executive; b. Detoit, Aug. 29, 1938; s. Myron Patrick and Vernice Beatrice (Smith) Coyle; children: Ian Patrick, Sean Patrick. BA, Dartmouth Coll., 1960; JD, Columbia U., 1964. Bar: NY 1965, Fla. 1971. Assoc. Breed, Abbott & Morgan, NYC, 1964—70, Courshon & Courshon, Miami Beach, Fla., 1970—74; mng. trustee First Mortgage Investors, Miami Beach, Fla., 1974—79; ptnr. Steel Hector & Davis, Miami, Fla., 1979—89; gen. counsel FPL Group, Inc. Fla. Power & Light Co., 1989—2005, sec. FPL Group Inc.; dir. Adelphia Comms. Corp., 1995—2004. Mem.: ABA, Miami Beach C. of C. (hon. lifetime trustee). Home: 2455 Snook Trl West Palm Beach FL 33410-1270

COYLE, FRANCIS SYLVESTER, III, management consultant; b. Orange, N.J. s. Francis S. and Aileen M. (McCormack) C.; m. Mary E. Kellenberg, Sept. 12, 1959; children: Kevin, Kathleen, John, Christopher, Timothy, Maureen. BA, Bklyn. Coll., 1955; BS, Pa. State U., 1962; MBA, So. Ill. U., 1976; MPA, U. So. Calif., 1987. Cert. govt. fin. mgr. Programmer State of Del., Dover, 1977-78, tng. & staff devel. officer Smyrna, 1978-79, dir. rsch. planning, 1979-80, asst. dir. ctrl. data processing Dover, 1980-85, policy & fin. analyst, 1985-87, fin. mgmt. specialist, 1987-90, tng. adminstr., 1990-98; pres. Coyle Mgmt. Cons., Inc., Dover, 1998—. Bd. dirs. Thomas More Acad., Dover, 1988—, Holy Cross Edn. Found., Dover, 1985—. Maj. USAF, 1955-76. Mem. Am. Soc. Pub. Adminstrn., Am. Meteorological Soc., Assn. Govt. Accts., KC. Office Phone: 302-697-0829. E-mail: cmci8@juno.com.

COYLE, JOSEPH THOMAS, psychiatrist; b. Chgo., Oct. 9, 1943; s. Joseph Thomas and Mercedes (Sartor) Coyle; m. Genevieve Sansoucy, Aug. 19, 1968; children: Andrew, Peter, David. AB, Coll. of the Holy Cross, 1965; MD, Johns Hopkins U., 1969; MA (hon.), Harvard U., 1991. Diplomate Am. Bd. Psychiatry and Neurology. Asst. prof. pharmacology Johns Hopkins Sch. of Medicine, Balt., 1974—76, asst. prof pharmacology and psychiatry, 1976—78, assoc. prof pharmacology and psychiatry, 1978—80, prof of neurosci., psychiatry and pharmacology, 1980—91, dir. divsn. child psychiatry, 1982—91, Disting. Svc. prof. of child psychiatry, 1985—91; Eben S. Draper prof. of psychiatry and neurosci. Harvard U., Boston, 1991—; chair consol. dept. psychiatry Harvard Med. Sch., Boston, 1991—2001. Co-dir. outpatient pharmacotherapy clinic Johns Hopkins Hosp., Balt., 1977—82; mem. sci. adv. bd. Pfizer Scholars Program, N.Y.C., 1989—94, John F. Merck Found., Boston, 1990—2000, Abbott Pharms., North Chicago, Ill., 1990—, Guilford Pharms., Balt., 1992—98. Contbr. articles to profl. jours.; editor: Archives of General Psychiatry, 2002—. Mem. adv. bd. NIMH, Washington, 1990—94. Recipient AE Bennett award, 1978, Gold Medal award, 1991, EA Strecker award, Inst. Pa. Hosp., 1993, Thomas Salmon medal, N.Y. Acad. Medicine, 1993, Passarow Found. award, 1997, Lieber award, Nat. Alliance Rsch. Schizophrenia and Depression, 2004. Fellow: Am. Acad. of Arts and Scis., Am. Psychiat. Assn. (Found. Fund prize 1985, Adolph Meyer award 1994, Kemp Fund award 1996); mem.: Inst. of Medicine of the Nat. Acad. Sci., Am. Soc. Pharmacology and Exptl. Therapeutics (John Jacob Abel award 1979), Am. Acad. Child and Adolescent Psychiatry, Am. Coll. Neuropsychopharmacology (pres. 2001, Effron award 1982), Soc. Neurosci. (pres. 1991—92, Spl. Achievement award 2001). Avocations: reading, fishing. Office: Harvard Med Sch Dept Psychiatry 115 Mill St Belmont MA 02478-1041 Business E-Mail: joseph_coyle@hms.harvard.edu.

COYLE, MARTIN ADOLPHUS, JR., lawyer, consultant; b. Hamilton, Ohio, June 3, 1941; s. Martin Adolphus and Lucille (Baird) C.; m. Sharon Sullivan, Mar. 29, 1969 (div. Dec. 1991); children: Cynthia Ann, David Martin, Jennifer Ann; m. Linda J. O'Brien, July 31, 1993 (div. July 1996); m. Sandra C. Lund, July 1998. BA, Ohio Wesleyan U., 1963; JD summa cum laude, Ohio State U., 1966. Bar: N.Y. 1967, Ohio 1966. Assoc. Cravath, Swaine & Moore, N.Y.C., 1966-72; chief counsel securities and fin. TRW Inc., Cleve., 1972-73, sr. counsel, asst. sec., 1973-75, asst. gen. counsel, asst. sec., 1976, asst. gen. counsel, sec., 1976-80, v.p., gen. counsel, sec., 1980-89, exec. v.p., gen. counsel, sec., 1989-97, exec. v.p., 1997-99; sec. TRW Found., Cleve., 1975-80, trustee, 1980-88. Sec. TRW Found., 1975-80, trustee, 1980-98. Co-inventor voting machine. Pres. Judson Retirement Cmty., 1986-88, trustee, 1986-90; trustee Berea Coll. 1989—, Chautauqua Found., 1999-2003, Chautauqua Inst., 1990-2000, Ohio Wesleyan U., 1992-2001, Gebbie Found., 2001-. Mem. ABA, Am. Soc. Corp. Secs. (pres. Ohio regional group 1978-80, nat. dir. 1981-87, nat. chmn. 1985-86), Assn. Gen. Counsel (exec. com. 1992-99, pres. 1995-97), Kiawah Island Club. E-mail: martycoyle@mac.com.

COYLE, MICHAEL LEE, lawyer; b. Mechanicsburg, Pa., Oct. 2, 1944; s. Patrick G. and Bertha M. C.; m. Kathleen J. West, July 15, 1967; children: Patrick M., Darren W. BS in Acctg., Utica Coll., 1966; JD, Syracuse U., 1971; LLM in Taxation, Georgetown U., 1975. Bar: N.Y. 1972, Conn. 1975, U.S. Tax Ct. 1975. Acct. Peat, Marwick, Mitchell & Co., Syracuse, N.Y., 1966, tax acct., 1969-71; atty., adviser interpretive div. Office Chief Counsel IRS, Washington, 1971-73; atty. adviser to judge U.S. Tax Ct., Washington, 1973-75; mem. firm Reid & Riege, P.C., Hartford, Conn., 1975—. Trustee U. Hartford Tax Inst., 1982-86; bd. dirs. adv. coun. Nat. Inst. State & Local Taxation, Old Lyme, Conn., 1987—. Mem., v.p., pres. St. Paul's Luth. Ch. Coun., Wethersfield, Conn., 1976-82, 87-92, 97-2000; bd. dirs. Children's Home Cromwell, Inc., Conn., 1980-88; mem. leadership Greater Hartford, 1978, Conn. Task Force Corp. Taxation; pres. Wethersfield Bus. & Civic Assn., 1978-80. With U.S. Army, 1966-68. Named one of Best Lawyers in Am., 1987—. Mem. ABA (chmn. sales and fin. transaction com., tax sect. 1983-85), Conn. Bar Assn. (tax exec. com., ltd. liability subcom. 1991—), Conn. Bus. & Industry Assn. (tax com. 1987—), Hartford Tax Study Group, Tax Club Hartford (pres.). Avocations: tennis, reading. Home: 144 Stonehill Dr Rocky Hill CT 06067 Office: Reid & Riege PC 1 Financial Plaza Fl 2100 Hartford CT 06103-3185 E-mail: mcoyle@reidandriege.com.

COYLE, ROBERT EVERETT, federal judge; b. Fresno, Calif., May 6, 1930; s. Everett LaJoya and Virginia Chandler C.; m. Faye Turnbaugh, June 11, 1953; children— Robert Allen, Richard Lee, Barbara Jean BA, Fresno State Coll., 1953; JD, U. Calif., 1956. Bar: Calif. Ptnr. McCormick, Barstow, Sheppard, Coyle & Wayte, 1958-82; chief judge U.S. Dist. Ct. (ea. dist.) Calif., 1990-96, sr. judge, 1996—. Former chair 9th Cir. Conf. of Chief Dist. Judges, chair 9th Cir. space and security com., mem. com. on state and fed. cts. Mem. Calif. Bar Assn. (exec. com. 1974-79, bd. govs. 1979-82, v.p. 1981), Fresno County Bar Assn. (pres. 1972). Office: US Dist Ct 5116 US Courthouse 1130 O St Fresno CA 93721-2201 Office Phone: 559-498-7318.

COYLE-REES, MARGARET MARY, chemist; b. Rochester, N.Y., June 10, 1960; d. Hughbert James and Patricia Ann (Crocker) Coyle; m. Wayne M. Rees, July 13, 1985; children: Sarah, William, Anna, Thomas. BS, U. Buffalo, 1982, PhD, 1988. Sr. rsch. scientist Procter & Gamble, Cin., 1988-94, SC

Johnson Wax & Son, Racine, Wis., 1994-97; tech. cons. Leifheit & Co., Racine, 1997—. Leader Girl Scouts U.S., 1992—94, 1999—. Mem. AAAS, N.Y. Acad. Scis., Am. Chem. Soc. Roman Catholic. Achievements include patents in field. Avocations: camping, bicycling, hiking, cooking, sewing. Home and Office: 3153 Rudolph Dr Racine WI 53406-1548 E-mail: mmcr@execpc.com.

COYNE, BRIAN J., pharmaceutical executive, researcher; b. Belfast, Northern Ireland, Dec. 5, 1961; s. Edward Anthony and Mary H. Coyne; m. Katharine B. Brunner, Apr. 11, 1992; children: Patrick Michael, Caroline Genevieve. BA, Ctrl. Conn. State U., New Britain, Conn., 1987; MA, Montclair State, Upper Montclair, N.J., 1995; MPA, Seton Hall U., South Orange, N.J., 2002. Cert. med. rep. Cert. Med. Rep. Inst., 1992, Coun. for Accreditation Pharm. Mfrs. Reps. of Canada Coun. for Continuing Pharm. Edn. of Can., 1997, Mem. Medical Reps. Inst. Ireland Med. Rep. Inst. of Ireland, 2000, Cert. Clin. Rsch. Assoc. Assn. of Clin. Rsch. Professionals, 2003, med. investigator Am. Coll. of Forensic Investigators, 2003. Country study mgr. The Clin. Resource Network, N.Y.C., 2003—04; sr. clin. rsch. scientist Novartis Pharmaceuticals Corp., East Hanover, NJ, 2004—. Mgr. clin. rsch. Knoll Pharm. Co., Mount Olive, NJ, 1988—2000, Cordis Corp., Warren, 2001—02; study mgr. North Am. ops. Aventis Pharmaceuticals Inc., Bridgewater, 2000—01; mgr. clin. ops. U.S. clin. rsch. assoc. Hemosol Inc., Parsippany, 2002—03. With USN, 1981—85. Decorated Battle E Ribbon U.S. Navy, Expeditionary medal, Rifle and Pistol Marksmanship medals, others; Fellowship, Royal Acad. Medicine, Ireland, 2002. Fellow: Royal Soc. Antiqueries Scotland; mem.: VFW, Am. Coll. of Forensic Examiners, Assn. of Mil. Surgeons of the US, Royal Soc. of Medicine, Am. Coll. of Clin. Pharmacology, Mil. History Soc. Ireland, U.S. Naval Inst., Soc. Mil. History, Am. Legion, Friendly Sons St. Patrick, Naval Order U.S. Avocations: running, weightlifting, history, scuba diving, reading.

COYNE, CAROL ANN, business owner, gemologist; b. L.A., Sept. 5, 1939; d. Arthur Leslye and Janet (Coniglio) Stevenson; divorced; children: Kevin Patrick, Cara Marie. BS, U. So. Calif., 1962. Owner Cara Creations, Ft. Worth, 1965—. Mem. Nat. Assn. Jewelry Appraisers, Women's Jewelry Assn. Roman Catholic. Office: Cara Creations PO Box 8052 Fort Worth TX 76124-0052

COYNE, CHARLES COLE, lawyer; b. Abington, Pa., Dec. 3, 1948; s. James Kitchenman Jr. and Pearl (Black) Coyne; m. Paula J. Latta, May 15, 1976; 1 child, Anna Elizabeth. BS in Econs., U. Pa., 1970; JD, Temple U., 1973. Bar: Pa. 1973, U.S. Supreme Ct. 1982, N.J. 1985. Intern Gen. Svcs. Adminstrn., Washington, 1971; counsel Hepburn Willcox Hamilton & Putnam, Phila., 1994—. Bd. dirs. George S. Coyne Chem. Co., Inc., Croydon, Pa., sec., 1973—; dir. Kitchenman Terminal Co. LLC; mng. dir. Cygnet Leasing Co. LLC. Assoc. editor: Temple Law Rev., 1972—73, columnist: Life in the Country, Ledger Newspaper Group, 1993—99. Chester County (Pa.) rep. Delaware Valley Regional Planning Commn., 1982—2003; mem. Chester County Health and Edn. Facilities Authority, 1982—, chmn., 1996—2000; bd. suprs. East Fallowfield Twp., Chester County, 1982—83; mem. panel U.S. Bankruptcy Trustees, 1991—93; mem. Chester County Pk. and Recreation Bd., 1998—2005; mem. racing com. Pa. Hunt Cup, 1992—; amb. People to People, Brazil, 2004; chmn. Greater Phila. Young Reps., 1975—76; Rep. candidate Pa. State Legislature, 1976; Phila. Rep. City Policy Com., 1975—77; chief counsel Jim Coyne for Congress Com., 1980, Re-Election Com., 1982. Recipient Disting. Young Rep. award, 1976; AIESEC scholar, U. Melbourne, 1968. Mem.: ABA, S.R. (bd. mgrs. 2000—03), Nat. Steeplechase Assn., Phila. Bar Assn., Pa. Bar Assn., Pa. Soc., U. Pa. Gen. Alumni Soc. (mem. alumni leadership coun., pres. class of 1970), Temple Law Sch. Alumni Assn., Quaker City Farmers Club, Union League, Capitol Hill Club, Lawyers Club Phila., Masons (master), Kappa Alpha Soc. Home: Sycamore Run Farm PO Box 155 Unionville PA 19375-0155 Office: Hepburn Willcox Hamilton & Putnam 1100 One Penn Ctr 1617 John F Kennedy Blvd Philadelphia PA 19103-1979 Office Phone: 215-568-7500.

COYNE, EDWARD JAMES, SR., international business educator; b. St. Louis, Sept. 25, 1930; s. Horace John and Bessie (Stinebaker) C.; m. Kathleen (Hayman), Sept. 9, 1952 (dec. April 1985); children: Edward James, Kevin Patrick, Shawn Thomas, Colin Mark, Kathleen Patrice (dec. Feb. 1968); m. Beulah (Shelton), April 19, 1986. BS, La. State U., 1952; MBA, Nova U., 1992; PhD, U. Bradford (Yorkshire, U.K.), 1994; LHD (hon.), Nova U., 1980. Gen. mgr., dir. Comalco Products, Pty., Sydney, Australia, 1966-73; pres. Kaiser Bauxite Co., Discovery Bay, Jamaica, 1974—86; v.p., gen. mgr., Rod, Bar, Wire Kaiser Aluminum & Chem., Oakland, Calif., 1986-90; exec., residence Nova U., Ft. Lauderdale, Fla., 1991-93; dir. MIBA program Nova Southeastern U., Ft. Lauderdale, 1993-96; acad. dean Am. Coll. Dublin, Dublin, 1997-98; vis. prof. Samford U., Birmingham, Ala., 1999—; CFO Connexxia, LLC, 2001—. Adv. bd. Inst. Internat. Edu., Southeastern Region, 1983-86, Ctr. Internat. Bus., U. Leeds, U.K., 1995—; vis. fellow U. Bradford, U.K., 1996—. Author: Targeting the Foreign Direct Investor, 1995, (chapt.) International Business Org., 1999; co-author: Human Resources: Caregiving Cancer Progression, 2004; contbr. articles to profl. jours. Vice-chmn. Agr. Mktg. Corp., Jamaica, 1981-86; chmn. Discovery Bay Water Co., Jamaica, 1974-80; vice-chmn. Aboukir Edu. & Industl. Inst., Jamaica, 1976-85; adv. bd. World Trade Council Ft. Lauderdale, 1995-96. Recipient Comdr. Order of Distinction, Govt. Jamaica, 1980; Sports Hall of Fame, Jackson-Madison County, Tenn., 1997. Mem. Acad. Internat. Bus., HR Devel. Internat. Jour. Republican. Roman Catholic. Avocations: reading, travel, teaching. Home: 2752 Berkeley Dr Birmingham AL 35242-4105 Office: Sch Bus Samford U 800 Lakeshore Dr Birmingham AL 35229-0001 Office Phone: 205-726-2041. Personal E-mail: ebcoyne@aol.com.

COYNE, FRANK J., insurance industry executive; b. 1948; BS, U. Scranton, 1970; JD, Duquesne U., 1973. Trial atty. U.S. Dept. Treasury, 1973-77; v.p., asst. gen. counsel Lynn Ins. Group, 1977-80; assoc. gen. counsel Reliance Ins. Co., 1980-83; v.p., gen. counsel PMA Ins. Co., 1983-85; from sr. v.p. to pres., COO Gen. Accident Corp. of Am. and subs., 1985-98; resigned Gen. Accident Ins. Co. Ins. Am., Inc., Phila., 1998; exec. v.p. Kemper Ins., Long Grove, Ill., 1998-99; pres. Ins. Svcs. Office, Inc., N.Y.C., 1999—. Pres., bd. dirs. Pa. Gen. Ins. Co., Potomac Ins. Co. Ill., Ga. Ins. Co. N.Y., PG Ins. Co. N.Y., Gen. Assurance Co.; bd. dirs. Silvey Cos., Hawkeye-Security Ins. Co., Oreg. Auto and North Pacific Ins. Cos., Pilot Ins. Co. (Can.), Mellon PSFS Bank, Ins. Fedn. Pa. Office: Insurance Services Office Inc Fl 12 545 Washington Ave Blvd Jersey City NJ 07310-1686 E-mail: fcoyne@iso.com.

COYNE, JUDITH, editor; With Glamour mag., 1986—98, sr. editor articles dept., 1989—92, exec. editor, 1992—98; editor-in-chief New Woman, 1998—2000; v.p., editor-in-chief Women.com networks, 2000—01; exec. dir. Good Housekeeping, 2001—. Office: Good Housekeeping 959 Eighth Ave New York NY 10019

COYNE, PATRICK IVAN, physiological ecologist; b. Wichita, Kans., Feb. 26, 1944; s. Ivan Lefranz and Ellen Lucille (Brown) C.; m. Mary Ann White, Aug. 22, 1964; children: Shane Barrett, Shannon Renee. BS, Kans. State U., 1966; PhD, Utah State U., 1970. R & D coord. U.S. Army Cold Regions Rsch. and Engring. Lab., Hanover, N.H., 1970-72; asst. prof. forestry U. Alaska, Fairbanks, 1973-74; plant physiologist, environ. scientist Lawrence Livermore (Calif.) Nat. Lab., 1975-79, cons., 1980—; rsch. plant physiologist USDA/ Agrl. Rsch. Svc., Woodward, Okla., 1979-85; prof., head Agrl. Rsch. Ctr. Kansas State U., Hays, 1985-94, prof., head Western Kans. Agrl. Rsch. Ctrs., 1994—. Mem. adv. coun. Kans. Geol. Survey, Lawrence, 1986-91. Contbr. 33 articles to profl. jours. Capt., U.S. Army, 1970-72. Mem. AAAS, Am. Soc. Agronomy, Soil Sci. Soc. Am., Crop Sci. Soc. Am., Soc. Range Mgmt., Coun. Agriculture Sci. and Tech., Hays Area C. of C. (bd. dirs. 1988-90), Rotary, Phi Kappa Phi, Gamma Sigma Delta, Sigma Xi. Republican. Mennonite Brethren Ch. Office: Kans State U Agrl Rsch Ctr 1232 240th Ave Hays KS 67601-9228

COYNE, STEPHEN B., education educator; b. Salem, N.J., May 8, 1950; s. James Richard and Louise Linneman (Baynes) C.; m. Susan Mary Kruml; children: Andrew, Laura. BA, Catawba Coll., 1972; MA, U. N.C., 1976; PhD, U. Denver, 1987. Reporter Thermal Belt News Jour., Columbus, N.C., 1976-78; instr. Isothermal C.C., Spindale, N.C., 1978-84; tchg. fellow U. Denver, 1984-87; assoc. prof. Morningside Coll., Sioux City, Iowa, 1988—. Author short stories, poems. N.J. State Coun. on the Arts Individual Artist fellow State of N.J., 1998; recipient New Stories from the South the Yrs. Best award Algonquin Books, 2001. Mem. MLA, Assoc. Writing Programs. E-mail: coyne@morningside.edu.

COYNE, THOMAS JOSEPH, economics professor, finance professor; b. Dec. 24, 1933; s. Thomas Joseph and Mary Germaine (Fox) C.; m. Patricia Anne Smith, June 8, 1957 (div. June 1986); children: Kathleen, Karen, Kevin, Kenneth, Thomas. BBA, Marshall U., 1958; MBA, Kent State U., 1961; PhD, Case Western Res. U., 1967; postgrad., U. Chgo., 1968, U. Mich., summers, 1972, 73. With B.F. Goodrich Co., Akron, Ohio, 1959-61, Robinson Clay Products Co., Akron, Ohio, 1961-63, C&O-B&O Ry., Cleve., 1963-65; instr. econs. Kent (Ohio) State U., 1963-67, instr. money and fin. mgmt., 1967—; asst. prof. econs., chmn. dept. Marshall U., Huntington, W.Va., 1967-69; prof. bus. econs. U. Akron, 1969-81; prof. fin. John Carroll U., Cleve., 1981-95. Owner The Coyne Trust, 1986-91; pres. Coyne & Assocs., Akron, 1980—, Coyne Pub. Co., 1991—; pub. The Coyne Quar., 1990—; corp. valuations, acquisitions; cons. in field; presenter seminars in fin. engring. and mgmt., Zagreb, Croatia Stock Exch., 1993; leader 1st del. in fin. to USSR, 1989; arbitrator Am. Arbitration Assn., Fed. Mediation and Conciliation Svc., 1968—, pres. 1979-81; pres. Summit Petroleum Corp., Akron; founder, pres. Cosntn. Endl. Assn., Inc., 2000—. Author: Understanding Managerial Economics, 1975, Managerial Economics: Analysis and Cases, 5th edit., 1984, Readings in Managerial Economics, 5th edit., 1992, License To Lie, 1997, 2000, How to Take Charge of Yourself, Your Money, Your Government, 1999; also articles and monographs; host half-hour weekly radio show, 1994; host one hour weekly radio show, 2001-2004; pub. (econ. commentaries) Coyne Quar., Online. V.p. rsch. Akron Regional Devel. Bd., 1975-78, chmn. taxation and legis. com., 1975-78, spkr. in field; candidate U.S. Senate, Ohio, 1994—. Served with inf., U.S. Army, 1952-54, Korea. Nat. City Bank Cleve. fellow, 1963-65; candidate Office of Gov., W. Va., 2004 Mem. Nat. Assn. of Securities Dealers Pub. Arbitrators, Sigma Phi Epsilon. Home: 535 Haskell Dr Akron OH 44333-2810 Business E-Mail: tom@coyne-assoc.com. *When God has given you a great deal, He expects a great deal of you. If you achieve everything you set out to achieve, you probably did not set out to achieve enough in the first place.*

COYNE, WILLIAM JOSEPH, former congressman; b. Pitts, Aug. 24, 1936; s. Phillip and Mary (Ridge) C. BS, Robert Morris Coll., 1965. Mem. Pa. Ho. of Reps., 1970-72; mem. Pitts. City Council, 1973-80, U.S. Congress from 14th Pa. dist., Washington, 1981—2002; mem. budget com.; mem. ways and means com. With AUS, 1955-57. Democrat. Roman Catholic.*

COYOTE, PETER (PETER COHON), actor; b. Colver, Pa., Oct. 10, 1941; m. Marilyn McCann, 1975 (div. 1998); 2 children; m. Stephanie Pleet, 1998. BA in English Lit., Grinnell Coll., 1964; student, San Francisco Actors Workshop. Theater appearances include The Red Snake, True West, The Abduction of Kari Swenson, Baby Girl Scott, (also dir.) The Minstrel Show, (also co-writer) Olive Pits; film appearances include Die Laughing, 1980, Tell Me a Riddle, 1980, Southern Comfort, 1981, E.T.: The Extra Terrestrial, 1982, Endangered Species, 1982, Timerider, 1982, Cross Creek, 1983, Stranger's Kiss, 1983, Slayground, 1983, Heartbreakers, 1984, The Legend of Billie Jean, 1985, Jagged Edge, 1985, Outrageous Fortune, 1987, Stacking, 1987, A Man in Love, 1987, Heart of Midnight, 1989, The Man Inside, 1990, Crooked Hearts, 1991, Bitter Moon, 1992, Kika, 1993, That Eye The Sky, 1994, Seeds of Doubt, 1996, Top of the World, 1997, Road Ends, 1997, Last Call, 1999, Patch Adams, 1998, More Dogs Than Bones, 1999, The Basket, 1999, Random Hearts, 1999, Erin Brockovich, 2000, Red Letters, 2000, Jack the Dog, 2000, Suddenly Naked, 2001, A Walk to Remember, 2002, Purpose, 2002, Femme Fatale, 2002, Northfork, 2003, Bon voyage, 2003, The Great Role, 2004, Shadow of Fear, 2004, Deepwater, 2005; TV appearances include Alcatraz: The Whole Shocking Story, 1980, The People vs. Jean Harris, 1981, Isabel's Choice, 1981, Best Kept Secrets, 1984, Scorned and Swindled, 1984, The Blue Yonder, 1984, Child's Cry, 1986, Sworn to Silence, 1987, Echoes in the Darkness, 1987, Unconquered, 1989, A Seduction in Travis County, 1991, Living a Lie, 1991, Keeper of the City, 1991, Buffalo Girls, 1995, Moonlight and Valentino, 1995, Seduced by Madness, 1996, Unforgettable, 1996, Dalva, 1996, (TV mini-series) The West, 1996, Two for Texas, 1998, Route 9, 1998, Execution of Justice, 1999, The Wednesday Woman, 2000, Midwives, 2001, Phenomenon II, 2003, (TV series) The 4400, 2004, The Inside, 2005. Office: Ofcl Internet Peter Coyote Fan Club 3425 Knox Pl Bronx NY 10467-2009 also: United Talent Agency 9560 Wilshire Blvd Beverly Hills CA 90211-1934*

COZAD, RACHAEL BLACKBURN, museum director; Exec. dir. Iris and B. Gerald Cantor Found., L.A., 1994—2001; dir. Kemper Mus. Contemporary Art, Kansas City, Mo., 2001—. Office: Kemper Mus Contemporary Art 4420 Warwick Blvd Kansas City MO 64111-1821 Office Phone: 816-753-5784. Business E-Mail: rbcozad@kemperart.org.

COZAN, LEE, clinical research psychologist; married, 1947. BA, Am. U., 1948; MA, George Washington U., 1951, PhD, 1964. Research psychologist U.S. Govt., Washington, 1954-64; pvt. practice psychology N.J., 1964-74; regional dir. Fla. Div. Mental Health, Ft. Lauderdale, 1974-76; mental hosp. adminstr. So. Fla. State Hosp., Hollywood, 1976-79; pres. Inst. Mental Health, Hollywood, 1979-81; dir. mental health program Fla. Dept. Health and Rehab. Services, Ft. Lauderdale, 1979-82; clin. psychologist Assocs. in Psychiatry, 1983-85; pres. Applied Psychology Corp., 1983-86, Children Residential and Day Treatment Ctr., Inc., 1987-96; health care cons. Fort Lauderdale, Fla., 1996—. Adj. prof. Fla. Atlantic U., 1974-79, Nova U., 1979-80 Editor: Jour. Indsl. Psychology, 1961-65, Jour. Engring. Psychology, 1963-68; cons. editor: Jour. Schizophrenia, 1970-71. Mem. Broward County (Fla.) Republican Exec. Com., 1976-80. Served with U.S. Army, 1941-46. Mem. APA, AAAS, Nat. Geog. Soc., Human Factors Soc., Fla. Psychol. Assn., Children's Hosp. Internat. Greek Orthodox. Achievements include research, publs. in psychology.

COZART, LEA ANNE, marketing professional, consultant; d. Aron Barney and Mildred Marie Cozart; life ptnr. Tina Rae Johnson. BA in Entertainment Prodn., U. Colo., 1991; MA in Orgnl. Mgmt., U. Phoenix, 1999. Cert. in tng. Mountain States Employers Coun., Colo., 2001. Pvt. practice cons., Colo. Springs, 2001—; tng. and implementation specialist WideOrbit, Inc., San Francisco, 2003; mktg. coord. Alliance Gen. Contractors, LLC, Colo. Springs, Colo., 2004—. Fundraiser Relay for Life Am. Cancer Assn., Colo. Springs, 2003—05; fundraiser Am. Heart Assn., Colo. Springs, 2004—05, Muscular Dystrophy Assn., Colo. Springs, 2004—05. Master: Soc. Change Mgmt. Profls. and Educators (assoc.). Avocations: martial arts, archaeology, guitar, outdoor adventuring, travel. Office: Alliance General Contractors LLC 5045 List Drive Colorado Springs CO 80919 Office Fax: 719-596-5969. Personal E-mail: leacozart@juno.com. E-mail: lcozart@agccolorado.com.

COZBY, RICHARD SCOTT, electronics engineer, military officer; b. Las Cruces, N.Mex., Apr. 13, 1961; s. Scott Dempsey and Elizabeth Ann (Carroll) Cozby; m. Maria (Jo) Blackwell, Dec. 28, 1984; children: Brenton Blackwell, Bradford Carroll. B in Engring., Vanderbilt U., 1983; diploma, U.S. Army Command Coll., 1994; MSA, Ctrl. Mich. U., 2002; diploma, Def. Sys. Mgmt. Coll., 2002. Commd. USAR, advanced through grade to lt. col.; comm. engr. U.S. Army Signal Corps, 1983—; electronics engr., chief, simulation and tech. divsn. Army Testing and Evaluation Command, Aberdeen Proving Ground, Md., 1988—, chief tech. mgmt. divsn., 1998—. U.S. Army prin. Mutli-Svc. Test Investment Rev. Com., Washington, 1990—95; bd. dirs. N.E. Md. Tech. Coun. Author: (book) Army GPS Test Results, 1984, Aquilla RPV Test Results, 1985. Chmn. Hickory Recreation Coun., Bel Air, 1998—; mem. outreach com. St. Margaret Parish, Bel Air, Md., 1989—95. Recipient Analyst of Yr., Army Rsch. Lab., 2003. Mem.: IEEE, Internat. Testing and Evaluation Assn. (chpt. pres. 1993, chpt. dir. 1994—), Harford Leadership Alumni Assn. (bd. dirs. 1996—, v.p. 1997—). Roman Catholic. Avocation: stamp collecting/philately. Office: CSTE-DTC-TT-M Aberdeen Proving Ground MD 21005 E-mail: rcozby@verizon.net.

COZEN, STEPHEN ALLEN, lawyer; b. Phila., Aug. 13, 1939; s. Samuel D. and Jean (Orlofsky) C.; m. Sandra Wexler, June 7, 1961; children: Sheri L., Lori S., Cathi A. BA with honors, U. Pa., 1961, LLB with honors, 1964. Bar: Pa. 1964, U.S. Dist. Ct. (ea., mid. and we. dists.) Pa. 1984, U.S. Ct. Appeals (3d and 9th cirs.) 1984, U.S. Ct. Claims 1984, U.S. Supreme Ct. 1984. Founder, chmn. Cozen and O'Connor, Phila., 1970—. Lectr. U. Pa.; bd. dirs. 1st Exec. Bank. Gen. editor: Insuring Real Property, 1989; contbr. numerous articles to profl. jours. Bd. dirs. Arthritis Ctr., Hahnemann U., Police Athletic League; trustee Fedn. Jewish Agys. Recipient Torch of Learning award Am. Friends of Hebrew U., 1984, Peace medal, 1991, State of Israel. Fellow Am. Bar Found., Am. Coll. Trial Lawyers; mem. ABA (vice chmn. ins. law com.), Pa. Bar Assn., Phila. Bar Assn., Am. Judicature Soc., Def. Rsch. Inst., Pa. Def. Inst., Pa. Bar Inst. (bd. dirs.), Fedn. Ins. and Corp. Counsel. Home: 1230 Mt Pleasant Rd Villanova PA 19085-2107 Office: Cozen and O'Connor The Atrium 1900 Market St Philadelphia PA 19103-3527

COZMUTA, IOANA, research scientist; d. Ileana Zorita and Augustin Ioan Cozmuta; m. Bogdan Craciun, 1999; 1 child, Amelia Teodora Craciun. PhD, U. Groningen, The Netherlands, 2001. Rsch. assoc. Calif. Inst. Tech., Pasadena, 2001—02, Stanford U., Palo Alto, Calif., 2002—03; rsch. scientist Eloret Corp, Sunnyvale, Calif., 2003—. Grantee Ubbo Emmius, U. Groningen, 1997-2001, Fantom Sch., 1998, 2001. Mem.: Biophysical Soc., ARCA. Achievements include research in indoor air quality, radon; molecular dynamics simulations, polymeric membranes; molecular dynamics simulations, nanocomposites; molecular dynamics simulations, DNA sequencing.

COZZENS, MIMI, actress, director; b. Bklyn. d. Milton L. Cozzens and Dorothy Pitt. Student, Emerson Coll., 1952—54; BA in Drama Speech, Hofstra Coll., 1956. Tchr., dir. Va. Ave. Project, LA, 1991—92; with Interact Theatre Co., 2005—. Actor: (TV series) Cold Case, The Practice, Will & Grace, Providence, 3rd Rock From The Sun, Seinfeld, Chgo. Hope, Seventh Heaven, The Drew Carey Show, Diagnosis Murder, Star Trek; (TV films) The Pandora Project, Perfect Prey, Tell Me No Secrets, Liz: The Elizabeth Taylor Story, Livewire, Daddy, Night Of The Cyclone, Spring Break; (Broadway plays) I Ought To Be In Pictures, Children Of A Lesser God, Same Time Next Year; (plays) The Dining Room, Mornings At Seven, Same Time Next Year, Prisoner Of Second Ave, Fallen Angels, Tribute, numerious regional prodns. Rep. Valley Theatre League, North Hollywood, Calif., 1992—94. Mem.: Women In Film (co-chmn. dirs. workshop 1990—96), Acad. TV Arts and Scis. Achievements include John Powers model since age 2 1/2; former champion water skier, 14 trophies in the 1950's. Avocations: water-skiing, scuba diving, sculpting.

CRABB, BARBARA BRANDRIFF, federal judge; b. Green Bay, Wis., Mar. 17, 1939; d. Charles Edward and Mary (Forrest) Brandriff; m. Theodore E. Crabb, Jr., Aug. 29, 1959; children: Julia Forrest, Philip Elliott. AB, U. Wis., 1960, JD, 1962. Bar: Wis. 1963. Assoc. Roberts, Boardman, Suhr and Curry, Madison, Wis., 1962-64; legal rschr. Sch. Law, U. Wis., 1968-70, Am. Bar Assn., Madison, 1970-71; US magistrate US Dist Ct (we. dist.) Wis., Madison, 1971-79; judge U.S. Dist. Ct. (we. dist.) Wis., Madison, 1979—, chief judge, 1980-96, 2002—. Mem. Gov. Wis. Task Force Prison Reform, 1971-73 Membership chmn., v.p. Milw. LWV, 1966-68; mem. Milw. Jr. League, 1967-68. Mem. ABA, Nat. Assn. Women Judges, State Bar Wis., Dane County Bar Assn., U. Wis. Law Alumni Assn. Office: US Dist Ct PO Box 591 120 N Henry St Madison WI 53701-0591

CRABB, VIRGINIA GEANY RUTH, librarian; b. Whittier, Calif., Dec. 30, 1951; d. Lawrence Guerro and Nellie Aguilar Gutierrez; m. Rod D. Crabb, Sept. 8, 1973; 1 child, Adam Matthew. AA in Fgn. Lang., Calif. State U., Fullerton, 1973. Children's librarian-sr. libr. asst. Orange County Libr., La Palma, Calif., 1975—76, Brea, Calif., 1976—81, sr. libr. asst. Mission Viejo, Calif., 1981—83, Orange County Libr.-University Park, Irvine, Calif., 1982—83, Orange County Libr., San Juan Capistrano, Calif., 1983—96; libr. - part time in absence of regular libr. Laguna Beach Sch. of Arts, Laguna Beach, Calif., 1988—88; sr. libr. asst. Orange County Libr., Garden Grove, Calif., 1996—98, Orange County Library-Costa Mesa, Costa Mesa, 1998—2001; children's librarian Orangewood Children's Home Libr., Orange, Calif., 2001—. Art asst. vol. Irvine Fine Arts, Irvine, Calif., 1985—85. Recipient Perspectives Study Program Cert., U. S. Ctr. for World Mission, 2003. Avocation: art travel. Personal E-mail: vrcrabb@ocpl.org.

CRABBS, ROGER ALAN, publishing executive, director, small business owner, military officer, educator; b. Cedar Rapids, Iowa, May 9, 1928; s. Winfred Wesley and Faye (Woodard) C.; m. Marilyn Lee Westcott, June 30, 1951; children: William Douglas, Janet Lee Crabbs Turner, Ann Lee Crabbs Menke. BA in Sci., State U. Iowa, 1954; MBA, George Washington U., 1965, DBA, 1973; M Christian Leadership, We. Sem., 1978. Commd. 2nd lt. USAF, 1950, advanced through grades to lt. col., 1968, Ret., 1972; prof. mgmt. U. Portland, Oreg., 1972-79; prof. bus. George Fox Coll., Newberg, Oreg., 1979-83; pres. Judson Bapt. Coll., The Dalles, Oreg., 1983-85. Pres. Host Pubs. Inc., pres., chmn. various corps., 1974-86; past chmn. nat. adv. bd. Travelhost, Inc.; cons. in field. Author: The Infallible Foundation for Management-The Bible, 1978, The Secret of Success in Small Business Management-Is in the Short Range, 1983; co-author: The Storybook Primer on Managing, 1976. Past pres. English Speaking Union, 1994-96, bd. dirs., 1994-97; bd. dirs. Christ Cmty. Ch., Conv. and Vis. Bur. of Washington County, 1986-2001, Oakhills Townhouse Assn., v.p., 1991-95; mem. Minority Conv. Tourism Adv. Coun., Oreg. Decorated Air Force Commendation medal with oak leaf cluster, Meritorious Service medal Dept. Def.; rated Command Air Force Missileman; recipient Jack Rosenberg Cmty. Svcs. award, 2000, regional, dist. and nat. awards SBA, Bonnie Hays Tourism award, 2001. Mem.: Soc. Advancement of Mgmt., Svc. Corps Ret. Execs., Am. Arbitration Assn., Acad. Mgmt., Assn. Atomic Vets., 51st Fighter Interceptor Wing Assn., Air Force Assn., Lang Syne Soc. of Portland, Portland Officers Club, Rotary (past pres.), Masons, Phi Mu Alpha, Delta Epsilon Sigma, Alpha Kappa Psi. Republican. Personal E-mail: leecrabbs@everdream.com. *A positive attitude, sincere interest in others and a sense of humility have been the building blocks of my personal philosophy. They have served me well through my three careers - professional military, university professor and publisher.*

CRABTREE, BEN C., neuromuscular therapy clinic director; b. Las Vegas, Sept. 11, 1964; s. Ben C. and Jaynelle (Felix) C.; m. Virginia Kathryn Vance, Feb. 7, 1988 (div. Nov. 1989); m. Tania Oylan Tason, May 5, 1992; children: Greta, Bryan. AS, Panama Canal Coll., La Boca, Rep. of Panama, 1993, Austin Peay State U., 1995; BBA, Our Lady of the Lake U., 1995. Cert. firearms instr.; registered massage therapist; cert. neuromuscular therapist; lic. massage therapy instr.; cert. neuromuscular therapy instr. Software tech., adminstr. asst. Ace Personal Health Care, Inc., San Antonio, 1994-95; dir. info. systems River City Fin. Health Group/Home Health Care Solutions, San Antonio, 1995; chief fin. officer, alt. adminstr. A&E Quality Home Health Care, San Antonio, 1996-99; pres. Oylan, Inc., San Antonio, 1997-99; pres., owner Antonian Bodyworks, 1999-2001; instr. neuromuscular therapy Neuromuscular Therapy Ctr. N.Mex., 2000—. Profl. adv. com. Silver Days Home Health Care, San Antonio, 1996-97, Responsive Health Svcs., 1997-99. Mem. Dist. 128 State Budget Adv. Com., San Antonio, 1995. Ssgt. U.S. Army, 1984-92. Mem.: Soc. Ortho-Bionomy Internat., Internat. Massage Assn., Tex. Action Shooting Club, U.S. Practical Shooting Assn. Avocations: practical shooting, web page design. Office: San Antonio Neuromuscular Therapy Ctr 11120 Wurzbach Ste 200 San Antonio TX 78230 E-mail: 4info@massagebyben.com.

CRABTREE, BEVERLY JUNE, retired dean; b. Lincoln, Nebr., June 22, 1937; d. Wayne Uniack and Frances Margaret (Wibbels) Deles Dernier; m. Robert Jewell Crabtree, June 1, 1958; children: Gregory, Karen. BS in Edn., U. Mo., 1959, MEd, 1962; PhD, Iowa State U., 1965. Tchr. home econs. area pub. schs., Pierce City and Sarcoxie, Mo., 1959-61; mem. faculty home econs. Mich. State U., East Lansing, 1964-67; assoc. prof. U. Mo., Columbia, 1967-72, coord. home econs. edn., 1967-73, prof., 1972-73, assoc. dean home econs., dir. home econs. extension programs, 1973-75; dean Coll. Home Econs. Okla. State U., Stillwater, 1975-87; dean Coll. Family and Consumer Scis. Iowa State U., Ames, 1987-97, ret., 1997. Mem. faculty Family Impact Seminar Inst. Ednl. Leadership, George Washington U., 1976-82, Cath. U. Am., 1982-87; mem. nat. panel cons. for Vocat. Ednl. Pers. Devel., 1969-70; mem. nat. com. on future of coop. extension USDA and Nat. Assn. State Univs. and Land Grant Colls., 1982; mem. joint coun. on food and agrl. scis., 1987-91. Contbr. articles in field to profl. jours. Gen. Foods fellow, 1963-64; recipient Centennial Alumni award Coll. Home Econs. Iowa State U., 1971, Alumni Citation of Merit, Coll. Home Econs. U. Mo., 1976, Profl. Achievement award Iow State U., 1983. Mem. Am. Home Econs. Assn. (pres. 1977-78, chmn. adv. coun. Ctr. for Family 1982-83, mem. coun. profl. devel. 1980-83, a leader to commemorate 75th anniversary 1984, pres. found. 1987-88, chair Coun. for Certification 1991-92, chair Coun. for Accreditation 1997-98, Disting. Svc. award 1993), Okla. Home Econs. Assn. (Profl. Achievement award 1983), Nat. Assn. State Univs. and Land Grant Colls. (mem. commn. home econs. 1981-84), Assn. Tchr. Educators, Home Econs. Edn. Assn., Nat. Coun. of Adminstrs. of Home Econs., Am. Ednl. Rsch. Assn., Am. Assn. Higher Edn., Nat. Assn. Tchr. Educators for Home Econs. (pres. 1969), Nat. Coun. on Family Relations, Mortar Bd., Golden Key, Omicron Nu, Phi Upsilon Omicron, Phi Delta Kappa, Omicron Delta Kappa, Pi Lambda Theta, Phi Kappa Phi, Gamma Sigma Delta. Methodist. Home: 3113 Rosewood Cir Ames IA 50014-4589

CRABTREE, DAVIDA FOY, minister; b. Waterbury, Conn., June 7, 1944; d. Alfred and Davida (Blakeslee) Foy; m. David T. Hindinger Jr., Aug. 28, 1982; stepchildren: Elizabeth Anne, David Todd. BS, Marietta Coll., 1967; MDiv, Andover Newton Theol. Sch., 1972; D of Ministry, Hartford Sem., 1989. Ordained to ministry United Ch. of Christ, 1972. Founder, exec. dir. Prudence Crandall Ctr. for Women, New Britain, Conn., 1973-76; min., dir. Greater Hartford (Conn.) Campus Ministry, 1976-80; sr. min. Colchester (Conn.) Federated Ch., 1980-91; bd. dirs. Conn. Conf. United Ch. of Christ, Hartford, 1982-90; conf. min. So. Calif. Conf., United Ch. of Christ, Pasadena, 1991-96, Conn. Conf., United Ch. of Christ, Hartford, 1996—. Rsch. assoc. Harvard Div. Sch., Cambridge, Mass., 1975—76. Author: The Empowering Church, 1989 (named one of Top Ten Books of Yr. 1990); editorial advisor Alban Inst., 1990-98. Bd. dirs. Hartford region YWCA, 1979-82, Christian Conf. of Conn., 1997—; trustee Cragin Meml. Libr., Colchester, 1980-91, Hartford Sem., 1983-91, Sch. of Theology at Claremont, 1993-96, Andover Newton Theol. Sch., 1997—; founder Youth Svcs. Bur., Colchester, 1984-89; pres. Creative Devel. for Colchester Inc., 1989-91; coun. Religious Leaders of L.A., 1991-96; v.p. Hope in Youth Campaign, 1992-96; dir. UCC Ins. bd., 1993-2000; bd. dirs. Amistad America, 1998—; trustee UCC Cornerstone Fund, 2000-04; chair Coun. of Conf. Mins., United Ch. of Christ, 2004—. Named one of Outstanding Conn. Women, UN Assn., 1987; recipient Antoinette Brown award, Gen. Synod, United Ch. of Christ, 1977, Conf. Preacher award, Conn. Conf. United Ch. of Christ, 1982, Woman in Leadership award, Hartford region YWCA, 1987, Pres.'s award, Conn. Coalition Against Domestic Violence, 1997, Somos Uno award, United Neighborhood Orgn., 1995, award, Vet. Feminists Am., 2005. Mem. Nat. Coun. Chs. (bd. dirs. 1969-81), Christians for Justice Action (exec. com. 1981-91). Mem. United Ch. Of Christ. E-mail: dfc@ctucc.org.

CRABTREE, JOHN MICHAEL, college administrator, consultant; b. Fostoria, Ohio, Nov. 11, 1949; s. John Dwight and Opal Marie (Tate) C.; m. Cheryl Lynn Wallace, July 6, 1974. AA in Music Edn., Mt. Vernon Nazarene Coll., 1970; B of Music Edn., So. Nazarene U., 1972, MA in Edn., 1976; postgrad., U. Okla., 1976. Sports info. dir. So. Nazarene U., Okla., 1971-80, dir. pub. rels., 1974-80, assoc. dean student devel., 1974-78, dir. alumni and media rels., 1980-89, adminstrv. asst. to pres., 1989-90, dir. univ. advancement, 1989, exec. dir., 1990-91, v.p., 1991-98, asst. to pres., 1998—. Adj. prof. mktg. So. Nazarene U., 1979-82; bd. rsch. advisors Governing Bd. Editors and Pub. Bd. The Am. Biographical Inst. Editor The Perspective, 1981-89. Chmn. United Fund Drive, Bethany, 1983; pub. rels. dir. B.U.I.L.D. (Bethany United Improvement League Downtown); mem. exec. bd. Bethany Main St.; exec. sec. Nazerene Officers Instl. Advancement, 1989-90; pres. Nazarene Officers Instl. Adv., 1996-2000; bd. dirs. Mabel Fry Meml. Libr., Yukon, Okla., 1990-94, So. Nazerene U. Found., 1993—, Okla. Planned Giving Coun, 2004—; mem. Okla. Friends of Libr., Okla Civic Music Assn., exec. bd. dirs.; mem. Oklahoma City Friends Eng., exec. bd. dirs.; mem. Real Effective Action Leadership; exec. bd. dirs. Oklahoma City 1st Nazarene Ch. Found Mem.: Oklahoma City Orch. League, Okla. Ind. Coll. Found., Okla. City C. of C. (pub. rels. and econ. devel. bds.), Sports Info. Dirs. Am. (ethics com. 1978—80, job attrition bd. 1980), Okla. Civic Music Assn. (bd. dirs.), Coun. Advancement and Support of Edn., Okla. Coll. Pub. Rels. Assn., Bethany C. of C., Assn. Fundraising Profls., Bethany Hist. Soc. (life), Oklahoma City Audubon Soc. (pub. rels. dir. wildlife film series 1974—93), Oklahoma City West Rotary, Kiwanis, Sigma Tau Delta. Republican. Avocations: photography, stamp collecting/philately, antique book collector. Office: So Nazarene U 6729 NW 39th Expy Bethany OK 73008-2605 E-mail: mcrabtre@snn.edu.

CRABTREE, ROBERT ALLEN, elementary school educator; b. Syracuse, N.Y., June 29, 1949; s. Donald John and Blossom (Allen) C. BA, SUNY, Fredonia, 1971; MS, SUNY, Cortland, 1975, cert. advanced study, 1990. Elem. tchr. North Syracuse (N.Y.) Cen. Schs., 1971—. Instr. West Genesee-Syracuse U. Tchg. Ctr., 1986. Pres. Dollars for Scholars, North Syracuse, 1993-99, 2002—; Dem. committeeman Town of Clay; vol. We Care Telephone Suicide Prevention Program, North Syracuse, 1989-2000. Recipient Outstanding Tchr. award Tech. Club of Syracuse, 1990, Syracuse Newspapers Golden Apple award, 1991, North Syracuse Tchr. of Yr. award, 1988. Mem. ASCD, NSTA, Assn. Math. Tchrs. of N.Y. State, Nat. Coun. Tchrs. Math., Sci. Tchrs. Assn. N.Y. State (chmn. ctrl. sect. 1992-96, Excellence in Sci. Tchg. award 1993), Optimist Club (v.p. 1991-92, bd. dirs. 1992, 2002—, pres. 1999-2000, lt. gov 2003—, Cmty. Svc. award 2002, NY Dist. Optimist of Yr. 2004). Democrat. Baptist. Avocations: swimming, bowling, jogging. Home: 102 Baxton St North Syracuse NY 13212-2002 Office: Cicero Elem Sch 5979 Rte 31 Cicero NY 13039-8890 E-mail: rcrabtr1@twcny.rr.com.

CRABTREE, ROBERT HOWARD, chemistry professor, consultant; b. Apr. 17, 1948; came to U.S., 1977, naturalized, 1985; s. Arthur and Marguerite (Vaniere) C. BA, Oxford U., 1970; PhD, Sussex U., Eng., 1973, DSc (hon.), 1985. Attache of rsch. Nat. Ctr. Sci. Rsch., Paris, 1975-77; asst. prof. chemistry Yale U., New Haven, Conn., 1977-83, assoc. prof., 1983-85, prof., 1985—. Office Phone: 203-432-3925. Business E-Mail: robert.crabtree@yale.edu.

CRACCHIOLO, JAMES M., diversified financial services company executive; Asset-mgmt. officer Shearson Lehman Brothers', 1982; pres. Am. Express Travel Related Svcs. Internat., 1998—2000; group pres. Am. Express Global Fin. Svcs., Mpls., 2001—. Bd. dirs. Tech Data Corp., 1999—. Office: Am Express Co 200 AXP Fin Ctr H27/52 Minneapolis MN 55474

CRACKEL, THEODORE JOSEPH, historian, consultant; b. Urbana, Ill., Sept. 10, 1938; s. Orville Lee and Aleta (Smith) C.; m. Kay Knight, Sept. 2, 1961 (div. 1972); children: Todd, Dana; m. Mai Thi Nguyen, Oct. 14, 1972 (div. 1991); children: John, Robert; m. Mary-Jo Kline, May 23, 1998. BA, U. Ill., 1962; MA, Rutgers U., 1971, PhD, 1985. Commd. 2nd lt. U.S. Army, 1962, advanced through grades to lt. col., 1978, tank unit comdr., 1963-66, advisor, 1966-67, 71-72; weapons sys. analyst Combat Devels. Command, Ft. Knox, Ky., 1967-69; asst. prof. history U.S. Mil. Acad., West Point, N.Y., 1972-75, 78-81; instr. Dept. Strategy U.S. Army Command and Gen. Staff Coll., 1975-77; dir. mil. history and strategy studies U.S. Army War Coll., Carlisle Barracks, Pa., 1981-83, ret., 1983; sr. fellow The Heritage Found., Washington, 1983-85; sr. cons. GE Co., Washington, 1985-87; exec. dir. Papers of the Comdg. Gens., 1988-93; dir., editor Papers of the War Dept. 1784-1800, 1993—2004. Vis. prof. history dept. U.S. Mil. Acad., West Point, N.Y., 2001-02; prof. U. Va., 2004— Author: The Army Additional Duty Guide, 1970, Mr. Jefferson's Army, 1987, The Illustrated History of West Point, 1991, History of the Civil Reserve Air Fleet, 1993, electronic edit., 1999, West Point: A Bicentennial History, 2002; contbr. articles on mil. and polit. history, def. orgn. reform to profl. jours.; editor: Papers of George Washington. Mem. Assn. Documentary Editors, Orgn. Am. Historians, Soc. Historians of Early Am. Republic, Army and Navy Club (Washington), Chi Psi. Office: Papers of George Washington U Va PO Box 400117 Charlottesville VA 22904-4117 Office Phone: 434-924-3569.

CRADDOCK, BANTZ J., career military officer; m. Linda Craddock; children: Zachary, Amanda. BS, W.Va. U., 1971; M of Mil. Arts and Sci., Army Command Gen. Staff Coll., 1984; graduate, US Army War Coll., 1993. Commd. Armor officer US Army, 1971; initial tour of duty 3d Armored Divsn., Germany; armor test officer US Army Armor and Engr. Bd., Ft. Knox, Ky.; tank comdr. 1st bn., 32d Armor, 3d Armored Divsn., Friedberg, Germany; systems analyst Engring divsn., Office of Program Mgr. Abrams Tank Sys., Warren, Mich., 1981, exec. officer to program mgr., 1982-85; exec. officer 4th Bn. 69th Armor 8th Infantry Divsn., Germany; dep. G-3, Ops. 8th Infantry Divsn. Hdqs.; comdr. 4th bn., 64th Armor 24th Infantry Divsn., Ft. Stewart, Ga., 1989; asst. chief of staff, G-3, Ops. 24th Infantry divsn., Ft. Stewart, Ga., 1991-93; comdr. 194th Separate Armored Brigade, Ft. Knox, 1993-95; asst. chief of staff, G-3 III Corps, Ft. Hood, Tex., 1995-96; asst. dep. dir. in J-5 Jt. Staff, Pentagon, 1996-98; asst. divsn. comdr. for maneuver 1st Infantry Divsn., Germany, 1998; comdr. US Forces for initial entry operation into Kosovo; commdg. gen. 7th Army Training Command, US Army Europe, 1999; comdr. 1st Infantry Divsn., 2000; sr. mil. asst. to sec. of def., 2002—04; comdr. US So. Command, 2004—. Decorated Valorous Unit award, Def. Disting. Svc. Medal, Disting. Svc. Medal, Silver Star, Def. Superior Svc. Medal with 1 Oak Leaf Cluster, Legion of Merit with 2 Oak Leaf Clusters, Bronze Star. Mem.: US Army Armor Assn. Office: US So Command 3511 NW 91st Ave Miami FL 33172

CRADDOCK, CAMPBELL (JOHN CAMPBELL CRADDOCK), geologist, educator; b. Chgo., Apr. 3, 1930; s. Alice Phillips; adopted by John and Bernice (Campbell) C.; m. Dorothy Dunkelberg, June 13, 1953; children: Susan, John, Carol. BA, DePauw U., 1951; MA, Columbia U., 1953, PhD, 1954. Geologist Shell Oil Co., N.Mex., Tex., Colo., Wyo., 1954-56; asst. prof. U. Minn., Mpls., 1956-60, assoc. prof., 1960-67; prof. geology U. Wis., Madison, 1967-96, prof. emeritus, 1996—, chmn. dept., 1977-80; leader Antarctic geologic field rsch. programs, 1959-69, geologist, 1980; leader Alaska Range field rsch. programs, 1968-81, Svalbard field rsch. programs, 1977-86. Cons. C.E. AUS, 1957—58, N. Star Rsch. Inst., 1965—68, Dept. State, 1976, Phillips Petroleum Co., 1980, Texaco, 1985; vis. scientist N.Z. Geol. Survey, 1962—63; lectr. Nanjing (China) U., 1981, Beijing U., 1981; chmn. panel polar geology and geophysics NRC, 1967—71, com. on polar rsch., 1967—71; convenor 3rd Internat. Symposium Antarctic Geology, Geophysics, Madison, Wis., 1977; mem. polar rsch. bd. NRC, 1978—82; U.S. mem. working group on geology Sci. Com. on Antarctic Rsch., 1967—81, chmn. group, 1973—80; co-chief scientist Leg 35 Deep Sea Drilling Project, 1974; chmn. Antarctic panel Circum-Pacific Map Project, 1979—90. Editor: Antarctic Geoscience, 1982; co-editor: Geologic Maps of Antarctica, Folio 12, Antarctic Map Folio Series, 1970, Initial Reports of the Deep Sea Drilling Project, Vol. 35, 1976, Geology and Paleontology of the Ellsworth Mountains, Antarctica, Geol. Soc. of Am. Memoir 170, 1992; contbr. articles to profl. jours. Higgins fellow, 1951-52, NSF fellow, 1952-53; Rsch. grantee, 1957-95; recipient U.S. Antarctic Service medal, 1968, Bellingshausen-Lazarev medal Soviet Acad. Scis., 1970, Alumni citation DePauw U., 1976 Fellow AAAS (steering com. geology and geography sect. 1996-98), Geol. Soc. Am. (chmn. North Ctrl. sect. 1982-83, chmn. structural geology and tectonics divsn. 1983-84, books editor 1982-88, Disting. Svc. award 1988); mem. Internat. Union Geol. Scis. (commn. on structural geology 1968-76, mem. commn. on tectonics 1976-85, del. Sci. Com. on Antarctic Rsch. 1974-87, mem. commn. on geologic map of world 1974-91, commn. v.p. for Antarctica 1979-91), Am. Geophys. Union, Am. Assn. Petroleum Geologists, Groupe Francais d'Etude de Gondwana (hon.), Phi Beta Kappa, Sigma Xi. Office: U Wis Dept Geology and Geophysics 1215 W Dayton St Madison WI 53706-1600

CRADDOCK, MARY SPENCER JACK, volunteer; b. Greensboro, Ala., Dec. 12, 1912; d. Theodore Henley Jack and Alice Searcy Ashley; m. George Barksdale Craddock, Feb. 1, 1941 (dec. Dec. 11, 1985); children: George B. Jr., Theodore J., Alice (Craddock) Massey. BA, Emory U., 1933. Pres. Lynchburg Jr. League, Va., 1944—45, Hillside Garden Club Va.; founder, bd. dirs. Seven Hills Sch., Lynchburg, 1959—70; Va. regent Gunston Hall Plantation, Commonwealth Va., 1980—92; pres. Family Svc., Lynchburg. Founder, bd. dirs. Lynchburg Mus. Sys., 1975—79; bd. dirs. Meals on Wheels, Lynchburg, 1993—96, Lynchburg Bicentennial Commn., 1973—76, Greater Lynchburg Cmty. Trust, 1991—99. Mem.: Nat. Soc. Col. Dames of Am. (Roll of Honor 1992—93), Garden Club Va., Boonsboro Country Club, Phi Beta Kappa. Episcopalian. Avocations: travel, bridge, reading, historic preservation. Home: 3249 Landon St Lynchburg VA 24503

CRAFORD, M. GEORGE, physicist, research administrator; b. Sioux City, Iowa, Dec. 29, 1938; BA, U. Iowa, 1961; MS, U. Ill., 1963, PhD in Physics, 1967. Mem. staff Monsanto, St. Louis, 1967-74, Palo Alto, Calif., 1974-79; mgr. R&D optoelec. divsn. Hewlett Packard, San Jose, Calif., 1979—2001; chief tech. officer Lumileds Lighting, San Jose, Calif., 2001—. Recipient Nat. Medal Technology, US Dept. Commerce, 2002. Fellow IEEE; mem. Nat. Acad. Engring. Achievements include development of visible light emitting diodes; nitrogen-doped GaAsP technology; first to develop AlInGaP LED's, AlGaAs and GaN products. Office: Lumileds Lighting LLC 370 W Trimble Rd San Jose CA 95131

CRAFT, CHERYL MAE, neurobiologist, anatomist, researcher; b. Lynch, Ky., Apr. 15, 1947; d. Cecil Berton and Lillian Lovelle C.; m. Laney K. Cormney, Oct. 14, 1967 (div. Sept. 1980); children: Tyler Craft Cormney, Ryan Berton Cormney (dec.); m. Richard N. Lolley (dec.). BS in Biology, Chemistry and Math., Valdosta State Coll., 1969; cert. in Tchg. Biology and Math., Ea. Ky. U., 1971; PhD in Human Anatomy and Neurosci., U. Tex., San Antonio, 1984. Undergrad. rsch. asst. Ea. Ky. U., Richmond, 1965-67; tchg. asst. dept. cell-structural biology U. Tex. Health Sci. Ctr., San Antonio, 1979-84; postdoctoral fellowship lab. devel. neurobiology NICHD and LMDB/NEI, Bethesda, Md., 1984-86; instr. dept. psychiatry U. Tex. Southwestern Med. Ctr., Dallas, 1986-87, asst. prof., 1987-91; dir. lab. Molecular Neurogenetics Schizophrenia Rsch. Ctr., VA Med. Ctr., Dallas, 1988-94; dir. Lab. Molecular Neurogenetics Mental Health Clinic Rsch. Ctr., U. Tex. Southwestern Med. Ctr., 1990-94; assoc. prof. U. Tex. Southwestern Med. Ctr., 1991-94; Mary D. Allen chair Doheny Eye Inst. U. So. Calif. Keck Sch. Medicine, L.A., Calif., 1994—, founding chmn. dept. cell and neurobiology, 1994—2004. Ad hoc reviewer NEI/NIH, Bethesda, 1993—; reviewer Molecular Biology, NSPB Fight for Sight Grants, 1991-94; STAR-sci. adv. bd. U. So. Calif./Bravo Magnet H.S., L.A., 1995—. Contbr. author: Melatonin: Biosynthesis, Physiological Effects, 1993; exec. editor Exptl. Eye Rsch. jour., 1993—; editor Molecular Vision. Recipient Merit award for rsch. VA Med. Ctr., 1992, 93, 94, nomination for Women in Sci. and Engring. award Dallas VA, 1992, 93; NEI fellow, 1986, NICHD/NIH fellow, 1986. Mem. AAAS, AAUW, Assn. for Rsch. in Vision and Ophthalmology (chair program planning com. 1991-94), Am. Soc. for Neurochemistry (Jordi Folch Pi Outstanding Young Investigator 1992), Sigma Xi (sec./treas. 1986-93, pres. 1993-94). Avocations: reading, travel. Office: U So Calif Keck Sch Medicine 1355 San Pablo St Rm 405 DVRC Los Angeles CA 90033 Office Phone: 323-442-6694. Personal E-mail: eyesightresearch@hotmail.com. Business E-Mail: ccraft@usc.edu.

CRAFT, DOUGLAS DURWOOD, artist; b. Greene, N.Y., Oct. 20, 1924; s. Harry Benjamin and Phoebe (Hotchkiss) C.; m. Elizabeth Louise Harms, Sept. 8, 1951. BFA, U. Chgo. and Art Inst. Chgo., 1950; MA in Painting, U. N.Mex., 1953. Grad. asst. U. N.Mex., 1951-52; assoc. prof. fine arts Sch. Art Inst., Chgo., 1957-65, Carnegie-Mellon U., Pitts., 1966-69; prof. fine arts Coll. New Rochelle, N.Y., 1970-91. Vis. artist in residence U. Ky., 1964, Cooper Union, N.Y.C., 1969-71, Sch. Visual Arts, N.Y.C., 1988; 1st Am. exch. prof., artist in residence Royal Coll. Art, London, 1964-65; guest artist curator Selected Women, Painters Castle Gallery, Coll. New Rochelle (N.Y.), 1982, Of Paper, Pigment and Glass, Castle Gallery, New Rochelle, 1987. One-man shows include Kasha Heman Gallery, Chgo., 1963, 61, U. N.Mex., 1964, 52, U. Ky., 1964, Travers Festival Gallery, Edinburgh, Scotland, 1965, Royal Coll. Art, London, 1964, Carnegie Mellon U., 1968, Mus. Art, Carnegie Inst., Pitts., 1968, Fischbach Gallery, N.Y.C., 1973, Jersey City Mus., 1978, 55 Mercer Gallery, N.Y.C., 1980, Bratton Gallery, Inc., N.Y.C., 1989, Coll. Ctr. Art Gallery, Coll. New Rochelle, 1989, Rosefsky Studio Art Gallery SUNY Binghamton, 1993, retrospective Butler Inst. Am. Art, Youngstown, Ohio, 1993, Paul McCarron Gallery, N.Y.C., 1995, Delaware Valley Arts Ctr., Narrowsburg, 1996, retrospective traveling exhbn. Makee Gallery, Canton, Mo., Gray Gallery, Quincy, Ill., Keokuk Art Ctr., Iowa, 1997, Paul McCarron Gallery, N.Y.C., 1996, 98, Del. Valley Arts Ctr., Narrowsburg, 2001, 2004, Gorshow Arch., N.Y.C., 2000, Mesaros Galleries, Butler Inst. Am. Art, Youngstown, 2005, others; exhibited in group shows at Rose Fried Gallery, N.Y.C., 1968, Montclair (N.J.) Art Mus., 1984, Traverse Gallery, Edinburgh, 1984, Studio K., Long Island City, N.Y., 1985, Castle Gallery, New Rochelle, N.Y., 1985-86, Jersey City Mus., 1987, Montclair Art Mus., 1987, Robeson Gallery, Rutger's U., Newark, 1987, N.A.M.E. Gallery, Chgo., 1988, Bratton Gallery, Inc., N.Y.C., 1988-89, Schick Art Gallery Skidmore Coll., 1995, Del. Arts Ctr. Gallery, 1995, Pavel Zoubok Gallery, N.Y.C., 2001-02, others; represented in permanent collections Smithsonian Instn., Washington, Art Inst. Chgo., U. Ky., Mus. Modern Art, N.Y.C., Whitney Mus. Am. Art, N.Y.C., U. N.Mex., Gill Libr. Coll. New Rochelle, Butler Inst. Am. Art, Youngstown, Ohio, Meml. Art Gallery, U. Rochester, N.Y., others; corp. collections; pvt. collections in U.S.A, Can., Eng. Scotland, France, Saudi Arabia, Japan. Bd. dirs. Castle Gallery, New Rochelle. Served with USNR, 1943-46. Recipient Logan bronze medal Art Inst. Chgo., 1966, Harry Allison Logan meml. award Chautauqua Art Assn., 1963, jury award in painting Carnegie Inst., 1968; Carr scholar U. Iowa, 1942-43; Carl Loeb fellow Syracuse U., 1950; grantee Richard A. Florsheim Art Fund, 1993. Home: PO Box 245 Jeffersonville NY 12748-0245 Studio: 21 Jefferson Ave Jeffersonville NY 12748

CRAFT, EDMUND COLEMAN, retired automotive parts manufacturing company executive; b. Plainfield, N.J., Dec. 23, 1939; s. Edmund Coleman and Ruth Irene (Morrell) C.; m. Gail Christensen; children: Edmund Coleman III, Elisabeth Gordon, William Todd. BS, Lycoming Coll., 1963; postgrad., Syracuse U., 1963-64; grad. exec. program, U. Minn., 1984. With Borg-Warner Corp., Detroit, adminstrv. asst. to chmn. Chgo., 1969-70; with Borg-Warner Ltd., Letchworth, Hertfordshire, Eng., 1970-75; v.p. hydraulics div. Borg-Warner, Wooster, Ohio, 1975-79; dir. hydraulics div. Donaldson Co. Inc., Mpls., 1979-83, v.p., 1983-2000; sr. advisor Global Aftermarket, 2000-2001; ret., 2001. Bd. dirs. Jr. Achievement of Upper Midwest Inc., 1993-2000, mem. exec. com., 1994-2000; divsn. chmn. United Way, Wooster, 1974. Mem. Automotive Filter Mfrs. Coun. (vice chmn. 1985-89, chmn. 1989-91, bd. dirs. 1991-2000), Dataw Island Club, Dataw Island Yacht Club. Republican. Presbyterian. Avocations: golf, power boating. E-mail: craft@islc.net.

CRAFT, LIZ, artist; b. LA, 1970; BA, Otis Parsons, 1994; MFA, UCLA, 1997. One-woman shows include, Richard Telles Fine Art, LA, 1998, Centrum fur Gegenwartskunst Oberosterreich, Linz, Austria, 2001, Galerie Nathalie Obadia, Paris, 2001, Public Art Fund, NY, 2002, A Real Mother For Ya, Sadie Coles HQ, London, 2002, Marianne Boesky Gallery, 2003, exhibited in group shows at Happy Trails, Coll. Creative Studies, U. Santa Barbara, 1999, Hot Spots, Weatherspoon Gallery, U. NC, 1999, Good Luck for You, Transmission Gallery, Edinburgh, 2000, Calif. Dreamin', Gallery Art, Carlsen Ctr., Johnson County Cmty. Coll., Kans. City, 2000, Young & Dumb, ACME, LA, 2001, Play it as it Lays, The London Inst. Gallery, 2002, Wheeling - Krad Kult Tour! Motorcycles in Art, Frankfurt am Main, Germany, 2002, 3-D, Friedrich Petzel Gallery, 2003, The Thought That Counts, Sister, LA, 2003, It's All An Illusion, Migros Museum fur Gegenwartskunst, Zurich, 2004, Whitney Biennial, Whitney Mus. Am. Art, 2004, Seeing Other People, 2004. Mailing: c/o Marianne Boesky Gallery 535 West 22st St New York NY 10011*

CRAFT, RANDAL ROBERT, JR., lawyer; b. Greenwood, Miss., Sept. 14, 1941; s. Randal Robert and Elizabeth (Nelson) C.; m. Irene Tichenor, Nov. 27, 1971; children: Elizabeth Napton, Sarah Nelson. BS in Aerospace Engring., U. Tex., 1964; JD, Georgetown U., 1968. Bar: Va. 1968, NY 1969, US Dist. Ct. (so. and ea. dists.) NY 1971, U.S. Ct. Appeals (2d cir.) 1975, US Supreme Ct. 1976, US Ct. Appeals (8th cir.) 1985, US Ct. Appeals (5th cir.) 1989, US Ct. Appeals (6th cir.) 1993. Assoc. Haight, Gardner, Poor & Havens, NYC, 1968-76, ptnr., 1976-97, chmn. litig. dept., 1995-97; ptnr. Holland & Knight, NYC, 1997—, litig. practice group leader. Gen. counsel AIAA, 1984-91; gen. counsel, bd. dirs., exec. com. NYC Ballet, 1978—. Author: (with others) Management of Complex Mass Tort Litigation, 1986, Aircraft Crash Litigation, 1984; co-author: The Government Contractor Defense, 1986; contbr. articles to profl. jours. Moderator Judson Meml. Ch., 1975-76; bd. dirs. NYC Ctr. Music and Drama, 1991—, U. Tex. Engring. Found. Adv. Coun., 2002—. Mem. ABA, Assn. of Bar of City of NY, Lawyers Alliance for NY (co-founder, chmn. 1970-71), Wings Club (bd. dirs. 1989-92, gen. counsel 1992—), Delta Upsilon. Republican. Baptist. Avocations: tennis, music. Office: Holland & Knight 195 Broadway 24th Fl New York NY 10007-3189 Office Phone: 212-513-3411.

CRAFT, ROBERT HOMAN, JR., lawyer; b. NYC, Sept. 24, 1939; s. Robert Homan and Janet Marie (Sullivan) C.; m. Margaret Jamison Ford, Feb. 6, 1971; children: Robert H. III, Gerard Ford. AB, Princeton U., 1961; BA, Oxford U., 1963; LLB, Harvard U., 1966. Bar: NY 1973, US Dist. Ct. (so. and ea. dists.) NY 1977, US Ct. Appeals (DC cir.) 1977, US Dist. Ct. DC 1978, US Ct. Appeals (2nd cir.) 1974, US Supreme Ct. 1977. Assoc. Sullivan & Cromwell, NYC, 1966-74; spl. asst. to under sec. of state for security assistance U.S. Dept. State, Washington, 1974-76; exec. asst. to chmn. SEC, Washington, 1976; ptnr. corp. and fin. Sullivan & Cromwell, LLP, Washington, 1977—, mng. ptnr. DC office, v.p. gen counsel. Bd. trustees Washington Nat. Opera, 1978—, pres. 1998-2002; dir. Coun. for Excellence in Govt., 1989—, Harvard Law Sch. Fund (nat. chair, 1997-99) Mem. ABA, DC Bar Assn., NY State Bar Assn., Assn. Bar City of NY, Am. Soc. Internat. Law, Met. Club (Washington), Chevy Chase (Md.) Club. Office: Sullivan & Cromwell LLP 1701 Pennsylvania Ave NW Washington DC 20006-5866 Office Phone: 202-956-7500. Office Fax: 202-293-6330. Business E-Mail: craftr@sullcrom.com.

CRAFTON-MASTERSON, ADRIENNE, real estate company executive; b. Providence, Mar. 6, 1926; d. John Harold and Adrienne (Fitzgerald) Crafton; m. Francis T. Masterson, May 31, 1947 (div. Jan. 1977); children: Mary Victoria Masterson Bush, Kathleen Joan, John Andrew, Barbara Lynn Harrison Student, No. Va. C.C., 1971-74; A in Biblical Studies, Christ to World Bible Inst., Jacksonville, Fla., 1992; A in Pastoral Leadership, Calvary Bible Inst., Jacksonville, Fla., 1993. Mem. staff Senator T.F. Green of R.I., Washington, 1944-47, 54-60, with U.S. Senate Com. on Campaign Expenditures, 1944-45; asst. chief clk. Ho. Govt. Ops. Com., 1948-49; clk. Ho. Campaign Expenditures Com., 1950; asst. appointment sec. Office of Pres., 1951-53; with Hubbard Realty, Alexandria, Va., 1962-67; owner, mgr. Adrienne C. Masterson Real Estate, Alexandria, 1968-82; pres. Adrienne Investment Real Estate (AIRE) Ltd., Alexandria, 1982-91; devel. staff writer Calvary Internat., Jacksonville, Fla., 1992-93; Adrienne Crafton-Masterson Real Estate, Winchester, Va., 1993-94, owner, prin., broker Haymarket, Va., 1994—. Pres. AIRE-Merkli developers, 1988-92; founder AIHRE USA, Inc., 1993—. Mem. adv. panel Fairfax County (Va.) Coun. on Arts, 1987-88;

founder, pres. Mt. Vernon/Lee Cultural Ctr. Found., Inc. 1984-92; mem. Haymarket (Va.) Hist. Commn., 1994-95, 97-2001, chmn., 1999-2001. Fellow Internat. Biog. Ctr. (dep. dir. gen.); mem. Internat. Orgn. Real Estate Appraisers (sr.), Nat. Assn. Realtors, No. Va. Assn. Realtors (chmn. comml. and indsl. com. 1982-83, cmty. revitalization com. 1983-84, pres. land comml. indsl. mems. 1985, v.p. land comml. and indsl. mems. 1989), Fairfax Affordable Housing Inc. (sec. 1990-91), Haymarket-Gainesville (Va.) Busl. and Profl. Assn. (bd. dirs. 1996-99, sec. 1998-99), Alexandria C. of C., Mt. Vernon/Lee C. of C., Friends of Kennedy Ctr. (founder), Optimist Club Gainesville-Haymarket (charter, bd. dirs. 1997-99). Office Phone: 727-723-7667. Personal E-mail: aihrecraft@earthlink.net.

CRAFT-ROSENBERG, MARTHA JANE, nursing educator, researcher; b. Downings, Mo., July 31, 1941; d. Harry R. and Emma (Bohi) Lewis; m. John Craft, Jan. 31, 1964 (dec.); 1 child, Jack; m. Guy Rosenberg, Oct. 24, 1993; children: Guy John, Gary Rosenberg. Diploma in nursing, Iowa Meth. Hosp. Sch. Nursing, 1962; BS, U. Iowa, 1970, MA, 1978, PhD, 1985. RN, Iowa. Staff/head nurse pediatrics U. Iowa Hosp./Clinics, Iowa City, 1962-64, asst. supr. pediatrics, 1964-66, supr. pediatrics, 1966-68, clin. nurse specialist, 1968-69, clin. nurse specialist neonatal, 1970-71; instr. Allen Meml. Hosp., Waterloo, Iowa, 1974-77; clin. nurse specialist II pediatrics U. Iowa Hosp./Clinics, Iowa City, 1977-80; asst. prof. nursing U. Iowa, Iowa City, 1980-86, assoc. prof. nursing, 1986-97, prof. nursing, 1997—. Editor: (two editions) Nursing Interventions for Infants and Children; contbr. articles to profl. jours. Grantee Robert Wood Johnson Found., 1987-88, Nat. Ctr. for Nursing Rsch., 1991-97, 2002—. Fellow: Am. Acad. Nursing; mem.: ANA (bd. dirs. Iowa chpt. 1986—87, coun. nurse researchers 1988—), Am. Children Acad. Nursing (expert panel 1998—2001, chair), Midwest Nursing Rsch. Soc. (Rschr. award 1996), N.Am. Nursing Diagnosis (pres.-elect, Unique Contribution award), Sigma Theta Assn. Avocations: piano, reading. Office: U Iowa Coll Nursing 344 Nursing Building Iowa City IA 52242-1121

CRAGIN, CHARLES LANGMAID, lawyer; b. Portland, Maine, Oct. 9, 1943; s. Charles Langmaid and Ruth (Meriam) C.; m. Maureen Patricia Ford, Oct. 8, 1994; children: Christine, Jean, Cathleen. BS, U. Maine, 1967, JD, 1970. Bar: Maine 1970, U.S. Dist. Ct. Maine 1970, U.S. Supreme Ct. 1974, U.S. Ct. Appeals (D.C. cir.) 1989, U.S. Ct. Vet. Appeals 1997. Assoc. Verrill & Dana, Portland, Maine, 1970-74, ptnr., 1974-90; chmn. U.S. Bd. of Vet.'s Appeals, Washington, D.C., 1991-97; counselor to undersec. U.S. Dept. VA, 1997, prin. dep. asst. sec. of def., Res. affairs, 1997-98, acting asst. sec. of def., res. affairs, 1998-2001; prin. dep. under sec. defense, personnel & readiness U.S. Dept. Defense, 1998-2001, acting under sec. def., personnel and readiness, 2001; ptnr. Blank Rome LLP, Washington, 2001—03; sr. v.p. nat. intelligence, security and response Sys. Planning Corp., Arlington, Va., 2003—. Contbr. articles to legal pubis. Rep. candidate for gov. Maine, 1982; bd. dirs., v.p. Margaret Chase Smith Found., Skowhegan, Maine, 1986—, Potomac divsn. AAA, 1992—; chmn. budget com. Rep. Nat. Com., 1984-90; mem. MaineCommn. on Govt. Ethics and Elections, 1986-88, Def. Adv. Com. on Women in Svcs.,1986-88; bd. dirs. U.S. Navy Meml. Found., 1989-2004, vice chmn., 2002-04. Capt. USNR; ret. Decorated Legion of Merit; named Outstanding Young Man Maine, Maine Jaycees, 1976; recipient Disting Svc. award U. So. Maine Alumni Assn., 1986, Exceptional Svc. award U.S. Dept. Vets. Affairs, 1997, Disting. Pub. Svc. award USCG, 2000, Nat. Pres.'s award Naval Res. Assn., 2000, Minuteman award Res. Officers Assn., 2000, Outstanding Svc. award Nat. Mil. Family Assn., 2000, Disting. Pub. Svc. medal Dept. Def., 2001, Decoration for Exceptional Civilian Svc., USAF, 2001, U.S. Army, 2001, Disting. Pub. Svc. medal U.S. Navy, 2001. Fellow Am. Acad. Hosp. Attys. (bd. dirs. 1979-82); mem. ABA, Maine Bar Assn. (Disting. Svc. award 1986), DC Bar Assn., Capitol Hill Club (Washington), Army and Navy Club (Washington). Roman Catholic. Avocations: skiing, wine collecting, amateur radio, gardening. Office: Sys Planning Corp 1000 Wilson Blvd 30th Fl Arlington VA 22209-2211 Office Phone: 703-351-8244. Business E-Mail: ccragin@sysplan.com.

CRAGNOLINO, GUSTAVO ADOLFO, research scientist; b. Marcos Juarez, Cordoba, Argentina, July 23, 1940; arrived in US, 1976; s. Roberto Clemente and Maria Antonia (Ferrer) Cragnolino; m. Aida Apter, Aug. 16, 1966; children: Ana, Ernesto. Licenciado in Chem. Scis., U. Buenos Aires, 1966, D in Chem. Scis., 1975. Rsch. assoc. Atomic Energy Commn., Buenos Aires, 1968—76; rsch. scientist Ohio State U., Columbus, 1976—86; assoc. scientist Brookhaven Nat. Lab., Upton, NY, 1986—88; sr. rsch. scientist Atomic Energy Commn., Buenos Aires, 1988—90; prin. scientist S.W. Rsch. Inst., San Antonio, 1990—95, staff scientist, 1995—2003, inst. scientist, 2003—05, tech. advisor, 2005—. Lectr., adv. Internat. Atomic Energy Agy., Vienna, 1994; presenter in field. Co-editor: Accelerated Corrosion Tests for Service Life Prediction of Materials, 1994, Scientific Basis for Nuclear Waste Management XXV, 2002, Corrosion Resistant Materials in Extreme Environments, 2005; co-author: ASME Handbook on Water Technology for Thermal Power Systems, 1998; contbr. articles to profl. jours. Fellow: Nat. Assn. Corrosion Engrs. Internat. (chmn. tech. com. 1996—98); mem.: Rsch. Com, ASTM Internat., Am. Nuc. Soc., Electrochem. Soc. Office: SW Rsch Inst 6220 Culebra Rd San Antonio TX 78238-5166 Office Phone: 210-522-5539. Business E-Mail: gcragno@swri.org.

CRAHALLA, JACQUELINE R., state representative; b. Phila., Oct. 8, 1940; m. Benjamin R. Crahalla; children: Benny, Richie(dec.). BA in English, Gwynedd-Mercy Coll. Supr. Lower Providence Twp.; twp. liaison Lower Providence Sewer Authority; Pa. state rep., 2002—. Mgr. corp. contbn. AstraZeneca; human health divsn. Merck & Co., Inc. Feature writer, weekly corr. (newpaper) Today's Post. Republican. Lutheran. Office: 161B East Wing Harrisburg PA 17120-2020

CRAHAN, JACK BERTSCH, retired manufacturing company executive; b. Peoria, Ill., Aug. 24, 1923; s. John F. and Ann B. (Bertsch) C.; m. Peggy Furey, Sept. 9, 1944; children: Patrick Michael, Colleen Mary, Kevin Furey. BS, U. Minn., 1948. With Flexsteel Industries, Inc., Dubuque, Iowa, 1948—50, plant mgr., 1950-54, gen. mgr., v.p., 1955-70, exec. v.p., 1970-84, pres., 1985-89, vice-chmn., COO, 1989-90, chmn., CEO, 1990-99; ret., 1999. Trustee United Steel Workers Am. Pension Fund, 1960—99; dir. Pres.'s Coun. for Phys. Fitness in Industry, 1970—74, Dubuque Bank & Trust, 1970—94; bd. dirs. Dubuque Racing Assn., 1987—2000. Bd. regents Loras Coll., 1967-80; bd. dirs. Xavier Hosp., 1969-78, Boys Club Am., 1981-99 . Served with USNR, 1942-43, with USMC, 1943-46, 51-52. Decorated D.F.C. (1), Air medal (3). Mem. Am. Furniture Assn. (bd. dirs. 1967-74). Republican. Roman Catholic. Home: 1195 Arrowhead Dr Dubuque IA 52003-8594 Office: Flexsteel Industries Inc Brunswick Indsl Block PO Box 847 Dubuque IA 52004-0847 Office Phone: 563-556-7730. Business E-Mail: jzemann@hersteel.com.

CRAIB, KENNETH BRYDEN, resource development executive, physicist, economist; b. Milford, Mass., Oct. 13, 1938; s. William Pirie and Virginia Louise (Bryden) C.; m. Gloria Faye Lisano, June 25, 1960; children: Kenneth Bryden, Judith Diane, Lori Elaine, Melissa Suzanne. BS in Physics, U. Houston, 1967; MA in Econs., Calif. State U., 1982; postgrad., Harvard U., 1989. Aerospace technologist NASA, Houston, 1962-68; staff physicist Mark Sys., Inc., Cupertino, Calif., 1968-69; v.p. World Resources Corp., Cupertino, 1969-71; dir. resources devel. divsn. Aero Svc. Corp., Phila., 1971-72; dir. ops. Resources Devel. Assocs., Los Altos, Calif., 1972-80, pres., CEO Diamond Springs, Calif., 1980-85; owner Sand Ridge Arabians, 1980-98; chmn., dir. Resources Devel. Assocs., Inc., 1982-86, Devel. Support Internat. Inc., Placerville, Calif., 1981-86; pres., chn., dir. RDA Internat., Inc., 1985-96, chmn., CEO, dir., 1995—2000; mgr. acad. affairs U. Phoenix, Sacramento, 2001—02, chmn. Coll. Undergrad. Bus. and Mgmt. Ft. Lauderdale, Fla., 2002—, prof., 2002—. Bd. dirs. Transatlantic Fisheries, Inc.; adj. prof. Sacramento City Coll., 1996—2001; prof. U. Phoenix, Sacramento, 1997—2002. Contbr. articles to profl. jours. Served with USAF, 1957-61. Recipient Sustained Superior Performance award NASA, 1966; NASA grantee, 1968. Mem. Am. Soc. Photogrammetry, Soc. Internat. Devel., Agrl. Rsch. Inst., Calif. Select Com. Remote Sensing, Internat. Assn. Natural Resources Pilots, Remote Sensing Soc. (coun.), Am. Soc. Oceanography (charter), Aircraft Owners and Pilots Assn., Gulf and Cribbean Fisheries Inst., Placerville C. of C., Harvard Alumni Assn., Exptl. Aircraft Assn., Asian Fisheries Soc. Office: U Phoenix Ft Lauderdale Campus 600 N Pine Island Rd Ste 500 Fort Lauderdale FL 33324 Mailing: 900 SW 74 Terr Plantation FL 33317 *What you do is not as important as how you do it, and the people whose lives you touch in the process.*

CRAIG, ALBERT MORTON, history professor, researcher; b. Chgo., Dec. 9, 1927; s. Albert Morton and Adda (Clendenin) C.; m. Teruko Ugaya, July 10, 1953; children— John, Paul. BS, Northwestern U., 1949; postgrad., Universite de Strasbourg, 1949-50, Kyoto U., 1951-53, Tokyo U., 1955-56; PhD, Harvard, 1959. Instr. U. Mass., 1957-59; instr. Harvard U., Cambridge, Mass., 1959-60, asst. prof., 1960-63, assoc. prof., 1963-67, prof., 1967—99, Harvard-Yenching prof. history, 1999—2005, Harvard-Yenching rsch. prof. history, 1999—; dir. Harvard-Yenching Inst., 1976-87. Author: Choshu in the Meiji Restoration, 1961, The Heritage of Chinese Civilization, 2001, The Heritage of Japanese Civilization, 2003, (with others) East Asia: The Modern Transformation, 1965, East Asia: Tradition and Transformation, 1973, 3d edit., 1989, The Heritage of World Civilizations, 1986, 7th edit., 2005; editor: Japan, A Comparative View, 1979; co-editor: Personality in Japanese History, 1970. Served with AUS, 1946-47. Mem. Assn. Asian Studies. Home: 172 Goden St Belmont MA 02478-2951 Office: 9 Kirkland Pl Cambridge MA 02138-2020 E-mail: acraig@Fas.Harvard.edu.

CRAIG, ANNA MAYNARD, financial educator, consultant; b. Columbus, Ohio, Sept. 2, 1944; d. David Stuart and Ann (Armstrong) C.; m. John D. Hogan, Nov. 26, 1976. BA cum laude, Smith Coll., 1966; MA, U. Wis., 1970, PhD, 1972. Chartered fin. analyst, CFP, enrolled agt., U.S. Treasury. Asst. prof. U. Ill., Chgo., 1971—75; vis. asst. prof. Ohio State U., Columbus, 1974—76; asst. prof. Ctrl. Mich. U., Mt. Pleasant, 1976—79; cons. Am. Productivity Ctr., Houston, 1979—81; adj. prof. Houston Bapt. U., 1980—86; adj. prof. Jones Grad. Sch. Adminstrn. Rice U., Houston, 1984; adj. prof. dept. fin. U. Ill., Champaign-Urbana, 1987—91; adj. faculty Goizueta Bus. Sch. Emory U., Atlanta, 1992—2000; faculty exec. and concentrated MBA program Ga. State U., 1992—93; faculty MBA program Poznan (Poland)/Ga. State U., 1997—; chief economist Encore Bank, Houston, 2001—. Bd. advisors Assn. for Internat. Exch. Students in Econs. and Commerce, U. Ill., 1987-91; advisor U. Ill. FMA Nat. Honor Soc., Fin. Club. Editor: (with John D. Hogan) Dimensions of Productivity Research, vol. 1, 1980, vol. II, 1981. Bd. dirs. Champaign-Urbana Symphony, 1987-91; trust mgmt. com. Univ. YWCA, Champaign, 1987-91. Ford fellow, U. Wis., 1970-72, NSF fellow, Stanford U., 1972; Fulbright scholar, 1966-67; named Outstanding Prof. Fin. U. Ill. Commerce Coun., 1987-88. Mem.: Smith Coll. Alumnae Assn. (chmn. spl. gifts 1983—86, class fund agt.), CFA Inst., Atlanta Soc. Fin. Analysts (trustee 2000—04, v.p. 2004, pres. 2004—), Am. Econ. Assn., Phi Beta Kappa, Fulbright Alumni Assn., Beta Gamma Sigma. Office: Gilnockie Assocs 3892 Byrnwyck Pl NE Atlanta GA 30319-1654

CRAIG, BENJAMIN LAWRENCE, lawyer; b. Great Falls, Mont., Mar. 15, 1931; s. Russell Edgar and Gladys Glenore (Chance) C.; m. Jeanne E. Higgins, Jan. 1, 1984; children— Russell Ivar, Pamela Sue. B.S. in Bus. Adminstrn., U. Mont., 1953; J.D., U. Denver, 1960. Bar: Colo. 1960, U.S. Dist. Ct. Colo. 1960, U.S. Ct. Appeals (10th cir.) 1960, U.S. Supreme Ct. 1966. Assoc. Cockrell, Quinn & Creighton and predecessor firm Henry, Cockrell, Quinn & Creighton and Henry & Adams, Denver, 1960—, ptnr., 1966—1996, gen. counsel, The Consolidated Mutual Water Co., 1996-204, arbitrator, mediator, 2004-. Pres. Pres.'s Roundtable Denver, 1975; bd. dirs. Boys Club Denver, Balarat Council. Served to col. USAFR, 1953-86. Mem. Denver Bar Assn., Colo. Bar Assn., ABA, Am. Judicature Soc., The Law Club Denver, Nat. Orgn. Legal Problems Edn., Nat. Sch. Bds. Assn. Council Sch. Attys. (chmn. 1973-75), Order of St. Ives Hon. Soc. Republican. Presbyterian. Clubs: Univ. (Denver), Army-Navy (Washington), Masons. Office: 1181 Pebble Beach Dr Mesquite NV 89027

CRAIG, CHARLES SAMUEL, marketing educator; b. Atlantic City, May 6, 1943; s. Charles Hays and Catherine Sara (McMullen) C.; m. Elizabeth Anne Coyne, Aug. 10, 1985; children: Mary Catherine, Caroline Elizabeth. BA, Westminster Coll., 1965; MS, U. R.I., 1967; PhD, Ohio State U., 1971. Mktg. rep. IBM, Providence, 1966—68; asst. dir. Mechanized Info. Ctr., Columbus, 1971—73; asst. prof. lib. adminstrn. Ohio State U., Columbus, 1971—73, asst. prof. mktg., 1972—74; asst. prof. mktg. Grad. Sch. Bus. and Pub. Adminstrn. Cornell U., Ithaca, NY, 1974—77, assoc. prof., 1977—79; from assoc. prof. mktg. Stern Sch. of Bus. to prof. NYU, 1979—, dir. entertainment, media and tech. program, 1999—, Catherine and Peter Kellner prof., 2001—. Bd. dirs. P&R Pub. Co., Phillipsburg, NJ; mem. exec. bd. Jour. Retailing, 1985—. Co-author: Consumer Behavior: An Information Processing Perspective, 1982; International Marketing Research, 1983, 3d edit., 2005, Global Marketing Strategy, 1995; co-editor: Personal Selling: Theory, Research and Practice, 1984, The Development of Media Models in Advertising, Repetition Effects over the Years, The Relationship of Advertising Expenditures to Sales, 1986; mem. edit. bd. Jour. Mktg. Rsch., 1978-85, Jour. Retailing, 1980-85, Jour. Advt. Rsch., 1994—, Internat. Jour. of Advt., 1997—; contbr. articles to profl. jours. NDEA fellow, 1969-71. Mem. Am. Mktg. Assn., Assn. Consumer Rsch., Acad. Internat. Bus., Phi Kappa Phi, Omicron Delta Epsilon, Psi Chi. Presbyterian. Home: 100 Bleecker St Apt 28D New York NY 10012-2207 Office: NYU 44 W 4th St New York NY 10012-1106

CRAIG, CYNTHIA MAE, mathematics professor; b. Brownsville, Tex., Jan. 22, 1951; d. Richard Virgil and Mae Margaret (Phillips) Cole; m. Daniel Baxter Craig, Jan. 15, 1971; children: Tammy Michelle Craig Black, Heather Elizabeth Craig Rios. BA, Augusta (Ga.) Coll., 1985, MEd, 1989, specialist in edn., 1993. Cert. devel. specialist; cert. tchr., Ga. Tchr. 5th-6th grade tchr. Blessed Sacrament Sch., El Paso, Tex., 1981-82; tchr. 4-8th grade honors math. St. Mary on the hill Cath. Sch., Augusta, Ga., 1985-87; tchr. Aquinas H.S., Augusta, 1987-88; asst. prof. of math. in learning support Augusta State U., 1989—, assoc. chair dept. learning support, 1998—2002, acting chair dept. learning supoort, 2002—04; dir., chair learning support Augusta State U. Coll., 2004—. Presenter at profl. confs. in field. Contbr. articles to profl. jours. Mem. ASCD, Ga. Assn. of Devel. Educators, Nat. Assn. for Devel. Edn., Phi Delta Kappa (newsletter editor 1990-93, v.p. membership 1993-94, newsletter editor 1989-92, 94-96, 97-98, found. rep. 1996-97, newsletter editor 1997-98, rsch. rep. 1998—). Avocations: reading, educational research, travel. Office: Augusta State U Learning Support 2500 Walton Way Augusta GA 30904-4562 Office Phone: 706-737-1685. Business E-Mail: ccraig@aug.edu.

CRAIG, DANIEL, actor; b. Chester, Eng., Mar. 2, 1968; 1 child. Grad., Guildhall Sch. Music and Drama. Actor: (films) The Power of One, 1992, A Kid in King Arthur's Court, 1995, Saint-Ex, 1996, Obsession, 1997, Love and Rage, 1998, Elizabeth, 1998, The Trench, 1999, I Dreamed of Africa, 2000, Some Voices, 2000, Lara Croft: Tomb Raider, 2001, Road to Perdition, 2002, Occasional, Strong, 2002, The Mother, 2003, Sylvia, 2003, Enduring Love, 2004, Layer Cake, 2004, The Jacket, 2005, Fateless, 2005; (TV films) Genghis Cohn, 1993, Sharpe's Eagle, 1993, Kiss and Tell, 1996, The Fortunes and Misfortunes of Moll Flanders, 1996, The Ice House, 1997, Shockers: The Visitor, 1999, Copenhagen, 2002, Archangel, 2005. Office: William Morris Agency Inc 1 William Morris Pl Beverly Hills CA 90212*

CRAIG, DAVID JEOFFREY, retired manufacturing company executive; b. Wyandotte, Mich., Sept. 29, 1925; s. Geoffrey F. and Catherine R. Craig; m. Shirley M. Lemhagen, Mar. 3, 1945; children: Susan Craig Noyes, Janice Craig Maggi, Sandra Barry, Jeffrey Allan. BS in Physics, U. Detroit, 1950, MS summa cum laude, 1951; postgrad., U. Mich., 1952-53. With The BOC Group, Murray Hill, N.J., 1956-90; dir. corp. planning and devel., 1970-71; group v.p., 1971-79; dep. group mng. dir. BOC Group plc, Surrey, Eng., 1979-83; mng. dir. engrng. and tech., 1983-90; dir. The BOC Group, Inc., BOC Group plc. Mem. Ticonderoga Country Club, Hobe Sound Golf Club. Home: 11430 SE Plandome Dr Hobe Sound FL 33455-7901

CRAIG, EDWARD VINCENT, orthopedic surgeon, educator; b. Bklyn., May 5, 1947; s. Edward Vincent and Lorraine (Youngkin) C.; m. Kathryn Ann Davis, July 4, 1982. BA, Princeton U., 1969; MD, Columbia U., 1973. Diplomate Am. Bd. Orthopaedic Surgery. Intern Columbia-Presbyn. Med. Ctr., N.Y.C., 1973-74, resident in internal medicine, 1975-76, resident in orthopaedic surgery, 1977-80, fellow in shoulder surgery, 1980-81, fellow in hand surgery, 1981-82; attending surgeon U. Minn. Hosp., Mpls., 1982-94, Hosp. Spl. Surgery, N.Y.C., 1994—, New York Hosp., N.Y.C., 1994—; prof. clin. surgery Cornell Med. Coll., N.Y.C., 1994—. Cons., designer Biomet Atlas Total Shoulder Replacement Sys., Warsaw, Ind., 1985—; cons. Minn. Twins Baseball Club, 1993-94. Author: The Shoulder, 1995, Clinical Orthopaedics, 1999, The Unstable Shoulder, 1999; contbr. articles to profl. jours. Bd. dirs. Waveny Day Care Ctr., New Canaan, Conn., 1996, New Canaan Country Sch., 2002, Juvenile Diabetes Found. Fairfield County, New Canaan Basketball Assn. Fellow Am. Acad. Orthopaedic Surgeons; mem. AMA, Am. Shoulder and Elbow Surgeons (pres. 1985—), Am. Orthopaedic Soc. for Sports Medicine (rsch. grantee 1995), Am. Soc. Surgery of the Hand, Am. Orthopaedic Assn. (ABC Traveling fellow 1980). Republican. Roman Catholic. Avocations: piano, skiing, golf, tennis, running. Office: Hosp Spl Surgery 535 E 70th St New York NY 10021-4872 also: 143 Sound Beach Ave Old Greenwich CT 06870 Office Phone: 212-606-1966. E-mail: craige@hss.edu.

CRAIG, GEORGE DENNIS, economics professor, consultant; b. Sept. 14, 1936; s. George S. and Alice H. (Childs) C.; m. Lelah Price, Aug. 21, 1984; children: R. Price Coyle, R. Nolan Coyle, Deborah L. Craig, W. Sean Coyle. BA, Wheaton Coll., 1960; MS, U. Ill., 1962, PhD, 1968. Asst. prof. econs. La. State U., Baton Rouge, 1965-69; assoc. prof. sch. bus. No. Ill. U., DeKalb, 1969-82; prof. econs., chmn. Oklahoma City U., 1982—. Cons. AT&T, Oklahoma City, 1984—. Contbr. articles to profl. jours. Mem. Am. Econs. Assn., So. Econs. Assn., Nat. Assn. Bus. Economists, Internat. Inst. Forecasting. Avocations: duplicate bridge, tennis. Home: 6915 Avondale Ct Oklahoma City OK 73116-5008 Office: 6421 Avondale Dr Ste 208 Oklahoma City OK 73116-6429 Office Phone: 405-842-8925. E-mail: craigg784@aol.com.

CRAIG, GORDON ALEXANDER, historian, educator; b. Glasgow, Scotland, Nov. 26, 1913; came to U.S., 1925; s. Frank Mansfield and Jane (Bissell) C.; m. Phyllis Halcomb, June 16, 1939; children: Susan, Deborah Gordon, Martha Jane, Charles Grant. BA, Princeton U., 1936, MA, 1939, PhD, 1941, DLitt (hon.), 1970; BLitt (Rhodes Scholar), Oxford U., Eng., 1938; DPhil (hon.), Free U. Berlin, 1983; HHD (hon.), Ball State U., 1984; DHL (hon.), Wake Forest U., 1988. Instr. history Yale U., New Haven, 1939-41; from instr. to prof. history Princeton U., N.J., 1941-61; prof. history Stanford U., Calif., 1961—, J.E. Wallace Sterling prof. humanities, 1969-79, J.E. Wallace Sterling prof. humanities emeritus, 1979—; prof. history Free U. Berlin, 1962—. Author: The Politics of the Prussian Army, 1640-1945, 1955, From Bismarck to Adenauer: Aspects of German Statecraft, 1958, Europe Since 1815, 1961, Europe Since 1815, 6th edit., 1983, The Battle of Königgrätz, 1964, War, Politics and Diplomacy: Selected Essays, 1966, Treitschke's History of Modern Germany, 1975, Economic Interest, Militarism and Foreign Policy: Essays of Eckart Kehr, 1977, Germany, 1866-1945, 1978, The Germans, 1982, Force and Statecraft: Diplomatic Problems of Our Times, 1983, The End of Prussia, 1984, Geld und Geist: Zürich im Zeitalter des Liberalismus, 1830-1896, 1988, The Triumph of Liberalism: Zürich in the Golden Age 1830-1869, 1989, Die Politik der Unpolitischen: Deutsche Schriftsteller und die Macht, 1770-1870, 1993, The Politics of the Unpolitical: German Writers and the Problem of Power, 1770-1871, 1995, Ueber Fontane, 1997, Theodor Fontane, Literature and History in the Bismarck Reich, 1999, Politics and Culture in Modern Germany: Essays From The New York Review of Books, 1999; assoc. editor, contbr.: Makers of Modern Strategy, 1943, Makers of Modern Strategy from Machiavelli to the Nuclear Age, 1986; joint editor, contbr.: The Diplomats, 1919-1939, 1953, The Diplomats, 1939-79, 1994; contbr. Geneva, Zurich, Basel: History, Culture and National Identity, 1994. Hon. mem. Berlin Hist. Commn., 1975—; polit. analyst Office Strategic Svcs., Dept. State, Washington, 1941-43; pub. mem. Fgn. Svc. Selection Bd., 1948-49; cons. U.S. Arms Control and Disarmament Agy., 1964-68; adv. coun. USAF Acad., 1968-73; adv. bd. USMC Hist. Sect., Washington, 1972-74. Capt. USMC, 1944-46. Named Hon. fellow, Balliol Coll., Oxford U., 1989; recipient Historikerpreis, Stadt Münster, Fed. Republic Germany, 1982, comdr.'s cross Legion of Merit, Fed. Republic Germany, 1984, Goethe medal, Goethe Inst., Fed. Republic Germany, 1987, Polit. Book prize, Ebert Stiftung, 1988, Max Geilinger prize, Max Geilinger Found., Zurich, 1991, Benjamin Franklin/Wilhelm von Humboldt prize, German-Am. Acad. Coun., 1999; fellow Guggenheim Found., 1969—70, 1982—83. Fellow Ctr. for Advanced Study in the Behavioral Scis., Bayerische Acad. Schönen Künste, Brit. Acad.; mem. Am. Acad. Arts and Scis., Am. Philos. Soc., Am. Hist. Assn. (pres. 1983), Internat. Com. Hist. Scis. (1st v.p. 1975-85), Coun. of Scholars of Libr. of Congress, Order pour le Merite fur Wissenschaften und Kunste (Germany), Phi Beta Kappa. Democrat. Presbyterian. Home: 451 Oak Grove Ave Apt B-2 Menlo Park CA 94025-3269 E-mail: professorgacraig@earthlink.net.

CRAIG, GREGORY BESTOR, lawyer, former government official; b. Norfolk, Va., Mar. 4, 1945; s. William Gregory and Lois (Bestor) C.; m. Margaret Davenport Noyes, July 27, 1974; children: William Eliot, Eliza Noyes, Margaret Bestor, Mary Duncan, James Gregory. AB magna cum laude, Harvard Coll., 1967; diploma in historical studies, Cambridge U., 1968; JD, Yale U., 1972. Bar: D.C. 1972, U.S. Ct. Appeals (D.C., 2d, 3d, 4th, 6th, 7th and 11th cirs.), U.S. Supreme Ct. Assoc. Williams Connolly & Califano, Washington, 1972-74; asst. fed. pub. defender U.S. Dist. Ct. Conn., 1974-76; assoc. Williams & Connolly, Washington, 1977-78, ptnr., 1979-84; sr. advisor on fgn. policy and def. Sen. Edward M. Kennedy, Washington, 1984-88; ptnr. Williams & Connolly, Washington, 1989-97; dir. Office of Policy and Planning Dept. of State, 1997—98, asst. to pres. and spl. counsel, 1998—99; ptnr. Williams & Connolly, Washington, 1999—. Tchr. trial practice Yale Law Sch., 1975-76, Harvard Inst. Trial Advocacy, 1980-84; chmn. Internat. Human Rights Law Group, 1989-96. Trustee Overseas Devel. Coun., 1993-96; vice chmn. Carnegie Endowment for Internat. Peace, 1990-97, 99—, Robert F. Kennedy Meml., 1989-97, 99—, Fgn. Student Svc. Coun., 1990-96, Mexican-Am. Legal Def. and Edn. Fund, 1995-97. Recipient John Harvard Scholar, Emmanuel Coll. Cambridge U., 1967—68. Mem. ABA, Phi Beta Kappa. Avocations: mountain climbing, hiking. Office: Williams & Connolly 725 12th St NW Washington DC 20005-5901 Office Phone: 202-434-5000. Personal E-mail: gcraig@wc.com.

CRAIG, HAROLD KENT, mechanical contracting executive, systems analyst; b. Columbus, Ohio, Nov. 21, 1956; s. Harold Harding and Mildred Annie (King) C.; m. Cathy M. Preslar, Nov. 19, 1979 (div. Sept. 2000); 1 child, Brian Scagel; m. Liann Craig Tabor, Oct. 24, 2000 (div. Dec. 2004); m. Kristi Linn Servies Rigg, May 14, 2005. Student, Goddard Coll., 1979. Lic. plumbing, boiler making, air conditioning, forced warm air heating; spl. elec. lic.; cert. exam proctor. V.p., project mgr. Craig Plumbing Co., Inc., Raleigh, N.C., 1972-95; v.p., project mgmt., sys. analyst Confluence Tech., Raleigh, NC, 1976—; sr. systems analyst Datasonix Inc., Smithfield, NC, 1980—83; heating, ventilation, air cond., plumbing and mech. cons. Valley Constrn. Co., Inc., Koslusco, Miss., 1985-86; sr. project mgr. and estimator Sneeden Mechanical Contractors, Inc., Wilmington, N.C., 1986-88; U.S. bus. agent The Circle Group, Arusha, Tanzania, 1974—; sr. estimator, sr. project mgr. Bay Mech. Inc., Raleigh, 1996—97; sr. project mgr., estimator Atlantic Coast Mech., Inc., Raleigh, 1997-98; sr. estimator, project mgr. Superior Plumbing & Mech., Inc., Wilson, NC, 1998—2003; sr. project mgr., estimator Raleigh Office Novak Mechanical, New Beun, NC, 2003—. Sys. cons. Consulting, Tech., and Design, Inc., Research Triangle Park, N.C., 1988-94; bd. dirs. N.C. Bldrs. Inst., Durham, N.C Author: Yes, the Sun Will Rise, 1979; editor Joe's Bozart mag., 1978; mem. editl. bd. In the Steps, 1976-81; contbr. articles to profl. jours.; contbg. editor, Contractor mag., 1998—. Mem. bd. adjustments Town of Cary (N.C.), 1981; mem. bd. Raleigh Artists' Cmty., 1974-79 Mem.: Am. Humanists Assn. (Humanists N.C. chpt. bd. dirs. 1974—81, editor The Tarheel Humanist newsletter 1975—78, named Humanist Adv. 1979). Home: 2008 Passaic Way Apex NC 27523 Mailing: PO Box 4153 Cary NC 27519-4153 Personal E-mail: hkcraig@gmail.com.

CRAIG, JAMES HICKLIN, fine arts consultant; b. Chester, S.C., July 23, 1937; s. John Edward and Una Bee (Martin) C. Student, U. S.C., 1955-56, Cin. Coll. Conservatory Music, 1956-59, Juilliard Sch. Music, 1960, Paris, 1960. Curator decorative arts N.C. Dept. Archives & History, Raleigh, 1962-64; grantee writing book on N.C. decorative arts Mus. So. Decorative Arts, 1964-65; prin. James Craig Fine & Decorative Arts, 1965-69; pres. Craig & Tarlton, Inc., Raleigh, 1969-85; fine arts cons. Independence, Va., 1985—. Bd. dirs. Sparta Mus. Project, Raleigh Chamber Music Soc., N.Y.C. Chamber Opera Theater, Mint Mus. of Art, Charlotte, trustee 2000—; cons. to N.C. Gov.'s Mansion bd.; mem. acquisitions com. Author: The Arts and Crafts in North Carolina 1699-1840, 1965 (listed by Montgomery as part of 100 best in field). Bd. dirs. Sparta (N.C.) Mus. Project. Avocations: art, antiques, gardening. Office: James Craig Fine Arts PO Box 397 Independence VA 24348-0397 E-mail: jim@jcraigart.com.

CRAIG, JAMES LYNN, physician, health services adminstrator; b. Columbia, Tenn., Aug. 7, 1933; s. Clifford Paul and Maple (Harris) Craig; m. Suzanne Anderson, July 20, 1957; children: James Lynn, Margaret; m. Roberta Annette Craig, May 17, 1980. Ed., Mid. Tenn. State U., 1953; MD, U. Tenn., 1956; MPH, U. Pitts., 1963. Diplomate Am. Bd. Preventive Medicine. Intern U. Tenn. Meml. Hosp., Knoxville, 1957; resident in occupl. medicine U. Pitts., 1962-64, TVA, Chattanooga, 1964-65, physician, 1966-69, chief med. officer, 1969-74; corp. med. dir. Gen. Mills Corp., Mpls., 1974-76, v.p. corp. med. dir., 1976-80, v.p., dir. health and human svcs., 1980-98; adj. clin. prof. U. Minn., Mpls., 1979—, chmn. cmty. adv. com. Ctr. for Environ. and Health Policy, 1994-97, mem. adv. coun. health in scis., 1992-95, chmn. adv. bd. Ctr. for Environ. and Health Policy, 1994-97; pres. Family and Preventive Health Svcs., Inc., Mpls., 1998—. Clin. instr. U. Tenn., Memphis, 1970—74, Meharry Med. Sch., Nashville, 1972—74; mem. adv. bd. to dir. Ctr. Disease Control and Prevention, 1996—99; nat. adv. bd. Internat. Health and Media Awards, 1996—. Contbr. articles to profl. jours. Bd. dirs. Mpls. Blood Bank, 1976—88, Minn. Safety Coun., 1981—90, Minn. Heart Assn., Mpls., 1976—87, Children's Heart Fund, 1976—88, Meth. Hosp. Found., 1979—87, Park Nicolett Med. Found., 1987—93, Altcare, 1983—95, Meth. Hosp. Health Assn., 1987—93, Minn. Wellness Coun., 1986—91, Health Sys. Minn. Assocs., 1993—94, Health Sys. Minn. Inst. Rsch. and Edn., 1996—2000, chmn., 1997—2000, Park Nicollet Inst., 2000—01; trustee Minn. Med. Found., 2001—; bd. dirs. Minn. Bible Coll., Rochester, 1978—83. Named Legacy Laureate, U. Pitts., 2000; recipient Cmty. Svc. award, Park Nicolett Med. Ctr., 1995, Knudsen award in occupl. medicine, Am. Coll. Occupl. and Environ. Medicine, 2000. Fellow: Am. Acad. Family Practice, Am. Acad. Occupl. Medicine (treas. 1982—83, sec. 1983—84, v.p. 1984—85, pres. 1986—87), Am. Occupl. Medicine Assn. (bd. dirs. 1974—78); mem.: AMA (alt. del. Ho. Dels. 1990—92, del. 1992—96, Recognition award 1975, 1978, 1981, 1985, 1989, 1993, 1996, 1999, 2002), Minn. Med. Found. (bd. dirs. 2001—), Emergency Physicians Assn. (bd. dirs. 1984—92), Mpls. Acad. Medicine (sec. 1983—85, pres. 1985—86), Minn. Acad. Medicine, North Ctrl. Occupl. Medicine Assn. (pres. 1977), Occupl. Health Inst. (chmn. 1983—84), Mpls. Kiwanis Club (bd. dirs. 2005—). Home: 10008 S Shore Dr Minneapolis MN 55441-5011 Office: PO Box 270330 Minneapolis MN 55427-6330 Office Phone: 612-669-3847. Personal E-mail: jimlcraig@aol.com. *The activities of my life are based on a balance between quality and acceptance.*

CRAIG, JAMES WILLIAM, physician, educator, dean; b. West Liberty, Ohio, Jan. 23, 1921; s. J. Frank and Clara Helen (Scarborough) C.; m. Helen Catherine Lang, Sept. 18, 1948 (dec.); children: Maribeth, Jon, William, Barbara; m. Wendy Burnip Johnson, June 23, 1972; stepchildren: Steven, Barbara, Philip, Laura Johnson. BS, Western Res. U., 1943, MD, 1945. Intern, asst. resident in medicine Presbyn. Hosp., N.Y.C., 1945-46, 48-50; fellow in medicine Western Res. U. Sch. Medicine, Cleve., 1950-52, from instr. to assoc. prof. medicine, 1952-72; assoc. dean Sch. Medicine U. Va., Charlottesville, 1972-89, prof. medicine, 1972-90, prof. emeritus, 1991—. Condr. research; contbr. articles on diabetes mellitus and intermediary metabolism to publs. Served with AUS, 1946-48. Recipient Lederle med. faculty award, 1962-64 Mem. Am. Inst. Nutrition, Ctrl. Soc. for Clin. Rsch., Med. Soc. Va., Phi Beta Kappa, Sigma Xi, Alpha Omega Alpha. Home: 101 Indian Spring Rd Charlottesville VA 22901-1019 E-mail: jwc9e@virginia.edu.

CRAIG, JAMES WILLIAM, lawyer; b. Manchester, N.H., June 2, 1951; s. William Henry and Felicia Agnes Craig; m. Sharon Elizabeth Moher, June 22, 1973; children: Molly, William. BA, Keene State Coll., N.H., 1973; MA, U. So. Calif., 1980; JD, Franklin Pierce Law Ctr., Concord, N.H., 1983. Bar: N.H. 1973, U.S. Ct. Appeals (1st cir.) 1983. From assoc. to ptnr. Craig, Wenners Craig and Capuchino P.A., Manchester, NH, 1983—; chair Manchester Conduct Bd., 1998—2002, 2004—. Pres. Serenity Pl. D&A Rehab., Manchester, 2000—; commr. Manchester Water Wks., 2001—; rep. NH Ho. of Reps., Concord, 1998—, Dem. leader, 2004—; bd. dirs. Easter Seals, Manchester, 1999—, Greater Manchester Mental Health Ctr., 1999—. Sgt. U.S. Army, 1977—80. Mem.: N.H. Trial Lawyers Assn., Manchester Bar Assn. (past pres.), N.H. Bar Assn., Queen City Rotary. Democrat. Avocations: golf, long distance running. Home: 233 Linden St Manchester NH 03104 Office: Craig Wenners Craig and Capuchino 84 Bay St Manchester NH 03104

CRAIG, JENNY, human services manager; b. New Orleans; d. James Yoric Guidroz and Gertrude Acosta; m. Sid Craig, 1979; children: Denise, Michele. Worked for Silhouette/Am. Health gym; owner Healthetic gym; from mgr. to nat. dir. ops. Body Contour, Inc.; co-founder Jenny Craig Inc., Australia, 1983—, entered US marketplace in LA, 1985, sold company, 2002. Achievements include providing a comprehensive weight mgmt. prog. designed by registered dietitians, psychologists and a med. adv. bd. to grow into one of the largest weight mgmt. cos. in the world; only weight mgmt. co. listed on N.Y. Stock Exch. Office: Jenny Craig Inc 5770 Fleet St Carlsbad CA 92008-4700

CRAIG, JOHN BRUCE, former ambassador, air transportation executive; BS, American U. With Sr. Fgn. Svc., dep. chief of mission, with Bur. Near Eastern Affairs Washington, dir. jr. officer divsn. Bur. of Pers., dir. Office of Arabian Peninsula Affairs, amb. Sultanate of Oman, 1998—2001; spl. asst. to Pres., mem. Nat. Security Council, sr. dir. for combating terrorism White House, Washington, 2001—03; v.p., Middle East internat. rels. Boeing Co., 2003—. Office: Boeing Company 100 N Riverside Plz Chicago IL 60606-1596*

CRAIG, JOHN TUCKER, economist, consultant; b. Bklyn., June 17, 1926; s. Clarence Tucker and Rena (Stebbins) C.; m. Ruth Doris Weiler, Aug. 5, 1950; children: Daniel, Thomas, Andrew, Paul. BA, Oberlin Coll., 1948; MPA, Princeton U., 1950; postgrad., Tufts U., 1966-67. With AID, 1950-80, program officer Tunis, Tunisia, 1967-68, Kathmandu, Nepal, 1968-71, internat. rels. officer Latin Am. Bur. Washington, 1971-74, program officer Port-au-Prince, Haiti, 1974-78, asst. dir. Georgetown, Guyana, 1978-80; cons. Silver Spring, Md., 1980-83; economist for agr. survey U. Md./Rwanda Agrl. Ministry, Kigali, Rwanda, 1983-86; chief party Assocs. in Rural Devel., Proje Sove Te, Burlington, Vt. and Camp Perrin, Haiti, 1988-90; cons. Washington, 1986—. Part-time fgn. affairs officer Freedom of Info., Dept. State. Editor: Haiti: Development Assistance Program, 1976, Guyana: Country Development Strategy Statement, 1980. With USN, 1944—46. Recipient Superior Honor Award, AID, 1980. Mem.: Am. Econ. Assn. Methodist. Avocations: hiking, swimming. Home and Office: Apt 502 4200 Massachusetts Ave NW Washington DC 20016-4752 Personal E-mail: johntcraig@comcast.net.

CRAIG, KERN WILLIAM, political science professor; b. Grand Island, Nebr., Jan. 19, 1946; s. Arthur E. and Marian E. Craig; m. Stacy J. Hazle, June 27, 1981; 1 child, Daniel A. BSc, Calif. State U.; MBA, Fairleigh Dickinson U.; PhD, U. Miss. Lic. contractor, ins. agt., Calif; registered Nat. Assn. Securities Dealers. With bus. mgmt. depts. various banks and oil cos., Calif., 030with; with Dept. Def.; mem. faculty U. Ark., Fayetteville, U. Miss., Oxford, U. Nebr., Omaha, U. No. Ala., Florence. Author: Empirical Tests of Dependency Theory, 1996, Policy Studies and Developing Nations, Vol. 6, 1999. Mem. Am. Polit. Sci. Assn., Soc. Exploration Geophysicists, Nat. Assn. Life Underwriters, ACLU, NRA, Profl. Assn. Diving Instrs., Am. Quarter Horse Assn., Am. Paint Horse Assn., Amnesty Internat. Libertarian. Episcopalian. Avocations: scuba diving, water-skiing, caribbean sailing, riding horses, playing tennis. Office: Wesleyan Coll Dept of Bus and Econ 4760 Forsyth Rd Macon GA 31210

CRAIG, L. CLIFFORD, lawyer; b. Ohio, Aug. 29, 1938; Student, Stanford U., 1957-59; BA, Duke U., 1961, LLB, 1964. Bar: Ohio. Ptnr. Taft, Stettinius & Hollister, Cin., 1971—. Fellow Am. Coll. Trial Lawyers; mem. ABA, Ohio Bar Assn., Cin. Bar Assn. Office: 425 Walnut St Ste 1800 Cincinnati OH 45202-3957 Office Phone: 513-381-2838. Business E-Mail: craig@taftlaw.com.

CRAIG, LARRY EDWIN, senator; b. Council, Idaho, July 20, 1945; m. Suzanne Craig; 3 children. BA, U. Idaho; postgrad, George Washington U. Farmer, rancher, Midvale area, Idaho; mem. Idaho Senate, 1974-80, 97th-101st Congresses from 1st Dist. Idaho, 1981-90, U.S. Senate, 1990—, mem. com. on judiciary, com. energy and natural resources, spl. com. on aging, vets. affairs, appropriations, chmn. subcom. on forests and pub. land mgmt., chmn. subcom. water and power. Chmn. Idaho Rep. State Senate Races, 1976-78, chmn. senate steering com.; mem. joint econ. com., com. veterans' affairs, subcom. energy R & D. Pres. Young Rep. League Idaho, 1976-77; mem. Idaho Rep. Exec. Com., 1976-78; chmn. Rep. Ctrl. Com. Washington County, 1971-72; advisor vocat. edn. in pub. schs. HEW, 1971-73; mem. Idaho Farm Bur., 1965-79. Served with U.S. Army N.G., 1970-72. Mem. NRA (bd. dirs. 1983—), Future Farmers of Am. (v.p. 1965). Republican. Methodist. Office: US Senate 520 Hart Senate Office Bldg Washington DC 20510-0001*

CRAIG, MARY LAURI, accountant; b. Helena, Mont., Jan. 19, 1936; d. Henry and Hilma (Newman) Lauri; m. William Craig (div. 1982); children: Nona Marie, Lauri Sue. BS cum laude, Rocky Mtn. Coll., 1973. CPA. Acct. various firms, Billings, Mont.; sole practice CPA Billings, 1973-78; dir. Mont. Dept. Revenue, Helena, 1979-81; sole practice CPA Helena, 1982—. Commr.'s adv. group IRS, Washington, 1994-96; exec. com. Multi-State Tax Commn., Denver. Co-author: Adventure Bound in Montana. Mem. Am. Soc. Women Accts. (pres. chpt. 100 1976), Mont. Soc. CPAs. Avocations: fly fishing, gold mining, woodworking, watercolors, music. Home and Office: 408 N Washington St Helena MT 59601-3911

CRAIG, PATRICIA, voice educator, opera singer; b. Kew Gardens, N.Y., July 21, 1943; d. William A. and Dorothy H. Duncklee; m. Donald E. Craig, July 23, 1966 (div. 1976); m. Richard Cassilly. BS in Music Edn., Ithaca Coll., 1965; postgrad., Manhattan Sch. Mus. Prin. artist N.Y.C. Opera, 1971-81, Met. Opera, 1978-91. Voice tchr. New Eng. Conservatory Music; condr. master classes various locations; advisor Longwood Opera; chair bd. overseers Opera Boston. Operatic debut as Marenka in The Bartered Bride, Met. Opera, 1978; appeared in Madama Butterfly, Carmen, La Boheme, I Pagliacci, The Rise and Fall of the City of Mahagonny, Les Dialogues des Carmelites, Pique Dame, Turandot, Peter Grimes, La Rondine, Zaza, Un Ballo in Maschera; appeared in maj. opera houses around the world. Home: 77 Pond Ave #1504 Brookline MA 02445 Office: New England Conservatory 290 Huntington Ave Boston MA 02115-5018 E-mail: casamaeda@aol.com.

CRAIG, PAUL MAX, JR., retired lawyer; b. Munich, Aug. 8, 1921; came to U.S., 1941; naturalized, 1944; s. Paul Max and Helen A. Craig; m. Leonie R. Hildebrand, June 26, 1962; children: Anthony P., Claudine A., Stephen P. BS in Elec. Engring., Worcester (Mass.) Poly. Inst., 1946; LLB, Georgetown U., 1950; LLM, George Washington U., 1952. Bar: D.C. 1950. Patent examiner U.S. Patent Office, Washington, 1946-50; patent advisor Office Chief Ordnance, Dept. Army, Washington, 1950-52; pvt. practice Washington, 1952—; ptnr. Craig & Antonelli (and predecessor firm), Washington, 1967-82, Craig & Burns, Washington, 1982-86, Barnes & Thornburg, Washington, 1986-88, Paul M. Craig, P.C., Washington, 1989-97; of counsel Dow, Lohnes & Albertson, 1989-92, affiliated with, 1992-95; of counsel Birch, Stewart, Kolasch & Birch, Falls Church, Va., 1995-97; pvt. practice Silver Spring, Md., 1998—; ret., 2005—. With USNR, 1944-46. Mem. Am., Inter-Am. bar assns., Am. Patent Law Assn., Assn. Internat. Pour la Protection de la Propriete Indsl., Licensing Execs. Soc., Am. Soc. Internat. Law, Assn. Trial Lawyers Am. Home: 207 Quaint Acres Dr Silver Spring MD 20904-2715 E-mail: pmcraig@starpower.net.

CRAIG, ROBERT H., historian, educator; s. Robert Hugh and Marion Grace Craig; m. Gail Marie Peterson, Aug. 3, 1963; children: R. Andrew, Ian Thomas. BA, U. Calif., 1964; MDiv, Union Theol. Sem., 1968; PhD, Columbia U., 1971. Philosophy instr. U. Maine, Orono, Maine, 1971—74; vis. asst. prof. Bucknell U., Lewisburg, Pa., 1976—78; vis. prof. Universidad Nacional de Costa Rica, Heredia, Costa Rica, 1978—82; vis. assoc. prof. Bucknell U., Lewisburg, Pa., 1983—86; asst. prof. Coll. of the Holy Cross, Worcester, Mass., 1986—90; assoc. prof. Mt. Union Coll., Alliance, Ohio, 1990—96; chair, prof. of history and internat. studies, dept. chair Coll. of St. Scholastica, Duluth, Minn., 1996—. Mem. Fulbright Bd., 2003—05. Author: Religion and Radical Politics, Protestantismo y Liberalism en America Latina; contbr. articles numerous profl. jours. (various literary awards). Recipient James A. Gathering Lectureship in Internat. Polit. award, Bucknell U., 1989; Joseph L. Blau fellowship, Columbia U., 1973-1974, Wye ellow, 1992, Summer Seminar grant, Am. Indian Ethnohistory, U. of Okla., NEH, 1995. Mem.: Bd. of the Minn. Chpt. of the Fulbright Assn. (bd. mem. 2003—04), Am. Hist. Assn. Home: 2408 Greysolon Rd Duluth MN 55812 Office: Coll St Scholastica Dept Hist 1200 Kenwood Ave Duluth MN 55811-4199 Office Phone: 218-723-6256. Office Fax: 218-723-6290.

CRAIG, SUSAN LYONS, library director; b. Barksdale Air Force Base, La., Feb. 23, 1948; BA, Trinity Coll., Washington, 1971; MSLS, Fla. State U., 1976; MBA, Rosary Coll., 1989. Pub. svcs. libr. St. Mary's Coll., Moraga, Calif., 1976-79; head pub. svcs. Hood Coll., Frederick, Md., 1979-85, Dominican U. (formerly Rosary Coll.), River Forest, Ill., 1985-87; dir. libr. Aurora (Ill.) U., 1987-97; dir. libr. and acad. info. svcs. Trinity Coll. Libr. (now Trinity U.), Washington, 1997—. Adj. assoc. prof Rosary Coll. Grad. Sch. Libr. and Info. Sci., 1990-97. Mem. ALA, Assn. Coll. and Rsch. Librs. (nat. adv. com., rep. Ill. chpt. 1991-95), Pvt. Acad. Librs. of Ill. (pres. 1994-96), Ill. Libr. Assn. (del. pre-White House Conf., Chgo., 1989-90), Beta Phi Mu, Phi Eta Sigma (hon.). Office: Trinity Univ Libr 125 Michigan Ave NE Washington DC 20017-1091 E-mail: Susancraig23@yahoo.com.

CRAIGHEAD, HAROLD G., physicist, educator; BS, U. Md., 1974; PhD, Cornell U., 1980. Mem. tech. staff Bell Telephone Labs., Holmdel, N.J., 1979-84; rsch. mgr. Bell Comms. Rsch., Red Bank, N.J., 1984-89; prof. Cornell U., Ithaca, NY, 1989—, dir. Sch. Applied and Engring. Physics, 1998—2000, dir. Naniobiotech. Ctr., 2000—01, 2002—, dean of engring., 2001—02. Dir. Nat. Nanofabrication Facility, Ithaca, 1989-95. Contbr. articles to profl. jours. Office: Cornell U Dept Applied Physics Clark Hall Ithaca NY 14853

CRAIGHEAD, JOHN EDWARD, pathology educator; b. Pitts., Aug. 14, 1930; s. Samuel Judson and Madeleine Rose (Schmalz) C.; m. Dorothy Ellen Ford, July 29, 1957 (div. July 1992); 2 children; m. Christina Ann Canon, Aug. 29, 1992; 7 children. BS, U. Utah, 1952, MD, 1956. Diplomate Am. Bd. Pathology, Nat. Bd. Med. Examiners (mem. pathology com. 1978-81). Intern ward med. svc. Barnes Hosp., St. Louis, 1956-57; jr. asst. resident in pathology Peter Bent Brigham Hosp., Boston, 1960-61, sr. asst. resident, 1961-62, chief resident, 1962-65, assoc. in pathology, 1965-68; asst. prof. pathology Harvard U. Med. Sch., Boston, 1963-66, assoc. prof., 1966-68, U. Vt. Coll. Medicine, Burlington, 1968-69, prof., 1969-72, chmn. dept. pathology, 1974-90. Attending physician Med. Ctr. Hosp. Vt., Burlington, 1970-94, Fletcher Allen Health Care, Burlington, 1995—; Harry B. Harding meml. lectr. Evanston (Ill.) Hosp., 1981; 4th ann. Karl Sohlberg lectr. U. Ill., 1981; Finlayson seminar lectr. McGill U., Montreal, Que., Can., 1987; George Hoyt Whipple lectr. U. Rochester, N.Y., 1989; assoc. mem. Commn. Viral Infections, Armed Forces Epidemiol. Bd., 1966-68; mem. adv. com. on infectious diseases Nat. Inst. Allergy and Infectious Diseases, 1971-75; mem. pathology A study sect. NIH, 1984-86, mem. nat. adv. environ. health scis. coun., 1985-89; mem. adv. com. Registry Comparative Pathology, Armed Forces Inst. Pathology, 1993-96; mem. Vt. Regional Cancer Ctr., 1988-91; mem. med. sci. adv. bd. Juvenile Diabetes Found., 1978-80; mem. residency rev. com. for pathology Accreditation Coun. for Grad. Med. Edn., 1979-83, vice chmn., 1982-84; dir. sci. program, chmn. environ. pathology task force Univs. Assoc. for Rsch. and Edn. in Pathology, 1991-98; mem. pulmonary panel Am. Registry Pathology, 1992-98. Editor: The Pathology of Environmental and Occupational Disease, 1995; mem. editl. bd. Lab. Investigation, Archives Pathology and Lab. Medicine, Human Pathology, Am. Jour. Pathology, 1980-92; contbr. numerous articles and abstracts to med. jours., chpts. to books. Surgeon USPHS, 1957-60. Recipient David Rumbough sci. award, U. Ill., 1976, Moses Barron award, Twin Cities Diabetes Assn., 1977; spl. fellow NIH, 1963; travel fellow Royal Soc. Medicine, 1971. Mem. AAAS, AMA (mem. coun. sci. affairs, mem. adv. panel on asbestos related diseases, chmn. 1982-83), Am. Acad. Pathology, Am. Assn. for Cancer Rsch., Am. Assn. Pathologists, Am. Soc. Clin. Pathologists (mem. basic sci. rsch. symposium com. 1978-82, H.P. Smith Meml. award 1987), Am. Thoracic Soc., Assn. Pathology Chairmen (past sec.-treas., v.p., pres. 1981-82), Internat. Acad. Pathology (councillor 1980-84), Coll. Am. Pathologists (mem. environ. resource com. coun. on pathology practice 1980-81), Am. Soc. for Virology, New England Soc. Pathologists (pres. 1980-81), Mass. Soc. Pathologists (mem. exec. com. 1967), Vt. Med. Soc., Chittenden County Med. Soc. Avocation: horticulture.

CRAIGHEAD, OWEN LINDSAY, writer; b. Cross River, NY, Aug. 30, 1934; d. Robert Feuchter Craighead and Alice Wilson; m. Janice Lee Rankin, Jan. 23, 1954; children: Carol Lee Yugovich, Thomas Wilson, Lauren Lindsay, William Owen. Owner Craighead Kennels, Cross River, NY; radio talk show host WGHQ, Kingston, NY; author and owner Crunk Publishing, Lubbock, Tex.; editor and founder Tom's E-zine for Am. Awareness. Author: (book) Skydivers Flying with their Pants, 1999, The Way It Is, Is, 2002, One of God's Salesmen, 2003, (advisory pamphlet) Home Buyer, Be Aware, 2003; prodr.(and dir.): (video) Skydiving, The New Frontier, 2003; author: (book) The Lethal Liberal Society in America, 2004. Vol. fireman South Salem Fire Dept., 1952—89, chmn., bd. fire commn., 1984—89; founder Lewisboro Vol. Ambulance Corp., 1977, pres., 1977—79, Lewisboro Lions Club, 1975—76; zone chmn. Saugerities Lions Club, 1992—93; sec. South Plains Lions Club, 2000—01; bulletin editor Lubbock Habitat for Humanity, 1999—2004; rep. candidate Lewisboro Town Bd., 1972; committeeman Lewisboro Rep. Com., 1977—85. Recipient Citizen of the Yr., Lewisboro C. of C., 1984, Lion of the Yr., Lewisboro Lions Club, 1984, Appreciation award, US Army Parachute Team Golden Knights, 1999. Mem.: Lewisboro Vol. Ambulance Corp. (life), South Salem Fire Dept. (life), Lions Internat. (life). Home: 8114 Temple Ave Lubbock TX 79401

CRAIGHEAD, RODKEY, banker, director; b. Pitts., July 24, 1916; s. Ernest S. and Florence L. (Rodkey) C.; m. Carol M. Price, June 26, 1943 (dec. June 1978); children: Rodkey, Virginia, Corinne; m. La Verne Hastings, Mar. 1979. BS, U. Pitts., 1942; postgrad., Grad. Sch. Banking, U. Wis., 1959-61. With Mellon Nat. Bank, Pitts., 1936-41; with Detroit Bank & Trust Co., 1946—, v.p., 1961-67, sr. v.p., 1967-69, exec. v.p., 1969-73, dir., 1971—, pres., 1974—, chmn., CEO, 1977—; pres., dir. Detroitbank Corp., 1974-81, chmn., CEO, 1977-81. Served to capt. AUS, 1942-46. Mem. Collier County Forum Club, Royal Poinciana Golf Club, Naples Athletic Club. Presbyterian. Home: 100 Glenview Pl #607 Naples FL 34108

CRAIGIE, JAMES R., consumer products company executive, former sports equipment apparel company executive; With General Foods and Kraft divsn. Phillip Morris, exec. v.p., pres. Beverage and Desserts divsn.; pres., CEO Spalding Sports Worldwide, Chicopee, Mass., 1998—2004, Church & Dwight Co., Inc., Princeton, 2004—. Mem.: bd. dirs., Church & Dwight Co., 2004-. Office: Church & Dwight Co Inc 469 N Harrison St Princeton NJ 08543-5297

CRAIL, FRANKLIN E., food products executive; b. N. Mex. married; 7 children. Student, San Diego State U. Systems analyst CIA; co-founder, pres. CNI Data Processing, Newport Beach, Calif.; co-founder Rocky Mountain Chocolate Factory, Durango, Colo., 1981; CEO, pres., dir. Rocky Mountain Chocolate Factory Inc., 1982—, chmn., 1986—. Dir. Volunteers of Am. Colo., 1994. Military intelligence, Vietnam War. Named one of fastest growing small public companies, Fortune mag., 2005. Office: Rocky Mountain Chocoloate Factory Inc 265 Turner Dr Durango CO 81301*

CRAIN, GAYLA CAMPBELL, lawyer; b. Cleburne, Tex., June 13, 1950; d. R. C. and Marilyn Ruth (McFadyen) Campbell; m. Howard Leo Crain, May 27, 1978; 1 child, Robert Leo. BA, Baylor U., 1972, JD, 1974. Bar: Tex. 1974, U.S. Dist. Ct. (no., ea., we., and so. dists.) Tex., U.S. Ct. Appeals (5th cir.) 1988, U.S. Ct. Appeals (10th cir.) 1994, U.S. Supreme Ct. 1999, U.S. Supreme Ct. 1999. Asst. counsel Trailways, Inc., Dallas, 1975-79; counsel Schering Plough, Inc., Kenilworth, NJ, 1979—81; assoc. Epstein Becker Green Wickliff & Hall, P.C., Ft. Worth, 1985-86, ptnr. Dallas, 1986—. Contbg. author: State by State Guide to Human Resources Law, 1990, 91; editl. adv. bd. Employee Rels. Law Jour., Tex. Employment Law, 1998. Trustee Dallas Bapt. U., 1989-97, 98—. Office: Epstein Becker Green Wickliff & Hall 500 N Akard St #2700 Dallas TX 75201-3306

CRAIN, JOHN WALTER, historian, educator; b. Amarillo, Tex., July 11, 1944; s. John Clyde and Roma (McDowell) C.; m. Mary Hemingway, Aug. 18, 1973; children: John Matthew, Sarah Hemingway, Margaret Aileen. BA, U. Tex., Austin, 1966; MA, S.W. Tex. State U., 1970; cert. arts adminstrn., Harvard U., 1975; cert. mus. mgmt., U. Calif.-Berkeley, 1979. Dir. Star of the Republic Museum, Washington-on-the-Brazos, Tex., 1971-76, Dallas Hist. Soc., 1976-90; chmn. Dallas County Hist. Commn., 1993-95. Cons. in field. Exec. dir. Summerlee Commn. on Tex. History, 1990-91; v.p., bd. dirs. program History Summerlee Found., Tex., 1990—, pres., 2004—; bd. dirs. Dallas County Hist. Found., Friends of Gov.'s Mansion; mem. adv. bd. Clements Ctr., So. Meth. U. Mem. Tex. State Hist. Assn. (hon., coun. 1994, exec. com., pres.), Conf. of S.W. Founds. (bd. dirs.), Tex. Map Soc. (bd. dirs., pres.), Philos. Soc. Tex. Methodist. Office: 5956 Sherry Ln Ste 610 Dallas TX 75225-8017

CRAIN, LINDA EARGLE, retired elementary school educator; b. Columbia, S.C., Apr. 7, 1947; d. Oscar Lawrence and Betty Anne (Johnson) Eargle; BA, U. S.C., 1969, MEd, 1979; 1 child, Melanie Denise. With Credit Bur. of Columbia, 1965-67; with Sears Roebuck & Co., Columbia, 1967-69; tchr. Irmo (S.C.) Elem. Sch., 1969-72, 74-80; tchr. Nursery Rd. Elem. Sch., Columbia, 1980-2001, ret., 2001; with Promissor Corp., 2003-04; receptionist State Farm Ins., 2004—. Named Tchr. of Yr., Nursery Rd. Elem. Sch., 1984. Mem. NEA, Irmo Chapin Edn. Assn. (past pres., v.p., sec.-treas., del.), S.C. Edn. Assn. (constitution com.). Ind. Baptist. Home: 313 Conover Rd Columbia SC 29210-3700 Office Phone: 803-781-7819.

CRAIN, MARY ANN, elementary school educator; b. Dallas, Sept. 5, 1951; d. Robert Lee and Mary Ann (T.) Crain. MusB in Edn., Fla. State U., 1973; MusM, Ohio State U., 1974; EdS, U. Ga., 1998. Cert. tchr. T-6, music, early childhood edn., mid. grades, ednl. leadership Ga. First clarinet Vienna Kursalon Orch., Vienna, 1975—77; band dir. Sch. Bd. of Broward County, Ft. Lauderdale, Fla., 1977—78; teller Fla. Coast Bank, Coral Springs, Fla., 1978—79; strings tchr., grades 6-7 DeKalb County Bd. of Edn., Decatur, Ga., 1979—82, band tchr., grades 6-7, 1982—86, classroom tchr., grades 4-7, 1986—96, math. specialist, grades 2-5, 1996—2000, early intervention math. and reading specialist, grades 2-5, 2000—02; math. specialist, grades K-5 Bethesda Elem. Sch., Lawrenceville, Ga., 2002—. Mem.: Phi Delta Kappa (chpt. v.p. for membership). Office: Bethesda Elem Sch 525 Bethesda Sch Rd NW Lawrenceville GA 30044 Personal E-mail: corkgrease@msn.com.

CRAIN, MARY TOM, volunteer; b. Vernon, Tex., Aug. 27, 1918; d. Samuel Asa Leland and Mary Verna (Johnson) Morgan; m. David Rasco, Dec. 24, 1941 (dec. Apr. 1955); children: Sarah M. Rasco Thomas, Mary Prudence Rasco Courtney; m. Sam H. Crain, Sept. 17, 1975 (dec. June 1980). Student, Stephens Coll., 1936-38, U. Tex., 1938-39; BS, U. Wis., 1941. Tchr. Williams Bay (Wis.) Schs., 1941; reporter Amarillo (Tex.) Globe News, 1957-65; exec. sec. Potter-Randall County Med. Soc., Amarillo, 1960-69; ret., 1969. Mem. lay adv. bd. St. Anthony's Hosp., Amarillo, 1957; mem. devel. bd. High Plains Hosp., 1995; coun. pres. Girl Scouts U.S., Amarillo, 1953-55; pres. Jr. League, Amarillo, 1956; bd. dirs. Amarillo Symphony, Art Mus., Panhandle Plains Hist. Soc., Amarillo Area Found., 1945—, Llano Cemetary; mem. City of Amarillo Park and Recreation Commn.; bd. dirs. Amarillo Coll. Found., Amarillo Pub. Libr., Art Force. Named Amarillo's Woman of yr., Beta Sigma Phi, 1955; named to Amarillo H.S. Hall of Fame, 1971. Methodist. Home: 3206 Amberwood Ln Amarillo TX 79106

CRAIN, VICTORIA LYNNE, nursing administrator; d. John Smith Crain and Carol Elaine Kohnfelder. BA in Psychology, Duquesne U., 1983; BSN, Duquesne U., 1988. Lic. psychiat. mental health nurse, ANA. Staff nurse Western Psychiat. Inst. and Clinic, Pitts., 1988—90, asst. nurse clin. mgr., 1990—93; clin. supr. Allegheny Neuropsychiat. Inst. and Clinic, Pitts., 1993; program mgr. Allegheny Neuropsychiat. Inst., Pitts., 1993—94; psychiat. team coord. Allegheny Gen. Hosp., Pitts., 1994—. Owner Pitts. Legal Nurse Consulting, 2004—. Child adv. Ct. Apptd. Spl. Adv., Pitts., 2001—05. Mem.: Am. Assn. of Legal Nurse Cons., Internat. Soc. Psychiat. Mental Health Nurses, Sigma Theta Tau. Avocations: gardening, hiking, swimming. Home: 109 Valonia St Pittsburgh PA 15220 Office: Pitts Legal Nurse Consulting 109 Valonia St Pittsburgh PA 15220 Office Phone: 412-921-7969. Personal E-mail: vcrn@comcast.net.

CRAINE, DALE THOMAS, music educator, department chairman; b. Wawautisa, Wis., Mar. 13, 1947; s. Larry and May Craine. BS in Music Edn., DePaul U., 1971; MA, Roosevelt U., 1986. Adminstr. Whittier/Hammond Elem., Chgo., 1971—79; dir. bands Farragut H.S., Chgo., 1979—80, Curic H.S., Chgo., 1980—2001; dir. bands, dept. chair Kelly H.S., Chgo., 2001—. Dir. All City Jazz Band, Chgo., 2003—. Musician: Chgo. Pops Wind Ensemble, 1990—. Mem.: Music Educators Nat. Conf., Chgo. Band Dir. Assn., Musician Union, Chgo. Tchrs. Union, Phi Beta Mu, Beta Phi Mu. Office: Kelly High Sch 4136 S California Ave Chicago IL 60632

CRAINE, THOMAS KNOWLTON, not-for-profit developer; b. Utica, N.Y., Apr. 19, 1942; s. Donald Holmes and Marjorie (Knowlton) C.; m. Susan Lynda Moseley, Dec. 21, 1966; children: Matthew Moseley, Tish Marjorie. BA, U. Rochester, 1964; MEd, SUNY, Buffalo, 1966, EdD, 1972. Dir. architecture and planning SUNY, Buffalo, 1968-72, asst. to pres., 1972-76, clin. assoc. prof., 1975-83, asst. v.p. acad. affairs, 1976-79; exec. v.p., assoc. prof. D'Youville Coll., Buffalo, 1979-83; pres. Loretto Heights Coll., Denver, 1983-88; v.p. instl. advancement and planning Iliff Sch. Theology, Denver, 1988-98; pres./CEO YMCA Met. Denver, 1998—2002, pres. emeritus, 2002—03; dir. N. Am. Urban Group of YMCA, 2003—. Evaluator North Cen. Assn. Instns. Higher Edn., 1984—, Assn. Theol. Schs., 1993—; cons. in strategic planning, bd. devel., fund raising. Mailing: YMCA of the USA 101 N Wacker Dr Chicago IL 60606 E-mail: tom.craine@ymca.net.

CRAKES, GARY MICHAEL, economics professor; b. Southington, Conn., July 2, 1953; s. Harry Fremont and Frances Katherine (Koth) C.; m. Deborah Jean MacArthur, Aug. 14, 1976; children: Andrew David, Jeffrey Alan, Timothy Scott. BA in Econs., Ctrl. Conn. State U., 1975; MA in Econs., U. Conn., 1976, PhD in Econs., 1984. Rsch. asst. Health Ctr. U. Conn., Farmington, 1976-79, vis. prof. Health Ctr., Sch. Dental Medicine, 1988, instr. Hartford, 1979-80; asst. prof. So. Conn. State U., New Haven, 1980-85, assoc. prof., 1985-89, prof., 1989—, chmn. dept. econs. and fin., 1991-96. Pres. Maher, Crakes & Assocs., Cheshire, Conn., 1987—; econ. expert witness. Contbr. articles to profl. jours. Mem. State of Conn. Sr. Economist Exam. Com., Hartford, 1987. Richard D. Irwin fellow Irwin Publ. Co., Homewood, Ill., 1983-84, U. Conn. fellow, 1983; recipient Univ. Tchr. of the Yr. award, 1987, Schs. of Bus. Outstanding Tchg. award, 1998; honored for pro bono work on behalf of World Trade Ctr. victim families, Assn. of Trial Lawyers of Am., 2004. Mem. AAUP, Am. Econ. Assn., Ea. Econ. Assn. Nat. Assn. Forensic Econ., Omicron Delta Epsilon (chpt. advisor). Democrat. Avocations: family activities, golf, fishing. Home: 860 Ward Ln Cheshire CT 06410-3363 Office: So Conn State U 501 Crescent St New Haven CT 06515-1330 Office Phone: 203-272-1205. Personal E-mail: gmcrks@aol.com.

CRAMBLETT, HENRY GAYLORD, pediatrician, virologist, educator; b. Scio, Ohio, Feb. 8, 1929; s. Carl Smith and Olive (Fulton) C.; m. Donna Jean Reese, June 16, 1960; children: Deborah Kaye, Betsy Diane. BS, Mt. Union Coll., 1950; MD, U. Cin., 1953. Diplomate Am. Bd. Pediatrics, Am. Bd. Microbiology, Am. Bd. Med. Specialists. Intern in medicine Boston City Hosp., Harvard Med. Svc., 1953-54; resident in pediatrics Children's Hosp., Cin., 1954-55; clin. rsch. assoc. Nat. Inst. Allergy and Infectious Diseases, Clin. Ctr., Bethesda, Md., 1955-57; chief resident, instr. dept. pediat. State U. Iowa, Iowa City, 1957-58, faculty, 1957-60, asst. prof., 1958-60; faculty Bowman Gray Sch. Medicine, 1960-64, prof. pediat., 1963-64, dir. virology lab., 1960-64; prof. pediat. Ohio State U., Columbus, 1964-95, prof. med. microbiology, 1966-95, exec. dir. Children's Hosp. Rsch. Found., 1964-73, chmn. dept. med. microbiology, 1966-73, dean Coll. Medicine, 1973-80, acting v.p. for med. affairs, 1974-80, v.p. health scis., 1980-83, Warner M. and Lora Kays Pomerene chair in medicine, 1982-95, assoc. to v.p. health svcs., to dean and prof. emeritus, 1984-95. Mem. Ohio State U. bd. trustees Cancer Hosp. Oversight Com., 1991-96, mem. Ohio Med. Bd., sec. 1984-92, past pres.; hosp. surveyor Joint Com. on Accreditation of Health Care Orgns., 1985-95; chmn. com. on cert., subcert. and recert. Am. Bd. Med. Specialists; mem. coms. on written exam., comprehensive qualifying evaluation program Nat. Bd. Med. Examiners; mem. Accreditation Coun. Continuing Med. Edn., chmn., 1980-83, 93-94, also mem. fin. com., 1993—, mem. strategic plan implementation com., 1993—, mem. external monitoring com., 1993—; mem. adv. com. on undergrad. med. evaluation; mem. Fedn. State Med. Bds., pres., 1976-82 (mem. Flex bd. 1983-91, chmn. 1985-91), mem. fin. audit com., 1991; chmn. Fed. Exam. Bd., 1991-92, cons., 1992—; mem. composite com. Fedn. of State Med. Bds. and Nat. Bd. of Med. Examiners, U.S. Med. Licensing Exam., 1990-96; Fedn. of State Med. Bds. observer Clin. Skills Assessment Alliance, 1990-95; bd. dirs. Ohio State U. Hosp., 1979-80; dir. med. and postgrad. med. edn. King Faisal Specialist Hosp., Riyadh, Saudi Arabia, 1983-84; mem. strategic planning task force CSAA, 1992-94; med. dir. Columbus Health Plan, 1995—. Trustee Children's Hosp. Rsch. Found., 1973-84, Children's Hosp., 1973-84, Children's Hosp., Inc., 1982-84. Recipient Hoffheimer prize U. Cin., 1953, Eben J. Carey award in anatomy, 1950, Rsch. Career Devel. award NIH, 1961-63; Henry G. Cramblett chair in medicine established at Ohio State U., 1988; Henry G. Cramblett Hall dedicated at Ohio State U., 1999. Fellow Am. Acad. Microbiology, AAAS; mem. So. Soc. Pediatric Rsch. (past pres.), Soc. Pediatric Rsch., Am. Pediatric Soc., Am. Acad. Pediat., Midwest Soc. Pediatric Rsch., Soc. Exptl. Biology and Medicine, Am. Soc. Microbiology, Alpha Omega Alpha. Achievements include research, publs. on medical licensure, medical staff hospital standards, etiologic assn. virus infections in illnesses of infants and children, estimation of importance of various viruses in morbidity and mortality in pediatric age group. Home: 2480 Sheringham Rd Columbus OH 43220-4274 Office: Ohio State U 1024 Cramblett Hall 456 W 10th Ave Columbus OH 43210-1240

CRAMER, BETTY F., life insurance company executive; b. Indpls., Dec. 9, 1920; d. Frank E. and Ethelyn L. (Jackson) C. BA, Butler U., 1943. Sec. to head pers. dept., payroll acct. Am. United Life Ins. Co., 1943-51; Sec. to v.p. and treas. Indpls. Life Ins. Co., 1951-69, supr. bond and stock acctg., 1969-75, securities asst., 1975-81, sec.-treas., 1981-89, ret., 1989. Advisor Jr. Achievement, Indpls., 1959-60; campaign chmn. United Way, 1980 Mem. Nat. Assn. Corp. Treas., Life Ins. Women's Assn. Indpls. (past v.p., pres.) Republican. Roman Catholic. Avocations: swimming, reading, travel. Home: 5158 N Central Ave Indianapolis IN 46205-1060

CRAMER, CHARLES LEONARD, economics educator; b. Chamois, Mo., Oct. 30, 1928; s. Charles C. and Matilda (Wenger) C.; m. Julia M. Koch, June 11, 1955; children: Christine, Keith, Caroline. BS, U. Mo.-Columbia, 1950, MS, 1954, PhD, 1960. Mem. faculty dept. agrl. econs. U. Mo., Columbia, 1960—92, chmn. dept., 1971-82, prof. agrl. econs., 1982—88, assoc. dean Coll. Agr., Food and Natural Resources, 1989—92. Served with U.S. Army, 1950-52. Mem. Am. Agrl. Econs. Assn. Lodges: Kiwanis. Presbyterian. Home: 309 Defoe Dr Columbia MO 65203-0209

CRAMER, DALE LEWIS, retired economics professor; b. Dixon, Ill., June 25, 1924; s. Ray C. and Rebecca (Levan) C.; m. Hula Jean Bond, Aug. 30, 1946; children: Becky Cramer McCarn, Craig Alan, Randall Scott. BS, Bradley U., 1949, MA, 1951; PhD, La. State U., 1958. Asst. prof. econs. La. State U., 1953-54, U. Tex.-El Paso, 1955-57, assoc. prof., 1957-58; assoc. prof. econs. U. Ala., 1958-63, prof., 1963-88, prof. emeritus econs., 1988—, head dept., 1968-72, acting head dept., 1981-82. Contbr. articles to profl. jours., books. Served with AUS, 1943-46. Earhart Found. fellow, 1954-55 Mem. Am., So. econ. assns., AAUP, Omicron Delta Epsilon, Beta Gamma Sigma. Home: 103 Riverdale N Tuscaloosa AL 35406-1818

CRAMER, DENNIS F., music educator, freelance/self-employed musician; b. McKeesport, Pa., Mar. 10, 1953; s. Robert T and Ruth V Cramer; m. Elizabeth A Michaliszyn, May 1, 1954. BS in Music Edn., Ind. U. of Pa., 1975, MA in Music, 1982. Permanent cert. music K-12 Dept. of Edn. Pa., 1979. Dir. of bands Ford City H.S., Pa., 1977—; prin. trombone Butler County Symphony Orch., Pa., 1986—. Music dir. Armstrong Concert Band, Kittanning, Pa., 1984—; trombonist, arranger, composer Ind. U. Pa. Trombone Choir, 1996—; trombonist Armstrong Brass Quintet, Kittanning, 1996—; instr. Pa. Trolley Mus., Washington, 1995—. Author: Trolleys of Armstrong County, Pennsylvania, 2000, Docent Manual for Pennsylvania Trolley Museum, 2001; host (TV films) Pennsylvania Cable Network Visits the Pennsylvania Trolley Museum, 1999, contbr. Pennsylvania Trolley Museum Calendar, 2001—; composer: (songs) Collected Works for Brass Quintet, 2003, Collected Works for Concert Band, 2004, (songs) Collected Works for Multiple Trombone, 2005; dir.: Public Concerts of Armstrong Concert Band, 1984—; contbr. articles to newspapers and jours. Mem. East Franklin Zoning Commn., Kittanning, Pa., 1980—90; pres. Armstrong Concert Band, Kittanning, 1998—2005. Served with US Army, 1975—75. Recipient Vol. in the Arts Award, WQED Multi-Media Pitts., 2001. Mem.: NEA, Armstrong County Band Dirs. Assn., Pa. Edn. Assn., Pa. Music Educators Assn. (bd. mem. 1988—90, dist. 3 pres. 1988—90), Am. Fedn. of Musicians, Internat. Trombone Assn., Music Educators Nat. Conf., Armstrong Edn. Assn., Pa. Trolley Mus., Phi Mu Alpha Sinfonia (life). Republican. Presbyterian. Avocations: photography, history. Home: 510 Sherwood Drive Kittanning PA 16201 Office: Ford City High School 1100 Fourth Avenue Ford City PA 16226 Office Phone: 724-763-5289. Personal E-mail: alto_trombone@hotmail.com. Business E-Mail: crad@asd.k12.pa.us.

CRAMER, DOUGLAS SCHOOLFIELD, broadcasting executive; b. Louisville, Aug. 22; s. Douglas Schoolfield and Pauline (Compton) C.; m. Joyce Haber, Sept. 25, 1966 (div. 1973); children: Douglas Schoolfield, III, Courtney Sanford. Student, Northwestern U., 1949-50, Sorbonne, Paris, 1951; BA, U. Cin., 1953; MFA, Columbia U., 1954. Prodn. asst. Radio City Music Hall, NYC, 1950-51; with script dept. Metro-Goldwyn-Mayer, 1952; mng. dir. Cin. Playhouse, 1953-54; instr. Carnegie Inst. Tech., 1955-56; TV supr. Procter & Gamble, 1956-59; broadcast supr. Ogilvy, Benson & Mather, 1959-62; v.p. program devel. ABC, 1962-66, 20th Century-Fox-TV, LA, 1966-68; exec. v.p. in charge prodn. Paramount TV, 1968-71; ind. producer, pres. Douglas S. Cramer Co., 1971—; exec. v.p. Aaron Spelling Prodns., 1976-87, vice-chmn., 1988-90. Exec. prodr.: Star Trek, 1968-69, Bridget Loves Bernie, CBS-TV, 1972-73, QB VII, 1973-74, Dawn: Portrait of a Teenage Runaway, NBC-TV, 1976, Danielle Steel's Fine Things, 1990, Kaleidscope, 1990, Changes, 1991, Daddy, 1991, Palomino, 1990-91, Secrets, 1991, Heart Beat, 1992, Star, 1993, Message to Nam, 1993, Vanished, 1995, Family Album, 1994, Perfect Stranger, 1994, No Greater Love, 1995, Mixed Blessings, 1995, Zoya, 1995, Family of Cops I & II, CBS-TV, 1995-96, The Ring, 1996, Remembrance, 1996, Full Circle, NBC-TV, 1996, Family of Cops III, 1999; co-exec. prodr.: Love Boat, ABC, 1977-86, Vegas, ABC, 1978-81, Wonder Woman, ABC, 1975-77, CBS, 1977-78, Dynasty, 1981-89, Hotel, 1983-87, Trade Winds, 1993; prodr.: (feature film) Sleeping Together, 1995; author: (plays) Call of Duty, 1953, Love Is A Smoke, 1957, Whose Baby Are You, 1963, Last Great Dish, 1994, Lust For Murder, 1995. Pres. Mus. Contemporary Art, LA, 1990-93, 1st vice-chair, 1993-96: bd. trustees, 1983-96; Internat. Coun. Mus. Modern Art, NYC, 1993—; pres., bd. trustees Douglas S. Cramer Found., 1993—; trustee MOMA NY, 1993—. Named one of Top 200 Collectors, ARTnews Mag., 2004. Mem. Univ. Club of NYC, Beta Theta Pi. Avocation: collector of contemporary art, especially 1960s & 1980s Am. Address: PO Box 713 Lakeville CT 06039-0713 Office: 160 E 72d St New York NY 10021*

CRAMER, EDWARD MORTON, lawyer, music company executive; b. N.Y.C., May 27, 1925; s. Israel and Elsie (Neuman) C.; m. Henrietta Pantel, 1973 (div.); children: Evin Joyce, Marjorie Sue, Charles Harris; m. Ethel Metzger, June 13, 1982. BA, Columbia U., 1947; LLB with distinction, Cornell U., Ithaca, N.Y., 1950; LLM, NYU, 1953; HHD (hon.), Lincoln (Ill.) Coll., 1982; LHD (hon.), Five Towns Coll., N.Y., 1998. Bar: N.Y. 1950, U.S. Supreme Ct. 1953. Teaching fellow NYU Sch. Law, 1950-51; assoc. Rosenman & Colin, N.Y.C., 1951-58; ptnr. Cramer & Hoffinger, N.Y.C., 1958-68; pres., CEO, Broadcast Music, Inc. (BMI), 1968-86; pvt. practice, N.Y.C., 1986—. Treas. Copyright Soc. U.S., 1963-68, 78-79, bd. editors bull., 1953-63; former mem. Peabody Awards Selection Com.; editor Cornell Law Quar. Trustee Congregation Adas Emuno; former trustee Tony Martell Found., Ford's Theater. Jr. grade lt. USNR, 1943—46. Recipient Spl. award Songwriters Guild Am., 1986, Spl. award Am. Composers Alliance, 1987, Spl. Peabody award, 1991; named Personality of Yr. Nat. Arts Club, 1972; Ed Cramer Day named in his honor, N.Y.C., 1979. Mem.: ABA (copyright com.), Practising Law Inst., Nat. Acad. Popular Music (trustee, bd. dirs. 1969—93, founding mem. Songwriters Hall of Fame, adv. com.), Internat. Confedn. Authoral Socs. (adminstrv. coun.), Broadcast Pioneers (pres. 1984, officer, bd. dirs. 1984—97), Nat. Music Coun. (v.p. 1968—86), Assn. Bar City NY (copyright com.), B'nai B'rith (pres. 1989—90, trustee, officer, pres. music and performing arts unit, Man of Yr. award 1979), Order of Coif. Jewish. Home: 254 Chestnut St Englewood NJ 07631-3134 Office: 110 E 59th St New York NY 10022-1304 Office Phone: 212-421-3350. *I'm not a creatively talented person but working with people who are, has given me a sense that I have shared their accomplishments.*

CRAMER, GAIL LATIMER, economist; b. Walla Walla, Wash., Sept. 27, 1941; s. Lawrence Theodore and Myrtle Pauline (Latimer) C.; m. Marilyn Jean Karlenberg, Aug. 31, 1963; children: Karilee, Bruce. BS, Wash. State U., 1963; MS, Mich. State U., 1964; PhD, Oreg. State U., 1968. Asst. prof. Mont. State U., Bozeman, 1967-72, assoc. prof., 1972-76, prof., 1976-86; L.C. Carter prof. U. Ark., Fayetteville, 1987-2000; prof., dept. head La. State U., 2000—. Vis. prof. Harvard U., Cambridge, 1974-75, Winrock Internat., Morrilton, Ark., 1980-81, U. Calif. Berkeley, 1993, Ohio State U., Columbus, 1994; bd. dirs. Internat. Agrl. Mgmt. Assn. Co-author: Grain Marketing, 1993, Agricultural, Economics and Agribusiness, 1997; editor Am. Agrl. Econs. Assn. Jour., 1999-2002. Bd. dirs. ARC, Bozeman, 1982-83, Bozeman Kiwanis Club, 1972-86 (Disting. Pres. 1983); mem. White House Agrl. commn. Washington. Recipient E.G. Nourse award, Am. Inst. Coop., Washington, 1968, Communication award, Am. Agrl. Econs. Assn., 1980, Rice Rsch. award, Tech. Workers, Little Rock, 1992, 1998, SAEA Lifetime Achievement award, 2002. Fellow: IAMA; mem.: Nat. Assn. Agrl. Econ. Administrators (pres. 2004—), Gamma Sigma Delta Internat. (Dist. Achievement Agrl. award). Avocations: basketball, running, writing. Office: La State U Dept Agrl Econs Baton Rouge LA 70808 Home: 13735 Clarendon Dr Baton Rouge LA 70810-3584 Business E-Mail: gcramer@agcenter.lsu.edu.

CRAMER, GRAYCE ELIZABETH, elementary school educator; b. Allegan, Mich., Dec. 14, 1945; d. Kenneth Murray and Doris Elizabeth Driver; m. Harry E. Cramer (div.); children: Julia Marie, Paul Allen, Rebekah Annette. BS summa cum laude in edn., Inda. U. Pa., 1991. Cert. tchr. Pa., 1991, collegiate profl. lic. Va., 1992. Libr. Hallstead Christian Acad., Hallstead, Pa., 1975—86; tchr. Northumberland Co. Pub. Sch., Heathsville, Va., 1992—2005, child study chair, 1999—2005. Cpt., relay for life team Am. Cancer Soc., Northumberland County, Va., 2000—05; mem. Team March of Dimes, Lancaster County, Va., 2002—05, Sherwood Forest Shores Assn. Bd. of Dirs., Reedville, Va., 2005. Mem.: Alpha Delta Kappa (historian 2004—06, recording sec. 2000—04). Bapt. Avocations: crocheting, gardening, reading, scrapbooks, walking. Home: 248 Berkshire Dr Reedville VA 22539 Office: Northumberland Elem Sch 757 Academic Ln Heathsville VA 22473 Office Phone: 804-580-8032. E-mail: graycecramer@wmconnect.com.

CRAMER, H. R. (HAL CRAMER), oil industry executive; BS in indsl. engring., Syracuse U., N.Y.; MBA, SUNY, Albany. With Mobil Oil, 1973; pres. Mobil South Inc.; v.p., Pacific Rim Mobil Corp., v.p. Europe Africa Mid. East mktg. and refining divsn., 1996—98; exec. v.p. and CFO Mobil Corp. (merged with Exxon), 1998—2000; v.p. Exxon Mobil Corp., 2000—; pres. ExxonMobil Fuels Mktg. Co., 2000—. Mem. exec. com. Mobil Oil. Office: Exxon Mobil Fuels Mktg 3225 Gallows Rd Fairfax VA 22037

CRAMER, HAROLD, lawyer; b. Phila., June 16, 1927; s. Aaron Harry and Blanche (Greenberg) C.; m. Geraldine Hassuk, July 14, 1957; 1 dau., Patricia Gail. AB, Temple U., 1948; JD cum laude, U. Pa., 1951. Bar: Pa. 1951. Law clk. to judge Common Pleas Ct. No. 2, 1953; mem. law faculty U. Pa., 1954; assoc. firm Shapiro, Rosenfeld, Stalberg & Cook, 1955-56, ptnr., 1956-67, Meslrov, Gelman, Jaffe & Levin, 1967-74, Mesirov, Gelman, Jaffe & Cramer, Phila., 1974-77, Mesirov, Gelman, Jaffe, Cramer & Jamieson, Phila., 1977-89, of counsel, 1996-2000; ret. ptnr. Schnader, Harison Segal & Lewis, 2000—; CEO Grad. Health System, Phila., 1989-96. Instr. Nat. Inst. Trial Advocacy, 1970-78; pres. Jewish Exponent, 1987-89, Times., 1987-89. Co-author: Trial Advocacy, 1968; contbr. articles to profl. jours. Chmn. bd. Eastern Pa. Psychiat. Hosp., 1974-81, Grad. Hosp., 1975-91; trustee Fedn. Jewish Agys., Jewish Publ. Soc., pres., 1996-98, chmn., 1998-2001. 1st lt. U.S. Army, 1951-53. Decorated Bronze Star. Fellow Am. Bar Found., Phila. Coll. Physicians; mem. ABA, Am. Law Inst., Pa. Bar Assn. (ho. of dels. 1966-75, 78—, bd. govs. 1975-78), Phila. Bar Found. (pres. 1988, trustee, pres. elect), Phila. Bar Assn. (bd. govs. 1967-69, chmn. 1969, vice chancellor 1970, chancellor 1972, editor The Shingle 1970-72, medal for extraordinary svc. to the bar 2003), U. Pa. Law Alumni Soc. (bd. mgrs. 1959-64, pres. 1968-70), Order of Coif (past chpt. pres., nat. exec. com. 1973-76), Tau Epsilon Rho (chancellor Phila. grad. chpt. 1960-62), Philmont Country Club, Pyramid Club, Greate Bay Golf Club. Home: 728 Pine St Philadelphia PA 19106-4005 Office: Schnader Harrison Segal & Lewis 1600 Market St Ste # 34 Philadelphia PA 19103-7501 Office Phone: 215-751-2312. Business E-Mail: hcramer@schnader.com.

CRAMER, HOWARD ROSS, geologist, environmental consultant; b. Chgo., Sept. 17, 1925; s. Don William and Esther Natalia (Johnson) C.; m. Ardis V. Lahann, Dec. 15, 1950 (dec. 1980); m. Themis Poulos, Dec. 5, 1982 BS (with honors), U. Ill., 1949, MS, 1950; PhD, Northwestern U., 1954. Registered geologist, Ga. Mem. faculty Franklin and Marshall Coll., 1953-58; asst. prof. geology Emory U., Atlanta, 1958-62, assoc. prof., 1962-76, prof., 1976-87, chmn. dept., 1981-87; cons. geology Ga. State U., Atlanta, 1988-91. Chmn. Ga. Bd. Registration Geologists, 1977-79; mem. Ga. Natural Areas Council, 1968-72. Contbr. articles to profl. jours., chapters to books. Served with AUS, 1943-46, to lt. USAR, 1948-53. Decorated Bronze Star; recipient Holgate prize Northwestern U., 1953, Cert. Commendation, Am. Assn. State and Local History, 1974, Honor award Am. Fedn. Mineralogy and Lapidary Socs., 1986. Fellow Geol. Soc. Am.; mem. Am. Assn. Petroleum Geologists, Nat. Assn. Geology Tchrs. (pres. Southeastern sect. 1971-73), Ga. Acad. Sci. (pres. 1964-65), Lambda Chi Alpha. Lodges: Ahepa. Greek Orthodox. Home: 2047 Deborah Dr NE Atlanta GA 30345-3917 Personal E-mail: hcramer@emory.edu.

CRAMER, JAMES DALE, physicist, scientific company executive; b. Canton, Ohio, Aug. 4, 1937; s. Dale and Vera Arlene (Lindower) C.; m. Geraldine M. Bendoski, July 20, 1957; children: Karen Lynn, Eric James. BS, Calif. State U., Fresno, 1960; MS, U. Oreg., 1962; PhD, U. N.Mex., 1969. Mem. tech. staff U. Calif., Los Alamos, 1962-70; v.p. Davis-Smith Corp., San Diego, 1970-73; mem. tech. staff Sci. Applications, Inc., LaJolla, Calif., 1970-73, group v.p. Albuquerque, 1973-80, dir., 1974-80; pres. Sci. & Engring. Assocs., Inc., Albuquerque, 1980—. Cons. in field; pres. Albuquerque Mus. Found., 1981-83. Contbr. articles to profl. pubs. Mem. Am. Phys. Soc., IEEE. Home: PO Box 30691 Albuquerque NM 87190-0691 Office: 6100 Uptown Blvd NE Ste 700 Albuquerque NM 87110-4174

CRAMER, JAMES PERRY, management strategist, architectural author, educator; b. Aberdeen, S.D., Aug. 7, 1947; s. Harry John and Carol B. (Bickel) C.; m. Corinne M. Aaker, Dec. 21, 1969; children: Ryan James, Austin Michael. BS, No. State U., Aberdeen, 1969; MA, St. Thomas U., St. Paul, 1974; planning cert., U. Minn., Mpls., 1976; bus. mgmt. cert., Wharton Sch. Bus., U. Pa., 1987. Dir., teaching faculty U. Minn., Mpls., 1974-76; dir. St. Louis Park Community Svcs., Minn., 1976-78; exec. v.p. Minn. Soc. Architects, Mpls., 1978-82; pres., chief exec. officer AIA Svc. Corp., Washington, 1982-86, also bd. regents; pres. Greenway Comms. Inc., 1994—. Pres. Am. Archtl. Found. and Octagon Mus., Washington, 1986-89; CEO AIA, Washington, 1989-94; group pub. Architecture Mag., 1982-88, pub. chmn., 1990-94; with Archtl. Tech. Mag., 1983-89; chmn. The Greenway Group; pres. Greenway Comm. Inc., 1994—; adj. prof. U. Hawaii Sch. Arch., 1999—. Pres. Coun. Archtl. Components, Washington, 1980-81; pres. Greenway Civic Assn., McLean, Va., 1986-88; trustee Nat. Bldg. Mus., Washington, 1989-94; chmn. Washington div. United Way Assn., 1992; White House liaison, 1988-95. Recipient Disting. Alumnus award No. State U., 1992, medal of Distinction, U. Minn., 1994; Richard Upjohn fellow; leadership fellow Western Behavioral Scis. Inst., 1998-. Mem. AIA (hon.; chmn. 1981-82, CEO 1989—, Spl. award 1982), Am. Soc. Assn. Execs. (cert. assn. exec.), Mag. Pubs. Am., Octagon Soc. (life hon.), Am. Archtl. Found. (life; pres. 1986-89, regent 1981-82, 86—), Am. Design Coun. (founder, bd. dirs. 1988-95), Soc. Archtl. Historians (bd. dirs. 1994-97), Design Futures Coun. (chmn. 1994—). Avocations: gardening, tennis, antiquarian books, design. Home: 2320 Littlebrooke Dr Dunwoody GA 30338-3156 Office: 30 Technology Pkwy S Ste 200 Norcross GA 30092-2925

CRAMER, JIM, online financial information executive; b. Feb. 1955; married. B in Govt., Harvard U., 1977; JD, Harvard Law Sch., 1984. Reporter Am. Lawyer, 1979-83; broker Goldman, Sachs & Co., NYC, 1984-87; founder Cramer & Co., NYC, 1987—2000; co-founder thestreet.com, NYC, 1996—, dir., market commentator, adv. to CEO, 2001—. Market's commentator CNBC's Squawk Box; co-host Am. Now; co-founder SmartMoney mag. Contbr. to NY mag.; author: Confessions of a Street Addict, 2002, You Got Screwed! Why Wall Street Tanked and How You Can Prosper, 2002. Office: thestreet.com 14 Wall St 15th Fl New York NY 10005

CRAMER, JOHN MCNAIGHT, lawyer; b. Lewistown, Pa., Sept. 23, 1941; s. John Mumma and Elaine Elizabeth (McNaight) C.; m. Susan Oakman, Nov. 26, 1966 (div. Mar. 1989); children: Natalie, Daniel, Melinda; m. Kay Stephenson, Apr. 8, 1989; children: Julia, Maria. AB, Juniata Coll., 1963; LLB, Harvard Law Sch., 1966. Bar: Pa. 1968. Law clk. U.S. Dist. Ct. So. Dist. N.Y., 1966-67; assoc. Reed Smith Shaw & McClay, Pitts., 1967-76, ptnr., 1976—2002, of counsel, 2002. Advocacy fellow Dickinson Sch. Law, Pa. State U., Carlisle, Pa., 1987-2002. Mem. editl. staff: Harvard Law Rev. Trustee Juniata Coll., Huntingdon, Pa., 1981—, sec., 1983—96, vice chair, 1996—97, chair, 1997—2001; bd. dirs. Ctrl. Pa. Food Bank, 1996—2001. Democrat. Home: Box 17 Old Trail Rd New Buffalo PA 17069 E-mail: crmfrm@earthlink.net.

CRAMER, KRISTEN M., music educator; b. Fort Benning, Ga., Aug. 19, 1969; d. Anthony C. and Linda M. Martin; m. William D. Cramer. BMus, Centenary Coll. La., 1991; MEd, La. State U., 1994. Cert. lifetime tchr. cert. Tex., 1991, adminstrv. cert. Tex., lifetime tchr. cert. La., 1991. Dir. choir Woodlawn H.S., Baton Rouge, 1991—95, Boswell H.S., Fort Worth, Tex., 1997—. Accompanist Broadmoor United Meth. Ch., Baton Rouge, 1993—95; pvt. instr., Fort Worth, 1995—; staff accompanist Tex. Christian U., Fort Worth, 1996—99; pvt. piano and voice instr. Master's Touch Sch. Music, Grapevine, Tex., 1997—; asst. mus. dir. First United Meth Ch., Baton Rouge, 1991—93. Singer: stage, TV, comml. jingles, 1993. Mem.: Tex. Gilbert and Sullivan Soc., Fort Worth Music Tchrs. Assn., Gospel Music Assn., Tex. Music Educators Assn., Nat. Assn. Tchrs. Singing. Republican. Avocations: exercise, singing, acting.

CRAMER, MARVIN EDWARD, internist, cardiologist; b. Wilmington, Dela., Dec. 27, 1943; MD, Jefferson Med. Coll., 1969. Diplomate Am. Bd. Internal Medicine, Am. Bd. Cardiology. Intern St. Lukes Med. Ctr., N.Y.C., 1969-70, resident in medicine, 1970-71, 73-74; fellow in cardiology Columbia-Presbyn. Med. Ctr., N.Y.C., 1974; pvt. practice Manhasset, N.Y. Assoc. attending physician North Shore Hosp., Manhasset; asst. prof. medicine NYU. Fellow Am. Coll. Cardiology; mem. AMA. Office: 450 Plandome Rd Manhasset NY 11030-1943

CRAMER, OWEN CARVER, classics educator; b. Tampa, Fla., Dec. 1, 1941; s. Maurice Browning and Alice (Carver) C.; m. Rebecca Jane Lowrey, June 23, 1962; children: Alfred, Thomas, Ethan, Benjamin AB, Oberlin Coll., 1962; PhD, U. Tex., 1973. Spl. instr. U. Tex., Austin, 1964-65; instr. in classics Colo. Coll., Colorado Springs, 1965-69, asst. prof. classics, 1969-75, assoc. prof. classics, 1975-84, M.C. Gile prof. classics, 1984—, dir. comparative lit., 1993—2002. Cons. humanist Colo. Humanities Program, Denver, 1982-83; vis. prof. U. Chgo., 1987-88; reader Advanced Placement Latin Exam., 1995-99; summer faculty Wyo. Humanities Coun. program, 2004; vis. faculty Whyming Humanities Coun. Summer Inst., 2004. Editorial asst. Arion, 1964-65; contbr. papers, articles on Greek lang. and lit. to profl. publs., 1974—; contbr. classical music revs. to Colorado Springs Sun, 1984-86. Chorus tenor Colo. Opera Festival, Colorado Springs, 1976-82; mem. El Paso County Dem. Ctrl. Com., Colo., 1968-88; ordained elder Presbyn. Ch., 1992; mem. alumni coun. Oberlin Coll., 1992-2002. Hon. Woodrow Wilson fellow, 1962; univ. fellow U. Tex., Austin, 1962-64 Mem. Am. Philol. Assn. (campus adv. svc. 1989, chmn. com. on smaller depts. 1979-80), Am. Comparative Lit. Assn., Classical Assn. Middle West and South, Modern Greek Studies Assn., Colo. Classics Assn., Round Table (Colorado Springs) Club,. Phi Beta Kappa. Home: 747 E Uintah St Colorado Springs CO 80903-2546 Office: Colo Coll Dept Classics Colorado Springs CO 80903 Office Phone: 719-389-6443. Business E-Mail: ocramer@coloradocollege.edu.

CRAMER, PHEBE, psychologist; b. San Francisco, Dec. 30, 1935; children: Mara, Julia. BA, U. Calif., Berkeley, 1957; PhD, NYU, 1962. Clin. psychologist Malmonides Hosp., Bklyn., 1962-63; asst. prof. Psychology Barnard Coll., N.Y.C., 1963-65; vis. asst. prof. Psychology U. Calif., Berkeley, 1965-70; assoc. prof. Psychology Williams Coll., Williamstown, Mass., 1970-73, prof. Psychology, 1973—. Pvt. practice in clin. psychology, Williamstown, 1970—; chief psychologist Berkshire Mental Health Ctr., Pittsfield, Mass., 1978-86. Author: (books) Word Association, 1968, Understanding Intellectual Development, 1972, The Development of Defense Mechanisms, 1991, Story-telling, Narrative, and the Thematic Apperception Test, 1996; mem. editl. bd. Jour. of Personality, 1987-96, assoc. editor, 1991-96; mem. editl. bd. Jour. of Personality Assessment, 1989—, European Jour. Personality, 2000—, Jour. Rsch. Personality, 2003—. Judge U.S. Figure Skating Assn., 1989—. Mem.: APA, Soc. Personality and Social Psychology, Soc. for Personality Assessment. Office: Williams Coll Dept Psychology Bronfman Sci Ctr Williamstown MA 01267 Home: 20 Forest Rd Williamstown MA 01267-2029 Business E-Mail: phebe.cramer@williams.edu.

CRAMER, ROBERT E., JR., (BUD CRAMER), congressman, lawyer; b. Huntsville, Ala., Aug. 22, 1947; 1 child, Hollan. BA in English, U. Ala., 1969, JD, 1972. Former prof. U. Ala. Sch. of Law; asst. dist. atty. Madison County, Ala., 1973—75, dist. atty., 1981—91; mem. U.S. Congress from 5th Ala. dist., 1991—. Mem. appropriations com. U.S. Ho. of Reps., subcom. on HUD, VA and IA, on the Interior, NASA. Mem. Nat. Legal Resource Cr. for Child Advocacy & Protection; co-founder Nat. Children's Advocacy Ctr.; adv. bd. mem. Nat. Ctr. for Missing and Exploited Children. Served in U.S. Army, 1972, served in USAR, 1976—78. Mem.: ABA, Ala. Dist. Atty. Assn. Democrat. Methodist. Office: US Ho of Reps 2368 Rayburn Ho Office Bldg Washington DC 20510-0105*

CRAMER, ROBERT VERN, retired college administrator, consultant; b. Fayetteville, Ark., Jan. 6, 1933; s. Paul and Fern (Way); m. M. Joan Sullivan, Sept. 6, 1953; children: Paula Jo, Melinda Kay, John Aaron. BA, Monmouth Coll., Ill., 1954; MA, U. Conn., 1964, PhD, 1965; LHD (hon.), Ill. Coll., 1985, Carroll Coll., 1988. Tchr. Monmouth Jr. HS, 1954—56; prin. Vandalia Elem. Sch., Ill., 1956—57; dir. publicity and publs. Monmouth Coll., 1957—59; dir. publs. and pub. info., also instr. journalism Millikin U., Decatur, Ill., 1959—61; v.p. Old Sturbridge Village, Mass., 1961—64; asst. dean, instr. Sch. Edn., U. Conn., 1964—65; v.p. Hanover Coll., Ind., 1965-68; pres. Northland Coll., Ashland, Wis., 1968—71, Carroll Coll., Waukesha, Wis., 1971—88, pres. emeritus, 1988—. Pres. Brunswick Pub. Charitable Found., Inc., Skokie, Ill., 1985-88; v.p. Wis. Found. Ind. Colls., 1969-71, pres., 1971-73, treas., 1973-76, sec., 1979-83; commr. Commn. Instns. Higher Edn., North Central Assn., 1972-76; v.p. Wis. Assn. Ind. Colls. and Univs., 1973-75, pres., 1985-87; bd. dirs. Payco Am. Corp., 1988-91; Council Ind. Colls, sec. 1979-81, vice chmn., 1981-83, chmn. 1983-85. Contbr. articles to profl. jours. Bd. dirs. Waukesha United Way, 1975-78, Waukesha Symphony, 1972-76, Waukesha Meml. Hosp., 1973-82, Lad Lake Residential Treatment Ctr. for Emotionally Disturbed Boys, 1974-78, Wis. Coun. on Econ. Edn., 1976-79; bd. dirs. Milw. chpt. ARC, 1973-81, vice chmn., 1978-80; mem. nexus com. Presbyn. Coll. Union, 1973-83; bd. dirs. Am. Coun. Edn., 1985-88; sec. Presbyn. Coll. Union, 1977-79, pres., 1979-81; trustee Columbia Coll. of Nursing, 1983-88, Hist. Preservation Soc. Durham, 1993-94; active Durham County Nursing Home Adv. Com., 1991-95, commr. Durham Hist. Preservation Com., 1992-97, Glaxo Welcome Instnl. Animal Care and Use Com., 1992-99. Recipient Outstanding Young Alumnus award Monmouth Coll., 1968, Disting. Alumnus award, 1980; named Ky. Col., 1975. Mem. Wis. Assn. Higher Edn. (exec. com., sec. 1972-73, pres. 1973-74), Delta Sigma Nu, Phi Delta Kappa, Theta Chi. E-mail: rvc-mjc@webtv.net.

CRAMER, SHARON F, education educator; d. Adolph and Gertrude Cramer; m. Leslie R Morris, Mar. 19, 1995. BA, Tufts U., 1970—71; MAT, Harvard U., 1971—72; PhD, NY U., 1973—84. Dir., title iv-c grant Porter County Spl. Edn. Coop., Valparaiso, Ind., 1978—81; dir., young children's program Youth Svc. Bur., Valparaiso, Ind., 1981—82; curriculum developer Shield Inst., Flushing, NY, 1982—85; from mem. faculty Dept. Exceptional Edn. to disting. svc. prof. Buffalo (N.Y.) State Coll., 1985—2005, disting. svc. prof., 2005—. Pres. Northeastern Ednl. Rsch. Assn., 2003; publ. chmn., divsn. of devel. disabilities Coun. for Exceptional Children, Reston, Va., 1997—2001, northeastern regional mem., divsn. of devel. disabilities, 1994—97, pres., NY state fedn. of chapters, NY, 1993—94. Author: (book) Collaboration: A Success Strategy for Special Educators, Student Information Systems: A Guide to Implementation Success. Recipient Burton Blatt Humanitarian award, Divsn. of Devel. Disabilities, Coun. for Exceptional Children, 2003. Mem.: Coun. for Exceptional Children (regional mem., sec. 1986—93, Svc. award, NY State Fedn. 1989), Phi Delta Kappa. Office: Buffalo State Coll 1300 Elmwood Ave Buffalo NY 14222 Office Phone: 716-878-4334.

CRAMER, THEODORE ROBERT, music educator; b. McKeesport, Pa., Mar. 13, 1950; s. Robert Theodore Cramer and Ruth Vivian Cramer (Roberts); m. Cynthia Marie Layfield, June 15, 1974; children: Timothy Theodore, Rebecca Marie. BS in music edn., Ind. U. of PA, 1968—73. PA Teacher Certification Pa., 1973. Band dir. Hampton Twp. Elem. Schools, Allison Park, Pa., 1973—77, Hampton Twp. H.S., 1977—90, Hampton Twp. Mid. Sch., 1990—. Mem. Allegheny Valley Band Directors Assn., Pa., 1977—, No. Area Honors Band Directors Assn., Allegheny County, Pa., 1999—. Mem./elder Plains Presbyn. Ch., Cranberry Township, Pa., 1978—2005; vol. band dir. and counselor Camping Assn. of the Presbyteries of Northwestern PA, Pa., 1973—2005; mem. Wildcat Regiment Civil War Brass Band. Recipient All Star Educator, U. of Pitts. Sch. of Edn., 1990. Mem.: NEA (assoc.), Pa. State Educators Assn. (assoc.), Music Educators Nat. Conf. (assoc.), Pennsylvania Music Educators Assn. (assoc.), Cranberry Twp. Area Lions Club (assoc.; sec.). Presbyn. Avocations: swimming, travel, history. Office Phone: 412-486-6000 x 2014. Personal E-mail: cramer@zbzoom.net.

CRAMER, WILLIAM ANTHONY, biochemistry and biophysics researcher, educator; b. NYC, June 11, 1938; s. Robert and Sylvia (Blumstein) C.; m. Hanni Aebersold, Sept. 11, 1964; children: Rebecca, Jean-Marc, Gabrielle, Nicholas. BS, MIT, 1959; MS, U. Chgo., 1960, PhD, 1965. NSF post doctoral fellow U. Calif., San Diego, 1965-67, rsch. assoc., 1967-68; asst. prof. dept. biol. scis. Purdue U., West Lafayette, Ind., 1968-73, assoc. prof., 1973-78, prof., 1978—, assoc. head dept., 1984-86, Henry Koffler prof. biol. scis. West Lafayette, Ind., 1995-2001, Henry Koffler Disting. prof. biol. scis., 2001—. Head panel predoctoral fellowships in biophysics and biochemistry NSF, 1979, mem. molecular biology panel, 1980-82, mem. cellular biochemistry panel, 1989-91; mem. panel competitive grants USDA, 1983-84; chmn. Gordon Confs. on Photosynthesis, 1990, Bioenergetics, 2001; mem. phys. biochemistry study sect. NIH, 1991-95. Author textbook on bioenergetics; editor: Archives Biochemistry and Biophysics, 1979—91, Biochem. Biophys. Acta, 1983—2003, Photosynthesis Rsch., 1989—98, Jour. Bioenergetics Biomembranes, 1991—, Biophys. Jour., 1999—2005, Biochem. Jour., 2001—04, Jour. Biol. Chemistry, 2002—; Bioenergetics sect. of Biophysics Textbook on-line (Biophysical Soc.), —; contbr. articles to profl. jours. Recipient Rsch. Career Devel. award, NIH, 1970—75, H.N. McCoy award for sci. achievement, Purdue U., 1988, Charles F. Kettering award, Am. Soc. Plant Physiologists, 1996; sr. EMBO fellow, U. Amsterdam, 1974—75, Alexander von Humboldt fellow, Max-Planck Inst., Frankfurt, 1992, John Simon Guggenheim fellow, 1992—93. Mem.: AAAS, Biophys. Soc. (chmn. bioenergetics subgroup 1989—92, organizing com. "Biophys. Discussions" 1992, program chair 40th ann. meeting 1996, coun. 1997—2001, rep. Fedn. Am. Socs. Exptl. Biology com. ethical issues genetic rsch. 1998, exec. coun. 1999—2001, pub. policy com. 1999—2005), Am. Soc. Biochemistry and Molecular Biology. Office: Purdue U Dept Biol Sci Lilly Hall of Life Sciences West Lafayette IN 47907 Office Phone: 765-494-4927. Business E-Mail: waclab@purdue.edu.

CRAMES, MICHAEL J., lawyer; b. NYC, Apr. 20, 1935; s. Paul and Regina (Haicken) C.; m. Elinor Weintraub, July 14, 1957; children: Michele Zenkel, Stefanie Solomon, Leslie Raiuer. BA, Amherst Coll., 1956; JD, NYU, 1961. Ptnr. Levin & Weintraub, Crames & Edelman, NYC, 1961-90, Kaye Scholer LLP, NYC, 1991—, mng. ptnr., 1993—, chmn. exec. com., 1993—97. Spkr. at seminars in field. Author: Fundamentals of Bankruptcy and Corporate Reorganization, 1998; contbr. articles to profl. jours. Recipient Judge Learned Hand Human Rels. award Am. Jewish Com., 1992; named Benjamin Wientraub lectr. Hofstra U. Sch. Law, 1985; honoree Bankruptcy and Reorgn. Group Lawyers Divsn. UJA Fedn., 1993. Mem. Assn. of Bar of City of NY (sec. 1969-71, chmn. bankruptcy and corp. reorgn. com. 1972-75), Fed. Bar Coun., Nat. Bankruptcy Conf. (exec. com. 1981-83), NY County Lawyers Assn., NY State Bar Assn., Westchester County Bar Assn., Am. Coll. Bankruptcy. Avocations: golf, bicycle riding, hiking, reading. Office: Kaye Scholer LLP 425 Park Ave New York NY 10022-3506 Office Phone: 212-836-8415. E-mail: mcrames@kayescholer.com.

CRAMP, LORI ANGELL, finance company executive; b. Kansas City, Mo., Apr. 17, 1955; d. William Greenleaf and Arline (Mullaney) Angell; m. John Stitzer, Aug. 13, 1977; children: Jeffrey William, Chelsea Angell, Trevor John. BA magna cum laude, Franklin & Marshall Coll., 1977; MBA, Harvard U., 1979. Mgmt. cons. Coopers & Lybrand Co., Washington, 1979-80, supr. mgmt. cons., 1980-81; supr. internal cons. Marriott Corp., Washington, 1981-82, mgr. internal cons., 1982-83, mgr. corp. fin., 1983-85, dir. corp. fin., 1985-86, v.p. corp. fin., 1987-89; v.p. project fin., 1990-92; sr. v.p. corp. and project fin. Coded Communications Corp., Carlsbad, Calif., 1994; sr. v.p., treas. Host Marriott Svcs. Corp., Bethesda, Md., 1995-99; exec. dir. Washington Ophthalmological Soc., 2004—. Treas. Churchill Sq. Homeowners Assn., Falls Church, Va., 1983; treas. Painted Rock PTA, 1992-93; mem. Painted Rock Sch. Site Coun., 1992-94, dist. rep. sch. site coun., 1993-94, mem. dist. math. adv. bd. 1994-95; bd. dirs. Marriott Employees Fed. Credit Union, 1996-99; pres. adv. sch. bd. Our Lady of Mercy Sch., 2001-04; bd dirs. Cath. Youth Orgn., Archdiocese Wash., 2002—. Mem. Phi Beta Kappa, Pi Gamma Mu. Avocations: skiing, tennis, in-line skating.

CRAMPTON, STUART JESSUP BIGELOW, physicist, researcher; b. N.Y.C., Nov. 3, 1936; s. Henry Edward and Harriet Elizabeth (Jessup) C.; m. Susan Harris, Dec. 29, 1961; children: David Stuart Jessup, Rebecca Lynn, Alexandra Lee. BA, Williams Coll., 1958; BA with honors, Worcester Coll., Oxford (Eng.) U., 1960, MA, 1965; PhD, Harvard U., 1964. NSF postdoctoral fellow Harvard U., 1964-65; mem. faculty Williams Coll., 1965—, prof. physics, 1975—, Barclay Jermain prof. natural philosophy, 1979—, chmn. dept. physics, 1970-77, chmn. dept. physics and astronomy, 1977-80; dir. Bronfman Sci. Ctr., 1988-90. Vis. prof. U. Paris VI, 1982-83; bd. dirs. Rsch. Corp.; former cons. Hughes Rsch. Labs.; vice chair Coun. on Undergrad. Rsch., 1988-89, chair 89-90, pres. 1990-91; cons. Sherman Fairchild Scientific Equipment Program; mem. bd. assessment physics labs. Nat. Inst. Stds. & Tech., 1994-99; provost Williams Coll., 1995-99. Author papers in field. Recipient NSF Faculty Profl. Devel. award, 1977-78; NATO sr. postdoctoral research fellow, 1975; grantee Nat. Bur. Stds.; grantee NSF; grantee Office Naval Rsch.; grantee NASA; Alfred P. Sloan rsch. fellow, 1967-69. Fellow Am. Phys. Soc. (councillor-at-large 1989-92, award for rsch. at undergrad. instn. 1989); mem. Sigma Xi, Sigma Phi. Episcopalian. Home: 54 Grandview Dr Williamstown MA 01267-2528 Office: Williams Coll Bronfman Sci Ctr 18 Hoxsey St Williamstown MA 01267-2518 Office Phone: 413-597-2247. Business E-Mail: scrampto@williams.edu.

CRAMTON, ROGER CONANT, lawyer, educator; b. Pittsfield, Mass., May 18, 1929; s. Edward Allen and Dorothy Stewart (Conant) C.; m. Harriet Cutter Haseltine, June 29, 1952; children: Ann, Charles, Peter, Cutter. AB, Harvard U., 1950; JD, U. Chgo., 1955; LLD, Nova U., 1980; MA (hon.), Oxford U., 1987. Bar: Vt. 1956, Mich. 1964, N.Y. State 1979. Law clk. to Hon. S.R. Waterman U.S. Ct. of Appeals (2d cir.), 1955-56; law clk. to assoc. justice Harold H. Burton U.S. Supreme Ct., 1956-57; asst. prof. U. Chgo., 1957-61; assoc. prof. U. Mich. Law Sch., 1961-64, prof., 1964-70; chmn. Adminstrv. Conf. of U.S., 1970-72; asst. atty. gen. Justice Dept., 1972-73; dean Cornell U. Law Sch., Ithaca, N.Y., 1973-80, Stevens prof., 1982—2002, Stevens prof. emeritus, 2002—. Mem. U.S. Commn. on Revision Fed. Ct. Appellate Sys., 1973-75; bd. dirs. U.S. Legal Svcs. Corp., 1975-79, chmn. bd., 1975-78; mem. U.S. Commn. on Jud. Discipline and Removal, 1991-93. Co-author: Conflict of Laws, 5th rev. edition, 1993, Law and Ethics of Lawyering, 4th rev. edit., 2005; editor Jour. Legal Edn., 1981-87; contbr. articles to profl. jours. Guggenheim fellow, 1987-88; recipient Rsch. award Am. Bar Found., 2000. Mem. ABA, Am. Law Inst. (council mem.), Assn. Am. Law Schs. (pres. 1985), Am. Acad. Arts and Scis., Order of Coif, Phi Beta Kappa. Congregationalist. Office: Cornell Law Sch Myron Taylor Hall Ithaca NY 14853-4901 Home: 475 Savage Farm DR Ithaca NY 14850-6508 Business E-Mail: rcc10@cornell.edu.

CRANDALL, BLANE MITCHELL, obstetrician, gynecologist; b. Atlanta, Ga., Dec. 4, 1970; s. Blane Milton and Doshie Ruth Crandall; m. Montese Marie Miller, June 12, 1993; children: Greyson Marie, Scarlett Cay. MD, U. Of South Fla., 1993—98. Ob-gyn. resident U. Chgo., 1998—2000, Northshore U., 2000—02; pvt. practice Blane M. Crandall, MD, Clinton, Okla., 2002—. Featured spkr. Symposium On Metal Ions In Biology And Medicine, Barcelona, 1996; vis. rschr. Royal Free Hosp., London, 1996; adj. prof. Southwestern Okla. State U., 2003—. Contbr. articles to profl. jours. Active mem. Noon Lions Club, Clinton, Okla., 2002—; vol. dr. Clinton Free Clinic, Okla., 2002—; bd. mem. Sunnyside Therapeutic Riding Ctr., Clinton, Okla., 2002—. Recipient Most Humanistic Resident, U. Of Chgo. Hospitals, 1999, Outstanding Tchg. award, 2000, Humanism And Excellence In Tchg. award, Arnold P. Gold Found., 2000, Physician's Recognition award, AMA, 2001, 2002, 2003. Fellow: Am. Coll. Of Obstetricians And Gynecologists; mem.: AMA, Soc. Of Med. Educators, Am. Assn. Of Gynecologic Laparoscopists, Nat. Assn. Of Doctors, Okla. State Med. Assn., Custer County Med. Soc. Avocations: travel, golf. Office: Blane M Crandall Md 611 Frisco Ave Clinton OK 73601

CRANDALL, IRA CARLTON, consulting electrical engineer; b. South Amboy, N.J., Oct. 30, 1931; s. Carlton Francis and Claire Elizabeth (Harned) C.; m. Jane Leigh Ford, Jan. 29, 1954; children— Elizabeth Anne, Amy Leigh, Matthew Garrett BS in Radio Engring., Ind. Inst. Tech., 1954, BS in Elec. Engring., 1958; BS in Electronics Engring., U.S. Naval Postgrad. Sch., 1962; PhD, U. Sussex, 1964; MA, Piedmont U., 1967, DSc (hon.), 1968; LLB, Blackstone Sch. Law, 1970; DLitt, St. Matthew U., 1970; EdD, Mt. Sinai U., 1972; Assoc. Bus., LaSalle U., 1975, B in Computer Sci., 1986; D. Internat. Rels., Australian Inst. for Coordinated Rsch., 1991. Tchr. Madison Twp. Pub. Schs., N.J., 1954-55; commd. ensign U.S. Navy, 1955, advanced through grades to lt. comdr., 1965, released to inactive duty, 1972; engring. cons. Concord, Calif., 1972—. Pres. 7C's Enterprises, Concord, 1972-96; v.p. Dickinson Enterprises, Concord, 1972-77, Williamson Engring., Inc., Walnut Creek, Calif., 1974-82; pres., chmn. bd. I.C. Crandall and Assocs., Inc., Concord and Westminster, Calif., Tigard, Oreg., 1976-82; pres. Internat. Rsch. Assocs., Concord, 1982-98; v.p. Gayner Engring. Inc., San Francisco, 1982-92; sr. engr. Ajmani Assoc., San Francisco, 1992-99, Syska and Hennesy, L.A., 1999-02. Vice pres. PTA, Concord, 1969; tribal organizer Mt. Diablo YMCA Indian Guide Program, 1971-74; pres. Mt. Diablo Unified Schs. Interested Citizens. Decorated Vietnamese Cross of Valor Fellow Am. Coll. Engrs.; mem. IEEE, U.S. Naval Inst. Am. Naval Assn., Assn. Elec. Engrs., Am. Inst. Tech. Mgmt. (sr.), Soc. Am. Mil. Engrs., Nat. Model Ry. Assn., Assn. Old Crows, Concord Homeowners Assn., Concord Chamber Singers, Concord Blue Devils, Scottish-Am. Military Soc., Am. Legion, Order of the Knights (knight), Templar of Jerusalem, Lofsensic Ursinius Order (knight commdr. 1991—), Pi Upsilon Eta, Gamma Chi Epsilon, Alpha Gamma Upsilon Republican. Methodist (adminstrv. bd. ch. 1971-76). Clubs: Navy League, Century. Lodge: Optimists (pres.) Home and Office: 5754 Pepperridge Pl Concord CA 94521-4821 Personal E-mail: ccrandall@yahoo.com.

CRANDALL, JOHN LYNN, retired insurance company executive, consultant; b. Chgo., Apr. 17, 1927; s. Paul Bertram and Olga (Bleich) C.; m. Irene Anze Ruenne, Dec. 26, 1973; children by previous marriage: Deborah Crandall Kulchar, Jeffrey, Lynne Crandall Blais; stepchildren: George Ruenne, Helgi Ruenne. BS in Fire Protection Engring., Ill. Inst. Tech., 1951. CPCU; cert. in gen. ins. Highly protected risk insp. FIA, Chgo., 1951-53, asst. engr. supr., 1953-56, engring. supr., 1956-59, underwriting supr., spl. agt., 1959-65; HPR engr., underwriter Kemper Group, Chgo., 1965-67, HPR sales specialist, 1967-71; asst. to dir. underwriting Protection Mut. Ins. Co., Park Ridge, Ill., 1971-73, v.p. underwriting, 1973-78, v.p., dir. underwriting, 1978-90; cons. Served with USN, 1945-46. Mem. Soc. Fire Protection Engrs. (charter), Soc. CPCU (chpt. pres. 1980-81, nat. dir. 1987-90, ethics com. 1990-97, sr. resource com. 1997-2000, chmn. sr. rsch. com. 2000-02, v.p. ch. coun. 1992-95, mem. sr. rsch. com. 2002—). Home: 811 Young St Galena IL 61036-1414 also: 9216 Spatterdock Ct Lakeland FL 33810-2344 Personal E-mail: jlc913@sbcglobal.net.

CRANDALL, MARIE, medical educator; b. Detroit, Mich., Nov. 18, 1969; d. John Crandall and Aggie Brown; life ptnr. David Ng. BA, U. Calif. Berkeley, 1991; MD, U. Calif. Los Angeles, 1996; MPH, U. Wash., 2002. General Surgery Am. Bd. of Surgery, 2001, Surgical Critical Care Am. Bd. of Surgery, 2003. Academic trauma surgeon; intern, resident Rush U., Chgo., 1996—2001; asst. prof. dept. surgery, asst. prof. dept. preventive medicine Northwestern U., 2003—. Adv. bd. mem. Albert Schweitzer Fellowship, Chicago, Ill., 2003; bd. mem. Chgo. Met. Battered Women's Network, Chicago, Ill., 2004. Loan Repayment Rsch. Grant, NIH, 2004-, Kathryn C. Bemmann Domestic Violence Investigative Grant, Am. Med. Women's Assn., 2004-. Mem.: Am. Cancer Soc. Liberal. Achievements include research in domestic violence and trauma,injury research. Avocations: travel, vegetarian gourmet food, reading, health & fitness. Office: NW U 201 E Huron Galter 10-105 Chicago IL 60616

CRANDALL, MICHAEL ALAN, music educator; b. Dunkirk, NY, Dec. 29, 1972; s. Renzo and Mary Lou Caniglia. MusB Edn., Ohio State U., 1996. Cert. tchr. Ohio. Choral dir. Teays Valley H.S., Ashville, Ohio, 1996—. Mem.: Am. Choral Dirs. Assn., Ohio Choral Dirs. Assn., Music Educators Nat. Conf., Ohio Music Educators Assn., Alumni Soc. of Franklin County, Ohio State Alumni Soc., Phi Mu Alpha Sinfonia. Democrat. Office: Teays Valley HS 3877 State Route 752 Ashville OH 43103 E-mail: mcrand1030@aol.com.

CRANDALL, STEPHEN HARRY, engineering educator; b. Cebu, Philippines, Dec. 2, 1920; s. William Harry and Julia Josephine (Kuenemann) C.; m. Patricia Estelle Stickel, Jan. 21, 1949; children: Jane S., William S. M.E., Stevens Inst. Tech., 1942; PhD, MIT, 1946. Registered profl. engr. Mem. staff radiation lab MIT, Cambridge, 1942-43, instr. math, 1944-46, asst. prof. mech. engring., 1947-51, assoc. prof., 1951-58, prof., 1958—, Ford prof. engring., 1975-91, prof. emeritus, 1991—, head div. applied mechanics, 1957-59, 61-67, head. div. mechanics and materials, 1968-71. Vis. prof. Marseille, France, 1960, U. Nat. Autonoma Mex., Mexico City, 1967, Ecole Nat. Superieure de Mecanique, Nantes, France, 1978, Fla. Atlantic U., 1993, Korean Advanced Inst. Sci. and Tech., 1996; exch. prof. Imperial Coll., London, 1949; NSF sci. faculty fellow, vis. scholar U. Calif., Berkeley, 1964-65; hon. rsch. assoc. Harvard U., 1971-72; Lady Davis vis. prof. Technion, Israel, 1987. Author: Engineering Analysis, 1956, Random Vibration in Mechanical Systems, 1963, (with others) Dynamics of Mechanical and Electromechanical Systems, 1968; editor: Random Vibration vol. 1, 1958, Random Vibration vol. 2, 1963, (with others) Mechanics of Solids, 1959, author (with others), 3d edit., 1978; contbr. artcles to profl. jours. Recipient ASCE Von Karman medal, 1984, Freudenthal medal, 1996, Alexander von Humboldt sr. U.S. scientist award, 1989; Fulbright fellow, London, 1949. Fellow AAAS, ASME (Worcester Reed Warner medal 1971, v.p. 1978-80, hon. mem. 1988, Timoshenko medal 1990, Den Hartog award 1991), Am. Acad. Arts and Scis., Am. Acoustical Soc. (Trent-Crede medal 1978), Am. Acad. Mechanics (pres. 1997, Disting. Svc. medal 1993); mem. NAS, NAE, NSPE, Soc. Indsl. and Applied Math., Am. Math. Soc., Am. Soc. for Engring. Edn., Internat. Union Theoretical and Applied Mechanics (chmn. U.S. del. 1974), Russian Acad. Engring. (fgn. mem.). Home: 25 Tabor Hill Rd Lincoln MA 01773-2905 Office: MIT/3-360 Dept Mech Engring Cambridge MA 02139 Office Phone: 617-253-2244. Personal E-mail: crandall@mit.edu.

CRANDELL, KENNETH JAMES, management consultant, entrepreneur; b. Ajax, Ont., Can., July 12, 1957; s. James Bauder Butterill and Barbara Joy Gillard; m. Christine Josephine McElhenney, July 28, 1984. B in Adminstrn. and B in Commerce, U. Ottawa, 1980; MBA, Fla. Atlantic U., 1982. CPA, Fla., Calif. Assoc. dir. entrepreneurial svcs. div. Ernst & Young, Ft. Lauderdale, Fla., 1982-88; founder, chmn., CEO NBS Cons. Group, Inc. dba New Bus. Strategies, Los Gatos, Calif., 1988—. Guest lectr. State Univ. System. Writer, co-producer TV series Florida Business Advisor, 1988; contbr. articles to mags. Recipient Up and Comer award, 1988. Mem. AICPA, Fin. & Adminstrn. Mgmt. in Entertainment, Fla. Inst. CPAs, Calif. Soc. CPAs, Am. Assn. Accts. (MAS divsn. 1980-93), Inst. Mgmt. Accts. (bd. dirs. Ft. Lauderdale 1983—, pres. 1988-89, bus. planning com. 1987-89), Can.-Am. C. of C. (co-founder), U. Miami Venture Coun. Forum, Gold Coast Venture Capital Club (v.p., bd. dirs. 1987-91, treas. 1987-88, co-editor newsletter 1987-89), Ft. Lauderdale C. of C. (chmn. venture capital activities 1986-88, small bus. coun. 1985-90), others. Avocations: ice hockey, published songwriter, reading. Office: NBS Cons Group Inc PMB #J 245 Mount Hermon Rd Ste M Scotts Valley CA 95066-4045 E-mail: james.crandell@newbizs.com.

CRANDELL, SUSAN, magazine editor; b. Troy, N.Y., July 31, 1951; d. Irwin Norton and Grace (Thompson) C.; m. Stephan Wilkinson, June 24, 1978; 1 child, Brook Crandell. BA in History cum laude, Middlebury Coll., 1973. Mng. editor Flying Mag., N.Y.C., 1973-79; editor-in-chief Direct Mag., N.Y.C., 1982-84; editor publ. devel. Comp-U-Card Internat., Stamford, Conn., 1985-86; editor custom media group Am. Express Publs., N.Y.C., 1986-90; exec. editor Travel & Leisure, N.Y.C., 1990-93; cons. editor Smart Money, N.Y.C., 1995, In Style, N.Y.C., 1993-95; exec. editor Ladies' Home Jour., N.Y.C., 1995-2000, MORE mag., N.Y.C., 1998—2000, editor, 2000—02, editor-in-chief, 2002—04. Office: More 125 Park Ave New York NY 10017-5529

CRANDLEMERE, ROBERT WAYNE, engineering executive; b. South Weymouth, Mass., Mar. 5, 1947; s. Robert Winton and Elizabeth Mildred (Smith) C.; m. Cynthia Robin Stoddard, May 18, 1980; children: Donna Marie, Raina Lee. A.E. in Chem. Tech., Franklin Inst. Boston, 1967; BS in Chemistry, Suffolk U., 1970, MS in Analytical Chemistry, 1975. V.p., chief chemist, lab. dir., dir. Briggs Engring. & Testing Inc., 1973-83; founder, prin., pres., CEO Cert. Engring. & Testing Co., Weymouth, Mass., 1983-92, R.W. Crandlemere & Assocs., Inc., Weymouth, Mass., 1993—2002; sr. mgr. Green Environ., Inc., Quincy, Mass., 2002—03; mgr. R.W. Crandlemere, LLC, Holbrook, Mass., 2003—. Former instr. environmental and phys. chemistry Suffolk U. Contbr. articles to profl. jours. Memm. ASTM (com. E50 on envrion. assessment, risk mgmt. and corrective action), Nat. Inst. Bldg. Scis. (com. on asbestos ops. and mgmt. programs). Home: 423 S Franklin St Holbrook MA 02343-1855 Office: 423 South Franklin St Holbrook MA 02343 Office Phone: 781-767-9490. Personal E-mail: rwaynecrandlemere@comcast.net.

CRANE, ARNOLD H., photographer; b. Chgo., July 17, 1932; s. Matthew and Dorothy Crane; m. Cynthia Crane, Jan. 24, 1988; 1 child, David. JD, DePaul U., 1954. Sr. counsel Arnold H. Crane & Assocs., Chgo., 1966—84. Mem. exhbn. com. Mus. Contemporary Art, Chgo., 1979—85; mem. media law rels. com. Chgo. Bar Assn., 1975—82; chmn. White House News Photog. Assn., Washington, 2000—01; adj. prof. Roosevelt U., Chgo., 1967—69; lectr., adj. prof. U. Mia, 1982—83. On the Other Side of the Camera, 1994 (Kodak award, 1995); photographer: (exhbns.). Recipient Fujifilm Photo Processing award, 2002. Home: 680 N Lake Shore Dr Chicago IL 60611

CRANE, BARBARA BACHMANN, photographer, educator; b. Chgo., Mar. 19, 1928; d. Burton Stanley and Della (Kreeger) Bachmann; children: Elizabeth, Jennifer, Bruce. Student, Mills Coll., 1945-48; BA in Art History, NYU, 1950; MS in Photography, Inst. Design, Ill. Inst. Tech., 1966. Prof. photography Sch. Art Inst. Chgo., 1967-93, prof. emeritus, 1993—; vis. prof. Phila. Coll. Art (now Univ. of the Arts), 1977, Sch. Mus. Fine Arts, Boston, 1979, Cornell U., Ithaca, N.Y., 1983; represented by Stephen Daiter Gallery, Chgo., Flatfile Photography Gallery, Chgo. Vis. prof. Bezalel Acad. Art and Design, Jerusalem, 1987. Author: (retrospective monograph) Barbara Crane: 1948-80, (exhbn. catalog) Barbara Crane: The Evolution of a Vision, 1983, Barbara Crane: Chicago Loop, 2002, Barbara Crane Urban Anomalies: Chicago, 2002, Barbara Crane Still Lifes: Natures Mortes, 2004, Barbara Crane: Grids, 2005. Fellow Photography fellow, NEA, 1975, 1988, Guggenheim Meml. fellow in photography, 1979—80; grantee, Polaroid Corp., 1979—95, Ill. Arts Coun., 1985, 2001. Mem.: Soc. Photog. Edn. (Nat. Honored Educator award 1993). Studio: 1015 W Jackson Blvd 1A Chicago IL 60607-2918 *Many of my photographic ideas have grown from chance or accident, both visually and technically, or from the subject matter itself. I welcome any unaccountable occurrence stemming from combinations of shutter speed, subject changes, technical happenings, or my mistakes. When such unpredictable pictures appear, I try to harness the visual episode by taking pictures that will allow the new experience to happen with intent. Fortunately, this way of working seems to expand my ideas and to continuously generate new visual experiences.*

CRANE, BARRY D., former federal agency administrator; Grad., USAF Acad.; PhD in Physics, U. Ariz. With Air Force Studies and Analyses Chief Tactical Br. USAF, 1983—86; specialist for electronic sys. Office of the Dir. of Def. Rsch. and Engring., 1987—91; project leader operational evaluation divsn. Inst. for Def. Analysis; dep. dir. for supply reduction Office Nat. Drug Control Policy Exec. Office of the Pres., Washington, 2002—04. Col. USAF, 1991.

CRANE, BENJAMIN FIELD, lawyer; b. Holden, Mass., May 5, 1929; s. Frederick Turner and Gertrude (Stange) C.; m. Sarah Anne Molloy, Feb. 8, 1959; children: Michael Turner, Elizabeth Loring, Susan Field. BA, U. Iowa, 1951; LL.B., NYU, 1954. Bar: N.Y. 1955. Assoc. Cravath, Swaine & Moore, N.Y.C., 1954-63, ptnr., 1963-94. Served with U.S. Army, 1946-47. Mem. Assn. of Bar of City of N.Y. Office: Cravath Swaine & Moore LLP Worldwide Plz 825 8th Ave New York NY 10019-7475

CRANE, CHARLES GRANT, financial analyst; b. Akron, Ohio, Nov. 22, 1959; s. Grant and Phyllis (Hamilton) C.; m. Leisa Beth Suhayda, July 2, 1983. AB, Dartmouth Coll., 1981, MBA, 1983. V.p. Oppenheimer and Co., Inc., N.Y.C., 1983-86, Prudential Bache Securities, N.Y.C., 1986-88, first v.p., 1988; dir. rsch. Spears Benzak Salomon & Farrell, N.Y.C., 1988—97, ptnr., 1989—2004; chief market strategist Key Asset Mgmt., 1997—2000; mng. ptnr., chief investment officer Victory SBSF Capital Mgmt. (formerly Spears Benzak Salomon & Farrell and Key Asset Mgmt.), 2000—04; co-founder Scotsman Capital Mgmt. LLC, 2004—. Speaker in field. Author: (newsletter) The Corner of Wall and Madison, 1984-88. Trustee HealthCare Chaplaincy, NY; dir. Habitat for Humanity, Portland, Maine; mem. MBA adv. bd. Amos Tuck Sch., Hanover, NH; mem. bd. advisors No. York County Family YMCA, Biddeford, Maine; treas. Pool Assoc., Biddeford, Maine. Named to All-Am. Research Team Instl. Investor; Edward Tuck Scholar Amos Tuck Sch., Hanover, N.H., 1983. Mem. Univ. Club, Abenakee Club, Phi Beta Kappa. Republican. Greek Orthodox. Avocations: golf, sea Kayaking, cooking, travel. Office: Scotsman Capital Mgmt 10 Rockefeller Plz 16th Fl New York NY 10020-1903 Office Phone: 212-713-7613.

CRANE, CHARLOTTE, law educator; b. Hanover, N.H., Aug. 30, 1951; d. Henry D. and Emily (Townsend) C.; m. Eric R. Fox, July 5, 1975; children: Hillary, Teresa. AB, Harvard U., 1973; JD, U. Mich., 1976. Bar: N.H. 1976, Ill. 1978. Law clk. to presiding judge U.S. Ct. Appeals (6th cir.), Detroit, 1976-77; law clk. to presiding justice U.S. Supreme Ct., Washington, 1977-78; assoc. Hopkins & Sutter, Chgo., 1978-82; asst. prof. Northwestern U., Chgo., 1982-86, assoc. prof., 1986-90, prof., 1990—. Contbr. articles to profl. jours. Mem. U.S. Women's Nat. Crew Team, 1976. Mem. ABA, Chgo. Tax Forum. Office: Northwestern U Sch Law 357 E Chicago Ave Chicago IL 60611-3059 Office Phone: 312-503-4528. E-mail: ccrane@law.northwestern.edu.

CRANE, DAVID, producer; With Bright-Kauffman-Crane Prodns., Burbank, Calif. Creator, prodr. Dream On, 1990-96 (Cable Ace award); creator, exec. prodr. Friends, 1994-2004 (Emmy nominee 1995, 96); writer, prodr. Couples, 1994; creator, exec. producer Veronica's Closet, 1997-2000; exec. prodr. Jesse, 1998-2000; co-writer (with Marta Kauffman) book and lyrics for the musical Personals (Outer Critics award, Drama Desk nomination). Office: Bright Kauffman Crane Prodns 4000 Warner Blvd Bldg 160 Burbank CA 91522-0001

CRANE, DAVID MICHAEL, prosecutor, former judge advocate, educator; b. Santa Monica, Calif., May 29, 1950; s. John Richard and Iris Joan (Nord) C.; m. Judith Anne Ponder, June 17, 1972; children: Katherine Carol, David Lewington. BGS summa cum laude, Ohio U., 1972, MA, 1973; JD, Syracuse U., 1980; postgrad., U. Va., 1985. Bar: N.D. 1981, U.S. Ct. Mil. Appeals 1981, U.S. Supreme Ct. 1985. With U.S. Army, 1972—96; sr. inspector gen., nat. security systems US Dept. Def, 1997—2002; chief prosecutor, Spl. Ct. for Sierra Leone UN, Freetown, 2002—05; prof. law Syracuse U., NY, 2005—. Contbr. articles to profl. jours. Mem. ABA, Assn. Trial Lawyers Am., Phi Alpha Theta, Omicron Delta Kappa. Democrat. Presbyterian. Avocations: running, reading. Office: Syracuse U Coll Law Syracuse NY 13244 Office Phone: 315-443-9541. Personal E-mail: dmcrane0617@yahoo.com.

CRANE, DAVID W., energy executive; BA, Princeton Univ.; JD, Harvard Univ. V.p. Asia-Pacific region ABB Energy Ventures; sr. v.p. global power group Lehman Bros., 1996—2000; COO Internat. Power PLC, 2000—02, CEO, 2003; pres., CEO, dir. NRG Energy, Princeton, NJ, 2003—. Sec. Elec. Power Supply Assn. Office: NRG Energy 211 Carnegie Ctr Princeton NJ 08540*

CRANE, DEBRA K., lawyer; b. 1957; BBA, U. Cinn.; JD, No. Kentucky U. Bar: 1996. Asst. treas. Ohio Casualty Corp., Fairfield, Ohio, 1996—99, v.p., 1999—2002, gen. counsel, 2000—, sr. v.p., sec., 2002—. Mem.: Assn. Corp. Counsel S.W. Ohio Chpt. Office: Ohio Casualty Corp 9450 Seward Rd Fairfield OH 45014-5456 Office Phone: 513-603-2400. Office Fax: 513-603-3179. E-mail: debra.crane@ocas.com.

CRANE, EDWARD HARRISON, III, academic administrator, financial analyst; b. LA, Aug. 15, 1944; s. Edward Harrison Jr. and Mary Barbara (Greene) C.; m. Kristina Knall; children: Geoffrey Harrison, Kathleen Wilder, Mary Adams. BS, U. Calif., Berkeley, 1967; MBA, U. So. Calif., 1968. Chartered fin. analyst. Portfolio mgr. Scudder, Stevens & Clark, Los Angeles, 1969-73; v.p. Alliance Capital Mgmt. Corp., San Francisco, 1973-75; nat. chmn. Libertarian Party, Washington, 1974-77; pres. Cato Inst., Washington, 1977—. Bd. Nat. Taxpayers Legal Fund, 1978-82. Pub. Inquiry mag., 1977-81, Regulation mag., 1990—; editor: Beyond the Status Quo, 1984, An American Vision, 1988, Market Liberalism, 1993; contbr. articles to profl. jours. Bd. dirs. Inst. Rsch. on Econs. of Taxation, 1988-92, Inst. Rsch. in Exptl. Econs., U.S. Term Limits, 1993—; bd. advisors Am. Inst. of Bus. and Econs. in Moscow. Inst. Chartered Fin. Analysts, Mont Pelerin Soc., Sigma Chi. Avocation: rowing. Office: Cato Inst 1000 Massachusetts Ave NW Washington DC 20001-5400 Home: 3239 Juniper Ln Falls Church VA 22044 Business E-Mail: ecrane@cato.org.

CRANE, FRANCES HAWKINS, artist, educator; b. July 8, 1928; d. Henry Cleo and Laura Elizabeth (Jenkins) Hawkins; m. Gene Calvin Crane, May 10, 1946; children: Cindie Crane Reynolds, Cheryl Crane Garcia. Student, Del Mar Coll., 1948; studied with, Frederick Taubes, N.Y.C. Exhibitions include Woodstone Gallery, Kerrville, Tex., Highland Mall Gallery, Austin, Tex., Prichard Gallery, Houston, Salado (Tex.) Gallery, Bellas Artes Gallery, Kerrville, Tex., Jerry Smith Gallery, Alice, Tex., Corpus Christi (Tex.) Mus., M. and N. Originals, Corpus Christi, Represented in permanent collections Corpus Christi Mus., Lyndon Baines Johnson Libr. Recipient, top awards local, state, nat., internat. shows. Mem.: Internat. Soc. Artists, Hill Country Arts Found., Intenat. Platform Assn., Nat. League Am. Pen Women, South Tex. Traditional Art Assn. Studio: 5058 Wingfoot Ln Corpus Christi TX 78413-2223 Home: 2802 Cimarron Blvd #210 Corpus Christi TX 78414

CRANE, FREDERICK BARON, retired music educator; b. Mount Pleasant, Iowa, Mar. 4, 1927; s. Baron Dana and Ruth Marie Crane; m. Lois Ann Zanger, Feb. 12, 1971; 1 child, Susan stepchildren: Mark, Reed, Robert; m. Lois Irene Russell, Aug. 15, 1956; 1 child, Elizabeth. BA, Carleton Coll., 1949; MA, U. Iowa, 1956, PhD, 1960. From tchg. asst. to prof. emeritus U. Iowa, Iowa City, 1957—94, prof. emeritus, 1994—; instr. Minot (N.D.) State Coll., 1957—58, SUNY, Binghampton, NY, 1960—63; asst. prof. La. State U., Baton Rouge, 1967—68. Author: Materials for the Study of the Fifteenth Century Basse Danse, 1968, Extant Medieval Musical Instruments: A Provisional Catalog by Types, 1972, Medieval Music: An Outline, 1974, A History of the Trump in Pictures: Europe and America, 2003; contbr. articles to profl. jours. With USN, 1945—46, with USN, 1951—52. Mem.: Soc. am. Music (program com. 1987, Lowens award com. 1989, 1997, chmn. program com. 1992), Am. Musicological Soc. (mem. coun. 1977—79, sec., treas. Gulf States chpt. 1965—67, program com. Midwest chpt. 1982—83), Am. Musical Instrument Soc. (bd. dirs. 1976—79, chmn. program 1977, chmn. nominating com. 1986), Internat. Jew's Harp Soc. Home: 601 Mt Whire St Mount Pleasant IA 52641

CRANE, HORACE RICHARD, physicist, researcher; b. Turlock, Calif., Nov. 4, 1907; s. Horace Stephen and Mary Alice (Roselle) Crane; m. Florence Rohmer LeBaron, Dec. 30, 1934; children: Carol Ann, George Richard, Janet(dec.). BS, Calif. Inst. Tech., 1930, PhD, 1934. Rsch. fellow Calif. Inst. Tech., 1934—35; mem. faculty U. Mich., Ann Arbor, 1935—, prof. physics, 1946—, chmn. dept. physics, 1965—72, George P. Williams Univ. prof., 1972—78, emeritus, 1978—. Rsch. assoc. (radar) MIT, 1940—41; physicist Carnegie Inst., Washington, 1941; project dir., proximity fuse project U. Mich., 1941—43, project dir., atomic energy project, 1943—45; cons. NDRC, 1941—45; mem. standing com. on controlled thermonuc. rsch. AEC, 1969—72; v.p. Midwestern Univs. Rsch. Assn., 1956—56, pres., 1957—60; mem. policy bd. Argonne Nat. Lab., 1957—67; bd. govs. Am. Inst. Physics, 1964—71, chmn., 1971—75; mem. Commn. on Human Resources, 1977—80; mem. Coun. for Internat. Exch. of Scholars, 1977—80. Author: (monthly series) How Things Work in the Physics Teacher, 1983—, How Things Work, 1992, Exhibits Guide, 1992, How to Build It, 1994; inventor, designer exhibits for hands-on type museums, 1981—; contbr. articles to profl. mags.; actor:. Recipient Davisson-Germer prize, 1967, Disting. Alumni medal, Calif. Inst. Tech., 1968, Disting. Svc. award, U. Mich., 1957, Nat. medal of Sci., 1986, Can-Doer award, Mich. Tech. Coun., 1993, Harris award, Rotary Internat., 1963, Henry Russel lectr., 1967. Fellow: AAAS, Am. Acad. Arts and Scis., Am. Phys. Soc.; mem.: NAS, Am. Assn. Physics Tchrs. (Oersted medal 1977, Melba Newell Phillips award 1988, pres. 1965), Sci. Rsch. Club (v.p. 1946—47, pres. 1947—48), Rsch. U. Mich. Club (pres. 1956—57), Sigma Xi. Achievements include invention of Race Track, a modified form of synchrotron for nuclear studies, 1946; early discoveries in field of artificially produced radioactive atoms, 1934-39; measurements of magnetic moment of free electron, 1950. Home: Fred Kitchens 66 Cavanaugh Lake Rd Chelsea MI 48118-9732

CRANE, HUGH WINGATE, railroad executive; b. Evergreen Park, Ill., Dec. 25, 1941; s. Hugh B. and Grace May (Wesche) C.; m. Kathy Ann Jent, Sept. 27, 1975; children: Steven Henry, Katie R. Student, DeVry, 1964, Milw. Sch. Engring., 1969. Tchr., mem. faculty Milw. Sch. Engring., 1966-71; engring. instr. Control Data Tech. Inst., Chgo., 1971-72; founder, chmn. bd., pres., chief engring. officer ARH, Ltd. dba Crab Orchard & Egyptian R.R., Marion, Ill., 1972—; vice-chmn. Regional Econ. Devel. Corp., Marion. Guest lectr. transp. and freight So. Ill. U., Carbondale, 1980. Author: (workbook) Engineering Descriptive Geometry, 1968, (textbook) Engineering Descriptive Geometry/Theory and Application, 1970. V.p. Lake Egypt Assn. Property Owners, Creal Springs, Ill., 1996-97. With ROTC, 1958-59. Recipient Sam Walton Cmty. Bus. Leader award, Marion, 1998; named Industrialist of Yr., Marion C. of C., 1993, Cert. of Appreciation, N.G. of Ill., 1995; transp. achievements recognized in U.S. congl. record U.S. Senator Paul Simon, 1994. Mem. Am. Rlwy. Engring. Assn., Am. R.R. Devel. Assn., Rotary. Avocations: boating, building large scale steam powered models. Office: Crab Orchard & Egyptian RR 514 N Market St Marion IL 62959-2300

CRANE, JAMESON, plastics manufacturing company executive; b. Columbus, Ohio, Mar. 14, 1926; s. Robert Sellers and Helen (Jameson) C.; m. Ann Burba, Sept. 17, 1948; children: Jameson Jr., Elizabeth Crane Westwater, Michael S., Sarah Crane MacPhail. BS, Ohio State U., 1947. Sales mgr. Columbus Coated Fabrics, 1948-60; pres. Crane Plastics Co., Columbus, Ohio, 1970-96; chmn., CEO Crane Group, Inc., Columbus, 1996—. Bd. dirs. Bank One Columbus NA, Morgan Lumber Co. Bd. dirs. Ohio State U. Found., 1991—. With USN, 1944-45. Mem. Columbus Club, Columbus Country Club, The Golf Club (Columbus), Lyford Cay Club (Nassau, Bahamas). Home: 299 N Parkview Ave Columbus OH 43209-1437 Office: Crane Group Inc 2141 Fairwood Ave Columbus OH 43207-1753

CRANE, LAURA JANE, retired chemist; b. Middletown, Ohio, Nov. 2, 1941; d. David R. and Frances T. (Watkins) Scott; m. Robert K. Crane, Apr. 13, 1972. BS, Carnegie Inst. Tech., 1963; MS, Harvard U., 1964; PhD, Rutgers U., 1972. Postdoctoral fellow Roche Inst. Molecular Biology, 1972-74, rsch. assoc., 1974-75; analytical chemist Eastman Kodak Co., Rochester, N.Y., 1962; asst. scientist Warner-Lambert Co., Morris Plains, N.J., 1965, 67-68; English tchr. Am. Sch., Manila, 1966; assoc. scientist W.R. Grace & Co., Clarksville, Md., 1969; sr. scientist diagnostic enzymology Warner-Lambert Co., 1975, group leader coagulation rsch., 1976-79; mgr. lab. products rsch. J.T. Baker Inc., Phillipsburg, N.J., 1979, asst. dir. R&D, 1980-85, dir. R&D, 1986-92; sr. dir. new product innovation Schering-Plough Health Products, Inc., Memphis, 1992-93, sr. dir. adv. products rsch. and new product innovation, 1993—2003, rsch. fellow, 2003—04, ret., 2004. Mem. faculty Seton Hall U., 1979; participant profl. symposia; mem. R&D coun. N.J., state sci. adv. coun. Rutgers U.; pres. Am. Clerical Soc. Memphis Section, 2005-, Delta Dressage Assn., 2005-; cons. in field. Contbr. editor sci. articles and books. US Dregsage Federation Bronze Medalist, 2003m, Armco Corp. scholar, 1959-63; Women's Dormitory Coun. scholar; William Connelly scholar; nat. Merit scholar; NSF fellow; DuPont fellow; NDEA fellow, 1969-72, others. Mem. AAAS, Am. Chem. Soc. (pres. Memphis chpt. 2005), U.S. Dressage Fedn., Delta Dressage Assn. (pres. 2005—), Arabian Horse Registry Assn., Al Khamsa Arabian Horse Breeders Assn. (pres.). Home: 7155 Highway 194 Williston TN 38076-3511 Office: Schering-Plough Health Products Inc 3030 Jackson Ave Memphis TN 38112-2020 Personal E-mail: ljcrane@bellsouth.net.

CRANE, MARK, lawyer; b. Chgo., Aug. 27, 1930; s. Martin and Ruth (Bangs) C.; m. Constance Bird Wilson, Aug. 18, 1956; children: Christopher, Katherine, Stephanie. AB, Princeton U., 1952; LLB, Harvard U., 1957. Bar: U.S. Dist. Ct. (no. dist.) Ill. 1957, U.S. Ct. Appeals (7th cir.) 1968, U.S. Ct. Appeals (9th cir.) 1972, U.S. Supreme Ct. 1978, U.S. Ct. Appeals (10th cir.) 1982, U.S. Ct. Appeals (fed. cir.) 1983, U.S. Ct. Appeals (6th cir.) 1995, U.S. Ct. Appeals (8th cir.) 1998. Assoc. Hopkins & Sutter, Chgo., 1957-63, ptnr., 1963-2001; of counsel Foley & Lardner, Chgo., 2001—. Adj. prof. Loyola U. Law Sch., 2000—; comml. arbitrator, mediator complex case panel Am. Arbitration Assn., Chgo., 1997—. Served to lt. (j.g.) USNR, 1952-54. Fellow Am. Bar Found., Am. Coll. Trial Lawyers (chmn. upstate Ill. com. 1997-99); mem. ABA (chmn. antitrust sect. 1986-87), Ill. Bar Assn. (chmn. fed. jud. appointments com. 1978-79, chmn. antitrust sect. 1970), Chgo. Bar Assn., 7th Cir. Bar Assn. (pres. 1984-85). Republican. Episcopalian. Home: 520 Hoyt Ln Winnetka IL 60093-2623 Office: The Quaker Oats Co 555 W Monroe St Chicago IL 60661-3716

CRANE, R.H., poet; b. Chgo., June 14, 1937; s. John and Helen Crane. BA in English, DePaul U., Chgo., 1972, MA in English, 1976. Founder, editor Veery, Chgo., 1991—. *"It is indeed a unique book, a new approach and fascinating concept. Who would ever dream of combining geometric drawings and poetry, especially in such harmony." —Renate Princess of Windisch-Graetz, Generalkonsulat der Bundesrepublik Deutschland, Letter of honor to R.H. Crane. "I would recommend this highly original art and art forms with great fervour." — John Bayley, Oxford University, The Daily Progress (Charlottesville). "Camera-ready pages of this original book will be displayed at the venue throughout January. It marks the unusual, and first, artistic union of poetry, drawing and geometry." Financial Times, London.* Author: Crossed Silver: Poems in Poetry, Drawing, and Geometry, 1992. Recipient Renate Princess of Windisch-Graetz, Generalkonsulat der Bundesrepublik Deutschland letter of honor for new and unique combining of poetry, drawing and geometry. Mem. Am. Philos. Assn. Office: Veery 333 N Michigan Ave Ste 2032 Chicago IL 60601-4102

CRANE, ROBERT KENDALL, engineering educator, researcher, consultant; b. Worcester, Mass., Dec. 9, 1935; s. Kendall Buck and Marjorie Armitage C.; m. Emma Ruth, June 15, 1957; children: Garry Robert, Susan Emma Crane Jennings, Katherine Anne Crane Kulas, Cynthia Elizabeth. BSEE, Worcester Poly. Inst., 1957, MSEE, 1959, PhD, 1970. Staff engr. MITRE Corp., Bedford, Mass., 1959-64; staff mem. Lincoln Lab. MIT, Lexington, 1964-76, cons., 1976-88; divsn. sr. scientist, dep. divsn. mgr. Environ. Rsch. and Tech., Inc., Concord, Mass., 1976-81; rsch. prof. Thayer Sch. Engring. Dartmouth Coll., Hanover, N.H., 1981-91; prof. meteorology, elec. engring. Coll. Geoscis. U. Okla., Norman, 1992-2000, prof. emeritus meteorology, elec. engring., 2000—. Cons. Raytheon Corp., Sudbury, Mass., 1981-87, Tech. Svc. Corp., Silver Spring, Md., 1988, Norden Sys., Melville, N.Y., 1988, Globalstar, San Jose, Calif., 1995-97, Applied Data Trends, Inc., 1996—2000, Teledesic Corp., 1997-99, Triton Network Sys., Inc., 1999, Hughes Network Sys., 1999-2000, Boeing Satellite Sys., 2001, Jet Propulsion Lab., 2004-05, Harris Corp., 2005. Contbr. over 100 tech. papers, reports to profl. jours. and other publs. Fellow IEEE (life, Disting. lectr. Antenna and Propagation Soc. 1988-91, adminstrv. com. 1985-87, wave propagation stds. com. 1971-92, assoc. editor Trans. Antennas and Propagation 1972-74), Internat. Sci. Radio Union (chmn. commn. F. 1987-90, vice comm. F. 1984-87), U.S. Nat. Com. Internat. Sci. Radio Union (chmn. 1985-87); mem. Am. Meterorol. Soc. (cert. cons. meterorologist, com. on radar meteorology 1981-83), Sigma Xi, Eta Kappa Nu. Avocations: hiking, skiing, photography. Home: 315 Forest Acres Rd New London NH 03257 also: 337 Lovewell Pond Rd Fryeburg ME 04037 Business E-Mail: bcrane@ou.edu.

CRANE, ROBERT MEREDITH, health facility administrator; b. Phila., Apr. 5, 1947; s. Frederick Barnard and Roberta Futhey C.; m. Susan Gail Dewald, May 5, 1973; 1 child, Alexis Meredith. BA, Coll. of Wooster, 1969; M Pub. Adminstrn., Cornell U., Ithaca, N.Y., 1971. Health planning specialist U.S. Dept. Health, Edn. and Welfare, Rockville, Md., 1971-73, tech. assistance bur. chief, 1973-76, regulatory methods bur. chief, 1976-77; sr. staff assoc. U.S. Ho. of Reps., Washington, 1977-79; dep. commr. N.Y. State Health Dept., Albany, 1979-82; dir. N.Y. State Office Health Sys. Mgmt., Albany, 1982-83; v.p. govt. rels. Kaiser Found. Health Plan, Oakland, calif., 1983-88, sr. v.p. nat. accts. and pub. rels., 1988-92, sr. v.p. quality mgmt., 1992-94, sr. v.p., chief adminstrv. officer, 1994-99, sr. v.p., rsch. and policy devel., dir. Inst. for Health Policy, 1999—2004; pres. Kaiser Permanente Internat., Oakland, 2004—. Bd. dirs. Acad. Health Svcs. Rsch. and Health Policy, 2000—; mem. Nat. Acad. Social Ins., 2000-03. Campaign cabinet United Way Bay area, 1989-90; steering com. Bay Area Econ. Forum, 1988-94, Bay Area Coun., 1991—; selection judge, preceptor Coro Found., San Francisco, 1985-86; chmn. bd. Alpha Ctr., 1992-98; co-chair conf. bd. Coun. of Shared Bus. Svcs. Execs., 1996—; trustee Employee Benefits Rsch. Inst. Sr. exec. fellow Harvard U., 1981. Mem. APHA (chmn. cmty. health planning sect. 1983-84, bd. govs. 1979-81), Am. Health Planning Assn. (bd. dirs. 1986-92). Presbyterian. Avocations: tennis, golf. Office: Kaiser Found Health Plan 1 Kaiser Plz Oakland CA 94612-3610

CRANE, ROGER RYAN, JR., lawyer; b. Washington, Mar. 28, 1946; s. Roger Ryan Crane and Jeanette (Hurlbut) Rosar. AB, Coll. of Holy Cross, 1968; JD, Fordham U., 1973; LLM, NYU, 1980. Bar: N.Y. 1974; U.S. Dist. Ct. (so. and ea. dist.) N.Y. 1974; U.S. Ct. Appeals (2nd cir.) 1974, (1st cir.) 1994. Assoc. Dunnington Bartholow & Miller, N.Y.C., 1973-79, Trubin Sillcocks Edelman, N.Y.C., 1979-81, ptnr., 1981—84; ptnr., head litig. dept. Bachner Tally Polevoy & Misher, N.Y.C., 1984-2000; co-mng. ptnr. N.Y. office McCarter & English, N.Y.C., 2000—02; ptnr. Nixon Peabody LLP, N.Y.C., 2002—. Contbr. articles to profl. jours. Mem. N.Y.C. Bar Assn. (prof. discipline com. 1996-99), Univ. Club N.Y., Tuxedo Club. Avocations: golf, tennis, fly fishing, riding. Office: Nixon Peabody 437 Madison Ave New York NY 10022 Office Phone: 212-940-3190, 212-940-3190. E-mail: rcrane@nixonpeabody.com.

CRANE, STEPHEN CHARLES, professional society administrator; b. Waterbury, Conn, Oct. 4, 1946; s. Homer and Edna Crane; children: Russell, Elizabeth. BA, Princeton U., 1969; MPH, U. Mich., 1973, PhD, 1981. Legis.

analyst, mgmt. intern Office of the Dir., NIH, Bethesda, Md., 1969; project dir. Columbia Rsch. Assocs., Inc., Cambridge, Mass., 1970; program analyst Office Asst. Sec. for Planning & Evaluation U.S. Dept. Health, Edn. and Welfare, 1972; grad. rsch. fellow Program Health Planning U. Mich.-Sch. Pub. Health, 1973, sr. rsch. assoc., rsch. assoc., grad. rsch. fellow, 1973-79, lectr. program and bur. hosp. adminstrn., 1979-80, asst. prof., lectr. dept. med. care orgn., 1980-83; asst. prof. Sch. Pub. Health Boston U., 1984-93, dep. chief health svc. sect. Sch. Pub. Health, 1988, asst. acad. v.p. for health affairs, 1986-88, dir. ednl. programs Health Policy Inst., 1983-90; v.p. Assn. for Health Svc. Rsch. & Found. for Health Svc. Rsch., Washington, 1990-93; program dir. Robert Wood Johnson Found. Investigator Awards in Health, 1992-93; exec. v.p. Am. Acad. Physician Asst., Alexandria, Va., 1993—. Investigator and presenter in field. Contbr. articles to profl. jours. Staff Mich. Pub. Health Statue Revision Project, 1975-78; cons. Spkr.'s Office, Mich. Ho. of Reps., Lansing, 1975-81; mem. adv. com. Mercy Coll. Physician Asst. Program, Detroit, 1979-83, Western Mich. Physician Asst. Program, Kalamazoo, 1981-85; staff Boston Mayor's Com. on Access to Health Care, 1984-86; mem. task force on access to health care Divsn. Alcoholism, Mass. Dept. Pub. Health, 1985-86; health care cons. Mass. Com. for the Medically Uninsured, 1985-86; cons. Gen. Assembly Task Force on Health Cost/Policies, Nat. Presbyn. Ch., 1985-91; corporator Milton Med. Ctr., 1988-90; mem. Commn. on Future of U. Detroit/Mercy. McConnell fellow Woodrow Wilson Sch., Princeton U., 1968; USPH Svc. fellow, 1972-73; Grad. Rsch. fellow Bur. Hosp. Adminstrn., Sch. Pub. Health, U. Mich., 1973-74; hon. fellow Mich. Acad. Physician Assts., 1977; recipient commendation Pub. Health Statue Revision Commn., 1979; Faculty Devel. grantee Ctr. for Rsch. on Learning and Teaching, U. Mich., 1982, John H. Romani Disting. Alumni award Mich. Sch. Pub. Health, 1996. Office: Am Acad Physician Asst 950 N Washington St Alexandria VA 22314-1534

CRANE, WILLIAM GRACE, lawyer; b. N.Y.C., Mar. 25, 1932; s. Thomas Francis and Rose (Illions) C.; m. Catherine A. Polsenski, Aug. 21, 1958; children: William Jr., Matthew, Genevieve, Bridget, James. BA, Manhattan Coll., 1953; JD, St. John's U., Bklyn., 1958. Bar: N.Y. Law clk. Ct. of Appeals N.Y., Albany, 1958-60; assoc. Gilbert & Segall, N.Y.C., 1960-61; law asst. 2d dept. Appellate Divsn., Bklyn., 1961-64; law clk. N.Y. Supreme Ct., White Plains, 1964-69; ptnr. Rosen, Crane & Wolfson, Poughkeepsie, N.Y., 1969-86, Crane Wolfson & Roberts, Poughkeepsie, 1986-91; prin. ct. atty. Surrogate's Ct. Dutchess county, Poughkeepsie, 1993-98; sole practitioner Poughkeepsie, 1991—. Law clk. Family Ct. Dutchess County, Poughkeepsie, 1973—93. Served with U.S. Army, 1955. Republican. Roman Catholic. Office: 11 Market St Ste 204 Poughkeepsie NY 12601-3215

CRANEFIELD, PAUL FREDERIC, physiology educator, pharmacologist; b. Madison, Wis., Apr. 28, 1925; s. Paul Frederic and Edna (Rothnick) C. Ph.B., U. Wis., 1946, PhD, 1951; MD, Albert Einstein Coll. Medicine, 1964. Fellow biophysics Johns Hopkins U., 1951-53; from instr. to assoc. prof. physiology State U. N.Y. Downstate Med. Center, N.Y.C., 1953-62; research fellow psychiatry Albert Einstein Coll. Medicine, 1960-64. Exec. sec. com. publs. and med. information, editor bull. N.Y. Acad. Medicine, 1963-66; adj. assoc. prof. pharmacology Columbia Coll. Physicians and Surgeons, 1964-75, adj. prof., 1975-96; assoc. prof. Rockefeller U., 1966-75, prof., 1975-96, prof. emeritus, 1996—. Author: (with Hoffman) The Electrophysiology of the Heart, 1960, Paired Pulse Stimulation of the Heart, 1968, (with C. McC. Brooks) The Historical Development of Physiological Thought, 1959, The Way In and the Way Out, 1974, The Conduction of the Cardiac Impulse, 1975, Claude Bernard's Revised Edition of his Introduction à L'Étude de la Médicine Expérimentale, 1976, (with Aronson) Cardiac Arrhythmias, The Role of Triggered Activity and Other Mechanisms, 1988, Science and Empire: East Coast Fever in Rhodesia and the Transvaal, 1991, Born Wanderer: The Life of Stanley Portal Hyatt, 1995; also numerous articles; editor: Two Great Scientists of the Nineteenth Century, 1982, Jour. Gen. Physiology, 1966-96; mem. editorial bd.: Circulation Research, Spl. Collections, Jour. of Electrocardiology; cons. editor: Internat. Microform Jour. Legal Medicine, 1969-77. Chmn. bd. dirs. LaMama Exptl. Theatre Club, 1965-69; chmn. bd. dirs. Circle Repertory Co., 1970-76, The Working Theatre; trustee Milton Helpern Library Legal Medicine. Recipient Einthoven medal U. Leiden, 1983, Disting. Scientist award N.Am. Soc. Pacing and Electrophysiology, 1994. Fellow N.Y. Acad. Medicine (medal 1988), Internat. Acad. History of Medicine; mem. Am. Physiol. Soc., Biophys. Soc., Am. Assn. History Medicine, Bibliog. Soc., Episcopal Actors Guild (mem. coun. 1990-92), Century Club, Players Club, Nat. Arts Club, Grolier Club, Coffee House Club, Cosmos Club (Washington), Savile Club (London). Home: 270 Madison Ave Rm 1207 New York NY 10016-0601

CRANER, LORNE WHITNEY, not-for-profit institute executive, former federal agency administrator; b. Bitburg AFB, Fed. Republic Germany; came to U.S., 1960; s. Robert Roger and Audrey Evelyn Craner. BA, Reed Coll., 1982; MA, Georgetown U., 1986. Staff asst. Congressman John McCain, Washington, 1983-84; legis. asst. Congressman Jim Kolbe, Washington, 1985, Congressman John McCain, Washington, 1986-87; staff Senate Cen. Am. observer Group, Washington, 1987-89; dep. asst. sec. for legis. affairs US Dept. State, Washington, 1989—92; dir. Asian Affairs NSC, Washington, 1992—93; vpres. prog. Int. Rep. Inst., Washington, 1993—95, pres., 1995—2001, 2004—; asst. sec. for democracy, human rights and labor U.S. Dept. State, Washington, 2001—04. Staff asst. George Bush for Pres., Alexandria, Va., 1980; mem. campaign staff John McCain for Senate, Phoenix, 1986. Mem.: Coun. on Fgn. Rels. Republican. Office: Internat Rep Inst 1225 Eye St NW Ste 700 Washington DC 20005

CRANFORD, JAMES MICHAEL, lawyer; b. Washington, Jan. 26, 1946; s. Jack and Wanda C.; m. Teresa, July 23, 1994; children: William Bodie, James Michael, Heather, Christopher. BA, Mercer U., 1978; JD, Woodrow Wilson U., 1984. Atty. pvt. practice, Macon, Ga., 1985—. Mem. city coun. Macon, 1995-99. Mem. Ga. Bar Assn., Ga. Trial Lawyers Assn., Ga. Assn. Criminal Defense Lawyers, Macon Bar Assn., Macon Assn. Criminal Defense Lawyers, Middle Ga. Trial Lawyers Assn. Episcopalian. Avocations: family, motorcycle racing, scuba diving, boxing, fishing. Home: 1842 Williamson Rd Macon GA 31206-3342 Office: 913 Washington Ave Macon GA 31201-6720 Office Phone: 478-746-0704.

CRANFORD, JOHN RINGER, physical scientist; b. Washington, Mar. 3, 1922; s. Walter Wilson and Delle Hout Cranford; m. Mary Knox Blandford, Dec. 4, 2001. BA, George Washington U., 1951. Phys. scientist US Info. Agy., Alexandria, Va. With USCG, 1940—43, NJ. Mem.: Mineral. Soc. DC. Meth. Avocations: geology, mineral collecting, singing. Home: 1994 Milboro Dr Rockville MD 20854

CRANFORD, PAGE DERONDE, lawyer; b. West Chester, Pa., Nov. 20, 1935; s. Joseph D. and Dorothy (Griffith) C.; m. Virginia Langen, Nov. 21, 1965; children: Elizabeth, Courtenay. BS, Washington and Lee U., 1958; JD, George Washington U., 1964; postgrad. in banking, Rutgers U., 1981. Bar: Md. 1964, D.C. 1965, Va. 1974, U.S. Ct. Appeals (D.C. cir.) 1965. Asst. v.p. Nat. Bank Washington, 1958-65; staff counsel U.S. Comptr. of Currency, Washington, 1965-66, regional adminstr. nat. banks Richmond, Va., 1966-72; sr. v.p., sec., gen. counsel Fidelity Am. Bank, Lynchburg, Va., 1972-75; assoc. Boothe, Prichard & Dudley, Fairfax, Va., 1975-76; corp. gen. counsel Va. Nat. Bankshares, Norfolk, Va., 1976-89; exec. v.p., gen. counsel Sorvan Fin. Corp, Norfolk, 1989-90, sr. exec. v.p., gen. counsel, 1990-91; sr. exec. v.p., gen. counsel, sec. C&S/Sovran Corp., Norfolk and Atlanta, 1990-92; ptnr. McGuire Woods Battle & Boothe, Norfolk, 1992-99, ptnr. in charge, 1992-96; of counsel McGuire Woods LLP, Norfolk, 2000—. Adj. prof. Sch. Law Regent U., Va. Beach, 1995-99, Sch. Law Coll. William and Mary, Williamsburg, Va., 1997-98. Trustee Richmond Montessori Sch., 1970-72, Lynchburg Montessori Sch., 1972-75, James River Day Sch., Lynchburg, 1973-75, Va. Symphony, Norfolk, 1984— . Served to capt. U.S. Army, 1958-66 Recipient Arthur S. Fleming award Jaycees, 1972 Mem. ABA (banking law subcom, corp. counsel subcom., bus. law sect.), Va. Bar Assn., Md. Bar Assn., D.C. Bar Assn., Town Point Club (Norfolk). Republican. Episcopalian. Office: McGuire Woods LLP 9000 World Trade Ctr 101 W Main St Ste 9000 Norfolk VA 23510-1655

CRANG, RICHARD FRANCIS EARL, botanist, writer, research scientist; b. Clinton, Ill., Dec. 2, 1936; s. Richard Francis and Clara Esther (Cummins) Crang; m. Linda L. Crang, Aug. 10, 1958 (div.). BS, Eastern Ill. U., 1958; MS, U. S.D., 1962; PhD, U. Iowa, 1965. Asst. prof. biology Wittenberg U., 1965-69; assoc. prof. biol. sci. Bowling Green State U., 1969-74, prof., 1974-80; prof. plant biology U. Ill., Urbana-Champaign, 1980—2002, assoc. head dept. plant biology, 1995-97, faculty fellow in acad. adminstrn., 1997-99, dir. Ctr. Elec. Microsci., 1980-92, prof. emeritus, 2002—. Adj. prof. anatomy Med. Coll. Ohio, 1974—80; summer rsch. prof. Lehman Coll., CUNY, Bronx, vis. prof. biol. sci., 1999—2005; vis. scientist Cambridge U., England, 1978—79, Komarov Bot. Inst., Warsaw U., Poland, 1993; rschr., collaborator in fungal adhesion Kaohsiung Med. Coll., Taiwan, China, 1988—90; lectr. in field. Author: (with A. Vassilyev) CD-ROM Text on Plant Anatomy, 2003; contbr. numerous articles to profl. jours. Mem. Statewide Democratic Support Group, Ill. Recipient Outstanding Faculty Rsch. Recognition awards Bowling Green State U., 1973, 75; grantee Paint Rsch. Inst., 1976-83, NSF, 1981-83, EPA, 1984-86, USDA, 1986-89, Internat. Plant and Pollution Lab., 1993-98; lifetime assoc. fellow Clare Hall, Cambridge, Eng. Mem. AAAS, Bot. Soc. Am., Internat. Soc. Environ. Botanists (advisor, life mem., inaugurated 1st internat. meeting, Lucknow, India, 1996, 2005), Microscopy Soc. Am. (nat. chmn. cert. bd. 1982-89, dir. USA local affiliates 1990-93, Disting. Svc. award 1994, Cecil Hall award for outstanding rsch. in biology with analytical microscopy 1994), Sigma Xi, Disciples Of Christ. Achievements include development of asynchronous learning techs. at college level by means of networked computers on World-Wide Web. Home: 3801 Clubhouse Dr #109 Champaign IL 61822-6400 Office: U Ill Plant Biology 505 S Goodwin Ave 665 Morrill Hall Urbana IL 61801-3707 Business E-Mail: r-crang@life.uiuc.edu.

CRÂNGANU, CONSTANTIN, engineer; s. Sterian and Ioana Crânganu; m. Veturia Stamatin; children: Dan, Andreea. MS, U. Bucharest, Romania, 1971—76, PhD, 1990—93, U. Okla., Norman, 1994—97. Geotechnical engr. Vaslui County, Romania, 1976—81; asst. prof. Iasi, Romania, 1981—93; rschr. U. Okla., Norman, 1997—2001; assoc. prof. CUNY, Bklyn Coll., 2001—. Fulbright vis. scientist U. Okla., Norman, 1993—94; asst. dir. Inst. for Exploration and Devel. Geoscis., Norman, Okla., 1998—2000; grad. dep. chair CUNY, Bklyn Coll., 2003—. Achievements include patents pending for Method for Producing Natural Gas from Gas Hydrates. Office: Bklyn Coll 2900 Bedford Ave Brooklyn NY 11210

CRANGLE, ROBERT D., lawyer, management consultant, entrepreneur; b. Putnam, Conn., May 5, 1943; s. Dale E. and Libbie S. (Krepela) C.; m. S. Jeanne Rose, June 6, 1968; children: Rob, Scott, Elenor, Bill, Kimball, Susan, Sara, Paul, Hally. BS in Nuclear Engring., Kans. State U., 1966; JD, Harvard U., 1969. Bar: Mass. 1969, Ill. 1974, Kans. 1987, U.S. Dist. Ct. Kans. 1987; cert. mgmt. cons. 1980. Sr. v.p. Harbridge House, Inc., Boston, 1969-84; pres., dir. Rose & Crangle, Ltd., Lincoln, 1984—; dir. Helisys Inc., L.A., 1985-99; ptnr. Metz and Crangle, Chartered, Lincoln, Kans., 1987—2003; elected Lincoln County Atty., 1997—2001; atty. Crangle Law Office, Lincoln, 2003—. Mem. faculty Bus. Sch., Ill. Inst. Tech., Chgo., 1984-87; dir. IIT Ctr. Rsch. on Indsl. Strategy and Policy, Chgo., 1984-87. Bd. dirs. Lake Bluff (Ill.) Sch. Bd., 1982-87, Farmers Nat. Bank, 1992-2004, Midwest Cmty. Bank, 2004—, adv. bd.; mem. Kans. Sci. and Tech. Coun., 1992-96; mem. Natural History Mus. Bd., 1995-98, Kans. Geol. Survey Adv. Com., 1995-2002. Recipient Meritorious Pub. Service award NSF, 1985. Fellow AAAS; mem. Kans. Bar Assn. (officer bus. law sect. 1993-97), N.W. Kans. Bar Assn., co-organizer Kans. Math and Sci. Edn. Coalition. Republican. Mem. Soc. Of Friends. Avocations: science policy, entrepreneurship. Office: Crangle Law Office Chtd 117 N 4th PO Box 285 Lincoln KS 67455-0285 also: Rose & Crangle Ltd PO Box 285 102 E Lincoln Av Lincoln KS 67455-0285 Office Phone: 785-524-5050. Business E-Mail: rcltd@nckcn.com.

CRANK, PATRICK J. (PAT CRANK), state attorney general; m. Anna Crank; children: Abbigail, Jerry, Zachary, Noah. BA, U. Wyo., 1982, JD, 1985. With Wyo. Atty. Gen. Office, 1985—86, Natrona County Dist. Atty. Office, 1987—90, US Atty. Office for Dist. Wyo., 1990—2002; atty. gen. State of Wyo., Cheyenne, 2003—. Democrat. Avocations: hunting, fishing, camping. Office: Atty Gens Office 123 Capitol 200 W 24th St Cheyenne WY 82002

CRANNEY, MARILYN KANREK, retired lawyer; b. Bklyn., June 18, 1949; d. Sidney Paul and Aurelia (Valice) Kanrek; m. John William Cranney, Jan. 22, 1970 (div. June 1975); 1 child, David Julian. BA, Brandeis U., 1970; MA in History, Brigham Young U., 1975; JD, U. Utah, 1979; LLM in Tax Law, NYU, 1984. Bar: N.Y. 1980, U.S. Dist. Ct. (so. and ea. dists.) N.Y. 1992. Assoc. Cravath Swaine & Moore, N.Y.C., 1979-81; 1st v.p., asst. gen. counsel Morgan Stanley Investment Advisors Inc., N.Y.C., 1981—2005; pvt. practice Bklyn., 2005—. Mem. Order of the Coif. Democrat. Jewish. Avocations: travel, reading.

CRANNY, THERESA M., veterinarian; b. Ames, Iowa, Dec. 10, 1965; d. Charles Joseph and Beverly Jean Cranny. BS in biology, Bowling Green State U., 1987; DVM, Ohio State U., 1991. Veterinarian Animal Clinic of Butler, Renfrew, Pa., 1991—93, Woodmar Animal Clin., Hammond, Ind., 1993—2000, Lincolnway Animal Hosp., Matteson, Ill., 2000—05, South Suburban Animal Clin., 2005—. Panelist Vet. Medicine Roundtable Discussion, 2002. Office: South Suburban Animal Clin 26611 N Dixie Hwy Perrysburg OH 43551 Office Phone: 419-872-0920. E-mail: tmcdvm@msn.com.

CRANSTON, HOWARD STEPHEN, lawyer, management consultant; b. Hartford, Conn., Oct. 20, 1937; s. Howard Samuel and Agnes (Corvo) C.; m. Karen Youngman, June 16, 1962; children: Margaret, Susan. BA cum laude, Pomona Coll., 1959; LLB, Harvard U., 1962. Bar: Calif. 1963. Assoc. MacDonald & Halsted, L.A., 1964-68; ptnr. MacDonald, Halsted & Laybourne, L.A., 1968-82, of counsel, 1982-86; pres. Knapp Comm., L.A., 1982-87, S.C. Cons. Corp., 1987—. Author: Handbook for Creative Managers, 1987. 1st lt. U.S. Army, 1962—64. Republican. Episcopalian. Office: 1613 Chelsea Rd # 252 San Marino CA 91108-2419 Personal E-mail: hscran@earthlink.net.

CRANSTON, JOHN WELCH, historian, educator; b. Utica, NY, Dec. 21, 1931; s. Earl and Mildred (Welch) C. BA, Pomona Coll., 1953; MA, Columbia U., 1964; PhD, U. Wis., 1970. Asst. prof. history West Tex. State U., 1970-74, U. Mo., Kansas City, 1970, Rust Coll., Holly Springs, Miss., 1974-80, assoc. prof., 1980-83; historian U.S. Army Armor Ctr., Ft. Knox, Ky., 1983-95; ret., 1995. Adj. prof. history and govt. Elizabethtown C.C., Ft. Knox, 1988-2002. Contbr. history articles to profl. lit. With U.S. Army, 1953-55. NEH fellow, summers 1976, 81. Mem. Am. Hist. Assn., Orgn. Am. Historians. Democrat. Episcopalian. Home: 900 E Harrison Ave Apt D-61 Pomona CA 91767

CRANSTON, MARY B., lawyer; b. Palo Alto, Calif., Dec. 29, 1947; d. James Alfred and Bettye (Luhnow) Bailey; m. Harold David Cranston, Aug. 15, 1970; children: Susan Anne, John David. AB in polit. sci., Stanford U., 1969, JD, 1975; MA in psychology, UCLA, 1970. Bar: Calif. 1975. Assoc. atty. Pillsbury, Madison & Sutro, San Francisco, 1975-82, ptnr., 1983—2001, firm chair, 1999—2001; (Pillsbury, Madison & Sutro merged with Winthrop, Stimson, Putnam & Roberts, 2001); ptnr. Pillsbury Winthrop LLP, San Francisco, 2001—, firm chair, 2001—04; (Pillsbury Winthrop LLP merged with Shaw Pittman LLP, 2005); firm chair Pillsbury Winthrop Shaw Pittman LLP, San Francisco, 2005—. Faculty The Rutter Group, 1984—, Calif. Continuing Edn. of the Bar, 1985—, Nat. Inst. Trial Advocacy, San Francisco, 1986—; bd. dirs. GrafTech Internat. Ltd., 1999—; Bay Area Coun., 1999—; editl. bd. Nat. Law Jour., 2004—. Contbr. articles to profl. journals. Trustee San Francisco Ballet, 1996, Stanford U., 2000—; mem. The Yosemite Fund; mem. nat. centennial com. Girl Scouts USA, 2001; bd. dirs. Legal Services for Children, San Francisco, 1983—87, San Francisco C. of C., 1999—2001; bd. dirs. hist. soc. US Dist. Ct. No. Dist. Calif., 2001—; bd. mem. Episcopal Charities, 2003—; exec. com. bd. visitors Stanford Law Sch., 1977—80, 1996—, chair bd. visitors, 2001; chair bd. advisors we. region Catalyst, 2004—; bd. governors Commonwealth Club of Calif. Named one of The 100 Most Influential Lawyers in Calif., LA Daily Jour., 1999—2002, The 50 Most Influential Bus. Women in the Bay Area, San Francisco Bus. Times, 1999—2003, The 100 Most Influential Lawyers in Am., Nat. Law Jour., 2000, The 2 Best Law Firm Leaders in the US, Of Counsel, 2002; recipient Stanford Associates Award for disting. svc., Stanford U., 1999, Disting. Jurisprudence Award, Anti-Defamation League, 2000, Award of Merit, Bar Assn. San Francisco, 2002, Athena Award, 2004. Fellow: Am. Coll. Trial Lawyers; mem.: Assn. Bus. Trial Lawyers (bd. dirs. 1993—97), Calif. State Bar (mem. com. on women 1986—89, chair sect. of antitrust and trade regulation 1998—99), ABA (mem. commn. on women 1993—2000, coun. mem. antitrust sect. 1994—97, officer antitrust sect. 1997—2000), Am. Law Inst., Stanford Alumni Assn. (bd. dirs. 1986—93, 2001—, pres. 1990), Cap & Gown (Stanford) (treas. 1974—75). Avocations: reading, sports. Office: Pillsbury Winthrop Shaw Pittman 50 Fremont St Ste 1474 San Francisco CA 94105 Office Phone: 415-983-1621. Office Fax: 415-983-1200. Business E-Mail: mary.cranston@pillsburylaw.com.*

CRANSTON, STEWART E., career officer; BA in Math., U. So. Calif., 1966; MBA, Auburn U., 1979; Grad., Air Command and Staff Coll., 1979; Diploma, Indsl. Coll. of Armed Forces, 1986; postgrad., Carnegie-Mellon U., 1989. Commd. 2d lt. USAF, 1966, advanced through ranks to lt. gen., 1997; various assignments to dep. chief of staff, test and opers. Hdqtrs. Air Force Material Command, Wright-Patterson AFB, Ohio, 1992-93; comdr. Air Force Devel. Test Ctr./Air Force Material Command, Eglin AFB, Fla., 1993-97; vice-comdr. Hdqtrs. Air Force Material Comman, Wright-Patterson AFB, Ohio, 1997—. Decorated Disting. Svc. medal, Legion of Merit, Disting. Flying Cross, Meritorious Svc. medal with four oak leaf clusters, Air medal with 15 oak leaf clusters, Air Force Commendation medal with oak leaf cluster, Republic of Vietnam Gallantry Cross with Palm, Vietnam Svc. medal with four svc. stars, others. Office: AFMC/CV 4375 Chidlaw Rd Ste 1 Wright Patterson Afb OH 45433-5066

CRAPARO, JOHN S., information technology executive; b. N.Y.C., Sept. 3, 1959; s. Francis Xavier Craparo, Jane Constance Licciardi. BA, Iona Coll., New Rochelle, N.Y., 1981; MS in Mgmt., Poly. U., Bklyn., 1990. Sr. v.p., chief tech. officer GE Capital Corp., Stamford, Conn., 1989—98; v.p. global info. tech. ops. Dell Computer Corp., Round Rock, Tex., 1998—; CIO Dell Fin. Svcs., Round Rock, 2002—. Assoc. prof. Pace U., White Plains, NY, 1990—; chancellor Continental U., Lemmon, SD, 1999—. Editor: (jour.) Journal of Continuing Professional Development, 1999; author: (book and software program) Trunkalculator: the telecommunications management tool, 1998. Torchbearer Salt Lake City Olympic Games, 2002; bd. dirs. and mentor Jr. Achievment of Ctrl. Tex., Austin, 1990—; mem. adv. bd. Pace U., White Plains, NY, 1997—; bd. dirs. ARC Ctrl. Tex.; ofcl. U.S. agt. U. of South Africa, Pretoria, South Africa, 1998—; mem. Catholic Hospitalier Order of the the Knights of Malta - Brotherhood of the Blessed Gerard, Mandeni, South Africa, 1998—. Capt. USAF Aux. Fellow Internat. Mgmt. Ctrs., 1999, N.Y.C. Sci. Found. fellow, Medgar Evers Coll. of CUNY, 1986—89; scholar N.Y. State Regent's scholar, SUNY, 1977—81. Fellow: Royal Soc. Arts; mem.: Assn. of Computing Machinery. Republican. Roman Catholic. Home: 5808 Misty Hill Cove Austin TX 78759

CRAPO, MICHAEL DEAN, senator, former congressman, lawyer; b. Idaho Falls, Idaho, May 20, 1951; s. George Lavelle and Melba (Olsen) C.; m. Susan Diane Hasleton, June 22, 1974; children: Michelle, Brian, Stephanie, Lara, Paul. BA Polit. Sci. summa cum laude, Brigham Young U., 1973; postgrad., U. Utah, 1973-74; JD cum laude, Harvard U., 1977. Bar: Calif. 1977, Idaho 1979. Law clk. to Hon. James M. Carter U.S. Ct. Appeals (9th cir.), San Diego, 1977-78; assoc. atty. Gibson, Dunn & Crutcher, L.A., 1978-79; atty. Holden, Kidwell, Hahn & Crapo, Idaho Falls, 1979-92, ptnr., 1983-92; mem. Idaho State Senate from 32A Dist., 1985—93, asst. majority leader, 1987—89; pres. Pro Tempore, 1989-92; congressman U.S. House of Reps., 2d Idaho dist., Washington, 1993—99; mem. commerce com., new mem. leader 103rd Congress, sophomore class leader 104th Congress, co-chair Congl. Beef Caucus, dep. whip western region U.S. House of Reps., Washington, vice chair energy and power subcom., strategic planning leader House Leadership 105th Congress, mem. house resources com., mem. commerce com., mem. resources com.; senator from Idaho U.S. Senate, 1999—, dep. whip 108th congress, chmn. subcom. on fisheries, wildlife and water, Senate environ and pub. works com., chmn. subcom. on forestry, conservation and rural revitalization, Senate agr. com., mem. banking, housing and urban devel. com., mem. small bus. com. Precinct committeeman Dist. 29, 1980-85; vice chmn. Legislative Dist. 29, 1984-85; Mem. Health and Welfare Com., 1985-89, Resources and Environ. Com., 1985-90, State Affairs Com., 1987-92; Rep. Pres. Task Force, 1989. Leader Boy Scouts Am., Calif., Idaho, 1977-92; mem. Bar Exam Preparation, Bar Exam Grading; chmn. Law Day.; Bonneville County chmn. Phil Batt gubernatorial campaign, 1982. Named one of Outstanding Young Men of Am., 1985; recipient Cert. of Merit Rep. Nat. Com., 1990, Guardian of Small Bus. award Nat. Fedn. of Ind. Bus., 1990, 94, Cert. of Recognition Am. Cancer Soc., 1990, Idaho Housing Agy., 1990, Idaho Lung Assn., 1985, 86, 89, Friend of Agr. award Idaho Farm Bur., 1989-90, medal of merit Rep. Presdl. Task Force, 1989, Nat. Legislator of Yr. award Nat. Rep. Legislators Assn., 1991, Golden Bulldog award Watchdogs of the Treas., 1996, Thomas Jefferson award Nat. Am. Wholesale Grocers Assn.-Ind. Food Distbrs. Assn., 1996, Spirit of Enterprise award U.S. C. of C., 1993, 94, 95, 96. Mem. ABA (antitrust law sect.), Idaho Bar Assn., Rotary. Republican. Mem. Lds Ch. Avocations: sports, backpacking, hunting, skiing. Office: US Senate 239 Dirksen Senate Ofc Bldg Washington DC 20510-0001*

CRAPOL, EDWARD P., history professor; b. Buffalo, Sept. 29, 1936; s. Paul H. and Emmi H. (klinger) C.; m. Jeanne Zeidler, Aug. 1, 1973; children: Heidi, Jennifer, Paul, Andrew. BA, SUNY, Buffalo, 1960; MS, Univ. Wis., 1964, PhD, 1968. Tchr. Amherst Ctrl. Jr. High Sch., Amherst, N.Y., 1961-63; instr. history Wis. State Univ., Eau Claire, Wis., 1966-67; asst. prof. history Coll. William and Mary, Williamsburg, Va., 1967-71, assoc. prof. history, 1971-77; exchange prof. history Univ. Exeter, Exeter, England, 1976-77; prof. history dept. Coll. William and Mary, Williamsburg, Va., 1978—, chmn. history dept., 1981-84, acting chmn. history dept., 1986-87, prof. history, 1994—2004, prof. emeritus, 2004—. Vis. faculty Utah State U., summer, 1972; reviewer grant proposals NEH, 1983—95; lectr. in field. Author: James G. Blaine: Architect of Empire, 1999; editor: Women and American Foreign Policy: Lobbyists, Critics, and Insiders, 1987, 1992, America for Americans: Economic Nationalism and Anglophobia in the Late Nineteenth Century, 1973; reviewer manuscripts for Diplomatic History, Journal of the Early Republic, Alfred A. Knopf, Scholary Resources, Greenwood Press, Kent State Univ. Press, D.C. Health, Univ. N.C. Press. Va. Found. for Humanities and Pub. Policy grant, 1983, NEH grant, 1984, 1986, Internat. Studies Curriculum Devel. grant Coll of William and Mary, 1987; Univ. Humanities fellow Coll. William and Mary, 1988; Thomas A. Graves Jr. award for Sustained Excellence in Teaching William and Mary Coll., 1991, Thomas Jefferson award Coll. William and Mary, 1992. Mem. Soc. Historians Am. Fgn. Rels., Orgn. Am. Historians, Am. Hist. Assn., Soc. Historians Early Am. Republic. Home: 148 Mimosa Dr Williamsburg VA 23185-4004 E-mail: edpcal@wm.edu.

CRAPON DE CAPRONA, COUNT NOËL FRANÇOIS MARIE, retired federal official; b. Chambery, Savoie, France, May 23, 1928; s. Denys and Eleanor Worthington (Mather) Crapon de Caprona; m. Barbro Sigrid Wenne, 1954; children: Guy, Yann. BA, Coll. St. Martin, Pontoise, France, 1946; LLB, U. Paris, 1952; diploma, Inst. Comparative Law, 1951; postgrad., Sch. Polit. Scis., 1952—54. Asst. mgr. Sta. Catalina Estancias, Argentina,

1947—48; editor dept. gen. affairs and info. FAO, UN, Rome, 1954—57; liaison officer for UN and various orgns. FAO Office Dir. Gen., 1957—65, chief reports and records, 1966—72, chief conf. ops. br., 1972—74; sec. gen. FAO Conf. and Coun., 1974—78; dir. FAO Conf., Coun. and Protocol Affairs, Rome, 1974—83. Author: The Longobards, A Tentative Explanation, 1995. Served with French Army, 1944. Recipient 25 Years of Svc. award, Silver medal, FAO, 1979, Medal of Honor, City of Salon de Provence, 1992. Mem.: Soc. in France of SAR, Alumni Assn. Ecole des Sciences Politiques, Alumni Assn. Coll. St. Martin. Roman Catholic. Achievements include research in early medieval history, especially Longobards. Office: 73-75 Lojovägen S-18147 Lidingö Sweden Address: Palais Hadrien Pl dei Tres Mast 83600 Port-Fréjus France

CRARY, MINER DUNHAM, JR., lawyer; b. Warren, Pa., Sept. 8, 1920; s. Miner D. and Edith (Ingraham) C.; m. Mary Chapman, Jan. 23, 1943; children: Edith Crary Howe, James G., Laura Crary Hall, Harriet Crary, Miner A. BA, Amherst Coll., 1942; MA, Harvard U., 1943, LLB, 1948. Bar: N.Y. 1949. Assoc. Curtis, Mallet-Prevost, 1949-61, ptnr., 1961-96, coun., 1996—. Trustee Am. U. in Cairo, 1959—, Heckscher Art Mus., Huntington, N.Y., 1968-85; trustee Sterling and Francine Clark Art Inst., Williamstown, Mass., 1974—; bd. dirs. Robert Sterling Clark Found., N.Y.C., 1972—; chmn. exec. com. alumni coun. Amherst Coll., 1961-68; chmn. Huntington Bd. Edn. and Ctrl. Sch. Dist. 2, 1961-67; acting village justice Village of Asharoken, Northport, N.Y., 1987-2002. Lt. USNR, 1942-45. Mem. ABA (real property and probate com.), N.Y. State Bar Assn. (taxation and estate com. 1973), Assn. of Bar of City of N.Y. (surrogate ct. com. 1969-73), Union League Club, Century Assn. Club. (N.Y.C.), Huntington Country Club. Office: Curtis Mallet-Prevost Colt 101 Park Ave Fl 34 New York NY 10178-0061 Office Phone: 212-696-6006. E-mail: mdcrary@aol.com, mcrary@cm-p.com.

CRASEMANN, BERND, physicist, researcher; b. Hamburg, Germany, Jan. 23, 1922; came to U.S., 1946, naturalized, 1955; s. Pablo Joaquin and Hildegard Carlota (Vorwerk) C. AB, UCLA, 1948; PhD, U. Calif.-Berkeley, 1953. With Lavadora de Lanas S.A., Viña del Mar, Chile, 1941-46; asst. prof. physics U. Oreg., Eugene, 1953-58, assoc. prof., 1958-63, prof., 1963-89, prof. emeritus, 1989—. chmn. dept., 1976-84, dir. Chem. Physics Inst., 1984-87. Guest assoc. physicist Brookhaven Nat. Lab., Upton, N.Y., 1961-62; vis. prof. U. Calif., Berkeley, 1968-69, Université Pierre et Marie Curie, Paris, 1977; vis. scholar Stanford U., 1983; cons. Lawrence Radiation Lab., 1954-68, physicist, 1968-69; mem. com. on atomic and molecular sci. NRC/Nat. Acad. Scis., 1976-82; vis. scientist NASA Ames Rsch. Ctr., 1975-76; mem. panel on radiation rsch. NRC, 1985-87, chair bd. on assessment of NIST programs panel on atomic molecular and optical physics, 1989-90; chair exec. com. Advanced Light Source Users, 1984-88, sci. policy bd., 1989-92; chair adv. bd. Basic Energy Scis. Synchrotron Radiation Ctr. Argonne Nat. Lab, 1991-93; mem. U. Chgo. Review Com. for Argonne Nat. Lab. Physics Divsn., 1993-98; U.S. advisor in physics U.S.-Mex. Found. for Sci., 1994-97. Author (with J.L. Powell): Quantum Mechanics, 1961; editor: Atomic Inner-Shell Processes, 1975, Atomic Inner-Shell Physics, 1985, Phys. Rev. A, 1992—; mem. editl. bd.: Phys. Rev. C, 1978, Atomic Data and Nuc. Data Tables, 1982—, mem. publs. bd.: Am. Inst. Physics, 1992—2000; contbr. articles to sci. jours. Mem. region XIV selection com. Woodrow Wilson Nat. Fellowship Found., 1959-61, 62-68. Recipient Ersted award for distinguished teaching U. Oreg., 1959; NSF research grantee, 1954-64; U.S. AEC grantee, 1964-72; NASA grantee, 1972-79; AFOSR grantee, 1979-86; NSF grantee, 1986-95. Fellow AAAS, Am. Phys. Soc. (chmn. div. electron and atomic physics 1981-82, councillor 1983-86, mem. com. on internat. sci. affairs 1997-2000, chmn. 2000); mem. ACLU, Am. Assn. Physics Tchrs. (pres. Oreg. sect. 1956-57), Croatian Acad. Scis. and Arts (corr. mem.), Sierra Club, Phi Beta Kappa. Office: U Oreg Dept Physics Eugene OR 97403-1274 Office Phone: 541-346-4754. Business E-Mail: berndc@uoregon.edu.

CRASWELL, RICHARD, law educator; b. 1954; BA in Economics, with high honors, Mich. State U., 1974; JD cum laude, U. Chgo., 1977. Atty. office policy planning FTC, 1977—81, atty. bur. competition and bur. economics, 1982, atty.-advisor to commr. David A. Clanton, 1982—83; asst. prof. U. So. Calif. Law Ctr., 1983—85, assoc. prof., 1985—88, prof. law, 1988—94, Carolyn Craig Franklin prof., 1991—94, assoc. dean, 1988—90; prof. law U. Chgo. Law Sch., 1994—98, Stanford Law Sch., 1998—, William F. Baxter - Visa Internat. prof. law, 2002—, assoc. dean, 1999—2001. Adj. prof. Georgetown U. Law Ctr., 1983; vis. prof. U. Chgo. Law Sch., 1987—88, Stanford Law Sch., 1993. Victor H. Kramer Fellow, Yale Law Sch. and Yale Instn. for Social & Policy Studies, 1981—82. Office: Stanford Law Sch Crown Quadrangle 559 Nathan Abbott Way Stanford CA 94305-8610 Office Phone: 650-725-8542. Office Fax: 650-723-8230. Business E-Mail: rcraswel@stanford.edu.*

CRATE, DARRELL W., investment company executive, political organization administrator; b. NY, 1968; m. Nancy Crate; 4 children. BA, Bates Coll.; MBA, Columbia U. Mng. dir. Fin. Inst. Group Chase Manhattan Corp.; sr. v.p., CFO Affiliated Mgrs. Group, Inc., Prides Crossing, Mass., 1998—2001, exec. v.p., CFO, 2001—, treas. Fin. chair Lt. Gov. Kerry Healey's campaign; chmn. Mass. Rep. Party, Boston, 2003—. Trustee Reservations, Brookwood Sch. Mem.: Aircraft Owners and Pilots Assn. (trustee). Office: Affiliated Mgrs Group, Inc 600 Hale St Prides Crossing MA 01965 also: Mass Rep Party 85 Merrimac St, Ste 400 Boston MA 02114-4728 Office Phone: 617-523-5005. Office Fax: 617-747-3000.*

CRATER, TIMOTHY ANDREWS, internist; b. Winston-Salem, N.C., Aug. 27, 1966; s. John Lee Crater and Nancy Denton Crater; m. Debra Marie Schuh, Feb. 14, 1992; children: Reed Brooks, Zoe Emerson, Grace Warren, Isabelle Holton. BA in History magna cum laude, Wake Forest U., 1989; student field arty. officers basic course, Ft. Sill Arty. Sch., Okla., 1990; officer's tng., U.S. Army Airborne Sch., Ft. Benning, Ga., 1990, 1st Infanty Divsn., 1991; MD, U. Kans., 1998. Commd. 2d lt. U.S. Army, 1989, advanced through grades to 1st lt., 1992, fire support officer hdqs. battery 1/5 field arty. Ft. Riley, 1990-91, fire direction officer bravo battery 1/5 field arty., 1991-92, targeting officer hdqs. battery 1/5 field arty., 1992-93; resigned, 1993; resident in internal medicine U. Ala. Birmingham Hosp., 1998-2001; staff physician internal medicine Hutchinson (Kans.) Clinic, 2001—, bd. dirs., 2004—; asst. med. dir. Harry Hynes Meml. Hospice, 2002—03; clin. asst. prof. internal medicine U. Kans. Sch. Medicine, Wichita, 2002—; asst. med. dir. Reno County Hospice, 2003—. Decorated Bronze Star medal, Army Commendation medal, Army Achievement medal with oak leaf cluster; fellow, Am. Coll. Physicians; History of Medicine grantee, U. Kans., 1995. Mem. AMA, ACP, VFW (life), Kans. Soc. SAR, Am. Mensa, Am. Legion, Officers of the 1st Divsn., Rotary (Hutchinson bd. dirs., Paul Harris fellow Rotary Internat.), Phi Beta Kappa, Phi Alpha Theta, Alpha Omega Alpha. Republican. Avocation: reading. Home: 3504 Thunderbird Dr Hutchinson KS 67502 Office: Hutchinson Clinic PA 2101 N Waldron Hutchinson KS 67502 Office Phone: 620-694-4224. E-mail: cratermd@aol.com.

CRAVCENCO, LUDMILA, academic administrator; b. Balts, Moldova, Oct. 16, 1963; arrived in U.S., 1998; d. Klaudia Rozneritsa; m. Sergei Cravcenco, Nov. 20, 1987; 1 child, Egor Cravenco. BE, Balts State U., 1985; MEd, Kent State U., 1995, PhD in Higher Edn. Adminstrn., 2004. Adminstr., tchr. English Balts High Sch., Moldova, 1985—87; tchr. English Balts Spl. English Sch., 1987—91; asst. prof. Balts State U., 1991—97; tng. coord. USAID, 1996—97; translator, interpretor, analyst Internat. Monetary Fund, 1997—98; rschr., grad. tchg. asst. Kent State U., Ohio, 1998—2004, adj. prof., 2004—05. Mem.: Nat. Assn. Fgn. Student Advisors, Am. Edn. Rsch. Assn., Am. Soc. Higher Edn., Phi Beta Delta. Avocations: hiking, dance, reading. Home: 9121 Ranch Rd #1301 Streetsboro OH 44241 Office Phone: 330-672-2580. Business E-Mail: lcravce1@sbcglobal.net.

CRAVEN, DONALD B., lawyer; b. Durham, N.C., Aug. 19, 1941; AB, U. N.C., 1963; LLB, Duke U., 1967; postgrad., Georgetown U. Bar: N.C. 1967, Va. 1973, D.C. 1975. Trial atty. tax divsn. U.S. Dept. Justice, 1968-73; assoc. asst. adminstr., acting asst. adminstr. Fed. Energy Adminstrn., 1974-75; mem. Miller & Chevalier Chartered, Washington; ptnr., civil and appellate litig. Akin Gump Strauss Hauer & Feld LLP, Washington, 2000—. Mem. editl. bd. Duke Law Jour., 1966-67. Mem. ABA, N.C. Bar Assn., Va. Bar Assn., N.C. State Bar, Va. State Bar, D.C. Bar, Bar Assn. of D.C., Phi Delta Phi (magister 1966-67). Office: Akin Gump Strauss Hauer & Feld LLP Robert S Strauss Bldg 1333 New Hamphire Ave NW Washington DC 20036-1564 Office Phone: 202-887-4000. Office Fax: 202-887-4288. E-mail: dcraven@akingump.com.

CRAVEN, FRANK JOHN, actor, playwright, poet; b. N.Y.C., Sept. 19, 1955; s. John and Dorothy (Langan) Craven; m. Fedora di Eugenio, June 12, 1991. Studied, HB Studio, NYC, 1977—79. Summer stock apprentice Corning Summer Theatre, 1981; drama coach Actors Youth Fund; columnist Streetnews, NYC. Prodr.: (documentaries) Conversations pour Picasso, Free Leonard Peltier Now! (writer/dir. Bronze, Worldfest, 2001, 2002), WTC RIP (Judges award, Hometown Video Fest, 1998, 1999); (TV series) What's Ailing/ Healing US America?; (TV films) The Clothes "Make" the Man (NY Film & Video Fest Best Costume award, 2001, Internet Cities Streamed TV award, 2001, Bronze Telly award, 00, 01, 02, 2003);, author plays, composer songs; actor: (films); (plays);, performer (m.c.) cabaret; model: prodr.: (screen play) Authority Vs. Majority (silver- comedy screenplay Worldfest Houston, 92), (staged at) Am. Theater of Actors, 1982, 1989; (TV films) The Terrorist Terrorized, "Criminal" Voices in the Wilderness, The Natural Law Party, Right Vs. Righteous. Mem.: AEA, AFTRA, SAG. Avocations: flamenco guitar, blues harmonica, painting, cartooning. Office: Authority vs Majority Prodn Co 300 E 52d St New York NY 10022 Office Phone: 212-967-7711 3259. E-mail: autvsmaj@aol.com.

CRAVEN, GEORGE W., lawyer; b. Louisville, Mar. 11, 1951; s. Mark Patrick and Doris Ann Craven; m. Jane A. Gallery, Aug. 16, 1980; children: Charles, Francis. Student, Sophia U., Tokyo, Japan, 1970-71; BA, U. Notre Dame, 1973; JD, Harvard U., 1976. Bar: Ill. 1976, U.S. Dist. Ct. (no. dist.) Ill. 1976, U.S. Tax Ct. 1977. Assoc. Sidley & Austin, Chgo., 1976—80; ptnr. Ogden & Robertson, Louisville, 1980—81; assoc. Mayer, Brown, Rowe & Maw, Chgo., 1981—82, ptnr., 1983—. Sec., United Way, Chgo., 1997—2003, bd. dirs., 2001-. Mem. ABA (sect. taxation), Coun. on Fgn. Rels. (Chgo. com. 1996—), Econ. Club Chgo. Roman Catholic. Office: Mayer Brown Rowe & Maw 71 S Wacker Dr Chicago IL 60606-4637 Office Phone: 312-701-7231. E-mail: gcraven@mayerbrown.com.

CRAVEN, JAMES MICHAEL (OMAHKOHKIAAYO I'POYI), economist, educator; b. Seattle, Mar. 10, 1946; s. Homer Henry and Mary Kathleen Craven; 1 child, Christina Kathleen Florindo-Craven. Student, U. Minn., 1966-68; BA in Sociology, BA in Econs., U. Manitoba, Winnipeg, Can., 1971, MA in Econs., 1974. Lic. pilot; cert. ground instr. Instr. econ. and bus. Red River C.C., Winnipeg, 1974-76; lectr. rsch. methods of stats. U. Manitoba, Winnipeg, 1977-78; instr. econ. and bus. Big Bend C.C., Moses Lake, Wash., 1980-81; planning analyst Govt. P.R., San Juan, 1984; prof. econs. and bus. Interam. U. P.R., Bayamon, 1984-85; instr. econs., lectr. history Green River C.C., Auburn, Wash., 1988-92; prof. dept. chair econs. Clark Coll., Vancouver, Wash., 1992—. Vis. prof. St. Berchman's U., Kerala, India, 1981, 83, 86, 91; instr. econs. Bellevue (Wash.) C.C., 1988-92; cons. Bellevue, 1988—, Irwin Pubs., 1995—. Inventor in field; contbr. articles to profl. jours. Platform com. mem. Wash. State Dem., Seattle, 1992; cons. Lowry for Gov. Campaign, Seattle, 1992; mem. (assoc.) Dem. Party Nat. Com., 1994-99; mem. Nat. Steering Com. for Re-election of Pres. Clinton, 1995-96; mem. Pres.'s Second Term Com., 1996-99; tribunal judge Inter-Tribal Tribunal on Residential Schs. in Can., Vancouver, 1998; mem. Blackfoot Nation. With U.S. Army, 1963-66. Recipient pilot wings FAA, 1988-92; Govt. Can. fellow, 1973-74. Mem. Assn. Northwest Econ. Educators, Wash. Edn. Assn., Assn. Nat. Security Alumni, Blackfoot Confederacy. Avocations: flying, languages, tennis, hiking. Home: 904 NE Minnehaha St Apt C9 Vancouver WA 98665-8732 Office: Clark Coll Dept Econs 1800 E Mcloughlin Blvd Vancouver WA 98663-3598 Office Phone: 360-992-2283. E-mail: jcraven@clark.edu, aradicalblackfoot@blogspot.com.

CRAVEN, JAMES W., conservator, educator; b. Ann Arbor, Mich., Oct. 17, 1931; s. George Ernest and Elsie (Wilkinson) Craven; m. Barbara Jean Cook (dec.); children: William, Pamela, Jane, Karen; m. Adela Pond Laporte, Aug. 7, 1982. Grad., Ann Arbor H.S., 1949. Apprentice bookbinder, journeyman bookbinder, supr. binding dept., document restoration specialist, book conservator U. Mich., Ann Arbor, 1949—. Author: Not Perfect But Just Right, 2004; co-author: Disaster Plan for the Bentley Library, 1976. Sgt. U.S. Army, 1951—54. Mem.: Midwestern Assn. Forensic Scientists, Libr. Binding Inst., Am. Inst. Conservation. Avocations: woodworking, horticulture, dogs. Office: U Mich Bentley Hist Libr 1150 Beal Ave Ann Arbor MI 48109

CRAVEN, PAMELA F., lawyer; b. Bloomfield, NJ, 1953; m. Bill Craven; 2 children. BA in English, U. Pa., 1974, JD, 1977; LLM in taxation, NYU, 1981. Bar: 1977. Assoc. McCarter & English, 1977—79, Coudert Brothers, 1979—82; asst. gen. counsel, asst. sec. NCR Corp., 1982—92; atty. AT&T, 1992—96; v.p. law Lucent Technologies Inc., Murray Hill, NJ, 1996—2000, sec., 1999—2000, v.p., gen. counsel, sec. Enterprise Networks Group, 2000; v.p., gen. counsel, sec. Avaya Inc., Basking Ridge, NJ, 2000—02, sr. v.p., gen. counsel, sec., 2002—. Bd. overseers U. Pa. Law Sch., 2004—; bd. managers U. Pa. Law Alumni Assn.; chair cmty. adv. bd. NJ Network. Recipient Alumni Award of Merit, U. Pa. Law Alumni Soc. Office: Avaya Inc 211 Mount Airy Rd Basking Ridge NJ 07920

CRAVEN, STEPHEN M., retired research chemist; b. Salem, NJ, July 30, 1944; s. John Richard and Helen Barbara (Orlowski) C.; m. Laura A. Blizzard, Mar. 6, 1971 (div. July 1984); children: Edward Marion, Theresae Marie. BA in Chemistry, Rutgers U., 1966; PhD in Phys.-Analytical Chemistry, U. S.C., 1970. Rsch. scientist Miami U., Wright-Patterson AFB, Ohio, 1970-72, rsch. assoc. Oxford, Ohio, 1972-73; sr. analytical chemist Akzona, Enka, N.C., 1973-75; rsch. assoc. Ohio U., Athens, 1975-76; sr. analytical chemist Monsanto Rsch. Corp., Miamisburg, Ohio, 1976-86; retired, 1986. Co-patentee in field. Co-recipient Nobel prize in physics, 2000. Mem. Cobletz Soc., Soc. for Applied Spectroscopy. Achievements include co-patent disclosure for new class of high electrical conducting (possible superconductor), and thermisters, low thermal conducting materials, new class of catalyst and new class of Lasant materials.

CRAVEN, WES, film director; b. Cleve., Aug. 2, 1939; m. Bonnie Broecker, 1964 (div.); children: Jonathan, Jessica; m. Mimi Craven, 1984 (div. 1987); m. Iya Labunka, Nov. 27, 2004. Co-owner prodn. co. Craven/Maddalena Films. Writer, editor, dir. (films) Last House on the Left, 1972, The Hills Have Eyes, 1977; 2d editor You've Got To Walk It Like You Talk It or You'll Loose That Beat, 1973; dir. (films) Deadly Friend, 1986, The Serpent and the Rainbow, 1988, Vampire in Brooklyn, 1995, Music of the Heart, 1999, Cursed, 2005, (TV films) A Stranger in Our House, 1978, Invitation to Hell, 1984, Chiller, 1985; actor: (films) The Fear, 1995, The Cutting Edge: The Magic of Movie Editing, 2004, (TV films) Shadow Zone: The Undead Express, 1996; actor, dir.: (films) Scream, 1996, Scream 2, 1997, Scream 3, 2000, Red Eye, 2005; writer: (films) A Nightmare on Elm Street 2: Freddy's Revenge, 1985, A Nightmare on Elm Street 4: The Dream Master, 1988, A Nightmare on Elm Street: The Dream Child, 1989, Freddy's Dead: The Final Nightmare, 1991, Freddy vs. Jason, 2003; writer, dir. (films) Deadly Blessing, 1981, Swamp Thing, 1982, A Nightmare on Elm Street, 1984; exec. prodr. (films) A Nightmare on Elm Street 3: Dream Warriors, 1987, Shocker, 1989, Night Visions, 1990, The People Under the Stairs, 1991, New Nightmare, 1994, The Outpost, 1995, Wishmaster, 1997, Carnival of Souls, 1998, Dracula 2000, (TV films) Laurel Canyon, 1993, Don't Look Down, 1998, They Shoot Divas, Don't They?, 2002, (TV series) Nightmare Cafe, 1992, Hollyweird, 1998-, author: (novel) The Fountain Society. Mem. Dirs. Guild Am. Avocation: birdwatching.*

CRAVENS, GARY DEAN, information scientist, physician; b. Phila., Oct. 18, 1953; s. Robert Walker and Mary Edna Cravens. BA, Ind. U., 1975, MS, 1979, MS, 1984, MS, 1992, MD, 1997. Computer programmer analyst Naval Surface Warfare Ctr., Crane, Ind., 1984—85; mathematician USAF Sch. Aerospace Medicine, San Antonio, 1985—87; advanced discipline specialist Vanguard Tech. Corp., Crane, 1987—88; resident Mayo Clinic, Rochester, Minn., 1999—2000; sr. informaticist Ingenix Health Intelligence, Eden Prairie, 2000—02; bioinformaticist Ind. U., Indpls., 2002—04; physician U. Pitts. Med. Ctr., 2004—. Contbr. articles to profl. jours. 2d lt. USAF, 1975-77. Med. Informatics fellow Ind. U., 1997-99. Mem. Am. Med. Informatics Assn. (reviewer 1998-99), World Future Soc., Alpha Omega Alpha. Avocations: travel, reading. Office: Dept Medicine U Pitts Med Ctr 200 Lothrop St Pittsburgh PA 15213

CRAVER, EARLENE, historian, educator; b. Fresno, Calif., Jan. 8, 1940; d. Earl H. Craver and Rose K. Gregorian; m. Axel Leijonhufvud, June 18, 1977; stepchildren: Gabriella Leijonhufvud, Christina Leijonhufvud. BA summa cum laude, Fresno State Coll., 1960; PhD, U. So. Calif., 1972. Instr. U. Calif., Riverside, 1968—70; asst. prof. U. Ky., Lexington, 1970—74; lectr. Calif. State U., Northridge, 1983, UCLA, 1983; vis. prof. U. Trento, Italy. Contbr. articles to profl. jours. Fellow, Nat. Def. Edn. Act, 1960—64, NEH, 1987—88. Mem.: Orgn. Am. Historians, Soc. Italian Hist. Studies, Am. Hist. Assn., Phi Kappa Phi.

CRAVER, JAMES BERNARD, lawyer; b. Morristown, N.J., July 20, 1943; s. Herbert Seward and Anne (Brady) C.; m. Elinor Ladd, Aug. 27, 1966; children: Elisabeth Ladd, Amy Richmond. AB cum laude, Harvard U., 1965; JD, U. Pa., 1970. Bar: N.Y. 1970, Mass. 1974, Ohio 1980. Assoc. Sullivan & Cromwell, N.Y.C., 1970-73; asst. counsel, asst. sec. Mass. Fin. Svcs. Co., Boston, 1973-76; gen. counsel, sec. Anchor Corp., Elizabeth, N.J., 1976-79; sec., sr. corp. counsel B.F. Goodrich Co., Akron, Ohio, 1979-84; ptnr. Baker & Hostetler, Columbus, 1984-90; sr. v.p., gen. coun. Signature Fin. Group, Inc., Boston, 1991-95; mng. dir. Eagle Instl. Fin. Svcs., Inc., Dover, Mass., 1995-2000; ptnr. Burns & Levinson, Boston, Mass., 2000—. Mem. N.Y. State Bar Assn., Mass. Bar Assn., Ohio Bar Assn., Boston Bar Assn., Sakonnet Golf Club (Little Compton, R.I.), Harvard Club of Boston, Harvard Club of Akron, Dedham (Mass.) Country and Polo Club. Home: PO Box 811 Dover MA 02030-0811 Office: Burns & Levinson 125 Summer St Boston MA 02110-1624 Fax: 617-345-3299. Office Phone: 617-345-3847. E-mail: jcraver@burnslev.com, jcraver@b-l.com.

CRAVEY, PAMELA J., librarian; b. Washington, Mar. 6, 1945; d. Jack M. and Marjorie M.W. Bristow; m. G. Randall Cravey; 1 child, Christopher B. BA, Baldwin Wallace Coll., 1967; MS, Fla. State U., 1968; PhD, Ga. State U., 1989. Libr., instr. Fla. State U., Tallahassee, 1968-69, U. Ga., Athens, 1969-72; asst. then assoc. libr. U. Ctrl. Fla., Orlando, 1973-75; asst. then assoc. prof., libr. Ga. State U., Atlanta, 1975-2000; pvt. practice $D, Decatur, 2000—. Author: Protecting Library Staff, Users, Collections, and Facilities, 2001; contbr. articles to profl. jours. and books. Libr. Svc. Enhancement Program grantee Coun. Libr. Resources; personal grantee Coun. Libr. Resources. Mem. ALA, Assn. Coll. Rsch. Librs. Home: 2413 Harrington Dr Decatur GA 30033-4903 Office: 2107 N Decatur Rd #308 Decatur GA 30033-5305 Office Phone: 404-636-6338. E-mail: pcraveyi2s@comcast.net.

CRAW, FREEMAN (JERRY), graphic artist; b. East Orange, N.J. s. Stanley Reston and Mildred (Godfrey) C.; m. Janet Secor Johnson (dec.); children: Peter (dec.), Stephanie (dec.). Grad., Cooper Union, degree (hon.), 1967. Artist Am. Colortype, Clifton, NJ, 1940-44; art dir. Tri-Arts Press, N.Y.C., 1944-65, art dir., v.p., 1956-65; prin. Freeman Craw Design, N.Y.C., 1965-81; mgr. graphics and prodn. Rockefeller U. Press, N.Y.C., 1981-86; prin. Freeman Craw, graphist, 1986—2001; pvt. practice Tinton Falls, NJ, 2001—. One-man shows include: Am. Type Founders, U. Ala., BBDO, N.Y.C., Carnegie-Mellon U., Cooper Union, Royal Coll. Art, London, Soc. Typog. Designers, London, Soc. Typog. Arts, Chgo., Rochester Inst. Tech., N.Y.; represented in permanent collections: Mus. Modern Art., N.Y.C., Cooper-Hewitt Mus., Smithsonian Instn., N.Y.C.; created 10 type faces. Mem. alumni adv. bd. Cooper Union, 1969-71. Recipient Goudy award Rochester Inst. Tech., 1981, Type Dirs. Club medal, 1988, Lernhardt award, 1966. Mem. Type Dirs. Club (bd. dirs. 1983-86), Art Dirs. Club, Guttenberg Mus. (hon.), Essex Skating Club (West Orange, N.J., hon.). Avocations: japanese prints, lectures. Office Phone: 732-918-8965.

CRAWFORD, B., lawyer; b. Tulsa, June 29, 1922; s. Burnett Hayden and Margaret Sara (Stevenson) C.; m. Carolyn McCann, June 5, 1946 (div.); m. Virginia Baker, July 23, 1970 (dec. June 1994); m. Melanie Crowley, Dec. 24, 1994; children: Margaret Louise Crawford Brucks, Robert Hayden. BA, U. Mich., 1944, JD, 1949. Bar: Okla. 1949, U.S. Dist. Ct. (no. dist.) Okla. 1949, U.S. Supreme Ct. 1954, U.S. Ct. Appeals (10th cir.) 1954, U.S. Dist. Ct. (so. dist.) Ill. 1959, U.S. Ct. Mil. Appeals 1959, U.S. Ct. Appeals (fed. cir.) 1959, U.S. Dist. Ct. (we. and ea. dists.) Okla. 1960, U.S. Tax Ct. 1967. Law clk. to chief judge U.S. Dist. Ct. (no. dist.) Okla., 1950-51; asst. city prosecuter City of Tulsa, 1951-52, alt. mcpl. judge, 1952-54; U.S. atty. No. Dist. Okla., 1954-58; asst. dep. atty. gen. U.S. Dept. Justice, 1958-60; sole practice Tulsa, 1960-77; sr. ptnr. Crawford Crowne and Bainbridge, Tulsa, 1981-96, The Law Office of B. Hayden Crawford, Tulsa, 1996—. Lectr. in field. Rep. nominee U.S. Senate from Okla., 1960, 62; Okla. mem. adv. com. U.S. Ct. of Appeals (10th circuit); active civic and mil. orgns. Served to Rear Adm. USNR, 1942-78. Decorated Legion of Merit, Purple Heart, Disting. Pub. Svc. medal, Dept. Def. Disting. Svc. award; recipient Okla. Minute Man award 1974. Fellow Am. Assn. Matrimonial Lawyers; mem. ABA, Okla. Bar Assn., Tulsa County Bar Assn., Assn. Trial Lawyers Am., Okla. Trial Lawyers Assn., U.S. Res. Officers Assn. (nat. pres. 1973-74), Phi Delta Theta, Phi Delta Phi, Tula Summit Club, Army and Navy Club (Washington), Garden of Gods Club (Colorado Springs, Colo.), So. Hills Country Club (Tulsa), Masons, Kiwanis (pres. 1969). Presbyterian. Home: 2300 Riverside Dr Tulsa OK 74114-2400 Office: 240 Mid-Continent Tower 401 S Boston Ave Tulsa OK 74103-4016

CRAWFORD, BRETT A., lawyer; BA in Journalism, La. State U., 1988; MBA, Dartmouth Coll., 1994; JD, Georgetown U., 2004, PhD candidate, 2006. Bar: Md. Cons. World Bank, Washington, 1989; assoc. coord. higher edn. transition team for Gov.-elect Mike Foster, La., 1995; co-owner, prin. cons. The Sequoia Group LLC, Baton Rouge; exec. dir. LA. Econ. Devel. Corp., 1996—97; undersec. revenue State of La., 1998—99, sec. revenue, 1999—2000; assoc. Sonnenschein Nath & Rosenthal LLP, Washington. Office: Sonnenschein Nath & Rosenthal LLP Ste 600, E Tower 1301 K St NW Washington DC 20005 Office Phone: 202-408-9238. Office Fax: 202-408-6399. Business E-Mail: bcrawford@sonnenschein.com.

CRAWFORD, BRUCE EDGAR, performing company executive; b. West Bridgewater, Mass., Mar. 16, 1929; s. Harry Ellsworth and Nancy (Morrison) C.; m. Christine Amelung, Feb. 1, 1958; 1 son, Robert Bosworth. BS in Econs., U. Pa., 1952. With Benton & Bowles, Inc., N.Y.C., 1954-58; v.p. Ted Bates & Co., N.Y.C., 1958-61; advt. dir. Chesebrough Ponds Inc., N.Y.C., 1961-63; with Batten, Barton, Durstine & Osborn, Inc., N.Y.C., 1963-85, pres., from 1978, BBDO Internat., N.Y.C., 1975-83, chief exec. officer, 1977-85, chmn., 1985; dir. Met. Opera Assn., from 1976, v.p., 1981, pres., 1984-85, gen. mgr., 1986-88; pres., chief exec. officer Omnicom Group, N.Y.C., 1989-97; chmn. Omnicom Group, Inc., N.Y.C., 1997—2002, Lincoln Center for the Performing Arts, N.Y.C., 2002—05. Served with U.S. Army, 1947-48. Mem.: Racquet and Tennis (N.Y.C.); Turf and Field. Republican.

CRAWFORD, CAREN LEE, computer engineer; b. Maywood, Calif., Sept. 1, 1954; d. Charles Earl and Wilma May (Flom) Hillhouse; m. Jimmie Crawford, Aug. 6, 1983. BA, Adams State Coll., 1976; AA, Western Nev. CC, 1980. CRP planner Bently Nev. Corp., Minden; MRB and source inspection coord. Apple Computer, Cupertino, Calif., 1981-83; quality assurance specialist Convergent Tech., San Jose, Calif., 1983-88; sr. project coord. Sun Microsystems, Mountain View, Calif., 1988-90, quality engr., 1990, sr. quality engr., 1991-97; s/w process engr. KLA-Tencor Corp., San Jose, 1997-98; sr. quality assurance analyst NET Delivery Corp, San Jose, 1999-00; sr. cons. DATATREND Info. Sys., Chgo., 2000; quality program mgr. Qwest Comms., Inc., Denver, 2000-01; br. office admin. Edward Jones, 2002—. Mem.:

APICS, Am. Soc. Quality Control (cert.), White Shine Jerusalem (worth shepardess 1981, Ruth 1972), Order Eastern Star. Home: 14871 Mariposa Ct Broomfield CO 80020-8742 Personal E-mail: carencrawford@earthlink.net.

CRAWFORD, CAROL GLORIA, mathematician, educator; b. Wilkes-Barre, Pa., Dec. 8, 1951; d. Harry H. and Gloria P. Crawford. BA in Math., Misericordia Coll., 1973; MA in Math., Georgetown U., 1975, PhD in Math., 1979. Prof. math. LeMoyne Coll., Syracuse, NY, 1979—81, U.S. Naval Acad., Annapolis, Md., 1981—. Mem. rev. panels NSF, 1997—99, 2003; v.p. faculty senate U.S. Naval Acad., 2001—03; presenter in field. Author: Math Without Fear, 1981; contbr. articles to profl. jours.; assoc. editor Am. Math. Monthly, 1984—86. Named rsch. fellow, USN, 1982, NASA, 1984; recipient Civilian Meritorious Svc. award and medal, USN, 1998; fellow, Inst. for Combinatorics, Winnipeg, Can., 1990; grantee, FBI, 1994—96, Office of Naval Rsch., 1994—96, NASA, 1994—96, David Taylor Rsch. Ctr., 1994—96, Carderock Divsn., 1994—96, Naval Air Warfare Ctr. Mem.: Math. Assn. Am. (regional chair, vice chair 1998—2000). Office: US Naval Acad Dept Math Annapolis MD 21402 Business E-Mail: cgc@usna.edu.

CRAWFORD, CAROL TALLMAN, law educator; b. Mt. Holly, NJ, Feb. 25, 1943; m. Ronald Crawford; children: Timothy, Jeffrey, Richard. BA, Mt. Holyoke Coll., 1965; JD magna cum laude, Washington Coll. Law, Am. U., 1978. Bar: Va. 1978, DC 1979. Legis. asst. to Senator Bob Packwood, Washington, 1969-75; assoc. firm Collier, Shannon, Rill & Scott, Washington, 1979-81; exec. asst. to chmn. FTC, Washington, 1981-83, dir. bur. consumer protection, 1983-85; assoc. dir. Office of Mgmt. & Budget, Washington, 1985-89; asst. atty. gen. legis. affairs U.S. Dept. Justice, Washington, 1989-90; commr. U.S. Internat. Trade Commn., 1991-2000; disting. vis. prof. law George Mason U., Arlington, Va., 2000-01. Bd. dirs. European Inst., Ind. Women's Forum, Smithfield Foods, Inc. Trustee Barry Goldwater Chair of Am. Instns., Ariz. State U., Phoenix, 1983—; chair internat. trade and investment subcom. Federalist Soc., 1998—99, chair internat. and nat. security sect., 1999—2003; mem. adv. com. NAFTA Labor Agreement, 2002—. Republican.

CRAWFORD, CINDY (CYNTHIA ANN CRAWFORD), model, actress; b. Dekalb, Ill., Feb. 20, 1966; d. Dan Crawford and Jennifer Moluf; m. Richard Gere, Dec. 12, 1991 (div. 1995); m. Rande Gerber, May 29, 1998; children: Presley Walker, Kaya Jordan. Student, Northwestern U. Model for Victor Skrebneski, 1984-86; signed with Elite Modeling Agy., 1986; spokesperson Revlon, 1989—, JH Collectibles, Pepsi Cola, Kay Jewelers, Blockbuster Video, others; host MTV's House of Style, 1989-95. Released Cindy Crawford Fragrance, 2003. First featured on cover Vogue, 1986; has appeared on covers of W, People, Harper's Bazaar, ELLE, Allure, many others; Actor: (films) Fair Game, 1995, 54, 1998, The Simian Line, 2000; (exercise videos): Cindy Crawford's Shape Your Body Workout, 1992, The Next Challenge Workout, 1993. Host: (TV specials) Sex With Cindy Crawford, 1998. Supporter breast cancer rsch.; active Leukemia Soc. of Am.

CRAWFORD, CURTIS J., computer and electronics company executive; CEO Zilog, Campbell, Calif.; pres., CEO XCEO, Inc.; dir. DuPont E.I. Nemours & Co.; CEO Onix Microsystems, Inc.; dir. Agilysis Inc., ITT, Inc. Trustee DePaul Univ. Office: DuPont EI Nemours 1007 Market St Wilmington DE 19898*

CRAWFORD, DAN, archivist; b. Waukesha, Wis., 1958; s. William John and Amata Irene Crawford. BA, Upper Iowa U., 1978; MLS, U. Wis., 1980. Univ. archivist Upper Iowa U., Fayette, 1976—78; book fair mgr. Newberry Libr., Chgo., 1995—; sec., bookkeeper Caxton Club, Chgo., 1995—2004, gen. mgr., 2004—. Author: Just As Leaf, 2004, Guile is Where it Goes, 2004, Authorella, 2003. Vol. Newberry Libr. Book Fair, Chgo., 1985—94. Named Author of the Month, Highlights for Children, 2001. Mem.: ALA, Mystery Writers Am., Caxton Club (treas. 2001—04). Office: The Newberry Libr 60 W Walton St Chicago IL

CRAWFORD, DAVID L., astronomer; b. Tarentom, Pa., Mar. 2, 1931; s. William Letham and A. Blanche (Livingstone) C.; m. Mary Louise Mueller, Aug. 16, 1940; children: Christine, Deborah, Lisa. PhD, U. Chgo., 1958. Rsch. asst. Yerkes Obs., Chgo., 1953-57; asst. prof. Vanderbilt U., Nashville, 1957-59; staff astronomer Kitt Peak Nat. Obs., Tucson, 1960-96, emeritus astronomer, 1997—. Rsch. asst. McDonald Obs., 1955-57; project mgr. Kitt Peak Nat. Obs., 1963-73, assoc. dir. rsch., 1970-73, head office univ. rels., 1984-85, head office of tech. transfer, 1993-95; exec. dir. Internat. Dark-Sky Assn., 1987—, pres. bd. dirs. GNAT, Inc., 1993—. Recipient outstanding svc. award Astron. League, 1992. Fellow AAAS (coun. 1986-89, com. on coun. affairs 1986-88), Illuminating Engring. Soc. N.Am. (roadway lighting com., outdoor environ. lighting impact com., sports lighting com.); mem. Am. Astron. Soc. (coun. 1972-75, Van Briesbrock award 1997), Astron. Soc. Pacific (bd. dirs. 1970-76, nominating com., publs. com.), Internat. Astron. Union (active numerous commns., exec. coms., past chmn. working group on amateur/profl. rels.). Avocations: travel, reading, teaching, trout fishing, photography. Office: IDA 3225 N First Ave Tucson AZ 85719 Office Phone: 520-293-3198. E-mail: crawford@darksky.org, ida@darksky.org.

CRAWFORD, DEWEY BYERS, lawyer; b. Saginaw, Mich., Dec. 22, 1941; s. Edward Owen and Ruth (Wentworth) C.; m. Nancy Elizabeth Eck, Mar. 24, 1973. AB in Econs., Dartmouth Coll., 1963; JD with distinction, U. Mich., 1966. Bar: Ill. 1967, U.S. Dist. Ct. (no. dist.) Ill. 1969. Assoc. Gardner, Carton & Douglas LLP, Chgo., 1969-74, ptnr., 1975—. Adj. prof. law, ITT, Kent Sch. Law, 1992—. Contbr. articles to profl. jours. Chmn. Winnetka (Ill.) Caucus Coun., 1988-89; governing mem. Chgo Symphony, Chgo. Bot. Garden; bd. govs. Winnetka Cmty. House. With U.S. Army, 1966-68, Vietnam. Mem. ABA, Chgo. Bar Assn., Am. Coll. Investment Counsel, Lawyers Club Chgo., Exec. Club Chgo. Republican. Congregationalist. Avocations: reading, music. Office: Gardner Carton & Douglas LLP 191 N Wacker Dr Ste 3700 Chicago IL 60606-1698 Office Phone: 312-569-1111. Business E-Mail: dcrawford@gcd.com.

CRAWFORD, DONALD WESLEY, philosophy educator, university official; b. Berkeley, Calif., July 30, 1938; s. Arthur Loyd and Josephine (Gareffa) C.; m. Sharon Dee Messenger, Nov. 5, 1960; children: Kathryn, Alison. BA, U. Calif., Berkeley, 1960; PhD, U. Wis., 1965. From tchg. asst. to dean U. Wis., Madison, 1962—89, dean Coll. Letters and Sci., 1989-92; asst. prof. U. Sask., Saskatchewan, Canada, 1965-68; vice chancellor acad. affairs U. Calif., Santa Barbara, 1992-93, exec. vice chancellor, 1993-98, prof., 1992—2004, prof. emeritus, 2004—, dir. London Ctr. for Edn. Abroad program, 1998-2000, dep. assoc. provost, 2001—. Author: Kant's Aesthetic Theory, 1974; editor Jour. Aesthetics and Art Criticism, 1989-93. Bd. dirs. Meriter Hosp., Madison, 1989-92, Santa Barbara Bot. Garden, 1993-98, U. Calif. Santa Barbara Found., 1992-98, U. Calif. Trust (U.K.), 2000—. NEH fellow, 1974. Mem. Am. Soc. for Aesthetic, Brit. Soc. for Aesthetic. Office: U Calif Dept Philosophy South Hall Santa Barbara CA 93106 E-mail: crawford@philosophy.ucsb.edu.

CRAWFORD, EDWIN MAC, pharmaceutical executive; b. 1949; m. Linda Crawford; children: Andrew, Ellen. BS, Auburn U., 1971. CPA. With Arthur Young & Co., 1971—77, 1978—81, Salem Nat. Corp., 1977—78, GTI Ltd., 1981—85, 1986, Oxylance Corp., 1985—86, Mulberry St. Investment Co., 1986—90; exec. v.p. hosp. ops. Charter Med. Corp., Atlanta, 1990—92; pres., COO Magellan (formerly Charter Med. Corp.), Atlanta, 1992—93, chair., pres., CEO, 1993—97; pres., CEO MedPartners, Inc., Birmingham, 1997—98; chmn., pres., CEO Caremark Rx, Inc. (formerly MedPartners), Birmingham, 1998—. Bd. dirs. Nashville Healthcare Coun., 2003—04, Pharm. Care Mgmt. Assn. Office: Caremark Rx Inc 211 Commerce St Nashville TN 37201

CRAWFORD, FELIX CONKLING, retired dentist; b. Jan. 11, 1938; DDS, U. Tex. Dental Br., Houston, 1963. Pvt. practice, Plainview, Tex.; ret. Pres. Rotary, Plainview, 1971-72, Plainview Country Club, 1973-74, Plainview C. of C., 1984; chmn. Tex. Dental Found., 1990-92. Named Outstanding Alumnus, U. Tex. Dental Br., 1996. Fellow: Internat. Coll. Dentists; mem.: ADA (chmn. ADPac 1994—95, vice chmn. coun. govt. affairs 1999—2000, 2d v.p. 2001—02), Tex. Dental Assn. (chmn. DenPac 1982—85, pres. 1988, Pres. award 1991, Disting. Svc. award 1994), Am. Coll. Dentists (chmn. Tex. sect. 1994), Acad. Gen. Dentistry.

CRAWFORD, FRANKLIN DAVID, publishing company executive; b. Denver, Aug. 9, 1928; s. Clifford Theodore and Sarah Ann (Fergeson) C.; m. Ruth Emilia Dallenbach, Oct. 19, 1957; children— Mark Franklin, Grant Robert. BA, Alma White Coll., 1953. Retail exec. Saks Fifth Av., N.Y.C., 1954-56, Federated Dept. Stores, N.Y.C., 1956-58, Allied Stores Corp., N.Y.C., 1958-61, J.C. Penney Corp., N.Y.C., 1961-63; owner, pres. Princeton Microfilm Corp., N.J., 1963—. Pres. Nat. Library Service Co., Princeton, 1974—. Chmn. bd. U.S. Hist. Documents Inst., Washington, 1970—; cons. Alma White Coll., Zarephath, N.J.; v.p., bd. dirs. Weaver Found., St. Louis, 1966—; mem. Internat. Tennis Found. and Hall of Fame, Inc. Served with USAF, 1946-49, 53-54. Mem.: Nassau, Beadensbrook, West Side Tennis. Republican. Home: PO Box 7006 Princeton NJ 08543-7006 Office: PO Box 2073 Princeton NJ 08543-2073 Office Phone: 800-257-9502. E-mail: fdc@princetonmicro.com.

CRAWFORD, FRED ALLEN, JR., cardiothoracic surgeon, educator; b. Columbia, S.C., Oct. 17, 1942; s. Fred Allen and Susan Valery Floyd C.; m. Mary Jane Dantzler, June 11, 1966; children: Fred Allen III, Mary Elizabeth. MD, Duke U., 1967. Diplomate Am. Bd. Surgery, Am. Bd. Thoracic Surgery. Intern Duke U. Med. Ctr., Durham, N.C., 1967-68, resident in surgery, 1971-76, instr. surgery, 1975-76; asst. prof. surgery, chief divsn. cardiac surgery U. Miss., Med. Ctr., Jackson, 1976-79; prof. surgery pediat., chief divsn. cardiothoracic surgery Med. U. of S.C., Charleston, 1979—, chmn. dept. surgery, 1988—. Contbr. numerous articles to profl. jours. Maj. U.S. Army, 1969-71. Decorated Bronze Star. Mem. ACS, Am. Surg. Assn., Charleston County Med. Soc., S.C. State Med. Assn., Soc. Thoracic Surgeons, So. Surg. Assn., So. Thoracic Surg. Assn., Am. Heart Assn., Am. Assn. Thoracic Surgery (pres. 2003), Am. Bd. Thoracic Surgery (bd. dirs. 1991-2002, chmn., 2001), Am. Coll. Cardiology, Phi Beta Kappa, Alpha Omega Alpha. Presbyterian. Office: 96 Jonathan Lucas St Rm 409 Charleston SC 29425-0001 Office Phone: 843-792-5897. Business E-Mail: crawfordf@musc.edu.

CRAWFORD, FRED LEE, public information officer; b. Spartanburg County, S.C., Aug. 30, 1928; s. Fred and Missouri (Plemmons) C. BA, Furnam U., 1957; MA, NYU, 1958; PhD with distinction, 1965; JD, U. S.C., 1970. Bar: S.C. Adminstr. Profl. Counseling Placement Lighthouse Internat., N.Y.C., 1962-66; commn. adminstr. S.C. Commn. for the Blind, Columbia, 1966-73; social security adminstr. supplemental security income planning specialist Social Security Adminstrn., Balt., 1973—, now sr. advisor to assoc. commr. for external affairs. Chmn., 1st pres. The Alliance Inc., Baltimore County, Md., 1979-83. Author: Career Planning for the Blind, 1965; co-author: (with Sidney Lirtzman) Counseling and Placement of Blind Persons in Professional Occupations, Practice and Research, 1965. Pres. Lions, Catonsville, Md., 1977-94. Baptist. Avocations: reading, volunteering in community, investments, business. Home: 908 Southridge Rd Baltimore MD 21228-1324 Office: Social Security Adminstrn 6401 Security Blvd Baltimore MD 21235-0001 E-mail: fred.l.crawford@ssa.gov.

CRAWFORD, HOWARD ALLEN, lawyer; b. Stafford, Kans., Aug. 4, 1917; s. Perry V. and Kate (Allen) C.; m. Millie Housewerth, Oct. 9, 1948; children: Catherine, Edward BS, Kans. State U., 1939; JD, U. Mich., 1942. Bar: Kans. 1942, Mo. 1943, U.S. Ct. Appeals (8th, 10th and D.C. cirs.), U.S. Supreme Ct. Mem. firm Lathrop and Gage, Kansas City, Mo., 1950-91; mng. ptnr. Lathrop and Norquist, Kansas City, Mo., 1970-85, ret., 1991. Dir. various cos. Mem. coun. City of Mission Hills, Kans., 1965-70 Mem. Lawyers Assn. Kansas City, Kansas City Club, Mission Hills Country Club. Home: 3103 W 67th Ter Shawnee Mission KS 66208-1857 Office: Lathrop and Gage 2345 Grand Blvd Fl 25 Kansas City MO 64108-2603

CRAWFORD, HUNT DORN, JR., retired military officer, educator, diplomat; b. Louisville, Dec. 25, 1948; s. Hunt Dorn Sr. and Carrol Frank (Watson) C.; m. Kate Kerr Delano, Aug. 1, 1970; children: Scott Holden, Carolyn Hunt. BS, U.S. Mil. Acad., 1970; MA and MS, Stanford U., Palo Alto, Calif., 1978; MPh, Columbia U., 1980; MMAS, Command & Gen. Staff Coll., 1985. Commd. 2d lt. U.S. Army, 1970, advanced through grades to lt. col., 1987; staff officer, comdr. 1st Inf. Div. Forward, Augsburg, Germany, 1970-73; staff officer Hdqrs. III Corps, Ft. Hood, Tex., 1974-75; from instr. to asst. prof. U.S. Mil. Acad., West Point, N.Y., 1978-81; staff prin. 1st Inf. Div. Forward, Goppingen, 1981-84; instr. Command & Gen. Staff Coll., Ft. Leavenworth, Kans., 1985-88; strategic analyst U.S. Army Concepts Analysis Agy., Bethesda, Md., 1988-91; ret. U.S. Army, 1992; polit./mil. affairs advisor U.S. Arms Control & Disarmament Agy., Washington, 1991-99, U.S. Dept. of State, Washington, 1999—. Mem. NATO arms control analysts group SHAPE Tech. Ctr., Hague, Netherlands, 1988-90; mem. conv. arms control work group Ctr. for Strategic and Internat. Studies, Washington, 1989-90; mem. arms control ad hoc study group Carnegie Endowment for Internat. Peace, Washington, 1990-92; mem. conventional arms control project Ford Found., 1993-96; adj. prof. polit. sci. U. Louisville, 1995—. Author: Conventional Armed Forces in Europe (CFE): A Review and Update of Key Treaty Elements, ann. 1991—; contbr. articles to profl. jours. and books. Decorated ACDA Meritorious honor award, Def. Superior Svc. medal, 5 M.S.M. awards. Mem. AAAS, Am. Polit. Sci. Assn., Acad. Polit. Sci., Internat. Inst. Strategic Studies, Internat. Studies Assn., Mil. Ops. Rsch. Soc. (bd. dirs. 1991-98, exec. coun. 1995-98), Inst. Ops. Rsch. and Mgmt. Scis., Phi Kappa Phi. Republican. Episcopalian. Avocations: bicycling, racquetball, aquaria. Home: 932 Audubon Pkwy Louisville KY 40213-1365 Office: US Dept of State 2201 St NW Washington DC 20520 Office Phone: 202-647-9407. E-mail: crawforddo@t.state.gov, dorncrawford@aol.com.

CRAWFORD, IAN, lawyer; b. Selkirk, Manitoba, Canada, Mar. 6, 1948; s. William McCulloch and Barbara Crawford; 1 child, Scott McCulloch. AB, Brown U., 1971; MA, U. Colo., 1979; JD, Suffolk U., 1984. Bar: Mass. 1985, U.S. Dist. Ct. Mass. 1985, U.S. Ct. Appeals (fed. cir.) 1990, U.S. Dist. Ct. (ctrl. dist.) Ill. 1991, U.S. Supreme Ct. 1991, U.S. Ct. Appeals (1st cir.) 1998. Assoc., ptnr. Hale and Dorr, Boston, 1984—92; mng. ptnr. Todd & Weld LLP, Boston, 1992—. Author: (book) Constitutional and Statutory Restriction on the Polygraph in Employment, 1979. Tutor and coach Citizens Sch., Boston; ct. apptd. spl. adv. Boston Juvenile Ct. Recipient Herbert & Sara Ehrman award, Mass. Citizens Against the Death Penalty, 1985, The 2000 Child Advocacy award, Mass. Soc. for the Prevention of Cruelty to Children, 2000, Mayor's award - Boston's Homeless, Boston Mayor Thomas Menino, 2004. Fellow: Boston Bar Found. (Citation of Outstanding Svc. to Children 2001); mem.: Boston Bar Assn. (chmn. various coms. 1996—2001), Mass. Bar Assn. Avocations: running, skiing. Office: Todd & Weld LLP 28 State St Boston MA 02109 Office Phone: 617-720-2626. Office Fax: 617-227-5777. Business E-Mail: icrawford@toddweld.com.

CRAWFORD, JACKIE R., retired federal agency administrator; m. Frances Lindsey; children: Jessica, Andrea, Katrina. BBA, Fla. State U., 1967; M in Acctg., Bowling Green State U., 1974; postgrad., Fed. Exec. Inst., Charlottesville, Va., 1988, Harvard U., 1991. CPA, Fla. Auditor Air Force Audit Agy., Eglin AFB, Fla., 1967-72, audit mgr. Wright-Patterson AFB, Ohio, 1972-77, supr. auditor L.A. AFB, 1977-79, Robins AFB, Ga., 1980-82, assoc. dir. weapon sys. audits Wright-Patterson AFB, Ohio, 1982-86, assoc. dir. acquisition, 1986-87, asst. auditor gen. acquisition and logistics audits, 1988-93; dir. acquisition support programs Dept. Def., Arlington, Va., 1987-88; auditor gen. of the Air Force The Pentagon, Washington, 1993—2001. Home: 233 Sweetwater Run Niceville FL 32578

CRAWFORD, JAMES DEE, chemical distribution executive; b. Boise, Idaho, June 23, 1950; s. Glen E. and Beverly J. (Thomas) C.; m. Diane E. Crawford (Ball), July 8, 1994. BBA, Boise State U., 1972. CPA, Idaho. Staff acct. J.R. Simplot Co., Boise, 1972-75, corp. acctg. mgr., 1975-79, asst. contr. Caldwell, Idaho, 1979-80; treas. SimCal Chem. Co., Fresno, Calif., 1980-83; dir. fin services J.R. Simplot Co., Boise, 1983-85, treas., 1995—97; CFO Wilbur-Ellis Co., San Francisco, 2000—; v.p., contr. J.R. Simplot Co., Boise, 1997—2000. Bd. dirs. Micron Tech., Inc., Boise, Investors Fin. Corp., Boise. Com. chmn. St. Alphonsus Found., Boise, 1985. Named one of Outstanding Young Men Am., Jaycees, 1974. Mem. AICPA, Idaho Soc. CPAs, Nat. Assn. Corp. Treas. Clubs: Crane Creek Country (Boise), City Club of San Francisco. Republican. Episcopalian. Avocation: golf.

CRAWFORD, JAMES DOUGLAS, lawyer; b. Phila., May 31, 1932; s. James A. and Katharine M. (Evenson) C.; m. Judith N. Dean, Apr. 29, 1977; 1 dau., Christopher Anne Crawford Samson. AB, Haverford Coll., 1954; LLB, U. Pa., 1962. Bar: Pa. 1963, D.C. 1979, U.S. Supreme Ct. 1968. Assoc. Montgomery, McCracken, Walker & Rhoads, Phila., 1962-66; asst. dist. atty. Phila., 1966-68; dep. dist. atty., chief appeals divsn., 1968-72; gen. counsel Redevel. Authority of City of Phila., 1972-74; ptnr. Schnader, Harrison, Segal & Lewis, Phila., 1974-97, sr. counsel, 1998—. Mem. adv. com. on appellate rules Pa. Supreme Ct., 1985-92; lectr. in law U. Pa., 1971-73; bd. dirs. Na. Assn. Law Placement, 1978-79; nat. chmn. ann. giving U. Pa. Law Sch., 1985-87. Editor in chief U. Pa. Law Rev., 1961-62. Mem. exec. com. Friends Phila. Mus. Art, 1980—86, fin. sec., 1981—82, co-chmn., 1982—84, mem. prints and drawing com., 1987—; treas. Hist. Soc. U.S. Ct. Appeals for 3d Cir., 1994—2000, pres., 2000—; bd. dirs. ACLU, 1978—, v.p., 1985—, bd. dirs. Pa. chpt., 1962—, v.p., 1980—85, pres., 1985—; bd. dirs., mem. exec. com. ACLU Greater Phila., 1972—, v.p., 1983—85; bd. dirs. Pub. Interest Law Ctr. Phila., 1980—90, mem. adv. bd., 1991—; bd. dirs. Citizens Crime Commn. Phila., 1986—96, Samuel S. Fleisher Art Meml., 1984—, pres., 1998—; bd. dirs. Print Club Phila., 1983—85, v.p., 1984—96, mem. adv. coun., 1997—. With U.S. Army, 1955—57. Fellow Am. Bar Found., Am. Coll. Trial Lawyers, Am. Acad. Appellate Lawyers; mem. Phila. Bar Assn. (gov. 1973-75, chmn. com. of censors 1972), Phila. Bar Found. (trustee 1987-93, sec. 1988-92), Am. Law Inst., Defender Assn. Phila. (bd. dirs. 1975—), Athenaeum Club, St. Andrews Soc., Order of Coif, Phi Beta Kappa. Republican. Presbyterian. Office: Schnader Harrison et al 1600 Market St Ste 3600 Philadelphia PA 19103-7287 also: 68 Rennie Ct 11 Upper Ground London SE1 9NZ England Personal E-mail: cd2018@aol.com. Business E-Mail: jcrawford@schnader.com.

CRAWFORD, JAMES LEROY, minister, retired theology studies educator; b. Tonkawa, Okla., Aug. 22, 1935; s. Leroy Jefferson and Beulah Lucille Crawford; m. Sammye Helen Henson, Jan. 26, 1957; children: James Jr., Joyce E. McCartney, Janet K. Austin. BA, Okla. Bapt. U., 1956; M Div., Southwestern Bapt. Theol. Sem., 1965, ThM, 1967, ThD, 1970. Ordained min. Bapt. Ch. Pastor S.E. Bapt. Ch., Muskegee, Okla., 1959—60, 1st So. Bapt. Ch., Rock Falls, Ill., 1960—61, Immanuel Bapt. Ch., Poteno, Okla., 1961—65, Mt. Gilead Bapt. Ch., Keiler, Tex., 1965—67, 1st Bapt. Ch., Alba, Tex., 1967—69; prof., ch. planter Internat. Mission Bd., So. Bapt. Ch., Richmond, Va., 1964—2001; ret., 2001; pastor Bapt. Spanish Ch., Olivet Bapt. Ch., Okla. City, 2005—. Adj. prof. Okla. Bapt. U., Shawnee, 2001—04; prof. Bapt. Theol. Sem., Los Teques, Venezuela, 1971—80, Los Teques, 1985—2000, pres., 1980—85, pres. emeritus, 1996. Author: (guide) Study Guide for the Old Testament, 1974, Biblical Introduction, 1996, (commendary series) Exegisis of the Book of Leviticus (in Spanish), 1998. Mem.: History Channel Club. Avocation: scroll sawing. Home: 5800 Melton Dr Oklahoma City OK 73132 Personal E-mail: jcraw822@aol.com.

CRAWFORD, JAMES WELDON, psychiatrist, educator, administrator; b. Napoleon, Ohio, Oct. 27, 1927; s. Homer and Olga (Aderman) C.; m. Susan Young, July 5, 1955; 1 child, Robert James AB, Oberlin Coll., 1950; MD, U. Chgo., 1954, PhD, 1961. Intern Wayne County Hosp. and Infirmary, Eloise, Mich., 1954-55; resident Northwestern U., Chgo., 1958-59, Mt. Sinai Hosp./Chgo. Med. Sch., 1959-60; practice medicine specializing in occupational, individual and family psychiatry Chgo., 1961—. Mem. staff St. Lukes-Presbyn. Med. Ctr.; clin. assoc. prof. dept. psychiatry Sch. of Medicine, U. Ill. at Chgo., 1970—; chair and assoc. prof. dept. psychiatry Ravenswood Hosp. Med. Ctr., 1973-79; chmn. J.W. Crawford Assocs., Inc., 1979-82; assoc. prof. depts. behavioral scis. and psychiatry Rush Med. Co. Contbr. articles to profl. jours. Bd. dirs. Pegasus Player, Chgo., 1978—96, chmn. bd. dirs., 1979-84; bd. dirs. Bach Soc., 1985-98; adv. Ill. Masonic Med. Ctr.; mem. health adv. com. Cook County (Ill.) Commr., 2003—; del. to Russia and the Ukraine with People-to-People Internat., 1993, del. to Kenya, 1995, del. to China, 1998. NIH Inst. Neurol. Diseases postdoctoral fellow, 1955-59. Fellow Am. Psychiat. Assn. (life, dist. mem.), Am. Orthopsychiat. Assn.; mem. AAAS, Am. Soc. Psychoanalytic Physicians, Nat. Coalition Mental Health Profls. and Consumers, Ill. Coalition Mental Health Profls. and Consumers (steering com.), Psychiat. Soc., Chgo. Assn. for Psychoanalytic Psychology, Nat. Coun. on Family Rels., Rotary (various coms. profl. rep.), Sigma Xi. Home and Office: 2418 Lincoln St Evanston IL 60201-2151 Office Phone: 847-869-3108. Personal E-mail: sjcrawf@aol.com.

CRAWFORD, JENNY LYNN SLUDER, medical/surgical nurse, educator; b. Asheville, NC, Oct. 14, 1952; d. Fletcher Sumpter and M. Orva (Yost) Sluder; m. Thomas Rodney Crawford, Jan. 21, 1984; children: Orva Marie, Sara Lynn. AA, Stephens Coll., 1972; BSN, Baylor U., 1974; MSN, U. NC, Charlotte, 1998. RN, Ola.; cert. med.-surg. nurse ANA. Staff nurse Comanche County Hosp., Lawton, Okla., 1974, VA Hosp., Asheville, 1975-77, VA Med. Ctr., Durham, NC, 1977-84, Presbyn. Hosp., Charlotte, NC, 1984-95; health occupations instr. Garinger HS, Charlotte, 1995—2002; health occupations inst. Independence HS, Charlotte, 2002—. Nursing instr. Presbyn. Hosp., Charlotte, 1989-95; instr. basic life support and CPR Am. Heart Assn., others. Mem.: ANA, Sigma Theta Tau. Avocations: camping, swimming, crosstitch, needlepoint, reading. Home: 8941 Dartmoor Pl Charlotte NC 28227-8983 Office Phone: 980-343-6900.

CRAWFORD, JOAN DAVIS, librarian; b. Shreveport, La., July 21, 1940; d. Earl J. and Eunice (Wiebracht) Davis; divorced; children: Kimberly Louise C. Eighmy, Christopher James. BA in Arts and Sci., U. Ala., 1962, MA in History, 1963; MA in Libr. Sci., U. So. Ala., 1976. Tchr. Meridian HS, Miss., 1962-63, Vigor HS, Prichard, Ala., 1963-64, Shaw HS, Mobile, 1964-66; attendance supr. Mobile County Pub. Schs., 1966-68; libr. Hollinger's Island Sch., 1976-86, UMS-Wright Prep Sch., 1983—. Deacon Springhill Presbyn. Ch., Mobile, Ala., 1983—85, 1987—90. Mem.: Ala. Libr. Assn., Internat. Reading Assn., Delta Kappa Gamma (pres. 1982—84). Avocations: reading, cross stitching, gardening. Office: UMS-Wright Prep Sch 65 N Mobile St Mobile AL 36607-3192

CRAWFORD, JOHN ANDREW, lawyer; b. Columbus, Ohio, Mar. 22, 1956; s. Thomas Michael and Nancy Jane (Keach) C.; m. Cheryl Ann, Fischer, Crawford, Aug. 8, 1981; children: Whitney, Mackenzie, Sam, Ellie. BA, Moorhead State U., 1978; JD, Ind. U., 1981. Bar: Ohio 1981. Assoc. Vorys, Sater, Seymour & Pease, Columbus, Ohio, 1981—84, McCamish, Ingram, Martin & Brown, Austin, Tex., 1984—87, Reese, Pyle, Drake & Meyer, Newark, Ohio, 1987—88, ptnr., 1989—. Pres. Granville (Ohio) Recreation Commn., 1991-93; v.p. Licking County bd. ARC; active Granville Village Exempted Sch. Dist. Bd. Edn., 2001—. Mem. Ohio Bar Assn., Ohio Assn. Civil Trial Attys., Kiwanis (pres. Granville club 1995-96). Office: Reese Pyle Drake & Meyer PO Box 919 Newark OH 43058-0919 E-mail: acrawford@rpdm.com.

CRAWFORD, JOHN EDWARD, geologist, consultant; b. Richmond, Va., June 6, 1924; s. James Henry and Loretta Ellen (Bankerd) C.; m. Mary Elizabeth Ayres, May 15, 1948; children: Michelle Lorraine, Caprice Lizette. BA, Johns Hopkins, 1947. Reg. geologist, Calif. Geologist uranium exploration program U.S. Geol. Survey, 1948-51; nat. stockpile materials specialist Munitions Bd., Office Sec. Def., 1951-53; prodn. engr. AEC, 1953-54; specialist on source, feed, fissionable materials Bur. Mines, 1954-57, nuclear tech. adviser to dir., 1957-60, chief nuc. engr. for atomic rsch. programs, 1960-63; dir. Marine Mineral Tech. Ctr., Tiburon, Calif., 1963-66; pres., founder Crawford Marine Specialists, Inc., San Francisco, also Suva, Fiji, 1966-76; pres. Earth Tech. Corp., San Rafael, 1973-77; mgr. geothermal rsch. programs and Salton Sea sci. drilling project U.S. Dept. Energy Ops. Office, Oakland, Calif., 1977-89; mgr. ops. and prin. geologist Western Geologic Resources, Inc., San Rafael, Calif., 1989-90; cons. geothermal and environ. affairs, 1990—; assoc., regional mgr. Western Ops. Earth Resources Internat., L.C., Carson City, Nev., 1994-2000. Author: Facts Concerning Uranium Exploration and Production, 1956; contbr. articles to govt. and profl. jours., Leaders in Am. Sci. Vol. VIII, 1968-69. Mem. Calif. Gov.'s Commn. Ocean Resources, 1966-67, Calif. Gov.'s Small Hydro Task Force, 1981-82. Served with AUS, 1943-46. Mem. Internat. Marine Minerals Soc. (Moore medal for excellence in devel. of marine minerals 1998), Geol. Soc. Am., Marine Tech. Soc. (past chmn. marine mineral resources com., past chmn. marine resources div.), Delta Upsilon. Home and Office: 1510 Valencia Ct Carson City NV 89703-2333

CRAWFORD, KENNETH CHARLES, retired academic administrator; b. Nokomis, Ill., Oct. 31, 1918; s. Charles Bryant and Blanche Dora (Gates) C.; m. Madge Marie Douglas, Aug. 23, 1942; 1 son, James Douglas. BA, Ill. Coll., 1946, SJD (hon.), 1970; JD, U. Va., 1951; grad., Command and Gen. Staff Coll., 1957, Army War Coll., 1962; MA, George Washington U., 1962. Bar: Va. 1951, Ga. 1967, Korean 1965, U.S. Supreme Ct. 1970, D.C. 1977. Commd. 2d lt. U.S. Army, 1942, advanced through grades to col., 1962; served in (F.A. and JAG Corps); tchr. legal subjects U. Md., U. Ga., Ga. State U., Nat. U., Washington, 1957-67; comdr. JAG Sch., 1967-70; ret., 1970; pres., CEO Ken Crawford Ednl. Inst., Inc., 1986-89. Editor: Laws of the Republic of Korea, 1964. Assoc. dir. edn. Southwestern Legal Found., Dallas, 1970-71, Atty. at Law, 1990-92; dir. edn. and tng. Fed. Jud. Ctr., Washington, 1971-86; cons. Fed. Jud. Ctr., 1986-87. Decorated Legion of Merit with 2 oak leaf clusters, Soldiers medal, Bronze Star, Belgian Fourragere, Disting. Citizen citation Ill. Coll., 1993. Mem. State Bar Va., Korean Bar, Order of Coif.

CRAWFORD, LESTER MILLS, JR., federal agency administrator; b. Demopolis, Ala., Mar. 13, 1938; s. Lester Mills and Susan Doris (Mitchell) C.; m. Catherine Walker, July 27, 1963; children: Catherine Leigh, Mary Stuart. D.V.M., Auburn U., 1963; PhD in Pharmacology, U. Ga., 1969; MDV. (hon.), Budapest U., Hungary, 1987. Pvt. practice vet. medicine, Meridian, Miss. and Birmingham, Ala., 1963-64; R & D staff agrl. divsn. Am. Cyanamid Co., Princeton, NJ, 1964-66, cons.; assoc. dean Coll. Vet. Medicine, U. Ga., 1970-75, head dept. physiology-pharmacology, 1980-82; dir. Ctr. Vet. Medicine, FDA, Dept. Health and Human Svcs., Rockville, Md., 1978—80, 1982—85; assoc. adminstr. food safety and inspection svc. USDA, Washington, 1986-87, adminstr., food safety and inspection svc., 1987-91; exec. v.p. sci. affairs Nat. Food Processors Assn., Washington, 1991-93; exec. dir. Assn. Am. Vet. Med. Colls., Washington, 1993—97, 2001—02; dir. Ctr. Food and Nutrition Policy, Georgetown U., Washington, 1997-2001; dir. Ctr. Food and Nutrition Policy Va. Tech., 2001—02; dep. commr. FDA, Dept. Health and Human Svcs., Rockville, Md., 2002—04, acting commr., 2004—05, commr., 2005—. Cons. pharm. industry, agribus. FDA, WHO; mem. Health Professions Commn., Pew Meml. Trust, 1990-93; bd. dir. Embrex Inc.; mem. sci. adv. bd. Inst. Food Tech., 1999-2002; chair, dept. phisiology-pharmacology, U. Ga. Contbr. sci. articles to profl. jours. Vice chmn. Codex Alimentarius Commn., 1991-93; bd. dir. Food and Drug Law Inst., 1988-2002; expert advisor food safety WHO. Recipient A.M. Mills award, 1979, K.F. Meyer award, 1980, U.S. Presdl. Rank award of Meritorious Exec., 1988, Disting. Alumnus award, Auburn U., 1989, Wooldridge Meml. medal, Brit. Vet. Assn., 1991, Commrs. Spl. citation FDA, award of merit, 1983. Fellow: Internat. Acad. Food Sci. and Tech., Royal Soc. Medicine (U.K.); mem.: NAS Inst. Medicine, AVMA, AAAS (com. scientific freedom and responsibility), Fedn. Am. Sch. Health Professions (pres. 1997), French Acad. Vet. (hon.), D.C. Vet Med. Assn., Nat. Acad. Practice, Cosmos Club (Washington), Phi Kappa Phi, Phi Zeta, Sigma Xi. Republican. Office: FDA Parklawn Bldg 14-71 HF-1 5600 Fishers Ln Rockville MD 20857 Office Phone: 301-827-2410, 301-827-2410. Office Fax: 301-443-3100. Business E-Mail: commissioner@fda.gov. *I have always predicated my own life on the certain knowledge that God is still at work in the world. I believe that every person carries a divine spark, and that the function of leadership is to ignite that spark. I furthermore believe that a Franciscan love of and respect for animals is a prerequisite for membership in the human race. And I believe that the true rewards in life are to be found in communion with family, friends and colleagues.*

CRAWFORD, LINDA SIBERY, lawyer, educator; b. Ann Arbor, Mich., Apr. 27, 1947; d. Donald Eugene and Verla Lillian (Schenck) Sibery; m. Leland Allardice Crawford, Apr. 4, 1970; children: Christina, Lillian, Leland. Student, Keele U., 1969; BA, U. Mich., 1969; postgrad., SUNY, Potsdam, 1971; JD, U. Maine, 1977. Bar: Maine 1977, U.S. Dist. Ct. Maine 1982, U.S. Ct. Appeals (1st cir.) 1983. Tchr. Pub. Sch., Tupper Lake, N.Y., 1970-71; asst. dist. atty. State of Maine, Farmington, 1977-79, asst. atty. gen. Augusta, Maine, 1979-95; prin. Linda Crawford and Assoc., 1985—, Litigation Consulting Firm, N.Y.C., 1986—. Legal adv. U. Maine, Farmington, 1975; legal counsel Fire Marshall's Office, Maine, 1980-83, Warden Svc., Maine, 1981-83, Dept. Mental Health, 1983-90, litigation divsn. 1990-95; tchg. team trial advocacy Law Sch., Harvard U., 1987—; lectr. Sch. Medicine Harvard U., 1991, 2004—; counsel to Bd. of Registration in Medicine, 1994-95; chmn. editl. bd. Mental and Physical Disability Law Reporter, 1993-95; arbitrator Am. Arbitration Assn., 1995—; facilitator Nat. Constrn. Task Force, St. Louis, 1995. Contbg. editor: Med. Malpractice Law and Strategy, 1997—, Managed Care Law Strategist, 1999—2002. Bd. dirs. Diocesan Human Rels. Coun., Maine, 1977-78, Arthritis Found., Maine, 1983-88; atty. expert commn. experts UN War Crime Investigation in the former Yugoslavia, 1994. Named one of Outstanding Young Women of Yr., Jaycees, 1981. Mem. ABA (com. on disability 1992-95), Nat. Assn. State Mental Health Attys. (treas. 1984-86, vice chmn. 1987-89, chmn. 1989-91), Nat. Health Lawyers Assn. Home and Office: 150 Orleans St PH 1 East Boston MA 02128 also: 45 Rockefeller Plz Fl 20 New York NY 10111-2099 Office Phone: 800-208-6117. Personal E-mail: lca@lcandassociates.com.

CRAWFORD, MARC, professional hockey coach; Head coach Quebec Nordiques, 1994-95, Colo. Avalanche, 1995-97, Vancouver Canucks, Vancouver, 1998—. Recipient Louis A.R. Pieri Meml. award, 1992-93, Jack Adams award, 1994-95; named NHL Coach of Yr. The Sporting News, 1994-95. Office: Vancouver Canucks 800 Griffiths Way Vancouver BC Canada V6B 6G1*

CRAWFORD, MARIA LUISA BUSE, geology educator; b. Beverly, Mass., July 18, 1939; d. William Theodore Buse and Barbara (Kidder) Aldana; m. William A. Crawford, Aug. 29, 1963. BA, Bryn Mawr Coll., 1960; postgrad., U. Oslo, 1960-61; PhD, U. Calif., 1965. Asst. prof. Bryn Mawr (Pa.) Coll., 1965-73, assoc. prof., 1973-79, prof., 1979-92, prof. environ. studies and sci., 1992—, William R. Kenan Jr. prof., 1985-92, chmn. dept. geology, 1976-88, 98—; mem. U.S. Nat. Com. Geology, 1994-97. Chmn. women geoscientists com. Am. Geol. Inst., 1976-77; mem. U.S. Nat. Com. Geochemistry, 1980-82; organizing com. 28th Internat. Geol. Cong., 1987-89. MacArthur fellow, 1993-98; grantee NASA, 1973-76, NSF, 1967—. Fellow Geol. Soc. Am. (councillor 1982-85), Mineral Soc. Am. (councillor 1989-92);mem. Mineral Assn. Can. (councilor 1985-87), Am. Geophys. Union, Norwegian Geol. Soc., Phila. Geol. Soc., Assn. Women in Sci. Office: Bryn Mawr Coll Dept Geology Bryn Mawr PA 19010 Office Phone: 610-526-5111. Business E-Mail: mcrawfor@brynmawr.edu.

CRAWFORD, MARY E., psychology educator; b. Pottsville, Pa., Aug. 16, 1942; d. Wallace Barckley and Mary c. (Drummer) Crawford; m. M.B. Whipple, June 3, 1962 (div. 1969); children: Mark, Mary; m. Roger J.S. Chaffin, Jan. 12, 1974; 1 child, Benjamin Crawford Chaffin. BS, West Chester (Pa.) Coll., 1963; MA, U. Del., Newark, 1972, PhD, 1975. Asst. prof. Buena Vista Coll., Storm Lake, Iowa, 1974-78; asst. prof. psychology West Chester U. of Pa., 1978-81, assoc. prof., 1981-84, prof. psychology, 1984-93; prof. psychology and grad. dir. women's studies U. S.C., Columbia, 1993—. Vis. prof. Trenton (N.J.) State Coll., 1989-90, Hamilton Coll., Clinton, N.Y., 1986-88. Book rev. editor Psychology of Women Quar., 1990—; editorial adv. bd. Feminism and Psychology, 1990—; co-editor: Gender and Thought, 1989; co-author: Women and Gender: A Feminist Psychology, 1992; contbr. articles to profl. jours. Fellow APA, Am. Psychol. Soc.; mem. Nat. Women's Studies Assn., Ea. Psychol. Assn., Sigma Xi. Office: U South Carolina Women's Studies 1710 College St Columbia SC 29201-3918

CRAWFORD, MICHAEL HOWARD, cardiologist, educator, researcher; b. Madison, Wis., July 10, 1943; s. William Henry and A. Kay (Keller) C.; m. Janis Raye Kirschner, June 23, 1968; children: Chelsea Susan, Dinah Jaye, Stuart Michael. AB, U. Calif., Berkeley, 1965; MD, U. Calif., San Francisco, 1969. Diplomate Am. Bd. Internal Medicine sub-bd. Cardiovasc. Disease. Med. resident U. Calif. Hosps., San Francisco, 1969-71; sr. med. resident Beth Israel Hosp., Boston, 1971-72; tchg. fellow Harvard Med. Sch., Boston, 1971-72; cardiology fellow U. Calif. Hosps., San Diego, 1972-74; asst. prof. medicine U. Calif. Sch. Medicine, San Diego, 1974-76, U. Tex. Health Sci. Ctr., San Antonio, 1976-78, assoc. prof. medicine, 1978-82, prof. medicine, 1982-89, Mayo Med. Sch., Minn., 2001—03, U. Calif., San Francisco, 2003—05, Lucie Stern chair cardiology; Robert S. Flinn prof. cardiology U. N.Mex. Sch. Medicine, Albuquerque, 1989—2001. Asst. dir. Ischemic Heart Disease Specialized Ctr. Rsch., San Diego, 1975—76; adj. scientist S.W. Found. Biomedical Rsch., San Antonio, 1980—89; co-dir. div. cardiology U. Tex. Health Sci. Ctr., San Antonio, 1983—89; chief div. cardiology U. N.Mex. Sch. Medicine, Albuquerque, 1989—2001; cons. cardiovasc. diseases Mayo Clinic, Scottsdale, Ariz., 2001—03; chief clin. cardiology U. Calif. San Francisco Med. Ctr., 2003—. Editor: Current Diagnosis and Treatment in Cardiology, 1995, 2d edit., 2004, Cardiology, 2001, 2d edit., 2003; editor Clinical Cardiology Alert newsletter, 1990—; cons. editor (periodical) Cardiology Clinics, 1989-; mem. editl. bd. Circulation Journal, 1990-99, Journal of American College in Cardiology, 1992-95, 2003-. Pres. Am. Heart Assn., San Antonio, 1981, Austin, Tex., 1987, chmn. coun. clin. cardiology, Dallas, 1989, pres., Albuquerque, 1995-96. Recipient Paul Dudley White award, Assn. Mil. Surgeons of U.S., 1981, Merit Review grant, Dept. VA, 1985—91, Rsch. Tng. grantee, Nat. Heart Lung Blood Inst., 1993—2004. Fellow: Am. Heart Assn., Am. Coll. Physicians, Am. Coll. Cardiology (bd. trustees 1998—2003); mem.: Western Assn. Physicians, Assn. Univ. Cardiologists (pres. 2005—), So. Soc. Clin. Investigation, Am. Soc. Echocardiography (bd. dirs. 1980—83). Avocation: skiing. Home: 3965 20th St San Francisco CA 94114 Office: U Calif 505 Parnassus Ave Box 0124 San Francisco CA 94143-0124 Office Phone: 415-502-8584.

CRAWFORD, MURIEL LAURA, lawyer, educator, writer; d. Mason Leland and Pauline Marie (Desllets) Henderson; m. Barrett Matson Crawford, May 10, 1959; children: Laura Joanne, Janet Muriel, Barbara Elizabeth. BA with honors, U. Ill., 1973; JD with honors, Ill. Inst. Tech., 1977; cert. employee benefit splst., U. Pa., 1989. Bar: Ill. 1977, Calif. 1991, U.S. Dist. Ct. (no. dist.) Ill. 1977, U.S. Dist. Ct. (no. dist.) Calif. 1991, U.S. Ct. Appeals (7th cir.) 1977, U.S. Ct. Appeals (9th cir.) 1991; CLU; chartered fin. cons. Atty. Washington Nat. Ins. Co., Evanston, Ill., 1977-80; sr. atty., 1980-81; asst. counsel, 1982-83; asst. gen. counsel, 1984-87; assoc. gen. counsel, sec., 1987-89; cons. employee benefit splst., 1989-91; assoc. Hancock, Rothert & Bushoft, San Francisco, 1991-92. Author: (with Beadles) Law and the Life Insurance Contract, 1989, (sole author) 7th edit., 1994, Life and Health Insurance Law, 8th edit., 1998; co-author: Legal Aspects of AIDS, 1990; contbr. articles to profl. jours. Recipient Am. Jurisprudence award Lawyer's Coop. Pub. Co., 1975, 2nd prize Internat. LeTourneau Student Med.-Legal Article Contest, 1976, LOMA FLMI Ins. Edn. award, 1999. Fellow Life Mgmt. Inst.; mem. Ill. Inst. Tech./Chgo.-Kent Alumni Assn. (bd. dirs. 1983-89, Bar and Gavel Soc. award 1977). Democrat.

CRAWFORD, NORMAN CRANE, JR., academic administrator, consultant; b. Newark, Oct. 30, 1930; s. Norman Crane and Anna (Wares) C.; m. Garnette Bell, June 25, 1955; children: Sally Jean, Ellen Ann. BS in Edn., Rutgers U., 1951, MEd, 1957; PhD, Northwestern U., 1966. Dir. scholarships Nat. Merit Scholarship Corp., Evanston, Ill., 1957-62; asst. dean arts and sci., asst. to provost U. Del., 1962-66, 67-70; acting dir. exams. Coll. Entrance Exam. Bd., N.Y.C., 1966-67; pres. Salisbury (Md.) State Coll., 1970-80, Drury Coll., Springfield, Mo., 1981-83; v.p. ops. Council for Advancement and Support Edn., Washington, 1985-87; interim pres. U. Maine, Farmington, 1987-88; v.p. pub. affairs Thomas A. Edison State Coll., 1989-91; cons. higher edn. Berlin, 1992—. Lt. j.g. USN, 1951-55. Joint recipient Higher Edn. Leadership award Gov. Del., Gov. Md., Gov. Va., 1974; named hon. trustee Ward Found. Wildfowl Art Museum, 1977. Mem. Phi Delta Kappa. Episcopalian. Home and Office: 108 Ocean Pkwy Ocean Pnes MD 21811-1644 E-mail: nccrawford@salisbury.edu.

CRAWFORD, PEGGY SMITH, design educator; b. Christiansburg, Va., Dec. 27, 1943; d. Andrew Morgan Smith and Margie Smith (Hill) Blakeslee; m. John Linnie Crawford, Jan. 12, 1963 (div. May 1979); children: John Christopher, James Andrew. Sec. Draper's Meadow EGA, Blacksburg, Va., 1983-85, 1999—, 2nd v.p., 1989-90; com. mem. Smithfield Needlework Exhibit, Blacksburg, 1986-87, com. chairperson, 1987-88; pres. Blue Ridge Embroiderer's Guild, Roanoke, Va., 1989-90; regional rep. Brazilian Dimensional Embroidery Internat. Guild, Washington, 1991—, sec., 1996-97. Tchr. Nat. Embroiderer's Guild Am., Inc. seminar, Greensboro, N.C., 1991, Reynolds Homestead, Critz, Va., 1993, Nat. Embroiderer's Guild Nat. Seminar, Williamsburg, Va., 1994, Brazilian Dimensional Embroidery Internat. Guild, Inc. seminars, 1994—, Oreg., 1999. Author: Stitching the Wildflowers of Virginia., 1992. Mem. Am. Needlepoint Guild, Blue Ridge Embroiderer's Guild, Drapers' Meadow Embroiderer's Guild Am., Inc., Brazilian Dimensional Embroidery Internat. Guild. Avocations: needlecrafts, sports, reading, hiking, music. Home: 206 Upland Rd Blacksburg VA 24060-5351 Office: Va Polytech and State U 1700 Pratt Dr Blacksburg VA 24060-6361

CRAWFORD, R. GEORGE, investment company executive, educator, filmmaker; b. Mpls., Oct. 30, 1943; s. Robert John and Agnes C.; m. M. Holly Shissler, May, 17, 1980; 1 child, Katherine Barnes. BA, Harvard U., 1965, JD, 1968. Bar N.Y. 1974, DC 1970, Calif. 1972, Ohio, 1969. Law clk. to Hon. Byron R. White U.S. Supreme Ct., Washington, 1968-69; staff asst. to President Washington, 1970-72; v.p. Archon, Inc., L.A., 1972—74; chair pvt. capital sect. Jones Day Reavis & Pogue, L.A., 1974—93; pres. Ilex Group, N.Y., 1997—; prof. Stanford (Calif.) U., 1993—2001; fellow NYU Med. Sch. Psychoanalytic Inst., 2004—. Rsch. fellow Hoover Instn., Stanford, Calif., 1994—97; fellow NYU Med. Sch. Psychoanalytic Inst., 2004—. Author: Derivatives for Decision Makers, 1996; contbr. articles to profl. jours. Pres. Fiduciary Found., N.Y., N.Y., 1992—; mem. supr. coun. Internat. Ctr. Not-for-Profit Law, Washington, 1998—. Fellow, Psychoanalytical Inst. NYU Med. Sch., 2004—. Mem. Internat. Corp. Governance Network (London, com. on governance stds. 1997—). Home: PO Box 677 Harrison NY 10528 Office: 985 Fifth Ave New York NY 10021 Business E-Mail: gc@iinc.us.

CRAWFORD, RAYMOND MAXWELL, JR., nuclear engineer; b. Charleston, SC, July 28, 1933; s. Raymond Maxwell and Mary Elizabeth (Bates) C.; m. J. Denise LeDuc, Mar. 10, 1951; children: Denis, Michael, Deborah, Peter, Elizabeth. BS, Wayne State U., 1958, MS, 1960; PhD, UCLA, 1969. Instr. Wayne State U., 1960-63; asst. prof. Calif. State U., Northridge, 1963-66; mem. tech. staff Atomics Internat., 1969-71; nuc. engr. Argonne Nat. Lab., Ill., 1971-74; assoc. and asst. head nuc. safeguards and licensing divsn. Sargent & Lundy, Chgo., 1974-80; v.p. Sci. Applications, Inc., Oak Brook, Ill., 1980-83; engring. dir. Nutech, Chgo., 1983-86; pres. Engring. Rsch. Group, Naperville, Ill., 1986—; mgr. spl. projects Fluor Daniel, Inc., 1988—2003; cons. Longenecker & Assocs., 2004—. Tech. cons. Atomic Power Devel. Assn., 1962-63; summer fellow NASA Lewis Rsch. Ctr., 1965-66. Contbr. articles to profl. jours. Scoutmaster, counsellor Boy Scouts Am., 1963—66; active YMCA, 1966—69, Recs. for Blind, 1964—65. Recipient numerous awards. Mem. Am. Nuclear Soc., Am. Inst. Chem. Engrs., Am. Chem. Soc., Nat. Soc. Profl. Engrs., Sigma Xi, Tau Beta Pi, Phi Lambda Upsilon. Home: 1005 Kennebec Ln Naperville IL 60563-1413 E-mail: ray.crawford@uclalumni.net.

CRAWFORD, RICHARD BRADWAY, biologist, biochemist, educator; b. Kalamazoo, Feb. 16, 1933; s. Kenneth and Alma (Smith) C.; m. Betty J. Jacobs, Jan. 30, 1954; children: Kathleen, Christine, Kevin, Nancy. AB, Kalamazoo Coll., 1954; PhD in Biochemistry, U. Rochester, 1959. Postdoctoral fellow U. Rochester, NY, 1959; instr. to assoc. prof. U. Pa., 1959-67; assoc. prof. to prof. biology Trinity Coll., Hartford, Conn., 1967-98, prof. emeritus, 1998—, chmn. dept., 1978-87, resuming chmn., 1996-97. Asst. dir., trustee Mt. Desert Island Biol. Lab., Salsbury Cove, Maine, 1966-82; vis. scientist Jackson Lab., Bar Harbor, Maine, 1988; vis. prof. biology U. Warwick, Eng., 1988; vis. prof. marine biology U. Calif. San Diego, 1974; vis. prof. U. Edinburgh, 1996; mem. faculty and curriculum com. Acadia Sr. Coll., 2000—, v.p. bd. dirs. Contbr. articles to profl. jours. Mem. Inlands, Wetlands and Water Courses Commn., Wethersfield, Conn., 1976-81, Wethersfield Conservation Commn., 1995-98; bd. dirs. Mt. Desert Island Hist. Soc., sec., 2001—; v.p. bd. dirs. Acadia Sr. Coll., 2003-. Mem. Rotary Club Hartford (pres. 1994-95), Mount Desert Island Rotary. Democrat. Congregationalist. Home: PO Box 826 Mount Desert ME 04660-0826

CRAWFORD, RICHARD EBEN, JR., retired investment advisor; b. Lake Forest, Ill., Dec. 24, 1930; s. Richard Eben Crawford and Alice B. (Appleton) Smith; m. Caroline Hellen Kelley, June 20, 1952 (div. 1980); children: Wes, John, J.D., Lindsay, Richard; m. Debbie Sum Chan, Feb. 1, 1985; children: Alexandra, Jessica. BA, Trinity Coll., Hartford, Conn., 1953; MBA, U. Pa., 1976. Various positions Minn. Natural Gas Co., St. Louis Park, Minn., 1957-69, pres., chief exec. officer, 1969-74; pres. Minn. Natural div. Minn. Gas Co., St. Louis Park, 1974-77; underwriter Conn. Gen. Life Ins. Co., Mpls., 1978-79; pres. Crawford Assocs., Tucson, 1980—85, Crawford Meml. Cemetery, Emlenton, Pa., 1986; founder Crawford Entrepreneurial Studies, LLC, 2002. Co-author: The Crawfords from Venango County, Pennsylvania, 1999. Area and state judge Career Devel. Conf. Ariz. Distbv. Edn. Clubs Am., 1986; vol. Mobile Meals program, Tucson, 1984-90; trustee St. Andrews Presbyn. Ch., Tucson, 1992-93, pre-sch. adv. bd., 1993; chartered mem. Presbyn. Ch. Am., 1998—; Rep. committeeman, 1992-94; chmn. Ariz. Advocacy Group for the US Pres. Line Item Veto. Capt. USAF, 1955-57. Mem. SAR (treas. Tucson chpt. 1991, 2d v.p. 1992, 1st v.p. 1994), Tuscon C. of C. (com. mil. affairs 1983-90), Pres.'s Club U. Ariz. Found., Skyline Country Club (tennis com. 1988-90), Wharton Club Ariz. (founder, pres. 1986-90), Greater Tuscon Econ. Coun. (agy. com. 1992-95), Toastmasters (pres. Aztec club 1984, 92, area gov. 1986-87, chmn. speechcraft com. 1987-88, Disting. Toastmaster, Catalina Foothills H.s. youth leadership pub. spkg. counselor 1995-96), Rotary (dist. treas. 1988-89, chmn. various coms.), Alpha Delta Phi. Avocations: genealogy, family history, tennis, fishing. Home and Office: 6550 N St Andrews Dr Tucson AZ 85718-2616 Personal E-mail: richardcrawford30@cox.net.

CRAWFORD, ROBERT JOHN, credit company executive; b. Cleve., Mar. 8, 1942; s. Robert John and Jean (Holmes) C.; m. Edna Jean Parker, June 14, 1975. AA, U. Alaska, Fairbanks, 1967, BE, 1971; HHD (hon.), London Inst. of Applied Rsch., 1975; BA/BS, SUNY, 1978. Pres. World Credit Corp., Wilmington, Del., 1972—; rep. in U.S. Hillcrest Worldwide Devel. Corp., S.A., Panama, 1988—; mediator Summit Ct. Sys., Akron, Ohio, 1994—. With U.S. Army, 1961—64. Mem. Mensa, Intertel, Internet Corp. Assigned Names and Numbers. Libertarian. Avocations: computers, real estate speculation. Home: 74 Maplewood Ave Akron OH 44313-6898 Office Phone: 866-866-6686. E-mail: A@att.net.

CRAWFORD, ROBERT W., JR., furniture rental company executive; b. Yonkers, N.Y., Oct. 19, 1938; BS, Dickinson Coll., 1960; MBA, U. Pa., 1963. Founder, chmn., CEO Brook Furniture Rental, Inc., Lake Forest, Ill. Trustee Field Mus. Inductee Chicagoland Entrepreneurial Hall of Fame, 1998. Mem. Nat. Recreation Found. (chmn., trustee), Internat. Furniture Rental Assn. (chmn., bd. dirs.), Chicagoland C. of C. (chmn. bd. dirs.), The Chgo. Club, The CEO Club, Execs. Club Chgo., Comml. Club Chgo., Econ. Club Chgo., Phi Kappa Sigma (Alumnus of Yr. award). Office: Brook Furniture Rental Inc 100 Field Dr Ste 220 Lake Forest IL 60045 E-mail: rwc@bfr.com.

CRAWFORD, ROY EDGINGTON, III, lawyer; b. Topeka, Dec. 23, 1938; s. Roy E. and Ethel Trula (Senne) C.; children: Michael, Jennifer. BS, U. Pa., 1960; LL.B., Stanford U., 1963. Bar: Calif. 1964, U.S. Ct. Mil. Appeals 1964, U.S. Tax Ct. 1969, U.S. Dist. Ct. (no. dist.) Calif. 1971, U.S. Ct. Claims 1974, U.S. Supreme Ct. 1979. Assoc. Brobeck Phleger & Harison, San Francisco, 1967-73, ptnr., 1973—2003; spl. counsel Heller Ehrman LLP, San Francisco, 2003—. Contbr. chpts. to books; bd. editors: Stanford U. Law Rev., 1962-63. Served to capt. AUS, 1964-67. Recipient award of merit U.S. Ski Assn., 1980. Mem. ABA (chmn. com. on state and local taxes 1979-81), Calif. State Bar Assn., San Francisco Bar Assn., Calif. Trout (bd. dirs. 1970-1992, v.p. 1975-94, sec.-treas. 1994-2001), The Nature Conservancy of Idaho (bd. dirs. 1994-2003), Yosemite Inst. (bd. dirs. 1997—), Beta Gamma Sigma. Office: Heller Ehrman LLP 333 Bush St San Francisco CA 94104 Office Phone: 415-772-6705. Business E-Mail: roy.crawford@hellerehrman.com.

CRAWFORD, SANDRA KAY, lawyer; b. Sept. 23, 1934; d. Obie Lee and Zilpha Elizabeth (Ash) Stalcup; m. William Walsh Crawford, Dec. 21, 1968; children: Bill, Jonathan, Constance, Amelia, Patrick. BA, Wellesley Coll., 1957; LLB, U. Tex., 1960. Bar: Tex. 1960, U.S. Supreme Ct. 1965, Colo. 1967, Ill. 1974. Asst. v.p.-legal Hamilton Mgmt. Corp., Denver, 1966—68; v.p., gen. counsel, sec. Transamerica Fund Mgmt. Corp., L.A., 1968; cons. to law dept. Met Life Ins. Co., N.Y.C., 1969—71; counsel Touche Ross & Co., Chgo., 1972—75; v.p., assoc. gen. counsel Continental Ill. Bank, Chgo., 1975—83; sr. div. counsel Motorola, Inc., Schaumburg, Ill., 1984; sr. counsel, asst. sec. Sears Roebuck & Co., 1985—90. Mem.: ABA, Tex. Bar Assn., Colo. Bar Assn., Ill. State Bar Assn., Beach Club (Palm Beach), Everglades Club. Home: 100 Royal Palm Way Apt G5 Palm Beach FL 33480-4270

CRAWFORD, SHEILA JANE, elementary education librarian, reading consultant; b. Beckley, W.Va., Mar. 1, 1943; d. Roger and Ruth (Ashworth) Crawford; m. Lloyd E. Johnston, June 4, 1966 (dec.); 1 child, Jacqueline; m. Troy Thomason, June 28, 2000. BA, Tenn. Tech. U., 1963; MA in Christian Edn., Seabury Western Theol. Sem., 1965; MS in Curriculum and Instrn., U. Tenn., Martin, 1989; EdD in Instrn. and Curriculum Leadership, U. Memphis, 1994; postgrad., San Jose State U., U. Calif., Berkeley, U. Utah, Tex. Woman's U. Cert. tchr. Tenn. Dir. Christian edn. St. Luke's Episcopal Ch., Rochester, Minn., 1965-66; elem. tchr. Santa Catalina Sch. Girls, 1967-69, Rowland-Hall St. Mark's Sch., Salt Lake City, 1968-69, Union City (Tenn.) Christian Sch., 1984-87; libr. Dept. Edn. U. Tenn. at Martin, 1987-89; rsch. asst. U. Memphis, 1989-92, adj. prof., 1996; prof., edn. dept. chair Lane Coll., Jackson, Tenn., 1992-94; reading tchr., drama club sponsor Ashland (Miss.) Mid. Sch., 1994-95; workshop presenter Jackson, Tenn., 1989-96; ednl. cons. Delta Faucet of Tenn. divsn. Masco Corp., Jackson, 1995—; homebound tchr. Jackson-Madison County Schs., 1996-97; instr., libr. LaGrange-Moscow (Tenn.) Sch., 1997-99; libr. Lauderdale Sch., Memphis. Mem. campus All Stars, Honda, Jackson, Tenn., 1992—93; cons. in field. Contbr. articles to profl. jours. Mem. story telling conf. Internat. Assn. Sch. Librs., Dublin, 1999, 2004. Mem. AAUW, DAR, Nat. Libr. Assn., Ch. and Synagogue Libr. Assn., Order Eastern Star (worthy matron 1980-81), Sch. Libr. Assn., Internat. Reading Assn., Sigma Tau Delta, Kappa Delta Pi Anglican. Achievements include research in the effect of chess on predicting and summarizing skills; Presentation of For You Stories from Primary Children in Memphis to Children in Ireland in the International Association of School Librarians Storytelling Convention in Dublin. Office Phone: 901-365-4863. Personal E-mail: crawfords444@cs.com.

CRAWFORD, STEPHEN, think tank executive; b. Doylestown, Pa., Nov. 22, 1942; m. Liliane Pasquale Floge; 1 child, Pascal Hoang. BA, Cornell U., 1964; MBA, U. Pa., 1971; PhD, Columbia U. Former exec. dir. Gov.'s Work Force Investment Bd., State of Md., Balt., Albert Einstein Instn., Ctr. Internat. and Security Studies, U. Md.; v.p., sec., treas. Nat. Policy Assn., Washington, 2000—. Dem. candidate for U.S. House 6th dist., Md., 1996; mem. Frederick County (Md.) Bd. of Edn. Served with U.S. Army, 1964-67. Personal E-mail: scrawford@nga.org.

CRAWFORD, STEPHEN S., diversified financial services company executive; b. May 20, 1964; BA, U. Va., 1986. With mgmt. investment banking divsn. Morgan Stanley Dean Witter, N.Y.C., 1986-98, mng. dir., 1998—2000, chief strategic and adminstrv. officer, 2000—01; pres., CFO Morgan Stanley, 2001—04, exec. v.p., chief adminstrv. officer, 2004—05, co-pres., 2005, mem. bd. & mgmt. com. with joint responsibility Institutional Securities Group, Individual Investor Group and Investment Mgmt., 2005, bd. dirs., 2005. Bd. dirs. Nat. Ctr. for Learning Disabilities, New York Philharmonic. Mem.: The Ctr. for Excellence in Acctg. and Security Analysis, Columbia Bus. Sch. (adv. bd. mem. 2003—).*

CRAWFORD, STEVEN ALAN, physician; b. Houston, July 25, 1953; s. Warren Donovan and Helen Elizabeth; m. Linda Deanna Tunmire, May 23, 1981; children: Tiffany, Thomas. BA, Claremont McKenna Coll., 1975; MD, U. Ill., 1979. Diplomate Am. Bd. Family Medicine. Resident McLennan County Family Medicine Residency Program, Waco, Tex., 1982; fellow Waco Faculty Devel. Ctr., 1983; assoc. dir. O.U. Coll. Med. Shawnee FM Residency, Shawnee, Okla., 1982-84; asst. prof. family medicine U. Okla., Okla. City, 1982-89; co-dir. family medicine Occ Med. Okla. U. Health Scis. Ctr. Residency, Okla. City, 1987-89; clinical assoc. prof. Coll. Medicine Okla. U. Health Scis. Ctr., Okla. City, 1989-95, vice chair, prof. family and preventive medicine, 1995-98, interim chair, prof., 1998-99, chair, prof., 1999—. Physician Okla. City clinic, 1989-98; pres. Okla. Acad. Family Physicians, 1994. Contbr. chpts. to books, article to profl. jour. Mem.: Okla. City Clin. Soc. (pres. 2005), Okla. County Med. Soc. (pres. 2002). Avocations: racquetball, sports cars. Office: OUHSC Family and Preventive Med 900 NE 10th St Oklahoma City OK 73104-5420 Office Phone: 405-271-4224. E-mail: steve-crawford@ouhsc.edu.

CRAWFORD, SUSAN, library director, educator, editor, writer; b. Vancouver, B.C., Can. d. James Y. and S. Young; m. James Weldon Crawford, July 5, 1955; 1 son, Robert James. BA, U. B.C., 1948; MA, U. Toronto, 1950, U. Chgo., 1954, PhD, 1970. With bur. libr. and indexing svc. ADA, 1954-56; with office exec. v.p. AMA, Chgo., 1956-60, dir. divsn. libr. and archival svcs., 1960-81; assoc. prof. Sch. Libr. Sci., Columbia U., N.Y.C., 1972-75; prof., dir. Sch. Medicine Libr. and Biomed. Comm. Ctr. Washington U., 1981-92; adj. prof. U. Ill., Chgo., 1994—. Author over 160 books and articles; mem. editl. bd. Med. Socioecon. Rsch. Sources, Index to Sci. Revs., Jour. Am. Soc. Info. Sci., Med. Libr. Assn. News, Health and Info. Librs., Budapest, Health Librs. Rev., London, Health Info. and Librs. Jour., Oxford, Eng., 2003—; assoc. editor Jour. Am. Soc. Info Sci., 1979-82; editor Med. Info. Sys., 1988-90; editor-in-chief Jour. Med. Libr. Assn., 1982-88, 91-92. Bd. regents Nat. Libr. Medicine, NIH, 1971-75; mem. bd. overseers for univ. librs. Tufts U., 1988-89 Janet Doe hon. lectr., 1983; recipient Disting. Alumni award U. Toronto, 1987, Grad. medal U. Toronto, 1989. Fellow AAAS (chmn. coms.), Med. Libr. Assn. (life, Eliot award 1976, chmn. com. on surveys and stats. 1966-75, publs. panel 1977-80, chmn. consulting editors panel 1981-88, 91-92, spl. award to editor of bull. 1988, Noyes award 1992, Pres.'s award 1992, Centennial award), Med. Libr. Assn. (100 Most Notable 1998); mem. ALA, Soc. Social Studies Sci., Am. Soc. Info. Sci. (chmn. med. info. sys. 1987-88, outstanding splty. group award 1988, 89, bd. and program chair Chgo. chpt. 1993-95), Am. Med. Informatics Assn., Acad. Health Info. Profls. (disting. mem.), European Assn. Health and Info. Librs. (U.S. rep. 1989-94), Sigma Xi (chmn. coms.). Home: 2418 Lincoln St Evanston IL 60201-2151 Office Phone: 847-869-3108. Personal E-mail: sjcrawf@aol.com.

CRAWFORD, SUSAN JEAN, federal judge; b. Pitts., Apr. 22, 1947; d. William Elmer Jr. and Joan Ruth (Bielau) C.; m. Roger W. Higgins; 1 child, Kelley S. BA, Bucknell U., 1969; JD, New Eng. Sch. Law, 1977. Bar: Md. 1977, D.C. 1980, U.S. Ct. Appeals for Armed Forces 1985, U.S. Ct. Appeals (4th cir.) 2003, U.S. Supreme Ct. 1993. Tchr. history, coach Radnor (Pa.) H.S., 1969-74; assoc. Burnett & Eiswert, Oakland, Md., 1977-79; ptnr. Burnett, Eiswert and Crawford, Oakland, 1979-81; prin. dep. gen. counsel U.S. Dept. Army, Washington, 1981-83, gen. counsel, 1983-89; insp. gen. U.S. Dept. Def., Arlington, Va., 1989-91; judge U.S. Ct. Appeals for the Armed Forces, Washington, 1991-99, 2004—, chief judge, 1999—2004. Asst. states atty. Garrett County, Md., 1978-79; instr. Garrett County C.C., 1979-81. Del. Md. Forestry Adv. Commn., Garrett County, 1978-81, Md. Commn. for Women, Garrett County, 1980-83; chair Rep. State Cen. Com., Garrett County, 1978-81, Bucknell U., 1988—, chair bd. trustees, 2003—; trustee New Eng. Sch. Law, 1989—. Mem. FBA, Md. Bar Assn., D.C. Bar Assn., Edward Bennett Williams Am. Inn of Ct. Presbyterian. Office: US Ct Appeals Armed Forces 450 E St NW Washington DC 20442-0001

CRAWFORD, TOMMY F., career officer; AA, N.Mex. Mil. Inst., 1970; BA, N.Mex. State U., 1972; student pilot tng., Laughlin AFB, Tex., 1972-73; student, Squadron Officer Sch., 1976, Air Command and Staff Coll., 1978, Air War Coll., 1994; MS in Computer Info. Sys., Boston U., 1994. Commd. 2d lt. USAF, 1972, advanced through grades to brig. gen., 1998; pilot 390th Tactical Fighter Squadron, Mountain Home AFB, Idaho, 1973-75, various positions, 1977-81; pilot 429th Tactical Fighter Squadron, Nellis AFB, Nev., 1975-77; instr. pilot, weapons and tactics officer 4450th Tactical Group, Nellis AFB, Nev., 1981-84; air staff spl. projects officer Hdqs. USAF, Washington, 1984-88; stationed at RAF Lakenheath, Eng., 1988-91, Taif, Kingdom Saudi Arabia, 1990-91; chief spl. weapons sect., mil. asst. Supreme Allied Comdr. Europe Supreme Hdqs. Allied Powers Europe, Mons, Belgium, 1991-93; pilot, dir. combat ops. and dep. comdr. 607th Air Ops. Group, Osan Air Base, S. Korea, 1994-95, pilot, comdr., 1995-97; insp. gen. Hdqs. Pacific Air Forces, Hickam AFB, Hawaii, 1996-97; comdr. 354th Fighter Wing, Eielson AFB, Alaska, 1997—99; dep. dir. ops. in nat. sys. support Nat. Reconnaissance Off., Pentagon, Washington, 1999—2000; dir. joint matters, dep. chief of staff, air and space ops. hqtrs. USAF, Washington, 2000—01; dep. chief, ctrl. security svc. NSA, Ft. George G Meade, Md., 2001—03; commander AF command and control and intelligence surveillance and reconnaissance ctr., Langley AFB, Va., 2003—. Decorated D.F.C. with oak leaf cluster, Legion of Merit, Air medal with oak leaf cluster. Office: Commander AF Command and Control Langley AFB Hampton VA 23665-2292

CRAWFORD, WILLIAM DAVID, office equipment company executive; b. Tuscaloosa, Ala., Jan. 19, 1947; s. Clarence W. and Louise (Hatcher) C.; m. Elaine Randall, July 21, 1977; 1 child, John Samuel. BS in Indsl. Mgmt., U. Ala., 1971; MBA, Jacksonville State U., 1974. Prodn. supr. Goodyear Tire & Rubber Co., Gadsden, Ala., 1971-77; mgmt. instr. U. Ala., Gadsden, 1975-77; various positions Mead-Hatcher, Inc., Buffalo, 1977-85, v.p., 1985-91, pres., CEO, 1991—2001; founder, pres. ErgoTeam, Ltd., 1999—. Bd. dirs., treas. Christian Found. for Performing Arts, 1992-99; bd. dirs. Athletes-in-Action, Buffalo, 1995-2001, Youth for Christ, Buffalo, 1996-2001; host com. Super Bowl Breakfast 2000, 01; bd. dirs. Oakbrook Condominium, Williamsville, NY, 1978-80, 87-90, pres., 1989-90. With USNR, 1964-80, Vietnam, 1967-68. Mem. Bus. Products Industry Assn. (various coms. 1983-2000, treas. 1997, vice chair 1998, chair 1999, bd. dirs. 1994-2000), Office Products Mfrs. Assn. (bd. dirs. 1986-96, treas. 1990-91, v.p. 1992, pres. 1993-94), SAR, U. Ala. Alumni Assn., Delta Chi. Republican. Protestant. Office Phone: 704-655-9147.

CRAWFORD, WILLIAM EDWARD, law educator; b. Key West, Fla., Dec. 15, 1927; s. John Felder and Elizabeth (Cooper) C.; m. Sandra Holmes Shuler, June 30, 1962; children: William, Jr., John F. II, Andrew. BA, La. State U., 1951, JD, 1955. Bar: La. 1955, U.S. Dist. Ct. (ea. dist.) La. 1955, U.S. Ct. Appeals (5th cir.) 1958. Pvt. practice, New Orleans, 1955-65; asst. dean, assoc. prof. La. State U. Law Sch., Baton Rouge, 1966-69, assoc. prof., 1969-71, prof., 1971—; dir. La. State Law Inst., Baton Rouge, 1978—. Spl. master U.S. Dist. Ct., Baton Rouge, 1973-76; cons. La. Assn. Bus. & Industry, Baton Rouge, 1988-92; cons. Gov. Foster, State of La., Baton Rouge, 1996—. Author: (book) La. Tort Law, 2000; editor: La. Code of Civil Procedure, 1982—2003, Stone, Tort Doctrine, 1982—2003, West La. Formulary, 2003; translator: La Nouvelle Code de Procedure Civile, 1978. With USAF, 1951-53. Named James J. Bailey Professor, La. State U. Ctr., 1987, named La. Bar Foundation Disting. Prof. of 2003. Fellow, La. Bar Found.; mem. La. State Bar Assn. Avocations: fishing, golf. Home: 7052 Highland Rd Baton Rouge LA 70808-6632 Office: LSU Law Ctr La State U Baton Rouge LA 70803-0001 Office Phone: 225-578-0204. E-mail: crawfordw@lsli.org.

CRAWFORD, WILLIAM WALSH, retired consumer products company executive; b. Clearwater, Fla., Oct. 7, 1927; s. Francis Marion and Frances Marie (Walsh) C. BS, Georgetown U., 1950; LL.B., Harvard, 1954. Bar: N.Y. 1955, Ill. 1972. Assoc. Sullivan & Cromwell, N.Y.C., 1954-58; counsel Esso Standard Oil, N.Y.C., 1958-60; ptnr. Alexander & Green, N.Y.C., 1960-71; v.p., gen. counsel Internat. Harvester Co., Chgo., 1971-76, v.p., gen. counsel, sec., 1976-80; sr. v.p. gen. counsel Kraft, Inc., Glenview, Ill., 1980-81; sr. v.p., gen. counsel, sec. Dart & Kraft, Inc., 1981-86, Kraft, Inc., 1986-88, sr. v.p., sec., 1988-89, ret., 1989. Mem. ABA, Ill. Bar Assn., Assn. Bar City N.Y., Am. Judicature Soc., Am. Law Inst., Assn. Gen. Counsel, Chgo. Club, Beach Club, Everglades Club, Old Guard Soc. Palm Beach Golfers.

CRAWFORD-LARSON, KRIS, minister; b. Port Lavaca, Tex., July 17, 1957; d. Fred Morris Thedford and Wanda Qualls; m. Stanley A. Larson, May 5, 2001; children: John Patrick Crawford, Carly Crawford, Tara Shea Crawford. BS in Home Econs., Tex. Tech. U., 1980; MDiv, Austin Presbytery Theol. Seminary, 1994. Ordained min. Mission Presbytery P.C., 1995. Assoc. pastor Grace Presbyn. Ch., Victoria, Tex., 1995—2001; pastor First Presbyn. Ch. P.C., Morrilton, Ark., 2001—. Leader Mission Trip to Kenya, 2001; mem. com. on ministry P.C. Presbytery Ark., 2002—03. Chair founding bd. dirs. Conway County Christian Clinic, Morrilton, Ark., 2003. Mem.: Rotary Internat. Avocations: scrapbooks, reading, walking. Office: First Presbyn Ch 105 W Church St Morrilton AR 72110 Office Phone: 501-354-2187.

CRAWFORD-MASON, CLARE WOOTTEN, television producer, journalist; b. Durham, N.C., July 22, 1936; d. Charles Thomas and Clare (Erly) Wootten; m. Robert Watts Mason; children: Victor Lawrence Crawford Jr., Charlene Elizabeth Crawford; stepchildren: John Mason, Robert Mason 3d. BA, U. Md., 1958. Reporter, columnist Washington Daily News, 1961-72; columnist Washington Star News, 1972-74; Washington bur. chief People mag., 1974-82; reporter, sr. prodr. NBC-TV, 1969-80; pres. CC-M Prodns. Inc., Washington, 1981—, managementwisdom.com. Prodr. 1st network documentary on spouse abuse NBC-TV, 1975 (blue ribbon San Francisco Film Festival), 1st network documentary on child sexual abuse NBC, TV, 1977, People of the Year (CBS), 1982, If Japan Can, Why Can't We, 1980 (Dupont award Columbia U. Sch. Journalism), It's Up to the Women, 1984, The Issues Hit Home, 1986, Windows on Women, 1986, How To Fix Up a Little Old American Town, 1987, Work Worth Doing, 1987 (Golden Eagle award Coun. on Internat. Non-theatrical Events), The Deming Library: Vols. I-27, Implementing Deming, vols. 1-4; co-author: Thinking About Quality, Progress, Wisdom and the Deming Revolution, 1995; prodr., dir. documentary series Quality of Else, 1991, W. Edwards Deming: The Prophet of Quality, 1994; co-author: Quality or Else: The Revolution in World Business, 1991; prodr. How Everyone Wins: Joy, Meaning and Profit in the Workplace, 1997, The Enneagram Nine Paths to a Productive and Fulfilling Life, 1999, Good News: How Hospitals Heal Themselves, 2005. Recipient Bill Pryor Meml. award, 1st prize Washington Newspaper Guild, 1966; Disting. Pub. Affairs Reporting award Am. Polit. Sci. Assn., 1967; Nat. Assn. Broadcasters award, 1971, 2 Emmy awards Nat. Acad. TV Arts and Scis., 1972, award for broadcast investigative reporting AAUW, 1972, award for investigative reporting Chesapeake Press Assn., 1971, Douglas Southall Freeman award for pub. service Va. Assn. Press Broadcasters, 1972; Washington Newspaper Guild award, 1974, Blue Ribbon Am. Film Festival, 1977, 1st place award Nat. Edn. Film Festival, 1985, documentary award Am. Women in Radio and TV, 1986, Golden Eagle award, 1986, 87, Award of Excellence Soc. Tech. Communication, 1988. Mem. AFTRA, SAG. Democrat. Roman Catholic. Office: 7755 16th St NW Washington DC 20012-1460 Office Phone: 202-882-7430.

CRAWLEY, CHERYL K., school system administrator; b. Stanley, Wis., Aug. 14, 1943; d. Donald Arthur and Margaret Banderob Schultze; m. Edward Todd Marckx, Mar. 23, 1996; 1 child, Damara Leanne Crawley Griffith. BS, Mont. State U., Bozeman, 1965; MA, Calif. State U., Hayward, 1976; CPhil, U. Calif., Berkeley, 1983. Cert. K-12 supt. Oreg., Mont. Dir. programs Hardin-Crow Agency-Ft. Smith Schs., Mont., 1978—82; asst. supt. Hardin-Crow Agency Ft. Smith Schs., Mont., 1983—86; dir. student svcs. Salem-Keizer Sch. Dist., Oreg., 1986—94; supt. Pub. Schs., Joseph, Oreg., 1994—97; supt. schs. The Dalles, Oreg., 1997—2004, Ross Valley, Marin County, Calif., 2004—. Mem. gov.'s task force Devel. Disabilities Svcs., Oreg., 1987—88; keynote spkr. Mont. Assn. for Bilingual Edn., 1987; mem. Horace Mann Soc. Pub. Edn., 1995—; chmn. resolutions com. Confederation Oreg. Sch. Adminstrs., 2002—03; bd. dirs. numerous non-profit orgns. Sr. examiner Baldridge Nat. Quality Award, Dept. Commerce, Washington, 2001—; fellow Leadership Am., Washington, 1997—, Leadership Mid-Columbia, Columbia Gorge, Oreg., 1998; govt. affairs com. C. of C., The Dalles, Oreg., 1999—2004; Oreg. econ. summit Oreg. Bus. Coun., 2002—03. Named Woman of Distinction, The Dalles Chronicle, 2001; recipient various grants, 1978—86. Mem.: NAFE, Am. Anthropol. Assn., Am. Assn. Sch. Adminstrs., Boardroom Bound, Rotary (The Dalles pres. 1998—99, Dist. 5100 area rep. 2001—04, Paul Harris fellow 2002, Presdl. Citation 1999). Avocations: photography, travel, environment, child advocacy. Office: Ross Valley Sch Dist 110 Shaw Dr San Anselmo CA 94960 Office Phone: 415-451-4060. Business E-Mail: crawley@marin.k12.ca.us.

CRAWLEY, DONTAE, foundation administrator, advocate; s. Donald Crawley and Valerie Lorraine Sneidman. BA, Ctrl. State U. Cmty. health surveyor Ryan White Title 1 Emergency Care Act Program, Washington; media specialist Corp. Nat. and Cmty. Svc., Nat. Svc. Trust. Adv. bd. mem. HRDI, Las Vegas; co-chmn. Ryan White Title 1 Las Vegas EMA Planning Coun., 2003—04, chmn. care strategies com., 2001—03; del. Jackson State U. Miss. Urban Rsch. Ctr., 2003—. African Am. team leader Rep. Nat. Com., Washington, 2000. Recipient Angel Heart award, Ryan White Title 1 Las Vegas EMA Planning Coun., 2003, Pub. Health Week Hero award, Clark County Health Dist., 2004; scholar, Save Aids Drug Assistance Program, 2005. Mem.: UN Assn. (assoc.; del. 2001). Baptist. Achievements include development of 5 year Comprehensive Care Plan for the State of Nevada to provide healthcare and support services that will improve and enhance the lives of persons infected and affected by HIV/AIDS. Avocations: tennis, movies, baseball. Office: Ryan White Title 1 Las Vegas EMA PC- 101 Conv Ctr Dr Ste 1125 Las Vegas NV 89109 Office Phone: 702-933-9603. Office Fax: 702-933-9602.

CRAWLEY, EDWARD FRANCIS, aerospace engineering educator; b. Boston, Sept. 7, 1954; s. Edward George and Dorothy Marie (Horgan) C. Student, Leningrad (USSR) State U., 1975; BS, MIT, 1976, MS, 1978, ScD, 1980. Asst. prof. MIT, Cambridge, 1980-86; aerospace engr. Johnson Space Flight Ctr., Houston, 1981; assoc. prof. MIT, Cambridge, 1986-90, dir. Space Engring. Rsch. Ctr., 1988-96, prof., 1990—, MacVicar faculty fellow dir. Sys. Design & Mgmt. Program, 1992—, dept. head, 1996—; co-exec. dir. Cambridge-MIT Inst. Vis. scholar Stanford U., Palo Alto, Calif., 1988; pres., CEO Sugarbush Soaring Assoc., Vt., 1987-90; chmn. Active Control Experts, 1992—. Assoc. editor Jour. of Intelligent Material Systems and Structures, 1988-95; author: over 50 jour. publs. Mem. presdl. adv. com. space sta. redesign, 1993, tech. and commercialization adv. com., NASA. NSF Presdl. Young Investigator, 1986. Fellow AIAA (assoc., assoc. editor Handbook of Astronautics 1988-92); mem. ASME (past chmn.), NAE (adv. space sta. com. 1987), Soaring Soc. Am. (chmn. structures materials panel). Office: Mass Inst Tech 77 Massachusetts Ave Bldg 33-207 Cambridge MA 02139 E-mail: crawley@mit.edu.*

CRAWLEY, VERNON OBADIAH, academic administrator; b. Oct. 22, 1936; s. Joseph and Ruth (Adkins) C.; m. Betty W. Wood, July 9, 1966; children: V. Alan, Vonda, Keith. BS in Chemistry, Va. State U., 1958; postgrad., Coll. William and Mary, 1962, Am. U., 1964; MEd, U. Va., 1965; EdD, Pa. State U., 1971. Chemist Stuart Products Co., Richmond, Va., 1958-61; tchr. sci. and math. Ruthville (Va.) High Sch., 1961-64; asst. prof. sci. dept. Morgan State U., Balt., 1965-69; instr. phys. sci. Towson State Coll., Balt., 1969; assoc. prof. chemistry, chmn. sci., math. and technologies Dundalk C.C., Balt., 1971-74; assoc. dean acad. affairs Mercer County C.C., Trenton, N.J., 1974-78; pres. St. Louis C.C. at Forest Park, 1978-91, Moraine Valley C.C., Palos Hills, Ill., 1991—. Acting dean James Kerney campus Mercer County C.C., Trenton, 1976-77; adminstrv. specialist in sci. NASA, Washington, summer 1966, 67, 68; cons. N. Cen. Assn., Coro Found. Adv. bd. mem. St. Francis Hosp., Blue Island, Ill.; fin. adv. com. mem. Ill. C.C. Bd.; chmn. Ill. Coun. C.C. Pres.; bd. dirs. Southwest YMCA, Alsip, Ill. Recipient Outstanding Svc. to Williams Cmty. Sch. award 8th Dist. Police Cmty.Youth Network Com., 1990, Assistance with Minority Tchr. Recruitment Program award St. Louis Area Pers. and Place Adminstrs., 1989, Outstanding Leadership award Nat. Coun. Black Am. Affairs, 1987, Citizenship award Wellston Sch. Dist., 1983, NSF Acad. Yr. award, 1964-65, Southern fellowship, 1965. Mem. League for Innovation in C.C. (bd. dirs.), Expanding Leadership Opportunities for Minorities in C.C. (nat. adv. group), Am. Assn. C.C. (bd. dirs., exec. bd.), Nat. Coun. on Black Am. Affairs (bd. dirs.), Econ. Devel. Corp. for Southwest Suburbs (bd. dirs.), Rotary Club Oak Lawn, Moraine Valley C.C. Found. (bd. dirs.), Mo. Assn. Community and Jr. Colls. (bd. dirs.), Mo. Coun. C.C. Pres./Chancellors (chmn. 1986-87, v.p. 1985-86, sec. treas. 1984-85), Sigma Xi, Phi Theta Kappa. Avocations: travel, reading, gardening. Home: 7841 Sioux Rd Orland Park IL 60462-1894 Office: Moraine Valley CC 10900 S 88th Ave Palos Hills IL 60465-2175

CRAWSHAW, RALPH, psychiatrist; b. N.Y.C., July 3, 1921; AB, Middlebury (Vt.) Coll., 1943; MD, N.Y. U., 1947. Diplomate: Nat. Bd. Med. Examiners, Am. Bd. Psychiatry and Neurology. Intern Lenox Hill Hosp., N.Y.C., 1947-48; resident Menninger Sch. Psychiatry, Topeka, 1948-50, Oreg. State Hosp., Salem, 1950-51; practice medicine specializing in psychiatry Washington, 1954; staff psychiatrist C.F. Menninger Meml. Hosp., Topeka, 1954-57; asst. chief VA Mental Hygiene Clinic, Topeka, 1957-60; staff psychiatrist Community Child Guidance Clinic, Portland, Oreg., 1960-63; founder, clinic dir. Tualatin Valley Guidance Clinic, Beaverton, Oreg., 1961-67; pvt. practice medicine, specializing in psychiatry Portland, 1960—2001; mem. staff Holladay Park Hosp., 1961—73. Lectr. dept. child psychiatry Med. Sch. U. Oreg., 1961-63, clin. prof. dept. psychiatry, 1976; lectr. Sch. Social Work, Portland State U., 1964-67; founder Benjamin Rush Found., 1968, pres., 1968—; founder Friends of Medicine, 1969, Ct. of Man, 1970, Club of Kos, 1974, Oreg. Health Decisions, 1983, Am. Health Decisions, 1989, Health Vol. Overseas, 1984; Sonian Machanic vis. prof. South African Coll. Medicine, 1993. Contbr. editor: AMA Jour. of Socio-Econs, 1972-75; Columnist: Prism mag, 1972-76, The Pharos, 1972—, Portland Physician, 1975, Western Jour. Medicine, 1980—; Contbr. articles to med. jours. Cons. Bur. Hearings and Appeals, HEW, 1964-90; cons. Albina Child Devel. Center, Portland, 1965-75, HEW Region 8 Health Planning, 1979; mem. Inst. Medicine, Nat. Acad. Sci., 1978, Oreg. Health Coordinating Council, 1979; Mem. Gov.'s Adv. Com. on Mental Health, 1966-72; ad hoc com. Nat. Leadership Conf. on Am. Health Policy, 1976, Gov.'s Adv. Com. on Med. Care to Indigent, 1976—; trustee Millicent Found., 1964-67, Multnomah Found. for Med. Care, 1977; pres. Bull Run Heritage Found., 1996; vis. scholar Center for Study Democratic Instns., 1969, Jack Murdock Charitable Trust, 1977, U.S.-USSR exchange scholar, 1973; founder Bull Run Heritage Found., 1996. Served with AUS, 1943-46; to lt., M.C. USN, 1951-54. Named Oreg. Dr./Citizen of Yr., 1978; U.S.-USSR rsch. scholar, 1973, 79; recipient I.N. Piragou medal for humanitarian Svcs., Russian Govt., 1992; Ralph Crawshaw Ann. Lectr. in Civic Medicine named in honor by Oreg. Found. for Med. Excellence, 1987. Fellow Am. Psychiat. Assn.; mem. AMA, APA, AAAS, Nat. Med. Assn., Oreg. Med. Assn. (trustee 1972—), Multnomah County Med. Soc. (pres. 1975), Royal Soc. Medicine, Inst. of Medicine of NAS, North Pacific Soc. Neurology and Psychiatry, Soc. for Psychol. Study Social Issues, Western European Assn. Aviation Psychology, Am. Med. Writers Assn., Portland Psychiatrists in Pvt. Practice (pres. 1971), Russian Acad. Natural Scis. (fgn. mem.), Alpha Omega. Home: 2884 NW Raleigh Portland OR 97210

CRAYBAS, JILL, professional tennis player; b. Providence, July 4, 1974; d. Norbert and Camille. Degree in telecom., U. Fla., 1996. Profl. tennis player, 1996—. Recipient Ranked #8 in U.S. 18s, 1992, NCAA Champion, 1996, Ranked #97, WTA, Ranked #14 Among U.S. Players, Highest Season Ending Singles Rank #57, 2002, 1WTA Tour Singles Title, Japan, 2002, 1 WTA Tour Doubles Title, Madrid, 2003, 2 ITF Women's Circuit Tour Titles, 8th Place Wimbledon, 2005. Office: WTA Tour Corporate Headquarters One Progress Plz Ste 1500 Saint Petersburg FL 33701*

CRAYPO, CHARLES, labor economics professor; b. Jackson, Mich., Jan. 3, 1936; s. Norman Laverne and Ann Marie (Bogdan) C.; m. Mary Louise Vaclavik, Sept. 6, 1958; children: Jack, Carrie, Susan. BA in Econs., Mich. State U., 1959, MA in Econs., 1961, PhD in Econs., 1966. Asst. prof. econs. U. Maine, Orono, 1966-67; assoc. prof. Mich. State U., East Lansing, 1967-72, Pa. State U., University Park, 1972-78, U. Notre Dame, Ind., 1978-82, prof., 1984-2000, prof., chmn. dept. econs., 1984-93; prof. Cornell U., Ithaca, N.Y., 1982-84. Bd. dirs. Bus. Devel. Com., South Bend, Ind.; dir. Bur. Workers Edn., U. Maine, Orono, 1966-67, Higgins Labor Rsch. Ctr., U. Notre Dame, 1993; mem. acad. evaluating com. Labor Studies Ctr., Empire State Coll., SUNY, 1980; mem. labor studies dept. Ramapo Coll., 1981; mem. indsl. rels. dept. LeMoyne Coll., Syracuse, N.Y., 1983, Bur. of Labor Edn., U. Maine, Orono; external rev. mem. Divsn. Labor Studies Ind. U., 1998-99; mem. Labor Rsch. Adv. Coun., Bureau Labor Statistics, U.S. Dept. Labor, 2000; lectr. in field; expert witness. Author: Economics of Collective Bargaining, 1986, Grand Designs, 1993; mem. editl. bd., bus. mgr. Labor Studies Jour., 1976-80, chmn. editl. bd., 1980-85; mem. editl. bd. Contbns. to Labor Studies, 1989-97; internat. mem. editl. bd. Indsl. Rels. Jour., 1989-2002; contbr. articles to profl. jours. Mem. acad. adv. com. Divsn. Labor Studies Ind. U., 1978-82, 84-92, 95-96. Served with USMC, 1953-55. Recipient Lilly Endowment, 1992, D. Dority Labor Rsch. Fund, Ganey Rsch. award, 2002; grantee NEH, 1981, Rsch. grant, Dept. Commerce, 1984. Mem.: Indsl. Rels. Rsch. Assn. Home: 50600 Sorrel Dr Granger IN 46530-8506 Office Phone: 574-631-6934. E-mail: craypo.3@nd.edu.

CRAYTON, ARNELL, secondary school educator; b. Galveston, Tex., Jan. 25, 1949; s. Arnell and Careline Crayton. BS, Tex. Christian U., 1971. Cert. educator Tex. Dir. planning and evaluation Gulf Coast Regional Mental Health and Mental Retardation Ctr., Galveston, 1972—74; acctg. supr. Allstate Ins. Co., Englewood, Colo., 1974—79; retail mgr. J C Penney, Houston, 1980—91, Dillards Dept. Stores, Houston, 1992—2003; tchr. Bellaire H.S., Bellaire, Tex., 2003—. Participant Park City Math. Inst., Inst. Advanced Sci., 2005. Parish social min. St. Vincents De Paul, Houston, 2004. Named Area Sales Mgr. of Quarter (8), Dillards Dept. Stores, 1994—2003; fellow Woodrow Wilson Found., 1971; Sherer Math. scholar, Tex. Christian U., 1970. Mem.: ASCD, Nat. Coun. Tchrs.Math. (life). Democrat. Roman Catholic. Avocations: music, reading, biblical studies. Home: 6824 Linden Houston TX 77087 Office: Bellaire HS 5100 Maple Bellaire TX 77401 Office Phone: 713-294-3704. Home Fax: 713-928-6382; Office Fax: 713-294-3704. Personal E-mail: a.crayton@worldnet.att.net.

CRAYTON, BILLY GENE, physician; b. Holden, Mo., May 15, 1931; s. John Reuben and Carrie Zona (Head) C. Student, Ctrl. Mo. State Coll., 1948-49; BS, Stetson U., 1958; postgrad., U. Kansas City, summer 1955; MD, U. Mo., 1962. Intern Mound Park Hosp., St. Petersburg, Fla., 1962-63;

practice gen. medicine Latham Hosp., Calif., Mo., 1963-64, Kelling Clinic and Hosp., Waverly, Mo., 1964-88, vice chief of staff, 1980-88; preceptor in cmty. health and med. practice U. Mo. Sch. Medicine, Waverly, 1968-88; sec., dir. Kelling Hosp., Inc., 1969-80; pres. Kelling Clinic, 1971-88; med. dir. Waverly Ambulance Co., 1985-86; pres. Riverview Heights, 1972-88. Advisor Mo. chpt. Am. Assn. Med. Assts., 1973-79. Adviser Explorer Post, Boy Scouts Am., 1968-70. Served with AUS, 1952-54. Fellow Am. Acad. Family Physicians. Baptist. Home: 1231 W 69th Ter Kansas City MO 64113-2054 Personal E-mail: bgcrayton@aol.com.

CREAGER, JOE SCOTT, geology and oceanography educator; b. Vernon, Tex., Aug. 30, 1929; s. Earl Litton and Irene Eugenia (Keller) C.; m. Barbara Clark, Aug. 30, 1951 (dec.); children: Kenneth Clark, Vanessa Irene; m. B. J. Wren, Sept. 5, 1987 (dec.); m. Eva R. Milligan, Mar. 18, 2001 (div.); m. Joanne L. Thronson, Aug. 7, 2004. BS, Colo. Coll., 1951; postgrad., Columbia, 1952-53; MS, Tex. A&M U., 1953, PhD, 1958. Asst. prof. dept. oceanography U. Wash., Seattle, 1958-61, assoc. prof., 1962-66, prof. oceanography, 1966-91, prof. geol. scis., 1981-91, prof. emeritus, 1991—, asst. chmn. dept. oceanography, 1964-65, assoc. dean arts and scis. for earth and planetary scis., 1966-95, assoc. dean for rsch., 1966-91, divisional dean emeritus, 1995—; program dir. for oceanography NSF, 1965-66; chief scientist numerous oceanographic expdns. to Arctic and Sub-arctic including Leg XIX of Deep Sea Drilling project, 1959-91. Vis. geol. scientist Am. Geol. Inst., 1962, 63, 65; U.S. Nat. coord. Internat. Indian Ocean Expedition, 1965-66; vis. scientist program lectr. Am. Geophys. Union, 1965-72; Battelle cons., advanced waste mgmt., 1974; cons. to U.S. Army C.E., 1976, U.S. Depts. Interior and Commerce, 1975; exec. sec., exec. com., chmn. planning com. Joint Oceanographic Insts. Deep Earth Sampling, 1970-72, 76-78; mem. evaluation com. Northwest Assn. Schs. and Colls., 1989-99. Mem. editorial bd. Internat. Jour. Marine Geology, 1964-91; assoc. editor Jour. Sedimentary Petrology, 1963-76; asst. editor Quaternary Research, 1970-79; contbr. articles to profl. jours. Skipper Sea Scout Ship, Boy Scouts Am., Bryan, Tex., 1957; coach Little League Baseball, Seattle, 1964-71, sec., 1971; cons. sci. curriculum Northshore Sch. Dist., 1970; mem. Seattle Citizens Shoreline Com., 1973-74, King County Shoreline Com., 1980. Served with U.S. Army, 1953-55. Colo. Coll. scholar, 1949-51; NSF grantee, 1962-82; ERDA grantee, 1962-64; U.S. Army C.E. grantee, 1975-82; Office of Naval Research grantee; U.S. Dept. Commerce grantee; U.S. Geol. Survey grantee. Fellow Geol. Soc. Am., AAAS; mem. Internat. Assn. Quaternary Research, Am. Geophys. Union, Internat. Assn. Sedimentology, Internat. Assn. Math. Geologists, Soc. Econ. Paleontologists and Mineralists, Marine Tech. Soc. (sec.-treas. 1972-75), Sigma Xi, Beta Theta Pi, Delta Epsilon. Home: 7449 NE 118th Pl Kirkland WA 98034 Office: U Wash PO Box 353765 Seattle WA 98195-3765 Personal E-mail: bjnjoe@att.net.

CREAMER, GERMAN GONZALO, financial consultant, educator; b. Caracas, Venezuela, Oct. 31, 1960; arrived in Ecuador, 1978; s. Claudio Creamer and Maria Del Carmen Guillen; m. Maria Consuelo Botero, June 19, 1992; children: Mateo, Carolina. BA in psychology, Cath. U. Ecuador, 1985, BA in Sociology, 1986; MA, U. Notre Dame, 1989, PhD in Econs., 1993; MSc in Fin. Engring., Columbia U., 2002. CFA. Dir. human resource dept. Constructora Elepeve, Quito, Ecuador, 1985-86; econ. advisor President of Ecuador, Quito, 1990-91; econs. program officer UN, Quito, 1992-93; assoc. prof., econs. coord. FLACSO, Quito, 1993-95; mgr. planning and econ. studies Banco del Pacifico, Guayaquil, 1996-97; prof. Catholic U, Guayaquil and Espol, 1995-97; vis. assoc. prof. fin. Bus. Sch., Tulane U., New Orleans, 1998—2002; adj. prof. bus. Tulane U., 2002—. Cons. UN, Equatorial Guinea, 1991, USAID, Quito, 1991, 94; Komex 1995, Urbana-World Bank, 2000; instr. Columbia U., 2002—. Author: Redistribution, Inflation, and Adjustment Policies, 1992, Predicting Performance and Quantifying Corporate Governance Risk for Latin American ADRs and Banks, 2004; co-author: La desarticulacion del Mundo Andino, 1986, Las economias Andinas, 1993, The Ecuadorean Participation in the Andean Pact, 1996, Ecuador en la Economía Mundial, 1997, The Cost of Hospital Cholera Treatment in Ecuador, 1999, Open Regionalism, Trade, Liberalization and the Role of Small Producers, 1999, Open Regionalism in the Andean Community: a trade flow analysis, 2003, Regionalismo Abierto en la Comunidad Andina, 2004, Predicting Performance and Quantifying Corporate Governance Risk for Latin American ADRs and Banks, 2004; contbr. articles to profl. jours. Fulbright scholar, N.Y., 1986, Inst. for Study of World Policies scholar, N.Y., 1988, MacArthur Found. scholar, U. Notre Dame, 1990, Kellogg Inst., 1989; grantee Bd. Regents, State of La., 1999. Mem. Am. Fin. Assn., Am. Assn. Artificial Intelligence, N.Y. Soc. Security Analysts, CFA Inst. Home: 150 Claremont Ave Apt 5D New York NY 10027 Office: 520 W 120th St #450 New York NY 10027 E-mail: gcreame@hotmail.com.

CREAMER, KATHY JAYNE, writer; b. Logansport, Ind., Dec. 10, 1959; d. James Hensley and Evelyn Lois (Good) Logan; m. Randall Wayne Creamer, Oct. 15, 1983; children: Jennifer Lois, Krysta Elizabeth. Lic., Beer Sch. Real Estate, 1987. Lic. real estate agt. Ind. Agt. Era Real Estate Co., Warsaw, Ind., 1987—88; referral agt. various real estate cos., Warsaw, 1988—89; freelance writer, 1992—. Author: (children's book) Case of the Missing Books, 1993, (novels) Shadows Dark, 1995. Vol. Am. Party, Ind., 1978; treas. sr. class Lakeland Christian Acad., Winona Lake, Ind., 1977—78. Republican. Baptist. Avocations: photography, quilting, reading, crafts, book collecting. Home: PO Box 184 Atwood IN 46502

CREAMER, PAULA, professional golfer; b. Mountain View, CA, Aug. 5, 1986; Golfer LPGA Tour, 2004—. Named Amateur of the Yr., Golf Digest, 2004, Golfweek, 2004, Player of the Yr., Am. Junior Golf Assoc., 2003; recipient Louise Suggs Rolex Rookie of the Year award, 2005. Achievements include first amateur to win the LPGA Final Qualifying Tournament, 2004; youngest person to win the LPGA Final Qualifying Tournament, 2004; 2 career LPGA tour victories; won her first tournament in Japan, the NEC Karuizawa; won 19 national championship, 11 Am. Junior Golf Assoc. tournaments. Office: Ladies Professional Golf Association 100 International Golf Drive Daytona Beach FL 32124*

CREAMER, ROBERT ALLAN, lawyer; b. Sept. 25, 1941; m. Joy A. Blakslee. BA, Northwestern U., 1963; LLB, Harvard U., 1967. Bar: Ill. 1967, U.S. Dist. Ct. (no. dist.) Ill. 1967, U.S. Ct. Appeals (7th cir.) 1969, U.S. Supreme Ct. 1976. Assoc. Keck, Mahin & Cate, Chgo., 1967—73, ptnr., 1974—93; v.p., loss prevention counsel Attys.' Liability Assurance Soc., Inc., Chgo., 1994—. Adj. prof. John Marshall Law Sch., Chgo., 1969—75, Northwestern U. Sch. Law, Chgo., 2000—. Mem.: ABA, Am. Law Inst., Ill. Bar Assn. (chmn. standing com. profl. conduct 1990—91, 1997—98), Chgo. Bar Assn., Northwestern U. Alumni Assn. (pres. 1990—94), Univ. Club (Chgo.), Cliff Dwellers Club (Chgo.), Lawyers Club Chgo. Democrat. Episcopalian. Home: 1500 Oak Ave Evanston IL 60201-4279 Office: Attys' Liability Assurance Soc Inc 311 S Wacker Dr Ste 5700 Chicago IL 60606-6629 Office Phone: 312-697-6944. Personal E-mail: racreamer@alas.com.

CREAN, PETER THOMAS, lawyer; b. N.Y.C., Feb. 14, 1955; s. Thomas D. and Dorothy (Barry) C.; m. Stefanie Lewand, May 26, 1979; children: T.R., Patrick, Rosemary. AB in Politics, U. Mass., 1977; JD, Fordham U., 1981. Bar: N.Y. 1982, U.S. Dist. Ct. (ea. and so. dists.) N.Y. 1982, U.S. Supreme Ct. 1995. Ptnr. Martin, Clearwater & Bell, N.Y.C., 1981—. Bd. trustees St. Agnes Hosp., White Plains, NY. Mem. N.Y. State Bar Assn., Assn. Bar City N.Y., Def. Rsch. Inst., Am. Health Lawyers Assn., Assn. Healthcare Risk Mgrs. Office: Martin Clearwater & Bell 220 E 42nd St New York NY 10017-5806

CREASIA, JOAN CATHERINE, dean, nursing educator; b. Burlington, Vt., Aug. 14, 1941; d. Ramon J. and Marjorie E. (Rising) LaBelle; m. Donald A. Creasia, June 29, 1963; children: Karen, Tracey. BSN, U. Vt., 1964; MSN, U. Tenn., 1978; PhD, U. Md., 1987. Staff nurse psychiat. unit Mass. Mental Health Ctr., Boston, 1964-65; instr. D'Youville Sch. Nursing, Cambridge, Mass., 1965-66; staff nurse Boston Lying-In Hosp., 1966-67; staff nurse med. surg. units Norwood (Mass.) Hosp., 1967-70; staff nurse, nursing supr. Oak Ridge (Tenn.) Hosp., 1971-74; staff nurse, supr. Frederick (Md.) Meml. Hosp., 1977-78, 86-92; instr. in nursing U. Tenn., Knoxville, 1974-77; rsch. asst. U. Md., Balt., 1980-83; instr., coord., asst. prof. med. surg. nursing Frederick (Md.) C.C., 1978-80, 81-83; asst. prof., coord. RN-BSN program U. Md. Sch. Nursing, Balt., 1983-90, assoc. prof., chair RN-BSN/MS programs, 1990-94, dir. statewide programs, 1991-94; assoc. dean for acad. programs and interim dean Med. U. of S.C. Coll. Nursing, Charleston, 1994-95; dean, Coll. Nursing, U. Tenn., Knoxville, 1995—. Cons. in field. Author: Conceptual Foundations of Professional Nursing Practice, 1991, 96 (Book of Yr. award Am. Jour. Nursing 1992), Conceptual Foundations: The Bridge to Professional Nursing Practice, 2001; contbr. articles to profl. jours. and books. Recipient Outstanding Achievement in Indirect Nursing Rsch. award, 1987, Nat. Rsch. Svc. award, 1982, 83, Profl. Nurse Traineeship award, 1981, Outstanding Leadership award Md. Nurses Assn., 1990. Mem.: ANA, Am. Assn. Colls. Nursing (bd. dirs.), Nat. League Nursing, Phi Kappa Phi, Sigma Theta Tau. Home: 605 Scotswood Cir Knoxville TN 37919-7457 Office Phone: 865-974-7583. Personal E-mail: dcreasia@aol.com. Business E-Mail: jcreasia@utk.edu.

CREASY, CHARLES L., creative director; b. Sumner Co, Tenn., Nov. 27, 1946; s. Charles E. and Vernie D. (Simpson) C.; m. Edythe Marnelle Davis, Sept. 10, 1966; children: Charles Jr., Chanda, Christopher. Student, Tenn. Tech. U., Cookeville, 1964-66, Harris Sch. Advt. Art, Nashville, 1969, John Pike Watercolor Sch., Woodstock, N.Y., 1969-70. Artist Eric Erickson & Assoc., Nashville, 1969-71; sr. art dir. Lee Harrison Advt., Nashville, 1971-72; creative dir. Nitro Lube Corp., Nashville, 1973-75; owner Chuck Creasy Design, Nashville; v.p. creative dir. Holder, Kennedy, Dye & Bell, Nashville, 1978-79; v.p. creative group head Eric Ericson & Assoc., 1980-84; became v.p. creative dir. Brumfield-Gallagher, Inc., Nashville, 1985; now ptnr., creative dir. Dye, Van Mol & Lawrence Pub. Relations, Nashville. Com. mem. Middle Tenn. Council Boy Scouts Am., Nashville 1986--; pres. The Creative Forum, Nashville 1987--. Designer Annual Report, Middle Tenn. Council BSA 1987 (awarded N.Y. Art Dir. Show Cal. Design Annual award); Creative Designer: Numerous Diamond awards, local and regional. Creative Dir. for Print & Design Reagan/Bush Campaign, Wash. 1984; Mem. Rep. Nat. Com., Wash. 1984—; Pres. Creative Forum 1987—. With U.S. Army 1966-68. Recipient Eagle Scout award Boy Scouts Am., Nashville 1962, Elder St. Luke Cumberland Presbyn. Ch., Madison 1979. Mem. Nashville Advt. Fed., Scuba Club Nashville (Pres. 1986). Republican. Southern Baptist. Avocations: scuba diving, watercolorist, antique collecting, salt water fishing. Office: Dye Van Mol & Lawrence Pub Relations 209 7th Ave N Nashville TN 37219-1802 Home: 1609 Riverchase Blvd Madison TN 37115-2056

CREATH, CURTIS JANSSEN, pediatric dentist; b. Lynwood, Calif., Mar. 10, 1958; s. Ronald J. and Madelyn W. (Chryst) C.; m. Deborah Ann Lipari, June 23, 1990; 1 child, Andrew. Student, UCLA, 1976-81; DMD, Oral Roberts U., 1985; MS, U. Ala., 1988. Asst. prof. Sch. Dental Medicine SUNY, Stony Brook, 1988-91, Sch. Dentistry U. Ala., Birmingham, 1991-94; staff pediat. dentist Family Cental Care Assocs., Cin., 1994-95; pvt. practice Milford, Ohio, 1995—. Team leader dental mission trips to Mex., Jamaica, Peru, 1982-84. Contbr. chpt. to: Special and Medically Compromised Patients in Dentistry, 1989, Clark's Clinical Dentistry, Vol. 2, 1994; contbr. articles, revs. on tobacco control, pediat. dentistry, and preventive medicine to profl. jours. Mem. ADA, Am. Acad. Pediat. Dentistry (mem. edn. com.), Am. Assn. Dental Schs. (v.p. 1986-88), Ala. Soc. Pediat. Dentistry (sec.-treas. 1992-94), Christian Med. and Dental Soc., Omicron Kappa Upsilon. Republican. Presbyterian. Avocations: vocal music, preaching, missionary work, woodworking, gardening. Home: 6514 Tulip Ct Liberty Township OH 45044-9726 Office: 1106-C Main St PO Box 267 Milford OH 45150-0267 Personal E-mail: curtjcre@aol.com.

CREATURA, MARK ANTHONY, lawyer; b. Conn., 1959; AB, Harvard U., 1980; JD, U. Calif., Berkeley, 1985. Bar: Calif. 1985. Atty. Troy & Gould, L.A., 1985-93; v.p., gen. counsel Urethane Technologies, Inc., Santa Ana, Calif., 1993-96; sr. v.p., gen. counsel Consumer Portfolio Svcs., Inc., Irvine, Calif., 1996—. Office: Consumer Portfolio Svcs Inc 16355 Laguna Canyon Rd Irvine CA 92618-3801 Office Phone: 888-785-6691. E-mail: creaturamark@yahoo.com.

CREAVEN, PATRICK JOSEPH, pharmacologist; b. Eng., Jan. 31, 1933; MB, BS, St. Mary's Hosp. Med. Sch., U. London, 1956, PhD, 1964. House surgeon Bedford Gen. Hosp.; also house physician Barnet Gen. Hosp., Eng., 1956-57; asst. lectr. biochemistry U. London, St. Mary's Hosp. Med. Sch., 1963-64, lectr., 1964-66; chief biochemistry Tex. Rsch. Inst. Mental Sci., 1966-69; head, pharmacology lab. Nat. Cancer Inst., VA Med. Oncology Br., 1969-75; assoc. chief, cancer rsch. clinician Roswell Park Meml. Inst. (now Roswell Park Cancer Inst.), Buffalo, 1975-79, chief cancer rsch. clinician, 1979—, chmn. dept. clin. pharmacology and therapeutics, 1979-89, chief div. clin. pharmacology and therapeutics, Dept. Medicine, 1989-91, sr. investigator dept. investigational therapeutics, 1991—; dir. Phase I Program Roswell Park Cancer Inst., 2001—; rsch. prof. medicine dept. medicine SUNY Med. Sch., Buffalo, 1994—. Contbr. articles to profl. jours. Fellow Am. Coll. Clin. Pharmacology, Royal Soc. Health; mem. Am. Assn. Cancer Rsch., Am. Soc. Clin. Oncology, Am. Soc. Pharmacology and Exptl. Therapeutics, Am. Soc. Clin. Pharmacology and Therapeutics. Office: Roswell Park Cancer Inst Elm And Carlton St Buffalo NY 14263-0001 Office Phone: 716-845-8451. Business E-Mail: patrick.creaven@roswellpark.org.

CREECH, JOHN LEWIS, botanist, consultant; b. Woonsocket, R.I., Jan. 17, 1920; s. Edward and Bessie (Faulkner) C.; m. Amy Elizabeth Wentzel, Feb. 14, 1942 (dec. Apr. 1984); children: Diane, Victoria, John; m. Elaine E. Godden Innes, July 10, 1984 (dec. July 2003). BS in Horticulture, U. R.I., 1941; MS in Horticulture, U. Mass., 1947; PhD in Botany, U. Md., 1953. Instr. horticulture U. Mass., Amherst, 1946-47; horticulturist Office Plant Exploration, Agrl. Rsch. Svc. USDA, 1947-50, asst. chief new crops rsch. br. Agrl. Rsch. Svc., 1958-66, chief br. Agrl. Rsch. Svc., 1966-72, scientist nat. program staff Agrl. Rsch. Svc., 1972-73; dir. U.S. Nat. Arboretum, Washington, 1973-80, N.C. Arboretum, 1987-88. Sr. adviser Internat. Bd. for Plant Genetic Resources; negotiator Bicentennial gift of Nat. Bonsai Collection from people of Japan; developer Nat. Herb Garden; program dir. for conservation of plant genetic materials Internat. Biol. Program, NAS; mem. panel FAO, 1966-74; preparer U.S. position paper for Stockholm Conf. on the Environment; adj. prof. biology U. N.C., Asheville; bd. dirs. N.C. Arboretum, Asheville, interim dir., 1986-87; U.S. judge Internat. Flower & Garden Expo, Japan, 1990; leader 9 plant expeditions Japan, China, Taiwan, USSR, Nepal, 1955-78; co-chmn. Genetic Resource Team, China, 1974; rev. nat. gen. resource program USDA, NAS, 1988-92; cons. Time-Life Books for Children, 1993; cons. in horticulture; leader hort. tours; mem. sci. & edn. com. Internat. Dendiology Soc. Author: The Bonsai Saga, 2001; co-author: Brocade Pillow, 1984, Garden Shrubs and Their Histories, 1992. Capt. U.S. Army, 1941-45, prisoner of war, ETO. Decorated Silver Star, Bronze Star; recipient Gold medal Scott Found., Gold medal Garden Club Am., Gold Seal medal Nat. Coun. State Garden Clubs, Thomas Roland medal Mass. Hort. Soc., Silver medal FAO-UN, Hort. medal Fedn. Garden Clubs N.Y., Norman J. Colman award Am. Nurserymans Assn., Hutchinson medal Chgo. Bot. Garden/Chgo. Hort. Soc., 1987, Gold medal and cert. of merit City of Kurume, Japan, 1988, Veitch Meml. medal Royal Hort. Soc., U.K., 1992, Award of Merit, Am. Assn. Bot. Gardens and Arb., 2000, Prs. award U. R.I., 2002; grantee Merrill Found., 1976, Nat. Geog. Soc., 1978, Japan Found., 1982; selected to give Morrison Meml. lecture. Mem. Am. Genetics Assn. (bd. dirs., Meyer medal), Am. Hort. Soc. (pres. 1954-56, profl. citation, Liberty Hyde Bailey medal 1989), Internat. Dendrology Soc. (v.p. 1989—), Sigma Xi, Phi Kappa Phi, Pi Alpha Xi. Republican. Episcopalian. Achievements include introduction of several plant varieties. Fax. Personal E-mail: jlcreech@teleplex.net.

CREECH, SHARON, children's author; b. South Euclid, Ohio; d. Arvel and Ann Creech; m. Lyle Rigg; children: Rob, Karin. BA, Hiram Coll.; MA, George Mason U. Editl. asst., indexer Congl. Quarterly, Washington; rschr. Libr. Congress. Author: Recital, Nickel Malley, Walk Two Moons, 1994 (School Library Journal Best Book of 1994, ALA Notable Children's Book Award, 1995, John Newbery medal 1995), Absolutely Normal Chaos, 1995, Pleasing The Ghost, 1996, Chasing Redbird, 1997, Bloomability, 1999, The Wanderer, 2000 (Newbery honor), Fishing in the Air, 2000, A Fine, Fine School, 2001, Love That Dog, 2001, Ruby Holler, 2002, Heartbeat, 2004. Office: care HarperCollins Children's Bks c/o Author Mail 1350 Ave of the Americas New York NY 10019

CREED, CHRISTIAN CARL, lawyer, investigator; b. Alexandria, La., Oct. 31, 1963; s. George Alton and Mickey (Svebek) C.; m. Catherine Campball, Aug. 12, 1995. BA, La. State U., 1985; JD, Loyola U., New Orleans, 1995. Bar: La. 1995, U.S. Dist. Ct. (we., mid., and ea. dists.) La. 1995, U.S. Dist. Ct. (no. and so. dists.) Miss. 1998, U.S. Ct. Appeals (5th cir.) 1995. Assoc. Boles, Boles & Ryan, Monroe, La., 1995-98; mng. ptnr. Creed & Creed, Monroe, La., 1998—. Author, contbg. editor (newsletter) Young Lawyers Newsletter, 1997-98. Mem. adv. bd. Salvation Army, Monroe, 1997—; mem. cabinet United Way, Monroe, 1998-99, bd. dirs., 2000—; mem. fundraising com. Boy Scouts Am. Mem. ABA, La. Bar Assn., 4th Jud. Dist. Ct. Bar Assn. (exec. com.), Baton Rouge Bar Assn., La. Trial Lawyers Assn. (bd. govs.), Am. Inns of Ct. (Fred Fudickar chpt. 1995—), Monroe C. of C. (state and fed. govt. com.), Kiwanis Internat., Ducks Unlimited (sponsorship com.), Rotary Internat., Phi Delta Phi (life mem.). Office: Creed & Creed 1805 Tower Dr Monroe LA 71201-4964 E-mail: law@creedlaw.com.

CREED, ROBERT PAYSON, SR., retired literature educator; b. Phila., Apr. 22, 1925; s. Edward E. and Blanche H. (Southerland) Creed; m. Catherine Hilton, Oct. 9, 1987; children from previous marriage: Mary Louise, Robert Payson. BA, Swarthmore Coll., 1948; MA, Harvard U., 1949, PhD, 1956. Instr. Smith Coll., Northampton, Mass., 1952-56; from asst. prof. to assoc. prof. Brown U., Providence, 1956—65; assoc. prof. SUNY, Stony Brook, 1965-67, prof., 1967-69; prof. English U. Mass., Amherst, 1969-97, prof. emeritus, 1997—, dir. grad. studies in English, 1969-72, prof. English and comparative lit., 1980-90, chmn. comparative lit. dept., 1980-85. Cons. G&C Merriam Co., Springfield, Mass., 1955—56; featured storyteller Ann. Nat. Storytelling Festival, Jonesborough, Tenn., 1985, Jonesborough, 92; nat. vis. prof. Paul Valery U., Montepellier, France, 1987; disting. faculty lectr. U. Mass., Amherst, 1993—94. Writer, chief performer Beowulf, Sta. WNYC pub. radio, 1979 (award Corp. Pub. Broadcasting); author: (book) Reconstructing the Rhythm of Beowulf, 1990; featured performer Asheville (N.C.) Poetry Festival, 1994. Bd. dirs. Arcadia Players Baroque Orch., Chorus and Chamber Ensemble, Northampton, Mass., pres., 1995—98; mem. Corp. Boston Early Music Festival, 2002—. With USNR, 1943—46, served to lt. (j.g.) USNR, 1949. John Simon Guggenheim fellow, 1962—63, NEH fellow, Yugoslavia, 1976, Inst. Advanced Studies Humanities fellow, Edinburgh U., 1976, Am. Coun. Learned Soc. grantee, 1978. Mem.: AAAS, MLA (life), Archaeol. Inst. Am. (exec. coun. Western Mass. Soc. 1996—), European Soc. Study Cognitive Sys., Lang. Origins Soc., Nat. Storytelling Assn., N.Y. Acad. Scis., Internat. Soc. Anglo-Saxonists. Home: 5 Kinder Ln Shutesbury MA 01072-9762 Business E-Mail: creed@english.umass.edu. *Though a professor of literature, I have become more and more deeply concerned with oral traditions. Behind surviving traditions-indeed, behind literature-lie tens of thousands of years of what we may call Memorable Speech, some of which survives embedded in early texts. Back of Memorable Speech lies the origin of human language. Through the study of (sound-) patterned Memorable Speech, I am trying to work back towards the beginning of language, our most adaptive and humanizing invention.*

CREED, WILLIAM STUART, film company executive; b. Detroit, Feb. 1, 1941; s. William T. and Mae Clara Creed; m. Jeannetta L. Imbler, Feb. 4, 1960 (div. 1979); children: Debra, William, Lori; m. Mary Ann Dingess, 1982 (div. 1991); m. Sharon Groones, Nov. 13, 2003. V.p. regional Telecom Inc., Charlotte, NC; regional dir. CRG Prod., Cocoa, Fla.; pres. Encore Prod., Detroit. Author: Comes The End, 2002. Councilman, Romeo, Mich., 1977. Staff sgt. USAF, 1959—73, Germany. Mem.: Theta Beta Phi (pres.). Republican. E-mail: wcreed@hotmail.com.

CREEDON, GERALDINE, state legislator; b. Springfield, Mass., Sept. 26, 1945; m. Robert Stanton Creedon Jr.; children: Jennifer, Robert S. BA, Emmanuel Coll., 1967. Vice chair edn. Mass. Ho. of Reps., Boston, mem. house ways and means com., mem. election laws, mem. Dist. 11, 1995—. Mem. Brockton (Mass.) City Coun., 1992-95, pres., 1995; bd. dirs. Charity Guild, 1990-97; mem. Dem. City Com. Roman Catholic. Office: Mass State Legis Rm 473G State House Boston MA 02133 Office Phone: 617-722-2070.

CREEDON, JEREMIAH F., aeronautical research laboratory administrator; BSEE, U. RI, 1961, MSEE, 1963, PhD in Elec. Engring., 1970; M Mgmt. Sci., Stanford U., 1983. Rsch. engr. navigation and guidance rsch. br., instrument rsch. divsn. NASA Langley Rsch. Ctr., Hampton, Va., 1963-70, head control and info. sys. sect., 1970-79, asst. head avionics tech. rsch. br., 1979-82, chief flight control sys. divsn., 1982-85, head flight sys. directorate, 1985-94, dir. aeros. program group, 1994-96, dir. Airframe Sys. Program Office, 1996, dir. Ctr., 1996—2002; assoc. admin., Aerospace Tech. NASA HQ, Washington, 2002—. Advisor to adminstr. on programs NASA. Contbr. articles to sci. jours. Recipient presdl. rank meritorious exec. in sr. exec. svc., 1989 & 2001, disting. exec., 1995; Sloan Fellow, Stanford U., 1982-1983. Fellow AIAA. Office: NASA HQ 300 E St SW Washington DC 20546

CREEL, HAROLD JENNINGS, JR., federal commission administrator, lawyer; b. Florence, S.C., July 1, 1957; s. Harold Jennings Sr. and Dorothy Louise (Fenters) C. BA in Polit. Sci., Wofford Coll., 1979; JD, U. S.C. Law Sch., 1982. Bar: La. Assoc. Courtenay, Forstall, Grace & Hebert, New Orleans, 1982-83; atty./advisor NOAA, Washington, 1983-89; sr. counsel subcom. of com. on commerce, sci. and transp. U.S. Senate - Mcht. Marine Subcom., Washington, 1989-94; commr. Fed. Maritime Commn., Washington, 1994-96, chmn., 1996—2002, commr., 2002—. Nominee Fed. Maritime Comm., U.S. Pres. Mem. La. State Bar Assn. Democrat. Avocations: fishing, gardening. Office: Fed Maritime Commn 800 N Capitol St NW Washington DC 20211-0001*

CREEL, JOHNNIE LARGUIER, real estate broker; d. Calvin Woodbridge and Iris Vine Larguier; m. Bryant Lawrence Creel, Aug. 10, 1988; children: Burton Larguier Cooper, Sarah Cabell Cooper. BA in Psychology, La. State U., 1970. Accredited buyers agt., cert. residential specialist. Examiner, asst. supr. Social Security Disability, Baton Rouge, 1970—71, 1972—83; investigator Alcoholic Beverage Control, Baton Rouge, 1971—72; auditor, investigator La. Real Estate Commn., Baton Rouge, 1983—88; broker Coldwell Banker Wallace & Wallace Realtors, Knoxville, Tenn. Mem. Susan G. Komen Race for Cure, Knoxville, 2000—03, Tenn. Human and Animal Bonding, Knoxville, 1998—2002; mem. guild Knoxville Mus. Art. Mem.: Knoxville Area Assn. Realtors (dir. 2000—, chair cmty. involvement com. 1998—2000), Tenn. Assn. Realtors, Nat. Assn. Realtors. Avocations: art, travel, entertaining, cooking. Office: Coldwell Banker Wallace & Wallace 140 Major Reynolds Pl Knoxville TN 37922 Office Fax: 865-558-8128. Business E-Mail: johnnie@johnniecreel.com.

CREEL, LUTHER EDWARD, III, lawyer; b. Huntsville, Ala., Sept. 23, 1937; s. Luther Edward and June (Oldacre) C.; m. Nan Dee McHalek, Apr. 11, 1974; children by previous marriage: Scott Mitchell, Todd Oldacre. AB in Psychology, George Washington U., 1959; JD, So. Methodist U., 1963. Bar: Tex. 1963. Pvt. practice, Dallas, 1963—; chmn. Creel & Atwood (and predecessors), Dallas, 1971-96; of counsel Malouf, Lynch, Jackson, Kessler & Collins, Dallas, 1996-98; chmn. Creel, Sussman & Moore, Dallas, 1998—2002; ptnr. Creel & Moore, 2002—. Pres., chmn. The Pines Camp, 1999—2001; lectr. in bankruptcy and reorgn. law. Contbr. articles to profl. jours. Chmn. Ford Debtor Assistance Program, 1995-98. Mem. Dallas Bar Assn. (chmn. bankruptcy sect. 1972), State Bar Tex. (cert. bus. bankruptcy specialist 1989-2003, chmn. bankruptcy com. 1979-81, exec. com. bankruptcy sect. 2002—), Am. Bankruptcy Inst. (co-founder, pres. 1982-87, vice-chmn. 1987-96, bd. dirs. 1982-2000, chmn. 1996-98, chmn. emeritus

1998-2000), Am. Coll. Bankruptcy (co-founder, fellow, pres. 1996-97), John C. Ford Inn of Ct. (master, exec. com. 1999-2004), GTG Tex. Longhorn Assn. (pres. 1998-2000), Internat. Tex. Longhorn Assn. (bd. dirs.). Republican. Baptist. Home: 20487 Marinias Rd Trinidad TX 75163 Office: Creel Sussman & Moore 8235 Douglas Ave Ste 1100 Dallas TX 75225-6011 Office Phone: 214-378-8270. Personal E-mail: creel3@aol.com.

CREEL, MICHAEL ALLEN, energy executive; b. Lake Charles, La., Dec. 27, 1953; s. Harold Lee and Reba (Harkens) Creel; m. Kathy Roberts, Nov. 26, 1977; children: Michael Andrew, Matthew Robert. BS in Acctg., McNeese State U., 1975. CPA Tex. Contr. Guaranty Fed. Savs. Loan Assn., Lake Charles, 1973-76, Houston 1st Am. Savs., 1976-80; mgr. cash adminstrn. Coastal Corp., Houston, 1980—81, mgr. cash control, 1981-82, project leader corp. fin., 1982-84, mgr. fin. planning, 1984-86, dir. fin. planning, 1986-91; dir. corp. fin. Enron Corp., Houston, 1991-93, gen. mgr. corp. fin., 1994-95; v.p., treas. NorAm Energy Corp., Houston, 1995-97; sr. v.p. fin. Tejas Energy LLC, Houston, 1997, sr. v.p., chief fin. officer, 1998-99; sr. v.p. Enterprise Products Co., Houston, 1999—2001, CFO, 1999—, exec. v.p., CFO, 2001—. Mem.: AICPA, Fin. Execs. Internat., Tex. Soc. CPAs, Nat. Eagle Scout Assn. Home: 223 N Tranquil Path Dr The Woodlands TX 77380-2759 Office: Enterprise Products Co PO Box 4324 Houston TX 77210-4324 Office Phone: 713-880-6500. Business E-Mail: mcreel@eprod.com.

CREEL, THOMAS LEONARD, lawyer; b. Kansas City, Mo., June 21, 1937; s. Thomas Howard and Elizabeth Alberta (Sharon) C.; m. Carol M. Plaisted, Nov. 26, 1992; children: Charles, Andrew, Andrea, Thomas, Joseph, Lauren. BS, U. Kans., 1960; LLB, U. Mich., 1963. Bar: Mich. 1963, N.Y. 1967, D.C. 1983, U.S. Supreme Ct. 1973, Ct. Mil. Appeals, 1964, U.S. Patent and Trademark Office 1965. Assoc. Kenyon and Kenyon, N.Y.C., 1966-74, ptnr., 1974-92, Kaye, Scholer, Fierman, Hayes & Handler, N.Y.C., 1992—2001, Goodwin Procter LLP, N.Y.C., 2001—. Faculty lectr. Columbia U. Sch. Law, N.Y.C., 1984-2001. Editor: Guide to Patent Arbitration, 1987. Capt., U.S. Army, 1963-66. Mem. ABA, N.Y. Intellectual Property Law Assn. (past pres.), Am. Intellectual Property Assn. Home: 104 Cedar Cliff Rd Riverside CT 06878-2606 Office: Goodwin Procter LLP 599 Lexington Ave New York NY 10022 Office Phone: 212-813-8866. E-mail: tcreel@goodwinprocter.com.

CREEL MIRANDA, SANTIAGO, Mexican government official; b. Mexico City, Dec. 11, 1954; Grad., U. Nacional Autónoma Mex., Mexico City; postgrad., U. Mich. Bar: (Mex.). Lawyer, Mexico; prof. Autonomous Technol. Inst. Mex.; sec. Vuelta periodical; founder Este País mag.; citizen advisor Gen. Coun. Fed. Electoral Inst., 1994—96; fed. dep. LVII Legislature, 1997; 1st chmn. Com. Govt. and Constitutional Issues; joined Nat. Action Party (PAN), 1999, cand. to head of govt. of Fed. Dist., 1999; std. bearer Alliance for Change; sec. of govt. for Mexico, Mexico City, 2000—. Nat. and internat. election overseer; organizer plebiscite, 1993. Mem.: Coll. Lawyers, Assn. Unity Our Am., Mexican Acad. Human Rights. Office: Abraham Gonzalez 48 PB Col Juraz 06600 Mexico City Mexico E-mail: scree12003@hotmail.com.

CREEM, CYNTHIA STONE, state legislator, lawyer; BSBA, JD, Boston U. Mem. Mass. Senate, Boston, 1998—. Mem. criminal justice Mass. State Senate, election laws com., fed. fin. assistance com., local affairs com. Mem. Newton Bd. Aldermen, Gov.'s Coun. Fellow Women's Bar Assn.; mem. Mass. Bar Assn. Democrat. Office: Mass State Senate State House Rm 416B Boston MA 02133 E-mail: cynthia.creem@state.ma.us.

CREEMER, LAWRENCE CAMILLO, chemist; b. Detroit, Aug. 12, 1962; s. John Lawrence and Joann Creemer; m. Laura Jean Clayton, June 6, 1987; children: Cassidy Noel, Andrew Christian. BS, Mich. Technol. U., Houghton, 1980—84; MS in Chemistry, Purdue U., Indpls., 1985—89. Rsch. asst. Mich. Technol. U., Houghton, 1983—84; chemist Merrell Dow Rsch. Inst., Indpls., 1984—89; assoc. organic chemist Eli Lilly and Co., Indpls., 1989—93, asst. sr. organic chemist, 1993—98; assoc. sr. organic chemist Elanco Animal Health, Eli Lilly and Co., Greenfield, Ind., 1998—2003, group leader, sr. organic chemist, 2003—04, rsch. scientist, 2004—. Adj. instr. U. Indpls., 1992—94. Contbr. articles to profl. jours., chapters to books. Independent. Achievements include patents in field. Avocations: woodworking, home improvement, photography. Home: 1763 N James Blvd Greenfield IN 46140 Office: Eli Lilly and Co 2001 W Main St Greenfield IN 46140

CREENAN, KATHERINE HERAS, lawyer; b. Elizabeth, N.J., Oct. 7, 1945; d. Victor Joseph and Katherine Regina (Lederer) Petervary; m. Edward James Creenan; 1 child, David Heras. BA, Kean Univ., 1968; JD, Rutgers U., 1984. Bar: N.J. 1984, Maine 1996, N.Y. 2005, U.S. Dist. Ct. N.J. 1984, U.S. Ct. Appeals (3d cir.) N.Y., 2005. Various tchg. positions including, Union and Stanhope, N.J., 1968-81; law clk. to presiding judge Superior Ct. of N.J. Appellate Div., Newark, 1984-85; assoc. Lowenstein, Sandler, Kohl, Fisher & Boylan, Roseland, N.J., 1985-88, Kirsten, Simon, Friedman, Allen, Cherin & Linken, Newark, 1988-89, Whitman & Ranson, Newark, 1989-93; sr. atty. Whitman Breed Abbott & Morgan LLP, Newark, 1993-99; sr. staff assoc. Skadden, Arps, Slate, Meagher & Flom LLP, Newark, 1999—2004, NYC, 2004—. Mem. ABA, N.J. State Bar Assn. Office: Skadden Arps Slate Meaghar & Flom LLP Four Times Sq New York NY 10036-6522 Office Phone: 212-735-2832. Business E-Mail: kcreenan@skadden.com.

CREER, THOMAS LASELLE, psychologist, educator, writer; b. Lund, Idaho, Nov. 2, 1934; s. Laselle Lewis Creer and Naomi Johanna Jones; m. Patricia P. Plummer, July 7, 1961; children: Jennifer, Matthew. BS, Brigham Young U., 1956; Master's, Utah State U., 1961; PhD in Psychology, Fla. State U., 1967. Lic. psychologist Colo. Prof. psychology Ohio U., Athens, 1980—96; pres. Creer Sys., Inc., Provo, Utah, 1995—2002. Co-exec. dir. Nat. Asthma Ctr., Denver, 1977—80. Author: (books) Chronically-Ill and Handicapped Children, 1976, Asthma Therapy: A Behavioral Health Care System for Respiratory Disorders, 1979, Self-Management of Chronic Disease, 1986, Psychology of Adjustment, 1997, Respiratory Disorders and Behavioral Medicine, 2002; contbr. numerous articles, revs., and chpts. in field. Bd. dirs. Am. Lung Assn. Ohio, Columbus, 1983—93, Am. Lung Assn. Utah, 2002—; pres. Am. Lung Assn., Utah, 2004—05. With U.S. Army, 1956—58. Recipient Pre-doctoral Internship award, VA, 1966—67; fellow Pre-doctoral fellow, U.S. Pub. Health Svc., 1963—66. Liberal. Avocation: reading. Home: 144 E 4620 N Provo UT 84604 Office: Creer Sys Inc 144 E 4620 N Provo UT 84604 Personal E-mail: tcreer@comcast.net.

CREGIER, DON MESICK, historian, educator, researcher, consultant; b. Schenectady, N.Y., Mar. 28, 1930; s. Harry Mesick and Marion (Shovea) C.; m. Sharon Kathleen Ellis, June 29, 1965. BA, Union Coll., 1951; MA, U. Mich., 1952; PhD, Columbia Pacific U., 1999. Instr. history U. Tenn., Knoxville, 1956—57; asst. prof. history Baker U., Baldwin City, Kans., 1958—61, Keuka Coll., Keuka Park, NY, 1962—64, St. John's U., Collegeville, Minn., 1964—65, St. Dunstan's U., Canada, 1966—69; assoc. prof. history U.P.E.I., Charlottetown, 1969—85, prof., 1985—96, adj. prof., 1996—2002. Salvage editor, rsch. cons., 1996—. *Author of over 150 articles and reviews, Cregier continues his research into early twentieth-century British and Irish history, and is canvassing a possible venture into fiction. His current writing project is a biography of Frederick E. Guest (1875-1937), cousin and friend of Sir Winston Churchill, British army officer in the Boer War and World War I, political advisor to Prime Minister David Lloyd George between 1917 and 1921, and air minister in 1921-22. Based in rural Prince Edward Island, Cregier keeps in touch with colleagues, clients, and the wider world through the Internet.* Author: Bounder from Wales: Lloyd George's Career before the First World War, 1976, Novel Exposures: Victorian Studies Featuring Contemporary Novels, 1979, Chiefs Without Indians: Asquith, Lloyd George and the Liberal Remnant (1916-1935), 1982, The Decline of the British Liberal Party: Why and How?, 1985, Freedom and Order: The Evolution of Liberalism and the Liberal Party in Great Britain Before 1868, 1988; co-author: The Rise of the Global Village, 1988; editor Quest for Edn., 1966-67; fgn. book rev. editor Can. Rev. Studies in Nationalism, 1996-98; abstracter ABC-Clio Info. Svcs., 1978—; assessor Internat. Rev. Periodical Lit., 1988-89; contbr. articles to profl. jours. Social Scis. and Humanities Rsch. Coun. Can. grantee, 1984-86; Mark Hopkins fellow, 1965-66, Can. Coun. fellow, 1972-73. Mem.: Soc. Acad. Freedom and Scholarship, Nat. Assn. Scholars, Nat. Coalition Ind. Scholars, Can. Assn. Univ. Tchrs., Am. Hist. Assn., Assn. Contemporary Historians, The Hist. Soc. N.Am. Conf. on Brit. Studies, Mark Twain Soc., Internat. Churchill Soc., Oxford Club, Pi Gamma Mu, Phi Kappa Phi, Phi Beta Kappa, Phi Sigma Kappa. Office: PO Box 1100 Montague PE Canada COA 1RO E-mail: dcregier@upei.ca.

CREHAN, JACQUELYN R., dean; b. Baton Rouge, La., Oct. 13, 1945; s. Samuel J. and Rae S. Romeo; m. James Crehan; children: Jeffrey, Jayme. AA, Montery Peninsula Coll., 1980; BS, So. Ill. U., 1986, MS, 1988; PhD, U. NE Lincoln, 1996. Learning disability specialist U. Nebr. Omaha, Omaha, 1992—93, dir. career svcs., svcs for students with disabilities, 1997—99; vis. prof. Western Mich. U., Kalamazoo, 1999—2000; asst. prof. SD State U., Brookings, SD, 2000—01; dean student svcs. Our Lady of the Lake Coll., Baton Rouge, 2001—. Pastoral coun. of minstries St. Patrick Cath. Ch., Baton Rouge; bd. dirs. Make-A-Wish Found., Anchorage. Editor: (newsletter) CECP Pride; publisher: newspaper Latest at the Lake, 2004—. Named Outstanding Working Woman of Terra Haute, Ind. Assn. Bus. Profl. Women. Mem.: La. Cath. Campus Min., Assn. of Higher Edn. Disabilities, Nat. Assn. Student Personnel Assoc., Omicron Tau Theta, Sigma Chpt., Chi Sigma Iota. Cath. Avocations: travel, golf. Office: Our Lady of the Lake Coll 7434 Perkins Rd Baton Rouge LA 70808 Office Phone: 225-768-1713. Office Fax: 225-214-1945. E-mail: jcrehan@ololcollege.edu.

CREHAN, JOSEPH EDWARD, lawyer; b. Detroit, Dec. 8, 1938; s. Owen Thomas and Marguerite (Dunn) C.; m. Sheila Anderson, Nov. 6, 1965; children: Kerry Marie, Christa Ellen. AB, Wayne State U., Detroit, 1961; JD, Ind. U., 1965. Bar: Ind. 1965, Mich. 1966, U.S. Supreme Ct. 1984. Pvt. practice, Detroit, 1966-68; assoc. Louisell & Barris (P.C.), 1968-72; ptnr. Fenton, Nederlander, Dodge, Barris & Crehan (P.C.), 1972-74, Barris & Crehan (P.C.), 1975-88; pvt. practice Bloomfield Hills, Mich. and Naples, Fla., 1977—. Mem. Am. Trial Lawyers Assn. Roman Catholic. Home and Office: 827 Bentwood Dr Naples FL 34108-8204

CREHORE, CHARLES AARON, lawyer; b. Lorain, Ohio, Sept. 15, 1946; s. Charles Case and Catherine Elizabeth Crehore; 1 child, Charles Case II. BA, Wittenberg U., 1968; postgrad., U. Mich., 1968—69, Cleve. State U., 1972—73; JD, U. Akron, 1976; diploma mgmt. mgrs. program, Pa. State U., 1983. Bar: US Patent Office 1975, Ohio 1976, US Dist Ct (no dist) Ohio 1976, US Ct Appeals (DC cir) 1977, US Tax Ct 1977, US Supreme Ct 1980, US Ct Appeals (fed cir) 1982. Assoc. chemist B.F. Goodrich Co., Akron, 1969-70, chemist, 1970-72, sr. chemist, 1972, patent atty. trainee, 1972-74, sr. patent atty. trainee, 1974-75, patent assoc., 1975-76, patent atty., 1976-79; atty. regulatory affairs The Lubrizol Corp., Wickliffe, Ohio, 1979-81, corp. counsel environment, health and safety, 1981-85, sr. corp. counsel, 1985-94, counsel, 1994-99; patent atty. Hudak and Shunk Co., L.P.A., 2000; of counsel Ulmer & Berne, LLP, 2000—. Guest lectr, moot ct judge Case Western Res Univ, 1983—; spkr. Calif Inst Bus Law, Ohio, 1991, Northeast Ohio Software Asn, 2001—, Lakeland Cmty. Coll., 2001—, Media Profls. Conf., 2002—; adv bd applied environ mgmt program Lake Erie Col, 1991—94. Grantee, Kennedy Found, 1968—69; scholar, Delta Sigma Phi Found, 1968—69. Mem.: ABA, Cleve. Bar Assn., Ohio State Bar Assn., Cleve. Intellectual Property Law Assn., Am. Intellectual Property Law Assn., Greater Cleve. Internat. Lawyers Group, Phi Alpha Delta. Home: PO Box 466 Wickliffe OH 44092-0466 Office: Penton Media Bldg 1300 E 9th St Ste 900 Cleveland OH 44114 E-mail: ccrehore@aol.com.

CREIGHTON, JOANNE VANISH, academic administrator; b. Marinette, Wis., Feb. 21, 1942; d. William J. and Bernice Vanish; m. Thomas F. Creighton, Nov. 9, 1968; 1 child, William. BA with honors, U. Wis., 1964; MA, Harvard U., 1965; PhD, U. Mich., 1969. From instr. to prof. English Wayne State U., Detroit, 1968—85, assoc. dean liberal arts, 1983—85; dean arts and scis., prof. English U. N.C., Greensboro, 1985—90; v.p. acad. affairs, provost, prof. English Wesleyan U., Middletown, Conn., 1990—94, interim pres., 1994—95; prof. English, pres. Mt. Holyoke Coll., South Hadley, Mass., 1995—. Author: William Faulkner's Craft of Revision, 1977, Joyce Carol Oates, 1979, Margaret Dabble, 1985, Joyce Carol Oates: Novels of the Middle Years, 1992. Grantee, Am. Coun. Learned Socs. Mem.: Phi Kappa Phi, Phi Beta Kappa. Home: 45 College St South Hadley MA 01075-1403 Office: Mount Holyoke Coll Office of Pres 50 College St South Hadley MA 01075-1423

CREIGHTON, NEAL, retired army officer; b. Ft. Sill, Okla., July 11, 1930; s. Neal and Charlotte (Gilliam) C.; m. Joan Hicks, Aug. 1, 1958; children: Linda, Lisa, Neal. BS, U.S. Mil. Acad., 1953; student, U. Madrid, 1959-60; MA, Middlebury Coll., 1961; grad., U.S. Army Command and Staff Coll., 1967, U.S. Army War Coll., 1970. Commd. 2d lt. U.S. Army, 1953, advanced through grades to maj. gen.; troop assignments, 1953-59; from instr. to asst. prof. fgn. lang. U.S. Mil. Acad., 1960-63; staff officer So. Command Panama, 1964-66; squadron comdr., 1967-68; mil. asst. Office of Sec. Army Washington, 1970-72; comdr. Combined Arms Tng. Center Germany, 1973-74; brigade comdr., 1974-76; dep. dir. Ops. and Readiness Directorate, Dept. Army, 1977-78; comdr. 1st Inf. Divsn. Germany, 1978-80; dep. chief of staff Allied Forces Central Europe, Brunssum, Netherlands, 1980; comdg. gen. 1st Inf. Divsn. Ft. Riley, Kans., 1982-84; ret. U.S. Army, 1984; administrator Robert R. McCormick Trust Founds., Chgo., 1985; pres., CEO R.R. McCormick Tribune Found., Chgo., 1986-99; pres. Westminster Coll., Fulton, MO, 1999-2000; exec. dir. Liberty Meml., Kansas City, Mo., 2001—02. Decorated Disting. Service Medal, Silver Star medal, Bronze Star medal, Air medal. Mem. Chgo. Coun. on Fgn. Rels., Nat. Strategy Forum. Episcopalian. Office: 4600 E 63rd Trfy Kansas City MO 64130-4529 E-mail: nealc@crosslink.net.

CREIGHTON, SUSAN J., elementary school educator; d. Robert E. and Ariel I. Stuckey; m. Larry R. Creighton, June 12, 1976; children: Ashley J., Robert C. BS in Edn., Ea. Ill. U., Charleston, 1976. Elem. tchr. St. Joseph Cmty. Sch., Ill., 1976—80, Newton Sch. Dist., 1980—85, Belle Valley Dist. 119, Belleville, 1985—. Adv. bd. Ill. Regional Office Edn., Belleville, 1998—2000; mem. quality rev. team Ill. State Bd. Edn., Springfield, 1997—2000; presenter Ill. Edn. Tech., Chgo., 2000, Nat. Edn. Conf., 2001; co-dir. musical Belle Valley South, 2003—. Recipient Excellence in Tchg. award, Emerson Elect., 1994. Mem.: Ill. Reading Coun., Belle Valley Edn. Assn. (pres. 1993—94). Avocations: golf, reading, swimming, dance. Office: Belle Valley Elem Sch N 100 Andora Dr Belleville IL 62221-4399

CRELLIN, ALAN W., air transportation executive; married; 2 children. Mgmt. positions Pacific S.W. Airlines (acquired by US Airways Inc.), 1971—88; joined US Airways, Inc., Arlington, Va., 1988—95, v.p. ground svcs., 1995—2000, sr. v.p. customer svc., 2000—02, exec. v.p. ops., 2002—. Police officer, L.A. With USMC. Office: US Airways 2345 Crystal Dr Arlington VA 22227

CREMER, THOMAS GERHARD, music educator; b. New Brunswick, N.J., May 23, 1961; s. Gerhard Josef and Lois Elaine (Cottrell) C.; m. Eva Almira Vivanco Vargas, Feb. 8, 1986. MusB magna cum laude, U. Mass., 1983; MusM, U. Ky., 1989; DMA in Conducting, U. S.C., 2004. Cert. music tchr., Mass., N.Y., Va., Ky., Ga., S.C. Music tchr. Athol-Royalston (Mass.) Schs., 1983-84; music tchr., band dir. Am. Sch. Lima, Peru, 1984-87; instr. tuba, euphonium U. Ky., Lexington, 1988-89; hon. asst. conductor Fitchburg (Mass.) State Coll., 1989-90; dir. bands, music instr. Warwick Acad., Bermuda, 1990-95; dir. nat. band Columbia Columbia Inst. Culture, Bogota, 1995; low brass instr. Augusta State U., 1996—2001; brass instr., asst. band dir. U. S.C., Aiken, 1998—; music dir. Jenkins County Middle Sch. and H.S., Millen, Ga., 1996-98; band dir. Burke County Mid. Sch., Ga., 2002—03, Cross Creek HS, Augusta, Ga., 2003—. Vis. prof. music, dir. faculty quintet Nat. Conservatory, Lima, 1985-87; tubist Nat. Symphony Peru, Lima, 1985-87; mem. Bermuda Secondary Sch. Curriculum Com., Warwick, 1991-94; asst. band dir. South Aiken High Sch., 1998-2001. Contbg. editor: Tuba Reference Guide, 1993; contbg. reviewer T.U.B.A. Jour., 1988, 94. Adv. All-City Music Fest, Lima, 1985-87. Recipient Diploma of Honor, West German Embassy in Peru, 1986; Acad. Excellence fellow U. Ky., 1988. Mem.: Music Tchrs. Nat. Assn., Music Educators Nat. Conf. (v.p. Bermuda chpt., pres. 1992—94), Internat. Trombone Assn., World Assn. Symphonic Bands Ensembles, Internat. Tuba Euphonium Assn., Shriners, Masons, Phi Kappa Lambda, Phi Delta Kappa. Roman Catholic. Avocations: golf, reading, motorcycling, travel. Home: 3328 Tanglewood Dr Augusta GA 30909-2455 Office Phone: 706-772-8140 ext. 226. E-mail: tgcremer@juno.com, thomasc@usca.edu.

CREMINS, JAMES SMYTH, lawyer; b. Washington, June 11, 1921; m. Mary Louise Gallagher (dec.); 5 children. AB with honors, U. Mo., Columbia, 1943; JD, U. Va., 1949. Asst. gen. counsel CSX Corp., Richmond, Va., 1980-85. Treas. Dem. Party Va., 1977-89. Contbr. articles to legal jours. Lay min. St. Mary's Ch., Richmond, 1968-85; bd. visitors U. Va., 1984-88, Pres.'s Roundtable JMU, 1985-90; mem. adv. bd. St. Gertrude H.S., Richmond, 1984-88; past instnl. rep. Robert E. Lee coun. Boy Scouts Am.; mem. fin. coun. Richmond Cath. Diocese, 1978—; trustee Commonwealth Cath. Charities, 1981—; bd. dirs. Maymont Found., 1976-89; mem. State Dem. Steering Com., 1972-89, State Dem. Ctrl. Com., 1972-89. Lt. USNR, 1943-46. Recipient Brotherhood award, Nat. Conf. Christians and Jews, 1985. Fellow: Am. Bar Found.; mem.: KC (4h degree Knight equesteian Order of the Holy Sepulchre of Jerusalem 1998), ABA, Am. Judicature Soc. (bd. dirs. 1973—77), Richmond Bar Assn. (chmn. corp. counsel sect. 1964—65), Va. Bar Assn., Ancient Order Hibernians (charter mem. Maj. James Dooley Divsn. 1), Nat. Soc. SAR (trustee 1989—90), Navy League U.S. (Judge adv. Richmond coun. 1985—89), Va. Soc. SAR (pres. 1988—89), Phi Delta Phi, Omicron Delta Kappa (hon.), Alpha Tau Omega.

CREMISIO, MATTHEW C., music educator, musician; b. Troy, N.Y., June 13, 1973; s. Leonard S. and Sharon M. Cremisio. BS in Music Edn., Crane Sch. of Music, 1995; MA in Jazz Studies, Coll. of St. Rose/ Eastman Sch. Music, 2000. Cert. permanent cert. music tchr. K-12. Dir. bands Shenendehowa H.S. East, Clifton Park, NY, 1998—; music faculty, drumset instr., jazz ensemble II dir. Coll. of St. Rose, Albany, NY, 1999—. Performing artist, educator Yamaha Corp. of Am., Buena Park, Calif., 1995—, Pro-Mark Corp., Craighead, Tex., 1995—, Sabian Cymbals, Marshfield, Mass., 1997—. Writer, reviewer: Jazz Player Mag. Mem.: N.Y. State Sch. Music Assn., Tri-M Internat. Music Honor Soc. (chpt. advisor 2002), Percussive Arts Soc., Internat. Assn. Jazz Educators, Music Educators Nat. Conf. Office: Shenendehowa H S 970 Rt 146 Clifton Park NY 12065 Home: 25 Talon Dr Niskayuna NY 12309-1840 Office Phone: 518-371-6000 61472. E-mail: yamadrum@nycap.rr.com.

CRENNEL, ROMEO, professional football coach; b. Lynchburg, Va. m. Rosemary Crennel; 3 children. BA physical Ed., MA, Western Kentucky Univ. Grad. asst. Western Kentucky Univ., 1970, defensive line coach, 1971—74; defensive asst. Texas Tech Univ., 1975—77; defensive ends coach Univ. of Miss., 1978—79; defensive line coach Ga. Tech Univ., 1980; special teams, defensive asst. coach NY Giants, 1981—82, spl. teams coach, 1983—89, defensive line coach, 1990—92, New England Patriots, 1993—96, NY Jets, 1997—99; defensive coordinator, line coach Cleve. Browns, 2000; defensive coordinator New England Patriots, 2001, 2004, defensive coordinator, defensive line coach, 2002—03; head coach Cleve. Browns, 2005—. Achievements include mem. Super Bowl Champion New York Giants, 1986, 1990, New England Patriots, 2001, 2003, 2004. Office: c/o Cleveland Browns 76 Lou Groza Blvd Berea OH 44017*

CRENSHAW, ALBERT BURFORD, journalist; b. Lexington, Va., Oct. 4, 1942; s. Ollinger and Marjorie (Burford) C.; m. Margaret Alice Price, Aug. 11, 1973; children— David Ollinger, Caroline Abbey AB, Harvard U., 1964; MS, U. Va., 1966; MS in Journalism, Columbia U., 1967. Reporter Washington Daily News, 1969-71, asst. city editor, 1971-72; asst. nat. editor Washington Post, 1972-76, night nat. editor, 1977-82, real estate editor, 1982-85, asst. fin. editor, 1985-88, fin. reporter, columnist, 1988—. Served with U.S. Army, 1967-69 Mem.: Harvard (N.Y.C.); Nat. Press (Washington). Home: 321 E Capitol St SE Washington DC 20003-3808 Office: Washington Post 1150 15th St NW Washington DC 20071-0002

CRENSHAW, ANDER, congressman, lawyer; b. Jacksonville, Fla., Sept. 1, 1944; m. Kitty, 1971; children: Sarah, Alex. BA, U. Ga., 1966; JD, U. Fla., 1970. Mem. Fla. Ho. of Reps., 1972—78; candidate Fla. Sec. of State, 1978, US Senate, 1980; mem. Fla. State Senate, Fla., 1986—94, Rep. leader, 1990—92, pres., 1993; sr. v.p. Donaldson, Lufkin and Jenrette, 1990—95, William R. Hough & Co., 1995—; mem. U.S. Congress from 4th Fla. Dist., 2001—. Mem. Congressional com. Armed Svcs., 2003— Budget, 2001—, Appropriations, Veterans' Affairs, Rep. policy; subcom. Mil. Rsch. and Devel., Mil. Installations and Facilities, Mil. Quality of Life, Foreign Ops., Homeland Security, Health, Benefits; appt. Asst. Majority Whip; rep. to House of GOP leadership. Mem. Fla. Ethics com., Fla. Constitution Revision com. Republican. Episcopalian. Office: US Ho of Reps 127 Cannon Ho Office Bldg Washington DC 20515-0904*

CRENSHAW, BEN, professional golfer; b. Austin, Tex., Jan. 11, 1952; m. Julie Ann; children: Katherine Vail, Claire Susan, Anna Riley. Grad., U. Tex. Mem. U.S. World Amateur Cup Team, 1972; mem. U.S. Ryder Cup, 1981, 83, 87, 95; profl. golfer, 1973—; U.S. team capt. Kirin Cup, 1988; team capt. Ryder Cup Team, 1999. Winner San Antonio Open, 1973, Western Amateur open match and medal plan champion, 1973, Bing Crosby Nat. Pro-Am., Ohio Kings Island Open, Hawaiian Open, 1976, Colonial Nat. Invitational, 1977, NCAA Championship, 1971, 72, 73, Irish Open, 1976, Phoenix Open, 1979, Walt Disney World Team Championship, 1980, AnheuserOBusch Classic, 1980, Tex. State Open winner, 1980, Ryder Cup, 1981, 83, 87, Byron Nelson Classic, 1983, Masters tournament, 1984, PGA Sr. Event Jeremy Ranch Shoot-Out teameed with Miller Barber, 1985, Buick Open, 1986, Vantage Championship, 1986, USF&G, 1987, Doral Ryder Open, 1988, World Cup, 1988, Western Open, 1992, Masters winner Augusta Nat. Golf Club, 1995, Masters Tournament, 1995, Ryder Cup, 1999, admitted to World Golf Hall of Fame, 2002. Mem. Profl. Golfers Assn. Am. Office: PO Box 50568 Austin TX 78763-0568*

CRENSHAW, EDWARD LEE, SR., aviation electronics technician; b. Shelby, N.C., Oct. 31, 1946; s. William and Ida Mae Crenshaw; m. Linda F. Yates, June 15, 1986; children: Edward Lee Jr., Kevin William, Bryant E. Yates. Lic. airframe and powerplant FAA/FCC. Airline servicer, customer svc. agt. aviation maintenance tech, avaition electronic tech. Eastern Air Lines Inc., United Air Lines Inc., Miami, San Francisco, Seattle, 1970—. Dir. BWI Chess Club, Balt., 1979—83. Author: (novels) ATC Emergency Code 7700 (10th Ann. Writers Digest Participation Cert., 2001), Deadly Satellites, 2004. Tchr. Local Union 141 Chess Club, San Francisco, 1992—96. Lt. cpl. USMC, 1964—68. Decorated Sharpshooter, Nuc. Biol. Chem. specialist USMC. Mem.: Assn. Writers and Writing Programs, Writers Cir. Home: 110 Sw 313th St Federal Way WA 98023 Office: United Air Lines Inc Seattle Tacoma Internat Airport Seattle WA 98158 Office Phone: 253-946-4549. E-mail: EL@fictionwritersplus.com.

CRENSHAW, FRANCIS NELSON, retired lawyer; b. Washington, Dec. 9, 1922; s. Russell Sydnor and Sally Nelson (Robins) C.; m. Jane Elizabeth Treadwell, Aug. 20, 1949 (dec. June 1993); children: Elizabeth, Page, Marian; m. Anne Alfriend Abbitt, July 12, 1997. Grad., St. George's Sch., 1939; BA, U. Va., 1943, LLB, 1948. Bar: Va. 1948. Ptnr. Baird, White & Lanning, Norfolk, 1952-55, Baird, Crenshaw & Lanning, Norfolk, 1955-60, Baird, Crenshaw & Ware, Norfolk, 1960-68, Crenshaw, Ware & Johnson, Norfolk, 1968-89, Crenshaw, Ware & Martin, Norfolk, 1989-99; ret., 1999. Mem. Va. Bd. Bar Examiners, 1973-90, pres., 1983-90. Mem. Norfolk City Sch. Bd., 1955-64, chmn., 1962-64; bd. visitors Old Dominion U., 1968-76, rector, 1972-76; mem. bd. commrs., Ea. Va. Med. Authority, 1966-68. Served with

USNR, 1943-46. Decorated Bronze Star. Fellow ABA, Va. Law Found.; mem. Va. Bar Assn. (chmn. exec. com. 1988-89), Va. State Bar (chmn. sr. lawyers sect. 1998-99; editor sr. lawyers newsletter 1999-2002), Norfolk-Portsmouth Bar Assn. (pres. 1967), Maritime Law Assn. Home: Unit 208 305 Brooke Ave Norfolk VA 23510 Office: 1200 Bank Am Bldg Norfolk VA 23510

CRENSHAW, HORACE, JR., military officer; b. Meridian, Miss., Dec. 6, 1970; s. Horace Cremshaw Sr. and Sarah R. Crenshaw; m. Trina Lavorn Johnson (div.); 1 child, Nilah Iman; m. Rhonda Latrice Crenshaw, Sept. 25, 2004. BA Polit. Sci., Tuskegee U., Ala., 1994; MA Internat. Rels., Webster U., St. Louis, 1999. Mgr. Red Lobster, Jackson, Miss., 1995—96; commd U.S. Army, 1993, advanced through grades to capt., 1995, supply and svcs. officer 329th q.m. bn. St. Louis, 1996—99; student Combined Logistics Capts., Fort Lee, Va., 1999—2000; ops. officer 361st Q.M. Bn, Montgomery, Ala., 2000—02; company commdr. 233rd q.m. co. (PS), Phila., 2002—04; planner/team chief Army Material Command, Ft. Belvoir, Va., 2004—. Mem.: Mil. Officers Assn., Masons, Kappa Alpha Psi. Achievements include successfully directed procuring, storing and shipping over 100 million gals. of fuel during Iraqi war. Avocations: basketball, golf, reading, running. Home: Apt C 5703 Woodlawn Cable Dr Alexandria VA 22309 Office: US Army Material Command Bldg 464 6000 6th St Fort Belvoir VA 22060 Office Phone: 703-806-4405 4750. Fax: 703-806-2078. E-mail: armynupe6@msn.com.

CRENSHAW, KIMBERLE WILLIAMS, law educator; b. 1959; BA, Cornell U., 1981; JD, Harvard U., 1984; LLM, Wis. U., 1985. Law clk. to Hon. Shirley S. Abrahamson Wis. Supreme Ct., 1985-86; asst. prof. UCLA, 1986-89, acting prof., 1989, prof. law, Columbia U., NYC. Co-founder African-American Policy Forum, 1996. Co-author: Words that Wound: Critical Race Theory, Assaultive Speech and the First Amendment, 1993, Critical Race Theory, 1995; contbr. articles to law jours. Office: UCLA Sch Law 405 Hilgard Ave Los Angeles CA 90095-9000 also: 435 W 116th St New York NY 10027 E-mail: crenshaw@law.columbia.edu, crenshaw@law.ucla.edu.*

CREPPEL, CLAIRE BINET, hotel owner; b. New Orleans, Nov. 30, 1936; d. Albert Leo and Leocadie (Dominique) Binet; m. Jacques Jules Creppel, Feb. 2, 1957; children: Ingrid, Foster, Collette and Gregg (twins), Lisa, Morgan. BA in English, U. Southwestern La., 1971; MEd in Guidance/Counseling Psychology, Loyola U., New Orleans, 1975; postgrad. adminstrn., mgmt., supervision, Tulane U., New Orleans, 1978. Instr. English and Spanish Booker T. Washington Sr. High Sch., 1972-74, instr. English and reading, 1974-76, guidance counselor, 1976-77; intervention counselor Sophie B. Wright Middle Sch., 1977-79; owner, gen. mgr. Columns Hotel, New Orleans, 1980—; owner Woodland Plantation, 1997—. New Orleans regional dir. La. Coun. on Child Abuse, 1985—87; v.p. bd. Barataria Terrebne Estuary Found. (Save the Wetlands), 2000—02; mem. adv. bd. Le Petite Thetre du Vieux Carre, 2000—; mem. citizens adv. bd. Jo Ellen Smith Hosp.; mem. task force Ct. Appointed Spl. Advocate; bd. dirs. So. Repertory Theatre of New Orleans, Odyssey House, Bravo, Arts Coun., Overture to the Cultural Season, pres., 1997—98. Named one of Top Exec. Women New Orleans, 1990, one of Top Women New Orleans Bus. Owners, 1997. Mem. Am. Pers. and Guidance Assn., AAUW, La. Pers. and Guidance Assn., Orleans Sch. Counselors Assn., St. Charles Ave. Bus. Assn., Street Car Inns, Fgn. Rels. Assn. New Orleans, Am. Heart Assn. (pres. elect, New Orleans chpt.), Kappa Delta Pi, Sigma Delta Pi. Republican. Roman Catholic. Avocations: preservation projects, real estate market, scuba diving, snow and water skiing, travel. Home: 7927 St Charles Ave New Orleans LA 70118-2724 Office: Columns Hotel 3811 Saint Charles Ave New Orleans LA 70115-4681 E-mail: clairecreppel@aol.com.

CREQUE, LINDA ANN, educational consultant association executive, former education commissioner; b. N.Y.C. d. Noel and Enid Louise (Schloss) DePass; m. Leonard J. Creque, July 29, 1967; children: Leah Michelle, Michael Gregory. BS, CUNY-Queens, 1963, MS, 1969; PhD, U. Ill., 1986. Tchr. 2d grade Bd. Edn., N.Y.C., 1963, tchr. demonstrations, team tchr., 1964-65, master tchr., 1965-66; elem. tchr. P.S. 69, Jackson Hgts., N.Y., 1963-67; tchr. English Cath. U., Ponce, P.R., 1967; cmty. exch. elem. tchr. grades K-6 Ponce, 1966-67; tchr. 4th grade Dept. Edn., V.I., 1967-69, tchr. remedial reading, master tchr., 1968-69; program coord. Project HeadStart, V.I., 1969-73, coord. Inst. Developmental Studies, 1970-71, acting dir., 1972-73; prin. Thomas Jefferson Annex Primary Sch., St. Thomas, V.I., 1973-80, Joseph Sibilly Elem. Sch., St. Thomas, 1980-87; commr. edn. Dept. Edn., St. Thomas, 1987-94; founder, pres. V.I. Inst. for Tchg. and Learning, St. Thomas, 1995—; pres. LCe Cons. Cons. Edn. Devel. Ctr., Mass. Nat. SSI Project, 1992-93, Coll. V.I., 1978; mem. exec. com., bd. overseers Regional Lab. Ednl. Improvement NE and Islands, Andover, Mass., 1988-92; bd. dirs. V.I. Pub. TV; mem. exec. bd. Leadership in Edn. Adminstrv. Devel., V.I., 1989—; op-ed columnist V.I. Daily News; presenter, keynote spkr. confs. in field. Contbr. articles to profl. publs. Trustee U. V.I., 1989—; mem. V.I. Residential Task Force for Human Svcs., 1989-94, V.I. Labor Coun.; bd. dirs. Nat. Urban Alliance for Effective Edn. Tchrs. Coll. Columbia U., N.Y.C., 1993—, Cultural Inst. V.I., 1989-94; mem. cultural endowment bd., V.I., 1989-94; mem. governing bd. East End Health Ctr., 1979-80; mem. Gov.'s Conf. Librs., 1978. Grantee V.I. Coun. on Arts Ceramics for Primary Children, 1974-78, Comprehensive Employment and Tng. Act, 1977, NSF, 1989-93, Carnegie Found., 1988-90; recipient award NASA, award St. Thomas-St. John Counselors Assn., 1988, Ednl. Excellence award Harvard U. Prins. Ctr., Ill. Edn. Svc. Ctr., 1975, Outstanding Leadership award FEMA, 1990, Disting. Svc. award Edn. Commn. of U.S., 1991, Outstanding Svc. award Coun. of Chief State Sch. Officers, 1995. Mem. LWV, St. Thomas Reading Coun., Nat. Assn. Tchrs. Math., Edn. Commn. of States (commr. 1987-93, steering com. 1988-92, internal audit com. 1988, policies priority com. 1991, exec. com. 1992, alt. steering com. 1991-94), Coun. Chief of State Sch. Officers (chair extra jurisdictions com., bd. dirs., task force early childhood edn., ednl. equity com., restructuring edn. com.), Phi Kappa Phi, Kappa Delta Pi, Phi Delta Kappa. Office: VI Inst for Tchg and Learning PO Box 301954 St Thomas VI 00803-1954

CRESS, CECILE COLLEEN, retired librarian; b. Colorado Springs, Colo., Feb. 26, 1914; d. John Leo and Elizabeth Veronica (Rouse) Haley; m. Arthur Henry Cress, May 8, 1937 (div. 1960); children: Ronnie Lou Kordick, Dan, Elaine. BA, Adams State Coll., 1936; MA in English, Colo. Coll., 1964; MLS, Denver U., 1970. 5th grade tchr. Westcliffe (Colo.) Elem., 1953-56; English tchr. Penrose (Colo.) H.S., 1956-59; English-social studies tchr. Excelsior Jr. H.S. Dist. 70, Pueblo, Colo., 1959-64; libr. Pueblo County H.S. Dist. 70, Pueblo, 1964-80, Nat. Coll./Pueblo Br., 1980-91; cataloger in libr. Pueblo C.C., 1992-95. Tutor adult literacy program South Cen. Bd. Coop. Svcs., 1991. Recipient Ace of Clubs award Am. Contract Bridge League, 1988, 89. Mem. Pueblo Ret. Sch. Employees (v.p. 1990-92, pres. 1982-84, state bd. 1982-86, sec. 1995-97), Colo. Libr. Assn., Unit 367 Am. Contract Bridge Assn., Irish Club Pueblo (pres. 1995-96), Welsh Terrier Club Colo., Alpha Delta Kappa (Pueblo chpt., pres. 1976-78, state historian 1980-82, state bd. 1980-82, rec. sec. 1994-98), Am. Contract Bridge League (v.p. unit 367 1998-2000). Democrat. Roman Catholic. Avocations: duplicate bridge, welsh terriers, travel. Home: Apt 417 755 Epps Bridge Pkwy Athens GA 30606 E-mail: cccress@cs.com.

CRESSEY, BRYAN CHARLES, venture capitalist; b. Seattle, Sept. 28, 1949; s. Charles Ovington and Alice Lorraine (Serry) C.; m. Christina Irene Petersen, Aug. 19, 1972; children: Monique Joy, Charlotte Lorraine, Alicia Lin. BA, U. Wash., 1972; MBA, JD, Harvard U., 1976. Bar: Wash. 1976, Ill. 1977. Sr. investment mgr. First Chgo. Investment Corp., Chgo., 1976-80; prin. Golder, Thoma, Cressey, Fauner, Inc., Chgo., 1980—; prnt. Thoma, Cressey Equity Ptnrs., 1998—. Chmn., bd. dirs. Cable Design Techs., Inc.; bd. dirs. Am. Habilitation, Inc., Houston, Assistive Tech., Ill., Clarion tech., Ill., Select Med., Harrisburg, Pa., Boston. Author: (theatrical play) Explosions. Bd. dirs. Infant Welfare Soc., Chgo., 1984—, Jr. Achievement, Chgo. Inductee Entrepreneurial Hall of Fame, 1998. Home: 500 W County Line Rd Barrington IL 60010-9629 Office: Thoma Cressey Equity Partners 9200 Sears Tower Chicago IL 60606

CRESSY, DAVID SARRAT, lawyer; b. New Orleans, July 6, 1937; s. Louis Villere and Nellie Marie C.; m. Barbara Mequet, Apr; 4, 1964 (div. Jan. 35, 1984); children: David, Andree Landry, Paul, Suzanne Brown; m. Laura Sutis Cressy, June 28, 1984; children: Nicolas Villere, Jordan Cheval. BS, U. Southwestern La., Lafayette, 1963; JD, Loyola U., New Orleans, 1967. City atty. City of New Orleans, 19687-78; pvt. practice Mandeville, New Orleans, 1978-96; city atty. City of Mandeville, La., 1996—. Trustee Wisner Found., New Orleans, 1972-76, New Orleans Mus. Art, 1975-76; commr. City park Bd. Commrs., New Orleans, 1973-76. With USAF, 1957-59. Fellow La. Law Found., La. State Bar Assn. Democrat. Avocations: sailing, horseback riding. Home: 132 Coffee St Mandeville LA 70448 Office: City of Mandeville 3101 East Causeway Mandeville LA 70448

CREUHERAS, SANTIAGO, social scientist; b. Guadalajara, Jalisco, Mex., June 30, 1974; s. Santiago Creuheras and Maryger Diaz. BA in Econs., U. Americas, Puebla, Mex., 1997; M in Liberal Arts in History, Harvard U., 2000, grad. cert. spl. studies in mgmt., M in Liberal Arts in Govt., Harvard U., 2001. Internat. affairs intern Embassy of Mex., Washington, 1997; legis. intern Rep. Joseph J. Kennedy's Office, Washington, 1997; rsch. asst. J.F.K. Sch. of Govt., Harvard U., Cambridge, 2000—; internat. internship program dir. David Rockefeller Ctr., Harvard U., Cambridge, 2000—01; regional econ. devel. dir. Ministry Econ. Devel., Puebla, Mexico, 2001—, regional econ. devel. gen. coord., 2002—04; gen. coord. social devel. Ministry Social Devel., 2004—. Mem. Harvard U. Mex. Assn. (sr. mem.), Harvard Club of Boston, Acad. of Polit. Sci. Roman Catholic. Avocations: swimming, travel, opera, golf. Office: Ministry Social Devel 4 Oriente #806 Puebla Mexico Home: Prol Sauces 2709 Puebla Mexico Office Phone: 52 222 2467994. E-mail: screuheras@post.harvard.edu.

CREUTZ, EDWARD CHESTER, physicist, museum director; b. Beaver Dam, Wis., Jan. 23, 1913; s. Lester Raymond and Grace (Smith) C.; m. Lela Rollefson, Sept. 13, 1937 (dec. Feb. 1972); children: Michael John, Carl Eugene, Ann Jo Carmel Creutz Cosgrove; m. Elisabeth B. Cordle, Oct. 5, 1974. BS, U. Wis., 1936, PhD, 1939. From rsch. assoc. to instr. physics Princeton U., 1939-41; physicist NDRC, 1941-42; physicist metall. lab. U. Chgo., 1942-44; physicist Manhattan Project, Los Alamos, 1944-46; assoc. prof. Carnegie Inst. Tech., Pitts., 1946—48, prof., head dept. physics, dir. Nuc. Rsch. Ctr., 1948—55; dir. John Jay Hopkins Lab. for Pure and Applied Sci., 1955-59; dir. rsch. Gen. Atomic Divsn. Gen. Dynamics Corp., San Diego, 1955-59, v.p. R&D, 1959-67, Gulf Gen. Atomic, San Diego, 1967-70; asst. dir. NSF, Washington, 1970-77, acting dep. dir., 1976-77; dir. Bernice Pauahi Bishop Mus., Honolulu, 1977-84, cons., 1984—. Mem. sea water conversion com. Water resources Ctr., U. Calif.-Berkeley, 1958-68; adv. com. office Sci. Pers. NRC, 1960-63; mem. exec. coun. Argonne Nat. Lab. (1946-51); cons. NSF, 1950-68; scientist-at-large Project Sherwood divsn. rsch. AEC, 1955-56; mem. com. sr. reviewers Dept. Energy, 1972-79, fusion power coordinating com., 1971-79; cons. Oak Ridge Nat. Lab., 1946-58; adv. panel gen. scis. Dept. Def., 1959-63; rsch. adv. com. electrophysics NASA, 1964-71, tech. adv. com., 1971-77; adj. prof. physics and astronomy U. Hawaii, 1977-87; adj. prof. physics U. Calif., San Diego, 1987—. Co-editor: Handbuch der Physik, vols. 14, 15; mem. editl. bd. Ann. Rev. Nuclear Sci., 1961-66, 72-75, Handbook of Chemistry and Physics, 1961-71; mem. editorial bd.: Interdisciplinary Science Reviews, London, 1976—; editl. adv. com. ann. revs.: Nuclear Sci. and Engring., 1959-72. Bd. dirs. San Diego Hall Sci. and Planetarium, v.p., 1956-70; v.p. San Diego Industry-Edn. Coun., 1956-65; mem. adv. coun. Dept. Edn. San Diego County. Fellow AAAS, Am. Phys. Soc. (NRC rep. 1956-57), Am. Nuclear Soc.; mem. NAS, Am. Assn. Physics Tchrs., Phys. Soc. Pitts. (pres. 1949), Am. Inst. Physics (dir.-at-large bd. govs. 1965-68) Home: PO Box 2757 Rancho Santa Fe CA 92067-2757 Office Phone: 858-736-4980.

CREW, SPENCER, museum administrator; b. Poughkeepsie, N.Y., Jan. 7, 1949; s. R. Spencer and Ada Lee (Scott) C.; m. Sandra Lorraine Prioleau, June 19, 1971; children: Alika, Adom. BA, Brown U., 1971; MA, Rutgers U., 1973, PhD, 1979. Asst. prof. U. Md. Baltimore County, Catonsville, 1978-81; historian Nat. Mus. Am. History, Smithsonian Instn., Washington, 1981-87, curator, 1987-89, chmn. dept. social and cultural history, 1989-91, dep. dir., acting dir., 1991-94, dir., 1994—2001; exec. dir., CEO Nat. Underground R.R. Freedom Ctr., 2001—. Commr. Md. Commn. on Afro-Am. History and Culture, Annapolis, 1990—; hist. cons. Nat. Civil Rights Mus., Memphis, 1987-91; cons. Civil Rights Inst., Birmingham, Ala., 1991-94; bd. dirs. Nat. History Day, 1994—. Exhbns. include Field to Factory: Afro-Am. Migration, 1915-40, 1987 (award 1988), Go Forth and Serve: Black Land Grant Colls., 1990. Bd. trustees Brown U., 1995—; adult leader Bapt. Youth Fellowship, St. John Ch., Columbia, Md., 1989-91; asst. coach Columbia Basketball Assn., 1990-92. Recipient Osceola award Delta Sigma Theta, 1988, Cert. award Smithsonian Instn., 1989, 90, 91, 92, Svc. award Assn. for Study of African Am. Life and History, 1994, Robert A. Brooks award Smithsonian Instn., 1994. Mem. African Am. Mus. Assn. (2d v.p. 1989-91), Orgn. Am. Historians (editl. bd. 1989-92), Am. Assn. Mus. (bd. dirs.), Nat. Coun. History Edn. (bd. trustees. 1995—), Am. Hist. Assn. (exhibit rev. co-editor 1990-95), Oral History in Mid Atlantic Region (exec. bd. 1987-90). Office: Nat Underground RR Freedom Ctr 50 E Freedom Way Cincinnati OH 45202

CREWDSON, JOHN MARK, journalist, writer; b. San Francisco, Dec. 15, 1945; s. Mark Guy and Eva Rebecca (Doane) C.; m. Prudence Gray Tillotson, Sept. 11, 1969; children: Anders Gray, Oliver McDuff. AB in Econs. with gt. distinction, U. Calif., Berkeley, 1970; postgrad. studies in politics, Oxford (Eng.) U., 1971-72. Reporter N.Y. Times, Washington, 1973-77, nat. corr Houston, 1977-82; nat. news editor Chgo. Tribune, 1982-83, met. news editor, 1983-84, west coast corr. L.A., 1984-90, nat. corr. Washington, 1990-96, sr. writer, 1996—2002, sr. corr., 2002—. Author: The Tarnished Door, 1983, By Silence Betrayed, 1988, Science Fictions, 2002. Recipient Bronze medallion Sigma Delta Chi, 1974, Goldberg award N.Y. Deadline Club, 1977, Page One award N.Y. Newspaper Guild, 1977, Pulitizer prize for nat. reporting, 1981, Polk award for med. reporting L.I. U., 1990, William H. Jones award for investigative reporting, 1990, 95, 97, Peter Lisagor award Chgo. Headline Club, 1997. Office: Chgo Tribune 1325 G St NW Washington DC 20005-3104 Business E-Mail: jcrewdson@tribune.com.

CREWE, ALBERT VICTOR, physicist, researcher, artist; b. Bradford, Yorkshire, Eng., Feb. 18, 1927; came to U.S., 1955, naturalized, 1961. s. Wilfred and Edith Fish (Lawrence) C.; m. Doreen Blunsdon, Apr. 9, 1949; children: Jennifer, Sarah, Elizabeth, David. BS in Physics, U. Liverpool, Eng., 1947, PhD, 1951; degree (hon.), Lake Forest Coll., 1972, U. Mo., 1972, Elmhurst Coll., 1972, U.Liverpool, 2001. Asst. lectr. U. Liverpool, Eng., 1950-52, lectr., 1952-55; rsch. assoc. U. Chgo., 1955-56, asst. prof., 1956-58, assoc. prof., 1958-63; prof. dept. physics Enrico Fermi Inst., 1963-71, dean phys. scis. divsn., 1971-81; also William Wrather Disting. Svc. prof. physics, 1958-61; emeritus, 1996—; dir. particle accelerator divsn. Argonne Nat. Lab., 1958-61, dir., 1961-66; pres. Orchid One Corp., 1987-90. Chmn. Chgo. Area R&D Coun. Recipient Outstanding Local Citizen in Field of Sci. award Chgo. Jr. Assn. Commerce and Industry, 1961; Outstanding New Citizen of Year award Citizenship Coun. Chgo., 1962; award for outstanding achievement in field of sci. Immigrant's Service League, 1962; Man of Year in Rsch. award Indsl. Rsch., Inc., 1970; Michelson medal Franklin Inst., 1977; Duddell medal Inst. of Physics, 1980. Fellow Am. Phys. Soc., Royal Microscopical Soc. (hon.), Chinese Electron Microscope Soc. (hon.); mem. NAS, Sci. Rsch. Soc. Am., Electron Microscopy Soc. Am. (Disting. Svc. award 1976), N.Y. Microscope Soc. (Abbe award 1979), Am. Acad. Arts and Scis., Palette and Chisel Acad. (artist mem.). Achievements include research on electron optics, design of electron microscopes, first images of single atoms. Home: 8 Summitt Dr Chesterton IN 46304-1024 E-mail: crewe@midway.uchicago.edu.

CREWE, NANCY MOE, psychologist, educator; b. Mpls., Aug. 27, 1939; d. Arnold O. and Ruby V. Moe; m. James C. Crewe (div.); 1 child, Laurel; m. John Pond. BA, U. Minn., 1961, MA, 1964, PhD, 1967. Lic. psychologist, Mich. Staff psychologist Am. Rehab. Found., Mpls., 1966-69, Robbinsdale (Minn.) Sch. Dist., 1969-71; asst. prof. psychology U. Minn., Mpls., 1971-78, assoc. prof. psychology, 1978-87; postdoctoral fellow New England Rehab. Hosp., Boston, 1985-86; prof. Mich. State U., East Lansing, 1987—. Co-author: Employment After Spinal Cord Injury, 1978, Psychology of Disability, 2004; co-editor: Independent Living for Disabled People, 1983. Bd. dirs. Accessible Space, Mpls., 1980-82, Met. Ctr. for Ind. Living, Mpls., 1983-85; bd. dirs., chairperson Comprehensive Svcs. for Disabled Citizens, Mpls., 1980-87, Capital Area Ctr. for Ind. Living, 2000—. Recipient Disting. Faculty award, Mich. State U., 1997, Roger Barker Disting. Career award, 2001. Fellow: APA (pres. divsn. 22 1987—88, Disting. Contbns. to Rehab. Psychology award 1993, Roger Barker Disting. Career award 2001); mem.: ACA, Nat. Coun. Rehab. Edn. (Disting. Career in Rehab. Edn. award 2004), Nat. Rehab. Assn., Am. Rehab. Counseling Assn., Am. Assn. Spinal Cord Injury Psychologists and Social Workers (bd. dirs. 1995—98, Disting. Svc. award 1990), Am. Congress Rehab. Medicine (Licht award 1981, Disting. Mem. award 1990), Phi Beta Kappa. Office: Mich State Univ 459 Erickson Hall East Lansing MI 48824-1034 Business E-Mail: ncrewe@msu.edu.

CREWS, FREDERICK CAMPBELL, humanities educator, writer; b. Phila., Feb. 20, 1933; s. Maurice Augustus and Robina (Gaudet) C.; m. Betty Claire Peterson, Sept. 9, 1959; children: Gretchen Detre, Ingrid Márquez. AB, Yale U., 1955; PhD, Princeton U., 1958. Faculty U. Calif., Berkeley, 1958—, instr. in English, 1958-60, asst. prof., 1960-62, assoc. prof., 1962-66, prof., 1986-94, vice-chair for grad. studies, 1988-92, chair dept., 1992-94; prof. emeritus, 1994—. Mem. study fellowship selection com. Am. Coun. Learned Socs., 1971-73; mem. selection com. summer seminars Nat. Endowment for Humanities, 1976-77; Ward-Phillips lectr. U. Notre Dame, 1974-75, Dorothy T. Burstein lectr. UCLA, 1984; Frederick Ives Carpenter vis. prof. U. Chgo., 1985; Lansdowne visitor U. Victoria, 1987-88; John Dewey lectr., 1988, Nina Mae Kellogg lectr. Portland (Oreg.) State U., 1989; mem. exec. com. bd. dirs. Mark Twain Project, 1984-94; faculty rsch. lectr. U. Calif., Berkeley, 1991-92; David L. Kubal Meml. lectr. Calif. State U., L.A., 1994; mem. sci. and profl. adv. bd. False Memory Syndrome Found., 1994—; mem. exec. coun. Com. for Sci. Investigation of Claims of the Paranormal, 2000—. Author: The Tragedy of Manners, 1957, E.M. Forster: The Perils of Humanism, 1962, The Pooh Perplex, 1963, The Sins of the Fathers, 1966, The Patch Commission, 1968, The Random House Handbook, 1974, 6th edit., 1992, Out of My System, 1975, Skeptical Engagements, 1986, 2000, The Critics Bear it Away, 1992, Postmodern Pooh, 2001; co-author: The Borzoi Handbook for Writers, 1985, 3d edit., 1993; prin. author: The Memory Wars, 1995; editor: The Red Badge of Courage (Crane), 1964, Great Short Works of Nathaniel Hawthorne, 1967, Starting Over, 1970, Psychoanalysis and Literary Process, 1970, The Random House Reader, 1981, Unauthorized Freud, 1998; mem. contbg. bd. editors The Common Review, 2000—. Recipient Essay prize Nat. Endowment Arts, 1968, Disting. Tchg. award U. Calif., Berkeley, 1985, Spielvogel Diamonstein PEN prize, 1992; named Fulbright lectr. Turin, Italy, 1961-62; fellow Am. Coun. Learned Socs., 1965-66, Ctr. for Advanced Study in Behavioral Scis., 1965-66, Guggenheim Found., 1970-71, Am. Acad. Arts and Scis., 1992. Fellow: Coun. for Sci. Medicine and Mental Health. Home: 636 Vincente Ave Berkeley CA 94707-1524 E-mail: fredc@berkeley.edu.

CREWS, FULTON TIMM, pharmacology educator; b. Raleigh, N.C., July 2, 1949; BS, Syracuse U., 1971; PhD in Pharmacology, U. Mich., 1978. Staff fellow sect. on pharmacology NIMH, Bethesda, Md., 1978-80; asst. prof. pharmacology Coll. Medicine U. Fla., Gainesville, 1980-85, assoc. prof., 1985-90, prof., 1990-94; prof., dir. pharmacology dept. U. N.C., Chapel Hill, 1995—. Dir. Ctr. for Neurobiology of Aging, 1989—, Ctr. for Alcohol Rsch., 1992—. Contbr. to books: Apomorphine and Other Dopaminomimetics, Vol. 2: Clinical Pharmacology, 1981, Phospholipids in the Nervous System, Vol. 1: Metabolism, 1982, Biochemistry of S-Adenosylmethionine and Related Compounds, 1982, Advances in Pharmacology and Therapeutics II, Vol. 2: Neurotransmitters receptors, 1982, Aging of the Brain, Vol. 22, 1983, Methods in Neurobiology: Vol. 1, Brain Neuro-transmitters and Neuromodulator Receptor Methodologies, 1984, Phospholipids in the Nervous System, Vol. 2. Physiological Roles, 1985, Phospholipids and Cellular Regulation, Vol. 1, Phospholipid Research and the Nervous System, Vol. 4, 1986, Treatment Development Strategies for Alzheimer's Disease, 1986, Alcohol and Alcoholism, 1987, Progress in Catacholamine Research, 1988, Psychoneuroendocrinology of Aging: Basic and Clinical Aspects, 1988, Biochemical and Molecular Pathology, 1989, Biomedical and Social Aspects of Alcohol and Alcoholism, 1988, Molecular Mechanisms of Alcohol, 1989, Neurochemical Aspects of Phospholipid Metabolism, 1989, Novel Approaches to the Treatment of Alzheimer's Disease, 1989, New Issues in Neurosciences: Basic and Clinical Approaches, 1990, Molecular Biology and Physiology of Insulin and Insulin-like Growth Factors, 1991, The Treatment of Dementias: A New Generation of Progress, 1991, Phospholipids and Signal Transduction, 1993, Handbook Med. Consequences Alcohol and Drug Abuse, 2003; also articles. Recipient U. Fla. Merit Teaching award, 1990; NIH fellow U. Mich., 1973-78, NIMH fellow, 1978-80; grantee NSF, 1981-84, Nat. Inst. on Aging, 1982-83, Nat. Ins. on Alcohol Abuse and Alcoholism, 1982—, Am. Fedn. for Aging, 1983-84, GREC, 1984-85, NIH, 1984—; Grass traveling scientist, 1987. Mem. AAAS, Am. Coll. Neuropsychopharmacology, Am. Soc. for Pharmacology and Exptl. Therapeutics, Internat. Soc. for Neurochemistry, N.Y. Acad. Scis., Rsch. Soc. on Alcoholism, Soc. for Neuroscience. Office: U NC Skipper Bowles Ctr Alcohol Studies Cb 7178 Thurston Bowles Bldg Chapel Hill NC 27599-7178

CREWS, KENNETH DONALD, law educator, legal consultant, dean; b. Fairborn, Ohio, Feb. 14, 1955; s. Ralph Wilson and Betty Jo (Anderson) C.; m. Elizabeth Dellvera St. Clair, July 24, 1982; 2 children: Veronica St. Clair Crews, Arthur Wilson Crews. BA, Northwestern U., 1977; JD, Washington U., 1980; PhD, UCLA, 1990. Bar: Calif. 1980. Pvt. practice, L.A., 1980—90; legal cons., 1990—; assoc. prof. bus. law San Jose State U., 1990—94; assoc. prof. law, libr. and info. sci. Ind. U., 1994—2000, prof., 2000—; assoc. dean faculties Ind. U.-Purdue U. Indpls., 1994—, Samuel R. Rosen prof. of law, 2003—. Exec. dir., co-founder Los Angeles Venture Assn., 1984-85; visitor Max Planck Inst., Munich, 2001, Munich Intellectual Property Law Ctr., 2003-. Author: Edward S. Corwin and the American Constitution, 1985, University Copyright Policies, 1987, Copyright, Fair Use, and the Challenge for Universities, 1993, Copyright Law and Graduate Research, 2000, Copyright Law for Librarians and Educators, 2000, 2d edit., 2005; editor: Corwin's Constitution, 1986. Counsel Wesley Found. Serving UCLA, 1983-90. Disting. scholar UCLA Alumni Assn., 1986; Assn. Coll. Rsch. Libraries Dissertation fellow 1989; Faculty Study grantee German Acad. Exchange Svc., 2000; recipient Disseration award Assn. for the Study of Higher Edn., 1990. Mem. ABA, ALA (Patterson Copyright award, 2005), Calif. Bar Assn. (chmn. history of law com. 1985-86), Am. Assn. Law Librs. Avocations: camping, hiking, bicycling, architecture. Office: Indiana Univ Sch Law 530 W New York St Indianapolis IN 46202-3225

CREWS, THOMAS RAYMOND, lawyer; b. Banks, Miss., May 2, 1925; s. Oscar Raymond Crews and Sarah Myrtle Pentecost; m. Gloria Rhea Stuart, Dec. 19, 1959. BA, U. Ill., Champaign, 1949; LLB, U. Miss., Oxford, 1951. Bar: Miss. 1951, US Dist. Ct. (no. and so. dists.) Miss. 1951, US Supreme Ct. 1980, US Ct. Appeals (5th cir.) 1983. Mem. Alexander & Crews, Jackson, Miss., 1960—63, Thompson, Alexander & Crews, Jackson, Miss., 1963—97, Watkins & Eager PLLC, Jackson, Miss., 1997—2004. Editor: Miss. Law Jour., 1950. Capt. USAF, 1943—53, Japan. Mem.: Miss. Oil & Gas Lawyers Assn., Miss. Bar Found., Hinds County Bar Assn. (pres. 1989), Jackson Ctrl. Lions Club (pres. 1993), River Hills Tennis Club (pres. 1999). Republican. Meth. Avocation: tennis. Office: Watkins & Eager PLLC 400 E Capitol St Ste 300 Jackson MS 39201 Office Fax: 601-354-3623.

CREWS, WILLIAM EDWIN, lawyer; b. Cin., Oct. 29, 1944; s. Donald Luther and Mary Ruth (Gardiner) C. BA, Miami U., Oxford, Ohio, 1966; JD with honors, George Washington U., 1969. Bar: Ohio 1971, Ga. 1978, U.S. Dist. Ct. (no. dist.) Ga. 1978, U.S. Ct. Appeals (11th cir.) 1978. Assoc. Hausser & Atkinson, Marietta, Ohio, 1971-74; asst. counsel Union CommerceBank, Cleve., 1974-76; asst. corp. counsel Trust Co. Ga., Trust Co. Bank Atlanta, 1976-84; assoc. corp.counsel Trust Co. Ga., Trust Co. Bank, Atlanta,

1984-94; sr. atty. SunTrust Banks, Inc., Atlanta, 1994—. Mem. ABA, State Bar Ga. Office: SunTrust Banks Inc 25 Park Pl NE Atlanta GA 30303-2900 Home: 7765 S Biloxi Way Aurora CO 80016-7101

CREWS, WILLIAM ODELL, JR., religious organization administrator; b. Houston, Feb. 8, 1936; s. William O. Sr. and Juanita (Pearson) C.; m. Wanda Jo Ann Cunningham; 1 child, Ronald Wayne. BA, Hardin Simmons U., 1957, HHD, 1987; BDiv, Southwestern Bapt. Theol. Sem., 1964; DD, Calif. Bapt. Coll., 1987; DMin, Golden Gate Bapt. Theol. Sem., 2000. Ordained to ministry Bapt. Ch., 1953. Pastor Grape Creek Bapt. Ch., San Angelo, Tex., 1952-54, Plainview Bapt. Ch., Stamford, Tex., 1955-57, 1st Bapt. Ch., Sterling City, Tex., 1957-60, 7th St. Bapt. Ch., Ballinger, Tex., 1960-65, Woodland Heights Bapt. Ch., Brownwood, Tex., 1965-67, Victory Bapt. Ch., Seattle, 1967-72, Met. Bapt. Ch., Portland, Oreg., 1972-77; dir. comm. N.W. Bapt. Conv., Portland, 1977-78; pastor Magnolia Ave Bapt. Ch., Riverside, Calif., 1978-86; pres. Golden Gate Bapt. Theol. Sem., Mill Valley, Calif., 1986—2003, chancellor, 2003—. Pres. N.W. Bapt. Conv., Portland, 1974-76, So. Bapt. Gen. Conv. Calif., Fresno, 1982-84. Trustee Fgn. Mission Bd., Richmond, Va., 1973-78, Golden Gate Bapt. Theol. Sem., 1980-85, Marin Cmty. Hosp. Found., 1992-95; bd. dirs. Midway Seatac Boys Club, Des Moines, 1969-72, Marin Gen. Hosp., 1998-2004, North Bay Coun., 1998—. Mem. Marin County C. of C. (bd. dirs. 1987-95), Midway C. of C. (bd. dirs. 1968-72), Rotary (bd. dirs. San Rafael chpt. 1992—, pres. Portland club 1975-76, pres.-elect Riverside club 1984-85). Baptist. Home: 3505 NW 9th Ave Camas WA 98607 Office: Golden Gate Bapt Theol Sem 3200 NE 109th Vancouver WA 98632 Office Phone: 360-882-2176. Business E-Mail: billcrews@ggbts.edu.

CRIANCAMILLI, ANDREW A., retail executive; Pres., COO Perry Drug Stores; with U.S. Kmart, Troy, Mich., 1995—, pres., gen. merchandise mgr., 1997—.

CRICHTON, DOUGLAS BENTLEY, editor, writer; b. Petersburg, Va., Sept. 12, 1959; s. James Bentley and Marjorie Ulalier (Robertson) C.; m. Virginia Elizabeth Munsch, Sept. 5, 1981; children: Christopher Winfield, Alexander Douglas, William Perry, Susannah Elizabeth. BA in English, U. Va., 1981. Reporter Richmond (Va.) Times-Dispatch, 1982-84; reporter, editor AP, Dallas, 1984-88; mng. editor, then editor Am. Way Mag., Dallas, 1988-93; exec. editor, then editor, v.p. Cooking Light Mag., Birmingham, Ala., 1993-2001; v.p., editor Health Mag., Birmingham, Ala., 2001—. Judge Maggie awards Western Pub. Assn., L.A., 1989-93. Named Va. Young Journalist of Yr., UPI, 1983; recipient over 150 awards for editl. and artistic excellence; scholar James Hay Found., 1980. Mem. Am. Soc. Mag. Editors, Assn. Food Journalists. Office: Health 2100 Lakeshore Dr Birmingham AL 35209

CRICHTON, FLORA CAMERON, volunteer, former foundation administrator; b. Waco, Tex. d. William Waldo and Helen Emelyn (Miller) Cameron; m. John H. Crichton, 1989; children: Ike Simpson Kampmann III(dec.), Megan Cameron Kampmann. Dir., mem. exec. com. Certain-Teed Corp., 1971—78; exec. com. San Antonio World's Fair, 1968. Mem. Pres.'s Mission to Latin Am., 1969; U.S. del. Inter-Am. Commn. Women, 1969—72; mem. nat. adv. coun. Georgia O'Keefe Mus.; mem. citizens stamp adv. commn. U.S. Postal Svc., 1969—71; cons. Bur. Inter-Am. Affairs, Dept. State, 1972—75; pres. Flora Cameron Found.; trustee Trinity U., San Antonio, 1965—, chmn., 1976—78; trustee Sweet Briar Coll., 1969—78; mem. Pres.'s Commn. German-Am. Tricentennial, 1983—84;bd. govs. East-West Ctr., Honolulu, 1989—92; vice chmn. exec. com. Tex. Rep. Party, 1958—60; del. Rep. Nat. Conv., 1960, 1964, alt. del., 1968, sec. platform com., 1960; mem. Rep. Nat. Fin. Com., 1965—, pres., chmn., 1976—78; vice chmn. nat. fin. com. George Bush for Pres., 1987—88; mem. Tex. Rep. Nat. Com., 1960—65; former mem. bd. dirs. San Antonio Art Inst., Sch. Am. Rsch., Santa Fe; former mem. nat. coun. Met. Opera. Mem.: San Antonio Jr. League, Colonial Dames Am. Home: 315 Westover Rd San Antonio TX 78209-5653 Office: 5701 Broadway St San Antonio TX 78209-5722

CRICHTON, MARY CHRISTINA, foreign language educator; b. Toronto, Ont., Can., Sept. 6, 1925; came to U.S., 1954; d. John Archibald and Annie Christina (Willison) C. BA, U. Toronto, 1947, MA, 1950; PhD, U. Wis., 1954. Lectr. in German McMaster U., Hamilton, Ont., 1947-50; instr. in German U. Wis., Madison, 1954-55, U. Mich., Ann Arbor, 1955-59, asst. prof. German, 1959-65, assoc. prof. German, 1965—95, assoc. prof. emeritus, 1995—. Subscription editor: Mich. Germanic Studies, 1983—2001; co-translator: Rainer Maria Rilke, Duino Elegies, 2003; contbr. articles to profl. jours. Mem. AAUP (sec. Mich. chpt. 1984-89, pres. 1989-92, treas. 1994—), Am. Assn. Tchrs. German, Modern Lang. Assn., Am. Soc. for Eighteenth Century Studies, Internat. Vereinigung für Germanistik. Methodist. Avocations: choral singing, organic gardening, photography, yoga. Office: Dept Germanic Langs & Lits Univ Mich Ann Arbor MI 48109-1275 E-mail: mcrichto@umich.edu.

CRICHTON, MICHAEL (JOHN MICHAEL CRICHTON), writer, film director; b. Chgo., Oct. 23, 1942; AB summa cum laude, Harvard U., 1964, MD, 1969. Postdoctoral fellow Salk Inst., La Jolla, Calif., 1969-70. Vis. writer MIT, Cambridge, 1988; vis. lectr. Cambridge U., 1965; creator, co-exec. prodr. TV show ER, 1994. Creator, co-exec., prodr.: ER, 1994; author: (as Jeffrey Hudson) A Case of Need, 1968 (Edgar award Mystery Writers of America 1968); (as John Lange) Odds On, 1966, Scratch One, 1967, Easy Go, 1968, Zero Cool, 1969, The Venom Business, 1969, Drug of Choice, 1970, Grave Descend, 1970, Binary, 1972; The Andromeda Strain, 1969, Five Patients, 1970 (Writer of the Year award Assn. American Medical Writers 1970), (with Douglas Crichton) Dealing: Or, The Berkeley to Boston Forty-Brick Lost-Bag Blues, 1971, The Terminal Man, 1972, The Great Train Robbery, 1975 (Edgar award Mystery Writers of America 1979), Eaters of the Dead, 1976, Jasper Johns, 1977, rev. edit., 1994, Congo, 1980, Electronic Life, 1983, Sphere, 1987, Travels, 1988, Jurassic Park, 1990, Rising Sun, 1992, Disclosure, 1994, Lost World, 1995, Airframe, 1996, Timeline, 1999, Prey, 2002, State of Fear, 2004 (Publishers Weekly bestseller list); screenwriter, dir. film Westworld, 1973, Coma, 1978, The Great Train Robbery, 1979, Looker, 1981, Runaway, 1984; dir. film Pursuit, 1972, Physical Evidence, 1989; co-screenwriter Jurassic Park, 1993, Rising Sun, 1993; co-screenwriter, co-writer Twister, 1996; co-prodr. (film) Disclosure, 1994, Sphere, 1998, 13th Warrior, 1999, Timeline, 2003. Mem. bd. overseers Harvard U. Recipient George Foster Peabody award ER, 1995, Emmy Best Dramatic series ER, 1996, Best Long Form Television Script for ER, Writer's Guild Am., 1995, Acad. Motion Pictures Arts and Scis. Tech. Achievement award for pioneering computerized motion picture budgeting and scheduling, 1995; Henry Russell Shaw traveling fellow, 1964-65. New ankylosaur named in honor Crichtonsaurus bohlini, 2003. Mem. Authors Guild (coun. 1995—), Writers Guild Am. West, Dirs. Guild Am., PEN Am. Ctr., Acad. Motion Picture Arts and Scis.; bd. dirs. Internat. Design Conf. at Aspen, 1985-91, Western Behavioral Scis. Inst., La Jolla, 1986-91; Phi Beta Kappa. Avocation: computer games. Office: Constant C Prodns Ste 433 2118 Wilshire Blvd Santa Monica CA 90403

CRICHTON, THOMAS, IV, lawyer; b. Shreveport, La., Dec. 2, 1947; BS, La. State U., 1969, JD, 1972. Bar: Tex. 1972, La. 1972, D.C. 1988. Mem. Vinson & Elkins, LLP, Dallas, co-head Tax Law Sect. Adj. prof. sch. law U. Houston, 1978-86. Mem. Order of Coif, Beta Alpha Psi, Beta Gamma Sigma, Omicron Delta Kappa, Phi Kappa Phi. Office: Vinson & Elkins LLP 3700 Trammell Crow Ctr Dallas TX 75201-2975 also: Vinson & Elkins LLP 2500 First City Tower 1001 Fannin St Ste 3300 Houston TX 77002-6706 also: Vinson & Elkins LLP 1455 Pennsylvania Ave NW Fl 7 Washington DC 20004-1008 Office Phone: 214-220-7984. Business E-Mail: tcrichton@velaw.com.

CRIDER, RUDYARD LEE, psychotherapist; b. Abilene, Kans., Oct. 16, 1942; s. Clarence A. and Myrtle (Cox) C.; m. Doris Elaine Heisey, Aug. 3, 1962; 1 child, Michele Renee. BA, Messiah Coll., 1971; MS, Shippensburg U., 1978. Cert. clin. mental health counselor; nat. cert. counselor; cert. diplomate in psychotherapy; lic. profl. counselor. Mental health worker King's View Hosp., Reedley, Calif., 1966-68; crisis intervention counselor Holy Spirit Hosp. Mental Health, Camp Hill, Pa., 1974-78, sr. psychotherapist, 1978—, asst. coord. outpatient svcs., 1989—2001, program supr. behavioral health svcs., 2001—; pvt. practice psychotherapy, 1992—. Sr. peer reviewer Holy Spirit Hosp. Mental Health, Camp Hill, 1990-96, quality assurance com., 1990—, clin. site supr., 1983—, mem. extended mgmt. team, 1994—. Recipient Recognition for Outstanding Svc. award Cumberland Perry County Mental Health-Mental Retardation Program, 1993. Mem. Acad. Clin. Mental Health Counselors, Am. Counseling Assn., Am. Mental Health Counselors Assn., Am. Psychotherapy Assn., Pa. Counselors Assn., Pa. Psychol. Assn. Lutheran. Avocations: photography, bicycling, hiking, drawing, backpacking. Home: 438 Parkside Rd Camp Hill PA 17011-2127 Office: Holy Spirit Hosp 21st St Camp Hill PA 17011 E-mail: RCrider@HSH.org.

CRIDER, RUSSELL J, pediatric orthopedic surgeon; b. St. Louis, Mo. s. Russell Jackson and Jane Alger Crider; m. Coleen Francis Hagart, Dec. 9, 1989; children: Tiffany, Katherine. BA, Carlton Coll., 1960—64; MD, Baylor Med. Sch., 1964—68. Diplomate Am. Bd. of Orthop. Surgeons, 1977. Pediat. orthop. surgeon Shriner's Children Hosp., San Francisco, 1975—80, NY U., 1980—89; assoc. team physician San Diego Chargers, 1970—91; co-dir. Children's Orthop. Combined San Francisco Orthop. Residency Program, 1990—92; dir. pediat. orthop. North Shore Univ. Hosp., Manhasset, NY, 1994—2000, chief divsn. of orthop. surgery, 1997—98; attending orthop. surgeon Miami Children's Hosp., Fla., 2000—02; clin. assoc. prof. orthop. surgery NY U., 1998—. Contbr. articles to profl. jours.; co-author (with R.G. Wilber): MRI in Spinal Injury, 1991. Major USAF, 1970—72, Eglia Air Force Base. Fellow: Am. Acad. Orthop. Surgery; mem.: Pediat. Orthop. Soc. of North Am. Avocations: scuba diving, tennis, golf. Personal E-mail: rjcridermofc@msn.com.

CRIER, CATHERINE, newscaster; b. Dallas; BA in Polit. Sci., Univ. Tex.; JD, So. Meth. Univ., Dallas. Asst. dist. atty., felony chief prosecutor Dallas Co. Dist. Atty. Off., 1978—81; civil litig. atty. Dallas, 1982—84; former judge 162nd Dist. Ct. Tex., 1984-89; anchor Cable News Network, 1989-92; corr. ABC 20/20, 1993-95; news corr. ABC News, 1995—98; anchor, Crier Report Fox News, 1998—99; exec. editor, legal news specials Court-TV, 1999—, host, Catherine Crier Live, 2001—. Author: The Case Against Lawyers, 2002 (NY Times bestseller); co-author (with Cole Thompson): A Deadly Game: The Untold Story of the Scott Peterson Investigation, 2005 (NY Times bestseller). Named one of the Dynamic Dozen, TV Guide Mag., 1990, Twenty Young Lawyers Who Make a Difference, ABA Barrister Mag., 1990; recipient Outstanding Young Tex. Ex award, Univ. Tex., Austin, 1990, Les Femmes du Monde award, Dallas Coun. on World Affairs, 1996, Emmy award, 1996, duPont-Columbia award, 2001, two Gracie Allen awards, Found. Am. Women in Radio and TV. Avocations: golf, scuba diving, raising, training Arabian horses. Office: Courtroom TV Network LLC Frnt 2 600 3rd Ave New York NY 10016 Business E-Mail: info@criercommunications.com.*

CRILE, SUSAN, artist; b. Cleve., Aug. 12, 1942; d. George Jr. and Jane (Halle) C.; m. Joseph S. Murphy, May 18, 1984. Student, NYU; BA, Bennington Coll., 1965. Mem. faculty Fordham U., N.Y.C., 1972-76, Princeton (N.J.) U., 1974-76, Sarah Lawrence Coll., Bronxville, N.Y., 1976-79, Sch. Visual Arts, N.Y.C., 1976-82, Barnard Coll., N.Y.C., 1983-86, Hunter Coll., N.Y.C., 1983—. Travelling rep. to Hungary and Portugal with exhbn. Am. Paintings in the Eighties, Internat. Comm. Agy., Washington, 1981; resident-in-painting Am. Acad. in Rome, 1990. One-woman shows include Kornblee Gallery, NYC, 1971-73, Fischbach Gallery, NYC, 1974-75, 77, Brooke Alexander Gallery, NYC, 1975, Phillips Collection, Washington, 1975, New Gallery, Cleve., 1977, Ctr. Gallery Bucknell U., Lewisburg, Pa., 1978, Droll Kolbert Gallery, NYC, 1978, 80, Ivory Kimpton Gallery, San Francisco, 1981, 84, 88, Van Straten Gallery, Chgo., 1983, Lincoln Ctr. Gallery, NYC, 1983, Cleve. Ctr. for Contemporary Art, 1984, Nina Freundenheim Gallery, Buffalo, NY, 1980, 84, Graham Modern, NYC, 1985, 87-88, 90, Adams Middleton Gallery, Dallas, 1986, Gloria Luria, Bay Harbor Island, Fla., 1987-88, 90, St. Louis Art Mus., 1994, Blaffer Gallery- U. Houston, 1994, Univ. Art Mus. U. So. Calif., Long Beach, 1994, Fed. Reserve Bd., Washington, 1995, Herbert Johnson Mus. Cornell U., Ithaca, NY, 1995, Middlebury (Vt.) Coll. Mus. Art, 1995, James Graham & Sons, NYC, 1995, 98, 2001, Nat. Coun. for Culture, Art and Letters, Kuwait City, Kuwait, 1996, U. Ariz. Mus. Art., Tucson, 2003, James Graham and Sons, NYC, 2004; exhibited in group shows at Whitney Mus. Art, NYC, 1972, 82, Indpls. Mus. Art, 1972, 74, Kent State U., 1972, Art Inst. Chgo., 1972, Corcoran Gallery Art, Washington, 1973, Va. Mus. Fine Arts, 1975, U.S.I.A., 1979, Grey Art Gallery, NYC, 1979, 83, Janie C. Lee Gallery, Houston, 1979, Meml. Art Gallery, U. Rochester, 1980, Bklyn. Mus., 1980-81, 83, Carnegie Inst., Pitts., 1981, Inst. Contemporary Art, 1981, Am. Acad. Arts and Letters, 1983, 94, 99, Weatherspoon Gallery, Greensboro, NC, 1984, Columbus (Ga.) Mus. Arts and Sci., 1985, Queens Mus., 1986, Portland (Maine) Mus. Art, 1986, Mus. Fine Arts, Boston, 1986, Cleve. Mus. Art, 1987, Mt. Holyoke Coll. Art Mus., South Hadley, Mass., 1987, Hudson River Mus., 1988, Bowdoin Coll. Mus. Art, Brunswick, Maine, 1992, Denver Art Mus., 1993-94, Am. Acad. Arts & Letters, NYC, 1994, Fla. Internat. U., Miami, 1995, James Graham & Sons, NYC, 1997, 99, 2003, Times Sq. Gallery, NYC, 2000, Art in Gen., NYC, 2000, U. Ariz. Mus. Art, Tempe, 2001, Smith and Eds, Palo Alto, Calif., U. Colorado Springs, Colo., 2002, Lehman Coll. Art Gallery, NYC, 2004; poster commn.: Live from Lincoln Ctr., NYC, 1980, Mostly Mozart, 1985, IBM Gallery Aci. & Art, NYC, 1989, Nat. Gallery Art, Washington, 1989, Detroit Inst. Art, 1991, Nat. Mus. Women in the Arts, Washington, 1991, William Proctor Art Gallery, Bard Coll., Annandale-on-Hudson, NY, 1992, Bowdoin Coll. Mus. Art, Brunswick, Maine, 1992, Andre Emmerich Gallery, NYC, 1992, Denver Art Mus., 1993, Cleve. Ctr. for Contemporary Art, 1993; represented in permanent collections Albright-Knox Art Gallery, Buffalo, Bklyn. Mus., Mus. Art Carnegie Inst., Pitts., Guggenheim Mus., NYC, Hirshhorn Mus., Washington, Met. Mus. Art, NYC, Phillips Collection, Washington, Cleve. Mus. Art, Libr. Congress, Washington, Denver Mus. Art, Middlebury Coll. Mus. Art, Ariz. State U. Art Mus., Tempe, Bowdoin Coll. Mus. Art, Brunswick, Fed. Res. Bd., Washington, Portland Mus., Weatherspoon Art Gallery, Greensboro. Trustee Bennington Coll., 1979-81; active Yaddo Corp., 1986—, bd. dirs., 1991—. Resident grantee Yaddo, 1970-71, 74-75, 78, MacDowell Colony, 1972, grantee Ingram Merrill Found., 1972; fellow Nat. Endowment for Arts, 1982, 89-90. Home: 168 W 86th St New York NY 10024-4033

CRILLEY, JOSEPH JAMES, artist; b. Phila., Jan. 8, 1920; s. James John and Anna (Spoerl) C.; m. Marion Gertrude Haly, Jan. 31, 1948 (div.); children: Pamela, Geraldine, Candace, Joseph; m. Suzanne Corlette, Aug. 16, 1982. Student, Phila. Coll. Art, 1937—41. Art tchr. New Hope (Pa.)-Solebury High Sch., 1955-61; photographer William J. Keller, Inc., Buffalo, 1960-71. Photographer: New York, Island of Islands, 1965; one-man exhibn. Lambertville (N.J., 1976-80, 82-85, Coryell Gallery, Lambertville, 1981, Kiski Sch., Saltsburg, Pa., 1985, Genest Gallery, Lambertville, 1986-90, Phila. Sketch Club, 1990, Gratz Gallery, New Hope, 2001—; exhibited in group shows at Nat. Acad. of Design, N.Y.C., Phila., Art and Alliance, Phila. Mus. of Art, Michener Art Mus., Doylestown, Pa., Mystic, Conn., others; represented in permanent collections at Kiski Sch., Atlantic Salmon Mus., Cape Breton, N.S., Can., Australia, France, others. Capt. AUS, 1942-45, ETO. Recipient 64 awards including Best of Show, 1983, New Hope Borough Seal, 1984, New Hope Arts Commn. Competition, 3 Gold medals, 1980-95, DaVinci Art Alliance Phila., Award of Excellence, 1991, 29th Mystic Internat., Conn., Anthony Cirino award 1992, Grumbacher Gold medal, 1996, Audubon Artists, N.Y., 15 awards 1962-95 Salmagundi Club, N.Y., 3 awards 1985-95, Phila. Sketch Club, Pa. Mem.: Salmagundi Club, DaVinci Art Alliance., Phila. Sketch Club, Audubon Artists. Avocations: fly fishing, skiing.

CRILLY, EUGENE RICHARD, engineering consultant; b. Phila., Oct. 30, 1923; s. Eugene John and Mary Virginia (Harvey) C.; m. Alice Royal Roth, Feb. 16, 1952. Degree of Mech. Engr., Stevens Inst. Tech., 1944, MS, 1949, U. Penn., 1951; postgrad., UCLA, 1955—58. Sr. rsch. engr. N.Am. Aviation, LA, 1954-57, Canoga Park and Downey, Calif., 1962-66; process engr. Northrop Aircraft Corp., Hawthorne, Calif., 1957-59; project engr., quality assurance mgr. HITCO, Gardena, Calif., 1959-62; sr. rsch. splist. Lockheed-Calif. Co., Burbank, Calif., 1966-74; engring. specialist N.Am. aircraft ops. Rockwell Internat., El Segundo, Calif., 1974-89. Author tech. papers. Mem. nat. com. 125th Anniversary Founding of Stevens Inst. Tech. in 1870. Served with USNR, 1943-46; comdr. Res. ret. Mem. Soc. for Advancement Material and Process Engring. (chmn. LA chpt. 1978-79, gen. chmn. 1981 symposium exhbn., nat. dir. 1979-86, treas. 1982-85, Award of Merit 1986), Naval Inst., Naval Res. Assn., VFW, Mil. Order World Wars (adj. San Fernando Valley chpt. 1985, 2d vice comdr. 1986, comdr. 1987-89, vice comdr. West, Dept. Ctrl. Calif., 1988-89, comdr. Cajon Valley San Diego chpt. 1990-92, adj./ROTC chmn. region XIV 1990-91, comdr. Dept. So. Calif. 1991-93, vice comdr. region XIV, 1992-93, dep. comdr. Gen. Staff Officer region XIV 1993-94, comdr. region XIV, 1994-95, Disting. Chpt. Comdr. Region XIV 1990-91, treas. region XIV 1998-99, treas. San Diego chpt. 1999-2000), Former Intelligence Officers Assn. (treas. San Diego chpt. one 1990-94), Mil. Officers Assn. Am. (treas. Silver Strand chpt. 1992-2000, 04-, asst. treas. San Diego nat. conv. 2000), Navy League U.S. (treas. Coronado coun. 1997-2001, bd. dirs. 2004-), Naval Order U.S., Naval Intelligence Profls. Assn., Brit. United Svc. Club LA, Marines Meml. Club (San Francisco), Coronado Round Table, Hammer Club of San Diego, Sigma Xi, Sigma Nu. Republican. Roman Catholic. Home and Office: 276 J Ave Coronado CA 92118-1138 Office Phone: 619-435-3778. Personal E-mail: genecrilly@aol.com.

CRIM, FORREST FLEMING, JR., chemist, educator; b. Waco, Tex., May 30, 1947; s. Forrest Fleming Sr. and Almanor Adair (Chapman) C.; m. Joyce Ann Wileman, June 21, 1969 (div.); 1 child, Tracy F. BS, Southwestern U., 1969; PhD, Cornell U., 1974. Staff mem. Engring. Rsch. Ctr. Western Electric Co., Princeton, N.J., 1974-76; postdoctoral staff mem. Los Alamos (N.Mex.) Sci. Lab., 1976-77; from asst. prof. to assoc. prof. Dept. Chemistry U. Wis., Madison, 1977-84, prof. Dept. Chemistry, 1984—. Mem. rev. panel, Dept. of Energy Combustion Rsch. Facility, 1983-85, chmn., 1985, review com., Chemistry Dept., Brookhaven Nat. Lab., 1989; mem. Nat. Rsch. Coun. Workshop on the Chemistry Dept. of the Future, 1987; chmn. Gordon Rsch Conf. on Atomic and Molecular Interactions, 1988; external adv. com. of the Chemical and Laser Scis. Divsn., Los Alamos Nat. Lab., 1990—; rev. com. Associated Univs. Chemistry Dept., Brookhaven Nat. Lab., 1990—; mem. Nat. Rsch. Coun. Panel on Future Opportunities in Atomic, Molecular, and Optical Sci., 1991—. Editorial bd. internat. revs. Phys. Chemistry, 1990—, editorial adv. bd. Ency. of Applied Physics, 1989—, Jour. Phys. Chemistry, 1987-93; contbr. articles to profl. jours. Fellow Alfred P. Sloan Rsch., 1981-83, fellow AAAS, 1995, fellow Am. Acad. Arts and Scis., 1998; named Camille and Henry Dreyfus Tchr.-Scholar, 1982, Helfaer Prof. Chemistry, 1985-91, Robert A. Welch Foun. lectr., 1989, Bayer-Mobay lectr., U. N.H., 1991, Malcolm Dole Disting. lectr., Northwestern U., 2000; recipient Alexander von Humnboldt Sr. U.S. Scientist award, 1986, Southwestern Univ. Alumni Assn. Citation of Merit, 1987, Max Planck award Alexander von Humboldt Soc., 1993. Fellow Am. Phys. Soc. (Earl K. Plyler Prize Selection Com. 1992—, Earle K. Plyler Molecular Physics prize 1998); mem. AAAS, NAS, Am. Chem. Soc. (chmn. Symposium on State-to-State Chemistry 1986, vice-chmn. Phys. Chemistry Div. 1986-87, chmn.-elect 1987-88, chmn. 1988-89, chmn. Task Force to Monitor Jour. of Physical Chemistry 1990-91), Optical Soc. of Am. (Quantum Electronics and Laser Scis. com. 1990-91). Office: Univ Wis Dept Chemistry 1101 University Ave Madison WI 53706-1322

CRIMANDO, THOMAS IGNATIUS, history educator; b. Batavia, N.Y. s. Gasper Joseph and Joan (Hilbert) C. BA in History cum laude, St. John Fisher Coll., 1976; MA in European History, U. Rochester, 1977, PhD in Early Modern European History, 1984. Lectr. history Nazareth Coll., Rochester, N.Y., 1985-88; adj. faculty history Rochester Inst. Tech., 1987-2001, SUNY, Brockport, 1988-2001, 2003. Vis. asst. prof. history SUNY, Brockport, 2001—03, adj. faculty history, 2002, Rochester Inst. Tech., 2002. Contbr. articles and revs. to profl. jours., articles to reference works. Named to Hall of Fame, Notre Dame H.S., Batavia, N.Y., 2001; recipient John A. Murray award, St. John Fisher Coll., 1976. Mem.: Nat. Geog. Soc., Eire Philatelic Soc., Vatican Philatelic Soc. (pres.), Western Front Assn., Am. Philatelic Assn., Phi Alpha Theta, Pi Gamma Mu. Roman Catholic. Avocation: stamp collecting/philately. E-mail: tcrimand@brockport.edu.

CRIMINALE, WILLIAM OLIVER, JR., applied mathematics professor; b. Mobile, Ala., Nov. 29, 1933; s. William Oliver and Vivian Gertrude (Skeetoe) C.; m. Ulrike Irmgard Wegner, June 7, 1962; children: Martin Oliver, Lucca. BS, U. Ala., 1955; PhD, Johns Hopkins U., 1960. Asst. prof. Princeton (N.J.) U., 1962-68; assoc. prof. U. Wash., Seattle, 1968-73, prof. oceanography, geophysics, applied math., 1973—, chmn. dept. applied math., 1976-84. Cons. Aerospace Corp., 1963—65, Boeing Corp., 1968—72, AGARD, 1967—68, Lenox Hill Hosp., 1967—68, ICASE, NASA Langley, 1990—2003; guest prof., Canada, 1965, 2001, France, 1967—68, Germany, 1973—74, Sweden, 1973—74, Scotland, 1985, 89, 91, England, 90, 91, Stanford U., 1990, Brazil, 92, 2001, Italy, 1999, Crete, 2005; Nat. Acad. exch. scientist USSR, 1969, 72. Author: Stability of Parallel Flows, 1967, Theory and Computation in Hydrodynamic Stability, 2003; contbr. articles to profl. jours. Served with U.S. Army, 1961-62. Boris A. Bakmeteff Meml. fellow, 1957-58, NATO postdoctoral fellow, 1960-61, Alexander von Humboldt Sr. fellow, 1973-74, Royal Soc. fellow, 1990-91. Fellow Am. Phys. Soc.; mem. Am. Acad. Mechanics, Am. Geophys. Union, Fedn. Am. Scientists. Home: 1635 Peach Ct E Seattle WA 98112-3428 Office: U Wash Dept Applied Math Box 352420 Seattle WA 98195-2420 Office Phone: 206-543-9506. Business E-Mail: lascala@amath.washington.edu.

CRIMLISK, JANE THERESE, probation officer; b. Boston, Dec. 2, 1945; d. Herbert Leo and Grace Beatrice (McGilvray) C. AS, Aquinas Coll., Newton, Mass., 1968; BA in Sociology cum laude, Boston Coll., 1974; MS in Bus. Edn., Suffolk U., Boston, 1978; MEd in Rehab. Counseling, U. Mass., 1991, Cert. of Advanced Grad. Study, 1995. Tchr. religious edn., 1965-88, 93—; legal sec. Hale, Sanderson, Byrnes & Morton, Boston, 1968-69; sec. Boston Coll. Law Sch., Chestnut Hill, 1969-74, Life Resources, Inc., Boston, 1974-75; tchr. Archbishop Williams High Sch., Braintree, Mass., 1975-78; exec. sec. Cramer Electronics, Newton, Mass., 1978-79; jud. sec. Com. of Mass. Ct. Systems, Boston, 1979-95; probation officer Probate and Family Ct., Boston, 1995—; tchr. adult edn. Aquinas Coll., Milton, 1989—. Vol. counselor Pregnancy Help, Brighton, Mass., 1992, Arthur Clark for U.S. Congress campaign, Newton, 1980, Marian Walsh for State Senate campaign, 1992, 94, Mass. Citizens for Life. Mem. Boston Coll. Alumni Assn. (bd. dirs. 1982-84), Boston Coll. Evening Coll. Alumni Assn. (bd. dirs., past pres.), Aquinas Coll. Alumni Assn. Democrat. Roman Catholic. Avocations: swimming, ice skating, crewel, cross stitch, music. Home: 416 Belgrade Ave Apt 25 West Roxbury MA 02132-1540 Office: Probate and Family Ct Dept 24 New Chardon St Boston MA 02114-4703

CRIMMINS, CATHY ELIZABETH, writer; b. East Orange, N.J., Aug. 22, 1955; d. David Joseph Crimmins and Elizabeth Ann (Kelly) Lancaster; m. David Ledger, Oct. 5, 1973 (div. 1978); m. Alan Steven Forman, May 31, 1982; 1 child, Kelly Crimmins. BA in English, Rutgers U., 1976; MA in English, U. Pa., 1978. Author: Curse of the Mommy, 1993, When My Parents Were My Age, They Were Old, 1995, Where Is the Mango Princess?, 2000; co-author: Newt Gingrich's Bedtime Stories for Orphans, 1995. Lit. fellow Pa. Coun. on the Arts, 1989. Mem. Am. Soc. Journalists and Authors. Avocations: gardening, singing. Home: 843 N Las Palmas Ave Los Angeles CA 90036-3515

CRIMMINS, PAMELA LEE, artist, educator; b. N.Y.C., Mar. 9, 1961; d. Kevin Bates and Cynthia (Crump) C.; m. Carl Lawrence Gable, May 13, 1989 (div. Sept. 1999); children: Lucinda, Kevin. Student, Univ. Coll., Cork, Ireland, 1981-82; BA cum laude, Yale U., 1984. Photographer U.S. Embassy, Rabat, Morocco, 1984-85; dir., co-dir. Young Artists Painting Workshop, N.Y.C., 1986-91; tchr. Silvermine Sch. Art, New Canaan, Conn., 1996—,

Studio In A School, N.Y.C., 1997—. One-person shows include Littlejohn Contemporary, N.Y.C., 2003; exhibited in group shows at Pierogi 2000 Gallery, Bklyn., 1997, 98, Small Works Gallery, Las Vegas, Nev., 1998, Ten-In-One Gallery, N.Y.C., 2001, Pensacola (Fla.) Mus. Art, 2002. Pres. PTA, Children's Workshop Sch., N.Y.C., 1995-96; mem. edn. com. Grace Ch. Sch., N.Y.C., 1999—; bd. dirs. Artists Alliance, Inc., N.Y.C. Grantee Pollock-Krasner Found., 1997, Gottlieb Found., 1997. Democrat. Roman Catholic.

CRIMMINS, PHILIP PATRICK, retired metallurgical engineer, lawyer; b. Poughkeepsie, N.Y., Aug. 1, 1930; s. Philip Patrick and Eva (Booth) C.; m. Janet E. Ballou, Feb. 14, 1953; children: Lisa Jane, Philip Patrick, Michael Mathew. BS, MIT, 1952; MS, Wayne State U., 1959; JD, U. Pacific, 1972. Registered profl. metall. engr. Metall. engr. Ford Motor Co., Livonia, Mich., 1954-58; dir. engring. Aerojet Space Boosters, Sacramento, 1958—95; ret. Served with AUS, 1952-54. Recipient William Sparagen award Am. Welding Soc., 1968 Calif. Fellow Am. Inst. Chemists; mem. Am. Soc. Metals, Fed., Am., Calif. bar assns. Home: 9113 Rosewood Dr Sacramento CA 95826-4526

CRINO, MARJANNE HELEN, anesthesiologist; b. Rochester, N.Y., Aug. 18, 1933; d. Michael Jay and Helen Barbara (Kennedy) C.; m. Michael Anthony La Iuppa, Nov. 12, 1960 (dec. Feb. 1996); children: James Michael, Barbara Helen, John Christopher. BS, Coll. St. Teresa, 1955; MD, Med. Coll. Wis., 1959; MA in Theology, St. Bernard's Inst., 1991. Diplomate Nat. Bd. Med. Examiners. House staff Genesee Hosp., Rochester, 1959-61; perinatal mortality rsch., resident in anesthesiology Jackson Meml Hosp.-U. Miami, 1962-65; attending staff in anesthesiology Genesee Hosp., Rochester, N.Y., 1969-2000; mem. exec. com., med. staff sec., 1980, 82; acting chmn. dept. anesthesiology Genesee Hosp., Rochester, N.Y., 1989, 91, chmn. pain control com., 1989-95; clin. instr. anesthesiology U. Rochester Sch. Medicine, 1983—. Cons. anesthesiology Rochester Psychiat. Ctr., 1975-85; instr. anesthesiology U. Miami Sch. medicine, 1966, 67; attending staff anesthesiology Jackson Meml. Hosp., Miami, 1966, 67. Mem. adv. bd. Isaiah House Hosp., 1994-2000, com. Pittsford (N.Y.) Rep. Party, 1970's-80's; vol. chaplain Genesee Hosp. Mem. N.Y. State Soc. Anesthesiologists (bd. dirs., vice spkr. 1983-86, del. 1971-82, 87-2002), Am. Soc. Anesthesiologists (del. 1979-86, 97), AMA, N.Y. State Med. Soc., Med. Soc. County of Monroe, Rochester Acad. Medicine, Cath. Physicians Guild Rochester (bd.dirs., pres. 1988-89), Margaret Roper Guild (pres. 1975-76), Cath. Women's Club (Diocese of Rochester). Roman Catholic. Avocations: reading, gardening, music. *Whether you are dealing with a large group, a small gathering or a single person, don't worry about the impression you are making or how uncomfortable you are. Try to find some way to make the others comfortable. You will never go wrong.*

CRIPPEN, TIMOTHY ALAN, sociology educator; b. Ft. Wayne, Ind., June 1, 1952; s. Raymond R. and Wilda E. Crippen; m. Pamela A. Crippen, Mar. 3, 1973. AB, Ind. U., 1974; MA, U. Tex., 1976, PhD, 1982. Asst. prof. sociology U. Mary Washington, Fredericksburg, Va., 1982-88, assoc. prof. sociology, 1988-94, prof. sociology, 1994—. Author: Crisis in Sociology, 1999; contbr. articles to profl. jours. Mem. AAAS, Am. Sociol. Assn., Assn. for Politics and Life Scis., Human Behavior and Evolution Soc., So. Sociol. Soc., Phi Kappa Phi. Office: U Mary Washington Dept Sociology and Anthropology Fredericksburg VA 22401 Office Phone: 540-654-1503. Business E-Mail: tcrippen@umw.edu.

CRIPPS, DEREK J., retired dermatologist, educator; b. Sept. 17, 1928; s. Edmund James and Susan Ann (Mayell) C.; m. Eileen Wright, Dec. 21, 1963; children: Andrew, Alasdair, Annabelle, Amanda. MB BS, U. London, 1953, MD, 1965; MS, U. Mich., 1961. Diplomate Am. Bd. Dermatology. Resident in dermatology U. Mich., 1959-62; asst. prof. medicine U. Wis., Madison, 1965-68, assoc. prof. medicine, 1968-72, prof., head dermatology, 1972-2000, emeritus prof. medicine, 2001—; ret., 2001. Cons. for sunscreens FDA, 1974-85. Author: Royal Navy Ships, Captains, and Stations Vol. I 1773-1972, 2003, Vol. II 1793-1800, 2003, Steel's List of the Royal Navy Ships Commanders and Stations: 1793-1805, 2004; conbr. over 100 articles to profl. jours. Mem. Great Brit. Nat. Swimming Team, 1950-51; surgeon lt. Royal Navy, 1954-58. Recipient Merit award AMA, 1968; grantee EPA, Porphyria in Turkey, 1979-84, NIH, 1965-84, Action spectra and Biochemistry of Photodermatoses. Fellow ACP; mem. Am. Acad. Dermatology (photobiology com., pres. 1976, Exhibit Gold award 1975), Brit. Dermatologic Assn., Ctrl. Soc. for Clin. Rsch., Soc. for Investigative Dermatology, Royal Soc. of Medicine, Wis. Dermatological Soc. (pres. 1976). Avocations: swimming, travel. Office: UW Health Dept Derm One South Park 7th Fl Madison WI 53715 Office Phone: 608-287-2620. Personal E-mail: drdjc727@aol.com.

CRIPPS, RICHARD E., diversified financial services company executive; Degree, James Madison U., 1979. Cert. fin. analyst. From stockbroker to chief mkt. strategist Legg Mason Wood Walker Inc., Balt., 1979—97, chief mkt. strategist, 1997—. Mem.: Balt. (Md.) Security Analysts Soc. Office: Legg Mason 100 Light St Baltimore MD 21202-1099

CRISCI, MATHEW G., marketing executive, writer; b. N.Y.C. s. Mathew Anthony and Frances (Coscia) C.; m. Mary Ann, Nov. 14, 1968; children: Mathew Joseph, Mark David, Mitchell Justin. BS, Iona Coll. Sr. v.p. Young & Rubicam, Inc., N.Y.C. and Sydney, Australia, 1968-82; exec. v.p., COO, bd. dirs. Integrated Barter Internat., N.Y.C. and L.A., 1982-85; sr. v.p., gen. mgr., bd. dirs. Chiat/Day Advt. Inc., San Francisco, 1986-90; exec. v.p., mng. dir. Lowe Lintas Worldwide, N.Y.C., 1991-97; exec. v.p., chief mktg. officer Alton Entertainment Co., L.A., 1997—2001, also bd. dirs.; chief mktg. officer Asset Mktg. Sys., San Diego, 2001—. Author: Observations of a Kind, 1998, Fanny, I Love You, 2003, This Little Piggy, 2004. Office: Asset Mktg Sys 9715 Business Park Ave San Diego CA 92131 Office Phone: 888-303-8755. Business E-Mail: mcrisci@assetmarketingsystems.net.

CRISCIONE, JEAN CAROL, literature and language educator; d. Enrico Salvatore Criscione and Jean Anziano. BA, Sacred Heart U., Fairfield, Conn., 1967; MA, U. Bridgeport, 1972. Cert. tchr. Conn., 1972. Tchr. English, sci. and theology Most Precious Blood sch., Trumbull, Conn., 1967—68; tchr. St. Patrick Sch., Bridgeport, 1970—72; tchr. English Read Mid. Sch., 1972—79; tchr. English and reading Ctrl. H.S., 1979—. Chaplain Delta Alpha Tau, Fairfield, Conn., 1963—67; mem. St. Theresa Ch., Trumbull. Recipient Journalism award. Mem.: Bridgeport Edn. Assn. (life). Independent. Roman Catholic. Avocations: writing, gardening, crafts, gourmet cooking, travel. Office: Ctrl HS 1 Lincoln Blvd Bridgeport CT 06606 Office Phone: 203-576-7377.

CRISE, ROBERT D., JR., mathematics professor; s. Robert D. and Fran Crise. BS in Math., U. Calif., 1977; MA in Math., Calif. State U., 1985. Assoc. prof. math. Crafton Hills Coll., Yucaipa, Calif., 2000—. Mem.: AMA, Math. Assn. Am., Am. Math. Assn. of Two Yr. Colls., Calif. Math. Counsel of CC's South (student liaison 2004). Office: Crafton Hills Coll 11711 Sand Canyon Rd Yucaipa CA 92399-1799 Office Phone: 909-389-3382.

CRISER, MARSHALL M., lawyer, retired academic administrator; b. Rumson, N.J., Sept. 4, 1928; s. Marshall and Louise (Johnson) C.; m. Paula Porcher, Apr. 27, 1957; children: Marshall III, Edward, Mary, Glenn, Kimberly, Mark. BSBA, U. Fla., 1951, LLB, 1951 (replaced by J.D., 1967). Bar: Fla. 1951. Pvt. practice, Palm Beach, 1953-84; ptnr. Gunster, Yoakley, Criser & Stewart, 1955-84; atty. Palm Beach County Sch. Bd., 1958-64; pres. U. Fla., Gainesville, 1984-89, pres. emeritus, 1989—; shareholder Mahoney, Adams & Criser, Jacksonville, Fla., 1989-97; of counsel McGuire Woods, LLP, Jacksonville, 1998-2000, ret. ptnr., 2000—. Dep. chmn. Rinker Group Ltd., 2003—; chmn. bd. dirs. Rinker Materials, Corp., 1989-2002; mem. pres.'s coun. NCAA, 1986-87; chmn. Installment Land Sales Bd., 1963-64, chmn. Acad. Task Force rev. tort and ins. law, Fla., 1986-88, The Emerald Funds; chmn. bd. trustees Emerald Fund, 1997-98; mem. Scripps Fla. Funding Corp., 2004—, chmn., 2004—. Bd. dirs. Univ. Med. Ctr., Jacksonville, 1989-96, Shands at Jacksonville Hosp., 1999-2002, M.E. Rinker Found., 1998—; bd. dirs. Shands Tchg. Hosp., Gainesville, Fla., pres., 1984-89, bd. dirs., 1996-2001; bd. govs. Good Samaritan Hosp., West Palm Beach, pres., 1979-84; mem. Fla. Bd. Regents, 1965, 71-81, chmn., 1974-77, Bus.-Higher Edn. Forum, 1987-89; trustee Collins Ctr., 1989-99; pres., chmn. Alliance for World Class Edn., Duval County, 1998-2001; chmn. Fed. Crt. Adv. Group Mid. Dist. of Fla., 1991-96; trustee U. Fla., 2001-03, chmn., 2001-03; mem. Fla. Fed. Jud. Nominating Com., 2001-05; mem. Gov.'s Med. Malpractice Task Force, 2002—03. With U.S. Army, 1951-53. Fellow Am. Bar Found.; mem. Fla. Coun. 100 (chmn. 1979-80), ABA (ho. dels. 1968-72), Fla. Bar (gov. 1960-68, pres. 1968-69), Fla. Blue Key, Phi Delta Phi, Sigma Nu. Office: 100 NW 20th St Gainesville FL 32603 Business E-Mail: mcriser@uff.ufl.edu.

CRISHAM, THOMAS MICHAEL, lawyer; b. Chgo., June 7, 1939; s. John and Ellen (Moore) C.; m. Catherine Marie Schaab, Oct. 2, 1965; children: Catherine Marie, Megan, Maura. BBA, Loyola U., 1962, JD cum laude, 1965. Bar: Ill. 1965, U.S. Dist. Ct. (no. dist.) Ill. 1965, U.S. Supreme Ct. 1971, U.S. Ct. Appeals (7th crct.) 1978. Ptnr. Hinshaw & Culbertson, Chgo., 1965-95; sr. ptnr. Quinlan & Crisham, Ltd., Chgo., 1996—2001, Crisham & Kubes, Ltd., Chgo., 2001—. Mem. editl. bd. Ins. Outlook, Colorado Springs, Colo., 1990; pres. Def. Rsch. and Trial Lawyers Inst., Chgo., 1989, chmn. bd., 1990; mem. advisors Expert Evidence Reporter, Colorado Springs, 1990. Contbg. author: Abortion and Social Justice, 1973, Human Life: Our Legacy and Our Challenge, 1975, Architect and Engineer Liability: Claims Against Design Professional, 1987, Prosecuting and Defending Insurance Claims, 1989. Bd. dirs. Wendy Will Case Cancer Rsch. Found., Boys' Hope Scholars. With USMCR, 1959-60. Fellow Am. Coll. Trial Lawyers, Internat. Soc. Barristers; mem. ABA, Am. Bd. Trial Advs. (diplomate), Def. Rsch. Inst. (pres. 1989-90, chair 1990-91), Internat. Assn. Def. Counsel, Ill. Bar Assn., Trial Lawyers Club Chgo. (pres. 1975-76), Soc. Trial Lawyers Ill., Appellate Lawyers Assn., Assn. Def. Trial Lawyers, Am. Inns of Ct., Chgo. Bar Assn. Roman Catholic. Office: Crisham & Kubes Ltd 30 N Lasalle St Ste 2800 Chicago IL 60602-2511 Office Phone: 312-917-8460. E-mail: tcrisham@crishamlaw.com.

CRISMAN, C. BENJAMIN, JR., lawyer; BA, Syracuse U., 1970; JD, Creighton U., 1975. Bar: DC, NY, Nebr. Spl. asst. US atty. Ea. Dist. Va., 1977; trial atty., antitrust divsn. US Dept. Justice, 1975—78; practice leader for antitrust Skadden, Arps, Slate, Meagher & Flom LLP, Washington. Sr. editor Creighton Law Review; contbr. articles to profl. jours. Office: Skadden Arps Slate Meagher & Flom LLP 1440 New York Ave NW Washington DC 20005 Office Phone: 202-371-7330. Office Fax: 202-661-8212.

CRISMAN, MARY FRANCES BORDEN, librarian; b. Tacoma, Nov. 23, 1919; d. Lindon A. and Mary Cecelia (Donnelly) Borden; m. Fredric Lee Crisman, Apr. 12, 1975 (dec. Dec. 1975). BA in History, U. Wash., 1943, BA in Librarianship, 1944. Asst. br. libr. in charge work with children Mottet br. Tacoma Pub. Libr., 1944-45, br. libr., 1945-49, br. libr. Moore br., 1950-55, asst. dir., 1955-70, dir., 1970-74, dir. emeritus, 1975—; mgr. corp. libr. Frank Russell Co., 1985-96, ret., 1997. Chmn. Wash. Cmty. Libr. Coun., 1970-72. Hostess program Your Libr. and You, Sta. KTPS-TV, 1969-71. Mem. Highland Homeowners League, Tacoma, 1980—, incorporating dir. 1980, sec., registered agt., 1980-82; mem. Denham West Condominium Assn., Sun City, Ariz., 1995—, chair by laws com., 1999, sec., 2002-05 Mem. ALA (chmn. mem. com. Wash. 1957-60, mem. nat. libr. week com. 1965, chmn. libr. adminstrn. divsn. nominating com. 1971, mem. ins. for librs. com. 1970-74, vice chmn. libr. adminstrn. divsn. personnel adminstrn. sect. 1972-73, chmn. 1973-74, mem. com. policy implementation 1973-74, mem. libr. orgn. and mgmt. sect. budgeting acctg. and costs com. 1974-75), Am. Libr. Trustee Assn. (legis. com. 1975-78, conf. program com. 1978-80, action devel. com. 1978-80), Pacific N.W. (trustee divsn. nominating com 1976-77), Wash. Libr. Assn. (exec. bd. 1957-59, state exec., dir. Nat. Libr. Week 1965, treas., exec. bd. 1969-71, 71-73), Urban Librs. Coun. (editl. sec. Newsletter 1972-73, exec. com. 1974-75), Ladies Aux. to United Transp. Union (past pres. Tacoma), Friends Tacoma Pub. Libr. (registered agt. 1975-83, sec. 1975-78, pres. 1978-80, bd. dirs. 1980-83), Smithsonian Assocs., Nat. Railway Hist. Soc., U. Wash. Alumni Assn., U. Wash. Sch. Librarianship Alumni Assn. Clubs: Quota Internat. (sec. 1957-58, 1st v.p. 1960-61, pres. 1961-62, treas. 1975-76, pres. 1979-80) (Tacoma). Home: 9054 N 109th Ave Sun City AZ 85351-4676

CRISMOND, LINDA FRY, public relations executive; b. Burbank, Calif., Mar. 1, 1943; d. Billy Chapin and Lois (Harding) Fry; m. Donald Burleigh Crismond, 1965 (dec.). BS, U. Calif.-Santa Barbara, 1964; M.L.S., U. Calif.-Berkeley, 1965. Cert. county libr., Calif., assn. exec. Reference libr., EDP coordinator San Francisco Pub. Library, 1965—72; head acquisition San Francisco Pub. Libr., 1972-74; asst. univ. libr. U. So. Calif., L.A., 1974-80; chief dep. county libr. L.A. County Pub. Libr., L.A., 1980-81, county libr. Downey, 1981-89; exec. dir ALA, Chgo., 1989-92; v.p. public rels. Profl. Media Svc. Corp., Chgo., 1992-98; v.p. pub. rels. Follett Media Distbn., Crystal Lake, Ill., 1999—2003; nat. media cons. BWI, Lexington, Ky., 2003—. Western rep. quality control council Ohio Coll. Libr. Ctr., Columbus, 1977-80; mem. Am. Nat. Standards Inst., N.Y.C., 1978-80; bd. councillors U. So. Calif. Sch. Libr. and Info. Mgmt., 1980-83; adv. bd. mem. UCLA Libr. Sch., 1981-89; chmn. bd. dirs. L.A. County Pub. Libr. Found., 1982-85; mem. OCLC Users Coun., 1988-89; mem. exec. com. L.A. County Mgmt. Coun., 1986-88, pres., 1988; cons. libr. Trinity Coll., 1995-99; prin. The Charleston Group, Inc., 1996—. Author: Directory of San Francisco Bay Area, 1968, Against All Odds, 1994; editor: Urban Librs. Coun. Exch., 1994—, The Charleston Report, 1996-99. Bd. dirs. So. Meth. U. Libr., 1992-98. Named Staff Mem. of Year San Francisco Pub. Libr., 1968 Mem. ALA, Calif. Libr. Assn. (council 1980-82), Calif. County Libr. Assn. (pres. 1984), L.A. County Mgmt. Assn. (pres. 1988). Home: 303 Mariner Dr Tarpon Springs FL 34689-5840

CRISP, FRED, retired publishing executive; m. Betty, Sept. 2, 1956; children: Michele Crisp Narron, Fred Durham III. Student, Mars Hill Coll., N.C.; BA, U. N.C. Advtsg. salesman Charlotte (N.C.) Observer, 1957-59, Virginian Pilot and Ledger Star, Norfolk, Va., 1959-68; advtsg. dir. The No. Va. Sun, Arlington, 1968-69; retail advtsg. mgr. The News and Observer Publ. Co., Raleigh, N.C., 1969-76, advtsg. dir., 1976-85, dir. sales, mktg., 1985-87, v.p. sales, mktg., 1987-90, v.p. gen. mgr., 1990-96, assoc. publ., 1996, pres., publ., 1997-2000. Mem. First Presbyn. Ch. Raleigh; bd. dirs. N.C. Citizens for Bus. and Industry, United Way, Downtown Raleigh Alliance; past bd. dirs. Theatre in the Park, Wake County Boys' Club; past vice chmn. adv. bd. Salvation Army; mem. presdl. bd. advisors Mars Hill Coll.; bd. dirs. bd. vis. journalism and mass comm. U. N.C., v.p. Sch. Journalism and Mass Com. Found.; bd. trustees Peace Coll.; mem. Peace Coll. Found. Bd. Recipient Silver Medal awrd Am. Advtsg. Fedn., 1979; inducted to N.C. Advtsg. Hall of Fame, 1991. Mem. Am. Advtsg. Fedn. (past gov. N.C.), Internat. Newspaper Advtsg. and Mktg. Execs. (hon. life, past pres.), Mid-Atlantic Newspaper Advtsg. and Mktg. Execs. (hon. life), N.C. Retail Merchant Assn. (bd. advisors), N.C. Press Assn. (past pres.), Newspaper Assn. Am. (past mem. exec. bd.), Distributive Edn. Clubs Am. (hon. life), Mid-Atlantic Newspaper Advtsg. and Mktg. Execs. (past pres.), Triangle Advtsg. Fedn. (past pres.), Raleigh Sales and Mktg. Execs., Inc. (past bd. dirs.). Avocation: golf. Office: McClatchy Newspapers 215 S McDowell St PO Box 191 Raleigh NC 27602-9150

CRISP, SANDRA SUE, procurement analyst; b. Jefferson City, Sept. 13, 1941; d. William Frederick and Marguerite Walter (Wilson) Meyer; m. Samuel Henry White, Sept. 20, 1965 (div. Feb. 1982); 1 child, Janelle Lynn; m. Richard Leslie Crisp, Apr. 26, 1982. BSBA, Lincoln U., 1963; MS in Mgmt., Naval Postgrad. Sch., 1996. Missile components buyer McDonnell/Douglas Corp., St. Louis, 1977-78; contract specialist U.S. Army Aviation R&D Command, St. Louis, 1978-80; contracting officer U.S. Army Aviation Materiel Command, St. Louis, 1980-82; chief facilities and materials br. U.S. Army-Europe, Frankfort, Germany, 1982-83, chief host nations br., 1983-85; spl. tech. asst. to dir. comml. activities Asst. Sec. of Army for Installations, Logistics & Environ., Arlington, Va., 1985-87; spl. tech. asst. to U.S. Army Competition Adv. Gen. Asst. Sec. of Army for Rsch., Devel. and Acquisition, Arlington, 1987-92; dep. chief of staff for procurement, prin. asst. contracting U.S. Army Depot Sys. Command, Chambersberg, Pa., 1992-95; chief ammunition procurement divsn. U.S. Army Indsl. Ops. Command, Rock Island, Ill., 1995-98; chief acquisitions policy divsn. U.S. Army Ops. Support Command, Rock Island, Ill., 1999—2001, command ombudsman, competition advocate, 2002—04. Mem. Nat. Contract Mgmt. Assn. (pres. Monterey chpt. 1995-96, edn. chair Quad City chpt. 1997-99), Nat. Def. Indsl. Assn. (bd. dirs. 1996—), U.S. Army Acquisition Corp. (sect. Army award for Professionalism in Contracting 1998), Women in Def. (founder, 1st pres. Ill.-Iowa chpt. 2001—). Avocations: volksmarching, needlecrafts, gardening, reading, golf. Home: 209 Ashbrook Dr Enterprise AL 36330 E-mail: rlsscrisp@centurytel.net.

CRISPIN, ANDRE ARTHUR, diversified financial services company executive; b. Brussels, Aug. 23, 1923; came to U.S., 1947; naturalized Am. citizen; m. Sylvia Clevenger; 5 children. Ed., U. Louvain, Belgium, 1943. V.p. Am. Supply and Equipment Co., Houston, 1947-48; chmn. Crispin Co., Houston, 1949—; hon. consul-gen. Belgium; ret. hon. consul-gen. Past chmn. bd. trustees so. region Inst. Internat. Edn.; mem. Citizens Environ. Coalition; past pres. Music Guild Houston; past chmn. bd. trustees Awty Internat. Sch. With Belgian Army, 1940, 44-46; chmn. emeritus Houston Counsular Ball, mem. Senate of Internat. Jr. C. of C. Decorated officier Ordre de Leopold II, Civic Cross 1st class, officier Ordre de Leopold ler (Belgium); chevalier Legion d'Honneur (France), Commdr.'s Cross Order of the Crown (Belgium), 1997; named one of 5 Outstanding Young Texans, 1953; recipient Houston Internat. Svc. award, 1986, medal of City of Bordeaux, Disting. Counselor award Pres. George H. Bush. Mem. Nat. Assn. Steel Pipe Distbrs. (past pres., bd. dirs.), Academie Internationale du Vin, Alliance Française de Houston (past pres., dir., exec. com.), Commanderie de Bordeaux d'Amerique (grand maitre emeritus, gov.), Commanderie de Bordeaux du Texas à Houston (founder, past maitre, commandeur), Commanderie du Bontemps, de Medoc et de Graves (France, commandeur d'honneur), German Wine Soc., Prodhomme, Jurade de St. Emilion Stylobate, Piliers Chablisiens, Compagnon de Loupiac, Echevin, Lussac Puisseguin St. Emilion, Lalande de Pomerol, Hospitaliers de Pomerol, Downtown Houston Assn., Belgian-Am. C. of C. (past bd. dirs.), French-Am. C. of C. (past pres. Houston chpt., dir.), Houston C. of C. (now named Greater Houston Partnership, bd. dirs. world trade divsn., internat. bus. com., past chmn.), Jr. C. of C. (internat. senator 2001), World Trade Assn. (past pres., dir.), Petroleum Club of Houston (past dir., past 1st v.p.). Home: One Crestwood Dr Houston TX 77007 Office: Crispin Co 2009 Lubbock St Houston TX 77007-7621 Office Phone: 713-224-8000. E-mail: andrecris@crispinco.com.

CRISPIN, PATRICIA LYNNETTE, social worker; b. Akron, Ohio, Apr. 29, 1969; d. Eddie Mae Robinson. BA, BA, Cleve. State U., Cleveland, OH, 1997; Masters Edn., Cleve. State Univeristy, Cleveland, OH, 2000. Intern East Cleve. Straight Talk, Cleveland, Ohio, 1996—96; instr. Urban League Cleve., Cleveland, Ohio, 1997—98, adminstrv. asst., 1997—98; spl. student asst. dean Cleve. State U. Dept. Student Life, Cleveland, Ohio, 1997—98; retention specialist Mt. Sinai Employment Moblzn., Cleveland, Ohio, 2000—01; program dir. Mt. Sinai Project Synergy, Cleveland, Ohio, 2001—01; staff asst. NASA, Cleveland, Ohio, 2001—01, SEMAA, Cleveland, Ohio, 2001—01, Tri-C, Cleveland, Ohio, 2001—01; americorp vista North East Ohio Coalition for the Homeless, Cleveland, Ohio, 2002—. Vol. coord. Cleve. State U. Black Studies Dept., Cleveland, Ohio, 1999—99, Rock N' Roll Hall of Fame, Cleveland, Ohio, 1999—99; event coord. Cleve. State U. Black Studies Dept., Cleveland, Ohio, 2000—01; notary pub. Nat. Assn. Notary Publics, Cleveland, Ohio, 2000—. Mem., sec., treas. Cleve. State U. NAACP Chpt., Cleveland, Ohio, 1989—97; advisor Cleve. State U. NAACP, Cleveland, Ohio, 1998—2001. Recipient Coloster B. Currant award, Nat. Hdqs. NAACP, 1993; scholar James Doodman scholarship, Cleve. State U., 1995, scholarship, Zeta Phi Beta Sorority Inc., 1999. Mem.: Cleve. State U. NAACP (advisor 1998—2001), Nat. Assn. Student Pers. Administrators, Order Ea. Star, Zeta Phi Beta Sorority Inc. (advisor 1998—2001, ednl. 2000). Christian. Avocations: writing, poetry, reading, entertainment business, planning events. Office: Ultimate Connexions PO Box 6792 Cleveland OH 44101 Personal E-mail: plcrispine@hotmail.com.

CRISS, CECIL M., chemistry professor; b. Wheeling, W.Va., Apr. 22, 1934; s. Cecil M. and Anna (Reece) C.; m. Laura Hopkins, Aug. 18, 1958; children: Cecil M. III, Laura Anna. AB, Kenyon Coll., 1956; PhD, Purdue U., 1961. Asst. prof. U. Vt., Burlington, 1961—65, U. Miami, Coral Gables, Fla., 1965—69, assoc. prof., 1970—75, prof., 1976—, chmn. dept., 1984—91, interim chmn. dept., 2002—04. Vis. scientist U. Lund, Sweden, 1977-78; vis. prof. Calif. State Coll., San Diego, 1978; program officer NSF, Washington, 1982-83; vis. scholar U. Del., 1992. Recipient Fla. award Fla. Sect. Am. Chem. Soc. Mem. Am. Chem Soc., Sigma Xi, Phi Lambda Upsilon. Episcopalian. Home: 4910 San Amaro Dr Coral Gables FL 33146-1632 Office: Dept Chemistry U Miami Coral Gables FL 33124 Office Phone: 305-284-6614. Business E-Mail: ccriss@umiami.ir.miami.edu.

CRISSMAN, JOHN D., former dean, pathologist; b. Detroit, Feb. 3, 1939; children: John, Allison. SBME, MIT, 1961; MD, Western Res. U., 1966. Physician U. Cin., 1974-81, Wayne State U., Detroit, 1981-87, Henry Ford Hosp., Detroit, 1987-90; prof., chmn. dept. pathology Wayne State U., Detroit, 1990—99; interim dean Wayne St. Univ. Sch. of Med., 1999—2000, dean, 2000—04. Chief pathologist Detroit Med. Ctr. Hosps., 1990—2000. Capt. USAF, 1968—70.

CRISSMAN, KATHERINE KOLB, counseling administrator; b. Jamestown, N.Y., Sept. 8, 1979; d. Harry Herb, Jr. and Stephanie Viola (Stowell) Kolb; m. Jason Earl Crissman, Aug. 11, 2001. BA, Messiah Coll., Grantham, Pa., 1997—2001; MEd, Ind. U. Pa., 2001—02, Ednl. Specialist Cert. in Sch. Psychology, 2002—04. Cert. sch. psychologist NASP, 2004, Commonwealth of Pa., 2004, Dept. Pub. Instrn. N.C., 2004. Sch. psychology intern Greater Latrobe Sch. Dist., Pa., 2003—04; sch. psychologist Gaston County Sch. Dist., Gastonia, NC, 2004—. Assessment adminstr. PsychCorp, San Antonio, 2004—. Vol. youth advisor Locust Grove Ch. of the Brethren, Johnstown, Pa., 2001—04; vol. group leader, Friday Night Kids New Day Corp., Johnstown, Pa., 2003—04. Mem.: NASP, Phi Kappa Phi. Office: Gaston County Sch Dist 730 W Garrison Blvd Gastonia NC 28052

CRIST, CHARLES (CHARLIE CRIST), state attorney general; b. Altoona, Pa., July 24, 1956; Student, Wake Forest U., 1974-76; BS in Govt., minor in edn., Fla. State U., 1978; JD, Samford U., 1981. Mem. Fla. State Senate, Tallahassee, 1992—98; dep. sec. Fla. Dept. Bus. and Profl. Regulation, 1999—2000; atty. gen. State of Fla., 2003—. Mem. Subcom. D. Criminal Justice Ways and Means Com., 1996-98, Judiciary Com., 1996-98, Govtl. Reform and Oversight Com., 1996-98, Criminal Justice Com., 1996-98; chmn. Exec. Bus., Ethics and Elections Com., 1996-98; former state dir. U.S. Sen. Connie Mack; chmn. anti-trust adv. com. Sen. Connie Mack's Baseball Anti-Trust Adv. Com.; mem. Sen. Connie Mack's Fed. Jud. Adv. Com.; mem. ethics com. Fla. Bar. Mem. Pinellas County Rep. Exec. Com., Area Agy. on Bay Mgmt.; mem. adminstrv. bd. First United Meth. Ch.; mem. Booster Fla. State U.; bd. dirs. Found. for Fla.'s Future, Op. PAR, Police Athletic League; mem. adv. com. Tampa Bay MDA. Recipient Phil Piton award for svc. Major League Baseball, Leadership St. Petersburg, Roll Call award Fla. C. of C., 1993, PACE award, 1993, Legis. award Pinellas Sch. Adminstrs., 1993, Fla. Assn. Sch. Adminstrs., 1993, Fla. Sheriffs Assn., 1994, 96, Govt. award Urban League, 1995, Senatorial Leadership award Fla. Prosecuting Attys. Assn., 1995, Legis. Conservation award Fla. Conservation Assn., 1996, Disting. Legislator award Fla. Police Benevolent Assn., 1996; named Conservationist Legislator of Yr. Fla. Wildlife Fedn., 1995, Legislator of Yr. Police Benevolent Assn., 1995, Hon. Sheriff, 1995. Fellow Am. Swiss Assn.; mem. ABA, Am. Lung Assn. (mem. pres.'s coun. Pinellas County), Fla. Conservation Assn., St. Petersburg C. of C., Pinellas Pk. C. of C., Hillsborough Bar Assn., St. Petersburg Bar Assn., Rep. Nat. Lawyers Assn. (bd.

govs.), Suncoasters Civic Club, Rotary, Suncoast Tiger Bay Club (bd. dirs., True Grit award). Republican. Methodist. Avocations: water-skiing, reading, jogging. Office: Office of Atty Gen State of Fla The Capitol PL-01 Tallahassee FL 32399-1050

CRIST, CHRISTINE MYERS, consulting executive; b. Harrisburg, Pa., Feb. 5, 1924; d. John Eyster and Eunice Horton (Ingham) Myers; m. Robert Grant Crist, June 25, 1949; children: Catherine Ingham Crist Marcson, Jessica Rogers Crist, Robert Jeffrey Myers Crist. BA, Dickinson Coll., 1946. Reporter The Patriot, Harrisburg, Pa., 1946-49; editor West Shore Times, Lemoyne, Pa., 1964-65; adminstr. arts in edn. Pa. Dept. Edn., Harrisburg, 1974-77, dir. leadership in arts edn., 1977-79; press sec. gov.'s office Pa. Commn. for Women, Harrisburg, 1980-83, dir. Gov.'s Commn. for Women, 1983-87; exec. dir. com. for women Evang. Luth. Ch. in Am., Chgo., 1987-90; ptnr. Crist and Crist, Cons., Camp Hill, Pa., 1990—. Mem. State Employees Retirement Bd., 1986-88; state coord. We the People Edn. Program. Editor: Song As A Measure of Man, 1975 (excellent pub. 1975). Mem. Camp Hill (Pa.) Sch. Bd., 1967-73, Capital Area Intermediate Bd., Lemoyne, Pa., 1970-73; pres. Camp Hill (Pa.) Civic Club, 1970-72, women's orgn. Trinity Lutheran Ch., 1999; chair Ch. in Society, Lower Susquehanna Synod, Evang. Lutheran Ch. in Am.; mem. coun. Trinity Congregation, 1991-94; mem. Harrisburg Choral Soc., Dickinson Alumni Coun., 1992—; bd. dirs. Women's Polit. Network Pa., Camp Hill Cmty. Found., 1996—; mem. candidacy bd. Luth. Ch., 1992—; Pa. bd. Common Cause, 1997—; mem. Envision Capital Region Task Force, 2000-02; mem. Nat. Assn. Comms. for Women, 1987. Recipient Women in Comms. Freedom of Info. award, 1982, Great Commicators award, 1985, Pa. Women's History award, Pa. Com. for Women, 2003, Women Inventing Future award, Cumberland County, 2003. Mem. Monday Club, Cumberland County Fedn. Women's Clubs (pres. 1996—), Coll. Club Harrisburg (pres. 2004—). Lutheran. Home and Office: Crist and Crist 1915 Walnut St Camp Hill PA 17011-3854 Personal E-mail: camcrist@paonline.com.

CRIST, JUDITH, film and drama critic; b. N.Y.C., May 22, 1922; d. Solomon and Helen (Schoenberg) Klein; m. William B. Crist, July 3, 1947 (dec. Apr. 1993); 1 son, Steven Gordon. AB, Hunter Coll., 1941; tchg. fellow, State Coll. Wash., 1942-43; MSc in Journalism, Columbia, 1945; DHL (hon.), SUNY, New Paltz, 1994. Civilian instr. 3081st Army AFB Unit, 1943-44; reporter N.Y. Herald Tribune, 1945-60, editor arts, 1960-63, assoc. theater critic, 1957-63, film critic, 1963-66; film, theater critic NBC-TV Today Show, 1963-73; film critic World Jour. Tribune, 1966-67; critic-at-large Ladies Home Jour., 1966-67; contbg. editor and film critic TV Guide, 1966-88; founding film critic N.Y. mag., 1968-75; film critic The Washingtonian, 1970-72, Palm Springs Life, 1971-75; contbg. editor, film critic Saturday Rev., 1975-77, 80-84, N.Y. Post, 1977-78, MD/Mrs., 1977—, 50 Plus, 1978-83, L'Officiel/USA, 1979-80; arts critic Sta. WWOR-TV, 1981-87; critical columnist for Coming Attractions, 1985-93; cons. editor Hollywood Mag., 1985-93; contbg. editor Columbia Mag., 1993-95. Instr. journalism Hunter Coll., 1947, Sarah Lawrence Coll., 1958-59; assoc. journalism Columbia Grad. Sch. Journalism, 1958-62, lectr. journalism, 1962-64, adj. prof., 1964—. Author: The Private Eye, The Cowboy and the Very Naked Girl, 1968, Judith Crist's TV Guide to the Movies, 1974, Take 22: Moviemakers on Moviemaking, 1984, rev. edit., 1991; contbr. articles to nat. mags. Trustee Anne O'Hare McCormick Scholarship Fund. Named to 50th Anniversary Honors List, Columbia Grad. Sch. Journalism, 1963, Hunter Alumni Hall of Fame, Hunter Coll., 1973; recipient Page One award, N.Y. Newspaper Guild, 1955, George Polk award, 1950, Newswomen's Club of N.Y. award, 1955, 1959, 1963, 1965, 1967, Edn. Writers Assn. award, 1952, Alumni award, Columbia Grad. Sch. Journalism, 1961, Centennial Pres.'s medal, Hunter Coll., 1970, Hall of Fame award for outstanding profl. achievement, 2003, Grad. Sch. Journalism's Faculty and Alumni award, Columbia U., 1998, Univ. Alumni Fedn. medal for conspicuous svc., 2003. Mem.: Soc. of the Silurians, Columbia Journalism Alumni Exec. Com. (pres. 1967—70), Sigma Tau Delta. Office: 180 Riverside Dr New York NY 10024-1048 *Care about people-not things.*

CRIST, PAUL GRANT, lawyer; b. Denver, Sept. 9, 1949; s. Max Warren and Marjorie Raymond (Catland) C.; m. Christine Faye Clements, June 4, 1972; children: Susan Christine, Benjamin Warren, John Willis. BA, U. Nebr., 1971; JD cum laude, NYU, 1974. Bar: Ohio 1974, U.S. Ct. Mil. Appeals 1975, Calif. 1976, U.S. Dist. Ct. (no. dist.) Ohio 1979, U.S. Ct. Appeals (6th cir.) 1982, U.S. Dist. Ct. (no., ea., so. and ctrl. dists.) Calif. 2003, U.S. Ct. Appeals (9th cir.) 2003. Assoc. Jones, Day, Reavis & Pogue, Cleve., 1974, 78-83, ptnr., 1984—. Rsch. editor NYU Law Rev., 1972-74. Capt. JAGC, USAF, 1974-78. Decorated Meritorious Svc. medal. Fellow Am. Coll. Trial Lawyers; mem. State Bar Calif., Order of Coif. Democrat. Presbyterian. Office: Jones Day North Point 901 Lakeside Ave Cleveland OH 44114 Office Phone: 216-586-3939. Business E-Mail: pgcrist@jonesday.com.

CRIST, WILLIAM MILES, dean, pediatrician, educator; b. Florence, S.C., July 21, 1943; s. Harry Brogan and Rosemary (Reid) C.; m. Helen Lucille Valle, June 5, 1971; 1 child, Brian. BA cum laude, Cen. Meth. Coll., 1965; MD, U. Mo., 1969. Intern in pediatrics Mott Children's Hosp., Ann Arbor, Mich., 1969-70; resident fellow in pediatrics and pediatric hematology St. Louis Children's Hosp., 1971-72; trainee Nat. Cancer Inst. Wash. U. Sch. Medicine, St. Louis, 1974-75; asst. prof. pediatrics U. Ala., Birmingham, 1975-78; assoc. scientist Comprehensive Cancer Ctr. U. Ala., Birmingham, 1975-78; acting dir., then dir. hematology/oncology Children's Hosp. U. Ala., Birmingham, 1976-85; prof. pediatrics, dir. pediatrics, hematology/oncology U. Tenn., Memphis, 1985—2000; chmn. dept. hematology/oncology St. Jude Children's Rsch. Hosp., Memphis, 1985—94, dep. dir., 1994—97; chair dept. pediats. and adolescent medicine Mayo Clinic, Rochester, 1997—2000; dean U. of Missouri-Columbia Sch. of Med., 2000—. Mem. Children's Oncology Group, 1976—. Maj. USAF, 1972-74. Mem. Am. Soc. Hematology, Sigma Epsilon Pi, Omicron Delta Kappa. Office: U Missouri Columbia Sch Med One Hospital Dr Columbia MO 65212

CRISTE, MIRLA, theater educator, director, choreographer; b. Davao City, Mindanao, Philippines, July 24, 1962; d. Federico Ines and Ruby Leah Agnir. MFA, U. Calif., Irvine, 1998. Vis. asst. prof. Oberlin Coll., Ohio, 2000—02, Hamilton Coll., Clinton, NY, 2003—04; grad. faculty, Dept. Theatre and Film Studies U. Georgia, Athens, Ga., 2004—. Actor: (original broadway cast) Miss Saigon. Mem.: SAG, Am. Fedn. of TV and Radio Artists, Actors Equity Assn., Am. Mensa. Democrat. Mem. United Ch. Of Christ. Avocations: concert dance, music composition, visual arts, writing, travel. Office: U of Georgia Dept of Drama and Theatre Athens GA 30602 Office Phone: 800-784-1431.

CRISTELLA, ARLEEN KARIMA, artist, writer, consultant; b. Phila., Dec. 20, 1941; d. Michael Amerigo and Helen Peter (Azar) C. Student, Pa. State U., 1960-61; student, Phila. Coll. Textiles & Sci., 1962-65, U. Okla., 1967-69; Student, Marywood Coll., 1977-78; BS in Theology, Calvary Bible Inst., 1985, PhD in Psychology, 1987. Represented in permanent Annenberg collection; also collections of family of Robert E. Lee, Mrs. Anwar Sadat, Omar Sharif, Sophia Loren. Activist anti-poverty, civil rights, human rights and peace movements, 1956-93; originator Am. Expressionism Art Movement, 1989-93; life mem. Deborah Hosp. Found.; advisor White House Commn. on Human Rights, 1996-98, White House Commn. on Civil Rights, 1997-98; mem. Ocean County (N.J.) Human Rels. Commn., So. Ocean County Hosp. Found., Asian-Pacific Employment Program, Assn. Improvement of Minorities, World Affairs Coun. Phila.; Dem. candidate 3d dist. NJ US Congress, 1998. Mem. AAUW, UDC (assoc.), Internat. Platform Assn.

CRISTESCU, NICOLAIE DAN, engineering educator; b. Chelmenti, Romania, Feb. 17, 1929; married (dec.); 1 child. Diplomat, Bucharest U., Romania, 1951, docent, 1967; PhD, Romanian Acad., 1955. Asst. prof. U. Bucharest, Romania, 1951-55, lectr., 1955-57, assoc. prof., 1957-66, prof., 1966-92, dept. chmn., 1982-90, pres., 1990-92; vis. grad. rsch. prof. U. Fla., 1970-76, grad. rsch. prof. dept. aerospace engring. mechanics and engring. sci. Gainesville, 1992—. Vis. prof. Johns Hopkins U., Balt., 1968-69, Drexel U., Phila., 1969; lectr. in field. Author: Dynamic Problems in Theory of Plasticity, 1958, The Mechanics of Extensible Strings, 1964, Dynamic Plasticity, 1967, 70 (in Japanese), Introduction to Rate-Dependent Plasticity (A Dynamic Approach), 1971, Rock Mechanics, 1983, 2d edit., 1984, supplemental 1988, Mechanics of Composite Materials, 1983, Rock Rheology, 1989, Rock Mechanics-Rheology Aspects, 1990, Rock Viscoplasticity, 1992, Viscoplasticity of Geomaterials, 1994, (with I. Suliciu) Viscoplasticity, 1976, 82, (with S. Cleja-Tigolu) Theory of Plasticity with Application to Metal Working, 1985, (with U. Hunsche) Time Effects in Rock Mechanics, 1998, (with E.M. Craciun and E. Soos) Mechanics of Elastic Composites, 2004; contbr. articles to profl. jours.; sr. editor: Internat. Jour. Plasticity; mem. editl. bd. Internat. Jour. Mechanical Sci., Mechanics Rsch. Comm., Mechanics of Cohesive-Frictional Materials and Structures, others. Fellow Romanian Acad., Acad. Europaea; mem. ASME (Arpad L. Nadai award 1995), Soc. Scholars, Internat. Soc. Interaction of Mechanics and Maths. (founder), Am. Rock Mechanics Assn. (founder), Am. Acad. Mechanics, Soc. Exptl. Stress Analysis, Group Français de Rheology, Internat. Assn. Computer Methods and Advances in Geomechanics, Internat. Soc. Rock Mechanics, Tau Beta Pi, Sigma Xi. Achievements include research in mechanics of solid deformable bodies, theory of plasticity, rheology, rock and soil mechanics, mechanics of powder-like materials. Office: U Fla 231 Aerospace Bldg PO Box 116250 Gainesville FL 32611-6250 Office Fax: 352-392-7303. Business E-Mail: cristesc@ufl.edu.

CRISTINI, VITTORIO, education educator, researcher; arrived in US, 1995; m. Jennifer Cristini; 1 child, Giovanni. Laurea in nuclear engring. summa cum laude, La Sapienza, Rome, 1994; MS, Yale U., 1996, MPh, 1998, PhD in Chem. Engring., 2000. Postdoctoral assoc. chem. engring. and materials sci. U. Minn., Mpls., 2000—02, postdoctoral assoc. Inst. Math. and its Applications, 2001—02, vis. asst. prof. math., 2002; asst. prof. biomed. engring. U. Calif., Irvine, 2002—, asst. prof. math., 2003—; pres., co-founder Advanced Biomed. Techs., LLC, 2004—. Vis. asst. prof. chem. engring. U. Naples, Italy, 2005; cons. ORQIS Med., Lake Forest, Calif., 2004—. Contbr. articles to profl. jours. Recipient Andreas Acrivos Dissertation Award in Fluid Dynamics, Americal Phys. Soc., 2000; grantee, NSF, 2003—05; rsch. scholar, Minn. Supercomputing Inst., U. Minn., 2001. Achievements include development of First computer simulators of cancer progression and response to therapy. Office Phone: 949-824-9132. Business E-Mail: cristini@math.uci.edu.

CRISTOL, A. JAY, federal judge; b. Fountain Hill, Pa., Feb. 25, 1929; s. Samuel and Mae (Stein) C.; m. Eleanor Rubin; children: Stephen Michael, David Alan. BA, U. Miami, 1958, LLB, 1959, PhD, 1997. Bar: Fla. 1959. Spl. asst. to Atty. Gen. of Fla., Tallahassee, 1959-65; sr. ptnr. Cristol, Mishan, Sloto, Miami, 1959-85; judge U.S. Bankruptcy Ct., Miami, 1985-93, chief judge, 1994-99, trustee Miami, 1982-84, chief judge emeritus, 1999—. Adj. prof. U. Miami Law Sch.; bd. govs. 11th cir. Nat. Conf. Bankruptcy Judges; bankruptcy rules adv. com. Jud. Conf. of U.S., 1995-2001; bankruptcy com. U.S. Ct. Appeals (11th cir.), 1996-2002; tchr. bankruptcy law to judges in Czech Republic, Slovenia, Thailand, Russia, India, Malaysia, Hong Kong, South Africa. Bd. trustees U. Miami, 1988-90, Coral Gables; bd. dirs. ARC, Miami, 1989—, Wings Over Miami Aviation Mus., 2001—. Capt. USNR, 1951-89. Fellow Am. Coll. Bankruptcy; mem. ABA, Am. Bankruptcy Inst., Nat. Conf. Bankruptcy Judges, Bankruptcy Bar Assn. (so. dist. of Fla.), Fla. Bar Assn., Dade County Bar Assn. Avocations: water-skiing, windsurfing, flying, reading. Office: US Bankruptcy Ct 1412 Fed Bldg 51 SW 1st Ave Miami FL 33130-1669 Office Phone: 305-714-1770.

CRISTOL, STANLEY JEROME, chemistry professor; b. Chgo., June 14, 1916; s. Myer J. and Lillian (Young) C.; m. Barbara Wright Swingle, June 1957; children: Marjorie Jo, Jeffrey Tod, Kurt W. Swingle, Sharon S. Metcalf, Larry M. Swingle. BS, Northwestern U., 1937; MA, UCLA, 1939, PhD, 1943. Rsch. chemist Std. Oil Co., Calif., 1938-41; rsch. fellow U. Ill., 1943-44; rsch. chemist U.S. Dept. Agr., 1944-46; asst. prof., then assoc. prof. U. Colo., 1946-55, prof., 1955—, Joseph Sewall Disting. prof., 1979—, chmn. dept. chemistry, 1960-62, grad. dean, 1980-81. Vis. prof. Stanford U., summer 1961, U. Geneva, 1975, U. Lausanne, Switzerland, 1981; with OSRD, 1944-46; adv. panels NSF, 1957-63, 69-73, NIH, 1969-72 Author: (with L.O. Smith, Jr.) Organic Chemistry, 1966; editorial bd., Chem. Revs., 1957-59, Jour. Organic Chemistry, 1964-68; contbr. rsch. articles to sci. jours. Guggenheim fellow, 1955-56, 81, 82; recipient James Flack Norris award in phys.-organic chemistry, 1972, Alumni Merit award Northwestern U., 1987. Fellow AAAS (councilor 1986-92); mem. NAS, AAUP, Am. Chem. Soc. (chmn. organic chemistry div. 1961-62, adv. bd. petroleum rsch. fund 1963-66, coun. policy com. 1968-73), Colo.-Wyo. Acad. Sci., Royal Soc. Chemistry, Phi Beta Kappa, Sigma Xi, Phi Lambda Upsilon. Home: 2918 3d St Boulder CO 80304-3041 Office: U Colo Dept Chemistry-Biochemistry Cb 215 Boulder CO 80309-0215 E-mail: stanley.cristol@durango.net.

CRISWELL, ELEANOR CAMP, psychologist; b. Norfolk, Va., May 12, 1938; d. Norman Harold Camp and Eleanor (Talman) David; m. Thomas L. Hanna. BA, U. Ky., 1961, MA, 1962; EdD, U. Fla., 1969. Asst. prof. edn. Calif. State Coll., Hayward, 1969; prof. psychology, former chair Calif. State U., Sonoma, 1969—. Faculty adviser Humanistic Psychology Inst., San Francisco, 1970-77; dir. Novato Inst. Somatic Rsch. and Tng.; editor Somatics jour.; cons. Venturi, Inc., Autogenic Sys., Inc.; clin. dir. Biotherapeutics, Kentfield Med. Hosp., 1985-90; founder Humanistic Psychology Inst. (now Saybrook Grad. Sch.), 1970. Author: How Yoga Works, 1987, Biofeedback and Somatics, 1995; co-editor: Biofeedback and Family Practice Medicine, 1983; patentee optokinetic perceptual learning device. Mem. APA (past pres. divsn. 32), Biofeedback Soc. Calif. (past pres.), Assn. for Humanistic Psychology (past pres.), Somatic Soc. (pres.), Equine Hanna Somatics (founder), Internat. Assn. Yoga Therapists (sec./treas.). Office: Novato Inst 1516 Grant Ave #212 Novato CA 94945 Office Phone: 415-897-0336. Business E-Mail: ecriswel@ix.netcom.com.

CRISWELL, STEPHEN, astronomer; Program mgr. Fred Lawrence Whipple Obs., Amada, Ariz. Project mgr. Very Energetic Radiation Imaging Telescope Array Sys. (VERITAS), a collaboration which pioneered the Imaging Atmospheric Cherenkov Technique for the detection of very high energy (VHE) gamma rays. Office: Fred Lawrence Whipple Obs PO Box 6369 Amado AZ 85645-6369 E-mail: scriswell@cfa.harvard.edu.

CRITCHETT, HUGH ADAMS, minister; b. Holister, Mich., Jan. 4, 1914; s. Carl and Anna Eliza (Coffin) C.; m. Edith Elizabeth Hoppner, Nov. 10, 1935; children: Herbert Adams, Elizabeth Critchett DeBerry. AB, Nebr. Wesleyan U., 1937; ThM, Iliff Sch. Theology, Denver. Ordained deacon, 1940, ordained elder, 1942, The Meth. Ch. Pastor Meth. Epis. Ch., Nemaha, Nebr., 1935-36, Palmyra, Nebr., 1936-37, Kowa County Parish/The Meth. Ch., Eads, Colo., 1938-42, The Meth. Ch., Yuma, Colo., 1942-45, Monte Vista, Colo., 1946-52, Montclair, Denver, 1952-61, dist. supt. Pueblo, Colo., 1961-67, pastor Westminster, Colo., 1967-71, First United Meth. Ch., Pueblo, 1971-76, Brighton (Colo.) United Meth. Ch., 1976-79, Beulah (Colo.) United Meth. Ch., 1981-92. Author: (book) His Final Days, 1995. Mem. Masons, Scottish Rite, Kiwanis. Home: 100 San Carlos Rd Apt 230 Pueblo CO 81005-2654

CRITCHLOW, CHARLES HOWARD, lawyer; b. Morristown, NJ, Nov. 23, 1950; s. George F. and Florence Critchlow; m. Mary Ellen Donnelly (dec.); children: Katharine F., Mary E.G. BA, Yale U., 1972; JD, Columbia U., 1975. Bar: N.Y. 1976, U.S. Dist. Ct. (so. and ea. dists.) N.Y. 1976, U.S. Ct. Appeals (2d cir.) 1982, U.S. Ct. Appeals (3d and 10th cirs.) 1991, U.S. Supreme Ct. 1993, U.S. Ct. Appeals (5th cir.) 1994, U.S. Ct. Appeals (4th cir.) 1995, U.S. Ct. Internat. Trade 1996, U.S. Ct. Appeals (Fed. Cir.) 1996. Assoc. Lord, Day & Lord, N.Y.C., 1975-85, ptnr., 1985-86, Coudert Bros. LLP, N.Y.C., 1986—. Contbr. to Antitrust Law Developments; contbr. articles to profl. jours. Active Yale Alumni Fund; mem. Yale Alumni Schs. Com. Mem.: ABA. Office: Coudert Bros LLP 1114 Avenue of the Americas New York NY 10036-7703 Office Phone: 212-626-4496. Business E-Mail: critchlowc@coudert.com.

CRITCHLOW, DONALD THOMAS, history professor; b. Pasadena, Calif., May 18, 1948; s. Patrick B. Critchlow and Anne Dawson Marchinton; m. Patricia Elizabeth Powers Feb. 18, 1978; children: Angieszka A., Magdalena D. BA magna cum laude, San Francisco State U., 1970; MA, U. Calif., Berkeley, 1972, PhD, 1978. Asst. prof. North Central Coll., Naperville, Ill., 1978-81, U. Dayton, Ohio, 1981-83; assoc. prof. Notre Dame U., South Bend, Ind., 1983-91; prof., dept. chair St. Louis U., Mo., 1991—, pres. Inst. for Polit. History, 1999—. Grad. dir. Phi Alph Theta, U. Dayton, U. Notre Dame; mem. Ill. steering com. OAH Conf. on the Promotion of History, Wesleyan U., Bloomington, Ill., 1980; program co-dir. Conf on Evolution of Fed. Social Policy, U. Notre Dame, South Bend, Ind.; guest scholar The Brookings Instn. 1976-77, Woodrow Wilson Internat. Ctr. Scholars/Guest Scholars, 1984-85, fellow 1996-97; vis. prof. U. Warsaw, 1988-89; summer fellow NEH, 1980, Rockefeller, 1983, 94. Author: Phyllis Schlafly and Grassroots Conservatism: A Woman's Crusade, 2005, (monographs) Brookings Institution 1916-1952 Expertise and Public Interest in a Democratic Society, 1985, Studebaker: The Life and Death of an American Corporation, 1852-1963, 1996, Intended Consequences: Birth Control, Abortion and the Federal Government in Modern America, 1999; co-author (with William Rorabaugh) Paula Baker, America's Promise, 2005; editor: Socialism in the Heartland: The Midwestern Experience, 1986, A History of the United States I-V, 1995, The Politics of Abortion and Birth Control in Historical Perspective, 1996; co-editor (with Ellis Hawley), Federal Social Policy: The Historical Dimension, 1989, Poverty and Public Policy in Modern America, 1989, With Us Always: Private Charity and Public Welfare in Historical Perspective, 1998; contbr. chpts. to books and revs. and articles to profl. jours, presented papers at profl. confs., nat. and internat., 1981—; founding editor Jour. of Policy History; gen. editor Critical Issues in Policy History, Critical Issues in History, Cambridge Essential Histories. Named USIA Disting. Lectr., 1988-89, grantee, 1995; fellow Fulbright Scholars Program, 1997-98, USIA China Spkrs. Program, 1999. Office: St Louis U History Dept 221 N Grand Blvd Saint Louis MO 63103-2006

CRITELLI, MICHAEL J., lawyer, manufacturing executive; b. 1948; BA, U. Wis., 1970; JD, Harvard U., 1974. Bar: Ill. 1974, N.Y. 1982. Assoc. Ross & Hardies, Chgo., 1974-76, Schwartz & Freeman, Chgo., 1976-79; counsel Pitney Bowes, Inc., 1979-83, sr. counsel, 1983-84, asst. gen. counsel, 1984-86, assoc. gen. counsel, 1986-88, v.p., sec., gen. counsel, 1988, chief pers. officer, 1990-94, vice chmn., 1994—, chmn., CEO, 1996—. Office: Pitney Bowes Inc 1 Elmcroft Rd Stamford CT 06926-0700*

CRITELLI, NICHOLAS (NICK), lawyer, barrister; Founder Law Chambers of Nicholas Critelli PC, Des Moines, IA, and London, Eng., 1967—. Admitted to practice U.S. Supreme Ct. Recipient InnovAction award, Coll. of Law Practice Mgmt., 2004. Mem.: Iowa Acad. Trial Lawyers (past pres.), Iowa State Bar Assn. (pres. 2004). Avocation: amateur radio. Office: Critelli Law Ste 950 317 Sixth Ave Des Moines IA 50309-4128 also: Barrister's Chambers 9 Stone Bldgs Lincoln's Inn London WC2A 3NN England

CRITES, CARL D., auditor; b. Cushing, Oklahoma, Aug. 13, 1956; s. Paul W. and Anna F. Crites; m. Sue B. Britton, Dec. 20, 1986; 1 child, Courtney B. BS in Elec. Engring. Tech., Okla. State U., 1986; MS in Mgmt., So. Nazarene U., 1994; MBA, Okla. City U., 1998. Audio visual technician White Ho. Comm. Agy., Washington, 1975—78; sound technician Tele Hifi, Tulsa, 1980—84; sr. assoc. systems engr. E-Systems, ETAG, Fairfax, Va., 1987—89; systems engr., paws support team leader Eagle Tech., Fairfax, 1989—92; v.p. Okla. ops. Potomac Systems Engring., Okla. City, 1992—95; staff engr. BDM Internat., Okla. City, 1995—97; yr. 2000 project mgr. U. Okla., Norman, 1997—99; sr. assoc. PriceWaterhouseCoopers, Okla. City, 1999—2001; info. systems audit supr. The Hertz Corp., Okla. City, 2001—; sr. info. sys. auditor Kerr-McGee Corp., 2003—. Bd. dirs. Mid. Earth Child Devel. Ctr., Norman, Okla., 1996—99, mem. fund raising com., 2000—05; info. systems audit cons., Okla. City, 2002—03. Served in U.S. Army, 1975—78. Mem.: Inst. Internal Auditors (cert. internal auditor), Info. Systems Control and Audit Assn. (cert. info. sys. auditor). Democrat. Avocation: auto racing. Home: 1608 Old Farm Rd Norman OK 73072 Office: Kerr-McGee 123 Robert S Kerr Oklahoma City OK 73125

CRITES, RICHARD DON, lawyer; b. Sept. 3, 1943; s. Ewell Barnett Crites and Frances Loretta (Prichard) Castro; m. Annabel Lee Sheilds, June 1964 (div. 1976); children: Amy Lee, Jonathon Peter; m. Judith Jean Gildig, May 30, 1976 (div. 1997); children: Kimberly Ann, Kevin John; m. Carrie M. Roat, June 2004. BA, Ariz. State U., 1965; JD, U. Ariz., 1968. Bar: Ariz., Mo. U.S. Dist. Ct., No. Dist. of Tex., U.S. Ct. of Appeals, 8th Cir., U.S. Ct. of Appeals, 9th Cir. Assoc. Knez & Glatz, Tucson, 1968—73; ptnr. Knez, Glatz & Crites, Tucson, 1973—78; chief counsel City Utilities, Sprinfield, Mo., 1978—79; pvt. practice Sprinfield, 1979—. Referee Pima County Juvenile Ct., Tucson, 1972—76; instr. Mo. Sheriff's Tng. Acad.; dep. sheriff Mo. Sheriff's Office, Stone County, 2003—, PvLaski County, 2004. Contbr. articles to law revs. Recipient Excellence in Ins. Law award, Bancroft-Whitney Co., 1967, Excellence in Criminal Law award, 1968. Mem.: Greene County Bar Assn., Mo. Bar Assn., Ariz. Bar Assn., Royal Order of Jesters, Optomists, Shriners, Elks. Republican. Presbyterian. Home and Office: 2045 S Glenstone Ste 201 Springfield MO 65804 Office Phone: 417-887-8351. E-mail: rcrites1@mindspring.com.

CRITES, RICHARD RAY, financial planner, investment advisor, financial services company executive; b. Rapid City, SD, Aug. 29, 1952; s. Charles Dayton and Marcia Ann (Heil) C.; m. Randel E. Golobic, Dec. 27, 1980 (div. May 1988); m. Ellen L. Edmondson, Mar. 13, 1998. B of Liberal Studies, U. Okla., 1975; MS, Stanford U., 1978; cert. sr. security checker, Advanced Orgn. L.A., 1987, cert. false purpose rundown auditor, 1988. Cert. staff status II, exec. status I, Am. St. Hill Orgn., exec. dir. full hat course Celebrity Ctr. Internat., 1992; cert. in ins.: series 7 securities lic., series 63, series 24 gen. securities principal lic., series 66 investment adv. rep. lic.; cert. life and disability ins., Fla.; lic. mortgage broker, Fla. From nat. sales trainer to regional sales mgr. Continental Mktg. Corp., Detroit, 1975—80; pres., CEO Retail Packaging Specialists, Inc., San Mateo, Calif., 1982-86; owner, CEO Miracle Method of San Mateo, Inc., 1985-87, Miracle Method of Beverly Hills, Inc., L.A., 1987-90, Miracle Method of So. Calif., Inc., L.A., 1986-92, Miracle Method of No. Calif., Inc., L.A., 1988-89; v.p., treas., chmn. bd. Miracle Method of the U.S., Inc., L.A., 1988-92; pres., chmn. bd. Internat. Miracle Method Appearance Ctrs. Pacific, Inc., L.A., 1988-92, Internat. Miracle Method Ctrs. Equip. & Supply, Inc., L.A., 1989-92; pres., chmn. bd. dirs. Miracle Method of the U.S., Inc., L.A., 1992-96; gen. mgr. Stellar Mgmt. Co., L.A., 1993-96; mng. mem. Stellar Mgmt. LLC, 1996—; securities prin. WMA Securities, Inc., Norcross, Ga., 1996—2002; mgr. br. office Graham Group Mortgage Corp., 2001—; registered rep., br. office supr., investment advisor rep. CapWest Securities, 2002; investment adv. rep., registered rep. SAL Fin. Svcs., Inc., Birmingham, Ala., 2002—04; securities prin., br. office mgr. Equity Leadership Securities Group, Inc., 2004—. Trustee New Civilization Found., 1996—. Mem. Citizen's Commn. on Human Rights, Citizens for an Alternative Tax System. Mem. Internat. Assn. Scientologists (sponsor), Assn. for Better Living Through Edn. Republican. Scientologist. Avocations: skiing, jazz vocal music, tennis, camping, flying. Office: Stellar Mgmt LLC 600 Bypass Dr Ste 106 Clearwater FL 33764 E-mail: rickcrites@usa.net.

CRITES, STEPHEN DECATUR, religion philosopher, educator; b. Elida, Ohio, July 27, 1931; s. Beryl Anderson and Martha Crites; m. Gertrud Elizabeth Bremer, Sept. 11, 1955 (div. June 1990); children: Dorothea, Stephanie, Lilian, Hannah; m. Ann Lindberg, Dec. 26, 1990. BA, Ohio Wesleyan U., 1953; BD, Yale U., 1956, MA, 1959, PhD, 1961; student, U. Heidelberg, Germany, 1959-60. Ordained to ministry United Meth. Ch., 1956. Minister Grace Meth. Ch., Southington, Conn., 1956-58; instr. philosophy and religion Colgate U., 1960-61; asst. prof. religion Wesleyan U., Middletown, Conn., 1961-66, assoc. prof., 1966-69, prof., 1969-2001, prof. philosophy, 1991-2001, prof. emeritus, 2001—. Author: In the Twilight of Christendom: Hegel vs. Kierkegaard on Faith and History, 1972, Dialectic and Gospel in the Development of Hegel's Thinking, 1998; translator: Kierkegaard, Crisis in the Life of an Actress and Other Essays on Drama, 1967; editor:

Studies in Religion, Am. Acad. Religion monograph series, 1971-79. Mem. Am. Acad. Religion, Soc. for Values in Higher Edn. Home: 281 Beaver Brook Rd Lyme CT 06371-3203 Office: Philosophy Dept Wesleyan U Middletown CT 06457 Business E-Mail: scrites@wesleyan.edu.

CRITOPH, EUGENE, retired physicist, nuclear energy industry executive; b. Vancouver, B.C., Can., Mar. 29, 1929; s. Dennis Basil and Lilian Sarah Critoph; m. Mary Elizabeth Ivens, Feb. 9, 1952 (dec. Oct. 2000); children: Christopher Michael, Stephen Bard, Eugene Mark, Boyd. B in Applied Sci., U. B.C., 1951, M in Applied Sci., 1957. Physicist Chalk River (Ont., Can.) Nuc. Labs., Atomic Energy of Can. Ltd., 1953-67, br. head, reactor physics, 1967-75, dir. fuels and materials div., 1975-76, dir. advanced projects and reactor physics div., 1976-79, v.p., gen. mgr., 1979-86; v.p. strategic tech. mgmt. Atomic Energy of Can. Ltd. Rsch. Co., Ottawa, Ont., 1986-92. Mem., sec., chmn. European-Am. Com. on Reactor Physics, 1962-69. Co-author, coord. Canada Enters the Nuclear Age, 1997. Mem. Can. Nuclear Soc. (W.B. Lewis medal 1986).

CRITTENDEN, DANIELLE ANN, writer, journalist; b. Toronto, Ont., Can., Apr. 20, 1963; d. Maxwell John Crittenden and Yvonne Ann (Wilson) Worthington; m. David Jeffrey Frum, June 26, 1988; children: Miranda Ann, Nathaniel Saul. Reporter Toronto Sun, 1983-86; founding editor Women's Quar., Arlington, Va., 1994-99; columnist The Nat. Post, N.Y.C., 1999—. Author: What Our Mothers Didn't Tell Us: Why Happiness Eludes the Modern Woman, 1999. Jewish. Office: c/o Simon & Schuster 1230 Avenue Of The Americas New York NY 10020-1513

CRITTENDEN, JOHN CHARLES, engineering educator; b. Nov. 12, 1949; BS in Chem. Engrng., U. Mich., 1971, MS in Civil and Environ. Engrng., 1972, PhD in Civil and Environ. Engrng., 1976. Sr. v.p. Limno-Tech, Inc., Ann Arbor, Mich., 1975-77; asst. prof. civil and environ. engrng. Wash. State U., Pullman, 1977-78; asst. prof. civil engrng., environ. engrng. sect. U. Ill., Urbana, 1978-79, Mich. Tech. U., Houghton, 1979-81, assoc. prof. civil engrng., environ. engrng. sect., 1981-84, adj. prof. chem. engrng., 1981-84, prof. civil and environ. engrng., 1984—. Dir. Ctr. for Clean Indsl. and Treatment Techs., Houghton, 1992—; presdl. prof. civil engrng. CenCITT Mich. Tech. U., 1988—. Mem. AIChE, ASCE (Rudolph Hering award 1980, Walter L. Huber rsch. prize 1991), Am. Acad. Environ. Engrs., Water Pollution Control Fedn., Internat. Soc. Humic Substances, Assn. Environ. Engrng. Profs., Am. Water Works Assn. (publs. award 1989), Am. Chem. Soc. Achievements include patents in field. Office: Mich Tech U Dept Civil & Environ Engr 1400 Townsend Dr Houghton MI 49931-1200

CRITTENDEN, LAURA ANN, academic administrator; d. Richard Joseph and Elvira Louise Kirkpatrick; m. Jason Christopher Crittenden, Dec. 7, 2001; 1 child, Abigail Marie. AA in Gen. studies, Germanna C.C., Locust Grove, Va., 1989; BA in English, U. Md. Asian divsn., Okinawa, Japan, 1992; MA in English, Miss. State U., 1997, PhD in higher Edn. Adminstrn., 2001. Instr. English as second lang. World Edn. Ctr., Okinawa, 1992—95; tchg. asst. freshman English Miss. State U., Mississppi State, 1995—98, instr. English composition, 1998—99, English instr. devel. English, 1999, ednl. leadership rsch. asst., 1999—2001, program coord. cmty. coll. studies, 2001—02, mgr. acad. outreach, 2002—. Ad hoc mem. Miss. State U.'s Grad. Coun., 2003—; mem. interview com., program coord. Search for Child Devel. Assoc. Degree Program, 2002—; chair Instrnl. Design Unit Proposal Com., 2002; presenter profl. seminars, condr. workshops in field. Contbr. articles to profl. jours.; reviewer: textbooks The Right Tools for the Right Job: Building Communication Skills, 2001, Policy Studies for Educational Leaders, 2000, student evaluation rev. Bedford/St. Martin's Press, 1998. Ofcl. judge Miss. Region V Sci. and Engrng. Fair, 2004. Recipient grants in field. Mem.: LERN, MidSouth Partnership for Rural C.C.s (mem. adv. bd. 2001), Assn. for Continuing Higher Edn., Partnership for Adult Continuing Edn., Nat. Univs. Degree Consortium (bd. dirs. 2002—04), So. Regional Electronic Bd. for Digital Content, U. Md. Alumni Assn. (life), Miss. State U. Alumni Assn. (life), Starkville Arts Coun. (co-chair talent show 1999), Miss. State U. Bulldog Club, Alpha Theta Chi, Phi Delta Kappa (evaluator essay scholarship awards 1998—2000, cert. instr. leadership studies 2002), Sigma Tau Delta (v.p. 1998), Zeta Tau Alpha. Avocations: skiing, reading, writing, horseback riding. Office: Miss State U 1 Barr Ave Mississippi State MS 39762

CRITTENDEN, MARTHA A., rehabilitation services professional; b. Georgiana, Ala., Nov. 2, 1957; d. Walter Ray and Martha Pugh C. AA, Lomax - Hannon Jr. Coll., Greenville, Ala., 1978; BS, Troy State U., 1987, MS, 1993. Cert. counselor Am. Counseling Assn./Ala. Alochol and Drug Abuse Assn.; cert. instr. HIV & AIDS, ARC; cert. criminal justice addiction profl., Ala. Patient care asst. Jackson Hosp., Montgomery, Ala., 1978-89, psychiat. tech., 1989-90; drug program specialist Bullock County Correctional, Union Spring, Ala., 1990-95; drug treatment counselor Montgomery Cmty. Based Facility, Mt. Meigs, Ala., 1995-99, Ala. Dept. Corrections, Birmingham, 1999-2000; disability specialist Ala. Dept. Edn. Birmingham Disability Determination Svcs., 2000—. Vol. Neighbors Who Care, 1999; tchr. Bethel Full Gospel Ch., Montgomery, 1986—, Faith Chapel Christian Ctr. Ch., 1986—. Recipient Supr. of Yr. award Ala. Dept. Corrections, 1994. Mem. Ala. Alcohol and Drug Abuse Assn., Ala. Dept. Corrections (supr. 1990-95, Supr. of Yr. 1994), Addiction and Offender Counselors, Gamma Beta Phi. Avocations: reading, church, friends, walking or jogging, school. Office: Birmingham Disability Determination Svcs PO Box 830300 Birmingham AL 35283 also: Faith Chapel Christian Ctr 800 Quebec St Birmingham AL 35224-1571 Home: 140 Shady Acres Rd Alabaster AL 35007-4631

CRITTENDEN, MARY LYNNE, science educator; b. Detroit, Oct. 27, 1951; d. William and Marie (Ryall) C. BS, Wayne State U., 1974; MS, U. Detroit, 1984; postgrad., Wayne State U., 1991—, 1997—. Tchr. sci. Detroit Bd. Edn., 1974-77, Highland Park (Mich.) C.C., 1980—. Faculty rschr. Air Force program Wright Patterson AFB, Dayton, Ohio, 1991; speaker Mich. Ednl. Occupational Assn., 1989, Liberal Arts Network Devel., Lansing, Mich., 1990, 95; presider Qualities Edn. Minorities, Math., Sci. Engrng. Conf., Detroit, 1996; adj. prof. U. Detroit, 1996-97. Author ednl. materials; contbr. to profl. publs. Mem. AAAS, Am. Chem. Soc. (outreach program 1992—), Civic Ctr. Optimist Club (bd. dirs. 1991-94, coord. scis. 1990-94), Mich. C.C. Biologists, Human Anatomy and Physiology Soc. Achievements include development of successful paradigm and teaching methods to make science palatable to urban community college students, modeling normal values in humans and some rodents applicable to physiologically-based pharmacokinetics. Office: Highland Park Schs 20 Bartlett St Highland Park MI 48203-3720

CRITTENDON, DONNA ELIZABETH, customer service administrator; b. San Diego, Aug. 3, 1954; d. Clayton Thomas and Bessie Mae Foster; m. Paul Gregory Crittendon, Mar. 14, 1955; children: Orin, Michelle. AA, Sacramento City Coll., 1975; BS in Bus. Adminstrn., U. Phoenix, Sacramento, 1999. Tchr. asst. Sutter County Schs., Yuba City, Calif., 1976, media clk. Comprehensive Employment Training Act program, 1977—79; svc. rep. Pacific Gas and Electric, Marysville, Calif., 1979—, safety coord., 1998—, Cordaptix trainer, 2002. United Way chairperson Pacific Gas and Electric Co., Marysville, 1998—; voter registration vol. Sutter County, Yuba City, Calif., 2000; corp. sec., treas., bookkeeper, media person Christ Temple Cmty. Ch., 1976—; vol. Women's Ministry at Convelesant Home, 1999—. Mem.: Calif. Dist. Coun. (sec./treas. 2001—, dist. #5 2001—03). Apostolic. Avocations: creating media, sewing, bookkeeping, gardening, cooking.

CRIVELLO, ANTHONY, actor; b. Milw., Aug. 2, 1955; s. Vincent J. and Josephine (Mussomeli) C. Student, Marquette U. Appearences include (theatre) Frankie and Johnny in the Clair de Lune, Hamlet, The Lover, Big Time, Teahouse of the August Moon, 3 Guys Naked from the Waist Down, The Juniper Tree, Star-Spangled Girl, Mr. Roberts, The Long Christmas Dinner, The Matchmaker, A Streetcar Named Desire, (Broadway) Evita, Les Miserables, The News (Carbonelle award 1985), Measure for Measure, Kiss of the Spider Woman, 1993 (Best Actor in Musical Tony award 1993), Zhivago, 2005;(TV) Law and Order, Miami Vice, Dark Justice, Murder in Black and White, (films) Spellbinder, 1988, Crocodile Dundee II, 1988, Shakedown, 1988, Slaves of New York, 1989, The Lost Capone, 1991, The Bet, 1993.*

CRNEKOVIC, VICTORIA ESTEFANIA, biologist, educator; b. Buenos Aires, Mar. 12, 1950; arrived in U.S., 1958; d. Steven and Rudolfina Crnekovic; children from previous marriage: Ryan Haney, Joseph Postula, Stefanie Postula, Danielle Postula. BS, U. Ill., 1972, MS, 1976. Med. technician Rush-Presbyn.-St. Luke's Hosp., Chgo., 1969—73; instr. Parkland Coll., Champaign, Ill., 1975—77, 1989—2001, assoc. prof., 2001—; rsch. specialist U. Ill., Urbana, 1977—79; tchr. Unity HS, Tolono, Ill., 1979—80. State sci. fair judge Ill. Jr. Acad. Sci., Champaign, 1975—; sponsor Girls Engring., Math. & Sci., Champaign, 1999—2000. Mem.: Ill. Assn. CC Biologists, Nat. Assn. Biology Tchrs. Avocations: ballroom dancing, motorcycling, gardening. Office: Parkland Coll 2400 W Bradley Ave Champaign IL 61821 Office Phone: 217-373-3731. Business E-Mail: vcrnekovic@parkland.edu.

CROAN, ROBERT JAMES, music critic; b. N.Y.C., Apr. 30, 1937; s. Sydney Joseph and Sylvia (Zorn) C. BA, Columbia U., 1958, MA, 1959; PhD, Boston U., 1968. Prof. voice Duquesne U. Sch. of Music, Pitts., 1962-2000, chmn., 1983-2000; ret. Pitts. Post-Gazette, 1999, music critic, 1964-99, sr. editor, 1999—. Mem. Music Critics Assn. N.Am. (chmn. ednl. activities 1978-90, pres. 1997-2001), Nat. Assn. Tchrs. of Singing. Democrat. Avocations: travel, culinary arts. E-mail: rcroan@lycos.com.

CROCE, ARLENE LOUISE, critic; b. Providence, May 5, 1934; d. Michael Daniel and Louise Natalie (Pensa) C. Student, Women's Coll., U. N.C., 1951-53; BA, Barnard Coll., 1955. Founder, editor Ballet Rev., 1965-78; dance critic New Yorker mag., 1973-98. Dance panelist Nat. Endowment for Arts, 1977-80. Author: The Fred Astaire & Ginger Rogers Book, 1972, Afterimages, 1977, Going to the Dance, 1982, Sight Lines, 1987, Writing in the Dark, Dancing in the New Yorker, 2000. Recipient AAAL award 1979, award of Honor for Arts and Culture Mayor N.Y.C., 1979, Janeway prize Barnard Coll., 1955; Hodder fellow Princeton U., 1971; Guggenheim fellow, 1972, 86, NEH fellow 1992, Nat. Arts Journalism Program sr. fellow, 1999. Office: New Yorker Mag 4 Times Sq New York NY 10036-6561 Office Phone: 212-286-2860.

CROCE, CARLO M., research scientist; b. Milan; MD summa cum laude, U. Rome, 1969. Assoc. scientist Wistar Inst. Biology and Anatomy, Phila., 1970—80; assoc. dir. Wistar Inst., 1980—88; Wistar prof. genetics U. Pa., 1980—88; dir. Fels Inst. Cancer Rsch. and Molecular Biology Temple U., 1988—91; dir. Kimmel Cancer Thomas Jefferson U., 1991—2004; dir. human cancer genetics program and chmn. dept. molecular virology, immunology, and med. genetics Ohio State U., 2004—. Recipient Pezcoller AACR award, Am. Assn. Cancer Rsch., 1999, Charles M. Mott prize, Gen. Motors Cancer Rsch. Found. Mem.: Nat. Acad. Sci., Acad. Nat. Sci. Italy. Office: Ohio State Univ 400 W 12th Ave Columbus OH 43210

CROCK, STANLEY MILES, journalist; b. New Bedford, Mass., Apr. 6, 1950; s. Max and Lillian Rose (Kivowitz) C.; m. Pamela J. Brown, Mar. 21, 1987; children: Russell, Meryl. BA, Columbia Coll., 1972; MS in Journalism, Northwestern U., 1973; JD, Columbia U., 1977. Reporter AP, Chgo., 1973, Palm Beach Post, West Palm Beach, Fla., 1973-74, Wall St. Jour., Washington, 1978-82; cons. Worldwide Info. Resources Ltd., Washington, 1982-83; editor McGraw-Hill World News, Washington, 1983-86; news editor Bus. Week, Washington, 1986-95, chief diplomatic corr., 1995—. Pres. Rollingwood Citizens Assn., Chevy Chase, Md., 1993-94; comptr. Temple Sinai, Washington, 2001-03, sec., 2003-04. Jewish. Avocation: golf. Home: 7016 Western Ave Chevy Chase MD 20815-3111 Office: Bus Week 1200 G St NW Ste 1100 Washington DC 20005-3844 Office Phone: 202-383-2202. E-mail: stan_crock@businessweek.com.

CROCK, WINIFRED WOODARD, director, music educator, conductor, musician; d. James Phillips and Winifred Harris Woodard; m. Steven Neil Crock; 1 child, William. MusB, So. Ill. U., 1982; MusM, Kent State U., 1985; grad., Suzuki Talent Edn. Inst., 1984. Cert. Kodaly Kodaly Ctr. of Am., 1985. Tchr. Suzuki violin So. Ill. U., E String Prep Program, Edwardsville, 1977—82; with Kent State U., Cmty. Music Sch., Ohio, 1983—85; violin tchr. St Louis Conservatory Sch. Arts, St Louis, 1987—95; orch. dir., tchr. Pky. Sch. Dist., Chesterfield, 1987—; pvt. studio violin tchr., 1986—. Lectr., clinician Memphis U., 1990—; tchg. clinician Nat. New Zealand Suzuki Inst.; suzuki clinician numerous schs. & Insts., 1987—; orch. condr. numerous guest performances, 1987—. Contbr. articles to profl. jours. Recipient Nat. Tchr. Team, USA Today Newspaper, 1998, Pillar Pky. award, Pky. Sch. Dist., 1998, Merit award, Mo. Music Educators Assn., St. Louis, 1998, Grammy Gold Signature award and Grantgrantee, Grammy Found., 2000, Mo. Pvt. Tchr. Yr. award, Am. String Teachers Assn. Mo. Chpt., 2001. Mem.: Am. String Teachers Assn. (Mo. chpt. bd. mem. 2004), Internat. Suzuki Assn., Music Educators Nat. Conf., Suzuki Assn. Ams. (life; nat. com. chair). Office: Parkway Central High School 369 N Woods Mill Road Chesterfield MO 63017 Office Phone: 314-415-7935. Personal E-mail: wwcpchorch@hotmail.com.

CROCKER, BARBARA JEAN, clinical nurse specialist; b. Worcester, Mass., Oct. 13, 1942; d. Roy A. and Mildred E. (Ewing) Benson; m. David L. Crocker, Aug. 29, 1964; children: Beth, Mark, Matthew. Diploma, Henry Heywood Meml. Hosp., Gardner, Mass., 1963; BS, Anna Maria Coll., Paxton, Mass., 1982, MS in Nursing, 1985. Cert. infection control nurse. Staff nurse Worcester Hahnemann Hosp., 1965-72, nursing supr., 1972-81, infection surveillance nurse, 1981-85; nurse epidemiologist The Med. Ctr.-Hahnemann, Worcester, 1985-92; infection control practitioner U. Mass. Meml. Health Care, Worcester, Mass., 1992—2002, clin. nurse specialist, 2002—. Mem. Henry Heywood Meml. Hosp. Alumnae Assn.

CROCKER, CHARLES ALLAN, lawyer; b. Waco, Tex., May 26, 1940; s. Wiley Vernon and Edith Mae Crocker; m. Mary Ann Herndon, Sept. 1, 1962; children: Cathryn Ann, Amy Lynn. BBA, Tex. Tech. U., 1962; LLB, U. Tex., 1965. Bar: Tex. 1965, U.S. Tax Ct. 1979, U.S. Dist. Ct. (so. dist.) Tex. 1980, U.S. Ct. of Appeals (fed. cir.) 1984, U.S. Claims Ct. 1981; cert. estate planning and probate. Estate tax examiner IRS, Houston, 1965-72; acct. Peat, Marwick, Mitchell, Houston, 1972-74; atty. Baker & Botts, Houston, 1974-86, Hendricks Mgmt. Co., Houston, 1986-87; pvt. practice Houston, 1987—. Dir. Houston Estate and Fin. Forum, 1976-80, Pinnacle Mgmt. and Trust Co., Houston, 1996—. Mem. Winedale (Tex.) Adv. Coun., 1997—. Mem. ABA, Houston Bar Assn. (probate sect.). Avocations: golf, skiing. Office: 2001 Kirby Dr Ste 1100 Houston TX 77019-6081 Office Phone: 713-524-2181. E-mail: charles@pdg.net.

CROCKER, CHESTER ARTHUR, diplomat, federal agency administrator; b. N.Y.C., Oct. 29, 1941; s. Arthur M. and Clare V.; m. Saone Baron, Dec. 18, 1965; children: Bathsheba, Karena, Rebecca. BA, Ohio State U., 1963; MA in Internat. Studies, Johns Hopkins U., 1965, PhD, 1969. News editor Africa Report, 1968-69; lectr. Am. U., 1969-70; staff officer NSC, 1970-72; dir. M.S. in Fgn. Svc. program Georgetown U., Washington, 1972-78, dir. African studies Ctr. for Strategic-Internat. Studies, 1976-81, disting. prof. diplomacy Sch. Fgn. Svc., 1989-98, James R. Schlesinger prof. strategic studies, 1998—; asst. sec. state African affairs, 1981-89. Cons. in strategy and negotiation; chmn. Africa working group Reagan campaign, 1980; coord. for Africa Bush campaign; bd. dirs. A.S.A. Ltd., Good Governance Group Ltd., Henry-Dunant Ctr. for Humanitarian Dialogue, Nat. Def. U., U.S. Inst. Peace, Universal Corp., First Africa Group, Ltd. Author: High Noon in Southern Africa, 1992, Managing Global Chaos, 1996, Herding Cats: Case Studies in International Mediation, 1999, Turbulent Peace: The Challenges of Managing International Conflict, 2001, Taming Intractable Conflicts: Mediation in the Hardest Cases, 2004, others; contbr. articles to profl. jours. Recipient Disting. Svc. award Sec. State, 1988, Presdl. Citizen's award, 1989 Mem. Coun. Fgn. Rels., Internat. Inst. Strategic Studies, Am. Acad. Diplomacy, Cosmos Club, Tahawus Club. Republican. Office: Georgetown U Sch Fgn Svc Intercultural Ctr Rm 813 Washington DC 20057-0001 Office Phone: 202-687-5074. Business E-Mail: crockerc@georgetown.edu.

CROCKER, EVELYNE MARIE, retired physical education educator; b. Hollis, Okla., Mar. 13, 1936; d. Horace Norton Crocker and Maezell Elizabeth Tarr; m. Kenneth D. Burgess-Bean, May 6, 1956 (div. 1980); children: R. N. Burgess-Bean, K.R. Burgess-Bean, W. R. Burgess-Bean. Student, Cisco Jr. Coll., N.Mex. State U. Cert. Medical Specialist 1956. Governess Brown Family, Snyder, Tx, 1954—55, The Burgess-Bean Family, Maryville, Tn, 1956—68; instr. phys. edn. Bishop Bryan Cath. H.S., Port Arthur, Tex., 1968—69; governess The Hitch Family, Albany, Tex., 1981—82; owner, operator Bean's Lawn and Landscape Co., 1982—; proprietor King Crocker Am. Boers, Abilene, Tex., 1997—2001, Crocker Scouting Svc., Abilene, Tex., 2000—01. Author (web sites): Texann Prairie Land Country, 1996. Vol. state coord., owner Tex. Am. Local History Net; webmaster, author A.M. Crocker -1720 rootsweb.com project; vol. county coord., webmaster TXGenWeb projects; den leader, coach Scouting, Maryville, Tenn., 1977—79. Pfc WAC, 1955—57. Recipient Cold War Cert., Sec. War, 2000. Mem.: Founding Families of the State of S.C. Before Statehood, Tex. Sheriff Assn. (assoc. Appreciation award 1999, 2000, 2001). Spiritualist. Avocations: historical re-enactment, genealogy, photography, preservation. Personal E-mail: texannusa36@yahoo.com.

CROCKER, IAN, Olympic athlete; b. Portland, Maine, Aug. 31, 1982; Mem. U.S. Olympic Swim Team, Sydney, 2000, Athens, 2004. Recipient Gold medal 4x100m medley relay, Sydney Olympic Games, 2000, 4x100m medley relay, Athens Olympic Games, 2004, Silver medal, 100m butterfly, Bronze medal, 4x100m freestyle relay, Athens Olympic Games, 2004; youngest man in U.S. history to break 1 minute, 50 seconds in 200-meter freestyle. holds world record in 100m fly, America records 50m, 100m, 100y fly. Office: USA Swimming 1 Olympic Plz Colorado Springs CO 80909-5746

CROCKER, MATTHEW HALLOWELL, historian, educator, writer, researcher; b. Providence, Ri, Aug. 25, 1962; s. John, Jr. and Elinor Winslow Crocker; m. Susan Duff Wilcox, July 16, 2000; 1 child, Samuel Winslow. Bachelor of the Arts, Macalester Coll., St. Paul, MN, 1980—84; MA, U. of Mass., Amherst, Amherst, MA, 1989—93, PhD, 1993—97. History tchr. Walnut Hill Sch., Natick, Mass., 1985—89; prof. of history Keene State Coll., Keene, NH, 2000—. Bd. of reviewers Hist. Jour. of Mass. History, Westfield, Mass., 1998—. Author: (historical monograph) The Magic of the Many: Josiah Quincy and the Rise of Mass Politics in Boston, 1800-1830, (scholarly article) Journal of the West, Massachusetts Politics: Selected Historical Essays; contbr. scholarly presentation New England Historical Association Conference, scholarly presentation Institute for Massachusetts Studies Conference. Mem.: New Eng. Hist. Assn., Orgn. of Am. Historians, Am. Hist. Assn. Democrat-Npl. Episcopalian. Avocations: sailing, squash, tennis. Office: Keene State College 229 Main St Morrison Hall Keene NH 03435

CROCKER, RAY DEAN, musician, musical director; b. Ft. Worth, Nov. 1, 1949; s. Ben Raglin and Nancy Mahota (Potts) C.; m. Emily Janice Holt. Student, Tex. Christian U., 1967-69; MusB, North Tex. State U., 1974, MusM, 1977. Pianist Casa Manana Musicals, Ft. Worth, 1979-83; mus. asst. Opera Theatre U. North Tex. (formerly North Tex. State U.), Denton, 1980-81, instr. music, 1983-84; staff accompanist Tex. Womans's U., Denton, 1982-85; mus. dir. Surflight Summer Theatre, Beach Haven, N.J., 1984-85; asst. condr. 42nd St., nat. tour, 1985-86; mus. dir. Dallas Repertory Theatre, 1986-89, Sacramento Music Circus, 1988-90, Oscar's Place Dinner Theatre, Milw., 1990, 42d St. European Tour Co., 1991-97, Great Lake Opera, Milw., 1992. Bd. dirs. Paint It Yellow Prodns., Inc., pres., 1999-2004 Composer: Twas the Night Before Christmas, 1983, Frosty the Snowman, 1985, others; condr.: Dreamgirls, 1988 Mem. ASCAP, Am. Fedn. Musicians, Dramatists Guild, Phi Mu Alpha, Kappa Kappa Psi, Alpha Psi Omega. Home: 2764 N 90th St Milwaukee WI 53222-4609 E-mail: dcrocker@paintityellow.org, dcrocker@operamail.com.

CROCKER, RICHARD LINCOLN, retired music educator; b. Roxbury, Mass., Feb. 17, 1927; s. Richard Whitney Crocker and Constance Homer; m. Joy Rush, July 24, 1948; children: Nathaniel, David Laramie, Martha Wells; m. Gloria Andersen Pihl, Aug. 1, 1977. BA, Yale Coll., 1950; PhD in Music, Yale U., 1957. Asst. prof. dept. music Yale U., New Haven, 1957—63; prof. dept. music U. Calif., Berkeley, 1963—94; ret. Author: The Early Medieval Sequence, 1977, Introduction to Gregorian Chant, 2000. Fellow, Guggenheim Found., 1969. Mem.: Am. Musicol. Assn. (hon. Einstein award 1966, Kinkeldey award 1977). Avocations: yachting, woodworking, gardening. Home: 1643 Walnut St Berkeley CA 94709

CROCKER, RYAN C., ambassador; b. Spokane, Wash., June 19, 1949; married. BA, Whitman Coll., 1971; postgrad., Univ. Coll., Dublin, Ireland. Fgn. svc. officer US Consulate, Khorramshahr, Iran, 1972—74; econ. commercial officer Am. Embassy, Doha, Qatar, 1974—76, chief econ. /commercial section US interests section Baghdad, 1978—81, chief polit. sect. Beirut, 1981-84; dep. dir. Office Israel and Arab-Israeli Affairs, US Dept. State, Washington, 1985-87; polit. counselor Am. Embassy, Cairo, 1987-90; US amb. to Lebanon, US Dept. State, Beirut, 1990-93, US amb. to Kuwait Kuwait City, 1994-97, US amb. to Syria, Damascus, 1998—2001, interim envoy to Afghanistan Kabul, 2002, dep. asst. sec., Near Eastern Affairs Washington, 2001—03; dir. governance Coalition Provisional Authority, Baghdad, Iraq, 2003; internat. affairs adv. Nat. War Coll., 2003—05; US amb. to Pakistan US Dept. State, Islamabad, Pakistan, 2004—. Mailing: US Ambassador 81 Islamabad Pl Washington DC 20521-8100*

CROCKER, THOMAS DUNSTAN, economics professor; b. Bangor, Maine, July 22, 1936; s. Floyd M. and Gloria F. (Thomas) C.; m. Sylvia Fleming, Dec. 31, 1961 (div. Sept. 1986); children: Sarah Lydia, Trena Elizabeth; m. Judith Powell, Sept. 9, 1989. AB, Bowdoin Coll., 1959; PhD, U. Mo., 1967. Asst. prof. econs. U. Wis., Milw., 1963-70; assoc. prof. U. Calif., Riverside, 1970-75; prof. U. Wyo., Laramie, 1975-2001, chairperson dept. econs. and fin., 1991-93, dir. Sch. Environment and Natural Resources, 1993-98, J.E. Warren distng. prof of Energy and Environment, 1997—, disting. prof. emeritus, 2001—. Rsch. assoc. U. Calif., Berkeley, 1973, Pa. State U., 1974; cons. Asarco, Inc., 1985—89, Mathtech, Inc., Princeton, NJ, 1987—88, Princeton, 1999—2001, Indsl. Econs., Inc., Cambridge, Mass., 1998—99, Shea and Gardner, Washington, 1989, Arco, Inc., 1992, A. Coors Co., 1992, Eastern Rsch. Group, 1997; mem. sci. adv. bd. EPA, Washington, 1973—76; mem. panel on long range transport issues U.S. Congress, Washington, 1981; mem. Gov.'s Competition Rev. Com., State of Wyo.; mem. panel NSF, 2002—03. Co-author: Environmental Economics, 1971; author, editor: Economic Perspectives on Acid Deposition Control, 1984; editorial coun. Jour. Environ. Econs. and Mgmt., 1973-88, 95-99; contbr. articles to profl. jours. Mem. com. impacts pollution on agriculture Orgn. for Econ. Cooperation and Devel., Paris, 1987-88. Grantee, NSF, 1968, 1973, 1981, EPA, 1971, 1976—85, 1997—; scholar, Fulbright Found., 2001—. Mem.: European Assn. Environ. Resource Econs., Assn. Environ. Resource Econs. (contributed papers com. 1989, Rsch. of Enduring Quality award 2002), Am. Econ. Assn. (mem. awards structure com. 1981—83), The Nature Conservancy. Republican. Avocations: skiing, bicycling, travel, trekking, rafting. Office: Univ Wyo Dept Econs Laramie WY 82071 Office Phone: 307-766-6423. Business E-Mail: tcrocker@uwyo.edu.

CROCKER, THOMAS EDWARD, lawyer; b. Washington, June 9, 1949; s. Thomas Edward and Miriam (Hedges) C.; m. Elizabeth Jane Lichte, Apr. 7, 1990; 1 child, Edward Day Hedges. AB, Princeton U., 1971; JD, Columbia U., 1974. Bar: D.C. 1976, U.S. Ct. Appeals (D.C. cir.) 1976. Assoc. Hunton & Williams, Washington, 1974-76; fgn. svc. officer U.S. Dept. of State, 1976-81; assoc. Quarles & Brady, Washington, 1981-83; atty. Shaw, Pittman, Potts & Trowbridge, Washington, 1983—96; ptnr., co-chmn., internat. trade and regulatory group Alston & Bird LLP, Washington, 1996—. Contbr.

articles to profl. jours. Mem. ABA, Va. Bar Assn., D.C. Bar, Met. Club, Chevy Chase Club, Princeton Club of N.Y.C. Episcopalian. Avocations: reading, history, writing, fly fishing. Office: Alston & Bird LLP 10th Fl 601 Pennsylvania Ave Washington DC 20004-2601 Office Phone: 202-756-3318. Office Fax: 202-756-3333. Business E-Mail: tcrocker@alston.com.

CROCKER, WILLIAM HENRY, ethnologist, researcher; b. San Francisco, Aug. 20, 1924; s. William Willard and Ruth (Hobart) C.; m. Roma Dillon Smyth, Apr. 11, 1969 (div. Nov. 1983); 1 child, Myles Hobart; m. Jean Galloway Thomas, Dec. 19, 1987. BA, Yale Coll., 1950; MA, Stanford U., 1953; PhD, U. Wis., 1962. Curator Smithsonian Inst., Washington, 1962-93, emeritus curator, 1993—. Author: The Canela: An Ethnographic Introduction, 1990; co-author: The Canela: Kinship, Ritual and Sex. Trustee World Learning, Inc., Brattleboro, Vt., 1974-92. Cpl. U.S. Army, 1943-46. Mem. Bohemian Club, Cosmos Club. Democrat. Avocation: photography. Home: 4 Chalfont Ct Bethesda MD 20816-1805 Office: Smithsonian Inst Dept Anthropology MRC 112 Washington DC 20560-0112

CROCKER, WILLIAM HENRY, school director, music educator; b. Wichita, Kans., Nov. 27, 1948; s. William Henry Crocker and Roberta Jean Halley; m. Marilyn Beth Riley, May 31, 1970; children: Jonathan Riley, Jennifer Marie, Mary Elizabeth Schlegel, David Allen. B in Music Edn., Emporia (Kans.) State U., 1972. Chmn. Jefferson Montessori Fine Arts H.S., Rigby, Idaho, 2001—; owner Crocker Music Studio, Iona, Idaho, 1985—. Author: (short story) Miracle of the Loaves, 1992 (Mentor Mag. Mentor award, 1992); musician: (solo performance) Philip Glass Violin Concerto, 1995; composer (author, dir.): (musical play) Zarahemla, 2001. Founder, original dir. Salina (Kans.) Symphony Young Artists Competition, 1987—89; violist Idaho Falls Symphony Orch., 2001—05, Snake River Symphony Orch., Idaho Falls, 2001—05; strings specialist Idaho Falls Youth Arts Coun., 2002—04. Named Outstanding Friend of the Orch., Salina Ctrl. Orch., 1987. Mem.: Lions (v.p. 2003—05). Mem. Lds Ch. Avocations: genealogy, hiking, counseling, public service. Home: Box 352 Iona ID 83427 Office Phone: 208-745-1334. Personal E-mail: wmtwilde@msn.com.

CROCKETT, ANDREW DUNCAN, bank executive; b. Mar. 23, 1943; s. Andrew and Sheilah (Stewart) C.; m. Marjorie Hlavacek, 1966; 3 children. Ed., Queens' Coll., Cambridge U., Eng., Yale U. Staff member Internat. Monetary Fund, 1972-89; exec. dir. Bank of England, London, 1989—93; gen. mgr. Bank Internat. Settlements, Basel, Switzerland, 1994—2003; pres. J.P. Morgan Chase Internat., N.Y.C., 2003—. Chmn. Fin. Stability Forum, 1999-2003, mem. board of trustees Internat. Acctg. Standards Board. Contbr. articles to profl. jours. Avocations: reading, golf, tennis. Office: JP Morgan Chase Internat 15th Fl 277 Park Ave New York NY 10017-2014

CROCKETT, CLAUDE HOWARD, surgeon; b. Bristol, Va., Feb. 9, 1936; BA, U. Va., 1957, MD, 1961. Diplomate Am. Bd. Facial Plastic and Reconstructive Surgery, Am. Bd. Cosmetic Surgery, Am. Bd. Otolaryngology-Head and Neck Surgery. Intern U. Fla., Gainesville, 1961-62; resident Richmond (Va.) Meml. Hosp., 1962-63; preceptor in gen. surgery Shaw AFB Hosp., Sumter, S.C., 1963-65; resident U. Va. Hosp., Charlottesville, 1965-68; with Bristol Regional Med. Ctr., Tenn.; chief staff Bristol Ambulatory Surg. Ctr., 1995; asst. clin. prof. Ea. Tenn. State U. Med. Ctr. Mem. ACS, Am. Acad. Cosmetic Surgery (pres.), Am. Acad. Facial Plastic and Reconstructive Surgery, Am. Acad. Otolaryngology Head and Neck Surgery, Am. Soc. Liposuction Surgery (treas., trustee). Office: 350 Blountville Hwy Ste 205 Bristol TN 37620-1671

CROCKETT, DODEE FROST, brokerage house executive; b. Oklahoma City, Oct. 19, 1956; d. Carl S. Frost and Mikki (Matheny) Marcus; m. Billy Crockett. M in Theol. Studies, So. Meth. U., 2003. 1st v.p., wealth mgmt. advisor Merrill Lynch Pvt. Client, Dallas, 1980—. Bd. dirs. North Dallas Shared Ministries, 1988-91, Ronald McDonald House of Dallas, 1992—, Dallas Social Venture Ptnrs., 2003—, chair of bd., 2005; trustee Dallas Opera, 1991—; exec. bd. Perkins Sch. Theology, So. Meth. U., Dallas, 2003-; found. adv. bd. Dallas Found.; pres. Cir. Shared Housing Ctr., Dallas. Mem. Nat. Assn. Securities Dealers (gen. securities prin., mcpl. securities rulemaking bd. prin., registered options prin., bd. arbitrators), NYSE (com. mem.), Merrill Lynch Dirs. Cir., Park Cities Exch. Club (charter). Office: Merrill Lynch Pierce Fenner and Smith 2000 Premier Pl 5910 N Central Expy Ste 2000 Dallas TX 75206-5152

CROCKETT, DONALD HAROLD, composer, music educator; b. Pasadena, Calif., Feb. 18, 1951; s. Harold Brown and Martha Amy C.; m. Karen Anne Gallagher Crockett, Nov. 11, 1972 (div. 1986); 1 child: Katherine Jane Crockett; m. Vicki Lyn Ray, June 6, 1988. MusB, U. So. Calif., 1974, MusM, 1976; PhD, U. Calif., Santa Barbara, 1981. Composer-in-residence Pasadena Chamber Orch., 1984-86, L.A. Chamber Orch., 1991-97. Asst. prof. U. So. Calif., L.A. 1981-84, assoc. prof., 1984-94, prof. 1994—; music dir., condr. U. So. Calif. Contemporary Music Ensemble, L.A., 1984—, Xtet, 1992-; sr. composer-in-residence Chamber Music Conf. and Composers Forum of the East, 2002—. Composer: Celestial Mechanics oboe and string quartet, 1990, Array string quartet number 1, 1987, Roethke Preludes for Orchestra, 1994, Concerto for Piano and Wind Ensemble, 1988, Scree for cello, piano and percussion, 1997, Island for concert band, 1998, The Falcon's Eye for solo guitar, 2000, Cascade for orchestra, 2001, Blue Earth for orchestra, 2002, The Ceiling of Heaven for piano quartet, 2004. Recipient Friedheim award Kennedy Ctr., Washington, 1991, Aaron Copland award Copland House, 1998, Sylvia Goldstein award Copland House, 2003; Goddard Lieberson fellow Am. Acad. Arts and Letters, N.Y.C., 1994; Nat. Endowment for the Arts grantee, Washington, 1993; artists' fellow Calif. Arts Coun., 1999. Mem. BMI, Am. Music Ctr., Am. Composers Forum, Phi Kappa Phi. Avocations: reading, backpacking, skiing. Office: Univ Southern Calif Thornton School Of Music Los Angeles CA 90089-0851 E-mail: dcrocket@usc.edu.

CROCKETT, FRANK MCCLUNG, arts educator, retired music educator; b. Jonesville, Va., July 25, 1921; s. Frank McClung Crockett and Elizabeth Wynn; m. Wanda Hill, Dec. 28, 1983; m. Betty Jean Weldon (dec.); 1 child, Lisa. BS Violin, Juilliard, N.Y., 1949; MM, U. Tex., Austin, Tex., 1952; EdD Music Edn., U. Ill., Urbana, Ill., 1960. Cert. T7 Tchg.at doctoral level Ga., 1986. Instr. of violin and viola Edinboro State Teachers Coll., Edinboro, Pa., 1949—50; coord. string project U. Tex., Austin, Tex., 1950—52; coord. string instrn. U. Miss., Oxford, Miss., 1952—54; assoc. prof. music U. So. Miss., Hattiesburg, Miss., 1954—58; coord. arts and humanities Ga. Dept. of Edn., Atlanta, 1958—86. Pres. So. Divsn. Music Tchrs. Nat. Assn., 1960—62; chmn. Nat. Interscholastic Activities Commn. of Music Educators, 1957—60; chmn. nat. com. on music tchg. Music Tchrs. Nat. Assn., 1964—67; exec. sec. Ga. Music Coun., Ga., 1960—86; organizer, condr. South Miss. Youth Orch.; guest faculty, conductor U. Tex., U. Mich., U. Ala., U. Fla. State., Va. Music Camp, Nat. Music Camp Interlochen, Mich. Author: Organizing String Programs; contbr. Ga. Govs. Honors Program, scientific papers. Vol. Atlanta Symphony Orch., 1995—2004; pres. Atlanta Music Club, 1991—94. T-5 U.S. Army, 1943—46, European Theater. Recipient Disting. Career Award, Ga. Music Educators Assn., Bicentennial Award, Ga. C. of C., 1974 1975 1976, Disting. Svc., Atlanta Music Club; Danforth Tchr. Study Grant, Danforth Found. Mem.: Am. String Tchrs. Assn. (pres. 1991—94), Music Educators Nat. Conf., Ga. Music Educators Assn. (Disting. Career Award 1999). Achievements include development of music program for Ga. Govs. Honors Program. Avocations: travel, music, coaching chamber music. Home: 2553 Rivermont Cir Kingsport TN 37660

CROCKETT, GEORGE EPHRIAM, secondary school educator; b. Chgo., July 5, 1940; s. Edmund and Ethel Teva (Cowan) C.; m. Ethelene Standifer, Nov. 25, 1968; children: Patricia Johnson, Ronald O'Neal, Michael O'Neal. BS, Ill. State U., 1964; MA in History, Northeastern Ill. U., 1981; postgrad., U. Ill., Champaign. Cert. tchr., Ill. History tchr. John Marshall Metro High Sch., Chgo., 1964—, chmn. social studies dept., 1992—. Tng. specialist John Marshall Metro Evening High Sch., 1966-69, counselor, 1980-83; cons. curriculum guide Chgo. Bd. Edn., 1970. Active Cen. Meml. Bapt. Ch., Chgo., 1957—; mem. com. explorer scouts Boy Scouts Am., 1977-79; mem. Citi-Educators Team Project, DePaul U., 1989. Recipient Tchr. of Yr. award Chgo. Bd. Edn., 1974, Black Educator award Push Found., 1977, Blum-Kovler Ednl. Found. award, 1984, merit award N. Eastern Ill. Alumni, 1985, Midwest Community award, 1990—. Mem. Ill. Coun. Social Studies, Chgo. Social Studies, Chgo. Afro-Am. Tchrs. Assn., Chgo. Area Alliance Black Sch. Educators, NAACP, Nat. Urban League, Midwest Community Coun., Operation Push, So. Christian Leadership Conf. Avocations: reading, sports, public speaking, gardening. Home: 3130 W Fulton St Chicago IL 60612-1728 Office: John Marshall Met High Sch 3250 W Adams St Chicago IL 60624-2901

CROCKETT, JOAN M., human resources executive; B in Polit. Sci., John Carroll Univ., 1972. Underwriter, various positions in human resources Allstate Ins. Co., 1973—94, sr. v.p. human resources, 1994—. Bd. dirs. INROADS; adv. bd. Univ. Ill. Chgo. Internat. Student Exchange Program; ptnr., bd. dirs. Ctr. for Human Resource Mgmt. Univ. Ill., gov. coun. Good Shepherd Hosp., Barrington, Ill. Named Human Resource Exec. of Yr., Human Resource Exec. mag., 1997. Mem.: Nat. Acad. Human Resources. Office: Allstate Corp 2775 Sanders Rd Northbrook IL 60062-6127 Office Phone: 847-402-5000. Office Fax: 847-326-7519.*

CROCKETT, LISA (ELIZABETH) JEAN, psychology professor; d. Robert Oscar and Jean Andrus Crockett; m. Allan Lee McCutcheon, May 25, 1985. BA, U. Pa., 1978; PhD, U. Chgo., 1986. Asst. prof. human devel. Pa. State U., State College, 1987—93, assoc. prof. human devel., 1993—96; assoc. prof. psychology U. Nebr., Lincoln, 1996—2000, prof. psychology, 2000—, assoc. dean, 2000—02, assoc. vice chancellor for rsch., 2002—05. Assoc. editor Jour. Rsch. on Adolescence, 1999—2004; co-editor: (books) Pathways through Adolescence, Negotiating Adolescence in Times of Social Change; contbr. articles to jours. including Devel. Psychology, Jour. Rsch. Adolescence; contbr. chapters to books. Recipient Jeanne Humphrey Block Dissertation award, Henry A. Murray Ctr., 1984, Dorothy Barnes award for Excellence in Tchg., Coll. Health and Human Devel., 1993, award for best article of 1999, Jour. Sex. Rsch., 2000; grantee, NIH, 1995—97, 2001—04; Summer fellow, Ctr. for Advanced Study in Behavioral Scis., 1990. Mem.: Soc. for Rsch. in Child Devel., Soc. for Rsch. on Adolescence. Avocations: travel, music, gardening. Office: U Nebr-Lincoln 319 Burnett Hall Lincoln NE 68588-0308

CROCKETT, ROBERT YORK, architect; b. West Covina, Calif., Nov. 27, 1962; s. Bob York and Carolyn Kathleen (McLellan) C. BArch, U. So. Calif., 1985; Masters, UCLA, 1994. Registered architect, Calif., Nev., Ariz., Miss., La. Designer TNT Architecture Internat., Malibu, Calif., 1983-85, Pace Group, L.A., 1985-87; architect in pvt. practice L.A., Calif., 1988—. Bd. dirs. (P.A.C.E.) Planning Architecture Consulting Engring., Phoenix. Avocations: music, art, sailing, golf. Office: 373 South Doheny Dr Ste A Beverly Hills CA 90211

CROCKETT ALDRIDGE, ETHEL STACY, librarian; b. Mt. Vernon, N.Y., Jan. 19, 1915; d. Henry Pomeroy and Marian (Putnam) Stacy; m. Clement Wirt Crockett, Aug. 17, 1936 (div. July 1969); children: Patricia Crockett Johnson, Richard; m. Jack Howard Aldridge, June 22, 1973. BA, Vassar Coll., 1936; MA, San Jose State Coll., 1962; postgrad., U. Calif., Berkeley, 1964-65, San Francisco State Coll., 1966. Children's librarian Corning (N.Y.) Meml. Library, 1958; catalog librarian Sequoia Union High Sch., Redwood City, Calif., 1960-61; gen. reference librarian, instr. San Jose (Calif.) City Coll., 1962-68; dir. library services City Coll. San Francisco, 1968-72; dir. Inst. Effective Use of Paraprofls. in Libraries, summer 1971; Calif. State librarian Sacramento, 1972-80. Chmn. Chief Officers of State Libr. Agys., 1974-75; mem. Nat. Coun. on Ednl. Stats., 1975-78; mem. adv. group on the Libr. to Libr. of Congress, mem. adv. coun. Ctr. for the Book, 1980-90; mem. vis. com. Stanford U. Librs., 1975-82, bd. dirs., 1990-91; mem. adv. coun. Stanford Libr. Assocs., 1978-92. V.p. Sir Francis Drake Commn., 1974-80; bd. dirs., treas. Seadrift Property Owners Assn., Stinson Beach, Calif.; bd. dirs. Strybing Arboretum Found., San Francisco; mem. edn. com. Strybing Arboretum Soc., San Francisco, 1987-90; bd. dirs. Pacific Horticulture Found., spl. events chmn., 1982-87; bd. dirs. San Francisco Mus. Art, Stinson Beach Cmty. Ctr.; mem. U. Calif.-Santa Cruz Arboretum Soc., 1987-91; bd. dirs., chmn. investment and fin. coms. West Marin Sr. Svcs., 1988-91; bd. dirs., chmn. investment and membership coms. Allied Arts of Stinson Beach; bd. dirs. Stanford U. Libr. Assocs., 1990-91; mem. Fine Arts Mus. San Francisco Belvedere-Tiburan Aux., 1995—. Mem. ALA, Book Club of Calif. (bd. dirs. 1982-86, 90-94, v.p. 1983-87), Calif. Libr. Assn., Calif. Inst. Librs. (pres. 1973-79), Strybing Arboretum Soc. (edn. com. San Francisco chpt. 1988-90), Master Gardener (Marin County, Calif.), Colophon Club. Clubs: Colophon. Home: 6 N Point Cir Belvedere CA 94920-2454 *My interest as state librarian was to provide excellent library service to all Californians. By aiding and encouraging all libraries to open their collections to patrons beyond their boundaries, I wished to see the great resources of California libraries available to all. My goal was to enable all kinds of libraries to work together cooperatively so that a book need be catalogued only once for all libraries, and so materials can be shared to avoid expensive, duplicative purchases. Thus, the library user would be better served while the cost of service stays within a reasonable limit.*

CROCKETT-WOJCIESKOSKI, BARBARA ANASTASIA, psychiatrist, educator; b. Chester, Pa., Feb. 23, 1943; d. Leon Joseph Wojcuchoski and Helen Julia Forenny; children: Barbara C., Christine A. BA, U. Pa., 1964; MD, Hahnemann U., 1968. Physician Duke U. Med. Ctr., Durham, NC, 1997—99, asst. clin. prof. psychiatry, 2003—; dir. rsch. moods U. N.C., Chapel Hill, NC, 1997—2004. Co-author: A PA Textbook Anxiety Disorders, 2001. Fellow, Duke U., 1997—99. Office: Duke Univ Med Ctr Dept Psychiatry PO Box 3516 Durham NC 27710-0001

CROFT, CANDACE ANN, psychology professor, academic administrator, small business owner; b. Lancaster, Wis., Jan. 14, 1957; d. Wilford Stanley and Myrna Viola Croft. BA, St. Olaf Coll., 1979; MS, U. Ariz., 1980; PhD, Pa. State U., 1984. Psychotherapist Forrester Clinic, Chgo., 1984-86; dir. rsch. on child and adolescent health Am. Acad. Ped., Elk Grove Village, Ill., 1986-92; dir. rsch. and sci. affairs Am. Acad. Orthop. Surgeons, Rosemont, Ill., 1992-94; sr. program assoc. Aon Found., Chgo., 1994-95; dir. Strong Spirit Wellness Ctr., Chgo., 1995-96; adj. prof. DePaul U., Chgo., 1993-96; assoc. prof. psychology, chmn. dept. psychology Clarke Coll., Dubuque, Iowa, 1996—2003, chair instl. rev. bd., 2000—03; dean Health & Human Svc. Occupations, SW Tech. Coll., Fennimore, Wis., 2003—; pres. Tabankhu, LLC, 2005—. Textbook reviewer McGraw-Hill, 1998-2003; media contact Nat. Coun. Family Rels., St. Paul, 1998—, Clarke Coll.-Fox-40, Dubuque, Iowa, KWWL Channel 7, Dubuque, Iowa; adv. Clarke Coll.; owner Heart Light Shing Author: Annalia's Simply Splendid, 2003, Growing Good Hearts: The Rooting Years, 2005; contbr. articles to sci. and profl. jour.; exec. producer film Heart of the Matter, 1991 (bronze award Houston Internat. Film Festival 1991); contbr. column to on-line pub., Living With Heart, 2002— Mem. liturg. ministry St. Mary's Ch., Platteville, Wis., 1999—2001. Mem. Nat. Coun. Family Rels. (cert. family life educator, sect. religion and the family, sect. on family and health), Assn. Humanistic Psychology, Inst. Noetic Scis., Assn. for Transpersonal Psychology, Nat. Coalition for Campus Children's Ctrs., Nat. Assn. for the Edn. of Young Children, Phi Kappa Phi, Omicron Nu. Avocations: writing, music, aerobics, swimming, photography. Home: 119 North Monroe Lancaster WI 53813 Office: SW Tech Coll 1800 Bronson Blvd Fennimore WI 53809 Personal E-mail: cacroft@pcii.net.

CROFT, DANIEL THOMAS, music educator; b. Pittsburgh, Pa., Oct. 15, 1951; s. Joseph Donald and Evelyn Marie Croft; m. Dawna LaRae Ainsworth, June 21, 1974; children: Daniel T., LaRae Marie. BS Music Ed., Clarion Univ., Clarion, PA, 1973. Band dir. North Star Area Sch. Dist., Boswell, Pa., 1973—. Founder/condr. Somerset County Cmty. Band, Somerset, Pa., 1988—; founder Somerset Alliance Ch. Band, Somerset, Pa.; faculty Clarion Univ. Summer Band Camp, Clarion, PA, 1975-1990. Tennis instr.; founder, dir. First Christian Ch. of Somerset Adult and Youth Bands; music ministry Chs.; referee Somerset Youth Basketball Assn., Somerset, Pa., 1982, pres., 1998. Recipient Grant B. Miller award-Man of the Yr., Somerset Chamber of Commerce, 1994. Mem.: Somerset County Music Educators Assn., PA State Educators Assn., PA Music Educators Assn., Music Educators Nat. Conf. (rep. to state music leadership conf.). R-Consevative. Christian. Avocation: raising cocker spaniels. Home: 262 Marker Dr Somerset PA 15501 Office: North Star Area School Dist 400 Ohio St Boswell PA 15531 E-mail: croft@shol.com.

CROFT, GEORGE T., physicist; b. Washington, Sept. 29, 1926; s. William Thomas and Georgietta (Lyon) C.; m. Geraldine Frizzel (div. Feb. 1995); children: Linda Marie, David Thomas, John Frizzell Croft; m. Nancy Mitchell, Aug. 14, 1996. BS in Physics, Western Md. Coll., Westminster, 1948; PhD in Physics, U. Pa., 1953. Rsch. physicist McGraw-Edison, West Orange, N.J., 1953-58; dir. R&D and staff engring. Pitney Bowes, Stamford, Conn., 1958-70; v.p. corp. R&D and staff engring. Addressograph-Multigraph, Cleve., 1970-76; v.p. R&D Am. Optical, Southbridge, Mass., 1976-80; pres. Technol. Resources Mgmt. Group, Hilton Head Island, S.C., 1980-87; dir. Coll. of Hilton Head U. S.C., Hilton Head Island, 1983-85; instr. physics and math. Savannah (Ga.) Tech. Inst., 1987-95; asst. adj. prof. physics U. S.C., Beaufort, 1995—. Pres. Intellectual Resources Group, Inc., 1992—; mem. adv. coun. to dean engring. U. Mass., Amherst, 1978-83; mem. R&D coun. Am. Mgmt. Assn., 1975-1980; mem. corp. assoc. adv. com. Am. Phys. Soc., 1977-80. Author: Three Diminsional Analytic Geometry, 2000; contbr. articles to profl. jours. Served with USNR, 1945-46, PTO. Mem. IEEE, Am. Phys. Soc. Achievements include staffing and organizing 3 research and development labs and establishing product development and related research programs in them; product development in office equipment and optical equipment industries; patents on safe hand gun locks. Home: 22 Coventry Ct Bluffton SC 29910-5706 E-mail: geotomirg@aol.com.

CROFT, HARRY ALLEN, psychiatrist; b. Houston, July 2, 1943; s. Louis and Ida (Kaplan) C.; m. Benay Bleacher, Dec. 27, 1964; children— Jamie Sue, Bradley Lane, Chasen Ashley. BS, So. Meth. U., 1964; MD, U. Tex. at Galveston, 1968. Intern Brackenridge Hosp., Austin, 1968-69; resident in obstetrics and gynecology U. Tex. Med. Br., 1969-70, resident in psychiatry, 1970-73; dir. methadone program Galveston County, Tex.; dir. sex therapy program U. Tex., Galveston, 1972-73; commd. capt. U.S. Army, 1973, advanced through grades to maj., 1975; chief (Mental Hygiene Service, Brooke Army Med. Center), Houston, 1973-76; pvt. practice, 1976—; med. dir. San Antonio Psychiat. Rsch. Ctr., 1988—. Clin. asst. prof. psychiatry and ob-gyn. Med. Sch. San Antonio, 1973-75; columnist San Antonio Express-News, 1975-76; weekly contbr. Sta. KMOL-TV (NBC) newscast, also KENS TV, 1988-90, KMOL TV, 1990-92; dir. rsch. and edn. Covenant Behavioral Health. Contbr. articles to profl. jours. Recipient physician's recognition award AMA, 1974, awards for med. TV work Nat. Healthcare Assn., 1988, Women in Comm., 1988; Meritorious Svc. medal U.S. Army, 1976, Ware 1st place audio-visual award Dept. Army, 1976, Gov.'s award State of Tex., 1991, award City of San Antonio, award Acad. Radio and TV Health Comm., Jules Bergman award-Broadcaster of Yr. award, 1995, Best Radio Show In U.S., Nat. Mental Health Assn., 1996; named Honoree, Am. Heart Assn., 2003. Mem. Am. Psychiat. Assn. (award 1991), Tex. Med. Assn. (award 1988), Am. Soc. Sex Educators, Counselors and Therapists, Am. Soc. Addiction Medince (cert. addictionist). Home: 12738 Hunters Chase St San Antonio TX 78230-1930 Office: 8038 Wurzbach Rd Ste 570 San Antonio TX 78229-3815 Office Phone: 210-692-1222. E-mail: hacmd@aol.com.

CROFT, KATHRYN DELAINE, social worker, consultant; b. Eastover, S.C., Jan. 13, 1944; d. Randolph and Ethel (Williams) Lloyd; m. Daniel Marranzini, June 26, 1987. BS, Wilberforce U., 1965; MS, Columbia U., 1982, New Sch. for Social Rsch., 1988. Cert. social worker, N.Y. Exec. dir. Family Dynamics, Inc., N.Y.C., 1987—92; asst. provost Columbia U., N.Y.C., 1992—94; commr. N.Y.C. Child Welfare Adminstrn., N.Y.C., 1994—96; dir. ops. Just One Break, Inc., N.Y.C., 1997—2000, exec. dir., 2000—02; chief program officer ARC Greater N.Y.C., 2002—04; adminstrv. dir. supported housing and real property Women-in-Need, Inc., 2004—. Cons. various nonprofit orgns., N.Y.C., 1996—. Bd. dirs. Artsgenesis, N.Y.C., 1993—, chmn., 1996-99; bd. dirs. Ackerman Inst., N.Y.C., 1997-2000. Recipient scholarships New Sch. for Social Rsch., 1985-88, Columbia U., 1978-82. Mem. NAFE, Assn. Black Women in Higher Edn. Avocations: travel, reading, photography.

CROFT, TERRENCE LEE, lawyer, mediator, arbitrator; b. St. Louis, Apr. 13, 1940; s. Thomas L. and Anita Belle Croft; m. Merry Patton, July 9, 1977; children: Michael, Shannon, Kimberly, Kristin, BethAnn, Katherine. AB, Yale U., 1962; JD with distinction, U. Mich. Law Sch., 1965. Bar: Mo. 1965, U.S. Dist. Ct. (ea. dist.) Mo. 1965, Ga. 1970, Fla. 1970, U.S. Ct. Appeals (5th, 8th and 11th cirs.) 1970, U.S. Supreme Ct. Assoc. Coburn, Croft & Kohn, St. Louis, 1965-69, Hansell, Post, Brandon & Dorsey, Atlanta, 1969-73; ptnr. Huie, Sterne & Ide, Atlanta, 1973-78, Kutak, Rock & Huie, Atlanta, 1978-83; shareholder Griffin, Cochrane & Marshall, Atlanta, 1983-93; ptnr. King & Croft LLP, Atlanta, 1994—. Mediator Henning Mediation & Arbitration Svc., Atlanta, 1996—. Fellow Am. Coll. Civil Trial Mediators; mem. ABA (ho. of dels. 1993-99), State Bar Ga. (bd. govs. 2002-, chair alt. dispute resolution sect.), Atlanta Bar Assn. (pres., sec., treas. bd. dirs. 1986-99, chmn., bd. dirs. litigation sect. 1982-86, pres. Alt. Dispute Resolution Lawyers sect. 1996-97, Charles Watkins award), Atlanta Coll. Arbitrators and Mediators (founder), Atlanta Bar Found. (pres. 1998-2003), Ga. Trial Lawyers Assn., Lawyers Club Atlanta, Old War Horse Lawyers Club. Episcopalian. Avocations: hiking, shooting, motorcycling, reading. Home: 2580 Westminster Heath NW Atlanta GA 30327-1449 Office: King & Croft LLP 707 The Candler Bldg 127 Peachtree St NE Atlanta GA 30303-1810 Fax: 404-577-8401. Office Phone: 404-577-8400. Business E-Mail: tlc@king-croft.com.

CROFT, VICKI FAYE, librarian; b. St. Lous, Jan. 13, 1948; d. Floyd Merle Keating and Vivian W. Keating Sorensen; m. James Vernon Croft, June 1, 1971. BS, Dana Coll., 1970; MLS, U. Ill., 1970. Asst. sci. libr. U. Nebr., Lincoln, 1971—76; head health scis. libr. Wash. State U., Pullman, 1976—. Chmn. Contributed Papers First Internat. Conf. on Animal Health Info. Profls., Reading, England, 1992; mem. planning com. 4th and 5th Internat. Conf. Animal Health Info. Profls., 2003—05. Editor: Pets sect. Mags. for LIbrs., 1982, 1986, 1989. Mem.: Acad. Health Info. Profls. (disting.), Pacific NW LIbraries Assn., Wash. Med. Librs. Assn. (exec. bd. 1984—85), Nebr. Libr. Assn. (sec.-treas. coll. and rsch. sect. 1973—74), Med. Libr. Assn. (sec.-treas. vet med. librs. sect. 1985—86, chmn. 1986—87, sect. coun. 1988—91, treas. 1994—96, chair 2004, cert., mem. Pacific NW chpt. treas. 1994—96, chmn. 2004). Lutheran. Home: Health Scis PO Box 2015 Pullman WA 99165-6512 Office: Wash State U Health Scis Libr 170 Wegner Hl Pullman WA 99164-6212 Office Phone: 509-335-5544. E-mail: croft@vetmed.wsu.edu.

CROFTS, ANTONY RICHARD, biochemistry and biophysics educator; b. Harrow, Eng., Jan. 26, 1940; came to U.S., 1978; s. Richard Basil Iliffe and Vera Rosetta (Bland) C.; m. Paula Anne Hinds-Johnson, June 7, 1969 (div. 1981); 1 child, Charlotte Victoria Patricia; 1 adopted child, Rupert Charles; m. Christine Thompson Yerkes, Dec. 23, 1982; children: Stephanie Boynton, Terence Spencer. BA, U. Cambridge, Eng., 1961, PhD, 1965. Asst. lectr. dept. biochemistry U. Bristol, Eng., 1964-65, lectr., 1966-72, reader, 1972-78; prof. biophysics U. Ill., Urbana-Champaign, 1978—, prof. microbiology, 1992-99, chmn. biophysics divsn., 1978-91, assoc. dean Coll. Liberal Arts & Scis., 1996-98, prof. biochemistry, 1998—. Mem. organizing com. 4th Internat. Congress Photosynthesis, Reading, Eng., 1977, 7th Internat. Congress Photosynthesis, Providence, 1986, Table Ronde, Rousel-UCLA Forum, Paris, 1985; vis. prof. Coll. de France, 1983; Lans Ernster Meml. Lecture, Stockholm U., 2005; lectr. in field. Contbr. numerous articles, revs., etc., in area of biophysics, photosynthesis and bioenergetics; mem. editl. bd. Biochem. Jour., U.K., 1971-72, Biochimica Biophysica Acta, Holland, 1972-77, jour. Bacteriology, 1979-83, Archives Biochemistry and Biophysics, 1980-85. Major scholar nat. sci. U. Cambridge, 1958-61, U. Ill. scholar, 1989-92; grantee U.S. Dept. Energy, 1982-96, Guggenheim Found., 1985, NSF, NIH, U.S. Dept. Agr., 1979—. Fellow AAAS; mem. Biophys. Soc., Am. Soc.

Biochemistry and Molecular Biology, Am. Soc. Plant Physiologists (Charles F. Kettering award 1992). Avocations: windsurfing, skiing, fishing, sailing. Office: U Ill Dept Biochemistry 419 Roger Adams Lab Box B4 600 S Mathews Ave Urbana IL 61801-3602 Office Phone: 217-333-2043. Business E-Mail: a-crofts@life.uiuc.edu.

CROHN, MAX HENRY, JR., lawyer; b. Asheville, N.C., Feb. 4, 1934; s. Max Henry and Edith Pearl (Hoffman) C.; m. Barbara Jean Morris, Jan. 28, 1960; children: David Michael, Edith Ann, Randal Morris. BA in Polit. Sci, U. N.C., 1955; LL.B., Georgetown U., 1961. Bar: D.C. 1961, N.C. 1977, N.Y. 1986. Practiced in, D.C., 1961-68; trial atty. Bur. Restraint of Trade, 1963-65; atty. adviser to chmn. FTC, 1965-66; asso. mem. firm Arnold & Porter, Washington, 1966-68; asso. counsel R.J. Reynolds Industries, Inc., Winston-Salem, N.C., 1968-75, asst. gen. counsel, 1975-78; sec. R.J. Reynolds Tobacco Co., 1971-81, gen. counsel, 1978-81; ptnr. Jacob, Medinger and Finnegan, 1981-95. Former chmn. bd. dirs. Forsyth County Econ. Devel. Corp., 1975-78. Served to lt. (j.g.) USNR, 1955-58. Mem. ABA. Home: 517 Redbud Rd Chapel Hill NC 27514-1710

CROISETIERE, JACQUES M., chemicals executive; m. Marthe Croisetiere. BS in Fin., U. Montreal, 1985. Fin. staff Master Card divsn. Bank of Montreal; dir. fin. Canadelle, Inc., 1983—90; from v.p. fin. Can. Salt to v.p., gen. mgr. plastic additives, biocides and sealants Morton Internat., Inc., 1990—98; v.p. Rohm and Haas Co., 1999—, CFO Phila., 2003—. Office: Rohm and Haas Co 100 Independence Mall W Philadelphia PA 19106-2399

CROISSANT, WILLIAM GEORGE, music educator; b. Kane, Pa., Oct. 24, 1941; s. Clifford Charles and Mildred Harriet Croissant; m. Patricia Evelyn Croissant, Jan. 16, 1964; children: Jennifer Louise, George William. BS, Pa. State U., 1963, MEd, 1968; MA, Indiana U. of Pa., 1998. Music tchr., dir. bands Ellwood City (Pa.) schs., 1966—70, Huntingdon (Pa.) schs., 1971—2003, Trumansburg (NY) schs., 1963—66. Guest condr., Pa., NJ, Md., 1998—. Composer: (choral composition) Crossing the Bar, Stopping By Woods, 1999, Red Rose, 1999, Tears, Idle Tears, 2000. Vol. Cadets of Bergen County Drum and Bugle Corps, Allentown, Pa., 1985—. Recipient Russell W. Galt award for excellence in tchg., Susquehanna U., 1991. Mem.: NEA, Conductors Guild, Am. Fedn. Musicians, Alumni Blue Band Assn. (bd. dirs. 2003—05), Pa. Music Educators Assn. (dist. pres. 1980—82), Pa. State Edn. Assn. Home: PO Box 451 Huntingdon PA 16652

CROLEY, STEVEN P., law educator; AB, U. Mich.; JD, Yale U.; PhD, Princeton U. Bar: Mich., Pa. Law clk. to Judge Stephen Williams US Ct. Appeals, DC Cir.; prof. law U. Mich. Law Sch., Ann Arbor, 1993—, assoc. dean academic affairs, 2003—. Cons. Adminstrn. Conf. of US, US Dept. Labor, Mich. Law Revision Commn. Contbr. articles to law jours. Recipient William Jennings Bryan Prize, John M. Olin Prize, Benjamin Scharps Prize; James B. Angell Scholar. Mem.: ABA (mem. Adminstrv. Law & Regulatory Practice Sect.). Office: U Mich Law Sch 333 Hutchins Hall 625 S State St Ann Arbor MI 48107-1215 Office Phone: 734-647-3729. Office Fax: 734-763-7415. E-mail: scroley@umich.edu.

CROLL, JILLIAN KATHLEEN, dietician, researcher; b. Moorhead, Minn., Sept. 12, 1970; m. Walter Charles Croll, Dec. 31, 2000. BA, U. St. Thomas, St. Paul, Minn., 1992; MS, U. Vt., Burlington, Vt., 1994; MPH, U. Minn., Mpls., 1999, PhD, 2003. Clin. dietitian Rutland Regional Med. Ctr., Rutland, Vt., 1995—97; rsch. clin. practice dir. Eating Disorders Inst., St. Louis Park, Minn., 1999—, clin. dietitian St. Louis Park, Minn., 1999—. Fellow U. Minn., Mpls., 1998—2000. Grantee Residential Eating Disorder Treatment Outcome Study, Blue Cross Blue Shield Found. of Minn., 2003, Family Practice Physician Assessment: Eating Disorder Assessment and Treatment, Pk. Nicollet Found., 2002. Mem.: SCAN, Am. Dietetic Assn., Acad. for Eating Disorders. Office: Eating Disorders Inst 6490 Excelsior Blvd Ste 315E Saint Louis Park MN 55426 Business E-Mail: crollj@parknicollet.com.

CROMARTIE, ROBERT SAMUEL, III, thoracic surgeon; b. Fayetteville, N.C., Dec. 25, 1943; s. Robert Samuel Jr. and May Hunter (Cook) C.; m. Mary Elaine Collier; children: Robert Samuel IV, David Alan, Kimberly Elaine. AB in Chemistry, U. N.C., 1965, MD, 1969. Diplomate Am. Bd. Surgery, Am. Bd. Thoracic Surgery, Am. Bd. Laser Surgery. Intern in surgery U. Miami, 1969-70, resident in gen. surgery, 1972-74, La. State U., New Orleans, 1974-76; resident in thoracic surgery Med. U. S.C., Charleston, 1976-78; asst. prof. surgery Ind. U. Med. Ctr., Indpls., 1978-80; thoracic and cardiovasc. surgeon Tampa (Fla.) Gen. Hosp., 1980-81, Meml. Hosp., Ormond Beach, Fla., 1981—, Columbia Med. Ctr., Daytona, Fla., 1981—99, chief of surgery, 1996-97; thoracic and cardiovasc. surgeon, chief thoracic surgery Halifax Hosp., Daytona Beach, 1984—, Peninsula Med. Ctr., Ormond Beach, Fla., 1993—, Fla. Hosp. Flagler, Palm Coast, Fla., 2002—. Contbr. articles to profl. jours. Del. Fla. Med. Assn., 1992, 93, 94. Served to capt. U.S. Army, 1970-72. Decorated Bronze Star. Fellow ACS, Am. Coll. Chest Physicians, Internat. Coll. Surgeons; mem. AMA, So. Thoracic Surg. Assn., Soc. Thoracic Surgeons, James D. Rives Surg. Soc., Am. Heart Assn., Soc. Critical Care Medicine. Avocations: skiing, racquetball, writing. Home: 236 John Anderson Dr Ormond Beach FL 32176-5706 Office: Coastal Cardiovasc & Thoracic Assocs 588 Sterthaus Ave Ormond Beach FL 32174-5128 Office Phone: 386-672-9501. E-mail: samcromartie@mac.com.

CROMARTIE, WILLIAM JAMES, medical educator, researcher; b. Garland, N.C., May 19, 1913; s. Robert Samuel and Mary Blanche (Jester) C.; m. Josephine Colter Rule, Nov. 19, 1945; children: William James, Robert Colter, Mary Blanche, John Benjamin, Martha Anne. Student, Presbyn. Jr. Coll., 1929-30, U. N.C., 1931, U. Ala., 1931-33; MD, Emory U., 1937. Diplomate Am. Bd. Internal Medicine. Intern Emory U. divsn. Grady Hosp., Atlanta, 1937-38; resident Vanderbilt U. Hosp., Nashville, 1938-40; instr. pathology Vanderbilt U., 1939-41; asst. prof. bacteriology and medicine U. Minn., Mpls., 1949-50, assoc. prof., 1950-51; assoc. prof. bacteriology and medicine U. N.C., Chapel Hill, 1951-59; chief divsn. infectious diseases, dept. medicine N.C. Meml. Hosp., Chapel Hill, 1952-65, chief of staff, 1967-72; prof. microbiology-immunology-medicine U. N.C., Chapel Hill, 1959-85, prof. emeritus, 1985—. Mem. adv. panel microbiology Office Naval Rsch., Washington, 1950-55; mem. Nat. Bd. Med. Examiners, Phila., 1966-68; mem. infectious disease adv. com. NIH, Bethesda, Md., 1971-75. Mem. bd. govs. Capital Health Planning Agy., Durham, N.C.; mem. exec. com. Regional Med. Program N.C., 1972-76; mem. intelligence mission investigating German rsch. on biol. warfare. Maj. U.S. Army, 1942-46, ETO. Decorated Legion of Merit; named Alumni Disting. Prof. U. N.C., 1980 Fellow ACP, Am. Acad. Microbiology (chmn. bd. govs. 1974-75); mem. Soc. Am. Microbiologists (mem. coun. 1974-75), Am. Assn. Pathologists, Infectious Disease Soc. Am., U. N.C. Med. Alumni Assn. (Disting. Faculty award 1983, Disting. Svc. award 1989). Democrat. Home: 437 Cedar Club Cir Chapel Hill NC 27517 Office: U NC Sch Medicine Dept Microbiology and Immunology 804 FLOB 23L-H Chapel Hill NC 27514

CROMBIE, DOUGLASS DARNILL, aerospace communications system engineer; b. Alexandra, New Zealand, Sept. 14, 1924; arrived in U.S., 1962, naturalized, 1967; s. Colin Lindsay and Ruth (Darnill) C.; m. Pauline L.A. Morrison, Mar. 2, 1951. BSc, Otago U., Dunedin, New Zealand, 1947, MSc, 1949. New Zealand nat. rsch. fellow Cavendish Lab., Cambridge, England, 1958-59; head radio physics divsn. New Zealand Dept. Sci. and Indsl. Rsch., 1961-62; chief spectrum utilization divsn., chief low frequency group Inst. Telecom. Scis., Dept. Commerce, Boulder, Colo., 1962-71, dir. inst., 1971-76; dir. Inst. Telecom. Scis., Nat. Telecom. and Info. Adminstrn., Boulder, 1976-80; chief scientist Nat. Telecom. and Info. Agy., 1980-85; sr. engrng. specialist Aerospace Corp., LA, 1985—. Served with New Zealand Air Force, 1943-44. Recipient Gold medal Dept. Commerce, 1970, citation, 1972. Fellow IEEE; mem. NAE. Home: 524 Standard St El Segundo CA 90245-3039 Office: The Aerospace Corp PO Box 92957 Los Angeles CA 90009-2957

CROMER, DON M., secondary school educator, music educator; b. La Mesa, Calif., Dec. 16, 1958; s. David W. and Carolyn M. Cromer; m. Cynthia S. Sowers, Aug. 14, 1984; children: Danielle May, Jeffrey Robert. MusB in Edn., U. Fla., 1981, MusM, 1993. Cert. profl. tchr. Fla. Dept. Edn., 2003. Dir. mid. sch. band Ft. Clarke Mid. Sch., Gainesville, Fla., 1997—98, Ft. McCoy Sch., 2000—. Bd. mem. Gainesville Symphony Orch., 1997—99. Mem.: Music Educators Nat. Conf., Fla. Bandmaster Assn., Fla. Music Educators Assn., Phi Mu Alpha Sinfonia, Kappa Kappa Psi (hon.). Independent. Methodist. Avocations: travel, racquetball, music. Office: Fort McCoy Sch One Cougar Ct Fort Mc Coy FL 32134 Office Phone: 352-318-7898.

CROMER, DONALD L., aerospace and electrical engineer; b. Grand Junction, Colo., Jan. 23, 1936; BS in Engrng., U.S. Naval Acad., 1959; MSEE, U. Denver, 1969. Commd. 2d lt. USAF, advanced through grades to lt. gen., 1988; mem. staff Project Gemini NASA; mem. staff Satellite Data Systems program office; directorate of space Hdqrs. USAF; sec. Air Force Spl. Projects Office; responsible for payloads on space shuttle Dept. Def., 1984—86; comdr. Space and Missile Test Orgn., Vandenberg AFB, 1986—88, Space Sys. Divsn., 1988—91; v.p. Hughes Electronics; pres. Hughes Space and Comms. Co. Bd. dirs. Draper Labs., Aerospace Corp., Global Crossings, Universal Space Networks. Recipient Schriever award. Mem.: AIAA, Internat. Acad. Aeronautics, Calif. Space Authority (bd. dirs.), Air Force Assn. (life).

CROMLEY, ALLAN WRAY, retired journalist; b. Topeka, Apr. 11, 1922; s. Frank George and Elsie May (Leedom) C.; m. Marian Minor, Jan. 30, 1949; children: Kathleen, Janet, Carter. BS in Journalism, U. Kans., 1948. Reporter Kansas City Kansan, 1948-49, Oklahoma City Times, 1949-53; Washington bur. chief Daily Oklahoman and Oklahoma City Times, 1953-87; sr. corr. Washington bur. Daily Oklahoman, 1987-95; ret., 1995. Sec. standing com. corrs. House and Senate Galleries, 1961. Bd. visitors U. Okla., 1970-72; trustee William Allen White Found. U. Kans., 1978-90; bd. dirs. Nat. Press Found., 1987-99, Battle of the Bulge. With AUS, 1943-45, ETO. Mem.: Nat. Gridiron Club (pres. 1978), Nat. Press Club (pres. 1968). Home: 3320 Stoneybrae Dr Falls Church VA 22044-1222 Personal E-mail: alcromley@aol.com.

CROMLEY, BRENT REED, lawyer, state senator; b. Great Falls, Mont., June 12, 1941; s. Arthur and Louise Lilian (Hiebert) C.; m. Dorothea Mae Zamborini, Sept. 9, 1967; children: Brent Reed Jr., Giano Lorenzo, Taya Rose. AB in Math., Dartmouth Coll., 1963; JD with honors, U. Mont., 1968. Bar: Mont. 1968, U.S. Dist. Ct. Mont. 1968, U.S. Ct. Appeals (9th cir.) 1968, U.S. Supreme Ct. 1978, U.S. Ct. Claims 1988, U.S. Ct. Appeals (D.C. cir.) 1988. Law clk. to presiding justice U.S. Dist. Ct. Mont., Billings, 1968-69; assoc. Hutton & Sheehy and predecessor firms, Billings, 1969-77, ptnr., 1977-78, Moulton, Bellingham, Longo & Mather, P.C., Billings, 1979—, also bd. dirs.; mem. Mont. Ho. of Reps., 1991-92, Mont. Senate, 2003—; pres. State Bar Mont., 1998-99. Contbr. articles to profl. jours. Mem. Yellowstone Bd. Health, Billings, 1972—; chmn. Mont. Bd. Pers. Appeals, 1974-80. Mem. ABA (appellate practice com.), ACLU, Internat. Assn. Def. Counsel, State Bar Mont. (chmn. bd. trustees 1995-97, trustee 1991—, pres. 1998-99), Yellowstone County Bar Assn. (various offices), Internat. Assn. Def. Counsel, Christian Legal Soc., Internat. Brotherhood of Magicians, Kiwanis. Avocations: running, magic, public speaking. Home: 235 Parkhill Dr Billings MT 59101-0660 Office: Moulton Bellingham Longo & Mather PC 27 N 27th St Ste 1900 Billings MT 59101-2399 E-mail: Cromley@moultonlawfirm.com.

CROMLEY, JOANNE T., retired music educator; b. Newport, R.I. d. Richard Frank and Regina Hilger Trufant; m. Luther Allen Cromley, June 8, 1974. B, Mansfield (Pa.) U., 1971; M, Pa. State U., 1975. Music tchr. East Lycoming Sch. Dist., Hughesville, Pa., 1971—2004. Mem.: Pa. Music Educators Assn., Music Educators Nat. Conf., Beta Sigma Phi. Republican. Methodist. Avocations: golf, swimming, travel. Home: 308 Sherman St Muncy PA 17756 E-mail: duckey6400@suscom.net.

CROMLEY, JON LOWELL, lawyer; b. Riverton, Ill., May 23, 1934; s. John Donald and Naomi M. (Mathews) C. JD, John Marshall Law Sch., 1966. Bar: Ill. 1966. Real estate title examiner Chgo. Title & Trust Co., 1966-70; pvt. practice Genoa, Ill., 1970—; mem. firm O'Grady & Cromley, Genoa, 1970-96. Bd. dirs. Citizen's First Nat. Bank, 1984-92, Kingston Mut. Ins. Co., Genoa Main St., Inc. Mem.: ABA, DeKalb County Bar Assn., Chgo. Bar Assn., Ill. State Bar Assn. Home: 130 Homewood Dr Genoa IL 60135-1260 Office Phone: 815-784-5895. E-mail: jcromley@msn.com.

CROMLEY, RAYMOND AVOLON, syndicated columnist; b. Tulare, Calif., Aug. 23, 1910; s. William James and Grace Violet (Bailey) C.; m. Masuyo Marjorie Suto (dec. Apr. 1946); m. Helen Sue Holcomb (dec. July 1967); children: Donald Stowe, Helen Sue, Jessica Lynn, Linda Grace, William Holcomb, Mary Ann, John Austin. BS in Physics, Calif. Inst. Tech., 1933; student, Japanese Lang. Inst., Tokyo, 1936-39, Strategic Intelligence Sch., Washington, 1954. Reporter Pasadena (Calif.) Post, 1928-34, Honolulu Advertiser, 1934-35, Flintridge Sch., Pasadena, 1935-36; reporter, then financial editor Japan Advertiser, Tokyo, 1936-40; editor Trans Pacific (econ. and financial weekly), 1938-40; with Wall St. Jour., 1938-55; Far Ea. corr., 1938-47; Washington corr., 1947-55; sci. editor radio program Monitor, 1955-56; econ. and financial commentator NBC radio, 1956-57; asst. producer CBS Radio, 1957-58; mil. analyst Newspaper Enterprise Assn., 1958-64; pres. Cromley News-Features, 1976—; syndicated columnist, 1964—. Asst. logic, freshman English Calif. Inst. Tech., 1928-30; lectr. Air War Coll., 1952, 54, Dept. State Fgn. Service Inst., 1955, 65-67; cons. guerilla war, Asian politics, 1952— Author: Veterans Benefits, 1966, 2d edit., 1970, 3d edit., 1973, rev. edit., 1975, Educational Benefits, 1968, Ariwara Narihira and Japanese Poetry of the Heian and Nara Periods. Chmn. dist. bds. charter rev. Boy Scouts Am., 1956-60; sec. bishop's com. pastoral benefits Va. Conf. Meth. Ch., 1967-68; organizer com. estatlishment Martha Washington Libr., Mt. Vernon, Va., 1954; chmn. Inter-ch. Coun. Teen Activities and Teen Clubs, Mt. Vernon, 1955-57, World Coun. Youth, 1932-35. Prisoner of war, 1941-42; col. AUS, 1943-46; comdg. officer U.S. Mil. and Dept. State mission to Mao-Tse-tung's hdqs., Yenan, Communist China. Decorated Legion of Merit, Bronze Star medal. Mem. Nat. Trust for Historic Preservation, Asiatic Soc. Japan, State Dept. Corrs. Assn. (pres. 1954-55), White House Corrs. Assn., Ret. Officers Assn., Smithsonian Assocs., Nat. Archives Assn., Nat. Press Found., Am. Fgn. Svc. Assn., Nat. Press Club Washington, Assn.Corcoran Gallery Art, Sigma Delta Chi, Pi Kappa Delta. Republican. Methodist (lay spkr., Sunday sch. tchr.). Clubs: Tokyo Correspondents (exec. com. 1947); Overseas Writers (Washington). Home and Office: Hollin Hills 1912 Marthas Rd Alexandria VA 22307-1952 *All great religions have one common theme -- Do unto others as you would have them do unto you. Some express it, do not do unto others what you would not want them to do unto you. I have seen the power of these beliefs first hand among ordinary men and women in Japan, Korea, China, Vietnam, Laos, Thailand, Bangladesh, India, Cuba, Mexico.*

CROMWELL, ADELAIDE M., sociology educator; b. Washington, Nov. 27, 1919; d. John Wesley Jr. and Yetta Elizabeth (Mavritte) Cromwell; 1 child, Anthony C. Hill. AB, Smith Coll., 1940; MA, U. Pa., 1941; cert. in Social Work, Bryn Mawr Coll., 1943; PhD, Radcliffe Coll., 1952; LHD (hon.), U. Southwestern Mass., 1972, George Washington U., 1989, Boston U., 1995. Mem. faculty Hunter Coll., 1942—44, Smith Coll., 1945—46, Boston U., 1951—85, prof. sociology, 1971—85, dir. Afro-Am. studies, 1969—88, prof. emerita sociology, 1985—; mem. faculty Harvard U. Ext., 1965—66. Mem. adv. com. vol. fgn. aid AID, 1964-80; mem. NEH, 1968-70; adv. com. corrections Commonwealth Mass., 1955-68; mem. commn. instns. higher edn., 1973-74; adv. com. to dir. IRS, 1970-71, to dir. census, 1972-75. Bd. dirs. Wheelock Coll., 1971-74, Nat. Ctr. Afro-Am. Artists, 1971-80, African Am. Scholars Coun., 1971—, Nat. Fellowship Fund, 1974-75, Mass. Hist. Commn., 1993; bd. dirs. Sci. and Tech. for Internat. Devel., 1984-86; mem. exec. com. Am. Soc. African Culture, 1967. Mem. AAAS, African Studies Assn. (bd. dir. 1966-68), Am. Acad. of Arts and Scis., Am. Sociol. Assn., Coun. on Fgn. Affairs (bd. fgn. scholarships 1980-84), Mass. Hist. Soc., Phi Beta Kappa. Home: 51 Addington Rd Brookline MA 02445-4519

CROMWELL, FLORENCE STEVENS, occupational therapist; b. Lewistown, Pa., May 14, 1922; d. William Andrew and Florence (Stevens) Cromwell. BS in Edn., Miami U., Oxford, Ohio, 1943; BS in Occupl. Therapy, Washington U., St. Louis, 1949; MA, U. So. Calif., 1952; cert. in health facility adminstrn., UCLA, 1978. Mem. staff, then supervising therapist Los Angeles County Gen. Hosp., 1949—53; occupl. therapist Goodwill Industries, L.A., 1954—55; staff therapist Vis. Nurse Assn., Phila., 1955—56; rsch. therapist United Cerebral Palsy Assn., L.A., 1956—60; dir. occupl. therapy Orthopaedic Hosp., L.A., 1961—67; coord. occupl. therapy Rsch. and Tng. Ctr. U. So. Calif. Med. Sch., L.A., 1967—70; assoc. prof. U. So. Calif., L.A., 1970—76, acting chmn. dept. occupl. therapy, 1973—76, mem. adv. bd. project SEARCH, Sch. Medicine, 1969—72; founding editor Occupl. Therapy in Health Care jour., 1984—88, editor emerita, 1988—. Assoc. dir. L.A. Job Corps Ctr., 1977—78; cons. in edn. and program devel., 1976—95; freelance editor, 1986—. Author: Manual for Basic Skills Assessment, 1960; contbr. articles to profl. jours. Mem. scholarship com. L.A. March of Dimes, 1963—70; mentor U. Tex.-Galveston Class 1990 Occupl. Therapy; bd. dirs. Am. Occupl. Therapy Found., 1965—69, v.p., 1966—69; bd. dirs. Nat. Health Coun., 1975—78. Served to lt. (j.g.) WAVES USNR, 1943—46. Recipient Disting. Alumni award, Washington U., 1978, Disting. Lectr., Calif. Occupl. Therapy Found., 1986. Fellow: Am. Occupl. Therapy Assn. (pres. 1967—73, Pres.'s WLWest commendation AOTA-AOTF 1999); mem.: Assn. Schs. Allied Health Professions (dir. 1973—74), Coalition Ind. Health Professions (chmn. 1973—74), So. Calif. Occupl. Therapy Assn. (pres. 1950—51, 1975—76), Inst. Medicine NAS (emerita 2002), Cwen, Kappa Kappa Gamma, Kappa Delta Pi, Mortar Bd.

CROMWELL, JAMES, actor; b. L.A., Jan. 27, 1940; s. John Cromwell and Kay Johnson; m. Anne Ulvestad, 1977 (div. 1986); 3 children; m. Julie Cobb, May 29, 1986. Student, Carnegie Inst. Tech. Actor (films) Murder by Death, 1976, The Cheap Detective, 1978, The Man with Two Brains, 1983, Tank, 1984, Revenge of the Nerds, 1984, Oh, God! You Devil, 1984, The House of God, 1984, Explorers, 1985, Revenge of the Nerds II: Nerds in Paradise, 1987, The Rescue, 1988, The Runnin' Kind, 1989, Pink Cadillac, 1989, The Babe, 1992, Romeo is Bleeding, 1993, Babe, 1995 (Oscar award nominee for best supporting actor), Star Trek: First Contact, 1996, Eraser, 1996, Owd Bob, 1997, The People vs. Larry Flynt, 1996, The Education of Little Tree, 1997, L.A. Confidential, 1997, Snow Falling on Cedars, 1998, Deep Impact, 1998, Species II, 1998, Babe: Pig in the City, 1998, Winter, 1998, The General's Daughter, 1999, The Green Mile, 1999, Space Cowboys, 2000, Spirit: Stallion of the Cimarron (voice), 2002, Sum of All Fears, 2002, The Nazi, 2002, Blackball, 2003, The Snow Walker, 2003, I, Robot, 2004, The Longest Yard, 2005; (TV series) All in the Family, 1971, Hot L. Baltimore, 1975, The Nancy Walker Show, 1976, The Last Precinct, 1986, Easy Street, 1986, Mama's Boy, 1988, Walking After Midnight, 1999, Citizen Baines, 2001, Six Feet Under, 2004-05; (TV miniseries) Once an Eagle, 1976, Dream West, 1986, Fail Safe, 2000, The Magnificent Ambersons, 2002, RFK, 2002, A Death in the Family, 2002, Angels in America, 2003; (TV movies) The Girl in the Empty Grave, 1977, Deadly Game, 1977, A Christmas Without Snow, 1980, The Rainmaker, 1982, Spraggue, 1984, Alison's Demise, 1987, China Beach, 1988, Christine Cromwell: Things That Go Bump in the Night, 1989, Miracle Landing, 1990, In a Child's Name, 1991, Revenge of the Nerds III: The Next Generation, 1992, The Shaggy Dog, 1994, Revenge of the Nerds IV: Nerds in Love, 1994, RKO 281, 1999, Fail Safe, 2000, The Magnificent Ambersons, 2002, Salem's Lot, 2004; (TV guest appearances) The Rockford Files, 1974, Barney Miller, 1977, 1979, 1981, M*A*S*H, 1977, Three's Company, 1977, Eight is Enough, 1979, Little House on the Prairie, 1980, Dallas, 1984, 1985, Hardcastle and McCormick, 1985, Scarecrow and Mrs. King, 1986, Star Trek: the Next Generation, 1990, 1993, Home Improvement, 1994, Picket Fences, 1995, The Client, 1996, ER, 2001, Enterprise, 2001, 05, The West Wing, 2004.*

CROMWELL, OLIVER DEAN, investment banker; b. Cleve., Sept. 19, 1950; s. Oliver and Mildred Jeanette (Galko) C.; m. Sheila Lea Terry, May 19, 1984; children: Ashley Melissa, Oliver Spencer. AB, Brown U., 1972; MBA, Harvard U., 1976. CFA. Trust adminstr. Bankers Trust, N.Y.C., 1973-74; assoc. Donaldson, Lufkin & Jenrette, N.Y.C., 1976-79, v.p., 1980-84, sr. v.p., 1985-87, Oppenheimer & Co. Inc., N.Y.C., 1987-88; 1st v.p. Paine Webber, N.Y.C., 1988-90; founder, pres. Bentley Assocs. L.P., N.Y.C., 1990—; pres. Bentley Securities Corp., N.Y.C., 1991—. Co-author: Leading Investment Bankers: The Art & Science of Investment Banking, 2002. Co-chmn. N.Y. met. area com. Brown Campaign, 1992—94; class '72 v.p. Brown U., 1997—; major gifts com. Harvard Bus. Sch. 20th Reunion, 1995—96; exec. com. Brown ann. fund Riverdale County Sch., 2000—03, 2005—. Recipient Alumni Svc. award Brown U., 1990. Mem. Assn. for Investment Mgmt. and Rsch., N.Y. Soc. Security Analysts, Securities Industry Assn. N.Y. (exec. com. 1987-90), Assn. Corp. Growth, Assn. Alumni Brown U. (co-head class agt. ann. fun. 1983-87, exec. com., bd. dirs. 85-87, steering com. 5 yr. reunion fund 85-87, exec. com. ann fund 91-93, co-chmn. 20 yr. reunion fund 91-92, co-chmn. 25 yr. reunion fund 96-97, bd. govs. 97-98, co-chmn. 30 yr. reunion fund 2001-02, exec. com. ann. fund leadership coun. 04—), Aston Martin Owners Club-East, Maserati Club Am., Rolls Royce Owners Club (bd. dirs. 1992-93), Bentley Drivers Club (U.K.), Brown U. Club N.Y.C. (bd. dirs. 1983-95, treas. 1984-89, v.p. 1989-91, pres. 1991-93), Harvard Bus. Sch. Club. N.Y. Home: 4 Eastway Bronxville NY 10708-4302 Office: Bentley Assocs LP 101 Park Ave 22d Fl New York NY 10178-0002 Office Phone: 212-972-8700. Business E-Mail: odcromwell@bentleylp.com.

CRON, KENNETH D., information technology executive; BA in Psychology, U. Colorado. Pres. publishing CMPMedia Inc. (now CMP Media LLC), Manhasset, NY, 1978—99; chmn., CEO Uproar Inc. (later acquired by Flipside), NYC, 1999—2001; CEO Flipside Network (div. of Vivendi Universal Games, Inc.), NYC, 2001; chmn., CEO Vivendi Universal Games, Inc. (div. of Vivendi Universal, S.A.), Los Angeles, Calif., 2001; interim COO Vivendi Universal Entertainment, NYC, 2002; bd. dirs. Computer Associates Internat., Inc., Islandia, NY, 2002—, interim CEO, 2004—05; chmn. Midway Games, Inc., Chgo. Office: Computer Assoc Internat Inc One Computer Plaza Islandia NY 11749 also: Midway Games Inc 2704 W Roscoe St Chicago IL 60618*

CRON, STEVEN MICHAEL, lawyer; b. LA, Feb. 17, 1948; BA, UCLA, 1970; JD, U. Calif., Hastings Coll. Law, 1973. Bar: Calif. 1974. Dep. pub. defender LA County Pub. Defender's Office, 1974—80; ptnr. Cron, Israels & Stark, Santa Monica, Calif. Adj. prof. Pepperdine U. Sch. Law; legal commentator Fox News, CNN, MSNBC. Mem.: Nat. Assn. Criminal Defense Lawyers, Calif. Attys. for Criminal Justice, Nat. Conf. Bar Pres., State Bar Calif. (mem. Com. Profl. Responsibility and Conduct), LA County Bar Assn., Santa Monica Bar Assn. (mem. bd. trustees 1987—94, pres. 1992—93), Zeta Beta Tau. Office: Cron, Israels & Stark 1541 Ocean Ave Ste 200 Santa Monica CA 90401 Office Phone: 310-421-9888. Personal E-mail: smcron@aol.com.

CRON, THEODORE OSCAR, writer, editor, educator; b. Newton, Mass., June 20, 1930; s. Jacob and Anna Ruth (Siegel) C.; m. Rosalie Heilpern, Jan. 17, 1954 (dec. Dec. 1998); children: Elizabeth Daryl Koozmin, Adam David. AB, Harvard U., 1952, MAT, 1954. Asst. commr. FDA, Washington, 1965-68; cons., writer Cron Comm., Chevy Chase, Md., 1969-77, 91—; dir. info. FTC, Washington, 1977-79; speech writer Office of Surgeon Gen., Washington, 1979-89; dir. info. Nat. Assn. Elem. Sch. Prins., Alexandria, Va., 1989-91; editor Better Ways to Health, Chevy Chase, 1995-96. Adj. prof. journalism George Washington U., Washington, 1979-96; writer, editor NIH, Bethesda, Md., 1991—, Nat. Health Svc. Corps, Bethesda, 1992—, NSF, Washington, 1993—, Cardiology Rsch. Found., Washington, 1995—, Nat. Acad. Scis., 1996—, Magnificent Pubs., 1998—. Author: Portrait of Carnegie Hall, 1966; contbr. articles to profl. jours. Chmn. bd. dirs. Edn. Study Ctr., Washington, 1968-73; trustee Intermet, Washington, 1971-75; bd. dirs. Nat. Coalition Consumer Edn., Madison, N.J., 1989-94. Recipient Spl. award Assn. Am. Indian Physicians, 1985, Freedom Found. at Valley Forge award 1989. Mem. Washington Ind. Writers, D.C. Sci. Writers Assn., N.Y. Acad. Sci. Avocation: watercolor painting. Home: 5517 Trent St Chevy Chase MD 20815-5511 Office Phone: 301-718-4688. E-mail: tedcron@aol.com.

CRONAN, JOHN EMERSON, microbiologist; b. Long Beach, Calif., Dec. 2, 1942; s. John Emerson Cronan and Matilda Marceline; m. Elizabeth Ann Johnson; children: Mark Robert, Glen Emerson. BA, Calif. State U., Northridge, 1965; PhD, U. Calif., Irvine, 1968. Asst. prof. molecular biophysics and biochemistry Yale U, New Haven, 1970—74, assoc. prof. molecular biophysics, 1974—78; prof. microbiology U. Ill., Urbana, 1978—, prof. biochemistry, 1987—, head dept. microbiology, prof. microbiology alumni, 2004—. Cons. E. I. DuPont Demours, Wilmington, Del., 1984—88, BASF, Ludwigshaffen, Germany, 1994—96, Monsanto, St. Louis, 1994—98, Wacker Chemie, Munich, 2001—, LG Life Science, Taejon, 2000—, Dupont, Wilmington, 1983—87, Monsanto, St. Louis, 1993—98, Advanced Medicine, Inc., South San Francisco, 2001—, Kosan Biosciences, Hayward, 2000—, Surromed, Moutain View, 2001—. Recipient MERIT award, NIH, 1993—, Biogen Award in Bacterial Physiology, Biogen, SA, 1984; scholar Univ. scholar, U. Ill., 1992. Home: 305 W High St Urbana IL 61801 Office: Univ Illinois 601 S Goodwin Ave Urbana IL 61801 Business E-Mail: j-cronan@life.uiuc.edu.

CRONAUER, GAIL ANN, theater educator, actress; d. Arline Searfoss and Joseph Jacob Cronauer; m. Mark Allyn Hougland, Apr. 23, 1974; children: Adam Cronauer Hougland, Noah Cronauer Hougland. MFA in acting, Case Western Res. U., 1971—73. Asst. prof. theatre Ill. State U., Normal, 1973—75, Webster Coll., St. Louis, 1975—76, U. Wis., Green Bay, 1976—79, So. Meth. U., Dallas, 1979—85; prof. theatre Collin County C.C., Plano, Tex., 1992—. Freelance theatre artist, Dallas, 1985—92. Actor: (plays) Hedda Gabler, The Night of the Iguana, The Seagull, All's Well That Ends Well, The Sisters Rosensweig, Fool for Love, The Norman Conquests, Better Half Dead, Therese Raquin, Othello, Much Ado About Nothing, Romeo and Juliet, Wolf At the Door, The Stick Wife, On The Verge, Getting Out (Dallas Critics award, 1980), A Shayna Maidel; (films) The Newton Boys, Carried Away, JFK, Learning Curve, Murder in the Heartland, Unspoken Truth, A Mother's Gift; (plays) Richard III; dir.: Horton Foote Trilogy, Boy Gets Girl, The Learned Ladies, Macbeth, Buried Child, Picnic, All in the Timing, The Three Sisters, The Heiress, You Can't Take It With You, Sketches and Strings, The Time of Your Life, Twelfth Night. Recipient Ambassador award for svc., CCCCD. Mem.: SAG, Actors Equity Assn. (mem. liasion com. 1996—2004), Women in Film. Office: Collin County Cmty Coll 2800 E Spring Creek Pkwy Plano TX 75074 Office Phone: 972-881-5125. Office Fax: 972-881-5103. Personal E-mail: cronhoug@flash.net. E-mail: gcronauer@ccccd.edu.

CRONCE, PAUL CALVIN, retired dermatologist; b. Trenton, NJ, Dec. 25, 1931; s. Paul I. and Rachie Cathryn (Allen) C.; m. Nancy Elizabeth Dorrien, Aug. 27, 1960 (div. Aug. 1979); children: Paul Allen, Charles Scott, Thomas Taylor. BA summa cum laude, Duke U., Durham, N.C., 1954; attended, Duke U. Grad. Sch. Arts & Scis., Durham, N.C., 1954-55; MD, Duke U. Sch. Medicine, Durham, N.C., 1960. Diplomate Am. Bd. Dermatology, 1965. Rotating med. intern USPHS Hosp., Boston, 1960-61, acting dermatology resident Staten Island, 1961—62, dermatology resident, 1962—65, asst. chief dermatology, 1965—66; vis. fellow in dermatology Columbia-Presbyn. Med. Ctr., N.Y.C., 1964-65; ptnr. Alden & Cronce Dermatology, Atlanta, 1966-73; pres. and treas. Alden Dermatology Assocs., P.A., Atlanta, 1973-99; ret., 1999. Instr. medicine, dermatology Emory U. Sch. Medicine, 1967-71, asst. clin. prof. dermatology, 1971-78, assoc. clin. prof. dermatology, 1978-89, clin. prof. dermatology, 1989-2001, prof. emeritus dermatology, 2001-. Contbr. articles to profl. jours. Fellow Am. Acad. Dermatology; mem. Southeastern Dermatological Assn., Ga. Soc. Dermatologists (vice chmn. 1971), Med. Assn. Ga., Internat. Soc. Dermatologic Surgery, Atlanta Dermatological Assn. (sec.-treas. 1967, pres. 1968), Med. Assn. Atlanta, Phi Beta Kappa, Alpha Omega Alpha. Republican. Presbyterian. Avocations: travel, gardening.

CRONE, ALAN GRADY, lawyer; b. Memphis, July 20, 1965; s. James Gerard and Dorothy Williams Crone; m. Allison S. Crone, July 8, 1989; children: James, Charles, Margaret. BA, U. Memphis, 1987, JD, 1990. Bar: U.S. Dist. Ct. (we. dist.) Tenn. 1991, U.S. Dist. Ct. (ea. and we. dists.) Ark. 1991, U.S. Dist. Ct. (ctrl. dist.) Tenn. 1995, U.S. Multi-Dist. Litigation Panel 1996, U.S. Ct. Appeals (6th cir.) 1998, U.S. Ct. Appeals (8th cir.) 2000, U.S. Supreme Ct. 2000. With Armstrong, Allen, Prewitt, Gentry, Johnston & Holmes, Memphis, 1990—91, Fisher, Avery, Yawn & Futris, Memphis, 1992—93, Apperson, Crump, Duzane & Maxwell, Memphis, 1994; apptd. chief counsel Tenn. Dept. Employment Security, 1995; asst. Shelby County atty., 1996—; co-founder, mng. mem. Crone & Mason, PLC, Memphis, 1995—. Spkr. profl. assn. convs.; panelist Nat. Fedn. Ind. Businesses Small Bus. Summit, Nashville, 1999, Am. Soc. Indsl. Security, Program on Profl. Investigations, St. Louis, 2000; campaign mgr. Salvaggio for Congress, Memphis, 1994. Frequent commentator on legal and polit. issues various local TV and radio news programs, Memphis, 1998—. Spl. judge Shelby County Gen. Sessions and City of Memphis Ct.; chmn. Rep. Party of Shelby County, 1999—; campaign counsel Congressman Ed Bryant, 1994, fin. com., 1994; steering com. Rep. Party of Shelby County, 1991—95; bd. dirs. Family Svcs. of Mid-South, 1996—98, Fire Mus. Memphis, 1998—2001, treas., 1999—2000. Mem.: ABA (litigation sect., coms. on pretrial practice and procedure and class s), Def. Rsch. Inst., Tenn. Def. Lawyers Assn., Ark. Bar Assn., Tenn. Bar Assn., Memphis Bar Assn. Roman Catholic. Office: Crone & Mason PLC 8 S 3d St 5th Fl Memphis TN 38103 E-mail: acrone@cronemason.com.

CRONE, EUGENE N., addictions specialist, retired educator; b. Newton Falls, Ohio., Apr. 17, 1929; s. Clarence Bennet and Violet Richards Crone. BM, Youngstown U., 1954; MA, Columbia U., 1958; PhD, Nat. U. Grad. Studies, Dallas, 1974. Cert. addiction profl., MAC-master addiction counselor, nat. cert. addiction counselor II, internat. cert. alcohol and drug counselor. Tchr., prof. various pub. schs. and colls., 1952—78; dir. addictions Horizon Psychiatric Hosp., Clearwater, Fla., 1978—95, Nat. Deaf Acad., Mt. Dora, Fla., 1995—, La Amistad Health Svcs., Maitland, Fla., 1999—2003; with Nat. Deaf Acad., Mt. Dora, Fla., 2003—. Presenter in field. Author: They Hear Through Their Eyes, 2003; contbr. articles to profl. jours. PFC U.S. Army, 1950—52. Recipient Profl. of Yr. Nat. award, NAADAC Nat. Conv., 1997, Profl. of Yr. award, Fla. NAADAC, 1996. Mem.: NAADAC, Addiction Profls. of Fla., Internat. Cert. Alcohol & Drug Counselors (presenter). Methodist. Home: 1001 Bristol Lake Rd #212 Mount Dora FL 32757 Office: Nat Deaf Acad 19650 US Hwy 441 Mount Dora FL 32757

CRONE, JOHN THOMAS, IV, portfolio manager, financial analyst; b. Nassau, Bahamas, May 8, 1969; came to U.S., 1971; s. John Thomas III and Kathryn (Abbott) C.; m. Tanya Melich Crone, May 3, 1997; children: Daisy Kathryn, Anne. BA, So. Meth. U., 1992. Rsch. asst. San Antonio Capital Mgmt., 1992-94; sales trader Bursa-Mex. Cast Bolsa, Mexico City, 1994-95; rsch. analyst Temp. Global Advisors, Nassau, 1995-2000; v.p., portfolio mgr. Templeton Global Advisors, Nassau, 2000—. Mem. Bahamas Soc. Fin. Analysts, Lyford Cay Club, Phi Delta Theta (v.p. 1990-91). Episcopalian. Office: Templeton Global Advisors PO Box 7759 Nassau The Bahamas E-mail: jcrone@templeton.com.

CRONENWETT, JACK LEMOYNE, vascular surgeon educator; b. Ludington, Mich., Dec. 13, 1946; s. Jack L. and K. Marie (Grundmark) C.; m. Linda R. Houk, 1969 (div. 1980); children: Sara, Molly; m. Debra A. Cote, Sept. 26, 1981. BS, U. Mich., 1969; MD, Stanford U., 1973. Diplomate in gen. surgery and vascular surgery Am. Bd. Surgery. Resident in gen. surgery U. Mich., Ann Arbor, 1973-79; resident in vacsular surgery U. Tenn., Memphis, 1979-80; asst. prof. surgery U. Mich., Ann Arbor, 1980-84; assoc. prof. surgery Dartmouth Coll., Hanover, N.H., 1984-89, prof. surgery, 1989—. Editor Jour. Vascular Surgery, 2003—. Mem. Am. Surg. Assn., New Eng. Soc. Vascular Surgery (sec. 1991-96, pres. 1997-98), Soc. Vascular Surgery (recorder 1996-2001, pres. 2002-03), Soc. Univ. Surgeons, Ea. Vascular Soc., Midwestern Vascular Soc., New Eng. Surg. Soc., Assn. Program Dirs. in Vascular Surgery (sec.-treas. 1993-97, pres. 2000-02). Office: Dartmouth-Hitchcock Med Ctr 1 Medical Center Dr Lebanon NH 03756-0002 Office Phone: 603-650-8670. E-mail: j.cronewett@hitchcock.org.

CRONENWETT, LINDA HOUK, dean; BSN, U. Mich., 1966, PhD in nursing, 1983; MSN in maternal-child nursing, U. Washington, 1970. Dir. profl. nursing, dir. nursing rsch. and edn. Mary Hitchcock Meml. Hosp., Lebanon, N.H., Dartmouth-Hitchcock Med. Ctr., Lebanon; mem. faculty U. Mich., U. N.H., Dartmouth U.; with U. N.C., Chapel Hill, 1998—, dean Sch. Nursing, 1999—. Mem. editl. bd. Jour. Nursing Measurement. With USN. Recipient Disting. Profl. Svc. award Assn. Women's Health, Obstetric and Neonatal Nurses, 1993, Disting. Scholar Nursing award NYU, 1997. Fellow Am. Acad. Nursing. Office: U NC Sch Nursing CB 7640 Carrington Hl Chapel Hill NC 27599-0001

CRONHOLM, LOIS S., academic administrator; b. St. Louis, Aug. 15, 1930; d. Fred and Emma (Tobias) Kisslinger; m. James Cronholm, Sept. 15, 1965 (div. 1974); children: Judith Frances, Peter Foster, Mark Steven Feldman; m. Stuart E. Neff, Apr. 11, 1975. BA, U. Louisville, 1962, PhD, 1966. Asst. prof. biology dept. U. Louisville, 1973-76, assoc. prof., 1976-80, dean arts and scis., 1979-85, prof., 1980-85; dean arts and scis., prof. Temple U., Phila., 1985-92; sr. v.p. acad. affairs, prof. Baruch Coll., CUNY, 1992-98, interim pres., 1998-99; CEO Ctr. for Jewish History, N.Y.C., 1999—2001; sr. v.p., chief operating officer CCNY, 2001—. Bd. dirs. J. History Ideas, 1987—93. Contbr. articles to profl. jours. Chmn. Human Relations Commn., Louisville, 1976-79; group capt. Dems., Valley Station, Ky., 1975-78; sec. Grass Roots Dem. Club, Valley Station, 1975; chmn. Southwestern Jefferson County Econ. Devel. Com., Valley Station, 1983-84; pres. Hampden-Booth Theater Libr., 1997-99. Recipient Pre-Doctoral fellowship NIH, 1963-66, Post-Doctoral fellowship NIH, 1967-70. Mem. Nat. Assn. Land Grant and Urban Univs. (chmn. com. arts and scis. 1987-89, bd. dirs. divsn. urban affairs 1988-90, sec. bd. dirs. internat. divsn. 1991-92), Coun. Colls. Arts and Scis. (bd. dirs. 1987-90, pres.-elect 1989-90, pres. 1990-91, chair commn. on faculty recruitment ethics 1991-93), Players Club N.Y.C. (sec. bd. 1994). Democrat. Jewish. Avocations: gardening, cooking. Office Phone: 212-650-7309. Business E-Mail: lcronholm@ccny.cuny.edu.

CRONIN, BONNIE KATHRYN LAMB, museum director; b. Mpls., Mar. 11, 1941; d. Edwin Rector and Maude Kathryn (MacPherson) Lamb; m. Barry Jay Cronin, Jan. 23, 1963 (div. Feb. 1972); 1 son, Philip Scott. BA, U. Mo., 1963, BS, 1964; MS, Ill. State U., 1970. Copywriter Neds & Wardlow Advt., Columbia, Mo., 1962-64; tchr. Columbia Sch. Sys., 1964-68, Normal (Ill.) Sch. Sys., 1968-69; asst. gen. mgr. Sta. WGLT, Normal, 1969-70; dir. devel. Radio Sta. WBUR, Boston, 1970-71, program dir., 1971-75, gen. mgr., 1975-78; dir. pub. rels. Joy of Movement Ctr., 1978-80; dep. scheduler Anderson for Pres., 1980; scheduler Spaulding for Gov., 1980-81; dir. scheduling John Kerry Campaign, 1982; dir. of scheduling Mass. Lt. Gov.'s Office, dir. ops., 1983-84; dep. campaign mgr. Kerry for Senate Com., 1984; dir. ops. Senator John Kerry, Washington, 1985-86, dir. constituency outreach Boston, 1986-92, exec. asst., 1992-95; chief staff to Senator John Kerry Boston, 1995-97; dir. devel. and pub. affairs Working Capital, 1997-2001; dir. found. rels. USS Constn. Mus., 2001—. Chair Mass. Micro Enterprise Coalition, 2000-01. Commr. Melrose Human Rights Commn., Mass., 2004—; active Melrose Econ. Devel. Coun., 2002—04. Mem.: Mass. Broadcasters Assn. (dir. 1973—78, chair scholarship com., pub. svc. com., adminstrv. oversight com.), Polymnia Choral Soc. (pres. 2002—04), Nat. Pub. Radio (dir. 1974—77, chairperson devel. com.). Office: Box 1812 Boston MA 02129 Office Phone: 617-426-1812. E-mail: bonniemelrose@aol.com.

CRONIN, DANIEL ANTHONY, emeritus archbishop; b. Boston, Mass., Nov. 14, 1927; s. Daniel George and Emily Frances (Joyce) Cronin. STL, Gregorian U., 1953, STD summa cum laude, 1956; LLD, Suffolk U., Boston, 1969, Stonehill Coll., North Easton, 1971. Ordained priest Roman Catholic Ch., 1952. Attache Apostolic Internunciature, Addis Ababa, Ethiopia, 1957—61, Secretariat of State, Vatican City, 1961—68; named Monsignor by His Holiness Pope John XXIII, 1962; named titular bishop of Egnatia and aux. bishop of Boston, 1968—70; Episcopal ordination from Archbishop of Boston Richard Cardinal Cushing, 1968; pastor St. Raphael Ch., Medford, Mass., 1968—70; bishop Fall River, Mass., 1970—92; archbishop of Hartford Conn., 1992—2003; archbishop emeritus of Hartford, 2003—. Mem.: KC (Father Michael J. McGivney award 1999). Office: 134 Farmington Ave Hartford CT 06105-3723*

CRONIN, DOREEN, writer, former lawyer; b. Queens, N.Y. m. Andrew Cronin. Grad., Pa. State U., St. John's U. Former comml. and civil litigation atty., NY; children's book author, 2000—. Author: Click, Clack, Moo: Cows That Type, 2000 (Caldecott Honor, 2000, Red Clover award, N.Y. Times best-seller, Cuffie award, Simington Black Honor, BookSense Honor, The Bill Martin Jr. award Kans. Reading Assn., 2003, The Charlotte award NYSRA, 2002, The Md. Sunflower award, 2002, The Smart award, 2002), Giggle, Giggle, Quack, 2000, Diary of a Worm, 2003, Duck for President, 2004 (Book Sense Book of Yr. for children's illustrated book, 2005). Office: Simon & Schuster Childrens Pub 1230 Ave of the Americas New York NY 10020*

CRONIN, JAMES WATSON, physicist, researcher; b. Chgo., Sept. 29, 1931; s. James Farley and Dorothy (Watson) Cronin; m. Annette Martin, Sept. 11, 1954; children: Catheryn, Emily, Daniel Watson. AB, So. Methodist U. (1951); PhD, U. Chgo.; D (hon.), U. Paris, 1995, U. Leeds, 1996, Univ. Pierre & Marie Curie, 1994; DSc (hon.), U. Leeds, 1996. Asst. physicist Brookhaven Nat. Lab., 1955—58; asst. prof. Princeton, 1958—65, prof. physics, 1965—71; prof. physics and astronomy U. Chgo., 1971—, prof. emeritus physics and astronomy. Loeb lectr. physics Harvard U., 1967; participant early devel. spark chambers; co-discoverer CP-violation, 64; lectr. Nashima Found., 1993; rschr. Internat. Ctr. Sci. Rsch. Contbr. articles to sci. jours. Decorated chevalier Legion of Honor (France); recipient Rsch. Corp. Am. award, 1967, John Price Wetherill medal, Franklin Inst., 1976, E.O. Lawrence award, ERDA, 1977, Nobel prize for Physics, 1980, Nat. medal of Sci., 1999; fellow Guggenheim, 1982—83; Sloan fellow, 1964—66, Guggenheim fellow, 1970—71. Mem.: NAS (coun. mem.), Russian Acad. Sci. (foreign mem.), Am. Phys. Soc., Am. Acad. Arts and Scis., Am. Philos. Soc. Achievements include showing that in rare instances subatomic particles called K mesons violate CP symmetry during their decay. Office: U Chgo Enrico Fermi Inst 5630 S Ellis Ave Chicago IL 60637-1433 E-mail: jwc@uchep.uchicago.edu.*

CRONIN, JEROME JOSEPH, JR., marketing educator, consultant; b. Springfield, Ohio, Apr. 27, 1952; s. Jerome Joseph Cronin and Edith E. Markley; m. Kern S. Westerberg, Oct. 9, 1976 (div. Aug. 1980). BS in Mktg., Wright State U., 1974; MBA, U. Dayton, 1976; PhD in Mktg., The Ohio State U., 1981. Vis. asst. prof. The Ohio State U., Columbus, 1981—82; asst. prof. U. Ky., Lexington, 1982—86; from asst. prof. to prof. Fla. State U., Tallahassee, 1986—94, prof., 1994—2002, Carl DeSantis Prof. Bus. Adminstrn., 2002—. Dir. edn. and tng. The Mktg. Inst. Fla. State U., 1997—; cons. Internat. Taxi & Literary Found., Raleigh, N.C., 1999-2001, Southwest Bell, San Antonio, Tex., 2000-01, Fla. Dept. Transportation, Tampa, 1997-2001, Ameritech, Chgo., 2000. Contbr. articles to profl. jours. Panel mem. Ctr. Clean Air Policy, Washington, 1999-2001, Transportation Rsch. Bd., Washington, 1999-2000, State of Ariz., Phoenix, 2000. Mem. Soc. Mktg. Advances, Am. Mktg. Assn., Acad. Mktg. Sci. Democrat. Roman Catholic. Avocations: baseball, travel, photography. Home: 3701 Sally Ln Tallahassee FL 32312 Office: Fla State Univ Coll of Business Tallahassee FL 32306 E-mail: jcronin@cob.fsu.edu.

CRONIN, PATRICIA ROMERO, computer company executive; m. Kevin Cronin; children: Briana, Meaghan, Alyse. BSc, U. Santa Clara; MBA, Golden Gate U. Dir. worldwide mktg., database products IBM, 1994, dir. mktg. strategy and bus. devel., 1996, gen. mgr. global ins. solutions, 1997, v.p. Olympic tech. integration, 1999; current v.p. transformation initiative IBM Global Svc. Mem. Pan Am. Roundtable; with Nat. Charity League; co-chair LaFamilia; bd. mem. Jr. Achievement. Named Elite Hispanic Woman, Hispanic mag., 2002; named one of 100 Top Latinas, 2003; recipient Exec. Excellence award, 1st female recipient, HENAAC, 2001. Avocation: playing and coaching soccer. Office: IBM Corp 4000 Executive Pkwy Ste 300 San Ramon CA 94583

CRONIN, PHILIP MARK, lawyer; b. Boston, July 21, 1932; s. Herbert Joseph and Elizabeth Ann (Sullivan) C.; m. Paula Cook Budlong, June 8, 1957; children: Thomas B., Philip S. AB, Harvard U., 1953, LLB, 1956. Bar: Mass. 1956. Sr. ptnr. firm Withington, Cross, Park & Groden, Boston, 1956-89, Peabody & Arnold, Boston, 1989—. Pres., pub. Harvard mag., 1971-78; city solicitor, Cambridge, Mass., 1968-72. Mng. editor: Mass. Law Rev, 1976-81; editor-in-chief, 1981-90; editor Mass. Legal History Jour., 1996—. Trustee Harvard Crimson, 1972—; pres. Cambridge Homes, 1991-94; overseer Mass. Supreme Jud. Ct. Hist. Soc., 1994—, editor jour., 1995—. Home: 3 Lincoln Ln Cambridge MA 02138-3351 Office: 30 Rowes Wharf Boston MA 02110-3339 Office Phone: 617-951-2100.

CRONIN, ROBERT LAWRENCE, painter; b. Lexington, Mass., Aug. 10, 1936; s. Daniel Augustus and Eileen Ursula (Keating) C.; m. Constance Marie Nelson, June 27, 1964 (div. 1974). BFA, R.I. Sch. Design, 1959; MFA, Cornell U., 1962. Tchr. Mich. State U., East Lansing, 1965-66, Bennington (Vt.) Coll., 1967-68, Brown U., Providence, 1969-71; tchrs. Sch. Worcester (Mass.) Art Mus., 1972-80. One-man shows Mus. Art Carnegie Inst., Pitts., 1981, Sculpture Ctr. Gallery, N.Y.C., 1981, Gimpel Fils Gallery, London, 1982, Gimpel & Weitzenhoffer Gallery, N.Y.C., 1982, 84, 87, 89, Watson de Nagy Gallery, Houston, 1983, 86, Gimpel-Hanover Galerien, Zurich, 1983, Clark Gallery, Lincoln, Mass., 1983, 85, 87, Janet Steinberg Gallery, San Francisco, 1985, Galerie Esperanza, Montreal, 1985, 87, Klonaridis Gallery, Toronto, 1984, 85, 87, 88, 89, Galerie Keeser-Bohbot, Hamburg, Germany, 1987, 89, Alice Simsar Gallery, Ann Arbor, Mich., 1988, Yoh Art Gallery, Osaka, 1989, Gallery Hiro, Tokyo, 1989, Helander, Gallery, Palm Beach, Fla., 1990, Fitchburg (Mass.) Art Mus., 1990, Munson Gallery, New Haven, 1991, Sound Shore Gallery, Stamford, Conn., 1992, Virginia Lynch Gallery, Tiverton, R.I., 1996, 98, Dillon Gallery, N.Y.C., 1996, 99, Tremaine Gallery, Hotchkiss Sch., Lakeville, Conn., 1999, Joseph Rickards Gallery, N.Y.C., 2001, Dillon Gallery, Oyster Bay, N.Y., 2002, Brown U. Hillel, Providence, 2004, Kouros Gallery, N.Y.C., 2004; represented in permanent collections Bklyn. Mus., Mus. Fine Arts, Boston, Mus. Art, U. Okla., Mus. Art, Carnegie Inst., Mus. Art, R.I. Sch. Design, Nat. Air and Space Mus., Mus. Fine Arts, Springfield, Worcester Art Mus., Worcester Polytech. Inst., De Cordova Mus., Nat. Acad. Design, N.Y.C. Recipient 1st prize for painting Boston Fine Arts Festival, 1963; recipient awards Mass. Artists Found., 1975, 79; individual support grantee Adolph and Esther Gottlieb Found., 1991. Mem. Nat. Acad. Design. Home: PO Box 74 Falls Village CT 06031-0074

CRONIN, THOMAS EDWARD, former academic administrator; b. Milton, Mass., Mar. 18, 1940; s. Joseph M. and Mary Jane Cronin; m. Tania Zaroodny, Nov. 26, 1966; 1 child, Alexander. AB, Holy Cross Coll., 1961; MA, Stanford U., 1964, PhD, 1968; LLD (hon.), Marietta Coll., 1987, Franklin Coll., 1993; DHL (hon.), Whitman Coll., 2005. Tchg. fellow Stanford U., Calif., 1962—64; staff mem. The White House, Washington, 1966—67; faculty mem. U. N.C., 1967—70; staff fellow Brookings Instn., 1970—72; faculty mem. Brandeis U., Waltham, Mass., 1975—77, U. Del., Newark, 1977—79; McHugh prof. of Am. instns. The Colo. Coll., Colorado Springs, 1985—93, acting pres., 1991; pres. Whitman Coll., Walla Walla, Wash., 1993—2005. Bd. dirs. Cascade Natural Gas Co.; moderator Aspen Inst. Exec. Sems., 1975—; pres. CRC, Inc., 1980—, Presidency Rsch. Group, 1981—82; cons. in field; guest polit. analyst various tv programs; mem. Wash. Com. Humanities. Author: The State of the Presidency, 1980, Direct Democracy, 1989, Colorado Politics and Government, 1993, The Paradoxes of the American Presidency, 1998, 2004. Dir. IES Chgo., Monterey Inst. Internat. Studies, 2002—; bd. dirs. Inst. Am. Univs. Mem.: Inst. Edn. Internat. Students, Western Polit. Sci. Assn. (pres. 1993—94), Am. Polit. Sci. Assn. (exec. com. 1990—92), C. of C., Pi Sigma Alpha. Avocations: tennis, hiking.

CRONIN, TIMOTHY CORNELIUS, III, computer manufacturing executive; b. Manchester, N.H., Sept. 26, 1927; s. Timothy Cornelius and Ann Frances (Meaney) C.; m. Gloria Mara, June 8, 1949 (dec. Sept. 1984); children: Gloria Ann, Constance, Timothy, Barbara, Mary, Thomas; m. A. Jeanine Wallis, June 15, 1991; children: Erik Wallis, Dana Wallis. BS, U.S. Mil. Acad., 1949; MBA, Ohio State U., 1952. Commd. 2d lt. USAF, 1949, advanced through grades to capt., 1956, resigned, 1956; mgr., v.p. Honeywell, Inc., Mpls. and Wellesley, Mass., 1956-71; v.p. Addressograph Multigraph, Cleve., 1971-74; chmn., CEO Inforex, Inc., Burlington, Mass., 1974-79; cons. in field Waltham, Mass., 1980-82; v.p. Wang Labs., Lowell, Mass., 1983-87; pres., CEO Wang Fin. Info. Svcs. Corp., N.Y.C., 1987-90, Digitran, Inc., Englewood Cliffs, N.J., 1990-91; ret., pvt. investor, 1991. Decorated Legion of Merit. Mem. Computer Industries Assn. (exec. com. 1975-79), Assn. Industries Mass. (bd. dirs. 1976-79). Republican. Roman Catholic. Home: 31 Shaw Dr Bedford NH 03110-6050

CRONK, LEONARD, management consultant; b. Paterson, NJ, Apr. 19, 1943; s. Leonard and Ruth (Brewer) Cronk; m. Martha Fanning, Aug. 21, 1965 (div. 1998); children: Catherine Cronk Clifford, Martha Brewer; m. Hisayo Arikawa, Oct. 25, 1998. BS in Indsl. Engring., Cornell U., 1965, M in Indsl. Engring., 1966, MBA, 1967. Cert. mgmt. cons., mgmt. acctg., securities registrations. Mem. ops. rsch. staff Mobil Corp., N.Y.C., 1967-69; from cons. to sr. mgr. Price Waterhouse, N.Y.C., 1969-79; mgr. fin. systems Kennecott Corp., Stamford, Conn., 1979-82; v.p. Kidder, Peabody, N.Y.C., 1982-87, Merrill Lynch, N.Y.C., 1987-91; mgmt. cons. Rowayton, Conn., 1991—; v.p. Manley Mktg., Greenwich, Conn. Adv. bd. Belle Haven Land Assn., Greenwich, Conn., 1983-85, bd. dirs., 1986-89; bd. dirs. Belle Haven Club, Greenwich, 1990-94. Mem.: Wilson Cove Yacht Club (bd. dirs. 2003—). Republican. Episcopalian. Avocations: playing trumpet, tennis. Home: 110 Leroy Ave Darien CT 06820 Office Phone: 203-655-3961. E-mail: leonardcronk@sbcglobal.net.

CRONK, WILLIAM F., III, food products executive; b. 1943; m. Janet Cronk; 3 children. Pres., dir. Dreyer's Grand Ice Cream, Inc., Oakland, Calif., 1977—2004, ret., 2004. Mem. adv. bd. Haas Bus. Sch. U. Calif., Berkeley. Nat. commr. Boy Scouts Am.; mem. Nat. Recreation Lakes Study Commn.

CRONKHITE, ALESIA J., insurance agent, investment advisor; d. Candy and Warren Mercer, Kris Mercer (Stepmother); m. Adrian B. Cronkhite; children: Jakob, Alaina. Lic. Lutcf Colo., 2004. Sales rep. Mut. of Omaha, Colorado Springs, Colo., 1994—. Mem.: Million Dollar Round Table, Rotary of Interquest Colo., Housing and Builing Assn. (assoc.). Office: Mutual of Omaha Ins Co 1115 Elkton Dr Ste 402 Colorado Springs CO 80907 Office Phone: 719-532-1990 222. Office Fax: 719-532-9693.

CRONKITE, WALTER, radio and television news correspondent; b. St. Joseph, Mo., Nov. 4, 1916; s. Walter Leland and Helen Lena Cronkite; m. Mary Elizabeth Maxwell, Mar. 30, 1940 (dec. Mar. 15, 2005); children: Nancy Elizabeth, Mary Kathleen, Walter Leland III. Student, U. Tex., 1933—35; LLD, Rollins Coll., 1966, Bucknell U., Syracuse U.; LHD, Ohio State U.; hon. degree, Am. Internat. Coll., Harvard U. News writer, editor Scripps-Howard, also UP, Houston, Kansas City, Dallas, Austin, El Paso; UP war corr., 1942—45; fgn. corr., reopening burs. in Amsterdam, Brussels, chief corr. Nuremberg war crimes trials, bur. mgr., Moscow, 1946—48; lectr., mag. contbr., 1948—49; CBS-News corr., 1950—81; spl. corr., 1981—; mng. editor CBS Evening News with Walter Cronkite, 1962—81. Chmn. The Cronkite Ward Co., 1993—; host spl. Universe, CBS, The Holocaust: In Memory of Millions, The Discovery Channel, 1993; anchor for TV news spls. Vietnam: A War That is Finished, 1975, In Celebration of US, 1976, Our Happiest Birthday, 1977, The President in China, 1975, Solzhenitsyn: 1984 Revisited. Author: Eye on the World, 1971, The Challenges of Change, 1971, A Reporter's Life, 1996, Around America, 2002; co-author: South by Southeast, North by Northeast, Westwind; prodr.(host): The e Reports (12 episode series for Discovery Channel), 1994—96, Cronkite Remembers (8 part series for CBS and Discovery Channel), 1996. Recipient Cable Ace award for best program interviewer, 1993, Peabody award, 1962, 1981, Emmy awards, William A. White award for journalistic merit, 1969, George Polke Journalism award, 1971, Gold medal, Internat. Radio and TV Soc., 1974, Alfred I. DuPont-Columbia U. award in broadcast journalism, 1978, 1981, Presdl. medal of Freedom, 1981. Mem.: Assn. Radio News Analysts,

Acad. Arts and Scis. (pres. nat. acad. N.Y. chpt. 1959, Gov.'s award 1979), Bohemian Club, N.Y. Yacht Club, Nat. Press Club, Overseas Press Club, Explorers Club, Chi Phi. Avocation: sailing. Office: CBS Inc 51 W 52nd St Ste 1934 New York NY 10019-6119*

CRONON, E(DMUND) DAVID, JR., historian, retired educator; b. Mpls., Mar. 11, 1924; s. Edmund David and Florence Ann (Meyer) C.; m. Mary Jean Hotmar, May 13, 1950; children: William John, Robert David. Student, Macalester Coll., 1942-43; AB, Oberlin Coll., 1948; AM, U. Wis., 1949, PhD, 1953; postgrad., Manchester (Eng.) U., 1950-51. Instr., then asst. prof. history Yale U., 1953-59; assoc. prof., then prof. history U. Nebr., 1959-62; prof. history U. Wis., Madison, 1962-94, dean Coll. Letters and Sci., 1974-89, chmn. dept., 1966-69, dir. Inst. Research in Humanities, 1969-74, prof., dean emeritus, 1994—; lectr. for State Dept., Europe and Near East, 1966. Fulbright-Hays lectr. Moscow State U., 1974 Author: Black Moses: The Story of Marcus Garvey and the Universal Negro Improvement Association, 1955, Josephus Daniels in Mexico, 1960, Government and the Economy: Some Nineteenth Century Views, 1960, Contemporary Labor-Management Relations, 1960, The Cabinet Diaries of Josephus Daniels, 1913-1921, 1963, Labor and the New Deal, 1963, Twentieth Century America; Selected Readings, 2 vols, 1965-66, The Political Thought of Woodrow Wilson, 1965, Marcus Garvey, 1973, The University of Wisconsin: Politics, Depression, and War, 1925-45 (with John W. Jenkins), 1994, (with John W. Jenkina) The University of Wisconsin: Renewal to Revolution, 1945-71. Mem. exec. com. Wis. Am. Revolution Bicentennial Commn.; adv. bd. Franklin D. Roosevelt Library, 1971-76, Wis. Humanities Com., 1973-77, Council for Internat. Exchange Scholars, 1977-80; mem. Commn. Instns. Higher Edn. N. Central Assn. Colls. and Schs., 1978-82, cons., examiner, 1970—; bd. dirs. Council of Colls. of Arts and Scis., 1978-80, pres., 1981-82; mem. Commn. Arts and Scis., Nat. Assn. State Univs. and Land Grant Colls., 1984-88; trustee Ripon Coll., 1976-91. Served to 1st lt., inf. AUS, 1943-46. Fulbright fellow, 1950-51; Stimson fellow, 1958-59 Fellow Soc. Am. Historians; mem. Am. Hist. Assn., Orgn. Am. Historians (exec. bd.), Wis. Hist. Soc. (bd. curators, pres.), So. Hist. Soc. (exec. coun., bd. editors), Madison Opera (bd. dirs., v.p., pres.), Phi Beta Kappa (nominating com. United chpts. 1985-91), Blackhawk Club, Univ. Club. Unitarian Universalist. Home: 5601 Varsity Hl Madison WI 53705-4653 Business E-Mail: edcronon@wisc.edu.

CRONON, WILLIAM, history professor; b. New Haven, Sept. 11, 1954; m. Nancy Elizabeth Fey. BA in History, English with honors, U. Wis., 1976; MA in Am. History, Yale U., 1979, M of Philosophy in Am. History, 1981, PhD in Am. History, 1990; DPhil in Brit. History, Oxford U., 1981. Asst. prof. history Yale U., New Haven, 1981-86, assoc. prof., 1986-91, prof., 1991-92, mem. studies in environment program creation com., 1983-84, co-chair studies environment program, 1989-92, dir. grad. studies, history dept., 1990-92; Frederick Jackson Turner chair of history, geography, and environ. studies U. Wis., Madison, 1992—, dir. honors program Coll. Letters and Sci., 1996-98, Vilas rsch. prof., 2003—; found. fac. dir. Chadbourne Residential Coll., 1997-2000. Asst. Am. sec. Rhodes Scholarship Trust, 1978-80, Wis. state sec., 1993-98; cons. in field; mem. adv. bd. The History Tchr., 1986-2000. Rhodes Dist. chmn., 2002-. Author: Changes in the Land: Indians, Colonists and the Ecology of New England, 1983 (Valley Forge honor cert. 1984, Soc. Colonial award citation of honor 1984, Francis Parkman prize 1984), Nature's Metropolis: Chicago and the Great West, 1991 (Chgo. Tribune Heartlaand prize 1991, Bancroft prize 1992, George Perkins Marsh prize 1993); editor: (with Miles and Gitlin) Under an Open Sky: Rethinking America's Western Past, 1992, Uncommon Ground: Rethinking the Human Place in Nature, 1995; mem. bd. editors Forest and Conservation History, 1986-91; also articles; gen. editor Weyerhaeuser Environ. Books, U. Wash. Press, 1993—. Bd. dirs. Conn. Fund for Environ., 1986-91, v.p., 1987-89; mem. adv. bd. TV series Am. Experience Sta. WGBH-TV; trustee Conn. Nature Conservancy, 1989-91; bd. dirs., mem. com. on problems and policy Social Sci. Rsch. Coun., 1991-96, chairperson com. on problems and policy, 1994-96. Rhodes scholar Oxford U., 1976-78; fellow Danforth Found., 1976-82, Newberry Libr., 1980, Mellon Found., 1982-83, Morse fellow Yale U., 1985-86, MacArthur Found., 1985-90, Whitney Humanities Ctr., 1987-89, fellow U. Calif. Humanities Rsch. Inst., 1994, Guggenheim fellow, 1995. Mem. AAAS, Am. Hist. Assn. (Robinson prize com. 1990), Am. Philos. Soc. (v.p. profl. divsn. 2002—), Orgn. Am. Historians (chmn. Curti prize com. 1987-88), Forest History Soc. (bd. dirs.), Econ. History Assn., Agrl. History Soc., Ecol. Soc. Am., Western Hist. Assn. (conv. program com. 1987, chmn. 1991-92), Assn. Am. Geographers, Am. Studies Assn., Am. Anthrop. Assn., Wilderness Soc. (gov. coun. 1995—), Am. Soc. for Ethnohistory, Chgo. Hist. Soc., Am. Antiquarian Soc., Soc. Am. Historians, Phi Beta Kappa (William C. DeVane award Yale chpt. 1988), Phi Kappa Phi, Phi Eta Sigma. Office: U Wis Dept History 3211 Humanities 455 N Park St Madison WI 53706-1405 Home: 2027 Chadbourne Ave Madison WI 53726-4046 Office Phone: 608-265-6023. Business E-Mail: wcronon@wisc.edu.

CRONSON, MARY SHARP, foundation administrator; Prod., works & process Guggenheim Mus., NYC; pres. Evelyn Sharp Found. Bd. trustee Solomon R. Guggenheim Mus., NYC; secy. NYC Opera. Office: Guggenheim Museum 107 Fifth Ave New York NY 10128-0173 Office Phone: 212-423-3500. Office Fax: 212-423-3650.*

CRONSON, ROBERT GRANVILLE, lawyer; b. Chgo., Dec. 23, 1924; s. Berthold A. and Ethel (Larson) C.; m. Agnes L. Diaz; children from previous marriage: Karen, Christopher, Keelyn, Morgan, Seth. AB in Econs., Dartmouth Coll., 1947; JD, U. Chgo., 1950. Bar: Ill. 1950. Atty. Daily, Dines, Ross & O'Keefe, Chgo., 1951-53; ptnr. DeBoice, Greening, Ackerman & Cronson, Springfield, Ill., 1957-60; asst. sec. of state of Ill. Springfield, 1958-64; sr. vp., sec. The Chgo. Corp., Chgo., 1965-73; assoc. prof. pub. adminstrn. Roosevelt U., 1973-74; adj. prof. adminstrn. Sangamon State U., 1983-87; auditor gen. State of Ill., 1974-92; retired, 1992. Mem. exec. com. post audit sect. Nat. Conf. State Legislatures, 1976-85, Nat. Assn. State Auditors, Comptrs. and Treasurers, 1979-81, and Nat. Intergovtl. Audit Forum, 1974-76; mem. Midwest Intergovtl. Audit Forum, 1974-92; adv. com. govt. acctg. standards Govt. Acctg. Stds. Bd. 1984-85. Chmn. Midwest Vehicle Proration Compact, 1959-61, Ill. Securities Adv. Com., 1964-73; chmn. William H. Chamberlain Scholarship Fund, Sangamon State U., 1972-85. Cpl. USMCR, 1942-46. Recipient Fin. Mgmt. Improvement (Scantlebury) award, U.S. Govt., 1980. Mem. Midwest Securities Commrs. Assn. (chmn. 1959-64), Securities Industry Assn. Am. (chmn. state legislation com. 1970-72), Nat. State Auditors Assn. (pres. 1980-81), Pi Alpha Alpha (hon.), Phi Kappa Psi. Republican. Congregationalist. Office Phone: 217-546-1330. Personal E-mail: jsnoopus@warpnet.net.

CRONYN, MARSHALL WILLIAM, chemistry educator; b. Oakland, Calif., June 22, 1919; s. George William and Lura (Miller) C.; m. Vesta Elizabeth Wetterborg, Feb. 27, 1942 (dec. June 1997); children: Evan (dec.), Gail, Lori. BA, Reed Coll., 1940; PhD in Chemistry, U. Mich., 1944. Research asso. penicillin project OSRD-Com. on Med. Research, U. Mich., Ann Arbor, 1944-46; Am. Chem. Soc. post-doctoral fellow U. Calif. at Berkeley, 1946-48, instr., 1948-49, asst. prof., 1949-52, Reed Coll., Portland, Oreg., 1952-56, assoc. prof., 1956-60, prof., 1960-89; prof. emeritus —, 1989—; chmn. dept. chemistry Reed Coll., 1966-73, v.p., provost, 1982-89, v.p., provost emeritus, 1989—. Mem., cons. Medicinal Chemistry Panel USPHS, 1961-66; H.V. Tartar vis. lectr. U. Wash., 1953. Research and publs. in field. NIH research fellow Cambridge, Eng., 1960-61 Fellow AAAS, Am. Chem. Soc., N.Y. Acad. Sci., Sigma Xi. Clubs: Portland City. Home: 3232 NW Luray Ter Portland OR 97210-2723

CROOK, CHARLES SAMUEL, III, lawyer; b. Des Moines, Iowa, Oct. 24, 1944; s. Charles Samuel, Jr. and Gertrude A. (Nichols) Crook; children: Donald, Michael, Brian, Nicole. BA, Drake U., 1969, JD, 1971. Bar: Iowa 1971. Law clk. to chief dist. judge U.S. Dist. Ct. (so. dist.), Iowa, 1971—73; pros. atty. Polk County Atty.'s Office, Des Moines, 1973—76; ptnr. Beving, Swanson & Forrest, P.C., Des Moines, 1976—83; pvt. practice Des Moines, 1983—. Lectr. Des Moines Area CC, 1979; assoc. prof. med. jurisprudence U. Osteo. Health Scis. Contbr. articles to profl. jours. Leader Cub Scouts Am., Des Moines. With U.S. Army, 1963—66. Mem.: ABA, Nat. Bd. Trial Advocacy (cert. 1981—86), Polk County Bar Assn., Iowa Bar Assn. Democrat. Roman Catholic. Home: PO Box 721 Des Moines IA 50303-0721 Office: Fleming Bldg 218 6th Ave Ste 1100 Des Moines IA 50309-4005

CROOK, DON RAY, artist, art director; b. La Crosse, Wis., July 24, 1934; s. Raymond Onto and Eleanor Johana Crook; m. Leah Marie Crook, 1954 (div. 1978); children: Kim, Kelley, Kerry, Kirsten, Korinne; m. Sharon marie Crook, May 15, 1980 (div. 1990); m. Shirley Larane Crook, Apr. 15, 1992. Student, Yakima (Wash.) Valley Coll., 1954-56. Art dir. Payless Drug, Yakima, 1960-64, KIMA TV, Yakima, 1965-70, Kwik Lok Corp., Yakima, 1971—. Commd. works include The Spokane Indian Wars, The Modac War Series for Favell Mus. Klamath Falls, Oreg., The Trail of Tears, Bowles Agy., Nashville, The End of the Oreg. Trail, State of Oreg. and City of Dalles, murals for Kittitas County Fair, Ellensburg, Wash; represented in pvt. collections including Gov.'s Mansion, State of Nev. Recipient 26 Best of Show awards, Best Painting award (3) Russell Show, Gt. Falls, Mont., Heritage award, Favell Mus., others. Mem. Elks. Republican. Home: 223 Parsons Ave Yakima WA 98908-1734 Office: Kwik Lok Corp 2712 S 16th Ave Yakima WA 98903 E-mail: don@ixpnet.com.

CROOK, ROBERT WAYNE, retired portfolio manager; b. Hartford, Conn., Apr. 6, 1936; s. William Gregor and Laura Foster (Keenan) C.; m. Leslie C. Rischer, Oct. 22, 1988; children from previous marriage: Robert Wayne, Laura Sigrid. AB, Harvard U., 1959; postgrad., U. Va. Sch. Law, 1962. With White, Weld & Co., Inc., Boston, 1961—78, v.p., 1971—75, 1st v.p., 1975—78; pres., dir. White Weld Money Market Fund, Boston, 1974—78, White Weld Govt. Fund, Boston, 1977—78; with Merrill Lynch Asset Mgmt., Inc., Boston, 1978—2001, v.p., 1981—89, sr. v.p., 1989—2001; v.p. Merrill Lynch Funds Distbr., Inc., 1978—89, sr. v.p., 1989—2001; pres., trustee Merrill Lynch Funds for Instns. Series, Boston, 1978—2001, Merrill Lynch Tax-Exempt Fund, 1983—2001; mng. dir. Merrill Lynch Investment Mgrs., 1997—2001; ret., 2001. Served with U.S. Army, 1960. E-mail: jeyhue99@adelphia.net.

CROOKALL, SIMON, performing company executive; b. Cheshire, England, Oct. 1, 1960; arrived in U.S., 2005; MA in Econs., Cambridge (Eng.) U., 1982. From academic asst. to mgr. front ho. Royal Scottish Acad. Music and Drama, Glasgow, Scotland, 1983—87, mgr. front ho., 1987—89; gen. mgr. The Queen's Hall, Edinburgh, 1995—96; chief exec. Royal Scottish Nat. Orch., Glasgow, 1995—96, 1997—2004; pres., CEO Indpls. (Ind.) Symphony Orch., 2005—. Dep. lt. City Glasgow, 2004; mem. panel Arts and Bus. New Ptnrs. Mem.: Assn. Brit. Orchs. (chmn. 2001—04), Westbourne Gardner's Assn. (treas.), Order St. John (music com.). Office: Indianapolis Symphony Orch 32 E Washington St Ste 600 Indianapolis IN 46204

CROOKE, PHILIP SCHUYLER, mathematics professor; b. Summit, N.J., Mar. 10, 1944; s. Philip Schuyler Jr. and Emma T. C.; m. Barbara E. Carey, Aug. 31, 1968; children: Philip Alexander, Cornelia Elizabeth. BS, Stevens Inst. Tech., 1966; PhD, Cornell U., 1970. Asst. prof. math. Vanderbilt U., Nashville, 1970-76, assoc. prof., 1976-86, prof., 1986—, prof. edn. secondary, 1995—. Vis. fellow Cornell U., Ithaca, N.Y., 1982. vice dir., Biomath Study Group, 2001— .vice chmn. Dept. Math., 2003— . Contbr. articles to profl. publs. Mem. Am. Math. Soc. Home: 611 Cantrell Ave Nashville TN 37215-1020 Office: Vanderbilt U Dept Math Nashville TN 37240-0001

CROOKE, ROBERT ANDREW, media consultant, writer, educator; b. Bklyn., Apr. 17, 1947; s. Henry A. and Theresa E. (Dougherty) C.; m. Angela Keller Lynch, Sept. 13, 1969; 1 child, Sean Peter. BA in English, Providence Coll., 1969; MA in English, Fordham U., 1974. Sports reporter, columnist L.I. Press, Jamaica, N.Y., 1969-75; profl. radio, TV, ednl. film script writer N.Y.C., 1976-79; assoc. editor Mag. Age, N.Y.C., 1979-81; reporter, contbg. editor L.I. Bus. Newsweekly, Ronkonkoma, N.Y., 1981-86; sr. acct. exec. Howard J. Rubenstein, N.Y.C., 1986-87; dir. media rels. Reuters Am., Inc., N.Y.C., 1987-94; v.p. comm. Reuters New Media, N.Y.C., 1994-96; v.p. media rels. Reuters Am. Holdings, Inc., N.Y.C., 1996-2000; mng. dir. Broadgate Consultants Inc., N.Y.C., 2000-01; media cons. Makinson Cowell (US) Ltd., 2001—. Adj. instr. English Suffolk County C.C., Selden, N.Y., 1972-76; lectr. Sch. Journalism, U. Nebr., 1998-99, Sch. Journalism, U.S.C., 2000; adj. prof. pub. affairs NYU, 1998-2000. Author: (history) Between Ocean and Empire, 1985; (poetry) West Hills Rev., 1986, 87; (fiction) American Family, 2004. Office: PO Box 392 334 Main St S Bridgewater CT 06752-1537 E-mail: rcrooke@msn.com.

CROOKE, STANLEY THOMAS, pharmaceutical executive; b. Indpls., Mar. 28, 1945; m. Nancy Alder (dec.); 1 child, Evan; m. Rosanne M. Snyder. BS in Pharmacy, Butler U., 1966; PhD, Baylor Coll., 1971, MD, 1974. Asst. dir. med. rsch. Bristol Labs., N.Y.C., 1975-76, assoc. dir. med. rsch., 1976-77, assoc. dir. R&D, 1977-79, v.p. R&D, 1979-80, Smith Kline & French Labs., Phila., 1980-82; pres. R&D Smith Kline French, Phila., 1982-88; chmn. bd., CEO ISIS Pharms., Inc., Carlsbad, Calif., 1989. Chmn. bd. dirs. GES Pharms., Inc., Houston, 1989-91; adj. prof. Baylor Coll. Medicine, Houston, 1982, U. Pa., Phila., 1982-98; chmn. bd. dirs. GeneMedicine, Houston, 1996-98; bd. dirs. Calif. Healthcare Inst., 1993-2003, Indsl. Biotech. Assn., Washington, Idun Pharms., San Diego 1997-2002, Epix Med., Cambridge, Mass., 1996—, BIO, Washington, 1993-94; mem. sci. adv. bd. SIBIA, La Jolla, Calif. 1992-99; adj. prof. pharmacology UCLA, 1991, U. Calif. San Diego, 1994; bd. dirs. Synsorb Biotech Inc., Calgary, Can., 1999-2002; bd. dirs. Axon Instruments, Inc., Foster City, Calif. 1999-2004, Valentis, Inc., Burlingame, Calif., 1999-2002, Antisense Therapeutics Ltd., Toorak, Victoria, Australia, 2002—, Applied Molecular Evolutions, Inc., San Diego, Calif., 2001-02, Biocom/San Diego, Calif., 2003—; mem. arts and scis. adv. coun. No. Ariz. U., 2002- Mem. editl. adv. bd. Molecular Pharmacology, 1986-91, Jour. Drug Targeting, 1992; editl. bd. Antisense Rsch. and Devel., 1994; sect. editl. bd. for biologicals and immunologicals Expert Opinion on Investigational Drugs, 1995. Trustee Franklin Inst., Phila., 1987-89; bd. dirs. Mann Music Ctr., Phila., 1987-89; children's com. Children's Svcs., Inc., Phila., 1983-84; adv. com. World Affairs Coun., Phila. Recipient Disting. Prof. award U. Ky., 1986, Julius Stermer award Phila. Coll. Pharmacy and Sci., 1981, Outstanding Lectr. award Baylor Coll. Medicine, 1984. Mem. AAAS, Am. Assn. for Cancer Rsch. (state legis. com.), Am. Soc. for Microbiology, Am. Soc. Pharmacology and Exptl. Therapeutics, Am. Soc. Clin. Pharmacology and Therapeutics, Am. Soc. Clin. Oncology, Indsl. Biotech. Assn. (bd. dirs. 1992-93). Achievements include numerous patents in field. Office: ISIS Pharms Inc 1896 Rutherford Rd Carlsbad CA 92008-7208 E-mail: scrooke@isisph.com.

CROOKS, NEIL PATRICK, state supreme court justice; b. Green Bay, Wis., May 16, 1938; s. George Merrill and Aurelia Ellen (O'Neill) C.; m. Kristin Marie Madson, Feb. 15, 1964; children: Michael, Molly, Kevin, Kathleen, Peggy, Eileen. BA magna cum laude, St. Norbert Coll., 1960; JD, U. Notre Dame, 1963. Bar: Wis. 1963, U.S. Supreme Ct. 1969. Assoc. Cohen and Parins, Green Bay, 1963; ptnr. Cohen, Grant, Crooks and Parins, Green Bay, 1966-70; sr. ptnr. Crooks, Jerry, Norman and Dilweg, Green Bay, 1970-77; judge Brown County (Wis.) Ct., 1977-78, Brown County (Wis.) Cir. Ct., 1978-96; justice Wis. Supreme Ct., Madison, 1996—. Instr. bus. law U. Wis., Green Bay, 1970-72; mem. faculty Wis. Jud. Coll., 1982. Editor Law Rev. Notre Dame, 1962-63. Pres. Brown County United Way, 1976-78; chmn. Brown County Legal Aid, 1971-73; mem. Northeast Criminal Justice Coord. Coun., 1973-85; pres. St. Joseph Acad. Sch. Bd., 1987-89. Capt. U.S. Army, 1963-66. Recipient Human Rights award Baha'i Community of Green Bay, 1971, Disting. Achievement award in Social Sci. St. Norbert Coll., 1977 award of Yr. U. Notre Dame, 1978, Brown County Vandalism Prevention Assn. award, 1982, W. Heraly MacDonald award Brown County United Way, 1983, Community Svc. award St. Joseph Acad., 1989, Alma Mater award St. Norbert Coll., 1992, Disting. Alumnus of Yr. award Notre Dame Acad., 2002; named Wis. Trial Judge of the Year Wis. Chpt. Am. Bd. of Trial Advocates, 1994. Mem. ABA (law sch. evaluator legal edn. and admissions sect.), FBA, State Bar Wis., Brown County Bar Assn. (pres. 1977), Wis. Acad. Trial Lawyers, Wis. Law Found. (bd. dirs., mem. exec. com.), Assn. of Women Lawyers for Brown County, Dane County Bar Assn., James E. Doyle Am. Inn of Ct., Wis. Jud. Coun., Notre Dame Law Assn. (dir.). Roman Catholic. Home: 5329 Lighthouse Bay Dr Madison WI 53704-1113 Office: PO Box 1688 State Capitol 16 E Madison WI 53701 Office Phone: 608-266-1883. E-mail: patrick.crooks@wicourts.gov.

CROOKS, ROSELYN JUNE, artist, writer; b. Lancaster, Ohio, Sept. 15, 1924; d. Ralph E. and Mildred Cecelia (Lutz) Sieber; m. J. Robert Crooks, Apr. 7, 1951 (dec. Dec. 1988); children: John R., Kimberly K. BFA, Ohio State U., 1946, postgrad., 1947. Illustrator Curtiss-Wright Corp., Columbus, 1944; advt.-display mgr. Hickle's Dept. Store, Lancaster, Ohio, 1947—48; pvt. practice Tucson, 1951—. Spkr. in field. One-woman shows include Skyline Country Club Gallery, Tucson, Ariz., 1980, 1982, 1983, 1986, 1999, 2001, 2005, exhibited in group shows at Tucson (Ariz.) Mus. Art, 1970, 1972, So. Ariz. Watercolor Guild, 1994, 1998, Skyline Country Club Gallery, 1984, 1986, 1987, 1992, 1992, 1995, 1995, 1998, 2000, 2002, 2004. Founder Skyline Art Group, 2004. Mem.: Skyline Art Group (founder 2004), So. Ariz. Watercolor Guild, Soc. Southwestern Authors (assoc.), Tucson (Ariz.) Mus. Art. Avocations: crossword puzzles, bridge, reading, travel. Home: 5822 N Placita Bacanora Tucson AZ 85718 Personal E-mail: roselynjc@aol.com.

CROOKSTON, R. KENT, agronomy educator; b. Magrath, Alta., Can., Mar. 8, 1943; s. Bryan Grant and Lisadore (Brown) C.; m. Gayle Loraine Jones, June 22, 1966; children: Rebecca, Casey, Polly, Daniel, Elizabeth, Emily, Sadie. BS, Brigham Young U., 1968; MS, U. Minn., 1970, PhD, 1972. Postdoctoral fellow Agr. Can., Lethbridge, Alta., 1972; rsch. assoc. Cornell U., Ithaca, N.Y., 1972-74; from asst. prof. to prof. U. Minn., St. Paul, 1974—82, dir. sustainable agr. program Coll. Agr., 1988-92, head dept. agronomy, 1990-98. Adj. prof. Inst. Agronomique Et Veterinaire Hassan II, Rabat, Morocco, 1984—; dean Coll. Biology and Agr., Brigham Young U., Provo, Utah, 1998-2005. Author rsch. manuscripts. With Can. armed forces, 1962. Fellow Am. Soc. Agronomy, Crop Sci. Soc. Am.; mem. Coun. Agrl. Sci. and Tech. Avocations: painting, woodworking, writing, photography. Home: 1055 N 1100 E Orem UT 84097-4390 Office: College of Biology and Agriculture 301 WIDB Brigham Young Univ Provo UT 84602-5250 Office Phone: 801-422-3963. Business E-Mail: kent_crookston@byu.edu.

CROOM, FREDERICK HAILEY, academic administrator, mathematician, educator; b. Lumberton, NC, Aug. 6, 1941; s. Robert DeVane and Anna Roslyn (Currie) Croom; m. Henrietta Brown, Aug. 17, 1963 (div. May 2000); children: Elizabeth Bonner, Frederick Hailey; m. Nancy Mishoe Brennecke, June 1, 2002; children: Alexander McMillan, Augustus Brennecke. BS, U. N.C., 1963, PhD, 1967. Asst. prof. math. U. Ky., Lexington, 1967-71, U. of the South, Sewanee, Tenn., 1971-74, assoc. prof., 1974-81, prof., 1981—, dir. Summer Sch., 1980-88, assoc. dean, 1984-88, provost, 1989-2001. Author: (book) Basic Concepts of Algebraic Topology, 1978, Principles of Topology, 1989. Pres. Tenn. Coll. Assn., 1999—2000; bd. dirs. St. Andrews-Sewanee Sch., 1981—86, Tenn. Found. Ind. Colls., 1996—99; trustee U. of the South, 1983—85. Fellow Woodrow Wilson, 1963, NSF, 1963—67. Mem.: AAUP, Mat. Assn. Am., Am. Math. Soc., Sigma Xi. Episcopalian. Office: U South University Ave Sewanee TN 37383-0001 Office Phone: 931-598-3385. Business E-Mail: fcroom@sewanee.edu.

CROOM, SYLVESTER, football coach; b. Tuscaloosa, Ala., Sept. 25, 1954; m. Jeri Croom; 1 child, Jennifer. BA in History, U. Ala., 1975, MA in Ednl. Adminstrn., 1977. Ctr. New Orleans Saints, 1975; grad. asst. U. Ala., 1976, linebackers coach, 1977—86; running backs coach Tampa Bay (Fla.) Buccaneers, 1987—90, Indpls. (Ind.) Colts, 1991, San Diego (Calif.) Chargers, 1992—96; offensive coord. Detroit (Mich.) Lions, 1997—2000; running backs coach Green Bay (Wis.) Packers, 2001—03; head football coach Miss. State U., 2003—. Office: Athletic Dept Miss State Univ PO Box 5327 Mississippi State MS 39762

CROPP, LINDA W., city official; b. Atlanta, Oct. 5, 1947; m. Dwight S. Cropp; children: Allison, Christopher. BA, Howard U., 1969, MA, 1971. Former pub. sch. tchr. and guidance counselor; mem.-at-large City Coun., Washington, 1990-98, chmn., 1999—, past chair human svcs. com., past chair regional authorities com., mem. pub. svc. com., mem. govt. ops. and self-determination com. Rep. Ward 4 Bd. Edn., 1979, past v.p., pres.; past mem. Washington Met. Area Transit Authority; active Rock Creek Civic Assn., Travelers Aid Soc., Girl Scouts Nation's Capital, Jr. Achievement; mem. adv. bd. United Negro Coll. Fund. Office: Council DC 1350 Penn Ave NW Washington DC 20004 Office Phone: 202-724-8032. E-mail: lcropp@dccouncil.us.

CROPPER, SUSAN PEGGY, veterinarian; b. N.Y.C., Feb. 11, 1941; d. Eli and Ruth (Rader) Abrahams; divorced; 1 child, Tracy Lynn. BS, Kans. State U., 1962, DVM, 1964. Assoc. veterinarian Asbury Park (N.J.) Animal Hosp., 1964-65; instr. in Vet. Sci. Kans. State U., Manhattan, 1965-66; owner, veterinarian Markle (Ind.) Vet. Clinic, 1966-71, Meisels Animal Hosp. Clinic, Elmwood Park, N.J., 1971-73, Ridgewood (N.J.) Animal Hosp., 1973-75, Cropper House Call Practice, Wyckoff, N.J., 1975—. Editor Nat. Assn. Women Vets., 1966-68; mem. Audibon Soc. Mus. Natural History. Co-author: Loving and Losing a Pet; editor WJMA Jour., 1973; photographer: Best Diving Spots in Western Hemisphere, 1987. Leader Brownie troop Girl Scouts U.S., Glen Rock, N.J., 1976-77, Wyckoff, 1977-83; chairperson No. Jersey Tridents, Ridgefield, N.J., 1985-86. Mem. AVMA, Soc. Aquatic Vet. Medicine (treas.), No. N.J. Vet. Med. Assn. (pres. 1972-73), Met. Vet. Med. Assn., N.Y. Zool. Soc., Van Saun Zool. Soc., N.J. Acad., Ski and Scuba Club of Westwood, North Jersey Tridents Club (Ridgefield, chair 1985-86, Millennial Cert. for philanthropic recognition). Avocations: scuba diving, underwater photography, travel, racquetball, markmanship practice. Office: 310 Newtown Rd Wyckoff NJ 07481-2608 Office Phone: 201-444-6254. Personal E-mail: dvm2go@optonline.net.

CROPSEY, JOSEPH, retired political science professor; b. NYC, Aug. 27, 1919; s. Gustave and Margaret C.; m. Lilian Crystal Levy, Nov. 4, 1945; children: Seth, Rachel Cropsey Simons AB, Columbia U., 1939, A.M., 1940, PhD, 1952; DHL (hon.), Colo. Coll., 1989. Tutor, asst. prof. CCNY, 1946-57; instr. polit. sci. New Sch. Social Rsch., N.Y.C., 1949-54; asst. prof. U. Chgo., 1958-64, assoc. prof., 1964-70, prof., 1970-85, Disting. Svc. prof., 1985-89, prof. emeritus, 1989—; ret., 1989. Author: Polity and Economy, 1957, Political Philosophy and the Issues of Politics, 1977, Plato's World, 1995; editor: Ancients and Moderns, 1964; co-editor, co-author: History of Political Philosophy, 1963 Served to 1st. lt. U.S. Army, 1941-46, PTO, ETO Office: U Chgo 5828 S University Ave Chicago IL 60637-1515

CRORY, ELIZABETH L., retired state legislator; b. Gardner, Mass., Sept. 12, 1932; d. James Quaiel and Mary (Reilly) Lupien; m. Frederick E. Crory, Aug. 21, 1954; children: Thomas, David, Ellen, Ann, Edward, Stephen. AB, U. Mass., 1954; MALS, Dartmouth Coll., 1975. Tchr. Amherst (Mass.) Schs., 1954, Lyme (N.H.) Schs., 1972-76; mem. N.H. Ho. of Reps., 1977-87, 92-96, mem. commerce/consumer affairs com., 1977-87, 93-96, mem. spl. com. on med. malpractice, 1984; exec. dir. Children's Ctr. of Upper Valley, 1986-90. Bd. dirs. Mascoma Savs. Bank. Mem. character and fitness com. N.H. Supreme Ct., 1998-2005; chair N.H. Health Svcs. Planning and Rev. Bd., 1999-2005; bd. dirs. Kendal at Hanover, 2001—. Roman Catholic. Home: 40 Rip Rd Hanover NH 03755-1614

CROSBY, BERNA, freelance/self-employed writer; b. Twin Falls, Idaho, Oct. 27, 1947; d. Harry L. and Virginia Lee Dodson (Stepmother); m. Jerry W. Crosby Sr., July 29, 1969; children: Jerry W. Crosby Jr., Cameron Jason Linde. AAS in Tech. Writing, Chattanooga State Tech. CC, 1993—95. Freelance tech. writer, Collegedale, Tenn., 1996—; peer counselor; asst. dir. and office mgr. Tri-state Resource And Advocacy For Ind. Living, Chattanooga, 1987—92; pvt. sec. Signal Centers, Chattanooga, 1986—87. Cons. Outreach and Needs Assessment Task Group, Ga. Adv. Coun. for Tech. Resources, Atlanta, 1991—93. Author: (short stories) One Moment for a Lifetime, The Cycle of Motherhood, (novels) Dreamer, Connected, (poem)

Daily Living (Editor's Choice Award, 1998). Chmn. Chattanooga Com. on Disability Awareness, 1994—96; student rep. Chattanooga State Tech. CC Affirmative Action Com., 1994—95; adv. bd. mem. Chattanooga State Tech. CC Adaptive Computer Lab; pres. SE Tenn., NE Ga. Chpt., Muscular Dystrophy Assn., 1989—90. Recipient State Vol. Adv. Yr., Tenn. Conf. on Social Welfare, 1995, Governor's Trophy Tenn. Disabled Citizen Yr., Governor's Com. on Employment of Persons with Disabilities, 1989, Handicapped Profl. Woman Yr., Chattanooga Area Com. on Employment, 1986. Seventh-Day-Adventist. Avocations: singing, reading, surfing, figure skating, martial arts. Home: PO Box 1417 Collegedale TN 37315-1417 Personal E-mail: bdcrosby@juno.com.

CROSBY, DAVID S, finance educator, consultant; b. St. George, Utah, June 4, 1938; s. Samuel Wallace and Mae (Dodds) C.; m. Anna Jo Hovermale, Apr. 15, 1962 (dec.); children: Anna Danisha, Mae Melinda. BS, Am. U., 1962; MA, U. Ariz., 1964, PhD, 1966. Stats. prof. Am. U., Washington, 1966—2003, stats. prof. emeritus, 2004—; cons. NOAA, Washington, 1968—, Nat. Environ. Satellite Data Info. Svc., Washington, 1968—2001. Contbr. over 20 articles to sci. jours. Mem. Phi Beta Kappa, Sigma Xi. Home: 51 Independence St Berkeley Springs WV 25411 Office: Am U 4400 Massachusetts Ave NW Washington DC 20016-8200 E-mail: dcrosby@american.edu.

CROSBY, DEBORAH BERRY, artist; b. Gulfport, Miss., Oct. 9, 1930; d. Thomas Davis and Deborah Bennett (Hewes) Berry; m. Charles E. McHale Jr., Nov. 23, 1950 (div. 1952); 1 child Deborah Bennett McHale; m. Hueston T. Fortner, Jr., Mar. 17, 1957 (div. 1963); 1 child, Hueston G. Fortner; m. Richard Louis Crosby, Dec. 27, 1981. BA, Sophie Newcomb Coll., 1951; MA, Ind. State U., 1968; postgrad., Utah State U., 1969, Tulane U., 1979; BA (hon.), U. New Orleans, 1984. Educator Wesleyan Coll., Rocky Mt., N.C., 1969-70; prof. Spanish, Bay de Noc Coll., Escanaba, Mich., 1970-72; instr. yoga, Spanish, U. So. Miss.-Gulf Park Campus, Long Beach, 1972-78, Miss. Gulf Coast Jr. Coll. Dist., Keesler AFB Ctr., 1972-78; instr. reading, English, Miss. Gulf Coast Jr. Coll. Dist.-Jefferson Davis Campus, Keesler AFB Ctr., 1972-78; freelance artist Metairie, La., 1988—. Vis. artist at various galleries. One-woman shows include Dixie Art Co., Jefferson, La., 1990, World Trade Ctr., New Orleans, 1993—2005, Reginelli's Eating Gallery, 1994, Marceline Bonorden Fine Arts Gallery, 1998, 1999, Agora Gallery, Soho, N.Y.C., 2000, Movie Pitchers, 2000—01, Ambassador Hotel, New Orleans, 2002—04, Leahy Gardens, Covington, La., 2005, exhibited in group shows at Artists Showroom Gallery, 1993—95, Rivertown Art Gallery, Kenner, La., Slidell Cultural Ctr., La. State Archives, Baton Rouge, La., Martin Hall, U. of Mobile, Ala., George E. Ohr Arts and Cultural Ctr., Biloxi, Miss., Stamford (Conn.) Mus., Havre de Grace (Mich.) Mus., West Wind Gallery, Casper, Wyo., Jefferson SQ, Klamath Falls, Oreg., Destrehan (La.) Plantation, Lexington (Ky.) Mus., Falls River Mills, Calif., Our Lady of the Rosary Gallery, NOLA Pitot Historic Ho., New Orleans, Marceline Bonorden Fine Arts Gallery, Agora Gallery, Soho, N.Y.C., The Purple Mullet Gallery, Ala., Serenity Gallery, The Artisan Mkt., Riverview Gallery, Zigler Art Mus., Jennings La., Regional Art Ctr., Hammond, La., 2004, New Orleans Mus. Art, Amsterdam Whitney Internat. Fine Arts Gallery, Inc., NYC, 2002—05, New Orleans Art Assn. Fine Arts Festival (1st place), St. Charles Art Assn. (1st place), Metairie Art Guild, 1996 (1st place), Oil Met. Art Guild (1st place), Grumbacher (1st, 2d and 3d place, 2002), Rivertown Gallery, Kenner, La., 2005, Represented in permanent collections World Trade Ctr., prin. works include Juvenile Diabetes Assn., 2001, Exhibited in group shows at WTC, New Orleans, 1995—2001; designer, executor (cover chess book) The Art of Bisguier, 2003; coloring book for Children's Life on a Louisiana Plantation, 2005. Chmn. auction Heart Ambs., 1995; mem. Ladies Leukemia League, 1994-, program chmn., 1996; mem. Goodwill Industries VS, 1995-2002, BRAVO Ballet, 1995—; fiesta hostess Napoleon's Home, Spring Fiesta Assn., 2002, 05; bd. dirs. Profl. Women's Adv. ABI, Inc., 2003, East Jefferson Hosp. Aux., 2005—; active Contemporary Arts Ctr. NOLA, 2003, 05, New Orleans Arts Coun., 2003—; appt. bd. dirs. East Jefferson Gen. Hosp. Aux., 2005. Named Sweetheart, Local Br. Am. Heart Assn. Heart Ambs., 2001; recipient Lyricist award, U. New Orleans, 1984, Spl. Painting award, Winsor-Newton, 1994, Great Lady award, New Orleans Met. area by East Jefferson Hosp. Aux., 2000. Mem. Nat. League Am. Pen Women (chaplain 1996—, v.p. 1998-2000), New Orleans Art Assn. (v.p. 1995-98), Le Petit Art Guild (program chair 1995-97, Le Grand chairperson, 1995-2003, officer 1995-97), St. Charles Art Assn. (pres. 1994-95, Artist of Yr. award 1991-92), Nat. Mus. Women in the Arts, Newcomers Club Avocations: yoga, community activist, languages, travel, songwriting. Home: 5600 Kawanee Ave Metairie LA 70003-1414 Office Phone: 504-455-1275.

CROSBY, FRED MCCLELLAN, retail executive; b. Cleve., May 17, 1928; s. Fred Douglas and Marion Grace (Naylor) Crosby; m. Phendalyné D. Tazewell, Dec. 23, 1958; children: Fred, James, Llionicia. Grad. HS. V.p. Seaway Flooring & Paving Co., Cleve., 1959-63; chmn., CEO Crosby Furniture Co., Inc., Cleve., 1963—. Vice chmn. bd. dirs. First Bank Nat.; bd. dirs. Budget Rent-A-Car Sys., Surveyors Telecom., Inc.; bd. dirs., chmn. First Intercity Banc Corp. Commr. Nat. Small Bus. Adv. Coun., 1980; bd. dirs. Forest City Hosp. Found., Cleve. State U. Found., Greater Cleve. Growth Assn., 1971—90, 1993—, Coun. Smaller Enterprise, 1973—80, Goodwill Industries, 1973—80, 1997—, Woodruff Hosp., 1975—82, Cleve. Devel. Found., Pub. TV, Sta. WVIZ-TV, Cleve.-Cuyahoga Port Authority, 1986—90; bd. dirs., treas. Urban League Cleve., 1971—78; chmn. Minority Econ. Devel. Corp., 1972—83; chmn. bd. dirs. Glenville YMCA, 1973—76; dir. adv. coun. Ohio Bd. Workmen's Compensation, 1974—82; trustee Cleve. Play House, 1979—87, Eliza Bryant Health Care Ctr., 1984—86, Cleve. Small Bus. Incubator, 1986—90, Better Bus. Bur., 1995—, Ohio Motorist, 1993—, Murtis H. Taylor Mental Health, Metro Hosp. Sys. Found.; mem. adv. coun. Small Bus. Assn.; mem. adv. bd. Salvation Army, 1980; commr. Ohio State Boxing Commn., 1984—94, Pvt. Industry Coun., 1985; county commrs. appointee Cmty. Adv. Bd.; mem. Cleve. Opera Coun., 1987—89; Gov. Voinovich appointee to minority devel. fin. adv. bd., 1996—; bd. advs. Antioch Coll. With U.S. Army, 1950—52. Named Family of the Yr., Cleve. Urban League, 1971; recipient award bus. excellence, Dept. Commerce, 1972, Presdl. award, YMCA, 1974, Gov. Ohio award cmty. action, 1973, 1st Class Leadership, Cleve., 1977. Mem.: NAACP (v.p. Cleve. 1969—78, exec. dir.), Ohio Home Furnishings and Appliance Assn. (pres. 1981—87), Ohio Coun. Retail Mchts. (chmn. 1991—93), Am. Auto Assn. (corp. mem.), Cleve. C. of C., Univ. Club (Cleve.), Braternahl Club, Harvard Bus. Sch. Club, Mid-Day Club, Rotary, Clevelander, Exec. Order Ohio Commodore. Office: 12435 Saint Clair Ave Cleveland OH 44108-2013 Office Phone: 216-541-5040. Personal E-mail: phendaly@aol.com.

CROSBY, GLENN ARTHUR, chemistry professor; b. nr. Youngwood, Pa., July 30, 1928; s. Edwin Glenn and Bertha May (Ritchey) C.; m. Jane Lichtenfels, May 29, 1950; children: Brian, Alan, Karen. BS, Waynesburg Coll., 1950; PhD, U. Wash., 1954. Rsch. assoc. Fla. State U., Tallahassee, 1955-57, vis. asst. prof. physics, 1957; asst. prof. chemistry U. N. Mex., Albuquerque, 1957-62, assoc. prof. chemistry, 1962-67; prof. chemistry and materials sci. Wash. State U., Pullman, 1967—2001, chmn. chem. physics program, 1977-84, prof. emeritus, 2001—. Mem. adv. com. Rsch. Corp., Tucson, 1981—88, 1990—92; vis. prof. phys. chemistry U. Tubingen, Germany, 1964; vis. prof. physics U. Canterbury, Christchurch, New Zealand, 1974; Humboldt sr. scientist, vis. prof. phys. chemistry U. Hohenheim, Germany, 1978—79; mem. commn. on life scis. NRC, 1991—96, com. on programs for advanced study math and sci. in U.S. h.s., 1999—2001. Author: Chemistry: Matter and Chemical change, 1962; also numerous sci. and sci.-related articles Recipient U.S. Sr. Scientist award Humboldt Found., Fed. Republic Germany, 1978-79, Catalyst award Chem. Mfrs. Assn., 1979, Disting. Alumnus award Waynesburg Coll., 1982, Wash. State U.Faculty Excellence award in instrn., 1984, Wash. State U. Faculty Excellence award for pub. svc., 1989, Disting. Prof. award Wash. State U. Mortar Bd., 1990, Pres.'s medallion Waynesburg Coll. for disting. lifetime sci. and ednl. achievement, 1998; named Prof. of Yr., U. N.Mex., 1967; NSF fellow U. Wash., Seattle, 1953-54; Rsch. Corp. Venture grantee, 1960; Fulbright fellow, 1964. Fellow: AAAS, Wash. Sci. Tchrs. Assn. (Outstanding Coll. Sci. Tchr. award 1975), Inter-Am. Photochem. Soc.; mem.: Nat. Sci. Tchrs. Assn., Am. Phys. Soc., Am. Chem. Soc. (numerous activities including chmn. divsn. chem. edn. 1982, chmn. com. on edn. 1990—91, bd. dirs. 1994—2002, We Conn. sect. Vis. Scientist award 1981, nat. award in chem. edn. 1985, Harry and Carol Mosher award Santa Clara Valley sect. 1998, Divsn. Chem. Edn. Outstanding Svc. award 2003), Sigma Xi, Sigma Pi Sigma, Phi Kappa Phi. Home: 1208 E Excelsior Rd Spokane WA 99224-9257 E-mail: gac@wsunix.wsu.edu.

CROSBY, IVAN KEITH, cardiac surgeon, educator; b. Brisbane, Queensland, Australia, Mar. 11, 1938; s. Robert William James and Ivy Katherine Crosby; m. Roberta Brunfeldt, Oct. 30, 1971; children: Katherine Anne, Ivan Keith Michael, Kristen Anne. Asst. prof. to assoc. prof. to prof., surgery U. Va., Charlottesville, 1972—84; co-dir. heart transplantation Baylor U. Med. Ctr., Dallas, 1984—86; chief, cardiac surgery Forsyth Med. Ctr., Winston-Salem, NC, 1987—2000; prof., surgery U. Va., 2000—. Co-dir., heart ctr. U. Va., 2000—. Contbr. articles various profl. jours. Named Best Dr. in N.C., 1998, Best Dr. in Va., 2003; recipient, Am. Bd. of Surgery, 1971, Am. Bd. of Thoracic Surgery, 1972; James IV Travelling scholar, James IV Surg. Assn. of U.S., Gt. Britain and Ireland. Fellow: ACS; mem.: So. Surg. Assn., Soc. for Vascular Surgery, Internat. Soc. for Cardiovasc. Surgery, Am. Assoc. for Thoracic Surgery. Achievements include patents for Pericardioscope . Office: U Va Dept of Surgery Box 800679 Charlottesville VA 22908 E-mail: icrosby@virginia.edu.

CROSBY, JACQUELINE GARTON, newspaper editor, journalist; b. Jacksonville, Fla., May 13, 1961; d. James Ellis and Marianne (Garton) Crosby. ABJ, U. Ga., 1983; MBA, U. Cen. Fla., 1987. Staff writer Macon Telegraph & News, Ga., 1983-84; copy editor Orlando Sentinel, Fla., 1984-85; dir. spl. projects Ivanhoe Communications, Inc., Orlando, Fla., 1987-89; producer spl. projects Sta. KSTP-TV, Mpls., 1989-94; asst. news editor Star Tribune Online, Mpls., 1994—2003, reporter, 2003—. Recipient award for best sports story Ga. Press Assn., 1982; award for best series of yr. AP, 1985, Pulitzer prize, 1985 Mem. Quill Avocations: competing in triathlons, playing electric bass, tutoring, reading. Home: 5348 Drew Ave S Minneapolis MN 55410-2006 Office: Star Tribune 425 Portland Ave Minneapolis MN 55488-0001

CROSBY, JOHN BARTLETT, lawyer, health science association administrator; b. South Bend, Ind., Mar. 25, 1947; s. John Strong and Dorothy (Bartlett) C.; m. Mary Jo Knaup, Dec. 27, 1969; children: Lara, Patrick, Anne. BA in History, Washington U., St. Louis, 1969; JDS cum laude, Ohio State U., 1972. Assoc. Thompson & Mitchell, St. Louis, 1972-77; adminstrv. asst. Congressman Richard A. Gephardt, Washington, 1977-81; dir. Project Hope Ctr. for Health Info., Millwood, Va., 1982-83; sr. v.p. and gen. counsel Nat. Assn. of Ind. Insurers, Des Plaines, Ill., 1983-89; sr. v.p. health policy AMA, Chgo., 1989-97; exec. dir. Am. Osteo. Assn., Chgo., 1997—. Bd. dirs. Nat. Health Coun. Mem. ABA, Mo. State Bar Assn. E-mail: jcrosby@osteopathic.org.

CROSBY, JOHN GRIFFITH, investment banker; b. Bayshore, N.Y., Feb. 10, 1943; s. Gordon Josiah and Ruth Louise (Plante) C.; m. Joan Louise Kelly, July 10, 1965; children: Bruce, Brian, David. BA with distinction, Lafayette Coll., 1965; MBA, Harvard U., 1969. V.p., stockholder, dir. Kidder, Peabody & Co. Inc., N.Y.C., 1969-80; mng. dir. Merrill Lynch & Co., N.Y.C., 1980-90; ptnr. The Lodestar Group, 1990-93; mng. dir. LSG Advisors, 1993-95; chmn., pres. Madison Ptnrs., Inc., 1995—. Author: Private Placement Market Review, 1975-81. Class fund mgr. Lafayette Coll., 1969-90, mem. leadership coun., 1997-2001; bd. deacons Presbyn. Ch., Madison, N.J., 1972; campaign chmn. Madison YMCA, 1975; coach Little League, 1977-84; treas. troop 125 Boy Scouts Am., 1984-87; bd. dirs. asst. treas. Am. Coun. Arts, 1987-90; pres. PTO, 1979-80. 1st lt. U.S. Army, 1965-67, Vietnam. Decorated Bronze Star medal. Mem.: Eagle Scout, Orchid Island Golf and Beach Club (bd. govs.). Home (Winter): 534 White Pelican Cir Vero Beach FL 32963-9561 Home (Summer): 5972 Lake Shore Dr Bolton Landing NY 12814-4521 Personal E-mail: nuinweh@aol.com.

CROSBY, MARENA LIENHARD, retired academic administrator; b. Shreveport, La., Mar. 2, 1948; d. John Joseph and Clara Curtis (Lawton) L.; m. H.W. Patrick Obrien, Sept. 23, 1977; m. John L. Crosby, Nov. 23, 1997. MEd, U. New Orleans; JD, Loyola U., New Orleans. Bar: La. 1971; lic. profl. counselor, La.; diplomate Am. Coll. Profl. Mental Health Practitioners. Instr. Delgado C.C., New Orleans, 1973-80, counselor, 1980-86, coord. testing, 1986-88, dir. admissions, 1988-90, dir. counseling and mktg., 1990-93, dir. degree audit program, 1993-97, asst. to v.p. student affairs, 1997-98, ret., 1998. Mem. DAR, FBA, ACA, Internat. Assn. for New Sci., Assn. for Rsch. and Enlightenment, Am. Psychotherapy Assn., Inst. Noetic Scis., Theosophical Soc. Am., Family Mediation Coun., La. Bar Assn., La. Notary Assn., La. Assn. Spiritual and Religious Values in Counseling, Assn. for Spiritual. Ethical and Religious Values in Counseling, New Orleans Bar Assn., New Orleans Womens Opera Guild, New Orleans Mus. Art, Colonial Dames, Magna Charta Dames. Republican. Avocations: reading, piano. E-mail: cmloc18@aol.com.

CROSBY, MICHAEL P., science administrator; BS, MS with honors, Old Dominion U.; PhD in Marine-Estuarine-Environ. Sci., U. Md. Various sci. positions Nat. Marine Fisheries Svc., U.S. Army Corps Engrs., Nat. Cancer Inst., NIH; numerous faculty positions U. S.C., Coastal Carolina U., U. Charleston, Salisbury State U.; exec. dir. sci. bd. Nat. Oceanic and Atmospheric Adminstrn., nat. rsch. coord. ocean and coastal resource mgmt., chief scientist sanctuaries and reserves, sr. adv. internat. sci. policy under sec. office internat. affairs; sr. sci. adv. marine and coastal ecosystems U.S. Agency Internal Devel.; exec. officer, dir. Nat. Sci. Bd., 2003—. Mem. numerous nat. and internat. sci. panels and adv. coms. Reviewer, panelist: numerous sci. jours.; editor: numerous books and manuals on marine protected areas and coral reefs. Grantee NSF, Nat. Oceanic and Atmospheric Adminstrn., EPA, DOD, USAID, others. Fellow: Royal Linnean Soc. London; mem.: AAAS, Pacific Congress Marine Sci. and Tech., Sci. Rsch. Soc., Estuarine Rsch. Fedn., Nat. Shellfisheries Assn., Coastal Soc., Nat. Areas Assn., Sigma Xi. Office: Nat Science Bd 4201 Wilson Blvd Arlington VA 22230 Office Phone: 703-292-7000. E-mail: mcrosby@nsf.gov.

CROSBY, NORMAN LAWRENCE, comedian; b. Boston, Sept. 15, 1927; s. John and Ann (Lansky) C.; m. Joan Crane Foley, Nov. 1, 1966; children: Daniel Joseph, Andrew Crane. Student, Mass. Sch. Art, Boston. Ind. comedian, entertainer, 1947—. Nat. spokesman Anheuser-Busch Natural Light Beer. Began work as comedian in New Eng. clubs, frat. and polit. dinners, numerous civic and charity functions; N.Y.C. debut Latin Quarter; several appearances London Palladium, regular appearances at all major hotels in Las Vegas, numerous other night clubs, concert halls, theaters, TV variety and panel shows; host: (syndicated TV series) Norm Crosby's Comedy Shop; nat. co-host on Jerry Lewis Muscular Dystrophy Assn. Telethon. Nat. hon. chmn. better Hearing Inst., Washington; trustee Hope for Hearing Found., UCLA; sponsor Norm Crosby Ann. Celebrity Golf Tournament benefitting City of Hope. With USCG, 1945-46. Recipient Jack Benny Comedy award Authors and Celebrities, 1981, Star on Hollywood (Calif.) Walk of Fame, Hollywood C. of C., 1982, Lifetime Achievement award in Entertainment, Touchdown Club, Washington, 1988, Victory award, Kennedy Ctr. Pres. George Bush, 1991; honored by USO and given privilege of laying wreath at tomb of Unknown Soldiers, Washington, 2001; named Internat. Variety Clubs Man of Yr., 1986. Mem. Friars Club (N.Y.C., L.A.; 20th term Internat. Amb. of Good Will for City of Hope), Masons, Shriners. Jewish.

CROSBY, PETER ALAN, management consultant; b. Santa Barbara, Calif., Oct. 20, 1945; s. Harold Bartley and Margaret Maida (Peterson) C.; m. Stephanie Jay Ellis, Dec. 20, 1969; children: Kelly Michelle, Michael Ellis. BS in Engring., U. Calif., Berkeley, 1967; MS in Ops. Rsch., Stanford U., 1969; ED, Stanford Bus. Sch., 1971. Cert. mgmt. cons. Logistics inventory analyst Ford Motor Co., Palo Alto, Calif., 1967-71; corp. ops. planning analyst FMC Corp., San Jose, Calif., 1972; assoc. mgmt. cons. A.T. Kearney, Inc., San Francisco, 1972-75; mgr. materials mgmt. cons. svcs. Coopers & Lybrand, Los Angeles, 1976-78; ptnr. gen. cons. unit (Case & Co.) Towers Perrin Forster & Crosby, L.A., 1978-81; prin. Crosby, Gustin, Rice & Co. (CGR Mgmt. Cons.), 1981—. Dir. Carbide Products Internat. Co. Mem. adv. bd. dirs. Stanton Chase. Mem. Coun. Logistic Mgmt., Inst. Mgmt. Cons. (past pres.), Food Cons. Group, Assn. for Corp. Growth, Phi Gamma Delta. Office: CGR Mgmt Consultants Ste 1900 1901 Avenue Of The Stars Los Angeles CA 90067-6020 Office Phone: 310-553-6837. Personal E-mail: crosbycgr@cs.com. Business E-Mail: petecrosby@cgrmc.com.

CROSBY, RALPH WOLF, communications executive; b. Annapolis, Md., Dec. 16, 1933; s. Raymond Thomas and Lillian Sylvia (Wolf) C.; m. Carlotta Stafford, June 16, 1958; children: Laura Crosby Avallone, Raymond, Belinda Crosby Butler. BS in Journalism, U Md., 1956. Reporter, editor Balt. News-Am., 1956-60; bur. editor Iron Age Mag., Washington, 1960-65, Med. Econs. mag., Washington, 1966-67; assoc. editor Kiplinger's Changing Times, Washington, 1967-70; exec. v.p. Annapolis Harbour House, Inc., 1970-86; chmn., CEO Crosby Mktg. Comm., Annapolis, 1972—. Bd. dirs. Annapolis Bank and Trust Co. Editor (book) Person to Person Management, 1966; contbr. articles to numerous mags. including N.Y. Times Mag. Bd. govs. U. Md. Coll. Journalism, 2005—. Recipient Jesse H. Neal editorial award, 1966. Mem. Md. Direct Mktg. Assn., Advt. Assn. Balt., Greater Annapolis C. of C. (pres. 1975-76, hall of fame 2005), Annapolis Bus. Coalition (pres. 1983-84), Nat. Press Club, Annapolis Touchdown Club (pres. 1976), U. Md. Coll. Journalism (bd. govs., 2005—), U. Md. Dean's First Edit. Club (chmn. 1986—, named Cool. of Journalism Alumnus of the Yr. 2005), Annapolitan Club. Democrat. Avocation: tennis. Home: 139 Wallace Manor Rd Edgewater MD 21037-1205 Office: Crosby Mktg Comms 705 Melvin Ave Ste 200 Annapolis MD 21401-1544 Office Phone: 410-626-0805.

CROSBY, THOMAS MANVILLE, JR., lawyer; b. Mpls., Oct. 9, 1938; s. Thomas M. and Ella (Pillsbury) C.; m. Eleanor Rauch, June 12, 1965; children: Stewart, Brewster, Grant, Brooke. BA, Yale U., 1960, LLB, 1965. Bar: Minn. 1965. Assoc. Faegre & Benson, Mpls., 1965-72, ptnr., 1965—. Served to lt. USNR, 1960—62. Office: Faegre & Benson 2200 Wells Fargo Ctr 90 S 7th St Ste 2200 Minneapolis MN 55402-3901 Office Phone: 612-766-8605. Business E-Mail: tcrosby@faegre.com.

CROSBY, THOMAS W., computer scientist; b. Boston, Apr. 17, 1942; s. Thomas W. and Dorothy Crosby. AA, Dean Jr. Coll., 1962; BA, Mich. State U., 1964; MBA, Babson Coll., 1980. From software engr. to mgr. array application performance engring. EMC Corp., Westboro, Mass., 1974—. Mem. IEEE, VFW, Vets of Vietnam. Office: EMC Corp 4400 Computer Dr Westborough MA 01580-0001 Office Phone: 508-898-7188.

CROSBY, WILLIAM DUNCAN, JR., lawyer; b. Louisville, Ky., Sept. 1, 1943; s. William Duncan and Lucille (Edwards) C.; m. Constance Elaine Frederick, June 2, 1973; children: William Duncan III, Lelia Margaret. BA, Yale U., 1965; JD, Columbia U., 1968. Bar: Ky. 1968, U.S. Dist. Ct. D.C. 1971, U.S. Supreme Ct. 1977. Rep. chief counsel Com. on Rules U.S. Ho. of Reps., Washington, 1972-94, chief counsel Com. on Rules, 1995-99; v.p., COO The Solomon Group, Washington, 1999—2001; exec. dir. The Livingston Solomon Group, LLC, Washington, 2002—03; prin. The Livingston Group, LLC, Washington, 2003—05, cons., 2005—; pres. The Crosby Group, LLC, Washington, 2005—. Chmn. Dranesville Dist., Fairfax County (Va.) Rep. Party, 1987-89; mem. Fairfax County Rep. Com., 1981—, chmn. fin. com., 2003—04. Lt. (j.g.) USNR, 1968-71. Mem. ABA, FBA, Ky. Bar Assn., D.C. Bar, The Federalist Soc., Columbia Law Sch. Alumni Assn. of Washington (pres. 1987-89). Republican. Baptist. Avocation: swimming. Home: 920 Mackall Ave Mc Lean VA 22101-1618 Office: The Livingston Group LLC 499 S Capitol St SW Ste 600 Washington DC 20003 Office Phone: 202-289-9881. Personal E-mail: billcrosby1@aol.com. Business E-Mail: bcrosby@livingstongroupdc.com.

CROSHERE, AUSTIN, professional basketball player; b. L.A., May 1, 1975; Student, Providence, 1997. Power forward Ind. Pacers, 1997—. Office: Ind Pacers 125 S Pennsylvania St Indianapolis IN 46204

CROSLEY, DAVID RISDON, chemical physicist; b. Webster City, Iowa, Mar. 4, 1941; s. Carlton Whitley and Helen Elizabeth (Mingle) C.; m. Barbara DeVries, Sept. 7, 1963 (div. 1985); 1 child, Stephen Risdon. BS, Iowa State U., 1962; MA, Columbia U., 1963, PhD, 1966. Postdoctoral fellow Joint Inst. Lab. Astrophysics, Boulder, Colo., 1966-68; prof. U. Wis., Madison, 1968-75; rsch. chemist Ballistic Rsch. Lab., Aberdeen, Md., 1975-79; program mgr. SRI Internat., Menlo Park, Calif., 1979-88, assoc. lab. dir., 1988-95, lab. dir., 1995—2001, sr. staff scientist, 2001—. Cons. Battelle, Columbus, Ohio, 1975-81, Sci. Applications Internat. Corp., La Jolla, Calif., 1982-86, NASA, Washington, 1984-89; vis. prof. Ruhr U., Bochum, Fed. Republic of Germany, 1988, U. Paris, Orsay, France, 1989, U. Bielefeld, Germany, 1997, U. Leeds, Eng., 2004. Editor: Laser Probes of Combustion Chemistry, 1980; contbr. over 190 articless to sci. jours. NSF grad. fellow, 1964-66. Fellow Am. Phys. Soc., AAAS; mem. Am. Chem. Soc., Combustion Inst., Am. Geophysical Union, Pi Mu Epsilon, Phi Lambda Upsilon, Sigma Chi. Democrat. Achievements include research in laser-induced fluorescence spectroscopy, quantum state specific collisional energy transfer, gas-phase reaction kinetics and laser-based diagnostic techniques, environmental monitoring and applications to small molecules important in the chemistry of combustion, the atmosphere and materials processing. Office: SRI Internat Molecular Physics Lab Menlo Park CA 94025 Office Phone: 650-859-2395. Business E-Mail: david.crosley@sri.com.

CROSLEY-MAYERS, DIANE, social worker; b. South Gate, Calif., June 22, 1954; d. Curtis and Olevia Frances (Boson) Richardson; m. Hilton Charles Crosley, May 28, 1977 (dec. Mar. 1986); 1 child, Hillary Calida Crosley; m. Robert Alonzo Mayers Jr., June 12, 1993. BA, Calif. State U., L.A., 1976; MPA, Pepperdine U., 1977; HROD, U. San Francisco, 1995. Supr., counselor L.A. Job Corps, 1976-77; program dir. Travis AFB, Calif., 1981-85; advocacy specialist Solano Napa Area Agy. Aging, Vallejo, Calif., 1984; group counselor Solano County Health & Social Svcs. Dept., Vallejo, Calif., 1984-85; sr. social worker Solano County Health & Social Svcs. Dept., Fairfield, Calif., 1985—98; human resources generalist City of Vacaville, Calif., 1993—98; human resources analyst City of Oakland, Calif., 1998—2001; sr. personnel analyst Napa County, Calif., 2001—02; diversity cons. U.S., 2003—; personnel analyst II City of Vallejo, Calif., 2003—. Cons. Mary Kay Cosmetics, Suisun, Calif., 1982-86; gust lectr. Solano C.C., Suisun, Calif., 1993—; affirmative action rep. Solano County, Fairfield, 1996; com. chair Black Adoption Fair, Countra Costa, Calif., 1994; core group adv. bd. Solano County Health & Social Svcs., Fairfield, 1995-98. V.p. Local 535 State Calif., 1996; mem. Dem. Nat. Com., 1992—; com. chair Solano County Grand Jury, 2003-04; mem. Human Resources Coun. Recipient Appreciation cert. USAF, 1995, Recognition cert. Calif. State Legislature, 1996. Mem.: NOW, Internat. Pers. Mgmt. Assn. (v.p. pers. testing coun. bd.), Delta Sigma Theta (2d v.p. 2003—04, 1st v.p. 2004—). Avocations: swimming, skiing, reading. Office: City Vallejo Human Resources Dept 555 Santa Clara St Vallejo CA 94590 Office Phone: 707-648-4365.

CROSMAN, CHRISTOPHER BYRON, museum director; b. Chgo., June 25, 1946; s. John Byron and Leila (Pomeroy) C.; m. Janet Thomas, Dec. 28, 1968; 1 child, Anne. BA, Washington and Lee U., 1968; postgrad., Oberlin Coll., 1970-72. Educator Albright-Knox Gallery, Buffalo, 1972-84; dir. Heckscher Mus., Huntington, N.Y., 1984-88, Farnsworth Art Mus., Rockland, Maine, 1988—. Panelist N.Y. State Coun. on Arts, N.Y.C., 1982-85; mem. adv. coun. adult learning, N.Y. Dept. Edn., Albany, 1982-85; bd. dirs. Gallery Assn. N.Y. State, Hamilton, 1986-88, Maine Coast Artists, Rockport, 1988—; treas. L.I. Mus. Assn., 1987-88. Co-author: From Museums, Libraries and

Galleries: Artists on Tape, 1984; contbr. articles to profl. jours.; co-producer video documentaries, 1974-84; curator exhbns. Mem. Am. Assn. Mus., Maine League Hist. Socs. and Mus., Rotary. Office: Farnsworth Art Mus 16 Museum St Rockland ME 04841-0466*

CROSS, ALVIN MILLER (AL CROSS), journalist; b. Knoxville, Tenn, Apr. 24, 1954; s. Perry Martin and Winnie Cook (Miller) C.; m. Patricia Hodges, June 19, 1976. BA in Mass Comm., Western Ky. U., 1978; postgrad., Poynter Inst. Media Studies, 1999. Sports reporter Clinton County News, Albany, Ky., 1965—71; announcer WANY Radio, Albany, 1968-75; advt. mgr., reporter, editor College Heights Herald, Bowling Green, Ky., 1973-74; editor and gen. mgr. The Reporter, Monticello, Ky., 1974-75; asst. mng. editor Logan Leader & News-Democrat, Russellville, Ky., 1975-77; editor Leitchfield Gazette, Grayson County News-Gazette, Ky., 1977-78; reporter Courier-Journal, Louisville, 1978-88, polit. writer, 1989—2004, polit. columnist, 1999—2004; dir. Inst. for Rural Journalism and Cmty. Issues U. Ky., Lexington, 2004—. Contbg. author: Campaigns and Elections: Contemporary Case Studies, 2002, Kentucky Governors, 2004, Kentucky 24/7, 2004. Rep. acad. coun. Associated Student Govt. We. Ky. U., 1972-73; bd. dirs. Sigma Delta Chi Found, 2001—. Recipient Founder's award Foothills Festival Inc., Albany, 1989, Outstanding Print Journalist in Ky. and Adjoining States award journalism dept. Western Ky. U., 1995, Deadline Reporting award Metro Louisville Journalism, 1989, 92, Column Writing award, 1989, Continuing Coverage award, 1992, 95. Mem. Soc. Profl. Journalists (regional dir. 1987-89, v.p. Louisville chpt. 1983-84, pres. 1984-85, chmn. nat. com. Project Watchdog 1995-99, nat. sec.-treas. 1999-2000, pres.-elect 2000-01, pres. 2001-02, Outstanding Newspaper in Region 5 award 1974), Ky. Hist. Soc., Filson Hist. Soc, Com. Concerned Journalists, Western Ky. U. Alumni Assn. Baptist. Avocations: reading, gardening, boating, touring. Home: 123 W Todd St Frankfort KY 40601-2825 Office: U Ky 122 Grehan Bldg Lexington KY 40506-0042 Office Phone: 859-257-3744. E-mail: al.cross@uky.edu.

CROSS, AUREAL THEOPHILUS, geology and botany educator; b. Findlay, Ohio, June 4, 1916; s. Raymond Willard and Myra Jane (Coon) C.; m. Christina Aleen Teyssier, Mar. 11, 1945; children: Timothy Aureal, Christina Avonne Cross Collier, Jonathan Ariel, Cheryl Aleen (Mrs. Richard M. Bowman), Christopher Charles. BA, Coe Coll., 1939; MS in Botany, U. Cin., 1941, PhD in Botany and Paleontology, 1943. Instr. to asst. prof. U. Notre Dame, 1942—46; NRC fellow in geology, 1943-44; paleobotanist; Ctrl. Expt. Sta., U.S. Bur. Mines, Pitts., 1945; asst. prof. dept. geology U. Cin., 1946-49, asst. prof. dept. botany, 1948-49; part-time geologist Geol. Survey Ohio, 1946-51; coal geologist and paleobotanist W.Va. Geol. and Econ. Survey, 1949-57; assoc. prof. to prof. dept. geology U. W.Va., 1949-57; sr. rsch. engr. Pan Am. Petroleum Corp. Rsch. Center, Tulsa, 1957-61, supr. tech. group and rsch. group, 1959-61; prof. dept. geology Mich. State U., East Lansing, 1961-86, prof. dept. botany and plant pathology, 1961-86, prof. emeritus East Lansing, 1987—. Prof. ecology U. Alaska, 1971; research palynologist U. So. Calif., 1972; Morton vis. prof. Ohio U., Athens Ohio, 1981; Nathaniel S. Shaler Disting. lectr. U. Ky., 1991; UNESCO adviser U. grants commn. India Coal Programs, 1983; Calcutta adviser geology dept. Jadavpur U., India, 1983. Editor: Palynology in Oil Exploration, 1964, Compte Rendu 9th Internat. Congress Carboniferous Stratigraphy and Geology, vol. 4, Econ. Geology: Coal, Oil and Gas, 1985; co-editor: Coal Resources and Research in Latin America, 1978, World Class Coal Deposits, Internat. Jour. Coal Geology, 1993; assoc. editor: Fossil Spores and Pollen, 55 vols, 1956-87; contbr. numerous articles, abstracts and revs. to profl. jours. Chmn. citywide rally Fellowship Christian Athletes, Tulsa, 1960; mem. nat. council U.P. Men, 1966-68, 74-84; active Boy Scouts Am., YMCA, others. Named Seward Meml. lectr. Sahni Inst. Palaeobotany, 1985, J. Sen Meml. lectr., 1985, Disting. lectr. Am. Assn. Petroleum Geologists, 1964, Outstanding Educator Am. Assn. Petroleum Geologists Ea. Sect., 1987, Outstanding Educator, 2005; recipient Gordon H. Wood Jr. Meml. award, 1993, John T. Galey medal, 1995. Mem. Am. Assn. Stratigraphic Palynologists (hon.; medal of Excellence in Edn. 1999), Bot. Soc. Am. (chmn. paleobotany sect. 1953, 77, grantee 1954, Disting. Svc. Paleobotany award 1985), Geol. Soc. Am. (Gilbert H. Cady Coal Geology award 1987, chmn. coal geology divsn. 1966, chmn. North Ctrl. sect. 1969-70, exec. sec. sect. 1971-80, grantee 1951), Soc. Econ. Paleontologists and Mineralogists (chmn. rsch. com. 1961-62, councillor in paleontology 1971-73, numerous other internat., nat. and regional profl. assns. Presbyterian. Home: 529 N Harrison Rd East Lansing MI 48823-3015 Office: Mich State Univ Dept Geol Scis East Lansing MI 48824 Fax: 517-353-8787. E-mail: cross1@msu.edu.

CROSS, BONHAM E(LWOOD), retired newspaper account executive; m. Marie Swanberg; children: Randi Lawrence, David. News photographer Star Tribune, Mpls., then with advt. dept.; ret. Chmn. Minn. Coun. for Hearing Impaired, interim exec. dir., 1991; mem. adv. com. Metro Regional Svc. Ctr. for Hearing Impaired; mem. Legis. Coalition for Hearing Impaired. Named Man of Yr., Minn. Assn. Deaf Citizens, 1987; recipient Virginia McKnight Binger award in Human Svc., 2002, also various awards for news photography. Avocation: flying. Home: 3662 Shady Oak Rd Minnetonka MN 55305-4223 Personal E-mail: bonhamc@worldnet.att.net.

CROSS, BRUCE MICHAEL, lawyer; b. Washington, Jan. 30, 1942; AB magna cum laude, Dartmouth Coll., 1964; JD magna cum laude, Harvard U., 1967. Bar: Wash. 1967. Law clk. to Hon. Frank P. Weaver Supreme Ct. Wash., 1967-68; mem. Perkins Coie LLP, Seattle, 1969—. Office: Perkins Coie LLP 1201 3rd Ave Fl 40 Seattle WA 98101-3099 Office Phone: 206-359-8453. Business E-Mail: bcross@perkinscoie.com.

CROSS, CHRISTOPHER T., educational association administrator, consultant; b. Lakewood, Ohio, May 30, 1940; s. Sterling Leonard and Virginia Mae (Taylor) C.; m. Constance Heatherly Woods, Aug. 26, 1961 (div. 1981); children: H. Allyson (dec.), Dana M., Charles M.B.; m. Diane Stricklan DeRoche, June 11, 1982; 1 child, Charles. BA in Polit. Sci., Whittier (Calif.) Coll., 1962; MA, Calif. State Coll., L.A., 1969. With Dept. HEW, Washington, 1969-70, dep. asst. sec. for legislation, 1970-73; sr. ednl. cons. U.S. Ho. of Reps., Washington, 1973-77, Rep. staff dir., com. on edn. and labor, 1977-78; dir. Washington Office ops. Abt Assoc., Inc., 1978-80; mktg. mgr. fed. govt. Westinghouse Info. Svc., Washington, 1980-82, mgr. fed. svc., 1982-83; pres., COO Univ. Rsch. Corp., Chevy Chase, Md., 1983-89; asst. sec. for ednl. rsch. and improvement U.S. Dept. Edn., Washington, 1989-91; dir. Am. Inst. Rsch., 1993—; chmn. Cross & Joftus, LLC, 2004—. Exec. dir., edn. initiative The Bus. Roundtable, 1991-94; pres. Coun. for Basic Edn., 1994-2001; mem. Nat. Edn. Commn. on Time and Learning, 1992-94; mem. Md. State Bd. Edn., 1993-97, pres. 1994-97. Contbr. articles to profl. jours. Trustee Whittier Coll., 1999—; chair Nat. Coun. Edn. & Human Devel. George Washington U., 2000-02. Mem. Profl. Svc. Coun. (exec. com. 1981-86, trustee), Coun. Excellence in Govt. Congregationalist. Home: 109 Sunhaven Rd Danville CA 94506 Office Phone: 925-314-1863. Business E-Mail: chris@edstrategies.net.

CROSS, DAVID RUSK, farmer, livestock raiser; b. Larned, Kans., July 25, 1952; s. Charles Rusk and Mary Helen (Gatterman) C.; m. Linda Rae Wheeler, Nov. 3, 1974; children: Aaron R., Carolyn R., Aimee E. BS in Agr., Fort Hays State U., 1974; AI Tech. Course, Kans. State U., 1988. Ptnr. Cross Bros., Lewis, Kans., 1974-94; bd. dirs. Home State Bank, Lewis, 1979-94, chmn. of the bd., 1991-94; bd. dirs. Star Alfalfa, Inc., Lewis, 1986—; pres. Cross Bros., 1994—; sec. Plaza Cattle Feeders, Inc., 1992—. Mem. adv. bd. Kennedy & Coe, LLC, Pratt, Kans., 1996—, class II grad. Wheat Industry Leaders of Tomorrow, St. Louis, 1998-99; panelist Kans. Farmer Mag., 1996—. Mem. sch. bd. United Sch. Dist. 503, Lewis, Kans., 1986-88; cub master Boy Scouts Am., Cub Pack 238, Lewis, Kans. 1987-89; mem. com. Troop 238 Boy Scouts Am., Lewis, 1989-96; trustee United Meth. Ch., 1994—; precinct com. Ctrl Com. Kans. Reps., Edwards County, Kans., 1984-91, chmn. 1996—; first dist. del. Kans. Rep. Party, Topeka, 2003; chmn. Edwards County Leadership, Kinsley, Kans., 1995-98. Recipient 20th N.Am. Big Game award, Boone and Crockett Club, 1987; owner Res. Champion Live, Heifer Beef Empire Days, Garden City, Kans., 1988. Mem. Nat. Cattleman's Beef Assn. (agr. policy com. 1995—), Kans. Livestock Assn. (bd. dirs. 1978-80, water com. 1994—, vice chmn. 1996-2002, policy and resolutions com., 1997—, cow, calf stocker coun. exec. com. 1999—), Kans. Assn. Wheat Growers (Edwards County chmn., 1994-95, bd. dirs. 1996—, state sec. 2002-03), Masons (master). Avocations: hunting, collecting western memorabalia. Home: RR 1 Box 22 Lewis KS 67552-9520 E-mail: crossbro@ruraltel.net.

CROSS, DEWITTE TALMADGE, III, radiologist; b. Birmingham, Ala., Feb. 28, 1953; s. DeWitte T. Jr. and Virginia G. Cross; m. Anne Haney, Apr. 19, 1980; children: Courtney Elizabeth, Kevin Andrew. BA, Vanderbilt U., 1975; MD, U. Ala., 1980. Diplomate Am. Bd. Radiology. Commd. ensign USN, 1976, advanced through grades to lt. commdr., 1987, intern, gen. med. officer San Diego and N.Y.C., 1980-82; residency in radiology Nat. Navel Med. Ctr., Bethesda, Md., 1982-85; head radiology Naval Hosp., Memphis, 1985-87; fellow in neuroradiology N.Y. Med. Coll., N.Y.C., 1987-88, Columbia U., N.Y.C., 1988-89, asst. prof., 1989-91; dir. interventional neuroradiology Washington U., St. Louis, 1991—. Chmn. radiation safety oversight com. Barnes-Jewish Hosp., St. Louis, 1998—2002, chmn. procedural sedation com., 2002—. Contbr. author: Abram's Angiography, 1996; contbr. articles to profl. jours. Mem. neighborhood coun. City of Clayton, Mo., 1998-2000. Mem. AMA, Am. Soc. Interventional and Therapeutic Neuroradiology, Am. Soc. Neuroradiology, Am. Coll. Radiology, Radiol. Soc. N.Am. Presbyterian. Avocations: exercise, movies, cars. Office: Washington U Med Ctr Dept Radiology Campus Box 8131 510 S Kingshighway Saint Louis MO 63110 Office Phone: 314-362-5950. E-mail: crossde@wustl.edu.

CROSS, EASON, JR., architect; b. Bisbee, Ariz., Nov. 14, 1925; s. Eason and Olive (Hardwick) C.; m. Diana Johnson, June 17, 1950; children: Ben, Becca, Amy, Susan. BA, Harvard U., 1949, MArch, 1951. Assoc. Charles M. Goodman, Washington, 1952-59, Keyes, Lethbridge & Condon, 1959-61; ptnr. Cross & Adreon, Arlington, Va., 1961-87; pres. Va. Architects Accord P.C., Alexandria, 1989—; prin. Cross Assocs., Alexandria, Va., 1987—. Patentee fastenings and furniture. Pres. Hollin Hills Cmty. Assn., 1978; chmn. Fairfax County Appeals Bd., 1970-80; pres. Old Dominion DESA, 1997-98, Purysburg Preservation Found., 1998—. With USNR, WWII. Recipient Ware prize, 1950, Washington Bd. Trade design award, 1965, Bethesda-Chevy Chase C. of C. design awards, 1966, 67; House and Home awards AIA, 1965-66; Mid-Atlantic Region design awards, 1967-, 69; Nat. Honor award, 1968; Nat. Honor award Am. inst. Steel Constrn., 1967; 4 awards HUD-Washington Ctr. Urban Studies furniture competition, 1971; Frameworks Home Desing Merit award, 1995; Fairfax County Exceptional Design award 1985, 87, N.V. CAA Design award 1999. Fellow AIA, Housing Competition ADPSR winner 1993; mem. Va. Soc. AIA (Energy award 1979, Design award 1986, Noland medal 1994), Harvard Club, Fox Club, Ga. Salzburger Soc. Purysburg Found., Ricochet Club. Episcopalian. Home: 2309 Glasgow Rd Alexandria VA 22307-1821 Personal E-mail: easonc@earthlink.net.

CROSS, EUNICE D., elementary school educator; b. Foley, Minn, May 28, 1932; d. William Joseph and Elizabeth Agnes Latterell; m. Alan Viking Cross; children: Carol, Michael, Mari, Elizabeth, Jon, Catherine. BS, St. Cloud State U., 1956, MS, 1964. Rural sch. tchr. Dist. Common Sch. 51, North Benton, Minn., 1958-59; tchr. 4th grade Ind. Dist. 51, Foley, 1960-64, tchr. 1st grade, 1964-66, tchr. 6th grade, 1966-85, Chpt. I tchr., 1985-96, chairperson Chpt. 1 dept., 1986—98. Sec. Benton unit Am. Cancer Soc., 1985—89, pres., 1989—2004, daffodil chairperson, 1986—2004; mem. Foley Pub. Sch. Bd., 1999—2004, treas., 2001—04; mem. Foley Connection Team, 1987—99, Foley Found., 2003—04. Recipient Leadership in Edn. Excellence award Ctrl. Minn. Edn. Rsch., 1996. Mem.: Minn. Sch. Bd. Assn. (del. to assembly 2003—04), Ret. Tchr. Assn. Ctrl. Minn. (v.p. 1998—2003), Foley Edn. Assn. (pres. 1970—85, Tchr. of Yr. 1971). Democrat. Roman Catholic. Home: 50 6th Ave Foley MN 56329 E-mail: alanv@cloudnet.com.

CROSS, GEORGE ALAN MARTIN, biochemistry professor, researcher; b. Cheadle, Cheshire, Eng., Sept. 27, 1942; s. George Bernard and Beatrice Mary (Horton) C.; 1 child, Julia Elizabeth. BA, Cambridge (Eng.) U., 1964, PhD, 1968. Scientist Med. Rsch. Coun., Cambridge, 1970-77; dept. head Wellcome Found. Rsch. Labs., Kent, Eng., 1977-82; Andre and Bella Meyer prof. molecular parasitology Rockefeller U., N.Y.C., 1982—, dean grad. and postgrad. studies, 1995-99. Cons. Wellcome Found., Eng., 1982-87, World Health Orgns., Geneva, 1983-87, New Eng. Biolabs., Beverly Mass., 1985-99. Contbr. articles to profl. jours. Recipient Paul Ehrlich prize, 1984, Chalmers medal Royal Soc. of Tropical Medicine, 1983; named Fleming Lectr. Soc. for Gen. Microbiology, 1978. Fellow The Royal Soc. (Leeuwenhoek Lectr. 1998). Office: The Rockefeller Univ 1230 York Ave New York NY 10021-6399 E-mail: gamc@mail.rockefeller.edu.

CROSS, J. BRUCE, lawyer; b. Sharon, Pa., Oct. 6, 1949; s. John Lantz and Agnes (Bruce) C.; children: Lantz Davis, Heather Lynn. BA, U. Notre Dame, 1971; JD, U. Ark., 1974. Bar: Ark. 1974, U.S. Ct. Appeals (8th cir.) 1979, U.S. Supreme Ct. 1980. Ptnr. House, Holmes and Jewell, Little Rock, 1974-90, Cross and Gunter, P.A., Little Rock, 1990, McGlinchey Stafford Lang, Little Rock, 1991-97, Cross, Gunter, Witherspoon & Galchus, P.C., Little Rock, 1997—. Chpt. atty. Ark. Subcontractors Assn., Little Rock, 1987-90; mem. young execs. coun. Associated Gen. Contractors, 1989. Contbr. to profl. publs. Active Big Bros. Ark., Little Rock, 1976-87; pres., bd. dirs. Ark. divsn. Nat. Soc. to Prevent Blindness, 1987-90; bd. dirs. Urban League Ark., 1989, Ark. Constrn. Edn. Found., Boy Scouts Am., 2004-05, Single Parent Schlarship Fund of Pulaski County, 2004-05; nat. bd. dirs. Associated Builders and Contractors Am., 1999-2001; active Leadership Hot Springs, Habitat for Humanity, Youth Home; bd. mem. Single Parent Scholarship Fund, 2004-05, Boy Scouts Am., 2004-05, Mus. of Discovery, 2005. Recipient Pres.'s award Nat. Soc. to Prevent Blindness. Mem. Ark. Hospitality Assn. (bd. dirs. 1988-89), Ark. Subcontractors Assn., Assoc. Bldrs. and Contrs. (pres. 1999-2000), Ark. Bar Assn. (past chmn. labor sect.), Ark. Ready Mixed Concrete Assn., Little Rock C. of C. (ptnrs. in edn. com. 1989-90), ABA (sect. labor and employment law com. on labor arbitration and the law of collective bargaining agreements 1981-99, com. on devel. of the law under the NLRA 2000—), Greater Hot Springs C. of C., Notre Dame Club Ark. (pres.). Roman Catholic. Office: Cross, Gunter, Witherspoon & Galchus PC 500 President Clinton Ave Ste 200 Little Rock AR 72201-1747 E-mail: jbcross@cgwg.com.

CROSS, JAMES EDWARD, electrical engineering educator; b. Hampton, Va., May 29, 1937; s. Julia Ann-Cross Morgan; m. Velta Rose Jones, Dec. 1, 1965; children: Michael Levi, Andre Lene, Michelle Monique-Cross Brown. Diploma in radio, TV and electronics, DeVry Tech. Inst., 1956; BE sci. in Elec. Engring., Johns Hopkins U., 1960; MSEE, La. State U., 1967; postgrad. in elec. engring., U. of Fla., 1972; student in Elec. Engring., La. State U., 1973; BTh, Christian Bible Coll., Baton Rouge, La., 1982, ThM, 1984, ThD, 1987. Asst. prof. in elec. engring. So. U., Baton Rouge, 1962—64, chmn. elec. engring. dept., 1964—91, assoc. prof. of elec. engring., 1991—. Mem. tech. staff Western Electric Co., Allentown, Pa., 1970, GE Rsch. Ctr., Schenectady, NY, 1971, Westinghouse Corp., Youngwood, Pa., 1965, Western Electric Co., Atlanta, 1966, Autonetics divsn. N.Am. Rockwell, Anaheim, Calif., 1968, Radiation Inc., Melbourne, Fla., 1969; tchg. assoc. U. Fla., Gainesville, 1971—72; vis. lectr. La. State U., Baton Rouge, 1972—73, rsch. asst., 1973; NASA/ASEE summer faculty fellow Langley Rsch. Ctr., Hampton, Va., 1974; mem. tech. staff Bell Labs., Holmel, NJ, 1979, IBM, Charlotte, NC, 1981, Caterpillar, Inc., Peoria, Ill., 1990; rschr. Air Force Rsch. Lab., Wright-Patterson AFB, Ohio, 2002; reviewer, evaluator of proposals NSF, Washington, 1987—. Co-author tech. papers to confs. Mem. Baton Rouge Coun. on Human Rels., La., 1969—; mem., sec. Christian Bible Coll., 1964—2001; mem. deacon bd. Mt. Pilgrim Bapt. Ch., Baton Rouge, 1964—; mem. La. Coun. on Human Rels., Lafayette, La., 1990—. Capt. res. Army Corp of Engrs., 1960—62, Heidelberg, Germany. Grantee, Air Force Rsch. Lab., 1996—99, La. Bd. of Regents, 1989—90, Raytheon Co., 2000—02. Mem.: AAUP (pres. of local chpt. 1969—71), IEEE (life), Am. Soc. for Engring. Edn., Early Risers Kiwanis Club, Am. Legion, Masons (sec., Hon. Worshipful Master, Twilight Lodge # 166). Democrat. Baptist. Home: 13608 Alba Dr Baker LA 70714 Office Phone: 225-775-4153. Personal E-mail: cross4153@aol.com.

CROSS, JEFFREY D., lawyer, electric power industry executive; b. Painesville, Ohio, Apr. 28, 1956; BA summa cum laude, U. Cin., 1978, JD, 1982. Bar: Ohio 1982. Atty. Am. Electric Power Co. Inc., Columbus, Ohio, 1984—87, sr. atty., asst. sec., 1987—94, asst. gen. counsel, 1994—2000, gen. counsel AEP Resources Inc. subsid., 1994, v.p. AEP Resources Inc., 1996, sr. v.p., dep. gen. counsel, 2000, sr. v.p., acting gen. counsel, 2000—01, sr. v.p., gen. counsel, 2001—04, dep. gen. counsel, 2004—. Mem. legal com. Edison Electric. Trustee ProMusica Chamber Orch. Mem.: ABA (vice chair corp. governance com. pub. utility, comm., transp. law sect), Columbus Bar Assn., Ohio State Bar Assn., Energy Bar Assn., Ctrl. Ohio Breathing Assn. (trustee), Phi Beta Kappa. Office: Am Electric Power Co Inc Legal Dept 1 Riverside Plz Columbus OH 43215-2373

CROSS, JOHN HENRY, parasitologist, educator; b. Lynn, Mass., Sept. 25, 1925; s. John Cross and Helena Barnes; children: John, Kelley. AB, Miami U., Ohio, 1953; MA, Miami U., 1955; PhD, U. Tex, Galveston, 1958. Assoc. prof. U. Ark., Little Rock, 1960—66; scientific dir. US Navel Med. U., Taipei, Taiwan, 1966—84; prof. Uniformed Svcs. U., Bethesda, Md., 1984—. With USN, 1942—50. Mem.: Am. Soc. Paracitologists. Office: Uniformed Svcs Univ Health Scis Jones Bridge Rd Bethesda MD 20814

CROSS, JOSEPH RUSSELL, JR., retired law librarian; b. Bennettsville, S.C., July 29, 1945; s. Joseph Russell and Julia Rogers C.; m. Inez Mary Robinson, May 12, 1973; children: David Sebastian, Sarah Harrington. BA, Wofford Coll., 1967; MLn, Emory U., 1972; JD, U. S.C., 1978. Bar: S.C. 1978. Tchr. Cross (SC) Schs., 1967-68, 70-71; reference librarian U. SC, Columbia, 1972-75; head of pub. svcs. U. SC Law Library, 1978—, assoc. dir., 1997—2002, law libr. emeritus, 2002—, acting dir., 1983-84, 97-98. Served as staff sgt. U.S. Army, 1968-70, Vietnam. Mem. ABA, S.C. Bar Assn., Am. Assn. Law Libraries, S.C. Library Assn. Democrat. United Methodist. Home: PO Box 305 Cross SC 29436-0305 Office: U SC Coleman Karesh Law Library Columbia SC 29208-0001

CROSS, KATHRYN PATRICIA, education educator; b. Normal, Ill., Mar. 17, 1926; d. Clarence L. and Katherine (Dague) C. BS, Ill. State U., 1948; MA, U. Ill., 1951, PhD, 1958; LLD (hon.), SUNY, 1988; DS (hon.), Loyola U., 1980, Northeastern U., 1975; DHL (hon.), De Paul U., 1986, Open U., The Netherlands, 1989. Math. tchr. Harvard (Ill.) Community High Sch., 1948-49; rsch. asst. dept. psychology U. Ill., Urbana, 1949-53, asst. dean of women, 1953-59; dean of women then dean of students Cornell U., Ithaca, N.Y., 1959-63; dir. coll. and univ. programs Ednl. Testing Svc., Princeton, N.J., 1963-66; rsch. educator Ctr. R&D in Higher Edn. U. Calif., Berkeley, 1966-77; rsch. scientist, sr. rsch. psychologist, dir. univ. programs Ednl. Testing Svc., Berkeley, 1966-80; prof. edn., chair dept. adminstrn., planning & social policy Harvard U., Cambridge, Mass., 1980-88; Elizabeth and Edward Conner prof. edn. U. Calif., Berkeley, 1988-94, David Pierpont Gardner prof. higher edn., 1994-96. Mem. sec. adv. com. on automated personal data sys. Dept. HEW, 1972-73; del. to Soviet Union, Seminar on Problems in Higher Edn., 1975; vis. prof. U. Nebr., 1975-76; vis. scholar Miami-Dade C.C., 1987; trustee Carnegie Found., 1999—, Berkeley Pub. Libr., 1998-2002; spkr., cons. in field; bd. dirs. Elderhostel. Author: Beyond the Open Door: New Students to Higher Education, 1971; author: (with S. B. Gould) Explorations in Non-Traditional Study, 1972; author: (with J. R. Valley and Assocs.) Planning Non-Traditional Programs: An Analysis of the Issues for Postsecondary Education, 1974; author: Accent on Learning, 1976, Adults as Learners, 1981; author: (with Thomas A. Angelo) Classroom Assessment Techniques, 1993; author: (with Mimi Harris Steadman) Classroom Research, 1996; author: (with Elizabeth Barkley and Claire Major) Collaborative Learning Techniques: A Handbook for College Faculty, 2005; contbr. articles, monographs to profl. publs., chapters to books; mem. editl. bd. several ednl. jours., cons. editor (ednl. mag.) Change, 1980—. Active Nat. Acad. Edn., 1975—, Coun. for Advancement of Exptl. Learning, 1982-85; trustee Bradford Coll., Mass., 1986-88, Antioch Coll., Yellow Springs, Ohio, 1976-78; mem. nat. adv. bd. Nat. Ctr. of Study of Adult Learning, Empire State Coll.; mem. nat. adv. bd. Okla. Bd. Regents; mem. higher edn. rsch. program Pew Charitable Trusts; mem. vis. com. Harvard Grad. Sch. Edn., 1998—; bd. dirs. Elderhostel, 1999—; trustee Berkeley Pub. Libr., 1999—, Carnegie Found., 1999—. Mem. Am. Assn. Higher Edn. (bd. dirs. 1987—, pres. 1975, chair 1989-90), Am. Assn. Comty. and Jr. Colls. (vice chair commn. of future comty. colls.), Carnegie Found. Advancement of Tchg. (adv. com. on classification of colls. and univs.), Nat. Ctr. for Devel. Edn. (adv. bd.), New Eng. Assn. Schs. and Colls. (commn. on instns. higher edn. 1982-86), Am. Coun. Edn. (commn. on higher edn. and adult learner 1986-88). Business E-Mail: patcross@berkeley.edu.

CROSS, LESLIE ERIC, electrical engineering educator; b. Leeds, Eng., Aug. 14, 1923; came to U.S., 1961. s. Charles Eric and Alice Emily (Plant) C.; m. Lorna Lucilla Fish, Apr. 1, 1950; children: Peter Charles, Matthew John, Daniel Eric, Rebecca Lorna, Rachel Jean, Elizabeth Mary. B.Sc., PhD, Leeds U.; D.Sc. (hon.), Xian Jiaotong U. ICI fellow Leeds U., 1951-54; rsch. scientist Elec. Rsch. Assn., Eng., 1954-61; assoc. prof. Pa. State U., University Park, 1961-65, Evan Pugh prof. elec. engring., 1965—, formerly dir. Materials Research Lab.; Evan Pugh prof. elec. engring. Am. U., 1985—. Recipient John Jeppson medal, 1984; Ross Coffin Purdy award, 1985, MRS medal, 1992. Fellow Am. Inst. Physics, Am. Ceramics Soc. (electronics award 1968), IEEE, Optical Soc. Am.; mem. Japan Phys. Soc., Nat. Acad. Engring. Office: Pa State U Materials Rsch Inst Rm 187 University Park PA 16802 Home: 305 Windmere Dr Apt 322 State College PA 16801-7687

CROSS, MARCIA, actress; b. Marlborough, Mass., Mar. 25, 1962; d. Mark and Janet Cross. Grad., Julliard Sch., NYC; M in Psycology, Antioch U., LA, Calif. Actress (TV series) The Edge of Night, 1984, One Life to Live, 1986—87, Another World, 1986, Knots Landing, 1991—92, Melrose Place, 1992—93, 1994—97, Everwood, 2003—04, Desperate Housewives, 2004— (co-recipient, Outstanding Performance by an Ensemble in a Drama Series, Screen Actors Guild award, 2005), (TV films) Brass, 1985, The Last Days of Frank and Jesse James, 1986, Pros & Cons, 1986, Almost Grown, 1988, Storm and Sorrow, 1990, M.A.N.T.I.S, 1994, All She Ever Wanted, 1996, Target Earth, 1998, Eastwick, 2002, (TV miniseries) George Washington II: The Forging of a Nation, 1986, (films) Bad Influence, 1990, Ripple, 1995, Female Perversions, 1996, Always Say Goodbye, 1996, Dancing in September, 2000, Living in Fear, 2001, Bank, 2002, The Wind Effect, 2003; performer: (plays) La Ronde, Twelfth Night, Gentleman of Verona; guest appearances Tales From the Darkside, 1986, Cheers, 1989, 1990, Booker, 1989, "Who's the Boss?", 1989, Doctor Doctor, 1989, Quantum Leap, 1990, Jake and the Fatman, 1991, Murder, She Wrote, 1992, Herman's Head, 1992, Raven, 1993, Ned and Stacey, Burke's Law, 1995, Seinfeld, 1997, The Outer Limits, 1999, Boy Meets World, 1999, Touched by an Angel, 1999, Profiler, 2000, Spin City, 2000, Ally McBeal, 2000, Strong Medicine, 2001, CSI: Crime Scene Investigation, 2001, The King of Queens, 2002, 2003, Life & Style, 2004, "Corazón, Corazón", 2005. Address: Desperate Housewives Touchstone Television 100 Universal City Plaza Bldg 2128 Ste G Universal City CA 91608*

CROSS, MEREDITH B., lawyer; b. Oct. 14, 1957; BA cum laude, Duke Univ., 1979; JD, Vanderbilt Univ., 1982. Bar: Ga. 1983, DC 1998. Law clk. Judge Albert J. Henderson, US Ct. Appeals (11th cir.); atty. fellow Div. Corp. Fin., SEC, Washington, 1990—92, chief counsel, 1992—94, assoc. dir., Internat. Corp. Fin. & Small Bus. sect., 1994, dep. dir., 1994—98; ptnr. Wilmer Cutler Pickering Hale & Dorr, Washington, 1998—, co-chmn. Corp. dept. Frequent speaker at securities law conferences. Mem.: Order of the Coif. Office: Wilmer Cutler Pickering Hale & Dorr 1899 Pennsylvania Ave NW Washington DC 20006 Mailing: Wllmer Cutler Pickering Hale & Dorr 2445 M St NW Washington DC 20037 Office Phone: 202-663-6644. Office Fax: 202-663-6363. Business E-Mail: meredith.cross@wilmerhale.com.

CROSS, RICHARD JOHN, bank executive; b. Denver, May 22, 1929; s. Arthur Chester and Gertrude Eva (Ryan) C.; m. Mildred Louise Mouton, Jan. 19, 1957; children: John Charles, Carolyn Louise, Paul Arthur. BS, U. Colo., 1950; M.B.A, Wharton Sch. Finance U. Pa., 1955. With Lloyds Bank Calif., 1962-81, exec. v.p., 1974-81; mng. ptnr. Cross Investment Co., 1971—. Dir. bus. program Woodbury U., L.A., 1985-87; adj. prof. fin. and mgmt., 1987-97; chmn. bd. Highland Fed. Bank; adv. bd. Archdiocese of L.A. Dept. Detention Ministries, 1991-97; bd. dirs. Atwater Park Ctr., treas. 2001—, chmn., 2004—. Mem. bd. councilors U. So. Calif. Andrus Gerontology Ctr., 2001—. Served with USN, 1950—53. Fellow Royal Soc. Arts; mem. Calif. Bankers Assn., So. Calif. Trust Officers Assn., Delta Tau Delta, Phi Epsilon Phi. Clubs: Sutter (Sacramento); Jonathan (Los Angeles); Oakmont Country (Glendale, Calif.). Democrat. Roman Catholic. Home: 1430 Greenbriar Rd Glendale CA 91207-1256 E-mail: richjero@yahoo.com.

CROSS, ROBERT CLARK, journalist; b. Cheboygan, Mich., May 12, 1939; s. Warren Clark and Meryle M. (Allaire) Cross; m. Juju Lien; children: Gabriel Francis, Amy Lien. BA in Journalism, Wayne State U., 1962. Writer, researcher Newsweek mag., 1962; reporter, editor Chgo. Tribune, 1962-66, 67-82, assoc. editor mag., 1973-82, writer, 1982—; reporter Newsday, 1966-67; travel writer, 1992—. Recipient Gold and Silver Lowell Thomas awards Soc. of Am. Travel Writers, 1995, 2000, 04. Office: 435 N Michigan Ave Chicago IL 60611-4066 Business E-Mail: bcross@tribune.com.

CROSS, ROBERT FRANCIS, commissioner; b. Port Jervis, N.Y., Dec. 17, 1950; s. Francis Stuart and Rita Clotilde (Beilman) C.; m. Sheila Lynne Cochrane, Sept. 24, 1983. AA, Orange County Coll., Middletown, N.Y., 1971; BS, SUNY, Albany, 1973; MA, SUNY, New Paltz, 1976. Reporter, photographer The Union-Gazette, Port Jervis, 1974-76; Albany (N.Y.) bur. chief Ottaway News Svc., 1976-78; Albany corr. The Wall St. Jour., 1976-78; sci. editor N.Y. State Dept. Environ. Conservation, Albany, 1978-83, spl. asst. to commr., 1983-85, exec. asst. to commr., 1985-87, asst. commr., 1987-95; commr. City of Albany Dept. of Water, 1996—. Author: Sailor in the White House: The Seafaring Life of FDR, 2003; contbr. articles to mags. and profl. jours. Mem. N.Y. State Gov.'s Task Force on the Del. Water Gap Nat. Recreation Area, 1973; chmn. People United to Restore the Environment, Orange County Coll., 1970-71, Mayor's Task Force on Water Resources; chmn. bd. Albany Port Dist. Commn.; bd. trustees Destroyer Escort Hist. Mus.; mem. Albany City Planning Bd., 1995-96; mem. Minisink Valley Hist. Soc., Albany Inst. History and Art, Nantucket Hist. Assn., Dorflinger-Suydam Wildlife Sanctuary. Mem. Am. Philatelic Soc., Nantucket Wharf Rat Club, Franklin and Eleanor Roosevelt Inst. Democrat. Roman Catholic. Avocations: writing, reading, history. Home: 977 Washington Ave Albany NY 12206-1431 Office: City of Albany Dept Water Supply 35 Erie Blvd Albany NY 12204-2593

CROSS, ROBERT LOUIS, realtor, landscape architect, land use planner, writer, real estate appraiser; b. Alton, Ill., Aug. 9, 1937; s. Louis William and Marion (Hanna) C.; m. Paula Sutton, June 8, 1958 (div. June 1970); children: Britomart, Christopher, Amoret; m. Carolee Sharko, May 5, 1990. BA, U. Kans., 1959, MA, 1961; grad., UCLA, 1969, Realtors Inst., L.A., 1980. Lectr. English lang. U. Kans., Lawrence, 1959-60, Washburn U., Topeka, Kans., 1960-61; editorial-mktg. rep. Prentice-Hall, Inc., Englewood Cliffs, N.J., 1962-64; dir. pub. info. Forest Lawn Meml. Pk., Glendale, Calif., 1964-68; account exec. pub. rels. J. Walter Thompson, L.A., 1968-70; sr. account exec. pub. rels. Botsford Ketchum, L.A., 1970-71, Harsh, Rotman & Druck, L.A., 1971-72; pres. Crossroads Combined Comm., L.A., 1973-80; real estate agt. Carmel (Calif.) Bd. Realtors, 1979—; gen. ptnr. Crossroads Design Ltd., Big Sur, Calif., 1990—; co-owner Big Sur Properties. Cons. Watts Mfg. Corp., L.A., 1970-73, U.S. Office Edn., Washington, 1971, U.S. Dept. Interior, Washington, 1972, Calif. State Coastal Commn., San Francisco, 1980-85; land use advisor Puakea Bay Ranch, Hawaii, dir., 2005—. Author: Henry Miller: The Paris Years, 1991; assoc. editor Calif. Life Mag., 1976; contbr. IN Monterey Mag., 1977, Big Sur Mag., 2004; real estate editor Monterey Life Mag., 1978. Pres., dir. Big Sur Hist. Soc., 1980-90, Coastlands Mut. Water Co., Big Sur, 1984—2004; co-founder Dialogue for Big Sur, 1984; dir. Big Sur Natural History Assn., 1984-86; founding docent Dept. Pks. and Recreation, Pt. Sur Historic State Park, Big Sur, 1987; active ARC Disaster Svcs.; founder Big Sur Cmty. Action Team. With U.S. Army, 1961-63. Mem. Agora Internat. Press Corps, Archeol. Inst. Am., Nat. Assn. Realtors, Am. Soc. Landscape Architects, Nat. Assn. Real Estate Appraisers (cert.), Calif. Assn. Realtors, Monterey County Assn. Realtors (Multiple Listing Svc. Sales award 1980), Carmel Multiple Listing Svc., Big Sur Grange, Coast Property Owners Assn., Environ. Assesment Assn. (cert.). Avocations: art, travel, automobiles, music, reading. Office Phone: 808-443-4964.

CROSS, ROBERT WILLIAM, lawyer, venture capitalist; b. Balt., Oct. 9, 1937; s. Rosamond and Mildred (Fowler) C.; m. Deanna Louise Deerr, Feb. 7, 1965; children Ann Elizabeth, Robert William II. BSBA, Washington U., St. Louis, 1962; JD, Washington U., 1964. Bar: N.Y. 1964. Assoc. Winthrop, Stimson, Putnam & Roberts, N.Y.C., 1964-68; gen. counsel Electronic Data Systems Corp., Dallas, 1968-69; pres. R.W. Cross & Co., Dallas and N.Y.C., 1970-90; chmn., CEO Cross Tech. Inc., N.Y.C., also Solebury, Pa., 1990—; pres., CEO Nanophase Tech. Corp., Romeoville, Ill., 1993-98; pres., COO Vcapital Inc., Chgo., 1999—2002; pres., CEO Vcapital Securities, Chgo., 2000—02; chmn., CEO DigitalWork, Inc., Chgo., 2003—05; CEO Patron Sys., Inc., 2005—; ptnr. Batterson, Cross, Ventura, 2005—. Mem. adv. bd. Apex Venture Fund, 2003—. With USMC, 1957—63. Mem.: Bus. Execs. for Nat. Security, Marine Corps Assn., Union League Club Chgo., Univ. Club NY, Omicron Delta Kappa. Republican. Home: PO Box 200 Solebury PA 18963-0200 Office: Cross Tech Inc 6475 Upper York Rd Solebury PA 18963 Business E-Mail: rcross@crosstechnologiesUS.com.

CROSS, SANDRA KAY, primary school educator; b. Des Moines, Iowa, Nov. 8, 1948; d. Shirley Emmett and Catherine M. Baughman; m. Gregory P. Cross, Jan. 30, 1970; children: Stephanie R., Brian J., Andrew S. M in Reading K-12, Westfield (Mass.) State Coll., 1978. Cert. profl. tchr. Fla. Dept. Edn., Commonwealth of Mass. Tchr. Springfield (Mass.) Pub. Schs., 1970—72, New Braintree (Mass.) Elem. Sch., 1974—75, Quaboag Regional H.S., West Brookfield, 1977—79, Inverness (Fla.) Primary Sch., 1981—. Sec. Citrus County Math Coun., Inverness, 1993—2002; co-founder Citrus County Sweet Adeline Singing Group. Contbr. computer edn. portfolio. Organizer free dinner for vets. and their families Inverness Primary Sch., 1995—2005, organizer vets. day program, 1995—2005; leader troop 302 Cub Scouts, Inverness, 1987—89; founder pre-kindergarten edn. class Our Lady of Fatima, Inverness, 1982—84, dir. children's choir, 1983—85; bd. dirs. Boy Scout Troop 302, Inverness, 1988—94; organizer children to participate in the Vets.Day parade Inverness Primary Sch., 2003. Recipient Americanism award, VFW Post 4337, 2000, Nat. award, Fleet Res. Assn. #186, 1999, Appreciation of Support for our Vets. award, Vets. Appreciation Week Com., 2002. Mem.: Fla. Parent Tchr. Assn. (licentiate), Inverness Primary Parent Tchr. Assn. (assoc.; tchr. liaison 1981—2005). Office: Inverness Primary Sch 206 S Line Ave Inverness FL 34452 Office Phone: 352-726-2632. Home Fax: 352-726-1883; Office Fax: 352-726-1883. Personal E-mail: mom4sba@earthlink.net. E-mail: crosss@citrus.k12.fl.us.

CROSS, SHELLEY ANN, neurologist, neuro-ophthalmologist; b. Beacon, N.Y., Dec. 2, 1948; d. A.J. and Anna L. (Geering) C. AB, Wellesley (Mass.) Coll., 1970; MD, Med. Coll. Pa., 1975. Intern Montreal (Can.) Gen. Hosp., 1975-76; resident in medicine Royal Victoria Hosp., Montreal, Can., 1976-78; resident in neurology Mass. Gen. Hosp., Boston, 1978-81; fellow in neuro-ophthalmology Bascom Palmer Eye Inst., Miami, Fla., 1981-82; cons. in neurology Mayo Clinic, Rochester, Minn., 1982—. Contbr. articles to profl. jours. Fellow ACP, Royal Coll. Physicians, N.Am. Neuroophthalmological Soc., Am. Acad. Neurology and Psychiatry. Avocations: classical music, travel, literature, languages. Office: Mayo Clinic Dept Neurology Rochester MN 55905-0001

CROSS, STEVEN JASPER, finance educator; b. Hohenwald, Tenn., Apr. 19, 1954; s. Thomas Edward and Eula Mae Cross; m. Patricia Aldas, Jan. 6, 1995. BS, Mid. Tenn. State U., 1976, MAT, 1980, DA, 1984. Sales rep. U. Ford Inc., Murfreesboro, Tenn., 1976; ins. underwriter Continental Ins., Inc., Nashville, 1976—77; credit rep. SunAm, Inc., Murfreesboro, 1977—78; instr. mgmt. Dyersburg (Tenn.) State C.C., 1980—81; instr. econs. Motlow State C.C., Tullahoma, Tenn., 1981—83, asst. prof. econs., 1983—85; assoc. prof. fin. Delta State U., Cleveland, Miss., 1985—88, prof. fin., chmn. divsn. econs. and fin., 1988—91; dean Sch. Bus., prof. bus. Troy State U., Dothan, Ala., 1991—97, prof. fin., 1997—. Contbr. articles to profl. jours. Mem. AAUP, NEA, Am. Fin. Assn., Am. Econ. Assn., Delta Mu Delta. Home: 112 Wentworth Dr Dothan AL 36305-6906

CROSS, THEODORE LAMONT, publisher, author; b. Newton, Mass., Feb. 12, 1924; s. Gorham Lamont and Margaret Moore (Warren) C.; m. Sheilah Burr Ross, Sept. 16, 1950 (div. 1972); children: Amanda Burr, Lisa Warren; m. Mary Warner, 1974. Grad., Deerfield Acad., 1942; AB, Amherst Coll., 1946; LLB, Harvard U., 1950. Bar: Mass. 1950, N.Y. 1953. With Hale and Dorr, Boston, 1950-52; chmn. bd., CEO Warren, Gorham & Lamont, Inc., 1980-83; chmn. Faulkner & Gray, Pubs., 1985-92, Hanover Pub., Inc., 1985—; editor in chief Bus. and Soc. Rev., 1971—; editor Jour. of Blacks in Higher Edn., 1993—. Cons. HEW, Fed. Office Econ. Opportunity, 1964-69; pub. gov. Am. Stock Exchange, 1972-77; bd. dirs. Inst. for Sci. Info., 1988—; lectr. on inner city econs. and minority econ. devel. Harvard, Cornell U., U. Va. Author: Black Capitalism: Strategy for Business in the Ghetto (McKinsey Found. book award 1969), (with Mary Cross) Behind the Great Wall, 1979, The Black Power Imperative, 1984, Birds of the Sea, Shore and Tundra, 1989; founder: Atomic Energy Law Jour., 1959; editor Harvard Law Rev., 1948-50. Trustee Amherst Coll., chmn. investment com., 1976-88; trustee Folger Shakespeare Libr., Princeton U. Press, Inst. Advanced Study, Nat. Humanities Ctr., John Simon Guggenheim Meml. Found.; mem. Coun. Fgn. Rels.; dir. Legal Def. Fund, NAACP, Century Assn., N.Y.C. With USNR, 1945-46. Mem. Coun. on Fgn. Rels. (treas.), Am. Philos. Soc. Home: 1 Campbelton Cir Princeton NJ 08540 Office: 200 W 57th St New York NY 10019-3211

CROSS, WILLIAM DENNIS, lawyer; b. Tulsa, Nov. 7, 1940; s. John Howell and Virginia Grace (Ferrell) C.; m. Peggy Ruth Plapp, Jan. 30, 1982; children: William Dennis Jr., John Frederick. BS, U.S. Naval Acad., 1962; JD, NYU, 1969. Bar: N.Y. 1970, U.S. Dist. Ct. (so. and ea. dists.) N.Y. 1970, U.S. Ct. Appeals (2d cir.) 1970, U.S. Supreme Ct. 1974, Calif. 1977, U.S. Dist. Ct. (ctrl. dist.) Calif. 1977, U.S. Ct. Appeals (9th cir.) 1977, U.S. Ct. Appeals (5th, 10th and 11th cirs.) 1981, Mo. 1982, U.S. Dist. Ct. (we. dist.) Mo. 1982, U.S. Ct. Appeals (8th cir.) 1989, U.S. Ct. Appeals (fed. cir.) 1992, U.S. Dist. Ct. Ariz. 1997, U.S. Dist. Ct. Colo. 1997, U.S. Dist. Ct. Kans. 1998. Commd. ensign USN, 1962, advanced through ranks to lt., 1965, resigned, 1966; assoc. Cravath, Swaine & Moore, N.Y.C., 1969-76, Lillick, McHose & Charles, L.A., 1976-77; asst. gen. counsel FTC, Washington, 1977-82; of counsel Morrison & Hecker, Kansas City, Mo., 1982-83, ptnr., 1983—2002, Stinson Morrison Hecker, 2002—. Staff mem. NYU Law Rev., 1967-69, editor, 1968-69; assoc. editor Antitrust Mag. Mem. ABA, Calif. Bar Assn., Mo. Bar Assn., Assn. Bar City N.Y., Kansas City Bar Assn., Lawyers Assn. Kansas City. Home: 1223 Huntington Rd Kansas City MO 64113-1347 Office: Stinson Morrison Hecker LLP 1201 Walnut St STe 2800 Kansas City MO 64106-2150 Office Phone: 816-691-2708. Business E-Mail: dcross@stinsonmoheck.com.

CROSSAN, JOHN ROBERT, lawyer; b. Buckhannon, W.Va., May 31, 1947; s. Thomas Benjamin Jr. and Margaret Windsor (Hicks) C.; m. Monique Margaretha Scheen, Dec. 22, 1973; children: Ashley Margaret, Aubry Kelly. BS with honors, U. Va., 1969; JD, U. Chgo., 1974. Bar: Ill. 1974, U.S. Dist. Ct. (no. dist.) Ill. 1974, (ctrl. dist.) Ill. 1998, U.S. Ct. Appeals (4th and 10th cirs.) 1978, U.S. Ct. Appeals (7th cir.) 1979, U.S. Ct. Appeals (fed. cir.) 1983, U.S. Supreme Ct. 1985, U.S. Ct. Appeals (6th cir.) 1989. Staff atty. Ill. Task Force N.E. Ill. Pub. Transp., Chgo., 1972-73; assoc. Hill, Van Santen, Steadman, Chiara, Chgo., 1973-77; assoc., then ptnr. Cook, Wetzel and Egan, Ltd., Chgo., 1978-88; counsel Willian, Brinks, Hofer, Gilson and Lione, Chgo., 1989-90; ptnr. Brinks, Hofer, Gilson & Lione, Chgo., 1991-97, Chapman and Cutler, Chgo., 1998—. V.p. Va. Engring. Found., 1998—2000, pres., 2000—02. Author: Quick Guide to the Patent Law, 1994; contbr. articles to profl jours. Pres. aux. bd. Chgo. Architecture Found., 1983-85. Mem. ABA, Am. Intellectual Property Lawyers Assn., Chgo. Yacht Club. Home: 2825 N Cambridge Ave Chicago IL 60657-6018 Office: Chapman and Cutler, LLP 111 W Monroe St Ste 1700 Chicago IL 60603-4080 Office Phone: 312-845-3420. Personal E-mail: jrcrossan@hotmail.com. Business E-Mail: crossan@chapman.com.

CROSSER, CARMEN LYNN, marriage and family therapist, social worker, consultant; b. Iowa Falls, Iowa, Jan. 17, 1970; d. Gary Laverne Sr. and Karen Dorothy (Ulrich) C. AA, Ellsworth C.C., 1990; BS, Iowa State U., 1993; MSW, U. Iowa, 1995; postgrad., U. Chgo., 1998—. Lic. clin. social worker, marriage and family thrapist, Ill.; cert. brief therapist, ACSW. Grad. teaching asst. U. Iowa, Iowa City, 1994-95; mental health therapy intern Mid-Eastern Cmty. Mental Health Ctr., Iowa City, 1994-95; clin. social worker Sinnissippi Ctrs., Inc., Dixon, Ill., 1995-97; family therapist Ctr. for Counseling, DeKalb, Ill., 1997—. Cons. sexual abuse svcs. Sinnissippi Ctrs. Inc., 1997—98; rsch. asst. U. Chgo., 1998—2000, tchg. asst., 1999—2001; revs. asst. Jour. of Marital and Family Therapy, 1999—2000; adj. prof. Dominican U., River Forest, Ill., 2002—. Mem. Dekalb Area Women's Ctr., 1997—2000; mem. instnl. rev. bd. No. Ill. U., DeKalb, 1997—2000. All-Am. scholar, 1995. Mem. ACA, NASW, NOW, Am. Soc. Prevention Cruelty Animals (voting mem.), Am. Assn. Marriage and Family Therapy (clin. mem.), Am. Coll. Counselors, Internat. Assn. Marriage and Family Counselors, Ill. Soc. Clin. Social Work, Assn. Play Therapy, Nat. Fedn. Socs. for Clin. Social Work, Golden Key, Phi Kappa Phi, Phi Alpha. Office: Ctr for Counseling 14 Health Svcs Dr Dekalb IL 60115 E-mail: c-crosser@uchicago.edu.

CROSSFIELD, ALBERT SCOTT, aeronautical science consultant, pilot; b. Berkeley, Calif., Oct. 2, 1921; s. Albert Scott and Lucia (Dwyer) C.; m. Alice Virginia Knoph, Apr. 21, 1943; children: Becky Lee, Thomas Scott, Paul Stanley, Anthony Scott, Sally Virginia, Robert Scott. BS in Aero. Engring., U. Wash., 1949, MS in Aero. Sci., 1950; D.Sc. (hon.), Fla. Inst. Tech., 1982. Lic. pilot. Mem. U. Wash. staff charge wind tunnel operation, 1946-50; aerodynamicist, project engr., also pilot research airplanes X-1, X-4, X-5, D-558-I and II, X-F-92, F-102, F-100, F-86, NACA, 1950-55; participation proposal, design, 1st pilot X-15 research aircraft, design specialist, also chief engring. test pilot Los Angeles div. N.Am. Aviation, Inc., 1955-61, dir. test and quality assurance, space and info. systems div., 1961-66, tech. dir. research and engring., space and info. systems div., 1966-67; v.p. flight research and devel. div. Eastern Air Lines, Miami, Fla., 1967-71, staff v.p. transp. systems devel. Washington, 1971-74; sr. v.p. Hawker Siddeley Aviation Inc., Washington, 1974; tech. cons. House Com. on Sci. and Tech., Washington, 1977-93. Spl. work on the WS-131b, Apollo, Saturn S-II, Paraglider programs. Author: Always Another Dawn, 1960; also articles. Mem. aviation and space hist. preservation com. Calif. Mus. Found., mem. Aerospace Walk of Honor, City of Lancaster, 1990. Lt. USN, 1942-46, WWII, USNR. Recipient Lawrence Sperry award Inst. Aero. Sci., 1954, Octave Chanute award, 1958, Flight Achievement award Am. Astronautics Soc., 1959, Astronautics award Am. Rocket Soc., 1960, Commendation award County L.A. Bd. Suprs., 1960, Internat. Clifford B. Harmon Trophy, 1961, Achievement award Nat. Aeronautics Assn., 1961, Collier Trophy, 1961, Charter award, 1963, Elder Statesman of Aviation award, 1983, Godfry Cabot award Aero Club New England, 1961, John J. Montgomery award Nat. Soc. Aerospace Profls., 1962, Kitty Hawk Meml. award City of L.A., 1969, Al J. Engel award We. Res. Hist. Soc., 1983, Meritorious Svc. to Aviation award Nat. Bus. Aircraft Assn., 1984, Disting. Alumnus award U. Wash., 1986, Crown Cir. award Nat. Congress Aviation and Space Edn., 1988, A. Scott Crossfield Elem. Sch. award Fairfax County Sch. Bd., 1988, Bernt Balchin Trophy, N.Y. State Air Force Assn., 1988, Glenn A. Gilbert Meml. award Air Traffic Control Assn., 1990, Aerospace Walk of Honor, City of Lancaster, Calif., 1990, Disting. Pub. Svc. medal NASA, 1993, Cert. of Appreciation, FAA, 1993, Ho. of Reps., 1993, Gold Air medal Fedn. Aeronautique Internat., Sun City, South Africa, 1995, Ray Lien award Internat. Sport Aviation Mus. and Sun 'N Fun, 1999, Ray Lien award for aviation edn. excellence, 2000, Glenn L. Martin medal, 2000, Lifetime Achievement award Nat. Air & Space Mus., 2000, Crystal Eagle award Aero Club No. Calif., 2002, Gathering of Eagles Recognition USAF, 2003, Aerospace Laureate, Aviation Week and Space Tech., 2004, CAP Disting. Svc. award, 2004; named Lareate for Aeronatics/Propulsion, Aviation Week and Space Tech., 1959, 2003; inducted into Nat. Aviation Hall of Fame, 1983, Internat. Aerospace Hall of Fame, 1963, Internat. Space Hall of Fame, 1988, Va. Aviation Hall of Fame, 1998; AIAA hon. fellow; named One of 100 Pilots of the Century, 2003 Fellow AIAA (hon., chmn. flight test tech. com. 1963-64, Disting. lectr. 1987, 88, 89, Pathfinder award 1999, hon. 1999), Soc. Exptl. Test Pilots (co-founder, chmn. East Coast sect. 1976-77, past exec. advisor, Ivan C. Kincheloe award 1960, Ray E. Tenhoff award 1978), Inst. Aerospace Scis., Aerospace Med. Assn. (hon.); mem. Am. Soc. Qualtiy Control (sect., chmn. L.A. 1964-66, Outstanding Contbn. to Quality Control award 1967), Flying Physicians Assn. (hon., Man of Yr. 1961), Exptl. Aircarft Assn. (hon., Svc. to Sport Aviation award 1979, cert. of appreciation 1982), First Flight Soc. (life), Sterman Alumnus Club, Mustang Pilot Soc. (charter), OX-5 Club, Nat. Aviation Club (pres. 1983, gov. emeritus, Achievement award 1960), Nat. Space Club (Dr. Wernher von Braun Space Flight trophy), Order of Daedalians (hon.), Sigma Xi, Tau Beta Pi. Republican. Episcopalian. Home: 12100 Thoroughbred Rd Herndon VA 20171-2009 Office Phone: 703-860-4223. Personal E-mail: sxfield@msn.com.

CROSSGROVE, ROGER LYNN, art educator; b. Farnam, Nebr., Nov. 17, 1921; s. Lynn Everett and Iva Ellen (Spangler) Crossgrove; children: Christopher, Catherine, Cory, Carolyn, Camilla, Carl. BFA, U. Nebr., 1946—49; MFA, U. Ill., 1951. Instr. to prof. Pratt Inst., Brooklyn, NY, 1953—68; prof. art U. Conn., Starrs, Conn., 1968—88. One-man shows include Roger L. Crossgrove, Three Decades: Works on Paper and Photographs, The William Benton Mus. of Art, 1991, Roger L. Crossgrove, Selected Works: Photographs 1978-1993, Artworks Gallery, 1993, Works on Paper: Selected Monotypes and Photographs by Roger L. Crossgrove, Homer Babbidge Libr., 1995, Solo Show: Roger L. Crossgrove, The Slater Meml. Mus., 1996, New Works on Paper: Monotypes and Photographs, Ellen Traut Collection, 1997, Diverse Affinities - Monotypes and Photographs, Works on Paper 1958-1998, Artworks Gallery, 1998, Diverse Affinities II - Monotypes and Photographs, U. Conn. Hartford Campus, 1999, others, Represented in permanent collections. Staff sgt. U.S. Army, 1942—46, Japan, Phillippines. Mem.: Conn. Watercolor Soc., Conn. Acad. of Fine Arts, Artworks Gallery. Democrat. Home: 362 Gurleyville Rd Storrs Mansfield CT 06268

CROSSLEY, FRANCIS RENDEL ERSKINE, former engineering educator; b. Quarndon Derby, Eng., July 21, 1915; came to U.S., 1937, naturalized, 1957; s. Erskine Alick and Edith Mary (Helme) C.; m. Mary Eleanore de Lacy Bernadotte Coyne, Aug. 23, 1941 (dec. May, 1, 1998); children: Phyllis de Lacy Mervine, Michael Francis Erskine Crossley; m. Virginia Morss Galpin, Aug. 31, 1999. BA in Mech. Scis., Cambridge (Eng.) U., 1937; MA, Cambridge U., Eng., 1941; D Engring., Yale U., 1949. Asst. prof. mech. engring. Yale U., New Haven, 1944-55, fellow Branford Coll., 1948-65, assoc. prof., 1955-65; vis. fellow U. Manchester (Eng.) Inst. Sci. and Tech., 1965; prof. mech. engring. Ga. Inst. of Tech., Atlanta, 1966-69, U. Mass., Amherst, 1970-78, prof. civil engring., 1978-80, prof. emeritus, 1980—. Fulbright lectr. Technische Hochschule Munich, 1962-63, Tech. U. Bucharest, Romania, 1976; mem. U.S. del. forestry energy divsn. Internat. Energy Agy., Ottawa, Helsinki, Dublin, 1977-79; initiated talks with Soviet Acad. Scis. for U.S.-USSR exch. of info. on space flight, 1970; staff scientist Conn. State Legislature, Hartford, 1981-83. Author: Dynamics in Machines, 1954; editor-in-chief Mechanism and Machine Theory, 1971-73; founder, editor Jour. Mechanisms, 1966-71; editor Proceedings Internat. Conf. on Mechanisms, 1961; designer mech. robot's 3-fingered hand for NASA Space Flight Ctr., 1973-74. Chmn. solid waste mgmt. commn. Town of Branford, Conn., 1985-86, bd. edn., 1987-92. Recipient sr. scientist award von Humboldt Found., Germany, 1975-76. Fellow ASME (life, chmn. mechanisms conf. Atlanta 1968, legis. fellow 1981-83, Centennial medal 1980, Machine Design award 1991); mem. Verein Deutscher Ingenieure (hon.), Internat. Fedn. for Theory Machines and Mechanisms (hon., founding com., author constn., 1st v.p. 1967-75), Crossley Motors Centennial, Eng.

CROSSLEY, FRANK ALPHONSO, retired metallurgical engineer; b. Chgo., Feb. 19, 1925; s. Joseph Buddie and Rosa Lee (Brefford) C.; m. Elaine J. Sherman, Nov. 23, 1950 (dec. 1996); 1 child, Desne Adrienne. BSChemE, Ill. Inst. Tech., 1945, MS in Metall. Engring, 1947, PhD in Metall. Engring, 1950. Instr. Ill. Inst. Tech., Chgo., 1948-49; prof. foundry engring., head dept. foundry engring. Tenn. Agrl. and Indsl. State U., 1950-52; sr. scientist Ill. Inst. Tech. Rsch. Inst., 1952-66; sr. mem. rsch. lab. Lockheed Missiles & Space Co., Palo Alto, Calif., 1966-74, mgr. dept. producibility and standards, 1974-78, mgr. dept. missile body mech. engring., 1978-79, cons. engr. missile systems div. Sunnyvale, Calif., 1979-86; dir. rsch. propulsion materials Aerojet Propulsion Rsch. Inst., 1986-87, rsch. dir. materials applications, 1987-90; tech. prin. Aerojet Propulsion div. GenCorp, Sacramento, 1990-91; ret., 1991. Contbr. articles to metall. jours. and symposia. Served to ensign (D)L USNR, 1944-46, PTO. Recipient GenCorp Aerojet 1990 R.B. Young Tech. Innovation award. Fellow Am. Soc. for Metals Internat.; mem. AIAA (mem. materials tech. com. 1979-81), Minerals, Metals and Materials Soc. of AIME (chmn. titanium com. 1974-75), Sigma Xi. Congregationalist. Achievements include patent on Transage titanium alloys and grain refiner for titanium alloy castings; research in titanium alloys; diffusion bonding of metals and alloys. Home: 44 Goodnow Ln Framingham MA 01702-5505 Personal E-mail: dac9fac78@aol.com. *Choose well how your time is spent. Time spent doing one thing is time that cannot be spent doing something else.*

CROSSMAN, WILLIAM WHITTARD, retired wire cable and communications executive; b. Mineola, NY, Aug. 10, 1927; s. Homer Danforth and Emily May (Whittard) C.; m. Mary DeJesu, Dec. 6, 1952; children: William Whittard Jr., Lindsay Maria, Michael DeJesu. BS in Engring. Sci., U. Miami, 1949. West coast mgr., gen. mgr. HiTemp Wires div. Simplex Wire & Cable Co., 1955-69; pres. surprenant divsn. ITT Corp., 1969-74, pres. royal electric divsn. Pawtucket, R.I., 1974-77, group gen. mgr. N.Y.C., 1977-85, v.p., 1979-87, chmn. and group exec. comm. and info. svcs. Secaucus, N.J., 1985-88, sr. v.p., 1987-88, ret., 1988. With USNR, 1945-46, USAF, 1951. Mem.: Owls Head Harbor. Republican. Episcopalian. Home: 24 White Oak Shade Rd New Canaan CT 06840 Home (Summer): 563 Owls Head Harbor Rd Addison VT 05491 Home (Winter): 2871 N Ocean Blvd 226M Boca Raton FL 33431

CROSSON, FREDERICK JAMES, retired dean, humanities educator; b. Belmar, N.J., Apr. 27, 1926; s. George Leon and Emily (Bennett) Crosson; m. Mary Patricia Burns, Sept. 5, 1953; children: Jessica, Christopher, Veronica, Benedict, Jennifer. BA, Cath. U. Am., 1949, MA, 1950; postgrad., U. Paris, 1951-52; PhD, U. Notre Dame, 1956. From instr. to assoc. prof. U. Notre Dame, Ind., 1953—66, prof., 1966—, O'Hara Disting. prof. philosophy, 1976-84, Cavanaugh Disting. prof. humanities, 1984—98, dean Coll. Arts and Letters, 1968-76. Author: (book) The Modeling of Mind, 1963, Philosophy and Cybernetics, 1967, Science and Contemporary Society, 1967; editor: Review of Politics, 1976—83. With USN, 1943—46. Mem.: North Ctrl. Assn. (exec. commr. 1984—89), Am. Cath. Philos. Assn. (pres. 1990—91), Am. Philos. Assn., Phi Beta Kappa (senator 1982—2000, v.p. 1994—97, pres. 1997—2000). Home: 51997 Heather Cv South Bend IN 46635-1074 Office: Coll Arts and Letters U of Notre Dame Notre Dame IN 46556

CROSWELL, KATRINA ANTOINETTE, writer; b. Chgo., Mar. 2, 1963; d. Bettye Jean Yeatman. Student, Columbia Coll., 2000—. Asst. Hillel Found., Washington, 1998—99; program asst. Met. Planning Coun., Chgo., 1998—. Author: (novels) To Whom Much Is Given, 2002, (short stories) In the Wind, 2003, (poems) Awakening (Editor's Choice award Internat. Libr. of Poetry, 2003), LONG LIFE short stories, 1999; co-author: American Poetry Anthology, 1989. Mem.: Acad. Am. Poets (assoc.). Baptist. Avocations: music, art, nature. Personal E-mail: Katant1@aol.com.

CROTEAU, MAUREEN ELIZABETH, journalism educator; b. Hartford, Conn., Feb. 1, 1949; d. Maurice Joseph and Muriel Lucille (Follert) C.; m. Wayne Worcester. BA, U. Conn., 1971; MS, Columbia U., 1973. Reporter Hartford (Conn.) Times, 1971-72; editor Hartford (Conn.) Courant, 1973-76; reporter, editor Providence (R.I.) Jour., 1976-83; freelance journalist, 1983—; dept. head, prof. journalism dept. Univ. Conn., Storrs, 1983—. Bd. dirs. Conn. Found. for Open Govt., Hartford, The New London Day newspaper. Co-author: Shipwrecked in the Tunnel of Love, 1983, The Essential Researcher, 1993. Mem. Assn. for Edn. in Journalism & Mass Communications, Soc. Profl. Journalists, Investigative Reporters and Editors. Office: Journalism Dept 337 Mansfield Rd Storrs Mansfield CT 06269-9015

CROTHERS, DANIEL J., State Supreme Court Justice; b. Fargo, ND, Jan. 3, 1957; BA, U. ND, 1979, JD, 1982. Bar: N.Mex. 1982, ND 1983. Law clk. NM Ct. Appeals, 1982—83; asst. states atty. Walsh County, ND, 1983; former ptnr. Nilles, Hansen & Davies Ltd., Fargo; assoc. justice ND Supreme Ct., 2005—. Adj. prof. real estate law Moorhead State U., 1986—89, natural resources law, 1988. Staff mem. Univ. ND Law Rev., 1980—82. Mem.: ND Bar Assn. (pres. 2001—02). Office: ND Supreme Ct State Capitol Bismarck ND 58505-0530*

CROTTY, PAUL A., federal judge, lawyer; b. Buffalo, Apr. 1, 1941; BA, U. Notre Dame, 1962; LLB, Cornell U., 1967. Bar: N.Y. 1967, U.S. Dist. Ct. (so. dist.) N.Y. 1969, U.S. Ct. Appeals (2d cir. 1970, U.S. Supreme Ct. 1972. Law clk. to Hon. Lloyd F. MacMahon U.S. Dist. Ct. (so. dist.) N.Y., 1967-69; assoc. Donovan Leisure Newton & Irvine, N.Y.C., 1969—74, ptnr., 1976—84, 1988—93; commr. N.Y.C. Office Fin. Svcs., 1984, N.Y.C. Dept. Fin., 1984-86, N.Y.C. Dept. Housing Preservation and Devel., 1986-88; corp. counsel City of N.Y., 1994—97; group pres. Verizon Communications, 1997—2005; judge U.S. Dist. Ct. (so. dist.) N.Y., 2005—. Chmn. N.Y.C. Employees Retirement System, 1984-86, N.Y.C. Housing Devel. Corp., Housing N.Y. Corp., 1986-88. Lt. (j.G.) USNR, 1962-64. Mem. Assn. of Bar of City of N.Y., Order of Coif. Office: US Courthouse 500 Pearl St New York NY 10007*

CROTTY, ROBERT BELL, lawyer; b. Dallas, Aug. 16, 1951; s. Willard and Betty (Bell) C.; m. Sarah (Smith), Mar. 8, 1980; children: Robert Edwin, Rebecca Bell. BA, Va. Mil. Inst., 1973; JD, U. Tex., 1976. Bar: Tex., 1976; US Dist. Ct. (no., so. and ea. dists.) Tex., 1977; US Ct. Appeals (5th cir.), 1978. Assoc. Akin, Gump, Strauss, Hauer, and Feld, Dallas, 1976-82, ptnr., 1983-92, hiring ptnr., 1988-91; prin. McKool Smith, P.C., Dallas, 1992-94; ptnr. Crotty & Johansen, LLP, Dallas, 1995—. Vis. bd. Va. Mil. Inst., 1995-99. Mem. Leadership Dallas, 1981; dir. Salesmanship Club, 1989—90, 1994—95, 2001—02, Va. Mil. Inst. Alumni Assn., 1991—95, Highland Park Ind. Sch. Dist. Edn. Found., 1991—97, 2004—, pres., 1997—2000; chmn. bd. dir. Salesmanship Club Youth & Family Ctr., Inc., 2001—02; chmn. G.T.E. Byron Nelson Classic, 1995; bd. dir. Goodwill Industries of Dallas, Inc., 2002—; pres. Dallas Bus. League, 1983, Big Bros. Big Sisters Met. Dallas, 1987—88. First lt. U.S. Army, 1976, first lt. USAR, 1973—81. Fellow Tex. Bar Found. (sustaining life), Dallas Bar Found. (sustaining life, pres. fellows 1999-2000); mem. Dallas Bar Assn., Tex. Law Rev. Assn. (life), State Bar Tex., Northwood Club (pres. 2003). Avocations: golf, reading, hunting, hiking. Office: Crotty & Johansen LLP 2311 Cedar Springs Rd Ste 250 Dallas TX 75201-7810 Office Phone: 214-922-7555. E-mail: bcrotty@crojolaw.com.

CROTTY GUILE, JULIANNE MARIE, composer, educator, musician, writer; b. Omaha, Mar. 13, 1956; d. Richard and Beverly Ruth (Dillon) Crotty; m. Peter John Guile. BA, NYU, 1986; MA in English, U. Nebr., 1992; postgrad., 2001—. Singer Western Australian Opera, Perth, 1987-88; prof. English and Humanities U. Nebr., 1989-93, Metro C.C., Omaha, 1991-93, Coll. St. Mary's, Omaha, 1994; prof. English Buena Vista Coll., Iowa, 1996; prof. music Phoenix Acad., 1997; dir. Noteworthy Music, Omaha, 1992—. Composer "Children's Stories and Songs" to commemmorate Duchesne Choir reunion, 1974, Crest of Cedar, 1994 (music award 1996); poet, author: Love From The Inside Out, 1988 (poetry award 1989). Mem. Nat. Coun. Boys Town, Omaha, 1994; cantor, pianist St. Stephen the M., Nebr. Churches, 1974—. Recipient Stuart Creativity award Duchesne Acad., Omaha, 1974. Mem. Nat. Music Tchrs. Assn. (Omaha chpt.), Omaha Musicians Union. Avocations: sailing, walking, swimming. E-mail: jcrottyg@aol.com.

CROUCH, GARY CLINTON, financial management company executive, accountant; b. Wichita, Kans., Aug. 26, 1956; s. John Clinton and Patricia Roslyn (Reynolds) C.; m. Cindy Ranell Johnson, June 5, 1982; 1 child, Christina N. BA in Theology, Oral Roberts U., 1978, BS in Acctg., 1982. CPA, Okla; cert. Microsoft profl., info. tech. profl. Clk. Holloway Acctg., Tulsa, 1978-82; pvt. practice Tulsa, 1982—2001; pres. AlterComp Mgmt., Inc., Tulsa, 1986-96; sec.-treas. Smoke Foods, Ltd., Tulsa, 1991-94; pres. Crouch, Slavin & Co., PC, Tulsa, 1996—. Treas. Sertoma Handicapped Opportunity Program Found., Inc., Tulsa, 1986-88; bd. dirs. Evangelistic Temple, 1994— Mem. AICPA, Okla. Soc. CPAs (mgmt. adv. com. 1985-88, mgmt. of an acctg. practice com. 1992-98, tech. com. 2001—), Soc. for Human Resource Mgmt. (Okla. human resource conf. com. 2000, 02), Tulsa Area Human Resources Assn. (treas. 2003—), Sertoma (v.p. Tulsa chpt. 1986-87, treas. 1985-91). Republican. Office: 1799 E 71st St Tulsa OK 74136-5108 E-mail: gcrouch@crouchslavin.com.

CROUCH, JACK DYER, II, federal official, former ambassador; b. 1958; m. Kristin Crouch; children: Lara, Jake. BA in Internat. Relations, MA, Ph.D, U. So. Calif. Advisor for U.S. Del. to Nuclear and Space Arms Talks U.S. Arms Control and Disarmament Agy., 1985—86; mil. legis. asst. to Sen. Malcolm Wallop US Senate, 1986—90; assoc. prof. dept. def. & strategic studies S.W. Mo. State U., Springfield, Mo., 1993—2001; dep. asst. sec. def. for internat. security policy US Dept. Def., Washington, 1990—92, asst. sec. for internat. security policy, 2001—03; US amb. to Romania US Dept. State, Bucharest, 2004—05; asst. to the Pres. The White House, Washington, 2005—; dep. nat. security advisor NSC, Washington, 2005—. Co-founder PalmGear.com. Office: National Security Coun 1600 Pennsylvania Ave NW Washington DC 20500

CROUCH, PETER E., engineering educator; b. Newcastle-Upon-Tyne, Eng. BSc in engrng. sci., U. Warwick, Eng., 1973, MSc in control theory, 1974; PhD in applied sciences, Harvard U., 1977. Lectr. in control theory dept. elec. engrng. U. Warwick, England, 1977—85, acting dir. Control Theory Ctr., 1983—84; rsch. assoc. divsn. applied sciences Harvard U., 1982; vis. assoc. prof. dept. math. Ariz. State U., 1984—85, assoc. prof. dept. elec. and computer engrng., 1985—88, prof. dept. elec. engrng., 1988—, acting chair dept. elec. and computer engrng., 1988—89, dir. Ctr. for Systems Sci. and Engrng., 1989—95, chair dept. elec. engrng., 1992—95, dean Ira A. Fulton Sch. Engrng., 1995—. Assoc. editor Jour. of Math. Control and Info., 1984—, Systems and Control Letters, 1988—93, Math. of Control, Signals and Systems, 1989—, Jour. of Dynamical and Control Systems, 1994—; mem. bd. Internat. Performance Conf. on Computers and Comm., 1995—; mem. bd. advisors Inst. Systems & Robotics, Portugal, 1995—. Author: numerous papers and jour. articles. Recipient Hartree Premium Award, Instn. Elec. Engineers, 1982; Frank Knox Meml. Fellowship, 1974—76. Fellow: IEEE (assoc. editor Transactions on Automatic Control 1986—88, assoc. editor at large 1995—); mem.: Ariz. Soc. Profl. Engineers, Am. Soc. Engrng. Edn., Soc. Indsl. and Applied Math., Am. Math. Soc. Office: Ariz State U Ira A Fulton Sch Engrng PO Box 875506 Tempe AZ 85287-5506

CROUCH, RICHARD EDELIN, lawyer; b. Arlington, Va., Dec. 3, 1940; s. Howard Fairfax and Helen Nora (Edelin) Crouch; m. Mary Blake French, Feb. 6, 1965; children: John Howard, Virginia Elizabeth. AB, Coll. William and Mary, 1962, JD, 1964. Bar: Va. 1964, U.S. Ct. Mil. Appeals 1965, U.S. Dist. Ct. (ea. dist.) Va. 1970, U.S. Ct. Appeals (DC cir.) 1970, U.S. Supreme Ct. 1970, U.S. Ct. Appeals (4th cir.) 1972. Assoc. Crouch & Crouch, Arlington, 1964; editor U.S. Law Week & Criminal Law Reporter, Washington, 1968-74; prin. Crouch & Crouch, Arlington, 1974—. Cons. editor legal svcs. Bur. Nat. Affairs, Inc., Washington, 1981—84. Mng. editor: Family Law Reporter, 1974—81; author: The Rights of Homemakers in Virginia, 1977, Interstate Custody Litigation, 1981. Capt. U.S. Army, 1964—68. Mem.: ABA, Loudoun County Preservation Soc., Fairfax County Hist. Soc., Arlington Hist. Soc., King and Queen County Hist. Soc., Internat. Soc. Family Law, Am. Acad. Matrimonial Lawyers, Internat. Acad. Matrimonial Lawyers, Va. State Bar (bd. govs. family law sect. 1988—92, chmn. 10th dist. disciplinary com. 1988—89), SCV. Episcopalian. Home: 2624 18th St N Arlington VA 22201-4049 Office: 2101 Wilson Blvd Ste 950 Arlington VA 22201-3051 Office Phone: 703-528-6700.

CROUCH, STANLEY, writer, musician; b. L.A., Dec. 14, 1945; Playwright, actor under Jayne Cortez, 1965-67; drummer with pianist Raymond King, 1966; drummer, bandleader with Quartet, Black Music Infinity, 1967—; instr. Claremont Coll., Calif., 1969-75. Columnist L.A. Free Press, The Cricket, SoHo Weekly News; jazz critic Village Voice; contbg. editor New Republic, 1990—; co-founder, artistic dir. Lincoln Ctr. jazz program. Author: Ain't No Ambulances for No Nigguhs Tonight, 1972, Notes of a Hanging Judge: Essays and Reviews, 1979-1989, 1990, The Artificial White Man: Essays on Authenticity, 2004; composer: Future Sallie's Time, Chicago for Bobby Seale, The Confessions of Father None, Flying Through Wire, Attica in Black September, Noteworthy Lady; albums include Now Is Another Time, Past Spirits. MacArthur grantee, 1993; recipient Jean Stein award Am. Acad. Arts and Letters, 1993. Office: Lincoln Ctr for Performing Arts Jazz Program 70 Lincoln Center Plz New York NY 10023-6548

CROUSE, CAROL K. MAVROMATIS, elementary school educator; d. George and Helen (Captis) Mavromatis; m. David Crouse (dec. 1998). BS in Edn., Temple U., 1972, MEd in Curriculum and Instrn., 1981. Elem. tchr. grades 1, 3, 4, 5, Upper Darby (Pa.) Sch. Dist., 1974—, mem. Sci. Curriculum Writing Commn., 1974—99. Mem. Excellence in Edn. Team, Hillcrest Elem. Sch., Pa., 1987; cert. NASA Lunar Rock and Meteorite Edn. Program, 1993—; tchr. adv. bd. Phila. Zoo, 1995—; mem. writing and evaluation team Schuylkill Valley Nature Ctr., 1993-94; Highland Park Elem. Sch. Learn and Serve Cmty. Svc. Ctr., Kids Care Club, 2000-2002, Safety Patrol Advisor, 2002—. Recipient Howard W. McComb award, Temple U. Phi Delta Kappa, 1981. Mem.: NSTA, ASCD, Upper Darby Recreation Tennis Players (tournament co-dir. 1983—92, Recreational Summer Camp supr. 2004—). Home: 122 Crestview Rd Upper Darby PA 19082

CROUSE, ERIN ELIZABETH, academic administrator; b. Burlington, Vt., Mar. 17, 1979; d. Roger Leslie and Judy Wiley Crouse. MEd, SUNY, Potsdam, N.Y., 2003. Cert. tchr. N.Y., 2003. Dir. residence hall SUNY, Potsdam, 2001—04, U. Mass., Lowell, 2004—. Presdl. scholar, Elmira Coll., 1997—2001. Mem.: Am. Coll. Pers. Assn. Home: PO Box 1007 Lowell MA 01853 Office: UMass Lowell One University Ave Lowell MA 01854 Office Phone: 978-934-6419. Personal E-mail: erin_crouse@uml.edu.

CROUSE, JERRY K., energy company executive; b. Jan. 1964; m. Ann Crouse. Former v.p., contr. Tenaska Energy, Omaha, CFO, 2003—. Office: Tenaska Energy 1044 N 115th St Ste 400 Omaha NE 68154 Office Phone: 402-691-9500. Office Fax: 402-691-9575. E-mail: power@tenaska.com.

CROUT, DANIEL WESLEY, lawyer; b. Covington, Ky., Jan. 26, 1937; s. Charles Wesley and Mary Margaret (Meier) C.; m. Nancy Ann Keys, July 20, 1968; children: Amy Marie, Steven Wesley. BA, Villa Madonna Coll., 1959; JD, Chase Law Sch., 1975. Bar: Ky. 1975, Ohio 1976, U.S. Dist. Ct. (ea. dist.) Ky. 1976, U.S. Ct. Appeals (6th cir.) 1977, U.S. Supreme Ct. 1982. Surg. tech. Children's Hosp. Rsch. Found., Cin.; spl. agt. Ky. Dept. Alcoholic Beverage Control, Frankfort, 1968-77; pvt. practice Covington, 1975—. Rsch. asst. Christ Hosp. Inst. Med. Rsch., Cin., 1959—; salesman Gene Snyder Realty, Erlanger, Ky., Austin Mann Realty, Erlanger, 1972. Active Kenton County (Ky.) Bd. Adjustment, 1992-2000; candidate dist. judge, Kenton County, 1977, 87. Mem. Ky. Bar Assn., Kenton County Bar Assn. (Cert. of Merit 1984), Kenton County Fraternal Order Police. Avocations: flower gardening, photography.

CROUT, ELIZABETH ROOP, retired educator; b. Linwood, Md., Aug. 25, 1925; d. John Daniel and Edith Elizabeth (Pfoutz) Roop; m. Alan Lee Crout, Mar. 31, 1951; children: J. Daniel, Peter A., John W., Ruth Ann. BS in Gen. Edn., Manchester Coll., North Manchester, Ind., 1948; postgrad., Miami U., Oxford, Ohio, 1963-87. Med. technologist State of Md., Sykesville, 1945-46, Ch. of Brethren, Castañer, P.R., 1946-47, Middletown (Ohio) Hosp., 1949-53, Hughes Hosp., Hamilton, Ohio, 1956-63; tchr. Middletown Bd. Edn., 1964-87; ret., 1987. Prayer warrior Oasis Ch., 1980—, Living World Ch., 1980—; chmn. Aglow treas., 1988-2005; tutor, Trenton, Ohio, 1987—. Mem. AAUW. Mem. Full Gospel Ch. Avocations: sewing, visiting sick and shut-ins. Home: 5389 Wayne Madison Rd Trenton OH 45067-9548

CROUT, J(OHN) RICHARD, pharmacologist, researcher; b. Portland, Oreg., Dec. 30, 1929; s. John Shaw and Georgia Crout; m. Carol Jean Keith, June 19, 1954; children: Linda Jane, Keith Richard, Andrew Richard. AB, Oberlin Coll., 1951; MD, Northwestern U., 1955, MS, 1956; DMed (hon.), U. Uppsala, Sweden, 1977. Intern Passavant Meml. Hosp., Chgo., 1955-56; asst. resident in internal medicine VA Rsch. Hosp., Chgo., 1956-57; clin. assoc. Nat. Heart Inst., Bethesda, Md., 1957-60; asst. resident in Medicine NYU-Bellevue Med. Ctr., N.Y.C., 1960-61; USPHS fellow, instr. pharmacology Harvard U., 1961-63; asst. prof. pharmacology and internal medicine U. Tex. Southwestern Med. Sch., Dallas, 1963-65, assoc. prof., 1965-70; prof. pharmacology and medicine Mich. State U., 1970-71; dep. dir. Bur. Drugs FDA, Rockville, Md., 1971-72, dir. office sci. evaluation Bur. Drugs, 1972-73, dir. Bur. Drugs, 1973-82; dir. Office of Med. Applications of Rsch. NIH, 1982-84; v.p. med. and sci. affairs Boehringer Mannheim Pharms., 1984-94; scholar in residence Inst. Medicine, 1994-95; pres. Crout Cons., Bethesda, 1994—. Mem. drug resch. bd. NAS-NRC; cons. WHO, 1974—84; trustee U.S. Pharmacopeia, 1985—95; mem. coms. Inst. Medicine, 1990, 1992—93, 1998, 2000; bd. dirs. Trimeris. Contbr. articles to profl jours. Served to sr asst surgeon USPHS, 1957—60, asst surgeon gen USPHS, 1976—84. Recipient Dist Serv Award, USPHS, 1977, Spec Citation, Comnr FDA, 1981, 1982, Distinguished Career Award, Drug Info Asn, 1994, Oscar B Hunter Award in Therapeutics, Am Soc Clin Pharmaceutical and Therapeutics, 1997; scholar Burroughs Wellcome, 1965—70. Fellow: ACP; mem.: Soc Clin Trials, Heart Asn, Am Soc Clin Pharmacology and Therapeutics, Am Soc Clin Investigation, Am Soc Pharmacology and Experimental Therapeutics, Am Fedn Clin Research, Phi Beta Kappa, Alpha Omega Alpha. Home and Office: 5300 Alta Vista Rd Bethesda MD 20814-1629 Office Phone: 301-897-3860. E-mail: jrcrout@aol.com.

CROUTHAMEL, JEAN, computer scientist; d. Philip and Jean Preston; m. Russel Crouthamel, Dec. 24, 1977. Computer Programming Certification Gwynedd Mercy Coll., 1979. Programmer HMIC, 1979—85, Merck & Co., West Point, Pa., 1985—93, programmer analyst, 1987—93, sr. programmer analyst, 1993—97, project manger, 1997—. Achievements include first to Implemented the first central repository of non-clinical study data retaining historical data as well as data transmitted from laboratories globally.

CROUTHAMEL, THOMAS GROVER, SR., editor, consultant; b. Berkeley, Calif., Sept. 10, 1930; s. Martin Luther and Elizabeth (Grover) C.; m. Madalene Donati, Sept. 6, 1954; children: Thomas Grover Jr., Annalise. BS, Thiel Coll., 1953. Sr. drug investigator FDA, L.A. and Edison, N.J., 1958-81; pres. Thomas G. Crouthamel, Inc., Bradenton, Fla., 1981—; ptnr. Crouthamel & Crouthamel, Bradenton, 1983-93; treas. Crouthamel Enterprises, Inc., Liberty Hill, Tex., 1986-92; sr. editor Keystone Press, Bradenton, 1982—. Author: Auditing EtO, 1982, It's OK, 1986, A History of Trailer Estates, 1987; When the Unthinkable Happens, 1995; contbr. articles to profl. jours. Cubmaster Boy Scouts Am., Pomona, Calif., 1963, committeeman, Spotswood, N.J., 1968-76, adult adviser Explorer Post, 1976-79; trustee Spotswood Libr. Bd., 1970-79; co-leader Compassionate Friends, Sarasota, Fla., 1984-90, chpt. advisor, facilitator, Englewood, Fla., 1989-91. With U.S. Army, 1953-55. Mem. Internat. Narcotics Officers Assn., The Authors Guild, Toastmasters (pres. 1969-71), Masons (high priest local chpt. 1967), FDA Alumni Assn., T.E. Masonic Square Club (pres. 2002, 2003). Avocations: travel, reading, fishing. Office: PO Box 6163 Bradenton FL 34281-6163

CROUTHER, MICHELE JEAN, history educator, literature and language educator; b. Moberly, Mo., Oct. 30, 1950; d. Patricia Ruth Clark-Wedding; m. Charles Edward Crouther, Sr., Dec. 29, 1990; m. Jennifer Lee Jokerst. A in Gen. Edn., Moberly Jr. Coll., 1970; B in Secondary Edn., Southwest Mo. State U., 1974; MA in lit., Southeast Mo. State. U., 1997. Cert. lifetime tchg. State of Mo. English tchr. Southland C9 Sch. Dist., Cardwell, Mo., 1975—77; English, history tchr. Mt. View, Birch Tree Sch. Dist., Mt. View, Mo., 1977—80; English tchr. Dora (Mo.) Sch. Dist., 1981—86; English, hist. tchr. St. Genevieve R -II Sch. Dist., St. Genevieve, Mo., 1986—; adj. prof. St. Louis U., 1996—. English dept. chairperson Ste. Genevieve R-II, Ste. Genevieve, Mo., 1999—; MAP sr. leader Regional Profl. Devel. Com., Southeast Mo. State U., Cape Girardeau, Mo., 2000—. Percussionist Ste. Genevieve Municipal Bd., Ste. Genevieve, Mo., Ste. Genevieve Wind Ensemble, Ste. Genevieve, Mo. Mem.: Mo. State Tchrs. Assn., Found. for the Restoration of Ste. Genevieve, Delta Kappa Gamma. Democrat. Avocations: crossword puzzles, reading, golden retrievers. Home: 955 Cedar Ln Sainte Genevieve MO 63670 Office: Ste Genevieve R II Sch Dist 715 Wash Sainte Genevieve MO 63670 E-mail: mcrouther@stegen.k12.mo.us.

CROW, F. TRAMMELL, real estate company executive; Chmn. bd. Trammell Crow Co., Dallas. Bd. dirs. Jones-Blair Co., Inc. Office: Trammell Crow Co 3500 Trammell Crow Ctr 2001 Ross Ave Ste 3400 Dallas TX 75201-2998

CROW, HAROLD EUGENE, physician, educator; b. Farber, Mo., Jan. 17, 1933; s. Leslie J. and Laura L. (Sparks) C.; m. Mary Kay Krenke, July 5, 1974; children: Janet L., Jason P. MD, U. Mo., 1963. Diplomate Am. Bd. Family Practice, Am. Bd. Med. Examiners. Intern E.W. Sparrow Hosp., Lansing, Mich., 1963-64; pvt. practice medicine specializing in family practice Lansing, 1964-70; dir. family practice residency E.W. Sparrow Hosp., Lansing, Mich., 1970-82; chmn. dept. family and community medicine Sch. Medicine, U. Nev., Reno, 1982-87, dir. office Rural Health Sch. Medicine, 1984-87; med. dir. S.W. Med. Assocs., Reno, 1987-88; dir. Lynchburg (Va.) Family Practice Resident Program, 1988-96; patient advocate Cons. for Caring, Sun City Center, Fla., 1996—98; dir. Outer Banks Edn. and Program Devel. Project, East Carolina U. Sch. Medicine, Nags Head, NC, 1999—. Dir. Outer Banks Edn. and Program Devel. Project. Developer non-rotational residency model for family practice tng., tng. model for rural med. practice; innovator computerized health info. systems for family physicians. Numerous civic activities. With U.S. Army, 1955-57. Mem. Am. Coll. Physician Exec., numerous profl. assns. Presbyterian. Home: 408 Stoneham Dr Sun City Center FL 33573-5841 *Not being hampered by Dogma, but being freed up by curiousity. Not being a heavy handed teacher, but a caring helper of learning; that's the essense of a successful innovator and educator.*

CROW, JAMES FRANKLIN, retired genetics educator; b. Phoenixville, Pa., Jan. 18, 1916; s. H. Ernest and Lena (Whitaker) C.; m. Ann Crockett, Aug. 9, 1941; children: Franklin, Laura, Catherine. AB, Friends U., 1937; PhD, U. Tex., 1941; DSc. (hon.), U. Chgo., 1991. Instr., then asst. prof. zoology Dartmouth U., 1941-48; faculty U. Wis., 1948—, prof. genetics, 1954-86, chmn. dept. med. genetics, 1958-63, 65-71, acting dean sch. medicine, 1963-65, prof. emeritus, 1986—. Chmn. genetics study sect. NIH, 1965-68 Author: Genetics Notes, 8th edit, 1983, Introduction to Population Genetics Theory, 1970, Basic Concepts in Population, Quantitative and Evolutionary Genetics, 1986, also articles. Chmn. mammalian genetics study sect. NIH, 1985-88. Mem. Nat. Acad. Scis. (chmn. com. genetic effects atomic radiation 1960-63, 70-72, chmn. com. chem. environ. mutagens 1980-83), Japan Acad. (fgn. mem.), Genetics Soc. Am. (pres. 1960), Am. Soc. Human Genetics (pres. 1963), Royal Soc. (fgn. mem.). Home: 24 Glenway St Madison WI 53705-5206 E-mail: jfcrow@facstaff.wisc.edu.

CROW, MARTHA ELLEN, lawyer; b. Bryan, Tex., Dec. 7, 1944; d. Elvin Earl and Walteen (Daly) Burnett; m. Michael Paine Crow, Apr. 20, 1968; children: Jennifer Johanna, Emily Jeanne, Bryan Jacob. BA, Baker U., 1966; JD magna cum laude, Washburn U., 1992. Bar: Kans. 1993. Tchr., jr. high Shawnee Mission Schs., Johnson County, Kans., 1966-68; legal intern Speaker's Office Kans. Legislature, Topeka, 1991; law clk. Freilich, Leitner, Shortlidge and Carlisle, Kansas City, Mo., 1992-93; planning cons. Kans. Dept. Health and Environment, Topeka, 1993-95; ptnr. Crow, Clothier & Assocs., Leavenworth, Kans., 1995—. Comments editor: Washburn Law Jour., Vol. 31, 1991-92. Mem. Kans. Ho. of Reps., 41st dist., 1996—, agenda chair Ho. Dems., 2001—; mem. Kans. Continuing Legal Edn. Commn., 1993—99, chmn., 1997—99; bd. dirs., founding mem. Leadership Leavenworth, 1988-90; chmn., vice chmn. Leavenworth City Planning Commn., 1978-90, 94-96; v.p. to pres. Leavenworth Bd. Edn., 1983-96; chmn. Leavenworth Bd. Zoning Appeals, 1979-89, 94-96; pres. Downtown Leavenworth Revitalization, Inc., 1988-90, Leadership Kans. Class of 1986; bd. dirs. YWCA, 1974-82, pres., 1977-79; bd. dirs. Leavenworth C. of C., women's divsn., 1980-86, Baker U. Alumni Assn., 1978-80, Mother to Mother Ministry, 1996—, Richard Allen Cultural Ctr., 2000-, Northeast Kans. Mental Health and Guidance Ctr., 1997—2003; co-chmn. residential divsn. United Way Drive, 1977, 78, numerous others. Recipient Michaud, Cordry, Michaud, Hutton scholarship, Wichita, Kans., 1991, scholarship Washburn Law Sch., 1991. Mem. ABA, Kans. Bar Assn., Kans. Trial Lawyers Assn., Washburn Sch. of Law (women's legal forum), Phi Kappa Phi, Phi Delta Phi, Phi Gamma Mu, Delta Delta Delta, PEO. Democrat. Methodist. Home: 1200 S Broadway St Leavenworth KS 66048-3118 Office: Crow Clothier & Assocs PO Box 707 302 Shawnee St Leavenworth KS 66048-2063 Office Phone: 913-682-0166.

CROW, MICHAEL, academic administrator; BA in polit. sci. & environ. studies, Iowa State U., 1977; doctorate in pub. adminstrn., Syracuse U. Exec. vice provost Columbia U., prof. sci., tech. policy; prof. tech. mgmt. Iowa State U., dir., inst. phys. rsch. & tech; pres. Ariz. State U., 2002—. Contbr. articles to jours.; editor numerous books. Office: Az State U PO Box 872203 Tempe AZ 85287-2203

CROW, MICHAEL P., lawyer; b. Fort Sill, Okla., Jan. 22, 1945; BA, Baker Univ., Kans., 1967; JD, Washburn Univ., Topeka, 1973. Mng. ptnr. Crow, Clothier & Bates, Leavenworth, Kans., 1974—. Law clerk Hon. Arthur J. Stanley Jr., U.S. Dist. Ct., 1974—75; lectr., judicial process Wichita State Univ., 1976—77; mcpl. judge, Basehor, Kans., 1976—79, Linwood, Kans., 1977—79; atty. Delaware Twp., Kans., 1977—79; city atty. Tonganoxie, Kans., 1977—2004, Linwood, Kans., 1988—; state rep. Kans. Ho. of Reps., 1978—82; atty. Linwood Civil Svc. Commn., Kans., 1988. Lt. U.S. Army, 1967—70. Mem.: Assn. of Trial Lawyers of Am., Kans. Trial Lawyers Assn. (bd. dir. 1989—, treas. 1995—96), Am. Bar Assn., Leavenworth County Bar Assn. (pres. 1981—82, bd. dir. 1990—94), Kans. Bar Assn. (bd. gov. 1995—, sec. 2001—02, v.p. 2002—03, pres. 2004—05), Phi Alpha Delta. Office: Crow Clothier & Bates 302 Shawnee PO Box 707 Leavenworth KS 66048

CROW, PAUL ABERNATHY, JR., retired minister; b. Birmingham, Ala., Nov. 17, 1931; s. Paul Abernathy and Beulah Elizabeth (Parker) C.; m. Mary Evelyn Matthews, Sept. 11, 1955; children: Carol Ann, Stephen Paul, Susan Margaret. BS, U. Ala., 1954; BD, Lexington Theol. Sem., 1957; STM, Hartford Sem. Found., 1958, PhD, 1962; postdoctoral studies, Oxford U., 1967-68, U. Geneva, Ecumenical Inst. Bossey, 1981, 87; DD, Phillips U., 1983, Bethany Coll., 1983, Yale U., 1986, Va. Theological Sem., 1987; DHL, Lynchburg Coll., 1997. Ordained to ministry Disciples of Christ, 1957. Minister in various Disciples congregations, Ala., Ky., 1953—57; min. First Congl. Ch., Hadley, Mass., 1957-61; assoc. prof. ch. history Lexington Theol. Sem., 1961-66, prof., 1966-68; Am. Assn. Theol. Schs. vis. fellow Oxford U., 1967-68; gen. sec. Consultation on Ch. Union, Princeton, N.J., 1968-74; pres. Coun. on Christian Unity, Indpls., 1974-98; vis. lectr. Princeton Theol. Sem.,

1969-78; affiliate prof. Christian Theol. Sem., 1974—. Vis. prof. Lexington Theol. Sem., 2001-; mem. ctr. com. World Coun. Chs., exec. com., faith and order plenary commn., 1975-98; vice moderator Faith and Order Commn., 1992-98; del. faith and order confs., St. Andrews, Scotland, 1960, Montreal, Que., Can., 1963, Bristol, Eng., 1967, Louvain, Belgium, 1971, Accra, Ghana, 1974, Bangalore, India, 1978, Lima, Peru, 1982, Stavanger, Norway, 1985, Budapest, Hungary, 1989, Santiago de Compostela, Spain, 1993, Moshi, Tanzania, 1996, Kuala Lumpur, Malaysia, 2004; del. World Coun. Chs. assembly Uppsala, Sweden, 1968, Nairobi, Kenya, 1975, Vancouver, Can., 1983, Canberra, Australia, 1991, Harare, Zimbabwe, 1998; del. ch. union confs., Limuru, Kenya, 1970, Toronto, Ont., Can., 1975, Colombo, Sri Lanka, 1981, Potsdam, German Democratic Republic, 1987, Ocho Rios, Jamaica, 1995, WCC World Missionary Conf., San Antonio, Tex., 1989; mem. exec. com. Consultation on Ch. Union; chmn. Disciples of Christ del., 1974-98, mem. exec. com., mem. gen. bd. Nat. Coun. Chs., 1974-98; co-chmn. Disciples of Christ-Roman Cath. Internat. Bilateral, 1977-2002; co-chmn. Disciples-Russian Orthodox Internat. Bilateral, co-chmn. Disciples-Reformed Internat. Bilateral, Disciples-Finnish Luth.; gen. sec. Disciples Ecumenical Consultative Coun., 1975-98 Author: Where We Are in Church Union, 1965, The Ecumenical Movement in Bibliographical Outline, 1965, No Greater Love: The Gospel and Its Imperatives, 1967, Church Union at Mid-Point, 1972, Christian Unity: Matrix for Mission, 1982, The Anatomy of a Nineteenth Century United Church, 1983, The Vision of Christian Unity: Essays in Honor of Paul A. Crow, Jr., 1997; author: (with James Duke) The Church for Disciples of Christ, 1998; contbr. over 300 articles to maj. scholarly jours. and ency.; editor: Mid-Stream: An Ecumenical Jour., 1974—99. Bd. dirs., moderator Ecumenical Inst., Bossey, 1974-83; trustee Disciples of Christ Hist. Soc Recipient Disting. Alumni award Hartford Sem. Found., 1986, Ecumenical Svc. award Nat. Workshop on Christian Unity, 1998, Focolare Internat. Luminos (Light) of Christian Unity award, 1998, Ecumenism award Washington Theol. Consortium, 2004; Jacobus fellow Hartford Sem. Found., 1958. Mem. Nat. Assn. Ecumenical Officers (pres. 1988-93), Am. Soc. Ch. History, North Am. Acad. Ecumenists, Societas Oecumenica, Fellowship of St. Alban and St. Sergius, Nassau Club (Princeton, N.J.), Indianapolis Athletic Club, Omicron Delta Kappa, Theta Phi, Pi Kappa Phi. Democrat. Home: 7215 Vauxhall Rd Indianapolis IN 46250-2737

CROW, SAM ALFRED, judge; b. Topeka, May 5, 1926; s. Samuel Wheadon and Phyllis K. (Brown) Crow; m. Ruth M. Rush, Jan. 30, 1948; children: Sam A., Dan W. BA, U. Kans., 1949; JD, Washburn U., 1952. Ptnr. Rooney, Dickinson, Prager & Crow, Topeka, 1953—63, Dickinson, Crow, Skoog & Honeyman, Topeka, 1963—70; sr. ptnr. Crow & Skoog, Topeka, 1971—75; part-time U.S. magistrate, 1973—75; U.S. magistrate, 1975—81; judge U.S. Dist. Ct. Kans., Wichita, 1981—92, Topeka, 1992—96, sr. judge, 1996—. Bd. rev. Boy Scouts Am., 1960—70, cubmaster, 1957—60; chmn. Kans. March of Dimes, 1959, bd. dirs., 1960—65, Topeka Coun. Chs., 1960—70; mem. Kans. Hist. Soc., 1960—; pres., v.p. PTA; bd. govs. Washburn Law Sch. Alumni Assn., 1993—99; mem. vestry Grace Episcopal Ch., Topeka, 1960—65. Col. JAGC USAR, ret. Named to, Topeka H.S. Hall of Fame, 2000; recipient Washburn U. Sch. Law Disting. Svc. award, 2000. Fellow: Kans. Bar Found.; mem.: ABA (del. Nat. Conf. Spl. Ct. Judges 1978), Topeka Lawyers Club (sec. 1964—65, pres. 1965—66), Wichita Bar Assn., Topeka Bar Assn. (chmn. jud. reform com., chmn. bench and bar com., chmn. criminal law com., Disting. Svc. award 2000), Nat. Assn. U.S. Magistrates (com. discovery abuse), Kans. Trial Lawyers Assn. (sec. 1959—60, pres. 1960—61), Kans. Bar Assn. (chmn. mil. law sect. 1965, 1967, 1970, trustee 1970—76, chmn. mil. law sect. 1972, 1974, 1975), Shawnee Country Club, Shriners (Shriner of Yr. 2005), Am. Legion, Sigma Alpha Epsilon, Delta Theta Phi. Office: US Dist Ct 444 SE Quincy St Topeka KS 66683

CROW, SHERYL, singer, songwriter, musician; b. Kennett, Mo., Feb. 11, 1962; Degree in classical piano, U. Mo., 1984. Backup singer Bad tour Michael Jackson, 1987; backup singer The End of the Innocence tour Don Henley, 1989; also backup singer George Harrison, Joe Cocker, Stevie Wonder, Rod Stewart. Singer: (albums) Tuesday Night Music Club, 1993, Sheryl Crow, 1996, The Globe Sessions, 1998, Sheryl Crow and Friends: Live in Central Park, 1999, C'mon, C'mon, 2002 (Grammy award best female rock vocal performance, 2003), Live at Budokan, 2003, (songs) Leaving Las Vegas, 1994, All I Wanna Do, 1994 (Grammy awards for Record of Year and Female Pop Vocal, 1995), Strong Enough, 1994, Can't Cry Anymore, 1995, Everyday Is a Winding Road, 1996, If It Makes You Happy, 1996, My Favorite Mistake, 1998, Anything But Down, 1999, Soak up the Sun, 2002; singer: (with Kid Rock) Picture, 2001; participant Lilith Fair, 1998, 1999. Recipient Grammy award for Best New Artist, 1995, Favorite Female Artist award Pop or Rock, Am. Music Awards, 2004, Favorite Artist award Adult Contemporary Music, 2004.

CROW, TODD WILLIAM, pianist; b. Santa Barbara, Calif., July 25, 1945; s. Andrew and Grace (Platt) C.; m. Linda Goolsby; children: Evelyn, Daniel. BA, U. Calif., Santa Barbara, 1967; MS, Juilliard Sch., 1968. Prof. music, chmn. music dept. Vassar Coll., Poughkeepsie, N.Y., 1969—; music dir. Mt. Desert Festival of Chamber Music, Northeast Harbor, Maine, 1996—. Editor: Bartók Studies, 1976; contbr. articles to profl. jours. and The Compleat Brahms, 1999; performed with Composers String Quartet, Concord String Quartet, Brentano String Quartet, Miami String Quartet, Shanghai Quartet, Borromeo String Quartet, St. Luke's Chamber Ensemble and Aspen Wind Quintet; concert pianist appearances in N.Am., S.Am. and Europe, including Met. Mus., N.Y., Avery Fisher Hall, N.Y., Weill Recital Hall, N.Y., Nat. Gallery of Art, Washington, South Bank, London, Concertgebouw, Amsterdam, Bard Music Festival, Casals Festival, Maverick Concerts, Music Mountain; debuts: London, Wigmore Hall, 1975, London orchestral, Barbican Hall with London Philharmonic, 1986, N.Y., Alice Tully Hall, 1982, New York orchestral Carnegie Hall with Am. Symphony, 1992; chamber music with Walter Trampler, Nathaniel Rosen, Eugene Drucker, David Krakauer, Mark Peskanov, and Benny Goodman; radio broadcasts include BBC, Sta. WQXR, Sta. WNCN, Sta. WNYC; rec. (compact disc) Schubert piano sonatas, Haydn piano sonatas, Berlioz/Liszt Symphonie fantastique, works of S. Taneyev, E. Toch Piano Concerto No. 1 (with NDR Symphony Orch., Hamburg), (with M. Shuman) complete music for cello and piano by Mendelssohn and piano music of Dohnányi. Scholarships S. D. Epstein Found., 1958-63, Pillsbury Found., 1967, 68; recipient Disting. Alumni award U. Calif., 1986; winner Young Artists Competition, Santa Barbara Symphony Orch., 1960. Mem. The Liszt Soc. (London).

CROWDER, LENA BELLE, retired special education educator; b. Winston-Salem, N.C., Apr. 4, 1931; d. Henry Lee and Janie (Woods) Thomas; m. Raymond Crowder, June 12, 1954; 1 child, Rayonette Janease. BS in Edn., Winston Salem State U., 1952; MS in Edn., Agrl. and Tech. Coll., 1959. Cert. elem. edn. tchr., N.C. Tchr. 1st grade Early County Sch. Sys., Blakely, Ga., 1953-56; tchr. kindergarten Thomas-Anderson Kindergarten, Winston-Salem, 1956-57, 58-60, 61-62; tchr. 1st grade Beaufort (S.C.) County Schs., 1957-58; tchr. Chapel Hill (N.C.) City Sch. System, 1960-61, Forsyth County Sch. System, Winston-Salem, 1961-62, 1962-67, Winston-Salem/Forsyth County Schs., 1967-93, ret., 1993. Precinct election recorder Winston-Salem/Forsyth County Election Bd., 1961; fin. sec. Mt. Zion Bapt. Ch. Sunday Sch., Winston Salem, 1977—; supporter Crisis Control Ministry, Winston-Salem, 1982—; participant neighborhood watch system Winston-Salem Police Dept.; chair sch. involvement projects ARC, 1991-92. Mem. NEA, Nat. Assn. Univ. Women, Coun. Exceptional Children, Nat. Women of Achievement (life, rec. sec. S.E. region 2000—, S.E. bd. dirs., Winston-Salem bd. dirs., Annie Lee Smith award 2003), Assn. Classroom Tchrs., Winston-Salem State U. Alumni & Friends (recording sec. 2003-04). Democrat. Home: 1140 Rich Ave Winston Salem NC 27101-3432

CROWDER, LILLIE MAE BROWN, retired architectural engineer; b. Georgetown, S.C., May 31, 1936; d. Moses and Maude (Session) Brown; m. Charles Lamar Crowder, Apr. 16, 1960 (div. Feb. 1972); children: Barney, Frederick. BS in Archtl. Engring., S.C. State U., 1958; postgrad., Tuskegee Inst., 1960, Inst. Design and Constrn., 1961, 63; diploma in archtl. drafting, CUNY, 1971; MA in Urban Edn., L.I. U., 1981. Rated aero. engr./jr. archtl. engr. U.S. Civil Svc. Commn. Draftperson David Byrd Assoc., Washington, 1958-59; tchr. Choppee H.S., Georgetown, 1958-60; draftperson Big 6 Press, N.Y.C., 1960-62; sr. warrant officer N.Y. Telephone Co., N.Y.C., 1963-64; chief draftsperson Wilbur Smith & Assoc. C.E., Manhattan, N.Y., 1964-67; asst. architect sch. planning and rsch. Bklyn. Bd. Edn., 1967-71, edn. facility coord. facilities planning divsn., 1971-84, archtl. faculty coord. divsn. spl. edn., 1984-90, sr. project liaison divsn. sch. facilities, 1990-98. Jr. engr. N.Y.C. Resignalization Study, 1959-60; organized 1st mech. drawing dept. at Choppee H.S. Spkr: Women History Month, 1998, Bus. and Profl. Women, N.Y.C.; Author: Essence of a Dream (featured in Sotheby's 8th Annual exhbn. of art by N.Y.C. pub. sch. tchrs. and students, 1998; contbr. poems to profl. publs. Trustee Salem United Meth. Ch., N.Y.C., 1972; bd. dirs. Lewis H. Latimer Fund, Inc., Flushing, N.Y., 1982—, Human Resource Ctr./St. Albans, Queens, N.Y., 1984; mem. adv. com. Black Am. Heritage Found. Music History Arch. York Coll., 1995—; women's com. Local 375, Architects and Engrs.; borough pres. Bklyn. Citation Achievement Field Edn. & Arch., Queens Black History Month-Mary McLeod Bethune Celebration; guest spkr. Women History Program, 1998, fed. women's com. Social Security Adminstrn. Recipient Disting. Alumni award S.C. State U., 1981, Nat. Assn. Equal Oppty. Higher Edn., 1982, Quarter Century award Black Am. Heritage Found., 1993, Positive Image award Key Women of Am.; L.B. Crowder Day proclaimed borough pres., city coun., Queens, 1993 (cited in Jet Magazine and Congl. Record 1993, 94), award Borough Pres. of Queens; 1st woman in N.Y.C. to receive archl. drafting license; architecture achievement citation Borough Pres. of Brooklyn, N.Y.; Black history month citation Borough Pres., Queens. Mem. New Yorkers for Inclusive Edn. Curriculum, United Fedn. Tchrs., S.C. State U. Club (exec. bd., sec. 1976-81), Delta Sigma Theta Sorority, Inc. Democrat. Avocations: painting, piano, poetry, composing, writing lyrics. Home: PO Box 401 PO Box 635-91 W B Middle Island NY 11953-0401

CROWDER, RICHARD MORGAN, pilot; b. Wurzburg, Bavaria, Germany, July 22, 1963; (parents Am. citizens); s. Richard Thomas and Margaret Taylor (Rainey) C. BS, U. Minn., 1986; postgrad., U. Colo., 1995-96. Capt., pilot Classic Aviation, Mpls., 1985-87; pilot Air South, Homestead, Fla., 1987, AVAir, Raleigh, N.C., 1987-88, Am. Eagle, Dallas, 1988-89, USAir, Arlington, Va., 1989-92, United Airlines, Chgo., 1992—. Republican. Presbyterian. Avocations: reading, running, bible study, trap shooting, foreign travel.

CROWDUS, GARY ALAN, film company executive; b. Lexington, Ky., Jan. 2, 1945; s. Charles Dallas and Bess May (Rice) C. BFA, NYU Inst. Film and TV, 1969. Founding editor Cineaste mag., N.Y.C., 1967—; assoc. editor Film Society Review, N.Y.C., 1968-72; v.p. Tricontinental Film Ctr., N.Y.C., 1972-79, Unifilm Inc., N.Y.C., 1979-80; gen. mgr. The Cinema Guild, Inc., N.Y.C., 1981—2004; dir. mktg. and publicity First Run/Icarus Films, Inc., Bklyn, 2004—. Mem. U.S. Conf. on Alternative Cinema, N.Y.C., 1978-79; mem. internat. adv. com. Internat. Documentary Film Week, 1989. Co-author: (with others) Quinze and de Cinema Mondial, 1975, The Documentary Tradition, 1979, The Cineaste Interviews, 1983, New Challenges for Documentary, 1988, Film and Politics in the Third World, 1988, Celluloid Power: Social Film Criticism from The Birth of a Nation to Judgement at Nuremberg, 1992, The Political Companion to American Film, 1994, The Cineaste Interviews, Vol. 2, 2002. Mem. Assn. Ind. Video and Filmmakers, Internat. Documentary Assn. Home: 116 Saint Marks Pl Apt 8 New York NY 10009-5856 Office: Cineaste Mag Art Politics Cinema 304 Hudson St New York NY 10013 also: FirstRun/Icarus FilmsI 32 Court St 21st Fl Brooklyn NY 11201 Office Phone: 212-366-5720, 718-488-8900. Business E-Mail: cineaste@cineaste.com.

CROWE, CAMERON, screenwriter, film director; b. Palm Springs, Calif., July 13, 1957; Student, Calif. State U., San Diego. Writer Rolling Stone mag., N.Y.C. Scripts include Fast Times at Ridgemont High, 1982, The Wild Life, 1984, Elizabethtown, 2005; screenwriter, dir.: Say Anything, 1989, Singles, 1992, Jerry Maguire, 1996; writer, prodr., dir. Almost Famous, 2000, Vanilla Sky, 2001; actor: American Hot Wax, 1978; creative cons.: (TV series) Fast Times, 1986. Office: c/o Robert Bookman Creative Artists Agy 9830 Wilshire Blvd Beverly Hills CA 90212

CROWE, CAMERON MACMILLAN, chemical engineering professor; b. Montreal, Que., Can., Oct. 6, 1931; s. Ernest Watson and Marianne (Macmillan) C.; m. Jean Margaret Gilbertson, Feb. 15, 1969. Student, Royal Mil. Coll., 1948-52; B.Eng., McGill U., 1953; PhD, Cambridge (Eng.) U., 1957. Sr. devel. engr. DuPont of Can., Maitland, Ont., 1957-59; mem. faculty dept. chem. engring. McMaster U., Hamilton, Ont., 1959—, assoc. prof., 1964-70, prof., 1970-96, prof. emeritus, 1996—, chmn. dept., 1971-74. Author: (with others) Chemical Plant Simulation, 1971; Assoc. editor: Canadian Jour. Chem. Engring, 1975-81. C.D. Howe Meml. fellow Rice U., Houston, 1967-68; Athlone fellow, 1953-55 Fellow Chem. Inst. Can.; mem. Am. Inst. Chem. Engrs., Can. Soc. Chem. Engring. (bd. dirs. 1984-87, v.p. 1990-91, pres. 1991-92). Home: 821 Glenwood Ave Burlington ON Canada L7T 2J8 Office: Chem Engring Dept McMaster U Hamilton ON Canada L8S 4L7

CROWE, EDITH LOUISE, librarian; b. Buffalo, N.Y., Nov. 12, 1947; d. Harold Peter and Edith Louise (Robinson) C. BA in Art History with honors, SUNY, Buffalo, 1970; MLS, SUNY, Geneseo, 1971; MA in Humanities, Calif. State U., Dominguez Hills, 1980. Libr. San Jose (Calif.) State U., 1971-75, 77—, Calif. State U., Hayward, 1976-77. Book reviewer Art Documentation, 1988—. Contbr. articles to profl. jours. Mem. ALA, Nat. Women's Studies Assn., Art Librs. Soc. (chair No. Calif. chpt. 1982-83, 93), Mythopoeic Soc. (exec. bd. 1998—), Phi Beta Kappa. Democrat. Avocations: illustration, creative writing. Office: San Jose State U King Libr 1 Washington Sq San Jose CA 95192-0028 Business E-Mail: edith.crowe@sjsu.edu.

CROWE, FLETCHER S., research and development company executive; b. Ponca City, Okla., Aug. 9, 1944; s. Fletcher S. Crowe, Jr. and Marjorie M. Crowe; m. Rita Riedel, Dec. 31, 1965 (div. Feb. 20, 1986); children: Fletcher Scotty, Wesley Ried, Derek Andy. PhD, Fla. State U., 1973. Dir. rsch. Office of Gov., Tallahassee, 1971—83; dir. of it r & d Equifax, Atlanta, 1987—93; pres. PARANETICS, Atlanta, 1993—. Asst. prof. Fla. Atlantic U., Boca Raton, Fla., 1987—88; dir. bus. devel. SAIC, Atlanta, 2002—04. Author: River of a Thousand Years: History of the Sandford, Sanford, Standefer, Standifer Family. Dir. rsch. Steve Pajcic for Gov., Jacksonville, Fla., 1982—82, Fred Schultz for US Senate, Jacksonville, 1968—70; bd. dirs. Boca Raton (Fla.) Unitarian Ch., 1986—87, N.W. Unitarian Ch., Atlanta, 1990—91. Recipient Outstanding Proposal award, U. Fla. Coll. of Engring., 1987; scholar, Ford Found., Stetson Univ., 1964. Mem.: Atlanta Artificial Intelligence Soc. (pres. 1990—92), Boca Raton Mus. Art (v.p. 1987—88). Democrat. Unitarian. Achievements include development of applications of high-performance artificial intelligence to very large databases; applications of neural network technology to commerical database applications; design of applications of neural networks to detection of heart conditions prior to chronic symptoms. Avocations: running, writing. Home: 1045 Riverbend Club Dr Atlanta GA 30339 Personal E-mail: fletchercrowe@charter.net.

CROWE, JAMES JOSEPH, lawyer; b. New Castle, Pennsylvania, June 9, 1935; s. William J. and Anna M. (Dickson) C.; m. Joan D. (Verba), Dec. 26, 1959. BA, Youngstown State U., 1958; JD, Georgetown U., 1963. Bar: Va. 1963, Ohio 1966. Atty. SEC, Washington, 1964-65, Gen. Tire and Rubber Co., Akron, Ohio, 1965-68; sr. atty. Eaton Corp., Cleve., 1968-72; sec. gen. counsel U.S. Shoe Corp., Cin., 1972-95, v.p., 1975-95; ptnr. Kepley, Gilligan, and Eyrich, Cin., 1996-2000; counsel Thompson Hine LLP, Cin., 2001—. Chmn. divsn. Fine Arts Fund, 1976; trustee Springer Ednl. Found., 1978-84, Cin. Music Festival Assn., 1980-86, 96-2003; group chmn. United Way, 1980; mem. pres. coun. Coll. Mt. St. Joseph, 1985-88; trustee Tennis for Charity Inc., 1986—, Playhouse in the Park, 1990-96, Greater Cin. Ctr. for Econ. Edn., 1992-96, Leadership Cin., Class XIV, 1990-91; trustee Cin. Nature Ctr., 1993-2000, chmn. 1996-98; bd. visitors U. Cin. Coll. Law, 1993-2002; trustee Invest in Neighborhoods, 1982-89, pres. 1984-86; trustee Cin. Hort. Soc., 1996-2002, World Piano Competition, 1999—. 2d lt. U.S. Army, 1958-59. Mem. Cin. Bar Assn., Cin. Country Club, Met. Club, Univ. Club. Office Phone: 513-352-6641. Personal E-mail: jcrowe7246@aol.com.

CROWE, JAMES QUELL, communications executive; b. Camp Pendleton, Calif., July 2, 1949; s. Henry Pierson and Mona (Quell) C.; m. Pamela L. Powell, June 20, 1986; children: Sterling, Angela, James Michael. BS in Mech. Engring., Rensselaer Poly. Inst., 1972; MBA, Pepperdine U., 1982. Project engr. Cozzolino Constrn. Co., Port of Albany, N.Y., 1971-73; ind., cons. engr. Albany, 1973-74; engr. Morrison-Knudsen, Saratoga, N.Y., 1974-75, project engr. Washington, 1975-76, project mgr. various cities, 1976-80, v.p. ops. Boise, 1980-83, group v.p. power, 1983-86; pres. Kiewit Indsl. Co., Omaha, 1986—91. Chmn., CEO MFS Comms. Co., Inc., Omaha, 1988-97; chmn. WorldCom, Inc., 1997; CEO, dir. Level 3 Comms., Inc., 1997—; dir. RCN Corp., Commonwealth Tel. Mem. Am. Nuclear Soc. Office: Level 3 Comm Inc 1025 Eldorado Blvd Broomfield CO 80021*

CROWE, JEFFREY C., transportation executive, federal agency administrator; b. 1946; m. Mary Crowe; 1 child. BA, Drake U. Regional mgr. Pacific Mountain Express, 1967-81; v.p. ops. Allstate Trucking, 1981-82; pres. Ind. Freightway, 1982-89; pres., CEO, chmn. Landstar Sys. Inc., 1989—2004, chmn., 2004—. Chmn. Nat. Defense Transp. Assoc., 1993—; bd. mem. US Chamber of Commerce, 1998—, vice chmn., 2002, chmn., 2003—. Recipient Silver award, Wall Street Transcript, 1994, Gold award, Transp. CEO of the Yr., 1995, Transp. CEO of the Yr., Financial World Mag., 1995, Nat. Transp. award, 1996. Office: Landstar System Inc 13410 Sutton Park Dr S Jacksonville FL 32224-5270 also: US Chamber of Commerce 1615 H St NW Washington DC 20062

CROWE, JOHN T., lawyer; b. Cabin Cove, Calif., Aug. 14, 1938; s. J. Thomas and Wanda (Walston) C.; m. Marina Protopapa, Dec. 28, 1968; 1 child, Erin Aleka. BA, U. Santa Clara, 1960, JD, 1962. Bar: Calif. 1962, U.S. Dist. Ct. (ea. dist.) Calif. 1967. Lawyer, Visalia, Calif., 1964—; ptnr. Crowe, Mitchell & Crowe, 1971-85. Bd. dirs. Willson Ranch Co., pres. 1997—; referee State Bar Ct., 1976-82; gen. counsel Sierra Wine, 1986-96. Bd. dirs. Mt. Whitney Area coun. Boy Scouts Am., 1966-85, pres., 1971, 1972, bd. dirs. Sequoia coun., 2003—; bd. dirs. Visalia Associated In-Group Donors (now United Way Tulare County), 1973-81, pres., 1978-79; bd. dirs. Tulare County Libr. Found., 1997—, Mineral King Dist. Assn., 2002—; mem. Visalia Airport Commn., 1982-90; Army Res. Forces Policy Com., 1995-99, chmn., 1997-99; bd. dirs. Mineral King District Assn., 2002-. 1st lt. U.S. Army, 1962-64, maj. gen. Res., 1960-62, 1964-99. Decorated DSM with oak leaf cluster, Legion of Merit with oak leaf cluster, Meritorious Svc. medal with 3 oak leaf clusters, Army Commendation medal; named Young Man of Yr., Visalia, 1973; Senator Jr. Chamber Internat., 1970; recipient Silver Beaver award Boy Scouts Am., 1983, Rudder medal Assn. U.S. Army, 1999; named to Sr. Army Res. Comdrs. Assn. Hall of Fame, 2003. Mem. ABA, Tulare County Bar Assn., Nat. Assn. R.R. Trial Counsel, State Bar Calif., Assn. U.S. Army (bd. dirs. 2000—, No. Calif. state pres. 2001—), Visalia C. of C. (pres. 1979-80), Rotary (pres. 1980-81), Visalia Country Club. Republican. Roman Catholic. Home: 3939 W School Ave Visalia CA 93291-5514 Office Phone: 559-734-0747.

CROWE, ROBERT WILLIAM, lawyer, mediator; b. Chgo., Aug. 20, 1924; s. Harry James and Miriam (McCune) C.; m. Virginia C. Kelley, Mar. 25, 1955 (dec. Feb. 1976); children— Robert Kelley, William Park; m. Elizabeth F. Roenisch, Oct. 22, 1977. AB, U. Chgo., 1948, JD, 1949. Bar: Ill. 1949. Practice in, Chgo., 1949-57; with R.R. Donnelley & Sons Co., Chgo., 1957-83, sec., 1965-83, v.p., 1970-83; chmn. Resolve Dispute Mgmt. Inc., Chgo., 1983-92; pres. Dearborn Inst. for Conflict Resolution, Chgo., 1992-94. Dir. Peoria Jour. Star, Inc., 1972-95. Bd. dirs. Chgo. Child Care Soc., 1963—; trustee Christian Century Found., 1966—; vis. com. U. Chgo. Divinity Sch. Served to 1st lt. USAAF, 1943-45. Decorated Air Medal with 5 oak leaf clusters. Mem. ABA, Chgo. Bar Assn., Lawyers Club Chgo., Econ. Club (Chgo.), Univ. Club (Chgo.). Presbyterian. Home and Office: 1228 Westmoor Rd Winnetka IL 60093-1845 Office Phone: 847-446-7054. Personal E-mail: rwcrowe@sbcglobal.net. *Cultivate a sense of gratitude as an approach to all of life, for the gift of life itself and for the potential for finding something joyful, empowering or at least instructive in every circumstance. These are the seeds for sharing the best of one's life with others.*

CROWE, RUSSELL, actor; b. Wellington, New Zealand, Apr. 7, 1964; m. Danielle Spencer, Apr. 7, 2003; 1 child, Charles Spencer. Actor: (plays) Grease, Rocky Horror Picture Show; (films) The Crossing, 1993, The Quick and the Dead, 1995, Proof, 1995, Romper Stomper, 1995, Rough Magic, 1995, Virtuosity, 1995, Under the Gun, 1995, Heaven's Burning, 1997, Breaking Up, 1997, L.A. Confidential, 1997, Mystery Alaska, 1999, The Insider, 1999 (Nat. Soc. of Film Critics award for best actor, 2000, Acad. Award nomination for best actor, 2000), Gladiator, 2000 (Academy award for best actor, 2002, Blockbuster Entertainment award, 2001, Broadcast Film Critics Assoc. award, 2001, Empire award, 2001, London Critics Circle award, 2001, Santa Fe Film Critics Circle award for best actor, 2001), Proof of Life, 2000, A Beautiful Mind, 2001 (Acad. award nomination for best actor, 2002, Golden Globe for best actor in a drama, 2002, SAG award for best actor, 2002, BAFTA Film award for best actor, 2002), Master and Commander: The Far Side of the World, 2003 (Golden Globe nomination for best actor in a drama, 2004), Cinderella Man, 2005; dir.: 60 Odd Hours in Italy, 2002; dir., prodr.: Texas, 2002; singer: 30 Odd Foot of Grunts. Named one of 50 Most Powerful People in Hollywood, Premiere mag., 2004, 2005; recipient Global Achievement award, Australian Film Inst., 2001. Address: c/o Shirley Pearce Bedford & Pearce Mgmt Party Ltd 2/263-269 Alfred St PO Box 171 Cammeray North Sydney 2062 Australia also: William Morris Agency 151 El Camino Dr Beverly Hills CA 90212*

CROWE, THOMAS LEONARD, lawyer; b. Amsterdam, N.Y., Aug. 3, 1944; s. Leonard Hoctor and Grace Agnes (O'Malley) C.; m. Barbara Ann Hauck, Aug. 2, 1969; children: Patrick, Brendan. AB, Georgetown U., 1966, JD, 1969. Law clk. to chief judge U.S. Dist. Ct. (no. dist.), Elkins, W.Va., 1969-70; trial atty. U.S. Dept. Justice, Washington, 1970-72; asst. U.S. atty. Balt., 1973-78; chief of criminal divsn. U.S. Atty.'s Office, Balt., 1977-78; ptnr. Cable, McDaniel, Bowie & Bond, Balt., 1979-91, McGuire, Woods, Battle & Boothe, Balt., 1991-95; of counsel Monshower & Miller, LLP, Columbia, Md., 1996-98; pvt. practice Balt., 1998—. Mem. jud. conf. U.S. Ct. Appeals for 4th Cir. Fellow Md. Bar Found.; mem. Fed. Bar Assn. (pres. Balt. chpt. 1981-82), Md. Bar Assn., Barristers Club (pres. 1990-91),. Democrat. Roman Catholic. Home: 11 Osborne Ave Baltimore MD 21228-4935 Office: Law Offices of Thomas L Crowe 1622 The World Trade Ctr 401 E Pratt St Baltimore MD 21202-3117 Office Phone: 410-685-9428. E-mail: tom.crowe@verizon.net.

CROWE, THOMAS RAIN, poet; b. Chgo., Aug. 23, 1949; s. Norman and Marilyn (King) Dawson; m. Nan Watkins; 1 child, Chris. BA in Sociology and Anthropology, Furman U., 1972. Editor Beatitude Mag. and Press, San Francisco, 1974—79, Katuah Jour., Asheville, NC, 1983—89; pressman Sylva (NC) Herald, 1989—93; publ., editor New Native Press, Cullowhee, NC, 1993—; prodr. Fern Hill Rcords, Cullowhee, 1995—. Lectr. SC Govs. Sch. for the Arts, Greenville, 1989—92; adv. bd. Nat. Humanities Faculty, Raleigh, NC, 1988—89; book reviewer in field. Author: The Laugharne Poems, 1998, Zoro's Field: My Life in the Appalachian Woods, 2005; editor: Writing the Wind: The New Celtic Poetry, 1998; translator: Drunk on the Wine of the Beloved: 100 Poems of Hafiz, 2002; writer, dir. (ballet, opera) The Eyes of the Butterfly, 1988. Founder, dir. San Francisco Internat. Poetry Festival, 1976; dir. Project to Protect Native Am. Sacred Sites, Cullowhee, 1988—96; interim dir. Western NC Alliance, Asheville, 1990; bd. dirs. Canary Coalition, Sylva, 2001, Artists and Musicians United for a Safe Environment, Raleigh, 1986. Recipient Thomas F. Dill Poetry prize, NC Poetry Soc., 1986, Tchr. Recognition award, Nat. Found. for Advancement in the Arts, 1996—97, Internat. Merit award, Atlanta Rev., 1996, Publ. Book of

Yr. award, Appalacaian Writers Assn., 1995. Mem.: Appalachian Coll. Assn. (lectr. 2003—04). Office: New Native Press PO Box 2554 Cullowhee NC 28723 Office Phone: 828-293-9237. Business E-Mail: newnativepress@hotmail.com.

CROWE, WILLIAM JAMES, JR., former Chairman of the Joint Chiefs of Staff, international consultant; b. La Grange, Ky., Jan. 2, 1925; s. William James and Eula (Russell) C.; m. Shirley Mary Grennell, Feb. 14, 1954; children: William Blake, James Brent, Mary Russell. BS, U.S. Naval Acad., 1946; MA in Edn., Stanford U., 1956; PhD in Politics (Harold W. Dodds fellow), Princeton U., 1965. Advanced through grades to adm USN, 1960, ret., 1989, Commd. ensign, 1946, comdg. officer U.S.S. Trout, 1960—62; comdr. Submarine Div. 31 San Diego, 1966-67; sr. adviser Vietnamese Navy, 1970-71; dep. to Pres.'s Spl. Rep. for Micronesian Status Negotiations, 1971-73; dep. dir. strategic plans CNO Staff, 1973-75; dir. East Asia and Pacific region Office of Sec. of Def. Washington, until 1976; comdr. Middle East Force Bahrain, 1976-77; dep. chief naval ops. plans and policy Washington, 1977-80; comdr.-in-chief Allied Forces So. Europe, 1980-83; comdr.-in-chief Pacific, 1983-85; chmn. Joint Chiefs of Staff, 1985-89; prof. geopolitics U. Okla., Norman, 1989-94; chmn. Fgn. Intelligence Adv. Bd., Washington, 1993-94; U.S. amb. to U.K. US Dept. State, London, 1994-97. Counselor Ctr. for Strategic and Internat. Studies, Washington, 1989-94; prof. U. Okla., 1989-94. Author: Line of Fire, 1993; co-author: Reducing Nuclear Danger: The Road Away from the Brink, 1993; author supr. ops. plan for repatriation of U.S.S. Pueblo crew. Trustee Princeton U., 1995-2000; dir. USNA Found., 1998—. Decorated Defense DSM with three oak leaf clusters (Dept. Def.), Navy DSM with two oak leaf clusters (USN), DSM (U.S. Army, USAF, USCG), Legion of Merit, Bronze Star with combat V, Air medal with six oak leaf clusters, Presdl. Medal of Freedom. Mem. U.S. Naval Inst., Am. Polit. Sci. Assn., Internat. Studies Assn., Coun. on Fgn. Rels., Washington Inst. Fgn. Affairs, Phi Gamma Delta, Phi Delta Phi. Office: Global Options 1615 L St NW Ste 300 Washington DC 20036-5655

CROWE, WILLIAM JOSEPH, librarian; b. Boston, Feb. 27, 1947; s. William J. and Mary (Dawley) C.; m. Nancy P. Sanders, June 10, 1978; children: Katherine. BA in European history with highest honors, Boston State Coll., 1968; MLS, Rutgers U., 1969; PhD in Adminstrn. Acad. Librs., Ind. U., 1986. Cataloger Boston Pub. Libr., 1969-70, asst. to acquisitions libr., 1970-71; coord. processing Ind. U. Librs., Bloomington, 1971-76, asst. to dean univ. librs., 1977-79; mgmt. intern U. Mich. Libr., Ann Arbor, 1976-77; asst. to dir. librs. Ohio State U., Columbus, 1979-83, asst. dir. librs. adminstrn. and tech. svcs., 1983-90; dean librs. U. Kans., Lawrence, 1990-96, vice chancellor, dean, 1996-99, libr. Spencer Rsch. Libr., 1999—. Trustee Online Computer Lit. Ctr., 1996—. Contbr. articles to profl. jours. Sr. fellow UCLA, 1991. Mem. ALA, Kans. Libr. Assn., Beta Phi Mu, Phi Alpha Theta. Home: 910 E 850th Rd Lawrence KS 66047-9578 Office: U Kans Spencer Rsch Libr Lawrence KS 66045-7616 Office Phone: 785-864-4970. Business E-Mail: wcrowe@ku.edu. *We must work to expand the next generation's opportunity for education--to foster greater equality of intellectual privilege.*

CROWE-HAGANS, NATONIA, manufacturing executive, engineer; b. Chgo., Feb. 10, 1955; d. Benjamin Kermit and Natalie (Williams) Crowe; m. Louis Fisher (div.); children: Sean Crowe, Tamara Fisher; m. William Hagans. AA, Vets. Hosp., Chgo., 1977; BSEE, U. Ill., Chgo., 1983; MS in Mgmt., Maryville U., 1988. Cert. mgr. Institute of Certified Professional Managers. Cert. mgr. Corning Glass Works, Bluffton, Ind., 1980; intern Corning (N.Y.) Glass Works, 1981-82; assoc. engr. McDonnell Douglas, St. Louis, 1983-84, engr., 1984-85, sr. engr., 1986-87, laser team leader, 1987-88, staff mgr. Huntington Beach, Calif., 1988-89; mgr. quick response ctr. Loral Electro-optical Sys., Pomona, Calif., 1989, mgr. mfg. svcs., 1989-91, mgr. material control svcs., 1991-92, program mgr., 1992-93, mgr. prodn., 1993-94; mgr. mfg. engr. Rockwell Automation, Allen Bradley, Milw., 1994-97, dir. electro-mech. ops., 1994-97; dir. ops. overhaul and repair United Techs.-Hamilton Std., Windsor Locks, Conn., 1997—2001; pres., CEO Crystal Vision, Windsor, Conn., 2001—02; site mfg. dir. Honeywell Space Systems and Defense, 2002—. Bd. dirs. Matarah Industries. Mem. Womens Aux., Yorba Linda, Calif., 1989, Illiteracy Com., St. Louis, 1984, PTA, Corona, Calif., 1991. Named to Acad. Women Achievers, 1999. Mem. NAFE, Nat. Soc. Black Engrs. (co-founding mem. Gateway chpt. 1987-88, Svc. award 1988), Nat. Mgmt. Assn. (sec., com. mem., numerous awards 1990), Profl. Dimensions, Assn. Mfg. Excellence, Assn. of Women Achievers. Avocation: writing science fiction. Home: 4294 Auston Way Palm Harbor FL 34685- E-mail: natoniac@tampabay.rr.com.

CROWELL, CRAVEN H., JR., retired federal agency administrator; b. Nashville, Aug. 27, 1943; s. Craven H. and Addie Ailene (Cooper) Crowell; m. Fredricka Friedli, Nov. 27, 1970; 1 child, Stephanie Kaye. BA, Lipscomb U., 1965. Reporter, city editor Nashville Tennessean, 1964-77; press sec. Senator Jim Sasser, 1977-80, chief of staff, 1989-93; dir. info. Tenn. Valley Authority, Knoxville, 1980-87, v.p. govtl. and pub. affairs Nashville, 1987-89, chmn. bd. dirs., 1993-2001; ret., 2001. Mem. exec. com. Nuc. Energy Inst.; past chmn. bd. dirs., mem. exec. com., mem. bd. adv. coun. Electric Power Rsch. Inst.; bd. dirs. EPRI Worldwide, eVionyx, Utility Automation Integration. Hon. pres. Hohai U., China, 1997. With USMC, with USNR. Named Alumnus of the Yr., Lipscomb U., 1995; recipient Nat. Headliner award, 1969. Mem.: Econ. Club N.Y., Pi Delta Epsilon. Democrat. Mem. Ch. Of Christ. Personal E-mail: cravencrowell@aol.com.

CROWELL, DAVID HARRISON, retired biomedical researcher; b. Trenton, Nj, July 19; m. Doris Collins; children: Michael David, Sandra Crowell Lupton, Shannon Kathleen Atkinson, Megan Crowell Sheridan. Ph. D., State U. of Iowa, Iowa City, Iowa, 1946—50. Internship-fellowship U. Iowa 49;Yale 66, Scientist Commd. Corps,USPHS, 1954. Rsch. cons. Straub Clinic and Hosp., Honolulu, Hawaii, 1983—; prin. investigator Kapiolani Med. Crnter, Honolulu, 1991—2002; rsch. cons. Nat'l Inst. Health, Washington, DC, 1973—89; prof. emeritus U. of Hawaii, Honolulu. Author: (scientific articles) Psychophysiology; dir.(researcher): (experimental studies) Scientific Articles (Continuing Grants), 1963). 1st lt. Ordnance Dept., U. Grantee Clin Home Infant, Clin. Study, Nichd, Nih, 1999-2000. Fellow: Amer Psychol. Assn., Amer Assn Adv Sci. (life); mem.: Amer. Acad. Sleep Medicine, Population Assoc Am. (assoc.), Hawn Acad Sci. (assoc.; pres. 1953—54), Soc Rsch Child Devel (assoc.), Amer Acad Sleep Med (assoc.), Amer Clin Neurophysiology Soc (assoc.), Sigma Xi (assoc.).

CROWELL, JOAN, writer, composer; b. N.Y.C., N.Y., June 6, 1921; d. Samuel A. and Margaret (Seligman) Lewisohn; m. David G. Crowell, Dec. 17, 1972; m. Sydney Simon (div.); children: Mark, Teru, Rachel, Nora, Juno. BA, Bennington Call, Vt.; MA, N.Y. U., N.Y.C.; student theory and harmony, Eastern Suffolf Sch. of Music; student composition and orchestration, Julliard, N.Y.C. Tchr. English N.Y. U., 1944—66; writer and composer. Treas. Partisan Rev., PEN Am. Ctr., N.Y.C., 1970—73. Author (as Joan Simon): Portrait of a Father, 1960, Fort Dix Stockade, 1972; composer: (Operas) The Bell Witch of Tennessee, 1985, The Heights; author: (English librettos) Orfeo by Gluck, Lelio by Berlioz; composer: Wallace Stevens Song Cycle, Arondissement, 1988, Song from the Wasteland, 1989, Brief Prolegomena to the 14 Kinds of Nothing, 1992, Wind Songs, 1991 (hon. mention Composers Guild, 1991), author (as Joan Simon or Joan Crowell) poems and articles; composer: Holes and Antimatters, 1993. Pres. Friends of Danile Dolci; founder Rockland Country Day Sch. Recipient editors Choice award, Poetry.com, 2003. Avocations: ping pong/table tennis, travel.

CROWELL, JOHN B., JR., lawyer, former government official; b. Elizabeth, N.J., Mar. 18, 1930; s. John B. and Anna B. (Trull) C.; m. Rebecca Margaret McCue, Feb. 13, 1954; children— John P., Patrick E., Ann M. AB, Dartmouth Coll., 1952; LL.B., Harvard U., 1957. Bar: N.J. bar 1958, Oreg. bar 1959. Law clk. to Judge Gerald McLaughlin U.S. Ct. Appeals, Newark, 1957-59; atty. Ga.-Pacific Corp., Portland, Oreg., 1959-72; gen. counsel La.-Pacific Corp., Portland, 1972-81; asst. sec. for natural resources and environment Dept. Agr., Washington, 1981-85; ptnr. Lane Powell Spears Lubersky, Portland, 1986-98, of counsel, 1998—. Served with USN, 1952-54. Mem. Am. Ornithologists Union, Wilson Ornithol. Soc., Cooper Ornithol. Soc., Soc. Am. Foresters, Soil Conservation Soc. Am. Clubs: Univ. (Portland). Republican. Presbyterian. Home: 1185 Hallinan Cir Lake Oswego OR 97034-4970 Office: Lane Powell 601 SW 2nd Ave # Ste #2100 Portland OR 97204-3154 Office Phone: 503-778-2172. Business E-Mail: crowellj@lanepowell.com.

CROWELL, JOHN C(HAMBERS), geology educator, researcher; b. State College, Pa., May 12, 1917; s. James White and Helen Hunt (Chambers) C.; m. Betty Marie Bruner, Nov. 22, 1946; 1 child, Martha Lynn Crowell Bobroskie. BS in Geology, U. Tex., 1939; MA in Oceanographic meteorology, Scripps Inst. Oceanography UCLA, 1946; PhD in Geology, UCLA, 1947; DSc (hon.), U. Louvain, Belgium, 1966. Geologist Shell Oil Co., Inc., Ventura, Calif., 1941-42; from instr. to prof. geology UCLA, 1947-67, chmn. dept., 1957-60, 63-66; prof. geology U. Calif., Santa Barbara, 1967-87, prof. emeritus, 1987, rsch. geologist Inst. for Crustal Studies, 1987—. Chmn. Office of Earth Scis., NRC, Nat. Acad. Scis., 1979-82. Served to capt. U.S. Army USAAF, 1942-46. Fellow AAAS, Geol. Soc. Am. (Penrose medal 1995), Am. Acad. Arts and Scis.; mem. Am. Assn. Petroleum Geologists, Am. Geophys. Union, Nat. Acad. Scis. Achievements include special research in structural geology, tectonics, interpretation sedimentary rocks, studies Andreas fault system, California tectonics, ancient glaciation, continental drift. Office: 300 Hot Springs Rd Apt 99 Santa Barbara CA 93108 Office Phone: 805-969-8218. E-mail: crowell@geol.ucsb.edu.

CROWELL, KENNETH E., lawyer, chemical engineer; b. Kearny, N.J., Dec. 29, 1957; s. Earl L.S. and Moira Parker (Foster) C.; m. Liliana Mino, June 24, 1990. BS in Biology, Allegheny Coll., 1979; BSChemE, N.J. Inst. Tech., 1984, MS in Chem. Engring., 1992; JD, Rutgers U., 1997. Registered profl. engr., N.J.; bar: N.J., N.Y. Tech. sales rep. patent and trademark Armak divsn. Akzo N.V., Chgo., 1979-82; prodn. mgr. Drew Chem. divsn. Ashland Oil, Kearny, N.J., 1984-87; sr. chem. engr. Jacobs Engring. Group, Mountainside, N.J., 1987-92; sr. environ. engr. Schering Plough Corp., Union, N.J., 1992-94; assoc. Milbank, Tweed, Hadley & McCloy LLP, N.Y.C., 1997-2000, Hopgood, Calimafde, Judlowe & Mondolino, LLP, N.Y.C., 2000—02, Morgan Lewis & Bockius, N.Y.C., 2002—. Author: Handbook of Biotechnology, 1997. Mem. ABA, AIChE, N.Y. State Bar Assn., Bar Assn. of City of N.Y., Order of the Coif, Tau Beta Pi. Avocation: fly fishing. Home: 40 Mitchell Rd Gillette NJ 07933-1428 Office: Morgan Lewis & Bockius LLP 101 Park Ave New York NY 10166 E-mail: Kcrowell@morganlewis.com.

CROWELL, REBECCA A., artist; b. Liberty, N.Y., June 13, 1954; d. Dorothy Furber and Aron Leavitt Crowell; m. Donald B Ticknor, Nov. 15, 1975; children: Benjamin F, Ross L. MFA-Painting, Ariz.State U., Tempe, 1985. Vis. artist and exhbn. juror U. of Wis.-Stout, Menomonie, Wis., 1992, U.of Wis.-La Crosse, 1994; artist in residence Ctr. D'Art I Natura, Farrera, Catalonia, Spain, 2001; featured artist Portal Wis. website (juried, state-sponsored), Madison. Exhibitions, Circa Gallery, Mpls., exhibition, Personal Journeys, The Phipps Ctr. Arts, Hudson, Wis., No. Nat. Competition, Rhinelander, Wis., Suzanne Kohn Gallery, St. Paul, Minn., U. Wis., Platteville, AGA Ctr. for Arts, Appleton, Wis., U. Wis., La Crosse, Eau Claire, The Walker Gallery, Chgo., Landscape: Wisconsin, U. Wis., Eau Claire, Art Contemporani de Muntanya, Universitat de Lleida, Catalunya, Spain, U. Minn., Morris, Sharon Park Gallery, Menlo Park, CA, Phipps Ctr. for Arts, Paine Art Ctr. and Arboretum, Oshkosh, Wis., Neolandscape, Union St. Gallery, Chgo. Heights, Ill., Vaguely Familiar, Galleria Mesa, Ariz., Represented in permanent collections Ceridean Corp., Mpls., U. Wis., Wis. Dept. Tranps., U. Minn., Midwest Banking Ctr., St. Louis, Enterprise Bank, Clayton, Mo. Grantee Project Grant, Wis. Arts Bd., 1989, Ruth Chenven Grant, Ruth Chenven Found., 1990, Travel Grant, Wis. Arts Bd., 1998. Avocations: travel, cooking. Home: N45355 Isom Rd Osseo WI 54758 Personal E-mail: crowellart@yahoo.com.

CROWELL, WILLIAM BRADFORD, management consultant; s. William Ernest and Joanne Bradford Whitney Crowell; m. Kimberley Holdridge Bensen, July 12, 1999; 1 child, Anna. BS, USMMA, NY, 1988; MS, Mass. Inst. Tech., 1992. Cons. Mercer Mgmt. Cons., Inc., Lexington, Mass., 1995—98; CEO E-Sys., Inc., Dennis, Mass., 1998—. Active Old Kings Hwy. Regional Hist. Dist. Com., Dennis, Mass., 2001. Lt. USNR.

CROWL, JOHN ALLEN, retired publishing company executive; b. Winchester, Va., Aug. 10, 1935; s. John Decatur and Cora Elizabeth (LLoyd) C.; m. Dana Jane Bernasek, Aug. 27, 1960 (div. 1986); 1 son, Patrick Joseph; m. Gaal Shepherd, Feb. 10, 1988. BA, U. Md., 1957, MA, 1961; LhD (hon.), Lebanon Valley Coll., 1993. Instr. Staunton (Va.) Mil. Acad., 1958-59; asst. dir. pub. rels. Johns Hopkins U., Balt., 1961-64; assoc. dir. Editl. Projects for Edn., Inc., Balt. and Washington, 1964-75, v.p., 1975-78; assoc. editor Chronicle of Higher Edn., Washington, 1966-72, mng. editor, 1972-79, pub., 1978-91, v.p., 1979-92. Founder Thistle Hill Publs., 2000—. Contbg. editor: Vt. Mag., 1995—2001; mem. editl. adv. bd. Vt. Life mag., 2002—; dir.: Vt. Pub. Radio, 2004—. Trustee Vt. Folklife Ctr., 1994-99, Vt. Arts Coun., 1994-98; trustee Planned Parenthood of No. New Eng., 1994-2000, chair 1997-99. With U.S. Army, 1958. Recipient Edn. Writers award AAUP, 1971. Home: Thistle Hill North Pomfret VT 05053 Office Phone: 802-457-2050. Personal E-mail: crowl1@earthlink.net.

CROWL, SAMUEL RENNINGER, former university dean, English language educator, author; b. Toledo, Oct. 9, 1940; s. Lester Samuel and Margaret Elizabeth (Renninger) C.; m. Susan Richardson, Dec. 29, 1963; children: Miranda Paine, Samuel Emerson. AB, Hamilton Coll., 1962; MA, Ind. U., 1969, PhD, 1970. Resident lectr. Ind. U., Indpls., 1967-69; asst. prof. English, Ohio U., Athens, 1970-75, assoc. prof., 1975-80, prof., 1980—, dean Univ. Coll., 1981-92, trustee prof. Eng., 1992—; cons. NEH, Washington, 1980—; observer Royal Shakespeare Co. Mem. Ohio Humanities Coun., 1985-91, Ohio Student Loan Commn., 1985-88. Author: Shakespeare Observed: Studies in Performance on Stage and Screen, 1992, Shakespeare at the Cineplex, 2003; co-author: Ohio University's Educational Plan, 1977-78; contbr. articles to profl. and Shakespearian jours. Recipient O'Bleness award for pub. broadcasting Ctr. Telecommunications, Ohio U., 1976, several awards disting. teaching. Fellow Royal Soc. Arts (London); mem. Nat. Assn. Univ. and Gen. Coll. Deans (pres. 1991—), Nat. Humanities Faculty, Ohio Shakespeare Assn. (founding mem.), Ohio U. Alumni Assn. (hon.), Univ. Club (Chgo.), Phi Kappa Phi. Avocations: Royal Shakespeare Co., Detroit Tigers. Office: Ohio U Eng Dept Ellis Hall Athens OH 45701 Office Phone: 740-593-2838.

CROWLEY, ARTHUR EDWARD, JR., lawyer; b. Rutland, Vt., Oct. 18, 1928; s. Arthur Edward and Mildred (Gilfeather) C.; m. Marcia Colby Smith, July 29, 1961 (div. 1984); children: Robert, David, Andrew, Christopher; m. Mary Rommele, Feb. 21, 1987. Student, Boston U., 1947-50, student, 1953-56. Bar: Vt. 1958. Pvt. practice, Rutland, 1959; dep. atty. gen. State of Vt., Montpelier, 1960-61; state's atty. Rutland County, 1961-65; ptnr. Bishop & Crowley, 1965-77, Keyser Crowley Banse & Facey, 1977-84. Corp. counsel City of Rutland, 1965-67. Mem. Vt. Rep. State Com., 1961-71(chmn. exec. com., 1963-67); chmn. Rutland County Rep. Party, 1961-71; alderman City of Rutland, 1987-95; trustee Vt. State Colls., 1979-85, Coll. St. Joseph, 1987-92. Served with AUS, 1951-53. Mem. Rutland County Bar Assn. (pres. 1983-84), Vt. Bar Assn., Am. Legion, Rutland Region C. of C. (dir. 1967-71). Roman Catholic. Office: 56 1/2 Merchants Row Ste 310 Rutland VT 05701-5907

CROWLEY, CYNTHIA JOHNSON, secondary school educator; b. Summit, N.J., June 28, 1930; d. Theodore Eames and Frances Lysett (Wetmore) J.; m. Robert J. Crowley, Sept. 6, 1952 (dec.); children: David Cochrane II, Cynthia Wetmore. BA, U. Pa., 1952; MA, Fairleigh-Dickinson U., 1980. Cert. English tchr., N.J. Tchr. econs. and reading St. Mary's Sch., Peekskill, N.Y., 1952-53; tchr. humanities Henry Hudson Regional Sch., Highlands, N.J., 1969-92, coord. gifted program, 1983-92. Pres. Associated Ednl. Svcs.; with N.J. Curriculum Revision Project; adv. bd. mem. Women's Athletics U. Pa., N.J. Coun. U.S. Congl. Awards Program; ednl. cons.; cons., lectr. creative writing workshops; mem. secondary sch. admissions com. U. Pa. Prodr. TV Tutor Series for Home and Schs. Former mem. Atlantic Highlands (N.J.) Bd. Edn., also past pres.; mem. adv. bd. Women's Athletic bd. U. Pa., 1992—, chair, 1999—; former mem. exec. com. Monmouth County Sch. Bds. Assn. Team Room named in her honor U. Pa., Palestra, 1997; named to Hall of Fame, U. Pa., 1998; recipient U. Pa. Alumni award, 1997, Alumni Merit award U. Pa., 2004 Mem. ASCD, Nat. Coun. Tchrs. English, Nat. Acad. TV Arts and Scis. (N.Y. chpt.), Gifted Educators (exec. com. 1986—), Alumni Pres.'s Coun. Ind. Secondary Schs. (life, past pres.), Phi Delta Kappa. Home and Office: 245 Shore Rd Westerly RI 02891-3707

CROWLEY, DANIEL FRANCIS, JR., transportation and logistics executive; b. Yonkers, N.Y., Oct. 23, 1949; s. Daniel F. and Margaret M. (Murphy) C.; m. Karen E. Williams, Dec. 18, 1982; children: Daniel, Ryan. BA in Lit., Columbia U., 1971, MBA in Fin., 1973. Mem. audit staff Arthur Andersen & Co., N.Y.C., 1973-78, audit mgr. London, 1978-81; dir. internal audit IMS Internat. Inc., London, 1981-82, contr. pharmacy svcs. divsn., 1982-83; exec. v.p., bd. dirs. Pharmassist, Inc., Dallas, 1983-84; sr. mgr. Coopers & Lybrand, N.Y.C., 1985-90; v.p. audit Grand Met. Food Sector, Mpls., 1990-91; v.p., contr. Grand Met./Green Giant USA, Mpls., 1991-92; v.p., ops. contr. Grand Met./Pillsbury, Mpls., 1992-93, v.p. reengring., 1993-95; v.p., contr. food sector Grand Met, London, 1995; dir. Pearle Vision, Inc., 1995-97; sr. v.p., CFO, Pearle Vision/Grand Met, Dallas, 1995-97; v.p. planning Frito-Lay Internat., Plano, Tex., 1997-98; exec. v.p., CFO BAX Global/Pittston, 1998—. Bd. dirs. Pearle Vision, Inc., 1995-97; treas. Grand Met/Pearle Found., Dallas, 1995-97. Treas. Grand Met/Pillsbury Found., Mpls., 1991-93. Mem. AICPA. Home: 3815 Vista Azul San Clemente CA 92672-4543 Office: BAX Global 440 Exchange Irvine CA 92602-1309

CROWLEY, DAVID JEREMIAH, psychiatrist, neurologist; b. Lynn, Mass., Jan. 6, 1941; s. John J. and Mary T. (McGillicuddy) C.; m. Martha Cotter, Apr. 15, 1967; children: Maureen, David Jr., Kevin. AB, Holy Cross Coll., 1962; MD, Tufts U., 1966. Diplomate Am. Bd. Neurology and Psychiatry. Intern St. Elizabeth's Hosp., Brighton, Mass., 1966-67, resident in internal medicine, 1967-69; resident in neurology New England Med. Ctr., Boston, 1969-72; pvt. practice Essex Neurol. Assn., Salem and Lynn, Mass., 1972—. Mem. AMA, Am. Acad. of Neurology, Mass. Med. Soc. Roman Catholic. Avocations: music, sports. Home: 4 Wilson Rd Gloucester MA 01930-1478 Office: Essex Neurol Assocs 225 Boston St Ste 3 Lynn MA 01904-3169 Office Phone: 781-595-6833.

CROWLEY, JAMES WORTHINGTON, retired lawyer, investor, financial consultant; b. Cookville, Tenn., Feb. 18, 1930; s. Worth and Jessie (Officer) C.; m. Laura June Bauserman, Jan. 27, 1951; children: James Kenneth, Laura Cynthia; m. Joyce A. Goode, Jan. 15, 1966; children: John Worthington, Noelle Virginia; m. Carol Golden, Sept. 4, 1981. BA, George Washington U., 1950, LLB, 1953. Bar: D.C. 1954. Underwriter, spl. agt. Am. Surety Co. of N.Y., Washington, 1953-56; adminstrv. asst., contract adminstr. Atlantic Rsch. Corp., Alexandria, Va., 1956-59, mgr. legal dept., asst. sec., counsel, 1959-65, sec., legal mgr., counsel, 1965-67, Susquehanna Corp. (merger with Atlantic Rsch. Corp.), 1967-70; pres., dir. Gen. Communication Co., Boston, 1962-70; v.p., gen. counsel E-Systems, Inc., 1970-95, sec., 1976-95; ret., 1995; ind. cons. bus. and fin., investor Dallas, 1995—. V.p., asst. sec., dir. Cemco, Inc.; v.p., dir. TAI, Inc., Serv-air, Inc., Greenville, Tex., Engring. Rsch. Assocs., Inc., Vienna, Va., HRB Systems, Inc., State Coll., Pa.; mem. adv. bd. sec. Internat. and Comparative Law Ctr.; v.p., sec., dir. Advanced Video Products, 1992-95; v.p., sec., gen. counsel E-Systems Med. Electronics, Inc., 1992-95. Mem. Am. Soc. Corp. Secs. (pres. Dallas regional group 1988-89, nat. dir. 1989-92), Inf. Mus. Assn., Nat. Security Indsl. Assn., Mfrs.' Alliance for Productivity and Innovation (mem. law coun.), Omicron Delta Kappa, Alpha Chi Sigma, Phi Sigma Kappa. Republican. Baptist. Home and Office: 16203 Spring Creek Rd Dallas TX 75248-3116 Personal E-mail: jwcrowle@ix.netcom.com.

CROWLEY, JOHN CRANE, real estate developer; b. Detroit, June 29, 1919; s. Edward John and Leah Helen (Crane) C.; m. Barbara Wenzel Gilfillan, Jan. 12, 1945; children: F. Alexander, Leonard, Philip, Eliot, Louise, Sylvia. BA with high honors, Swarthmore Coll., 1941; MS, U. Denver, 1943. Asst. dir. Mcpl. Fin. Officers Assn., Chgo., 1946-48; So. Calif. mgr. League Calif. Cities, Los Angeles, 1948-53; mgr. City of Monterey Park, Calif., 1953-56. Founder, exec. v.p. Nat. Med. Enterprises, L.A., 1968; pres. Ventura Towne House (Calif.), 1963-96; mem. faculty U. So. Calif. Sch. Pub. Adminstrn., 1950-53; bd. dirs. Regional Inst. of So. Calif., The L.A. Partnership 2000, Burbank-Glendale-Pasadena Airport Authority; commr. Bob Hope Airport. Trustee Pacific Oaks Friends Sch. and Coll., Pasadena, 1954-57, 92-98, Swarthmore Coll., 1987—; bd. dirs. Pasadena Area Liberal Arts Ctr., 1962-72, pres., 1965-68; bd. dirs. Pacificulture Found. and Asia Mus., 1971-76, pres., 1972-74; bd. dirs. Nat. Mcpl. League, 1986-92, AAF Rose Bowl Aquatics Ctr., 1997—; chmn. Pasadena Cultural Heritage Commn., 1975-78; city dir. Pasadena, 1979-91; mayor City of Pasadena, 1986-88; bd. dirs. Western Justice Ctr., 1992—, v.p., 1995—, LA County Commn. on Efficiency and Economy, 1994—; mem. L.A. County Commn. on Local Govt., 2000—. Sloan Found. fellow, 1941-43; recipient Arthur Nobel award City of Pasadena. Mem. Am. Soc. Pub. Adminstrn. (local chpt., Winston Crouch award 1990), Internat. City Mgmt. Assn., Nat. Mcpl. League (nat. bd. 1980-92, Disting. Citizen award, 1984), Inst. Pub. Adminstrn. (sr. assoc.), Phi Delta Theta. Democrat. Unitarian Universalist. Home: 615 Linda Vista Ave Pasadena CA 91105-1122 Office Phone: 626-795-8221.

CROWLEY, JOHN FRANCIS, III, university dean; b. New Haven, Jan. 29, 1945; s. John Francis Jr. and Anna Cecil (Elliott) C.; m. Alice Ann Kennedy, Dec. 26, 1970; children: John Francis IV, Sarah Ann. MA in Regional and City Planning, U. Okla., 1973, PhD in Urban Geography, 1977. Dir. planning Seminole, Okla.; chief planner Okla. State Parks, 1973—74; asst. prof. environ. design U. Ga., Athens, 1974—78, prof., dean Coll. Environ. and Design, 1996—; exec. dir. Tulsa Metro Area Planning Commn., 1978—80; v.p., devel. Williams Realty Corp., Tulsa, 1980—87; pres. Urbantech Inc., Tulsa, 1987—; dir. Okla. Dept. of Transp., Oklahoma City, 1993—95. Bd. dirs. Downtown Tulsa Unltd., 1983-89; chmn. Sales Tax Overview Com., Tulsa, 1988-90; sec. bd. trustees Tulsa County Pub. Facilities Authority, 1983-96. 1st lt. U.S. Army, 1965-69. Sara Moss faculty fellow U. Ga., 1976. Fellow Am. Inst. Cert. Planners; mem. Am. Soc. Landscape Architects, Am. Planning Assn., Nature Conservancy, Urban Land Inst., Transp. Rsch. Bd. Democrat. Roman Catholic. Avocations: art, sports, travel. Home: 335 Crystal Ct Athens GA 30606-3245 Business E-Mail: jcrowley@uga.edu.

CROWLEY, JOHN WILLIAM, literature and language professor; b. New Haven, Dec. 27, 1945; s. John Adam and Mary T. (McKenna) C.; m. Sheila A. Myers, Mar. 17, 1967 (div. 1977); children: Matthew, Anne; m. Susan Wolstenholme, May 27, 1978 (div. 2001); children: Raphael, Mary; m. Emily T. Smith, Nov. 23, 2001. BA, Yale U., 1967; MA, Ind. U., 1969, PhD, 1970. Asst. prof. English Syracuse (N.Y.) U., 1970-74, assoc. prof., 1974-79, prof., 1979—2002, dir. humanities doctoral program, 1985—88, 1996—2002, dir. grad. studies, 1986-89, chair, 1989—92; prof. U. Ala., Tuscaloosa, 2002—, chair dept., 2002—03. Author: George Cabot Lodge, 1976, The Black Heart's Truth, 1985, The Mask of Fiction, 1989, The White Logic, 1994, The Dean of American Letters, 1999, Bill W. and Mr. Wilson, 2000; co-author: Drunkard's Refuge, 2004; editor: New Essays on Winesburg, Ohio, 1990, Genteel Pagan, 1991, The Sunnier Side, 1996, The Rise of Silas Lapham, 1996, Drunkard's Progress, 1999; co-editor: The Haunted Dusk, 1983. Hon. Woodrow Wilson fellow, 1967; NDEA fellow, 1967-70; Nat. Endowment for Humanities summer stipend, 1975 Mem.: Phi Beta Kappa. Democrat. Home: 1900 Woodridge Rd Tuscaloosa AL 35406 Office: Dept of English U Ala Tuscaloosa AL 35487-0244 Office Phone: 205-348-8522. Business E-Mail: jcrowley@english.as.ua.edu.

CROWLEY, JOSEPH, congressman; b. Queens County, N.Y., Mar. 16, 1962; BA, Queens Coll., 1985. Mem. N.Y. State Assembly, 1987-98, U.S. Congress from 7th N.Y. dist., Washington, 1999—; mem. internat rels. com., fin. svcs. com. Former mem. standing com. in banking N.Y. State Assembly, elec. law com., consumer affairs com., labor & housing com., ways and means com., chmn. racing & wagering com Mem. Cavan Men's Assn., VFW, K. of C. Democrat. Office: US Ho of Reps 312 Cannon Ho Office Bldg Washington DC 20515 Address: 7409 37th Ave Ste 306B Jackson Heights NY 11372-6303*

CROWLEY, JOSEPH NEIL, academic administrator, political scientist, educator; b. Oelwein, Iowa, July 9, 1933; . James Bernard and Nina Mary (Neil) C.; m. Johanna Lois Reitz, Sept. 9, 1961; children: Theresa, Neil, Margaret, Timothy. BA, U. Iowa, 1959; MA, Calif. State U., Fresno, 1963; PhD (Univ. fellow), U. Wash., 1967. Reporter Fresno Bee, 1961-62; asst. prof. polit. sci. U. Nev., Reno, 1966-71, asso. prof., 1971-79, prof., 1979—, chmn. dept. polit. sci., 1976-78, pres., 1978-2000, pres. emeritus, regents prof., 2000—; interim pres. San Jose State U., 2003—04. Bd. dirs. Citibank Nev.; policy formulation officer EPA, Washington, 1973-74; dir. instl. studies Nat. Commn. on Water Quality, Washington, 1974-75. Author: Democrats, Delegates and Politics in Nevada: A Grassroots Chronicle of 1972, 1976, Notes From the President's Chair, 1988, No Equal in the World; An Interpretation of the Academic Presidency, 1994, The Constant Conversation: A Chronicle of Campus Life, 2000; editor: (with R. Roelofs and D. Hardesty) Environment and Society, 1973. Chair Nev. Rhodes Scholar Comm., 1988—2000, mem., 2002—04; mem. coun. NCAA, 1987—92, mem. pres.' commn., 1991—92, pres., 1993—95; bd. dirs. Nat. Consortium for Acads. and Sports, 1992—; bd. dirs. campaign chmn. No. Nev. United Way, 1985; bd. dirs. campaing chmn., 1997—2002; bd. dir. Collegiate Women Sports Awards; mem. Commn. on Colls., 1980—87; mem. adv. commn. on mining and minerals rsch. U.S. Dept. Interior, 1985—91. Recipient Thornton Peace Prize U. Nev., 1971, Humanitarian of Yr. award NCCJ, 1986, Alumnus of Yr. award Calif. State U., Fresno, 1989, ADL Champion of Liberty award, 1993, Disting. Alumni award U. Iowa, 1994, Giant Step award Ctr. for Study of Sport in Soc., 1994, William Anderson award AAHPERD, 1998, Lifetime Achievement award Nat. Consortium for Acads. and Sports, 2001, Nev Arts and Humanities award for pub. svc., 2000, Nev. Edn. Hall of Fame, 2003; Nat. Assn. Schs. Pub. Affairs and Adminstrn. fellow, 1973-74. Mem.: Nat. Assn. State Univs. and Land Grant Colls. (bd. dirs. 1999-2000 1999—2000). Office: U Nev Mail Stop 310 Reno NV 89557 Office Phone: 775-784-1500. Business E-Mail: crowley@unr.edu.

CROWLEY, JUANITA A., lawyer; b. Jan. 11, 1953; BA, Trinity Coll., 1974; JD, Georgetown Univ., 1977. Bar: DC 1977. Law clk. Judge Herbert F. Murray, US Dist. Ct. (Md. dist.), 1977—78; ptnr., co-chmn. Litigation dept. Wilmer Cutler Pickering Hale & Dorr, Washington. Prof. Nat. Inst. Trial Advocacy, Boulder, Colo. Editor (exec.): Georgetown Law Jour. Mem.: ABA, Phi Beta Kappa. Office: Wilmer Cutler Pickering Hale & Dorr 2445 M St NW Washington DC 20037 Office Phone: 202-663-6207. Office Fax: 202-663-6363. Business E-Mail: juanita.crowley@wilmerhale.com.

CROWLEY, WILLIAM C., retail executive; BS in Psychology, Yale U., 1979. With Goldman Sachs, 1986—99; pres., chief ops. officer Investments, Inc., 1999—2003; sr. v.p. fin. Kmart Corp., 2003—. Office: Kmart Corp 3100 W Big Beaver Rd Troy MI 48084

CROWLEY, WILLIAM FRANCIS, JR., endocrinologist, educator; b. Meriden, Conn., Dec. 28, 1943; s. William Francis and Kathryn (Kiernan) C.; m. Nancy Marie Colwell; children: William Francis III, Sean Timothy, Regan Elizabeth, Colin Colwell. BA (honors curriculum), Holy Cross Coll., Worcester, Mass., 1965; MD, Tufts U., 1969. Diplomate Am. Bd. Internal Medicine. Intern Mass. Gen. Hosp., Boston, 1969-70, asst. resident in medicine, 1970-71, sr. resident in medicine, 1973-74, clin. and rsch. fellow in endocrinology, 1974-76; instr. medicine Harvard Med. Sch., Mass. Gen. Hosp., 1976-80; asst. prof. medicine Harvard Med. Sch., Boston, 1980-84, assoc. prof., 1984-92, prof. medicine, 1992—. Chief reproductive endocrine unit Mass. Gen. Hosp., 1984—, attending physician, 1988—, dir. clin. rsch., 1996—; dir. Vincent Rsch. Labs., 1987-90, dir. Harvard Reproductive Endocrine Sci. Ctr. 1991—; adv. bds. NIH, FDA, 1979—; lectr. in sci. writing, Harvard U., 1974-76; vis. prof. Yale U., 1982, Duke U., 1983, N.Y. Obstet. Soc., 1983, George Washington U., 1985, U. Miami, 1989; Goldfarb lectr., Vanderbilt U., 1989; Leathem lectr., Rutgers U., 1981; Israel Mackler lectr. Albert Einstein Coll. Medicine, 1982; lectr. Mayo Clinic, 1990, U. Chgo., 1990, U. Va., 1994, Northwestern U., 1995; invited speaker Laurentian Hormone Conf., 1984, 90; Winkler Meml. lectr. U. Buffalo, 1989; cons. Study Sect., Ctr. for Population, 1979-80, Contract Adv. Bd. Contraceptive Devel. Br., Nat. Inst. Child Health and Human Devel., NIH, 1979—; dir. Mass. Gen. Hosp. Reproductive Endocrine Scis. Ctr.-NIH Ctrs. of Reproductive Excellences, 1991, Nat. Ctr. Infertility Rsch., Mass Gen Hosp., 1991—, NIH Tng. Grant in Reproductive and Devel. Biology, 1991; mem. Ptnrs. Rsch. Coun., 1994—; dir. clin. rsch. MGH, 1995—; mem. sci. adv. bd. PRACIS Pharm. Co., 1996—, Ligand Pharm. Co., 1997-2000. Editor: (with J.G. Hofler) The Episodic Secretion of Hormones, 1987; contbr. articles to profl. jours.; mem. editorial bds. numerous profl. and sci. jours. including Jour. Clin. Endocrinology and Metabolism, 1983-87, Neuroendocrinology, 1987—, Acta Endocrinologica, 1983—, Internat. Jour. Fertility, 1985—, Annals Internal Medicine, 1986—, Endocrinology, 1988—, Molecular and Cellular Neuroscis., 1989—. Mem. Union of Concerned Scientists, Planned Parenthood, RESOLVE (physicians' bd.); founder Acad. Health Ctr. Clin. Rsch. Forum, 1996. Lt. USNR, 1971-73. Recipient Mentoring award Women in Endocrinology, 2000; Daland fellows Am. Philos. Soc., 1975-78; NIH grantee, 1979—. Fellow Royal Coll. Physicians (hon.); mem. ACP, Am. Fedn. Med. Rsch., Soc. for Study Reprodn., Am. Soc. Clin. Investigation, Assn. Am. Physicians, Endocrine Soc. (pres. 2000-01, Presdl. lectr. 1996, pres. 2001, Clin. Investigator award 2000, Fred Conrad Koch award 2005), Peripatetic Soc., Interurban Club, Mass. Med. Soc., Am. Fertility Soc., Am. Fedn. Clin. Rsch., Inst. Medicine (clin. rsch. roundtable 2000—), N.Y. Acad. Scis., Hyannisport Country Club (Mass.). Avocations: tennis, skiing, walking, reading, golf. Office: Mass Gen Hosp Reproductive Endocrine Scis Ctr Bartlett Hall Ext 5 Boston MA 02114

CROWN, DAVID ALLAN, criminologist, educator; b. Long Beach, N.Y., Sept. 13, 1928; s. John and Florence (Coe) C.; m. Maria Braml, Feb. 13, 1954; children: Ingrid, Eric. BS, Union Coll., 1948; M in Criminology, U. Calif., 1960, D in Criminology, 1969. Spl. agt. CIC, 1951-53; asst. dir. San Francisco Indentification Lab., U.S. Postal Inspection Service, 1957-67; dir. Questioned Document Lab., Records Analysis Group, Dept. Army, Washington, 1967-72, Questioned Documents Staff, INR/DDC, U.S. Dept. State, Washington, 1972-77; chief Questioned Documents Lab., Office of Tech. Services, 1977-82. Lectr. Chabot Coll., Hayward, Calif., 1966-67, Georgetown U., Washington, 1973; adj. prof. Am. U., Washington, 1971-80; professorial lectr. George Washington U., 1973-77, Antioch Sch. Law, 1977-1981; guest lectr. FBI Acad., Quantico, Va.; pres. Crown Forensic Labs., Inc.; chmn. recert. com. Am. Bd. Forensic Document Examiners. Author: The Forensic Examination of Paints and Pigments, 1968; co-author: Forensic Science, 1982, Legal Medicine, 1985, Forensic Handwriting Examination, 1993; contbr. articles to profl. publs.; mem. editl. bd.: Jour. Forensic Scis., 1971-73, Internat. Jour. Forensic Document Examiners; book rev. editor, 1973-74, assoc. editor, 1974-84. Pres. Temple Bat Yam, Sanibel, Fla., 1996-98. Mem. Am. Acad. Forensic Scis. (chmn. questioned document sect. 1969-70, exec. com. 1970-74, pres. 1974-75), Am. Soc. Questioned Document Examiners (chmn. accreditation com. 1969-70, sec.-treas. 1976-78, pres. 1980-82), ASTM (chmn. questioned document com. 1970-71, vice chmn. 1972), Forensic Sci. Found. (dir. 1971-72, trustee 1973-75). Home: 3344 Twin Lakes Ln Sanibel FL 33957-5528 Office Phone: 239-395-1900.

CROWN, ERIC J., information systems executive; BSc in Bus. Computer Info. Sys., Ariz. State U., 1984. Chmn., CEO, founder Insight Enterprises, Tempe, Ariz., 1988—. Office: Insight Enterprises 6820 S Harl Ave Tempe AZ 85283-4318 E-mail: ecrown@insight.com.

CROWN, JAMES SCHINE, investment company executive; b. Chgo., June 25, 1953; s. Lester and Renée (Schine) Crown; m. Paula Anne Hannaway, June 27, 1985; children: Victoria, Hayley, Andrew, Summer Olivia. BA, Hampshire Coll., 1976; JD, Stanford U., 1980. Bar: Ill. 1980. V.p. Salomon Bros. Inc., N.Y.C., 1980-85; gen. ptnr. Henry Crown and Co., Chgo., 1985—. Bd. dirs. Gen. Dynamics Corp., Falls Church, Va., JPMorgan Chase & Co., Sara Lee Corp. Chmn. bd. U. Chgo.; Trustee Mus. Sci. and Industry, Chgo., Orchestral Assn., Chgo. Mem.: Ill. State Bar Assn. Office: Henry Crown and Co 222 N La Salle St Chicago IL 60601-1003

CROWN, JOHN WALTER, vocational education supervisor; b. Waverly, Va., Dec. 13, 1937; s. Wilburt Herman and Martha Ann (Holmes) B. BS in Vocat. Indsl. Edn., Va. State U., 1968; MEd in Vocat. Indsl. Edn., Pa. State U., 1970; cert. advanced study in edn., Johns Hopkins U., 1973; PhD in Vocat. Indsl. Edn., Pa. State U., 1976. Cert. tchr., advanced profl., prin., supr., supt., vocat. edn., Md. and Pa. Drafting instr. Peabody Sr. High Sch., Petersburg, Va., 1962-63; electronics instr. Hampstead Hill Jr. High Sch., Balt., 1965-66, Calverton Jr. High Sch., Balt., 1966-73, dep. prin., 1975-80; vice prin. Carver Vocat. Tech. Sr. High Sch., Balt., 1975; ednl. specialist Balt. City Pub. Schs., 1974, coord., 1980-84, div. specialist, 1984-89, curriculum specialist, 1989-93; prin. House One Rowland Intermediate Sch., Harrisburg, Pa., 1993-94; coord. profl. pers. devel. Pa. State Dept. of Edn., Harrisburg, 1994—2003, coord. profl. pers. devel. and acting mgr., divsn. product devel., 2001—. Instr. Va. State U., Petersburg, 1962-63, Coppin State Coll., Balt., 1972-73; mem. Balt. City Adv. Coun. on Vocat. Edn. and trade adv. subcoms. With U.S. Army, 1963-65. Named to Va. State U. Sports Hall of Fame. Mem. Am. Vocat. Edn. Assn., Nat. Assn. Indsl. and Tech. Edn., Pub. Schs. Adminstrs. and Suprs. Assn., Johns Hopkins Alumni Assn., Pa. State U. Alumni Assn., Va. State U. Alumni Assn., Iota Lambda Sigma, Phi Delta Kappa. Methodist. Avocations: sports, reading, travel, writing, gardening. Home: 5914 Charnwood Rd Baltimore MD 21228-1205 Office: Pa State Dept Edn Bur of Career and Tech Edn 333 Market St Harrisburg PA 17101-2210 E-mail: jobrown@state.pa.us.

CROWN, LESTER, manufacturing executive; b. Chgo., June 7, 1925; s. Henry and Rebecca (Kranz) C.; m. Renee Schine, Dec. 28, 1950; children: Steven, James, Patricia, Daniel, Susan, Sara, Janet. BS in Chem. Engring., Northwestern U., 1946; MBA, Harvard U., 1949. Instr. math. Northwestern U., 1946-47; v.p., chem. engr. Marblehead Lime Co., 1950-56, pres., 1956-66, also bd. dirs.; v.p. Material Svc. Corp. subs. Gen. Dynamics Corp., Chgo., 1953-66, pres., 1970-83, chmn., 1983—, also bd. dirs.; bd. dirs. Gen. Dynamics Corp.; pres. Henry Crown & Co., Chgo., 1969—2002, chmn., 2002—, also bd. dirs. Bd. dirs. Maytag Corp.; ptnr. Yankee Global Enterprise, 1973-; chmn. Comml. Club Chgo., 2005-. Trustee, vice chmn. Aspen Inst. Humanistic Studies, Northwestern U., Michael Reese Found.; bd. dirs. Lyric Opera Corp., Children's Meml. Med. Ctr., Jewish Theol. Sem., Jerusalem Found.; mem. bd. govs. Weizmann Inst. of Sci./Tel Aviv U.; chmn. Chgo. Coun. on Fgn. Rels., 2004—. Mem. Am. Acad. Arts and Scis., Lake Shore Country Club, Northmoor Country Club, Old Elm Club, Standard Club, Econ. Club (dir. 1972), Chgo. Club, Comml. Club, Mid-Am. Club (Chgo.), John Evans Club of Northwestern U., Tau Beta Pi, Pi My Epsilon, Phi Eta Sigma. Office: Material Svc Corp 222 N La Salle St Ste 1200 Chicago IL 60601-1087 also: Gen Dynamics Corp 2941 Fairview Park Dr Falls Church VA 22042-4510

CROWN, MICHELE FLEURETTE, lawyer; b. NYC, Nov. 16, 1943; d. Louis and Sophia C.; m. Norman R. Williams, Dec. 2, 1972; children: Zachary Crown Williams, Oliver Crown Williams. BA, Queens Coll., CUNY, 1965; JD, Brooklyn Law Sch., 1967. Bar: N.Y. 1968, D.C. 1969. Trial atty. FTC, Washington, 1967-72, 1975-79; gen. counsel Am. Meat Inst., Washington, 1979-82; of counsel Perito, Duerk & Pinco, Washington, 1982-84, Olsson, Frank & Weeda, Washington, 1984—, Venable LLP, Washington, 2001—. Author reports to Congress; contbr. articles to profl. jours. Mem. ABA, FDLI (mem. academic oversight com.), Pi Sigma Alpha. Office: Venable LLP 575 7th St NW Washington DC 20004 Office Phone: 202-344-4778. Office Fax: 202-344-8300. Business E-Mail: mfcrown@venable.com.

CROWN, ROBERTA, artist, educator; b. N.Y.C., Sept. 9, 1946; d. Louis and Sophia (Siegal) C. B.A., Queens Coll., M.A., 1970. Art tchr. N.Y. Bd. Edn., N.Y.C., 1969—. One-woman shows include: Harbor Sq., Washington, 1970, Andalusia Arts, Inc. Gallery, N.Y.C., 1974, Women's Studio Workship Gallery, Rosendale, N.Y., 1988, Queens Coll. Art Ctr., Flushing, N.Y., 1989, Dag Jammaraskjold Tower, N.Y.C., 1997, Uniproperty Gallery, N.Y.C., 1998; group shows include: Air Naval Res. Show (1st prize oils, 3d prize watercolors), 1969, East Meadow Outdoor Show, N.Y.C., 1970, Aorta, East Hampton, N.Y., 1971, United Art Group, N.Y.C., 1976, WIA Gallery, N.Y.C., 1978, 79, 80, Bklyn. Coll. (2d prize oils), 1978, One Hundred Artists Show, N.Y.C., 1979, Picture Show Gallery, N.Y.C., 1979, Contemporary Arts Ctr., 1980, Fed. S.I. Artists, Lever House, N.Y.C., 1980, Fine Arts Gallery Ocean County Coll., 1980, Panassus Gallery, Woodstock, N.Y., 1980, Gallery 14, Copenhagen, 1980, Newhouse Gallery, 1981, Queens Mus., 1981, 84, Off the Wall Show, 1982, Cork Gallery, 1983, 84, 86, 87, Nugent Gallery, Marymount Manhattan Coll., 1983, 84, Garcia Gallery, Bronx, N.Y., 1983, City Gallery, N.Y.C., 1984, Franklin Furnace, N.Y.C., 1984, Lehigh U., Bethlehem, Pa., 1984, Chgo. Gallery, U. Ill., 1984, Tokyo Met. Mus., 1984, Arsenal Gallery, 1984, 86, Art and Design High Sch., N.Y.C., 1985, Janco-Dada Mus., Ein-Hod, Israel, 1985, Passaic Community Coll., Patterson, N.J., 1986, Todd Capp Gallery, N.Y.C., 1986, Castillo Gallery, N.Y.C., 1987, WRIC Ctr., 1987, Appalachian State U., Boone, N.C., 1988, Transco Energy Gallery, Houston, 1988, Rice Gallery, 1991, Sotherby's, 1991, Nat. Mus. Women in Arts, 1991, NAWA Traveling Show, 1992, Tesori Gallery, 1993; one-woman shows include: Harbor Sq., Washington, 1970, Andalusia Arts, Inc. Gallery, N.Y.C., 1974, Women's Sutdio Workshop Gallery, Rosendale, N.Y., 1988, Queen Coll. Art Ctr., 1989, others. Mem. Women in the Arts Found., Inc. (exec. coordinator 1980—), Women Caucus in Art, N.Y. State Assn. Tchrs. Art. Studio: 365 Canal St New York NY 10013

CROWN, ROBERTA LILA, artist; BA, Queens Coll., MA, 1970; postgrad., Triangle Work Shop, Pine Plains, N.Y., 1987. One woman shows include Queens Coll. Art Ctr., Flushing, N.Y., 1989, Women's Studio Workshop Gallery, Rosendale, N.Y., 1988, Andalusia Arts, Inc. Gallery, N.Y.C., 1974, Harbor Sq., Washington, 1970; exhibited in corp. collections at ABC-TV, Joseph Gray & Co., Arkwin Industries, Inc., NBC-TV, 20th Century-Fox TV; exhibited in numerous group shows. Mem. Women in the Arts Found., Inc. (exec. coord.), Artists Equity, Nat. Assn. Women Artists, Women's Caucus for Art. Home and Office: 1175 York Ave New York NY 10021-7169

CROWN, TIMOTHY A., computer technology company executive; BS in Bus. and Computer Sci., U. Kans., 1986. Adminstrv. analyst NCR Corp., 1986-87; various positions to pres. Insight Enterprises, Tempe, Ariz., 1988-89, co-CEO, co-chmn., 1994—, now chmn. Ind. computer bus. cons., 1987-88. Office: Insight Enterprises 6820 S Harl Ave Tempe AZ 85283

CROWNER, DEE KAY, library administrator; b. Spirit Lake, Jan. 15, 1946; d. Harold Raymond Crowner and Kathryn Margaret Louise Hinkey. BA in Libr. Sci., U. No. Iowa, 1969. Media specialist Nashua (Iowa) Pub. Schs., Alden (Iowa) Pub. Schs., Berkley & Co., Spirit Lake, Iowa, Stylecraft Furniture, Milford, Iowa, Nat. Computer Sys., Iowa City, AT&T, Cedar Rapids, Iowa, MCI, Cedar Rapids; libr. dir. North Liberty (Iowa) Cmty. Libr., 1987—. Past mem. conf. planning com. State Libr. Iowa, mem. accreditation com. Author: (monthly news column) Bookends; newsletter editor Iowa Pub. Libr. Forum. Mem. Big Bros./Big Sisters. Mem. ALA, Iowa Small Libr. Assn. (pres., newsletter editor), Iowa Libr. Assn. (membership com., past mem. govtl. affairs com., children's and young people's roundtable and conf. planning com.), Pub. Libr. Assn., Iowa Libr. Adminstrn. and Mgmt. Assn., Johnson County Pub. Libr. Assn. (chair), North Liberty Optimists. Avocations: reading, theater, restaurants, movies, travel. Office: North Liberty Cmty Libr 520 W Cherry St North Liberty IA 52317-9797 E-mail: nlcl@zeus.ia.net.

CROWSON, HENRY LAWRENCE, mathematician, educator; b. Okeechobee, Fla., Apr. 16, 1927; s. Ernest Hubbard and Mary Elizabeth Crowson; m. Betty Mae George, June 16, 1951; children: Lawrence George, James Maxwell, Timothy David. BChemE, U. Fla., Gainesville, 1953, MS in Math., 1955, PhD in Math., 1959. Cert. engr. in tng., Fla. Asst. prof. U. Fla., Gainesville, 1958-60; advisory mathematician IBM Corp., Gaithersburg, Md., 1960-72; sr. mathematician CACI Corp., Arlington, Va., 1975-77; assoc. prof. U. P.M., Saudi Arabia, 1977-79, U. Houston, 1982-86, TIEC/MUCIA, Shah Alam, Malaysia, 1986-89, Tex. A&M Internat. U., Laredo, 1990-98. Cons. Bell Labs., CACI, Vitro Labs., Cornell U., others, 1955—. Reviewer books and math. texts, 1965-68. Mem. Am. Math. Soc., Sigma Xi, Pi Mu Epsilon. Republican. Avocations: reading, music, composing poetry. Home: 10127 Falls Rd Potomac MD 20854-4107

CROWSON, JAMES LAWRENCE, lawyer, academic administrator, finance company executive; b. Duncan, Okla., Aug. 3, 1938; s. George L. and Emry Elifair (McKee) C.; children from previous marriage: James Lawrence Jr., Jason Phillips, Kristan Fair Nickel; m. Linda Sue Crowson, Mar. 2, 1986; stepchildren: Chadwick Lanier Johnson, Kim Johnson Osborn. BA in English Lit., U. Okla., 1960; LLB, So. Meth. U., 1963. Bar: Tex. 1963. Legis. counsel Tex. Legis. Coun., Austin, 1966-67; dir. hearings Tex. Water Quality Bd., Austin, 1967-68, chief legal officer, 1967-68, dir. hearings and enforcement, 1969-70; adminstrv. asst. Office of Gov., Austin, 1968-69; univ. atty. U. Tex. System, Austin, 1970; asst. to pres. U. Tex., Austin, 1970-71, Dallas, 1971-74, v.p., 1974-77, exec. v.p., 1977-80; vice chancellor, gen. counsel U. Tex. System, Austin, 1980-87; sr. v.p., gen. counsel Lomas Fin. Group, Dallas, 1987-94, exec. v.p., 1994-95; pvt. investment practice Dallas, 1995-96; dep. chancellor adminstrn. Tex. Tech. Univ. System, Lubbock, 1996—2002. Sec. Tex. Higher Edn. Found., 1988-1996, Higher Edn. Legis. Polit. Action Com., 1987-1996; vice chmn. HCB Enterprises Inc., 1995—; bd. dirs. KOHM Pub. Radio Sta., 1997-99, Tex. Univs. Health Plan, 1998-2002; bd. dirs. Market Lubbock, Inc., 1997-99, v.p. 1999. Trustee Alliance for Higher Edn., 1991-96, Dallas Edn. Ctr., 1995-96. Capt. U.S. Army, 1963-66. Mem. Mortgage Bankers Assn. Am. (mem. legal issues com., mem. legis. com.), U.S. C. of C. (mem. edn. employment and tng. com., mem. labor rels. com., mem. S.W. pub. affairs task force). Office: 5109 82d St Ste 7 # 258 Lubbock TX 79424 Office Phone: 806-793-0203. Personal E-mail: crowsonj@swbell.net.

CROWSON, WATIE DEE, foundation administrator, poet, lyricist; b. Vian, Okla., Aug. 29, 1953; s. Harvey and Gussie B. Crowson; m. Sandra G. Brewster, Aug. 26, 1972 (div. June 1974); m. Sharon K. Moody, Mar. 27, 1979 (div. Aug. 1979); life ptnr. Alice F. Allen; 1 child, Regina Lea. Student, Carl Albert U. Former welder, iron worker, home builder, power plant operator, lakes and park ranger asst.; legis. chmn. DAV, Sallisaw, Okla., 1998—. Second vice comdr. Disabled Am. Vets. Chpt. 83, Post 27; With USN, 1974-75. Mem. Am. Legion (Honor Guard, legis. chmn.), USS Kitty Hawk Assn, Marble City Citizen Bank, Seyquayah county Hist. Soc., VFW. Independent. Avocations: guitar, gardening, cooking, reading, landscaping. Home: Apt E 210 N Walnut Sallisaw OK 74955

CROWTHER, RICHARD LAYTON, architect, consultant, researcher, author, lecturer; b. Newark, Dec. 16, 1910; s. William George and Grace (Layton) C.; m. Emma Jane Hubbard, 1935 (div. 1949); children: Bethe Crowther Allison, Warren Winfield, Vivian Layton; m. 2d Pearl Marie Tesch, Sept. 16, 1950. Student, Newark Sch. Fine and Indsl. Arts, 1928-31, San Diego State Coll., 1933, U. Colo., 1956. Registered architect, Colo. Prin. Crowther & Marshall, San Diego, 1946-50, Richard L. Crowther, Denver, 1951-66, Crowther, Kruse, Landin, Denver, 1966-70, Crowther, Kruse, McWilliams, Denver, 1970-75, Crowther Solar Group, Denver, 1975-82, Richard L. Crowther FAIA, Denver, 1982—. Vis. critic, lectr. U. Nebr., 1981; holistic energy design process methodology energy cons. Holistic Health Ctr., 1982-83; adv. cons. interior and archtl. design class U. Colo., 1982-83, Cherry Creek, Denver redevel., 1984-88, Colo. smoking control legislation, 1985, interior solar concepts Colo. Inst. Art, 1986, Bio-Electro-Magnetics Inst., 1987-88; mentor U. Colo. Sch. Architecture, 1987-88. Author Sun/Earth, 1975 (Progressive Architecture award, 1975), rev. edit., 1983, reprint, 1995, Affordable Passive Solar Homes, 1983, reprint, 1996, Paradox of Smoking, 1983, Women/Nature/Destiny: Female/Male Equity for Global Survival, 1987, (monographs) Context in Art and Design, 1985, Existence, Design and Risk, 1986, Indoor Air: Risks and Remedies, 1986, Human Migration in Solar Homes for Seasonal Comfort and Energy Conservation, 1986, 88, Ecologic Architecture, 1992, Ecologic Digest, 1993, Ecologic Connections, 1996, Colorado Architect Monographs on Environmental Themes, 1998, Environmental Sustainability, 1999. NSF grantee, 1974-75; archtl. plans, drawings, photographs, ecol. and solar writings in archibes of western history dept. Denver Pub. Libr., 2002. Fellow AIA (commr. research, edn. and environ. Colo. Central chpt. 1972-75, bd. dirs. chpt. 1973-74 AIA Research Corp. Solar Monitoring Program contract award, spkr. and pub. Colo. Ecologic Connections open forum 1996). Achievements include ecologic bio-toxic and bio-electromagnetic research; donating architectural plans, renderings, and photographs in Western History to the Denver Pub. Libr. *Inner awareness, relevancy, persistence and adaptiveness are all that we have in a world of vanity, variety and change.*

CROXTON, JACK SANDERS, dean, consultant; b. Auburn, Ind., Aug. 3, 1949; s. Jack Anderson and Virginia Sanders Croxton; m. Mary Martha Miller, Dec. 31, 1973; children: Jessica Loring, Jennifer Allison, Joshua Benjamin. BS in Gen. Bus., Miami U., 1971, PhD in Social Psychology, 1979. Rsch. psychologist Nat. Inst. Occupl. Safety and Health, Cin., 1978—79; asst. prof. dept. psychology SUNY, Fredonia, NY, 1979—85, assoc. prof. dept. psychology, 1985—93, prof. dept. psychology, chair dept. psychology, 1990—99, dir. office campus assessment, 1999—2002, interim dean Coll. Natural and Social Scis., 2004—. External program reviewer SUNY, Albany, 2002—03; cons. Chautauqua County Sch. to Work Consortium, Jamestown; instr. Burgas Free U., Burgas, Bulgaria; vis. assoc. prof. Princeton U., NJ, 1987—88. Contbr. articles to profl. jours. Sch. bd. mem. Fredonia Ctrl. Schs., 1996—97. Recipient Rsch. Opportunity award, NSF, 1987, Pres.'s award Excellence in Tchg., SUNY, Fredonia, 1991; fellow, Princeton U., 1987—88; Fullbright fellow, 2000. Mem.: Midwestern Psychol. Assn., Ea. Psychol. Assn., Sigma Xi, Beta Gamma Sigma, Phi Beta Kappa. Avocations: travel, kayaking, hiking. Home: 22 Gillis St Fredonia NY 14063 Office: SUNY Thompson Hall Fredonia NY 14063 Office Phone: 716-673-3129. Office Fax: 716-673-3332. Personal E-mail: jackcroxton@hotmail.com. E-mail: jack.croxton@fredonia.edu.

CROXTON, PAMELA JOYCE, language educator, educational association administrator; b. Columbus, Ga., May 21, 1963; d. David Austin and Judith Louise (Doman) C. BA, Messiah Coll., Grantham, Pa., 1985. Cert. tchr., Pa. Student work-study supr. Messiah Coll., 1985-88; tchr. English, English Lang. Inst., Urumqi, Xinjiang, People's Republic China, 1988-90; instr. in ESL York (Pa.) County Literacy Coun., 1991—, ESL program coord., 1992—; subs. tchr. York City Sch. Dist./Christian Sch. of York, 1991—; ESL program coord. York County Literacy Coun., 1992—; ESL tchr. Dallastown Mid. Sch., 1992—. Speaker to various chs.; mem. York (Pa.) Ch. Volleyball League, 1986—; ESL instr. and vol. immigration and refugee svcs., Cath. charities, Harrisburg. Mem. Nat. Coun. Tchrs. English, Internat. Fellowship Alliance Profls. (assoc.), Teaching English to Students of Other Langs., ASCD. Mem. Christian and Missionary Alliance Ch. Avocations: volleyball, biking, reading, photography. Home: 2720 Steeple Chase DR York PA 17402-8529

CROYLE, BARBARA ANN, health facility administrator, director; b. Knoxville, Tenn., Oct. 22, 1949; d. Charles Evans and Myrtle Elizabeth (Kellam) C. BA cum laude in Sociology, Coll. William and Mary, 1971; cert. corp. tax and securities law, Inst. Paralegal Tng., 1971; JD, U. Colo., 1975; cert. program mgmt. devel., Colo. Women's Coll., 1980; MBA, U. Denver, 1983. Bar: Colo. 1976. Paralegal Holland & Hart, Denver, 1972-73; law clk. Colo. Ct. Appeals, Denver, summer 1976; assoc. firm Shaw Spangler & Roth, Denver, 1976-77; mgr. acquisitions/lands Petro-Lewis Corp., Denver, 1977-85; mgr. strategic planning Westinghouse, Transp. Divsn., Denver, 1985-87;

mng. dir. Benefit Resource Mgmt. Group (subs. Blue Cross We. Pa.), 1987-92; COO, v.p. D.T. Watson Rehab. Hosp., 1992-93; v.p. ambulatory care svcs., compliance officer Franciscan Med. Ctr., Dayton campus, Ohio, 1994-2000; exec. dir. Swedish Am. Ctr. for Complementary Medicine, Rockford, Ill., 2000—02; v.p., legal advisor Peninsula United Meth. Homes, Inc., Hockessin, Del., 2003—. Tchr. oil and gas law Colo. Paralegal Inst., 1978, 79; arbitrator Am. Arbitration Assn.; mediator Dayton Mediation Ctr. Mem. ABA, Del. Bar Assn., Inst. Noetic Scis., Am. Coll. Healthcare Execs. Home: 150 Mercer Mill Rd Landenberg PA 19350 Office: Peninsula United Meth Home 726 Loveville Rd Hockessin DE 19807 Office Phone: 302-235-6823. E-mail: bcroyle@earthlink.net.

CROYLE, ROBERT T., federal agency administrator, psychologist, educator; b. Seattle, Jan. 19, 1956; s. William R. and Elcena (Torrance) C.; m. Carol Jackson, Aug. 8, 1981; children: Kaitlin, Thomas. BA, U. Wash., 1978; PhD, Princeton U., 1985. Asst. prof. Williams Coll., Williamstown, Mass., 1983-86; vis. investigator Hutchinson Cancer Rsch. Ctr., Seattle, 1986-89; assoc. prof. U. Utah, Salt Lake City, 1989—98; assoc. dir., behavioral rsch. program, div. cancer control & population sciences Nat. Cancer Inst., 1998—2002, dir., div. cancer control & prevention science, 2003—. Editor: Mental Representation in Health and Illness, 1991. Office: Nat Cancer Inst 6130 Exec Blvd Rm 6138 Exec Plz N Rockville MD 20852

CROZIER, SCOTT A., lawyer; b. 1950; BA, Ariz. State U., 1975, JD, 1978. Bar: Ariz. 1978. Asst. counsel Talley Industries, Inc., 1980-87; sr. counsel, dir. environ. svcs. dept. Phelps Dodge Corp., 1987-90, assoc. gen. counsel, dir., 1990-91, v.p., gen. counsel, 1991—99; sr. v.p., gen. counsel PetSmart, Inc., 1999—, corp. sec., 2000—. Former enforcement atty. securities div. Ariz. Corp. Commn.; former special asst. atty. gen. Ariz. Atty. General's Office. Office: PetSmart Inc 19601 N 27th Ave Phoenix AZ 85027

CRUDEN, JOHN CHARLES, lawyer; b. Topeka, Feb. 23, 1946; s. George Harry and Agnes (Telban) C.; m. Sharon Lynn Holland, June 15, 1968; children: Kristen, Heather. BS, U.S. Mil. Acad., 1968; JD, U. Santa Clara, 1974; MA, U. Va., 1975; grad., Gen. Staff Coll., 1982. Bar: Calif. 1975, DC 1979, U.S. Supreme Ct. 1979. Commd. 2d lt. U.S. Army, 1968, advanced through grades to col., 1987, with airborne, ranger, spl. forces Germany, Vietnam, 1968-71, clk. Calif. Supreme Ct., 1974, prosecutor, 1975-76, chief litig. br. Hdqrs. Europe, 1976-78, sr. trial atty. comml. br. litig. divsn., 1978-79, gen. counsel Def. Nuc. Agy., 1979-80; prof., chief Adminstrv. and Civil Law divsn. Judge Adv. Gen.'s Sch., Charlottesville, Va., 1982-85; staff Judge Adv. Europe, 1985-87; spl. counsel to asst. atty. gen. civil divsn. U.S. Dept. Justice, 1987-88; chief legis. counsel Dept. Army, 1988-91; chief environ. enforcement sect. Environ. & Natural Resource divsn. U.S. Dept. Justice, Washington, 1991-95, dep. asst. atty. gen., 1995—2001, acting asst. atty. gen., 2001—02, dep. asst. atty. gen., 2002—, pres., 2005—. Contbr. articles to profl. jours. Fellow, Army War Coll., 1988. Mem. ABA (coun. sect. on environment, energy and resources 2002-, vice chmn. adminstrv. law and gen. practice sect. 1985-88, vice chmn. fed. legis. com. 1989-92, adv. com., standing com. on law and nat. security 1988-94), FBA (Younger Fed. Lawyers award 1981), JAG Sch. Alumni Assn. (pres. 1982-85), DC Bar Assn. (bd. govs. 2001—, pres.-elect 2004-05, pres. 2005—), Calif. Bar Assn. Office: US Dept Justice 950 Pennsylvania Ave Washington DC 20530-0001 Business E-Mail: john.cruden@usdoj.gov.

CRUDEN, ROBERT WILLIAM, botany educator; b. Cleve., Mar. 18, 1936; m. Diana Benedict Loeb, Dec. 21, 1967; children: Nathalie Rebecca, Lyda Marie; m. Diana Ruth Gannett, July 1996. AB, Hiram (Ohio) Coll., 1958; MS, Ohio State U., Columbus, 1960; PhD, U. Calif., Berkeley, 1967. Asst. prof. U. Iowa, Iowa City, 1967-71, assoc. prof., 1971-78, prof., 1978-99, prof. emeritus, 1999—. Acting dir. Iowa Lakeside Lab., Wahepton, 1989-94, past asst. dir.; adj. prof. U. Mich, Ann Arbor, 2001- Editor Ecol. Soc. Am., 1983-86; editl. bd. Madrono; contbr. numerous articles to profl. jours. Mem. pres.'s coun. on sci. initiatives Hiram Coll., 1994—. Recipient J.J. Turner award Hiram Coll., 2001. Fellow Iowa Acad. Sci.; mem. AAAS, Am. Soc. Plant Taxonomists, Bot. Soc. Am., Ecol. Soc. Am., Iowa Acad. Sci., Soc. for the Study of Evolution, Assn. for Tropical Biology, New Eng. Bot. Soc. Home: 550 Woodhill Dr Saline MI 48176 Personal E-mail: robert-cruden@uiowa.edu.

CRUDUP, PAMELA TRACY PARHAM, science educator, writer; 1 child, Courtney Allison. Cert. cardiovasc. technologist, Shelby State Coll., 1996; BS in Biology, BS in Secondary Edn., Crichton Coll., 2001; MS in Pub. Health, Walden U., 2005. Cardiovasc. technologist, catheter lab. mgr. Meth. Hosp., Somierville, Tenn., 1995—96, radiology physician liaison Memphis, 1996—2004. Instr. anatomy/physiology, Memphis, 2001—. Author: The Hat Box, 2003, The Mist of Mineral Springs, 2004. Mem.: NEA, Endometriosis Assn. (West Tenn. support group leader), Assn. Pub. Health, Authors for Charity, Nat. Trust for Hist. Preservation. Republican. Baptist. Avocations: travel, antiques, tennis, walking, writing. E-mail: InstructorCrudup@aol.com.

CRUESS, RICHARD LEIGH, orthopedic surgeon, dean; b. London, Ont., Can., Dec. 17, 1929; s. Leigh S. and Martha A. (Peever) C.; m. Sylvia Crane Robinson, May 30, 1953; children: Leigh S., Andrew C. BA, Princeton U., 1951; MD, Columbia U., 1955; DSc (hon.), U. Laval, 2004. Diplomate Am. Bd. Orthopedic Surgery. Intern Royal Victoria Hosp., Montreal, Que., 1955-56, resident surgery, 1956-57, N.Y. Orthopedic Hosp., 1959-60, asst. resident orthopedic surgery, 1960-61, resident orthopedic surgery, 1961-62, Annie C. Kane fellow orthopedic surgery, 1961-62; research asso. depts. orthopedic surgery and biochemistry Columbia U., N.Y.C., 1962-63; John Armour Travelling fellow, 1962-63; Am.-Brit.-Can. Travelling fellow, 1967; practice medicine specializing in orthopedic surgery Montreal, 1963-95; orthopedic surgeon Royal Victoria Hosp., orthopedic surgeon-in-charge, 1968-81, asst. surgeon-in-chief, 1970-81; chief surgeon Shriner's Hosp. for Crippled Children, Montreal, 1970-82; prof. surgery McGill U., Montreal, 1970—, chmn. div. orthopedic surgery, 1976-81, dean faculty medicine, 1981-95, prof. Ctr. for Med. Edn., 1995—. Hon. cons. orthopedic surgery Queen Elizabeth Hosp., 1972-95; mem. clin. grants com. Med. Rsch. Coun., 1972-75, mem. coun., 1980-86, mem. exec., 1983-86. Contbr. articles on surgery to profl. jours.; mem. editl. bd. Jour. Internat. Orthopedics, 1976-85, Jour. Bone and Joint Surgery, 1977-83, Current Problems in Orthopedics, 1977-83, Jour. Orthopaedic Rsch., 1986-88. Served to lt. M.C., USN, 1957-59. Decorated mem. and officer Order of Can., officer Order of Que. Fellow Royal Coll. Physicians and Surgeons Can. (chief examiner orthopedic surgery 1970-72), ACS, Am. Acad. Orthopedic Surgeons, Royal Soc. Can.; mem. Can. Orthopedic Assn. (sec. 1971-76, pres. 1977-78), Can. Orthopedic Rsch. Soc. (pres. 1971-72), Am. Orthopedic Rsch. Soc. (pres. 1975-76), Am. Orthopedic Assn., Ann. Orthopedic Surgeons Province Que. (treas. 1971-72), Société Française de Chirurgie Orthopedique (hon.), McGill Osler Reporting Soc., Assn. can. Med. colls. (pres. 1987-89). Home: Apt 903 2333 Sherbrooke St W Montreal PQ Canada H3H 2T6 Office: McGill U 1110 Pine Ave W Montreal PQ Canada H3A 1A3 Office Phone: 514-398-7331. E-mail: richard.cruess@mcgill.ca.

CRUICKSHANK, JOHN DOUGLAS, publishing executive; b. Toronto, Ont., Can., Apr. 7, 1953; s. Norman and Jean (McPherson) C.; m. Jennifer Hunter; children: Simone, Noah. BA with honors, U. Toronto, 1975. Reporter The Kingston Whig-Standard, Canada, 1977-79, The Montreal Gazette, 1979-81; edn. writer The Globe & Mail, Toronto, 1981-82, Queen's Park writer, 1982-85, bur. chief Vancouver, 1985-88, editorial writer Toronto, 1988-90, assoc. editor, 1990-92, mng. editor, 1992-95; editor-in-chief The Vancouver Sun, 1995-2000; v.p. editl. Chgo. Sun-Times, 2000—03, pub., 2003—; COO Chgo. Group Hollinger Internat. Inc., 2003—. Office: Chgo Sun-Times 401 N Wabash Ave Chicago IL 60611*

CRUIKSHANK, JOHN W., III, insurance agent; b. Sharon, Pa., Aug. 22, 1933; s. John W. and Jeannette Sprague (Lane) C.; m. Myrna Jean Wright, Nov. 25, 1960; children: Nancy Lynn, David Wright. BA, Princeton U., 1955. CLU. Group ins. sales rep. Conn. Gen. Life Ins. Co., Hartford, also Chgo., 1955-56; spl. agt. Northwestern Mut. Life Ins. Co., Chgo., 1959—, pres. Spl. Agts., Inc., 1983-84, faculty advanced planning sch. Northbrook, Ill., 1978-97; pres. Assn. of Agts. Northwestern Mut. Life, 1994-95. Pres. Million Dollar Round Table Found., 1988—89; divisional v.p. Million Dollar Round Table, 1976—77, 1986—87, 1992—93, exec. com., 1994—98, pres., 1996—97; trustee Life Underwriter Tng. Coun., 1997—2001. Bd. dirs. Life and Health Ins. Found. for Edn., 1997—2003, chmn., 2002; bd. dirs. North Shore Sr. Ctr., 2001—; trustee Pikeville (Ky.) Coll., 1969—75, The Am. Coll., 2001—02; pres. Nat. Coun. United Presbyn. Men, 1971—72; elder United Presbyn. Ch. in U.S.A., 1975—, mem. gen. assembly mission coun., 1972—78; chmn. mission divsn. Presbytery of Chgo., gen. coun., 1966—67, 1980—84; bd. dirs. Vocation Agy., Presbyn. Ch. in U.S.A., 1982—87. Named one of Most Outstanding Life Underwriters in the U.S. for decade of 1990s, Leaders Mag., 1999; recipient Cir. of Life award, Million Dollar Round Table Found., 1998, Huebner Scholar award, Am. Soc. CLU and ChFC, Chgo., 1995, Disting. Citizen award, Ill. St. Andrew Soc., 1998, Grauer Disting. Svc. award, Chgo. Chpt. Fin. Svc. Profls., 2000. Home: 1412 Ridge Rd Northbrook IL 60062-4628

CRUIKSHANK, THOMAS HENRY, energy services and engineering executive; b. Lake Charles, La., Nov. 3, 1931; s. Louis James and Helene L. (Little) Cruikshank; m. Ann Coe, Nov. 17, 1955; children: Thomas Henry Jr., Kate Martin, Stuart Coe. BA, Rice U., 1952; postgrad., U. Tex., 1952—53, U. Houston, 1953—55. CPA Tex.; bar: Tex. Accountant Arthur Andersen & Co., Houston, 1953-55, 58-60; mem. firm Vinson & Elkins, Houston, 1961—69; v.p. Halliburton Co., Dallas, 1969—72, sr. v.p., 1972—80, exec. v.p., 1980, pres., CEO subs. Otis Engring. Corp., 1980—81, pres., 1981—83, pres., CEO, 1983-89, chmn., CEO, 1989—95, dir., 1977—95. Former bd. dirs. Williams Cos., Goodyear Tire & Rubber Co.; former mem. Nat. Petroleum Coun.; policy com. Bus. Roundtable; dir. Lehman Bros. Holdings, Inc. Trustee Calif. Inst. Tech., 1991—95; nat. bd. dirs. Jr. Achievement, 1976—95, chmn., 1989—90; bd. dirs. Up With People, 1998—2000; Pres. Jr. Achievement, Dallas, 1974—76, chmn., 1976—78. Lt. (j.g.) USNR, 1955—58. Mem.: Am. Petroleum Inst., Tex. Bar Assn., ABA, Pine Valley Golf Club, Eldorado Country Club (Calif.), Grandfather Golf and Country Club (N.C.), Dallas Country Club. Home: 4201 Lomo Alto Dallas TX 75219 Office: 5949 Sherry Ln Dallas TX 75225-6532

CRUISE, DAVID M., SR., management consultant; BA in Bus. Adminstrn. Mktg., Samford U.; MS, Jefferson State Coll. Sales mgr. life and health divsn. Travelers Ins. Co.; sales mgr. St. Paul Cos.; mgr. major accts. and mktg. dir. Blue Cross Blue Shield Fla., Jacksonville, 1985—88; v.p. CompBenefits Corp., Atlanta, 1988—95; pres., CEO David M. Cruise Corp., Tampa, 1995—. Cons. in field; pilot's adv. bd. on avionics Honeywell, 2003. Chmn. Gainsville (Fla.) Regional Airshow Consortium, Inc., Heart of Fla. Airshow, 2005, Magical Night of the Arabian Horse, 1998; adv. bd. Amazon Vision Ministries; pres. City of Lake Mary Cmty. Assn., Fla.; police pension bd., charter rev. com. City of Lake Mary; com. chmn. Ctrl. Fla. US Bicentennial Celebration; transp. com. Ctrl. Fla. Goals 2000; tenant com. Orlando Exec. Airport, Fla.; active State of Ala. Citizen's Hwy. Commn.; exec. com. precinct chmn. Seminole County Rep. Party. Mem.: Alachua Arabian Horse Assn. (dir.). Avocation: flying. Home: 14606 NW 154th Terr Alachua FL 32615

CRUISE, TOM (THOMAS CRUISE MAPOTHER IV), actor; b. Syracuse, N.Y., July 3, 1962; s. Thomas C. III and Mary Lee Mapother; m. Mimi Rogers, May 9, 1987 (div. Feb. 4, 1990); m. Nicole Kidman, Dec. 24, 1990 (div. Aug. 8, 2001); adopted children: Isabella Jane Kidman, Connor Antony Kidman Grad. H.S., Glen Ridge, N.J. Actor: (films) Endless Love, 1981, Taps, 1981, The Outsiders, 1983, Losin' It, 1983, Risky Business, 1983 (Golden Globe nomination for best actor in a motion picture comedy/musical, 1984), All the Right Moves, 1983, Legend, 1985, Top Gun, 1986, The Color of Money, 1986, Cocktail, 1988, Rain Man, 1988, Born on the Fourth of July, 1989 (Golden Globe award for best actor in a motion picture drama, 1990, Acad. award nomination for best actor, 1990), Far and Away, 1992, A Few Good Men, 1992 (Golden Globe nomination for best actor in a motion picture drama), The Firm, 1993, Interview with the Vampire, 1994, Jerry McGuire, 1996 (Golden Globe award for best actor, 1997, Acad. Award nomination for best actor, 1997), Eyes Wide Shut, 1998, Magnolia, 1999 (Golden Globe award for best supporting actor in a motion picture, 2000, Acad. Award nomination for best supporting actor, 2000), Minority Report, 2002, Collateral, 2004, War of the Worlds, 2005; actor, prodr.: (films) Mission Impossible, 1996, Mission Impossible II, 2000, Vanilla Sky, 2001, The Last Samurai, 2003 (Golden Globe nomination for best actor, 2004); actor, writer: (films) Days of Thunder, 1990; prodr.: (films) Without Limits, 1998; exec. prodr.: (films) The Others, 2001, Narc, 2002, Shattered Glass, 2003. Named one of 50 Most Powerful People in Hollywood, Premiere mag., 2004—05; recipient Star on the Hollywood Walk of Fame, John Huston Award for Artists Rights, The Artists Rights Found., 1998.*

CRULL, JAN, JR., lawyer; b. The Netherlands; s. Jan Crull and Frederika Minderop. *Both parents were scions of Nederland's Patriciaat and Adelsboek families. According to the Dutch CBG, their families and their extended ones have been interwoven with the history, culture, and commerce of Holland for five centuries and also European history (e.g., in 1814, Dr. Wolter Crull married Scheltina van Broeckhuysen, great granddaughter of Anna Bentinck, a sister of Hans Willem Bentinck, 1st Earl of Portland, whose great grandson was a British Prime Minister, great-great grandson the 1st Governor General of India, and great-great-great-great-great granddaughter was Elizabeth A.M. Bowes-Lyon, Queen consort of George VI of Great Britain).* Grad., Lake Forest Acad.; student, Northwestern U.; BA with hons., Dalhousie U., 1975; MA, Purdue U., 1977, U. Chgo., 1984; JD, Tulane U., 1990. Intern GGvA, NYC, 1973—74; tchg. asst., grad. instr. Purdue U., 1975—76; asst. to OOTC, NYC, 1978; asst. to chpt. pres. Ramah Navajo Reservation, Pinehill, N.Mex., 1979—80; profl. staff mem. U.S. Ho. of Reps., Washington, 1981; asst. money mgr. Gulf and Occidental Investment Co. SA, Geneva, 1982, 1985—86, 1989, counsel, advisor, 1990—91; counsel, co-prin. SandCru, Inc., Chgo., 1992—; pres., gen. counsel Vigil Film Prodn. Co., L.A. and Sacramento, Calif., 1993—97; dir./counsel Von Quesar Holdings, OHG, Vienna, 1994—98, Beeltsnijder KG, Berlin, 1995—97. Developer (films) What About My Friend's Children, 1973, Not in Fiction Only: There and Here Also, 1974, A Free People, Free to Choose, 1992—93, AIDDS: American Indians' Devastating Dilemma Soon, 1993, To Mute Them Once Again, 1994, Indian Buckaroos, 1996. Author provisions for First Reauthorization of Tribally Controlled Cmty. Coll. Assistance Act 97th U.S. Congress; author spl. provisions for Native Ams. in Libr. Svcs. Constrn. Act 97th - 98th U.S. Congress. Nominee Rockefeller Pub. Svc. award, 1981. Mem.: ABA, Chgo. Coun. on Fgn. Rels., Chgo. Bar Assn., Ill. State Bar Assn., 1781 Club Netherlands Antilles, Quadrangle Club Chgo., Phi Kappa Psi. Mem. Protestant Dutch Reformed Church. Office: SandCru Inc PO Box 6637 Chicago IL 60680-6637

CRUM, ALBERT BYRD, psychiatrist, consultant; b. Omaha, Nov. 17, 1931; s. J. Rufus and Alberta (McCreary) C.; m. Rosa Maria Hennessy y Sinclair; children: Rosa Maria Crum O'Brien, Elsie Crum McCabe, Alberta Crum Fousek. BS, U. Redlands, Calif., 1953, DSc (hon.), 1974; MD, Harvard U., 1957; MS, NYU, 1987. Diplomate Am. Bd. Forensic Medicine, in Psychotherapy Am. Psychotherapy Assn., Am. Bd. Forensic Examiners. Med. intern Columbia U. divsn. Bellevue Med. Ctr., N.Y.C., 1957—58; rsch. fellow, psychiat. resident Creedmoor Inst. for Psychobiol. Studies, Queens Village, NY, 1958—59; chief, neuropsychiatric svcs. Continental Air Command Hdqs. 2500 USAF Hosp., 1959-61; psychiat. resident Columbia U. Psychiat. Inst. of Columbia-Presbyn. Hosp., N.Y.C., 1961—63; pvt. practice Brooklyn Heights, NY, 1963—. Co-chmn. U.S. Coordinating Commn. for Nomination of His Holiness the Dalai Lama of Tibet for the Nobel Peace Prize, Brooklyn Heights, 1986; chmn. Human Behavior Found., Brooklyn Heights, 1968—; chmn. selection com. Human Behavior Found.'s Albert Schweitzer Humanitarian Award, Brooklyn Heights, 1986—; expert Nat. Forensic Ctr.; pres. Stress Watchers, Inc., The ProImmune Co., LLC., Y.F. One/N.Y., Ltd., 1991—; advisor Office of Tibet, N.Y.C., 1984—; clin. prof. mgmt. sci., adj. prof. anatomy and neuroanatomy NYU, 1987-2002. Author: The 10-Step Method of Stress Relief: Decoding the Meaning and Significance of Stress, CRC Press, 2000; contbr. articles and abstracts to profl. jours. Bd. dirs. Albert Schweitzer Fellowship, N.Y.C., 1982—; bd. dirs. Burdick Internat. Ancestry Library, Sarasota, Fla., 1985—; mem., chn., bd. advisors NYU's Coll. of Dentistry, N.Y.C., 1988-96; mem. Bklyn. Heights Assn., 1970-96; class agent Harvard Med. Sch. Class of 1957; pres. Stress Watchers, Inc. Capt. USAF, 1959-61. Recipient Disting. Svc. award Bklyn. Jr. C. of C., 1966, Bicentennial award Nat. Jogging Assn., 1976; Citizen of Yr. award, Achievements in Medicine and Human Understanding, Bklyn. Philharm., 1986; named Disting. Lectr., NYU Coll. Dentistry, Omicron Kappa Upsilon lectr., 1986. Fellow Royal Coll. Physicians and Surgeons in Psychiatry; mem. Sci. Rsch. Soc. (life), Am. Acad. of Forensic Scis. (assoc.), Nat. Bd. Med. Examiners, Med. Coun. of Can., Am. Acad. Clin. Psychiatrists, Am. Physicians Art Assn., Harvard Med. Soc., Harvard Club of N.Y., MENSA (life, nat. coord. 1980-84), Phi Beta Kappa (councillor 1981-84), Sigma Xi (life) Achievements include patents for nutritional or therapeutic composition; nutritional or therapeutic supplement and method. Avocations: jogging, studying world religions, history, leadership. Home: 10 Center St Rhinebeck NY 12472 Office Phone: 845-876-3222. Personal E-mail: albertbcrum@frontierne.net.

CRUM, JAMES FRANCIS, waste recycling company executive; b. Pitts., July 23, 1934; s. Frank J. and Martha (Huffman) C.; m. Madeleine Jones, July 3, 1957 (dec. Feb. 2001); children: Cynthia Anne, James Joseph. BMechE, U. Rochester, 1956. Trainee to supt. transp. U.S. Steel Corp., Braddock, Pa., 1959-74, supt. transp. South Chgo., Ill., 1974-75, supt. operating maintenance, 1975-76, asst. divsn. supt. iron Gary, Ind., 1976-83; divsn. mgr. iron. U.S. Steel div. USX, Gary, 1983-88; exec. v.p., COO McGraw Construction Co., Middletown, Ohio, 1988-92; from dir. bus. devel. to v.p. ops. Nat. Recovery Systems, East Chicago, Ind., 1992-99, pvt. practice Flossmoor, Ill., 1999—. Adv. coun. South Suburban Hosp., 1993—; cons. in field. Vol. U. Rochester Admissions Network, N.Y., 1987—; cons. Clean City Coalition, Gary, 1988-90; bd. dirs. South Suburban Hosp. Found. Mem. AIME, Eastern States Blast Furnace Assn., Western States Blast Furnace Assn. (bd. dirs. 1985-88), Assn. Iron & Steel Engrs. Republican. Roman Catholic. Avocations: golf, photography, foreign travel, stained glass. Home: 736 Central Park Ave Flossmoor IL 60422-2220 E-mail: jfcrum@aol.com.

CRUM, JOHN KISTLER, management consultant; b. Brownsville, Tex., July 28, 1936; s. John Mears and Mary Louise (Kistler) C. BS, U. Tex., 1960, PhD, 1964; grad. Advanced Mgmt. Program, Harvard U., 1975. Research fellow Robert A. Welch Found., 1962-64; asst. editor Am. Chem. Soc., Washington, 1964-65, assoc. editor, 1966-68, mng. editor, 1969-70, group mgr. jours., 1970, dir. books and jours. div., 1971-75, treas., chief fin. officer, 1975-80, dep. exec. dir. and chief operating officer, 1981-82, exec. dir., 1983—2003; pres., CEO Quinta Assocs., LLC, 2004—. Chmn. bd. Centcom Ltd., 1983-2003, Sci. Info. Internat., Ltd., 1995-2003; chmn. governing bd. Chem. Abstracts Svc., 1991-1996, ACS publs., 1997-2003; mem. U.S. nat. com. Internat. Union Pure and Applied Chemistry; sr. mem. Con. Bd.; mem. Bretton Woods Com., 2002—; bd. dirs. Consumers Union of U.S., 1991-93. Contbr. articles to profl. jours. Fellow Washington Acad. Scis.; mem. Royal Chem. Soc. (London), Am. Chem. Soc., Am. Soc. Assn. Execs., Coun. Engring. and Sci., Soc. Execs., Assn. Sci. Soc. Editors, N.Y. Acad. Scis., Chem. Soc. Washington, Cosmos Club, City Club, Univ. Club (Washington), Chemists Club (N.Y.), Sigma Xi, Phi Theta Kappa. Republican. Home: PO Box 780 Cobbs Creek VA 23035 Office Phone: 703-528-0321. Business E-Mail: j_crum@acs.org.

CRUM, LAWRENCE LEE, banking educator; b. Brownsville, Tex., July 25, 1933; s. John Mears and Mary Louise (Kistler) Crum. BBA with highest honors (Alpha Kappa Psi scholar 1954), U. Tex., Austin, 1954, MBA, 1956, PhD, 1961; postgrad., Carnegie-Mellon U., 1962, Harvard U., 1965. Ayres fellow Am. Bankers Assn., 1966; asst. prof., then assoc. prof. U. Fla., 1959-65; mem. faculty U. Tex., Austin, 1965—, prof. fin., 1969-82, Tex. Commerce Bancshares Centennial prof. comml. banking, 1982-94, Tex. Commerce Bancshares Centennial prof. emeritus, 1994—, chmn. dept. fin., 1969-76, fellow, Ben F. Love chair in bank mgmt., 1991-93, dir. banking program, 1980-92. Chmn. bd. dirs. San Antonio br. Fed. Res. Bank, Dallas, 1980-86; cons. in comml. banking field; loan com. Franklin Lindsay Student Aid Fund, 1980-94. Author: Time Deposits in Present Day Commercial Banking, 1964, Transition in the Texas Commercial Banking Industry, 1970; co-author: The Development of State-Chartered Banking in Texas, 1978, Competition for the Commercial Banking Industry in the Establishment and Operation of an Electronic Payments System, 1971; contbr. articles to profl. jours. Fellow, Ford Found., 1963—64. Mem. Am. Fin. Assn., Am. Econ. Assn., Fin. Mgmt. Assn., Beta Gamma Sigma, Phi Kappa Phi. Republican. Presbyterian. Home: 3920 Sierra Dr Austin TX 78731-3912 Office: U Tex CBA 6 222 Austin TX 78712

CRUMB, GEORGE HENRY, composer, educator; b. Charleston, W.Va., Oct. 24, 1929; s. George Henry and Vivian (Reed) C.; m. Elizabeth May Brown, May 21, 1949; children: Elizabeth Ann, David Reed, Peter Stanley. B.Mus., Mason Coll., 1950; M.Mus., U. Ill., 1952; postgrad. (Fulbright fellow), Hochschule für Musik, Berlin, Germany, 1955-56, Berkshire Music Center, Tanglewood, Mass., summer 1955; D.Mus. Arts, U. Mich., 1959. Instr. theory Hollins Coll., Va., 1958-59; asst. prof. composition and piano U. Colo., 1959-64; creative asso. composition State U. N.Y. at Buffalo, 1964-65; asst. prof. composition U. Pa., Phila., 1965-66, asso. prof., 1966-71, prof., 1971—, Annenberg prof., 1983—. Composer: String Quartet, 1954, Sonata; for solo violoncello, 1955; Variazioni; for large orch., 1959; Five Pieces; for piano, 1962, Night Music I; for soprano, keyboard and percussion, 1963; Four Nocturnes Night Music II; for violin and piano, 1964; Madrigals, Books I and II; for solo voice and instruments, 1965; Eleven Echoes of Autumn; for violin, alto flute, clarinet and piano, 1966; Echoes of Time and the River, 1967 (Pulitzer prize 1968); for orch. Songs, Drones and Refrains of Death for baritone and electric instruments; U. Iowa commn., 1968, Madrigals, Books III and IV; for soprano and instruments, 1969; Night of the Four Moons; for alto and instruments, 1969; Black Angels (Thirteen Images from the Dark Land); for electric string quartet, U. Mich. commn., 1970; Ancient Voices of Children; for soprano and instruments, Coolidge Found. commn., 1970; Vox Balaenae; for electric flute, electric cello and electric piano, 1971; Lux Aeterna; for soprano, sitar, bass flute and two percussionists, 1971; for amplified piano Makrokosmos, Vol. I, 1972, Vol. II, 1973; Makrokosmos, Vol. I Music for a Summer Evening; for 2 amplified pianos and percussion, Fromm Found. commn., 1974; Dream Sequence; for violin, cello, piano, percussion and glass-harmonica, 1976; Star-Child: A Parable; for Solo Soprano, Antiphonal Children's Voices, Bell Ringers and Large Orch., Ford Found. Commn., 1977; Celestial Mechanics, Cosmic Dances; for Amplified Piano, 4-Hands, 1979; Apparition; elegiac songs and vocalises for soprano and amplified piano, 1979; A Little Suite for Christmas, A.D. 1979, 1980, Gnomic Variations for Piano, 1981, Pastoral Drone for Organ, 1982, Processional for piano, 1983, A Haunted Landscape for Orchestra, 1984, The Sleeper for Soprano and Piano, 1984, An Idyll for the Misbegotten for Flute and Drums, 1985; Federico's Little Songs for Children for Soprano, Flute and Harp, 1986, Zeitgeist for two amplified pianos, 1987, Easter Dawning for Carillon, 1991; also commns. Koussevitzky Found., 1964, Bowdoin Coll., 1965, U. Chgo., 1966; Quest, 1994 for guitar and chamber ensemble, Mundus Canis for Guitar and Percussion, 1997, for amplified piano, Eine Kleine Mitternachtmusik, 2002, Unto the Hills, 2002 for voice, percussion quartet and amplified piano, Otherworldly Resonances, 2002, A Journey Beyond Time, 2003, The River of LIfe, 2003. Edward MacDowell Colony medal, Peterborough, 1995. Mem. B.M.I., Nat. Inst. Arts and Letters, German Acad. Arts (hon.), Bavarian Acad. Fine Arts, Am. Acad. Arts and Scis., Pi Kappa Lambda, Phi Mu Alpha. Office: U Pa Music Bldg Philadelphia PA 19104

CRUMBAUGH, JAMES CHARLES, retired psychologist; b. Terrell, Tex., Dec. 11, 1912; s. Charles Miller and Hallie Virginia (Dansby) C.; m. Edna Mae Bailey, 1938 (dec. 1946); 1 child, Charles; m. Teresa Amanda Croteau, June 14, 1975 (dec. Feb. 1989); m. Lois Dickson Hicks, Nov. 10, 1992. AB, Baylor U., 1935; AM, So. Meth. U., 1938; PhD, U. Tex., 1953. Lic. psychologist, Miss.; cert. logotherapist. Psychologist, tchr. Memphis State U.,

1947-56; chmn. Dept. Psychology MacMurray Coll., Jacksonville, Ill., 1957-59; rsch. dir. Bradley Ctr., Inc., Columbus, Ga., 1959-64; staff psychologist VA Med. Ctr., Augusta, Ga., 1964-65, Gulfport, Miss., 1965-80; so. regional dir. Inst. Logotheraphy, Berkeley, Calif., 1980—. Rsch. cons. Internat. Graphoanalysis Soc., Chgo., 1968—. Author: Counseling for Graphoanalysts, 1970, Everything to Gain, 1973; co-author: Logotherapy, 1980; sr. author (with M.T. Manolick) The Purpose-in-Life Test, 1965; co-editor: Primer of Projective Techniques, 1990. With U.S. Army air Corps, 1941-45. Rsch. fellow Duke U., 1954-55. Mem. APA, Miss. Psychol. Assn. (Kinlock Gill award 1989), Southeastern Psychol. Assn., So. Soc. Philosophy and Psychology, Psi Chi. Roman Catholic. Avocation: writing. Home: 140 Balmoral Ave Biloxi MS 39531-4701 Office: 140A Balmoral Ave Biloxi MS 39531-4701 E-mail: texasjim2@aol.com, texasjim2004@hotmail.com.

CRUMBLEY, DONALD LARRY, finance educator, writer; b. Kannapolis, N.C., Jan. 18, 1941; s. Carl Donald and Velvia (Kelly) C.; m. Donna Darlene Loflin, Aug. 31, 1963; children: Stacey Lynn, Dana Lea, Heather Ann. BS cum laude, Pfeiffer U., 1963; MS, La. State U., 1965, PhD, 1967. CPA NC, cert. forensic acct.; diplomate Am. Bd. Forensic Accts. Grad rsch. asst. La. State U., Baton Rouge, 1963-65, tchg. asst., 1965-66; asst. prof. acctg. Pa. State U., State College, 1967-69; staff acct. Arthur Andersen & Co., N.Y.C., 1969-70; adj. asst. prof. NYU Grad. Sch. Bus., 1970; faculty resident Laventhol & Horwath, 1972; assoc. prof., dir. M. Bus. Taxation program U. So. Calif., LA, 1973-74, U. Fla., Gainesville, 1970-73, 74-75; prof. Tex. A&M U., College Station, 1975-97, Shelton prof. taxation, 1984-97; KPMG endowed prof. La. State U., Baton Rouge, 1997—. Newspaper and mag. columnist; creator Soc. for a Return to Acad. Stds., 1993—. Author: Financial Management of Your Coin-Stamp Estate, 1978, Practical Guide to Preparing a Federal Gift Tax Return, 1981, Readings in Selected Tax Problems of the Oil Industry, 1982, Handbook of Accounting for Natural Resources, 1986, Handbook of Estate Planning, 1988, Handbook of Governmental Accounting and Finance, 1988, 1992, Handbook of Financial Management for Banks, 1988, The Ultimate Rip-off: A Taxing Tale, 1999, Accosting the Golden Spire, 1989, Handbook on Financial Aspect of Divorce and Separation, 1989, Keys to Understanding the Financial News, 2000, Keys to Estate Planning and Trusts, 1989, Keys to Personal Financial Planning, 1991, Keys to Surviving a Tax Audit, 1991, Handbook of Natural Gas Accounting, 1991, Keys to Understanding Social Security Benefits, 1992; co-author: Donate Less to the IRS, 1981, Readings in Oil Industry Accounting, 1980, Estate Planning: A Guide for Advisers and Their Clients, West's Federal Taxation, 4 vols., Trap Doors and Trojan Horses, 1991, Financial Analysis, 1994, How To Manage Corporate Cash, 1994, Costly Reflections in a Midas Mirror, 1995, Barron's Guide to Tax Terms, 1995, Activity Based Costing, 1995, Deadly Art Puzzle: Accounting for Murder, 1996, The Bottom Line is Betrayal, 1995, Non-profit Sleuths: Follow the Money, 1997, Simon the Incredible: A Novel, 1998, Chemistry in Whispering Caves, 1998, Computer Encryptions in Whispering Caves, 1999, The Big R: An Internal Auditing Action Adventure, 2000, U.S. Master Auditing Guide, 2d edit., Forensic and Investigating Accounting, 2003; contbr. chpts. to books, articles to profl. publs.; editor Oil, Gas & Energy Quar., 1977—, Jour. Forensic Acctg., 1999—; co-editor Tex. Tax Services, 1983—; cons. editor Lawyers and Judges Pub. Co., Tucson; contbg. editor Hard Facts and Tax Angles; mem. editl. bd. Jour. Petroleum Acctg., Jour. Managerial Issues, Jour. East-West Bus., Forensic Examiner, Acctg. Educators' Jour., Acctg. Rev.; mem. editl. adv. bd. Advances in Acctg. Named to Alumni Hall of Fame, A.L. Brown H.S., 1972; recipient Contbn. to Cmty. award Sta. WRUF, 1972; Coll. Bus. Adminstrn. Rsch. award Tex. A&M U., 1982; Ford Found. grantee, 1966-67; Disting. Alumni award Pfeiffer Coll., 1972; Arthur Young rsch. grantee, 1984-85. Mem. Am. Taxation Assn. (pres. 1974-75, trustee 1975-77, founder), Am. Inst. CPA's, Am. Acctg. Assn., Nat. Taxation Assn., Am. Tax Assn. (founding pres.), Govt. Fin. Officers' Assn., Tex. Soc. CPA's, La. Soc. CPA's, Numis. Lit. Guild, Order of Sundial, Phi Kappa Phi, Beta Gamma Sigma, Beta Alpha Psi. Methodist. Office: La State U Dept Acctg 3101 CEBA Bldg Baton Rouge LA 70803-0001 Office Phone: 225-578-6231. Business E-Mail: dcrumbl@lsu.edu.

CRUMBLEY, ESTHER HELEN KENDRICK, retired real estate agent, retired secondary school educator, councilman; b. Okeechobee, Fla., Oct. 3, 1928; d. James A. and Corrine (Burney) Kendrick; m. Chandler Jackson, Oct. 24, 1949 (dec.); children: Pamela E., Chandler A., William J. BS in Math. Edn., Ga. So. Coll., 1966; M in Math., Jacksonville (Fla.) U., 1979. Cert. secondary edn. tchr., Ga. Secondary edn. tchr. Camden County Bd. Edn., St. Mary's, Ga., 1958-92, ret.; realtor Watson Realty, St. Mary's, 1985-98, ret., 1998. Dept. chairperson Camden H.S., St. Mary's, 1966-72. Reporter: for hometown newspaper. Councilwoman City of St. Mary's, 1979-86, mayor pro tem, 1981-86. Mem. Camden Ga. Assn. Educators (pres. 1976, sec.-treas. 1977-78, star tchr. 1972), PAGE (biog. com. rep. 1984-92, 1992 retired, named outstanding 8th dist. bldg. rep.), Camden Gen. Mcpl. Assn. (pres., sec.-treas. 1979-88), fin. and budget coms.), Math. Assn., Internat. Platform Assn. Internat. Dictionary Ctr., ABI. Republican. Baptist. Avocations: reading, art. Home: RR 3 Box 810 Folkston GA 31537-9729 *Hard work, perseverance and determination will get you to any goal in life. Put God first, country and family in that order. Can't should not be in your vocabulary.*

CRUMBLING, DEANA MARIE, environmental scientist; b. Moses Lake, Wash., Oct. 2, 1958; d. Dean Arthur and Fayalene Rae (Kunkel) C. AA in Life Scis., Harrisburg Area C.C., 1986; BA in Psychology, BS in Biochemistry, Lebanon Valley Coll., 1989; MS in Environ. Sci., Drexel U., 1997. Med. technologist several hosps., Pa., Va., 1977-87; rsch. technician Weiss Ctr. Rsch./Geisinger Clinic, Danville, Pa., 1988-89; chemist United Tech. Assn., Hershey (Pa.) Foods, 1989-90; environ. chemist Pa. Dept. Environ. Resources, Harrisburg, 1990-91; rsch. asst. Drexel U., Phila., 1991-93; med. technologist West Jersey Health System, Voorhees, N.J., 1991-97; asst. environ. scientist Woodward-Clyde Cons., Phila., 1995-96; lab. mgr., mem. adj. faculty Sch. Sci. and Health, Phila. Coll. Textiles and Sci., 1996-97; phys. scientist Superfund Remediation and Tech. Innovation EPA, Washington, 1997—. Gay-rights activist, spokesperson Pa. Justice Campaign, Harrisburg, 1990, 91. Recipient Andrew Bender Meml. Chemistry award Lebanon Valley Coll., Annville, Pa., 1989, Jean O. Love Meml. award Psychology, 1989. Mem. AAAS, Am. Chem. Soc., Am. Inst. Biol. Sci., Soc. Environ. Toxicology and Chemistry, Environ. Def. Fund, Natural Resources Def. Coun., Sierra Club. Democrat. Avocations: canoeing, camping, needlecrafts, snorkeling. Office: EPA (5102G) 1200 Pennsylvania Ave NW Washington DC 20460 Home: 4534 Eaton Pl Alexandria VA 22310-2028 Office Phone: 703-603-0643. Business E-Mail: crumbling.deana@epa.gov.

CRUMLEY, DAVID OLIVER, publishing executive, writer, corporate executive; b. New Orleans, May 18, 1949; s. David Shiffer III and Martha Ann (Carey) C. BA, Tulane U., 1974. Sec., editor The Social Dir. of Greater New Orleans, Inc., 1975-77, pres., pub., 1977-92. Pres. Laser Documentation Inc. Author, historian: Reflection of Life in New Orleans: Architecture & Interior Decoration as Historical, Social & Cultural Commentary, 1970; pub., author: Mardi Gras in New Orleans 1971, 1971; researcher Town & Country, 1979. Historian hist. marker Ashland Plantation, 1969, La Maison Blanche Plantation, 1974; co-founder Soc. Huguenot A Nouvelle, New Orleans, 1973, The Grand Priory of the South, The Mil. and Hospitaller Order of St. Lazarus of Jerusalem, New Orleans, 1976; vestry Mt. Olivet Episc. Ch., 1971-90, jr. warden of vestry, 1976-88, sr. warden of vestry, 1989. Internat. Rels. scholar Tulane U., 1974. Mem. Sons of the Revolution (genealogist La chpt. 1974-88), Societe Huguenot A Nouvelle Orleans (bd. dirs. 1973—), Soc. of the War of 1812 (vice-genealogist La. chpt. 1974-80), Royal Soc. of St. George (bd. dirs. New Orleans chpt. 1974-76), Soc. Colonial Wars (dep. genealogist La. chpt. 1974-77, 79-88, genealogist La. chpt. 1977-79), SAR (genealogist George Washington chpt. 1986-87), La. Hist. Soc., Masons. Avocation: reading. Office: Social Dir of Greater New Orleans Inc 4403 Maple Leaf Dr New Orleans LA 70131-7455

CRUMLEY, JAMES ROBERT, JR., retired bishop; b. Bluff City, Tenn., Mar. 30, 1925; s. James Robert and Ida Frances (Fine) C.; m. Sara Annette Bodie, May 26, 1950; children: Frances Crumley Holman, James Robert, Jeanne Crumley Lindemann. BA, Roanoke Coll., 1948, DD (hon.), 1973; MDiv, Luth. Theol. So. Sem., Columbia, S.C., 1951; DD (hon.), Newberry (S.C.) Coll., 1971, Augustana Coll., 1982, Muhlenberg Coll., Allentown, Pa., 1983; LLD (hon.), Susquehanna U., Selinsgrove, Pa., 1977; LHD (hon.), Lenoir-Rhyne Coll., Hickory, N.C., 1979; LittD (hon.), Bethany Coll., 1981; LHD (hon.), Manhattan Coll., 1984, U. S.C., 1987. Ordained to ministry Luth. Ch., 1951. Pastor chs. in, Greenville and Oak Ridge, Tenn., Savannah, Ga., 1951-74; sec. Luth. Ch. in Am., N.Y.C., 1974-78, bishop, 1978-88. Vis. prof. ecumenism Luth. Theol. So. Sem., Columbia, S.C., 1988, ret., 1993. Lutheran. Home: 362 Little Creek Dr Leesville SC 29070-9379 E-mail: jcrum362@aol.com.

CRUMLEY, MARTHA ANN, charity fundraising executive; b. New Orleans, Aug. 8, 1910; d. Mark Oliver and Mary Elizabeth (Schroder) Carey; m. David Shiffer Crumley III, May 7, 1947; 1 child, David Oliver. Pres., chief exec. officer Westbank Acad., Gretna, La., 1953-68; sr. v.p. The Social Directory Greater New Orleans, Inc., 1975-92, pres., 1992-94. Pres. Algiers Little Theatre, New Orleans, 1930; tchr. speech and drama YWCA, New Orleans, 1938-39, producer, dir. plays, 1938-39; prs. Krewe of Aparamest, New Orleans, 1938; chmn. fundraising New Orleans Philharmonic Symphony, New Orleans, 1967; mem. women's vol. com. New Orleans Mus. Art, 1967-68; dir. sr. and jr. choir Mt. Olivet Episcopal Ch., New Orleans, 1922-83, mem. altar guild, 1922-83; pres. Mt. Olivet's Women Aux., New Orleans, 1950; mem. women's guild New Orleans Philharmonic. Mem. DAR, English Speaking Union, La. Landmark Soc., Friends of the Cabildo, Children of the Am. Revolution (sr. prs. 1969), Colonial Dames XVII Century (pres. La. chpt. 1977). Home: 4403 Maple Leaf Dr New Orleans LA 70131-7455

CRUMLEY, ROGER LEE, surgeon, educator, otolaryngologist; b. Perry, Iowa, Oct. 8, 1941; s. Dwight Moody and Helen Ethelwyn (Anderson) C.; m. Janet Lynn Conant, Nov. 13, 1987; children: Erin Kelly Helen, Danielle Nicole. BA, Simpson Coll., 1964; MS, U. Iowa, 1975, MD, 1967; MBA, U. Phoenix, 1999. Diplomate Am. Bd. Otolaryngology (dir. 1992—2004). Intern L.A. County Gen. Hosp., 1967-68; resident in surgery Highland-Alameda Hosp., Oakland, Calif., 1968-69; bn. surgeon 1st Marine Div., Vietnam, 1968-69; resident in otolaryngology U. Iowa, Iowa City, 1971-75; chief otolarygology San Francisco Gen. Hosp., 1975-81; assoc. prof., then prof. U. Calif., San Francisco, 1981-87, prof., chief otolaryngology-head and neck surgery Irvine, 1987—. Guest prof. Humboldt U., East Berlin, 1982, M.S. McLeod vis. prof. S. Australian Postgrad. Edn. Ctr., Adelaide, 1988; treas., pres. Am. Acad. Facial Plastic Surgeons, 1994-95, Triological Soc., 2002-03; McBride lectr. U. Edinburgh, 1998. Contbr. articles and book chpts. to profl. publs. With USN, 1969-71, Vietnam. Recipient Alumni Achievement award Simpson Coll., 1984. Fellow ACS, Am. Acad. Otolaryngology (bd. dirs. 1988—, award 1989); mem. Soc. Univ. Otolaryngologists, Triological Soc. (pres. 2002-), Bohemian Club (San Francisco), Center Club (Costa Mesa, Calif.). Republican. Methodist. Avocations: music, piano, jazz flûgelhorn, running, skiing. Office: U Calif-Irvine Med Ctr Dept Otolaryngology Head & Neck 101 The City Dr S Orange CA 92868-3201 Office Phone: 714-456-5750. Business E-Mail: rcrumley@uci.edu.

CRUMP, CLAUDIA, geographer, educator; BS in Elem. Edn., Western Ky. U., 1952; MS in Elem. Edn., Ind. U., 1957, EdD in Elem. Edn., 1969. Co-author: Teaching for Social Values in Social Studies, 1974, Indiana Map Studies, 1983, Indiana Yesterday and Today, 1985, Teaching History in the Elementary School, 1988, People in Time and Place: Indiana Hoosier Heritage, 1992. Recipient First Educator of Yr. award, Nat. Coun. Internat. Visitors, 2005. Home: 309 Whippoorwill Hts New Albany IN 47150-4255 Office: Ind U Southeast Sch Edn New Albany IN 47150 E-mail: ccrump700@cs.com.

CRUMP, GERALD FRANKLIN, retired lawyer; b. Sacramento, Feb. 16, 1935; s. John Laurin and Ida May (Banta) C.; m. Glenda Roberts Glass, Nov. 21, 1959; children: Sara Elizabeth, Juliane Kathryn, Joseph Stephen. AB, U. Calif., Berkeley, 1956; JD, U. Calif., 1959; MA, Baylor U., 1966. Bar: Calif. 1960. Dep. county counsel L.A. County, 1963-73, legis. rep., 1970-73, chief pub. works div., 1973-84, sr. asst. county counsel, 1984-85, chief asst. county counsel, 1985-97; ret., 1997. Lectr. Pepperdine U., 1978, U. Calif., 1982. Former v.p. San Fernando Valley Girl Scout Coun. Served to capt. USAF, 1960-63; to maj. gen. USAFR, 1963-95, ret.; mobilization asst. to the JAG. Decorated DSM, Legion of Merit. Mem. ABA, State Bar Calif., L.A. County Bar Assn. (past chmn. trustee govtl. law sect., past mem.exec. com. litig. sect.), Air Force Assn., Res. Officers Assn., Phi Alpha Delta, Delta Sigma Phi. Home: 4020 Camino De La Cumbre Sherman Oaks CA 91423-4522

CRUMP, JOHN, lawyer; Exec. dir. Nat. Bar Assn., Washington. Office: Nat Bar Assn 1225 11th St NW Washington DC 20001-4217*

CRUMP-CAINE, LYNN, food service executive; Mgmt. trainee McDonald's Corp., Oakbrook, Ill., 1975—77, various regional dept. head positions Norfolk, Nashville, S. Fla., 1977—85, head worldwide restaurant systems and U.S. restaurant systems, 1985—97, regional v.p. Atlanta region Oakbrook, 1997—2001, exec. v.p. worldwide ops. and systems, 2001—. Mem. adv. bd. Women Looking Ahead News Magazine; bd.dirs. Goodman Theater, Chgo. Recipient Outstanding Bus. and Profl. award, Dollars and Sense, 1991. Mem.: NAFE, McDonald's Black Employee Network. Office: McDonald's Corp McDonald's Plz Oak Brook IL 60523

CRUMPTON, HANK (HENRY CRUMPTON), federal agency administrator; b. Athens, Ga. BA in Polit. Sci., U. N. Mex.; M in Internat. Pub. Policy, John Hopkins U. Dep. chief internat. terrorism ops. FBI U.S. Dept. Justice, Washington, 1998—99; dep. chief counter terrorism ctr., spl. ops. CIA, 1999—2001, chief nat. resources divsn., 2003—05; amb. at large, coord. counter terrorism dept. U.S. Dept. State, 2005—. Recipient George H.W. Bush award for excellence in counter terrorism, Sherman Kent award, Donovan award, others. Office: US Dept of State Harry S Truman Bldg 2201 C Street NW Rm 2509 Washington DC 20520 Office Phone: 202-647-9892. Office Fax: 202-647-9256.*

CRUMPTON, P. SUE, think-tank executive; d. Lee Homer Englett and Sally Belle Scott; children: Danie Sue King, Nicholas Mark, William Paul. Pub. Adminstrn., Pk. U., Parkville, Mo., 2003—. Coord. East Ctrl. Bd., Kans. City, Mo., 1972—76; svc. mgr. Youth Diversion Project of City of Kans. City, Kans. City, Mo., 1976—80; mediator/arbitrator Justice Ctr./Kans. City Human Rels. Dept., Kans. City, Mo., 1977—84; program dir. Minute Cir. Friendly Ho., Kans. City, Mo., 1980—85; exec. dir. Ho. of Ruth, Claremont, Calif., 1985—91; dir. agy. rels. Arrowhead United Way, San Bernardino, Calif., 1990—91; exec. dir. LA Shanti, L.A., 1991—98, Nebr. AIDS Project, Omaha, 1998—2001; dir. of ops. Met. Luth. Ministry, Kans. City, Mo., 2000—01; exec. dir. Columbus AIDS Task Force, Columbus, Ohio, 2001—03; coord. AYUSA, Kansas City, Mo., 2003—04; exec. dir. Cmty. Svcs. League, Independence, Mo., 2004—. Ohio statewide hiv/aids coordinating coun. State of Ohio Health Dept., Columbus, Ohio, 2002—03; bd. mem. AIDS Action Coun., Washington, LA HIV Planning Coun., L.A., Calif., 1992—95, So. CA Coalition on Battered Women, Santa Monica, Calif., 1985—92; chair coun. of exec. Mt. Baldy United Way, Ontario, Calif., 1987—89; bd. mem. State of Calif. Office of Criminal Justice Tech. Adv. Com., Sacramento, 1990—90; mem. San Bernardino County FEMA Bd., Ontario, Calif., 1989—91; bd. mem. & chair program com. United Svcs. of Greater Kans. City, Kans. City, Mo., 1979—84. Bd. mem./chair of program com. united svc.; cmty. activist hiv/aids svcs. Recipient Commendation City of Kans. City, Key to the City, 1984, Commendation Jackson County, Mo., 1984, Commendation City of W. Hollywood Calif., Commendation City of Independence, Mo., 1984, Commendation Clay County, Mo., 1984, Commendation Cass County, Mo., 1984. Mem.: Am. Soc. of Pub. Adminstrn. (assoc.). Liberal. Unity. Avocations: reading, art, movies, writing. Office: Cmty Svcs League 300 W Maple Independence MO 64051 Home Fax: 816-252-9906. Personal E-mail: psuec@earthlink.net. Business E-Mail: crumptons@communityserv.org.

CRUNDWELL, DUNCAN JAMES, electronics executive; b. Maidstone, Kent, Eng., Mar. 18, 1957; arrived in US, 1995; s. James Stanley and June (Reid) Crundwell; m. Bridgette Grieve, Dec. 24, 1983 (div. Jan. 1995); 1 child, Ben; m. Natasha Shankova, May 12, 1995. BSME, Brunel U., London, 1979; MBA, Henley Mgmt. Coll., Eng., 1996. Charterd engr. Student engr. Dowty Group, Cheltenham, Eng., 1975-79; chief engr. Yamco, London, 1979-80; tech. mgr. Bandive, London, 1980-84; custom projects mgr. Solid State Logic, Oxford, Eng., 1984-86, systems mgr., 1986-88, product group mgr., 1988-90; mng. dir. Solid State Logic Organ Systems, Brandon, Eng., 1990-95, CEO, pres. Detroit, 1995—2002, 1602 Group LLC, Alexandria, Va., 2002—; founding ptnr. People Going Global LLC, 2000—. Tchr. Opening Windows Engring., Oxford Schs., 1988—91; client, project mgr. new hdqs. bldg. Solid State Logic. Prodr.: (radio program) Glad to Be Gay or Not?, 1977 (UK Local Radio award, 1977). Recipient award, Royal Inst. Brit. Archs., 1989, Dir. Gen.'s cert., Engring. Coun., London, 1990. Mem.: Instn. Mech. Engrs. (chmn. YM panel 1988—89, sec. 1987—88, Outstanding Project Work award 1979). Anglican. Achievements include inventor in field. Avocations: photography, architecture, music, fine art. Home: 1501 N Highview Ln # 412 Alexandria VA 22311-2036 Office: 1602 Group LLC 4900 Seminary Rd Ste 560 Alexandria VA 22311-1009

CRUSE, FREDRICH JAMES, lawyer; b. Marysville, Calif., Sept. 7, 1947; s. Monta Parish and Jennie Ruth (Cudworth) C.; m. Nancy Kay Kress, Dec. 30, 1967; 1 child, Jason Alan. AB, William Jewel Coll., 1969; JD, U. Mo., Kansas City, 1973; postdoctoral, U. Va., 1974-75. Bar: Mo. 1974, U.S. Dist. Ct. (we. dist.) Mo. 1974, U.S. Ct. Mil. Appeals 1975, U.S. Dist. Ct. (ea. dist.) Mo. 1977, U.S. Supreme Ct. 1977, Ill. 1982, Utah 1987, U.S. Dist. Ct. Utah 1987, U.S. Dist. Ct. (cen. dist.) Ill. 1989. Pub. defender 10th Jud. Cir., Hannibal, Mo., 1977-80; sole practice Hannibal, 1981-87; ptnr. Cruse, Dempsey, Dempsey & Riggs, P.C., Hannibal, 1987-95; prin. The Cruse Law Firm, P.C., 1995—. V.p. Mo. State Pub. Defender's Assn., Jefferson City, 1979; pres. Mark Twain Area Title Ins. Co., Hannibal, 1986-98. Pres., drive chmn. United Way of Hannibal, 1978-80; dist. chmn., scoutmaster, varsity coach Boy Scouts Am., Hannibal, 1979—, mem. exec. bd. Great Rivers coun.; atty. City of Hannibal, 1981-85. Capt. JAGC, USMC, 1974-77. Recipient Vigil Honor Order of Arrow, Boy Scouts Am., 1984, Dist. Award of Merit, Mark Twain dist., Boy Scouts Am., 1985, Scoutmaster Award of Merit, 1989, Silver Beaver award, 1997. Mem. ABA, Ill. State Bar Assn., Utah Bar Assn., Nat. Assn. Bankruptcy Trustees (bd. dirs. 1990-2002, sec., treas. 1992-94), Mo. Bar Assn. (chmn. econs. and methods of practice com. 1984-87, chmn. non-urban lawyer com. 1982-84), Mo. Trial Lawyers Assn., Kiwanis (Disting. Pres. award 1980-81). Democrat. Mem. Ch. LDS. Avocations: restoring old houses, backpacking. Home: 9 Stillwell Pl Hannibal MO 63401-3462 Office: 718 Broadway PO Box 914 Hannibal MO 63401-0914 Office Phone: 573-221-1333. Business E-Mail: fcruse@cruselaw.com.

CRUSE, HOWARD, writer, illustrator; b. Birmingham, May 2, 1944; s. Jesse Clyde and Irma Russell Cruse; life ptnr. Ed Sedarbaum, Apr. 15, 1979. BFA, Birmingham-So. Coll., 1968. Staff artist WAPI-TV, Birmingham, 1964—65, The Birmingham News, 1967—68; art dir. & puppeteer WBMG-TV, 1969—73; actor & scenic artist Atlanta Children's Theatre, Atlanta, 1973—74; prodn. artist The Luckie Co., Birmingham, 1975—76; art dir. Starlog Mag., N.Y.C., 1977—78; cartooning instr. NY Sch. Visual Arts, 2001—03. Author (illustrator): Wendel All Together, Barefootz Funnies, Tops & Button, Stuck Rubber Baby (Eisner award, 1996, Harvey award, 1996), Early Barefootz, Wendel On The Rebound, Dancin' Nekkid With The Angels, Wendel, Loose Cruse, Count Fangor; co-author, illustrator (with Jeanne E. Shaffer) The Swimmer with a Rope in his Teeth. Individual activist Gay Rights Movement, N.Y.C., 1977—2003. Co-recipient Stonewall Award, 1994. Avocations: playwright, stage director, actor. Home: PO Box 100 North Adams MA 01247 Personal E-mail: howard@howardcruse.com. E-mail: howardcruse@verizon.net.

CRUSE, JULIUS MAJOR, JR., pathologist, educator; b. New Albany, Miss., Feb. 15, 1937; s. Julius Major and Effie (Davis) C. BA, BS with honors, U. Miss., 1958; DMS with honors, U. Graz, Austria, 1960; MD, U. Tenn., 1964, PhD in Pathology (USPHS fellow), 1966, USPHS postdoctoral fellow, 1964-67; DD (hon.), Gen. Theol. Sem., N.Y., 1999. Prof. immunology and biology Grad. Sch. U. Miss., 1967—74, prof. pathology, 1974—, assoc. prof. microbiology, 1974—, dir. grad. studies program in pathology, 1974—, dir. clin. immunopathology, 1978—, dir. immunopathology sect., 1978—, dir. tissue typing lab., 1980—, assoc. prof. medicine, 1989—, disting. prof. history medicine Med. Sch., 2003—, Guyton disting prof., 2004—. Lectr. pathology U. Tenn. Coll. Medicine, 1967-74; adj. prof. immunology Miss. Coll., 1977-1992; mem. NIH study section on transplantation immunology, 1992; mem. sci. adv. bd. Immuno Tech. Corp., L.A.; active FDA Expert Panel on Alternatives to Silicone Breast Implants, 1994—. Author: Immunology Examination Review Book, 1971, rev. edit., 1975, Introduction to Immunology, 1977, Principles of Immuno-pathology, 1979; editor-in-chief Immunologic Rsch., 1981—, Pathology and Immunopathology Rsch., 1982-90, Concepts in Immunopathology, 1985—, The Year in Immunology, 1984—, Pathobiology: Jour. Immunopathology, Molecular and Cellular Biology, 1990-98, Exptl. & Molecular Pathology, 1999—, Transgenics: Biological Analysis Through DNA Transfer, 1992-; immunology cons.: Dorland's Illustrated Medical Dictionary, 1967-1994; contbns. to Microbiology and Immunology; editor Immunomodulation of Neoplasia, Antigenic Variation: Molecular and Genetic Mechanisms of Relapsing Disease, 1987, Autoimmunoregulation and Autoimmune Disease, 1987; The Year in Immunology, vol. 1, 1984-85, vol. 2, 1985-86, The Year in Immunology, vol. 3, 1987, The Year in Immunology, vols. 4, 5, 1988, vol. 6, 1989-90, Genetic Basis of Autoimmune Disease, 1988, Cellular Aspects of Autoimmunity, 1988, Therapy of Autoimmune Diseases, 1989, B Lymphocytes: Function and Regulation, Conjugate Vaccines, 1989, Molecules and Cells of Immunity, 1990, Immunoregulation and Autoimmunity, 1986, Organ-Based Autoimmune Diseases, 1985, Autoimmunity: Basic Concepts, Systemic and Selected Organ-Specific Diseases, 1985, Clinical and Molecular Aspects of Autoimmune Diseases, 1990, Immunoregulatory Cytokines and Cell Growth, 1989, Complement Profiles, 1992; co-editor: Self-Nonself Discrimination in the Immune System, 1992, Complement Profiles, vol. 1, 1992, Illustrated Dictionary of Immunology, 1995, 2d edit., 2003, Atlas of Immunology, 1998, 2d edit., 2003, Immunology Guidebook, 2004, T.S. Eliot Bibliography, 2003, Historical Atlas of Immunology, 2005; contbr. chpts. to books and articles to profl. jours; editor-in-chief: Experimental and Molecular Pathology, 1999—. Recipient Pathologists award in continuing edn. Coll. Am. Pathologists-Am. Soc. Clin. Pathologists, 1976; Julius M. Cruse collection in immunology established in his honor Middleton Med. Libr., U. Wis., Madison, 1979, Julius M. Cruse collection of T.S. Eliot's works, St. Mark's Libr., Gen. Theol. Sem. (Episcopal), N.Y.C., Julius M. Cruse collection in history of immunology Rowland Med. Libr., U. Miss. Med. Ctr., 2004; Wilson Found. grantee, 1990-95, 93-94, 95-98, 99-2003; B.S. Guyton lectr. on history of medicine, 1998; Fulbright scholar U. Graz, Austria, 1958-60. Fellow AAAS, Royal Soc. Medicine, Royal Soc. Promotion Health, Am. Acad. Microbiology, Am. Soc. for Histocompatibility and Immunogenetics (chmn. publs. com. 1987-95, councillor 1997-99, historian 2000—), Intercontinental Biog. Assn.; mem. AMA (Physicians Recognition award 196-75), Clin. Immunology Soc., Am. Inst. Biol. Scis., Am. Soc. Clin. Pathologists, Can. Soc. Microbiologists, N.Y. Acad. Scis. Exptl. Biology and Medicine, Am. Diabetes Assn., Soc. Francaise d'Immunologie, Reticuloendothelial Soc., Transplantation Soc., Electron Microscopy Soc. Am., Am. Assn. History Medicine, The Paul Ehrlich Soc., Am. Soc. Investigative Pathology, Am. Assn. Pathologists, Am. Chem. Soc., Brit. Soc. Immunology, Can. Soc. Immunology, Am. Soc. Microbiology, Internat. Acad. Pathology, Am. Assn. Immunologists (historian 1990—), T.S. Eliot Soc., Sigma Xi, Phi Kappa Phi, Phi Eta Sigma, Alpha Epsilon Delta, Gamma Sigma Epsilon, Phi Chi. Anglo-Catholic. Office: U Miss Med Ctr Dept Pathology 2500 N State St Jackson MS 39216-4500 Office Phone: 601-984-1565. Business E-Mail: jcruse@pathology.umsmed.edu.

CRUSEMANN, F. ROSS (FREDERICK ROSS CRUSEMANN), advertising agency official; b. Ft. Worth, Nov. 9, 1953; s. Frederick Ross and Louise (Russell) C. BA, Austin Coll., 1975; MBA, Tex. Christian U., 1977. Supr. Ben

E. Keith Co., Ft. Worth, 1977-78; project dir. Parmer Cos., Ft. Worth, 1978-80; mktg. mgr. Shoreline Products, Ft. Worth, 1980-85; mktg. cons. Dallas, 1986; mgr. programs visibility FW divsn. Gen. Dynamics, Ft. Worth, 1986-89; dir. mktg. Motel 6, Dallas, 1989-94; v.p. Peter A. Mayer Advt., Baton Rouge, 1994—2003; sr. v.p. mktg. Dalla Conv. and Visitors Bur., 2003—. Sponsor Spl. Olympics Internat., Washington, 1992-94, Dallas Symphony Assn., 1992—, Sta. KERA-PBS Affiliation, Dallas, 1993—. Recipient Commendation award Radio Advt. Bur., N.Y.C., 1993; named Am. Advt. Assn. Ad Person of Yr., New Orleans Ad Club, 1998 Mem. Am. Mktg. Assn. (Tomy award 1989), Assn. Nat. Advertisers (com. chmn. 1989—), Travel Industry Assn. (com. mem. 1992—, nat. conf. planning com. 1992—, POW WOW internat. planning com. 1993—), Am. Hotel and Motel Assn. (comms. com. 1991—), Hotel Sales and Mktg. Assn. Internat. (Adrian award 1989—). Avocations: skiing, water-skiing, bicycling, cooking. Home: 7110 Twin Tree Ln Dallas TX 75214-1938 Office: Dallas Conv and Visitors Bur 325 N St Paul St Ste 700 Dallas TX 75201 Office Phone: 214-571-1075. E-mail: rcrusemann@dallascvb.com.

CRUSIE, JENNIFER, writer, literature educator; b. Wapakoneta, Ohio, Sept. 17, 1949; d. Jack Eldon and JoAnn Katherine Smith; m. Mollie Amanda Smith. BS in Art Edn., Bowling Green (Ohio) State U., 1973; MA in Feminist Criticism, Wright State U., 1986; MFA in Fiction, Ohio State U., 1996. From elem. art coord. to HS English tchr. Beavercreek (Ohio) Schs., 1977—87, HS English tchr., 1987—92; instr. Ohio State U., Columbus, Ohio, 1992—. Instr. Antioch Coll., Yellow Springs, Ohio, 1985; English tchg. asst. Wright State U., Fairborn, Ohio, 1985—87; instr. Ohio State U., 1987, Antioch Coll., 2001. Author: Manhunting, 1993, Getting Rid of Bradley, 1994, Strange Bedpersons, 1995, What the Lady Wants, 1996, Anyone But You, 1997, The Cinderella Deal, 1996, Trust Me On This, 1997, Tell Me Lies, 1998, Crazy For You, 1999, We Come To Temptation, 2000, Fast Women, 2001, Faking It, 2002; contbr. essays to mags., 1996. Mem.: Author's Guild, Romance Writers of Am. (pub. author liason 1998, nat. bd. dirs. 1999—2000, Rita award 1995). Office: c/o Jane Rotrosen Agency 318 E 51st St New York NY 10022

CRUSTO, MITCHELL FERDINAND, lawyer, educator; b. New Orleans, Apr. 22, 1953; BA magna cum laude, Yale U., 1975; BA, Oxford U., Eng., 1980, MA, 1985; JD, Yale U., 1981. Bar: La. 1982, Mo. 1984, Ill. 1985. Law clk. to Hon. John M. Wisdom U.S. Ct. Appeals (5th cir.), New Orleans, 1981-82; assoc. Jones, Walker, Waechter, Pointevent, Carrere & Denegre, New Orleans, 1982-84; sr. v.p., gen. counsel, asst. corp. sec. Stifel, Nicolaus & Co., Inc., St. Louis, 1984-88; CEO Crusto Capital Resources, Inc., St. Louis, 1988-89; assoc. dep. adminstr. for fin., investment and procurement U.S. Small Bus. Adminstrn., Washington, 1989-91; dir. corp. environ. policy Monsanto Co., St. Louis, 1991-93; sr. mgr. Arthur Andersen Environ. Svcs., Chgo., 1993-95; prof. Loyola Sch. Law, New Orleans, 1995—. Vis. prof. Vt. Law Sch., summers 2000-2003, Washington U. Sch. Law, summer 1999; mem. faculty Washington U., St. Louis, 1985-89, St. Louis U. Law Sch., 1987-88, Webster U., St. Louis, 1986; securities advisor to sec. of state State of Mo., 1986-89; lectr. legal divsn. Securities Industry Assn., 1986-88; mem. Pres. Clinton transition team natural resource cluster EPA, 1992; owner Angelic Asset Mgmt., 1998—. Contbr. articles in newspapers, mags., jours. Mem. ABA, La. Bar Assn., Mo. Bar Assn., Ill. Bar Assn., Middle Temple (London). Home: PO Box 791719 New Orleans LA 70179-1719 Office: Loyola U Sch Law 7214 Saint Charles Ave # 901 New Orleans LA 70118-3538 Office Phone: 504-861-5743. Business E-Mail: mfcrusto@loyno.edu.

CRUTCHER, MICHAEL BAYARD, lawyer, consumer products company executive; b. Seattle, Apr. 7, 1944; s. M. Bayard and Marjorie (Sandstrom) C.; m. Judith Johnston, Aug 26, 1967; children: Alexandra, Andrew, Charles. BA, Yale U., 1966; JD, Harvard U., 1969. Bar: Wash. 1969, Ky. 1990. Assoc. Preston, Thorgrimson, Ellis & Holman, Seattle, 1969-73, ptnr., 1974-89; sr. v.p., gen. counsel, sec. Brown-Forman Corp., Louisville, 1989—2003, vice chmn., gen. counsel, sec., 2003—. Bd. dirs. Distilled Spirits Coun. U.S., 1991-99, chmn., 1992-94; chmn. Internat. Ctr. Info. on Beverage Alcohol, 1994-95, Internat. Ctr. Alchohol Policy, 1996-97, Louisville Fund for Arts, 2004-; trustee Bellarmine U., 2003-. Mem. Jefferson Club, Owl Creek Country Club, Persimmon Ridge Golf Club. Republican. Office: Brown-Forman Corp 850 Dixie Hwy Louisville KY 40210-1091 Office Phone: 502-774-7631.

CRUTCHER, RONALD ANDREW, music educator, academic administrator; b. Cin., Feb. 27, 1947; s. Andrew James and Burdella (Miller) C.; m. Betty Joy Neal, Nov. 24, 1979; 1 child, Sara Elizabeth. BM, Miami U., 1969; M in Musical Arts, Yale U., 1972; Diploma, State Acad. Music, Frankfurt, Germany, 1976; D in Musical Arts, Yale U., 1979. Cello instr. Bonn Sch. Music, Germany, 1973-76; asst. prof., head string program Wittenberg U. Sch. of Music, Springfield, Ohio, 1977-79; asst. prof. U. NC, Greensboro, 1979-84, assoc. prof., coord. string area, 1984—88, acting asst. vice chancellor academic affairs, 1988-89, assoc. vice chancellor academic affairs/faculty devel. and instrn., 1989-90; v.p. academic affairs, dean of conservatory, mem. chamber and cello music faculties Cleve. Inst. Music, 1990-94; dir. Sch. of Music U. Tex., Austin, 1994—99, Marie and Joseph D. Jamail Sr. Regents Prof. in Fine Arts, 1994—98, Florence Thelma Hall Chair in Music, 1998—99; provost, exec. v.p. academic affairs, prof. music Miami U., Ohio, 1999—2004; pres. Wheaton Coll., Norton, Mass., 2004—. Bd. dirs. Chamber Music Am., NY, 1993—01, v.p., 1994-96, pres., 1996-2000; bd. dirs. Fulbright Assn., 1998-2002, OhioLINK, 1999-; bd. dirs. Assn. Am. Colls. and Univs., 2000-, mem. exec. com., 2003-, chair, 2005—; mem. coun. acad. affairs Nat. Assn. State Univs. and Land Grant Colls., 2001-04, vice chair 2004-05, chair 2005-; bd. dirs. Cin. Opera Assn. 2001-04; mem. commn. on accreditation Nat. Assn. Schs. Music, Reston, Va., 1993—99; mem. adv. coun. Chgo. Civic Orch., 1994—96; mem. exec. com. Austin Symphony Orch., 1994—99; trustee Cavani Quartet, 1994-; trustee Musical Arts Assn./Cleve. Orch., 1993—96, internat. trustee, 1996- . Contbr. articles to jours. in field; Carnegie Hall debut, 1985; cellist The Klemperer Trio, 1980—. Alumni adv. coun. Yale Sch. Music, 2000—02. Recipient Outstanding Svc. to Strings award, NC Chpt. Am. String Tchrs. Assn., 1983, Cultural Excellence award, Cleveland Music. Sch. Settlement, Cert. Merit, Yale Sch. Music Alumni Assn., 2000; Woodrow Wilson fellow, 1969, Ford Found. fellow, 1969, Lucy G. Moses fellowship, Yale U., 1971-72, Fulbright fellow, Germany, 1972-74. Mem. Philos. Soc. Tex., Cum Laude Soc., Phi Beta Kappa (pres. 1987-89), Pi Kappa Lambda (pres. 1988-90), Phi Kappa Phi (Centennial Excellence Award, 1997), Sigma Pi Phi, Gamma Gamma Boulé, Alpha Phi Alpha. Avocations: fitness, cooking, bicycling, travel. Office: Wheaton Coll 115 Park Hall E Main St Norton MA 02766-2322 Office Phone: 508-286-8244. Business E-Mail: crutcher_ronald@wheatoncollege.edu.

CRUTCHFIELD, GEORGE THOMAS, journalism educator; b. Sutton, W.Va., Sept. 11, 1933; s. Harry Lee and Grace Rae (Gibson) C.; m. Carmen Rhodes, Aug. 28, 1955 (dec. Oct. 30, 1966); children: Lisa Susan, Laurence Steven; m. Frances Bailey, May 6, 1995; 1 stepchild, Henry Ruffin Broaddus. BS, Fla. So. Coll., 1955, DHL (hon.), 1990; MS, Fla. State U., 1959; postgrad., Syracuse U., 1959—63. Writer, editor Braxton Dem., Sutton, 1953-55; dir. pub. rels. Athens (Ala.) Coll., 1955-57; writer AP, Tallahassee, 1957-59; copy editor Syracuse (N.Y.) Post-Std., 1959-63; dir. coll. rels. Emory (Va.) & Henry Coll., 1963-65; asst. prof. U. S.C., Columbia, 1965-70; prof., dir. Sch. Mass. Comms. Va. Commonwealth U., Richmond, 1970-99; disting. prof., endowed chair in mass comms. Fla. So. Coll., Lakeland, 1999—2001. Educator-in-residence Richmond Newspapers, Inc., 1989-90. Bd. dirs. Better Bus. Bur., Richmond, 1991-2001, Va. Inst. Pastoral Care, Richmond, 1997—; bd. dirs. Tuckahoe Little League, Richmond, 1972-92, pres., 1978-79; bd. govs. Va. Home for Boys, Richmond, 1998—; exec. dir. N.Y. State Soc. Newspaper Editors, Syracuse, 1960-63, S.C. Scholastic Press Assn., Columbia, 1965-68; mem. exec. bd. Heart of Virginia coun. Boy Scouts Am., 1989—, v.p., 1989-2004. Recipient Communicator of Achievement award Va. Press Women, 1992, Disting. Alumnus award Fla. So. Coll., 1992, Silver Antelope award Boy Scouts Am., 1999; named to Va. Comms. of Fame, 1990. Mem. Soc. Profl. Journalists (George Mason award 1982), Fine Creek Club, Kappa Tau Alpha (nat. pres. 1986-88). Episcopalian. Avocations: camping, backpacking. Home: 1196 Huguenot Tr Midlothian VA 23113 E-mail: oldscouts2@aol.com.

CRUTCHFIELD, JAMES N., publishing executive; b. McKeesport, Pa., Dec. 7, 1947; m. Cynthia L. Parish; 1 child. BA in Journalism, Duquesne U., 1992. Reporter Pitts (Pa.) Press, 1968-71; pub. info. officer Pitts. Model Cities Program., 1971; reporter Pitts. Post-Gazette, 1971-76, Detroit Free Press, 1976-79; press. sec. for U.S. Sen. Carl Levin of Mich., 1979-81; chief of bur. Free Press., Lansing, Mich., 1981-83; asst. city editor, dep. city editor, dept. mng. editor Free Press, Lansing, Mich., 1983-89; mng. editor Akron (Ohio) Beacon Jour., 1989—93; exec. editor Press-Telegram, Long Beach, Calif., 1993—98; gen. man. Akron (Ohio) Beacon Journal, 1999—2001, pres., 2001—, pub., 2001—. Mem. bd. John S. and James L. Knight Found., United Way Summit County. Mem.: Ohio Newspaper Assn., Asian Am. Journalists Assn., Nat. Assn. Minority Media Execs., Nat. Assn. Black Journalists, Am. Soc. Newspaper Editors.

CRUTCHFIELD, JONATHAN ERIC, conductor, director; b. Winston-Salem, N.C., Nov. 12, 1959; s. Marvin Rudolph and Virginia Evangeline (Tucker) Crutchfield. MusB in Piano, So. Wesleyan U., 1982; MusM in Choral Conducting, Fla. State U., 1984; Mus D in Choral Conducting, So. Bapt. Theol. Sem., Louisville, 1994. Dir. choral activities So. Wesleyan U., Central, SC, 1984—87; organist, music assoc. First Bapt. Ch., Huntsville, Ala., 1994—96, Chattanooga, 1996—2002; dir. Sch. Fine Arts, Chattanooga, 1996—2002; min. music and worship Highland Bapt. Ch., Louisville, 2003—. Choral dir. Ind. U. S.E. Composer: Look, ye Saints, the Sight is Glorious, 1995, Make Our Church One Joyful Choir, 2002. Mem.: Am. Choral Dirs. Assn. (chair music r&s choir 2003—05), Am. Guild Organists. Office: Highland Bapt Ch 1101 Cherokee Rd Louisville KY 40204

CRUTCHFIELD, KRISTEN LEIGH, education educator; d. Thomas Paul and Carol Ann Crutchfield. BA, Greensboro Coll., 2004; MEd, N.C. State U., 2004. Coll. rels. student worker, office pub. info. student worker Greensboro Coll., NC, 2000—04; waterfront dir. Tarheel Triad Girl Scout Coun., Greensboro, 2002—03; leaders in tng. counselor YMCA Camp Hanes, King, NC, 2004—04; women in sci. and engring. grad. asst. N.C. State U., Raleigh, 2004—. Mem.: Am. Coll. Pers. Assn., Alpha Xi Delta (founding sister).

CRUTCHFIELD, WILLIAM RICHARD, artist, educator; b. Indpls., Jan. 21, 1932; s. William C. and Vera Eleanor (Wiggam) Neidlinger; m. Barbara Jean Seaman, June 14, 1964. B.F.A., Herron Sch. Art, Ind. U., 1956; M.F.A., Tulane U., 1960. Instr. Herron Sch. Art, Ind. U., Indpls., 1963-65; asst. prof. Mpls. Coll. Art and Design, 1966-67, chmn. found. studies, 1966-67. Author: Owl Feathers, 1975, (film) William Crutchfield, Sage of Machine Wit, 1973, Crutchfield, A Recollection of the Future, 1977; principal works include Alphabet Spire, Corbins Corner, Conn., 1974, Countdown, Short Hills, N.J., 1980, Punctuation Spire, Herron Sch. Art, Ind. U., Indpls., 2002, Wish, Glen Burnie, Md., 1986, The Importance of Being A Bubble, Ft. Lauderdale/Hollywood Internat. Airport, Ft. Lauderdale, Fla., 1989, Fifty Years of Flight, SAS Hdqs., Stockholm, 1996. Served with U.S. Army, 1957-59. Recipient Mary Milliken award Herron Sch. Art, 1956, Mayor's award for outstanding achievement in arts, L.A., 1988; Fulbright scholar, 1961; named Disting. Artist of Los Angeles 100 Club, Music Center, 1982 Home: 2011 S Mesa St San Pedro CA 90731-5515

CRUTHIRD, ROBERT LEE, sociology educator; b. Dec. 10, 1944; s. Harvie and Mary Florence (Black) Cruthird; m. Julie Mae Boyd, Dec. 17, 1965 (div.); 1 child, Robert Lee; m. Jeanette M. Williams. BA, U. Ill., Chgo., 1976; PhD, Heed U., 1994. Correctional counselor Ill. Dept. Corrections, Joliet, 1977—78; instr. in sociology Kennedy-King Coll., Chgo., 1978—80, 1981—84, asst. prof., 1984—87, assoc. prof., 1987—, chmn. social sci. dept., 1996, dir. instnl. rsch., 1980—81. With Chgo. State U., 1982, U. Chgo., 1986. Author: Black Rural-Urban Migration 1915-50, 1984, Remedial/Developmental Instructions in Classroom, 1987. With U.S. Army, 1965—67. Named Most Disting. Advisor Ill., 1989; recipient Monarch award in edn., Alpha Kappa Alpha, 1999, crime and delinquency rsch. tng. fellowship, U. Ill.-Chgo., 1976—77, NEH fellowship, U. Wis., 1983. Mem.: Assn. Study of Afro-Am. Life and History, Nat. Assn. Devel. Edn., Assn. Instl. Rsch., Am. Sociol. Assn., U. Ill. Chgo. Alumni Assn. (life), Phi Theta Kappa (named to Ill. Hall of Honor 1984, 1986, 1988, hon. scholar 23d ann. inst., hon. scholar 24th ann. inst. 1991), Alpha Phi Alpha (life). Democrat. Baptist. Home: 259 E 107th St Chicago IL 60628-3668 Office: Kennedy-King Coll 6800 S Wentworth Ave Ste 350 Chicago IL 60621-3728

CRUVER, SUZANNE LEE, communications executive, writer; b. Indpls., Mar. 24, 1942; d. William Edward and Margaret Rosetta (McArtor) Ozzard; m. Donald Richard Cruver, June 9, 1963 (div. Feb. 1989); children: Donald Scott, Kimberly Sue, Brian Richard. BA in English, Rutgers U., 1964; postgrad., Rice U., 1990—. Asst. dir. pub. rels. dept. Upsala Coll., East Orange, N.J., 1964-65; asst. planner, pub. editor N.J. Divsn. State & Regional Planning, Trenton, 1967-68; realtor Vonnie Cobb Realtors, Houston, 1979-81; owner Sugar Land Comm., 1980-94; exec. v.p., mktg. mgr. Photoflight Aviation Corp., Sugar Land, Tex., 1982; exec. v.p., artist mgr. H. McMillan Orgn., Inc., Sugar Land, 1983-85; account exec. Mel Anderson Comm., Inc., Houston, 1986; exec. dir. Ft. Bend Arts Coun., Sugar Land, 1986-87; dir. resource devel., vol. svcs., pub. info. Richmond (Tex.) State Sch., Tex. Dept. Mental Health/Mental Retardation, 1987-93; dir. corp. and found. giving Meml. Found., Meml. Healthcare Sys., Houston, 1993-94; owner SLC Comms., Houston & Englewood, Fla., 1994-2000; mktg. coord., pub. info. officer Gulf Coast Workforce Bd. Houston-Galveston Area Coun., 2000—. Mem. adv. bd. Ft. Bend Regional Coun. on Alcoholism and Drug Abuse, Rosenburg, Tex., 1989—. Writer, editor: PATCH Handbook: A Parent to Parent Guide to Texas Children's Hospital, 1983, Ft. Bend mag., 1985-86; book editor, contbg. writer: Fort Bend County, Texas - A Pictorial History, 1996. Pres. Ft. Bend Arts Coun., Ft. Bend County, Tex., 1987-89; founding dir. PATCH, Tex. Children's Hosp., Houston, 1982; mem. adv. bd. Challenger Ctr. of Ft. Bend; committeeman Houston Livestock Show & Rodeo, 1996—; co-coord. 25th Anniversary of lunar landing celebration and internat. space expo, Houston, 1994; bd. dirs. United Way South Sarasota County. Mem. NAFE, Nat. Soc. Fundraising Execs., Women in Comm., Ft. Bend Profl. Women, Pub. Rels. Soc. Am., Houston (Tex.) Advt. Fedn., Houston World Trade Assn., Ft. Bend C. of C., Rosenberg/Rich C. of C., Leadership Tex. Alumni Assn., Exch. Club of Sugar Land, Ft. Bend Exch. Club (charter bd. mem.). Republican. Presbyterian. Avocations: travel, scuba diving, golf, dance, photography. Business E-Mail: sue.cruver@theworksource.org.

CRUZ, CORINA, mathematician, educator; d. Mario and Cora De Los Santos; m. Senon Cruz, May 31, 1997; 1 child, Marcus Zenon. BSc in Edn., Tex. Tech U., 1984. Cert. tchr. Tex. State Bd. Edn., 1984. Tchr. fifth grade Lubbock (Tex.) Ind. Sch. Dist., 1984—86; tchr. math 5th grade Roosevelt Ind. Sch. Dist., Lubbock, Tex., 1986—. Tchrs. rep. Hunt Elem. Sch., Lubbock, 1984—85; head Dept. Math. Roosevelt Elem., 2000—, lead tchr. grade level, 1999—. Nominee Presdl. award for Math. and Sci. Tchg., 2004. Mem.: South Plains Coun. Math. Tchrs., Tex. Coun. Math. Tchrs., Tex. Classroom Tchrs. Assn. Business E-Mail: ccruz@roosevelt.esc17.net.

CRUZ, JARROD NIBALDO, director; b. Key West, Fla., Mar. 28, 1977; s. Nick and Debra May Cruz. BA in Polit. Sci., U. Tenn., Knoxville, 2002. Residence hall dir. Office Residence Life Lyndon State Coll., Lyndonville, Vt., 2002—04; grad. residence dir. Office Housing and Residence Life Ind. U. Pa., 2004—. Lesbian, gay, bisexual and transgender rsch. Recipient citation Extraordinary Leadership and Svc., U. Tenn., 2002. Mem.: Am. Coll. Pers. Assn. (assoc.), Lambda Theta Phi (life). Office: Ind Univ Pa B-31 Clark Hall 1090 South Dr Indiana PA 15705 Office Phone: 724-357-3052. Personal E-mail: volgrad02@hotmail.com.

CRUZ, JOSE BEJAR, JR., engineering educator; b. Bacolod City, Sept. 17, 1932; came to U.S., 1954, naturalized, 1969; s. Jose P. and Felicidad (Bejar) C.; m. Stella E. Rubia; children by previous marriage: Fe E. Cruz Langdon, Ricardo A., Rene L., Sylvia C. Cruz Loebach, Loretta C. Cruz Spray. BSEE summa cum laude, U. Philippines, 1953; MS in Elec. Engring., MIT, 1956; PhD in Elec. Engring., U. Ill., 1959. Lic. profl. engr., Ill., Ohio. Instr. elec. engring. U. Philippines, Quezon City, 1953-54; rsch. asst. MIT, Cambridge, 1954-56, vis. prof., 1973; from instr. to assoc. prof. U. Ill., Urbana-Champaign, 1956-65, prof. elec. engring., 1965-86, assoc. mem. Ctr. Advanced Study, 1967-68; rsch. prof. Coordinated Sci. Lab., 1965-86; prof. dept. elec. and computer engring. U. Calif., Irvine, 1986-92, chmn. dept., 1986-90; prof. elec. engring. Ohio State U., Columbus, 1992—2004, dean Coll. Engring., 1992-97, Howard D. Winbigler chair in engring., 1997—2004, dist. prof. engring., 2004—. Vis. assoc. prof. U. Calif., Berkeley, 1964-65; vis. prof. Harvard U., 1973; pres. Dynamic Sys.; theory com. Am. Automatic Control Coun., 1967; gen. chmn. Conf. on Decision and Control, 1975; mem. profl. engring. exam. com. State of Ill., 1984-86; mem. Nat. Coun. Engring. Examiners, 1985-86; project adv. group on engring. and sci. edn. project Dept. Sci. and Tech., Republic of The Philippines, 1993-98. Author: (with M.E. Van Valkenburg) Introductory Signals and Circuits, 1967, (with W.R. Perkins) Engineering of Dynamic Systems, 1969, Feedback Systems, 1972, translated into Chinese, 1976, Polish, 1977, System Sensitivity Analysis, 1973, (with M.E. Van Valkenburg) Signals in Linear Circuits, 1974, translated into Spanish, 1978; Assoc. editor: Jour. Franklin Inst, 1976-82, Jour. Optimization Theory and Applications, 1980—; series editor Advances in Large Scale Systems Theory and Applications; contbr. articles on network theory, automatic control systems, system theory, sensitivity theory of dynamical systems, large scale systems, dynamic games and dynamic scheduling in mfg. systems to sci., tech. jours. Recipient Purple Tower award Beta Epsilon U., Philippines, 1969, Diamond award, 1999, Curtis W. McGraw Rsch. award Am. Soc. for Engring. Edn., 1972, Halliburton Engring. Edn. Leadership award, 1981, Most Outstanding Alumnus award U. of the Philippines Alumni Assn. Am., 1989, Most Outstanding Overseas Alumnus Coll. Engring., U. of the Philippines Alumni Assn., 1990, Richard E. Bellman Control Heritage award Am. Automatic Control Coun., 1994, others Fellow AAAS (sect. com. for sect. on engring. 1991-94, sec. 1998-2003, chmn.-elect 2003-04, chmn. 2004-05, ret. chair 2005-, mem. coun. 2005-) Am. Soc. Engring Edn. (awards policy com., Ternan awards com.), IEEE (chmn. linear sys. com., group on automatic control 1966-68, assoc. editor Trans. on Circuit Theory 1962-64), Am. Soc. Engring. Edn.; mem. Control Sys. Soc. (adminstrv. com. 1966-75, 78-80, v.p. fin. and adminstrv. activities 1976-77, pres. 1979, chmn. awards com. 1973-75, ednl. activities bd. 1973-75, editor Trans. on Automatic Control 1971-73, tech. activities bd. 1979-83, chmn. 1982-83, v.p. tech. activities 1982-83, edn. med. com. 1977-79, dir. 1980-85, vice-chmn. publs. bd. 1981, chmn. 1984-85, chmn. panel of tech. editors 1981, chmn. TAB periodicals com. 1981, chmn. PUB. Soc. publs. com. 1981, v.p. publ. activities 1984-85, exec. com. 1982-85, Richard M. Emberson award 1989), Philippine Engrs. and Scientists Orgn., Nat. Acad. Engring., Nat. Acad. Sci. & Tech., U.S. Nat. Acad. Engring. (peer com. for electronics engring. 1982, 2000-04, vice-chmn. 2002-03, chmn. 2003-04, com. on nat. agenda for career-long edn. for engrs. 1986-88, membership com. 1987-90, 2003—, acad. adv. bd. 1994-97, com. on diversity in engring. workforce 1999-2001), Nat. Acad. for Sci. and Tech. (corr.), Philippine-Am. Acad. Sci. and Engring. (founding mem. 1980, pres. 1982, chmn. bd. dirs. 1998-2000, Founders Lecture award 2001), Internat. Fedn. Automatic Control (chmn. theory com. 1981-84, vice-chmn. tech. bd. 1984-87, policy com. 1987-93, vice-chmn. 1993, 99, chmn. 1996, congress internat. program com.), Philippine Engrs. and Scientists Orgn., Sigma Xi, Phi Kappa Phi, Eta Kappa Nu. Roman Catholic. Achievements include introduction of concept of comparison sensitivity in dynamical feedback systems, of leader-follower strategies in hierarchical engineering systems; development of synthesis methods for time-varying systems. Office: Ohio State Univ Dept Elec & Computer Engring 2015 Neil Ave Columbus OH 43210-1272 Office Phone: 614-292-1588. Personal E-mail: jbcruz@ieee.org. Business E-Mail: cruz@ece.osu.edu.

CRUZ, MICHELE ANNETTE, graphic arts executive; b. Elyria, Ohio, Mar. 1, 1964; d. Daniel Tristian and Donna Marie (Wolff) Carpenter; m. Derrick Ralph Cruz (div.); 1 child, Jasper Jonas. Attended, Bridgewater Coll., 1984; BA, Wake Forest U., 1986. Sports, photo, news editor The Nashville Graphic, Nashville, NC, 1986—88; asst. dir. pub. info. Nash County Schs., Nashville, NC, 1988—89; pub. editor, designer Rocky Mt. C. of C., Rocky Mt., NC, 1989—90; dir. pub. info., art instr. NC Wesleyan Coll., Rocky Mt., 1990—95; art, photography tchr. Rocky Mt. Sr. HS, Rocky Mt., 1995—98; co-owner Cruz Gallery of Fine Art, Tarboro, NC, 1998—99; graphic arts dir. Carolina Industl. Resources, Rocky Mt., NC, 1998—2003, flexographic quality control mgr., 2001—03; owner, graphic designer C2 Printing and Design, Inc., Nashville, 2003—. Graphic arts tech. trainee Am. Press, Inc., Gordonsville, Va., 1980—82; pressman, bindery worker Carolina Office Equip. Co., Rocky Mt., 1984; pub. relations dir. Rocky Mt./Nash Spl. Olympics, Rocky Mt., 1987—89. Editor (designer): (catalogue) African-American Quilts, NC Wesleyan Coll., 2003; exhibitions include Mims Gallery, NC Wesleyan Coll., Rocky Mt., NC, 1999, selected copperwork, Rose Hill Plantation, Nashville, NC, 2001—02, Via Cappaccino Coffeehouse, Rocky Mt., NC, 2001—02. Vol. reader Down East Radio Reading Svc., Rocky Mt., NC, 2002—; chair of pub. edn. com. Cause and Concern, Battleboro, NC, 2001—; curator Quigless Clinic Hosp. Hist. Exhibit, Tarboro, NC, 2000—; vol. counselor Big Bros/Big Sisters of Nash and Edgecombe Counties, Rocky Mt., 1986—2000; ch. liaison Rocky Mt. Pregnancy Ctr., Rocky Mt., 1990—; youth bible tchr. Temple Bible Ch., Rocky Mt., 1989—2002. Recipient Newspaper Design award, NC Sch. Pub. Relations Assn., 1988, 3rd Place Overall award, Icarus Internat. Art. Competition, 2002. Mem.: Temple Bible Ch., NC Wesleyan Archaeological Soc., U. and Coll. Designers Assn., Tar River Chorus. Avocations: writing, photography, reading, bible study. Home: 209 Regency Dr Nashville NC 27856 Office: C2 Printing and Design Inc PO Box 746 208 W Washington St Nashville NC 27856 Office Phone: 252-459-0049, 252-442-8833. Office Fax: 252-459-0048, 252-442-7952. E-mail: c2pd@earthlink.net, isaiah35@earthlink.net.

CRUZ, PENELOPE, actress; b. Madrid, Apr. 28, 1974; d. Eduardo and Encarna Cruz. Studied classical ballet, Nat. Conservatory, Madrid. Actor: (TV films) Framed, 1992; (films) El Laberinto griego, 1991, Belle époque, 1992, Jamón, jamón, 1992, La Ribelle, 1993, La Celestina, 1996, Más que amor, frenesí, 1996, Et Hjørne af paradis, 1997, Carne trémula, 1997, Abre los ojos, 1997, Don Juan, 1998, The Man with Rain in His Shoes, 1998, Talk of Angels, 1998, La Niña de tus ojos, 1998, The Hi-Lo Country, 1998, Todo sobre mi madre, 1999, Volavèrunt, 1999, Woman on Top, 2000, All the Pretty Horses, 2000, Blow, 2001, Captain Corelli's Mandolin, 2001, Sin noticias de Dios, 2001, Vanilla Sky, 2001, Waking Up in Reno, 2002, Masked and Anonymous, 2003, Fanfan la tulipe, 2003, Gothika, 2003, Noel, 2004, Head in the Clouds, 2004, Sahara, 2005. Founder Sabera Found.*

CRUZ, ROBYN FLAUM, research scientist; b. Atlanta, July 13, 1954; d. Norman Herman and Jean Miller Flaum; m. Mario Cruz. BS, Vanderbilt U., 1975; MA, NYU, 1981; PhD, U. Ariz., 1995. Nat. cert. counselor. Rsch. specialist Nat. Ctr. for Neurogenic Comm. Disorders, U. Ariz., Tucson, 1994—99; dir. rsch. COPE Behavioral Svcs., Inc., Tucson, 1999—2002; dir. creative and expressive art therapy Western Psychiat. Inst. & Clinic, Pitts., 2002—. Co-Editor American Journal of Dance Therapy, American Dance Therapy Association, Columbia, MD, 1997—2001; adj. asst. prof. dept. ednl. psychology U. Ariz., 1997—2000; adj. faculty mem. grad. creative arts therapy program Pratt Inst. of Arts, N.Y.C., 2000—. Contbr. rsch. articles to profl. jours.; editor in chief: The Arts in Psychotherapy, 2002—. Mem.: APA, Am. Dance Therapy Assn. (cert., v.p. 2002—). Home: 5900 Jackson St Pittsburgh PA 15206 Office: Western Psychiat Inst & Clin Univ Pitts Med Ctr 3811 O'Hara St Pittsburgh PA 15213 E-mail: robyncruz@stargate.net, cruzrf@msx.upmc.edu.

CRUZ, TED, lawyer; s. Rafael Bienvenido and Eleanor Elizabeth (Darragh) Cruz; m. Heidi Suzanne Nelson, May 27, 2001. AB cum laude, Princeton U., Princeton, NJ., 1992; JD magna cum laude, Havard Law Sch., Cambridge, Mass., 1995. Bar: Tex. 1997, D.C. 1998. Law clk. U.S. Ct. Appeals 4th Cir., Washington, 1995—96, U.S. Supreme Ct., Washington, 1996—97; atty. Cooper, Carvin, and Rosenthal, Washington, 1997—99; domestic policy advisor Bush - Cheney 2000, Austin, Tex., 1999—2000; assoc. dep. atty. gen. U.S. Dept. of Justice, Washington, 2001; dir. of policy Fed. Trade Comm., Washington, 2001—03; solicitor gen. of Tex. Austin, Tex., 2003—; adj. prof. U. Tex. Sch. of Law, 2004—. Bd. dirs. Criminal Justice Legal Found. Editor: (primary) Harvard Law Rev., 1995, (exec.) Harvard Jour. of Law and Pub. Policy, 1995, (co founding) Harvard Latino Law Rev. Dept. Justice Coord. Bush Cheney Transition Team, Washington, 2001; atty. Bush Cheney Presdl. Recount, Fla., 2000; acive Bush-Cheney '04; dir. Tex. Mavericks. Recipient U.S. Nat. Champion Debate Team, Am. Parliamentary Debate Assn., 1992, U.S. Nat. Champion Spkr., 1992, Ranked #1 Spkr. in No. Am., No. Am. Debate Championship, 1992, Best U.S. Supreme Ct. Merits Brief award, Nat. Assn. Attys. Gen., 2003, 2004. Mem.: Tex. Rev. of Law and Politics (steering com.), Tex. Lycenn (dir., v.p.), Tex. Hispanic Alliance Progress (chmn.). Republican. Achievements include twice named 100 Most Influential Hispanics, Hispanic Business Mag; named to 20 young Hispanics to watch, 1999, Newsweek Mag; named to 50 Most Influential People in Poltics, 2001, George Mag. Office: Office of Atty Gen PO Box 12548 Austin TX 78711 Office Phone: 512-936-1700.

CRUZ, WILFREDO VARGAS, software safety and reliability consultant; b. Metro-Manila, The Philippines, Nov. 27, 1942; came to U.S., 1967; s. Alfredo Cordova and Presentacion (Vargas) C.; m. Florita Vedoya Salandanan, July 30, 1979; children: John Christopher, Charles Wesley. BSEE, U. the East, Manila, 1964. Cons. Braun Global Svcs. Inc., Arabian Am. Oil Co., Dharan, Saudia Arabia, 1977-83, Lockheed Space Ops. Co., Titusville, Fla., 1984-89, Lockheed Engrng. and Scis. Co., Moffett Field, Calif., 1989, Westinghouse Marine Divsn., Sunnyvale, Calif., 1989-91, Ralph M. Parsons Co., Pasadena, Calif., 1991-92, Boeing Aerospace Ops., Inc., Moffett Field, 1994, Hernandez Engrng., Inc., Moffett Field, 1995, Lockheed Martin Def. Sys., Pittsfield, Mass., 1996, United Def. LP, Mpls., 1996, Boeing Def. and Space Co., Chatsworth, Calif., 1996-98, Hunterskil Howard Internat. Ltd., London, 1998-2000. CEO, founder Euro-Asean-Am. Found., Hengelo, The Netherlands, 1998. Specialist 5 U.S. Army, 1967-70. Mem. Sys. Safety Soc. Home: 17895 Calle Barcelona Rowland Heights CA 91748-2533 E-mail: will.cruz@wxs.nl, wvcruz1227@aol.com.

CRUZ, WILHELMINA MANGAHAS, critical care physician, educator; b. Bulacan, Philippines, July 20, 1942; d. Rectorino Bernardo and Mercedes Correa (Mangahas) C.; m. Antonio I. Lee, May 28, 1977; children: Richard Anthony, Alexander Victor. AA, U. Santo Tomas, The Philippines, 1960, MD, 1965. Diplomate in internal medicine and critical care medicine Am. Bd. Internal Medicine; diplomate Am. Bd. Nephrology. Intern Meml. Hosp., Albany, N.Y., 1967-68; resident in internal medicine Coney Island Hosp., Bklyn., 1968-71; fellow in nephrology VA Hosp., Bronx, 1971-72, SUNY Downstate Med. Ctr., Bklyn., 1972-73; staff physician King's County Hosp. Ctr., Bklyn., 1973-76; coord. in medicine Kingsbrook Jewish Med. Ctr., Bklyn., 1976—. Assoc. med. dir. ICU Drs. Cmty. Hosp., Lanham, Md., 1977-99, med. dir. critical care svcs., 1999—; clin. asst. prof. SUNY Downstate Med. Ctr., 1977—. Mem. ACP, Med. and Chirurg. Soc. Md., Prince George's Med. Soc., Soc. Critical Care Medicine, Philippine Med. Assn. Washington. Roman Catholic. Office: 7700 Old Branch Ave Ste D205 Clinton MD 20735-1611 Office Phone: 301-868-3858.

CRUZ, ZOE, diversified financial services company executive; b. Feb. 2, 1955; m. Ernesto Cruz. BA in Literature, Harvard U., 1977, MBA, 1982. With Morgan Stanley, 1982—, v.p., 1986—88, prin., fixed income, 1988—90, mng. dir., fixed income, 1990—93, co-chief, fgn. exch., 1993—2000, head of worldwide fixed income, fgn. exch. and commodities, 2000—05, co-pres., 2005, acting pres., 2005—, bd. dirs., 2005—. Named one of Most Powerful Women, Forbes mag., 2005. Office: Morgan Stanley 1585 Broadway New York NY 10036*

CRUZAN, CLARAH CATHERINE, dietician; b. Cushing, Okla., Mar. 17, 1913; d. Ulysses Grant and Mamie Amanda (Montgomery) C. BS, Okla. State U., 1941; MS, U. Iowa, 1942. Lic. dietitian, Okla., 1984. Instr. household sci. Okla. State U., Stillwater, 1942-43, instr. home econs. edn., 1947-49; cons. dietitian Rest Haven Nursing Home, Cushing, Okla., 1967-91. Sec. Cushing Sr. Citizens Steering Coun., 1972-91; reporter Okla. Pioneer club, Cushing, 1973-85; precinct election judge, 1989-94. 1st lt. U.S. Army, 1943-46, ETO. Decorated Bronze Star. Mem. AAUW (life, treas. 1970-72, pres. 1974-75), Am. Dietetic Assn., Okla. Heritage Assn., Iris Garden Club (pres. 1971-73), Eastside Garden Club (reporter 1970-75), Omicron Nu, Phi Kappa Phi. Republican. Presbyterian. Home: 201 W Van Buren St Broken Arrow OK 74011-6639

CRUZ-CONNERTON, MAYRA, elementary school educator; d. Louis Cruz and Maria Christina Quiñones-Cruz; m. Christopher Charles Connerton, Aug. 29, 1998; children: Isabella Maria Connerton(dec.), Julian Christopher Connerton, Gabriel Ryan Connerton. BA in English Lit., Georgian Ct. Coll., 1993, postgrad., 1994—. Tchr. Atlantic City (N.J.) Bd. Edn., 1997—. Author: When Children Go to Heaven, 2004. Named Gov.'s Tchr. of Yr., State of N.J., 1998—99. Democrat. Roman Catholic. Avocations: reading, writing.

CRUZ-ROMO, GILDA, soprano; b. Guadalajara, Jalisco, Mexico; came to U.S., 1967; d. Feliciano and Maria del Rosario (Diaz) C.; m. Robert B. Romo, June 10, 1967. Grad., Coll. Nueva Galicia, Guadalajara, 1958; student, Nat. Conservatory of Music of Mexico, Mexico City, 1962-64. Tchr. voice U. Tex., Austin, 1990—. Assoc. prof., coach, voice tchr. U. Tex., Austin, 1990—. With, Nat. and Internat. Opera, Mexico City, 1962-67, toured, Australia, N.Z., S.Am., with, Dallas Civic Opera, 1966-68, N.Y.C. Opera, 1969-72, Lyric Opera Chgo., 1975, Met. Opera debut as Madama Butterfly, 1970, leading soprano, 1970—, appeared in U.S. and abroad including Covent Garden, La Scala, Vienna State Opera, Rome Opera, Paris Opera, Florence Opera, Torino Opera, Verona Opera, Portugal, Buenos Aires, others, concert appearances in U.S., Can., Mexico; U.S. rep. World-Wide Madama Butterfly Competition, Tokyo, 1970; La Scala rep. in: Aida, USSR, 1974; appeared on radio, TV; filmed and recorded: Aida, with Orange Festival, France, 1976; roles include Aida, Madama Butterfly, Suor Angelica, Tosca, Odabella in Attila; Manon Lescaut, Leonora in Il Trovatore; Norma; Maddelena in Andrea Chenier; Desdemona in Otello; Donna Anna in Don Giovanni; Santuzza in Cavalleria Rusticana; (title role) La Gioconda; Adriana Lecouvreur; Luisa Miller; Elisabetta in Don Carlo; Margherite in Faust; Venus in Tannhauser; Giorgetta in Il Tabarro; also roles in Macbeth, Turnadot, Norma, Medea; recipient Gold medal in Fine Arts, Mexico. Named Winner Met. Opera Nat. Auditions, 1970, Best Singer, 1976—77, honoree, Opera Guild of San Antonio, 2003; recipient Critics award, Union Mexicana de Cronistas de Teatro y Musica, 1973, Minerva al Arte award, Mexico, 1991, Silver Bird award, Govt. of Jalisco, Mexico, 1998, season Cronistas de Santiago de Chile, 1976, Baccarat 2001 award, The Licia Albanese-Puccini Found., 2001, Lifetime Achievement award, Nat. Opera Assn., 2003, Pedro Sarquis Merrewe Found., 2004. Personal E-mail: bobgilda2@sbcglobal.net.

CRYAN, RICHARD JAMES, JR., academic administrator; b. Buffalo, Nov. 28, 1955; s. Richard James Sr. and Geraldine C.; m. Lee Ann Cryan; children: Richard, Christine, Sean, Amy, Jonathan, Sharon. BS, Heritage Coll., 1983; M in Christian Edn., Freedom U., 1996, EdD in Higher Edn., 1994. Dir. N.Y. Inst. Theology, Buffalo, 1985-2001; lt. gen., pres., chancellor Kings Coll. War, Buffalo, 2001—. Author: The Art of Makahiya, God's Purpose and Plan, 2000, Heritage Preparatory Academy, 2000, New York Institute of Theology, 2000, The Professional Lies of Modern Educators and Pastors, 2000, Kings College of War, 2000, Renew Counseling Institute, 2002, United States of America Bible Society, 2003. Avocation: makahiya (black belt ninth degree). Office: Kings Coll War 1911 Seneca St Buffalo NY 14210 Home: 395 North St #16 Yale MI 48097-2976

CRYER, PHILIP EUGENE, endocrinologist; b. El Paso, Ill., Jan. 5, 1940; s. Clifford Eugene and Carol Ruth (Cherry) C.; m. Susan Odette Shipman, Dec. 23, 1963 (div. May 1990); children: Philip Clifford, Justine Laurel; m. Carolyn Elizabeth Havlin, Sept. 16, 1994. BA, Northwestern U., 1962, MD, 1965; MD (hon.), U. Copenhagen, 2000. Diplomate Am. Bd. Internal Medicine, diplomate Am. Bd. Endocrinology and Metabolism. Intern Barnes Hosp., St. Louis, 1965-67; fellow in endocrinology Barnes Hosp./Washington U., 1967-68, resident in medicine, 1968-69, 71-72; investigator Naval Med. Rsch. Inst., Bethesda, Md., 1969-71; from instr. to assoc. prof. Washington U. Sch. Medicine, St. Louis, 1971-80, prof., 1981—, Irene E. and Michael M. Karl prof. endocrinology/metabolism, 1995—, dir. gen. clin. rsch. ctr., 1978—, dir. div. endocrinology, diabetes and metabolism, 1985—2002. Connaught-Novo lectr. Can. Diabetes Assn., 1987; Pimstone lectr. Soc. Endocrinology, Metabolism and Diabetes, South Africa, 1989; Kellion lectr. Australian Diabetes Soc., 1992; Plenary lectr. Japan Diabetes Soc., 1994, plenary lectr. Argentine Diabetes Assn., 1998, plenary lectr. Asean Fed. Endocrine Socs., 1999. Author: Diagnostic Endocrinology, 1976, Diagnostic Endocrinology, 2d edit., 1979, Hypoglycemia, 1997, also 74 book chpts.; editor: Diabetes; mem. editl. bd.: Jour. Clin. Investigation, Am. Jour. Physiology; contbr. over 300 articles to profl. jours. Lt. comdr. M.C. USNR, 1969—71. Recipient Rorer Clin. Investigator award Endocrine Soc., 1988, Rumbaugh Sci. award Juvenile Diabetes Found., 1989, Banting medal Am. Diabetes Assn., 1994, Excellence in Clin. Rsch. award NIH, 1994, Claude Bernard medal European Assn. Study Diabetes, 2001; Am. Diabetes Clin. Rsch. grantee, 1988-, NIH Rsch. grantee, 1980—. Fellow ACP; mem. Am. Fedn. Clin. Rsch. (councilor 1979-80), Am. Soc. Clin. Investigation (v.p. 1985-86), Assn. Am. Physicians, Am. Diabetes Assn. (pres. 1996-97), Phi Beta Kappa, Alpha Omega Alpha. Office: Washington U Sch Medicine 660 South Euclid Ave Box 8127 Saint Louis MO 63110 Office Phone: 314-362-7635. Business E-Mail: pcryer@wustl.edu.

CRYER, RODGER EARL, educational administrator; b. Detroit, Apr. 2, 1940; AB in Fine Arts, San Diego State U., 1965; MA in Edn. Adminstrn., Stanford U., 1972; PhD in Psychol. Svcs. Counseling, Columbia-Pacific U., 1985; Cert. Credit Union Dir., London Sch. of Bus., 2000. Cert. tchr., N.J., Calif.; cert. gen. adminstrn., Calif. Spl. asst. to commr. N.J. State Dept. Edn., Trenton, 1967—68; cons. N.J. Urban Sch. Devel., Trenton, 1969—70; mgmt. cons. Rodger E. Cryer, Co., Pinole, Calif., 1970—73; adminstrv. asst. Franklin McKinley Sch. Dist., San Jose, Calif.; pres. Chief Exec. Tng. Corp., San Jose, 1981—82; prin. McKinley Sch., 1986—91, Hellyer Sch., 1991—96. Bd. instl. rev. Calif. State Dept. Edn. Accreditation Commn., 1996—; adj. prof. Nat. U., San Jose, 1996—; ptnr. Guided Learning Enterprises, chmn.; bd. dirs. Commonwealth Cen. Credit Union, Our City Forest, Inc., 1994-98. Contbr. articles to profl. jours. Bd. dirs., pres. Friends of San Jose Beautiful, Inc., 1994-95; adv. com. City of San Jose Bicycle, 1994-95; pres. Friends of Evergreen Libr., 2000-01. Mem.: Calif. Sch. Pub. Rels. Assn. (pres. 2001—), Nat. Sch. Pub. Rels. Assn. (sec. 1975—86), The Villages Golf and Country Club (rules com. 2002—04, landscape com. 2005—). Home: 6328 Whaley Dr San Jose CA 95135-1447 E-mail: rodgerbella@yahoo.com.

CRYER, THEODORE HUDSON, ophthalmologist, educator; b. Chgo., May 8, 1946; s. Arthur William and Maxine (Ritter) Cryer; children: Timothy Hudson, Jordan Tinley, Megan Elizabeth, Rebecca Jeanne. AB in Chemistry, Taylor U., 1968; MD, U. Md., 1972. Diplomate Am. Bd. Ophthalmology. Straight med. intern South Balt. Gen. Hosp., 1972-73, jr. asst. resident, 1973-74; asst. resident U. Md. Hosp., Balt., 1974-76, resident, 1976-77; pvt. practice Waynesboro, Pa., 1977—, Westminster, Md., 1977-85. Instr. U. Md. Sch. Medicine, 1979—91, clin. asst. prof. medicine, 1991—; chmn. com. ethics Waynesboro Hosp., 1984, trustee, 1991—97, chmn. com. quality assurance, 1996—97, v.p. mem. staff, 1988—89, 1999, pres., 1990—91, 2000—01, treas. med. staff, 2001—03, chmn. com. credentialing, chmn. bylaws com., 2003—, chief of surgery, 1992—96, 2004—. Clk. session Westminster Reformed Presbyn. Ch., 1980—83; trustee Christ United Meth. Ch., 1997—2000. Fellow: ACS, Am. Acad. Ophthalmology; mem.: AAAS, AMA, Opthal. Assn. Rsch. to Prevent Blindness, Nat. Soc. to Prevent Blindness (charter mem.), Pa. Acad. Otolaryngology and Ophthalmology, Md. Eye Physicians and Surgeons, Franklin County Med. Soc., Pa. Med. Soc. Republican. Methodist. Office: 1647 E Main St Waynesboro PA 17268-1874 Office Phone: 717-762-1158. Office Fax: 717-762-8858. Personal E-mail: thcryer@earthlink.net.

CRYSTAL, BILLY, comedian, actor; b. Long Beach, N.Y., Mar. 14, 1947; s. Jack and Helen C.; m. Janice Goldfinger; children: Jennifer, Lindsay. Student, Marshall U., Nassau Community Coll; BFA in TV & Film Direction, N.Y.U., 1970. House mgr. for play You're a Good Man Charlie Brown, 1971; mem. group 3's Company; later solo appearances as stand-up comedian; TV appearances include (series) Soap, 1977-81, The Billy Crystal Comedy Hour, 1982, Saturday Night Live, 1984-85; exec. prodr., writer Midnight Train to Moscow, 1989 (Emmy award outstanding writing 1989), HBO series Sessions, 1991; TV films include SST-Death Flight, 1977, Human Feelings, 1978, Breaking Up Is Hard to Do, 1979, Enola Gay, The Men, The Mission, The Atomic Bomb, 1980; dir., prodr. 61, 2001; motion pictures include Rabbit Test, 1978, (voice) Animalympics, 1979, This Is Spinal Tap, 1984, Running Scared, 1986, The Princess Bride, 1987, Goodnight Moon, 1987, Throw Momma from the Train, 1987, (also prodr., co-screenwriter) Memories of Me, 1988, When Harry Met Sally..., 1989 (Am.Comedy award funniest actor in a motion picture 1989), (also exec. prodr., story) City Slickers, 1991 (Golden Globe nomination best actor 1991, Am. Comedy award 1991), (also dir., writer, prodr.) Mr. Saturday Night, 1992, City Slickers II: The Legend of Curley's Gold, 1994, (also dir., prodr., writer) Forget Paris, 1995, Hamlet, 1996, Father's Day, 1997, Deconstructing Harry, 1997, My Giant, 1998, Analyze This, 1999, The Adventures of Rocky & Bullwinkle, 2000, America's Sweethearts, 2001, (voice) Monsters, Inc., Mike's New Car, 2002, (also exec. prodr.) Analyze That, 2002, (voice) Howl's Moving Castle, 2004; theatre performances include 700 Sundays, 2005 (Outer Critics Cir. award, outstanding solo performance, 2005, Tony award for best spl. theatrical event, 2005, Drama Desk award, outstanding solo performance, 2005); host (HBO) Comic Relief, 1986, (TV host) Grammy Awards, 1988, 89, Acad. Awards, 1990-93, 96-98, 2000, 2004 (Emmy award outstanding performance in special events, 1989, Emmy award outstanding writing, 1991, Emmy award outstanding indiv. performance, 1991, 98), Saturday Night Live: 25th Anniversary, 1999, AFI's 100 Years, 100 Laughs: America's Funniest Movies, 2000; author: (with Dick Schaap) Absolutley Mahvelous, 1986, I Already Know I Love You, 2004; recording You Look Mahvelous, 1985. Mailing: c/o Broadhurst Theatre 235 W 44th St New York NY 10036*

CRYSTAL, J. SCOTT, publishing executive; BS, State Univ. of NY, Binghamton, NY. Mktg., sales mgmt. The New York Times Co., USA Today, Hearst Corp., 1982—92; western advt. dir. Nat. Geog. Soc., Inc., 1992—94, v.p. & pub. dir., 1994—2000; exec. v.p., pub. dir. Consumer Mag. Group, Ziff Davis Media, Inc., 2000—01; pres., CEO Gruner & Jahr USA Bus. Innovator Group, 2001—02; pub./exec. v.p. Gemstar - TV Guide, NY, 2002—. Recipient Advt. Hall of Achievement, Am. Advt. Fed. In his new role, Mr. Crystal will be responsible for mng. the sales and mktg. teams for all of TV Guide's print publ. and online platform. Office: Gemstar TV Guide Internat Inc 4th Floor 1211 Avenue of the Americas 28th Fl New York NY 10036-8701 Office Phone: 212-853-7310. Office Fax: 212-852-7323.*

CRYSTAL, JAMES WILLIAM, insurance company executive; b. NYC, Oct. 9, 1937; s. I. Frank and Evelyn G. Crystal; m. Jean Crystal; children: James F., Sanford F., Jonathan F. BS, Trinity Coll., 1958. With Royal Globe Ins. Group, N.Y.C., 1956; underwriter Home Ins. Co., N.Y.C., 1957, spl. agt. San Francisco, 1958-59; chmn., CEO Frank Crystal & Co. Inc., N.Y.C., 1960—. Chmn. bd. F.F.H. Ins. Co., N.E. Inst. Co.; bd. dirs. Atlantic Internat. Ins. Co., Auto Resources, Inc. Vice chmn. Mt. Sinai Med. Ctr.; trustee Mt. Sinai NYU Health Orgn., N.Y.C., Mt. Sinai Med. Sch. Mem.: Nat. Assn. Casualty and Surety Agts., Wings Club N.Y., Century Country Club, India Ho. Club N.Y., N.Y. Stock Exch. Lunch Club, Harmonie Club. Republican. Home: 875 Park Ave New York NY 10021-0341 Office: Frank Crystal & Co 32 Old Slip New York NY 10005 Office Phone: 212-504-5999. Business E-Mail: jwc@fcrystal.com.

CRYSTAL, JONATHAN ANDREW, executive recruiter; b. New Rochelle, NY, May 18, 1943; s. Robert Garrison and Luella (Peters) C.; m. Pamela Paterson, July 31, 1965; children: Alexandra, Laura, Elizabeth, Matthew. BSBA, Northwestern U., 1965; MBA in Fin., Columbia U., 1971. Mktg. rep. Texaco, Inc., 1965-66; trainee Chase Manhattan Bank, 1971; assoc. corp. fin. Drexel Burnham & Lambert, Inc., 1971-73; acct. officer Citicorp, N.Y.C., 1973-77, asst. v.p., 1975-77, v.p., regional treas. mgr. Houston, 1977-80; prin. Russell Reynolds & Assocs., Houston, 1980-88, SpencerStuart, Houston, 1988—, chmn. audit com., 1997-98. Guest lectr. bus. schs. of Rice U., U. Houston, U. St. Thomas; spkr. in field. Contbr. articles to profl. jours. Adv. bd. Ctr. for Bus. Ethics U. St. Thomas, 1998—. Lt. (j.g.) USN, 1966-69. Named one of Top 200 Recruiters in the U.S. The Career Makers, 1990. Mem. Houston Forum (bd. govs. 1992-2000, exec. com. 1995-2000), Spring Branch Edn. Found. (bd. dirs. 1993-2001, exec. com. 1994-2000, vice-chmn., 1999-2000), Univ. Club, Galveston (Tex.) Country Club. Office Phone: 713-225-1621. Business E-Mail: jcrystal@spencerstuart.com.

CSAKI, CSABA, physicist; b. Budapest, Hungary, Dec. 13, 1969; arrived in US, 1993; s. Csaba and Borbala (Munkacsi) Csaki; m. Zsuzsanna Tonkovics, Sept. 19, 1992; children: Agnes, Zoltan. BSc, Eotvos U., Budapest, 1993; PhD, MIT, 1997. Miller Rsch. fellow U. Calif., Berkeley, 1997—99; J.R. Oppenheimer fellow Los Alamos Nat. Lab., N.Mex., 1999—2001; asst. prof. physics Cornell U., Ithaca, NY, 2002—. Author over 60 jour. articles, over 3000 citations of articles. Named Outstanding Jr. Investigator, US Dept. Energy, 2001; recipient 1st prize ann. essay competition, Gravity Rsch. Found., 2001, 3d prize Physics Olympics, Bad Ischl, Austria, 1988. Mem.: Am. Phys. Soc. Office: Cornell U Dept Physics Ithaca NY 14853 Office Phone: 607-254-8935.

CSASZAR, PETER, software engineer; b. Budapest, Hungary, 1967; arrived in U.S., 1992; BEE, Tech. U. Budapest, 1989; PhD in Computer Sci., U. Ill., Chgo., 1998. Software engr. MMG Automation Works, Budapest, 1991-92, Motorola, Inc., Schaumburg, Ill., 1998—2002, Lawrence Technol. U., Southfield, Mich., 2002—. Author: Object-Oriented Simulator Design for an Automated High-Speed Modular Placement Machine Family, 1999, Optimization of a High-Speed Placement Machine Using Tabu Search Algorithms, 2000, Tabu Search for Rugged Search Spaces with Multiple Symmetric Basins, 2001. Mem.: IEEE. Business E-Mail: csaszar@ltu.edu.

CSERE, CSABA, magazine editor; b. Cleve., June 16, 1951; s. Zoltan and Theresa (Balazs) Csere; m. Mary Patricia O'Brien, July 6, 1975; 1 child, Madeline Christine. BS, MIT, 1975. Design engr. Data Gen. Corp., Southboro, Mass., 1975—77, Ford Motor Co., 1978—80; tech. editor Car and Driver mag., 1980—87, tech. dir., 1987—93, editor-in-chief, 1993—. Mem.: Am. Soc. Mag. Editors, Soc. Automotive Engrs. Office: Car and Driver Hachette Filipacchi Mags Inc 2002 Hogback Rd Ann Arbor MI 48105-9795 Office Phone: 734-971-3600. Office Fax: 734-971-9188.*

CSERR, ROBERT, psychiatrist, physician, hospital administrator; b. Perth Amboy, N.J., May 29, 1936; s. Frank Joseph and Helen (Bodzany) C.; m. Helen Fitzgerald, May 28, 1962; 1 dau., Ruth. AB magna cum laude, Harvard U., 1958, MD, 1962. Med. intern U. Va. Hosp., 1962-63; resident, fellow in psychiatry Mass. Gen. Hosp., Harvard Med. Sch., 1963-66; alcohol coordinator Mass. Gen. Hosp., 1967-68, clin. assoc. psychiatry, 1968—; asst. supt. Medfield State Hosp., Harding, Mass., 1968-70, supt., 1970-74, area program dir., 1970-74; dir. Outlook Psychiat. Facility, Hampstead, N.H., 1974-76; med. dir. Charles River Hosp., Wellesley, Mass., 1976-80, psychiatrist-in-chief, 1980-87, Hahnemann Hosp., Boston, 1982—; med. dir. Taunton Hosp. and Regional Svc. Ctr., 1990-92; assoc. med. dir. psychiatry PHCS, Lexington, Mass., 1991-93, v.p., med. dir. mental health svcs. Waltham, Mass., 1993-96. V.p. clin. affairs Cmty. Care Systems Inc., 1979-86, sr. cons., 1986—; asst. clin. prof. psychiatry Boston U. Sch. Medicine, 1968-74, assoc. clin. prof., 1979—; asst. psychiatrist Beth Israel Hosp., 1970—; lectr. in psychiatry Harvard Med. Sch., 1972-89; cons. Med. Mgmt., Managed Care Programs, 1986—. Pres. Medfield Found.; bd. overseers Mt. Desert Island Biol. Lab. Served with AUS, 1966-68. Mem. Am. Coll. Mental Health Adminstrn., Mass. Med. Soc., BCN Med. Soc. Office: 707 Green Acres North Dighton MA 02764

CSIKSZENTMIHALYI, MIHALY, psychology professor; b. Fiume, Italy, Sept. 29, 1934; came to U.S., 1956; s. Alfred and Edith (Jankovich) C.; m. Isabella Selega, Dec. 30, 1961; children: Mark, Christopher. BA, U. Chgo., 1960, PhD, 1965. Reporter European News Service, Rome, 1952-56; free-lance artist Rome, 1954-56; translator U.S.A. Pubs., Chgo., 1958-64; prof. sociology Lake Forest (Ill.) Coll., 1965-70; prof. psychology human devel., edn. U. Chgo., 1971—. Adv. bd. Ency. Britannica, Chgo., 1985—, J.P. Getty Mus., Malibu, Calif., 1985—. Author: Beyond Boredom and Anxiety, 1975, Flow: The Psychology of Optimal Experience, 1990, The Evolving Self, 1993, Creativity, 1996, Finding Flow in Everyday Life, 1997, Good Business, 2003; (with others) The Creative Vision, 1976, The Meaning of Things, 1981, Being Adolescent, 1984, Optimal Experience, 1988, Television and the Quality of Life, 1990, The Art of Seeing, 1990, Talented Teenagers, 1993, Creating Worlds, 1994. Fulbright Sr. scholar, 1984, 1990, Fellow Ctr. for Advanced Studies in the Behavioral Sci., 1994-95. Fellow Am. Acad. Arts and Scis., Am. Acad. Edn., Am. Acad. Leisure Scis., Am. Acad. Polit. and Social Scis.; mem. Quadrangle Club. Avocations: mountain climbing, reading, art, chess. Home: 700 Alamosa Dr Claremont CA 91711 Office: 1021 N Dartmouth Ave Claremont CA 91711 Office Phone: 909-607-3307. Business E-Mail: miska@cgu.edu.

CSONKA, PAUL L., theoretical physicist, educator; b. Budapest, Hungary, Aug. 10, 1938; came to U.S., 1957; s. Pal Csonka and Margit Warga; m. Martha E. C.; children: Emese C., Paul J., Livia M. PhD, Johns Hopkins U., 1963. Postdoctoral fellow Lawrence Livermore (Calif.) Nat. Lab., 1964-66; NSF postdoctoral fellow CERN Labs., Geneva, Switzerland, 1966-68; prof. physics U. Oreg., Eugene, 1968—, dir. Robert D. Clark Honors Coll., 1997-2000. NORDITA vis. prof. to Scandinavia, 1972-73; dir. Inst. of Theoretical Sci., U. Oreg., 1977-79. Alfred P. Sloan fellowship, 1970-72; recipient Fulbright Sr. Rsch. award Budapest, Hungary, 1993, 94. Office: U Oreg Dept Physics Eugene OR 97403 Business E-Mail: pcsonka@oregon.uoregon.edu.

CSÖRGÖ, MIKLOS, mathematics and statistics educator; b. Egerfarmos, Hungary, Mar. 12, 1932; arrived in Can., 1957, naturalized, 1962; s. Miklos and Ilona (Veres) Csörgö; m. Anna Eszter Toth, Aug. 10, 1957; children: Adria, Lilla. BA, Karl Marx U. Econs., Budapest, Hungary, 1955; MA, McGill U., 1961, PhD, 1963. Instr., postdoctoral fellow Princeton U., NJ, 1963—65; asst. prof. McGill U., Montreal, Canada, 1965—68, assoc. prof., 1968—71; vis. prof. U. Vienna, 1969—70; assoc. prof. math. and stats. Carleton U., Ottawa, Canada, 1971—72, prof., 1972—, co-dir. Lab. for Rsch. in Stats. and Probability, 1983—. Vis. prof. U. Utah, 1991—92. Author (with P. Révész): Strong Approximations in Probability and Statistics, 1981; author: Quantile Processes with Statistical Applications, 1983; author: (with others) An Asymptotic Theory for Empirical Reliability and Concentration Processes, 1986; author: (with L. Horváth) Weighted Approximations in Probability and Statistics, 1993; author: (with L. Horvath) Limit Theorems in Change-Point Analysis, 1997; assoc. editor The Annals of Probability, 1979—81, mem. editl. bd. Stats. and Decisions, 1981—2002, Jour. Multivariate Analysis, 1986—87. Fellow, Can. Coun., 1969—70, 1976—77, Killam sr. rsch. fellow, 1978—79, 1979—80. Fellow: Inst. Math. Stats., Royal Soc. Can.; mem.: Hungarian Acad. Sci. (external mem.), Internat. Statis. Inst., Bernoulli Soc., Statis. Soc. Can., Can. Math. Soc., Am. Math. Soc. Office: Carleton U Lab Rsch in Stats 1125 Colonel By Dr Ottawa ON Canada K1S 5B6 E-mail: mcsorgo@math.carleton.ca.

CSURGAI-SCHMITT, JACQUELINE, musician, educator; b. Detroit, Mar. 30, 1943; d. Alfred Nichols Schmitt and Evelyn Margarite Churgay. MusB in Piano Performance, Mich. State. U. Hon. Coll., 1965; MusM in Piano Performance, Indiana U., 1967. Piano instr. No. Va. CC, Alexandria, 1971—73, George Mason U., Fairfax, 1973—81; pianist Detroit, 1988—2004, Dearborn Symphony, 1994—2005. Cons. to injured pianists, 1984—2004; instr. workshops for music tchr. orgns., 1984—; co-founder Pianist's Com. Technique Movement Wellness, 1996—2000; spkr. in field; instr. Marygrove Coll., Detroit, 2004—. Author: Mind and Body for Optional Performance, 2002; contbr. chapters to books. Recipient Mayor's Arts award, 1998. Mem.: Tuesday Musicale Detroit (pres. 1998—2001, performing mem. 1996—2004), Pi Kappa Lamda, Delta Omicron.

CUA, ANTONIO S., philosopher, educator; b. Manila, July 23, 1932; arrived in U.S., 1953, naturalized, 1971; s. Oh and Chio (So) Cua; m. Shoke-Hwee Khaw, June 11, 1956; 1 child, Athene K. BA, Far Eastern U., Manila, 1952; MA, U. Calif, Berkeley, 1954; PhD, U. Calif., Berkeley, 1958. Tchg. asst. U. Calif. Berkeley, 1955—58; instr., asst. prof. Ohio U., 1958-62; prof., chmn. dept. philosophy SUNY Coll. at Oswego, 1962-69; prof. philosophy Cath. U. Am., Washington, 1969-96, prof. emeritus, 1996—. Vis. prof. U. Mo., Columbia, 1974—75, U. Hawaii, 1976—77; vis. professorial lectr. Nat. Cheng-chi U., Taiwan, 1993, Nat. Tsinghua U., Taiwan, 1995. Author: Reason and Virtue: A Study in the Ethics of Richard Price, 1966, Dimensions of Moral Creativity: Paradigms, Principles, and Ideals, 1978, The Unity of Knowledge and Action: A Study in Wang Yang-ming's Moral Psychology, 1982, Ethical Argumentation: A Study in Hsün Tzu's Moral Epistemology, 1985, Moral Vision and Tradition: Essays in Chinese Ethics, 1998, Human Nature, Ritual and History: Studies in Xunzi and Chinese Philosophy, 2005; editor: Encyclpedia of Chinese Philosophy, 2003; co-editor: Jour. Chinese Philosophy; assoc. editor: Internat. Jour. Philosophy Religion, mem. editl. bd.: Am. Philos. Quar., 1972—2002, Philosophy East and West, 1985—2003, Dao: A Jour. Comparative Philosophy; contbr. articles to profl. jours. Mem.: Aristolelian Soc., Mind Assn., Soc. Asian and Comparative Philosophy (pres. 1978—79), Internat. Soc. Chinese Philosophy (pres. 1984—86), Am. Philos. Assn. Office: Cath U Am Sch Philosophy Washington DC 20064-0001 Mailing: 7525 Cayuga Ave Bethesda MD 20817 Personal E-mail: antoniocua@msn.com. Business E-Mail: cua@cua.edu.

CUADRA, CARLOS ALBERT, library and information scientist, consultant; b. San Francisco, Dec. 21, 1925; s. Gregorio and Amanda (Mendoza) C.; m. Gloria Nathalie Adams, May 3, 1947; children: Mary Susan Cuadra Nielsen, Neil Gregory, Dean Arthur. AB in Psychology with highest honors, U. Calif., Berkeley, 1949, PhD in Psychology, 1953. Staff psychologist VA, Downey, Ill., 1953-56; with Sys. Devel. Corp., Santa Monica, Calif., 1957-78, mgr. libr. and documentation sys. dept., 1968-70, mgr. edn. and libr. sys. dept., 1971-74; gen. mgr. SDC Search Svc., 1974-78; founder Cuadra Assocs., L.A., 1978—. Founder, editor: Ann. Rev. of Info. Sci. and Tech., 1964—75; contbr. articles to profl. jours. Mem. Nat. Commn. Librs. and Info. Sci., 1971-84. Served with USN, 1944-46. Recipient Merit award Am. Soc. Info. Sci., 1968, Best Info. Sci. Book award Am. Soc. Info. Sci., 1969, Miles Conrad award Nat. Fedn. Abstracting and Info. Svcs., 1980, Roger Summit award Assn. Ind. Info. Profls., 2001; named Disting. Lectr. of Yr., Am. Soc. Info. Sci., 1970, hon. fellow Nat. Fedn. Abstracting and Info. Svcs., 1997. Mem. Info. Industry Assn. (bd. dirs., Hall of Fame award 1980), Chem. Abstracts Soc. (governing bd. 1991-96), Am. Chem. Soc. (governing bd. pub. 1997-2000), Phi Beta Kappa. Home: 13213 Warren Ave Los Angeles CA 90066-1750 Office: Cuadra Associates 11835 W Olympic Blvd Ste 855 Los Angeles CA 90064-5001

CUALING, HERNANI DEL MUNDO, physician, researcher; s. Pablo Mateong and Flor Del Mundo Cualing; m. Rawia Salem Yassin, Dec. 20, 1989; children: Kareem Yassin Khozaim, Phillip, Andrew. BS, U. Philippines, 1974, MD, 1978. Diplomate Am. Bd. of Pathology, 1991. Chief resident Nassau County U. Med. Ctr., East Meadow, NY, 1990—91; fellow dept. pathology Ind. U. Med. Ctr., Indpls., 1991—92; asst. prof. U. Cin. Med. Ctr., 1992—2002; assoc. prof. dept. pathology U. Cin., 2002—02; assoc. prof. U. South Fla./Moffitt Cancer Ctr., Tampa, 2002—. Consulting hematopathology staff VA Med. Ctr., Cin., 1993—2002; med. dir. U. Cin. Med. Ctr., 1993—96, Diagnostic Immunology and Flow Cytometry Interpretation of Leukemias and Lymphomas, Diagnostic Flow Cytometry by Health Alliance, 2000—02; med. dir. immunohistochemistry/histology Moffitt Cancer Ctr. and Rsch. Inst., Tampa, Fla., 2002—. Period furniture, Queen Anne Desk; contbr. articles to profl. jours. Mem. U. Philippines Med. Alumni Soc., Tampa, Fla., 2002—03. Recipient First prize Paper, Fla. Soc. Pathologists, 2004, Tchr. of Yr., U. South Fla. Pathology Residents, 2004; grantee Biomedical Engring. of Leukemia/Lymphoma, Whitaker Found., 1997-2000; Pioneering grant, U. Cin. Biomed. Engring., 1994. Fellow: Coll. Am. Pathologists (assoc.); mem.: Soc. Applied Immunohistochemistry (assoc.), Internat. Soc. Optical Engring. (assoc.). R-Liberal. Catholic. Achievements include invention of Computerized Aided Counting of Immunostained cells. Avocations: woodworking, sailing. Home: 18804 Chaville Rd Lutz FL 33558 Office Phone: 813-979-3914. E-mail: cualinhd@moffitt.usf.edu.

CUARON, ALFONSO, film director; b. Mexico City, Mex., Nov. 28, 1961; Student, Cooperative Universataria Edigtrice Cagliaritana, Mex. 1st asst. dir.: (films) Gaby, A Love Story, 1987; Romero, 1989; dir.: Cuarteto para el fin del tiempo, 1983, A Little Princess, 1995 (L.A. Film Critics New Generation award), Great Expectations, 1998, Harry Potter and the Prisoner of Azkaban, 2004, (TV episode) Fallen Angels, 1993 (CableACE award), Cita Con La Muerte, 1989; prodr.: (films) Me La Debes, 2001, The Assassination of Richard Nixon, 2004; dir., prodr. (films) Love in the Time of Hysteria, 1991, dir., prodr., writer Y Tu Mama Tambien, 2001 (Best Screenplay award Venice Film Festival, L.A. Film Critics award, Ind. Spirit award for Best Fgn. Film), dir., writer The Children of Men, 2002.

CUATRECASAS, PEDRO MARTIN, research biochemist, pharmaceutical executive; b. Madrid, Sept. 27, 1936; came to U.S., 1947; s. Jose and Martha C.; m. Carol Zies, Aug. 15, 1959; children: Paul, Lisa, Diane, Julia. AB, Washington U., St. Louis, 1958, MD, 1962; DSc honoris causa, U. Barcelona, 1984, Mt. Sinai Sch. Medicine, 1985, U. Buenos Aires, 1990, U. Naples, Italy, 1990. Intern, then resident in internal medicine Osler Svc. Johns Hopkins Hosp., 1962-64, asst. physician, 1972-75; clin. asso., clin. endocrinology br. Nat. Inst. Arthritis and Metabolic Diseases, NIH, 1964-66; spl. USPHS postdoctoral fellow Lab. Chem. Biology, 1966-67, med. officer, 1967-70; professorial lectr. biochemistry George Washington U. Med. Sch., 1967-70; assoc. prof. pharmacology and exptl. therapeutics, assoc. prof. medicine, dir. div. clin. pharmacology, Burroughs Wellcome prof. clin. pharmacology Johns Hopkins U. Med. Sch., 1970-72, prof. pharmacology and exptl. therapeutics, assoc. prof. medicine, 1972-75; v.p. rsch., devel. and med. Wellcome Rsch. Labs.; dir. Burroughs Wellcome Co., Research Triangle Park, N.C., 1975-86; sr. v.p. R&D Glaxo Inc., 1986-89; also bd. dirs. Glaxo Inc., Glaxo Internat. Rsch., Ltd., London, 1986-89; pres. pharm. rsch. divsn., and co. v.p. Warner-Lambert Co., Ann Arbor, Mich., 1989-97; ind. pharm. rsch. cons. Rancho Santa Fe, Calif., 1997—; prof. dept. medicine & pharm. U. Calif., San Diego, 1997—. Adj. prof. Duke U. Med. Sch., 1975-89; adj. prof., mem. adv. com. cancer rsch. program U. N.C. Med. Sch., 1975-90; adj. prof. dept. pharm. and medicinal chemistry, U. Mich., 1990-97; bd. dirs. Alliance Pharms.; mem. FDA sci. bd., 1994-98. Editor: Receptors and Recognition Series, 1975-98, Jour. Solid-Phase Biochemistry, 1975-80, Handbook of Experimental Pharmacology, 1984-99, Internat. Jour. Biochemistry, 1973, Molecular and Cellular Endocrinology, 1973-77, Biochimica Biophysica Acta, 1973-79, Life Scis., 1978-88, Neuropeptides, 1979-99, Jour. Applied Biochemistry, 1978-91, Cancer Research, 1980-81, Jour. Applied Biochemistry and Biotech., 1980—98, Toxin Revs., 1981-90, Biochem. Biophys. Rsch. Comms., 1981-94; contbr. articles to profl. jours. Active Am. Diabetes Assn., 1972—, PMA Commn. on Drugs and Rare Diseases, 1982-89; bd. dirs. Burroughs Wellcome Fund, 1975-86. Recipient John Jacob Abel prize, 1972, Laude prize Pharm. World, 1975, Beerman award Soc. Investigative Dermatology, 1981, Isco award U. Nebr., 1985, Dupont Splty. Diagnostics award Clin. Ligand Assay Soc., 1986, Alumni Achievement award Washington U. Sch. Medicine, 1987, Wolf Found. prize in medicine, 1987, N.C. Gov.'s medal award in sci., 1988, Achievement award Soc. for Biomolecular Screening, 1999, Johns Hopkins U. Disting. Alumnus award, 2000; FDA Commr.'s Spl. citation, 1997, City of Medicine award (disting. achievement in medicine), 1998; inducted into Johns Hopkins Soc. Scholar, 1990. Fellow Am. Acad. Arts. and Scis.; mem. Am. Soc. Biol. Chemists, Nat. Acad. Scis., Inst. Medicine of Nat. Acad. Scis. (governing council 1988-96), Am. Soc. Pharmacology and Exptl. Therapeutics (Goodman and Gilman award 1982), Am. Soc. Clin. Investigation, Am. Soc. Clin. Rsch., Spanish Biochem. Soc., Md. Acad. Scis. (Outstanding Young Scientist of Year 1970), Am. Cancer Soc., Endocrine Soc., Am. Chem. Soc., Am. Diabetes Assn. (Eli Lilly award 1975), Am. Diabetes Assn., Sigma Xi. Personal E-mail: pedrocuatrecasas@znet.com.

CUBA, BENJAMIN JAMES, lawyer, mediator; b. Dec. 12, 1936; s. Ben and Patricia (Machalek) C.; m. Bernadette Theresa Haney, Sept. 4, 1964; children: Benjamin Courtney, Tristan Konrad. AA, Temple Coll., 1957; BBA, U. Tex., 1959; JD, Baylor U., 1963. Bar: Tex. 1964, U.S. Dist. Ct. (we. dist.) Tex. 1970, U.S. Ct. Appeals (5th and 11th cirs.) 1981, U.S. Supreme Ct. 1978. Assoc. Law Offices of Jarrard Secrest, Temple, Tex., 1964-66; ptnr. Secrest & Cuba, Temple, Tex., 1966-68; sr. ptnr. Cuba & Cuba and predecessor firms, Temple, Tex., 1968—. Dir. founding trustee, atty. Inst. for Humanities at Salado, Tex., 1980—, founding trustee, legal counsel First House, Inc., Temple, 1981-86; legal counsel, mem. cmty. adv. bd. Jr. League of Bell County, Inc. (and predecessor org. Svc. League of Temple, Inc.), 1976—; v.p. Temple Indsl. Devel. Corp., 1984-89; pres. Trailblazer Corp., 1973-. Fellow Tex. Bar Found. (life); mem. Bell-Lampasas-Mills Counties Bar Assn. (pres. 1973-74), State Bar Tex., U. Tex. Ex Student's Assn., Baylor Law Alumni Assn., Quarterback Club (dir. 1984, 85), Phi Delta Phi. Lutheran. Office: Cuba & Cuba PLC 18 S Main St Ste 802 Temple TX 76501-7608 Office Phone: 254-778-1824. Business E-Mail: benjamin@cuba-law.com.

CUBA, LEE, dean; BS in Sociology and Urban Studies, So. Meth. U., 1976; MA, Yale U., 1977, MPhil, 1978, PhD, 1981. Instr. sociology U. Alaska, 1979, Yale U., 1981; mem. faculty Wellesley (Mass.) Coll., 1981—, assoc. dean of coll., 1995—99, dean of coll., 1999—. Chair dept. sociology Wellesley U., 1992—95, assoc. dir. writing program, 1993—95. Author: Identity and Community on the Alaskan Frontier, 1987, A Short Guide to Writing About Social Science, 4th edit., 2001; contbr. numerous articles to profl. jours. Grantee, NIH, Nat. Inst. Aging, NIMH, Alfred P. Sloan Found. Mem.: Phi Beta Kappa. Office: Wellesley Coll Office of Dean of Coll 106 Central St Green Hall Rm 345 Wellesley MA 02481

CUBA, STANLEY L., government official; b. Denver, Apr. 30, 1948; s. Frank L. (Czuba) Cuba and Wanda Helen Kugaczewska; m. Ewa Zofia Galkowska, Sept. 18, 1998. BA in Polit. Sci., Europe-Columbia U., 1970; cert. in East European studies, Inst. on East Cen., 1972; MA in History, Columbia U., 1978. Assoc. conf. coord. Polish Inst. Arts and Scis., N.Y.C., 1970-72; asst. to pres. Kosciuszko Found., N.Y.C., 1972-79; assoc. dir. Andre Zarre Gallery, N.Y.C., 1980-82; transl. Denver, 1983-90; ct. clk. II Denver County Ct., 1986-90; cert. investigator Mayor's Office of Contract Compliance, Denver, 1990-2000; prevailing wage investigator auditor's office Denver Internat. Airport, 2000—. Mayor's Office of Contract Compliance liaison to Asian C. of C., Denver, 1993-2000; presenter in field. Author: (exhbn. catalogs) Stefan Mrozewski (1894-1975) Wood Engravings: A Posthumous Exhibition, 1976, Jozef Pankiewicz (1886-1940): A Loan Exhibition of Oils, Watercolors, Sketches and Graphics, 1978, Hussars and the Crescent: The Polish Relief of Vienna, 1983, The Art of Jozef Bakos: An Early Modernist, 1891-1977, 1988, Colorado Women Artists, 1859-1950: An Unprecedented Exhibition of Women Artists Living or Working in Colorado from 1859 to 1950, 1989, Jan Sawka: A Selected Retrospective, 1990, The Art of Jozef Bakos: Selections from the Estate of Jozef Gabryel Bakos, 1992, Olive Rush: A Hoosier Artist in New Mexico, 1992, John F. Carlson and Artists of the Broadmoor Art Academy, 1999; co-author: (book) Great Drawings of the 20th Century, 1981, The Colorado Book, 1993, The Art of Charles Partridge Adams, 1993, (exhbn. catalogs) George Luks: An American Artist, 1987, Pikes Peak Vision: The Broadmoor Art Academy, 1919-1945, 1989, Hayes Lyon: A Colorado Regionalist (1909-1987), 1991; contbr. to Allgemeines Kunstler Lexikon, 1998-99, also to exhbn. catalogs and mags. Mem. Denver Cath. Archdiocesan Adv. Coun., 1999-2002, photo/art acquisitions com. We. History Dept. Denver (Colo.) Pub. Lib.; mem. Denver Cath. Archdiocesan Due Process Panel, 2003-; mem. mus./gallery com. Arvada (Colo.) Ctr. for Arts and Humanities, 1990-2002. Recipient Bicentennial Recognition of Exhbn. Curated on History of Polish Cmty. in Colo., 1859-1876, Colo. Bicentennial Commn./Denver Mayoral Bicentennial Commn., 1976; Interpreter grantee Ford. Found./Citizens Exch. Corps, 1969, Polonian Rsch. Ctr. grant Jagiellonian U., Krakow, 1980. Mem. Polish Nat. Alliance (lodge 134, v.p. 1990-96, fin. sec. 1996-98), Polish Am. Hist. Assn. (mem., chmn. award com. 1979-83, Rev. Joseph Swastek prize 1984), Polish Inst. Arts & Scis., Kosciuszko Found. Democrat. Roman Catholic. Avocations: collecting art, travel, attending art exhibitions, concerts, and theater, films. Home: 2643 Utica St Denver CO 80212-3007 Office Phone: 303-342-2710. Personal E-mail: s.cuba@worldnet.att.net.

CUBAN, LARRY, education educator, researcher; b. Passaic, N.J., Oct. 31, 1934; s. Morris and Fanny (Janofsky) C.; m. Barbara Joan Smith, June 15, 1958; children: Sondra, Janice. BA in History, U. Pitts., 1955; MA in History, Case-Western Res. U., 1958; PhD, Stanford U., 1974. Cert. tchr., Calif., D.C., Pa. Biology tchr. McKeesport (Pa.) Pub. Schs., 1955-56; social studies tchr. Cleve. Pub. Schs., 1956-63; master tchr. history Washington D.C. Pub. Schs., 1963-65, dir.Cardozo project in urban tchg., 1965-67, social studies tchr., 1967-68, 70-72, dir. staff devel., 1968-70; supt. Arlington (Va.) Pub. Schs., 1974-81; prof. Stanford U. Sch. Edn., 1981—2001. Cons. in field. Author: To Make a Difference: Teaching in the Inner City, 1970, Teachers & Machines, 1986, How Teachers Taught, 2d edit., 1993, Why Is It So Hard to Get Good Schools?, 2003; co-author: (with David Tyack) Tinkering Toward Utopia, 1995, How Scholars Trumped Teachers, 1999, Oversold and Underused: Computers in Schools, 2001, The Blackboard and the Bottom Line: Why Schools Can't Be Businesses, 2004. John Hay Whitney Found. fellow, 1960-61; fellow Ctr. for Advanced Studies in Behavioral Scis., 1999-2000; Rsch. grantee Nat. Inst. Edn., 1980, Spencer Found., 1988. Mem. Am. Ednl. Rsch. Assn. (pres. 1990-91), History Edn. Soc., Phi Delta Kappa. Avocation: bicycling. Home: 2846 Kipling St Palo Alto CA 94306-2429 Office: Stanford Univ Sch of Edn Stanford CA 94305 Business E-Mail: cuban@stanford.edu.

CUBAN, MARK, professional sports team executive, Internet company executive; b. Pitts. m. Tiffany Stewart, Sept. 21, 2002; 1 child. Grad., Indiana U., 1981. Founder MicroSolutions (sold to CompuServe), 1983-90; pres. Radical Computing; co-founder broadcast.com (sold to Yahoo!), 1995—99; owner, mng. ptnr. Dallas Mavericks, 2000—; co-founder, pres., chmn. HDNet, 2001—; chmn., co-owner Magnolia Pictures, Landmark Theaters; chmn., majority owner Rysher Entertainment. Exec. prodr.: Godsend, 2004; exec. prodr.: Criminal, 2004; co-exec. prodr.: Star Search, 2002—04; exec. prodr.: Searching for Debra Winger, 2002; host: (TV series) The Benefactor, 2004. Founder Mark Cuban Found., The Fallen Patriot Fund, 2003—. Named one of Forbes 400 Richest Americans, Forbes Mag., 2000—. Office: Dallas Mavericks The Pavillion 2909 Taylor St Dallas TX 75226

CUBAS, JOSE M(ANUEL), advertising agency executive; b. Matanzas, Cuba, Mar. 1, 1930; came to U.S., 1960; s. Jose M. and Luisa M. (Ruiz) C.; m. Edith Perez, Apr. 26, 1952; children: Mercedes, Alina. Student, U. Havana Law Sch. Pres. Publicidad Siboney, S.A., Havana, 1953-60, San Juan, P.R., 1962-84, Internat. Mktg. and Advt. Services Corp., Fla., 1979-84; pres., CEO Foote Cone & Belding-Latin Am., N.Y.C., 1985-86, pres., 1987-97; chmn., CEO Siboney USA, Miami, Fla., 1998—. Mem. Internat. Advt. Assn., U.S.-Hispanic C. of C. (recipient awards). Republican. Roman Catholic. Avocations: travel, swimming, tennis. Office: Siboney USA 1401 Brickell Ave Ste 1100 Miami FL 33131-3504

CUBBAGE, ELINOR PHILLIPS, English language educator; b. Milford, Del., Apr. 4, 1948; d. Thomas Allen and Katheryn Augusta (Schaeffer) Phillips; m. James Stephenson, July 11, 1970; children: Kate Allen, Benjamin David. BA, U. Del., Newark, 1970; MS, Ea. Conn. State Coll., 1975; EdD, U. Md., 1993. Tchr. English Vernon (Conn.) H.S., 1971-75; prof. English Wor-Wic C.C., Salisbury, Md., 1977—, chairperson honors program, 1997—, chief writer Middle States Report, 1994-95, 99—. Adj. prof. Salisbury State U., 1975, 99—; rsch. coord. Nat. Ctr. for Devel. Edn., 1990-91. Editor-in-chief Student Creative Arts Mag., 1987—; contbr. articles, poetry to profl. jours. Mem. praise and worship team The Way, Salisbury, Md., 2001— NEH grantee, 1994-95. Mem. Nat. Coun. Tchrs. English, Tchrs. of English in the Two-Yr. Coll. (sec. of exec. bd. 1985-97). Avocation: creative writing. Home: 7180 Rockawalkin Rd Hebron MD 21830-1177 Office: Wor-Wic Cmty Coll 32000 Campus Dr Salisbury MD 21804-1485

CUBBEDGE, CAROLYN SUE HALE, minister; b. Lily, Ky., July 8, 1949; d. Jesse Edward and Freda Green Hale; m. James Edward Cubbedge, Nov. 30, 2003. BA cum laude, Georgetown Coll., 1971, MA in Edn., 1979; MDiv, Lexington Theol. Sem., 1994. Tchr. Lakota H.S., West Chester, Ohio, 1971—78; dir. student activities Georgetown (Ky.) Coll., 1978—85, dean student life, 1985—91; assoc. pastor Faith Bapt. Ch., Georgetown, 1991—92; comm. coord. Ky. Bapt. Fellowship, Lexington, Ky., 1993—97; dir. continuing edn. Lexington Theol. Sem., Lexington, 1994—95; chaplain/houseparent Quest Farm, Georgetown, 1996—97; mgr. Bob W. Brown Housing for Handicapped, Lexington, 1997—99; pastor Meml. Bapt. Ch., Savannah, Ga., 1999—. Coord. coun. Coop. Bapt. Fellowship, Atlanta, 1991—96; bd. dir. Morningstar Treatment Svcs., Brunswick, Ga. Co-author: Reflections, 1992—. Bd. mem. Habitat of Savannah, Ga., 2001—04. Named Woman of Yr., Georgetown Woman's Club, 1996. Mem.: Bapt. Women in Ministry (pres. 1992—93, bd. dir. 2000—, interim editor Folio 2001—02). Democrat. Baptist. Avocations: computerized embroidery, reading. Office: Meml Bapt Ch 6500 Habersham St Savannah GA 31405

CUBELL, HOWARD ALAN, lawyer; b. Brookline, Mass., Dec. 23, 1948; s. Robert and Mildred (Sugarman) C.; m. Ivy Beth Wiener, May 2, 1972; children: Michael and Daniel (twins). BA, U. Mich., 1970; JD, Boston, 1973; postgrad., NYU, 1973-76. Bar: N.Y. 1973, Mass. 1975. Assoc. Skadden, Arps, Slate, Meagher & Flom, N.Y.C., 1972-73, Debevoise & Plimpton, N.Y.C., 1973-75; ptnr. Goodwin Procter LLP (formerly Goodwin, Procter & Hoar), Boston, 1975—; chair, tax practice group Goodwin Procter LLP, Boston. Editor articles Boston U. Law Rev., 1972-73. Mem. ABA (tax sect.), Internat. Bar Assn., Boston Bar Assn. (co-chmn. internat. tax subcom. tax sect.). Office: Goodwin Procter LLP Exchange Pl 53 State St Boston MA 02109-2803 Office Phone: 617-570-1560. Office Fax: 617-523-1231. Business E-Mail: hcubell@goodwinprocter.com.

CUBEÑAS, JOSÉ ANTONIO, social worker, consultant; b. Manzanillo, Oriente, Cuba, Sept. 27, 1925; came to U.S., 1961; s. José Amador Cubeñas and Maximina Peluzzo; m. Elsie Mujica, Sept. 22, 1979. LLD, U. Havana, 1950; MA in Spanish, St. John's U., 1975. Practice law, Cuba, 1950-60; co-founder Fundación Cultura Hispánica, N.Y.C., 1980—. Author: Rubén Darío: Restaurador de la conciencia de armonía del mundo, 1975, Spanish and Hispanic Presence in Florida - The Oliveros House, 1979, Pandemocracia: La solución política de Iberoamérica?, 1991; contbr. articles to profl. and polit. jours. Cand. N.Y. State Assembly, 1994; mayor City of Manzanillo, Cuba 1959; co-founder Hispanic sect. of N.Y. State Rep. Party, 1980. Mem. Acad. Norteamericana de la Lengua Española, Círculo de Escritores y Poetas Iberoamericanos de N.Y. Republican. Roman Catholic. Avocations: soccer, history, literature. Office: Empress Travel 161 Dreiser Loop Bronx NY 10475

CUBIN, BARBARA LYNN, congresswoman; b. Salinas, Calif., Nov. 30, 1946; d. Russell G. and Barbara Lee (Howard) Sage; m. Frederick William Cubin, Aug. 1; children: William Russell, Frederick William III. BS in Chemistry, Creighton U., 1969. Chemist Wyo. Machinery Co., Casper, Wyo., 1973-75; social worker State of Wyo.; office mgr. Casper, Wyo.; mem. Wyo. Ho. Reps., 1987-92, Wyo. Senate, 1993-94; pres. Spectrum Promotions and Mgmt., Casper, 1993-94; at-large repr. U.S. Ho. Reps. from Wyo., Washington, 1995—; mem. resources com., energy and commerce com. Mem. steering com. Exptl. Program to Stimulate Competitive Rsch. (EPSCOR); mem. Coun. of State Govts.; active Gov.'s Com. on Preventive Medicine, 1992; vice chmn. Cleer Bd. Energy Coun., Irving, Tex., 1993—; chmn. Wyo. Senate Rep. Conf., Casper, 1993—; mem. Wyo. Rep. Party Exec. Com., 1993; pres. Southridge Elem. Sch. PTO, Casper, Wyo. Toll fellow Coun. State Govts., 1990, Wyo. Legislator of Yr. award for energy and environ. issues Edison Electric Inst., 1994. Mem. Am. Legis. Exch. Coun., Rep. Women. Republican. Avocations: duplicate bridge, golf, singing, reading, hunting. Office: US House of Reps 1114 Longworth House Office Bldg Washington DC 20515-5001*

CUBITTO, ROBERT J., lawyer; b. Globe, Ariz., Aug. 1, 1950; s. Claude A. and Arizona C. (DiMario) C. BA, U. Ariz., 1972, BSBA, 1974; JD, Harvard Law Sch., 1976. Bar: Mass. 1977, N.Y. 1979, U.S. Dist. Ct. (so. and ea. dists.) N.Y. 1979, U.S. Tax Ct. 1979. Cons. Boston Cons. Group, 1976-78; assoc. Debevoise & Plimpton LLP, N.Y.C., 1978-84, ptnr., 1985—. Bd. dirs. Met. Opera, 2005—. Mem. ABA, NY State Bar Assn. (exec. com. tax sect. 1987-88), Assn. of Bar of City of NY, Harvard Club NYC (asst. treas. 1985-89, bd. mgrs. 1990-93), The Club of Turtle Bay (treas. 1994-97, pres. 1998—), The Met. Opera (bd. dirs. 2005-). Office: Debevoise & Plimpton LLP 919 3rd Ave New York NY 10022-3904 Office Phone: 212-909-6338.

CUCCO, ULISSE P., retired obstetrician, gynecologist; b. Bklyn., Aug. 19, 1929; s. Charles and Elvira (Garafalo) C.; m. Antoinette DeMarco, Aug. 31, 1952; children— Carl, Richard, Antoinette Marie, Michael, Frank, James BS cum laude, L.I. U., 1950; MD, Loyola U., Chgo., 1954. Diplomate Am. Bd. Ob-Gyn. Intern Nassau County Hosp., Hempstead, N.Y., 1954-55; resident in ob-gyn Lewis Meml. Mercy Hosp., Chgo., 1955-58; practice medicine specializing in ob-gyn Des Plaines, Ill., 1960—. Past pres. med. staff, chmn. dept. ob-gyn. Holy Family Hosp., Des Plaines, Ill.; clin. asst. prof. Stritch Sch. Medicine, Loyola U. Contbr. articles to med. jours. Mem. ACS, Am. Fertility Soc., Ctrl. Assn. Ob-Gyn., Ill. Med. Soc., Chgo. Med. Soc., Chgo. Gynecol. Soc. (past pres.), Chgo. Inst. Medicine, Sunset Ridge Country Club. Roman Catholic. Home: 665 Midfield Ln Northbrook IL 60062-5507

CUCIN, ROBERT LOUIS, plastic surgeon, lawyer; b. N.Y.C., Apr. 17, 1946; s. Robert and Julia C. BA magna cum laude, Cornell U., 1967, MD, 1971; JD, Fordham U., 1985; MBA, Columbia U., 2003. Bar: N.Y. 1983, N.J. State Sureme Ct., Washington Ct. of Appeals; bd. cert. legal medicine, diplomate Am. Bd. Surgery, Am. Bd. Plastic Surgery, lic. physician NJ, N.Y. State, Calif., Va., gen. socs. prin.; securities license series 4, 7, 24, 27 and 63. Intern Cornell-N.Y. Hosp., N.Y.C., 1971-72, resident in gen. surgery, 1972-76, resident in plastic surgery, 1977-79; fellow in surgery Meml.-Sloan Kettering Found., 1972-76, 77-79; practice medicine specializing in plastic surgery Columbia MBA, N.Y.C., 1979—; instr. surgery Cornell U. Med. Coll., 1980—; asst. attending plastic surgeon Beth Israel North, N.Y. Downtown Hosp., 1979—, N.Y. Hosp., 1980—, Drs. Hosp., 1987—. Pres. Esquire Cadillac Limousine Svc. Inc., 1977—93, Beaux Arts Holdings, 1979—, Rocin Labs., Inc., 1981—; pres., CEO Biosculpture Tech., Inc., 2001—. Author: The Kindest Cut, Keeping Face, Medical Malpractice: Handling Plastic Surgical Cases; contbr. articles to profl, jours. Mem. N.Y. County Health Svc. Rev. Orgn., 1976—; founder, dir Rocin Found. for Plastic Surg. Rsch., 1979—; Maj. M.C., USAF, 1976-77; Japan. Fellow: ACS, Am. Coll. Legal Medicine, Internat. Coll. Surgeons; mem.: ABA, ATLA, AMA (Physicians Recognition award 1978, 1981), N.Y. Acad. Scis., N.Y. County Med. Soc. (health systems, pub. rels., peer rev. coms.), N.Y. State Med. Soc., Royal Soc. Medicine, Am. Soc. Plastic and Reconstructive Surgery, Am. Mensa, Cornell Club, N.Y. Athletic Club, Le Club, Phi Beta Kappa. Republican. Office: 120 Central Park S New York NY 10019-1560 Office Phone: 212-586-9500.

CUCULLU, SANTIAGO, artist; b. Buenos Aires, 1969; BFA, Hartford Art Sch., 1992; MFA, Mpls. Coll. Art & Design, 1999. One-man shows include Solo Show, Boom Gallery, Mpls., 1999, Art Houston, Barbara Davis Gallery, Houston, 2002, Wiyya To Hell Owwa That, Julia Friedman Gallery, Chgo., 2003, Art Basel Miami: Art Statements, Barbara Davis Gallery, Houston, 2003, Arco: Madrid Project Room, Julia Friedman Gallery, Chgo., 2004, Mori Art Mus., Tokyo, 2004, Hammer Mus., LA, 2004, exhibited in group shows, Escacio de Pensamiento, Bueno Aires, Argentina, 1995, Dumb & Evil, Calhoun Sq. Gallery, Mpls., 1998, Push, Pull Pop, 1999, XL, Weinstein Gallery, Mpls., 2000, 13 From Mpls., Mpls., 2002, Fresh-The Altoids Collection, Mus. Contemporary Art, NY, 2003, Works on Paper, Blum & Poe Gallery, LA, 2003, How Latitudes Become Forms, Walker Art Ctr., Mpls., 2004, Whitney Biennial, Whitney Mus. Am. Art, 2004. Jerome Emerging Artist Fellowship, Mpls. Coll. Art & Design, 2000. Office: c/o Julia Friedman Gallery 118 North Peoria Chicago IL 60607*

CUDAHY, RICHARD D., federal judge; b. Milw., Feb. 2, 1926; s. Michael F. and Alice ((Dickson)) Cudahy; m. Ann (Featherston), July 14, 1956 (dec. 1974); m. Janet (Stuart), July 17, 1976; children: Richard D., Norma K., Theresa E., Daniel M., Michaela A., Marguerite L., Patrick G. BS, U.S. Mil. Acad., 1948; JD, Yale U., 1955; LLD, Ripon Coll., 1981, DePaul U., 1995, Wabash Coll., 1996, Stetson U., 1998. Bar: Conn. 1955, D.C. 1957, Ill. 1957, Wis. 1961. Commd., 2d. lt. U.S. Army, 1948, 1st. lt., 1950; law clk. to presiding judge U.S. Ct. Appeals (2d cir.), 1955—56; asst. to legal adv. Dept. State, 1956—57; assoc. Isham, Lincoln, and Beale, Chgo., 1957—60; pres. Patrick Cudahy, Inc., Wis., 1961—71, Patrick Cudahy Family Co., Wis., 1968—75; ptnr. firm Godfrey and Kahn, Milw., 1972; commr., chmn. Wis. Pub. Svc. Commn., 1972—75; ptnr. Isham, Lincoln, and Beale, Chgo. and Washington, 1976—79; judge U.S. Ct. Appeals (7th cir.), Chgo., 1979—94, sr. judge, 1994—. Lectr. law Marquette U. Law Sch., 1962—66; vis. prof. law U. Wis., 1966—67; prof. lectr. law George Washington U., Washington, 1978—79; adj. prof. DePaul U. Coll. Law, 1995—. Commr. Milw. Harbor, 1964—66; pres. Milw. Urban League, 1965—66; trustee Environ. Def. Fund, 1976—79; chmn. DePaul U., Human Rights Law Inst., 1990—98; mem. adv. com. Ctr. for Internat. Human Rights, Northwestern U., 2000—; mem. vis. com. U. Chgo. Div. Sch.; chmn. Wis. Dem. Party, 1967—68; Dem. candidate for Wis. Atty. Gen., 1968. Mem.: ABA (spl. com. on Energy Law 1978—84, pub. utility sect. coun. group), DC Cir. Apptd. Ind. Counsel (spl. divsn. 1998—2002), Ill. Bar Assn., DC Bar Assn., Am. Inst. for Pub. Svc. (bd. selectors 1973—98), Fed. Judges' Assn. (bd. dirs. 1993—96), Chgo. Bar Assn., Wis. Bar Assn., Am. Law Inst., Cath. Theol. Union (trustee emeritus), Lawyers Club, Chgo. (pres. 1992—93). Office: US Ct Appeals 219 S Dearborn St Ste 2648 Chicago IL 60604-1874

CUDAK, GAIL LINDA, lawyer; b. Bellville, Ill., July 13, 1952; d. Robert Joseph and Margaret Lucille Cudak; m. Thomas Edward Young, Sept. 15, 1979. BA, Kenyon Coll., 1974; JD, Case Western Res. U., 1977, MBA, 1991. Bar: Ohio 1977, U.S. Dist. Ct. (no. dist.) Ohio 1977, U.S. Ct. Appeals (6th cir.) 1977, U.S. Ct. Appeals (fed. cir.) 1989. Assoc. Fuerst, Leidner, Dougherty & Kasdan, Cleve., 1977-79; staff atty. The B.F. Goodrich Co., Akron, Ohio, 1979-84, sr. corp. counsel Independence, Ohio, 1985-89, divsn. counsel Brecksville, Ohio, 1990-98, group counsel, 1998-99; sr. attorney Eaton Corp., Cleve., 1999—. Trustee Great Lakes Theater Festival, 1996—, mem. exec. com.; fundraiser Ohio Found. Ind. Colls., 1993—. Mem.: ABA, Cleve. Internat. Lawyers Group, Cleve. Bar Assn. (chair corp. sect.), Ohio State Bar Assn. Home: 12520 Edgewater Dr Apt 1405 Lakewood OH 44107-1639 Office: Eaton Corp 1111 Superior Ave E Cleveland OH 44114-2507

CUDDY, DANIEL HON, bank executive; b. Valdez, Alaska, Feb. 8, 1921; s. Warren N. and Lucy C.; m. Betty Puckett, Oct. 6, 1947; children: Roxanna, David, Gretchen, Jane, Lucy, Laurel. BA, Stanford U., 1946; LLD (hon.), U. Alaska, 2000. Bar: Alaska 1948. Pvt. practice, Anchorage, 1948-53; pres. First Nat. Bank Anchorage, 1951—, chmn. bd.; consul for the Netherlands, 1975—85. With U.S. Army, World War II, ETO. Named Alaskan of Yr., 2002. Office: First Nat Bank 101 W 36th Ave Anchorage AK 99503-5904

CUDE, THOMAS BRET, real estate broker; b. Evanston, Ill., Dec. 30, 1958; s. Herman (Bud) Earl Cude and Anne Carolyn McGuire; m. Susan Lynn Butterworth, Nov. 30, 1985; 1 child, Cassandra (Cassy) Leigh. BS in Agrl. Bus., Murray State U., Ky, 1981. Accredited farm mgr. Am. Soc. Of Farm Managers And Rural Appraisers/ Ill., 2000, cert. crop advisor Am. Soc. Of Agronomy/ill., 1997. Dist. sales mgr. Pioneer Hi-bred Internat., Inc., Iuka, Ill.; sr. farm mgr./ real estate broker Farmers Nat. Co., Nashville, Ill., 1993—. Mem. of leadership team Lighthouse Cmty. Ch., Nashville, Ill., 2003; treas. St. Louis Agribus. Club, 2003—04, 1st v.p., 2005—; bldg. com. chair Hickory Lake Subdivsn., Nashville, Ill., 1994; parent rep. Nashville Swim Team, Nashville, Ill., 1999; team rep. Shawnee Conf. Swim Conf., Pickneyville, Ill., 2002. Mem.: Ill. Soc. Of Profl. Farm Mgrs. and Rural Appraisers (com. mem. 1999), Murray State Agr. Alumni Assn (life; pres-elect, pres., past pres 1997—2000), Alpha Zeta (life), Alpha Gamma Rho (life; alumni bd. 2002). Southern Baptist. Avocations: golf, basketball. Home: 27 Hickory St Nashville IL 62263 Office: Farmers National Co Po Box 248 Nashville IL 62263-0248 Office Phone: 618-327-9242. Personal E-mail: bcude@farmersnational.com.

CUDKOWICZ, LEON, medical educator; b. Lodz, Poland, Jan. 18, 1923; came to U.S., 1956; s. Mauryce and Masza (Malynski) C.; m. Margaret Chandler, Mar. 14, 1950 (div. July 1981); children: Alexander, Penelope; m. Teresa Cuiza de Alfaro, Jan. 18, 1986. BS, U. London, 1946, MD, 1951. James Hudson Brown fellow Yale U. Sch. Medicine, 1956-58; registrar St. Thomas Hosp., U. London, 1958-59; asst. prof. then assoc. prof. medicine Dalhousie U., Halifax, N.S., Can., 1960-69; prof. medicine Thomas Jefferson U., Phila., 1970-74; prof., chmn. Wright State U., Dayton, 1974-79, King Faisal U., Dammam, Saudi Arabia, 1979-81; prof. medicine U. Cin., 1981-95, prof. emeritus, 1995—. Author: Human Bronchial Circulation, 1970; contbr. more than 100 articles to profl. jours. Capt. RAMC, 1946-49. NIH sr. internat. fellow, 1974—75. Fellow Royal Coll. Physicians, Nat. Pediat. Soc. Bolivia (hon.). Avocations: writing, mountain climbing, gardening, travel. Home: Yonder Hill Farm Highland OH 45132 Office: U Cin Sch Medicine 253 Bethesda Ave Cincinnati OH 45229-2827

CUEBAS IRIZARRY, ANA E., director; b. Mayaguez, P.R., Apr. 29, 1944; d. Francisco Cuebas and Isidora Irizarry. BA in Econ., Coll. Agr. & Mechanics Arts, Mayaguez, 1965; MLA, Pratt Inst., 1967; MPA, U. P.R., Rio Piedras, 1972; postgrad., U. P.R., San Germán, 2001—. Head reference collection Gen. Libr. U. P.R., Mayaguez, 1972—75, dir. pub. svcs., 1975—78, dir. documentation ctr. and cultural promotion, 1978—79, head purotorrican collector, 1978—80, head serials dept., 1980—86, project dir. title III Aguadilla, 1986—88, dir. continuing edn. and profl. studies, 1988—. Part-time prof. U. P.R., Mayaguez, 1972—82, mem. libr. personal com., Aguadilla, 1988—, coord. students deanship, 1990—, pres. continuing edn. dirs. com., Rio Piedras, PR, 1994—97; mem. consultive bd. Coun. Superior Edn., Rio Piedras, 1995; trustee Consorcio del Noroeste. Author: (book) Diccionario de siglas en uso en PR, 1979, En busca de una bibliografía para Mayagüez, 1982; contbr. articles to profl. jours. Mem. Cultural: Eugenio María de Hostos, Mayaguez, 1985—94. Recipient Spl. recognition, Altrusa Internat. Mayaguez, 1996—98, plaque of Recognition, Sindrome Down Assn., 2002, 2004, Altrusa Internat. Ing. 14th Dist., 1992—94, cert. of Recognition, Coun. Superior Edn. P.R., 2002; grantee, 2002, P.R. Humanities Endowment, 1998, Consejo de Desarrollo Ocupacional y Recursos Humanos, 1998, Works Rights Adminstrn., 2000, Dept. Edn., Rincón Sch. Dist., 2002, Dept. Edn., P.R., 2002, San Sebastián Sch. Dist., P.R., 2002. Mem.: PR ASCD, ASCD, Puertorrican Assn. Continuing Edn., Asociación Puertorriqueña Educación Continua, Phi Delta Kappa. Avocations: cooking, reading, Three Kings collector. Home: 626 Yaurel ST Mayaguez PR 00682-6233 Office: U PR Bell St Aguadilla PR 00604-0160 Personal E-mail: a_cuebas@hotmail.com.

CUELLAR, HENRY, congressman, lawyer; b. Laredo, Tex., Sept. 19, 1955; s. Martin and Odilia (Perez) C. BS, Georgetown Univ., 1978; JD, Univ. Tex., 1981; MA, Tex. A&M Univ., 1982; PhD Government, Univ. Tex., 1998. Bar: Tex. 1981, U.S. Dist. Ct. (so. dist.) Tex. 1981, U.S. Ct. Internat. Trade, 1981, U.S. Ct. Appeals (5th cir.) 1981. Atty. Henry Cuellar Law Office, Laredo, Tex., 1981—; customs broker Laredo, Tex., 1983—; mem. Tex. Ho. Rep., 1987—2001; sec. of state Tex., 2001; mem. U.S. Ho. Rep., 109th Congress, 28th Dist. Tex., 2004—. Mem. Tex. Ho. Reps., 1986—, chmn. internat. trade between Tex. and Mex. commn.; adj. prof. internat. comml. law Laredo State U., 1984-86; instr. state and nat. govt. Laredo Jr. Coll., 1982-86; speaker in field. Pres. bd. dirs. Laredo Legal Aid Soc. Inc., 1982-84, Laredo Vol. Lawyers Program Inc., 1982-83, Internat. Good Neighbor Council, 1984-85; treas. bd. dirs. Stop Child Abuse and Neglect, 1982-83, adv. bd., 1984—; state legal advisor Am. GI Forum of Tex., 1986-88; bd. dirs. United Way. 1982-83. Named one of Outstanding Young Men Am., 1982, 86. Mem. ABA, Tex. Bar Assn., Inter-Am. Bar Assn., Laredo Young Lawyers Assn. (pres. 1983-84), Kiwanis (bd. dirs. Laredo 1982-83). Democrat. Roman Catholic. Avocations: reading, karate. football, weightlifting. Office: US Ho of Reps 1404 Longworth Ho Office Bldg Washington DC 20515-4328 Office Phone: 202-225-1640.*

CUESTA, GEORGE MICHAEL, psychologist, clinical neuropsychologist, rehabilitation psychologist; b. N.Y.C., Feb. 3, 1955; s. Alex Cuesta Jr. and Theresa Aragon Torres. BS, U.S. Mil. Acad., 1978; MEd, Boston U., 1985; PhD, Calif. Sch. Profl. Psychology, Alameda, 1995. Lic. psychologist, N.Y. Counseling psychologist VA, Washington, San Francisco, 1985-88; psychology intern St. Mary's Med. Ctr., San Francisco, 1988-90; clin. psychologist Letterman Army Med. Ctr., San Francisco, 1990-91; psychol. asst. pvt. practice, San Francisco, 1988-97; postdoctoral fellow in neuropsychology San Francisco Gen. Hosp. and Med. Ctr., 1996-97; postdoctoral fellow in brain injury rehab. NYU Med. Ctr., N.Y.C., 1997; clin. neuropsychologist Kingsbrook Jewish Med. Ctr., Bklyn., 1997-99; dir. rehab. psychology and neuropsychology svcs. The Burke Rehab. Hosp., White Plains, NY, 1999—; clin. asst. prof. neuropsychology dept. neurology and neurosci. Weill Med. Coll. of Cornell U., 1999—. Capt. U.S. Army, 1978—85, Capt. Med. Svc. Corps USAR, 1999—. Decorated Meritorious Svc. medal, Army Commendation medal. Mem.: APA, N.Y. State Psychol. Assn., Am. Coll. Forensic Examiners, Internat. Neuropsychol. Soc., Nat. Acad. Neuropsychology. Avocations: skiing, bicycling, running, hiking, movies, theater, travel. Office: The Burke Rehab Hosp 785 Mamaroneck Ave White Plains NY 10605-2523 Office Phone: 914-597-2889. E-mail: gcuesta@burke.org.

CUEVAS, EDUARDO SAMANIEGO, internist; b. Manila, Oct. 7, 1958; came to U.S., 1985; s. Porfirio Carmona and Erlinda Samaniego Cuevas; m. Gigi Mariette Delos Reyes, Aug. 19, 1985; children: Elizabeth Grace, Edilene Gayle, Edward Gabriel, Emmanuel Gregory. BS in Psychology, U. of the Philippines, Quezon City, 1979; MD, Feu Inst. of Medicine, Manila, 1983. Diplomate Am. Bd. Internal Medicine. Intern San Juan de Dios Hosp., Pasay City, The Philippines, 1983-84, surg. resident, 1985; internal medicine resident Bklyn. Hosp. Ctr., 1989-92; pvt. practice Tacoma, 1992—. Dir., chair membership com. Southcare HMO, Tacoma, 1995—98; mem. policy bd. Doctors Health Plan, Auburn, Wash., 1996—98; mem. exec. com., chair pharmacy and therapeutics com. Puget Sound Hosp., Tacoma, 1996—97; mem. oper. bd., bd. mem. Physicians Health Network, Tacoma, 2001—03. Reviewer, contbr. Am. Bd. Internal Medicine, 1997—. With U.S. Army, 1986-88. Recipient Army Achievement award, 1988. Mem.: ACP-ASIM, AMA (Physicians Recognition award 1999—), Catholic Physicians Guild of Washington, Filipino Am. Physicians of Wash., Tacoma Acad. Internal Medicine, Pierce County Med. Soc., Wash. State Med. Assn., Beta Sigma (grand princep 2001—03). Avocations: piano, travel. Home: 6306 89th Ave W University Place WA 98467-1644 Office: Allenmore Med Ctr 1901 South Union St Ste A-114 Tacoma WA 98405 Office Phone: 253-472-8389. Personal E-mail: edcuevas@aol.com.

CUEVAS, KIMBERLY LYNETTE, secondary school educator; d. Warren Briggs and Sherryann Oakley; m. David Miguel Cuevas, May 9, 1992; children: Michael, Nicholas. BA, Ea. Mich. U., 1992. Tchr. Spanish Pearson Edn. Ctr., Reford, Mich., 1992—95, Redford (Mich.) Union H.S., 1995—. Avocations: reading, rollerblading. Office: Redford Union High Sch 17711 Kinloch Redford MI 48240-2295

CUFFE, STAFFORD SIGESMUND, business, technology, manufacturing & management consultant; AAS in Electronics Engring. Tech., N.Y.C. Coll. Tech., 1976; B of Engring. Tech., CCNY, 1977; MSA in Bus./Mgmt. Adminstrn., Cen. Mich. U., 1993; PhD in Applied Mgmt. and Decision Sci., Walden U., 1996. Project engr. PPG Industries, Wichita Falls, Tex., 1977—79; sr. mfg. engr. glass divsn. Ford Motor Co., Mich. and Okla., 1979—95; pres., cons. Cuffe & Assocs., Inc., Bloomfield Hills, Mich., 1996—. Cons in e-commerce, e-bus., info. tech., lean mfg., mgmt., curriculum devel., assessment tools; adj. prof. distance learning MBA program U. Dallas, 2000—02; adj. prof. Capella U., Sch. Bus. Adminstrn., Minn., 2000—04, Baker Coll., Ctr. for Grad. Studies, Mich., 2000—; assoc. prof. Touro U. Internat., Sch. Bus., Calif., 2003—; adj. prof. PhD program Nova Southeastern U., Sch. Bus. and Entrepreneurship, Fla., 2004—. Mem.: IEEE, Assn. for Info. Sys., Am. Mgmt. Assn., Soc. Mfg. Engrs. Avocations: golf, tennis, cross country skiing. Office: Cuffe & Assocs Inc PO Box 7123 Bloomfield Hills MI 48302-7123 Office Phone: 248-557-8541. E-mail: caimmts@aol.com.

CUI, HONGLIANG, engineering company executive, researcher; b. Hegang, Heilongjiang, China, July 7, 1965; s. Guanglin Cui and Jinyu Wang; m. Junxiu Zhu, May 15, 1965; 1 child, Weiqi. PhD, Stevens Inst. of Tech., 2004. Dir., engr. Shenyang Aircraft Rsch. Inst., China, 1986—95; with Inst. of Space and Aero. Sci. / U. Tokyo, Shagamihara, Japan, 1996—99; rschr. ABB Robotics, Windsor, Conn., 2000—04; exec. mgr. NDT, East Windsor, Conn., 2004—. Mem.: AIAA, ASME. Buddhist. Achievements include development of China fighter structure design; composite aircraft structure design; research in kinematics and error modeling of parallel robot; patents pending for six degrees of freedom measuring system. Office Phone: 201-216-5579. Home Fax: 860-233-8853; Office Fax: 201-216-8315. Personal E-mail: hcui1@stevens.edu.

CUI, JIANMIN, neuroscientist, educator; s. Silan Cui and Shuzhen Hong; m. Jingyi Shi, Aug. 29, 1986; children: Kevin Jiaqi, Amy Hanqi. BS, Peking U., Beijing, 1983, MS, 1986; PhD, SUNY, Stony Brook, 1992. Postdoctoral assoc. SUNY, Stony Brook, NY, 1992—94; postdoctoral fellow Stanford U., Palo Alto, Calif., 1994—98; asst. prof. Case Western Res. U., Cleve., 1999—2004; Spencer T. Olin assoc. prof. Washington U., St. Louis, 2004—. Mem.: Soc. Gen. Physiologists, Soc. for Neurosci., Biophys. Soc. Office: Wash U St Louis 290 C Whitaker Hall One Brookings Dr Saint Louis MO 63130 E-mail: jcui@biomed.wustl.edu.

CUIFFO, FRANK WAYNE, lawyer; b. Houston, Oct. 13, 1943; s. Richard and Helen (Giaco) C.; m. Barbara Joyce Streeter, Nov. 26, 1966; children: Karen, Deborah, Richard, Steven. BS, U. Notre Dame, 1964; JD, Fordham U., 1967. Bar: N.Y. 1967. Assoc. Pennie & Edmonds (formerly Pennie, Edmonds, Morton, Taylor & Adams), N.Y.C., 1967-69; sr. assoc. Emmet, Marvin, & Martin, N.Y.C., 1969-74, Golenbock & Barell, N.Y.C., 1974-78; mng. ptnr. Carro, Spanbock, Kaster & Cuiffo, N.Y.C., 1978-93; chmn. real estate dept., exec. com. Donovan, Leisure, Newton & Irvine, N.Y.C., 1993-98; ptnr. McDermott, Will & Emery, N.Y.C., 1998—. Mem. ABA, U.S. Patent Bar, N.Y. State Bar, Siwanoy Country Club, South Seas Club. Office: McDermott Will & Emery 50 Rockefeller Plz Fl 12 New York NY 10020-1600 E-mail: fcuiffo@mwe.com.

CULBERSON, GARY MICHAEL, hotel manager; b. Jackson, Miss., Sept. 16, 1955; s. William James and Peggy Ann (Pickett) C.; m. Mary Lee Yadron, May 8, 1986; children: Ashley Victoria, Brent Michael. Student, Miss. State U., 1973-78. Cert. hotel adminstr. Resident mgr. Kingston Plantation, Myrtle Beach, S.C.; exec. asst., mgr. Brown Palace Hotel, Denver; mng. dir. Tremont Hotel, Chgo., 1991; gen. mgr. Embassy Suites Hotel, Denver, 1996-97; hotel mgr. Casino Magic Hotel, Biloxi, Miss., 1997—2002; v.p. Beau Rivage Resort, Biloxi, 2002—. Mem.: So. Innkeepers (v.p. 2001—), Miss. Hotel and Lodging Assn. (v.p. 2001—02, pres. 2002—03, Gen. Mgr. of Yr. 2002), Miss. Gulf Coast Hotel and Motel Assn. (v.p. 1998—99, pres. 2000—02), Confrerie de la Chaine des Rotisseurs (Maitre of Table Restaurateur 1991—92), Mensa. Avocations: skiing, golf. Office: Beau Rivage Resort 3903 Cabildo Pl Ocean Springs MS 39564 E-mail: mculberson@beaurivage.com.

CULBERSON, JOHN A., congressman, lawyer; b. Houston, June 24, 1956; m. Belinda Burney, Dec. 1989; 1 child: Caroline Virginia. BA in history, Southern Meth. U.; JD, South Tex. Coll. Law. Assoc. civil defense atty. Lorance & Thompson, 1985—; mem. Tex. House of Reps., 1986-2000, U.S. Congress 7th Tex. dist., 2001—, mem. house appropriations com., vice chair, nat. rep. congressional com. Mem. Congressional com. Steering, Budget, Edn. and Workforce, Transportation and Infrastructure; served on House Environ. Regulation and Corrections com., House Public Edn. and Natural Resources com.; selected as House Rep. Whip. Mem. United Meth. Church. Office: US Ho of Reps 1728 Longworth Ho Office Bldg Washington DC 20515-4307*

CULBERT, DAVID HOLBROOK, historian, educator, editor, writer; b. San Antonio, July 7, 1943; s. Robert William Culbert and Dorothy Fairfax Kift; m. Lubna Aranki, May 26, 1979. Student, Mozarteum, Salzburg, Austria, 1963-64; BA, Oberlin Coll., 1966; MusB, Oberlin Conservatory Music, 1966; PhD, Northwestern U., 1970. Asst. prof. history Yale U., New Haven, Conn., 1970-71, La. State U., Baton Rouge, 1971-76, assoc. prof. history, 1976-84, prof. history, 1984—. Author: News for Everyman, 1976, Mission to Moscow, 1980; editor-in-chief: Film and Propaganda in America, 5 vols., 1990—93; editor (with John Chambers): World War II, Film and History, 1996; editor: (with Nicholas Cull and David Welch) Propaganda and Mass Persuasion: A Historical Encyclopedia (1500 to the Present), 2003; editor: (with K. R. M. Short) Cambridge Studies in the History of Mass Communications, 1999—; editor: (with David Welch) Studies in Propaganda, 1999—; editor: Hist. Jour. Film, Radio and TV, 1992—; contbr. articles to profl. jours.; dir. hist. rsch., assoc. prodr.: (films) Huey Long, 1985; co-prodr.: Television's Vietnam: The Impact of Media, 1986; hist. cons.: Die Macht der Bilder: Leni Riefenstahl, 1993; sr. cons.: (TV miniseries) Dawn of the Eye, 1998. Organist-choirmaster St. James Episcopal Ch., Baton Rouge, 1981—. Fellow, Woodrow Wilson Ctr. Scholars, 1976—77, Nat. Humanities Inst., Yale U., 1977—78; Vis. fellow, Inst. Advanced Study, 1995. Mem.: Internat. Assn. Media and History (coun., pres. 1987—89), Am. Hist. Assn. (chmn. John O'Connor Prize com. 2000—01), Orgn. Am. Historians (1st chmn. com. radio-TV-film media, 1st chmn. Erik Barnouw Prize com. 1981—84), Grolier Club, City Club Baton Rouge, Phi Beta Kappa, Pi Kappa Lambda. Republican. Home: 2933 Reymond Ave Baton Rouge LA 70808 Office: Dept History La State U 224 Himes Hall Baton Rouge LA 70803 Office Phone: 225-578-4471. Personal E-mail: dhculbert@aol.com.

CULBERTSON, FRANCES MITCHELL, psychology professor; b. Boston, Jan. 31, 1921; d. David and Goldie (Fishman) Mitchell; m. John Mathew Culbertson, Aug. 27, 1947; children: John David, Joanne, Lyndall, Amy. BS, U. Mich., 1947, MS, 1949, PhD, 1955. Diplomate Am. Bd. of Profl. Psychology; lic. psychologist, Wis. Clin. child psychologist Wis. Diagnostic Ctr., Madison, 1961-65; chief clin. psychologist dept. child psychiatry U. Wis., Madison, 1965-66; resident rsch. psychologist NIMH, Berkeley, Calif., 1966-67; psychologist Madison Pub. Schs., 1967-68; prof. psychology U. Wis., Whitewater, 1968-88, prof. emeritus, 1988—; psychologist Mental Health Assocs., Madison, 1987—2003. Clin. psychologist Counseling and Psychotherapy Assn., Madison, 1982-87; clin. hypnotherapy cons. Family Achievement Ctr., Oconomowoc, Wis., 1984-89; cons. Wis Disability Determination Bur., 2001—. Author: Voices in International School Psychology, 1985; contbr. chpts. to books, articles to profl. jours. Mem. Dane County Mental Health Bd., Madison, 1980-82. Fellow: APA (bd. conv. affairs 1990—94, pres. sect. clin. psychology women 1991—92, coun. rep. liaison and bd. mem. internat. psychology divsn. 52 1997—97, chmn. membership com., coun. rep. psychol. hypnosis divsn. 1998—99, coun. rep. internat. psych. divsn., coun. mem. 1999—2003, bd. dirs. internat. psych. divsn. 2003—, bd. dirs. divsn. 52 2003—, Contbn. award for internat. achievement 1994, Divsn. 1 Eminent Woman in Psychology award 1999, Divsn. 52 Career award for outstanding contbns. to internat. psychology 1999); mem.: Madison Hypnotherapy Soc. (pres. 1986—94), Brazilian Soc. Clin. Psychology (hon. pres. 1979), Wis. Psychol. Assn. (pres. divsn. psychol. hypnosis 1991—99), Internat. Coun. Psychologists (pres. 1979), Internat. Soc. Clin. Psychology (founding co-chair 1997—98, treas. 1997—), Internat. Assn. Applied Psychology Divsn. Applied Gerontology (pres.-elect 1994—98, exec. bd. mem. 1995—, pres. 1998—2003, past pres. 2003—), Phi Kappa Phi, Pi Lambda Theta, Sigma Xi. Avocations: skiing, walking, hiking, reading, gardening. Home: 8301 Old Sauk Rd Apt 323 Middleton WI 53562-4394 Office: Capitol Assoc LLC 440 Science Dr #200 Madison WI 53711 Office Phone: 608-238-5176. Personal E-mail: franculb@aol.com.

CULBERTSON, JACK ARTHUR, education educator; b. Nickelsville, Va., July 16, 1918; s. Otto Cecil and Lola Kate (Fuller) C.; m. Mary Virginia Pond, Aug. 12, 1952; children: Karen Anne Hasselo, Margaret Lynn. AB in Edn., Emory and Henry Coll., 1943; MA in German, Duke U., 1946; PhD in Edn. Adminstrn., U. Calif., Berkeley, 1955. Cert. tchr., sch. adminstr., Va., Calif. Tchg. prin. Scott County Sch. Sys., Gate City, Va., 1937—41, Jewell Ridge (Va.) Sch. Sys., 1941—42, Tazewell (Va.) County Sch. Sys., 1947—49; H.S. tchr. Mineral Springs (N.C.) Sch. Sys., 1943—44; tchr. jr. H.S. El Centro (Calif.) Sch. Sys., 1949—51; sch. supt. Ellwood Sch. Dist., Goleta, Calif., 1951—53; prof. U. Oreg., Eugene, 1955—59; exec. dir. Univ. Coun. for Edn. Adminstrn., Columbus, 1959—81; prof. Ohio State U., Columbus, 1981—86, emeritus prof., 1986—. Cons. W.K. Kellogg Found., Battle Creek, Mich., 1968, Ford Found., N.Y.C., 1967; advisor Edn. Commn. States, Denver, 1967, Pan Am. Union, Washington, 1968; founder 1st Internat. Intervisitation Program in Edn. Adminstrn., 1966; spkr. OAS, Brasilia, Brazil, 1968, Australian Coun. for Edn. Rsch., Sydney, 1967, German Assn. for Tng. Sch. Adminstrs., 1975. Author: Building Bridges, 1995; co-author: Administrative Relationships, 1960, Preparing Educational Leaders for the Seventies, 1969. Recipient Commonwealth Fellow award Commonwealth Coun. for Edn. Adminstrn., 1978, Roald F. Campbell Lifetime Achievement award Univ. Coun. for Edn. Adminstrn., 1993. Mem. Am. Edn. Rsch. Assn. (v.p. 1964-66), Am. Assn. Sch. Adminstrs. (adv. commn. 1974-76), Nat. Coun. for Profs. of Edn. Adminstrn. (exec. com. 1957-60, Living Legends award 1999-2000), Nat. Soc. for Study of Edn. (co-editor yearbook 1986). Avocations: reading, television, card playing. Home: 145 Montrose Way Columbus OH 43214-3634

CULBERTSON, JANET LYNN, artist; b. Greensburg, Pa., Mar. 15, 1932; d. Joseph F. and Helen C. (Moore) Culbertson; m. Douglas I. Kaften, Sept. 30, 1964. BFA, Carnegie Inst. Tech., 1953; MA, NYU, 1963. Instr. art Pace Coll., N.Y.C., 1964-68, Pratt Art Inst., Bklyn., 1973; assoc. prof. Southampton Coll., 1976; drawing instr. Parrish Art Mus., 1979. Exhibited one-woman shows 20th Century West Gallery, N.Y.C., 1967, Molly Barnes Gallery, L.A., 1970, Midtown Gallery, Atlanta, 1971, Lerner-Misrachi Gallery, N.Y.C., 1971, Lerner-Heller Gallery, N.Y.C., 1973, 75, 77, Tower Gallery, Southampton, N.Y., 1976, Benson Gallery, Bridgehampton, N.Y., 1978, 81, 89, Interart Gallery, N.Y.C., 1979, Harriman Coll., N.Y., 1980, Nardin Gallery, N.Y.C., 1981, Aronson Gallery, Atlanta, 1982, Harrisburg State Mus. Pa., 1988, Women Artists Series Rutgers U., N.J., 1988, Carnegie Mellon U., Pitts., 1991, Acme Art Co., Columbus, Ohio, 1992, Islip (N.Y.) Mus., 1992, Suffolk Coll., Riverhead, N.Y., 1996, Stone Quarry Art Park, Cazenovia, N.Y., 1996, Wave Hill, Bronx, N.Y., 1997, Atelier A/E Gallery, N.Y.C., 1997, U. Alaska, Anchorage, 1997, Nat. Acad. Scis., Washington, 1998, Hoyt Mus., New Castle, Pa., 1998, U. Nebr., Omaha, 2002, Huntington Arts Coun. Gallery, N.Y., 2002-03, Cambridge Multicultural Arts Ctr., 2003, Nat. Mus. of Women in the Arts, Washington, 2004, Nassau County Mus., Hewlett-Woodmere Libr. Gallery, 2004, Ill. Ctrl. Coll., Ohio, 2005, East End Arts, Riverhead, NY,

2005; two-women shows Women's Art Ctr., San Francisco, 1975; four-women show Heckscher Mus., Huntington, N.Y., 1980; numerous group exhbns.from 1953 to present including most recently Parrish Art Mus., Southampton, N.Y., 2000, N.J. Ctr. Visual Arts, Summit, 2000, Toxic Landscapes, Puffin Found. traveling exhib., Morning, Noon and Night, The Long Island Mus. of Stony Brook, N.Y., Earth 2002, U. Miami Coral Gables, Denise Bibro Fine Art, N.Y.C., 2002, Soho Photo, N.Y.C., 2002, Savannah Coll. Art and Design, Ga., 2002, Long Beach Found. for Arts, NJ, 2002, Antioch Coll., Ohio, 2004, others; contbr. collage to Attica Book, 1972; contbr. articles to profl. jours., prodr. and contbr. Heresies #13 mag. Creative Artists Pub. Svc. grantee, 1979. Recipient Shirk Meml. award for oil painting Nat. Assn. Women Artists, Inc., 1993, first place award Notorious L.I. exhibit Hillwood Art Mus., Brookville, N.Y., 1994, Purchase award Hoyt Art Inst., 1995, Purchase award Nassau County Mus. Art, 1997, Print Ctr. Excellence award, Phila., 2001; fellow Ossabaw Found., 1981, Dorland, 1983, Ucross Found., 1989, 99, Blue Mt. Found., 1991, 94, 96, 2000, 02, VCCA Ctr. Found., Ragdale Found., 1984, 2001; Ludwig Vogelstein grantee, 2004, Puffin grantee, 2004. Home: PO Box 455 Shelter Island Heights NY 11965 Personal E-mail: jculbertson@att.net.

CULBERTSON, JOHN DENNIS, counselor; b. Greenville, S.C., Aug. 18, 1947; s. John Bolt and Ellie (Barbare) C.; B.S., U. S.C., 1969; M.S., N.D. State U., 1978; Ph.D. (scholar), U. N.D., 1982; nat. cert. counselor, nat. cert. sch. counselor, Nat. Bd. Cert. Counselors, lic. profl. counselor, S.C.; m. Eunice Virginia Watson, June 7, 1969; children: John David, Ellen Barbare. Cert. sch. counselor Nat. Bd. for Cert. Counselors; lic. profl. counselor, S.C. Commd. 2d lt. U.S. Air Force, 1969, advanced through grades to capt., 1973; squadron exec. officer Minot AFB, N.D., 1975-77, resigned, 1977; grad. asst. U. N.D., Grand Forks, 1978; grad. asst., intern The Counseling Center, U. S.C., Columbia, 1978-79; pvt. practice counseling, Columbia, 1978, Florence, S.C., 1979-88; elem. sch. counselor, Florence, 1979-88, discussion leader students, staff, faculty; high sch. counselor, Florence, 1988-90, Newberry, SC, 1994-2001; H.S. guidance dir., Silver Bluff, 2001-04; ret.; adj. faculty mem. Piedmont Tech. Coll.; founder Counseling and Ednl. Cons., 1980. Vol. group leader Parenting Skills, Columbia Area Council on Child Abuse; vol. profl. leader Parents Anonymous, Florence. Mem. NEA, SCEA, Am. Counseling Assn., S.C. Assn. Counseling and Devel. (treas. 1985-86, Profl. Service award 1986), Am. Sch. Counselors Assn., S.C. Counseling Assn. (treas. 1985-86, profl. svc. award 1986), S.C. Sch. Counselors Assn., Assn. for Specialists in Group Work, Nat. Council on Measurement in Edn., S.C. Assn. for Measurement and Evaluation in Guidance, Assn. for Non-White Concerns in Personnel and Guidance, S.C. Assn. for Non-White Concerns in Personnel and Guidance, S.C. Assn. for Humanistic Edn. and Devel. (sec. 2003), Am. Legion, others. Methodist. Home: 295 Pine Ridge Rd Edgefield SC 29824 E-mail: johnculbertson@hotmail.com.

CULBERTSON, LESLIE S., computer company executive; Bachelor's, Lewis and Clark U., 1971. Cost mgr. British Petroleum/Standard Oil Ohio; acctg. mgr., controller Intel, Santa Clara, Calif., 1979—98, dir. corp. fin., 1997—, v.p., co-dir. materials orgn., 1998—2000, v.p., gen. mgr. sys. mfg., 2000—. Office: Intel 2200 Mission Coll Blvd Santa Clara CA 95052*

CULBERTSON, RICHARD ALLEN, healthcare educator, health facility administrator; b. Fremont, Ohio, Aug. 13, 1946; s. Raymond Clark and Ruth Elizabeth Culbertson; m. Linnea VanDyne, July 11, 1970 (div. Dec. 1981); m. Susan Mary Leary, May 3, 1986. BA, Lawrence U., 1967; MDiv, Harvard U., 1970; M in Health Adminstrn., U. Minn., 1973; PhD, U. Calif., San Francisco, 1993. Cert. healthcare exec. Am. Coll. Health Execs. Asst. prof. U. Minn., Mpls., 1976—78; dep. dir., COO St. Paul-Ramsey Med. Ctr., 1978—84; hosp. dir., CEO Kaiser Found. Hosp., LA, 1984—87; dir. adminstrn. U. Calif. San Francisco Med. Group, 1987—92; assoc. dean, vice chancellor U. Wis., Madison, 1992—95; assoc. prof., dir. Ind. U., Indpls., 1995—97; assoc. prof. Tulane U., New Orleans, 1997—. Chmn. bd. dirs. Aurora HealthCare Inc., Milw., 1994—; mem. governing bd. Touro Infirmary, New Orleans, 2004—; cert. site reviewer NCAA, Indpls., 2001—; chair senate com. on intercollegiate athletics Tulane U., 2002—, spl. asst. to pres. for NCAA cert., 1999—2002. Contbg. author The Nation's Health, 6th edit., 2001; contbr. articles to profl. jours. Mem. Mardi Gras Krewe of Mid-City; pres. Humane Soc. Ramsey County, St. Paul, 1981—84; mem., bd. dirs. Touro Found., New Orleans, 2004—; bd. dirs. Wis. Profl. Rev., Madison, 1994—95, Eldercare Dane County, Madison, 1994—95, Touro Found., New Orleans, 2004—. Named Emerging Leader in Healthcare, Healthcare Forum, San Francisco, 1986; recipient Spurgeon award for cmty. svc., Explorer Scouts, St. Paul, 1983; Nat. Leader fellow, W.K. Kellogg Found., 1985—88. Mem.: U. Minn. Pres. Club, Harvard Club (La.), Delta Omega Soc. (Eta chpt.), Phi Beta Kappa (La. Alpha chpt.), Beta Theta Pi. Avocations: swimming, intercollegiate athletics, dance organizations patron, Tae Kwon Do. Office: Tulane U Sch Pub Health 1430 Tulane Ave SL-29 New Orleans LA 70112 Office Phone: 504-988-6247. Business E-Mail: rculber@tulane.edu.

CULHANE, HIND RASSAM, psychologist, educator, historian; b. Mosul, Iraq, Feb. 20, 1939; came to U.S., 1955; d. Noel Michael and Sophie (Bakhazy) Rassam; m. John William Culhane, Aug. 27, 1960; children: Michael Noel, T.H. AA, Cazenovia (N.Y.) Jr. Coll., 1957; EdD (hon.), Cazenovia (N.Y.) Coll., 2005; BA, Rockford Coll., 1959, MA, 1963; MEd, Columbia U., 1988, EdD, 1992; M Pedagogy (hon.), Mercy Coll., 1998. Edn. coord. Head Start, Chgo., 1965-69, Westchester County, NY, 1969-77; assoc. dean grad. program L.I. U., Dobbs Ferry, NY, 1976-82; asst. prof. Mercy Coll., Dobbs Ferry, 1982-92, assoc. prof., assoc. chair social scis. divsn., 1992—2002, co-chair, social scis. divsn., 2003—; sr. edn. adv. Revitalization of Iraq, Sch. and Stabilization of Edn. (R.I.S.E.) U.S. State Dept., Baghdad, 2003—04; adv. Iraqi Min. of Edn., Strategic Planning for Future of Tchr. Tng. in Iraq, 2004; tchr. trainer Creative Assoc. Internat., Iraq, 2003—04; cons. U.S. State Dept. Mid. East Edn. Project Initiative, Oman, 2005. Adj. prof. Mercy Coll., Dobbs Ferry, 1970-76; guest lectr. The U. Baghdad (Iraq), 1981-84, Rock Valley Coll., Rockford, Ill., 2003; campus coord. Woodrow Wilson fellows program Mercy Coll., 1990-97; group dynamics leader NAIM Found. Workshop, Washington, 1992-93; guest psychologist Mental Health Hour Arabnet radio, Washington, 1994-95; psychologist, admissions com. U. Poznań (Poland) Med. Sch., 1994—; commentator on Arab film, CUNY TV, 1998, commentator on overthrow of Saddam Hussein, Phil Donahue TV show, 2003; edn. evaluator for Sultan of Oman, Creative Assn. Internat., 2005. Author (Arab film history) East/West, An Ambiguous State of Being, 1995; vocalist Arabic songs, U.S. State Dept. Rock and Roll Tours of Syria and Kuwait with U.S. Rock Band Circus Guy, 2003-04; contbr. article to Ency. Modern Mid. East, 1996. Mem. Arab-Am. Anti-Defamation League, Washington, 1987—. Nat. Multicultural Faculty Devel. fellow, 1995-97; Nat. fellow Tchg. for a Change, C.C. of Aurora, Colo., 1995; Fulbright Scholar to Syria, 2000—. Mem. Psi Chi, Delta Pi. Avocations: collecting Arab songs, world travel, environmental concerns. Office: Social Scis Bldg Mercy Coll 555 Broadway Dobbs Ferry NY 10522-1134 Business E-Mail: hculhane@mercy.edu.

CULHANE, JOHN JOSEPH, lawyer; b. Yonkers, NY, Apr. 24, 1945; s. John Jospeh and Anna Rita (Merrins) Culhane. BS with honors, St. Peters Coll., 1968; JD with honors, Fordham U., 1973. Bar: NJ 1973, Wis. 1975, US Ct. Appeals 7th cir. Chief prosecutor, Weehawken, NJ, 1973—75; ptnr. Howard, Peterman & Eisenberg, Milw., 1975-80; dep. gen. counsel Schlitz Brewing Co., Milw., 1980—82; assoc. gen. counsel, asst. sec. Stroh Brewing Co., Detroit, 1982-83; v.p., gen. counsel Pabst Brewing Co., Milw., 1983—86; sr. fin. counsel Coca-Cola Co., Atlanta, 1986—92, gen. counsel N.Am. group, 1992—98; gen. counsel, corp. sec. Coca-Cola HBC, London, 1998—2001, Coca-Cola Bottlers' Sales and Services Co., 2001—04; spl. counsel Coca-Cola Enterprises Inc., 2001—04, interim gen. counsel Atlanta, 2004, sr. v.p., gen. counsel, 2004—. Dir. US Brewers Assn., 1983—85, Future Milw. Com., 1983—85. Mem.: Milw. Bar Assn., Wis. Bar Assn., NJ Bar Assn., ABA. Roman Catholic. Office: Coca-Cola Enterprises Inc 2500 Windy Ridge Pkwy Atlanta GA 30339

CULHANE, JOHN WILLIAM, journalist, writer, film historian; b. Rockford, Ill., Feb. 7, 1934; s. John William and Isabel June (Fissinger) C.; m. Hind Noel Rassam, Aug. 27, 1960; children: Michael Noel, T.H. BS, St. Louis U., 1956; cert. in advanced internat. reporting, Columbia U., 1966. Reporter St. Louis (Mo.) Globe Dem., 1955; daily columnist, reporter Rockford Register-Republic, 1956-61; reporter, feature writer, fgn. corr. Chgo. Daily News, 1962-66; assoc. editor Newsweek mag., N.Y.C., 1966-71; freelance journalist N.Y. Times mag., others, N.Y.C., 1971-85; roving editor Reader's Digest, Pleasantville, N.Y., 1985-93; roving writer Johimith Robidoux Prodns., 1994—. Jury chmn. 2d N.Y. Internat. Animation Film Festival, 1974; lectr., Northwestern U., 1995, NYU, 1996; lectr. film festival, Mulhouse, France, 1990, Am. animation U.S. State Dept., Damascus, Syria, 2001, Art Inst. Pitts., 2001, spirituality in animation Marble Collegiate Ch., N.Y.C., 2002, Linc Svcs., Atlantis Resort, The Bahamas, 2003, Iranian Animation Retrospective, Columbia U., 2003, Peter Ellenshaw, spl. effects wizard NYU, 2005; moustro-of-ceremonies Mickey Mouse's 50th Birthday Retrospective and Whistle-Stop Train Tour Across the U.S., 1978; guest clown Ringling Bros., Barnum and Bailey Circus, 1974-84; instr. 1st course in history of animation for coll. credit Sch. Visual Arts, N.Y.C., 1972; sr. lectr. animation history U. Arts, Phila., 1997-98, NYU, 1997—, Fashion Inst. of Tech., N.Y.C., 2000—, Mercy Coll. Digital Arts Ctr., White Plains, N.Y., 2003—; vis. artist Disney Inst., Fla., 1999—; writer Richard Williams Animation, London, 1973; Salvador Dali's Hundreth Birthday lecture: Dali told me about Destino, Dobbs Ferry, N.Y. Public Libr., 2004; invitee Newsweek 'Glory Days' Reunion, Union League Club, N.Y., 2004; moderator, lectr. in field. Author: (critical essays) Walt Disney, 1972, Special Effects in the Movies, 1981, Walt Disney's Fantasia, 1983, The American Circus: An Illustrated History, 1990 (Washington Irving Book Selection Westchester Libr. Assn. 1991), Disney's Aladdin: The Making of an Animated Film, 1992, Fantasia 2000: Visions of Hope, N.Y. Hyperion, 1999, (documentaries) The Making of Aladdin: A Whole New World, 1992, Backstage at Disney's 1983, The Making of The Jungle Book, 1997, Walt Disney: The Man Behind the Myth, 2001; co-author: The Art of the Muppets, 1980, (TV spls.) Noah's Animals, 1974, King of the Beasts, 1976, Last of the Red Hot Dragons, 1980; contbr. The 50 Greatest Cartoons, 1994; voice of cartoon dragon, moderator: (coll. tour) Disney on Film: A Forum on Animation and Fantasy Filmmaking, 1981; co-prodr. (documentary) Circus!, 1983; commentator (documentaries) Fantasia: The Making of a Masterpiece, 1991, Jungle Book, 1993, Frank and Ollie, 1995, (TV spl.) The Flying Wallendas: Legends on the High Wire, 1998, The Making of BAMBI: A Prince is Born, 2005; writer (TV spl.) Illusionist David Copperfield Vanishes the Statue of Liberty, 1983, (feature films) Something Wicked This Way Comes, 1983, The Thief and the Cobbler, 1995; (CD-ROM essay) Walt Disney's Snow White and the Seven Dwarfs, 1998, (essays) The Disney Century, Fantasia Set for a New Millennium, 1998, "Charlie Brown: A Boy for all Seasons" N.Y. Mus. of Broadcasting, 1984, others; model for Mr. Snoops character Walt Disney's The Rescuers, 1977, model for 2nd Disney character, Flying John in "Rhapsody in Blue" in "Fantasia 2000". Master-of-ceremonies Winnebago County Sesquicentennial, Rockford, 1968; mem. Clearwater Assn. (author: PCBs: The Poison That Won't Go Away). Served with AUS, 1957-58. Recipient 4 1st Prize awards Ill. AP, 1960, 61, 63, 64, St. Louis U. Alumni Merit award as writer and film historian, 1982; Ford fellow Columbia U., 1965-66; Ill. Humanities Coun. grantee, 1991; Woodrow Wilson fellow in writing and film history, 1993. Mem. Writer's Guild Am., Clearwater Assn., Alpha Sigma Nu, Sigma Delta Chi (2 awards for pub. service journalism 1964, 69). Avocations: global travel, environment. Office: care Joelle Delbourgo Assocs 450 7th Ave Ste 3004 New York NY 10123-3004

CULICK, FRED ELLSWORTH CLOW, engineering educator, physics professor; b. Wolfeboro, N.H., Oct. 25, 1933; s. Joseph Frank and Mildred Beliss (Clow) C.; m. Frederica Mills, June 11, 1960; children: Liza Hall, Alexander Joseph, Mariette Huxham. Student, U. Glasgow, Scotland, 1957-58; SB, MIT, 1957, PhD, 1961. Rsch. fellow Calif. Inst. Tech., Pasadena, 1961-63, asst. prof., 1963-66, assoc. prof., 1966-70, prof. mech. engring. and jet propulsion, 1970-97, Richard L. and Dorothy M. Hayman prof. mech. engring., 1997—, prof. jet propulsion, 1997—. Cons. to govt. agys. and indsl. orgns. Fellow AIAA, Internat. Acad. Astronautics; mem. Internat. Fedn. Astronautics, Am. Phys. Soc. Home: 1375 Hull Ln Altadena CA 91001-2620 Office: Calif Inst Tech Caltech 205-45 207 Guggenheim Pasadena CA 91125 Office Phone: 626-395-4783. Business E-Mail: fecfly@caltech.edu.

CULIVER, ELIZABETH ANN, elementary school educator; b. Goresville, Ill., July 10, 1942; d. Milton E. Sr. and Alyene Claudis (Grise) Terry; m. Walter Roderick Culiver, Oct. 29, 1960; children: Terry Scott, Richard Wilson, Lisa Dawn Russell. Student, U. So. Ind., 1979, MA, 1983. Cert. endorsement reading and gifted edn. tchr., Ind. Tchr. 8th grade Vanderburgh County, Evansville, Ind., 1979-80, tchr. kindergarten, 1980-83, tchr. mid. sch., 1983-84, tchr. 5th grade, 1984—. Adj. prof. U. So. Ind., 1992. Mem. alumni bd. dirs. U. So. Ind., Evansville, 1989—, econ. adv. bd., 1990—. Mem. Ind. Reading Assn., Evansville Tchr. Assn., Evansville Area Reading Assn., Kappan, Kappa Delta Pi (pres. 1978-79). Republican. Southern Baptist. Avocations: reading, golf, antique collector, cooking. Home: 8666 Flintlock Dr Newburgh IN 47630-9334 Office: Hebron Elem Sch 4400 Bellemeade Ave Evansville IN 47714-0618

CULKIN, CHARLES WALKER, JR., retired trade association administrator; b. Aug. 22, 1947; s. Charles Walker and Helen Elizabeth (Wilson) C.; m. Carolyn DeWayne Franklin, Apr. 5, 1974; children: David Laurence Franklin, Kimberly Anne Franklin. A in Bus. Adminstrn., Benjamin Franklin U., 1968, BA in Comml. Sci., 1970. Asst. auditor United Va. Bank, Vienna, 1967—70; sr. asst. dir. U.S. GAO, Washington, 1970—97; exec. dir. Assn. Gov. Accts., Washington, 1997—2003; ret., 2003. Chmn. Pacific Emerging Issues Conf., Honolulu, 1982; spkr. confs. and seminars; founder, incorporator Reston Commuter Bus., Inc., 1971, treas., dir., 1971-78. Pub. The Jour. Govt. Fin. Mgmt., 1997-2003; contbr. articles to profl. jours. Recipient RCB Bd. Dirs. award 1978. Outstanding Achievement award Fairfax County (Va.) Bd. Suprs., 1978, Nat. Pres. award Am. Soc. of Mil. Comptr., 1999, 2003. Mem. Am. Assn. for Budget Program Analysis, Inst. Internal Auditors (sec. no. Va. chpt. 1984-86), Assn. Govt. Accts. (dir. Hawaii chpt. 1981-84, conf. mgr. fed. leadership conf. 1994, No. Va. chpt. 1991—, Nat. AGA Spl. Recognition award 1988, 90, 93, President's award 1992, 95-96, Outstanding Mem. award 1983, nat. treas.-elect, 1995-96, nat. treas. 1996-97, Edn. award 1994), Nat. Assn. Accts. (no. Va. Chpt. dir. 1977-78, v.p. 1979-80), Benjamin Franklin U. Alumni Assn. (pres. 1988-92, Outstanding Leadership award 1991, Bd. Govs. Svc. award 1992, Disting. Alumni award, 1995), George Washington U. Gen. Alumni Assn. (dir. 1991-92, Vol. of Yr. award 1992), KC (Coun. #3358 dep. grand knight 2004-2005, grand knight 2005—). Roman Catholic. Home: 5351 Fox Run Rd Sarasota FL 34231-7348 Personal E-mail: cinandchas@comcast.net.

CULKIN, MACAULAY, actor; b. N.Y.C., Aug. 26; s. Christopher "Kit" and Pat Culkin; m. Rachel Miner, 1998 (div. 2000). Student, St Joseph's Sch. of Yorkville, N.Y.C., George Balanchine's Sch. of Ballet. Appeared in TV commercials; films include Rocket Gibraltar, 1988, Uncle Buck, 1989, See You In The Morning, 1989, Jacob's Ladder, 1990, Home Alone, 1990, My Girl, 1991, Only the Lonely, 1991, Home Alone 2: Lost In New York, 1992, The Good Son, 1993, George Balanchine's The Nutcracker, 1993, Getting Even With Dad, 1994, The Pagemaster, 1994, Richie Rich, 1994, Party Monster, 2003, Saved!, 2004; appeared in Michael Jackson's Black or White video, 1991; voice of Nicholas McClary on Wishkid cartoon, 1991-92. Office: William Morris Agy care Brian Gersh 151 S El Camino Dr Beverly Hills CA 90212-2775

CULL, ROBERT ROBINETTE, manufacturing executive; b. Cleve., Sept. 24, 1912; s. Louis David and Wilma Penn (Robinette) C.; m. Gay Cornwell, Oct. 4, 1986. BS in Physics, M.I.T., 1934. Supr. Eastman Kodak Co., Rochester, N.Y., 1934-39; asst. to gen. mgr. Cleve. Chain & Mfg. Co., 1940-45; partner Tenna Mfg. Co., Cleve., 1945-56; pres. Tenatronics Ltd., Newmarket, Ont., Can., 1956—, Sterling Mfg. Co., Cleve., 1960—. Trustee Garden Center Greater Cleve., 1975-80, pres., 1979-80; trustee Musical Arts Assn. of Cleve. Orch., 1976—2003. Mem. IEEE, Cleve. Engring. Soc., Sigma Psi. Clubs: Hermit, Union.

CULLARI, SALVATORE SANTINO, clinical psychologist, educator, writer; b. Caroniti, Calabria, Italy, Apr. 1, 1952; came to U.S., 1955; s. Carmelo and Carmela (Cullari) C.; m. Kathryn Plesce, Apr. 26, 1985; children: Catherine, Dante. BA, Kean Coll., 1974; MA, Western Mich. U., 1976, PhD, 1981. Lic. psychologist, Pa., W.Va. Dir. psychology White Haven (Pa.) Ctr., 1982—83; psychologist Danville (Pa.) State Hosp., 1983—84; coord. of psychology Harrisburg (Pa.) State Hosp., 1984—86; prof., chair dept. psychology Lebanon Valley Coll., Annville, Pa., 1986—2003, prof. emeritus, 2003—. Cons. Bur. Disability Determination, Harrisburg, 1987—. Author questionaire acad. social evaluation scales, 1990, Treatment Resistance, 1996; editor Found. of Clin. Psychology, 1998, Counseling and Psychotherapy, 2001; contbr. numerous articles to profl. jours. Mem. APA, Assn. Advancement of Behavior Therapy, Pa. Psychol. Assn. (pres. 2005-, Psychology in the Media award 2003), Soc. for the Exploration of Psychotherapy Integration. Business E-Mail: cullari@lvc.edu.

CULLEN, CHARLES THOMAS, historian, librarian; b. Gainesville, Fla., Oct. 11, 1940; s. Spencer L. and Blanche J. Cullen; m. Shirley Harrington, June 13, 1964; children: Leslie Lanier, Charles Spencer Harrington. BA, U. of South, 1962; MA, Fla. State U., 1963; PhD, U. Va., 1971; HHD (hon.), Lewis U., 1987; DLitt (hon.), U. South, 1994; LLD (hon.), John Marshall Law Sch., 1995; DHist (hon.), Lincoln Coll., 2000. Asst. prof. history Averett Coll., 1963-66; assoc. editor Papers of John Marshall Inst. Early Am. History and Culture, Williamsburg, Va., 1971-74, co-editor, 1974-77, editor, 1977-79; lectr. history Coll. William and Mary, 1971-79; sr. research historian, editor Papers of Thomas Jefferson Princeton (N.J.) U., 1979-86; pres., libr. Newberry Library, Chgo., 1986—2005, pres., libr. emeritus, 2005—. Mem. N.J. Hist. Commn., 1985-86, Nat. Hist. Publs. and Records Com., 1990—; mem. adv. bd. Abraham Lincoln Presdl. Libr. and Mus., 2002-04. Trustee Thomas Jefferson Found., 2004—. Nat. Hist. Publs. and Records Commn. fellow, 1970-71. Mem. Assn. Documentary Editing (pres. 1982-83), Orgn. Am. Historians, Am. Hist. Assn., Am. Antiquarian Soc., Heartland Lit. Soc. (pres. 1994—), The Poetry Found. (vice chmn. 1998-2005), Ind. Rsch. Librs. Assn. (pres. 2000—03), Caxton Club, Grolier Club. Office: Newberry Libr 60 W Walton St Chicago IL 60610-7324

CULLEN, EDWARD PETER, bishop; b. Phila., Mar. 15, 1933; Student, St. Charles Borromeo Sem., Overbrook, Pa.; MSW, U. Pa., 1970; M in Edn., LaSalle U., 1971; MDiv, St. Charles Borromeo Sem., 1974. Ordained priest Roman Cath. Ch. 1962. Asst. pastor St. Maria Goretti Ch., Hatfield, St. Bartholomew Ch., Phila.; chaplain to Sisters of Mercy Merion Motherhouse; chaplain St. Edmond's Home for Children, See of Allentown; titular bishop Diocese of Paria, 1994—; aux. bishop Diocese of Phila., 1994—99; bishop Diocese of Allentown, Pa., 1998—. Mem. Cath. Social Svcs. Named Hon. Prelate to His Holiness Pope John Paul II, 1982. Office: Diocese of Allentown PO Box F Allentown PA 18105-1538*

CULLEN, JACK JOSEPH, lawyer; b. Sept. 20, 1951; s. Ray Brandes (stepfather) and Helen Cullen; m. Deborah L. Vick, Oct. 28, 1978; children: Cameron, Katherine. BA, Western Wash. State Coll., 1973; JD, U. Puget Sound, 1976. Bar: Wash. 1977, U.S. Dist. Ct. (we. dist.) Wash. 1977, U.S. Dist. Ct. (ea. dist.) Wash. 1977, U.S. Tax Ct. 1984, U.S. Ct. Appeals (9th cir.) 1980. Staff atty. Wash. State Bar Assn., Seattle, 1977-79; assoc. Hatch & Leslie, Seattle, 1979-85, mng. ptnr., 1985-91; ptnr. Foster Pepper & Shefelman, Seattle, 1991-96, mng. ptnr., 1996—2002, mng. chair, 1991—. Spkr. in field. Co-author: Prejudgment Attachment, 1986. Active Frank Lloyd Wright Bldg. Conservancy, 1989—; trustee Seattle Repertory Theater, 1999-2002. Mem. ABA (bus. law sect.), Am. Bankruptcy Inst., Wash. State Bar Assn. (creditor-debtor sect., chair exec. 1982-90, spl. dist. counsel 1988—, hearing officer 1990), Seattle-King County Bar Assn. (bankruptcy rules subcom. 1988-90), Vancouver-Seattle Involvency Group (charter mem. 1990—), U.S. Sport Parachuting Team (nat. and world champions 1976, instrument rated pilot). Office: Foster Pepper & Shefelman PLLC 1111 3rd Ave Ste 3400 Seattle WA 98101-3299 E-mail: jc@foster.com.

CULLEN, JAMES D., lawyer; b. St. Louis, May 18, 1925; s. James and Frances C. Cullen; m. Joyce Marie Jackson, Aug. 19, 1950 (div.); children: Mary Lynn Cullen Walsh, James D., Michael Parnell, Carol Cullen Bernstein. LLD, St. Louis, 1948. Bar: Mo. 1948. Pvt. practice law, St. Louis. Bd. dirs. Gen. Protestant Children's Home, Richard Greene Co. 1st lt. USAF, 1943—45. Mem.: ABA, Lawyers Assn. St. Louis, St. Louis Bar Assn., Mo. Bar Assn. Roman Catholic. Office: 16 Berkshire Saint Louis MO 63144

CULLEN, JAMES G., telecommunications industry executive; b. 1942; Married. BA, Rutgers U., 1964; Postgrad., M.I.T. With NJ Bell Tel. Co., Newark, 1964, pres., CEO, 1989—93; pres. Bell Atlantic Corp., 1993—95, vice chmn., 1995—98, pres., COO, 1998—2000. Bd. dir. Nuestar Inc., Johnson & Johnson Inc., Prudential Life Ins. Co.; dir., non-exec. chmn. Agilent Technologies Inc. Office: Agilent Technologies Inc 395 Page Mill Rd Palo Alto CA 94306*

CULLEN, JEAN (JOHN) THOMAS, writer; b. Nurenberg, Germany, June 21, 1949; s. George Thomas Cullen and Hortense Marie-Madelaine Didier; m. Carolyn Ann Jones; 1 child, Andrew Francis. BA in English, U. Conn., 1972; MSBA, Boston U., 1980; BBA in Computer Info. Systems, Nat. U., San Diego, 1984. Adminstr. U.S. Army, Kaiserslautern, Germany, 1975—80. Author: A Walk in Ancient Rome, 2005, (novels) Nob Hill, 2003, Robinson Crusoe 1000000 A.D., 2003, The Generals of October, 2004, Nebula Express, 2004, The Christmas Clock, 2004, Invasion of the Mushroom People, 2006. A.g. U.S. Army, 1975—80, Kaiserslautern, West Germany. Democrat. Roman Catholic. Office: Saint Ronan St Atelier 6549 Mission Gorge Rd PMB 260 San Diego CA 92120 Office Phone: 619-501-4196. E-mail: publishers@cox.net.

CULLEN, MARK RICHARD, medical educator; b. Phila., Feb. 25, 1950; AB with honors, Harvard Coll., 1971; MD, Yale U., 1976. Resident Yale-New Haven Hosp., 1976-79, chief resident, 1979-80; dir. Yale-New Haven Occupl. and Environ. Medicine program Yale U. Sch. Medicine, 1980—, asst. prof. medicine, 1980-85, assoc. prof. medicine and epidemiology, 1985-93, prof. medicine and pub. health, 1993—. Vis. prof. U. Zimbabwe Faculty Medicine, 1988; cons. in field. Author: Clinical Occupational Medicine, 1986, Occupational Medicine: State of the Art Reviews, 1987, Textbook of Clinical Occupational and Environmental Medicine, 2004; contbr. articles to profl. jours., chpts. to books. Mem. Assn. Occupl. and Environ. Clinics (interim bd. dirs. 1986-88), Inst. Medicine, Inst. Medicine Bd. Health Sci. Policy. Office: Yale Occupl & Environ Medicine Program Yale U Sch Medicine 135 College St Ste 3D New Haven CT 06510-2483 Office Phone: 203-785-6434. E-mail: mark.cullen@yale.edu.

CULLEN, ROBERT JOHN, financial planner, investment advisor; b. York, Pa., Feb. 14, 1949; s. John Joseph and Florence Susanne (Staab) C.; m. Elizabeth Maule, Oct. 20, 1984; 1 child, Michael Joseph. BA, Winona (Minn.) State U., 1972. CFP; registered investment advisor. Editor-in-chief Overseas Life, Leimen, Fed. Republic of Germany, 1978-80; feature editor L.A. Daily Commerce, 1980-83; pres. HighTech Editorial, L.A., 1983-99; fin. planner Cullen Fin. Svcs. Inc., Upland, Calif., 1989—; br. mgr. LPL Fin. Computer editor Plaza Communications, Irvine, Calif., 1984-91; founder Saving Mom and Dad Inst., 2004—. With U.S. Army, 1974-78, ETO. Mem. Inst. of Cert. Fin. Planners, Calif. Advs. Nursing Home Reform. Avocations: creative writing, public speaking. Office: Cullen Fin Svcs 818 N Mountain Ave Ste 102 Upland CA 91786-4164

CULLEN, THOMAS FRANCIS, JR., lawyer; b. Scranton, Pa., Mar. 23, 1949; s. Thomas Francis Cullen Sr.; m. Elizabeth Davis, Mar. 2, 1985; children: Elizabeth Mellody, Thomas McDonough, Samuel Fisher, William Eroe. AB magna cum laude, Harvard U., 1971, JD magna cum laude, 1974. Bar:DC 1975, US Dist. Ct. Md. 1975, US Dist. Ct. Pa. 1979, US Supreme Ct. 1983, US Ct. Appeals (DC, 2d, 4th, 7th and 10th cirs.), US Tax Ct., US Ct. Claims. Law clk. U.S. Ct. Appeals, Balt., 1974-75; assoc. Jones, Day, Reavis & Pogue, Washington, 1975-80; ptnr. Jones Day, Washington, 1981—, and chair, firmwide litigation practice. Editor Harvard U. Law Rev. Mem. Am. Bar Found. Office: Jones Day 51 Louisiana Ave NW Washington DC 20001-2113 Office Phone: 202-879-3924. Office Fax: 202-626-1700. Business E-Mail: tfcullen@jonesday.com.

CULLER, ARTHUR DWIGHT, language educator; b. McPherson, Kans., July 25, 1917; s. Arthur Jerome and Susanna (Stover) C.; m. Helen Lucile Simpson, Sept. 14, 1941; children: Jonathan Dwight, Helen Elizabeth. BA, Oberlin Coll., 1938; PhD, Yale U., 1941. Instr. English Cornell U., 1941-42; instr., then asst. Yale U., 1946-55; prof. English, 1958-85; chmn. English dept., 1971-75. Assoc. prof. English U. Ill., 1955-58 Author: The Imperial Intellect; A Study of Newman's Educational Ideal, 1955; Editor: (J.H. Newman) Apologia pro Vita Sua, 1956, (with G.P. Clark) Student and Society, 1959, Poetry and Criticism of Matthew Arnold, 1961, Imaginative Reason: The Poetry of Matthew Arnold, 1966, The Poetry of Tennyson, 1977, The Victorian Mirror of History, 1986 Fulbright fellow in Eng., 1950-51; Guggenheim fellow, 1961-62, 76; NEH fellow, 1979-80 Mem. Am. Acad. Arts and Scis., MLA, Phi Beta Kappa. Home: 200 Leeder Hill Dr Apt 518 Hamden CT 06517-2723

CULLER, JONATHAN DWIGHT, English language educator; b. Cleve., Oct. 1, 1944; s. Arthur Dwight and Helen Lucille (Simpson) Culler; m. Cynthia Chase, Dec. 27, 1976. BA, Harvard U., 1966; BPhil, St. John's Coll., Oxford, Eng., 1968, DPhil, 1972. Fellow Selwyn Coll. Cambridge (Eng.) U., 1969-74; fellow Brasenose Coll., lectr. French Oxford U., 1974-77; vis. prof. French and comparative lit. Yale U., New Haven, 1975; prof. English and comparative lit. Cornell U., Ithaca, NY, 1977—, chair dept. comparative lit., 1993-96, 2004—, chmn. dept. English, 1996-99, sr. assoc. dean, Coll. Arts & Scis., 2000—03. Dir. Soc. Humanities Cornell U., Ithaca, 1984—93. Author: (book) Flaubert: The Uses of Uncertainty, 1974, Structuralist Poetics: Strucutralism, Linguistics and the Study of Literature, 1975 (James Russell Lowell prize MLA, 1975), Ferdinand de Saussure, 1976, The Pursuit of Signs: Semiotics, Literature, Deconstruction, 1981, On Deconstruction: Theory and Criticism after Structuralism, 1982, Roland Barthes, 1983, Framing the Sign: Criticism and Its Institutions, 1988, Literary Theory: A Very Short Introduction, 1997; translator: Jacques Derrida's Memoires for Paul de Man, 1986; editor: The Harvard Advocate, Centennial Anthology, 1966, Grounds of Comparison: Around the Work of Benedict Anderson, 2003, Just Being Difficult: Academic Writing in the Public Arena, 2003; adv. editor: New Literary History, 1972—, PTL, 1976—79, mem. editl. bd.: Diacritics, 1974—; editor, 1994—. Fellow Guggenheim, 1979—80, NEH, 1987—88; scholar Rhodes, 1966—69. Mem.: ACLS (bd. dirs. 2005—), MLA (mem. adv. bd. publs. 1978—81, exec. coun. 1985—88, 1990—91), Am. Comparative Lit. Assn. (v.p. 1997—99, pres. 1999—2001), Semiotic Soc. Am. (v.p. 1987, pres. 1988). Office: Cornell U Dept English Lit Ithaca NY 14853 E-mail: jdc9@cornell.edu.

CULLIGAN, JENINE ELIZABETH, curator; b. Lexington, Ky., Dec. 15, 1959; d. Justin Francis and Beverly Elizabeth Culligan; m. Philip Allen Adkins, May 19, 2001. BA in Art History, U. Ky., 1984; MA in Art History/Mus. Studies, Case Western Res. U., 1987. Summer mus. intern U. Ky. Art Mus., Lexington, 1983; tchg. asst. Case Western Res. U./CMA, Cleve., 1985—87; mus. intern Cleve. Mus. Art, 1986—87; summer mus. intern Nat. Gallery Art, Washington, 1987; asst. edn. coord. U. Ky. Art Mus., Lexington, 1987—88; assoc. curator for exhbns. Del. Art Mus., Wilmington, 1988—99; sr. curator Huntington Mus. Art, W.Va., 1999—. Regional rep. curators commn. Mid-Atlantic Assn. Museums, 1991—94; cmty. adv. com. Del. Art Mus., Wilmington, 1991—96; juror various art exhbns., 1990—; panel moderator; lectr. in field. Editor, contbr.: exhbn. catalogs. Vol. Lexington Humane Soc., Ky., Tri-State Bird Rescue, Newark, Ind. Dogs Inc., Chadds Ford, Pa. Recipient Anne Worthington Callahan award, U. Ky., 1984; Stone fellowship, Case Western Res. U., 1985—87. Mem.: Coll. Art Assn., Assn. of Art Mus. Curators, Am. Assn. Museums (Travel award 1990). Office: Huntington Mus Art 2033 McCoy Rd Huntington WV 25701

CULLIGAN, KEVIN JAMES, lawyer; b. Monticello, N.Y., Sept. 11, 1954; s. James Robert and Ann Audrey Culligan; m. Nancy Jean Segal, Aug. 10, 1980; children: Ryan James, Katherine Lynn, Casey Ann. AB in Biology, Colgate U., 1976; JD, Cornell U., 1980. Bar: N.Y. 1981, U.S. Dist. Ct. (so. and ea. dists.) N.Y. 1981, U.S. Ct. Appeals (fed. cir.), U.S. Dist. Ct. (we. dist.) N.Y. 1988, U.S. Supreme Ct. 1998. Mem. ABA, N.Y. Intellectual Property Law Assn., Assn. of the Bar of the City of N.Y. Home: 41 Kent Dr Cortlandt Mnr NY 10567-6232 Office: Fish & Neave 1251 Avenue of the Americas New York NY 10020-1105 E-mail: kculligan@fishneave.com.

CULLIGAN, PATRICK JOHN, obstetrician, urogynecologist, surgeon, researcher; s. Thomas Michael and Lois Fern Culligan; m. Kimberly D Dovey, May 20, 1995; children: Molly Elizabeth children: Brian Thomas, Clare Dovey. BS, Ga. Inst. of Tech., 1989; MD, Mercer U., 1993. Diplomate Am. Bd. of Obstetrics and Gynecology, 2001. Resident ob-gyn. Greenville (S.C.) Hosp. Sys., 1993—97; fellow urogynecology and reconstructive pelvic surgery Northwestern U. Med. Sch., Evanston, Ill., 1997—99; asst. prof. of ob-gyn. U. of Louisville (Ky.) Health Scis. Ctr., 1999—, assoc. prof. of ob-gyn., 2002—; v.p. U. OB-GYN Assocs., PSC, Louisville, 2002. Cons. Domain Associs., LLC, Princeton, NJ, 1994—; bd. dirs. U. OB-GYN Found., Inc. Co-author: Urogynecology and Reconstructive Pelvic Surgery, 2002; contbr. articles to profl. jours. Bd. dir. Girls on the Run, Louisville, 2001. Recipient Thompson A Gailey award for academic achievement, Greenville Hosp. Sys. Dept. of OB-GYN, 1997, Faculty Devel. award, Berlex Found., 2002. Fellow: ACS (assoc.), Am. Coll. of Ob-Gyn. (assoc. grantee 1999); mem.: Am. Urogynecologic Soc. (assoc.; pub. rels. com. mem. 2001—02), Soc. of Gynecologic Surgeons (assoc.), Young President's Org. Republican. Roman Catholic. Avocations: tennis, skiing, bicycling, travel. Office Phone: 502-629-2184. Business E-Mail: culligan@mybladdermd.com.

CULLINA, WILLIAM MICHAEL, lawyer; b. Hartford, Conn., July 22, 1921; s. Michael Stephen and Margaret (Carroll) C.; m. Gertrude Evelyn Blasig, Apr. 29, 1961; children: William Gregory, Kevin Michael, John Stephen, Susan Margaret. AB, Catholic U. Am., 1942; LLB, Yale U., 1948. Bar: Conn. bar 1948. Assoc. Murtha Cullina LLP, Hartford, 1948—, ptnr., 1952-91, of counsel, 1992—. Bd. dirs. St. Francis Hosp. and Med. Ctr., 1968-2002, hon. dir., 2002—; trustee St. Joseph Coll., 1986-98, trustee emeritus, 1998—; bd. govs. The Hartford Club, 1984-89, chair, 1987-88. Served with USNR, 1942-46. Fellow Am. Bar Found.; mem. ABA, Conn. Bar Assn., Hartford County Bar Assn., Hartford Tennis Club, Country Club of Farmington, Knight of St. Gregory, Phi Beta Kappa. Roman Catholic. Office: Murtha Cullina LLP City Pl 185 Asylum St Ste 29 Hartford CT 06103-3469

CULLINAN, BERNICE ELLINGER, education educator; b. Hamilton, Ohio, Oct. 12, 1926; d. Lee Alexander and Hazel (Berry) Dees; m. George W. Ellinger, June 5, 1948 (div. 1966); children: Susan Jane Ellinger, James Webb Ellinger; m. Paul Anthony Cullinan, June 9, 1967 (div. 1994); m. Kenneth Seeman Giniger, Apr. 13, 2002. BS, Ohio State U., 1948, MA, 1951, PhD, 1964. Cert. elem. educator Ohio, N.Y. Tchr. Maple Pk. Elem. Sch., Middletown, Ohio, 1944-46, Trotwood (Ohio) Elem. Sch., 1946-47, Columbus (Ohio) Pub. Schs., 1948-50, Upper Arlington (Ohio) Pub. Schs., 1950-52; instr. Ohio State U., Columbus, 1959-64, asst. prof., 1964-67, Ohio State U./Charlotte Huck prof. children's lit., 1997; assoc. prof. NYU, N.Y.C., 1967-72, prof. reading, 1972-97, prof. emeritus, 1998—; editor-in-chief Wordsong Books, Honesdale, Pa., 1990—. Chair selection com. Ezra Jack Keats New Writer award, 1984—2000; exec. sec. English Stds. Project, 1993—94. Author (with Lee Galda): Lit. and the Child, 1989, 5th edit., 2002; author: Children's Lit. in the Classroom: Weaving Charlotte's Web, 1989, 2d edit., 1994, Read to Me: Raising Kids Who Love to Read, 1992, 2d edit., 2000, Let's Read About: Finding Books They'll Love to Read, 1993; author: (with Brod Bagert) Helping Your Child Learn to Read, 1993; author: (with Dorothy Strickland and Lee Galda) Lang. Arts: Learning and Tchg., 2003; author: (with L. Galda and D. Strickland) Lang., Literacy and the Child, 1993; author:, 2002; author: (with Marilyn Scala and Virginia Schroder) Three Voices: Invitation to Poetry Across the Curriculum, 1995; author: 75 Authors and Illustrators Everyone Should Know, 1994; author: (with David Harrison) Poetry Lessons That Dazzle and Delight, 1999; editor: Children's Lit. in the Reading Program, 1987, Invitation to Read: More Children's Lit. in the Reading Program, 1992, Black Dialects and Reading, 1974, Fact and Fiction: Lit. Across the Curriculum, 1993, Children's Voices, 1993, Pen in Hand, 1993, A Jar of Tiny Stars, 1996; editor: (with Diane Person) The Continuum Encyclopedia of Children's Literature, 2003; editor: (with Bonnie L. Kunzel and Deborah A. Wooten) The Continuum Encyclopedia of Young Adult Literature, 2005; author (with M. Jerry Weiss): Books I Read When I Was Young, 1980; author: (with Carolyn Carmichael) Literature and Young Children, 1977; author: Children's Literature in the Classroom: Extending Charlotte's Web, 1993; mem. editl. bd. Nat. Coun. Tchrs. English, Champaign, Ill., 1973—76, New Adv., 1987—99, Ranger Rick Mag., 1992—; contbr. articles to profl. jours. Adv. bd. Reading Rainbow, 1979—, Sta. WGBH-TV, 1989—; mem. selection com. Caldecott award ALA, Chgo., 1982—83; trustee Highlights Children Found., 1993—. Named Outstanding Educator in Lang. Arts, Nat. Coun. Tchrs. English, 2003; named to Ohio State U. Coll. Edn. Hall of Fame, 1995; recipient Ind. U. Citation for outstanding contbn. to literacy, 1995. Mem.: Reading Hall of Fame (pres. 1998—99, inducted 1989), Internat. Reading Found. (trustee 1984—91, Jeremiah Ludington award 1992), Internat. Reading Assn. (bd. dirs. 1979—84, pres. 1984—85, chair Tchrs. Choices 1988—91, chair spl. svc. award selection com. 2005—, Arbuthnot award for outstanding tchr. children's lit. 1989). Avocations: tennis, reading for pleasure, poetry. Home: 1045 Park Ave Apt 6A New York NY 10028 Office: 3 Tudor Ln Sands Point NY 11050-1104 Office Phone: 212-369-7899. Personal E-mail: BerniceCullinan@verizon.net.

CULLINEY, JOHN JAMES, radiologist, educator; b. N.Y.C., Oct. 17, 1955; s. Michael and Marion (Dakowski) C.; m. Margaret Mary Steinhardt, Oct. 11, 1986. BS, Rutgers U., 1977, MS, 1981; MD, U Medicine and Dentistry N.J., 1984. Diplomate Am. Bd. Radiology, Nat. Bd. Med. Examiners. Intern physician Med. Coll. of Pa. Hosp., Phila., 1984-85; resident physician U. Medicine & Dentistry N.J., Newark, 1985-89, asst. prof. clin. diagnostic radiology, chief uroradiology, 1990-92; fellow body imaging, instr. diagnostic radiology Hahnemann U. Hosp., Phila., 1989-90; clin. instr. diagnostic radiology, chief cross-sect. imaging Mercy & Moses Taylor Hosps. affiliates Temple Med. Sch., Scranton, Pa., 1992-2001; pres. Radiol. Cons. Inc., 1999-2001; radiologist and radiation safety officer Kauai Med. Clinic, Hawaii, 2001—, chmn. dept. radiology, 2004—, vice chmn. dept. radiology, 2002—03, bd. dirs., 2002—; mem. KMC Physicians Adv. Group, 2005. Bd. dirs. Radiol. Cons., Inc., Dunmore, Pa., 1994-2001; co-dir. Phoenix Vascular Lab.; dir. radiology Mercy Hosp. Scranton, Clin. Vascular Lab. Mem. AMA, AAUP, Am. Coll. Radiology, Am. Soc. Breast Imagers, Roentgen Soc. N.Am., KC. Roman Catholic. Avocations: amateur radio technician class, skiing. Home: 2940 Kanani St Lihue HI 96766 Office: Kauai Med Clinic 3-3420 Kuhio Hwy Ste B Lihue HI 96766 E-mail: culliney@aol.com.

CULLITON, BARBARA J., publishing executive; b. Buffalo, May 2, 1943; Grad., Vassar Coll. Founder, dep. editor and head editl. ops. N.Am. Nature Publs. Nature Medicine, Structural Biology, Nature Genetics., 1991—99; founder, sci. comm. and exec. editor GeneWire.com Celera Genomics, 1999—2001; v.p. for pub. The Inst. for Genomic Rsch., Rockville, Md., 2001—; editor-in-chief Genome News Network, Rockville, 2001—. Times Mirror vis. prof. and dir. Writing About Sci. The Writing Seminars, Johns Hopkins U., Balt., 1990—98; advisor Am. Bd. Internal Medicine; adv. com. Knight Journalism Fellows, MIT, Cambridge; journalism advisor Fulbright Scholars program; advisor Sound Print, the radio series; panelist Sci. Jour., a Pub. Broadcasting prodn. Editor (founding editor-in-chief): Nature Genomics, Nature Structural Biology, Nature Medicine. Bd. overseers Darmouth Med. Sch. Co-recipient George Polk award for journalism. Mem.: Coun. for Advancement of Sci. Writing (pres. 1985—89, bd. dirs.), Nat. Assn. Sci. Writers (pres. 1981—82), Inst. of Medicine of NAS (mem. governing coun.), Italian Soc. for Molecular Medicine (hon.), Sigma Xi (hon.). Episcopalian. Office: Genome News Network 9712 Medical Center Dr Rockville MD 20850 Home: 5020 Easterngate NW Washington DC 20016

CULLMAN, HUGH, retired tobacco company executive; b. N.Y.C., Jan. 27, 1923; s. Howard S. and Elsie (Gottheil) C.; m. Nan Alva Ogburn, May 12, 1951; children: Katherine Victoria, Hugh Jr., Alexandra Miriam. BS, U.S. Naval Acad., 1945. With Benson & Hedges, 1949-54, mgr. research, 1952-54; with Philip Morris Inc., 1954—, treas., 1959-60, v.p., asst. chief ops., 1960-64, exec. v.p. ops., 1966—, also bd. dirs.; exec. v.p. Philip Morris Internat., 1965, pres., 1967-78, also bd. dirs.; group exec. v.p. Philip Morris Inc., 1978-84; chief exec. officer Philip Morris U.S.A., 1978-84; vice chmn. Philip Morris Cos. Inc., 1985-88. Sr. trustee U.S. Coun. for Internat. Bus.; bd. dirs. N.C. Cmty. Found.; mem. adv. bd. Duke U. Marine Lab; emeritus mem. Tyron Palace Commn. Lt. USN, 1945—47, PTO, Lt. USN, 1951—52, Europe. Address: 821 Front St Beaufort NC 28516-2230

CULLOM, WILLIAM OTIS, industrial designer, retired trade association executive; b. Huntsville, Ala., Mar. 20, 1932; s. Otis McKinley and Elna (Reese) C.; m. Caryl James, May 26, 1956; children: Cheryl Ann Cullom Stewart, Jennifer James Cullom Barksdale. BS, Fla. State U., 1958. Fingerprint expert FBI, 1950-52; asst. bus. mgr. Fla. State U., 1954-64; with Ryder Truck Rental Inc., Miami, Fla., 1964-79, exec. v.p. mktg., 1979; pres., chief operating officer Jartran, Inc., Coral Gables, Fla., 1979-81; pres. Greater Miami C. of C., 1981—2004; founder WOC Consulting Co., 2004—, ret., 2005; pvt. practice Burnsville, 2005—. V.p. Orange Bowl Com., 1992—. Sec., bd. dirs. Miami-Dade Coll. Found.; mem. cabinet exec. com. Beacon Coun. United Way, Miami, 1974-80; trustee Bethune Cookman Coll., Daytona Beach, Fla., Barry U., St. Thomas U., Miami-Dade C.C. Found.; past chmn. bd. trustees Fla. State U; chmn. adminstrv. bd. Kendall Meth. Ch.; mem. pres.'s adv. com. Fla. Meml. Coll., Miami; bd. dirs. Bapt. Hosp. Found., Coconut Grove Playhouse, Goodwill Industries, Salvation Army; v.p. Orange Bowl Com.; chmn. bd. trustees Fla. State U. Found., 1994-95; chmn. Greater Miami Chamber Coalition. With U.S. Army, 1952-54. Recipient Miami Black Bus. Cmtys. Econ. Unity award, 1984, Anti Defamation League Human Rels. award, 1992, Disting. Cmty. Svc. award, 1998, Cedars Found. Concern award, 1994, NCCJ Humanitarian award, 1995, Silver Medallion award Greater Miami NCCJ, Citizen of Yr. award Greater Miami Rotary Club, Club at Dornal award, Life Achievement award Nat. PTA, Sand in My Shoes award, 2003, Carrfour Supportive Housing highest award, 2003, Lifetime Achievement award Human Svcs. Coalition, 2003, Daily Point of Light award, Pres. George Sr. and George W. Bush, 2004; named South Fla. Scout of Yr., Scouts Internat. in South Fla., 1997. Mem. Am. Trucking Assn., Truck Leasing and Renting Assn. (pres. Fla. chpt. 1972-73), Fla. State U. Nat. Alumni Assn. (pres.), Miami Hist. Assn., Brickell Club, Univ. Club, Riviera Country Club, City Club, Bankers Club, Ocean Reef Yacht Club, Gov.'s Club (Tallahassee), Dearing Bay Yacht Club, Biscayne Bay Yacht Club, Mountain Air Country Club (Burnsville, NC), Rotary, Doral Country Club (mem. of bd. Doral Golf Championship). Democrat. Methodist. Office: Greater Miami C of C 1601 Biscayne Blvd Miami FL 33132-1224 Home and Office: 55 Cullom Chapel Road Burnsville NC 28714

CULLUM, BRIAN MICHAEL, science educator; b. Bel Air, Md., July 15, 1972; s. Neil and Mattie Cullum; m. Dimitra Stratis-Cullum, June 9, 2001. AA in chemistry, Harford C.C., 1992; BS in chemistry, Frostburg State U., 1994; PhD in chemistry, U. SC, 1998. Postdoctoral fellow Oak Ridge (Tenn.) Nat. Lab., 1999—2002; asst. prof. chemistry U. Md. Balt. County, 2002—. Chair Smart Med. and Biomedical Sensor Tech. Conf., 2003—; project cons. NATO Science for Peach Program, Brussels, 2004. Contbr. articles various profl. jours. Recipient Rsch. and Devel. 100 award, R & D Mag., 2003. Mem.: Soc. for Applied Spectroscopy. Office: U Md Balt County 1000 Hilltop Cir Baltimore MD 21250 Office Fax: 410-455-2608. E-mail: cullum@umbc.edu.

CULLUM, JOHN, actor, singer; b. Knoxville, Tenn., Mar. 2, 1930; m. Emily Frankel; 1 child, John David. BA, U. Tenn. Former tennis player and real estate salesman. N.Y. debut with Shakespearewrights, 1957; joined N.Y. Shakespeare Festival, 1960; Broadway debut in Camelot, 1962; played Laertes in Hamlet, 1964; other Broadway appearances include On A Clear Day You Can See Forever, 1965 (Theatre World award 1965), Man of La Mancha, 1966, 1776, 1969, Vivat! Vivat Regina, 1972, Shenandoah, 1975 (Tony award as best actor 1975), The Trip Back Down, 1977, On the Twentieth Century, 1978 (Tony award as best actor in musical 1978), Deathtrap, 1979, Whistler, 1981 (Drama Desk award), Private Lives (with Richard Burton and Elizabeth Taylor), 1983, Doubles, 1985, The Boys in Autumn (with George C. Scott), 1986, Purlie, 2005; other leading roles include plays Hamlet, Cyrano de Bergerac; film appearances include: All the Way Home, 1963, Hawaii, 1966, 1776, 1972, The Prodigal, 1982, Sweet Country, 1985, Marie, 1985, The Boys in Autumn (with George C. Scott), 1986, Ricochet River, 1998, Held Up, 1999, Urinetown, 2003, Candide, 2005; concert readings include The Golden Apple, 2005; appeared in TV movie A Man Without a Country, 1973, The Day After, 1984, Shootdown, 1988, With a Vengeance, 1992, Inherit the Wind, 1999, also public TV movies Summer, 1980, Carl Sandburg, 1981; TV series include: Buck James, 1987-88, Northern Exposure, 1990-95 (Emmy nomination, Supporting Actor - Comedy, 1993), ER, 1994, To Have & To Hold, 1998; TV appearance in All My Children, 1997; spokesman for arts and entertainment cable TV, Victorian Days. Served with U.S. Army. Office: care Internat Creative Mgmt 8942 Wilshire Blvd Beverly Hills CA 90211-1934*

CULLUM, LEE BROOKS, journalist; b. Dallas, Mar. 18, 1939; d. Charles Gillespie and Garland Chapman Cullum; m. James Howard Clark Jr., June 29, 1962 (div. June 1976); 1 child, James Howard Cullum Clark. Student, Sweet Briar Coll.; BA, So. Meth. U., 1961; DHL (hon.), Monterey Inst. Inter. Studies, 1997, U. Puget Sound, 2002. Reporter, then exec. prodr. and on-air moderator Newsroom Sta. KERA-TV, Dallas, 1970-76, v.p. program devel., 1976-81; account exec. Hill & Knowlton, Dallas, 1981-82; editor D Mag., Dallas, 1982-85; dir. client svcs. Hill & Knowlton, Dallas, 1985-86; editor editl. page Dallas Times Herald, Dallas, 1986-91; commentator Newshour with Jim Lehrer (formerly Macneil-Lehrer Newshour), Washington, 1988—2001; contbg. columnist Dallas Morning News, Dallas, 1992—; commentator All Things Considered Nat. Pub. Radio, 1994—2000; commentator Morning Edition, KERA-FM, 2000—. Bd. dirs. Coun. Fgn. Rels., N.Y., Pacific Coun. Internat. Policy, L.A., Sammons Found., Dallas. Author: Genius Came Early: Creativity in the Twentieth Century, 1999. Bd. dirs. S.W. Legal Found., Dallas, 1995-99, The Hockaday Sch., Dallas, 1997-2003; bd. visitors Internat. Programs Ctr., Okla. U., 1997—; mem. Am. Coun. on Germany; mem. Nat. Com. on U.S.-China Rels., InterAm. Dialogue Dallas Inst. for Humanities and Culture fellow; recipient Matrix award Women in Comms., 1977, 85, J. B. Marryatt award Dallas Press Club, 1996. Mem.: Nat. Conf. Editl. Writers. Episcopalian. Avocations: the arts, travel, books. E-mail: lcullum@swbell.net.

CULMER, LEOME FRANCES, volunteer; b. Miami, Fla., July 19, 1925; d. Arthur Francis and Manette Aileen Scavella; m. John Edwin Culmer, July 3, 1947 (dec. June 18, 1963); children: Francena Culmer-Brooks, John E., Angela M., Lona Culmer-Schellbach, James A. BS, Bethune-Cookman Coll., 1949. Cert. tchr. Exhibit chair, 100-Yr History of St. Agnes' Episcopal Ch., 1998. Rschr., writer African Am. com. Dade Heritage Trust; program chmn. African Am. Com. Commemorative Svc.; script writer African Am. Com.; mem. City of Miami Cemetery Task Force, Dade Heritage Trust, Hist. Mus. So. Fla.; trustee, bd. dirs., chmn. spkrs.' bur. Black Archives Found., Inc.; former bd. dirs. Children's Home Soc. Fla.; mem. Oral History com. Va. Key Beach Park Trust, mem., oral history com.; co-parliamentarian, diocesan exec. bd. Order of Daus. of the King; pres. St. Cecelia's chpt. Episcopal Ch. Women; parish historian, vacation bible sch. tchr., mem. exec. bd., parish coun. St. Agnes' Episcopal Ch.; mem. Union of Black Episcopalians; former mem. com. Fla. Coun. Chs.; former mem. archives and records com. Diocese of S.E. Fla. Named Citizen of the Day, Black Archives, Citizen of Yr., King of Clubs, 2000; recipient Congl. Nat. Parents' Day awrd, 1995, Woman of Distinction award, Miami-Dade Pub. Schs., 2000, Woman of Impact award, Miami-Dade Coalition Women's History, Black Archives Founder's award medallion, 2002, award of appreciation, BellSouth, 1997—98, cert. appreciation, Dade County Pub. Schs. Sch. Vol. Program, Spl. Black Woman cert. appreciation, Miami-Dade Pub. Libr. Sys., Outstanding Cmty. Svc. award, Women's C. of C., Patronal Appreciation award, St. Agnes' Episcopal Ch., 1983, Resolution, Chpt. of Trinity Episcopal Cathedral, Pres.' cert. AAUW, cert. appreciation, Booker T. Washington Sr. H.S., Black Archives, cmty. svc. award, Dade County Pub. Sch., award of excellence for cmty. svc., Collegians Club, Inc., rector's award, dedicated and devoted svc. award, cert. commendation, St. Agnes' Episcopal Ch., cert. honor, Fla. State Tchrs. Reunion Assn., Outstanding Cmty. Svc. award, Women's C. of C., Citizen of Day award, Miami-Dade County, Proclamation of Appreciation for Cmty. Svc., Miami-Dade County Office of Mayor, 2001, Enid C. Pinkney Humanitarian award, 2001, commendation, City of Miami, 2001, Recognition Award, Nat. Pres. of Order of Daughters of King, Miami-Dade Preservation Bd., numerous others. Mem.: AAUW, Bethune-Cookman Coll. Alumni Assn., Soc. Episcopal Historians and Archivists. Episcopalian. Avocations: research, writing, preservation activism, history. Home: 1434 NW 55th Terr Miami FL 33142 Personal E-mail: amculmer@aol.com.

CULNON, SHARON DARLENE, reading specialist, special education educator; b. Balt., Apr. 20, 1947; d. Clayton Claude and Ann (McIntyre) Legg; m. Allen William Culnon, July 9, 1975. BA in Elem. Edn., U. Mich., 1972; MAT in Reading Edn., Oakland U., 1980; cert. Learning Disabilities, Ariz. State U., 1983. Cert. K-8 edn., K-12 reading specialist, K-12 learning disabilities specialist. Tchr. Mt. Morris (Mich.) Consolidated Schs., 1972—77; reading specialist Paradise Valley Schs., Phoenix, 1978—87, learning disabilities specialist, 1987—90, tchr., 1990—2000. Mem. Kachina Jr. Women's Club, Phoenix, 1980-83, sec., 1981-82. Recipient Learning Leader/dist. award Paradise Valley Bd. of Edn., Phoenix, 1986. Mem. Phi Delta Kappa (historian 1987-88). Presbyterian. Avocations: travel, wildlife viewing and study, reading, pets, photography. Home: 9035 N Concho Ln Phoenix AZ 85028-5318

CULP, CHARLES WILLIAM, lawyer; b. Louisville, Nov. 13, 1931; s. Charles Cantrell and Carolyn Marticia (O'Bannon) C.; m. Elisabeth Martha Stoker, Sept. 22, 1962; children: Charles Cantrell, Virginia Sheldon. BA, Yale U., 1953; JD, Harvard U., 1958. Bar: Ind. 1958. Ptnr. Cadick, Burns Duck & Peterson, Indpls., 1958-81, Shortridge & Culp, Indpls., 1981-88; pvt. practice Indpls., 1988—. Mem. Traders Point Hunt, Lawyers Club, Univ. Club, Dramatic Club. Home: 9251 Spring Forest Dr Indianapolis IN 46260-1267 Office Phone: 317-634-3700. E-mail: cwculp@ameritech.net.

CULP, DONALD ALLEN, lawyer; b. Atchison, Kans., June 13, 1938; s. Roy Allen and Audrey Mae (Moyer) C.; m. Judy Wayne Smith, Sept. 10, 1966; children: Brian David, Matthew Allen, Lindsey Beth. Bar: Kans. 1965, Mo. 1987. Ptnr. Culp & Sheppard, Overland Park, Kans., 1969-79; gen. counsel Electronic Realty Assn., Overland Park, Kans., 1979-87; v.p., gen. counsel Signature Foods, Inc., Kansas City, Mo., 1987-89; ptnr. Shughart, Thomson & Kilroy, Overland Park, 1989-97, Blackwell, Sanders, Pepper, Martin, Kansas City, Mo., 1997—. Pres. Am. Cancer Soc., Overland Park, 1970-73, hon. life mem., 1981—; elder Rolling Hills Presbyn. Ch., Overland Park, 1972-80; pres., bd. dirs. Shawnee Mission Bd. Edn., Overland Park, 1975-83; bd. dirs. Overland Park C. of C., 1978-81. Mem. ABA, Kans. Bar Assn., Mo. Bar Assn., Johnson County Bar Assn. Republican. Presbyterian. Avocations: bicycling, race walking. Home: 9609 W 104th St Shawnee Mission KS 66212-5606 Office: Blackwell Sanders Peper Martin PO Box 419777 2300 Main St Ste 1100 Kansas City MO 64108-2416 Office Phone: 816-983-8115. Business E-Mail: dculp@blackwellsanders.com.

CULP, FAYE BERRY, state legislator; b. Kilmichael, Miss., Dec. 6, 1939; d. Otis Milton and Drapa (Clark) Berry; m. James H. Culp, Dec. 28, 1966; children: James Jr., David. BS in Bus. Edn., Miss. U. for Women, 1961; postgrad., Ga. State U., 1965-66; M, U. South Fla., Tampa, 1993. Tchr. Atlanta Pub. Schs., 1961-66; ednl. svcs. rep. IBM, San Francisco, 1966, Poughkeepsie, N.Y., 1967-68; real estate salesperson Yates Realty, Tampa, 1975-79; mem. sch. bd. Hillsborough County, Tampa, 1988-92; mem. Fla. Ho. of Reps., Tallahassee and Tampa, 1994—, majority whip, 1996-98. Chair Joint Ho. and Senate Com. for Legis. Info. Tech. Resources Procedural Coun., mem. edn., appropriations, tourism coms.; mem. State Task Force for Tech. Fla. Sch. Bds. Assn.; chmn. legis. subcom. on spl. legislation, chmn. bylaws com. Fla. Sch. Bds. Assn.; mem. State Instrnl. Coun. Textbook Selection; chmn. juvenile justice com. Fla. Ho. Reps, 2005—. Asst. dir. Theatre Atlanta prodns.; dir., prodr. musicals First United Meth. Ch., Tampa. Mem. Govs. Task Force for Prevention Teen-Age Suicides; del. Fla. Fedn. Rep. Women's Conv.; 1st pres. Child Abuse Coun. Aux.; pres. Hillsborough Women's Rep. Club, Tampa Realistic Artists, Inc., United Meth. Women, 1st United Meth. Ch., Tampa, Plant High Sch. Parent Student Tchrs. Assn.; v.p. various PTAs; area v.p. Hillsborough County Coun.; juvenile protection chmn. Hillsborough PTA County Coun.; youth coord., bd. trustees First United Meth. Ch.; bd. mem. Nat. Coun. Christians and Jews, Coun. Downtown Chs.; treas. West State Archaeol. Soc.; chmn. internat. affairs Tampa Civic Assn.; leader, den mother Cub Scouts; chmn. Just Friends Mentoring Program; bd. mem., officer Friends of Pub. Edn.; chmn. Masterpiece Morning. Named Woman of Distinction Girl Scouts Am., Tampa, Pacesetter in Ky. So. Women in Pub. Svc., 1997, Disting. Alumni of Yr. U. South Fla. Coll. Fine Arts, Tampa, 1997, Legislator of Yr. Internat. Coun. Shopping Ctrs., Orlando, Fla., 1997, 2003, One of Top 40 Legislators, Fla. C. of C., 1997, Legislator of Yr. Fla. Sch. Bds. Assn., 1997, Alliance Homeowners Assn., 2003, Elected Official of Yr, Tampa Rep. Women, 2004; recipient over 150 awards in photography, 40 awards in painting, 3 awards in poetry, others. Mem. LWV, Nat. Order Women Legislators (stakeholder, regional dir. nat. conf., nat. pres. 2004—), Nat. Found. Women Legislators (chmn.), PEO (chpt. historian), Miss. U. for Women Alumni Assn. (pres. Suncoast chpt.), Fla. Ho. Reps. (vice chmn. gen. edn., children's svs.), Hillsborough County Pres. Roundtable, Greater Tampa C. of C. (mem. edn. coun.), South Tampa C. of C., Greater Town n' Country C. of C., Lamplighters, Red Cross Angels, Friends of the Arts, Fla. Orch. Guild, Port Tampa Civic Assn., Alpha. Republican. Methodist. Avocations: photography, painting, travel. Office Phone: 813-272-2920. Personal E-mail: faye.culp@myfloridahouse.gov.

CULP, GORDON LOUIS, consulting engineer, management consultant; b. Topeka, Dec. 30, 1939; s. Russell Louis and Dorothy Marion (Wilson) C.; m. Rosemary Anne Smith, Apr. 7, 1990. BS in Civil Engring., U. Kans., 1961, MS in Environ. Health Engring., 1962; MA in Applied Psychology, U. Santa Monica, 1991. Registered profl. engr., Calif., Nev., Wash., Oreg.; cert. Myers Briggs practitioner MBTI Cert. Program, Gainsville, Fla. San. engr. USPHS, Cin., 1962-64, CH2M/Hill Engrs., Corvallis, Oreg., 1964-66; rsch. engr. Neptune Microfloc, Corvallis, 1966-70; rsch. mgr. Battelle N.W., Richland, Wash., 1970-71; regional mgr. CH2M/Hill Engrs., Reston, Va., 1971-73; pres. Culp, Wesner Culp (acquired by HDR Engring. 1986), Cameron Park, Calif., 1973-93, Smith Culp Consulting, Las Vegas, Nev., 1993—. Author: New Concepts in Water Purification, 1974, Handbook of Advanced Wastewater Treatment, 1978, 2d edit., 2001, Managing People (including Yourself) for Project Success, 1991,The Lead Dog Has the Best View: Leading Your Project Team to Success, 2005, others; assoc. editor Jour. Engring. Mgmt. Named one of four Outstanding Graduates in Hist. of Civil Engrg. Program, U. Kans. Mem. ASCE, Am. Water Works Assn., Water Pollution Control Fedn., Am. Acad. Environ. Engrs., Assn. Psychol. Type, Rotary (pres. 1977-78). Office: Smith Culp Consulting 653 Ravel Ct Las Vegas NV 89145-8628 Office Phone: 702-360-1120. Business E-Mail: gordon@smithculp.com.

CULP, H. LAWRENCE, manufacturing executive; BA in Econs., Wash. Coll., 1985; MBA, Harvard U., 1990. Product mgr. Veeder-Root, 1990, v.p. mktg. and sales, pres., 1993—95; group exec., corp. officer Danaher Corp., 1995—99, exec. v.p., 1999—2000, COO, 2000—01, CEO, pres., 2001—. Office: 2099 Pennsylavania Ave NW Washington DC 20006-1813

CULP, JOE C(ARL), electronics executive; b. Little Rock, July 23, 1933; s. Charles Carl and Doris Evelyn (Jackson) C.; m. Norma Carol Kennan, Jan. 26, 1954; 1 dau., Karen Gay Culp Ashorn. BSEE, U. Ark., 1955. Staff asst. to exec. v.p. Collins Radio, Dallas, 1967—68; with Rockwell Internat., Dallas, 1968—88, dir. data sys. mktg., 1968—71, dir. mktg. transmission sys. divsn., 1971—78, v.p. Latin-Am. divsn., 1978—80, v.p., gen. mgr. transmission sys. divsn., 1980—82, pres. telecom. group, 1982—88; pres., CEO Lightnet, Rockville, Md., 1988—89; exec. v.p. Comm. Transmission Inc., Austin, Tex., 1989—90. Pres. Culp Comm. Assocs., Austin, 1990—; bd. dirs. March Networks, Brecon Ridge Mfg. Sys. Chmn. engring. bd. advisors U. Tex., Arlington, 1984; bd. advisors Coll. Engring. U. Ark., Fayetteville, 1982. Named Disting. Grad., Coll. Engring. U. Ark., 1981, Disting. Engr., U. Tex., Arlington, 1984. Mem. Electronic Industry Assn. (bd. govs. 1984-88), U.S. Tel. Suppliers Assn. (dir. 1984-88), Ind. Tel. Pioneers. Republican. Methodist. Office: Culp Comm Assocs Inc 2305 Barton Creek Blvd #20 Austin TX 78735

CULP, KRISTINE ANN, dean, theology studies educator; B in Gen. Studies with distinction, U. Iowa, 1978; MDiv, Princeton Theol. Sem., 1982; PhD in Religion, U. Chgo., 1989. Vis. instr. theology St. Paul Sch. Theology, Kansas City, Mo., 1985-86, instr. theology, 1986-89, asst. prof. theology, 1990-91; dean Disciples Div. House U. Chgo., 1991—, sr. lectr. theology Div. Sch., 1991—. Contbr. articles to profl. jours. Office: U Chgo Disciples Divinity House 1156 E 57th St Chicago IL 60637-1536 also: The Divinity Sch-U Chgo Swift Hall S-406 1025 E 58th St Chicago IL 60637-1509

CULP, MICHAEL BRONSTON, investor, writer, publisher; b. NYC, June 17, 1952; s. Robert Walter and Anna Lee (Filtzer) C.; m. Deborah T. Bronston. BA in Econs. cum laude, CUNY, 1973; CFA, U. Va., 1979. Securities analyst Standard & Poor's, N.Y.C., 1974—79; v.p., securities analyst E. F. Hutton & Co., Inc., N.Y.C., 1979—82; v.p., sr. securities analyst Prudential Securities Inc., N.Y.C., 1982-86, sr. v.p., mng. dir. rsch., 1986-94, sr. v.p., dir. global rsch., 1994-97, bd. dirs., 1986-91, oper. coun., 1991-97, chmn. stock selection com., 1989-97, chmn. equity devel. com., 1991-97, equity transactions bd., 1994-97, investment banking com., 1994-97; mem. investment com. Roman Arch Fund, 1996-97; mng. dir., dir. rsch., mem. oper. com. PaineWebber Inc., N.Y.C., 1997-2000, also bd. dirs., 1997-2000; pres. Michael Culp & Co., Inc., N.Y.C., 2000—01, Mecox Bay Press LLC, 2002—; dir., mem. audit com. The Nat. Rsch. Exch. and Nat. Rsch. Std., 2004—. Author: Conflicted, A Novel, 2003. Mem. Pubs.' Mktg. Assn., N.Y. Soc. Security Analysts, Fin. Analysts' Fedn., Inst. CFAs, Internat. Soc. Fin. Analysts, Assn. for Investment Mgmt. and Rsch., Mensa, Phi Beta Kappa, Omicron Delta Epsilon. Home: 11 Jule Pond Dr Southampton NY 11968 also: 350 East 79th Street New York NY 10021

CULP, MILDRED LOUISE, corporate financial executive; b. Ft. Monroe, Va., Jan. 13, 1949; d. William W. and Winifred (Stilwell) C. BA in English, Knox Coll., 1971; AM in Religion and Literature, U. Chgo., 1974, PhD The Com. on History of Culture, 1976. Faculty, adminstr. Coll., 1976—81; dir. Exec. Résumés, Seattle, 1981—; pres. Exec. Directions Internat., Inc., Seattle, 1985—2000, Clive, Iowa, 2000—03, Crete, Ill., 2003—. Mem. MBA mgmt. skills adv. com. U. Wash. Sch. Bus. Adminstrn., 1993; spkr. in field; contract rschr. U.S. Army Recruiting Command, 1997. Author: Be WorkWise: Retooling Your Work for the 21st Century, 1994; columnist Seattle Daily Jour. Commerce, 1982-88; writer Singer Media Corp., 1991-98, Worldwide Media, 1999-2002, Globalvision, Inc., 2002—, WorkWise syndicated column, 1994—, Universal Press Syndicate, 1997-2001, WorkWise Interactive syndicated column, 2004-, WorkWise Advice column, 2003-04; WorkWise Internet audio program, 2000—; featured on TV and radio; contbr. articles to profl. jours.; presenter WorkWise Report, Sta. KIRO, 1991-96 Admissions counselor U. Chgo., 1981—; mem. Nat. Alliance Mentally Ill, 1984-91; mem. (life) A.M.I. Hamilton County, 1984—; founding mem. People Against Telephone Terrorism and Harassment, 1990; co-sponsor WorkWise award, 1999-2000. Recipient Alumni Achievement award Knox Coll., 1990, 8 other awards; named Hon. Army Recruiter. Mem.: U. Chgo. Puget Sound Alumni Club (bd. dir. 1982—86), Knox Coll. Alumni Network. E-mail: culp@workwise.net.

CULPEPPER, DAUNTE, professional football player; b. Jan. 28, 1977; Football player Minn. Vikings, 1999—. Named to NFL Pro-Bowl, 2000, 2003—04; recipient Breakthrough Athlete of the Yr. award, ESPY, 2000. Achievements include set NCAA record for single season completion percentage (.736), 1998; drafted by MLB NY Yankee's, 1995. Office: Minn Vikings 9520 Viking Dr Eden Prairie MN 55344*

CULPEPPER, JETTA CAROL, librarian; b. Murray, Ky., Oct. 17, 1946; BS, Murray State U., 1968, MA, 1969; MLS, George Peabody Coll., 1972, EdS, 1975. Cataloger Murray (Ky.) State U., 1969-78, head edn. libr., 1978-79, head acquisitions dept., 1980-92, head media resources dept., 1993-94, collection analysis libr., 1994-97, spl. programs libr., 1997—2004, interim dir. curriculum Materials Ctr. Coll. Edn., 2004—. Gender equity grantee Dept. Adult and Tech. Edn., Cabinet for Workforce Devel. of Ky., 1993-94, 94-95. Mem. ALA, Coll. and Rsch. Librs., Southeastern Librs., Ky. Libr. Assn., First Dist. Libr. Assn. (sec.). Office: Murray State Univ Alexander Hall Rm 311 Murray KY 42071-3340 Office Phone: 270-762-4276.

CULPEPPER, JO LONG, retired librarian; b. Franklin, Va., Mar. 10, 1945; d. Sidney Earl and Fannie Lou (Flythe) Long; m. Britton Barclay Culpepper, Jr., Aug. 19, 1967; children: Britton B. III, Edmond Scott, Lou Ann. BS, Radford (Va.) U., 1967; MS, Old Dominion U., 1983. Min. of activities Westmoreland Bapt. Ch., Huntington, W.Va., 1967-70; libr. Walter Cecil Rawls Libr. and Mus., Courtland, Va., 1971-79, Hunterdale Elem. Sch., Franklin, Va., 1979—2005, ret., 2005. Dir. Sunday sch. Franklin Bapt. Ch., 1988-98, bd. deacons, 1994-97; trustee Walter Cecil Rawls Libr. and Mus., 1985-89; troop leader Boy Scouts Am. Mem. Va. Ednl. Media Assn., Franklin/Southampton Reading Coun., Va. Reading Coun. Avocations: scouting, reading, bowling, camping. Home: 401 Trail Rd Franklin VA 23851-2909 Personal E-mail: britt_jo_culpepper@hotmail.com.

CULPEPPER, MARY KAY, publishing executive; With Weight Watchers; exec. dir. Coastal Living, 2000—01; editor Cooking Light Mag., 2001—, v.p., 2002—. Office: Cooking Light Magazine P O Box 62376 Tampa FL 33662*

CULPEPPER, WARREN LEIGH, management consultant; b. Atlanta, Jan. 30, 1942; s. Harry Stuart and Alma Elaine (Payne) C.; m. Suzanne Elizabeth Hooper, Nov. 28, 1964 (dec. June 1982); children: Warren Leigh, Jonathan Lane; m. Cathryn Lee Thrasher, Aug. 27, 1995. BA cum laude, U. of the South, 1964. CLU. Agt. Mass Mutual Life Ins. Co., Nashville, 1964-67; sys. engr. IBM, Atlanta, 1967-70; dir. customer svcs. Info. Sys. Am., Atlanta, 1970-79; CEO Culpepper and Assocs., Inc., Atlanta, 1979—. Bd. dirs. Geac Computers, Ltd., Toronto, Ont., Can., Reaction Design, San Diego. Pub., editor The Culpepper Letter, 1979-98, Software Pricing Trends, 1981, 84, 87, 90, 93, Software Industry Compensation Library, annually 1982-99, Financial Operating Ratios for Software Companies, 1990, 92, 94, 96, 98. Vestry St. Patricks Episcopal Ch., Dunwoody, Ga., 1980-83. Staff sgt. Air Nat. Guard, 1964. Republican. Episcopalian. Avocations: hiking, genealogy. Home: 10436 Big Canoe Jasper GA 30143-5125 Fax: 520-441-5114. E-mail: warren@culpepper.com.

CULTON, PAUL MELVIN, retired counselor, educator, interpreter; b. Council Bluffs, Iowa, Feb. 12, 1932; s. Paul Roland and Hallie Ethel Emma (Paschal) C. AB, Minn. Bible Coll., 1955; BS, U. Nebr., Omaha, 1965; MA, Calif. State U., Northridge, 1970; EdD, Brigham Young U., 1981. Cert. tchr., Iowa. Tchr. Iowa Sch. for Deaf, Council Bluffs, 1956-70; ednl. specialist Golden West Coll., Huntington Beach, Calif., 1970-71, dir. disabled students, 1971-82, instr., 1982-88; counselor El Camino Coll., Via Torrance, Calif., 1990-93, acting assoc. dean, 1993-94, counselor, 1994-97, lectr., 1997—2005. Interpreter various state and fed. cts., Iowa, Calif., 1960-90; asst. prof. Calif. State U., Northridge, Fresno, Dominguez Hills, 1973, 76, 80, 87-91, L.A., 1999-2005; vis. prof. U. Guam, Agana, 1977; mem. allocations task force, task force on deafness, trainer handicapped students Calif. C.C.s, 1971-81 Editor: Region IX Conf. for Coordinating Rehab. and Edn. Svcs. for Deaf proceedings, 1970, Toward Rehab. Involvement by Parents of Deaf conf. proceedings, 1971; composer Carry the Light, 1986. Bd. dirs. Iowa NAACP, 1966-68, Gay and Lesbian Cmty. Svcs. Ctr., Orange County, Calif., 1975-77; founding sec. Dayle McIntosh Ctr. for Disabled, Anaheim and Garden Grove, Calif., 1974-80; active Dem. Cent. Com. Pottawattamie County, Council Bluffs, 1960-70; del. People to People N.Am. Educators Deaf Vis. Russian Schs. & Programs for Deaf, 1993. League for Innovation in Community Coll. fellow, 1974. Mem. Calif. Assn. Postsecondary Edn. and Disability (founding v.p.), Registry of Interpreters for Deaf, Am. Sign Lang. Tchrs. Assn., Nat. Assn. Deaf. Mem. Am. Humanist Assn. Avocations: vocal music, languages, community activism, travel, politics. Home: 692 N Adele St #29 Orange CA 92867 E-mail: pmculton@joimail.com.

CULVAHOUSE, ARTHUR BOGGESS, JR., lawyer; b. Athens, Tenn., July 4, 1948; s. Arthur Boggess and Ruth Webb (Wear) C.; m. Pamela Smith Comparato, Apr. 29, 2001; children: Sarah Abbott, Arthur Boggess (dec.), Elizabeth Louise, Anne Pierce. BS, U. Tenn., 1970; JD, NYU Sch. Law, 1973, Root-Tilden Scholar. Bar: Tenn. 1973, Calif. 1977, D.C. 1977. Hief legis. asst. and counsel to U.S. Sen. Howard H. Baker, Jr., Washington, 1973-76; assoc. O'Melveny & Myers LLP, Washington, 1976-81, ptnr., 1982-84, 89—, chmn., 2000—, chair policy com.; ptnr. Vinson & Elkins, Washington, 1984-87; counsel to the Pres. The White House, Washington, 1987-89; mem. adminstrv. conf. of the U.S., 1989—94. Mem. bd. visitors U.S. Naval Acad., 1989—91; mem. Fed. Adv. Com. on Nuclear Failsafe and Risk Reduction, 1990—92; chmn. bd. dirs. Regulatory DataCorp, Internat. LLC. Bd. trustee Brookings Inst. Recipient Presdl. Citizen's medal, 1989, Def. Dept. Disting. Svc. medal. 1992. Republican. Episcopalian. Office: O'Melveny & Myers LLP 1625 Eye St NW Washington DC 20006 Office Phone: 202-383-5388. Office Fax: 202-383-5414. Business E-Mail: aculvahouse@omm.com.

CULVER, CHESTER J. (CHET CULVER), state official, educator; s. John and Ann (Cooper) Culver; m. Mari Thinnes Culver. BA in Polit. Sci., Va. Polytechnic Inst. and State U., 1988; MA in Tchg., Drake U., 1994. Tchr. HS govt., history, coach Hoover HS, Des Moines; investigator Atty. Gen.'s Office; sec. of state State of Iowa, 1999—. Established Iowa Student Polit. Awareness Club; elder mem. Ctrl. Presbyn. Ch. Mem.: Iowa State Edn. Assn. (Fulbright Meml. Fund Tchrs. scholarship 1997), Coun. State Govts., Elections Task Force, New Millenium Youth Initiative, Presdl. Caucuses and Primaries Com., Elections and Voter Participation Com., Nat. Assn. Secs. State, State Records Mgmt. Com., State Voter Registration Commn. (chmn.), Exec. Coun. (chmn.). Democrat. Prebyterian. Office: Office of Secretary of State State House Des Moines IA 50319-0001 Business E-Mail: sos@sos.state.ia.us.

CULVER, CURT S., diversified financial services company executive; BA in Real Estate with honors, MS in Urban Land Econ. with honors, Univ. Wis., Madison. Joined Mortgage Guaranty Ins. Corp. (subs. MGIC Investment Corp.), Milw., 1982, COO, 1996—99, pres., 1996—, CEO, 1999—; also pres. MGIC Investment Corp., Milw., 1999—, CEO, 2000—, chmn., 2005—. Named one of Most Powerful People in Am., Forbes mag. Office: MGIC 250 E Kilbourn Ave Milwaukee WI 53202 Office Phone: 414-347-6480.*

CULVER, DAN LOUIS, federal agency administrator; b. Savannah, Ga., Dec. 7, 1957; s. Louis and Jean Culver. BS in Mktg., U. Tenn., 1981; postgrad., Air Force Acad., 1982, Cornell U., 1985; BS in Edn. and Tng., U. W. Fla., 1995, MEd in Orgnl. Devel. and Leadership, 1998. Cert. tchr. Fla. Logistics support officer USAF, Ft. Walton Beach, Fla., 1982-86; mgmt. assoc. Barnett Bank, Ft. Walton Beach, Fla., 1987-89; program adminstr. disaster relief SBA, Atlanta, 1989—. Diplomatic observer UN, N.Y.C.; promoter lectrs., entertainers and authors. Pioneered automation of airforce support ops., 1982—84. Vol. disaster relief for victims of Hurricane Hugo, Charleston, SC, 1989, Hurricane Andrew, Miami, Fla., 1992, Miss. River flood, 1993, L.A. earthquake, 1994, World Trade Ctr. destruction, N.Y.C., 2001, Hurricanes Charley and Ivan, 2004; bd. dirs. non-profit orgns. Recipient Comdr.-in-Chief's Spl. Recognition for Excellence award, Pres. Ronald Reagan, 1986. Mem.: Asia Soc., Internat. Parliament Safety and Peace, Maison Internat. des Intellectuels, Internat. Platform Assn., Order of Knight Templars. Avocations: flying, skiing, sailing. Mailing: 2045 Mt Zion Rd #120 Morrow GA 30260

CULVER, JULIE MARIE, publishing executive; b. Washington, Sept. 16, 1978; d. James Andrew and Nancy Neese Culver. BA, Middlebury Coll., 2000. Prodn. editor Samuel French, Inc., N.Y.C., 2000—01; fgn. rights mgr., lit. agt. Lowenstein-Yost Assoc., N.Y.C., 2002—. Rec. sec. Horatio St. Assn., N.Y.C., 2002—03. D-Liberal. Office: Lowenstein-Yost Assoc 121 W 27th St Apt 5A New York NY 10001 Office Phone: 212-206-1630.

CULVER, MICHAEL PATRICK, music educator, composer; b. Memphis, Oct. 24, 1948; s. Charles Lawrence and Ruth Enid (Boone) Culver; m. Linda Marie Szymanski, Dec. 17, 1966; children: Erik-Jon, Ezra Charles, Soren Bernard. A in Music, Ulster County C.C., 1975; BA in Music Composition, Empire State Coll., 1989; MFA in Music Composition, Bard Coll., 1993. Tutor, evaluator Empire State Coll., New Paltz, NY, 1992—96; pvt. practice Bloomington, NY, 1975—96. Composer: Dadaloop, for magnetic tape, 1979, Ontic Emanations: music for piano, 1980—87, 2 Etudes for Electronic Sound Sources, 1990, Four Georgics for String Quartet, 1991, Medium of Exchange, for flute, cello, piano, 1992, 1980—87, Her Sleeping Form Shifting, for oboe, viola, piano, 1994, Stevedores, for violin, bass clarinet, piano, 1996, Pronaos: Structural Trio for Seven Instruments, 1998, Occasional Chairs: 10 trio sonatas, 2002, Non Liquet, for String Quartet, 2004, Itinerary, for tape recorder and piano, 2004. Home: PO Box 69 Bloomington NY 12411 Office Phone: 845-338-3652.

CULVERWELL, ALBERT HENRY, historian; b. Portland, Oreg., Jan. 28, 1913; s. John Albert and Nettie L. (Kingery) C.; m. Ethel E. Klein, Aug. 17, 1941 (dec.); children: Cheryl Evelyn, John Albert; m. Eleanor M. Liere, May 6, 1986 (dec.). Scholarship student in stagecraft, color and design, Cornish Sch., Seattle, 1935-36; BA, U. Wash., Seattle, 1936, MA, 1941; postgrad., Am. U., Wash. State U. Mem. faculty Whitworth Coll., Spokane, Wash., 1941-42, 46-50; civilian U.S. Naval Air Sta., Seattle, 1942-45; safety engr., asst. dir. personnel Pacific Car & Foundry Co., Renton, Wash., 1945-46; instr. social sci. Wash. State U., Pullman, 1949-50; asst. prof. history Western Wash. State Coll., Bellingham, 1950-53; historian, supr. interpretation Wash. State Parks, Olympia, 1953-62; chief br. interpretive services Region 4, U.S. Forest Service, Ogden, Utah, 1962-68; dir. Eastern Wash. State Hist. Soc., Spokane, 1968-82; pres. Wash. Art Consortium, 1979-82. Mem. Wash. Archives Adv. Bd., 1977-82, Adv. Coun. Preservation of Hist. Sites and Bldgs., 1968-78, com. to develop Hist. Interpretive Ctr., Wash. State Capitol Bldg., 1983-84; mem. design com. Main St. Program, San Jacinto, Calif., 1988-91; vol. art assoc. in support and adminstrn. Fine Arts Gallery, Mt. San Jacinto Coll., 1988-98; vol. history assoc. in preservation and interpretation of Estudillo Mansion in San Jacinto, 1993-98, pres. Resident Coun. SunWest Village, Hemet, CA, 1998-99. Author articles in field, also, film and TV scripts. Elder United Presbyn. Ch. U.S.A., 1942—; adminstrv. adv. com. Sheldon Jackson Jr. Coll., Sitka, Alaska, 1961-63; bd. dirs. Westminster Found., 1961-62; mem. Woodway (Wash.) Planning Commn., 1961-63, Wash. Gov.'s Adv. Coun. on Observance Civil War Centennial, 1961; Gov. Wash. Coun. Boundary Survey Centennial, 1961. Recipient cert. of commendation Am. Assn. State and Local History, 1965 Mem. Am. Assn. Museums (pres. Western regional conf. 1969-71), Orgn. Am. Historians, Pacific N.W. Hist. Soc., Idaho Hist. Soc., Utah Hist. Soc., Westerners, Phi Sigma Kappa, Pi Sigma Alpha. Clubs: Rotary. Home: 973 Sunwest Dr Hemet CA 92545-1626 *In my life I have striven to achieve something positive in whatever I have done. Success depends on faith in myself as well as in someone greater than I, and, to an extent, with those with whom I have worked. This has brought a measure of patience to me which has made it possible to accept setbacks which make achievement slow. But when one has gained confidence and patience, success is often achieved.*

CULWELL, CHARLES LOUIS, retired manufacturing company executive; b. Putnam, Tex., Apr. 26, 1927; s. Willie and Ila Alberta (Crosby) C.; m. Virginia Green, June 10, 1949; children: Andrew Scott, Perry Neal, Curtis Austin, Travis Lee. BSEE, U.S. Naval Acad., 1949; MS in Mgmt., U.S. Naval Postgrad. Sch., 1969. Commd. ensign U.S. Navy, 1949, advanced through grades to capt., 1969; service in Korea and Vietnam; comdg. officer Naval Supply Center, Oakland, Calif., 1975-76; ret., 1976; asst. to pres., then v.p. Purex Corp., 1976-79; group v.p., gen. mgr. indsl., instl. and comml. products Purex Industries, Inc., Lakewood, Calif., 1979-84, v.p., asst. to CEO Carson, Calif., 1984-86, Purex Industries Liquidation, Carson, Calif., 1986-87, ret., 1987. Decorated Legion of Merit, Bronze Star with combat V, Meritorious Svc. medal. Mem. U.S. Naval Acad. Alumni Assn. Baptist. E-mail: chasvaculw@aol.com.

CULY, DOUGLAS G., mechanical engineer, consultant; b. Medford, Oreg. BSME, Oreg. State U.; MS in Indsl. Engring., MBA in Indsl. Engring., Ariz. State U. Registered profl. engr., Wash. Project and function mgmt. and engring. fin. ops. various aircraft engine prodn. enterprises, 1960—93; dir. Engring. Aviation Cons. Resources, 1993—. Author seminars on econs. of gas turbines and risk analysis, fin. modeling high tech. activities. Contbr. articles to profl. jours. and encyclopedias Cons. project bus. Jr. Achievement Mem. ASME (chmn. Ariz. sect. 1996—97), AIAA, Soc. Automotive Engrs. (chmn. Ariz. sect. 1980-81, mem. sects. bd. 1981-85. chmn. life cycle cost com. 1987-94), Toastmasters (club pres. Phoenix 1983, dist. treas. 1982-83). Office: Aviation Cons Resources 1408 E Whalers Way Tempe AZ 85283-5503

CUMMING, ALAN, actor; b. Perthshire, Scotland, Jan. 27, 1965; m. Hilary Lyon, 1985 (div. 1993). BA, Royal Scottish Acad. Music and Drama. Actor: (Broadway plays) Cabaret (Tony Drama desk award, 1998, NY Free Press award, Outer Critics Circle award, others); (films) Prague, 1992, Second Best, 1994, Circle of Friends, 1995, GoldenEye, 1995, Burn Your Phone, 1996, Emma, 1996, Spice World, 1997, For My Baby, 1997, Romy and Michele's High School Reunion, 1997, Buddy, 1997, Urban Folk Tales, 1999, Plunkett & MaCleane, 1999, Eyes Wide Shut, 1999, Titus, 1999, Company Man, 2000, Get Carter, 2000, The Flintstones in Viva Rock Vegas, 2000, Spy Kids, 2001, Josie and the Pussycats, 2001, Spy Kids 2: Island of Lost Dreams, 2002, Nicholas Nickleby, 2002, Cinemagique, 2002, X2, 2003, Spy Kids 3-D: Game Over, 2003, (voice) Garfield, 2004, Mr. Ripley's Return, 2004, Son of the Mask, 2005; actor, dir., writer, prodr.: The Anniversary Party, 2001 (Excellence in Filmaking award Nat. Bd. Rev.); actor, dir., writer: (TV films) Butter, 1994; actor, dir.: (films) Wedding Photo, 2005; actor: (TV films) Accidental Death of an Anarchist, 1983 (Laurence Olivier award for Comedy Performance of Yr., 1991), The Last Romantics, 1991, Bernard and the Genie, 1991, The Airzone Solution, 1993, Micky Love, 1993, (voice) Black Beauty, 1994, That Sunday, 1994, Annie, 1999, Zero Effect, 2002, The Goodbye Girl, 2004; (TV series) The High Life, 1994, (voice) God, the Devil, and Bob, 2000, Shoebox Zoo, 2004; author: (novels) Tommy's Tale, 2002. Named to Vanity Fair Hall of Fame; recipient Immigrant Achievement award, NY, 2001.*

CUMMING, GRAEME SHAW, ecologist, educator; b. Cape Town, Cape Province, South Africa, May 11, 1973; s. David Hugh Cumming and Margaret Shaw Cumming (nee Thomson). BSc with honors, Rhodes U., Grahamstown, 1996; DPhil, U. Oxford, Eng., 1999. D.H. Smith postdoctoral fellow U. of Wis., Madison, 1999—2001; asst. prof. U. of Fla., Gainesville, Fla., 2001—. Contbr. articles to profl. jours. Recipient Ralf Yorque Meml. prize, Jour.: Ecology and Soc., 2003; scholar Rhodes scholar, Rhodes Trust, 1996—99. Mem.: Resilience Alliance, Ecol. Soc. of Am. Office: University of Florida 308 Newins-Ziegler Hall Gainesville FL 32611-0430

CUMMING, IAN M., holding company executive; b. 1940; BA, U. Kans., 1964; MBA, Harvard U., 1970. Chmn., dir. Leucadia Nat. Corp., NYC, 1978—; chmn. FINOVA, 2001—. Bd. dir. Skywest Inc., HomeFed. Office: Leucadia National Corp 315 Park Ave S Fl 20 New York NY 10010-3686*

CUMMING, ROBERT EMIL, editor, writer; b. Lincoln, Nebr., June 2, 1933; s. Eugene Earl and Christiana (Jensen) C. Student, U. Nebr., 1955; Music Ed. (Presser Found. scholar), Nebr. Wesleyan U., 1956. With Music Jour. mag., N.Y.C., 1958-75, editor in chief, 1964-75; with Weekly Reader Corp. (formerly Xerox Edn. Publs. and Field Publs.), 1977-97; founder, pres. Conn. Singers Agy., 1997—. Theater editor Middlesex mag., 1995—97, The Trumpeter, 1997—, critic Hometown News Pubs., 1999—2002; critic, condr., singer, stage dir. Village Light Opera Group, Hunter Coll., N.Y.C., Cmty. Opera, Little Orch. Soc.; founder-mem. Singing Editors, nationally concertized, 1974-76; toured U.S. and Can. as stage dir. Naughty Marietta, Little Orch. Concerts, 1976; compiler, editor: The Power of Music by Dmitri Shostakovich, 1968, They Talk About Music, 1971-72; editor Spl. Librs. Assn. Bull., Publ. Divsn., 1989—, Life is a Poem, 1999; composer children's operettas Rumplestiltskin, 1952, Song of Andorra, 1953; songs: God Is My Salvation, 1954, How Sly, 1954, Ya Gotta Have Love, 1955, The Hills of Sand, 1969; ann. music report for Living History of the World, 1967-68; contbr. articles to profl. jours. Mem. East Haddam Hist. Soc., 1977—, pres., 1998—2004, exec. dir., 2005—; dir. East Lyme Arts Coun., 1990—93; bd. dirs. U. Conn. Gilbert and Sullivan Summer Prodns., 1985—88. Mem. N.Y. Gilbert and Sullivan Soc. (pres. 1967-69), Conn. Gilbert and Sullivan Soc. (founder, dir. 1980—), Conn. Sinfonia Soc. (founder), So. Conn. Libr. Coun. (bd. dirs. 1986-89), Conn. Critics Circle. Episcopalian. Home: PO Box 196 East Haddam CT 06423-0196 Office: PO Box 294 Moodus CT 06469-0294 Personal E-mail: singers.agency@snet.net. *I have developed an awareness of the need for: enough strength to overcome loneliness; enough ego to communicate well; enough vision to perceive the need; enough ambition to overcome laziness; enough drive to complete what is begun; enough compassion to wish to help; enough insight to grow humility; enough talent to be grateful; enough intelligence to remain practical; enough wisdom to be open; enough sensitivity to be myself; enough pain to keep in balance; enough pleasure to retain my humor; enough culture to be knowing; enough honesty to admit ignorance; enough love to appreciate symbols; enough religion to sense God.*

CUMMING, ROBERT HUGH, artist, photographer; b. Worcester, Mass., Oct. 7, 1943; s. Robert H. and Evelyn (Schold) C. B.F.A., Mass. Coll. Art, 1965; M.F.A., U. Ill., 1967. Lectr. UCLA Extension, 1974-77, Otis Art Inst., Los Angeles, 1975-76, Calif. Inst. Arts, Valencia, 1976-77; asst. prof. U. Calif.-Irvine, 1977-78; assoc. prof. U. Hartford, West Hartford, Conn., 1978-86. Juror, cons. U.S. Eye Exhibit Winter Olympics, Lake Placid, N.Y., 1979; vis. artist Polaroid Corp., Cambridge, Mass., 1979, traveling retrospective through Australian Gallery Dirs. Coun., Sydney, Australia, 1979 Exhibited retrospective show, Friends of Photography, Carmel, Calif., 1979, Travelling retrospective show, Brisbane, Sydney, Melbourne, Adelaide, and Burney, Australia, 1979, one man shows, Castelli Gallery, N.Y.C., 1982, 85, 86, 88, 91, Werkstatt fur Photographie, Berlin, 1982, Whitney Mus. Am. Art, 1986, Hirshhorn Mus., Washington, 1988; retrospective exhbns. include San Diego Mus. of Contemporary Art, Boston Mus. of Fine Arts, Houston Contemporary Arts Mus., 1993-94. Recipient Awards in Visual Arts, Winston-Salem, N.C., 1984, Creative Arts award Brandeis U., 1985; grantee Nat. Endowment for Arts, 1972, 75; John S. Guggenheim fellow, 1980; fellow Japan-U.S. Friendship Commn., 1981

CUMMING, THOMAS ALEXANDER, brokerage house executive; b. Toronto, Ont., Can., Oct. 14, 1937; s. Alison A. and Anne B. (Berry) C.; m. E. Mary Stevens, Mar. 12, 1965; children: Jennifer, Allison, Katy. BAS, U. Toronto, 1960. Registered profl. engr., Can. With Bank of Nova Scotia, 1965-88; spl. rep. Toronto, 1965-68; br. mgr. Dublin, Ireland, 1969-71, London, 1971-75; v.p. Calgary, Alta., Can., 1975-80; sr. v.p. Calgery, Alta., Can., 1980-85, Toronto, 1986-88; pres., CEO Alta. Stock Exchange, Calgary, 1988-99. Bd. dirs. YMCA of Calgary Found., Pengrowth Energy Trust, Western Lakota Energy Svcs., Inc.; chair Canadian Investor Protection Fund, Balancing Pool. Mem. Assn. Profl. Engrs., Calgary C. of C. (pres. 1991), Calgary Golf and Country Club, Calgary Petroleum Club. Home and Office: 2906 10th St SW Calgary AB Canada T2T 3H2

CUMMINGS, ALEXANDER B., JR., food products executive; BS in Fin. and Econs., No. Ill. U.; MBA in Fin., Atlanta U. Former v.p. fin. The Pillsbury Co.; former region mgr. Nigeria The Coca-Cola Co., former pres. North and West Africa divsn., pres., COO Africa Group, 2001—, exec. v.p. corp., 2002—. Chmn. The Coca-Cola Africa Found.; mem. Ctr. for Global Devel. Commn. on U.S. Policy toward Low-Income Poorly Performing States; bd. dirs. Africa-Am. Inst., Corp. Coun. on Africa, U.S.-Egypt Bus. Coun.; past bd. dirs. Sabathani Cmty. Ctr., Mpls. Office: The Coca-Cola Co PO Box 1734 Atlanta GA 30301

CUMMINGS, ANDREA J., lawyer; b. 1967; BA in Polit. sci., BS in Journalism, Boston U., 1990; JD, U. Va., 1995. Bar: Tex. 1995, Calif. 1999, Ill. 2000. With Locke Purnell Rain Harell, Tex., 1995—97, Weil, Gotshall Manges LLP, 1997—98, Nomura Asset Capital Corp., 1998—99, Gray Cary Uare Freidenrich, 1999—2000, Sidley Austin Brown & Wood LLP, Chgo., 2000—, ptnr., 2003—. Office: Sidley Austin Brown and Wood Bank One Plz 10 S Dearborn St Chicago IL 60603

CUMMINGS, CHARLES WILLIAM, otolaryngologist, educator; b. Boston, Nov. 16, 1935; s. Harry Blanchard and Madge (Frey) C.; m. Jane Drake Cummings, July 1, 1983; children— Charles William, Lee Blanchard, Evelyn Howard. AB, Dartmouth Coll., 1957; MD, U. Va., 1961. Intern Mary Hitchcock Meml. Hosp., Hanover, N.H., 1961-62; resident otolaryngology Harvard U. Med. Sch., 1965-68; assoc. prof. otolaryngology Upstate Med. Sch., SUNY, Syracuse, 1976-78; prof., chmn. dept. otolaryngology-head and neck surgery U. Wash. Med. Sch., Seattle, 1978-91, Johns Hopkins Hosp. and Med. Ctr., Balt., 1991—93; disting. svcs. prof., med. dir. Johns Hopkins Internat. Chief staff Johns Hopkins Hosp., 1996-98; bd. dirs. Am. Bd. Otolaryngology Author: Atlas of Laryngeal Surgery; co-author: Comprehensive Text of Otolaryngology-Head and Neck Surgery; contbr. sci. articles to profl. jours. Served to capt., M.C. USAF, 1963-65. Mem. ACS (chmn. adv. coun.), Soc. Head and Neck Surgeons, Am. Soc. for Head and Neck Surgery (sec., pres.), Soc. Univ. Otolaryngologists, Assn. Acad. Depts., Otolaryngology (past pres.), Triological Soc., Laryngological Soc., Bronchoesophagological Soc. (past pres.), Am. Acad. Otolaryngology-Head and Neck Surgery (bd. dirs., past pres.). Episcopalian. Office: Johns Hopkins U Dept Otolaryngology/Head/Neck/Surgery 601 N Caroline St Baltimore MD 21287-0006 Office Phone: 410-955-7400. Business E-Mail: ccummings@jhmc.edu.

CUMMINGS, DAVID WILLIAM, artist, educator; b. Okmulgee, Okla., July 15, 1937; s. Harold Raymond and Mildred Delores (Smith) C.; m. Marcia Mills Laging, June 20, 1964 (div. 1970); m. Beatrice M. Mady, Oct. 2, 1981. BFA, Kansas City Art Inst., 1963; MFA, U. Nebr., 1967. Prof. SUNY, New Paltz, 1964-70, CUNY, 1971-89; adj. instr. Wagner Coll., S.I., N.Y., 1970-71; adj. prof. St. Peter's Coll., Jersey City, 1985—2003; adj. faculty Parson School of Design, New School U., 2004—; adj asst. prof. Raritan Valley Coll., Somerville, NJ, 2004. Vis. prof. NYU, 1980-82, SUNY, Purchase, 1984, Rochester (N.Y.) Inst. Tech., 1983, U. N.D., Grand Forks, 1982, Colo. Mountain Coll., Vail, 1975-84. One-man shows include Katz Galleries, N.Y.C., 1970, Henri Gallery, Washington, 1969-70, Allan Stone Gallery, N.Y.C., 1974-77, Gallery Alexandra Monett, Brussels, 1975, 77, 78, Sebastian/Moore Gallery, Denver, 1978, Ericson Gallery, N.Y.C., 1981, U. N.D., Grand Forks, 1981, Shahin Requicha Gallery, Rochester, N.Y., 1983, La Petite Galeria, Bayonne, N.J., 1986, Gallery Jupiter, Little Silver, N.J., 1987, A.M.B. Galleries, Hoboken, N.J., Cabrillo Coll. Gallery, Aptos, Calif., 1991, Clin. Ctr. Galleries, NIH, Bethesda, Md., 1993, Rabbet Gallery, New Brunswick, N.J., 1996, St. John's U., Jamaica, N.Y., 1999, Johnson and Johnson Galleries, New Bruswick, N.J., 2001. Served with U.S. Army, 1957-59. Wood Found. fellow, 1966-67, N.J. State Coun. of Arts fellow, 1985, 91; Ford Found. grantee, 1963.

CUMMINGS, ELIJAH E., congressman; b. Balt., Jan. 18, 1951; BS, Howard U., 1973; JD, U. Md., 1976. Bar: Md. 1976. Atty. priv. practice, 1980—96, Md. Gen. Assembly, 1982; mem. Md. Ho. of Dels., Annapolis, 1983—96, vice chmn. constl. and adminstrv. law com., 1987—96, chmn. com. econ. devel., 1996, vice chmn. house econ. matters com., 1994—96, speaker pro tempore, 1995—96; mem. transp. subcom. for coast guard and maritime transp., mem. transp. subcom. for water resources and environ. 104th-108th Congress from 7th Md. dist., 1996—; mem. govt. reform com. and transp. infrastructure com. Chmn. Md. Legis. Black Caucus; chmn. Gov.'s Commn. on Black Males, 1990—; pres. Bancroft Lit. Soc., Congressional Black Caucus Found. (first vice chmn., bd. dirs., now chair) 1998, chmn., 2003-. Named Outstanding U.S. Student Govt. Leader Royal Arts Soc. of London. Mem.: Md. Bar Assn. Democrat. Office: US Ho of Reps 2235 Rayburn Ho Office Bldg Washington DC 20515-2007*

CUMMINGS, FRANK, lawyer; b. N.Y.C., Dec. 11, 1929; s. Louis and Florence (Levine) Cummings; m. Jill Schwartz, July 6, 1958; children: Peter Ian, Margaret Anne. BA, Hobart Coll., 1951; MA, Columbia U., 1955, LLB, 1958. Bar: N.Y. 1959, D.C. 1963. Adminstrv. asst. to U.S. Senator Jacob Javits, 1969-71; minority counsel com. labor and pub. welfare U.S. Senate, Washington, 1965-67, 71-72; assoc. Cravath, Swaine & Moore, N.Y.C., 1958-63, Gall, Lane & Powell, Washington, 1967-68, ptnr., 1972-75, Marshall, Bratter, Greene, Allison & Tucker, Washington, 1976-85, Nossaman, Keurger & Knox, 1982-83, Cummings & Cummings, P.C. and predecessor firm, 1983-86, LeBoeuf, Lamb, Greene & MacRae, LLP, Washington, 1986-2000, of counsel, 2000—. Lectr. law Columbia U. Law Sch., 1970-74, U. Va. Sch. Law, 2000—; adj. prof. Georgetown U. Law Sch., 1983-86; chmn. Am. Law Inst.-ABA Ann. Course ERISA Litigation, 1989—, Employment and Labor Rels. Law for Corp. Coun. and Gen. Practitioner, 1978—; mem. pub. adv. coun. employee welfare and pension benefit plans Dept. Labor, 1972-74; mem. adv. bd. Pension Reporter Bur. Nat. Affairs. Author: Capitol Hill Manual, 1976, Capitol Hill Manual, 2d edit., 1984, Pension Plan Terminations-Single Employer Plans, 3rd edit., 2002, Multiemployer Plans, 2d edit., 1986; articles editor: Columbia U. Law Rev., 1957—58. Fellow Am. Coll. Employee Benefits Counsel; mem. ABA (chmn. com. pension, welfare and related plans 1976-79), Am. Law Inst. (advisor to restatement of employment law 2002—), Bar Assn. D.C. (chmn. com. labor rels. law 1972-73), Cosmos Club, Phi Beta Kappa. Office: LeBoeuf Lamb Greene & MacRae LLP 1875 Connecticut Ave NW Washington DC 20009-5728 Home: 800 25th St NW Washington DC 20037 Office Phone: 202-986-8022. Business E-Mail: fcumming@llgm.com.

CUMMINGS, FREDERIC ALAN, lawyer; b. Mobile, Ala., Sept. 5, 1944; s. J. V. and Alice Cummings; children: Christian Gordon, Sara Elise, Alice Kate Griffith, James Cale, Camille Pichard. BS in Econs., Auburn U., 1967; JD, Fla. State U., 1975. Bar: Fla. 1976, U.S. Ct. Appeals (11th cir.), U.S. Dist. Ct. (mid. and no. dists.) Fla. Ptnr. Holland & Knight, Tallahassee, 1975-86, Cummings, Lawrence & Vezina PA, Tallahassee, 1986-97, Cummings & Snyder PA, Tallahassee, 1997-2000, Smith, Currie & Hancock LLP, Tallahassee, 2001—. Office: Smith Currie & Hancock LLP PO Box 589 Tallahassee FL 32302-0589 Office Phone: 850-878-3700.

CUMMINGS, JOAN E., health facility administrator, educator; BA, Trinity Coll., 1964; MD, Loyola U., 1968. Diplomate Am. Bd. Internal Medicine, Geriatric Medicine. Med. intern St. Vincent Hosp., Worcester, Mass., 1968-69; med. resident Hines VA Hosp., Hines, Ill., 1969-71, sr. resident in nephrology, 1971-72, ambulatory care svc. chief gen. med. sect., 1971-84, med. dir., hosp. based home care, 1972-87, chief, intermediate care svc., 1984-87, assoc. chief of staff, extended care and geriatrics, 1987-90, med. dir., extended care center, 1987-90, dir., 1990—; asst. prof. clin. medicine U. Ill., 1976-82, Loyola U., 1983-91, assoc. prof. clin. medicine, 1991—; network dir. Dept. Vet. Affairs, Hines, Ill., 1995—2005. Mem. ad hoc com. on primary care U. Ill., 1980-82, coll. edn. policy com. U. Ill., 1980-82, State Ill. Emergency Med. Svc. Coun., 1981-83, Comprehensive Health Ins. Plan Bd. State Ill., 1990—, Med. Licensing Bd. State Ill., 1992—, exec. com. Chgo. Fed. Exec. Bd. State Ill., 1992—; program dir. Loyola/Hines Geriatric Fellowship Program, 1987-90. Contbr. to profl. mags. and jour. Recipient Disting. Svc. award Abraham Lincoln Sch. Med. Univ. Ill., 1979, 81, Leadership award VA, 1980, Certificate of Appreciation award VA, 1980, Laureate award Am. Coll. Physicians, 1990. Fellow ACP; mem. AMA (Ill. delegation 1985—, vice speaker ho. of dels. 1987-89), Chgo. Med. Soc. (pres. Hines-Loyola br. 1982-83), Ill. State Med. Soc. (trustee 1984—, chmn. com. on Ill. med., 1988—, spkr. ho. of dels. 1989-91, exec. com., 1989-91, policy com., 1989—), Chgo. Geriatric Soc., Am. Geriatric Soc. Office: 772 St Charles Rd Glen Ellyn IL 60137 E-mail: joanecum@msn.com.

CUMMINGS, JOHN W., diversified financial services company executive; BA in Econs., Fairfield U. Various mgmt. positions Merrill Lynch & Co., Stamford, Conn., 1981—2002, CEO, 2002—03, sr. v.p. N.Y.C., 2002—, head global tech. & svcs., 2003—. Bd. dirs. Depository Trust & Clearning Corp., Merrill Lynch Fin. Data Scvs, Inc. Office: Merrill Lynch & Co 4 World Fin Ctr New York NY 10080

CUMMINGS, JOSEPHINE ANNA, writer, consultant, advertising executive; b. Gainesville, Fla., July 12, 1949; d. Robert Jay and Marcella Dee (Mount) Cummings. ABJ./Design cum laude, U. Ga., Athens, 1971; MA, NYU, 1999. Copywriter William Cook, Jacksonville, Fla., 1971-73; creative dir. Leo Burnett, Chgo., 1973-76; sr. v.p., group creative dir. D. D. B. Needham, Chgo., 1976-84; sr. v.p., creative dir. Saatchi-Saatchi, N.Y.C., 1984; sr. v.p., sr. creative dir. Ted Bates, N.Y.C., 1984; exec. v.p., chief creative officer Tracy-Locke, Dallas, 1985-87; exec. v.p., exec. creative dir. Bozell, Chgo, 1989; exec. v.p., creative dir. Y&R, N.Y.C., 1990-92; pres. The Joey Co., N.Y.C., 1992—. Author: (play) Azaleas, 1988, (short story collection) Crimes of Passion, 1988, (childrens' book) The Hospital is a Funny Place, 1988, (short film) Night Magic, 1989. Named as creator One of Hundred Best TV Commls. Advt. Age, 1978-79, one of Advt. 100 Best Advt. Age, 1986, one of People to Watch Fortune mag., 1986, Ad Age one of Best and Brightest, N.Y. Mem. Amelia Earhard, Ninety Niners Club, N.Y. Women in Film. Avocations: reading, writing, juggling. Office: The Joey Co Ste 656S 55 Washington St Brooklyn NY 11201 E-mail: joey@thejoeycompany.com.

CUMMINGS, JUDY ANNETTE, retired secondary education educator; b. Denver, May 27, 1943; d. John Joseph and Garnett Edwana (Ferry) Leuthard; m. Ernest LeRoy Cummings, Aug. 6, 1965; 1 child, Scott Joseph. BS in Edn., Black Hills State U., Spearfish, S.D., 1971. Cert. tchr., Wyo. Clk. Workmen's Compensation, Denver, 1961-62, Wood Product Co., Berkeley, Calif., 1962, Denver Pub. Sch. Sys., 1964-65; clk.-typist Martin Marietta Corp., Waterton, Colo., 1962-64; sec. Yardney Electric Corp., Pawcatuck, Conn., 1965; substitute tchr. Campbell County Sch. Dist., Gillette, Wyo., 1970-73, tchr. bus. edn., 1973-97, ret., 1997. Dir. drug free sch. program Campbell County H.S., 1993—, quality sch. team, 1995-96, sch. improvement com., 1995-96; sec. CAMPCO Credit Union Bd.; alt. mem. Liaison Com. for Salaries and Benefits; mem. Elem. Sch. Keyboarding Task Force. Mem. adv. com. Juvenile Detention-Treatment Ctr., Gilette, 1993. Recipient plaque as outstanding bus. educator Campbell County H.S., 1991, named Tchr. of Yr., 1994, 96-97. Mem. NEA, Am. Vocat. Assn. (life), Wyo. Edn. Assn., Wyo. Bus. Edn. Assn. (membership chmn. 1985), Wyo. Vocat. Assn. (membership chmn. 1985), Campbell County Edn. Assn. (membership chmn.), Nat. Bus. Edn. Assn., Campbell County Vocat. Assn. (sec.), Campbell County C. of C. (adv. bd. 1982-84), Wyo. Coaches Assn., Future Farmers Am. (hon., cert. of appreciation), Molly Reds Red Hat Soc. (Queen Mom, 2005—), Alpha Delta Kappa (past pres.). Republican. Methodist. Avocations: reading, crocheting, embroidery, cross-stitching, travel. Home: 1183 Country Club Rd Gillette WY 82718-5512 Office: Campbell County HS 1000 Camel Dr Gillette WY 82716-4950 Personal E-mail: jcummings@vcn.com.

CUMMINGS, KAREN SUE, retired corrections classification administrator; b. Ft. Wayne, Ind., July 15, 1939; d. Floyd Henry and Mary Emma (Wolfe) Kneller; m. Oswald Wade Cummings, Feb. 16, 1962; children: Ruth Marie Cummings Everett, John Phillip. BA, Bethal Coll., 1976; MA, Webster U., 1989; grad., Corrections Mgmt. Sch., La., 1991. Sub. tchr. various sch., Mishawaka, Ind., La., 1978-82; classification dir. Work Tng. Facility North La. Dept. Corrections, Pineville, La., 1978-82; eligibility worker Office of Family Security, Alexandria, La., 1982-84; classification officer Work Tng. Facility North La. Dept. Corrections, Pineville, 1984-92, classification dir. Work Tng. Facility North, 1992—, ret., 2002—. Big sister Big Bros./Big Sisters, Mishawaka, 1974-76, Pineville, 1990-91. With USAF, 1957-65. Mem. Am. Correctional Assn., So. States Corrections Assn. Republican. Baptist. Avocation: travel. Office: 1519 Dupree Rd Pineville LA 71360-8718

CUMMINGS, KENNETH ILA, coroner, medical examiner; b. Athens, La., Mar. 14, 1936; s. Otto L. and Idelle (James) C.; m. (div. 1981); children: Alison, Courtney, Kurt, Emily; m. Sandra Tipton Gamble, July 2000. BS in Liberal Arts, La. Tech. U., 1958; MD, La. State U., New Orleans, 1962; M in Dermatology, Tulane U., 1966. Diplomate Am. Acad. Dermatology. Intern Confederate Meml. Med. Ctr., Shreveport, La., 1962-63; resident Tulane U. Charity Hosp. of La., New Orleans, 1963-66; chief resident dermatology La. State U. Sch. Med., New Orleans, 1965-66; clin. prof. dermatology La. State U. Med. Sch., Shreveport, 1968-87; chief resident dermatology Tulane U. Med. Sch., New Orleans, 1965-66, Charity Hosp. La., New Orleans, 1965-66; instr. U.S. Naval Aerospace Med. Inst., Pensacola, Fla., 1966-68; pvt. practice Shreveport, La., 1968-87; coroner, med. examiner Bienville Parish, Arcadia, La., 1987-96. Fed. referee disability cases U.S. Govt., Shreveport, 1972—. Author: (novel) Poppies in the Field, 1998, Next to Nod, 2000; contbr. articles to profl. jours. Lt. comdr. USNR, 1966-68. Recipient Award for Surg. Treatment for Baldness Tex. Med. Assn., 1967, Peterkin prize La. Dermatol. Soc., 1966. Mem. SAG, Am. Acad. Dermatology, La. State Med. Soc., Shreveport Med. Soc., La. Coroners Assn., Screen Writers Guild. Democrat. Episcopalian. Avocations: nusmismatics, fiction writing, movie acting, freelance work. Home: 3072 Hazel St Arcadia LA 71001-4100 E-mail: cumm3399@bellsouth.net.

CUMMINGS, LESLIE EDWARDS, university administrator; b. Modesto, Calif., Feb. 17, 1951; d. George Robert and Mary Lou (Bomberger) Edwards; m. William Theodore Cummings Jr., Mar. 12, 1977. BS in Home Econs., Ariz. State U., 1974, MS in Agr., 1977, D in Pub. Adminstrn., 1990. Intern General Mills, Inc., Golden Valley, Minn., 1968; diet technician Mesa Luth. Hosp., Ariz., 1972—73; salesperson Romney Products, Inc., 1974; auditor pharm. ins. Pharm. Card Sys., Inc., 1974—76; mem. chain hdqrs. staff Fry's Supermarkets, Inc., 1977; adj. instr. foodsvc. Auburn U., Ala., 1978—79, from asst. mgr. to mgr. Campus Ctr. Foodsvcs., 1979—80; analyst customer support WANG Labs., Inc., 1981—83; asst. prof. U. Nev., Coll. Hotel Adminstrn., Las Vegas, 1983—87, assoc. prof., 1987—93, prof., 1993—2000; adminstrn. instrnl. tech. U. Houston, Clear Lake, 2000—. Presenter Hotel-Motel Expo, 1985, So. Nev. Dietetics Assn. and So. Nev. Home Econs. Assn., Las Vegas, 1986, Inst. Food Technologists, Las Vegas, 1987, Universidad Madre y Maestra System, Santo Domingo, Dominican Republic, 1987, Internat. Assn. Hospitality Accts., Las Vegas, 1986, Foodsvc. and the Environment, Scottsdale, Ariz., 1990, State of Ariz. Dietetics Assn., Scottsdale, 1991, Assn. for the Study of Food and Soc., Tucson, 1991, ASPA, Las Vegas, 1991, Foodsvcs. Sys. Beyond 2000 Conf., Israel, 1992, Gaming Educator's Conf., Las Vegas, Hospitality Info. Tech. Assn., New Orleans, 1995, Environments for Tourism Conf., Las Vegas, 1996, Internat. Hospitality Tech. Conf., Nashville, 1996; panelist, spkr. in field of applied tech. and gaming trends. Author: (textbook) (with Lendal Kotschevar) Nutrition Management for Foodservices, 1989, Instructor's Manual for Nutrition Management for Foodservices, 1989; contbr. numerous articles on hospitality applications of tech. and distance edn. to acad. jours. Vol. Women's Resource Network Career Event, Annual Nev. Gov.'s Conf. for Women. Recipient Nat. Assn. Schs. Pub. Adminstrn. dissertation award, 1990, Boyd Rsch. award, 1991, Ace Denken Disting. Rsch. award, 1996-98; fellow Rotary Internat., 1978. Mem. ASPA, Am. Dietetic Assn. (treas. environ. nutrition dietetic practice group 1992-95, registered dietitian), Inst. Internal Auditors (cert.), Coun. on Hotel, Restaurant and Instnl. Edn., Phi Beta Kappa, Phi Kappa Phi, Pi Alpha Alpha. Avocations: horse training, learning about plants and animals, listening. Office: U Houston Clear Lake 2700 Bay Area Blvd # 291 Houston TX 77058-1002 E-mail: cummings@cl.uh.edu.

CUMMINGS, MARTIN MARC, medical educator, physician, academic administrator; b. Camden, NJ, Sept. 7, 1920; s. Samuel and Cecelia (Silverman) Cummings; m. Arlene Sally Avrutine, Sept. 27, 1942; children: Marc Steven, Lee Bernard, Stuart Lewis. BS, Bucknell U., 1941, DSc, 1969; MD, Duke U., 1944, DSc (hon.), 1985; DHL (hon.), Georgetown U., 1976; DSc (hon.), U. Nebr., Emory U.; MD (hon.), Karolinska Inst., 1972, U. Lvov, 1975. Diplomate Am. Bd. Microbiology. Intern, resident Boston Marine Hosp., 1944—46; resident Tb Grasslands Hosp., Valhalla, NY, 1946—47; dir. Tb evaluation lab. Communicable Disease Ctr., USPHS, Atlanta, 1947—49; instr. medicine Emory U. Sch. Medicine, 1948—50, assoc. medicine, 1950—52, asst. prof., 1953; chief Tb sect., also dir. Tb rsch. lab. VA Hosp., Atlanta, 1949—53; dir. rsch. svcs. VA Ctrl. Office, Washington, 1953—59; prof. microbiology, chmn. dept. Okla. U. Sch. Medicine, 1959—61; chief Office Internat. Rsch., NIH, USPHS, 1961—63; dir. Nat. Libr. Medicine, 1964—84, dir. emeritus, 1984—; cons. Coun. on Libr. Resources, 1984—, chmn., bd. dirs., 1994—96. Assoc. dir. rsch. grants NIH, 1963—64; chmn. com. med. rsch. Nat. Tb Assn., 1958—59; chmn. panel Sarcoidosis NRC-NAS, 1958—60; dist. prof. cmty. medicine Georgetown U. Sch. Medicine, 1986—90. Author (with Dr. H.S. Willis): Diagnostic and Experimental Methods in Tuberculosis, 1952, The Economics of Research Libraries, 1986; editor: Influencing Change in Research Libraries, 1989; contbr. chpt. on Tubercle Bacilli Diagnostic Procedures and Reagents, 1950. Served with AUS, 1943—44. Recipient Exceptional Svc. award, VA, 1959, Disting. Svc. award, HEW, 1968, Rockefeller Pub. Svc. award, 1973, Disting. Achievement award, Modern Medicine, 1976, Disting. Svc. award, Am. Coll. Cardiology, 1978, John C. Leonard award, Assn. Hosp. Med. Edn., 1979. Fellow: AAAS, Phila. Coll. Physicians, Med. Libr. Assn., Royal Soc. Medicine, N.Y. Acad. Medicine (hon.); mem.: NAS, Inst. Medicine, Am. Fedn. Clin. Rsch., Am. Soc. Clin. Investigation (sr.). Home: 700 John Ringling Blvd Apt 1407 Sarasota FL 34236-1555 E-mail: martincummings@comcast.net.

CUMMINGS, MAXINE GIBSON, elementary school educator; b. Tupelo, Miss., Oct. 7, 1940; d. T. Ruben and Maggie (Ruff) Gibson; m. Willie B. Cummings, Aug. 15, 1964; 1 child, Stanley. BS, Barber-Scotia Coll., Concord, N.C., 1962; MA, Northeastern Ill. U., Chgo., 1974. Cert. tchr., N.C., Ill. Tchr. Walter Reed Elem. Sch., Chgo., 1963-75, reading tchr., 1975-82, social studies tchr., 1982-85; reading resource tchr. Arna Bontemps Sch., Chgo., 1985-91, ESEA lab. tchr., 1991—; Title I reading/math tchr. St. Sabina Acad., Chgo. Mentor tchr. Tchrs. for Chgo. Program, Arna W. Bontemps Sch. Site, 1996—; counselor Westside YWCA, Chgo., 1963-68; chmn. reading com. Bontemps Sch., 1986-92, chmn. activity com., 1992-93; mentor tchr. Bontemps Tchrs. for Chgo. Program; mem. staff devel. team Reading Tchrs. Acad. for Profl. Growth, Chgo. Bd. Edn.; Title I tchr., presenter in field. Contbr. articles to profl. jours. Vol., Edna White Century Garden; sec. S.W. Morgan Park Civic Assn., Chgo., 1990-92; block rep. Neighborhood Watch Program, Chgo., 1989-90; trustee, elder Morgan Park Presbyn. Ch., peace and justice com., mem. choir; Great Books Discussion leader Walker Br. Libr., 1999; race rels. com. Beverly/Morgan Park Neighborhood-Task Force; coord. garden site Metra Train Sta., hist. rschr. family reunions. Recipient Regional Cmty. Gardening award, Morgan Park Neighborhood, Chgo., 1998, Mayor Daley's Landscpae Improvement Program award, 1999, 2d place award, City Scape Gardening Corner, Chgo., 1999; grantee, Chgo.-Incentive, 1987, NEH, 1984, Northeastern Ill. U., 1980. Mem. Minority Students of Chgo. Area (recruiter), Barber-Scotia Alumni Club (sec. 1989-92), Pi Lambda Theta. Avocations: biking, walking, reading, travel, gardening. Home: 11116 S Longwood Dr Chicago IL 60643-4043 Office: St Sabina Acad 7801 S Throop St Chicago IL 60620- Office Phone: 773-535-3596. E-mail: mcummings@cps.k12.il.us.

CUMMINGS, MEGAN DOROTHY, computer scientist, consultant; b. Amity, Oreg., Sept. 1, 1979; d. Lawrence Newell and Christine C Cummings. BS in Computer Info. Sci., So. Oreg. U., 2002. Computer scientist Newtec, Ft Huachuca, Ariz., 2002—; prin., owner Integral Solutions, Hereford, Ariz., 2004—. Mary Roby scholar, U. Ariz., 1997—98. Mem.: MENSA, CAP. Republican. Avocations: aviation, fitness competitions, creative writing, languages - russian, mathematics. Office: Newtec EPG 2000 Arizona St Sierra Vista AZ 85635 Office Phone: 520-533-8210. Personal E-mail: megan.cummings@gmail.com.

CUMMINGS, NICHOLAS ANDREW, psychologist; b. Salinas, Calif., July 25, 1924; s. Andrew and Urania (Sims) C.; m. Dorothy Mills, Feb. 5, 1948; children: Janet Lynn, Andrew Mark. AB, U. Calif., Berkeley, 1948; MA, Claremont Grad. Sch., 1954; PhD, Adelphi U., 1958. Chief psychologist Kaiser Permanente No. Calif., San Francisco, 1959-76; pres. Found Behavioral Health, San Francisco, 1976—; chmn., CEO Am. Biodyne, Inc., San Francisco, 1985-93, Kendron Internat., Ltd., Reno, Nev., 1992-95; chmn. Nicholas & Dorothy Cummings Found., Reno, 1994—; chmn., pres. U.K. Behavioural Health, Ltd., London, 1996-98; Disting. prof. U. Nev., 1997—; chmn., CEO DynaMed Integrated Care, Inc., 1998—. Co-dir. South San Francisco Health Ctr., 1959-75; pres. Calif. Sch. Profl. Psychology, L.A., San Francisco, San Diego, Fresno campuses, 1969-76; chmn. bd. Calif. Cmty. Mental Health Ctrs., Inc., L.A., San Diego, San Francisco, 1975-77; pres. Blue Psi, Inc., San Francisco, 1972-80, Inst. for Psychosocial Interaction, 1980-84; mem. mental health adv. bd. City and County San Francisco, 1968-75; bd. dirs. San Francisco Assn. Mental Health, 1965-75; pres., chmn. bd. Psycho-Social Inst., 1972-80; dir. Mental Rsch. Inst., Palo Alto, Calif., 1979-80; pres. Nat. Acads. of Practice, 1981-93. Served with U.S. Army, 1944-46. Fellow APA (dir. 1975-81, pres. 1979); mem. Calif. Psychol. Assn. (pres. 1968). Office: Nicholas & Dorothy Cummings Found 4781 Caughlin Pkwy Reno NV 89509 Office Phone: 775-826-3311. Personal E-mail: cummfound@aol.com.

CUMMINGS, PATRICIA ANNE (FELICITAS CRUZ), writer, journalist, poet; b. El Paso, Tex., Nov. 19, 1963; d. Herman Charles Cummings and Felicia Cruz. Diploma, Inst. Children's Lit., 1989, 92, 96. Cert. associated journalist. Poet World Poetry, L.A., 1980-85; poet, editor Poets Inc., El Paso, 1985-88; pvt. practice El Paso, 1993—. Instr. poetry Cath. Ch., El Paso, 1992—, instr. writing, 1993—. Author: I Will Sail My Vessel, 1993 (1st Pl. 1994); author numerous poems. Recipient Golden Poet award Poetry World, 1985, 86, Silver Poet award Poetry World, 1989, Editor's Choice award Internat. Poetry Hall of Fame, 1991; named Outstanding Journalist, City News Svc., 1992. Mem. Am. Acad. Poets (contbg. mem.), Poetry Soc. Am. (contbg. mem.). Democrat. Roman Catholic. Avocations: motocross, arenacross, supercross. Home: 6231 Trowbridge Dr El Paso TX 79905-2115

CUMMINGS, PEGGY ANN, counseling administrator; b. Plainfield, NJ, May 18, 1957; d. Peter James Cummings and Marjorie Ann Pope. MA in Student Pers. Svcs., Rowan U., 1986, BA in Spl. Edn., 1979; AS in Restaurant Mgmt., Restaurant Sch. Phila., 1989. Cert. tchr. of handicapped NJ, lic. profl. counselor NJ, nat. cert. counselor, nat. cert. dietary mgr., cert. food mgr./operator Pa., student pers. svcs. NJ, supr. NJ. Sch. counselor Montgomery Twp. Sch. Dist., Skillman, NJ, 1999—, spl. edn. tchr., 1995—99; dist. mgr. Nutrition Mgmt. Svcs. Co., Kimberton, Pa., 1994—95, food svc. dir., 1990—94; spl. edn. tchr. Haddon Heights Sch. Dist., NJ, 1979—88; dir., camp Jotoni Somerset County Assn. for Retarded Citizens, Manville, NJ, 1979—82. Co-pres. MTEA Challenger Little League, Montgomery Twp., NJ, 2002—. Author (school guidance department member) school guidance curriculum, grades 3-4; contbr. workshop presentation Character Education Conference, Central NJ; co-author (character education committee member): (elementary character education curriculum) Montgomery Township Character Education Curriculum. Sch. rep. Rocky Hill/Montgomery Twp. Mcpl. Alliance, Belle Mead, NJ, 2002—03; donor membership Sharing Network Organ and Tissue Donation Svcs., Springfield, NJ, 2001—; vol. MTEA Challenger Little League, Belle Mead, 2001—; contbr. Samaritan Interim Homeless Program, Somerville, NJ, 2001—. Mem.: PTA, NEA, Am. Assn. Marriage and Family Therapists (student mem.), N.J. Edn. Assn., N.J. Sch. Counselor Assn. (Somerset County Counselor of Yr. 2002—03), Am. Sch. Counselor Assn., Kappa Delta Pi, Gamma Tau Sigma, Mortar Bd. Achievements include development of Elementary School Peer Mediation Student Leader and Peer Partners Programs. Avocations: golf, swimming, hiking, gardening, bicycling. Home: 423 Jackson Ave Manville NJ 08835 Office: Montgomery Township School District 1014 Rte 601 Skillman NJ 08558 E-mail: pcummings@mtsd.k12.nj.us.

CUMMINGS, SANDRA EILEEN, medical products executive; d. Edwin T. Cummings and Regina E. DeVecchis; m. Richard S. Surwit; children: Daniel Surwit, Sarah Surwit. BA, Wake Forest U., 1973; MA, Middlebury Coll., 1977; MBA, U. N.C., 1983. Mktg. mgmt. Nortel Networks, Research Triangle Park, NC, 1983—96; pres. ZyCare, Inc., Chapel Hill, NC, 1996—. Chairperson Sch. Governance Coms., Chapel Hill, 1993—2003. Small Bus. Innovation and Rsch. Fast Track grant Nat. Heart and Lung Inst., NIH, 2001—04. Achievements include patents for computer programs for remote managment of patients with chronic conditions; research in The CoagCare Anticoagulation Management System. Office: ZyCare Inc 3804 Sweeten Creek Rd Chapel Hill NC 27514

CUMMINGS, STEPHEN EMERY, investment banking executive; b. Atlanta, May 27, 1955; s. Robert Emery and Catherine Brierly (Longyear) C.; m. Karen Lee Ludwick, Feb. 21, 1981; children: William Ludwick, Stephen Clifton, Caroline Margret, Russell Ludwick, Lee Wyman. BA in Adminstrv. Sci., Colby Coll., Waterville, Maine, 1977; MBA, Columbia U., N.Y.C., 1979. V.p. Kidder, Peabody & Co., Inc., N.Y.C., 1979-85; with Bowles Hollowell Conner & Co. (merged with First Union), Charlotte, 1985—98, chmn., CEO, 1993—98; Managing Director and Head of Mergers and Acquisitions First Union Corp. (now Wachovia Corp.), 1998—99, Managing Director, Co-Head Investment Banking Group, 1999—2000; sr. exec. v.p., co- head Corporate and Investment Banking division Wachovia Corp., 2000—04, sr. exec. v.p., head Corporate and Investment Banking division, 2004—. George F. Baker scholar Colby Coll., 1977. Mem. Beta Gamma Sigma. Republican. Episcopalian. Office: Wachovia Corp 1 Wachovia Ctr Charlotte NC 28288

CUMMINGS, WILLIAM KENNETH, sociology educator; b. Raleigh, N.C., Oct. 18, 1943; s. Ralph Waldo and Mary Catherine (Parrish) C.; m. Fumiko Kimura, Jan. 26, 1969; children: Yujin K., Seijin K. BA, U. Mich., 1965; MA, Harvard U., 1968, PhD, 1972. Assoc. prof. U. Chgo., 1972-77, 81; project officer Ford Found., 1977-81; sr. fellow East-West Ctr., 1982-84; sr. analyst NSF, 1984-86; project coord. Harvard Inst. Internat. Devel., Cambridge, Mass., 1987-93; prof., dir., Ctr. for Asian Studies SUNY, Buffalo, 1993-94, dir. Ctr. for Comparative and Global Studies Edn., 1994—. Author: Education and Equality in Japan, 1980, Educational Policies in Crisis, 1987, Profiting from Education, 1990. Rsch. grantee Social Sci. Rsch. Coun., 1973, Japan Found., 1975, Nat. Inst. Edn., 1975, U.S.-Japan Friendship Commn., 1989. Office: SUNY Baldy 428 Buffalo NY 14260-0001

CUMMINGS ROCKWELL, PATRICIA GUILBAULT, psychiatric nurse; b. Ludlow, Mass., June 22, 1939; d. Lee Allen and Mavis Isabella (White) Guilbault; m. Philip W. Cummings, Oct. 23, 1960 (dec. Jan. 1978); children: Sharon Ellen Timmons, Geoffrey Scott Cummings, Susan Mavis Lornitzo, Lee Millett Cummings, Mary Rockwell Thon; m. William Leonard Rockwell Jr., Aug. 18, 1990. ADN, Vt. Coll., 1982; BSN, Norwich U., 1987. RN, Vt. Staff nurse Ctrl. Vt. Hosp. Nursing Home, Berlin, 1982-84, 87—; staff psychiat. nurse Va. Hosp. Ground East, White River Junction, Vt., 1987-94; owner Globe Travel, Bradford, Vt., 1988-94; rschr. Norwich U., Northfield, Vt., 1988—. Nurse-entrepeneur Globe Travel, 1988—. Tchr. adult edn. ARC, Bradford, Vt., 1988, 89; dir. Vt. Lakes and Pond Assn.; v.p. Vale Hospice Internat.; dir. Fedn. Vt. Lakes and Ponds Inc. Mem. ANA (nat. and Vt. chpts.), AAUW, New Eng. Hist. Geneal. Soc. Avocations: writing, travel, medical genealogy, genetics and genealogy. Home: 307 Godfrey Rd East Thetford VT 05043-9517 Office Phone: 802-785-4812. E-mail: patsy@together.net, patsy@valehospice.org.

CUMMINS, ANN, literature and language professor, writer; d. Cyril P. and Barbara R. Cummins; m. Steven Evans Willis, Apr. 14, 2001. MA, Johns Hopkins U., Balt., 1987; MFA, U. Ariz., Tucson, 1989. Prof. creative writing No. Ariz. U., Flagstaff, 1989—. Author: Red Ant House. Mem. No. Ariz. Book Festival, Flagstaff. Fiction fellow, Ariz. Commn. on the Arts, 1990, 1994, Lit. fellow, Lannan Found., 2002—03. Office: No Ariz U Box 6032 Flagstaff AZ 86011 Office Phone: 928-523-7304. E-mail: ann.cummins@nau.edu.

CUMMINS, CHRISTOPHER C., chemistry professor; b. Boston, Feb. 28, 1966; AB, Cornell U., 1989; PhD, MIT, 1993. Prof. chemistry, rschr. MIT, Cambridge, Mass. Contbr. articles to profl. publs. Recipient Alan T. Waterman award, NSF, 1998. Achievements include research in new methods for inorganic synthesis; the synthesis, isolation and characterization of unusually reactive transition metal and actinide complexes of unique design and construction; the activation of ubiquitous small molecules including dinitrogen; the assembly of novel functional groups containing both transition metals and main group elements; development of new reagents for organic synthesis. Office: MIT Dept Chemistry Rm 2-227 77 Massachusetts Ave Cambridge MA 02139-4301 E-mail: ccummins@mit.edu.

CUMMINS, DELMER DUANE, academic administrator, historian; b. Dawson, Nebr., June 4, 1935; s. Delmer H. and Ina Z. (Arnold) C.; m. Darla Sue Beard, Oct. 6, 1957; children: Stephen Duane, Cristi Sue, Caroline Renee. BS, Phillips U., Enid, Okla., 1957; MA, U. Denver, 1965; PhD, U. Okla., 1974; LLD, Williams Woods Coll., 1979; HHD (hon.), Phillips U., 1983; DLitt (hon.), Chapman U., 1996. Tchr., Jefferson County Pub. Schs., Denver, 1956-67; mem. faculty Oklahoma City U., 1967-77, Darbeth-Whitten prof. history, 1974-77, curator George Shirk Collection, 1977. Chmn. dept. history Oklahoma City U., 1969—72; dir. Robert A. Taft Inst. Govt., 1972—77; pres. Bethany (W.Va.) Coll., 1988—2002, pres. emeritus, 2002—; pres. Brite Div. Sch., 2002—03; vis. scholar in history Johns Hopkins U., 2002—. Author: The American Frontier, 1968, Origins of the Civil War, 1971;: 2d edit., 1978, The American Revolution, 1968, Contrasting Decades, 1920's and 1930's, 1972;: 2d edit., 1978, Consensus and Turmoil, 1972, William R. Leigh: Biography of a Western Artist, 1980, A Handbook for Today's Disciples, 1981, 3d edit., 2003; author: (with D. Hohweller) An Enlisted Soldier's View of the Civil War, 1981, 3d edit., 2003; author: (with others) Seeking God's Peace in a Nuclear Age, 1985; author: The Disciples Colleges: A History, 1987, The Search for Identity, Disciples of Christ-The Restructure Years, 1987, Dale Fiers: Twentieth Century Disciple, 2003; editor: The Disciples Theol. Digest, 1986—88, Biography of Alexander Campbell, 2004; contbr. articles to profl. jours. Active Pitts. Opera Bd., 1996—2001; moderator, active multiple nat. bds. and task forces Christian Ch., 1993—95; bd. dirs. Disciples of Christ Hist. Soc., pres., 2004—05; pres. divsn. higher edn. Christian Ch., 1978—88; trustee Culver-Stockton Coll., 1978—88, Tougaloo Coll., 1978—88, vice chmn., 1985—88; Danforth assoc., 1976—78. Mem. Okla. Humanities Coun.(grantee 1974), Phillips U. Alumni Assn. (pres. 1975-76), Nat. Assn. Ind. Colls. and Univs. (secretariat, policy comm. 1990-94), chair pres.'s athletic conf. 1990-92), W.Va. Assn. Ind. Colls. (chair 1994-97, chair east ctrl. coll. consortium 1997-98), Co. Ind. Colls. (bd. dirs. 1998-01). Home: 255 Sears Ln Swanton MD 21561 E-mail: d.cummins@mail.bethanywv.edu, d_cummins@gcnetmail.net.

CUMMINS, H. E. BUD, III, prosecutor; b. Enid, Okla., Aug. 6, 1959; BS, U. Ark., 1981, JD, 1989. Clk. U.S. Dist. Judge Stephen Reasoner, U.S. Magistrate John Forster Jr.; chief legal counsel Gov. Mike Huckabee; atty. Little Rock; U.S. atty. Ea. Dist. Ark., 2001—. State dir. Nat. Fedn. Ind. Bus. Republican. Methodist. Office: Ea Dist Ark PO 1229 Little Rock AR 72203

CUMMINS, HERMAN ZACHARY, physicist; b. Rochester, N.Y., Apr. 23, 1933; s. Louis H. and Rhoda Edith (Kitay) Kominz C.; m. Marsha Z. Hirsch, Aug. 18, 1963. BS, MS, Ohio State U., 1956; Diplome d'Etudes Superieures, U. Paris, 1957; PhD, Columbia U., 1963; D honoris causa, U. P. et M. Curie, 1999. Rsch. assoc. Columbia U., N.Y.C., 1963-64; asst. prof. physics Johns Hopkins U., Balt., 1964-67, assoc. prof., 1967-69, prof., 1969-71; prof. physics NYU, 1971-73; disting. prof. physics City Coll., CUNY, 1973—2004, prof. emeritus, 2004—. Guggenheim fellow, 1984-85; Sloan fellow, 1969-72; recipient von Humboldt Sr. Rsch. award, 1998. Fellow Am. Phys. Soc., N.Y. Acad. Scis., Am. Assn. Adv. Sci.; mem. NAS, Am. Acad. Arts and Scis. Achievements include research in laser light scattering physics; phase transitions and critical phenomena; laser Doppler velocimetry; solid state and biophysics; liquid-glass transition; alloy solidification and pattern-forming instabilities. Office: City Coll CUNY Dept Physics New York NY 10031 Office Phone: 212-650-6921. E-mail: cummins@sci.ccny.cuny.edu, hzcummins@aol.com.

CUMMINS, JAMIE JOANN DAVIS, school counselor; b. Honolulu, Oct. 27, 1975; d. Stephen E. and Kathleen M. Davis; m. Kenneth V. Cummins, July 1, 2000; 1 child, Connor N. B in Mus. Edn., Wartburg Coll., 1998; MS, Calif. Luth. U., 2004. Music tchr. Liberty Mid. Sch., Mo., 1998—99, Marion Ind. Schs., Iowa, 1999—2000, Mt. Gleason Mid. Sch., L.A., 2000—04; sch. counselor Monroe HS, L.A., 2004—.

CUMMINS, JOSEPH M., biotechnology company executive; DVM, Ohio State U., 1966; PhD in Microbiology, U. Mo., 1978. Chmn. bd. dirs. Amarillo Bioscis., Inc., Amarillo, Tex., 1984—, pres., 1994—, CFO, 1998—. Contbr. over 40 articles to profl. jours.; patentee in field. Office: 4134 Business Park Dr Amarillo TX 79110-4225

CUMMINS, KENNETH WILLIAM, ecologist, educator; b. Chgo., Ill., Mar. 28, 1933; s. Charles Alfred and Mary Grace Cummins; m. Margaret Ann Wilzbach, June 21, 1985; children: Michael Scott, Steven Mathew, Paul Trevor. BA, Lawrence U., Wis., 1955; MS, U. Mich., 1957, PhD, 1961. Postdoctoral instr. U. Mich., Ann Arbor, Mich., 1961—62; asst. prof. Northwestern U., Evanston, Ill., 1962—63; asst, assoc. prof. U. Pitts., 1963—68, 1989—93; assoc. prof., prof. Mich. State U., East Lansing, Mich., 1968—78; prof. Oreg. State U., Corvallis, Oreg., 1978—84, U. Maryland, Frostburg, Md., 1984—89; dist. scientist South Fla. Water Mgmt. Dist., West Palm Beach, Fla., 1994—2000. Adj. prof. Humboldt State U., Arcata, Calif., 2000—; dir. Inst. River Ecosystems Humboldt State U., Arcata, 2004—. Editor, author An Intro to Aquatic Insects of N.Am., 1996; contbr. articles to profl. jours. Recipient Disting. Scientist, N.Am. Benthological Soc. Avocations: fishing, hockey, camping. Office: Humboldt State Univ Inst for River Ecosystems 592 14th St Arcata CA 95521 Office Phone: 707-825-7350.

CUMMINS, PAUL ZACH, II, insurance company executive; b. Fitchburg, Mass., May 1, 1936; s. Paul Z. and Camille M. (Hook) C.; children: Paul Zach III, Colleen Elizabeth. BS, U.S. Naval Acad., 1958, MS, 1964; MBA, Syracuse U., 1973. Mgr., engrng. liaison Carrier Corp., Syracuse, N.Y., 1969-73; mgr. systems, mfg. group Republic Steel Corp., Youngstown, Ohio, 1973-74, mgr., bus. planning, 1974-76; dir. adminstrn. planning Republic Builders Products Corp., Atlanta, 1976-77; dir. corp. strategy and devel. Blue Cross/Blue Shield Md., 1978-89, cons. internal ops., 1989-92; ind. cons., 1992—. Instr. U.S. Naval Acad., Annapolis, 1964-65. Past chmn., mem. Md. Gov.'s Vietnam and Disabled Vets. Bus. Resource Coun., SBA Adv. Bd. Balt Dist. With USN, 1958-69. Decorated Joint Svc. Commendation medal. Mem. U.S. Naval Acad. Alumni Assn., Am. Legion, Kiwanis (past pres. Liverpool, N.Y., past pres. Camillus, N.Y.), Optimist. Methodist. Home: 16933 Flickerwood Rd Parkton MD 21120-9767

CUMMINS, RICHARD WILLIAM, academic administrator, writer; b. Cleveland, Ohio, June 12, 1957; s. Robert Vernon and Rita Camille Cummins; m. Margaret Ann Woods, Dec. 16, 1994; children: Eleanor Artemis, Isaac James. BA in English Lit., U. Cin., 1982; MFA, U. Ariz., 1985. V.p. instrn. Columbia Basin Coll., Pasco, Wash., 2002—04, acting pres., 2004—. Pres. Columbia Basin Advanced Tech. Ctr., LLC, Pasco, 2000—02. Co-author: Reading, Writing, and the World Wide Web; section editor: jour. Technology Source. Mem. Applied Process Engrng. Lab., Richland, Wash., 2003—04, Tri-Cities Enterprise Ctr., Richland, 2000—04. Mem.: Kiwanis. Office: Columbia Basin Coll 2600 N 20th Ave Pasco WA 99301 Office Phone: 509-547-0511. Personal E-mail: rcummins@columbiabasin.edu.

CUMMINS, WILMA JEANNE, actress; b. Guthrie, Okla., Sept. 25, 1927; d. Chauncey Dewitt and Etta (Marshall) Anderson; m. Joseph Sylvester Cummins, May 24, 1952; children: Jeanetta Kay Arnold, Bunny Gail Cline, Mary Jo Stoops, Susan Dee. BA, Phillip's U., 1948; MA, U. Tulsa, 1980. Cert. tchr., lic. real estate broker. Ops. base payload control United Air Lines, Denver, 1948-50; lab. tech. Barnes Hosp., St. Louis, 1950; elem. tchr. Kans., Mo., 1951-53; actress Gaslight Dinner Theatre, Tulsa, 1984, Discoveryland's Okla., Prattville, 1985; tchr. Tulsa Pub. Schs., 1970-78; part time tchr. Tulsa Jr. Coll., 1987-89; freelancer in TV and radio SAG, AFTRA, Dallas, Tulsa, 1991—. Real estate broker, Tulsa, 1981—93. Performer: (radio) Grasso's Barn Dance Festival, 1950; actor: (films) The Ripper, 1985, UHF, 1988, Christmas Child, 2003; (TV series) Rosie O'Donnell Show, 1997, America's Funniest People, 1991, Howie Mandel Show, 1999, Tonight Show with Jay Leno, 2001, 30 Seconds to Fame, 2002, Lawrence Welk Champagne Theatre, 1997, Spotlight Theatre, 1983—, (commercial) Tex. Transp. Inst., 2002. Vol. Gilcrease Mus., Tulsa, 1995—2002; pres. Internat. Club, Tulsa, 1996, Pan-Am. Round Table, Tulsa, 1990, Altrusa Club, Tulsa, 1985, Christian Women's Fellowship, 1983, Conversing Couples, 1986—, Pro-Am., 2001—02. Recipient 1st pl. monologue, Internat. Platform Assn., 1989, 2d pl., 1991, 1st pl., Srs. Take Ctr. Stage, Welk Resort, 2000. Republican. Methodist. Avocations: theater, commercials. Office Phone: 918-628-1359. E-mail: wilmajeannecummins@att.net.

CUMMIS, CLIVE SANFORD, lawyer; b. Newark, Nov. 21, 1928; s. Joseph Jack and Lee (Berkie) C.; m. Ann Denburg, Mar. 24, 1956; children: Andrea, Deborah, Cynthia, Jessica. AB, Tulane U., 1949; JD, U. Pa., 1952; LL.M., N.Y. U., 1959. Bar: N.J. 1952. Law sec. Hon. Walter Freund, Appellate Div., Superior Ct., 1955-56; partner firm Cummis & Kroner, Newark, 1956-60; chief counsel County and Mcpl. Law Revision Commn., State of N.J., Newark, 1959-62; partner firm Schiff, Cummis & Kent, Newark, 1962-67, Cummis, Kent, Radin & Tischman, Newark, 1967-70; sr. v.p., dir. Cadence Industries, N.Y.C., 1967-70; dir. Plume & Atwood Industries, Stamford, Conn., 1969-71; chmn., chmn. emeritus Sills Cummis Epstein & Gross, P.C., Newark, 1970—; exec. v.p. law and corp. affairs, sec. Park Place Entertainment corp., Las Vegas, Nev., 1999—2001; vice chmn. bd. dirs. Caesars Entertainment, Inc., Las Vegas, Nev., 2000—05. Dir. Essex County State Bank, Financial Resources Group; instr. Practising Law Inst. Chief counsel County and Mcpl. Revision Commn., 1959-62, N.J. Pub. Market Commn., 1961-63; counsel Bd. Edn. of South Orange and Maplewood, 1964-74, Town of Cedar Grove, 1966-70, Bd. Edn. of Dumont, 1968-72; mem. com. on rules and civil practice N.J. Supreme Ct., 1975-78. Assoc. editor N.J. Law Jour., 1961—. Trustee Newark Beth Israel Med. Ctr., 1965-75, Northfield YM-YWHA, 1968-70, U. Medicine and Dentistry NJ, 1980-84, Newark Mus., NJ Performing Arts Ctr., Blue Cross and Blue Shield NJ, 1983-93, Found. U. Medicine and Dentistry NJ, 1999—; gen. coun. NJ Turnpike Authority, 1990-94; bd. overseers U. Pa. Law Sch., 1991-96; bd. govs. Daus. Israel Home for Aged, 1968-70; active NJ Commn. on Statue of Liberty; pres.'s coun. Tulane U., 1992—; pres. bd. dirs. Tulane Assocs., 1994-96; Pres.'s commn. on White House Fellows, 1993-2001; dir. NJ Regional Planning Assn., Horizon Found., NJ, 2004—, Flame of Charity Found., 2005—. Recipient 1st Ann. Judge Learned Hand award Am. Jewish Com., 1994, First Ann. Disting. Citizen award N.J. Med. Sch., 2002. Fellow Am. Bar Found.; mem. ABA, Am. Law Inst. (life, bd. dirs.), Am. Judicature Soc., U. Pa. Law Sch. Alumni Soc. (pres.), NJ Bar Assn., Essex County Bar Assn., NY Athletic Club (NYC), Greenbrook County Club (North Caldwell, NJ), Stockbridge Golf Club (Mass.). Democrat. Jewish. Office: Sills Cummis Epstein & Gross PC One Riverfront Pl Newark NJ 07102 Office Phone: 973-643-5499. Business E-Mail: ccummis@sillscummis.com.

CUNDIFF, EDWARD WILLIAM, retired marketing educator; b. Long Beach, Calif., Sept. 28, 1919; s. Harry Thomas and Martha Magdalene (Koltes) C.; m. Margaret Wallace Stroud, Sept. 8, 1956; children: Richard Wallace, Gregory Edward, Geoffrey William. BA, Stanford, 1940, MBA, 1942; Ed.D., 1952; Ford Fellow, Harvard Sch. Bus. Adminstrn., 1956. Retailing exec., 1946-48; instr. mktg. San Jose State Coll., 1949-52; asst. prof., later asso. prof. mktg. Syracuse U., 1952-58, asst. dean, 1954-58; prof. mktg., chmn. dept. mktg. adminstrn. U. Tex., 1958-73, assoc. dean Grad. Sch. Bus., 1973-76; L.J. Buchan distinguished vis. prof. U. Tex. at San Antonio, 1976-77; Charles C. Kellstadt prof. mktg. Emory U., 1977-87; John A. Beck Centennial prof. comm. U. Tex., Austin, 1987-94, John A. Beck emeritus prof. comm. dept. advt., 1994-96, emeritus prof. mktg., 1996—; ret., 1994. Vis. prof. mktg., Fontainebleau, France, Palermo, Sicily, 1960-61. Author: (with R.R. Still) Sales Management: Decisions, Policies and Cases, 5th edit, 1988, Basic Marketing: Concepts, Environment, and Decisions, 1964, rev. edit., 1970, Essentials of Marketing, 1966, 3d edit., 1986, (with R.R. Still and N.A.P. Govoni) Fundamentals of Modern Marketing, 3d edit, 1980, (with Marye Hilger) Marketing in the International Environment, 2d edit., 1988; editor: Jour. Mktg, 1973-76. Served to lt. (s.g.) USNR, World War II. Mem. Am. Mktg. Assn. (v.p. 1980—), So. Mktg. Assn. (pres. 1967-68), Beta Gamma Sigma, Delta Sigma Pi, Theta Chi. Home: # 1281 4100 Jackson Ave Apt 229 Austin TX 78731-6038 Office: U Tex Coll Communication Austin TX 78712 Personal E-mail: ecundiff@sbcglobal.net.

CUNDIFF, VICTORIA ANNE, lawyer; b. Denver, Jan. 25, 1955; d. Jerome W. and Anne (O'Rourke) C. BA summa cum laude, U. Denver, 1977; JD, Yale U., 1980. Bar: N.Y. 1981, U.S. Dist. Ct. (so. and ea. dists.) N.Y. 1981, U.S. Ct. Appeals (2nd cir.) 1984, U.S. Ct. Appeals (3rd cir.) 1988, U.S. Supreme Ct. 1991. Assoc. Breed Abbott & Morgan, N.Y.C., 1980-82, Milgrim Thomajan & Lee, P.C., N.Y.C., 1982-87, mem., 1987-92; ptnr. Paul, Hastings, Janofsky & Walker, N.Y.C., 1992—, chairperson intellectual property practice group. Author: Maximum Security: How to Prevent Departing Employees From Putting Your Trade Secrets to Work for Your Competitors, 1992; contbg. editor Intellectual Property Law. Bd. dirs. Yale Law Sch. Fund. Mem. ABA (mem. com. on intellectual property litigation 1988—, chairperson subcom. on trade secrets litigation 1990—, mem. com. on pre-trial practice and discovery 1988—, lectr. ABA Nat. Inst. on Corp. Litigation), N.Y. State Bar Assn. (chair com. trade secrets 1992—), Assn. of Bar of City of N.Y. (mem. com. on sci. and law, 1991—, com. trademarks and unfair competition 1987-90, chair PLI program on trade secret protection and litigation 1992). Avocations: art history, historic preservation. Office: Paul Hastings Janofsky & Walker LLP 399 Park Ave Fl 30 New York NY 10022-4697 Office Phone: 212-318-6030. Office Fax: 212-230-7643. Business E-Mail: victoriacundiff@paulhastings.com.

CUNEO, ANTHONY DANIEL, artist, educator; s. Paul Kleist and Mary Louise Cuneo; children: Paul Benjamin, Sarah Beatrice. MFA, U. Pa., 1981. Chmn. Dept. Fine and Perfoming Arts Montclair (N.J.) Kimberley Acad., 1992—. One-man shows include Amos Eno Gallery, N.Y., The Watchung Arts Center, The Bruce S, Kershner Gallery, Fairfield (Conn.) Pub. Libr., exhibitions include Gallery 10 Ltd., Washington, D.C., Amos Eno Gallery, N.Y., ARC Gallery, Chgo., Ill., The Baird Ctr., South Orange, N.J., 750 Gallery, Sacramento, Calif., Krasdale Gallery, White Plains, N.Y., Bromfield Gallery, Boston, Mass., Artists' Choice Mus., N.Y.C., N.Y. Finalist Excellence in Secondary Tchg. award, Princeton (N.J.) U., 2002; recipient First Pl. award, Watchung Arts Ctr., 1997; Benjamin Franklin scholar, U. Pa., 1974—79. Office Phone: 973-509-4866. E-mail: acuneo@montclairkimberley.org.

CUNEO, DENNIS CLIFFORD, automotive company executive; b. Ridgway, Pa., Jan. 12, 1950; s. Clifford Francis and Erma Theresa (Nissel) C.; m. Bonnie Frances Mish, Aug. 18, 1972; children: Corinne, Kyle, James. BS, Gannon U., 1971; MBA, Kent State U., 1973; JD, Loyola U., New Orleans,

1976. Bar: D.C. 1977. Trial atty. U.S. Dept. Justice, Washington, 1976-80; assoc. Arent, Fox, Kintner, Plotkin & Kahn, Washington, 1980-84; gen. counsel New United Motor Mfg. Inc. joint venture GM-Toyota, Fremont, Calif., 1984-88, v.p. legal and govt. affairs, 1988-90, v.p. corp. planning and legal affairs, 1990-92, v.p. corp. planning and external affairs, corp. sec., 1992-96; sr. v.p. legal, environ., external affairs Toyota Motor Mfg. N.Am., 1996-2000, sr. v.p., 2000—. Chmn. Calif. Workside Rsch. Com., Sacramento, 1988—96; lectr. exec. program U. Calif., Davis, 1988—95; lectr. internat. motor vehicle program MIT, Berlin and Beijing, 1994; mem. Gov. Pete Wilson Trade Mission to Asia, 1993; bd. dirs. Toyota Motor Corp. Svcs., Inc., 1996—99; mem. Cin. Bus. Com.; mem. gov.'s econ. adv. com., Frankfort, Ky., 2001—. Campaign chmn. United Way, Alameda County, 1993-95, No. Ky. United Way, 2000; co-chmn. Blue Ribbon com. to Save the Oakland A's, 1994; vice chmn. Alameda County Econ. Devel. Bd., Oakland, 1990-96, Team Calif., Sacramento, 1994; bd. visitors Loyola Law Sch., 1987-95; mem. Calif. Select Com. on Jud. Retirement, 1993; mem. steering com. Bay Area Coun., San Francisco, 1990-95, Bay Area Dredging Coalition, San Francisco, 1991-96; mem. Statewide Pupil Assessment Rev. Panel, Sacramento, 1996-97; bd. dirs. Oakland-Alameda County Coliseum, 1995-97, Cin. United Way, 1997—, Bay Area Regional Tech. Alliance, Oakland, 94-96; mem. flood relief cabinet ARC, 1997; mem. Gov.'s Task Force on Child Devel., Frankfort, Ky., 1999— . Mem.: ABA, Calif. Mfrs. Assn. (vice chmn. 1994—99, pres. Calif. manufactures svcs. corp. 1996—97), Nat. Mfrs. Assn. (chmn. human resources policy group 1999—, bd. dirs., exec. com.), Oakland Football Mktg. Assn. (pres. 1995—96), Greater Cin. C. of C. (bd. dirs. 1998—), No. Ky. C. of C. (bd. dirs. 1997—98), Assoc. Industries Ky. (bd. dirs. 1999—), Cin. Club, Metro. Club (bd. dirs. 1999—). Avocations: skiing, model trains. Office: Toyota Motor Mfg NAm 25 Atlantic Ave Erlanger KY 41018-3188

CUNEO, DONALD LANE, lawyer, educator; b. Alameda, Calif., Apr. 19, 1944; s. Vernon Edmund and Dorothy (Lane) c.; m. Frances Susan Huze, Aug. 8, 1981; children: Kristen Marie, Lane Michael. BA, Lehigh U., 1966; JD, MBA, Columbia U., 1970. Bar: N.Y. 1971, D.C. 1992, U.S. Claims Ct. 1972, U.S. Tax Ct. 1972, U.S. Dist. Ct. (so. dist.) N.Y. 1973, U.S. Dist. Ct. (no. dist.) 1978, U.S. Dist. Ct. D.C. 1992, U.S. Ct. Appeals (2nd cir.) 1979, U.S. Ct. Appeals (D.C. cir.) 1992, U.S. Ct. Internat. Trade 1979, U.S. Ct. Appeals (fed. cir.) 1979, U.S. Supreme Ct. 1979. Assoc. Shearman & Sterling, N.Y.C., 1971-79, ptnr., 1979-93; pres., CEO Internat. House, 1993—. Sec., trustee Internat. House, N.Y.C., 1977-93; pres. Morningside Area Alliance, N.Y.C., 2000—03. Author: (with others) Prevention and Prosecution of Computer and High Technology Crime, 1988; contbr. articles to profl. jours. Reginald Heber Smith Cmty. Lawyer fellow U.S. Govt., 1970-71. Mem. Coun. Fgn. Rels. Avocations: sports, travel. Home and Office: Internat House 500 Riverside Dr New York NY 10027-3916 E-mail: dcuneo@ihouse-nyc.org.

CUNHA, MARK GEOFFREY, lawyer; b. Lexington, Mass, Sept. 26, 1955; s. John Henry and Dolores (DeRosas) C.; children: Celine Yvonne, Nicholas Brian. AB magna cum laude, Cornell U., 1977; JD, Stanford U., 1980. Bar: N.Y. 1981, U.S. Dist. Ct. (so. and ea. dists.) N.Y. 1981, U.S. Ct. Appeals (2nd cir.) 1991, U.S. Tax Ct. 1992, U.S. Supreme Ct. 1996, U.S. Ct. Appeals (3d cir.) 2001. Intern The White House, Washington, 1979-80; assoc. Simpson Thacher & Bartlett, NYC, 1980-88, ptnr., 1989—. Mediator comml. divsn. NY State Supreme Ct., NY County, 1996—; bd. dir. legal svc. for NYC, 1997—. Bd. dir. NY Lawyers for Pub. Interest, 1989-2004; trustee Inst. for Ednl. Achievement, 1995—, Lycee Francais NY, 1998—. Recipient Outstanding Vol. Lawyers award Legal Aid Soc., 1990, Pro Bono award NY County Lawyers Assn., 1991. Mem.: Assn. Bar City NY (v.p., chmn. exec. com., chmn. com. on legal assistance, chmn. del. to NY State Bar Assn. Ho. of Dels., steering com. on legal assistance), NY State Bar Assn. (exec. com. on comml. and fed. litigation sect.), Internat. Bar Assn., ABA, Phi Beta Kappa. Democrat. Home: 1150 Fifth Ave Apt 3A New York NY 10128-0724 Office: Simpson Thacher & Bartlett 425 Lexington Ave New York NY 10017-3954 Office Phone: 212-455-3475. Business E-Mail: mcunha@stblaw.com.

CUNNINGHAM, ALICE WELT, law educator; b. Washington, Aug. 18, 1949; d. Samuel Louis and Beatrice (Boxer) Welt; m. Daniel Paul Cunningham, Aug. 10, 1975; adopted children: Stephen Paul, Philip James 1 child, Samuel Paul (dec.). BA summa cum laude, Yale U., 1971; JD, Harvard U., 1974; MA in Math. Edn., postgrad., Columbia U., 2001. Bar: N.Y. 1975, Calif. 1975, U.S. Dist. Ct. (no. dist.) Calif. 1975, U.S. Ct. Appeals (fed. cir.) 1980, U.S. Tax Ct. 1976. Assoc. Shearman & Sterling, N.Y.C., 1974-75, Heller Ehrman, White & McAuliffe, San Francisco, 1975-78, Debevoise & Plimpton, N.Y.C., 1978-83; assoc. prof. N.Y. Law Sch., N.Y.C., 1983-86. Contbr. articles to profl. jours. Mem.: ABA, Assn. Bar City N.Y., N.Y. State Bar Assn., Kappa Delta Pi, Phi Beta Kappa. Personal E-mail: acunnin167@aol.com.

CUNNINGHAM, ANDREA LEE, public relations executive; b. Oak Park, Ill., Dec. 15, 1956; d. Ralph Edward and Barbara Ann C.; m. Rand Wyatt Siegfried, Sept. 24, 1983. BA, Northwestern U., 1979. Feature writer Irving-Cloud Pub. Co., Lincolnwood, Ill., 1979-81; account exec. Burson-Marsteller Inc., Chgo., 1981-83; group account mgr. Regis McKenna Inc., Palo Alto, Calif., 1983-85; founder, owner, pres. Cunningham Communication Inc., Santa Clara, Calif., 1985—. Mem. Am. Electronics Assn., U.S. C. of C., Young Pres.' Orgn., Software Pubs. Assn., Boston Computer Soc., Leadership Calif., U.S. Cambridge C. of C. Republican. Avocations: running, roller skating, aerobics, racquetball.

CUNNINGHAM, ANTHONY WILLARD, lawyer; b. Lakeland, Fla., Nov. 10, 1931; s. Elmo and Anna Catherine Cunningham; m. Kathleen, 1960 (div. 1974); children: Matthew, Tracy, Melisse, Megan, Joshua, Alexandra; m. Robin Richards, Nov. 22, 1980. LLB, U. Fla., 1962. Bar: Fla. 1963, U.S. Dist. Ct. (mid. dist.) Fla. 1964, U.S. Ct. Appeals (5th cir.) 1964, U.S. Supreme Ct. 1975. Assoc. Fishback, Davis, Dominick & Troutman, Orlando, Fla., 1962-64, Nichols, Gaither, Beckham, Colson, Spence & Hicks, Miami, Fla., 1964-65, Orlando and Tampa, Fla., 1965-67; prin. Wagner, Cunningham, Vaughan & McLaughlin, P.A., Tampa, 1967-92, Cunningham Law Group, P.A., Tampa, 1992—. 1st lt. USAF, 1951-56. Mem. ATLA (bd. govs. 1979—90, 95), Trial Lawyers Pub. Justice (bd. dirs. 1986—, pres. elect 1990-91, pres. 1991-92), Acad. Fla. Trial Lawyers (bd. dirs., past pres. 1971—). Democrat. Avocations: boating, fishing, skiing. Office: Cunningham Law Group 601 Bayshore Blvd Ste 750 Tampa FL 33606-2760 Office Phone: 813-258-0333. E-mail: awc8669@aol.com.

CUNNINGHAM, ATLEE MARION, JR., aeronautical engineer; b. Corpus Christi, Tex., Aug. 17, 1938; s. Atlee Marion and Carlos Dean (Shepherd) Cunningham; m. Diana Wahl Bonelli, July 17, 1976; children from previous marriage: Christopher Atlee Acie, Scott Patrick, Sean Michael. BSME, MSME, U. Tex., 1961, PhD, 1966. Rsch. scientist Def. Rsch. Lab., Austin, Tex., 1965; engring. staff specialist Gen. Dynamics Corp., Ft. Worth, 1965—93, Lockheed Corp., Ft. Worth, 1993—95, Lockheed Martin, 1995—, sr. prin. rsch. engr., sr. tech. fellow, 2002—. Vis. indsl. prof. So. Meth. U. Inst. Tech., Dallas, 1969—70; vis. assoc. prof. aero. engring. U. Tex., 1978—; lectr. in aeroelasticity Nat. Cheng Kung U., Taiwan, 1984, U. Tex., Arlington, 1990—; cons. NASA, USAF, USN, U. Tex.; cons. on aeroelastic and vibration issues for Lockheed Martin F-16, C-130J, F-22 and F-35 aircraft. Contbr. articles to profl. jours. V.p. Tex. Fine Arts Assn., Ft. Worth, 1972. Served with USN, 1962—64. Recipient NASA Cert. of Recognition for tech. publ., 1980, Achievement award, Gen. Dynamics, 1980, 1983, 1989; Welding Rsch. Assn. fellow, 1961—62. Fellow: AIAA (assoc.; tech. reviewer jours.); mem.: Sigma Xi. Achievements include innovations in subsonic, transonic and supersonic steady and oscillatory aerodynamics method; major contributions to aeroelastic developments and improvements for Gen. Dynamics F-16 and F-111, F/A-22 and F-35 aircrafts; development of new methods for predicting high angle of attack aerodynamics in subsonic and supersonic flows; steady and unsteady force testing techniques for aerodynamic investigations using water tunnels, new concepts and methods for nonlinear aeroelasticity; pioneered new technology development for unsteady separated flows and buffeting on aircraft maneuvering at high angle of attack involving support of Air Force; Navy; NASA; Nat. Aerospace Lab. (Netherlands); Lockheed Martin; U. Tex., Austin; patents in field. Home: 4932 Black Oak Ln Fort Worth TX 76114-2936

CUNNINGHAM, CHARLES BAKER, III, manufacturing executive; b. St. Louis, Oct. 1, 1941; s. Charles Baker C. and Mary Blythe (Cunningham); m. Georganne Rose, Sept. 17, 1966; children: Margaret B., Charles B. IV. BS, Washington U., St. Louis, 1964; MS, Ga. Inst. Tech., 1966; MBA, Harvard U., 1970. Dir. fin. The Cooper Group, Raleigh, N.C., 1972-75, v.p. adminstrn., 1975-77; v.p. devel. Cooper Industries Inc., Houston, 1977-79, v.p. ops., 1980-82, exec. v.p., 1982-93, pres. Indsl. Equipment Group, 1979-80; chmn., pres., CEO Belden Inc., 1993—. Served to 1st lt. U.S. Army, 1966-68, Iran. Decorated Army Commendation medal Office: Belden Inc 7701 Forsyth Blvd Ste 800 Saint Louis MO 63105-1861 E-mail: baker.cunningham@belden.com.

CUNNINGHAM, CHARLES ERNEST, physics educator; b. Long Beach, Calif., May 26, 1964; s. Charles Owen and Mary Catherine Cunningham; m. Paula Lynn Shanklin, Sept. 6, 1986. BS in Physics, Harvey Mudd Coll., Claremont, Calif., 1986; MS in Physics, Stanford U., 1987, PhD in Physics, 1992. Tchg. asst. Stanford (Calif.) U., 1987-88, rsch. asst., 1986-92; postdoctoral rschr. Lawrence Livermore (Calif.) Nat. Lab., 1992-93, guest rschr., 1993-94; asst. prof. physics Grinnell (Iowa) Coll., 1993-2000, assoc. prof., 2000—, chmn. physics dept., 2002—. Vis. rschr. Iowa State U., 2000-01; vis. prof. Nanjing (China) U., 2004-05. Contbr. articles to profl. jours. Recipient Cottrell Coll. Sci. award Rsch. Corp., 1994-96, 2003-05; NSF fellow, 1986-89, Harris fellow, 1996-97. Mem. AAUP, Am. Phys. Soc., Am. Assn. Physics Tchrs., Coun. Undergrad. Rsch., Nat. Soc. Black Physicists, Sigma Xi. Office: Grinnell Coll Physics Dept Grinnell IA 50112

CUNNINGHAM, CHESTER GRANT, writer; b. Shelby, Nebr., Dec. 9, 1928; s. Merle B. and Hazel May Cunningham; m. Rose Marie Wilholt, Jan. 18, 1953; children: Gregory Merle, Scott Douglas, Chistine Ann. BA, Pacific Univ., Forest Grove, Oreg., 1950; MA, Columbia Univ., N.Y., 1954. Reporter News Times, Forest Grove, Oreg., 1950—51; city editor Evening Observer, La Grande, Oreg., 1953—54. Syndicated newspaper column 40 newspapers, 1961—81. Author: (novels) (308 books) 145 western, 20 hist. many action war, adventure and spy books. Organized, leader Writers Workshop, San Diego; organizer San Diego Book Awards. Sgt. FC U.S. Army, 1950—52, Korea. Recipient Writer of the Yr., SD Writers Monthly, 1995, Lola award, San Diego Libr., 2001. Achievements include sold first novel in 1968. Home and Office: 8431 Beaver Lake Dr San Diego CA 92119

CUNNINGHAM, COLLEEN LYNN, language educator; d. Robert F. and Patricia E. Cunningham. BA in Spanish & Bus., Wash. & Jefferson Coll., 2000. Cert. tchg. 2001. Tchr. Spanish West Allegheny HS, Imperial, Pa., 2001—.

CUNNINGHAM, ELDON LLOYD, artist, educator; b. Colby, Kans., Mar. 2, 1956; s. Gordon Keith and Annie (Gardner) C.; m. Allison Mary Cunningham, May 29, 1982; 1 child, Kevin Lloyd. BFA, Wichita State U., 1979; MFA, U. Colo., 1982. Grad. instr. U. Colo., Boulder, 1980—81; master printer Master Edits. Ltd., Englewood, Colo., 1982—84; instr. Univ. Without Walls-Laretto Hts. Coll., Denver, 1984; prof. art Met. State Coll., Denver, 1983—, chmn. dept. art, 1998—. Author: Printmaking: A Primary Form of Expression, 1992; dir., publ. (video) Nat. Printmaking Slide Video Exch., 1990; one-man shows include Wichita State U., 1995, U. Wyo., 1997, Laredo Coll., Tex, 2004. Mem. Coll. Art Assn., Mid.-Am. Print Coun. (pres. 1994-96, bd. dirs.), So. Graphics Coun. Mem. Ch. Brethren. Avocations: water gardening, beer brewing. Office: Met State Coll CB 59 PO Box 173362 Denver CO 80217-3362

CUNNINGHAM, FRANCIS, artist; b. NYC, Jan. 18, 1931; s. Francis de Lancey and Marcia (Davis) C.; m. Katharine Spalding, Sept. 18, 1954; children: Marcia, Katharine. AB, Harvard Coll., 1953; student, The Art Students League, 1955-59. Tchr. CCNY, 1962-65, Bklyn. Mus. Art Sch., 1962-80, The Art Students League N.Y., 1980-83; founder, co-dir. The New Bklyn. Sch. Life Drawing, Painting & Sculpture, 1980-83; founder, co-dir. N.Y. Acad. Art, 1983-85. One man shows include Waverly Gallery, N.Y.C., 1964, Harry Salpeter Gallery, N.Y.C., 1966, The Berkshire Mus., Pittsfield, Mass., 1969, Distelheim Galleries, Chgo., 1970, Michelson Gallery, Washington, 1971, Welles Gallery, Lenox, Mass., 1971, Hirschl & Adler Galleries, N.Y.C., 1967, 70, 75, New Bklyn. Sch. Life Drawing, Painting and Sculpture, N.Y.C., 1982, Danish Consulate, N.Y.C., 1987, Marsh Gallery U. Richmond, Va., 1989, Gallerihuset, Copenhagen, Denmark, 1995, First St. Gallery, N.Y.C., 1995, Pro Persona Gallery, Stockholm, Sweden, 1998, Laurel Tracey Gallery, 2000, 02, 03, 04; exhibited in group shows at Nat. Acad. Design, The Tel Aviv Museum of Art, 1999, Fedn. Modern Painters, N.Y.C., 2001, Art Students League of N.Y., 2001, Galerie Susanne Ho/Jriis, Copenhagen, Denmark, 2002, numerous others. Capt. USMCR, 1953-57. Recipient Purchase award Berkshire Mus., 1968, Peebles award, 1965, Benjamin West Clinedinst medal Exceptional Artistic Merit Artists' Fellowship, 2004; Louis Comfort Tiffany Found. grantee, 1973; artist in residence The Sense of Place, Manhattan, Kans., 1974; named Nat. Academician, Nat. Acad. Design, 1994; fellow, Bogliasco Found., 1997. Mem. Audubon Artists (bd. dirs. 1988—, Salmagundi award 1973, Minnie Stern award 1977, cert. of merit 1980, Joseph Raskin award 1985), Century Assn. Home and Office: 789 W End Ave New York NY 10025-5469

CUNNINGHAM, GARY H., lawyer; b. Grand Rapids, Mich., Jan. 11, 1953; s. Gordon H. and Marilyn J. (Lookabill) C.; children: Stephanie M., Gregory H. B.Gen. Studies, U. Mich., 1975, MA, 1977; JD, Detroit Coll. Law, 1980. Bar: Mich. 1980, U.S. Dist. Ct. Mich. 1983, U.S. Ct. Appeals (6th cir.) 1986, U.S. Ct. Appeals (Fed. cir.) 1990, U.S. Supreme Ct. 2004. Law clk. and estate adminstr. U.S. Bankruptcy Ct., Ea. Dist. Mich., Detroit, 1980-83; assoc./ptnr. Schlussel, Lifton, Simon, Rands, Galvin & Jackier, Southfield, Mich., 1983-90; ptnr./shareholder Kramer Mellen, P.C., Southfield, Mich., 1990-95; prin. shareholder Strobl Cunningham & Sharp, P.C., Bloomfield Hills, Mich., 1995—. Sr. staff mem. Detroit Coll. of Law Rev., 1978-80; contbr. articles to profl. jours. Mem. ABA (bus. law sect.), Fed. Bar Assn. (chmn. bankruptcy sect. 1989-91), Oakland County Bar Assn. (bus. law com.), State Bar of Mich. (mem. corp., fin. and bus. law sect.), Am. Bankruptcy Inst. (sponsor), Comml. Law League of Am., Detroit Econ. Club, Detroit Inst. Arts, Delta Theta Phi. Avocations: sailing, skiing, tennis. Home: 3399 Roxbury Dr Troy MI 48084-2613 Office: Strobl Cunningham & Sharp PC 300 E Long Lake Rd Ste 200 Bloomfield Hills MI 48304-2376 Office Phone: 248-540-2300. E-mail: gcunningham@stroblpc.com.

CUNNINGHAM, GORDON ROSS, finance company executive; b. Toronto, Nov. 15, 1944; s. Wendell Carson and Catherine Ann C.; m. Patricia Dorothy Westheuser, Dec. 22, 1966; children: Kristyn Catherine, Kaleigh Ann, James Gordon. BA, U. Toronto, 1966, LLB, 1969; LLD (hon.), U. Victoria, 1995. Bar: Ont. 1971. With Tory, Tory, DesLauriers & Binnington, Toronto, 1971-76; ptnr. Toronto, 1977-84; exec. v.p., COO Trilon Fin. Corp., Toronto, 1984-88, pres., COO, 1988-89, bd. dirs.; pres., CEO London Life Ins. Co. and London Ins. Group Inc., 1989-96; pres. Cumberland Asset Mgmt. Corp., 1997—. Pres., dir. Fairmoor Holdings Inc.; bd. dirs. Intertape Polymer Group, Inc., Allied Properties Real Estate Investment Trust. Former nat. corp. campaign chmn. Diabetes Can. Mem. Can. Bar Assn., Can. Life and Health Ins. Assn. (past chmn.), Upper Can. Law Soc., Rosedale Golf Club, Univ. Club, Devil's Glen Ski Club, Mad River Golf Club, Portmarnock Golf Club (Dublin), Ristigouche Salmon Club. Avocations: golf, squash, fishing, tennis, skiing. Office: Cumberland Asset Mgmt Corp M99 Yorkville Ave Toronto ON Canada M5R 3K5 Office Phone: 916-929-1090.

CUNNINGHAM, GUNTHER, professional football coach; m. Rene Cunningham; children: Natalie, Adam. BS in Gen. Sci., U. Oreg., 1969. Football coach U. Oreg., 1969-71, U. Kar., 1972, Stanford (Calif.) U., 1973-76, U. Calif., 1977-80; coach defensive line, linebackers CFL's Hamilton Tiger Cats, 1981; defensive line coach Balt. Colts, 1982-84; mentor defensive line San Diego Chargers, 1985-90; coach linebackers Oakland (Calif.) Raiders, 1991, defensive coord., 1992-93, defensive line, 1994; defensive coord. Kansas City (Mo.) Chiefs, 1995-98, head coach, 1999—2001, defensive coord., 2004—; coach linebackers Tenn. Titans, Nashville, 2002—04. Office: c/o Kansas City Chiefs One Arrowhead Dr Kansas City MO 64129

CUNNINGHAM, JACQUELINE LEMMÉ, psychologist, educator, researcher; b. Biddeford, Maine, Apr. 22, 1941; d. S. James and Alice (Fréchette) Lemmé; m. Seymour Cunningham II, Dec. 16, 1960 (dec. 1987); children: Macklin Todd, Danielle, Alyssa. BA in Psychology cum laude, U. Maine, Orono, 1963; MS in Psychology, U. South Ala., 1983; PhD in Ednl. Psychology, U. Tex., 1994. Tchr. Mobile (Ala.) Pub. Schs., 1976-81; psychology intern Devereux Found., Devon, Pa., 1988-89; fellow in developmental disabilities Children's Hosp. Harvard Med. Sch., Boston, 1990; prof. U. S.D., Vermillion, 1994-95; fellow in pediat. neuropsychology Children's Nat. Med. Ctr., George Washington U. Med. Ctr., Washington, 1995—97; psychologist pvt. practice, Wilmington, Del., 1997—2000, Children's Hosp. of Phila., Phila., 2000—. Cons. in field. Contbr. articles to profl. jours., chapters to books. Mem. Am. Psychol. Assn. (outstanding dissertation of yr. award 1994), Internat. Neuropsychol. Soc., Nat. Acad. Neuropsychology, Soc. History Behavioral Scis., Phila. Neuropsychology Soc. (bd. dirs. 1998-2002), Phi Kappa Phi. Avocations: travel, writing. Office: Children's Hosp of Phila 34th St & Civic Ctr Blvd Philadelphia PA 19104 Business E-Mail: cunningham@email.chop.edu.

CUNNINGHAM, JAMES BLAIR, former ambassador; b. Sept. 2, 1952; s. Blair Walter and Julia Katherine (Knowles) C.; m. Leslie Ann Genier, Aug. 9, 1975; children: Emma Julianne, Abigail Kathleen. B of Polit. Sci. and Psychology cum laude, Syracuse U., 1974. Staff asst. to the amb., polit. officer fgn. svc. U.S. Embassy, Stockholm, 1975-77; dep. Spanish affairs officer U.S. State Dept., Washington, 1977-79, sec. affairs, 1979-81; polit.-mil. affairs officer U.S. Embassy, Rome, 1981-85; U.S. mission NATO, 1985-88; dir. pvt. office of NATO sec. gen. Manfred Woerner Brussels, 1988-90; dep. polit. counselor U.S. mission to UN U.S. Dept. State, Washington, 1990-92, dep. dir. office of European security and polit. affairs, 1992-93, dir. office of European security and polit. affairs, 1993-95; dep. chief of mission U.S. Embassy, Rome, 1996—99; dep. U.S. rep., amb. to UN, N.Y.C., 1999—2004.

CUNNINGHAM, JAMES GERALD, JR., transportation company executive; b. Morristown, NJ, Aug. 5, 1930; s. James Gerald and Kathryn Virginia (Cannon) C.; m. Marilyn Swanson, Sept. 22, 1956; children: Kathleen, Jean Marie, Barbara, James Gerald, III, Carl. BS in Civil Engring, Newark Coll. Engring., 1952. Civil engr. Pa. R.R., 1952-54; trainmaster Erie-Lackawanna R.R., 1956-62; divsn. mgr., dir. transp. Consol. Freightways, Menlo Park, Calif., 1962-69; sr. v.p., dir. REA Express, Inc., N.Y.C., 1969-75; also dir. REA Holding Corp.; pres., dir. Gateway Transp. Co., La Crosse, Wis., 1976-78; gen. mgr. intermodal ops. Consol. Rail Corp., Phila., 1978-79; pres., CEO PTL Truck Line LLC, Phila., 1980—. Served with Transp. Corps AUS, 1953-55. Mem. Am. Trucking Assn. (chmn. met. planning orgn. task force, exec. com.), Equipment Interchange Assn. (exec. com., past pres.), Intermodal Transp. Assn. (exec. com., past pres.), Aronimink Country Club. Home: 3505 Saint Davids Rd Newtown Square PA 19073-1417 Office: PTL Truck Line LLC 320 King of Prussia Rd Radnor PA 19087 E-mail: msclpwr@netcarrier.com.

CUNNINGHAM, JANIS ANN, lawyer; b. Seattle, May 13, 1952; d. Luvern Victor and Anna Jane (Bierstedt) Rieke; m. D. John Cunningham, June 10, 1972; children: Emily Jane, Laura Christine. BS with honors, U. Wis., Milw., 1973; JD, U. Wash., 1976. Bar: Wash. 1976, U.S. Dist. Ct. (we. dist.) Wash. 1976, U.S. Ct. Appeals (9th cir.) 1976. Law clk. to Hon. Eugene A. Wright U.S. Ct. Appeals (9th cir.), Seattle, 1976-77; assoc. Karr, Tuttle, & Campbell, Seattle, 1977-84; ptnr. Karr, Tuttle, Koch, Campbell, Mawer & Sax, Seattle, 1984-89; ptnr., Personal Planning Area Perkins Coie LLP, Seattle, 1989—. Lectr. community property law U. Wash., Seattle, 1984, mem. estate planning coun. adv. bd., 1984-85. Co-author: Washington Practical Probate, 1982, 5th rev. edit., 1988; editor in chief U. Wash. Law Rev., 1975-76. Mem. estate plnning com. Am. Heart Assn., Seattle, 1978; bd. dirs. Community Services for the Blind, Seattle, 1977-79. Fellow Am. Coll. Trust and Estate Counsel; mem. Wash. State Bar Assn. (Real Property, Probate & Trust Section, exec. com. 1988-95, chmn. 1993-94), Seattle Estate Planning Coun., King County Bar Assn. (Real Property, Probate & Trust Section, pres 1986-87), Order of Coif. Republican. Lutheran. Avocations: family, hiking, canoeing. Office: Perkins Coie LLP 1201 3rd Ave Fl 40 Seattle WA 98101-3029 Office Phone: 206-583-8660. Office Fax: 206-359-9000. Business E-Mail: jcunningham@perkinscoie.com.

CUNNINGHAM, JESSIE JEROME, real estate investor, import/export company executive, entrepreneur, small business owner; b. Miami, Fla., Oct. 10, 1963; s. Jesse James and Racheal Mae Cunningham. Student, Morristown Coll., 1989—91, Knoxville Coll., 1992—93. CEO, founder Cunningham Family Enterprises and subs. The Midnight Mail Order Almanac Co., The Last Watch Ministry, Cunningham Ventures and Realty, Twilight Prime HDDT TV Motion Picture Studies of Burbank, Calif., Phila., 1993—. Author: (novels) The Flame of Silence Jones Book One/Ever Prevailing Enemy!, 2001, Insights for Our Days and Time, 2002, Trilogy of the Gods, 2002. Mem.: Internat. Traders, Soc. Seven Pillars, Phi Beta Lambda (Omega Lambda chpt.). Avocations: running, travel, painting, sculpting, acting. Office: PO Box 8016 Philadelphia PA 19101 Office Phone: 877-896-9723. Personal E-mail: jjc@cfe.net.

CUNNINGHAM, JOEL LUTHER, academic administrator; b. Mooresville, NC, Jan. 11, 1944; s. Elbert Claxton and Ruth Morton (Journey) Cunningham; m. Trudy Bender, June 12, 1965; children: Nancy Elizabeth, Susan Ruth. BA, U. Tenn., Chattanooga, 1965; MA, U. Oreg., 1967, PhD, 1969. Asst. prof. math. U. Ky., Lexington, 1969—74; dean continuing edn. U. Tenn., Chattanooga, 1974—79; acad. v.p. Susquehanna U., Selinsgrove, Pa., 1979—84, pres., 1984—2000; vice-chancellor, pres. U. South, Sewanee, Tenn., 2000—. Chmn. Nat. Assn. Coll. and U. Commn. Policy Analysts, 1996—98, with, 1998—99, 2002—; treas. Tenn. Ind. Coll. Assn., 2005—, Appalachian Coll. Assn., 2005—; trustee Assn. of Episcopal Coll., 2000—, chair, 2002—; bd. dirs. Sunbury (Pa.) Hosp., 1992—98; mem. nat. adv. com. Woodrow Wilson Fedn., 1995—; pres. Sunbury (Pa.) Hosp., 1998—2000, Coll. and U. Anglican Commn., 2001—, treas., 2002—; mem. St. Mary's Conf. Ctr., 2000—. Fellow Woodrow Wilson fellow, 1965, Am. Coun. on Edn. fellow, 1976—77. Mem.: Soc. for Values in Higher Edn. (bd. dirs. 1992—99, v.p. 1994—95, pres. 1995—99), Am. Assn. for Higher Edn., Math. Assn. Am., Am. Math. Soc., Sigma Chi (chmn. bd. leadership tng. 1977—87, treas. 1987—89, v.p. 1989—91, pres. 1991—93, Internat. Balfour award 1965), Sigma Xi. Episcopalian. Home: PO Box 3326 Sewanee TN 37375 Office: U South Office VC & Pres 735 University Ave Sewanee TN 37383 E-mail: jcunning@sewanee.edu.

CUNNINGHAM, JOHN RANDOLPH, project manager; b. Alexandria, La., July 17, 1954; s. John Adolphus and Zelma Audrey (Cox) C.; m. Teresa Ellen Toms, Jan. 22, 1977. BS in Computer Sci., La. Tech. U., 1976; masters cert. in project mgmt., George Washington U., 1999. Cert. project mgmt. profl. Customer support specialist South Ctrl. Bell Tel. Co., New Orleans, 1977-81; data comm. designer Weyerhaeuser, Tacoma, 1981-87, acct. rep., 1987-89, planning mgr., 1989-92, EDI project leader, 1992-2000, capacity planning mgr., 2001—; project mgr. Vision Compass, Inc., Seattle, 2000, Network Commerce, Seattle, 2000-01. Adv. bd. U. Wash., Seattle, 1989-94; spkr. fin. EDI confs. Contbr. articles to profl. jours. Vol. Big Bros., Tacoma, 1989—99, Wash. State First Responder, 1989—2000; instr. CPR, 1999—2000; instr. neighborhood emergency tng., 1999—2000; instr. emergency first aid, 2001—. Mem. NRA, Computer and Automated Systems Assn. (treas. 1991-95, pres. 1995-99), Project Mgmt. Inst., Indsl. Computing Soc.,

Instrument Soc. Am., Toastmasters Internat., Upsilon Pi Epsilon. Republican. Baptist. Home: 319 SW 328th St Federal Way WA 98023-5645 Business E-Mail: randy.cunningham@weyerhaeuser.com.

CUNNINGHAM, JOSEPH NEWTON, JR., cardiothoracic and vascular surgeon; b. Selma, Ala., Mar. 10, 1940; s. Joseph N. and Velma (Greenfield) C.; m. Bonnie Halper; children: Teri, Lori, Stephanie, Jessica, Gaynor, Joseph, Daniel. BS, U. Ala., 1962; MD, Med. Coll. Ala., 1966. Attending surgeon divsn. thoracic surgery NYU Med. Ctr., N.Y.C., 1974-82, Bellevue Hosp., N.Y.C., 1974-82, Manhattan VA Hosp., N.Y.C., 1974-82, Beekman-Downtown Hosp., N.Y.C., 1977-83, St. Vincent's Hosp. and Med. Ctr., N.Y.C., 1977-90; chmn. dept. surgery Maimonides Med. Ctr., Bklyn., 1982—, chief divsn. cardiothoracic surgery, 1982-88, 99—; attending surgeon dept. surg. svcs. Coney Island Hosp., Bklyn., 1982—, Bklyn. VA Hosp., 1982—, Kings County Hosp., Bklyn., 1985—; attending surgeon, dir. divsn. cardiothoracic surgery SUNY Health Sci. Ctr., Bklyn., 1985—. Contbr. numerous chpts. to textbooks in field. Rsch. fellow in surgery Parkland Meml. Hosp./U. Tex. Southwestern Med. Sch., Dallas, 1966-72; dir. Berg Lab. for Cardiothoracic Rsch. NYU Med. Ctr., N.Y.C., 1975-82; dir. lab. for surg. rsch. Edward Neimeth Inst. Med. Rsch. Maimonides Med. Ctr., 1982—. Grantee USPHS, 1966-72, NIH, 1981-84, 93-96, Maimonides Med. Ctr. R&D Found., 1990-93, 94-95, N.Y. Cardiac Ctr., 1993-96. Fellow ACS (mem. com. on applicants L.I. dist.), N.Y. Acad. Medicine; mem. Am. Heart Assn., Soc. Thoracic Surgeons, Am. Surg. Assn., Am. Coll. Chest surgeons, Am. Assn. Thoracic Surgery, Internat. Soc. Cardiovascular Surgery, Am. Soc. Artificial Internal Organs, N.Y. Acad. Scis., N.Y. Surg. Soc., N.Y. Cardiovascular Soc., N.Y. Cardiol. Soc., N.Y. Heart Assn. Coun. on Rsch., N.Y. Soc. Thoracic Surgery (pres. 1990), N.Y. Soc. Surgeons, Bklyn. Surg. Soc. (pres. 1989). Office: Cardiothoracic Surg Assoc 4802 10th Ave Brooklyn NY 11219-2844

CUNNINGHAM, JOYCE WENTWORTH, retired secondary school educator; b. Sanford, Maine, Aug. 29, 1930; d. Norman Lowd and Helen Martha (Dunnells) Wentworth; m. Ralph Clifford Cunningham, Feb. 6, 1954; children: Cynthia, Alan. BS in Edn., Gorham (Maine) State Tchrs. Coll., 1951. Cert. elem., secondary, occupl. English, and social studies tchr. Mass. Tchr. social studies City of Wallingford, Conn., 1951-54; tchr. English Town of Westboro, Mass., 1956-57; tchr. Town of Grafton, Mass., 1968-74, Assabet Valley Regional Vocat. Sch. Dist., Marlboro, Mass., 1974-90, lead tchr., 1978-90, tchr. bus. communications Assabet Valley Regional Vocat. High Sch., 1979-82, trainer, 1982-85; ret. Docent Willowbrook Mus. Village, Newfield, Maine, 2005—; dir. Christian edn. Bangor (Maine) Theol. Sem., 1999. Named Disting. Tchr. of the Yr.; recipient Horace Mann award, Commonwealth of Mass., 1986—87, 1987—88, Outstanding Instrnl. Materials for Profl. Devel. award, Am. Vocat. Assn. Mem.: NEA (life), PEO, Mass. Coun. Tchrs. English, New Eng. Assn. Tchrs. English. Methodist. Avocations: reading, decorative painting, golf, bridge. Home: PO Box 868 Acton ME 04001-0868 Personal E-mail: joycliffe@yahoo.com.

CUNNINGHAM, JUDY MARIE, lawyer; b. Durant, Okla., Sept. 7, 1944; d. Rowe Edwin and Margaret (Arnott) C. BA, U. Tex., 1967, JD, 1971; postgrad., Schiller Coll., Heidelberg, Fed. Republic Germany, 1976. Bar: Tex. 1972. Quizmaster U. Tex. Law Sch., Austin, 1969-71; rschr. Tex. Law Rev., Washington, 1970; staff atty. Tex. Legis. Coun., Austin, 1972-75; adminstrv. law judge, dir. sales tax div., assoc. counsel Comptr. of Pub. Accounts, Austin, 1975-85; owner, editor J.C. Law Publs., Austin, 1986—; pvt. practice Austin, 1986—. Author: (with others) Texas Tax Service, 1985; pub., editor, contbr. (newsletter) Tex. State Tax Update, 1986—; contbr. articles to Revenue Adminstrn.; assoc. editor Tex. Law Rev., 1968-71. State del. Dem. Party, Ft. Worth, 1990, county del., Austin, 1972, 88, 90, 92; vol. numerous Dem. campaigns, Austin, 1972-90. Mem. Industry Practitioners Liaison Group (comptr. pub. accts.), State Bar Tex. (taxation sect.), Austin (Tex.) Bar Assn. (bus. corp. and taxation sect.), Tex. Taxpayers and Rsch. Assn. Avocations: travel, cooking, reading mysteries, photography, swimming. Office: 4905 W Park Dr Austin TX 78731-5535 Office Phone: 512-459-3810. Personal E-mail: judymcunningham@earthlink.net.

CUNNINGHAM, JULIA WOOLFOLK, author; b. Spokane, Oct. 4, 1916; d. John George and Sue (Larabie) C. Grad., St. Anne's Sch., Charlottesville, Va., 1933. Author: (juveniles): The Vision of Francois the Fox, 1960, Dear Rat, 1961, Macaroon, 1962, Candle Tales, 1964, Dorp Dead, 1965 (Children's Spring Book Festival award), Violet, 1966, Onion Journey, 1967, Burnish Me Bright, 1970, Wings of the Morning, 1971, Far in the Day, 1972, The Treasure Is the Rose, 1973, Maybe, A Mole, 1974, Come to the Edge, 1977 (Christoper award 1978), Tuppenny, 1978, A Mouse called Junction, 1980, Flight of the Sparrow, 1980 (Commonwealth Club Calif. award, Honor Book award Boston Globe), The Silent Voice, 1981, Wolf Roland, 1983, Oaf, 1986, (with Betsy Hearne) Dorp Dead, 2002; (poetry) Shadow Heart, 1999, The Stable Rat and Other Christmas Poems, 2001, Cicada, 2001. Mem. Authors Guild. Home: Rancho Santa Barbara 333 Old Mill Rd Space 88 Santa Barbara CA 93110-4429

CUNNINGHAM, JULIAN ANTONIA, retired protective services official; b. Mobile, Ala., Oct. 24, 1954; s. Booker Telefaro Cunningham Jr. and Julia Aldonia Cunningham; 1 child, Tüvora Chanel Cook. Grad. h.s., Mobile. Salesman Treadwell Ford, Mobile, 1976, Al Trovinger Ford, Mobile, 1977; lt. Ala. Security Police & K9, Mobile, 1978—80; clk. U.S. Census Bur., Mobile, 1980; merchant civilian USN, Bayonne, NJ, 1985; ret. Radio operator, basic obedience trainer Mobile Ala. Security Police, 1979; chief usher Rock of Faith Bapt. Ch., 1998, trustee, 2001. With USNR, 1972—78. Democrat. Baptist. Avocations: dog training, horses. Home: 1150 Freeman St Mobile AL 36605

CUNNINGHAM, KEITH ALLEN, nuclear energy industry executive, accountant, lawyer, engineer; b. Weaver, W.Va., Aug. 21, 1922; s. James Arthur and Blanche (Proudfoot) C.; m. Jeanne Antoinette Viquesney, June 6, 1942; children: Keith Allen, Kathe Jan. BSBA, W.Va. U., 1948, JD, 1951. Bar: W.Va. 1951; CPA, Mich., Ohio, N.Y., Ind., La. Bldg. constrn. engr. Gibbs & Hills, Inc., N.Y.C., 1942-43; pvt. practice Belington, W.Va., 1952; assoc. Touche, Niven, Bailey & Smart, CPAs, Detroit, 1952-60; ptnr.-in-charge Dayton (Ohio) office Touche, Ross, Bailey & Smart, 1960-65, dir. adminstrn. and office ops., 1965-67, exec. adminstrv. ptnr., vice chmn. bd. dirs., 1967-70; pres. Energy Conversion Devices, Inc., Troy, Mich., 1969-72, dir., 1969-74; exec. v.p. United Nuclear Corp., Falls Church, Va., 1973-75, pres., CEO, 1975-84, chmn. bd., 1982-84, also dir. Chmn. bd., CEO Atlis Systems, Inc., Atlis Cons. Group, Atlis Fed. Svcs., Inc., Atlis Legal Info. Svcs., Inc., Atlis Micrographics Svcs., Inc., Atlis Pub. Svcs., Inc., 1984—; dir. Clevepak Corp.; chmn. bd. Atlis Corp.; lectr. W.Va. Tax Inst. Mem. Coun. for Reorgn. Ohio State Govt., 1963-64; treas. Mich. Employers Umployment Compensation Bur., 1957-60; mem. adv. com. Mich. Security Commn., 1958-60. Served with USAAF, 1943-46. Mem. AICPAs, Am. Acctg. Assn., Nat. Assn. Accts., Mich. Soc. CPAs, Ohio Soc. CPAs (dir.), N.Y. Soc. CPAs, N.J. Soc. CPAs, Mich. Bar Assn., W.Va. Bar Assn., Detroit Bar Assn., Mining Club (N.Y.C.), Detroit Athletic Club, Petroleum Club, Albuquerque Country Club, Congl. Country Club, Farmington Country Club (Charlottesville, Va.), Vero Beach Country Club, Phi Beta Kappa, Phi Delta Phi. Methodist. Home: 12208 Meadow Creek Ct Potomac MD 20854-1408 also: 653 Lake Dr Vero Beach FL 32963-2166 Office: 8728 Colesville Rd Silver Spring MD 20910-3918 E-mail: kac@atlis.com.

CUNNINGHAM, LEEANN, assistant prosecutor; b. Denville, NJ, Nov. 18, 1961; d. William Thomas and Patricia Carole Cunningham; m. Keith Henry Melofchik; children: Megan Patricia Melofchik, Carleigh Joan Melofchik. BA in Polit. Sci., Pa. State U., 1984; JD, Vt. Law Sch., 1987. Legal intern Hon. Donald G. Collester, Jr., and Hon. Herbert S. Friend, Morristown, NJ, 1986; legal intern, mem. ho. and senate judiciary coms. Legis. Coun. Vt. Legislature, Montpelier, 1987; jud. clk. Hon. Paul Bangiola, J.S.C., Morristown, 1987—88; litigating atty. James, Wyckoff, Vecchio & Pitman, Denville, NJ, 1988—90, Gebhardt & Kiefer, Clinton, NJ, 1991—94; atty. Law Office of LeeAnn Cunningham, Esq., Long Valley, NJ, 1994—2000; asst. prosecutor Warren County Prosecutor's Office, Belvidere, NJ, 2000—05, Essex County Prosecutor's Office, Newark, 2005—. Co-author: (legal treatise) New Jersey Practice, Family Law and Practice Section, 1999. Leader troop 518 Morris Area Girl Scouts, Long Valley, NJ, 2003—05; elder Long Valley Presbyn. Ch., 1998—2000. Mem.: Warren County Bar Assn., Nat. Dist. Attys. Assn., Lady Blue and Gold, Pa. State U. Alumni Assn. (life). Methodist. Avocations: hiking, skiing, tennis. Office: Essex County Prosecutor's Office 50 Wetmarket St Newark NJ 07102 Office Phone: 973-621-4560. Office Fax: 908-475-6350. E-mail: appeal@co.warren.nj.us.

CUNNINGHAM, LOUIS ERNEST, physician, cardiologist; b. Jackson, Tenn., May 7, 1951; s. LeRoy and Alice (Brown) C.; divorced; 1 child, Candance Nicole; divorced, 1 child, Avery Alice Cheatman Cunningham. BS cum laude, Lane Coll., 1973; MS, Ohio State U., 1974; MD, Meharry Med. Ctr., 1979. Diplomate Am. Bd. Internal Medicine. Intern Tulane, New Orleans, 1979-80, Hubbard Hosp., Nashville, 1980-81, instr., 1982-83, chief resident, 1982-83; asst. prof. medicine Meharry Med. Coll., Murfreesboro, Tenn., 1983; resident Harlem Hosp., N.Y.C., 1985-87; med. dir., owner Mid-South Heart Ctr., P.C., Jackson, Tenn., 1993—. Chmn. Am. Heart Assn., Jackson, Tenn., 1994; bd. trustees Lane Coll., Jackson, 1995—. Fellow Am. Coll. Cardiology; mem. AMA, Nat. Med. Assn., Tenn. Med. Assn., M.V. Lynk Med. Soc. (sec. 1995—), Alpha Phi Alpha. Avocations: jazz music, classical music, rhythm and blues music. Office: Mid South Heart Ctr PC 48 Medical Center Dr Jackson TN 38301-3947

CUNNINGHAM, MARY ELIZABETH (MARY CUNNINGHAM-LUSBY), physician; b. Newark, Apr. 21, 1931; d. William Rutherford and Mary Agnes Veronica (Harvey) C.; m. Perry Minor Lusby, Nov. 30, 1996. AB, Mount Holyoke Coll., 1953; MS, U. Ill., 1957; PhD, U. Oregon, 1964; MD, U. Conn., 1982. Diplomate Am. Bd. Emergency Medicine. Sr. physicist Lawrence Livermore Nat. Lab., Livermore, Calif., 1964-78; residency in emergency medicine Mich. State U. Affiliated Hosp., 1982—85, chief resident, 1984—85; sr. physician The Permanente Med. Group, Sacramento, 1985—96, ret., 1996, vol. physician, 1996—. Cons. emergency medicine King Faisal Specialist Hosp. and Rsch. Ctr., Jeddah, KSA, 2000-01. Contbr. articles to profl. jours. Physician Flying Samaritans-Mother Lode chpt., Sonoma, Calif., 1991—. Fellow Am. Coll. Emergency Physicians; mem. AMA (Calif. chpt.), CAL-ACEP, Am. Physical Soc., Calif. Med. Assn., N.Y. Acad. Scis., Phi Beta Kappa, Sigma Xi (grant-in-aid-of-rsch. award 1963-64). Roman Cath. Office: Kaiser Permanente Med Ctr 6600 Bruceville Rd Sacramento CA 95823-4671

CUNNINGHAM, MERCE, dancer; b. Centralia, Wash. Student, Cornish Sch.; PhD (hon.), U. Ill.; DFA (hon.), Wesleyan U., 1995. Own dance co., 1953—; tchr. Sch. Am. Ballet, 1948-51; propr. own dance sch. N.Y.C., 1959—. Dancer with company on world tour, 1964, S.Am. tour, 1968, numerous tours including U.S., Europe, Far East, Australia, South Am., others, choreographer The Seasons, 1947, Sixteen Dances for Soloist and Company of Three, 1951, Septet, 1953, Minutiae, 1954, Suite for Five, 1956, Nocturnes, 1956, Rune, 1959, Crises, 1960, Aeon, 1961, Story, 1963, Winterbranch, 1964, Variations V, 1965, How to Pass, Kick, Fall and Run, 1965, Place, 1966, Canfield, 1969, Tread, 1970, Second Hand, 1970, Signals, 1970, Landrover, 1972, Changing Steps, 1975, Solo, 1975, Un Jour ou Deux, 1973, Sounddance, 1975, Rebus, 1975, Torse, 1976, Squaregame, 1976, Travelogue, 1977, Inlets, 1977, Fractions, 1977, Exchange, 1978, Locale, 1979, Duets, 1980, Channels/Inserts, 1981, Trails, 1982, Quartet, 1982, Coast Zone, 1983, Roaratorio, 1983, Pictures, 1984, Doubles, 1984, Phrases, 1984, Native Green, 1985, Arcade, 1985, Points in Space, 1986, Fabrications, 1987, Shards, 1987, Five Stone Wind, 1988, Cargo X, 1989, August Pace, 1989, Polarity, 1990, Neighbors, 1991, Trackers, 1991, Beach Birds, 1991, Loosestrife, 1991, Change of Address, 1992, Touchbase, 1992, Enter, 1992, Doubletoss, 1993, CRWDSPCR, 1993, Ocean, 1994, Ground Level Overlay, 1995, Windows, 1995, Rondo, 1996, Installations, 1996, Scenario, 1997, Pond Way, 1998, BIPED, 1999, Interscape, 2000, Way Station, 2001, Loose Time, 2002, Fluid Canvas, 2002, Split Sides, 2003. Decorated Comdr. Order of Arts and Letters Legion of Honor France; recipient Gold medal, Internat. Festival Dance, 1966, Grand prix, Belgrade Internat. Theatre Festival, 1972, Creative Arts award, Brandeis U., 1973, Capezio award, 1977, Samuel H. Scripps/Am. Dance Festival award, 1982, Mayor's award of honor for arts and culture, N.Y.C., 1983, Kennedy Ctr. honors, 1985, Laurence Olivier award, 1985, Meadows award for Excellence in Arts, So. Meth. U., 1987, Nat. Medal of Arts, 1990, Digital Dance Premier award, 1990, Wexner prize, Wexner Ctr. for Arts, Columbus, Ohio, 1993, Golden Lion award, Venice Biennale, 1995, Nellie Cornish Arts Achievement award, Cornish Coll. of Arts, Seattle, 1996, Medal of Distinction, Barnard Coll., 1997, Grand Prix, SACD, France, 1997, Belknap award in Humanities, Princeton U., 1998, Key to City, Montpellier, France, 1999, Established Artists award, Bagley Wright Fund, Seattle, 1998, Isadora Duncan award for Lifetime Achievement in Dance, Nat. Dance Week, San Francisco, 1999, Premio Tani, Rome, 1999, Handel Medallion, N.Y.C., 1999, Nijinsky Spl. prize, Monaco, 2000, Dorothy and Lillian Gish prize, 2000; MacArthur Found. fellow, 1985. Mem.: Am. Acad. and Inst. Arts and Letters (hon.). Office: Cunningham Dance Found 55 Bethune St New York NY 10014-2010 Office Phone: 212-255-8240. E-mail: info@merce.org.

CUNNINGHAM, MICHAEL GERALD, composer, music educator; b. Warren, Mich., Aug. 5, 1937; s. Edmund John and Mary Ann (Etienne) C. MusB, Wayne State U., 1959; MusM, U. Mich., 1961; MusD, Ind. U., 1973. Accompanist, music dir. dance dept. Wayne State U., Detroit, 1961, 64-67, instr. music dept., 1967-69; teaching asst. Ind. U. Sch. Music, Bloomington, 1969-71; lectr. music theory U. Kans. Sch. Fine Arts, Lawrence, 1972; asst. prof. Conservatory Music, U. Pacific, Stockton, Calif., 1973; prof. music theory and composition U. Wis., Eau Claire, 1973—. Author: The Inner World of Traditional Theory, 1989, The Romantic Century, 2000, Progressive Bach, 2001, Divisional Counterpoint, 2004; composer: numerous compositions. With U.S. Army, 1962-63. Mem. ASCAP (ann. stipend 1969—), Wis. Alliance Composers, Sigma Alpha Iota. Office Phone: 715-836-4172. Business E-Mail: cunninmg@uwec.edu.

CUNNINGHAM, MILAMARI ANTOINELLA, anesthesiologist; b. Cody, Wyo., Oct. 4, 1949; d. Milo Leo and Mary Madeline (Haley) Olds; m. Michael Otis Webb, June 4, 1970 (div. Feb. 1971); m. James Kenneth Cunningham, June 14, 1975. BA with honors, U. Mo., 1971, MD, 1975. Diplomate Am. Bd. Anesthesiologists. Intern and resident U. Mo., Columbia, 1975-78; jr. ptnr. Anesthesiologist, Inc., 1979-82, ptnr., 1982-86; owner Cunningham Anesthesia, 1986—; dir. anesthesia dept. Ellis Fischel Cancer Ctr., 1991-92; acting chief anesthesia Harry S. Truman Meml. Vets. Hosp., 1994-95. Mem. med. staff Columbia Regional Hosp., U. Mo. Hosp. and Clinics, Columbia; mem. rev. com. Mo. Health Facilities, 2001—. Mem. editl. bd.: Mo. Medicine Jour., 2001. Active Mo. Med. Polit. Action Com., 1991-2000, Friends of Music, Friends of Libr., Boone County Fair, 1978-94, with ham breakfast divsn., 1978-85, with draft horse and mule show, 1986-88; Mo. bd. dirs. A Call to Serve, 1996-2004, program mgr., 2004. Fellowship Am. Coll. Anesthesiologists, 1977; named Lifetime Senator, World Nations Congress, 2003. Mem.: AMA (Physicians Recognition award 1978, 1985, 1987, 1991, 1995), Vis. Nurses Assn. (bd. dirs. 1982—89, chair 1984—86, adv. bd. 1989—93), Am. Soc. Anesthesiologists (alt. dir. dist. 17 2003, Mo. dist. dir. 2003—05), Mo. State Med. Assn. (commn. econs. third party payors 1986—89, chair 1989, Mo. health facilities rev. com. 2001—), Boone County Med. Soc. (membership chair 1982—84, alt. del. 1986, sec.-treas. 1996, bd. dirs. 1996—99, pres. 1998, del. various yrs. including 1996—2004), Mo. Soc. Anesthesiologists (v.p. 1986—87, pres. elect 1987—88, pres. 1988—89, del. 1989—98, spkr. ho. dels. 1992—2002, del. 2000, del 2000—02), Phi Beta Kappa. Home and Office: 8202 S Bennett Dr Columbia MO 65201-9178 E-mail: mila@tranquility.net.

CUNNINGHAM, NOËL B., law educator; b. 1944; BS, CCNY, 1967; MA, U. Conn., 1971, JD, 1974; LLM in Taxation, NYU, 1975. Bar: Conn. 1974, NY 1975. Instr. NYU Sch. Law, NYC, 1975-78, asst. prof., 1978-82, assoc. prof., 1982-86, prof. law, 1986—, dir. grad. tax program, 1988—95. Atty.-adviser US Dept. Treasury, 1980-82. Mem. Phi Kappa Phi. Office: NYU Sch Law Vanderbilt Hall Rm 430G 40 Washington Sq S New York NY 10012-1099 Office Phone: 212-998-6159. E-mail: nbc@juris.law.nyu.edu.*

CUNNINGHAM, PARIS LYNN, systems administrator, consultant; d. Harvey Edward Thomas and Doris Mercedes Cunningham; life ptnr. Richard Dale Stueven, Oct. 31, 1995. BS in Computer sci., U. Phoenix. Cert. Beer Judge Cert. Program, 2002. Mgr. global stds., database programmer Genentech, Inc, South San Francisco, Calif., 1983—96; sr. dba Am. Med. Security, Green Bay, Wis., 1999—2002; prin. cons. Oracle Corp, Iselin, NJ, 2002—. Alt. brewer Egan's Brewing, DePere, Wis., 1998—2001. Doll artist (create and sell collectible dolls) Mademoiselles Magnifiques. Mem.: Oracle Clin. Users Group (corr.). Libertarian. Home and Office: 3022 14th St Columbus NE 68601 Office Phone: 715-377-6205. Personal E-mail: paris@we7cats.com.

CUNNINGHAM, PATRICIA ANN CAHOY, band director, musician; d. Arnold Stephan Cahoy and Carolyn Ann Thiry; m. Gregg A. Cunningham, July 30, 1988. MusB Edn., U. No. Iowa, Cedar Falls, Iowa, 1980; MusM, Boston U., Boston, Mass., 1997. Band dir. Allamakee Cmty. Sch., Waukon, Iowa, 1981—81, Ventura Cmty. Sch., Ventura, Iowa, 1981—83, Ctrl. City Cmty. Sch., Central City, Iowa, 1983—85, Merrimack Cmty. Sch., Merrimack, NH, 1986—. Prin. clarinetist N.H. Philharm. Orch., Manchester, NH, 1985—; clarinetist New Eng. Wind Symphony, Manchester, NH, 1985—, New Eng. Symphony Orch., North Conway, NH, 1998—, Granite State Symphony, Concord, NH, 2000—02, Gt. Waters Music Festival Orch., Wolfeboro, NH, 1999—, North End Marching Band, Boston, 2001—. Musician: (featured soloist) North Iowa Wind Ensemble, N.H. Philharmonic Orch. Music merit badge advisor Boy Scouts, Nashua, NH, 1990; sec. N.H. Philharm. Orch., Manchester, NH, 1987—95. Scholar Meritorious Performer, Boston U., 1996. Mem.: NEA (assoc.), Merrimack Teachers' Assn. (assoc.), N.H. Music Educators' Assn., Internat. Clarinet Assn. (assoc.), Nat. Band Assn. (assoc.), Iowa Bandmasters' Assn. (assoc.), Pi Kappa Lambda (assoc.). Achievements include Merrimack High School Band receives top ratings at competitions. Avocations: travel, gardening, tennis. Office: Merrimack H S 38 McElwain St Merrimack NH 03054 Business E-Mail: patricia.cunningham@merrimack.k12.nh.us.

CUNNINGHAM, PAUL GEORGE, minister; b. Chgo., Aug. 27, 1937; s. Paul George Sr. and Naomi Pearl (Anderson) C.; m. Constance Ruth Seaman, May 27, 1960; children: Lori, Paul, Connie Jo. BA, Olivet Nazarene U., 1960; BDiv., Nazarene Theol. Sem., 1964; DD, Mid Am. Nazarene Coll., 1975. Sr. pastor Coll. Ch. of the Nazarene, Olathe, Kans., 1964-93; gen. supt. Internat. Ch. of the Nazarene, 1993—. Adv. bd. Kansas City Dist. Ch. of the Nazarene, Overland Park, Kans., 1971-93; trustee Mid Am. Nazarene Coll., Olathe, 1971—; chmn. book com. Nazarene Pub. House, Kansas City, Mo., 1974-90; pres. gen. bd. Internat. Ch. of the Nazarene, Kansas City, 1985-93. Police chaplain Olathe (Kans.) Police Dept., 1975-93; adv. bd. Good Samaritan Ctr., Olathe, 1990—. Recipient Disting. Svc. award Jaycees, Olathe, 1967, Paul Harris fellow Rotary Internat., Olathe, 1989. Mem. Nat. Assn. Evangs., Rotary. Mem. Ch. Of The Nazarene. Home: 12543 S Hagan Ln Olathe KS 66062-6075 Office: Ch of the Nazarene 6401 Paseo Blvd Kansas City MO 64131-1213 Business E-Mail: pcunningham@nazarene.org.

CUNNINGHAM, RANDY, congressman; b. LA, Dec. 8, 1941; m. Nancy Jones; children: Todd, April, Carrie. BA, MA, U. Mo., 1967; MBA, Nat. U. Lt. commander U.S. Navy, 1966—68; mem. U.S. Congress from 50th (formerly 44th) Calif. dist., 1991—; mem. intelligence com.; mem. appropriations com. Flight instr. Top Gun Prog., Miramar Naval Air Station; founder Top Gun Enterprises, 1987—; dean Sch. Aviation, Nat. U., 1988—89. Commdg. officer USN, 1966—87. Republican. Office: US Ho Reps 2350 Rayburn Ho Office Bldg Washington DC 20515-0551

CUNNINGHAM, ROBERT JAMES, lawyer; b. Kearney, Nebr., June 27, 1942; m. Sara Jean Dickson, July 22, 1967. BA, U. Nebr., 1964; JD, NYU, 1967, LLM in Taxation, 1969. Bar: N.Y. 1967, Ill. 1969, U.S. Dist. Ct. (no. dist.) Ill. 1969, U.S. Ct. Claims 1970, U.S. Tax Ct. 1970, U.S. Ct. Appeals (D.C. cir.) 1972, U.S. Ct. Appeals (9th cir.) 1975, U.S. Ct. Appeals (7th cir.) 1979, U.S. Ct. Appeals (fed. cir.) 1982. Instr. law NYU, N.Y.C., 1967-69; assoc. Baker & McKenzie LLP, Chgo., 1969-74, ptnr., 1974—. Spkr. in field. Contbr. articles to profl. jours. Mem. ABA, Ill. Bar Assn., Chgo. Bar Assn. Office: Baker & McKenzie LLP One Prudential Plz 130 E Randolph Dr Ste 3900 Chicago IL 60601-6342 Office Phone: 312-861-2931. E-mail: robert.j.cunningham@bakernet.com.

CUNNINGHAM, ROBERT JOSEPH, bishop; b. Buffalo, N.Y., June 18, 1943; Ordained priest Buffalo, N.Y. Bishop Diocese of Ogdensburg, NY, 2004—. Office: Diocese of Ogdensburg PO Box 369 622 Washington St Ogdensburg NY 13669-0369

CUNNINGHAM, ROBERT L., JR., lawyer; b. Charlotte, NC, 1947; Student, Université de Montpellier, France, 1967—68; BA cum laude, Davidson Coll., 1969; JD, Columbia Univ., 1972. Bar: NY 1973. Ptnr., co-chair, lending/structured fin. practice worldwide/Asia Jones Day, NYC. Mem., Latin Am. practice Jones Day, mem., energy practice. Fluent in French. Office: Jones Day 222 E 41st St New York NY 10017-6702 Office Fax: 212-755-7306. Business E-Mail: rcunningham@jonesday.com.

CUNNINGHAM, RONNIE WALTER, venture capitalist; b. Creston, Iowa, Mar. 16, 1932; s. Walter Wilfred and Gladys (Backen) C.; m. Dorothy League, Dec. 27, 1997; children: Brian Keith, Kimberly Ann. BS in Physics, UCLA, 1960, MA, 1961; advanced mgmt. program, Harvard Grad. Sch. Bus., 1974. Rsch. asst. Planning Rsch. Corp., Westwood, Calif., 1959-60; physicist RAND Corp., Santa Monica, Calif., 1960-64; astronaut NASA, 1964-71; crew member of first manned Apollo spacecraft Apollo 7; chief, Skylab br., 1968-71; sr. v.p. Century Devel., 1971-74; pres. Hydrotech Devel. Co., Houston, 1974-76; sr. v.p. 3D/Internat., Houston, 1976-79; founder The Capital Group, Houston, 1979-86; mng. ptnr. Genesis Fund, 1986-98. Bd. dirs. numerous tech. based cos.; mem. adv. bd. Nat. Renewable Energy Lab.; lectr. in field. Author: The All American Boys, 1977; host radio talk show Lift-Off to Logic, 1998—. Judge Rolex awards for enterprise, 1984. With USNR, 1951-52, fighter pilot USMCR, 1952-74, col. ret. Recipient NASA Exceptional Service medal, also; Haley Astronautics award; Profl. Achievement award UCLA Alumni, 1969; Spl. Trustee award Nat. Acad. Television Arts and Scis., 1969; medal of valor Am. Legion, 1975; Outstanding Am. award Am. Conservative Union, 1975, George Haddaway award, 2000; named to Internat. Space Hall of Fame, Houston Hall of Fame, Astronaut Hall of Fame, 1997. Fellow Am. Astronautical Soc.; mem. Soc. Exptl. Test Pilots, Am. Inst. Aeros. and Astronautics, Assn. Space Explorers-U.S.A., Am. Geophys. Union, Sigma Pi Sigma. Office: 2425 West Loop S Ste 200 Houston TX 77027-4207

CUNNINGHAM, SONIA MICHELLE, personnel director; d. Ulysses and Cora Burnside Cunningham; 1 child, Bryant Scott Cheek Jr. BA, Clemson U., 1991, M in Secondary Edn., 1993; MA, U. SC, 1997; D in Ednl. Adminstrn., SC State U., 2004. Cert. sch. supt. Tchr. English Laurens (SC) Dist. 55 HS, 1991—99, Greenville (SC) County Schs., 1999—2002, asst. prin., curriculum coord., 2002—04; dir. pers. svcs. Anderson (SC) Sch. Dist. 5, 2004—. Ray A. Croc scholar, 1988, Literacy grantee, Laurens County Literacy Assn., 1995, 1997. Mem.: ASCD, SC Assn. Sch. Administrators, Delta Sigma Theta (life). Home: 104 Bonaire Pointe Anderson SC 29621 Office: Anderson Sch Dist 5 400 Pearman Dairy Rd Anderson SC 29625

CUNNINGHAM, STACY R., music educator; d. Rosemary J. Cunningham. BA in Music Edn., North Ctrl. Coll., 2001. Tchr. Plainfield HS, Ill., 2001—02, Leyden HS, Franklin Park, Ill., 2002—. Dir. music Queen of Peace HS,

Burbank, Ill., 2004—. Mem.: IAJE (assoc.), Ill. Music Educator Assn. (assoc.; vocal jazz chair (dist. 1) 2004—05), Am. Choral Dirs. Assn. (assoc.). Greek Orthodox. Home: 2815 W 91 St Evergreen Park IL 60805 Personal E-mail: iteachsinging@hotmail.com.

CUNNINGHAM, STANLEY LLOYD, lawyer; b. Durant, Okla., Feb. 7, 1938; s. Stanley Ryan and Hazel Dell (Dillingham) C.; m. Suzanne Yerger, Sept. 18, 1960; children: Stanley William, Ryan Yerger. BS in Geology, U. Okla., 1960, LLB, 1963. Bar: U.S. Dist. Ct. (we. dist.) Okla. 1963; U.S. Ct. Appeals (10th cir.) 1965; U.S. Supreme Ct. Okla. 1963. Atty. Phillips Petroleum Co., Oklahoma City, 1963-64, Bartlesville, Okla., 1964-71; counsel McAfee, Taft, et al., Oklahoma City, 1971—. Lectr. U. Okla. Coll. Law, Norman, 1977, 79, S.W. Legal Found., Dallas, 1986, 89. Contbr. articles to profl. jours. Layreader All Souls' Episcopal Ch., Oklahoma City, 1972-75. 1st lt. USAFR, 1963-72. Harry J. Brown scholar, U. Okla., 1960—63. Mem. ABA, Fed. Energy Bar Assn., Am. Soc. Internat. Law, Geological Soc. Am., Alumni Adv. Coun., U. Okla. Assoc., Oklahoma City Golf & Country Club, Order of Coif, Phi Alpha Delta, Sigma Gamma Epsilon. Republican. Episcopalian. Avocations: golf, reading. Office: McAfee & Taft 2 Leadership Sq Fl 10 Oklahoma City OK 73102 Office Phone: 405-235-9621.

CUNNINGHAM, SUE J., artist; b. Newton, Ill., Oct. 19, 1932; d. Harvey Eugene and Shirley Hazel Huddlestun; m. William Dean Cunningham (dec.); 1 child, Steven Dean. Student, So. Ill. U., 1958—60, Millikin U., 1961—. Free-lance newspaper illustrator, Decatur, Ill., 1967—80; free-lance watercolorist, 1981—. Ofcl. artist USCG, 1985—. Just What You've Always Wanted... Another Cookbook, 1977, Just in Case You Need... Another Cookbook, 1981, one-woman shows include Carl Sandburg Coll., Galesburg, Ill., 1984, Jeffrey's Gallery, Springfield, Ill., 1985, Paris Art Ctr., Ill., 1986, Garden Club Decatur, 1988, exhibited in group shows at Millikin U., Decatur, 1984, Ariz. Artists Alliance, Phoenix, 1991, exhibitions include Ky. Mus. Art, Owensboro, 1982, Ind. Mus. Arts, Evansville, 1983, Herbert Georg Profl. Art Gallery, Springfield, Ill., 1984, Am. Acad. Art, N.Y.C., 1984, U. Ky. Art Mus., Lexington, 1984, Tarble Arts Ctr, Charleston, Ill., 1985, Intarent. Trade Mart, New Orleans, 1985, Ind. Mus. Arts and Sci., 1986, 1992, Okla. Art Ctr., Oklahoma City, 1986, Mo. Mus. Art, Springfield, 1987, Sheldon Swope Art Mus., Terre Haute, Ind., 1988, Mo. Athletic Club, St. Louis, 1988, Firehouse Gallery, Springfield, Ill., 1990, Springfield Art Assn., Ill., 1991, numerous others, Represented in permanent collections Acton Acton Meyer and Smith, Danville, Ill, Blank, Wasselink and Cook Assocs., Decatur, Bristol-Myers Co., Evansville, Comfort Inns, First Nat. Bank, Mattoon, Ill, Herald and Rev. Newspaper, Decatur, Hillside Acad., Ill., Mead Johnson and Co., Evansville, Mut. Home and Savings, Decatur, Quaker Oats Co., Danville, Roland and Co., Tom Lange Co., Inc., Springfield, Ill., U.S. Coast Guard, Washington, V.A. Kibler Assocs., Newton, Craig and Craig Law Offices, Mattoon; featured artist, author The Watercolor Page, Am. Artist Mag., 1986. Recipient Merit award, Mid-Am. Biennial, Ky. Mus. Art, 1982, Award of Excellence, St. Louis Art Affair, 1985, Merit award, Watercolor Ill., Ea. Ill. U., 1985, 1987, 1987, St. Louis Artists Guild, 1986, 1987. Mem.: St. Louis Artists Guild (mem. art sect.), Barn Colony Artists, Nat. Mus. Women in Arts (charter), Nat Watercolor Soc. (regional rep. 1987—91), Am. Watercolor Soc. (assoc.), Ky. Watercolor Soc. (assoc.). Methodist. Avocations: writing, golf, dance, hiking, birdwatching, sports. Home: 112 Manchester Dr Decatur IL 62526

CUNNINGHAM, SUSAN KATHRYN, secondary school educator; b. Oak Ridge, Tenn., Oct. 3, 1954; d. George Wilmot and Inez Kathryn (Williams) Smith; m. John Alan Cunningham, Aug. 6, 1977; children: Jodi Megan, Bradyn Alan. Student, U. San Francisco, 1972; BSEd in Art, Ohio U., 1976, M in Elem. Edn., 1992. Tchr. art Laurelville and Salt Creek Elem. Schs., Circleville, Ohio, 1976-84, McDowell Exch. Sch., Circleville, 1984-93, Logan Elm H.S., Circleville, 1993-99; art tchr. Smith and Mount Logan Mid. Schs., Chillicothe Sch. Sys., 1999—2001, Chillicothe H.S., 1999—; chair dept. art Chillicothe City Schs., 1999—. Mem. art and environ. com. St. Peters Ch., Chillicothe, Ohio, 1982—; mem. bd. edn. Bishop Flaget Sch., Chillicothe, 1987-91; chmn. art dept. Logan Elm Sch. Dist., 1990—. Author, artist: (children's book) Adventures of Simba, 1977; artist: Eat Right Day and Night, 2002; artist: Bookworm game boards, 1995, 96. Mem., artist Jr. Civic League, Chillicothe, 1990-97; liturgical artist St. Peters Ch., Chillicothe, 1982—. Grantee Martha Holden Jennings, Logan Elm H.s., 1990, McDowell Exch. Sch., 1989, Ohio State Grant and Laurelville Salt Creek Elem., 1977. Mem. Nat. Art Edn. Assn., Ohio Edn. Assn., Ohio Art Edn. Assn., Ohio Crafts Coun., Logan Elm Classroom Tchrs. Assn., Chillocothe Edn. Assn. (bldg. rep. 2004). Democrat. Roman Catholic. Avocations: painting, drawing, piano, gardening, papermaking. Home: 49 Rookwood Dr Chillicothe OH 45601-3085 Office: Chillicothe HS 381 Yoctangee Pky Chillicothe OH 45601

CUNNINGHAM, TERENCE THOMAS, III, hospital administrator; b. Bell, Calif. BS in Microbiology, Calif. State U., Long Beach; MA in Hosp. Adminstrn., George Washington U., Washington, 1974. Commd. 2d lt. USAF, advanced through grades to col., 1989; adminstrv. resident MacDill Hosp., Tampa, Fla., 1973-74; adminstr. Rhein-Main Clinic, Frankfurt, Germany, 1974-79; hosp. cons. Air Force Med. Inspection Ctr., San Bernardino, Calif., 1979-81; CFO David Grant Med. Ctr., Fairfield, Calif., 1981-82; CEO Torrejon Hosp., Madrid, 1982-85; COO, CFO and materials officer Office Command Surgeon, Hdqrs. Mil. Airlift Command, Bellville, Ill., 1985-87; CEO Wright Patterson Med. Ctr., Dayton, Ohio, 1987-92; adminstr. Wilford Hall Med. Ctr., San Antonio, 1992-94; v.p. adminstrn. Johns Hopkins Hosp., Balt., 1994-2000; pres. Ben Taub Gen. Hosp., Houston, 2000—. Instr. grad. program health care adminstrn. Chapman Coll., Calif., 1981-82; preceptor grad. students in hosp. and health care adminstrn. Xavier U., Cin., 1987—, Baylor U., San Antonio, 1988—, George Washington U., Washington, 1995—, Johns Hopkins U., Balt., 1995—; asst. clin. prof. Wright State U. Sch. Medicine, Dayton, Ohio, 1990—; assoc. prof. Dept. Health Policy and Mgmt. Johns Hopkins U. Sch. Pub. Health and Hygiene; clin. instr. Baylor Coll. Medicine, 2001; adj. prof. Grad. Sch. Mgmt., Rice U., Houston, 2003—; cons. Surgeon Gen. USAF, 1986—. Book reviewer Hosps. and Health Svcs. Adminstrn., Jour. Quality Assurance, Mil. Medicine; mem. editl. bd. Frontiers of Health Svcs. Mgmt., Health Adminstrn. Press. Bd. dirs. Am. Red Cross, Houston. Fellow Am. Coll. Healthcare Execs. (various coms., regent to U.S. Air Force); mem. Ohio Hosp. Assn. (chmn. accreditation com.), Greater Dayton Area Hosp. Assn. (bd. dirs.), Tex. Hosp. Assn. (mem. edn. com., Disaster Readiness Task Force), Assn. Mil. Surgeons U.S. (Young Fed. Healthcare Adminstr. of Yr. 1983, Fed. Healthcare Adminstr. of Yr. 1989, Sr. Fed. Healthcare Adminstr. of Yr. 1992), Interagy. Inst. Fed. Health Care Alumni Assn. Avocations: bicycling, photography, sailing, reading. Address: 1919 Spann St Houston TX 77019

CUNNINGHAM, TESS, marketing professional; b. Milw., May 5, 1949; d. Andrew Michael and Marie Magdalene (Fuchs) Weber; m. John B. Cunningham, Sept. 12, 1970 (div.); children: Misty, Jordan, Lauren. Student, Chattanooga State U. Art cons., divsn. mgr. CI Internat. and Regency Galleries, Athens, 1982-89; sales assoc., pub. rels. mgr., fin. mgr. Heyward Allen Motor Co., Athens, 1987-91; telemarketing assoc., cons. Dial Am., Athens, 1994-95; owner mktg., media and pub. rels. cons. Tess Cunningham Cons., Atlanta, 1993—; dir. mktg., owner Paradigm Racing, Atlanta, 1995—. Dir. mktg. Visual Comms., Atlanta, 1998—; pub. rels. cons. Pineapple Pub. Rels., Atlanta, 1998-99; owner Paradigm Mktg., 1999—. Facilitator planning com. Athens-Clarke Tomorrow, Athens, 1993; art com., co-chair Athens Internat. Art Festival, Athens, 1994; v.p. Forging New Tomorrows, Atlanta, 1994-98—; bd. dirs., com. chmn. Alliance Theatre Guild, 1995—; mem. steering com. Earth Keepers; bd. dirs. Illian Adoption, Inc. Mem. NATAS, Women of the So. Region (mktg. and fund raising cons. 1998), Cystic Fibrosis Found., AIDS Walk Atlanta, Freedom Found. of Valley Forge. Avocations: stained glass, boating, racing, hiking, movies. Home and Office: 132 Shadybrook Dr Athens GA 30605-2416

CUNNINGHAM, TOM ALAN, lawyer; b. Houston, Nov. 5, 1946; s. Warren Peek and Ellen Ardelle (Benner) Cunningham; m. Jeanne Adrienne Moran, July 21, 1972; 1 child, Christopher Alan. BA, U. Tex., 1968, JD, 1974. Bar: Tex. 1974, U.S. Dist. Ct. (so. dist.) Tex. 1976, U.S. Dist. Ct. (no. dist.) Tex. 1982, U.S. Dist. Ct. (we. dist.) Tex. 1984, U.S. Ct. Appeals (5th and 11th cirs.) 1981, U.S. Ct. Appeals (8th cir.) 1919. Ptnr. Fulbright & Jaworski L.L.P., Houston, 1974—98; founding ptnr. Cunningham, Welsh, Darlow, Zook & Chapoton, L.L.P., Houston, 1998—. Bd. trustee Children's Charity Fund, Houston, 1983—88; active South Tex. Ctr. Legal Responsibility; mem. exec. com., bd. dirs. Assn. for Cmty. TV. Lt. (j.g.) USNR, 1969—72. Fellow: Houston Bar Found., Tex. Trial Lawyers Assn., Am. Coll. Trial Lawyers, Am. Bd. Trial Advs., Tex. Bar Found. (life; chmn. bd. trustees, adv. bd., chair 1995—, chair bd. trustees 1995—, chair Lola Wright com., adv. bd., new fellows com., awards com., pub. com., bd. dirs., ct. ruels com.), Am. Bar Found.; mem.: CPR Inst. for Dispute Resolution, Resolution Forum, Inc. (pres.), Tex. Empowerment Network (bd. dirs.), Tex. Ctr. Legal Ethics and Professionalism, Tex. Assn. Def. Counsel, Tex. Bd. Legal Specialization, State Bar Tex. (chmn. spl. com. on lawyer adt. and solicitation 1982, chmn. dist.4H grievance com. 1982—88, bd. dirs. 1989—92, chair bd. dirs. exec. com. 1991—92, chair com. for lawyer discipline 1992—94, chair gen. counsel adv. com., exec. com., ct. rules com., Pres.'s award 1983, Pres.'s citation for meritorious svc. 1991, Pres.'s spl. recognition for meritorious svc. 1993, 1994, nominee Outstanding Young Lawyer 1981), Houston Bar Assn. (professionalism com., chmn. constn. bicentennial com., arbitration com., membership com., Pres.'s award 1988), Am. Arbitration Assn. (panel of arbitrators), ABA (arbitration com. 1995—, litigation sect., discovery com., forum com. constrn. industry, alternate dispute resolution com.), Lakeside Country Club, Coronado Club, Houston Club, Phi Delta Phi. Home: 10811 Pine Bayou St Houston TX 77024-3018 Office Phone: 713-255-5500. Business E-Mail: tcunningham@cdzc.u.com.

CUNNINGHAM, WARD (HOWARD G. CUNNINGHAM), application developer; b. May 26, 1949; m. Karen Cunningham; 2 children. BS in Interdisciplinary Engring., MS in Computer Sci., Purdue Univ. Prin. engr. Tektronix Rsch. Lab.; dir., rsch., devel. Wyatt Software; founder Cunningham & Cunningham, Portland, Oreg.; and architect, Platform Architecture Group Microsoft Corp., Redmond, Wash., 2003—. Founding mem. Hillside Group, Inc., 1993—. Co-author (with Bo Leuf): The Wiki Way: Quick Collaboration on the Web, 2001. Achievements include development of of WikiWiki concept, 1995 ("Wiki" means quick in Hawaiian); of software devel. methodology: Extreme Programming; and holder of several patents. Office: Cunningham & Cunningham Ste 4 7830 SW 4th Ave Portland OR 97219 also: Platform Architect Group Microsoft Corp One Microsoft Way Redmond WA 98052 Office Phone: 503-245-5633. Business E-Mail: ward@c2.com.*

CUNNINGHAM, WILLIAM FRANCIS, JR., literature and language professor, academic administrator; b. Holyoke, Mass., Feb. 9, 1931; s. William Francis and Constance Emma (Cox) C.; m. Eleanor Mary Bissonette, Dec. 27, 1956; children— Margaret Ann, William John, Mary Elizabeth. AB, Holy Cross Coll., 1954; MA, Boston Coll., 1956; PhD, U. Pitts., 1961; DHL honoris causa, Le Moyne Coll., 1994. Asst. prof. English, Duquesne U., 1955-63; prof. Le Moyne Coll., 1963-78; prof. English Creighton U., 1978—, dean Coll. Arts and Scis., 1978-87, acting v.p. for acad. affairs, 1986-87, v.p. acad. affairs, 1987-93, spl. asst. to pres., 1993-96; dean emeritus, 1994—; ret., 1997. Danforth assoc., 1974—. Contbr. articles on 18th-century Brit. lit. to profl. jours. Mem. Coll. Bd. (coun. on coll.-level svcs., exec. com. Midwestern regional assembly 1980-84), Am. Soc. 18th-century Studies.

CUNNINGHAM, WILLIAM HENRY, retired food products executive; b. Oxnard, Calif., Dec. 2, 1930; s. William Henry and Carrie Edna (Wilson) C.; m. Carmen Nelson Alden, Jan. 19, 1957; children: Nelson, Clifford, Cynthia. BA, U. Calif., Santa Barbara, 1952; B of Foreign Trade, Am Grad. Sch. Internat. Mgmt., 1958. With Colgate-Palmolive Internat., N.Y. and Colombia, El Salvador, 1958-63; mktg. cons. Anderson, Clayton Co., Mexico City, Buenos Aires and Lima, 1963-66; mgr. consumer divsn. Cyanamid, Buenos Aires, 1966-69; dir. mktg. and sales Alimentos Kraft, Caracas, Venezuela, 1969-74; gen. mgr. Panama and Cen. Am. Panama and Ctrl. Am. Kraft Foods, Inc., 1974-80; pres. Alimentos Kraft Alimentos Kraft Foods, Inc., Venezuela, 1980-86; v.p., dir. Kraft Foods, Inc. Kraft Gen. Foods, Walt Disney World, Fla., 1986-92. V.p., dir. The Land, Epcot Ctr., Walt Disney World, Fla. Stewareship chmn. St. Lukes Meth. Ch., Windermere, Fla., 1991-92; vol. Inter Exec. Svc. Corp. for assignment in L.Am. to help local industry, 1993, assignment to Bogota Colombia, 1994, Ctrl. Russia, 1996; vol. Second Helping; Spanish transl. Free Clinic, Deep Well; pres. Hosp. Aux., Hilton Head, S.C. 2002-03. Recipient Tribute Appreciation award U.S. State Dept., 1980, Order of Vasco Nunez de Balboa, Govt. Panama, 1980, First Class Work Merit award Govt. Venezuela, 1985, Jonas Mayer Disting. Alumni award Thunderbird Grad. Sch. for Internat. Mgmt., 1997, Citizen's Honor award Hilton Head. Mem. Am. C. of C. (pres., founder Panama City chpt. 1979, sec. Caracas 1986), Am. Soc. (pres. Panama City chpt. 1977), Walt Disney World Participant Assn. (pres. 1990-91), U. Calif. Alumni Assn. (bd. dirs. Santa Barbara 1992-98, chair awards, nominated Lifetime Achievement award 2004), Bear Creek Golf Club, Hilton Head. Democrat. Methodist. Avocations: golf, tennis. Home: 11 Bear Creek Dr Hilton Head Island SC 29926-1904 Personal E-mail: CarmenAC@adephia.net.

CUNNINGHAM, WILLIAM HUGHES, retired academic administrator, marketing professional, educator; b. Detroit, Jan. 5, 1944; married; 1 child BA, Mich. State U., 1966, MBA, 1967, PhD, 1971, LLD (hon.), 1993. Mem. faculty U. Tex., Austin, 1971—, assoc. prof. mktg., 1973-79, prof., 1979—, assoc. dean grad. programs, 1976-82, Foley/Sanger Harris prof. retail merchandising, 1982-83, acting dean Coll. Bus. Adminstrn. and Grad. Sch. Bus., 1982-83, dean, 1983-85, pres., 1985-92, Centennial Chair Bus. Edn. Leadership, 1983-85, Regents Chair Higher Edn. Leadership, 1985-92, Lee Hage and Joseph D. Jamail Regents Chair Higher Edn. Leadership, 1992-2000, James L. Bayless Chair for Free Enterprise, 1988—; chancellor U. Tex. Sys., Austin, 1992-2000. Bd. dirs. Jefferson-Pilot Corp., John Hancock Funds, S.W. Airlines Co., Introgen Therapeutics, Hayes Lemmerz Internat., LIN TV; mem. corp. Conf. Bd. Author: (with W.J.E. Crissy and I.C.M. Cunningham) Selling: The Personal Force in Marketing, 1977, 2d edit. (with D.W. Jackson and Cunningham), 1988, Effective Selling, 1977, Spanish edit., 1980, (with S. Lopreato) Consumers' Energy Attitudes and Behavior, 1977, (with Cunningham) Marketing: A Managerial Approach, 1981, 2d edit. (with Cunningham and C. Swift), 1988, (with R. Aldag and C. Swift) Introduction to Business, 1984, 3d edit. (with R. Aldag and S. Block), 1992, 4th edit. (with R. Aldag and M. Stone), 1995, (with B. Verhage and Cunningham) Grondslagen van het Marketing Management, 1984, (with R. Aldag and S. Block) Business in a Changing World, 1992, also monographs and articles; editor Jour. Mktg., 1981-84. Bd. dirs. Houston Area Rsch. Coun., 1984; mem. Mental Health/Mental Retardation Legis. Oversight Com., 1984; mem. adv. bd. Found. for Cultural Exch./The Netherlands-U.S.A.; bd. dirs. Lyndon Baines Johnson Found. Recipient Tchg. Excellence award U. Tex. Coll. Bus. Adminstrn., 1972, Alpha Kappa Psi, 1975, Hank and Mary Harkins Found., 1978, Disting. Scholastic Contbn. award Coll. Bus. Adminstrn. Found. Adv. Council, 1982, Disting. Alumnus award Coll. and Grad. Sch. Bus., Mich. State U., 1983, 93, Tree of Life award Jewish Nat. Fund, 1992; named among top 20 profs. Utmost Mag., 1982; Rsch. grant Univ. Rsch. Inst., 1971-73, Latin Am. Inst., 1972, So. Union Gas Energy, 1975-76, ERDA, 1976 Mem. Am. Inst. for Decision Scis., Am. Mktg. Assn., Assn. Consumer Rsch., So. Mktg. Assn., S.W. Social Sci. Assn., Phi Kappa Phi, Omicron Delta Kappa Office: U Tex PO Box E Austin TX 78713 Office Phone: 512-232-7540. Business E-Mail: connie@po.utexas.edu.

CUNNINGHAM-RUNDLES, CHARLOTTE, physician, immunobiology educator, researcher; b. Ann Arbor, Mich., July 12, 1943; d. R. Wayne Rundles and Mary Alice (Cunningham) Cunningham-Rundles; m. James B. Bussel, Nov. 13, 1982; 1 child, A. Christine. BS, Duke U., 1965; MD, Columbia U., 1969; PhD, NYU, 1974. Diplomate Am. Bd. Internal Medicine. Intern Bellevue Hosp., NYU, N.Y.C., 1969-70, resident, 1970-72; with dept. immunology NYU Med. Ctr., 1972-74; assoc. Sloan Kettering Inst., N.Y.C., 1974-86, dir. biochem. immunology, 1982-86; assoc. attending physician Meml. Hosp., N.Y.C., 1978-86, adj. assoc., 1986—; prof. biochemistry, medicine and pediatrics Mt. Sinai Med. Ctr., N.Y.C., 1986—, assoc. prof. Immunobiology Inst., 1986—; prof. Immunology Inst., 1994—. Bd. dirs. Immunodeficiency clinic; speaker various nat. and internat. mtgs. on immunology, program dir., Allergy Immunology Fellowship, 2001-, mem. blood safety adv. com. FDA, 2002-04; bd. med. advisors Primary Immunodeficiency Found., 1988—, Modell Found., 1989—; adv. NASA Contbr. numerous articles to sci. and med. jours., chpts. to books. Recipient Lifetime Achievement award Modell Found.; grantee NIH, Nat. Cancer Inst., Am. Cancer Soc., Nat. Found. March of Dimes, Multiple Sclerosis Soc. Fellow ACP; mem. Am. Fedn. Clin. Rsch., Am. Assn. Immunologist, Mucosal Immune Soc., Clin. Immunology Soc. (pres. 2003-04), The Harvey Soc. Episcopalian. Avocations: painting, drawing, computer graphics. Office: Mt Sinai Med Ctr 1 Gustave L Levy Pl New York NY 10029-6500

CUNNYNGHAM, JON, economist, information systems educator; b. Jefferson City, Mo., Mar. 3, 1935; s. Wilkie Burford and Modesta (Gutierrez) C.; m. Nancy Lou Bonte, June 21, 1958 (dec. 1981); children: Kathryn Lisa, Karen Elizabeth, Kristin Anne; m. Mary Ellen Eschbach, Dec. 11, 1982 (div. Dec. 1994); children: Jason B., Ian Michael. BA, Oberlin Coll., 1957; PhD, U. Chgo., 1964. Instr. U. Chgo., 1961-62; asst. prof. econs. Columbia U., N.Y.C., 1963-65, assoc. prof., 1965-66, Ohio State U., Columbus, 1966-68, prof., 1969-88, chmn. econs. dept., 1968-76, Mershon policy economist, 1976-80, prof. information systems, 1981-88; dir. Found. for Electronic Pub., 1990-93; founder Star Nest Light Ctr., 1993—96; dir. Star Gate Enterprise, 1997—2001, Emergent Process Enterprise, 2002—. Econ. statistician U.S. Bur. Census, Washington, 1962-63; research assoc. Nat. Bur. Econ. Research, 1963-68; dir. Fin. Research Ctr., Columbus, 1967-75; dir. research Applied Info. Techs. Research Ctr., Columbus, 1987-89. Ford Found. Faculty Research fellow, 1965-66 Mem. AAAS, Am. Econ. Assn., Am. Soc. for Cybernetics (treas. 1981-82, pres. 1983-85), Am. Statis. Assn., Econometric Soc., Soc. for Gen. Sys. Rsch. (treas. Ctrl. Ohio chpt. 1977-78, pres. 1978-79), Internat. Standards Orgn. JTC1/SC18 (chmn. TG5 1991-94, convenor WG5 1992-94), Accredited U.S. Standards Com. X3VI. Home: 3680 Waldo Pl Columbus OH 43220-2216 Business E-Mail: cunnyngham@osu.edu.

CUNO, JAMES, museum director; b. St. Louis, Apr. 6, 1951; married; 2 children. BA in History, Willamette U., 1973; MA in Art History, U. Oreg., 1978; MA in Fine Arts, Harvard U., 1980, PhD in Fine Arts, 1985. Asst. curator prints Fogg Art Mus., Harvard U., Cambridge, Mass., 1980-83; asst. prof. dept. art Vassar Coll., Poughkeepsie, N.Y., 1983-86; dir. Grunwald Ctr. for Graphic Arts, UCLA, 1986-89; dir. Hood Mus. Art, Dartmouth Coll., Hanover, N.H., 1989-91; dir. Univ. Art Mus. Harvard U., Cambridge, Mass., 1991—2003; dir. Courtauld Institute of Art, London, 2003—04; pres., Eloise W. Martin dir. Art Inst. of Chgo., 2004—. Trustee Wadsworth Atheneum; panelist NEH, NEA; mem. pub. grant adv. com. Getty Grant Program, 1991-96; mem. vis. com. J. Paul Getty Mus. Author, editor exhbn. catalogues (with others) Foirades/Fizzles: Echo and Allusion in the Art of Jasper Johns, 1987, Politics and Polemics: French Caricature and the Revolution, 1789-1799, 1988, Scenes and Sequences: Recent Monotypes by Eric Fischl, 1990, Jonathan Borofsky: Prints and Multiples, 1982-91, 1991, The Popularization of Images: Visual Culture Under the July Monarchy, 1994; contbr. articles to profl. jours. Mem. Assn. Art Mus. Dirs. (trustee, pres.). Office: Art Inst of Chgo 111 S Michigan Ave Chicago IL 60603-6110*

CUOMO, ANDREW, former secretary of housing and urban development; b. Dec. 6, 1957; s. Mario M. and Matilda (Raffa) Cuomo; m. Kerry Kennedy, 1990 (div.); 3 children. BA, Fordham U., 1979; JD, Albany Law Sch., 1982. Asst. dist. atty. Dist. Atty's Office, Manhattan; ptnr. Blutrich, Falcone and Miller, N.Y.C.; chmn. N.Y.C. Commn. on the Homeless, 1991-93; asst. sec. cmty. planning and devel. HUD, Washington, 1993-97, sec., 1997-2001. Pub. spkr. The Allen Agy.; vis. fellow Inst. of Politics, Harvard U. Author: Crossroads: The Future of Am. Politics, 2003. Campaign mgr. Mario M. Cuomo for Gov. N.Y., 1982; founder, pres. H.E.L.P., 1986, founder Genesis, 1992. Recipient Good Neighbor award ARC, Outstanding Comty. Svc. award Latin Soul, 1988, Man of the Yr. award Coalition of Italian Am. Orgns., 1988, Ed Sulzberger award, Our Town newspaper, 1989, Pub. Svc. award Coun. of Jewish Orgns., 1989, Disting. Comty. Svc. award NYU, 1991, Bard award, 1992, Albert Einstein award, 1993, Encore Heart to Heart award, 1994, Innovation Am. Govt. award John F. Kennedy Sch. Govt. Harvard U., 1996. Office: Island Capital 717 5th Ave 18th Fl New York NY 10022

CUOMO, MARIO MATTHEW, lawyer, former governor; b. Queens County, N.Y., June 15, 1932; s. Andrea and Immaculata (Giordano) Cuomo; m. Matilda Raffa, June 5, 1954; children: Margaret Cuomo Maier, Andrew, Maria Cuomo Cole, Madeline Cuomo O'Donoghue, Christopher. BA summa cum laude, St. John's Coll., 1953; LLB cum laude, St. John's U., 1956. Bar: NY 1956, U.S. Dist. Ct. (no. dist.) NY 1957, U.S. Dist. Ct. (so. dist.) NY 1998, U.S. Supreme Ct. 1960, U.S. Dist. Ct. (ea. dist.) NY 1962, U.S. Ct. Appeals (2d cir.) 1967. Confidential legal asst. to Hon. Adrian P. Burke, NY State Ct. Appeals, 1956—58; assoc. Corner, Weisbrod, Froeb and Charles, Bklyn., 1958—63; ptnr. Corner, Cuomo & Charles, 1963—75; sec. of state State of NY, 1975—79, lt. gov., 1979—83, gov., 1983—94; ptnr., now of counsel Wilkie Farr & Gallagher, N.Y.C., 1995—. Mem. faculty St. John's U. Sch. Law, 1963—73; counsel to cmty. groups, including Corona Homeowners, 1966—72; charter mem. First Ecumenical Commn. of Christians and Jews for Bklyn. and Queens, NY. Author: Forest Hills Diary: The Crisis of Low-Income Housing, 1974, Diaries of Mario M. Cuomo, Campaign for Governor, 1982; co-author: Lincoln on Democracy, 1990, More Than Words, 1993, The New York Idea: An Experiment in Democracy, 1994, Reason to Believe, 1995, The Blue Spruce, 1999; contbr. articles to legal publs. Spkr. keynote address Dem. Nat. Conv., San Francisco, 1984, nominating address Dem. Nat. Conv., N.Y.C., 1992. Recipient Rapallo award, Columbia Lawyers Assn., 1976, Dante medal, Italian Govt.-Am. Assn. Tchrs. Italian, 1976, Silver medallion, Columbia Coalition, 1976, Pub. Adminstr. award, C.W. Post Coll., 1977, Theodore Roosevelt award, Internat. Platform Assn., 1984. Mem.: ABA, Am. Judicature Soc., Assn. of Bar of City of NY, Queens County Bar Assn., Nassau Bar Assn., Bklyn. Bar Assn., NY State Bar Assn., Cath. Lawyers Guild of Queens County (pres. 1966—67), St. John's U. Alumni Fedn. (chmn. bd. 1970—72), Skull and Circle. Home: 50 Sutton Pl S New York NY 10022-4167 Address: Wilkie Farr & Gallagher 787 7th Ave Rm 203 New York NY 10019-6018

CUOZZO, STEVEN DAVID, newspaper editor; b. NYC, Jan. 17, 1950; s. Joseph and Lillian (Picini) C.; m. Jane Hershey, Nov. 29, 1980 BA in English, SUNY, Stony Brook, 1971. Arts and leisure editor NY Post, NYC, 1978-80, asst. mng. editor features, 1980-91, mng. editor, 1991-93, exec. editor, 1993—, also food critic. Author: It's Alive: How America's Oldest Newspaper Cheated Death and Why It Matters, 1996. Office: NY Post 10th Fl 1211 Avenue Of The Americas New York NY 10036 E-mail: scuozzo@nypost.com.*

CUPOLO, NANCY, education educator, department chairman; d. George B. and Alice T. Burke; m. Frank P. Cupolo; children: Lisa, Andria. BSc in Edn., Russell Sage Coll., 1975, MSc in Edn., 1977. Cert. spl. edn. educator N.Y., 1977. Asst, N.Y. State Edn. Dept., Albany, NY, 1978—80; prin., owner Flower Hill Day Care and Nursery, Troy, NY, 1981—91; pvt. practice cons. Children First: Ednl. and Behavioral Consultation Svcs., Troy, 1981—; assoc. prof. Hudson Valley C.C., Troy, 1989—, chmn. Dept. Edn., 2003—. Instr. Russell Sage Coll., Troy, 1977—89; mem. adv. bd. After Sch. Programs Troy (N.Y.) City Schs. Contbr. articles to profl. jours. and newspapers;, author manuels in field. Recipient Elizabeth Ann Seton award, 1995, Chancellor's award, N.Y. State, 1999. Mem.: Nat. Assn. C.C. Tchr. Edn. Programs, Nat. Assn. Edn. Young Children, Sch. Age Child Care Network, Coun. Exceptional Children, Assn. Retarded Citizens. Home: 13 Staulters Farm Rd Ballston Spa NY 12020 Office Phone: 518-629-7250.

CUPP, DAVID FOSTER, photographer, journalist; b. Derry Twp., Pa., Feb. 4, 1938; s. Foster Wilson and Elizabeth (Erhard) C.; m. Catherine Lucille Lum, Nov. 20, 1965; children: Mary Catherine, David Patterson, John. BA in Journalism, U. Miami (Fla.), 1960. Staff photographer Miami News, 1960-63, Charlotte (N.C.) Observer, 1963-66; photographer, writer Internat. Harvesters, Chgo., 1966-67; picture editor Nat. Geog. Mag., Washington, 1967, photographer, 1967-69; picture editor Detroit Free Press, 1969; writer, photographer Denver Post, 1969-77; freelance writer, photographer, 1977-88; dir. photography Press-Enterprise, Riverside, Calif., 1988-90; instr. photojournalism, dept. journalism U. Mo., Columbia, 1990; instr. Sch. Vis. Communication Ohio U., Athens, 1991-92; working book author Cupp Design, Inc., Atlanta, 1993; graphics editor Ft. Lauderdale (Fla.) Sun-Sentinel, 1993-94; freelance writer & photographer Hilliard, Ohio, 1994—; pres., creative dir. Photos Online, Inc., Hilliard, 1995—; pres. Half Moon Pub., LLC, Hilliard, 2003—. Tchr. jr. and sr. h.s.-adult classes, including Journalist-in-the-schs., pilot program, Aurora, Colo., 1974-76, Nat. Endowment Arts poet-in-residence 5 Colo. schs.; photography aboard Voyager Spacecraft Co-author Search and Rescue Dogs, 1988; contbg. author: Nat. Geog. books; co-author: Cindy, a Hearing Ear Dog, The Animal Shelter, All Wild Creatures Welcome; contbr. article, photographs to popular mags. Bd. dirs. Friends of Children of Vietnam, adoption agy., 1973. Mem. Nat. Press Photographers Assn. (named Nat. runner-up Photographer of Year 1965, 72, named Regional Photographer of Year 1974, 2d Pl. News Picture Story award 1974, 3rd Pl. Sports Picture Story award 1974, McWilliams award for picture story 1974, McWilliams award for single picture 1974-75, 2d Home, Family Picture Story award 1972, co-chmn. nat. conv.), Colo. Press Photographers Assn. (v.p.), Am. Soc. Mag. Photographers. Home: 4508 Swenson St Hilliard OH 43026-3811 E-mail: pol@columbus.rr.com. *I don't think it's possible to sum life up in a few sentences, life is too complex, but if I were to try, I would have to say that I try to live my life in such a way that my children have pride in me, what I do, and how I do it. I don't feel I can tell my children to be honest, then I be dishonest, or tell them to have compassion, while I have none. I cannot punish a child for doing something at night, that I do during the day. In short, I try to be the person that I would want my children to be.*

CUPP, GARLAND, computer company executive; Exec. vice-pres., CIO Travel Related Services Div. Am. Express; dir. bus. services McDonnell Douglas Automation Co.; chmn. Apex Mortgage Co.; bd. mem. Edmond Bank & Trust; chmn. bd. dir. BMC Software, Inc., 1989—. Office: BMC Software Inc 2101 City West Blvd Houston TX 77042-2827 Office Phone: 713-918-8800. Office Fax: 713-918-8000.*

CUPP, ORVILLE SHAWN, military officer; s. Wayne Wine and Susan Auville Cupp; m. Kimberly Teagle, June 27, 1987; 1 child, Kayla Christine. BS in Agr. Edn., Va. Tech, 1985, MS in Vocat. Edn., 1986; M in Mil. Art and Sci., US Army Command and Gen. Staff Coll., 2002. Asst. prof. US Army Command and Gen. Staff Coll., Ft. Leavenworth, Kans., 2001—05. Contbr. articles to profl. jour. including US Army Profl. Jour. Adult leader Girl Scouts, Ft. Leavenworth, Kans., 2002—04. Lt. col. U.S. Army, 1986—2005, US, Germany, Desert Shield/Desert Storm, Korea, Kosovo. Mem.: VFW (assoc.), US Army Ordnance Corps Assn. (assoc.). Home: 412 Grant Ave Fort Leavenworth KS 66027-1331 Office: US Army Command & Gen Staff Coll 1 Reynolds Ave Fort Leavenworth KS 66027 Office Phone: 913-684-2983. Personal E-mail: orville.cupp@leavenworth.army.mil.

CUPP, ROBERT ERHARD, golf course architect, land use planner; b. Lewistown, Pa., Dec. 27, 1939; s. Foster Wilson and Elizabeth (Erhard) C.; m. Glenda Dell, Aug. 26, 1962 (div. 1983); children: Robert E. II, Caren E., Laura G.; m. Pamela Patricia Amy, Dec. 27, 1986. BA, U. Miami, Coral Gables, Fla., 1962; MA, U.S. Army, Anchorage, 1966. Art dir. Jefferson, Inc., Miami, 1966-67; golf profl. Colonial Palms Country Club, Miami, 1967-68, Crooked Creek Country Club, Miami, 1968-69; pvt. practice golf course architect Miami, 1969-72; golf course architect Golden Bear Enterprises, North Palm Beach, Fla., 1972-86; pvt. practice golf course architect Atlanta, 1984—. Sr. designer Jack Nicklaus Design, North Palm Beach, 1972-86; pres. Cupp Design, Inc., Atlanta, 1984—. Designed East Sussex (Eng.) Nat. Golf Club, site of 1993-94 European Open Championship (Best New Golf Course, Golf Monthly), Pumpkin Ridge Golf Club, Portland, Oreg., Site of 1996 U.S. Amateur Championship, 1992 & 2003 U.S. Women's Open Championship, 2000 U.S. Boys and Girls Nat. Champtionship, Old Waverly Golf Club, West Point, Miss. (Top 100 Golf Course in U.S., Golf Digest, Site of U.S. Women's Open Championship), Settindown Creek Golf Club, Atlanta, (site of U.S. Nike Tour Championship, 1995, 96, and U.S. Women's Amateur Championship 2005), Pumpkin Ridge, Ghost Creek, 1992 (Best New Course, Golf Digest), Western Gales, Osceola, Mich., 1993, Indianwood, Lake Orion, Mich., 1988 (Runner up Best New Course, Golf Digest), Pumpkin Ridge, Witch Hollow, Portland, 1992, Old Waverly, West Point, 1989, Big Sky Country Club, Pemberton, B.C., Can., 1994, Crosswater Golf Club, Sunriver, Oreg., 1995 (Best New Course 1995), Hawks Ridge, Atlanta, 2000 (Best New Course runner up Golf Digest), others. Served to capt. U.S. Army, 1963-66. Named Golf World/Golf Digest Designer of Yr., 1992, Top 100, Golf Digest. Office: Cupp Design Inc 5457 Roswell Rd NE Ste 103 Atlanta GA 30342-1900 also: Bob Cupp Inc PO Box 191581 Atlanta GA 31119-1581 E-mail: cuppdsgn@aol.com.

CUPPLES, STEPHEN ELLIOT, lawyer; b. St. Louis, Feb. 20, 1955; children: Christina, James, Catherine, Stephanie, Alex. AB summa cum laude, U. Mo., 1976, JD summa cum laude, 1979. Bar: Mo. 1979, U.S. Dist. Ct. (ea. dist.) Mo. 1979, U.S. Ct. Appeals (8th cir.) 1980, U.S. Tax Ct. 1981, U.S. Claims Ct. 1985. Assoc. Peper, Martin, Jensen, Maichel and Hetlage, St. Louis, 1979-84; ptnr. Cupples & Cupples, P.C., St. Louis, 1985, Cupples, Edwards, Cooper & Singer, St. Louis, 1985-86, Lashly & Baer, P.C., St. Louis, 1987-95, Thompson Coburn LLP, St. Louis, 1995—. Bd. dirs. Estate Planning Coun. of St. Louis, 1992-, pres. 2002-03. Fellow Am. Coll. Trust and Estate Coun.; mem. ABA, Mo. Bar Assn., Bar Assn. Met. St. Louis (chmn. taxation sect. 1988-89), Young Lawyers Tax Club (chmn. 1983-87), Phi Beta Kappa, Phi Kappa Phi. Office: Thompson Coburn LLP One US Bank Plaza Ste 2600 Saint Louis MO 63101-1693 Office Phone: 314-552-6027. Business E-Mail: scupples@thompsoncoburn.com.

CURB, JESS DAVID, medical educator, researcher; b. Raton, N.Mex., Dec. 29, 1945; s. Leslie Calvin and Evelyn Lula (Lindley) C.; m. Beatriz Lorenza Rodriquez; children: Jess Calvin, William Noa, Maria Lorenza, Isabel Alani. BA, U. Colo., 1967; MD, U. N.Mex., 1971; MPH, U. Tex., Houston, 1974. Diplomate, cert. geriatric medicine Am. Bd. Internal Medicine. Intern Harlem Hosp., Columbia U., N.Y.C., 1971-72; rsch. assoc. U. Tex. Sch. Pub. Health and Medicine, Houston, 1973-76, asst. prof., 1978-80; resident internal medicine Northwestern U. Sch. Medicine, Chgo., 1976-78; asst. prof. Baylor Coll. Medicine, Houston, 1980-83; assoc. prof. U. Hawaii, Honolulu, 1983-85, prof., 1985-87; assoc. dir. Nat. Inst. on Aging, Bethesda, Md., 1986-89; prof. geriatric medicine, chief Divsn. Clin. Epidemiology U. Hawaii, Sch. Medicine, Honolulu, 1989—; CEO, med. dir. Pacific Health Rsch. Inst., 1995—2003, pres., 2003—. Contbr. articles to profl. jours. Grantee Honolulu Heart Program, Nat. Heart, Lung and Blood Inst., Honolulu, 1989-2003, Hawaii Asia Aging Study, Nat. Inst. on Aging, Honolulu, 1994-2002, Women's Health Initiative, NIH, Honolulu, 1994-, Family Blood Pressure Program, 1995—. Fellow ACP, Am. Heart Assn. (coun. on epidemiology); mem. Am. Geriatric Soc. Office: Pacific Health Research Inst 846 South Hotel St Ste 301 Honolulu HI 96813 Office Phone: 808-524-4411. Business E-Mail: jdcurb@phrihawaii.org.

CURCIO, CHRISTOPHER FRANK, recreation director; b. Oakland, Calif., Feb. 3, 1950; s. Frank William and Virginie Theresa (Le Gris) C. BA in Speech/Drama, Calif. State U., Hayward, 1971; MBA in Arts Adminstrn., UCLA, 1974; MPA in Pub. Policy, Ariz. State U., 1982. Intern John F. Kennedy Ctr. for Arts, Washington, 1973; gen. mgr. Old Eagle Theatre, Sacramento, 1974-75; cultural arts supr. Fresno Parks and Recreation Dept., 1975-79; supr. cultural and spl. events Phoenix Parks & Recreation Dept., 1979-87, budget analyst, 1987, mgmt. svcs. adminstr., 1987-97, dep. dir., 1997—. Mgmt. and budget analyst City of Phoenix, 1985; grants panelist Phoenix Arts Commn., 1987, Ariz. Commn. on Arts, 1987-88; voter Zony Theatre Awards, 1991-92; freelance theater critic, 1987-89; theater critic Ariz. Republic, 1990-98, 2004—, PHX Downtown, 1997-98, CityAZ, 1997-98, Ariz. Foothills Mag., 1998-2002, Sunday Showtunes Broadway's Biggest Hits, 1998-2000, In Theater Mag., 1999-2000, Variety, 1995—, KBAQ-FM Radio, 1999—, Broadway's Biggest Hits, 2000—, Ariz. Producton Assn., 2002—. Active Valley Leadership Program, Phoenix, 1987—, Valley Big Bros./Big Sisters, 1980-94; chair allocation panel United Way, 1990-92; sec. Los Olivos Townhome Assn., Phoenix, 1986-92. Mem. Am. Soc. Pub. Adminstrn., Nat. Recreation and Park Assn., Am. Theatre Critics Assn., Internat. Theater Critics Assn., Ariz. Park and Recreation Assn. Republican. Avocations: theater history, writing, reading, cooking, gardening. Office: Phoenix Parks & Recreation Dept 200 W Washington St Fl 16 Phoenix AZ 85003-1611 Office Phone: 602-262-4987. Personal E-mail: criticrep@aol.com. Business E-Mail: chris.curcio@phoenix.gov.

CURCIO, MARIA, mathematics educator; d. Leoluca and Josephine De-Luca; m. Bart John Curcio, Aug. 15, 1970; children: Bart, Laura. BA, Queens Coll., 1988, MS, 1991. Tchr. math. Herricks High Sch., NY, 1988—90, Hewlett High Sch, 1990—. Recipient Herb Fremont award, Queens Coll., 1988. Avocation: golf. Office: George W Hewlett High Sch 60 Everit Ave Hewlett NY 11557

CURFMAN, DAVID RALPH, neurosurgeon, educator, civic leader, musician; b. Bucyrus, Ohio, Jan. 2, 1942; s. Ralph Oliver and Agnes Mozelle (Schreck) C.; m. Blanche Lee Anderson, June 6, 1970. Student, Capital U., 1960—62; AB, Columbia Union Coll., 1965; MS, George Washington U., 1967, MD, 1973. Diplomate Nat. Bd. Med. Examiners. Asst. organist, choirmaster Peace Luth. Ch., Galion, Ohio, 1956-62; bus. mgr. Mansfield/Galion Ambulance Svc., Galion, 1962-66; with news divsn. Sta. WTOP-TV, CBS, Washington, 1965; choirmaster, assoc. organist Grace Luth. Ch., Washington, 1966-73, historian, curator, 1969—; tchg. fellow in anatomy George Washington U., Washington, 1966-67, gen. surgery intern, 1973-74, resident in neurol. surgery, 1974-78, clin. instr. neurol. surgery, 2000—, asst. clin. prof., 2001—; resident in neuropathology Armed Forces Inst. Pathology, Washington, 1975; resident in pediatric neurol. surgery Children's Hosp. Nat. Med. Ctr., Washington, 1976; tchg. fellow in anatomy Georgetown U., Washington, 1967-69, clin. instr. neurol. surgery, nuerol. surgeon, 1978—. Chief divsn. neurol. surgery Jefferson Hosp., Alexandria, Va., 1989-93, Washington Hosp. Ctr. Soc., 1992—, oper. room com. 1998-2003; vice-chmn. bylaws com. Providence Hosp., 1987-95, chief of neorosurgery divsn.; panelist ann. meeting ethical issues in neurol. surgery Am. Assn. Neurol. Surgery; guest spkr. Nat. Youth Leadership Forum, 1996—. Chmn., chief author: Physician's Reference Guide for Medicolegal Matters, 1982, Nat. Capital Astronomers' Association, 1986-87. Elected mem. DC Rep. Com., 1988-94; bd. dirs., historian The Christmas Pageant of Peace, Inc., Washington, The Leo Sowerby Found.; pres., bd. govs. Nat. Columbus Celebration Assn. Hon. mem. Quiz Kid Show, 1953; recipient Found. award Cathedral Choral Soc., 1997, Medal of Honor Nat. Soc. DAR, 2004. Mem.: SAR (bd., DC Soc. 1997—), AMA (Phys. Recognition award 1983—), Order of Merovingian Dynasty (founding mem., surgeon gen.), DC Soc. (bd. mgmt.), Order of the Crown in Am., Assn. Mil. Surgeons U.S. (Continuing Edn. Neurosurgery award 1993—), Washington Acad. Neurosurgery (pres. 2004—), Am. Coll. Legal Medicine, Congress Neurol. Surgeons (joint sect. neuro-trauma and critical care), Pan Am. Med. Soc. (mem. exec. bd. 1993—97, pres. 1997—), Med. Soc. DC (chmn. medicine and religion com. 1981—83, chmn. medico-legal com. 1986—88), Am. Soc. Law, Medicine and Ethics, Assn. Am. Med. Colls. (nat. student chmn. rules and regulations com. 1971—73), Heredity Soc. Cmty. USA, Nat. Gavel Soc., St. Andrew's Soc. (Washington), Hymn Soc. Am., Pilgrim Soc. Plymouth Mass. (Plymouth, Mass.), Order Three Crusades (1096-1192), The Baronial Order of Magna Carta, Mil. Hospitaller Order Saint Lazarus Jerusalem (knight), U.S. Capitol Hist. Soc. (founding supporting mem., trust mem., bd. dirs.), Nat. Cathedral Assn., Cathedral Choral Soc. (repertoire chmn. 1981—82, v.p. bd. trustees 1981—83, pres. 1984—86, found. award 1977), Am. Guild Organists (dean DC chpt. 1974—76, publicity chmn. nat. conv. 1982, state chmn. 1984—91, nat. com. long-range devel. 1990—96), Internat. Congress Organists (Washington program chmn. 1977), Royal Sch. Ch. Music (Eng.), Order of the Crown of Charlemagne (surgeon gen.), Nat. Soc. Ams. Royal Descent (councillor), Order of Ams. of Armorial Ancestry (chaplain), Nat. Soc. Children Am. Revolution (pres. Ohio 1963—64, hon. sr. nat. v.p. 1999—2004, sr. nat. officers. club historian 2003—, sr. nat. 2d v.p. 2004—, hon. Ohio pres.), Gen. Soc. Sons of the Revolution (chmn. bicentennial commemorative com. death of Gen. George Washington 1999, NY and DC bd. 2002—, 3d v.p.), Hereditary Order Descendants of the Loyalists and Patriots of the Am. Revolution, Baronial Order of Magna Charta, Sons and Daus. of Colonial and Antebellum Bench and Bar, Samuel Victor Constant Soc., Order of Washington, Hospitaller Order of St. John (hon.; knight), Osler Soc., Galion Hist. Soc. (charter), Continental Soc. Sons Indian Wars, Order Sancti Constantini Magni, Colonial Order of the Acorn NY, Vet. Corps Arty. State NY, Am. Revolution Soc., Soc. of 1812, Nat. Soc. Children Am. Colonists (pres. gen. 2003—), Mil. Order Loyal Legion U.S. (Aide-de-Camp to comdr.-in-chief), Sons Am. Colonists (surgeon gen. 1997—2005, lt. gov. gen. 2005—), Soc. Colonial Wars (surgeon 1997—), Order of Indian Wars in the U.S. (historian 1999—), Am. Polit. Items Collectors Assn., Sons/Daus. of the Pilgrims (historian gen. 1999—2001, first dep. gov. gen. 2003—, dep. gov. gen. 2003—05), Lincoln Birthday Nat. Commemorative Com (master of ceremonies 1995—99, vice chmn.), Sons of Union Vets. Civil War (chmn. hist. Meml. Day observances), Sovereign Mil. Order Temple of Jerusalem (grand chirurgeon emeritus, grand comdr., Order of Merit), Mil. Order of the Crusades, Soc. War 1812 (surgeon gen., 1st v.p. DC chpt., dist. dep. pres. gen., Md. chpt.), Columbus Philatelic Soc., Crawford County Coin Club (charter mem.), George Washington U. Club, Elks (Galion Lodge No. 1191), Sigma Xi (pres. George Washington U. chpt. 1981—82), Phi Delta Epsilon (life). Home: 4201 Massachusetts Ave NW Washington DC 20016-4701 Office: 3301 New Mexico Ave NW Ste 210 Washington DC 20016-3622 Office Phone: 202-244-6302.

CURFMAN, FLOYD EDWIN, retired engineering educator; b. Gorin, Mo., Nov. 16, 1929; s. Charles Robert and Cleo Lucille (Sweeney) C.; m. Eleanor Elaine Fehl, Aug. 5, 1950; children: Gary Floyd, Karen Elaine. BSCE, U. Mo., 1958; BA in Math. Edn., Mt. Mary Coll., 1988. Registered profl. engr., Wis., Mo.; cert. tchr. Wis. Forest engr. U.S. Forest Svc., Rolla and Harrisburg, Mo., Ill., 1958-70, engrng. dir. Milw., 1970-84, chief tech. engr. Washington, 1984-86; tchr. Wauwatosa (Wis.) High Sch., 1987-89, Our Lady of Rosary, Milw., 1989-96; retired, 1996. Author: (booklet) Forest Roads-R-9, 1973; co-author: (tng. manual) Transportation Roads, 1966. Co-leader Boy Scouts Am., Harrisburg, 1958-62; activities coord. Cmty. Action Com., Brookfield, 1970-76; bike and hiking trails com. City of Brookfield (Wis.), 1982-83; program chair Math Counts, 1982. With U.S. Army, 1952-54. Mem. ASCE (program chair, Letter Nat. award 1970), NSPE (coms. 1970-86), Nat. Coun. Tchrs. Math., Wis. Soc. Profl. Engrs. (pres. Milw. chpt. 1982-83, State Recognition award 1983). Avocations: travel, auto trips, reading. Home: 1755 N 166th St Brookfield WI 53005-5114

CURIE, CHARLES G., federal agency administrator; b. Ind. m. Candace Curie. Grad., Huntington Coll., 1977; Masters Degree, U. Chgo., 1979. Cert. Acad. Cert. Social Workers. Pres., CEO Helen H. Stevens Cmty. Mental Health Ctr., Carlisle, 1988—90; dir. risk mgmt. svcs. Henry S. Lehr Inc., Bethlehem, Pa., 1990—95; exec. dir., CEO Sandusky Valley Ctr., Tiffin, Ohio; dep. sec. for mental health and substance abuse svcs. Dept. Pub. Welfare, State of Pa., 1995—2001; adminstr. Substance Abuse and Mental Health Svcs. Adminstrn. U.S. Dept. HHS, Rockville, Md., 2001—. Chmn. Greater Carlisle United Way Annual Campaign; mem. adv. bd. Tiffin Mercy Hosp.; pres. Huntington Coll. Student Union; senate mem. Huntington Coll. Bd. Trustees; pres. Alpha Sigma Eta; past mem. bd. dirs. Greater Carlisle C. of C. Mem.: Rotary Internat. Office: US Dept Health and Human Svcs Substance Abuse & Mental Health Svcs Adm 1 Choke Cherry Rd Rockville MD 20857 E-mail: charles.curie@samhsa.hhs.gov.

CURINGTON, THOMAS FRANKLIN, III, photographer, writer; s. Thomas Franklin Curington Jr. and Kitty Sue Garrett. BS in psychology, Ga. Coll. and State U., 1993, MS in psychology, 1996. Mental health counselor Baldwin State Prison, Milledgeville, Ga., 1996—97. Democrat.

CURL, LAYTON SETH, psychologist, consultant, educator; b. Batesville, Ark., Apr. 3, 1976; s. Eric Lynn and Rita Kay Curl. Diploma in Asian studies, Kansai Gaidai U., Japan, 1997; BA in Psychology, Lyon Coll., Batesville, AR, 1998; MA in Exptl. Psychology, U. Miss., Oxford, 2000, PhD in Social and Cross-Cultural Psychology, 2002. Instr. English Kansai Gaidai U., Kyoto, 1996—97; instr. psychology U. Miss., Oxford, 1998—2002; mng. editor Internat. Jour. Intercultural Rels., Hilo, Hawaii, 2000—02; prof. cross-cultural psychology Hobart and William Smith Colleges, Geneva, NY, 2002—04; prof. social psychology Met. State Coll. Denver, 2004—. Mem. Human Rights Campaign, New York City, 2000. Scholar, Dept. of Higher Edn. & Century Tube Corp., 1996. Fellow: Internat. Assn. Intercultural Rels. (assoc.); mem.: Asian Assn. Social Psychologists, Internat. Assn. Cross-Cultural Psychology. Democrat. Home: 855 Pennsylvania St #206 Denver CO 80203 Office: Dept Psychology Metropolitan State Coll Denver Campus Box 54 PO Box 173362 Denver CO 80217-3362 Office Phone: 303-556-3025. Business E-Mail: lcurl@mscd.edu.

CURL, LEIGH ANN, orthopedist, surgeon; b. 1963; d. Frank and Barabara Curl. Bachelors, U. Conn., 1985; MD, Johns Hopkins U., 1989. Intern, reisdent Johns Hopkins Hosp., Balt.; fellow in sports medicine and shoulder surgery Hosp. for Spl. Surgery, Cornell U., N.Y.C., 1994—95; asst. prof. orthop. surgery and sports medicine U. Md. Med. Sys.; head team physician U. Md. Terrapins, 1997—2002; Balt. asst. prof. orthop. surgery Johns Hopkins Hosp., Balt., 2002—; team orthop. surgeon Balt. Ravens (NFL), 2001—; orthopedic surgeon Johns Hopkins Bayview Med. Ctr., Balt. Vol. team physician USA Women's Basketball, USA Women's Rugby and Johns Hopkins U. Named GTE Acad. All-Am. (twice), Big East Scholar-Athlete of Yr. (twice); inducted into, GTE Acad. Hall of Fame, 1998. Fellow: Am. Acad. Orthop. Surgery. Office: Johns Hopkins Bayview Med Ctr 4940 Eastern Ave Baltimore MD 21224 Office Phone: 410-847-3517.

CURL, ROBERT FLOYD, JR., chemistry professor; b. Alice, Tex., Aug. 23, 1933; s. Robert Floyd and Lessie (Merritt) Curl; m. Jonel Whipple, Dec. 21, 1955; children: Michael, David. BA, Rice U., 1954; PhD, U. Calif., Berkeley, 1957; D (hon.), U. Buenos Aires, 1997; D, U. Littoral, 2002. Rsch. fellow Harvard U., Cambridge, Mass., 1957—58; from asst. prof. chemistry to prof. Rice U., Houston, 1958—2003, Kenneth S. Pitzer-Schlumberger prof. natural scis., 2003—05, Kenneth S. Pitzer-Schlumberger emeritus prof. natural scis., 2005—; master Lovett Coll., 1968—72, u. prof., 2003—05, prof. emeritus, 2005—. Vis. rsch. officer NRC Can., 1972—73; vis. prof. Inst. Molecular Sci., Okazaki, Japan, 1977, U. Bonn, 1985; Erskine fellow U. Canterbury, 1999; hon. prof. USTC, 2002—. Contbr. articles to profl. jours. Co-recipient Nobel prize in Chemistry, 1996; named to, Tex. Sci. Hall of Fame; recipient Clayton prize, Instn. Mech. Engrs., London, 1958, Internat. New Materials prize, Am. Phys. Soc., 1992, Alexander von Humboldt sr. U.S. scientist award, 1984, Order of Golden Plate, 1997, Achievement award, Am. Carbon Soc., 1997, Tex. Disting. Scientist award, 1997, Johannes Marcus Marci award in spectroscopy, 1998, Madison Marshall award, 1998, Space Act award, 1998, Centenary medal, Royal Soc. Chemistry, 1999, Forschungspreis Chemie, U. Bochum, 2004; fellow NSF, Alfred P. Sloan, 1961—63, NATO postdoctoral, 1964. Fellow: Am. Acad. Arts and Scis., Am. Optical Soc., Royal Soc. of New Zealand (hon.); mem.: NAS, European Acad. Scis., Arts and Letters (titulaire mem.), Am. Chem. Soc., Sigma Xi, Phi Beta Kappa. Methodist. Home: 1824 Bolsover Rd Houston TX 77005-1728 Office: Rice University PO Box 1892 6100 Main St Houston TX 77005-1892 Office Phone: 713-348-4816. E-mail: rfcurl@rice.edu.

CURL, SAMUEL EVERETT, retired dean, agriculturist, consultant; b. Ft. Worth, Dec. 26, 1937; s. Henry Clay and Mary Elva (Watson) C.; m. Betty Doris Savage, June 6, 1957 (div.); children: Jane Ellen, Julia Kathleen, Karen Elizabeth; m. Mary Behrends Reeves, Sept. 11, 1993; stepchildren: Ryan Andrew, Shelly Lyn. Student, Tarleton State Coll., 1955-57; BS, Sam Houston State U., 1959; MS, U. Mo., 1961; PhD, Tex. A&M U., 1963. Mem. faculty Tex. Tech U., Lubbock, 1961, 63-76, 79-97, tchr., rschr. animal physiology and genetics, 1963-76, asst., assoc. and interim dean Coll. Agrl. Sci., 1968-73, assoc. v.p. acad. affairs, prof., 1973-76, dean Coll. Agrl. Scis. and Natural Resources, prof., 1979-97; pres. Phillips U., Enid, Okla., 1976-79; agrl. cons., 1964-76; dean and dir. divsn. agrl. scis. and natural resources Okla. State U., Stillwater, 1994—2004; ret., 2004; past pres. So. Assn. Agrl. Scientists. Bd. dirs. Am. Distance Edn. Consortium, Okla. Sci. and Tech. R&D Bd., Food and Agr. Ednl. Info. Sys., Okla. Youth Expo.; past chmn. So. Region Adminstrv. Heads, So. Region Adminstrv. Heads Liaison to Coun. on Agrl. Rsch., Ext. and Tchg.; mem. adminstrv. com. Okla. State U. Sch. Internat. Studies; former bd. dirs. Mid Am. Internat. Agrl. Consortium, 1997—2002, past chmn., 1998—99, 2001—02; mem. Gov.'s Task Force on Agrl. Devel. in Tex., 1982—83, 1988, Tex. Crop and Livestock Adv. Com., 1985—91, Tex. Agrl. Resources Protection Authority, 1989—97, Tex. Agribus. Rsch. Promotion Coun., 1995—97, Okla. State Com., Exptl. Program to Stimulate Competitive Rsch.; del. Eisenhower Consortium for Western Environ. Forestry Rsch., 1979—84; mgmt. com. S.W. Consortium on Plant Genetics and Water Resources, 1984—97, chmn., 1989—95; mem. USDA Nat. Planning Com. on Hispanic Minority Recruitment, 1988—93; trustee Consortium for Internat. Devel., 1979—97, mem. exec. com., 1981—84, 1986—87, 1989—90; former mem. High Plains Rsch. Coord. Bd., So. Regional Coun., U.S. Joint Coun. Food and Agrl. Scis.; former trustee Water Inc.; chmn. agrl. and natural resources program rev. task force Sam Houston State U., 1982—83; mem. adv. com. Sch. Agr. Angelo State U., 1989—95; mem. 1995 farm bill task force Tex. Dept. Agr., 1994—95; chair agrl. team Okla. Govs. EDGE project; adj. faculty mem., outreach coor. Tarleton State U., Stephenville, Tex.; cons. in field. Author: (with others) Progress and Change in the Agricultural Industry, 1974, Food and Fiber for a Changing World, 1976, 2d edit., 1982; contbr. 95 articles to profl. jours. Pres. Lubbock Econ. Coun., 1982; bd. dirs. Market Lubbock Econ. Devel. Corp., 1995-97; former mem. bd. overseers Ranching Heritage Assn.; mem. Goals for Lubbock: A Vision into the 21st Century Com., 1995-96; elder Westminster Presbyn. Ch., Lubbock, 1994-97; 2d lt. U.S. Army, 1959, capt. USAR. Danforth Assn. fellow, 1964-76, Am. Coun. Edn. fellow, 1972-73; recipient Disting. Alumnus award, Faculty-Alumni Gold medal U. Mo., 1975, Outstanding Agr. Alumnus award Sam Houston State U., 1986, Disting. Alumnus award, 1993, Tex. Citation for Outstanding Svc. award Tex. 4-H Found., 1987, Tex. 4-H Alumni award, 1993, Disting. Svc. award Vocational Agrl. Tchrs. Assn. Tex., 1987, Blue and Gold Meritorious Svc. award Tex. Future Farmers of Am., 1988, Tex. State degree Future Farmers Am., 1988, Area Disting. Svc. award Vocat. Agr. Tchrs., 1987, Okla. Hon. State degree Future Farmers Am., 2002. Mem.: Profl. Agrl. Workers Tex. (bd. dirs., Disting. Svc. to Tex. Agr. award 1984), Coun. Adminstrv. Heads of Agr., Nat. Assn. State Univs. and Land-Grant Colls. (exec. com. bd. agr. 1994—97, 1998—2001), Assn. U.S. Univ. Dirs. Internat. Agrl. Programs, Am. Assn. Univ. Agrl. Adminstrs., Am. Soc. Animal Sci. (program com. Biennial Symposium on Animal Reprodn. 1972—76, reviewer Jour. Animal Sci.), Lubbock C. of C. (chmn. agr. task force, chmn. rsch. com. 1981—86, bd. dirs. 1988—92, water com., legis. affairs com., agr. com., gubernatorial appointments task force), West Tex. C. of C. (former bd. dirs., chmn. agrl. and ranching com.), Century Club, Centennial Rotary (hon.), Okla. State U. Alumni Assn., Lubbock Rotary Club (bd. dirs., 1st v.p.), Sirloin Club Okla., Sigma Xi, Gamma Sigma Delta, Phi Kappa Phi, Omicron Delta Kappa, Farmhouse Frat. (assoc.). Methodist. Home: 8703 Claremont Dr Granbury TX 76049 Office Phone: 405-776-1285. E-mail: samcurl@charter.net.

CURLANDER, PAUL JOSEPH, technology executive; b. Balt., Dec. 15, 1952; BSEE, U. Colo., 1974; MSEE, MIT, 1977, PhDEE, 1979. Elec. engr. gen. products divsn. IBM, Boulder, 1974—78, staff printer tech. group office product divsn., 1978—85, product mgr. laser printers, 1985-86, product mgr. letter quality printers info. products divsn., 1986-89, dir. printer products, 1989-91; gen. mgr. Lexmark Printer Bus., 1991-93; v.p., gen. mgr. printing sys. bus. Lexmark, Lexington, Ky., 1993-95, exec. v.p. ops., 1995-97, pres., COO, 1997-98, pres., CEO, 1998—, chmn., 1999—. Contbr. articles to profl. jours.; patentee in field. Office: Lexmark Internat Inc 740 New Circle Rd NW Lexington KY 40550

CURLE, ROBIN LEA, computer software industry executive; b. Denver, Feb. 23, 1950; d. Fred Warren and Claudia Jean (Harding) C.; m. Lucien Ray Reed, Feb. 23, 1981 (div. Oct. 1984). BS in Bus. Comm., U. Ky., 1972. Systems analyst 1st Nat. Bank, Lexington, Ky., 1972-73, SW BancShares, Houston, 1973-77; sales rep. Software Internat., Houston, 1977-80; dist. mgr. UCCEL, Dallas, 1980-82; v.p. and gen. mgr. Southeastern region Info. Sci., Inc., Atlanta, 1982-83; v.p. sales and mktg. TesserAct, San Francisco, 1983-86, Foothill Rsch., San Francisco, 1986; pres., founder Curle Cons. Group, San Francisco, 1986-89; mgr. strategic mktg. MCC, Austin, Tex., 1989-90; founder, exec. v.p. Evolutionary Tech., Inc., Austin, 1991-99; pres., CEO Journée Software, Austin, 1999-2000; founder, mng. dir. CEO Partnerships, Austin, 2000—02; pres., CEO Zebra Imaging, 2002—. Bd. dirs. Evolutionary Techs. Internat., Austin Software Coun., Tex. Property and Casualty, Zebra Imaging, Govs. Bus. Coun.; adv. bd. 360 Summit; dir. adv. bd. U. Tex. Engring. Sch. Recipient Ma Ferguson award Exec. Women Internat. 1997, Grad of Yr. award Nat. Bus. Incubator Assn. 1996, Profiles in Power award, 1999, Entrepreneur of Yr. award 360 Summit Adv. Bd.; feature in Forbes Mag., 1996, Entrepreneur Mag., 1997; named top 50 most prestigious people Digital South; profile documentary Entrepreneurial Revolution, 1997, Inc 500 List, 1997, 98. Mem. U. Ky. Alumni Assn., Women in Tech., Women of Austin, Software Exec. Com., Inc. 500 Cos., Austin C. of C. (bd. dirs.), Delta Gamma (pres. 1969). Republican. Avocations: scuba diving, running, skiing, cooking. Home: 7009 Quill Leaf Cv Austin TX 78750-8306 Office Phone: 512-583-1222. Personal E-mail: rcurle@zebraimaging.com. E-mail: rcurle@austin.rr.com.

CURLEE, J. MATTHEW, musician, director; b. Greensboro, NC, Apr. 26, 1976; s. John T. and Ellen H. Curlee; m. Alisa F. Rathjen, Dec. 20, 1998. MusB, Eastman Sch. Music, 1999, MA, 2000. Cert. performer Eastman Sch. Music, 1999. Asst. organist Peachtree Presbyn. Ch., Atlanta, 2001—02; organist, dir. music St. Joseph's Cath. Ch., Penfield, NY, 2002—. Internat. concert artist, 1996—. Musician, prodr. (album) Mackerel Sky, Syntax; musician: (album) An Austrian Neurotic in Graf Kaiserling's Court. Vol. EMT Penfield Ambulance, 2000—05. Finalist Calgary Internat. Organ Competition, Calgary Internat. Organ Festival, 1998; recipient Grand Prix Chartres award, Concours Internat. D'Orgue, 1996. Mem.: Am. Guild Organists. Office: Suigeneris Creative Prodns PO Box 99 Penfield NY 14526 Office Phone: 585-764-0856.

CURLER, JEFFREY H., packaging manufacturing executive; Various positions Bemis Co., Inc., Mpls., 1973—, pres., 1995—, COO, 1998-2000, CEO, 2000—, also chmn. Office: Bemis Co Inc 222 S 9th St Ste 2300 Minneapolis MN 55402-4099*

CURLEY, EDWIN MUNSON, philosophy educator; b. Albany, N.Y., May 1, 1937; s. Julius Edwin and Gertrude E.; m. Ruth Helen Snyder, Dec. 12, 1959; children: Julia Anne, Richard Edwin. BA, Lafayette Coll., 1959; PhD, Duke U., 1963. Asst. prof. philosophy San Jose State Coll., 1963-66; research fellow Australian Nat. U., Canberra, 1966-68, fellow, 1968-72, sr. fellow, 1972-77; prof. philosophy Northwestern U., 1977-83, U. Ill.-Chgo., 1983-93, U. Mich., 1993—. Author: Hellenistic Philosophy, 1965, Spinoza's Metaphysics, 1969, Descartes Against the Skeptics, 1978, The Collected Works of Spinoza, vol. 1, 1985, Behind the Geometrical Method, 1988, A Spinoza Reader, 1994, Hobbes' Leviathan, 1994; Am. co-editor Archiv für Geschichte der Philosophie, 1979-95; contbr. articles to profl. jours. Fellow AAAS; mem. Am. Philos. Assn. (v.p. ctr. divsn., 1989-90, pres. 1990-91). Home: 2645 Pin Oak Dr Ann Arbor MI 48103-2370 Office: U Mich Dept Philosophy 2215 Angell Hall Ann Arbor MI 48109 Business E-Mail: emcurley@umich.edu.

CURLEY, JOHN FRANCIS, JR., mutual fund executive; b. Wollaston, Mass., July 24, 1939; s. John Francis and Ann (Omar) C.; m. Loretta Mae O'Keeffe, Oct. 20, 1962; children: William Laurance, Edward Reid, David Neil. Grad., Phillips Acad.; AB, Princeton U., 1960; MBA, Harvard U., 1962. With Paine, Webber, Jackson & Curtis, Inc., N.Y.C., 1964—, gen. ptnr., 1969-72, exec. v.p., 1972-77, pres., 1977-80, chmn. fin. com., 1980-82; vice-chmn. bd. Legg Mason, Inc., Balt., 1982-98, Legg Mason Wood Walker, Inc., Balt., 1982-98. Chmn. bd. dirs. Legg Mason Mutual Funds, 1982-; bd. govs. Investment Co. Inst., ICI Mut. Ins. Co., 1994-98, Sellinger Sch. Bus., 1995-98. 1st lt. AUS, 1962-64. Mem. Securities Industry Assn. (dir., exec. com. 1978-80), Investment Assn. N.Y. (past pres.). Office: Legg Mason Wood Walker Inc 100 Light St Baltimore MD 21202-1099

CURLEY, THOMAS, newspaper executive; b. Easton, Pa., July 6, 1948; s. John Joseph and Emily Dixon (Sprague) Curley; m. Marsha Stanley, Sept. 14, 1974; children: Laura Stanley, Melinda Burke. BA in Polit. Sci., La Salle U., 1970; MBA, Rochester Inst. Tech., 1977. Reporter The News Tribune, Woodbridge, NJ, 1967, 1968, reporter, copy editor, 1970—72; night city/suburban editor The Times-Tribune, Rochester, NY, 1972—76; dir. info. Gannett Co., Inc., Rochester, 1976—80, dir. rsch., 1980—82; editor Norwich (Conn.) Bulletin, 1982—83; pub. The Courier-News, Bridgewater, NJ, 1983—85; exec. v.p. USA Today, Washington, 1985—86, pres., 1986—89, pres., COO, 1989—91, pres., pub., 1991—2003; sr. v.p. Gannett Co., Inc., 1998—; pres., CEO The Associated Press, NYC, 2003—. Trustee LaSalle U., Phila., 1987—, Rochester Inst. Tech., Ronald McDonald House Charities; former chmn. Am. Advertising Fed. Hall of Fame; mem. exec. bd. Ad Council. Pres. Ctrl. Jersey C. of C., Plainfield, NJ, 1984—85; exec. v.p. United Way Somerset Valley, Bridgewater, 1985; bd. dirs. Assn. for Retarded Citizens, Manville, NJ, 1983—85. Recipient Alumnus of Yr. award, Rochester Inst. Tech., 1986; Pub. Opinion Rsch. fellow, Northwestern U., 1976. Office: The Associated Press 50 Rockefeller Plz Flr 7 New York NY 10020-1605

CURLEY, WALTER JOSEPH PATRICK, diplomat, investment banker; b. Pitts., Sept. 17, 1922; s. Walter Joseph and Marguerite Inez (Cowan) C.; m. Mary Walton, Dec. 18, 1948; children: Margaret Cowan, Walter Joseph, Patrick III, John Walton (dec. 2003), James Mellon (dec. 1994). BA, Yale U., 1944; cert., U. Oslo, 1948; MBA, Harvard U., 1948; LLD (hon.), Trinity Coll., Dublin, Ireland, 1976. Mgr. Caltex Oil Co., India, 1948-52, 1952-55, N.Y.C., 1955-57; v.p. San Jacinto Petroleum, 1957-60; ptnr. J.H. Whitney Co., 1961-75. Commr. pub. events, chief protocol City of N.Y., 1973-74; amb. to Ireland, 1975-77, amb. to France, 1989-93; prin. W.J.P. Curley, 1978—; pres. Curley Land Co., Pitts., 1993—; chmn. internat. adv. bd. Sotheby's, 1999—. Author: Letters From The Pacific, 1965, Monarchs in Waiting, 1974, Vanishing Kingdoms, 2004. Trustee Buckley Sch., 1960-75, Miss Porter's Sch., Farmington, Mass., 1965-74, Barnard Coll., 1966-75, N.Y. Pub. Libr., 1972-75, The Frick Collection, 1993-2004; hon. chmn. French-Am. Found., N.Y., 1993—. Decorated Bronze Star; Cloud and Banner (Republic of China); comdr. French Legion of Honor. Mem. Coun. Fgn. Rels., Yale Club, Knickerbocker Club, Links Club, Racquet and Tennis Club, Rolling Rock Club (Ligonier, Pa.), Kildare St. Club (Dublin), Bedford Golf and Tennis Club, Traveller's Club (Paris), Seminole Golf Club (Palm Beach, Fla.). Office: 645 Fifth Ave 18th Fl New York NY 10022 E-mail: curleywjp@aol.com.

CURLOOK, WALTER, management consultant; b. Coniston, Ont., Can., Mar. 14, 1929; s. William and Stephanie (Acker) C.; m. Jennifer Burak, May 28, 1955; children: Christine, William Paul, John Michael, Andrea. BA in Sci., U. Toronto, 1950, MA in Sci., 1951, PhD, 1953, DEng (hon.), 2002; DSc (hon.), Laurentian U., 1983. Postdoctoral fellow Imperial Coll. Sci. and Tech., London, 1954; rsch. metallurgist Inco, Sudbury, Canada, 1954-59, supr. rsch. sta. Port Colborne, Canada, 1959-60, supr. rsch. Copper Cliff, Canada, 1960-64, asst. to gen. mgr., 1964-69, v.p. adminstrv. and engring. svcs., 1973-74, v.p. NYC, 1974-77; dir. tech. COFIMPAC, Paris, 1969-72; sr. v.p. prodn. Inco Metals Co., Toronto, 1977-80, pres., chief exec. officer, 1980-82; exec. v.p. Inco Ltd., Toronto, 1982-91, vice chmn., 1991-94, dir., 1989-94; pres. Inco Gold Co., Toronto, 1987-89; pres. commr. P.T. Inco, Indonesia, 1990-93; pres., dir. gen. Goro Nickel, S.A., Noumea, New Caledonia, 1992-97. Disting. adj. prof. U. Toronto, 1999—; mem. Nat. Adv. Com. Mining Industry, 1980-94; mem. Premier's Coun. Econ. Renewal, 1991-94. Patentee in field. Bd. dirs. Cambrian Found., Sudbury, 1983; first chmn. bd. Cambrian Coll. Applied Arts and Tech., Sudbury, Ont., 1967. Named to Can. Mining Hall of Fame, 1997; recipient McCharles prize, U. Toronto, 1989, Charles F. Rand medal, AIME, 2002. Fellow Can. Acad. Engring.; mem. Assn. Profl. Engrs. of Ont., Metall. Soc. of Can. Inst. Mining and Metallurgy (Airey award 1979, Platinum medal 1994), Mining Assn. Can. (bd. dir. and past chmn.), Sci. North (hon. life Sudbury chpt. 1988), Ont. Mining Assn. (past pres.), Order of Can. Home and Office: 25 Cluny Dr Toronto ON Canada M4W 2P9 Office Phone: 416-934-1048.

CURMANO, BILLY X., art director; b. Milwaukee, Wis., Feb. 1, 1949; s. Nicholas Daniel and Marion J. (Peot) Curman. BFA, U.Wis., 1973, MS, 1977; sculpture program, Art Students League N.Y., 1982. Prodr. dir. cert. Hollywood Film Inst. L.A., Calif., 2001. Editor Wis. art guild news Wis. Art Guild, Milw., 1973—75; dir. Broadway Galleries, Milw., 1976—77; art coord. S.E. Librs. Cooperating, Rochester and ten county region, Minn., 1979—81; dir. XART and Art Works USA, Rushford, Minn., 1979—. Vis. artist U. Hawaii, Honolulu, 1993, U. N.C., Chapel Hill, 1995, Ill. State U., Normal, Ill. Solo exhbn., Progression, Selections from Objects; soloist, dir., prodr. (performance and documentary video) Swimming the Mississippi (Hampton award, 2002), (performance with documentary video) The Fire Bearer, composer/soloist (compact disc) Billy X: Solo Set. Pres. Winona Arts Ctr., 2001—04; corr. Found. Cmty. Artists, N.Y.C., 1980—82; steering com. Wis. Art Guild, Milwaukee, 1973—76. Specialist 4th class e-4 Army Airborne, 1967—69, USA and Vietnam. Recipient Billy X. Curmano Day St. Louis, Mayor's Proclamation, St. Louis, 1992, Billy X. Curmano Day New Orleans, Mayor's Proclamation New Orleans, 1997, Hon. City Councilman, Memphis City Coun., 1995, Hon. Citizen Greenville, Mayor Greenville, Miss., 1996; fellow Interdisciplinary Art fellowship, McKnight Found., 1997. Mem.: Coll. Art Assn. Achievements include represented the USA with paintings in the III Vienna Graphikbiennale, Albertina Museum/Vienna Secession, Vienna, Austria 1977; first person in recorded history to swim the Mississippi River from source to gulf in a 2, 367.4 performance and environmental statement, Swimmin' the River (1987-1997); Death Valley Desert Classic, 40 day juice and water only performance art fast in Death Valley, CA (1999-2000). Avocations: hiking, biking, camping, reading, canoeing. Home: 28401 Hartwood Dr Rushford MN 55971 Office: XART Exptl Art Rsch Terminal Art Works USA Rushford MN 55971 Office Phone: 507-864-2716. Personal E-mail: billyx@acegroup.cc.

CURNAN, SUSAN P., social policy and management educator, consultant; b. Hyde Park, N.Y., Mar. 7, 1949; d. Charles Agustus and Mildred (Kron) C. BA cum laude, Stony Brook U., 1971; MS, SUNY, New Paltz, 1972; MFS, Yale U., 1978. Cert. tchr. K-12. Rsch. assoc. Yale U., New Haven, 1976-78; dir. New England Non-Profit Corp., Vt., 1978-82, Brandeis U. Ctr. for Youth and Comtys., Waltham, Mass. Co-founder, pres. ER's Kitchen Cabinet, spec. food co., 2001. Co-pub. CYD Jour.; contbr. articles to profl. jours. Trustee Taconic Found., N.Y.C., 1987—93; co-founder, chmn. Inst. for Just Cmtys., 2001. Fellow Berkley Coll. Yale U., 1985, 88; Grad. fellow Yale U., 1976-78; recipient Key to City and Cert. Hon. Citizenship, New Orleans Mayor and City Coun., 1991, Outstanding Young Woman in Am. award, 1982. Home: 174 Boston Post Rd Sudbury MA 01776-3102 Office: Brandeis U 60 Turner St Waltham MA 02453-8923

CURNOW, KATHY, art historian, educator; BA in Art History magna cum laude, Pa. State U., 1974; MA in Art History, Ind. U., 1980, PhD in Art History, African Studies, 1983. Prin. lectr. dept. design Nigerian TV Coll., Jos Plateau State, 1983-85, head dept. gen. studies, sr. lectr., 1985-88; exec. asst. Am. Found. Negro Affairs, Nat. Edn. Rsch. Fund, Phila., 1988-89; vis. asst. prof. dept. art Cleve. State U., 1990-91, asst. prof., 1991-94, assoc. prof., 1995—. Grad. asst. Ind. U., Bloomington, 1978-80; adj. asst. prof. U. Pa., Phila., 1989-91; vis. asst. prof. dept. art Lincoln U., Pa., 1989-90, dept. humanities U. Arts, Phila., 1990; lectr. Met. Mus. Art, N.Y.C., 1990; vis. Fulbright assoc. prof. U. Benin, Benin City, Nigeria, 1997-98. Author: (chpt.) Communications Training and Practice in Nigeria, 1987, Kulte, Kunstler, Könige in Afrika, 1997; contbr. articles to profl. jours. Recipient Nigerian Learning Materials award, 1987, Nat. Merit award Nigerian Festival TV Programming, 1987; Westinghouse scholar, 1973; Ind. U. fellow, 1977-80; grantee Rsch. Challenge, 1992, Social Sci. Rsch. Coun., 1993, NEH, 1993-98, Fulbright award, 1997-98. Mem. African Studies Assn. (arts coun., textbook writing com. 1991-93, bd. dirs. 1993-97, chair book prize com. 1994-95, sec.-treas. 1995-97), African Studies Assn., Coll. Art Assn., Delta Studies Assn., Midwest Art Historians Assn., Sierra Leone Studies Assn. Avocation: writing fiction. Office: Cleve State U Art Dept 111 AB Cleveland OH 44115

CURNUTTE, MARY E., artist; b. Valera, Tex., Dec. 15, 1920; d. Robert Franklin and Mary Elizabeth (Walker) Line; m. James Richard Curnutte, Oct. 14, 1950 (dec. Feb. 1972); 1 child, Sandra Elizabeth; m. Robert Frederick Furman, Apr. 27, 1985 (dec. Apr. 2003). Grad. h.s., 1936. Bookkeeper, sec. drug stores, 1942-49, NCO Club, Goodfellow AFB, San Angelo, Tex., 1949-51; bookkeeper Boyce Hardware and Fuel Oil, Portsmouth, Va., 1953; artist/logs/filing Christian Broadcasting Network, Portsmouth, 1972-73; tchr. art Frederick Mil. Acad., Portsmouth, 1978-82, Alliance Christian Sch., Portsmouth, 1981-85; artist and pvt. tchr. art and music, restorer of art Portsmouth, 1959-89; artist Winter Haven, Fla., 1989—. Recipient Silver Cup award Alliance Christian Sch., 1984. Mem.: DAV Aux., Nat. Assn. Ret. Fed. Employees, Nat. Mus. Women in the Arts (charter). Baptist. Avocations: photography, swimming, fishing, music, travel.

CURNYN, KATHLEEN MARIE, elementary school educator; b. N.Y.C., July 20, 1943; d. James Aloysius and Sarah Marie (Wamsganz) C. BA, Georgian Ct. Coll., 1970; MA, Seton Hall U., 1973; MPS, Loyola U., 1987. Cert. elem. tchr., N.J., media specialist, adminstr. Tchr. 4th grade St. James Sch., Red Bank, N.J., 1964-65; tchr. 4th-8th grades St. Mary Sch., South Amboy, N.J., 1965-69; tchr. 7th grade St. John Sch., Lambertville, N.J., 1969-71; tchr. 8th grade O. L of Victories Sch., Sayreville, N.J., 1971-72; prin. 1-8 grades St. Ann Sch., Keansburg, N.J., 1972-80; tchr. 8th grade Sacred Heart Sch., South Plainfield, N.J., 1980-83; tchr. 7th grade Holy Spirit Sch., Perth Amboy, N.J., 1983-84; asst. supt. Diocese of Newark, 1984-86; regional supr. Diocese of Bklyn., 1986-90; prin. St. Matthew Sch., Edison, N.J., 1990—. Mem. ASCD, Nat. Cath. Educators. Roman Catholic. Office Phone: 732-985-6633.

CUROL, HELEN RUTH, librarian, English language educator; b. Grayson, La., May 30, 1944; d. Alfred John and Ethel Lea (McDaniel) Broussard; m. Kenneth Arthur Curol, June 25, 1967 (div. 1988); children: Edward, Bryan. BA, McNeese State U., 1966; postgrad., L.I. U., 1969—70; MLS, La. State U., 1987. Tchr., libr. Cameron Parish Schs., Grand Lake, La., 1966—67; media specialist Brentwood Sch. Dist., NY, 1967—69; sch. libr. Patchogue H.S., NY, 1969—70, 1976—95; reference libr., mgr. circulation dept. McNeese State U., Lake Charles, La., 1976—96; test adminstr. Edn. Testing Svc., Princeton, NJ, 1987—95; asst. prof. McNeese U., 1989—95; owner Curol Consulting, Lake Charles, 1995—2002; head adult svcs. Laman Pub. Libr., North Little Rock, Ark., 1996; media libr., tech. rep. LaGrange H.S., Lake Charles, 1997—2004; libr. cons. Calcasieu Parish Sch. Sys., La., 2004—. Rschr. Boise Cascade, DeRidder, La., 1987-88, Vidtron, Dallas, 1990-92, Nat. Archives, Washington, 1989; cons. Cmty. Housing Resource Bd., Lake Charles, 1988-93, Boyce Internat. Engrs., Houston, 1988-89, La. Pub. Broadcasting, Baton Rouge, 1989; devel. cons. Calcasieu Women's Shelter, 1988-92; reference cons. Calcasieu Parish Pub. Libr., 1990-95; presenter at confs. Sr. arbitrator Better Bus. Bur., Lake Charles, 1986-95; local facilitator La. Com. for Fiscal Reform, Lake Charles, 1988; state bd. dirs. PTA, Baton Rouge, 1981-83, LWV La., Baton Rouge, 1983-85; chairperson budget panel com. United Way S.W. La., Lake Charles, 1992-94, bd. dirs., 1995-96; judge La. region IV Social Studies Fair, 1979-89; program spkr. region IV tng. conf. HUD, El Paso, 1992; rep. on Nat. Taxpayer Advocacy Panel, 2002-05, to La.'s Virtual Libr. Commn., 2000—; mem. I-10 Petrochemical Industry's Citizen Adv. Panel, 2003—; apptd. City of Lake Charles Alcohol Rev. Bd., 2003-05 Named Citizen of the Day, Sta. KLOU, 1978; grantee La. Endowment for Humanities, 1987, La. Divsn. Arts, 1989, Fair Housing Initiative Program, 1990, HUD, 1992, La. Ctr. Women and Govt. of Nicholls State U., 1993. Mem. ALA (sec. coun. 1988-90, chairperson coun. 1990-91), AAUW (chairperson intellectual freedom com. 1988-89), La. Libr. Assn. (chairperson reference group 1988-90), La. Assn. Coll. and Rsch. Librs. (chairperson 1995-96), Ark. Libr. Assn., McNeese U. Alumni Assn., S.W. La. C. of C. (legis. com. 1992), Krewe du Feteurs (Mardi Gras Ct. Duchess 1992), Beta Sigma Phi (pres. Lake Charles chpt. 1983-84), Beta Phi Mu. Republican. Lutheran. Address: 1005 Cherryhill St Lake Charles LA 70607-4911 Office: Calcasieu Parish School Board's Library Services 2423 6th St Lake Charles LA 70601 Office Phone: 337-437-1211.

CUROTT, DAVID RICHARD, physics professor; b. Passaic, NJ, June 3, 1937; s. Frank L. and Mathilda (Esser) C.; m. Janice F. Warren, July 31, 1982; children: Lisa-Anne, Michael Williams. BS, Stevens Tech., Hoboken, N.J., 1959; MA, Princeton U., 1962, PhD, 1965. Teaching asst. Princeton (N.J.) U., 1965-67; asst. prof. Wesleyan U., Middletown, Conn., 1967-75; assoc. prof. U. North Ala., Florence, 1975-79, prof. physics, 1979-99, planetarium dir., 1980-99, prof. emeritus, 1999—. Contbr. articles to profl. jours. Vol. Florence Pub. Libr., Florence, Ala., 2001—05. Recipient NASA traineeship, 1962. Mem. Am. Assn. Variable Star Observers (pep adv. com. 1991-94), S.E. Physics Assn. Avocations: astronomy, playing recorder and oboe, genealogy.

CURPHEY, THOMAS JOHN, chemist, researcher; b. N.Y.C., Oct. 7, 1934; s. Theodore Joscelyn and Aies Curphey; m. Marilyn Gomulka, Aug. 2, 1959; children: Linda Lee, Alison. AB, Harvard U., 1956, PhD, 1960. Rsch. assoc. U. of Wis., Madison, Wis., 1960—62; instr. in chemistry Yale U., New Haven, 1962—64; asst. prof. of chemistry St. Louis U., St. Louis, 1964—68, assoc. prof. of chemistry, 1968—73, prof. of chemistry, 1973—74; adj. prof. of chemistry Dartmouth Coll., Hanover, NH, 1974—2003; sr. rsch. assoc. Dartmouth Med. Sch., Hanover, NH, 1974—80, rsch. assoc. prof. of pathology, 1980—85, rsch. prof. of pathology, 1985—2003, rsch. prof. pathology emeritus, 2003—. Cons. Crime Lab, St. Louis Met. Police, St. Louis. Contbr. articles to profl. jours. Grantee More than 30, NIH, NSF, 1962 - 2002. Mem.: Am. Chem. Soc. (treas. St. Louis sect. 1971—72, dir. 1974—75, chmn. organic tropical group 1966—67). Home: 12 Dresden Rd Hanover NH 03755 Office: Dartmouth Med Sch Hanover NH 03755 Office Phone: 603-650-1972. Business E-Mail: tjcu@dartmouth.edu.

CURRAN, CHARLES EDWARD, theology studies educator, priest; b. Rochester, N.Y., Mar. 30, 1934; s. John F. and Gertrude (Beisner) C. BA, St. Bernard's Coll., 1955; Licentiate in Sacred Theology, Pontifical Gregorian U., Rome, 1959, STD, 1961, Acad. Alfonsiana, 1961; PhD (hon.), U. Charleston, 1987, Concordia Coll., Portland, 1992. Ordained priest Roman Cath. Ch., 1958. Prof. moral theology St. Bernard's Sem., Rochester, 1961-65; from asst. prof. to prof. Cath. U. Am., Washington, 1965-87; vis. Kaneb prof. Cath. studies Cornell U., Ithaca, N.Y., 1987-88; vis. Brooks prof. Religion U. So. Calif., L.A., 1988-89, vis. Firestone prof. Religion, 1989-90; vis. Goodwin-Philpott eminent scholar in Religion Auburn (Ala.) U., 1990-91; Elizabth Scurlock U. prof. of human values So. Meth. U., Dallas, 1991—. External examiner in Christian ethics U. W.I., 1982-86; lectr. in field. Author: Christian Morality Today, 1966, A New Look at Christian Morality, 1968, Contemporary Problems in Moral Theology, 1970, Catholic Moral Theology in Dialogue, 1972, The Crisis in Priestly Ministry, 1972, Politics, Medicine and Christian Ethics: A Dialogue with Paul Ramsey, 1973, New Perspectives in Moral Theology, 1974, Ongoing Revision: Studies in Moral Theology, 1976, Themes in Fundamental Moral Theology, 1977, Issues in Sexual and Medical Ethics, 1978, Transition and Tradition in Moral Theology, 1979, Moral Theology: A Continuing Journey, 1982, American Catholic Social Ethics: Twentieth Century Approaches, 1982, Critical Concerns in Moral Theology, 1984, Directions in Catholic Social Ethics, 1985, Directions in Fundamental Moral Theology, 1985, Faithful Dissent, 1986, Toward an American Catholic Moral Theology, 1988, Sexualitat and Ethik, 1988, Tensions in Moral Theology, 1988, Catholic Higher Education, Theology, and Academic Freedom, 1990, The Living Tradition of Moral Theology, 1992, The Church and Morality: An Ecumenical and Catholic Approach, 1993, History and Contemporary Issues: Studies in Moral Theology, 1996, The Origins of Moral Theology in the U.S.: Three Different Approaches, 1997, Moral Theology at the End of the Century, 1999, The Catholic Moral Tradition Today: A Synthesis, 1999, Catholic Social Teaching 1891-Present: A Historical, Theological, and Ethical Analysis, 2002, The Moral Theology of Pope John Paul II, 2005; also articles; (with others) Dissent In and For the Church: Theologians and Humanae Vitae, 1969, The Responsibility of Dissent: The Church and Academic Freedom, 1969; editor: Absolutes in Moral Theology?, 1968, Contraception: Authority and Dissent, 1969, Moral Theology: Challenges for the Future, 1990; co-editor book series: (with Richard A. McCormick) Readings in Moral Theology: No. 1: Moral Norms and Catholic Tradition, 1979, No. 2: The Distinctiveness of Christian Ethics, 1980, No. 3: The Magisterium and Morality, 1982, No. 4: The Use of Scripture in Moral Theology, 1984, No. 5: Official Catholic Social Teaching, 1986, No. 6: Dissent in the Church, 1988, No. 7: Natural Law and Theology, 1991, No. 8: Dialogue About Catholic Sexual Teaching, 1993, Feminist Ethics and the Catholic Moral Tradition: Reading in Moral Theology No. 9, 1996, John Paul II and Moral Theology: Readings in Moral Theology, 1998, The Historical Development of Fundamental Moral Theology in The United States: Readings in Moral Theology, 1999, The Catholic Church, Morality, and Politics: Readings in Moral Theology, 2001, Readings in Moral Theology,2003, 04. Am. Assn. Theol. Schs. fellow, 1971; Georgetown U. Kennedy Ctr. for Bioethics scholar, 1972; named ABC-TV person week, 1986. Mem. Cath. Theol. Soc. Am. (pres. 1969-70, John Courtney Murray award 1972), Soc. Christian Ethics (pres. 1971-72, mem. editorial bd. Ann. 1991—), Am. Theol. Soc. (pres. 1989-90), Coll. Theology Soc. (Pres. award, 2003). Avocations: golf, swimming, reading. Home: 4125 Woodcreek Dr Dallas TX 75220-5074

CURRAN, DANIEL J., academic administrator, sociologist, educator; b. Phila. m. Claire M. Renzetti; children: Sean, Aidan. B in Sociology, St. Joseph's U., Phila., 1973; M in Sociology, Temple U., 1978; PhD in Sociology, U. Del., 1980. Joined St. Joseph's U., Phila., 1979, faculty positions dept. sociology, chair dept. sociology, 1988—92, dean Coll. Arts and Scis., 1994—97, v.p. acad. affairs, 1997—2002, exec. v.p., 1999—2002; pres. U. Dayton, Ohio, 2002—, prof. sociology, 2002—. Concurrent professorship Nanjing (China) U.; mem. task force on sports wagering NCAA, 2004—; mem. Ohio Aerospace and Def. Adv. Coun.; bd. dirs. Dayton Devel. Coalition. Author: Dead Laws for Dead Men, 1993; co-author (with Claire M. Renzetti): Social Problems: Society in Crisis Women, Men and Society, Contemporary Societies: Problems and Prospects Criminology, Living Sociology, Theories in Crime. Bd. dirs. St. Joseph's Carpenter Soc. Recipient Eternal Flame award for Holocaust edn., 2002; Fulbright Sr. scholar, U. Melbourne, Australia, 1990. Mem.: Dayton Area C. of C. (mem. exec. com.). Office: Univ Dayton 300 College Pk Dayton OH 45469

CURRAN, DARRYL JOSEPH, photographer, educator; b. Santa Barbara, Calif., Oct. 19, 1935; s. Joseph Harold and Irma Marie (Schlagel) C.; m. Doris Jean Smith, July 12, 1968. AA, Ventura Coll., 1958; BA, UCLA, 1960, MA, 1964. Designer, installer UCLA Art Galleries, 1963-65; mem. faculty Los Angeles Harbor Coll., 1968-69, UCLA Ext., 1972-79, Sch. Art Inst. Chgo., 1975; prof. art Calif. State U., Fullerton, 1967-2001, chmn. art dept., 1989-99; curator various shows, 1971—. Bd. dirs. Los Angeles Center Photog. Studies, 1973-77, pres., 1980-83; juror Los Angeles Olympics Photog. Commns. Project, 1983. One-man shows include U. Chgo., 1975, U. R.I., 1975, Art Space, L.A., 1978, Photoworks Gallery, Richmond, Va., 1979, Alan Hancock Coll., Santa Maria, Calif., 1979, G. Ray Hawkins Gallery, L.A., 1981, Portland (Maine) Sch. Art, 1983, Grossmont Coll., San Diego, 1982, (retrospective) Chaffey Coll., Alta Loma, Calif., L.A. Ctr. for Photog. Studies, 1984, U. Calif. Ext. Ctr., San Francisco, 1986, Cuesta Coll., San Luis Obispo, Calif., 1992, Cypress Coll., 1993, Tex. Woman's U., Denton, 1997, Irvine Valley Coll., 1997, Ellen Kim Murphy Gallery, Santa Monica, 2000, William Marten Gallery, Rochester, N.Y., 2001, No. Ky. U., 2002, Carnegie Art Mus., Oxnard, Calif., 2003; two-person show No. Ky. U., 1995; group exhbns. include Laguna Mus. Art, San Francisco, 1992, Friends of Photography, San Francisco, 1993, U.S. Info. Agy. Empowered Images, 1994—, USIA, Jan Abrams Gallery, L.A., 1995; group exhibns. include Mt. St. Mary's Coll.,

1997, Ranch Santiago Coll., 1997; represented in permanent collections Mus. Modern Art, Royal Photog. Soc., London, Nat. Gallery Can., Ottawa, Mpls. Inst. Art, Oakland Mus., U. N.Mex., UCLA, Seagram's Collection, N.Y.C., Mus. Photog. Arts, San Diego, Phila. Mus. Art, J. Paul Getty Mus., Phila. Mus. Art, San Francisco Mus. Art. Bd. dirs. Cheviot Hills Home Owners Assn., 1973. Served with U.S. Army, 1954-56. Recipient Career Achievement award Calif. Mus. Photography, 1986; NEA Photographers fellow, 1980; Honored Educatior award Soc. Photographic Edn., 1996. Mem. Soc. Photog. Edn. (dir. 1975-79, honored educator 1996). Home: 10537 Dunleer Dr Los Angeles CA 90064-4317 Personal E-mail: localdj@mindspring.com. *I am an artist with abstract expressionist sympathies who chooses to use the photographic medium in its broadest definition.*

CURRAN, EMILY KATHERINE, museum director; b. Boston, Mar. 27, 1960; d. George Morton and Gloria Rose (Martino) C.; m. John Vincent Callahan, Oct. 8, 1989; 1 dau., Clara Huiru. AB in Fine Arts, Bard Coll., 1982; MS in Mus. Leadership, Bank Street Coll., 1992. Sr. developer The Children's Mus., Boston, 1982-88; dir. edn. The Old South Meeting House, Boston, 1988-92, exec. dir., 1992—. Vis. cmty. artist Great George's Project, Liverpool, Eng., 1983. Author: Science Sensations, 1989, An Architectural History of the Old South Meeting House, 1995. Bd. dirs. Freedom Trail Found., Boston, 1992-97; elected mem. Colonial Soc. Mass., 1996—; mem., exec. com. mem. cmty. adv. bd. WGBH, Boston, 1996-99, vice chair, 1998-99. Mus. edn. fellow Bank Street Coll., 1989-91. Fellow Mass. Hist. Soc.; Mem. Am. Assn. Mus., Am. Assn. State and Local History, New Eng. Mus. Assn., Boston Mus. Educators' Roundtable (chair steering com. 1989-91). Office: Old South Meeting House 310 Washington St Boston MA 02108-4616

CURRAN, J. JOSEPH, JR., state attorney general; b. West Palm Beach, Fla., July 7, 1931; s. J. Joseph Sr. and Catherine (Clark) Curran; m. Barbara Marie Atkins, 1959; children: Mary Carole, Alice Ann, Catherine Marie, J. Joseph III, William A.(dec.). LLB, U. Balt., 1959. Bar: Md. 1959, U.S. Dist. Ct. Md., U.S. Supreme Ct. 1987. Mem. Md. House of del., 1958—63; State senator from Md., 1963—82; lt. gov. State of Md., 1983—87, atty. gen. Balt., 1987—. Mem. Md. Regional Planning Coun., 1963—82. Mem.: Balt. Bar Assn., Md. Bar Assn. Democrat. Office: Office of Atty Gen 200 Saint Paul Pl Baltimore MD 21202-2002*

CURRAN, JAMES W., epidemiologist, educator, academic administrator; b. Monroe, Mich., Sept. 16, 1944; married; 2 children. BS, U. Notre Dame, 1966; MD, U. Mich., 1970; MPH, Harvard U., 1974. Rsch. instr. dept. preventive and cmty. medicine U. Tenn. Med. Sch., 1971—73; career devel. tng. Ctr. Disease Control, USPHS, 1973—75; asst. commr. health med. svc. Columbus (Ohio) City Health Dept., 1975—78; chief oper. rsch. br. Venereal Disease Control Ctr. Disease Control and Prevention, 1978—82; dir. Acquired Immune Deficiency Syndrome Activ, 1982—84; chief AIDS br. Divsn. Viral Diseases, Ctr. Infectious Diseases, 1984—85; dir. WHO Referal Ctr. AIDS & Retroviruses, 1985—92; assoc. dir. human immunodeficiency virus/AIDS Ctr. Disease Control and Prevention, 1992—95; dean Rollins Sch. Pub. Health Emory U., Atlanta, 1995—. L. Vernon Scott lectr. U. Okla. Health Sci. Ctr., 1985; Verna & Mars lectr. Baylor Coll. Medicine, 1988; Oliver Cope lectr. Mass. Gen. Hosp., 1988; clin. rsch. investigator Venereal Disease Br., Ctr. Disease Control, 1971—73; med. dir. Influenza Immunization Program, Franklin County, 1976—77; clin. rsch. investigator, coord. Oper. Rsch. Bd., Venereal Disease Control Divsn., Ctr. Disease Control, 1975—78; clin. asst. prof. dept. preventive ve and cmty. medicine Coll. Medicine, Ohio State U., 1976—79; John Forbes fellow infectious disease Fairfield Hosp., Melbourne, Australia, 1985; vis. prof. Coll. Medicine, U. Ill., 1988; asst. surgeon gen. USHPS, 1991. Recipient William C. Watson Jr. award, 1987. Fellow: Am. Epidemiol. Soc., Am. Coll. Preventive Medicine, Infectious Disease Soc. Am.; mem.: AAAS, Am. Venereal Disease Assn., Inst. Medicine-NAS, Sigma Xi. Office: Emory U Rollins Sch Pub Health 1518 Clifton Rd NE Rm 1820 Atlanta GA 30322-4201

CURRAN, JAN BARER, writer, editor, public relations executive; b. Walla Walla, Wash., May 2, 1937; d. David and Dora (Copeland) Barer; m. Alan Goldberg, June 16, 1957 (div. 1974); children: Lee Goldberg, Karen Goldberg Dinino, Linda Goldberg, Tod Goldberg; m. Don Curran, Dec. 27, 1976 (div. 1978). Student, U. Wash., 1958. Soc. editor, feature writer Lesher Comms., Walnut Creek, Calif., 1976-81; freelance feature writer Oakland (Calif.) Tribune, San Francisco Chronicle, 1981-85; feature writer Diablo Valley Mag., San Francisco Bay area, Calif., 1982-83; author HBJ, N.Y.C., 1976-80; editor Santa Barbara Writer's Conf., 1980-95; pub. rels. cons. Jan Curran Pub. Rels., Walnut Creek/Palm Springs, Calif., 1974-95; soc. editor, columnist The Desert Sun, Palm Springs, 1987—. Cons. Watts Industries, Oakland, Calif., 1983-84, San Ysidro Ranch, Santa Barbara, 1975-89, Bay Area Optometric Soc., San Francisco Bay area, 1980-84, Cancer Care Corp., Salt Lake City, 1985-87; mem. adv. bd. Open Space Found., Walnut Creek, 1983-85, Walnut Festival, Walnut Creek, 1984-85; speaker San Diego Writers Conf., 1984-87, Romance Writers of Am. Conv., San Diego, 1984, The Springs, Rancho Mirage, Calif., 1990, Lions Clubs, Kiwanis and Rotary, Palm Springs, 1992, 93, 94. Author: The Statue of Liberty is Cracking Up, 1978, 79 (Honorarium San Diego Writers Conf., Merit award Santa Barbara Writers Conf., Gov.'s award/State of Wash., Walla Walla Pub. Libr. award); columnist: (newspaper) The Contra Costa Times, 1977, 78 (Outstanding Achievement award, Oakland Airport Achievement award); author, feature writer book and mag. articles, 1979 (Merit award Santa Barbara Writers Conf.). Mem. adv. bd. Am. Heart Assn., Walnut Creek, 1974-76, Am. Cancer Soc., Walnut Creek, 1979-82; bd. dirs. Vision Coun. San Francisco Bay Area, 1980, Nat. Panhellenic Couns., San Francisco Bay area, 1974-77, West Coast Opera League, Palm Springs, 1994-95, Palm Springs Youth Ctr., 1993, 94, 95; vol. tchr. Mt. Diablo Sch. Dist., Walnut Creek, 1976, speaker, 1975-80; leader 4-H, Walnut Creek, 1974; ADL chmn. B'nai Brith, Oakland, 1965; founding mem. Lupus Support Group, San Francisco Bay area, 1976; mem. bd. dirs. pub. info. Contra Cost Unit Am. Cancer Soc.; model Fashion Show for Desert Hosp., Palm Springs, 1991; celebrity participant Cerebal Palsy Telethon, Palm Springs, 1989-92; interviewee radio and TV Lupus Pub. Info., Cathedral City, Rancho Mirage, Palm Desert, Palm Springs, 1992; speaker Children's Orthopedic Hosp., Palm Springs, 1994, Desert Hosp., 1993. Named Princess: Mardi Gras Ball, San Francisco Children's Hosp., 1974, Woman of Yr., San Francisco Panhellenic, 1975, 76, Woman of Distinction, Friends of Hebrew U., 1991; recipient Proclamation of Honor, Congressman Al McCandless, Riverside County, 1992; Jan Curran Day named in her honor City of Palm Springs, 1992, A Salute to Jan Curran, A Woman of Valour, Nat. Jewish Hosp., Denver, 1992. Mem. So. Calif. Book Publicists, Young Profls. (McCallum Theater, Bob Hope Cultural Ctr. Desert Hosp., Desert Mus.), U. So. Calif. Law League of the Desert, Santa Barbara Screenwriters Assn., U. Wash. Alums, Wash. State U. Alums (hon. cougar award), Desert Press Club, Womens Press Club (Press Woman of the Yr.). Avocations: reading, gardening, swimming, travel. Home: 2157 Casitas Way Palm Springs CA 92264-8213 Office: The Desert Sun 750 N Gene Autry Trl Palm Springs CA 92262-5463

CURRAN, JOSEPH PATRICK, lawyer; b. Providence, Apr. 25, 1951; s. Joseph Patrick and Susan (Donohue) C.; m. Sheila Jane McGowan, July 14, 1974; children: Christopher, Peter. BA, Holy Cross Coll., 1973; MA, London Sch. Econs., 1974; JD, U. Mich., 1978. Bar: R.I. 1978. Spl. asst. to gen. counsel Office of Sec. USN, Washington, 1978-81; assoc. Hinckley, Allen & Snyder, Providence, 1981-86; ptnr. Hinckley, Allen & Snyder, Providence, 1986—. Editor U. Mich. Law Rev., 1976-78. Pres. Improvise Inc., Providence, 1989—. Lt. USN, 1978-81. Mem. ABA, R.I. Bar Assn., Order of Coif. Home: 232 Taber Ave Providence RI 02906-3351 Office: Hinckley Allen Snyder 1500 Fleet Ctr Providence RI 02903-2319 Office Phone: 401-274-2000. E-mail: jcurran@haslaw.com.

CURRAN, LEIGH, actress, playwright; b. Santa Barbara, Calif., Dec. 5, 1943; d. John Van Benschoten and Barbara (Hansl) Griggs; m. Edward Herrmann, Sept. 9, 1978. Grad., Am. Mus. and Dramatic Acad., 1964. Mem. L.A. Women's Shakespeare Co., 1992—. Actress: (Broadway debut) How Now, Dow Jones, Lunt-Fontanne Theatre, 1968, (stage prodns.) The Lunch Girls, 1977 (also author), 'night, Mother, 1985, Stitchers and Starlight Talkers, 1986, Walking The Blonde, 1989 (also author), The 52nd Street Project, 1987-91, (feature films) I Never Promised You a Rose Garden, 1977, Reds, 1981, (TV series) Adam's Rib, 1974, St. Elsewhere, 1985, Another World, 1986, L.A. Law, 1991, West Wing, 2002, Judging Amy, 2002 author: (play) Alterations, Useful Trash, Zone 13 Hair, Michelle Hammer, Girl Detective, Destiny, Destiny, Destiny, Pressed Against Strangers; (teleplays) The Paper Chase, St. Elsewhere; artistic dir. The Virginia Avenue Project, 1991—. Mem. AFTRA, Actors' Equity Assn., Screen Actors Guild, Writers Guild, Dramatists Guild, Women in Film. Office: 3782 Redwood Ave Los Angeles CA 90066 Office Phone: 310-264-4224.

CURRAN, MARY, lawyer; b. NYC, Aug. 29, 1947; d. Philip Joseph and Catherine Mary (Galvin) C.; m. John Michael Quigley, Feb. 4, 1978; children: Oliver, Jane-Claire. AB, Fordham U., 1969; JD, Yale U., 1981; PhD, Columbia U., 1992. Bar: Calif. 1981, U.S. Dist. Ct. (no. and ctrl. dists.) Calif. 1981, 90. Asst. prof. Yale U., New Haven, 1975-79; assoc. McCutchen, Doyle, Brown & Enersen, San Francisco, 1981-84; sr. atty. Dean Witter Reynolds, Inc., San Francisco, 1984-85, v.p., 1985-87, asst. gen. counsel, 1987-92, sr. v.p., assoc. gen. counsel, 1992-97; gen. counsel, sr. v.p. Morgan Stanley Dean Witter Online, San Francisco, 1997—2002; mng. dir., gen. counsel Sutton Place Mgmt., LLC, San Francisco, 2002—. Mem. ABA, State Bar Calif., Bar Assn. San Francisco (cert. of commendation 1990-91). Office: Sutton Place Mgmt LLC 433 California St 11th Fl San Francisco CA 94104 Business E-Mail: mcurran@forwardmgmt.com.

CURRAN, MICHAEL J., finance company executive; Grad., Collgate U. Sr. v.p. Fleet Bank, 1993—99; dir. global svcs. FleetBoston Fin. Corp., 1999—. Mem. Fleet's Adv. Group, Fleet's Corp. Diversity Coun., Fleet's eCatalyst Exec. Panel. Office: FleetBoston Fin Corp 100 Federal St Boston MA 02110

CURRAN, MICHAEL J., Stock Exchange executive; BA in economics, Dickinson Coll., Carlisle, Pa., 1976. Sys. engr. Electronic Data Sys., 1977; mgr. info. sys. Peat, Marwick, Mitchell & Co.; mgr. Info. Tech. Resources & Strategic Planning Apollo Computer; ptnr. Coopers & Lybrand, 1986—93; sr. positions most recently COO Zurich Scudder Investments Inc., 1993—2001; CIO Boston Stock Exch., 2001—04, CEO and acting chmn., 2004—. Adv. bd. Hickory Hill Ventures LLC. Office: Boston Stock Exch 100 Franklin St Boston MA 02110 Office Phone: 617-235-2000. Office Fax: 617-235-2200.

CURRAN, M(ICHAEL) SCOT, lawyer; b. Dayton, Ohio, Feb. 7, 1952; s. John J. Curran and Patricia (Ludwig) Curran Schaffner; m. Ellen L. O'Leary, Apr. 22, 1978; children: Allison M., Scot Michael. BA, Washington & Jefferson U., 1974; JD, U. Pitts., 1977. Bar: Pa. 1977, U.S. Dist. Ct. (we. dist.) Pa. 1977, U.S. Ct. Appeals (3d cir.) 1977. Assoc. Lawrence R. Zewe Law Office, Washington, Pa., 1977-80; ptnr. Clarke & Curran, Washington, Pa., 1980-83, Saxton & Curran, Washington, Pa., 1983-86, M. Scot Curran & Assocs., Washington, Pa., 1986—. Bd. dirs. Mental Health/Mental Retardation, Washington, 1983-85; chmn. Civil Rights Com., Washington, 1988, mem., 1989-99; co-chmn. Profl. Awareness Com., Washington, 1989-99. Fellow SW Pa. Acad. Trial Lawyers (past pres. 1997); mem. Pa. Bar Assn., Pa. Trial Lawyers Assn., Washington County Bar Assn. Avocations: reading, golf. Office: M Scot Curran & Assoc 11 S College St Washington PA 15301-4821

CURRAN, MICHAEL WALTER, research scientist; b. St. Louis, Dec. 6, 1935; s. Clarence Maurice and Helen Gertrude (Parsons) Curran; m. Jeanette Lucille Rawizza, Sept. 24, 1955 (div. 1977); children: Kevin Michael, Karen Ann, Kathleen Marie(dec.), Kimberly Elizabeth; m. Mary Jane Lemanek, Aug. 18, 1981. BS, Washington U., St. Louis, 1964. With Monsanto Co., St. Louis, 1953-65, supervisory positions dept. adminstrv. services, 1956-64, rsch. technician inorganic chems. divsn., 1964-65; sr. ops. rsch. analyst Pet Inc., St. Louis, 1965-68; pres., CEO, dir. Decision Scis. Corp., St. Louis, 1968—. Former mem. adv. bd. Entrepreneurial Bus. Ctr., U. Mo., St. Louis; judge Tech. Excellence Awards, St. Louis, 2002—04. Co-author: (book) Handbook of Budgeting, 1981, Handbook of Budgeting, 4th edit., 1999, Effective Project Management Through Applied Cost and Schedule Control, 1996; editor: Professional Practice Guide to Risk, Vols. 1-3, 1998; contbr. articles to profl. jours.; developer theories of bracket budgeting and range estimating. Adviser Jr. Achievement, St. Louis, 1958—59; active United Way, 1958—62. Mem.: Soc. Cost Estimating and Analysis, Project Mgmt. Inst., Assn. Advancement Cost Engrng. (chmn. risk mgmt. com. 1991—, mem. editl. adv. com. 1997—, Tech. Excellence award 2000), Ops. Rsch. Soc. Am., Inst. Mgmt. Scis. (chmn. St. Louis chpt. 1971—72), Intertel, Mensa, Alpha Sigma Lambda, Sigma Xi. Office: Decision Scis Corp PO Box 28848 Saint Louis MO 63123-0048 Office Phone: 314-739-2662.

CURRAN, PAUL SAETHER, lawyer; b. Mauston, Wis., Nov. 24, 1960; s. Thomas John and Collette Mary (Saether) C. BA, Marquette U., 1983, JD, 1986. Bar: Wis. 1986, U.S. Dist. Ct. (ea. and we. dists.) Wis. 1986. Assoc. Merten & Schwemer, S.C., Milw., 1986-89, Gray & End, Milw., 1990-94. Instr. Cardinal Stritch Coll., Milw., 1987-94. Mem. Wis. Bar Assn., Delta Theta Phi, Phi Sigma Tau (v.p. 1982-83). Republican. Roman Catholic. Avocations: hunting, fishing, basketball. Home: 324 Tremont St Mauston WI 53948-1306 Office: Curran Hollenbeck & Orton SC 111 Oak St PO Box 140 Mauston WI 53948-0140

CURRAN, PHYLLIS MARIE, counselor; b. Cleve., Jan. 22, 1933; d. Herbert Charles Eisele and Edna Marie Huesman; m. James Francis Curran, Dec. 27, 1955 (div. Dec. 30, 1985); children: Debbie, Sean, Terry, Holly. Lic. ind. chem. dependency counselor Ohio, internationally cert. alcohol and drug counselor. Sec.-counselor Chisholm Ctr., Cleve., 1982—84; counselor, clin. dir. Stella Maris Detox Ctr., Cleve., 1984—90; clin. dir., counselor, cofounder Freedom House Inc., Cleve., 1991—98; co-founder Ed Keating Ctr. Inc., Cleve., 1998—, dir. program, 1998—, counselor, 1998—. Mem.: Ohio Chem. Dependency Profls. Bd., Nat. Assn. Alcoholism and Drug Abuse Counselors. Democrat. Roman Catholic. Office: Ed Keating Ctr Inc PO Box 770108 Cleveland OH 44107

CURRAN, ROBERT BRUCE, lawyer; b. Charleston, W.Va., July 2, 1948; s. Bruce Frederick and Hazel Viola (Hoy) C.; children: Michael Robert, Laura Elizabeth, Emily Ann. BA, U. Del., 1971; JD, U. Md., 1974. Bar: Md. 1974. Ptnr. Frank, Bernstein, Conaway & Goldman, Balt., 1974-92, Whiteford Taylor & Preston, Balt., 1992—. Co-author: Tax Planning Forms for Businesses and Individuals, 1985. Mem. Md. Bar Assn. (sec. and treas. taxation sect. 1985-86, chmn. taxation sect. 1987-88). Office: Whiteford Taylor & Preston 7 Saint Paul St Baltimore MD 21202-1626 Office Phone: 410-347-9472. Business E-Mail: rcurran@wtplaw.com.

CURRAN, THOMAS, molecular biologist, educator; b. Broxburn, West Lothian, Scotland, Feb. 14, 1956; came to U.S., 1982; s. Thomas and Jane Holden (McGovern) C.; m. Frances Ko-Fang Yao, Dec. 27, 1979; 1 child, Sean Philip. BS, U. Edinburgh, Scotland, 1978; PhD, U. Coll. London, 1982. Postdoctoral fellow Salk Inst., San Diego, 1982-84; sr. scientist Hoffman-La Roche Inc., Nutley, N.J., 1984-85; asst. mem. Roche Inst. Molecular Biology, Nutley, 1985-86, assoc. mem., 1986-88, full mem., 1988-95, head dept., 1989-92, assoc. dir., 1991-95; adj. prof. Columbia U., N.Y.C., 1989-95; mem. and chmn. dept. devel. neurobiology St. Jude Children's Rsch. Hosp., Memphis, 1995—. Mem. adv. bd. study sect. NIH, Washington, 1991-94, Damon Runyan/Walter Winchell Cancer Rsch. Fund, N.Y.C., 1992—96 Merton F. Utter Meml. lectr. Case Western Res. U., 1992. Editor: The Oncogene Handbook, 1988, Origins of Human Cancer, 1991; contbr. over 150 articles to sci. jours. and books. Recipient Young Scientist award Passano Found., 1992, Rita Levi Montalcino Lecture award Fidia Rsch. Found., 1992, Glasgow U.-Tenovus-Scotland medal, 1992, Litchfield Lecture award Oxford U., 1994, Golgi award Italian Acad. Neurosci. and Camillo Golgi Found., 1994.; Imperial Cancer Rsch. Fund grantee. Fellow AAAS, Am. Acad. Microbiology; mem. Am. Assn. for Cancer Rsch. (Rhoads award 1993, pres.-elect 1999), Am. Soc. for Cell Biology, Am. Soc. Biochemistry and Molecular Biology, Soc. for Neurosci., Harvey Soc. Roman Catholic. Achievements include discovery and characterization of fos oncogene which causes bone tumors in mice; demonstration that fos gene expression is increased rapidly in many cell types treated with agents associated with mitogenesis, differentiation and stimulation of neurons, fos encodes DNA binding protein that functions in transcriptional regulation in association with the product of the jun oncogene, identification of gene responsible for the mouse, neurodevelopmental mutation reeler. Office: St Jude Childrens Rsch Hosp 332 N Lauderdale St Memphis TN 38105-2729

CURRERI, PETER WILLIAM, health facility administrator, consultant; b. Milw., Sept. 2, 1936; s. Anthony Rudolph and Dorothea Christiana (Heubsch) C.; m. Patricia Ann Egry, Aug. 14, 1958 (div. 1975); children: Charles Anthony, James Bradley, Regina Dawn. BA, Swarthmore Coll., 1958; MD, U. Pa., 1962. Intern Hosp. of U. Pa., 1962-63, resident in surgery, 1963-68; asst. prof. surgery U. Tex., Southwestern MEd. Ctr., Dallas, 1971-74; assoc. prof. surgery U. Wash. Med. Sch., Seattle, 1974-77; prof. surgery Cornell U. Med. Ctr., N.Y.C., 1977-81; prof., chmn. surgery U. South Ala. Med. Sch., Mobile, 1981-88; pres. Strategem of Ala., Inc., Daphne, 1988—2003. Mem. surgery anesthesiology and trauma study sect. NIH, Washington, 1980-84, chmn., 1986-88; commr. Physician Payment Rev. Commn., Washington, 1988-97; mem. Medicare Payment Adv. Com., 1997-99. Contbr. articles to profl. jours. Lt. col. U.S. Army, 1968-71. Decorated Meritorious Svc. medal; recipient Rsch. Career Devel. award NIH, 1972, Curtis P. Artz award Am. Trauma Soc., 1989. Mem. Am. Assn. for Surgery of Trauma (pres. 1989-90), Am. Burn Assn. (pres. 1983-84), Am. Coll. Surgeons (sec. bd. govs. 1987-89), Halstead Surg. Soc. (pres. 1988-89), Soc. Univ. Surgeons (pres. 1980-81), Assn. Acad. Surgery (recorder 1972-74). Baptist. Avocations: golf, hunting, walking. Office: Strategem Inc 26064 Capital Dr Ste A Daphne AL 36526-6166 Office Phone: 251-625-2205. Personal E-mail: curcur@msn.com.

CURREY, CECIL BARR, retired history professor; b. Clarks, Nebr., Nov. 29, 1932; s. Cecil Chalmers Currey and Edith Estelle Barr; m. Laura Gene Hewett, Aug. 14, 1952; children: Samuel Bowman, Anne Estelle, Laura Alise. BA, Ft. Hays State U., 1958, MS, 1959; PhD, U. Kans., 1965. From asst. to assoc. prof. history Nebr. Wesleyan U., Lincoln, 1964—67; prof. mil. history U. So. Fla., Tampa, 1967—2001, prof. emeritus, 2002—. Vis. prof. U. Nebr., 1966-67; vis. prof. mil. history U. Hawaii, Honolulu, summers 1991, 92; ednl. cons., 1967-98; mil. analyst Desert Shield/Desert Storm, various T.V. stas., 1990-91; invited spkr. Viet Nam Fgn. Ministry, Hanoi, 1988. Author: Road to Revolution: Benjamin Franklin in England, 1765-1775, 1968, Follow Me and Die: The Destruction of an American Division in World War II, 1984, Edward Lansdale: The Unquiet American, 1989, Victory at Any Cost: The Genius of Viet Nam's General Vo Nguyen Giap, 1996 (Pulitzer nomination 1997), Long Binh Jail: An Oral History of the U.S. Army's Notorious Prison in Viet Nam, (novel) Innocence Dies, 1999, A Time to Remember, 2004; contbr. to books, encys., and dictionaries, over 25 articles to profl. publs. Col. USAR, 1953-92. Grantee U. So. Fla. Rsch. Found., 1988, 89; recipient Disting. Alumni award Ft. Hays State U., 1975. Mem. Assn. 3d World Studies (book prize 1997). Avocation: travel. Home: 3330 Crenshaw Lake Rd Lutz FL 33548 E-mail: cbcthor123@aol.com.

CURREY, PATRICIA L., small business owner, financial planner; b. Youngstown, Ohio, May 20, 1954; d. Robert George and Betty Lou (Stiver) Alm; m. John Douglas Potter, June 21, 1975 (div. Feb. 1987); m. John Raymond Currey III, Aug. 17, 1991; 1 child. BSBA, Miami U., 1976; M in Gen. Adminstrn., U. Md., 1989; grad., Coll. Fin. Planning, 1996. Cert. employee benefit specialist, cert. fin. planner. Profit sharing analyst Booke & Co., Winston-Salem, N.C., 1977-78; indsl. engring. tech. Cons. and Designers, Inc., Winston-Salem, N.C., 1978-79; allocations unit supr. Wachovia Bank & Trust Co., Winston-Salem, 1979-80, asst. v.p. employee benefit plans dept., 1980-82, 84-85; v.p., group head, employee benefit trust group Nations Bank Trust, Balt., 1985-90, v.p., new bus. devel. personal trust unit, 1991-95; v.p. trust bus. devel. Farmers Bank of Md., Annapolis, 1995-96; v.p., mgr. trust mktg. and sales 1st Va. Bank, 1996-99; prin. Currey Fin. Consulting, LLC, Annapolis, 1999—. Evening lectr. asset mgmt. Anne Arundel C.C., 1994. Fin. com., bd. trustees Indian Creek Sch., 2004—. Mem. Fin. Planning Assn., Meml. Hosp. Easton (planned gifts com. 1991—), Salisbury State U. (chmn., planned gifts com. 1993-95), Anne Arundel Med. Ctr. (planned gifts com. 2000—), Natl. Assn. Personal Fin. Adv. Republican. Avocations: gardening, golf.

CURREY, THOMAS ARTHUR, ophthalmologist; b. Itawamba County, Miss., July 9, 1933; s. Charles Edward and Anna L. (Williams) C; m. Carol Ann Clabough, Nov. 7, 1959; children: Thomas A. Jr., C. Russell. Degree, U. Miss., 1955; MD, U. Tenn., 1958. Diplomate Am. Bd. Ophthalmology. Intern City of Memphis Hosps., 1958-59; resident in ophthalmology U. Tenn., Memphis, 1962-65; pvt. practice Memphis, 1965—; mem. staff St. Francis Hosp., 1965—, pres. med. staff, 1985. Assoc. instr. ophthalmology dept. family practice, 1990—, asst. clin. instr. ophthalmology U. Tenn., 1965—. Fellow ACS; mem. Tenn. Med. Assn. (v.p. 1987), Tenn. Acad. Ophthalmology (pres. 1975), Memphis & Shelby County Med. Soc. (treas. 1983-86). Office: Eye Specialists Assoc PC 1900 Kirby Pky Memphis TN 38138-3690 Office Phone: 901-754-0930. Personal E-mail: tcurrey901@aol.com.

CURRID, MICHAEL, finance educator, consultant, real estate developer; b. Dublin, Sept. 22, 1945; arrived in U.S., 1976; s. Patrick G. Currid and Mary O'Driscoll; m. Aideen M. O'Sullivan, Dec. 29, 1973; children: Elizabeth, Evan, Sarah. BS, U. Coll., Dublin, Ireland, 1966, BSc, 1969; MA, Trinity Coll., Dublin, Ireland, 1970, W.Va. U., 1978; PhD, U. Pitts., 1980; MBA, Duquesne U., 1981. Assoc. prof. bus. adminstrn. Susquehanna U., Selinsgrove, Pa., Gannon U., Erie, Pa. Brig. gen. Irish Army. Avocation: poker. Home: PO Box 279 Riverside PA 17868 Office: Gannon Univ 129 Mill St Danville PA 17821-1996 Office Phone: 570-275-5099.

CURRIE, BARBARA FLYNN, state legislator; b. LaCrosse, Wis., May 3, 1940; d. Frank T. And Elsie R. (Gobel) Flynn; m. David P. Currie, Dec. 29, 1959; children: Stephen Francis, Margaret Rose. AB cum laude, U. Chgo., 1968, AM, 1973. Asst. study dir. Nat. Opinion Rsch. Ctr., Chgo., 1973-77; part time instr. polit. sci. DePaul U., Chgo., 1973-74; mem. Ill. Ho. of Reps., 1979—, chmn. House Dem. Study Group, 1980-83, asst. majority leader, 1993, asst. minority leader, 1995, majority leader, 1997. V.p. Chgo. LWV, 1965-69; mem. Hyde Park-Kenwood Cmty. Conf., Ind. Voters of Ill., Ill. Conf. Women Legislators, Ind. Precinct Orgn., Hyde Park Coop. Soc., Ams. for Dem. Action., Women United for S. Shore. Named Best Legislator Ind. Voters of Ill., 1980, 82, 84, 86, 88, 90, 92, 94, 96, 98, Best Legislator Ill. Credit Union League, Outstanding Legislator Ill. Hosp. Assn., 1987; Legislator of Yr. Ill. Nurses Assn., 1984, Nat. Assn. Social Workers, 1984, Ill. Women's Substance Abuse Coalition, 1984; recipient Leon Despres award, 1991, Ill. Environ. Coun. award, Ill. Women's Polit. Caucus Lottie Holman O'Neill award, Susan B. Anthony award, honor award Nat. Trust Historic Preservation; awards Welfare Rights Coalition of Orgns., Ill. Pub. Action Coun., Chgo. Heart Assn., BEST BETS award Nat. Ctr. Policy Alternatives, 1988, Svc. award Nat. Ctr. for Freedom of Info. Studies, 1989, Beautiful Person award Chgo. Urban League, 1989, Friend of Labor award Ill. AFL-CIO, 1990, Ill. Maternal and Child Health Coalition award, 1990, Ill. Hunger Coalition award, 1991, Cert. of Appreciation SEIU Local 880, 1989, March of Dimes, 1988, Chgo. Tchrs. Union, Ill. Hosp. Assn., Ptnr. Vision award Families' and Children's AIDS Network, Woman of Vision award Womens' Bar Assn. Ill., 1997, Nat. Elected Pub. Offcl. award Nat. Assn. Social Workers, 1997, Outstanding Working Woman of Ill. award Ill. Fedn. Bus. and Profl. Women, Dist. Pub. Health Legislator award Am. Pub. Health Assn., 1999, Legis. award Ill. Primary Health Care Assn., 2002, others. Mem.: LWV, ACLU (bd. dirs. Ill.). Office: Ill Gen Assembly 300 State House Springfield IL 62706-0001 Office Phone: 773-667-0550.

CURRIE, BRUCE, artist; b. Sac City, Iowa, Nov. 27, 1911; s. Malcolm and Clara Mabel (Austin) C.; m. Ethel Magafan, June 30, 1946; 1 dau., Jenne Magafan. Student, Northwestern U., 1930-32, U. Chgo., 1932-33. One-man shows include Am. embassy, Athens, Greece, 1952, Ganso Gallery, N.Y.C., 1953, 54, Roko Gallery, 1958, 60, Albany Inst. History and Art, 1958, Ulster County C.C., Kingston, N.Y., 1967, Joseloff Gallery, U. Hartford, 1968, Schenectady Mus., 1970, Jacques Seligmann Galleries, N.Y.C., 1978, Midtown Galleries, N.Y.C., 1980, 83, retrospective exhbns. Woodstock (NY) Artists Assn., 1993, Windham (NY) Fine Arts, 2004, 20th Century Contemporaries Gallery, Hudson, NY, 2005; represented in permanent collections SUNY-Albany, Dwight Art Meml., Mt. Holyoke Coll., Colorado Springs Fine Arts Ctr., Butler Inst. Am. Art, Kalamazoo Inst. Arts, N.A.D., Ulster County C.C., Kingston, Berkshire Cmty. Coll. Served with USAAF, 1942-45, ETO. Decorated European - African - Middle Ea. Theater ribbon with 1 Silver and 1 Bronze Battle Star; recipient Purchase award Henry Ward Ranger Fund, N.A.D., 1964, 75, Clarke prize, 1966, Benjamin Altman figure prize, 1979, Gold medal of honor Nat. Arts Club, 1964; Albany Inst. History and Art award, 1967, Berle award Berkshire Art Assn., 1967, purchase award, 1973, Soletsky award Nat. Soc. Painters in Casein and Acrylic, 1973, Grumbacher award, 1974, John J. Newman Meml. award, 1976, Wallach Meml. award, 1980, Wright Meml. prize Cooperstown Art Assn., 1978, grand prize, 1981, also others. Mem. NAD (acad.), Audubon Artists (life, Medal of Honor 1963, 82, 98, Joseph Raskin Meml. award 1987, Ralph Fabri Medal of Honor 1989, Emily Lowe award 1990, Silver medal 1998Richeson award 2000, Salmagundi award 2002), Am. Watercolor Soc. (Silver medal 1958, Emily Lowe award 1968, Whitney award 1975, Winsor-Newton award 1981, Mario Cooper award 1985, Elsie and David WU Ject-Key Meml. award 1997), Adirondack Nat. Exhbn. of Am. Watercolors (Martin award 1988, Smith Packing Co. award 1990), Conn. Acad. Fine Arts (prize for Painting, 1965, Charles Noel Flagg Meml. prize 1968). Home: 72 Boggs Hill Rd Woodstock NY 12498-2706 Office Phone: 845-679-2170.

CURRIE, CAMERON MCGOWAN, federal judge; b. 1948; BA, U. S.C., 1970; JD with honors, George Washington U., 1975. Tchr. Moultrie H.S., Mt. Pleasant; law intern to magistrate judge Hon. Arthur L. Burnett U.S. Dist. Ct. D.C., 1973-74; atty. Arent, Fox, Kintner, Plotkin & Kahn, Washington, 1975-78; asst. U.S. Atty. Office U.S. Atty., Washington, 1978-80, Columbia, S.C., 1980-84; magistrate judge U.S. Dist. Ct. S.C., Columbia, 1984-86; pvt. practice Columbia, 1986-89; chief dep. atty. gen. Office Atty. Gen., State of S.C., Columbia, 1989-94; judge U.S. Dist. Ct. S.C., Columbia, 1994—. Adj. prof. in trial advocacy Sch. Law U. S.C., 1986-89. Assoc. editor SEC No Action Letters Index, 1972-73. Bd. dirs. Wings, Inc., 1986-94, sec., 1992-94. Mem. S.C. Bar, D.C. Bar, S.C. Women Lawyers Assn., Fed. Judges Assn., John Belton O'Neall Inn of Ct. Office: US Dist Ct 901 Richland St Columbia SC 29201

CURRIE, DAVID PARK, law educator; b. Macon, Ga., May 29, 1936; s. Gillette Brainerd and Elmyr (Park) C.; m. Barbara Suzanne Flynn, Dec. 29, 1959; children: Stephen Francis, Margaret Rose. BA, U. Chgo., 1957; LLB, Harvard U., 1960. Bar: Ill. 1963. Law clk. to Hon. Henry J. Friendly U.S. Ct. Appeals (2d cir.), N.Y.C., 1960-61; to Hon. Felix Frankfurter U.S. Supreme Ct., Washington, 1961-62; asst. prof. law U. Chgo., 1962-65, assoc. prof., 1965-68, prof., 1968—, Edward H. Levi Disting. Svc. prof., 1991—. Vis. prof. Stanford (Calif.) U. Law Sch., 1965, U. Mich. Law Sch., Ann Arbor, 1964, 68, U. Hanover, Germany, 1981, U. Frankfurt, Germany, 1986, U. Heidelberg, Germany, 1989, U. Tubingen, Germany, 1996, U. Aix-Marseille, France, 1998; coord. environ. quality State of Ill., Chgo., 1970; chmn. Ill. Pollution Control Bd., Chgo., 1970-72. Author: Cases and Materials on Federal Courts, 1968, 4th edit., 1990, On Pollution, 1975, On Conflict of Laws, 1968, 6th edit., 2001, Federal Jurisdiction in a Nutshell, 1976, 81, 90, 99, Air Pollution: Federal Law and Analysis, 1981, Constitution in the Supreme Court, 2 vols., 1985, 1990, Constitution of the Federal Republic of Germany, 1994, Constitution in Congress, 4 vols., 1997, 2001, 05. Mem. Am. Acad. Arts and Scis. Office: U Chgo Law Sch 1111 E 60th St Chicago IL 60637-2776 Business E-Mail: david_currie@law.uchicago.edu.

CURRIE, EARL JAMES, transportation executive; b. Fergus Falls, Minn., May 14, 1939; s. Victor James and Calma (Hammer) Currie; m. Kathleen P. Phalen, June 3, 1972; children: Jane, Joseph. BA, St. Olaf Coll., 1961; cert. in transp., Yale U., 1963; PMD, Harvard U., 1974. With Burlington No. Inc., 1964-85, asst. v.p. St. Paul, 1977-78, Chgo., 1978-80, v.p., gen. mgr. Seattle, 1980-83, sr. v.p. Overland Park, Kans., 1983-85; pres. Camas Prairie R.R., Lewiston, Idaho, 1982-83, Longview Switching Co., Wash., 1982-83, Western Fruit Express Co., 1984-85; exec. v.p. ops. Soo Line R.R. Co. & Rail Units, 1986-89; v.p. engring. CSX Transp. Co., Jacksonville, Fla., 1989-92, v.p., chief transp. officer, 1992-95; v.p. planning, chief safety officer Wis. Ctrl. Ltd., 1996-99; sr. v.p. ops. Rail World, Inc., 1999—2001; mng. dir. Estonian Rlwy. Sys., Tallinn, 2001—02; cons. rlwy. ops. and maintenance, 2002—. Bd. dirs. Belt Ry. Co. Chgo., Terminal R.R. Assn., St. Louis, Norfolk and Portsmouth Ry. Co. Bd. dirs. United Way, King County, Wash., 1980—83, Corp. Coun. Arts, Seattle, 1980—83, Jr. Achievement, 1980—82, North Shore Scenic R.R., 1999—, Hist. Union Depot, 2003—, Lake Superior Mus. Transp., 1986—89, 1999—, pres., 2001—; mem. Mpls. Neighborhood Employment Network; bd. dirs. James J. Hill Reference Libr., 2000—; trustee St. Martins Coll., Lacey, Wash., 1982—83. Mem.: Roadmasters Assn., Internat. Assn. R.R. Oper. Officers, Am. Assn. R.R. Supts. (bd. dirs. 1979—80), Am. Rlwy. Engring. and Maintenance Assn., Am. Rlwy. Engring. Assn. (bd. dirs. 1989—92), St. Olaf Coll. Alumni Assn. (bd. dirs. 1993—97), Seattle C. of C. (bd. dirs. 1980—83). Home: PO Box 2827 Warba MN 55793-2827

CURRIE, FERGUS GARDNER, performing arts educator; b. Chgo., June 29, 1931; s. Neill Roswell and Ruth (Anderson) C. BS, Davidson Coll., 1953; MA, U. Mo., 1957; EdD, Columbia U., 1963. Instr. Columbia U., N.Y.C., 1957-61, CUNY, 1961-64, asst. prof. speech and theatre, 1966-69; asst. exec. sec. Speech Assn. Am., N.Y.C., 1964-66; dir. theatre Ga. Inst. Tech., Atlanta, 1970-72, Emory U., Atlanta, 1972-82; pres. Atlantis Prodns., Inc., Atlanta, 1977-86; coord. arts mgmt. U. So. Fla., Tampa, 1985-86; ctrl. regional dir. Actor's Equity Assn., Chgo., 1986-96; ptnr. Theatre Mgmt. Assocs., Chgo., 1996—; prof. theatre, dir. sch. theatre Ill. State U., 1997—. Assoc. producer Centauri Films, Washington, 1983-84; guest dir. Okla. Theatre Ctr., Oklahoma City, 1982, Fort Wayne Civic Theatre, 1984, Kanahwa Players, Charleston, W.Va., 1984; artist in residence Ga. Council for Arts, Atlanta, 1982-84. Creator musical revues: From Harlem to Broadway, 1981; Harlem Nocturen, 1983, Sweet Auburn, 1985. V.p. DeKalb Coun. for Arts, Decatur, Ga., 1980-82; bd. dirs. Ill. Arts Alliance, 1988—. 1st lt. inf. U.S. Army, 1954-56. Gregory scholar, 1956. Mem. Screen Actors Guild (pres. Ga. br. 1983-85), Actors' Equity Assn., AFTRA (Atlanta chtp. pres. 1983-85, nat. merger com. 1982-87), Am. Coun. of the Arts, Ill. Arts Alliance, Assn. of Theatre in Higher Edn. (gov. bd. conf. chair, 1996-97), Nat. Assn. Schs. Theatre (chair ethics com. 1999—), Nat. Theatre Conf., Mid-Am. Theatre Conf. (pres. 1999-2002), Ill. Theatre Assn. (chair conf. 1999), Phi Gamma Delta (treas. 1952-53). Democrat. Presbyterian. Avocations: writing, golf.

CURRIE, JANET M., economics professor; b. Kingston, Ont., Can., Mar. 29, 1960; came to U.S., 1983; d. Kenneth Lyell and Edrith Delores Currie; m. William Bentley MacLeod, May 18, 1996; children: Joana Marion, Daniel Bentley. BA, U. Toronto, 1982, MA, 1983; PhD in Econs., Princeton U., 1988. Asst. prof. econs. UCLA, 1988-91, MIT, Cambridge, Mass., 1992, assoc. prof. econs., 1993, UCLA, 1994-95, prof. econs., 1995—. Panel mem. NAS, Washington, 1998-99, 2000-01, NSF, Washington, 1998-2001; rsch. assoc. Nat. Bur. Econ. Rsch., 1995—; mem. Brookings Roundtable on Children and Families, 1998—; affiliate Joint Ctr. Poverty Rsch., 1998—; cons. RAND, 1993—. Author: Welfare and the Well Being of Children, 1994; contbr. chpts. to books, articles to profl. jours.; co-editor Jour. Labor Econs., 1994-2000; mem. edit. bd. Quar. Jour. Econs., 1995—; assoc. editor Jour. Health Econs., 2000—02. Alfred P. Sloan Found. fellow, 1993-95, Olin fellow Nat. Bur. Econ. Rsch., 1993, Can. Inst. Advanced Rsch. fellow, 1998-2000. Avocation: gardening. Office: UCLA Dept Econs 405 Hilgard Ave Los Angeles CA 90095-1477

CURRIE, JOHN THORNTON (JACK CURRIE), retired investment banker; b. Houston, Aug. 4, 1928; s. John Felix and Irma Lillian (Haxthausen) C.; m. Dorothy Lee Peek, May 30, 1959; children: Harriss Thornton, Laura Graef. BA, U. Tex., 1949, BBA, 1950. Salesman Harris, Upham & Co., N.Y.C. and Houston, 1950-52; ptnr. Moreland, Brandenberger & Currie, Galveston, Tex., 1955-60; pres., bd. dirs. Moroney, Beissner & Co., Inc., Houston, 1960-74; sr. v.p., bd. dirs. Rotan Mosle Inc., Houston, 1974-81, chmn., 1981-83; vice chmn. Rotan Mosle Fin. Corp., Houston, 1984; mng. dir. Mason Best Co., Houston, 1984-86. Bd. dirs. family mut. funds managed by Am. Nat. Ins. Co., Galveston, Artspace Inc., Mpls., Minn., Internat. Exec. Svc. Corps.; rep. Muslim Comml. Bank, Karachi, Pakistan, 1992, Govt. of Lithuania, Vilnius, 1993, Capital Ptnrs., Bratislava, Slovakia, 1997. Trustee Holly Hall, Houston, 1968-73, Harris and Eliza Kempner Fund, Galveston, Tex., 1975—; mem. devel. bd. U. Tex. Health Sci. Ctr., Houston, 1978-89, U. Tex. Med. Br., Galveston, 1992—; mem. Chancellor's Coun. U. Tex. System; established Mary Tucker Currie Professorship, Tex. A&M U.; 1st lt. U.S. Army, 1952-54. Mem.: Yacht Club (Galveston), Krewe of Momus Galveston, Galveston Artillery Club, Houston Country Club. Republican. Episcopalian. Avocations: sailing, hunting, history. Home: 323 Longwoods Ln Houston TX 77024-5615 Office: 520 Post Oak Blvd Ste 125 Houston TX 77027-9495 Office Phone: 713-552-0033. *The acquisition of material goods makes life comfortable. Love received and given is the only real hallmark of a successful life.*

CURRIE, LARRY LAMAR, insurance agent; b. Rome, Ga., Dec. 30, 1946; s. Kaylor and Mary R. (Lee) C.; m. Linda Marie Warner, Nov. 9, 1968; children: Kristin Denise, Jeremy Scott, Matthew Lamar. Student, U. N.D., 1968-69, Gadsden State Coll., 1972-73; MS in Mgmt., Am. Coll., 1997. CLU, 1987; cert. facilitator Covey Leadership; registered rep. Agt. State Farm Ins., Millbrook, Ala., 1974-81, agy. mgr. Alexandria City, Ala., 1981-88, agy. dir. Birmingham, Ala., 1988-96, agy. field exec., 1996—. Mem. adv. bd. East Tallapoosa County Med. Ctr., Dadeville, Ala., 1987-88. Editor: Multiline Family Practice, 1995-98. Mem. adv. bd. U. Ala.-Birmingham, Golden 100 Club, 1993-94; high sch. econs. cons. Jr. Achievement, 1996-98; mem. adv. bd. Project Kids in Distress, 1997-98; bd. dirs. Kid One Transport, 1998-2001; bd. dirs. N.E. Ala. Boys and Girls Club; exec. com. mem. Shelby County Rep. Party, 1998-2001; mem. Pres. Bush's Bus. Com., 2002—. Mem. Nat. Assn. Life Underwriters, Autauga-Elmore County Life Underwriters (pres. 1978-79), Birmingham Assn. Life Underwriters (bd. dirs. 1996-97), Soc. Fin. Svc. Profls. (chair leadership and mgmt. sect.), N.E. Ala. Ins. and Fin. Assn. (bd. dirs. 2002-05), Pres.'s Cir. Am. Coll., Porsche Club Am. Republican. Roman Catholic. Avocations: jogging, sailing. Home: 524 Marsh Ln Oxford AL 36203-3967 Office: 1130 Quintard Ave Anniston AL 36201

CURRIE, LLOYD ARTHUR, nuclear scientist, educator; b. Portland, Oreg., Mar. 14, 1930; s. Stuart G. and Twilla L. Currie; m. Barbara B. Currie, June 27, 1959; children: Susan J., John S., Douglas W., Kenneth E. SB in Chemistry, MIT, Cambridge, Mass., 1952; PhD in Phys. Chemistry, U. Chgo., 1955. Asst. prof., chemistry Pa. State U., State College, 1955—62; rsch. chemist Nat. Bur. Stds., Gaithersburg, Md., 1962—85, leader, atmospheric chemistry group, 1985—94, fellow, 1994—, scientist emeritus, 2000—. Co-initiator Internat. Nuc. Sci. and Engring. Program, Pa. State U., State College, 1957—61; professorial lectr. Am. U., Washington, 1963—64; vis. prof. U. Ghent, Belgium, 1970—71, U. Berne, Switzerland, 1970—71; Commerce sci. fellow U.S. Ho. of Reps., Washington, 1974—75; faculty mem. NATO Advanced Study Inst., Cosenza, Italy, 1983; titular mem. Internat. Union of Pure and Applied Chemistry, 1984—2001, fellow, 2002—; cons. Internat. Atomic Energy Agy., Vienna; mem., chmn., nat. adv. bd. Nat. Ocean Scis. Accelerator Mass Spectrometry Lab., Woods Hole, Mass., 1990—95; mem. Internat. Steering Com. for Black Carbon Reference Materials, 1999—; mem., attribution sci. panel U.S. Interagy., 2003—04. Mem. editl. bd. Analytical Letters, Jour. of Chemometrics, editor, author Nuclear and Chemical Dating Techniques: Interpreting the Environmental Record, 1982, Detection in Analytical Chemistry: Importance, Theory, and Practice, 1988; contbr. articles to profl. jours.; author: Seminal, 1968 (Most Cited Work on Detection and Quantification Limits in Chem.). Recipient Silver Medal, U.S. Dept. Commerce, 1980, Gold Medal, 1989, I.M. Marci Medal, Czech Spectroscopic Soc., Czech Acad. Scis., 2002, NIST Gallery of Disting. Engrs., Scientists and Adminstrs., 2004—; grantee, U.S. Air Force, 1956—60, NSF, 1999—2000, EPA, 1980—88, NASA, 1990—95; sci. and tech. fellow, U.S. Dept. Commerce, 1974. Fellow: Am. Inst. Chemists (life); mem.: European Geosciences Union, Am. Geophys. Union, Am. Chem. Soc., Sigma Xi. Achievements include research in the development and application of micro-radiocarbon measurements fr the apportionment of fossil and biomass cabonaceous particles in the atmosphere. Avocations: instrumental music, skiing, sailing, swimming, travel. Home: 215 Rolling Rd Gaithersburg MD 20877 Office: Nat Inst of Standards and Tech Stop 8370 100 Bureau Dr Gaithersburg MD 20899-8370 Office Phone: 301-975-3919. Personal E-mail: lloyd.currie@alum.mit.edu.

CURRIE, MALCOLM RODERICK, aerospace executive, automotive executive, research scientist; b. Spokane, Wash., Mar. 13, 1927; s. Erwin Casper and Genevieve (Hauenstein) C.; m. Sunya Lofsky, June 24, 1951; children: Deborah, David, Diana; m. Barbara L. Dyer, Mar. 5, 1977. AB, U. Calif., Berkeley, 1949, MS, 1951, PhD, 1954. Rsch. engr. Microwave Lab., U. Calif. at Berkeley, 1949-52; elec. engring. faculty microwave lab. U. Calif., Berkeley, 1953-54; lectr. UCLA, 1955-57; rsch. engr. Hughes Aircraft Co., 1954-57, v.p., 1965-66; head electron dynamics dept. Hughes Rsch. Labs., Culver City, Calif., 1957-60, dir. physics lab. Malibu, Calif., 1960-61, asso. dir., 1961-63, v.p., dir. rsch. labs., 1963-65, v.p., mgr. R & D divsn., 1965-69; v.p. R & D Beckman Instruments, Inc., 1969-73; undersec. rsch. and engring. dept. Office Sec. Def., Washington, 1973-77; pres. missile sys. group Hughes Aircraft Co., Canoga Park, Calif., 1977-83, exec. v.p., 1983-88, CEO, chmn. bd. dirs., 1988—, also bd. dirs.; pres., CEO Delco Electronics Corp., 1986-88. Chmn., CEO Hughes Aircraft Co., 1988—92, chmn. emeritus, 1992—; CEO Currie Techs. Inc., 1997—, Med-Electvic, 2001—; bd. dirs. Innovative Micro Techs., LSI Logic Corp., Inamed Corp., Regal One, Enova Sys. Corp.; bd. overseers Keck Med. Sch., U. So. Calif.; trustee U. So. Calif., 1989—, chmn., 1995—2000. Contbr. articles to profl. jours.; patentee in field. Mem. adv. bd. U. Calif., Berkeley, UCLA, Galaxy Edn. Inst., Calif. Coun. Sci. and Tech.; former chmn. bd. trustees U. So. Calif., 1989; trustee Howard U., 1989-92, UCLA Found.; bd. dirs. western region United Way, 1987; coord., head U.S. Savs. Bond Dr., So. Calif., 1991. With USNR, 1944-47. Decorated comdr. Legion of Honor France; named Nation's Outstanding Young Elec. Engr. Eta Kappa Nu, 1958, one of 5 Outstanding Young Men of Calif. by Calif. Jr. C. of C., 1960; recipient Nat. Achievement medal Am. Elec. Assn. 1992, Goddard Astronautics award AIAA, Chester Nimitz award U.S. Navy League, 192, Thomas White award USAF, 1992. Fellow IEEE (Founders award 1995), AIAA (pres. 1994, Goddard Astronautics award), AAAS, Royal Aeronautic Soc., Am. Acad. Arts and Scis.; mem. NAE, Am. Phys. Soc., Berkeley Fellow, Commn. on Competitiveness, Calif. Coun. on Sci. and Tech. (co-chair project Calif.), Cosmos Club, Phi Beta Kappa, Sigma Xi, Lambda Chi Alpha. Home: 28780 Wagon Rd Agoura Hills CA 91301-2732 Office Phone: 818-707-8652. Personal E-mail: mrcurrie@sbcglobal.net.

CURRIE, NANCY JANE, astronaut; b. Wilmington, Del., Dec. 29, 1958; m. David W. Currie; 1 child. BA in Biol. Scis., Ohio State U., 1980; MS in Safety, U. So. Calif., 1985; D in Indsl. Engring., U. Houston, 1997. Neuropathology rsch. asst. Ohio State U. Coll. Medicine; commd. 2nd lt. U.S. Army, 1981, helicopter instr. pilot, sect. leader, platoon leader, brigade flight standardization officer, master army aviator; flight simulation engr. shuttle tng. aircraft NASA Johnson Space Ctr., Houston, 1987, astronaut, 1991, flight crew rep. for crew equipment, lead for remote manipulator sys., spacecraft communicator, flight engr. mission specialist on STS-57, 1993, flight engr. mission specialist on STS-70, 1995, flight engr. mission specialist on STS-88, 1998, flight engr. mission specialist on STS-109, 2002, chief astronaut office robotics br. Mem. Army Aviation Assn. Am., Ohio State U. and ROTC Alumni Assns., Inst. Indsl. Engrs., Human Factors and Ergonomics Soc., Phi Kappa Phi. Avocations: weightlifting, running, swimming, scuba diving, skiing. Office: NASA Lyndon B Johnson Space Ctr Houston TX 77058

CURRIE, PHILIP JOHN, research paleontologist, educator, museum curator; b. Toronto, Ont., Can., Mar. 13, 1949; children: Tarl, Devin, Brett. BSc, U. Toronto, 1972; MSc, McGill U., 1975, PhD in Biology, 1981. Curator paleontology Provincial Mus. Alta., Edmonton, Canada, 1976-81; mus. curator Palaeontology Mus. and Rsch. Inst., Drumheller, Canada, 1981-82; asst. dir. rsch. Tyrrell Mus. Palaeontology, Drumheller, Canada, 1982-89, head dinosaur rsch., 1989—2005, U. Alberta, Canada, 2005—. Sec. Alta. Paleontology Adv. Com., 1977-89; treas. Palaeontology Can., 1981-84. Author: Flying Dinosaurs, 1991, Dinosaur Renaissance, 1994; co-author: The Great Dinosaurs, 1994, 101 Questions About Dinosaurs, 1996, Troodon, 1997, Albertosaurus, 1998, Centrosaurus, 1998, Sinosauropteryx, 1999; co-editor: Dinosaur Systematics, 1990, Dinosaur Encyclopedia, 1997, Newest and Coolest Dinosaurs, 1998, Flying Dragons-Studies on the Transitions from Dinosaurs to Birds, 2003, Dinosaur Provincial Park, A Spectacular Ancient Ecosystem Revealed, 2005; contbr. articles to profl. publs.; featured in numerous articles and programs. Recipient Commendation medal 125th Anniversary of Govt. of Can., 1993, Sir Frederick Haultain award Govt. of Alta., 1988, Michel Halbouty award Am. Assn. Petroleum Geologists, 1999. Fellow Royal Soc. Can.; mem. Soc. Vertebrate Paleontology (program officer 1985-87, conf. chmn. 1988, conf. chmn. Mesozoic Terrestrial Ecosystems 1987), Paleontol. Soc., Can. Soc. Petroleum Geologists, Am. Soc. Zoologists, Sigma Xi. Achievements include research in fossil reptiles including Permian Sphenacodonts from Europe and United States; Permian eosuchians from Africa and Madagascar; Jurassic and Cretaceous dinosaurs from Canada, Argentina and Asia and their footprints. Office: Univ Alberta Biological Sciences CW 405 11145 Saskatchewan Dr T6G 2E9 Edmonton Canada

CURRIE, ROBERT, communications executive; b. Plainfield, N.J., July 30, 1959; s. Ashton Markoe and Evelyn Margaret (Gautreau) C.; m. Suzanne Jean Morris, Oct. 18, 1987; 1 child, Claire MacPherson Currie; 1 stepchild, Hilary Buchanan Boller. BS in Mktg. cum laude, Fairleigh Dickinson U., 1981, MA in Corp. and Orgnl. Comms., 1996. Journalist Foster Pubs., Scotch Plains, NJ, 1979-81; internat. specialist Hoechst Celanese Corp., Bridgewater, NJ, 1981-89, mktg. coord. Summit, NJ, 1989—96; dir. global comms. GAF Corp., Wayne, NJ, 1996—98; v.p., chief commn., pub. affairs officer J.M. Huber Corp., Edison, NJ, 1998—. V.p. HCC Sci. and Tech. Co., Inc., Bridgewater, 1989-92. Producer/dir. film: Trade Secrets and Technology, 1991 (Disting. Achievement award Am. Soc. Indsl. Security); editor (book): With Sword and Harp, 1992, (website) clancurrie.com; writer/dir. films: Winning Strategies, 1993 (Bronze medal N.Y. Festival, Bronze plaque Columbus Internat. TV Festival), The Pipes of Christmas, 2002, 03, 05 (Telly award); prodr. Tartan Day on Ellis Island, 2002—, The Crafter's Song (documentary short film); prodr. exhbn. The Life and Legacy of John Muir, 2005. Pres. Clan Currie Soc. Summit, N.J., 1990—; dir. Bonnie Brae Scottish Games, Millington, N.J., 1985-88, U.S. Equestrian Team - Horse Trials, Gladstone, N.J., 1990-91; chmn. Ethnic Adv. Coun. State N.J., 1993—; hon. plankowner USS John Paul Jones, Scottish Heritage U.S.A.; chmn. NJ Nat. Tartan Day.; bd. dirs. Save Ellis Island! Found.; mem. N.J. Gov.'s Adv. Com. on Preservation and Use of Ellis Island, 1998-2000. Recipient James S. Cogswell Outstanding Indsl. Secruity Achievement award Dept. Def., 1992, World Pairs Driving Championship, Gladstone, N.J., 1993, 10 Telly awards for broadcast and non-broadcast TV programming, 1993-2002, Outstanding Ethnic Leader of NJ, 1999. Fellow Soc. Antiquaries, Friends of Order of the Garter; mem. St. Andrew's Soc. of N.Y., Coun. Comm. Mgmt., Pub. Rels. Soc. Am., Nat. Investor Rels. Inst., Am. Soc. Media Photographers, Finlaggan Trust. Avocations: golf, photography, genealogy, music. Home: PO Box 541 Summit NJ 07902-0541 Office: JM Huber Corp 333 Thornall St Edison NJ 08837-2220 E-mail: clancurrie@mail.com.

CURRIE, ROBERT EMIL, retired lawyer; b. Jackson, Tenn., Oct. 10, 1937; s. Forrest Edward Currie and Mary Elizabeth (Nuckolls) Empson; m. Brenda Ray Eddings, July 2, 1960; children: Cheryl Lynn, Forrest Clayton, Kristin Emil. BS with distinction, U.S. Naval Acad., 1959; LLB cum laude, Harvard U., 1967. Bar: Calif. 1967, U.S. Ct. Appeals (9th cir.) 1970, U.S. Supreme Ct. 1979. Assoc. Latham & Watkins, L.A., 1967-75, ptnr. Costa Mesa, Calif., 1975—2003, mng. ptnr., 1993—96; ret., 2003. Dir. Constl. Rights Found., Orange County, Calif., 1986-91; lawyer rep. 9th Cir. Jud. Conf., 1991-93. Mem. exec. com. Orange County coun. Boy Scouts Am., Costa Mesa, 1982-95. Capt. USNR, 1955-83. Recipient Silver Beaver award Boy Scouts Am., Orange County coun., 1991. Fellow Am. Coll. Trial Lawyers; mem. Orange County Bar Assn. (dir. 1984-91), U.S. Supreme Ct. Hist. Soc. (chmn. So. Calif. 1992-93), Orange County Bar Found. (dir. 1999—). Home: 24 Pinehurst Ln Newport Beach CA 92660 Business E-Mail: robert.currie@lw.com.

CURRIE, RUSSELL, composer, educator; b. North Arlington, NJ, Apr. 3, 1954; s. James Andrew and Mary Allan (Fleming) Currie; m. Julie Currie, Apr. 1, 2002. Studied at, Mannes Coll. Music (with Alfred Mann), 1977; BA, Bklyn. Coll., 1981; MA, Eastman Sch. Music, 1996. Piano and theory instr. Packer Coll. Inst., 1982—84; adminstrn. dir. Haydn-Mozart Chamber Orch., 1982—84; project dir. The Poetry Project, NYC, 1983—85; artistic dir. ORRA, Inc., 1988; electronic music studio tchg. asst. for Alan Schindler, 1991—92; composition instr. Eastman Sch. Music, 1993—94; coord. Eastman Sch. of Music Composition, 1993—94; theory instr. for undergraduates U. Rochester, 1996; new music adv. The Am. Music Ctr., 1996—97; music dir. Edgar Allan Poe Soc. of Prague, 1997—99; dir. of electronic/midi studio Fieldston Sch., 1998—; artistic dir. New Opera Theatre Ensemble of Scotland, 1998—. Lectr. on new chamber music Orra Chamber Ensemble, 1988—91; guest lectr./pvt. lessons Royal No. Coll. Music, 1993—94, Cheatham's Sch. Music, 1993—94; com. on acad. integrity Eastman Sch. Music, 1993; guest composer seminar Royal Scottish Acad. of Music and Drama, 1996; guest composer seminar and lectr. London Coll. of Music, 1997. Condr. Opera Theatre of Rochester, ORRA Chamber Orch., Golden Fleece, Haydn-Mozart Chamber Orch., Am. Opera Projects, Bronx Arts Ensemble, Eastman Sch. Music; composer: Mackintosh's Lament, 1995, Dreams, 1995, Walk Me Home, 1993, Caliban, 1992, Rimshot, 1989, A Dream Within A Dream, 1984, The Cask of Amontillado, 1982, (film score) The Bunker, 2000, Dizzy Horse, 1995, The Black Cat, 1993, Azul, 1988, (prodn.) Perfect Roses, 1981, The Heart of the City, 1979, (chamber/orch. music) Frozen Motion, 1988, Wet on Wet, 1998, Dreams, 1997, Quiet Thoughts, 1996, Seasons of a Day, 1994, Coronach, 1994, Galvanic Music, 1993, Sonatina for Violin and Piano, 1990, Ancient Dances, 1988. Recipient ASCAP spl. awards, 1985—2003, Composer Assistance award, Am. Music Ctr., 1985, NY State Coun. on the Arts Individual Artists award, Nat. Endowment of the Arts, 1988, Grad. award, Eastman Sch. Music, 1991—94; Glasgow City Coun. Dept. of Performing Develop. grant, 1998—99.

CURRIE, STEVEN RAY, artist; b. Flint, Mich., Sept. 1, 1954; s. Richard Lee and Gwen Laurie (Cummings) C.; m. Annette Marie Davidek, July 27, 1985. BFA, U. Mich., 1977; MFA, Yale U., 1984. One man shows include Borgenicht Gallery, N.Y.C., 1988, 90, 92, 93, Ctr. Contemporary Art, Chgo., 1989, 91, Weatherspoon Art Gallery, Greensboro, N.C., 1995, Revolution Gallery, Detroit, 1995, Littlejohn Contemporary, N.Y.C., 1997; group shows include Boise (Idaho) Art Mus., 1994, Faulconer Gallery, Grinnell (Iowa) Coll., 2001, 80 Washington Sq. East Galleries, NYU, N.Y., 2002; represented in various mus. collections including Bklyn. Mus., Modern Art Mus. Ft. Worth, Walker Art Ctr., Mpls., Met. Mus. Art, N.Y.C., Albright-Knox Art Gallery, Buffalo, Orange County Mus. Art, Newport Beach, Calif. NEA fellow, 1988, N.Y. Found. Arts fellow, 1990, 97.

CURRIE, WILLIAM G., forest products executive; b. Youngsville, N.Y., 1947; Degree, Hope Coll., 1969. With Universal Forest Products, Grand Rapids, Mich., 1971—, pres., 1983—90, pres., CEO, 1990—2000, vice chmn., CEO, 2000—. Office: Universal Forest Products Inc 2801 E Beltline NE Grand Rapids MI 49525*

CURRIER, MIKE, elementary school educator, writer; b. Omaha, June 21, 1943; s. Melvin Ellis and Margaret (Morris) Currier; m. Linda K. White, Sept. 3, 1999; children: Melanie E. McQueen, Kjirsten L. Wellman, Marshall E., Merrill P. BS Elem. Edn. in Humanities, U. Omaha, 1965, MS in Edn. in

Reading, 1968; PhD in Edn., U. Nebr., 1977. Cert. elem. tchr. Tex., reading, English, social studies tchr. Tex., ESL Tex., mid. mgmt. adminstr. Tex. 6th grade tchr. Coun. Bluffs (Iowa) Cmty. Schools, 1965—67, reading clinician, 1969—70; reading cons. Ednl. R & D Ctr., Pipestone, Minn., 1968; assoc. prof. elem. edn. Peru (Nebr.) State Coll., 1970—73; ednl. specialist: rural edn. Edn. Svc. Unit #2, Fremont, Nebr., 1973—74; assoc. prof. of early childhood edn. Ft. Hays (Kans) State U., 1974—83; tng. devel., presenter Performance Learning Systems, Inc, Arlington, Tex., 1983—93; spl. edn. and preschool cons. Region XI Ednl. Svc. Ctr., Fort Worth, 1994—96; curriculum specialist Castleberry Ind. Sch. Dist., Fort Worth, Tex., 1996—99; classroom tchr. Springtown (Tex.) Intermediate Sch., 1999—. Ednl. cons., trainer State Departments Edn., 1969—2005; pres. Nebr. State Reading Assn., Omaha, 1976—77. Author: (manual) 5 Fingers: Games to Motivate the Growing Reader, Creating Effective Classroom Environments, (text) The Unordinary Classroom, Kindergarten: A Lily Pad or a Launching Pad, Teaching with M-powerment, The Write way to Teach Penmanship. Mem.: Nat. Assn. Edn. for Young Children (bd. dirs. Kans. chpt. 1979—84), Nat. Coun. Tchrs. English, Internat. Reading Assn. Republican. Baptist. Avocations: 1st century biblical history, etymology, computing, throwing pottery, raising orchids. Home: 7344 Chambers Ln Fort Worth TX 76179-2960 Office Phone: 817-220-1219. Personal E-mail: curriern@charter.net. E-mail: mcurrier@springtownisd.net.

CURRIS, CONSTANTINE WILLIAM, university president; b. Lexington, Ky., Nov. 13, 1940; s. William C. and Mary (Kalpakis) C.; m. Roberta Jo Hern, Aug. 9, 1974. BA, U. Ky., 1962, EdD, 1967; MA, U. Ill., 1965. Vice pres., dean of faculty Midway (Ky.) Coll., 1965-68; dir. ednl. programs W.Va. Bd. Edn., Charleston, 1968-69; dean student pers. programs Marshall U., Huntington, W.Va., 1969-71; v.p., dean of faculty W.Va. Inst. Tech., Montgomery, 1971-73; pres. Murray (Ky.) State U., 1973-83, U. No. Iowa, 1983-95, Clemson U., 1995-99, Am. Assn. State Colls. and Univs., 1999—. Chmn. emeritus Am. Humanics Inc. Trustee Midway Coll., Allen Coll. Nursing; charter mem. adv. coun. Nat. Small Bus. Devel. Ctr. Recipient Algernon S. Sullivan medallion U. Ky., 1962; named outstanding young man in Ky., Jaycees, 1974, U. Ky. Alumni Hall of Fame, 2000. Mem. Phi Beta Kappa, Omicron Delta Kappa, Sigma Chi. Greek Orthodox. Office: Am Assn State Colls and Univs 1307 New York Ave NW Washington DC 20005 *I am very grateful for what America has given me. As the son of a Greek immigrant who possessed neither education nor a command of the English language, I am keenly aware of the opportunities a government of and for the people affords its citizens. If there is any quality to which I attribute what success I have achieved it would be that of an abiding devotion to the "public interest" rather than allowing my decisions to be determined by vested or parochial interests.**

CURRIVAN, JOHN DANIEL, lawyer; b. Paris; s. Gene and Rachel Currivan; m. Patrice Salley; children: Christopher, Melissa. BS with distinction, Cornell U.; MS, U Calif.-Berkeley; MS, U. West Fla.; JD summa cum laude, Cornell Law Sch., 1978. Bar: Ohio 1978. Mng. ptnr. S.W. Devel. Co., Kingsville, Tex., 1971-76; note editor Cornell Law Rev., Ithaca, N.Y., 1977-78; prosecutor Naval Legal Office, Norfolk, Va., 1978-79, chief prosecutor, 1979-81; sr. atty. USS Nimitz, 1981-83; trial judge Naval Base, Norfolk, 1983-84; tax atty. Jones, Day, Reavis & Pogue, Cleve., 1984-88, ptnr., 1989—. Adj. prof. law Case Western Res. U. Sch. Law, 1997—2003; chmn. Cleve. Tax Inst., 2005. Author: (with Rickert) Ohio Limited Liability Companies, 1999. Comdr. USN, 1969-84. Recipient Younger Fed. Lawyer award FBA, 1981. Mem. ABA, Nat. Assn. Bond Lawyers, Order of Coif, Tau Beta Pi, Eta Kappa Nu, Phi Kappa Phi. Home: 12700 Lake Ave Ste 2105 Lakewood OH 44107-1506 Office: Jones Day Reavis & Pogue 901 Lakeside Ave E Cleveland OH 44114-1190 Office Phone: 216-586-7262. Business E-Mail: jdcurrivan@jonesday.com.

CURRY, ADAM CLARK, television personality, radio personality, computer programmer, computer technology company executive; b. Washington, Sept. 3, 1964; s. Jay Curry; m. Patricia Paay, 1989; 1 child, Christina. Host, music television program Countdown, Netherlands, 1972—87; video jockey Music Television (MTV), 1987—94, host, Top 20 Countdown, 1987—91; drive-time host WHTZ, NYC, 1989; host HitLine USA, Headbangers Ball, 1988—90; host, co-exec. prodr. radio show Adam Curry's Top 30 Hit List, 1993; host of several other radio and television programs broadcast station Veronica, Netherlands, 2003—04; founder OnRamp, Inc. (sold to THINK New Ideas, Inc (also co-founder), 1994—96; chief technology officer THINK (merged with Answerthink, Inc.), 1996—99. Contbr. BloggerCon 2004, Stanford Law Sch. Guest appearances (TV) Circus of the Stars Gives Kids the World, 1993; guest appearances (TV) Swamp Thing; guest appearances (TV) Another World, (TV Series) Adam's Family, 2003, Pulse, 2004; actor: The Weight of Water, 2000; prodr., presenter The Daily Source Code (dailysourcecode.com), prodr., host, writer The Buzz, presenter curry.com, iPodder.org, host Podshow.com, Sirius Satelite Radio, 2005—. Nominee Rave award in Tech., WIRED, 2005. Achievements include key player in the development and promotion of the concept of Podcasting. Mailing: Sirius Satellite Radio Inc 1221 Avenue of the Americas 36th Fl New York NY 10020 E-mail: adam@curry.com.*

CURRY, ALAN CHESTER, insurance company executive; b. Columbus, Ohio, Oct. 15, 1933; s. Harold E. and Martha (Dew) C.; children: Diane, Thomas, Timothy, Jeffrey. Student, U. Ill., 1951-52; EdB, Ill. State U., 1957. Various actuarial positions State Farm Mut. Automobile Ins. Co., Bloomington, Ill., 1952-70, v.p., actuary, 1970-97. Bd. dirs. State Farm Gen. Ins. Co. Fellow Casualty Actuarial Soc. (dir. 1970-73, 87-90); mem. Am. Acad. Actuaries (dir. 1977-80), Midwestern Actuarial Forum (pres. 1972-73), Shriners, Pi Gamma Mu, Pi Omega Pi, Kappa Delta Pi. Home and Office: 7 Canterbury Ct Bloomington IL 61701-3401 Office Phone: 309-662-8689.

CURRY, ALTON FRANK, lawyer; b. Dallas, Aug. 21, 1933; s. William Hadley and Myrtle Estelle (Posey) McKinney; m. Carole B. Piepgrass, Feb. 14, 1960 (div. Nov. 1979); children: Robyn, Mark, John; m. Ann O. Williams, Apr. 12, 1980. BA, Baylor U., 1958, LLB, 1960. Bar: Tex. 1960. Assoc. Fulbright & Jaworski, Houston, 1960-70, ptnr., 1970-98; spl. asst. to Atty. Gen. of Tex., 1964-65, 71-72. Trustee Found. for Bus., Politics and Econs., 1979-92, A.A. White Inst.; chmn. adminstrv. bd. Methodist Ch. Cpl. U.S. Army, 1953-55. Fellow Tex. Bar Found. (sustaining life); mem. ABA, Tex. Bar Assn., Houston Bar Assn., Baylor Law Alumni Assn. (dir. 1977-79, pres. 1979-80), Phi Alpha Delta, Houstonian Club (trustee 1980-83), Coronado Club, Masons. Home: 2707 Weslayan St Houston TX 77027-5123 Office: Fulbright & Jaworski 1301 Mckinney St Houston TX 77010-3031

CURRY, ANN, correspondent, anchor; b. Agana, Guam, Nov. 19, 1956; d. Robert Paul and Hiroe (Nagase) Curry; m. Brian Wilson Ross, Oct. 21, 1987; children: Anna McKenzie, William Walker. Student, U. Oreg., 1974—78. Reporter Sta. KTVL-TV, Medford, Oreg., 1978—81; reporter, weekend anchor Sta. KGW-TV, Portland, Oreg., 1981—84; reporter Sta. KCBS-TV, L.A., 1984—90; corr., anchor NBC News at Sunrise NBC News, N.Y.C., 1991—96; news anchor Today Show, 1997—. Nominee Emmy award, 1985, 1986, 1987, 1988; recipient Golden Mike award, RTNA, 1986, 1987, 1989, Cert. Excellence award, AP, 1987, 1988, Greater L.A. Press Club, 1987, Superior Reporting award, NAACP, 1989, Emmy award, Acad. TV Arts and Scis., 1987, 1989, Nat. award, AAJA, 2000, AmeriCares Humanitarian Medal award, 2002. Avocation: art history. Office: NBC News 30 Rockefeller Plz # 374E New York NY 10112-0002*

CURRY, CARLTON E., broadcast executive, councilman; b. Lizton, Ind., Mar. 4, 1935; m. Ann Merritt, 1957. BS, Purdue U., 1958. Registered profl. engr., Ind., cert. profl. logistician. Program adminstr. Allison Gas Turbine divsn. GM, 1966-79, staff systems analyst, 1979-83, mgr. mktg. program, 1983-85, dir. logistics support, 1985-90; cons., 1990-93; pres. SaniServ, Inc., 1990-96, Curry Inc., 1997—. Chmn. Cable Franchise Bd., 1996-2002. City councilman, Indpls., 1983-99; bd. dirs. Dept. of Waterworks, 2002; dir. contracts & ops. Dept. of Waterworks, 2002—. With USN, 1958-66, USAR, 1956-63. Mem. AIAA, Am. Water Works Assn., Soc. Logistics Engrs., Lions, Kiwanis. Republican. Baptist. Personal E-mail: accurry2@comcast.net.

CURRY, CLIFTON CONRAD, JR., lawyer; b. Tampa, Fla., July 8, 1957; s. Clifton C. and Louise (Owens) C.; m. Teresa D. Cox, Dec. 22, 1979; children: Mary Beth, Clifton C. III, Colton Cox. BS, Fla. State U., 1979; JD, Stetson U., 1981. Bar: Fla. 1982, U.S. Dist. Ct. (mid. dist.) Fla. 1982. Assoc. Mark R. Horwitz, P.A., Orlando, Fla., 1981-83; pres. Tittsworth and Curry, P.A., Brandon, Fla., 1984—, Curry and Assocs., P.A., Brandon, 1991—. Bd. dirs. Kiwanis Children's Clinic, 1988-90; vol. Missing Children's Help Ctr.; bd. dirs. Big Bros./Big Sisters, 1985-88, Rough Riders, 1987—, Brandon Outreach Clinic; chmn. Brandon Walk, March of Dimes Birth Defects Found., 1989; gen. coun. Grand Lodge of Fla. Masons, Egypt Temple Shrine, Tampa, Fla., 1996-97; active various polit. campaign coms. Recipient Alice Be. Thompkins Community Svc. award, 1991; named hon. mayor City of Brandon, 1985-86; recipient svc. award Brandon Lions Club, 1985. Mem. ABA, Assn. Trial Lawyers Am., Fla. Bar Assn., Hillsborough County Bar Assn., Brandon Bar Assn., Acad. Fla. Trial Lawyers, Brandon C. of C. (pres. 1989, bd. dirs. 1987-91, chmn. exec. bd. 1990-91, Small Bus. Leader of Yr. 1990), Kiwanis Club Brandon (past bd. dirs., pres. 1988-89), Krewe of Venus King's Guard (bd. dirs.), Fla. State Alumni Assn., Brandon Yacht Club, Ducks Unlimited, YMCA Century Club, Masons, Shriners, Scottish Rite, York Rite. Office: Curry and Assocs PA 750 W Lumsden Rd Brandon FL 33511-6217

CURRY, DALE BLAIR, retired journalist; b. Memphis, May 30, 1941; d. Hamilton Minter and Doris (Terry) Blair; m. Douglas Hester Curry, Dec. 21, 1963; children: Jennifer, Elizabeth. BA, U. Miss., 1963. Reporter The Commerical-Appeal, Memphis, 1962-63, Atlanta Constn., 1963-65, The States-Item, New Orleans, 1969-72, The Morning Advocate, Baton Rouge, 1974-76, 82-84; food editor The Times-Picayune, New Orleans, 1984—2004; columnist New Orleans Mag.; food and travel freelance writer. Elder St. Charles Ave. Presbyn. Ch., New Orleans, 1984-87, 91-94. Recipient award AP, UPI, New Orleans Press Club; named among Top 50 alumni 50th Anniversary U. Miss. Sch. Journalism, 1998. Mem. Assn. Food Journalists (pres. 1994-96), Theta Sigma Phi (Alumni of Yr. U. Miss. chpt.). E-mail: dalecurry2004@yahoo.com.

CURRY, DANIEL FRANCIS MYLES, filmmaker; b. N.Y.C., Sept. 22, 1946; s. John Joseph Curry Jr. and Florence Cecelia (Rattler) Curry; m. Ubolvan Chaiwatana, July 27, 1972; children: Devin, Daniel. BA in Fine Arts, minor in Theatre, Middlebury Coll., 1968; MFA in Film and Theatre, Humboldt State U., 1979. Vol. cmty. devel. U.S. Peace Corps, Khon Kaen, Thailand, 1969—71; writer-dir. ednl. TV Ministry of Edn., Govt. of Thailand, Bangkok, 1971—72; freelance filmmaker/artist/designer various clients Bangkok, 1972—74; instr. fine arts Cape Cod Community Coll., West Barnstable, Mass., 1974—77; instr. film and theatre Humboldt State U., Arcata, Calif., 1977—79; visual effects artist Universal Studios Hartland Facility, North Hollywood, Calif., 1979—80; art dir. Modern Film Effects, Hollywood, Calif., 1980—85; v.p., dir. creative svcs. Cinema Rsch. Corp., Hollywood, 1985—88; visual effects producer-dir. Star Trek, the Next Generation, Paramount Pictures, Hollywood, 1987—; pres. O.M.R. Prodns., Manhattan Beach, Calif., 1989—. Supr., title designer: Star Trek IV; Top Gun; Flash Dance; Fatal Attraction; Cujo; The Blob; Rocky IV; Cobra; Staying Alive; Tootsie; Risky Business; Amadeus; The Right Stuff; Mommie Dearest; Uncommon Valor; Pure Luck; Back to School; Raging Bull; Class; Cool World; Captured; Christine; Body Double; Flashpoint; Tiger Town; Invasion U.S.A.; Fast Forward; Bolero; Wild Thing; Pray for Death; Days of Thunder; Indian Jones & The Temple of Doom; Star Trek, Generations; visual effects prodr.: 6th Season Star Trek, The Next Generation (best spl. visual effects Emmy award, 1992); Star Trek Deep Space Nine, 1993—; Star Trek Voyager, 1995— (Emmy award). Nominee Emmy award, 1989, 1990; recipient Emmy award for spl. visual effects, Acad. TV Arts and Scis., 1992, 1994, Internat. Monitor award, 1996. Mem.: Am. Soc. Cinematrographers, Am. Film Inst., Soc. Motion Picture and TV Engrs., Acad. TV Arts and Scis. Fluent in Thai and Lao.

CURRY, EMMA BEATRICE, elementary school educator; b. Commerce, Ga., July 7, 1927; d. John Henry and Annie Bell (Wilkins) Thomas; m. Harvey Curry, Aug. 4, 1946; children: Gloria Dawn, Harvey Nathaniel, Norbert. BA in Psychology, U. Hawaii, 1971; MEd, counseling degree, Boston U., 1973; postgrad., U. So. Calif., Heidelberg, 1981; postgrad. in fine arts, City Coll., Heidelberg, 1986; postgrad., U. Md., Woxton Coll., Eng., U. Calif., Berkeley. Cert. tchr. social studies, N.J., English, cosmetology, psychology, social studies, DOD. Substitute tchr. Waupahu (Hawaii) H.S. and Leilehua (Hawaii) H.S., 1961-67, DOD, Augsberg, Germany, 1967-69; tchr. Mannheim Am. H.S., Germany, 1971-73, 1977-99; substitute tchr. Pennsauken (N.J.) Ctrl. Elem. Sch., 2000—. Author: (poetry) Feelings: Contemporary Verse, 1999. Bd. dirs. PTA, Mannheim Am. H.S., 1985-86, multicultural chairperson, 1971-73, 77-99; choir condr., soloist Meth. Ch., Wahiwai, 1964, Augsberg, Germany, 1968-69; Sunday sch. tchr. arts and crafts ch., Dachau, Germany, 1955-59. Mem. Nick Virgilio Haiku Assn. Democrat. Methodist. Avocations: poet, artist, sculpturing, piano, guitar. Home: 4716 Temple Hills Rd Temple Hills MD 20748

CURRY, ESTELLA ROBERTA, education educator, consultant; d. John Henry and Grace Gannon; m. Carl Alton Curry, Apr. 7, 1950 (dec. Feb. 1986); children: John, Carl, Carla, David. BS cum laude, Ohio U., 1968, postgrad., 1973—2002; MA, Marshall U., 1969, postgrad., 1971—73. Cert. elem. tchr. Ohio, 1961, sch. counselor Ohio, 1969, sch. psychologist Ohio, 1973. Middle sch. tchr. South Point (Ohio) Local Schs., 1961—64, elem. sch. tchr., 1964—68, elem. guidance counselor, 1969—72; grad. asst. Marshall U., Huntington, W.Va., 1968—69; sch. guidance counselor Fairland Local Schs., Proctorville, Ohio, 1972—73; G.E.D. adminstr., coordinator of psychological svcs., sch. psychologist/counselor Lawrence County Ednl. Svc. Ctr., Ironton, Ohio, 1973—. Therapist, clin. supr. Prestera Mental Health Ctr., Huntington, 1991—96; instr. Ohio U., Ironton, 1999—; ednl. cons. Oakridge Treatment Ctr., Ironton, 1999—. Mem.: Sch. Psychology Assn. South Ea. Ohio, Ohio Sch. Psychologist Assn., Coun. for Exceptional Children. Avocations: reading, travel, cooking, art collecting, gardening. Home: 3964 County Rd 15 South Point OH 45680 Office: Lawrence County Ednl Svc Ctr 111 S 4th St Ironton OH 45638

CURRY, JANE LOUISE, writer; b. East Liverpool, Ohio, Sept. 24, 1932; d. William Jack and Helen Margaret (Willis) C. Student, Pa. State U., 1950-51; BS, Indiana U. of Pa., 1954; postgrad., UCLA, 1957-59; AM, Stanford U., 1962, PhD, 1969; student, U. London, 1961-62, 65-66. Tchr. art East Liverpool schs., 1955, L.A. schs., 1956-59; teaching asst. dept. English Stanford (Calif.) U., 1959-61, 64-65, acting instr., 1967-68, instr., 1983-84, lectr., 1987. Storyteller, 1962—. Author: Down from the Lonely Mountain, 1965, Beneath the Hill, 1967, The Sleepers, 1968, The Change-Child, 1969, The Daybreakers, 1970, Mindy's Mysterious Miniature, 1970, Over the Sea's Edge, 1971, The Ice Ghosts Mystery, 1972, The Lost Farm, 1974, Parsley Sage, Rosemary and Time, 1975, The Watchers, 1975, The Magical Cupboard, 1976, Poor Tom's Ghost, 1977, The Birdstones, 1977, The Bassumtyte Treasure, 1978, Ghost Lane, 1979, The Wolves of Aam, 1981, Shadow Dancers, 1983, The Great Flood Mystery, 1985, The Lotus Cup, 1986, Back in the Beforetime, 1987, Me, Myself and I, 1987, The Big Smith Snatch, 1989, Little Little Sister, 1989, What the Dickens?, 1991, The Great Smith House Hustle, 1993, The Christmas Knight, 1993, Robin Hood and his Merry Men, 1994, Robin Hood in the Greenwood, 1995, Moon Window, 1996, Dark Shade, 1998, Turtle Island, 1999, A Stolen Life, 1999, The Wonderful Sky Boat, 2001, The Egyptian Box, 2002, Hold Up the Sky, 2003, Brave Cloelia, 2004, The Black Canary, 2005. Office: Simon & Schuster Children's Publ Divsn 1230 Ave of Ams New York NY 10020

CURRY, JOHN JOSEPH, historian, educator; b. Westwood, Mass., Oct. 7, 1970; s. John Joseph and Joan Marie Curry; m. Suna Curry, Feb. 18, 2001. BA, Northwestern U., 1992; MA in Arabic Lang., Ohio State U., 1998, PhD in History, 2005. Grad. tchg. assoc. The Ohio State U., Columbus, Ohio, 1998—2003, student sect. leader, 2004—; instr. Bowling Green State U., 2005—. Grantee, Title VI, U.S. Govt., 1995—98, 2001—02, The Am. Rsch. Inst. Turkey, 2000—01; Presdl. fellowship, The Ohio State U., 2003—04. Mem.: The Am. Hist. Assn. (assoc.), Mid. East Studies Assn. (assoc.). Office: The Ohio State University 230 W 17th Ave Columbus OH 43202 Office Phone: 614-804-1823. Office Fax: 614-292-2282. Personal E-mail: curry.83@osu.edu. E-mail: curry83@yahoo.com.

CURRY, JOHN MICHAEL, investment banker; b. Buffalo, N.Y., Dec. 30, 1942; s. John Vincent and June (Eisele) C.; m. Thea Adrian KIrk, July 12, 1969 (div. 1982); children: John Adrian, James Prescott; m. Margaretta Buckley, Mar. 17, 1990; 1 child, Michael Jeremiah. BA, U. San Francisco, 1968; MBA, Harvard U., 1970; postgrad., Suffolk U., 1971. Cert. property mgr.; registered rep. and gen. securities rep.; registered fiduciary and investment adviser, registered securities prin. Developer Devel. Corp. Am., Boston, 1970-73; founder, chmn. APT Fin. Svcs., Inc., Boston, 1977—, Am. Securities Team, Inc., Boston, 1992—, Am. Properties Team, APT Asset, Boston, 1987—; chmn. Am. Devel. Team, 1985-92, Am. Realty Team, Fla., 1994—, Infrastructure Repair Technologies, 1998—. Bd. dirs. six corps.; Boston rep. Taylor Woodrow PLC, London, 1983-85. Vol. various fed., state, local polit. orgns. and campaigns. Sgt. U.S. Army, 1961-64. Recipient Modernization award Building Mag., 1980-81, Outstanding Restoration award Lowell C. of C., 1981, Nat. Jewish Life award, 1987. Mem. Harvard Club (Boston), various securities firms orgns. Avocations: scuba diving, Karate, golf. Office Phone: 781-935-4200. E-mail: jcurry@aptfin.com.

CURRY, JOHN PATRICK, insurance company executive, management consultant; b. Logan, W.Va., May 3, 1934; s. Albert Bruce and Mary Naomi (Shugert) C.; m. Patricia Jean Blessington, Oct. 26, 1956; children: Joseph Patrick, Mary Patricia, Kathleen Anne, Carmen Frances, John Gregory. Student, St. Charles Coll., Catonsville, Md., 1949-52; BA, U. Notre Dame, 1956; MS in Ops. Rsch., Western Mich. U., 1976. Lic. prof. cons., Mich. Agt. Conn. Mut. Life Ins. Co., 1959-65; gen. agt. Occidental Life Ins. Co., L.A., 1965-66; pres. Investment Assocs. Inc., L.A., 1966-69; gen. agt. Fed. Life Ins. Co., Peoples Home Life Ins. Co. and Home Assurance Cos., 1969-71; actuarial cons. Am.-Brit. Ins. & Annuity Co. Ltd. (Bermuda), Battle Creek, Mich., 1979-87, mgmt. cons., 1971-88; owner, mgr. Nat. Search Cons., exec. search firm, Kalamazoo; owner, operator Curry Supply Co., Portage, Mich., 1978-83; pres. The Consulting Group Inc. (Del.), Kalamazoo, 1985—93, JPC Holding, Inc., 1993—. Pres. The Pilot Co., Turks and Caicos Islands, 1985-90; dir. Anglo-Am. Ins. Co., Ltd. (Bermuda), 1979-87. With U.S. Army, 1957—59. U. Notre Dame scholar, 1952-56; Pat O'Brien scholar, 1956. Mem.: Rep. Pres.'s Round Table, Sertoma Club (charter dir. Kalamazoo club 1961—64). Republican. Roman Catholic. Home: 7226 Rockford St Portage MI 49024-4122 Office: The Consulting Group Kalamazoo MI 49024 Office Phone: 269-978-0824. E-mail: jpcurry@charter.net, jpchinc@hotmail.com.

CURRY, JOHN WESLEY, retired secondary school educator; b. Canton, Ill., Nov. 13, 1948; s. Wesley LeRoy and Clara Mae (Hysler) C.; m. Francene Elizabeth Anderson, July 12, 1970; children: Jennifer, Robert, Rachel. BS, Ill. State U., 1970; MA, Sangamon State U., 1980. Tchr. math., coach Athens (Ill.) H.S., 1970—2004, tchr. math., athletic dir., 1978—95, tchr. math., coach, 1983—94; ret., 2004. Asst. mgr. Illini Sporting Goods, Springfield, Ill., 1977-78; evening instr. Lincoln Land Community Coll. Sunday sch. tchr. Athens United Meth. Ch., 1973-2004, bd. dirs., 1973—, chmn. bd., 1978-81, 99-2003, lay leader, 1972-78, 81-2000, 2002-04, chmn. bd. trustees, 1982-83. Recipient Those Who Excel award of merit, Ill. State Bd. Edn., 1995. Mem. ASCD, NEA (life), Nat. Coun. Tchrs. Math., Ill. Coun. Tchrs. Math., Ill. Edn. Assn., Ill. Basketball Coaches Hall of Fame. Methodist. Home: 14280 Prairie Trl Athens IL 62613-7639

CURRY, JULIE A., state official; b. Granite City, Ill., June 7, 1962; 1 child, Evan Curry-Dennison. BA, Eastern Ill. U., 1984, MA, 1985. Ill. state rep. Dist. 101, 1995—2003; deputy chief staff, economic devel. and labor State of Ill., 2003—. Democrat. Office: 207 State Capitol Bldg Springfield IL 62706*

CURRY, KATHLEEN BRIDGET, retired librarian; b. Parnell, Iowa, May 19, 1931; d. John Michael and Ellen Theresa (Clear) Curry. BSLS, Marycrest Coll., 1953. Head libr. Moline (Ill.) Sr. HS, 1953-90; ret., 1990. Part-time libr. Moline Pub. Hosp. Sch. Nursing, 1957—66; mem. sch. nursing libr. St. Anthony's Hosp., Rock Island, Ill., 1955; hist. libr. Rock Island Hist. Libr., Moline, 1956—59; libr. Black Hawk Coll., Moline, 1958—59. Guild mem. Quad City Symphony Orch., Davenport, 1972—; bd. dirs. Quad City Arts Coun., Davenport, 1990, Miss Black Hawk Coll., Moline, 1986—; exec. bd. Miss Iowa Pageant, Davenport, 1987—. Recipient Disting. Svc. award, Moline HS PTA, 1983, Marycrest Coll., 1987. Mem.: AAUW, NEA, Iowa Libr. Assn., Moline Edn. Assn., Ill. Sch. Libr. Assn., Ill. Edn. Assn., Zonta Internat., Delta Kappa Gamma. Democrat. Roman Catholic. Avocations: playing the piano, cooking. Home: 3646 71st St Ct Moline IL 61265-1833 E-mail: gmedhus@aol.com.

CURRY, MICHAEL JAMES, history educator; b. Chgo., Sept. 12, 1950; s. James Thomas and Winnefred Rose Curry; m. Lianne E. Curry, Nov. 16, 1974; children: Thomas, Joseph, William, Marci. BA, Loras Coll., 1974; MS, Western Ill. U., 1986. Tchr., coach Freeport Cath. Schs., Ill., 1974—86, Aurora Ctrl. Cath. H.S., Ill., 1987—. Chair social studies dept. Aurora Ctrl. Cath. H.S. Named Coach of Yr., Football Coaches Assn. Republican. Roman Catholic. Avocations: reading, music, book clubs. Home: 723 Fifth St Aurora IL 60505 Office: Aurora Ctrl Cath HS 1255 N Edgelawn Aurora IL 60506 Office Phone: 630-907-0095. Business E-Mail: mcurry@auroracentral.com.

CURRY, MICHAEL W., secondary school educator; b. Moses Lake, Wash., 1964; s. John Edson Curry and Margaret Lynn (Ziegenfus Phearner) Bierce; m. Nancy J. Lutz, Aug. 4, 1984; children: Jessicah Joy, Christa Noel. Degree, Chinen Go Ju Ryu Dojo, Spokane, 1987; AS, Spokane Falls C.C., 1987; AA, Big Bend C.C., Moses Lake, 1989; BA, Ctrl. Wash. U., 1991; MEd, Heritage U., 1998. Produce, diary mgr. Royal Excell, Royal City, Wash., 1987—89; tchr. Wahluke H.S., Mattawa, Wash., 1991—94, Manson (Wash.) Jr./Sr. H.S., 1984—97, Lake Chelan (Wash.) H.S., 1997—2005, journalism tchr., 1997—98, photo, art, Spanish tchr., 1997—2005. Author: Chicken Soup of the Grandparents' Soul, 2002, Celebrate Poetry, 2002; actor: (summer theatre) Steven Spielberg's Always, 1989. Mem. Northshore Bible, Manson, 2001—. Named Tchr. of Yr., Lions, Manson and Chelan, Wash., 1996; named one of Top Ten Poets, Poeticpower. Mem.: NEA, Wash. Farm Bur., Wash. Educators Assn. Avocations: photography, watercolors, reading. Office: Lake Chelan High Sch PO Box 369 215 W Webster Chelan WA 98816 Office Phone: 509-682-4061. Personal E-mail: arkanjel@hotmail.com.

CURRY, NANCY ELLEN, psychologist, psychoanalyst, educator; b. Brockway, Pa., Jan. 26, 1931; d. George R. and Mary F. (Covert) C. BA, Grove City Coll., 1952; MEd, U. Pitts., 1956, PhD, 1972; grad., Pitts. Psychoanalytic Inst., 1988, grad. child analytic program, 1992. Lic. psychologist, Pa. Tchr. public schs., East Brady and Oakmont, Pa., 1952-55; presch. demonstration tchr. Arsenal Family and Children's Center, U. Pitts., 1955-79, assoc. dir., 1971-79; from instr. in psychiatry to prof. child devel. Sch. Social Work, U. Pitts, 1957-93; prof. emeritus Sch. Social Work, U. Pitts.; also mem. faculty U. Pitts Sch. Medicine, Sch. Edn., Sch. Health Related Professions.; pvt. practice in psychanalysis and psychotherapy; ret., 2000. Supr., cons., 1957-58; Fulbright exchange tchr. North Oxford Nursery Sch., Oxford, Eng., 1957-58; vis. prof. Oreg. State U., summer, 1964, Ariz. State U., summer, 1969; assoc. dir. early childhood project Edn. Professions Devel. Act, U.S. Office of Edn., 1970-74; cons. in field. Co-producer 12 films on children's play; co-author Beyond Self-esteem, 1990; editor The Feeling Child; author numerous articles on child devel. Mem. APA, Assn. Child Psychoanalysis, Am. Psychoanalysts Assn. Home: 149 Shadow Ridge Dr Pittsburgh PA 15238-2133 E-mail: NCU149@aol.com.

CURRY, PAUL RUSSELL, protective services official, lobbyist; b. Portland, Oreg; s. Russell John and Elma Arlene Curry; m. Kathryn Gene, Nov. 3, 1972; children: Heather Marie Curry Sharpe, Emily Kathryn Ackerman Hodges. AA in Police Sci., San Bernardino (Calif.) Valley Coll., 1974; BS in Pub. Mgmt., Pepperdine U., 1975. Dep. sheriff San Bernardino County Sheriff, 1970—, from detective to lt., 1976-97. Chair legis. com. Calif. Peace Officers Assn., Sacramento, 1995-2002, chmn. legal svc. program, 1992—; author child pornography increased penalty legis., 1994-98, pub. records act modification, 1992-99, civil easement law, 1998-2002; bd. dir. Calif. State U. Athletic Assn., San Bernardino, 1996—; chmn. Citizens for Good Govt., Fontana, Calif., 1998—. With USN, 1965-69. Recipient Micky Rainey award Calif. Peace Officers Assn., 1997. Mem. Am. Soc. Indsl. Security (chpt. pres.), Calif. State Sheriff's Assn. (assoc.), 1st Amendment Coalition, Am. Legion, Footprinters, Derby Club. Republican. Roman Catholic. Avocations: woodworking, vintage automobiles. Office: San Bernardino County Sheriff's Dept 655 E 3d St San Bernardino CA 92415 E-mail: paulcurry@usa.net.

CURRY, RAYMOND HOWARD, physician; b. Lexington, Ky., June 5, 1956; s. Howard Jr. and Venita (Dawson) C. AB, U. Ky., 1977; MD, Washington U., St. Louis, 1982. Diplomate Am. Bd. Internal Medicine. Resident in internal medicine McGaw Med. Ctr. Northwestern U., Chgo., 1982-85; internist Northwestern Med. Faculty Found., Chgo., 1985—; instr. Northwestern U. Med. Sch., Chgo., 1985-89, asst. prof., 1989-96, assoc. prof., 1996—2002, prof., 2002—, dir. undergrad. edn. dept. medicine, 1992—98, exec. assoc. dean, 1998—; mem. staff Northwestern Meml. Hosp., Chgo., 1985—; pres. McGaw Med. Ctr. NW U., 2004—. Mem. ACP, Soc. Gen. Internal Medicine, Am. Acad. Physician and Patient, Phi Beta Kappa. Office: Northwestern U Feinberg Sch of Medicine 303 E Chicago Ave Chicago IL 60611

CURRY, THOMAS J., former state agency administrator, federal agency administrator; Grad. summa cum laude, Manhattan Coll.; JD, New Eng. Sch. Law. Bar: Mass., Conn. Atty. Mass. Sec. of State's Office, 1982; asst. gen. counsel Commonwealth of Mass.-Divsn. Banks, 1986—87, first dep. commr. banks, 1987—94, acting commr. banks, 1994-95, commr. banks, 1995—2003. Mem. state liaison com. Fed. Fin. Instn. Exam. Coun., 1996—2003; chmn. regulatory com. Conf. of State Bank Suprs., 2000—03; mem., bd. dirs. FDIC, Washington, 2004—. Mem. Phi Beta Kappa. Office: FDIC 550 17th St NW Rm 6098 Washington DC 20429-9990 Office Phone: 202-898-3957.*

CURRY, TIM, actor; b. Cheshire, Eng., Apr. 19, 1946; s. James and Patricia Curry. Attended, U. Birmingham, Eng. Stage performances include A Mid-Summer Night's Dream, The Rocky Horror Show, Amadeus, The Pirates of Penzance, Me and My Girl, My Favorite Year; films The Rocky Horror Picture Show, 1975, The Shout, 1980, Times Square, 1980, Annie, 1982, The Ploughman's Lunch, 1984, Clue, 1985, Legend, 1986, Pass the Ammo, 1988, The Hunt for Red October, 1990, Oscar, 1991, (voice) Ferngully...The Last Rainforest, 1992, Passed Away, 1992, Home Alone 2: Lost in New York, 1992, Loaded Weapon 1, 1992, The Three Musketeers, 1993, The Shadow, 1994, Congo, 1995, Lovers' Knot, 1995, (voice) The Pebble and the Penguin, 1995, Muppet Treasure Island, 1996, McHale's Navy, 1997, (voice) Rugrats Movie, 1998, The Titanic Chronicles, 1999, Jackies Back, 1999, Pirates of the Plain, 1999, Charlie's Angels: The Movie, 2000, Sorted, 2000, Lion of Oz, 2000, Four Dogs Playing Poker, 2000, (voice) Rugrats in Paris: The Movie Rugrats II, 2000, Ritual, 2000, Scary Movie 2, 2001, The Scoundrel's Wife, 2002, (voice) The Wild Thornberrys Movie, 2002, (voice) I, Crocodile, 2002, (voice) Rugrats Go Wild, 2003, Kinsey, 2004, Baily's Billion$, 2005, (voice) Valiant, 2005; TV appearances Oliver Twist, 1982, Stephen King's It, 1990, (voice) Peter Pan and the Pirates, 1991 (Emmy award), Family Affair, 2002-03; numerous voices in TV series including Fish Police, 1992, Tales From the Crypt (Death of Some Salesman), 1993 (Emmy nomination, Guest Actor - Drama, 1994), Earth 2, 1994, (voice) Superhuman Samurai Syber-Squad, 1994, Aaahh!! Real Monsters, 1994, The Mask, 1995, Toonstruck, 1996, Story of Santa Claus, 1996, Quack Pack, 1996, Mighty Ducks, 1996, Bruno the Kid, 1996-97, Jumanji, 1996-99, Lexx: The Dark Zone, 1997, The Wild Thornberrys, 1998, The Net, 1998, Mattimeo: A Tale of Redwall, 2000; albums: Read My Lips, 1978, Fearless, 1979, Simplicity, 1981, The Best of Tim Curry, 1989. Office: William Morris Agency c/o Elyse Scherz 151 S El Camino Dr Beverly Hills CA 90212-2775*

CURRY, TONI GRIFFIN, counseling center executive, consultant; b. Langdale, Ala., June 23, 1938; d. Robert Alton and Elsie (Dodson) Griffin; m. Ronald William Curry, June 13, 1959 (div. 1972); children: Christopher, Catherine, Angela. BA, Ga. State U., 1962; MSW, U. Ga., 1981. Lic. clin. therapist; cert. addictions counselor. Tchr. DeKalb County Bd. Edn., Atlanta, 1962-63; counselor Charter Peachford Hosp., Atlanta, 1974-79; dir. aftercare, 1976-79; dir. aftercare and occupational svcs. Ridgeview Inst., Atlanta, 1979-82; owner, dir., adminstr., counselor Toni Cury and Assocs., Inc., Atlanta, 1982—. Cons., lectr. to numerous cos. and orgns.; mem. adv. bd. Peachford Hosp., Atlanta, 1982-87, Rockdale House, Conyers, Ga., 1981—, Outpatient Addictions Clinics Am., 1983-85; bd. dirs. Employee Assistance Programs Inst.; lectr. local, nat. and internat. confs. Cloud's House, Wilshire, Eng., 1986; founder Internat. Recovery Ctr., Cannes, France, 1990; founder, bd. dirs. Anchor Hosp., 1985-93; seminars on addiction in Italy and Switzerland; pres., mem. exec. bd. Ga. Employee Assistance Programs Forum, Atlanta, 1981-86; appointed to Gov.'s Advisory Coun. on Mental Health, Mental Retardation and Substance Abuse, 1984, Gov.'s Commn. Drug Awareness and Prevention, 1986; chairperson Ga. Gov.'s Driving Under Influence of Alcohol Assessment Task Force; adv. bd. Hawthorne House; presenter European Conf. Drugs and Alcohol, Edinburgh, Scotland; faculty Southeastern Conf. Alcohol and Drugs, 1996; annual presenter So. Coastal Conf., Jekyll Is., Ga., 1996—; mem. steering com. personnel programs Delta Air Lines, 1992—. Vol. My Sister's Ho. Mem. Nat. Assn. Social Workers, Ga. Addiction Counselors Assn. (dir. 1982-86), Ga. Citizens Coun. Alcoholism, Employee Assistance Programs Assn., Assn. Behavioral Therapists, Nat. Assn. Alcoholism and Drug Abuse Counselors, Mems. Guild of High Mus. Art, Kappa Alpha Theta. Home: 7245 Chattahoochee Bluff Dr Atlanta GA 30350-1071 Office: 4546 Barclay Dr Atlanta GA 30338-5802

CURRY, WILLIAM SIMS, county official; b. Mt. Vernon, Washington, Feb. 6, 1938; s. Eli Herbert Curry and Winona Geraldine Davis; m. Kirsten Ingeborg Arms, May 20, 1971; children: William II, Kevin, Randal, Kim Cannova, Derek. BS in Bus. Mgmt., Fla. State U., 1967; MBA, Ohio State U., 1968. Cert. profl. contracts mgr. Asst. purchasing officer Stanford (Calif.) Linear Accelerator Ctr., 1977-80; subcontract adminstr. Lockheed Missiles & Space Co., Sunnyvale, Calif., 1980-81; materials mgr. Altus Corp., San Jose, Calif., 1981-86; purchasing mgr. Litton Electron Devices, San Carlos, Calif., 1986-95, Comms. & Power Industries, Palo Alto, Calif., 1995-97; contracts mgr. Landacorp, Chico, Calif., 1998; purchasing svcs. mgr. Butte County, Oroville, Calif., 1998-01, dep. adminstrv. officer, 2001—, gen. svcs. dir., 2001—. Bd. dirs. Industry Coun. for Small Bus. Devel., Sunnyvale, 1992-97, v.p. programs, 1992-93, exec. v.p., 1994-95, pres., 1995-97. Contbr. articles to profl. jours. Capt. USAF, 1955-77. Decorated Meritorious Svc. medal with one oak leaf cluster, USAF, 1977. Fellow Nat. Contract Mgmt. Assn.; mem. Calif. Assn. Pub. Purchasing Officers, Am. Mensa, Beta Gamma Sigma. Republican. Avocations: chess, writing, bicycling. Home: 17 Northwood Commons Pl Chico CA 95973-7213 Office: Butte County 3-A County Center Dr Oroville CA 95965-3334 E-mail: bnkcurry@sbcglobal.net.

CURSON, THEODORE, musician; b. Phila., June 3, 1935; s. Leroy and Reava (Paige) C.; m. Marjorie N. Goltry, Apr. 1, 1967; children: Charlene, Theodore II. Student, Mastbaum Sch., Granoff Music Conservatory, Phila., 1952-53. Mem. Charles Mingus' Jazz Workshop, 1959-60. Guest instr. U. Vt. Festival of Contemporary Music, 1968; instr. music Warsaw U.; pres. Nosruc Pub. Co., from 1961. Trumpeter with Max Roach, Philly Joe Jones, Cecil Taylor, Eric Dolphy, 1960—63; musician: appeared on radio, TV, clubs, jazz festivals include Riga, Latvia, Tallinn, Estonia, Vienna, France, NorthSea, The Hague, Nice, Jazz Yatra, India, Antibes, Aix en Provence, Lugano, Bologna, Macerata, Prague, Bled, Warsaw, Molde, Kongberg, Ahus, Laren, Pori, Caracas, Amsterdam, 1964, U.S. festivals New Music Across America, Birdland, Newport/N.Y., Newport Rebels Festival, univ. concerts include Princeton U., U. Wis., Baton Rouge, Columbia U., N.Y.U., Hobart Coll., We. Wash. Coll., Grinnell Coll., U. Calif., Santa Monica and Berkeley, U. Vt., toured India, Middle East and N. Africa for State Dept., 1980, toured Siberia, 1996; guest soloist Norddeutscher Rundfunk TV, star PBS TV show Jazz Set, 1972, star, with NOS Dutch TV (jazz video) Last Date; composer: Nosruc Waltz, 1960, Flatted Fifth, 1960, The Leopard, 1964, Straight Ice, 1965, Typical Ted, 1970, Reava's Waltz, Airi's Tune, Searchin for the Blues, Lost Her, 1987; musician: (recording) Plenty of Horn, 1961, Fire Down Below, 1963, Tears for Dolphy, 1976, 1994, New Thing and Blue Thing, 1965, Urge, 1966, Ode to Booker Ervin, 1970, Pop Wine, 1972, Quicksand, 1975, Jubilant Power, 1976, Blue Piccolo, 1976, Flip Top, 1977, Typical Ted, 1977, The Trio, 1979, I Heard Mingus, 1980, Snake Johnson, 1981, Round Midnight, 1990, Cattin' Curson, 1993, Traveling On, 1997, Sugar'n Spice, 1999, Pori Jazz, 2001, Face to Face, 2002, (music for films) Teorema, 1968, Notes for a Film on Jazz, 1968, The Brown Bunny, 2003; dir.: Blue Note Open Jam, 1984—93, Trumpets Open Jam, 2003—05. Named New Star Monterey Jazz Festival 1962, winner Trumpet sect. Down Beat Internat. Critics Poll, 1966, Ted Curson & Co. winner Down Beat Reader's Poll, 1978, named New Jazz Artist Jazz Podium, Germany; recipient L.I. Musicians Soc. award 1970, Pori (Finland) City Standard 1978, Keys to City, 1998, Paul Robeson Community Arts award Jersey City Pub. Libr., 1994. Mem. Am. Fedn. Musicians.

CURT, CAROL LYNN, psychologist, consultant; b. Chgo., Jan. 31, 1956; d. Charles Curt and Edith M. Elling; m. Robert James Moretti, 1986. BS, Loyola U., Chgo., Ill., 1977, MA, 1982, PhD, 1987. Lectr., dept. psychology Loyola U., Chgo., 1980—84; lectr. dept. psychology Barat Coll., Lake Forest, Ill., 1981; statistician, author Profl. Rsch. Analysts, Chgo., 1980—84; human factors specialist AT&T, Naperville, Ill., 1986—96, Lucent Technologies, Naperville, Ill., 1996—2000; sr. voice user interface designer Nuance Comm., Chgo., 2000—. Presenter in field. Contbr. articles to profl. jours. Mem.: Human Factors and Ergonomics Soc. Home and Office: 3458 N Normandy Chicago IL 60634 Office Phone: 773-725-1286.

CURT, DENISE MORRIS, painter, photographer; b. New Haven, Nov. 15, 1936; d. Bertrand and Anna Geraldine (Fiak) Rocheleau; m. John Morris, Oct. 4, 1954 (dec.); children: Tyler John, Cynthia Leigh Morris Bell; m. Albert A. Curt, 1973 (div. 1981). Student of Louis Crescenti, Orange, Conn., 1950-52; student, Whitney Sch. Art, New Haven, 1950, Luchetti Sch. Art, 1951, Paier Sch. Art, Hamden, Conn., 1951. Interior designer State of Conn., Hartford, 1972-75; dir. Meet The Artists and Artisans, Milford, 1962—. One-woman shows Gull Gallery, Provincetown, Mass., Chapelle Jean Cocteau, Villefranche Sur Mer, France, Garfield Galleries, Orange, Conn., Yale U., Stratford Gallery, Stevenson (Md.) Galleries, also others; represented in numerous pvt. and pub. collections throughout world. Lectr. to numerous civic orgns.; mem. Vis. Artists in Schs., 1970—; commr. Conn. Commn. on Arts, 1974-79; photography chmn. Milford Fine Arts Coun., New Haven Arts Coun.; bd. dir. Milford Hosp. Aux.; mem. Literacy Vols., Milford. Recipient award Mystic Art Festival, 1969, Sterling House Art Show, 1985, Glastonbury Art Guild, 1988. Mem. Guilford Art League (bd. dir. 1975-80), Nat. League Am. Pen Women (category painting, bd. dirs. Fairfield chpt., art chair), Conn. Classic Arts, Milford Hist. Soc., Yale U. Gallery, Met. Mus. Art. Republican. Congregationalist. Avocations: renaissance and baroque music, antiques, foreign travel. Home and Office: Meet the artists & Artisans 41 Green St Milford CT 06460-4709 Office Phone: 203-874-5672. E-mail: ctlimner@snet.net.

CURTIN, BRIAN JOSEPH, ophthalmologist; b. N.Y.C., July 25, 1921; s. James Joseph and Julia Margaret (Smith) C.; m. Claire Margaret Flood, June 18, 1955; children: Edward Brian, James Martin, Thomas Hayes, Deirdre Claire. BS, Fordham U., 1942; MD, NYU, 1945. Intern St. Vincent's Hosp., N.Y.C., 1945-46; resident surgeon Manhattan Eye, Ear and Throat Hosp., 1950-53, asst. attending surgeon, asso. attending surgeon, 1953-74, surgeon dir., 1974-89, surgeon dir. emeritus, 1990—, pres. med. bd., 1977-79, vice chmn. dept. ophthalmology, 1983-89, med. dir., 1989-91; attending ophthalmologist, chief svc. Misericordia-Lincoln Affiliated Hosps., 1958-79; attending ophthalmologist N.Y. Hosp., 1969-84; assoc. attending ophthalmologist Columbia Presbyn. Med. Ctr., 1985-92; asst. prof. clin. ophthalmology NYU, 1954-70; assoc. prof. clin. ophthalmology Cornell Med. Coll., 1970-84, Columbia U. Coll. Physicians and Surgeons, 1985-98; pvt. practice N.Y.C. Med. adv. bd. Eye Bank for Sight Restoration, N.Y.C., 1978-90, chmn., 1988-90; attending ophthalmologist, chmn. dept. St. Clare's Hosp. and Health Ctr., 1978-81. Author: The Myopias: Basic Science and Clinical Management, 1985; mem. editorial bd. Cornea, 1981-85; contbr. chpts. to textbooks, articles to med. jours. With U.S. Navy, 1946-48. Recipient Achievement award Fordham U., 1976. Mem. ACS, AMA, AAAS, Am. Ophthalmol. Soc., N.Y. State Med. Soc., N.Y. County Med. Soc., N.Y. Acad. Medicine, N.Y. Acad. Scis., Am. Acad. Ophthalmology, N.Y. Ophthal. Soc. (v.p. 1981-82, pres. 1982-83), Am. Eye Study Club. Home: 4402 Theall Rd Rye NY 10580-1480 Personal E-mail: bcurti@hotmail.com.

CURTIN, CONSTANCE O'HARA, language educator, writer; b. NYC, Mar. 11, 1927; d. V. Winthrop and Belle Callum O'Hara; m. David Yarrow Curtin, July 1, 1950; children: Susan M., David F., Jane C. Jones. *Husband, David Y. Curtin, was a professor of chemistry, emeritus from University of Illinois, 1951-1988. Daughter, Susan McLean Curtin, received a BA, MS, and PhD in Psychology from the University of Oregon. She is now a psychologist in a private practice in Eugene, Oregon. Son, David Ferris Curtin received a BA and Med in educational psychology, research evaluation, and measurement statistics from the University of Georgia. He is a network administrator at the Frank Porter Graham Child Development Institute at the University of North Carolina. Daughter, Jane Curtin Jones, volunteers at the Harold Washington Library at Northwestern Memorial Hospital.* AB, Mt. Holyoke Coll., Mass., 1948; MA in Chemistry, Columbia U., 1950, PhD in Chemistry, 1953; MAT in Russian, U. Ill., Urbana, 1966. Author of cyrillic alphabet lesson PLATO (Programmed Logic for Automatic Tchg. Ops.), U. of Ill., Urbana, Ill., 1966—89; author of Russian reading program PLATO, U. of Ill., 1966—89, author of lab. material for slavic 101-104, 1966—82; tchr. of Russian U. H.S., U. of Ill., 1966—89; ret. Project dir. Apple Edn. Found., Urbana. Author (cd) Russian Alphabet Program for TRS80, Apple II and IBM PC; author: (cd) Language Review Packets for Apple II and IBM; author: (software designer) (cd for lang. learning) Conversations Around the World: in French, German, Russian, Spanish. Recipient Outstanding Tchr. of Russian, Ill. Fgn. Lang. Assn., 1986; NEH grant, Apple Edn. Found. Mem.: Am. Assn. of Tchrs. Slavic and East European Langs. (sec., treas., v.p., pres. 1980—85), Phi Beta Kappa. Home: 12114 Lakewood Court Fort Myers FL 33908

CURTIN, DANIEL JOSEPH, JR., lawyer; b. San Francisco, Jan. 7, 1933; s. Daniel Joseph and Nell Helen (Lenihan) Curtin; m. Myrtle Rose Wanke, Feb. 7, 1959; children: Kathleen Mary, Patricia, Thomas, Carol. AB in Polit. Sci., U. San Francisco, 1954, JD, 1957. Asst. sec. State Senate Calif., Sacramento, 1959; cons., counsel Assembly Com. on Local Govt., Sacramento, 1959-60; dep. city atty. City of Richmond, Calif., 1961-65; city atty. City of Walnut Creek, Calif., 1965-82; with Williams, Caploe, Robbins & Curtin, Benicia, Calif., 1983-84; ptnr. McCutchen, Doyle, Brown & Enersen, Walnut Creek, 1984—2001; counsel Bingham McCutchen, 2002—. Mem. bd. advisors environ. affairs Boston Coll. Sch. Law, 1987—; mem. State Sen. Housing Adv. Task Force, 1983—84; instr. continuing edn. bar U. Calif. Extension, 1973—, 1975, 82, 88, Golden Gate U. Sch. Law, 1979—82, John F. Kennedy U. Sch. Law, Walnut Creek, 1983—90, U. San Francisco Sch. Law, 1988—92. Contbr. articles to profl. jours. Lt. U.S. Army, 1958—64. Named City Atty. of the Yr., 1971, others; recipient Disting. Leadership award, Nat. Planning award, Am. Planning Assn., 1988. Mem.: ABA (chmn. land use, planning and zoning com. 1976—78, vice chair 1999, coun. chair 2001—02, sect. state and local govt. law, Jefferson Fordham Lifetime Achievement award 2003), Nat. Inst. Mcpl. Law Officer (chmn. zoning and planning com. 1969—79, regional v.p. 1979—82, Lifetime Achievement in Mcpl. Law Charles S. Rhyne award), Calif. State Bar Assn. (mem. exec. com., real property law sect. 1988—91, mem. com. environ. 1977—80), League of Calif. Cities (pres. city atty.'s dept. 1973—74), Calif. Pk. and Recreation Soc., Lambda Alpha. Democrat. Roman Catholic. Avocation: gardening. Office: Bingham McCutchen 1333 N Calif Blvd Ste 210 PO Box V Walnut Creek CA 94596-4534 Office Phone: 925-975-5351. Office Fax: 925-975-5390. Business E-Mail: daniel.curtin@bingham.com.

CURTIN, GARY LEE, air force officer; b. Washington, Apr. 24, 1943; s. Thomas Francis and Lois Sarah (Hall) C.; m. Karen Marcella Reinmann, Nov. 26, 1966; children: Jennifer Lynne, Scott Marshall. BS in Aerospace Engring., U. Md., 1965; MS in Econs., S.D. State U., Ellsworth AFB, 1970. Commd. 2d lt. USAF, 1965, advanced through grades to maj. gen., 1992; launch officer 44th Strategic Missile Wing, Ellsworth AFB, 1965-70; intelligence officer Pacific Air Forces, Udorn, Thailand, Hickam AFB, Hawaii, 1971-75; internat. polit. affairs staff officer Hdqrs. USAF/Dep. Chief of Staff, Plans Pentagon, Washington, 1976-80; comdr. 400th Strategic Missile Squadron, Warren AFB, Wyo., 1980-82; dir. Intercontinental Ballistic Missile requirements Hdqrs. Strategic Air Command, Offutt AFB, Nebr., 1983-86; comdr. 90th Strategic Missile Wing, Warren AFB, Wyo., 1986-88; dir. comd. control Hdqrs. SAC, Offutt AFB, 1988-90; Joint Chiefs of Staff rep. to START negotiations Joint Staff, Geneva, 1990-91; dep. dir. for internat. negotiations Joint Staff/J-5/Pentagon, Washington, 1991-93; dir. of intelligence U. S. Strategic Command, Offutt AFB, Neb., 1993-95; dir. Def. Nuclear Agy./Def. Spl. Weapons Agy., Alexandria, Va., 1995-98; sr. v.p. Def. Group Inc., 1998—. Mem. Air Force Assn., Tau Beta Pi, Omicron Delta Epsilon. Avocations: computers, travel, reading, model aircraft. Office: Defense Gp Inc 2034 Eisenhower Ave Ste 115 Alexandria VA 22314-4678 E-mail: gary.curtin@defensegp.com.

CURTIN, JANE THERESE, actress, writer; b. Cambridge, Mass., Sept. 6, 1947; d. John Joseph and Mary Constance (Farrell) C.; m. Patrick F. Lynch, Apr. 31, 1975. AA, Elizabeth Seton Jr. Coll., 1967; student, Northeastern U., 1967-68. Appeared in plays The Proposition, Cambridge and N.Y.C., 1968-72, Last of the Red Hot Lovers touring co., 1973; Broadway debut in Candida, 1981; author, actress Off-Broadway mus. rev. Pretzels, 1974-75; star TV series NBC Saturday Night Live, 1975-79, Kate & Allie, 1984-88, Working It Out, 1990, 3rd Rock from the Sun, 1996-2001 (Golden Satellite for best actress 1996); appeared in films including Mr. Mike's Mondo Video, 1979, How to Beat the High Cost of Living, 1980, O.C. and Stiggs, 1987, Coneheads, 1993, Antz, 1998; TV films include Divorce Wars-A Love Story, 1982, Suspicion, 1988, Maybe Baby, 1988, Common Ground, 1990, Tad, 1995, Christmas in Washington, 1996, Catch a Falling Star, 2000; TV guest appearance Recess, 1997. Recipient Emmy nomination, 1977, 87; Emmy awards for outstanding actress in comedy series, 1984, 85 Mem. Screen Actors Guild, Actors Equity, AFTRA. Office: ICM care Boaty Boatwright 40 W 57th St Fl 16 New York NY 10019-4098

CURTIN, JOHN JOSEPH, JR., lawyer; b. Englewood, N.J., Mar. 12, 1933; s. John Joseph and Marion (Walsh) C.; m. Mary Daly, Sept. 27, 1958; children: Kevin Joseph, Catherine Mary, Joseph Patrick, Ann Mary, Daniel Joseph. AB magna cum laude, Boston Coll., 1954, JD, 1957; LLM, Georgetown U., 1959. Bar: Mass. 1957, D.C. 1959, U.S. Supreme Ct. 1961. Atty. US Dept. Justice, Washington, 1957-59; assoc. firm Hogan and Hartson, Washington, 1959-61; atty. Office of U.S. Atty., Boston, 1961-64; chief civil divsn., 1963-64; assoc. then ptnr. Bingham McCutchen LLP (formerly Bingham, Dana & Gould), Boston, 1964—. Instr. Boston Coll. Law Sch., 1965—; lectr. Harvard U. Law Sch., 1977-82; bd. dirs. Nat. Consumer Law Ctr., 1994—. Trustee Regis Coll., 1977-83, Newton Coll. Sacred Heart, 1973-75; mem. local govt. adv. com. Commonwealth of Mass., 1978; mem. Town Mtg., Wellesley, Mass., 1970-79, moderator, 1979-84, chmn. adv. com., 1974-75, chmn. town improvements coordinating com., 1977-79, chmn. capital budgeting and investment com., 1979-80; chmn. bd. advisors Boston Coll. Law Sch., 1997—; exec. com. mem. Ctr. for Public Resources, 1994—. Recipient Lifetime Achievement award, Am. Lawyer mag., 2005 Mem. ABA (chmn. sect. litigation 1984-85, pres. 1990-91, chmn. working group state justice initiatives, 1994-97, chmn. coalition for justice 1997—), Boston Bar Assn. (pres. 1979-81, chmn. task force profl. fulfillment, 1996—), Am. Bar Found., Am. Law Inst., Greater Boston Legal Svcs. (bd. dirs. until 1990), Boston Coll. Alumni Assn. (v.p., pres. 1975-76), Mass. Assn. Town Fin. Fin. Com. (pres. 1978), Nat. Assn. Pub. Interest Law, Fellowships for Equal Justice (pres. 1992-95), Nat. Legal Aid and Defender Assn. (bd. dirs. 1990—). Office: Bingham McCutchen LLP 150 Federal St Fl 15 Boston MA 02110-1745 E-mail: jjcurtin@bingham.com.

CURTIN, LAWRENCE N., lawyer; b. Glen Ridge, N.J., Apr. 29, 1950; BS with honors, Fla. State U., 1972; JD with honors, Fla. State U. Coll. Law, 1976. Bar: Fla. 1976, U.S. Dist. Ct. (No. Dist.) Fla., U.S. Ct. Appeals (4th, 5th, 11th and D.C. cirs.). Law clerk to Hon. William Stafford U.S. Dist. Ct. (No. dist.) Fla., 1976-78; exec. ptnr. Holland & Knight, Tallahassee. Mem. Law Review, 1975-76; co-author: Surface Water Pollution Control, vol. 1, 1986-96; contbr. articles to profl. jours. Mem. ABA (litig., corp., bus. and banking sects.), Fla. Bar (chmn. energy law com. 1983-84, mem. administrv. and environ. and land use law sect., natural resources law), Tallahassee Bar Assn., Beta Gamma Sigma, Sigma Iota Epsilon. Office: Holland & Knight LLP PO Drawer 810 315 S Calhoun St Ste 600 Tallahassee FL 32301-1897 Office Phone: 850-224-7000, 850-425-5678. E-mail: larry.curtin@hklaw.com.

CURTIN, PETER J., lawyer; b. Cincinnati, Ohio, Sept. 18, 1967; BA summa cum laude, U. Cincinnati, 1988; JD magna cum laude, Georgetown U., 1991. Bar: DC 1991, US Army Ct. of Military Review 1992, US Ct. of Appeals, Fourth Circuit 1993, US Dist. Ct., Md. 1998, US Ct. of Appeals, Federal Circuit 2002, US Dist. Ct., DC 2004. Former military prosecutor; former special asst. US atty. 6th Military Judicial Circuit, Ea. Dist., NC; assoc., intellectual property litigation Venable LLP, Washington, ptnr., intellectual property litigation, 2001—. Capt. U.S. Army, 1992—95. Mem.: ABA (mem. litigation, intellectual property & criminal justice sections), Am. Intellectual Property Law Assn., Federal Circuit Bar Assn., DC Bar Assn. Office: Venable LLP 575 7th St NW Washington DC 20004 Office Phone: 202-344-8187. Office Fax: 202-344-8300. Business E-Mail: pjcurtin@venable.com.

CURTIN, PHYLLIS, music educator, dean, vocalist; b. Clarksburg, W.Va. d. E. Vernon and Betty R. (Robinson) Smith; m. Eugene Cook, May 6, 1956 (dec.); 1 child, Claudia Madeleine. BA, Wellesley Coll., 1943. Prof. Yale Sch. Music, New Haven, 1974-83; master Branford Coll. Yale U., New Haven, 1979-83; dean Coll. Fine Arts, prof. music Boston U., 1983-91, prof. music, 1983—, dean emerita, prof. music, 1991—; artist-in-residence Tanglewood Music Ctr., Tanglewood, Lenox, Mass., 1965—. Named Amb. for the Arts; tchr. master classes U.S., Can., Beijing, Moscow. Recital debut Town Hall, NYC, 1950, opera debut, NYC Opera in U.S. premiere of The Trial, 1953, recitals throughout, U.S. and fgn. countries; soprano soloist leading symphony orchestras; performer, tchr., Aspen Mus. Festival, 1953-57, appeared as Cressida in, Walton's Troilus and Cressida in, NY premiere, 1955; title role in Floyd's: Susannah, world premiere, Tallahassee, 1956; title role in: Darius Milhaud's Medea, U.S. premiere, Brandeis U., 1955; world premiere Floyd's opera Wuthering Heights, 1958, Floyd's Passion of Jonathan Wade, 1959, Flower and Hawk, 1971; U.S. Premier Peter Grimes, 1946; leading soprano: Vienna Staatsoper, 1960, 61; debut as Fiordiligi in Cosi Fan Tutte, Met. Opera Co., 1961, La Scala Opera, Milan, 1962; U.S. premiere Benjamin Britten's War Requiem, with Boston Symphony, 1963; world premiere of Darius Milhaud's opera La Mére Coupable, Geneva, 1966; U.S. premiere Dimitri Shostakovitch's Symphony No. 14, with, Phila. Orch., 1971. Recipient Alumnae Achievement award, Wellesley Coll., Nadia Boulanger Achievement award, Longy Sch. Music, Letter of Distinction for Svc. to Am. Music, Am. Music Ctr., Lifetime Achievement award, Nat. Opera Assn., 2005. Home: 9 Seekonk Rd Great Barrington MA 01230-1558 Personal E-mail: curtinphyllis@msn.com.

CURTIN, RICHARD DELMAR, counselor, private practice investigator; b. Bronx, N.Y., Feb. 4, 1963; s. Ernest F. Jr. and Carol Anne (Seman) Nygard. BA in Sociology, Wagner Coll., 1985. With Norman Jaspan Assoc. Managerial Cons., N.Y.C., 1985-87, The Argus Agy., Chgo., 1987-89, Judson Sch., Phoenix, 1990; counselor Oak Creek Ranch Sch., Sedona, Ariz., 1990—. Pvt. practice investigator, Phoenix, 1990—; v.p. P. C. Enterprises, Phoenix, 1990—. Author poetry. Avocations: hunting, shooting, fishing, literary discussion.

CURTIN, SUSAN ELIZABETH, artist, art educator; b. Bryn Mawr, Pa., Nov. 21, 1951; d. Samuel Clarke and Eliza Myers Miller; m. Joseph William Curtin, June 23, 1972; children: Sheila Elizabeth, Maeve Mara. Cert. in Painting, Pa. Acad. Fine Arts, Phila., 1974; student, Rosemont Coll., Siena and Florence, Italy, 1987; four week studio fellow, Vt. Studio Ctr., Johnson, Vt., 1992, four week studio fellow, 1994, four week studio fellow, 1995; student, U. Arts., Phila., 1997. Drawing instr. night Main Line Sch., Radnor, Pa., 1985—86; drawing and painting instr. Chester County Art Assn., West Chester, Pa., 1987—2002; pastel workshop instr. Del. County Art League, Haverford, Pa., 1991; children's art instr. Vt. Studio Ctr., 1994, So. Home Svcs., Phila., 1995—97; sr. art instr. West Chester Sr. Ctr., West Chester, 2000; children's art instr. Domestic Violence Ctr., West Chester, 2001—02. Artist-in-residence Wetherill Sch. Upland-Chester Sch. Dist., Pa., 1993. Exhibited in group shows at Pa. Acad. Fine Arts, 1989 (Mary Butler Meml. Fund. purchase prize, 1989), Woodmere Art Mus., 1990 (Endowment Fund 1st prize, 1990), Wayne Art Ctr., 1993 (1st prize, 1993), Md. Fedn. Art, 1996 (Juror's Choice award, 1996), Main Line Ctr. Arts, Haverford, Pa., 2001 (1st prize, 2001). Grantee grant to paint mural, Phila. Found.-Creative Artists Network, 1998, grant to teach sr. citizens, Phila. Found.-Chester County Art Assn., 2000, grant to teach children, 2001—02. Mem.: Main Line Ctr. Arts, Wayne Art Ctr., Creative Artists Netowrk (assoc.). Democrat. Episcopalian. Avocations: beekeeping, gardening, doves, chickens, dogs. Home: 822 Spruce Avet West Chester PA 19382-5413

CURTIN, THOMAS LEE, ophthalmologist; b. Columbus, Ohio, Sept. 9, 1932; s. Leo Anthony and Mary Elizabeth (Burns) C.; m. Constance L. Sallman; children: Michael, Gregory, Thomas, Christopher. BS, Loyola U., L.A., 1954; MD, U. So. Calif., 1957; cert. navy flight surgeon, U.S. Naval Sch. Aerospace Med., 1959. Diplomate Am. Bd. Ophthalmology. Intern Ohio State U. Hosp., 1957-58; resident in ophthalmology U.S. Naval Hosp, San Diego, 1961-64; pvt. practice medicine specializing in ophthalmology Oceanside, Calif., 1967—. Mem. staff Tri City, Scripps Meml. hosps.; sci. adv. bd. So. Calif. Soc. Prevention Blindness, 1973-76; bd. dirs. North Coast Surgery Ctr., Oceanside, 1987-96; cons. in field. Trustee Carlsbad (Calif.) Unified Sch. Dist., 1975-83, pres., 1979, 82, 83; trustee Carlsbad Libr., 1990-99, pres., 1993, 98. Officer, MC, USN, 1958-67. Mem. AMA, Calif. Med. Assn., San Diego County Med. Soc., Am. Acad. Ophthalmology, Aerospace Med. Assn., San Diego Acad. Ophthalmology (pres. 1979), Calif. Assn. Ophthalmology (bd. dirs.), Carlsbad Rotary, El Camino Country Club. Repubican. Roman Catholic. Office: 3231 Waring Ct Ste S Oceanside CA 92056-4510 Office Phone: 760-724-1800.

CURTIN, TIMOTHY JOHN, lawyer; b. Detroit, Sept. 21, 1942; s. James J. and Irma Alice (Sirotti) C.; m. B. Colleen Lindsey, July 11, 1964; children: Kathleen, Mary. BA, U. Mich., 1964, JD, 1967. Bar: Ohio 1968, Mich. 1970, U.S. Dist. Ct. (so. dist.) Ohio 1968, U.S. Dist. Ct. (we. dist.) Mich. 1970, U.S. Dist. Ct. (ea. dist.) Mich. 1980, U.S. Dist. Ct. Del. 1996, U.S. Dist. Ct. (no. dist.) Ill. 1999, U.S. Ct. Appeals (6th cir.) 1968. Assoc. Taft, Stettinius & Hollister, Cin., 1967-70, McCobb, Heaney & Van't Hof, Grand Rapids, Mich., 1970-72; ptnr. Schmidt, Howlett, Van't Hof, Snell & Vana, Grand Rapids, 1972-83, Varnum, Riddering, Schmidt & Howlett, Grand Rapids, 1983—. Contbr. articles to legal publs. Treas. Kent County Dem. Com., 1976-78, chmn. 3rd Dist. Dem. Com., 1993—. Mem. ABA, Mich. Bar Assn., Grand Rapids Bar Assn., Fed. Bar Assn., Am. Bankruptcy Inst., Egypt Valley C.C. Democrat. Roman Catholic. Avocations: travel, fishing. Office: Varnum Riddering Schmidt & Howlett Box 352 333 Bridge St SW Grand Rapids MI 49501-0352 Office Phone: 616-336-6440. Business E-Mail: tjcurtin@varnumlaw.com.

CURTIS, ALTON KENNETH, film company executive, clergyman; b. June 14, 1939; s. Alton T. and Althea A. Curtis; m. Dorothy Stevenson, Aug. 27, 1961; children: William Kenneth, Karen Althea. BA, Gordon Coll., 1961; MDiv, Gordon Conwell Theol. Sem., 1964, DD, 1987; PhD, Walden U., 1976; postgrad., Boston U., 1966-69, Pa. State U., 1971. Ordained to ministry Am. Bapt. Chs., 1964. Dir. comms. City Mission Soc., Boston, 1967-68; media cons. Am. Bapt. Chs., 1968-70; gen. mgr. Creative Venture Assocs., Valley Forge, Pa., 1970-72; pres. Gateway Films, Inc., Worcester, Pa., 1972—. Chmn. Curtis Mark Comms., Lansdale, Pa., 1980-85, Vision Video, Inc., Worcester, 1981—; adj. faculty mem. Gordon Conwell Theol. Sem., Boston Theol. Inst., Harvard Div. Sch., 1965-67; adj. faculty Ea. Coll., St. Davids, Pa., 1974—; adj. faculty, prof. ch. history Ea. Bapt. Theol. sem., Pa., 1986-87, chmn., pres. Friends of the Libr., 1991-95; vis. prof. Inst. Youth Ministries, Colorado Springs, Colo., 1991; cons. Stratetic Careers Project, 1990-95. Author: Dates with Destiny, 1991, 92, From Christ to Constantine, 1991; founder, pub., editor Christian History mag., 1982-89, sr. editor, 1990—; editor, pub. (periodicals) Glimpses, Pastor's Notes, 1990—; writer, prodr. (film) First Fruits, 1982; prodr., dir., author The Good Seed, 1985; assoc. prodr. Shadowlands, 1986 (Internat. Emmy); writer, prodr. Comenius, 1987, (TV documentary series) The Trial and Testimony of the Early Church, 1989 (Gold medal Houston Internat. Film Festival, Chris award Columbus Film Festival, Angel award Religion in Media, Best Series award Christian Visual Media Internat.), (TV series) Discovering the Bible, 1995; prodn. assoc., cons. (TV documentary series) Mine Eyes Have Seen the Glory, 1992; prodr., host Refamation Overview, 1994; prodr., dir. (video documentary series) Jesus The New Way (Gold award Flagstaff Internat. Film Festival 1998, Chris award Columbus Internat. Film Festival); exec. prodr. (film) Candle in the Dark, 1998 (Gold award Christian Broadcasting Commn. of U.K. 1998, Gold award Worldfest Houston, 1999); co-prodr. film So Who Is This Jesus?; editl. dir. Pocket Classics; contbr. articles on mass media and religion to mags. Mem. adv. bd. Episcopal Radio-TV Found., 1991-96; bd. dirs. Martin Luther Acad., Wittenberg, Germany, Christianity Today Inc. v.p. Internat. Christian Visual Media Assn., 1993-94; sr. pastor Lower Providence Bapt. Ch., Collegeville, Pa., 1977-80; pres. Christian History Inst., 1983—; instr. YMCA Handicapped Persons Swimming Program, Lansdale, Pa., 1986-97. Recipient Best Screenplay of Yr. award and Best Film of Yr. award Acad. Christian Cinemagraphic Arts, 1983, Chris award Columbus Film Festival, Gold award Houston Internat. Film Festival, Silver award Charleston Internat. Film Festival, Best Series award Internat. Christian Visual Media. Mem. Montgomery County Bar Assn. Found. (bd. dirs. 1988—), Phi Alpha Chi. Office: Gateway Films Inc PO Box 540 Worcester PA 19490-0540

CURTIS, ANN B., utilities executive; Mgr., adminstr. Gibbs & Hill, Inc.; v.p. mgmt. and fin. svcs. Calpine Corp., 1984—92, sr. v.p., 1992—98, dir., 1996—, exec. v.p., sec., 1998—, vice chmn., 2002—. Office: Calpine 50 W San Fernando St 5th Fl San Jose CA 95113

CURTIS, ANTHONY R., political science professor; b. Marietta, Ohio, Oct. 31, 1940; s. Edwin Wyatt and Charlotte Suder Curtis; m. Judith Genevicz Curtis, Feb. 11, 1977. BA in journalism, Penn State U., 1967, MA in polit. sci., 1970; PhD in mass comm., Union Inst. & U., 1997. Asst. prof. Penn State U., U. Pk., Pa., 1971—77; v.p. TAB Books, Blue Ridge Summit, Pa., 1978—81; asst. prof. Hood Coll., Frederick, Md., 1981—84; pres. ARCSoft Publishers, Woodsboro, Md., 1981—92; instr. Salisbury State U., Salisbury, Md., 1992—97; assoc. dean Union Inst. & U., Cin., 1997—2002; prof. U. NC, Pembroke, NC, 2002—. Author: Space Almanac, 1989; editor: (online mag.) Space Today Online, 1994—; author: (cd rom book) Space: A Visual History of Manned Spaceflight, 1998. Mem. Raleigh Tavern Soc., Colonial Williamsburg Found., Williamsburg, Va., 1981—89. Recipient Apple Dist. Educator, Apple Computer, 2000—, Ednl. Adv., Am. Radio Relay League, 2000—, NASA Solar Sys. Ambassador, NASA Jet Propulsion Lab, 2002—. Mem.: Hist. of Sci. Soc., Friends of the UNCP Libr. (bd. pres. 2005—06), Radio Amateur Satellite Corp., Highland Soc., Scotland Meml. Hosp. Found., W.A.R. Goodwin Soc., Colonial Williamsburg Found. Avocations: stamp collecting/philately, model railroading, amateur radio. Home: 8000 Carnostie Dr Laurinburg NC 28352 Office: U NC PO Box 1510 Pembroke NC 28372 Office Phone: 910-521-6616. Office Fax: 910-522-5795. E-mail: acurtis@uncp.edu.

CURTIS, ARNOLD BENNETT, retired lumber company executive; b. Astoria, Oreg., May 5, 1940; s. Arnold Bennett and Irja Virginia (Thompson) C.; m. Erica Katherine Mitchell, Dec. 23, 1985; children: Braden Thomas, Bryce Bennett. BS, Oreg. State U., 1962. Brewing chemist Gen. Brewing, San Francisco, 1962-67; v.p. N.W. Hardwoods, Inc., Portland, Oreg., 1967-71, pres., 1971-80, also bd. dirs.; pres. N.W. Hardwoods divsn. Weyerhauser Co., Federal Way, Wash., 1980-97, v.p. Hardwood Bus. Group, 1990-98; ret., 1998. Bd. dirs. Puyallup Internat. Inc., Weyerhaeuser New Zealand Ltd., Pine Solutions Australia; chmn. bd. dirs. Columbia Forest Products, 2001. Mem. adv. bd. Ctr. Retail and Bus. Market Strategy. Mem. Hardwood Mfrs. Assn. (dir., exec. com. 1985-95, pres. 1993). *When you commit yourself to an answer it's best to always tell the truth - then you never have to worry about remembering what you said.*

CURTIS, C., hotel executive; BS, Cornell U.; MBA; PhD (hon.), Johnson U., Wales U., Niagara U. With Hyatt Hotels, Four Seasons; mgmt. exec. Radisson Hotels Worldwide/Carlson Hospitality, 1989—92; from exec. v.p. to pres., CEO Country Hospitality Worldwide, 1993—2002; pres., COO Carlson Cos., Minnetonka, Minn., 2003—. Bd. dirs. Conrad Hilton Coll., U. Houston, Houston. Bd. dirs. Greater Twin Cities United Way, Walker Art Ctr., Mpls. Named Global Leader for Tomorrow, World Econ. Forum, 2003; recipient Lifetime Achievement award, Hospitality Industry Diversity Inst., 2002. Mem.: World Travel and Tourism Coun. (exec. com.), Travel Bus. Roundtable.

CURTIS, CHARLES EDWARD, Canadian government official; b. Winnipeg, Man., Can., July 28, 1931; s. Samuel and May (Goodison) C.; m. Hilda Marion Simpson, Oct. 30, 1954; 1 dau., Nancy Maude. C.A., U. Manitoba, 1955. Chartered acct. Dunwoody & Co., Winnipeg, 1949-54; chief assessor nat. revenue, income tax bd. Province of N.B., Can., 1954-67; asst. dep. min. budget fin. and adminstrn. Province of Man., Winnipeg, 1967-75, dep. min., 1976-96. Past CEO Man. Energy Authority; acting CEO MTX subs. Man. Telephone Sys.; mem. investment coms. Superannuation Bd., WPG Found., Manitoba Mus. Man & Nature, Law Soc. Manitoba; exec.-in-residence faculty of mgmt. U. Man.; dir. Mizuao Corp. Bank (Can.). Fellow Can. Inst. Chartered Accts. (past chmn. pub. sector acctg. and audit standards com.); mem. Man. Inst. Chartered Accts. (pres. 1975-76), Law Soc. of Man. (lay bencher), Order of Man., Rotary (hon. treas. 1974-2000), Man. Club. Home: 596 South Dr Winnipeg MB Canada R3T 0B1 Office: Provincial Govt Province MN 109-450 Broadway Ave Winnipeg MB Canada R3C 0V8

CURTIS, CHARLES G., JR., lawyer; BA History, magna cum laude, Harvard Univ., 1978; JD, The Univ. of Chicago Law School, 1982. Bar: Wis., Am. Bar Assoc., U.S. Supreme Ct., U.S. Ct. appeals, 7th cir., U.S. Dist. Ct., Nr. N.Y. Law Clerk Senior Judge David L. Bazelon, U.S. Ct. of Appeals, 1982—83, Justice William J. Brennan, Jr., U.S. Supreme Ct., 1984; ptnr. Foley & Lardner; atty., Co-Chair Appeals and Strategy Heller, Ehrman, White, & McAuliffe LLP, 2001—. Named one of The Best Lawyers in Am., 2003—04. Office: Heller Ehrman 1 Main St Ste 201 Madison WI 53703 Fax: 608-663-7499. Office Phone: 608-663-7480. E-mail: ccurtis@hewm.com.

CURTIS, CYRIL DEAN, retired physicist; b. Albion, Ill., Sept. 18, 1920; s. Benjamin H. and Zella Vieve (Tait) C.; m. Helen Ulrey, Apr. 16, 1948; children: Jonathan, Christopher. BS, Mckendree Coll., 1943; MS, U. Ill., 1947, PhD, 1951. Assoc. scientist Argonne Nat. Lab., Lemont, Ill., 1951-53; asst. prof. Vanderbilt U., Nashville, 1953-59; physicist Midwestern Univs. Rsch. Assn., Madison, Wis., 1959-67; scientist Fermi Nat. Accelerator Lab., Batavia, Ill., 1967-86; cons. Loma Linda (Calif.) U., 1984-90; ret. Contbr. articles to profl. jours. 1st lt. USAAF, 1943-46. Mem. AAAS, Sigma Xi. Methodist. Achievements include patents for neutron counter, high voltage electric generator. Home: 144 W Main St Albion IL 62806-1008

CURTIS, DOLORES ROGERS, writer; b. Columbus, Ohio, Apr. 16, 1929; d. Charles William and Lillian Beatrice Rogers. Student, Ctrl. State U., Xenia, Ohio, 1956—57; B.Elem.Edn., Ohio State U., 1963; attended, John Carroll U., 1980. Bookkeeper Spiegel's, Chgo., Kronfeld's, Manhattan, NY; libr. U.S. Govt. Facility, Columbus; sec. to traveling entertainer, 1949—54; tchr. Columbus Pub. Schs., 1963—68, Cleve. Bd. Edn., 1968—93. Author: Rhyming Pretzels, 2002. Avocations: reading, art, playing piano and organ, writing.

CURTIS, DOUGLAS HOMER, small business owner; b. Jackson, Mich., July 19, 1934; s. Homer K. and Luella D. (Hall) C.; m. Jean A. Breaux; children: Rebecca, Linda, Colleen, Robert. BA, Park Coll., Parkville, Mo., 1956. With Gen. Electric Co., 1958-69, mgr. Boston region Gen. Electric Supply Co. div., 1967-69; v.p. fin. and adminstrn. internat. Data Corp., Boston, 1969; v.p. fin. Franklin Electric Co. Inc., Bluffton, Ind., 1969-80; pres. Curtis Assocs., Inc., Bluffton, 1980-82; pres., COO Satelco, Inc., San Antonio, 1983-84; v.p. adminstrn. Lyall Electric Co., Kendallville, Ind., 1984-86; pres., owner Flexible Personnel Group of Cos., Inc., Ft. Wayne, Ind., 1987-97, Nat. On-Site Pers., 1991-2001, HR America, 1992—, On-Site Med. Staffing, 2000—. Bd. dirs. Wabash Valley Mfg., Inc., Silver Lake, Ind., Sentry Points; pres. Wells County (Ind.) Hosp. Authority, 1974-75 Served to capt. USMCR, 1956-58. Mem. Nat. Assn. Securities Dealers (vicechmn. fin. 1980, chmn. fin. com. 1980), Fin. Execs. Inst. (chpt. dir. 1975) Office: 1833 Magnavox Way Fort Wayne IN 46804-1539 Office Phone: 260-436-3878. Business E-Mail: dcurtis@hramerica.net.

CURTIS, EDWARD JOSEPH, JR., gas industry executive, management consultant; b. Boston, May 26, 1942; s. Edward Joseph and Violet Ella (Upton) C.; m. Virginia Carolyn Fye, May 6, 1976; children: Jane Mercedes, Sherri Jean, Virginia Amy. BSChemE, Worcester Polytech., 1964, MSChemE, 1966. Engr. Cabot Corp., Boston, 1966-68; mgr. corp. devel. Distrigas Corp., Boston, 1968-72; pres. E.J. Curtis Assocs., Inc., York Harbor, Maine, 1972—. Pres. Pine Hill Assocs., Inc., Hollis, N.H., 1976-80; ptnr. ABC Mgmt. Systems, Bellingham, Wash., 1977-82; mng. ptnr. Essex Cons. Svcs., Boston, 1981-82; bd. dirs. SEMCO Energy Inc. Pres. York Harbor Neighborhood Assn., 1989-92. Mem. AIChE, Am. Gas Assn., New Eng. Gas Assn. (bd. dirs. 1988-91, 95-2001), Soc. Gas Lighting, Assn. Energy Engrs., Internat. Assn. Energy Economists, Guild Gas Mgrs., York Golf and Tennis Club, Rosedale Golf and Country Club, Agamenticus Yacht Club, York Harbor Reading Rm., Theta Chi. Republican. Mem. Congl. Ch. Avocations: sailing, skiing, golf, computer science, music.

CURTIS, FRANK R., lawyer; b. Valley Stream, N.Y., Sept. 27, 1946; s. Frank and Rosalind (Vreeland) Curtis; m. Cynthia Mary Knapik, May 14, 1977; children: Lauren Josephine, Frank Edward, Michael Bennett. AB magna cum laude, Harvard Coll., 1968; JD, Yale U., 1971. Bar: N.Y. 1972, U.S. Dist. Cts. (so. and ea. dists.): N.Y. 1973, U.S. Ct. Appeals (2d cir.): 1975. Assoc. Hellerstein Rosier & Rembar, N.Y.C., 1971—73; ptnr. Rembar Wolf & Curtis, NY, 1974—77, Rembar & Curtis, N.Y.C., 1978—. Lectr. PLI, N.Y.C., 1980, N.Y.C., 88. Trustee North Salem Free Libr., NY, 1983—91. Mem.: N.Y. State Bar Assn., Copyright Soc. of the U.S.A., Assn. of Bar of City of N.Y. (sec. com. on copyright 1979—80), Harvard Club, Phi Beta Kappa. Home: PO Box 908 2 Juengstville Rd Croton Falls NY 10519-0908 Office: Rembar & Curtis 19 W 44th St New York NY 10036-6070 Office Phone: 212-575-8500.

CURTIS, J. VAUGHAN, lawyer; b. Lexington, Ky., June 2, 1951; Student, Centre Coll.; BA, U. Ky., 1973, MA, 1975, JD with distinction, 1978. Bar: Ga. 1978, Ky. 1980. Atty. The White House, Ford Adminstrn.; joined Alston & Bird LLP, Atlanta, 1978—, ptnr., healthcare, corp. group Atlanta & NYC. Lead articles editor Ky. Law Jour., 1977-78. Mem. State Bar Ga., Ky. Bar Assn., Atlanta Bar Assn., Order of Coif., Phi Delta Phi. Office: Alston & Bird LLP One Atlantic Ctr 1201 W Peachtree St NW Atlanta GA 30309-3424 Office Phone: 404-881-7397. Office Fax: 404-881-7777. Business E-Mail: vcurtis@alston.com.

CURTIS, JAMES EDWARD, III, legal commentator; b. LA; married; 3 children. BA in Spanish lit., U. Calif., San Diego; JD, Calif. Western Sch. Law. Bar: Calif. 1989; cert. master and rescue diver. Legis. aide Calif. State Senator Diane Watson; prosecutor Riverside Country Dist. Atty. Office; radio talk show host In Your Defense, KUCR Radio, 1993; legal commentator Court TV (during O.J. Simpson Criminal Trial), 1995; host Curtis Court, Court TV, 1999—. Legal commentator The O'Reilly Factor, FOX News, Cold Pizza, ESPN2. Recipient Beacon award, 2004. Achievements include recognized by NY Branch of NAACP for Lifetime Commitment to human and civil rights through his work in media and the courts, 2003. Avocations: tennis, golf, chess. Office: Court TV 600 Third Ave 3rd Fl New York NY 10016 Office Phone: 212-973-2800. Business E-Mail: trialheat@courttv.com.

CURTIS, JAMES RICHARD, writer, editor; b. LA, Nov. 16, 1953; s. Richard Borah and Dorothy Dawn Curtis; m. Debra Reed, June 7, 1978 (div. 1992); m. Kim Geary, Jan. 1, 1994. AA in Telecommunications, Fullerton Coll., 1974; BA in Communications, Calif. State U., 1979. Instructional designer Insgroup, Inc., Huntington Beach, Calif., 1979-80; sr. tech. writer MSI Data Corp., Costa Mesa, Calif., 1981-83, dir. corp. communications, 1983-85; dir. communications Calif. Dental Health Plan, Tustin, 1986-90; v.p. comm. and product coordination Dental Health Plan Am., Tustin, 1990—94; freelance mktg. cons. Brea, Calif., 1995—. Author: Between Flops, 1982, James Whale: A New World of Gods and Monsters, 1998, W.C. Fields: A Biography, 2003.; editor: The Creative Producer, 1993, Featured Player, 1996 Mem.: Authors Guild Am. Home: 658 Magnolia Ave Brea CA 92821-6552 Office Phone: 714-990-4858.

CURTIS, JAMES THEODORE, lawyer; b. Lowell, Mass., July 8, 1923; s. Theodore D. and Maria (Souliotis) Koutras; m. Kleanthe D. Dusopol, June 25, 1950; children: Madelon Mary, Theodore James, Stephanie Diane, Gregory Theodosius, James Theodore Jr. BA, U. Mich., 1948; JD, Harvard U., 1951; ScD (hon.), U. Mass., 1972. Bar: Mass. 1951. Assoc. Adams & Blinn, Boston, 1951-52; legal asst., asst. atty. gen. Mass., 1952-53; pvt. practice law Lowell, 1953-57; sr. ptnr. firm Goldman & Curtis, and predecessors, Lowell and Boston, 1957—. Elected mem. Lowell Charter Commn., 1969—71; del. Dem. Party State Convs., 1956—60; chmn. Greater Lowell Heart Fund, 1967—68; mem. adv. bd. Salvation Army, sec., 1956—58; mem. Bd. Higher Edn. Msss., 1967—72; bd. dirs. U. Mass. Rsch. Found., Lowell, 1965—72, Merrimack Valley Health Planning Coun., 1969—72; trustee U. Mass., Lowell, 1963—72, chmn. bd., 1968—72. With 10th mt. divsn. U.S. Army, 1943—45, spl. agent counter intelligence corps. U.S. Army, 1945—46. Decorated Knight Order Orthodox Crusade Holy Sepulcher. Mem.: ATLA, ABA, U. Mich. Alumni Assn., Harvard Law Sch. Alumni Assn., Am. Judicature Soc., Mass. Acad. Trial Lawyers, Middlesex Conty Bar Assn., Mass. Bar Assn., DAV, Lowell Hist. Soc., Harvard Club (Lowell, pres. 1969—71, bd. dirs.), Masons, Delta Epsilon Pi. Home: 111 Rivercliff Rd Lowell MA 01852-1471 Office: Goldman & Curtis PC 144 Merrimack St Ste 444 Lowell MA 01852-1789 Office Phone: 978-454-8804. Business E-Mail: jcurtis@goldman-curtis.com.

CURTIS, JAMIE LEE, actress; b. L.A., Nov. 22, 1958; d. Tony Curtis and Janet Leigh (dec. 2004); m. Christopher Guest, Dec. 18, 1984; children: Annie, Thomas. Student, U. Pacific, Stockton, Calif., 1976. Actress: (films) Halloween, 1978, The Fog, 1980, Prom Night, 1980, Terror Train, 1980, Halloween II, 1981, Road Games, 1981, Trading Places, 1983, Love Letters, 1984 Grandview USA, 1984, The Adventures of Buckaroo Banzai: Across the 8th Dimension, 1984, Perfect, 1985, Welcome Home, 1986, A Man in Love, 1987, Amazing Grace and Chuck, 1987, Dominick and Eugene, 1988, A Fish Called Wanda, 1988, Blue Steel, 1990, Queens Logic, 1991, My Girl, 1991, Forever Young, 1992, My Girl 2, 1994, Mother's Boys, 1994 True Lies, 1994 (Golden Globe award Best Actress - Musical or Comedy), House Arrest, 1996, Ellen's Energy Adventure, 1996, Fierce Creatures, 1997, Homegrown, 1998, Halloween H2O, 1998, Virus, 1999, Drowning Mona, 2000, The Tailor of Panama, 2001, Daddy and Them, 2001, Rudolf the Red-Nosed Reindeer and the Island of Misfit Toys (voice), 2001, Halloween: Resurrection, 2002, Freaky Friday, 2003, Christmas with the Kranks, 2004; (TV movies) Colombo: Bye-Bye Sky-High I.Q. Murder Case, 1977, Death of a Centerfold: The Dorothy Stratten Story, 1981, Money on the Side, 1982. As Summers Die, 1986, The Heidi Chronicles, 1995, Nicolas' Gift, 1998;(TV series) Operation Petticoat, 1977-78, She's in the Army Now, 1981, Anything but Love, 1990-93, Pigs Next Door, 2000; (TV appearances) Quincy, 1977, Hardy Boys/Nancy Drew Mysteries, 1977, Charlie's Angels, 1978, The Love Boat, 1978, Buck Rogers in the 25th Century, 1979, The Drew Carey Show, 1996; dir.: Anything But Love, 1990; author (children's books): When I Was Little: A Four-Year-Old's Memoir of Her Youth, 1993, Today I Feel Silly, 1998, Where Do Balloons Go? An Uplifting Mystery, 2000, I'm Gonna Like Me: Letting Off a Little Self-Esteem, 2002, It's Hard to Be Five, 2004. Office: Creative Artists Agy c/o Rick Kurtzman 9830 Wilshire Blvd Beverly Hills CA 90212-1804*

CURTIS, JOHN J., medical educator; b. Rochester, N.Y., Jan. 16, 1944; s. John Joseph and Mabel (Leatherman) C.; m. Vicky Burleson, Oct. 2, 1987. BS, U. Scranton, 1966; MD, Georgetown U., 1970. Diplomate Am. Bd. Internal Medicine, Am. Bd. Nephrology. Asst. prof. medicine U. Ky. Med. Ctr., Lexington, Ky., 1974-79; assoc. prof. medicine U. Ala., Birmingham, 1979-85, prof. medicine, 1985—, prof. surgery, 1991—, Endowed prof. transplant surgery, 1991—, dir. The Transplant Ctr., 1999—. Program dir. Gen. Clin. Rsch. Ctr., Birmingham, 1988-98; mem. med. adv. bd. Ala. Kidney Found., Birmingham, 1989—. Asst. editor Am. Jour. Kidney Diseases, 1987-92; transplantation editor (book) Yearbook of Nephrology, 1992-96. 1st lt. USAR, 1970-72. Mem. Am. Soc. Nephrology, Internat. Soc. Nephrology, The Transplantation Soc., Am. Soc. Transplant Physicians, European Dialysis & Transplant Assn. Office: U Ala Birmingham Divsn Nephrology THT 643 1530 3D Ave S Birmingham AL 35294-0006

CURTIS, JOHN JOSEPH, lawyer, writer; b. Fairmont, W.Va., Nov. 23, 1942; s. John Joseph and Marie Francis (Christopher) C.; m. Shirley Ann Slater, Oct. 15, 1971 (div. June 1993); children: Christopher, Kevin. AB, U. W.Va., 1964, JD, 1967. Bar: W.Va. 1967, Ill. 1972, Calif. 1979. Pvt. practice law, South Charleston, W.Va., 1967-68; chief counsel, asst. dir. W.Va. Tax Dept., Charleston, 1968-71; tax atty. Sears, Roebuck & Co., Chgo., 1971-73; chief tax counsel, dir. taxes Pacific Lighting, L.A., 1973-87; ptnr. Baker & Hostetler, L.A., 1987-93, Law Offices of John Curtis, L.A., 1994—. Author: The Code, 2004. Com. mem. Pasadena Tournament Roses, 1978-93. Lt. comdr. USNR, 1968-80. Mem. ABA, L.A. County Bar Assn. (chmn. com. 1989), Calif. Bar Assn., Inst. Property Tax, So. Calif.Tax Fund. (pres. 1990-96), L.A. Taxpayers Assn. (pres. 1990-95), Calif. Taxpayers Assn. (pres. 1987-88). Avocations: skiing, scuba, fishing. Office: 2 Arado Rancho Santa Margarita CA 92688-2749 Office Phone: 949-888-9157. E-mail: jcurtis595@aol.com.

CURTIS, KATHERINE LANAE, pharmacist; b. Bossier City, La., Apr. 4, 1973; d. Clarence Rayson III and Sara Vernelda White; m. Juvar Nakia Curtis, Jan. 26, 2003; 1 child, Juvar Pierre. Assoc. Electronics, C.C. Air Force, Randolph AFB, Tex., 1997; BS, Wayne State U., 2001, D Pharmacy, 2003. Registered pharmacist Mich. Pharmacy intern Bon Secour Hosp., Grosse Pointe, Mich., 1999—2001, VA Hosp., Detroit, 2000—03, Meijer's Pharmacy, Livonia, Mich., 2001—03; pharmacist Walgreens, Detroit, 2003; staff pharmacist Semper Care Hosp., Kalamazoo, 2003—04, A&P Great Atlantic Tea Co., Detroit, 2004—. Counselor Camp Tomahawk, Enid, Okla., 1996; vol. Vol. Impact, Detroit, 2001—03; med. min. Straight Gate Ch., Detroit, 1999—2001. With USAF, 1994—97. Mem.: Wayne State Alumni Assn., Am. Pharm. Assn. Democrat. Mem. Full Gospel Ch. Avocations: reading, writing, singing. Personal E-mail: katherin_curtis@sbcglobal.net.

CURTIS, LORETTA O'ELLEN, retired construction executive; b. Washington, Pa., Apr. 5, 1937; d. Monroe and Mildred (Carr) Bogan; m. Joseph H. Dudley (div. Oct. 1964); children: Ronald S., Joseph T., Mildred M.; m. Wayne J. Curtis (dec. 12/98). AS, Franklin U., 1983, BS, 1989; Grad., Columbus Leadership Program, 1991; grad., Premier Sch. of Travel, 1996. With Bur. Employment Svcs., Columbus, Ohio, 1962-87, examiner, equal employment opportunity officer, 1983-87, ret., 1987; v.p. Aries Constrn., Inc., Columbus, 1988-91, pres., 1991-96; ret., 1996. Mediator small claims divsn. Franklin County; tour leader GLAMER; chmn. Sch. of Ushering ICUA (Interdenominational Church Ushers Assn.), Columbus, substitute tchg., Columbus Pub. Schs., 1999—. Mem. Interdenominational Ch. Ushers Assn. Columbus. Mem. NAFE, Nat. Assn. Parliamentarians (profl. registered parliamentarian), Nat. United Ch. Ushers Assn. (bd. mem.), Ohio Assn. Colored Women (treas. 1990-94), Ohio Assn. Parliamentarians (pres. 1989-90), Interdenominational Ch. Ushers Assn. (pres. Columbus chpt. 1977-84, Plaque 1989), Mayme Moore Club (pres. 1990-93, cert. 1989). Avocations: cooking, reading, golf, volunteering. Home: 2257 Century Dr Columbus OH 43211-1919

CURTIS, MARVIN VERNELL, music educator; b. Chgo., Feb. 12, 1951; s. John Wesley Jr. and Dorothy Marva Curtis. MusB, North Park Coll., 1972; MA, Presbyn. Sch. Christian Edn., 1974; EdD, U. of Pacific, 1990. Asst. prof. music Calif. State U.-Stanislaus, Turlock, 1988-91; assoc. prof. music Va. Union U., Richmond, 1991-94, Lane Coll., Jackson, Tenn., 1995-96, Fayetteville (N.C.) State U., 1996—2002, prof., chmn. dept. performing and fine arts, 2002—; asst. dean Coll. Humanities and Social Sci., 2005—. Music advisor In Harmony series Richmond Symphony, 1996-99. Composer City on the Hill written for 1st Inauguration of Pres. Clinton, 1993; contbr. articles to profl. jours. Bd. dirs. Fayetteville Symphony, 1998—, 1st v.p., 2001; bd. dirs. Cmty. Concert Series, 1998-99; chmn. Dept. Performing and Fine Arts, 2002-05 Recipient Key to City, Savannah, Ga., 1992, Medallion of City of Richmond, Mayor's Office, 1993, Outstanding Rsch. award Nat. Assn. for Equal Opportunity, 1992, Edn. and Cultural Devel. award Cumberland Regional Improvement Corp., 2000, Noah Ryder Composer award Norfolk State U. Alumni Assn., 2000. Mem. Music Educators Nat. Conf., Nat. Coun. for Black Studies, Am. Choral Dirs. Assn. Democrat. Home: 4911 Cooper Rd Fayetteville NC 28311-0823 E-mail: mcurtis@uncfsu.edu.

CURTIS, MARY E. (MARY CURTIS HOROWITZ), publishing executive; d. Lloyd E. and Jean Curtis; m. Irving Louis Horowitz, Oct. 30, 1979 AB cum laude, Washington U., St. Louis, 1968. Editl. dir. Transaction Pubs., New Brunswick, N.J., 1968-74, exec. v.p., 1987-97, pres., 1997—, chmn. bd. dirs., 1994-97; editor in chief Praeger Pubs. subs. CBS Ednl. Pub., N.Y.C., 1974-79; v.p., pub. periodicals John Wiley and Sons, N.Y.C., 1979-87; v.p. Scripta Technica subs. John Wiley and Sons, Washington, 1984-87; mem. mgmt. bd. MIT Press, 1998—; vice chair, trustee Horowitz Found. for Social Policy, 1998—. Chair adv. com. Serials Industry Systems, 1985-88; dir. Transaction Pubs. (U.K.) Ltd.; lectr. in field. Contbr. articles to profl. jours. Mem. Soc. Scholarly Pubs. (bd. dirs. 1984-88), Assn. Am. Pubs. (Freedom to Read com.). Jewish. Business E-Mail: mcurtis@transactionpub.com.

CURTIS, MARY LOUISE, artist, educator; b. Houston, Mar. 20, 1928; d. Frank Tracy and Louise (White) Burtle; m. Robert Allen Curtis, June 26, 1946; 1 child, William Allen. BLS magna cum laude, St. Edward's U., 1979; postgrad., Austin (Tex.) Community Coll., 1979-80. Adminstrv. asst. State Bd. Ins., Austin, 1967-80; freelance tchr. drawing, watercolor Austin, 1980—; owner, artist Curtis Art, Austin, 1980—. Spkr. various charities and art groups, Tex., 1980—; tchr. watercolor and drawing classes on radio, Austin, 1989-90; comml. artist, fabric designer clothing; tchr. adult art edn. Lady Bird Johnson Wildflower Ctr., 1995—; tchr. watercolor and pastels Largo Vista (Tex.) Arts Assn., 2001—; tchr. pub. and pvt. classes in pastels and watermedia, Wildlife Refuge, 2002-03; freelance art materials factory rep., tchr., demonstrator; tchr. media classes, tchr. assisted living residence, Round Rock, Tex., 2005—. Exhibited in gallery and one-person shows, internat. art sales, pvt. and corp. collections, 1981—; rsch., design cover, illustrator for hist. novels; illustrator Grasses and Plants; represented in permanant collection at City of Austin History Ctr., Camp Mabry Armed Forces Mil. History Mus., Austin, Tex., Unity Ch. of the Hills, Austin, U.S. Dept. Interior Fish and Wildlife Svc., Balcones Canyonlands Nat. Wildlife Ctr.; bird and landscape artist Nat. Wildlife Refuge; contbr. articles to profl. jours. Bd. dirs. Hancock Recreation Ctr., Austin, 1982-83, Austin Artist Harvest, Austin C. of C., 1984-8. Native Plant Soc. Tex., 1984-85; artist State Tex. Sesquicentennial, Austin, 1984-86, Sonora Hist. Mus. (contbr. 2 original water colors), Sonora Courthouse, Sutton County; vol. artist Nat. Wildflower Rsch. Ctr., Austin, 1985—, Keep Austin Beautiful artist, 1994—; sec. Balcones Canyonlands Nat. Wildlife Refuge, 2001-02, bd. dirs., 2003, vol. artist second-day cachet envelopes March Fed. Refuges Centennial Celebration; vol. artist songbird festival Lago Vista C. of C., 2003; vol. facilitator mktg. and activities Brookdale-The Island on Lake Travis Retirement Resort, Largo Vista. Mem. Nat. Mus. Women in the Arts (charter), Capital Arts Soc. (pres. 1990-91), Waterloo Watercolor Group (chmn. art show 1982), San Antonio Watercolor Group, Lake Travis Art League (Bluebonnet Bash com. 1995), Heritage Soc. Austin (hist. archtl. illustrations 1996), Am. History Club Austin (artist-officer), Austin Pastel Soc. (charter). Avocations: public speaking, brochure illustration, posters for charity, historical research, flower gardening. Home: 7701 Rialto Blvd # 1116 Austin TX 78735 Office Phone: 512-891-0247. E-mail: Mary@curtisweb.com.

CURTIS, ORLIE LINDSEY, JR., lawyer; b. Hutchinson, Kans., Feb. 27, 1934; s. Orlie Lindsey and Lillian Esther (Barnes) C.; m. Idella Mae Krueger, June 5, 1955; children: Elizabeth, Victoria. BA with high distinction, Union Coll., Lincoln, Nebr., 1954; MS, Purdue U., 1956; PhD, U. Tenn., 1961; JD, U. So. Calif., 1977. Bar: Calif. 1977. Group chief Oak Ridge Nat. Lab., 1956-63; lab. dir., sci. fellow Northrop Corp., Hawthorne, Calif., 1963-77; ptnr. firm Kroloff, Belcher, Smart, Perry & Christopherson, 1980—. Vis. lectr. physics U. Calif., Berkeley, 1970-71; adv. bd. physics dept. U. Ky., 1970-73; lectr. Nat. Symposia Products Liability and Ins. Law. Author: Point Defects in Solids, 1975; contbr. articles to profl. jours.; patentee in field. Bd. dirs. So. Calif. Conf. Seventh-day Adventists, 1970-74, Newbury Park Acad., 1970-74, Lodi Acad., 1979-84, No. Calif. Conf. Seventh-day Adventists, 1980-86, 95—, Dameron Hosp. Found., 1985-2000, N.Am. Divsn. Seventh-day Adventists, 1997—. Fellow Am. Phys. Soc., IEEE (chmn. radiation effects com. 1970-73); mem. Assn. Def. Coun. No. Calif., Def. Rsch. Inst., State Bar Calif., San Joaquin County Bar Assn., Adventist Attys. Assn. (pres. 1983-84), Internat. Assn. Def. Counsel, Order of Coif, Am. Bd. Trial Advocates.

CURTIS, PAUL JAMES, theater director; b. Boston, Aug. 29, 1927; s. Lawrence D. and Madeleine Maria (Schwager) C. Studied directing with Erwin Piscator, New Sch. for Social Rsch., 1947-49. Dir. Deal Conservatory Theatre, 1948; founder, dir., performer Am. Mime Theatre, N.Y.C., 1952—; founder Am. Mime, Inc., N.Y.C., 1970—, Internat. Mimes & Pantomimists, 1972-74; chmn. mime dept. Am. Acad. Dramatic Arts, N.Y.C., 1956-71; lectr. emeritas Cornell U., Ithaca, NY, 1969-89. Instr. mime Bennington (Vt.) Coll., Jacob's Pillow Dance Festival, Mass., Ohio U., Austin Coll., Goodman Sch. Drama, Chgo., Pace U., N.Y.C., Hunter Coll., N.Y.C., Met. Opera Ballet Sch., N.Y.C., New Sch. Social Rsch., N.Y.C., Gene Frankel Theatre Workshop, N.Y.C., Guggenheim Mus., N.Y.C., Johns Hopkins U., Balt., Am. Conservatory Theatre, San Francisco, Circle in Sq. Theatre Sch., N.Y.C., Sarah Lawrence Coll., N.Y., D'Youville Coll., N.Y., Lincoln Sch., Calif., Fairleigh Dickinson U., N.J., Stockton State Coll. N.J., Rutgers U., New Brunswick, N.J., Clarke Ctr., N.Y.C., Guggenheim Mus., N.Y.C., The Family, N.Y.C., Johns Hopkins, Balt., R.I. Sch. Drama, Am. Conservatory Theatre Arts Guild, N.J., Brown U., R.I., Seven Arts Ctr., N.Y.C., Rye H.S., N.Y., Footlight Ranch, Pa., Ohio U., Austin Coll., Tex., Internat. Dance Sch., N.Y.C., Mamaroneck Sch. Performing Arts, N.Y., The Leonardo's, Paris; Am. mime course established at Salle Pleyel, Paris, 1998, 59 Rivoli Chez Robert, Electron Libre, Paris workshops, 2000. TV appearances NBC Exploring the Performing Arts, 1963, NBC Profile on the Arts, 1966, Nippon TV Japan, 1970, NBC To Tell The Truth, 1973, NY Live Cable TV, 1974, NBC Today Show, 1975, WNYC-TV, 1975, 1978, ABC Kids Are People Too, 1978, WNEW Broadway Extra, 1978, ABC The Last Word, 1983, TV appearance Documentary Film on the American Mime Theatre, 2003; author: (textbook) American Mime, the Medium, 1952, (plays) The Pinball Machine, 1953, Fate, 1953, The Tell Tale Heart, 1953, Escapade, 1953, The Demon Lover, 1953, Of Identity, 1953, Once Upon An Island, 1954, Monolotry, 1954, The Triple Goddess, 1954, The Western, 1954, Improvisation, 1955, Presentation, 1955, Eden, 1956, Abstraction, 1956, Commedia, 1956, Dreams I, 1958, The Scarecrow, 1962, Dreams II, 1962, The Godstuff, 1962, The Lovers, 1963, Birds, 1965, Female, 1967, Light, 1968, Hurly-Burly, 1969, Evolution, 1973, Sludge, 1974, Six, 1975, Work in Progress, 1976, Abstraction, 1977, The Unitaur, 1982, Peepshow, 1988, Pageant, 1989, Music Box, 1991, Couplings, 1999. With USN, 1944—46. Mem. AEA, AFTRA, Nat. Movement Theatre Assn. Office: Am Mime Theatre 61 4th Ave Fl 2 New York NY 10003-5204 Office Phone: 212-777-1710. Personal E-mail: ammime@aol.com. Business E-Mail: Mime@Americanmime.org.

CURTIS, PAULA ANNETTE, elementary and secondary education educator; b. Natrona Heights, Pa., Apr. 16, 1953; d. Stephen John and Josephine Kathleen (Killian) C. BS In Edn., Geneva Coll., 1974; postgrad., U. Vt., 1975, Pa. State U., New Kensington, 1978. Cert. religious edn. tchr., Pitts. Diocese. Tchr. Transfiguration Sch., Russellton, Pa., 1979—, dir. religious edn., 1995-98; tchr. continuing edn. C.C. of Allegheny County, Pitts., 1992—, Pa. State U., New Kensington, 1988—; tchr. O'Mara Driving Sch., Lower Burrell, Pa., 1976—, Lenape Votech., 1990—; CCD tchr. Transfiguration Sch., Russellton, 1995-97, head tchr., head fine arts dept., 1995-97, head Spanish dept. K-8, 1979—. Chmn. vision and values in Pitts. Diocese, Transfiguration Sch., 1980-97; CCD tchr. St. Clement Parish, Tarentum, Pa., 1986-92, dir. religious edn., 1987-92; dir. religious edn. St. Joseph Parish, Natrona, Pa., 1992-93; product tester Nat. Family Opinion Poll, 1987—; model Van Enterprises, Cranberry, Pa., 1989-92; tchr. driver edn. Plum (Pa.) Sr. H.S., 1996-98; Act 48 presenter for Penn Hills Sch. Dist. and Pitts. Diocesan Schs., 2002—; freelance model, Fashion Bug, 1998—. Vol. Help Beautify the Cmty. with Art, Russellton. Mem. Nat. Cath. Educators Assn., Nat. English Tchrs. Assn. Democrat. Roman Catholic. Avocations: craft designs, needle work, collecting reptiles, collecting and breeding tropical birds, breeding shih-tzus. Home: 211 W 9th Ave Tarentum PA 15084-1241 Office: Transfiguration Sch CCD Office 100 Mckrell Rd Russellton PA 15076-1100 Office Phone: 724-265-3350.

CURTIS, PHILIP KERRY, lawyer; b. Mineola, New York, Nov. 6, 1945; s. William Kerry and Cherry (Smith) C.; m. Janet (McDowell), Sept. 9, 1970; 1 child, Kerry Bowen. BA, Dartmouth Coll., 1968; JD, Harvard Law Sch., 1971; MBA, Harvard U., 1974. Bar: N.Y., 1971; Ga., 1976. Assoc. White and Case, N.Y.C., 1971-72, Hansell and Post, Atlanta, 1975-76; counsel, asst. to pres. Wiggins and Assoc., Atlanta, 1976-82; exec. v.p. Coers, Steinemann, and Co., Atlanta, 1982-84; exec. v.p., ptnr. Western Devel. South East, Atlanta, 1984-87; ptnr., sr. v.p. Charter Properties, Inc., Atlanta, 1987-93; exec. v.p. JDN Realty Corp., Atlanta, 1994-96; pres. Habersham Ptnr., Atlanta, 1996—2002; ptnr. Matteson Ptnr., Atlanta, 2002—. Vis. lectr. real estate, Kennesaw Coll., Grad. Bus. Sch., 1992-93. Elder Peachtree Presbyn. Ch., Atlanta, 1983-86; dir. Met. Arts Found., Atlanta, 1983-87; 1st lt., USAR, 1971-78. Mem. German Club (pres. 1986), Harvard Club of Ga., Cherokee Town and Country Club, Buckhead Rotary, Dartmouth Club of Ga. (pres. 1982-84, Club of Yr. 1984), Harvard Bus. Sch. Club of Atlanta (pres. 1982-83), Atlanta Forum, Army and Navy Club, Civil War Roundtable, Ravinia Club Ga., SAR (1st v.p.), Sigma Chi Club Atlanta (bd. dir. 1985-86), Old Guard. Republican. Home: 3111 Arden Rd NW Atlanta GA 30305-1916 Office: Two Ravinia Dr Ste 310 Atlanta GA 30346

CURTIS, RONALD CALVIN, music educator; b. Harrison, Ark., Feb. 6, 1939; s. Donald Calvin and Alice Cora (Waters) Curtis; children: Derek, Steffanie, Ryan. BS in Edn., U. Mo., 1964; MEd, Lindenwood Coll., St. Charles, Mo., 1989. Band dir. Ralls County RIII Schs., Center, Mo., 1964-66, Lincoln County RIX Schs., Troy, Mo., 1966-72, St. Clair (Mo.) Sch. Dist., 1974-75, Union (Mo.) RXI Sch. Dist., 1975-80, Francis Howell Sch. Dist., St. Charles, 1980—. Adjudicator Mo. state band contests; judge numerous marching contests, Mo., La., Ky.; guest condr. various conf. bands, Mo. Named Man of the Yr., Troy C. of C., 1969; named to Greater St. Louis Metro Band Dirs. Hall of Fame, 2001; recipient Outstanding Educator award, Union Jr. C. of C., 1980. Mem.: Mo. Bandmasters Assn., Mo. Music Educators Assn., Phi Beta Mu. Avocations: fishing, camping. Home: 371 Rose Ln Foristell MO 63348-2500 Office: Francis Howell HS 7001 S Highway 94 Saint Charles MO 63304-2201

CURTIS, SHERRY LYNN, education educator; b. Winchester, Ky., July 8, 1954; d. Obert G. and Betty (Lainhart) L. BA cum laude, Ky. Christian Coll., 1976; BA, Ea. Ky. U., 1977, MEd, 1986; PhD, Ohio U., 1997. Cert. secondary sch. counselor, secondary sch. history tchr., Ky. Tchr., residence hall supr. Mt. Mission Sch., Grundy, Va., 1977-79; dir., instr. adult edn. program Ky. River Foothills Devel. Coun., Irvine, 1979-80; adminstr., tchr. Lexington (Ky.) Christian Sch., 1980-86; tchr., counselor Lexington Day Treatment Ctr., 1986-88; prof. tchr. edn. Ky. Christian Coll., Grayson, 1988-94, v.p. student life, 1994—. Mem. Christian Ch. Home and Office: Ky Christian Coll 100 Academic Pkwy Grayson KY 41143-1123 E-mail: slcurtis@email.kcc.edu.

CURTIS, SUSAN GRACE, lawyer; b. N.Y.C., Apr. 24, 1950; d. Henry G. and Helen Curtis; m. Robert Y. Pelgrift Jr., June 8, 1974; children: Robert III, Henry, Victoria. A.B., Yale Coll., 1971; J.D., Columbia U., 1974. Bar: N.Y. 1975, U.S. Ct. Appeals (2d cir.) 1975. With Lord, Day & Lord, N.Y.C., 1974-79, Shearman & Sterling, N.Y.C., 1979-84, Proskauer, Rose, 1984-87, 93-98; ptnr. Epstein, Becker & Green, N.Y.C., 1987-93; of counsel White & Case, N.Y.C., 1998—; adj. asst. prof. law NYU Sch. Law, 1995-98; mem. faculty Practising Law Inst., 1990—. Contbg. editor: Jour. Pension Planning and Compliance, 1991—; mem. editl. adv. bd. BNA Pension Reporter, 1993—, tax mgmt. adv. bd., 1993—; contbr. articles to profl. jours. Mem. ABA (com. employee benefits), N.Y. State Bar Assn. (com. employee benefits), Assn. Bar City N.Y. (sec. com. employee benefits 1987-90). Office: White & Case Bldg Ll 1155 Avenue Of The Americas New York NY 10036-2787

CURTIS, SUSAN M., lawyer; b. Nashville, 1956; BA summa cum laude, U. Tenn., Knoxville; JD, Vanderbilt Univ., 1981. Bar: NY 1982. Ptnr., structured fin. Skadden, Arps, Slate, Meagher & Flom, N.Y.C. Mem.: Phi Beta Kappa. Office: Skadden Arps Slate Meagher & Flom 4 Times Sq New York NY 10036 Office Phone: 212-735-2119. Office Fax: 917-777-2119. Business E-Mail: scurtis@skadden.com.*

CURTISS, CAROL PERRY, health facility administrator, consultant, nurse; b. Worcester, Mass., Dec. 9, 1946; d. Joseph Anthony and Marjorie Ruth (Riedle) Perry; m. Jack Daniel Curtiss, Feb. 8, 1970; children: Paul Daniel, Jennifer Perry. Diploma in nursing, Mass. Gen. Hosp. Sch. Nursing, Boston, 1967; BS, Am. Internat. Coll., Springfield, Mass., 1978; MSN, Yale U., 1981. RN Mass. Staff nurse Franklin Med. Ctr., Greenfield, Mass., 1970, Greenfield Ob-Gyn. Assocs., 1972-74, Greenfield Vis. Nurses, 1974-75; instr. Slim Living Program YMCA, Greenfield, 1977-78; instr. nursing Greenfield C.C., 1978; asst. prof. nursing Elms Coll., Chicopee, Mass., 1981-84; oncology program mgr. Franklin Med. Ctr, Greenfield, 1986-93; cancer care cons. Curtiss Cons., Greenfield, 1981—. Mem. faculty Greenfield C.C., 1985—87; vis. lectr., clin. instr. Fitchburg (Mass.) State Coll., 1985—86; vis. lectr. Elms Coll., Chicopee, Mass., 1984—85; mem. adj. faculty SUNY, 1987—90, U. Mass., Amherst, 1989—2005; peer reviewer Agy. for Health Care Policy and Rsch., Cancer Pain Gidelines, HHS, 1993; presenter in field, U.S. and abroad, 1981—; adj. faculty Sch. Nursing U. So. Ind.; adj. clin. instr. Tufts U. Sch. Medicine, 2005—. Co-author: Cancer Doesn't Have to Hurt, 1997; guest editor Oncology Nursing Forum, 1993; contbr. articles to profl. jours. Bd. dirs. Franklin County, Am. Cancer Soc., Greenfield, 1979-95, mem. nurse and social work scholarship com., 1988-96, nursing com. liaison, 1990-98; mem. steering com. Mass. Cancer Pain Initiative, 1988-90, 2002—, liaison, 1990-97, cons. chmn., 2002—; trustee Oncology Nursing Found., 1995-2000. Recipient Am. Alliance of Cancer Pain Initiatives award, Dahl Lectureship: Leadership in Systems Change, Am. Alliance of Cancer Pain Initiatives, 2003. Mem.: Internat. Union Against Cancer, Am. Soc. Pain Mgmt. Nurses, Am. Pain Soc., Internat. Union Against Cancer (U.S. com. 1992—2000), Oncology Nursing Soc. (mem. numerous sub coms. 1987—, mem. numerous subcoms. 1987—, pres.-elect 1991—92, 1991—92, corp. adv. bd. 1991—93, 1991—93, bd. dirs. 1991—, 1991—, nat. pres. 1992—93, Oncology Nursing Press pres. 1992—94, pres. Oncology Nursing Press 1992—94, pres. 1993—94, co-chair conf. on pain 1994, Disting. Svc. award 1999), Am. Soc. Pain Mgmt. Nurses (Master Faculty 2005—), Am. Pain Soc., Sigma Theta Tau. Avocations: biking, skiing, tennis, carpentry. Home: 73 James St Greenfield MA 01301-3607 Office Phone: 413-774-5238. E-mail: carol.curtiss@verizon.net.

CURTISS, CHARLES FRANCIS, chemist, educator; b. Chgo., Apr. 4, 1921; s. Ralph Charles and Camille (Guthormsen) C.; m. Lois Pauline Hruska, Mar. 23, 1946; children: Larry A., Glenn D., Ned S. BS, U. Wis., 1942, PhD, 1948. Faculty U. Wis., 1949—, prof. chemistry, 1960-89, emeritus, 1989—. Author: (with others) Molecular Theory of Gases and Liquids, 1954, Dynamics of Polymeric Liquids, 1977, 87; also research papers. Fellow Am. Phys. Soc., AAAS; mem. Am. Chem. Soc. Home: 6317 Keelson Dr Madison WI 53705-4368 Business E-Mail: curtiss@chem.wisc.edu.

CURTISS, ELDEN FRANCIS, archbishop; b. Baker, Oreg., June 16, 1932; s. Elden F. and Mary (Neiger) C. BA, St. Edward Sem., Seattle, MDiv, 1958; MA in Ednl. Adminstrn, U. Portland, 1965; postgrad., Fordham U., U. Notre Dame. Priest Roman Cath. Ch., 1958. Campus chaplain, 1959—68; supt. schs. Diocese of Baker, Oreg., 1962—70; pastor, 1968—70; mem. ecumenical ministries State of Oreg., 1972; pres., ector Mt. Angel Sem., Benedict, Oreg., 1972—76, mem. bd. regents, 1976—93; mem. pastoral svcs. Oreg. State Hosp., Salem, 1975—76; bishop Diocese of Helena, Mont., 1976—93; archbishop Archdiocese of Omaha, 1993—. Chmn. bd. Boys Town USA, Cath. Mut. Relief Soc. Am.; mem. Pontifical Coun. for Family, Rome; Episcopal advisor Serra Internat. Mem.: Nat. Cath. Ednl. Assn. (bishops and pres's com. coll. dept., Outstanding Educator 1972). Office: Archdiocese of Omaha 100 N 62nd St Omaha NE 68132-2702*

CURTISS, JEFF, industrial company executive, lawyer; BSBA, U. Nebr., 1970, JD, 1971; LLM in Taxation, Washington U., St. Louis, 1975. Bar: Nebr., Colo., Ill., Mo.; CPA, Colo. Various devel. positions to v.p. fin. G.D. Searle & Co., 9 yrs; CFO, Coleman Co.; exec. v.p., CFO, bd. dirs. Heritage Media, Dallas; CFO, sr. v.p. Browning-Ferris Industries, Inc., Houston, 1992-99, Svc. Corp. Internat., Houston, 2000—. Office: Svc Corp Internat PO Box 130548 1929 Allen Pkwy Houston TX 77219-0548 Mailing: PO Box 3151 Houston TX 77253-3151

CURTISS, RICHARD HOLDEN, magazine editor, writer; b. Grand Rapids, Mich., June 13, 1927; s. Fred Adelbert and Alma Clement (Holden) C.; m. Donna Jean Bourne, June 18, 1950; children: Diana Ruth Sreebny, Delinda Louise Hanley, Andrew Bourne, Raymond Holden. BA in Journalism, U. So. Calif., L.A., 1949. Reporter OMGUS Observer, Berlin, Germany, 1946-47; editor/reporter Whittier (Calif.) Star Reporter, 1949-50; newsman UP, L.A., 1950-51; pubs. officer U.S. Embassy, Djakarta, Indonesia, 1951-53, press attache Ankara, Turkey, 1957-59, Baghdad, 1963-66, pub. affairs officer Damascus, Syria, 1966-67, counselor for pub. affairs Beirut, 1973-76; info. officer Am. Consulate Gen., Stuttgart, Germany, 1954-56; newswriter USIA, Washington, 1959-62, program coord. Near East, South Asia, 1967-69, dep. asst. dir. Near East, North Africa, 1976-78, chief insp., 1979-80; dir. Voice of Am. Program Ctr., Rhodes, Greece, 1970-73; exec. dir. Am. Edn. Trust, Washington, 1981—. Exec. editor Washington Report on Mid. East Affairs, 1983—; founding dir. Mid.-East Policy Coun., Washington, 1981-82, Coun. for Nat. Interest, Washington, 1985-86. Author: A Changing Image: American Perceptions of the Arab-Israel Dispute, 1982, 2d edit., 1986, Stealth Pacs: Lobbying Congress for Control of U.S.-Mid. East Policy, 1990, 4th edit., 1996; co-editor: Seeing the Light: Personal Encounters with the Middle East and Islam, 1997; contbr. numerous articles to profl. jours. Recipient Edward R. Murrow award for excellence in pub. diplomacy Fletcher Sch. for Law and Diplomacy, 1976, Superior Honor award USIA, 1976, Lifetime Achievement award Am.-Arab Anti-Discrimination Com., 1992, Achievement award Ptnrs. for Peace, 1993, Dedicated Svc. award Islamic Assn. for Palestine in N.Am., 1994, Lifelong Dedication award United Muslims of Am., 1994, Cert. of Appreciation The Jerusalem Fund for Edn. and Cmty. Devel. and Ctr. for Policy Analysis on Palestine, 1995, They Dared to Speak Out award Coun. for Nat. Interest, 1995, Voice of Conscience of Am. Journalism award Am. Muslim Alliance, 1998, Cmty. award for journalism Coun. on Am. Islamic Rels., 1999, Constn. to World Awareness award Solidarity for Palestinian Human Rights Orgns. of McGill and Concordia Univs., Montreal, Liberty and Justice award Am. Muslim Coun., Muslim Am. Soc., and United Assn. for Studies and Rsch., 1999. Mem. Nat. Press Club. Avocations: archaeology, paleontology, environmental protection, human rights. Office: American Educational Trust 1902 18th St NW Washington DC 20009-1707 E-mail: wrmea@aol.com.

CURTISS, ROY, III, life sciences professor; b. May 27, 1934; m. Josephine Clark, Dec. 28, 1976; children: Brian, Wayne, Roy IV, Lynn, Gregory Clark, Eric Garth, Megan Kimberly. BS in Agr., Cornell U., 1956; PhD in Microbiology, U. Chgo., 1962; DSc (hon.), So. Ill. U., Edwardsville, 2003. Instr., rsch. asst. Cornell U., 1955-56; jr. tech. specialist Brookhaven Nat. Lab., 1956-58; fellow microbiology U. Chgo., 1958-60, USPHS fellow, 1960-62; biologist Oak Ridge Nat. Lab., 1963-72; lectr. microbiology U. Tenn., Oak Ridge, 1965-72, lectr. Grad. Sch. Biomed. Scis., 1967-69, prof., 1969-72, assoc. dir., 1970-71, interim dir., 1971-72; Charles H. McCauley prof. microbiology U. Ala., Birmingham, 1972-83; sr. scientist Inst. Dental Rsch., 1972-83, Comprehensive Cancer Ctr., 1972-83, dir. molecular cell biology grad. program, 1973-82; dir., sr. scientist Cystic Fibrosis Rsch. Ctr., 1981-83; prof. cellular and molecular biology Sch. Dental Medicine Washington U., St. Louis, 1983-91, George William and Irene Koechig Freiberg prof. biology, 1984—2005, chmn. dept. biology, 1983-93, dir. Ctr. Plant Sci. and Biotech., 1991-94, George William and Irene Koechig Freiburg prof. emeritus, 2005—; prof. life scis. Ariz. State U., 2004—; co-dir. Ctr. Infectious Diseases and Vaccinology, Biodesign Inst., Ariz. State U., 2004—. Mem. Ctr. for Infectious Disease, Washington U., St. Louis; vis. prof. Instituto Venezolana de Investigaciones Cientificas, 1969, U. P.R., 1972, U. Católica de Chile, 1973, U. Okla., 1982; recombinant DNA molecule program adv. com. NIH, 1974-77, genetic basis disease rev. com., 1979-83, chmn., 1981-83, vaccine study panel, 2001-04, chmn. bacterial biodefence rev. com., 2003-2004; genetic biology com. NSF, 1975-78; mem. diseases rsch. adv. bd. Midwest Regional Ctr. Excellence in Biodefense and Emerging Infections, 2003-2005 Editor: Jour. Bacteriology, 1970-76, Infection and Immunity, 1985-92, Escherichia coli and Salmonella: Cellular and Molecular Biology, 1993-96, exec. editor-in-chief, 2000—. Active Oak Ridge City Coun., 1969-72, Cystic Fibrosis Found., rsch. devel. program rev. com. 1984-89, Conf. Rsch. Workers on Animal Diseases, Heiser Found. Sci. Adv. Bd., 1996-2004; bd. dirs. Am. Type Culture Collection, 1989-99, presdl. adv., 2003—; bd. dirs. Whitfield Sch., 1997-2005, exec. com., 2002-2005; founder, dir. and sci. adv. MEGAN Health, Inc., 1992-2000, v.p. rsch., 1998-99; mem. Mo. Seed Capital Investment Bd., 2000-03. Recipient Sardinia Sci. award, 2003; named Mo. Inventor of Yr., 1997. Fellow: AAAS, Acad. Sci. St. Louis, Am. Acad. Microbiology; mem.: NAS, Internat. Soc. Vaccines, World Health Orgn. (steering com. immunology of TB 1982—85), Coun. Advancement Sci. Writing (dir. 1976—82, v.p. 1978—82), N.Y. Acad. Scis., Am. Soc. Microbiology (parliamentarian 1970—75, dir. 1977—80, editl. bd. ASM News 1987—99, dir. 1989—94, 1999—2004), Soc. Gen. Microbiology, Internat. Soc. Mucosal Immunology, Am. Assn. Avian Pathologists, Genetics Soc. Am. (chmn. genetics stock ctrs. com. 1987—89), Gateway Strikers Soccer Club (pres. 1995—2001, chmn. bd. dirs. 2001—05, founder), Sigma Xi. Home: 6732 N Joshua Tree Ln Paradise Valley AZ 85253-3245 Office: CIDV The Biodesign Inst Ariz State U Tempe AZ 85287-5401

CURTISS, THOMAS, JR., lawyer, educator; b. Buffalo, Nov. 4, 1941; s. Thomas and Hope (Middleton Plumb) C. BA, Yale U., 1963; JD, Harvard U., 1970. Bar: Calif. 1971. Assoc. Musick, Peeler & Garrett, L.A., 1970-72, Macdonald, Halsted & Laybourne, L.A., 1972-76, ptnr., 1976-88, Kindel & Anderson, L.A., 1992-96, McKenna & Cuneo, L.L.P., L.A., 1996—2002; prin. Rodi, Pollock, Pettker, Galbraith & Cahill, a law corp., 2000—. Adj. prof. Loyola U., L.A. Law Sch., 1982-93, 99. Mem. editl. bd. L.A. Lawyer, 1992-93; contbr. articles to profl. jours. Mem. vestry Trinity Episc. Ch., L.A., sr. warden, 1982, 84-86; mem. Commn. on Ordained Ministry, Diocese of L.A., 1983-88; legal com. Music Ctr. Found., 1988-94, dir. Cath. Ctr. St. Paul, 1989-94, treas., 1989-95; mem. AIDS Interfaith Coun. So. Calif., Inc., 1989-91; Class of 1959 agt. Phillips Exeter Acad., 1994-98; dir. Mental Health Assn., L.A. County, 1996-97. Maj., USMCR, 1963-78. Fellow Am. Coll. Trust and Estate Counse; mem. ABA (mem. sect. real property, probate and trust law), L.A. County Bar Assn. (chmn. exec. com., probate and trust law sect. 1991-92), The Calif. Club, State Bar of Calif. (bd. of legal specialization, cert. specialist, estate planning, trust and probate law). Republican. Home: 2250 Micheltorena St Los Angeles CA 90039-3021 Office Phone: 213-438-5207. E-mail: tcurtissj@sbcglobal.net.

CURTIS-TWEED, PHYLLIS MARIE, humanities educator; d. Cecil Morris and Alice Marie Curtis; m. Nicholas Genevieve-Tweed, May 30, 1992; 1 child, Lauren Genevieve-Tweed. BA, U. Md., College Park, 1978, MEd, 1985; PhD, Emory U., 1993. Rsch. assoc., instr. in psychology dept. of psychiatry Harvard Med. Sch., Judge Baker Children's Ctr., Boston, 1995—2001; assoc. prof., dir., freshman yr. program Medgar Evers Coll. of CUNY, Bklyn., 2001—. Contbr. entry, articles to profl. publs. Leader Reach Out and Touch/Macedonia AME Ch., Flushing, NY, 2002. Recipient post-doctoral fellowship in psychology dept. psychiatry, Harvard U., 1993—95, Rsch. award, Childrens Studies at Harvard U., 1998—99, U.S. Achievement Acad. Nat. award, 1994; grantee, NIMH, 1995—2001. Mem.: Assn. for Moral Edn. (exec. bd. mem. 2005—). African Methodist Episcopal Church. Avocations: reading, writing, travel. Office: Medgar Evers Coll 1650 Bedford Ave Brooklyn NY 11225 Office Phone: 718-270-4960. E-mail: ptweed@mec.cuny.edu.

CURTMAN, TERESA GAYLE, music educator; b. Dexter, Mo., Sept. 24, 1970; d. Earl Edward and Judith Carole Slaughter; m. Jason Daniel Curtman, May 14, 2001; children: Brent Cameron, Hannah Grace. AA, Three Rivers C.C., Poplar Bluff, Mo., 1998; B in Music Edn., S.E. Mo. State U., Cape Girardeau, Mo., 2000. Cert. music tchr. Music tchr. grades K-8 Twin Rivers Sch. Dist., Fisk, Mo., 2000—. Mem.: Music Educators Nat. Conf. (sec./treas. 1997—2000).

CURTS, HAROLD LAYNE, construction executive; b. Dallas, Oct. 30, 1957; s. Harold Franklin and Betty Ann (Moulton) C.; m. Trina Elizabeth Roach, Aug. 16, 1980; children: Steven Robert, Valerie Layne. AA in Design and Drafting, Mountain View Coll., 1978; AA in Civil Constrn., Tarrant County Coll., 1985; BS, Letourneau U., 1994. Project engr. Broyles & Broyles, Inc., Ft. Worth, 1978-80; project mgr. Precision Concrete and Constrn., Inc., Dallas, 1980-81; constrn. mgr. Methodist Hosps. of Dallas, 1981-83; v.p. constrn. Medco Constn., Baylor Health Care System, Dallas, 1983-85; v.p. design and constrn. The Centra Group, Ft. Worth, 1985-91; pres. Tech. Interiors, Ft. Worth, 1991—. Mem. ASCE, Tex. Assn. Hosp. Engrs., Nat. Eagle Scout Assn. Republican. Baptist. Avocations: travel, fishing. Office: Technical Interiors PO Box 14824 Fort Worth TX 76117-0824 Office Phone: 817-589-7985. Personal E-mail: pickup83@aol.com.

CURTZ, CHAUNCEY S.R., lawyer, real estate company executive; b. Ann Arbor, Mich., July 14, 1954; s. Thaddeus Bankson and Rebecca Parkhill (Reeve) C.; m. Brenda Lee Kyriss, Sept. 2, 1976; children: Lydia Lorraine, Charles Edward. Student, Georgetown U., 1972-73; BS, McGill U., 1976; JD, U. Wis., 1981. Bar: Wis. 1981, Ky. 1981, U.S. Dist. Ct. (ea. dist.) Ky. 1981, U.S. Ct. Appeals (6th cir.) 1983, U.S. Supreme Ct. 1986, U.S. Dist. Ct. (we. dist.) Ky. 1993. Assoc. Wyatt, Tarrant & Combs, Lexington, Ky., 1981-87, ptnr., 1987-97; counsel Dinsmore & Shohl, Lexington, 1997—; sr. v.p. ops., gen. coun. Big Sandy Mgmt. Co., Inc., Lexington, 1997—2002; pres., CEO, chmn. bd. Beaver Dam Coal Co., Hartford, Ky., 2000—02; bd. dirs., pres., gen. counsel Coal Energy Investments & Mgmt., LLC, 2002—. Bd. dirs., sec. Curtz & Shine, Inc., Lexington, 1985—; bd. dirs., pres. CSR Curtz, Inc., Lexington, 1997—. Contbr. articles to profl. jours.; contbg. author: UK/CLE Practitioners Manual, 1989. Chmn. Lexington Arts & Cultural Coun., 1995-96, chmn., 2003-04; bd. dirs. Lexington Philharmonic, 1996-97, Lexington Children's Theatre, 1997-99; mem. Pritchard Com. Acad. Excellence, Lexington, 1995-98; trustee Energy and Mineral Law Found., 2000—, mem. exec. com., 2001-04, asst. sec., 2003-04, trustee Nat. Coun. Coal Lessors, 2003-2004; mem. adv. com. Gov.'s Sch. for Arts, 2001-02. Mem. Lexington Coal Exchg. Avocations: travel, gardening, cooking, wine. Office: Dinsmore & Shohl 250 W Main St Ste 1400 Lexington KY 40507-1735 Office Phone: 859-425-1000. E-mail: curtz@dinslaw.com.

CURWEN, RANDALL WILLIAM, journalist, editor; b. Hazel Green, Wis., Apr. 18, 1946; s. Charles William and Theda (Hillary) C. BS, U. Wis., 1968. Reporter Rockford (Ill.) Morning Star, 1968-69, copy editor/asst. city editor, 1969-72; copy editor Chgo. Today, 1972-74; copy editor/asst. sect. editor Chgo. Tribune, 1974-80, assoc. features editor, 1980-91, co-editor evening edit., 1992, travel editor, 1992—. Recipient 1st place headline writing award Ill. UPI, 1977, Johnrae Earl award Chgo. Tribune, 1979, 96, Soc. Am. Travel Writers Ctrl. States award for best travel sect., 1994, 99, 2001, 02. Mem. Soc. Am. Travel Writers (Lowell Thomas award for best travel sect. 1995, 97), Nat. Lesbian and Gay Journalists Assn. Avocations: travel, baseball, video. Home: 930 W Roscoe Rear Coachhouse Chicago IL 60657 Office: Chgo Tribune Co 435 N Michigan Ave PO Box 25340 Chicago IL 60625-0340

CURZAN, MYRON PAUL, lawyer; b. N.Y.C., May 13, 1940; s. Lee and Hannah Rose (Tannenbaum) C.; m. Mary Hannah Curzan; children: Elisabeth, Anne, Katherine. BA, Columbia U., 1961, LLB, 1965; MA, Yale U., 1962. Bar: Calif. 1966, D.C. 1969. Clk. to chief justice Calif. Supreme Ct., 1965-66; legis. asst. to Senator Robert F. Kennedy Washington, 1966-67; ptnr. Arnold & Porter, Washington, 1967-91; CEO APCO Assocs., The Arnold & Porter Cons. Group, 1984-88; pres., CEO MPC & Assocs., Inc., 1984-91, chmn. bd., 1991-96; pres., CEO UniDev, LLC, 1996—; CEO Nat. Captioning Inst., 1996-98. Vice-chmn. bd. Conn. Mut. Life Ins. Co., 1991-93; counsel Arnold & Porter, 1993-98; bd. dirs. Rocky Mountain Inst., E Source Inc., Internat. Inst. for Energy Conservation. Contbr. articles to profl. jours. Address: 6404 Garnett Dr Chevy Chase MD 20815-6616 Office Phone: 301-656-7742. E-mail: mcurzan@univer.com.

CURZON, SUSAN CAROL, academic administrator; b. Poole, Eng., Dec. 11, 1947; came to U.S., 1952. d. Kenneth Nigel and Terry Marguerite (Morris) C. AB, U. Calif., Riverside, 1970; MLS, U. Wash., 1972; PhD, U. So. Calif., 1983. Spl. libr. Kennecott Exploration, San Diego, 1972-73; various positions L.A. County Pub. Libr., 1973-89; dir. libr. Glendale (Calif.) Pub. Libr., 1989-92; dean univ. libr. Calif. State U., Northridge, 1992—, 1992—. Cons. Grantsmanship Ctr., L.A., 1981-83; vis. lectr. Grad. Sch. Libr. and Info. Sci. UCLA, 1986-92. Author: Managing Change, Managing the Interview. Libr. of the Year, Libr. Jour., 1993. Mem. ALA, Calif. Libr. Assn. Democrat. Avocations: history, horses. Office: Calif State U Libr Office of the Dean 18111 Nordhoff St Northridge CA 91330-8326 Office Phone: 818-677-2271.

CUSACK, JOAN, actress; b. NYC, Oct. 11, 1962; d. Richard and Nancy C.; m. Richard Burke 1993; 2 children. BA, U. Wis., 1985. Stage appearances include Road, 1988, Brilliant Traces, 1989, Cymbeline, 1989; TV appearances include Saturday Night Live (regular 1985-86 season), The Mother, 1994, What About Joan, 2001-02, A Very Merry Muppet Christmas, 2002; film appearances include Cutting Loose, 1980, My Bodyguard, 1980, Class, 1983, Grandview USA, 1984, Sixteen Candles, 1984, The Allnighter, 1987, Broadcast News, 1987, Stars and Bars (aka An Englishman in New York), 1988, Married to the Mob, 1988, Working Girl, 1988 (Acad. award nominee best supporting actress 1989), Say Anything, 1989, Men Don't Leave, 1989, My Blue Heaven, 1990, The Cabinet of Dr. Ramirez, 1991, Hero, 1992, Toys, 1992 (also musician), Addams Family Values, 1993, Corrina, Corrina, 1994, Nine Months, 1995, Two Much, 1996, Mr. Wrong, 1996, A Smile Like Yours, 1997, In and Out, 1997, Grosse Pointe Blank, 1997, Arlington Road, 1999, Runaway Bride, 1999, (voice) Toy Story 2, 1999, Arlington Road, 1999, Cradle Will Rock, 1999, High Fidelity, 2000, Where the Heart Is, 2000, School of Rock, 2003, Looney Toons-Back in Action, 2003, Raising Helen, 2004, The Last Shot, 2004, Ice Princess, 2005. Office: United Talent Agy Inc 9560 Wilshire Blvd Fl 5 Beverly Hills CA 90212*

CUSACK, JOHN, actor; b. Evanston, Ill., June 28, 1966; s. Richard and Nancy Cusack Co-owner New Crime Productions. Actor: (films) Class, 1983, Sixteen Candles, 1984, Grandview USA, 1984, The Sure Thing, 1985, Journey of Natty Gann, 1985, Better Off Dead, 1985, Stand By Me, 1986, One Crazy Summer, 1986, Broadcast News, 1987, Hot Pursuit, 1987, Eight Men Out, 1988, Tapeheads, 1988, Say Anything, 1989, Fatman and Little Boy, 1989, The Grifters, 1990, True Colors, 1991, Shadows and Fog, 1992, Roadside Prophets, 1992, The Player, 1992, Map of the Human Heart, 1992, Bob Roberts, 1992, Money for Nothing, 1993, Bullets Over Broadway, 1994, The Road to Wellville, 1994, Floundering, 1994, City Hall, 1995, (voice) Anastasia, 1997, Con Air, 1997, Hellcab, 1997, Midnight in the Garden of Good and Evil, 1997, This is My Father, 1998, The Thin Red Line, 1998, Pushing Tin, 1998, Being John Malkovich, 1999, Live of the Party, 2000, Ango, 2000, America's Sweethearts, 2001, Serendipity, 2001, Identity, 2003, Runaway Jury, 2003, Must Love Dogs, 2005; actor, dir., writer Grosse Pointe Blank, 1997; prodr., actor Arigo, 1998, Max, 2002; actor, writer High Fidelity, 2000, The Cradle Will Rock, 1999; prodr. Cosmic Banditos, 2002, 2.2, 2002. Office: William Morris Agy 151 El Camino Dr Beverly Hills CA 90212*

CUSACK, JOHN T., lawyer; b. Sept. 10, 1958; BS magna cum laude, Drew Univ., 1980; JD, George Washington Univ., 1983. Bar: NY 1984, Ill. 1986. Ptnr. chair fin., fin. svcs. and bankruptcy DLA Piper Rudnick Gray Cary, Chgo. and NYC. Mem.: ABA, Chgo. Bar Assn., Ill. State Bar Assn. Office: DLA Piper Rudnick Gray Cary 1251 Ave of the Americas New York NY 10020-1104 also: DLA Piper Rudnick Gray Cary Ste1900 203 N LaSalle St Chicago IL 60601-1293 Office Phone: 212-835-6049, 312-368-4049. Office Fax: 312-236-7516. Business E-Mail: john.cusack@piperrudnick.com.

CUSACK, JOHN THOMAS, lawyer; b. Oak Park, Ill., June 22, 1935; s. Thomas Jr. and Clare (Hock) C.; m. Mary Louise Coughlin, Nov. 1, 1969; children: John, James, Mary Helen, Cathleen. AB cum laude, U. Notre Dame, 1957; JD, U. Mich., 1960; postgrad., Harvard U., 1961-62. Bar: Ill. 1960, U.S. Dist. Ct. (no. dist.) Ill. 1961, U.S. Dist. Ct. (no. dist.) Ind. 1983, U.S. Tax Ct. 1984, U.S. Ct. Appeals (7th cir.) 1973, U.S. Ct. Appeals (5th and 9th cirs.) 1975, U.S. Ct. Appeals (3d cir.) 1986, U.S. Ct. Appeals (10th cir.) 1987, U.S. Ct. Appeals (11th cir.) 1988, U.S. Supreme Ct. 1966. Trial atty. antitrust div. U.S. Dept. Justice, 1962-70; assoc. Gardner, Carton & Douglas, Chgo., 1970-74, ptnr., 1974—, chmn. litigation dept., 1978-86, chmn. antitrust practice group, 1986—. Contbr. articles to legal jours. Trustee Fenwick H.S. 1st lt. JAGC, USAR, 1963-67. Mem. ABA (antitrust and litigation sect., health law com. 1960—), Chgo. Bar Assn., Law Club City Chgo. Roman Catholic. Home: 1030 Franklin Ave River Forest IL 60305-1340 Office: Gardner Carton & Douglas 191 N Wacker Dr Ste 3700 Chicago IL 60606-1698 E-mail: jcusack@gcd.com.

CUSACK, THOMAS JOSEPH, retired banker; b. N.Y.C., Aug. 12, 1938; s. Thomas Joseph and Josephine (Mingalone) C.; m. Elizabeth Mary McAuliffe, June 4, 1960; children: Thomas, Elizabeth, Bridget. BBA, St. Francis Coll., 1968; grad., Stonier Grad. Sch. Banking, New Brunswick, N.J. Asst. v.p. Irving Trust Co., N.Y.C., 1959-79; v.p., sr. ops. mgr. Mellon Bank Internat., N.Y.C., 1979-83, gen. mgr., 1983-85; v.p., sr. ops. mgr. Creditanstalt, Greenwich, Conn., 1985-90, v.p. planning and devel., 1990-93, v.p., COO, 1993-94, sr. v.p., COO, 1995-98; ret., 1998. U.S. rep. Swift Documentary Credit Working Group, Brussels, Belgium, 1983-85; mem. Payments and Settlement Systems Com., Bankers Assn. Fgn. Trade, 1983-85. Fin. com., trustee St. Vincent DePaul Roman Cath. Ch., Elmont, N.Y., 1988—. Mem.K.C.(4th deg.), U.S. Coun. on Internat. Banking (chmn. 1987-88). Avocations: camping, touring. Home: 10 John Ave Elmont NY 11003-1916 Personal E-mail: tjccat@optonline.net. *If we all would realize that the only lasting thing we leave in this world is our reputation, what a better world this would be.*

CUSH, JOHN PATRICK, priest, theology studies educator; b. Bklyn., Jan. 20, 1972; s. Edward Joseph Cush and Catherine Mary Flynn. BA in Philosophy and English, St. John's U., Jamaica, NY, 1994; STB in Theology, Gregorian U., Rome, 1997, STL in Theology, 1999. Parochial vicar Good Shepherd Roman Cath. Ch., Bklyn., 1998, St. Helen Roman Cath. Ch., Howard Beach, NY, 1999—2004; chaplain St. Edmund's H.S., Bkln., 1999—2000; instr. deacon program Diocese of Bklyn., 1999—2000, 2005—, mem. Cath.-Luth. bilaterals, 2000—, censor of books, 2001—; faculty Cathedral Prep. Sem., Elmhurst, NY, 2004—. Theology instr. Diocesan Pastoral Inst. for Formation of Lay Ecclesial Ministers, 2001—; presenter ministry workshops Diocesan Liturgical Commn., 2002—; spiritual dir. permanent diaconate, Diocese Bklyn., 2002—. Contbr. articles to Bklyn. Tablet. Mem.: Am. Cath. Philos. Assn., Canon Law Soc. Am., Cath. Biblical Assn. Am. Office: Cathedral Prep Sem 56-25 92nd St Elmhurst NY 11373

CUSHING, DIANE T., voice educator; b. Holden, Mass., Aug. 15, 1955; d. Toivo V. and Impi E. Tammi; m. Theodore S. Cushing, June 3, 1978; children: Emily T., Olivia D. M in Conducting, Syracuse U., 1978; M in Vocal Performance, Boston Conservatory, 1990; MusB in Music Edn., Anna Marie Coll., 1977. Pvt. practice, Gardner, 1981—; music tchr. Mt. Wachusett CC, Gardner, Mass., 1981—87, dir. youth choir, 1991—2004; prof. voice Keene (NH) State Coll., 1997—. Dir., founder Greater Gardner Cmty. Choir, 1991—; dir. choral activities Gardner Sch. Sys., 1992—2004; lectr. in field. Minister music Bethany Bapt. Ch., Gardner, 1981—96. Mem.: Nat. Assn. Tchrs. Singing. Avocations: tennis, running. Home: 24 Jackson Park Gardner MA 01440 Office Phone: 978-407-4632. Personal E-mail: tcush81247@aol.com.

CUSHING, MARK L., lawyer; BA with honors, Stanford U., 1975; JD, Willamette U., 1981. Spl. asst. to Gov. Oreg.; ptnr. & litig. Tonkon, Torp, Galen, Marmaduke and Booth, LLP, Portland, Oreg., Ball, Janik and Novak, LLP, Portland, Oreg.; sr. v.p. Video Lottery Technologies Inc., 1993—94; pres. Automated Wagering Internat. Inc., 1994; asst. to chmn. Lynch Corp., Greenwich, Conn., 1996; pres. St. George Crystal, Jeanette, Pa., 1999; of counsel Winstead Sechrest & Minick PC, Austin, Tex., 2001—02, ptnr. Washington, 2002—04, chair govt rels. and pub. policy sect.; mem. Winstead Consulting Group LLC; ptnr., pub. law & policy strategies group Sonnenschein Nath & Rosenthal LLP, Washington, 2004—. Office: Sonnenschein Nath & Rosenthal LLP Ste 600, E Tower 1301 K St NW Washington DC 20005 Office Phone: 202-408-9205. Office Fax: 202-408-6399. Business E-Mail: mcushing@sonnenschein.com.

CUSHING, SARA ELIZABETH, language educator, writer; b. Richmond, Va., July 7, 1950; d. William Routledge and Sara Margie (Williams) C. BA, Duke U., 1972; MS, SUNY, Cortland, 1978. Cert. tchr. secondary English, N.Y. Adminstrv. asst. Duke Players/Duke U., Durham, N.C., 1970-72; substitute tchr. Maine-Endwell and Union Endicott Schs., Endicott and Endwell, N.Y., 1972-73; tchr. English and drama John F. Kennedy High Sch., Richmond, Va., 1973-75; project coord. Alekna Constrn., Endicott, 1975-77; tchr. English Vestal (N.Y.) Sr. High Sch., 1977-78, Greene (N.Y.) Jr.-Sr. High Sch., 1978-88; writer, editor, writing cons., 1981—; instr. English Piedmont Tech. Coll., Greenwood, SC, 1988—, computer lab. mgr., weekend coord. coll., 1988—2002; cons. Time to Celebrate, 2003—04. Rental agt. Drucker and Falk, Richmond, 1974-75; liaison/amb. to Lander Coll., Greenwood, 1990-91, co-chmn. Praxis Conf., 1990-91; team leader S.C Advanced Technol. Edn. Exemplary Faculty Team, 1995-98, Ad-hoc Workplace Rsch. Team Leader, 1996-97. Author: (textbook) You, Too, Can Write, 1990, 4th edit., 1998. Named Faculty Educator of Yr., Piedmont Tech. Coll., 2002; recipient summer seminar stipend, NEH, Atlanta, 1984. Mem. Ea. Regional Competency-Based Edn. Consortium (bd. dirs., conf. chair 1999-2000, treas. 2001-2004), Greene Tchrs. Assn. (pres. 1983-85, mem. negotiating team 1984-86), SC Tech. Educators Assn., Phi Theta Kappa (hon.), AAUP. Avocations: writing, gardening, reading, dramatics, pets. Home: 709 Logan Ct Greenwood SC 29646 Office: Piedmont Tech Coll PO Box 1467 Greenwood SC 29648-1467 Office Phone: 864-941-8452. Business E-Mail: cushing.s@ptc.edu.

CUSHING, STEVEN, linguist, educator, writer, researcher, consultant; b. Brookline, Mass., June 25, 1948; s. Alfred Edward and Evelyn Cushing. SB, MIT, 1970; MA, UCLA, 1972, PhD, 1976. Rsch. asst. MIT, 1967-70, UCLA, 1973-74; instr. U. Mass., Boston, 1974-75, Roxbury C.C., Boston, 1975-77; rsch. staff Higher Order Software Inc., Cambridge, Mass., 1976-82; rsch. assoc. Rockefeller U., N.Y.C., 1979; from master lectr. to assoc. prof. Boston U., 1986-94; rsch. fellow NASA-Ames Rsch. Ctr., Mountain View, Calif., 1987-88, Stanford U., Palo Alto, Calif., 1987-88, NASA-Langley Rsch. Ctr., Hampton, Va., 1989; asst. prof. St. Anselm Coll., Manchester, N.H., 1983-85, Stonehill Coll., North Easton, Mass., 1985-89; adj. prof. Union Inst. Grad. Sch., Cin., 1994—; lectr. Boston U., 2002—, Northeastern U., Boston, 2003—; instr. Mass. Sch. Law, 2002—, Hingham HS, Mass., 2003—, Belmont Hill Sch., Mass., 2004—. Mem. bd. editl. commentators The Behavioral and Brain Scis., 1978—; chmn. software design Internat. Conf. Sys. Scis., Honolulu, 1978; mem. 1st fgn. del. USSR Acad. of Scis., 1989; session chmn. session on internat. comm. Internat. Pragmatics Conf., Kobe, Japan, 1993; invited spkr. Internat. Conf. on Maritime Edn. and Tng., Rijeka, Croatia, 1999. Author: Quantifier Meanings: A Study in the Dimensions of Semantic Competence, 1982, Fatal Words: Communication Clashes and Aircraft Crashes, 1994, Japanese edit., 2001; assoc. editor Language, 1998-2000; contbr. articles to profl. jours. and mags. Mem. nat. exec. coun. Nat. Ethical Youth Orgn., 1965—66; fiddler Strathspey and Reel Soc. N.H. Recipient New Eng. Regional award Future Scientists of Am., 1965, 1st pl. award U.S. Nat. Scottish Fiddle Composition Competition, 1996; NSF grantee, 1965, 70-71, NIMH grantee, 1970-71, NDEA grantee, 1970-73; Woodrow Wilson Found. fellow, 1970-71, NASA Summer Faculty fellow, 1987-89; rsch. affiliate MIT, 1978-79, Boston U., 1986-88. Mem. Linguistic Soc. Am., Nat. Ctr. for Sci. Edn., Internat. Pragmatics Assn. Home: 20 Parks Dr Sherborn MA 01770 E-mail: stevencushing@alum.mit.edu.

CUSHMAN, BARRY, law educator; b. Columbus, Ohio, 1960; BA, Amherst Coll., 1982; MA, JD, U. Va., 1986, PhD, 1995. Bar: W.Va. 1986, Calif. 1987. Law clk. to Hon. Richard Neely W.Va. Supreme Ct. of Appeals, Charleston, 1986—87; assoc. Riordian & McKinzie, LA, 1987—88; Samuel I. Golieb fellow in legal history NYU Sch. Law, 1990—91; asst. prof. St. Louis U. Sch. Law, 1991—95, assoc. prof., 1995—98; prof. U. Va. Sch. Law, 1998—, Elizabeth A. & Richard D. Merrill rsch. prof., 1999—2002, now Percy Brown, Jr. prof. law and history, dir. program on legal and constitutional history. Author: Rethinking the New Deal Court: The Structure of a Constitutional Revolution, 1998 (Littleton-Griswold Prize in Am. Law and Soc., Am. Hist. Assn., 1998). Recipient All-Univ. Tchg. Award, U. Va., 2003. Mem.: Am. Soc. Legal History (bd. dirs., exec. com.). Office: U Va Sch Law 580 Massie Rd Charlottesville VA 22903-1789 Office Phone: 434-924-7371. E-mail: bjc2r@virginia.edu.

CUSHMAN, HELEN MERLE BAKER, retired management consultant; b. Perth Amboy, N.J. d. Ivan F. and Lucile (Atkinson) Baker; m. Robert Arnold Cushman, June 2, 1945; children— Lucinda Ann, Robert Rorem. AB in History, Barnard Coll., 1942; postgrad., NYU, 1944. Route analyst intelligence divsn. Air Transport Command, Washington, 1943-44; personnel asst. Gen. Cable Corp., N.Y.C., 1944-45; sr. staff asst. to chmn. bd. Trans World Airlines, N.Y.C., 1945-50; pres. H.M. Baker Assocs., Westfield, N.J., 1958-93; ret., 1993. Past archivist-historian N.J. chpt. Am. Records Mgmt. Assn. Author: ARMA-New Jersey, The Founding Years, 1972, A History of Shreve, Crump and Low, 1974, Butterick and the Story of Sewing, 1975, The Anniversary Manual, 1976, Gears, Machines, Systems, 1978, Mountainside Chapel: Yesterday, Today, Tomorrow, 1981, Serving Westerly Since 1800, 1985, The Mill on the Third River, 1992, From Seed to Harvest, 1993, The Church at the Crossroads, 1999, Walter's World: Memoirs of W.E. Atkinson 1856-1944, 2004; editor, pub. Ministry Press, The Bus. History Letter; contbr. to Am. Archivist. Recipient Lit. award Am. Records Mgmt. Assn., 1972. Mem.: PEO Sisterhood (pres. chpt. AE,.Princeton N.J.), various hist. socs., Newcomen Soc., Barnard Coll. Club North Ctrl. NJ (past pres.). Address: 321 Sharon Way Monroe Township NJ 08831-1561

CUSHMAN, JOHN C., III, real estate company executive; Grad., Colgate U., 1963; grad. advanced mgmt. program, Harvard U. Co-founder Cushman Realty Corp., 1963—78, Cushman Winery Corp., 1972, dir., CEO; chmn. Cushman & Wakefield, Inc., L.A., 2001—, also bd. dirs. Bd. mem. Culinary Holdings Inc., D.A. Cushman Realty Corp., Inglewood Pk. Cemetery, La Quinta Corp., La Quinta Properties, Inc., Callaway Golf Co. Mem.: L.A. Turf Club (bd. mem.). Office: Cushman Wakfield Inc 601 S Figueroa St Los Angeles CA 90017

CUSHMAN, KAREN LIPSKI, writer; b. Chgo. married; 1 child, Leah. BA in English/Greek, Stanford U., 1963; MA in Human Behavior, USIU, 1977; MA in Mus. Studies, JFK U., 1987. Faculty mus. studies dept. John F. Kennedy U., San Francisco. Author: Catherine, Called Birdy, 1994, The Midwife's Apprentice, 1995 (John Newberry award 1996), The Ballad of Lucy Whipple, 1996, Matilda Bone, 2000, Rodzina, 2003. Office: 17804 Thorsen Road Sw Vashon WA 98070

CUSHMAN, MARGARET JANE, herbalist, nurse; b. Pahokee, Fla., Nov. 17, 1948; d. Edmund Francis and Mary Margaret (Adams) C. Diploma in nursing, Johns Hopkins Hosp., l969; BSN, U. Pa., 1972; MSN, Yale U., 1976; MS in Herbal Medicine, TAI Sophia Inst., 2004; postgrad., U. Mass., 2004—. Asst. dir. nursing St. Joseph's Hosp., Phila., 1972-74; asst. dir. Regional Vis. Nurse Agy., North Haven, Conn., 1976-78; exec. dir. Waterbury (Conn.) Vis. Nurse Assn., 1978-82; exec. v.p. VNA Health Care, Inc., Plainville, Conn., 1982-86; pres. Vis. Nurse And Home Care, Inc. (name changed to VNA Health Care, Inc.), Plainville, Conn., 1986-98; CEO Home Care U. Nat. Assn. for Home Care, Washington, 1998—2002; v.p. Nat. Assn. Home Care, Washington, 1999—2002; exec. dir. Home Healthcare Nurses Assn., Nat. Assn. for Home Care, 1999—2002; editor-in-chief Caring Mag., Nat. Assn. for Home Care, 1999—2002; editl. cons. Caring Mag., 2003; clin. herbalist and cons. Herbs and Health LLC, Freeport, Maine, 2004—. Asst. clin. prof. Yale U. Sch. Nursing, New Haven, 1978-99, assoc. clin. prof., 1999—; asst. clin. prof. U. Tex. Sch. Nursing, San Antonio, 1990-97; cons. U. S.C. Sch. Nursing, 1987-89, U. Tex. Sch. Nursing, San Antonio, 1989-90; corporator Am. Savs. Bank, 1993-98, Hartford Hosp., 1993—, Hosp. for Special Care, 1994-98. Contbg. author: Home Health Administration, 1988; mem. editl. adv. bd. Home Healthcare Nurse, 1988-95; co-editor Certification for Home Care/Hospice Execs. Study Guide; contbr. articles to profl. jours. Mem. Conn. Gov.'s Blue Ribbon Com. to Investigate Nursing Home Industry in Conn., Hartford, 1975-77; mem. nat. adv. com. Ctr. for Health Policy Rsch., Denver, 1989-94; mem. Conn. Award for Excellence Health Adv. Task Force, 1993-94; sec. Found. for Hospice and Home Care, 1989-95; mem. joint adv. coun. and pub. health adv. coun. Conn. Dept. Pub. Health and Addiction Svcs., 1994-95; bd. dirs. St. Mary's Hosp., Waterbury, Conn., 1996-98, Health Tech, 1997-98. Robert Wood Johnson/Nat. League for nursing fellow, 1975, fellow Found. for Hospice and Home Care, 1992; recipient Andrew Veckerelli prize Yale U. Sch. Nursing, 1976, Disting. Alumni award, 1986, Creative Thinking Assn. Tribute, 1990, Leadership award Conn. Assn. for Home Care, 1995. Fellow Am. Acad. Nursing; mem. ANA, Acad. Health, Ea. Nursing Rsch. Soc., Am. Herbalists Guild, Inst. of Noetic Scis., Creative Thinking Assn., Nat. League for Nursing (nat. adv. coun. home health outcome study 1989-93), Nat. Assn. Home Care (chmn. 1986-88, sec. 1984-86, 91-94, vice chair 1995-98, Mem. of Yr. award 1984, 97, Virginia

Henderson award for excellence in nursing 1997), Conn. Assn. Home Care (sec. 1981-85), Greater Hartford C. of C. (women execs. com. 1990-98), Coastal Ctr. for Entrepreneurship, Alumni Assn. Leadership Greater Hartford, Maine Women's Network, Sigma Theta Tau. Avocation: herb gardening. Home: 75 Shore Dr Freeport ME 04032 Office Phone: 207-865-6444.

CUSHMAN, PAUL, physician, educator; b. N.Y.C., Feb. 4, 1930; m. Paulette Bessire; children: Paul, III, Clare Hepburn. BA, Yale U., 1951; MD, Columbia U., 1955. Intern Barnes Hosp., St. Louis, 1955-56; asst. resident Strong Meml. Hosp., Rochester, N.Y., 1956-57, 1959-61; asst. resident attending physician St. Lukes Hosp., N.Y.C., 1961-77; instr. Columbia U, N.Y.C., 1961-65, asst. prof. medicine, 1965-77; assoc. prof. medicine, pharmacology, psychiatry Med. Coll., Wis., Milw., 1977-81; from assoc. prof. to prof. medicine, pharmacology and psychiatry Med. Coll. Va., Richmond, 1982-87; prof. psychiatry, prof. clin. medicine NYU, 1987-90; prof. psychiatry SUNY, Stony Brook, 1990—. Bd. dirs. Cathedral Ch. St. John the Divine, Episcopal Mission Soc., Milw. Found. Capt. USAF, 1957-59. Recipient Caleb Fiske prize, 1967; Henry E. Sigerist prize Yale U., 1973. Fellow ACP, Am. Coll. Clin. Pharmacology; mem. AAAS, Endocrine Soc., Am. Physiol. Soc., Am. Fedn. Clin. Rsch., Union Club, St. NIcholas Soc., Ch. Club, Century Assn., New Eng. Soc., Pilgrim Soc. Episcopalian.

CUSHMAN, VALERIE JEAN, athletic director; b. Rome, N.Y., Oct. 25, 1962; d. Robert Harley and Peggy Ann C. BS in Edn., SUNY, Cortland, 1984; MS in Edn., East Stroudsburg U., 1988; PhD in Higher Edn., Syracuse U., 2000. Tchr. John Coleman H.S., Kingston, N.Y., 1984-87; tchr., coach Vassar Coll., Poughkeepsie, N.Y., 1988-97; athletic dir. Randolph Macon Woman's Coll., Lynchburg, Va., 1997—. Mem. Nat. Assn. Collegiate Women Athletic Adminstrs. (nominating com. 1996-97), Nat. Collegiate Athletic Assn. (nominating com. 1997—). Office: Randolph Macon Womans Coll 2500 Rivermont Ave Lynchburg VA 24503-1555 Home: 103 Woodville Dr Forest VA 24551-2504

CUSHWA, PATRICIA K., commissioner; b. Aug. 1938; m. Victor Cushwa (dec.); 3 children. BA, MA, Hood Coll. Mem. Md. State Senate, 1990; chair, commr. Md. Parole Commn., 1992—2004; commr. U.S. Parole Commn., 2004—. Adj. faculty mem. Hagerstown C.C.; established Ctr. Against Spousal Abuse, Washington County; former mem. Md. Human Relations Commn., Md. State Sch. Bd. Mem. bd. trustees Hagerstown C.C., 2003—. Democrat. Office: US Dept Justice 950 Pennsylvania Ave, NW Washington DC 20530-0001 Office Phone: 301-492-7014. Business E-Mail: patricia.cushwa@usdoj.gov.

CUSHWA, WILLIAM WALLACE, retired machinery parts company executive; b. Youngstown, Ohio, Aug. 15, 1937; s. Charles Benton Jr. and Margaret Elizabeth (Hall) C.; m. Anna Jean Schuler, Feb. 4, 1961; children: Elizabeth Ann, William W. Jr., Margaret Louise, David Frederick, Anne Jennifer. BA in English, U. Notre Dame, 1959; MBA, Case Western Res. U., 1975. Systems analyst Comml. Shearing, Inc., Youngstown, Ohio, 1960-67, asst. to sec.-treas., 1967-77, asst. treas., 1969-966, dir. corp. planning, 1977-81, v.p. planning, 1981-96, also bd dirs. Pres. Youngstown Area Urban League, 1975-78; trustee St. Elizabeth Hosp. Med. Ctr., Youngstown, 1975-95, treas., 1986-92, Walsh U., 1999—; chmn. fund drive United Negro Coll. Fund, Youngstown, 1978; treas. Hospice of Youngstown, 1980-87; bd. dirs. South Bend Symphony Orch., 2003—, Real Svc., 2005—; co-chmn. cmty. adv. coun. U. Notre Dame, 2003—. Roman Catholic.

CUSICK, ALAN PHILIP, lawyer, educator; b. Providence, July 6, 1948; s. Alan Philip Sr. and Nancy Taylor (Mc Enerney) C.; m. Judith Eileen Kiersky, June 20, 1978 (div. July 1984); m. Shirley Ann Mulholland, Dec. 28, 1985. BA, Brown U., 1970; JD, Georgetown U., 1977; LLM in Tax with honors, Golden Gate U., 1995. Bar: R.I. 1977, U.S. Dist. Ct. R.I. 1977, Calif. 1979, U.S. Dist. Ct. Calif. 1979, Colo. 1995. Atty. Law Offices of Alan P. Cusick Sr., Providence, 1977-78; trial atty. Crawford & Valerian, Lafayette, Calif., 1979-94; pvt. practice, Denver, 1995—. Adj. faculty John F. Kennedy Sch. Law, Walnut Creek, Calif., 1983-90, Golden Gate U. Law Sch., San Francisco, 1984-85; instr. advanced legal rsch. and writing Calif. State U., Hayward, 1988-90; panelist and lectr. Nat. Bus. Inst., 1997. Rsch. asst.: (book) Federal Income Taxation of Corporations and Shareholders, 1977; author material for seminars. Pres. Markham Farms Homeowners Assn., Longmont, Colo., 1996-97. Comdr. USN, 1970-74. Recipient citation for lifesaving USS Niagara Falls, 1971; Merit scholar Golden Gate U., 1995. Mem. Calif. Bar Assn., Colo. Bar Assn., VFW, Navy League of U.S. (pres. Denver coun. 1996—). Avocations: hiking, gardening, collecting political americana. Home: 1452 Cherrywood Way Longmont CO 80501-3065 Office: 2441 Darts Cove Way Mount Pleasant SC 29466-8121

CUSICK, PATRICIA A., information technology executive; b. Scranton, Pa., Nov. 5, 1948; BS in Math., Marywood Coll., Scranton, 1970. Plant mgr., sys. supplies IBM, dir., info. sys. and logistics for comm. product group; dir., computer integrated mfg., mktg. & devel. IBM U.S.; dir., acct. technical programs IBM at Fort Motor Co.; mgr., info. tech. Digital Equipment Corp., Maynard, Mass.; joined Xerox Corp., 1991, v.p., info. mgmt., bus. group ops., v.p. & chief info. officer Webster, NY, 1999—. Named Woman of Yr. in Bus. and Industry, Raritan Valley C. of C., 1984, one of top tech. innovators, Info. Week mag., 2004. Office: VP & CIO Xerox Corp M/S 102-12A 800 Phillips Rd Webster NY 14580

CUSSEN, JUNE, book publisher, editor-in-chief; d. Thomas Miller and Rose Stephens; m. David Martin Cussen; children: Thomas David, Sarah Rose. BA, Northwestern U., 1966; MA, San Francisco State U., 1967; MS, U. Calif., Berkeley, 1969. Co-pub., exec. editor Pineapple Press, Inc., Sarasota, Fla., 1982—. Business E-Mail: june@pineapplepress.com.

CUSSLER, CLIVE ERIC, author; b. Aurora, Ill., July 15, 1931; s. Eric E. and Amy (Hunnewell) C.; m. Barbara Knight, Aug. 28, 1955; children: Teri, Dirk, Dana. Student, Pasadena City Coll., 1949-51; PhD in Maritime History, N.Y. State Maritime Coll., 1997. Owner Bestgen & Cussler Advt., Newport Beach, Calif., 1961-65; creative dir. Darcy Advt., Hollywood, Calif., 1965-67; chmn. Nat. Underwater and Marine Agy. Author: (novels) The Mediterranean Caper, 1973, Iceberg, 1975, Raise the Titanic!, 1976, Vixen 03, 1978, Night Probe, 1981, Pacific Vortex, 1982, Deep Six, 1984, Cyclops, 1986, Treasure, 1988, Dragon, 1990, Sahara, 1992, Inca Gold, 1994, Shock Wave, 1995, Sea Hunters, 1996, Flood Tide, 1997, Clive Cussler & Dirk Pitt Revealed, 1998, Atlantis Found, 1999, Valhalla Rising, 2001, Serpent, 1999, Blue Gold, 2000, Fire Ice, 2002, Sea Hunters II, 2002, White Death, 2003, Golden Buddha, 2003, Trojan Odyssey, 2003, Sacred Stone, 2004, (with Dirk Cussler) Black Wind, 2004 (Publishers Weekly Bestseller); (with Paul Kemprecos) Lost City, 2004 (Publishers Weekly Bestseller), Polar Shift, 2005, Dark Watch, 2005. Served in USAF, 1950-54. Recipient Disting. Svc. award, Nat. Maritime Hist. Soc., Navy Meml. Heritage award, Nat. Trust for Hist. Preservation award, numerous advt. awards. Fellow Nat. Soc. Oceanographers, N.Y. Explorers Club (Lowell Thomas Underwater Explorers award), Royal Geog. Soc. London, Classic Car Club Am. Achievements include discovery of over 60 historic shipwrecks.

CUSSLER, EDWARD LANSING, JR., chemical engineer, educator; s. Edward Lansing and Eleanor Christine (Lloyd-Jones) C.; m. Elizabeth Campbell Beidler. BS in Chem. Engring., Yale U., 1961; MS in Chem. Engring., U. Wis., 1963, PhD, 1965; DSc honoris causa, U. Lund, 2002. Rsch. asst. U. Wis., Madison, 1961—65, postdoctoral fellow, 1961—65, U. Adelaide, Australia, 1965-66, Yale U., 1966-67; asst. prof. Carnegie-Mellon U., 1967-70, assoc. prof., 1970-73, prof., 1973-80, U. Minn., Mpls., 1980—. Mem. editl. bd. Jour. Membrane Sci., 1975—, AIChE, 1996—. Recipient William H. Frances S. Ryan award Carnegie-Mellon U., 1975, George Taylor Tchg. award U. Minn., 1987, Separations Sci. award ACS, 2002, Separations Sci. award NAE, 2002. Mem. NAE, AIChE (Alan P. Colburn award 1975, bd. dirs. 1989-92, v.p. 1993, pres. 1994, W.K. Lewis award 2001), Am. Assn. Engrs. Soc. (chair 1996). Office: U Minn Chem Engring Dept 421 Washington Ave SE Minneapolis MN 55455-0373 Office Phone: 612-625-1596. E-mail: cuss1001@umn.edu.

CUSSON-CAIL, KATHLEEN, consulting company executive; b. Manchester, N.H., Mar. 17, 1971; m. Alan Cail, Feb. 26, 2000. AS in Archtl. Engring. Tech., N.H. Tech. Inst., 1994; BS in Mgmt., Franklin Pierce Coll., 1995, MBA, 2000. Lic. securities, life, property, casualty. Personal fin. analyst Primerica Fin. Svcs., Nashua, NH, 1996—2003; instructor Introduction to Windows and Word Processing, Adult Comm. Education program Merrimack Sch. District, 2000—02; prin., owner Aggregate Bus. & Comm. Cons., Inc., Manchester, NH, 2002—, Collabresource, Manchester, 2002—, Ideal Instr., Manchester, 2002—. Vol. Vt. Adaptive Ski and Sport, 1996—98, Jerry Lewis Labor Day Telethon, 1998—2003, Riverfest, 1999. Recipient Good Citizenship award DAR, 1985. Avocations: volleyball, horseshoes, motorcycling, winter hiking. Office: Aggregate Business & Communication Cons Inc 1361 Elm Street Ste 208 Manchester NH 03101

CUSTER, CHARLES FRANCIS, lawyer; b. Hays, Kans., Aug. 19, 1928; s. Raymond Earl and Eva Marie (Walker) C.; m. Irene Louise Macarow, Jan. 2, 1950; children: Shannon Elaine, Charles Francis, Murray Maxwell, Kelly Sue. AB, U. Chgo., 1948, JD, 1958. Bar: Ill. 1958, U.S. Dist. Ct. (no dist.) Ill. 1971, U.S. Supreme Ct. 1991. Assoc. Meyers & Matthias, Chgo., 1958-72; pvt. practice Chgo., 1972-78; ptnr. Vedder, Price, Kaufman & Kammholz, Chgo., 1978-98, of counsel, 1998—. Arbitrator, mediator. Past dir. Family Care Svcs., Chgo. Mem. ABA (mem. fed. regulation of securities and devels. in investment svcs. coms., dispute resolution sect.), Chgo. Bar Assn. (mem. securities law com., mem. investment cos. subcom., alternative dispute resolution com.), Cliff Dwellers (past officer and dir.). Avocations: music, theater. Home: 5210 S Kenwood Ave Chicago IL 60615-4006 Office: Vedder Price Kaufman & Kammholz 222 N La Salle St Ste 2600 Chicago IL 60601-1100 Office Phone: 312-609-7545.

CUSTER, JOHN CHARLES, portfolio manager; b. Chgo., Aug. 30, 1934; s. John Howard and Irene Lillian (McGovern) C.; m. Barbara Ann Welcher, Sept. 5, 1959 (dec. Sept. 1996); 1 child, John Thomas. AB, Ind. U., 1956; MHA, U. Minn., 1966; grad., Harvard U., 1975. Asst. adminstr. Johns Hopkins Hosp., Balt., 1966-67; clin. adminstr. Kaiser Permanente Med. Care Program, Oakland, Calif., 1967-69, dir. materials, 1969-70, mgr. health plan Cleve., 1970-74, v.p., health plan mgr., 1974-79; v.p. Kaiser Permanente Adv. Svcs., Oakland, 1979-84; pres., CEO Keystone Health Plan, Camp Hill, Pa., 1984—87, Custer & Assocs., Hummelstown, Pa., 1987—92; investment broker Legg Mason Wood Walker, Inc., 1992—. Lectr. U. Minn. Grad. Sch. of Pub. Health, Mpls., 1981-85, Harvard U. Grad. Sch. of Pub. Health, Boston, 1977-80. Chmn. Pa. Assn. HMO's, Harrisburg, 1984-86. 1st lt. U.S. Army, 1956-58, col. USAR. Mem. APHA, Am. Coll. Health Care Execs., Am. Hosp. Assn., Med. Group Mgmt. Assn., Internat. Fedn. of Employee Benefit Plans, Pa. State C. of C. (health care cost contain com.), Pa. State Dept. of Pub. Welfare (health care adv. subcom. 1984-85), Oakmont Homeowners Assn. (pres.), Hershey Golf Club (trustee 2004—), Cosmos Club (Washington), Army-Navy Club (Washington), Harvard Club (N.Y.C.), Elks, Delta Upsilon. Episcopalian. Home: 589 Lovell Ct Hummelstown PA 17036-9156 Office: 214 Senate Ave Ste 700 Camp Hill PA 17011-2382 Fax: (717) 737-0800. Office Phone: 717-737-6500. E-mail: jccuster@leggmason.com.

CUSTODIO, ANGEL MANUEL, engineering company executive; s. Angel Custodio and Juana Guzman; m. Maria Soledad Collazo, May 25, 1980; children: Marie Angelic, Gian Carlo. BSME, U. PR, 1981. Registered profl. engr., PR State Dept., 1984. Dir. maintenance mgmt. Yonkers Industries Inc., Cary, NC, 1983—; engring. and maintenance mgr. Warner Lambert Inc., Fajardo, PR, 1983—87; pres. A. Custodio Engring. Consultants, Caguas, PR, 1987—2003. Author: (technical book) Know and Understand Centrifugal Pumps. Deacon, counselor Iglesia Torre Fuerte, Caguas, PR, 1997—2005. Mem.: ASME (assoc.), PR Engr. & Surveyor Coll. (assoc.; sec. mech. engrs. inst. 1988—90). Evangelical. Avocations: dance, travel. Home: 2d 2P-15 Mirador de Bairoa Caguas PR 00725-1022 Office: Yonkers Industries Inc Tetuan St #201B Old San Juan PR 00902-3416 Office Phone: 787-721-1222. Home Fax: 787-721-1222; Office Fax: 787-721-1229. Personal E-mail: acustodio@libertypr.net. E-mail: acustodio@yonkersindustries.com.

CUSTURERI, MARY CATHERINE FOCA, literature educator; b. Jersey City, Dec. 28, 1929; d. Joseph and Rosa (Scala) Foca; m. Domenick Custureri, July 31, 1948; children: Frank, Richard. BS, Fla. Atlantic U., 1969, MEd, 1972, EdS, 1986, EdD, 1989. English lectr. Embry Riddle Aeronautical U., Daytona Beach, Fla.; lectr., coll. instr., 1999—. Tchr.-trainer learning strategies, speaker at confs. in field and at Internat. Reading Assn., Nat. Coun. of Tchrs. of English. Instructional Strategies: Helping all Students Succeed, 2004; contbr. articles to profl. jours. Grantee Palm Beach County Edn. Found., 1985, Fla. Atlantic U., 1980, Cardinal Newman H.S., Latner Found., Nat. Cath. Edn. Assn., Good Sam Wallmart. Mem. Internat. Reading Assn. (spkr. 1988), Nat. Cath. Edn. Assn., Fla. Reading Assn., Nat. Coun. Tchrs. English (spkr.), Fla. Writers Assn., Assn. for Supervision and Curriculum Devel. (spkr. various confs.), Fla. Devel. Assn. (spkr. 2003), Delta Kappa Gamma (North Palm Beach chpt., spkr.). Roman Catholic.

CUSUMANO, CHRISTOPHER ROBERT, language educator, musician; b. N.Y., July 28, 1944; s. Robert Manon and Violet Rita Cusumano. BA in Spanish, CW Post Coll., 1966, MA in English Edn., 1982. Cert. tchr. Spanish and English N.Y. Tchr. Huntington (N.Y.) H.S., 1966—2000; organist U.S. Merchant Marine Acad., Kings Point, NY, 1978—, dir. chapel music, 1978—, instr. English, 2001—. Adv. Key Club Huntington (N.Y.) H.S., 1969—97. Contbr. articles to profl. jours. Mem.: Reed Organ Soc., Organ Hist. Soc., Am. Guild Organists (mem. jet placement Nassau County 1965—). Home: 273 West Neck Rd Huntington NY 11743-2460 Office: US Merchant Marine Academy 300 Steamboat Rd Kings Point NY 11024

CUSUMANO, JAMES ANTHONY, filmmaker, retired recording industry executive; b. Elizabeth, N.J., Apr. 14, 1942; s. Charles Anthony and Carmella Madeline (Catalano) Cusumano; m. Jane LaVerne Melvin, June 15, 1985 (dec. June 2001); children: Doreen Ann, Polly Jean; m. Inez Sipulova, July 9, 2003. BA, Rutgers U., 1964, PhD, 1967; grad. Exec. Mktg. Program, Stanford U., 1981, Harvard U., 1988. Mgr. catalyst rsch. Exxon Rsch. and Engring. Co., Linden, N.J., 1967-74; pres., chief exec. officer, founder Catalytica Inc., Mountain View, Calif., 1974-85, chmn., 1985-2000, also bd. dirs.; pres., CEO, bd. dirs. Catalytica Fine Chems., Inc., Mountain View, Calif., 1993-97; chmn., CEO, bd. dirs. Catalytica Pharms., Inc., 1997-99, chmn., chief strategic officer, 1999-2000; pres., CEO, founder Chateau Wally Films LLC, Ojai, Calif., 2000—; exec. dir. Chateau du Catalyst Found., 2002—; vice chmn. World Bus. Acad. Bd. dir. Ojai Film Festival, Croma Business Acad., Croatia; advisor Fulbright scholar program Inst. Internat. Edn.; mem. dean's adv. bd. Rutgers U., 1997—; mem. com. on catalysts and environ. NSF; exec. briefings with Pres. George Bush and Cabinet mems., 1990, 92; bd. dirs. Catalytica Advanced Techs., Inc.; dir. Croma Bus. Acad., Zagreb, Croatia, 2004—; spkr. in field; lectr. in field. Author: Catalysis in Coal Conversion, 1978, (with others) Critical Materials Problems in Energy Production, 1976, Advanced Materials in Catalysis, 1977, Liquid Fuels from Coal, 1977, Kirk-Othmer Encyclopedia of Chemical Technology, 1979, Chemistry for the 21st Century, Perspectives in Catalysis, 1992, Science and Technology in Catalysis 1994, 1995; contbr. articles to profl. jours., chpts. to books; founding editor Jour. of Applied Catalysis, 1980; exec. prodr. feature film: What Matters Most, 2001; exec. prodr. documentary film: One Tough Biscotti: A Woman, A Film and A Fight, 2001; rec. artist with Royal Teens and Dino Take Five for ABC Paramount, Capitol and Jubilee Records, 1957-67; single records include Short Shorts, Short Shorts Twist, My Way, Hey Jude, Rosemarie, Please Say You Want Me, Lovers Never Say Goodbye; albums include The Best of the Royal Teens, Newies But Oldies; cd's for Global Children's Charities, Oldies for Youngies, 2004; appeared in PBS TV prodn. on molecular engring., Little by Little, 1989. Recipient Surface Chemistry award Continental Oil Co., 1964; Henry Rutgers scholar, 1963, Lever Bros. fellow, 1965, Churchill Coll. fellow Cambridge Univ., 1992. Mem.: ASCAP, AIChE, World Future Soc., Smithsonian Assocs., Pres.'s Assn., Am. Mus. Natural History, Soc. Organic Chems. MFrs. (bd. dirs. 1996), N.Y. Acad. Scis., Am. Phys. Soc., Am. Chem. Soc. (planetary lectr. to chem. educators nat. meeting 1994), Phi Lambda Upsilon, Sigma Psi. Roman Catholic. Achievements include 20 patents in catalysis and surface science. Office: Chateau Wally Films LLC Ste 236 428 Bryant Cir Ste 236 Ojai CA 93023 Home: Dr Zikmunda Wintra 5 160 00 Prague 6 Czech Republic Personal E-mail: jim@catalyst.cz. Business E-Mail: jim@chateauwallyfilms.com.

CUSWORTH, CHRISTYL J., conservator, artist; b. Neptune, NJ, Mar. 14, 1963; d. Christopher and Dorothy Cusworth. BA, Coll. N.J., 1986; student, Am. Coll. Greece, Athens, 1984; sculpture student, U. New Orleans, 1994. Registered profl. assoc. Am. Inst. for Conservation of Hist. and Artistic Works. Artist, bronze caster Antietam, Trenton, NJ, 1987—91; paintings conservator, artist Christyl Cusworth Paintings Conservator, Lambertville, NJ, 1995—. Bronze caste, art installer Artist Julian Schnabel, NYC, 1989—90; apprentice, artist Salah Hudson Conservation Studio, New Orleans, 1991—95; art installer Artist/Photojournalist Melina Mara, Washington, 2003. Oil painting, Star night over Lambertville (Bob and Joyce Byers award, 2004). Office: Christyl Cusworth Paintings Conservator 28 N Union St Lambertville NJ 08530 Personal E-mail: cus@pil.net.

CUTCHINS, CLIFFORD ARMSTRONG, IV, lawyer; b. Norfolk, Va., May 13, 1948; s. Clifford Armstrong III and Ann (Woods) Cutchins; m. Jane McKenzie, Aug. 14, 1971; children: Sarah Helen, Ann Woods. BA, Princeton U., 1971; JD, MBA, U. Va., 1975. Bar: Va. 1975, US Dist. Ct. Ea. Dist. Va. 1975, US Ct. Appeals 4th Cir. 1975. Assoc. McGuire, Woods, Battle & Boothe (now McGuireWoods LLP), Richmond, Va., 1975—82, ptnr., 1982—90, 2001—, now chair firm corp. services dept.; sr. v.p., gen. counsel, sec. James River Corp. Va., Richmond, 1990-97, Ft. James Corp., Deerfield, Ill., 1997-2000. Bd. dirs. Arts Coun. Richmond, 1980-86, Richmond Heart Assn., 1980-83, St. Catherine's Sch., Richmond, 1983-86, Richmond Ballet, 1986-88, Richmond Children's Mus., 1986-94, Richmond on the James, 1986-88, Hist. Richmond Found., 1990-94, Richmond Met. Blood Svc., 1995-97, Kohl Children's Mus., Wilmette, Ill., 1998-2000, Richmond First Tee, 2001-, The Nature Conservancy Va. Chpt., 2002-, Assn. for Corp. Growth, Richmond; bd. trustees Henrico Doctors' Hosp., 1986-, Va. Commonwealth U. Sch. Engring. Found., 1997-. chmn. Fort James Found., 1997-2000. Mem.: Va. Bar Assn., Commonwealth Club (bd. dirs. 1983—86, 1996—97), Kinloch Golf Club, Country Club Va. (bd. dirs. 1990—93, 2003—). Republican. Baptist. Avocations: golf, travel, reading. Office: McGuireWoods LLP One James Ctr 901 E Cary St Richmond VA 23219-4030 Office Phone: 804-775-4720. Office Fax: 804-225-5344. E-mail: ccutchins@mcguirewoods.com.

CUTHBERTSON, GILBERT MORRIS, political science professor; b. Warrensburg, Mo., Nov. 20, 1937; s. Gilbert and Marion Darlington (Morris) C. BA, U. Kans., 1959; PhD, Harvard U., 1963. Asst. prof. Rice U., Houston, 1963-68, assoc. prof., 1968-77, prof., 1977—. Resident assoc. Will Rice Coll., Houston, 1964—. Author: (book) Political Myth and Epic, 1975, (monographs) Political Power, 1968, Myth, Power, Value, 1982; co-author: Teacher Immortal, 1984. Mem. curator's bd. Mus. of Printing History. Recipient George R. Brown lifetime award for excellence in tchg., 1993; Summerfield scholar U. Kans., 1955-59; Woodrow Wilson fellow Harvard U., 1959-63; Wilson C. Morris fellow. Mem. Am. Polit. Sci. Assn., Scottish Heritage Found. (bd. dirs. Great Scot award), River Oaks Rotary (bd. dirs., Paul Harris fellow), Knife and Fork Club, Phi Beta Kappa (past pres. chpt.), Pi Sigma Alpha, Sigma Tau Gamma, Delta Phi Alpha. Democrat. Presbyterian. Avocation: bridge. Office: Rice U Dept Polit Sci Houston TX 77251-1892 Office Phone: 713-348-3363. E-mail: poli@rice.edu.

CUTHBERTSON, SUE ELLEN, secondary school educator; b. Greensboro, N.C., Jan. 25, 1944; d. Hugh Henry and Goldia Mae (Graham) Smith; m. Larry Evan Cuthbertson, June 4, 1966; children: Brian David, Grant Evan, April Dawn. BS, E. Carolina U., 1966; MA, U. N.C., 1982. Cert. tchr. Tchr. New Bern (N.C.) City Schs., 1966—68, Broward County Schs., Chocowinity, NC, 1968—70, Hollywood (Fla.) Hills HS, 1971—72, Guilford County Schs., Greensboro, NC, 1973, 1989—2000, Wake County Pub. Schs., Raleigh, NC, 2000—. Chairperson region Dept. Pub. Dist. Vocat. Edn., 1977—88. Tchr. Greensboro Pks. and Recreation, 1975—80. Mem.: NEA, Assn. Colls. Tchr. Edn., N.C. Assn. Colls. Tchr. Edn. (mem. resolutions com. 2000—03), N.C. Edn. Assn. Southern Baptist. Avocations: sewing, cake decorating, exercise. Office: Broughton HS 723 Saint Marys St Raleigh NC 27606

CUTHRELL, CARL EDWARD, retired clergyman, lawyer, educator; b. Norfolk, Va., Aug. 13, 1934; s. Cecil Edward and Edna Catherine (Kirby) C.; m. Naomi Lorene Marshall, Dec. 23, 1960; children: Byron Eugene, Benjamin Dean. LLB, LaSalle U. Law Sch., Chgo., 1959; diploma Egyptian studies, Oriental Inst., U. Chgo., 1960; BD, Brantridge Forest Sch., Eng., 1970; MA in Med. History, Sussex (Eng.) Coll. Tech., 1972; MA in Classical Studies, Christ Ch. Coll., Oxford, Eng., 1973; diploma Germanic langs., Heidelberg (Fed. Republic Germany) U., 1975; BA, Upper Iowa U., 1979; MA, Covington Theol. Sem., 1982; BRE, Cen. Bapt. Bicle Coll., 1989. Pvt. practice, Hampton, 1960—; ordained to ministry Evang. Friends Ch., 1972; pastor Rescue (Va.) Friends Ch., 1968-96. Mem. faculty dept. theology, Norfolk extension Washington Bible Coll., Lanham, Md., dept. spl. programs/history Coll. William and Mary, Williamsburg, Va., dept. secular studies Cen. Bapt. Bible Coll., Hampton, Va. Author: Ancient Mummies, 1967, Paul's Voyage, 1971; Contbr.: lit. criticisms to Times Herald Newspaper; also numerous short stories. Bd. dirs. Nat. Philatelic Inst.; trustee Quincy Coll., 1970, Nat. Coll. Surgeons Hall of Fame, 1972. Served with M.C. AUS, 1950-57, Korea. Decorated Silver Star; recipient Scouter's award medal Boy Scouts Am., 1956, Silver Beaver award, 1976, Nat. Tchrs. medal Freedoms Found., 1973, Peace medal UN, 1973, Good Citizenship medal SAR, 1976 Mem. U.S. Capital, Nat. hist. socs., S.R., Sons Confederate Vets., Christian Educators Assn., Va. Herpetological Soc., Mil. Order Stars and Bars. Republican. Home: 307 Agusta Dr Newport News VA 23601-1436 Personal E-mail: carloreneva@aol.com.

CUTI, ANTHONY J., consumer products company executive; b. 1946; BA, Rutgers U., 1967; MBA, Fairleigh Dickinson U., 1970. Fin. analyst CIBA Geigy Corp., 1967-70; auditor Arthur Anderson & Co., 1970-72; v.p. fin. Revlon, Inc., 1972-84, Bristol Meyers Co., 1984-90; exec. v.p., CFO Supermarkets Gen. Holdings Corp., Woodbridge, N.J., 1990-93, pres., CFO, 1993—; chmn., pres, CEO Duane Reade, NYC. Office: Duane Reade Inc 440 9th Ave New York NY 10001-1620*

CUTLER, ALEXANDER MACDONALD, manufacturing executive; b. Milw., May 28, 1951; s. Richard Woolsey and Elizabeth (Fitzgerald) C.; m. Sarah Lynn Stark, Oct. 11, 1980; children: David Alexander, William MacDonald. BA, Yale U., 1973; MBA, Dartmouth Coll., 1975. Fin. analyst Cutler-Hammer, Milw., 1975-77, bus. group contr., 1977-79; contr. custom distbn. and control divsn. Eaton Corp., Atlanta, 1979-80, plant mgr. custom distbn. and control divsn., 1981-82, mgr. custom distbn. and control divsn., 1982-83, mgr. power distbn. divsn. Milw., 1984-85, gen. mgr. indsl. control and power distbn., 1985-86, pres. controls group Cleve., 1986-91, exec. v.p. ops., 1992-93, exec. v.p., COO controls, 1993-95, pres., COO, 1995-2000, chmn., CEO, 2000—, bd. dirs. Bd. dirs. Axcelis Techs., 2000-. Bd. dirs. United Way Svcs. Cleve., N.E. Ohio Coun. on Higher Edn., 1993-97, Greater Cleve. Growth Assn., 2001-04, Cleve. Tomorrow, 2000-04, Greater Cleve. Roundtable, 2000-04; class agt. alumni fund Loomis Chaffee Sch., Windsor, Conn., 1969—; bd. dirs. alumni fund Yale U., New Haven, 1974-89; trustee The Cleve. Play House, 1987—2002, Gt. Lakes Mus., Inc., 1988-91, Mus. Natural History, Cleve., 1989-97; bd. overseers Amos Tuck Sch. Bus. Dartmouth Coll., 1996—; trustee Loomis Inst., 2003-; active Keycorp., 2000—, Bus. Roundtable, 2002—; chmn. Greater Cleve. Partnership, 2004—. Mem. Nat. Elec. Mfrs. Assn. (bd. govs. 1987-99, indsl. automation divsn. 1986-90, treas. 1993-95, bd. govs. 1996-99), Elec. Mfrs. Club (bd.

dirs.), Yale U. Alumni Assn. (pres. Cleve. chpt. 1991-93, exec. com. of vis. com. Weatherhead Sch. Mgmt. 1993-2002, Yale devel. bd. 1998—), Chagrin Valley Hunt Club. Avocation: tennis. Office: Eaton Corp 1111 Superior Ave Eaton Ctr Cleveland OH 44114-2584

CUTLER, AMY, artist; b. Poughkeepsie, NY, 1974; Attended, Staatliche Hochschule für Bildende Künste, Germany, 1994—95, Cooper Union Sch. Art, NY, 1997, Skowhegan Sch. Painting & Sculpture, 1999. Exhibitions include, Miller Block Gallery, Boston, 2000, Dialogues: Amy Cutler/David Rathman, Walker Art Ctr., Mpls., 2002, Inst. Contemporary Art, Phila., 2002, Once Upon A Time, Kohler Art Center, Sheboygan, Wis., 2003, Kemper Museum of Contemporary Art, Kansas City, Mo., 2004, exhibited in group shows at Small Works, 80 Washington Square East Galleries, NY, 1998, Art for Parks, Bklyn. Mus., 1999, Summer Voices, Miller Block Gallery, Boston, 1999, Rural Crossing, 195 Bedford Avenue, NY, 1999, Artists in the Marketplace, Bronx Mus., 2000, Terrors and Wonders: Monsters in Contemporary Art, De Cordova Museum & Sculpture Park, Lincoln, Mass., 2001, Stranger Than You, New Langton Arts, San Francisco, 2001, Works on Paper, The Weatherspoon Art Museum, Greensboro, NC, 2002, Rendered, Sara Meltzer Gallery, NY, 2003, Open House: Working in Bklyn., Bklyn. Mus. Art, 2004, Whitney Biennial, Whitney Mus. Am. Art, 2004, The Drawn Page, Aldrich Mus. Contemporary Art, Ridgefield, Conn., 2004, About Painting, Tang Mus., Saratoga Springs, NY, 2004. Roma Hort Mann Found. Grant, 1999. Office: c/o Whitney Museum American Art 945 Madison Ave New York NY 10021*

CUTLER, BERNARD JOSEPH, editor-in-chief, writer; b. N.Y.C., May 26, 1924; s. Joseph Louis and Sophie (Appel) C.; m. Carol Ann Rataic, Mar. 6, 1948. BSME, Pa. State Coll., 1945. Reporter Pitts. Press, 1945-51; reporter N.Y. Herald Tribune, 1951-56, Moscow corr., 1956-58, chief Paris bur., 1958-60, mng. editor European edition Paris, 1960, editor European edition, 1961-66; European corr. Scripps-Howard Newspapers, Paris, 1966-69, fgn. editl. writer Washington, 1969-72, chief editl. writer, 1972-80, editor-in-chief, 1980-89, fgn. affairs columnist, 1989-95. Author: Reactionary! Sgt. Lloyd W. Pate's Story, 1956. Recipient Disting. Alumni award Pa. State U., 1972. Mem.: Gridiron, National Press. Office: 2735 P St NW Washington DC 20007-3065

CUTLER, BRUCE, lawyer; b. Brooklyn, New York, Apr. 29, 1948; BA, Hamilton College, 1970; JD cum laude, Brooklyn Law School, 1974. Bar: NY 1975, U.S. Supreme Ct. 1979, U.S. Ct. Appeals (2nd cir.) 1982. Supervising sr. trial atty. Homicide Bureau, New York, 1974—81; deputy chief Court Bureau, Office of the Dist. Atty., Kings County, NY; attorney Slotnick & Baker, 1981—87; pvt. practice, 1987—. Author: (novels) Closing Argument: Defending (and Befriending) John Gotti, and Other Legal Battles I Have Waged, 2003. Recipient American Jurisprudence Award in Criminal Law. Office: 260 Madison Ave New York NY 10016

CUTLER, CAROL ANN, food writer, consultant; b. Pitts. d. John Michael and Stella (Kope) Rataic; m. B.J. Cutler, Mar. 6, 1948. Student, U. Pitts., 1945—46, Hunter Coll., 1953, U. Paris-Sorbonne, 1959—60, Le Cordon Bleu, Paris, 1962—66; diploma, Ecole des 3 Gourmandes, Paris, 1967. Art critic Paris Herald Tribune, 1959-69; European corr. Art in Am., N.Y.C., 1963-71; cons. Nat. Gallery Art, Washington, 1970, Met. Mus. Art, N.Y.C., 1971; food columnist Washington Post, 1971-73; pub. affairs officer Nat. Portrait Gallery, Washington, 1974-78; chief food cons. Time-Life Books, Alexandria, Va., 1978-86; syndicated columnist Copley News Service, San Diego, 1986—. Restaurant critic, Dossier, Washington, 1988, Washington Bus. Forward, 1999-2002. Author 8 cookbooks including The Six-Minute Souffle and Other Culinary Delights, 1976 (Tastemaker award); freelance author and food cons. Mem. Am. Wine Soc., Am. Inst. Wine and Food, Les Dames d'Escoffier (pres. 1983-84), Les Cercle des Goumettes. Avocations: music, touring architectural sites. Home and Office: 2735 P St NW Washington DC 20007-3065 Office Phone: 202-333-8051. E-mail: cabjcutler@earthlink.net.

CUTLER, EVERETTE WAYNE, history professor; b. Beaumont, Tex., Nov. 29, 1938; s. Homer Everette and Mary Abbie (Osborne) C.; m. Leta Harriet Rush; 1 child, Lori Catherine. BA, Lamar U., 1959; BD, So. Meth. U., 1964; MA, U. Tex., 1967, PhD, 1971. Rsch. assoc. U. Tex., Austin, 1965-67, U. Ky., Lexington, 1970-75; assoc. prof. history Vanderbilt U., Nashville, 1975-87; rsch. prof. history U. Tenn., Knoxville, 1987—. Dir. Polk Project, Vanderbilt U., Nashville, 1975-87, Polk Project, U. Tenn., 1987—. Asst. editor Southwestern Hist. Quar., 1965-67; asst. editor: Papers of Henry Clay, vols. 4 and 5, 1970-75; editor: Correspondence of James K. Polk, vols. 5-10, 1975—, North for Union, 1986. Pres. Nashville Symphony Chorus, 1982-83; vestry St. George's Episc. Ch., Nashville, 1984-87; dir. Tenn. Pres. Trust, 1991—; commodore Concord Yacht Club, 2000-02. Grantee NEH, 1984, 88-96, 2002-03, Nat. Hist. Publs. and Records Commn., 1975—, Tenn. Hist. Commn., 1975—. Mem. Am. Hist. Assn., Orgn. Am. Historians, So. Hist. Assn., Assn. for Documentary Editing, Interscholastic Sailing Assn. (dir. bd. 2003—), Phi Kappa Phi, Alpha Tau Omega. Democrat. Episcopalian. Avocations: choral music, sailing, fiction writing. Home: 7901 High Heath Knoxville TN 37919-4410 Office: U Tenn Hoskins Libr 216 Knoxville TN 37996-0001 Office Phone: 865-974-0662. Business E-Mail: wcutler@utk.edu.

CUTLER, HOLLIE SHAWN, lawyer; b. Bklyn., June 23, 1955; d. Jay B. and Randy R. Cutler. BS, U. Md., 1977; JD, U. San Diego, 1980. Bar: Calif. 1980, U.S. Dist. Ct. (so. dist.) Calif. 1980, Md. 1982, U.S. Dist. Ct. Md. 1982. Asst. pub. defender Pub. Defender's Office, Annapolis, Md., 1982-85; sole practice law Annapolis, 1985-2000; ptnr. Cutler & Lipsetts, Annapolis, 2000—. Instr. U. Md., College Park, 1983-85, Anne Arundel C.C., 1987-88. Lectr. separation and divorce YWCA, Annapolis, 1985—; vol. pro bono domestic violence, Anne Arundel County; vol. program dir. Md. Therapeutic Riding, 1997—. Mem. Md. Bar Assn. (vice chair com. on resolution of fee disputes 2000—), Anne Arundel County Bar Assn. (family law subcom. sec. 1996—), Women's Bar Assn. (directory chair 2000—). Democrat. Avocations: dressage, scuba. Office: Cutler & Lipsetts LLC 7 Willow St 101 Annapolis MD 21401-3112

CUTLER, JOHN EARL, landscape architect; b. Houston, Nov. 21, 1943; s. John Cecil and Dorothy Evelyn (Hewett) C.; m. Paula Helene Murdy, Dec. 27, 1969; children: Christian Hewett, Leigh Helene. BS in Landscape Architecture, Tex. A&M U., 1967. Registered landscape arch., Tex. Landscape arch. Caudill Rowlett Scott, Houston, 1968-69, Marmon Mok Green, Houston, 1969-70; campus landscape arch. U. Houston, 1970-74; ptnr., landscape arch. Office of George Porcher, Houston, 1974-79; prin., landscape arch. The SWA Group, Houston, 1979—. Bd. dirs. Trees for Houston, 1984—. Recipient Oustanding Alumni award, Tex. A&M U., 2004. Fellow Am. Soc. Landscape Archs. Avocations: sailing, checker automobiles. Home: 2235 Bartlett St Houston TX 77098-5201 Office: The SWA Group 1245 W 18th St Houston TX 77008-3392 Office Phone: 713-868-1676. Business E-Mail: jcutler@swagroup.com.

CUTLER, KENNETH ALAN, lawyer, educator; b. Hollywood, Fla., Feb. 14, 1960; s. Leon Jay and Adrienne Taylor Cutler; m. Sharon Sue Weinstein, Dec. 22, 1984; children: Douglas Benjamin, Samantha Jaime. BA, U. Fla., 1982; JD, Nova U., Fla., 1985. Bar: Fla. 1986, U.S. Dist. Ct. Bench and Trial Bar 1991; cert. court arbitrator. Law clk. to assoc. Hollander and Assocs., Hollywood, Fla., 1984—87; assoc. to ptnr. Pyszka & Kessler, Ft. Lauderdale, 1987—96; ptnr. Goldman, Daszkal, Cutler, Bolton & Kirby, Deerfield Beach, Fla., 1996—. Adj. prof. Fla. Atlantic U., Boca Raton, 2003—04. Pres. Friends of Parkland (Fla.) Libr., 2001—; judge Broward County Teen Ct., Deerfield Beach, Fla., 2000—; pack founder, leader Cub Scout Troop 201, Coral Springs, Fla., 1995—98; reader Palm Beach County Lit. Coalition, Boca Raton, Fla., 2001, Palm Beach County, Boca Raton, Fla., 2002, Palm Beach County Lit. Coalition, 2003, Palm Beach County, 2005. Mem.: Palm County Bar, Broward County Bar, Assn. Trial Lawyers of Am., Acad. Fla. Trial Lawyers. Avocations: reading, genealogy, watercolor painting, fishing. Office: Goldman Daszkal Cutler Bolton & Kirby 1630 W Hillsboro Blvd Deerfield Beach FL 33442 Office Phone: 954-428-9333. Office Fax: 954-428-9338. Business E-Mail: kcutler@goldmandaszkahl.com.

CUTLER, KENNETH BURNETT, lawyer, investment company executive; b. Muskegon Heights, Mich., June 19, 1932; s. Stanley and Lucile (Miles) C.; m. Cecelia Bilsly, Mar. 9, 1967; children: Kenneth Burnett, Randall Miles, Cynthia Bilsly, Robert Appleby, Jeffrey Lamont Derrick. BBA, U. Mich., 1954, JD, 1957. Bar: Mich. 1957, N.Y. 1960. Assoc. Dewey Ballantine, Bushby, Palmer & Wood, N.Y.C., 1957-66; v.p., gen. counsel The Lord Abbett Managed Funds, N.Y.C., 1966—72; ptnr., gen. counsel Lord, Abbett & Co., N.Y.C., 1972-97. Mem.: NASD (arbitration bd. 1976—), Palmas Del Mar Country Club (P.R.), Bronxville Field Club, Winged Foot Golf Club, Met. Club (N.Y.C.), Phi Delta Phi, Delta Tau Delta. Avocations: golf, tennis, skiing. Home: 10 Westway Bronxville NY 10708-4311

CUTLER, LAURENCE STEPHAN, architect, museum program director, advertising executive, educator; b. New Haven, Conn., Aug. 27, 1940; s. Hermann Shepard and Doris Winifred Cutler; m. Sherrie Stephens, Jan. 24, 1967 (div. 1992); children: A. Maximilian S., Zachary Wolf S.; m. Judy Goffman, Feb. 7, 1995; stepchildren: Jennifer Paige Greenawalt, Andrew Douglas Goffman. BA, U. Pa., 1962; MArch, Harvard U., 1966, MArch in Urban Design, 1967. Nationally cert. architect. Founder, co-prin. ECODESIGN, Cambridge, 1966; with ECODESIGN subs. Combustion Engring., Inc., 1972—79; founder C-E Tec Internat., Inc., 1972-79, ECODESIGN/SPC Internat., 1979—82; with Architects Collaborative, Eero Saarinen & Assocs.; group dir. Lodigiani U.S.A. Ltd., 1985-87, also bd. dirs. Prof. MIT, 1967-72, Harvard U., 1965-73, R.I. Sch. Design, 1965-68; group dir. N.Am. Gold Greenless Trott (USA) Holdings, Inc., London, 1988-91; adv. dir. Emery Roth Architects, 1984-90. Prin. archtl. works include Chase Manhattan Bank Hdqrs. for Caribbean, St. Thomas, Ballys Park Pl. Casino Hotel, Sugarloaf/USA Ski Area, Maine, fire and police complex, Westford Mass., Lockhart Gardens Shopping Ctr., U.S. Virgin Islands, Am. Embassy housing, Lagos, Nigeria; author: (with Albert G.H. Dietz) Industrialized Building Systems for Housing, 1971, (with Sherrie Stephens Cutler) Recycling Cities for People: The Urban Design Process, 1976, 3d edit., 1983, Handbook of Housing Systems for Designers and Developers, 1974, (with Judy Cutler) Parrish & Poetry, 1995, 99, Maxfield Parrish: A Retrospective, 1996, 99,(with Judy Cutler) Maxfield Parrish, 2000, 04. Incorporator Cambridge Sch. Weston; founder, trustee The Woodbridge Found.; adv. dir. Am. Illustrators Gallery, N.Y.C., 1984—, founder, chair ARTShows and Products, Corp., 1993—, Maxfield Parrish Orgn.; officer Paul Cezanne Family Orgn., Inc.; founder, chair Nat. Mus. Am. Illustration, Newport, R.I., 1998—; chair Am. Civilization Found., 1998—. Recipient Alpha-Rho Chi Gold medal Harvard U., 1966, Engring. Excellence award Colo. Cons. Engrs. Coun., 1973, Design and Environment award, 1975, Design Arts Program award NEA, 1980; Milton Fund grantee, Harvard U., 1966, Fulbright-Hays grantee, India, 1968. Mem. AIA (Regional Honors award 1974, 75), Royal Inst. Brit. Architects, Am. Soc. Planning Ofcls., Nat. Coun. Archtl. Registration Bds., Harvard Club N.Y., Nat. Arts Club, Carnegie Club, Skibo Castle Scotland, Carnegie-Abbey (Portsmouth, R.I.). Address: 18 E 77th St Apt 2A New York NY 10021-1700 also: Vernon Ct Bellevue Ave Newport RI 02840 Office Phone: 401-851-8949 10. E-mail: lcutler@americanillustration.org.

CUTLER, LEONARD SAMUEL, physicist; b. LA, Jan. 10, 1928; s. Morris and Ethel (Kalech) C.; m. Dorothy Alice Pett, Feb. 13, 1954; children: Jeffrey Alan, Gregory Michael, Steven Russell, Scott Darren. BS in Physics, Stanford U., 1958, MS, 1960, PhD, 1966. Chief engr. Gertsch Products Co., LA, 1948-56, v.p. R & D, 1956-57; with Hewlett-Packard Co., Palo Alto, Calif., 1957-99, dir. physics rsch., 1969-85, dir. instruments and photonics lab., 1985-87, dir. superconductivity lab., 1987-89, disting. contbr., 1989-99; disting. contbr. tech. staff Agilent Techs., 2000—04, disting. fellow tech. staff, 2004—. Mem. adv. panels Nat. Bur. Stds.; cons. Kernco, Inc., Danvers, Mass., 1982—, others. Patentee in field. Served with USNR, 1945-46. Recipient Achievement award Indsl. Rsch. Inst., 1990, Indsl. Applications prize Am. Inst. Physics, 1993. Fellow IEEE (Morris Leeds award 1984, Rabi award 1989), Am. Phys. Soc.; mem. AAAS, NAE, Sigma Xi. Home: 26944 Almaden Ct Los Altos CA 94022-4349 Office: Agilent Techs PO Box 10350 Palo Alto CA 94303-0867 Business E-Mail: len_cutler@agilent.com.

CUTLER, MIRIAM, lawyer; b. Cambridge, N.Y., Nov. 20, 1953; d. Howard Bernard and Elaine (Niewood) C.; m. Horacio Gustavo Ferrari, Mar. 26, 1985; children: Alejandro Eric Ferrari, Corinne Bianca Ferrari. BA cum laude, Barnard Coll., 1976; JD, Yeshiva U., 1980. Bar: D.C. 1981, Va. 1986; cert. guardian ad litem Commonwealth Va., 1994-98, family mediator, Supreme Ct. Va., 1996-98. Assoc. Ginsburg, Feldman, Weil & Bress, Washington, 1980-82, Weil, Gotshal & Manges, Washington, 1982-83, Mudge Rose Guthrie Alexander & Ferdon, Washington, 1983-86; ptnr. Braverman and Cutler, Arlington, Va., 1986-88; pvt. practice Arlington, 1988—. Civil magistrate, 1994—. Contbr. articles to profl. jours. Bd. dirs. Friends of Argus and Aurora House, 1993-97; bd. dirs. Walter T. McCarthy Libr., 1992-96, sec., 1992-94. Mem. Am. Immigration Lawyers Assn., Va. State Bar (4th dist. com. sect. I 1998-04, vice chair 1999-02, chair 2002-04), Arlington County Bar Assn. (mem. mediation task force and section 1994-97, treas. 1995-97, chair family law sect. 1997-2000, co-chair ct. 2001—). Office: 2009 14th St N Ste 508 Arlington VA 22201-2514 Office Phone: 703-525-8515.

CUTLER, NORMAN BARRY, funeral service executive; b. Chgo., Mar. 5, 1942; s. Jerome and Hannah (Feinberg) C.; m. Gail Weinstein, June 30, 1965; children: Brett, Rebecca. BSBA, Northwestern U., 1964, MBA, 1965. Mgmt. trainee First Nat. Bank Chgo., 1965-66; ptnr. Chgo. Jewish Funerals, Buffalo Grove, Ill., 1966-98; pres., CEO Weinstein Family Svcs., Inc. (formerly Weinstein Bros. Inc.), Wilmette, Ill., 1966-99; pres. Levitt-Weinstein, Inc., North Miami Beach, Fla., 1979-97; exec. v.p. Beth David Meml. Gardens, Hollywood, Fla., 1985-97, Mt. Nebo Meml. Gardens, Miami, Fla. Gen. ptnr. Wilmette Computer Assocs., Dixie Ptnrs., N.M.B. Assocs.; faculty Worsham Coll., Skokie, Ill., 1981-82. Gen. co-chmn. Channel 11 Pub. TV Auction, 1974-75; bd. govs Congregation Am Ahalom, Glencoe, Ill., v.p., pres., 1986-88; bd. dirs. North Suburban Jewish Cmty. Ctr., 1975-85, also past pres.; pres. ctrl. bd. dirs. Jewish Cmty. Ctrs., Chgo.; pres. Bernard Horwich Jewish Cmty. Ctr., 1993—; bd. govs. Nat. Found. Funeral Svc., Des Plaines, Ill., 1991-93; bd. dirs. Writers Theatre of Ill., 1999—. Mem. Jewish Funeral Dirs. Am. (pres. 1985-86, bd. govs.), Acad. Profl. Funeral Svc. Practice (pres. 1988-89), B'nai B'rith (v.p.).

CUTLER, RICHARD W., lawyer; b. New Rochelle, N.Y., Mar. 9, 1917; s. Charles Evelyn and Amelia (MacDonald) C.; m. Elizabeth Fitzgerald, Oct. 18, 1947; children: Marguerite Blackburn, Alexander MacDonald, Judith Elizabeth. BA, Yale U., 1938, LLB, 1941. Bar: Conn. 1941, N.Y. 1942, Wis. 1950, D.C. 1975, U.S. Supreme Ct. 1980. Practiced in, NYC, 1941—49, Milw., 1949—87; assoc. Donovan, Leisure, Newton & Lumbard, 1941—42; atty. Legal Aid Soc., 1946—47, RCA Comm., Inc., 1947—49; ptnr. Quarles & Brady, and predecessors, 1954—87; gen. ptnr. Sunset Investment Co., Milw. Author: Zoning Law and Practice in Wisconsin, 1967, Greater Milwaukee's Growing Pains, 1950-2000: An Insider's View, 2001, Counter-spy: Memoir of a Counterintelligence Officer in World War II and the Cold War, 2004. Chmn. Milw. br. Fgn. Policy Assn., 1951-53; pres. Childrens Service Soc. Wis., 1961-63, Neighborhood House, 1971-74; sec. Southeastern Wis. Regional Planning Commn., 1960-84, Yale Devel. Bd., 1973-79; bd. dirs. Wis. Dept. Resource Devel., 1967-68; Met. Milw. Study Commn., 1957-61; bd. dirs. Milw. Innovation Ctr., 1985-89, pres., 1984-85, exec. v.p., 1985-89; bd. dirs. Greater Milw. Com., 1982-89. Capt. USAAF, 1943-46 and OSS, 1944-46. Recipient Disting. Leadership award Am. Planning Assn., 1992. Mem. ABA, Wis. Bar Assn., Milw. Club, Milw. Country Club, Town Club, Phi Beta Kappa. Presbyterian. Home: 938 W Shaker Cir Mequon WI 53092-6032 Office: 411 E Wisconsin Ave Milwaukee WI 53202-4461 Office Phone: 414-277-5811. E-mail: rwc@quarles.com.

CUTLER, RONNIE, artist; b. N.Y.C. d. Leo and Sarah (Saks) C.; m. Mar. 1, 1951 (dec. May 1990). Student, Columbia U., 1955—56, Bklyn. Mus. Art, 1958, Art Students League, NYC, 1959—60. Exhibited in group shows William Whipple Mus. and Gallery Southwest State U. Minn., 2005, Internat. Works on Paper, Watercolor, 2003, Monique Goldstorm Gallery, N.Y.C., 2002, Whitney Mus. Am. Art, 1954, Am. Watercolor Soc. 132d Ann. Internat., 1999, 2000, 133d Ann. Internat., 2000, Delgado Mus. Art, New Orleans, 1955, Berkshire Mus. Art, Pittsfield, Mass., 1955, 56, Bklyn. Mus., 1956, 58, Riverside Mus. Art, N.Y.C., 1957, Springfield (Mass.) Mus. Art, 1957, Nat. Acad. Art, N.Y.C., 1958, Provincetown (Mass.) Art Assn. and Mus., 1993, 57th Ann. Aubudon Artists, 1999; permanent collection Southwest State U., 2003. Recipient Sherwood prize in oil, Silvermine Guild Artists, 1955, 1st prize, Riverside Mus. Art, 1957, alumni purchase award, Art Students League, 1960, 1st ptize in oil, So. Berkshire Assn., 1979, 1st prize in oil, 1980, Painters and Sculptors Soc., 1955, Frederix/Tara prize, Audubon Artists 58th Ann., First prize Oil Works on Canvas, Pen and Brush, NYC, 2003. Mem. Am. Watercolor Soc. Internat., Salmagundi Club (Thomas E. Picard award). Home: 175 W 12th St Apt 11J New York NY 10011-8206 Office Phone: 212-242-7934.

CUTLER, STEPHEN JOEL, sociologist, educator; b. Lawrence, Mass., Jan. 1, 1943; s. Lewis J. and Minnie C.; m. Karan Elizabeth Davis, Apr. 25, 1968; children: Ellen Min, Timothy Spence. BA, Dartmouth Coll., 1964; MA, U. Mich., 1965, PhD, 1969. Faculty Oberlin Coll., Ohio, 1969-84, prof. sociology-anthropology, 1979-84, chmn. dept., 1979-82; prof. sociology, Bishop Robert F. Joyce Disting. Prof. gerontology U. Vt., Burlington, 1984—, dir. Ctr. Study of Aging, 1993-96. Sr. fellow Ctr. Study Aging and Human Devel., Duke U., 1975-76; adv. bd. nat. data program social scis. Nat. Opinion Rsch. Ctr., 1980-85; mem. human devel. and aging study sect. NIH, 1979-84, 88-92, chmn., 1990-92; vis. scholar Oreg. State U., 2002; Fulbright scholar, 2003—. Co-author: Middle Start: An Experiment in the Educational Enrichment of Young Adolescents, 1978; co-editor: Major Social Problems: A Multidisciplinary View, 1979, Promoting Successful and Productive Aging, 1995; assoc. editor Gerontol. Monographs, 1976-82; mem. editl. bd. Internat. Jour. Aging and Human Devel., 1980—, Jour. Gerontology, 1981-86, Rsch. on Aging, 1982—, Am. Jour. Alzheimer's Disease, 2002—; editor Jour. Gerontology: Social Scis., 1990-93. Grantee, NIMH, NSF, NIH, Alzheimer's Assn.; Woodrow Wilson fellow, 1965, Univ. scholar, 2000—01, Fulbright scholar, 2003—04. Fellow Gerontol. Soc. Am. (exec. com. behavioral and social scis. sect. 1979-81, chmn. 1987, coun. mem. 1986-88, pres.-elect 1997, pres. 1998); mem. Am. Sociol. Assn. (coun. sect. on aging 1982-84, chmn.-elect 1993-94, chmn. 1994-95), Assn. for Gerontology in Higher Edn. (bd. dirs., exec. com. 1985-87, 95-97, Clark Tibbitts award 2001). Home: 54 Sleepy Hollow Rd Essex Junction VT 05452-2712 Office: U Vt Dept Sociology Burlington VT 05405-0001 Business E-Mail: scutler@uvm.edu.

CUTLER, STEPHEN M., lawyer, former federal agency administrator; b. 1961; BA summa cum laude, Yale U., 1982; JD, Yale Law Sch., 1985. Law clk. to Hon. Dorothy W. Nelson US Ct. Appeals (9th cir.), 1985—86; assoc. Wilmer Cutler & Pickering, 1987—93, ptnr., 1993—98; dep. dir. enforcement Securities and Exchange Commn. (SEC), Washington, 1999—2001, acting dir. enforcement, 2001, dir. enforcement, 2001—05; ptnr. Wilmer Cutler Pickering Hale & Dorr, Washington, 2005—. Vis. fellow Ctr. Law in Pub. Interest, 1986—87. Editor: Yale Law Jour. Recipient Chmn. award Excellence, 1999, 2000, 2003. Office: Wilmer Cutler Pickering Hale and Dorr 2445 M St NW Washington DC 20037 E-mail: stephen.cutler@wilmerhale.com.*

CUTLER, TIMOTHY SPENCE, music educator, composer; b. Oberlin, Ohio, Feb. 2, 1973; s. Stephen Joel and Karan Elizabeth Cutler; m. Ann Christine Fisher, July 24, 2004. MusB, Oberlin Conservatory of Music, Ohio, 1995; PhD, Yale U., New Haven, 2000. Expert U.S. Chess Fedn. Grad. asst. Yale U., New Haven, 1997—2000; asst. prof. music Austin Coll., Sherman, Tex., 2000—. Founder and editor Internet Music Theory Database, 2003—; prin. second violin Sherman Symphony Orch., Sherman, Tex., 2000—; grading com. Advanced Placement Music Theory Exam, Princeton, NJ, 2000—; composer-in-residence Denison Heritage Performing Artists, Denison, Tex., 2001—; music divsn. editl. bd. Learning Object Learning Activities Project, Wesleyan, Conn., 2004—; presenter to profl. confs. Composer: Four Songs for Tenor and Piano (Included in ERM Media's CD-series Masterworks of the New Era, 2004), Symphony (Oberlin Conservatory, First Prize, Symphonic Composition, 1995), The Last Performance (Oberlin Conservatory, First Prize, Chamber Composition, 1995); contbr. articles to profl. jours. Henry and Lucy Moses fellowship, Yale U., 1996, Mellon Summer Rsch. fellowship, 1999, Tech. grantee, Associated Colls. of the South, 2003, 2005. Mem.: Tex. Soc. Music Theory (program com. 2001), Coll. Music Soc., Soc. Music Theory, Orpheus Alliance, Pi Kappa Lambda. Avocation: chess. Office: Austin Coll Ste 61634 900 N Grand Sherman TX 75090 Office Phone: 903-813-2462.

CUTLER, WALTER LEON, diplomat, foundation executive; b. Boston, Nov. 25, 1931; s. Walter Leon and Esther Dewey (Bradley) C.; m. Sarah G. Beeson, Mar. 16, 1957 (div. 1981); children: Allen Bradley, Thomas Gerard.; m. Isabel K. Brookfield, Nov. 28, 1981. BA, Wesleyan U., Middletown, Conn., 1953; MA, Fletcher Sch. of Law & Diplomacy, 1954. Joined U.S. Fgn. Service, 1956; vice consul Am. consulate Yaounde, Cameroon, 1957-59; fgn. affairs officer Dept. State, Washington, 1959-60, staff asst. to sec. of state, 1960-62; 2d sec. Am. Embassy Algiers, Algeria, 1962-65; prin. officer Am. Consulate Tabriz, Iran, 1965-67; polit. officer, 1st sec. Am. Embassy Seoul, Korea, 1967-69, Saigon, Vietnam, 1969-71; spl. asst. for Vietnam Peace Negotiations U.S. Dept. State, 1971-73; mem. Sr. Seminar in Fgn. Policy, 1973-74; dir. Office Ctrl. African Affairs, 1974-75; amb. to Zaire, 1975-79; amb.-designate to Iran, 1979; prin. dep. asst. sec. for congl. rels. Dept. State, Washington, 1979-81; amb. to Tunisia, 1982-84, Saudi Arabia, 1984-87, 1988-89; rsch. prof. diplomacy Georgetown U., Washington, 1987-88; pres. Meridian Internat. Ctr., Washington, 1989—; spl. emissary for sec. gen. UN, N.Y.C., 1994. Served with U.S. Army, 1954-56. Recipient Disting. Alumnus award Wesleyan U., 1983, King Abdul Aziz award Saudi Arabia, 1986, Presdl. Performance award, 1986, 87, Wilbur J. Carr award U.S. Dept. State, 1989, Dir. Gen.'s Cup award, 1993; decorated Order of the Leopard, Zaire, 1979. Mem. Coun. Fgn. Rels., Am. Fgn. Svc. Assn., Am. Acad. Diplomacy, Washington Inst. Fgn. Affairs, Mid. East Inst., Am. Tunisian Assn. (hon. com. The Am. Coms. on Foreign Rels.), Nat. Coun. for Internat. Visitors (mem. adv. coun.), Met. Club. Office: Meridian Internat Ctr 1630 Crescent Pl NW Washington DC 20009-4004

CUTLIP, RANDALL BROWER, retired psychologist, university president emeritus; b. Clarksburg, W.Va., Oct. 1, 1916; s. M.N. and Mildred (Brower) C.; m. Virginia White, Apr. 21, 1951; children: Raymond Bennett, Catherine Baumgarten. AB, Bethany Coll., 1940; cert. indsl. pers. mgmt., So. Meth. U., 1944; MA, East Tex. U., 1949; EdD, U. Houston, 1953; LLD, Bethany Coll., 1965, Columbia Coll., 1980; LHD, Drury Coll., 1975; ScD, S.W. Bapt. U., 1978; LittD, William Woods U., 1981. Tchr. adminstr. Tex. pub. sch., 1947-50; dir. tchr. placement U. Houston, 1950-51, supr. counselling, 1951-53; dean students Atlantic Christian Coll., Wilson, NC, 1953-56, dean, 1956-58; dean personnel, dir. grad. divsn. Chapman U., Orange, Calif., 1958-60; pres. William Woods Coll., Fulton, Mo., 1960-81, pres. emeritus, 1981—; trustee William Woods U., Fulton, Mo., 1981-85, 92—. Chmn. bd. dirs. Mo. Colls. Fund, 1973-75; chmn. Mid-Mo. Assn. Coll., 1972-76; bd. dir. Marina del Sol, bd. pres., 1985-90, 92-95. Mem. visitors' bd. Mo. Mil. Acad., 1966-70, chmn., 1968-72; trustee Schreiner Coll., Kerrville, Tex., 1983-92, Amy Shelton McNutt Charitable Trust, 1983—, Permanent Endowment Fund, 1987-96, Scholarship Found. and Res. Fund of Christian Ch., 1992-96, Christian Found., 1990—; bd. dir. Univ. of the Americas, 1984-96, exec. v.p., 1985-96; bd. dirs. Tex. State Aquarium, 1994, exec. com., 1994—, pres. 1998; elder emeritus Christian Ch., bd. dir., exec. com. Recipient McCubbin award, 1968, Delta Beta Xi award, 1959 Mem. Am. Pers. and Guidance Assn., Alpha Sigma Phi, Phi Delta Kappa, Kappa Delta Pi, Alpha Chi. Address: 1400 Ocean Dr Corpus Christi TX 78404-2109

CUTNAW, MARY-FRANCES, retired communications educator, writer, editor; b. Dickinson, N.D., June 15, 1931; d. Delbert A. and Edith (Calhoun-Pritchard) C. BS, U. Wis., 1953, MS, 1957, postgrad., 1957—68. Life tchg. license in speech, English and French, Wis. Vol. tchr. Vocat. Sch. for World War II Displaced Persons, Stevens Point, Wis., 1951-52; speech tchr. Pulaski H.S., Milw., 1953-55; tchg. asst. dept. speech U. Wis., Madison, 1956-57, spl. asst. Sch. Edn., summer 1957; instr. speech U. Wis.-Stout, Menomonie, 1957-58, dean of women, 1958-59, asst. prof. speech, 1959-64, assoc. prof. speech, 1964-74, prof. emeritus, 1974—. Comm. and pers. cons., St. Paul, 1974—; writer, editor, pub. New Legal Press, 1995—. Author: How to Settle a Living Trust, 1996, 4th edit., 2003. Organizer, past advisor Young Dems., Menomonie, 1959—; founder Edith and Kent Cutnaw Scholarship, U. Wis., Stevens Point, 1960—; bd. dirs. Blaisdell Place, Mpls., 1980-85. Hon. scholar U. Wis., Madison, 1959-60, 67-68. Mem. ACLU, NOW, Internat. Platform Assn., Nat. Women's History Mus., Wis. Acad. Arts and Scis., Wis. Women's Network, Progressive Roundtable (Mpls.), Calhoun Beach Club (Mpls.), Amnesty Internat., World Jewish Congress (charter), U. Club St. Paul, Greenpeace, Dunn County Humane Soc., Sierra Club, Soc. for Prevention of Cruelty to Animals, Humane Soc. U.S., Gamma Phi Beta, Phi Beta, Sigma Tau Delta, Pi Lambda Theta. Roman Catholic. Avocations: ecology, civil rights, animal rights, consumer protection, health and wellness. Office: New Legal Press PO Box 282 Menomonie WI 54751-0282 Business E-Mail: cutnawm@uwstout.edu.

CUTRELL, CHARLES C., III, lawyer; b. Great Falls, Mont., Aug. 23, 1954; BA in gov. & econ., Oberline College, 1976; JD, U. Va., 1981. Assoc. Gaston & Snow, Boston, 1981—86; v.p., counsel The Boston Co., 1986—94; with State Street Corp., Boston, 1994—, exec. v.p., gen. counsel, sec., 2004—. Mem.: Am. Bankers Assn., Boston Bar Assn., Securities Assn., Greater Boston Legal Svcs. Office: State Street Corp 225 Franklin St Boston MA 02101 Home: 26 Orient Ave Newton Center MA 02459 Office Phone: 617-786-3000. Office Fax: 617-664-4006.

CUTRER, FRED MICHAEL, neurologist; b. Jackson, Miss., July 16, 1956; s. Hugh Lowery and Rose (Wilson) C.; m. Lucinda Jane Turley, May 28, 1994. BMus, Belhaven Coll., 1978; MMus, Am. Conservatory of Music, 1980; MD, U. Miss., 1988. Diplomate Am. Bd. Psychiatry and Neurology. Intern U. Miss. Med. Ctr., Jackson, 1988-89; resident in neurology UCLA, 1989-92; fellow in neurology-migraine mechanisms Mass. Gen. Hosp./Harvard Med. Sch., Boston, 1992-94; asst. in neurology Mass. Gen. Hosp., Boston, 1994—; instr. in neurology Harvard Med. Sch., 1994—. Cons. Glaxo Pharms., Raliegh-Durham, 1995—; vis. migraine faculty Annenberg Ctr.-Eisenhower, Rancho Mirage, Calif., 1995—. Assoc. editor Up to Date in Neurology, 1995; author: Massachusetts General Hospital Handbook of Pain Management, 1995, Headache, 1996; editl. bd. Contemporary Neurology, 1995. Missions com. Trinitarian Congrl. Ch., Concord, Mass., 1995—. Recipient Clin. Investigator Devel. award Nat. Inst. for Stroke and Neurologic Disease, 1995; Glaxo fellowship Glaxo Pharms., 1992-93. Mem. Am. Acad. Neurology, Am. Assn. for the Study of Headache (Harold Wolff award 1996), Internat. Headache Soc. Avocations: music, print collecting, weightlifting, gardening. Office: Mass Gen Hosp 149 13th St # 6403 Charlestown MA 02129-2020

CUTRONE, RONNIE BLAISE, artist; s. Mario and Elvira; m. Kelly Cutrone (div.). Student, Sch. Visual Arts, 1966—70. Asst. to Andy Warhol Warhol Studio, N.Y.C., 1972—82; artist, 1982—. Front cover, New, Used, and Improved - Art for the 80s, by Michael McKenzie, 1988, back cover, Pop Art - A Continuing History by Marco Livingstone, 2001, cover, Pop Art by Lucy Lipard, 2000, exhibitions include Whitney Mus. Independent. Avocation: Ikebana (study of human behavior). Home and Studio: 274 Lake Dr Lake Peekskill NY 10537 Office Phone: 845-526-1121.

CUTSHALL-HAYES, DIANE MARION, elementary school educator; b. Pitts., Jan. 15, 1954; d. William Edward and Irma Delores (Marion) Snowden; m. John Steven Baran, Jan. 11, 1975 (div. 1982); 1 child, Allison Rae; m. Dean F. Cutshall, Dec. 17, 1989. BA, Eureka Coll., 1975; BS, Ind. U., Ft. Wayne, 1986. First grade tchr. Hoover Elem. Sch., Schaumburg, Ill., 1976-79, Indian Meadows Elem. Sch., Ft. Wayne, Ind., 1979-80, 82-86, Perry Hill Elem. Sch., Ft. Wayne, 1981-82; second grade tchr. Indian Meadows Elem. Sch., Ft. Wayne, 1986—. Tchr. rep. State Ill. Rsch. Adv. Coun., 1991; active ISTEP Blue Ribbon Commn., Ill., 1989, State Ill. Lang. Arts Adv. Commn., 1988, Project REAP Adv. Bd., 1988. Spl. events chair Greater Ft. Wayne (Ind.) Crime Stoppers, 1992-95; active YMCA Camp Potawotami, Ft. Wayne, 1993—, Eureka Coll. Alumni Assn., 1992—, pres., 1995—. Christa McAuliffe fellow State of Ind., 1987; recipient Excellence in Edn. award Inst. Copy Corp., 1988, Outstanding Young Alumna award Eureka Coll., 1990, Armstrong Tchr. Educator award, 1998; named Ind. State Elem. Tchr. of Yr., 1993. Mem. Nat. Coun. Tchrs. Math., Internat. Reading Assn., Tchrs. Applying Whole Langs. Lutheran. Avocations: inline skating, racquetball, reading, walking. Home: 5809 Eagle Creek Dr Fort Wayne IN 46814-3207 Office: Indian Meadows Elem Sch 4810 Homestead Rd Fort Wayne IN 46814-5461

CUTSHAW, KENNETH ANDREW, lawyer; b. Knoxville, Tenn., Sept. 2, 1953; s. Harvey Audley and Frankie Janelle (Temple) C.; m. Diane Dracos. BA, U. Tenn., 1975, JD, 1978; LLM, Am. U., 1987. Bar: Tenn. 1978, D.C. 1987, U.S. Dist. Ct. (mid. dist.) 1978, Tenn., (ea. dist.) 1978, Tenn. Supreme Ct. 1978, U.S. Supreme Ct. 1987, U.S. Fed. cir., 1991. Sr. atty. State of Tenn. Legis., Nashville, 1979-80, The 1982 World's Affair, Knoxville, 1980-83, cons., 1984; campaign mgr. for candidate U.S. Senate, 1983-84; asst. dep., asst. sec. import adminstrn. Dept. Commerce, Washington, 1985-87, chief of staff export adminstrn., 1987-89, dep. asst. sec. export enforcement, 1989-91; ptnr. Miller & Steuart, Washington, 1991-93; pres. Global Trading Ptnrs., Inc., Washington, 1991-93; of counsel Troutman Sanders, LLP, Atlanta, 1993-95, Smith Gambrell & Russell, LLP, 1995-99; ptnr. Holland & Knight, LLP, Atlanta, 1999—. Mem. U.S. Govt. Industry Adv. Com. on Customs and Trade, 1994-96; adj. prof. Ga. State U., 1997—, Emory U., 2002—, Ga. Tech., 2005—; hon. counsul Govt. of India; mng. dir. India, China Am. Inst.; Georgia; ptnr. KBS India. Author: Tennessee Criminal Law Statutes, 1980; co-author: Doing Business in China, 1995, Doing Business in Russia, 1999, Doing Business in India, 2001; contbr. articles to profl. jours. Vice chmn., exec. com. Tenn. Rep. Party, 1982-85; internat. chmn. Boy Scouts Am., Atlanta; mem. Bretton Woods Com.; co-chmn. Awakening Weekend; dir. Ctr. Global Bus. Leadership, 2002-. Roddy Acad. scholar U. Tenn., 1971-72. Mem. ABA, Internat. Bar Assn., Ga. Bar Assn., Atlanta Bar Assn., Tenn. Bar Assn. (com. chmn. 1983-84), D.C. Bar Assn., Am. Coun. Young Polit. Leaders (bd. dirs., co-chmn.), Coun. on Fgn. Rels., Atlanta Round Table (chmn.), World Trade Ctr. (bd. dirs.), Elks, Sigma Chi. Baptist. Avocations: flying, skiing, hiking, cultural events, golf. Home: 4417 Dunmore Rd Marietta GA 30068-4224 Office: Holland & Knight LLP One Atlantic Center 1201 W Peachtree St NW Ste 2000 Atlanta GA 30309-3453 Office Phone: 404-312-5544. E-mail: ken.cutshaw@hklaw.com, ken@cutshaw.net.

CUTTER, CURTIS CARLY, consulting company executive; b. Sacramento, Oct. 27, 1928; s. Curtis Harold and Leita (Carly) C.; m. Christiane Kühne, Jan. 29, 1965; children: Colette, Curtis Brooks, Lucho Antonio, Kai Kirsten, Sasha Christiana, Knut Carly. AB, U. Calif., Berkeley, 1951; cert., U. Geneva, 1955; MA, Stanford U., 1969. Consular officer Am. Embasssy, Phnom Penh, Cambodia, 1957-59; U.S. del. to UN and Trusteeship Coun., 1959-62; polit. officer Am. Embassy, Lima, Peru, 1962-65; chief Office Peruvian Affairs, State Dept., Washington, 1965-67; U.S. del. OAS, 1967-68; prin. officer Am. Consulate, Porto Alegre, Brazil, 1969-70; polit. officer Am. Embassy, Madrid, 1970-72; prin. officer, consul gen. Am. Consulate Gen., Seville, Spain, 1972-75; dep. dir. Office UN Polit. Affairs, 1975-77; acting dep. asst. sec. for congl. rels., 1977-78; pres. Interworld Cons., 1978-93, chmn., 1994—. Pres. ChinaMetrik, 1988-98; mng. dir. IMS ChinaMetrik Ltd., 1998-2003; sr. cons. Nat. Dem. Inst. Bd. dirs. China Med. Tribune; dir. AMS Found., Asian Am. Civic Assn. Boston. Capt. AUS, 1951-53. Recipient State Dept. award for heroism, 1970, State Dept. Meritorious Honor award, 1971; Woodrow Wilson fellow, 1983-94. Mem. Am. Fgn. Svc. Assn., Asian American Civic Assn., Union League (N.Y.C.), Nat. Press Club (Washington), Alpha Delta Phi. Address: 175 Commonwealth Ave Boston MA 02116-2215 Office Phone: 617-867-0061. E-mail: curtcutter@aol.com.

CUTTER, DAVID LEE, pharmaceutical company executive; b. Oakland, Calif., Jan. 3, 1929; s. Robert Kennedy and Virginia (White) C.; m. Nancy Lee Baugh, Sept. 14, 1950; children: David Lee, Jr., Thomas White, William Baugh, Steven Kennedy, Michael Lee. Student, U. Calif.-Berkeley, 1947; AB, Stanford U., 1950, MBA, 1952. C.P.A., Calif. Staff accountant Webb & Webb, C.P.A.'s, San Francisco, 1952-54; with Cutter Labs., Inc., 1954-84, pres., 1967-74, chmn., 1974-80, vice-chmn., 1980-82; sr. cons., 1982-84. Active various cmty. drives; mem. Citizens Com. to Study Discrimination in Housing, Berkeley, 1961-62; troop committeeman Boy Scouts Am., 1964-74; v.p. Mt. Diablo Coun., 1975-77, pres., 1978-80, bd. dirs., 1975—; bd. dirs. Golden Gate Scouting, 1978-90, pres. 1980-84; bd. dirs. Park Hills Homes Assn., 1961-63, HEALS, Emeryville, Calif., 1980-87, Alameda County (Calif.) Taxpayers Assn., 1967-69, Insts. Med. Scis., San Francisco, 1974-76, San Francisco Bay Area Coun., 1968-84, pres. Cutter Found., 1967-86; trustee United Way of Bay Area, 1981-86, Miles Found., 1986-92; mem. adv. bd. Herrick Hosp., 1968-76, trustee, 1976-84, pres. bd. trustees, 1978-84; mem. Accrediting Commn. on Edn. in Health Svcs. Adminstrn., 1982-88, adv. coun. Sch. Bus., San Francisco State Coll., 1966-70; bd. dirs. Alta Bates Health Sys., 1984-95, Alta Bates Med. Ctr., 1988-95, chmn., 1991-95, East Bay Cmty. Found., 1984-89, Hosp. Coun. No. Calif., 1983-89, Pathology Inst., 1986-90; bd. dirs. Acute Care Affiliates, 1987-89, chmn. 1988-89, Calif. Healthcare System, 1992-95; bd. govs. Vol. Trustees Not-for-Profit Hosps., 1989-95, vice chmn. 1990-92, treas. 1993-95; bd. dirs. Rossmoor Med. Ctr., 2000—03, chmn., 2000—03 Recipient Silver Beaver award, James E. West fellow Boy Scouts Am., 1982. Mem. AICPA, Stanford Alumni Assn., Berkeley C. of C. (dir. 1977-83, v.p. 1978-83), Rotary (Paul Harris fellow 1990), Delta Upsilon. E-mail: Davcutter@aol.com.

CUTTING, HEYWARD, designer, planner; b. N.Y.C., Dec. 3, 1921; s. Heyward and Constance (Roberson) C.; m. Jeremy Hohenstein, 1948 (div. 1978); children: Heyward, Francis Brockholst, William Bayard; m. Joan Faulkner Randell, Nov. 3, 1979; Stepson, Thomas William Randell. Grad., Eton, 1939; student, Harvard, 1939-41; B.Sc., Ill. Inst. Tech., 1953. Ptnr. Chermayeff & Cutting (architects and indsl. designers), 1954-56; pvt. practice architecture Cambridge, 1957; mem. Geometrics, Inc. (architects, engrs. and cons. specialized structures), Cambridge, 1958-68, 73-86; pvt. practice cons., 1986—. Asst. dir. adminstrn. Mus. Fine Arts, Boston, 1968-73, trustee, 1961-68, 73-78 Former trustee Mt. Auburn Hosp., Cambridge; past mem. vis. com. dept. archaeology, also dept. fine arts Harvard U. Served to maj. KRRC, 60th Rifles Brit. Army, 1941-45, Egypt, Italy. Mentioned in despatches. Mem.: Tavern (Boston). Home and Office: 377 Main St Concord MA 01742-2340

CUTTING, LAURIE E., psychology professor, researcher; b. Washington, Oct. 2, 1970; d. James Hulbert Barnes and Mary Dorthea Little Cutting; m. Pete Finis Long, Feb. 26, 2000. BA, Am. U., 1993; MA, Northwestern U., 1995, PhD, 1997. Clinic supr. Northwestern U., Evanston, Ill., 1994-97; postdoctoral fellow Johns Hopkins Sch. Medicine, Balt., 1997-99; ednl. and learning disabilities specialist Washington, 1997—; instr. Kennedy Krieger Inst./Johns Hopkins Sch. Medicine, Balt., 1997-99, asst. prof., 2000—. Mem. Gen. Clin. Rsch. Ctrs. Adv. Com., Balt., 2000—. Contbr. chpt. to book, articles to profl. jours. Grantee Dept. Def., 2000—. Mem. APA, Coun. for Exceptional Children (Dissertation of Yr. award 1998), Internat. Dyslexia Assn., Soc. for Sci. Study of Reading, Soc. for Rsch. in Child Devel., Jr. League. Episcopalian. Avocations: biking, running, skiing, reading. E-mail: cutting_l@yahoo.com, cutting@kennedykrieger.org.

CUTTING, MARSHA LEE, hospital chaplain; b. Madison, Wis., Mar. 3, 1947; d. Leland David and Beth B. (Evans) C. BS, U. Wis., Stevens Point, 1976; MDiv, Yale U., 1980; cert. in pastoral counseling, Postgrad. Ctr. Mental Health, 1995. Ordained to ministry Presbyn. Ch., 1981. Interim pastor Ross Meml. Presbyn. Ch., Binghamton, N.Y., 1980-81; pastor Stephentown (N.Y.) Federated Ch., 1981-86; music dir. The Ark, Troy, N.Y., 1987-90, Rensselaer (N.Y.) Summer Theater Program, 1988; interim assoc. pastor First Presbyn. Ch., Albany, N.Y., 1987-88; Protestant chaplain Russell Sage Coll., Troy, 1987-90, Capital Dist. Psychiat. Ctr., Albany, N.Y., 1987—, 4 Winds, Saratoga, N.Y., 1995-98; co-pastor Woodside Presbyn. Ch., Troy, 1992-94. Chair chaplaincy commn. Capitol Area Coun. Chs., Albany, 1996-98; sec. bd. mgrs. Jour. Pastoral Care Pubs., Decatur, Ga., 1996-99; mem. commn. on chaplaincy cert. N.Y. State Cmty. of Chs., Albany, 1995—; mem. publs. coun. Coll. of Chaplains, Schaumburg, Ill., 1994-98. Singer, songwriter cassette: Dancing With Grace, 1989. Mem. women's concerns team Synod of N.E., Syracuse, N.Y., 1981-83, mem. worship team, Morristown, N.J., 1992; mem. women's concerns team Albany Presbytery, 1982-85, chair, 1983-85, mem. com. on ministries for peace and justice, 1990-96, chair, 1995-96, trustee, 1997-99; del. gen. assembly United Presbyn. Ch. (USA), Phoenix, 1984. Recipient Spl. Opportunity Stipend Rensselaer County Coun. for Arts, 1992; honored at ann. banquet Interndenominational Ministries Conf., 1997. Mem. APA, Am. Assn. Pastoral Counselors (cert.), Assn. Mental Health Clergy (cert. chaplain, sec. 1996-98), Assn. Profl. Chaplains (bd. cert. chaplain), N.Y. State Chaplains' Assn. (v.p. 1995-97), N.Y. State Assn. Protestant Chaplains, Psychol. Assn. NE N.Y., Presbyn. Health, Edn. and Welfare Assn. Avocations: folk music, sailboat racing. Office: Capital Dist Psychiat Ctr 75 New Scotland Ave Albany NY 12208-3412 also: 256 Marginal St Boston MA 02128-2800 E-mail: mcutting@mindspring.com.

CUTTING, MARY DOROTHEA, audio and audio-visual communications company executive; b. N.Y.C., Feb. 20, 1943; d. Elliotte Robinson and Mary Dorothea (Clarke) Little; m. James H. B. Cutting, July 18, 1964; children—Gwendolyn Louise, Laura Elizabeth. Student Whitman Coll., 1960-62; B.A. in English Lit., U. Wash., 1964. Tchr. English, Severna Park High Sch., Md., 1965-66; remedial reading substitute tchr. St. Patrick's Day Sch., Washington, 1976-77; v.p. mktg. The Cutting Corp., Washington, 1978—; bd. dirs. Potomac Talking Book Svcs, Inc., 1990—; Editor children's cassettes: Fisher-Price Toys Spellbinder Series, 1983 (Consumer Com. of Ams. for Democratic Action award for being one of nation's 6 best toys for under $5 1983). Vol. chmn., bd. dirs. Washington Assn. for TV and Children, 1977. Mem. Internat. Assn. Bus. Communicators, Jr. League Washington (bd. dirs. 1977). Republican. Episcopalian. Office: 4940 Hampden Ln Ste 300 Bethesda MD 20814-2945

CUTTLER, CHARLES DAVID, art historian, educator; b. Cleve., Ohio, Apr. 8, 1913; s. Morris Joseph and Nettie (Wolff) Cuttler; m. Betty Iverson Monroe, Jan. 4, 1989; 1 child, Judith Ann. BFA, Ohio State, 1935, MA, 1937; PhD, NYU, 1952. Asst. instr. Ohio State U., Columbus, Ohio, 1935—37; tchr. art hist. U. Colo., Boulder, Colo., 1938; asst. prof. Mich. State U., E. Lansing, Mich., 1947—57; assoc. to prof. U. Iowa, Iowa City, 1957—83; ret., 1983. Eng., designer Allen Kauderer Engring., Detroit, 1940—47. Mem.: Midwest Art History Soc. (co-founder, first pres.). Home: 1691 Ridge Rd Iowa City IA 52245-1628 E-mail: charles-cuttler@iowa.edu.

CUTTS, CHARLES EUGENE, retired engineering educator; b. Sioux Falls, S.D., May 15, 1914; s. Charles Clifford and Ethel May (Gardner) C.; m. Jane Bebensee, Mar. 16, 1946; children: George Gardner, Elizabeth Anne. B.C.E., U. Minn., 1936, MS in Civil Engring, 1939, PhD, 1949. Registered profl. engr., Minn., Fla., Mich. Instrumentman Milw. R.R., 1936- 38; teaching asst. dept. civil engring. U. Minn., 1938-39, instr., asst. prof., 1946-50; engr. C.F. Haglin & Sons, summer 1939; asst. prof. dept. civil engring. Robert Coll., Istanbul, Turkey, 1939-42; engr. Braithwaite Co., Ltd., Iskenderun, Turkey, summer 1942, 43; assoc. prof., assoc. rsch. engr. U. Fla., 1950-53; engr. Engring. Scis. Program NSF, Washington, 1953-56; profl. lectr. civil engring. George Washington U., 1955-56; prof., chmn. dept. civil engring. Mich. State U., 1956-69, prof., 1969-84, prof. emeritus, 1984—; ret., 1984. Cons. U. Minn. Morocco Project, 1986. Author: Structural Design in Reinforced Concrete, 1954, other tech. publs. Served to maj. C.E. AUS, 1943-46; lt. col. Res. ret. Mem. Nat. Acad. Scis. (fellowship com. 1961-63), ASCE (chmn. com. on mech. properties of materials 1965, pres. Mich. sect. 1967, chmn. com. on engring. edn. 1969-70), Am. Concrete Inst., Am. Soc. Engring. Edn. (chmn. civil engr. div. 1965-66, v.p. 1970—, chmn. constn. and bylaws com. 1981-83), Engrs. Coun. Profl. Devel. (chmn. region 5 1972-73), Nat. Soc. Profl. Engrs., Tau Beta Pi, Chi Epsilon. Home: 4599 Ottawa Dr Okemos MI 48864-2028 Office: Civil Engring Mich State Univ East Lansing MI 48824 Office Phone: 517-349-9590.

CVENGROS, JOSEPH MICHAEL, manufacturing company executive; b. Pana, Ill., Oct. 8, 1931; s. Joseph John and Mary Bernice (Sturgeon) C.; m. Mary Elizabeth Ainsworth, Feb. 11, 1956; children: Joseph J., Mary E., Andrew T., Katherine A., J. Michael, Robert A., David L., Susan M. BABS, Washington U., St. Louis, 1955; MBA, Northwestern U., 1960. Pers. mgr. Continental Baking Co., Chgo., 1956-57; asst. to chmn. bd. dirs. Automatic Canteen Co. divsn. ITT, Chgo., 1957-65; cons. Spencer Stuart and Assoc., Chgo., 1965-68; investor High Tech., Inc., Chgo., 1968—; chmn. bd. dirs., CEO Anaconda Metal Hose divsn. Anamet, Inc., Glen Ellyn, Ill., 1984—. Fellow Econ. Club Chgo. Office: Anamet Inc 739 Roosevelt Rd Ste 204 Glen Ellyn IL 60137-5873

CVETANOVICH, DAN L., lawyer; b. Wheeling, W.Va., Oct. 2, 1952; s. Louis J. and Nila J. (Hall) Cvetanovich; m. Sharon M. Smith, Sept. 8, 1979; children: Gregory L., Steven W. BA, West Liberty State Coll., 1974; JD, Harvard U., 1977. Bar: Ohio 1977, U.S. Dist. Ct. (so. dist.) Ohio 1978, U.S. Ct. Appeals (6th cir.) 1980, U.S. Dist. Ct. (no. dist.) Ohio 1984, W.Va. 1985, U.S. Dist. Ct. (so. dist.) W.Va. 1985, U.S. Ct. Appeals (4th cir.) 1986, U.S. Dist. Ct. (we. dist.) Tex. 1998, U.S. Dist. Ct. (no. dist.) W.Va. 2001. Assoc. Bricker & Eckler, Columbus, Ohio, 1977-82, ptnr., 1983-87, Arter & Hadden LLP, Columbus, 1987—2003; mem. Bailey Cavalieri LLC, Columbus, 2003—. Mem.: ABA, Columbus Bar Assn., W.Va. State Bar, Ohio State Bar Assn. Republican. Avocations: hunting, fishing, golf. Office: Bailey Cavalieri LLC One Columbus 10 W Broad St 21st Fl Columbus OH 43215-3422 Office Phone: 614-229-3291. Business E-Mail: Dan.Cvetanovich@baileycavalieri.com.

CWIAK, CARRIE ANN, obstetrician, gynecologist; b. San Diego, Calif., Mar. 13, 1970; life ptnr. Chad Huot. BA, U. San Diego, 1992—92; MD, St. Louis U. Sch. Medicine, 1997; MPH, Emory U. Sch. Pub. Health, Atlanta, 2003. Lic. Ga., 2001. Family planning clin. care and rsch. fellow Dept. Gynecology and Obstetrics Emory U., Atlanta, 2001—03, asst. prof., 2003—. Family planning specialist. Co-author: Managing Contraception. Recipient Rsch. award in contraception, Am. Coll. Obstetricians and Gynecologists and Organon Inc., 2002—03. Mem.: Assn. Reproductive Health Profls., Am. Coll. Obstetricians and Gynecologists. Achievements include design of (with Oreg. Health and Sci. U.) interactive lecture teaching contraception to medical students. Office: Emory Univ Dept GYN/OB 49 Jesse Hill Jr Dr Atlanta GA 30303 Office Phone: 404-778-1385.

CWIKLA, RICH I., secondary school educator; Secondary tchr. West Fargo (N.D.) High Sch. Recipient Tchr. Excellence for N.D. award Internat. Tech. Edn. Assn., 1992. Office: West Fargo High Sch 801 9th St E West Fargo ND 58078-3100

CYCHOLL, TASHA NICOLE, lawyer; b. Chgo., Sept. 16, 1974; d. William Gustav and Gail Ann Cycholl. BA, Ariz. State U., 1996, JD, 1999. Bar: Ariz. 1999, U.S. Dist. Ct. Ariz. 1999. Atty. Rhees Hopkins & Kreamer, Phoenix, 1999—2001, Low & Childers, PC, Phoenix, 2001—. Mem.: Ariz. Women Lawyers Assn. (young lawyers divsn., dir. Maricopa county bar, domestic violence com. 1999—). Office: Low & Childers PC 2999N 44th St Ste 250 Phoenix AZ 85018 Office Phone: 602-266-1166. Business E-Mail: tcycholl@lowchilders.com.

CYGANOWSKI, MELANIE L., bankruptcy judge; b. Chgo., June 8, 1952; d. Daniel F. and Sophia A. C.; married, 1989. AB in anthropology, Grinnell Coll., 1974; postgrad. in urban devel., Cornell U., 1975; JD magna cum laude, SUNY, Buffalo, 1981. Bar: N.Y. 1982, U.S. Supreme Ct., U.S. Ct. Appeals (2d cir.), U.S. Dist. Ct. (so., ea. and we. dists.) N.Y. Coord. program planning, planner, cons. dept. community devel. and human resources City of Buffalo, N.Y., 1974-78; dir. individual referral program Broadway-Filmore Area Coun., Inc., Buffalo, 1978-79; summer assoc. Hodgson, Russ, Andrews, Wood & Goodyear, Buffalo, 1980; law clk. to Hon. Charles L. Brieant U.S. Dist. Ct. (so. dist.) N.Y., 1981-82; litigation assoc. Sullivan & Cromwell, N.Y.C., 1982-89; sr. atty. Milbank, Tweed, Hadley & McCloy, 1989-93; judge U.S. Bankruptcy Ct. (ea. dist.) N.Y., Ctrl. Islip, 1993—. Adj. prof. law bankruptcy program St. John's U. Sch. Law. Contbr. articles to legal jours. Fellow Am. Bar Found, ABA; mem., Nat. Conf. Bankruptcy Judges, N.Y. State Bar Assn. Roman Catholic. Avocations: bicycling, gardening, fishing. Office: US Bankruptcy Ct The Long Island Fed Ct 290 Federal Plz Central Islip NY 11722 Office Phone: 631-712-5682. Business E-Mail: melanie_cyganowski@nyeb.uscourts.gov.

CYLKE, FRANK KURT, librarian; b. New Haven, Conn., Feb. 13, 1932; s. Frank Anton and Helen Mary (Callahan) C.; m. Mary Elizabeth Newhouse, Dec. 28, 1962; children: Frank Kurt, Mary Amanda, Virginia Ann. BA, U. Conn., 1954; M.L.S., Pratt Inst., 1957; postgrad., Fairfield U., Am. U., Georgetown U. Libr. Graham-Eckes Sch., Palm Beach, Fla., 1957-58; reference libr. Bridgeport (Conn.) Pub. Libr., 1958-62; head pub. svc. New Haven Pub. Libr., 1962-65; asst. libr. Providence Pub. Libr., 1965-68; chief libr. rsch. U.S. Office Edn., 1968-69; exec. dir. fed. libr. com. Libr. of Congress, 1970-73; dir. nat. libr. svc. for blind, physically handicapped Library of Congress, 1973—. Instr. Grad. Libr. Sch. U. R.I., 1967-68; instr. Grad. Libr. Sch. Cath. U. Am., 1974—, bd. visitors, 1980—; exec. sec. panel edn. & tng. Com. Sci. and Tech. Inst.; chmn. librs. tech. com. Met. Washington Coun. Govts., 1970-71; sec. U.S. Book Exch., 1972-74; sec.-treas. Joint Venture Pub. Activity, 1970-74; mem. E. Greenwich (R.I.) Free Libr. Corp., 1967—; adv. bd. Ednl. Resources Info. Ctr./Clearinghouse Libr. and Info. Sci., 1970-72; bd. visitors Grad. Sch. Libr./Info. Sci., Pratt Inst., 1980—. Editor: Captains Shelf, 1964-66, FLC Newsletter, 1970-73, Library Service for the Blind and Physically Handicapped: An International Approach, 1979, Recipient Va. Cultural Laureate, 1992, Dayton M. Forman Meml. award Can. Nat. Inst. for the Blind, 1996, Newel Perry award Nat. Fedn. of Blind, 2005; grantee U.S. Office Edn., 1972 Mem.: KC, ALA (Joseph W. Lippincott award 1992, F.J. Campbell medal 1975—76), Friends of Librs. for Blind in N.Am. (founder, ex-officio bd. dirs.), Internat. Fedn. Libr. Assns. (founder, chmn. sect. for blind), World Blind Union, Am. Soc. Info. Sci. (sec. 1874—1975), Spl. Librs. Assn. (chpt. pres. 1975—76), Dinghy Cruising Assn., Shenandoah Nat. Park Assn., Mystic Seaport (pilot), Crow's Nest (St. John's, Nfld.), Mansion House Yacht Club, Fed. City Club, Ancient Order of Hibernians, Knights of Columbus. Roman Catholic. Avocations: sailing, birding. Home: PO Box 192 Great Falls VA 22066-0192 Office: Libr of Congress Nat Libr Svc for the Blind 1291 Taylor St NW Washington DC 20542-0002 Office Phone: 202-707-5104. Personal E-mail: kurt.cylke@verizon.net. Business E-Mail: fcyl@loc.gov.

CYMBLER, MURRAY JOEL, corporate financial executive; b. Germany, July 20, 1948; U.S., 1949; s. Harry and Adele C.; m. Carol Horowitz, Nov. 23, 1972; children: Adam, Robyn. BA, Hunter Coll., 1970. Tchr. N.Y. Bd. Edn., Bronx, 1970-71; contract analyst The Equitable Life Assurance Soc., N.Y.C., 1972-86; chmn., CEO Astro-Stream Corp., Levittown, N.Y., 1986-91; mgr. fin. Landmark Plaza Properties Corp., Sayville, N.Y., 1991-99; gen. mgr. Intown Theaters, Sayville, 1999—2000, supr., 1998—2000; fin. sales Met Life, 2001, Nat. Life, 2002. Achievements include invention of Orbi Sport-toy, 1985. Office: Orbico Inc 133 Ronni Dr East Meadow NY 11554-1330

CYMROT, MARK ALAN, lawyer; b. Queens, NY, Oct. 8, 1947; s. Irwin Maurice and Anne (Kipnis) C.; m. Janinne Dall' Orto; children: Isaac, Erin, Isabella. BA, George Washington U., 1969; JD, Columbia U., 1972. Bar: D.C. 1973, N.Y. 2000. Trial lawyer civil divsn. U.S. Dept. of Justice, Washington,

1972-77; sr. litigator Consumers Union of U.S. Inc., Washington, 1977-79; spl. litigation counsel civil divsn. U.S. Dept. of Justice, Washington, 1979-83; ptnr. Cole Corette & Abrutyn, Washington, 1983-91, Baker & Hostetler LLP, Washington, 1991—. Contbr. articles to profl. jours. Named one of Best Lawyers in Washington, Washingtonian Mag. Avocations: photography, writing, golf, tennis. Office: Baker & Hostetler LLP 1050 Connecticut Ave NW Washington DC 20036-5304 Office Phone: 202-861-1677. Business E-Mail: mcymrot@bakerlaw.com.

CYNADER, MAX SIGMUND, psychology professor, physiology educator, researcher; b. Berlin, Feb. 24, 1947; arrived in Can., 1951; s. Samuel and Maria (Kraushar) C.; m. Ann Lynn Langford, Sept. 26, 2004; children: Madeleine Maria, Rebecca Kay, Alexandra Josephine. BSc, Mc Gill U., Montreal, Que., Can., 1967; PhD, MIT, 1972. Fellow neuroanatomy Max-Planck Inst. Psychiatry, Munich, 1972-73; asst. prof. psychology Dalhousie U., 1973-77, assoc. prof., 1977-81, assoc. prof. physiology, 1979-84, prof. psychology, 1981-84, Killam rsch. prof., 1984-88, prof. physiology, 1984-88; prof. psychology U. B.C., 1988—, prof. physiology, 1988—, prof. dept. ophthalmology, 1988—, dir., 1988-99; dir. Brain Rsch. Ctr., U. B.C. and Vancouver Hosp. and Health Scis. Ctr., 1997. Mem. pres.'s workshop on five yr. plan strengthening sci. support in Can. Natural Scis. and Engring. Rsch. Coun. Can., 1984, workshop for Steacie fellows, 1988; mem. task force on curriculum devel. in Can. neurosci., 1984; mem. spl. adv. panel on rsch. preparedness USAF, 1985; rep. Internat. Human Frontiers Sci. program Med. Rsch. Coun. Can., 1988; mem. grants com. behavioural scis. Med. Rsch. Coun. Can., program grants com. 1989—; referee senate rev. grad. program in neurosci. U. Western Ont., 1989; mem. math., computational and theoretical spl. rev. com. NIMH, 1989—; external reviewer Med. Rsch. Coun. Can., Alta. Heritage Fund Med. Rsch., NIH, NSF, USAF Office Sci. Rsch., Multiple Sclerosis Soc. Can., Vancouver Found., March of Dimes, Fight for Sight; CRC chair in brain devel., 2001-06. Mem. editorial bd. jours. Behavioral Brain Rsch., Clin. Vision Scis., Concepts in Neurosci., Devel. Brain Rsch., Exptl. Brain Rsch., Neural Networks, Visual Neurosci.; mem. adv. bd. series Rsch. Notes in Neural Computing; contbr. articles to profl. jours. Recipient Killam Rsch. prize U. B.C., 1989—; E.W.R. Steacie fellow Natural Sci. and Engring. Rsch. Coun. Can., 1979, Can. Inst. Advanced Rsch. fellow, 1986—, Bank of Montreal fellow Can. Inst. for Advanced Rsch., 1998; grantee Med. Rsch. Coun. Can., 1973—, Natural Sci. and Engring. Rsch. Coun. Can., 1975—, NIH, 1978-81, Killam Rsch. Prof., 1984, B.C. Sci. & Tech. Champion, 2004. Fellow Can. Inst. Advanced Rsch., Royal Soc. Can.; mem. Soc. Neurosci. (Halifax chpt., pres. 1985, edn. com. 1986-89), Can. Assn. Neurosci. (pres. 1986), Assn. Rsch. Otolaryngology, Assn. Rsch. in Vision and Opthalmology, Can. Physiol. Soc., Internat. Brain Rsch. Orgn., Internat. Soc. Devel. Neurosci., Internat. Strabismol. Assn., World Fedn. Neuroscientists. Achievements include being named semifinalist Can. Astronaut program, 1983. Office: U BC Vancouver Hosp Brain Rsch Ctr 2211 Wesbrook Mall Vancouver BC Canada V6T 2B5 Business E-Mail: cynader@brain.ubc.ca.

CYPERT, JIMMY DEAN, lawyer; b. Springdale, Ark., May 24, 1934; s. Burl Irvin and Ora Opal (Sisco) C.; m. Gaye Annette Warren, Aug. 26, 1956; children: Julie Jan, Jamie Ann. BS, U. Ark., 1956, LLB, JD, 1959. Bar: Ark. 1959. Assoc. Crouch, Jones & Blair, Springdale, 1959-60; ptnr. Crouch, Blair, Cypert & Waters, Springdale, 1960-91, Cypert, Crouch, Clark & Harwell, Springdale, 1991—. Bd. dirs., pres. Westwood Inc., Indsl. Leasing Inc., TC Investments; bd. dirs. 1st Nat. Bank. Pres. Washington County Young Democrats, 1962; bd. dirs. United Fund, 1962; pres., bd. dirs. Springdale Bd. Edn., 1966-73; bd. dirs. Washington County Sch. for Retarded Children, 1967-70; mem. hon. coun. U. Ark. Sch. Law., 1958; trustee Springdale Meml. Hosp., 1976—. Capt. U.S. Army, 1956-58. Recipient Disting. Svc. award Springdale Jaycees, 1963; named one of Outstanding Young Men of Am., U.S. Jaycees, 1963. Mem. ABA (Outstanding Lawyer-Citizen award 1985-86), Ark. Bar Assn. (exec. com., ho. of dels. 1976-78, chmn. exec. com. 1978, pres. 1981-82), Washington County Bar Assn., Internat. Platform Assn., Ark. Young Lawyers Assn. (pres. 1962), Springdale C. of C. (dir. 1964-70, pres. 1966, Outstanding Svc. award 1968, Outstanding Citizen award 1984), Elks, Kiwanis, Sigma Nu, Alph Kappa Psi. Methodist (chmn. bd.). Home: 109 Woodcliff Cir Springdale AR 72764-3603 Office: 111 S Holcomb St Springdale AR 72764-4441

CYPSER, DARLENE ANN, lawyer, film producer, writer; b. Tulsa, Jan. 3, 1958; d. Donald A. and Evelyn D. (Carrigan) Chappell; 1 child, Christopher A. BA, U. Okla., 1980, JD, 1986. Bar: N.Y. 1987, Colo. 1988. Pvt. practice, Boulder, Colo., 1988-99. Pres. The Midgard Corp., 1999—, Inferno Film Prodns., 1999—. Contbr. articles to profl. jours. Vol. Boulder County Legal Svcs., 1987-99, Legal Aid Soc. Westchester County, White Plains, N.Y., 1986-87; bd. dirs. Nyx Net, 1997-. Mem. Am. Geophys. Union, Colo. Film and Video Assn. Avocations: macrame, hiking, photography, cooking. Office: 6529 Lakeside Cir Littleton CO 80125 Business E-Mail: darlene@themidgardcorp.com.

CYR, ARTHUR I., political science professor, economics professor; b. LA, Mar. 1, 1945; s. Irving Arthur and Frances Mary Cyr; children: David Arthur, Thomas Harold, James Price. BA, UCLA, 1966, MA, 1967; AM, Harvard U., 1969, PhD, 1971. Teaching fellow Harvard U., 1970-71; program officer internat. and edn.-rsch. divs. Ford Found., 1971-74; asst. prof., adminstr. UCLA, 1974-76; program dir. Chgo. Coun. Fgn. Rels., 1976-81, v.p., 1981-96; pres., CEO, World Trade Ctr. Assn., Chgo., 1996-98; Clausen disting. prof. polit. econ. and world bus. Carthage Coll., Kenosha, Wis., 1998—; dir. Clausen Ctr. World Bus., 2000—. Author: Liberal Politics in Britain, 1977, rev. edit., 1988, British Foreign Policy and the Atlantic Area, 1979, U.S. Foreign Policy and European Security, 1987, After the Cold War—American Foreign Policy, Europe and Asia, 1997, rev. edit., 2000, Taiwan: The Commercial State, 2003, rev. edit., 2005; contbr. articles to profl. jours. Served with USAR, 1966—73. Mem. Internat. Inst. Strategic Studies, Royal Inst. Internat. Affairs, Royal United Sen. Inst., Am. Polit. Sci. Assn., Coun. Fgn. Rels., Century, Phi Beta Kappa. Office: Carthage Coll Clausen Ctr Kenosha WI 53140-1994 Business E-Mail: acyr@carthage.edu.

CYR, CONRAD KEEFE, federal judge; b. Limestone, Maine, Dec. 9, 1931; s. Louis Emery and Kathleen Mary (Keefe) Cyr; m. Judith Ann Pirie, June 23, 1962 (dec. Mar. 1985); children: Keefe Clark, Jeffrey Louis Frederick; m. Diana Kathleen Sanborn, Sept. 25, 1987. BS cum laude, Holy Cross Coll., 1953; JD, Yale U., 1956; LLD (hon.), Husson Coll., 1991. Bar: Maine 1956. Pvt. practice, Limestone, 1956—59; asst. U.S. atty., Bangor, Maine, 1959—61; pvt. practice Winchell & Cyr, Bangor, Maine, 1961—62; judge U.S. Bankruptcy Ct., Bangor, 1961—81, U.S. Dist. Ct., Bangor, 1981—83, chief judge, 1983—89; judge U.S. Fgn. Intelligence Surveillance Ct., 1987—89, U.S. Ct. Appeals (1st cir.), Boston, 1989—97, sr. judge, 1997—. Standing spl. master U.S. Dist. Ct., Maine, 1974—76; chief judge Bankruptcy Appellate Panel Dist., Mass., 1980—81; mem. Jud. Council (1st cir.), 1987—; com. on adminstrn. of bankruptcy sys. Jud. Conf. U.S., 1987—. Founder, editor-in-chief: Am. Bankruptcy Law Jour., 1970—81, contbg. author, editor: Collier on Bankruptcy, vol. 10. Steering com. U.S. AID Project for Assisting Bankruptcy and Reorgn. Procedures in Ctr. and Ea. Europe; treas. Limestone Rep. Com., 1958; chmn. budget com. Town of Limestone, 1959. Named one of Outstanding Young Men of Maine, 1963; recipient cert. of appreciation, Kans. Bar Assn., 1979, U. Maine, 1983, Nat. Judge's Recognition award, Nat. Conf. Bankruptcy Judges, 1979, Key to Town Limestone, 1983. Fellow: Am. Coll. Bankruptcy, Maine Bar Found. (charter); mem.: ABA, John Ballou Am. Inn of Ct., Aroostook Bar Assn., Am. Judicature Soc., Nat. Bankruptcy Conf. (exec. bd. 1974—77), Nat. Conf. Bankruptcy Judges (pres. 1976—77), Penobscot Bar Assn., Maine Bar Assn., Limestone C. of C. (pres.). Roman Catholic.*

CYR, J. V. RAYMOND, telecommunications industry executive; b. Montreal, Que., Can., Feb. 11, 1934; s. Armand and Yvonne (Lagace) Cyr; m. Marie Bourdon, Sept. 1, 1956; children: Helene, Paul Andre. Student, Ecole Poly.; BSc, U. Montreal, 1958; postgrad., Bell Labs., NJ, Nat. Def. Coll., 1972—73; LLD (hon.), Concordia U., Montreal, 1988. With Bell Can., 1992-96, engr., 1958-65, staff engr. Montreal, 1965-70, from v.p. ops. staff region to v.p., 1973-75, pres., 1983-85, chmn., pres., CEO, 1985-87, chmn. bd. dirs., 1987-89, pres., 1983-85, chmn., pres., CEO, 1985-87, chmn. bd., 1987-89, chief engr. Quebec City, 1970-73, from exec. v.p. to v.p. adminstrn., 1975-83, chmn., 1992-96; with BCE, Inc. (formerly Bell Can. Enterprises), 1987-93, pres. Montreal, 1987-88, pres., CEO, 1988-89, also bd. dirs., chmn., pres., CEO, 1989-90, chmn., CEO, 1990-92, chmn., 1992-93, dir., sr. advisor to chmn.'s office, 1993-97; chmn. Montreal Trust, 1989-90. Bd. dirs. Can. Nat., SR Telecom., ART Advanced Rsch. & Techs. Inc., Polyvalor Inc., G.T.C. Transcontinental Ltd., IsacSoft Techs. Inc., Fonds de Solidarite des Travailleurs du Que., Triton Electronik Inc., Old Port of Montreal Corp. Inc., Transp. Can. Pipelines, chmn. bd., 1989—92. Past chmn. Jr. Achievement Can., Montreal Mus. Contemporary Art, Opera de Montreal; assoc. gov. U. Montreal. Named chair in mgmt. in his honor, Ecole Polytechnique, Laureate Personnalite, 125th Anniversaire de l'Ecole Polytechnique, 1998; recipient Gold Medal award, Can. Egnrs., 1987, Ordre du Mérite des Diplîes, U. Montreal, 1988, Laureate of Prix des comm. du Que., 1990, Mgmt. Achievement award, McGill U., 1991, Gt. Montrealer award, 1991, Commemorative medal, 125th Ann. Confederation Can., 1992. Mem.: Can. Acad. Engring. (founding), Islemere Club, St. James Club, St. Denis Club. Roman Catholic. Avocations: golf, swimming. Office: 1050 Beaver Hall Hill 19th Montreal PQ Canada H2Z 1S4 Office Phone: 514-870-8799. Office Fax: 514-870-4136.

CYR, MICHELE GAIL, internist, hospital administrator, dean; m. Gregory Towne; 1 child, Benjamin Towne. BA magna cum laude, Bowdoin Coll., 1976; MD, Dartmouth Med. Sch., 1979. Dir. divsn. gen. internal medicine R.I. Hosp., Providence, 1991—, Meml. Hosp. R.I., Pawtucket, 1991—. Health columnist McCall's Mag., 1985—2000; assoc. dean grad. med. edn. Brown Med. Sch., Providence, 1997—; spokesperson Nat. Yogurt Assn., 2000—03; assoc. dean women in medicine Brown Med. Sch., Providence, 2003—. Co-author: (health book) The New Truth About Menopause; contbr. articles to profl. jours. Recipient Influential Women R.I., Perishable Theater, 2002. Mem.: Soc. Gen. Internal Medicine (career support task force 2004). Office: RI Hosp DGIM 593 Eddy St Jane Brown Ground 0100 Providence RI 02903 Office Phone: 401-444-8537. Home Fax: 401-444-3056; Office Fax: 401-444-3056. E-mail: michele_cyr@brown.edu.

CYRUS, CYNTHIA J., dean, music educator; b. Seattle, Sept. 2, 1963; d. John D. and Virginia J. Cyrus; m. Thomas B. Dowling; children: Amelia Berle, Nathaniel Berle, Nissa Berle. BA, Pomona Coll., 1984; MA, U. N.C., 1987, PhD, 1990. Vis. asst. prof. U. Rochester, NY, 1991—92, SUNY, Stony Brook, NY, 1992—94; asst. prof. Blair Sch. Music Vanderbilt U., Nashville, 1994—2001, assoc. prof., 2001—, assoc. dean Blair Sch. Music, 2004—. Mem. adv. bd. rsch. jour. Vanderbilt U., 2004—; session organizer Internat. Medieval Congress, Kalamazoo, 2001—04; lectr. in field. Editor: Online Reference Book for Medieval Studies, 1997—, De tous biens plaine: 28 Settings of Hayne, 2000; contbr. articles to profl. jours. Organizer Bellevue Project-Oriented Unschoolers, Nashville, 2002—. Recipient Friends of Libr. award, Pontifical Inst. Mediaeval Studies, Toronto, Can., 2000; fellow, The Ohio State U., 1990—91; grantee, Univ. Rsch. Coun., 1995—96, Vanderbilt U., 1996, NEH, 2004; Joseph E. Pogue fellowship, U. N.C., 1984—88. Mem.: Internat. Machaut Soc. (webmaster 2002—03, bd. dirs. 2002—), Coll. Music Soc. (campus rep. 2002—04), Am. Musicological Soc. (mem. com. moderated elec. discussion list 2002—, chmn. program com. 1995—96), Medieval Acad. Am. Office: Blair School Music Vanderbilt Univ 2400 Blakemore Ave Nashville TN 37212 Office Phone: 615-322-7693.

CYS, RICHARD L., lawyer; b. Boulder, Colo., Oct. 9, 1944; BS with honors, U. Colo., 1966; JD, Georgetown U., 1969. Bar: D.C. 1969. Law clk. to Hon. John Pratt D.C., 1969-70; asst. U.S. atty. D.C., 1970-77; mem. Davis Wright Tremaine LLP, Washington. Mem. ABA, D.C. Bar, Bar Assn. D.C. Office: Davis Wright Tremaine LLP 1500 K St NW Ste 450 Washington DC 20005-1272 Office Phone: 202-508-6617.

CYWAR, ADAM WALTER, engineering executive; b. Kearny, N.J., Mar. 14, 1937; s. Adam Benjamin and Sophie Julia (Kurak) C.; m. Gloria Ella Beresford, Mar. 29, 1956 (div. May 1973); children: Victoria Cywar, Douglas A., Sophia; m. Rose Barter Tubb, May 11, 1973. BSME, N.J. Inst. Tech., Newark, 1960, MSMgtE, 1965. Design engr. Colgate-Palmolive, Jersey City, N.J., 1956-60; indsl. engr. Lionel Corp., Hillside, N.J., 1960-63; sr. engr. IBM Corp., Boca Raton, Fla., 1963-93; pres. Adam Cywar Indsl. Engr., Austin, Tex., 1993—. V.p. info. sys. RPM Assocs., Georgetown, Tex., 1993-97; founder IBM Worldwide Activity Based Mgmt. Competency Ctr. Author: Handbook of Industrial Engineering, 1982 (IBM Achievement award 1983). Chmn. Town of Poughkeepsie Rep. Com. to Elect Jim Buckley, 1968. Mem. ASME (sr. mem.), Inst. Indsl. Engrs. (sr., treas. 1975-90, dir. honors and awards 1970-75, Disting. Svc. award 1977). Avocations: writing, industrial engineering research. Home and Office: Adam Cywar Indsl Engr 4307 Las Palmas Dr Austin TX 78759-5062 Personal E-mail: acywar@yahoo.com.

CZACHOR, BRUCE, lawyer, consultant; b. Bklyn., May 7, 1961; BA in Polit. sci., SUNY, Binghampton, 1983; JD magna cum laude, NY Law Sch., 1987. Bar: NY 1988, NJ 1988, DC 1989, Calif. 2004. Letter of credit analyst Chase Manhattan Bank, NYC, 1983-84; law clk. to Hon. George Gallagher US Ct. Appeals (DC cir.), Washington, 1987-88; law clk. to Hon. Judge John Reilly; ptnr. Shearman & Sterling LLP, NYC & Toronto, 1988—94, mng. ptnr. Menlo Park, Calif., co-mng. ptnr. San Francisco. Mem. ABA, NY Bar Assn., NJ Bar Assn. Republican. Office: Shearman & Sterling LLP 1080 Marsh Rd Menlo Park CA 94025-1022 also: Shearman & Sterling LLP 525 Market St San Francisco CA 94105 Office Phone: 650-838-3632. Office Fax: 650-743-6630. Business E-Mail: bczachor@shearman.com.

CZAJA, ALBERT JOSEPH, physician, educator; b. Phila., Feb. 17, 1943; s. Albert Joseph and Lillian Teresa Czaja; m. Herschel Carpenter, Jan. 13, 1969; children: Christopher Albert, Jonathan Joseph. AB, Dartmouth Coll., 1965, BMS, 1966; MD, Harvard U., 1968. Diplomate Am. Bd. Internal Medicine, Am. Bd. Gastroenterology. Intern Phila. Gen. Hosp., 1968-69, resident in medicine, 1969-72; staff gastroenterologist Burn Unit USA Insts., San Antonio, 1972-75; NIH rsch. fellow Mayo Clin., Rochester, Minn., 1975-77, gastroenterology cons., 1977—; prof. medicine Mayo Med. Sch., Rochester, Minn., 1986—. Editor: Chronic Active Hepatitis, 1986, Autoimmune Hepatitis, 2002. Maj. USMC, 1972-75. Recipient Meritorius Svc. medal USA Med. Corps, 1975. Fellow ACG, Am. Coll. Gastroenterology; mem. Am. Gastroenterol. Assn. (Disting. Achievement award 1997), Am. Assn. Study Liver Diseases, Internat. Assn. Study Liver Diseases, Am. Soc. Gastrointestinal Endoscopy. Avocations: sailing, opera. Office: Mayo Clin 200 1st St SW Rochester MN 55905-0001

CZAJKA, JAMES VINCENT, architect; b. Lackawanna, NY, Dec. 6, 1950; s. Joseph Martin and Livia Maria (Jengo) C. BS in Art and Design, MIT, 1972, MArch, 1975. Registered architect, NY. Asst. prof. architecture SUNY, Buffalo, 1975-79; architect Ehrenkrantz Group Architects and Planners, N.Y.C., 1979-84, Beyer, Blinder, Belle Architects and Planners, N.Y.C., 1984-91, assoc., 1987-91, studio dir., 1988-91; pvt. practice N.Y.C., 1991-92; prin. Allanbrook Benic Czajka Architects & Planners, N.Y.C., 1993-2001, James Vincent Czajka Architects, N.Y.C., 2001—. Prin. works include Baird Point Amphitheater, SUNY, Buffalo, 1978, Social Security Adminstrn. Bldg., Queens, N.Y., 1982, Paul Klapper Hall, Queens Coll., 1986, N.Y. Hall Sci. Master Plan, Queens, N.Y., 1992, Am. Acad. Arts and Letters Master Plan, 1994, St. Joseph Parish Master Plan, Queens, 1994, World Monuments Fund Hdqrs., Manhattan, 1995, Loyola Sch. Sci. Ctr. renovation, Manhattan, 1996, Rutgers Ch. renovation, Manhattan, 1997, Bklyn. Conservatory of Music renovation, 1998, Blue Heron Arts Ctr., Manhattan, 1999, Preissner House, East Hampton, N.Y., 2000, Conard House, Manhattan, 2000, The Rockwell Mus. of Western Art, Corning, N.Y., 2001, N.Y. Soc. Libr. Master Plan, 2002, Lefferts Homestead Children's Mus., Bklyn., 2002, Elephant House Renovation, Bronx Zoo, 2003, Myerson House, Amagansett, N.Y., 2004, Third St. Music Sch. Master Plan, Manhattan, N.Y., 2005 Mem. AIA, Nat. Coun. Archtl. Registration Bds. (cert.). Avocation: piano. Home: 303 E 84th St Apt 2F New York NY 10028-4435 Office: 611 Broadway Rm 817 New York NY 10012-2608 Office Phone: 212-475-1112. Business E-Mail: jvc@jvcarchitects.com.

CZAJKOWSKI, EVA ANNA, aerospace engineer, educator; b. New Britain, Conn., Sept. 4, 1961; Student, Yale U., 1978; BS in Aero. Engring. cum laude, M in Aero. Engring., Rensselaer Poly. Inst., 1983; SM in Aeronautics and Astronautics, MIT, 1985; PhD in Aerospace Engring., Va. Poly. Inst. and State U., 1988. Registered profl engr, NY. Student trainee U.S. Govt., Washington, 1981-82; intern N.Y. State Assembly, Albany, 1983; teaching asst. Rensselaer Poly. Inst., Troy, N.Y., 1983, rsch. asst. U.S. Army Rsch. Office Ctr. Excellence, 1982-83; engring. analyst Pratt & Whitney Aircraft, West Palm Beach, Fla., 1984; rsch. asst. Gas Turbine and Plasma Dynamics Lab., Cambridge, 1984-85; from rsch. asst., tchg. asst. dept. aerospace & ocean engring. to sr. engring. and tech. mgr. Va. Poly. Inst. and State U., Blacksburg, 1985—2005, sr. engring. and tech. mgr., 2005—. U.S. dels. eleven European nations, 1991—2005. Author: (book) Russian Aeronautical Test Facilities, 1994; contbr. scientific papers confs, articles profl jours and ency. Assoc mem Nat Air and Space Mus, Am Mus Natural History; vol. New Britain Gen Hosp, 1977—79. Decorated dame commandeur Ordre Souvereign Militaire de la Milice du Saint Sepulcre; named, Souverain Order Knights Justice; named to World Order Sci.-Edn.-Culture, 2002; recipient Medal Hon. Sci. Award, Bausch & Lomb, 1978, Internat. Woman Yr., 1991—92, 1996—97, Joseph B. Platt Award, 1997, Scientist Yr., 2001, Int. Sci. Medal, 2001, Albert Schweitzer Medal Sci. and Peace, 50th Anniversary of Nobel Peace prize, Albert Schweitzer Internat. Univ. Found., 2004; fellow Amelia Earhart, Zonta Int., 1983—85, Prat Presdl. Eng. Program, 1985—88; scholar, Unico Nat., 1979—80, Am. Helicopter Soc. Vertical Flight Found., 1983. Mem.: NAFE, AIAA, London Diplomatic Acad., N.Y. Acad. Scis., Nat. Space Soc., World Found. Successful Women, Internat. Platform Assn., Planetary Soc., Polish Rotorcraft Assn., Am. Helicopter Soc., Am. Astronaut Soc., Sovereign Order Knights of Justice (named Dame Comdr. 2004), World Order Sci.-Edn.-Culture (named Dame 2002), Confederation Chivalry (named Dame Comdr. 1990), Gamma Beta Phi, Tau Beta Pi, Phi Kappa Phi, Sigma Gamma Tau, Sigma Xi. Avocations: art, horseback riding, piano, flying private plane, sailing. Home: 170 Carlton St New Britain CT 06053-3106

CZAJKOWSKI-BARRETT, KAREN ANGELA, human resources specialist; b. Bklyn., Sept. 13, 1957; d. Frank Henry and Cecilia (Artowicz) Czajkowski; div. Mar. 1992; children: Jennifer Marie, Michael Joseph. BSBA, Fairfield U., 1979; MBA, Sacred Heart U., 1984. Office systems analyst Union Trust Co., Stamford, Conn., 1979-80, sr. office systems analyst, 1980-81; ops. analyst Homequity, Inc., Wilton, 1981-82, project leader human rels. dept., 1982-85, organization devel. cons., 1985-87; tng. and devel. cons. People's Bank, Bridgeport, Conn., 1987-90; mgr. human resource planning and devel. Pitney Bowes Mgmt. Svcs., Stamford, 1990-93, dir. human resources planning and devel., 1993-98; regional learning mgr. Hewitt Assocs. LLC, Rowayton, Conn., 1998—2003, human resources ops. mgr., bus. cons., 2003—. Adj. instr. Sacred Heart U., Bridgeport, 1987. Sec. Cub Scouts Adv. Com., 1991-92; mem. regional bd. Conn. Fedn. Cath. Sch. Parents, 1993-94; treas. St. Theresa Sch.-Home Sch. Assn., 1994-96. Recipient Nash Engring., 1979; named Bus. Advisor of Yr., INROADS/Fairfield-Westchester Counties, Inc., 1993. Mem. ASTD, Am. Mgmt. Assn., Human Resource Planning Soc. Exec. Women's Golf Assn. Home: 28 Wendover Rd Trumbull CT 06611-1530 Office: Hewitt Assocs LLC 45 Glover Ave Norwalk CT 06850

CZAKO, ALAN H., human resources specialist, benefits compensation analyst; b. N.Y.C., Dec. 17, 1942; s. Joseph H. Czako and Dorothy Alfonso; m. Sara Saed, Jan. 10, 1981; m. Susan A. Lieberman, Dec. 23, 1967 (div.); children: Michael S., Brian M., Adam S., Michele A. Weinstein. BS, Bklyn Coll., 1967; MA, New Sch. for Social Rsch., N.Y.C., 1971; post grad., Teachers Coll. Columbia U., N.Y.C., 1971—73. Diplomate profl. counseling Int'l Acad. of Behavioral Medicine, Counseling, and Psychotherapy, 1991; sr. profl. human resources Human Resources Certification Inst., 1991, cert. compensation profl. WorldatWork Soc. of Cert. Professionals, 2001. Asst. pers. dir. Jersey City Job Corps Ctr. for Women, 1969—71; EEO specialist to sr pers. specialist to mgr, manpower planning Navy Exch. Svc. Command, Bklyn., 1971—81, pers. mgr. San Diego, 1981—82, Subic Bay, Philippines, 1982—83, sr. pers. specialist S.I., NY, 1983—85; regional human resources mgr. Navy Exch. Field Support Office, Norfolk, Va., 1985—94; assoc. dir. benefits Navy Exch. Svc. Command, Virginia Beach, 1994—96, dir. human resources svc. ctr., 1994—96, assoc. dir. labor and employee rels., 1994—96; human resources mgr. Sheraton Chapel Hill Hotel, NC, 1997—98; selection specialist PHE, Inc., Hillsborough, 1998—99; compensation specialist Navy Exch. Svc. Command, Virginia Beach, 1999—2001; compensation cons. Conectiv, Wilmington, Del., 2001—03; compensation mgr. County of Chester, West Chester, Pa., 2003—. Mem. planning coun. Bayside H.S., Virginia Beach, Va., 1999—2001; vol. Chester County Rep. Com., West Chester, Pa., 2003—; dir. Navy Exch. Ret. Employees Assn, Virginia Beach, Va., 1997—2001. Mem.: WorldatWork (formerly Am. Compensation Assn), Soc. for Human Resource Mgmt., Chester County Consistory Club, Am. Legion Post No. 134, Scottish Rite Valley of Reading (choir mem. 2004—), Masonic Lodge No. 322. Office: County of Chester 34 W Gay St West Chester PA 19380 Office Phone: 610-344-5351. Office Fax: 610-344-5489. E-mail: aczako@chesco.org.

CZARNECKI, ANTHONY J., correction administrator, educator; b. Mt. Vernon, N.Y., Aug. 28, 1948; s. Stanley and Lucy (Calabrese) C.; m. Lorraine Portman, Oct. 9, 1971; children: David, Pamela. BA, Iona Coll., 1970; MA, John Jay Coll., 1975; MPA, Pace U., 1990. Probation officer, sr. probation officer, tng. dir. Westchester County Probation Dept., White Plains, N.Y., 1970-83; chief of staff Westchester County Correction Dept., Valhalla, NY, 1983—. Adj. prof. criminal justice Westchester C.C., Valhalla, 1976—, Iona Coll., New Rochelle, N.Y., 1981—. Editor-in-chief Jour. Probation and Parole, 1980-82; contbr. articles to profl. jours. Recipient Disting. Alumnus award, John Jay Coll. Criminal Justice, 2003. Mem. Am. Correctional Assn. (chmn. com. profl. ethics 2004—), Am. Probation and Parole Assn. (Probation officer Yr. award 1981), Am. Soc. Pub. Adminstrn., Middle Atlantic States Correctional Assn. (pres. 1997-99, trustee 1979—, Achievement award 1989, Leadership award 1997, Founders award 2000), N.Y. State Probation Officers Assn. (pres. 1978-80). Roman Catholic. Office: Westchester County Correction Dept PO Box 389 Hdq Bldg Valhalla NY 10595-0389 Office Phone: 914-231-1102.

CZARNECKI, GERALD MILTON, investment banker, venture capitalist; b. Phila., Mar. 22, 1940; s. Casimir M. and Rose-Mary (Grajek) C.; m. Lois Rae DiJoseph, July 9, 1965; 1 dau., Robyn Alexandra. BS, Temple U., 1965; MA, Mich. State U., 1967; LHD (hon.), Nat. U., 1994. C.P.A., Ill., Tex. With Continental Bank, Chgo., 1968-79, v.p., operating gen. mgr. trust ops. and gen. mgr. corp. svcs., 1971-78; pres. Fla. Computing Svcs., 1979; exec. v.p. Houston Nat. Bank, 1979-82; sr. v.p. fin. Republic Bank Corp., 1982-83, exec. v.p., 1983-84; pres., CEO Altus Bank, 1984-87; chmn., chief exec. officer Bank of Am. Hawaii, Honolulu, 1987-93; sr. v.p. human resources and adminstrn. IBM Corp., Armonk, N.Y., 1993-94; pres. UNC Inc., Annapolis, Md., 1994-95; chmn., CEO Deltennium Group, Inc., Boca Raton, Fla., 1995—, Renaissance, Inc., 1999—2001, also bd. dirs. Mem. faculty DePaul U., Chgo., 1975-78; adj. prof. econs. Houston Bapt. U., 1980-82; mem. faculty Bank Adminstrn. Inst., 1978-85, Grad. Sch. Banking, U. Wis., 1979-86; chmn. bd. dirs. Inroads, Inc./Chgo., 1977-79, Inroads, Inc./Houston, 1981 vis. prof. Jones Sch. Bus., Rice U., 1980; adj. prof. policy and strategy So. Meth. U., 1983-84; mem. adv. com. Banking Ctr., Tex. So. U., 1980-82; chmn. securities processing sub-com. Am. Nat. Standards Inst., 1974-79, mem. Tuskegee Inst. State Adv. Coun., 1984-87; treas., mem. exec. com., bd. dirs. Nat. Coun. Savs. Instns., 1984-90; pres. thrift adv. coun. Fed. Res. Bd., 1986-90; bd. dirs. State Farm Ins. Cos.; chmn. bd. dirs. Great Clips Mid-Atlantic, Inc., 1997—2004, Deltennium Corp., 1996—; bd. dirs. State Farm Banks, ATM Nat., Inc.; chmn. bd. Renaissance, Inc., 1999-2004; mgr. bd. dirs., chmn. audit com. Del Global Techs. Inc. Contbr. articles to profl.

publs. Bd. dirs., treas. Hawaii Theatre Ctr., 1988-93; bd. dirs. Honolulu Econ. Devel. Corp., 1988-93, Nature Conservancy Hawaii, 1988-93, U. Hawaii Pres.' Coun., 1988-93, Aloha United Way, 1988-93; mem. Bus. Roundtable of Hawaii, 1989-93; chmn. Mil. Affairs Coun., 1992-93; mem. exec. and policy coms. Bus. Coun. N.Y. State, 1993-94; mem. adv. bd. Corp. Leadership Coun., 1993-94; nat. bd. dirs. Jr. Achievement, 1993—; trustee, vice chmn. Nat. U., 1994—, chair Nat. Leadership Inst, 2005—, InPractice, Inc., 2004—; bd. dirs. Jr. Achievement Worldwide, 1994—. Mem. AICPA, Am. Bankers Assn. (chmn. securities processing com. 1974-77, trust ops. com. 1978, mem. exec. com. ops. and automation div. 1980-83, rsch. com.), Am. Econ. Assn., Nat. Assn. Corp. Dirs. (bd. dirs. D.C. chpt. 1999—), Tex. Soc. CPAs, Fin. Execs. Inst., Consumer Bankers Assn. (bd. dirs. 1986-89), N. Am. Soc. Corp. Planners (bd. dirs. Dallas Chpt. 1982-83), Assn. for Corp. Growth, Orgn. Resource Counselors, Inc., Hawaii C. of C. (bd. dirs. 1988-89, chmn. bd. 1990-92), Omicron Delta Epsilon, Alpha Delta Phi. Office Phone: 561-620-2356. Business E-Mail: gmc@deltennium.com.

CZARNECKI, RITA MARIE, music educator, pianist; b. Akron, Ohio, Sept. 6, 1939; d. Charles Paul and Mary Margaret (Gerhart) Reymann; m. John Teddy Czarnecki, Oct. 22, 1982; 1 child, Annemarie. BA, Kent State U., 1961; MusM, Ind. U., 1966. Tchr. piano, music edn. pvt. practice, Akron, Ohio, 1967—. Lectr. music U. Akron, 1978-89; judge Nat. Guild Piano Tchrs. Mem. Nat. Guild Piano Tchrs., Ohio Music Tchrs. Assn. (publicity chmn. 1994-96), Friends of Music, Tuesday Mus. Club Akron, Delta Omicron, Pi Kappa Lambda. Avocations: homemaking, gardening, cooking, reading. Home: 154 Hollywood Ave Akron OH 44313-6750

CZARNY, FRANK SILVEY, social services administrator, consultant; b. Cincinnati, OH, Nov. 28, 1951; s. Doris Majura Harris, Frank Henry Harris. Bachelors of Arts in Psychology, Miami University, Oxford, Ohio, 1969—73, Masters of Arts in Teaching, 1973—75; Master of Arts in Organizational Development, Fielding Graduate Institute, Santa Barbara, CA., PhD in Human and Organizational Systems, 1998—2000. Social Problems Specialist Rockbridge Communications, Seattle, 1994—2002; Faculty, Undergraduate and Graduate Business Administration University of Phoenix, Seattle. President, Diversity Committee US West Communications, Carrier and Information Provider Division, Denver, 1993—94; Public Relations Correspondent US West Communications, 102+ Committee, Denver, 1989—90; Urban League Corporate Representative US West Communications, Carrier and Information Provider Division, Denver, 1993—94. Author: (Children's Paleontology Workshop) "Cookie Monsters", 1987 (Denver Natural History Museum Honorarium, 1987); performer: Cin. Youth Sumphony, 1968—69, Cin. All-City Youth Symphony, 1969. Workshop Presenter: "Communities of Faith and Public Education" Washington Education Association, Seattle; Member West Seattle Chamber of Commerce, Seattle, 2001—02. Recipient President's Club award, US West Communications Carrier and Information Provider Division, 1990; scholar Kenneth Kinnard scholarship, Kenneth Kinnard Found., 1969—73, Hebrew U. Summer Studies scholarship, Cin. Colored Woman's Assn., 1968. Mem.: NAACP, Urban League, American Black Anthropologists, American Anthropological Association. Avocation: RV, Snow Shoe, Ski, Hike. E-mail: fczarny@cox.net.

CZECH, MARK LYLE, music educator; b. Mpls., Minn., Mar. 6, 1962; s. Lyle John Czech, Evelyn Mae Czech; m. Heather Caech, Sept. 16, 1998; children: Dilan Michael, Connor James, Lindsay Rae. BS in Liberal Arts, Golden Valley Luth. Coll., 1983; BA in Music Edn., Augsburg Coll., 1985; MA in Curriculum and Instrn., U. St. Thomas, 1986. Tchr. orchestra Hopkins Pub. Schs., Hopkins, Minn., 1985—. Home: 660 Shawnee Woods Rd Medina MN 55340

CZEPIEL, LORI ANNE, lawyer; b. Chgo., Aug. 23, 1963; BA in economics, Northwestern U., 1981—84; JD cum laude, Boston U. Sch. of Law, 1984—87. Counsel, assoc. Skadden, Arps, Slate, Meagher & Flom LLP, Los Angeles, 1987—97; ptnr. Sidley Austin Brown & Wood LLP, New York, NY, 1997—. Current dir. and v.p., etc. prior roles Northwestern Alumni Assn., Evanston, Ill., 1998—2003; exec. bd. mem. and pac fundraising chair Young Executives of Am., Los Angeles, 1996—97; mem. Northwestern U. Coun. of 100, Evanston, Ill., 1998—2003. Mem.: Assn. of the Bar of the City of NY, ABA. Office: Sidley Austin Brown & Wood LLP 787 Seventh Ave New York NY 10019 Business E-Mail: lczepiel@sidley.com.

CZESTOCHOWSKI, JOSEPH STEPHEN, museum administrator; b. Bklyn., Aug. 6, 1950; s. Joseph Stephen and Julia (Skowron) C.; m. Debra J. Nicholson, Nov. 18, 1972; 1 child, J. F. Stefan Parker. Diploma, Jagiellonian U., Poland, 1971; BA, U. Ill., 1971, MA, 1973. Curator of collections Brooks Mus. Art, Memphis, 1973-75; dir. Decker Gallery, Md. Inst., Balt., 1975-78; exec. dir. Cedar Rapids (Iowa) Mus. Art, 1978-94; dir. The Dixon Gallery and Gardens, Memphis, 1994—. Sr. examiner Accreditation Commn. of the AAM; field reviewer Inst. Mus. Svcs.; govt. and art com. Assn. Art Mus. Dirs. Monographs include The Pioneers, 1977, Polish Posters, 1979, The Combined Works of Arthur B. Davies, 1980, Prints by Childe Hassam, 1980, John S. Curry and Grant Wood - A Portrait of Rural America, 1981, The American Landscape Tradition 1738-1965, 1982, Marvin D. Cone - An American Tradition, 1985, Arthur B. Davies - Catalogue Raisonne of Prints, 1988, Degas Complete Sculptures, 2002, Georgia O'Keeffe: Visions of the Sublime, 2004. Mem. adv. bd. Krannert Art Mus. Fellow Vatican Mus. and Smithsonian Inst., 1976, Smithsonian Instn., 1977-79; recipient first Nancy Hanks Meml. award for profl. excellence Am. Assn. Mus., 1985. Mem. Am. Assn. Mus. Dirs., Internat. Coun. Mus., The Kosciuszko Found. (trustee 1988-96), The Polish Inst. Arts and Scis. in Am., Inc. (trustee 1986—), Ctr. for the Study of the Presidency (trustee), Coll. Liberal Arts and Scis. U. Ill. Alumni Assn. (trustee 1994—), Rotary Internat. Office: Internat Arts 319 Goodwyn St Memphis TN 38111-3311 E-mail: interarts@parkers.com.

CZUMA, STANISLAW J., historian; b. Warsaw, Oct. 26, 1935; s. Wladyslaw and Wanda Ligon Czuma; m. Ingrid Zollinger; 1 child, Lesley Breitner. BA, Jagiellon U., 1953, MA, 1957; grad. studies, Banares Hindu U., 1958—59, Calcutta U., 1958—59, Sor Bonne, 1960—61; PhD, U. Mich., 1961—68. Rsch. asst. U. Mich., Ann Arbor, Mich., 1963—68; post doctoral intern Clev. Mus. of Art, Cleve., 1968—69; curator, asian art Bklyn. Mus. Art, Bklyn., 1969—72; prof. Asian art Case Western Reserve U., Cleve., 1972—2000; cuartor, Indian & SE Asian Art Cleve. Mus. Art, Cleve., 1972—. Office: Cleve Mus Art Assn Dept 111150 Cleveland OH 44106 Office Phone: 216-707-2230. Business E-Mail: sczuma@clevelandart.org.

DAAB-KRZYKOWSKI, ANDRE, pharmaceutical and nutritional manufacturing company administrator; b. Warsaw, May 16, 1949; came to U.S., 1973, naturalized, 1981; s. Aleksy Czeslaw Crest Polkozic and Zofia (Dyszkiewicz crest Kudrys) Krzykowski; 1 child, Cecylia. MSChemE, Tech. U., Warsaw, 1973; MBA, Memphis State U., 1979. Rsch. chemist Schering-Plough, Memphis, 1974-77; process control mgr. Ralston Purina Co., Memphis, 1977-80; dir. pharm. projects Bristol-Myers Squibb Co., Mayaguez, P.R., 1980-90; process devel. group mgr. R&D Ross Labs. divsn. Abbott Labs., 1990—. Patentee in field. Served to 2d lt. Polish Army Res. Mem. Am. Mgmt. Assn., Am. Chem. Soc., Toastmasters (pres. local chpt. 1986). Republican. Lutheran. Avocations: sailing, scuba diving, Karate. Office: Ross Labs 625 Cleveland Ave Columbus OH 43215-1724 Office Phone: 614-624-3966. Business E-Mail: andre.daab-krzykowski@abbott.com.

DAANE, JAMES DEWEY, banker; b. Grand Rapids, Mich., July 6, 1918; s. Gilbert L. and Mamie (Blocksma) D.; m. Blanche M. Tichenor, Apr. 28, 1941 (div. 1952); 1 dau., Elizabeth Marie Daane Mallek; m. Onnie B. Selby, Jan. 23, 1953 (dec. Dec. 1961); m. Barbara W. McMann, Feb. 16, 1963; children: Elizabeth Whitney, Olivia Quartel. AB magna cum laude, Duke U., 1939; MPA, Harvard U., 1946, D in Pub. Adminstrn. (Littauer fellow), 1949. With Fed. Res. Bank, Richmond, Va., 1939-60, asst. v.p., 1953-57, v.p., 1957-60, also cons. to pres. bank, adviser to pres. Mpls., 1960; asst. to sec. treasury, 1960-61; dep. undersec. treasury for monetary affairs, 1961-63; mem. bd. govs. Fed. Reserve System, Washington, 1963-74; vice chmn. bd. dirs. Commerce Union Bank, Sovran Bank/Cen. South, Nashville, 1974-78; chmn. internat. policy com. Commerce Union Corp., 1978-87; dir. Nat. Futures Assn., Ill., 1983—2002; chmn. internat. policy com Sovran Fin. Corp., Nashville, 1988; chmn. money market com. Commerce Union Bank, 1974-87; chmn. money market com. cen. S. Sovran Bank, 1988-90. Assoc. economist Fed. Open Market Com., 1955-56, 58-59; chief IMF Fiscal Mission to Paraquay, 1950-51; vice chmn. Tennessee Valley Bancorp. Inc., 1975-78; Frank K. Houston prof. banking and fin. Owen Grad. Sch. Mgmt., Vanderbilt U., 1974-85, Valere Blair Potter prof. banking and fin., 1985-89, Frank K. Houston prof. emeritus, 1989—, Alan R. Holmes prof. econs. Middlebury Coll., 1991-93; bd. dirs. Chgo. Bd. of Trade, 1979-82; prof. fin. Vanderbilt U. Editor: (with David C. Colander) The Art of Monetary Policy. Bd. advisers Patterson Sch. Diplomacy and Internat. Commerce, U. Ky. Mem. J.F. Kennedy Sch. Govt. Assn. of Harvard U., Am. Econ. Assn., Am. Finance Assn. Home: 102 Westhampton Pl Nashville TN 37205-3439 Office: Vanderbilt U Owen Grad Sch Mgmt 401 21st Ave N Nashville TN 37203 Office Phone: 615-322-3632. E-mail: dewey.daane@owen.vanderbilt.edu.

DAARSTAD, ERIK, cinematographer; b. Fjotland, Norway, June 27, 1935; arrived in U.S., 1953; s. Even Olsen Daarstad and Margit Elida Johnsen; m. Louanne Jo Frye, July 6, 1963; children: Kari Ann, Heather Britt, Erik Even. BA, U. So. Calif., 1957. Pres. Stadmor Film Co., Inc., Manhattan Beach, Calif., 1966—76; dir. photography Nat. Geog. Soc., Metro-Goldwyn-Mayer, Walt Disney; dir. photograph PBS, Am. Film Found., Saul Bass & Assocs., others. Dir. photography: (documentaries) The Exiles, 1961 (Golden Ducat award); Why Man Creates, 1969 (Acad. award); The Great Whales, 1978 (Emmy award); Four Stones for Kanemitsu, 1974 (Acad. award nomination); The Incredible Machine, 1975 (Acad. award nomination); Notes on the Performing Arts, 1977 (Acad. award nomination); Never Give Up, 1995 (Acad. award nomination); Sing!, 2002 (Acad. award nomination); Mysteries of the Mind, 1980 (Emmy award); Superliners: Twilight of an Era, 1980 (Emmy award, Peabody award). Bd. dirs. Pend Oreille Arts Coun., 1999—2001, Bonner County Hist. Soc., 2001—03, Panida Theater, 2004—. With U.S. Army, 1959—61. Named Citizen of Yr., Sandpoint (Idaho) C. of C., 2002; recipient Cert. Commendation, Am. Assn. State and Local History, 2003. Democrat. Avocations: skiing, photography. Home: 1504 Northshore Dr Sandpoint ID 83864 Fax: 208-263-5790. Personal E-mail: eriklou@bossig.com.

DABBAGH, MAHMOUD, language educator, researcher; b. Damascus, Syria, Aug. 14, 1964; s. Anwar Al Dabbagh and Najah al Zaim; m. Rana Dabbagh, May 30, 2005; 1 stepchild, Hilal Alsibai; children: Maher, Dania. BA, MA with honors, U. Damascus, 1987; degree in extensive studies, with highest distinction, Sorbonne Paris V, 1990; PhD with highest distinction, Sorbonne Paris III, 1997. Cert. translator Arabic-French-English French Translators' Assn. Secondary sch. tchr. Umar Bin Abdel-Aziz Sch., Damascus, 1986—87; accredited translatory interpreter Tenth Mediterranean Games, Damascus, Syria, 1987; French tchr. For Adults Lang. Sch., Paris, 1991; interpreter, sales rep. Orient-Export, Paris, 1988—98; translator Al-Farabi Pub. Ho., Damascus and Paris, 1999; postdoctoral rschr. Sorbonne Ctr. Arabic Studies, Paris, 1997—99; Arabic instr. Mil. Linguists-Joint Lang. Ctr., Augusta, Ga., 2002; adj. lectr. course bldg. French, Arabic SUNY, Brockport, 2002—, Nazareth Coll., Rochester, 2002—. Author (translator): The Non-Observance of the Four Doctrines: The Most Dangerous Heresy that Threatens Divine Law, 1999. Mem.: French Translators Assn., French Embassy Cultural Ctr., Alliance Francaise (Rochester), Cercle Francais Nazareth Coll. Avocations: reading, computer science, literary theory. Office: SUNY Fgn Lang and Lit 350 New Campus Dr Brockport NY 14420-2914 Home: 2025 E Henrietta Rd Apt 1 Rochester NY 14623 Office Phone: 585-265-9654. Personal E-mail: mdabbagh@rochester.rr.com. Business E-Mail: mdabbagh@brockport.edu.

DABDOUB, PAUL OSCAR, academic administrator; b. La Lima, Honduras, July 7, 1946; came to U.S., 1955; s. Jacob Abraham and Helen (McNabb) D.; m. Lorrie Suzanne Shell, Aug. 9, 1993; children by previous marriage: Desiree, John Kelly, Paul Jacob. B of Bible, Open Bible Coll., 1983; student, Liberty U., 1979; M of Theology, D of Pastoral Theology, Andersonville Bapt. Sem., 1996. Fin. mgr. 3d Nat. Bank, Nashville, 1973-78; min. Mooring Bapt. Ch., Tiptonville, Tenn., 1978-79, Kinfolks Ridge Bapt. Ch., Caruthersville, Mo., 1979-80; min., founder Victory Bapt. Ch., Caruthersville, 1980-91; adminstr., founder, min. Victory Bapt. Acad., Caruthersville, 1984—91; min. Ridge Meml. Bapt. Ch., Slidell, La., 1991—; sci. instr. Northlake Christian Sch., Covington, La., 1991. Founder, pres., instr. Slidell Bapt. Sem., 1994—. Avocation: wild turkey hunting. Home: 106 Jane St Slidell LA 70461 Office Phone: 985-726-9600. Personal E-mail: bpdkjvi@aol.com.

DABERKO, DAVID A., banker; b. Hudson, Ohio, 1945; BA, Denison U., 1967; MBA, Case Western Res. U., 1970. Mgmt. trainee Nat. City Bank, Cleve., 1968-72, asst. v.p., 1972-73, v.p. bank investment divsn., dept. head met. lending divsn., 1973-80, sr. v.p. corp. banking, 1980-82, pres., 1987-93; exec. v.p. corp. banking Nat. City Corp., Nat. City Bank, Cleve., 1982-85; pres., bd. dirs. Nat. City Bank (formerly BancOhio Nat. Bank), Columbus, 1985-87; dep. chmn. Nat. City Corp., Cleve., 1987-93, pres., CEO, 1993-95, chmn., CEO, 1995—. Dir. Fed. Res. Bank, Cleve. Trustee Cleve. Tomorrow, Greater Cleve. Growth Assn., Case Western Res. U., Hawken Sch., Neighborhood Progress, Univ. Cir. Inc., Univ. Hosp. Health Sys.; co-chair Harvest for Hunger Campaign, 1992, 93. Mem. Bankers Roundtable. Office: Nat City Corp National City Center 1900 E 9th St Cleveland OH 44114-3401

DABERKOW, CHRISTINE, management consultant; b. Washington, June 7, 1977; d. Stan and Julie Daberkow. BS in Acctg. (hon.), U. Md., 1999. Cert. Govt. Fin. Mgr., 2001. Acct./sales Book Makers Internat., Riverdale, Md., 1994—95; acct. Office of Dr. Jeanne Chamberlain, Columbia, Md., 1996—97; acctg. intern Orbital Scis. Corp., Germantown, Md., 1997—97, Gonzalez & Assocs., Pub. Accts., Riverdale, Md., 1998—98, ARINC, Annapolis, Md., 1998—99; tax acct. Peacock, Condron, Anderson, & Co., CPA Firm, Columbia, Md., 1998—99; interviewer/survey adminstr. R.O.W Scis. and Fed. Data Corp., Rockville, Md., 1999—99; tutor University Park, Md., 1996—; mgmt. cons. Price WaterhouseCoopers Consulting, Arlington, Va., 1999—. Mem.: Inst. Mgmt. Accts. Roman Catholic. Avocations: travel, swimming. Office: Price Waterhouse Coopers Consulting 1616 North Fort Myer Dr Arlington VA 22209 Office Phone: 703-741-1559. Home Fax: 703-322-2819. Personal E-mail: christine.nasser.daberkow@us.pwcglobal.com.

DABICH, ELI, JR., insurance company executive; b. Chgo., June 7, 1939; s. Eli and Helen (Radakovich) D.; m. Eileen Dabich, June 8, 1963; children: Michael, Charles, Mary, Kathleen BS, U.S. Naval Acad., 1963; MS, George Washington U., 1970. Mktg. rep. IBM, Balt., 1970-74; sr. v.p. adminstrn. Sun Life, Atlanta, 1974-82; sr. exec. v.p. adminstrn. and fin. Md. Casualty Co., Balt., 1982-88; nat. dir. ins. cons. Coopers & Lybrand, N.Y.C., 1988-90; sr. v.p. Nationale Nederlanden, Washington, 1990-93; sr. v.p., chief adminstrv. officer TIG Ins. Co., 1993-95; pres. Synergy 2000 Inc., 1995—. Bd. dirs. Ivans. Pres. Oak Hill Elem. Sch., PTA, Severna Park, Md., 1970; sec. U.S. Naval Acad., Annapolis, Md., 1963-70; bd. dirs. Ins. Tech., Securities Software & Cons. Capt. USN, 1963-85. Home: 2815 Cox Neck Rd Chester MD 21619-2345 Office Phone: 410-643-5563.

DABINETT, DIANA FRANCES, artist; d. Leslie Frank and Ivy Annie May; m. Patrick Dabinett, Aug. 1969; children: Emily Thomas. BA in fine arts, U. Cape Town, 1963. H.S. art tchr., Zimbabwe, 1965-66; H.S. English tchr., 1967-69; asst. curator London (Ont.) Art Gallery, 1969-73. Visual arts advisor, adv. panel Fed.-Prov. Cultural Agreement, Nfld., Canada, 1992—2000; Can. artists rep., Nfld. and Labrador, 1980—97; artist in residence, Hopedale, Labrador, 1988—99, Gros Morne Park, Nfld., 2001. One-woman shows include St. John's, 1989-92, Lunenberg, N.S., 1992, Christina Parker Fine Art St. John's, 1994, 98, 2000, 02, 04, Can. Embassy Tokyo, 2001, Can. Embassy Washington, 2003, Argyle Fine Art Gallery, Halifax, 2003, Prince Edward Island, Can., 2004; two-person exhbn. Pathways, 1997-99; exhibited in group shows at Discovery Travelling Maritimes, 1997; commd. works at Birthing Ctr. and Cancer Ctr., Cmty. Hosp. of the Monterey Peninsula, St. Lawrence Hosp. and Labrador Health Ctr., Newfoundland, N.S. Health and Welfare Dept. Halifax; illustrator: Icebergs-Castles in the Sea, 2000; collection HRH Queen Elizabeth II. Mem.: Canadian Soc. Water Colour Painters. Avocations: reading, snow shoeing, hiking. Address: Box 1005 Torbay NL Canada A1K 1K9 Business E-Mail: dianadabinett@nl.rogers.com.

DABNEY, H. SLAYTON, JR., lawyer; b. Charlottesville, Va., Sept. 14, 1949; s. Hovey S. and Patricia S (Schmidt) D.; m. Donna C. Warns, Jan. 14, 1983; children: Slayton, Kate, Andrew. BA, U. Va., 1971, JD, 1974. Bar: Va. 1974, U.S. Dist. Ct. (ea. and we. dists.) Va., U.S. Bankruptcy Ct. (ea. and we. dists.) Va., U.S. Ct. Appeals (4th cir.), U.S. Dist. Ct. D.C. Ptnr. King & Spalding, LLP, N.Y.C. Mem. ABA, Am. Bankruptcy Inst. Office: King & Spalding LLP 1185 Avenue of the Americas New York NY 10036-4003 Office Phone: 212-556-2287. Business E-Mail: sdabney@kslaw.com.

D'ABRAMO, LOUIS R., zoologist, educator; s. Louis J. and Mary A. D'Abramo; children: Jason E., Erin M. BA, Assumption Coll., Worcester, Mass., 1974, Doctorate (hon.); PhD, MPhil, Yale U., 1979. Postgrad. rsch. nutritionist U. Calif., Davis, 1979—84; prof. Miss. State U., 1984—. Named Disting. Prof., Miss. State U., 2003; named to Hall of Fame, Waterbury, Conn., Silas Bronson Libr., 2004; recipient John Grisham Master Tchr. award, Miss. State U., 2000—01, Exemplary Svc. award, World Aquaculture Soc., 2003. Achievements include patents for formulated diet for larval fish and crustaceans. Office: Miss State Univ Box 9690 Mississippi State MS 39762 Office Phone: 662-325-7492. Office Fax: 662-325-8726. Personal E-mail: ldabramo@cfr.msstate.edu.

DABROWSKA, DOROTA MARIA, statistician, educator; b. Warsaw, Dec. 10, 1954; arrived in U.S., 1981, naturalized, 1992; d. Emma Katalin Juhasz-Dabrowska and Cyryl Alfons Dabrowski. MA in Math., Warsaw U., 1978; PhD in Stats., U. Calif., Berkeley, 1984. Rsch. assoc. Polish Acad. Sci., Warsaw, 1978—81; asst. prof. Carnegie-Mellon U., Pitts., 1984—88, UCLA, 1988—91, assoc. prof., 1991—96, prof., 1996—. Assoc. editor: Jour. Multivariate Analysis, 1999—, Lifetime Data Analysis, 2002—, Annals of Statistics, 2004—; contbr. articles to profl. jours. Recipient Evelyn Fix Meml. medal, U. Calif., 1984; grantee, NSF, 1989—2003, NIH, 1995—2003; Earl C. Anthony fellow, U. Calif., 1981—82, Regents fellow, 1982—83, UC Presdl. fellow, 1986—88. Fellow: Inst. Math. Stats.; mem.: Biometric Soc., Bernoulli Soc., Am. Statis. Assn. Roman Catholic. Avocations: music, travel, art. Office: Univ Calif LA Sch Pub Health/Biostatistics Los Angeles CA 90095-1772

DABROWSKI, EDWARD JOHN, television technical director; b. Chgo., Nov. 16, 1957; s. Edward J. and Justina J. (Grilc) D. BS in Elec. Engring., Ill. Inst. Tech., Chgo., 1979. Engr. Sta. WMAQ-TV, Chgo., 1976-83, tech. dir., 1983—; engr.-in-charge The Jenny Jones Show, 1995. Tech. dir. (NBC afternoon spl.) The Sixth Street Kids, 1984, (WMAQ-TV docu-drama) Fast Break to Glory: Dusable Panthers, 1988, Chgo. Sisslin (Chgo. Emmy award 1989), Chgo. Bears Pre-Season football, 1993, Engring. Devel. Group, 1996—. Emmy nomination, Chgo. Chpt., 1998; recipient Emmy award, 2000, 03; 1999 Millennium Spl. Coverage award, Tech. award Chgo. Marathon 2002 Mem. IEEE, Soc. Broadcast Engrs., NATAS (Emmy nominations Chgo. chpt. 1986), Nat. Assn. Broadcast Employees and Technicians (steward Chgo. chpt. 1981-87, mobilization coord. Chgo. 1994-95), Natl. Assn. of Broadcast Employees and Technicians, Broadcasting and Cable Television Workers Sector of the Communications Workers of Amer., AFL-CIO Steward and Exec. Bd. Mem. Chgo. Local 41 1999—, Am. Radio Relay League (life), Chgo.-Suburban Radio Assn., Mus. Broadcast Comm. (charter), Am. Fraternal Union, Slovene Nat. Benefit Soc. (rec. sec. lodge 449, pres. Chgo. dist. 2003—) Democrat. Roman Catholic. Avocations: amateur radio, photography. Office: Sta WMAQ-TV NBC Tower 454 N Columbus Dr Chicago IL 60611-5514 Office Phone: 312-836-5522. E-mail: edward.dabrowski@nbc.com.

DABROWSKI, THADDEUS E., art educator, art consultant, painter; b. Bronx, N.Y., July 17, 1945; s. Theodore J. and Wanda K. (Curylo) D.; m. Althea M. Smith, May 17, 1970; children: Veronika D. Bulkin, Sibyl T. Jayne. BBA, U. Mass., 1968, MFA, 1970, MEd, 1972. Tech. specialist U. Mass., Amherst, 1972-78, adminstrv. asst., 1978-95, textbook adminstr., 1995—2001, adj. lectr. art, 1981—; art edn. cons., 2001—. Pres., v.p., treas. Leverette (Mass.) Artists and Craftsmen, 1982—; mem. Pub. Arts Commn., Amherst, 1990-94; cons. Nat. Edn. Systems, Amherst, 2001—. Solo exhbns. include Campus Cinema, Hadley, Mass., 1968, U. Mass. Student Union Gallery, Amherst, 1970, Leverett (Mass.) Crafts and Art Ctr., 1990, Burnett Gallery, Jones Libr., Amherst, 1995; showcase artist New Eng. Arts Festival, U. Mass., 1983. Loaned exec., mem. cabinet United Way of Hampshire, Amherst, 1987-2002; mem. Commonwealth of Mass. Employees Charitable Campaign Com., 1987—, Region 4 Charity Application Rev. Com., 1987-2003; elected town meeting mem. Town of Amherst, 2001—. Recipient Milton Bradley award Springfield (Mass.) Art League, 1976. Mem. NEA, Nat. Art Edn. Assn., Mass. Tchrs. Assn., Mass. Assn. for Ednl. Tech. (charter), Univ. Staff Assn. (steward, chief steward 1995-02), Rotary (sec. Amherst 1989-91, v.p. 1991-92, pres. 1992-93, Paul Harris fellow 1984—). Avocations: classic automobile preservation, piano, computer systems. Home: 9 Squire Ln Amherst MA 01002-3232 Office: U Mass Dept Art Amherst MA 01003 Business E-Mail: thaddeus@art.umass.edu.

D'ABRUZZO, STEPHANIE, actress; Grad., Northwestern U. Actor: (off-broadway plays) Avenue Q, 2003 (Drama Desk nominee, 2003); (TV series) Sesame Street, 1993—, The Wubbulous World of Dr. Seuss, 1996—98, Oobi, 2003—04, (voice actor) Sheep in the Big City, 2000—01, The Book of Pooh, 2000—01, Proof of Life on Earth, 2005,: (films) The Adventures of Elmo in Grouchland, 1999, Sesame Street 4D, 2003; (Broadway plays) Carnival, 2002, Chess, 2003—, Avenue Q, 2003 (Tony nominee, 2004, Theatre World award, 2004, Outer Critics Circle Special Ensemble award). Office: Golden Theater 252 W 45th St New York NY 10036

DACBERT-FRIESE, SHARYN VARHELY, social worker, evangelist; b. Utica, N.Y., Dec. 10, 1947; d. Henry Alexander Varhely and Elouise Fulmore; m. Thomas Jewett Mitchell III, Oct. 20, 1968 (div. Dec. 1982); children: Sharyn Mitchell Wallace, James Bailey Mitchell, Jaclyn Ashley Mitchell; m. Guenther Roland Friese, Dec. 16, 1998. BA, U. Ala., 1968; MSW, Our Lady of the Lake U., San Antonio, Tex., 1991. Lic. master social worker Advanced Clin. Practitioner, 1991, cert. clin. supr. 1998, LCSW 2003. Entrepreneur, Laredo, Tex., 1972—85; founder, owner Jacob's Well, Laredo, Tex., 1980—87; corp. v.p. Dacbert Music Co., San Antonio, 1992—94; individual and family psychotherapist Fuller & Assocs., San Antonio, 1991—94; pvt. practice San Antonio, 1994—; sr. pastor, founder, pres., chmn. Sheepgate Fellowship, San Antonio, 1997—; dir., founder, pres., chmn. Christian Family Counseling Ctr., San Antonio, 1997—. Radio personality, counselor Sta. KSLR-AM, San Antonio, 1997—2001; individual and family psychotherapist Adult Parent Child, San Antonio, 1991—92. Contbr. articles to profl. jours. Mem.: NASW, Nat. Assn. Bus. and Profl. Women, Am. Assn. Christian Counselors, Play Therapy Assn., Tuesday Musical Club. Avocations: painting, camping, drawing, cooking, quilting. Office: Christian Family Counseling Ctr PO Box 460686 San Antonio TX 78246 Office Phone: 210-533-9250. Personal E-mail: sdacbert1@aol.com.

D'ACCONE, FRANK ANTHONY, music educator; b. Somerville, Mass., June 13, 1931; s. Salvatore and Maria (DiChiappari) D'A. Mus. B., Boston U., 1952, Mus.M., 1953; A.M., Harvard U., 1955, PhD, 1960. Asst. prof. music SUNY at Buffalo, 1960-63, assoc. prof., 1964-68; prof. music UCLA, 1968-94, chmn. dept., 1973-76; chmn. faculty UCLA (Coll. Fine Arts), 1976-79; chmn. dept. musicology UCLA, 1989-93. Vis. prof. music Yale U., 1972-73 Author: The History of a Baroque Opera, 1985, The Civic Muse, 1997; editor: Music of the Florentine Renaissance, vols. 1-12, 1967-94; gen. editor Corpus Mensurabilis Musicae, 1986-2001; co-editor Musica Disciplina, 1990-2001; contbr. articles to profl. jours. Fellow Am. Acad. Rome,

1963-64, Fulbright Found., 1963-64, NEH, 1975; recipient G.K. Delmas Venetian Studies award, 1977, J.S. Guggenheim Found. award, 1980, Internat. Galilei prize, Pisa, 1997. Fellow Am. Acad. of Arts and Scis.; mem. Am. Musicol. Soc. (dir. 1973-74), Internat. Musicol. Soc. Home: 725 Fontana Way Laguna Beach CA 92651-4010 Office: U Calif Dept Music Los Angeles CA 90024

DACEK, JOANNE CAROLE, psychologist; b. Oceanside, N.Y., July 26, 1963; d. Gerald S. and Teresa E. (Iusi) Martinis; m. Stephen T. Dacek, Jan. 17, 1988; children: Stephen Thomas, Mark Brendan, Megan Michelle, Phoebe Lauren, Benjamin Ryan. BA, Adelphi U., 1984; MS, Syracuse U., 1987; MA, Sem. of Immaculate Conception, 1995. Cert. sch. psychologist. Psychologist Greece (N.Y.) Ctrl. Schs., 1987-90, Bellmore (N.Y.) Union Free Sch. Dist., 1990-95; chair C.S.E., Bellmore (N.Y.) Unified Sch. Dist., 1995—98. Office: Bellmore Unified Sch Dist 2750 S Saint Marks Ave Bellmore NY 11710-5016

DACEY, PAUL, artist; b. Toledo, July 16, 1960; s. Eleanor Dacey. BFA in Painting, Cleve. Inst. Art, 1984; course, Artists Environ. Found., 1982, Lacoste Summer Arts Program, France, 1982. Artist (commns.) Nokia US Hdqrs., Dallas, 1999, Credit Suisse First Boston, London, 1999—2000, US Embassy, Ottawa, Can., 1999, Kampala, Uganda, 2000, (prin. works) Maxwell Davidson Gallery, NYC, Morgan Lehman Gallery, Lakeville, Conn., (one-man shows) Reconfigured, Interchurch Ctr., NYC, 1996, Wash. Square Windows, N.Y.U., 1998, World Without End, St. Peter's Ch., 1999, Maxwell Davidson Gallery, N.Y.C., 1999, Manifest Destiny, Maxwell Davidson Gallery, 2001, (group shows) ADAA, Art of the 20th Century, NYC, San Francisco Art Expo, Art Chgo., Art Miami, Art Cologne, Maxwell Davidson Gallery, Nancy Hoffman Gallery, N.Y.C., Qualita Fine Art, Las Vegas, Washington Sq. East Gallery, NYU, Art L.A., Kunstverein Neuenhaus, Germany, 101 Calif., San Francisco, Toledo Mus. Art, Ohio, (permanent collections) Cleary Gottlieb, Steen & Hamilton, NYC, Progressive Mayfield Village, Ohio, Dechart, Price & Rhoads, NYC, Novell, San Jose, Toledo Mus. Art, featured (book authored by Fre Ilgen) ART? No Thing! (Analogies between Art, Science, Philosophy). Ellen Battell Stoeckel fellow, Yale U., 1983. Home and Office: Apt 23 35-21 80th St Jackson Heights NY 11372 Office Phone: 718-457-6637. Personal E-mail: pauldacey@earthlink.net.

DACH, LESLIE ALAN, public relations company executive; b. N.Y.C., Apr. 17, 1954; s. Joseph and Edith (Lipsyzc) D.; m. Mary Ann Dickie, Nov. 19, 1983; children: Jonathan Alexander, Eliza May. BS in Biology, Yale U., 1975; MPA, Harvard U., 1981. Staff scientist Environ. Def. Fund., Washington, 1977-79; assoc. dir. Nat. Audubon Soc., Washington, 1981-84, legis. dir., 1984-87; dir. scheduling Mondale-Ferraro campaign, Washington, 1984; spl. asst. to chmn. U.S. Senate Agr. Com., Washington, 1987; dir. comm. Dukakis for Pres., Boston, 1987-88; sr. v.p. Edelman Pub. Rels., Washington, 1989-90, exec. v.p., 1990-96, vice chmn., 1996—. Office: Edelman Pub Rels 1875 Eye St NW Ste 900 Washington DC 20006-5422

DACHOWSKI, PETER RICHARD, manufacturing executive; b. Hillingdon, Middlesex, Eng., June 2, 1948; came to U.S., 1969; s. Teodor and Mary D.; m. Victoria Kaplan, May 1, 1977. MA in Econs. with first class honors, Queens' Coll., Cambridge, Eng., 1969; MBA, U. Chgo., 1971. Fin. analyst Exxon Corp., 1971-73; mgr. Boston Cons. Group, 1973-76; asst. treas. CertainTeed Corp., Valley Forge, Pa., 1976-78, asst. to CEO, 1979-80; v.p. planning and devel. CertainTeed Co., Valley Forge, Pa., 1980-81, v.p., treas., 1981-83, v.p., compt., 1983-85; v.p., pres. Roofing Products Group, 1985-90, Vinyl Bldg. Products Group, Valley Forge, 1987-90; sr. v.p., pres. Exterior Products Group, 1990-93, exec. v.p., 1994—96, pres., CEO, 2004—. Mem. corp. devel. staff Saint Gobain, Paris, 1978—79; pres. Worldwide Insulation Saint-Gobain, 1996—2004; adv. coun. U. Chgo. Grad. Sch. Bus., 2001—; bd. dirs. Ball Hort. Co., C&D Techs. Mem. Joint Ctr. Housing Studies Harvard U., 1990-; trustee Internat. House of Phila., 1994-96, 2004-; bd. dirs. Phila. Orch. Assn., 2002—, Nat. Bldg. Material Distbrs. Assn., 2005—. Recipient Wall St. Jour. award Dow Jones-Chgo., 1971. Mem.: Union League Phila., Alliance Francaise Phila. (trustee 1994—96), Brit.-Am. C. of C., World Pres. Orgn., Beta Gamma Sigma. Avocations: travel, listening to live music, sailing, scuba diving. Home: 321 Woodmont Cir Berwyn PA 19312-1431 Office: CertainTeed Corp PO Box 860 Valley Forge PA 19482-0860 Office Phone: 610-341-7749.

DACHTYL, CARY, music educator; b. Cleve., Oct. 4, 1957; s. Edward Joseph Dachtyl and Sophia Catherine Januszok; m. Linda Lee Dauwalder, Feb. 11, 1989. BS in Math., Baldwin-Wallace Coll., 1978, MusB in Music Edn., 1979; MusM in Percussion, MA in Math Edn., Ohio State U., 1984, PhD in Music, 1993. Cert. tchr. music Ohio Dept. Edn., tchr. math. Ohio Dept. Edn. Instr. computer graphic arts Columbus (Ohio) State C. C., 1978—79; tchr. math and music Elyria (Ohio) West H.S., 1979—82; network mgr. Ohio Divsn. Securities, Columbus, 1993—2002; instr. percussion Kenyon Coll., Gambier, Ohio, 2000—. Dir. music Welsh Hills Symphony Orch., Granville, Ohio, 2002—, bd. dirs. Mem.: Percussive Arts Soc. (pres. Ohio chpt. 2004—), Am. Fedn. Musicians (assoc.). Roman Catholic. Avocations: audio recording, woodworking, travel. Personal E-mail: cdachtyl@earthlink.net.

DACIER, PAUL T., electronics company executive, lawyer; b. Boston, Dec. 21, 1957; BA, Marquette U., 1980, JD, 1983. Bar: Wis. 1983, Mass. 1995. Assoc. counsel Apollo Computer, Inc., 1984-85, counsel, 1985-87, sr. counsel, 1987-89; corp. counsel EMC Corp., 1990—92, gen. counsel, 1993—, v.p., 1993—2000, sr. v.p., 2000—. Mem. Mass. Bar Assn., State Bar Wis. (v.p., gen. counsel). Office: EMC Corp PO Box 368 171 South St Hopkinton MA 01748-2222

DACKAWICH, S. JOHN, sociology educator, academic administrator; b. Loch Gelley, W.Va., Jan. 31, 1926; s. Samuel and Estelle (Jablonski) D.; m. Shirley Jean McVay, May 20, 1950; children: Robert John, Nancy Joan. BA, U. Md., 1955; PhD, U. Colo., 1958. Instr. U. Colo., 1955-57, Colo. State U., 1957-59; prof., chmn. sociology Calif. State U., Long Beach, 1959-70, prof. sociology Fresno, 1970-94, chmn. dept., 1970-75, prof. sociology emeritus, 1994—. Pvt. practice survey rsch., 1962-. Author: Sociology, 1970, The Fiery Furnace Effect, 2000; contbr. articles and rsch. papers to profl. publs. Mem. Calif. Dem. Ctrl. Com., 1960-62; co-dir. Long Beach Ctrl. Area Study, 1962-64, Citizen Participation Study, Fresno. With USMCR, 1943-46, U.S. Army, 1950-53. Mem. Am. Sociol. Assn., Pacific Sociol. Assn. Home: 5841 W Judy Ct Visalia CA 93277-8601 Office: Calif State U Dept Sociology 5340 N Campus Dr Fresno CA 93740-8019

DACONTI, JOSE RAFAEL, electric power industry executive, consultant; b. Recife, Brazil, Oct. 6, 1954; arrived in U.S., 2001; s. Jose Daconti Neto and Inalda Viegas Daconti; m. Liege Carolina Riker Daconti, July 18, 1981; children: Leticia Riker, Leonardo Riker, Renata Riker. MSEE with honors, Fed. Engrng. Sch. Itajuba, Brazil, 1986. Cert. specialist in electric power sys., Fed. Engrng. Sch. Itajuba, 1981. Engr. CHESF, Recife, 1978—98; ind. cons. Recife, 1998—2001; exec. cons. Siemens Power Techs. Internat., Schenectady, NY, 2001—. Hubert H. Humphrey fellow, U.S. Congress, Cornell U., 1997. Mem.: CIGRE (disting mem.), IEEE (Schenectady chmn. PES chpt.), Sigma Xi. Office: Siemens PTI 1482 Erie Blvd Schenectady NY 12301-1058 Office Phone: 518-395-5090. Personal E-mail: daconti@ieee.org.

DACORTE, ALLAN FRANCIS, financial consultant; b. Evergreen Park, Ill., June 30, 1946; s. Cyrus (Pat) DaCorte and Helen Regina Nachman. BA, Maryknoll Coll., 1969; MDiv, Cath. Theol. Union, Chgo., 1971. Ordained priest Roman Cath. Ch., 1971. Dir. candidate formation Franciscan Friars, Joliet, Ill., 1989—96, dir. fin. St. Louis, 1996—2002. Cons. Order of Friars Minor, Rome, 1989—91. Contbr. Ratio Formationis, 1992. Trustee Quincy (Ill.) U., 1988—93, 1999—2002, Padua HS, Parma, Ohio, 1997—99. Mem.: Franciscan English Spking Conf. Treas., Nat. Assn. Treas. Religious Insts. (exec. com. 2000—02, pres. 2002—, bd. dirs. 1999—2002). Roman Catholic. Avocations: music, travel, sports. Home: 3140 Meramec St Saint Louis MO 63118 Office: Franciscan Friars Office Fin 3140 Meramec St Saint Louis MO 63118 Office Phone: 314 353-7470.

D'ADDARIO, ALICE MARIE, retired school system administrator; b. N.Y.C., Feb. 9, 1942; d. Ralph and Rose Marie (Ventigmiglia) DeMartino; m. Joseph L. D'Addario, June 27, 1964; children: Joseph R., Paul T. BS in Social Studies, St. John's U., 1962, MS in Secondary Edn., 1963; MA in Liberal Studies, NYU, 1981. Cert. sch. adminstr., secondary educator of English and Social Studies, N.Y. Tchr. social studies So. Huntington Schs., Huntington Station, NY, 1963-83; dept. chair Walt Whitman H.S., Huntington Station, 1983—2005. Adj. prof. Adelphi U., Garden City, N.Y., 1989-02, inservice instr. S. Hungington Tchr. Ctr., 2002—; tchg. adv. panelist, program reviewer America, Pathways to the Present, Prentice Hall, 1998, program reviewer, tchr. adv. panel World History, Connections to Today, 1999; counselor Ind. Coll., 1988—; mem. ednl. leadership coun. Malloy Coll. Author: Writing Across the Curriculum, 1988, Participationin Government-A Guide for Teachers I, 1989, II, 1991, Asian Studies Elective Curriculum. PTA pres. P.S. 144 Queens, 1981-83, Russell Sage Jr. High Sch. 190, Queens, 1983-85, Parents Assn. Hillcrest H.S., Queens, 1986-88, Queen's Confederation of Parents, 1987-88. Recipient Parent Svc. award Hillcrest H.S., Queens, 1986-88, Profl. Recognition award Bd. Edn. South Huntington Schs., 1983, Tchr. of Yr. award Walt Whitman H.S. Parent Assn., 1984, Spl. Tchrs. Are Recognized award Cornell U., 1992, Dartmouth Coll. Freshman Tchr. Recognition award, 1994, Outstanding Social Studies Supr. award L.I. Coun. for the Social Studies, 1997, Disting. Dept. Leader award Molloy Coll., 2004. Mem. L.I. Council for the Social Studies, Assn. Sch. Adminstrs., So. Huntington Chairperson Assn. (v.p. 1985-87, pres. 1987—). Democrat. Roman Catholic. Avocations: reading, theater, art museums, bicycling, jogging. Home: 68-47 Harrow St Flushing NY 11375-5157 Personal E-mail: aljog29@aol.com.

DADDARIO, RICHARD, chief financial officer, accountant; b. Windsor, Conn., June 17, 1947; s. Albert R. and Mamie (Castelleneta) D.; m. Patricia M. Melnyk, Oct., 1970; children: Gregory, Kristen. BS in Econs. and Fin., U. Hartford, Conn., 1969, MS in Acctg., 1975. CPA, Conn. Group life and health ins. underwriter Travelers Ins. Co., 1969-76; sr. audit mgr. Arthur Andersen & Co., 1976-83; dir. fin. acctg. Hartford Ins. Group, 1948; v.p., corp. controller Primerica Corp., Teaneck, N.J., 1985-89; sr. v.p., corp. controller Mut. of N.Y., Teaneck, 1989-90. Mem. AICPAs, Fin. Execs. Inst. Office: Mut of NY Glenpointe Centre West Teaneck NJ 07666

DADISMAN, JOSEPH CARROL, newspaper executive; b. Statesboro, Ga., May 24, 1934; s. Howard Dean and Mary Lou (Moore) D.; m. Mildred Jean Sparks, Aug. 19, 1956; children: David Carrol, Ellen Clarice. AB, U. Ga., 1956. Reporter, editorial writer, mng. editor Augusta (Ga.) Chronicle, 1956-66; editor Marietta (Ga.) Daily Jour., 1966-72; mng. editor Macon (Ga.) News, 1972-74; exec. editor, v.p. Columbus (Ga.) Ledger-Enquirer, 1974-80; gen. mgr. Tallahassee Dem., 1980-81, pub., pres., 1981-97; Knight Internat. Press fellow to Russia, 1998. Pres. adv. bd. U. Ga. Sch. Journalism, 1979-81, Fla. A&M U. Sch. Journalism, 1988-90; pres. Jr. Achievement of Columbus-Phenix City, 1977-78, United Way of Leon County, 1985-86, Ga. AP Assn., 1976-77; pres. Cmty. Found. of North Fla., 1997-2001. Served with AUS, 1957-59. Recipient Pub. Svc. award Cobb County C. of C., 1968, Fearless Editl. award Ga. Press Assn., 1963, Outstanding Alumnus award U. Ga. Sch. Journalism, 1994, Disting. Leader award Tallahassee Area C. of C., 1995, meritorious achievement award Fla. A&M U., 1996, Knight-Ridder excellence award in cmty. svc., 1997; named Young Man of Yr., Augusta Jaycees, 1962. Mem. Am. Soc. Newspaper Editors, Fla. Press Assn. (bd. dirs. 1984-86, v.p. 1986-87, pres. 1987-88), So. Newspaper Pubs. Assn. (bd. dirs. 1989-92), Econ. Club Fla. (pres. 1993-94, chmn. 1995-97), Orange Bowl Com., Governors Club (bd. dirs. 2000-02, pres. 2002), Killearn Country Club, Capital Tiger Bay Club, Rotary. Methodist. Home: 1235 Live Oak Plantation Rd Tallahassee FL 32312-2509 E-mail: jcdadisman@aol.com.

DADO, DIANE VALENTINA, plastic and reconstructive surgeon; b. Chgo., Feb. 14, 1952; d. Ralph N. and Violet M. Dado; 1 child, Joseph. BA, St. Xavier Coll., Chgo., 1973; MD, Loyola U., Maywood, Ill., 1976. Cert. Am. Bd. Plastic and Reconstructive Surgeery. Intern in surgery Loyola U. Med. Ctr., Maywood, Ill., 1976-77, resident in surgery, 1977-79, resident plastic surgery, 1979-82; fellow plastic surgery Children's Meml. Hosp., Chgo., 1982-83; instr. surgery Stritch Sch. Medicine Loyola U., Maywood, 1983, asst. prof. surgery, 1983-89, prof. surgery, pediatrics, 1989—. Mem. plastic surgery rsch. coun. Loyola U. Cleft Palate/Craniofacial Team, 1983—; attending physician Loyola U. Med. Ctr. div. Plastic Surgery, 1983—, children's Meml. Hosp. div. plastic surgery, 1983—. Contbr. articles to profl. jours. Mem. Am. Soc. Plastic and Reconstructive Surgeons, Am. Acad. Pediatrics, ACS, Am. Cleft Palate Assn., Ill. Assn. Craniofacial Teams, Chgo. Soc. Plastic Surgery, Can. Soc. Plastic Surgeons, Desmond A. Kernahan Soc. (founding). Avocations: martial arts, scuba diving, sailing, skiing. Office: Loyola U Med Ctr 2160 S 1st Ave Maywood IL 60153-3304

DADRIAN, VAHAKN NORAIR, retired sociology educator; b. Istanbul, Turkey, May 26, 1926; came to U.S., 1947, naturalized, 1961; s. Hagop and Mayreni (Der Garabedian) D. Ed. (Alexander von Humboldt fellow), U. Berlin, Germany, U. Vienna, Austria; ed. (scholar), U. Zurich, Switzerland; MA, Wayne State U., 1950; PhD (Reynolds fellow), U. Chgo., 1954. Asst. prof. sociology Washington Coll., Chestertown, Md., 1955-56, Boston U., 1957-59; rsch. fellow Harvard Ctr. for Middle Eastern Studies, 1961-62; sr. analyst dept. strategic studies div. missiles and space Raytheon, 1962-63; lectr. Boston Coll., 1963-65; asso. prof. Wis. State U., Superior, 1965-67, Fla. Atlantic U., 1967-68, prof., 1968-70, SUNY, Geneseo, 1970-91; dir. genocide study project H.F. Guggenhiem Found., Conesus, N.Y., 1991—. Vis. scholar Mass. Inst. Tech. Ctr. Internat. Studies, 1960-61; guest rschr. Inst. for Rsch. on Soviet Union, Munich, Germany, summer 1962; participant, Am. Sociol. Assn. grantee 6th World Congress of Sociology, Evian, France, fall 1966; vis. prof. Duke, summer 1971; dir. genocide study project NSF, 1977—; lectr. at univs., confs. and on TV in, U.S., Europe, Soviet Union, S.Am. Contbg. author: World Book Ency., 1972—, Encyclopedia of Genocide, 1999, Encylopedia Mondiale des génocides, 2001, Encyclopedia of Genocide and Crimes Against Humanity, 2005; Cons. editor: Internat. Jour. Contemporary Soc; translator, editor: United and Independent Turania (Zarevand), 1971; Contbr. articles to profl. jours., newspapers. Recipient Wis. U. Bd. Regents award, 1966, St. Vardan medal for scholarship in field of Soviet nationalities Cardinal Aghadjanian, Rome, 1968, Ellis Island medal of honor, 2005, Lifetime Achievement award Internat. Assn. Genocide Scholars, 2005, Lifetime Achievement award Scholars Conf. on the Holocaust and the Churches, 2005; grantee Harvard Lab. Social Rels., 1959, Am. Philos. Soc., 1961, Am. Com. Travel, 1962, Wenner-Gren Found., 1963, 65, Am. Coun. Learned Socs., summer 1966, NSF, 1968, 73, 76, SUNY, 1974, H.F. Guggenheim Found., 1990-91. Mem. Delta Tau Kappa (hon.) Home: PO Box 99 Conesus NY 14435-0099 Office: Genocide Rsch Zoryan Inst PO Box 99 Conesus NY 14435-0099

DADY, ROBERT EDWARD, lawyer; b. N.Y.C., Nov. 11, 1936; s. Edward Joseph and Florence (Scheidt) D.; m. Mollie D. Richman; children: Michael, Andrew, Rachel. BA, Queens Coll., 1958; LLB, Fordham U., 1961. Bar: N.Y. 1962, Fla. 1974. Asst. gen. counsel The Equity Corp., N.Y.C., 1962-66; gen. atty. ITT_Levitt and Sons, Inc., Washington, Lake Success, N.Y., 1966-70; sr. v.p.-legal First Realty Investment Corp., Miami Beach, Fla., 1970-71; v.p.-legal, sec. Cavanagh Cmtys. Corp., Miami, Fla., 1971-75; ptnr. Mann & Dady, P.A., Miami, 1975-80, Mann, Dady, Corrigan & Zelman, P.A., Miami, 1980-83, Dady, Siegfried & Kipnis, P.A., Miami, 1984-85; pvt. practice Miami, 1985-87; ptnr. Kimbrell and Hamann, P.A., 1987-89; shareholder Popham, Haik, Schnobrich & Kaufman, Ltd., 1990-96; of counsel Fieldstone, Lester, Shear & Denberg, Coral Gables, Fla., 1996—. Past adj. prof. law U. Miami Sch. Law.; bd. dirs. Spectrum Programs, Inc., pres., 1984-86, Spectrum Found., Inc., pres. 1988—. Author: Land Acquistion and Development, 1975. Bd. dirs., exec. comm. Miami Coalition for a Safe and Drug Free Cmty., 1992-99; vice-chmn. Childrens Home Soc. Found. Miami, 1993-96, bd. dirs., 1993-2004; appointed to (by gov.) Fla. Jud. Nom. Com., 1995-98; bd. dirs. Wellness Cmty., Greater Miami, 2001—. Mem. Nat. Land Coun. (pres. 1974-81, vice chmn. bd. dirs. 1973—), Builders Assn. So. Fla. (life dir., gen. counsel 1982-2001), ABA (environ. law com., timesharing and recreation law com., vice chmn. 2004), Fla. Bar Assn. Democrat. Home: 8440 SW 143rd St Miami FL 33158-1457 Office: Fieldstone Lester Shear & Denberg Sun Trust Plaza 201 Alhambra Cir Ste 601 Coral Gables FL 33134-5107 Office Phone: 305-357-1001. Business E-Mail: bd@flsdlaw.com.

DAEHN, GLENN STEVEN, materials scientist; b. Chgo., July 4, 1961; s. Ralph Charles and Beverly S. (Shanske) D.; m. Margaret A. Burkhart, Oct. 25, 1987; children: Andrew Joseph, Katrin Ellen, Matthew Charles. BS, Northwestern U., 1983; MS, Stanford U., 1985, PhD, 1988. Rsch. asst. Stanford U., Palo Alto, Calif., 1983-87; asst. prof. dept. materials sci. and engrng. Ohio State U., Columbus, 1987-92, assoc. prof. dept. materials sci. and engring., 1992-96, Fontana prof. dept. materials sci. and engring., 1996—. Co-founder, v.p. technology Excera Materials Group, 1992—. Co-editor: Modeling the Deformation of Crystalline Solids, 1991. Named Nat. Young Investigator, NSF, 1992; recipient Young Investigator award Army Rsch. Office, 1992, R.L. Hardy Gold medal TMS, 1992, Marcus Grossman award ASM Internat., 1990. Mem. ASM Internat., Am. Ceramic Soc., Materials Rsch. Soc., Minerals, Metals and Materials Soc. Achievements include description and practical applications of how temperature changes accelerate the deformation of composite materials; co-development of new class of ceramic-metal composites; development of hyperplasticity --practical application of extended metal ductility observed at high velocity. Home: 2076 Fairfax Rd Upper Arlington OH 43221-4319 Office: Ohio State U Materials Sci Dept 2041 N College Rd Columbus OH 43210-1124 Office Phone: 614-292-6779. Business E-Mail: Daehn.1@osu.edu.

DAEMMRICH, HORST SIGMUND, German language and literature educator; b. Pausa, Germany, Jan. 5, 1930; s. Arthur M. and Gertrud A. (Orlamunde) D.; m. Ingrid H. Guenther, June 10, 1962; children: JoAnn, Arthur. AB, Wayne State U., 1958, MA, 1959; PhD, U. Chgo., 1964. Instr. U. Chgo., 1961-62; asst. prof. Germanic langs. and lits. Wayne State U., Detroit, 1962-66, assoc. prof., 1967-70, prof., 1971-80; prof., chair U. Pa., 1981-98. Resident dir. Jr. Year Inst. at U. Freiburg, Germany, 1972-73 Author: The Shattered Self, 1973, Literaturkritik in Theorie und Praxis, 1974 (with Ingrid Daemmrich) Wiederholte Spiegelungen, Themen und Motive in der Literatur, 1978, Karl Krolow, 1980, Wilhelm Raabe, 1981, Themes and Motifs in Western Literature: A Handbook, 1987, Themen und Motive in der Literatur, 1987, 2d edit, 1995, Spirals and Circles: A Key to Thematic Patternn in Classicism and Realism, 2 vols., 1994, Themen and Motive in der Literatur, Handbuch, 1995; editor: The Challenge of German Literature, 1971, Studies on Themes and Motifs in Literature, 1990; gen. editor: Studies on Themes and Motifs in Literature, 1991-2005, 76 vols.; contbr. articles to profl. jours. Mem. Am. Soc. Aesthetics, Acad. Lit. Studies, Am. Lessing Soc., Am. Assn. Tchrs. German (mem. commn. on higher edn. 1974—), Am. Comparative Lit. Assn., MLA (sec. and chmn. 19th century lit. 1972-73), Midwest MLA (sec., chmn. modern Germanic lit. 1966-67), Phi Beta Kappa. Home: 307 Suffolk Rd Flourtown PA 19031-2119 Office: U Pa Dept Germanic Langs Philadelphia PA 19104-6305

DAENZER, BERNARD JOHN, insurance company executive, consultant, legal association administrator; b. N.Y.C., Jan. 15, 1916; s. Bernard Cornelius and Amelia Catherine (Heinze) D.; m. Valerie Antoinette Lee, June 8, 1941 (dec. Feb. 29, 2004); children: Peter, Jean Daenzer Aiken, John, Richard (dec.). AB, Fordham Coll., 1937, LL.D., 1942, Coll. Ins. N.Y.C., 1981. Spl. agt. Loyalty Group, Westchester, N.Y., 1937-43; with Security-Conn. Group, 1943-57, exec. v.p., 1955-57; pres. Wohlreich & Anderson Ltd., Cranford, N.J., 1957-81. Dir. Alexander Howden Group Ltd., London, 1968-81; underwriter Lloyds of London, 1968—; dir. emeritus RLI Corp., Peoria, Ill., 1972-2003. Columnist: Weekly Underwriter, 1964-86; Author publs. in field. Trustee Loman Found., Malvern, Pa. Served with USNR, 1944-46. Mem.: Soc. Chartered Property and Casualty Underwriters, Coll. Ins. N.Y.C., Racquet Club, Card Sound Country Club, Ocean Reef Club. Republican. Roman Catholic. Office: Ocean Reef 29 Angelfish Cay Dr Key Largo FL 33037-5271 Fax: 305-367-3354. Office Phone: 305-367-2925. E-mail: bjdlondon@aol.com.

DAETWILER, KIRBY DEAN, history educator; b. Wichita, Kans., June 15, 1961; s. Maurice Dean and June Ilo Daetwiler. BS, Kans. State U., 1989. History educator Unified Sch. Dist. 259, Wichita, Kans., 1998—. Mem. Republican Nat. Com., Washington, 2004. Mem.: Assn. for Supervision and Curriculum Devel., Phi Kappa Phi. Presbyterian. Avocations: digital photography, horsemanship. Home: 618 Barlow St Wichita KS 67207

DAFERMOS, CONSTANTINE MICHAEL, applied mathematics professor; b. Athens, Greece, May 26, 1941; came to U.S., 1964; s. Michael Constantine and Sophia (Raptarchis) D.; m. Stella Theodoracopoulos, Sept. 6, 1964; children: Thalia, Michael. Diploma, Athens Nat. Tech. U., 1964; PhD, Johns Hopkins U., 1967. Fellow Johns Hopkins U., 1967-68; asst. prof. Cornell U., 1968-71; assoc. prof. Brown U., 1971-76, prof. applied math., 1976—. Univ. prof., 1988—, dir. Lefschetz Ctr. for Dynamical Systems, 1988-94. Author: Hyperbolic Conservation Laws in Continuum Physics, 2000; mem. editl. bd. Archive for Rational Mechanics and Analysis, 1972—, Jour. of Thermal Stresses, 1978-2000, Quar. Applied Math., 1985—, Math. Modeling and Numerical Analysis, 1986-96, Proc. Royal Soc. Edinburgh, 1987—, Advances Math. Applied Sci., 1989—, Math. Models and Methods, 1990-97, Comm. on Applied Nonlinear Analysis, 1995—, Ricerche di Matematica, 1997—, Jour. Am. Math. Soc., 1999—, Revista Matematica Complutense, 2000, Jour. Dynamics and Differential Equations, 2002--; contbr. articles to profl. jours. NSF grantee, 1970—, Office Naval Rsch. grantee, 1972-80, 92—, USAF grantee, 1972-73, U.S. Army grantee, 1973-96. Mem. Soc. Natural Philosophy (treas. 1975-76, chmn. 1977-78), Am. Math. Soc., Acad. of Athens, Am. Acad. Arts and Scis. Office: Brown U Lefschetz Ctr Dynamical Sys 182 George St Providence RI 02912-9056 E-mail: dafermos@dam.brown.edu.

DAFFORN, GEOFFREY ALAN, biochemist; b. Cunningham, Kans., Feb. 4, 1944; s. Francis Elston and Anna Elizabeth Dafforn; m. Gail McLaughlin, July 14, 1973; 1 child, Christine Elizabeth. BA cum laude, Harvard U., 1966; PhD, U. Calif., Berkeley, 1970. Postdoctoral fellow U. Calif., Berkeley, 1973; asst. prof. U. Tex., Austin, 1974; from asst. prof. to assoc. prof. Bowling Green (Ohio) State U., 1974-81; sr. chemist Syva Co., Palo Alto, Calif., 1982-87, rsch. fellow, 1987—, group mgr., 1999—2000; prin. scientist Nugen Techs., San Carlos, Calif., 2001—. Author articles and abstracts; patentee in field. Grantee Army Rsch. Office, 1979-82, Am. Chem. Soc., 1975-80. Mem. AAAS, Am. Chem. Soc., Sierra Club. Office: Nugen Techs 821 Indsl Rd Unit A San Carlos CA 94070

DAFFRON, MARYELLEN, retired librarian; b. Richmond, Va., Nov. 12, 1946; d. William Charles and Ellen (Ahern) D. BA, Coll. Mt. St. Joseph on Ohio, Cin., 1968; MLS, Drexel U., 1970. Libr. Richmond Pub. Libr., 1969-73, FMC, Washington, 1973—93; with U.S. Immigration and Naturalization Svc. Office of Gen. Counsel, Washington, 1993—2003; law libr. Office of Prin. Legal Advisor, U.S. Immigration and Customs Enforcement, Washington, 2003—05, ret., 2005. Vol. No. Va. Hotline, Arlington, 1974-79. City of Richmond fellow, 1968. Mem. Law Libr. Soc. Washington, Beta Phi Mu. Roman Catholic.

DAFNOS, MARTHA JO, music educator; b. Richmond, Ind., Aug. 6, 1952; d. Fred E. and Edna M. (Neukam) Philhower; m. Thomas M. Dafnos, Feb. 7, 1975; 1 child, Sarah Jean. BS, U. INdpls., 1974; MA, Ball State U., 1979; postgrad., Met. Opera NY, 1991—94. Music tchr. Grissom Elem. Sch., Muncie, Ind., 1976—84; music specialist, tchr. Sand Creek Intermediate Sch., Noblesville, Ind., 1987—; asst. condr. Indpls. Children's Choir Butler U., 1991—96. Condr., dir.: original opera. Local chmn. America's Jr. Miss Scholarship Program, Noblesville, 1999—2001. Grantee, McDonald's Corp., 2001. Mem.: Ind. Music Educators Assn., Ind. Orff Schulwerk Assn., Music Educators Nat. Conf., Kappa Kappa Kappa. Avocations: gardening, needlecrafts, scrapbooks. Home: 11644 Horizon Ct Fishers IN 46038

DAFOE, WILLEM, actor; b. Appleton, Wis., July 22, 1955; s. William Dafoe; 1 child. Student, U. Wis. Mem. Theatre X theatrical co., 1975, co-founder, The Wooster Group theatrical co., N.Y.C., 1977—. Actor (feature films) The Loveless, 1983, The Hunger, 1983, New York Nights, 1984, Roadhouse 66, 1984, Streets of Fire, 1984, To Live and Die in L.A., 1985, Platoon, 1986 (Acad. award nomination 1987), The Last Temptation of Christ, 1988, Off Limits, 1988, Mississippi Burning, 1988, Triumph of the Spirit, 1989, Born on the Fourth of July, 1989, Cry-Baby, Flight of the Intruder, Wild at Heart, 1990, White Sands, 1992, Light Sleeper, 1992, Body of Evidence, 1992, Far Away So Close!, 1993, The Night and the Moment, 1994, Clear and Present Danger, 1994, Tom and Viv, 1995, Victory, 1995, The English Patient, 1996, Basquiat, 1996, Speed 2: Cruise Control, 1997, Affliction, 1997, New Rose Hotel (also co-prod.), 1998, Lulu on the Bridge, 1998, eXisten Z, 1998, American Psycho, 1999, The Boondock Saints, 1999, Bullfighter, 2000, The Animal Factory, 2000, Shadow of the Vampire, 2000 (Oscar Nominee for Best Actor in a Supporting Role, 2000), The Gangs of New York, 2000, Pavillion of Women, 2001, Edges of the Lord, 2001, Spider-Man, 2002, Auto-Focus, 2002, Finding Nemo (voice only), 2003, Once Upon A Time in Mexico, 2003, Camel Cricket City (voice only), 2003, The Reckoning, 2004, The Clearing, 2004, Spider-Man 2, 2004, The Life Aquatic with Steve Zissou, 2004, The Aviator, 2004, Ripley Under Ground, 2005, Control, 2005, xXx: State of the Union, 2005; TV appearances: The Hitchhiker, 1985, The Simpsons (voice only), 1997. Only actor to ever be nominated for an Oscar for playing a vampire.*

DAFOE, WILLIAM ALFRED, surgeon; b. Wautoma, Wis., July 21, 1917; s. George Eber And Gertrude (Collins) D.; m. Muriel Isabel Sprissler, July 13, 1942; children: Barbara, Nancy, Diane, Donald, Richard, Jane, Willem, Sarah. BA, U. Wis., 1937; MD, Harvard U., 1940; MS in Surgery, U. Minn., 1947. Diplomate Am. Bd. Surgery. Intern Faulkner Hosp., Boston, 1941; resident Boston City Hosp., 1942-44; surg. fellow Mayo Clinic, Rochester, Minn., 1944-47; pvt. practice Appleton, Wis., 1947-85, Orlando, Fla., 1985—. Fellow Am. Coll. Surgeons; mem. AMA, Wis. Surg. Soc., Southeastern Surg. Congress. Avocations: gardening, fishing. Home and Office: 1915 N Forest Ave Orlando FL 32803-1520 Office Phone: 407-894-5552. Personal E-mail: willz23@aol.com.

DAFT, DOUGLAS N., retired beverage company executive; b. Sydney, Australia, 1944; m. Delphine Daft; 2 children. BA in Mathematics, U. New Eng., 1969; Grad., U. New South Wales. Planning officer Coca-Cola Co., Sydney, Australia, 1969—71, asst. to regional. mgr. Indonesia, 1971—75, mgr. planning & spl. products Sydney, 1975—77, mgr. mktg. & planning Coca-Cola Far East Ltd. Hong Kong, 1977—78, regional mgr. E Asia region, 1978—82, v.p. Coca-Cola Far East Ltd., 1982—84, pres. ctrl. pacific divsn., 1984—87, sr. v.p. pacific group, 1987, pres. north pacific divsn., 1988—91, pres. pacific group, 1991—95, pres., mid. & far east and Africa groups, Schweppes divsn., 1995—99, pres., COO, 1999—2000, chmn., CEO, 2000—04. Bd. dirs. Sun-Trust Banks, The McGraw-Hill Cos. Inc., 2003—, Wal-Mart Stores Inc., Ctr. for Strategic & Internat. Studies; bd. trustees Emory U., The Am. Assembly.

DAG-ELLAMS, IDRIS, neurosurgeon; b. Agenebode, Edo, Nigeria, Oct. 2, 1949; s. Alhassan Garba and Rekyia (Aigbona) E.; m. Ugonwa Okpara; children: aisha, Nkechi, Naema, Ayman. Grad., Christiana Albertina U., Kiel, Germany, 1979, MD, 1982. Resident, rsch. fellow Justus Liebig U. Hosp., Giessen, Germany, 1979-85; cons., sr. lectr. Ahmadu Bello U. Hosp., Zaria, Nigeria, 1985-89; neurosurgeon King Khalid Hosp., Najran, Saudi Arabia, 1989-90; cons. Kign Abdul Aziz Hosp., Jeddah, Saudi Arabia, 1990-91; locum sr. cons. King Fahd Hosp., Hofuf, Saudi Arabia, 1991-92; sr. cons. Al-Noor Specialist Hosp., Makkah, Saudi Arabia, 1993—, head dept. neurosurgery, 1993—, chmn. surg. divsn., 1993-99, dep. chief med. dir., 1993-99. Chmn., exec. dir. Nanfield Inc., Mississauga, Can., 1999. Contbr. articles to profl. jours. Fellow West African Coll. Surgeons; mem. AAAS, N.Y. Acad. Scis., Nigeria Med. Assn. Germany (pres. 1982-85), Rotary. Avocation: reading. Fax: 905-816-0281. E-mail: idris_dr@yahoo.com, iyaghumeh@hotmail.com, nanfield1@rogers.com.

DAGENHARDT, GLYNN ANTHONY, secondary school educator; b. Houma, La., May 23, 1956; s. Lloyd Francis and Yvonne Marie Dagenhardt; m. Jean Carol Schexnayder; 1 child, Julie. BME, Nicholls State U., 1975—90. Tchr. Houma Jr. High, Houma, La., 1990—. Office: Houma Junior High School 315 St Charles St Houma LA 70360 Office Phone: 985-879-4259. Office Fax: 872-1511. E-mail: gdagenhardt@tpsb.net.

DAGENHART, LARRY JONES, lawyer; b. Taylorsville, N.C., July 20, 1932; s. Luther Jones and Louise (Icenhour) D.; m. Sarah Katheryne Petty, June 23, 1956; children: Katie Dagenhart Satterwhite, Mary Louise Dagenhart Culpepper, Larry Jones Jr. BS, Davidson (N.C.) Coll., 1953, LLD, 2003; LL.B., NYU, 1958. Bar: N.C. 1958. Pvt. practice, Charlotte, 1958—; of counsel Helms, Mulliss & Wicker, Charlotte. Bd. dirs. Cannon med. rsch. ctr., 1994—2001. Trustee Davidson Coll., 1970-2002, chmn., 1998-2000; trustee U. N.C., Wilmington, 1997-2005, chmn., 2001, chmn., chancellor search com., 2002; trustee Kate B. Reynolds Trust, 1990-96; bd. dirs. N.C. Citizens for Bus. and Industry, 1995-2001; past chmn. Charlotte C. of C., 1983, Charlotte Arts and Scis. Coun., 1976-77, Mecklenburg County Bar Assn., 1974-75, Charlotte United Way, 1978, Found. for the Carolinas, 1987-89, Charlotte Country Day Sch., 1985-87, Charlotte City Club, 1979, Charlotte World Affairs Coun., 1996-98, Ben Craig Incubator Ctr., 1998-2002 Named George F. Baker scholar, 1949-53, Root-Tilden scholar, 1953-58; fellow Am. Bar Found., 1970—; recipient Harold Josephson award, Charlote World Affairs Coun. award, 2002 Mem.: Am. Law Inst. Democrat. Lutheran. Home: 1601 Biltmore Dr Charlotte NC 28207-2611 Office: Helms Mulliss & Wicker PO Box 31247 Charlotte NC 28231-1247 E-mail: larry.dagenhart@hmw.com.

DAGER, WILLIAM ERLING, pharmacist, educator; b. Long Beach, Calif., Oct. 20, 1958; s. William Elwood and Olivia G. Dager; m. Karen Renee Helmle, Aug. 31, 1985; children: William Randall, Jessica Lynn, Laura Michelle. PharmD, U. Calif., San Francisco, 1985. Cert. Residency Cert. U. Calif. Davis Med. Ctr., 1986, Nephrology Preseptorship U. Calif. of Pitts., 1995. Pharmacist specialist U. Calif. Davis Med. Ctr., Sacramento, 1986—. Fellow Calif. Soc. of Hosp. Pharmacists, Calif., 1992—; clin. prof. of pharmacy U. Calif. Sch. Pharmacy, San Francisco, 2000; assoc. clin. prof. medicine U. Calif. Davis Sch. Medicine, 2000; affiliate acls facility Am. Heart Assn., Calif.; presenter in field. Mem. editl. bd. Annals Pharmacotherapy, Jour. Cardiovascular Pharmacology and Therapeutics, ClotCare Online Resource; contbr. articles to profl. jours. Founding mem. Shingle Springs (Calif.) Adv. Com., 2000—02. Mem.: Sacramento Valley Soc. Health-Sys. Pharmacy, Internat. Soc. on Thrombosis and Haemostasis, Am. Coll. Clinical Pharmacy, Am. Soc. Health-Sys. Pharmacy, Calif. Soc. Health-Sys. Pharmacy, Sacramento Valley Coral Soc. Orch. Achievements include research in clinical pharmacokinetic observations; anticoagulation approaches; clinical pharmacology. Avocations: skiing, house restoration, trumpet music. Office: U Calif Davis Medl Ctr 2315 Stockton Blvd Sacramento CA 95817 Personal E-mail: william.dager@ucdmc.ucdavis.edu.

DAGGER, RICHARD KEITH, political science and philosphy educator; b. Cape Girardeau, Mo., Oct. 23, 1948; s. Richard Ball Dagger and Julia Bea Verhines; m. Barbara Ann Duepner, Oct. 17, 1946; children: Emily Abbott, Elizabeth Bennett. BA, U. of Missouri-St. Louis, 1966—70; PhD, U. of Minn., 1970—76. Prof., polit. sci. and philosophy Ariz. State U., 1976—. Dir., program in philosophy, politics, and law Barrett Honors Coll., Ariz. State U., 2001—; faculty fellow Ctr. for Ethics and Pub. Affairs, Tulane U., 2005—. Author: (book) Civic Virtues: Rights, Citizenship, and Rep. Liberalism (Elaine and David Spitz Award, Conf. for the Study of Polit. Thought, 1999); co-author: Polit. Ideologies and the Dem. Ideal; co-editor: Ideals and Ideologies: A Reader. Hubert H. Humphrey Fellow, U. of Minn., 1972—73. Mem.: Conf. for the Study of Polit. Thought, Am. Soc. for Polit. and Legal Philosophy, Am. Polit. Sci. Assn. (program com. 1993—94, 2000—01). Roman Catholic. Office: Arizona State U Dept of Polit Sci Tempe AZ 85287-3902 E-mail: rdagger@asu.edu.

DAGI, TEODORO FORCHT, neurosurgeon, educator, venture capitalist; s. Ira and Lora Forcht Dagi; m. Linda Rabinowitz, Sept. 4, 1982; children: Lora Rabin, Ariella Rabin, Alexander Forcht. AB, Columbia U., 1967; MD, MPH, Johns Hopkins U., 1971; MTS, Harvard U., 1975; MBA, U. Pa., 1995. Diplomate Am. Bd. Neurol. Surgery, Nat. Bd. Med. Examiners. Asst. prof. surgery and anatomy, neurosurgeon Georgetown U. Hosp., Washington, 1980—85; adj. prof. law Georgetown U. Law Ctr., Washington, 1981—88; assoc. clin. prof. neurosurgery Uniformed Svcs. U. Health Scis., Bethesda, Md.; clin. prof. of surgery Med. Coll. Ga., Augusta, Ga.; vis. prof. mgmt. Dupree Sch. Ga. Inst. Mgmt., Atlanta, 1998; mng. ptnr. Cordova Ventures, Atlanta, 1997—. Bd. dirs. Ga. Biomedical Partnership, Atlanta, Atherogenics, Inc., Alpharette, Ga.; dir. program in entrepreneurship Wharton Sch. U. Pa., Phila.; cons. in neurosurgy Fed. Aviation Adminstrn., Washington, 1990—; mem. Res. Coun. of the US, Washington, 1982—85. Editor: A History of Neurological Surgery, 1997, A History of Neurosurgical Technique, 2001, Jour. Med. Humanities; mem. editl. bd. Jour. Clinical Ethics, Jour. Biolaw and Bus.; contbr. Pres. Ga. Neurosurg. Soc., Atlanta, 1999—2000; bd. dirs. SE Entrepreneur Found., Atlanta, 2000—02, Wellness Found., Atlanta, Atlanta Biotechnology Network, Atlanta; pres., bd. dirs. Harvard Club Ga., Atlanta; pres. Johns Hopkins Sch. Hygiene and Pub. Health Alumni Assn., Atlanta. Lt. col. MC U.S. Army, 1985—2000. Fellow, Neuroresearch Soc., 1971—72, Joseph P. Kennedy, Jr., Found., 1973—75, Coll. Critical Care Medicine, 1995; scholar Borsa Scolastica, Govt. of Italy, 1967; Travelling fellow, Mendeleyeff Fund, 1968. Fellow: ACS (exec. com., chmn., new technologies com., com. on perioperative care), Coll. Critical Care Medicine; mem.: Congress Neurol. Surgery, Am. Assn. Neurol. Surgeons (bd. dirs. 1999—2001, sect. chair, com. chair, chmn. ethics com.). Achievements include design of device for cortical stimulation of the brain to control intractable epilepsy; development of mobile intensive care units after civil disasters; research in anatomy and function of the limbic system. Home: 423 Commonwealth Ave Newton Center MA 02459 Office Phone: 404-386-0947. Business E-Mail: tdagi@post.harvard.edu.

DAGIT, CHARLES EDWARD, JR., architect, educator; b. Phila., July 1, 1943; s. Charles E. and Janet (Donnelly) D.; m. Alice M. Murdoch, June 3, 1967; children: Charles Edward, J. Murdoch. BA, U. Pa., 1965, B.Arch., 1967, M.Arch., 1968. Registered architect, Pa., N.Y., N.J., Conn., Va., Md., Vt. Designer Henry D. Dagit & Sons, Phila., 1965-68, Mitchell, Giurgola Assocs., Phila., 1968-69; project designer Henry D. Dagit & Sons, Phila., 1969-70; ptnr. Dagit Saylor Architects, Phila., 1970—. Adj. asst. prof. Sch. Arch. and Engring., Temple U., 1973-80; adj. prof. dept. arch. Phila. Coll. Art, 1979-80; vis. prof. U. Pa., 1980; prof. dept. arch. Drexel U. Prin. works include Peale House of Pa. Acad. Fine Arts (Design award Phila. chpt. AIA 1983, Merit award Pa. Mus. and Hist. Com.), Agrl. Arena at Pa. State U. (Silver medal Pa. State U. 1985, Design award Phila. chpt. AIA 1985), Spring Garden Health Ctr. (runner-up for Rudi Brunner award), Phoenix City Ctr. for Arts (NEA grant), 1983, Cumberland Union Bldg. Shippensburg U. (Phila. chpt. AIA Design award 1992, Design award PSA 1992), Bartram's Garden (Pa. Mus. and Hist. Commn. Preservation award 1993), Campus Ctr. Bldg. Haverford Coll. (Phila. chpt. AIA Design award 1994, Design award PSA 1994, F.W. Olin Bldg. (Phila. chpt. AIA Design award 1992, Design award PSA 1992), Pa. Ballet (Design award PSA 1989), Gwynedd Mercy Coll. Lourdes Libr. Addition (Phila. chpt. AIA Design award 1986), Magee Rehab. Hosp. (Phila. chpt. Design award 1984), Logan Mus. Anthropology, Beloit Coll. (Phila. chpt. AIA Design award 1995, Internat. Illumination Design award, Preservation award WI Preservation Trust 1995), Grove Hall, Coll. Bus. Bldg., Shippensburg U. (Design award Phila. chpt. AIA 1999). Pres. Gladwyne Civic Assn., 1981-82; pres. Friends of St. Christopher's Hosp., Phila., 1977-78; trustee Bryn Mawr. (Pa.) Country Day Sch., 1975-79; bd. dirs. Phila. Zool. Soc., 1979-87; pres. bd. trustees Gladwyne Libr. Bd., 1990-91; trustee Acad. Cmty. Music, 1997—. Recipient Design award Progressive Architecture, 1974, 40 Under 40 award A&U Mag., Japan, 1977, View of World Contemporary Architecture award Japan Architect, 1977; winner nat. design competition Cultural Arts Pavillion, Newport News, Va., 1985. Fellow AIA (Silver medal Phila. chpt. 1976, Gold medal 1978, pres.-elect Phila. chpt. 1989, pres. Phila. chpt. 1990, chair Nat. Design Conf. commn. on architecture for arts and recreation, Cin. 1976, chair Nat. Design Conf. commn. on design, Louis I. Kahn & Phila. Sch. 1991, chmn. designate commn. on design 1992, vice chmn. commn. design, 1993, chmn. commn. design 1994, AIA PA chmn. leadership forum 2003-04, vice chmn., 2003-04); mem. AIA PA PAC (chmn. 2005). AIA (Silver medal 1985), Soc. Coll.and U. Planners, Facilities Planning Acad., Downtown Club Phila. (bd. dirs. 1986-89), Merion Golf Club (Ardmore, Pa.), Mask and Wig Club, U. Pa. Spinx Sr. Soc. (bd. dirs. 1973-76), The Carpenter's Co. Republican. Roman Catholic. Home: 381 Williamson Rd Gladwyne PA 19035-1618 Office: Dagit Saylor Architects 100 S Broad St Ste 1100 Philadelphia PA 19110-1003 Business E-Mail: cdagit@dagitsaylor.com.

DAGLIS, LISA GENINE, law clerk to state supreme court justice; b. Northridge, Calif., Feb. 28, 1969; d. Abraham and Rosalynd Rohrberger; m. John P. Daglis, Apr. 21, 1988; 1 child, Brett John. AA pre law, Atlantic C.C., Mays Landing, N.J., 1985; BA Govt. and Politics, Widener U., Chester, Pa., 1997; JD, Widener U. Law Sch., Wilmington, Del., 2003. Bar: N.J. 2003. Staff S, Jersey Legal Svcs., Atlantic City, 2004; law clk. Superior Ct. N.J., Mays Landing, 2004—. Legal aid vol. South Jersey Legal Svcs., 2004; campaign vol. Rep. Club, Atlantic County, Hamilton Twp., NJ. Recipient Zelda K. Hermann award, Widener Sch. of Law, 2003. Mem.: ABA, U. S.Holocaust Meml. Mus. Soc., So. Poverty Law Ctr., Phi Kappa Phi. Avocations: sailing, interior decorating, painting. Office Phone: 609-909-8204.

D'AGNENICA, JILL MARIE, artist; b. Upland, Calif., June 30, 1964; d. Anthony Baron and Rosaria (Ruggeri) D'A.; m. John Michael Child, July 30, 1988; 1 child, Isabella Child. Student, U. Studi di Firenze, Florence, Italy, 1985-86; BA in History magna cum laude, UCLA, 1987; MFA in Visual Art, Claremont Grad. Sch., 1991. Guest artist So. Calif., 1993—, U. Ark., 1997, U. So. Calif., 2000, Coll. of the Canyons, 2001; ind. curator, 1996—. Works exhibited Margert Fowler Gardens, Claremont, Calif., 1990, Claremont Grad. Sch., 1991, U. N.Mex., Portales, 1992 (Best of Show 1992), Calif State U., Northridge, 1992, Robert Berman Gallery, Santa Monica, 1994, Lucky Nun Gallery, Silverlake, Calif., 1995, Rio Hondo Coll., LA, 1995, Mus. Civico, Padua, Italy, 1995, Ga. Mus. Art, Athens, 1995, LA Mcpl. Art Gallery, 1996, Mt. San Antonio Coll., Walnut, Calif., 1997, Mus. Italo-Americano, San Francisco, 1999, Robert Berman Gallery, Santa Monica, Calif., 2000, Internat. Exch. for Peace, LA, Tel Aviv, Italy, 2002, The Brewery Project, LA, 2003, Limbus Gallery, Tel Aviv, 2003, others; represented in pvt. collections Archer Sch. for Girls, LA, Commune di Gubbio, Italy, Westchester Pub. Libr., LA, Northridge Pub. Libr., LA. Recipient Rose award Downtown LA Breakfast Club, 1996, First prize Museo-Italo-Americano, 1997-98; Travel and Rsch. grantee Claremont Grad. Sch., 1991, grantee L.A. Contemporary Exhbns. Artist's Project,1994, City of LA Cultural Affairs, 1994-95, City LA Cultural Affairs, 2002. Mem. NOW, So. Calif. Women's Caucus for Art (exec. bd. dirs. 1992-94), Coll. Art Assn., Brewery Artwalk Assn. Home: # 020 2020 N Main St Ste 20 Los Angeles CA 90031-3254 Personal E-mail: jilldagnenica@yahoo.com.

DAGNON, JAMES BERNARD, human resources executive; b. St. Paul, Jan. 31, 1940; s. James Lavern and Margaret Elizabeth D.; m. Sandra Ann McGinley, June 4, 1960; children: Sheri T. Dagnon Tice, Terry J., Laurie M. Zinn, Diana L. Felner. BS in Bus. with distinction, U. Minn., St. Paul, 1979, cert. in Indsl. Rels., 1978. Various clerical positions No. Pacific Ry. Co., St. Paul, 1957-70; supr., then mgr. pers. rsch. and stats. Burlington No. R.R. Co., St. Paul, 1970, mgr. manpower planning, 1970-78, dir. compensation and orgnl. planning, 1978-81; asst. v.p. compensation and benefits Burlington No. Inc., Seattle, 1981-84, from v.p. labor rels. to exec. v.p. employee rels. Ft. Worth, 1984-95; sr. v.p. employee rels. Burlington No. Santa Fe Rlwy. Co., Ft. Worth, 1995-97; sr. v.p. people The Boeing Co., Seattle, 1997—2002; pres. Christian Living Inst., 2004. Bd. dirs. Inroads Inc., Seattle Inroads Inc.; chmn. Corp. Champions, Ft. Worth, 1994—96; trustee Cook-Ft. Worth Children's Med. Ctr., 1995—97; bd. dirs. United Way Met. Tarrant County, 1995—97, Wash. State Gov.'s Commn. on Higher Edn. in 2020; trustee Bellevue C.C., 1999—; bd. dirs., trustee Wash. Early Learning Found., 1999—2003; pres. Cath. Evang. Outreach, Seattle, 1981—84, Christian Living Inst., 2004—; bd. dirs. Western Wash. Cath. Charismatic Renewal, 2004—. Capt. USAR, 1957—70. Fellow Nat. Acad. Human Resources; mem. Beta Gamma Sigma. Republican. Avocations: scuba diving, photography. Home: PO Box 605 Medina WA 98039-0605

D'AGOSTINO, CLAUDIO, sculptor; b. Toronto, Can., Apr. 9, 1963; s. Natalina D'Agostino. Studied in sculpture, Studio of Ceramic Arts, El Cajon, 1987—97. Porcelaine, Presidential Flower Sculpture, Represented in permanent collections John D. Spreckels Sculpture, Spreckels Organ Pavillion, San Diego Balboa Park. Mem.: Nat. Sculpture Soc. (assoc.). Democrat. Achievements include design of porcelaine creations of realistic flowers. Address: PO Box 632992 San Diego CA 92163 Personal E-mail: claudiosculptor@hotmail.com.

D'AGOSTINO, JAMES SAMUEL, JR., corporate financial executive; b. Balt., July 4, 1946; s. James Samuel and Betty Ann (List) D'A.; m. Diane Martin Greener, Sept. 25, 1971; children: James Martin, Ann Diestel. BS in Econs., Villanova U., 1968; JD, Seton Hall Sch. Law, Newark, 1974; postgrad., Harvard U., 1993. Bar: N.J. 1974, Tex. 1979. Trust officer Fidelity Union Trust Co., Newark, 1968-73; asst. treas. The Chase Manhattan Bank, N.A., N.Y.C., 1973-76; v.p. Citibank/Citicorp, Houston, 1976-86; v.p., treas. Am. Gen. Corp., Houston, 1986-90, sr. v.p. investor rels., 1990-91, sr. v.p. adminstrn., 1991-93, exec. v.p. adminstrn., 1993; pres., CEO Am. Gen. Life and Accident Ins. Co., Nashville, 1993-95, chmn., CEO, 1995-97; pres. Am. Gen. Corp., Houston, 1997-98; vice-chmn., group exec. Consumer Fin. Am. Gen. Corp., Houston, 1998-99; chmn., pres., CEO Encore Bank, 1999—. Republican. Presbyterian. Office: Encore Bank 9 Greenway Plaza Ste 1000 Houston TX 77046 Office Phone: 713-787-3103. E-mail: jdagostino@encorebank.com.

D'AGOSTINO, RALPH BENEDICT, mathematician, statistician, educator, consultant; b. Somerville, Mass., Aug. 16, 1940; s. Bennedetto and Carmela (Piemonte) D'A.; m. Lei Lanie Carta, Aug. 28, 1965; children: Ralph Benedict, Lei Lanie Maria. AB, Boston U., 1962, MA, 1964; PhD, Harvard U., 1968. Lectr. math. Boston U., 1964-68, asst. prof., 1968-71, assoc. prof., 1971-76, lectr. law, 1975-91, assoc. dean Grad. Sch., 1976-78, prof. math. and stats., 1976—, prof. pub. health, 1982—, dir. data analysis and stats. Framingham Heart Study, 1985—, chmn. dept. math., 1986-91, dir. stats. cons. unit, 1986—, dir. Biostats MA/PhD Program, 1988—, prof. law, 1991—2004; adj. prof. Tufts U., 2004—. Exec. dir. data mgmt. and biostats. Harvard Clin. Rsch. Inst., 2002—; vis. lectr. Am. Statis. Assn., 1975-86, 88-92; vis. prof. biostats. clin. epidiology unit Univ. Hosp., Geneva, 1993; Rankin vis. prof. U. Wis., 1995; spl. lectr. clin. trials symposium U. Fla., 1995; vis. scientist NHLBI, 1993; Lowell Reed lectr. APHA, 1996; spl. scientist Boston City Hosp., 1981-95, Boston Med. Ctr., 1996—, New Eng. Med. Ctr., 1990—; mem. Health Inst. New Eng. Med. Ctr., 1990—; cons. stats. United Brands, 1968-76, Diabetes and Arthritis Control Unit, Boston, 1971-75, City of Somerville, Mass., 1972, ednl. Harvard U. Dental Sch., 1969, Lahey Clinic Found., 1973-85, Walden Rsch., 1974-79, FDA Biometrics Divsn. and Over-the-Counter Divsn., 1975—, Cardio and Renal Divsn. FDA, 1987—, Gastrointestinal Drug Divsn., FDA, 1994-96, Medical Devise Divsn. 1999-, Arnold & Porter, 1980, Bedford Rsch. Assn., 1976-81, Corneal Scis., 1976, Biotek, 1979-88, GCA, 1979-87, Lever Bros., 1982-87, Conrail, 1981, FBI, 1984, Ctr. Psychiat. Rehab., Boston U., 1985—, NIMH, 1985, Dade Clin. Assays, 1986-90, Millipore, 1983-92, VLI Corp., 1985-90, New Eng. Coll. Optometry, 1985-93, Dupont Corp., 1985, Bristol Myers, 1986, 93, Cheeseborough Ponds, 1987-96, med. decision making divsn. and health svcs. rsch. unit Tufts New Eng. Med. Ctr., 1986—, Am. Inst. Rsch. in Social Scis., 1983-88, New Eng. Rsch. Insts., 1987-92, Thompson Med., 1987-96, Merck, Sharpe and Dohme, 1988-94, Carter Ctr., Emory U., 1969-75, Unilever, 1991-96, Miles, 1991-95, Ultra Fem., 1991-93, Health Effects Inst., 1992—, Forsyth Dental Clinic, 1992-93, 95—, Bard Vascular, 1990-95, Ultra Slim Fast, 1990-95, Block Med., 1993-95, Bayer Pharm., 1993-98, Astra Pharm., 1993-97, Cytyc, 1993-97, Regua, 1994-96, SmithKline Beechman, 1994-95, Proctor and Gamble, 1994-96, 2000—, Sandoz, 1994-96, R W Johnson Pharms., 1997, Mass. Med. Assistance, 1995-97, Cambridge Heart, 1996—2000, Merck/ Johnson & Johnson, 1999—, Aventis, 2000—, Ajinomoto, 2000, Discovery Lab, 2000— Pfizer, 2000-; mem. various FDA coms. including fertility and maternal health drugs adv. com, 1978-81, life support subcom., 1979-81, drug abuse adv. com., 1987-90, gastrointestinal drugs adv. com., 1990-94, nonprescriptive drug adv. com., 1995—, chair, 1996-98; cons. various FDA coms., Cardio-Renal com., 1995-, arthritis com., 1997-; mem. task force on design and analysis of dental and oral rsch., 1979—, Harvard U. health tech. com., 1986-90; mem. Honolulu Heart Study Adv. Com., NIH, 1989-96, Balt. Longitudinal Study of Aging Adv. Com., 1990, NIH Consensus Panel on Liver Transplantation, 1983, Consensus Panel on Fresh Frozen Plasma, 1984, Consensus Panel on Geriatric Assessment Methods for Clin. Decision Making, 1987; mem. task force Office Tech. Assessment, 1980; mem. consensus panel on intraoral techniques ADA, 1990; mem. study sect. Agy. for Health Care Policy and Rsch., 1990-94; mem. Bethesda Conf. on Matching Intensity of Risk Factor Mgmt. With the Hazard for Coronary Disease Events, 1996; prin., co-prin. investigator or sr. statistician on grants Nat. Ctr. Health Svcs. Rsch., 1976-82, NHLBI, 1982—, USAF, 1980-85, Nat. Cancer Inst., 1985—, Nat. Inst. Criminal Justice, 1982-85, Nat. Ctr. Child Abuse and Neglect, 1982-85, Robert Wood Johnson Found., 1981-85, Social Security Adminstrn., 1982-86, 90-93, Motor Vehicles Mem. Assn., 1987, NIOSH, 1985, Nat. Insts. Aging, 1986—, Agency for Health Care Policy and Rsch., 1989—; grant and contract reviewer NAS, 1979—, Nat. Ctr. Health Svcs. Rsch., 1976, 89, NIH, 1983, NSF, 1987-95, AHCPR, 1990; co-prin. investigator Framingham Heart Study, 1993-; chair spl. emphasis panel reviewing small bus. grant proposal Nat. Inst. Dental Rsch., 1996. Author: (with E.E. Cureton) Factor Analysis, An Applied Approach, 1983, (with Shuman and Wolf) Mathematical Modeling, Applications in Emergency Health Services, 1984, (with Stephens) Goodness of Fit Techniques, 1986, (with D. Schiff) Practical Engineering Statistics, 1996, (with Sullivan and Beiser) Introductory Applied Biostatistics, 2004; assoc. editor Am. Statistician, 1972-76, Jour. Am. Statis. Assn., 1993-96; editor Emergency Health Svc. Rev., 1981-88, Stats. in Medicine (biostat. tutorials), 1993—, Stats. in Medicine, 1997—; mem. editl. bd. Biostatistica, 1990-99, Jour. Hypertension, 2004-; book reviewer Houghton-Mifflin, Holden, Day, Duxbury Press, Prentice Hall, 1969; contbr. articles to profl. jours.; co-developer instrument for predicting acute ischemic health disease, stroke health risk appraisal function and coronary heart disease risk assessment function. Recipient Spl. citation FDA Commr., 1981, 95, Metcalf awrd for excellence in teaching Boston U., 1985; Am. Heart Assn. fellow, 1991; pre-doctoral fellow NIH, 1962-68. Fellow Am. Statis. Assn. (pres. Boston chpt. 1972, v.p. 1971, mem. nat. coun. 1973-75, vis. lectr. 1976-78, 80—, Statistician of Yr. Boston chpt. 1993, chmn. sect. Health Policy Stats. 1996, chmn. sect. Epidemiology 2003); mem. APHA (Lowell Reed lectr. 1996, chmn. sect. emergency health svcs. 1982-83, governing coun. 1983-85), Am. Heart Assn. (mem. cardiovasc. epidemiology coun.), Inst. Math. Stats., Am. Soc. Quality Control, Biometrics Soc. (mem. regional adv. com. 1989-94), Phi Beta Kappa, Sigma Xi. Roman Catholic. Home: 5 Everett Ave Winchester MA 01890-3523 Office: Boston U Statistics & Cons Unit 111 Cummington St Boston MA 02215-2411 Office Phone: 617-353-2767. Business E-Mail: ralph@bu.edu.

DAGSTINE, LAWRENCE, writer, artist; b. N.Y., Mar. 25, 1974; s. Joel and Claudia Dagstine; life ptnr. Student, ICS Sch. Journalism, 1996. Novelist, short story writer Lawrence Dagstine, New York, 1996—. Author: (novel) Espionage First, Spencer Prague, (novel-length short story collection) Death of the Common Writer, (novelette) The Illusion of Lewis Carroll (Best Short Story, 2002); webzine, SOBER-The Devil's Punchbowl, N.Y., 1989—95 (One of the Two Hundred Biggest Graffiti Art Webzines in World, 2002); author: (novels) Allegiance to Arms. Freedom Socialist. Achievements include creating a webzine for showcasing the work of talented graffiti/urban artists worldwide.

DAGUE, PAIGE ANDREA, school counselor; d. Donald Edward and Mary Lou Louise Harr; m. James Lowell Dague, Feb. 25, 1989; children: Jameson Atticus, Elaina Faith Hatfield, Cooper Marcus. BA in Social Sci., St. Xavier U., 1992; MA in Psychology and Counseling, Govs. State U., 2000, MA in Ednl. Adminstrn., 2004. Guidance counselor Lincoln-Way Sch. Dist., New Lenox, Ill., 2000—03, Homewood-Flossmoor Dist. 233, 2003—05, chair dept., 2005—. Mem. counseling adv. bd. Govs. State U., University Park, Ill., 2002—03. Mem.: ASCD, Am. Ednl. Rsch. Assn., I-Care Ill. Avocation: writing children's books. Office: Homewood-Flossmoor High Sch 999 Kedzie Ave Homewood IL 60430

DAGUISAN, JANEL, biomedical engineer, electronics and computer educator, music producer; b. Port-Au-Prince, Haiti, July 31, 1964; arrived in U.S., 1984; s. Hermann and Marie-Anne Antoinette (Duvernois) Daguisan; m. Guerline M. Petit-Homme, Jan. 4, 1992; children: Michael, Patricia, Tamarra, Zachary. Degree in electronic engring., Nat. Inst. Profl. Formation, Port-Au-Prince, 1983. Electronic technician Van's Electronics, Great Neck, NY, 1986—87, Apex Electronics, Bristol, Pa., 1987—90; mgr., owner J & F Electronics, Phila., 1991—97; master electronic technician Circuit City, Bristol, 1997—99; electronics and computer instr. CHI Inst., Southampton, Pa., 1999; electronic engring. mgr. Visual Sound, Broomall, Pa., 2000—01; biomed. engring. mgr. Kennedy Health Systems, Stratford, NJ, 2001—. Author: Electronique, 1983, (poems) Mes Poemes, 1982; author, prodr. Les Chansons de Janel, 1989; prodr.: (music album) I Love You Lord. Humanitarian trip vol. Healing the Children, Quito, Ecuador, 2003; exec. mem. Internat. Visitors' Coun., Phila., 1996. Mem.: Phila. Area Med. Instrumentation Assn., Internat. Soc. Cert. Electronic Technicians. Avocations: composing and producing music, writing poetry, billiards. Office: Kennedy Health Systems 18 E Laurel Rd Stratford NJ 08084

DAGUM, CAMILO, economist, educator; b. Argentina, Aug. 11, 1925; arrived in Can., 1972, naturalized, 1978; s. Alexander and Nazira (Hakim) D.; m. Estela Bee, Dec. 22, 1958; children: Alexander, Paul, Leonardo. PhD (gold medal summa cum laude), Nat. U. Cordoba, 1949, degree (hon.), 1988, U. Bologna, 1988, U. Montpelier, France, 1995; D (hon.), U. Naples, 2004. Mem. faculty Nat. U. Cordoba, 1950-66, prof. econs., 1956-66, dean Faculty Econ. Scis., 1962-66; sr. rsch. economist Princeton U., 1966-68; prof. Nat. U. Mex., 1968-70; vis. prof. Inst. d'Etudes du Devel. Econ. and Social U. Paris, 1967-69, U. Iowa, 1970-72; prof. econs. U. Ottawa, Ont., Can., 1972-91, chmn. dept., 1973-75, mem. acad. senate, 1981-84, bd. govs., 1983-84, prof. emeritus, 1992—. Prof. stats. and econs. U. Milan, 1990-94, chmn. Inst. Quantitative Methods, 1993-94; prof. econs. and stats. U. Bologna, Italy, 1994-02; pres. Cordoba Inst. Social Security, 1962-63; cons. to govt. and industry, 1956—; rsch. prof. U. Rome, 1956-57, London Sch. Econs., 1960-62, Inst. Sci. Econmique Appliquèe, Coll. France, 1965; vis. fellow Birkbeck Coll., U. London, 1960-61, Australian Nat. U., 1985; guest scholar Brookings Instn., 1978-79; vis. prof. U. Siena, Italy, 1987, 88, U. Rome, 1989; spkr. in field. Author books on eocn. theory; editor econ. and statis. jours.; contbr. articles to profl. jours. Mem. Acad. Coun. Rsch. Ctr. on Income Distbn., U. Siena, 1986—, Sci. Com. on Econ. Rsch. and Analysis Program, U. Montreal, 1992-96, Sci. Adv. Com. U. Bologna, Buenos Aires. Res. officer Argentina Army, 1948. Decorated Pro-Patria Gold medal, 1948; hon. prof. Inst. Advanced Studies, Salta, Argentina, 1972; extraordinary prof. Cath. U. Salta, 1981; elected mem. Accademia di Scienze e Lettere, Istituto Lombardo, 1992—. Fellow Acad. Sci. of Bologna; mem. Internat. Inst. Sociology, Internat. Statis. Inst., Statis. Soc., Econ. Soc., Econ. History Soc. Argentina, U.S. Eastern Econ. Assn., Econometric Soc., Am. Statis. Assn., Am. Econ. Assn., Can. Econ. Assn., Can. Statis. Soc., Assn. Social Econs., N.Y. Acad. Scis. Roman Catholic. Home: 318 Stewart St Ottawa ON Canada K1N 6K6 Office: U Ottawa Faculty Social Scis Dept Econs 550 Cumberland St POB 450 Station A Ottawa ON Canada K1N 6N5 also: U Bologna Dept Statis Scis Via delle Belle Arti 41 40126 Bologna Italy Office Phone: 1-613-562-5753. E-mail: dagum@stat.unibo.it.

DAHAN, MICHAEL HAIM, obstetrician, gynecologist, researcher; b. Montreal, Quebec, Canada, Oct. 12, 1970; arrived in US, 1992; s. Simon Dahan and Barbara Rissman; m. Leah Terry Litvin, Mar. 3, 2003; 1 child, Shimon Yehuda. BA with great distinction, McGill U., Montreal, Can., 1992; MD, SUNY, Stony Brook, 1996. Lic. med. Dr. N.Y., 1996. Resident obstetrics and gynecology L.I. Coll. Hosp., Bklyn., 1996—2000; fellow reproductive endocrinology and infertility U. Calif. San Diego, La Jolla, Calif., 2000—03; asst. prof. Wash. U., St. Louis, 2003—04; rsch. scholar women's reproductive health Stanford U., Calif., 2005—. Named one of Top Am. Obstetricians and Gynecologist, Consumers' Rsch. Coun. Am., 2004—; named to Wyeth-Ayerst Reporter Program, 2002 ASRM Nat. Meeting, Orlando Fla., Am. Soc. Reproductive Medicine Ann. Mtg., 2002; recipient Adminstrv. Chief Resident, LI Coll. Hosp., 1999-2000, James McGill Academic Scholarship, Faculty Scholar, Excellence in Tchg. award, Dept. Obstetrics and Gynecology Wash. U., 2003—04; grantee Ruth L. Kirschtein Nat. Rsch. Svc. award, U.S. Pub. Health Svc., 2001—02, Wash. U. OB-GYN Dept., 2003—04, McGill U., 1991; scholar, 1989, 1990; Women's Reproductive Health Rsch. scholar, Nat. Inst. Child Health and Human Devel. NIH, 2005—, Women's Reproductive Health Rsch. scholar, NIH, 2005—, Ted Adams scholar, Pacific Coast OB-GYN Soc., 2002, Eli Lilly scholar, Am. Soc. Reproductive Medicine, 2001, 2003. Fellow: Am. Coll. of Onstetrics and Gynecology (assoc.), Endocrine Soc. (assoc.), Am. Soc. for Reproductive Medicine (assoc.); mem.: Soc. For Reproductive Endocrinology and Infertility (assoc.; assoc. com. co-chair 2002—03, assoc. com. chmn. 2003—04). Avocations: restoring antique toys, running, weight lifting, enjoying my children. Office: Stanford University 300 Pasteur Dr (A370) Stanford CA 94305 Office Phone: 650-724-4683. Office Fax: 650-723-7737.

DAHAN, RENE, oil industry executive; b. Aug. 26, 1941; Diploma in nautical sci., Sch. Hydrogeography, Bordeaux, France. Process technician Esso, Rotterdam, The Netherlands, 1963-73, mgr., 1973-74, mgr. refining dept., 1974-77; head corp. planning divsn. Esso Europe, London, 1977-78, mgr. natural gas dept., 1978-81; dep. mgr. petroleum products dept. Exxon Corp., 1981-83; exec. v.p. Esso B.V., Breda, The Netherlands, 1983-85, pres. CEO, 1985-91; exec. v.p. ECI, 1991-92; corp. v.p., pres. ECI Exxon Corp., 1992-95, sr. v.p., 1995-98, Exxon Mobil Corp., 1999—. Mem. internat. adv. bd. Inst. Empresa.; acting chmn. supervisory bd. Ahold, 2004—; supervisory bd. VNU NV, TPG NV, Aegon NV; internat. advisory bd. CVC Capital Ptnr.; bd. dir. Jr. Achievement Internat.; bd. trustees US Coun. Internat. Bus. Office: Exxon Mobil Corp 5959 Las Colinas Blvd Irving TX 75039-2298

DAHEIM, MARY RENE RICHARDSON, writer; b. Seattle, Nov. 7, 1937; d. Hugh Emery and Monica Mary (Dawson) Richardson; m. David Charles Daheim, Dec. 18, 1965; children: Barbara, Katherine, Magdalen. BA in Communications, U. Wash., 1960. Mng. editor Anacortes (Wash.) Am. Bull., 1960; mgr. Pacific NW Bell Tel. Co., Seattle, 1960-66; reporter, columnist Port Angeles (Wash.) Evening News, 1966-69; pub. rels. cons. Pacific N.W. Bell, U.S. West, Seattle, 1969-86; writer Seattle, 1983—. Author: Love's Pirate, 1983, Destiny's Pawn, 1984, Pride's Captive, 1986, Passion's Triumph, 1988, King's Ransom, 1990, Improbable Eden, 1991, Just Desserts, 1991, Fowl Prey, 1991, Holy Terrors, 1992, Gypsy Baron, 1992, Alpine Advocate, 1992, Dune to Death, 1993, Alpine Betrayal, 1993, Bantam of the Opera, 1993, The Alpine Christmas, 1993, A Fit of Tempera, 1994, The Alpine Decoy, 1994, Major Vices, 1995, The Alpine Escape, 1995, Murder, My Suite, 1995, The Alpine Fury, 1995, Auntie Mayhem, 1996, The Alpine Gamble, 1996, Nutty as a Fruitcake, 1996, The Alpine Hero, 1997, September Mourn, 1997, The Alpine Icon, 1997, The Alpine Journey, 1998, Wed and Buried, 1998, Snow Place to Die, 1998, The Alpine Kindred, 1999, Legs Benedict, 1999, The Alpine Legacy, 1999, Creeps Suzette, 2000, Suture Self, 2001, Silver Scream, 2002,Alpine Obituary, 2002, This Old Souse, 2004, The Alpine Pursuit, 2004, Hocus Croakus, 2004, The Alpine Quilt, 2005, Dead Man Docking, 2005. Mem. Romance Writers Am., Mystery Writers Am., Authors Guild. Roman Catholic. Avocations: gardening, reading, history, travel, opera. Mailing: c/o Maureen Moran Agency Park West Station PO Box 20191 New York NY 10025*

DAHILL, THOMAS HENRY, artist, educator; b. Cambridge, Mass., June 22, 1925; s. Thomas Henry Dahill and Helen Agnes Ireland. BS in Chemistry, Tufts Coll., 1949; diploma in painting, Sch. of Mus. of Fine Arts, Boston, 1953, 5th-yr. cert., 1954; student, Harvard Summer Sch., 1953; MA (hon.), Emerson Coll., Boston, 1967. Instr. art history Tufts U., Medford, Mass., 1944—45, 1959—65, lectr. art history and drawing Naples, Italy, 1966; instr. dept. drawing Sch. of Mus. of Fine Arts, Boston, 1953—55, 1958—69; prof., chmn. fine arts Emerson Coll., Boston, 1961—94. Resident MacDowall Colony, Peterborough, NH, 1958; participant IAMCR Conf. UNESCO, Sao Paulo, Brazil, 1989. Mural, LifeCycle, 1957, Dock, Canal Mus., Billerica, Mass., 2005, portrait, Dr. and Mrs. James Jackson, 1990, exhibitions include Boston Arts Festival, 1954, 1955, 1956, USIA Graphics to Near East and Asia, 1958, Carl Siembab Gallery, Fogg Mus., Boston Pub. Libr., Lenin Libr., also collections. Pres., dir. Lend-a-Hand Charity, Boston, 1968—2005; guest sec. of culture Moscow, 1974; dir. Soc. for Propagation of Bible for Indians and Others in N.Am., Boston, 1970—. 2d lt. USAF, 1943—46, PTO. Recipient Abbey Meml. fellowship, Am. Acad. in Rome, 1955—57; scholar, Skowhegan (Maine) Sch. Painting and Sculpture, 1952, Sch. Mus. Fine Arts, Boston, 1950. Mem.: Harvard Mus. Soc., Medici Soc., Middlesex Canal Assn. (v.p., dir. 1990—), St. Botolph Club (mem. arts com. 1989). Avocations: swimming, travel, writing poetry. Home: 223 Broadway Arlington MA 02474

DAHIYA, RAJBIR SINGH, mathematics professor, researcher; b. Rattangarh, Haryana, India, Dec. 3, 1940; came to U.S., 1968; s. Ram S. and Kesar (Devi) D.; m. Krishna Tavathia, Dec. 11, 1966; children: Madhu, Ranjan. PhD, Birla Inst. Sci. and Tech., Pilani, India, 1967. Lectr. Birla Inst. Sci. and Tech., 1967-68; asst. prof. math. Iowa State U., Ames, 1968-72, assoc. prof., 1972-78, prof., 1978—. Reviewer math. revs. Zentrallblat; referee applied math. jours. Contbr. over 150 rsch. papers on delay and advanced differential equations, transform theory and spl. functions to U.S., European and Australian profl. jours. Mem. Am. Math. Soc., Soc. Indsl. and Applied Math. Democrat. Hindu. Home: 3144 Sycamore Rd Ames IA 50014-4510 Office: Iowa State U Dept Math Ames IA 50011-0001

DAHL, ANDREW WILBUR, health services executive; b. N.Y.C., Feb. 19, 1943; s. Wilbur A. and Margret L. Dahl; m. Janice White, Sept. 4, 1965; children: Kristina, Jennifer, Meredith. BS, Clark U., 1968; MPA, Cornell U., 1970; ScD, Hohns Hopkins U., 1974. Staff asst. Md. Comprehensive Health Planning Agy., Balt., 1970-72; dir. planning St. John Hosp., Detroit, 1972-79; exec. v.p., COO St. John Health Corp., Detroit, 1979-85; pres., CEO United Health Sys., Detroit, 1983-88; v.p. devel. Hosp. Corp. Am. Mgmt. Co., 1988-90; pres., CEO IVF America Inc., Greenwich, Conn., 1990-94, Health-Net, Kansas City, 1994-2000, Evolution Benefits Corp., Avon, Conn., 2000—. Bd. dirs. AVAX Techs., Inc.; mem. adv. bd. Clark U. Grad. Sch. Mgmt.; instr. U. Mich. Bur. Hosp. Adminstrn., 1981—88. Bd. dirs. Detroit Sci. Ctr., 1984-91; mem. Nat. Com. for Quality Health Care, Washington, 1984-89; bd. dirs. Forum Health Care Planning Kansas City (Mo.) Mus., 1995—. Served with USN, 1965-67. Recipient Disting. Svc. award Mich. Jaycees, 1977, Outstanding Contbns. to Profl. Mgmt. award Cornell U., 1980. Fellow Am. Coll. Healthcare Execs.; mem. AAAS, APHA, Am. Hosp. Assn. (rehab sect. bd.), Am. Assn. Health Plans, Internat. Health Econs. and Mgmt. Inst., Hallbrook Country Club, Cornell Club N.Y. Methodist. Office: 22 Waterville Rd Avon CT 06001 E-mail: awdahl@yahoo.com.

DAHL, ARLENE, actress, writer, apparel designer, cosmetics executive; b. Mpls., Aug. 11, 1928; d. Rudolph and Idelle (Swan) D.; m. Marc A. Rosen; children: Lorenzo Lamas, Carole Christine Holmes, Stephen Andreas Schaum. Student, U. Minn., 1943-44, Mpls. Inst. Art, 1945, Minn. Coll. Music, 1944, Minn. Bus. Coll., 1944. Pres. Arlene Dahl Enterprises, 1952-67; v.p. Kenyon & Eckhart, 1967-72; pres. Woman's World divsn. Kenyon & Eckhart Advt. Agy., 1967-72; nat. beauty and health advisor Sears Roebuck Co., 1970-75; internat. dir. Sales and Mktg. Execs. Internat., 1972-75; fashion dir. O.M.A., 1975-78; pres. Dahlia Parfums, Inc., 1975-80, Dahlia Prodns., Inc., 1978-81, Dahlmark Prodns., 1981—; pres., CEO Scandia Cosmetics, Ltd., 1978-80; pres., chmn. Lasting Beauty Ltd., 1986—. Author: Always Ask a Man, 1965, 12 Beautyscope books, 1968, rev. edit., 1978, Arlene Dahl's Secrets of Hair Care, 1969, Arlene Dahl's Secrets of Skin Care, 1972, Beyond Beauty, 1980, Arlene Dahl's Lovescopes, 1983, Arlene Dahl's Weekly Astro Forecast, yearly from 1991-2004, Arlene Dahl's Hollywood Horoscope internat. syndicated weekly column, 1990—; actress: (Broadway plays) including Mr. Strauss Goes to Boston, Questionable Ladies, Cyrano de Bergerac, Applause (Tony award musical), (films) including (debut) My Wild Irish Rose, The Bride Goes Wild, Reign of Terror, A Southern Yankee, Ambush, The Outriders, Three Little Words, Watch the Birdie, Scene of the Crime, Inside Straight, No Questions Asked, Desert Legion, Slightly Scarlet, Sangaree, Caribbean Gold, Jamaica Run, Diamond Queen, Here Come the Girls, Bengal Brigade, Kisses for My President, Woman's World, Journey to the Center of the Earth, Wicked as They Come, She Played with Fire, Les Poneyettes, Du Blé Enliases, The Land Raiders, The Way to Kathmandu, Fortune Is a Woman, The Big Bank Roll, Who Killed Maxwell Thorn?, Midnight Warrior, 1991, (TV shows) Lux Video Theatre, 1952-53, guest starring appearances on The Love Boat, Fantasy Island, Love American Style, One Life to Live, 1981-84, Night of 100 Stars, 1983, Happy Birthday Hollywood, 1987, All My Children, 1995, Renegade, 1995, 96, 97, Air America, 1999; hostess (TV series): Pepsi-Cola Theatre, 1954, Opening Night, 1958, Arlene Dahl's Beauty Spot, 1966, Arlene Dahl's Starscope, 1979-80, Arlene Dahl's Lovescope, 1980-82; played throughout U.S. in One Touch of Venus, The Camel Bell, Blithe Spirit, Liliom, The King and I, Roman Candle, I Married an Angel, Bell, Book and Candle, Applause, Marriage Go Round, Pal Joey, A Little Night Music, Forty Carats, Life with Father, Murder Among Friends, Dear Liar; nightclub acts Flamingo Hotel, Las Vegas, Latin Quarter, N.Y.C., musical stage appearances: Carnegie Hall, 1997, London Paladium, 1992, 1998, Salute to MGM Musicals; internat. syndicated beauty columnist Chgo. Tribune/ N.Y. News Syndicate, 1950-70, Arlene Dahl's Lucky Stars Column, Globe Communications, 1988-90, Arlene Dahl's Starscope Weekly Column, 1991, 92, 93, 94, 95, 96, 97, 98, 99, 2000, 01, 02, 03, 04, Horoscope Yearly Forecast 1991-2002; designer sleepwear for A.N. Saab & Co., 1952-57, In Vogue with Arlene Dahl (Vogue Patterns), 1980-85, Arlene Dahl Pvt. Collection Jewelry, 1989-94, Arlene Dahl's Jewels of Fortune Home Shopping Network, 1996. Hon. life mem. Father Flannagan's Boys Town; internat. amb. Pearl Buck Found.; founder, pres. Broadway Walk of Stars Found., Inc.; bd. dirs. Hollywood Mus. Recipient 10 Box Office Laurel awards, Hollywood Walk of Fame Star, 1961, Coup de Chapeau Deaville Film Festival award, 1982, 92; named Best Coiffed, Heads of Fame awards, 1967-72, 80; named Woman of the Yr., Advt. Club of N.Y.C., 1969, Mother of the Yr., 1982, Lifetime Achievement award WorldFest, 1994, Leadership in the Arts, 1997; named to Scandinavian Hall of Fame, 1997. Fellow: Vesterheim Norwegian/Am. Found. (life); mem.: UNIFEM, NATAS (trustee), Film Soc., Edward Grieg Soc., Authors Guild, Acad. Motion Picture Arts and Scis. (vice chair N.Y. spl. events), Acad. TV Arts and Scis. (bd. govs., v.p.), Smithsonian Assocs., Nat. Trust for Hist. Preservation, Commanderie de Bordeaux (N.Y.), Commanderie de Bontemps du Medoc et Graves, France. Office: Dahlmark Prodns PO Box 116 Sparkill NY 10976-0116

DAHL, EVERETT E., lawyer; b. Sandy, Utah, June 21, 1923; m. Ann Kosovich, June 21, 1947; children: Annette, EvAnn. BS, U. Utah, 1947, JD, 1949. Bar: Utah 1949, U.S. Dist. Ct. Utah 1959, U.S. Ct. Mil. Appeals 1959, U.S. Supreme Ct., U.S. Ct. Appeals (10th cir.). Commd. 2d lt. U.S. Army, 1943, advanced through grades to col., ret., 1975; pvt. practice Midvale, Utah, 1949—. Mayor City of Midvale, 1986-94; exec. sec. Midvale C. of C., 1950-60; bd. dirs. Rsch. Inst., 1955—; pres. Palo Verde Park, Inc., Safford, Ariz., 1970's; chmn. Salt Lake County Coun. Govts., South Valley Emergency Ctr.; bd. dirs. Trans Jordan Landfill. Mem. Res. Officers Assn. (life, dept. comdr. nat. exec. com.), Amvets (dept. pres. nat. exec. com. 1993—), VFW, Phi Kappa Phi. Avocations: fishing, golf. Office: 49 W Center St Midvale UT 84047-7451 Office Phone: 801-255-6834.

DAHL, GERALD LUVERN, psychotherapist, educator; b. Nov. 10, 1938; s. Lloyd F. and Leola J. (Painter) Dahl; m. Judith Lee Brown, June 24, 1960; children: Peter, Stephen, Leah. BA, Wheaton Coll., 1960; MSW, U. Nebr., 1962; PhD in Psychotherapy (hon.), Internat. U. Found., 1987. Diplomate Am. Psychotherapy Assn. Juvenile probation officer Hennepin County Ct. Svcs., 1962—65; cons. Citizens Coun. on Delinquency and Crime, Mpls., 1965—67; dir. patient svcs. Mt. Sinai Hosp., Mpls., 1967—69; clin. social worker Mpls. Clinic of Psychiatry, 1969—82, G.L. Dahl & Assocs., Inc., Mpls., 1983—. Assoc. prof. social work Bethel Coll., St. Paul, 1964—83; spl. instr. sociology Golden Valley Luth. Coll., 1974—83; pres. Strategic Team-Makers, Inc., 1985—; adj. prof. U. Wis., River Falls, 1988—90. Author: Why Christian Marriages Are Breaking Up, 1979, Everybody Needs Somebody Sometime, 1980, How Can We Keep Christian Marriages from Falling Apart, 1988, The Sandwich Generation, 1995; contbr. articles to profl. jours. Founder, bd. stewards Family Counseling Svc., Minn. Bapt. Conf., 1994—; bd. dirs. Edgewater Bapt. Ch., 1972—75, chmn., 1974—75; vice chmn. bd. stewards Minnetonka Bapt. Ch., 1995. Mem.: AAUP, Am. Assn. Behavioral Therapists, Pi Gamma Mu. Office: 7575 Golden Valley Rd Ste 130 Golden Valley MN 55427 Office Phone: 763-542-1199. Personal E-mail: jerryd@stmi.biz.

DAHL, GORDON B., economics professor; BA, Brigham Young U., Provo, Utah, 1993; PhD, Princeton U., Princeton, N.J., 1998, MA, 1995. Asst. prof. U. Rochester, Rochester, NY, 1998—2004, assoc. prof., 2004—. Faculty rsch. fellow Nat. Bur. of Econ. Rsch., Cambridge, Mass., 2003—. Contbr. articles pub. to profl. jour. Fellow NSF Fellowship for Grad. Study, NSF. Office: Univ Rochester Harkness Hall Rochester NY 14627

DAHL, JEFFREY A(LAN), lawyer; b. Salt Lake City, July 31, 1953; s. Alan Craven and Dorothy (Beckstead) D.; m. Julie Ann Jelte, Jan. 3, 1975; children: Erika Dahl Price, Hillary Dahl Murphy, Miriam Dahl Padilla, Katherine, Alan J., Spencer C. BS magna cum laude, U. Utah, 1976; JD cum laude, Brigham Young U., 1979. Bar: N.Mex. 1979, U.S. Dist. Ct. N.Mex. 1979, U.S. Ct. Appeals (10th cir.) 1985. Assoc. Lamb, Metzgar and Lines (now Lamb, Metzgar, Lines & Dahl), Albuquerque, 1979-84, ptnr., 1984—. Mem. faculty U. Phoenix, Albuquerque, 1985-95. Com. mem. Boy Scouts Am. Rio Grande dist., Albuquerque, 1983; mem. exec. bd. Great Southwest Coun., 1991-2001. Recipient Christenson Meml. award Brigham Young U., 1979; named Outstanding Faculty Mem. U. Phoenix, 1987, 91. Mem. ABA, N.Mex. Bar Assn. (chmn. employment law divsn. 1998-2000), Albuquerque Bar Assn., Alliance Francaise, Phi Beta Kappa, Phi Kappa Phi. Mem. Lds Ch. Avocations: running, biking, swimming, backpacking, skiing. Home: 6216 Dellyne Ct NW Albuquerque NM 87120-2048 Office: Lamb Metzgar Lines & Dahl PA PO Box 987 300 Central SW Albuquerque NM 87103 Office Phone: 505-247-0100. E-mail: jad@lamblaw.com.

DAHL, JOHN CLARENCE, JR., academic administrator; b. Indpls., Jan. 10, 1948; s. John C. and Dorothy L. (Reed) D.; m. Vickie E. Eckert, Oct. 18, 1980; children: Jennifer, Bradley. BS in Bus., Ind. U., 1970, MS in Edn., 1972, EdD, 1982. Asst. univ. registrar, dir. admissions Ind. U., Bloomington, 1971-80; assoc. vice chancellor, registrar Ind. U.-Purdue U. Ft. Wayne, 1980—. Mem. adv. com. Ind. Commn. for Higher Edn., Indpls., 1982; presenter workshops in field. Mem. Am. Assn. Collegiate Registrars and Admissions Officers (various coms. 1975-87), Assn. for Instnl. Rsch., Soc. for Coll. and Univ. Planning. Office: Ind-Purdue U Ft Wayne 2101 E Coliseum Blvd Fort Wayne IN 46805-1445 E-mail: dahl@ipfw.edu.

DAHL, JOYLE COCHRAN, lawyer; b. Oakland, Calif., Oct. 5, 1935; s. Carl Arthur and Jane Virginia (Cochran) D.; m. Dawn Adele Wood, Aug. 16, 1959; children: Brenda Loreen, Peter Carl. BS, U. Oreg., 1957, LLB, 1959; LLM, NYU, 1964. Bar: Oreg. 1959, U.S. Supreme Ct. 1963. Trial atty. tax div. Dept. Justice, Washington, 1960-63; ptnr. Duffy, Georgeson, Dahl et al, Portland, Oreg., 1964-76, Dahl, Zalutsky, Nichols et al, Portland, 1976-79, Tonkon, Torp, Galen et al, Portland, 1979-85; sr. ptnr. Schwabe Williamson & Wyatt, Portland, 1985—. Bd. dirs. Portland Fixture Ltd. Partnership, Peter Jacobsen Prodns., Portland, Jour. Graphics, Inc. Contbr. numerous articles on taxation to profl. jours. Bd. dirs. Portland Youth Philharmonic, 1989-90, Oreg. Sports Hall of Fame, Delauney Mental Health Ctr., Portland, 1974-80; adv. bd. Salvation Army, The Children's Course, 1995-. Mem. Oreg. Bar Assn. (chmn. tax sect. 1972), Estate Planning Coun. Oreg., Waverley Country Club (Portland, v.p. 1984), Thunderbird Country Club (Rancho Mirage, Calif., pres. 2000), Oreg. Golf Club (West Linn, pres. 1994-95), Multnomah Athletic Club (Portland, v.p. 1979). Republican. Presbyterian. Avocation: golf. Home: 1111 SW Myrtle Dr Portland OR 97201-2270 Office: Schwabe Williamson & Wyatt 1211 SW 5th Ave Ste 1800 Portland OR 97204-3713 Office Phone: 503-222-9981.

DAHL, LAWRENCE FREDERICK, chemistry educator; b. Evanston, Ill., June 2, 1929; s. Lawrence Gustave and Anne (Stuessy) D.; m. June Lomnes, Sept. 1, 1956; children: Larry, Eric, Christopher (dec.). BS in Chemistry, U. Louisville, 1951; PhD, Iowa State U., 1956; DSc (hon.), U. Louisville, 1991. Postdoctoral fellow Ames (Iowa State U.) Lab. AEC, 1957; from instr. to assoc. prof. chemistry U. Wis., Madison, 1957-64, prof., 1964—. R. E. Rundlechair, 1978—, Hilldale chair and prof., 1991—. Brotherton rsch. prof. U. Leeds, 1983 Recipient Inorganic Chemistry award Am. Chem. Soc., 1974, Disting. Alumnus award U. Louisville Coll. Letters and Sci., 1990, Sr. U.S. Scientist Humboldt award Alexander von Humboldt Stiftung, 1985, R.S. Nyholm medal Royal Soc. Chemistry, 1985, P. Chini medal Italian Soc. Chemistry, 1989, J.C. Bailar Jr. medal U. Ill., 1990, F. Basolo medal Northwestern U., 1995, Hilldale award in phys. scis. U. Wis., 1994, Willard Gibbs medal, Chgo. sect. Am. Chem. Soc., 1999, Pioneer award, Am. Inst. Chemists, 2000; named to Hon. Order Ky. Cols., 1982; Alfred P. Sloan fellow, 1963-65, U. Louisvlle Coll. Letters and Sci. fellow, 1990. Fellow AAAS, N.Y. Acad. Sci., Am. Acad. Arts and Scis.; mem. NAS. Home: 4817 Woodburn Dr Madison WI 53711-1345 Office: Univ of Wis Madison Dept of Chemistry 1101 University Ave Madison WI 53706-1322 Fax: 608-262-6143. E-mail: dahl@chem.wisc.edu.

DAHL, MARK VICTOR, dermatologist, educator; b. Mpls., Aug. 24, 1942; s. Victor E. and Edith M. D.; m. Arlene C., July 1, 1966; children: Kristian Mark, Jonathan Mark. BA, Wesleyan U., 1964; MD, U. Minn., 1968. Diplomate in dermatology Am. Bd. Dermatology, 1980, in immunodermatology Am. Bd. Dermatology, 1986. Intern U. Ore. Med. Sci. Ctr., Portland, 1968-69; fellow in dermatology U. Copenhagen, 1969-70; rsch. assoc. Walter Reed Army Med. Ctr., Washington, 1970-72; resident dermatology U. Calif., San Francisco, 1972—74; from asst. prof. to prof. dermatology U. Minn. Med. Sch., Mpls., 1974—2000, chmn. dept. dermatology, 1995—2000; prof., chmn. dept. dermatology Mayo Clinic, Scottsdale, Ariz., 2000—04, prof. emeritus, 2000—. Pres. Mark Dahl & Assocs., Inc., 1994-2002. Author: Clinical Immunodermatology, 1981, 3d edit., 1996, Common Office Dermatology, 1983, Clinical Dermatology, 1990, 3d edit., 2003, Dermatology, 1991; mem. editl. bd. jours. in field; contbr. articles to profl. jours. Founder Camp Discovery for children with severe skin diseases. Maj. M.C., U.S. Army, 1970-72. Mem. ACP, Am. Soc. Allergy and Immunology (pres. 1981-82), Am. Acad. Dermatology (hon., pres. 1993-94, Henry Stelwagen award 1972, Gold Triangle award 1998, Gold medal 2002), Am. Dermatology Assn., Assn. Profs. Dermatology, Internat. Soc. Dermatology, Soc. Investigative Dermatology (hon., v.p. 1994-95), Br. Dermatol. Assn., Mex. Acad. Dermatology, Can. Dermatol. Assn., Minn. Dermatol. Assn., Phoenix Dermatol. Soc., South Africa Dermatology Soc., Pacific Dermatology Soc Office: Mayo Clinic Scottsdale 13400 Shea Blvd Scottsdale AZ 85259 Office Phone: 480-301-6169. Business E-Mail: dahl.markv@mayo.edu.

DAHL, ROBERT ALAN, political science professor; b. Inwood, Iowa, Dec. 17, 1915; s. Peter Ivor and Vera (Lewis) D.; m. Mary Louise Bartlett, 1940 (dec. 1970); children: Ellen Kirsten, Peter Bartlett (dec.), Eric Lewis, Christopher Robert; m. Ann Goodrich Sale, 1973. AB, U. Wash., 1936; PhD, Yale U., 1940; LLD (hon.), U. Mich., 1985, U. Alaska, 1987; D of Philosophy (hon.), U. Oslo, 1994; LLD (hon.), Law Sch. for Social Rsch., 1996, Harvard U., 1998; D honoris causa, U. Madrid Complutense, 2001; LLD, Grinnell

Coll., 2001; LittD, Columbia U., 2005. Mgmt. analyst USDA, 1940; economist Office Prodn. Mgmt., Office Price Adminstrn. and Civilian Supply, War Prodn. Bd., 1940-42; faculty Yale U., 1946—, Eugene M3yer prof. polit. sci., 1955-64, Sterling prof. polit sci., from 1964, Ford Rsch. prof., 1957-58, chmn. dept. polit. sci., 1957-62. Lectr. polit. sci., Flacso, Santiago, Chile, 1967; pres. Am. Polit. Sci. Assn., 1967. Author: Congress and Foreign Policy, 1950, (with E. Browne) Domestic Control of Atomic Energy, 1951, (with C.E. Lindblom) Politics, Economics and Welfare, 1952, A Preface to Democratic Theory, 1956, (with Haire and Lazarsfeld) Social Science Research on Business, 1959, Who Governs?, 1961, Modern Political Analysis, 1963, Political Oppositions in Western Democracies, 1966, After the Revolution?, 1970, Polyarchy: Participation and Opposition, 1971, Regimes and Oppositions, 1972, Democracy in the United States, 1972, (with E.R. Tufte) Size and Democracy, 1973, Dilemmas of Pluralist Democracy, 1982, A Preface to Economic Democracy, 1985, Controlling Nuclear Weapons, 1985, Democracy, Liberty and Equality, 1986, Democracy and the Critics, 1989, The New American Political (Dis) Order, 1994, Toward Democracy: A Journey Reflections: 1940-1997, 1997, On Democracy, 1999, Politica e virtu, 2001, How Democratic Is the American Constitution?, 2002, Intervista sul Pluralismo, 2002. With U.S. Army, 1943-45. Decorated Bronze Star with cluster; Cavaliere of Republic of Italy, 1988; recipient Woodrow Wilson prize, 1963, 90, Talcott Parsons prize, 1977, Wilbur Lucius Cross medal, 1986, Elaine and David Spitz award, 1991; Guggenheim fellow, 1950, 78, fellow Ctr. for Advanced Study in Behavioral Scis., 1955-56, 67. Fellow Am. Acad. Arts and Scis. (Talcott Parsons prize 1977); mem. NAS, Am. Philos. Soc., Am. Polit. Sci. Assn. (pres. 1966-67, Woodrow Wilson prize 1963, James Madison prize 1978, Gladys Kammerer award 1983, Benjamin Lippincott award 1989, Johan Skytte prize 1995), New Eng. Polit. Assn. (pres. 1951), ACLU, Brit. Acad., Phi Beta Kappa. Home: 17 Cooper Rd North Haven CT 06473-3001 Office Phone: 203-432-5283. E-mail: robert.dahl@yale.edu.

DAHLBERG, ALBERT EDWARD, biochemistry professor; b. Chgo., Sept. 19, 1938; s. Albert Archer and Thelma Elizabeth (Ham) D.; m. Pamela Kathy Voth, June 29, 1963; children: Albert Andrew, Krista Katherine, Paul Eric BS, Haverford Coll., 1960; MD, U. Chgo., 1965, PhD in Biochemistry, 1968. Rsch. assoc. Nat. Cancer Inst.-NIH, Bethesda, Md., 1967-70; European Molecular Biology Orgn. fellow Molecular Biol. Inst., U. Aarhus, Denmark, 1970-72; prof. biochemistry Brown U., Providence, 1972—, chmn. dept. biochemistry, 1985, 87. Vis. prof. U. Wis., Madison, 1978-79; v.p. rsch. Mora Pharms., Inc., Miami, Fla., 1983—; founder, bd. dirs. Milkhaus Lab. Inc., Delanson, N.Y., 1993—; mem. bd. sci. counselors divsn. cancer biology diagnosis and ctrs. Nat. Cancer Inst., 1992-95; mem. Corp. of Haverford Coll., 1995—. Contbr. articles to profl. jours., chpts. to books NIH grantee, 1972—; recipient USPHS Rsch. Career Devel. award NIH, 1975-80 Fellow AAAS, Am. Soc. Microbiology; mem. Am. Soc. Biochemistry and Molecular Biology (sec. 2001—04), The Monroe Inst. Mem. Society Of Friends. Home: 554 Wayland Ave Providence RI 02906-4723 Office: Brown U Dept Molecular and Cell Biology and Biochemistry Dept Biochemistry Box G- j4 Providence RI 02912 Office Phone: 401-863-2223. E-mail: Albert_Dahlberg@Brown.edu.

DAHLBERG, ALFRED WILLIAM, electric company executive; b. Atlanta, 1940; BS in Bus. Admin., Ga. State U., 1970. Meter installer Georgia Power, 1961; pres., CEO Southern Co. Services, 1985, Georgia Power, 1988; pres. Southern Co., Atlanta, 1994—2001, chmn., CEO, 1995—2001; chmn. Mirant Corp., 2000—. Bd. dir. Equifax, Inc. Bd. Councilors Carter Ctr.; mem. Ga. State U. Alumni Assn. Named Man of the Year, Georgia Trend mag., 1994, Georgia's Most Respected CEO, 1996; recipient Salute to Greatness award, King Center, 1997. Mem.: US C. of C. (bd. mem., exec. com.). Office: Mirant 1155 Perimeter Ctr West Atlanta GA 30338

DAHLBERG, CARL FREDRICK, JR., entrepreneur; b. New Orleans, Aug. 20, 1936; s. Carl Fredrick and Nancey Erwin (Jones) D.; m. Constance Weston, Dec. 30, 1961; children: Kirsten Erwin Dahlberg Turner, Catherine Morgan Dahlberg Stokes. BSCE, Tulane U., 1958; MBA, Harvard U., 1964. Regional mgr. bond dept. E.F. Hutton & Co., Inc., New Orleans, 1965-67; chmn. exec. com. Dahlberg, Kelly & Wisdom, Inc., New Orleans, 1967-71; pres. St. Mary Galvanizing Co., Inc., New Orleans, 1971-2000, chmn., 2000—; pres. The South Coast Co., LLC, 2004—. Co-organizer, dir. Charter Med. Corp., 1969-72; adv. dir. Rathborne Cos., 1985-91; with Internat. Trade Mart, 1974-89, mem. exec. com., 1981-84, treas., 1983-84; consul gen. of Monaco, New Orleans, 1981-98; treas. Consul Corps of New Orleans, 1990-94. Co-author: Hydrochloric Acid Pickling, 1979. Trustee Metairie Park Country Day Sch., New Orleans, 1976-85, treas., 1980-82, chmn., 1982-84; trustee Eye, Ear, Nose and Throat Hosp., New Orleans, 1980-96, mem. exec. com., 1980-83; trustee Eye, Ear, Nose and Throat Found., 1980-83, U. South, Sewanee, Tenn., 1984-90; bd. dirs. New Orleans Tech. Coun., 1993-98, Mus. Arts Soc. New Orleans, 2000—; vis. com. Monroe libr. Loyola U., New Orleans, La., 2002-; vestryman Christ Ch. Cathedral, New Orleans, 1981-85. With U.S. Army, 1958-59. Mem. ASCE, Nat. Assn. Mfrs. (bd. dirs. 1997-2003), Venerable Order Hosp. of St. John of Jerusalem, Mil. and Hospitaller Order St. Lazarus, Order of Merit of Italian Republic, Order of Grimaldi (Monaco), New Orleans Country Club, Pickwick Club, Army and Navy Club (Washington), The Brook Club (N.Y.C.). Republican. Episcopalian. Home: 199 Audubon Blvd New Orleans LA 70118-5538 Office: 201 Saint Charles Ave Ste 2531 New Orleans LA 70170-1000 Office Phone: 504-599-5960. E-mail: fritzdahl@aol.com.

DAHLBERG, ERIC ROSS, music educator; b. Mpls., Nov. 7, 1962; s. Jerome E. and Marilyn D. Dahlberg; m. Suzanne Marie Parenteau, May 22, 1993; children: Madeline Rae, Heather Marie. MusB, U. Minn., 1985, MEd, 1999. Lic. tchr. State Minn., cert. environ. edn. Hamline U., 2002. Pvt. instrumental music instr., Minn., 1985—; instr. longterm band, strings, classroom music Hopkins Pub. Schools #270, Golden Valley, Minn., 1985—86; dir. orch. Oskaloosa (Iowa) Cmty. Schs., 1987—90; tchr. instrumental music St. Paul Pub. Schools #625, St. Paul, 1993—. Mem. cello sect. Bloomington Symphony Orch., Minn., 1990—2000; condr. Rondo Cmty. Orch. (formerly 'Capitol Hill Symphony'), St. Paul, 1995—2000, Woodbury Youth Orch., 2001—. Writer (article) Gopher Music Notes, photographer (photograph/color print) Voyage Through Time, Lasting Illusions, Champion, Ramsey County Fair, 2004, Reserve Champion, Wash. County Fair, 2003, 2005. Recipient Champions Ribbon for photography, Ramsey County Fair, Reserve Champion Ribbon for photography, Wash. County Fair. Mem.: Minn. Music Educators Assn. (Minn. All State Orch. award 1979—81), Minn. Band Dirs. Assn., Music Educators Nat. Conf. (no. state coord. - student chpt. 1984—85). Achievements include Have held the position of 'Principal Cello' for the following orchestras:Armstrong Sr. H. School; University of Minnesota, Duluth, Symphony Orchestra & Chamber Orchestra; Oskaloosa Community Orchestra; Currently hold a 'Brown Belt' in karate. Have won 1st, 2nd, and/or 3rd place trophies at 'Green, Blue and Red' belt levels at local karate tournaments. Avocations: photography, Karate, fishing, alpine skiing, travel. Office: Linwood A+ Elem School 1023 Osceola Ave Saint Paul MN 55105

DAHLBERG, KENNETH C., engineering executive; b. Camden, N.J., Oct. 19, 1944; BSEE, Drexel U., 1967; MSEE, U. So. Calif., 1969; student, UCLA bus. sch.for advanced edn. for execs. Various engring., program mgmt., leadership positions Hughes Electronics Corp., 1967, corp. v.p.; sr. v.p. Hughes Aircraft Co.; pres., COO Raytheon Sys. Raytheon Co., Washington, 1997—2000, exec. v.p. bus. devel., 2000—03; exec. v.p. Gen. Dynamics; pres., CEO Sci. Applications Internat. Corp., San Diego, 2003—, chmn., 2004—. Mem. IEEE, Am. Soc. Naval Engrs., Nat. Def. Indsl. Assn. (bd. dirs.), Surface Navy Assn., U.S. Navy League (life), Assn. U.S. Army. Office: Sci Applications Internat Corp 10260 Campus Point Dr San Diego CA 92121*

DAHLBERG, MARK L., music educator, elementary school educator; b. Chgo., Dec. 21, 1965; s. Ted and Joan Dahlberg; m. Melissa Dahlberg, Mar. 4, 1995. B of Music Edn., Fla. State U., 1991; MS, Nova U., 2004. Educator music Cypress Lake High Sch., Ft. Myers, Fla., 1991—2001, Ft. Myers High Sch., 2001—. Office: Ft Myers High Sch 2635 Cortez Blvd Fort Myers FL 33901

DAHLBURG, JOHN-THOR THEODORE, news correspondent; b. Orange, N.J., Apr. 30, 1953; s. Donald Russell and Madeline (Blackadore) D.; m. Yvonne Michelle Bastien, Nov. 18, 1980; children: Cecile, Charlotte. BA summa cum laude, Washington and Lee U., 1975; LLD with highest honors, U. Toulouse, France, 1980. Reporter, pub. affairs dir. Sta. WLUR-FM, Lexington, Va., 1971-75; stringer Lynchburg (Va.) News, 1974-75; news clk., intern Time Mag., Paris, 1974; reporter, editor Boca Raton (Fla.) News, 1980-81; newsman AP, Miami, Paris, 1981-83, editor, fgn. desk N.Y.C., 1984-86, corr. Moscow, 1986-90, L.A. Times, Moscow, 1990-93, bur. chief New Delhi, 1993-96, Paris, 1996-2001, Miami, 2001—. Journalistes en Europe fellow, 1983-84; recipient George Polk award L.I. U., 1993, Excellence citation Overseas Press Club Am., 1993, Hal Boyle award, 1996, Cert. of Merit AP News Execs. Coun., 1993, Robert F. Kennedy Journalism award, 1996, Soc. Profl. Journalists award for internat. reporting, 1997; named finalist Pulitzer Prize in internat. reporting, 1992, 93. Mem.: Soc. Profl. Journalists (bd. dirs. South Fla. chpt.). Avocations: Model T Ford restoration, rowing. Office: LA Times 3050 Biscayne Blvd Ste 500 Miami FL 33137

DAHLE, CAROL JO, secondary school educator, director; b. St. Cloud, Minn., Dec. 29, 1951; d. Calvin John and Kathleen Florence Repulski; m. Thomas Alan Dahle, June 30, 1953; 1 child, Stephen Thomas. BMus in Applied Music, NW State U., Natchitoches, La., 1974; BS in Music Edn., St. Cloud State U., 1976; postgrad., U. Wis., River Falls, 1977. Band, choir dir. Allen HS, Robeline, La., 1975—76; mid. sch./jr. high choir dir., tchr. Hudson (Wis.) Sch. Dist., 1976—. Active Phipps Ctr. for the Arts, Hudson, 1985—, music dir. for musicals, 1980, past pres.; choir dir. Trinity Luth. Ch., Hudson, 1984—. Recipient Star Excellence award, Hudson Edn. Found., 1998. Mem.: St. Croix Valley Mus. Edn. Assn. (treas., pres. 1976—, sec.), Wis. Sch. Music Assn., Wis. Choral Dirs. Assn. (guest dir. Singing in Wis. music festival 1996, rep. N.W. dist. 2001—05, 5 Star award 2003, named Outstanding Mid. Level Choir Dir. 2004, 5 Star award 2004, 2005). Democrat. Lutheran. Avocations: reading, gardening, travel. Office: Hudson Mid Sch 1300 Carmichael Rd Hudson WI 54016

DAHLE, JOHANNES UPTON, retired academic administrator; b. Ada, Minn., Nov. 28, 1933; s. Upton Emmanuel and Marte (Goli) D.; m. Arlene Isabel Powell, Dec. 27, 1956; children: Randall Douglas, Lisa Johanna. BS, U. Minn., 1956, MA, 1966. Choral dir. U. Minn., Mpls., 1960-62-63-66; dir. choirs Macalester Coll., St. Paul, 1962-63; dir. student activities and univ. programs U. Wis., Eau Claire, 1966-71, dir. univ. ctrs., 1971-84, dir. devel., 1984-95, ret., 1995. Pres., dir. Eau Claire Conv. Tourism Bur., 1979-84; v.p., dir. Eau Claire Regional Arts Coun., 1982-84; bd. dirs. United Way of Eau Claire; mem. Plymouth Congrl. Ch., Mpls. Capt. USAF, 1956-60. Mem. Internat. Assn. Coll. Unions, Coun. for Advancement and Support Edn., Kiwanis (pres. Eau Claire chpt. 1975-76), Phi Kappa Phi (sec. 1982-84), Omicron Delta Kappa (sec. 1981-84), Phi Mu Alpha Sinfonia. Home: 1929 Hunter Hill Rd Hudson WI 54016-5818

DAHLEN, ERIC REYNOLDS, psychology professor; s. Dennis and Susan Dahlen. PhD, Colo. State U., 1999. Lic. Psychologist Miss., 2001. Asst. prof. U. So. Miss., Hattiesburg, Miss., 1999—. Dir. Cmty. Counseling & Assessment Clinic, Hattiesburg, Miss., 2002—. Contbr. chapters to books, articles to profl. jours. Grantee CEMRRAT Grant for Minority Recruitment, Retention, and Tng., APA, 2004—05. Mem.: APA, Assn. of Dirs. Psychology Tng. Clinics, Assn. for Advancement of Behavior Therapy, Southeastern Psychol. Assn. Office: Univ So Miss 118 College Dr #5025 Hattiesburg MS 39406-5025 Office Phone: 601-266-4601. E-mail: eric.dahlen@usm.edu.

DAHLGREN, CARL HERMAN PER, performing company executive, educator; b. N.Y.C., July 2, 1929; s. Harry W.A. and Ester Florence (Carlson) D.; m. Ella Kate Bowes, Oct. 8, 1960; children: Robert C., John L., Per M., Eva B. MusB, Westminster Choir Coll., Princeton, N.J., 1954. Project dir. Benson & Benson, Princeton, 1954-55; asst. head spl. research and analysis Gallup & Robinson, Princeton, 1956-57; v.p., artist mgr. Columbia Artists Mgmt., Inc., N.Y.C., 1958-68, dir., 1962-68; v.p. Hurok Concerts, Inc., N.Y.C., 1968-70, assoc., 1970-74; pres. Dahlgren Arts Mgmt., Inc., Denver, 1970-78; sr. ptnr. Dahlgren, Schiffmann & Assocs., N.Y.C., 1978-80; assoc. prof. arts adminstrn. U. Cin., 1978—, acting head broadcasting divsn., 1979-80. Dir. masters program in arts adminstrn. Coll. Conservatory of Music, 1978—, prof., 1989—, prof. emeritus, 1992; prin. Dahlgren & Yaffe, Arts Cons., 1992; acting exec. dir. Assn. for Advancement of Arts Edn., Cin., 1995-96; mem. faculty senate U. Cin., 1988-90. Co-founder, exec. dir. Westminster Choir Coll. Alumni Fund Assn., 1954-59; mgr. Princeton Symphony Orch., 1957-59; gen. mgr., dir. Central City (Colo.) Opera House, 1970-72; bd. dirs. Gilpin County Arts Assn., 1970-76; bd. dirs., sec. Colo. Celebration of Arts, 1974-76; pres. Classic Choral, 1975-78, Cin. Chamber Orch., 1982-91; trustee Westminster Choir Coll., 1967-74. With AUS, 1947-49. Decorated knight 1st Class Order of Lion, Finland; recipient Merit award Westminster Choir Coll. Mem. AAUP (v.p. U. Cin. chpt. 1990-92), Assn. Arts Adminstrn. Educators (trustee 1988, pres. 1990), Am. Assn. Mus., Faculty Club U. Cin. Episcopalian. Home: 3750 E Via Palomita Unit 1202 Tucson AZ 85718 E-mail: chpdahl@theriver.com.

DAHLGREN, DOROTHY, museum director; b. Coeur d'Alene, Idaho; BS in Museology and History, U. Idaho, 1982; M in Orgnl. Leadership, Gonzaga U., 1998. Dir. Mus. North Idaho, Coeur d'Alene, 1982—. Mem. Kootenai County Hist. Preservation Comm. Author: (with Simone Carbonneau Kincaid) In All the West No Place Like This: A Pictorial History of the Coeur d'Alene Region, 1996. Mem. no. region com. Idaho Heritage Trust. Office: Mus N Idaho PO Box 812 Coeur D Alene ID 83816 Office Phone: 208-664-3448. E-mail: dd@museumni.org.

DAHLIN, DONALD C(LIFFORD), academic administrator; b. Ironwood, Mich., June 18, 1941; married; 2 children. BA magna cum laude in history, Carroll Coll., 1963; PhD in Govt. (Univ. Departmental fellow), Claremont Grad. Sch., 1969; fellow in ct. mgmt., Inst. Ct. Mgmt., 1980. Asst. prof. govt. U. S.D., Vermillion, 1966-70, assoc. prof., 1970-75, prof., 1975—, dir. criminal justice studies program, 1972-75, 78-89, chmn. dept. polit. sci., 1978-89, 95-98, fellow Pres.'s office, 1984-85, interim v.p. acad. affairs, 1988-90, acting dean continuing edn., 1995, v.p. acad. affairs, 1997—2004, ret., acting pres., 2002. Mgmt. analyst Law Enforcement Assistance Adminstrn., Dept. Justice, Washington, 1970-71; sec. S.D. Dept. Public Safety, Pierre, 1975-78; lectr., cons. in field; mem. S.D. Human Resource Cabinet Sub-Group, 1975-78, chmn., 1977-78; mem. S.D. Planning Commn., 1975-78; adv. bd. Criminal Justice Statis. Analysis Center, 1975-78; chmn. S.D. Criminal Justice Commn., 1976-78; mem. U. So. Calif. Criminal Justice Tng. Center Planning Com., 1977-79, U. S.D. Research Inst. Adv. Panel, 1978-80, Gov.'s Corrections Task Force, 1987; mem. acad. resource council S.D. Planning Agy., 1978-79; chmn. S.D. County Commr.'s Juvenile Justice Com., 1986-89; chmn. S.D. Youth Advocacy Project; mem. Commn. on Advancement of Fed. Law Enforcement, 1997-99, constitutional revisino commn., 2004—. Author: Models of Court Management, 1986; contbr. articles to profl. publs. Recipient Sustained High Performance award Law Enforcement Assistance Adminstrn., 1971, Disting. Safety Svcs. award S.D. Auto Club, 1978, Disting. Faculty award U. S.D., 1980, Friend of Law Enforcement award S.D. Peace Officers, 1983; Haynes Found. rsch. fellow, 1965-66; ASPA fellow, 1970-71; Bush Leadership fellow, summer 1975; Law Enforcement Edn. Program grantee, 1972-75; S.D. Criminal Justice Commn. grantee, 1972-74, 72-75; Criminal Justice Standards and Goals for S.D. grantee, 1974-75; Criminal Justice Data Collection grantee, 1974-75. Mem. ASPA (pres. Siouxland chpt. 1980-81, exec. bd. dirs. and sec./treas. criminal justice adminstrn. sect.), Am. Polit. Sci. Assn., Am. Judicature Soc. Home: 608 Poplar St Vermillion SD 57069-3529 Office: U SD Polit Sci Vermillion SD 57069 Office Phone: 605-677-5116. Business E-Mail: ddahlin@usd.edu.

DAHLING, GERALD VERNON, lawyer; b. Red Wing, Minn., Jan. 11, 1947; s. Vernon and Lucille Alfrieda (Reuter) D.; m. Edell Marie Villella, July 26, 1969; children: David (dec.), Christopher, Elizabeth, Mary. BS, Winona (Minn.) State Coll., 1968; MS, U. Minn., 1970; PhD, Harvard U., 1974; JD, William Mitchell Coll. of Law, 1980. Bar: U.S. Patent Office 1979, Minn. 1980, Ind. 1980, Pa. 1997, U.S. Dist. Ct. (so. dist.) Ind. 1980. Patent atty. Eli Lilly and Co., Indpls., 1980-84, mgr. biotech. patents, 1984-86, asst. patent counsel biotech., 1986-89, asst. patent counsel biotech. and fermentation products, 1990, asst. gen. patent counsel, 1991-95; dir. intellectual property Pasteur Mérieux Connaught, Lyon, France and Swiftwater, Pa., 1995-97, corp. v.p., dir. intellectual property, 1997-98, sr. v.p. intellectual property Lyon, France, 1998-99, Rhone Poulenc Rorer, Collegeville, Pa., 1998—99; sr. v.p., global patents Aventis Pharms., Bridgewater, NJ, 2000—05; v.p., gen. counsel, global patent litigation and lifecycle mgmt. Sanofi-Aventis, 2005—. Mem. ABA, Ind. Bar Assn., Pa. Bar Assn., Am. Intellectual Property Law Assn., Intellectual Property Owners Assn. (bd. dirs.), INTERPAT. Democrat. Roman Catholic. Office: Rt 202-206 PO Box 6800 Bridgewater NJ 08807-0800 also: Sanofi-Aventis 13 Pont Pasteur 69348 Lyon France

DAHLK, THOMAS HARLAN, lawyer; b. Madison, Wis., Aug. 22, 1952; s. Harlan Edward and Ardys (Hanson) D.; m. Janice Kay Larson, Dec. 21, 1973; children: Lesley Anne, Thomas Larson. BA with distinction, U. Wis., 1974; JD magna cum laude, Creighton U., 1977. Bar: Nebr. 1977, Nebr. Supreme Ct. 1977, U.S. Dist. Ct. (Nebr., Okla., Iowa, Minn., Ariz., Ga., Fla., Kans., we. dist. Mo., so. dist. NY), U.S. Ct. Appeals (8th, 10th, 11th cir.), U.S. Supreme Ct. 1992. Assoc. Fitzgerald and Brown, Omaha, 1977-83, ptnr., 1983—88; ptnr. Lieben Dahlk Whitted Houghton Slowiaczek & Jahn, 1988-98; ptnr., bus. & comml. litig. Blackwell Sanders Peper Martin LLP, 1998-, Omaha office mng. ptnr. 2003-. Adj. faculty Creighton Law Sch., Omaha, 1981—. Trustee Brownell-Talbot Sch., Omaha; gov. mem. Omaha Symphony. Contbr. articles to legal publs., lead articles editor Creighton Law Rev. Fellow Nebr. bar Found.; mem. ABA (com. fed. securities regulation 1982—), Nebr. Bar Assn. (chmn. mentoring com. 2001-03), Nebr. Assn. Trial Attys., Omaha Bar Assn. Lutheran. Office: Blackwell Sanders Peper Martin LLP Ste 2100 1620 Dodge St Omaha NE 68102 Office Phone: 402-964-5031. Office Fax: 402-964-5050. Business E-Mail: tdahlk@blackwellsanders.com.

DAHLSTROM, BECKY JOANNE, journalist; b. Olympia, Wash., Sept. 24, 1957; d. Timothy Craddick and Shirleen (Stout) Roan; m. Kenneth W. Dahlstrom, Mar. 17, 1978 (div. Aug. 1984); children: Levi, Olivia; m. Robert Salley, Sr., Feb. 21, 1986 (div. Sept. 1994); 1 child, Robert, Jr. Student, Am. Coll., 1985-86. Writer Hospital, 1988-89; admitting clerk County Ventura (Calif.) Healthcare Agy., 1989—. Writer, editor West Fork (Ark.) Elem. Sch., 1970-73. Author: (poem) My Authority, 1980 (Hon. mention 1980). Mem. Future Bus. Leaders Am. Republican. Baptist. Avocations: drawing, writing, horseback riding, ceramics.

DAHLSTROM, PATRICIA MARGARET, real estate appraiser; b. L.A., Calif., Apr. 29, 1951; d. Colin Rose, Jr. and Patricia Rose; m. David Keith Dahlstrom, July 15, 1989; m. Peter Klaus Reese, Dec. 3, 1972 (div. Dec. 31, 1983); 1 child, Steven Eric Reese. BA in Urban Econ. Geography, Calif. State U., Northridge, 1976, MA in Urban Econ. Geography, 1984; BSN, UCLA, Westwood, Calif., 1995, MSN, 1997. Cert. profl. logistician, Soc. of Logistics Engrs., 1987; RN Calif., 1995, lic. Nurse Practitioner, Bd. of Registered Nursing, Calif., 1997, cert. Pediatric Nurse Practitioner, Nat. Certification Bd. of Pediatric Nurse Practitioners, 1997. Instr. Moorpark (Calif.) Coll., 1977—78; rsch. analyst Natelson Co., Westwood, Calif., 1976—78; logistics engr. Litton, Data Systems Divsn., Van Nuys, Calif., 1980—84; program mgr. Micom, Simi Valley, Calif., 1984—86; logistics engr. Allied Signal, Ocean Systems, Sylmar, Calif., 1986—87; logistics engr./project lead Litton, Data Systems Divsn., Van Nuys/Agoura Hills, Calif., 1987—91; PNP Children's Hosp., Los Angeles, Calif., 1997—98, Lavin and VanDopp, MDs, Tarzana/Van Nuys, Calif., 1998—99, Kaiser Permanent, Panorama City, Calif., 2000—01; part-time faculty instr. Calif. State U., Dept. Health Scis., Northridge, 1998—2002; appraiser Graphic Appraisal Svcs., Sherman Oaks, Calif., 2003—; tchg. asst. UCLA Sch. Nursing, Westwood, Calif., 1995—97. Workshop leader Profls. Plus Networking Group, Lancaster, Calif., 1991—92; cons. AMEX, Compton, Calif., 1986—86. On-screen nurse practitioner & co-author: (instructional video) Physical Assessment: Head to Toe Examination in 45 Minutes. Fundraiser Am. Stroke Assn., L.A., Calif., 2003; pres. Calif. Coalition of Nurse Practitioners, Region 16, San Fernando Valley, 1999—2000; sec. Calif. Coalition of Nurse Practitioners, Region 13, L.A., 1998—99; ch. coun. Ch. of the Foothills, Sylmar, Calif., 2002—. Fellow: Nat. Assn. of Pediatric Nurse Practitioners; mem.: Soc. for Adolescent Medicine, Am. Acad. of Pediat., Calif. Coalition of Nurse Practitioners, Golden Key, Sigma Theta Tau. Democrat. Lutheran. Avocations: travel, walking marathons, reading, gardening, music, theater, movies.

DAHLSTROM, WILLIAM GRANT, psychologist, educator; b. Mpls., Nov. 1, 1922; s. Arthur William and Elizabeth Priscilla (Baker) D.; m. Leona Erickson, Sept. 3, 1948; children: Amy Louise, Eric Lee. Student, UCLA, 1940-41; BA cum laude, U. Minn., 1944, PhD in Psychology, 1949. Instr. psychology U. Minn., 1946-48, Ohio Wesleyan U., 1948-49; vis. asst. prof. State U. Iowa, 1949-53, research assoc., summer 1957; assoc. prof. psychiatry and psychology, dir. psychol. svcs. Meml. Hosp. U. N.C., Chapel Hill, 1953-56; assoc. prof. psychology U. N.C., 1956-60, research assoc. psychiatry, 1956-60, prof. psychology, 1960-87, Kenan prof. psychology, 1987-93, Kenan prof. emeritus, 1993—, 1993—, clin. prof. psychology in dept. psychiatry, 1960—; research prof. Inst. for Research in Social Sci., 1960—, chmn. dept., 1971-76. Vis. scholar U. Calif., Berkeley, 1968, 76-77; field dir. Child Study Center U. N.C., 1962-63; chmn. mental health study sect. NIH, 1966-67 Author: (with G.S. Welsh) An MMPI Handbook, 1960, rev. edit. (with G.S. Welsh and L.E. Dahlstrom) Vol. I, 1972, Vol. II, 1975, (with E.E. Baughman) Negro and White Children, 1968, (with L.E. Dahlstrom) Basic Readings on the MMPI, 1980, (with D. Lachar and L.E. Dahlstrom) MMPI Patterns of American Minorities, 1986. Co-editor: (with J.W. Thibaut) Jour. Personality, 1959-60; Cons. editor: Jour. Cons. Psychology, 1964-78, Jour. Abnormal Psychology, 1964-70, Psychosomatic Medicine, 1982—; Contbr. articles to profl. jours. NIMH sr. postdoctoral fellow Menninger Found., Topeka, Kans., 1967-68; Co-recipient Anisfield-Wolf award for outstanding contbn. to race relations Sat. Rev. Lit., 1968; Hargrove award N.C. Found. for Research in Mental Health, 1987. Fellow Soc. Personality Assessment, APA (Disting. Profl. Contbn. to Knowledge award 1991), AAAS, N.Y. Acad. Scis.; mem. Am. Psychosomatic Soc.; Sigma Xi. Democrat. Home: 750 Weaver Dairy Rd Apt 188 Chapel Hill NC 27514-1441

DAHM, WERNER K., aerodynamicist; Chief aerodynamicist George C. Marshall Space Ctr., mem. Von Braun Rocket Team, NASA. Recipient applied Aerodynamics award AIAA, 1997, NASA Exceptional Svc Medal, 2004. Office: NASA George C Marshall Space Flight Ctr Bldg 4203 MSFC Mailstop EV01 Huntsville AL 35812

DAHN, JEFF RAYMOND, physics professor; b. Bridgeport, Conn., Jan. 9, 1957; arrived in Can., 1970; s. Raymond Charles and Margery (Halsted) D.; m. Katherine Mary Lillian Macdonald, July 1, 1987 (div.); children: Hannah, Tara, Jackson. BSc in Physics with honors, Dalhousie U., Halifax, N.S., Can., 1978; MSc in Physics, U. B.C., Vancouver, Can., 1980, PhD in Physics, 1982. Rsch. assoc. Nat. Rsch. Coun. Can., Ottawa, Ont., 1982-83, mem. continuing staff, 1983-85; project leader materials sci. Moli Energy Ltd., Vancouver, 1985-87, rsch. dir., 1987-90; assoc. prof. physics Simon Fraser U., Burnaby, B.C., 1990-94, prof. physics, 1994-96; prof. physics and chemistry Dalhousie U., Halifax, 1996—, Can. rsch. chair, 2003—. Cons. Moli Energy (1990) Ltd., 1990-96, 3M Co., 1996—. Contbr. more than 290 sci. papers to profl. jours.; patentee in field. Recipient Medal for Innovation in Physics from Can. Assn. Physicists, 1987, Herzberg medal Can. Assn. Physicists, 1996, Gold medal B.C. Sci. Coun., 1996. Fellow Royal Soc. Can.; mem. Am. Phys. Soc.,

Electrochem. Soc. (Lash Miller award Can. sect. 1993, Battery divsn. Rsch. award 1996), Internat. Battery Materials Assn. (Rsch. award 1995). Avocations: woodworking, basketball, hiking in mountains. Office: Dalhousie U Dept Physics Halifax NS Canada B3H 3J5 Office Phone: 902-494-2991. E-mail: jeff.dahn@dal.ca.

DAHNK, JEAN PATRICIA, lawyer; b. 1958; BS in Bus. Adminstrn., George Washington U.; JD, Coll. William and Mary. Bar: Va. 1986. Ptnr. Glover & Dahnk, Fredericksburg, Va. Mem.: Va. State Bar (pres.-elect 2002, pres. 2003). Office: Glover and Dahnk PO Box 207 Fredericksburg VA 22404-0207

DAHRENDORF, LORD RALF GUSTAV, sociologist, educator; b. Hamburg, Germany, May 1, 1929; s. Gustav and Lina (Witt) D.; m. Christiane Klebs, April, 2004. PhD, U. Hamburg, 1952, London Sch. Econs., 1954; 26 hon. degrees from various univs. Privatdozent sociology U. Saar, Fed. Republic Germany, 1957; fellow Ctr. for Advanced Studies in Behavioral Scis., Palo Alto, Calif., 1957-58; prof. sociology U. Hamburg, 1958-60, U. Tubingen, 1960-66; prof. U. Constance, 1966-69, dean faculty social scis., 1966-67; mem. Fed. Parliament Govt. of Fed. Republic Germany, 1969-70; parliamentary sec. of state in German Fgn. Office, 1969-70; mem. Commn. of the European Cmtys., 1970-74; dir. London Sch. Econs., 1974-84; warden St. Antony's Coll., Oxford, 1987-97; mem. House of Lords, London, 1993—, chmn. delegated powers select com., 2002—; rsch. prof. Social Sci. Ctr., Berlin, 2005—. Trustee Ford Found., 1976-87; mem. Coun. of Brit. Acad., 1980-83, House of Lords, 1993—; chmn. bd. Friedrich-Naumann Stiftung, 1982-87, Delegated Powers Select com., 2002—. Author: Marx in Perspective, 1953, Industrie-und Betriebssoziologie, 1956, Class and Class Conflict, 1959, Die angewandte Aufklä rung, 1963, Gesellschaft und Demokratie in Deutschland, 1965, Pfade aus Utopia, 1967, Essays in Theory of Society, 1968, Konflikt und Freiheit, 1972, Plä doyer für die Europä ische Union, 1973, The New Liberty, 1975, Life Chances, 1980, On Britain, 1982, Die Chancen der Krise, 1983, The Modern Social Conflict, 1988 (all transl. into many langs.), Reflections on the Revolution in Europe, 1991, LSE: A History of the London School of Economics 1895-1995, 1995, Morals, Revolution and Civil Society, 1997, After 1989, 1997, Liberal und unabhängig, Gerd Bucerius und seine Zeit, 2000, Universities after Communism, 2000, Über Grenzen, 2002, Auf der Suche nach einer neuen Ordnung, 2003, Der Wiederbeginn der Geschichte, 2004. Mem. Hansard Soc. of Electoral Reform, 1975-76; mem. Royal Commn. on Legal Svcs., 1976-79; mem. Com. to Rev. the Functioning of Fin. Instns., 1977-80; mem. German PEN Ctr., 1971—. Decorated knight comdr. Order Brit. Empire, also by decorated by govts. of Senegal, Luxembourg, Fed. Republic Germany, Austria, Belgium, Italy. Fellow Anglo German Soc. (presidium), British Acad., Royal Soc. Arts, Royal Coll. Surgeons (hon.); mem. AAAS (hon.), NAS (fgn. assoc.), Am. Philos. Soc., Royal Irish Acad. (hon.), others. Office: House of Lords London SW1A 0PW England

DAHSE, KENNETH WILLIAM, photographer, writer, educator; b. Teaneck, N.J., May 3, 1949; s. William Charles Dahse and Dorothy Rose Devine; m. Carol Salminen (div.); 1 child, Lisa; m. Linda Jewell, Feb. 23, 1974; 1 child, Shannon. BA, Montclair State U., 1972, MA, 1977. Secondary educator Bogota (N.J.) Pub. Schs., 1977—; adj. instr. Bergen C.C., Paramus, N.J., 1991—. Author: RVing America's Backroads, 1989, The Hell Riders, 2005; contbr. articles to jours. including Am. Legion, Trailer Life, Motorcycle Tour & Cruiser, Motor/Home, Rider, Roadbike, Family Motor Coaching. Environ. activist C.L.E.A.N., Inc., Ringwood, N.J. Mem. N.J. Edn. Assn., Bogota Edn. Assn. (pres., 1995-2004), Sierra Club, Appalachian Mt. Club. Avocations: motorcycle riding, backpacking, hiking, kayaking.

DAI, KUN, research scientist; b. Qingdao, Shandong, China, Apr. 20, 1970; arrived in U.S., 2000; s. Jizhang Dai and Fangzong Wang; m. Shangming Li, Feb. 7, 1996. BS, Qingdao U., China, 1992; MS, Harbin Inst. Tech., China, 1994, PhD, 1997, U. Conn., 2005. Rsch. assoc. Harbin Inst. Tech., China, 1997—2000; rsch. asst. U. Conn., Storrs, 2000—. Contbr. articles to profl. jours. and conf. procs. Recipient Best Poster award, 14th SEF Symposium, U. Tex., 2003, Nat. Collegiate Engring. award, U.S. Achievement Acad., 2003, Outstanding Grad. Student award, Materials Sci. and Engring., U. Conn., 2004. Mem.: Minerals, Metals & Materials Soc., Am. Soc. for Metals, Alpha Sigma Mu. Avocations: soccer, table tennis, fishing, hiking. Home: 1 Northwood Rd Apt 87 Storrs Mansfield CT 06268 Office: Univ Conn 97 N Eagleville Rd U-3136 Storrs Mansfield CT 06269 Office Phone: 860-486-4410. E-mail: kundai@gmail.com.

DAI, YINGCONG, historian, educator; d. Wensai Dai and Shengmei Liu; m. Ming Jian. PhD, U. Wash., 1996. Assoc. prof. William Paterson U., Wayne, NJ, 1998—. Contbr. articles to profl. jours. Hiao scholar, U. Wash., 1991—92, 1992—93, Small grantee, Assn. Asia Studies, 2001. Mem.: Chinese Mil. History Soc., Am. Hist. Assn., Assn. Asian Studies, Phi Alpha Theta. Office Phone: 973-720-2816.

DAICHI, TOTTORI, academic administrator, trade association administrator, accountant, lawyer; b. Fukuoka, Japan, Feb. 5, 1980; arrived in US, 2001; s. Takayuki (Stepfather) and Kikuko Tottori (Stepmother), Kazuko Tottori. MBA in Acctg., Americana U., USA, 2002; AS in Fin., Am. Mgmt. and Bus. Adminstrn. Inst. and U., 2003; PhD in Tax Law (hon.), St. Regis U., Liberia, 2003; DBA (hon.), St. Bernard U. Seborga, Italy, 2005. CPA Calif.; registered home inspector, Housing Inspection Found., cert. constrn. inspector, Assn. Constrn. Inspectors, constrn. project mgr., Assn. Constrn. Inspectors; registered property mgmt. dir. Japan, lic. real estate broker Japan, cert. property mgr. Japan; adminstrv. atty., Japan, enrolled agt., IRS; ordained minister Universal Ministries; sr. valuer Internat. Real Estate Inst., environ. inspector Environ. Assessment Assn., testing specialist Environ. Assessment Assn., remediation specialist Environ. Assessment Assn., rev. appraiser Nat. Assn. Rev. Appraisers and Mortgage Underwriters. CEO Bill Cashman and Co., NY, 2003—; full prof. St. Regis U., Liberia, 2003—05; pres. St. Bernard U. Seborga, Italy, 2004—; trade attache' Seborga Bus. Ctr., Principality of Seborga, Italy, 2004—; full prof. James Monroe U., Liberia, Liberia, 2004—. Rsch. and study Ctrl. Sch. of Plitics of Liberal Dem. Party, Japan, 2004; bishop Universal Ministries, Japan. Recipient Order of Knight, Ethiopian Order of St.Mary Zion, 2004, Insignia for Social and Cultural Achievement, Principality of Seborga, 2004. Mem.: Internat. Real Estate Inst., Housing Inspection Found., Nat. Assn. of Rev. Appraisers and Mortgage Underwrithers, Environ. Assessment Assn., Assn. of Constrn. Insp., Info. Sys. and Contorol Assn., Assn. of Cert. Fraud Examiners, Ethiopian Royal Order of St.Mary Zion, Order of St.Lazaro (Order of Knight 2004), The Imperial Soc. of St. George of Lalibela, Assn. of Frendship for Seborga, Japan. Achievements include Knight Order from Ethipia Royal Family; Insignia from Principality of Seborga. Personal E-mail: dtottori@hotmail.com.

DAICOFF, SUSAN (SUSAN DAICOFF DUNN), law educator; b. Chgo., July 5, 1962; d. George Ronald and Mary Jane (Swaim) D.; m. Robert Lewis Harding, Oct. 1, 1983 (div. Mar. 1990); m. Gordon Victor Monday, Dec. 12, 1992 (div. Mar. 1994); m. Robert Neal Baskin Jr., June 22, 1996 (div. 2001); children: Arizona Gray, Graylin Diana: m. Kevin Emmett Dunn, Jan. 01, 2005. BA in Math., U. Fla., 1980, JD with honors, 1983; LLM in Taxation, NYU, 1985; MS in Clin. Psychology, U. Ctrl. Fla., 1992. Bar: Fla. 1984. Atty. Smith, Mackinnon, Mathews et al., Orlando, Fla., 1985-88; author Tax Practice Series, Tax Mgmt., Orlando, 1989; counselor III Project III of Ctrl. Fla., Orlando, 1991-92; asst. rsch. assoc. team performance lab. U. Ctrl. Fla., Orlando, 1992-93; atty. in taxation, corporate law and psychology Barnett, Bolt, Kirkwood & Long, Tampa, 1993-94; asst. prof. law Capital U. Law Sch., Columbus, Ohio, 1995-2000; assoc. prof. law Fla. Coastal Sch. Law, Jacksonville, 2000—03, prof., 2003—. Adj. instr. Valencia Cmty. Coll., Orlando, 1988; mental health counselor intern Response, Inc., Sexual Assault Ctr., Orlando, 1992-93. Wallace scholarship NYU, 1984-85. Mem. Order of Coif, Phi Beta Kappa. Office: Fla Coastal Sch Law 7555 Beach Blvd Jacksonville FL 32216-3000 E-mail: sdaicoff@fcsl.edu.

DAIDONE, LEWIS EUGENE, finance company executive; b. Perth Amboy, N.J., Aug. 6, 1957; s. Eugene John and Gertrude Rose (Sawyer) D.; m. Kathleen Eleanor Ward, May 11, 1985; children: Eugene Joseph, Brittany Nicole, Lewis Peter. BA, Rutgers U., 1979, MBA, 1980. CPA, N.Y., N.J. Sr. acct. Ernst & Young, N.Y.C., 1980-82; asst. controller Reserve Group, N.Y.C., 1982-84; mgr. commodity acctg. Dean Witter Reynolds, N.Y.C., 1984; v.p., treas., sec. Cortland Distbrs., Inc., Hackensack, N.J., 1984-89; sr. v.p., CFO Cortland Fin. Group, Inc., Hackensack, NJ, 1984—89; mng. dir., CFO mutual funds Salomon Smith Barney, Inc., N.Y.C., 1990—2004; sr. v.p., dir. Smith Barney Fund Mgmt. LLC, N.Y.C., 1990—2004; sr. v.p., treas. Smith Barney Funds., Inc., N.Y.C., 1990—2004, Smith Barney Money Funds, Inc., N.Y.C., 1990—2004, Smith Barney Muni Funds, N.Y.C., 1990—2004, Smith Barney Tax-Free Money Fund, N.Y.C., 1990—2004, Smith Barney Intermediate Mcpl. Fund, N.Y.C., 1992—2004, Smith Barney Mcpl. Fund, Inc., N.Y.C., 1992—2004, Smith Barney High Income Opportunity Fund, Inc., N.Y.C., 1993—2004; chmn. Global Horizon Investment Series, Brit. West Indies, 1992—2000, Smith Barney Internat. Funds, Luxembourg, 1993-97; and exec. of 150 other investment cos. with Salomon Smith Barney. Head funds adminstrn. Citigroup Asset Mgmt., 1998-2004; CFO LOG-NET, Inc., 2005—; v.p., treas. Cortland Trust, Inc., Hackensack, 1984-89; cons. in field. Trustee Wyndmoor Condominium Assn., Woodbridge, N.J. Named one of Outstanding Young Men Am., U.S. Jaycees, 1979. Fellow N.J. State Soc. CPAs; mem. AICPA, N.Y. State Soc. CPAs, Beta Gamma Sigma. Avocations: golf, racquetball. Office: LOG-NET Inc 230 Half Mile Rd Red Bank NJ 07701

DAIKER, PAUL B., lawyer; b. Oxford, Ohio, Nov. 6, 1967; s. Donald A. and Victoria A. Daiker; m. Elizabeth A. Salzarulo, June 24, 1995. BA, Vanderbilt U., 1990; JD, Cleve. State U., 1993. Bar: Ohio 1993, U.S. Dist. Ct. (no. dist.) Ohio 1996, U.S. Ct. Appeals (6th cir.) 1996. Assoc., trail lawyer Zukerman & Assocs., Cleve., 1993-96; shareholder, ptnr. Zukerman & Daker Co., LPA, Cleve., 1996—; prosecutor Village of Moreland Hills, Ohio, 1996-00. Office: Zukerman & Daker Co LPA 2000 E 9th St Ste 700 Cleveland OH 44115-1301

DAIL, JOSEPH GARNER, JR., judge; b. Elloree, S.C., June 15, 1932; s. Joseph Garner and Esther Vernette (Harbort) D.; m. Martha E. MacReynolds; children: Edward Benjamin, Mary Holyoke. BS, U. N.C., 1953, JD with honors, 1955. Bar: N.C. 1955, Va. 1976. Pvt. practice, Washington, 1959-76; ptnr. Croft, Dail & Vance (and predecessor), 1966-76; sole practitioner McLean, Va., 1976—83; counsel Gabeler, Ward & Griggs, 1983-87; judge U.S. adminstrv. law Fresno, Calif., 1987-94, San Francisco, 1994-97, Tampa, 1997-99; sr. U.S. adminstrv. law judge, 1999—2005. Assoc. editor: N.C. Law Rev, 1954-55. Lt. USNR, 1955-59; capt. Res. (ret.). Mem. N.C. Bar Assn., Va. Bar Assn., Transp. Lawyers Assn. (Disting. Svc. award 1976), Order of Coif, Phi Beta Kappa. Republican. Home: 103 Masters Ln Safety Harbor FL 34695-3722 Personal E-mail: macdail@aol.com.

DAILEY, DANIEL OWEN, artist, educator, product designer; b. Phila., Feb. 4, 1947; s. David Bireley and Barbara Tarleton (Tricebock) D.; m. Linda MacNeil, Aug. 19, 1977; children: Allison MacNeil, Owen MacNeil. B.F.A., Phila. Coll. Art, 1969; M.F.A., R.I. Sch. Design, Providence, 1972. Tchr., fellow MIT Ctr. for Advanced Visual Studies, Cambridge, 1975-80; founder, prof. glass program Mass. Coll. Art, Boston, 1973-89; mem. faculty Pilchuck Glass Sch., Stanwood, Wash., 1974—; designer, artist Cristallerie Daum, Paris and Nancy, France, 1975—; designer Steuben Glass, Corning, N.Y., 1982—. Tchr. glass R.I. Sch. Design, 1970-72, Haystack Mountain Sch. Crafts, Deer Isle, Maine, 1976—; owner Dan Dailey Inc., Kensington, N.H., 1977—; mem. faculty Mass. Coll. Art, 1989—; bd. govs. Mus. Arts and Design, N.Y.C., 2000—. One-man and group shows throughout U.S. and Europe, 1970—; represented in permanent collections Renwick Gallery, Smithsonian Inst., Washington, Toledo Mus. Art, J.B. Speed Mus., Louisville, Creative Glass Ctr. Am., Millville, NJ, Morris Mus., Morristown, NJ, Royal Ont. (Can.) Mus., Met. Mus. Art, NYC, Smithsonian Inst., Washington, Corning (NY) Mus. Glass, Huntington (W.Va.) Mus., New Indian Mus., Flagstaff, Ariz., Les Archives Daum, Nancy, France, U. Ill. Art Gallery, Normal, Brockton (Mass.) Art Mus., Nat. Gallery Victoria, Melbourne, Australia, Nat. Mus. Modern Art, Kyoto, Japan, St. Louis Mus. Art, High Mus. Art, Atlanta, Phila. Mus. Art, Kestner Mus., Hannover, Fed. Republic Germany, Mus. Art, Darmstatt, Fed. Republic Germany, Indpls. Mus. Art, Mus. Arts & Design, NYC, LA County Mus. Art, Mus. des Arts Decoratifs, Paris, Boston Mus. Fine Arts, Detroit Inst. Art, Yokohama Mus. Art, Japan, Mus. Design et Dárts Appliques Contemporairs, Lausanne, Switzerland, Wheaton Mus., Millville, NJ, Milw. Mus. Art, Boca Raton (Fla.) Mus. Art, Carnagie Mus. Art, Pitts., Racine Art Mus., Wis., Currier Gallery of Art, Manchester, NH, Darmstatt Mus., Germany, Dayton Art Inst., Ohio, Greatest Bar on Earth, Windows on the World Corp., One World Trade Ctr. Towers, NYC, Hunter Mus. Am. Art, Chattanooga, Tenn., Pilchuck Glass Collection at City Centre and U.S. Bank Centre, Seattle, WA, Pacific First Ctr., Seattle, Rockefeller Ctr. Corp., NYC, Chase Manhattan Bank Collection, NYC, Town of Vail, Colo., Toyama Inst. Glass, Toyama City, Japan, Visions, NYC, Mus. Art Royal Ontario Mus., Toronto, Can., Renwick Gallery, Smithsonian Inst., Washington; exhibitions include Renwick Gallery, 1987, Smithsonian Inst., 1987, Mus. Am. Art, 1987, Habatat Galleries, Boca Raton, 1987-2005, Leo Kaplan Modern, NYC, 1990-2005; commns. include Jasper's Restaurant, Boston, Dreyfus Corp. Hdgrs., Met Life Bldg., NYC, Children's Hosp., Boston, No. Essex County Courthouse, Newburyport, Mass., Rockefeller Ctr., Rainbow Room, NYC, Commonwealth Energy Svcs. Corp. Hdqrs., Cambridge, Mass., Town of Vail, Colo., 1992-2005, LA County Mus., 1993, pvt. residence, Zurich, Switzerland, NYC, Boca Raton (Fla.) Mus. Art, Windows on the World, NY, 1996, 92d St. Y, NYC, 1998, Mayo Clinic, Rochester, 2001, Restaurant Daniel, NYC, 2002, Providence Performing Arts Ctr., 2004; represented in pvt. collections. Trustee Haystack Mountain Sch., Deer Isle, Maine, 1983-92, Urban Glass; nat. adv. bd. U. Arts, Phila., 1989—, Renwick Gallery, Smithsonian Instn., Washington; bd. govs. Mus. Arts and Design, NYC, 2000— Fulbright Hayes fellow Venice, Italy, 1972-73; Glass fellow NEA, 1979, Masters fellow Creative Glass Ctr. Am., 1989, Mass. Coun. for Arts, 1980, 85-87, MIT Ctr. Advanced Visual Studies fellow, 1975-79, Grad. Tchg. fellow RISD, 1970-72, fellow award Am. Craft Coun., 1998; recipient Libensky award Chateau St. Michelle Vineyards and Winery, 2000, Masters of the Medium award Renwick Smithsonian, 2001, Pres. Disting. Artist award U. of the Arts, Phila., 2001, Art of Liberty award Nat. Liberty Mus Fellow Am. Craft Coun.; mem. Glass Art Soc. (pres., chmn. bd. dirs. 1980-82, hon. life). E-mail: studio@idandailey.com.

DAILEY, DARREN, conductor; b. Newark, June 1, 1967; MusB in Edn., Westminster Choir Coll., 1989; MusM, Hayes Sch. Music Appalachian State U., 1998. Dir. music St. Patrick Ch., Fayetteville, Mass., 1991—2003; artistic dir. Boston Children's Chorus, Boston, 2003—. Mem.: Am. Choral Dirs. Assn. Office: Boston Children's Chorus 105 Chauncy St 7th fl Boston MA 02111 Office Phone: 617-778-2242.

DAILEY, DIANNE K., lawyer; b. Great Falls, Mont., Oct. 10, 1950; d. Gilmore and Patricia Marie (Linnane) Halverson. BS, Portland State U., 1977; JD, Lewis & Clark Coll., 1982. Assoc. Bullivant, Houser, Bailey, et. al., Portland, Oreg., 1982-88, ptnr., 1988—, pres., 2002—. Contbr. articles to profl. jours. Mem.: ABA (chair task force on involvement of women 1990—93, governing coun. 1992—99, liaison to commn. on women 1993—97, vice chair tort and ins. practice sect. 1995—96, chair-elect tort and ins. practice sect. 1996—97, standing com. environ. law 1996—99, chair tort and ins. practice sect. 1997—98, chair sect. officers conf. 1998—2001, governing coun. 2003, del. 2003, property ins. law com., ins. coverage litigation com., chair task force CERCLA reauthorization, law practice mgmt. sect., comm. com.), Fedn. Ins. and Corp. Counsel, Def. Rsch. Inst., Internat. Assn. Def. Counsel, Multnomah Bar Assn. (bd. dirs. 1994—95), Oreg. State Bar, Wash. Bar Assn. Office: Bullivant Houser Bailey 300 Pioneer Tower 888 SW 5th Ave Ste 300 Portland OR 97204-2089 Office Phone: 503-499-4430. Business E-Mail: dianne.dailey@bullivant.com.

DAILEY, GARRETT CLARK, publisher, lawyer; b. Bethesda, Md., Mar. 22, 1947; s. Garrett Hobart Valentine and Margaret (Clark) Dailey; m. Carolynn Farrar, June 21, 1969; children: Patrick, Steven. AB, UCLA, 1969; MA, Ariz. State U., 1974; JD, U. Calif., Davis, 1977. Bar: Calif. 1977, U.S. Dist. Ct. (no. dist.) Calif. 1969. Assoc. Stark, Stewart, Simon & Sparrowe, Oakland, Calif., 1977-80; ptnr. Davies & Dailey, Oakland, 1980-85, owner, 1986-90; ptnr. Blum, Davies & Dailey, Oakland, 1985-86; pres., pub. Attys. Briefcase, Inc., Oakland, 1989—, pres., CEO, 1989—. Lectr. U. Calif. Davis Sch. Law, 1988-90, Golden Gate U. Grad. Sch. Taxation, San Francisco, 1986—. Author: SupporTax, 2001, Dissomaster, 2004; co-author: Attorney's Briefcase, Calif. Family Law, 1990—, Calif. Evidence, 1993—, Children and the Law, 1992—, Calif. Lawgic Marital Termination Agreements, 1996—, Calif. Divorce Guide, 1997—, Lawgic Premarital Agreements, 1997— Bd. dirs. Amigos de las Americas, San Ramon Valley, Calif., 1980-85, Rotary 517 Found., Oakland, 1985, Kid's Turn, 1993. Recipient Hall of Fame award Calif. Assn. Cert. Family Law Specialists, 1995, Spencer Brandeis award LA County Bar Assn., 2003. Fellow Am. Acad. Matrimonial Lawyers; mem. Assn. Cert. Family Law Specialists (Hall of Fame award 1995). Democrat. Congregationalist. Home: 1651 W Livorna Rd Alamo CA 94507-1018 Office: Attys Briefcase Inc 2915 McClure St Oakland CA 94609 Office Phone: 510-465-3920. E-mail: briefcase@aol.com.

DAILEY, JAMES RICHARD, lawyer; b. Erie, Pa., Aug. 15, 1935; s. Fred and Elinor (Casey) D.; m. Mary Alice Sedelmeyer, July 13, 1963 (dec. Feb. 2001); children: Timothy, Kathleen, Brian. PhilB, U. Detroit, 1957; JD, Dickinson Sch. Law, 1961. Bar: Pa. 1961, U.S. Dist. Ct. (we. dist.) Pa. 1962, U.S. Ct. Appeals (3d cir.) 1968. Asst. Dist. Atty. Office, Erie, Pa., 1966-71, 81-88; sole practitioner Daily Karte & Villella, Erie, 1968—. 2d lt. U.S. Army, 1957-58. Mem. Pa. Bar Assn. Republican. Roman Catholic. Office: Dailey Restifo & Dailey 900 State St Ste 310 Erie PA 16501-1427 Office Phone: 814-453-4651.

DAILEY, JANET, writer; b. Storm Lake, Iowa, May 21, 1944; d. Boyd and Louise Haradon; m. William Dailey; 2 stepchildren. Student pub. schs., Independence, Iowa. Sec., Nebr., Iowa, 1963-74. Author: No Quarter Asked, 1976, After the Storm, 1976, Boss Man From Ogallala, 1976, Savage Land, 1976, Land of Enchantment, 1976, Fire and Ice, 1976, The Homeplace, 1976, Dangerous Masquerade, 1977, Night of the Cotillion, 1977, Valley of the Vapors, 1977, Fiesta San Antonio, 1977, Show Me, 1977, Bluegrass King, 1977, A Lyon's Share, 1977, The Widow and the Wastrel, 1977, Giant of Mesabi, 1978, The Ivory Cane, 1978, The Indy Man, 1978, Darling Jenny, 1978, Reilly's Woman, 1978, To Tell the Truth, 1978, Sonora Sundown, 1978, Big Sky Country, 1978, Something Extra, 1978, Master Fiddler, 1978, Beware of the Stranger, 1978, The Matchmakers, 1978, For Bitter or Worse, 1979, Green Mountain Man, 1979, Six White Horses, 1979, Summer Mahogany, 1979, Touch the Wind, 1979, Strange Bedfellow, 1979, Low Country Liars, 1979, Sweet Promise, 1979, For Mike's Sake, 1979, Sentimental Journey, 1979, A Land Called Deseret, 1979, The Bride of the Delta Queen, 1979, Tidewater Lover, 1979, Lord of the High Lonesome, 1980, Kona Winds, 1980, The Boston Man, 1980, The Rogue, 1980, Bed of Grass, 1980, The Thawing of Mara, 1980, The Mating Season, 1980, Southern Nights, 1980, Ride the Thunder, 1980, Enemy in Camp, 1980, Difficult Decision, 1980, Heart of Stone, 1980, One of the Boys, 1980, Wild and Wonderful, 1981, A Tradition of Pride, 1981, The Traveling Kind, 1981, The Hostage Bride, 1981, Dakota Dreamin', 1981, For the Love of God, 1981, Night Way, 1981, This Calder Sky, 1981, Lancaster Men, 1981, Terms of Surrender, 1982, With a Little Luck, 1982, Wildcatter's Woman, 1982, Northern Magic, 1982, That Carolina Summer, 1982, This Calder Range, 1982, Foxfire Light, 1982, The Second Time, 1982, Mistletoe and Holly, 1982, Stands a Calder Man, 1983, Separate Cabins, 1983, Western Man, 1983, Calder Born, Calder Bred, 1983, Best Way to Lose, 1983, Leftover Love, 1984, Silver Wings, Santiago Blue, 1984, The Pride of Hannah Wade, 1985, The Glory Game, 1985, The Great Alone, 1986, Heiress, 1987, Rivals, 1989, Masquerade, 1990, Aspen Gold, 1991, Tangled Vines, 1992, Riding High, 1994, The Proud and The Free, 1994, Touch the Wind, 1994, Summer Mahogany, 1995, Legacies, 1996, Homecoming, 1997, Illusions: A Novel, 1997, The Prodigal Daughter, 1998, This Calder Sky, 1999, Calder Pride, 1999, A Capital Holiday, 2001, Green Calder Grass, 2002 Happy Holidays, 2004. Recipient Golden Heart award Romance Writers Am., 1981, Romantic Times Contemporary award, 1983.

DAILEY, JOHN REVELL, museum administrator, former career officer; b. Quantico, Va., Feb. 17, 1934; s. Frank Galvin and Flora (Revell) D.; m. Mimi Leni Rodian, July 11, 1964; children: Lisa Charlotte, Patrick Dailey. BS, U. Calif., L.A., 1956. Commd. 2d lt. USMC, 1956, advanced through grades to gen.; retired, 1992; assoc. dep. adminstr. NASA, 1992-1999; dir. Smithsonian Nat. Air and Space Mus., Washington, 2000—. Contbr. articles to Marine Corps Gazette. Mem. Marine Corps Assn. (pres. 1991—). Avocation: golf. Home: Quarters 1 Marine Barracks Washington DC 20390-0001 Office: Nat Air and Space Museum 7th & Independence Ave SW Washington DC 20560-0001*

DAILEY, MACEO CRENSHAW, JR., humanities educator; b. Norfolk, Va., July 4, 1943; s. Maceo Crenshaw Dailey, Sr. and Marguerite Britton; m. Sandra Prettyman, Feb. 13, 1967 (div. Apr. 1, 1998); children: Michael, Christopher, Crenshaw, Cameron, Cranston; m. Sondra Elise Banfield, June 7, 2003. BS, Towson State U., 1967; MA, Morgan State U., 1971; PhD, Howard U., 1983. Instr. African Am. studies Smith Coll., Northampton, Mass., 1976—80; lectr. dept. history Howard U., Washington, 1981—82; assoc. prof. dept. history Boston Coll., 1982—87, Spelman Coll., Atlanta, 1988—93, Morehouse Coll., Atlanta, 1993—96; dir. African Am. studies U. Tex., El Paso, 1996—. Sr. editor Marcus Garvey and UNIA Editl. Project UCLA, 1980—81; vis. lectr. Black studies Brown U., Providence, 1986—87; cons. Atlanta History Ctr., Smithsonian Mus.; spkr. in field. Co-editor (with K. Navarro): Wheresoever My People Chance to Dwell: Oral Interviews with African American Women of El Paso, 2000; asst. editor: Jour. Negro History; co-editor (with R. Winegarten): Tuneful Tales, 2002; contbr. chapters to books, articles to profl. jours. Bd. dir. El Paso Symphony Orch., 2000—; commr. Tex. Juneteenth Commn., Austin, 2000—; chair bd. dir. Tex. Coun. for Humanities, Austin, 2003—. Recipient Alex W. Bealer prize, Atlanta Hist. Soc. Mem.: Nat. Coun. for Black Studies, Inc., Assn. for the Study of Afro Am. Life and History, Am. Hist. Assn. Avocations: reading, travel, music, drama. Home: 508 Tawny Oak Pl El Paso TX 79912 Office: Univ Tex El Paso 500 University Ave El Paso TX 79968 Office Phone: 915-747-8650. E-mail: mdailey@utep.edu.

DAILEY, THOMAS HAMMOND, retired surgeon; b. Orange, N.J. s. Louis Bird and Evelyn (Hammond) D.; m. Denise Benzacar Dailey, Aug. 22, 1959; children: Andrea, Erika, Seth. AB, Princeton U., 1957; MD, Cornell U. Med. Coll., 1961. Assoc. prof. clin. surgery Columbia U. Coll. Phys. and Surg., N.Y.C., 1991; sr. attending dept. surgery St. Luke's-Roosevelt Hosp. Ctr., N.Y.C., 1982, dir. divsn. colon and rectal surgery, 1990-96, chief med. officer, 1996-99; clin. prof. surgery Columbia U. Coll. Phys. and Surg., N.Y.C., 1997-99; ret., 1999. Pres. med. bd. St. Luke's-Roosevelt Hosp., N.Y.C., 1989-91; v.p. Rsch. Found. of Am. Soc. Colon and Rectal Surgeons, pres., 1995-98. Pres. Am. Soc. Colon and Rectal Surgeons Rsch. Found., 1995—; bd. dirs. Riverside Symphony Orch., N.Y.C., 1998-2003. Capt. M.C., U.S. Army, 1966-68, Vietnam. Mem. Med. Strollers, Physician's Sci. Soc., N.Y. Soc. of Colon and Rectal Surgeons (pres. 1979-81).

DAILY, FRANK J(EROME), lawyer; b. Chgo., Mar. 22, 1942; s. Francis Jerome and Eileen Veronica (O'Toole) D.; m. Julianna Ebert, June 23, 1996; children: Catherine, Eileen, Frank, William, Michael. BA in Journalism, Marquette U., 1964, JD, 1968. Bar: Wis. 1968, U.S. Dist. Ct. (ea. dist.) Wis. 1968, U.S. Dist. Ct. (we. dist.) Wis. 1971, U.S. Dist. Ct. (ctrl. dist.) Ill. 1990, U.S. Dist. Ct. (ea. dist.) Mich. 1994, U.S. Ct. Appeals (7th cir.) 1977, U.S. Ct. Appeals (3d and 5th cirs.) 1985, U.S. Ct. Appeals (4th, 6th, 8th, 9th, 10th, 11th cirs.) 1990, U.S. Supreme Ct. 1998, U.S. Dist. Ct. (no. dist.) Ill. 1999. Assoc. Quarles & Brady, Milw., 1968-75, ptnr., 1975—. Lectr. in product liability law and trial techniques Marquette U. Law Sch., U. Wis., Harvard U.;

lectr. seminars sponsored by ABA, State Bar Wis., State Bar S.D., State Bar S.C., Product Liability Adv. Coun., Chem. Mfrs. Assn., Wis. Acad. Trial Lawyers, Trial Attys. Am., Marquette U., Southeastern Corp. Law Inst., Risk Ins. Mgmt. Soc., Inc.; life mem. pres.'s coun. Wake Forest U., U. Dayton, Boston Coll. Author: Your Product's Life Is in the Balance: Litigation Survival-Increasing the Odds for Success, 1986, Product Liability Litigation in the 80s: A Trial Lawyer's View from the Trenches, 1986, Discovery Available to the Litigator and Its Effective Use, 1986, The Future of Tort Litigation: The Continuing Validity of Jury Trials, 1991, How to Make an Impact in Opening Statements for the Defense in Automobile Product Liability Cases, 1992, How Much Reform Does Civil Jury System Need, 1992, Do Protective Orders Compromise Public's Right to Know, 1993, Developments in Chemical Exposure Cases: Challenging Expert Testimony, 1993, The Spoliation Doctrine: The Sword, The Shield and The Shadow, 1997, Trial Tested Techniques for Winning Opening Statements, 1997, Litigation in the Next Millennium -- A Trial Lawyer's Crystal Ball Report, 1998, What's Hot and What's Not in Non-Daubert Products Liability In the Seventh Circuit, 1998. Commr. for chief judge Milwaukee County, Wis., 2001; bd. visitors Wake Forest U. Law Sch.; bd. trustees U. Ala. Law Sch. Named Marquette U. Law Alumnus of Yr., 2000. Fellow Internat. Acad. Trial Lawyers; mem. ABA (past co-chair discovery com. litigation sect., vice chmn. products, gen. liability and consumer law com. of sect. tort and ins. practice, litigation sect. and mfrs. liability subcom.), ATLA, AAAS, Trial Atty. of Am., Wis. Bar Assn., Milw. Bar Assn., 7th Cir. Bar Assn., Am. Judicature Soc., Def. Rsch. Inst., Supreme Ct. Hist. Soc., Indsl. Truck Assn. (lawyers com.), Am. Law Inst., Product Liability Adv. Coun., Am. Agrl. Law Assn., Wis. Acad. Trial Lawyers, Assn. for Advancement of Automotive Medicine (life), Nat. I-Club U. Iowa, U. Ala. Nat. Alumni Assn., Circle of Champions. Roman Catholic. Office: Quarles & Brady 411 E Wisconsin Ave Ste 2040 Milwaukee WI 53202-4497 Office Phone: 414-277-5381. E-mail: fjd@quarles.com.

DAILY, GRETCHEN CARA, ecologist, environmental services administrator; b. Washington, Oct. 19, 1964; d. Charles Dennis and Suzanne Rachel (Schubert) D. BS, Stanford U., 1986, MS, 1987, PhD, 1992. Ctr. for Conservation Biology/Nature Conservancy fellow Stanford (Calif.) U., 1988-92; Winslow/Heinz postdoctoral fellow U. Calif., Berkeley, 1992—; assoc. prof. biology Stanford (Calif.) U., dir., Tropical Rsch. Program, Ctr. for Conservation. Sci. advisor IPAT Prodns. (film), Stanford, 1995—. Author (with PR Ehrlich & AH Ehrlich) The Stork and the Plow: The Equity Solution to the Human Dilemma, 1995, (with Katherine Ellison) The New Economy of Nature: The Quest to Make Conservatoin Profitable, 2002; Contbr. over 50 articles to profl. jours. Recipient Frances Lou Kallman award Stanford U., 1992, 21st Century Scientist award, 2000; Named Pew scholar in conservation and environ., Pew Found., 1994, Fellow, Aldo Leopard Leadership Program, 1999, Smith Sr. Scholar, The Nature Conservancy, 2003 Mem. Rocky Mtn. Biol. Lab; Fellow, Am. Acad. Arts & Sciences, 2005 Office: Stanford U Ctr Conservation Biology 385 Serra Mall Stanford CA 94305 E-mail: gdaily@stanford.edu.

DAILY, THOMAS A., lawyer; b. Ft. Smith, Ark., Jan. 8, 1946; BA, U. of the South, 1967; JD with honors, U. Ark., 1970. Bar: Ark. 1970. Ptnr. Daily & Woods PLLC, Ft. Smith, Ark. Mem.: ABA, Ark. Bar Assn. (pres.-elect 2002, pres. 2003). Office: Daily & Woods PLLC PO Box 1446 623 Garrison Ave #600 Fort Smith AR 72902-1446

DAIM, TUGRUL UNSAL, technology management specialist, educator; b. Istanbul, May 22, 1967; s. Turhan Hasan and Tulay Ayse D.; m. Yonca Tarman. BS, Bogazici U., Istanbul, 1989; MSc, PhD, Portland State U., 1998. Program mgr. Intel Corp., Hillsboro, Oreg., 1995—. Adj. prof. Portland State U., 1997—, Oreg. Grad. Inst. Sci. and Tech., Beaverton, 1999—; cons. KOC Corp., Istanbul, 1992-93, Turkpetrol Corp., Istanbul, 1993-96. Contbr. articles to profl. jours., chpts. to books. Pres. Turkish Am. Students Cultural Assn., Portland, 1993-95, Suadiye LEO Club, Istanbul, 1989. Mem. IEEE, Am. Soc. Engring. Mgmt., Nat. Geographic Soc., Internat. Assn. Mgmt. Tech., Product Devel. Mgmt. Assn., Inst. Ops. Rsch. and Mgmt. Sci., Portland Downtown Lions Club (dir. 1995-96), Omega Rho (pres. chpt. 1995-97), Sigma Xi, Tau Beta Pi. Avocations: european comics, soccer, tennis, gourmet cooking. Office: Intel Corp JF1-231 25th Ave Hillsboro OR 97124 Home: 16125 SW Kessler Tigard OR 97224 Fax: 503-725-4667. Office Phone: 503-806-2791. E-mail: tugrul@emp.pdx.edu, tugrul.u.daim@intel.com.

DAIN, TODD, secondary school educator, football coach; s. Claude Wesley and Sandra Sue Dain; m. Jessica Rulon, July 4, 1998; children: Andie Elizabeth, Ashton Leigh, Brock Marcus. BS in Edn., Emporia (Kans.) State U., 1994, MS in Ednl. Adminstrn., 2000. Cert. tchr. Kans., 1994, secondary edn. administr. Kans., 2000. Head track and asst. football coach Shawnee Mission West H.S., Overland Park, Kans., 1995—2000; head football coach Shawnee Mission East H.S., Prairie Village, Kans., 2000—02, Olathe (Kans.) N.W. H.S., 2002—. Office: Olathe Northwest High School 21300 College Boulevard Olathe KS 66061 Office Phone: 913-780-7150. Office Fax: 913-780-7159.

DAINES, N. GEORGE, lawyer; b. 1949; m. Mindy Daines; 6 children. BA, Utah State U.; JD, Yale U. Bar: Utah 1976. Chief judge U.S. Ct. Appeals (10th Cir.); ptnr. Barrett & Daines, Logan, Utah; atty. Cache County, 2003—. Tchr. bus. and real estate law Utah State U.; founder, prin. owner Cache Valley Bank; bd. dirs. Utah Prosecution Coun. Mem. bd. editors: Yale Law Jour. Active in the historical renovation of prime historic sites in Cache Valley. Mem.: Utah State Bar (mem. exec. com., jud. evaluation com., pres.-elect 2003—04, pres. 2004—). Office: Cache County Atty 11 W 100 North Logan UT 84321 Office Phone: 435-716-8361. Office Fax: 435-716-8381. E-mail: george@legal.state.ut.us.

DAINES, ROBERT M., law educator; married; 5 children. BA in Am. Studies, BS in Economics, Brigham Young U., 1989; JD, Yale U., 1992. Law clk. to Hon. Ralph K. Winter US Ct. Appeals 2nd Cir., 1992—93; assoc. in leveraged fin. Goldman Sachs & Co., 1993—97; asst. prof. law NYU Sch. Law, 1997—99, assoc. prof., 2000—02, prof., 2002—04; vis. Olin fellow Columbia Law Sch., 1999; Pritzker prof. law and bus. Stanford Law Sch., 2004—. Vis. prof. Yale Law Sch., 2001. Office: Stanford Law Sch Crown Quadrangle 559 Nathan Abbott Way Stanford CA 94305-8610 Office Phone: 650-736-2684. Business E-Mail: daines@stanford.edu.*

DAISS-HURLEY, MARGARET DEAN, writer; b. Framingham, Mass., June 19, 1952; d. Robert Charles Jr. and E. Nancy (Hayes) Dean; m. John Linforth Daiss, June 22, 1974; children: Elisabeth Linforth Jee Youn Daiss, Samuel Hayes Young Min Daiss. BA in English/Fine and Applied Arts, Wellesley Coll., 1974; MS in Edn., SUNY, Brockport, 2005. Curator Balt. Mayor's Office, 1979-80; pub. rels. dir. Arts for Greater Rochester, 1982-83; writer editor Rochester Inst. Tech., 1986-88; writer WordSmart, Rochester, 1989-90; writer, press sec. Monroe County, Rochester, 1990-91; writer self employed, Rochester, 1991-97; English tchr. Rochester City Sch. Dist. 7-12, 1999—. Contbr. essays to Ms. Parenting, Yosung Shinmun, others; contb. essay to Best Am. Essays; presenter in field. Mem. Rochester City Planning Commn., 1986-88. Freedom Forum grantee, 1995. Home: 180 Burwell Rd Rochester NY 14617-

DAISY, KYRAN MAXWELL, artist, writer; s. Maureen Cecile and Maxwell Lawrence Daisy. BA in Psychology, Boston U., 1993—97. Grad. Gemologist Gemological Inst. of Am. (GIA), 2000. Pres., CEO Designs By Kyran, N.Y.C., 2001—. Author (artist): (book) Can't Nobody Take Me Away!; designs by kyran print collection, Can't Nobody Take Me Away! collection, Conversations collection; author: (book) Conversations. Mem.: ASCAP, Nat. Acad. Rec. Arts and Sci. (assoc.). Avocations: travel, music, art, writing, archery. Office Phone: 866-295-9726. Business E-Mail: kyran@designsbykyran.com.

DAITZ, RONALD FREDERICK, lawyer; b. N.Y.C., Sept. 1, 1940; s. Abraham and Anne (Birnbaum) D.; m. Linda Fay Rosenberg, Aug. 2, 1964; children: Paul Bennett, Charles Spencer. AB, Amherst Coll., 1961; LLB, Harvard U., 1964. Bar: N.Y. 1966, Colo. 1964, U.S. Dist. Ct. Colo. 1964, U.S. Ct. Appeals (10th cir.) 1964, U.S. Dist. Ct. (so. dist.) N.Y. 1979. Assoc. Henry & Adams, Denver, 1964-65; from assoc. to ptnr. Weil, Gotshal & Manges LLP, N.Y.C., 1965—. Mem. ABA (fed. regulation of securities com., bus. law sect. 1979—), Am. Coll. Comml. Fin. Lawyers, N.Y. State Bar Assn. (mem. com. securities regulation, bus. law sect. 1984—, chmn. 1990-93, sec. bus. law sect. 1994-95, 2d vice-chair and fiscal officer 1995-96, mem. exec. com. 1991-2001, 1st vice chair 1996-97, chair 1997-98), Assn. Bar City N.Y. (com. corp. law 1975-77, 87-88, 95-97). Office: Weil Gotshal & Manges LLP 767 5th Ave Fl Concl New York NY 10153-0119 Office Phone: +44 207 903-1404.

DAJANI, JARIR SUBHI, retired civil engineer, consultant; b. Jerusalem, Apr. 5, 1940; s. Subhi T. and Lisa (Stori) D.; m. Rihab Dajani, Aug. 23, 1965; children: Jumana, Subhi, Dina. B in Civil Engring., Am. U. Beirut, 1961; MS, Stanford U., 1966; PhD, Northwestern U., 1971. Project engr. Assoc. Consulting Engrs., Lebanon, Saudi Arabia, 1961-65; assoc. prof. Civil Engring. and Policy Scis. Duke U., Durham, NC, 1971—76; assoc. prof. Civil Engring. Stanford (Calif.) U., Calif., 1976-82; cons. Amman, Jordan, 1980-82; adv. Abu Dhabi Fund For Devel., 1982—2004; ret., 2004. Cons. US Agy. for Int. Devel., 1976-82, World Bank, Washington, 1979. Office Phone: 703-567-3600. Personal E-mail: jarir_d@hotmail.com.

DAJANI, VIRGINIA, arts association administrator; Exec. dir. Am. Acad. Arts and Letters, N.Y.C., 1990—. Office: Am Acad Arts and Letters 633 W 155th St New York NY 10032-7501 Office Phone: 212-368-5900. E-mail: academy@artsandletters.org.

DAJNOWICZ, JAN, software and hardware designer, researcher; arrived in US, 1998; BSc in Electronics and Telecomm., Silesian Tech. U., Gliwice, Poland, 1995. Engr. Welding Inst., Gliwice, 1982—92, group leader, 1992—95, head computer sci. dept., 1995—98; programmer JLA, Park Ridge, NJ, 1998—2001; I/T specialist IBM Corp., Armonk, NY, 1998—2004, Southbury, Conn., 2005—. Cons./programmer AVREX, Gliwice, 1990-93, Technologia, Gliwice, 1993-95, Gambit, Gliwice, 1995-98, IBM-Armonk, 1998—. Inventor in field; contbr. chpt. to book, articles to profl. jours. Recipient Silver medals, Eureka, Brussels, 1995, 96, 97, award of gt. invention competition Ministry Environ. Protection Natural and Forest, Warsaw, 1997. Mem.: N.Y. Acad. Scis., NY Acad. Scis., Am. Assn. Artificial Intelligence. Avocations: Karate, Japanese and Chinese cultures. E-mail: jandajno@us.ibm.com.

DAKAI, STEVEN HENRY, alcohol/drug abuse services professional; b. Wausau, Wis., Aug. 19, 1952; s. Henry George and Carol Ruth Dakai; m. Brenda Joyce Dakai, June 2, 1984; children: Amanda J., Julia E., Rebecca R. BS in Sociology, Ashington U., 2000; Date in addictive disorders, Brening Inst., 2003. Cert. chem. dependency counselor, relapse counselor, bd. cert. interventionist, grief recovery specialist. Contractor, Phoenix, 1970—85; adult trainer State of Ariz., Phoenix, 1985—96; behavioral tech. Devereaux, Phoenix, 1996—98; practicum Salvation Army, Phoenix, 1997—98; counselor Maniilaq Assoc., Kotzebue, Alaska, 1998—. Author: (book) Sand Paintings, 2001, Looking Out My Backdoor, 2001. Scoutmaster Boy Scouts Am., Phoenix, 1970—82; pres. PTA, Phoenix, 1985—86; trustee Christ Ch., Phoenix, 1984—86, facilitator 12 steps, 1987—89. Named Wildlife Educator of the Yr., Wildlife Fedn., 1992. Mem.: Alaska Chem. Dependency Counselors Assn., Am. Coun. Ethics, Grief Recovery Inst., Nat. Assn. Drug Abuse Counselors. Republican. Lutheran. Home: PO Box 836 Kotzebue AK 99752 Office: Maniilaq Assoc PO Box 256 Kotzebue AK 99752

DAKE, MARCIA ALLENE, retired nursing educator, dean; b. Bemus Point, N.Y., May 22, 1923; d. Earl B. and Bernice DeLeo (Haskin) D. Diploma, Crouse Irving Hosp., 1944; BS, Syracuse U., 1951; MA, Columbia U., 1955, EdD, 1958. RN. Sch. nurse tchr. various locations, 1946—48; chmn. health dept. SUNY, Oneonta, 1952—56; dean coll. nursing U. Ky., Lexington, 1958—72; dir. dept. nursing edn. ANA, Kansas City, 1972-74; project dir. program devel. nursing ARC, Washington, 1975—79; dir. nursing edn. James Madison U. Coll. Nursing, 1979—81; prof. dean Coll. Nursing, 1981—88; ret., 1988. Editor, resident photographer: Greenspring Village Photo Directories, 2000—; programmer, host Closed Circuit TV Studio, 2000—. Mem. Ky. Bd. Nursing Edn. Nurse Registration, 1969-72, pres., 1970-72; pres. Va. Coun. Deans of Baccalaureate Nursing Programs, 1981-84; nurse officer Civil Def. Otsego County, N.Y., 1953-56; mem. Def. Adv. Com. on Women in Svcs., 1963-65; mem. Ky. Comprehensive Health Planning Coun., 1968-71; pres. Ky. League for Nursing, 1961-65; bd. dirs. Cmty. Ch. Coll., Sun City Ctr., Fla., 1989-92, Sun City Ctr. Guardianship Found., 1990-98; trustee United Cmty. Ch., Sun City Ctr., 1993-96, chmn. pers. com., 1994-96, fin. com., 1994-95, vice chmn. bd. trustees, 1995-96, stewardship com., 1996, mem. pastoral rels. com., 1996—, mem. long range planning com., 1996-97, chmn. pastoral rels. com., 1998—; sec. Caloosa Women's Golf Assn., Sun City Ctr., 1991-92; treas. Greater Sun City Ctr. Disaster Coun., 1992-94; mem., vice chmn. resident adv. com. Greenspring Village, Springfield, Va., 1999-2000, corr. sec. resident adv. com., 2001; prodr., host Channel 6 T.V Greenspring Village, 2001-. 1st lt. U.S. Army Nurse Corps., 1945—46. Fellow Nat. League Nursing; mem. ANA, Va. Nurses Assn. (pres. dist. 9 1983-85), Va. Soc. Profl. Nurses (treas. 1983-88), Va. Assn. Colls. of Nursing (sec. 1980-82, pres. 1982-85), Alliance of Nursing Orgns. (chmn. Va. 1985-88), LWV, Delta Kappa Gamma, Kappa Delta Pi, Pu Lambda Theta. Address: 222 7442 Spring Village Dr Springfield VA 22150-4444 Personal E-mail: mdake@aeitv.net.

DAKIN, CHRISTINE WHITNEY, dancer, educator; b. New Haven, Aug. 25, 1949; d. James Irving, Jr. and Jean Evelyn (Coulter) Crump; m. Robert Ford Dakin, June 21, 1969 (div. Sept. 1982); m. Stephen J. Mauer, Aug. 1, 1985. Student, U. Mich., 1967-71; D of Arts (hon.), Shenandoah U., 1996. Performer, teacher Ann Arbor Dance Theater, Mich., 1965-71; tchr. Ann Arbor Pub. Schs., 1967-70, Lincoln Ctr. Inst., N.Y.C., 1978, Guanajuato U., Mex., 1982; vis. artist USIA Vladivastock, Vladivastock, Russia, 1992; ArtsLink grantee, vis. artist Vladivastock, 1996; tchr., faculty advisor, choreographer Ballet Nacional de Mex., 1993—, U. Colima, Mexico, 2000—; vis. artist USIA Ballet Contemporaneo, Buenos Aires, 1993; prin. dancer Martha Graham Dance Co., N.Y.C., 1976—. Dancer, rehearsal dir. Pearl Lang. Dance Co., 1972-76, Kazuko Hirabayashi Dance Co., 1974-76; faculty Martha Graham Sch., 1972—, Juilliard Sch., 1992—, Alvin Alley Am. Dance Ctr., 1989-93. Appeared in: It's Hard to Be a Jew, 1972, The Dybuk, 1975; appeared (with Martha Graham Dance Co.) Covent Garden, London, 1976, Met. Opera, 1980, Bklyn. Acad. Music, 1994, Sta. WNET Dance in Am. Series, 1979; Young Artist in Performance at The White House, Sta. WNET, 1982, (with Rudolph Nureyev) Paris Opera, Berlin Opera, 1984, N.Y. State Theater, 1985; NHK Film, Japan, 1990, Paris Opera Film, 1991, (documentary film) Les Printemps du Sacre, 1993; assoc. founder Buglisi/Foreman Dance, 1994, (with Buglisi/Foreman Dance) Runes of the Heart, Kennedy Ctr., 1997; assoc. artistic dir. Martha Graham Dance Co., 1997, artistic dir., 2001. Am. Dance Festival scholar, 1969, Garcia-Robles Sr. scholar Fulbright Found., 1999; recipient award Dance Mag., 1994, U. Mich. Alumni award, 2000, Bessie award, 2004; grantee Rockefeller U.S.-Mex. Fund for Culture, 1997-98, 2001. Mem. Am. Guild Mus. Artists (life, bd. govs.) Office: Martha Graham Dance 344 East 59th Street New York NY 10022 Business E-Mail: cdakin@marthagrahamdance.org.

DALAI, TARUN K., geochemist, researcher; s. Purna C. and Gourilata Dalai; m. Meetu Agarwal, June 28, 2003. BS, Ravenshaw Coll., 1993; M in Tech., U. Roorkee, 1996; PhD in Geology, Phys. Rsch. Lab., 2001. Post doctoral fellow Ocean Rsch. Inst., U. Tokyo, 2002—04, Dept. Geology & Geophysics, U. Hawaii, Honolulu, 2004—. Recipient Young Scientist medal, Indian Nat. Sci. Acad., 2005. Mem.: Am. Geophys. Union. Hindu. Achievements include research in Using dissolved Rhenium (Re), provided first estimates of release flux of CO_2 via weathering of organic rich sediments in the Ganga and Yamuna basins in the Himalaya; A study on geochemistry of Molybdenum in a tropical estuary that revealed that suboxic diagenesis in sediments and pore water transport is an important and hitherto unrecognized source of Mo; Provided quantitative and qualitative estimates that silicate rocks are the dominant source of radiogenic Sr isotope (87Sr) to the rivers draining the southern slopes of the Himalaya; Showed that Os isotopic composition (187Os/188Os) of seawater during the last glacial cycle was lower relative to the interglacial period; Established that marine Os isotopic composition can be used as a powerful tool for chemostratigraphy of global events. Avocations: swimming, reading. Office: U Hawaii POST 707 1680 East West Rd Honolulu HI 96822 Office Phone: 1-808-956-0720. Office Fax: 1-808-956-5512. E-mail: dalai@hawaii.edu.

DALAL, MAYUR THAKORBHAI, charitable estate planner; b. Bombay, Apr. 1, 1958; came to U.S., 1988; m. Thakorbhai H. and Jaya T. (Rokadia) D.; m. Madhavi M. Shah, Dec. 8, 1985; children: Sagar, Reema. BS with honors, St. Xavier's, Bombay, 1978; B.Tech., Bombay U., 1981; MBA, Bajaj Inst. of Mgmt. Studies, Bombay, 1986. Mgmt. trainee A. Sarabhai Enterprises Ltd., Bombay, 1981-82, asst. mktg. exec., 1982-83; product mgr. Corn Products div. of CPC Internat., Bombay, 1983-86; mktg. mgr. Foods and Inns Ltd., Bombay, 1986-88; registered rep. Equitable Fin. Co., N.Y.C., 1988-91; asst. agy. mgr. The Equitable Cos., Lake Success, N.Y., 1991—, dist. mgr., 1994-98; CEO Legacy Planning Group LLC, 1998—. Mem. Assn. Advanced Life Underwriters, Fin. Planner Assn., Million Dollar Round Table (Top of Table award), Nat. Assn. Philanthropic Planners. Home: 30 Hunt Ct Jericho NY 11753-1139 Office: Legacy Planning Group LLC 1111 Marcus Ave #100 New Hyde Park NY 11042

D'ALBANI, THOMAS LAURANCE, lawyer; b. Oak Park, Ill., May 12, 1951; s. Thomas James and Joyce M. (Bender) D'A.; m. Jane Grace Killgore, Feb. 9, 1980; children: Lindsay Anne, Jeffery Thomas. BS, U. Ill., 1973; JD, Ill. Inst. Tech., 1977. Bar: Ill. 1977, U.S. Dist. Ct. (no. dist.) Ill. 1977, Minn. 1980. Ptnr. Cann Haskell D'Albani, et al, Bemidji, Minn., 1980—. Bd. dirs. JEDC. Mem. Minn. State Bar Assn., Bemidji C. of C. (bd. dirs.), Rotary Internat., Ducks Unltd. (bd. dirs.). Republican. Lutheran. Avocations: fishing, hunting, farming. Home: 205 7th St Bemidji MN 56601

DAL COL, RICHARD HERBERT, cardiothoracic surgeon; b. Amityville, N.Y., May 18, 1956; s. Rino Angelo and Joan Dal Col; m. Kathleen Ciancetta Dal Col, Aug. 24, 1985; children: Devan, Alexis, Brendan. BS, Le Moyne Coll., 1978; MD, Albany (N.Y.) Med. Coll., 1982. Diplomate Am. Bd. Surgery, 1990, cert. Am. Bd. Thoracic Surgery, 1992. Internship Albany Med. Ctr. Hosp., 1982—83, residency, 1983—87, fellowship in cardiothoracic surgery, 1987—90; cardiothoracic surgeon Albany (N.Y.) Cardiothoracic Surgeons, 1990—. Fellow: ACS; mem.: Soc. Thoracic Surgeons. Avocations: fishing, skiing. Home: 28 East Ridge Rd Loudonville NY 12211 Office: Albany Cardiothoracic Surgeons 317 S Manning Blvd Ste 240 Albany NY 12208 Office Phone: 518-591-2200.

DALE, BRENDA STEPHENS, gifted and talented educator; b. Hickory, N.C., Sept. 24, 1942; d. John Doyle and Bertha (Barger) Stephens; m. James Darrell Dale, June 13, 1964; children: Ginger Leigh Rizoti, Jami Lynne Price. BS in English, Appalachian State U., 1964, MA in Reading Edn., 1977; cert. edn. academically gifted, Lenoir Rhyne, Hickory, N.C., 1982. H.S. tchr. Moore County Schs., Carthage, N.C., 1964, Asheboro (N.C.) City Schs., 1964-65; 8th grade tchr. Davidson County Schs., Thomasville, N.C., 1967-68; reading specialist Randolph County Schs., Trinity, N.C., 1970-72, Wilkes N.C. Schs., Wilkesboro, 1972-82, tchr. acad. gifted, 1982—. Tchr. Davidson County C.C., Lexington, N.C., 1965-68, Wilkes C.C., Wilkesboro, 1982-87, 97—; adult literacy tutor, 1997-99. Edn. chair, bd. dirs. Am. Cancer Soc., North Wilkesboro, N.C., 1985-90; mem. Wilkes Regional Med. Ctr. Aux., 1992—; adminstrv. coun. Wilkesboro Meth. Ch., 1997-1999; vol. Samaritan's Purse, 1997-99, 2005—. Tchr. scholar fellow N.C. Ctr. for Advancement of Tchg., Western Carolina U., 1990; recipient C.B. Eller Tchg. award C.B. Eller Found., 1991; finalist Gifted Tchr. of Yr. N.C., 2003 Mem. AAUW (charter, fundraiser 1977-78, bd. dirs., chmn. edn. found. 1992-96), NEA, N.C. Assn. Educators (state del. 2002, intellectual profl. devel. com. 2003—), Internat. Reading Assn. (sec. 1985-86), Mary Hemphill Svc. Group, So. Appalachian Leadership on Cancer, Lynnwoode Recreation Club, United Meth. Women (dist. membership chair Western N.C. conf. 1996-97, nominating com. 1997-98), Alpha Delta Kappa. Methodist. Avocations: writing, reading, piano. Home: 187 Laurel Mountain Rd North Wilkesboro NC 28659-8122 Office: Wilkes County Schs Main St Wilkesboro NC 28697

DALE, DAVID C., physician, educator; b. Knoxville, Tenn., Sept. 19, 1940; s. John Irvin and Cecil (Chandler) D.; m. Rose Marie Wilson, June 22, 1963 BS magna cum laude, Carson-Newman Coll., 1962; MD cum laude, Harvard U., 1966. Intern and resident Mass. Gen. Hosp., 1966-68; resident U. Wash. Hosp., Seattle, 1971-72; clin. assoc. NIH, 1968-71; prof., assoc. chmn. dept. medicine U. Wash., Seattle, 1976-82, dean Sch. of Medicine, 1982-86. Contbr. numerous articles to profl. jours. Served to comdr. USPHS, 1968-70, 72-74 Mem. Am. Soc. Hematology, Assn. Am. Physicians, Am. Soc. for Clin. Investigation, ACP Avocations: woodworking, gardening, backpacking, sports. Office: U Wash Sch Medicine PO Box 356422 Seattle WA 98195-6422 Business E-Mail: dcdale@u.washington.edu.

DALE, ERWIN RANDOLPH, retired lawyer, writer; b. Herrin, Ill., July 30, 1915; s. Henry and Lena Bell (Campbell) D.; m. Charline Vincent, Aug. 27, 1955; children: Allyson Ann (Mrs. Earl A. Samson III), Kristan Charline (Mrs. Victor L. Zimmermann). BA, U. Tex., El Paso, 1937; JD, U. Tex., 1943. Bar: Tex. 1943, D.C. 1953, Mich. 1956, N.Y. 1960. Atty. IRS, 1943-56, chief reorgn. and dividend br., 1954-56; legal staff Gen. Motors Corp., 1956-57; ptnr. Chapman, Walsh & O'Connell, N.Y.C. and Washington, 1957-59, Hawkins, Delafield & Wood, N.Y.C., 1959-84; of counsel Hutchison, Price, Boyle & Brooks, Dallas, 1985-86, Jenkens, Hutchison & Gilchrist, Dallas, 1986, Hutchison, Boyle, Brooks & Dransfield, Dallas, 1986—87, ret., 1987—. Lectr. tax matters; dir. Md. Electronics Mfg. Corp., 1948-58; dir., treas. The Renaissance Corp., 1968-72; dir., asst. treas. Shancom Reconstrn. Corp., 1968-72, Newhaven Corp., 1968-72 Author numerous articles on fed. tax matters; bd. editors: Tex. Law Rev., 1941-42, 42-43. Mem. ABA (chmn. com. consol. returns sect. taxation 1959-60), Tex. Bar Assn., Mich. Bar Assn., N.Y. State Bar Assn. (chmn. corp. tax com. tax sect. 1967-68, mem. exec. com. 1968-70), Tax Inst. Am. (bd. dirs. 1967-69, treas. 1966), Assn. of Bar of City of N.Y., Nat. Tax Assn., Nat. Assn. Bond Lawyers, Am. Coll. Tax Counsel, Ex-Students Assn. U. Tex., Ex-Students Assn. U. Tex., El Paso, Bronxville Field Club (N.Y.), Masons. Home: 10 Holly Ln Darien CT 06820-3303 Home Fax: 203-662-9386. Personal E-mail: erdale@aol.com.

DALE, JOHN SORENSEN, investment company executive, portfolio manager; b. Mpls., Sept. 30, 1945; s. John Sorensen and Ruth Elaine (Bergstrom) D.; m. Cheryl Lee Woolley, June 19, 1965; children: John, Christopher. BA in Mktg. and Humanities, U. Minn., 1968. CFA. Securities analyst, portfolio mgr. Norwest Corp., Mpls., 1968-78, v.p., sr. trust investment strategist, 1978-84, sr. v.p., mgr. equity advisors, 1984-87; sr. v.p., sr. portfolio mgr. Peregrine Capital Mgmt., Mpls., 1987—. Fellow Inst. Chartered Fin. Analysts; mem. Assn. Investment Mgmt. and Rsch., Twin Cities Soc., Security Analysts, Internat. Soc. Fin. Analysts. Avocations: travel, fishing, hunting. Office: Peregrine Capital Mgmt LaSalle Plz Ste 1850 8th and LaSalle Minneapolis MN 55402-2018

DALE, JUDY RIES, religious organization administrator, consultant; b. Memphis, Dec. 13, 1944; d. James Lorigan and Julia Marie (Schwinn) Ries; m. Eddie Melvin Ashmore, July 12, 1969 (div. Dec. 1983). BA, Rhodes Coll., 1966; M in Religious Edn., grad. specialist in religious edn., So. Bapt. Theol. Sem., 1969. Cert. tchr. educable mentally handicapped, secondary English, adminstrn. and supervision spl. edn. EMH tchr., curriculum writer, tchr. trainer Jefferson County Bd. Edn., Louisville, 1969-88, edn. cons., 1988-90; dist. coord. Gt. Lakes dist. Universal Fellowship Met. Cmty. Chs., Louisville, 1990—2002. Lectr. U. Louisville, 1976—77, 1987—90, Jefferson CC,

Louisville, 1987—93; mem. program adv. com. Internat. Conf. Spl. Edn., Beijing, 1987—88; mem. faculty Samaritan Inst. Religious Studies, 1992—98. Editor, writer: A Manual of Instructional Strategies, 1985, Handbook for Begining Teachers, 1989. Bd. sec. Com. Ten, Inc., Louisville, 1987—91; v.p. GLUE, 1988—92, pres., 1992—94; mem. steering com. Ky. Fairness Alliance, 2005—, treas., 2005—; mem. membership com. Cmty. Health Trust, 1991—94; chair acad. affairs com. Samaritan Inst. Religious Studies, 1996—97, trustee, 1992—98; mem. programs and budget divsn. Universal Fellowship Met. Cmty. Chs., 1990—97, counsel, 1990—2002, active women's secretariat steering com., 1991—95, mem. core team, 1993—2000, chair, 1997—2000, fin. team, 2000—, bd. adminstrn., 2003—, chmn. risk mgmt. team, 2003, sec., 2004—, chair, 2005—, dist. coord. Gt. Lakes dist. Named Outstanding Elem. Tchr. Am., 1975; recipient Hon. Order of Ky. Cols., 1976, MCC Disting. Lay Leadership award, 1999. Mem.: ACLU, NOW, AAUW, Ky. Coun. Exceptional Children (bd. dirs. 1978—90, Mem. of the Yr. 1987), Coun. Exceptional Children (keynote spkr., mem. exec. com. 1984—88, internat. pres. 1986—87, bd. govs. 1981—88), Women's Alliance, Parents, Family and Friends Lesbians and Gays, Nat. Gay & Lesbian Task Force, Nat. Ctr. Lesbian Rights, Internat. Platform Assn., Gay and Lesbian Assn. Anti-Defamation, Lambda Legal Def. and Edn. Fund, Phi Kappa Phi. Democrat. Avocations: reading, handwork. Home and Office: 1300 Ambridge Dr Louisville KY 40207-2410 Personal E-mail: judydale13@aol.com.

DALE, ROBERT GORDON, investment company executive; b. Toronto, Ont., Can., Nov. 1, 1920; s. Gordon McIntyre and Helen Marjorie (Cartwright) D.; m. Mary Austin Babcock, Apr. 3, 1948; children: Robert Austin, John Gordon. Ed., U. Toronto Schs., 1930-39, Trinity Coll.; student, U. Toronto, 1939-40. Cert. in bus. adminstrn., 1946. With Maple Leaf Mills, Ltd., Toronto, 1947—, plant mgr., 1957-61, gen. product mgr., 1961-65, asst. to pres., 1965-67, exec. v.p., 1967-68, chmn., pres., chief exec. officer, 1968-86, dir.; chmn. Upper Lakes Group Inc., Toronto, 1993—95; dep. chmn. Upper Lakes Group, Inc., Toronto, 1996—; pres. Pinedale Investments Inc., Toronto, 1994—. Hon. pres. Air Cadet League Can.; past chmn. Ont. Provincial Com.; trustee United Comty. Fund Greater Toronto; past chmn. bd. govs. Can. Corps Commissionaires, Canadian Exec. Svc. Orgn.; bd. dirs. Sunnybrook Med. Ctr.; past pres. Branch 165 Royal Can. Legion. With RCAF, 1940-45. Decorated D.F.C., Can. Forces Decoration, Disting. Service Order. Mem. Phi Kappa Pi. Clubs: Rosedale Golf, Nat, Royal Can. Mil. Inst., Empire. Conservative. Anglican. Office: Upper Lakes Group Inc 49 Jackes Ave Toronto ON Canada M4T 1E2 Personal E-mail: dalerobertg@hotmail.com.

DALE, SHARON KAY, real estate broker; b. San Francisco, July 14, 1940; d. Terrill Odin and Alice Ernestine (Anthony) Glenn; divorced; 1 child, Kimberly Kay. AS, Fresno City Coll., Calif., 1982; student, Calif. State U., Fresno, 1983—. Lic. real estate broker, Calif. Sales assoc. Red Carpet Realtors, Fresno, 1974-77; broker, owner U.S. Cities Realtors, dba, Pierson & Planamento, Inc., Fresno, 1977-80; broker assoc. Easterbrook Constrn., Fresno, 1980-81, 1983-84; exec. sec. Valley Med. Ctr., Fresno, 1981—96; broker Assoc. Adanalian & Jackson Real Estate, Fresno, 1981—83, 1984—85. Dir. div. II U.S. Cities Realtors, Inc. No. Calif, Nev., 1978-80. Vol. St. Agnes Service Guild, Fresno, 1974—, Mental Health Assn., Fresno, 1982-83, Ednl. T.V. Channel 18, Fresno,1983, Valley Med. Ctr. Aux., Fresno, 1985-96, Holiday Guild Children's Hosp. Ctrl. Calif., 2000—. Mem. Fresno County, City C. of C. (Ambassadors Club), Calif. Assn. Realtors, Fresno Bd. Realtors, Multiple Listing Svc., Nat. Bd. Realtors, Fresno State Alumni Assn., Sierra Sport & Racquet Club (Fresno, Calif.) (charter mem.). Republican. Avocations: golf, tennis, photography, travel. Home: 5099 W Shields Ave Fresno CA 93722-9751 Office: Adanalian & Jackson Real Estate 1515 W Shaw Ave Fresno CA 93711-3503

DALE, SHIRLEY MARIE, protective services official; b. Camden, Ala., Aug. 22, 1959; children: Velda Venessa, Teresa Almeta. Diploma, William J. Jones, 1977; BA in Polit. Sci., U. Detroit Mercy, 1994. Clk. typist, data entry, sec. Designers, Detroit, 1981; switchboard operator We. Temp. Svc., Detroit, 1984—86; police cpl. Wayne County Sheriff's, Detroit, 1986—; assoc. prodr. studio/porta pak workshop Barden Cablevision, 1989. Avocation: songwriting. Office: Wayne County Sheriff Dept 1441 St Antoine Detroit MI 48226 Home: 15467 Heyden Detroit MI 48223 Office Phone: 313-224-2407. E-mail: s-marie@msn.com.

DALE, T.D., architectural firm executive; CEO, pres. Dale & Assocs., P.A., Jackson, Miss. With Sch. Architecture Adv. Coun. Mem.: Miss. State Bd. Architecture (sec., treas. 1986, pres. 1992), Am. Inst. Architects Miss. (bd. dir. 1996, chmn. 1996, sec. treas. 1997, chmn. state conv. 1999). Office: Dale and Assocs PA 120 N Congress St Ste 110 Jackson MS 39201-2683*

DALE, WILLIAM BROWN, economist, consultant; b. Detroit, Mar. 24, 1924; s. William Holl and Grace May (Brown) D.; m. Deborah Jane Parry, July 27, 1946 (dec. July 2, 1997); children: William P., Susan D., Christopher A., Judith A., Katherine S.; m. Joy Peabody Ogden, Nov. 19, 1999. BA with honors, U. Mich., 1944; MA, Fletcher Sch. Law and Diplomacy, 1947, PhD candidate, 1948. Internat. economist U.S. Treasury, 1948-56; program mgr. internat. research Stanford Research Inst., 1956-61; U.S. exec. dir. Internat. Monetary Fund, Washington, 1962-74, dep. mng. dir., 1974-84; cons. internat. fin. Served with USN, 1944-46. Mem. Council Fgn. Relations, Phi Beta Kappa. Democrat. Home: 6008 Landon Ln Bethesda MD 20817-6218

DALEN, JAMES EUGENE, cardiologist, educator; b. Seattle, Apr. 1, 1932; s. Charles A. and Muriel E. (Joanise) Robinson. BS, Wash. State U., 1955; MA, U. Mich., 1956; MD, U. Wash., 1961; MPH, Harvard U., 1972. Intern and asst. med. resident Boston City Hosp., 1961—63; sr. resident New Eng. Med. Ctr., Boston, 1963—64; rsch. fellow in cardiology Harvard Med. Sch., Peter Bent Brigham Hosp., Boston, 1964—67, assoc. dir. cardiovasc. lab., 1967—75; instr., asst. prof., assoc. prof. medicine Harvard Med. Sch., 1967—75; chmn. dept. cardiovasc. medicine U. Mass. Med. Sch., 1975—77, prof., chmn. dept. medicine, 1977—88; physician-in-chief U. Mass. Hosp., 1977—88; acting chancellor U. Mass., Worcester, 1986—87; editor Archives Internal Medicine, 1987—2004; dean, vice provost med. affairs U. Ariz. Coll. Medicine, Tucson, 1988—95, dean, v.p. health scis., 1995—2001. Mem. editl. bd. Jour. AMA, 1987—2004; contbr. articles to profl. jours. With USN, 1951—53. Mem.: ACP, Am. Coll. Chest Physicians (pres. 1985—86), Am. Coll. Cardiology, Assn. Univ. Cardiologists. Home: 5305 N Via Velazquez Tucson AZ 85750-5989 Office: 1840 E River Rd Ste 120 Tucson AZ 85718 Office Phone: 520-577-8180. Personal E-mail: jamesdalen@yahoo.com.

D'ALENE, ALIXANDRIA FRANCES, human resources professional; b. Buffalo, Oct. 21, 1951; d. Fern (Hill D'A. BA, Canisius Coll., Buffalo, 1973, MS, 1975, MBA, 1980. Tchr. Buffalo pub. schs., 1973-76; pers. cons. Sanford Rose Assocs., Williamsville, N.Y., 1976-78; mgr. benefits adminstrn. Svc. Sys. Corp., Clarence, N.Y., 1978-80; mgr. employee rels. Del. Monte Corp., Walnut Creek, Calif., 1980-82; human resource mgmt. cons. H.R.S., Inc., Winston-Salem, N.C., 1982-87; corp. pers. specialist Advance Stroes Co., Inc., Roanoke, Va., 1987-90; pers. dir. Alfred (N.Y.) U., 1990-94; dir. human resources Framtone Connectors USA, Inc., Norwalk, Conn., 1994—; mgr. Lord Corp., Shelton, Conn., 1994-96; dir. human resources Energy Scis., Inc., Wilmington, Mass., 1999—. Mem. Assn. Pers. Adminstrs., Indsl. Pers. Soc., Coll. and U. Pers. Assn., Phi Alpha Theta. Episcopalian. Home: 250 Lynnfield St # A Peabody MA 01960-4921 Office: 42 Industrial Way Wilmington MA 01887-4605 Office Phone: 978-694-9000. E-mail: tighee@comcast.net.

DALES, SAMUEL, microbiologist, virologist, educator; b. Warsaw, Aug. 31, 1927; emigrated to Can., 1948, naturalized, 1953; s. James and Helen (Ochs) D.; m. Laura L.R.J. Fischer, Dec. 28, 1952 (dec.); children: Adam Charles, Pamela Ann. BA with honors, U. B.C., 1951, MA, 1953; PhD, U. Toronto, 1956. Postdoctoral fellow Nat. Cancer Inst. Can., 1957-60; rsch. assoc., asst. prof. Rockefeller U., N.Y.C., 1960-66; assoc. mem., mem., chief cytobiology Pub. Health Rsch. Inst. City of N.Y., Inc., 1966-76; prof. U. Western Ont., Can., London, Can., 1975-93, prof. emeritus, 1993—, chmn. microbiology and immunology, 1975-80. Research prof. NYU Med. Sch., 1969-75; mem. adv. bd. spl. virus cancer program Nat. Cancer Inst., NIH, 1969-73; mem. virology study sect. NIH, 1971-75, ad hoc, 1977, 79; mem. sci. adv. bd. Banting Rsch. Found., 1978-80; mem. rev. panels virology and cancer USPHS, Med. Rsch. Coun. Can.; adj. prof. Rockefeller U., 1996—. Author: Biology of Poxviruses, 1981; mem. editl. bd. Virology, 1963—, Jour. Cell Biology, 1973-76, Intervirology, 1973-91, Virus Rsch., 1983-92, Microbial Pathogenesis, 1985—, Jour. Virology, 1989-97, Ency. Virology, 1990-95; contbr. sci. articles and revs. to profl. publs. Fellow Royal Soc. Can.; Macy Found. scholar, 1981-82; rsch. grantee USPHS; rsch. grantee Med. Rsch. Coun. Can.; rsch. grantee Multiple Sclerosis Soc. Fellow AAAS; mem. Fedn. Am. Socs. for Exptl. Biology, Harvey Soc., Am. Soc. Cell Biology, N.Y. Soc. Electron Microscopy (coun. 1968-70), Amyotrophic Lateral Sclerosis Soc. An. (sci. adv. bd.) Home: 262 Central Park W Apt 4C New York NY 10024-3512 Personal E-mail: drssdfr@aol.com.

D'ALESANDRO, PHILIP ANTHONY, parasitologist, immunologist, retired medical educator; b. Bound Brook, N.J., Apr. 2, 1927; s. Philip and Antoinette Ann (Vaccaro) D'A.; m. Rosemary Natale Falzarine, Nov. 25, 1961. BSc, Rutgers U., 1952, MSc, 1954; PhD, U. Chgo., 1958. Rsch. assoc. U. Chgo., 1958-59; assoc. prof. Rockefeller U., N.Y.C., 1959-75; assoc. prof., acting head divsn. tropical medicine Columbia U., N.Y.C., 1975-92, emeritus prof., 1992—. Chmn. tropical medicine and parasitology study sect. NIH, Bethesda, Md., 1976-80. Author: (with others) Immunity to Parasitic Animals, 1970, Pathogenicity of Trypanosomes, 1979, Parasitic Protoza, Vol. 1, 1991; editor Jour. Protozoology, 1980-88; contbr. articles to profl. jours. Sgt. U.S. Army Air Corps, 1945-46. Grantee NIH, 1972-90, 79-82. Fellow AAAS; mem. Phi Beta Kappa. Avocations: antique cars, model railroading, photography. E-mail: pdalesand@aol.com.

D'ALESSANDRI, ROBERT M., dean; b. N.Y.C., June 26, 1945; m. Elaine D'Alessandri; 2 children. BA, Fordham U., 1967; MD, N.Y. Med. Coll., 1971. Diplomate Am. Bd. Internal Medicine, Am. Bd. Infectious Diseases. Intern dept. medicine Met. Hosp., N.Y.C., 1971—72; fellowship divsn. infectious diseases U. Fla., Gainesville, 1974—76, resident dept. medicine, 1976—77; instr., chief resident dept. medicine W.Va. U. Sch. Medicine, 1977—78, asst. prof. dept. medicine, 1978—81, assoc. prof. dept. medicine, 1981—84, prof. dept. medicine, 1985—, chief sect. of comprehensive medicine dept. medicine, 1979—87, assoc. dean ambulatory svcs. dept. medicine, 1987—90, dean Sch. of Medicine dept. medicine, 1989—2004; v.p. for health scis. W.Va. U., 1992—; pres. Blanchette Rockefeller Neurosciences Inst. Bd. dirs. Nat. Bank of W.Va., Morgantown, MountainView Regional Rehab. Hosp., W.Va. U. Rsch. Corp., Chestnut Ridge Psychiat. Hosp., W.Va. U. Hosps., W.Va. U. Med. Corp., Morgantown HealthRight Clinic, Morgantown Hospice; commentator Sta. WNPB, W.Va. Pub. Radio; host weekly Doctors on Call; weekly med. corr. Sta. WCHS-TV, Charleston, Sta. WDTV, Clarksbur, Sta. WTRF, Wheeling; elected shc. medicine rep. Univ. Faculty Senate, 1980-84; chair credentials com. W.Va. Hosps., 1984-85, med. exec. bd. chair 1985-86, chair infection control com., 1985-86, exec. com. chair 1986-87, mem. 1983-87, chair hosp. med. records com., 1986-87, chair hosps. patient care rev. com., 1986-87, chair ambulatory care bldg. com., 1987-89, chair dean's com. VA Med. Ctr., Martinsburg, 1991—, Clarksburg, 1989—; chair sch. of medicine edn. adv. coun. W.Va. U. Health Scis. Ctr., 1989—, chair sch. of medicine exec. faculty, 1989—, chair health scis. ctr. exec. com., 1992—; coord. intro. clin. medicine dental studies, 1979-84, coord. intro. to clin. medicine, phys. diagnosis course, 1979-84; spl. lectr. Guiyang (China) Med. Coll., 1988, Hangzhou (China) Red Cross Hosp., 1988. Contbr. numerous articles to profl. jours. Bd. dirs. Monongalia Arts Ctr., Morgantown, 1989—. Mem. AMA, Am. Coll. of Physicians, Infectious Diseases Soc., Soc. for Gen. Internal Medicine, Nat. Rural Health Assn., W.Va. State Med. Assn., Monongalia County Med. Soc. Office: RC Byrd Health Scis Ctr 1150 Health Scis N PO Box 9000 Morgantown WV 26506-9000*

D'ALESSANDRO, DAVID C., lawyer; b. Det., Mich., Mar. 17, 1969; s. Robert and Antoinette D'Alessandro. BA, Boston Coll., 1991; JD, U. of Mich., 1994. Bar: Tex. 1994. Atty. Gardere & Wynne, Dallas, 1994—96, Vinson & Elkins, 1996—2002, ptnr., 2003—. Co-author (legal treatise) Tax Management Portfolio - Qualified Retirement Plans. Mem.: Nat. Assn. of Stock Plan Profls., Dallas Bar Assn. Employee Benefits and Exec. Compensation Sect. Office: Vinson & Elkins 3700 Trammell Crow Ctr Dallas TX 75201 Office Phone: 214-220-7890. Office Fax: 214-999-7890. E-mail: ddalessandro@velaw.com.

D'ALESSANDRO, DAVID FRANCIS, insurance company executive; b. Utica, N.Y., Jan. 6, 1951; s. Dominick Vincent and Rosemary (Pallaria) D'A.; children: Michael, Andrew. BA, Utica Coll. of Syracuse U., 1972. Account supr. Daniel J. Edelman Inc. Pub. Rels., 1972-74; info. programs mgr. svc. bur. Control Data Corp., 1974-77, comm. mgr. data svcs., 1977-79, gen. mgr. comml. credit, 1980-84; asst. v.p. Citibank Comm. Svcs., 1979-80; v.p. John Hancock Fin. Svcs., Boston, 1984-85, sr. v.p., 1985-88, pres. corp. sector, mem. mgt. com., 1988-91, sr. exec. v.p. retail sector, 1991—, pres., CEO, 1996—, also bd. dirs. Trustee, mem. exec. com. Wang Ctr. for Performing Arts, Boston, 1989—; chmn. Harvard U. Kennedy Sch. Govt., 1990—; bd. trustees Syracuse U., 1990—, Utica (N.Y.) Coll., 1988—. Office: John Hancock Fin Svcs John Hancock Pl Boston MA 02117

D'ALESSANDRO, DOMINIC, financial executive; b. Italy, Jan. 18, 1947; arrived in Can., 1954; 3 children. BSc., Loyola Coll., 1967; postgrad., McGill U., 1971. Acct. Coopers & Lybrand, 1968-75, dep. mgr. Paris office, 1970-71; asst. contr. GenStar, Ltd., 1975; from dir. fin. to gen. mgr. GenStar, Saudi Arabia, 1976-79; v.p. Materials and Constrn. Group, San Francisco, 1979-81; dep. contr. Royal Bank of Can., Toronto, 1981, v.p. and contr., 1982, sr. v.p., 1983-87, exec. v.p. fin., 1987; pres., CEO Laurentian Bank of Can., 1988, Manulife Fin., Toronto, 1994—; also bd. dirs. ManuLife Fin., Toronto. Adv. bd. Lazard Can., Ltd., Willis Inc.; vice chmn. bd. Can. Coun. Chief Execs.; past chmn. Canadian Life and Health Ins. Assn. Mem. Bus. Coun. on Nat. Issues; chmn. United Way of Greater Toronto, 1998. Fellow Inst. Chartered Accts. (chartered). Office: Manulife Financial 200 Bloor St E Toronto ON Canada M4W 1E5

D'ALESSANDRO-FERNANDEZ-PHILLIPS, GINA, elementary school educator; b. Englewood, N.J., Oct. 21, 1964; d. Daniel J. and Eleanor L. (Allen) D'Alessandro. BA in Psychology, Rutgers Coll., 1986; cert., Trenton State Coll., 1987; MA in Urban Adminstrn. Supr., Jersey City State Coll. Tchr. Christopher Acad., Scotch Plains, N.J., asst. dir. summer camp; tchr. Toms River (N.J.) Regional Schs.; lead tchr. sci. Intermediate East, Toms River, 1988—. Asst. dir. sci. fair Intermediate East. Coach girls basketball, cheerleading. Audubon scholar, 1991. Mem. Rutgers Alumni Assn., SSTOP Team mem.; Save the Manatee Club, World Wildlife Fedn. Avocations: reading mystery novels, bowling, boating. Home: 1200 Riviera Ave Toms River NJ 08753

DALESSIO, DONALD JOHN, internist, neurologist, educator; b. Jersey City, Mar. 2, 1931; s. John Andrea and Susan Dorothy (Minotta) Dalessio; m. Jane Catherine Schneider, Sept. 4, 1954 (dec. Mar. 1998); children: Catherine Leah, James John, Susan Jane. BA, Wesleyan U., 1952; MD, Yale U., 1956. Diplomate Am. Bd. Internal Medicine. Intern N.Y.C. Hosp., 1956—57, asst. resident in medicine and neurology, 1959—61; resident in medicine Yale Med. Ctr., 1961—62; pres. med. staff Scripps Clinic, La Jolla, Calif., 1974—78; chmn. dept. medicine Scripps Clin., La Jolla, 1974—89, chmn. emeritus, 1989—, cons., 1982—, pres. med. group, 1980—81; clin. prof. neurology U. Calif., San Diego, 1973—. Physician in chief Green Hosp., La Jolla, 1974—89; pres. Am. Assn. Study Headache, Chgo., 1974—76; chmn. Fedn. We. Soc. Neurology, Santa Barbara, Calif., 1976—77; Musser-Burch lectr. Tulane U., 1979; Kash lectr. U. Ky., 1979. Author: (book) Wolff's Headache, 7th edit., 2001, Approach to Headache, 1973, Approach to Headache, 6th edit., 1999; editor: Headache jour., 1965—75, 1979—84, Scripps Clinic Personal Health Letter; mem. editl. bd. Jour. AMA, 1977—87; columnist: San Diego Tribune. Pres. Nat. Migraine Found., Chgo., 1977—79. Capt. U.S. Army, 1957—59. Recipient Disting. Alumnus award, Wesleyan U., 1982. Fellow: ACP; mem.: World Fedn. Neurology (Am. sec. 1980—90, rsch. group migraine), Am. Acad. Neurology (assoc.), La Jolla Beach/Tennis Club, La Jolla Country Club. Avocations: tennis, squash, piano. Home: 8891 Nottingham Pl La Jolla CA 92037-2131 Office: Scripps Clinic & Rsch Found 10666 N Torrey Pines Rd La Jolla CA 92037-1092

D'ALESSIO, FREDERICK D., telecommunications company executive; b. N.J. BSEE, MS in Engring., N.J. Inst. Tech.; MBA, Rutgers U. With N.J. Bell, from 1971; v.p. ops. and engring. Bell Atlantic Corp., 1990-91; pres., CEO, Bell Atlantic-Md., Inc., 1991-95; pres. Bell Atlantic-Consumer Svcs., Arlington, Va., 1995—, group pres. N.Y.C.; pres. advanced svcs. Verizon Comms., Inc., N.Y.C. Non-exec. dir. Spirent PLC, 2004—, Network Equipment Technologies, Inc., 2005—. Bd. govs. Nat. Aquarium, Balt.; bd. dirs. Balt. Symphony Orch., Greater Balt. Com., Inc., Kennedy Krieger Inst.; trustee Goucher Coll. Office: Verizon Comms Inc 1095 Avenue Of The Americas New York NY 10036-6704*

DALEY, ARTHUR JAMES, retired magazine publisher; b. St. Paul, Aug. 15, 1916; s. John and Mary (Mayer) D.; m. Lorayne Mary Mongan, June 7, 1941; children: Michael, Kay. Student pub. schs., Fond du Lac, Wis. Advt. salesman Fond du Lac Commonwealth Reporter, 1936, sports editor, 1937-40; sports writer Green Bay (Wis.) Press-Gazette, 1941-43, sports editor, 1946-68, telegraph, picture editor, 1968-78; pub. Green Bay Packer Yearbook, 1960-83, assoc. pub., 1984-88, ret., 1988; columnist Green Bay Packer Report, 1974—. Mem. Wis. Hall of Fame Com. Served with AUS, 1943-46, ETO. Inducted into Green Bay Packer Hall of Fame, 1993. Mem. Pro Football Writers Am., Nat. Football League Alumni Assn., Oneida Golf and Country Club. Home: 1146 Highview Ln Green Bay WI 54304-2222

DALEY, CHARLES MIKE, consumer products company executive; b. Boston, June 7, 1936; s. Francis Daniel and Kathleen (Gillin) Daley; m. Janet Marie Richards, Aug. 24, 1957; children: Stephen M., Kevin F., Thomas P., Mary E. BS, Boston Coll., 1958. With S. S. Kresge Co., Boston and Burlington, Vt., 1958-59; sales staff Libby McNeill & Libby, 1960-63; account exec. J. Daren & Sons, Norwich, Conn., 1963-66; CEO, pres., treas. Daley Care Mgmt. Co., Boston, 1966-88; CEO, chmn., treas. Lojack Corp., Westwood, Mass., 1986—2001, cons., 2001—. Bd. dirs., v.p., pres., chmn. Mass. Fedn. Nursing Homes, Boston; v.p., pres. Mass Health Coun., Boston; bd. advisors Bit Group, 2002—. Pres. Norwich (Conn.) Jaycees, 1964—65; v.p. Conn. Jaycees, state chmn., 1964—66; v.p., nat. dir., pres., chmn. Mass. Jaycees, 1966—72; co-chair 150th anniversary com. YMCA, 2001—02, vice chmn., 2002—; bd. dirs., mem. exec. com. Greater Boston YMCA, 1997—; mem. exec. com. Inner City Scholarship Fund, 1998—; trustee, vice chmn., chmn. Emmanuel Coll., Boston, 1993—; bd. dirs. Cathedral H.S., 2003—, trustee, 2003; mem. nat. devel. bd. Boston Coll., nat. campaign com.; chmn. patrons com. Boston Coll. McMullen Mus. Art. Named Man of the Yr., Norwich C. of C., 1965, Disting. Nursing Home Adminstr., Boston chpt. Am. Coll. Nursing Home Adminstrs. Mem.: Cathedral HS Bd., Boston Coll. Alumni Assn., Bonita Country Club, Oyster Harbors Country Club (bd. govs. 2003—), Boston Coll. Club (founder, trustee 1997—). Roman Catholic. Avocations: music, walking, art and antique collecting. Home: 60 Elm St Canton MA 02021-1230 Office Phone: 781-251-4244.

DALEY, GEORGE QUENTIN, hematologist, biomedial research scientist; b. Catskill, N.Y., Nov. 13, 1960; s. Frank Leonard and Natalie Alcine (Evans) D. AB, Harvard U., 1982; PhD in Biology, MIT, 1989; MD summa cum laude, Harvard U., 1991. Diplomate Am. Bd. Internal Medicine. Chief resident in internal medicine Mass. Gen. Hosp., Boston, 1994-95; fellow Whitehead Inst., Cambridge, Mass., 1995; clin. rsch. fellow hematology/oncology Children's, Brigham, Women's and Dana Farber Cancer Ctr. Inst.; assoc. prof. Harvard Med. Sch., 2002—; with divsn. hematology/oncology Children's Hosp., Boston, 2003—, assoc. dir. stem cell/devel. biology rsch. Chmn. pre-med. adv. com. Quincy House, Harvard U., Cambridge, 1987-95. Contbr. articles to sci. jours. Recipient rsch. award for Clin. Trainees NIH, 1992, Burroughs-Wellcome Fund Career award, Scholar award, Leukemia and Lymphoma Soc. Am., Pioneer award, NIH, 2004; nat. scholar Harvard U., 1978-91. Mem. AAAS, Am. Soc. Clin. Investigation. Achievements include creation of mouse model for chronic myelogenous leukemia; research in stem cells of the blood to define the molecular basis for human leukemia; self-renewal and differentiation of human ES cells, target directed chemotherapy for chronic myelogenous leukemia (CML); germ cell development (germ cell research cited a "Top Ten" breakthrough by Science magazine). Office: Childrens Hosp Boston 300 Longwood Ave Karp-7 Boston MA 02115 Office Phone: 617-919-2013. Office Fax: 617-730-0222.

DALEY, HENRY J., lawyer; b. Boston, Mass. BS, Worcester Polytechnic Inst., 1978; PhD in Physics, U. Arizona, 1984; JD, Northeastern U., 1996. Bar: Mass. 1997, DC 1999, US Patent and Trademark Office. Former rsch. scientist Daresbury Lab., England, MIT, Lincoln Lab.; former assoc. Pillsbury Winthrop, Va., ptnr. Washington, 2002—05; ptnr., intellectual property group Venable LLP, Washington, 2005—. Former visiting scholar Yale U., Kernfysisch Versneller Inst., Netherlands. Office: Venable LLP 575 7th St NW Washington DC 20004 Office Phone: 202-344-4362. Office Fax: 202-344-8300. Business E-Mail: hjdaley@venable.com.

DALEY, LINDA, lawyer; b. Newark, N.J., Jan. 19, 1954; d. Charles and Margaret Mongiovi; m. Rodger Cleveland Daley, Oct. 7, 1978. Student, Upsala Coll., 1971—74; BS, Regis Coll., 1975; JD, U. of Denver, 1982. Bar: Colo. 1982. Loan svc. clk. World Savs. & Loan Assn., Denver, 1975—76; rschr. Eleanor Roosevelt Inst. for Cancer Rsch., Denver, 1976—79; legal asst. Robert T. Hinds, Jr. & Associates, P.C., Littleton, Colo., 1979—82, assoc., 1982—86; law clerk to Hon. Donald P. Smith Colo. Ct. Appeals, 1987—89; assoc. staff atty. Colo. Ct. of Appeals, Denver, 1989—95, dep. chief staff atty., 1995—. Contbr. articles to profl. jours. Mem.: Colo. Bar Assn. (Amicus com.), YMCA, Denver Law Jour., Phi Beta Kappa. Avocations: walking, pets, knitting, crocheting. Business E-Mail: linda.daley@judicial.state.co.us.

DALEY, MICHAEL JOSEPH, lawyer; b. Phila., Aug. 9, 1955; s. Robert Charles and Agnes Theresa (Brophy) D. BA with honors, U. Denver, 1977; JD, Loyola U., Chgo., 1980. Bar: Ill. 1980, U.S. Dist. Ct. (no. dist.) Ill. 1980, Trial Bar (no. dist.) Ill. 1983, U.S. Ct. Appeals (7th cir.) 1985, U.S. Supreme Ct. 1985, U.S. Dist. Ct. (no. dist.) Ind. 1994, U.S. Tax Ct. 1994. Asst. state's atty. Cook County State Atty.'s Office, Chgo., 1981-83; assoc. Nisen & Elliott, Chgo., 1983-86, ptnr., 1986—. Instr. trial advocacy Loyola U. of Chgo., 1986—, Nat. Inst. Trial Advocacy, 2000-. Recipient Lewis Powell Medal for Advocacy, Am. Coll. Trial Lawyers, 1980, Robert Bellarmine award Loyola U. Chgo., 1995. Mem. Bar Assn. 7th Fed. Cir., Assn. of Transp. Practitioners, Nat. Assn. R.R. Trial Counsel, Union League Club Chgo. Avocations: skiing, bicycling, golf. Office: Nisen & Elliott 200 W Adams St Ste 2500 Chicago IL 60606-5283 E-mail: mdaley@nisen.com.

DALEY, PAMELA, diversified services, technology and manufacturing company executive; b. Springfield, Mass., Oct. 1, 1952; d. Edward Murray and Elizabeth Bloom Daley; m. Randall Lee Phelps, Aug. 26, 1995. AB summa cum laude in Romance Langs. and Lit., Princeton U., 1974; JD magna cum laude, U. Pa., 1979. Bar: Pa. 1979, N.Y. 1991. Lectr. partnership taxation law U. Pa., Phila., 1982-89; assoc. tax sect. Morgan, Lewis & Bockius, Phila., 1979-86, ptnr., 1986-89; tax counsel GE, Fairfield, Conn., 1989-91, v.p., sr. counsel for transactions, 1991—2004, v.p. bus. devel., 2004—. Bd. outside advisor Va. Tax Review assn., 1982-92. Editor-in-chief U. Pa. Law Review; contbr. articles to profl. jours. Trustee MacDuffie Sch., Springfield, 1986-92; bd. govs. Pa. Economy League, 1986-89; mem. bd. overseers Law Sch. U. Pa., 1999—; bd. dirs. G.E. Found., 1999—, Genworth Fin., Inc.; bd. dirs. World Wildlife Found., 1999—. Teaching fellow Salzburg Seminar on Am. Law and Legal Instns., 1986; named to Acad. Women Achievers YWCA, 1992. Mem. Order of Coif, Phi Beta Kappa. Office: GE 3135 Easton Tpke # E3 Fairfield CT 06828

DALEY, PAUL PATRICK, lawyer; b. Boston, July 10, 1941; s. Patrick Joseph and Catherine Josephine (Ford) D.; m. Barbara Sabin, May 24, 1980; 1 child, Patrick. AB, Boston Coll., 1963; MBA, JD, Harvard U., 1973. Bar: Mass. 1973, U.S. Ct. Appeals (1st cir.) 1974, U.S. Dist. Ct. (Mass.) 1974, U.S. Ct. Appeals (5th cir.) 1980, U.S. Supreme Ct. 1980, N.Y. 1983, U.S. Ct. Appeals (2d cir.) 1998. Assoc. Hale and Dorr LLP, Boston, 1973-78; jr. ptnr. Hale and Dorr, Boston, 1978-82; sr. ptnr. Wilmer Cutler Pickering Hale and Dorr LLP, Boston, 1982—. Lectr. CLE programs. Assoc. editor Mass. Law Rev., 1998—; contbr. articles to profl. jours. Trustee Mass. Sch. Profl. Psychology, Boston, 1985-2003, chair, 1994-2003; trustee St. Sebastians Sch., Needham, Mass. 1981-1982, Naval War Coll. Found., 1996—, pres., 2000-02, chmn., 2002-04; bd. dirs. Am. Sail Train Assn., Newport, R.I., 1982-86. Capt. USNR, 1963-94, Vietnam 1965-67. Decorated DFC, Air Medals (16), Navy Commendation medal with Combat V, Vietnamese Air Gallantry Cross. Fellow Am. Coll. Bankruptcy; mem. ABA, Mass. Bar Assn. (past chmn. bus. bank com., bus. law sect., fee arbitation bd.), Boston Bar Assn. (coun.), Am. Bankruptcy Inst., Nat. Def. U. Found., U.S. Naval Inst., Naval Res. Assn., Assn. Naval Aviation, Tailhook Assn., Comml. Law League, Navy League, Windsor Club (Waban, Mass.), Brae Burn Country Club, Wardroom Club. Democrat. Roman Catholic. Avocations: flying, scuba diving, biking, reading, theater. Home: 9 Crofton Rd Waban MA 02468-1931 Office: Wilmer Cutler Pickering Hale and Dorr LLP 60 State St Boston MA 02109-1816 Office Phone: 617-526-6720. Office Fax: 617-526-5000. Business E-Mail: paul.daley@wilmerhale.com.

DALEY, RICHARD MICHAEL, mayor; b. Chgo., Apr. 24, 1942; s. Richard J. and Eleanor (Guilfoyle) D.; m. Margaret Corbett, Mar. 25, 1972; children: Nora, Patrick, Elizabeth. BA, DePaul U., Chgo., 1964, JD, 1968. Bar: Ill. 1969. Ptnr. Simon and Daley, Chgo., 1970-72, Daley, Riley & Daley, Chgo., 1972-80; mem. Ill. State Senate, 1973-80, chmn. Judiciary I Com., 1975, 77; state's atty. Cook County, Ill., 1980-89; mayor Chgo., 1989—; pres. U.S. Conf. Mayors, 1996. Headed the US Conf. Mayors, 1996. Bd. dirs. Little City Home; mem. Citizens Bd. U. Chgo.; mem. adv. bd. Mercy Hosp., Chgo.; bd. mgrs. Valentine Boys Club; active Nativity of Our Lord Parish, Chgo. Named Outstanding Leader, Ill. Assn. Social Workers, 1978, Outstanding Legislator of Yr., Lt. Gov. Sr. Legis. Forum, 1979, Outstanding Leader in Revision of Ill. Mental Health Code, Ill. Assn. Retarded Citizens, 1979, Municipal Leader of Yr., American City and County mag., 1997, Pub. Official of Yr., Governing mag., 1997, Politician of Yr., Library Jour., 1997; recipient Golden Rule plaque, Chgo. Boys Club Am., Education Excellence award, Nat. Conf. for Cmty. and Justice, 1999, Pub. Svc. Leadership award, Nat. Coun. for Urban Econ. Develop., 1999, J. Sterling Morton award, Nat. Arbor Day Found., 1999, Keystone award, Am. Architectural Found., 1999, Martin Luther King/Robert F. Kennedy award, Coalition to Stop Gun Violence/Education Fund To End Handgun Violence, 1999, Openlands Project Conservation Leadership award, 2000, National Trust's Trustee's award for Outstanding Achievement in Pub. Policy, 2000, National Trust for Historic Preservation National Preservation award, 2000, 2002, Ill. Coalition Against Domestic Violence (ICADV) Human Dignity award, 2001, Chgo. Innovation award, Sun-Times, 2002, Extreme City 'Digie' (Digital Innovation) award, 2002, Waste Management, Inc. Top honors in City Livability award, US Conf. of Mayors, 2002. Mem. Chgo. Bar Assn., Ill. State Bar Assn., ABA, Cath. Lawyers Guild. Democrat. Roman Catholic. Office: Office of the Mayor City Hall Rm 507 121 N La Salle Chicago IL 60602-1202*

DALEY, ROBERT EMMETT, retired foundation executive; b. Cleve., Mar. 13, 1933; s. Emmett Wilfred and Anne Gertrude (O'Donnell) D.; m. Mary Berneta Fredericks, June 7, 1958; children: Marianne Fredericks, John Gerard. BA in English, U. Dayton, 1955; MA in Polit. Sci., Ohio State U., 1968, MA in Pub. Adminstrn., 1976. Local govt. reporter, Washington corr., fin. editor Jour. Herald, Dayton, Ohio, 1957-65, pub. affairs reporter, 1967; staff writer Congressional Quar., Inc., Washington, 1966; pub. affairs reporter Dayton Daily News, Dayton, 1969; dir. pub. affairs & comm. Charles F. Kettering Found., Dayton, 1977-94, ret., now assoc., 1994—. Part-time copy boy, sports reporter Jour. Herald, Dayton, 1953-55. Past pres., bd. trustees St. Joseph Home for Children; former mem. adv. bd. Ctr. for Religious Telecomms., U. Dayton; traveling press sec. sen. candidate John J. Gilligan, 1968, for gubernatorial candidate, 1970-71, asst. to Gov. Gilligan, 1971-75; media rels. dir. Nat. League of Cities, Washington, 1976-77; mem. Montgomery County Hist. Soc.; past mem. Ind. Sector Pub. Info. & Edn. Com. With U.S. Army, 1955-57. Mem. Pub. Rels. Soc. Am., Soc. Profl. Journalists, Nat. Press Club, KC, Ancient Order Hibernians. Roman Catholic. Home: 888 Cranbrook Ct Dayton OH 45459-1525 Office: Charles F Kettering Found 200 Commons Rd Dayton OH 45459-2788 Office Phone: 937-434-7300. Business E-Mail: daley@kettering.org.

DALEY, RON (RONALD EUGENE DALEY), playwright, poet, theater director, theater producer; b. Washington, Sept. 24, 1945; s. Russell Eugene and Dorothy Sybil (Krouse) D.; m. Virginia Ann Bean, Nov. 7, 1986; children: Jackson Phillip Wesley, Bryan Augustin, Geoffrey Eugene. BA in Philosophy, North Park Coll., 1967; MA in English with honors, Roosevelt U., 1968; MA in Drama, Syracuse U., 1975. founder ACT-Argyle, 1999—. Instr. English/Philosophy Malcolm X C.C., Chgo., 1968-70, Orange County C.C., Middletown, N.Y., 1970-73; English N.Y.C. C.C., Bklyn., 1975-78; dir., designer various theatre companies, 1978-80; producer Jerron Prodns., N.Y.C., 1980-81; assoc. artistic dir. New World Theatre, N.Y.C., 1981-82; artistic dir. Nat. Shakespeare Co., N.Y.C., 1982-85; resident dir., producer Riverside Shakespeare Co., N.Y.C., 1986; exec. dir. RED Prodns., Argyle, Wis., 1985—. Guest dir. Broom St. Theatre, Madison, 1987-94, Classic Theatre, N.Y.C., 1979-84, AMDA Studio One, N.Y.C., 1977-78, Camden (Maine) Shakespeare Festival, 1979, Mercury Players, Madison, 1994—. Author of plays off Broadway including Beyond the Veil, Damphools and Wowsers, Argyle Wisconsin 53504, In the Matter of John David Hutchins, It's Gotta Be the Shoes, Nobody Dies, 5:45, Badger Orpheus, The Third Blackhawk War, Journeys with Nanabozo, The Abrazo, The Knight of the Burning Pestle, The Red Palace; editor Amphibious Maneuvers. Prodr. Free Shakespeare in the Parks, N.Y.C., 1986. Mem Soc. of Stage Dirs. and Choreographers, Dramatists Guild, U.S. Holocaust Meml. Mus., ACLU. Avocations: fishing, gardening, carpentry. Home: PO Box 196 Argyle WI 53504-0196

DALEY, RUTH MARGARET, advertising agency administrator; b. Buffalo, Apr. 12, 1950; d. Russell Short and Emma Pleasant (Wear) Garrick; m. Jeffrey George Vanghel (dec. 1988); m. Patrick L. Daley. Student, Villa Maria Coll., Buffalo. Sec. McKesson & Robbins Drug Co., Cheektowaga, N.Y., 1972-78; sales rep. Nasco Inc., Springfield, Tenn., 1978-80; telemktg. sales rep. L.M. Berry & Co., Amherst, N.Y., 1980-81, mgr. telemktg. sales unit, 1981-83, mgr. telemktg. sales dept., 1984-90; mgmt. cons. Ameritech, Troy, Mich., 1990-92; mgr. tng. White Directory Pub. (The Talking Phone Book), Buffalo, 1992—2002, telephone sales mgr., 2002—. Grad. asst. Dale Carnegie Inst., Buffalo, 1985. Avocations: dance, reading, travel. Home: 66 Parktrail Ln Buffalo NY 14227-2545 Office: The Talking Phone Book 1945 Sheridan Dr Buffalo NY 14223-1203 Office Phone: 716-875-9100 x142. Business E-Mail: rdaley@talkingphonebook.com.

DALEY, SUSAN JEAN, lawyer; b. New Britain, Conn., May 27, 1959; d. George Joseph and Norma (Woods) Daley. BA, U. Conn., 1978; JD, Harvard U., 1981. Bar: Ill. 1981. Assoc. Altheimer & Gray, Chgo., 1981-86, ptnr., 1986—2003, Perkins Coie LLP, Chgo., 2003—. Mem.: ABA (real property, probate and trust law sect. 1983—, employee benefits com. taxation sect. 1984—, chmn. welfare plans com. real property, probate and trust law sect. 1989—95, chmn. employee benefits, securities law com. taxation sect. 2001—), Chgo. Coun. Fgn. Rels., Chgo. Bar Assn. (chmn. employee benefits divsn. fed. taxation com. 1985—86, chmn. employee benefits com. 1990—91, chmn. fed. taxation com. 1992—93), Ill. Bar Assn. (chmn. employee benefits divsn. fed. taxation sect. 1984—86, chmn. employee benefits sect. 1995—96), Nat. Assn. Stock Plan Profls. (pres. Chgo. chpt. 1995—). Avocation: marathons. Home: 1636 N Wells St Apt 415 Chicago IL 60614-6009 Office: 131 S Dearborn St STE 1700 Chicago IL 60603-5559 Office Phone: 312-324-8645. Business E-Mail: SDaley@perkinscoie.com.

DALEY, THOMAS P., marketing professional, sales executive; BS in Mktg., Boston Coll., 1988. Sales mgr. LoJack Corp., Boston, 1989—90, dir. sales and mktg. N.Y. and N.J., 1990—94, gen. sales mgr. mid-Atlantic, 1994—99, gen. mgr. mid-Atlantic and Ga., 1999—2001; bus. devel. Hotels.com, Washington, Dallas and Miami, 2002—. Vice chmn. nat. fin. com John Kerry for Pres., 2002—04, advisor social issues. Address: Apt 1306 1200 N Veitch St Arlington VA 22201

DALEY, VETA ADASSA, educational administrator; b. St. Elizabeth, Jamaica, Jan. 14, 1953; came to U.S., 1981; d. Waldemar and Princess (Bartley) Solomon; m. Vincent Daley, Jan. 27, 1973; children: Yuland, Angelo. Cert. in edn., U. W.I., Jamaica, 1978; BS, Westfield (Mass.) State Coll., 1987, MEd in Adminstrn., 1991. Tchr. Ministry Edn., Jamaica, 1972-81, Forest Park Jr.-Mid. Sch., Springfield, Mass., 1987-92; grad. asst. Westfield State Coll., 1988-90; asst. prin. Duggan Mid. Sch., Springfield, 1992-94; prin. John F. Kennedy Mid. Sch., Springfield, 1994—. Mem. Mass. Curriculum Adv. Commn., Malden, 1992—. Advisor Jamaica Festival Commn., Mandeville, 1973-80, Jamaica 4-H Clubs, 1970-76; vice chmn. adminstrv. bd. Wesley United Meth. Ch., Springfield, 1988—, pres. Meth. Women, 1991-93; chmn. Liberian Christian Fund, Springfield, 1990, New Eng. Conf. United Meth. Women, 1994; mem. African Task Force-R.I., 1991—. Recipient Outstanding Achievement award Jamaica 4-H Clubs, 1975, Outstanding Achievement in Edn. award Jamaican Cmty., Springfield, 1992, citation Mass. Ho. of Reps., 1992. Mem. New Eng. League Mid. Schs., Springfield Adminstrv. Assn., Jack and Jill Am. (pres. Springfield chpt. 1992—, Disting. Mother of Yr. award ea. region 1994). Home: 81 Embury St Springfield MA 01109-1847 Office: John F Kennedy Mid Sch 1385 Berkshire Ave Indian Orchard MA 01151-1819

DALEY, VINCENT RAYMOND, JR., real estate company executive, consultant; b. Evanston, Ill., June 21, 1940; s. Vincent R. and Carole V. Daley; m. Viola (Vi) Elizabeth Bursiek, May 6, 1967; children: Kathleen Marie, Colleen Patricia. AA, Lincoln Coll., 1961; BS, Loyola U., Chgo., 1963; student in real estate, Roosevelt U., 1964. From salesman to store mgr. Sears Roebuck & Co., Chgo., 1962—73; v.p., cons. Kencoe Corp., Des Plaines, Ill., 1973—74; pres. Daley & Assocs., Chgo., 1974—; chmn. Wacker Real Estate Svcs., Chgo., 1997—. Chmn. Wacker Mgmt. Corp., Chgo. State legis. asst. 8th Legis. Dist., Chgo., 1985—93; mem. econ. devel. com. State of Ill., Springfield, 1985—88; bd. trustees Lincoln Col. Chartered Lincoln U., 2001—. Chgo. Bd. Realtors (life, bd. dirs.), Nat. Assn. Realtors (bd. regents), Ill. Assn. Realtors (bd. dirs.), Realtors Land Inst. (bd. govs.), CCIM Inst., Internat. Real Estate Fed. (sr. cert. valuerer, registered internat. mem., cert. investment finnancier). Democrat. Roman Catholic. Avocation: travel. Home: 1807 N Orleans St Chicago IL 60614-5325 Office: Wacker Real Estate Svcs 400 N Michigan Ave Ste 600 Chicago IL 60611-4129 Office Phone: 312-787-7554. E-mail: vincevidaley@aol.com.

DALEY, WILLIAM M., former federal government official; b. Aug. 8, 1948; m. Loretta Daley; 3 children. BA, Loyola U., 1970; LLB, John Marshall Law Sch., Chgo., LLD (hon.), 1975. Bar: Ill. 1975. With Daley and George, Chgo.; ptnr. Mayer, Brown & Platt; vice chmn. Amalgamated Bank, Chgo., 1989, pres., COO, 1990-93; atty., advisor to Mayor Richard M. Daley, Chicago, 1993—97; sec. Dept. Commerce, Washington, 1997-2000; chmn., v.p. Al Gore's presidential campaign, 2000; vice chmn. Evercore Capital Partners L.P., 2000—01; pres. SBC Communications, 2001—04; chmn. elect mid-western operations J.P. Morgan Chase & Co., 2004—. Bd. dirs. Merck & Co., Boston Properties, Coun. Foreign Rels., John F. Kennedy Ctr. Performing Arts, Com. US-China Foreign Relations; spl. counsel to Pres. for NAFTA. Served in Army Nat. Guard & Air Nat. Guard, 1970—76. Recipient St. Ignatius award fro Excellence in the Practice of Law, 2995, World Trade award World Trade Ctr., Chgo., 1994, World Standards Day 2002 Hon. Chair & Ron Bown award, Alliance for Telecomm. Industry Solutions. Office: SBC Comm 175 E Houston San Antonio TX 78205

DAL FABBRO, MARIO, author, sculptor; b. Cappella Maggiore, Treviso, Italy, Oct. 6, 1913; came to U.S., 1948, naturalized, 1951; s. Pietro and Luigia Fiorina (Gava) Dal F.; m. Helen Dall'Antonia, May 9, 1944; 1 child, Sulvia Dal Fabbro Nucera. BFA, Inst. Indsl. Art, Venice, Italy, 1935; MFA, Magistero of Art, Venice, 1937. Author on furniture design and constrn., 1950-69; designer furniture, 1938-66; sculptor-in-residence Fairfield, Conn., 1968—. One-man shows include Allentown (Pa.) Art Mus., 1972, Kemerer Mus., Bethlehem, Pa., 1976, Mus. Sci. and Industry, Bridgeport, Conn., 1978, Nat. Art Ctr., N.Y., 1979, Silvermine Guild Ctr. for Arts, New Canaan, Conn., 1980, Civic Biblioteca and Museo, Vittorio Veneto, Italy, 1980, Stamford (Conn.) Mus. and Nature Ctr., 1982; exhibited in group shows at Nat. Exhbn. Mini-Painting and Sculpture, Trieste, V Bienal Internacional del'Arte en Los Deportes, Barcelona, Mus. Phila. Civic Ctr., Conn. Acad. Fine Arts, Wadsworth Anthenaeum, Hartford, Conn., Nat. Exhbn. Salmagundi Club, N.Y.C., Nat. Exhbn. Audubon Artists, N.Y.C., Woodmere Art GAllery, Phila., 1974, Galleria Sant Ambroeus, Milan, Italy, 1982, also numerous group shows in Brazil, Can., Argentina and throughout U.S.; represented in permanent collections Nat. Mus. Art, Sao Paulo, Brazil, Kemerer Mus., Allentown Art Mus., Italian Cultural Ctr., Stone Park, Chgo. Civic Mus., Treviso, Civic Mus. Vittorio, Veneto, Mus. de Bellas Artes, Cordoba, Argentina, Civic Mus. Modern Art, Trieste; author: Costruzione e Funzionalita del Mobile Moderno, 1950, Furniture for Modern Interiors, 1954, How to Build Modern Furniture, 1957, Upholstered Furniture, 1969. Served with Italian Army, 1941-43. Recipient Silver medal Nat. Italian Am. Artists in U.S., 1978-79, Gold medal Nat. Art Exhbn. Boito-Polpet, Belluno, Italy, 1981, several Best in Show awards; named Artist of Yr., Fairfield, 1986. Mem. Silvermine Guild Ctr. for the Arts. Democrat. Roman Catholic. Home: 67 Sherman Ct Fairfield CT 06430-5827

DALIA, VESTA MAYO, artist; b. Atlanta, Aug. 14, 1932; d. Frank and Winnifred (Layton) Mayo; m. William Barber Macke, May 30, 1952 (div. 1971); children: William Barber Jr., Michael Mayo, Vesta Melissa, Mary Sue Macke Mullen; m. Joseph William Dalia, Aug. 31, 1973 (dec. 1990); stepchildren: Joseph W. Jr., Jeffrey Meade, Denise Marie Dalia Cooper, Nancy Dalia Cook. Student, U. Ga. Tchr. art Cen. Piedmont Coll., Charlotte, N.C. Exhibited art in shows in Charlotte and Atlanta. Bd. dirs., officer Caribbean Condo; poll worker Fla. elections. Mem. Nat. Tole and Decorative Painters (past pres. Dogwood chpt., recipient Golden Palet award 1990), Missle Tole Decorative Painters, Team Network S.E. Painters, Weinman Mineral Mus., West Fulton Owls Club, Frog Club, Zoo Atlanta, Friendship Force, Native Atlantans Club, The Etowah Found. NATAS (Atlanta chpt.), NRA, Ga. Ensemble Theatre. Republican. Episcopalian. Home: 2814 S Peninsula Dr Daytona Beach FL 32118 E-mail: vdalia@cfl.rr.com.

DALIANIS, LINDA STEWART, state supreme court justice; BA cum laude, Northeastern U., 1970; JD, Suffolk U., 1974, JD (hon.), 2001. Bar: N.H. 1974, U.S. Dist. Ct. N.H. 1974, U.S. Supreme Ct. 1974. Pvt. law practice, Nashua, NH, 1974-79; marital master NH Superior Ct., 1979-80, assoc. justice, 1980—2000, chief justice, 2000; assoc. justice NH Supreme Ct., Concord, 2000—. Chair Interbranch Criminal and Juvenile Justice Com.; mem. Edn. Coms. N.H. Supreme and Superior Cts., Northern New Eng. Jud. Edn. Com.; mem. Jud. Adv. Com. N.H. Dept. Corrections; mem. Marital Masters Com., Alternative Dispute Resolution Com. N.H. Supreme Ct. First woman to hold seat on N.H. Supreme Ct. Office: Supreme Ct Bldg One Noble Dr Concord NH 03301-6160

DALINKA, MURRAY KENNETH, radiologist, educator; b. Bklyn., May 13, 1938; s. Joseph and Gertrude (Cohen) D.; m. Janice L. Kolber, Feb. 28, 1982; 1 son, Bradford Gordon; children by previous marriage: Ilene, Ian Scott. BS, U. Mich., 1960, MD, 1964. Diplomate Am. Bd. Radiology. Intern Pa. Hosp., Phila., 1964-65; resident in radiology Montefiore Hosp., N.Y.C., 1965-68; instr. radiology Harvard Med. Sch., 1970-71; from asst. prof. to assoc. prof. radiology Thomas Jefferson U. Hosp., Phila., 1971-76, prof., 1976—; chief orthop. radiology Hosp. U. Pa., 1976—. Chief diagnostic radiology Thomas Jefferson U. Hosp., Phila., 1974-76; . cons.hila. Naval Hosp., 1974-79, Walson Hosp., Ft. Dix Army Base, 1972-77. Author: Arthography, 1980, Symposium on Orthopedic Radiology, 1983; mem. editorial bd. Bone Syllabus IV, 1982—, Skeletal Radiology, 1982—, Conversations in Radiology, 1977-79; guest editor Emergency Medicine Clinics of North America, Vol. 3, 1985; editor: (with J.J. Kaye) Radiology in Emergency Medicine Clinics in Emergency, Vol. 3, 1984, (with J. Edeiken and D. Karasick) Edeiken's Roentgen Diagnosis of Diseases of Bone, 4th edit. Served to capt. USAF, 1968-70. James Picker research fellow, 1972-73 Mem. Internat. Skeletal Soc. (past pres.), Radiol. Soc. N.Am. (Outstanding Educator award 2003), Am. Coll. Radiology (chmn. panel on musculoskeletal imaging, mem. task force on appropriateness criteria/diagnostic patient care guidelines), Phila. Roentgen Ray Soc. (past pres.). Home: 318 S 21st St Philadelphia PA 19103-6531 Office: U Pa Hosp Dept Radiology 3400 Spruce St Philadelphia PA 19104-4206 E-mail: dalinka@oasis.rad.upenn.edu.

DALIS, IRENE, mezzo soprano, performing arts association administrator; b. San Jose, Calif., Oct. 8, 1925; d. Peter Nicholas and Mamie Rose (Boitano) D.; m. George Loinaz, July 16, 1957; 1 child, Alida Mercedes. AB, San Jose State Coll., 1946; MA in Teaching, Columbia U., 1947; MMus (hon.), San Jose State U., 1957; studied voice with, Edyth Walker, N.Y.C., 1947-50, Paul Althouse, 1950-51, Dr. Otto Mueller, Milan, Italy, 1952-72; MusD (hon.), Santa Clara U., 1987; DFA (hon.), Calif. State U., 1999. Prin. artist Berlin Opera, 1955-65, Met. Opera, N.Y.C., 1957-77, San Francisco Opera, 1958-73, Hamburg (Fed. Republic Germany) Staatsoper, 1966-71; prof. music San Jose State U., Calif., 1977—2004; founder, gen. dir. Opera San Jose, 1984—. Dir. Met. Opera Nat. Auditions, San Jose dist., 1980-88. Operatic debut as dramatic mezzo-soprano Oldenburgisches Staatstheater, 1953, Berlin Staedtische Opera, 1955; debut Met. Opera, N.Y.C., 1957, 1st Am.-born singer, Kundry Bayreuth Festival, 1961, opened, Bayreuth Festival, Parsifal, 1963; commemorative Wagner 150th Birth Anniversary; opened 1963 Met. Opera Season in Aida; premiered: Dello Joio's Blood Moon, 1961, Henderson's Medea, 1972; rec. artist Parsifal, 1964 (Grand Prix du Disque award); contbg. editor Opera Quar., 1983. Recipient Fulbright award for study in Italy, 1951, Woman of Achievement award Commn. on Status of Women, 1983, Pres.'s award Nat. Italian Am. Found., 1985, award of merit People of San Francisco, 1985, San Jose Renaissance award for sustained and outstanding artistic contbn., 1987, Medal of Achievement Acad. Vocal Arts, 1988; named Honored Citizen City of San Jose, 1986; inducted into Calif. Pub. Edn. Hall of Fame, 1985, others. Mem. Beethoven Soc. (mem. adv. bd. 1985—), San Jose Arts Round Table, San Jose Opera Guild, Am. Soc. Univ. Women, Arts Edn. Week Consortium, Phi Kappa Phi, Mu Phi Epsilon. Office: Opera San Jose 2149 Paragon Dr San Jose CA 95131 Office Phone: 408-437-4450. E-mail: dalis@operasj.org.

DALLARA, CHARLES H., think-tank executive, financial analyst; b. Spartanburg, S.C. m. Carolyn Gault; children: Stephen, Emily. BS in Econs., U. S.C., 1970; MA, Tufts U., 1975, MA in Law and Diplomacy, 1976, PhD, 1986; LLD (hon.), U. S.C., 1990. Various positions Dept. Treasury; U.S. alt. exec. dir. IMF, 1982-83, dep. asst. set. treas., 1983-85, exec. dir., 1984-89, sr. dep. asst. sec. treasury internat. econ. policy, 1985-88, asst. sec. treasury for policy devel., sr. adv. policy, 1988-89; mng. dir. J.P. Morgan & Co., 1991-93, Inst. Internat. Fin., 1993—, also bd. dirs. With USN, 1970-74. Office: IIF Ste 8500 2000 Pennsylvania Ave NW Washington DC 20006-1852

DALLAS, DOROTHY BENZ, painter, printmaker; b. 1930; d. John Jacob and Elsie Bertha (Bruns) Benz; m. Donald Peter Dallas, Sept. 1, 1952; children: Diana, Bruce, Linda, Andrew. Cert. in interior design, Pratt Inst., 1950, BFA, 1978, MFA, 1981. Interior designer Voorhees, Walker, Smith, Smith, Haines, N.Y.C., 1950-55; pvt. practice interior designer N.Y.C., 1955-63. One-woman shows include Dwight/Englewood Sch., 1981, Pratt Inst., Bklyn., 1981, Interchurch Ctr., N.Y.C., 1983, Old Ch. Cultural Ctr., Demarest, N.J., 1983, St. Peter's Ch., N.Y.C., 1987, Johnson & Johnson, New Brunswick, N.J., 1989; group shows include Summit Art Ctr., 1981, Monmouth Mus., 1982, 89, Bergen Mus., Paramus, N.J., 1983, Nat. Arts Club, N.Y.C., 1984, N.J. Watercolor Soc., 1988, Noyes (N.J.) Mus., 1989, Nat. Assn. Women Artists, 1989, Ednl. Testing Ctr., Princeton, N.J., 2005. Recipient 3d prize Painter and Sculptors Soc., 1982, 3d prize Garden State Watercolor Soc., 1984, 1st prize Hudson River Regional, 1989. Mem. Nat. Assn. Women Artists (2d prize 1984, Witte award 1986, Grumbacher award 1988), Am. Watercolor Soc. (Millard Sheets medal 2004), Art Ctr. Water Color Affiliates (founder, sec. 1978-87, pres.), N.J. Watercolor Soc. (membership chmn. 1981—, Members Show 1st prize 1981), Catherine Lorillard Wolfe Art Club (bd. dirs. 1982-89, pres. 1989—, Zahn award 1988, Gold medal 1998), Salmagundi Club Republican. Lutheran. Avocations: gardening, sailing, snorkeling. Home: 378 Eastwood Ct Englewood NJ 07631-3109

DALLAS, H. JAMES, textiles executive; b. Lithonia, Ga., Aug. 1, 1958; BS in Acctg., U. S.C., 1983; MBA, Emory U., 1994. Equipment cleaner Pepperidge Farms, Aiken, SC, 1981—83; br. auditor C & S Nat. Bank, 1983—84; cost acct. Gypsum divsn. Ga.-Pacific Corp., 1984—85, programmer corp. info. tech., 1985—87, analyst corp. info. tech., 1987—89, mgr. info. sys.-transp. divsn., 1989—92, gen. mgr. transp. divsn., 1992—94, dir. strategy and planning corp. info. tech., 1994—96, group dir. bldg. products mfg. info. tech., 1996—98, group dir. bldg. products mfg. and distbn. info. tech., 1998—2000, v.p. bldg. products distbn. sales and logistics Mid-Atlantic and S.E. regions, 2000—01, pres. lumber, 2001—02, v.p., CIO info. tech., 2002—. Mem. adv. bd. Habitat for Humanity, Atlanta; mem. exec. com. Nat. Eagle Leadership Instn.; mem. resource devel. com. Cool Girls; mem. CIS adv. bd. Kennesaw State U.; former mem. assoc. com. Interdenominational Theol. Ctr. Office: Georgia-Pacific Corp 133 Peachtree St NE Atlanta GA 30303

DALLAS, SANDRA, writer; b. Washington, June 11, 1939; d. Forrest Everett and Harriett (Mavity) Dallas; m. Robert Thomas Atchison, Apr. 20, 1963; children: Dana Dallas, Povy Kendal Dallas. BA, U. Denver, 1960. Asst. editor U. Denver Mag., 1965-66; editl. asst. Bus. Week, Denver, 1961-63, 67-69, bur. chief, 1969-85, 90-91, sr. corr., 1985-90; freelance editor, 1990—2001. Book reviewer Denver Post, 1961—, regional book columnist, 1980—. Author: Gaslights and Gingerbread, 1965, rev. edit., 1984, Gold and Gothic, 1967, No More Than 5 in a Bed, 1967, Vail, 1969, Cherry Creek Gothic, 1971, Yesterday's Denver, 1974, Sacred Paint, 1980, Colorado Ghost Towns and Mining Camps, 1985, Colorado Homes, 1986, Buster Midnight's Cafe, 1990, reissued, 1998, The Persian Pickle Club, 1995, The Diary of Mattie Spenser, 1997, Alice's Tulips, 2000, The Chili Queen, 2002, The Quilt that Walked to Golden, 2004, New Mercies, 2005; editor: The Colorado Book, 1993; contbr. articles to popular mags. Bd. dirs. Vis. Nurse Assn., Denver, 1983—85, Hist. Denver, Inc., 1979—82, 1984—87, Rocky Mountain Quilt Mus., 2001—04, Historic Georgetown, Inc., 2002—05. Recipient Wrangler award Nat. Cowboy Hall of Fame, 1980, Lifetime Achievement award Denver Posse of Westerners, 1996, disting. svc. award U. Colo., 1997; named Colo. Exceptional Chronicler of Western History by Women's Library Assn. and Denver Pub. Library Friends Found., 1986; finalist Spur award We. Writers of Am., 1998, recipient, 2003, finalist Willa award Women Writing the West, 2000, 2003, Colo. Book awards, 2000, Mt. Plains Booksellers award, 2003, Benjamin Franklin award Ind. Book Pub. Assn., 2005 Mem. Women's Forum Colo., Denver Woman's Press Club, Western Writers Am. (Spur award 2003), Women Writing the West. Democrat. Presbyterian. Home and Office: 750 Marion St Denver CO 80218-3434

DALLAS, SATERIOS (SAM DALLAS), aerospace engineer, researcher, consultant; b. Detroit, May 9, 1938; s. Peter and Pauline (Alex) D.; m. Athena Ethel Spartos, July 12, 1964; children: Gregory Dean, Paula Marie. BS in Aero. Engring., U. Mich., 1959, BS in Engring. Math., 1960; MS in Astrodynamics, UCLA, 1963, PhD in Engring., 1968. Rsch. engr. astrodynamics dept. Jet Propulsion Lab., Pasadena, Calif., 1965-78, supr. tech. group mission design, 1978-82, flight engring. office mgr. Voyager Project, 1982-84, sci. and mission design mgr. Magellan Project, 1984-89, tech. mgr. spacecraft analysis, 1989-90, mission mgr. Mars Observer Project, 1990-93, mission mgr. Mars Global Surveyor Project, 1994-97, mission mgr. space interferometry mission, 1997-99, flight project mentor, 2002—04, cons., 2004—. Instr. Pepperdine U., Malibu, Calif., 1973-75; lectr. on space missions Kennedy Space Ctr., Cape Canaveral, Fla., 1988, Australian Dept. Industry, Tech. and

Commerce, Canberra, 1988, USAF-CAP-PLR Ctr. Aerospace Edn., Las Vegas, Neb., 1991. Author: Progress in Astronautics and Aeronautics, 1964, Natural and Artificial Satellite Motion, 1979; contbr. articles to sci. jours. Coach Glendale (Calif.) Little League, 1979-82; com. mem. troop 125 Boy Scouts Am., Glendale, 1980. Recipient Apollo achievement award NASA, 1969, cert. of recognition, 1974, Laurels award Aviation Week, 1989, 94, Exceptional Achievement award NASA, 1998. Mem. AIAA, Am. Astron. Soc. (astrodynamics tech. com. 1970-80). Republican. Greek Orthodox. Avocations: skiing, hiking, woodworking, tennis, computer applications development. Home: 3860 Karen Lynn Dr Glendale CA 91206-1218 E-mail: ssd1938@hotmail.com.

DALLAS, TERRY G., gas industry executive; b. Fulton, Ky. BS in Civil Engring., Ga. Inst. Tech., 1973; MBA in Fin., U. Calif., LA, Calif., 1979. With Civil Engr. Corp. USN; from mgr. fin. control and planning to sr. v.p. ARCO Brit., Ltd., 1988—96, sr. v.p., 1996—2000; exec. v.p. Unocal, El Segundo, Calif., 2000—, CFO, 2000—. Mem. mgmt. com. Unocal.

DALLEK, ROBERT, history professor, historian; b. Bklyn., May 16, 1934; s. Rubin and Esther (Fisher) Dallek; m. Ilse F. Shatzkin, Nov. 20, 1959 (dec. Oct. 1962); m. Geraldine R. Kronmal, Aug. 22, 1965; children: Matthew J., Rebecca R. BA, U. Ill., 1955; MA, Columbia U., 1957, PhD, 1964. Lectr. history CCNY, 1959-60; instr. history Columbia U., N.Y.C., 1960-64; from asst. prof. to prof. UCLA, 1964—94, prof., 1994, vice-chmn. dept. history, 1972-74; prof. history Boston U., 1996—. Rsch. assoc. So. Calif. Psychoanalytic Inst., L.A., 1981—85; Commonwealth Fund lectr. Univ. Coll., London, 1984; Thompson lectr. U. Wyo., Laramie, 1986; Charles Griffin lectr. Vassar Coll., Poughkeepsie, NY, 1987; George W. Littlefield lectr. U. Tex., Austin, 1990; vis. Harmsworth prof. Oxford U., England, 1994—95; cons. ABC, N.Y.C., 1981—82, Ednl. Film Ctr., Annandale, Va., 1988, Sta. KCET-TV, L.A., 1988, KERA-TV, Dallas, 1989—91; vis. prof. history Dartmouth Coll., 2004. Author: Democrat and Diplomat: the Life of William E. Dodd, 1968, Franklin D. Roosevelt and American Foreign Policy, 1932-1945, 1979, The American Style of Foreign Policy: Cultural Politics and Foreign Affairs, 1983, Ronald Reagan: The Politics of Symbolism, 1984, Lone Star Rising: Lyndon Johnson and His Times, 1908-1960, 1991, Hail to the Chief: The Making and Unmaking of American Presidents, 1996, Flawed Giant: Lyndon Johnson and His Times 1961-1973, 1998, An Unfinished Life: John F. Kennedy, 1917-1963, 2003, Lyndon B. Johnson: Portrait of a President, 2003; editor: 3 books; contbr. article to profl. jours. Mem. adv. com. on diplomatic documents Dept. State, Washington, 1985—88; mem. adv. com. Mayor Tom Bradley, L.A., 1986; mem. adv. com. on ethics L.A. City Coun., 1989—90; bd. dirs. FDR and Eleanor Roosevelt Inst., 2003—, Nat. Portrait Gallery, 2003—04. Grantee Montgomery fellow, Dartmouth Coll., 2005; John Simon Guggenheim fellow, 1973—74, sr. fellow, NEH, 1976—77, Humanities fellow, Rockefeller Found., 1981—82, Am. Coun. Learned Socs. fellow, 1984—85, Rsch. grant, Eleanor Roosevelt Inst., 1976—77, Lyndon B. Johnson Found., 1984—85, 1988—89, Montgomery fellow, Dartmouth Coll., 2004. Fellow: Am. Acad. Arts and Scis., Soc. Am. Historians (pres. 2004—); mem.: Com. on History Second World War, Soc. for Historians of Am. Fgn. Rels. Home: 2138 Cathedral Ave NW Washington DC 20008-1502 Office Phone: 202-588-8963.

DALLEN, RUSSELL MORRIS, JR., investment company executive, lawyer, publishing company executive; b. Biloxi, Miss., Jan. 20, 1963; s. Russell Morris and Faye Annette (Werner) D.; m. Claire Lucia (Hodgson), May 27, 1995; children: Allegra Julia Faye, Arabella Sarah Emma. BA in econ. and polit. sci., U. Miss., 1985; M in internat. affairs, Columbia U., 1987; diploma in internat. law, Nottingham U., Eng., 1988; BA in jurisprudence, Oxford U., Eng., 1990, MA in law, 1994. Fgn. corr. Newsweek, London, 1990-91; sr. fellow, dir. UN Assn., USA, N.Y.C., 1991-93; assoc. Morgan Stanley and Co., Inc., N.Y.C., 1994-96; ptnr. Stires, O'Donnell and Co., Inc., 1996-99, Brisbane, Mendez de Leon and Co., Fahnestock and Co.,Inc., Oppenheimer and Co., Inc., 2000—; pres., editor in chief The Daily Jour., 2003—. Co-author: Revitalizing The United Nations, 1993; Issues Before the United Nations, 1989, A Global Agenda, 1992; contbr. articles to profl. jour. Bd. dirs. Venezuelan-Am. Amistad Assn., 2005—; bd. govs. Harold W. Rosenthal Fellowship, Washington, 1985—; exec. com. Manhattan coun. Boy Scouts Am., N.Y.C., 1992—; vol. Big Bros. and Big Sisters, N.Y.C., 1992—. Recipient Ner Tamid Leadership Award; Nat. Jewish Com. on Scouting, 1979; Kluwer Internat. Law Award, 1990; Article of Yr. Award Common Market Law Rev.; named Century III Leader, 1981; Harry S. Truman scholar, 1983; U.K. Fgn. and Commonwealth Office scholar, 1987; Harold Rosenthal Fellow, 1985; Am. Fellow European Communities, 1986; Ctr. Fellow Ctr. for Study of Presdy., 1985. Mem. N.Y. State Bar Assn.; N.Y. County Lawyers Assn. (chmn. sub-com. 1992—); Oxford and Cambridge Club; Squadron A Club; Cornell Club; Landsdowne Club. Avocations: sailing, flying, riding. Home: M365 PO Box 3340 New York NY 10185-3340 Office Phone: 212-227-1492. E-mail: rmdallen@aol.com.

DALLER, MORTON FRANKLIN, lawyer, writer; b. Phila., Nov. 2, 1938; s. George Morton and Claire (Stritzinger) D.; m. Heide Tilda Schroeder, Dec. 23, 1966 (dec. Oct. 1982); children: Adam, Sarah; m. Margaret Ann O'Donnell, Aug. 11, 1983; children: Zachary, Nicholas. BA magna cum laude, Brown U., 1960; LLB, U. Pa., 1963. Bar: Pa. 1964, U.S. Dist. Ct. (ea. dist.) Pa. 1964, U.S. Dist. Ct. (mid. dist.) Pa. 1976, U.S. Dist. Ct. (we. dist.) Pa. 1990, U.S. Ct. Appeals (3d cir.) 1964. Assoc. Rawle & Henderson, Phila., 1964-70, ptnr., 1970-94, Daller Greenberg & Dietrich, Ft. Washington, Pa., 1994—. Regional consel Firestone & Brush Wellman. Editor-in-chief: Product Liability Desk Reference, 1990, Tort Law Desk Reference, 2000. Mem. Phila. Assn. Def. Counse. (pres. 1990, dir. 1990-93), Phi Beta Kappa. Republican. Methodist. Avocation: sportsman. Home: 514 Edann Rd Glenside PA 19038-1405 Office: 161 Washington St Conshohocken PA 19428-2083 E-mail: mdaller@dallergreenberg.com.

D'ALLESANDRO, DAVID F., insurance company executive; b. Utica, N.Y., Feb. 6, 1951; children: Michael, Andrew. BS in Pub. Rels. and Journalism, Syracuse U., 1972. Reporter Gannett Newspaper, Utica, 1969; account supr. Daniel J. Edelman, Inc., N.Y., 1972; gen. mgr. Comml. Credit Co., N.Y., 1974-84; v.p. corp. comms. John Hancock Mut. Life Ins., Boston, 1984-86, sr. v.p. corp. comms., 1986-87, pres. corp. sector, 1988-91, sr. exec. v.p. retail sector, 1991—, mem. mgmt. com., 1989—, now pres., COO, also bd. dirs. Dir. John Hancock Freedom Securities, Boston, 1988—, John Hancock Subs., Inc., Boston, 1988—. Bd. advisors Red Auerbach Fund for Youth, Boston; chair Fenway Fantasy Day, Jimmy Fund, Boston; bd. dirs. Mass. Sports Partnership, The Kennedy Sch., Harvard U.; bd. trustees Syracuse U., Boston U.; chmn. bd. The Wang Ctr. Named one of 100 Most Powerful People in Sports, Sporting News, 1996, Marketer of Yr., ADWEEK Mag., 1986. Office: John Hancock Fin Svcs John Hancock Place Boston MA 02117-0111*

DALLEY, GEORGE ALBERT, lawyer, consultant; b. Havana, Cuba, Aug. 25, 1941; s. Cleveland Ernest and Constance Joyce (Powell) D.; m. Pearl Elizabeth Love, Aug. 1, 1970; children: Jason Christopher, Benjamin Christian. AB, Columbia U., 1963, JD, MBA, Columbia U., 1966. Bar: N.Y. 1966, D.C. 1971, U.S. Supreme Ct. 1972. Asst. to pres. Met. Applied Rsch. Ctr., N.Y.C., 1967-69; counsel The Children's Found., Washington, 1970-71; assoc. counsel Stroock and Stroock and Lavan, Washington, 1970-71, Com. on Judiciary, U.S. Ho. of Reps., Washington, 1971-72; adminstrv. asst. to Rep. Charles B. Rangel, N.Y.C., Washington, 1973-77, counsel, staff dir., 1985-89; dep. asst. sec. for human rights and social affairs Bur. Internat. Orgns. Affairs Dept. State, Washington, 1977-80; mem. CAB, 1980-82; dep. dir. Mondale for Pres. Com., Washington, 1983-84; counsel, staff dir. Congressman Charles B. Rangel, U.S. Ho. of Reps., Washington, 1985-89; sr. v.p. Neill and Co., Washington, 1989-93; ptnr. Neill, Dalley, Carroll, Nealer and Assevero, Washington, 1992-93; sr. ptnr. Holland and Knight, Washington, 1993—2001; counsel, and staff dir. to Congressman Charles Rangel, Washington, 2001—. Adj. prof. Am. U. Sch. Law. Mem. legal adv. com. Dem. Nat. Com., 1975-76; bd. dirs. Africare, TransAfrica; Joint Ctr. for Polit. and Econ. Studies Internat. Inst., Jamaica Nats. Devel. Found. Mem. ABA, Nat. Bar Assn., Fed. Bar Assn., Nat. Conf. Black Lawyers, Cosmos Club, Coun. Fgn. Rels. Home: 1328 Vermont Ave NW Washington DC 20005-3607 Office: Rm 2354 US House Rep Washington DC 20515 Personal E-mail: gdalley@aol.com.

DALLMAN, MARY F., physiologist, science educator; BA in Chemistry, Smith Coll., 1956; PhD in Physiology, Stanford U., 1967; postgrad., Swedish Royal Vet. Sch., 1968, U. Calif., San Francisco, 1969—70. Lectr. U. Calif. Dept. Physiology, San Francisco, 1970—72, aast., 1972—76, assoc. prof., 1976—81, prof., 1981—, vice-chair, 1987—. Assoc. editor Am. Jour. Physiol.: Endocrnology and Metabolism, 1979—85, Steroids, 1919—87, Am. Jour. Physiol.: Regulatory, Integrative and Comparative Physiology, 1990—92; contbr. articles to profl. jours. Recipient Am. Diabetes Rsch. award, 1996. Mem.: NIH (mem. endocrine study sect. 1977—81, mem. diabetes, digestive, kidney grants rev. subcom. 1988—92, chair 1992—93), Internat. Soc. Neuroendocrinology (pres. 1996), Women in Endocrinology (pres. 1993—95). Office: U Calif Dept Physiology Box 0444 HSW 747 513 Parnassus Ave San Francisco CA 94143

DALLMANN, DANIEL F., artist, educator; b. St. Paul, Mar. 21, 1942; BS, Minn. State U., 1965; MA, U. Iowa, 1968, M.F.A., 1969. Prof. Tyler Sch. Art, Phila., 1969—. One-man shows include Schoelkopf Gallery, N.Y.C., 1980, 84, 87, J. Rosenthal Fine Arts, Ltd., Chgo., 1989, Tatischeff Gallery, N.Y.C., 1993, Davidson Gallery, Seattle, 1994, Payne Gallery of Moravian Coll., Bethlehem, Pa., Kendall Gallery of Miami-Dade Coll., Miami, Fla., 1997, Dartmouth Coll. Hanover N.H., Lied Art Gallery, Creighton U., Omaha, 1998, Charles More Gallery, Phila., 2000-02; exhibited in group shows, including Allan Frumkin, N.Y.C., 1982, Berkshire Mus., Pittsfield, Mass., 1983, Hudson River Mus., Yonkers, N.Y., 1984, 86, San Francisco Mus. Modern Art, 1985, Orlando (Fla.) Mus. Art at Loch Haven, 1986, NAD, N.Y.C., 1988, NAS, Washington, 1989, Md. Inst., Balt., 1990, So. Alleghenies Mus. Art, Loretto, Pa., 1992, 93, Forum Gallery, N.Y.C., 1994, Smith Coll., Northampton, Mass., 1996, Hackett-Freedman Gallery, San Francisco, 1998, Art Inst. Chgo., 1999, Emporia (Kans.) State U., 2000, Frye Mus. of Art, Seattle, 02; represented in permanent collections Woodmere Art Mus., Phila., J.B. Speed Mus., Louisville, Nat. Mus. Am. Art, Washington, Art Inst. Chgo., Amity Art Found., Woodbridge, Conn., also corp. collections. Office Phone: 215-782-2837. E-mail: dallmann@temple.edu.

DALLMANN, WILLIAM CHARLES, speech educator, writer; b. Detroit, Nov. 16, 1929; s. Bertram and Lillian Dallmann; m. Constance Joan Covington; children: Shane, Alan, Lara. AB in Speech and Drama, San Francisco State U., 1957, MA in Drama, 1963; PhD in Speech Pathology, Purdue U., 1973. Cert. Am. Speech Hearing and Lang. Assn. Prof. communicative disorders Valparaiso (Ind.) U., 1964—84; Ju-Jutsu sensei Pacific Acad. Life Arts, Monterey, Calif., 1984—89; freelance writer Monterey, 2001—. Pvt. investigator Wittlinger Agy., Indpls., 1982—84; speech pathologist, clin. hypnotist Counseling Assocs., Valparaiso, 1976—81, exec. dir., 1976—81; dir. Speech Lang. Clinic, Valparaiso, 1964—84. Author: The Children of Prometheus, 1999, 2 Kill or Not to Kill, 2001. With USN, 1948—49, 1st lt. U.S. Army, 1951—53, Korea. Mem.: ACLU, Inst. Gen. Semantics, Vets. for Peace (pres. chpt.), Amnesty Internat., 25th Infantry Divsn. Assn. (life). Lutheran. Avocations: reading, languages, quantum physics, theology, semantics. Home: 4080 Los Altos Drive Pebble Beach CA 93953 Personal E-mail: raven@redshift.com.

DALLMEYER, ROBERT FREDERICK, museum administrator; b. Pittsfield, Mass., Jan. 1, 1938; s. Frederick Charles and Madeline Rita (Morrissey) D.; children: Kimberly Ann Kapelson, Kristen Elizabeth Nimr. BA in Sociology and English, U. Mass., 1959. Dir. tech. presentations United Tech., Hartford, Conn., 1960-82; v.p. Elec. Convention Mgmt., L.A., 1982-83; pres. Event Exhbn. Enterprises, L.A., 1983; v.p. Brussels Exhbn. Ctr.; owner, founder Robert Dallmeyer Internat., L.A., 1984—. Pres. Sterling Gavin Assocs., Conn., 1975—77; cons. Monterrey (Mex.) Conv. and Visitors, Bastizan Data Systems, Calif. Restaurant Assn., 2000; pres. adv. bd. Project Return, L.A., 1994—; instr. event mgmt. George Washington U., Washington, 1999—. Author: International Exhibition Handbook, 1980, Snapshots, 1984, (booklet) Successful Logistics, 1999; columnist (mag.) Ideas mag., 1982—. Bd. dirs., v.p. U. Mass. Alumni, Amherst, 1965-72, U. Mass. Found., Amherst, 1972-78; bd. dirs. Hill Ctr., Hartford, 1976-79. Recipient Disting. Svc. award U. Mass., 1981. Mem.: Ctr. Exhbn. Industry Rsch. (bd. dirs. 1976—), Trade Show Exhibitors Assn. (chmn., Pres. award 1979, 1979, Disting. Svc. award 1983, Life Mem. award 2001), Internat. Assn. Exhbn. Mgrs. (chmn.). Avocations: theater, music, bicycling, teaching. Home: 357 S Curson Ave Ste 5D Los Angeles CA 90036 E-mail: dallmeyer@cs.com.

DALLOS, PETER JOHN, neurobiologist, educator; b. Budapest, Hungary, Nov. 26, 1934; arrived in US, 1956, naturalized, 1962; s. Ernest and Maria Dallos; m. Joan Usis, Aug. 18, 1977; 1 child by previous marriage, Christopher. Student, Tech. U. Budapest, 1953-56; BS, Ill. Inst. Tech., 1958; MS, Northwestern U., 1959, PhD, 1962. Rsch. engr. Am. Machine and Foundry Co., 1959; cons. engr., 1959-60; mem. faculty Northwestern U., 1962—, prof. audiology and elec. engring., 1969—, prof. neurobiology and physiology, 1981—, chmn., 1981-84, 86-87, assoc. dean Coll. Arts and Scis., 1984-85, John Evans prof. neurosci., 1986—, Hugh Knowles prof. audiology, 1994—2003. Vis. scientist Karolinska Inst., Stockholm, 1977-78; chmn. behavioral and neuroscis. rev. panel No. 5 Nat. Inst. Neurol., Communicative Disorders and Stroke, NIH, 1982-85, mem. nat. adv. council, 1984-87 Author: The Auditory Periphery: Biophysics and Physiology, 1973; editor: The Cochlea, 1996; contbr. articles to profl. jours. Recipient 12th ann. award Beltone Inst. Hearing Rsch., 1977, Internat. prize Amplifon Rsch. and Study Ctr., 1984, Senator Jacob Javits Neurosci. Investigator award, 1984, Honors of Assn. award Am. Speech-Lang.-Hearing Assn., 1994, Bekesy medal of Acoustical Soc. Am., 1995, Sigma Xi Disting. Nat. lectr., 1997-98, Acta Otolaryngologica Internat. prize, 1997, Kresge-Mirmelstein prize La. State U., 2000; Guggenheim fellow, 1977-78; McKnight sr. fellow, 1997-2000. Fellow IEEE (life), AAAS, Acoustical Soc. Am., Am. Acad. Arts and Scis.; mem. Soc. for Neurosci., Assn. for Rsch. in Otolaryngology (pres. 1992-93, award of merit 1994), Collegium Otolaryngologicum Amicitae Sacrum, Hungarian Acad. Scis. (hon.; Guyot prize 2004, Hugh Knowles prize 2005), Sigma Xi, Tau Beta Pi, Eta Kappa Nu. Office: Northwestern U 2240 Campus Dr Evanston IL 60208-0837 Business E-Mail: p-dallos@northwestern.edu.

DALLURA, SAL ANTHONY, physician; b. Flushing, N.Y., Nov. 7, 1960; s. Russ and Mayann (Taranto) D.; m. Donna Ann Baldassare, Aug. 6, 1983 (div. Mar. 1993); children: Christopher Anthony, Corinne Elizabeth; m. Stacy Elizabeth Carberry, July 1, 1995 (div. Jan. 1999); 1 child, Matthew Anthony; m. Tammy L. Chance, Dec. 27, 1999. BS in Pre-Profl. Studies cum laude, U. Notre Dame, 1982; D of Osteo. Medicine with honors, N.Y. Coll. Osteo. Medicine, 1986. Diplomate Am. Acad. Family Physicians, 1990, 96, 2002. Mng. ptnr. Flashner Med. Ptnrship., Babylon, N.Y., 1989-91; assoc. physician Moriches Med. Care, Center Moriches, N.Y., 1989-91, Digiovanna, Massepequa Park, N.Y., 1991-92, Tippecanoe Family Physicians, Tipp City, Ohio, 1992-98, Milton Union Med. Ctr., West Milton, Ohio, 1998-2000; physician mng. ptnr. After Hours Family Care, Tipp City, 1994-98; physician Upper Valley Profl. Corp., 1994-2000, Kenbrook Med. Ctr., 2000—02, St. Marys (Ohio) Family Practice, St. Marys, Ohio, 2002—. Expert witness malpractice def., case revs., depositions, testimony for family practice. Recipient Excellence in Gastroenterology award, 1986. Fellow Am. Acad. Family Practice; mem. Am. Osteo. Assn., OH Osteo. Assn., Alpha Epsilon Delta. Republican. Roman Catholic. Avocations: model railroading, coin and stamp collecting, reading, audio and video entertainment, computer research. Office: 1300 Greenville Rd Saint Marys OH 45885-2427 Office Phone: 419-394-4813. E-mail: sdallura@bright.net, sdallura@nktelco.net.

DALLY, JAMES WILLIAM, mechanical engineering educator, consultant; b. Sardis, OH, Aug. 2, 1929; s. William Hiram and Martha (Siebert) D.; m. Anne Evangeline Tziritas, Dec. 22, 1955; children: Lisa, William, Michelle. BSME, Carnegie Mellon U., 1951, MSME, 1953; PhD, Ill. Inst. Tech., 1958. Registered profl. engr., Md. Asst. dir. rsch. Armour Research Found., Chgo., 1961-64; prof. Ill. Inst. Tech., Chgo., 1964-71; prof., chmn. dept. U. Md., College Park, 1971-79; dean Coll. Engring. U. R.I., Kingston, 1979-82; mgr. mech. devel. IBM, Manassas, Va., 1982-84; prof. mech. engring. U. Md., College Park, 1984-97. Disting. vis. prof. USAF Acad., 1995-96; mem. tech. assessment bd. Army Rsch. Lab., 1997-2000; pres. College House Enterprises, LLC, 1998—. Author: Experimental Stress Analysis, 2005, Photoelastic Coatings, 1977, Engineering Measurements, 1984, 2nd edit., 1993, Packaging Electronic Systems, 1990, Introduction to Engineering Design, Book 8, 2004, Product Engineering and Manufacturing, 1998, Design Analysis of Structural Elements, 3rd edit., 2003, 4th edit., 2004; contbr. articles. Recipient Boeing Outstanding Educator award, 1996. Fellow ASME, Am. Acad. Mechanics (bd. dirs. 1984-88, pres. 1990-91, Disting. Svc. award 2004), Soc. Exptl. Mechanics (hon., pres. 1970-71, Murray lectureship 1979, Past Pres. award 1971, M.M. Frocht award 1976, Hetenyi award 1995, F.G. Tatnall award 2001, Charles E. Taylor award 2002); mem. Nat. Acad. Engring., U.S. Nat. Com. Theoretical and Applied Mechanics (chmn. 1982-84, vice-chmn., 1984-86). Achievements include patents in field. Office Phone: 865-558-6111. Personal E-mail: jdally0829@comcast.net.

DALPINO, IDA JANE, retired secondary school educator; b. Newhall, Calif., Oct. 20, 1936; d. Bernhardt Arthur and Wahneta May (Blyler) Melby; m. Gilbert Augustus, June 14, 1963 (div. 1976); 1 child, Nicolette Jane. BA, Calif. State U., Chico, 1960; postgrad., Sacramento State, 1961—65, Sonoma State, 1970—71; MA, U. San Francisco, 1978. Cert. cmty. counselor, learning handicapped, c.c. instr., exceptional children, pupil pers. specialist, secondary tchr., resource specialist. Tchr. Chico High Sch., 1959-60; counselor Mira Loma High Sch., Sacramento, 1960-66; tchr. ESL Phoenix Ind. High Sch., 1968-69; resource specialist Yuba City (Calif.) High Sch., 1971-2000; ret., 2000. English tchr. Rough Rock Demonstration Sch., summers, 1975, 76. Office sec. Job's Daus., North Bend, Oreg., 1953—; active Environ. Def. Fund, Centerville Hist. Assn., Chico, 1991—. Mem. NEA, Calif. Tchrs. Assn., Chico State Alumni Assn., Sierra Club, Nature Conservancy, Audubon, Greenpeace, Sigma Kappa Alumni. Democrat. Mem. Science of the Mind Church. Avocations: reading, ecology, genealogy. Home: 6 Navajo Ln Corte Madera CA 94925 Personal E-mail: idajane@comcast.net.

DAL PORTO, MARK DANIEL, music educator; b. Sacramento, July 29, 1955; s. Dante and Shirley Louise Dal Porto. BA, Calif. State U., Sacramento, 1978, MA, 1981; DMA, U. Tex., 1985. Vis. asst. prof. music Tex. State U., San Marcos, 1987—89; from asst. prof. to assoc. prof. music No. State U., Aberdeen, SD, 1989—94, Tex. Woman's U., Denton, 1994—2001; assoc. prof. music Ea. N.Mex U., Portales, 2001—. Presenter at confs. and meetings. Author: (music composition) Galactica for Symphonic Wind Ensemble (Pub. by So. Music Co., 2001), Spring, the Sweet Spring for Choir with Piano Accompaniment (Winner of Denton Cmty. Chorus Composition Contest, 2001), Domestic Suite: Scenes and Memories from Childhood for Piano Solo, 2001, When Your Song Rang Out to Me, 2003 (Vanguard Premiers Choral Composition Contest, 2004), Song of the Night for Oboe, Voice, and Piano, 2004. Mem.: ASCAP (Royalties 1986 - present), Soc. Composers, Inc., Coll. Music Soc., Am. Music Ctr., Am. Composer's Forum. Home: 1116 Gemini Drive Portales NM 88130-6134 Office: Eastern New Mexico University Department of Music Station 16 Portales NM 88130 Office Phone: 505-562-2271. Personal E-mail: mark.dalporto@enmu.edu.

DALRYMPLE, DONALD (DACK) WYLIE, lawyer; b. Bloomington, Ill., June 3, 1947; s. Franklin Wells and Mary June (Endsley) Shearer; m. Marcia Bresee Dalrymple, Sept. 8, 1979; children: Daylen Lee, Lauren Wells. BS, Centre Coll., 1969; postgrad., Stetson U., 1969-72; JD magna cum laude, U. Balt., 1973. Bar: D.C. 1975, Fla. 1974. Legis. asst. to U.S. Rep. Paul Rogers, Washington, 1970—; counsel subcom. on health and environ., com. on energy & commerce U.S. Ho. of Reps., Washington, 1973-79; dir. med. govt. relations Am. Cyanamid Co., Washington, 1979-94; sr. v.p. Ketchum Govt. & Pub. Rels., Washington, 1995-96; ptnr. Bailey & Dalrymple, Washington, 1997-2000; prin. Dalrymple & Assocs., Washington, 2001—. Served to specialist grade 4 USAR, 1970-76. Mem. ABA, Fla. Bar Assn., D.C. Bar Assn., Heiusler Legal Hon. Soc., Sigma Alpha Epsilon, Phi Alpha Delta. Presbyterian. Home: 2801 34th Pl NW Washington DC 20007-1406 Office: Dalrymple & Assocs LLC Ste 300 1926 N St NW Washington DC 20036-1615 E-mail: dackdal@erols.com.

DALRYMPLE, GARY BRENT, research geologist; b. Alhambra, Calif., May 9, 1937; s. Donald Inlow and Wynona Edith (Pierce) D.; m. Sharon Ann Tramel, June 28, 1959; children: Stacie Ann, Robynne Ann Sisco, Melinda Ann Dalrymple McGurer. AB in Geology, Occidental Coll., 1959; PhD in Geology, U. Calif., Berkeley, 1963; DSc (hon.), Occidental Coll., Los Angeles, 1993. Rsch. geologist U.S. Geol. Survey, Menlo Park, Calif., 1963-81, 84-94, asst. chief geologist we. region, 1981-84; dean, prof. Coll. Oceanic and Atmospheric Sci., Oreg. State U., Corvallis, 1994-2001, dean and prof. emeritus, 2001—. Vis. prof. sch. earth scis. Stanford U., 1969-72, cons. prof., 1983-85, 90-94; disting. alumni centennial spkr. Occidental Coll., 1986-87. Author: Potassium-Argon Dating, 1969, Age of Earth, 1991, Ancient Earth, Ancient Skies, 2004; contbr. chpts. to books and articles to profl. jours. Fellow NSF, 1961-63; recipient Meritorius Svc. award U.S. Dept. Interior, 1984, Public Svc. award Geological Soc. Am., 2001, Nat. medal Sci., 2003. Fellow Am. Geophys. Union (pres.-elect 1988-90, pres. 1990-92), Am. Acad. Arts and Scis.; mem. NAS (chair geology sect. 1997-2000), Am. Inst. Physics (bd. govs. 1991-97), Consortium for Oceanographic Rsch. and Edn. (bd. govs. 1994-2001), Joint Oceanographic Inst. (bd. govs. 1994-2001, chair 1996-98). Achievements include discovery that the earth's magnetic field reverses polarity and determination of time scale of these reversals for the past 3.5 million years; development of ultra-fast high-sensitivity thermoluminescence analyzer for studying lunar surface processes; development and refinement of K-Ar and 40 Ar/39 Ar dating methods and instrumentation, continuous laser probe for determining ages of microgram-sized mineral samples; research on volcanoes in the Hawaiian-Emperor volcanic chain, chronology of lunar basin formation, development and improvement of isotopic dating techniques and instrumentation, geomagnetic field behavior, plate tectonics of the Pacific Ocean basin, evolution of volcanoes, various aspects of Pleistocene history of the western U.S. Home: 1847 NW Hillcrest Dr Corvallis OR 97330-1859 Personal E-mail: brentandsharon@comcast.net.

DALRYMPLE, JACK, lieutenant governor; b. Minneapolis, Minn., Oct. 16, 1948; m. Betsy Dalrymple; 4 children. BA, Yale U., 1970. Farmer, 1970—; state rep. dist. 22, 1985—2001; lt. gov. State of N.D., 2001—. Chmn. appropriations com. N.D. Ho. Reps.; bd. dirs. Prairie Pub. TV, N.D. State U. Devel. Found., Golden Growers Coop.; mem. Edn. Broadcasting Coun.; co-founder Share House Inc. Recipient Outstanding Young Farmer award, 1983. Mem. Cass Coounty Rural Water Users Assn. (past bd. dirs.), Casselton Econ. Devel. Found., Univ. Pres. Agr. Club (pres.), Durum Growers Assn. (bd. dirs.), Jaycees. Republican. Address: PO Box 220 Casselton ND 58012-0220 Office: 600 E Boulevard Ave Bismarck ND 58505

DALRYMPLE, THOMAS LAWRENCE, retired lawyer; b. Wellsburg, W. Va., May 20, 1921; s. Lawrence Chester and Ethel May (Taylor) D.; m. Marjorie May Keeler; children: Bruce Lawrence, Dale Brian. AB, U. Mich., 1943, JD, 1947. Bar: Ohio 1947, U.S. Supreme Ct. Practiced in, Toledo, 1947-96; assoc. Williams, Eversman & Morgan and successor firms, 1947-50, Welles, Kelsey, Fuller, Harrington & Seney and successor firms, 1950-52; ptnr. Fuller & Henry and predecessor firms, 1953-96. Mem. Trout Unltd., Toledo Mus. Art. Served to capt. inf. AUS, 1943-46. Decorated Combat Inf. badge, Silver Star medal, Purple Heart. Fellow Am. Coll. Trial Lawyers, Am. Bar Found., Ohio Bar Found.; mem. Order of Cof, Phi Beta Kappa. Home: 4307 Stannard Dr Toledo OH 43613-3636

DALSIMER, ANTHONY STEARNS, retired foreign service officer, educator; b. N.Y.C., July 30, 1935; s. Allan Furth Dalsimer and Helen Stearns; m. Isabel Ann Price (div.); m. Marilyn Nowak (div.); children: Allyn Ann, Melanie, Heather. BA, Grinnell Coll., 1957; MA, Fletcher Sch. Law & Diplomacy, 1958; postgrad., Stanford U., 1971-72, Howard U., 1973-75; MS, U. D.C., 1991. Staff econ. office Dept. of State, Washington, 1960, officer in charge Guinea and Dahomey, 1971-73, divsn. chief Exch. North and West Africa, 1973-75, divsn. chief Cultural Exch. So. and East Africa, 1975-77, dir. rsch. for Africa, 1985-88, dir. Office Ctrl. African Affairs, 1988-91, dir. Office Hist. Document Rev., 1994-97; vice consul/econ. officer Am. Embassy, Ouagadougou, Upper Volta, 1961-63, vice consul Bamako, Mali, 1965, comml. attache Kinshasa, Zaire, 1967-69, dep. chief of mission Ndjamena, Chad, 1977-79, counselor polit. affairs Kinshasa, Zaire, 1979-81, dep. chief of mission Ouagadougou, Burkina Faso, 1981-84, counselor for labor affairs Paris, 1991-94; gen. mgr. Dalsimer Florist, Cedarhurst, N.Y., 1963-64; vice consul Am. Consulate, Hargeisa, Somalia, 1966-67, consul Bukavu, Congo, 1969-70; adj. faculty African history, internat. rels., govt. and politics U. South Fla., Sarasota, 1997—. Lectr. Elder Hostels Eckerd Coll., 2001—. Vol. ARC, Helen Payne Sch. Mem.: Fgn. Svc. Ret. Assn. Fla. (bd. dirs.), Diplomats and Consular Officers, Am. Fgn. Svc. Assn., Greencroft Condo Assn. (pres. 2001—). Democrat. Unitarian Universalist.

DALTAS, ARTHUR JOHN, management consultant, software services manager; b. Mpls., Aug. 5, 1945; s. John Howard Locken and Adella Marie (DeChaney) D.; stepfather, John Paul Daltas; m. Ellen Causey Peckham, Feb. 23, 2001; children: Alexander, Andrew, Elizabeth; stepchildren: Samuel Peckham, Anne Peckham. BA, Coll. St. Thomas, 1968; MBA with high honors, Boston U., 1973. Tchr. U.S. Dept. Def., Frankfurt, Germany, 1970-71; treas., mgr. Cambridge (Mass.) Comm. Group, Inc., 1973-78; v.p. The MAC Group/Gemini Inc., Cambridge, 1978-84; founder, pres. The Mgrs. Group, Concord, Mass., 1984-87; prin., chmn. Concord Cons. Group, 1987-2000. Pres. Exec. Advisors Corp., 1997, Global Svcs. Offerings Mgmt., Progress Software Corp., 2000. Contbg. author: Implementing Strategy, 1982, Marketing Management, 1991; contbr. articles to various publs. Bd. dirs. Make a Wish Boston, 1991-96; asst. scoutmaster Boy Scouts Am., 1999-2002; deacon, standing com. Hancock Ch., 2000—. With U.S. Army, 1968-70. Mem. Nat. Alumni Coun. Boston U., SMG Alumni Bd. Dirs. Boston U., Beta Gamma Sigma. Avocations: skiing, hiking, golf. Office: Progress Software Corp 14 Oak Park Bedford MA 01730

DALTON, CHERYL RENEE, entrepreneur; b. Jersey City, May 16, 1960; d. Ronald McGowan and Marie Funchess; m. Allen Brett Dalton, Sept. 3, 1995; children: Sha-nia Nell Smith, Ebony Elisa Casley 1 stepchild, Ebony Johnsen. Student, Barnwell Vocat. Sch., 1992. Cert. nursing asst., S.C. Pvt. nurse Atty. George Crawford, Orangeburg, SC, 1992—95; nursing asst. Dehec Home Health, 1992—95; asst. dir. CMC Group Home, 2004—. Founder, dir. Edisto Fork Family Info. Referral, Orangeburg, 2003—. Author: A Path From Destruction (Then & Now), 2001; writer poetry for gospel songs:. Mem.: NAACP, Order Ea. Star. Methodist. Achievements include patents pending for adhesive weave. Avocation: softball. Home and Office: 356 Cimmaron St Orangeburg SC 29115 Office Phone: 803-533-5599. E-mail: cheryldalton@peoplepc.com, orangeburgrenee@aol.com.

DALTON, CLAUDETTE ELLIS HARLOE, anesthesiologist, educator, dean; b. Roanoke, Va., Jan. 18, 1947; d. John Pinckney and Dorothy Anne (Ellis) Harloe; m. Henry Tucker Dalton, May 17, 1973 (div. 1979); 1 child, Gordon Tucker; m. H. Christopher Alexander, III, Apr. 29, 2000. BA, Sweet Briar Coll., 1969; MD, U. Va., 1974. Resident in anesthesiology U. N.C., Chapel Hill, 1974—77; med. edn. Lenoir County Meml Hosp./East Carolina U., Kinston, 1978—80; med. edn. in intensive care Presbyn Hosp., Charlotte, NC, 1981—82; practice anesthesiology Charlotte Eye, Ear, Nose and Throat Hosp., 1982—85, Medivision of Charlotte and Orthopedic Hosp. of Charlotte, 1985—89; asst. prof. U. Va. Health Scis. Ctr., Charlottesville, Va., 1992—; dir. Office of Cmty. Based Med. Edn., Charlottesville, 1994—; asst. dean for cmty. based med. edn. U. Va., Charlottesville, 1996—, med. dir. Pre-Anesthesia Clinic, 1996—, asst. prof. anesthesiology and med. edn., 1996—. Mem. adv. bd. Nat. Bd. Med. Examiners, 2004; bd. dirs., mem. exec. com. Accreditation Coun. Continuing Med. Edn., 2004; mem. Va. Bd. Medicine, 2005—. Author: emergency med. svc. tng. program, 1961, patient edn. materials for illiterate patients, 1979—. Bd. dirs. Charlottesville Family Svcs., Family Svcs. Albemarle County, 1992—93, Coun. Aging, Am. Cancer Soc.; exec. dir. Cmty. Involvement Coun. Lenoir County, Kinston, 1979; county coord. Internat. Yr. of Child, Kinston, 1979; bd. dirs. U. Va. Women's Ctr., 1996—, Lenoir County CC; mem. sch. medicine com. women U. Va. Med. Sch. Named Commencement spkr., U. Va. Sch. Medicine Graduation, 1993; recipient Gov.'s award, State of N.C., 1980, cert. of merit for svc. to children, N.C. Dept. Human Resources, Outstanding Tchg. award, U. Va. Sch. Medicine, 1993, Sharon L. Hostler U. Va. Outstanding Woman in Medicine award, 2002. Mem.: AMA, Va. Soc. Anesthesiology, Albemarle County Med. Soc., Med. Soc. Va. (bd. dirs. Va. Health Quality Coun. 1995—97, chair ad hoc com. on telemedicine 1996—99, 2d v.p. 1998—99, chair scope of practice com. 1999—2002, dist. dir. 1999—, editor med. news Va. Med. Quar., mem. legis. com., mem. health access com., mem. strategic planning and implementation com., mem. women's com., mem. med. affairs com., mem. bd. medicine adv. com., Cmty. Svc award 2003), Alpha Omega Alpha, U. Va. Med. Alumni Assn. (assoc. bd. dirs. 1989—92, chair women in medicine leadership conf. 1998—99). Avocations: natural history, environment, dance, writing, gardening. Office: U Va Med Sch PO Box 800325 Charlottesville VA 22908-0325

DALTON, DAN R., finance educator, former dean; BA, Calif. State U., 1970, MS, 1975; PhD, U. Calif., Irvine, 1979. Owner retail bus. Middle Earth, 1971—73; owner D&H Industries, 1971—73; mem. staff GE; faculty mem. UCLA, Santa Ana Coll., Calif. State U. Long Beach, Kelley Sch. Bus. Ind. U., Bloomington, Ind., 1979—, assoc. dean for academic affairs, Samuel and Pauline Glaubinger Prof. Mgmt., 1995—98, dean, 1997—2004, Harold A. Poling Chair in Strategic Management, 1998—, dean emeitus, 2004—; dir., Inst. for Corp. Governance, 2004—. Contbr. numerous articles to profl. jours. Recipient numerous awards and citations for excellence in tchg. Office: Indiana Univ Kelley School Business 1309 E 10th St Bloomington IN 47405-1701

DALTON, DAVID ROBERT, chemistry professor; b. Chgo., Nov. 16, 1936; s. William Edward and Ethel (Shaykin) D.; m. Cecile Kaplan, Aug. 31, 1958; children: Nathaniel, Rachel, Aaron. BA, Northwestern U., 1957; PhD, UCLA, 1962. Chemist G. D. Searle & Co., Skokie, Ill., 1958-63, Monsanto Rsch. Corp., Dayton, Ohio, 1963-64; postdoctoral instr. Ohio State U., Columbus, 1964-65; asst. prof. chemistry Temple U., Phila., 1965-68, assoc. prof. chemistry, 1968-73, prof. chemistry, 1973—, assoc. dean rsch. and grad. studies, 1993-95, chmn. dept. chemistry, 2000—03, Honors prof., 2005. Cons. Noramco, Wilmington, Del., 1987—, Auxillium Pharm. Co., 99—, McNeil Pahrm. Co., 99—, Inkine Pharm. Co., 99—. Author: The Alkaloids, 1979, Organic Chemistry in the Lab, 1979. Recipient Scroll award Am. Inst. Chemists, 1982, Section award undergrad. edn. Am. Chem. Soc., 2003; named Hons. Prof. 2005, Temple U., 2005 Mem.: AAAS, Am. Chem. Soc. (Undergrad. Edn. award 2003, Temple U. Hon. Prof. of Year 2005). Home: 143 Gulph Hills Rd Radnor PA 19087-4615 Office: Temple U 13th And Norris St Philadelphia PA 19122 Office Phone: 215-204-7138. Business E-Mail: david.dalton@temple.edu.

DALTON, DENNIS GILMORE, political science professor; b. Morristown, N.J., Mar. 12, 1938; s. Andrew John and Emily Snow (Smith) D.; m. Sharron Louise Scheline, May 22, 1961; children: Kevin Andrew, Shaun Michael. BA, Rutgers U., 1960; MA, U. Chgo., 1962; PhD, U. London, 1965. Lectr. politics U. London, 1965-69; Ann Whitney Olin prof. polit. sci. Barnard Coll., Columbia U., N.Y.C., 1969—. Condr. series of e-seminars Nonviolent Power, M.K. Gandhi, M.L. King, Jr. and Nonviolent Resistance Around the World, Columbia U. Digital Knowledge, 2002. Author: Indian Idea of Freedom, 1982, Mahatma Gandhi: Nonviolent Power in Action, 1993; editor: States of South Asia, 1983, Mahatma Gandhi: Selected Political Writings, 1996. Mem. War Resisters League, N.Y.C., 1969— . Recipient Emily Gregory Disting. Teaching award, 1978; Am. Coun. Learned Socs. grantee, 1975, Am. Philos. Soc. grantee, 1975; Am. Inst. Indian Studies fellow, 1974; Fulbright scholar to Nepal, 1994-95. Home: 390 Riverside Dr Apt 3e-1 New York NY 10025-1867 Office: Columbia Univ Barnard Coll 606 W 120th St New York NY 10027-5706 Office Phone: 212-854-8422. E-mail: ddalton@barnard.edu. *My research for the last four decades on the life and thought of Mahatma Gandhi has convinced me that his example carries universal implications for the study of conflict resolution. The theory and practice of nonviolence offer us today a system of values and a hope for the future that should serve to inspire humanity.*

DALTON, HARLON L., law educator; AB, Harvard U., 1969; JD, Yale U., 1973. Bar: NY 1973, US Supreme Ct. 1979, Conn. 1983. Law clk. to Judge Robert L. Carter; with Legal Action Ctr., 1973—79, Office of Solicitor Gen., US Dept. Justice; assoc. prof. law Yale U., New Haven, 1981—90, prof. law, 1990—. Bd. dirs. Legal Affairs. Author: AIDS and the Law, 1987, AIDS Law Today, 1993, Racial Healing, 1995. Bd. dirs. Ctr. for Contemplative Mind in Soc.; priest, assoc. rector Episcopal Ch. of St. Paul and St. James. Office: Yale Law Sch PO Box 208215 New Haven CT 06520 E-mail: harlon.dalton@yale.edu.

DALTON, HARRY JIROU, JR., (JERRY DALTON), public relations executive; b. San Antonio, Feb. 7, 1927; s. Harry Jirou and Dorothy Bess (Black) D.; m. Marion Packard Hume Dalton, Aug. 21, 1954; children: Cynthia Kay, Robert Hume, Steven Jirou. BBA in Advt., U. Tex., 1949, postgrad., 1949-50, Boston U., 1958, U. Nebr., Omaha, 1958-60. Commd. 2d lt. USAF, 1950, advanced through grades to brig. gen., 1975; from assoc. to dir. corp. com. EDS Corp., Dallas, 1980-84; mgr. corp. comm. The LTV Corp., Dallas, 1984-92, Vought Aircraft Co., Dallas, 1992-93; pvt. practice as pub. rels. counsel Dallas, 1994—. Named Outstanding Govt. Pub. Info. Officer Aviation/Space Writers Assn., Washington, 1974. Fellow Pub. Rels Soc. Am. (pres. 1990); mem. Tex. Pub. Rels. Assn. (Outstanding Pub. Rels. Practitioner in Tex. award 1989, Silver Spur award 1991). Presbyterian. Home and Office: 6411 Laurel Valley Rd Dallas TX 75248-3904 Office Phone: 972-960-0145. E-mail: jerrydalton@sbcglobal.net.

DALTON, HOWARD EDWARD, retired accounting executive; b. N.Y.C., June 28, 1937; s. Edward R. and Josephine J. Dalton; m. Elizabeth J. Jeronimus; children: Kevin, Kathleen. BSBA, Holy Cross, 1959. CPA. Ptnr. KPMG, Mpls., 1959-87; sr. v.p., chief acctg. officer St. Paul Cos., Inc., 1987-98. Treas., dir. Cath. Charities, Mpls., 1978-2000; rep. U.S. on ins. steering com. Internat. Acctg. Stds. Com. Avocations: golf, travel. Address: 9943 E Chuckwagon Ln Scottsdale AZ 85262 E-mail: hedalton10@aol.com.

DALTON, JAMES BRADLEY, III, geophysicist; b. Memphis, June 26, 1964; s. James Bradley, II and Patricia Dalton; m. Li-Yun Hsiao, Oct. 7, 2000; 1 child, Jascha Hsiao Roy Owens. BS in Physics, BS in Computer Sci., Washington U., St. Louis, 1987; MS in Geophysics, U. Colo., 1996, PhD Astrophysical, Planetary and Atmosphere Sci., 2000. Math. analyst Synernet Corp./NASA-Ames, Mountain View, Calif., 1987—92; geophysicist U.S. Geol. Survey, Denver, 1993—95, 1996—2001; rsch. assoc. Nat. Acad. Scis./NASA-Ames, Mountain View, 2001—03; prin. investigator SETI Inst./NASA-Ames, Mountain View, 2003—. Cons. Lockheed-Martin Advanced Tech. Ctr., Palo Alto, Calif., 2004—05. Reviewer: TERC Astrobiology Curriculum, 2001. Nat. Merit scholar, 1982—86. Mem.: Am. Geophys. Union, Am. Astron. Soc., Sierra Club. Avocations: hiking, camping. Office: NASA Ames Rsch Ctr MS 245-3 Moffett Field CA 94035

DALTON, JAMES EDGAR, JR., health facility administrator; b. Gretna, Va., Sept. 17, 1942; married. Bachelors degree, Randolph-Macon Coll., 1964; Masters degree, Va. Commonwealth U., 1966. Adminstrv. resident Lynchburg (Va.) Gen. Hosp., 1965-66, adminstrv. asst., 1966-69, asst. adminstr., 1969-70; adminstr. Princeton (W.Va.) Cmty. Hosp., 1970-72; regional adminstr. Humana Inc., Dallas, 1972-73, regional v.p. Tampa, Fla., 1973-76; dir. hosp. svcs. Am. Medicorp Inc., Atlanta, 1976-77, Dallas, 1977-78; v.p. Hosp. Corp. Am., Nashville, 1978-79, Arlington, Tex., 1979-87, HealthTrust, Inc., Arlington, 1987-89, Nashville, 1989-90; pres., CEO Quorum Health Group, Inc., Brentwood, Tenn., 1990-2001; pres. Edinburgh Assocs., Inc., 2001—. Home and Office: 6505 Edinburgh Dr Nashville TN 37221-3707

DALTON, JOHN JOSEPH, lawyer; b. NYC, Feb. 7, 1943; s. John Henry and Anna Veronica D.; m. Martha Warren Egan, Feb. 24, 1968; children: Martha G., J. Michael, W. Brian. BBA, Fairfield U., 1964; JD, Northwestern U., 1967. Bar: Ill. 1967, Ga. 1970, U.S. Dist. Ct. (no. and mid. dists.) Ga., U.S. Dist. Ct. (no. dist.) Ill., U.S. Ct. Appeals (2d, 4th, 5th, 7th, 10th and 11th cirs.), U.S. Tax Ct., U.S. Supreme Ct. Atty. Clausen, Miller, Gorman, Caffrey & Witous, Chgo., 1967-69; ptnr. Troutman Sanders (formerly Troutman, Sanders, Lockerman & Ashmore), Atlanta, 1970—. Chmn. bd. Atlanta Vol. Lawyers Found., 1993. With U.S. Army, 1968-69. Fellow: Am. Bar Found., Am. Coll. Trial Lawyers (regent 2001—, chmn. bd. Ga. justice project 2003—04); mem.: Atlanta Bar Assn. (dir.), Highlands Country Club, Peachtree Golf Club, Piedmont Driving Club. Office: Troutman Sanders 600 Peachtree St NE Ste 5200 Atlanta GA 30308-2216 Office Phone: 404-885-3120. Office Fax: 404-885-3900. Business E-Mail: john.dalton@troutmansanders.com.

DALTON, KATHLEEN, history professor; BA with in History with honors, Mills Coll., 1970, MA, 1975; PhD, Johns Hopkins U., 1979. Cecil F.P. Bancroft instr. history and social scis. Phillips Acad., Andover, Mass., 1980—; instr. A.L.M. program Harvard U. Ext. Sch., 1997—99. Adj. prof. dept. history Am. U., Washington, 1979—80; cons. Nat. Park Svc. Orgn. Am. Historians Pub. History Office, 2002—05, cons. historian, rschr., writer in field, fellow, 2005—. Author: Theodore Roosevelt: A Strenuous Life, 2002, A Portrait of a School: Coeducation at Andover, 1986; co-author: Between the Wars, 1978; contbr. articles to profl. jours. Fellow, Charles Warren Ctr. Studies Am. History, Harvard U., 1996—97. Mem.: Coord. Coun. Women History, Orgn. Am. Historians. Home: 41 Salem St Andover MA 01810 Office Phone: 978-749-4000. Business E-Mail: kdalton@andover.edu.

DALTON, MARTHA GOMER, music educator; d. Roy Paul and Gladys Gomer; m. Ronnie Thomas Dalton, Oct. 15, 1977; children: John, James, Stephen. MusB, Trevecca Nazarene U., 1976; MusM in Vocal Performance, Miami U., 1994; MusM in Vocal Pedagogy, Roosevelt U., 2004. Grad. tchg. asst. Miami U., Oxford, Ohio, 1991—92; prof. music Olivet Nazarene U., Bourbonnais, Ill., 1996—. Mem.: Nat. Assn. Tchrs. Singing, Am. Choral Dirs. Assn. Office: Olivet Nazarene U One University Ave Bourbonnais IL 60914 Business E-Mail: mdalton@olivet.edu.

DALTON, PETER JOHN, electronics executive; b. Feb. 5, 1944; s. Peter J. and Rita Dalton; m. Pat Hubbard, Sept. 29, 1991; children: Kelley, Kathy, Amy. BS in Acctg., LaSalle U., 1966. Cost acct. Johnson & Johnson, New Brunswick, N.J., 1966-68; div. adminstr. M/A Com., Sunnyvale, Calif., 1968-70; contr., treas. Wilsey Corp., Oakland, Calif., 1975-80; chmn., pres. KLM Electronics, Inc., Morgan Hill, Calif., 1980-85, Harlan & Dalton, Burlingame, Calif., 1986-91; pres. EPRO Corp., San Jose, Calif., 1988-91, RJE Comms., Sunnyvale, Calif., 1990-92; pres., CEO Am. Quality Mfg., 1991-93; mng. ptnr. Dalton Ptnrs., 1991—. Pres. No. Distribution, San Jose, 1993-96; pres., CEO Morpheus Lights, 1996-99; bd. dirs. Simco Electronics, Santa Clara, BASC, Wood Assocs., Strasbaugh Inc.; CEO Clickhome, Dalton Ptnrs. Contbr. articles to popular mags. Home and Office: 14467 Oak St Saratoga CA 95070-6025 Office Phone: 408-234-1415. Personal E-mail: wgkw@aol.com.

DALTON, ROBERT EDGAR, retired mathematician, computer scientist; b. Boston, May 2, 1938; s. Robert Evelyn and Mildred Louise (Zoellick) D.; m. Sally (Turner), Sept. 12, 1961 (div. 1977); children: Stephen Howard, Alena Lynn BS in Math., U. Chgo., 1959; MS in Applied Math., N.C. State U., 1961, PhD in Applied Math., 1964; MS in Computer Sci., Fla. State U., 1982. Systems analyst RCA Svc. Co., Cocoa Beach, Fla., 1964—65; mem. tech. staff TRW Systems Group, Cocoa Beach, Fla., 1965—71; ops. rsch. analyst Naval Underwater Systems Ctr., West Palm Beach, Fla., 1971—79; grad. tchg. asst. Fla. State U., Tallahassee, 1980—81; asst. prof. Am. U., Washington, 1981—83; mem. tech. staff Mitre Corp., Greenbelt, Md., 1983—85; prin. investigator Vitro Corp., Silver Spring, Md., 1985—93; sr. software devel. engr. Raytheon Co., Bedford, Mass., 1995—2003. Adj. prof. Fla. Inst. Tech., 1964-68, Fla. Atlantic Univ., 1979. Contbr. chapters to books, articles to journals. Sec., U.S. Jaycees, Boynton Beach, Fla., 1974; chmn. U. Chgo. Alumni Fund, Palm Beach County, Fla., 1975-79. Recipient Spl. Achievement Award Naval Underwater Sys. Ctr., 1974, 76. Achievements include rsch. in underwater acoustics, knowledge acquisition and learning, computer games, pattern recognition, knowledge based sys. devel., and decision support with fuzzy logic. Home: 201 G Chadwick Ct Hendersonville NC 28739

DALTON, RONNIE THOMAS, theology educator; b. Dayton, Ohio, Apr. 25, 1953; s. Merl Thomas and Luttie (Scrimager) D.; m. Martha Gomer, Oct. 15, 1977; children: John Thomas, James Douglas, Stephen Wade. AA, Mt. Vernon Nazarene Coll., 1973; BA, Trevecca Nazarene Coll., 1975; MDiv, Nazarene Theol. Sem., 1979; D Ministry, Vanderbilt U., 1984. Ordained to ministry Ch. of Nazarene, 1983. Pastor Ch. of Brethren, St. Joseph, Mo., 1977-78; assoc. pastor Grace Nazarene Ch., Chattanooga, 1979-80; v.p. Nazarene Youth Internat., Dist. E. Tenn., 1982-84; teaching asst. Vanderbilt Div. Sch., Nashville, 1983-84; pastor West View Nazarene Ch., Lebanon, Tenn., 1980-85, Montana Ave Nazarene Ch., Cin., 1985; prof. practical theology Olivet Nazarene U., Bourbonnais, Ill., 1993—, dir. Ch. Growth Rsch. & Resource Ctr., 1995-97, chair master of pastoral counseling and master of ch. mgmt. programs, 1996—2002, chair master of min., dir. Inst. Pastoral Leadership, 1996—2002. Adj. prof. religion Mt. Vernon Nazarene Coll.; dir. mins. tng. seminars Antioch U. Mem. Am. Acad. of Religion, Religious Rsch. Assn., Wesleyan Theol. Soc. Avocations: computer programming and design, golf, antique auto rebuilding. Home: 1454 Westminster Ln Bourbonnais IL 60914-1636 Office: Olivet Nazarene U One Univ Ave Bourbonnais IL 60914-0592 Office Phone: 815-939-5264. Business E-Mail: rdalton@olivet.edu. *The challenge of holiness is to reconcile our experiences of Being in the World and those of Being in Christ. It is an ethic which is both personal and social, attained by both personal struggle and Divine gift.*

DALTON, STEPHEN, molecular cell biologist; b. Birmingham, Eng., June 7, 1961; s. Bernard George and Valerie Margaret Dalton; m. Dawn Harvey, Feb. 18, 1987. PhD, U. Adelaide, Australia, 1988. Assoc. prof. U. Ga., Athens, 2003—. Finalist GRA Eminent scholar, Ga. Rsch. Alliance, 2003—05. Achievements include research in stem cells. Office: U Ga 425 River Rd Athens GA 30602

DALTON, TIMOTHY JOHN, economics professor; b. Moline, Ill., May 4, 1966; s. William Louis and Barbara JoAnn Dalton; m. Nina Kristiina Lilja, July 28, 2000; 1 child, Amelia Maria. AB, Columbia U., 1988; MS, U. of Ill., Urbana, 1991; PhD, Purdue U., 1996. Iprodn. economist West Africa Rice Devel. Assn., Bouake, Cote d'Ivoire, 1996—99; assoc. prof. U. Maine, Orono, Maine, 1999—. Contbr. articles to profl. jours. Grantee, Internat., Fed., State and Industry Source, 1999—. Mem.: Internat. Assn. Agrl. Economists, N.E Agrl. and Resource Econ. Assn., Am. Assn. of Agrl. Econs. Office: Univ Maine 5782 Winslow Hall Orono ME 04469-5782

DALTREY, ROGER, musician; b. London, Mar. 1, 1944; s. Harry and Irene D.; m. Jacqueline Jan. 29, 1964 (div. 1968); m. Heather Taylor (July 19, 1971); children: Simon, Mathias, Rosie Lea, Willow Amber, Jaimie. Vocalist with musical group The Who, 1965-83; recs. include (solo albums) Daltrey, Ride A Rock Horse, Parting Should Be Painless, 1984, Under a Raging Moon, 1985, Can't Wait to See the Movie, 1987, Rocks in the Head, 1992, Martyrs & Madmen, 1997, (albums with The Who) My Generation, 1965, Happy Jack, 1966, The Who Sell Out, 1967, Magic Bus: The Who on Tour, 1968, Tommy, 1969, Live at Leeds, 1970, Who's Next, 1971, Meaty, Beaty, Big and Bouncy, 1972, Quadrophenia, 1973, Odds & Sods, 1974, Who By Numbers, 1975, Who Are You, 1978, The Kids Are All Right, 1979, Quadrophenia (soundtrack album), 1979, Hooligans, 1981, Face Dances, 1981, It's Hard, 1982, Who's Last, 1984, Whos's Better Who's Best, 1989, Who's Missing (1965-72), The Chieftains: An Irish Evening, Celebration-Music of Pete Townsend, 1994; exec. prodr. (films) Quadrophenia, 1979; appearance (films) Woodstock, 1970, Tommy, 1975, Lisztomania, 1975, The Kids are Alright, 1979, The Legacy, 1979, McVicar, 1980 (also prodr.), Three Penny Opera, 1988, Cold Justice, 1989, Mack the Knife, 1989, Buddy's Song, 1990 (also prodr.), If Looks Could Kill, 1991, Lightning Jack, 1994, Message to Love: The Isle of Wright Festival, 1996, Like It Is, 1998, Best, 2000, Chasing Destiny, 2001, .com for Murder, 2002; (TV movie) The Wizard of Oz in Concert, 1995, The Magical Legend of the Leprechauns, 1999, Dark Prince: The True Story of Dracula, 2000; (video) Classic Albums-The Who: Who's Next, 1999, (voice) The Wheels On the Bus Video: Mango and Papaya's Animal Adventures, 2003, (voice) The Wheels On the Bus Video, 2004; performed vocals for film Quicksilver, 1986; TV appearances include: The Comedy of Errors, BBC-TV, 1984, The Beggar's Opera, BBC-TV, 1984, BBC-TV series, 1988, (TV miniseries) Pirate Tales, 1997, Leprechauns, 1999, Rude Awakening, 1999, 2000, The Simpsons, 2000, That '70s Show, 2002. Inducted into Rock & Roll Hall of Fame, 1990. Office: WEA/Atlantic 75 Rockefeller Plz New York NY 10019-6908

DA'LUZ VIEIRA-JONES, LORRAINE CHRISTINE C., acupuncturist, researcher; b. London, Apr. 30, 1955; arrived in U.S., 1999; d. Archibald Carlyle and Christine Heather Da Luz Vieira; m. Schuyler M. Jones, Dec. 23, 1998; children: Jesse Christopher, Cassandra Laurie. Licentiate in Acupuncture, C.T.C.M., Leamington Spa, Eng., 1983, B in Acupuncture, 1986, M in Acupuncture, 1989; M in Anthropology, Oxford (Eng.) U., 1994, MPh in Med. Anthropology, 1995, DPhil, 1999; DOM (hon.), Chelsea (England) U., 2004; diploma in Acupuncture (hon.), 2002. Lectr. Coll. Traditional Chinese Medicine, England, 1985-96; cons. Drug and Alcohol Rehab. Centre, London, 1994-97; pvt. practice acupuncturist Oxford, 1982—99, Wichita, Kans., 2000—. Cons. to various clinics, Canada, United States, Europe, 1983—, England, 1987—; lectr. hosps., England, 1984—, Acad. 5 Element Acupuncture, Miami, Fla., 2002—; lectr., cons. 10 hosps., China, 1993; adj. prof. WSU, Kans. Bd. dirs. O.A.C.M., Oxford, England, 1981, W.I.S.E., Netherlands, 1979—82. Grantee, Oxford U., 1997. Fellow: Am. Assn. Integrative Medicine, Am. Integrative Medicine Assn.; mem.: Traditional Acupuncture Soc., Brit. Acupuncture Coun., Am. Assn. Oriental Medicine. Avocations: travel, reading, cooking, tapestry, music. Mailing: 1570 N Ridgewood Dr Wichita KS 67208 Office Phone: 316-841-4745. Personal E-mail: drlorijones@cs.com.

DALVI, HEMLATA CHINTAMAN, psychiatrist; arrived in U.S., 1979; d. Yashvantrao Narayan and Tara Yashvantrao Chaubal; m. Chintaman Mukundrao Dalvi, Feb. 28, 1979; 1 child, Amish. MBBS, Govt. Med. Coll., Surat, Gujarat, India, 1979. Diplomate Am. Bd. Psychiatry and Neurology. Unit chief, psychiatrist Woodhill Med. Mental Health Ctr., Bklyn., 1993—2002; mem. faculty psychiatry Brookdale U. Hosp., Bklyn., 2002—03; unit chief, psychiatrist Interfaith Med. Ctr., 2003—04; attending psychiatrist Creedmoor Psychiat. Ctr., Queens Village, NY, 2004—. Named one of Am.'s Top Psychiatrist, Consumers Rsch. Coun. Am., 2002—03, 2004—05; scholar, Mahila Jidyalay, Gujarat, 1971. Mem.: Am. Assn. Physicians from India, Am. Psychiat. Assn. Office: Creedmoor Psychiat Ctr 80-45 Winchester Blvd Queens Village NY 11427

DALY, BENEDICT DUDLEY THOMAS, JR., cardiothoracic surgeon; b. Boston, Nov. 28, 1939; s. Benedict Dudley Thomas and Alice Margaret (Groden) D.; m. Joan Marie Behenna, Sept. 25, 1971; children: Jennifer, Benedict, Matthew. AB, Georgetown U., 1961; MD, Boston U., 1965. Intern, Boston City Hosp., 1965-66, resident, 1966-72; assoc. surgeon Tex. Heart Inst., Houston, 1972-75; dir. cardiothoracic surgery St. Elizabeth Hosp., Brighton, Mass., 1976-78; surgeon New Eng. Med. Ctr., Boston, 1978-87, sr. surgeon, 1987—; chief cardiothoracic surgery VA Med. Ctr., Boston, 1987-2002, Newton Wellesley Hosp., 1986-93; clin. dir. gen. thoracic surgery Boston Med. Ctr., 2002-, dir. Ctr. Thoracic Oncology, 2003-; assoc. prof. Tufts U., Boston, 1976-84, prof. cardiothoracic surgery, 1984-02, prof. cardiothoracic surgery Boston U. Sch. Medicine, 2003. Contbr. articles to profl. jours. NIH-NHLBI grantee, 1978-84; Am. Heart Assn. grantee, 1973-74. Fellow ACS, Coll. Chest Physicians, Am. Coll. Cardiology; mem. Soc. Thoracic Surgeons, Am. Assn. Thoracic Surgery. Home: 12 Wildwood Cir

Wellesley MA 02482-6465 Office: Boston Med Ctr Ctr Thoracic Oncology Robinson B405 88 E Newton St Boston MA 02118 Office Phone: 617-638-5600. E-mail: benedict.daly@bmc.org.

DALY, CHARLES ARTHUR, health facility administrator; b. Hartford, Conn., Aug. 22, 1945; s. Robert William and Josephine Frances (Gustafson) D.; m. Leslie Jane Lane, Nov. 5, 1967; children: Cheryl, Christopher. BA, Yale U., 1967; MHA, U. Mich., 1974. Mgr. Blue Cross and Blue Shield of Mich., Detroit, 1974-83; v.p. Del. Valley Hosp. Coun., Phila., 1984-96, Health Visions, Inc., Pennsauken, NJ, 1996-97, South Ctrl. Health Planning Coun., Brick, NJ, 1997-98, Health Resources and Svcs. Adminstrn., Rockville, Md., 1999. Bd. dirs. Health Strategy Network, Phila., Phila. AIDS Consortium, Phila. Health Mmgt. Corp.; mem. Phila. Emergency Med. Svcs. Coun., 1984-96. Lt. USN, 1967-72. Fellow Am. Coll. Healthcare Execs., Coun. Excellence in Govt. Avocations: swimming, golf, baseball. Home: 501 Kegworth Ct Severna Park MD 21146-1720 Business E-Mail: cdaly2@hrsa.gov.

DALY, CHARLES ULICK, foundation executive; b. Dublin, May 29, 1927; came to U.S., 1934, naturalized, 1940; s. Ulick deBurgh and Violet (Sealy-King) D.; m. Mary Larmonth, June 11, 1949 (dec.); children: Michael, Douglas; m. Christine Sullivan, Nov. 5, 1988; children: Charles, Kevin. BA in Internat. Rels., Yale U., 1949; MS in Journalism, Columbia U., 1959. Mgr. then v.p. Mexican subs. Pacific Molasses Co., San Francisco, 1949-50, 52-58; congl. fellow Am. Polit. Sci. Assn., 1959-60; editor Stanford U., Calif., 1961; staff asst. Pres. Kennedy and Pres. Johnson, 1962-64; v.p. U. Chgo., 1964-71; v.p. govt. and cmty. affairs Harvard U., Cambridge, Mass., 1971-76; editor Media and the Cities, The Quality of Inequality, Urban Violence; pres. Joyce Found., Chgo., 1978-86; dir. John F. Kennedy Found., Boston, 1988-2001, dir. emeritus, 2001—. Mem. Lloyd's of London, 1976—; freelance writer, 1958—. Mem. Commn. on Adminstrv. Rev., U.S. Ho. of Reps.; chmn. Donor's Forum, Chgo., 1980; bd. dirs. Am. Ireland Fund, Ind. News and Media, Ireland. With USNR, 1945-46; USMCR, 1950-52. Decorated Silver Star, Purple Heart. Mem. Bantry Golf Club (Ireland), Bantry Sailing Club (Ireland), Boca Grande Club (Fla.), Wightman Tennis Club. Home: 32 Forest Ridge Rd Weston MA 02493

DALY, CHERYL, broadcast executive; b. Providence, Apr. 20, 1947; d. Francis Patrick and Mary Ann (Wallis) D.; m. Arthur James Generas, July 18, 1970; 1 child, Caroline. BA, Rutgers U., 1969; postgrad., New Sch. for Social Rsch., 1975-78. Account exec. Phil Dean Assocs., N.Y.C., 1969—72; dir. pub. rels. Kirkland Coll., Clinton, 1972—75; mgr. press svcs. CBS Radio, N.Y.C., 1976—80; assoc. dir. internal comm. CBS, Inc., 1980—81, dir. corp. info., 1981—83; v.p. pub. rels. Group W Satellite Comm., 1984—95, sr. v.p. pub. rels., 1995—97, CBS Cable, 1997—2000; sr. v.p. comm. TNN, MTV Networks, 2000—01; v.p. media relations MSNBC, 2002; pub. rels. cons. N.Y.C., 2002—. Examiner Westinghouse Quality Awards, Pitts., 1990. Recipient Best Co. Comm. award Cable TV Bus., 1986, Mktg. award Westinghouse Broadcasting Co., 1991. Mem. Cable TV Pub. Affairs Assn. (bd. dirs. 1985-87), Media Mommies (co-founder 1987). Democrat. Roman Catholic. Home: 1 W 67th St New York NY 10023-6200 Office: One West 67 St New York NY 10023-6200 E-mail: dcheryl311@aol.com.

DALY, DANIEL LEE, librarian; b. Iowa City, Iowa, May 19, 1953; s. James and Ruth Ann Daly; m. Elizabeth Karen Bylander, May 5, 1984; children: Megan Mariah, Tomas James. Cert. libr. State Libr. Iowa, 1987. Libr. IIHR Hydroscience & Engring., Iowa City, 1986—. Prodr.: (films) Friends of Old Time Music Fiddler's Picnic, (and creator): (TV series) Space Heaters (Best Pub. Access Program award, 1982). Mem. Commn. on Cmty. Needs, Iowa City; mem. parish coun. St. Patricks Ch., Iowa City. Mem.: A.F.S.C.M.E, County Johnson Irish, Johnson County Songbird Project, Iowa Bibliophiles, VOIC Underground Radio Conspiracy. Democrat. Achievements include design of floor plan and layout for four successive generations of facilities for the literature collections of the Iowa Institute of Hydraulic Research, now known as IIHR - Hydroscience & Engineering; development of the IIHR Bibliographic database, a unique, searchable listing of some 100, 000 titles in the hydrosciences available to students, faculty and researchers of the Institute. Home: 2325 Mayfield Road Iowa City IA 52242-1585 Office: IIHR Hydroscience & Engineering 300 South Riverside Drive Iowa City IA 52242-1585 Office Phone: 319-335-5221. Home Fax: 319-335-5238; Office Fax: 319-335-5238. Personal E-mail: dan-daly@uiowa.edu.

DALY, DONALD F., retired engineering company executive; b. Morristown, N.J., Jan. 10, 1933; s. John F. and Sophie E. (Podeski) D.; m. Bennie L. London, Nov. 2, 1963; children: Stephen, David, Eric. ME, Stevens Inst. Tech., 1955. Equipment engr. Corning (N.Y.) Glass Works, 1955-56; sales engr. Mundet Cork, 1958-60; process engr. Thiokol Chem. Corp., 1961-65; dir. engring. Syntex Corp., 1966-78; v.p., project mgr. Indsl. Design Corp., 1978-2000; dir. Tech. Design & Constrn. Co., Portland, Oreg., 1992-94; ret., 2000. Republican. Avocations: golf, skiing, horse ranching.

DALY, GAIL M., law librarian, educator; b. Detroit; BA in Edn., U. Mich., 1968, MA in Libr. Sci., 1969; JD, U. Minn., 1989. Former assoc. dir. U. Minn. Law Sch. Libr.; assoc. dean for libr. and tech., assoc. prof. law So. Meth. U. Dedman Sch. Law, Dallas. Former mng. editor Minn. Law Rev.; vis. assoc. law Rsch. Librs. Group Stanford U., Mountain View, Calif.; mem. Nat. Mus. and Libr. Svcs. Bd., Washington, 2004—. Mem.: ABA, Am. Assn. Law Librs., Assn. Am. Law Schs. Office: So Meth Univ Underwood Law Libr 6550 Hillcrest Ave Dallas TX 75275

DALY, GEORGE GARMAN, former college dean, educator; b. Painesville, Ohio, Oct. 5, 1940; s. George Ferdinand and Helen May (Garman) D.; m. Barbara Leigh Anthony, Mar. 13, 1977. AB, Miami U., Oxford, Ohio, 1962; MA, Northwestern U., 1965, PhD, 1967. Asst. then assoc. prof. Miami U., Oxford, 1965-69; asst. prof. U. Tex., Austin, 1969-70; asst. prof., then prof. U. Houston, 1971-77, dean Coll. Social Sci., 1979-83; dean Coll. Bus. U. Iowa, Iowa City, 1983-93; dean Stern Sch. Bus. NYU, NYC, 1992—2002. Sr. economist Exec. Officer Pres., Washington, 1974; economist Fed. Energy Agy., Washington, 1975-76; adv. bd. Ctr. Pub. Policy, Houston; exec. dir., investor-edn. plan, SEC, 2004. Mem. Am. Econs. Assn., Public Choice Soc., Phi Beta Kappa, Beta Gamma Sigma Home: 29 Washington Sq W Apt 10A New York NY 10011-9128 Office: Mgmt Ctr NYU 44 W 4th St New York NY 10012-1106 E-mail: gdaly@stern.nyu.edu.

DALY, GLORIA HUME, performing company executive; b. Apr. 16, 1934; d. Wilbur Harrison and Virginia Ellies Hume; m. Clark V. Daly (div.); children: Jeffrey Christopher, Sarah. Student, Ohio Wesleyan U., 1952—54; BA, Ohio State U., 1956. Dir. spl. events Nat. Coun. Chs., N.Y., 1956—58; prin., owner Pickwick Papers, Basking Ridge, NJ, 1963—69; cons. spl. events Dave Ellies Design, N.Y., 1965—70; exec. dir. Bravo Arts, Richmond, Va., 1974—81; dir. mktg. Hilton Head (S.C.) Playhouse, 1983—87; dir. spl. events, devel. Cultural Coun. Arts, Hilton Head, 1986—96; exec. dir. Hilton Head (S.C.) Orch., 1989—. Committeman Somerset Hills Rep. Club, Basking Ridge; elder Basking Ridge (N.J.) Presbyn. Ch.; chmn. Hilton Head (S.C.) Presbyn. Ch.; bd. dirs. Hope Cottage, Hilton Head Island, SC, 2005—; co-chmn. Greater Island Com. Named Leader in Arts, Carolina Morning News; named one of Citizens of Yr., Hilton Head (S.C.) Monthly. Mem.: DAR, Hilton Head Island (S.C.) C. of C. (co-chmn. arts and cultural com.), Rotary (mem. spl. events com. 1995—), Pi Beta Phi. Home: PO Box 6428 Hilton Head Island SC 29938 Office: Hilton Head Orchestra PO Drawer Hilton Head Island SC 29938

DALY, JOHN M., surgeon, educator; b. Phila., Dec. 10, 1947; m. Mary F. Bonner, Aug. 1971; children: John M. Jr., William L., Brian P., Timothy J., Patrick T., Maureen P. BA cum laude, LaSalle Coll., 1969; MD, Temple U., 1973. Diplomate Am. Bd. Surgery. Intern Hermann Hosp. U. Tex. Med. Sch., Houston, 1973-74; resident in gen. surgery U. Tex. Med. Sch., Houston, 1974-78, chief resident in gen. surgery, 1977-78, instr. surgery, 1978; faculty assoc. in surgery M.D. Anderson Hosp., Houston, 1978-79; asst. prof. surgery U. Tex. Med. Sch., Houston, 1978-80, M.D. Anderson Hosp. and Tumor Inst., Houston, 1979-80; assoc. attending surgeon Meml. Sloan-Kettering Cancer Ctr., NYC, 1980-85; prof. surgery, chief div. surgical oncology U. Pa., Phila., 1986—93; asst. prof. surgery Weill Med. Coll. of Cornell U., NYC, 1980-81, Lewis Atterbury Stimson prof., 1993—2002, prog. dir., gen. surgery residence prog., 1993—2002, chair, surgery dept., 1993—2002; surgeon-in-chief NY Presbyterian Hosp., 1993—2002; dean Temple U. Med. Sch., 2002—. Vis. assoc. physician Rockefeller U. Hosp., N.Y.C., 1980; asst. mem. Sloan-Kettering Inst., 1981-84, assoc. mem., 1984-85; assoc. attending physician N.Y. Hosp., 1983; Jonathan E. Rhoads prof. surgery U. Pa. Sch. Medicine, Phila., 1986; cons. in surgery Meml. Sloan-Kettering Cancer Ctr., N.Y.C., 1986. Contbr. numerous articles in sci. and profl. jours. Rsch. grantee Smith Kline and French, 1967; named one of Outstanding Young Men of Am., 1972; recipient Rsch. award So. Med. Soc., 1974, Resident Rsch. award, 1977-78, George Waldren award for Outstanding Chief Resident in Surgery, U. Tex. Med. Sch., 1978, Sam E. Roberts Nutrition Found. medal U. Kans. Sch. Medicine, 1981. Mem. AMA (Joseph B. Goldberger Rsch. award 1970-72), Am. Cancer Soc. (bd. dirs. Phila. divsn., nominating com., profl. edn. com., pub. edn. com., Clin. Rsch. award 1977-78, jr. faculty clin. fellowship 1979-82), ACS (Schering Rsch. award 1977-78), AAAS, Am. Assn. Cancer Rsch., Am. Gastroent. Soc., Am. Soc. for Parenteral and Enteral Nutrition (program chmn. 4th clin. congress, chmn. edn. com. 1980-81, treas. and exec. com. 1981-83, pres. 1985-86), Am. Soc. Clin. Oncology, Am. Soc. Clin. Nutrition, Am. Surg. Assn., Assn. Acad. Surgery (program com. 1979-80, 80-81, com. on issues 1980-82, nominating com. 1983-84, council-man 1984-86), Collegium Internationale Chirurgiae Digestivae, Fedn. Am. Socs. Exptl. Biology and Medicine, Am. Inst. Nutrition, Internat. Soc. Surgery, Internat. Soc. Parenteral Nutrition, N.Y. Cancer Soc., N.Y. Surg. Soc., Phila. Acad. Surgery, Phila. Coll. Physicians, Soc. Surgery of Alimentary Tract, Soc. Clin. Surgery, Soc. Surg. Oncology (pres. 2002-03), Soc. Univ. Surgeons. Clubs: Surg. Biology III. Office: Temple U Sch Medicine 3400 N Broad St Philadelphia PA 19140

DALY, JOHN PATRICK, professional golfer; b. Carmichael, Calif., Apr. 28, 1966; m. Sherrie Daly; 3 children. Student, U. Ark. Profl. golfer PGA Tour, 1991—. Winner golf tournaments including PGA Championship, 1991, B.C. Open, 1992, Bell South Classic, 1994, Brit. Open, 1995, Buick Invitational, 2004; mem. Dunhill Cup, 1993, 98, 2000. Address: care PGA Am 100 Avenue Of Champions Palm Beach Gardens FL 33418-3653

DALY, JOSEPH LEO, law educator; b. Phila., July 31, 1942; s. Leo Vincent and Genevieve Delores (McGinnis) D.; m. Kathleen Ann Dolan, July 24, 1965; children: Michael, Colleen. BA, U. Minn., 1964; JD, William Mitchell Coll. Law, 1969. Bar: Minn. 1969, U.S. Dist. Ct. Minn. 1970, U.S. Supreme Ct. 1972, U.S. Ct. Appeals (8th cir.) 1973, U.S. Ct. Appeals (D.C. cir.) 1974; cert. mediator and arbitrator alternative dispute rev. bd. Minn. Supreme Ct. Ptnr. Franke & Daly, Mpls., 1969-74; prof. law Hamline U. Sch. Law, St. Paul, 1974—. Arbitrator Am. Arbitration Assn., N.Y.C., 1980—, U.S. Fed. Mediation and Conciliation Svc., Washington, 1988—, for the states of Minn., Hawaii, Idaho, Ind., Mass., Mich., N.D., Pa., Oreg., Wisc., V.I and City of L.A.; arbitrator Bur. Mediation Svcs., St. Paul, 1978—; vis. scholar Ctr. for Dispute Resolution, Willamette U., Salem, Oreg., 1985; facilitator Minn. Internat. Health Vols., Kenya, 1985; observer Philippine Constl. Conv., Manila, 1986; participant European Arab Arbitration Congress, Bahrain, 1987; human rights investigator in the Philippines, 1989; vis. scholar U. Oslo, 1990, 91, 92, 96, 97; lectr. on trial skills for human rights lawyers, The Philippines, 1989; lectr. to leaders at Site 2 Cambodian Refugee Camp, Thai/Cambodian border, 1989; lectr. U. Cluj-NAPACA, Romania, 1991; vis. lectr. for developing countries Internat. Bar Assn., 1991-92; lectr. U. Tirana, Albania, 1992, London, 1993, Nat. Econs. U., Hanoi, Vietnam, 1993, 94, Danang (Vietnam) Poly. U., 1993, Ho Chi Minh Econs. U., Saigon, Vietnam, 1993, U. Hanoi Law Sch., 1994, U. Modena, Italy, 1994, Hanoi, Danang and Saigon, 1995, Phnom Penh, Cambodia, 1995, Hong Kong, 1996, Shenzhen, China, 1996, Oslo, Norway, 1996, Karolinska Inst., Stockholm, 1997; vis. prof. So. Cross U., Lismore, Australia, 1998, 99, U. Bergen, Norway, 1999, Tongji U., Shanghai, China, 1999, U. Saigon, Vietnam, 1999, 2000; cons. Chua U., Tokyo, 2001; team leader UN Devel. Programme mid-term evaluation of UN project, Vietnam, Hanoi, 2001; vis. prof. U. Queensland, Brisbane, Australia, 2001, 02, 2003, 2004; Fulbright scholar U. Montevideo, Uruguay, 2002, 2003, 2004. Co-author: The Law, the Student and the Catholic School, 1981; co-author, editor: The Student Lawyer: A High School Handbook of Minnesota Law, 1981, rev. edit., 1986, Strategies and Exercises in Law Related Education, 1981, International Law, 1993, The American Trial System, 1994, International Commercial Negotiation and Arbitration, 2001, Leading American Attorneys in ADR, 2003; contbr. more than 50 articles to profl. jours. Mem. Minn. Legislature Task Force on Sexual Exploitation by Counselors and Therapists, St. Paul, 1984-85, Nat. Adv. Com. on Citizen Edn. in Law, 1982-85; bd. dirs. Scenic Am., Washington, 1989-92. Recipient Spurgeon award Mayor and Citizens of St. Paul and Indianhead Scouting, 1983; named a Leading Am. Atty. in Alternative Dispute Resolution: Employment Law; fellow U. Miss. Law Sch.; Fulbright sr. specialist, 2005. Mem. ABA (contbg. editor Preview of U.S. Supreme Ct. Cases mag. 1984—), Internat. Bar Assn. (London, vis. lectr. for devel. countries 1991—), Minn. State Bar Assn., Minn. Lawyers Internat. (human rights com., rep. to Philippine Constl. Conv. 1986), St. Paul Athletic Club, Phi Alpha Delta. Avocations: jogging, sailing. Office: Hamline U Sch Law 1536 Hewitt Ave Saint Paul MN 55104-1205 Office Phone: 651-523-2121. Business E-Mail: jdaly@gw.hamline.edu.

DALY, KENDRA LEE, oceanographer, educator; d. Daniel Leo and Elaine Loretta Daly. BS, U. Wash., 1973, MS, 1990; PhD, U. Tenn., 1995. Oceanographer U. Wash., Seattle, 1973—91; program dir. NSF, Arlington, Va., 1997—2001; prof. U. South Fla., St. Petersburg, Fla., 2001—. Contbr. articles to profl. jours. Recipient Antarctic Svc. medal, NSF, 1984; grantee, NSF, Nat. Oceanic and Atmospheric Adminstrn.; Hollaender Disting. Post-doctoral fellowship, Dept. of Energy, 1995—97. Mem.: AAAS, Ocean Rsch. Interactive Obs. Networks (excutive steering com. 2004—), Dynamics Earth and Ocean Sys., U.S. Nat. Global Ocean Ecosystem Dynamics (exec. steering com. 2004—, steering com. 2002—), The Am. Geophys. Union, The Oceanography Soc., Am. Soc. Limnology and Oceanography. Achievements include research in polar ecosystems. Office: University of South Florida 140 Seventh Ave S Saint Petersburg FL 33701 Office Phone: 727-553-1041. Office Fax: 727-553-1189. E-mail: kdaly@marine.usf.edu.

DALY, MARY C., dean, law educator; BA, Thomas More Coll., 1969; JD cum laude, Fordham U. Sch. Law, 1972; LLM in Comparative Law, NYU Sch. Law, 1975—78. Assoc. Rogers & Wells, 1973—75; asst. U.S. Atty. Civil Div., 1975—80; chief of civil div. U.S. Atty. Office, So. Dist. N.Y., 1981—83; prof. Fordham Law Sch., 1983—2004, co-dir. Louis Stein Ctr. for Law and Ethics, dir. Grad. Prog., James H. Quinn Prof. Legal Ethics; dean, John V. Brennan Chair Law and Ethics St. John's U. Sch. Law, 2004—. Grantee Zichkla Fellow, Université de Paris, Faculté de Droit, 1973. Mem.: ABA (reporter Commn. Multidisciplinary Practice 1998—2000, mem. Out-of-the Box Com.), Fed. Bar Coun. (trustee 1997—2004), Assn. Bar N.Y.C. (chair Com. Profl. and Judicial Ethics 1996—99, mem. Delegation to Chile, Rwanda and Brazil 2002—03). Office: St Johns U Sch Law 8000 Utopia Parkway Jamaica NY 11439 E-mail: dalym@stjohns.edu.

DALY, MIRIAM SHAMER, retired family physician; b. Balt., Jan. 26, 1925; d. Maurice Emory and Bertha (Tapman) Shamer; m. Harold L. Daly, Jr., June 28, 1948 (dec. July 2, 1989); children: John, Martha, Thomas, David. AB, Goucher Coll., 1946; MD, U. Md., 1950. Diplomate Am. Bd. Family Practice. Intern Luth. Hosp. of Md., Balt., 1950-51, resident, 1951-52; clinic physician Balt. City Health Dept., Md. State Health Dept., 1952-55; practicing physician Balt., 1952-55; physician pvt. practice Albion, Mich., 1955-93; ret., 1993. Leader, camp counsellor Girl Scouts, South Ctrl. Mich., 1955—, pres. Irish Hills Coun., 1993-97, bd. dirs., 1990-97; bd. dirs. Albion Ambulance Svc., 1989-95, ARC Calhoun County chpt., 1993—, Great Lakes Region Blood Svcs., ARC, 1994-95; mem. lay bd. Albion-Homer United Way, 1989-, pres., 2001, 2002; coord. Albion ARC blood drives, 1994-. Recipient Girl Scouts Thanks Badge, Irish Hills Girls Scouts Coun., 1983, 1993, Cmty. Recognition award, Albion Coll., 1996, Athena award, Greater Albion C. of C., 2000. Mem. AMA, NAACP (exec. bd. 2005—), Mich. State Med. Soc. (Frederick and Besse Moulton Plessner Meml. award 1996), Calhoun County Med. Soc., Am. Acad. Family Practice, Mich. Acad. Family Practice, S.W. Mich. Perinatal Assn., AAUW, Rotary Club, Sweet Adlines. Avocations: piano, photography, gardening, gardening. Personal E-mail: msdaly@hotmail.com.

DALY, PATRICK F., real estate executive, architect; b. Chgo., Jan. 25, 1949; s. John F. and Margaret M. (Gleason) D.; m. Shirley J. Kumis, June 25, 1971; children: Sean P., James P. BArch with honors and distinction, BA in Archtl. History with honors and distinction, U. Ill., Chgo., 1972. Cert. architect. Chmn. bd. Dalan Realty Corp., Chgo., 1980—, Dalan Devel. Corp., Chgo., 1986—; pres. Dalan/ Jupiter, Inc., Chgo., 1987—; mng. ptnr. Rising Sun Riverboat Casino and Resort, LLC, Chgo., 1995—; chmn. The Daly Group LLC, 1995—. Bd. dirs. Private Bancorp Inc., Private Bank & Trust Co., Chgo., Affiliated Network Svc., Inc.; vice chmn. bd. mgrs. U. Ill. Rsch. Parks, LLC, 2003-. Contbr. articles to profl. jours. Chmn. Ill. Ambs., Chgo., 1990-98; vice chmn. Met. Pier & Expn. Authority, Chgo., 1985-2002; commr. Nat. Adv. Commn. U.S. Dept. Labor, Washington, 1991-93; trustee Fund Am. Studies, 1993—, Univ. Ill. Found., 1993—, dir. emeritus 1999; trustee Inst. Cmty. Empowerment, 1991-98; trustee Chgo. Acad. Scis., 2001—, chmn., 2002—; chmn. Chancellor's Corp. adv. com. U. Ill., Chgo., 1995-2004; adv. bd. mem. Ind. Univ. Ctr. Real Estate Studies, 1994—, Roosevelt U. Sch. Real Estate, 2000—; dir. U.S. Com. for UNICEF/Chgo., 1996—, U.S.O., Chgo.; chmn. U. Ill. Alumni Assn., 1997-99; mem. leadership com. United Way, 1998; mem. coun. Brookings Instn.; co-chmn. Chgo. Am. Heartwalk, Am. Heart Assn., 2002. Recipient Alumni Achievement award U. Ill., 1993, City Ptnr. award, 2004; inducted into Chgo. Area Entrepreneurship Hall of Fame, 2002. Mem. Alpha Rho Chi. Office: The Daly Group 20 N Wacker Dr Ste 1500 Chicago IL 60606-2903 Business E-Mail: pdaly@thedalygroup.com.

DALY, PAUL SYLVESTER, former mayor, retired academic administrator, management consultant; b. Belmont, Mass., Jan. 8, 1934; s. Matthew Joseph and Alice Mary (Hall) D.; m. Maureen Teresa Kenny, May 25, 1957; children: Judith Mary, Paul S. Jr., Susan Marie, John Joseph, Maureen Hall. BS in Engring. Sci., Naval Postgrad. Sch., 1968; MBA, U. W. Fla., 1971. Commd. ensign USN, 1955; advanced through grades to capt., 1979; coll. dean Embry-Riddle Aero. U., Daytona Beach, Fla., 1979—81, chancellor Ariz., 1981—95; mayor City of Prescott, Ariz., 1996—99; mgmt. cons., 1999—; legis. affairs cons. Lectr. seminars, 1979-85; cons. British Aerospace, 1979-84, McDonnell Douglas, 1979-84, IBM, 1983-84; sr. faculty U. Phoenix, 1983-86. Bd. dirs. Yavapai Regional Med. Ctr., Prescott, Ariz., 1983-86, Prescott C. of C., 1982-84; chmn. Ariz. State Bd. Pvt. Postsecondary Edn.; pres. Ind. Coll. and Univs. of Ariz., Phoenix, 1982—; pres., founder West Yavapai County Am. Heart Assn. Chpt., chmn. affiliate of Am. Heart Assn./Ariz. Decorated Legion of Merit. Mem. Ret. Officers Assn. Republican. Roman Catholic. Avocation: sports. Personal E-mail: daly@myway.com.

DALY, ROBERT ANTHONY, international relief organization executive, former professional sports team executive, retired film company executive; b. Bklyn., Dec. 8, 1936; s. James and Eleanor Daly; m. Carole Bayer; 1 stepchild, Cristopher Bacharach; children: Linda Marie, Robert Anthony, Brian James. Student, Bklyn. Coll.; PhD in Fine Arts (hon.), Am. Film Inst.; DHL (hon.), Trinity Coll. From dir. bus. affairs to v.p. bus. affairs, to exec. v.p. CBS TV Network, 1955—80; pres. CBS Entertainment Co., 1977—80; chmn., CEO Warner Bros., Burbank, Calif., 1982—94; chmn., co-CEO Warner Music Group, 1995—99; chmn., CEO, mng. ptnr. L.A. Dodgers, 1999—2004; chmn. Save the Children Fedn., Inc., Westport, 2005—. Bd. dirs. Am. Film Inst. Trustee Am. Film Inst. Mem.: NATAS, Hollywood Radio and TV Soc., Motion Picture Pioneers, Acad. Motion Picture Arts and Scis. Roman Catholic. Office: 10877 Wilshire Blvd #610 Los Angeles CA 90024 also: Save the Children 2000 M St NW Ste 500 Washington DC 20036

DALY, TOM, county official; BA, Harvard U., 1976. Elected mem. City Coun. of Anaheim, Calif., 1988, elected mayor, 1992—2001; clk. recorder Orange County, Calif., 2002—. Trustee Anaheim Union High Sch. Dist., 1985—88; mem. Anaheim Libr. Bd., 1985—88; mem. adv. bd. Anaheim Boys and Girls Club; mem. bd. dirs. cmty. support group Anaheim Meml. Hosp.; bd. dirs. Orange County Transp. Authority, Urban Water Inst. Office: 12 Civic Ctr PO Box 238 Santa Ana CA 92702 Office Phone: 714-834-2248. E-mail: tom.daly@rec.ocgov.com.

DALY, TYNE, actress; b. Madison, Wis., Feb. 21, 1946; d. James Daly and Hope Newell; m. Georg Stanford Brown (div.); children: Alyxandra, Kathryne, Alisabeth. Student, Brandeis U., Am. Music and Dramatic Acad. Performed at Am. Shakespeare Festival, Stratford, Conn.; appeared on Broadway in Gypsy, 1990, 91 revivals, The Seagull, 1992; films include Angel Unchained, 1970, The Enforcer, 1976, The Entertainer, 1976, Speed Trap, 1977, Telefon, 1977, Zoot Suit, 1982, The Aviator, 1985, Movers and Shakers, 1985; made TV debut in series The Virginian; guest appearances in various TV series including Veronica's Closet, 1996, appearances in TV series include Cagney & Lacey, 1982-88 (Emmy awards 1983, 84, 85, 88), Christy, 1994, (Emmy award 1996), Judging Amy, 1999-, (Emmy award best sup. actress, 2003); TV films include In Search of America, 1971, A Howling in the Woods, 1971, Heat of Anger, 1972, The Man Who Could Talk to Kids, 1973, Larry, 1974, Intimate Strangers, 1977, Better Late Than Never, 1979, The Women's Room, 1980, A Matter of Life and Death, 1981, The Great Gilly Hopkins, 1981, Your Place or Mine, 1983, Kids Like These, 1987, Stuck With Each Other, 1989, The Last to Go, 1990, Face of a Stranger, 1991, On the Town, 1993, Scattered Dreams, 1994, Colombo: Bird in the Hand, 1994, Bye Bye Birdie, 1994, Columbo: Undercover, 1994, The Forget-Me-Not Murders, 1994, Cagney and Lacey: The Return, 1994, Cagney and Lacey: Together Again, 1995, A Perfect Mother, 1996, Autumn Heart, The Simian Line, Shades of Gray, Three Secrets, Tricks, 1997, The Perfect Mother, 1997, Vig, 1998, Execution of Justice, 1999, The Wedding Dress, 2001; appearance one-woman show Mystery School. Recipient Tony award for Mama Rose role in Gypsy, 1990. Address: 272 S Lasky Dr Unit 402 Beverly Hills CA 90212-3671

DALY, WALTER JOSEPH, medical educator; b. Michigan City, Ind., Jan. 12, 1930; m. Joan Brown, June 12, 1953; children: Lois Kay, Alice Louise. AB, Ind. U., 1951, MD, 1955, ScD, 1998. Diplomate Am. Bd. Internal Medicine. Intern Ind. U., 1955-56, resident, 1956-57, 59-62, instr. medicine, 1962-63, asst. prof., 1963-65, assoc. prof., 1965-68, prof., 1968-77, John B. Hickam prof., 1977-80, J.O. Ritchey prof., 1980-95, J.O. Ritchey prof. emeritus, 1995—; chmn. dept. medicine, 1970-83; dean Sch. Medicine, 1983-95; dean emeritus Ind. U., 1995—. Dir. Regenstrief Inst. Health Rsch., 1976-83. Capt. M.C., U.S. Army, 1957-59. Master ACP (gov. 1980-84), Am. Physiol. Soc., Ctr. Soc. Clin. Rsch. (pres. 1980-81), Am. Soc. Clin. Investigation, Am. Clin. and Climatol. Assn. (v.p. 2004-05), Assn. Am. Physicians. Office: Ind U Sch Medicine 1120 South Dr Indianapolis IN 46202-5135 Office Phone: 317-274-7109.

DALY, WILLIAM JOSEPH, lawyer; b. Bklyn., Mar. 19, 1928; s. William Bernard and Charlotte Marie (Saunders) D.; m. Barbara A. Longenecker, Nov. 19, 1955; children: Sharon, Nancy, Carol. BA, St. John's U., 1951, JD, 1953. Bar: N.Y. 1954, U.S. Dist. Ct. (so. and ea. dists.) N.Y. 1958, U.S. Ct. Mil. Appeals 1969, U.S. Ct. Claims 1969, U.S. Tax Ct. 1969, U.S. Supreme Ct. 1973. Assoc. Garvey & Conway, Esquires, N.Y.C., 1954-55, Wing & Wing, Esquires, N.Y.C., 1955-58; ptnr. Daly Lavery & Hall, Esquires and predecessors, Ossining, N.Y., 1958—. Adj. prof. law Mercy Coll., Dobbs Ferry, N.Y. V.p. Legal Aid Soc., Westchester County, N.Y., 1983—; mem. 9th Jud. Dist. Grievance Com., 1981-89, chmn. 1988-89; spl. referee in disciplinary procs.; trustee Supreme Ct. Libr. at White Plains, 1985—. With U.S. Army, 1946-48; ret. col. JA-AUS, 1978; mem. Hall of Fame U.S. Army Officer Cand. Sch., Ft. Benning, Ga. Fellow Am. Bar Found., N.Y. Bar Found.; mem. ABA, N.Y. State Bar Assn. (ho. of dels. 1977-89, 90-96, exec. com. 1983-89, 90-96, v.p. 1985-89, 90-96), Westchester County Bar Assn. (pres. 1979-81, dirs. coun. 1981—), Westchester County Bar Inst. (bd. dirs. 1982-98), Ossinging Bar Assn. (pres. 1966-67), ATLA, N.Y. State Trial Lawyers Assn., Res. Officers Assn. U.S., Skull and Circle, Phi Delta Phi. Roman Catholic. Home: 232 Hunter Ave Sleepy Hollow NY 10591-1317 Office: 73 Croton Ave Ste 209 Ossining NY 10562-4971 Office Phone: 914-941-7000.

DALY-GAWENDA, DEBRA, health facility administrator, nursing educator; b. Chgo., Aug. 30, 1956; m. Tom Gawenda; children: Christopher, Haley, Zachary. Diploma, Michael Reese Hosp. Sch. Nsg., 1978; AA in Liberal Arts, Richard J. Daley Coll., 1982; BSN, Rush U., 1983; MS, U. Ill., Chgo., 1984. RN, Ill. Staff nurse emergency room Rush Med. Ctr., Chgo., Mercy Hosp. and Med. Ctr., Chgo.; asst. prof. Rush. U., Chgo.; dir. employee & corp. health svcs. Rush-Presbyn.-St. Luke's Med. Ctr., Chgo. Lectr. in field. Author 2 books; contbr. articles to profl. publs. Mem. NAFE, Nat. Wellness Inst., Am. Assn. Occupl. Health Nurses, Internat. Platform Assn., Ill. Hosp. Assn. Occupl. Health Nurses (pres.), Ill. Coun. Nurse Mgrs., Worksite Wellness Coun. Ill. (bd. dirs.), Sigma Theta Tau (mem. nominating com.). Home: 11580 Circle DR Burr Ridge IL 60527-8012

DALZELL, RICK, information technology executive; BS in Engring., US Mil. Acad. Bus. devel. mgr. E-Sys., Inc., 1987—90; with info. sys. divsn. Wal-Mart Stores, Inc., 1990—94, v.p. info. sys., 1994—97; v.p., chief info. officer Amazon.com, Seattle, 1997—2000, sr. v.p., chief info. officer, 2000—01, sr. v.p. worldwide arch. and platform software, chief info. officer, 2001—. With U.S. Army, 1983—90. Office: Amazon.com 1200 12th Ave S Seattle WA 98144

DALZELL, ROBERT FENTON, JR., historian, educator; b. Cleve., Apr. 28, 1937; s. Robert Fenton and Lucile (Cain) D.; m. Lee Baldwin, June 18, 1960; children: Frederick, Jeffery, Victoria, Alex. BA, Amherst Coll., 1959; MA, Yale U., 1962, PhD, 1966. Instr. history Yale U., New Haven, 1962-66, asst. prof., 1966-70; assoc. prof. history Williams Coll., Williamstown, Mass., 1970-75, prof., 1975-77, Ephraim Williams prof. Am. history, 1977—2003, Willmott Family Third Century prof., 2003—, chmn. Am. civilization program, 1981—91, dep. coll. marshal, 1984—87, coll. marshal, 1987—95. Vis. prof. U. Va., 1985-86; mem. Mmass. Found. Humantities and Pub. Policy, 1982-89, v.p. 1987-88; trustee Hist. Deerfield, 1983-2003, Bennington Mus., 2000-02. Author: American Participation in the Great Exhibition of 1851, 1960, Daniel Webster and the Trial of American Nationalism, 1973, Enterprising Elite: The Boston Associates and the World They Made, 1987, (with Lee B. Dalzell) George Washington's Mount Vernon: At Home in Revolutionary America, 1998. Morse fellow, 1968-69, Guggenheim fellow, 1973-74, Charles Warren fellow, 1973-74, Williams Coll. Ctr. for Humanities and Social Scis. fellow, 1990; Mass. Soc. of the Cin. George Washington Disting. Prof., 1998-2003. Fellow Mass. Hist. Soc.; mem. Orgn. Am. Historians, Colonial Soc. Mass., Am. Studies Assn., Berkshire County Hist. Soc. Office: Williams Coll Stetson Hall Williamstown MA 01267 Office Phone: 413-597-2316. E-mail: rdalzell@williams.edu.

DAM, KENNETH W., law educator, former federal agency administrator; b. Marysville, Kans., Aug. 10, 1932; s. Oliver W. and Ida L. (Hueppelsheuser) D.; m. Marcia Wachs, June 9, 1962; children: Eliot, Charlotte. BS, U. Kans., 1954; JD, U. Chgo., 1957; LLD (hon.), New Sch. Social Rsch., 1983. Bar: N.Y. State 1959. Law clk. to justice U.S. Supreme Ct., 1957-58; assoc. Cravath, Swaine & Moore, N.Y.C., 1958-60; faculty U. Chgo. Law Sch., 1960-82, prof., 1964-71, 74-82, Harold J. and Marion F. Green prof., 1976-82, provost, 1980-82, Max Pam prof. Am. and fgn. law, 1992—2001, 2003—04, sr. lectr., 2004—; dep. sec. U.S. Dept. State, 1982-85; v.p. law and external rels. IBM Corp., 1985-92; pres., CEO United Way Am., 1992; dep. sec. U.S. Dept. Treasury, Washington, 2001—03, acting sec., 2002—03; sr. fellow Brookings Instn., 2003—. Asst. dir. nat. security and internat. affairs Office Mgmt. and Budget, 1971-73; exec. dir. Coun. Econ. Policy, 1973; vis. prof. U. Freiburg, Germany, 1964; adv. bd. BMW of N.Am., 1990-95. Author: The GATT: Law and International Economic Organization, 1970, Oil Resources: Who Gets What How?, 1976, The Rules of the Game: Reform and Evolution in the International Monetary System, 1982, The Rules of the Global Game: A New Look at U.S. International Economic Policymaking, 2001; co-author: Federal Tax Treatment of Foreign Income, 1964, Economic Policy Beyond the Headlines, 1977, 2d edit., 1998; co-editor: Cryptography's Role in Securing the Information Society, 1996; chair bd. advisors Fgn. Affairs jour., 1997-2001. Bd. dirs. Am. Coun. on Germany, 1986-95, Am.-China Soc., 1989-99, Atlantic Coun., 1985-92, 2004—, Coun. on Fgn. Rels., 1992-2001, Chgo. Coun. on Fgn. Rels., 1992-2001; trustee Brookings Inst., 1989-2001, 03-; co-chmn. Aspen Strategy Group, 1991-2001. Mem. Am. Acad. Arts and Scis., Am. Acad. Diplomacy, Am. Law Inst., Aspen Strategy Group, Met. Club (Wash.), Quadrangle Club., The Nat. Acad. (sci., tech. and law panel, 2003-), Shadow Fin. Regulatory Com., Munich Intellectual Property Law Ctr. (trustee, 2004-). Office: U Chgo Law Sch 1111 E 60th St Chicago IL 60637 Office Phone: 773-702-0216. Business E-Mail: kdam@law.uchicago.edu.

DAMADIAN, RAYMOND VAHAN, biophysicist; b. N.Y.C., Mar. 16, 1936; s. Vahan and Odette (Yazedjian) Damadian; m. Elizabeth Donna Terry, June 4, 1960; children: Timothy, Jevan, Kiera. BS in Math., U. Wis., 1956; MD, Albert Einstein Coll. Medicine, 1960. Univ. rsch. fellow in biophysics Harvard U., Cambridge, Mass., 1963—65; sr. investigator Sch. Aerospace Medicine, USAF, 1965—67; asst. prof. SUNY, Bklyn., 1967—71, assoc. prof., 1971—80; pres., chmn. Fonar Corp., Melville, NY, 1978—. Career investigator Health Rsch. Coun., N.Y.C., 1967—72. Capt. USAF, 1963—65. Named to National Inventors Hall of Fame, 1989; recipient Lawrence Sperry award, 1984, Nat. medal of Tech., 1988. Mem.: AAAS, Biophys. Soc., Am. Chem. Soc., Sigma Xi. Achievements include development of MRI (detecting cancer in tissue). Office: Fonar Corp 110 Marcus Dr Melville NY 11747-4292

DAMAN, ERNEST LUDWIG, mechanical engineer; b. Hannover, Germany, Mar. 14, 1923; came to U.S., 1940, naturalized, 1944; s. Fritz and Ruth Edith (Meyer) Dammann; m. Jan. 20, 1945 (div.); children: Diane Cathrine, Cynthia Ruth, Bruce Hershey; m. Dorothy Russo, June 21, 1980; stepchildren: Christopher Walsweer, Jonathan Walsweer. BS in Mech. Engring, Poly. Inst. Bklyn., 1943. With Foster Wheeler Corp., Livingston, N.J., 1947—; dir. rsch. Foster Wheeler Energy Corp., Livingston, N.J., 1960-73, v.p., 1973-81, sr. v.p., 1981-88; chmn. Foster Wheeler Devel. Corp., Livingston, N.J., 1977-88, chmn. emeritus, 1988—; chmn., chief exec. officer HDS Fibers Inc., 1986-89; tech. exec. Exec. Office of Pres., The White House, Washington, 1995-97. Chmn. Nat. Materials Property Data Network, Inc., 1986-94; mem. sci. and tech. info. bd. NRC, 1989-91; lectr. in field. Patentee in field. Chmn. Westfield (N.J.) Democratic Com., 1956-60, Westfield Area Com. for Human Rights, 1962-68; mem. Westfield Charter Study Commn., 1964. Served with U.S. Army, 1944-46. Decorated Bronze Star. Fellow: ASME (pres.-elect 1987, pres. 1988—89), AAAS; mem.: NAE, United Engring. Trustees (bd. dirs. 1989—92, trustee 1989—2000, chmn. 1993), Am. Assn. Engring. Socs. (chmn. engring. roundtable 1993, bd. dirs.), Welding Rsch. Coun. (chmn. 1985), Westfield Tennis Club, Pi Tau Sigma. Achievements include development of advanced naval propulsion machinery, fluidized bed combustion, fast breeder reactor steam generators and intermediate heat exchangers; patents for energy conversion processes and heat system. Home: PO Box 1944 Edgartown MA 02539-1944 Office: Foster Wheeler Corp 12 Peach Tree Hill Rd Livingston NJ 07039-5701 Office Phone: 508-627-8323. Personal E-mail: damande@att.net. *As a naturalized citizen my life has been influenced by my strong admiration for American Democracy and all that it implies.*

DAMAN, HARLAN RICHARD, allergist, educator; b. NYC, Nov. 1, 1941; s. D. Leon and Frances (Weissler) D. AB cum laude, Harvard U., 1963; MD, Albert Einstein Coll. Medicine, 1967. Diplomate Am. Bd. Pediat., Am. Bd. Allergy and Immunology. Intern, then resident Yale-New Haven Hosp. and Med. Ctr., 1967-69; fellow in allergy and clin. immunology Nat. Jewish Hosp. Rsch,. Ctr., U. Colo. Med. Ctr., Denver, 1971-73; pvt. practice, Yonkers, NY, 1974—. Instr. Albert Einstein Coll. Medicine, N.Y.C., 1974-81; clin. asst. prof. pediat. Albert Einstein Coll. Medicine, N.Y.C., 1981—; dir. pediatric allergy clinic Bronx Mcpl. Hosp. Ctr., 1982-92; mem. Mt. Sinai Med. Ctr. and Sch. Medicine, 1976-90. Co-editor: Psychobiologic Aspects of Allergic Disorders, 1986; contbg. author: Outpatient Medicine, 1980; contbr. articles on pulmonary function testing in asthmatic disorders to med. jours. Maj. M.C., USAF, 1969-71. Fellow Am. Acad. Pediat., Am. Coll. Allergy, Asthma and Immunology, Am. Coll. Chest Physicians, Am. Acad. Asthma, Allergy and Immunology; mem. N.Y. Allergy Soc., Westchester Allergy Soc. (dir. ednl. program 1978-79, treas. 1980-81, pres. 1982-83), Westchester Acad. Medicine. Office: 769 Kimball Ave Yonkers NY 10704-1534

DAMARLA, THYAGARAJU, electronics engineer; b. Mangalagiri, India, Aug. 2, 1948; s. Ramakantha Rao and Ramulamma Damarla; m. Komala Bai Sriperambuduru, Oct. 20, 2001; m. Rohini Velagapudi, Dec. 9, 1973 (div. May 17, 2001); children: Chanakya Chakravarthy, Mahendra. BSc with honors, Indian Inst. of Tech., 1965—68, BS in Tech. with honors, 1968—71, MS in Tech., 1971—73; PhD, Boston U., 1983—87. Sr. engr. Indian Space Rsch. Orgn., Sriharikota, India, 1973—79; sr. rsch. engr. Indian Inst. of Tech., 1979—82; rsch. asst. ECE Dept., Boston U., 1983—87; asst. prof. EE Dept., U. of Ky., 1987—94; rsch. assoc. NRC, Washington, D.C., DC, 1994—96; electronics engr. U.S. Army Rsch. Lab., Adelphi, Md. Nrc advisor U.S. Army Rsch. Lab., Adelphi, Md., 1996—. Contbr. articles to profl. jours. Tutor High Point H.S., Beltsville, Md., 2001—05. Recipient Governor's Vol. Svc. Cert., Govt. of Md., 2004. Mem.: IEEE. Hindu. Achievements include patents for; invention of methods and computer programs for minimizing logic circuit design using identity cell; implementation of signature analysis for analog and mixed signal circuits; a built-in self test method for identification of faulty chips in multi chip modules. Avocations: gardening, tennis, golf, skiing. Home: 9812 Robinson Blvd Laurel MD 20723 Office Phone: 301-394-1266. Personal E-mail: tdamarla@hotmail.com.

DAMASHEK, PHILIP MICHAEL, lawyer; b. N.Y.C., May 18, 1940; s. Jacob and Esther (Sassower) D.; m. Judith Ellen Gold, Dec. 3, 1967; children: Alan S., Jonathan S., Harris R. BBA, U. Miami, 1964. Bar: N.Y. 1969, U.S. Dist. Ct. (so. and ea. dists.) N.Y. 1977. Lawyer Cosmopolitan Mut. Ins. Co., N.Y.C., 1969—70, Schneider, Kleinick, Weitz & Damashek, 1971—73; sr. ptnr. Philip M. Damashek, P.C., N.Y.C., 1974—89; ptnr. Damashek, Godosky & Gentile, 1989—94; mng. ptnr. Schneider, Kleinick, Weitz, Damashek & Shoot, 1994—2000, Cochran Firm Schneider, Kleinick, Weitz, Damashek & Shoot, 2000—02, Schneider, Kleinick, Weitz & Damashek, 2002—. Chmn. Combined Bar Assns. Jud.Screening Panel, N.Y.C., 1983—88; legis. appointment mem. Com. to Rev. Audio-Visual Coverage of Ct. Procs., 1993—94; exec. apptd. to govs. N.Y. Jud. Screening Com., 1997—; adv. bd. N.Y. Israel Econ. Devel. Partnership, 1997—; apptd. Com. on Case Mgmt. Office of Ct. Adminstrn., Cts. of State of N.Y., 1993—, Task Force on Reducing Litigation Cost and Delay, 1st Jud. Dist., 1996—, Differentiated Case Mgmt. Project, Kings County, 1996—, Alt. Dispute Resolution Adv. Com. N.Y. State Unified Ct. Sys., 1999—, N.Y. State Jud. Salary Commn., 1997—, N.Y. State CLE Bd., 1997—, charter bd. mem., 1997—2000; trustee N.Y. Law Sch., 1996—; malpractice panel Supreme Ct. of the State of N.Y., County of N.Y., 1990—91; dir. and v.p. for govt. rels. Respect for Law Alliance, Inc., 1995—; adv. com. on the jud. N.Y.C. Mayor, 2002—03; mem. bus. adv. bd. First Nat. Bank of L.I., 2003. Named Lawyer of Yr., Inst. Jewish Humanities, 1990, Lawyer of the Yr., UJA Fedn., 1993. Mem. ABA, Am. Bd. Trial Advs. (advocate), Am. Judicature Soc., Am. Bar Found., Assn. Trial Lawyers Am. (life, Wiedemann Wysocki citation of excellence 1990, bd. govs. 1990-92, state rels. com. 1990-92, no-fault coordinating com. 1990-92), N.Y. State Bar Assn. (ct. adminstrn. com., com. jud. adminstrn. 1990-94), Assn. of Bar of City of N.Y., N.Y. State Trial Lawyers Assn. (trustee 1989-91, pres. 1990-91, bd. dirs., co-chmn. law pac 1997—, N.Y. Law Schs. Lifetime Achievement award 2000, Ann. Philip M. Damashek Lifetime Achievement award 2003), Assn. Trial Lawyers City N.Y. (bd. dirs.), N.Y. County Lawyers Assn., Jewish Lawyers Guild (bd. govs.). Office: Schneider Kleinick Weitz & Damashek 233 Broadway Fl 5 New York NY 10279-0599 Office Phone: 212-431-9100.

DAMASKA, MIRJAN RADOVAN, law educator; b. Brezice, Slovenia, Oct. 8, 1931; came to U.S., 1972; s. Radovan and Ljerka (Tkalcic) D.; m. Marija Brkoevic, Aug. 10, 1960. LL.M., U. Zagreb, Croatia, 1956; D.Jurisprudence, Ljubljana Law Sch., 1960; LL.M., U. Zagreb, Croatia, 1956. Prof. law U. Zagreb, 1960-72, acting dean Law Sch., 1970-71; prof. law U. Pa. Law Sch., Phila., 1972-76; Ford Found. prof. law Yale U. Law Sch., New Haven, 1976-95, Sterling prof. law, 1996—; cons. Author: Position of the Criminal Defendant, 1962, Faces of Justice and State Authority, 1986, (with Schlesinger, Baade & Herzog) Comparative Law, 1988, Evidence Law Adrift, 1997; contbr. articles to profl. jours. Nat. Found. for Study of Humanities fellow, 1978-79 Fellow Am. Acad. Arts and Scis.; mem. Am. Assn. for Comparative Study of Law, Internat. Acad. Comparative Law. Office: Yale Law Sch PO Box 208215 New Haven CT 06520 E-mail: mirjan.damaska@yale.edu.*

D'AMATO, ALFONSE M., lawyer, senator; b. Bklyn., Aug. 1, 1937; m. Penelope Ann Collenburg, 1960 (div. 1995); children: Lisa, Lorraine, Daniel, Christopher. BS, Syracuse U., 1959, JD, 1961. Bar: N.Y. 1962. Adminstr., Nassau County, N.Y., 1965-68; receiver of taxes Town of Hempstead, L.I., N.Y., 1971-77, presiding supr., vice chmn. county bd. suprs., 1977-80; U.S. senator from N.Y., 1981-98; lawyer, comm. Fox News, 1999—; mng. dir. Park Strategies LLC, 1999—. Chmn. banking, housing and urban affairs com., mem. fin. com., caucus on internat. narcotics control; co-chmn. U.S. Commn. on Security and Coperation in Europe. Author: Power, Pasta, and Politics, 1996. Mem. Island Park Vol. Fire Dept. Mem. Lions, Sons of Italy, KC. Roman Catholic. Avocations: reading, piano. Office: Park Strategies LLC 101 Park Ave, Ste 2506 New York NY 10178*

D'AMATO, ANTHONY, law educator; b. NYC, Jan. 10, 1937; s. Anthony A. and Mary (DiNicholas) D'A.; m. Barbara W. Steketee, Sept. 4, 1958; children: Brian, Paul. BA, Cornell U., 1958; JD, Harvard U., 1961; PhD, Columbia U., 1968. Bar: NY 1963, US Supreme Ct. 1963, US Tax Ct. 1987. Instr. Wellesley Coll., 1963-66; of counsel S.W. Africa Cases, N.Y.C., 1965-66; Woodrow Wilson fellow U. Mich., Ann Arbor, 1966-67; Leighton prof. law Northwestern U. Law Sch., Chgo., 1968—. Author: The Concept of Custom in International Law, 1971, (with O'Neil) The Judiciary and Vietnam, 1972, (with Hargrove) Environment and the Law of the Sea, 1976 (with Wasby and Metrailer) Desegregation from Brown to Alexander, 1977, (with Weston and Falk) International Law and World Order, 1980, 2d edit., 1990, Jurisprudence: A Descriptive and Normative Analysis of Law, 1984, International Law: Process and Prospect, 1987, 2d edit., 1995, How to Understand the Law, 1989, (with Jacobson) Justice and the Legal System, 1992, International Law Anthology, 1994, International Law Coursebook, 1994, International Environmental Law Anthology, 1995, International Law and Political Reality, 1995, Analytic Jurisprudence Anthology, 1995, International Intellectual Property Anthology, 1996, Introduction to Law and Legal Thinking, 1996, International Law Studies, 1996, International Law Studies, 1997, International Intellectual Property Law, 1997, European Union Law Anthology, 1998, The Alien Tort Claims Act: An Analytical Anthology, 1999, International Intellectual Property Coursebook, 2000, International Law Sources: Collected Papers, Vol. 3, 2004; bd. editors Am. Jour. Internat. Law, 1981-95. Recipient Annual Book award Am. Soc. Internat. Law., 1981, Carl L. Fulda award for Outstanding Contbn. to Internat. Law, 1988. Mem. Internat. Law Assn., Am. Soc. Legal and Polit. Philosophy (chair inter-bar study group on ind. of lawyers and judges), ABA (coun. internat. law and practice), Am. Soc. Internat. Law (chair human rights interest group). Home: 5807 Lakeshore Dr N Holland MI 49424-1019 Office: Northwestern U Sch Law 357 E Chicago Ave Chicago IL 60611-3059 E-mail: a-damato@law.northwestern.edu. *All goals in life pale in comparison to the one issue of transcendant planetary importance: preventing nuclear war. We must establish mutually stable deterrence systems to prevent the temptation to initiate a nuclear attack. As a student of international and constitutional law, I pledge to use whatever I have learned in order to promote the recourse to law and justice that may help to establish conditions of international stability and trust.**

D'AMATO, ANTHONY ROGER, recording industry executive; b. N.Y.C., Jan. 21, 1931; s. Agostino and Luisa (Galiani) D'A.; m. Gabrielle Hilton, June 26, 1958; children— Luisa, Jennie, Tania, Joanna, Antonia. BA in Music and English Lit. cum laude (Founders Day award 1956), N.Y. U., 1956; MI.A. (teaching fellow), Brandeis U., 1957. Artist and repertoire dir. stereophonic div. Decca Record Co., Ltd., Eng., 1958-78; pres. TDA Prodns. Ltd., N.Y.C., 1978—; exec. dir. Winnipeg (Man., Can.) Symphony Orch., 1979-80; v.p. artist and repertoire AudioFidelity Enterprises, N.Y.C., 1980-81; mng. dir. Mantovani Prodns., Mantovani Orch., N.Y.C., 1982—. Mng. cons. Leopold Stokowski, 1964-72 Served with USMCR, 1951-53. Recipient Grand Prix du Disque, Charles Cros award rec., 1969 Mem. Assn. Cultural Execs. Can., Winnipeg C. of C., Phi Beta Kappa.

D'AMATO, FRANCES LOUISE, art educator, psychology professor; b. N.Y.C., Mar. 30, 1943; d. Louis and Frances Anna (O'Resto) D'Amato; m. Lewis M. Smoley, Sept. 17, 1977 (div. Mar. 1988). BS in Edn., SUNY, Oswego, 1964; MEd, Hofstra U., Hempstead, N.Y., 1969; MA in Orgnl. Psychology, Columbia U., 1986, MA in Art Edn., 1991. Cert. tchr. K-6, N.Y. Tchr. 5th grade Farmingdale (N.Y.) Pub. Schs., 1965-67; reading supr. Lynbrook (N.Y.) Pub. Schs., 1967-69; reading coord. Am. Cmty. Sch., Beirut, 1969-71; internal tng. cons. Chase Manhattan Bank, N.Y.C., 1971-73; asst. v.p. CIT Fin. Corp., N.Y.C., 1973-78; v.p. human resources Am. Mgmt. Assn., N.Y.C., 1978-81; cons. Tree Group, N.Y.C., 1981—; prof. art Caldwell C.C., Hudson/Boone, N.C., 1988-95; prof. art and psychology Catawba Valley C.C., Hickory, N.C., 1991-95; tchr. printmaking Spirit Square, Charlotte, 1998—. Cons., spkr. Women's Resource Ctr., Hickory, 1990-96; cons. exec. program Columbia U. Bus. Sch., 1981-82; cons. Frye Regional Hosp., Seminar on Assertiveness Tng., 1994; organizer Advent Retreat Cath. Conf. Ctr., Hickory, 1993-96; spkr. various seminars, 1994, 96; conf. leader Dreams Visions of the Night seminar Belmont Abbey Coll. Conf. Ctr., 1995, 96, Stress Reduction seminar, 1996; spkr. in field Author: Benjaman and the Tent, 1986; editor OD Network Newsletter, 1983-87, EIC Intelligence, 1987-90; contbr. articles to profl. publs. Grassroots grant participant N.C. Arts Coun., Boone, 1988-90; participant Blue Ridge Leadership Challenge, Boone, 1990-91; organizer Visual Art Tchrs., Valle Crusis, N.C., 1991; alumni bd. dirs. SUNY-Oswego, 1974-84; coord. bereavement coun. St. Gabriels Ch., Charlotte, 2001—; counselor chs., schs. and orgns; personal trainer, 1999—. Recipient Printmaking award Caldwell Arts Coun., Lenoir, N.C., 1989. Mem. ASTD (bd. dirs. 1975-77, mem. awards com. 1980-81), Nat. Art Edn. Assn. (conf. organizer 1991), OD Network (steering com. 1972-84), Kappa Delta Pi. Avocations: printmaking, writing, reading, swimming, sports. Home: 1140 Knollwood Drive Claremont NC 28610 Office: 2214 E 7th St Apt C Charlotte NC 28204-3387 Office Phone: 704-379-7923. E-mail: fldamato@yahoo.com.

DAMAZ, PAUL F., architect; b. Portugal, Nov. 8, 1917; came to U.S., 1947, naturalized, 1953; s. Pierre L. and Maria A. (Leite) D.; m. Solange Guillon, Dec. 26, 1981. BA in Architecture, Ecole Speciale d'Architecture, 1941; M. Town Planning, U. Paris, Sorbonne, 1946. Archtl. designer UN Hdqrs., N.Y.C., 1948-51, Harrison & Abramowitz, N.Y.C., 1951-53; chief designer Cajetan Baumann, N.Y.C., 1953-61; ptnr. Damaz & Weigel, N.Y.C., 1962-76; pres. Adasco Tech Internat., N.Y.C., 1976-81; prin. Paul Damaz Assos., East Hampton, N.Y., 1981—. Design critic Columbia, 1953; writer, critic, lectr. maj. univs. and TV. Dir. N.Y. Fine Arts Fedn.; Mem. nat. panel arbitrators Am. Arbitration Assn. Author: Art in European Architecture, 1956, Art in Latin American Architecture, 1962. Capt. French Army, 1939—45, POW in Germany. Fellow AIA; mem. French Ordre des Architectes, Archtl. League N.Y. (past v.p., Arnold W. Brunner award 1958), Mcpl. Arts Soc., French-Am. Soc., Am. Inst. Planners. Office: 218 Old Stone Hwy East Hampton NY 11937-1621

D'AMBOISE, CHRISTOPHER, ballet dancer, artistic director, choreographer; b. NYC, Feb. 4, 1960; s. Jacques and Carolyn (George) d'A; married; children Josephine and Shelby. Mem. co. NYC Ballet, 1978—; artistic dir., pres. Pa. Ballet, 1990-94. Debut in The Nutcracker; dance appearances also include Stars and Stripes, Four Temperaments, Mozartiana, Tango, Interplay, Fancy Free, Dancers at a Gathering, Piano Pieces, The Gershwin Concerto, On Your Toes, Song and Dance; choreographed Da Mummy, Nyet Mummy, Runaway Train, The Golden Mean, Sacred and Profane, The Planets, Franklin Court, Bounding Lane, The Seven Deadly Sins, You Never Know, 2005; author: Leap Year: A Year in the Life of a Dancer, 1982.*

D'AMBRA, THOMAS E., pharmaceutical executive; m. Constance D'Ambra; children: Abigail, Geoffrey, Agatha. BA in Chemistry, Coll. Holy Cross, Worcester, Mass., 1978; D in Organic Chemistry, MIT, 1982. Mem. medicinal chemistry dept. Sterling Winthrop, 1982—89; co-founder Coromed, Inc., Albany, NY, 1989—91; founder, CEO, chmn. Albany Molecular Rsch., Inc., Albany, NY, 1991—. Office: Albany Molecular Rsch Inc 21 Corporate Cir Albany NY 12212-5098

DAMBRANS, VERENA STELPS, music educator; b. Liepaja, Latvia, Jan. 28, 1931; arrived in U.S., 1950; d. Alexander and Marta Stelps; m. Juris Dambrans, Dec. 23, 1956. BS, Ctrl. Mich. U., 1952; MusM, U. Mich., 1953. Prof. music, chmn. piano dept. Capital U., Columbus, Ohio, 1956—93; adjudicator piano competitions, lectr., solo, ensemble and chamber music performer, 1993—. Lectr. in field. Organist Luth. Ch., Columbus, Ohio, 1961—. Mem.: Women in Music Columbus (pres. 1995—97, 25 Year Svc. award), Music Tchrs. Nat. Assn., Ohio Music Tchrs. Assn. (com. chair, chairperson scholarships, 25 Year Svc. award), Am.-Latvian Assn. (chairperson arts coun.). Avocations: skiing, golf, gardening, reading. Home: 668 Founder Ridge Dr Gahanna OH 43230

D'AMBROSIO, CHARLES ANTHONY, SR., economist, educator; b. Chgo., Aug. 31, 1932; s. Anthony and Della (Malpede) D'Ambrosio; married; children: Michael, John. BS, Loyola U., Chgo., 1955; MS, U. Ill., 1958, PhD, 1962. Asst. prof. fin. U. Wash., Seattle, 1960-63, assoc. prof., 1963-70, prof., 1970-90. Fin. cons.; dir. research found. Inst. for Chartered Fin. Analysts. Author: Principles of Modern Investments, 1976; editor in chief Fin. Analysts Jour., 1982—92. Bd. dirs. Inst. for Quantitative Research in Fin. Mem. Am. Fin. Assn., Western Fin. Assn. (pres. 1980-82), Am. Econ. Assn., Seattle Soc. Analysts, Fin. Mgmt. Assn. (pres.-elect 1988-89, pres. 89-90). Roman Catholic. Office: 1000 8th Ave Apt A1307 Seattle WA 98104-4228

DAME, CATHERINE ELAINE, acupuncturist; b. Holyoke, Mass., Oct. 1, 1951; d. Josaphat Charles and Lillian Geneva (Archer) Boulanger; m. William Henry Dame, Jan. 9, 1970 (div. May 1999); 1 child, Cristinna Lian. Acupuncture Diplomate, N.E. Sch. Acupuncture, Watertown, Mass., 1992; student, Ind. U., 1988-93; MEd, Cambridge Coll., 1994. Lic. acupuncturist, Mass.; nat. bd. cert. in acupuncture. Dept. mgr. Zayre Dept. Store, Chicopee, Mass., 1969; retail sales clk. Woodward & Lothrop Store, Alexandria, Va., 1971-72; dept. mgr. Steiger Dept. Store, Enfield, Conn., 1972-73; retail sales clk. Point Dept. Store, Ft. Walton Beach, Fla., 1973-74; assembly, repair mfg. Texas Instruments, Ft. Walton Beach, 1974-75; tller Third Nat. Bank, Springfield, Mass., 1975-81, customer svc. rep., 1981-82; teller Bank of N.E./Fleet Bank, Springfield, 1990-93; owner, mgr. Acupuncture Svcs., Chicopee, 1994—. Cons. Cambridge Coll., Springfield, Mass., 1994-95; bus. office liaison Cambridge Coll., 1995-98; Traditional Chinese Med. tour, China, 2001. Mem. People to People Internat. Mem.: Acupuncture Soc. Mass., Bus. and Profl. Trade Exch., Nat. Commn. for Cert. of Acupuncturists Directory, Am. Assn. Oriental Medicine, Chicopee C. of C., Kings Bridge Equine Rescue, Inc., Granby Regional Horse Coun. Office: Acupuncture Svcs Chicopee 665 Prospect St Chicopee MA 01020-3064

DAME, RICHARD FRANKLIN, marine biology educator; b. Charleston, S.C., Nov. 16, 1941; s. Richard F. and Laurie M. (Heisser) D.; m. Amanda M. Roberts, Apr. 29, 1967; children: Caroline, Elizabeth. BS, Coll. of Charleston, 1964; MA, U. N.C., 1967; PhD, U. S.C., 1971. Tchr. St. Andrews High Sch., Charleston, 1966-68; prof. Coastal Carolina Coll. U. S.C., Conway, 1971-90, Palmetto prof., 1990—; dir. ecosystems program NSF, Washington, 1992-93, ecology cluster leader, 1993-94. Cons. Smithsonian Instn., Washington, 1985,

U. Md., Solomons Island, 1991; panel mem. NSF, Washington, 1986, 89, 90, 2005; keynote speaker European Marine Biology Symposium, 1991. Author, editor: Marsh Estuarine Systems Simulation, 1979, Ecology of Marine Bivalves: A Ecosystem Approach; author newspaper/TV course Oceans and Man, 1980, The Role of Bivalve Filter Feeders in Estuarine and Coastal Ecosystem Processes, 1993, Comparative Roles of Estuarine Feeders and Ecosystems, 2005; contbr. articles to profl. jours. Vestry Trinity Episcopal Ch., Myrtle Beach, S.C., 1979-81; bd. dirs. Litchfield Beaches Homeowners Assn., Pawleys Island, S.C., 1974-76. Named one of Outstanding Young Men Am., 1975, Disting. Alumnus Coll. Charleston, 1989; fellow Belle Baruch Found., 1970-71. Mem. AAAS, Am. Soc. Limnology and Oceanography, Estuarine Rsch. Fedn., Southeastern Estuarine Rsch. Soc. (pres.-elect 1994-95, pres. 1996-98), Sigma Xi. Achievements include being first to measure oyster metabolism and growth; research in the importance of oyster reefs to estuarine water quality, Outwelling hypothesis, influence of oyster reefs on water chemistry, estuarine continuum theory. Office: Dept Marine Sci Coastal Carolina Univ Conway SC 29526 Office Phone: 843-349-2216.

DAME, WILLIAM PAGE, III, bank executive, educational administrator; b. Balt., July 6, 1940; s. William Page and Harriet Carrington (Brent) D.; m. Laura Jacqueline Cordier, June 28, 1968 (div. 1975); children: William Page IV, Laura Alexandra; m. Beverly Ann Reece, July 4, 1998. BA, U. Va., 1963. Ofcl. asst., asst. treas. Bankers Trust Co., N.Y.C., 1963-68, dep. rep. Tokyo, 1968-70, asst. treas. N.Y.C., 1970-71; asst. v.p. Franklin Nat. Bank, N.Y.C., 1971-72, regional rep. Singapore, 1972—74; v.p. Riggs Nat. Bank, Washington, 1974-76, Security Pacific Nat. Bank, L.A., 1976-77, San Francisco, 1977-79, Sydney, Australia, 1979-80, J. Henry Schroder Bank and Trust Co., N.Y.C., 1981-82; sr. v.p. Palmer Nat. Bank, Washington, 1982-84; v.p. Sovran Bank, Arlington, Va., 1985-86; chief fin. officer DITT, Inc. subs. Electricité de France, Washington, 1986-88; v.p. Am. Security Bank, Washington, 1988-91; internat. fin. cons. Washington, 1991-93; adminstr. Grace Episc. Day Sch., Silver Spring, Md., 1993-95, Evergreen Sch., Kensington, Md., 1995-98, Alexandria Country Day Sch., Alexandria, Va., 1998—2002; asst. headmaster Lyndon Inst., Lyndon Ctr., Vt., 2002—. Corporator Passumpsic Savs. Bank, St. Johnsbury, Vt., 2004—. Sr. warden St. Paul's Episc. Ch., Washington, 1995-96; dir. The Woodley Ensemble, Washington, 1997-2002, The Piggery Theater, North Hatley, Que., 2003—04, North Hatley Club, 2003—. Mem. Soc. Colonial Wars, Am. Bus. Coun.-Singapore (founding mem.), World Affairs Coun., Asia Soc., Old Asian Hands Soc., BT Alumni Assn., Soc. of the Cin., North Hatley Club, Tanglin Club, Singapore Cricket Club, U. Club Montreal. Democrat. Episcopalian. Home: 235 Skyline Dr Lyndonville VT 05851 Office: College Rd Box 127 Lyndon Center VT 05850 Personal E-mail: chantman@charter.net. Business E-Mail: pdame@lyndon.k12.vt.us.

DAMELIN, STEVEN BENJAMIN, mathematician, educator; b. Nov. 1, 1968; married; 3 children. BS in Math., U. Witwatersrand, 1991, MS in Pure Math., 1993, PhD, 1996. Rsch. assoc. U. Witwatersrand, South Africa, 1995—2000; asst. prof. math. Ga. So. U., Statesboro, 2000—04, assoc. prof. math, 2004—; IMA new dirs. prof. U. Minn., 2005—. Vis. prof. U. South Fla., Tampa, 1997; vis. asst. prof. math. Pa. State U., 1999—2000; rschr. in field.; spkr. in field. Co-editor: Boundary Value-Problems and Orthogonal Polynomials, 2002; contbr. more than 40 sci. papers profl. jours. Fellow, FRD, 1996—97, Univ. Liecster, 2005—; grantee, Ctr. Applicable Analysis and Number Theory, 1996—97, U. South Fla., 1997, Belgian FWO Rsch. Project, 1997, U. Witwatersrand, 1998—99, Ga. So. Found., 2000—03, Ga. So. U., 2000—02; Rosterholtz Mem. scholar, 1994, EPSRC vis. fellow, U. Leicester, 2005—. Achievements include research in applied analysis, finite fields. Office: Ga So U Dept Math Scis PO Box 8093 Statesboro GA 30460-8093

D'AMELIO, FRANK ANTHONY, communications company executive; b. Jersey City, Dec. 9, 1957; s. Joseph and Rose (Giordano) D'A.; m. Carmel Rachel Zampaglione, Mar. 31, 1984. BS, St. Peter's Coll., 1979; MBA, St. John's U., 1983. Asst. fin. analyst AT&T Bell Labs., Short Hills, NJ, 1979-80, sr. asst. fin. analyst, 1980-81, supr. payroll dept., 1981-82, fin. analyst, 1982-83, supr. fin. services, 1983-84, property mgr., 1984, mgr., services and personnel div., 1984-85, mgr. engring., adminstrn., 1985-86, mgr. facility ops. Murray Hill, NJ, 1986-88, mgr. govt. systems fin. and corp. customer relations Short Hills, NJ, 1988—94; controller AT&T Network Systems, 1994—96, CFO, 1996—98; exec. v.p., CFO Lucent Technologies, Murray Hill, NJ, 2001—. Mem. Bldg. Owner's Mgmt. Assn. Republican. Roman Catholic. Avocations: weightlifting, football, basketball, real estate, water sports. Office: Lucent Technologies 600 Mountain Ave New Providence NJ 07974*

DAMERIS, THAD THANO, lawyer; b. Houston, Tex., Feb. 27, 1960; BBA, So. Methodist Univ., 1982; JD with honors, Univ. Tex., 1986. Bar: Tex. 1986, US Dist. Ct. (no., so., ea., we. dist. Tex., Ariz., so., no. dist. Calif., DC, so., ea. dist. NY, we. dist. Ark.), US Ct. Appeals (5th, 8th, 9th cir.), US Supreme Ct. Ptnr., co-leader Aviation Aerospace & Transp. industry team Pillsbury Winthrop Shaw Pittman, Houston. Contbr. articles to profl. jours. Fellow: Tex. Bar Found., Houston Bar Found.; mem.: ABA (chmn. Aviation & Space Law com., vice chmn. Aviation Litigation com., co-chmn. mfg. div. Forum on Air & Space Law), Am. Bd. Trial Advocates, Internat. Bar Assn., Am. Soc. Internat. Law, NTSB Bar Assn., Def. Rsch. Inst., Lawyer Pilot Bar Assn., Tex. Assn. Def. Counsel, State Bar Tex. Office: Pillsbury Winthrop Shaw Pittman 22nd Fl 909 Fannin St Houston TX 77010 Office Phone: 713-425-7322. Office Fax: 713-425-7373. Business E-Mail: thad.dameris@pillsburylaw.com.

DAMERST, WILLIAM, language educator, humanities educator; b. Pelham, Mass., Aug. 21, 1923; s. Steven M. and Clara (Peterson) Damerst; m. Dorothy Blackburn, Feb. 16, 1946 (dec. 2001); children: Jeffrey W., Laura Barron, Gail Pashek. Student, Amherst Coll., 1941—43, student, 1945—46, Mich. State U., 1943; BS, U. Ill., 1946; MA, U. Mass., 1955. Officer family bus., 1946—55; instr. English Pa. State U., University Park, 1955—60, asst. prof., 1960—65, assoc. prof., 1965—72, prof., 1972—85, prof. emeritus, 1985—. Cons. Gulf Oil Corp., Phila., Gulf R&D Co., Phila., GE Co., Erie, Pa., St. Joseph Lead Co., Monaca, Pa. Author: (text) Good Gulf Letters and Reports, 1959, Resourceful Business Communication, 1965, Clear Tech. Reports, 1972, Clear Tech. Comm. 3d edit., 1990, (novel) Joey, Joe, and Joseph, 2001. 1st lt. USAF, 1943—45. Decorated Air medal with 5 oak leaf clusters; grantee, Gulf Aid to Edn., 1959, 1960. Address: 705 Jerdon Cir North Myrtle Beach SC 29582

DAMES, LUELLA B., music educator, director; b. O'Fallon, Mo., Jan. 24, 1933; d. Eugene Clarence Dames and Frances Luella Albers. BS, U. Mo., 1967; MS, Ind. State U., 1968; M in Christian Spirituality, Creighton U., 1977; MS in Edn., Washington U., 1988. Tchr. Sisters of Most Precious Blood, O'Fallon, 1951—67, vocation dir., 1968—78; guidance counselor St. Elizabeth Acad., St. Louis, 1968—70; theology tchr. St. Mary's Coll., O'Fallon, 1978—81; dir. music and liturgy St. Incarnate Word Ch., Chesterfield, Mo., 1982—88, St. Charles (Mo.) Borromeo Ch., 1988—90, St. Mary's Inst., O'Fallon, 1990—. Preacher Precious Blood Missions, Chgo., 2004—05. Mem.: Am. Guild Organists, Nat. Pastoral Musicians, Pi Lambda Theta. Roman Catholic. Avocations: classical music, reading, crossword puzzles. Home: 204 N Main St O Fallon MO 63366

DAMIANO, BETH CAROLE, special education educator; b. Vineland, NJ, Sept. 17, 1963; d. John Edward Giacometti, Jr. and Nancy Carole Giacometti; m. James Damiano, Nov. 2, 1991; 1 child, Dennis James stepchildren: Nicole Nowak, Jimmy. A in Occupl. Therapy, Wesley Coll., Dover, Del., 1983; BA/Tchr. of Handicapped, Glassboro State Coll., NJ, 1986. Spl. edn. tchr. Cumberland Regional HS, Seabrook, NJ, 1986—2005. Avocations: needlepoint, camping. Office: Cumberland Regional HS PO Box 5115 Seabrook NJ 08302

DAMIANOS, SYLVESTER, architect, sculptor; b. McKeesport, Pa., Dec. 31, 1933; s. Tsambikos and Melanie (Barboteau) D.; m. Eva Lu Spears, Dec. 28, 1957; children: Lynne Lucille, Laurie Elizabeth, Leigh Ann. BArch, Carnegie Inst. Tech., 1956; postgrad., Tech. Inst. Delft, Netherlands, 1957. Registered arch., Pa. Assoc. ptnr. Celli-Flynn, McKeesport, Pa., 1960-67; prin. Damianos & Pedone, Pitts., 1967-79; pres. Damianos & Assocs., Pitts., 1979-89; chmn. Damianos Brown Andrews Inc., Pitts., 1989-95; pres. Damianos + Anthony, Pitts., 1995—, Damianosgroup, 2001—. Pres. Pitts. Plan for Art, 1960-82; bd. dirs. Action-Housing, Inc. Arch. bldg. renovation, 601 Grant St. Office Bldg. (Design 1993); exhibited works of sculpture, Mus. Art Carnegie Inst., 1975, Westmoreland County Mus. Art, 1966, N.Y.C., London. Chmn. planning com. Borough of Edgewood, Pa., 1976-77, mem. coun., 1977-81; bd. dirs. Met. Pitts. Pub. Broadcasting, Am. Wind Symphony, Pitts., 1975-76; sec. Pitts. Art Commn., 1970-78; chmn. bd. regents Am. Archtl. Found., 1991-94; chair pub. art adv. com. Pitts. Cultural Trust, 1994—, co-chair dist. design com., 2005— Fulbright grantee USIS, Netherlands, 1956 Fellow AIA (regional dir. 1985-87, v.p. 1988, 1st v.p. 1989, nat. pres. 1990, pres. Pitts. chpt. 1980, vice chancellor Coll. of Fellows 2002, chancellor elect 2001, chancellor 2002-03, Kemper award 1996, Medal of Distinction, Pa. chpt. 1997), Fedn. Archs. Republic Mex. (hon.), Royal Can. Inst. Archs. (hon.), Japan Inst. Archs. (hon.); mem. Pa. Soc. Archs. (bd. dirs., v.p. svcs.), Pitts. Archtl. Club (pres. 1963-64), Soc. Sculptors (dir. 1977-79), Assoc. Artists Pitts. (pres., dir. 1963-65, 93—), Edgewood Club (pres., dir. 1969-75). Greek Orthodox. Home: 328 Locust St Pittsburgh PA 15218-1457 Office: Damianos & Anthony 4617 Winthrop St Pittsburgh PA 15213-3718 E-mail: syl@damianosgroup.com.

D'AMICO, ANTHONY VICTOR, radiation oncologist; b. N.Y.C., June 9, 1961; BS in Physics, MIT, BS in Nuclear Engring., MS in Nuclear Engring., MIT, 1984, PhD in Radiation Physics, 1986; MD, U. Pa., 1990. Diplomate Am. Bd. Radiology. Intern Pa. Hosp., Phila., 1990-91; resident in radiation oncology Hosp. of U. Pa., Phila., 1991-94; asst. prof. radiation oncology Harvard U. Med. Sch., Boston, 1994—, assoc. prof. radiation oncology; chief genitourinary radiation oncology Dana-Farber Cancer Inst. Mem. AMA, Am. Radium Soc., Am. Soc. Clin. Oncology, Am. Soc. for Therapeutic Radiology and Oncology, Am. Urol. Assn., Mass. Med. Soc., Alpha Omega Alpha. Office: Dana Farber Cancer Inst Brigham and Womens Hosp 44 Binney St Tower L2 Boston MA 02115

DAMICO, DAVID A., lawyer; b. Pitts., Apr. 15, 1959; BS magna cum laude, Wash. and Jefferson Coll., 1981; JD, U. Pitts. Sch. Law, 1984. Bar: Pa. 1984, Ohio 1991, US Supreme Ct., US Ct. Appeals, Third and Sixth Circuits. Founding ptnr. Burns, White & Hickton LLC, 1987—. Past v.p. Nat. Assn. Railroad Trial Counsel (NARTC). Named to Pa. Super Lawyers, Phila. Mag., 2004. Mem.: ABA, Ohio Bar Assn., Pa. Bar Assn., Allegheny County Bar Assn. Office: Four Northshore Ctr 106 Isabella St Pittsburgh PA 15202 Office Phone: 412-394-2508, 412-995-3208. Business E-Mail: dadamico@bwhllc.com.

DAMICO, DEBRA LYNN, college official, English and French educator; b. Passaic, N.J., Apr. 15, 1956; d. Nicholas Biagio and Eleanore Lorraine (Hugle) D. BA, Montclair State U., 1978, MA, 1989. Cert. tchr., N.J, reading specialist. Tchr. St. Francis Sch., Hackensack, NJ, 1978—79, Saddle Brook (N.J.) H.S., 1979-80, St. Dominic Acad., Jersey City, 1980-84; tchr. adult basic edn., gen. edn devel. and ESL, Montclair State U., 1974—2001, coord. EXCEL program, 1993—2001; internat. student advisor Manhattan Coll., Bronx, N.Y., 1984—, ESL instr., 1986—, instr. French, 1998—. Instr. Writing Inst. Adult Edn. Resource Ctr., Jersey City State Coll., 1987—; Outstanding Internat. Student advisor, 1989—. Mem. Dist. Wide Curriculum Council, Lodi, N.J., 1977-78; ch. cantor and musician. Named Outstanding Young Woman Am., 1986; grantee, Assn. Internat. Educators, 1985—86. Mem. Nat. Assn. Tchrs. of English as a Fgn. Lang., N.Y. Tchrs. of ESL, Assn. of Internat. Educators, Metro-Internat., Am. Assn. Tchrs. French, NAFSA:Assn. of Internat. Educators, Kappa Delta Pi, Pi Delta Phi. Democrat. Roman Catholic. Avocations: singing, playing and teaching guitar, cantor and musician at church. Office: Manhattan Coll 4513 Manhattan College Pkwy Bronx NY 10471-4998 Fax: 718-862-8016. Business E-Mail: debra.damico@manhattan.edu.

D'AMICO, FRANCINE J., political scientist, educator; b. Geneva, N.Y., July 29, 1958; d. Francis J. and L. Bernadette (Roesch) D'Amico; m. Douglas J. Roll, July 17, 1982; children: James F. D'Amico Roll, Patrick C. D'Amico Roll. BA in English and Polit. Sci., William Smith Coll., 1980; MA in Govt., Cornell U., 1985, PhD in Govt., 1989. Asst. prof. Ithaca (N.Y.) Coll., 1987—93, Hobart & William Smith Colls., Geneva, NY, 1994—97; lectr. SUNY, Cortland, 1998—2001; asst. prof. polit. sci. Syracuse (N.Y.) U., 2000—04, assoc. prof. polit. sci., dir. undergrad. studies internat. rels., 2004—. Vis. rsch. fellow peace studies program Cornell U., Ithaca, 1993—96, vis. asst. prof. dept. govt., 1996—97; vis. asst. prof. LeMoyne Coll., Syracuse, 1999—2000, asst. prof. polit. sci., 1999—2004; dir. under grad studies in internat. rels. LeMonne Coll., 2004; presenter/lectr. in field. Co-editor: Women, Gender & World Politics, 1994, Women in World Politics, 1995, Gender Camouflage: Women and the U.S. Military, 1999; contbr. articles to profl. jours. Chair Town of Geneva Dem. Com., 2000—02; candidate N.Y. State Assembly 129th Dist., 2002. Mem.: Women in Internat. Security, Am. Polit. Sci. Assn., Internat. Studies Assn. (rep. at large, exec. coun. 2002—). Democrat. Roman Catholic. Office: The Maxwell Sch Internat Rels Syracuse U Syracuse NY 13244-1020

DAMICO, JOSEPH F., medical products executive; BA, James Madison U., 1976, MBA in Mgmt. and Mktg., 1977. Sales rep. to various mgmt. positions Am. Hosp. Supply Corp. (now merged with Baxter), 1979-87; former group v.p. to pres. divsns. Baxter Internat., Inc., 1987-93; former pres., COO Allegiance Corp., 1996—98; group pres. Cardinal Health, Dublin, Ohio, 1996—; founding partner, operating principal Roundtable Healthcare Partners, Lake Forest, Ill.; chair. Vanguard Med. Concepts. Bd. dirs. Xillix Technologies Corp., Richmond, B.C., Lake Forest Hosp., Ill., Health Industry Mfrs. Assn., Washington, The Baxter Allegiance Found., Deerfield, Ill., Coll. of Lake County, Grayslake, Ill. Office: Roundtable Healthcare Partners 272 E Deerpath Rd, Ste 350 Lake Forest IL 60045

D'AMICO, MICHAEL, architect, urban planner; b. Bklyn., Sept. 11, 1936; s. Michael and Rosalie (Vinciguerra) D'Amico; m. Joan Hand, Nov. 26, 1955; children: Michael III, Dion Charles. BArch, U. Okla., 1961; postgrad., So. Meth. U. Sch. Law, 1962—63, Coll. Marin, 1988—89, San Francisco Law Sch., 1994—. Supr. advanced planning sect. Dallas Dept. City Planning, 1961—63; designer, planner in charge Leo A. Daly Co., San Francisco, 1963—66; project planner Whisler, Patri Assocs., San Francisco, 1966—67; arch., urban planner D'Amico & Assocs., San Francisco, NY, Guam, 1967—73; pres. D'Amico & Assocs., Inc., Mill Valley and San Francisco, Calif., and Guam, 1973—, Jericho Alpha Inc., 1979—82, Alpha Internet Sys., Inc., 1996—. Cons. arch., planner City of Seaside, Calif., 1967—72, 1979—81, 1989—; cons. urban devel., Eureka, Calif., 1967—82; cons. planner, Lakewood, Calif.; redevel. cons., Daly City, Calif., 1975—77; redevel. advisor Tamalpais Valley Bus. Assn., 1975—77; archtl. and hist. analyst Calif. Dept. Transp., 1975—77; agt. Eureka, Calif., Coastal Commn., 1977—79; devel. cons. City of Scotts Valley, 1977—95, City of Suisun, 1988—89, City of Union City, 1989—91. Mem. steering com. San Francisco Joint Com. Urban Design, 1967—72. Recipient 1st prize, Port Aransas (Tex.) Master Plan Competition, 1964, Design award, Karachi Mcpl. Authority, 1987, Merit award, St. Vincent's/Silveira. Mem.: AIA (inactive, Cmty. Design award 1970), Solar Energy Soc. Am., World Future Soc., Calif. Assn. Planning Cons. (sec.-treas. 1970—72), Am. Planning Assn., Am. Inst. Cons. Planners. Office: 525 Midvale Way Mill Valley CA 94941-3705 Business E-Mail: alphais@alphais.com.

D'AMICO, SANDRA HATHAWAY, art educator; b. Torrington, Wyo., Dec. 3, 1954; d. Stanley Knapp and Roberta Harley Hathaway; m. John Chris D'Amico, May 24, 1980; children: Andrew, Christine. BFA, U. Denver, 1977; M of Humanities, U. Colo., Denver, 1998. Tchr. art Aurora (Colo.) Pub. Schs., 1977—81; artist-in-residence Wilder Elementary Sch., Littleton, 1988—90; art tchr. on spl. assignment Littleton Pub. Schs., 1989—90; tchr. art Creekside Elem. Sch., Aurora, 1990—92, Laredo Mid. Sch., 1992—98, Smoky Hill H.S., 1998—. Visual arts coord. Smoky Hill H.S., Aurora, Colo., 2000—. Mem.: ArtSource Colo. (adv. coun., chair staff devel. 2003—), Colo. Art Edn. Assn. (Outstanding H.S. Art Educator 2003). Office: Smoky Hill HS 16100 E Smoky Hill Rd Aurora CO 80015

DAMJANOV, IVAN, pathologist, educator; b. Subotica, Yugoslavia, Mar. 31, 1941; came to U.S., 1967; s. Milenko and Ana (Pavkovic) D.; m. Andrea Zivanovic, Jan. 18, 1964; children: Nevena, Ivana, Milena. MD, U. Zagreb (Croatia), 1964, PhD, 1971. Lic. physician, Croatia, Pa., Kans.; diplomate Am. Bd. Pathology. Intern Gen. Hosp., Zagreb, 1964-65; resident in pathology U. Zagreb, 1966-67; intern in pathology Cleve. Met. Gen. Hosp., 1967-68; resident in pathology Mt. Sinai Hosp., N.Y.C., 1968-69; asst. in pathology U. Zagreb, 1969-71; postdoctoral fellow Fels Rsch. Inst., Temple U., Phila., 1971-72; asst. prof. pathology U. Zagreb, 1972-73; from asst. prof. to assoc. prof. U. Conn., Farmington, 1973-77; from assoc. prof. to prof. Hahnemann Med. Coll. and Hosp., Phila., 1977-86; prof. pathology Jefferson Med. Coll. of Thomas Jefferson U., Phila., 1986-94; prof. pathology, chmn. U. Kans. Sch. Med., Kansas City, 1994-98, prof. pathology, 1998—. Cons. pathologist VA Hosp., Newington, Conn., 1975-77, Cancer Info. Dissemination and Analysis Ctr. for Virology, Immunology and Cancer-Related Biology, Franklin Inst., Phila., 1977-82, VAMC, Kansas City, Mo., 1995—, Pathology Stedman's Med. Dictionary, Phila., Pa., 2001—; mem. group for rsch. in pathology edn. U. Iowa, 1977-82; ad hoc reviewer, mem. site vis. teams and study sects. NIH, Bethesda, Md., 1978—; mem. basic sci. merit award bd. VA, 1989-92; mem. Croatian Acad. Arts and Scis., 1992; mem. coun. U.S.-Can. Acad. Pathology, 1996-99. Mem. editl. bd. Ultrastructural Pathology, 1985-96, Virchows Archiv, 1986—2003, In Vivo, 1988—, Modern Pathology, 1989—, Hosp. Physician, 1990-96, Human Pathology, 1991—, Croatian Med. Jour., 1992-, Lab. Investigation, 1994—, Pathology Rsch. Practice, 1998-2002, Jour. Urologic Pathology, 1991-2000, Internat. Jour. Devel. Biology, 2005-, Ann. Clin. Lab. Sci., 2005-, editor-in-chief, 2000-02; mem. editl. adv. bd. Am. Registry of Pathology, Washington, D.C., 2000—; assoc. editor Lab. Investigation, 1982-94; regional editor N.Am. Differentiation, 1985-96; co-editor Anderson's Pathology, 10th edit., 1996; mem. editl. rev. group chair for pathology/surg. pathology Doody's Health Sciences Book Rev. Jour., 1998—. Recipient Christian R. and Mary F. Lindback award for disting. teaching Jefferson Med. Coll., Phila., 1988. Mem. Am. Soc. Investigative Pathology, Internat. Acad. Pathology, European Soc. Pathology. Office: U Kansas Sch Med Dept Pathol & Lab Med 3901 Rainbow Blvd Kansas City KS 66160-0001 Office Phone: 913-588-7090. Personal E-mail: idamjanov@kc.rr.com. Business E-Mail: idamjanov@kumc.edu.

DAMJANOVICH, CHASLAV M. (CASEY DIAMOND), filmmaker, television producer, writer; b. Ohrid, Yogoslavia, Sept. 25, 1932; arrived in U.S., 1973; s. Milan S. Damjanovich and Darinka Dj. Kosanovic; m. Ljiljana Jankovic (div.); m. Lana Grant (div.); 1 child, Srdjan C. Diploma in English Lit. and Lang., U. of Philosophy, Belgrade, Yugoslavia, 1955, diploma in Comparative World Lit., 1960. WW2 UFA news rsch. Cinematique, Belgrade, Serbia and Montenegro, 1954—55, mgr., 1956—58; filmmaker Avala Film, 1959—72; sr. broadcasting prodr. Broadcast Bd. of Gov. (formerly Voice of Am.), Washington, 1984—. Cons. on Yogoslav history U.S. Congress, Washington, 1984—87; writer newspaper Liberty, Serbia and Montenegro, 1985—91. Prodr.: (films) The Gangsters, 1959—73; dir.: Operation Cross Eagles, 1969; writer-dir.: Bomb at 10:10, 1968 (Golden Globe nominee, 1969); The Last Train to Berlin, 1970; (TV series) The Frontier Remote, 1982; dir.: (TV commls.); co-dir.: (films) Guestarbeiter, 1959—73, Window to the World, 1959—73; writer-translator: Majestic, 1991. Capt. Yugoslavian Army, 1959—60. Named Best VOA Prodr. European divsn., 1987. Republican. Avocations: Sumerian mythology, development of religious propaganda, development of mythology. Office: VOA 333 Constitution Ave SW 20024

DAMMERMAN, DENNIS DEAN, diversified technology and services company executive; b. Fairfield, Iowa, Nov. 4, 1945; s. Morris Melvin and Mary Louise (Watson) D.; m. Patricia Anne Bryk, July 9, 1967; children: Dwight David, Heather Lynne. BS, U. Dubuque, 1967. Fin. mgmt. trainee GE, 1967-69, corp. auditor, 1969-74, mgr. acquisitions analysis, lighting bus. group, 1974-76, mgr. ops. analysis, consumer products and services sector, 1976-78; v.p., comptr. Gen. Electric Credit Corp., Stamford, Conn., 1978-81; v.p. Comml. Fin. Svcs., 1981, Real Estate Fin. Svcs. div., 1981-84; sr. v.p. fin., CFO GE, 1984—98, vice chmn., 1998—; chmn., CEO, Capital Svcs., Stamford, 1998—; chmn., CEO Kidder, Peabody Group, Inc., 1994—95. Mem. bd. dirs. GE, 1994—. Trustee Fairfield U., Fin. Acctg. Found.; bd. dirs. U. Dubuque. Mem. Coun. Fin. Execs., Fin. Execs. Inst., Officers Conf. Group. Republican. Office: GE Capital Svcs 260 Long Ridge Rd Stamford CT 06927*

DAMODARAN, PURUSHOTHAMAN, research engineer, educator; s. K. M. and Maleswari Damodaran; m. Shanthi Muthuswamy; 1 child, Anand Purushothaman. B of Engring., U. Madras, 1994; MS, No. Ill. U., 1997; PhD, Tex. A&M U., 2002. Cert. engr., Tex., 1999. Rsch. asst. Tex. A&M U., College Station, 1997—2000, lectr., 2000—02; rsch. asst. prof. SUNY, Binghamton, 2002—. Prin. investigator SUNY, 2002—; rschr. in field. Contbr. articles to profl. jours. Recipient Outstanding Svc. award, No. Ill. U., 1996; fellow, Tex. A&M U., 1997—98. Mem.: INFORMS, Alpha Pi Mu (treas. 1996—97). Achievements include research in sponsored industry funding for over $400k per annum. Office: Sys Sci and Indsl Engring SUNY Binghamton NY 13902-6000 Office Phone: 607-777-4281. Business E-Mail: pdamodar@binghamton.edu.

DAMON, EDMUND HOLCOMBE, retired plastics company executive; b. St. Louis, Aug. 5, 1929; s. Ralph Shepard Damon and Harriet (Dudley) Holcombe; m. Florence Elizabeth Drake, Apr. 14, 1956; children: Elizabeth, Leslie. BA, Amherst Coll., 1951; MA, U. Bridgeport, 1991. Contr., treas. Strategic Materials Corp., N.Y.C., 1955-63; ops. analyst Norton Co., Troy, N.Y., 1964-65; v.p. corp. devel. Singer Co., Stamford, Conn., 1965-82; pres., chief exec. officer Pantasote Inc., Greenwich, Conn., 1983-89. Elder First Presbyn. Ch., Greenwich, 1970-88; bd. dirs. Child Guidance Ctr., Stamford, 1983-84, Fairfield County Cmty. Found., exec. com., 1991-97; pres. Greenwich United Way, 1986-92, Greenwich Cmty. Fund, 1992-97; bd. dirs., vice chmn. Greenwich chpt. ARC, 1989-92; mem. ARC N.E. regional commn., 1992-93; chmn. adminstrv. coun. First Ch. of Round Hill, Greenwich, 1989-97; bd. dirs. United Way, York County, Maine, 1998—2004, Brick Store Mus., Kennebunk, Maine, 1998-2000; adminstrv. coun. Ch. on Cape, Cape Porpoise, Maine, 1997-98. Mem. Webhannet Golf Club (Kennebunk, Maine). Home: 5 Annies Way Kennebunk ME 04043-7533 Personal E-mail: nomade@adelphia.net.

DAMON, JOHNNY, professional baseball player; b. Ft. Riley, Kans., Nov. 5, 1973; m. Michelle Mangan, Dec. 30, 2004. Baseball player Kansas City (Mo.) Royals, 1995—2000, Oakland A's, 2001, Boston Red Sox, 2002—. Author (with Peter Golenbock): Idiot: Beating the Curse and Enjoying the Game of Life, 2005. Named to MLB All-Star game, 2002, MLB All-Star Game, 2005. Achievements include led Am. League in runs (136), stolen bases (46), 2000; mem. World Series Champion Boston Red Sox, 2004. Office: c/o Boston Red Sox 4 Yawkey Way Boston MA 02215

DAMON, MATTHEW PAIGE, actor; b. Cambridge, Mass., Oct. 8, 1970; Actor: (films) Mystic Pizza, 1988, School Ties, 1992, Geronimo: An American Legend, 1993, Courage Under Fire, 1996, Glory Daze, 1996, Chasing Amy, 1997, The Rainmaker, 1997 (nominee Blockbuster Entertainment award Favorite Actor-Drama), Rounders, 1998, Saving Private Ryan, 1998 (nominee SAG award Outstanding Performance by a Cast), The Talented Mr. Ripley, 1999 (nominee Best Performance by Actor in Motion Picture Drama Golden Globe award, 2000), Dogma, 1999, All the Pretty Horses, 1999, Titan A.E. (voice), 2000, The Legend of Bagger Vance, 2000, Jay and Silent Bob Strike Back, 2001, The Majestic (voice), 2001, Oceans Eleven, 2001, Gerry, 2002, The Bourne Identity, 2002, Spirit: Stallion of the Cimarron (voice), 2002, Confessions of a Dangerous Mind, 2002, Stuck on You, 2003, Eurotrip, 2004, The Bourne Supremacy, 2004, Ocean's Twelve, 2004, The Brothers Grimm, 2005; actor, writer (film) Good Will Hunting,

1997 (nominee SAG award Outstanding Performance by a Male Actor in a Leading Role, MTV Movie awards Best Kiss, Best Male Performance, Best On-Screen Duo, ALFS award London Critics Cir. Actor of Yr., Screenwriter of Yr., Writers Guild Am. Screen award Best Screenplay written directly for screen, Golden Satellite award Best Action in Motion Picture, Golden Globe award Best Performance by an Actor in a Motion Picture-Drama, 3d pl. Boston Soc. Film Critics award Best Screenplay, Blockbuster Entertainment award Favorite Actor-Video, Oscar award Best Actor, Golden Satellite award Best Motion Picture Screenplay, Golden Globe award Best Screenplay-Motion Picture, Fla. Film Critics Cir. award Newcomer of Yr., Chgo. Film Critics Assn. award Most Promising Actor, BFCA award Breakthrough Artist, Berlin Internat. Film Festival Silver Berlin Bear award Outstanding Single Achievement, Oscar award Best Writing, Screenplay Written Directly for Screen), actor, exec. prodr. The Third Wheel, 2002; exec. prodr.: (films) Speakeasy, 2002, The Battle of Shaker Heights, 2003; prodr.: Stolen Summer, 2002; (TV series) Project Greenlight, 2001—, Push, Nevada, 2002. Named one of 50 Most Powerful People in Hollywood, Premiere mag., 2005. Office: c/o Endeavor Talent Agency LLC 9701 Wilshire Blvd 10th Fl Beverly Hills CA 90210*

DAMON, WILLIAM VAN BUREN, developmental psychologist, educator, writer; b. Brockton, Mass., Nov. 10, 1944; s. Philip Arthur and Helen (Meyers) D.; m. Wendy Obernauer (div. 1982); children: Jesse Louis, Maria; m. Anne Colby, Sept. 24, 1983, 1 child, Caroline. BA, Harvard U., 1967; PhD, U. Calif., Berkeley, 1973. Social worker N.Y.C. Dept. Social Svcs., 1968-70; prof. psychology Clark U., Worcester, Mass., 1973-89, dean Grad Sch., 1983-87, chmn. dept. edn., 1988-89; Disting. vis. prof. U. P.R., 1988; prof., chair edn. dept. Brown U., Providence, 1989-92, prof., Mittlemann Family dir. Ctr. for Study of Human Devel., 1993-98, univ. prof., 1997-98; fellow Ctr. for Advanced Study in the Behavioral Scis., 1994-95; prof., dir. Ctr. on Adolescence Stanford (Calif.) U., 1997—. Sr. fellow Hoover Instn., 1999—; mem. study sect. NIMH, Bethesda, Md., 1981-84; cons. State of Mass., 1976, State of Calif., 1978, Allegheny County, Pa., 1979, Pinellas County, Fla., 1990, Com. of Va., 1993, Hawaii, 1995, Children's TV Workshop, 1991-09, Annenberg Adv. Coun. on Excellence in Children's TV, 1996-99, Project for Excellence in Journalism, 2000-; mem. nat. adv. bd. Fox Family TV Network, 1998-2001. Author: Social World of the Child, 1977, Social and Personality Development, 1983, Self-Understanding in Childhood and Adolescence, 1988, The Moral Child, 1988, Child Development Today and Tomorrow, 1989, Some Do Care, 1992, Greater Expectations, 1995 (Parent's Choice Book award, 1995), The Youth Charter, 1997, Handbook of Child Psychology, 1998;: Good Work, 2001, Bringing in a New Era in Character Education, 2002, Noble Purpose, 2003, The Moral Advantage, 2004; editor: New Directions for Child Devel., 1978—. Trustee Bancroft Sch., Worcester, Mass., 1982-84; mem. adv. bd. Ednl. Alliance, 1991—; mem. bd. advisors John Templeto Found., 2005—. Grantee Carnegie Corp., N.Y.C., 1975-79, 97—, Spencer Found., 1980, 92-96, 98-2001, N.Y. comty. Trust, 1984-88, Inst. Noetic Scis., 1988-90, MacArthur Found., 1990-95, Pew Charitable Trusts, 1990-95, 98-2000, Ross Inst., 1996—, Hewlett Found., 1997—, The Templeton Found., 1998—, Atlantic Philanthropies, 2003-. Mem. APA, Jean Piaget Soc. (bd. dirs. 1983-87), Am. Ednl. Rsch. Assn., Soc. for Rsch. in Child Devel., Nat. Acad. Edn., Harvard Clubs of N.Y. and Boston. Republican. Episcopalian. Office: Stanford U Ctr on Adolescence Cypress Bldg C Stanford CA 94305-4145 Office Phone: 650-725-8205. Business E-Mail: wdamon@stanford.edu. *Learn to thrive on the risks and challenges themselves rather than merely on the prospects of winning; expect that every right and privilege must be vigorously defended; and through it all never give up the principle of common decency.*

DAMRON, BRIAN ALAN, music educator, musician; b. Topeka, Kans., Feb. 14, 1973; s. Steve and Nancy Damron. Degree in music edn., Case Western Res. U. Dir. of instrumental music James Hubert Blake H.S., Silver Spring, Md., 2002—. Mem.: Md. Music Educators Assn., Internat. Assn. of Jazz Educators, Music Educators Nat. Conf. Office: James Hubert Blake High School 300 Norwood Road Silver Spring MD 20905 Office Phone: 301-879-1339. Office Fax: 301-879-1306. E-mail: brian_damron@fc.mcps.k12.md.us.

DAMROSCH, LORI FISLER, law educator; b. Santa Monica, Calif., Nov. 4, 1953; d. Peter D. and Jean (Bauer) Fisler; m. David Damrosch, May 18, 1974; children: Diana Helen, Eva Katherine, Peter Leopold. BA summa cum laude, Yale U., 1973, JD, 1976. Bar: Conn. 1976, DC 1980, NY 1982, US Supreme Ct. 1982. Law clk. US Dist. Ct., New Haven, 1976-77; atty. US Dept. State, Washington, 1977-80; assoc. Sullivan & Cromwell, NYC, 1981-84; assoc. prof. law Columbia U. Sch. Law, NYC, 1984-89, prof. law, 1989—, Henry L. Moses prof. law and internat. organ., 1999—. Mem. adv. com. internat. law U.S. Dept. State, Washington, 1986—. Editor: The International Court of Justice at a Crossroads, 1987 (recipient Am. Soc. Internat. Law cert. of merit 1988); bd. editors Am. Jour. Internat. Law, 1990—; co-author: United States Law of Sovereign Immunity, 1983, Law and Force in the New International Order, 1991, Collective Restraint: Intervention in Internal Conflicts, 1993. Mem. Human Rights Watch, N.Y.C., 1987-. Recipient Superior Honor award Dept. State, Washington, 1980. Mem. ABA, Am. Soc. Internat. Law (exec. coun. 1985-88, Francis Deak Prize 1981), Assn. of Bar of City of N.Y. (sec. internat. law com. 1981-84), Phi Beta Kappa. Home: 138 St Johns Pl Brooklyn NY 11217-3402 Office: Columbia Law Sch Jerome L Greene Hall 435 W 116th St New York NY 10027-7297 E-mail: damrosch@law.columbia.edu.*

DAMROW, RICHARD G., marketing executive; s. Donald C. and V. June (Miller) D.; m. Mary Jen Bear, Sept. 1, 1995; children: Andrew, Anthony, Adam, Deborah, Scott. BA cum laude, Hastings Coll., 1970; postgrad., Creighton U., 1970-72. Cert. bus. communicator. Pub. rels. assoc. Western Electric Co., Omaha, 1970-71; mgr. employee and pub. rels. Gate City Steel Corp., Omaha, 1971-72; advt. mgr. Ag-tronic, Inc., Hastings, Nebr., 1972-74; v.p. Fletcher/Mayo Assocs., St. Joseph, Mich., 1974-80; pres. Mark Morris & Co., Mpls., 1980-82; sr. v.p., mng. dir. Carmichael Lynch Advt., Mpls., 1982-86, exec. v.p., 1989-92, Miller Meester Advt., Mpls., 1986-89, CMF&Z, Cedar Rapids, Iowa, 1992-94; founding ptnr. Contract Mktg. Assocs., 1994-95; exec. v.p., chief mkg. officer The AdTrack Corp., Cedar Rapids, Iowa, 1995-97; chief mktg. officer Davis, Jones, Lamb Ins., Cedar Rapids, 1997, Net Worth Advisors, Cedar Rapids, 19998—. Mem. M.W. Direct Mktg. Assn., Bus. Mktg. Assn., Nat. Agrimktg. Assn., Direct Mktg. Assn. Republican. Presbyterian. Home: 2700 Granite Ct NE Cedar Rapids IA 52402-3324 Office: Net Worth Advisors PO Box 10260 Cedar Rapids IA 52410-0260

DAMSBO, ANN MARIE, psychologist; b. Cortland, N.Y., July 7, 1931; d. Jorgen Einer and Agatha Irene (Schenck) D. BS, San Diego State Coll., 1952; MA, U.S. Internat. U., 1974, PhD, 1975. Diplomate Am. Acad. Pain Mgmt., Am. Coll. Forensic Examiners, Am. Bd. Psychol. Spltys. Commd. 2d lt. U.S. Army, 1952, advanced through grades to capt., 1957; staff therapist Letterman Army Hosp., San Francisco, 1953—54, 1956—58, 1961—62, Ft. Devers, Mass., 1955—56, Walter Reed Army Hosp., Washington, 1958—59, Tripler Army Hosp., Hawaii, 1959—61, Ft. Benning, Ga., 1962—64; chief therapist U.S. Army Hosp., Ft. McPherson, Ga., 1964—67; ret. U.S. Army, 1967; med. missionary So. Presbyn. Ch., Taiwan, 1968—70; psychology intern So. Naval Hosp., San Diego, 1975; pre-doctoral intern Naval Regional Med. Ctr., San Diego, 1975—76, postdoctoral intern, 1975—76, chief, founder pain clinic, 1977—86. Adj. tchr. U. Calif. Med. Sch., San Diego; lectr., U.S., Can., Eng., France, Australia; cons. forensic hypnosis to law enforcement agys.; approved cons. in hypnosis. Contbr. articles to profl. jours., chapters to books. Tchr. Sunday Sch. United Meth. Ch., 1945—; Rep. Nat. Candidate Trust Presdl. adv. com., platform planning commn. at-large-del.; ARC psychology vol. Naval Hosp., San Diego. Fellow Am. Soc. Clin. Hypnosis (psychology mem.-at-large, exec. bd. 1989-90), San Diego Soc. Clin. Hypnosis (pres. 1980); mem. AAUW, Am. Phys. Therapy Assn., Calif. Soc. Clin. Hypnosis (bd. govs.), Am. Soc. Clin. Hypnosis Edn. Rsch. Found. (trustee 1992-94), Internat. Platform Assn., Ret. Officers Am., Ret. Officers Assn. (bd. dirs. Hidden Valley chpt., rep. presdl. task force, pres. adv. com.), Toastmasters (local pres.), Job's Daus. Republican. Home and Office: 1062 W Fifth Ave Escondido CA 92025-3802 Office Phone: 760-745-6640. *A purpose in life is essential to happiness. Success is a matter of making the most of the talents we are given, not receiving greater talents. Time is the most important gift. We can ill afford to waste it or wish it away. All accomplishment is meaningless unless one walks in harmony and fellowship with her maker and her fellow human beings. I am grateful to my parents and teachers for their examples and for providing me the opportunity for self-actualization.*

DAMSEL, CHARLES H., JR., lawyer; b. Apr. 30, 1929; s. Charles H. and Dorothy Mae (Carter) Damsel; m. Margaret W. Damsel, Aug. 25, 1951; children: Charles H. III, Cherie Damsel Boone. BSBA, U. Fla., 1950, JD, 1956. Bar: Fla. 1956, U.S. Dist. Ct. Fla. 1956, U.S. Ct. Appeals (5th cir.) 1958, U.S. Supreme Ct. 1969, U.S. Ct. Appeals (11th cir.) 1981, cert.: Fla. (civil trial lawyer), adv.: Nat. Bd. Trial Advocacy, diplomate: Nat. Bd. Trial Advocacy, civil mediator: Fla. Supreme Ct., diplomate: Am. Bd. Trial Advocates. Assoc. Gurney, McDonald & Handly, Orlando, Fla., 1956—58; mem. Jones & Foster, P.A., West Palm Beach, Fla., 1958—86, Damsel & Gelston, P.A., 1987—98; sole practitioner, 1999—. Contbr. articles to profl. jours. Served with U.S. Army, 1951—53. Mem.: ABA, ATLA, Palm Beach County Econ. Coun., Am. Arbitration Assn., Def. Rsch. Inst. (area chmn.), Fedn. Ins. Counsel (v.p. 1978—79), Fla. Bar (bd. of legal specialization, exec. coun. trial lawyers sect.), Fed. Bar Assn. (pres. local chpt. 1977), Fla. Def. Lawyers Assn. (pres. 1976—77), Palm Beach County Trial Lawyers Assn., Palm Beach County Bar Assn. (pres. 1971), Fla. Blue Key (pres. 1954), Masons, Kappa Sigma, Pi Epsilon Delta, Alpha Phi Omega, Alpha Kappa Psi, Phi Delta Phi. Republican. Presbyterian. Office: 1803 S Australian Ave Ste A West Palm Beach FL 33409 Office Phone: 561-296-9390. Office Fax: 561-296-9396. Personal E-mail: cdamsel@aol.com.

DAMSGAARD, KELL MARSH, lawyer; b. Darby, Pa., May 16, 1949; s. Kjeld and Dorothy (Fanck) D.; m. Katherine Elizabeth Stark, June 17, 1972; children: Peter Kjeld, Christopher William, David Zentner. BA cum laude, Yale U., 1971; JD, U. Pa., 1974. Bar: Pa. 1974, U.S. Dist. Ct. (ea. dist.) Pa. 1975, U.S. Ct. Appeals (3d cir.) 1984, U.S. Ct. Appeals (D.C. cir.) 1989, U.S. Ct. Appeals (8th cir.) 1990, U.S. Ct. Appeals (10th cir.) 1991, U.S. Ct. Appeals (9th cir.) 2003, U.S. Supreme Ct. 1991. Law clk. to judge Superior Ct. of Pa., Phila., 1974-75; assoc. Morgan, Lewis & Bockius LLP, Phila., 1975-81, ptnr., 1981—, firm adminstrv. ptnr., 1996—. Fellow Am. Coll. Trial Lawyers; mem. ABA, Phila. Bar Assn. Avocations: skiing, jogging, tennis, antiques. Office: Morgan Lewis & Bockius LLP 1701 Market St Philadelphia PA 19103-2903 Office Phone: 215-963-5592. Office Fax: 215-963-5001. Business E-Mail: kdamsgaard@morganlewis.com.

DAMSKI, MEL, film director; b. N.Y.C., July 21, 1946; Ed., Colgate U. Dir.: (TV films) Long Journey Back, 1978, The Child Stealer, 1979, A Perfect Match, 1980, Word of Honor, 1981, American Dream, 1981, For Ladies Only, 1981, The Legend of Walks Far Woman, 1982, An Invasion of Privacy, 1983, Attack on Fear, 1984, Badge of the Assassin, 1985, A Winner Never Quits, 1985, Hero in the Family, 1986, The Three Kings, 1987, Murder by the Book, 1987, Happy Togeterh, 1989, Everybody's Baby: The Rescue of Jessica McClure, 1989, The Girl Who Came Between Them, 1990, Blood River, 1991, Wild Card, 1992, Back to the Streets of San Francisco, 1992, The Care and Handling of Roses, 1996, Their Second Chance, 1997, Still Kicking: The Fabulous Palm Springs Follies, 1997, (TV series) Barnaby Jones, 1973-80, Bionic Woman, 1976-78, Kaz, 1978-79, Picket Fences, 1992-96, Class of '96, 1993, Hearts of the West, 1993-94, Chicago Hope, 1994-2000, Nowhere Man, 1995-96, American Gothic, 1995-96, Early Edition, 1996-2000, The Practice, 1997-2004, Any Day Now, 1998-2002, Jack & Jill, 1999-2001, Ally, 1999-2000, Young Americans, 2000, Boston Public, 2000-04, Kevin Hill, 2004-05, Darcy's Wild Life, 2004-, Beautiful People, 2005-, (films) Yellowbeard, 1983, Mischief, 1985, Murder by the Book, 1986. Mem. Dirs. Guild Am.*

DAMSON, BARRIE MORTON, oil and gas exploration company executive; b. N.Y.C., Jan. 29, 1936; s. Harry and Ethel (Brody) Damson; m. Joan Selig, Feb. 29, 1972; children: Blair, Laura, Bethany. AB, Harvard U., 1956; LLB, NYU, 1959. Bar: N.Y. 1959. Pres. Damson Petroleum Corp., N.Y.C., 1963-69, Bronco Oil Corp., Midland, Tex., 1965-69, Delta Minerals Inc., Lake Charles, La., 1967-69; pres., chmn. bd. Damson Oil Corp., N.Y.C., 1969-91. Pres., chmn. bd. First Crescent Corp.; chmn. Crescent Natural Resources, Inc.; bd. dirs., chmn., nominating com. Am. Stock Exch., 1981—91, bd. govs., chmn. audit com.; chmn. Damson Natural Resources, Inc., 1991, Damson Investment Group, Inc., European Am. Oil Co., Inc., 1991—94, Stagebill, 1993; bd. dirs. United Gas Holding Corp., 1993—97. Chmn. bd. mem. N.Y.C. Econ. Devel. Corp., 1992—96; dir. Robert Steel Found. for Pediat. Cancer Rsch., 1995; bd. trustees Hosp. Spl. Surgery, 2002; mem. Am. Bus. Conf., 1980—94; mem. Dean's Coun. Harvard Sch. Pub. Health. Mem.: Bar. Assn. N.Y., Harvard Club. Address: 1095 Pequot Ave Southport CT 06890-1421

DAN, ASIT, computer scientist, research scientist; arrived in US, 1982; s. Joy Krishna and A. L. Dan; m. Karen Frazier, Aug. 31, 1996; children: Indra Neil, Ariana Kajolee. BTech, Indian Inst. Tech., Kharagpur, India, 1982; MS, U. Mass., 1985, PhD, 1990. Rsch. staff mem. IBM Rsch., Hawthorne, NY, 1990—. Author: (book) Multimedia Servers Applications, Environments and Design, 2000, Performance Analysis of Data Sharing Environments (ACM Disting. Dissertation Hon. Mention, 1992); contbr. book chpt. Recovery In Database Management Systems, book chpt. Multimedia Technologies and Applications for the 21st Century, book chpt. Multimedia Information Storage and Management, book chpt. The Internet and Telecommunications: Architectures, Technologies, and Business Developments, articles to profl. jours. Mem.: IEEE, ACM. Achievements include patents for in the areas of multimedia servers, transaction processing architectures and B2B integrations. Home: 6 Heritage Dr Pleasantville NY 10570 Office: IBM T J Watson Rsch Ctr 19 Skyline Dr Hawthorne NY 10532

DAN, BERNARD W., stock company executive; b. Chgo. BS in Acctg., St. John's U., Collegeville, Minn. With Nat. Futures Assn., 1983—85; adminstrv. mgr. oper. activities Cargill Investor Svcs., Ltd., London, 1986—89, adminstrv. mgr. N.Y.C., 1989—91, asst. v.p., 1991—93, v.p., 1993—94; dir. Cargill Investors Svcs. (Singapore) Pty. Ltd., 1994—97; v.p., Global Head of Execution Cargill Investors Svcs., Chgo., 1997—98; pres., CEO Cargill Investor Svcs., Chgo., 1998—2001; exec. v.p. Chgo. Bd. of Trade, 2001—02, pres., CEO, 2002—. Gov. Bd. of Trade Clearing Corp., mem. bd. govs., 1st vice chmn. Office: Chicago Bd of Trade 141 W Jackson Blvd Chicago IL 60604-2994*

DAN, JOHNSON, state representative; b. Hays, Kans., Aug. 18, 1936; m. Gwen Dan, 1958; 2 children. BS, MS in Indsl. Arts, Ft. Hays State U. Tchr. Ft. Hays State U., 1961—69; mem. Kans. Ho. of Reps., 1997—. Lt. col. USAR, 1954—77, ret., 1977. Mem.: Kans. Livestock Assn., Ellis County Farm Bur., Ellis County Hist. Soc., Epsilon Pi Tau, Phi Kappa Phi. Republican. Episcopalian. Office: 426-S State Capitol 300 SW 10th Ave Topeka KS 66612 Address: PO Box 247 Hays KS 67601

DAN, MICHAEL T., security firm executive; Pres., CEO Brink's Inc., 1993—; chmn., pres., CEO The Brink's Co., Richmond, Va., 1998—. Office: Brink's Co 1801 Bayberry Ct PO Box 18100 Richmond VA 23226-8100*

DANA, DAVID, law educator; BA summa cum laude, Harvard U.; JD magna cum laude, Harvard U, 1988. Law clerk Hon. Betty Fletcher, U.S. Court of Appeals for the Ninth Circuit, 1988—89; assoc. Wilmer, Cutler & Pickering, 1989—91; attorney Environmental and Natural Resources Division, U.S. Dept. of Justice, 1991—93; prof., assoc. prof. law Boston U. School of Law, 1993—98; prof. law Northwestern U., 1999—, assoc. dean for faculty research. Office: Institute for Policy Research Northwestern University 2040 Sheridan Road Evanston IL 60208 E-mail: d-dana@northwestern.edu.

DANA, EDWARD RUNKLE, retired physician; b. Columbus, Ohio, May 20, 1919; s. Lowell Brockway and Helen (Runkle) D.; m. Lorraine Kirschner, Aug. 2, 1945; children— Edward R., H. Richard. AB, Wesleyan U., 1941; MD, Johns Hopkins U., 1944. Diplomate: Am. Bd. Radiology. Intern Univ. Hosps., Cleve., 1944-45; resident radiology Johns Hopkins Hosp., 1947-50; dir. radiology Mercy Hosp., Balt., 1950-64; asst. prof. radiology Johns Hopkins Med. Sch., 1960-68, asso. prof., 1968-69; chief diagnostic radiology Orange (Calif.) County Med. Ctr., 1969—2005; asso. prof. radiology U. Calif. Med. Sch., Irvine, 1969-79, prof., 1979—2005, joint prof. gastroenterology, 1969—2005, chief gastrointestinal radiology, 1976-77, co-chief, 1977—2005; co-dir. swallowing ctr. U. Calif. Med. Ctr., Coll. Medicine, Irvine; ret., 2005. Cons. gastroent. radiology Long Beach (Calif.) VA Hosp., 1974— Contbr. articles to profl. jours. Served to capt. M.C. U.S. Army, 1945-47. Named Tchr. of Yr. U. Calif. Irvine Coll. Med., 1996. Mem. Soc. Gastrointestinal Radiologists, Mensa, Sigma Chi, Phi Chi. Clubs: Md. Home: 2523 Altamar Dr Irvine Cove Laguna Beach CA 92651

DANA, F(RANK) MITCHELL, theatrical lighting designer; b. Washington, Nov. 14, 1942; s. John Daskum Mitchell and Elizabeth Francis (Woods) D.; m. Wendy Karen Bensinger, Dec. 31, 1967; children: Scott Cameron, Ian Michael. BFA, Utah State U., 1964; MFA, Yale Drama Sch., 1967. Asst. to Jo Mielziner, N.Y.C., 1968-69; tech. dir. Yale Drama Sch., New Haven, Conn., 1970-71; assoc. lighting dir. Ferd Manning, N.Y.C., 1978-88. Guest lectr. U. Wash., So. Meth. U., San Francisco State U.; lectr. Mason Gross Sch. Arts, Rutgers U., 1982-97, asst. prof., 1997-99, assoc. prof., 2000—. Prodn. mgr.: Stratford Festival, Pitts. Civic Light Opera; prodn. supr. Yale Repertory Theatre; lighting designer: Broadway Plays include The Freedom of the City, 1974, Once in a Lifetime, 1978, Inspector General, 1978, Man and Superman, 1978, The Suicide, 1980 (Drama Logue award), Mass Appeal, 1981, Monday After the Miracle, 1982, The Babe, 1984, Oh Coward, 1986; off-Broadway Plays include Three Acts of Recognition, 1982, A Coupla White Chicks, 1980, Mass Appeal, 1980, Oh Coward, 1981, Calling in Crazy, 1969, Songs My Mother Never Sang Me, 1982, Husbandry, 1984, A Hell of a Town, 1984, The Ninth Step, 1984, Daughters, 1986, Cold Sweat, 1988, Other People's Money, 1989, King Fish, 1991, Lust 1995, PaPa 1996, Pete 'n' Keely, 2000, Rounding Third, 2003; operas World Premier of Harriet: The Woman Called Moses, Orphee, Patricia II, Tempest 94, Turandot, Royal Opera, Covent Garden, 1984, Olympic Arts Festival, 1984, L.A. Rondine, N.Y.C. Opera, 1984, Magic Flute, 1985, Merry Widow, 1986, Cleve. Symphony, Un Ballo in Maschera Va. Opera, 1985, Opera Festival of N.J., 1989-2001 Turandot, Royal Opera/Covent Garden at Wembly Arena, 1991, Carmen for L.A. Opera and Seville Expo92, La Traviata for Barcelona's Gran Licieu, 1992; Makropolous Case, Traviata, Midsummer Night's Dream, 1992, Elgato Montez, Madama Butterfly, Faust, Electra, Don Giovanni, L.A. Opera, 1994, Ky. Opera, 1999—, other opera cos.; also Pitts. Civic Light Opera, 1973-74, 79, 84-87; tours Hello Dolly, 1981, Mass Appeal, 1982, Guys and Dolls, 1984, George M., Jesus Christ Superstar, 1985, Stop the World, 1986, Other People's Money, Okla., 1990; regional theaters Am. Conservatory Theatre, 1972-80, BAM Theatre Co., 1977, 78, 80, 81, Goodman Theatre, 1973-82, McCarter Theatre, 1969-71, 82, 86-90, Nat. Arts Ctr., Ottawa, 1982-84, others including Mark Taper Forum, Paper Mill Playhouse, Phila. Drama Guild, Va. Mus. Theatre, Crossroads Theatre Co., Geva Theater, Folger Theater, Hartford Stage Co., Interact Theatre, Ala. Shakespeare Co., Cin. Playhouse, St. Louis MUNY, Syracuse Stage, 1984, 87, 96, Seattle Repertory, Stratford Shakespeare Festival, Studio Arena Theatre, Stratford Festival Theatre, Roundabout Theatre, 1987, 88, George Street Playhouse, Interact Theatre Co., Derby Playhouse (U.K.). Mem. Internat. Alliance Theatrical Stage Employees, United Scenic Artists USA 829 (lighting trustee 1970-72, 96-2003, nat. v.p. 2002--). Republican. Office: 221 W 82d St New York NY 10024-5406 Office Phone: 212-873-1229. E-mail: fmdld@earthlink.net.

DANA, HOWARD H., JR., state supreme court justice; m. Susan Dana. Grad., Bowdoin Coll., 1962; J.D., M.A., Cornell, 1966; M Jud. Process, Univ. Va., 1991. Law clerk Judge E.T. Gignoux, Maine; atty. Verill & Dana, Maine; assoc. justice Maine Supreme Ct., Portland, 1993—. Bd. dir Legal Svcs. Corp., 1982, bd. dir., 1990—93; vice chmn. Just. Action Group; chmn. Ct. Alternative Dispute Resolution Conf.; co-chmn. JAG Self Representation Task Force; liason Maine Sup. Jud. Ct. to Lawyers Fund for Client Protection. Mem.: ABA (bd. gov. 2002—). Office: Maine Supreme Judicial Ct 142 Federal St PO Box 368 Portland ME 04112-0368*

DANA, LAUREN ELIZABETH, lawyer; b. Hollywood, Calif., Sept. 30, 1950; d. Franklin Eugene and Margaret Elizabeth (Nixon) D.; m. Andrew Russell Willing, May 25, 1986; 1 child, Matthew Barkan Willing. BA cum laude, Calif. State U., Northridge, 1973; JD cum laude, Southwestern U., 1982. Bar: Calif. 1982, U.S. Dist. Ct. (cen. dist.) Calif. 1983, U.S. Ct. Appeals (9th cir.) 1983, U.S. Supreme Ct. 1987. Assoc. Law Office Andrew R. Willing, L.A., 1982-84; dep. atty. gen. Calif. Dept. Justice-Atty. Gen., L.A., 1984—. Temporary judge L.A. Mcpl. Ct. Assoc. editor legal update Police Officer Law Report, 1986-87. Recipient Am. Jurisprudence Book award Lawyers Coop. Pub. Co., 1980, Am. Jurisprudence Book award in Evidence, 1980. Mem.: ABA, Los Angeles County Bar Assn. (conf. of dels. 1998—), L.A. World Affairs Coun., Women Lawyers Assn. L.A., U.S. Supreme Ct. Hist. Soc., Selden Soc., Constnl. Rights Found., Am. Judicature Soc., Alliance for Children's Rights, Women of Pasadena, The Da Camera Soc., Town Hall, Phi Alpha Delta. Avocations: reading, music, collecting books on english history, travel, french. Office: Calif Dept Justice 300 S Spring St Los Angeles CA 90013-1230

DANA-DAVIDSON, LAOMA COOK, English language educator; b. Herndon, W.Va., Nov. 23, 1925; d. Virgil A. and Latha (Shrewsbury) Cook; m. William J. Davidson, Apr. 1946 (div. 1971); 1 child, Deborah Davidson Bollom. BE, Marshall U., 1946; MA in Adminstrn., Azusa U., 1981. Cert. tchr., Calif. Tchr. Cajon Valley Union Sch. Dist., El Cajon, Calif., 1958—, San Diego Diocese. Master tchr. to 50 student tchrs. Author: Reading series used in dist., 1968. Former pres. El Cajon Rep. Women Federated; chaplin San Diego County Rep. Women; mem. El Cajon Hist. Assn.; v.p. Cajon Valley Union Sch. Bd.; active literacy program Rolling Readers; mem. Spa-Wars Edn. Com. for Navy Relocation; mem. Alcohol and Drug Prevention Task Force; recent candidate Calif. State Assembly; apptd. hon. chmn. reflectice com. promoting art, music, dance and phys. edn. PTA Coun., 2000. Recipient sabbatical to study British Schs. Cajon Valley Union Sch. Dist., 1977-78. Mem. AAUW (pres. 1964-66, edn. com. 1993-94, policy com., women's issuees com., Chris Lynn Downey rsch. and projects award 1996), League of Women Voters, Grossmont Concert Assn., La Mesa C. of C. (edn. rep. Cajon Valley Sch. Dist.), Delta Kappa Gamma, Phi Delta Kappa. Avocations: travel, writing, reading, tennis, theater. Office: 609 Ecken Rd El Cajon CA 92020-7312 Fax: (619) 447-4512.

DANAHAR, DAVID C., academic administrator, historian, educator; b. Dobbs Ferry, N.Y., Sept. 29, 1941; s. Walter Vincent and Catherine Marie (Charles) Danahar; m. Cecelia Upritchard, Aug. 24, 1985; children: Deirdre, Rebecca, Michael. BA, Manhattan Coll., Bronx, N.Y., 1963; MA, U. Mass., 1965, PhD, 1970. Instr. U. Mass., Amherst, 1969-70; asst. prof. SUNY, Oswego, 1970-73, assoc. prof., 1973-84, prof., 1984-85; dean Coll. Arts and Scis., prof. history Fairfield (Conn.) U., 1985-92; provost, acad. v.p. Loyola U., New Orleans, 1992-2001; pres. S.W. Minn. State U., 2001—. Vis. prof. U. Pisa, Italy, 1971—72. Contbr. articles to profl. jours. Mem. Fairfield 2000, 1983—88; bd. dirs. New Orleans Mus. Art, 1993—95; mem. Pres.'s Coun. NCAA II, 2005—. Grantee, SUNY Rsch. Found., 1971—73, NEH, 1983—88, others, 1985—; Univ. fellow, U. Mass., 1966—69, Rsch. fellow, Am. Coun. Learned Socs., 1975—76. Mem.: Am. Assn. Higher Edn., Conf. Ctrl. European History, Coun. Colls. Arts and Scis., Am. Conf. Acad. Deans, Am. Hist. Assn. Avocations: travel, sailing. Office: Southwest Minn State U 1501 State St Marshall MN 56258 Office Phone: 507-537-6272. Business E-Mail: danahar@southwestern.edu.

DANAHER, JAMES WILLIAM, retired federal agency administrator; b. St. Marys, Ohio, Feb. 20, 1929; s. William Louis and Cora Caroline (Hausfeld) D.; m. Ellen Serena Martin, Feb. 5, 1972; children— Patrick

Brendan, Kathryn Annette BS in Econs., Villanova U., 1952; MA in Psychology, Ohio State U., 1958; grad., Fed. Execs. Inst., 1978; Indsl. fellow, Linacre Coll./Oxford U., 2000. Lic. comml. pilot. Rsch. assoc. Courtney & Co., Phila., 1958-62; v.p., rsch. scientist Matrix Rsch. Corp., Arlington, Va., 1962-70; chief human factors divsn. Nat. Transp. Safety Bd., Washington, 1970-76, from chief operational factors divsn. to dir. bur. techn., 1976-85, chief operational factors and human performance divsn., 1985-98; ret., 1998. Aviation safety cons., 1998—; mem. four study coms. for Nat. Rsch. Coun., Nat. Acad. of Scis., 1994—. Contbr. articles to profl. jours. Bd. dirs. Alexandria Soccer Assn., Va., 1983-86; v.p. Charles Barrett Sch. PTA, Alexandria, 1983-84. Capt. USNR, 1952-76. Mem. Human Factors and Ergonomics Soc., Internat. Soc. Air Safety Investigators, Naval Res. Assn. (life), K.C. Roman Catholic. Avocations: long distance running, skiing, golf. Home: 717 S Overlook Dr Alexandria VA 22305-1215 E-mail: jwdanaher@aol.com.

DANAHER, JOHN ANTHONY, III, prosecutor; b. New Haven, Conn., Aug. 22, 1950; s. John Anthony Jr. and Grace Elizabeth (Burkett) D.; m. Anne Elizabeth Morrison, May 11, 1985; children: Ceara Morrison Danaher, Brendan Ahearn, Austin Spellman, Mary Kate Shea. Awd, Fairfield U., 1972; MA, U. Hartford, 1977; JD, U. Conn., 1980. Bar: Conn. 1980; U.S. Dist. Ct. Conn. 1980; U.S. Ct. Appeals (2d cir.) 1982; U.S. Supreme Ct. 1987. Law clk. to hon. judge T. Emmet Clarie U.S. Dist. Ct. Conn., Hartford, Conn., 1980-81; trial atty. Day, Berry & Howard, Hartford, Conn., 1981-86; prosecutor U.S. Atty.'s Office, Hartford, Conn., 1986—; former U.S. atty. U.S. Atty.'s Office Ct. Dist. Editor Conn. Law Rev. 1978-80. Mem. Red Cross blood svcs. com., Hartford, 1981-85; active Conn. Rivers Coun., Boy Scouts Am., 1994—. Recipient Disting. Svc. award Atty. Gen. of U.S., Washington, 1990; 14 Superior Achievement awards Dept. of Justice, Hartford, 1988, 90-2000. Mem. Fed. Bar Assn. (pres. Hartford County chpt. 1985-86). Office: US Attys Office Ct Fin Ctr 157 Church St PO Box 1824 New Haven CT 06508

DANAHER, MALLORY MILLETT (MALLORY JONES), actress, photographer, film producer, theater producer; b. St. Paul, 1939; d. James Albert and Helen Rose (Feely) Millett m. Thomas C. Danaher, Mar. 1985; 1 child by previous marriage, Kristen Vigard. BA, U. Minn. CFO Sheets & Co., N.Y.C., Happy Camper, N.Y.C., Everwarm, Inc., Mallory Inc. Actress: original cos. of Annie, The Best Little Whorehouse in Texas; stage roles: Dodsworth, Berkshire Theatre Festival; House of Blue Leaves; Hedda Gabler; Kennedy's Children (dir. Olympia Dukakis); Edward Albee's Everything in the Garden (dir. Shelley Winters); Lincoln Ctr. Libr. Theatre; Stella; Cocteau's one-character play The Human Voice at Deutsches-Haus, NYU; Full Moon and High Tide; (off-Broadway prodn.) Loose Connections, Judith Anderson Theatre; actor: (TV series) Love of Life, Another World, Hunter, Thirtysomething, Superior Court, Divorce Court, The Judge, Eischied: Only the Pretty Girls Die (NBC Movie of the Week); (films) Tootsie, Hell Hath No Fury with Barbara Eden, Alone in the Dark; exhibitions include Third Eye Gallery, NYC, Modernage Discovery Gallery, Gallery of St. Clement's; author: Fatherless Child, numerous poems; co-prodr.: (films) Three Lives; prodr.: (Broadway plays) Epic Proportions; exec. prodr., lead actress: Deleting Spam. Active Creative Coalition, NY Theatre. Mem.: Ctr. for Study of Popular Culture (bd. dirs.), Am. Women's Econ. Devel., Nat. Assn. for Self-Employed, Women in Theatre, Legatus, The Actors Studio (chmn. auditions), The Friars Club.

DANAS, ANDREW MICHAEL, lawyer; b. Redwood City, Calif., Apr. 25, 1955; s. Michael George and Marjorie Jean (Bailey) D.; m. Barbara C. Matthews. BA in Polit. Sci. and History, U. Conn., 1977; JD, George Washington U., 1982. Bar: DC 1982, US Dist. Ct. (DC cir.) 1983, US Dist. Ct. Md. 1987, US Ct. Appeals (Fed. cir.) 1984, US Ct. Appeals (11th cir.) 1987, US Ct. Appeals (3d and 4th cirs.) 1988, US Ct. Appeals (6th cir.) 1990, US Ct. Appeals (2d cir.) 1998, US Ct. of Claims 1984, US Supreme Ct. 1994, US Ct. of Internat. Trade 2003. Atty. Assn. Am. R.R., Washington, 1983-84; assoc. Grove Jaskiewicz & Cobert, Washington, 1984-90, Ptnr., 1991—. Contbg. author: Freewheeling; author legal column Intermodal Reporter, 1986-94; contbr. articles to profl. jour. Exec. com. Friends Assisting the Nat. Symphony, Washington, 1996-97. Mem.: ABA, Transp. Lawyers Assn. (chmn. legis. com. 1995—98, co-chmn. 1999—2001, co-chmn. antitrust com. 2003—, Disting. Svc. award 1996), Transp. Law Inst. (chair 1993—94), Euro-Am. Lawyers Group (mgmt. com. 2000—, sec. 2002—), Internat. Bar Assn., Mensa, Univ. Club (Washington) (mem. internat. com.), Phi Alpha Theta. Avocations: skiing, music, travel. Home: 621 Tivoli Psge Alexandria VA 22314-1932 Office: Grove Jaskiewicz and Cobert 1730 M St NW Ste 400 Washington DC 20036-4579 Office Phone: 202-296-2900 x219. Business E-Mail: adanas@gjcobert.com.

DANBY, F. WILLIAM, dermatologist, educator; s. Charles W.E. and M. Lucy (Bunny) Danby; m. Lynette Joan Margesson, June 26, 1975; children: Dawn Lynette, Claire Somerset. MD, Queen's U., Kingston, Ont., Can., 1967. Diplomate Am. Bd. Dermatology. Intern Vancouver Gen. Hosp., Canada, 1967—68; resident St. Francis Hosp., Honolulu, 1969, Kingston Gen. And Hotel Dieu Hosp., Kingston, Canada, 1969—70, U. Toronto Hosp., 1970—73; asst. prof., chair divsn. dermatology Queen's U., Kingston, 1978—97; lectr. Dartmouth Med. Sch., Hanover, NH, 1999—. Contbr. articles to profl. jours. Exec. com. N.H. Physicians Orgn., Manchester, 2004. Fellow: Royal Coll. Physicians and Surgeons Can.; mem.: Can. Dermatology Assn. (sec.-treas. 1987—92, pres. 1996—97), Am. Acad. Dermatology. Independent. Achievements include research in linking dairy consumption to acne. Avocations: skiing, shooting. Office: FWD MD and LJM MD Pa 721 Chestnut St Manchester NH 03104-3002 Office Phone: 603-668-0858.

D'ANCA, JOHN ARTHUR, psychotherapist, educator; b. Chgo., Apr. 19, 1950; s. John Joseph and Josephine Rose (Bartolotta) D.; m. Carol Amendola; 1 son, Matthew John; stepdaughters, Ingrid, Heidi. BA, DePaul U., 1972; MA, Governors State U., 1975; CAS, No. Ill. U., 1978, EdD, 1982; PsyD, Chgo. Sch. Profl. Psychology, 1996; studied, Harvard U., 1994-95. Cert. eye movement desensitization and reprocessing; lic. clinician, Ill. Mem. counseling faculty Fenwick H.S., Oak Park, Ill., 1973-75; instr. psychology, counselor Triton Coll., River Grove, Ill., 1975-78; assoc. dir. Ball Found., Glen Ellyn, Ill., 1978-79; prof. student devel. Oakton Coll., Des Plaines, Ill., 1979—; pvt. practice psychology Park Ridge, Ill., 1975—. Extern John J. Madden Mental Health Ctr., Dept. of Psychiatry Chgo. Osteo. Hosp.; intern in psychology svc. Edward Hines Jr. VA Hosp., Hines, Ill., 1990—; mem. staff Bayside Clinic, Kenosha, Wis., 1993-97, mem. staff, psychiat. svcs., 1998—; cons. Molex Internat., 1986; lectr. in field; cons. Ill. Dept. Edn., Am. Med. Technologists, Goodwill Industries Internat.; cons., expert witness Ill. Dept. Profl. Regulation. Contbr. articles to profl. jours. Bd. dirs. Chgo. Bd. of Mental Health, Northwest, 1974-75; mem. Oakton Coll. Crusade of Mercy Appeal, 1982; eucharistic min. Roman Cath. Ch. Sears grantee, 1986—; recipient NISOD award for Coll. Tchg. Excellence, U. Tex., Austin, 2003. Mem. NEA, APA, Internat. Soc. Traumatic Stress Studies (presenter 1996), Ill. Edn. Assn., Am. Soc. Clin. Hypnosis, Soc. Clin. and Experimental Hypnosis, Joint Civic Commn. Italian Americans, Midwest Psychol. Assn., N.Am. Assn. Adlerian Psychology, Ill. Guidance and Pers. Assn., Ill. Coll. Pers. Assn., Phi Delta Kappa. Home: 935 Evergreen Way Highland Park IL 60035-3739 Office: 1600 E Golf Rd Des Plaines IL 60016-1234 E-mail: johnd@oakton.edu.

DANCE, FRANCIS ESBURN XAVIER, communications educator; b. Bklyn., Nov. 9, 1929; s. Clifton Louis and Catherine (Tester) D.; m. Nora Alice Rush, May 1, 1954 (div. 1974); children: Clifton Louis III, Charles Daniel, Alison Catherine, Andrea Frances, Frances Sue, Brendan Rush; m. Carol Camille Zak, July 4, 1974; children: Zachary Esburn, Gabriel Joseph, Caleb Michael, Catherine Emily BS, Fordham U., 1951; MS, Northwestern U., 1953, PhD, 1959. Instr. speech Bklyn. Adult Labor Schs., 1951; instr. humanities, coord. radio and TV U. Ill. at Chgo., 1953—54; instr. Univ. Coll. U. Chgo., 1958; asst. prof. St. Joseph's (Ind.) Coll., Ind., 1958—60; asst. prof., then assoc. prof. U. Kans., 1960—63; mem. faculty U. Wis., Milw., 1963—71, prof. comm., 1965—71, dir. Speech Comm. Ctr., 1963—70; prof. U. Denver, 1971—, John Evans prof., 1995—; prof. homiletics St. John Vianney Theol. Sem., 2002—. Content expert and mem. faculty adv. bd. to Internat. U. on Knowledge Channel, 1993-95; cons. in field. Author: The Citizen Speaks, 1962, (with Harold P. Zelko) Business and Professional Speech Communication, 1965, 2d edit., 1978, Human Communication Theory, 1967, (with Carl E. Larson) Perspectives on Communication, 1970, Speech Communication: Concepts and Behavior, 1972, The Functions of Speech Communication: A Theoretical Approach, 1976, Human Communication Theory, 1982, (with Carol C. Zak-Dance) Public Speaking, 1986, Speaking Your Mind, 1994, 2d edit., 1996; editor Jour. Comm., 1962-64, Speech Tchr., 1970-72; adv. bd. Jour. Black Studies; editl. bd. Jour. Psycholinguistic Rsch; contbr. articles to profl. jours. Bd. dirs. Milw. Mental Health Assn., 1966-67. 2d lt. AUS, 1954-56. Knapp Univ. scholar in comm., 1967-68; recipient Outstanding Prof. award Std. Oil Found., 1967; Master Tchr. award U. Denver, 1985, Univ. Lectr. award U. Denver, 1986. Fellow Internat. Comm. Assn. (pres. 1967); mem. Nat. Comm. Assn. (pres. 1982), Psi Upsilon. Office: U Denver Dept Human Comm Studies Denver CO 80208-0001 *Life should include a personal commitment to excellence with a corresponding humane tolerance for failure in self or in others. A belief in the progressive acquisition of autonomy can help guide both personal and professional decisions.*

DANCER, MARK RICHARD, lawyer; b. Toledo, Nov. 18, 1960; s. Richard E. Dancer and Mary Jane Strausser; m. Teresa Catherine Craft, Oct. 7, 1989; children: Rebecca, Jessica. BA, U. Colo., 1983; JD, Ohio State U., 1986. Bar: Calif. 1987, Mich. 1993, U.S. Dist. Ct. (ea. and we. dists.) Mich. 1994, U.S. Ct. Appeals (6th cir.) 1994, U.S. Ct. Appeals (fed. cir.) 1998. Assoc. McClutchon, Black et al, L.A., 1987-89, McClintock, Weston et al, L.A., 1989-91, Hill, Wynne, Troop et al, L.A., 1991-93; ptnr. Dingeman, Dancer & Christopherson, P.L.C., Traverse City, Mich., 1993—. Former arbitrator Am. Arbitration Assn., Southfield, Mich., 1994; mediator 13th Jud. Cir., Traverse City, 1993, 46th Jud. Cir., Gaylord, Mich., 1996, 19th Jud. Cir., Manistee, 1997, 33rd/57th Jud. Cirs., Charlevoix/Emmet, 1997, U.S. Dist. Ct., Grand Rapids, 1997. Mem. ABA, ATLA, State Bar Calif., State Bar Mich., Mich. Trial Lawyers Assn., Grand Traverse-Antrim-Leelanau Bar Assn., Phi Beta Kappa. Office: Dingeman Dancer & Christopherson PLC 100 Park St Traverse City MI 49684

DANCEWICZ, JOHN EDWARD, investment banker; b. Boston, Mass., Feb. 12, 1949; s. John Felix and Teresa Sophia (Lewandowski) D.; m. Barbaragail Jarrett, Jan. 23, 1971; children: John Lawrence, Jill Elizabeth, Jenna Gail. BA in Econs., Yale U., 1971; MBA, Harvard U., 1973. Project adminstr. fin., cons. Nat. Shawmut Bank Boston, 1972-73; v.p., founder, mgr. U.S. investment banking Continental Ill. Nat. Bank Chgo., 1973-82; sr. mng. dir., mgr. corp. fin. Bear Stearns & Co. Inc., Chgo., 1982-96; founder, mng. ptnr. DN Ptnrs. LLP, DN Ptnrs. LP and DN Ptnrs. LP II, 1996—. Chmn. bd. dirs. Ctrl. Can Co., Inc., FCL Graphics, Inc., Aztec Outdoor Advt. Co.; adv. dir. PPI, Inc., Crysteel, Inc.; dir. Primco-Greenleaf LLC, Country Pure Foods, Inc. Contbr. articles to profl. jours. Active schs. com., Yale U., spl. gifts com., chmn. 25th reunion fundraising, sec. class 1971; sec. Harvard Bus. Sch. sect.; mem. spl. gifts com. Harvard Bus. Sch. Found. Recipient Pres.'s award, Yale Alumni Assn. Mem. Scholarship and Guidance Assn. (bd. dirs., v.p. 1982—), Lake Forest H.S. Ice Hockey Assn. (pres.), Harvard Bus. Sch. Club Chgo., Econ. Club, Univ. Club, East Bank Club, Mid-Am. Club. Home: 969 Spring Ln Lake Forest IL 60045-2302 Office: 77 W Wacker Dr Ste 4550 Chicago IL 60601 Office Phone: 312-332-7960. Business E-Mail: info@dupartners.com.

DANCEY, CHARLES LOHMAN, retired newspaper executive; b. Pekin, Ill., Nov. 28, 1916; s. Albert Duane and Bertha (Lohman) D.; m. Nina Evelyn Manker, Dec. 10, 1944; children: Richard, Burt Lee, Clinton Dancey. BS, U. Ill., 1938. Reporter Peoria (Ill.) Star, 1938-40, Peoria Jour., 1946-50; editor Peoria Jour. Star, 1958-80, asst. pub., 1980-87, cons., 1987-96, dir., 1993-96; dir., exec. bd. Dirksen Congrl. Rsch. Ctr., 1994-99, ret., 1999. Owner rep., mgmt. bd. WTVH-TV, Peoria, 1956-58 Ill. state comdt. Marine Corps League, 1947; City councilman, commr. fire and plice, Pekin, 1946-50. Col. USMCR, 1941-46, 50-51. Recipient Peoria chpt. B'nai B'rith Citizenship award, 1964 Mem. Inter-Am. Press Assn. (dir., exec. bd.), Am. Soc. Newspaper Editors. Clubs: Mason. Home: 419 Haines Ave Pekin IL 61554-4229 E-mail: china@dpc.net.

DANCO, LÉON ANTOINE, management consultant, educator; b. NYC, May 30, 1923; s. Léon A. and Alvira T. (Gomez) D.; m. Katharine Elizabeth Leck, Aug. 25, 1951; children: Suzanne, Walter Ten Eyck. AB, Harvard, 1943, MBA, 1947; PhD, Case Western Res. U., 1963. Asst. to divsn. pres. Interchem. Corp., N.Y.C., 1947-50; sales promotion mgr. Risdon Mfg. Co., Waterbury, Conn., 1950-55; mgmt. cons. Cheshire, Conn., 1955-57; prof., assoc. dir. mgmt. program Case Inst. Tech., Cleve., 1957-58, lectr., 1959—; mgmt. cons. L.A. Danco & Co., 1957—; lectr. John Carroll U., Cleve., 1959-66, prof., dir. mgmt. confs., 1966—. Vis. prof. econs. Cleve. Inst. Art, 1966-69, Kent State U., 1966-67; exec. dir. Univ. Svcs. Inst., Cleve., 1967-69, pres., 1969—, chmn., 1989—; pub. The Family in Business (newsletter), 1978—; pres. Center for Family Bus., 1978—, chmn. Ctr.for Family Bus., 1991. Author: Beyond Survival-A Business Owners Guide for Success, 1975, Inside the Successful Family Business, 1979, Outside Directors in the Family Owned Business, 1981, Someday It'll All Be...Whose?, 1990; (in French) L'Entreprise Familiale, 1998; (in Spanish) La Empresa Familiare, 1998; syndicated columnist: It's Your Business, 1973—. Lt. (j.g.) USCG, 1942-46, PTO. Mem. Am. Econ. Assn. Home: 32000 Fairmount Blvd Pepper Pike Cleveland OH 44124 Office: Ctr for Family Bus PO Box 24219 Cleveland OH 44124-0219 Office Phone: 440-460-3377. Personal E-mail: grummi@aol.com. *Whatever success we may achieve in this life will come from the purpose to which we put God's priceless gift of time.*

DANDASHI, S. ALEXANDER-LEVI, research scientist, government and business advisor; b. July 20, 1959; came to U.S., 1982; naturalized, 1989; 1 child, Leonard Levi. BSCE, George Washington U., 1987, Applied Scientist in Gen. Ops. Rsch., 1992; MSME in Aeronautics, Astronautics and Rocket Propulsion, George Washington U. & NASA, 1989; MSc in Math., Oxford (Eng.) U., 1994. Designer-analyst, design div. George Washington U., Washington, 1985-89, head design div., 1989-91, doctoral fellow, 1992-93, applied scientist, sci. rsch. assoc., 1992-93; vice chmn. FANEX Australia Pty. Ltd., Brisbane, Australia, 1995-96, Japan, 1996-97, 1997-98, dir. Brisbane, 1994-98; pres., CEO Lynk Internat. Group, N.Y.C., Beverly Hills, Paris, 2000—. Co-founder, dir. ICQA Pty. Ltd., Brisbane, Australia, 1995-98, pres., CEO, 1995-96, dir. mktg. and client rels. in Japan, 1996-97; vis. scientist Kyoto (Japan) U., 1996-97; advisor external, polit. rels. Establishment Le Jour. du Parlement, France, 1999-2002, bus. devel., pub. rels. BDA Comm., France, 2000—, advisor for Le Comité de Miss France, Paris, 2000-2002; mem. bd. dirs. FANEX Party Ltd., ICQA Party Ltd., FANEX USA, Inc., 1994-2000. Mem. AAAS, AIAA (sr.), Ops. Rsch. Soc. Am., Inst. Mgmt. Sci., Fedn. Am. Scientists, Am. Jewish Hist. Soc., Oxford Soc., N.Y. Acd. Sci., Masons, Sigma Xi, Omega Rho (v.p. 1993-94), Sigma Gamma Tau. Office: Ste 15 G 20 River Rd New York NY 10044 Office Phone: 212-750-3772, 310-801-8585. Office Fax: 212-750-3990.

DANDEKAR, SWATI, state representative; b. Mar. 1951; arrived in US, 1973; m. Arvind Dandekar; children: Ajai, Govind. BS in Chem. & Biology, Nagpur (India) U., 1971; postgrad. diploma in Dietetics, Bombay U., 1972. Mem. Iowa Ho. Reps., DesMoines, 2003—, mem. appropriations com., mem. econ. growth com., mem. edn. com. Active Linn-Mar Cmty. Sch. Dist. Bd. Edn., 1996—, Vision Iowa Bd., 2000—; bd. dir. Iowa Assn. Sch. Bds., 2000—; bd. dirs. Liars Holographic Radio Theatre, 2001—. Recipient JC Penney Edu. Golden Rule award, 2000. Mem.: Jr. League Cedar Rapids (pres. sustainers, chair diversity com.). Office: State Capitol East 12th and Grand Des Moines IA 50319 Office Phone: 515-281-3221. E-mail: swati.dandekar@legis.state.ia.us.*

DANDO, WILLIAM ARTHUR, academic administrator, geography and geology educator; b. Newell, Pa., June 13, 1934; s. Carl Frederick and Myrtle Jane (Foster) D.; m. Caroline Zaporowsky, July 19, 1958; children: Christina Elizabeth, Lara Margaret, William Arthur II. BS, Calif. U. Pa., 1959; MA, U. Minn., 1962, PhD, 1969. Vis. instr. U. Manitoba, Winnepeg, Can., 1961; instr. U. Md., College Park, 1965-66, lectr., 1967-69, asst. prof., 1970-75; assoc. prof. U. N.D., Grand Forks, 1975-80, prof., 1980-89, chair geography, 1977-82; prof. Ind. State U., Terre Haute, 1989—2002, chair geography, geology and anthropology, 1989—2002, dir. Sr. Scholar Acad., 2002—. Prin. investigator NSF Meteorology-Climatology Project, 1985-92, NIH Multiple Sclerosis Project, 1988-91, NSF Phys. Geography Inst., 1992-96, Dept. Edn. Project GEO, 1992-97, Geo-Technology-GIS Project, 1995-2000. Author: Introduction to Maryland, 1970, The Geography of Famine, 1980, Food and Famine, A Reference, 1991, Russia and the Independent Nations of the Former USSR: Geofacts and Maps, 1995; editor: Innovations in Land Use Management, 1977, World Hunger and Famine, 1995, Russia, 2003; author numerous articles and revs. Pres. Univ. Luth. Ch., Grand Forks, 1979, Christus Rex Luth. Campus Ministry, 1979-87, N.D. Luth. Campus Ministry Com. 1986-88; chairperson fin. com. Trinity Luth. Ch., Terre Haute, 1992-97, v.p., 1996-97. Recipient Disting. Tchg. Achievement award Nat. Coun. for Geographic Edn., 1986, 98, Burlington Northern Found. Faculty Achievement award, 1988, Illustrious Alumni Calif. State U. award, 1976, Ind. State U. Pres. award, 1997, Ind. State U. Disting. Prof. award, 2000. Mem. Assn. Am. Geography (chair Mid. Atlantic divsn. 1973-74, chair Great Plains-Rocky Mt. divsn. 1978-80, chair West Lakes divsn. 1994-95, regional councillor 1997-2000, West Lakes divsn. Disting. Svc. award 2002), Nat. Coun. for Geog. Edn. (annual meeting chair 1998), Assn. N.D. Geographers (pres. 1976-80), Geography Educators Network Ind. (dir. devel. 1991-2000), Sigma Xi (U. N.D. chpt. pres. 1986-87, Ind. State U. chpt. v.p. 1991-92, pres. 1992-93, Individual Excellence in Scientific Rsch. award 1983). Lutheran. Avocations: trout fishing, hiking, automobile restoration. Home: 7785 S Carlisle Rd Terre Haute IN 47802-9343 Office: Ind State U Sr Scholar Acad Terre Haute IN 47809-0001

D'ANDREA, VINCENT CHARLES, postal clerk; b. Newport, RI, Apr. 9, 1958; s. John Raymond and Ruth Rosabel D'Andrea. A, Cameron U., 1981; B, Salve Regina U., 1990. With mil. police U.S. Army, 1977—86, R.I. N.G., 1986—94; with U.S. Post Office, Providence, 1995—. Sgt. U.S. Army, 1977—86. Recipient S.W. Asian Campaign medal, U.S. Army, 1991, Kuwait Liberation medal, 1991. Mem.: NRA, TREA, VFW, Am. Postal Workers Union, Labor Notes, AmVets, Planetary Soc., Elks, Am. Legion. Republican. Roman Catholic. Avocations: coin collecting/numismatics, sports memorabilia, autograph collecting. Home: 2 Elliott Pl Newport RI 02840-1804 Office: US Post Office 24 Corliss St Providence RI 02904

DANDRIDGE, LENOR, paralegal; d. LeRoy and Lucille Dandridge; 1 child, LaMont Warren. Student, Malcolm X Coll., 1976—79, Roosevelt U., 1979—83, Harold Washington Coll., 2002—. Owner Dandridge Tutoring and Mentoring, Chgo., 1998—. Author: (children's coloring book) Color N History, 1992, poetry. Cons., vol. Home-Along-With Home, Chgo., 1987—; tutor, mentor YMCA, Chgo., 1998, Hull House, Chgo., 2002; vol., asst. Play and Learn Daycare, Burham, Ill., 1999—; respite worker Ada S. McKinley, Chgo., 2002; vol. Lincoln Park Zoo, Chgo., 2003. Avocations: writing, bowling, modern jazz dancing, exercising. Home and Office: Dandridge Tutoring and Mentoring Svcs 2309 E 79th St #205 Chicago IL 60649-5015

DANE, JEFIC, internist; b. Zenica, Bosnia-Herzegovina, May 11, 1972; s. Dimitrije and Jelena Jefic; m. Dijana Bozic, Oct. 2, 1997. MD, U. Novi Sad Med. Sch., Novi Sad, Serbia, 1997. Cert. ECFMG Ednl. Commn. for Fgn. Med. Graduates, 2000, diplomate Internal Medicine Am. Bd. of Internal Medicine, 2004. Internal medicine resident St John Hosp. and Med. Ctr., Detroit, 2001—04, chief med. resident, 2004—. Recipient Dawson Award for Med. rsch., South-East Mich. Ctr. for Med. Edn., 2004. Mem.: ACP (assoc.). Office: St John Hosp and Med Ctr Divsn Cardiology 22151 Moross Rd STe 126 Detroit MI 48236 Office Phone: 313-343-4612. Office Fax: 313-343-7784.

DANE, STEPHEN MARK, lawyer; b. Chillicothe, Ohio, Mar. 27, 1956; s. Clyde and Rita M. (Murray) D.; m. Kim P. Piatt, July 7, 1979; children: Tara, Adam, Shannon, Alexandra, Courtney. BS with honors, U. Notre Dame, 1978; JD magna cum laude, U. Toledo, 1981. Bar: Ohio 1981, U.S. Ct. Appeals (6th and 10th cirs.) 1982, U.S. Dist. Ct. (no. dist.) Ohio 1983, U.S. Dist. Ct. (no. dist.) Tex. 1983, U.S. Ct. Appeals (5th cir.) 1984, U.S. Supreme Ct. 1985, U.S. Ct. Appeals (7th cir.) 1993. Law clk. U.S. Ct. Appeals (6th cir.), Cin., 1981-82; ptnr. Cooper & Walinski, Toledo, 1986—2004; atty. Relman & Assoc., Washington, 2005—. Judge pro tempore Perrysburg Mcpl. Ct., 1990—. Recipient Fair Housing award HUD, 1996, Spirit of Wood County award, 1988, Pub. Interest Law award Equal Access to Justice Com., 2000, Fair Housing award Oho Civil Rights Commn. 2001; named Lawyer of Yr. Lawyers Weekly, 1998; named to St. John's Jesuit H.S. Hall of Fame, 1991. Mem. ABA, Ohio State Bar Assn., Toledo Bar Assn. (chmn. fed. ct. com. 1987-89, trustee 2001--), Wood County Bar Assn. Roman Catholic. Home: 501 Hickory St Perrysburg OH 43551-2206 Office: Relman & Assoc 1225 19th St NW Washington DC 20036-2456 Office Phone: 202-728-1888. Business E-Mail: sdane@relmanlaw.com.

DANES, CLAIRE, actress; b. NYC, Apr. 12, 1979; d. Chris and Carla Danes. Attended, Lee Strasberg Theater Inst., Yale U., 1998—2002. TV role as Angela Chase in series My So-Called Life, ABC, 1994-95 (nominee Emmy award for Best Lead in Drama Series 1995, Golden Globe award for Best Actress ina Drama 1995); appeared in HBO spl. More Than Friends: The Coming Out of Heidi Leiter, 1994; guest appearances on TV series Law and Order, 1990; film appearances include: Dreams of Love, 1992, 30, 1993, Little Women, 1994, Dead Man's Jack, 1994, How to Make an American Quilt, 1995, Home for the Holidays, 1995, The Pesky Suitor, 1995, I Love You, I love You Not 1996, To Gillian on Her 37th Birthday, 1996, as Juliet in William Shakespeare's Romeo and Juliet, 1996, Mononoke-hime (voive only), 1997, U-Turn, 1997, The Rainmaker, 1997, Les Misérables, 1998, Polish Wedding, 1998, The Mod Squad, 1998, Brokedown Palace, 1999, Hercules (voice only), 1998, Igby Goes Down, 2002, The Hours, 2002, It's All About Love, 2003, Terminator 3: Rise of the Machines, 2003, The Rage in Placid Lake, 2003, Stage Beauty, 2004, Shopgirl, 2005; NYC Theatre appearences include Christina Olson: American Model, 2005. Named one of 50 most beautiful people in the world, People mag., 1997.

DANFORD, MARY ANN WENTWORTH, elementary school educator; b. Montgomery, Ala., Sept. 25, 1973; d. Ruby Lyn and Wiley Lewis Wentworth; m. Phillip Allen Danford, Feb. 15, 1997; 1 child, Audrey Dianne. M in elem. edn., Ala. State U., 1996—98; BS in elem. edn., Troy State U., 1993—95; AA, Lurleen B. Wallce C.C., 1991—93. Cert. Master Level in Adminstrn. & Supervision 2005. Fourth grade tchr. W. O. Parmer Elem. Sch., Greenville, Ala., 1995—96, second grade tchr., 1996—99; first grade tchr. East Three Notch Elem. Sch., Andalusia, Ala., 1999—2000; Ala. reading initiative reading coach Andalusia Elem. Sch., Ala., 2000—. Consulting Ala. Reading Initiative, 2001—05. Bd. mem. Wiregrass Writing Project, Troy, Ala., 2004—05. Mem.: Internat. Reading Assn. R-Consevative. Southern Baptist. Office: Andalusia Elementary Sch 1501 West ByPass Andalusia AL 36420 Office Phone: 334-222-1224. E-mail: danfordm@andalusia.k12.al.us.

DANFORTH, ARTHUR EDWARDS, finance executive; b. Cleve., Jan. 23, 1925; s. Arthur Edwards and Jane (Hillyard) D.; m. Elizabeth Wagley, Mar. 17, 1956; children: Hillyard Raible, Nicholas Edwards (dec.), Jonathan Ingersoll, Elizabeth Wagley, Michael Stowe. BA, Yale U., 1948. With Hayden Miller Co., Cleve., 1949-54, First Nat. City Bank (predecessor to Citibank N.A.), N.Y.C., 1954-63, asst. mgr. Buenos Aires office, 1959-61; treas. Bunge Corp., N.Y.C., 1963-65; sr. v.p., treas. Colonial Bank & Trust Co., Waterbury, Conn., 1965-70; chmn., CEO Farmers Bank of Del., Wilmington, 1970-76; prin. Danforthgroup, New Canaan, Conn., 1976-98; ret., 1998. Past bd. dirs. United Way of Del., Boys Club of Wilmington, Grand Opera House Inc. of Del., NCCJ, Audubon Soc. Conn., Greater Wilmington Devel. Coun. Ensign USNR, 1943-46. Mem.: Quail Valley Golf Club (Vero Beach, Fla.), Yale Club (N.Y.C.), Nantucket Yacht Club, Sankaty Head Golf Club.

DANFORTH, DAVID NEWTON, JR., surgeon, oncologist; b. N.Y.C., June 25, 1942; s. David Newton and Gladys Margaret (Blaine) D.; m. Anne Walker Nickson, Apr. 13, 1985; 1 child, Laura. BA, Northwestern U., Evanston, Ill., 1965; MD, Northwestern U., Chgo., 1971; MS, U. N.Mex., Albuquerque, 1967. Diplomate Am. Bd. Surgery. Intern, then resident Cornell Med. Ctr., N.Y.C., 1971-74, 77-79; clin. assoc. NIH, Bethesda, Md., 1974-77; surg. fellow M.D. Anderson Hosp., Houston, 1979-80; sr. staff fellow NIH, Bethesda, 1980-82; sr. investigator Nat. Cancer Inst., NIH, Bethesda, 1982—. Editor: Diagnosis and Management of Breast Cancer, 1988; contbr. articles to profl. jours. Served to lt. comdr. USPHS, 1974-76. Fellow Am. Cancer Soc., 1979-80. Fellow ACS, Soc. Surg. Oncology, Am. Soc. Clin. Oncology, Am. Assn. Cancer Rsch., Endocrine Soc. Republican. Episcopalian. Avocations: travel, sports, reading. Home: 7301 Meadow Ln Chevy Chase MD 20815-5009 Office: Nat Cancer Inst Surgery Br Bldg 10 Rm 2B38 Bethesda MD 20892 Business E-Mail: David_Danforth@nih.gov.

DANFORTH, ELLIOT, JR., medical educator; b. Bainbridge, N.Y., Oct. 21, 1933; s. Elliot and Ellen (Roberts) D.; m. Joan C. Garrett, Dec. 26, 1959; children: Kimberly H., Noel, Peter E. AB, Dartmouth Coll., 1956; MS, Ohio State U., 1958; MD, Albany (N.Y.) Med. Coll., 1962. Resident Dartmouth Affliated Hosps., Hanover, N.H., 1962-65; instr. Dartmouth Med. Sch., Hanover, 1965-66; rsch. internist Walter Reed Army Inst. Rsch., Washington, 1966-70; asst. prof. U. Vt. Coll. Medicine, Burlington, 1970-74, assoc. prof., 1974-79, prof., 1979-94, prof. emeritus, 1993—, dir. clin. rsch. ctr., 1980-93, chief divsn. endocrinology, metabolism and nutrition, 1990-93; dir. Sims Obesity/Nutrition Rsch. Ctr., 1992-93; exec. dir. cardiovasc. metabolic rsch. Lederle Labs., Am. Cyanamid Co., 1993-95; med. cons. to pharm. industry, 1996—; pres., CEO Beartown Pharma, Underhill, Vt., 1998—. Cons. Walter Reed Gen. Hosp. Mem. editl. bd. J. Clin. Endocrinology and Metabolism, Jour. Gerontology, Obesity Rsch., Jour. Gerontology: Biol. Scis.; contbr. articles to profl. jours. Served to cpt. U.S. Army, 1966-68. NIH grantee, Washington, 1970-94. Mem. AAAS, Endocrine Soc., Am. Diabetes Assn., Am. Thyroid Assn., Am. Fedn. Clin. Rsch., Soc. Exptl. Biology and Medicine (mem. editl. bd. procs., coun. mem.), Internat. Assn. for Study of Obesity, N.Y. Acad. Scis., N.Am. Assn. Study Obesity. Avocations: travel, farming, fishing. Home and Office: 84 Beartown Rd Underhill VT 05489-9365 Office Phone: 802-899-2349. Personal E-mail: edanforth@adelphia.net.

DANFORTH, JOHN CLAGGETT, lawyer, former ambassador, former senator; b. St. Louis, Sept. 5, 1936; s. Donald and Dorothy (Claggett) D.; m. Sally B. Dobson, Sept. 7, 1957; children: Eleanor, Mary, Dorothy, Johanna, Thomas. BA with honors, Princeton U., 1958; BD, LLB, Yale U., 1963, MA (hon.); LHD (hon.), Lindenwood Coll., 1970, Ind. Central U.; LLD (hon.), Drury Coll., 1970, Maryville Coll., Rockhurst Coll., Westminster Coll., Culver-Stockton Coll., St. Louis U.; DD (hon.), Lewis and Clark Coll.; HHD (hon.), William Jewell Coll.; STD (hon.), Southwest Bapt. Coll.; hon. deg., Va. Theol. Sem., 1990, Holy Cross Coll., 1992, Harris Stowe Coll., 1992, Wash. U., 1995, U. Mo., 1995. Bar: NY 1963, Mo. 1966, DC 1994. With firm Davis Polk Wardwell Sunderland & Kiendl, NYC, 1964-66; ptnr. Bryan, Cave, McPheeters and McRoberts (now Bryan Cave LLP), St. Louis, 1966—68, 1995—2004, 2005—; atty. gen. State of Mo., 1969-76; US senator from Mo., 1976-94; spl. presidential envoy to Sudan Khartoum, 2001—02; permanent US rep. UN, 2004—05; ordained deacon Episc. Ch., 1963, priest, 1964; asst. rector NYC, 1963-66; assoc. rector Clayton, Mo., 1966-68, Grace Ch., Jefferson City, 1969; hon. assoc. St. Alban's Ch., Washington, 1977-94. Chmn. Mo. Law Enforcement Assistance Council, 1973-74; asst. chaplain Meml. Sloan-Kettering Cancer Ctr. of N.Y.C.; asst. rector Ch. of Epiphany in N.Y.C., Ch. of St. Michael and St. George, Clayton, Mo.; hon. canon Christ Ch. Cathedral, St. Louis. Republican nominee US Senate, 1970; assoc. rector Ch. of the Holy Communion, Univ. City, Mo., 1995—. Recipient Disting. Svc. award St. Louis Jr. C. of C., 1969, Disting. Missourian and Brotherhood awards NCCJ, Presdl. World Without Hunger award, 1985, Disting. Lectr. award Avila Coll., Chancellors medal UMKC, 1995; named Outstanding Young Man Mo. Jr. C. of C., 1968, St. Louis Man of Yr., 1994; Alumni fellow Yale U., 1973-79 Mem. Mo. Acad. Squires, Alpha Sigma Nu (hon.), bd. dirs., Dow Chemical Co., 1996-, Met. Life Insurance Co., 2000-. Republican. Office: Bryan Cave LLP One Met Sq 211 N Broadway Ste 3600 Saint Louis MO 63102-2750 E-mail: johncdanforth@bryancave.com.

DANFORTH, WILLIAM HENRY, retired academic administrator, physician; b. St. Louis, Apr. 10, 1926; s. Donald and Dorothy (Claggett) D.; m. Elizabeth Anne Gray, Sept. 1, 1950; children: Cynthia Danforth Prather, David Gray, Maebelle Reed, Elizabeth D. Sankey. AB, Princeton U., 1947; MD, Harvard U., 1951. Intern Barnes Hosp., St. Louis, 1951—52, resident, 1954—57; now mem. staff; asst. prof. medicine Washington U., St. Louis, 1960—65, assoc. prof., 1965—67, prof., 1967—, vice chancellor for med. affairs, 1965—71, chancellor, 1971—95, chmn., bd. trustees St. Louis, 1995—99, vice-chmn. bd. trustees, chancellor emeritus, 1999—. Pres. Washington U. Med. Sch. and Assoc. Hosps., 1965-71; program coord. Bi-State Regional Med. Program, 1967-68; dir. Energizing Holdings; chmn. bd. dirs. Donald Danforth Plant Sci. Ctr. Trustee Danforth Found.; trustee Am. Youth Found., 1963—, Princeton U., 1970-74; pres. St. Louis Christmas Carols Assn., 1958-74, chmn., 1975—; co-chair Barnes/Jewish Hosp., 1996-2002; bd. dirs. BJC Health Systems, 1996-2002. Named Man of Yr., St. Louis Gloe-Democrat, 1978. Fellow: AAAS, Am. Acad. Arts and Scis.; mem.: Inst. Medicine. Home: 10 Glenview Rd Saint Louis MO 63124-1308 Office: Washington U West Campus Campus Box 1044 7425 Forsyth Blvd Ste 262 Saint Louis MO 63105-2161

DANFORTH-MORNINGSTAR, ELIZABETH, obstetrician, gynecologist; b. Sioux Falls, S.D., July 3, 1951; d. George Jonathan and Mina (Schumacher) Danforth; m. John Wesley Morningstar III, May 29, 1976; children: John Wesley Morningstar IV, George Danforth, Charles Alexander. BA, Grinnell (Iowa) Coll., 1972; MD, Med. Coll. Va., Richmond, 1976. Intern Strong Meml. Hosp.-U. Rochester, 1976-77, resident ob/gyn, 1977-80; MD Genesee Hosp., Rochester, N.Y.; clin. assoc. prof. U. Rochester Sch. Medicine. Pres. Women Gynecology and Childbirth Assocs., 1989—; adv. bd. Rochester Individual Practice Assocs. Adv., mem. Monroe County Bd. for Infant Mortality, Rochester, N.Y. Mem. Monroe County Med. Soc., Am. Coll. Obstetricians/Gynecologists. Home: 55 Babcock Dr Rochester NY 14610-3304

DANG, CHI VAN, hematology and oncology educator; b. Saigon, Vietnam, Nov. 2, 1954; came to U.S., 1967; s. Chieu Van and Nga Ngoc (Nguyen) D.; m. Mary Doreen Seeley, May 18, 1985; children: Eric Van, Vanessa Marie. BS in Chemistry, U. Mich., 1975; PhD in Chemistry, Georgetown U., 1978; MD, Johns Hopkins U., 1982. Diplomate Am. Bd. Internal Medicine, Am. Bd. Med. Oncology. Resident in internal medicine Johns Hopkins Hosp., Balt., 1982-85; fellow in hematology and oncology U. Calif., San Francisco, 1985-87; asst. prof. medicine Johns Hopkins U., 1987-91, assoc. prof., 1991-97, assoc. prof. oncol., pathology, molecular biology & genetics, 1995-97, dir. hematology, 1993—2003, prof. medicine, oncology, and pathology, 1997—, prof. cell biology, 2001—, dep. dir. basic rsch., dept. medicine, 1996-99, co-dir. immunology and hematopoiesis, oncology, 1998-2000; vice dean rsch. Johns Hopkins Sch. Medicine, 2000—. Mem. oncological scis. path B NIH, Bethesda, Md., 1993-97; cons. Abbott Lab., 2002, Novartis, East Hanover, N.J., 1993-98, Genentech, South San Francisco, Calif., 1995; sci. adv. bd. Lion Pharm. Corp., Balt.; mem. bd. scientific counselors Nat. Cancer Inst. Contbr. articles to Nature, Molecular and Cellular Biology, Genes and Devel.; mem. editl. bd. Jour. Clin. Invest., 1998—, Neoplasia, 1999—; mem. editl. bd. Cancer Rsch., 2000—, sr. editor, 2003—. Scholar Leukemia Soc. Am., 1992-97, Stohlman scholar award Leukemia Soc. Am., 1996, Merit award NIH/NCI, 1999. Mem. Assn. Am. Physicians, Am. Soc. for Clin. Investigation (pres. 2002-03), Phi Beta Kappa, Alpha Omega Alpha, Phi Lambda Upsilon. Avocations: india ink sketching, poetry. Home: 217 Upnor Rd Baltimore MD 21212-3425 Office: Johns Hopkins U Sch Med Ross 1025 720 Rutland Ave Baltimore MD 21205-2109 Business E-Mail: cvdang@jhmi.edu.

DANG, HAI, geographer; b. Saigon, Vietnam, Apr. 15, 1968; s. Tru Tran (adoptive father) and Dan Dang; m. Hong Kim Tran, Sept. 10, 1992; children: Bao Dang, Thanh Dang. MS, Fla. State U., 1993; postgrad., Touro U., 2002. Cert. Microsoft profl. Geographical info. sys. specialist Gulf Coast Elec. Coop., Panama City, Fla., 1999—. Bd. dirs., Capital City Action Agy., Tallahassee, 1994-95. Republican. Roman Catholic. Avocation: travel. Fax: (850) 265-3634.

DANG, JOANNA, marketing professional; b. San Francisco, Calif., June 12, 1972; d. Carl and Munsie Chan. BS in Mktg., Calif. State U., 1995, MBA, 1999. Mktg. specialist IA Corp., Emeryville, Calif., 1996-98; product mktg. specialist GST Telecom., San Francisco, 1998-99; mktg. comms. mgr. Eilink Corp., Fremont, Calif., 1999-2000, Sensiva, Inc., Mountain View, Calif., 2000—01; sr. Marcom programs mgr. Integrated Device Tech., Inc., Santa Clara, 2001—03; realtor Prudential Calif. Realty, 2003—. Mktg. cons. Venturetec, Inc., Bangkok, Thailand, 1997. Mem. Calif. State U. Hayward Alumni Assn., Pi Sigma Epsilon (v.p. human resource 1997-98). Republican. Roman Catholic. Avocations: cross country running, biking, tennis, photography.

DANG, TUAN DUC, optometrist; b. Saigon, Vietnam, Jan. 30, 1969; arrived in U.S., 1975; s. Trinh Duc Dang and Nhu Lan (Thi) Nguyen; m. Bich Ha Thi Nguyen, Dec. 31, 1999. BS, U. Houston, 1991, MBA, 1994, OD, 2001. Cert. therapeutic optometrist, optometric glaucoma specialist Tex., Calif. Vietnamese med. interpreter M.D. Anderson Cancer Ctr., Houston, 1992—94; project dir. Asian Am. Health Coalition, Houston, 1996—97; program coord. R&D Inst., Houston, 1995—96; divsn. officer, staff optometrist Naval Med. Ctr., San Diego, 2001—. Adj. clin. asst. prof. U. Houston, Coll. Optometry, 2003—; adj. clin. instr. So. Calif. Coll. Optometry, Fullerton, 2002—, Pa. Coll. Optometry, Elkins Park, 2002—. Contbr. articles to profl. jours. Vision coord. Health Edn. for Asian League, Houston, 1998—2001; pub. health coord. Vietnamese Am. Cmty. Health Network, Houston, 1995—98. Lt. USN, 2001—. Fellow: Am. Contacat Lens Soc., Am. Acad. Optometry; mem.: Mil. Officers Assn. Am., Am. Optometric Assn., Golden Key. Avocations: camping, fishing, basketball. Office: Naval Med Ctr 34800 Bob Wilson Dr San Diego CA 92134-5000

D'ANGELO, CHRISTOPHER SCOTT, lawyer; b. Phila., Aug. 30, 1953; s. George Anthony and Antonia Scott (Billett) D'A.; m. Betsy Hart Josephs, May 22, 1982; children: John Robert, Christopher Hart, Caroline Colt, Jennifer Scott. BA with honors and distinction, U. Va., 1975, JD, 1978. Bar: Pa. 1978, U.S. Dist. Ct. (ea. dist.) Pa. 1978, (mid. dist.) Pa. 1992, U.S. Ct. Appeals (3d cir.) 1978, U.S. Supreme Ct. 1981. From assoc. to ptnr. Montgomery, McCracken, Walker & Rhoads, LLP, Phila., 1978—, chmn., product liability and mass tort sect., 1996—. Sustaining mem. Products Liability Adv. Coun., 1985—, case selection com. 1988-91, experts com., 1991—, restatement project com., 1993-2000, bd. dirs., 1998-2002, aggregation of claims project com., 2005—; mem. Am. Law Inst., 1996—, mem. consultative group-products liability, mem. consultative group-Aggregation of Claims, mem. consultative group-trusts, 1996—; lectr., writer in law internet and tech. matters Co-founder The Declaration (U. Va. newsweekly), 1973-75; Editor: Counsel Table, 1990-94; contbr. articles to law jours. Mem. Internat. Vis. Ctr., Phila., 1982—, bd. dirs., 1987-90, chmn. long range fin. com., 1987-89, counsel for COMPASS (young profl. and spl. events div. of ctr.), 1982-89, exec. com., 1982-89; mem. selection com. Jefferson Scholars U. Va., Phila., 1980-84, chmn., 1981-82; fundraiser U.S. Ski Team, Phila., 1979-90, chmn., 1982-83, 87; fundraiser Acad. Natural Scis., Phila, 1979-88; trustee Episcopal Acad., Merion, Pa., 1988-91, 92—, mem. fin. com., 1988-91, 92-97, 2000—, property com., 1998—, exec. com., 1999—; chmn. ann. giving campaigns Episcopal Acad., 1983-88; bd. mgrs. Episc. Acad. Alumni Soc., Merion, Pa., 1983-92, treas., 1984-85, v.p. 1985-88, pres. 1988-91; treas., exec. com., bd. dirs. Phila. Art Alliance, 1980-86; bd. dirs. English Speaking Union U.S., 1979-82, chmn. young mem. group, 1980-83; bd. dirs. English Speaking Union Phila., 1980-88, chmn. fin. com., 1985-88; counsel honor com. and judiciary com. U. Va., 1976-78; mem. nominating com. St. Christopher's Ch., Gladwyne, Pa., 1989-91; fundraiser Friends Sch., Haverford, Pa., 1987-89; lay reader The Ch. of the Redeemer, Bryn Mawr, Pa., 1992—, mem. capital campaign, 1993-1995, head usher, 1993-2001, chmn. Stewardship Com., 1997-98, vestry, 1997-2000; mem. trophy com. Devon (Pa.) Horse Show, 1978—; mem. com. Benjamin Franklin Inst. Nat. Meml. Awards, 1995-98, bd. dirs. Haverford Civic Assn., 2004-. Mem. ABA (mem. sect. litigation, products liability com., sect. internat. law, corp. counsel com.), Pa. Bar Assn. (exec. com. young lawyers divsn. 1979-85, probate sect. 1979—, litigation sect. 1979—), Phila. Bar Assn. (probate sect. 1979—), Products Liability Adv. Coun. (mem. Am. Law Inst. com., 1993-2000, mem. case selection com., 1988-91, mem. experts com. 1991—, bd. dirs. 1998-2002), Def. Rsch. Inst. (products liability com., bus. litigation com., drug and med. device com., co-chmn European Corporate Outreach Com. 2002, vice chmn. internat. law com. 2001-03, chmn. 2003-05), Fedn. Def. and Corp. Counsel (mem. computers and tech. com., products liability com.), Internat. Assn. Def. Counsel, (bd. dirs. 2004-, mem. products liability com., mem. bus. litigation com., chmn. 2001-2003, drug and med. device com., complex class action com., multi-nat. litigation com., vice chmn., 2003-05), computer and tech. com., author newsletters and jour. articles), Acad. Natural Scis., Anthenaeum, Phila. Mus. Art, Phila. Zoo, Merion Cricket Club (Haverford), Penn Club, IV St. Club, The Assemblies, Phila. Club Republican. Avocations: sailing, photography, travel, squash. Office: Montgomery McCracken Walker & Rhoads LLP 123 S Broad St Fl 24 Philadelphia PA 19109-1099 Office Phone: 215-772-7397. E-mail: cdangelo@mmwr.com.

D'ANGELO, JOSEPH FRANCIS, publishing company executive; b. Astoria, N.Y., July 4, 1930; s. Frank and Matilda (Oliveri) D'A.; m. Marcia Elaine Mackie, Mar. 4, 1965; children: Elena, Joseph Francis. BBA, St. John's U., 1952; PhD (hon.), St. John's U., William Penn Coll. Mem. Haskins & Sells CPAs, N.Y.C., 1952-61; treas., contr. internat. ops. Borden Co., Panama and P.R., 1961-65; from v.p. to pres. King Features Syndicate divsn. Hearst Corp., N.Y.C., 1973-96, chmn., 1997—; resident contr., 1965-73; bus. mgr., 1968-73; gen. mgr., 1973-75; pres., dir. King Features Syndicate, Inc., 1973-97. Pres., bd. dirs. Cowles Syndicate Inc., 1986-97, NAS, Inc., 1987-97; chmn. King Features Syndicate, Inc., Cowles, Inc., NAS, Inc., 1997—. Mem. Com. of 300 Archdiocese of N.Y.; bd. dirs. Alcoholism Coun. Greater N.Y.; trustee Emerson Coll., Boston, North Shore Univ. Hosp., pres. Mus. Cartoon Art and Hall of Fame, Boca Raton, Fla., Bd. of Trade. Mem. Artists and Writers Assn., Nat. Cartoonists Soc., Newspaper Features Coun., N.Y. Newspaper Pubs. Assn., N.Y. State Soc. Newspaper Editors, So. Newspaper Pubs. Assn., Sigma Delta Chi, Dutch Treat Club, Friars Club, N.Y. Athletic Club, Overseas Press Club, Wheatley Hills Golf Club, Knights of Malta. Republican. Roman Catholic. Office: King Features Syndicate Inc 959 Eighth Ave New York NY 10019 Business E-Mail: jdangelo@hearst.com.

D'ANGELO, RENÉE YOUNG, special education educator; d. William and Iva Mae Young; m. Thomas C. D'Angelo, Aug. 15, 1981. BS, Ea. Nazarene Coll., 1981; MS, Nova U., 1991. Cert. profl. educator's cert. Fla., elem. edn. Fla., emotionally handicapped Fla., specific learning disabilities Fla., English to spkrs. of other langs. Fla. Tchr. specific learning disabilities Palm Beach County Schs., Belle Glade, Fla., 1986—88, tchr. emotionally handicapped, 1988—92, Loxahatchee, Fla., 1992—95, pre-kindergarten tchr. of autistic, 1995—. Recipient Seldon Waldo Meml. award, Fla. Jr. C. of C., 1998. Mem.: Royal Palm Beach Jaycees (sec. 1995—97, pres. 1997—98, mgmt. v.p. 1998—99), Palm Beach County Chpt. 200, Coun. for Exceptional Children (sec. Palm Beach County chpt. 2001—02, pres. Palm Beach County chpt. 2003—04). Avocations: reading, travel, cooking, walking.

D'ANGELO, ROBERT WILLIAM, lawyer; b. Buffalo, Nov. 10, 1932; s. Samuel and Margaret Theresa Guercio D'A.; m. Ellen Frances Neary, Sept. 17, 1959; children: Christopher Robert, Gregory Andrew. BBA, Loyola U., L.A., 1954; JD, UCLA, 1960. Bar: Calif. 1960; cert. specialist taxation law. Practiced in, L.A., 1960-89; mem. firm. Myers & D'Angelo, Pasadena, Calif., 1967—. Adj. prof. law, taxation Whittier Coll. Sch. of Law., 1981. Served to capt. USAF, 1954—57. Mem. ABA, AICPA, State Bar Calif., L.A. County Bar Assn., Wilshire Bar Assn., Pasadena Bar Assn., Calif. Soc. CPAs, Am. Assn. Atty. CPAs, Calif. Assn. Atty. CPAs (pres. 1980), Phi Delta Phi, Alpha Sigma Nu. Home: 1706 Highland Ave Glendale CA 91202-1265 Office: 301 N Lake Ave Ste 800 Pasadena CA 91101-4108 Office Phone: 626-792-0007. Personal E-mail: m-dlaw@pacbell.net.

D'ANGELO, STARLYN D., museum director, curator; b. Loveland, Colo., Sept. 13, 1970; d. Jimmy L. Brunmeier and Carrie L. Vaughn; m. John Christopher D'Angelo. BA, Colo. State U., 1993; MA, SUNY, 1997. Curator Old Stone Fort Mus., Schoharie, NY, 1998—2000, Shaker Mus. and Libr., Old Chatham, NY, 2000—03; exec. dir. Shaker Heritage Soc., Albany, NY, 2003—. Bd. dir. Upstate History Alliance, Oneonta, NY, Mohawk River Cmty. Ptnrs., Colonie, NY. Avocations: hiking, yoga. Office: Shaker Heritage Society 875 Watervliet Shaker Rd Albany NY 12211

D'ANGELO, THOMAS J., not-for-profit developer, financial consultant; b. Paterson, N.J., July 31, 1941; s. Stephen and Ann D'Angelo; m. Patricia LaGatutta, Nov. 15, 1998; m. Ruth D'Angelo (div.); children: Christine, Thomas. BA in econ., Fairleigh Dickinson U., Teaneck, N.J., 1968. Credit supr. Irving Trust Co., N.Y.C., 1965—68; sr. regional mgr. Summit Bank, Princeton, NJ, 1968—99; pres., CEO Charitable Emporium.Com, Inc., Newark, 1999—. Adv. coun. Independence Cmty. Bank, Newark, 2001—. Exec. com., bd. dirs. New Cmty. Found.; bd. trustees Essex County Work Force Investment Bd., Essex County Econ. Devel. Corp. Meadowlink; bd. dirs. Althea Gibson Found., chmn. fund raising gala, 1999—2000; bd. dirs. Hispanic Am. C. of C. Found., chmn. fund raising gala, 2002; first v.p., bd. dirs. Meadowlands C. of C. Nat. guard, 1960—66, Lodi, N.J. Recipient Bus. & Cmty. Leadership commendation, Meadowlands Regional C. of C., 1996, Outstanding Achievement award, Girl Scout Coun. Bergen County, Paramus, N.J., 1999, Gov. Adv. Coun. Volunteerism and Cmty. Svc., 2003—04. Avocations: golf, music. Home: 3 Diamond Ct Glen Rock NJ 07452 Business E-Mail: tj@cecharity.com.

D'ANGELO MELBY, DONNA MARIE, lawyer; BA, U. Calif., 1972; JD, Calif. Western Sch. Law, 1978. Bar: Calif. 1979. Ptnr. Sonnenschein, Nath & Rosenthal LLP, L.A. Apptd. Jud. Sect. Adv. Panel; spkr. in field. Contbr. articles to profl. jours. Bd. dirs. Wellness Cmty. Foothills. Named one of Top 30 Women Litigators, L.A. and San Francisco Daily Jour., 2002, 2003, 2004, 100 Most Influential Attys. in Calif., L.A. Daily Jour., San Francisco Recorder, 2004, Top 5% So. Calif. Super Lawyers, Los Angeles Mag. & Law and Politics, 2004, 2005. Fellow: Internat. Soc. Barristers, Am. Coll. Trial Lawyers; mem.: ABA (mem. litigation sect., labor sect., employment sect), Fedn. Def. and Corp. Counsel, Internat. Assn. Def. Counsel, Def. Rsch. Inst., State Bar Calif. (trustee legal svcs. trust fund commn. 1985—86, 1997), L.A. Bar Assn. (mem. labor and employment law sect.), Fed. Bar Assn., Women Lawyers Assn. L.A., Calif. Women Lawyers, Am. Bd. Trial Advocates (exec. com. L.A. chpt. 1995—, mem. pres.'s coun. 1997, co-chair civil justice and nat. office com. 2001, nat. bd. dirs., nat. pres. 2005, pres. L.A. chpt. 2004). Office: Sonnenschein Nath & Rosenthal LLP 601 S Figueroa St Ste 1500 Los Angeles CA 90017 Office Phone: 213-892-5027. Business E-Mail: dmelby@sonnenschein.com.

D'ANGIO, GIULIO JOHN, radiologist, educator; b. N.Y.C., May 2, 1922; s. Carlo and Rosa (Calderazzo) D'A.; m. Jean Chittenden Terhune, Aug. 27, 1955 (dec. Nov.11, 2004); children: Carl, Peter; m. Audrey Evans, Feb. 1, 2005. AB, Columbia U., 1943; MD, Harvard U., 1945; D. Medicine and Surgery (hon.), U. Bologna, 1983. Diplomate: Am. Bd. Radiology, Am. Bd. Therapeutic Radiology. Surg. intern Children's Hosp., Boston, 1945-46, tng. in pathology, 1948-49; resident in radiology Boston City Hosp., 1949-53; also mem. staff; radiation therapist Children's Hosp., Boston, 1956-62; researcher Donner Lab., also Lawrence Radiation Lab., U. Calif., Berkeley, 1962-63; dir. divsn. radiation therapy U. Minn. Med. Sch., 1964-68; chmn. dept. radiation therapy Meml. Hosp., N.Y.C., 1968-76; dir. children's cancer rsch. ctr. Children's Hosp., Phila., 1976-89; prof. radiation oncology Hosp. of U. Pa., Phila., 1976-92, vice chmn., clin. dir. dept. radiation oncology, 1989-92, prof. emeritus, 1992—; prof. pediatric oncology U. Pa. Med. Sch., Phila., 1976-92. Chmn. Nat. Wilms Tumor Study Com., 1968-91; past chmn. cancer clin. investigation rev. com. Nat. Cancer Inst. Editor-in-chief Med. and Pediat. Oncology, 1996-2003; contbr. numerous articles to med. jours. Capt. M.C. AUS, 1946-48. Decorated Commendation medal; recipient ann. award Am. Cancer Soc., 1978, Heath Meml. award M.D. Anderson Tumor and Cancer Inst., 1979, Gold medal Am. Soc. Therapeutic Radiation Oncologists, 1999, Gold medal Charles U., Prague, cert. merit Pres. Italian Republic, 2003, Charles U., 2003. Fellow Royal Coll. Radiology, Am. Acad. Pediatrics; mem. Am. Acad. Pediat. (past chmn. sect. oncology-hematology), AAAS, Am. Assn. Cancer Rsch., Am. Coll. Radiology, Am. Soc. Therapeutic Radiologists, Mass. Med. Soc., Pa. Med. Soc., Royal Soc. Medicine, Internat. Soc. Pediat. Oncology (pres. 1987), Radiol. Soc. N.Am., Am. Radium Soc., Soc. Pediat. Radiology, Phi Beta Kappa. Episcopalian. Home: 2010 Spruce St Philadelphia PA 19103 Office: U Pa Hosp Dept Radiation Oncology 3400 Spruce St Philadelphia PA 19104-4206

DANGOOR, DAVID EZRA RAMSI, consumer goods company executive; b. Teheran, Iran, Aug. 3, 1949; arrived in Sweden, 1950, came to U.S., 1987; s. Selim Eliaho and Ruth (Lehr) D.; m. Ida (Ide) Weitzen, May 24, 1992; children: Rebecca Frances, Diana Katherine, Louisa Faye, Selim Edward. Civilekonom (MBA), Stockholm Sch. Econs., Sweden, 1973. Asst. dir. Scandinavian Supplies AB, Stockholm, 1970-74; asst. corp. treas. AGA Group AB, Stockholm, 1974-76; asst. to. v.p. Philip Morris Europe, Middle East & Africa, Lausanne, Switzerland, 1976; dept. mktg. dir. Philip Morris Co. Germany, Munich, Fed. Republic Germany, 1977-80; area dir. No. Europe Seven Up Internat., London, 1980-84; pres. Benson & Hedges Can. Inc., Philip Morris Internat., Montreal, Que., Can., 1984-86; sr. v.p. mktg. Philip Morris USA, N.Y.C., 1987-92; exec. v.p. Philip Morris Internat., Rye Brook, N.Y., 1992—. Bd. dirs. Rothmans, Benson & Hedges, Inc., Toronto, 1987—; mem. bd. dirs. and exec. com. Swedish Am. C. of C., N.Y., 1996-2001, chmn., 1998-2001; bd. dirs. Fgn. Policy Assn. N.Y., 1997—. Exec. v.p. Student Assn. Palmgrenska Samskolan, Stockholm, 1966-68; bd. dirs. Student Assn. Stockholm Sch. Bus. Adminstrn. and Econs., 1969-72, Am. Scandinavian Found., 1999—; officer Royal Swedish Coast Art; exec. bd. dirs. Raoul Wallenberg Com. of U.S., 1990-93; trustee Arthur F. Burns Fellowships, 1997—; mem. internat. devel. com. Internat. Fedn. Multiple Sclerosis Socs., 1993-95. Fellow Amaranten, Sweden, 1971. Mem. Swedish Am. C. of C. (bd. dirs. exec. com. 1996—), Sallskapet Club (Stockholm), Hurlingham Club (London), Hillside Tennis Club (Montreal), Southampton (N.Y.) Bath and Tennis Club, The Tuxedo Park (N.Y.) Club. Avocations: squash, tennis, sailing, bridge.

DANGREMOND, DAVID W., art history educator; b. Norristown, Pa., June 8, 1952; s. James L. and Joan O. (Kross) D.; m. Mary Plant Spivy, Oct. 18, 1980; children: Saumel Plant Chapin, Augustus Welles Ewing. BA cum laude, Amherst Coll., 1974; MA, U. Del., 1976, Yale U., 1987, MPhil, 1990. Dir. Webb-Deane-Stevens Mus., Wethersfield, Conn., 1976-80, Bennington Mus., Vt., 1980-96; adj. prof. art history Trinity Coll., Hartford, Conn., 1996—. Adj. prof. art history U. Hartford, Conn., 1977-80; tutor Historic Deerfield, Mass., 1975; trustee Williamstown (Mass.) Regional Art Conservation Lab., 1981-86, 2001—, Florence Griswold Mus., Old Lyme, Conn., 1987—, v.p., 1992—; trustee Conn. Humanities Coun., 1997—, Essex Savings Bank, 2001—; mem. adv. bd. Gunston Hall Plantation, Lorton, Va., 1985—, Nat. Trust Hist. Preservation; dir. Attingham Summer Sch., Shropshire, Eng., 1980—; profl. adv. bd. Victoria Mus., Portland, Maine, 1985—; bd. overseers Strawberry Banke Mus., Portsmouth, N.H., 1987—, v.p., 1988-90; mem. exec. com. Yale U. Art Gallery Assocs., 1987-93; mus. cons. various mus., 1995; chmn. Newport Symposium, 2002—. Foreword author: Heritage Houses: the American Tradition in Connecticut 1660-1900, 1979; contbr. articles to jours. Bd. dirs. Hartford Architecture Conservancy, 1978-80; mem. adv. bd. Deacon John Grave Found.; mem. art and antiques coun. Conn. Pub. TV, Hartford, 1977-80; mem. concert com. Vt. Symphony Orch., 1980-86; trustee Musical Masterworks, 1992—, v.p. 1998—, pres. 2003—; div. head United Way Bennington County, 1982-84; del. Gov.'s Conf. on Future of

Vt.'s Heritage, Montpelier, 1982; sr. warden St. Peter's Episcopal Ch., 1985—; bd. govs. Hill-Stead Mus., Farmington, 1990—; trustee Wadsworth Atheneum, Hartford, 1991—, exec. com., 1995—, chmn. curatorial com., 1995—, chmn. ethics com. 1996—, v.p. 1998—; trustee Conn. Hist. Soc., 1989—, v.p. 2003—. Fellow Historic Deerfield, 1973; Winterthur fellow H.F. duPont Winterthur Mus., 1974-76; Sir George Trevelyan scholar Attingham summer sch., Shropshire, Eng., 1976; recipient: Disting. Advocate for the Arts award, Conn. Commn. on the Arts, 1999. Mem. Am. Assn. for State and Local History (state awards chmn.), New Eng. Mus. Assn. (exec. com. 1985-86), Am. Assn. Mus. (accreditation vis. com., mus. assessment program cons.), Am. Antiquarian Soc., Vt. Mus. and Gallery Alliance (pres. 1983-86), Greater Hartford Assn. of Historic Houses (bd. dirs.), Decorative Arts Soc., Am. Ceramics Circle, Coll. Art Assn., Soc. Archtl. Historians, Century Assn. (N.Y.C.), Knickerbocker Club (N.Y.C.), Grolier Club (N.Y.C.), Hartford Club, Old Lyme Country, Yale Club N.Y.C., Lawn Club (New Haven), Dauntless Club (Essex), Newport Reading Rm. Episcopalian.

DANI, sculptor, painter; b. L.A., Mar. 11, 1933; d. Gordon Hale and Gladys Christine Daniels; m. Lowell James Leyrer, Nov. 13, 1954; children: Jacque Sue Fait, Lori Kay Leyrer. Student, Pasadena City Coll., 1948—51, Laguna Beach Sch. Art, 1980, Orange Coast Coll., 1987—90, Calif. State U., Long Beach, 1990. Instr. art Pks. and Recreation, Costa Mesa, Calif.; tchrs. aide spl. edn. Newport/Mesa Unified Schs., 1968—73; corp. coord. Aminco Internat., Irvine, 1992—98; owner Studio Dani, Ramona, 1972—2005. Exhibitions include San Bernardino Mus. Art, Calif., 1976—79, U. Miss. Nat. Show, 1977, Nat. Acad. Design, N.Y., 1978, Hudson Valley Art Assoc., 1978, Sothby's, 1996, 1998. Pres. PTA Assn., Costa Mesa, 1965—66; co-chair Orange County Showcase, 2000; bd. dirs. Costa Mesa Sr. Ctr., 1999. Recipient Mrs. John Newington award, Hudson Valley Art Assn., N.Y., 1981, 1st Pl. Sculpture, Catharine Lorillard Wolfe Show, N.Y., 1995, Sculptor's award, Hillcrest Invitational, 1970, 1982, Art Fest award, Am. Artists Profl. League, 1998, H.A. Fadhi Sculpture award, 2002, Leila Gardin Sawyer Meml. award, 2002. Mem.: Acad. Fine Arts Found. (Rembrandt mem. 2002—04), San Vicente Valley Club (bd. dirs. 2004—, pres. 2005—), Salmagundo Club (exhibition 1996, pres. 2005—), Calif. Art Club (exhibition 2002, 2004, 2005). Republican. Methodist. Avocations: tennis, golf, swimming, walking. Office Phone: 760-787-9813.

DANIC, ROBERT IAN, application developer; b. Sarnia, Ont., Can., July 21; s. Jerry John Danic and Jane Sutton Weir. BA, Queens U., Kingston, Ont., 1981; MBA, York U., Toronto, 1985. Mktg. mgr. Georisk s.a., Brussels, 1987—88; mktg. support mgr. IP Sharp Assocs., Toronto, Canada, 1984—87; regional mgr. for securities markets Soc. for Worldwide Interbank Telecom-(S.W.I.F.T.), Brussels, 1988—90, sr. regional mgr. N.Y.C., 1990—93; mktg. mgr., global securities svc. Goldman Sachs & Co., N.Y.C., 1993—94; v.p., sales Braid Inc., N.Y.C., 1995—97; exec. v.p. sales and mktg. and ptnr. Electra Info. Systems, N.Y.C., 1997—. Home: 8 Gramercy Park S Apt 2A New York NY 10003-1725 Office: Electra Information Systems 381 Park Ave S Ste 1413 New York NY 10016-8806 Office Phone: 212-696-1595. Office Fax: 212-696-1595. E-mail: idanic@electrainfo.com.

DANIEL, ARLIE V., speech education educator; b. Spencer, Iowa, May 15, 1943; s. Arlie Verl and Eleanor Marie (Grover) D. AA, Iowa Lakes C.C., 1963; BA, Morningside Coll., 1965; MA, U. Iowa, 1978; PhD, U. Nebr., 1981. High sch. tchr. Missouri Valley (Iowa) Pub. Schs., 1965-68, Clinton (Iowa) Pub. Schs., 1971-78; dir. speech edn. East Cen. U., Ada, Okla., 1981—. Co-author: Project Text for Public Speaking, 6th edit., 1991; co-author chpt. in Basic Communication Course Annual, 1994; editor: Activities Integrating Oral Communication Skills for Students in Grades K-8, 1992; contbr. chpt. to Teaching and Directing the Basic Communication Course, 1993; contbg. author Creating Competent Communicators: Activities for Teaching, Speaking, Listening and Media Literacy in the K-12 Classroom, 2003. 1st lt. U.S. Army, 1968-71. Mem. AAUP, Assn. Tchr. Educators, Internat. Comm. Assn., Okla. Speech Theatre Comm. Assn. (pres. 1986-87, exec. sec. 1989-92, Outstanding Comm. Educator award 1985, Josh Lee Svc. award 1992, Spl. award for contbns. to profession 1994), Ctrl. States Comm. Assn. (life, exec. dir. 1994-97, v.p., 1997-98, pres. elect, 1998-99, pres. 1999-2000, past pres. 2000-2001, Outstanding Young Speech Tchr. award 1985), Nat. Comm. Assn. (life), Rotary Internat. (chair youth com. Ada chpt. 1994-2003, pres. elect 2002-03, pres. Ada 2003-04, v.p. 2004-2005, dist. 5770 Interact chair 1995-2003, Rotaract chair, 2003—), Pi Kappa Delta. Democrat. Methodist. Avocations: golf, bowling, wine making. Home: 1206 Tower Rd Ada OK 74820-6106 Office: East Cen U Communication Dept Ada OK 74820-6899 Office Phone: 580-310-5214. E-mail: adaniel@csca.ecok.edu.

DANIEL, BARBARA ANN, retired elementary school educator; b. La-Crosse, Wis., Mar. 22, 1938; d. Rudolph J. and Dorothy M. (Farnham) Beranek; m. David Daniel; children: Raychelle, Clarence, Bernadette, Brenda. BS in Edn. cum laude, Midwestern U., Wichita Falls, Tex., 1967; postgrad., U. Alaska, Fairbanks, Anchorage, Juneau, U. Alaska, Bethel. Cert. tchr., Alaska. Primary tchr. Bur. Indian Affairs, Nunapitchuk and Tuntutuliak, Alaska, 1967-70; tchr. Lower Kuskokwim Sch. Dist., Tuntutuliak, 1981—2003, English lang. leader grades k-12, 1995—2002, ret., 2003. Mem. lang. arts curriculum revision task force Lower Kuskokwim Sch. Dist., 1990; past mem. state bd. Academic Pentathlon, Alaska; past acad. decathlon, pentathlon coach, 1980's. Rsch. video rec. of elders in Alaskan village. Mem.: NEA, Alaska Coun. Tchrs. English. Home: 25 West Circle PO Box Wtl-8048 Tuntutuliak AK 99680

DANIEL, BARBARA ANN, realtor, advertising executive; b. Pineville, Ky., May 28, 1954; d. Charles Edward and Emma Walters; m. Michael Daniel, Dec. 23, 1973; children: Michael Alan, Charles Edward. A, S.E. C.C., Cumberland, Ky., 1992. Lic. real estate Tenn. Real Estate Commn., 2000. Receptionist Daniel Boone Clinic, Harlan, Ky., 1973—81; instrnl. tchr.'s aide Loyall (Ky.) Elem., 1986—89; tchr.'s aide, bus driver Ky. Cmty. Econ. Opportunity Coun./Head Start, Harlan, 1989—90; spl. edn. instrnl. aide Harlan (Ky.) Elem., 1991—92; 4-H asst. U. Ky. Coop. Ext. Svc., Harlan, 1992—93; advt. sales rep. Middlesboro (Ky.) Daily News, 1994—95, The Bargain Banner, Harlan, 1995—96, Powell Valley News, Pennington Gap, Va., 1996—. Affiliate broker The Realty Group, Tazewell, Tenn., 2000—01; realtor Rosenbalm Real Estate, 2001—. Author: (children picture book) Kara and the Butterfly. Writer/dir. plays Liggett (Ky.) Bapt. Ch., 1982—88, youth dir., 1982—88; vol. instrnl. tchr.'s aide Holy Trinity Sch., Harlan. Recipient Ready award (real estate advt. of distinction), Nat. Newspaper Am., 2001. Baptist. Avocations: painting, hiking, travel, bicycling. Mailing: PO Box 231 Middlesboro KY 40965-0231 Personal E-mail: daniel2@netcommander.com.

DANIEL, BETH, professional golfer; b. Charleston, S.C., Oct. 14, 1956; d. Robert and Lucia D. Grad., Furman U., 1978. Profl. golfer Ladies Profl. Golf Assn. tour, 1979—. Mem. U.S.A. World Cup Team, 1978, U.S.A. Solheim Cup Team, 1990, 92, 94, 96, 2000, 02, 03, LPGA Executive Com., 2002—03. Winner U.S. Amateur Title, 1975, 77; winner 33 LPGA events including World Series Women's Golf, 1980, 81, Columbia Savs. Classic, 1980, 82, LPGA Championship, 1990, Big Apple Classic, 1994; Named Rolex Rookie of Yr., 1979, Rolex Player of Yr., 1980, 90, 94, A.P. Female Athlete of Yr., 1990; recipient Vare Trophy, 1989, 90, 94, The Heather Farr Player Award, 2003. Achievements include being the leading money winner in LPGA, 1980, 81, 90; inducted into LPGA Tour Hall of Fame, 1999, inducted World Golf Hall of Fame, 2000; named in the top 50 LPGA Players All-time, 2000.

DANIEL, CHARLES DWELLE, JR., retired military officer; b. San Antonio, Oct. 30, 1925; s. Charles Dwelle and Jean Elizabeth (Stormont) D.; m. Ann Meredith Carter, June 7, 1946; children: Charles Dwelle III, Peter C. BS, U.S. Mil. Acad., 1946; MS, Tulane U., 1961, PhD, 1968; BA in Studio Art, Am. U., 1987. Joined U.S. Army; advanced through grades to maj. gen.; F.A. battery comdr. U.S. Army (3d inf. divsn.), Republic of Korea, 1950—52; adviser Ky. N.G., Louisville, 1953-55; F.A. missile officer 7th U.S. Army Europe, 1956-59; physicist Def. Atomic Support Agy., Washington, 1963-66; F.A. bn. and divsn. artillery comdr. 1st inf. divsn. Viet Nam, 1966-67; divsn. chief, dir. Office of Chief of U.S. Army R & D, 1968-71; commdg. gen. I Corps, Arty., Republic of Korea, 1971; dep. commdg. gen. Korean Support Command, 1971-72; dir. army rsch. Dept. Army, Washington, 1972-74, dir. combat support systems, 1974; dep. comdt. Nat. War Coll., Ft. McNair, Washington, 1974-75; spl. asst. to commdg. gen. U.S. Army Material Command, Alexandria, Va., 1975-77; commdg. gen. U.S. Army Electronics R & D Command, Adelphi, Md., 1977-79; ret., 1979. Dir. target acquisition BDM Corp., McLean, Va., 1979-80; cons. Burdeshaw Assocs., 1981—. Decorated D.S.M., Silver Star, Legion of Merit with oak leaf cluster, D.F.C., Bronze Star with 4 oak leaf clusters, Air medal with 16 oak leaf clusters, Joint Svc. Commendation medal, Army Commendation medal U.S., Vietnamese Cross of Gallantry with silver star; named Hon. Col. 33d Regiment, U.S. Field Artillery, 2003. Mem. SAR, Assn. U.S. Army, Assn. Grads. U.S. Mil. Acad. Home: 4904 Baltan Rd Bethesda MD 20816-2404 Office: Burdeshaw Assocs Ltd 4701 Sangamore Rd Bethesda MD 20816-2508

DANIEL, CHARLES TIMOTHY, transportation engineer, consultant; b. NYC, Aug. 3, 1958; s. John Carl and Eleanor (Sauer) D.; m. Melissa J. Sanft, Mar. 4, 1995. BA in Engring., Lafayette Coll., 1980; MS in Transp., MIT, 1982; MBA, NYU, 1991. Staff engr. George Beetle Co., Phila., 1983-84; project engr. Transamerica Leasing, Purchase, NY, 1984-87, mgr. tech. svcs. White Plains, 1987-89, engring. cons., 1989—. Treas. Midtown Daniel Corp., 1990—, pres., 1995—; mem. domestic freight container stds. subcom. Internat. Standardization Orgn. Tech. Com. on Freight Containers, 1986-88; bd. advisors Princeton Com. on Fgn. Rels., 2003—. Mem. alumni bd. Rutgers Preparatory Sch., Somerset, NJ, 1985—; bd. advisors Princeton Com. on Fgn. Rels.; county committeeman Middlesex County (N.J.) Dem. Orgn., 1992—. Mem. ASCE, Sigma Xi, Beta Gamma Sigma. Lutheran. Achievements include development of code structure for electronic data interchange of freight container chassis repair data. Home: 33 North Dr East Brunswick NJ 08816-1124 Office: Midtown Daniel Corp 645 Madison Ave Fl 20 New York NY 10022-1010 Personal E-mail: ctd095@earthlink.net.

DANIEL, COLDWELL, III, economist, educator, entrepreneur; b. New Orleans; s. Coldwell Jr. and Josephine Agnes (Weick) D.; children: Anne Alexis, Coldwell IV. BBA, Tulane U., 1949; MBA, Ind. U., 1950; PhD, U. Va., 1959; postdoctoral, U. Chgo., 1964-65. Instr. stats. U. Va., 1955-56; instr. econs. Pomona Coll., 1956-57; prof. econs., dept. chmn. U. So. Miss., 1958-65; prof. econs. U. Houston, 1965-70, U. Memphis, 1970—2004, prof. emeritus econs., 2004—. Rsch. coord. So. Calif. Rsch. Coun., 1956-57; vis. prof. La. State U., 1959; sr. Fulbright prof. econs. Dacca U., Bangladesh, 1961-62; Disting. Fulbright lectr. Shanghai Jiao Tong U., 2001; project dir. Miss. Test Facility Econ. Impact Study NASA, 1963; prin. The Anwell Co., Memphis, 1974—; disting. Fulbright lectr. Shanghai Jiao Tong U., 2001; candidate Fulbright Sr. Specialist Roster, 2002-, pres. Coastal Castles, Inc., 2004-. Author: Mathematical Models in Microeconomics, 1970; reader Jour. Econ. and Bus., 1991-2004, Social Sci. Jour., 1988-2004, Am. Jour. Econs. and Sociology, 1990-2004, Jour. Econ. Edn., 1997-2004, Internat. Econ. Jour., 1999-2004, Am. Econ. Rev., 2000; founder, chmn. bd. editors, The So. Quar., 1962-64; co-founder and manuscript rev. editor Jour. Econs. and Fin., 1977-91; mem. editl. bd. Jour. Econs. and Fin., 1991-94, Jour. Econs. and Fin. Edn., 2002-2004; assoc. editor for econs. Social Sci. Quar., 1968-70, mem. editl. bd., 1972-84; contbr. articles to profl. jours. Trustee Christ United Meth. Ch. With USAF, 1945-46; 1st lt. US Army, 1951-53. Decorated Bronze Star; NSF Sci. Faculty fellow, 1964-66. Fellow Acad. Econs. and Fin.; mem. Am. Econ. Assn., Pakistan Econ. Assn. (life), Southwestern Econs. Assn., Acad. Econs. and Fin. (co-founder, pres. 1977-78, area coord. Indsl. Orgn. and pub. Policy, 1990-94, Disting. Svc. award 1979, Cert. Appreciation 1981), Mo. Valley Econs. Assn. (pres. 1984-85, Meritorious Svc. award 1986), So. Econ. Assn., Atlantic Econ. Soc. (exec. com. 1991-94, area coord. Indsl. Orgn. and Pub. Policy 1989-94), The Raven Soc., Sigma Xi, Beta Gamma Sigma, Omicron Delta Kappa, Pi Kappa Pi, Omicron Delta Epsilon, Pi Gamma Mu, Delta Tau Kappa, Phi Beta Delta, Pi Sigma Epsilon, Delta Sigma Pi. E-mail: cdaniel1@memphis.edu.

DANIEL, DAVID EDWIN, academic administrator, civil engineer; b. Newport News, Va., Dec. 20, 1949; s. David Edwin and Betty Ruth (Aschenback) D.; m. Frances Louise Locker, June 12, 1971 (div.); children: Katherine Ruth, William Monroe; m. Susan Nielsen Brady, May 12, 1989; 1 child, Alexander David. BS, U. Tex., 1972, MS, 1974, PhD, 1980. Staff engr. Woodward-Clyde, San Francisco, 1974-77; asst. prof. U. Tex., Austin, 1981-85, assoc. prof., 1985-91, prof., 1991-96; prof., head dept. civil engring. U. Ill., Urbana, 1996-2001, dean Dept. Engring., Gutgsell Prof. Civil Engring., 2001—05; pres. U. Tex., Dallas, 2005—. Recipient Richard R. Torrens award Am. Soc. of Civil Engineers, 1995 Mem. ASCE (Norman medal 1975, Cross medal 1984, 2000, Middlebrooks award 1995), NAE. Office: Univ Texas Dallas Office of Pres PO Box 830688 Richardson TX 75083-0688 Business E-Mail: dedaniel@utdallas.edu.

DANIEL, ELNORA D., academic administrator; d. Stephen and Cecelia Bell; m. Herman Daniel, Mar. 25, 1961; 1 child, Michael. BS, N.C. Agrl. and Tech. U., Greensboro, 1964; MEd, Columbia U., N.Y.C., 1968; EdD, Columbia U., 1978. RN N.C., 1964. V.p. for acad. affairs Hampton U., Va., 1991—93, v.p. for health, 1994—95, exec. v.p. and provost, 1995—98; pres. Chgo. State U., 1998—. Bd. dirs. LaRabida Children's Hosp., Am. Assn. State Colls. and Univs. (AASCU), Am. Coun. Edn. (ACE), Commn. Adult Edn., Nat. Assn. Equal Opportunity Higher Edn. (NAFEO), Beverly Bank & Trust Co., Little Co. Mary Hosp., Seaway Nat. Bank; nat. adv. bd. Millennium Leadership Initiative Am. Assn. State Colls. and Univs. (AASCU). Contbr. articles to profl. jours., chpts. to books. Mem. LWV Chgo., 1999, Ill. Commn. 50th Anniversary Brown vs. Bd. Edn.; mem. advisory bd. Cmty Violence Prevention Program Ctrl State. U.; prin. mem. Chgo. United; mem. Econ. Club Chgo., Women's Network Chgo., Chgo. Consortium Higher Edn., Comml. Club Chgo., Univ. Club Chgo.; mem. women's bd. Field Mus. Ret. col. Nurses Corp. U.S. Army, 1991. Named to Hall of Fame, Today's Chgo. Woman, 2002; recipient Dir.'s Oustanding Achievement award, Ill., 2002. Fellow: Am. Acad. Nursing; mem.: Jr. Achievement Chgo. Independent. Office: Chicago State Univ 9501 S King Dr ADM/313 Chicago IL 60628 Office Phone: 773-995-2400. Business E-Mail: ed-daniel2@csu.edu.

DANIEL, HAROLD TURNER, JR., lawyer; b. Griffin, Ga., July 3, 1943; s. Harold Turner and Mary Pearl (Rowan) D.; m. Laurie Guiles Webb, oct. 3, 1981; children: Marian Amelia, Annie Laurie. BA, Emory U., 1965, JD, 1969. Bar: Ga. 1970, U.S. Supreme Ct. Assoc., ptnr. Webb, Parker, Young & Ferguson, Atlanta, 1970-77; ptnr. Webb, Young, Daniel & Murphy, Atlanta, 1977-81, Webb, Daniel & Betts, Atlanta, 1981-83, Webb & Daniel, Atlanta, 1983-94, Holland & Knight LLP, Atlanta, 1994—. Fellow Am. Bar Foun., Am. Coll. Trial Lawyers; mem. State Bar Ga. (pres. 1994-95), Lawyers Club Atlanta (pres. 1983-84). Office: Holland & Knight LLP 1201 W Peachtree St NW Atlanta GA 30309-3449 Business E-Mail: harold.daniel@hklaw.com.

DANIEL, J. CHRISTOPHER, health facility administrator, family medicine physician, military officer; b. Phila., Apr. 15, 1958; s. Frank V. and Regina Luff Daniel; m. Lorraine Yetsuko Higa, June 19, 1993; children: Penelope Nicole Michiko, Nicholas Wayne. AB cum laude, Princeton U., 1980; MD, Jefferson Med. Coll., Phila., 1984. Diplomate Am. Bd. Family Medicine (added qualification in adolescent medicine). Spl. asst. for health care matters Office of Sec. of Navy, Washington, 1981—82; basic surgery intern Naval Hosp., San Diego, 1984—85; flight surgeon U.S Naval Hosp., Subic Bay, Philippines, 1986—89, Fleet Composite Squadron FIVE, Naval Air Station Cubi Point, 1989—90; family practice resident Naval Hosp., Camp Pendleton, Calif., 1991—93; family physician U.S. Naval Hosp., Naval Air Station Sigonella, Italy, 1993—96; adolescent medicine fellow Naval Med. Ctr., San Diego, 1996—98; chief med. staff, family and adolescent medicine physician Naval Med. Clinic, Annapolis, Md., 1998—2002; exec. officer U.S. Naval Med. Rsch. Unit Two, Jakarta, Indonesia, 2002—04; commdg. officer Naval Submarine Med. Rsch. Lab., Groton, Conn., 2004—. Sr. med. officer, dir. Br. Med. Clinic, NAS Cubi Point, 1987—90; AHA ACLS affiliate faculty, program dir. U.S. Naval Hosp., Naval Air Station Sigonella, 1994—96; founder, dir. Travel Medicine Clinic, U.S. Naval Hosp., Naval Air Station Sigonella, 1994—96; co-founder, dir. San Diego H.S. Football Head Injury Project, 1997—98; clin. instr., dept. family and preventive medicine U. Calif., San Diego, 1997—98; assoc. prof. dept family medicine Uniformed Svcs. U. of Health Scis., Bethesda, Md., 1997—2002; mem. editl. adv. bd. Am. Family Physician, Leawood, Kans., 2002—. Capt. USN, 1980—. Named one of America's Top Family Drs., Consumer's Rsch. Coun. Am., 2002—03, 2004—05; recipient Outstanding Scholar Athlete award, Phila. Evening and Sunday Bull., 1976, 1st prize staff rsch. project, Naval Med. Ctr., San Diego, 1999. Fellow: Am. Acad. Family Physicians; mem.: Internat. Soc. Travel Medicine, Naval Submarine League, World Orgn. Family Drs., Aerospace Med. Assn. (life), Am. Coll. Physician Execs. (life), Uniformed Svcs. Acad. Family Physicians, Soc. for Adolescent Medicine (chair internat. adolescent health profls. in tng. 1996—98). Roman Catholic. Avocations: sports, travel. Office: Naval Submarine Med Rsch Lab Box 900 Groton CT 06349

DANIEL, JALEE LYNN, music educator; b. For Morgan, Colo., Nov. 26, 1974; d. James Lee and Susan K. Daniel. MusB, U. Northern Colo., 1998, MusM, 2004. Music dir. Bennett HS, Bennett, Colo., 1999—, Bennett Mid. Sch., Bennett, Colo., 1999—. Social com. chair, prin. adv. com. Bennett HS, Bennett, Colo., 2002—04; purcussionist Littleton Symphony Orch., Littleton, Colo., 2002—04; com. mem. Bennett Music Sch. Accountability Com., Bennett, Colo., 2004—. Host sch. Honor Choir, Colo. Music Dirs., Bennett, Colo., 2002—04. Named Colo. Tchr. of Yr., Colo. Dept. Edn., 2003; Sch. to Career grant, Bennett Sch. Dist., 1999. Mem.: Colo. Music Educators Assn., Music Educators Nat. Assn. Luth. Avocations: gardening, rollerblading, dance. Office: Bennett HS 1010 7th St Bennett CO 80102 Office Phone: 303-644-3234 x7402. E-mail: jaleedaniel@aol.com.

DANIEL, JAMES, curator, writer; b. Davidson County, N.C., June 6, 1916; s. James Manly and Bert (Fletcher) Daniel; m. Ramona Teijeiro, Apr. 15, 1939 (dec. May 2000); children: Jane Clare, Ramona Nina. AB, U. N.C., 1937; Nieman fellow, Harvard, 1942-43. Reporter Raleigh (N.C.) News & Observer, 1937-40, Washington Daily News, 1941, city editor, 1946-47; with Office War Info., CBI, 1943-45; Washington corr. Scripps-Howard Papers, 1948-56; contbg. editor Time mag., 1957-60; roving editor Reader's Digest, 1961-81; pres. Healing Springs Properties, Inc.; curator Weston (Conn.) Town Hall Art Collection, 1992—. Author: (with J. G. Hubbell) Strike in the West, The Complete Story of the Cuban Crisis, 1963; editor: Private Investment, The Key to International Development, 1958. Mem.: Harvard (N.Y.C.). Home: 183 Good Hill Rd Weston CT 06883-2312

DANIEL, JAMES RICHARD, accountant, corporate financial executive; b. Chgo., June 26, 1947; s. Elmer Alexander and June B. (Bush) D.; m. Marsha Ruth Stone, Nov. 8, 1969; children: Jennifer Rae, Michael James. BS in Acctg., U. Ill., 1970; MBA, Loyola U., 1974. CPA, Ill., La. Dir. fin. Baxter Travenol Labs., Chgo., 1974-79; corp. contr. Bio-Rad Labs. Inc., Richmond, Calif., 1979-81; v.p., treas., contr. Lykes Bros. Steamship Co. Inc., New Orleans, 1981-84; CFO SCI Systems Inc., Huntsville, Ala., 1984-91; sr. v.p., CFO Dell Computer Corp., Austin, Tex., 1991-93; exec. v.p., CFO, pres. hdqrs. support, treas. MicroAge, Inc., Tempe, 1993-2000; cons., 2000-01; sr. v.p., CFO PetsMart Inc., Phoenix, 2001. Mem. issuer affairs com. NASDAQ, 1995-2001. With U.S. Army, 1970-73. Recipient Outstanding Alumnus award Loyola U. Grad. Sch. Bus., 1995. Mem. AICPA. Republican. Home: 3858 E Cholla Ln Phoenix AZ 85028-5023 Office Phone: 928-684-6189. E-mail: jdanieletal@aol.com.

DANIEL, JOHN MORGAN, publisher, writer; b. Mpls., Nov. 22, 1941; s. Lewis Morgan and Hannah Neil (Mallon) D.; m. Karen Ann Mullenger, June 12, 1964 (div. 1970); children: Morgan Neil, Benjamin William Lewis; m. Susan Plumley, July 9, 1987. AB, Stanford (Calif.) U., 1964. Editor asst. Stanford U. Press., 1968-70; clerk, buyer Kepler's Books, Menlo Park, Calif., 1970-77; owner, pres. John Daniel Pubs. Svcs., Palo Alto, Calif., 1977-80; mgr. Wilbur Hot Springs (Calif.) Health Sanctuary, 1980-82; mgr., buyer Keplers Books, Los Altos, Calif., 1982-83; sales mgr. Capra Press, Santa Barbara, Calif., 1983-86; owner, pub. John Daniel & Co., Santa Barbara, 1986-90, Daniel & Daniel Pubs., Inc., Santa Barbara, 1990—. Bd. mem. Santa Barbara Writers Consortium, 1983-85; instr. UCLA Extension, 1991—; writer in residence Wilbur Hot Springs, 1980-82. Author: Play Melancholy Baby, 1986, The Woman By The Bridge, 1991, The Poet's Funeral, 2005. Wallace Stegner fellow Stanford U., 1967-68. Democrat. Office: PO Box 21922 Santa Barbara CA 93121-1922*

DANIEL, KAREN, engineering and design company executive; BS in Acctg., N.W. Mo. State, 1980; MS in Acctg., U. Mo., Kansas City, 1981. CPA. With KPMG Peat Marwick, 1981—92, Black & Veatch, Overland Park, Kans., 1992—, now CFO. Mem. bd. commrs. Kansas City Pks. and Recreation, 1999—2003; bd. dirs. Cmty. Found., Women's Employment Network, Black Econ. Union; mem. bd. regents N.W. Mo. State U., 2003—. Recipient Nat. Profl. Achievement award, Nat. Women of Color, 2002. Office: Black & Veatch 11401 Lamar Overland Park KS 66211

DANIEL, LEON, journalist; b. Etowah, Tenn., Aug. 8, 1931; s. Oscar Leon and Mary Nancy (Cook) D.; m. Carobel Heidt Calhoun, Oct. 26, 1963 (div.); 1 child, Lillian Fant. Student, U. Tenn., 1949-56. Reporter UP, Nashville, 1956-58; bur. mgr. UPI, Knoxville, Tenn., 1958-61, reporter Atlanta, 1961-66, corr. Saigon, 1966-67, Tokyo, 1967-70, mgr. for Thailand Bangkok, 1970-72, chief corr. for South Asia New Delhi, 1972-74, chief corr. for East Asia Manila, 1974, editor for Asia Hong Kong, 1974-77, editor for Europe London, 1977-80, nat. reporter Washington, 1980-87, mng. editor, internat., 1987-88, sr. editor, columnist, 1989-93; cons., columnist The Ind., Dhaka, Bangladesh, 1995. With USMC, 1950-53, Korea. Decorated Purple Heart. Mem. Phi Gamma Delta, Sigma Delta Chi. Democrat. Episcopalian. Home: 120 Turtle Creek Rd Charlottesville VA 22901-6763

DANIEL, MARGARET HAGEN, music and voice educator; b. Eau Claire, Wis., Sept. 9, 1949; d. Harold Odin and Genevieve (Kjendalen) Hagen; m. Douglas Vaughn Daniel, Aug. 9, 1975; children: Nathan Elliot, Adam Stuart, Jason Christopher (dec.). MusB in Voice, Wis. State U., Eau Claire, 1971; postgrad., Boston U., 1971; MusM in Voice, U. Wis., 1973; pvt. studies in piano and voice. Pvt. instr. piano, 1965-71; instr. music, voice U. Southwestern La., Lafayette, 1973-80, asst. prof. music, voice, class piano and music fundamentals, 1980-93, assoc. prof. music, voice, diction, pedagogy, 1993—; coord. vocal studies U. La., Lafayette (formerly U. Southwestern La.). Asst. to dir. Sch. Music, U. Southwestern La., 1991-95; guest faculty summer music symposium Kansas State U., 1994; adjudicator mus. competitions and auditions, 1974—; presenter vocal clinics Grace Presbyn. Ch., Lafayette, 1983, 85, Chorale Acadienne, Lafayette, 1985, 86, First Bapt. Ch., Lafayette, 1989, Cantors of St. Joseph Ch., Milton, La., 1991; guest artist Luther Northwestern Theo. Sem., St. Paul, 1991, McNeese State U., Lake Charles, La., 1993, Troy (Ala.) State U., 1993, Nicholls State U., Thibodaux, La., 1994-95, New Orleans, 1995, Houston, 1996, Monroe, La., 1996, Shreveport, La., 1997; lectr./recital performer So. Chpt. Coll. Mus. Soc., 1993, 95, 96, La. Music Tchrs. Assn., 1993, 95, 2003, 05, La. Music Educators Assn., 1994, 95. Performer operas, including Roméo et Juliette, 1973, Rigoletto, 1974, La Traviata, 1978, others, also leading roles in musicals; oratorios include Handel's Messiah, 1980, Haydn's The Creation, 1982, Brahms' Ein Deutsches Requiem, 1989, Mendelssohn's Elijah, 1992, others; contbr. articles to profl. publs. Dir. music summer bible sch. Grace Presbyn. Ch., 1986-90, dir. children's choir, 1987-88; mem. cultural arts com. Plantation Elem. PTO, 1991-93; team coord. Cajun Sports Assn., 1991-93, Lafayette Youth Soccer Assn., 1991-93; active L.J. Alleman Mid. Sch. PTO, 1992; guest soloist numerous chs., 1966—; organist Grace Presbyn. Ch., 1997-04. Recipient Cert. of Appreciation, Coun. Devel. of French in La., 1975, Plantation Elem. Sch., 1989, 90, 91, 92; music scholar U. Wis., Eau Claire, 1967-71. Mem. AAUP, Nat. Assn. Tchrs. of Singing (v.p. South La. chpt. 1988-90, pres. 1990-92), Music Educators Nat. Conf., La. Music Tchrs. Assn., Music Tchrs. Nat. Assn. (nat. cert.), Coll. Music Soc., Sigma Alpha Iota (life, pres. 1978-80, 87-88, editor 1983-85, faculty advisor 1980—, Sword of Honor 1982), Pi Kappa Lambda (pres. 1990-92), Phi Kappa Phi. Avocations: travel, camping, reading, sewing. Office: Univ. Louisiana-Lafayette PO Box 41207U Lafayette LA 70504-0001 Office Phone: 318-482-5202.

DANIEL, MARIAN PHILLIPS, language educator; b. Tulsa, Okla. d. Richard Tevier Daniel Jr. and Aena E. Martin. AA, Stephens Coll., Columbia, Missouri; BA in Romance Langs., U. Ark., 1964, MA in Spanish, 1967. Cert. secondary edn. Tex. Edn. Agy. Editor, translator El Ganadero Internacional, San Antonio, 1967—82; secondary edn. educator South San Antonio Ind. Sch. Dist., 1993—2002, N.E. Ind. Sch. Dist., San Antonio, 2002—04. Mem. Cherokee Nation, Osage Tribe of Indians. Mem.: Tex. Fgn. Lang. Assn. Roman Catholic. Avocations: swimming, scuba diving, travel, sailing. Office: St Philip's Coll 1801 Martin Luther King San Antonio TX 78203 Business E-Mail: mdaniel16@mail.accd.edu.

DANIEL, MARILYN S., lawyer; b. Tulsa, Okla., July 30, 1940; d. Basil M. and Kathryne (Shannon) Stewart; m. John A. Daniel, June 15, 1962; 1 child, John S. BA, Rhodes Coll., 1962; JD, U. Ky. Coll. of Law, 1976. Bar: Ky. Sec. math. tchr., 1962—71; legal clerk U.S. Dist. Judge, Lexington, Ky., 1977; asst. U.S. atty. U.S. Dept. Justice, Lexington, 1978—81; gen. counsel Mason & Hanger Corp., Lexington, 1982—, v.p. adminstrn., 1992—96, sr. v.p., 1996—99. Dir. The Mason Co., Lexington, 1990—99, Ky. Bar Assn. for Women, 1991—93; vol. dir. Maxwell St. Legal Clinic, 1999—. Mem. Fayette County Bd. Edn., 1985—88; trustee Transylvania Presbytery, 1985—98; elder Maxwell St. Presbyn. Ch., 1993—. Recipient Women of Achievement award YWCA, 1993. Mem. ABA, KBA (CLE chair ann. conv. 1992), Fayette County Bar Assn. (Henry T. Duncan award 1994. Avocations: gardening, cooking, hiking, quilting, handwork.

DANIEL, PATRICK D., energy executive; m. Dora Daniel; 2 children. BS chem. engring., Univ. Alta.; MS chem. engring., Univ. BC. Pres. IPL Energy U.S.; CEO Interprovincial Pipe Line Inc.; exec. v.p., COO energy transp. svc. Enbridge Energy, pres., COO, pres., CEO, 2001—. Office: Enbridge Energy 3000 Fifth Ave Pl 425 First St SW Calgary AB T2P 3L8 Canada*

DANIEL, ROBERT MICHAEL, lawyer; b. Rocky Mount, NC, Aug. 21, 1947; s. Harvey Derby and Edna Lois (McCullen) D.; m. Kaye Ruth Coates, Aug. 31, 1968; children: Robert M. Jr., John Matthew. AB in Econs., U. N.C., 1968, JD, 1971. Bar: N.C. 1971, Pa. 1976; U.S. Dist. Ct. (we. dist.) Pa. 1976; U.S. Tax Ct. 1979. Judge adv. U.S. Marine Corps., 1971-74; ptnr. Smith & Daniel, Pittsboro, N.C., 1974-75; trust officer Mellon Bank, N.A., Pitts., 1975-78; assoc. Buchanan Ingersoll, Pitts., 1978-82, ptnr., 1982—2001; dir. Cohen & Grigsby PC, Pitts., 2002—. Bd. dirs. Cohen & Grigsby, Pitts., 2002. Pres. Greater Pitts. coun. Boy Scouts Am., 1996-99, bd. dirs. N.E. region. Col. USMCR, 1966-98, ret. Fellow Am. Coll. Trust and Estate Counsel; mem. Pa. Bar Assn. (past chmn. real property, probate and trust law sect. 1998-99), Duquesne Club. Presbyterian. Avocations: travel, reading military history. Home: 1491 Redfern Dr Pittsburgh PA 15241-2956 Office: Cohen & Grigsby PC 11 Stanwix St 15th Flr Pittsburgh PA 15222-1319 Office Phone: 412-297-4989.

DANIEL, ROSS PRESTON, III, economist, educator; b. Beckley, W.Va., July 6, 1951; s. Ross Preston and Ruth Irene (Roby) Daniel. BA, Marshall U., 1973, MBA, 1975; MA, W.Va. U., 1979. Lectr. W.Va. U., Morgantown, 1981—82; asst. mktg. mgr. Mountaineer Mall, Morgantown, 1979—81; asst. prof. Nicholls State U., Thibodaux, La., 1982—85, U. Southwestern La., Lafayette, 1985—86; dir. Ctr. Econ. Edn. La. State U., Baton Rouge, 1986—91. Instr. So. U., Baton Rouge, 1996—2001; asst. prof. Baton Rouge C.C., 2002—; pres. J.B. Enterprises Photography, 1986—93, Buff Daniel Photography, 1986—; v.p. R.D. Software, Inc., Thibodaux, 1983—. Fellow, W.Va. U., 1976—77, 1977—81, Benedum rsch. fellow, 1976. Mem.: Am. Econ. Assn., Tau Kappa Epsilon. Episcopalian. Home: 5115 Highland Rd Apt 135 Baton Rouge LA 70808-6529 E-mail: buffland@excite.com.

DANIEL, ROYAL THOMAS, III, lawyer, mechanical engineer, accountant; b. Portsmouth, Va., July 30, 1956; s. Royal Thomas Daniel, Jr. and Lillian Martha (Ellis) Daniel; m. Holly Ann Walsh, Oct. 30, 1993; children: Andrew Joseph, Royal Thomas IV, James David. BS in Nuclear Engring., N.C. State U., 1978, MS in Indsl. Mgmt., 1980; MS in Acctg., Bentley Coll., 1985, MS in Computer Info. Systems, 1986; JD, Suffolk U., 1990; degree in Advanced Mgmt. Program, U. Pa., 2005. Bar: N.C. 1991, Mass. 1991, D.C. 1992, N.Y. 2003, N.J. 2003, U.S. Tax Ct. 1993, N.Y. 2003, N.J., 2003; registered profl. mech. and indsl. engr., Mass., N.C.; CPA, Md., N.C.; cogeneration profl. Assn. Energy Engrs. Sr. proposal engr. Combustion Engring. Power Sys., Inc., Windsor, Conn., 1979—80; coordinating specialist Boston Edison Co., 1980—85, power supply coord., 1985—92; prin. Daniel Law Offices, P.A., Raleigh, NC, 1992—94; v.p. PSEG Asia, Ltd., Hong Kong, 1994—2000; bd. dirs., v.p. Meiya Power Co. Ltd., Hong Kong, 1995—98, 2002—04; pres., bd. dirs. Energy Infrastructure Devel., Bangkok, 1998—2000; vice chmn. ops. and fin. Sri U-Thong, Bangkok, 1998—2000; corp. devel. PSEG Global LLC, NJ, 2000—01, U.S. bus. mgr., 2001—. Contbr. chapters to books. Exec. dir. Patriot's Path Coun. Boy Scouts Am., NJ. Mem. NSPE, ABA, Am. Inst. Certification of Computer Profls., Am. Arbitration Assn. (panel arbitrators), Nat. Assn. Accts. (cert. Inst. Cert. Mgmt. Accts.), NC Assn. CPA, N.C. Bar Assn., DC Bar Assn., Inst. Cert. Computer Profls. (cert. data processor, sys. profl.), Rotary, Order St. Patrick, Phi Delta Phi, Tau Beta Pi. Baptist. Home: 333 Boulevard Mountain Lakes NJ 07046-1517 Office Phone: 973-430-7286. Personal E-mail: royal_daniel@hotmail.com.

DANIEL, SAMUEL J., hospital administrator, medical educator; b. Leeward Islands, Sept. 13, 1950; MD, Columbia U., 1978. Diplomate Am. Bd. Internal Medicine, Am. Bd. Gastroenterology. Intern Roosevelt Hosp., N.Y.C., 1978—79, resident in internal medicine, 1979—80, St. Lukes-Roosevelt Hosp., N.Y.C., 1980—81, resident in gastroenterology, 1981—83; dir. medicine N. Gen. Hosp., N.Y.C., 1995—2001, CEO, 2001—. Asst. clin. prof. Columbia U.; assoc. clin. prof. Mt. Sinai Sch. Medicine, 2001—. Office: 1789 Madison Ave New York NY 10035 Address: 1879 Madison Ave New York NY 10035-3832 Office Phone: 212-360-5090. Business E-Mail: samuel.daniel@ngsc.org.

DANIEL, T., mime performer, theater director, choreographer; b. Chgo., Aug. 23, 1945; s. Theodore Charles and Thelma L. (Søderlind) Heagstedt; m. Laurie Willets, July 14, 1976. BS, Ill. State U., 1967, postgrad., 1969. Cert. Ecole Internat. de Mime. Performer, creator, artistic dir. T. Daniel Productions (Movement & Movement Theatre), Chgo., 1971—. Choreographer (film) Poltergeist III, 1988; choreographer, performer (video) Sweets for the Sweet, 1984; performer, creator (plays) Fantasmia, 1984, Merlin & The Color of Magic, 1986, Structures on Silence, 1988, The Magic of Mime, 1973, A World of Mime, 1971, ImVentionS, musical mims quartet, 2000 Home and Office: 6619 N Campbell Chicago IL 60645

DANIEL, THOMAS L., zoology educator; b. N.Y.C., Aug. 21, 1954; BS in Anthropology and Engring., U. Wis., 1976, MS in Zoology and Engring., 1978; PhD in Zoology, Duke U., 1982; postgrad., Calif. Inst. Tech. Myron A. Bantrell postdoctoral fellow in sci. and engring. Calif. Inst. Tech., 1982-84; asst. prof. dept. zoology U. Wash., Seattle, 1984-88, assoc. prof. dept. zoology, 1988-92, prof. dept. zoology, 1992—, Joan and Richard Komen Chair of Biol. External grad. faculty Oreg. State U., 1987—; mem. various coms. at U. Wash. including chair grad. admissions dept. zoology, 1989-91, chair grad. program dept. zoology, 1991-94, dir. math. biology tng. program, 1993—; panel mem. physiol. processes NSF, 1991—; presenter in field. Mem. editl. bd. Jour. Exptl. Biology, Cambridge U., 1988-90, 93—; contbr. articles to profl. jours. Grantee NSF, 1984-87, 88-91, 91-93, 93, U. Wash., 1987-88, J. Fluke Co., 1988, Reticon, Inc., 1988, Am. Soc. Zoologists Symposium on Efficiency in Organisms, 1988-89, Whitaker Found. for Biomed. Rsch., 1988-91, Howard Hughes Found., 1989-94, M.J. Murdock Meml. Trust, 1989-94, Apple Computer, 1991; MacArthur fellow, 1996. Office: U Wash Dept Zoology PO Box 351800 Seattle WA 98195-1800*

DANIEL, WALTER COOK, psychologist, educator, researcher; s. Arthur and Mary Cook; m. Becky Childers, Aug. 10, 1968; 1 child, Carrie Anderson. BA, So. Ill. U., 1967; MEd, U. Mo., 1969, PhD, 1974. Lic. psychologist Ark., 1976. Rehab. counselor Fulton (Mo.) State Hosp., 1969—71; prof. U. Ark., Fayetteville, 1974—. Contbr. chapters to books, articles to profl. jours. Mem. Commn. on Rehab. Counselor Certification, Rolling Meadows, Ill., 1992—97. Fellow: APA; mem.: Nat. Coun. on Rehab. Edn. (chair rsch. com. 1977—80, Rehab. Educator of Yr. 1994), Am. Rehab. Counseling Assn. (chair rsch. com., chair membership com., rsch. award 1977—92, James Garrett award for a disting. career in rehab. rsch. 1998, Rsch. awards 1977, 1980, 1983, Svc. award 1980, 1990, 1994). Home: 2308 Golden Oaks Fayetteville AR 72703 Office: Univ Ark 153 Graduate Education Fayetteville AR 72703 Office Phone: 479-521-6426. Office Fax: 479-575-3319.

DANIEL, WILBON HARRISON, history educator; b. Lynchburg, Va., Sept. 25, 1922; s. Benjamin Ernest and Annie (Coleman) D.; m. Margaret Anne Ferguson, May 30, 1950; 1 child, Anne Margaret. BA, Lynchburg Coll., 1944; BD, Vanderbilt U., 1946, MA, 1947; PhD, Duke U., 1957. Tchr. history Va. Intermont Coll., Bristol, 1947-54; instr. history U. Richmond, Va., 1956-57, asst. prof., 1957-62, assoc. prof., 1962-69, prof., 1969—, William Binford Vest prof. history, 1980-93, William Binford Vest prof. history emeritus, 1993—. Author: Bedford County, Va., 1840-60, 1985, Va. Baptists, 1860-1962, 1987, Southern Protestantism in the Confederacy, 1989, History at the University of Richmond, 1991, Jimmie Foxx, The Life and Times of a Baseball Hall of Famer, 1907-1967, 1996. Avocations: reading, travel, baseball, gardening. Home: 21 Bostwick Ln Richmond VA 23226-3106

DANIEL, WINIFRED YVONNE, elementary school educator; d. William Clair Goatley and Imogene Gregory Shelby; 1 child, Jacquelyn Marie. BS in Elem. Edn., Ctrl. State U., 1960. Profl. cert. elem. edn. Ohio. Tchr. grade 1 Cleve. Pub. Schs., 1960—72; tchr. grades 1 and 4 Maple Heights Pub. Schs., Ohio, 1972—77; tchr. grades 4-8 Warren City Schs., Ohio, 1977—2000. Substitute tchr. Warren City Schs., 2000—. Jennings scholar, Martha Holden Jennings Found., 1966—67. Mem.: Delta Sigma Theta. Baptist. Avocations: reading, baking, quilting.

DANIEL-DREYFUS, SUSAN B. RUSSE, information technology executive; b. St. Louis, May 30, 1940; d. Frederick William and Suzanne (Mackay) Russe; m. Don B. Faerber, Nov. 27, 1962 (div. Nov. 1968); 1 child, Suzanne Mackay; m. Marc Andre Daniel-Dreyfus, Aug. 9, 1969; 1 child, Cable Dunster. Student, Smith Coll., 1958-60, Corcoran Sch. Fine Arts, 1960-61, Washington U., St. Louis, 1961-62; MEd, Cambridge Coll., 1991. Mng. ptnr. Comm., Inc., 1980-82; asst. dir. Harvard Bus. Sch. Fund, Cambridge, 1982-86; pres. SCR Assocs. Corp., Cambridge, 1986—. Mem. bd. advisors Odysseum, Inc.; bd. dirs. Future Mgmt. Systems. Mem. St. Louis-St. Louis County White House Conf. on Edn., 1966-68; mem. Mo. 1st Gov.'s Conf. on Edn., 1966, 2d Conf., 1968; bd. dirs. Tunbridge Sch., 1973-78, St. Louis Smith Coll.; hon. bd. dirs. New Music Circle; mem. woman's bd. dirs. Washington U., New Music Circle, 1963-67; mem. woman's bd. Mo. Hist. Soc.; bd. dirs. Non-Partisan Ct. Plan for Mo., Young Audiences Inc., 1967-69; bd. dirs. Childrens Art Bazaar, 1968-70; founder St. Louis Opera Theater; chmn. Art. Mus. Bond Issue election St. Louis, 1966; jr. bd. dirs. St. Louis Symphony, 1966-68, Opportunities Indsl. Center, Boston; legis. chmn. bd. dirs. Boston LWV, 1969-72; mem. coun., bd. dirs. Jr. League Boston, 1970-72, 74-76, v.p. Bd. of Family Counseling Services-Region West, Boston, 1979—; pres. Family Counseling Bd., Brookline, Mass.; trustee Chestnut Hill Sch., Boston, Brookline Friendly Soc.; mem. steering com. ann. fund Boston Children's Hosp. Med. Center, 1980-84; v.p. Nat. Friends Bd., Joslin Diabetes Found., 1980-83; mem. corp. bd. Joslin Diabetes Ctr.; v.p. bd. dirs. Boston Ctr. Internat. Visitors, 1979-82; Boston bd. dirs. Mass. Soc. Prevention of Cruelty to Children, 1980-84; exec. v.p. Ctr. for Middle East Bus., 1978-82; pres. bd. Brookline Community Fund, 1984—; overseer Old Sturbridge Village, 1987—. Mem. Colonial Dames, Soc. Art Historians. Clubs: Women's City (dir., Boston); Vincent (dir.). Home: PO Box 638 Altona 3018 Australia

DANIELIDES, JOANNIE C., public relations executive; m. Nicholas Danielides; children: Philippe, Alexander. BA in art history, Finch Coll.; MA in art history, Queens Coll. With Met. Mus. Art, NYC, lectr.; with Ruder Finn, Burson-Marsteller, Ogilvy & Mather, Spencer & Rubinow; press sec. for Donna Hanover, others; founder, pres. Danielides Comm., 1986—. Bd. sec. Am. Farm Sch., 2005—. Recipient Media award, Am. Acad. Nursing, 1998. Mem.: NY Women in Comm (pres. 2003—04, found. pres. 2004—05). Office: Danielides Comm 9 E 53rd St New York NY 10022-4220 Office Phone: 212-319-7566. Business E-Mail: joannie@danielides.net.

DANIELL, HERMAN BURCH, pharmacologist; b. Cadwell, Ga., May 25, 1929; s. Walter and Ruby Florence (Burch) Daniell; m. Mickey Marucheau, May 24, 1952 (dec.); m. Lorraine Smith, June 30, 1957 (dec.); children: Kimberley Ann, Anthony Burch, Walter Herman. BS in Pharmacy, U. Ga., 1951, MS in Pharmacology, 1964; PhD in Pharmacology, Med. U. S.C., 1966. Owner-operator retail pharmacies, Savannah, Ga., 1953-62; instr. U. Ga., 1962-64; USPHS trainee Med. Coll. S.C., Charleston, 1964—66; mem. faculty Med. U. S.C., 1966-92, prof. pharmacology, 1978-92, prof. emeritus, 1992—. Contbr. articles to profl. jours. Served to capt. M.S.C. U.S. Army, 1951—53. Grantee, USPHS, 1966—85, S.C. Heart Assn., 1966—73. Mem.: Am. Soc. Pharmacology and Exptl. Therapeutics, Sigma Xi, Kappa Sigma, Rho Chi. Episcopalian. Home: 1549 Burningtree Rd Charleston SC 29412-2630

DANIELL, JERE ROGERS, II, retired historian; b. Millinocket, Maine, Nov. 28, 1932; s. Warren Fisher and Mary (Holway) D.; m. Sally Ann Wellborn, Dec. 1955 (div. 1969); children: Douglas, Alexander, Matthew; m. 2d Elena Lillie, July 19, 1969; stepchildren: Breena Daniell, Clifford Brodsky. AB, Dartmouth Coll., 1955; MA, Harvard U., 1962, PhD, 1964. Asst. prof. history Dartmouth Coll., 1964-69, assoc. prof., 1969-74, prof., 1974—2003, chmn. dept., 1979-83; class of 1925 prof., 1984—; head tutor Heritage Found., Old Deerfield, Mass., 1960-64; ret., 2003. Author: Experiment in Republicanism: N.H. Politics and the American Revolution, 1970, Colonial N.H.: A History, 1981; bd. editors: Univ. Press of New England, 1978-86. Served to lt (j.g.) USN, 1955-58. Mem. Colonial Soc. Mass., N.H. Hist. Soc. (bd. trustee 1979-86, 1999—), Vt. Hist. Soc., Maine Hist. Soc., Mass. Hist. Soc. Home: 11 Barrymore Rd Hanover NH 03755-2401 Office: Dartmouth Coll Dept History Hanover NH 03755 Office Phone: 603-646-2995. E-mail: jere.r.daniell@dartmouth.edu.

DANIELL, STEVEN J., language educator, department chairman; b. Lubbock, Tex., June 9, 1961; s. Thelon Max and Patricia Hayno Daniell; m. Lauren A. Brzeskiewicz, Feb. 16, 1991; 1 child, Madeleine Thelon. BA, Tex. Tech U., 1983; MA, U. Ill., 1987, PhD, 1991. Asst. prof. French Auburn U. Montgomery, 1991—96, assoc. prof. French, 1996—, head dept. internat. studies, 1999—. Field bibliographer MLA Internat. Bibliography, N.Y.C., 1995—; state adminstr. Nat. French Contest, Carbondale, Ill., 1996—. Mem.: Ala. Assn. Tchrs. French (pres. 1999—2001), Am. Assn. Tchrs. French (Contest Adminstr. of Yr., Nat. French Contest 2002), Assn. for Can. Studies in the US, Am. Coun. for Que. Studies. Unitarian Universalist. Avocations: writing, jogging, home renovations, cooking. Home: 2423 Agnew St Montgomery AL 36106 Office: AUM International Studies PO Box 244023 Montgomery AL 36124 Office Phone: 334-244-3239. Office Fax: 334-244-3177. Personal E-mail: txtech1983@yahoo.com. Business E-Mail: sdaniell@mail.aum.edu.

DANIELOVITCH, ISSUR See DOUGLAS, KIRK

DANIELS, ALBERTINA DIANA, secondary school educator; b. Jacksonville, Fla., Aug. 30, 1948; d. David and Petronita Josephine Daniels. BS, Edward Waters Coll., Jacksonville, 1971; MA in Tchg., Marygrove Coll., Detroit, 2003. Cert. notary pub. N.J., N.J. Dept. Banking and Ins. Prodr. Bus. edn. tchr. Camden City Sch. Dist., NJ, 1976—, resource tchr., 1991—96, GED examiner, 1998—2001, GED chief examiner, 2001—, career counselor, 1999—. Coord. food basket drive Cmty. Sharing and Caring, Camden, 1994—, sch. book asst., 1995—, summer food program asst., 1998—. Mem.: Camden Edn. Assn. (exec. bd. 2004—, chair sunshine com. 2005—), Women's Internat. Bowling Congress, Club Docetts, Order of Ea. Star (grand organizer 1988—, assoc. matron). Baptist. Avocations: bowling, sewing, reading, travel, computer programs. Office: Cmty Sharing and Caring Corp 2656 Baird Blvd Camden NJ 08105 Personal E-mail: tindaniels@aol.com.

DANIELS, ARLENE KAPLAN, sociology educator; b. N.Y.C., Dec. 10, 1930; d. Jacob and Elizabeth (Rathstein) Kaplan; m. Richard Rene Daniels, June 9, 1956. BA with honors in English, U. Calif., Berkeley, 1952; MA in Sociology, 1954, PhD in Sociology, 1960. Instr. dept. speech U. Calif., Berkeley, 1959-61; rsch. assoc. Mental Rsch. Inst., Palo Alto, Calif., 1961-66; assoc. prof. sociology San Francisco State Coll., 1966-70; chief Center for Study Women in Soc., Inst. Sci. Analysis, San Francisco, 1970-80; mem. faculty Northwestern U., Evanston, Ill., 1975-95, prof. dept. sociology, 1975-95, dir. Women's Studies, 1992-94, prof. emerita. Vis. prof. dept. sociology U. Calif., Berkeley, 1997—; cons. NIMH, 1971-73, NEH, 1975-80, Nat. Inst. Edn., 1978-82 Editor: (with Rachel Kahn-Hut) Academics on the Line, 1970; co-editor: (with Gaye Tuchman and James Benét) Hearth and Home: Images of Women in the Mass Media, 1978, (with James Benét) Education: Straightjacket or Opportunity?, 1979, (with Rachel Kahn-Hut and Richard Colvard) Women and Work, 1982, (with Alice Cook and Val Lorwin) Women and Trade Unions in Eleven Industrialized Countries, (with Teresa Odendahl and Elizabeth Boris) Working in Foundations, 1985, Invisible Careers, 1988, (with Alice Cook and Val Lorwin) The Most Difficult Revolution: Women in the Trade Union Movement, 1992; editor: Jour. Social Problems, 1974-78; assoc. editor: Contemporary Sociology, 1980-82, Symbolic Interaction, 1979-84, Am. Sociol. Rev., 1987-90. Trustee Bus. and Profl. Women's Rsch. Found. Bd., 1980-85, Women's Equity Action League Legal and Ednl. Def. Fund, 1979-81; mem. Chgo. Rsch. Assoc. Bd., 1981-87. Recipient Social Sci. Rsch. Council Faculty Rsch. award, 1970-71; Ford Found. Faculty fellow, 1975-76; grantee Nat. Inst. Edn., 1978-79, 1979-80, NSF, 1974-75, NIMH, 1973-74 Mem. Inst. Medicine NAS, Sociologists Women in Soc. (pres. 1975-76), Am. Sociology Assn. (coun. 1979-81, chmn. occupations and orgns. 1987, chmn. pubs. com. 1985-87, sec. 1992-95, Jessie Bernard award 1995), Soc. Study Social Problems (v.p. 1981-82, pres. 1987 Lee Founders award 1988), Soc. Study Symbolic Inter-Action. E-mail: akdaniels@aol.com.

DANIELS, CALLIE HARMON, mathematics professor; b. Fort Smith, Ark., July 6, 1967; d. James Gilbert and Patricia Cole Harmon; m. Kurtis James Daniels; children: Clayton James, Grady Luke. BS in Math. Edn., U. of Ozarks, 1989; MS, U. Mo., Rolla, 1991; MA in Secondary Edn., U. Mo., St. Louis, 2003. Prof. math. and stats. St. Charles C.C., St. Peters, Mo., 1992—. Named to Hall of Honor, Van Buren H.S. Adminstrn., 2003; recipient Young Alumni Svc. award, U. of Ozarks Alumni Bd., 1998. Mem.: Am. Assn. Two-Yr. Colleges, Math. Assn. Am., Mo. Math. Assn. Two-Yr. Colleges, Am. Statis. Assn. Home: 21 Trophy Buck Ln Foristell MO 63348 Office: St Charles CC 4601 Mid Rivers Mall Dr Saint Peters MO 63376 Office Phone: 636-922-8547. Personal E-mail: cdaniels@stchas.edu.

DANIELS, CAROLINE, publishing company executive; b. San Francisco, Dec. 11, 1948; d. William L. and Gladys Daniels; m. Jack Wernick, Nov. 30, 1985 (div.); children: Martin, Katherine. Student, U. Dijon, France, 1965; BA in Psychology, U. Colo., 1970; postgrad. mgmt. program, Harvard U., 1983-85. Export agt. Air Oceanic Shippers, San Francisco, 1972-73; library supr. Aircraft Tech. Pubs., San Francisco, 1973-75, ops. mgr., 1975-80, v.p., 1980-82, exec. v.p. Brisbane, Calif., 1982-84, pres., CEO, chmn. bd. dirs., 1984—. Pres. adv. bd. Embry Riddle Aero. U.; bd. dirs. Acad. Art U., San Francisco. Past mem. bd. dirs. Jr. Achievement of The Bay Area. Mem.: Gen. Aviation Mfg. Assn. (bd. dirs., exec. com., former chmn. pub. affairs com., chmn. safety affairs com.), San Francisco Opera Guild. Office: Aircraft Tech Pubs 101 S Hill Dr Brisbane CA 94005-1251 Home: Apt 1002 1000 Green St San Francisco CA 94133-3693 Office Phone: 415-330-9500.

DANIELS, CHARLIE, musician, songwriter; b. Wilmington, N.C., Oct. 28, 1936; Founder Charlie Daniels Memorabilia Mus., Nashville, 2001—. Mem. (band) Jaguar band, 1958—67, session man (in Nashville with Flatt and Scruggs) Marty Robbins, Claude King, Pete Seeger, Bob Dylan, others, founder, mem. (band) Charlie Daniels Band, 1971—, recorded for (record cos.) Kama Sutra and Sony/Epic Records, —, records include (albums) Te John, Charlie Daniels, 1971, Grease and the Wolfman, 1972, Uneasy Rider, 1973, Whiskey, 1974, Fire on the Mountain, 1974, Nightrider, 1975, Saddle Tramp, 1976, Volunteer Jam Capricorn, 1976, Volunteer Jam III and IV, 1978, Volunteer Jam VI, 1980, Volunteer Jam VII, 1981, High Lonesome, 1976, Whiskey, 1977, Midnight Wind, 1977 (Grammy award best single of yr. Devil Went Down to Georgia), Million Mile Reflections, 1979, Full Moon, 1980, Windows, 1982, Decade of Hits, 1983, Me and the Boys, 1985, Powder Keg, 1987, Homesick Heroes, 1988, Simple Man, 1989, Christmas Time Down South, 1990, Renegade, 1991, America, I Believe in You, 1993, All Time Greatest Hits, 1993, The Door, 1994, Same Ole Me, 1995, CDB Live, How Sweet the Sound, 2002, Redneck Fiddle Man, 2002, A Merry Christmas to All, 2002, Freedom and Justice For All, 2003, 1st Christian Album The Door, 1994, Super Hits, 1994, 2d Christian album Steel Witness, 1996, SONY Legacy releases 1st CDB box set, The Roots Remain, 1996, By the Light of the Moon, 1997, Road Dogs, 2000, founder (record label) Blue Hat debut for label, 1998, Fiddle Fire, 1998, Tailgate Party, 1999; songwriter:, songs recorded by (songs) Elvis Presley, Gary Stewart, Tammy Wynette, others; actor(appeared in): (TV films) PBS TV film The Lone Star Kid, 1986; also composed score; author: (short stories) The Devil Went Down to Georgia; songs This Ain't No Rag It's a Flag, 2001 (Biggest Single for CDB in 10 yrs.); Gospel album (albums) How Sweet The Sound: 25 Favorite Hymns and Gospel Greats; author: (handbook) Aint No Rag, 2003. Recipient 3 Country Music Assn. awards, 1979, Grammy award for best performance by a country group, 1980, Toys for Tots Man of Yr. award, 1992, Humanitarian award Country Radio Broadcasters Seminar, 1992; named Instrumentalist of Yr., Instrumental Group of Yr., Winner Acad. Country Music's Pioneer award, 1998, Winner TNN Music City News Living Legend award, 1999; named to Wilmington, NC, Walk of Fame, 2002. Office: The Charlie Daniels Band CDB Inc 17060 Central Pike Lebanon TN 37090-8019 Fax: 615-443-3140. E-mail: paulacdb@aol.com.

DANIELS, CHARLIE, state official; m. Patricia Burleson; children: Marsha, Chuck. Attended, So. Ark. U., U. Ark., Little Rock; LHD (hon.), Shorter Coll. With Ark. Electric Cooperatives; commr. state land State of Ark.; dir. Ark. Dept. Labor; Sec. of State Ark., 2003—. With Parker's Chapel Sch. Bd. Served USAF, served USAFR. Mem.: Nat. Assn. Secs. State, Ea. Land Resources Coun., Western States Land Commrs. Assn., Ark. Natural and Cultural Resources Coun., Natural Resources Com., State Bd. Apportionment, Info. Network Ark. Bd. Office: 256 State Capitol Bldg Little Rock AR 72201 Office Phone: 501-682-1010. Business E-Mail: cdaniels@sosmail.state.ar.us.

DANIELS, CHERYL LYNN, pediatrics nurse, case manager; b. Paterson, NJ, June 15, 1951; d. Nathan and Frances Avonna (Bradshaw) D. RN, Martland Hosp. Sch. Nursing, Newark, 1971; AAS in Health and Community Svc., NYU, 1984, BA in Journalism, 1987. Evening charge nurse Martland Hosp. Unit, Newark, 1971-73; staff nurse Heal Econs. Advancement League, Paterson, N.J., 1972-74; neonatal intensive care nurse St. Joseph's Hosp. & Med. Ctr., Paterson, N.J., 1973-77, charge nurse neonatal intensive care, 1977—79, pediat. neonatal ICU, 1979-89, intensive care nurse, pediatric HIV outpatient nurse, 1989-90; rsch. outpatient HIV/SJH case mgmt. nurse Aids Clin. Trial Group, 1990-2001; case mgr. outpatient pediat. HIV Clinic, 1989—; pediat. sedation nurse for CT scan procedures, 2001—02. Mentor Career Beginning Program, Paterson, 1988-90. Recipient Gobetz award, NYU, 1984. Mem. ARC, AACN (cert. pediat. nursing), Alpha Sigma Lambda. Baptist. Avocations: clarinet, swimming, reading, writing, painting. Office: Saint Joseph Hosp 703 Main St Paterson NJ 07503-2691 Office Phone: 973-754-4703. Business E-Mail: danielscheryl@msn.com.

DANIELS, DANIEL LLOYD, lawyer; b. New Milford, Conn., Nov. 17, 1962; s. C. Ross Jr. and Fayne M. (McGrath) D.; m. Jennifer A. Matteis, Aug. 27, 1988; children: Benjamin T., Elizabeth S. AB summa cum laude, Dartmouth Coll., 1984; JD cum laude, Harvard U., 1987. Bar: N.Y. 1988, Conn. 1991. Law clk. Mass. Supreme Ct., Boston, 1987-88; assoc. Sullivan & Cromwell, N.Y.C., 1988-89; prin. Settle Agy., Inc., Danbury, Conn., 1989-91; assoc. Cummings & Lockwood, Stamford, Conn., 1991-96, ptnr., 1997—. Contbg. author: The 401 (K) Plan Handbook, 1997. Mem. Danbury Econ. Devel. Commn., 1991; bd. dirs. Cmty. Ctrs., Inc., Grenwich, Conn., 1994-96, Cmty. Answers at Greenwich Libr., 1996—. Fellow Am Coll. Trust and Estate Counsel; mem. ABA, Conn. Bar Assn. (presenter 1996, mem. estates and probate exec. com. 1999—), N.Y. State Bar Assn., Stamford-Norwalk Regional Bar Assn., Harvard Law Sch. Assn. Conn. (trustee Stamford 1995—). Avocations: a capella singing, gilbert and sullivan, musical theater. Office: Cummings & Lockwood 4 Stamford Plz Stamford CT 06902-3834 E-mail: ddaniels@cl-law.com.

DANIELS, DAVETTA MILLS, principal; b. Austin, Tex., July 31, 1952; d. Carole Athene and David Crockett Hill; m. Ray McCoy Daniels, Feb. 17, 2001; 1 child, Joelle Devee Mills. EdD, Nova Southeastern U., 2003. Cert. tchr. Tex. Edn. Agy., 1978. Social work Houston Area Urban League, Houston, Tex., 1975—76; tchr. Houston Ind. Sch. Dist., Houston, Tex. Prin. Houston Ind. Sch. Dist., Houston, 1995—2003, Hartsfield Elem., Houston, Texas, Tex.; founder/dir. Nat. Counseling and Referral Svcs., Houston; presenter Oxford (Eng.) U., 1999. Greeter/welcomer Wheeler Ave. Bapt. Ch., Houston, 2002—03; bd. mem. Women's Ctr., Houston, 2000—02; dir. Pass It On Mentorship/Guidance Program for Male Students, Houston. Fellow: Tenn. State U. (life; sec. 1999—2002); mem.: NAACP, Tex. Assn. Secondary Sch. Prins. (Outstanding Prin. of Yr. 1999—2000), Phi Delta Kappa, Delta Sigma Theta, Alpha Kappa Alpha. Home: 12714 Water Oak Drive Missouri City TX 77489 Office: Hartsfield Elem Sch 5001 Perry St Houston TX 77021 Personal E-mail: ddaniel1@houstonisd.org.

DANIELS, DEBORAH JEAN, lawyer, former federal agency administrator; BA, De Pauw U., 1973; JD, Ind. U. Bar: Ind. 1977, admitted to practice: US Dist. Ct. (So. Dist.) Ind. 1977, US Ct. Appeals (7th Cir.) 1977, US Supreme Ct. 1987. Chief counsel, Marion County, Ind.; ptnr. Kreig DeVault, LLP, Indpls., 1991—96, 2005—; US atty. U.S. Dist. Ct. (So. Dist.) Ind., 1988—93; first dir. exec. office Weed and Seed US Dept. Justice, 1992—93, asst. atty. gen. justice programs Washington, 2001—05. Exec. dir. Greater Indpls. Progress Com., Inc., 1994—96. Office: Krieg DeVault LLP One Indiana Sq Ste 2800 Indianapolis IN 46204 Office Phone: 317-238-6253. Office Fax: 317-636-1507. E-mail: ddaniels@kdlegal.com.

DANIELS, DIANA M., lawyer, publishing executive; b. Dillon, Mont. BA, Cornell U., 1971; JD, Harvard U., 1974; M of City Planning, MIT, 1974; diploma, U. Edinburgh, Scotland, 1976. Bar: N.Y. 1975, U.S. Dist. Ct. (ea. and so. dists.) N.Y. 1975, U.S. Ct. Appeals (2d cir.) 1975, D.C. 1978, U.S. Supreme Ct. 1988. Assoc. Cravath, Swaine & Moore, N.Y.C., 1975-78; asst. counsel Washington Post newspaper, 1978-79; gen. counsel Washington Post Co., 1988-89, v.p., gen. counsel, 1989-91, v.p., gen. counsel, sec., 1991—; v.p., counsel Newsweek, N.Y.C., 1979-85, v.p., gen. counsel, 1985-88. Mem. legal adv. com. NYSE, 2003—. Trustee Cornell U., 1995-, ABA Mus. Law, 1997-04, Appleseed Found., 1998-2004, Ctr. Study of Presidency, 1997-01, Am. Law Inst., 2003-; mem. legal adv. com. NYSE, 2003-. Office: Washington Post Co 1150 15th St NW Washington DC 20071-0002

DANIELS, ELIZABETH, retired dentist; b. Sebastian, Fla., Sept. 1938; d. Lievi and Addie Daniels; m. Jesse Robinson; 1 child, Jennifer. BS in Biochemistry, Tenn. State U., 1958; MS in Biochemistry, Howard U., 1963; PhD in Organic Chemistry, U. Calif., Riverside, Calif., 1969; DMD, U. Conn., 1977. Lic. dentist Va., 1978. Tchr. Carver H.S., Delray Beach, Fla., 1960—61; med. chemist Pfizer Inc., Groton, Conn., 1968—73; assoc. prof. dentistry Meharry Sch. Dentistry, Nashville, 1977—85, assoc. dean acad. affairs, 1985—88; pvt. practice Portsmouth, Va., 1990—2005. Bd. dirs. Starbase Atlantis, Portsmouth, Va., Portsmouth (Va.) City Pub. Schs., Va. Sch. Bds. Assn., Charlottesville, Va. Bd. dirs. Empowerment Zone, 2000—. Fellow, NASA, 1964—68. Mem.: NAACP (pres. Portsmouth (Va.) chpt. 1996—), Va. Sch. Bds. Assn. (pres.-elect 2005), Nat. Dental Assn., John McGriff Dental Assn. (pres. 2001—03).

DANIELS, ELIZABETH ADAMS, English language educator; b. Westport, Conn., May 8, 1920; d. Thomas Davies and Minnie Mae (Sherwood) Adams; m. John L. Daniels, Mar. 21, 1942; children: John L., Eleanor B. (dec.), Sherwood A., Ann S. AB, Vassar Coll., 1941; A.M., U. Mich., 1942; PhD, N.Y. U., 1954. From instr. to prof. English Vassar Coll., Poughkeepsie, N.Y., 1948-85, dean freshmen, 1955-58, dean studies, 1965-73, chmn. dept. English, 1974-76, 81-84, acting dean faculty, 1976-78, chmn. self-study, 1978-80, Vassar historian, 1985—. Author: Jessie White Mario, Risorgimento Revolutionary, 1972, Main to Mudd, Bridges to the World, 1994, Main to Mudd, and More, 1996; co-author: (with Clyde Griffen) Full Steam Ahead in Poughkeepsie, The Story of Coeducation at Vassar 1966-74, 2000, (with Maryann Bruno) Vassar College 1861-2000, 2000, (with Ron Patkus, Kari Strickland and Marian Thomas) Administrative History of Vassar College, 2004; contbr. articles to publs. Bd. dirs. Alzheimer's Assn. Mid-Hudson Valley, World Affairs Coun. Hudson Valley. Recipient Grad. award Alumnae Assn. N.Y. U., 1954; Vassar fellow, 1941; Nat. Endowment Humanities summer stipend, 1981 Mem. MLA, AAUP, Poughkeepsie Tennis Club, Phi Beta Kappa. Democrat. Home: 56 Muirfield Ct Poughkeepsie NY 12603 Office: Vassar Coll PO Box 74 Poughkeepsie NY 12602-0074 *Growing up with intellectual ambitions, I was able to work out a very satisfactory career combining teaching, college administration, scholarship, family life, and a good marriage slightly forerunning the feminist movement of the late nineteen-sixties. I owe much of this to Vassar College, the first endowed woman's college in the U.S.*

DANIELS, GEORGE BENJAMIN, federal judge; b. Allendale, S.C., May 13, 1953; s. Rufus Jacob and Florence (Morten) D. Student, Suffield Acad., 1967-71; BA, Yale U., 1975; JD, U. Calif., Berkeley, 1978. Bar: D.C. 1978, N.Y. 1979, Calif. 1981, N.J. 1983, U.S. Supreme Ct. 1982; notary public, N.Y. Trial atty. criminal def. div. Legal Aid Soc. N.Y., N.Y.C., 1978-80; law clk. to presiding justice Calif. Supreme Ct., San Francisco, 1980-81; litigation atty. Skadden, Arps, Slate, Meagher & Flom, N.Y.C., 1981-83; asst. U.S. atty. U.S. Atty.'s Office, Bklyn., 1983-89; judge Criminal Ct. City N.Y., 1989-90; counsel to mayor City of N.Y., 1990-93; judge Criminal Ct., N.Y.C., 1993-95; justice Supreme Ct. N.Y., 1995-2000; judge U.S. Dist. Ct. (so. dist.) N.Y., 2000—. Adj. prof. Bklyn. Law Sch., 1988-91. Bd. trustees Suffield (Conn.) Acad., 1986—; bd. dirs. Andrew Glover Youth Program, N.Y.C., 1982—. Mem. ABA. Office: US Courthouse 40 Foley Sq New York NY 10007*

DANIELS, GWYNN MARIE, biologist; b. Mplis., Sept. 29, 1956; d. Larry Lyman and Alice Lorraine Bushnell; m. John William Lyngdal, Aug. 9, 1998. BS, St Cloud (Minn.) State U., 1991; PhD, Oreg. Health & Sci. U., 1999. Mgr. Taco John's, Rochester, Minn., 1975—84; dept. mgr. Target Stores, Duluth, Minn., 1985—87; rsch. asst. St Cloud (Minn.) State U., 1989—91; from grad. rsch. asst. to biosafety officer Oreg. Health & Sci. U., Portland, Oreg., 1991—2002, biosafety officer, 2002—; rsch. assoc. Portland (Oreg.) VA Med. Ctr., 2000—02. Contbr. articles to profl. jours. Bd. dirs. Operation Nightwatch, Portland, 1994—98. Grantee, NIH, 1989. Mem.: Am. Biol. Safety Assn. Office Phone: 503-494-0655.

DANIELS, JAMES DOUGLAS, retired academic administrator; b. Harmony, NC, Nov. 14, 1935; m. Marie Brown, Oct. 6, 1957; children: Christopher James, Gregory John, Susan Marie. AB, Davidson Coll., 1957; MA, U. N.C., 1962, PhD, 1968. Exec. tng. program Deering-Milliken Textile Corp., Gainesville, Ga., 1957-58; history instr. Hargrave Military Acad., Chatham, Va., 1961-62, chmn., divsn. social sci., 1962-65, dean students, summer sch., 1964-65; asst. prof. history Valdosta (Ga.) State Coll., 1968-71, assoc. prof. history, 1971-78, history prof., 1978, dean, sch. arts, sci., 1970-80; pres., prof. history Coker Coll., Hartsville, SC, 1981—2002; ret., 2002. Bd. dirs. Byerly Hosp., 1981-85; Sunday sch. tchr. First Presbyn. Ch. Hartsville, 1981—. Com. on ministry Pee Dee Presbytery of S.C., 1985—, moderator, 1985; adv. bd. Bank of Am., 1988—, Pee Dee Heritage, 1982—, Darlington County Mental Health Citizens, 1987—. With U.S. Army, 1958—60. NDEA fellow, U. N.C., 1966-68; recipient Man and Boy award Valdosta Boys' Club Bd. Dirs., 1970. Mem. Greater Hartsville C. of C. (bd. dirs. 1982-88, v.p. 1986, pres. 1987, chmn. bd. 1988), Hartsville H.S. Acad. Boosters Club and Band Boosters, Rotary (bd. dirs. 1982-99, Citizen of Yr. award 1989), Order of Palmetto, Omicron Delta Kappa. Presbyterian. Avocations: reading, fishing. Home: 206 Persimmon Fork Rd Blythewood SC 29016

DANIELS, JAMES MAURICE, retired physicist; b. Leeds, Eng., Aug. 26, 1924; emigrated to Can., 1953, naturalized, 1971; came to U.S., 1984, naturalized, 1992. s. Bernard and Mary Mahala (Proctor) D.; married; children: Ian Nicolas James, Maurice Edward Bruce. BA, Oxford (Eng.) U., 1945, MA, 1949, D.Phil., 1952. Exptl. asst. Radar R & D Establishment, Malvern, Eng., 1944-46; tech. officer explosives div. Imperial Chem. Industries, Ardeer, Scotland, 1946-47; rsch. fellow Clarendon Lab., Oxford (Eng.) U., 1952-53; asst. prof. physics U. B.C., Vancouver, Can., 1953-56, assoc. prof., 1956-60; UNESCO expert U. Buenos Aires, Argentina, 1958-59; prof. U. Toronto, Ont., Can., 1961-87, prof. emeritus, 1987—, chmn. dept. physics, 1968-73, chmn. dept. stats., 1983-84. Vis. prof. Instituto de Fisica, S.C. de Bariloche Argentina, 1960-61, Helsinki U. Tech., 1974, Columbia U., 1978-79, Princeton U., 1984-85, Ecole Normale Superieure Paris, 1985-86, Nat. Tsing Hua U., Hsinchu, Republic of China, 1990, 91-92; vis. disting. prof. Oakland U., Rochester, Mich., 1994-95; pres. U. Toronto Faculty Assn., 1976-77; v.p. Can. Assn. Univ. Tchrs., Ottawa, 1979-80; sec., treas. Can. Inst. Particle Physics, Ottawa, 1970-73. Author: Oriented Nuclei, Polarized Targets and Beams, 1965; contbr. numerous articles to profl. jours. Alfred P. Sloan fellow, 1962-65, Guggenheim fellow, 1978-79 Fellow London Phys. Soc., London Inst. Physics (chartered physicist), London Royal Soc. Arts, Royal Soc. Can.; mem. Can. Assn. Physicists, Am. Phys. Soc., N.Y. Acad. Scis., Can. Inst. Particle Physics (sec-treas. 1971-73), Can. Assn. Univ. Tchrs. (v.p. 1977-78). Achievements include patents for Doppler radar; instrument for measure the polarization of 3 He; first to first successful production of spatially oriented atomic nuclei; compressed spin-polarizedd 3 He; application of the Mossbauer effect for determining spin arrangements in magnetic materials. Personal E-mail: jmdaniels314@hotmail.com.

DANIELS, JAMES WALTER, lawyer; b. Chgo., Oct. 13, 1945; s. Ben George and Delores L. (Wolanin) D.; m. Gail Anne Rihacek, June 14, 1969; children: Morgan, Abigail, Rachel. AB, Brown U., 1967; JD, U. Chgo., 1970. Bar: Calif. 1970, U.S. Dist. Ct. (ctrl. dist.) Calif. 1970, U.S. Tax Ct., 1972, U.S. Supreme Ct. 1979. Assoc. firm Latham & Watkins, L.A. and Newport Beach, Calif., 1970-77, ptnr., 1977—. Arbitrator Orange County Superior Ct., Santa Ana, Calif., 1978—88, judge pro tem, 1979—87. Fin. dir. St. Elizabeth Ann Seton Parish, Irvine, Calif., 1975-82; sec. Turtlerock Tennis Com., Irvine, 1981-83, 86—, pres., 1985-86; bd. dirs. Turtlerock Terr. Homeowners Assn., 1983-85, 87-89. Mem. ABA, Internat. Coun. Shopping Ctrs., Center club, Irvine Racquet Club, Palm Valley Country Club. Democrat. Roman Catholic. Home: 19241 Beckwith Ter Irvine CA 92603 Office: Latham & Watkins 650 Town Center Dr Ste 2000 Costa Mesa CA 92626-7135 Office Phone: 714-540-1235. Business E-Mail: james.daniels@lw.com.

DANIELS, JEFF, actor; b. Athens, Ga., Feb. 19, 1955; m. Kathleen Treado, July 13, 1979; 3 children. Student, Cen. Mich. U. Apprentice Circle Repertory Co., N.Y.C.; founder Purple Rose Theatre Co., Chelsea, Mich. Actor: (stage prodns.) The Farm, 1976, My Life, 1977, Brontosaurus, 1977, Feedlot, 1977, Lulu, 1978, Slugger, 1978, The Fifth of July, 1978, 79, 80-81, Johnny Got His Gun, 1982 (Obie award), Three Sisters, 1982-83, The Golden Age, 1984, Short-Changed Review, Redwood Curtain, 1993, (feature films) Ragtime, 1981, Terms of Endearment, 1983, The Purple Rose of Cairo, 1985, Marie, 1985, Heartburn, 1986, Something Wild, 1986, Radio Days, 1987, The House on Carroll Street, 1988, Sweet Hearts Dance, 1988, Grand Tour, 1989, Checking Out, 1989, Arachnophobia, 1990, Welcome Home, Roxy Carmichael, 1990, Love Hurts, 1990, The Butcher's Wife, 1992, Gettysburg, 1993, Speed, 1994, Dumb and Dumber, 1994, Fly Away Home, 1996, 2 Days in the Valley, 1996, 101 Dalmations, 1996, Trial and Error, 1997, Pleasantville, 1998, My Favorite Martian, 1999, All the Rage, 1999, Chasing Sleep, 2000, Escanaba in da Moonlight, 2001 (also writer, dir.), Blood Work, 2002, The Hours, 2002, Gods and Generals, 2003, I Witness, 2003, Imaginary Heroes, 2004, Because of Winn-Dixie, 2005, The Squid and the Whale, 2005; (TV movies) A Rumor of War, 1980, An Invasion of Privacy, 1983, The Caine Mutiny Court Marshall, 1988, No Place Like Home, 1989, Disaster in Time, 1992, Redwood Curtain, 1995, The Crossing, 2000, Cheaters, 2000, The Goodbye Girl, 2004, The Five People You Meet in Heaven, 2004; playwright: Shoeman, 1991, The Tropical Pickle, 1992, The Vast Difference, 1993, Thy Kingdom's Coming, 1994, Escanaba in da Moonlight, 1995.*

DANIELS, JOHN HANCOCK, agricultural products company executive; b. St. Paul, Oct. 28, 1921; s. Thomas L. and Frances (Hancock) D.; m. Martha H. Williams, Dec. 23, 1942; children: Martha M., John Hancock, Jane P. Daniels Moffett, Christopher W. Student, St. Paul Acad., 1932-37; grad., Phillips Exeter Acad., 1939; BA, Yale, 1943; grad., Advanced Mgmt. Program, Harvard, 1957. With Archer-Daniels-Midland Co., Mpls., 1946-96, successively mem. staff linseed oil div., prodn. mgr. alfalfa divsn., mgr. feed divsn., v.p., dir., 1946-53, pres., dir., 1958-67, chmn., 1967-72, dir., mem. exec. com., 1972-96. With Mulberry Resources Inc. Author: Nothing Could Be Finer, 1996, Affectionately H, 1999, In The Boat, 2004. With Bus. Coun.; trustee Com. Econ. Devel.; chmn. 1972 Decatur United Way Campaign. Served from 2d lt. to capt. F.A., AUS, 1943-46. Decorated Bronze Star medal. Mem. Grolier Club, Elizabethan Club, Links Club (N.Y.C.), Mpls. Club, Woodhill (Minn.) Club, Sprindale Hall Club (Camden, S.C.), Grolier Club, Lafayette Club. Episcopalian. Home: Mulberry Plantation PO Box 1349 Camden SC 29020-1349 Personal E-mail: CDE322@aol.com.

DANIELS, JOHN PETER, lawyer; b. N.Y.C., Feb. 5, 1937; s. Jack Brainard and Isabelle (McConachie) D.; m. Lynn Eldridge, Aug. 28, 1978 (div. Jan. 1980); m. Susan Gurley, Apr. 1, 1983. AB, Dartmouth Coll., 1959; JD, U. So. Calif., 1963. Bar: Calif. 1964; diplomate Am. Bd. Trial Advocates. Assoc. Bolton, Groff and Dunne, L.A., 1964-67, Jones and Daniels, L.A., 1967-70, Acret and Perrochet, L.A., 1971-81; ptnr. Daniels, Baratta and Fine, L.A., 1982-99, Daniels, Fine, Israel & Schonbuch, L.A., 1999—. Mem. Assn. So. Calif. Def. Counsel (bd. dirs. 1975-80), Fedn. Ins and Corp. Counsel. Clubs: Wilshire Country (Los Angeles). Avocations: scuba diving, golf, hunting. Office: Daniels Fine Israel & Schonbuch 1801 Century Park E Fl 9 Los Angeles CA 90067-2302 Office Phone: 310-556-7900. Business E-Mail: daniels@dfls-law.com.

DANIELS, JOHN R., oncologist, educator; b. Detroit, May 9, 1938; BA, Stanford U., 1959, MD, 1964. Diplomate Am. Bd. Internal Medicine. Postdoctoral fellow dept. cell biology Albert Einstein Coll. Medicine, 1964; intern in medicine Stanford U. Sch. Medicine, 1964-65; rsch. assoc. Nat. Inst. Dental Rsch., NIH, 1966-69; sr. resident in medicine Stanford U. Sch. Medicine, 1969-70, instr. div. oncology, 1970-71, asst. prof. div. oncology, 1971-78, clin. assoc. prof. div. oncology, 1978-79; v.p. for sci. and tech. affairs Collagen Corp., 1978-79; CEO, dir. Target Therapeutics, 1985-89; assoc. prof. medicine div. oncology U. So. Calif. Sch. Medicine, L.A., 1979—, assoc. prof. radiology, 1990—. Bd. dirs. Collagen Corp. Contbr. over 85 articles to profl. jours.; 9 patents in field. Mem. Am. Assn. for Cancer Rsch., Am. Soc. Clin. Oncology. Home: 842 N Las Casas Ave Pacific Palisades CA 90272-2340 Office: Cohesion Technologies Inc 2500 Faber Pl Palo Alto CA 94303

DANIELS, JONATHAN PAUL, web architect; b. Davenport, Iowa, Sept. 30, 1964; s. John Paul and Francine Roberta (Piperata) D.; children: Reece, Chase. Front office mgr. Westin Hotel Vail, Vail, Colo., 1987-90; cons. PC Info. Ctr., Allentown, Pa., 1991-92; analyst Rodale Press, Emmaus, Pa., 1992-94, messaging engr., 1994-98, web engr., 1998-99; web developer Computer Aid, Allentown, 2000—02; web arch. Computer Aid, Inc., Allentown, 2002—04; info. archt. Roska Direct Mktg., Montgomeryville, Pa., 2004—. Cons. Rodale Inst. Exptl. Farm, Maxatawny, Pa., 1991-93; adv. East Penn Sch. Dist., Emmaus, 1995-2001. Democrat. Roman Catholic. Avocations: skiing, golf, softball, football, grateful dead. E-mail: jon@alumni.lehigh.edu.

DANIELS, KATHLEEN ANGELA, educational administrator; b. Detroit, Jan. 21, 1945; d. Leondro Cardinez and Lillian Mary (Murray) Castro; m. Donald W. Daniels, Jan. 30, 1971 (div. May 1983); 1 child, Donald. BA in Environ. Design, Wayne State U., 1967; student, U. Calif., L.A., 1969. Photographic artist Jana Taylor & Co., Venice, Calif., 1985-88; rep., founder Am. Child Found., Venice, 1986-88; exec. dir. Cmty. Assns. Inst., L.A., 1989—2000; interior plantscaper, owner Ms. Green Thumb, 2003—. Mem. NOW, Nat. Woman's Polit. Caucus, Nat. Assn. Female Execs., Am. Soc. Assn. Execs., Sierra Club, Nat. Dem. Club. Avocations: gardening, ceramic animal collector, reading, walking. Home and Office: Ms Green Thumb 1903 W 9th St San Pedro CA 90732-3303 Office Phone: 310-339-0898. E-mail: msgreenthumb8@yahoo.com.

DANIELS, KATRINA L., elementary school educator; b. Omaha, Nebr., May 31, 1980; d. Michael E. and Inga R. Daniels. BS, Peru State Coll., 2002; M summe cum laude in edn., U. Nebr., 2003. Page Omaha Pub. Libr., Omaha, 1997—2002; tchr. Millard Pub. Sch., Omaha, 2002—. Tutor, study ctr. Millard Pub. Sch., Omaha, 2004—, MIT cons., 2004—; knitting tchr. MPS-Neihardt Elem., Omaha, 2005—. Study Ctr. grant, Millard Edn. Found., 2004, Learning Bag grant, 2004. Mem.: NEA, Internat. Reading Assn., Phi Delta Kappa. Avocations: tennis, sewing, reading, aerobics, golf. Office Phone: 402-895-8360. E-mail: kldaniels@mpsomaha.org.

DANIELS, KURT R., speech and language pathologist; b. Chgo., Oct. 22, 1954; s. Donald R. and Phyllis D. (Lenz) D.; m. Renee Perry, July 5, 1980. BS, Ea. Ill. U., 1976, MS, 1977. Cert. clin. competence speech/lang. pathology; lic. speech/lang. pathologist, nursing home adminstr; tchr's. cert. spl. K-12th grades. Hearing and speech specialist Shapiro Devel. Ctr., Kankakee, Ill., 1977-80; dysphagia specialist lead profl. W.A. Howe Ctr., Tinley Pk., Ill., 1980—. Adv. bd. program in comm. disorders Govs. State U., clin. adj. prof.; cons., presenter in field Recipient Editor's Choice award Nat. Libr. Poetry, 1994, 95. Mem. Am. Speech, Lang. and Hearing Assn., Ill. Speech, Lang. and Hearing Assn., Internat. Soc. Poets, Chicagoland Dysphagia Forum (sec. 1998-2000) Achievements include research in dysphagia and developmental disabilities. Office: 7600 W 183d St Tinley Park IL 60477 Office Phone: 708-614-4355.

DANIELS, LEE ALBERT, state legislator; b. Lansing, Mich., Apr. 15, 1942; s. Albert Lee and Evelyn (Bousfield) D.; m. Pamela Mesha; children: Laurie Lynn, Rachael Lee, Julie, Thomas, Christina. BA, U. Iowa, 1965; JD, John Marshall Law Sch., 1967. Rep. precinct committeeman, 1965-74; mem. bd. auditors York Twp., Ill., 1966-73; vice chmn. York Twp. Rep. Comty. Orgn., 1973-74; former minority spokesman judiciary com. Ill. Ho. of Reps.; spl. asst. atty. gen., 1973-75; Ill. state rep. 46th Dist., 1975—, majority whip, 1981-82, minority leader, 1983-94, spkr. Ho., 1995—97. Full ptnr. Katten, Muchin & Zavis, 1984-91; ptnr. Bell, Boyd & Lloyd, Chgo., 1992— Trustee Elmhurst Hosp.; chmn. Ill. Rep. Party, 2001-2002. Recipient Everett McKinley Dirksen award, 1995; named one of Outstanding Legislators in Country, Nat. Rep. Legis. Assn., 1991, Legislator of Yr., Ill. Hosp. Assn., 1986, DuPage Mayors and Mgrs. Conf., 1995. Mem. ABA, Ill. Bar Assn., DuPage County Bar Assn., Shriners, Masons, Moose. Republican. Home: 105 S York Rd Ste 550 Elmhurst IL 60126 Office: 200 5N Stratton Springfield IL 62706-0001

DANIELS, MARTHA K., artist; b. Bklyn., Sept. 21, 1943; d. Clifford William and Martha Katherine (Kreiss) Kirmss; m. Willem-Hendryk Daniels (div. 1973). Studied, Cooper Union, N.Y.C., 1961—64; BFA in Ceramics and Art History, Metrop. State Coll., Denver, 1975. Represented in permanent collections Kaiser Permanente, Taco Bell Corp., Native Am. Rights Found., Boulder, Colo., Amoco Oil Corp., Vance Kirkland Mus., exhibitions include Ivan Spence Gallery, Ibiza, Spain, 1965, Spectrum Gallery, Estes Park, Colo., 1970, Lodestone Gallery, Boulder, Colo., 1970—72, Boulder Designer Craftsman, 1970—72, Sebastian-Moore Gallery, 1978—81, Wash. Art, Wash., D.C., 1978, Ludlow-Hyland Gallery, N.Y.C., 1982—83, Spark Gallery, Denver, 1983, 1986, Pirate Gallery, Denver, 1984—92, Cafe Noir, Brussels, Belguim, 1988—90, David Rago Gallery, Lambertville, N.J., 1988, Mino, Japan, 1989—90, Boulder Pub. Libr., 1992, Denver Art Mus., 1978, 1990, 1994, one-man shows include, 2000, exhibitions include Foothills Art Ctr., Golden, Colo., 1992, 1998, Savageau Gallery, Denver, 1993—98, Saks Galleries, 1994—95, Rocky Mountain Women's Inst., 1995, Sage Gallery, Santa Fe, 1996, Elizabeth Schlosser Gallery, Denver, 1996, William Havu Gallery, 1999, 2000, 2001, 2003, Internat. Mus. Ceramics, Faenza, Italy, 2003, Robert Nichols Gallery, Santa Fe, 2003, Vance Kirkland Mus., Denver, Colo., 2003, Denver Mus. Contemporary Art, 1997, 2002, 2003. Recipient Mayor's Award, Rocky Mountain Women's Inst., 1995; fellow, 1995, Colo. Coun. on the Arts, 2001; grantee, Denver Art Mus., 1999. Home and Studio: 2138 Marion St Denver CO 80205

DANIELS, MICHAEL PAUL, lawyer; b. Maplewood, N.J., Apr. 22, 1930; s. Samuel and Lena E. (Oxman) D.; m. Lora Lee, June 23, 1949 (div. Aug. 1964); children: Lisa J., Rachel L., Aaron N.; m. Elaine Makris, Sept. 1, 1964; children: Anthony P., Maria, Alexander P. BA, U. Chgo., 1949, JD, 1952; student, U. Tokyo Sch. Law, 1958-59. Bar: U.S. Ct. Appeals (D.C. cir.) 1955, U.S. Supreme Ct., U.S. Ct. Internat. Trade; U.S. Ct. Appeals (fed. cir.). Atty. U.S. Congl. Reference Service, Washington, 1955-56; assoc. Becker & Maguire, Washington, 1956-57, Stitt & Hemendinger, Washington, 1958-63; ptnr. Stitt, Hemindinger & Daniels, Washington, 1963-67, Daniels, Houlihan & Palmeter, Washington, 1968-84; ptnr., internat. dept. head Mudge, Rose, Guthrie, Alexander & Ferdon, Washington, 1984-95; ptnr. Graham & James, Washington, 1995-97, Powell Goldstein Frazer & Murphy, Washington, 1997—2000; ptnr., chmn. internat. trade group Loeffler Tuggey Pauerstein Rosenthal LLP, 2003—. Cons. Fasturn Inc., 2000—03. Served with U.S. Army, 1952-54, Korea. Decorated Meritorious Bronze Star; fellow Fulbright fellow. Mem. ABA, D.C. Bar Assn. Home: 5615 Bent Branch Rd Bethesda MD 20816-1049 Office Phone: 202-775-4427. Personal E-mail: MikeElaineDaniels@comcast.net. Business E-Mail: mdaniels@loefflerllp.com.

DANIELS, MITCHELL ELIAS, JR., governor, former federal agency administrator; b. Monongahela, Pa., Apr. 7, 1949; s. Mitchell Elias and Dorothy Mae (Wilkes) D.; m. Cheri Lynn Herman, May 20, 1978; children—Meagan, Melissa, Meredith, Margaret. AB, Princeton U., 1971; JD, Georgetown U., 1979. Bar: Ind. 1979. Exec. v.p. Campaign Communicators, Inc., Indpls., 1971-74; dep. to mayor City of Indpls., 1974-75; campaign mgr. Lugar for U.S. Senate, Indpls., 1976; adminstrv. asst. to U.S. Senator Dick Lugar U.S. Senate, Washington, 1977-83; exec. dir. Nat. Rep. Sen. Com., Washington, 1983-85; asst. to the Pres. The White House, Washington, 1985—87; CEO Hudson Inst., 1987—90; pres. N. Am. pharmaceutical ops. Eli Lilly and Co., 1993—97, sr. v.p. corp. strategy, policy, 1997—2001; dir. Office Mgmt. & Budget Exec. Office of the Pres., Washington, 2001—03; gov. State of Ind., Indianapolis, 2005—. Vice pres., trustee Am. Council Young Polit. Leaders, Washington, 1983—; mem. adv. com. Responsible Govt. for Am. Found., Washington, 1983—; bd. dirs. Fund for Hoosier Excellence, 1984—, Ind. Nat. Bank, Ind. Power & Light, Angie's List. Recipient Graham award Ind. Am. Legion, 1966, "Hero of the Taxpayer" award, American for Tax Reform, 2002, Chauncey Rose award, Rose-Hulman Inst. Tech., 2003; Presdl. scholar, 1967 Mem. Ind. Bar Assn. Clubs: Columbia (Indpls.). Republican. Presbyterian. Office: Office of Gov 206 State House Indianapolis IN 46204*

DANIELS, NORMAN, philosopher, educator; b. N.Y.C., June 30, 1942; s. Manus and Evelyn (Auerbach) D.; m. Anne L. Hooker; 1 child, Noah. AB summa cum laude, Wesleyan U., 1964; BA, MA, Balliol Coll., Oxford, Eng., 1966; PhD, Harvard U., 1970. Asst. prof. philosophy Tufts U., Medford, Mass., 1970-76, assoc. prof. philosophy, 1976-81, prof. philosophy, 1981—2002, chmn. philosophy dept., 1983—2002; prof., sch. of public health Harvard U., Boston, 2002—. Faculty Harvard extension, Cambridge, Mass., 1976—; vis. assoc. prof. bioethics Brown U., Providence, 1979; reviewer NEH, NSF, 1982-85; panel mem. NSF-NEH Ethics and Values in Sci. and Tech., 1982. Author: (book) Thomas Reid's Inquiry: The Geometry of Visibles and the Case for Realism, 1974, Reading Rawls: Critical Studies of John Rawls' A Theory of Justice, 1975, In Search of Equity: Health Needs and the Health Care System, 1983, Just Health Care, 1985, Am I My Parent's Keeper? An Essay on Justice Between the Young and the Old, 1988; editorial bd. Australasian Jour. Philosophy, Ethics, Jour. Medicine and Philosophy; editor (with Keith Lehrer) series of philosophy textbooks; referee Isis, Nous, Philos. Forum, Philos. Studies, Social Theory and Practice, Jour. Medicine and Philosophy, Bus. and Profl. Ethics Jour., Milbank Meml. Fund Quar., Philosophy and Econs., Philosophy and Phenomenology Research; reviewer Wadsworth Pub. Co., Dickenson, Prentice-Hall, Oxford, Princeton, Garland Pub. Co., Cornell U. Press, Rowman and Littlefield, Cambridge U. Press. Recipient George Plimpton Adams prize, 1970, Woodrow Wilson Career Devel. award, 1980, Mass. Found. Humanities and Pub. Policy and Matchette Found. award, 1980; Harvard Grad. Nat. fellow, 1966-69, NEH Individual fellow, 1977-78; grantee Marsden Found., 1966, Nat. Ctr. Health Svcs. rsch. grantee, 1978-79, 79-80, 80-81, 81-82, NEH, 1983-85, 89—, Retirement Rsch. Found., 1983-86, NSF, 1987, USPHS, 1989—. Mem.: Nat. Institute of Health, 1999-, AAAS, AAUP, Am. Philos. Assn., Philosophy of Sci. Assn., Phi Beta Kappa. Office: Harvard Sch Pub Health 665 Huntington Ave Rm 1104C Boston MA 02115

DANIELS, RANDY A., state official; married; 2 children. BA in Govt. and Journalism, So. Ill. U. Prof. adj. journalism CCNY, Columbia U.'s Grad. Sch. Journalism; reporter WVON Radio, Chgo., 1970—72; corr. CBS News, Chgo., 1972—77, fgn. corr. Kenya, 1977—80, nat. corr. N.Y.C., 1980—82; mng. editor Jacaranda Nigeria Ltd., 1982—84; dir. Comm. N.Y.C. Coun. Pres.'s Office, 1986—88; Press Sec. Prime Min. of Bahamas, 1988—92; v.p. Hirshfeld realty, N.Y.C., 1993—95; sr. v.p., dep. commr. econ. revitalization Empire State Corp. (ESDC), 1995—99; sr. v.p. Canyon Johnson Urban Fund, L.L.P., 1999—2001; sec. state State of N.Y., Albany, 2001—. Mem.: Exec. and Fin. Coms., SUNY Bd. Trustees (vice chmn., chmn. invetsment com., co-chmn. coms. on gen. edn. and charter schs.). Office: 41 State St 9th Fl Albany NY 12231-0001 Business E-Mail: info@dos.state.ny.us.

DANIELS, RICHARD J., publishing executive; BBA, Northeastern U., 1980; postgrad., Boston U. Cons. Andersen Consulting, 1980—83; joined as software analyst Boston Globe, 1983; dir. bus. devel. Affiliated Publications, also v.p. systems & tech. BPI Comm.; v.p. strategic planning Boston Globe, named sr. v.p., 1996, sr. v.p. sales & marketing, CFO, 1998—2000, sr. v.p. planning & ops., 2000—01; pres. Globe Newspaper Co. & Boston Globe, 2001—. Office: Boston Globe PO Box 2378 135 Morrissey Blvd Dorchester MA 02107-2378*

DANIELS, ROBERT E., child psychologist; b. Detroit, Nov. 19, 1970; s. Loren S. and Sharon E. Daniels; m. Amy L. Larmore, Aug. 21, 1999; children: Taylor Marie, Emma Elizabeth. BA Honors with Distinction, U. of Mich., 1992; PhD, Ill. Inst. of Tech., Chgo., 1999. Lic. clin. psychologist Dept. of Fin. and Profl. Regulation, Ill. Psychologist Rush Neurobehavioral Ctr., Skokie, Ill., 2000; exec. dir. Children's Clinic, LLC, Chgo., 2000—. Presenter Comparing Two Early Intervention Methods For Children With Autism: Full-day Preschool And Home-based Applied Behavior Therapy. Contbr. articles to profl. jours. Recipient Prin. Investigator grant, Jewish Fedn. of Met. Chgo. and Michael Reese Health Trust, 2001—05, Wash. Sq. Health Found., 2001—02, Prin. Investigator, Rush-Presbyn.-St. Luke's Med. Ctr., Inst. for Mental Well-Being, 1997—98, Morris E. Aderman Rsch. award, Ill. Inst. of Tech., 1995. Mem.: APA, Autism Soc. of Am., Internat. Dyslexia Assn., Ill. Psychol. Assn., Midwest Psychol. Assn., Psi Chi. Jewish. Avocations: travel, scuba diving, skiing. Office: Children's Clinic LLC Ste 100 1333 N Kingsbury St Chicago IL 606622 Office Phone: 312-587-1742. Office Fax: 312-944-8796. E-mail: rdaniels@chicagochildrensclinic.com.

DANIELS, ROBERT VINCENT, history professor, former state senator; b. Boston, Jan. 4, 1926; s. Robert Whiting and Helen Underwood (Hoyt) D.; m. Alice May Wendell, July 2, 1945; children: Robert H., Helen L. Turcotte, Irene L., Thomas L. AB, Harvard U., 1945, MA, 1947, PhD, 1951; LLD (hon.), U. Vt., 1994. Rsch. assoc. MIT, Cambridge, 1951-52; social sci. faculty Bennington (Vt.) Coll., 1952-53, 57-58; asst. prof. Slavic studies Ind. U., 1953-55; rsch. assoc. Columbia U., 1955-56; from asst. prof. history to prof. U. Vt., Burlington, 1956-88, prof. emeritus, 1988—, chmn. dept., 1964-69, dir. exptl. program, 1969-71; mem. Vt. Senate, 1973-82, asst. minority leader, 1977-80, minority leader, 1981-82. Chmn. Vt. Gov.'s Commn. Med. Care, 1974-75; mem. Vt. Health Policy Corp., 1977-80; mem. adv. com. on East Europe and USSR, Coun. on Internat. Exch. of Scholars, 1983-85; adv. coun. Ctr. for Internat. Polit. Studies, Rome, 1989—; mem. sister state com. Vt.-Karelia, 1991—, co-dir. self-govt. tng. program, 1993-94; dir. U. Vt. Petrozavodsk U. partnership program, 1994-95; mem. supervisory bd. Internat. Coop. Ctr. Karelian br. St. Petersburg Acad. Pub. Adminstrn. Author: The Conscience of the Revolution, 1960, Documentary History of Communism, 1960, rev. edit., 1993, The Nature of Communism, 1962, Studying History, 1966, Red October, 1967, The Russian Revolution, 1972, Fodor's Europe Talking, 1975, Russia-The Roots of Confrontation, 1985, Is Russia Reformable?, 1988, Year of the Heroic Guerrilla, 1989, Trotsky, Stalin and Socialism, 1992, The End of the Communist Revolution, 1993, Soviet Communism from Reform to Collapse, 1994, Russia's Transformation, 1997; editor: The University of Vermont: The First Two Hundred Years, 1991. Mem. Chittenden County (Vt.) Dem. Com., 1959—; mem. Burlington City Dem. Com., 1965—; chmn. policy and planning platform com. Vt. Dem. Party, 1962-66, 69-73, 76-80, mem. exec. com., 1981-85; alt. Dem. Nat. Conv., 1968; mem. Dem. Platform Com., 1980; bd. visitors USAF Acad., 1965-67. Ensign USNR, 1944-46. U.S.-Soviet Cultural Exch. scholar U. Moscow, 1966, USSR Acad. Scis. scholar, 1976, 84, 88; NEH fellow, 1971-72, Guggenheim fellow, 1980-81, Kennan Inst. fellow, 1985. Fellow Vt. Acad. Arts and Scis.; mem. Am. Hist. Assn. (pres. conf. Slavic and East European history 1976-77), Am. Assn. Advancement Slavic Studies (bd. dirs. 1968-71, v.p. 1991, pres. 1992, chmn. com. on govt. affairs 1993-94, Disting. Contbns. award 2001), Can. Assn. Slavists, Authors' Guild, Vt. Hist. Soc. (trustee 1968-71), Vt. Coun. World Affairs, Norwich Ctr./Bridges for Peace (bd. dirs. 1988-94), Harvard Club Vt. (pres. 1974-75). Home: 195 S Prospect St Burlington VT 05401-3519 Office: University of Vermont Dept Of History Burlington VT 05405-0001 Office Phone: 802-656-3180. Business E-Mail: rdaniels@zoo.uvm.edu.

DANIELS, RONALD DALE, conductor; b. San Mateo, Calif., Aug. 19, 1943; s. Worth W. and Margurite Pearl (Chandler) D.; 1 child, Ryan Stark. BMus, San Francisco Conservatory, 1968. Condr., music dir. Musical Arts of Contra Costa (Calif.) County, 1968-75, U. Calif., Berkeley, 1973-75, Contra Costa Symphony, 1976-79, Reno (Nev.) Philharm., 1979-98, conductor Laureate, 1998—. Guest conductor various orchs.; grants rev. cons. in field. With USMC, 1966. Recipient Lucien Wulsin award Baldwin Piano Co., Tanglewood Festival, 1968, Gov.'s Art award State of Nev., 1981. Avocations: ice skating, skiing, sailing, hiking. Office: Reno Philharm Assn Ste 3 925 Riverside Dr Reno NV 89503 Home: 703 Pat Ln Carson City NV 89701-5623

DANIELS, RONALD GEORGE, theater director; b. Niteroi, Rio de Janiero, Brazil, Oct. 15, 1942; arrived in U.S., 1991; s. Percy and Nellie (Chalmers) D.; m. Anjula Harman; children: Alexis, Eliena. Student, Fundacão Brasileira de Teatro, Rio de Janiero. Assoc. artistic dir. Am. Reperatory Theatre, Cambridge, Mass., 1991—96; head acting and directing programs Inst. for Advanced Theatre Tng. Harvard U., 1991—96. Hon. assoc. dir. Royal Shakespeare Co., Stratford-upon-Avon, London; lectr. Shakespeare Inst., U. Birmingham, Friends Royal Shakespeare Co., others. Dir.: (stage) Coriolanus, Major Barbara, Who's Afraid of Virginia Wolf, Sweeney Todd, Ghosts, Hamlet, Drums in the Night, The Samaritan, Time Travelers, The Long and Short and the Tall, The Word, Measure for Measure, Fear and Miseries of the Third Reich, The Insect Play, Twelfth Night, A Midsummer Night's Dream, Pillars of the Community, Man is Man, The Children's Crusade, Female Transport, Sgt. Musgreve's Dance, Into the Mouth of Crabs, By Common Consent, The Motor Show, Made in Britain, Bang, Afore Night Come, Bingo, Puntila and His Servant Matti, Ivanov, Destiny, T'is Pity She's a Whore, The Lorenzaccio Story, The Sons of Light, Pericles, The Suicide, Timon of Athens, Hippolytus, Camille, Hansel and Gretel, Peer Gynt, Romeo and Juliet, Ashes, The Beastly Beatitudes of Balthazar B, Across from the Garden of Allah, Playing with Trains, The Tempest, Julius Cesar, Maydays, Breaking the Silence, The Danton Affair, The Women Pirates, Real Dreams, They Shoot Horses, Much Ado About Nothing, The Plain Dealer, The Clockwork Orange, Earwig, Richard II, The Seagull, As You Like It, The Dream of The Red Spider, Silence, Cunning, Exile, Cakewalk, Henry IV parts I and II, The Cherry Orchard, Henry V, The Threepenny Opera, The Tempest, Slaughter City, Long Day's Journey into Night, Blinded by the Sun, Anthony and Cleopatra, The Shepherd King, One Flea Spare, Madama Butterfly, Henry V and Richard II, Richard III, Macbeth, Remember This, King Lear, Carmen, Hedda Gabler, The Feast of Snails, The Turn of the Screw, Sana que Sana, Havana is Waiting, Tosca, Cosi Fan Tutti, La Forza del Destino; exec. prodr. Lawn Dogs. Mem. Soc. Stage Dirs. and Choreographers, Dirs. Guild Gt. Britain, Am. Guild Musical Artists, Nat. Assn. Latino Ind. Prodrs.

DANIELS, SEAN E., music educator; s. Jimmy L. Daniels and Davora Daniels Jenkins; m. Sonya Lee Daniels; 1 child, Sean E. III. BA, Ala. State U., 1989; MusM, Ohio State U., 1991; MusD, U. N.C., 2004. Percussionist Montgomery (Ala.) Symphony Orch., 1986—89; percussion instr. Blue Lake Fine Arts Camp, Twin Lake, Mich., 1990; applied percussion instr. Stivers Mid. Sch. Arts, Dayton, Ohio, 1991—93; asst. band dir., applied percussion instr. Col. White H.S. Arts, Dayton, 1991—93; asst. prof. music, asst. dir. band Hampton (Va.) U., 1993—97; dir. bands Benedict Coll., Columbiz, SC, 1997—. With Va. Beach Symphony Orch., 1995—97; dir. coll. percussion ensemble Sinclair C.C., Dayton, 1992—93. Composer: Dawne for Solo Marimba, 2002. Founding dir. Hampton -Newport News All Area Percussion Ensemble, Va., 1994, Columbia Percussion Project, 2004. Mem.: Coll. Band Dir. Nat. Assn., Internat. Assn. Jazz Educators, Internat. Percussion Arts Soc. Avocations: bowling, reading, running. Office: Benedict Coll 1600 Harden St Columbia SC 29204

DANIELS, STEPHEN M., government official; b. Boston, Mar. 28, 1947; s. Everett Jerome and Helen Dorothy (Ettinger) Daniels; m. Maygene Louise Frost, June 25, 1972; children: Edward Frost, Leah Lillian. BA, Yale U., 1968, JD, 1972. Bar: Calif. 1972, DC 1973, U.S. Supreme Ct. 1980. Asst. to asst. sec. for legis. HEW, Washington, 1969-70; legis. analyst U.S. Office of Mgmt. and Budget, Washington, 1971; legis. asst. to Congressman U.S. Ho. Reps., Washington, 1972-73, with Com. on Govt. Ops., 1973-87, minority counsel Com. on Govt. Ops., 1980-87, minority staff dir. Com. on Govt. Ops., 1984-87; bd. contract appeals GSA, Washington, 1987—, chmn., 1992—. Treas. Capitol Hill Cmty. Found., Washington, 1999—. Commr. Congl. Softball League, Washington, 1977—81; pres. Capitol East Children's Ctr., Washington, 1982—83; trustee Capitol Hill Day Sch., Washington, 1988—92. Capt. USAR, 1970—71. Mem.: ABA, Calif. Bar Assn., D.C. Bar Assn., Fed. Bar Assn. Avocations: bicycling, baseball, home restoration, camping. Home: 816 Massachusetts Ave NE Washington DC 20002-6016 Office: 1800 F St NW Washington DC 20405-0001 Business E-Mail: stephen.daniels@gsa.gov.

DANIELS, SUSANNE, broadcast executive; m. Greg Daniels. Grad., Harvard U. Asst. mgr. devel. Broadway Video Entertainment, mgr. devel.; dir. variety, reality and specials ABC TV Network; dir. comedy devel. The Fox Broadcasting Co.; pres. entertainment, lifetime svcs. entertainment The WB Network, Burbank, Calif., 2005—. Spkr. in field; developer (for Lorne Michaels) Saturday Night Live, Kids in the Hall, Am. Detective, America's Funniest People, Living Single, Martin, Buffy the Vampire Slayer, Dawson's Creek, Felicity, Roswell, Angel, Gilmore Girls, 7th Heaven; responsible for overseeing (ABCs spls.) Academy Awards, Muhammad Ali's 50th Birthday Spl., Am. Comedy Awards. Bd. dirs. The Nat. Campaign to Prevent Teenage Pregnancy. Named in the Power Issue Entertainment Weekly, 1997, one of most powerful women in entertainment, The Hollywood Reporter, 1998, 1999, 2000. Mem.: Acad. TV Arts and Sci. Office: WB Network 4000 Warner Blvd Bldg 34R Burbank CA 91522*

DANIELS, SYDNEY ROBERT, theater director, educator; b. Sept. 16, 1941; s. James Monroe and Marie P. Daniels. BS in Edn., Ill. State U., Normal, 1963, MS in Edn., 1967. Art tchr. Wendell Phillips H.S., Chgo., 1965—67; instr. Harold Washington Coll., Chgo., 1967—70, asst. prof., 1971—89, assoc. prof., 1989—92, prof., 1992—. Tech. dir. theatre Harold Washington Coll., 1968—69, assoc. dir. theatre, 1969—74, dir. theatre, 1974—. Mem. Joseph Jefferson Theatre Awards Com., Chgo., 1970—. Recipient Excellence award, Nat. Inst. for Staff Devel., 1996, Alumni Achievement award, Ill State U. Alumni Assn., 1998, 25 Yr. Svc. award, Joseph Jefferson Theatre Awards Com., 2005. Roman Catholic. Avocations: painting, attending theatrical presentations, gardening, singing.

DANIELS, WILLIAM ANTHONY, lawyer, writer; b. San Francisco, Aug. 29, 1956; s. William Edward and Violetta (Remedios) D.; m. Cheryl Ann Cureton, June 21, 1986; children: William Anthony, Jennifer Ann. BA in Radio and TV, San Francisco State U., 1982; JD, Loyola U., L.A., 1994. Bar: Calif. 1994, US Dist Ct. Calif. 1994, US Ct. Appeals (9th cir.) 1994, US Supreme Ct. 00. Bus. reporter Daily Variety, Hollywood, Calif., 1984—90; sr. v.p. Near North Nat. Group, Beverly Hills, Calif., 1991—92; assoc. Paul & Janofsky, Santa Monica, Calif., 1994—99, Mazursky Schwartz & Angelo, 1999—2002, Mazursky & Schwartz, 2003; ptnr. Mazursky, Schwartz, Daniels & Bradley, 2004—. Recipient 1st prize Nathan Burkan Competition, ASCAP, N.Y.C., 1994. Mem. ATLA, Consumer Attys. Calif., Consumer Attys. L.A. (bd. govs. 2001—, editor-in chief CAALA Advocate 2002-03, chair Loyola Law Sch./CAPEF jury trial symposium com.), Cowboy Lawyers Assn. (bd. govs. 1998—, pres. 2002-03). Democrat. Roman Catholic. Office: Mazursky Schwartz Daniels & Bradley 10990 Wilshire Blvd # 1200 Los Angeles CA 90024 Office Phone: 310-478-5838. Business E-Mail: william.daniels@msdblaw.com.

DANIELS, WILLIAM BURTON, retired physicist, educator; b. Buffalo, Dec. 21, 1930; s. William C. and Sophia (Penner) D.; m. Adriana A. Braakman, Sept. 2, 1958; children: Charlotte Mary, William Fredrik, Donald Christopher. BS in Physics, U. Buffalo, 1952; MS, Case Inst. Tech., 1955, PhD, 1957. Instr. to asst. prof. Case Inst. Tech., 1957-59; rsch. scientist Union Carbide Corp., 1959-61; mem. faculty Princeton U., 1961-72, prof. solid state scis., 1967-72; Unidel prof. physics U. Del., Newark, 1972-2000, Unidel prof. emeritus, 2001—. Rsch. collaborator Brookhaven nat. Lab.; cons. U.S. Army Rsch. Lb.; guest scientist rsch. facility, Denmark, 1976; invité Coll. France, 1977; exch. prof. U. Paris, 1977; guest scientist IBM Zurich Lab., 1977; guest scientist Max Planck Inst. for Festkoerperforschung; vis. faculty Geophys. Lab., Carnegie Inst. of Washington, 2000. Recipient Alexander von Humboldt Sr. Scientist award, 1981, 92; John S. Guggenheim Meml. fellow, 1976-77. Fellow Am. Phys. Soc. Achievements include research in properties materials at high pressure, equation of state of solids, experimentation on solidified permanent gases, electronic structure of compressed solids, instrumentation high pressure research, non-linear optics. E-mail: Family_Daniels@yahoo.com.

DANIELSEN, ALBERT LEROY, economics professor, energy and utilities consultant; b. Council Bluffs, Iowa, May 26, 1934; s. Moroni Lloyd and Geneva Gale (Williford) Danielsen; m. Eleanor Jean Gibson, June 7, 1958; children: Bartley Roland, Lea Anne, Albert William. BS, Clemson U., 1960; PhD, Duke U., 1966. From asst. prof. to prof. econs. U. Ga., Athens, 1963—97, prof. emeritus, 1997—; dir. Office Internat. Market Analysis, U.S. Dept. Energy, Washington, 1976—78; pres. Nat. Bus. and Econ. Edn. Assocs. Inc., 1988—; dir. James C. Bonbright Utilities Ctr., U. Ga., 1991—. Econ. cons. on pvt. contracts, regulation, elec. restructuring and privitization Czech Republic, Egypt, India, Malasia, Panama and U.S.; testified before numerous regulatory agys.; dir. nat. utility confs., 1980—. Author: Evolution of OPEC, 1982, Principles of Public Utility Rates, 1988, OPEC, Encyclopedia Britannica, 2002; contbr. articles to profl. jours.; author: documents in field. Grantee, Social Sci. Rsch. Coun., 1982. Mem.: Am. Econs. Assn., Internat. Assn. Energy Economists (rep. Atlanta chpt., exec. com. 1981—99). Baptist. Avocations: swimming, golf. Office Phone: 706-546-6517. Personal E-mail: allele2@aol.com. Business E-Mail: bonbright@terry.uga.edu.

DANIELSON, GILBERT LAWRENCE, consumer products company executive; b. Monmouth, Ill., Aug. 22, 1946; BS, Drake U., 1968. With Arthur Andersen & Co., Chgo.; various sr. fin. positions; v.p. fin., CFO Aaron Rents, Inc., Atlanta, 1990-98, exec. v.p., CFO, 1998, also bd. dirs. Bd. dirs. Abrams Industries, Inc. 1st lt. U.S. Army, Vietnam. Office: Aaron Rents Inc 309 E Paces Ferry Rd NE Atlanta GA 30305-2377 Business E-Mail: Gil.Danielson@aaronrents.com.

DANIELSON, GORDON KENNETH, JR., cardiovascular surgeon, educator; b. Burlington, Iowa, Dec. 5, 1931; s. Gordon Kenneth and Helen H. (Hill) D.; m. Sondra Jean Bolich, Jan. 21, 1961; children: Gordon Kenneth III, Laura, Karen, Keith, Bruce, Susan, Jennifer. BA in Chemistry, U. Pa., 1953, MD (Pfizer, Senatorial, Clark scholar, Albert Einstein award 1956, Roche award 1956, Spencer Morris prize 1956), 1956, postgrad., 1960. Diplomate Am. Bd. Surgery, Am. Bd. Thoracic Surgery. Intern U. Mich. Hosp., Ann Arbor, 1956-57; asst. resident in surgery Hosp. of U. Pa., 1957-61, chief resident in surgery, 1961-62, gen. and thoracic surgeon, 1962-65, asst. chief surg. div. I, 1962-65; vis. fellow in thoracic surgery Thorax Kliniken, Stockholm, 1963-64; practice medicine specializing in thoracic and cardiovascular surgery Phila., 1963-65, Lexington, Ky., 1965-67, Rochester, Minn., 1967—2003. Assoc. prof. surgery U. Ky. Med. Sch.; also chief cardiac surgery Univ. Hosp., 1965-67; mem. faculty Mayo Grad. Sch. Medicine, Rochester, Minn., 1967-2003, prof. surgery, 1975—, Joe M. and Ruth Roberts prof. surgery, 1987-2004; past chmn. divsn. thoracic and cardiovascular surgery, cons. cardiovascular and thoracic surgery Mayo Clinic/Mayo Found., 1967-2003, St. Mary's Hosp., Meth. Hosp., Rochester, 1967-2003; Am. Heart Assn. vis. tchr., Singapore, 1975, Amman, Jordan, 1981, W.W.L. Glenn lectr., 1999. Editor: Cardiovascular Surgery, 1972—78; contbr. numerous articles to med. jours. Markle scholar in acad. medicine, 1962—67. Fellow ACS, Am. Coll. Cardiology; mem. Am. Assn. Thoracic Surgery, Am. Surg. Assn., Am. Heart Assn. (fellow coun. cardiovascular surgery), Soc. Thoracic Surgeons (a founder), Soc. Univ. Surgeons, Soc. Vascular Surgery, Mexican Soc. Cardiology (hon.), Assn. Thoracic and Cardiovascular Surgeons of Asia (hon.), India (hon.), Chile Soc. Cardiology and Cardiovascular Surgery (hon.), Colombian Soc. of Cardiology (hon.), Congenital Heart Surgeons Soc., Peruvian Soc. of Cardiology (hon.), Phi Beta Kappa, Alpha Omega Alpha. Achievements include being the 1st fellow in congenital heart disease U.S.-USSR Health Exchange Program, 1973. Home: 6000 16th Ave NW Rochester MN 55901-2107 Office: Mayo Med Ctr Plummer N-10 Rochester MN 55905-0001 Office Phone: 507-284-2691. Business E-Mail: danielson.gordon@mayo.edu.

DANIELSON, MARY ANN, communications educator; BSBA in Acctg., U. Nebr., Omaha, 1985, MA, 1989; PhD, U. Nebr., 1997. Assoc. prof. dept. communication studies Creighton U., Omaha, 1989—, chmn. dept. communication studies, 1997—2005, dir. forensics, 2001—03, interim dir. Office Excellence Tchg., Learning and Assessment, 2003. Mem. editl. rev. bd. Communication Studies, Communication Tchr.; mem. editl. rev. bd.: Jour. Cognative Affective Learning; author (with others): Handbook for Effective Business Communication, Preparing Youth to Excel in the Workplace, Selection from Speech Communication Teacher; contbr. articles to profl. jours. Chair bd. dirs. Luth. Tape Ministries, Blue Springs, Nebr., 1999—2000; treas., crisis communication St. Paul Luth. Sch., Omaha, 1991—2003. Recipient Disting. Svc. Award, Nebr. Intercollegiate Forensics Assn., 2000, Alumni Achievement award, U. Nebr. Omaha, 2002, Coll. award for Excellence in Oustanding Svc., 2004; grantee, Omaha Job Tng. Svcs., 2001; scholar Goodrich scholar, U. Nebr. Omaha, 1980—85, Forensics scholar, 1981—85; Curriculum Devel. grantee, Creighton U., 1993, AT-risk Youth Rsch. Project grantee, 1997, Core assessment grantee, 1998, At-Risk Youths' Employability grantee, 1999, Maj. Assessment grantee, 2000, Tchg. fellow, 2002—04, Bertha Clark Hughes Speech scholar, U. Nebr. Omaha, 1984—85. Mem.: Nebr. Intercollegiate Forensic Assn. (exec. sec. 1991—93), Assn. SJ Colls. and Univs. (chair, conf. host 2001—02), Ctrl. States Communication Assn. (chair local arrangements, orgnl. and profl. 1995—2003), Nat. Communication Assn. (legis. assembly mem., chair communication needs of students 2002—04). Office: Creighton U 2500 California Plz Omaha NE 68178 Office Phone: 402-280-2631. Business E-Mail: maddam@creighton.edu.

DANIELSON, NEIL DAVID, chemistry educator; b. Ames, Iowa, July 25, 1950; s. Gordon Charles and Dorothy Elisabeth (Thompson) D.; m. Elizabeth Moore, Aug. 4, 1979 (dec. July 28, 1986); 1 child, Glenn James; m. Kami Lee Park, Oct. 7, 1990; children: Kenneth Park, Alex Paul, Ryan Christopher, Evan Phillip. BS, Iowa State U., 1972; MS, Nebr. U., 1974; PhD, Ga. U., 1978. Asst. prof. Miami U., Oxford, Ohio, 1978-83, assoc. prof., 1983-91, prof., 1991—. Vis. scientist E.I. DuPont Co., Wilmington, Del., 1985-86; cons. Interaction Chems., Inc., Mountain View, Calif., 1983-91; sec. Ohio Valley Chromatography Symposium, 1988-96. Contbr. articles to Analytical Chemistry, Jour. Chromatography, Jour. Chromatographic Sci., Ency. Sci. & Tech., others. Achievements include research in high performance liquid chromatography, capillary electrophoresis and chemiluminescence. Office: Miami U Dept Chemistry and Biochem Oxford OH 45056 Office Phone: 513-529-2872. Business E-Mail: danielnd@muohio.edu.

DANIELSON, WALTER GEORGE, lawyer; b. Anaconda, Mont., July 3, 1903; s. John and Tekla Christina (Jonsson) Danielson; m. Beryl Marie Pearce, Aug. 17, 1935; children: Karin Lynn Godfrey, John Howard. LLB, U. Mont., 1929, JD (hon.), 1970; diploma of honor, Pepperdine U., 1980. Bar: Calif. 1929. Pvt. practice, L.A.; vice consul for Sweden, L.A., 1937—55, consul, 1955—69, consl gen., 1969—76, emeritus, 1976; sec. L.A. Consular Corps, 1976—. Trustee Luth. Hosp. Soc. So. Calif., L.A.; bd. dirs. Calif. Hosp. Decorated Knight Royal Order Vasa, comdr., Royal Order North Star, Sweden, officers cross Hungar7, Knight Royal Order St. Olav, Norway, Knight's cross 1st class Royal Order Dannebrog, Denmark. Mem.: L.A. Bar Assn., Calif. State Bar, Swedish Club, Vasa Order Am., Calif. Club. Home: 68 Fremont Pl Los Angeles CA 90005-3858 Office: Danielson & St Clair 68 Fremont Pl Los Angeles CA 90005-3858 Address: 1525 Granvia Altamira Palos Verdes Estates CA 90274

DANIKAS, DIMITRIOS, plastic surgeon; s. Charalambos and Anna D. MD, U. Patras Med. Sch., Patras-Rion, Greece, 1991. Resident dept. gen. surgery St. Andrews' Gen. Regional Hosp., Patras, Greece, 1992—94; intern N.Y. Hosp. Med. Ctr. Queens, Flushing, 1994—95; resident dept. surgery Monmouth Med. Ctr., Long Branch, NJ, 1995—2001; rschr. dept. plastic surgery, hand surgery/microsurgery So. Ill. U., Springfield, 2001—02; plastic surgeon dept. plastic surgery SUNY, Bklyn., 2002—03; plastic surgeon divsn. plastic surgery N.Y. Presbyn. Hosp., 2003—. Chief resident gen. surgery Beth Israel Med. Ctr., Newark, 2000—01, Monmouth Med. Ctr., Long Branch, NJ, 2000—01. Contbr. articles, chapters to books, presentations. Mem.: Med. Soc. Patras, N.Y. Med. Soc., Sangamon Med. Soc., Hellenic Med. Soc. N.Y., Am. Soc. Gen. Surgeons, Soc.Laparoendoscopic Surgeons (hon. Outstanding Laparoendoscopy award 2000), Soc. Am. Coll. Surgeons (assoc.; candidate). Avocations: history, philosophy. Home: 435 E 70th St Apt 7G New York NY 10021-5340 E-mail: ddanikas@yahoo.com.

DANILOV, VICTOR JOSEPH, museum administrator, educator, writer; b. Farrell, Pa., Dec. 30, 1924; s. Joseph M. and Ella (Tominovich) D.; m. Toni Dewey, Sept. 6, 1980; children: Thomas J., Duane P., Denise S. BA in

Journalism, Pa. State U., 1945; MS in Journalism, Northwestern U., 1946; EdD in Higher Edn., U. Colo., 1964. With Sharon Herald, Pa., 1942, Youngstown (Ohio) Vindicator, 1945, Pitts. Sun-Telegraph, 1946-47, Chgo. Daily News, 1947-50; instr. journalism U. Colo., 1950-51; asst. prof. journalism U. Kans., 1951-53; with Kansas City Star, 1953; mgr. pub. rels. Ill. Inst. Tech. and IIT Rsch. Inst., 1953-57; dir. univ. rels. and pub. info. U. Colo., 1957-60; pres. Profile Co., Boulder, Colo., 1960-62; exec. editor, exec. v.p. Indsl. Rsch. Inc., Beverly Shores, Ind., 1962-69, pub., exec. v.p., 1969-71; dir., v.p. Mus. Sci. and Industry, Chgo., 1971-77, pres., dir., 1978-87, pres. emeritus, 1987—. Dir. mus. mgmt. program U. Colo., 1987-2004, adj. prof., 1987-2004; rural industrialization adv. group Dept. Agr., 1967; mem. panel internat. transfer tech. Dept. Commerce, 1968; sci. info. com. NSF, 1969-72; chmn. Conf. on Implications Metric Change, 1972, Nat. Conf. Indsl. Rsch., 1966-70; chmn. observance Nat. Indsl. Rsch. Week, 1967-70; chmn. Midwest White House Conf. on Indsl. World Ahead, 1972, Internat. Conf. Sci. and Tech. Museums, 1976, 82; task force on fin. acctg. and reporting by non bus. orgns., others. Author: Public Affairs Reporting, 1955, Starting a Science Center, 1977, Science and Technology Centers, 1982, Science Center Planning Guide, 1985, Chicago's Museums, 1987, rev. edit., 1991, America's Science Museums, 1990, Corporate Museums, Galleries, and Visitor Centers: A Directory, 1991, A Planning Guide for Corporate Museums, Galleries, and Visitors Centers, 1992, Museum Careers and Training: A Professional Guide, 1994, University and College Museums, Galleries, and Related Facilities, 1996, Hall of Fame Museums: A Reference Guide, 1997, Colorado Museums and Historical Sites, 2000, Museums and Historic Sites of the American West, 2002, Sports Mus. and Halls of Fame Worldwide, 2005, also articles; editor: Crucial Issues in Public Relations, 1960, Corporate Research and Profitability, 1966, Innovation and Profitability, 1967, Research Decision-Making in New Product Development, 1968, New Products--and Profits, 1969, Applying Emerging Technologies, 1970, Nuclear Power in the South, 1970, The Future of Science and Technology, 1975, Museum Accounting Guidelines, 1976, Traveling Exhibitions, 1978, Towards the Year 2000, 1981; editor profl. procs. Trustee Women of the West Mus., 1991-99, v.p., 1991-99; trustee La Rabida Children's Hosp. and Rsch. Ctr., 1973-83; mem. U. Chgo. Citizens Bd., 1978-87. Mem. Am. Assn. Mus. (exec. com. 1976-77, bd. dirs. 1985-88, chmn. mus. studies task force 1988-89), AAAS, Assn. Sci.-Tech. Ctrs. (bd. dirs. 1973-84, sec.-treas. 1973-74, pres. 1975-76), Internat. Coun. Mus. (com. on sci. and tech. mus. 1972—, vice chmn. 1977-87, chmn. 1982-83, bd. dirs. 1985-88), Chgo. Coun. on Fine Arts (chmn. 1976-84), Ill. Arts Alliance (bd. dirs. 1983-86), Sci. Mus. Exhibit Collaborative (pres. 1983-86), Mus. Film Network (pres. 1984-86). Home and Office: 1426 Chicago Ave Evanston IL 60201 Office Phone: 847-328-5256.

DANILOVICH, JOHN J., ambassador; b. Calif., June 25, 1950; m. Irene Forte, Mar. 19, 1977; children: John Charles, Alice, Alexander. Grad., The Choate Sch., 1968; BA in Polit. Sci., Stanford U., 1972; MA in Internat. Rels., U. So. Calif., London, 1980. Ptnr., cons. The Eisenhower Inst., Washington, 1987—90; US amb. to Costa Rica US Dept. State, 2001—04, US amb. to Brazil, 2004—. Mem., exec. mgmt. bd. Interocean Shipping Group, 1977—88. Bd. dirs., chmn. transition com. Panama Canal Commn., 1991—96; former trustee Am. Mus. in Britain; former chmn. Republicans Abroad; former bd. dirs. Stanford U. Trust, U.S.-U.K. Fulbright Commn. Recipient Orden Nacional Juan Mora Fernandez award, Govt. Costa Rica. Mem.: Coun. on Fgn. Rels., White's (London), Pacific Union Club (San Francisco), K.M. Office: Amer Embassy Unit 3500 Apo AA 34030 Office Phone: 55-61-312-7588. Business E-Mail: danilovichjj@state.gov.

DANILOW, GREG A., lawyer; b. NYC, Feb. 23, 1949; BA cum laude, Lehigh U., 1970; JD, Fordham U., 1974. Law clerk to Judge John M. Cannella US Dist. Ct., So. Dist. NY, 1974—76; ptnr., co-head bus. and securities litigation dept. Weil, Gotshal & Manges LLP, NYC. Lectr. in field. Writing and rsch. editor Fordham Law Review, 1973—74. Office: Weil Gotshal & Manges LLP 767 Fifth Ave New York NY 10153 Office Phone: 212-310-8182. Office Fax: 212-310-8007. Business E-Mail: greg.danilow@weil.com.

DANISHEFSKY, SAMUEL J., chemistry professor; b. Bayonne, N.J., Mar. 10, 1936; BS, Yeshiva U., 1956; PhD in Chemistry, Harvard U., 1962. Fellow chemistry Columbia U., N.Y.C., 1961-63, prof. chemistry, 1963—; asst. to prof. chemistry U. Pitts., 1963-79; prof. chemistry Yale U., New Haven, Conn., 1979-93, chmn. dept. chemistry, 1981-88; chair, dir. bio organic chemistry Sloan Kettering Inst., 1993—, Kettering chair, dir. lab. Cons. Merck Sharp & Dohme, 1973—, GE Co., 1977—, vis. prof. Iowa State U., 1974, U. Calif., 1977, Rice U., 1977, Tex. A&M, 1986; vis. lectr. Tex., 1979. Recipient Wolf Foundation (chemistry) award Wolf Foundation, 1995, Claude S. Hudson award in Carbohydrate Chemistry, 1997, Tetrahedron prize, 1996. Fellow AAAS, Am. Acad. Arts and Sci.; mem. NAS, Am. Chem. Soc. (Arthur C. Cope award 1998, Claude S. Hudson Award in Carbohydrate Chemistry, 1997, Nichols medal 1999), Swiss Chem. Soc., Japanese Chem. Soc. Office: Sloan Kettering Inst 1275 York Ave New York NY 10021-6094

DANISI, JOHN J., philosopher, educator; b. Bklyn., Mar. 19, 1948; s. Jack F. and Mary (Kelly) D.; m. Carolyn S. Swallum, Sept. 30, 1989; children: Mary, Jacqueline. BA cum laude, St. Louis U., 1969; MA, NYU, 1974, PhD, 1993. Cert. secondary sch. tchr., Mo. Jr. high sch. tchr. Annunciation Sch., St. Louis, 1969-71; instr. St. Louis U., 1970; adj. asst. prof. dept. philosophy. NYU, 1982—. Contbr. articles to profl. jours. Invited del. Citizen Amb. Program People to People Internat.; Philosophy Edn. Del. to China, 1993, Edn. Delegation to Berlin, 1994, Spokane, 1994. Fellowship Andrew W. Mellon fellow, NYU, 1981, NYU fellow, 1978-82, A. Ogden Butler fellowship NYU, 1987; recipient William James Prize Essay Am. Philos. Assn. Eastern divsn. 1986. Mem. Am. Philos. Assn., Soc. for the Advancement of Am. Philosophy, Leibniz Soc. Home: 4445 Post Rd Apt 8H Riverdale NY 10471-3449 Office: NYU Dept Philosophy 503 Main Bldg New York NY 10003-6688

DANITZ, MARILYNN PATRICIA, choreographer, video specialist; b. Buffalo; BS in Chemistry, Le Moyne Coll.; MS in Chem. Engring., Columbia U. Artistic dir. High Frequency Wavelengths/Danitz Dances, 1976—. Assoc. prof. Tainan Cheng Chuan Coll., Taiwan, 1984; profl. dancer Ballet Mcpl. Strasbourg, France, Ballet Mcpl. Geneva, Switzerland; choreography commns. performances include The 11th Internat. Ballet Comp. Varna, Bulgaria, 1983, Tbilisi Ballet co., USSR, Nat. Ballet of Colombia, Nat. Inst. Arts, Taiwan, Nanatsudera Theatre, Nagoya, Japan, Shanghai Ballet and Shanghai Jiao Tung U., People's Republic of China, Nat. Cheng Kung Dance Group, Taiwan, Jacob's Pillow Dance Festival, Mass., 6th Internat. Dance Theatre Festival, Poland, 5th Anniversary Celebration Kannon Ctr., St. Petersburg, Russia, 15th Internat. Festival of Modern Choreography, Belarus, others; master choreography workshops include Ctrl. Ballet, Beijing, Chinese Cultural U., Taipei, Taiwan, Okuda Studio, Nagoya, Ballet Philippines, Manila, NSW Coll. Dance, Sydney, The Ballet Sch., Bogota, Colombia, Lublin, Lodz, Poznan and Bytom, Poland, Vitebsk, Belarus, others; video prodn. Real Art Ways Nat. Residency, funded by NEA, 1990; video art collaboration with Allen Ginsberg. Presentations include Internat. Conf. on Dance and Tech., 1993, Naropa Inst. 20th Anniversary Celebration, 1994; video work presented at Lincoln Ctr., N.Y.C., 1995, Hanyang U., Seoul, Korea, 1997, others; video work in permanent collection Lincoln Ctr. Dance Collection; TV prodns. of works include Nat. Broadcasting, Venezuela, Colombia, Bulgaria, Poland, Russia, Belarus, Pub. Broadcasting, Albany, N.Y.C., Mpls.; works performed by Nat. Ballet with the Nat. Philharm. Orch. of Colombia Gala Performance, 1984; co. tours include China, Japan, Taiwan, Europe, Hawaii, Philippines, Can, Europe, S.Am., Russia and Belarus; co-editor Branching Out, Oral Histories of the Founders of Six National Dance Orgns.; juror competitions. Recipient Outstanding Dance-Theater Work of 1986 award Dance Brew-ATV Cable Manhattan, award for disting. choreography Nat. Assn. Regional Ballet, 1982; Bessie Schoenberg Lab. for Experienced Choreographers Dance Theater Workshop; NIH fellow; Gold Medal scholar Conservatoire Geneve, N.Y. State Regents scholar, Le Moyne Coll. Chemistry scholar, others. Mem. Dance Theater Workshop, Am. Dance Guild (pres., editor Am. Dance, bd. dirs., nat. conf. planning com.), Soc. Dance History Scholars, Dance Films Assn., Congress on Rsch. in Dance Address: 560 Riverside Dr Apt 16E New York NY 10027-3208 also: PO Box 216 Sand Lake NY 12153-0216 also: 3200 Holly Rd Apt 2 Virginia Beach VA 23451-2926 Office Phone: 212-222-7204, 757-422-1240. E-mail: HFW2000@aol.com.

DANJCZEK, DAVID WILLIAM, manufacturing executive; b. Phillipsburg, N.J., Sept. 29, 1951; s. William Emil and Erna (Lob) D. BSFS, Georgetown U., 1973; postgrad., Waseda U., 1973-74, Loyola U., L.A., 1977-78. Contract adminstr. Aero Products, Woodland Hills, Calif., 1974-76, sr. contract adminstr., 1976-78; dir. internat. ops. Litton Industries, Washington, 1978-90, v.p. internat. bus., 1990-93; v.p. govt. and internat. affairs Western Atlas Inc., 1993-97; corp. v.p. Unova, Inc., Arlington, Va., 1997—; v.p. adminstrn. Mfrs. Alliance/MAPI, 2002—. Adj. prof. Georgetown U.; chmn. industry sector adv. com. U.S. Dept. Commerce; bd. dirs., past chair Exec. Coun. Diplomacy. Mem. Am. Countertrade Assn., Univ. Club., Washington Ind. Roundtable (sec., treas.). Roman Catholic. Avocations: squash, bridge. Office: 1525 Wilson Blvd Arlington VA 22209

DANJCZEK, MICHAEL HARVEY, social services administrator; b. Phillipsburg, N.J., May 9, 1949; s. William Emil and Erna (Lob) D.; m. Cynthia Ann Johanson, June 9, 1973; children: William Emil II, Liesel J., Rachel L., Peter L. BA in Urban Studies, Lehigh U., Bethlehem, Pa., 1972, MEd in Social Restoration, 1974, EdD in Ednl. Adminstrn., 1985; PhD (hon.), Lafayette Coll., 2000. Exec. dir. Lehigh Valley Opportunity Ctr., Bethlehem, Pa., 1972-74; pres., exec. dir. Children's Home, Easton, Pa., 1974—. Adj. prof. Lehigh County C.C., 1987-91, Grad. Sch., Jersey City State Tchrs. Coll., 1989-92; treas. Pa. Coun. Children's Svcs., 1982-84; mem. Commn. on Accreditation, Nat. Assn. Homes for Children, 1982-87, chmn. bd. dirs., 1997-98; mem. authority bd. Northampton C.C., 1983-95; v.p. Pa. Coun. Children's Svcs., 1985-87, bd. dirs., 1987-89; bd. dirs. Lehigh Valley Drug Treatment Program, 1986-88; mem. Ea. U.S. Svc. Coun. of Coun. on Accreditation Svcs. for Families and children, 1987-92; treas. Nat. Assn. Homes and Svcs. for Children, 1988-93, chmn. bd. dirs., 1997-98; bd. dirs. Twin Rivers Cmty. Bank, 1991-98, Coun. on Accreditation Svcs. for Family and Children, 1993-98, Vista Bank, 1998-2002. Asst. wrestling coach Lafayette Coll., 1974-76; mem. exec. com. Rep. party of Northampton County, 1975-76; bd. advisors Jr. League Lehigh Valley, 1975-77; chmn. profl. adv. com. Family and Child Welfare of Lehigh Valley Cmty. Coun., 1976; mem. adv. bd. Cath. Social Svcs., Diocese of Allentown, 1976-81; mem. Wilson Boro Sch. Bd., 1980-83; bd. dirs. Pa. Coun. Vol. Child Care Agys., 1980-84; bd. dirs. Helen Beebe Speech and Hearing Ctr., 1980-89, pres. bd. dirs., 1987-89; bd. dirs. Parents Anonymous Pa., 1981-90, pres. bd., 1981-85; gen. campaign chmn. United Way of Northampton and Warren Counties, 1982-83; bd. dirs. Great Valley Girl Scout Coun., 1983-89; chmn. Minsi Trail Drug Abuse Prevention Rally for Forks of Del., Boy Scouts Am., 1987; mem. St. Bernard's Ch. Parish Coun., 1991-93; chmn. elect, v.p. econ. devel. Two Rivers Area Commerce Coun., 1991-92; chmn. Northampton County Sports and Spl. Events Com., 1994-97; mem. governing bd., CEO, chmn. BallYard, Inc., 1994; mem. governing bd. St. Vincent's Home for Children, 1995-99; bd. chair Children's Coalition of the Lehigh Valley, 1998-99, Pa. Coun. Children's Svcs., 1998-2000; bd. dirs. Families Internat., 1998—2000, Alliance for Children and Families, 1998—2002; co-founder Pro Kids Alliance, 1994—, CEO Alliance for Children and Families of the Lehigh Valley, 1999—. Recipient Disting. Cmty. Svc. award Easton Area Jaycees, 1975, Disting. Svc. award Pa. Com. on Internat. Yr. of Child, 1979, Coll. Edn., Lehigh U., 1983, Disting. Alumni award Lehigh U., 1987, Gafney award Lehigh U. Assn. Ednl. Adminstrs., 1988, Pres. award for cmty. svc. Easton Area Sales and Mktg. Execs., 1990, Svc. to Mankind award Sertoma Club, 1991; inducted to Notre Dame H.S. Athletic Hall of Fame, 1990. Mem. Lehigh U. Alumni Assn. Home Club (bd. dirs. 1990—), Lehigh U. Alumni Assn. (bd. dirs. 1987-90), Northampton Country Club (bd. govs. 1985-94), Nat. Fellowship Child Care Execs. (exec. sec. 1993-98, pres. 1992-93), Two Rivers Area C. of C. (chmn. 1993-95), Rotary (past pres. Easton). Republican. Roman Catholic. Avocations: private pilot, golf, skiing, travel. Home and Office: Childrens Home Easton 2000 S 25th St Easton PA 18042 Office Phone: 610-258-2831. Business E-Mail: mhd@thechildrenshome.org.

DANK, LEONARD DEWEY, medical illustrator, audio-visual consultant; b. Birmingham, Ala., Dec. 21, 1929; s. George and Ellen (Balsam) D.; B.A. in Zoology, Cornell U., 1952; grad. Sch. Med. Illustration, Mass. Gen. Hosp., 1955; m. Beryl Eileen Jealous, Sept. 30, 1961; 1 dau., Amelia Theresa. Staff med. artist, plastic surgery clinic Manhattan Eye, Ear & Throat Hosp., 1955-57, Eye Bank for Sight Restoration, 1957-59; owner Leonard D. Dank Med. Illustration Studio, 1959-79; pres. Med. Illustrations Co., 1979— (all N.Y.C.); cons. med. illustrator St. Luke's Hosp., 1961-83, trans-vision div. Milprint, Inc., 1965—, Woman's Hosp., 1963-83, H.S. Struttman, Inc., 1964—, Home Library Press, 1960-70 (all N.Y.C.), Synapse Communications, Inc. (Conn.), 1973-75, Contemporary Orthopaedics and Contemporary Surgery, 1981-85, P.W. Communications, Inc., 1982-89, Esquire Mags. Health and Fitness Clinic, 1985-88, Whittle Communications, 1988—. Recipient 1st prize certificate merit A.M.A., 1959, 1st prize citation of merit in motion picture program A.C.S., 1959, 62; Better Teller award Assn. Indsl. Advertisers, 1973, Outstanding Sci. Book award for Children Nat. Sci. Tchrs. Assn., 1982, Cert. of Merit Soc. of Illustrators, 1986. Mem. Assn. Med. Illustrators, Guild Natural Sci. Illustrators. Roman Catholic. Co-author: Gynecologic Operations, 1978; med. illustrator for numerous med. books, jours., elementary textbooks, juvenile books, encys. Fax: 631-734-5496. Home and Office: PO Box 944 Cutchogue NY 11935-0944

DANKANYIN, ROBERT JOHN, international business executive; b. Sharon, Pa., Sept. 4, 1934; s. John and Anna (Kolesar) D.; m. Dorothy Jean Kuchel, Aug. 9, 1958 (div. June 1975); children: Douglas John, David Jay, Dana Jean; m. Georgia C. Oleson, Apr. 2, 1988 (dec. Sept. 1990); m. Charlene Marcella Bassett, May 16, 1998 BSCE, Pa. State U., 1956; MBA, U. So. Calif., 1961; MSEE, UCLA, 1963. Cert. level 2 Profl. Ski Instrs. Am. From mgr. mobile ICBM systems engring. dept. to mgr. space system lab. Hughes Aircraft Co., Culver City, Calif., 1956-68; program mgr. Litton Industries, Beverly Hills, Calif., 1968-70; v.p. program mgmt. Litton Ship Systems, Culver City, 1970-71, Litton Ship Sys., Pascagoula, Miss., 1971-73; asst. mgr. for U.S. Roland program, Canoga Pk., Calif. Hughes Aircraft Co., Culver City, Calif., 1975-77, asst. divsn. mgr. missile devel. div. Canoga Pk., Calif., 1977-84, mgr. land combat systems divsn. Culver City, Calif., 1984-86, group v.p. missile systems group, 1986-87; v.p., asst. group exec. missle systems group Canoga Park, Calif., 1987-88; v.p., asst. group exec. space and communication group, El Segundo, Calif. Hughes Aircraft Co., Culver City, Calif., 1988-89, corp. sr. v.p. diversification L.A., 1989-92, sr. v.p. bus. devel., 1992-93; sr. v.p., pres. Hughes Indsl. Electronics Co., L.A., 1993-95; group exec. Whittaker Corp., Westwood Village, Calif., 1973-75; pres., chmn. bd. Whittaker Cmty. Devel. Corp., Englewood, Colo., Knoxville, Tenn., Westwood Village, San Juan, P.R., 1973-75; internat. bus. and mgmt. cons., pres., CEO ITI, Malibu, Calif., 1995—. Chmn. Hughes Program Mgr. Devel. Course, L.A., 1976-88; chmn., bd. dirs. Light Valve Products, Inc., 1988-92, Hughes/Japan Victor Tech. Inc., 1992-95, Hughes Micro Electronics Ltd., Glenrothes, Scotland, Hughes Europa Ltd., Brussels, Belgium, 1993-95; bd. dirs. Hughes Environ. Sys., Inc., Long Beach, Calif.; Hughes España, Madrid, Spain, Aero Sys., Inc., Paris; mem. adv. bd. Pulse Link Inc., San Diego, 2002—; dir. several wholly owned subs. including Direct TV, Spectrolab, Hughes Network Sys., RF Identification Sys.; lectr., guest spkr., author on tech. mgmt.; bus. ventures, fgn. mktg., def. conversion, diversification and entrepreneurship. Editor Inter Fraternity/Sorority Newsletter Pa. State U., 1955-56. Chmn. indsl. and profl. adv. coun. Coll. Engring, Pa. State U.; ski instr. Bear Mountain Ski Resort, Big Bear Lake, Calif., 1990—; chmn. several indsl. task forces reporting to U.S. congl. coms. Voted Ordo Honorium by Kappa Delta Rho Fraternity, 1991, outstanding Engr. of the Yr. by Pa. State U., 1991; honored as outstanding engineering alumnus, 1992. Mem. Am. Def. Preparedness Assn. (bd. dirs. 1986-94, chmn. fin. com. 1990-94), Hughes Mgmt. Club, Aero Club So. Calif., Marina City Club, Riviera Country Club (bd. govs. 1999—2004), Calif. Yacht Club. Republican. Roman Catholic. Avocations: skiing, scuba diving, sailing, hiking, fishing, golf. Home: 20700 Rockpoint Rd Malibu CA 90265 Office Phone: 310-508-6863. E-mail: rdankanyin@aol.com.

DANKO, GEORGE, engineering educator; b. Budapest, Hungary, Apr. 3, 1944; came to U.S., 1986; s. Gyorgy and Ilona (Mihaly) D.; m. Eva Arvay, Dec. 14, 1976; 1 child, Reka. BSME, Tech. U. Budapest, 1968, PhD, 1976; MS in Applied Math., Eotovs U. of Scis., Budapest, 1975; PhD, Hungarian Acad. Scis., Budapest, 1985. Cert. Profl. Ski Instrs. Am. Assn. Asst. prof. Tech. U. Budapest, 1968-75, assoc. prof., 1979-86; fellow Hungarian Acad. Scis., Budapest, 1975-79; rsch. assoc. U. Nev., Reno, 1986-90, assoc. prof., 1990-95, prof. mining engring., 1995—. Cons. Sierra Sci., Reno, 1990—; chmn. High-Level Radioactive Waste Mgmt. Conf., 1991, 92; portrait artist, Reno, 1987-92. Co-author: Methods for the Calculation of Pipeline Transients, 1976, Warming-up and Cooling of Electrical Machinery, 1982; contbr. articles to profl. jours. Com. rep. Truckee River Steering Com., Reno, 1993-94. Grantee U.S. Bur. Mines, 1986-97, U.S. Dept. Energy, 1991—, Clarkson Co., 1992-98. Mem. ASME, ISES (internat. organizing com. 1993-94), IFAC (internat. program com. 1995—), Soc. Mining Engrs., Am. Nuclear Soc. Achievements include patents for methods and apparatus for the determination of the heat transfer coefficient, process and apparatus for the determination of thermophysical properties, underground cooling enhancement for nuclear waste repository, method and apparatus for underground nuclear waste repository, others. Office: U Nev Reno Mining Engring Dept 173 Reno NV 89557-0001

DANN, JOHN CHRISTIE, historian, library director; b. Wilmington, Del., May 3, 1944; s. C. Marshall and Catharine (Christie) D.; m. Orelia Sparrow, Jan. 24, 1970; children: Catharine Christie, Orelia Eliabeth. BA, Dickinson Coll., 1966; MA, Coll. William and Mary, 1970, PhD, 1975. Prof. history U. Mich., Ann Arbor, 1975—, curator of manuscripts William C. Clements Libr., 1971-77, dir. William C. Clements Libr., 1977—. Author: 101 Treasures, 1998; editor: The Revolution Remembered, 1980, The Nagle Journal, 1989; editor Am. Mag.; mem. various hist. and editl. bds. Mem. Dexter (Mich.) Village Coun., 1982-86. Mem. Cosmos Club (Washington), Azazels. Congregationalist. Avocations: fishing, golf. Home: 7580 4th St Dexter MI 48130-1424 Office: Clements Libr 909 S University Ave Ann Arbor MI 48109-1190

DANN, MARC, state senator; BA in History, U. Mich.; JD, Case Western Res. U. Atty.; state sen., dist. 32 Ohio State Senate, Columbus, 2003—, ranking minority mem., mem. agr., hwys and transp., judiciary civil justice, judiciary criminal justice, ways and means, and econ. devel. coms. Mem. regional bd. Anti-Defamation League; mem. bd. edn. Liberty Twp., Ohio, 2001—02. Named Legislator of the Yr., Ohio Farmers Union, 2005, Amvets, 2005; recipient Pro Bono award, Northeast Ohio Legal Svcs. Mem.: Mahoning and Trumbull County Bar Assns., Tobacco-Free Youth, Youngstown-Warren Regional C. of C., Jewish Cmty. Ctr. Democrat. Office: Senate Bldg Rm 057, Ground Fl Columbus OH 43215 Office Phone: 330-759-4155. Business E-Mail: dann32@maild.sen.state.oh.us.

DANN, MARY ROBERTS, music educator; b. Kalispell, Mont., Dec. 10, 1954; d. William Wicks and Philippa (Landry) Roberts; m. Paul Henry Dann, Mar. 31, 1984; children: Geoffrey Paul, Gregory Colin, Claire Elizabeth. B Music Edn., U. Mont., 1977; M Music Edn., U. Oreg., 1983. Cert. tchr. Nat. Bd. for Profl. Tchg. Stds. K-8 music tchr. Shelby (Mont.) Sch. Dist., 1977—80; 1-6 music tchr. Richland (Wash.) Sch. Dist., 1980—97, K-5 music tchr., 1997—. Adj. prof. Wash. State U., Richland, 1991—; music dir. summer showcase Columbia Basin Coll., Pasco, Wash., 1998—2001; tchr. Acad. Children's Theatre, Richland, 2001—; music dir. N.W. acting camp Acad. of Children's Theater, Richland, 2002—. Composer: (musical) Travel the U.S.A!, 1999. Team mgr. Tri-Cities Youth Soccer Assn., Pasco, 1997—99; costumer, music asst. Hanford Drama Dept., Richland, 2002—; cantor, music asst. Christ the King Parish, Richland, 1980—. Named Southwestern Wash. Regional Tchr. of YR., 2004—05; grantee, Lamb-Weston, Inc., 1999. Mem.: Music Educators Nat. Conf., Delta Kappa Gamma. Republican. Roman Catholic. Avocations: reading, sewing, crafts, gardening. Home: 1727 Hunt Ave Richland WA 99354 Office: Sacajawea Elem Sch 518 Catskill Richland WA 99354 Office Phone: 509-371-2680. E-mail: cggpmdann@netscape.net.

DANN, OLIVER TOWNSEND, psychoanalyst, psychiatrist, educator; b. Mansfield, Ohio, Aug. 10, 1935; s. Edward William and Mary Virginia (Townsend) D.; m. Linda Marie Schweers, July 15, 1961; children: Sara Katharine, Jonathan William Jenner, Luke Nathan Townsend, Jesse Charles. AB, Columbia U., 1958; MD, Yale U., 1962. Diplomate Am. Bd. Psychiatry and Neurology. Resident in psychiatry Sch. Medicine Yale U., New Haven, 1963-67, asst., assoc. prof. psychiatry Sch. Medicine, 1967-79; clin. prof. psychiatry Will Sch. Medicine U. Miami, Fla., 1980—; dir. Fla. Psychoanalytic Inst., 1997—2001, chair edn. com., 2003—. Pvt. practice, Miami, 1979—. Contbr. articles to profl. jours. Fellow APA (disting. life), Ctr. for Advanced Psychoanalytic Studies; mem. SAR, Am. Psychoanalytic Assn., Internat. Psychoanalytic Assn., Western New England Inst. Soc. Psychoanalysis, Balt.-Washington Inst. Soc. Psychoanalysis, Fla. Psychanalytic Inst. Soc. Found., Mayflower Soc., Jamestowne Soc., Huguenot Soc., Explorers Club, Phi Beta Kappa. Avocations: sailing, canoeing, hiking. Home and Office: 4550 SW 74th St Miami FL 33143-6271 Office Phone: 305-665-5677. Personal E-mail: lindadann@hotmail.com. E-mail: otdann@hotmail.com.

DANNEMILLER, JOHN C., transportation company executive; b. Cleve., May 17, 1938; s. John Charles and Jean I. (Bage) D.; m. Jean Marie Sheridan, Sept. 22, 1962; children— David, Peter BS, Case Western Res. U., 1960, MBA, 1964; postgrad., Stanford U., 1975, Columbia U., 1974, Tuck Exec. program Dartmouth Coll., 1976. Vice pres. foods div. Diamond Shamrock, 1978-81, dir. planning, 1981-83; v.p. SDS Biotech Corp., Cleve., 1984-85; group v.p. leasing group Leaseway Transp., Cleve., 1984-85, pres., chief operating officer, 1985-88, exec. v.p., chief oper. officer, 1988—; exec. v.p. Bearings Inc., Cleve., 1988—, now chmn., ceo, b d. dirs. Bd. dirs. Lamson & Sessions, Cleve., Star Bank, Cleve. Bd. dirs., advisor Jr. Achievement, Cleve., 1962-64; bd. dirs. Luth. Med. Found.; fund raiser United Way, Cleve. and St. Louis Mem. Bearing Speciality Assn., Cleve. Athletic Club, Lakewood Country Club, Union Club, Univ. Club, Beta Gamma Sigma. Republican. Presbyterian. Avocations: tennis, water-skiing, boating, skiing, golf. Office: Bearings Inc PO Box 6925 3600 Euclid Ave Cleveland OH 44115-2515

DANNENBERG, ARTHUR MILTON, JR., experimental pathologist, immunologist, educator; b. Phila., Oct. 17, 1923; s. Arthur Mansbach and Marion (Loeb) D.; m. Aileen Rose Hart, Mar. 30, 1948; children: Arlene Dannenberg Bowes, Andrew Loeb, Audrey Ann. AB, Swarthmore Coll., 1944; MD, Harvard U., 1947; MA, U. Pa., 1951, PhD, 1952. Diplomate: Nat. Bd. Med. Examiners. Intern Albert Einstein Med. Ctr., Phila., 1947-48; rsch. resident Children's Hosp., Phila., 1948-49; fellow Henry Phipps Inst. U. Pa., Phila., 1950-52, asst. prof., 1956-64; fellow U. Utah, 1952-54; assoc. prof. environ. health scis. Johns Hopkins U. Bloomberg Sch. Pub. Health, Balt., 1964-73, prof., 1973—, prof. joint faculty sch. medicine dept. pathology, 1976—. Mem. editl. bd. Am. Rev. Respiratory Diseases, 1973-75, 79-84, Infection and Immunity jour., 1976-78; contbr. articles to profl. jours. and chpts. to books. Lt. comdr. Med. Rsch. Unit 1, USN, 1954-56. Mem. Am. Soc. Investigative Pathology, Histochem. Soc., Am. Soc. Microbiology, Soc. for Leukocyte Biology (sec. 1975-76), Am. Assn. Immunologists, Am. Thoracic Soc., Soc. Investigative Dermatology. Office: Johns Hopkins U Bloomberg Sch Pub Health 615 N Wolfe St Baltimore MD 21205-2103 Office Phone: 410-955-3062. Business E-Mail: artdann@jhsph.edu.

DANNENBERG, KONRAD K., aeronautical engineer; b. Weissenfels, Germany, Aug. 5, 1912; came to U.S. 1945. s. Hermann and Klara (Kittler) D.; m. Ingeborg M. Kamke, Apr. 8, 1944 (dec.); 1 child, Klaus Dieter; m. Jacquelyn E. Staiger, Mar. 31, 1990. MS Engring., Techn. U., Hannover, Ger., 1938. Asst. Tech. U., Hannover, 1938, engr. Frankfurt, Ger., 1939; rschr. HAP-Peenemuende, Germany, 1940-45; mgr. U.S. Army Ordnance, Ft. Bliss,

Tex., 1945-50, ABMA, Huntsville, Ala., 1950-60, NASA/MSFC, Huntsville, 1960-73; assoc. prof. UTSI-U. Tenn., Tullahoma, 1973-78; cons. The Space & Rocket Ctr., Huntsville, 1978—. Author: In Memory of H. Oberth, 1990, Vahrenwald to Dresden, 1990; (with E. Stuhlinger) Rocket Center Peenemünde, 1993, Albert Püllenberg and the Gesellschaft für Raketenforschung, 1995, (with Donald Tarter) Mitchell R. Sharpe-Aerospace Historian, 1997. Lt. German Army, 1939-40. Recipient Meritorious Svc. award U.S. Army, 1960, Exceptional Svc. award NASA, 1969, Gov. of Ala. Commendation, 2002, Genesis award Ala. Info. Tech. Assn., 2004; Konrad K. Dannenberg scholar, 1992. Fellow AIAA (chpt. chmn. 1967, Durand lectr. pub. svc. 1990), Holger N. Toftoy award, Hermann Oberth award 1996); mem. Hermann Oberth Soc. (hon., Golden Hermann Oberth medal 1994), Nat. Space Soc. (charter), Am. Rocket Soc. (chmn. 1962). Lutheran. Achievements include patents in rocket engine design. Home and Office: 233 Cheswick Dr Madison AL 35757-8712 E-mail: konrad2@aol.com.

DANNENBERG, OTTO DOYLE, optometrist; b. Heber, Utah, June 21, 1925; OD, So. Calif. Coll. Optometry, 1948. Pvt. practice, Escondido, Calif., 1949—98. Chmn. avoidable blindness task force Rotary Internat., 2000—01; chmn. Internat. Eye Care Fellowship of Rotarians, 2004—05. Recipient Centennial Honor award, So. Calif. Coll. Optometry, 2004, Paul Yarwood award, Calif. Optometric Assn., 2004. Fellow: AAAS; mem.: Am. Acad. Optomery. Home: 340 Linwood St Escondido CA 92027

DANNER, BLYTHE KATHARINE, actress; b. Phila., Feb. 3, 1943; d. Harry Earl and Katharine D.; m. Bruce W. Paltrow, Dec. 14, 1969 (dec. Oct. 3, 2002); children: Gwyneth Kate, Jake, Laura. BA in Drama, Bard Coll., 1965, D.F.A. (hon.), 1981; L.H.D. (hon.), Hobart-Smith Coll., 1981. Appeared as Laura in Glass Menagerie, 1965; repertory at Theatre Co. Boston, The Knack, and 7 new Am. Plays, 1965-66; appeared as Helena in repertory Midsummer Night's Dream, Trinity Sq. Playhouse, R.I.; appeared as Irena in repertory Three Sisters, Trinity Sq. Playhouse, R.I., 1967; with Lincoln Ctr. Repertory Co. in Summertree, 1968, Cyrano de Bergerac, 1968, Elise in the Miser, 1969 (Theatre World award); appeared on Broadway as Jill Tanner in Butterflies Are Free (Tony award 1971); also appeared in Major Barbara, 1971, Twelfth Night, 1972, The Seagull, 1974, Ring Around The Moon, 1975, Betrayal, 1980 (Tony award nominee), Blithe Spirit, 1987, A Streetcar Named Desire, 1988, Sylvia, 1995, Moonlight, 1995; motion picture appearances include 1776, 1972, To Kill a Clown, 1972, Lovin' Molly, 1974, Hearts of the West, 1975, The Seagull, 1975, Futureworld, 1976, The Great Santini, 1980, Too Far to Go, 1982, Man, Woman, And Child, 1983, Brighton Beach Memoirs, 1986, Another Woman, 1988, Mr. and Mrs. Bridge, 1990, Alice, 1990, The Prince of Tides, 1991, Husbands and Wives, 1992, To Wong Foo, Thanks for Everything, Julie Newmar, 1995, The Myth of Fingerprints, 1997, The X Files, 1998, The Farmhouse, 1998, Forces of Nature, 1999, The Love Letter, Meet the Parents, 2000, The Invisible Circus, 2001, 3 Days of Rain, 2002, The Quality of Life, 2003, Sylvia, 2003, Meet the Fockers, 2004, (voice) Howl's Moving Castle, 2004; TV movies include To Confuse the Angel, 1970, Dr Cook's Garden, 1971, George M!, 1972, The Scarecrow, 1972, F. Scott Fitzgerald and "The Last of the Belles", 1974, Sidekicks, 1974, Eccentricities of a Nightingale, 1976, The Court-Martial of George Armstrong Custer, 1977, A Love Affair: Eleanor and Lou Gehrig, 1978, Are You in the House Alone?, 1978, Roots: The Next Generations, 1979, Too Far to Go, 1979, You Can't Take It With You, 1979, Inside the Third Reich, 1982, In Defense of Kids, 1983, Helen Keller-The Miracle Continues, 1984, Guilty Conscience, 1985, A Streetcar Named Desire, 1988, Tattinger's, 1988, Judgment, 1990, Never Forget, 1991, Cruel Doubt, 1992, Getting Up and Going Home, 1992, Homage, 1995, Saint Maybe, 1998, We Were the Mulvaneys, 2002, Back When We Were Grownups, 2004; TV series: Adam's Rib, 1973, Healthcare Crisis, 2000, Presidio Med, 2002-03, Huff, 2004. Recipient Theatre World award, 1969; Best Actress award Vevey Film Festival, Switzerland, 1982

DANNER, BRYANT CRAIG, lawyer; b. Boston, Nov. 18, 1937; s. Nevin Earle and Marjorie (Harms) D.; m. Judith I. Baker, Aug. 23, 1958; 1 child Debra Irene. BA, Harvard U., 1960, LLB, 1963. Bar: Calif. 1963, U.S. Dist. Ct. (cen. dist.) Calif. 1963. Assoc. Latham & Watkins, L.A., 1963-70, ptnr., 1970-92; sr. v.p., gen. counsel So. Calif. Edison Co., Rosemead, Calif., 1992-95, exec. v.p., gen. counsel, 1995—2005, Edison Internat., Rosemead, 2000—. Mem. L.A. County Bar Assn. (chmn. environ. sect. 1988-89). Avocations: fly fishing, astronomy. Office: Edison International 2244 Walnut Grove Ave Rosemead CA 91770-3714

DANNER, KATHLEEN FRANCES STEELE, federal official; b. Kansas City, Mo., Oct. 28, 1960; m. Steve Danner, Jan. 18, 1996. Admissions counselor N.E. Mo. State U., Kirksville, 1980-83, assoc. dir. admissions, 1983-86, programming coord. dept. pub. svcs., 1986-87; Iowa, N.H. dir. Gephardt for Pres., St. Louis, 1987-88; mem. Mo. Ho. of Reps., Jefferson City, 1988-94; state dir. Clinton for Pres., 1991-92; regional dir. U.S. Dept. HHS, Kansas City, Mo., 1994—, acting dir. intergovtl. affairs Washington, 1998—. Pres. Greater Kansas City Fed. Exec. Bd. Pres. Greater Mo. Found.; exec. com. Heart of Am. United Way; mem. White House Outreach Task Force on CHIP. Recipient Hammer award V.P. Gore, 1999, award for disting. svc. Sec. Shalala, 1998. Mem. Ctrl. Exch., Nat. Women's Polit. Caucus. Roman Catholic. Avocations: sports enthusiast, dance, reading, politics. Office: US Dept Health and Human Svcs 601 E 12th St Ste 210 Kansas City MO 64106-2826 Home: 306 Earnhardt Dr Branson MO 65616

DANNER, PATSY ANN, former congresswoman; b. Louisville, Ky., Jan. 13, 1934; d. Henry J. and Catherine M. (Shaheen) Berrer; children: Stephen, Stephanie, Shane, Shavonne.; m. C.M. Meyer, Dec. 30, 1982. Student, Hannibal-LaGrange Coll., 1952; BA in Polit. Sci. cum laude, N.E. Mo. State U., 1972. Dist. asst. to Congressman Jerry Litton, Kansas City, Mo., 1973-76; fed. co-chmn. Ozarks Regional Comm., Washington, 1977-81; mem. Mo. State Senate, 1983-1992, 103rd-106th Congress from 6th Mo. dist., 1993-2001. Mem. internat. rels. com., transp. and infrastructure com. Mem.: LWV (bd. mem., health chairwoman Columbia-Boone County, Mo.). Democrat. Roman Catholic.*

DANNHAUSER, STEPHEN J., lawyer; b. NYC, May 23, 1950; s. Frank A. and Irene (Tinney) Dannhauser; m. Mary Elizabeth Robinson, July 1, 1973; children: Benjamin, Todd, Jess. BA with honors, SUNY, Stonybrook, 1972; JD with honors, Bklyn. Law Sch., 1975. Bar: NY 1976. Atty. Weil Gotshal & Manges LLP, NYC, 1975—, exec. ptnr., 1989—2001, chmn., 2002—. Mem. NY Bar Assn. Com. to Enhance Diversity; mem., Internat. Policy Com. US C. of C. Mem., decisions editor: Bklyn. Law Rev., 1974—75. Pres. NY Police and Fire Widows' and Children's Benefit Fund, NYC, 1985—; chair, mem. various coms. Nat. Minority Bus. Coun., Assn. for the Help of Retarded Children, Catholic Charities, Covenant House, Legal Aid Soc., United Way, Ronald McDonald House, NY Blood Ctr., Boy Scouts Am., Police Athletic League and other orgns., NYC, 1993; chmn., bd. dirs. Boys and Girls Harbor, Inc., East Harlem, NY; hon. mem. Honor Legion of the Police Dept. City NY. Named Honorary Asst. Chief, Fire Dept. City NY; recipient award, Fed. Bar Coun. and its Pub. Svc. Com., NYC Police Dept. Bomb Squad, Ellis Island Medal of Honor, Founder's Medal, Boy's & Girl's Harbor, Inc., Chairman's award, Nat. Minority Bus. Coun., Michael Bolton Charities Lifetime Achievement award. Fellow: Am. Bar Found.; mem.: ABA (ABA Law Firm Pro Bono Project Adv. Com.). Avocations: running, golf. Office: Weil Gotshal & Manges LLP c/o Grace F Lopez 767 5th Ave 10th Flr New York NY 10153-0119 Office Phone: 212-310-8326. Office Fax: 212-310-8007. E-mail: stephen.dannhauser@weil.com.

DANOFF, DUDLEY SETH, surgeon, urologist; b. N.Y.C., June 10, 1937; s. Alfred and Ruth (Kauffman) D.; m. Hevda Amrani, July 1, 1971; children: Aurele, Doran. BA summa cum laude, Princeton U., 1959; MD, Yale U., 1963. Diplomate Am. Bd. Urology. Surg. intern Columbia-Presbyn. Med. Ctr., N.Y.C., 1963-64; resident in surgery Yale New Haven Med. Ctr., 1964-65; resident in urologic surgery Squier Urologic Clinic, Columbia-Presbyn. Med. Ctr., 1965-69; NIH trainee Francis Delafield Hosp., N.Y.C., 1969; asst. in urology Columbia U.Columbia-Presbyn. Hosp., N.Y.C., 1969; cons., surgeon New Orleans VA Hosp., 1970; asst. surgeon Tulane U., New Orleans, 1970; pvt. practice urologic surgery L.A., 1971—. Attending urologic surgeon Cedars-Sinai Med. Ctr., L.A., VA Hosp., L.A.; attending urologic surgeon, clin. faculty UCLA Author: (Book) Superpotency, 1998; contbr. articles to profl. jours. Bd. dirs. Tel-Hashomer Hosp., Israel, Christian Children's Fund, Beverly Hills Edn. Found.; trustee Anti-Defamation League; mem. prof. adv. bd. The Wellness Comty.; mem. nat. exec. bd. Gesher Found.; mem. adv. com., past pres. Med. divsn. L.A. Jewish Fedn. Coun.; mem. nat. leadership cabinet United Jewish Appeal; chmn. Am. Friends of Assaf Harofeh Med. Ctr., Israel; pres. western states region and internat. bd. govs. Am. Friends Hebrew U. Jerusalem; pres. western region Am. Commn. for Shaare Zedek Med. Ctr. Jerusalem. Recipient Excellence in Medicine award, Israel Cancer Rsch. Found., 1998. Fellow ACS; mem. AMA, Internat. Coll. Surgeons, Israeli Med. Assn., Am. Fertility Soc., Soc. Air Force Clin. Surgeons, Am. Urologic Assn., Societe International d'Urologie, Transplant Soc. So. Calif., Los Angeles County Med. Assn., Soc. for Laparoendoscopic Surgeons, Am. Technion Soc., Profl. Men's Club of L.A. (past pres.), Princeton Club So. Calif., Yale Club So. Calif., Hillcrest Country Club, Phi Beta Kappa, Sigma Xi, Alpha Omega Alpha, Phi Delta Epsilon (past pres., exec. com.). Jewish. Achievements include research in in Laparoscopic Urologic Procedures. Avocations: golf, swimming, reading, writing. Office: Cedars-Sinai Med Ctr Towers Ste 1W 8635 W 3d St Los Angeles CA 90048-5912 Office Phone: 310-854-9898. Office Fax: 310-854-0267. E-mail: danoff@aol.com.

DANOFF, ERIC MICHAEL, lawyer; b. Waukegan, Ill., June 30, 1949; m. Barbara Madsen, May 27, 1979; children: Nicholas Madsen Danoff, Alexander Madsen Danoff. AB, Dartmouth Coll., 1971; JD, U. Calif., Berkeley, 1974. Bar: Calif. 1974, U.S. Dist. Ct. (no., cen., ea. and so. dists.) Calif., U.S. Ct. Appeals (9th cir.), U.S. Supreme Ct. Assoc. Graham & James, San Francisco, 1974-80, ptnr., 1981-97, Kaye, Rose & Ptnrs., San Francisco, 1998-2001, Emard, Danoff, Port & Tamulski, LLP, San Francisco, 2001—. Contbr. articles to profl. publs. Mem. Maritime Law Assn. Office: Emard Danoff Port & Tamulski LLP Ste 400 49 Stevenson St San Francisco CA 94105 Office Phone: 415-227-9455. E-mail: edanoff@edptlaw.com.

DANOS, PAUL, dean, accounting educator; m. Mary Ellen Danos; children: Amanda, Melissa. BS in acctg., U. New Orleans, 1964, MBA in acctg., 1968; PhD in acctg., U. Texas, Austin, 1974. CPA La. Arthur Andersen & Co. Prof. Acctg. Sch. Bus. Adminstrn., U. Mich., 1985-95, dir. Paton Acctg. Ctr., 1988-91, sr. assoc. dean, 1992—95; dean, Laurence F. Whittemore prof. bus. adminstrn. Tuck Sch. Bus., Dartmouth Coll., Hanover, NH, 1995—. Bd. dirs. Grad. Mgmt. Admissions Coun.; chair LEAD Coun. Deans, 2002—. Author two text books; contbr. articles to profl. jours. Mem. Assn. to Advance Collegiate Schs. of Bus. (bd. dirs., sec.-treas., 2003-). Office: Tuck Sch Bus 100 Tuck Hall Hanover NH 03755-9027

DANOS, ROBERT MCCLURE, retired oil company executive; b. New Orleans, Dec. 9, 1929; s. Joseph A. and Muriel R. (McClure) D.; m. Barbara Umbach, Apr. 30, 1955; children: Robert M., Sally C., Susan M., Julie A., Richard F., Renee R. BS in Geology, Tulane U., 1950; MS, La. State U., 1952. Geologist Texaco, Inc., New Orleans, 1955-67, staff geologist Houston, 1967, divsn. geologist Tulsa, 1968-70, exploration mgr. Denver, 1970-80; sr. v.p. K N Energy, Inc., Lakewood, Colo., 1980-83; pres., CEO Midlands Energy Co., Lakewood, 1983-84; pres. McMoRan-Midlands Oil Co., New Orleans, 1984-86; pres., chief ops. officer McMoRan Oil & Gas Co., New Orleans, 1986-89; pres. Plains Petroleum Oper. Co., Lakewood, Colo., 1989-95; dir. Am. Exploration Co., Houston, 1996-97. 1st lt. U.S. Army, 1954. Mem. Am. Assn. Petroleum Geologists (del.), New Orleans Geolog. Soc. (v.p. 1965-67), Rocky Mountain Geolog. Assn., Bienville Club, Cherry Hills Country Club, Pickwick Club, Arlberg Club. Home: 124 High St Denver CO 80218-4018 E-mail: rmdanos@msn.com.

DANSBY, JOHN WALTER, retired oil industry executive; b. Logan, W.Va., Dec. 29, 1944; s. Charles Eugene and Lillian (Maggard) Dansby; m. Karen Navarin, June 20, 1970; children: Andrew, David. BS in Econs, U. Pa., 1966; MBA, Emory U., 1967; PhD in Econs, U. Ky., 1976. Fin. analyst Ashland (Ky.) Oil, Inc., 1970-71, staff economist, 1975-77, mgr. fed. energy programs, 1977-81, exec. asst., 1981, v.p. strategic planning, 1981-84, v.p. planning, 1984-92, adminstrv. v.p. and treas., 1992-98; ret., 1998. Part-time instr. No. Ariz. U., 2000—. Treas. Sedona Chamber Music Soc., 2000—. Home: 75 Rim Shadows Cir Sedona AZ 86336-2196

DANSBY, RONNIE, transportation executive; b. Washington, Oct. 14, 1961; s. William Dansby and Helen Beatrice Bruce; life ptnr. Alma Floyd; 1 child, Brian. Student, No. Va. C.C., Annandale, Virginia, 1987—89. Cert. comml. driving instr. Bus operator Transit Mgmt. of Alexandria, Va., 1984—88, rd. supr., 1988—99, safety and loss control coord., 1999—2002, safety mgr., 2002—; CEO and owner Key Destination Directory, Inc., 2002—. Chmn. safety and accident rev. com. Transit Mgmt. of Alexandria, 1999—. Inventor detailed info. database mgmt. sys., 1995 (US Patent, 2000). Baptist. Avocations: racquetball, weightlifting, travel, jogging, martial arts.

DANSE, ILENE HOMNICK RAISFELD, physician, educator, toxicologist; b. Bklyn. d. Jack and Henrietta Homnick; m. James Atherton Danse, Aug. 10, 1982; children: Arthur Raisfeld, Robin Raisfeld. BS, CUNY, 1960; MD, NYU, 1964; student, Pratt Inst., Art Students League, Bklyn. Mus. Art Sch. Diplomate Nat. Bd. Med. Examiners, Am. Bd. Internal Medicine, Am. Bd. Toxicology. Assoc. prof. internal medicine SUNY, Stony Brook, 1975-83, assoc. prof. pharmacology, 1977-83, dir. clin. pharmacology and toxicology Sch. Medicine, 1978-83; acting chairperson clin. pharmacology Northport VA Hosp., L.I., N.Y., 1978-83; sr. advisor Chevron Environ. Health Ctr., San Pablo, Calif., 1982-84; prin. ENVIROMED Health Svcs., Inc., Novato, Calif., 1984-99; ind. med. examiner toxicology and internal medicine Dept. Indsl. Rels., State of Calif., 1985—; assoc. clin. prof. dept. medicine div. occupl. and environ. medicine U. Calif., San Francisco, 1986—, assoc. clin. prof. dept. epidemiol. and preventive medicine Davis, 1991—. Cons. in fields of toxicology, pharmacology, environ., occupl. and internal medicine, 1984—; mem. bd. sci. advisors Am. Coun. Sci. and Health; mem. sci. rev. panel Hazardous Substances Data Base, Nat. Libr. Medicine. Author: Common Sense Toxics In the Workplace, 1991; contbr. articles to sci. publs. Mem. bd. sci. advisors Am. Coun. on Sci. and Health; mem. sci. rev. panel Hazardous Substances Data Base, Nat. Libr. of Medicine. Fellow ACP, Am. Coll. Clin. Pharmacology; mem. AAAS, Am. Acad. Clin. Toxicology, Am. Chem. Soc. (environ. health and safety sect.), Am. Coll. Occupl. Medicine, Am. Indsl. Hygiene Assn. (occupational medicine sect.), Am. Coll. Toxicology, Am. Soc. Pharmacology and Therapeutics, Soc. Toxicology, Western Occupational Med. Assn. Achievements include patent for epithelial cell growth-regulating composition containing polyamines, and method of its use.

DANSKY, IRA M., lawyer; b. N.Y.C. BS, U. R.I., 1967; JD, Vanderbilt U., 1970; LLM in Taxation, NYU, 1973. Bar: NY 1971, Conn. 1989. Exec. v.p., gen. counsel, sec. Jones Apparel Group, N.Y.C. Mem.: ABA, Conn. Bar Assn., N.Y. State Bar Assn. Office: Jones Apparel Group Legal Dept 1411 Broadway New York NY 10018 Business E-Mail: jdansky@jny.com.

DANSON, TED, actor; b. San Diego, Dec. 29, 1947; s. Edward B. and Jessica (McMaster) D.; m. Randall Lee Gosch, Aug. 1970 (div. 1975); m. Cassandra Coates, July 30, 1977 (div. 1993); children: Kate, Alexis; m. Mary Steenburgen, Oct. 7, 1995. Student, The Kent Sch., Conn., 1961-66, Stanford U., 1966-68, Carnegie-Mellon U., 1968-72. Tchr. The Actors' Inst., L.A., 1978. Off Broadway plays include: The Real Inspector Hound, 1972, Comedy of Errors, Comedians; actor (daytime dramas) The Doctors, Somerset, (TV films) The Women's Room, 1980, Once Upon a Story, 1980, Our Family Business, 1981, Cowboy, 1983, Something About Amelia, 1984, The Good Witch at Laurel Canyon, Gulliver's Travels; actor, producer: (TV film) When The Bough Breaks, 1986, We Are The Children, 1987; film appearances include: The Onion Field, 1979, Body Heat, 1981, Creepshow, 1983, A Little Treasure, 1985, A Fine Mess, 1986, Just Between Friends, 1986, Three Men and a Baby, 1987, Cousins, 1989, Dad, 1989, Three Men and A Little Lady, 1990, Made in America, 1993, Getting Even With Dad, 1994, Pontiac Moon, 1994, Loch Ness, 1995, Jerry & Tom, 1998, Homegrown, 1998, Thanks of a Grateful Nation, 1998, Saving Private Ryan, 1998, Becker, 1998, Mumford, 1999; star NBC TV series Cheers, 1982-1993 (Emmy award Best Comedy Actor, 1990, 1993, Golden Globe award 1990, 91), Ink, 1996, Anasazi Prodns., Becker, 1998-; (TV films) exec. producer When the Bough Breaks, 1986, We Are the Children, 1986, Walk Me to the Distance, 1989, Down Home, 1989, Mercy Mission: The Rescue of Flight 771, 1993, On Promised Land, 1994; (TV mini series) Gulliver's Travels, 1996, Living with the Dead, 2004. Recipient Presdl. End Hunger award AID, 1989, Am. Comedy Award, 1991, The Peoples Choice Award for Favorite Male TV Performer, 1992, Emmy for Best Actor in Comedy Series, 1990, 93, Golden Globe awards, 1985, 90, 91, Star on Walk of Fame, 1999. Office: care Creative Artists Agy c/o Josh Liberman 9830 Wilshire Blvd Beverly Hills CA 90212-1804

DANTO, ARTHUR COLEMAN, writer, philosopher, critic; b. Ann Arbor, Mich., Jan. 1, 1924; s. Samuel Budd and Sylvia (Gittleman) D.; m. Shirley Rovetch, Aug. 9, 1946 (dec. July 1978); children: Elizabeth, Jane; m. Barbara Westman, Feb. 15, 1980. BA, Wayne State U., 1948; MA, Columbia U., 1949, PhD, 1952; postgrad., U. Paris, 1949-50. Instr. U. Colo., Colo., 1950-51; mem. faculty Columbia U., 1952—, Johnsonian prof. philosophy, 1975-92, chmn. dept., 1979-87, co-dir. Ctr. for Study of Human Rights, 1978-92; prof. emeritus, 1992. Andrew W. Mellon Fine Arts lectr., 1995 Author: Analytical Philosophy of Knowledge, 1968, What Philosophy Is, 1968, Analytical Philosophy of Hist., 1965, Nietzsche as Philosopher, 1965, Analytical Philosophy of Action, 1973, Mysticism and Morality, 1972, Jean-Paul Sartre, 1975, The Transfiguration of the Commonplace, 1981 (Lionel Trilling Book prize 1982), Narration and Knowledge, 1985, The Philosophical Disenfranchisement of Art, 1986, The State of the Art, 1987, Connections to the World, 1989, Encounters and Reflections: Art in the Hist. Present, 1990 (Nat. Book Critics Circle Prize for Criticism, 1990), Beyond the Brillo Box: Art in the Post Hist. Period, 1992, Mark Tansey: Visions and Revisions, 1992, Robert Mapplethorpe, 1992, Embodied Meanings: Critical Essays and Aesthetic Meditations, 1994, Playing with the Edge: The Photographic Achievement of Robert Mapplethorpe, After the End of Art: Contemporary Art and the Pale of Hist., 1997 (Eugene Kayden prize 1997), The Body/Body Problem, 1999, Philosophizing Art, 1999, The Madonna of the Future, 2000, The Abuse of Beauty: Aesthetics and the Concept of Art, 2003, Unnatural Wonders: Essays in the Gap Between Art and Life, 2004; editor Jour. Philosophy, 1965—, pres., 1987—; art critic The Nation, 1984—; contbg. editor ARTFORUM; cons. editor for various other publs. Bd. dirs. Amnesty Internat., 1970-75, gen. sec., 1973. Served with AUS, 1942-45. Recipient prize for disting. criticism Mfr.-Hanover/Art World, 1985, George S. Polk award for criticism, 1985, Nat. Book Critics Circle prize for criticism, 1990, ICP Infinity prize for writing in photography, 1993, Prix Philosophie, 2003; fellow Fulbright Found., 1949, Guggenheim Found., 1969, 82, Am. Coun. Learned Socs., 1961, 70; Fulbright disting. prof. Yugoslavia, 1976; Phi Beta Kappa prof. Arts and Scis.; mem. Am. Philos. Assn. (v.p. 1969, pres. 1983), Am. Soc. Aesthetics (v.p. 1987, pres. 1989). Fellow AAAS; mem. Am. Philos. Assn. (v.p. 1969, pres. 1983), Am. Soc. Aesthetics (v.p. 1987, pres. 1989), Coll. Art Assn. (Frank Jewett Mather prize for criticism). Office: 420 Riverside Dr New York NY 10025-7773 Business E-Mail: acd1@columbia.edu.

D'ANTONI, DAVID J., chemicals executive; BS chem engring., Va. Polytechnic Inst.; MBA, Harvard Bus. Sch. Advanced Mgmt. Pres. Ashland Chems. Trustee Franklin Univ. Mem.: Auto Fin. Corp., Nat. Assn. Manufacturers (mem. bd. dir.). Office: Ashland Chem Co 5200 Blazer Memorial Pky Dublin OH 43017-5309*

D'ANTONI, MIKE, professional athletics coach; b. Mullens, W.Va., May 8, 1951; m. Laurel D'Antoni; 1 child, Michael. Basketball player Sacramento Kings, 1973-1975, San Antonio Spurs, 1975-76; past basketball player Milan Italian League, winner 2 European Cups, 2 InterContinental Cups Milan, coach Milan, 1990-93, head coach Milan, 1996-97, winner Italian Cup, 1997; dir. player pers. Denver Nuggets, 1997-98, head coach, 1998-99; scout San Antonio Spurs, 1999—2000; assist. coach Portland Trailblazers, 2000—01, Phoenix Suns, 2003—, head coach, 2003—. Named to Marshall U. Hall of Fame, 1997. Office: Phoenix Suns 201 E Jefferson St Phoenix AZ 85004

D'ANTONI, PHILIP, television producer; b. Bronx, N.Y., Feb. 19, 1929; s. Peter and Josephine (Elici) D'Antoni; m. Ruth Ann Wiederecht, Sept. 12, 1953; children: Christopher, Jeanne, Carol, James, Robert. Student, Fordham U., 1948-50. Prodn. asst., asso. producer CBS-TV, 1949-53; v.p., dir. Mut. Broadcasting Sys., 1955-61; pres. D'Antoni/Weitz TV Prodns. Prodr.: (TV series) Movin' On, 1961—73; (films) Bullitt, 1968, The French Connection, 1971 (Acad. award, 1971), (spls.) Elizabeth Taylor in London, 1964, Sophia Loren in Rome, 1965, Melina Mercouri in Greece, 1966, (dir): (films) The Seven Ups, 1974; (TV films) Strike Force, The Connection, Cabo, Inside-Outside, In Tandem, Rubber Gun Squad, 1974—77. Served with U.S. Army, 1946—48. Mem.: Motion Picture Acad., Screenwriters Guild, Dirs. Guild Am. Home: care of St Andrews G C 10 Old Jackson Ave Hastings On Hudson NY 10706

DANTZKER, GAIL D., academic administrator, consultant; children: Curtiss Phegley, Kenneth Phegley. BS Edn., Ind. State U., 1969, MS Edn., 1971; PhD, Loyola U.-Chgo. Exec. dir. of planning and assessment Tex. A&M U., Kingsville, 2004—. Sr. rsch. assoc. MLDCJC, McAllen, Tex. Office Phone: 361-593-4105.

DANTZLER, ANDREW ALAN, science administrator; b. Bethesda, Md., Mar. 25, 1962; s. Taft Earnest and Barbara Mae Dantzler; m. Wendy Lynne Bratzel, Aug. 24, 1985 (div. Sept. 1992); m. Erin E. O'Connor, June 26, 1994; children: Melanie Meade Celano, Nicholas Andrew, Wesley Stephen BS in Astronomy, U. Md., 1984. From optical engr. to asst. dir. Space Sci. Directorate NASA Goddard Space Flight Ctr., Greenbelt, Md., 1984—2001, asst. dir. Space Scis. Directorate, 2001—04; dep. dir. programs Solar Sys. Exploration Divsn. NASA HQ, 2004—. Avocations: Judo, chess, astronomy. Office: NASA Headquarters Code SE Washington DC 20546 Business E-Mail: Andrew.Dantzler@nasa.gov.

DANTZSCHER, JAMIE, gymnast; b. Canoga Park, Calif., May 2, 1982; d. John and Joyce Dantzcher. Student, UCLA, 2001—. Mem. U.S. Nat. Team, 1994—2001, U.S. Gymnastic Team, Sydney Olympics, 2000. Mem. Charter Oaks Gliders. Named NCAA Champion, All-around, Vault and Floor Competitions, 2002, NCAA Co-Champion, Uneven Bars, 2003; recipient 1st pl. vault, Coca-Cola Nat. Championships, 1995, 1st pl. all-around, City of Popes (France) Competition, 1996, 1st pl. (tied) vault, Am. Classic, 1998, 1st pl. uneven bars, John Hancock U.S. Gymnastics Championships, 1999. Address: c/o UCLA Athletic Dept JD Morgan Ctr PO Box 24044 Los Angeles CA 90024

DANZ, MICHAEL L., music educator; b. Oak Park, Ill., Apr. 1, 1977; s. James Michael and Mary (Marvine) Danz; m. Robyn Marie Obert, Mar. 15, 2003. A in Fine Arts, William R. Harper Coll., Palatine, Ill., 1998; MusB in Bus., Elmhurst Coll., 2000, MusB in Edn., 2003; MusM in Edn., Vandercook Coll. Music, 2005. Cert. music tchr. K-12 Ill. Musician, 1996—; pvt. music tchr. Shaumburg, Ill., 1996—2003; K-12 tchr. Lake Zurich (Ill.) Sch. Dist. 95, 2003—. Music instr. poverty-stricken areas Elmhurst Coll., Jamaica, 2002; music min. Summitview Christian Ch., Hoffman Estates, Ill., 2003—. Mem.: Music Educators Nat. Conf. Avocations: weightlifting, reading.

DANZA, TONY, actor; b. Bklyn., Apr. 21, 1951; m. Rhonda Yeoman (div.); 1 child, Marc Anthony; m. Tracy Robinson 1986; children: Katherine Anne, Emily Lyn. Grad., U. Dubuque. Began career as profl. boxer; appeared in films Hollywood Knights, 1980, Going Ape, 1981, Cannonball Run II, 1984, She's Out of Control, 1989, Angels in the Outfield, 1994, Dear God, 1996, Illtown, 1996, A Brookln State of Mind, 1997, Meet Wally Sparks, 1997, Glam, 1997, The Girl Gets Moe, 1997, A Brooklyn State of Mind, 1997,

Glam, 2001, Crash, 2004, The Whisper, 2004; TV series include Taxi, ABC, 1978-83, Who's the Boss?, ABC, 1984-92 (also dir.), Baby Talk, 1992, Hudson Street, 1995, The Tony Danza Show, 1997, Homewood P.I., 2000, Family Law, 2000-02; TV films include Doing Life, Wall of Tyranny, Single Bar, Single Women, Freedom Fighters (also exec. prodr.), Bob Hope: Laughing With the Presidents, 1996, 12 Angry Men, 1997, North Shore Fish, 1997, The Garbage Picking Field Goal Kicking Philadelphia Phenomenon, 1998, Noah, 1998, Stealing Christmas, 2003; co-exec. prodr. (TV films) Doing Life, 1986; exec. prodr. (TV films) The Whereabouts of Jenny, 1991, Bermuda Triangle, 1996, Sudden Terror: The Hijacking of School Bus #17, 1996, Crowned and Dangerous, 1997, (TV series) George, 1993, Hudson Street, 1995, (films) The Jerky Boys, 1995; host, co-exec. prodr. (TV series) The Tony Danza Show, 2004-; stage appearance Wrong Turn at Lungfish, 1993. Avocations: softball, running. Office: c/o ABC TV 57 W 66th St New York NY 10023-6298*

DANZBERGER, ALEXANDER HARRIS, retired chemical engineer, consultant; b. N.Y.C., Mar. 23, 1932; s. George Harris and Ruth P. (Alexander) D.; m. Jacqueline P. Pilcher, Mar. 12, 1954; children: Alison, Alexander, Diana, Robert; m. Anne Griggs Pierson, Apr. 23, 1977; stepchildren: Jennifer Pierson, Priscilla Pierson, Stephanie Pierson BSChemE, MIT, 1953. Registered profl. engr., Mass., Colo. Mem. staff Arthur D. Little Inc., Cambridge, Mass., 1953-60; engring. mgr. Linde div. Union Carbide Corp., Tonawanda, N.Y., N.Y.C., 1961-70; chief engr. Booz, Allen & Hamilton, Florham Park, N.J., 1971-72, Marcom Cons., N.Y.C., 1973-75; v.p. Hydrotechnic Corp., N.Y.C., 1976-81; mgr. pollution control group Dames & Moore, Golden, Colo., 1982-83; pres. Danzberger and Assocs., Inc., Lakewood, Colo., 1983—2004; ret. Adj. prof. dept. arts and scis. Johnson and Wales U., Providence, 2001—03. Served to 1st lt. U.S. Army, 1956-58. Recipient Kenneth B. Allen award N.Y. Water Pollution Control Assn., 1983. Fellow: AIChE; mem.: ASME (life), Masons. Republican. Presbyterian. Home and Office: 273 N Farm Dr Bristol RI 02809-1560 E-mail: aharrisd@aol.com.

DANZIG, FREDERICK PAUL, newspaper editor; b. Springfield, Mass., Sept. 17, 1925; s. Phillip and Sylvia (Levin) D.; m. Edith Goret, Mar. 16, 1952; children: Steven, Ellen Kay. BA, Washington Sq. Coll., NYU, 1949. Copy boy AP, N.Y.C., 1943; reporter Herkimer (N.Y.) Evening Telegram, 1949, Port Chester (N.Y.) Daily Item, 1950-51; reporter, columnist UPI, N.Y.C., 1951-62; sr. editor Advt. Age, N.Y.C., 1962-68, exec. editor, 1969-84, editor, 1984-94; contbg. editor, 1995—. Advt. newscaster Sta. WQXR, 1979-81, Sta. WMCA, 1982-86; adj. instr. New Sch. Social Rsch., N.Y.C.; pub. radio commentator, 1989-90; media cons. Comprehensive Cmty. Revitalization Program, N.Y.C, 1994-98; mem. adv. bd. Youth Law Ctr., Washington; dir. Greenshoe Inc., Southampton, N.Y. Author: (with Ted Klein) How to be Heard, 1974, Publicity, 1985. Served with inf. AUS, 1943-46. Decorated Bronze Star, Purple Heart; recipient Alumni Achievement award NYU, 1983. Mem. 29th Inf. Divsn. Assn., Amagansett Hist. Assn., The Battle of Normandy Found., U.S. Holocaust Meml. Mus., Internat. Mus. Cartoon Art (adv. bd.). E-mail: fredpep@aol.com.

DANZIG, WILLIAM HAROLD, marketing executive; b. Bklyn., Feb. 24, 1947; s. Sidney and Beatrice (Reiss) D.; m. Sheila Ring, Aug. 11, 1968; children: David Scott, Gregory Charles. BS in Acctg., Baruch Coll., 1969; MS in Edn., Long Island U., 1971; PhD, Am. Coastline U., 1996. Acct. JK Lasser, N.Y.C., 1972; tchr. N.Y.C. Bd. Edn., Queens, 1969-74; pres. Nat. Success Mktg. Inc., Ft. Lauderdale, Fla., 1969—. Sponsor Coop. Bus. Edn., Broward County, Fla., 1986; participant Bus. Expo, Ft. Lauderdale, 1985; cons. Mail Market Monitor, Ft. Lauderdale, 1988—, Gulfstream Pub., Ft. Lauderdale, 1988—. Co-author: You Deserve to be Rich, 1975, Play to Win, 1982; publisher (computer program) Turn Your Computer Into A Money Machine, 1994. Mem. Mail Order Bus. Bd., Greater Ft. Lauderdale C. of C., B'nai Brith (chpt. bd. dirs. 1976). Republican. Jewish. Office: PO Box 16180 Fort Lauderdale FL 33318-6180

DANZIGER, BRUCE EDWARD, civil engineer; b. N.Y.C., Feb. 14, 1964; s. Frederick Benjamin Danziger and Elise Lee (Saranow) Gold. BS in Archtl. Engring., Calif. Poly. U., 1988. Project engr. Ove Arup & Ptnrs., London, 1988-90, Sevilla, Spain, 1990-92, L.A., 1992-93, 2002—, N.Y.C., 1993-97, San Francisco, 1997—2002. Mem. faculty So. Calif. Inst. Architecture. Recipient 1st prize MakMax Membrane Design Competition, 1993, Hon. Mention award, 1995, 96. Office: Arup 2440 S Sepulveda Blvd Ste 180 Los Angeles CA 90064 Office Phone: 310-312-5040. Business E-Mail: bruce.danziger@arup.com.

DANZIGER, GLENN NORMAN, retired chemicals executive; b. N.Y.C., Apr. 7, 1930; s. Victor and Freda (Lazar) Danziger; m. Florence Spielvogel, June 7, 1953; children: Jill Marla Danziger Hetson, Amy L. Tenenbaum, Beth J. Keyes(dec.). AB, Columbia U., 1952, BSChE, 1953. Chemist Breinig Bros., Hoboken, NJ, 1955-61; v.p., tech. dir. Flood and Conklin, Newark, 1961-65; tech. sales rep. SEABORD Chem. Corp., Lodi, NJ, 1965-75; pres. Seaboard Sales Corp., Paterson, NJ, 1975—2002; ret., 2002. Author: Formulation of Organic Coatings, 1967. Lt. (j.g.) USNR, 1953—55. Jewish. Avocations: travel, golf, skiing, reading.

DANZIGER, JAMES NORRIS, political science professor; b. L.A., May 28, 1945; s. Edward and Beverly Jane Danziger; m. Lesley Robson, June 12, 1971; children: Nicholas James, Vanessa Margaret. BA, Occidental Coll., L.A., 1966; MA, Sussex U., Brighton, Eng., 1968; MA, PhD, Stanford U., 1974. Prof. polit. sci. U. Calif., Irvine, 1972—, chmn. dept. polit. sci., 1974-76, 81-83, 88-92, assoc. dean Sch. Social Scis., 1978-81, chmn. acad. senate, 1994-95, dean of undergrad. edn., 1995-99; rsch. assoc. Ctr. Rsch. Info. Tech. and Orgns., Irvine, 1974—, dir., 2000-01, assoc. dir., 2001—; scholar-in-residence LaVerne (Calif.) U., 1983-84. Vis. prof. U. Pitts., 1996, Aarhus (Denmark) U., 1985. Author: Making Budgets, 1978, Understanding the Political World, 1991, 7th edit., 2005; co-author: Computers and Politics, 1982, People and Computers, 1986; mem. editl. bd. Local Govt. Studies, 1981—; assoc. editor Social Sci. Computer Rev. Bd. dirs. South Laguna Civic Assn., 1983-86, chair South Laguna Annexation Task Force, 1986, bd. dirs. Irvine Campus Housing Authority, 1996-2004. Recipient Disting. Teaching award U. Calif., 1979, Daniel Aldrich disting. svc. award, 1997, Marshall scholar Govt. of U.K., 1966-68; named Disting. Faculty Lectr. U. Calif. Acad. Senate, 1987, IBM Faculty fellow, 2003—; NSF grantee, 1973-79, 80-83, 1996-98, 99—. Mem. Am. Polit. Sci. Assn. (Leonard White award 1974), ASPA (Marshall Dimock award 1977), Phi Beta Kappa (pres. local chpt. 1988-89, sec.-treas. local chpt. 1996-99, Pi Sigma Alpha (pres. local chpt. 1987—). Avocations: travel, basketball, literature. Office: U Calif Sch Social Scis Irvine CA 92697-5100 Office Phone: 949-824-5533. E-mail: danziger@uci.edu.

DANZIGER, LUCY, editor; married; 2 children. Grad., Harvard U. Reporter Star-Ledger, Newark, 1982—86; mag. assoc. editor, 1986—88; founding mng. editor 7 Days, 1988—90; exec. editor Manhattan, Inc., N.Y.C., 1990—92; freelance writer, 1992—95; freelance editor Allure; editor style and news dept. NY Times, N.Y.C., 1994—95; founding editor Women's Sports & Fitness, 1997—2001; editor-in-chief SELF mag., N.Y.C., 2001—. Office: Salf Mag 4 Times Sq New York NY 10036

DANZIGER, PETER, lawyer; b. N.Y.C., Jan. 5, 1949; s. Herbert and Eleanor (Rosner) D.; m. Joan Nelick, Aug. 15, 1970; children: Lisa, Carrie, Beth. BA, U. Vt., 1970; JD, Albany Law Sch., 1973; MS, SUNY, Albany, 1977. Bar: N.Y. 1974, U.S. Dist. Ct. (no. dist.) N.Y. 1974. Assoc. O'Connell and Aronowitz, Albany, N.Y., 1973-79, sr. ptnr., 1979—. Instr. Albany Law Sch., 1972-73, SUNY at Albany, 1978-88. Author: (book) Special Education Litigation, 1989, Tapping Officials Secrets, 1989—; author Albany Law Rev., 1972, (newspaper column) Legal Line, 1990-2000; contbr. Long Term Care Insurance in N.Y., 2000; editor: Representing People with Disabilities, 1989—. Legal counsel Jewish Family Svcs. of N.E. N.Y., Albany, 1977—. Named one of Best Lawyers in Am., Woodward/White Inc., 1991—. Mem. ABA, N.Y. State Trial Lawyers Assn., Am. Trial Lawyers Assn., N.Y. State Bar Assn. (chairperson com. on mental and phys. disabilities 1989-93). Office: O'Connell and Aronowitz 54 State St Albany NY 12207-1897

DANZIGER, RAPHAEL, political scientist, researcher; b. Haifa, Israel, June 26, 1944; came to U.S., 1968; s. Norbert and Hanna Danziger; m. Carla Danziger, June 12, 1970; children: Elon, Tamar. BA in Polit. Sci. and History Islamic Countries, Hebrew U., Jerusalem, 1965; MA in Near Ea. Studies, U. Wash., 1970; MA in European and Near Ea. History, Princeton U., 1972, PhD in Near Ea. Studies, 1974. Rschr. Shiloah Ctr. for Mid. Ea. Studies Tel Aviv (Israel) U., 1975-76; dep. dir. Inst. Mid. Ea. Studies U. Haifa (Israel), 1976-77; policy analyst commn. on internat. affairs Am. Jewish Congress, N.Y.C., 1981-86, asst. dir. commn. on internat. affairs, 1986-90; dir. rsch. and info. Am. Israel Pub. Affairs Com., Washington, 1990—. Cons. Hudson Inst., Croton-on-Hudson, N.Y., 1974-75; vis. rsch. fellow dept. history U. Bergen, Norway, 1980; vis. fellow dept. Near Ea. studies Princeton (N.J.) U., 1981; lectr. dept. Mid. East history U. Haifa, 1975-81; vis. asst. prof. dept. history U. Wash., Seattle, 1980-81; lectr. in field. Author: Abd al-Qadir and the Algerians: Resistance to the French and Internal Consolidation, 1977; editor Near East Report, 1992—; contbr. articles to profl. jours. Lt. Israeli Army, 1965-68. Mem. Mid. East Studies Assn., Mid. East Inst. Office: Am Israel Pub Affairs Com 440 1st St NW Ste 600 Washington DC 20001-2017 Office Phone: 202-639-5268. Business E-Mail: rdanziger@aipac.org.

DANZIS, ROSE MARIE, emeritus college president; b. Adrian, Pa. d. Paul A. and Josephine (Bugala) Manger; m. James Gordon Channing, Jan. 24, 1954 (dec. 1973); children: Rose Marie Buhrman, Lorraine Genieczko; m. Sidney Danzis, June 1, 1986. Diploma, Jersey City Hosp. Sch. Nursing, 1949; BS, N.Y. U., 1954; MA, Columbia U., 1961, M.Ed., 1971, Ed.D., 1973. Staff nurse, asst. supr. Pub. Health Nursing Svc., Jersey City, 1949-55; dir. health and recreation, clin. coordinator, asso. dir. nursing edn. Charles E. Gregory Sch. Nursing, Perth Amboy (N.J.) Gen. Hosp., 1958-66; chmn. dept. nurse edn., dir. health techs., dean div. health techs. Middlesex County Coll., Edison, N.J., 1966-78, pres., 1978-86; ret. Mem. Middlesex County Comprehensive Health Planning Coun., 1973-75, N.Y. Com. Regents External Degree in Nursing, 1972-80, Council on Continuing Edn. for Allied Health Pers., N.J.; Regional Med. Program, 1968-71; chmn. N.J. Health Professions Edn. Adv. Council, N.J. Dept. Higher Edn., 1979-82, chmn. nursing subcom., 1975-78; mem. health careers com. J.F. Kennedy Hosp., 1972-75; chmn. Middlesex County Coll. Assembly, 1975-77; mem. Pres.'s Adv. Com. Sch. Allied Health, Coll. Medicine and Dentistry of N.J., 1976-79; commr. Middle States Assn. of Colls. and Schs.; chmn. Commn. High Edn., 1984-85; mem. liaison com. Am. Assn. Cmty. and Jr. Colls. and Nat. League for Nursing, 1978-82; chmn. acad. affairs com. N.J. Coun. of C.C., pres., 1978-82; trustee Nat. Bank of N.J., 1979-81; exec. com. Acad. Pres.'s, Am. Assn. Community and Jr. Colls.; also exec. com. Internat./Intercultural Consortium. Contbr. articles to profl. jours. Recipient Torch of Liberty award Anti-Defamation League, 1981, Disting. Service award U. Medicine and Dentistry of N.J. Sch. Health Related Professions, 1983; named to Hall of Fame, Perth Amboy High Sch., 1985 Mem. Council of County Coll. Presidents, Am. Nurses Assn., Nat. League for Nursing, Am. Soc. Allied Health Professions, Am. Coun. on Edn., Am. Assn. Cmty. and Jr. Colls. (bd. dirs. 1984-86), Coll. Consortium for Internat. Studies., Jersey City Sch. Nursing Alumni Assn., N.Y. U. Alumni Assn., Tchrs. Coll., Columbia Alumni Assn., Kappa Delta Pi. Home: 5055 Collins Ave Apt 8C Miami Beach FL 33140 *An important principle, accepted early in my life, was that education is the key to a successful professional and personal life. I believe in goal-setting on a short term achievable basis, leading gradually to a higher long term goal. Upon making a decision regarding further study or accepting a position, total commitment is essential to success. I take my study and work seriously, but not myself. I truly enjoy all people and working with them.*

DANZL, DANIEL FRANK, emergency physician; b. Cin., Apr. 2, 1950; s. Frank Bernard and Mary Ellen (Doerger) D.; m. Joanna Colosimo Danzl, Nov. 25, 1978; children: Maggie, Julia. BS magna cum laude, U. Cin., 1972; MD, Ohio State U., 1976. Diplomate Am. Bd. Emergency Medicine. Intern St. Francis Med. Ctr., Peoria, Ill., 1976-77; resident in emergency medicine U. Louisville, 1977-79, asst. prof. emergency medicine, 1979-83, assoc. prof. emergency medicine, 1983-89, prof. emergency medicine, 1989-91, prof., chair, 1991—. Bd. dirs., councilman-at-large Univ. Assn. for Emergency Medicine, 1988-89, indsl./govtl. rels. com., 1984-85, nominating com., 1987-88; bd. dirs. Soc. for Acad. Emergency Medicine, 1989, mem. annals of emergency meidcine task force, 1989; bd. dirs. Am. Bd. Emergency Medicine, sec.-treas., 1995-96, pres.-elect, 1996-97, pres. 1997—, mem. ad hoc com., oral examiner, 1982—; mem. Com. to Advise the Nat. ARC, 1984-87; reviewer for various med. jours. Author book chpts., monographs and textbooks including Airway Management in the Trauma Patient in the Clinical Practice of Emergency Medicine, 1991; editl. bd. Jour. Emergency Medicine, 1983—, Poisindex-Emergindex, 1982—, Jour. Wilderness Medicine, 1991—; contbr. more than 70 articles to Jour. Wilderness Medicine, Jpur. Emergency Medicine, Annals of Emergency Medicine, Am. Jour. Emergency Medicine, others. Mem. Water Safety Com. Nat. Safety Coun.-Pub. Safety Div., 1981-84; alternate med. dir. Jefferson Vocat. Edn.-Louisville EMS Paramedic Tng. Program, 1989-90, 90-91. Recipient Silver Tongue Orator award Soc. Tchrs. of Emergency Medicine, 1986, 88; grantee Office of Naval Resources, 1983-85, Key Pharmaceuticals, 1985, Hoffman-LaRoche, Inc., 1988, 89. Fellow Am. Coll. Emergency Physicians (nat. coun. mem. 1981-93, reference com. mem. 1981, 85, 89, rsch. com. mem. 1982-83, 83-84); mem. AMA (Physician's Recognition awards), NAS, Am. Soc. Circumpolar Health, Soc. for Acad. Emergency Medicine (bd. dirs. 1989, task force 1989), Nat. Rsch. Coun., Undersea and Hyperbaric Oxygen Med. Soc., Ky. Chpt. Am. Coll. Emergency Physicians (councillor 1981-93, sec.-treas. 1983-84, pres.-elect 1984-85, pres. 1985-86), Wilderness Med. Soc., Phi Beta Kappa, Beta Theta Pi, Alpha Omega Alpha, Phi Eta Sigma. Roman Catholic. Achievements include research on hypothermia. Home: 4804 Smith Rd Floyds Knobs IN 47119-9238 Office: U Louisville Dept Emergency Med 530 S Jackson St Louisville KY 40202-1675 Office Phone: 502-588-5689.

DAO, HANH D., lawyer; b. Thu Duc, Vietnam, May 25, 1970; came to the U.S., 1975; s. Nhi V. Dao and Thu T. Nguyen; m. Lien B. Pham, Dec. 1, 1996; 1 child, Michael D. BS in Fin., Calif. Poly. U., Pomona, 1992; JD, Boston U., 1995. Bar: Calif., Cabazon Tribal Bar. Assoc. Law Office of Robert G. Johnson, Jr., Laguna Niguel, Calif., 1995-96; ptnr. Archer & Dao, Irvine, Calif., 1996—. Gen. counsel Internat. Female Boxers Assn., Palos Verdes, Calif., 1997—, The Pet Rescue Ctr., Inc., Indio, Calif., 1998—. Mem. ABA, Young Lawyers Assn. Roman Catholic. Avocations: tennis, golf. Office: 2127 E Ward Ter Anaheim CA 92806-3619

DAO, THUY DINH, personal care industry executive; b. Bac Ninh, Vietnam, Apr. 12, 1942; arrived in U.S., 1991, naturalized, 1997; s. Tan Dinh Dao, Thu Thi Pham, Hoi Thi Nguyen (Stepmother); m. Dung Ngoc Tran, Mar. 30, 1968; children: Thuy-Van, Khai, Tri. Baccalaureat 1st Degree, Tri-Duc Cath. Sch., Da-Lat, Vietnam, 1961; cert. Radio/TV Technician, Can-Tho U., Vietnam, 1987; cert. Computer/Elec. Cable Tech., Amtek Inst., Arlington, Va., 1992; former student, Lycee Yersin, Da-Lat. A+ cert. Nova C.C., Alexandria, Va., 2001, cert. nail tech. Falls Ch., Va. Interpreter, transplator U.S. Adv. Teams, Vietnam, 1965—70; tinsmith Vietnam, 1976—81; owner coffee shop Ho-Chi-Minh City, Vietnam, 1983—88; with Ritz Carlton Hotel Pentagon City, Arlington, Va., 1991—96; owner Elegant Nails, New Castle, Del., 1999—2000, mgr. Alexandria, 2001—02, Belle Beauté and Hollywood Image Inc., Wilmington, Del., 2003—, Bella Nails, Wilmington, 2003—04; asst. T&D Home Improvement, Inc., Falls Ch., Va., 2004—. Trader Fgn. Currency Agy., (IMEX Can Tho) Can Tho, Vietnam, 1981—82. Author: The Siren, 1980, numerous poems; contbr. articles to profl. jours. With Army South Vietnam, 1970—75. Fellow: Internat. Biog. Assn., Cambridge, England. Avocations: music, movies, travel, reading, sports. Office: T&D Home Improvement Inc 3059 Sleepy Hollow Rd Falls Church VA 22042 Personal E-mail: thuy.dao@worldnet.att.net.

DAOUD, ABRAHAM JOSEPH, IV, funeral director, former police officer; b. Miami Beach, Fla., Jan. 19, 1957; children: Joseph Abraham, Baileigh Patt. AS in Funeral Svcs., cert. police officer, Miami Dade C.C., 1980; cert. crime prevention, S.W. Tex. State U., 1981; BS, Barry U., 1992; MBA, U. Phoenix, 2004. Cert. police officer; lic. funeral dir., Fla., N.C., Tex. Pres. Daoud's, Inc., Miami Beach, Fla., 1974—76; coord. Fed. CETA Program, Miami Beach, 1978; aux. police officer Miami Beach Police Dept., 1976—79, police officer, 1979—86; v.p. Daoud Med. Ctr., Miami Beach, 1982—84; crime prevention officer Miami Beach Police Dept., 1980—82; funeral dir. Riverside Meml. Chapels, Miami Beach, 1981—86; with Guardian Plan Inc., 1986—89; regional mgr. Osiris Corp., 1988—95; regional v.p. S.E. U.S. Loewen Group, 1995—99; pres. Daoud Holdings, Inc., Pilot Mountain, NC, 1999—. Coord. Aux. Police, Miami Beach, 1981. Mem. Pilot Mountain Zoning Bd., 2004; chmn. Pilot Mountain United Way, 2003; mem. com. Habitat for Humanity, 2003—. Recipient cert. of appreciation Dade County Pharm. Assn., 1974, citation of appreciation Am. Legion, 1984, Outstanding Citizen award Miami Beach Taxpayers, 1986, Disting. Citizen award City of Miami Beach, 1986. Mem. Nat. Funeral Dir. Assn. (mem. comm. nat. com. 2001-), Pilot Mountain Merchant Assn. (pres. 2003), Miami Beach Police Athletic League (exec. dir. 1982-86, Fla. state pres. 1985, nat. v.p. 1986-87, 9 Svc. awards, Police Athletic League Recreation Hall dedication 1986), Fla. Police Athletic League (pres. 1983-87, Disting. Founder award 2004), Jaycees (pres. Miami Beach club 1984, mgmt. v.p. 1982, 83, Appreciation award 1984), Fraternal Order of Police, Internat. Assn. Chiefs of Police, Internat. Assn. Chiefs of Police, Gemological Internat. Assn., Miami Beach C. of C., Elks (Miami Beach) (trustee, Exalted Ruler 1985), Masons, Shriners, Optimists, Rotary. Avocations: reading, youth activities, community service, politics. Office: PO Box 37 Pilot Mountain NC 27041-0037 Office Phone: 336-368-2233. Personal E-mail: ajdaoud@aol.com.

DAOUST, DONALD ROGER, pharmaceutical executive, microbiologist, cosmetics executive; b. Worcester, Mass., Aug. 13, 1935; s. G. Arthur and Alice Anne (Lavalee) D.; m. Johanna K. Kalinoski, May 30, 1959 (div. 2003); children: Donna Jean, Stephen Michael, Sandra Marie; m. Barbara Neubert, 2005. BA, U. Conn., 1957; MS, U. Mass., 1959, PhD, 1962. Sr. rsch. microbiologist Merck Sharp & Dohme, Rahway, N.J., 1962-70, rsch. fellow, 1970-72, mgr. biol. quality control West Point, Pa., 1972-75; dir. quality control Armour Pharm. Co., Kankakee, Ill., 1975-76, v.p. quality assurance and regulatory compliance Phoenix, 1976-78; v.p., quality control Carter-Wallace, Inc., Cranbury, NJ, 1978—2001. Contbr. articles to profl. jours., chpts. to books; patentee in field. Mem. Borough Coun., South Plainfield, N.J., 1970-72; treas. George Washington coun. Boy Scouts Am., 1981-84, pres., 1984-87, area v.p., bd.dirs. NE region U.S., 1987—2004. Recipient Disting. Svc. award South Plainfield Jaycees, 1969, silver Beaver award Boy Scouts Am., 1988, Silver Antelope award N.E. region, 1992; named Outstanding Young Man, N.J. Jaycees, 1970. Mem.: AAAS, Pharm. Mfrs. Assn. (quality control adminstrn. 1979—82, adv. bd. 1982—94, vice chmn 1988—90, chmn. 1990—92), Am. Soc. for Quality Control, Am. Soc. Microbiology, Laurel Oak Country Club (Sarasota, Fla.). Avocations: golf, jogging, reading, gardening. Home: 3254 Chas MacDonald Dr Sarasota FL 34240 Personal E-mail: dondaoust@msn.com.

DAPPER, L. ROBERT, healthcare insurance company executive; Mgmt. Arthur Andersen; sr. v.p., human capital UnitedHealth Group, 2000—. Office: UnitedHealth Group Ctr 9900 Bren Rd E Minnetonka MN 55343

DAPRON, ELMER JOSEPH, JR., communications executive; b. Clayton, Mo., Jan. 14, 1925; s. Elmer Joseph and Susanna (Kruse) D.; m. Sharon Kay Neuling, Feb. 22, 1977 (dec. Apr. 1987). Employed in constrn., Fairbanks, Alaska, 1947-48; tech. writer-editor McDonnell-Douglas Corp., St. Louis, 1948-57; freelance writer Paris, 1957; with Gardner Advt. Co., St. Louis, 1960-78, v.p., 1969-78; sr. v.p. Kenrick Advt. Inc., 1978-83; pres. Cornucopia Communications, Inc., 1979—. Producer syndicated radio and TV show Elmer Dapron's Grocery List; advt. and mktg. cons. to govt. and industry; commentator The Grocery List Armed Forces Radio Network (worldwide); contbr. articles to publs. Mem. Nat. Dem. Com., candidate for Gov. of Mo., 1992; nat. pres. Iwo Jima Task Force Two, 1994—; nat. chmn. Korea Task Force 2000, 1997—. With USMCR, 1943-45, PTO, 50-51, Korea. Recipient advt. awards including New Filming Techniques award Internat.-Film Festival; hon. fellow Harry Truman Libr. Inst. Mem. Nat. Agrl. Mktg. Assn., Miss. Valley Farm Mktg. (Man of Yr. 1974), Assn. R.R. Advt. and Mktg. (nat. membership chmn.), Marine Corps League (nat. vice comdt. 1967-69, nat. press officer 4th Marine Div. Assn. 1989—, publicity chmn.), Media Club, St. Louis Track Club. Democrat. Office: 119 Lakeview Estates Dr Warrenton MO 63383-5258 Office Phone: 636-456-0154.

D'AQUINO, THOMAS, lawyer, educator, entrepreneur; b. Trail, B.C., Can., Nov. 3, 1940; m. Susan Marion Peterson, 1965. BA, U. B.C., 1962, LLB, 1965; LLB, LLM, U. London, 1967; LLD (hon.), Queen's U., 1996, Wilfred Laurier U. Adj. prof. law U. Ottawa, Canada; chmn. Intercounsel Ltd.; pres., chief exec. Can. Coun. Chief Execs. (CCCE), Ottawa, 1981—. Former exec. asst. to Fed. Min., spl. asst. to Prime Min., Can., 1969-72; internat. cons. firm in London and Paris, 1972-75; frequent guest lectr.; mem. Chmn's Internat. Adv. Coun. of the Am.'s Soc.; founding mem. Pacific Coun. on Internat. Policy; adv. bd. Lazard Can.; chmn. Nat. Gallery of Can. Found., N.Am. security and prosperity initiative, Can. Coun. Chief Execs. (CCCE), co-chmn. corp. govt. initiative. Co-author: Northern Edge: How Canadians Can Triumph in the Global Economy, 2001; contbr. articles to profl. jours. Mem. World Econ. Forum Geneva, Inst. for Strategic Studies, London. Mem. Can. Bar Assn., Internat. Bar Assn., B.C. Law Soc. Office: Can Coun Chief Execs 99 Bank St Ste 1001 Ottawa ON Canada K1P 6B9

DARAISEH, NANCY M., researcher, educator; arrived in U.S., 1994; d. Mohammad B. Daraiseh and Fathyah I. Sheboul. BS, Jordan U., Irbid, 1987—92; MS, U. Cin., 1995—99, D, 1999, PhD, 2004. Engr. Fernald Environ. Remediation Mgmt. Corp., Cin., 1996; fellowship Nat. Inst. Occupl. Safety and Health, 1996—2004; rsch., tchg. asst. U. Cin., 1999—2004, post doctoral rschr., 2004—. Contbr. articles to journals. Fellow Ednl. Rsch. Ctr. Grad. Fellowship, Nat. Inst. Occupl. Safety and Health, 1996 - present; grantee Pilot rsch. project grant, 1999-2003. Mem.: Am. Soc. Safety Engrs., Human Factors Ergonomics Soc., Inst. Indsl. Engineers, Alpha Pi Mu. Office: U Cin Po Box 210072 Cincinnati OH 45221-0072 Office Phone: 513-556-2643. Business E-Mail: nancydaraiseh@email.uc.edu.

DARBEE, PETER A., electric power company executive; b. 1954; BA in Econ., MBA, Darmouth Coll.; Nuclear Reactor Technology Program, MIT. Mgmt. Salomon Brothers, AT&T; investment banker, v.p. Goldman Sachs; v.p., CFO, controller Pacific Bell; v.p., CFO Advance Fibre Commns., Inc.; sr. v.p., CFO, treas. PG&E Corp., 1999—2005, pres., CEO, 2005—. Mem. San Francisco Com. on Jobs. Office: PG&E 1 Market Spear Tower San Francisco CA 94105*

DARBELNET, ROBERT LOUIS, automobile association executive; b. Portland, Maine, Dec. 14, 1951; s. Jean Louis and Elizabeth (Matheson) D.; m. Mary Ann McCaughey, Aug. 27, 1977; children: John Kevin, Mary Jennifer. LLB, Laval U., Quebec City, 1978. Dir. consumer protection dept. Que. (Can.) Automobile Club, Quebec City, 1973-76, dir. road and tech. svcs., 1976-78, dir. gen. ins. dept., 1978-79, asst. gen. mgr., 1980-83, dir. gen., 1983-90, pres., 1990-94. Tchr. bus. Coll. Sainte Foy (Que.), 1978—84, v.p., 1981—82, pres., 1982—86; bd. dirs. Ont. Corp., Muncie, Ind., ITS Am., vice chair, 2002; mem. Nat. Petroleum Coun.; pres. Alliance Internat. Tourisme, 2001—, chair mgmt. com., 2001—; chair world bd. Alliance Internat. Tourisme/Fedn. Internat. de'lAutomobile, 2002; mem. Fedn. Internat. del'Automobile Senate, 1997—. Mem. Fedn. Internat. de l'Automobile, Paris, 1990—, dep. pres., 2001—; bd. dirs. Corp. de la Salle Albert Rousseau, 1990—94, Enfant Jesus Hosp., 1993—94, Union Canadienne Ins., 1993—94; bd. govs. Coll. Sainte-Foy, 1980—88, bd. govs. alumni fund, 1980—88, v.p., 1982—88; trustee AAA Found. for Traffic Safety, 1990—, sec., 1993—94;

v.p. Internat. Tourism Commn., 1995—, world tng. coun., 1995—, mem. mgmt. com., 1995—. Mem.: Am. Automobile Assn. (pres., CEO 1994—). Office: 1000 Aaa Dr Heathrow FL 32746-5063*

D'ARBELOFF, ALEXANDER V., former electronics company executive; Co-founder Teradyne Corp., Boston, 1960—99, pres., 1971—96, CEO, 1971—97, chmn. bd. dirs., 1977—; hon. chair. MIT, Cambridge. Bd. dirs. Stratus Computer, Inc., BTU Internat., Inc., PRI Automation, Inc., GeoTel Comm. Corp. Chmn. bd. trustees MIT, Cambridge, 1997—. Office: 77 Massachusetts Ave E52-586 Cambridge MA 02139-4307 Office Phone: 617-253-4034.

DARBY, EDWIN WHEELER, retired columnist; b. Oakland, Md., Jan. 7, 1922; s. John Dade and Nell (Bosley) D.; children— Ann Wheeler, John Dade; m. Susan E. Kroening, Mar. 14, 1970; 1 son, George Kroening. BS in Journalism, Ohio U. White House corr. Time mag., 1948-55; midwest corr. Time and Fortune mags., 1956-58; financial editor, columnist Chgo. Sun-Times, 1958-95; ret., 1995. Author: The Fortune Builders, 1987. Recipient Marshall Field award, 1974, Loeb award, 1975 Mem. Tavern Club. Home: 2703 W Logan Blvd Chicago IL 60647-1831

DARBY, G(EORGE) HARRISON, lawyer; b. N.Y.C., Jan. 24, 1942; s. Stephen John and Madge B. (Leh) D. BA, Muhlenberg Coll., 1963; LLB, Bklyn. Law Sch., 1967. Bar: N.Y. 1967. Of counsel Jackson Lewis LLP, L.A. and other offices, 1967—. Mem. child adv. group Internat. Inst. of L.A., 1989-96. Office: Jackson Lewis LLP 725 South Figueroa St Los Angeles CA 90017-5408 Office Phone: 213-689-0404.

DARBY, JOSEPH BRANCH, JR., retired metallurgist, retired federal agency administrator; b. Petersburg, Va., Dec. 12, 1925; s. Joseph Branch and Jessie Catherine (Frazier) Darby; m. Eleanor Lee Daley, Mar. 25, 1951; children: Joseph III, John, Leslie, Peter. BS, Coll. William and Mary, 1948, Va. Poly. Inst., 1951; MS, U. Ill., 1955, PhD, 1958. Chemist Allied Chem. Corp., Hopewell, Va., 1948-49; devel. engr. Union Carbide Corp., Niagara Falls, NY, 1951-53; rsch. scientist Argonne (Ill.) Nat. Lab., 1958-86, assoc. dir. fusion energy program, 1974-78, assoc. dir. ocean thermal energy conversion, 1978-84; program mgr. basic energy scis. Office Energy Rsch., Dept. Energy, Washington, 1986-94; adj. prof. U. Va. Sch. Engring., Charlottesville, 1995-97; ret., 1997. Vis. sr. rsch. fellow U. Birmingham, England, 1970—71. Co-editor: The Electronic Structure of the Actinides and Related Properties, 2 vols., 1974; mem. adv. bd. Jour. Less-Common Metals, 1971—82, Materials Letters, 1988—92; co-editor: Jour. Nuc. Materials, 1971—74; chmn. bd. editors:, 1984—90; mem. adv. bd. Jour. Nuc. Materials, 1990—94; contbr. articles to profl. jours. Mem. nominating com. sch. bd., Wheaton, Ill., 1961—63, Bd. Trustees Coll. DuPage, 1963—65. With A.C. USMC, 1944—46. Recipient Loyalty award, U. Ill., Disting. Editor award, Materials Soc., 1994; Sci. Rsch. Coun. Sr. fellow, 1970—71. Fellow: Am. Soc. Metals (mem. energy coun. divsn., mem. nuc. metallurgy com.); mem.: AAAS, ASTM, Cape Cod Geneal. Soc. (co-pres. 1996—98), Fedn. Materials Socs. (bd. dirs. 1988—94), Am. Inst. Mining, Metall. and Petroleum Engrs., Metall. Soc., Sigma Xi, Sigma Gamma Epsilon, Alpha Sigma Mu, Tau Beta Pi. Presbyterian. Home: PO Box 655 25 Pine St Yarmouth Port MA 02675-1838 Personal E-mail: darbytn@capecod.net.

DARBY, MICHAEL RUCKER, economist, educator; b. Dallas, Nov. 24, 1945; s. Joseph Jasper and Frances Adah (Rucker) D.; children: Margaret Loutrel, David Michael; Lynne Ann Zucker-Darby, 1992; stepchildren: Joshua R. Zucker, Danielle T. Zucker. AB summa cum laude, Dartmouth Coll., 1967; MA, U. Chgo., 1968, PhD, 1970. Asst. prof. econ. Ohio State U., 1970-73; vis. asst. prof. econ. UCLA, 1972-73, assoc. prof., 1973-78, prof., 1978-87, 96—, prof. Anderson Grad. Sch. Mgmt., 1987-94, Warren C. Cordner prof. money and fin. mkts., 1995—, vice-chmn., 1992-93; dir. John M. Olin Ctr. for Policy, 1993—; assoc. dir. orgnl. rsch. program UCLA Inst. for Social Sci. Rsch., 1995—2000; assoc. dir. Ctr. Internat. Sci., Tech., Cultural Policy Sch. Pub. Affairs, UCLA, 1996—; rsch. assoc. Nat. Bur. Econ. Rsch., 1976-86, 92—; asst. sec. for econ. policy U.S. Dept. Treasury, Washington, 1986-89; mem. Nat. Commn. on Superconductivity, 1988-89; under sec. for econ. affairs U.S. Dept. Commerce, Washington, 1989-92; adminstr. Econs. and Stats. Adminstrn., 1990-92. V.p., dir. Paragon Industries, Inc., Dallas, 1964—83; mem. exec. com. Western Econ. Assn., 1987—90, v.p., 1998—99, pres.-elect, 1999—2000, pres., 2000—01; chmn. The Dumbarton Group, 1992—; adj. scholar Am. Ent. Inst. for Pub. Policy Rsch., 1992—; economist stats. income divsn. IRS, 1992—94; mem. regulatory coord. adv. com. Commodity Futures Trading Commn., 1992—96. Author: Macroeconomics, 1976, Have Controls Ever Worked: The Post-War Record, 1976, Intermediate Macroeconomics, 1979, 2d edit., 1986, The Effects of Social Security on Income and the Capital Stock, 1979, The International Transmission of Inflation, 1981, Labor Force, Employment, and Productivity in Historical Perspective, 1984, Reducing Poverty in America: Views and Approaches, 1996; editor Jour. Internat. Money and Fin., 1981-86, mem. editl. bd., 1986—; mem. editl. bd. Am. Econ. Rev., 1983-86, Contemporary Policy Issues, 1990-93, Contemporary Econ. Policy, 1994—, Internat. Reports, 1992—. Bd. dirs. The Opera Assoc., 1992—; mem. acad. adv. bd. Ctr. Regulation and Econ. Growth of the Alexis de Tocqueville Instn., 1993-96. Recipient Alexander Hamilton award U.S. Treasury Dept., 1989; sr. fellow Dartmouth Coll., 1966-67, Woodrow Wilson fellow, 1967-68, NSF grad. fellow, 1967-69, FDIC grad. fellow, 1969-70, Harry Scherman rsch. fellow Nat. Bur. Econ. Rsch., 1974-75, vis. fellow Hoover Instn., Stanford U., 1977-78. Mem. AAAS, Am. Econ. Assn., Am. Fin. Assn., Am. Statis. Assn., Am. Law & Econs. Assn., Nat. Assn. Bus. Economists, Royal Econ. Soc., So. Econ. Assn., Western Econ. Assn., N.Y. Acad. Scis., Capitol Hill Club (D.C.), Nat. Econ. Club. Episcopalian. Home: 18108 Meandering Way Dallas TX 75252-2763 Office: UCLA Anderson Grad Sch Mgmt Los Angeles CA 90095-0001

DARCHUN, LINO AUKSUTIS, real estate professional; b. Chgo., Mar. 4, 1942; s. Joseph and Ursula (Shimkus) D.; m. Mary Lynn Burchette, Nov. 11, 1983; 1 child, Matthew. Student, So. Ill. U., 1960-62, 65, U. Ill., Chgo., 1966; grad., Realtor Inst., 1991. Cert. residential specialist, residential broker, internat. property specialist. Agt. Ea. Airlines, Chgo., 1967-68; sta. mgr. World Airways, Oakland, Calif., 1968-71; mgr. The Bulls Restaurant-Nightclub, Chgo., 1971-73, pres., 1977-88; v.p. Leber-Darchun, Inc., Chgo., 1973-74; adminstr. dept. aviation City of Chgo., 1974-77; assoc. realtor Palormo Realty, Chgo., 1987-88, realtor, 1988-93, v.p., 1990-93; realtor Rubloff, Inc., Chgo., 1988-90; asst. br. mgr. Coldwell Banker Residential Lincoln Park, Chgo., 1993-95, br. mgr., 1995-97; broker assoc. Coldwell Banker Residential Real Estate, Chgo., 1997—. Chmn. com. Old Wicker Park, Chgo., 1972-73; vol. Grant Hosp., Chgo.; v.p. Lincoln Park Inter-Agy. Coun., 1988; mem. adv. bd., bd. dirs. Friends of Lincoln Park/Lakeview Schs.; mem. Chgo.-Vilnius (Lithuania) Sister City Com.; mem. adv. bd. Acapulco (Mex.) Children's Home. Sgt. U.S. Army, 1962-65. Fellow Internat. Real Estate Fedn.; mem. Nat. Assn. Realtors, Chgo. Assn. Realtors (chmn. 2004, mem. multiple listing svcs. com.), Grievance Com., Internat. Real Estate Fedn., Internat. Cmty. Affairs, Lincoln Park C. of C. (v.p. 1991—, chmn. human svcs. com. 1987—, bd. dirs.), Lincoln Park Zool. Soc., Lincoln Park Conservation Assn. (1st v.p. 1988, bd. dirs., v.p. 1998-2000), Chgo. Pub. Schs. Alumni Assn. Democrat. Unitarian Universalist. Avocations: travel, music, epicure, arts. Home: 2731 N Wilton Ave Chicago IL 60614-1423 Office: Coldwell Banker Residential Lincoln Park 1840 N Clark St Chicago IL 60614-5881 Office Phone: 312-397-3082. Business E-Mail: lino@linodarchun.com.

D'ARCY, GERALD PAUL, engineering executive, consultant; b. Jackson, Mich., June 6, 1933; s. Merlin Wellington and Jessie Elizabeth (Sober) D.; m. Dorothy Lee Cordell, Nov. 27, 1953; children: Sherry, Janet, Nancy, Deborah, Helen. BSMechE, U. Tex., 1956; MSMechE, U. Colo., 1962; PhD, U. Tex., 1973. Registered profl. engr., Tex. Commd. 2d lt. USAF, 1956, advanced through grades to col., ret., 1986; asst. chief soil and rock mechanics group Air Force Weapons Lab., Kirtland AFB, N.Mex., 1962-67; rsch. assoc. Lawrence Radiation Lab., Livermore, Calif., 1967-70; chief phys. & engring. scis. divsn. Air Force Systems Command, Andrews AFB, Md., 1973-74; chief guns, rockets & explosives divsn. Air Force Armament Lab., Eglin AFB, Fla., 1975-79; vice comdr., later comdr. Air Force Geophysics, Hanscom AFB, Mass., 1979-84; comdr., dir. Air Force Office of Sci. Rsch., Bolling AFB, 1984-86; v.p. Applied Rsch. Assocs. Inc., Albuquerque, 1986-94; ret., 1994. Mech. engring. vis. com. U. Tex., Austin, 1976-79. Inventor soil stress gage; author more than 20 articles. Decorated Legion of Merit; recipient Meritorious Svc. award for nuclear weapons devel. U. Calif., Livermore, 1970; named Disting. Engring. Grad. U. Tex., Austin, 1985. Mem.: U. Tex. Mech. Engring. Acad. Dist. Alumni, Phi Kappa Phi. Democrat. Methodist. Avocation: woodworking. Home: 808 Plantation Way Panama City FL 32404-8603 E-mail: utdeg@aol.com.

DARCY, KEITH THOMAS, finance company executive, educator; b. NYC, June 18, 1948; s. Donald and Geraldine (Kindermann) D.; m. Lynne Alison Cumming, June 17, 1972; children: Erin Lyn, Timothy James. BS in Econs., Fordham U., 1970; MBA, Iona Coll., New Rochelle, N.Y., 1974; postgrad., N.Y. Theol. Sem., 1988-89. With Bankers Trust Co., N.Y.C., 1970—77; v.p. Marine Midland Bank N.A., N.Y.C., 1977—82; CEO, IGM divsn. Gen. Reins. Corp., Stamford, Conn., 1982—83; dir. human resource divsn. Marine Midland Bank, N.Y.C., 1984—89; pres., CEO, The Leadership Group, Inc., N.Y.C., 1989—94; v.p., assoc. ethics officer Prudential Securities Inc., N.Y.C., 1994—96, sr. ethics advisor, 1996—97; assoc. dean, disting. prof. bus. Georgetown U., Washington, 1995—96; exec. v.p. office of the pres. IBJ Whitehall Bank and Trust Co., N.Y.C., 1997—2002; chmn. Darcy Ptnrs. Inc., Pound Ridge, NY, 2003—; exec. dir. Ethics Officer Assn., Waltham, Mass., 2005—. Adj. faculty Marymount Coll., 1978-96, Mercy Coll., 1975-96; faculty advanced exec. edn. Wharton, U. Pa., 1994—; faculty grad. mgmt. program Antioch U., Seattle, 1989-96; exec.-in-residence U. Md. Univ. Coll., 2004—; exec.-in-residence grad. program in human resources and orgnl. devel. and grad. program in orgnl. leadership Manhattanville Coll., Purchase, NY, corp. adv. bd., 1989—; exec. fellow Ctr. for Bus. Ethics, Bentley Coll., Waltham, Mass., 1993—, exec. com.; tchg. fellow Smith Sch. Bus., U. Md., College Park, 2002—; bd. dirs. Barat House, Purchase, NY; dir. emeritus Ethics Officer Assn.; steering com. Caux (Switzerland) Round Table, 1996-99; nat. adv. bd. Worktalk, 1999—; vice chmn. Ctr. for Values-Based Leadership, 1999-2004, chmn., bd. trustees BBB Found., 2001—; bd. dirs. E*Trade Bank, Arlington, Va., ETB Holdings Inc., Arlington, NY Nat. Bank, NYC; mem. com. on effects of mktg. on obesity in children and youth Inst. Medicine, Washington; faculty Insead, France and Singapore Co-author: Change Management, 1993, The Ethics Companion, 1999, The Crisis in Corporate Governance-HR's Role, 2003; mem. editl. bd., contbr.: At Work: Stories of Tomorrow's Workplace, 1992—; featured in The Ethical Edge, The Portable Executive, Merchants of Vision, Career Crossroads, Winning the People Wars, Survival Skills in the Fin. Svcs. Industry. Treas. Westchester County Rep. Com., White Plains, N.Y., 1979-89; asst. treas. N.Y. State Friends for Jim Buckley, 1976; dir. NCCJ, 1977-85; trustee Bedford Presbyn. Ch., N.Y., 1982-87, Better Bus. Bur. Found., N.Y., 2001—; mem. Westchester Blue Ribbon Commn. to Formulate County Housing Policy, 1979; trustee March of Dimes, Westchester, 1978-84, chmn. Exec. Walkathon, 1978-81. Mem. Ethics Officers Assn. (dir. emeritus, exec. dir.), Caux (Switzerland) Round Table (affil.), Soc. Friendly Sons of St. Patrick (pres. 1985) Home: Horseshoe Hl W Pound Ridge NY 10576 Office: 27 Horseshoe Hill W Pound Ridge NY 10576 Office Phone: 914-764-5600. E-mail: keith.darcy@ethicsinleadership.com.

D'ARCY, PAULA, writer; b. Fall River, Mass., Nov. 6, 1947; d. Raymond Vincent and Barbara (Waite) Pettine; m. Roy Thomas D'Arcy, Jan. 6, 1973 (dec. Aug. 1975); children: Sarah (dec.), Beth; m. Charles Granville Verge, Nov. 7, 1987. BA, Stonehill Coll., 1969; M in Counseling, U. N.H., 1970. Lic. allied mental health counselor. Counselor Mattatuck C.C., Waterbury, Conn., 1970-73; pvt. practice psychotherapy Newton, Mass., 1988—. Pub. author, 1979—, speaker, 1980—; cons. dept. ministry & guidance Peale Ctr. for Christian Living, Pawling, N.Y., 1981—. Author: Song for Sarah, 1979, Where the Wind Begins, 1984, When Your Friend is Grieving, 1990, Gift of the Red Bird, 1996, A New Set of Eyes, 2002, Seeking with All My Heart, 2003, Sacred Threshold, 2004. Mem. ch. Christian edn. com. Union Ch., Newton, 1993—, ch. search com., 1991-93. Mem. ACA, Internat. Graphoanalysis Soc. Avocations: reading, travel, biking, tennis, music. Office: 190 Scenic Hill Rd Kerrville TX 78028-9163*

DARCY, ROBERT EMMETT, political science and statistics professor; b. Elizabeth, N.J., Feb. 25, 1942; s. John William and Jane (Alton) D.; m. Lynne C. Murnane, Aug. 30, 1975; children: Mary Frances, Catherine Rose. BA, U. Wis., 1965; MA, U. Ky., 1970, PhD, 1971. Asst. prof. George Washington U., Washington, 1971—77, Okla. State U., Stillwater, 1977—80, assoc. prof. polit. sci. and stats., 1980—85, prof., 1985—90, Regents prof., 1991—. Expert witness on racial disparities, ballot and election procedures Atty. Gen., State of Okla., Oklahoma City, 1984-86, 91-95, 98, 2002, Ohio, 1991, N.H., 1995, 2004-05, N.C., 1998, N.Y., 1999, Fed. Dist. Ct., 2002, 03, 04, 05; vis. guest prof. U. Conn., 1984; mem. Okla. Commn. on Status Women, 1997—, co-chmn. summit 1997, 99; mem. Okla. Jud. Evaluation Commn., 1997-2001, Legis. Task Force on Jud. Selection, 1999-2000; vice chmn. gen. faculty Okla. State U., 2004-05, faculty coun., 2004-05, chair gen. faculty, 2005—, faculty coun., 2005—; lectr. in field. Author: Women, Elections and Representation, 1987, 90, 94, Guide to Quantitative History, 1995; editor Jour. Okla. Politics, 1991-99, 2004, Social Sci. Jour., 1983-85; contbr. articles to profl. jours. Recipient Liberty Bell award Okla. Bar Assn., 1999, Commendation, Okla. Ho. of Reps., 2000; Bruce fellow Keele U., Eng., 1998; vis. rsch. scholar Acad. Korean Studies, Seoul, 1983. Mem. AAUP (chpt. pres. 1984, 88), Polit. Studies Assn. Ireland, Am. Polit. Sci. Assn., Am. Assn. Pub. Opinion Rsch., Western Social Sci. Assn., Okla. Polit. Sci. Assn. (pres. 1992, Outstanding Okla. Polit. Scientist award 1993), So. Polit. Sci. Assn., Midwestern Polit. Sci. Assn. Republican. Home: 2215 W 5th Ave Stillwater OK 74074-2818 Office: Okla State U Dept Polit Sci Stillwater OK 74078-0001 Office Phone: 405-744-5641. Business E-Mail: bdarcy@okstate.edu.

DARCY, THOMAS E., science company executive; b. 1950; Mng. pntr. audit and bus. adv. svcs. tech. Pricewaterhouse Coopers LLP, pntr.; exec. v.p. and CFO Sci. Applications Internat. Corp., 2000—. Bd. dirs. Coll. Bus. Adminstrn., San Diego State U., ACCION San Diego; bd. mem. BICOM, San Diego, San Diego Econ. Devel. Assn. Office: 10260 Campus Point Dr San Diego CA 92121

DARDAI, SHAHID MOINUDDIN, computer science educator; b. India, May 11, 1940; Prof. computer sci. dept. Richard J. Daley Coll., Chgo., 1993—, data processing coord. Chairperson computer sci. dept. Richard J. Daley Coll., 1993—; adj. faculty math. and computer sci. dept. Chgo. State U., 1993—. Recipient Disting. Prof. award, City Coll. Chgo., 2000—01. Mem. Data Processing Mgmt. Assn., Phi Theta Kappa. Office: Richard J Daley Coll 7500 S Pulaski Rd Chicago IL 60652-1242 Fax: (312) 838-7524. E-mail: sdardai@hotmail.com, sdardai@ccc.edu.

DARDAS, ZISSIS, research scientist; s. Anastassios and Agnes Dardas; m. Athena Chryssanthakopoulou, June 21, 1987; children: Agnes, Anastassios, Marios Zissis. Diploma in Chem. Engring., Nat. Tech. U., Athens, Greece, 1986; PhD in Chem. Engring., Purdue U., West Lafayette, Ind., 1993; MS in Mgmt., Rensselaer Poly. Inst., Hartford, Conn., 2000. Rsch. assoc. dept. chem. engring. Worcester Poly. Inst., Mass., 1993—96; group leader phys. scis. United Technologies Rsch. Ctr., East Hartford, Conn., 1996—. Chmn. New Eng. Catalysis Soc., Worcester, Mass., 2002—03. Amb. United Way, Hartford, Conn., 2004—05. Recipient 1st award Math., Hellenic Orgn. Math., 1980, Outstanding Achievement award, United Technologies, 2000, 2002; grantee, Aristotle Onassis Found., Greece, 1987—90, Bodossakis Found., Greece, 1987—89; Rsch. fellow, Purdue U., 1987—93. Greek Orthodox. Achievements include research in desulfurizing gasoline or diesel fuel for use in internal combustion engines and fuel cells; diffusion bonding tooling with comformal cooling; advanced compact fuel processors and catalysts; development of in situ FTIR method for studying catalytic reactions under high temperature and pressure; patents in field; patents pending in field. Avocations: travel, astronomy, swimming. Office: United Technologies Rsch Ctr 411 Silver Ln East Hartford CT 06108 Office Phone: 860-610-7371. Office Fax: 860-610-7669. Personal E-mail: dardasz@att.net. E-mail: dardasz@utrc.utc.com.

DARDEN, BARBARA S., library director; b. Cleve., Apr. 6, 1947; d. Curley and Cora (Chambliss) Brown; m. Joseph S. Darden; children: Michelle, Crystal. BS, Ohio State U., 1967; MS in Ednl. Media, MLS, Kent State U., 1971; PhD, Rutgers U., 2002. Adminstrv. supr. Cleve. Pub. Schs., 1968-70; libr. Cuyahoga C.C., 1972-75, coord., 1975-77, interim dir., 1977-78, asst. dean, 1978-80, dir., 1980-84; dir. libr. Kean Coll., Union, N.J., 1984—. Cons. Dembsy Assocs., Boston, 1967-81; editl. cons. Max Pub. Co., N.Y.C., 1967-81; cons. reader U.S. Office Edn., Washington, 1979-80; editl. cons. Jossey-Bass Pub. Co., 1979. Cons. editor Probe, 1976, Sch. Media Ctr., 1968, Booklist, 1969; contbr. articles to profl. jours. Bd. dirs. N.J. Adv. Bd. on Status of Women, 1988, Africana Studies, 1988; mem. N.J. State Libr. Adv. Bd.; bd. dirs. N.J. Ednl. Activities Task Force Libr. Com. Recipient Phillips award Kent State U., 1970. Mem. ALA (chmn. pay equity com. 1996, chair LAMA-COLA 1999), Higher Edn. Reps., N.J. Acad. Libr. Network (chmn. 1987, bd. dirs. 1995—), Coun. N.J. Librs. (prs. 1987—), N.J. Libr. Assn., Oral History Soc., N.J. Hist. Soc., Libr. Adminstrn. Mgmt. Assn. (chair 1997-99, bd. dirs. 1999), Coun. N.J. Coll. and Univ. Libr. Dirs. (pres. 1999—), Jr. League (Cleve. vice chmn. 1981, 83), Concerned Parents Club (pres. 1984), Women's City Club (adv. bd. 1997—). Avocations: music, reading. Office: Kean Univ Libr Morris Ave Union NJ 07083

DARDEN, CALVIN, delivery service executive; b. Buffalo, Feb. 5, 1950; m. Patricia Gail Darden, Aug. 21, 1971; children: Ramarro, Tami, Lorielle. B in bus. mgmt., Canisius Coll., 1972; Exec. Devel. Consortium, Emory U., 1997. Dist. mgr. United Parcel Svc., North Jersey, 1984—86, Metro Jersey, 1986—91, Metro DC, 1991—93, v.p. Pacific region, 1993—95, v.p. corp. strategic quality coord., 1995—, sr. v.p. U.S. ops. Atlanta, 1997—; mem. UPS mgmt. com., 1997—, UPS bd. dirs., 2001—. Mem. bd. dirs. Target Corp., Coca-Cola Enterprises. Chair bd. trustees Atlanta Police Found.; mem. bd. trustees Canisius Coll.; mem. bd. dirs. Nat. Urban League. Named one of Fortune's 50 Most Powerful Black Execs. in Am. (ranked eighth). Mem.: United Way, 100 Black Men North Metro Atlanta. Office: United Parcel Svc 55 Glenlake Pkwy NE Atlanta GA 30328

DARDEN, CHRISTOPHER ALLEN, lawyer, actor, writer; b. Martinez, Calif., Apr. 7, 1956; m. Marcia Carter, Aug. 31, 1997. BA in Criminal Justice, Calif. State U., San Jose; JD, U. Calif., San Francisco, 1980. Bar: Calif. 1980. Former atty. Nat. Labor Rels. Bd.; former asst. head dep. in spl. investigations divsn. L.A. County Dist. Attys. Office, former dep. dist. atty. in maj. crimes divsn.; actor, writer, 1996—; faculty Calif. State Univ., Los Angeles, 1995; assoc. prof. law Sch. Law Southwestern U., L.A., 1996—99; atty. Darden & Assoc., Los Angeles, 1999—. Former legal commentator NBC & CNBC. Author: (with Jess Walter) In Contempt, 1996; author (with Dick Lochte) The Trials of Nikki Hill, 1999, L.A. Justice, 2000, The Last Defense, 2002, Lawless, 2004. Recipient Crystal Heart award, Loved Ones of Homicide Victims, 1998, Humanitarian of the Year, Eli Home, 2000. Mem.: Am. Trial Lawyers Assn., Nat. Bar Assn. (life). Office: Darden & Associates 5757 W Century Blvd Los Angeles CA 90045 Office Phone: 310-568-1806. Business E-Mail: dardenatty@aol.com.

DARDEN, CLAIBOURNE HENRY, JR., marketing research professional; b. Greensboro, N.C., June 26, 1943; s. Claibourne Henry and Gerry (Bonkemeyer); m. Anita McMurry; children: Claibourne III, Prentiss. BS, Washington & Lee U., 1966; MBA, Emory U., 1968. Pres. Darden Rsch. Corp., Atlanta, 1968—. TV commentator, spkr. in field. Bd. dirs. Nat. Wild Turkey Fedn., Edgefield, SC, 1985—2000, Quality Deer Mgmt. Assn., Watkinsville, Ga., 2001—, Ga. Conservancy, 1985—91, Washington & Lee Alumni Assn., Atlanta, 1986—87. Mem. Am. Mktg. Assn. (bd. dirs. Atlanta chpt. 1970-75, Mktg. Profl. of Yr. 1976), N.Y. Yacht Club, Druid Hills Golf Club. Presbyterian. Avocations: hunting, sailing, fishing. Office: Darden Rsch Corporation 1534 N Decatur Rd NE Atlanta GA 30307-1022

DARDEN, EDWIN SPEIGHT, SR., architect; b. Stantonsburg, N.C., Oct. 14, 1920; s. Edwin Speight and Sallie (Jordan) D.; m. s. Pauline K. Bartlett, Feb. 26, 1944; children: Edwin Speight III, Judith Ann, Diane Russell. BS in Archtl. Engring., Kans. State U., 1947. Registered architect, Calif. Assoc., Fred L. Swartz and William G. Hyberg, Fresno, Calif., 1949-59; ptnr. Nargis and Darden (Architects), Fresno, 1959-69; pres. Edwin S. Darden Assocs., Inc., Fresno, 1969-85, cons., 1985—. Bd. dirs. Murphy Bank; mem. state adv. bd. Office of Architecture and Constrn., 1970-78; cons. ednl. facilities, 1975—. Prin. works include Clovis (Calif.) High Sch., 1969, Clovis W. High Sch., 1976, Ahwahnee Jr. High Sch., Fresno, 1966, Tehipite Jr. High Sch., Fresno, 1973, Fresno County Dept. Health, 1978, Floyd B. Buchanan Edn. Ctr., Clovis, 1990. Served to 1st lt. C.E., AUS, 1942-46. Fellow AIA; mem. Sigma Phi Epsilon, Alpha Kappa Psi. Clubs: Fresno Rotary. Presbyterian. Office: Edwin S Darden Associates Inc 6790 N West Ave #104 Fresno CA 93711-1393 E-mail: esda@pacbell.net.

DARDEN, JOSEPH SAMUEL, JR., health educator; b. Pleasantville, N.J., July 25, 1925; s. Joseph Samuel and Blanche Catherine (Paige) D.; m. Barbara Cassandra Sellers, Dec. 30, 1955 (div. July 1979); 1 child, Michele Irene; m. Barbara L. Simpson, Oct. 21, 1987. AB, Lincoln U., 1948; MA, NYU, 1952, EdD (Danforth Found. fellow), 1963. Instr. biol. scis. Clark Coll., Atlanta, 1952-55; asst. prof. Albany (Ga.) State Coll., 1955-58, prof., 1959-64; asst. prof. Kean U. of N.J., Union, 1964-67, prof. health edn., 1970—2002, coord. health, 1977-79, chmn. dept. health and recreation, 1979-84, coord. health, 1984—2002, dir. minority enrollment, 1988-94, prof. emeritus, 2002—. Adj. prof. health Wagner Coll., S.I., N.Y., 1965-88; cons. N.J. Dept. Edn., 1968-73, 76-88. Author: (with others) Growth Pattern and Sex Education, 1967, Updated Supplement to Growth Pattern and Sex Education, 1972, Toward a Healthier Sexuality: A Book of Readings, 1997; editor, co-author: Critical Health Issues Reader, 2002. Bd. advisors Marylawn of Oranges, 1971-73; bd. dirs. N.J. Coun. Family Relations, 1981-83; trustee Planned Parenthood of Essex County, N.J., 1985—; trustee Planned Parenthood of Met. N.J, 1985-2003. With AUS, 1944-46. Recipient Alumni Achievement award, Lincoln U., 1993, Presdl. Excellence award, Kean U., 2002. Fellow Am. Assn. Health Edn. (charter), Am. Sch. Health Assn. (governing coun. 1970-73, Disting. Svc. award 1971); mem. AAHPERD (Eastern dist. v.p. for health edn. 1971-72, dist. pres. 1974-75, Eastern dist. rep. 1979-82, honor award Eastern dist. 1976, nat. honor award 1985, Outstanding Tchr. award Eastern dist. 1983, Charles D. Henry award 1988, Edwin B. Henderson award 1991), Assn. Advancement Health Edn. (dir. 1975-78, Profl. Svc. award 1990, presdl. citation 1996), N.J. Health Edn. Coun. (founder 1967, honor award 1975), N.J. Assn. Health, Phys. Edn. and Recreation (v.p. health edn. 1967-68, Honor fellow award 1972, Disting. Leadership award 1975), Alpha Phi Alpha. Home: 1416 Thelma Dr Union NJ 07083-6220 Office: Kean U NJ Union NJ 07083

DARDEN, LAURETTA, elementary school educator; b. Kinston, N.C., Dec. 1, 1956; d. Robert Lee and Sallie Lorraine Brown; m. Gregory Maurice Darden, July 2, 1988; 1 child, Loreal Sallie Lorraine. BA, Fayetteville State U., N.C., 1978. Elementary Education NJ., 1979, Nursery NJ. Elem. tchr. Paterson Bd. of Edn., Paterson, NJ, 1979—. Recipient Governor's Tchr. Recognition, Paterson Bd. of Edn., 2001, Mayor's Award (outstanding civic contbn.), Mayor Barnes Paterson, N.J., 2001, Golden Apple Award, The NJ. Herald News, 2002. Mem.: NJ. Edn. Assn. (assoc.), Paterson Edn. Assn. (assoc.), Alpha Kappa Alpha Sorority Inc. (life). Avocations: reading, sewing, drawing, travel. Personal E-mail: hunnybrown2@yahoo.com.

DARDEN, MARY LANDON, director, researcher; d. George Kemlo and Ruth Ann (Brewer) Landon; m. Robert Fulton Darden, Aug. 8, 1988; children: Daniel Landon Barkley, Rachel Anne Menjivar, Robert Van. Student, Sweet Briar Coll., Va., 1970—72, Tex. A&M U., 1973—74; BA in Sociology, U. Tex. Permian Basin, Odessa, 1975; MSEd in Wellness, Baylor U., 1991, postgrad., 2002—. Case worker and asst. emergency svcs. coord. Tex. Dept. Mental Health and Mental Retardation, Odessa, 1976—77; co-owner Aerobic Dancercise, Odessa, 1978—80; owner, pres. Mind & Body Prodns., 1981—94; grad. tchg. asst. Baylor U., Waco, Tex., 1989—91, lectr. dept. health, human performance and recreation, 1991, rsch. asst., 2002—, intern with provost, 2004; owner New Canaan Wellness, 1991—92; coord. avocational continuing edn., dir. wellness McLennan C.C., 1994—96, coord. cmty. programs, 1996—2002. Spkr. numerous confs. in field; sec. bd. dirs. Tex. Adminstrs. Continuing Edn., 1998—2000, chair nat. conf. welcome, 2001; nat. dir. cmty. svc. on bd. dirs. Nat. Coun. for Continuing Edn. and Tng., 2002—. Contbr. articles to profl. jours.; columnist Inside Running mag., 1982—84. 1st co-chair McLennan County Green Party, Tex., 2000—02; chair cabinet, moderator Seventh and James Bapt. Ch., Waco, 2005; chair bd. commrs. Waco Housing Authority, Tex., 2001. Recipient Pathfinder award in Athletics, Tex. Gov.'s Commn. for Women and YWCA, 1982, Nat. Exemplary Program award for cmty. svc., Nat. Coun. Continuing Edn. and Tng. USA, 2001, 1st pl. State award, Tex. Adminstrs. Continuing Edn., 2000, 2001. Mem.: Assn. for Study of Higher Edn., Coun. on Study of Cmty. Colls., Pi Lamda Theta. Democrat. Baptist. Avocations: travel, walking, reading, movies, fishing. Home: 118 N 30th St Waco TX 76710 Office: Baylor U Waco TX 76798 E-mail: mldarden@earthlink.net, Mary_Darden@baylor.edu.

DARDEN, WILLIAM HOWARD, JR., biology professor; b. Tuscaloosa, Ala., Apr. 25, 1937; s. William Howard and Jannie Belle (Herring) D.; m. Caroline Jackson, July 15, 1959; children: Leanne Carol, Michael Howard. BS, U. Ala., Tuscaloosa, 1959, MS, 1961; PhD, Ind. U., 1965. Asst. prof. biology U. Ala., Tuscaloosa, 1965-68, assoc. prof., 1969-73, prof., assoc. chmn. dept. biology, 1973-74, prof., chmn. dept. biology, 1974-96; prof. emeritus, 1996—. Contbr. articles to sci. jours. Bd. dirs. Springhill Lake Assn., 1980-85, So. Grass Tennis Club, 1979-81, Ala. Credit Union, 1987—. Predoctoral fellow NIH, 1963-65; grantee NSF, 1972, U. Ala., Tuscaloosa, 1965-71 Mem. Sigma Xi, Beta Beta Beta, Omicron Delta Kappa, Phi Kappa Phi. Am. Baptist. Home: 3628 Rainbow Dr Tuscaloosa AL 35405-5331 Office: U Ala PO Box 870344 Tuscaloosa AL 35487-0001 E-mail: dardoc@aol.com.

DARDICK, GEETA, writer, psychotherapist; b. St. Louis, July 15, 1942; d. Charles Kalman and Carol Jane (Kalish) Berger; m. Samuel Ian Dardick, Jan. 26, 1964; children: Caleb, Joshua, Samantha. Student, Wellesley Coll., 1960-62; BA, Wash. U., 1964; MA, U. San Francisco, 1993. Cert. marriage, family, and child counselor, Calif. Profl. writer, North San Juan, Calif., 1982—; psychotherapist, 1993—. Contbr. more than 100 articles to profl. publs. Co-founder FREED Ind. Living Ctr., Nevada City, Calif., 1985, bd. dirs., 1986-92. Recipent Commendation for Volunteerism Bd. Suprs., 1987. Mem. Am. Soc. Journalists and Authors, U.S. Tennis Assn. (capt. 1992-98), Nat. Depression Assn. (co-dir. depression screening day 1997), Toastmasters Internat. Avocations: tennis, the internet, skiing, journalism. Office Phone: 530-292-3059. E-mail: geeta@jps.net.

DARDICK, KENNETH REGEN, physician, educator; b. Bklyn., Oct. 16, 1946; s. Bruce S. and Leila Mae (Regen) D.; children from previous marriage: Lauren E., Jeremy S.; m. Judith Stein, 1996; stepchildren: Katherine Stein Stonebraker, Rachel Stein Stonebroker. AB cum laude, Dartmouth Coll., 1968, BMS, 1969; MD, Harvard U., 1971; D in Tropical Medicine and Hygiene, London Sch. of Hygiene and Tropical Medicine, 1989. Intern Cambridge (Mass.) Hosp., 1971-72, resident in internal medicine, 1973-74; resident in pediatrics Children's Med. Ctr., Boston, 1972-73; with USPHS, Rochester, N.Y., 1974-76; pres., med. dir. med. dental staff Westside Health Svcs., Rochester, N.Y., 1975-76; practice medicine specializing in internal medicine and family practice Storrs, Conn., 1976—. Mem. staff, chmn. dept. medicine Windham (Conn.) Cmty. Meml. Hosp., 1993-95, asst. chief med. staff, 1994-95, 2001-2002, chief med. staff, 2003-2004; asst. clin. prof. U. Conn. Med. Sch., Med. adv., Eastern Highland Health Dist., 1997—, dir. health, Windham, 1993-94; dir. of health, Mansfield, Conn., 1986-97, sch. physician, Mansfield, 1990-98; chmn. Hypertension Task Force, Am. Heart Assn., 1981-84; dir. Capital area IPA, 1987-88; mem. adv. bd. Conn. Datalink, 1994—; counselor Am. Com. on Clin. Tropical Medicine and Traveler's Health of the Am. Soc. of Tropical Medicine and Hygiene, 2002-2004 Author: Foreign Travel and Immunization Guide, 13th edit. Founder. pres. Conn. Safety Belt Coalition, 1984—; pres., med. dir. Immunization Alert, 1983-96; censor Windham County Med. Assn., 1992-94. Jeffrey Richardson fellow Harvard U., 1988; recipient Patient Care award for excellence in patient edn., 1983, 88. Fellow ACP (George C. Griffith Traveling scholar 1988), Royal Soc. Tropical Medicine, Am. Acad. Family Practice; mem. Am. Soc. Tropical Medicine and Hygiene. Office: Mansfield Profl Park Storrs Mansfield CT 06268

DARDIK, HERBERT, vascular surgeon, general surgeon; b. Long Branch, N.J., May 17, 1935; s. Morris and Sarah D.; m. Janet E. Goldstein, June 23, 1958; children: Alan, Michael, Sharon. BA magna cum laude, NYU, 1956, MD, 1960. Diplomate Am. Bd. Med. Examiners, Am. Bd. Surgery, cert. spl. competency in vascular surgery; lic. physician NJ, NY. Intern Montefiore Hosp. and Med. Ctr., N.Y.C., 1960-61, asst. surg. resident to chief surg. resident, 1961-65; instr. surgery Albert Einstein Coll. Medicine, N.Y.C., 1964-65, asst. prof. surgery, 1967-77; clin. assoc. prof. surgery N.J. Coll. Medicine, Newark, 1981-91; clin. prof. in surgery Sch. Medicine U. Pa., Phila., 1991—2002, clin. prof. surgery Sch. Medicine, 2003—; clin. prof. surgery Mt. Sinai Sch. Medicine, N.Y.C., 1991—; staff surgeon USAF Hosp. Andrews AFB, Washington, 1965-67; assoc. dir. surgery to dir. surgery Montefiore-Morrisania Affiliate, N.Y.C., 1967-71, cons. in surgery, 1971-76; assoc. attending surgeon Montefiore Hosp. and Med. Ctr., N.Y.C., 1970-77; cons. surgery North Ctrl. Bronx Hosp., NY, 1976; assoc. attending surgeon Englewood (NJ) Hosp., 1973-79, active attending surgeon and chief vascular surg. svc., 1979—, chief dept. surgery, 1984, 1995, 2000—. Sr. rsch. scientist Lab. for Exptl. Medicine and Surgery in Primates, NYU Med. Ctr., 1973-78; numerous visiting professorships, 1976-95, at Good Samaritan Hosp., Cin., U. Munich, U. Laval, Que., Can., Rigshospitalet, Copenhagen, Karolinska Inst., Stockholm, Semmelweis Med. U., Budapest, First Internat. Course on Vascular Traumatology, Mexico City, Inst. of Vascular Surgery of U. Milan, Groote Schuur Hosp., Cape Town, South Africa, U. Orange Free State, Bloemfontein, South Africa, Johannesburg Hosp. of U. of Witwatersrand, South Africa, Allegheny Gen. Hosp., Pitts., Wilmington (Del.) Med. Ctr., Mercy Hosp., Pitts., U. Cologne, Germany, Jewish Gen. Hosp., Montreal (Harry C. Vallon Vis. Prof.), U. Md., Balt., Maritime Vascular Soc., North Sydney Hosp., N.S., Can., Pa. Hosp., Phila., U. Colo. Health Sci. Ctr. and Affiliated Hosps., Denver, Mary Imogene Basset Hosp., Cooperstown, N.Y., Cooper Hosp./Univ. Med. Ctr., Camden, N.J., Gulf Coast Vascular Soc., Tulane U., La. State U. Ochsner Med. Clinic, New Orleans, St. Vincent's Med. Ctr., N.Y.C., U. Trondheim, Norway, Broadgreen Hosp., Liverpool, Eng., U. Colo. Rose Med. Ctr. (guest lectr.), Queen Elizabeth Hosp., Montreal, Wright State U., Dayton, Ohio, Cleve. Vascular Soc., N.Y. Meth. Hosp., Bklyn.; surgeon by invitation Mass. Gen. Hosp., Bosotn, 1979, Milan, 1981, Sydney, N.S., 1985, Colo. Health Sci. Ctr., 1985, U. Trondheim, 1992, Paul Brousse Hosp., Paris, 1995, Utrecht, The Netherlands, 1997; internat. adv. com. Internat. Vascular Symposium, London, 1981, Internat. Coll. Angiology, Athens, 1985, 14th World Congress Internat. Union Angiology, Munich, 1986. Contbr. over 300 articles and abstracts to profl. jours., chpts. to books; presenter in field; creator exhibits in field; dir. numerous symposia in field; patentee in field; editor SCVS Newsletter, 1987—; editl. bd. Jour. Englewood Hosp., 1989—, Fitness Swimmer, 1992-95, Vascular Forum, 1993-95, guest editor 1994, Vascular Surgery, 1995—; Creativity editor Jour. Am. Coll. Physician Inventors, 1992-95; invited reviewer Jour. Vascular Surgery, European Jour. Vascular Surgery, Am. Jour. Surgery. Capt. USAF Med. Corps, 1965-67. Recipient George Schwartz prize in biology, 1954, Wortis Biol. prize, 1956, Herbert Dardik awards, Ann. Vascular Fellows Abstract Presentation, Humanitarian award, Retired Sr. Vol. Program, 2001. Mem. ACS (bd. govs. 1991-94, adv. coun. vascular surg. 1995—), ACP, AMA (Hektoen Gold medal 1976), Assn. Acad. Surgery, Soc. Vascular Surgery, Internat. Soc. Cardiovasc. Surgery, Soc. Internat. de Chirurgia, Soc. Clin. Vascular Surgery (hon., various offices and coms., pres. 1984-85, exec. com. 1982—, Lifetime Achievement award 2001), Soc. Surgery of the Alimentary Tract, Am. Coll. Gastroenterology, Collegium Internat. Chirurgia Digestive, Am. Coll. Physician Inventors (founding mem., sec. 1992—), Eastern Vascular Soc. (adv. coun. 1991—, exec. com. 1996-95, pres. 1990-91), N.J. Vascular Soc. (pres.-elect 1983-84, pres. 1984-85, dir. exec. com. 1982-83, postgrad. surg. edn. award 1983), N.Y. Soc. Cardiovasc. Surgery, N.Y. Surg. Soc., Bergen County Med. Soc., Maine Vascular Soc. (hon.), Mex. Soc. Angiology (hon.), Israel Soc. Vascular Surgery (hon.), Rocky Mountain Vascular Soc. (hon.), Cleve. Vascular Soc. (hon.), Phi Beta Kappa. Office: Englewood Hosp & Med Ctr Dept Surgery 350 Engle St Englewood NJ 07631-1823 E-mail: hdardik@ehmc.com.

DAREN, SYLVIA, poet; b. N.Y.C., N.Y., Apr. 2, 1920; d. Louis Millman and Rose Beresnoger; m. Joseph Daren, Dec. 24, 1939; children: Edythe Hepner, Marsha. Student, grad. H.S., 1937. Lectr. Singles Group, N.Y.C.; poet laureat Temple Emeth; bd. mem. & by-law co-chair Temple Emeth Sisterhood; Instalation Chmn. Gold Coast Cancer Rsch. of Palm Greens, Women's Club of Palm Green; fund raising chair Delray B'nai B'rith; Poet and Mistress of Ceremonies Palm Greens Entertainers; actor, poet, story teller Yiddish Club of Palm Greens. Author (childrens poetry): Moses, The Hebrew Giant; author: (poetry book) How I Earned My Bachelor of Life Degree --You Can COunt Your Credits Too !!!; author: (plays and poetry) various including Temple Emeth of Delray Beach (Poet Laureat); co-dir.: Oakland Sr. Citizens -Oakland Jewish Ctr., 1962—80; editor (newspaper): Palms West O.R.T.; actor(co-author): (plays) My Unfair Lady. Leader Girl Scouts of Am., Queens, NY, 1953—54; vol. Creedmore Hosp., Queens; v.p. and trustee, adv. girls, fund raising, cmty. svc., jewish edn., Aid to Israel for Queens, vol. B'nai B'rith, Bayside, NY, 1953—2003, various Fla., 1953—2003; founder Marsha Daren Fund Long Island Jewish Med. Ctr., Long Island, 1975—89. Recipient Honorary Mem. of Am. Legion, Am. Legion, 1933, Honoree- This is Your Life, Oakland B'nai B'rith, 1959, Honoree, Org. of people Undaunted by Stroke, 1976, United Jewish Appeal & Federation of Jewish Philanthropies, 1976, Jewish Nat. Fund Temple Emeth, 0955—2003, Mem. award, B'nai B'rith Dist. 5, Woman of Achievement award, Women's League of Conservative Judaism, 2005. Mem.: Bowling League, B'nai B'rith. Jewish. Avocations: poetry, acting, bowling, golf, volunteering.

DARENSBOURG, MARCETTA YORK, chemistry professor; b. Artemus, Ky., May 4, 1942; m. 1967. BA, Union Coll., 1963; PhD in Inorganic Chemistry, U. Ill., Urbana, 1967. Asst. prof. inorganic chemistry Vassar Coll., 1967-69; asst. prof. SUNY, Buffalo, 1969-71; from asst. to assoc. prof. Tulane U., La., 1971-79, prof. inorganic chemistry, 1979—; prof. chemistry Tex. A&M U. Recipient Agnes Faye Rsch. award, 1981; Am. Chem Soc. award for Disting. Svc. in the Advancement of Inorganic Chemistry, 1995. Mem. Am. Chem. Soc. (chair-elect, chair inorganic divsn., Disting. Svc. award 1995), Sigma Xi. Office: Texas A & M U Dept Chemistry College Station TX 77843-0001

DARGAN, PAMELA ANN, systems engineer, consultant; b. Norfolk, Va. d. Thomas J. and Stana E. (Verich) Piazza; m. W. Scott Dargan, Dec., 1990. BS in Math., Va. Poly. and State U., 1979; MS in Computer Sci., George Mason U., 1993. Programmer Control Data Corp., Rockville, Md., 1979—80; tech. staff BDM Corp., McLean, Va., 1980—81, TRW Fed. Sys. Group, McLean, 1981—87; dep. program mgr. Mystech, Inc., Alexandria, Va., 1987—89; lead engr. MITRE Corp., McLean, 1989—98, prin., 2001—02, Litton Tasc, Inc., Chantilly, Va., 1998—2001; sr. cons. Scitor Corp., Chantilly, 2002—03; prin. sys. engr. SAIC, Reston, Va., 2003—. Program chair East Coast Artificial Intelligence Work Sta. Users Group, 1984-85; author on open sys. for internat. confs. and publs. Author: Open Systems and Standards for Software Product Development, 2005; contbr. chpts. to books, articles to profl. jours. Mem. IEEE, Assn. Computing Machinery, Internat. Coun. on Sys. Engrng. E-mail: pdargan@erols.com, pamela.a.dargan@saic.com.

DARIEN, STEVEN MARTIN, management consulting company executive; b. N.Y.C., Oct. 29, 1942; s. Leo and Laura Darien; m. Susan Ruth Kinsley, Nov. 29, 1942; children: Jodi Ellen, Andrew Todd. AB, Rutgers Coll., 1963; MBA, Columbia U., 1966. Claims settler Equitable Life, N.Y.C., 1963-64; mgmt. trainee Merck & Co., Inc., Rahway, N.J., 1966-69, mgr. coll. rels., 1969-74, exec. dir. pers. resources, 1974-79, exec. dir. U.S. Pers., 1979-85, v.p. employee rels., 1985-89, v.p. worldwide pres., 1989-90, v.p. human resources, 1990-96; pres. Darien Assocs., 1996-98; chmn., CEO The Cabot Adv. Group, Washington, 1998—. Bd. dirs. Somerset Hosp. Chmn. Olin Inst. for Employment Practice and Policy; chmn. Olin Found. for Employment Policy and Practice. Mem. Columbia U. Bus. Sch. Alumni Assn. (v.p.). Office Phone: 908-704-1888. E-mail: steve@sdarien.com.

DARIOTIS, TERRENCE THEODORE, lawyer; b. Chgo., Feb. 28, 1946; s. Theodore S. and Dorothy Mizzen D.; m. Jeanne Elizabeth Gibbons, Oct. 24, 1970; children: Sara, Kristin, Jennifer. BA in Philosophy, St. Joseph's Coll., Rensselaer, Ind., 1969; JD, Loyola U., Chgo., 1973; LL M. in Taxation, U. Fla., 2003. Bar: Ill. 1973, Fla. 1975, U.S. Tax Ct. 1993, U.S. Supreme Ct., 1978. Law clk. to presiding justice Appellate Ct. of Ill. (2d dist.), Waukegan, 1973-74; assoc. Keith Kinderman, Tallahassee, 1975-76; sole practitioner Tallahassee, 1976—82, 2000—; ptnr. Kahn and Dariotis, P.A., Tallahassee, 1982-96, Warfel, Goldberg, Dariotis, Waldoch & Olive, P.A., Tallahassee, 1996-00. Adj. prof. Fla. State U. Coll. Bus., 1987-93. Office: 1695 Metropolitan Cir Ste 6 Tallahassee FL 32308-3731 Office Phone: 850-523-9300. E-mail: tdariotis@nettally.com.

DARK, OKIANER CHRISTIAN, law educator; b. Petersburg, Va., Dec. 8, 1954; d. Marshall Taylor and Vivian Louise (Rier) Christian; m. Lawrence J. Dark, June 20, 1981; 1 child. BA magna cum laude, Upsala Coll., East Orange, N.J., 1976; JD, Rutgers U., Newark, 1979. Bar: Pa. 1979, N.J. 1979, U.S. Dist. Ct. N.J. 1979, U.S. Ct. Appeals (4th cir.) 1985, Va. 1988. Trial atty. antitrust div. U.S. Dept. Justice, Washington, 1979-84, trial atty. civil div., 1984; asst. prof. U. Richmond (Va.) Law Sch., 1984-87, assoc. prof., 1987-90, prof. antitrust, torts and white collar crime, 1990—97. Vis. prof., scholar Washington Coll. Law, Am. U., Washington, 1991-92; prof. Coun. on Legal Edn. Opportunity, Washington, 1985, 91, 92; asst. team leader southeastern regional program Nat. Trial Advocacy Inst., Chapel Hill, N.C., 1989, 90; cons. C.L. Harris & Assocs., Md., 1991—; speaker, panelist and workshop leader in field, asst. United States Atty Dist. Oreg., 1995-2001, prof. Howard U. Sch. Law, 2001—, assoc. dean acad. affairs, 2005—. Mem. adv. bd. Nat. Bar Assn. Mag.; contbr. articles to legal publs. Mem. Richmond Commn. to Study Minority Participation in Constrn. Industry, 1989-92; bd. dirs. Jewels of Ann Pvt. Day Sch., Washington, 1991-92, Daily Planet, Richmond, 1987-95, Va. League for Planned Parenthood, 1993-95, N.W. Health Found.; trustee YMCA Greater Portland, St. Paul's Coll., Lawrenceville, Va., 1989-95; trustee, chair minority affairs com. Law Sch. Admission Coun., 1991-95; assessment specialist United Way Greater Richmond, 1987-92, 2002—; commr. Montgomery County Commn. on Health, 2002-05 Recipient Disting. Educator award U. Richmond, 1990, 93, Disting. Faculty award Va. Women Attys. Assn. Found., 1991, Disting. Woman in Law award YWCA, 1991, Hope for People award Hope Fair Housing Ctr., Lombard, Ill., 1991, ann. Afro-Am. Achievement award Dale City Christian Ch., 1992, Award of Excellence, Nat. Alliance of Fair Housing Assn., 1997, Warren Rosarium Prof. Excellence award Howard U., 2005 Mem. ABA (former vice chmn. comml. torts subcom. torts and ins. sect., standing com. pub. edn. 2005—), Va. State Bar, Va. Bar Assn. (com. on lawyer professionalism), Old Dominion Bar Assn., Va. Assn. Black Women Attys. (bd. dirs.), Va. Womens Assn. Found. (bd. dirs.), Assn. Am. Law Schs., Women in Legal Edn. (minority affairs com. law sch. admission coun., com. torts, tchg. methods section, and ins. sect., antitrust and econ. regulation sect., chair), Oreg. State Bar (Oreg. Supreme Ct. gender fairness task force), Montgomery County Commn. on Health (vice chmn. 2004-05, chmn. mental health com. 2005—), Law Sch. Admission Coun. Bd. Trustees, Alpha Kappa Alpha. Baptist. Office: Howard U Sch Law Washington DC 20008 Office Phone: 202-806-8003. Business E-Mail: odark@law.howard.edu.

DARKO, DENIS F., research scientist, educator, physician; b. Indpls., July 13, 1947; s. Charles O. and Agnes Mary (Lauck) Darko; m. Ann Marie Barker, Oct. 15, 1983; children: Emily Marie, Roseann Michelle. BS in Physics, U. Notre Dame, 1969; MD, Ind. U., 1975. Diplomate Am. Bd. Psychiatry and Neurology. Staff rsch. assoc. biols. divsn. Eli Lilly Co., Indpls., 1970, U. Co. Sch. Medicine, 1971; resident physician family practice Maricopa County Hosp., 1975, Scottsdale (Ariz.) Meml. Hosp., 1975—76; resident physician psychiatry Good Samaritan Med. Ctr., Phoenix, 1977—80, chief resident in psychiatry, 1978—80; pvt. practice psychiatry Scottsdale, 1980—83; cons. psychiatrist Phoenix Indian Med. Ctr., 1980—81; supr. psychiatry residency program Maricopa County Med. Ctr., 1980—83; instr. family practice residency program Ariz. State U., 1980—83; fellow in consultation/liaison psychiatry U. Calif.-San Diego Med. Ctr., 1983—84, fellow in psychopharmacology and psychobiology Clin. Rsch. Ctr., 1984—85; asst. prof. psychiatry U. Calif., San Diego Sch. Medicine, 1985—92, assoc. adj. prof., 1992—2004, assoc. clin. prof., 2004—, chmn. diagnostic com. NIMH mental health clin. rsch. ctr., 1984—89, rsch. fellow in immunology and allergy divsn. immunology and allergy Dept. Pediats., 1985—87, chmn. resident rsch. com. dept. psychiatry, 1989—92; attending physician Univ. Hosp., 1985—94; ward chief San Diego VA Med. Ctr., 1985—87, staff psychiatrist, 1985—93, med. dir. mental health clinic, 1987—92, chief psychiat. emergency svc., 1988—92; dir. Mood Disorders Rsch. Clinic U. Calif. San Diego Sch. Medicine and San Diego VA Med. Ctr., 1987—90; med. dir. NIMH Mental Health Clin. Rsch. Ctr., 1987—88; vis. scientist Scripps Clinic and Rsch. Found. Dept. Neuropharmacology, 1990; assoc. adj. prof. Scripps Rsch. Inst. Dept. Neuropharmacology, 1991—92, assoc. prof., 1993—2002; attending physician Scripps Clin. Dept. Medicine, Divsn. Psychiatry, 1991—2002, head divsn. psychiatry and behavioral medicine, 1997—2002; head neuroimmunology lab., dept. neuropharmacology Scripps Rsch. Inst., 1993—2002; med. dir., v.p. Calif. Clin. Trials, LLC, 2002—03; dir. clin. rsch., neurosci. AstraZeneca PLC, Wilmington, 2003—. Chmn. grant application rev. com., dept. acad. affairs Scripps Clinic Found., 1995—2002; cons. Hybritech, 1991—94. Editl. reviewer: Am. Jour. of Psychiatry in Medicine, 1987—2002, Internat. Jour. of Psychiatry in Medicine, 1987—97, Jour. of Neuropsychiatry and Clin. Neuroscis., 1988—2002, Biol. Psychiatry, 1988, Behavioral Science, 1990—92. Recipient review article award, Am. Coll. Allergists, 1986; fellow, USPHS, 1972, ACP, 1988. Fellow: ACP, Am. Psychiat. Assn.; mem.: AAAS, Am. Acad. Sleep Medicine, West Coast Coll. Biol. Psychiatry, Psychoneuroimmunology Rsch. Soc. (founding), Soc. Biol. Psychiatry, Endocrine Soc., San Diego Soc. Psychiat. Physicians (chmn. membership com. 1991—94, treas. 1993—94), Calif. Psychiat. Assn. Office: AstraZeneca B2B-421 PO Box 15437 Wilmington DE 19850-5437 Home: 2 Pine Ln Chadds Ford PA 19317-9730 Office Phone: 302-885-4643 2297.

DARLING, ALBERTA HELEN, state legislator, art gallery director, marketing professional; b. Hammond, Ind., Apr. 28, 1944; d. Albert William and Helen Anne (Vaicunas) Statkus; m. William Anthony Darling, Aug. 12, 1967; children— Elizabeth Suzanne, William Anthony. BS, U. Wis., 1967. English tchr. Nathan Hale High Sch., West Allis, Wis., 1967—69, Castle Rock High Sch., Castle Rock, Colo., 1969—71; mem. Wis. State Assembly, 0990—1992, Wis. Senate from 8th dist., Madison, 1992—. Cons. orgn. devel., Milw., 1982—; dir. mktg. and communications Milw. Art Mus., 1981-88; exec. dir. mktg. architectural firm, 1988-90; State Rep. Wis., 1990—, mem. urban edn. com., children and human svcs. com., tourism com., homelessness com., teeenage pregnancy com., vice chmn. gov.'s housing policy commn., assembly coms. Pres. Community Action Seminar for Women, 1979-80; a founder Goals for Greater Milw. 2000, 1980-84; co-chair Action 2000, 1984-86; co-chmn. Icebreaker Am. Winterfestival; chmn. Community Action Seminar for Women, 1988; bd. dirs., exec. com. United Way, Milw., 1982-1992, chair project 1985, 1984-85, chmn. policy com. 1988; founder Today's Girls/Tomorrow's Women, Milw., pres. Jr. League Milw., 1980-82, Planned Parenthood Milw., 1982-84, Future Milw., 1983-85; vice chmn. State of Wis. Strategic Planning Council, 1988—, chmn. small bus./entrpreneur com.; mem. Greater Milw. Com.'s Mktg. Task Force, 1987-88; chmn. United Way Policy Com., 1987-88; participant Bus. Ptnrs. White House Conf., 1987; mem. summerfest adv. com. on Winter Festivals, 1989; founder Women's Fund of Milw. Found; active Juvenile Justice Leadership Com. Recipient Vol. Action award Milw. Civic Alliance, 1984, Community Service award United Way, 1984, Leader of Future award Milw. Mag., 1988, Nat. Assn. Community Leadership Orgn. award, 1986, Today's Girls/Tomorrow's Women Leadership award, 1987, Future Milw. Community Leadership award, 1988, Friend of Edn. Leadership award Head Start, 1994, William Steiger Humanitarian award, 1994. Mem. Greater Milw. Com., TEMPO Profl. Women, Am. Mktg. Assn. (Marketer of Yr. 1984), Pub. Relations Soc. Am., Ctr. for Pub. Representation (state bd. 1988), ARC (bd. dirs., exec. fin. coms. 1987—), Women's Fund (steering com. 1988), Internat. Assn. Bus. Communicators, Greater Milw. Com. Republican. Avocations: travel, art history, contemporary american literature, golf, tennis. Home: 1325 W Dean Rd Milwaukee WI 53217-2537 Office: State Capitol PO Box 7882 Madison WI 53707-7882 Office Phone: 608-266-5830. Business E-Mail: sen.darling@legis.state.wi.us.

DARLING, GEORGE CURTIS, minister, administrator; b. Xenia, Ohio, Nov. 23, 1928; s. Russell M. and Mary Elizabeth (Young) D.; m. Edna Pearlen Phillips, May 1, 1960; (div. Apr. 1973) 1 child, Curtis; m. Mary Elizabeth Miller, Oct. 24, 1952 (div. Aug. 1956), 1 child, Kirk; m. Evelyn Cornelia Woodfork, Apr. 10, 1976 (dec. Nov. 1998; m. Anna Jean Parks, Aug. 30, 2002. Adrloma in Theology, Am. Bapt. Theol. Sem., Dayton, Ohio, 1970. Ordained to ministry Bapt. Ch., 1963. Pastor 2nd Bapt. Ch., Del., Ohio, 1966-71; supply pastor Tabernacle Bapt. Ch., Columbus, Ohio, 1974; pastor Flintridge Bapt. Ch., Columbus, 1980-91; asst. pastor Peace Bapt. Ch., Columbus, 1993—. V.p. Springfield (Ohio) Dist. Sunday Sch. and Bapt. Tng. Union. Author: How to Find God, 1969. Bd. dirs., pres. Liberty Ctr., Delaware, Ohio, 1968-70; mem. Delaware County Community Action Orgn., 1967; vol. motivational spkr. to stroke patients, 1996—. With U.S. Army, 1950-52, Korea.; ret. USAF, 1988. Recipient Hon. Sci. award, Bausch & Lomb, 1946. Mem. Eastern Union Missionary Bapt. Assn. (statis. clk. Ohio 1981-85, 3d vice moderator 1985-87, 2d vice moderator, 1987-91), Columbus Bapt. Ministers and Laity Bible League (instr. 1987-96, parliamentarian 1999—). Home: 884 E Weber Rd Columbus OH 43211-1174 *On cloudy days when the sun is hidden from view, flying above the clouds enables one to see the brightness of the sun. When things go wrong in my life, I take a spiritual trip beyond the darkness of the moment into the sunlight of hope.*

DARLING, JOHN ARTHUR, music educator; b. Schenectady, NY, Jan. 11, 1957; s. Eleanor Meaux; m. Nancy Lee Paulson, Feb. 14, 1987; 1 child, Wesley Justin. B of liberal arts, U. of the State of NY, 1991—94; M of musical arts, Va. Commonwealth U., 1994—96; D of musical arts, Ohio State U., 1998—2001. Enlisted soldier U.S. Army, 1975—86, chief warrant officer, 1986—98; grad. asst. Ohio State U., 1998—2001; asst. dir. of bands Rutgers U., New Brunswick, NJ, 2001—03; asst. prof. of music Bismarck State Coll., Bismarck, ND, 2003—. Conductor (albums) Distinguished Music For Developing Bands, Vol. 4; prodr.: (compact disc) American Images, Rutgers Wind Ensemble. Chief warrant officer three U.S. Army, 1975—98. Mem.: Music Educator's Nat. Assn., Coll. Band Director's Nat. Assn., Nat. Band Assn. Home: 4501 37th Ave NW Mandan ND 58554 Office: Bismarck State Coll 1500 Edwards Ave Bismarck ND 58501 Office Phone: 701-224-5444. Personal E-mail: johnadarling@aol.com. E-mail: john.darling@bsc.nodak.edu.

DARLING, JOHN ROTHBURN, JR., business educator; b. Holton, Kans., Mar. 30, 1937; s. John Rothburn and Beatrice Noel (Deaver) D.; m. Melva Jean Fears, Aug. 20, 1958; children: Stephen, Cynthia, Gregory. BS, U. Ala., 1959, MS, 1960; PhD, U. Ill., 1967; PhD (hon.), Chung Yuan Christian U., Taiwan, 1998. Divisional mgr. J.C. Penney Co., 1960-63; grad. teaching asst. U. Ill., Urbana, 1965-66; asst. prof. mktg. U. Ala., Tuscaloosa, 1966-68; assoc. prof. mktg. U. Mo., Columbia, 1968-71; prof., adminstrn., coord. mktg. Wichita State U., 1971-76; dean, prof. mktg. Coll. Bus. Adminstrn. So. Ill. U., Carbondale, 1976-81; v.p. acad. affairs and rsch., prof. internat. bus. Tex. Tech U., Lubbock, 1981-86; provost, v.p. acad. affairs, prof. mktg. and internat.

bus. Miss. State U., Mississippi State, 1986-90; chancellor, disting. prof. internat. bus. La. State U., Shreveport, 1990-95; pres. Pittsburg (Kans.) State U., 1995-99, prof. mktg. and internat. bus., 1995-2000; vis. disting. prof. mktg. Rockhurst U., 2000—. Mktg. rsch. cons. Southwestern Bell, 1970; sr. v.p. Boothe Advt. Wichita, 1972; pres. Bus. Rsch. Assocs., 1972-76; cons. Bus. Rsch. Assocs., 1976-82; spl. cons. FTC, Washington, 1972-75, U.S. Dept. Justice, 1973-74, Atty. Gen., State of Kans., 1972-76, Dist. Atty. 18th Jud. Dist., Wichita, 1972-76, Maya Internat. Inc., Houston, 1995—, Morrison and Assocs., Inc., Shreveport, 1995-97; vis. disting. prof. internat. mktg. Helsinki Sch. Econs. and Bus. Adminstrn., 1993—. Author: (with Harry A. Lipson) Marketing Fundamentals, Text and Cases, 1980, (with Raimo Nurmi) International Management Leadership: The Primary Competitive Advantage, 1997; mem. bd. cons. editors Jour. Advt., 1984—; mem. editl. rev. bd. Jour. Internat. Bus. Studies, 1991—, Jour. Entrepreneurship, 1997—; contbr. articles to profl. jours. Bd. dirs. Outreach Found., 1973-79, v.p., 1975-77; trustee Graceland Coll., Lamoni, Iowa, 1976-82; mem. mgmt. com. Park Coll., Kansas City, 1976-79. Dist. Eagle Scout Awd., Boy Scouts Amer., 1998. Mem. Internat. Coun. Small Bus., Am. Mktg. Assn., Am. Mgmt. Assn., Acad. Internat. Bus., Am. Econs. Assn., Am. Arbitration Assn., (mem. nat. panel arbitrators and mediators 1993—), Nat. Assn. Intercollegiate Athletics (mem. governing bd. 1994-95), So. Bus. Adminstrn. Assn., So. Mktg. Assn., So. Econs. Assn., So. Assn. Colls. and Schs. (chair reaccreditation com. 1982-95, chair faculty qualifications criteria com. 1989-90, com. to rev. criteria for accreditation 1990-92, commr. 1992-95, Nat. Assn. State Univs. and Land-Grant Colls. (chair regional accreditation rev. com. 1989-90), Sales and Mktg. Execs. Internat., Beta Gamma Sigma, Phi Kappa Phi, Omicorn Delta Kappa, Phi Delta Kappa, Kappa Delta Phi, Mu Kappa Tau, Pi Sigma Epsilon, Alpha Kappa Psi, Chi Alpha Phi, Alpha Phi Omega, Phi Eta Sigma, Delta Mu Delta, Alpha Mu Gamma. Home: 12705 E 37th Terr Ct Independence MO 64055-3179 Office: Office of the President Pittsburg State Univ 1701 S Broadway St Pittsburg KS 66762-5856

DARLING, ROBERT EDWARD, theater director, costume designer; b. Oakland, Calif., Oct. 1, 1937; s. Irving Jackson and Helen Ellen (Hebel) D.; m. Ann Farris, Aug. 22, 1970. BA, San Francisco State U., 1959; M.F.A., Yale U. Sch. Drama, 1963; student, Bayreuth Festspiel Meisterclasse, 1965. Creative problem solving, idea design/graphic facilatation and transition mgr. MG Taylor Corp., 1984—; with Robert Darling & Assoc., Darling Assoc. Garden Design, 1991—, DTE Energy Learing Zone, 2000—01. Former mem. opera-musical theatre policy panel Nat. Endowment for Arts; panelist Nat. Opera Inst., Nat. Inst. for Music Theater, OPERA Am., 1997—. Designer, dir. numerous opera, theatre and ballet prodns. throughout U.S. and Can., 1960—; N.Y.C. debut with Another Evening with Harry Stoones, 1962; San Francisco Opera debut with L'Elisir d'Amore, 1967; Santa Fe Opera debut with Anna Bolena, 1970, Chgo. Lyric Opera debut with Don Carlo, 1972; N.Y.C. Opera debut with Der Fliegende Hollander, 1976, Hidden Valley Opera Don Giovanni, 1975, Seattle Opera Tannhaüser, 1984; dir. and designer world premiers of Medea, 1972, Colonel Johnathan the Saint, 1972, The Infanta, 1975, The Last of the Mohicans, 1976, The Face on the Barroom Floor, 1978, Soyazhe, 1979, Freddy the Leaf, 1987, 90-91, Recollections RLS, 1993, Williamstown Theatre Festival debut season J.B., 1963, Williamstown Theatre Festival: Marat/Sade, 1990, Speed The Plow, 1991, Miami City Ballet, Pan Nuit Suite, Jewels, 1993, debut Utah Festival Opera (Pagliacci, Gianni Schicchi), 1998; dramaturg-Coyote Tales Score, Kansas City Lyric Opera, 1998, Hidden Valley Opera La Boheme, 2002; artistic coord. Spring Opera Theatre, San Francisco, 1972, artistic adv. Kans. City (Mo.) Lyric Theatre, 1973; co-founder, prin. dir. Hidden Valley Opera Ensemble, Carmel, Calif., 1974-77; artistic dir. Central City Opera House Assn., Denver, 1977-82, Hidden Valley Opera, 1985-89, 2002—; illustrations, E.C. Schirmer, 2000; artistic prodr. Acorn Theatre, Washington, 1988—; site coord., founding mem. Alliance for New Music-Theater, 1994—, v.p. 2005; designs represented in collection Am. design Smithsomian Mus., Mus. of the City of N.Y., Prague Quadrennial Scenographic Design, 1987; contbr. articles to profl. jours. Mem. United Scenic Artists, Am. Guild Mus. Artists, Actors Equity-Can., OPERA Am., Logan Circle Assn., Washington Daffodil Soc. (past pres.). Democrat. Lutheran. Personal E-mail: darlingr@aol.com.

DARLING, ROBERT HOWARD, lawyer; b. Detroit, Oct. 29, 1947; s. George Beatson and Jeanne May (Mainville) D.; m. Cathy Lee Trygstad, Apr. 30, 1970; children: Bradley Howard, Brian Lee, Kara Kristine, Blake Robert. BS in Mech. Engring., U. Mich., 1969, MS in Mech. Engring., 1971; JD, Wayne State U., 1975. Bar: Mich. 1975, U.S. Dist. Ct. (ea. dist.) Mich. 1975, U.S. Ct. Appeals (6th cir.) 1975. Engr. Bendix Corp., Ann Arbor, Mich., 1970, Ford Motor Co., Dearborn, Mich., 1972-73; ptnr. Philo, Atkinson, Darling, Steinberg, Harper & Edwards, Detroit, 1975-81; sr. ptnr. Sommers, Schwartz, Silver & Schwartz, Southfield, Mich., 1981—. Assoc. editor Wayne State U. Law Review. Mem. ABA, Assn. Trial Lawyers Am., Mich. Trial Lawyers Assn. (exec. bd. 1981—, publs. chmn. 1981-85, products liability chmn. 1986—), Met. Detroit Trial Lawyers Assn., Oakland County Trial Lawyers Assn., State Bar Mich., Detroit Bar Assn., Plymouth Hist. Soc., Pi Tau Sigma. Avocation: golf. Home: 8785 Warren Rd Plymouth MI 48170-5119 Office: Sommers Schwartz Silver Schwartz 2000 Town Ctr Ste 900 Southfield MI 48075-1100 Address: 8785 Warren Rd Plymouth MI 48170-5119 E-mail: rdarling@s4online.com.

DARLING, SCOTT EDWARD, lawyer; b. L.A., Dec. 31, 1949; s. Dick R. and Marjorie Helen (Otto) D.; m. Cynthia Diane Harrah, June 1970 (div.); 1 child, Smokie; m. Deborah Lee Cochran, Aug. 22, 1981; children: Ryan, Jacob, Guinevere. BA, U. Redlands, 1972; JD, U.S.C., 1975. Bar: Calif. 1976, U.S. Dist. Ct. (cen. dist.) Calif. 1976. Assoc. atty. Elver, Falsetti, Boone & Crafts, Riverside, 1976-78; ptnr. Falsetti, Crafts, Pritchard & Darling, Riverside, 1978-84; pres. Scott Edward Darling, A Profl. Corp., Riverside, 1984—. Grant reviewer HHS, Washington, 1982-88; judge pro tem Riverside County Mcpl. Ct., 1980, Riverside County Superior Ct., 1987-88; bd. dirs. Tel Law Nat. Legal Pub. Info. System, Riverside, 1978-80. Author, editor: Small Law Office Computer Legal System, 1984. Bd. dirs. Youth Adv. Com. to Selective Svc., 1968-70, Am. Heart Assn. Riverside County, 1978-82, Survival Ministries, 1986-89; atty. panel Calif. Assn. Realtors, L.A., 1980—; pres. Calif. Young Reps., 1978-80; mem. GI Forum, Riverside, 1970-88; presdl. del. Nat. Rep. Party, 1980-84; asst. treas. Calif. Rep. Party, 1981-83; Rep. Congl. candidate, Riverside, 1982; treas. Riverside Sickle Cell Found., 1980-82, recipient Eddie D. Smith award; pres. Calif. Rep. Youth Caucus, 1980-82; v.p. Riverside County Red Cross, 1982-84; mem. Citizen's Univ. Com., Riverside, 1978-84, World Affairs Council, 1978-82, Urban League, Riverside, 1980-82. Calif. Scholarship Fedn. (life). Named one of Outstanding Young Men in Am., U.S. Jaycees, 1979-86. Mem. ABA, Riverside County Bar Assn., Speaker's Bur. Riverside County Bar Assn., Riverside Jaycees, Riverside C. of C. Lodges: Native Sons of Golden West. Avocations: skiing, swimming, reading. Office: 3697 Arlington Ave Riverside CA 92506-3938 Office Phone: 951-788-2889. Personal E-mail: scott@scottdarling.com. Business E-Mail: rivlaw@aol.com.

DARLING, STEPHEN EDWARD, lawyer; b. Columbia, S.C., Apr. 12, 1949; s. Norman Rushton and Elizabeth (Clarkson) D.; m. Denise Howell, June 30, 1979; children: Julia Hanley, Edward McCrady, Elizabeth Rushton. BS in Banking, Fin., Real Estate, Ins., U. S.C., 1971, JD, 1974. Bar: S.C. 1974, U.S. Dist. Ct. S.C. 1975, U.S. Ct. Appeals (4th cir.) 1975, U.S. Ct. Appeals (5th cir.) 1976, U.S. Supreme Ct. 1982, U.S. Ct. Appeals (3d cir.) 1999. From assoc. to ptnr. Sinkler, Gibbs & Simons, Charleston, S.C., 1974-87; ptnr. Sinkler & Boyd, Charleston, 1987-2000, Haynsworth Sinkler Boyd P.A., Charleston, 2000—. Mem.: ABA, Am. Bd. Trial Advs., Def. Rsch. Inst., Southeastern Admiralty Law Inst., Internat. Assn. Def. Counsel, Charelston County Bar Assn. (exec. com. 1989—90, 1992—93), S.C. Def. Trial Attys. Assn. (exec. com. 1994—99, sec. 2000, treas. 2001, pres.-elect 2002, pres. 2003), S.C. Bar Assn., Met. Exch. Club (Charleston). Episcopalian. Home: 23 New St Charleston SC 29401-2405 Office: Haynsworth Sinkler Boyd PA 134 Meeting St 3d Fl Charleston SC 29401 Office Phone: 843-722-3366. E-mail: sdarling@hsblawfirm.com.

DARLINGTON, DAVID WILLIAM, management consultant; b. Boston, Oct. 3, 1945; s. Horace and Maude Beatrice (Pfalzgraf) D.; m. Stacey A. Mitchell, May 24, 1986; children: Elizabeth Joy, Christine Rebecca. BS, Babson Coll., 1974; MBA, 1976; postgrad., Northeastern U., 1977-80. Planning engr. Stone & Webster Engring. Corp., Boston, 1974-75; project adminstr. Northrop Corp., Norwood, Mass., 1975-80; mgr. program adminstrn. internat. sys. dvisn. Sanders Assos., Inc., Nashua, NH, 1980-82, bus. mgr. Cons., program mgr., contr. Arthur D. Little, Cambridge, Mass., 1982-2002; fin. dir. ICF Cons., Inc., 2002-03; acctg. mgr. M/A-com Tyco Electronics, 2003—. With USN, 1964—71. Mem. Am. Prodn. and Inventory Control Soc. (cert.), Nat. Contract Mgmt. Assn. (cert.), Inst. Cost Analysis (cert.), Inst. Mgmt. Accts., Appalachian Mountain Club, Betta Gamma. Home: 378 Charles Bancroft Hwy Litchfield NH 03052-8033

DARLINGTON, DEMETRA BREWER, elementary school educator; b. Portsmouth, Va., Aug. 7, 1956; d. William Henry and Florence Roberta Hale Brewer; m. Jerome Lucius Darlington, June 16, 2000. BS in Home Econ., Norfolk State U., 1978. Tchr. Headstart, Arlington, Va., 1979—86; tchr., asst. dir. Learning Tree Day Care, Arlington, 1986—88; tchr. Creative Child Devel. Ctr., Washington, 1988—90; tchr., asst. dir. Hopkins House Assn., Alexandria, Va., 1990—95; dir., tchr. United Meth. Ch. of the Redeemer Child Devel. Ctr., Temple Hills, Md., 1995—97; tchr. D.C. Pub. Sch., 1997—. Baptist. Avocations: reading, sewing, cooking, sports. Home: 3702 Melrose Ave District Heights MD 20747 Office: Amidon Elem Sch 401 I St SW Washington DC 20024 Office Phone: 202-724-4867. E-mail: metrabre998@yahoo.com.

DARLINGTON, RICHARD BENJAMIN, psychologist, educator; b. Woodbury, NJ, Nov. 16, 1937; s. Charles Joseph and Eleanor (Collins) D.; m. Elizabeth Day, June 13, 1959; children: Jean Susan, Lois Heather. BA, Swarthmore Coll., 1959; PhD, U. Minn., 1963. Asst. prof. psychology Cornell U., Ithaca, N.Y., 1963-68, assoc. prof., 1968-80, prof., 1980—. Author: Radicals and Squares, 1975, (with others) Lasting Effects of Early Education, 1982, (with Patricia M. Carlson) Behavioral Statistics: Logic and Methods, 1987, Regression and Linear Models, 1990; contbr. articles to profl. jours.; contbr. chpts. to books. Project dir. Am. Friends Service Com., 1960, 61. Fellow NSF, 1959-60; fellow Woodrow Wilson Found., 1959-60; grantee HEW, 1977-81, Office of Edn., 1966-67, 70-71, Dept. of Labor, 1980-81 Fellow AAAS; mem. Phi Beta Kappa Mem. Soc. Of Friends. Home: 204 Fairmount Ave Ithaca NY 14850-4804 Office: Cornell Univ Dept Psychology Uris H Ithaca NY 14853 Business E-Mail: rbd1@cornell.edu.

DARLOW, GEORGE ANTHONY GRATTON, investor; b. Rochester, N.Y., June 16, 1938; s. Alfred Miltenberger and Lillian (Gratton) D.; m. Helen Julia Donovan, Mar. 2, 1971 (div.); 1 child, Gillian Darlow Jones; m. Christiana Sewall Alden (div.). BA, Yale U., 1961; JD, Columbia U., 1971; LLD, Yale U., 1979, Columbia U., 1979, U. Rochester, 1979, Sweet Briar Coll., 1979. Trustee Am. Indian Archeol. Inst., Washington, Conn., 1973-93; chmn., trustee Inst. Am. Indian Studies, Washington, Conn., 1993—. With USN, 1961-64; lic. capt. USCG. Mem. Colony Found. (trustee 1995—), Ancient Free Accepted Masons (32nd Degree), Rotary Internat., Berzelius Soc., Beta Theta Pi, Lions Club, Yale Club (N.Y.C.), Royal Palm Yacht Club, Mory's (New Haven). Republican. Episcopalian. Home: 18925 S River Rd Alva FL 33920

DARLOW, JULIA DONOVAN, lawyer; b. Detroit, Sept. 18, 1941; d. Frank William Donovan and Helen Adele Turner; m. George Anthony Gratton Darlow (div.); 1 child, Gillian; m. John Corbett O'Meara. AB, Vassar Coll., 1963; postgrad., Columbia U. Law Sch., 1964-65; JD cum laude, Wayne State U., 1971. Bar: Mich. 1971, U.S. Dist. Ct. (ea. dist.) Mich. 1971. Assoc. Dickinson, Wright, McKean, Cudlip & Moon, Detroit, 1971-78; ptnr. Dickinson, Wright, Moon, Van Dusen & Freeman and predecessor, Detroit, 1978—2001; sr. v.p. Detroit Med. Ctr., 2001—01; cons. mem. Dickinson, Wright PLLC, Detroit, 2002—04; counsel Varnum, Riddering, Schmidt & Howlett, LLP, 2005—. Bd. dirs. Internat Corp., chair corp. governance com., 2004-; adj. prof. Wayne State U. Law Sch., 1974-75, 96; commr. State Bar Mich., 1977-87, mem. exec. com., 1979-83, 84-87, sec. 1980-81, v.p., 1984-85, pres.-elect 1985-86, pres. 1986-87, coun. corp. fin. and bus. law sect. 1980-86, coun. computer law sect. 1985-88; mem. State Officers Compensation Commn., 1994-96; chair Mich. Supreme Ct. Task Force on Gender Issues in the Cts., 1987-89. Bd. dirs. Hutzel Hosp., 1984—2003, chair, 2002—03; bd. dirs. Mich. Opera Theatre, 1985—, mem. exec. com., 1992—; bd. dirs. Mich. Women's Found., 1986—91, Detroit Med. Ctr., 1990—2003, Marygrove Coll., 1996—, sec., 2003—; trustee Internat. Inst. Met. Detroit, 1986—92; trustee Mich. Met. coun. Girl Scouts USA, 1988—91; trustee Detroit coun. Boy Scouts Am., 1988—; mem. exec. com. Mich. Coun. Humnanities, 1988—92; mem. Blue Cross-Blue Shield Prospective Reimbursement Com., Detroit, 1979—81; v.p., mem. exec. com. United Found., 1988—95; mem. Mich. Gov.'s Bilateral Trade Team for Germany, 1992—98. Fellow Am. Bar Found. (Mich. State chair 1990-96); mem. Detroit Bar Assn. Found. (treas. 1984-85, trustee 1982-85), Mich. Bar Found. (trustee 1987-94), Am. Judicature Soc. (bd. dirs. 1985-88), Internat. Women's Forum (global affairs com. 1994-03), Women Lawyers Assn. (pres. 1977-78), Mich. Women's Campaign Fund (charter), Detroit Athletic Club. Democrat. Office: Fed Bldg Ste 400 200 E Liberty St Ann Arbor MI 48104 Address: Varnum Riddering Schmidt & Howlett LLP 39555 Orchard Hill Pl Ste 600 Novi MI 48375 Office Phone: 313-690-3054. Business E-Mail: jdarlow@varnumlaw.com.

DARMAN, RICHARD, investor, former government official; b. Charlotte, NC, May 10, 1943; m. Kathleen Emmet, Sept. 1, 1967; children: William Temple Emmet, Jonathan Warren Emmet, Christopher Temple Emmet BA cum laude, Harvard U., 1964, MBA, 1967, DSc (hon.); DLaw (hon.). Dep. asst. sec. HEW, Washington, 1971-72; asst. to sec. Dept. Def., Washington, 1973; spl. asst. to atty. gen. Washington, 1973; fellow Woodrow Wilson Internat. Center for Scholars, Washington, 1974; prin., dir. ICF, Inc., Washington, 1975, 77-80; asst. sec. Dept. Commerce, 1976-77; lectr. public policy and mgmt. Harvard U., 1977-80; asst. to Pres. Reagan, The White House, Washington, 1981-85; dep. sec. Dept. Treasury, 1985-87; mng. dir. Shearson Lehman Hutton Inc., N.Y.C., 1987-88; dir. office mgmt. and budget, mem. Pres. Cabinet The White House, Washington, 1989-93; prof. JFK Sch. Govt. Harvard U., 1998—2002; ptnr. The Carlyle Group, 1993—; chmn. bd. dir. AES Corp., Arlington, Va., 2003—. Bd. dirs. Frontier Ventures Corp., 1993—, AES Corp., 2002—, vice chmn., 2002, chmn., 2003—. Editor: Harvard Ednl. Rev, 1970; contbg. editor U.S. News & World Report, 1987-88; author: Who's in Control?, 1996; contbr. articles to profl. jours. Trustee Bennington Coll., 1974—75, The Brookings Inst., 1987—88; bd. dirs. Smithsonian Nat. Mus. Am. History, 2000—, vice chmn. bd., 2003—; trustee IXIS Funds, 1996—, Loomis Sayles Funds, 2003—; mem. overseers com. to visit Kennedy Sch. Govt. Harvard U., 1988—98, 2003—, Harvard Med. Sch., 1994—99. Office: The Carlyle Group 1001 Pennsylvania Ave NW Washington DC 20004-2505

D'ARMAND, JOHN BERGER, music educator; b. Knoxville, Tenn., Nov. 15, 1935; s. Roscoe Carlisle and Virginia Luck Berger d'Armand; m. Susanne Buchinger, Dec. 24, 1987; children: Cynthia Luck Sullivan, Jeannette Noël, Maureen. BS, U. of Tenn., 1954—58; MusB, Baldwin-Wallace Coll., 1960—63; MusM, U. of Ill., 1963—65; D of musical arts, U. of Cin., 1967—80; Kodály Diploma, U. of Calgary, 1982—84; Med, U. of Alaska, 1990—2004. Type A Teaching Certificate State of Alaska, 1999. Chorister Robert Shaw Chorale, NYC; artist in residence Concordia Coll., Moorhead, Minn., 1964—67; assoc. prof. of music U. of Mass., 1968—80; lectr. in music Wesleyan U., Middletown, Conn., 1970—72; music dir. WFCR, Amherst, Mass., 1973—75; prof. of music U. of Alaska, 1980—. Founder and exec. dir. Paul Ulanowsky Found. for Chamber Musicians, Deerfield, Mass., 1969—; voice coach Oren Brown Voice Seminar, Amherst, Mass., 1980; pres. of the faculty senate U. of Alaska, 1997—98. Singer: (rca victor choral recording) Bach: Mass in B minor (Grammy winner for best sacred choral rec., 1960). Recipient Independent Students Association Man of the Yr., U. Tenn., 1958, Baldwin-Wallace College Alumni Achievement award, 1984; scholarship, Berkshire Music Ctr. at Tanglewood, 1960, Oglebay Pk. Opera Workshop, Wheeling, W.Va., 1960, Performing Assistantship in opera performance, U. of Ill., 1963—64, scholarship, Yale Summer Sch. of Music and Art, 1967, Grad. Assistantship in opera and conducting, U. of Cin., 1967—68. Mem.: Pi Kappa Lambda, Delta Phi Alpha. Home: P O Box 210623 Auke Bay AK 99821-0623 Home Fax: 907-789-3981. Personal E-mail: jbd@gci.net.

DARMER, ELLEN SUZANNE, school system administrator; b. Arab, Ala., Nov. 28, 1951; d. Bennett Hurst and Edna Annie Ruth Darmer; divorced; children: Kristin Kara Toop, Destin William Toop. BA, U. Ala., 1973; MA, Ala. A&M U., 1976; EdD, Miami U., Oxford, Ohio, 1998. Cert. tchr. Ohio, prin. Ohio, supt. Ohio. Tchr. Guntersville (Ala.) City Schs., 1974—76; coord. coll. tutorial program U. Tenn., Chattanooga, 1986—87; prin. Hickory Valley Christian Sch., Chattanooga, 1987—91; tchr., coord. New Richmond (Ohio) Schs., 1991—98; fed. programs coord. South-Western City Schs., Grove City, Ohio, 1998—2000; asst. supt. Greenville (Ohio) City Schs., 2000—. Dir. summer camp for girls Culver (Ind.) Mil. Acad., 1987—91; adj. faculty U. Tenn., Chattanooga, 1984—86. Cons. for Unted Way Metro. Coun. for Cmty. Svcs., Chattanooga, 1987; exec. bd. Boys and Girls Club Am., New Richmond, Ohio, 1996—98; bd. dirs. Character Coun., Greenville, 2002—05. Grantee, Fed. Govt., 2000. Mem.: Ohio Assn. Adminstrs. State and Fed. Edn. Programs (com. practitioners adv. bd. for no child left behind 2003—05, pres. 2001—02), Buckeye Assn. Sch. Adminstrs., Kiwanis, Alpha Delta Kappa. Avocations: water sports, ballroom dancing, horticulture. Office: Greenville City Schs 215 W Fourth St Greenville OH 45331

DARMODY, STEPHEN JEROME, lawyer; b. Worcester, Mass., Nov. 28, 1957; s. Jeremiah and Anna Mae (Tangney) D.; m. Maureen Adelaide Miller, June 4, 1983; children: Caroline Marie, James Edward, Mary Grace. BS in Mgmt., USCG Acad., 1979; MBA in Fin./Investments, George Washington U., 1984, JD with honors, 1988, LLM with highest honors in Environ. Law, 1993. Bar: Va. 1988, D.C. 1989, U.S. Ct. Mil. Appeals 1989, U.S. Ct. Appeals (4th cir.) 1988, U.S. Ct. Appeals (D.C. cir.) 1994, U.S. Supreme Ct. 1994, N.C. 1996, Fla. 2001, U.S. Ct. Appeals (11th cir.) 2001. Commd. officer USCG, advanced through grades to comdr.; shipboard ops. officer USCG Cutter Acushnet, Gulfport, Miss., 1979-81; planning, programming and budgeting analyst USCG Hdqs., Washington, 1981-85, law clk., 1986-87; asst. dist. legal officer 8th Coast Guard Dist., New Orleans, 1988-92; staff atty. Coast Guard Environ. Law divsn., Coast Guard Hdqrs., Washington, 1993-95; asst. chief Coast Guard Office of Regulations and Adminstrv. Law, 1995-97; regional counsel Great Lakes U.S. Coast Guard, Cleve., 1997—, ret., 2001; atty. Shook, Hardy & Bacon, Miami, Fla., 2001—. Apptd. mil. judge for trials by court-martial, 1995. Spkr. The Admissibility of Expert Testimony, Am. Bar Assn., 2004, Regulatory Takings and the Environmental Law, The Federalist Soc., 2004, Toxic Torts, Civil Litigationand Market Responses, U. Fla, 2005; contbr. articles to profl. jours. Mem. sch. bd. St. Andrew's Elem. Sch., New Orleans, 1991-92, religion tchr., 1989-91. Recipient 2 Meritorious Svc. medals, 2 Commendation medals U.S. Coast Guard, 2 Achievement medals, Commandants's Letter of Commendation, 2 Vice Presdl. award for reinventing govt. Mem. ABA (Outstanding Young Coast Guard lawyer 1990-91), Va. State Bar, D.C. Bar Assn., Fla. Bar (mem. admiralty com. 2002—), N.C. Bar, Federalist Soc., Judge Advocates Assn. (bd. dirs. 1994-95, Outstanding Career Lawyer of Yr. 1996), Southeastern Admiralty Law Inst. Office: One Miami Ctr Ste 2400 201 Biscayne Blvd Miami FL 33132 Office Phone: 305-358-5171. E-mail: sdarmody@shb.com.

DARMSTANDLER, HARRY MAX, retired military officer; b. Indpls., Aug. 9, 1922; s. Max M. and Nonna (Holden) D.; m. Donna L. Bender, Mar. 10, 1957; children: Paul William, Thomas Alan. BS, U. Omaha, 1964; MS, George Washington U., 1965; grad., Nat. War Coll., 1965. Commd. 2d lt. USAAF, 1943; advanced through grades to maj. gen. USAF, 1973; served with 15th Air Force, 1943, 5th Air Force, Republic of Korea, 1952; comdr.-in-chief Pacific, 1960—63; served with joint chiefs of staff, 1965—68; supreme comdr. Allied Powers Europe, 1969—71; comdr. 12th Air Divsn. SAC, 1972, dep. chief of staff for plans, 1973; spl. asst. to chief of staff USAF, 1974—75; chmn. bd., CEO Rancho Bernardo Savs. Bank, San Diego, 1983—90; ptnr. Allied Assocs., Colorado Springs, Colo., 1968—, D & H Inc., Woodland Park, Colo., 1979—; founding ptnr. Assocs. Group, San Diego, 1995—. Cons. Mid East matters and bd. dirs. Palomar Pomerado Health Found, San Diego; bd. dirs. Clean Found., San Diego. Author numerous articles on nat. def. requirements. Elder, Rancho Bernardo Community Presbyn. Ch., San Diego. Decorated D.S.M. with oak leaf cluster, Legion of Merit with oak leaf cluster, D.F.C., Air medal with 3 oak leaf clusters; research fellow UCLA, 1969. Mem. AIAA, Order Daedalians, Soc. Strategic Air Command, Eagle Scout Alumni Assn., Bernardo Heights Country Club (San Diego, past pres.), Phi Tau Alpha. Home: La Jolla Village Towers 8515 Costa Verde Blvd #1707 San Diego CA 92122 Personal E-mail: dhank32@sbcglobal.net.

DARNALL, DARLEEN RENE, lawyer; b. Montebello, Calif., July 7, 1962; d. John Everett and Mary Irene Mock; m. Jeffrey Scott Darnall, Aug. 17, 1985 (div. Jan. 1998). BA, George Fox Coll., 1984; JD, U. Mich. Law Sch., 1989. Assoc. Honigman, Miller, Schwartz & Cohn, Detroit, 1989-90, Dykema Gossett, Detroit, 1990-92, Bullivant Houser, Portland, Oreg., 1992-95; assoc., ptnr. Davis Wright Tremaine, L.L.P., Portland, Oreg., 1995—. Pres., bd. dirs. Open Adoption and Family Svcs., Portland, 1995—; mem. bd, govs. Heart Rsch. Ctr., Oreg. Health Scis. U., Portland, 1998—. Mem. Mich. Bar Assn., Washington Bar Assn., Oreg. Bar Assn., Oreg. Women Lawyers. Democrat. Mem. Soc. Of Friends. Office: Davis Wright Tremaine 2300 First Interstate Tower 1300 SW 5th Ave Ste 2200 Portland OR 97201-5667 E-mail: darleendarnall@dwt.com.

DARNALL, ROBERTA MORROW, association executive; b. Kemmerer, Wyo., May 18, 1949; d. C. Dale and Eugenia Stayner (Christmas) Morrow; m. Leslie A. Darnall, Sept. 3, 1977; children: Kimberly Gene, Leslie Nicole. BS, U. Wyo., Laramie, 1972. Tariff sec., ins. adminstr. Wyo Trucking Assn., Casper, 1973-75; asst. clerical supr. Wyo. Legislature, Cheyenne, 1972-77, congrl. campaign press aide, 1974; pub. rels. dir. Casper, Wyo., Wyo. Rep. Ctr. Com., 1976-77; asst. dir. alumni rels. U. Wyo., 1977-81; exec. dir. Alumni Assn., 1981—. Bd. dirs. recognition and golf coms. Ivison Meml. Hosp. Found.; mem. Altar Guild, lector, usher, former acolyte, coord. St. Matthew's Ch. Mem. Higher Edn. Assn. Rockies, Am. Soc. Assn. Execs., Laramie C. of C. (past edn.com.), U. Wyo. Alumni Assn., Cowboy Joe Club, PEO (former courtesy com., officer). Republican. Episcopalian. Home: 15 Snowy View Ct Laramie WY 82070-5358 Office: 214 S 14th St Laramie WY 82070 Office Phone: 307-766-4166. E-mail: robbie@uwyo.edu.

DARNELL, JAMES EDWIN, JR., molecular biologist, educator; b. Columbus, Miss., Sept. 9, 1930; s. James Edwin and Helen (Hopkins) D.; m. Jane Roller, 1957; children: Christopher, Robert, Jonathan; m. Kristin Holby, 2002. BS, U. Miss., 1951; MD, Washington U., 1955, DSc, 1996. Intern Barnes Hosp., 1955-56; asst. to sr. surgeon USPHS, Bethesda, Md., 1957-60; asst. and assoc. prof. MIT, Cambridge, 1961-64; prof. Albert Einstein Coll. Medicine, N.Y.C., 1967, Columbia U., 1968-74, chmn. dept. biol. scis., 1971-74; Vincent Astor prof. Rockefeller U., N.Y.C., 1974—, v.p. acad. affairs, 1990-91. Co-author: (textbooks) General Virology, 1967, 77, Molecular Cell Biology, 1986, rev. edits., 1990, 1995, 2000, 03. Recipient H.T. Rickets award U. Chgo., 1979, Internat. award Gairdner Found., Toronto, Ont., Can., 1986, Paul Janssen prize in Advanced Biotech. and Medicine, 1994, Bertner award in cancer rsch., 1996, Passano award, 1997, Milstein award, 1997, City of Medicine, 1998, E.B. Wilson award, 1998, Lynen medal, 1999, Dickson Prize in Medicine, 1999, William B. Coley award, 1999, Gerald D. Aurbach lecture award The Endocrine Soc., 1999, Novartis/Drew award in biomed. rsch., 2000, N.Y. Acad. Medicine medal for disting. contbns. in biomed. sci., 2002, Albert Lasker award for Spl. Achievement in Med. Sci., 2002, Nat. Medal of Science award, 2002. Mem. NAS, Am. Acad. Arts and Scis. (award 1973), Royal Soc. (fgn.), Japanese Biochem. Soc. (hon.), Royal Swedish Acad. Aci. (fgn.), European Acad. Scis. Office: Rockefeller U Molecular Cell Biology 1230 York Ave New York NY 10021-6399

DARNELL, RILEY CARLISLE, state official, lawyer; b. Clarksville, Tenn., May 13, 1940; s. Elliott Sinclair and Mary Anita (Whitefield) D.; m. Mary Penelope Crockarell, June 2, 1963; children: Neil Whitefield, Duncan Edward, Mary Eve, Penelope Joy, Dawson Riley. BS, Austin Peay State U., 1962; JD, Vanderbilt U., 1965. Bar: Tenn. 1965. Gen. practice, Clarksville, 1965-66, 69—. Mem. Tenn. Ho. of Reps. from 67th Dist., 1971-80, treas. house-senate caucus, 1971-86, sec. house com. ways and means, chmn. joint house-senate fiscal rev. com., 1975-80; mem. Tenn. State Senate, 1980-92, chmn. transp. com., 1982-86, chmn. joint com. children and youth, 1987-89; senate majority leader, 1988-92; sec. of state State of Tenn., Nashville, 1993—. Served to Capt. JAGC, USAF, 1966-69. Fellow Tenn. Bar Found.; mem. ABA, Montgomery County Bar Assn., Tenn. Trial Lawyers, Tenn. Bar Assn., Nat. Conf. State Legislators (jud. task force), So. Lesig. Conf. (mem. fiscal affairs com.) Democrat. Mem. Ch. Of Christ. Office: State Capitol 1st Fl 600 Charlotte Ave Nashville TN 37243 Home: 817 Salisbury Way Clarksville TN 37043-5690 Office Phone: 615-741-2819. Business E-Mail: riley.darnell@state.tn.us.

DARNELL, WILLIAM HEADEN, chemical engineer, medical/surgical nurse, nursing educator; b. Roanoke, Va., May 14, 1925; s. William Lee and Edythe Headen (Scott) Darnell; m. Kathryn Jane McManaway, June 3, 1950; 1 child, William Jamison. BS, Va. Poly. Inst. and State U., 1950; MS, U. Wis., 1951, PhD, 1953; ASN, Tri-County Tech. Coll., 2004. RN S.C., 1989. Prodn. asst. Merck Pharm. Co., Elkton, Va., 1946; rsch. engr., supr. E.I. du Pont de Nemours Co., Wilmington, Del., 1953—60, nylon tech. supt. Victoria, Tex., 1960—63, devel. mgr. Wilmington, Del., 1963—68, rsch. mgr., 1968—72, lab. adminstr., 1972—77, environ. mgr., 1977—85; RN staff Oconee Meml. Hosp. Inc., Seneca, SC, 1989—2001; pvt. practice RN educator Salem, SC, 2001—04. Contbr. editor handbook Processing Thermoplastics, 1959, articles to profl. jours. Chpt. pres. Rotary Internat., Wilmington, 1970—71, dist. sec., NJ and Del., 1971—72; affiliate faculty Am. Heart Assn., Del. and Southeastern Pa., 1974—83; election judge Kennett Twp., Kennett Square, Pa., 1976—78; bd. dir. Am. Cancer Soc., Del., 1968—70; bd. dir. and pres. Advanced Life Support, Inc., West Grove, Pa., 1982—85, exec. dir., treas. and v.p.; exec. dir., treas., v.p., bd. dir. and pres. Hospice of the Foothills, Inc., Seneca, SC, 1987—98; v.p. and vice chmn. bd. dir. Hospice Found., 1998—2005. 2d Lt. U.S. Army, 1943—53, ATO, ETO, PTO. Recipient Best Tech. Paper award, AIChE, 1959, Silver Dove award, Hospice Found., 2004; fellow, NSF, 1952. Mem.: SAR (chpt. pres. 1997, Patriot award 1994), Nat. Soc. SAR (trustee 1996—97), S.C. Soc. SAR (state pres. 1994—96). Republican. Presbyterian. Avocations: music, furniture reproductions, swimming. Home: 7 Gybe Ho Ct Salem SC 29676

DARNTON, JOHN TOWNSEND, journalist; b. NYC, Nov. 20, 1941; s. Byron and Eleanor Kate (Choate) D.; m. Nina Jane Lieberman, Aug. 21, 1966; children: Kyra, Liza, James. BS, U. Wis., 1966. Reporter NY Times, NYC, 1968-75, br. chief Lagos, Nigeria, 1975-76, Nairobi, Kenya, 1976-79, Warsaw, 1979-82, Madrid, 1982-84, met. editor NYC, 1986-91, news editor, 1991-93, London corr., 1993-96, culture editor NYC, 1996—2003, assoc. editor, 2003—. Ferris prof. Princeton (N.J.) U., 1991-92. Author: Neanderthal, 1996, The Experiment, 1999, Muid Catcher, 2002, The Darwin Conspiracy, 2005. Recipient Pulitzer prize, 1982, George Polk award L.I. U., 1979, 82. Mem. Century Club. Office: NY Times Culture News Dept 229 W 43rd St New York NY 10036-3959

DARNTON, ROBERT CHOATE, historian, educator; b. NYC, May 10, 1939; s. Byron and Eleanor (Choate) D.; m. Susan Lee Glover, June 29, 1963; children: Nicholas Campbell, Catherine Choate, Margaret Townsend. BA, Harvard U., 1960; BPhil, Oxford U., Eng., 1962, DPhil, 1964. Reporter N.Y. Times, N.Y.C., 1964; jr. fellow Harvard U., 1964-68; asst. prof. history Princeton U., N.J., 1968-71, assoc. prof., 1971-72, prof., 1972—. Author: Mesmerism and the End of the Enlightenment in France, 1968, The Business of Enlightenment: A Publishing History of the Encyclopédie, 1775-1800, 1979 (Am. Hist. Assn. Leo Gershoy prize 1979), The Literary Underground of the Old Regime, 1982, The Great Cat Massacre and Other Episodes in French Cultural History, 1984 (LA Times book prize), The Kiss of Lamourette: Reflections in Cultural History, 1989, Edition et Sédition, L'univers de la littérature clandestine au XVIII e siècle, 1991 (Prix Chateaubriand), Berlin Journal, 1989-90, 1991, Gens de lettres, gens du livre, 1992, The Forbidden Best-Sellers of Pre-Revolutionary France, 1995 (Nat. Book Critics Circle award 1996), The Corpus of Clandestine Literature in France, 1995, Jacques-Pierre Brissot, His Career and Correspondence, 1779-1787, 2001, George Washington's False Teeth. An Unconventional Guide to the Eighteenth Century, 2003. Decorated officer Ordre des Arts et des Lettres, chevalier Légion d'Honneur, 1999; recipient Koren prize Soc. French Hist. Studies, 1973, MacArthur Found. prize, 1982, Gutenberg prize Internat. Gutenberg Soc. and City of Mainz, 2004 Fellow Am. Acad. Arts and Scis., Am. Philos. Soc., Brit. Acad. (corr. 2001); mem. Am. Hist. Assn. (pres.-elect 1998, pres. 1999-2000), Am. Soc. 18th-Century Studies (Clifford prize 1971, 73), Internat. Soc. 18th-Century Studies (pres. 1987-1992), Academia Europaea, Belgian Royal Acad. French Lang. and Lit. Office: Princeton U Dept History Princeton NJ 08540

DAROFF, ROBERT BARRY, neurologist, educator; b. NYC, Aug. 3, 1936; s. Charles and May (Wolin) D.; m. Jane L. Abrahams, Dec. 4, 1959; children: Charles II, Robert Barry, Jr., William Clayton BA, U. Pa., 1957, MD, 1961. Cert. in Neurology Am. Bd. Psychiatry and Neurology, 1969. Intern Phila. Gen. Hosp., 1961-62; resident in neurology Yale-New Haven Med. Center, 1962-65; fellow in neuro-ophthalmology U. Calif. Med. Center, San Francisco, 1967-68; prof. neurology, assoc. prof. ophthalmology U. Miami Med. Sch.; dir. ocular motor neurophysiology lab. Miami VA Med. Center, 1968-80; Gilbert W. Humphrey prof., chmn. dept. neurology Case Western Res. U. Med. Sch.; dir. dept. neurology Univ. Hosps., Cleve., 1980-93; prof. neurology Case Western U., 1980—, assoc. dean, 1994—2003, interim vice dean edn. and acad. affairs, 2004—; staff neurologist Cleve. VA Med. Ctr., 1980-93; chief of staff, sr. v.p. acad. affairs U. Hosp., Cleve., 1994—2003; chief med. officer St. Vincents Charity, St. Johns West Shore Hosps., 2004—. Med. sci. adv. bd., chmn. sci. program com. Myasthenia Gravis Found., 1984—87, exec. com., 1992—2003, sec., 1995—96, vice chair, 1997—99, chair, 1999—2001, chair nominating com., 2002—03; adv. bd. Nat. Multiple Sclerosis Found., 1988—90, Soc. Progressive Supranuclear Palsy, 1991—94; nat. adv. eye coun. sensory and motor disorders vision panel NIH, 1980—83; steering com. neurological disorders in comml. drivers U.S. Dept. Transp., chmn. task force, 1987; lectr. T.S. Srinivasan Endowment, Madras, India, 1994; Cumings lectr. Migraine Trust, London, 1994; lectr. Am. Coun. Headache Edn., 1996, vice chair, 2000—02; Soriano lectr., 2001; prof. (hon.) Astana-State Med. Acad., Kazakhstan, 1999; bd. advisors Capnia, Inc., 2000—. Book rev. editor: Neuro-ophthalmology, 1981-86, mem. editl. bd., 1987-2003; assoc. editor Jour. Biomed. Sys., 1970-72; editor Neurol. Progress, Anns. Neurology, 1981-84; editor-in-chief Neurology, 1987-96, sci. integrity adv., 2004-; co-editor World Neurology, 1991-98, editl. adv. bd. 1998—2003; mem. editl. bd. Archives of Neurology, 1976, Annals of Neurology, 1977-86, Neurology and Neurosurgery Update Series, 1978-93, Headache, 1980-86, sr. edit. advisor, 2004-; Contemporary Neurology Series, 1989-93, Neurosci., Saudi Arabia, 2003—, Practical Neurology, 2003—; mem. editl. coun. Neurologia Croatica, 1991—; mem. editl. com. Valeology, Kazakhstan, 2002-05; contbr. articles to profl. jours. Chmn. Young Tae Kwon Do Acad., North Miami, 1977-80; bd. dirs. Benign Essential Blepharospasm Rsch. Found., 1983-; trustee Fairhill Ctr. for Aging, 1988—, The Learning Corp., 1992-2000, Edison Bio Tech. Ctr., 1994-2001, Great Lakes Sci. Ctr., 1994-2001, Myasthenia Gravis Found. Am., 1999-2001; mem. tech. adv. coun. BIOMEC, Inc., 1999-; bd. trustees Greater Cleve. chpt. ARC, 1999-2005, mem. exec. com., 2000-03; mem. cmty. bd. St. Vincent Charity Hosp., 2003-, St. John West Shore Hosp., 2003-. With USAR, 1965—67. Recipient Ernst Jung-Medaille Für Medizin in Gold, 1993, Silver Jubilee Oration award Med. Coll. Trivandrum, India, 1994, John H. Budd Disting. Mem. award Cleve. Acad. Med., 2002, Disting. Grad. award U. Pa., 2003, Lifetime Achievement awaed, Neurisciences India Group, 2005. Fellow: Am. Headache Soc. (pres. 2002—04, bd. dirs., sec., John R. Graham Svc. Clin. Forum award 2005); mem.: AMA, Eastern Mediterranean Association of Med. Editors, World Assn. Med. Editors, Internat. Headache Soc., Neuromuscular Disease Assn. Romania (internat. sci. com. 1991—93), Acad. Med. Scis. Kazakhstan, Alliance Brain Initiatives (founding mem.), Dana Found., Asociación Colombiana Neurologia (hon.), Am. Neurol. Assn. (hon.); program adv. com. 1977—78, chmn. 1978, councillor 1980—82, membership adv. com. 1980—83, chmn. 1981—83, nominating com. 1984, chmn. Annals of Neurology oversight com. 1984—86, sec. 1985—89, pres.-elect 1989—90, pres. 1990—91, past pres. 1991—92), Am. Acad. Neurology (hon.; chmn. sci. program com. 1973—75, exec. bd. 1987—96, Netter lectr. 1989, pub. com. 1993—2001), Coun. Sci. Editors, World Fedn. Neurology (fin. com. 1985—, exec. com. Rsch. group on Neuro-Ophthalmology 1987—95, publs. com. 1987—, chmn. 1990—2001), Clin. Eye Movement Soc. (founder), Barany Soc., Internat. Neuro-Ophthalmology Soc. (organizing com. 1986), N.Am. Neuro-Ophthalmology Soc. (bd. dirs. 1986—94, chair cert. and accreditation com. 1997—98, publs. com. 1999—2001), Rocky Mountain Neuro-Ophthalmology Soc. (bd. dirs. 1980—86), Vietnam Vets Inst. (bd. scholars 1998—, eastern med. Assn. med. editors, ethics and scientific misconduct com. 2005, united coun. of neurolgic subspecialists, alternate dir. 2005—), Alpha Omega Alpha. Office: CASE Sch Medicine 10900 Euclid Ave Rm T101 Cleveland OH 44106-4994 Business E-Mail: rbd2@case.edu.

DA ROSA, ALISON, travel editor; Travel editor San Diego Union-Tribune. Office: San Diego Union-Tribune 350 Camino De La Reina San Diego CA 92108-3003

DARR, ALAN PHIPPS, curator, historian; b. Kankakee, Ill., Sept. 30, 1948; s. Milton Freeman, Jr. and Margaret (Phipps) D.; m. Mollie Hayden Fletcher, June 28, 1980; children: Owen, Alexander. BA, Northwestern U., 1970; MA, Inst. Fine Arts, NYU, 1975, PhD in Art History, 1980; Cert., Mus. Tng., Met. Mus. Art, 1976, Mus. Mgmt. Inst., U. Calif. Berkeley, 1980. Grad. intern Met. Mus. Art, NYC, 1976; instr. NYU, 1976; asst. curator Detroit Inst. Arts, 1978-80, assoc. curator, 1980-81, curator in charge European sculpture and decorative arts, 1981—, Walter B. Ford II Family curator European sculpture and decorative arts, 1997—; postdoctoral fellow Harvard U. Ctr. for Italian Renaissance Studies at Villa I Tatti, Florence, 1988-89; adj. prof. Wayne State U., Detroit, 1982—; Paul Mellon vis. sr. scholar Ctr. Advanced Study in Visual Arts, Nat. Gallery, Washington, 1994. Co-editor/co-author: Italian Renaissance Sculpture in the Time of Donatello, 1985-86, Donatello Studien, 1989, Verrocchio and Late Quattrocentro Italian Sculpture, 1992, The Dodge Collection of Eighteenth Century French and English Art in the Detroit Institute of Arts, 1996, Woven Splendor: Five Centuries of European Tapestry in the Detroit Institute of Arts, 1996, Catalogue of Italian Sculpture in the Detroit Inst. of Arts, 2 vols., 2002, The Medici, Michelangelo and the Art of Late Renaissance Florence, 2002, Large Bronzes in the Renaissance, Studies in the History of Art, vol. 64, Nat. Gallery of Art, 2003, others; contbr. articles to profl. jours. Nat. Endowment Arts Mus. Profls. Fellow, 1983; John J. McCloy fellow, 1980-81, Ford Found. fellow, 1975-78, Met. Mus. Art fellow, 1975. Office: Detroit Inst Arts 5200 Woodward Ave Detroit MI 48202-4094

DARR, ANN RUSSELL, poet, educator; b. Bagley, Iowa, Mar. 13, 1920; d. Henry Horton and Lessie Rebecca (Hooper) Russell; m. George Campbell Darr, Nov. 7, 1941 (div. Mar. 1981); children: Elizabeth Russell, Deborah Horton, Shannon Campbell. BA magna cum laude, State U. Iowa, 1941; postgrad., Harvard Coll., 1980, Am. U., 1981. Writer/actor NBC Radio, N.Y.C., 1941-43, 45-46; tape recs. for blind Libr. of Congress, Washington, 1950-60; instr. creative writing Poets in the Schs., Md., Va. and D.C., 1970-80, 92-93; co-dir. workshop Nethers (Va.) Arts Colony, 1979; poet/dir. Georgetown U., Washington, summer 1977-78; poet The Writers Ctr., Bethesda, Md., 1981—; adj. prof. dept. lit. Am. U., Washington, 1982—. Fine arts seminar poet Montgomery (Ala.) Seminars, summer 1975; poet-in-residence Columbia (S.C.) Coll., spring 1975, 76, Am. Wind Symphony aboard Point Counterpoint II, U.S., 1976, 86, Jamaica, 1981, Europe, 1989, Eckard Coll., St. Petersburg, Fla., spring 1977; workshop poet St. Mary's (Md.) Coll., spring 1981, 82, 94, 95, 98, 99; judge for poetry Eckerd Coll., St. Petersburg, Fla., 1977, Nat. Endowment for Arts, Washington, 1979, Radcliff Coll., Cambridge, Mass., 1980, New Eng. Poetry Soc., Boston, 1981; mem. lit. panel Nat. Endowment for Arts, 1979-80; mem. adv. com. Folger Libr. Poetry Series, Washington, 1974-96. Author: St. Ann's Gut, 1971, The Myth of a Woman's Fist, 1973, Cleared for Landing, 1978, Riding with the Fireworks, 1981, Do You Take This Woman..., 1986 (Pub. award 1986), The Twelve Pound Cigarette, 1991, Confessions of a Skewed Romantic, 1993, Flying the Zuni Mountains, 1994, Gussie, Mad Hannah & Me, 1999, Love In the Past Tense, 2000; editor: Hungry As We Are, 1995; author numerous poems, 1961-99; translator (with others) Reading the Ashes, 1978, (with others) After the First Rain, 1997; featured poet Nat. Mus. Radio and TV, 1997. Mem. election com. Somerset (Md.) Town Bd., 1975-79; vol. Arena Stage, Washington, 1949-52. With U.S. Army Airforce (Women's Airforce Svc. pilot), 1943-44, WWII. Recipient Bunting fellowship Radcliffe Coll., 1979-80, Discovery 70 award Poetry Ctr., N.Y.C., 1970, Yaddo fellowship Yaddo, 1979, 86, MacDowell fellowship MacDowell Found., 1979. Mem. White House Conf. for Poets, Poetry Soc. Am., Acad. Am. Poets, Phi Beta Kappa, Zeta Phi Eta. Avocations: flying, travel, acting, reading, collecting birds. Office: Am Univ 4400 Massachusetts Ave NW Washington DC 20016-8001 Home: Apt 803 900 N Lake Shore Dr Chicago IL 60611-1530

DARR, JAMES DANIEL, poet; b. Casper, Wyo., Jan. 29, 1980; life ptnr. JoAnn Marie Lehmann; 1 child, Taryn Sue Olson. Author: Poetry's New Leash on life, Path of Vampiric Verse, Poetry of the Soul, Search for Answers. Home: 809 W 10th Casper WY 82601

DARR, WALTER ROBERT, financial analyst; b. Phila., June 19, 1956; s. John Fluke, Sr. and Lois Marilyn (Fry) Darr. BS in Commerce, Rider U., Lawrenceville, N.J., 1978, MBA, 1991. Collateral analyst First Nat. Bank & Trust Co., Beverly, NJ, 1978-84, First Peoples Bank N.J., Westmont, 1984-88, loan rev. analyst, 1988-92; loan acctg. tech. N.J. Nat. Bank, Trenton, 1992-93; sr. credit analyst Carnegie Bank, N.A., Princeton, NJ, 1993-94, asst. cashier, sr. credit analyst, 1994-97; credit officer, credit dept. supr. Broad Nat./Independence Cmty. Bank, Newark, 1997-99; asst. sec., bus. banking divsn. Ind. Cmty. Bank, Newark, 1999-2000, asst. v.p. SBA lending, 2001—; sr. underwriter, bus. banking div. Summit Bank, Dayton, NJ, 2000-2001. Treas. Cinnaminson (N.J.) Bapt. Ch., 1983—87, deacon, 1988—89, 1993—94; chmn.-treas. Mercer County chpt. Child Evangelism Fellowship N.J., 1996—99; mem. Lewis Shearer Chorale/Garden State Chorale, NJ, 1982—94. Recipient Sch. award, Am. Legion Post, Medford, N.J., 1974. Mem.: Rider U. Alumni Assn. (bd. dirs. 2002—, sec. 2003—05), Gideons (camp pres. Mercer West, NJ 2002—05, pres. 2002—05, camp sec. 2005—). Republican. Baptist. Avocations: classic cars, bicycling, classical music, Victorian architecture. Home: 107 Manlove Ave Apt E-B Hightstown NJ 08520-3234 Office: Independence Community Bank 909 Broad St Newark NJ 07102 Personal E-mail: wdarr56@aol.com. Business E-Mail: wdarr@icbny.com.

DARRELL, EVELYN BOYDEN, psychologist, educator; b. Spring Lake, N.J. d. John and Ethel (Notis) Boyden; m. Thomas E. Darrell, Sept. 4, 1954 (div. Oct. 1972); 1 child, Michele Ann (dec.). AB, NYU, 1959, MA, PhD, 1961; hon. degree, Hamilton State Coll., 1970. Lic. psychologist, N.J., lic. sch. psychologist, N.J.; cert. tchr. psychology, N.J.; cert. neuropsychologist. Supr. testing Testing and Advisement Ctr., NYU, 1960-63, psychometrist, 1960-61; intern psychologist Bellevue Psychiat. Hosp., 1963-64; teaching asst. psychology dept. Grad. Sch. Edn. NYU, 1964-65; clin. psychologist charge adolescent girls svc. Bellvue Hosp., 1964—; rsch. assoc. charge testing NYU, 1966—; supervising clin. psychologist, clin. instr. dept. psychiatry NYU Med. Sch., 1968—. Clin. therapist, cons. St. Barnabas House, N.Y.C., 1974-76; cons. N.Y. State Office Vocat. Rehab., 1980-82, Diabetic Rsch. Project, N.Y. Med. Coll., Cornell U.; mem. child placement rev. bd. Superior Ct. N.J., 1981—. Contbr. articles to profl. jours. Del. Cen. Labor Coun., Dist. Coun. 37 AFL-CIO, mem. exec. bd. city psychologists local; bd. dirs. Montclair-N. Essex YWCA, 1973-88. Recipient Role Model award Coalition of 100 Black Women N.J., 1983, Cert. of Merit Superior Ct. Essex County, 1984. Mem. NAACP (sec. 1955-56, bicentennial chair 1963, Am. Psychol. Assn., Assn. Black Psychologists (treas. N.J. chpt. 1967-70), Iota Phi Lambda (pres. Phi chpt. 1966-69, Ea. region journalist 1972-74). Presbyterian. Avocations: writing, calligraphy. Home: 36 Hawthorne Pl Montclair NJ 07042-3229 Office: NYU Bellevue Med Ctr 1st Ave New York NY 10009

DARRELL, NORRIS, JR., lawyer; b. Berlin, May 10, 1929; s. Norris and Doris Clare (Williams) D. (parents Am. citizens); m. Henriette Maria Haid, July 31, 1962; 1 child, Andrew. AB, Harvard U., 1951, LL.B. cum laude, 1954. Bar: N.Y. 1955, U.S. Supreme Ct. 1965. Assoc. Sullivan & Cromwell, N.Y.C., 1956-65, ptnr., 1965-92, sr. ptnr. European office Paris, 1968-71, sr. counsel, 1993—. Bd. dirs. Lumina Found. for Edn., Inc., Indpls., Ind. Trustee Cold Spring Harbor Lab., Inc., 1974-81, United Student Aid Funds, Inc., Fishers, Ind., 1974-94, USA Group Inc., Fishers, Ind., 1993-2000, East Woods Sch., Oyster Bay, N.Y., 1974-79; hon. trustee Heckscher Mus., Huntington, N.Y. With U.S. Army, 1954-56. Fellow Am. Bar Found.; mem. Am. Law Inst., ABA, Assn. Bar City N.Y., Harvard Club N.Y., Pilgrims Club, River Club (bd. govs. 1978-98), Cold Spring Harbor Beach Club, Edgartown Yacht Club. Home: 44 Walnut Tree Ln Cold Spring Harbor New York NY 11724 Personal E-mail: norrisd482@aol.com.

DARROW, ARTHUR LLOYD, management consultant, educator; b. Anamosa, Iowa, Feb. 5, 1947; s. Lloyd S. and Thelma Cook Darrow; m. Susan Davenport Darrow, Nov. 9, 1980; children: Anne Clark, Paul Saver, Thomas I.A. BA, U. No. Iowa, 1969; MBA, Ctrl. Mo. State U., 1974; PhD, U. Iowa, 1982. Prof. mgmt. Bowling Green State U., Ohio, 1980—. Cons., prin. Orgn. and Change Mgmt. Specialist, Bowling Green, Ohio, 1980—. Author: (book) Managing Work Related Stress, 1994, The Duh Factor, 2005. Founding mgr. Bowling Green Symphony, Ohio, 2000; campaign advisor Darrow for Congress, Ohio, 1998. Capt. USAF, 1969—74. Mem.: Acad. Mgmt., Orgn. Devel. Network. Democrat. Unitarian-Universalist. Avocations: martial arts, guitar building, golf. Home: 1014 Partridge Ln Bowling Green OH 43402 Office: Bowling Green State Univ Dept Mgmt Bowling Green OH 43403

DARROW, EMILY M., public relations executive, writer; b. Kingston, N.Y., Sept. 21, 1964; d. H. Van Wyck and Marianne Darrow; m. Brendon Paul McCrane, Oct. 5, 2002. Student, Vassar Coll., 1983—84; BA, Hunter Coll., 1989; postgrad., Inst. of FIne Arts, NYU, 1992. Mus. mgr., edn. mgr. Hist. Hudson Valley-Montgomery Pl., Annandale-on-Hudson, NY, 1995; dir. pub. rels. and promotions Mohonk Mountain Ho., New Paltz, NY, 1997—98; pub. rels. assoc. Bard Coll., Annandale-on-Hudson, 1998—; asst. to exec. dir. Inst. Advanced Theology Bard Coll., Annandale-on-Hudson, 2001—. Rschr. Salander O'Reilly Gallery-Stuart Davis Catalogue Raisonne Project, N.Y.C., 1989—90; writer, rschr. Art Commn. City of N.Y., 1989—90; internship in pub. rels. Opera Garnier de Paris-Paris Opera Ballet, Paris, 1990—91, N.Y.C. Ballet, 1982—84; cons., writer Vikarmasila Found., N.Y.C., 1999—; mem. Woodstock Arts Bd., 2004—. Mem. Woodstock (N.Y.) Arts Bd., 2004—. Recipient Zabar grad. scholarship, Hunter Coll., 1989; fellow Leon Levy and Shelby White, Inst. of Fine Arts/NYU, 1990. Mem.: Coll. Art Assn. and Pub. Rels. Soc. Am., Jr. League Kingston (rec. sec. 1991—96, pub. rels. dir. 1991—96). Home: 250 Morton Rd Rhinebeck NY 12572 Office: Bard Coll Annandale Hotel Annandale On Hudson NY 12504 Personal E-mail: EMDarrow87@alum.vassar.edu.

DARROW, JILL E(LLEN), lawyer; b. NYC, Jan. 6, 1954; d. Milton and Elaine (Sklarin) D.; m. Michael V.P. Marks, May 14, 1987. AB in English, Barnard Coll., 1975; JD, U. Pa., 1978; LLM in Tax Law, NYU, 1983. Bar: Pa. 1978, NY 1979, US Tax Ct. 1982. Assoc. Shearman & Sterling, NYC, 1978-79, Rosenman & Colin, NYC, 1979-86, ptnr., 1987—2002, Katten Muchin Rosenman LLP, NYC, 2002—. Mem. ABA, NY State Bar Assn., Pa. Bar Assn., Phi Beta Kappa. Home: 300 Central Park W New York NY 10024 Office: Katten Muchin Rosenman LLP 575 Madison Ave Fl 12 New York NY 10022-2511 Office Phone: 212-940-7113. Business E-Mail: jill.darrow@kattenlaw.com.

DARROW, KURT L., manufacturing executive; BA, Adrian U. V.p. sales La-Z-Boy Inc., 1987—99, sr. v.p., sales & marketing, 1999—2001, pres., residential div., 2001—03, pres., CEO, 2003—. Office: La Z Boy Inc 1248 N Telegraph Rd Monroe MI 48162*

DARROW, MARIANNE ROSINA, speech pathology/audiology services professional, editor, writer; b. Kingston, N.Y., Dec. 11, 1925; d. Burton Jacob and Mary Anne Davis; m. H. Van Wyck Darrow, Jr., Nov. 24, 1963 (dec. July 1998); 1 child, Emily Marika. BA in English/Social Studies/Drama cum laude, SUNY, Albany, 1946; MA in Speech/Drama, Columbia U., 1952. Lic. speech-lang. pathologist N.Y., tchr. speech/hearing handicapped N.Y. Copywriter trainee J. Walter Thompson, N.Y.C., 1946—47; dancer Pitts. Ligth Opera Co., 1947, Touring Co., 1947—48; soc. editor Kingston (N.Y.) Daily Freeman, 1953—55; entertainment editor Ulster County Townsman, Woodstock, NY; pre-doctoral assoc. U. Wash. Speech and Hearing Clinic, Seattle, 1957—60; speech and hearing tchr. Kingston City Schs. Consol., 1960—64; speech-lang. pathologist Cerebral Palsy Ctr., Kingston, 1962, therapist, 1967—69; cons. Benedictine and Kingston Hosps., Kingston, 1967—72; speech cons. Ten Broeck Commons, Ulster, 2001—02; with Hutton Nursing Home, Kingston, 2002—03; speech cons. Ulster-Greene ARC, Kingston, NY. Actor: Coach House Players, 1951, Woodstock Playhouse, 1951; contbr. articles to profl. jours., to mags. including The Citizen, Antique Living. Chair pers. com. Kingston City Sch. Bd., 1970—75; founder pres. coun. PTA; chair environ. project group Against Spraying Pesticides, Hurley, 1993—; founder, mem. prevention group Benedictine Hosp., 1995; dir. entertainment Sapporo, Japan, Nurnberg, Germany, 1948—50. Named Citizen Adv. of Yr., Mid-Hudson Options Project, Inc., 2001. Mem.: AAUW, N.Y. State Speech Hearing Lang. Assn., Am. Speech/Lang./Hearing Assn., Hillside Acres Garden Club. Avocations: gardening, swimming, travel, lecturing. Home: 436 Old Rt 209 Hurley NY 12443

DARROW, WILLIAM RICHARD, retired pharmaceutical company executive, consultant; b. Middletown, Ohio, 1939; s. Richard William and Nelda D.; m. Janet Elizabeth Swan, 1964; children: James William, Susan Elizabeth, Margaret Ellen. BA, Ohio Wesleyan U., 1960; MD, Western Res. U., 1964; PhD in Pharmacology, Case-Western Res. U., 1969. Intern Univ. Hosps., Cleve., 1964; sr. clin. rsch. assoc. CIBA Pharm. Co., 1969, asst. dir. clin. pharmacology, 1969—70; dir. clin. pharmacology CIBA-GEIGY Corp., 1970—75, exec. dir. clin. rsch., 1975—76; sr. v.p. rsch., med. dir. Wallace Labs. divsn. Carter Wallace, Inc., Cranbury, NJ, 1976—80; med. dir. Schering Labs. divsn. Schering-Plough Corp., Kenilworth, NJ, 1980; v.p. med. and regulatory affairs Schering-Plough Rsch., Kenilworth, 1981—82; sr. v.p. med. ops. Schering-Plough Corp., Kenilworth, 1982—94, sr. med. advisor, 1994—2003; ret., 2003. Bd. dirs. AltaRex Corp., 2001-02; chmn. rsch. com. N.J. Health Scis. Group, 1973-76, mem. exec. com., 1973-74, 76-86, treas., 1977-80, v.p., 1980-86; mem. Bernards Twp. Bd. Health, 1979-93, v.p., 1980, pres., 1981-85, 86-93; chmn. Bernards Twp. Deer Study Task Force/ Deer Mgmt. Adv. Com., 1999—; bd. dirs. N.J. chpt. Arthritis Found., 1990-2004, exec. com., 1991-2004, vice chmn., 1995-97, chmn. bd. dirs., 1997-2001, past chmn., 2001-04; bd. dirs. Pharm. Ednl. and Rsch. Inst., 1993-2000, chmn. curriculum com., 1993-95; bd. dirs. Junior Achievement No. N.J., 1996; mem. sci. adv. bd. Clin. Rsch. Ctr. Robert Wood Johnson Med. Ctr., 1990-2000; mem. U.S. del. Internat. Conf. on Harmonization, 1991-99; mem. N.J. State Adv. Coun. on Arthritis, 2000-05. Recipient Roche award, 1962, Humanitarian of Yr. award Arthritis Found. N.J., 1994; USPHS postdoctoral fellow, 1965-69. Fellow: Royal Soc. Medicine, Am. Acad. Pharm. Physicians (life); mem.: AMA, Pharm. Rsch. Mfrs. Am. Found. (sci. adv. bd. 1990—, chmn. 1994—, chief sci. advisor 1997—), Pharm. Rsch. Mfrs. Am. (steering com. med. sect. 1984—96, program chmn. 1988—89, vice-chmn. 1989—90, chmn. 1990—92, past chmn. 1992—96), Drug Info. Assn., Lakeside Country Club (Penn Yan, N.Y.), Basking Ridge (N.J.) Country Club, Pi Delta Epsilon, Omicron Delta Kappa, Phi Rho Sigma, Phi Gamma Delta. Republican. Presbyterian.

DARSCH, NANCY, former professional basketball coach; b. Plymouth, Mass., 1951; BS, Springfield (Mass.) Coll., 1973. Coach Longmeadow (Mass.) H.S.; asst. coach U. Tenn., 1978-85; coach Ohio State U., 1985-97; head coach N.Y. Liberty, WNBA, 1997-98, Washington Mystics, WNBA, 1998—2000; asst. coach Minn. Lynx, 2003—. Coach U.S.A. Olympic trials, 1980, 88, U.S.A. Pan Am. Games trials, 1979, 83; head coach U.S.A. Jr. Nat. basketball team, 1990; asst. coach U.S. Olympic team, 1984, 96.*

DARSEY, JEROME ANTHONY (JERRY DARSEY), chemistry professor, consultant; b. Houma, La., Aug. 26, 1946; s. Elmer Joseph and Arline (Houghton) D.; m. Patricia Ann Bukowski, June 10, 1989; children: Brittany Angéle, Joseph Anthony, Mary Catherine. BS in Physics, La. State U., 1970, PhD in Chemistry, 1982. Asst. prof. chemistry and physics Gordon Coll. U. Ga. System, Barnsville, 1983-84; asst. prof. Tarleton State U./Tex. A&M U., Stephenville, Tex., 1984-88, assoc. prof., 1988-90; asst. prof. U. Ark., Little Rock, 1990-93, assoc. prof., 1993-96, prof., 1996—. Univ. scholar natural scis. Tarleton State U., Tex. A&M U., 1989-90; cons. Oak Ridge (Tenn.) Nat. Lab., 1990-95; co-chmn. 1st workshop neural network applications to material scis. Dept. Energy, 1994; chmn. 1st APS Symposium on Applications of Artificial Neural Networks to Chemical Systems; invited lectr. 21st Australian Polymer Symposium, 1996. Contbr. scientific papers to profl. jours. Named Outstanding Univ. Rschr., U. Ark., Little Rock, 1995, Outstanding Rschr. Coll. Sci. and Math., 1995, 2000; grantee Am. Chem. Soc., 1986, 90, NSF, 1992, 96, NASA, 1994-2001. Fellow AAAS; mem. Am. Chem. Soc. (chmn. Ark. sect. 1993), Am. Phys. Soc., Ark. Acad. Sci., S.W. Theoretical Chemistry Conf. (chmn. 1986-87), Tex. Acad. Sci. (vice chmn. chemistry divsn. 1986-87, chmn. 1987-88). Achievements include patents in field. Home: 1514 Alberta Dr Little Rock AR 72227-5803 Office: U Ark Dept Chemistry 2801 S University Ave Dept Little Rock AR 72204-1099 Office Phone: 501-569-8828. E-mail: jadarsey@ualr.edu.

DARST, BETTY JANE, historian, educator, dramatist; b. Columbus Grove, Ohio, Nov. 11, 1939; d. Edward and Mary Naomi Foulkes; m. John F. Darst, Dec. 17, 1993; children: Janet Moore, Diana Veid, Glenn Geiger. BS in Edn., Ohio No. U., 1960; cert. specialist media, Ohio U., 1979; MEd, U. Dayton, 1985. Social studies tchr. North Plainfield (N.J.) H.S., Greenhills-Forest Park City Schs.; media specialist West Muskingum Mid. Sch.; coord. media svcs. Franklin City Schs., 1980-89; supr. ednl. media Springfield (Ohio) City Sch. Dists., 1989—2002; pvt. practice Dayton, Ohio, 2003—. Adj. faculty Wright State U., 2003—; leader nat. workshop in children's lit.; presenter in field. Co-author: Speaking of Flying, 2000; creator: (video) Tour of Home: Wright Brothers; contbr. articles to profl. jours. Mem. Lima City Bd. Edn., 1976; pres. Greater Miami Valley Ednl. Tech., 1992-94; bd. dirs. Aviation Trail, Friendship Force, First to Fly Found.; mem. Wright Rsch. Com., Speaker Bur.- Ohio Humanities Coun. Mem. ALA, AASL, Phi Delta Kappa. Methodist. Achievements include listed as leading aviation performer. Avocation: living history presentations. Home: 2423 Brown Bark Dr Dayton OH 45431 Office Phone: 937-426-8114. E-mail: betty.darst@wright.edu.

DARST, DAVID MARTIN, investment banker, educator, writer; b. Knoxville; s. Guy Bewley and Susan Mary (McGinnis) Darst; m. Diane Wassman; children: Elizabeth Mathews, David Martin. BA, Yale U., 1969; MBA, Harvard U., 1971. Assoc. Goldman, Sachs & Co., N.Y.C., 1971-75, v.p., mgr., 1981—, v.p., resident mgr. Zurich, Switzerland, 1975-81, CFO global equities divsn., 1991—96; mng. dir. Morgan Stanley, N.Y.C., 1996—; founding pres. Morgan Stanley Investment Group, 1998—; dir. Morgan Stanley Trust Co., 1999—. Vis. lectr. Coll. and Sch. Mgmt., Yale U., New Haven, 1981—, Bus. Sch., Harvard U., Boston, 1987—. Author: The Complete Bond Book, 1975, The Handbook of the Bond and Money Markets, 1981, The Art of Asset Allocation, 2003, Mastering the Art of Asset Allocation, 2005; contbr. articles to profl. jours. Bd. dirs. Deer Park Assn., 1985—, pres., 1989—; bd. dirs. Can.-U.S. Found. Ednl. Exch., 1996—, Studetn Sponsor Partnership, 2002—; bd. profl. adv. N.Y.C. Ballet, 1997—; corp. adv. bd. Sch. Am. Ballet, N.Y.C., 2002—. William H. Donaldson Disting. Faculty fellow, Sch. Mgmt. Yale U., 1986—87. Mem.: Assn. Internat. Bond Dealers (mem. edn. com.), Yale Alumni Assn. Greenwich (bd. dirs. 1996—), Phelps Assn. (v.p., gov. 1974—), Yale Club N.Y.C. (coun. 1987—, chmn. fin. com. 1987—), Money Marketeers. Office: Morgan Stanley 4th Fl 1221 Ave of the Americas New York NY 10020-1001

DART, DEBORAH GORDON, artist; b. Princeton, N.J., Oct. 1, 1951; d. Henry Ward and Joyce V. (Switzgable) Gordon; m. John McRae Dart, Dec. 1, 1973; children: Sara M., Alexandra G. Student, Phila. Coll. Art, 1968—69, U. Miami, 1970—71, Ringling Sch. Art, 1971—73. Freelance artist, Sarasota, Fla., 1972—86, 1995—; contractor Renovation/Rehab. of Hist. and Non-Hist. Homes, Sarasota, 1983—91; v.p. John Ringling Ctr. Found., Sarasota, 1991—95. Illustrations published in New Yorker Mag., Bon Appetit Mag., Yankee Mag. Bd. dirs. City of Sarasota Hist. Preservation Bd., 1989-95, chair, 1992; bd. dirs. Sarasota County Hist. Commn., 1991-93; mem. Sarasota Alliance for Hist. Preservation, v.p., 1987—; mem. Hist. Soc. Sarasota County, v.p., 1986—; mem. Rosemary Cemetery Project, chair, vice chair, 1986-90; mem. Fla. Trust for Hist. Preservation, 1990-96, Preservation Action, 1994-96, Nat. Trust Hist. Preservation, 1990-96. Avocation: historic preservation activist. E-mail: artist@dagdart.com.

DART, JOHN SEWARD, journalist, writer; b. Peekskill, N.Y., Aug. 1, 1936; s. Seward Homer and Vella Marion (Haverstock) D.; m. Gloria Joan Walker, Aug. 31, 1957; children— Kim, John W., Randall, Christopher. BA, U. Colo., 1958. Staff writer UPI, Indpls. and L.A., 1961-65; sci. writer Calif. Inst. Tech., Pasadena, 1966-67; religion writer L.A. Times, 1967-98; news editor Christian Century mag., 2000—. Author: The Laughing Savior, 1976, The Jesus of Heresy and History, rev., expanded edit., 1988, Decoding Mark, 2003; co-author: Unearthing the Lost Words of Jesus, 1998; contbr. reports for Freedom Forum First Amendment Ctr., Vanderbilt U. Served with U.S. Army, 1958-61 Recipient Supple Meml. award Religion Newswriters Assn., 1980, Merrell Meml. award Jim Merrell Religion Liberty Found., 1980, William F. Leidt award Episcopal Ch., 1980, Angel award Religion in Media, 1985, News Reporting award Am. Acad. Religion, 2004; NEH fellow Stanford U., 1973-74, First Amendment Ctr. fellow Vanderbilt U., 1992-93. Mem. Soc. Profl. Journalists (chpt. pres. 1976), Religion Newswriters Assn. (pres. 1990-92), Soc. Bibl. Lit. (mem.-at-large exec. com. Pacific Coast region 1990-95). Home and Office: 12122 Bowmore Ave Northridge CA 91326-1002

DART, KENNETH, food container manufacturing executive; Pres., CEO Dart Container Corp., Mason, Mich. Office: Dart Container Corp 500 Hogsback Rd Mason MI 48854-9547

DARTER, JEFFREY ALLEN, data processing professional; b. Wichita, Kans., Jan. 31, 1958; s. Richard J. Darter and Elizabeth (Cannady) Baumgartner; m. Karen Darlene Dees; 1 child, Stephanie Elizabeth. Student, Palm Beach Atlantic Coll., 1976-79. Installer Teleprompter Cable TV, West Palm Beach, Fla., 1979-80, technician, 1980-83; prodn. coord. Group W Cable, West Palm Beach, 1983-84; coord. Palm-Comm Cable, Lake Worth, Fla., 1984-85; dir. engring. Palm Comm Cable, Lake Worth, Fla., 1985-87; branch mgr. Telesat Cablevision, Lake Worth, 1987-88; systems analyst RMS, 1988-91; info. tech. mgr. Palm Beach County Supr. Elections Office, 1991—. Assoc. info. tech. mgr. Broadcast Profls. Forum of Compuserve Computer Svc., Columbus, Ohio, 1986—87; cons. Palm Beach County Pub. Access, West Palm Beach, 1987—, West Palm Beach Pvt. Sch., 1987—91; mem. voter registration tech. adv. group, 2001—; chmn. Sequoia Customer Devel. Com., 2003—. Mem. com. Palm Beach Jr. Coll., West Palm Beach, 1986-87. Recipient Outstanding Citizen award Town of Palm Beach, Fla., 1984, Oracle Master certification Oracle Corp., 1993. Mem. Soc. Cable TV Engrs. Avocations: music, computers, photography. Office: Palm Beach County Elections 240 S Military Trl West Palm Beach FL 33415 E-mail: jdarter@hotmail.com.

DARTER, THOMAS EUGENE, JR., composer, musician, writer; b. Livermore, Calif., Feb. 13, 1949; s. Thomas Eugene and Vivian Lorene Darter; m. Sibyl Heishman, Dec. 3, 1977 (div. Feb. 1992); children: Erika Borges, Lisa, Allana; m. Karen Lucille Hogan, Sept. 21, 1996. BA summa cum laude, Cornell U., 1969, MFA, 1972, D in Musical Arts, 1979. Instr. music theory and composition Roosevelt U., Chgo., 1972-75; editor Keyboard Mag., Cupertino, Calif., 1975-85, mng. editor, 1991-94, editor San Mateo, Calif., 1994-97, pub., 1997-98; editor AfterTouch Mag., Buena Park, Calif., 1986-89; engring. publs. mgr. Coactive Networks, Sausalito, Calif., 2000-01; freelance musician, writer, 1998—. Dir. contemporary music ensemble Roosevelt U., Chgo., 1972-75; lectr. music/film dept. U. So. Calif., L.A., 1984-88; consulting editor Keyboard Mag., Cupertino, 1990-91. Composer, pianist Scatter: Manring Kassin Darter Live in San Francisco, 2002; arranger Monk Suite (Kronos Quartet), 1985, Music of Bill Evans (Kronos Quartet), 1986. 1st prize Nat. Fedn. Music Clubs, 1969, 71. Mem. Am. Fedn. Musicians, Phi Beta Kappa, Phi Kappa Phi. Home: 750 South L St Livermore CA 94550

DARVAROVA, ELMIRA, musician, concertmaster; b. Bulgaria; came to U.S., 1986; MusB, State Conservatory, Sofia, Bulgaria, 1977, MusM, 1979; certificate, Guildhall Sch. Music, London, 1982; artist's diploma, Ind. U., 1987. Concertmaster Plovdiv (Bulgaria) Philharm. Orch., 1979-86, Owensboro (Ky.) Symphony Orch., 1986-88, Evansville (Ind.) Philharm., 1987-88; artistic dir., concertmaster Evansville Chamber Orch., 1987-88; assoc. instr. violin Ind. U. Sch. Music, Bloomington, 1986-88; acting concertmaster Rochester (N.Y.) Philharm., 1988. Vis. lectr. Ind. U. Sch. Mus., 1988; guest concertmaster Columbus Symphony Orch., Columbus, Ohio, 1988; concertmaster Met. Opera Orch., NYC, 1989-2002, Chgo. Grant Park Symphony, 1990-2003; founding mem. New World Trio, 1991; performer at various recitals and concerts throughout the world. Recipient 1st medal internat. competition, Barcelona, Spain, 1979, hon. diploma, prize Tchaikovsky competition, Moscow, 1982, silver medal Viotti internat. competition, Vercelli, Italy, 1984, 3d prize internat. competition, Sion, Switzerland, 1985. Achievements include first woman concertmaster in Metropolitan Opera history. Avocations: reading, languages.

DARVILL, ALAN G., biochemist, botanist, educator; b. Redditch, Worchester, U.K., Jan. 27, 1952; came to U.S., 1976; s. Bryan Richard and Pamela Mary Darvill; m. Janet Elizabeth Jones, July 12, 1975; 1 child, Sarah Jayne. BS in Plant Biology, Wolverhampton Poly., U.K., 1973; PhD in Plant Physiology, Univ. Coll. Wales, Aberystwyth, 1976. Postdoctoral assoc. U. Colo., Boulder, 1976—78, sr. rsch. assoc., 1978—83, asst. prof. dept. molecular, cellular and devel. biology, 1983—84, assoc. prof., 1984—85; assoc. prof. dept. biochemistry and plant biology U. Ga., Athens, 1985—87, prof., 1988—2003, Regents prof., 2003—, assoc. dir. Complex Carbohydrate Rsch. Ctr., 1985—87, dir., 1987—, co-dir. Ctr. for Plant & Microbial Complex Carbohydrates, 1987—. Adminstrv. dir. NIH/NCRR rsch. resource Integrated Glycotech, 1999—; adminstrv. dir. NIH/NCRR integrated tech. Biomed. Glyconics, 2004—. Contbr. more than 195 articles to profl. jours. Mem. AAAS, Am. Chem. Soc. (exec. com. divsn. carbohydrate chemistry 1993—, chmn. divsn. carbohydrate chemistry 1994-95), Soc. for Complex Carbohydrates. Office: U Ga Complex Carbohydrate Rsch Ctr 315 Riverbend Rd Athens GA 30602-4712

DARWIN, DAVID, engineering educator, consultant; b. NYC, Apr. 17, 1946; s. Samuel David and Earle D.; m. Diane Marie Mayer, June 29, 1968; children: Samuel David, Lorraine Marie. BS in Civil Engring., Cornell U., 1967, MS in Structural Engring., 1968; PhD in Civil Engring., U. Ill., 1974. Lic. profl. engr., Kans. Asst. prof. civil engring. U. Kans., Lawrence, 1974-77, assoc. prof., 1977-82, prof., 1982—, Deane E. Ackers disting. prof. civil engring., 1990—, dir. Structural Engring. and Materials Lab., 1982—; dir. Infrastructure Rsch. Inst., 1998-2001. Cons. David Darwin, Lawrence, 1976—. Author: Steel and Composite Beams with Web Openings, 1990; co-author: Concrete, 2d edit., 2003, Design of Concrete Structures, 13th edit., 2004; contbr. articles to profl. jours. Mem. Uniform Bldg. Code Bd. Appeals, Lawrence, 1978-84. Capt. U.S. Army, 1967-72, Vietnam. Decorated Bronze Star with oak leaf cluster; recipient Miller award, U. Kans., 1986, Irvin Youngberg Rsch. Achievement award, 1992, Civil and Environ. Engring. Alumni Assn. Disting. Alumnus award, U. Ill., 2003; grantee, NSF, 1976—2003, Kans. Dept. Transp., 1980—82, 1990—, Air Force Office Sci. Rsch., 1985—92, Civil Engring. Rsch. Found., 1991—95, Fed. Hwy. Adminstrn., 1994—98, 2001—, SD Dept. Transp., 2001—, Nat. Coop. Hwy. Rsch. Program, 1994—95; Bellows scholar, 2001, Miller scholar, 2004. Fellow ASCE (editor Jour. Structural Engring. 1994-00, bd. govs. Structural Engring. Inst. 2000-04, treas., 2003-04, Kans. sect. v.p., pres.-elect 2001-02, pres. 2002-03, Huber Rsch. prize 1985, Moisseiff award 1991, state-of-the-art of civil engring. award 1996, 2000, Richard R. Torrens award 1997), Am. Concrete Inst. (pres. Kans. chpt. 1975, bd. dirs. 1988-91, 05-, v.p. 2005-, exec. com. 2005-, Bloem Disting. Svc. award 1986, Arthur R. Anderson award for disting. rsch. 1992, Structural Rsch. award 1996, Joe W. Kelly award); mem. AAAS, ASTM (award of appreciation 2003), Am. Soc. Engring. Edn., Am. Inst. Steel Constrn. (profl.), Prestressed Concrete Inst. (profl.), Post-Tensioning Inst. (profl.), Concrete Rsch. Coun. (chmn. 1990-96), Structural Engring. Inst. (bd. govs. 2000-04, treas. 2003-04), Phi Kappa Phi (pres. U. Kans. chpt. 1976-78). Democrat. Unitarian Universalist. Achievements include development of standard method of design for structural steel and composite beams with web openings. Avocations: swimming, walking. Office: U Kans Civil Environ and Archtl Engring Dept 2142 Learned Hall 1530 W 15th St Lawrence KS 66045-7609 Office Phone: 785-864-3827. E-mail: daved@ku.edu.

DARZYNKIEWICZ, ZBIGNIEW D., research scientist; b. Dzisna, Poland, May 12, 1936; came to U.S., 1969; s. Boleslaw and Waclawa D.; m. Elizabeth, June 20, 1966; children: Richard, Robert. MD, Sch. Medicine, Warsaw, 1960, PhD, 1966. Resident 4th City Hosp., Warsaw, 1960-62; assoc. prof. Cornell U. Grad. Sch. Medicine Sci., N.Y.C., 1978-88, prof. cell biology & genetics, 1988-90; prof. pathology & medicine N.Y. Med. Coll., Valhalla, 1990—, dir. cancer rsch. inst., 1990—. Vis. scientist Nobel Med. Inst., Karolinska U., Stockholm, 1968-70; assoc. mem. Sloan Kettering Cancer Ctr., N.Y.C., 1978-88, mem., 1988-90; cons. NASA, Houston, 1987-92. Editor/co-author 12 books; contbr. over 470 articles to profl. jours., chpts. to books; patentee in field. Recipient NIH/NCI Merit award, Bethesda, Md., 1987. Mem. Polish Acadm Scis. Office: NY Med Coll Brander Cancer Rsch Inst 19 Bradhurst Ave Hawthorne NY 10532-2140 Business E-Mail: darzynk@nymc.edu.

DAS, ANANYA, gastroenterologist, researcher; m. Madhumita Sinha; 1 child, Amit. MD, Postgrad. Inst. Med. Edn. & Rsch., 1990. Intern, resident SUNY, 1994—96; fellow Case Western Res. U., Cleve.; chief sect. gastrointestinal endoscopy Cleve. VA Med. Ctr, 2002—. Contbr. articles to profl. jours. Recipient Rsch. excellence in Gastroenterology and Liver Diseases award, 2003. Fellow: ACP. Office: Divsn Gastroenterology CWRU 11100 Euclid Ave Cleveland OH 44106 E-mail: ananya.das@med.va.gov.

DAS, ASHOKE KUMAR, internist, consultant; b. Calcutta, W. Bengal, India, Nov. 1, 1934; came to U.S., 1974; s. Srikrishna and Durgeshnandini (Bose) D.; m. Geeta Mukhopadhyay, Aug. 15, 1961 (dec. 1993); 1 child, Arnab. MBBS, Calcutta U., 1957, MD, 1962, PhD, 1971. Diplomate Royal Coll. Physicians London, Am. Bd. Internal Medicine. Rotating intern NRS Med. Coll. Hosp., Calcutta, 1956, resident, 1957-58; chief resident Stafford Gen. Infrimary U.K., 1970; chief resident internal medicine and cardiology Rush Green Hosp. U.K., 1971-74; attending physician Our Lady Mercy Med. Ctr., Bronx, 1976—; chief sect. internal medicine Morrisania Clin., Bronx, 1980-83; pvt. practice Bronx, 1983—; attending physician St. Barnabas Hosp., Bronx, 1983—, Bronx Lebanon Hosp. Ctr., 1983—. Clin. asst. prof. medicine N.Y. Med. Coll.; cons. in field. Indian Coun. Med. Rsch. grantee, 1958-59. Fellow ACP, Royal Coll. Physicians. (Eng.), Royal Soc. London; mem. AMA, N.Y. State Med. Soc., Bronx Med. Soc., U. Calcutta Med. Assn. Am., Assn. Physicians India (U.S.), Lions Club (mem. fundraising campaign 1995—, v.p. 1999, pres. 2001). Avocations: walking, travel. Office: 2940 Grand Course Bronx NY 10458 Office Phone: 718-933-6655.

DAS, GOKUL M., research scientist, educator; arrived in U.S., 1983; s. Sivarama Menon; m. Lekha G. Nair, Apr. 25, 1965; children: Anagha M., Ananth M. BSc, U. Calicut, Kerala, India, 1975, EdB, 1977; MSc, Jawaharlal Nehru U., New Delhi, India, 1979, MPhil, 1982; PhD, Baylor U., 1988. Head Gene Regulation Lab. Cancer Therapy & Rsch. Ctr., San Antonio, 1994—2000; mem. San Antonio Cancer Inst., 1995—2002; asst. mem. Roswell Pk. Cancer Inst., Buffalo, 2002—; sr. mem. SUNY, Buffalo, 2002—. Adj. asst. prof. U. Tex. Health Sci. Ctr., San Antonio, 1995—2000, asst. prof., 2000—02; cons. InCell, San Antonio, 1998—2002. Recipient Rsch. Excellence award, Mead Johnson, 1988; fellow, Leukemia Soc. Am., 1988; grantee, San Antonio Area Found., 1995, San Antonio Cancer Inst., 1995, Am. Cancer Soc., 1996, Cancer Ctr. Coun., 1998, Charlotte Geyer Found., 1999, Nat. Cancer Inst., NIH, 1999, Wendy Will Case Cancer Fund, 1999, U.S. Army Breast Cancer Rsch. Program, 2001; Jr. Rsch. fellow, U. Grants Commn., India, 1979—82, Sr. Rsch. fellow, 1982—83, Rsch. fellow, L.I. Biol. Assn., Merit scholar, Jawaharlal Nehru U., 1977—79. Mem.: AAAS, Am. Assn. for Cancer Rsch. Achievements include discovery of transcription of U6 gene by RNA ploymease III; U6 gene in fruit fly (drosophila); tRNA gene upstream of U6 gene cluster in fruit fly genome; alternatively spliced vaiant of human homeo domain protein Oct-1; p53 tumor suppressor protein induced in response to genomic damage is active for gene transcription; elucidated the mechanism underlying activation of a gene by an oncoprotein and a tumorsuppressor protein. Office: Roswell Pk Cancer Inst Elm & Carlton Sts Buffalo NY 14263 E-mail: gokul.das@roswellpark.org.

DAS, NIROD K., engineering educator; b. Puri, Orissa, India, Feb. 27, 1963; came to U.S., 1985; s. Binayak and Sailabala Das; m. Nibedita Mohanty, Jan. 16, 1993. B in Tech., Indian Inst. Tech., Kharagpur, 1985; MSEE, U. Mass., 1987, PhD in Elec. Engring., 1989. Rschr. Indian Space Rsch. Orgn., Bangalore, summer 1984; rsch. asst. antenna lab. U. Mass., Amherst, 1985-89, postdoctoral rsch. assoc., 1989-90; asst. prof. dept. elec. engring. Poly. U., Bklyn., 1990-97, assoc. prof., 1997—. Contbr. articles to profl. jours.; co-editor: Directions for the Next Generation of MMIC Devices and Systems, 1997. Mem. IEEE (editl. bd. IEEE Microwave Theory and Techniques Transactions 1991—, tech. program com. Microwave Theory and Techniques Symposia 1996—, RWP King Best Paper award Antennas and Propagation Soc. 1993), N.Y. Acad. Scis. Avocations: astronomy, photography, camping. Office: Poly U 6 Metrotech Ctr Brooklyn NY 11201 E-mail: ndas@photon.poly.edu.

DAS, SUJIT, policy analyst; b. Calcutta, India, May 11, 1958; came to U.S. 1980; s. Hari Mohan and Sandhya Rani Das; m. Suchita De, June 16, 1987; 1 child, Sreetham. BTech, Indian Inst. Tech., 1979; MS, U. Tenn., 1982, MBA, 1984. Sr. rsch. staff Oak Ridge (Tenn.) Nat. Lab., 1984—; vis. fellow Tata Energy Rsch. Inst., New Delhi, 1992-93. Contbr. articles to profl. jours. Mem. Soc. Automotive Engrs., Soc. for Internat. Devel. Achievements include research in plastics recycling, oil vulnerability, flood damage estimation, energy and environmental analysis, uranium assessment, assessment of advanced materials technologies and vehicle designs. Office: Nat Transp Rsch Ctr 2360 Cherahala Blvd Rm I-05 Knoxville TN 37932-6472 Business E-Mail: dass@ornl.gov.

DAS, SUMAN KUMAR, plastic surgeon, researcher; b. Calcutta, India, May 6, 1944; came to U.S., 1980; s. Bisweswar and Devi Rani (Ghosh) D.; m. Carole Ellen Simmons, July 10, 1976 (div. Apr. 1984); children: Louise Angelique, Natalie Krishna; m. Rosyln Tanner, Mar. 22, 1991. B of Medicine and Surgery, Calcutta (India) U., 1967; MD, Ednl. Commn. Fgn. Med. Grad., 1981. Diplomate Am. Bd. Plastic Surgery. Intern R.G. Kar Med. Coll. and Hosp., Calcatta, 1966-67, resident in gen. surgery, house officer, 1967-68; sr. house officer in accident and emergency, orthopaedics Royal Infirmary, Bolton, Lancs, Eng., 1968-69, house surgeon in gen. surgery, 1969-70; sr. house officer in gen. surgery Royal United Hosp., St. Martins's Hosp., Bath, Eng., 1970-72; house officer in medicine Whiston Hosp., Prescot, Liverpool, Eng., 1970; registrar in gen. surgery Frenchay Hosp., Bristol, Eng., 1972-73, sr. house officer in plastic surgery, 1973-74; registrar in plastic surgery Frenchay Hosp., Bristol, Eng., 1974, Royal Victoria Infirmary, Fleming Meml. Children's Hosp., Newcastle-Upon-Tyne, Eng., 1974-77; fellow in plastic and reconstructive surgery Hosp. for Sick Children, Toronto, Ont., Can., 1978; fellow in micro and hand surgery St. Vincent's Hosp., Melbourne, Australia, 1979-80, asst. plastic surgeon, 1979-80; rsch. assoc. in plastic surgery UCLA Med. Ctr., 1980-82; co-dir. microsurgery tng. program Harbor/UCLA Med. Ctr., 1980-82; dir. plastic surgery rsch. VA Wadsworth Med. Ctr., L.A., 1980-82; resident in plastic surgery U. Miss. Med. Ctr., Jackson, 1982-83, sr. and chief resident in plastic surgery, 1983-84; pvt. practice Jackson, 1984-86; chief and asst. prof. div. plastic surgery U. Miss. Med. Ctr., Jackson, 1986-87, chief and assoc. prof. div. plastic surgery, 1987-90, prof. plastic surgery, chief div. plastic surgery, chief, 1990-95, clin. prof. plastic surgery, 1995—. Cons. plastic surgery Miss. Bapt. Med. Ctr., River Oaks Hosp.; attending Meth. Rehab. Ctr., U. Miss. Med. Ctr., River Oaks East Hosp., St. Dominiso Hosp.; vis. prof. dept. surgery divsn. plastic surgery U. Calif., San Francisco, 1981, U. Ala., 1992; mem. patient care com. U. Miss., Jackson, 1990—92; pres. internet co. Nxmed.com. Inc., 1999—; dir. St. Dominic Ambulatory Surgery Ctr., 1999—; dir. outreach program St. Dominic Hosp.; med. dir. St. Dominic's Ambulatory Surgery Ctr., 1999—, pres., 2003—; presenter and exhibitor in field at numerous profl. meetings. Author: (with others) Manual of Operative Plastic and Reconstructive Surgery, 1980, Textbook of Surgery, 2nd edit., 1988, Ency. of Flaps, 1990; mem. editorial bd. So. Med. Jour., 1993-1999; contbr. articles to Brit. Jour. Surgery, Brit. Jour. Plastic Surgery, Indian Jour. Dermatology, Hand, Plastic Surgery Forum, Jour. Singapore Acad. Sci., Jour. Oral Surgery, Plastic Reconstrn. Surgery, Acta Anatomica, Jour. Clin. Pathology, others; inventor turmeric on wound healing. Pres. NxMed.com Internet Distant Edn., 2000—. Recipient prize North Eng. Surg. Soc., 1977, Plastic Surgery Ednl. Found. Rsch. grant 1983-84, other grants Eli Lilly 1989, Tyra, 1989, Collagen Corp. 1989, 90-91, NIH, 1989, Am. Soc. Aesthetic Plastic Surgery, 1990, 91. Fellow ACS, Royal Coll. Surgeons London, Royal Coll. Surgeons Edinburgh (traveling scholarship 1976); mem. AMA, AAAS, Am. Fedn. for Clin. Rsch., Am. Assn. Hand Surgery (rsch. grant com. 1990-91, chmn. rsch. grant com. 1992), Am. Assn. Acad. Plastic Surgeons (fellowship com. 1990), Am. Soc. Plastic and Reconstructive Surgeons, Am. Assn. Plastic Surgeons, Internat. Soc. Burn Injuries, Internat. Soc. Reconstructive Microsurgery, Internat. Soc. Surgery, Internat. Soc. Emergency Medicine and Critical Care (charter), Brit. Assn. Plastic Surgeons (best prize and cert. 1967), Brit. Soc. Surgery of Hands (European traveling scholarship 1977), Soc. N.Am. Skull Base Surgery (founding), Miss. State Med. Assn., Plastic Surgery Rsch. Coun., N.Y. Acad. Sci., S.E. Soc. Plastic and Reconstructive Surgeons (program com. 1990—, trustee 1997-2000, historian 2000-01, chmn. CME com. 1999--, asst. sec. 2001--), Miss. Acad. Scis. (chmn. 1992), Acad. Surg. Rsch., Assn. for Acad. Surgery, Southeastern Surg. Congress, Internat. Fedn. Surg. Colls., So. Med. Assn. (chmn. elect 1991, chmn. 1992), Lion's Club (Flora), Sigma Xi. Achievements include discovery that silicone does not elicit any change in T cell population; that capsular contracture with silicone implant is not an immunological effect; rsch. on best treatment for finger tip amputation in children, size and lengthening of human omentum, muscle transplantation by microvascular technique fatigue like normal muscle. Home: 242 Highland Hills Ln Flora MS 39071-9613 Office: 764 Lakeland Dr Ste 306 Jackson MS 39216-4616 Office Phone: 601-362-0611. Office Fax: 601-362-0192. Personal E-mail: Sushrata@aol.com.

DAS, T. K., management educator, consultant; b. Calcutta, India, July 8, 1938; BS with honors, U. Calcutta, 1957; MS, Jadavpur U., Calcutta, 1959; M in Mgmt., Asian Inst. Mgmt., Manila, 1977; PhD, UCLA, 1984. Cert. Assoc. of the Indian Inst. of Bankers. Various exec. positions State Bank of India, 1960-76; part-time asst. prof. mgmt. Calif. State U., L.A., 1980-83; asst. prof. strategic mgmt. Tex. Tech U., Lubbock, 1984-86; mem. doctoral faculty CUNY, 1987—; asst. prof. strategic mgmt. Baruch Coll., CUNY,

1987-89, assoc. prof., 1990-96, prof., 1997—; area coord. Strategic Mgmt. and Bus. & Soc., 1997—. Author: Human Resource Management and Productivity: State of the Art and Future Prospects, Vol. I: Focus on the United States, 1984, Vol. II: International Perspectives, 1985, The Subjective Side of Strategy Making: Future Orientations and Perceptions of Executives, 1986, The Time Dimension: An Interdisciplinary Guide, 1990; assoc. editor Rev. of Business Studies, 1992-94, Internat. Jour. Orgnl. Analysis, 1993-96; mem. editorial bd. Jour. Managerial Issues, 1991-94, Internat. Jour. Commerce & Mgmt., 1997—, Jour. Internat. Mgmt., 2000—; mem. acad. adv. bd. Jour. Mgmt. Studies, 2003—; sr. editor Orgn. Studies, 2004—; contbr. more than 120 articles to scholarly and profl. jours Recipient 1st prize Indian Inst. Bankers Prize Essay Competition, 1964, Charat Ram Found. award All India Mgmt. Assn., 1968; grantee CUNY Rsch. Found., 1993-94, 97-98, 98-99, 99-2000, 2001-02. Mem. Strategic Mgmt. Soc., Acad. of Mgmt., Inst. for Ops. Rsch. and the Mgmt. Scis., Soc. for Bus. Ethics, World Future Soc., Internat. Soc. for the Study of Time, Indian Inst. Bankers (life), Beta Gamma Sigma. Office: CUNY Baruch Coll Zicklin Sch Bus Dept Mgmt One Bernard Baruch Way Box B9-240 New York NY 10010-5585 Office Phone: 646-312-3634. E-mail: TK_Das@baruch.cuny.edu.

DASARI, GANESWARA R., oil industry executive; s. Venkat R and Seeta R Dasari; m. Usha S Chava, Dec. 22, 1996; children: Shobha, Shourav. B in engring. (hon.), Andhra U., 1984—88; M in tech., I I T Kharagpur, 1988—91; PhD, Cambridge U., 1991—96. Offshore engr. Fugro Ltd, London, 1996—97; rsch. assoc. Cambridge U., Cambridge, England, 1997—2000; asst. prof. Nat. Univ. of Singapore, 2000—03; sr. rsch. engr. ExxonMobil Upstream Rsch. Co., Houston. Cons. Drb Hicom, Kaulalumpur, Malaysia, 2000—. Mem.: ASCE (assoc.), Soc. of Petroleum Engineers (assoc.), Cambridge Commonwealth Trust (life), Cambridge Philos. Soc. (life). Achievements include research in role of geomechanics in reservoir engineering; development of methodology to predict mine burial for Office of Naval Research. Office: ExxonMobil Upstream Research Company 3120 Buffalo Speedway URC-N344 Houston TX 77252-2189 Office Phone: 713-431-4844. Business E-Mail: ganeswara.r.dasari@exxonmobil.com.

DASARO, JOSEPH LEONARD, art educator; b. Greensboro, N.C., Dec. 31, 1953; s. Nathan Anthony and Bernise Virginia Dasaro; m. Elizabeth Gail Herrage, Dec. 2, 1989; children: Katie, Stephen, Madeline. BS, Auburn U., 1978. Tchr., coach football and wrestling Gordon County Sch. Sys., Calhoun, Ga., 1978—79, Huntsville (Ala.) City Schs., 1979—. Dir. Ala. Sports Festival, Huntsville, 1988, 2003—04. Named Ala. Coach of Yr. (7 times), Nat. Coach of Yr. Mem.: NEA, Ala. Edn. Assn. Avocations: fishing, hiking, bicycling, drawing. Home: 1025 Bayfield Dr Huntsville AL 35802 Office: Grissom HS 7901 Baylie Cove Rd Huntsville AL 35802

DASBURG, JOHN HAROLD, restaurant executive; b. NYC, Jan. 7, 1943; s. Jean Henry and Alice Etta Dasburg; m. Mary Lois Diaz, July 6, 1968; children: John Peter, Kathryn. AA, U. Miami, 1963; BS in Indsl. Engring., U. Fla., 1966, MBA, 1971, JD, 1973. Bar: Fla. 1974; CPA, Fla., Md. Staff Peat Marwick Mitchell & Co., Jacksonville, Fla., 1973-78, tax ptnr. in charge, 1978-80; v.p. tax Marriott Corp., Washington, 1980-82, v.p. fin., 1982-84, sr. v.p., 1984-85, exec. v.p., CFO, chief real estate officer, 1985-88, pres. lodging group, 1988-89; pres., CEO Northwest Airlines, 1990-2001; chmn. Burger King Corp., Miami, Fla., 2001—03, pres., CEO, 2001—02; chmn., CEO, pres. Astar Air Cargo, Inc., Miami, 2003—. Bd. dirs. St. Paul Travelers Cos., WCI Cmtys., Inc., Winn Dixie Stores, Inc. Contbr. articles to profl. jours. Lt. (j.g.) USN, 1966-69, Vietnam. Republican. Roman Catholic. Office: Astar Air Cargo Inc 2 S Biscayne Blvd Ste 3663 Miami FL 33131 Office Phone: 305-982-0500.

DASCHER, PAUL EDWARD, dean, accounting educator; b. Oct. 1, 1942; s. Albert Jacob abd Ruth (Mountney) D.; m. Nancy Patricia Byrne; children: Mitchell Paul, Heidi Beth. BS, Pa. State U., 1964, MS, 1966, PhD, 1969. Instr. acctg. Pa. State U., 1968-69; asst. prof. acctg. Va. Poly. Inst., Blacksburg, 1969-71, assoc. prof. acctg., 1971-73; prof. acctg. Drexel U., Phila., 1973-93, dept. head, 1974-77, dean Coll. of Bus. and Adminstrn., 1977-93; dean Sch. Bus. Adminstrn. Stetson U., Deland, Fla., 1993—2004, prof. acctg., 1993—, M.E. Rinker, Sr. dist. prof., 2002—. Vis. prof. Northeastern U., Boston, 1976; cons. Price Waterhouse and Co., N.Y.C., 1974-75; lectr. in field. Co-author: Financial Accounting, 1980, 4th edit., 1995, Accounting Readings, 1982, Managerial Accounting, 1985, 11th edit., 2002; contbr. numerous articles to profl. jours. Fellow Price Waterhouse & Co., Armstrong Cork Co.; recipient Nat. Assn. Accts. Socio-Econ. Disting. Svc. award, 1973, 75, 81, Drexel U. Faculty Appreciation award, 1977, Commendation Phila. chpt. Pa. Inst CPA's, 1977, Cmty. Accts. Meritorious Svc. award, 1981; named one of Outstanding Young Men of Am., 1979. Mem. Am. Acctg. Assn., Fin. Execs. Inst., Inst. Mgmt. Accts. (nat. v.p. 1989-90), Accts. for Pub. Interest (pres. 1986-89), Alpha Kappa Psi, Beta Alpha Psi, Beta Gamma Sigma. Republican. Lutheran. Avocations: tennis, reading. Office: Stetson U Sch Bus Adm Deland FL 32723 Office Phone: 386-822-7404. E-mail: pdascher@stetson.edu.

DASCHLE, THOMAS ANDREW, former senator; b. Aberdeen, SC, Dec. 9, 1947; m. Linda Hall Daschle; children: Kelly, Nathan, Lindsay. BA, S.D. State U., 1969. Fin. investment rep.; chief legis. aide, field coordinator Sen. James Abourzek, 1973-77; mem. 96th-97th Congresses from 1st S.D. Dist., U.S. Ho. of Reps., 1979—87, 98th-99th Congresses at large, 1983-87; U.S. senator from S.D., 1987—2005; minority leader U.S Senate, 1996—2001, 2003—04, majority leader, 2001—03; spl. policy advisor Alston & Bird LLP, Washington, 2005—. Mem. agrl. nutrition and forestry com., mem. fin. com., rules com., co-chmn. Sen. Dem. steering and coord. com., co-chair Sen. Dem. tech. and comm. com., chmn. Sen. Dem. conf. com., co-chmn. Sen. Dem. policy com.; leader bipartisan effort; author, enforcer Agent Orange Act, 1991; authored, reformulated gasoline provisions of Clean Air Act Amendment 1990. Founder Am. Grown Found., 1987. Served to 1st lt. USAF, 1969-72. Recipient Nat. Commdr.'s award Disabled Am. Vets., 1980, Disting. Alumni award S.D. State U., 1997, VFW Congl. award VFW, 1997, Legislator of Yr. award Vietnam Vets. Am., 1997, Cert. Appreciation, Nat. Assn. Federally Impacted Sch., 1997, Congl. Leadership award Cmty. Anti-Drug Coalitions Am., 1997, Golden Triangle award Nat. Farmer's Union, 1997-98, Outstanding Vets. Adv. of Yr. award Disabled Am. Vets. Dept. S.D., 1998, Pres. Recognition award Nat. Indian Impacted Schs. Assn., 1998, Cert. Appreciation, Nat. Assn. Alcoholism and Drug Abuse Counselors, 1998, Diplomat award Rapid City C. of C., 1998, Disting. Svc. award Nat. Rural Electric Coop. Assn., 2000; named Outstanding Young Man of Yr., U.S. Jaycees, 1981, Friend of Edn., S.D. Edn. Assn., 1997, Person of the Yr., Nat. Assn. Concerned Vets., 1997, Legislator of Yr., Renewable Fuels Assn., 1998, Maj. Gen. Williamson's S.D. Nat. Guard Militia Man of 1998, S.D. Nat. Guard. Democrat. Roman Catholic. Office: Alston & Bird LLP 601 Pennsylvania Ave NW N Bldg 10th Fl Washington DC 20004 Office Phone: 202-756-3156. Business E-Mail: tom.daschle@alston.com.

DASGUPTA, AMITAVA, chemist, educator; b. Calcutta, India, May 6, 1958; came to U.S., 1980; naturalized U.S. citizen, 1996; s. Anil Kumar and Hasi Dasgupta. BS with honors, U. Calcutta, India, 1978; MS in Chemistry, U. Ga., 1981; PhD in Chemistry, Stanford U., 1986. Diplomate Am. Bd. Clin. Chemistry. Fellow in clin. chemistry U. Wash., Seattle, 1986-88; asst. dir. clin. chemistry U. Chgo., 1988-93; dir. clin. chemistry lab. U. N.Mex. Hosp., Albuquerque, 1993-97; assoc. prof. pathology and biochemistry U. N.Mex., Albuquerque, 1993-97; prof. pathology U. Tex.-Houston Med. Sch., 1998—. Lectr in field. Reviewer jours. Clin. Chemistry, Nephron, Jour. Liquid Chromatography; contbr. articles to Clin. Chemistry, Am. Jour. Clin. Pathology, Jour. Am. Soc. Nephrology, SYVA, 1990-91, Home Health Care, 1992-93. Fellow Nat. Acad. Clin. Biochemistry (Grannis award 1993); mem. Am. Assn. Clin. Chemistry, Acad. Clin. Labs. Physicians and Scientists. Hindu. Achievements include research in role of lipids and lipid peroxidation in the pathophysiology of disease; characterization of digoxin-like immunoreactive substance; drug-drug interaction and advantages of monitoring free drug concentrations. Office: U Texas Med School Dept Pathology 6431 Fannin St # Msb2292 Houston TX 77030-1501

DASGUPTA, INDRANIL, physician, educator; b. Barielly, India, May 24, 1960; came to the U.S., 1961; s. Sunil Pryia and Krishna Dasgupta. BA in Philosophy, Duke U., 1982; MPH in Internat. Health, Loma Linda U., 1987; cert. epidemiology, Johns Hopkins U., 1987; MBA in Fin., George Washington U., 1989; MD, St. George's (Grenada) U., 1994. Diplomate Am. Bd. Internal Medicine. Congl. intern U.S. Ho. of Reps., Washington, 1983; rsch. asst. Harvard Med. Sch., Boston, 1983-84, Dartmouth U. Med. Sch., Hanover, N.H., 1985-86; rsch. assoc. Loma Linda (Calif.) Sch. Pub. Health, 1986-87; congl. intern U.S. Senator Ed Kennedy, Washington, 1988-89; med. resident Med. Coll. Pa.-Hahnemann U. Hosps., Phila., 1995-98, rsch. assoc., 1998-99, geriatric fellow Phila., 1998-99; cardiology fellow Robert Wood Johnson Med. Sch. U. Medicine and Dentistry N.J., Camden, 1999—2002, rsch. assoc., 1999—2002; clin. asst. prof. divsn. cardiology Jefferson Med. Coll., Phila., 2002—; attending cardiologist Thomas Jefferson U. Hosp., Phila., 2002—. Contbr.: U.S. House Select Committee on Aging, 1983. Vol. Muscular Dystrophy Assn., Winston-Salem, N.C., 1981, U.S. Spl. Olympics, Wilmington, Del., 1985, Dem. Fund Raising, Washington, 1988. Fellow: Soc. Geriatric Cardiology; mem.: ACP, Am. Soc. Nuclear Cardiology, Internat. Soc. Heart and Lung Transplantation, NY Acad. Scis., NJ Acad. Sci., Nat. Assn. Advancement Sci., Am. Heart Assn., Am. Coll. Cardiology, Delta Omega, Sigma Alpha Epsilon. Democrat. Avocations: travel, sailing, snorkling, soccer. Home: 2528 Tigani Dr Wilmington DE 19808 Office: Thomas Jefferson U Hosp Jefferson Heart Inst 925 Chestnut St Mezzanine Level Philadelphia PA 19107 E-mail: indranildasgupta@aol.com.

DAS GUPTA, SUBAL, physics professor, researcher; b. Calcutta, India, Aug. 11, 1939; emigrated to Can., 1960; s. Subodh Chandra and Pritilata (Sen) Das G.; m. Sanjukta Sen Gupta, Aug. 12, 1965; children: Monidipa, Nandini. MSc, Calcutta U., 1959; PhD, McMaster U., 1963. Nat. Scis. and Engring. Rsch. Coun. Can. post-doctoral fellow AECL, Chalk River, Ont., Can., 1963-64; rsch. sci. Tata Inst. for Fundamental Rsch., Bombay, India, 1964-65; postdoctoral fellow in physics McGill U., Montreal, Que., Can., 1965-66, asst. prof. physics, 1967-71, assoc. prof., 1972-77, prof., 1978—, chair dept. physics, 1993-97, prof. physics, 1997—. Contbr. articles to profl. jours. Oper. grantee Nat. Sci. and Engring. Rsch. Coun., 1966—. Office: McGill U Dept Physics ERP 319 3600 University St Montreal PQ Canada H3A 2T8 Business E-Mail: dasgupta@physics.mcgill.ca.

DASGUPTA, SUBRATA, computer scientist, author; b. Calcutta, West Benga, India, Oct. 18, 1944; came to U.S., 1982; s. Satyabrata and Protima (Gupta) D.; m. Sarmistha Dasgupta, Jan. 18, 1970; children: Jaideep, Monish. BEE, U. Calcutta, 1967; MS, U. Alt., Edmonton, Can., 1974, PhD, 1976. Programmer, analyst IBM World Trade Corp., Calcutta, 1967-71; rsch. asst. Nat. Rsch. Coun. Can. postgrad. U. Alt., 1972-75; asst. prof. computer sci. Simon Fraser U., Vancouver, B.C., Can., 1975-79, Ohio State U., Columbus, 1979-80, U. Alt., Edmonton, 1980-82, U. Southwestern La., Lafayette, 1982-84, prof. elec. and computer engring., 1984—. Sr. visitor U. Cambridge, Eng., 1977; vis. fellow Wolfson Coll., U. Oxford, 1986; guest prof. German Sci. Found., U. Oldenburg, Fed. Republic of Germany, 1988; disting. visitor Simon Fraser U., Vancouver, 1990. Author: The Design and Description of Computer Architectures, 1984, Computer Architecture: A Modern Synthesis Vol. I, Foundations and Vol. II, Advanced, 1989, Design Theory and Computer Science, 1990; contbr. articles to profl. jours. Grantee NSF, 1985-89. Mem. IEEE, Assn. for Computing Machiner, Internat. Fedn. for Info. Processing, Sigma Xi (Outstanding rsch. award 1987). Avocations: English lit. and philosophy, classical and folk music films. Office: U Southwestern La Ctr Advanced Computer Study PO Box 44330 Lafayette LA 70504-0001

DASH, DAMON, broadcast executive, recording industry executive; b. Harlem, May 3, 1971; Co-founder, CEO Roc-A-Fella Enterprise (sold to Universal Music Group's Island Def Jam for $10 million), N.Y.C., 1995—2005; founder RocaWear, Damon Dash Music Group, 2005—. Actor: (films) Highlander: Endgame, 2000; prodr.: Backstage, 2000; writer, dir.: Paper Soldiers, 2002; prodr., actor State Property, 2002; Paid in Full, 2002; Death of a Dynasty, 2002; exec. prodr.: The Woodsman, 2004; appearing in reality show: The Ultimate Hustler, 2005. Office: Damon Dash Music Group 1501 Broadway New York NY 10036*

DASH, LEON DECOSTA, JR., journalist; b. New Bedford, Mass., Mar. 16, 1944; s. Leon DeCosta and Ruth Elizabeth (Kydd). BA, Howard U., 1968; DHD, Lincoln U., 1996. Reporter Washington Post, 1966—68, 1971—79, African bur. chief, 1979—83, with investigations desk, 1984—98; prof. journalism U. Ill., Champaign, 1998—99, Swanlund chair prof. journalism, 2000—01, Swanlund prof. journalism, 2001—; prof. journalism Ctr. Advanced Study, 2003—. Vis. prof. U. Calif.-San Diego, 1978. Author (with Ben H. Bagdikian): (book) The Shame of the Prisons, 1972; author: When Children Want Children: The Urban Crisis of Teenage Childbearing, 1989, Rosa Lee: A Mother and Her Family in Urban America, 1996 (Polit. Book award Washington Monthly Mag., 1997, 1st prize Harry Chapin Best Book award World Hunger Yr. Orgn., 1997). Vol. Peace Corps, Kenya, 1969—70. Co-recipient Editl. award for news series, Chesapeake AP, 1987, Editl. award, 1989; named one of Best 100 Works in 20th Century Am. Journalism for 8-part series Rosa Lee's Story for Washington Post, 1999; recipient George Polk Meml. award, Overseas Press Club, 1974, award for internat. news reporting, Washington-Balt. Newspaper Guild, 1974, hon. mention, 1975, Internat. Reporting award, Africare, 1984, Capitol Press Club, 1984, 1st Place Journalism award for gen. news, Nat. Assn. Black Journalists, 1986, Investigative Reporters and Editors award, 1987, 1st Prize award, Washington-Balt. Newspaper Guild, 1987, Pres.'s award, Washington Ind. Writers Assn., 1989, Martha Albrand Spl. Citation for Nonfiction, PEN, 1990, Pulitzer Prize for explanatory journalism, 1995, 1st Prize Robert F. Kennedy award for print journalism, 1995, Emmy award for pub. affairs, NATAS, 1996, Polit. Book award, The Washington Monthly mag., 1997, Prevention for a Safer Soc. award, Nat. Coun. on Crime and Delinquency for Rosa Lee book, 1997; Henry J. Kaiser Family Found. fellow, 1995—96. Office: U Ill Dept Journalism 119 Gregory Hall 810 S Wright St Urbana IL 61801-3644 Office Phone: 217-265-5055. Business E-Mail: leondash@uiuc.edu.

DASH, SANFORD MARK, aerospace scientist; b. N.Y.C., May 26, 1943; s. Jack and Rachael (Calamar) D.; m. Barbara Gaile Held; children: David, Kenneth, Jonathan, Naomi. BSME, CCNY, 1964; MS in Aeronautics and Astronautics, NYU, 1966, PhD in Aeronautics and Astronautics, 1969. Rsch. scientist Gen. Applied Sci. Labs., Westbury, N.Y., 1969-77; cons. Aero. Rsch. Assocs. Princeton, N.J., 1977-80; v.p., mgr. propulsive scis. divsn. Sci. Applications Internat. Corp., Princeton, N.J., 1980-94; pres., chief scientist Combustion Rsch. and Flow Tech., Inc., Pipersville, Pa., 1994—. Cons. in field. Contbr. over 250 articles to profl. pubs., chpts. to books. Recipient Cert. of Recognition, NASA, 1975, USAF, 1985. Fellow: AIAA (assoc.; chmn. aero-acoustics tech. com. 1997—99, Aerospace Profl. of Yr. 2002); mem.: NATO and Joint Army, Navy, NASA, Air Force Coms. Achievements include development of U.S. standard plume flowfield models for aircraft and missiles; rsch. on Nat. Aerospace Plane Program; formulation of jet noise reduction concepts for military aircraft; research on scramjet technology for next generation missile system. Business E-Mail: dash@craft-tech.com.

DASHE, JODI S., obstetrician, educator; d. Lewis B. and Gloria A. Dashe; m. Gad Ifrah, Sept. 5, 2002; 1 child, Jacob H. Ifrah. BA, U. Pa., 1988; MD, Yale U., 1992. Diplomate Am. Bd. of Obstetrics & Gynecology, 1999, cert. Maternal Fetal Medicine Specialist Am. Bd. of Obstetrics & Gynecology, 2001. Asst. prof. U. Tex. Southwestern Med. Ctr., Dallas, 1996—2002; assoc. prof. Coll. Medicine Drexel U., Phila., 2002—03; assoc. prof. U. Tex. Southwestern Med. Ctr., Dallas, 2003—. Fellow: Am. Coll. Ob-Gyn.

DASIGI, VENUGOPALA RAO, computer science educator; b. Khurda Road, Orissa, India, Nov. 8, 1957; came to U.S. 1982; s. Perraju and Savitri Devi (Jayanti) D.; m. Vijaya Lakshmi Kavuru, Aug. 6, 1982; children: Tara Srujana, Jay Viraj. B in Engring., Andhra U., 1979; MEE, Philips Internat. Inst., 1981; MS, U. Md., 1985, PhD, 1988. Programmer Philips Audio Div., Eindhoven, Netherlands, 1980, Philips Data Systems, Eindhoven, Netherlands, 1980-81; devel. engr. Philips India, Ltd., Pune, 1981-82; teaching asst. U. Md., College Park, 1982, rsch. asst., 1983-88; part-time instr. U. Coll., College Park, 1984-88; asst. prof. Wright State U., Dayton, Ohio, 1988-94; assoc. prof., grad. program dir. Sacred Heart U., Fairfield, Conn., 1994—. Travel grantee Internat. Joint Confs. on Artificial Intelligence, Inc., 1991, Fedn. Computing in the U.S., 1996, rsch. challenge grantee State of Ohio, 1990-91, Sm. Bus. Innovation Rsch., 1997, Dept. Energy and Air Force Office of Sci. Rsch. summer rsch. fellowship grantee, 1995, 96, 97. Mem. Assn. Computing Machinery, IEEE Computer Soc., Am. Assn. Artificial Intelligence (corr., mem. organizing com. workship 1991), Am. Soc. Info. Sci., Sigma Xi. Avocations: reading, amateur acting. Office: Sacred Heart U Dept Computer Sci and Info Tech Fairfield CT 06432-1000

DA SILVA, DELIO P., investment advisor; b. Macau, Portugal, Aug. 20, 1948; came to U.S., 1978; s. João Santos and Maria Dionizia Eusebio Pereira Da Silva; m. Rosalie R. P. Da Silva, June 1980 (div. Aug. 1986); children: Alexia C. P., Simone P. BS, U. London, 1977; MBA, U. Calif., Berkeley, 1983. Registered investment advisor. Negotiator Bank of Tokyo, San Francisco; fgn. trade advisor Bank of Brasil, San Francisco; fin. advisor bus. devel. Coast Savs. Bank, San Francisco; specialist fin. advisor Roberts & Ryan, San Francisco; investment fin. advisor Am. Express, San Francisco; investment and fin. advisor Associated Securities, San Francisco; registered investment advisor D.P. Da Silva (R.I.A.) & Co., San Francisco. V.p. Marin Cultural Ctr. and Mus., Ross, Calif., 1988; mem. adv. bd. Portuguese C. of C., San Jose, 1995. With M.P., 1970-72, Portugal. Mem. San Francisco Fine Arts Mus., Commonwealth Club, World Trade Club, Portuguese Athletic Club, Marin Cricket Club. Republican. Roman Catholic. Office: D P Da Silva (RIA) & Co Ste 200 Two Embarcadero Ctr San Francisco CA 94111

DA SILVA, ERCIO MARIO, physician; b. Catajuczes, Minas, Brazil; s. Mario and Rosa (Pinto) da S.; m. Doris Hale da Silva, Aug. 22, 1953; children: Robert, Suzanne. MD, U. Mines, Brazil, 1949. Diplomate Am. Bd. Colon Rectal Surgery. Physician U.S. Mil. Base, Columbia, S.C., 1988—. Mem. Am. Soc. Colon Rectal Surgery, Columbia Med. Soc. Home: 413 Brookshire Dr Columbia SC 29210-4203

DASILVA, WILLARD H., lawyer, educator; b. Freeport, N.Y., Oct. 17, 1923; BA, NYU, 1946; LLB, Columbia U., 1949. Bar: N.Y. 1949, U.S. Tax Ct. 1969, U.S. Supreme Ct. 1969. Pvt. practice, N.Y.C., 1969-70, Carle Place, N.Y., 1973-76, Garden City, NY, 1978—91; ptnr. Goodman & DaSilva, N.Y.C., 1970-73, DaSilva & Samuelson, Garden City, 1977, DaSilva & Keidel, Garden City, 1992—97, DaSilva, Garson & Hilowitz LLP, Garden City, 1998-99, DaSilva, Hilowitz & McEvily LLP, Garden City, 1999—. V.p. Marcus Bros. Textile Corp., N.Y.C., 1961-63; pres. Cortley Fabrics subs. Cone Mills Corp., N.Y.C., 1964-65; lectr. Columbia U. Law Sch., Bklyn. Law Sch., St. John's Law Sch., Cardozo Law Sch., Hofstra U. Law Sch., Touro Law Sch.; mem. faculty Practising Law Inst., N.Y.C., 1972—; mem. nat. panel arbitrators Am. Arbitration Assn., 1965-2001. Author: N.Y. Matrimonial Practice, 1980—; editor Matrimonial Law Jour., 1977-85, Fair Share mag., 1985-99, N.Y. Matrimonial Case Law, 1985—; editor-author Family Law Practice Systems Manual, 1982—; editor-in-chief N.Y. Domestic Rels. Reporter, 1992—; editor NY Bar Jour., 1999—; chmn. bd. editors The Matrimonial Strategist, 2003—; contbr. articles to law jours. Trustee NAFA Found., 1977-85; trustee North Shore U. Hosp., 1988-95, chmn. adv. bd. family in transition program, 1991—; atty. Edn. and Assistance Corp., 1992-97; bd. dirs. NY. Virtuosi Symphony Orch., 2002—. 2d lt. USAAF, 1942-46. Fellow ABA (coun. family law sect. 1992—, editor-in-chief Family Adv. 1981—), N.Y. State Bar Found.; mem. Am. Coll. Family Trial Lawyers (diplomate), Am. Acad. Matrimonial Lawyers (pres. 1982-84, bd. mgrs. 1977—), N.Y. State Trial Lawyers Assn., Am. Bar Found., N.Y. State Bar Assn. (CLE com. 1980-90, program chmn. family law sect. 1978-82, sec. gen. practice sect. 1994-95, chmn. matrimonial com. 1989—, coun. 1992—, chmn.-elect 1995-96, chmn. 1996-97, editor Jour. 2000—), Nassau County Bar Assn., Suffolk County Bar Assn. (chmn. family law sect. 1982-84), N.Y. Family Law Am. Inn of Ct. (master 1995—, sec./treas. 1999-2001, counsel 2001-03, pres. 2003-05), Internat. Soc. on Family Law, Am. Soc. Writers on Legal Subjects, Phi Beta Kappa. Office: 585 Stewart Ave Garden City NY 11530-4783 Office Phone: 516-222-0700.

DASKIN, MARK STEPHEN, engineering educator; b. Balt., Dec. 3, 1952; s. Walter and Betty Jane (Fax) D.; m. Babette Reva Levy, July 2, 1978; children: Tamar, Keren. BSCE, MIT, 1974; postgrad. study in Engring., Cambridge, England, 1975; PhD in Civil Engring., MIT, 1978. Tchg. asst. trans. sys. divsn. civil engring. MIT, Cambridge, 1976-77; asst. prof. civil engring. Univ. Tex., Austin, 1978-79, Northwestern U., Evanston, Ill., 1980-83, assoc. prof. civil engring., 1983-89, prof., 1989—, chair dept. indsl. engring. and mgmt. scis., 1995—2001. Author: Network and Discrete Location: Models, Algorithms and Applications, 1995; editor-in-chief Transp. Sci., 1991-94; assoc. editor Location Sci., 1991-2000; contbr. articles to profl. jours. Bd. dirs. North Suburban Synagogue Beth El, Highland Park, Ill., 1991-94. U. Tex. Bur. Engring. Rsch. granee, 1978-79, Northwestern U. Transp. Ctr. grantee, 1980, 81, NSF grantee, 1980-82, 84-90, 93-96, 95-98, 96-99, 1998-2002, 02-04, 05—, Urban Mass Transp. Adminstr. grantee, 1982-84, 84-85, United Parcel Svc. grantee, 1983-86, 91-92, Thermo-King Corp. grantee, 1990-91, 92-94, Heartland Blood Ctr. grantee, 1992, 96, grantee Office Naval Rsch., 2005, other grants; recipient Fulbright Rsch. award, 1989-90, Burlington No. Found. Faculty Achievement award, 1985, NSF Presdl. Young Investigator award, 1984, Scott Paper Leadership award, 1973-75, IIE Tech. Innovation award in indsl. engring., Fred C. Crane disting. svc. award; INFORMS fellow, 2004 Mem. Inst. Indsl. Engrs. (editor-in-chief IEE Transactions 2001—04, Fred C. Crane award for disting. svc. 2005), INFORMS (v.p. publs. 1996-99, pres.-elect 2005), Ops. Rsch. Soc. Am. (jour. editor 1991-94), Inst. Mgmt. Sci., Sigma Xi, Tau Beta Pi, Chi Epsilon. Avocations: swimming, photography. Office: Northwestern U Dept Indsl Engring Mgmt Sci Evanston IL 60208-0001 Office Phone: 847-491-8796. Business E-Mail: m-daskin@northwestern.edu.

DASKIVICH, ROBERTA SUSAN, elementary school educator; d. Robert Samuel and Sarah Ellison Tritinger; m. John Joseph Daskivich, July 27, 1968; children: Amy Lynne Daskivich Herrmann, Timothy John. BS in Edn., Ind. U. Pa., 1968; MEd, U. Pitts., 1971. Cert. tchr. Pa. Tchr. Hampton Twp. Sch. Dist., Allison Park, Pa., 1968—74; caseworker Pa. Welfare Dept., Pitts., 1988; tchr. Hampton Twp. Sch. Dist., 1988—. Team leader Lit. Team, Ctrl. Elem. Sch., Allison Park, 2003—05; mem. Western Pa. Writing Project, 2003—05; co-chair Pub. Team, Ctrl. Elem. Sch., 2005. Social com. chair, treas. Ingonar North Recreadion and Swim Club, Pitts., 1987—88; mem. chair McKnight Elem. PTA, 1985—88; pres., v.p., sec., treas. St. Alex Nevsky Womens Club, 1985—95. Mem.: Adult Book Club. Republican. Russian Orthodox. Avocations: reading, gardening, writing. Office: Ctrl Elem Sch 4100 Middle Rd Allison Park PA 15101

DASSANOWSKY, ROBERT VON, film producer, educator, editor, writer; b. NYC, Jan. 28, 1960; s. Elfi von Dassanowsky. Grad., Am. Acad. Dramatic Arts; BA with honors, UCLA, 1985, MA, 1988, PhD, 1992. Actor, 1975—; asst. prof. German, UCLA, 1992-93; asst. prof. German U. Colo., Colorado Springs, 1993-99, head German studies, 1993—, assoc. prof. German and film, dir. film studies, 1999—, interim chair dept. visual and performing arts, 2000-01, chair dept. langs. and cultures, 2001—. Author: (plays) The Birthday of Margot Beck, 1980, Briefly Noted, 1981, Vespers, 1982 (Beverly Hills Theatre Guild award 1984), Tristan in Winter, 1986, Songs of a Wayfarer, 1986, Coda, 1991, (criticism) Phantom Empires: The Novels of A. Lernet-Holenia and the Question of Postimperial Austrian Identity, 1996, Verses of a Marriage, Translation of Poetry Collection by Hans Raimund, 1996, Telegrams from the Metropole: Selected Poetry, 1999, Gale Encyclopedia of Multicultural America, 2nd edit., 2000; contbg. editl. advisor: International Dictionary of Films and Filmmakers, 4th edit., 2001, Mars in Aries, trans. of novel by A. Lernet-Holenia, 2003, Austrian Cinema: A History, 2005; founding editor Rohwedder: Internat. Jour. Lit. and Art, 1986-93; editor Pen Center mag., 1992-98; contbg. editor Osiris, Rampike, Adirondack Rev., Poetry Salzburg Rev.; mem. editl. bd. Modern Austrian Lit.,

1997-01; exec. prodr. The Nightmare Stumbles Past, 2002, Semmelweis, 2001, Wilson Chance, 2005; co-prodr. Epicure, 2002, Believe, 2003; columnist Celluloid Mag., Austria; mem. editl. bd. Modern Austrian Literature, 1997-2001; editl. adv. bd. Ariadne Press, 1999—; editor Press of South, 2004— Mem. Accademia Culturale d'Europa, Italy, Colo. Springs World Affairs Coun.; bd. dirs. The Internt. Exptl. Cinema Exposition, Denver Brit. Film Festival Decorated Order of the Vitez (Hungary); Cultural grantee City of L.A., 1990, 91, 92; Pres.'s Fund for Humanities grantee U. Colo., 1996, 2001; named Colo. Prof. of Yr., Carnegie Found./CASE, 2004; recipient Residency award Karolyi Found., France, 1979, Letters, Arts and Scis. Rsch. and Creative Work award U. Colo., 2002. Mem. MLA, PEN (West bd. dirs. L.A. 1992-99, founder and pres. Colo. chpt. 1994-99 2002-03), PEN Austria, Internat. Lernet-Holenia Soc. (v.p. 1998—), Austrian Am. Film Assn. (v.p. 1997—), Austria Mundi (U.S. rep. 2002—), Soc. Cinema and Media Studies, Poets and Writers, L.A. Poetry Festival, SAG, Concordia Assn. Journalists and Writers (Austria), Am. Coll. Heraldry (bd. govs. 2000—), European Acad. Arts and Scis., U.S. Fencing Assn., Constantinian Order St. George Office: U Colo Dept Langs and Cultures Colorado Springs CO 80933-7150 Office Phone: 719-262-3562. Personal E-mail: belvederefilm@yahoo.com.

DAS SARMA, SANKAR, physics professor; came to U.S., 1974; BS with honors, Calcutta U., 1973; MS, Brown U., 1976, PhD, 1979. Rsch. assoc. U. So. Calif., L.A., 1979-80; rsch. scientist Tech. U. Munich (Germany), 1980; rsch. assoc. U. Md., College Park, 1981-82, asst. prof., 1982-85, assoc. prof., 1985-87, prof., 1987—, disting. prof., 1995—. Gordon Godfrey Bequest prof. U. New South Wales (Sydney, Australia), 1992; vis. prof. U. Calif., Santa Barbara, 1992, U. Hamburg (Germany), 1985, IBM TJ Watson Rsch. Ctr., Yorktown Heights, N.Y., 1983. Contbr. over 200 rsch. articles to profl. publs. Benjamin West fellow Brown U., 1974, Royal Soc. Vis. fellow, 1988, Disting. Rsch. fellow U. Md., 1991. Fellow Am. Phys. Soc. Office: U Md Dept Physics College Park MD 20742-0001

DASSEL-STUKE, DONNA JANE, psychologist, educator; b. Evansville, Ind., Feb. 29, 1956; d. Forrest James Dassel and Doris Eileen (Edmonson) Vowels; m. Michael Charles Stuke, July 7, 1985; 1 child, James Conrad. Student, Harlayton Coll., 1976; BS cum laude, U. Evansville, 1977, MS, 1981; postgrad., Emporia State U., 1991—92. Cert. sch. psychologist 1988. Work adjustment supr. So. Ind. Rehab. Ctr., Boonville, 1978, work adjustment specialist, 1978—79; vocat. evaluator Rehab. Ctr., Evansville, 1979—81; intern Evansville Vanderburgh Sch., 1981; sch. psychologist Twin Lakes Coop., Clay Center, Kans., 1981—83, Marshall-Norman Coop., Seneca, 1983—99; substitute tchr. Holton, 1999—2005, Sabeting, 1999—2005, Fall City, Nebr., 1999—2005; prof. Highland C.C., Kans., 2000—05. Mem.: Kans. Assn. Sch. Psychologists, Nat. Assn. Sch. Psychologists, Delta Kappa Gamma, Alpha Lambda Delta. Democrat. Presbyterian. Avocations: piano, swimming, fishing, baseball, basketball. Home: 311 S Mathews St Bern KS 66408-0151

DASSO, JAMES DANIEL, lawyer; b. Columbus, Ohio, Dec. 30, 1960; s. Jerome J. Dasso and Patricia M. Conger; m. Kathleen H. Dasso, May 12, 1990; children: Lillian Mary, Margaret Elizabeth, Mary Kathleen, Thomas Jerome, Eleanor Hart. BA, U. Oregon, 1982; JD, U. Mich., 1986. Bar: Ill. 1987. Jud. clerk J. Edward Lumbard, U.S. Ct. Appeals, 2nd Cir., N.Y.C., 1986-87; assoc. Kirkland & Ellis, Chgo., 1987-93; ptnr. Phelan, Cahill & Quinlan, Chgo., 1993-96, Foley & Lardner LLP, Chgo., 1996—, co-chmn. appellate practice group. Office: Foley & Lardner LLP One IBM Plaza 330 N Wabash Ave Ste 3300 Chicago IL 60611-3603 Office Phone: 312-832-4501. Business E-Mail: jdasso@foley.com.

DASSO, JEROME JOSEPH, real estate educator; b. Neillsville, Wis., Jan. 12, 1929; s. Henry J. and Frances (Schweickert) D.; m. Patricia Mary Conger, June 13, 1959 (div. 1978); children: James Daniel, Mary Cecilia, Nancy Ann, Wendy Jo. BS, Purdue U., 1951; MBA, U. Mich., 1952; MS, U. Wis., 1960, PhD, 1964. Ptnr. Dasso Constrn. Co., Dubuque, Iowa, 1956-58; planner Franklin County, Columbus, Ohio, 1960-61; asst. prof. U. Ill., Urbana, 1964-66; vis. chairholder U. Hawaii, Honolulu, 1982-83; mem. faculty U. Oreg., Eugene, 1966-95, H.T. Miner chair in real estate, 1978-95, H.T. Miner chair emeritus, 1995—. Vis. prof. U. Wis., Madison, 1984; cons. Internat. Assn. Assessing Officers, Chgo., 1972-75; ednl. cons. Hawaii Real Estate Commn., Honolulu, 1982-83. Co-author: (S. Kahn, R. Nesslinger et a)l Principle of Right of Way Acquisition, 1972, (with G. Kuhn) Real Estate Finance, 1983, (with A.A. Ring) Real Estate Principles and Practices, 8th edit., 1977, 9th edit., 1981, 10th edit., 1985, 11th edit., 1989, (with Jim Shilling) 12th edit., 1995, Computerized Assessment Adminstration, 1973; contbr. numerous articles to various publs. Lt. USNR, 1952—60. Vivian Stewart vis. fellow Cambridge U., spring, 1987. Fellow Am. Inst. Corp. Asset Mgmt. (bd. govs. 1988-91), Homer Hoyt Inst. Adv. Studies Real Estate & Urban Land Econs.; mem. Real Estate Educators Assn. (pres. 1980-81, Outstanding Svc. award 1981, Disting. Career award 1989), Am. Real Estate and Urban Econs. Assn. (bd. dirs. 1974-77, 80-83), Real Estate Ctr. Dirs. Chairholders Assn. (pres. 1987-88), Am. Real Estate Soc. (life, bd. dirs. 1985-86, v.p. 1988-89, pres. elect 1989-90, pres. 1990-91), Am. Fin. Assn. (life), Nat. Assn. Realtors (edn. com. 1970-76), Internat. Real Estate Soc. (pres. 1994-95), VFW. Roman Catholic. Avocations: golf, skiing, hiking, photography.

DASTIN, BARRY L., lawyer; BA magna cum laude, Yale U., 1975; JD cum laude, Harvard U., 1978. Bar: NY 1979, Calif. 1985. Ptnr. corp. and fin. dept. Kaye Scholer LLP, LA. Office: Kaye Scholer LLP Ste 1700 1999 Ave of the Stars Los Angeles CA 90067 Office Phone: 310-788-1070. E-mail: bdastin@kayescholer.com.

DASTRUP-HAMILL, FAYE MYERS, city official; b. Sanford, Colo., Dec. 15; d. Earl Dixon and Kady Florence (Cornum) Faucett; m. Sherly K. Myers (dec.); children: Carla Pearce, Susan Kitley (dec.), Mary Jane James, Elizabeth Ireland; m. Merrill E. Dastrup, Sept. 22, 1972 (dec. July 1987); m. Wayne A. Hamill, Mar. 23, 1991. Student, L.D.S. Bus. Coll., 1934-35; grad., Dale Carnegie Inst., 1953; degree in mcpl. works adminstrn., Mt. San Antonio Coll., 1960; student, Syracuse U. Inst., 1968; degree in tech. reporting, Chaffey Coll., 1970. Legal sec. W. W. Platt, City Atty., Alamosa, Colo., 1935-40; sec. pub. works dept. City of Ontario, Calif., 1957-60, dep. city clk., dep. city treas., 1960-64, city clk., 1964-73, city coun. mem., mayor and mayor pro tem, 1974-92; mem. part 150 implementation com. Ontario Airport, Calif., 1993—, chmn. noise adv. com., dept. trans. State of Calif., 1994—. Sec. pers. dept. L.A. Housing Authority, 1948; mem. legis. subcom. So. Calif. Assn. Govts., chmn. hist. preservation and cultural arts com.; mem. revenue and taxation com. League of Calif. Cities, vice-chmn., chmn. Clks. Inst., gen. resolutions com., com. on environ. quality Inland Empire divsn.; chmn. San Bernardino County Planning Com., Criminal Justice; prese. So. Calif. City Clks. Assn., chmn. legis. com.; mem. exec. com. Valley Assn. of Cities; city coun. rep. Ontario Libr. Bd. Trustees. Escort sch. classes through City Hall; judge sci. fairs and sch. and comty. events; life mem. Friends of Ontario Libr.; mem., donor Friends of Mus. of History and Art, Ontario; pres., treas., trustee Ontario (Calif.) City Libr., 1993—; choir dir., life mem. Ch. of Jesus. Recipient plaque with gold gavel So. Calif. City Clks. Assn., 1972, Women Helping Women award Soroptomist Internat. of Ontario, 1981, 1990 Woman of Yr. award State Legislature, State of Calif., 1990, Woman of Achievement award 90s Women's Conf., 1990, 1994 YWCA Woman of Achievement award West End YWCA, 1994, Elizabeth S. Genee Lifetime Achievement award, West End YWCA, 1994, Bryce Denton award Mus. of History and Art, 1996, Outstanding Effort with Calif. Water plaque San Bernardino County Waterworks Dist. #8, 1986, Outstanding Svc. plaque Ontario Air N.G., 1990, Leadership plaque San Bernardino County Sheriff's Dept., 1993, Founding, Support and Encouragement of Crime Stoppers Spl. Recognition plaque Ontario Police Dept., 1993, Outstanding Comty. Svc. plaque U.S. Congressman Jay Kim, 1994, Plaque and Spl. Cert. congratulating receipt of Elizabeth Genee Lifetime Achievement award, 1994, Pub. Svc. Award trophy Adrian Meewis, 1972, plaque for dedicated and meritorious svc. to Ontario, as mayor City Coun. and City Clk., 1986, Lifetime Achievement plaque San Bernardino County Supr. Larry Walker, 1994, Svc. plaque South Coast Air Quality Mgmt. Dist., 1987, decorated plaque Salvation Army, 1992, others. Mem. Calif. Assn. Libr. Trustees and Commrs., Comty. Concert Assn. Pomona Valley (donor), Ontario C. of C. (life, Svc. Award plaque 1992), Musicians Club of Pomona Valley. Mem. Ch. of Jesus Christ of LDS. Avocation: vocal soloist. Home: 761 W Hawthorne St Ontario CA 91762-1510

DATA, ART J., information technology executive; B in Mech. Engring., Marquette Univ., 1972; MBA, DePaul Univ., 1985. With Danly Machine Tool Corp., 1968—75; joined Internat. Truck & Engine Corp. (operating co. of Navistar Internat. Corp.), Warrenville, Ill., 1975, various positions, including process engr. chief engr. computer tech., sr. project engr. for CAD engring., dir. bus. and tech. sys for engine group, 1975—93, v.p. info. tech., 1993—. Named one of the top tech. innovators, Info. Week mag., 2004. Mem.: Tech. Executives Club, AITP, SIM, Soc. of Mfg. Engineers, Soc. of Automotive Engineers. Office: Internat Truck & Engine Corp 4201 Winfield Rd PO Box 1488 Warrenville IL 60555

DATA, LINDA LASKI, music educator; b. Berwyn, Ill., Oct. 28, 1949; d. James J., Sr. and Mary K. Laski; m. Arthur J. Data, Nov. 4, 1978; children: Arthur III, Nicholas. BA, Coll. St. Teresa, Winona, Minn., 1971; MA, St. Xavier U., Chgo., 1994. Customer svc. rep. Kendall Co., Chgo., 1971—75; exec. sec. Ency. Britannica, Chgo., 1975—81; art history tchr. St. Gerald Sch., Oak Lawn, Ill., 1990—91; music tchr. St. Barnabas Sch., Chgo., 1995—96, St. Louis de Montfort Sch., Oak Lawn, Ill., 1996—97, Our Lady of the Ridge Sch., Chgo. Ridge, Ill., 1997—98, St. Edmund Sch., Oak Park, Ill., 1999—2004. Musician: Teresan Orch., 1967—70, Southwest Symphony Tng. Orch., 1996—98. Nominee Heart of the Schs., Archdiocese of Chgo., 2003. Mem.: Am. String Tchrs. Assn., Nat. Assn. for Music Educators, Kappa Gamma Pi, Kappa Delta Pi. Roman Catholic. Avocation: violin. Home: 131 Augusta Ln Palos Heights IL 60463-2919 Office: St George Sch 6700 W Oak Pk Ave Tinley Park IL 60477 E-mail: LD7078@aol.com.

DATARS, WILLIAM ROSS, physicist, researcher; b. Desboro., Ont., Can., June 14, 1932; s. Albert John and Leona Alberta (Fries) D.; m. Eleanor Wismer, 1959 (dec. Oct. 2002); children: Timothy, Andrew, David. B.Sc., McMaster U., Hamilton. Ont., 1955; M.Sc., 1956; PhD, U. Wis., 1959. Physicist Def. Research Bd., 1959-62; mem. faculty McMaster U., 1962—, prof. physics, 1969-96, prof. emeritus, 1996—. E.W.R. Steacie fellow, 1968-70 Fellow Royal Soc. Can., Am. Phys. Soc.; mem. Can. Assn. Physics Lutheran. Home: RR 2 Lynden ON Canada L0R 1T0 Office: McMaster U Dept Physics & Astronomy Hamilton ON Canada L8S 4M1 Business E-Mail: datars@mcmaster.ca.

DATCU, IOANA, artist; b. Bucharest, Romania, Apr. 22, 1944; d. Marin and Niculina Datcu; m. Vasile Porcisanu, Aug. 5, 1967 (div. 1983); 1 child, Isabelle Ioana. BA, Pedagogical Inst., Bucharest, 1967; BFA summa cum laude, U. Minn., 1987, MFA, 1991. Tchr. biology high sch., Argova, Preasna, Romania, 1967—74; photography asst. U. Minn., St. Paul, 1985—86; photographer civil rights dept. City Hall, St. Paul, 1986—87; darkroom supervisor Film in the Cities, St. Paul, 1987—88; gallery asst., curator Paul Whitney Gallery, St. Paul, 1987—91; art instr. Minn. Mus. Am. Art, St. Paul, 1993—94; instr. drawing & painting U. Minn., Mpls., 1996—97. One-woman shows include Flanders Contemporary Art, Mpls., 1994, Winona (Minn.) State U, 1995, Mont. State U., Billings, 1996, Ea. Wash. U., Cheney, 1996, Indpls. Art Ctr., 1996, Kansas City (Mo.) Artists Coalition, 1997, Grants Pass (Oreg.) Mus. Art, 1997, Trinity Presbyn. Ch., Denton, Tex., 1998, South Bend (Ind.) Mus. Art, 1998, U. Dayton, Ohio, 2000, Concordia U., Seward, Nebr., 2004, exhibited in group shows at North Park Coll., Chgo., 1991, Hist. Trinity, Detroit, 1993, 1995—96, Coll. St. Catherine, St. Paul, 1995, Barrett House Galleries, Poughkeepsie, N.Y., 1994, 1996, Minot (ND) State U., 1995, St. John's U., NY, 1995, Katherine E. Nash Gallery, Mpls., 1992, 1995—96, Focal Point Gallery, NYC, 1996, SoHo Photo Gallery, 1997, Greater Lafayette Mus. Art, 1997, Truman State U., Mo., 1998, McNeese State U., La., 1998, Attelboro (Mass.) Mus. Art, 1998—99, New World Art Ctr., NYC, 1999, Ctrl. Mo. State U., 1999, Am. Bible Soc. Gallery, NYC, 2000, Internat. Print Triennial, Cracow, Poland, 2000, Krakow Nürnberg, Messezentrum Mus., Germany, 2000, Jewish Cmty. Ctr. Greater New Haven, Woodbridge, Conn., 2001, Korean Cultural Ctr., LA, 2001, Open Studio Press, 1995, Images of the Spirit Traveling Exhibit, 1995—97, CIVA CODEX III traveling exhibit, 1997—2001, Grand Forks Art Gallery, Can., 2004, represented in, CD-Rom collections of Art Comms. Internat., 1995, Artmax Internat., 1995, Ency. Internat. Women Artists, Alliance Women Artists, 1997, New Art Internat., Book Art Press, 1997, Christianity and the Arts Jour., 1999, Bridge to the Future, 2000, The Missing Mary (by Charlene Spretnak), 2004, Faith and Vision: Twenty Five Years of Christians in the Visual Arts, 2005. Grantee Pollock-Krasner Found., 1992, Minn. State Arts Bd., 1994; Jerome Found. Residency fellow, 1994; McKnight Photography fellow, 1992, fellow Arts Midwest NEA, 1994-95, Clowes Fund regional residency fellow, Indpls., 1997; Vt. Studio Ctr. Residency award, Johnson, Vt., 1997. Mem. Christians in the Visual Arts, Nat. Assn. Women Artists, Inc. Mem. Eastern Orthodox Ch. Avocations: classical music, movies, yoga, books, animals. Home: 1028 E Justin St Sunsites AZ 85625 Office Phone: 520-820-1653. Personal E-mail: datcui@vtc.net. E-mail: ioanadatcu@yahoo.com.

DATE, ELAINE SATOMI, physiatrist, educator; b. San Jose, Calif., Feb. 19, 1957; BS, Stanford U., 1978; MD, Med. Coll. Pa., 1982. Diplomate of Nat. Bd. Med. Examiners. Diplomate Am. Bd. Phys. Medicine and Rehab. Dir. phys. medicine and rehab. Stanford (Calif.) U. Sch. Medicine, 1985—, rehab. medicine sect. chief, 1988-90, head phys. medicine and rehab. div., 1990—, assoc. prof. dept. functional rehab., 1995—; rehab. medicine chief Palo Alto (Calif.) VA Med. Ctr., 1988—. Fellow Am. Acad. Phys. Medicine and Rehab., Am. Assn. Electromyography and Electrodiagnosis. Avocations: reading, jogging.

DATIASHVILI, RAMAZI O., plastic surgeon; b. Kutaisi, Georgia, U.S.S.R., July 8, 1949; arrived in U.S., 1992; s. Otari Datiashvili and Meri Yakobashvili; m. Tatyana Y. Kharina, Apr. 24, 1981; 1 child, Meri. MD, 1st Moscow Med. Inst., 1972; DSc, USSR Nat. Ctr. Surgery, 1988. Diplomate Am. Bd. Plastic Surgery. Attending surgeon City Hosp. #51, Moscow, 1974—79, chief dept. microsurgery, 1979—81; jr. sci. worker to sr. sci. worker USSR Nat. Ctr. Surgery, Moscow, 1981—87, leading sci. worker, 1987—90, chief sci. worker, 1990—91; resident in gen. surgery Mt. Sinai Sch. Medicine, N.Y.C., 1996—99; resident in plastic surgery U. Med. and Dentistry NJ/NJ Med. Sch., Newark, 1999—2001; asst. prof. U. N.J. Med. Sch., Newark, 2001—. Author: Major Limb Replantations, 1991; contbr. articles to numerous profl. jours. Avocations: music, sports. Office: Univ NJ Dept Microsurgery Divsn Plastic Surgery Bergen St Ste 7200 Newark NJ 07103 Office Phone: 973-972-8092. Business E-Mail: datiasro@umdnj.edu.

DATTA, KOUSHIK, aerospace engineer, researcher; b. Lucknow, India, Dec. 7, 1958; arrived in US, 1980; s. Nepal Krishna and Tapati Datta; m. Stacy Budin, Mar. 7, 1986; children: Monica B., Nicholas B. B of Tech. in Mech. Engring., Indian Inst. Tech., Madras, India, 1980; MS in Ops. Rsch., U. Calif., Berkeley, 1981, PhD, 1989. Computer cons. U. Calif., Berkeley, 1983—85; planning engr. US Sprint, Burlingame, Calif., 1985—86; sr. engr. Gen. Atomics, San Diego, 1990—93; lead engr. Sverdrup Tech., Inc., Moffett Field, Calif., 1995—98; mgr. Ames office Bd. Sys., Inc., Moffett Field, Calif., 1998—2003; aero. engr. NASA Ames Rsch. Ctr., Moffett Field, 2003—. Earle C. Anthony fellow, U. Calif., 1980—81. Mem.: IEEE. Avocations: soccer, volleyball. Office: NASA Ames Rsch Ctr M/S 218-7 Moffett Field CA 94035

DATTA, SUDIP, finance educator; b. Kanpur, India, Feb. 2, 1962; s. Provash Chandra and Maya (Sinha) Dutta; m. Mai Elias Iskandar Datta, Mar. 26, 1993; children: Arun Basel, Anita Leela. BS in Econs., Presidency Coll., 1984; MA, SUNY Binghamton, 1987, PhD, 1989. Instr. SUNY, Binghamton, 1987-89; asst. prof. Bentley Coll., Waltham, Mass., 1989-95, assoc. prof., 1995-97, Robert and Julia Dorn prof. fin., 1997—2004; T. Norris Hitchman endowed chairholder, prof. fin. Sch. Bus. Adminstrn., Wayne State U., Detroit, 2004—. Contbr. articles to profl. jours. Fellow Am. Fin. Assn., Fin. Mgmt. Assn. (program com.), So. Fin. Assn. (program com.), We. Fin. Assn. Avocations: investing, travel, cooking, soccer, chess. Office: Wayne State Univ 5201 Cass Ave Prentis 216 Detroit MI 48202 Office Phone: 313-577-0408. Business E-Mail: sdatta@wayne.edu.

DATTA, SUKDEB, anesthesiologist, pain management specialist; b. Jamshedpur, India, June 6, 1967; s. Kartik Chandra and Bela Datta; m. Koel Chatterjee, Sept. 27, 1997. MBBS, NRS Med. Coll., Calcutta, India, 1989. Diplomate Am. Bd. Anesthesiology, Am. Bd. Pain Medicine, subspecialty cert. pain mgmt. Postgrad. trainee in surgery Calcutta (India) U., 1992-94; resident in surgery Nassau County Med. Ctr., East Meadow, N.Y., 1994-95; resident in anesthesiology New Eng. Med. Ctr., Boston, 1995-96, Cook County Hosp., Chgo., 1996-98, chief resident, clin. scientist, 1998-99, fellow pain mgmt. program, 1999-2000; asst. prof. U. Cin., 2000—04, Vanderbilt U., 2004—; chief pain mgmt. svcs. Tenn. Valley Healthcare Sys. Mem. spl. interest groups IASP, SIG. Author: Essentials of Practical Physiology and Viva in Physiology, 1987; contbr. articles to profl. jours.; mem. editl. adv. bd. Pain Physician Jour. Recipient Midwest Anesthesiology Residents Conf. award Ohio State U., Columbus, 1999, Sigma Xi award, 1999; named Best Meeting Sci. Abstracts, IARS Nat. Meeting, 2000. Mem. Am. Soc. Anesthesiologists, Internat. Anesthesia Rsch. Soc. (Best of Meeting award for sci. abstracts 74th Clin. and Sci. Congress 2000), Am. Soc. Regional Anesthesia, Ill. Soc. Anesthesiologists, Greater Cin. Pain Soc. (sec. 2002--), Internat. Spinal Intervention Soc., Internat. Assn. for Study of Pain, Am. Soc. Interventional Pain Physicians. Avocations: music, software. Office: VA Tenn Valley Healthcare Sys Pain Clinic 1310 24th Ave S Nashville TN 37212 Fax: 513-469-0476. Business E-Mail: sukdeb.datta@vanderbilt.edu. E-mail: sukdeb@hotmail.com.

DATTILO, THOMAS A., diversified corporation executive; BA, OH State U.; JD, U. Toledo; graduate of Advanced Mgmt. Program, Harvard Bus. Sch. Mem., corporate legal staff Dana Corp., 1977-82, with ins. operations dvsn., 1982-85, v.p. then gen. mgr., Precision Control Divsn., and other sr. mgmt. positions Laurinburg, NC, 1985—98; pres. and CEO Hayes-Dana Inc., St. Cahtarines, Ont., Can.; pres. Victor Reinz Products, N. Am., Lisle, Ill., 1997—; pres., sealing products group Dana Corp., Toledo, 1997—99; pres. and COO Cooper Tire and Rubber Co., Findlay, Ohio, 1999—2000, chmn., pres., CEO, 2000—. Mem.: Mfr. Alliance (vice chmn.), Rubber Mfr. Assn. (chmn.), Automotive Parts Manufacturer's Assn., Young President's Orgn. Office: Cooper Tire & Rubber Co 701 Lima Ave Findlay OH 45840-2388*

DATTNER, BENJAMIN, management consultant; BA, Harvard Coll., 1992; PhD, NYU, 1999. Prin. Dattner Cons., LLC, N.Y.C., 2001—. Alumni interviewer Harvard Coll., N.Y.C., 1994—2003. Mem.: Soc. for Indsl. and Orgnl. Psychology. Personal E-mail: bdattner@dattnerconsulting.com.

DATZ, ISRAEL MORTIMER, information systems specialist; b. N.Y.C., Feb. 11, 1928; s. A. Mark and Lillian (Barkin) D.; m. Gerd Elin Alme-Torkildsen, Apr. 30, 1956. BS, CCNY, 1950; postgrad., U. Bergen, Norway, 1951-55. Chief programming group Internat. Inst. Meteorology, Stockholm, 1958-59; head support svcs. sect. NASA Goddard Space Flight Ctr., Greenbelt, Md., 1959-61; mathematician Army Strategy and Tactics Analysis Group, Bethesda, Md., 1961-63; acting chief div. ops. analysis Dept. Commerce Maritime Adminstrn., Washington, 1963-64; head computer div. marine engring. lab. Annapolis (Md.) div. Naval Ship R & D Ctr., 1964-68, rsch. coord. math., 1968-72, tech. adv. ops. rsch., 1972-79; pvt. practice, 1979-84, 92—; chief studies and analysis U.S. Army Engr. Sch., Ft. Leonard Wood, Mo., 1984—92. Author: Planning Tools for Ocean Transportation, 1971, Power Transmission and Automation for Ships and Submersibles, 1975, Planning in a Military Context: An Army Perspective, 1998, Military Operations Under Special Conditions of Terrain and Weather, 2004; contbr. articles to profl. jours. Recipient summer stipend, Woods Hole Oceanographic Instn., 1949, rsch. stipend, The Geophysics Inst., Bergen, Norway, 1953. Fellow AAAS; mem. N.Y. Acad. Scis., Inst. Ops. Rsch. and Mgmt. Sci., Assn. Computing Machinery, Nat. Def. Indsl. Assn., Am. Soc. Naval Engrs., Marine Tech. Soc., Soc. Naval Architects and Marine Engrs., U.S. Naval Inst., Navy League U.S. Home and Office: 1343 California Dr Rolla MO 65401-4529 Office Phone: 573-341-3870. Personal E-mail: mortdatz@prodigy.net.

DAUB, HAL, former mayor, former congressman; b. Fayetteville, N.C., Apr. 23, 1941; s. Harold John and Eleanor M. (Hickman) D.; m. Mary Mernin; children: Natalie Ann, John Clifford, Tammy Renee. BSBA, Washington U., St. Louis, 1963; JD, U. Nebr., 1966. Bar: Nebr. 1966, U.S. Ct. Appeals (8th cir.), U.S. Ct. Customs and Patent Appeals, U.S. Supreme Ct. Assoc. Fitzgerald, Brown, Leahy, McGill & Strom, 1968-71; v.p., gen. counsel Standard Chem. Mfg. Co., 1971-80; mem. 97th-100th Congresses from 2nd Nebr. dist., 1981-1989, mem. ways and means com., subcoms. on health and social security; prin., nat. dir. fed. govt. affairs Deloitte & Touche Acctg. and Cons. Firm, 1981-94; mayor City of Omaha, 1995—2000; ptnr. Blackwell Sanders Peper Martin, LLP, 2001—04, of counsel, 2004—; pres., CEO Am. Health Care Assn., Washington, 2004—. Presdl. appointee Nat. Adv. Coun. on Pub. Svc., 1991—92; presdl. appointee chmn. Social Security Adv. Bd., 2001—, chmn., 2001—; prin. Coun. for Excellence in Govt.; staff intern to U.S. Senator Roman Hruska from Nebr., 1966; pres. Republican Mayors and Local Elected Ofcls., 1995—2001; adv. bd. U.S. Conf. Mayors, 1998—2001; chmn. pub. safety and crime prevention com. Nat. League of Cities, 1996—97. Mem. Congl. Regulatory Reform Task Force, 1981-83, Congl. Rep. Agrl. Task Force, 1981-88; co-founder Liability Ins. and Tort Reform Task Force, 1986; mem. exec. com. Rep. Nat. Congl. Com., 1981-88; co-founder, co-chmn. Budget Reform Task Force, 1981-84; jr. pres. Nebr. Founders' Day, 1971; jr. pres. Nebr. Founders' Day, 1971; mem. exec. com., bd. dirs. Combined Health Agys. Drive, 1976; nat. bd. dirs. Combined Health Agys. of Am., 2003—; pres. Douglas-Sarpy unit Nebr. Heart Assn.; bd. dirs. Metro Arts Coun., 1989-93; treas. Douglas County (Nebr.) Rep. Party, 1970-73, chmn., 1974-77; elder Presbyn. Ch. Capt. U.S. Army, 1963-68. Decorated Army Commendation medal with oak leaf cluster, Expeditionary medal; named Outstanding Nebraskan, 1966, Outstanding Vol. of Yr. award Douglas-Sarpy unit Nebr. Heart Assn., 1976, Disting. Eagle Scout; recipient Svc. award SAC, 1976, Leadership awards (4) Coalition for Peace Through Strength, Guardian of Small Bus. awards (4), 1981-88, Omaha C. of C. award, Watchdog of Treasury awards (5), 1981-88. Mem. Omaha Bar Assn., Nebr. Bar Assn., Nat. Assn. Credit Mgmt. (1st v.p. 1977), Res. Officers Assn., Am. Legion, 40 and 8, VFW, Urban League Nebr., Optimists, Masons (33d degree), Shriners, SAR, Kappa Sigma, Alpha Kappa Psi, Omicron Delta Kappa, Delta Theta Phi. Republican. Office: Am Health Care Assn 1201 L St Washington DC 20005 Office Phone: 202-898-2828. Personal E-mail: hdaub@ahca.org. Business E-Mail: hdaub@blackwellsanders.com.

DAUB, MATTHEW FORREST, artist, educator; b. NYC, Aug. 29, 1951; s. Alan J. and Sara Ann D.; m. Barbara Crawford, Aug. 1, 1971; children: Joshua, Sarah. Student, Pratt Inst., 1969-70; BA, So. Ill. U., 1981, MFA, 1984. From asst. prof. to assoc. prof. Kutztown (Pa.) U., 1987-95, prof., 1995—. Author: A Charmed Vision: The Art of Carolyn Plochmann, 1990; one-man shows include Sherry French Gallery, 1984, 86, 88, 91, 93, Jan Cicero Gallery, 1987-89, Evansville (Ind.) Museum Arts and Sci., 1994, Am. Acad. Arts and Letters, 1996, MB Modern Gallery, N.Y., 1998, Demuth Mus., Lancaster, Pa., 2000, Reading (Pa.) Pub. Mus., 2001; contbr. art to calendar Met. Mus. Art, 1991. Home: 920 N Richmond St Fleetwood PA 19522-1905 Office: Kutztown U Sharadin Art Bldg Kutztown PA 19530

DAUB, PEGGY ELLEN, library administrator; b. Bluffton, Ohio, Oct. 15, 1949; d. Perry J. and Olive L. (Hoover) D.; m. Jeffrey H. Cooper, Dec. 13, 1975; 1 child, William P. Cooper-Daub. MusB summa cum laude, Miami U., 1972; MA, Cornell U., 1975; MSLS, U. Ill., 1980; PhD, Cornell U., 1985. Acting asst. music libr. Yale U., 1980-81, head of music tech. svcs., rare books libr. Music Libr., 1981-82; head Music Libr. U. Mich., Ann Arbor, 1982-89, head Spl. Collections & Arts Librs., 1989-99, head Spl. Collections Libr., 2000—. Presenter Rare Books and Manuscript Sect. Pre-Conf., New Orleans, 1993, Bloomington, 1995 and others. Contbr. articles to profl. jours.

Co-clk. Ann Arbor Friends Meeting, 1997-2001. Travel grantee Ctr. for Internat. Studies, Cornell U., 1977. Mem. ALA (Assn. Coll. and Rsch. Librs. rare books and manuscripts sect., mem. task force on interlibr. loan 1991-93, mem. preconf. program planning com. 1992-94), Music Libr. Assn. (bd. dirs. 1985-87, mem. resource sharing and collection devel. com. 1982-91), Rsch. Librs. Group (chairperson music program com. 1985-87, mem. steering com. 1982-87), Am. Musicol. Soc. (mem. coun. 1988-91, mem. coun. com. on minorities/diversity 1988-91), Phi Beta Kappa. Mem. Soc. Of Friends. Office: U of Mich Spl Collections Libr 711 Graduate Libr Ann Arbor MI 48109-1205 Office Phone: 734-764-9377. E-mail: pdaub@umich.edu.

DAUBENAS, JEAN DOROTHY TENBRINCK, retired librarian, educator; b. N.Y.C., Apr. 04; d. Eduard J.A. and Margaret Dorothy (Schaffner) Tenbrinck; m. Joseph Anthony Daubenas, May 29, 1965. Grad., Am. Acad. Dramatic Arts, 1963; AB, Barnard Coll., Columbia U., 1962; MA, NYU, 1965; MLS, U. Ariz., 1972; PhD, U. Utah, 1986. Tchr. Beth Jacob Tchrs. Sem. Am., Bronx, N.Y., 1965-66; caseworker Dept. Social Svcs., N.Y.C., 1966-67; actress Boothbay (Maine) Playhouse, also others, 1967-70; reference libr. Ariz. State U., Tempe, 1972-75; grad. asst. U. Utah, Salt Lake City, 1976-77; asst. libr., asst. prof. libr. sci. Avila Coll., Kansas City, Mo., 1979-83; assoc. prof., libr. St. John's U., Jamaica, NY, 1983—99; ret., 2000. N.Y. State Regents scholar, 1958-61, U. Ariz. scholar, 1971-72. Mem. ALA, AAUP, Actors Equity Assn., Theatre Libr. Assn., Assn. Theatre in Higher Edn., Beta Phi Mu, Phi Kappa Phi. Roman Catholic.

DAUBERT, ERIK JOSEPH, organization administrator, consultant; b. Goshen, N.Y., June 21, 1966; s. Robert Louis and Madeline J.; m. Andrea Miele, Oct. 4, 1997. BA, U. N.C., Chapel Hill, 1989; postgrad. in non-profit mgmt., Duke U., 1992; MBA, Campbell U., 2002; postgrad., Stanford U., 2005. Cert. fund raising exec. Exec. dir. Eco-Logical, Durham, NC, 1991-95; v.p. devel. YMCA of Triangle Area, Raleigh, NC, 1996—; cons. ptnr. We Improve It. Cons. in field, Research Triangle Park, N.C., 1995—; mem. coun. N.Am. YMCA Devel. Officers, 2005—. Vice chair Sierra Club, Durham, 1991-93; pres. bd. dirs. Child Advocacy Commn., Durham, 1995-97; bd. dirs. Eno River Assn., 2003-05, chair. resource devel. com. Named Outstanding Vol., N.C. Pub. Allies, 1994, Cmty. Hero-Torchbearer, 1996 Olympic Games, 1996; recipient cert. merit The Nat. Arbor Day Found., 1993, 94; Stanford U. Grad. Sch Bus. Ctr. for Social Innovation fellow, 2005. Mem. Carolina Prospect Rsch. Assn. Avocations: canoeing, camping, bicycling, reading, people. Home: 2917 Beech Grove Dr Durham NC 27705 Office: YMCA of the Triangle Area 1601 Hillsborough St Raleigh NC 27605 Home Fax: 919-383-3092. E-mail: edaubert@weimproveit.com.

DAUBERT, HARLAN AARON, music educator, director; b. Suedburg, Pa. s. George Edward Daubert and Minnie Wagner; m. Jeanne Elizabeth Beaver, July 25, 1954; children: Suzanne, Nancy, Harlan, Alison, Christopher, Elizabeth, Aaron. BS, Lebanon Valley Coll., Annville, Pa., 1949; MS, Pa. State Coll., 1953; postgrad., Lehigh U., Bethlehem, Pa., 1962—63. Cert. tchr. Pa., supr. Pa. Tchr. music No. Lebanon Sch., Fredericksburg, Pa., 1949—60, dir. of music, 1960—86; dir. of music Zion Luth. Ch., Lebanon, Pa., 1960—. Named Paul Harris fellow, Lebanon Rotary Club, 1986; named to, Nat. Band Dir.'s Hall of Fame; recipient Outstanding Tchr. of Yr. award, Lebanon County, 1983, Outstanding Alumnus award, Lebanon Valley Coll., 1985, Excellence in Music award, Lebanon County Choral Soc., 1986. Mem.: Music Educators Nat. Coun., Profl. Music Educators Assn., Lions Club (Fredericksburg chpt.), Phi Beta Mu. Lutheran. Home: 273 W Main St Fredericksburg PA 17026 Office Phone: 888-459-2487. E-mail: jdaubert@paonline.com.

DAUBERT, MADELINE J., finance educator; b. Norwich, N.Y., Aug. 22, 1941; d. Clifford T. and Marian A. Jones; m. Robert Louis Daubert, 1959; children: David, Lisa, Erik. BS, SUNY, Cortland, 1962; MLS, SUNY, Albany, 1969. CPA, N.C.; cert. libr., sch. media specialist, N.Y. Libr. various pub. schs., N.Y., 1966-78; mgr. mgmt. acctg. Peoples Security Life Ins., Durham, N.C., 1983-84; sys. acct. N.C. Ctrl. U., Durham, 1985-90; owner Madeline J. Daubert, CPA, Durham and Hendersonville, N.C., 1987—. Adj. faculty Tex. Woman's U., Denton, 1990-91, U. South Fla., Tampa, 1993, U. N.C., Chapel Hill, 1995, 98; cons., workshop leader Libr. Congress, Washington, 1999; continuing edn. instr. Spl. Librs. Assn., Washington, 1995-2000; software cons. various univs., Tex., Tenn., Colo., N.C., 1990-91, U. N.C.-Asheville, 1987-89. Author: Financial Management for Small and Medium-Sized Libraries, 1993, Money Talk: Accounting Fundamentals for Special Librarians, 1995, Control of Administrative and Financial Operations in Special Libraries, 1996, Analyzing Library Costs, 1997. Trustee Keller (Tex.) Libr. Bd., 1991—92; mem. Village of Flat Rock Bd. of Adjustment, 2000—03, vice chmn., 2000—01; treas. Hendersonville Little Theater, 2002—03; dir. Cmty. Found. Henderson County, 2000—. Office: 428 Chaparral Ln Flat Rock NC 28731-9560

DAUCH, RICHARD E., automobile manufacturing company executive; b. 1942; BS, Purdue U., 1964. With Gen. Motors Corp., Detroit, 1964-75; group v.p. mfg. Volkswagen of Am., Detroit, 1976-80; v.p. Chrysler Corp., Detroit, 1980, exec. v.p. diversified ops., 1980-81, exec. v.p. stamping assembly diversified ops., 1981-84, exec. v.p. mfg., 1984-1994; co-founder, CEO Am. Axle and Mfg., Detroit, 1994—, pres., 1994—2001, chmn., 2001—. Recipient Eli Whitney Meml. Award Soc. Mfg. Engr., 1987, Ellis Island Medal of Honor, 1997; named Industry Leader of the Yr., Automotive Hall of Fame, 1997; Mfr. of the Yr., Mich. Mfg. Assn., 1997; Newsmaker of the Yr., Crain's Detroit Bus., 1998, World Trader of the Yr., Detroit Regional Chamber, 2002, Mich. Exec. of the Yr., Wayne State U. Coll. Bus. Adminstrn., 2002. Mem.: Nat. Assn. Mfr. (chairman 2003). Office: American Axle and Mfg 1840 Holbrook St Detroit MI 48212-3442

DAUCHER, DONALD A., lawyer; b. Buffalo, N.Y., Apr. 2, 1945; BS, U. Rochester, 1967; JD, Duke U., 1971. Bar: Calif. 1972. Mng. ptnr.-San Diego Office Paul, Hastings, Janofsky & Walker, San Diego. Mem. Order Coif, Beta Gamma Sigma. Office: Paul Hastings Janofsky & Walker LLP 3579 Valley Ctr Dr San Diego CA 92130 Office Phone: 858-720-2860. Office Fax: 858-720-2555. Business E-Mail: dondaucher@paulhastings.com.

DAUENHAUER, RICHARD LEONARD, writer; b. Syracuse, N.Y., Apr. 10, 1942; s. Leonard George and Jane Grier D.; m. Nora Marks, Nov. 1973. BA in Russian, Syracuse U., 1964; MA in German, U. Tex., 1966; PhD in Comparative Lit., U. Wis., 1975. Asst. prof. comparative lit. Alaska Meth. U., Anchorage, 1969-75; staff assoc. Alaska Native Found., Anchorage, 1976-78; assoc. prof. humanities Alaska Pacific U., Anchorage, 1979-83; program dir. Sealaska Heritage Found., Juneau, 1983-97; freelance writer, cons., 1997—2005; pres.'s prof. native langs. and culture U. Alaska, Juneau, 2005—. Author: Glacier Bay Concerto, 1980, Frames of Reference, 1987; author, editor For Healing Our Spirit: Tlingit Oratory, 1990; contbr. articles to profl. jours. Recipient Govs. award Arts, State Alaska, 1989, Am. Book award Before Columbus Found., 1991; named Poet Laureate of Alaska, 1981-88; Fulbright fellow, 1966. Home: 3740 N Douglas Hwy Juneau AK 99801-9420 E-mail: jfrld@uas.alaska.edu.

DAUER, DONALD DEAN, investment company executive; b. Fresno, Calif., June 1, 1936; s. Andrew and Erma Mae (Zigenman) D.; m. LaVerne DiBuduo, Jan. 23, 1971; children: Gina, Sarah. BS in Bus. Adminstrn., Calif. State U. Fresno; postgrad., U. Wash., 1964. Loan officer First Savs. and Loan, Fresno, 1961-66, v.p., 1966-71, sr. v.p., 1971-81, exec. v.p., 1978-81; pres. Uniservice Corp., Fresno, 1976-81, Don Dauer Investments, Fresno, 1981—; pres., chief oper. officer Riverbend Internat. Corp., Sanger, Calif., 1985-89. Chmn. bd. dirs. Univ. Savs. and Loan, 1991-92, acting pres., CEO, 1992; loan officer Norwest Mortgage, 1993-95; mgr. CMB Fin., 1995-96. Chmn. bd. dirs. City of Fresno Gen. Svcs. Retirement Bd., 1973-83, West Fresno Econ. and Bus. Devel. Program Bd., 1980-83; pres. bd. dirs. Cen. Calif. United Cerebral Palsy Assn., 1979-82; bd. dirs. Valley Children's Hosp. Found., Fresno, 1984-93; trustee, chmn. Valley Children's Hosp., 1987-93; bd. dirs. Youth for Christ USA, 1988-94, Twilight Haven Inc., 2000—; vice chmn. Riverbend Internat., 1975-91. Mem. Soc. Real Estate Appraisers (past pres.). Office: 2733 W Palo Alto Ave Fresno CA 93711-1110 Office Phone: 559-431-2764. E-mail: dddauer@yahoo.com.

DAUER, EDWARD ARNOLD, law educator; b. Providence, Sept. 28, 1944; s. Marshall and Shirley (Moverman) Dauer; m. Carol Jean Egglestone, June 16, 1966; children: E. Craig, Rachel P. AB, Brown U., 1966; LLB cum laude, Yale U., 1969; MPH, Harvard U., 2001. Bar: Conn. 1978, Colo. 1986. Asst. prof. law sch. U. Toledo, 1969-72; assoc. prof. law U. So. Calif., L.A., 1972-74; assoc. prof. Yale U., New Haven, 1975-85, assoc. dean, 1978-83, dep. dean Law Sch., 1983-85; dean, prof. U. Denver, 1985-90, dean emeritus, prof., 1991—. Of counsel Popham, Haik, Schnobrich and Kaufman, 1990—97; vis. scholar Harvard U. Sch. Pub. Health, 1996—2004; pres. CAEJAD Aviation Corp.; assoc. Health Care Negotiations Assocs., Inc. Author: (book) Materials on a Nonadversarial Legal Process, 1978, Conflict Resolution Strategies in Health Care, 1993, Manual of Dispute Resolution: ADR Law and Practice, 1994 (CPR Book award, 1994), Health Care Dispute Resolution, 2000; contbr. articles to profl. jours. Founder, pres. Nat. Ctr. Preventive Law; bd. dirs. New Haven Cmty. Action Agy., 1978—81; mem. Colo. Commn. Higher Edn., 1987—91; bd. dirs. Cerebral Palsy Found., Denver, 1989—, pres., 1992—95; commr. Colo. Advanced Tech. Inst., 1989—91. Recipient W. Quinn Jordan award, Nat. Blood Found., 1994, Paelia award, Harvard Sch. Pub. Health, 1996, Sanbar award, Am. Coll. Legal Medicine, 1999. Mem.: Am. Law Inst. (life), Met. Club, Cherry Creek Athletic Club, Order of Coif. Republican. Home: 127 S Garfield St Denver CO 80209 Office: U Denver Coll Law 2255 E Evans Ave Denver CO 90208 Office Phone: 303-871-6278. Business E-Mail: edauer@law.du.edu.

DAUER, SHEILA A., human rights program director; b. Phila., Pa., Oct. 17, 1943; d. Max G. and Sheila A. Dauer. BA in English, Temple U.; PhD in Anthropology, U. Pa. Asst. prof. anthropology Queens Coll. CUNY, 1971—73; asst. prof. anthropology Hunter coll. CUNY, 1973—74; exec. asst. to exec. dir. Amnesty Internat., N.Y.C, 1976—77, dir. country specialist program, 1977—81, acting nat. campaign dir., 1982—93, dir. women's human rights program, 1994—. Vis. lectr. Dartmouth Coll., Hanover, NH, 1975—76; vis. lectr. New Sch. for Social Rsch., N.Y.C., 1976—77; advisor Women Changing the World Series, the Feminist Press, 1999—; mem. adv. bd. Ctr. for Gender and Refugee Studies, Hastings Coll. Law, U. Calif., San Francisco, 2000—; participant in numerous internat. confs. on human rights in various roles including chair, 1991—. Contbr. articles to various publs., 1973—84. Recipient Aston scholarship, U. Pa., 1965—66; fellow for field rsch., NIMH, 1968—70, Dissertaion fellowship, Ford Found., 1974—75, Rsch. fellowship, NIMH, 1967—70. Fellow: Am. Anthrop. Assn. (mem. human rights com. 2000—02); mem.: Assn. for Feminist Anthropology. Office: Amnesty Internat USA 322 8th Ave 10th Fl New York NY 10001

DAUGAARD, DENNIS M., lieutenant governor; b. Garretson, S.D., June 11, 1953; m. Linda Kay Schmidt; 3 children. BS, U. S.D., 1975; JD, Northwestern U., 1978. Bar: S.D. Atty. Supena & Nyman, 1978-79, Shand Morahan & Co., 1979-81; bank trust officer 1st Bank S.d., 1981-90; devel. dir. Children's Home Soc., 1990—; mem. S.D. Senate from 9th dist., Pierre, 1997—2003; lt. gov. state of S.D., 2003—. Mem. Nat. Soc. Fund Raising Execs., S.D. Bar Assn., S.D. Planned Giving Coun., Siox Falls (S.D.) Estate Planning Coun., Rotary. Republican. Lutheran. Office: State Capitol Bldg 500 E Capitol Ave Pierre SD 57501-5070*

DAUGHENBAUGH, RANDALL JAY, retired chemical company executive, consultant; b. Rapid City, S.D., Feb. 10, 1948; s. Horace Allan and Helen Imogene (Reder) Daughenbaugh; m. Mary R. Wynja, Aug. 25, 1973; children: Jason Allan, Jill Christen. BS, S.D. Tech., 1970; PhD, U. Colo., 1975. Rsch. chemist Air Prod. and Chem., Allentown, Pa., 1975-80; rsch. dir. Chem. Exch. Industries, Boulder, Colo., 1980-83; pres. Hauser Chem. Rsch., Inc., Boulder, 1983-93, chief tech. officer, exec. v.p., 1993-99; ret. Contbr. articles to profl. jours. Named Engrepreneur of the Yr., Inc. Mag., 1992; recipient IR-100 award, R&D Mag., 1993. Mem.: Am. Chem. Soc. Achievements include patents in field. Home: 10755 Sheridan Lake Rd Rapid City SD 57702-6506 Personal E-mail: rjdaugh@rapidnet.com.

DAUGHERTY, F(RANCIS) MARK, music educator, conductor, theater director; b. Reading, Pa., May 28, 1951; s. Francis Rodman Daugherty and Lucy Eddinger. MusB, Eastman Sch. Music, 1973; MusM, Temple U, 1997; JD, Temple U., 1978. Bar: Pa. 1978. Editor Musicdata, Inc., Phila., 1984—99; tchg. asst. Temple U., 1995—97; tchr. Chestnut Hill Acad., 1997—. Artistic dir. Ambler Choral Soc., Pa., 1985—; accompanist Orpheus Club Phila., 1986—; dir. music Unitarian Soc. Germantown, 1983—; musical dir. Old York Rd. Temple Beth Am, Abington, 1984—; music dir. Camp Tecumseh, Center Harbor, NH, 1991—. Editor: (bibliographic reference) Sacred Choral Music In Print, 2nd Ed., Secular Choral Music In Print, 2nd Ed., Sacred Choral Music In Print, '92 & '95 Supps., Secular Choral Music In Print, '91 & '93 Supps, Organ Music In Print: '90 Supplement, Classical Vocal Music In Print, 1985 Supplement. Recipient Elaine Brown Tribute award, Boyer Coll. of Music, Temple U, 1996; fellow, Chorus Am., 1996; scholar, Boyer Coll. Music, Temple U., 1995—96, 1996—97. Mem.: Unitarian Universalist Musicians Network, Guild Temple Musicians, Am. Guild Organists, Am. Choral Dirs. Assn., The Musical Fund Soc., Pi Kappa Lambda. Avocations: travel, fitness, environmental conservation, world music. Home: 21 Leamy House 115 Roumfort Rd Philadelphia PA 19119 Office: Chestnut Hill Acad 500 West Willow Grove Ave Philadelphia PA 19118 Office Phone: 215-247-4700. Personal E-mail: fmdleamy@aol.com. Business E-Mail: mdaugherty@chestnuthillacademy.org.

DAUGHERTY, FREDERICK ALVIN, federal judge; b. Oklahoma City, Aug. 18, 1914; s. Charles Lemuel and Felicia (Mitchell) D.; m. Marjorie E. Green, Mar. 15, 1947 (dec. Feb. 1964); m. Betsy F. Amis, Dec. 15, 1965. LL.B., Cumberland U., 1933; postgrad., Oklahoma City U., 1934-35, LL.B. (hon.), 1974; postgrad., Okla. U., 1936-37; HHD (hon.), Okla. Christian Coll., 1976. Bar: Okla. 1937. Practiced, Oklahoma City, 1937-40; mem. firm Ames, Ames & Daugherty, Oklahoma City, 1946-50, Ames, Daugherty, Bynum & Black, Oklahoma City, 1952-55; judge 7th Jud. Dist. Ct., Oklahoma City, 1955-61; U.S. dist. judge Western, Eastern and No. Dists. Okla., Oklahoma City, 1961—; chief judge Western Dist. Okla., Oklahoma City, 1972-82. Mem. Fgn. Intelligence Surveillance Ct., 1981-88, Temporary Emergency Ct. Appeals, 1983-93, Multi dist. Litigation panel, 1980-90; mem. codes of conduct com. U.S. Jud. Conf., 1980-87. Active local ARC, 1956—, chmn., 1958-60, nat. bd. govs., 1963-69, 3d nat. vice chmn., 1968-69; active United Fund Greater Oklahoma City, 1957—, pres., 1961, trustee, 1963—; pres. Community Coun. Oklahoma City and County, 1967-69; exec. com. Okla. Med. Rsch. Found., 1966-69. With AUS, 1940-45, 50-52. Decorated Legion of Merit with 2 oak leaf clusters, Bronze Star with oak leaf cluster, Combat Infantrymans badge; recipient award to mankind Okla. City Sertoma Club, 1962, Outstanding Citizen award Okla. City Jr. C. ofC., 1965, Disting. Alumni citation Samford U., 1974, Disting. Svc. citation Okla. U., 1973, Constn. award Rogers State Coll., 1988, Pathmakers award Oklahoma County Hist. Soc., 1991; named to Okla. Hall of Fame, 1969, Okla. Mil. Hall of Fame, 2000. Mem. Fed. Bar Assn., Okla. Bar Assn., Am. Bar Found., Sigma Alpha Epsilon, Phi Delta Phi, Men's Dinner Club (Oklahoma City) (pres. 1966-69), Kiwanis (pres. 1957, lt. gov. 1959), Masons (33 degree, sovereign grand insp. gen. in Okla. 1982-86), Shriners, Jesters, Order of Coif (hon. mem. Okla. chpt.). Episcopalian (sr. warden 1957).

DAUGHERTY, JAMES G., music educator; b. Jefferson, N.C., Sept. 29, 1971; s. Henry Fred and Linda Mae Daugherty. MusB in Edn., Appalachian State U., 1993, MusM in Edn., 1994. Dir. of bands, instr. of music theory/history Cen. Davidson H.S., Lexington, NC, 1994—. Author: (master's thesis) An Historical and Analytical View of Five Compositions for Brass Ensemble As Presented In A Graduate Conducting Recital, 1994. Named Outstanding Young Educator, Lexington, N.C. Jaycees, 1997; recipient N.C. Tchg. Fellows scholarship, State of N.C., 1989, Citation of Excellence, Nat. Band Assn., 1998, Province Leadership award, Phi Mu Alpha, 1995. Mem.: N.C. Assn. of Educators, N.C. Bandmasters Assn. (bd. dirs. N.W. dist. 1996, treas. of N.W. dist.), N.C. Music Educators Assn., Music Educators Nat. Conf., Nat. Band Assn. (Citation of Excellence 1998), Am. Sch. Band Dirs. Assn., Phi Eta Sigma, Kappa Delta Pi, Phi Kappa Lambda, Phi Mu Alpha (v.p., sec., fraternal edn. officer 1990—93). Baptist. Home: 2788 NC Hwy 47 Lexington NC 27292 Office: Cen Davidson H S 2747 NC Hwy 47 Lexington NC 27292 Personal E-mail: conductor@lexcominc.net.

DAUGHERTY, KENNETH EARL, research company executive, educator; b. Pitts., Dec. 27, 1938; s. Thomas Hill and Laura Elizabeth (Schuda) D.; m. Joan Kay Ogrosky, Dec. 22, 1961; children: Brian Earl, Kirsten Kay. BS in Chemistry, Carnegie-Mellon U., 1960; PhD in Analytical Chemistry, U. Wash., 1964; M in Bus. Econs., Claremont Grad. Sch., 1971. Chemist Marbon Chem.-Borg Warner, Washington, W.Va., 1960; rsch. chemist Rohm and Haas Corp., Bristol, Pa., 1964; group leader, sr. staff Amcord, Riverside, Calif., 1966-71; assoc. prof. chemistry U. Pitts., 1971-73; dir. research and devel. Gen. Portland Inc., Dallas, 1973-77; dir. energy and materials sci. Inst. Applied Scis. North Tex. State U., Denton, 1977-79, prof. chemistry, 1979—2000, chmn. analytical divsn., 1980—95; owner TRAC Labs., Denton, 1981—. Pres., CEO, KEDS Inc., KD Cons., 1977—; adj. prof. chemistry U. Pitts., 1973-2000, North Tex. State U., Denton, 1974-2000; adj. faculty Army Command and Gen. Staff Coll., 1983—; cons. in field. Author numerous publs. in field; patentee in field. Col. U.S. Army, 1964—66, col. USAR, 1966—95. Decorated Army Commendation medal, Army Achievement medal, Army Meritorious Svc. medal; fellow DuPont, Shell Oil, Std. Oil, NSF, 1964. Fellow Am. Inst. Chemists; mem. Research Soc. Am., ASTM, Rilem, Nat. (transp. research bd.), NY Acad. Scis., Am. Ceramic Soc. (program chmn. 1986), Am. Chem. Soc. (chpt. pres. 1960, chmn. Dallas-Ft. Worth 1986), Applied Spectroscopy Soc., Soc. Petroleum Engrs., Soc. Plastics Engrs., Sr. Army Comdrs. Assn., Sigma Xi, Pi Kappa Alpha, Omicron Delta Epsilon, Phi Lambda Upsilon, Alpha Chi Sigma, Masons (32d degree), Shriners, Rotary. Republican. Methodist. Home: 1912 Hunskor Rd Oak Harbor WA 98277-8666 Personal E-mail: kedsinc@whidbey.net.

DAUGHERTY, LINDA HAGAMAN, real estate company executive; b. Denver, Jan. 25, 1940; d. Charles B. and Agnes May (Wall) Hagaman; m. Thomas Daniel Daugherty, Nov. 20, 1965; children: Patrick, Christina Marie. BS in Bus., U. Colo., 1961; postgrad., Tulane U., 1963-64, U. St. Thomas, 1990-91. Sr. systems analyst Lockheed Electronics NASA, Houston, 1966-73; sr. systems cons. TRW Systems Internat., Caracas, Venezuela, 1973-74; sy. systems cons. TRW Systems, L.A., 1974-75; mng. ptnr. Motivated Child Learning Ctrs., Katy, Tex., 1976—; pres. Nottingham Country Day Sch., Katy, 1977—; sr. systems analyst Intercomp, Houston, 1979-80; pres. Daugherty Fin. Svcs., Inc., Katy, 1979—91, Williamsburg Country Day Sch., Katy, 1983—. Mem. Epiphany Ch. Social Works Commn., San Antonio World Affair Coun.; pres. Mason Creek Women Reps. Club, Katy, 1980; treas. Nottingham Country Civic Club, Katy, 1979; mem. adv. bd. Nottingham Country Club, 1982—85; co-founder Friends of Archaeology U. St. Thomas, pres., 1991—93; pres., treas. Friends of Boerne Pub. Libr., 1997—99; asst. curator Archaeology Gallery, U. St. Thomas. Mem. Houston Archeology Soc., Tex. Archeology Soc., Archaeology Inst. of Am., Boerne Women's Club. Roman Catholic. Avocations: archaeology, bridge. Office: Motivated Child Learning Ctr PO Box 489 Boerne TX 78006-0489

DAUGHERTY, PATRICIA ANN, retired elementary school educator; b. Rockford, Ill., May 19, 1949; d. Bjarne John and Mary Rita (Ryan) Jacobsen; m. Greg A. Kramer, June 23, 1973 (div. Apr. 1988); 1 child, Josie Kramer. BS, No. Ill. U., 1971, MS, 1978. cert. elem. tchr., Ill., spl. edn. tchr., Ill. Tchr. Aurora (Ill.) East Sch. Dist., 1971—2004, ret., 2004; adj. faculty dept. edn. Aurora U., 2004—. Mem. choir Our Lady of Mercy Cath. Ch. Mem. AAUW (2d v.p. membership 2005—, gift honoree 1996), Am. Fedn. Tchrs. (bldg. rep. 1995-2004), Ill. Ret. Tchrs. Assn. Avocations: reading, gardening, skiing, golf. Home: 340 Inverness Dr Aurora IL 60504-6925

DAUGHERTY, PHYLLIS LYN, secondary school educator; d. E. Sexton and Myra Catherine Daugherty; m. Kendell C. McMillan, 1973 (div. 1993); children: Erin, Rachel; m. G. James Jackson Jr., 2003. BA in English and Secondary Edn., Harding U., 1973; MA in Pub. History, U. Ill., Springfield, Ill., 1997, MA in Edn. Leadership (Adminstrn.), 2003. Cert. secondary edn. (6-12) Ill., 1973, adminstrv. Ill., 2002. Educator Granite City (Ill.) Sch. Dist., 1973—79; permanent substitute Lafayette (La.) Parish Sch. Dist., 1984—87, Dept. Def., Wiesbaden, Germany, 1990—93, tchr. Taegu, Republic of Korea, 1997—98, Springfield (Ill.) Sch. Dist., 1993—97, 1998—2004, Collinsville (Ill.) Sch. Dist., 2004—. Transcriber: Lincoln's Legal Papers, 1996. Bd. dir. Sangamon County Hist. Soc., Springfield, 1997—98, Ill. Humanities Coun., Springfield, 1999—. Recipient Gulf War Commemorative medal, Dept. of Def. and Am. Red Cross, 1991; grantee LEAD grant, Readers Digest, 2002. Mem.: Ill. Principals Assn., Org. of Am. Historians, Phi Alpha Theta. Avocations: travel, cooking, gardening. Office: Collinsville HS 2201 S Morrison Collinsville IL 62234

DAUGHERTY, RUTH ALICE, religious association consultant; b. Shenandoah, Va., Feb. 21, 1931; d. Lee Earl and Lena Alice (Heishman) Sheaffer; m. Robert Mowery Daugherty, July 11, 1953; children: Carole Ruth Daugherty Haigh, Steven Robert, Beth Anne Daugherty Carr. AA, Shenandoah Jr. Coll., 1950; BA, Lebanon Valley Coll., 1952; HHD (hon.), Albright Coll., 1982, Shenandoah U., 1986. English and history tchr. Bruce H.S., Westernport, Md., 1952-53, Trotwood (Ohio) H.S., 1953-55; officer United Meth. Women, Pa., 1956-72, nat. pres., 1980-84, dir. women's divsn., 1976—84; mem. gen. coun. on ministries United Meth. Ch., 1972—76, nat. chair ministry study, 1984-92; nat. v.p. United Meth. Comm. Commn., 1984-88; v.p. United Bd. for Christian Higher Edn. in Asia, N.Y.C., 1984-87. M. faculty Drew Theol. Sem., 2001; cons. for gen. commn. Christian unity and interreligious concerns United Meth. Ch., 2001—04. Author: (booklet) United Methodist Women in Mission, 1994, (study guide) John Wesley Study, 1996, The Missionary Spirit: History of the Methodist Protestant Church, 2004. Trustee Lebanon Valley Coll., Annville, Pa., 1971—89; chair pers. com., chair mus. com. Scarritt-Bennett Ctr., Nashville, 1991—96, sec., 1996—99; pres. Lumina Bd., Lancaster, Pa., 1998—; co-chair addressing world and cmty. issues EPA Conf., 2000—04, del. to quad gen. confs., 1972—; sec. NE jurisdiction United Meth. Ch., 2003—; bd. dirs. United Meth. Pub. House, 2003—; chair policy program com., chair directions for the '90s United Bd. for Christian Edn. in Asia, 1990—98, trustee emeritus, 1998—; sec. trustees Ea. Pa. Conf. United Meth Ch., Valley Forge, 1992—98; gen. commn. Christian unity and interreligious concerns United Meth. Ch., 1992—2000, sec., 1996—2000, Otterbein dist. lay leader, 1998—2001, cons., 2000—04, bd. ordained ministry Ea. Pa. chpt., 2004—, mem. nat. adv. com. ch. and cmty. workers, 2004—, mem. 50th anniversary taks force ordination of women, 2002—. Recipient Disting. Alumni award Shenandoah U., 1996, Alumni award Lebanon Valley Coll., 1979, Woodrow B. Seals Laity award Perkins Sch. Theology, 1997, Anna Howard Shaw award Anna Howard Shaw Ctr., Boston U. Avocations: making yeast breads, making quilts, reading, gardening. Home: 1936 N Eden Rd Lancaster PA 17601-4952 Personal E-mail: rdaugherty@mycyberlink.net.

DAUGHERTY, SANDRA GAYE, artist; b. Casper, Wyo., May 26, 1946; d. Vernon H. and Edith Blanche (Massick) Anderson; m. Jim W. Bright, June 5, 1965 (div. Apr. 1975); 1 child, Joe W.; m. Roy Lawrence Daugherty, Aug. 11, 1975; 1 child, Kelly Gilbert. Student, Fresno State U., 1963—64, Casper Coll., 1964—65, Ea. Wyo. U., 1979—80. Cattle rancher, 1965—75; asst. mgr. Credit Bur., Douglas, Wyo., 1965—66; bookkeeper, teller, estates Converse County Bank, Douglas, 1966—74; oil field sec. Chinook, Douglas, 1974—75; co-owner Daugherty Constrn., Douglas, 1975—81; fire dispatcher/typist USDA-Forest Svc. Fed. Law Enforcement, Douglas, 1977—81, pub. info. officer, 1978—81; parent adv., counselor Govs. Coun. Devel. Disabilities, Cheyenne, Wyo., 1989—92; trust mgr. Blondin Revocable Trust, Casper, Wyo., 1993—98. Pres. Glenrock (Wyo.) Art Guild, 1977—78. Exhibitions include Gallery of The Yellowstone, Gardiner, Mont., 1975—76, West Wind Gallery, Casper, Wyo., 1977, Nat. Mus. Women in the

Arts, 1997—, Cheyenne Nat. Art Show, Cheyenne, Wyo., 2004, 2005. Active Rep. Nat. Com., Washington, 2002—. Mem.: NRA (mem. Internat. Legis. Com.). Methodist. Avocations: raising and training racehorses, hunting, fishing, antiques, birdwatching. Home: 76 St Hwy 319 Douglas WY 82633 Office Phone: 307-358-9257.

DAUGHTON, DONALD, lawyer; b. Grand River, Iowa, Mar. 11, 1932; s. F.J. and Ethel (Edwards) D.; m. Sally Daughton; children by previous marriage: Erin, Thomas, Andrew, J.P. BSc, U. Iowa, 1953, JD, 1956. Bar: Iowa, 1956, Ariz., 1958. Asst. county atty. Polk County, Des Moines, Iowa, 1956, 1958-59; atty. Snell & Wilmer, Phoenix, 1959-64, Browder and Daughton, Phoenix, 1964-65; judge Superior Ct. of Ariz., Phoenix, 1965-67, 97—; atty. Browder Gillenwater and Daughton, Phoenix, 1967-72, Daughton Feinstein and Wilson, Phoenix, 1972-86, Daughton Hawkins and Bacon, Phoenix, 1986-88; resident mng. ptnr. Brian Cave, Phoenix, 1988-92; atty. Daughton Hawkins Brockelman Guinnan and Patterson, Phoenix, 1992-97. Asst. county atty. Polk County, 1958-59 chmn. Phoenix Employees Relations Bd., 1976. Pres. Maricopa County Legal Aid Soc., 1971-73. 1st lt. JAG, USAF, 1956-58. Fellow Am. Bar Found., Ariz. Bar Found. (founder); mem. ABA (bd. govs. 1989-92, exec. com. 1991-92), State Bar Ariz. (chmn. pub. rels. com. 1980-84, jud. evaluation poll com. 1984-94), Iowa State Bar, Maricopa County Bar Assn. (bd. dirs. 1962-64), 9th Cir. Jud. Conf. (lawyer rep. 1981-84, 88), Nat. Acad. Arbitrators, Chartered Inst. Arbitrators, Univ. Club. Office: Superior Ct of Ariz 201 W Jefferson St Phoenix AZ 85003-2205

DAUGHTREY, MARTHA CRAIG, federal judge; b. Covington, Ky., July 21, 1942; d. Spence E. Kerkow and Martha E. (Craig) Piatt; m. Larry G. Daughtrey, Dec. 28, 1962; 1 child, Carran. BA cum laude, Vanderbilt U., 1964, JD, 1968. Bar: Tenn. 1968. Pvt. practice, Nashville, 1968; asst. U.S. atty., 1968—69; asst. dist. atty., 1969—72; asst. prof. law Vanderbilt U., Nashville, 1972—75; judge Tenn. Ct. Appeals, Nashville, 1975—90; assoc. justice Tenn. Supreme Ct., Nashville, 1990—93; circuit judge U.S. Ct. Appeals (6th cir.), Nashville, 1993—. Lectr. law Vanderbilt Law Sch., Nashville, 1975—82, adj. prof., 1988—90; mem. faculty NYU Appellate Judges Seminar, N.Y.C., 1977—90, N.Y.C., 1994—. Contbr. articles to profl. jours. Pres. Women Judges Fund for Justice, 1984—85, 1986—87; active various civic orgns. Named Woman of the Yr., Women Prof. Internat., 1976; recipient Athena award, Nat. Athena Program, 1991. Mem.: ABA (chmn. appellate judges conf. 1985—86, ho. of dels. 1988—91, chmn. jud. divsn. 1989—90, standing com. on continuing edn. of bar 1992—94, commn. on women in the profession 1994—97, bd. editors ABA Jour. 1995—2001, Margaret Brent award 2003), past mem., bd. visitors, Memphis State Sch. of Law, past mem., ed. bd., Judge's Journal, Lawyers Assn. for Women (pres. Nashville 1986—87), Nat. Assn. Women Judges (pres. 1985—86), Am. Judicature Soc. (bd. dirs. 1988—92), Nashville Bar Assn. (bd. dirs. 1988—90), Tenn. Bar Assn. Office: US Ct Appeals 300 Customs House 701 Broadway Nashville TN 37203-3944*

DAUM, BRYAN EDWIN, lawyer; b. Granite City, Ill., Sept. 14, 1949; s. Edwin Leo and Melba Louise (King) D.; m. Elizabeth Lanney, May 5, 1974; children: Andrea, Veronica, Benjamin. BA, Tex. Christian U., 1971; JD, U. Tex., 1979. Bar: Fla. 1979, Ariz. 1985, U.S. Ct. Appeals (5th and 11th cirs.) 1981, U.S. Ct. Appeals (9th cir.) 1985, U.S. Dist. Ct. Ariz. 1985. Assoc. Trenam, Simmons, Kemker, Scharf, Barkin, Frye & O'Neill, P.A., Tampa, Fla., 1979-85, Bilby & Shoenhair, P.C., Tucson, 1985-89, Snell & Wilmer, Tucson, 1989-91; pvt. practice Tucson, 1991—. Served with USN, 1972-76. Mem. ABA, Fla. Bar Assn., Ariz. Bar Assn., Order of Coif, Phi Beta Kappa. Home: 5735 N Camino Del Conde Tucson AZ 85718-4307 Office: 6262 N Swan Rd Ste 130 Tucson AZ 85718

DAUM, DAVID ERNEST, machinery manufacturing company executive; b. Pitts., July 31, 1939; s. Edward Charles and Esther (Horn) D.; children—Anjeanette R., Matthew C. BSE, Princeton U., 1960; MBA, U. Calif., Long Beach, 1972. Sales engr. Joy Mfg. Co., Seattle and San Francisco, 1960-68, dist. mgr. Mpls., 1968-70; pres. Sullair of So. Calif., Long Beach, 1970-75; v.p. Sullair Corp., Michigan City, Ind., 1975-85, Safway Steel Products, Milw., 1986-92; pres., owner Daum & Assocs., 1992—. Trustee, pres. Scaffolding, Shoring and Forming Inst. Am.; bd. dirs. Montessori Sch., Michigan City, 1970. Mem. Beta Gamma Sigma. Republican. Lutheran. Address: PO Box 1277 Friday Harbor WA 98250-1277 E-mail: daumicilio@prodigy.net.mx.

DAUM, JOHN F., lawyer; b. Washington, May 9, 1943; BA summa cum laude, Harvard U., 1965; LLB, Yale U., 1969. Bar: D.C. 1971, Calif. 1972. Ptnr. O'Melveny & Myers LLP, LA, mem. policy com. Lectr., fed. cts. and fed. jurisdiction U So. Calif. Law Sch. Mem. Yale Law Jour., 1967—69. Mem. ABA, LA County Bar Assn.(mem. com. of fed. procedure), Order of the Coif, Phi Beta Kappa. Office: O'Melveny & Myers LLP 400 S Hope St Los Angeles CA 90071-2899 Office Phone: 213-430-6111. Office Fax: 213-430-6407. Business E-Mail: jdaum@omm.com.

DAUM, JOHN LAVERN, retired band director, educator; b. Centralia, Ill., July 3, 1929; s. John Albert and Miriam Daum; m. Emma Elizabeth Kent, Oct. 17, 1954; children: John Thomas, Susan Lucille Daum-Bartling, Nancy Jane Daum-Durham, Brian Lee. AA in Edn., Centralia Jr. Coll., 1952; BA in Music Edn., So. Ill. U., Carbondale, 1954, MA in Music Edn., 1962. Band dir., tchr. Sch. Dist. 1, Vienna, Ill., 1954—58, Reorganized Dist. 1, Matthews, Mo., 1958—62, Cmty. Unit 1, Charleston, Ill., 1962—88; ret., 1988; band dir., originator Charleston Cmty. Band, 1977—2005; ret., 2005. Commr. Park & Recreation Adv., Charleston, 1990—2005; music adjudicator Ill. HS Assn., 1968—2005, Ill. Elem. Sch. Assn., 1968—2005. Leader Boy Scouts Am., staff Nat. Jamboree, 1977, 1981, 1985, 1989, 1993, 1997, 2001, 2005. Recipient Vigil Honor, Boy Scouts Am., 1980, Woodbadge, 1982, Silver Beaver award, 1985, Jefferson award, Am. Inst. Pub. Svc., 2004. Mem.: Nat. Fedn. HS Music Assn., Nat. Band Assn. Methodist. Home: 1600 C St Charleston IL 61920

DAUM, ROBERT CHARLES, investment banker; b. Phila., Aug. 13, 1952; s. Robert William and Lois Audrey (Bischoff) D.; m. Julie Ann Hembrock; children: Alexandra, Schuyler, Bailey. BA, Colgate U., 1974; MBA, Harvard U., 1978. Assoc. Dillon Read and Co., N.Y. and London, 1978-82; v.p. Merrill Lynch Capital Markets, N.Y. and London, 1982-88; mng. dir. Prudential Securities Inc., N.Y.C., 1988-93, UBS Warburg, N.Y.C., 1993-99; exec. v.p. elot, Inc., 2000—02; mng. dir. Growth Capital Ptnrs., N.Y.C., 2003—. Mem. Links, Racquet and Tennis Club, River Club, Tuxedo Club, Harvard Club NY, Racquet Club Phila., Alpha Tau Omega. Republican. Episcopalian.

DAUSSMAN, GROVER FREDERICK, electrical engineer, consultant; b. Warrick County, Ind., May 6, 1919; s. Grover Cleveland and Madeline (Springer) D.; m. Elli Margrite Kilian, Dec. 27. 1941; children: Cynthia Louise Daussman Quinn, Judith Ann, Margaret Elizabeth Daussman Davidson Cooper. Student, U. Cin., 1936-38, Carnegie Inst. Tech., 1944-45, George Washington U., 1948-56; BSEE, U. Ala., 1963, postgrad., 1963-64, 77, Indsl. Coll. Armed Forces, 1955, 63; PhD (hon.), Hamilton State U., 1973. Registered profl. engr., Ala., Va., D.C.; cert. fallout shelter analyst. Coop. engr. Sunbeam Elec. Mfg. Co., Evansville, Ind., 1936-38; engr., draftsman Phila. Navy Yard, 1941-42; resident engr., supr. shipbldg. USN, Neville Island, Pa., 1942-45; engr. Pearl Harbor Navy Yard, 1945-48; sect. head Bur. Ships USN, Washington, 1948-56; head guidance and control tech. liaison Army Ballistic Missile Agy., Huntsville, Ala., 1956-58, chief program coordination Guidance and Control Lab., 1958-60; chief program coordination Astronics Lab., Marshall Space Flight Ctr., Huntsville, 1960-63, dir's staff asst. for advanced rsch. and tech., 1963-70, engrng. cons., 1970—. Project dir. fallout shelter surveys Mil Dept. Tenn., 1971-73; head drafting dept. Alverson-Draughon Coll., Huntsville, 1974-77; instr. Ala. Christian Coll., 1977-79; engrng. draftsman Reisz Engrng., 1979; chief engr. Sheraton Motor Inn, 1979; sr. engr. Sperry Support Services, 1980; assoc. Techni-Core Profls., Huntsville, 1980-81; elec. engr. Reisz Engrng., Huntsville, 1981-86; tutor in mathematics, scis. and engrng. North Ala. Ctr. for Ednl. Excellence, Huntsville, 1986-2000, and U.S. Dept. Vet. Affairs, 2000-. Chmn. cmty. spl. gifts com. Madison County Heart Assn., 1965; active Population Action Coun., Huntsville Track Club, Mended Hearts, Inc., Prayer Power Club, Nat. Assn. Sr. Friends, Sierra Club; treas. Huntsville (Ala.) United Ch. of Christ, 1959-61; mem. ch. council St. John's United Ch., Cullman, Ala., 1964-66; sec. ch. council, program com. chmn. ch. council 1965-66; vice moderator Ala.-Tenn. Assn. 1965-68; bd. dirs. Southeast conf. 1965-66, mem. budget and finance com. 1965-66. Recipient Appreciation cert. North Ala. Ednl. Opportunity Ctr., Inc., 1987, 88, 89, 90, 91. Fellow: Explorers Club; mem.: ACLU, AARP, AIAA, NSPE (state dir. 1962—65, chpt. pres. 1966—67, state dir. 1968—71, 1985—91), AAAS, IEEE (life; sr. mem. sect. chmn. No. Ala. sect. 1961—62, founder, chmn. engrng. mgmt. chpt. 1964—65, mem. inst. rsch. com. 1965—67, mem. adminstrv. com. engrng. mgmt. soc. 1966—86, sec. soc. 1968—85, mem. Region 3 exec. com. 1969—79, mem. inst. bd. dirs., regional del. dir. S.E. region 1972—73, certs. of appreciation 1960—62, Centennial medal 1984, Centennial Hon.Role of Outstanding Vols 1986, Ednl. Activities award 1987), Jr. Engrng. Tech. Soc. (organizer local high sch. chpts.), U.S. Naval Inst., Am. Soc. Naval Engrs., Huntsville Assn. Tech. Socs. (sec. 1969—70, v.p. 1970—71, founder), Nat. Assn. Retarded Children, Internat. Platform Assn., Am. Def. Preparedness Assn. (post dir. Tenn. Valley 1963—66), Am. Inst. Urban and Regional Affairs, Ala. Soc. Profl. Engrs. (state dir. 1962—65, chpt. pres. 1966—67, state dir. 1968—71, regional Math Counts coord. 1981—91, state dir. 1985—91, state math. counts coord. 1988—89, Chtp. Engr. of Yr. 1968, 1982, Cert. of Appreciation 1982, Chtp. Engr. of Yr. 1989, Pres. award 1989), Planetary Soc. (charter), Hellenic Profl. Assn. Am. (hon.), MSFC Retirees Assn. (v.p. 1973—74, pres. 1974—75), Nat. Assn. Ret. Fed. Employees, Assn. U.S. Army, Missile, Space and Range Pioneers (life), Cousteau Soc., U. Ala. Alumni Assn., Redstone Arsenal Officers Club. Democrat. Office: 200 Westside Sq Ste 205 Huntsville AL 35801

DAUSTER, WILLIAM GARY, lawyer, economist; b. Sacramento, Nov. 25, 1957; s. William Joe and Marianne Dauster; m. Ellen Lisa Weintraub, May 10, 1986; children: Matthew Isaac, Natanya Miriam, Emma Sophia. BA in Econs., Polit. Sci. and Internat. Rels., U. So. Calif., 1978, MA in Econs., 1981; JD, Columbia U., 1984. Bar: N.Y. 1985, U.S. Dist. Ct. (so. and ea. dists.) N.Y. 1985, D.C. 1986, U.S. Supreme Ct. 1997. Assoc. Cravath, Swaine & Moore, N.Y.C., 1984-86; chief counsel com. on budget U.S. Senate, Washington, 1986-94, acting staff dir., chief coun., 1994, Dem. chief of staff, chief coun., 1995-97, Dem. dep. staff dir., gen. coun. com. labor & human resources, 1997, Dem. chief of staff, chief coun., 1997-98; counselor Wellstone Pres. Exploratory Com., Washington, 1998-99; dep. asst. to the Pres. for econ. policy, dep. dir. Nat. Econ. Coun., The White House, Washington, 1999-2000; sr. counselor to Senator Russ Feingold U.S. Senate, Washington, 2000—01, legis. dir., 2001—03. Dem. gen. coun. com. on fin. U.S. Senate, 2003, Dem. dep. staff dir., gen. coun., 2003—. Author: Congressional Budget Act Annotated, 1990, Budget Process Law Annotated, 1991, 1993; contbr. articles to profl. jours. Bd. visitors Columbia Law Sch., 1992—2000. Recipient Order of Palm, 1978, trustee scholarship, U. So. Calif., 1974, Harlan Fiske Stone scholar, 1982—84. Mem.: N.Y. Bar Assn., D.C. Bar Assn. Democrat. Jewish. Home: 9713 Connecticut Ave Kensington MD 20895-3528 Office Phone: 202-224-1965. Personal E-mail: bill_dauster@yahoo.com. Business E-Mail: bill_dauster@finance-dem.senate.gov.

DAUTARTAS, MINO F., physical chemist; b. Cleve., Oct. 5, 1952; s. Zigmas and Madeleine Dautartas; m. Barbara Ann Renner, June 26, 1976; children: Angela Madeleine, Jennifer Ileine. BS in Chemistry, Ohio State U., 1977; PhD in Analytical Chemistry, U. Minn., 1982. Fellow U. Minn., Mpls., 1977—82; prin. investigator Bell Labs., Breinigsville, Pa., 1982—2000; chief tech. officer Haleos, Blacksburg, Va., 2000—02, Luma Innovations, Blacksburg, 2002; prin., owner LightVortx, Blacksburg, 2002—03. Cons. MFD Consulting, Blacksburg, 2004—. Mem. City Coun., Alburtis, Pa., 1993—94. Mem.: IEEE (chmn. optoelectronicd com. 1998—2000, Outstanding Paper award 1993). Achievements include patents for 62 U.S. patents in fiberoptics & integrated optics; invention of low cost miniture laser package; development of laser package, provided 1/3 World Market and brought in $2Billion in Revenue to Lucent; first to invent organometalic solar cell without a semiconductor. Home and Office: MFD Consulting 2006 Sycamore Trail Blacksburg VA 24060 Office Phone: 540-953-2160. Office Fax: 540-953-2164. Personal E-mail: mino.dautartas@verizon.net.

DAUTEL, CHARLES SHREVE, retired mining company executive; b. Cleve., Apr. 5, 1923; s. Robert Poe and Frances (Shreve) D.; m. Isabell Francis Brown, June 11, 1947; children: Charles Warren, Louis Craig. BSc, Ohio U., 1948; JD, U. Cin., 1952. Bar: Ohio 1952. With Nichols, Wood, Marx & Ginter, Cin., 1952-55, Eagle-Picher Industries, Inc., Cin., 1955-88, asst. sec., asst. gen. counsel, 1958-70, sec., 1970-87, v.p., 1980-87. With AUS, 1942-46. Mem. Phi Delta Theta, Phi Delta Phi. Clubs: Hidden Valley Lake Country. Home: 1448 Brookridge Circle Dr Lawrenceburg IN 47025-9332

DAUTEN, DALE ALAN, newspaper columnist; b. Fairfield, Iowa, Sept. 30, 1950; s. Joel John and Jeri (Muck) D.; m. Sandy Kelley; children: Hilary, Trevor, Joel. BS, Ariz. State U., 1971, MS, 1972; postgrad., Stanford U., 1972-73. Rsch. analyst AMERCO, Phoenix, 1972-74; rsch. mgr. Armour-Dial Corp., Phoenix, 1974-75; v.p. Hollander Assn., Atlanta, 1975-80; owner, founder Rsch. Resources, Atlanta and L.A., 1980-88; columnist King Features, N.Y.C., 1992—; owner/founder The Innovators' Lab, 2002—. Cons., Tempe, Ariz., 1988—; syndicated columnist The Corporate Curmudgeon, 1992—, Kate & Dale Talk Jobs, 1996—. Author: Quitting, 1980, Taking Chances, 1986, The Max Strategy, 1996, The Gifted Boss, 1999. Mediator State Atty. Gen., Phoenix, 1992-98; commr. Tempe Planning and Zoning commn., 1993-98; v.p., bd. dirs. Tactile Mus. for the Blind, Tempe, 1995-2000, Tempe Dream Commn., 1999-2000. Office: c/o King Features 235 E 45th St New York NY 10017-3305 Office Phone: 480-839-8999. E-mail: dale@dauten.com.

DAUTH, FRANCES KUTCHER, journalist, editor; b. St. Louis, Aug. 20, 1941; d. David Jacob Kutcher and Dorothy Marie (Baugh) Hedges; m. Jerry Donald Dauth, July 5, 1964 (div. Dec. 1980). BA, U. Colo., 1963; cert. mgmt. program, Smith Coll., 1989. Staff writer Alameda (Calif.) Times Star, 1966—67, Contra Costa Times, Walnut Creek, Calif., 1968—69, Oakland (Calif.) Tribune, 1969—77; project editor San Francisco Examiner, 1977—82; asst. city editor Phila. Inquirer, 1982, dep. N.J. editor, 1983, suburban editor, 1984—85, city editor, 1985—89, nat. editor, 1989—91, fgn. editor, 1991—94, assoc. mng. editor, 1994—96; mng. editor Star Ledger, Newark, 1996—2004, editor editl. pages, 2004—. Office: Star Ledger Newark NJ 07102 Office Phone: 973-392-1536. Business E-Mail: fdauth@starledger.com.

DAVANT, JAMES WARING, investment banker; b. McComb, Miss., Dec. 1, 1917; s. Guy Hamilton and Em Reid (Waring) D.; m. Mary Ellis Westlake, Apr. 4, 1942; children: Mary Diane, John Hamilton, Patricia Jean (Mrs. Coleman Dupont Donaldson). Student, U. Va., 1939. With Paine, Webber, Jackson & Curtis, 1945—81, gen. ptnr., 1956—81, mem. policy com., 1963—81, mng. ptnr., 1964—81, pres., CEO, 1970—71, chmn. bd., CEO, 1971—80; chmn. Paine Webber Inc., 1974—81, ret., 1981. Chmn. Assn. Stock Exchange Firms, 1966-68; bd. dirs. N.Y. Stock Exchange, 1972-77, past chmn. cen. market com. Chmn. nat. adv. council Nat. Cystic Fibrosis Research Found.; bd. dirs. Securities Industry Assn., 1973-78, Manhattan Eye, Ear and Throat Hosp., Darden Sch., U. Va., 1978-1987; chmn. ctrl. market com. Stock Exchange. From aviation cadet to lt. comdr. USNR, 1940-46. Mem. Council Fgn. Relations, Econ. Club (chmn. 1976-77, trustee), Pilgrims of U.S., Bond Club (N.Y.C., gov. 1965—, pres. 1972—). Episcopalian. Office: 4600 N Ocean Blvd Boynton Beach FL 33435-7365

DAVATZES, NICKOLAS, retired broadcast executive; married; 2 children. BA, M, St. John's U. Various exec. positions Xerox Corp., 1965—75, v.p. sales and mktg., 1975—77; pres. Intext Comm. Sys., 1978—80; pres., CEO A&E TV Networks, N.Y.C., 1983—2005, CEO emeritus, 2005—. Mem. adv. bd. Colls. Bus. Adminstrn. St. John's U.; bd. govs. Banff TV Festival. Founder Conn. Found. Childhood Leukemia; trustee St. John's U. Formerly with USMC. Co-recipient Salute to Freedom award, USS Intrepid Found., 1995; named to Broadcasting and Cable Hall of Fame, 1999; recipient Hist. Found. Heritage award, USMC, Chevalier des Arts et Lettres, French Govt., 1989, Pres.'s award, Cable TV Pub. Affairs Assn., 1996, Vanguard award, Nat. Cable TV Assn., 1994, Hellenic Heritage Achievement award, Am. Hellenic Inst., 2000. Mem.: NATAS (dir. internat. coun.), Brit. Acad. Film and TV Arts (east coast, trustee).

D'AVELLA, BERNARD JOHNSON, JR., publishing executive, lawyer; b. Orange, N.J., Jan. 6, 1945; s. Bernard Johnson and Aida Santa (Magliacane) D'A.; m. Elaine Anne Benucci, Aug. 11, 1973; children: Bernard J. III, Anthony N. Student, Princeton U., 1962-66; AB, Rutgers U., 1970; JD, U. Penn., 1973. Bar: N.J. 1973, U.S. Dist. Ct. N.J. 1973. Assoc. atty. Hannoch Weisman, Newark, 1973-78, ptnr., dir. Newark, Roseland, Trenton, N.J., 1978-98, mng. ptnr., dir., 1980-91; pres., COO Prudent Pub. Co. and The Gallery Collection, Ridgefield Park, N.J., 1998—. Former class pres. Princeton U., mem. exec. com., 25th, 30th and 35th reunion coms., former chmn. Maclean fellow sel. com.; former treas., trustee The Joint Connection; chmn. emeritus bd. dirs. N.J. State Opera; former chmn. ethics commn. Borough of Roseland, N.J.; chmn. Juvenile Conf. Com. Twp. of Essex Fells, N.J. Sgt. U.S. Army, 1967-69. Decorated Bronze Star, Bronze Star with oak leaf cluster, Air medal, Army Commendation medal. Mem. ABA, N.J. State Bar Assn., Assn. Fed. Bar, Essex County Bar Assn., Princeton Alumni Assn. Essex County (exec. com., alumni schs. com., past pres.), Essex Fells Country Club, Fellsbrook Paddle and Tennis Club, Mantoloking Yacht Club (bd. govs.). Avocations: opera, house restoration and design, antiques and classic automobiles, tennis, golf. Office: Prudent Pub Co Inc 65 Challenger Rd 1st Fl Ridgefield Park NJ 07660-2111

DAVENPORT, ALAN GARNETT, civil engineer, educator; b. Madras, India, Sept. 19, 1932; came to Can., naturalized; s. Tom and May Davenport; m. Sheila Rand Smith, Apr. 13, 1957; children: Thomas Sidney, Anna Margaret, Andrew Hope, Clare Rand BA, Cambridge U., Eng., 1954, MA, 1958; MASc, U. Toronto, Ont., Can., 1957, DEng (hon.), 1989; PhD, U. Bristol, Eng., 1960; D. in Applied Sci. (hon.), U. Louvain, Belgium, 1979; D. in Tech. (hon.), Tech. U. Denmark, 1982; DSc (hon.), McGill U., Montreal, Que., Can., 1983, U. Toronto, Ont., 1989; DEng (hon.), Waterloo (Ont., Can.) U., 1986; DSc (hon.), U. Guelph, Ont., 1993, U. La Plata, Argentina, 1993; DEng, Carlton U., 1996, U. Bristol, 1998; DSc (hon.), U. Western Ontario, London, Canada, 2002. Lectr. U. Toronto, Ont., Can., 1955-57; research officer Nat. Research Council, Ottawa, Ont., Can., 1957-58; asst. prof., then prof. U. Western Ont., London, Can., 1960—, dir. Boundary Layer Wind Tunnel Lab., 1960—, rsch. dir. Inst. for Catastrophic Loss Reduction, 1999; dir. Ctr. for Studies in Constrn., 1990—. Cons. on numerous bldgs., bridges and towers, including World Trade Ctr., N.Y.C., CN Tower, Toronto, Sears Bldg., Chgo., Sunshine Skyway Bridge, Fla., Hong Kong and Shanghai Bank Bldg., Hong Kong, Bank of China Bldg., Hong Kong, Great Belt Bridge, Denmark, Normandy Bridge, France, Millau Viaduct, France. Editor: Can Jour. Civil Engrng., 1974-79, mem. editorial bd., 1979-81 Chmn. Can. nat. com. UN-Internat. Decade for Natural Disaster Reduction, 1993—. Decorated Order of Canada; named to Engrng. Hall of Distinction, U. Toronto, 1999; recipient Nobel prize, 1963, Cancam medal, Cancam 83, Saskatoon, Sask., Can., 1983, Queen Elizabeth medal, 1952—77, Gold medal, Inst. Structural Engrs., 1987, Oleg A. Kerensky medal, 1988, Ernest C. Manning award of distinction, Can. Confedn. medal, 1967—92, Killam prize, 1993, Can. Gold medal for sci. and engrng., Natural Sci. and Engrng. Rsch. Coun. Can., 1994, Gold ribbon d'Or award, French Autoroute Authority, Hellmuth prize for rsch., U. Western Ont., Otto H.G Flaschbart medal, Wind Engrng. Soc. Germany, Austria and Switzerland, 2000, John F. Kennedy medal, Engrng. Inst. Can., 2000, Albert Caquot prize, French Assn. Civil Engrs., 2001, Spl. Achievement award, Am. Inst. Steel Constrn., 2005. Fellow Can. Soc. Civil Engrng. (A.B. Sanderson award 1985), Engrng. Inst. Can. (Duggan medal 1960, Gzowski medal 1963, 78, Julian C. Smith medal), Royal Soc. Can. (Rutherford lectr. 1988); mem. Am. Meteorol. Soc., Can. Meteorol. Soc. (prize in Applied Meterology 1965), ASCE (State of Art Civil Engrng. award 1973, Can-Am Civil Engrng. award 1977, Jack Cermak medal, 2003), Assn. Profl. Engrs. Ont. (Silver medal 1977, Bell Canada Forum award, 1992), Internat. Assn. Bridge and Structural Engrng. (Award of Merit), Internat. Assn. Shell Structures (Tsubai prize 1997), Nat. Acad. Engrng. (fgn. assoc.), Can. Acad. Engrng. (founding mem., pres.), Royal Acad. Engrng. (fgn. mem.). Avocations: sailing, squash, tennis. Home: 412 Lawson Rd London ON Canada N6G 1X8 Office: U Western Ont Boundary Layer Wind Tunnel Lab Engrng Sci London ON Canada N6A 5B9 E-mail: agd@blwtl.uwo.ca.

DAVENPORT, ANN ADELE MAYFIELD, retired home care agency administrator; b. New Orleans, Nov. 12, 1941; d. Henry Louis and Myrtie Iola (Cason) Mayfield; m. John Wayne Davenport, June 18, 1966; children: Steven Lyle, Daniel Ryan, Elaine Adele. BA, Southeasten La. Coll., 1963; MA in Edn., George Peabody C., 1965; MA in Sociology, Tex. Tech. U., 1971. Tchr. various schs., 1963; instr. of sociology Tex. Tech. U., Lubbock, 1970—74, James Madison U., Harrisonburg, Va., 1981—82, Ga. So. Coll., Statesboro, 1982—84; 5th grade tchr. Bulloch County Schs., Statesboro, Ga., 1985—87; gerontology project coord. Dept. of Nursing Ga. So. Coll., 1987—89; project dir. Sr. Companion Program Ctr. for Rural Health and Rsch., Ga. So. U., Statesboro, 1988—93; instr. dept. health sci. edn. Ga. So. Coll., Statesboro, 1993—95; exec. dir. Ogeechee Home Health Agy., Statesboro, 1995—96, Homebound Svcs., Statesboro, 1996—2002; ret., 2002. Editor various newsletters, 1987-2002. Bd. dirs. Citizens Against Violence, Statesboro, 1987-88, Habitat for Humanity, 1990-2002; pres. Coun. on Children and Parents, Statesboro, 1988-89, 93-94; mem. steering com. Bulloch County Commn. on Human Svcs., 1989-2002; mem. adminstrv. bd. dirs., coun. on ministries, nominating com. Pittman Park United Meth. Ch.; pres. Ogeechee Wellness Coun., 1992-2002; bd. dirs. Ogeechee Home Health Agy., 1989-93. Mem. Ga. Rural Health Assn. (sec. 1988-89, editor state newsletter 1989-96), So. Sociol. Soc., Ga. Gerontol. Assn., Ga. Sociol. Assn., AAUW (newsletter editor Statesboro l987-89), Am. Soc. on Aging, Nat. Coun. on the Aging, Am. Rural Health Assn. Avocations: tennis, reading. Home: 1920 Hampton Way Ada OK 74820

DAVENPORT, ANNE MARILYN, dietician; b. Queens Village, N.Y., Nov. 29, 1947; d. Alfred Francis Morel and Charlotte Adelaide Ward; m. John Howard Pearson, June 27, 1981 (div. July 1989); m. Terry Del Davenport, Sept. 10, 1995. AA in Liberal Arts, So. Seminary Jr. Coll., Buena Vista, Va., 1967; BS in Math. & Secondary Edn., U. Mass., Amherst, 1969, MS in Nutrition & Computers in Nutrition, 1975. Math. tchr. Highland Falls H.S., NY, 1969—71; clin. dietician Aspen Valley Hosp., Colo., 1974—75; head clin. dietician Cabell Huntington Hosp., W.Va., 1977—78, St. Mary's Hosp. & Med. Ctr., Grand Junction, Colo., 1978—82; nursing home cons. Powell County Nursing Home, Deerlodge, Mont., 1989—94; adminstrv. cons., bookkeeper Nat. Housebuilders Constrn. Co., Victor, Mont., 1995—. Author: (sci. fiction) Earthero, 2000. Mem.: New World Order Ministry for World Peace, Mont. Dietetic Assn., Am. Dietetic Assn. Avocations: jogging, walking. Home: 260 Indian Prairie Loop Victor MT 59875 Office Phone: 406-642-6863.

DAVENPORT, BILL, sculptor; b. Greenfield, Mass., 1962; BFA in Sculpture, R.I. Sch. Design, 1986; MFA in Sculpture, U. Mass., 1990. One-man shows include Student Uniion Gallery, U. Mass., Amherst, 1990, Wierzbowski Gallery, Houston, 1993, Inman Gallery Viewing Room, Houston, 1994, 95, 99, Christinerose Gallery, N.Y.C., 1997, Good/Bad Art Collective, Denton, Tex., 1997, Sala Diaz, San Antonio, 1998, Angstrom Gallery, Dallas, 1999; group shows include Wheeler Gallery, Providence, R.I., 1984, Helme House Gallery, Kingston, R.I., 1985, Bristol (R.I.) Art Mus., 1986, Hampden Gallery, U. Mass., Amherst, 1988, 89, Art league Houston, 1991, Robinson Gallery, Houston, 1991, Cullen Ctr. Gallery, Houston, 1992, 94, Graham Gallery, Albuquerque, 1992, Allen Ctr. Gallery, Houston, 1992, Hillwood Art Mus., L.I. Univ., 1993, Inman Gallery, Houston, 1993, 94, 96, 98, Whitney Mus. Am. Art, 1993, Conduit Gallery, Dallas, 1994,

Lambert Hall, Houston, 1994, Ctr. Gallery, Bucknell U., Lewisburg, Pa., 1995, Lawndale Art Performance Ctr., Houston, 1995, U. Tex., San Antonio, 1995, San Antonio Mus. Art, 1995, Spanish Kitchen Gallery, L.A., 1996, Barry Whistler Gallery, Dallas, 1996, Cristinerose Gallery, N.Y.C., 1997, Arlington (Tex.) Mus. Art, 1997, Angstrom Gallery, Dallas, 1997, Austin (Tex.) Mus. Art, 1998, Smart Mus. Art, U. Chgo., 1998, City Gallery Chastain, Atlanta, 1998, Galveston (Tex.) Arts Ctr., 1998, Kohler Arts Ctr., 1999, Weatherspoon Art Gallery, U. N.C., 1999, Contemporary Art Collective, Las Vegas, 1999, Inman Gallery, Houston, 1999, 2001, Angstrom Gallery, Dallas, 1999, Homeroom Gallery, Munich, 2001, Angstrom Gallery, Dallas, 2003. Core fellow Mus. Fine Arts, Houston, 1990-92; Individual Artist grantee Cultural Arts Coun. Houston Harris County, 1996, Louis Comfort Tiffany grantee, 1997. Office: c/o Inman Gallery 1114 Barkdull St Houston TX 77006-6402

DAVENPORT, BRADFUTE WARWICK, JR., lawyer; b. Richmond, Va., Oct. 19, 1946; s. Bradfute Warwick and Martha (Orr) D.; m. Suzanne Jeannette Shepherd, May 3, 1987; children: Sarah Shepherd, Maria Byrd, John Sidney, Stephen Warwick, Kate Moore. BA, Yale U., 1969; JD, U. Va., 1972. Bar: Va. 1972, U.S. Supreme Ct. 1982, U.S. Ct. Appeals (4th cir.) 1975, U.S. Ct. Appeals (D.C. cir.) 1978, U.S. Dist. Ct. (ea. dist.) Va. 1973, U.S. Dist. Ct. (we. dist.) Va. 1982. Assoc. Mays & Valentine, Richmond, Va., 1972-78; ptnr., complex litig. Troutman, Sanders, Mays & Valentine, LLP, Richmond, Va., 1978—, and chair, ethics com. Mem. ABA, Va. Bar Assn., Va. State Bar, Def. Rsch. Inst., Va. Assn. Def. Attys., Va. Trial Lawyers Assn., Internat. Assn. Def. Counsel, Am. Arbitration Assn. Episcopalian. Office: Troutman Sanders LLP 1111 East Main St PO Box 1122 Richmond VA 23218-1122 Office Phone: 804-697-1311. Office Fax: 804-698-5159. Business E-Mail: brad.davenport@troutmansanders.com.*

DAVENPORT, DAVID, retired academic administrator, lawyer, public information officer; b. Sheboygan, Wis., Oct. 24, 1950; s. E. Guy and Beverly J. (Snoddy) D.; m. Sally Nelson, Aug. 13, 1977; children— Katherine, Charles, Scott. BA, Stanford U., 1972; JD, U. Kans., Lawrence, 1977. Bar: Calif. 1977, U.S. Dist. Ct. (so. dist.) Calif., 1977. Assoc. Gray, Cary, Ames & Frye, San Diego, 1977-78; min. Ch. of Christ, San Diego, 1979; law prof. Pepperdine U., Malibu, Calif., 1980—99, gen. counsel, 1981-83, exec. v.p., 1983-85, pres., 1985—2000. Co-author: Shepherd Leadership; contbr. Fed. Antitrust Law, 1985, articles to profl. jourls. Mem. Adminstrv. Conf. of U.S., Washington, 1984-86; bd. overseers Hoover Inst., Stanford U.; bd. dirs. L.A. World Affairs Coun., Nat. Legal Ctr. for Pub. Interest, Washington. Mem. Mchts. and Mfrs. Assn. Calif. (bd. dirs. 1985—), Am. Assn. Pres. of Ind. Colls. and Univs. (bd. dirs. 1985—, pres.), Young Pres. Orgn., Calif. C. of C. (bd. dirs.), Order of Coif. Republican. Office: Pepperdine U Office of President 24255 Pacific Coast Hwy Malibu CA 90263-0002 Business E-Mail: david.davenport@pepperdine.edu.

DAVENPORT, DENNIS LYNN, protective services official; b. Charleroi, Pa., July 12, 1947; s. Elmer Webb and Maude Elsie Davenport; m. Patricia Susan Davenport, May 10, 1980; children: Brian, Marc, Joshua. AA, Florissant (Mo.) Valley C.C., 1971; BA in Criminal Justice, U. Mo., St. Louis, 1976, MA in Criminology, 1993; grad., FBI Nat. Acad. Rsch. technician McDonnell Douglas, St. Louis, 1969-71; adminstrn. asst. to chief Clayton (Mo.) Police Dept., 1971—, accreditation mgr., 1997—. Sec. ops. planner Washington U. Presdl. Debate, St. Louis, 1992, 2000, safety com. chmn. St. Louis Art Fair, Clayton, 1993-2002, St. Louis Jazz Festival, Clayton, 2002. Contbr. articles to profl. jours. Booster Francis Howell Soccer, St. Charles, Mo., 1997-2001. Sgt. USAF, 1965-69, Vietnam. Recipient Fiction Writing award Springfield Writer's Conf., 1998. Mem. NRA, United Svcs. Orgn., Law Enforcement Orgn., FBI Nat. Acad. Assocs., Mo. Accreditation Coalition (sec., treas. 1999—), MidAm. Contingency Planning Forum, Civil War Preservation Trust, Friends of Nat. Parks at Gettysburg. Avocations: Civil War, hunting. Office: Clayton Police Dept 227 S Central Ave Clayton MO 63105

DAVENPORT, GERALD BRUCE, lawyer; b. Adrian, Mich., May 17, 1949; s. Bruce Nelson and Mildred Louise (Avis) D.; m. RoxAnn Ferguson, Dec. 27, 1975; children: Jonathan Gerald, Christopher Bruce, Timothy Charles. AB, U. Mich., 1971; JD, U. Tex., 1975. Bar: Tex. 1975, Okla. 1993. Pvt. practice Law Office of Gerald B. Davenport, Cedar Park, Tex., 1975-77; atty. Milchem Inc., Houston, 1977-81, Baker Hughes Prodn. Tools Inc., Houston, 1981-87; sr. atty. Baker Hughes Inc., Houston, 1987-88; gen. atty. environ. law Tex. Ea. Corp., Houston, 1988; atty. Browning-Ferris Industries, Houston, 1988-89, mgr. environ. law sect., 1989-92; asst. gen. counsel environ. law Mapco Inc., Tulsa, 1992-94; of counsel McKinney, Stringer & Webster, P.C., Tulsa, 1994-95; dir. Davenport & Williams, P.C., Tulsa, 1995-96; shareholder Hall, Estill, Hardwick, Gable, Golden & Nelson, P.C., Tulsa, 1996-99; of counsel Shipley, Jennings & Champlin, P.C., Oklahoma City, 1999—2002, Elias, Books, & Brown, PC, Oklahoma City, 2002—04, GBD Enterprises, Tulsa, 2004—. Contbr. articles to profl. jours. Mem. ABA, State Bar Tex. (environ. law sect.), Okla. Bar Assn. (environ. law sect.). Republican. Office: Ste 100 1648 S Boston Tulsa OK 74119 Office Phone: 918-582-1720. Business E-Mail: jerry_davenport@swbell.net.

DAVENPORT, JAMES GUYTHON, minister; b. Columbia, N.C., Sept. 15, 1932; s. Llewellyn Harrison and Lillian Mae (Brickhouse) D.; m. Bethany Lavinia Sawyer, Nov. 23, 1956 (div. July 1983); 1 child, Kathleen Nina Davenport Ingram; m. Jacqueline Ann Wilson, Aug. 5, 1983; children: Daniel, Jeffrey, Jack, Jerry. AA, Chowan Coll., 1963; BA, Miss. Coll., 1965; MDiv, Southeastern Bapt. Theol. Sem., 1968; Clin. Pastoral Edn. Cert., Cen. State Hosp., Milledgeville, Ga., 1971; DD, Bethany Theol. Sem., 1991. Ordained to ministry So. Bapt. Conv., 1963; cert. hosp., instnl., mil. chaplain. Pastor Holy Grove Bapt. Ch., Powellsville, N.C., 1963, Siloam Bapt. Ch., Windsor, NC., 1965-68, Fellowship Bapt. Ch., Ettrick, Va., 1968-70, 71-83, Dinwiddie (Va.) Bapt. Ch., 1983-85, McKenney (Va.) Bapt. Ch., 1983-95; ret.; intrum pastor Arvon Bapt. Ch., Arvonia, Va., 2001—03, Mt. Tabor Bapt. Ch., New Canton, Va., 2003—. Substitute tchr. Dinwiddie County Sch. Bd., 1985-95; chaplain CAP, Hopewell, Va., 1969-83, Ettrick-Matoaca rescue Squad, 1973-74, Petersburg (Va.) Correctional Ctr., 1974-83; staff counselor Southside Area Counseling Svc., Petersburg, 1968-91. Vol. fireman St. Brides Fire Dept., Chesapeake, Va., 1959-61; mem. Ettrick-Matoaca Rescue Squad, 1968-74, Planning Commn., McKenney, 1989-94; election ofcl. Dinwiddie County, 1985-95; chaplain Petersburg FOP, 1975-80 (Outstanding Svc. plaque 1977); election official Buckingham County, 1996. Mem. Petersburg Bapt. Assn. (sec. 1974). Home: RR 1 Box 5160 Dillwyn VA 23936-8752 Office Phone: 804-983-1269. *I have found that all too often when people want to change their life for the better they depend only on their own will power and never realize that God has given us the power of the Holy Spirit to work with ours in our transformation.*

DAVENPORT, KIRK ADDISON, lawyer; b. Sept. 20, 1959; s. William and Gertrude (Perkins) D.; children: Lydia, Addison. BA, Brown U., 1981; JD, U. Mich., 1984. Bar: N.Y. 1984. Ptnr. Latham & Watkins, N.Y.C., 1985—. Office: Latham & Watkins 885 3rd Ave Ste 1000 New York NY 10022-4834

DAVENPORT, LAWRENCE FRANKLIN, academic administrator; b. Lansing, Mich., Oct. 13, 1944; s. Theodore and Bernice (Alexander) D.; m. Cecelia Jackson, Sept. 24, 1966; children— Laurence, Anita, Anthony BA, Mich. State U., 1966, MA, 1968; Ed.D., Fairleigh Dickinson U., 1975; MS, Leicester Univ., Eng., 2002. V.p. devel. Tuskegee Inst., Ala., 1972-74; pres. ednl. complex San Diego C.C., 1974-79, provost, 1979-81; assoc. dir. ACTION, Washington, 1981-82; asst. sec. U.S. Dept. Edn., Washington, 1982-87; asst. sec. mgmt. and adminstrn. U.S. Dept. Energy, Washington, 1987-89; assoc. vice chancellor U. Calif., San Francisco, 1989-92; pres. Lawrence Davenport & Assocs., Mercer Island, Wash., 1989—2003; CFO, Seattle Pub. Schs., 1992-94; v.p. fin. and ops., CFO Milton Hershey (Pa.) Sch., 1994-2000; sr. v.p. Antin Neher Assocs., Hershey, 2000—01; dep. chief adminstrv. officer U.S. Ho. of Reps., 2001—02; exec. dir. Hale House Ctr. Inc., N.Y.C., 2002—04; exec. v.p., COO Fla. Atlantic U., Boca Raton, 2004—. Co-author (with Petty): Career Education and Minorities, 1973. Presbyterian. Personal E-mail: lfdavenport@adelphia.net.

DAVENPORT, LEE LOSEE, physicist; b. Schenectady, N.Y., Dec. 31, 1915; m. Anne S. Davenport, 1944; children: Jeanne Treder, Carol Davenport. BS, Union Coll., 1937; MS, U. Pitts., 1940, PhD in Physics, 1946. Rsch. assoc. radar MIT, Cambridge, Mass., 1941-46; rsch. fellow constrn. cyclotron Harvard U., Cambridge, Mass., 1946-50; exec. v.p. Perkin-Elmer Corp., Norwalk, Conn., 1950-57; pres. Sylvania Corning Nuclear Corp., Bayside L.I., N.Y., 1957-60; v.p. planning Sylvania Elec. Prodn., Inc., N.Y.C., 1960-62; pres. GTE Labs, Inc., Stamford, Conn., 1962-77; v.p., chief scientist GTE, 1977-80, cons. telecomm., 1980—. Asst. dir. Electronics Rsch. Lab., U. Pitts, 1946, corp. dir., 1980-92. Fellow IEEE, Am. Phys. Soc. (life); mem. Nat. Acad. Engring., Sci. Rsch. Soc. Am. Home: 61 Winding Ln Greenwich CT 06831-3704 E-mail: lld@sanglier.net.

DAVENPORT, LINDSAY, professional tennis player; b. Palos Verdes, Calif., June 8, 1976; d. Wink and Ann Lindsay; m. Jon Leach, 2003. Profl. tennis player, 1993—. Mem. U.S. Women's Olympic Tennis Team, Atlanta, 1996, Sydney, 2000, U.S. Fed Cup Team, 1993—2000, 2002. Named Rookie of the Yr., TENNIS Magazine, 1993, World Team Tennis, 1993, MVP, 1997, Player of the Year, TENNIS Magazine, 1998, Tour Player of the Year, WTA, 1998, 1999. Achievements include winner, gold medal, U.S. Women's singles, Atlanta Olympic Games, 1996; singles champion, U.S. Open, 1998, Wimbledon, 1999, Australian Open, 2000; doubles champion, Roland Garros (with Mary Jo Fernanadez), 1996, U.S. Open (with Jana Novotna), 1997, Wimbledon (with Corina Morariu), 1999; WTA Tour Champion, 1999; winner, 48 career singles titles, 35 doubles titles, WTA Tour. Office: US Tennis Assn 70 W Red Oak Ln White Plains NY 10604-3602

DAVENPORT, LINNEA MAIBRIT, design educator; b. Jorhat, India, Dec. 26, 1928; arrived in U.S.A., 1942, permanent resident; d. Victor Hugo and Cora Stella (Walter) Sword; m. Ernest Davenport, 1949 (div. 1981); children: Eric Ross, Karla Ray, Kristin Kay; m. Ken Farley, 1986 (div. 1991). BA, Linfield Coll., Oreg., 1949. Decorator/ sales Nico Dept. Store, Salem, Oreg., 1979—81, Rainbow Furniture, Salem, 1981—86; tchr., interior design Salem/ Keizer Sch., 1991—93, Mt. Hood C.C., Gresham, Oreg., 1986—, Portland C.C., Oreg., 1996—, Chemeketa C.C., Salem, 2001—. Author: The Gemstones, 2003, Kathleen, 2004. Vol. Elsinore Hist. Theatre, Salem, 1998—, Deepwood Hist. Estate, 1998—.

DAVENPORT, MARGARET ANDREWS, lawyer; b. Nov. 1, 1961; BA magna cum laude, Amherst Coll., 1983; JD, U. Chgo., 1987. Bar: NY 1988. Assoc. Debevoise & Plimpton LLP, NYC, 1987—95, ptnr., 1995—, co-head pvt. equity group. Mem.: ABA, Assn. of Bar City of NY. Office: Debevoise & Plimpton LLP 919 Third Ave New York NY 10022-3904 Office Phone: 212-909-6667. Office Fax: 212-909-6836. E-mail: madavenport@debevoise.com.

DAVENPORT, PAUL, economics professor; BA in Econs. with gt. distinction/honors, Stanford U., 1969; MA, U. Toronto, 1970, PhD, 1976, LLD (hon.), 2000, U. Alta., 1994; PhD (hon.), Internat. U. Moscow, 2002. Prof. econs. McGill U., Montreal, Que., Can., 1972-89, assoc. dean grad. studies, 1982-86, vice prin. planning and computer svcs., 1986-89; pres., vice chancellor U. Alta., Edmonton, Alta., Can., 1989-94, U. Western Ont., London, Can., 1994—. Chair Assn. Univs. and Colls. Can., 1997-99, Coun. Ont. Univs., 1999-2001. Editor: (with Richard H. Leach) Reshaping Confederation: The 1982 Reform of the Canadian Constitution, 1984; contbbg. author Renovating the Ivory Tower, 2002. Chair United Way Campaign, 2005. Decorated Chevalier Legion of Honor (France); Officer Order of Can. Mem.: Am. Econ. Assn., Can. Assn. Economists, Phi Beta Kappa. Office: U Western Ont Office of Pres Stevenson-Lawson Bldg London ON Canada N6A 5B8 Office Fax: 519-661-3106. E-mail: pdavenpo@uwo.ca.

DAVENPORT, RAY CHARLES, artist, lithographer; b. Rockville Center, NY, May 5, 1926; s. Raymond Forbes D.; m. Lula Kate Chatham, Dec. 28, 1946; children: Louise, Raymond, Susan. Student in Advt. Design, Pratt Inst., Bklyn., 1948; student in Lithography, U. S.C., 1980. Draftsman B.L. Montague Co. Inc., Sumter, S.C., 1951-57; comml. artist Sumter, S.C.; illustrator 9th Air Force, Shaw AFB, S.C., 1959-61; advt. mgr. B.L. Montague Co. Inc., Sumter, 1961-65; mgr. printing dept. Osteen-Davis Printing Co., Sumter, 1965-75; artist, lithographer Sumter, 1975—. Exhibitions include Sumter Gallery Art, 1991 (1st pl.), 2004. Chmn. Sumter County Cultural Commn., 1977; chmn., bd. dirs. Sumter Gallery of Art, 1980; mem. acquisitions com. S.C. Arts Commn., Columbia, 1981. Sgt. U.S. Army Air Corps, 1944-45. Recipient Best in Show award S.C. State Fair Art Dept., 1992, Nat. Merit award Mod. Maturity Mag., 1990, 1st place award S.C. Festival Flowers, 1989. Mem. Nat. Soc. Painters in Casein and Acrylic (Ralph Fabri award 1973, Mordecai Newman award 1995), Allied Artists Am. (Atto Newer award 1983, Gloria Benson Stacks award 1985), S.C. Watercolor Soc. (Winsor and Newton award 1981), Artists Guild Columbia (Best in Show award 1981), Sumter Artists Guild (1st place award 1978), Guild S.C. Artists (pres. 1989). Office Phone: 803-481-2604. E-mail: rdavenport@sc.rr.com.

DAVENPORT, RICHARD LEE, music educator; b. Osak Harbor, Wash., Dec. 7, 1966; s. Jack C. and Janice B. Davenport; m. Tanya M. Oswald; 1 child, Richard W. MusB in Edn., Fla. State U., 1988, MS in Ednl. Leadership, 1999. Cert. profl. tchr. Fla. Assoc. band dir. Marianna (Fla.) H.S., 1989—93; band dir., music tchr. Graceville (Fla.) H.S., 1993—99; band dir. Chipley (Fla.) H.S., Fla., 1999—. Sch. adv. coun. chmn. Graceville H.S., 1995—99; sch. adv. coun. faculty rep. Chipley H.S., 1999—2002; band adjudicator Fla. Bandmasters Assn., 2002; min. music Damascus Bapt. Ch., Graceville, 1995—99; dir. music and edn. First Presbyn. Ch., Marianna, 1990—93. Mem.: Music Educators Nat. Conf., Fla. Music Educators Assn., Fla. Bandmasters Assn. (dist. 2 chmn. 1999—, 10 Yr. Superior award 2002). Baptist. Office: Chipley High School 1535 Brickyard Rd Chipley FL 32428

DAVENPORT, WILLIAM WEEKS, retired pilot, retired military officer; b. Jacksonville, Fla., Apr. 2, 1926; s. Boswell Utz and Pauline Genereaux Davenport; m. Ada Lee Byrd (div.); children: Carroll Ann, Virginia Lee; m. Candy Jeanie Rivera, Aug. 19, 1984; 1 child, James William. AA, Princeton U., 1948. Commd. ens. USN, 1944, advanced through grades to lt. comdr., ret.; capt., flight mgr., chief pilot Am. Airlines, Washington, ret.; ops. inspector FAA, Washington, ret. Author: Foleyisms, 1982. Recipient Commendation for sailboat rescue, USCG, 1984. Master: Masons (32d degree); mem.: Washington D.C. Hangar. Republican. Episcopalian. Home: 2502 Wood Fern Ct Reston VA 20191 Home Fax: 703-391-9082. Personal E-mail: BillDavenport747@aol.com.

DAVERNE, STEVEN RICHARD, advertising director, artist, illustrator, behavior analyst; b. Patuxant, Md., July 10, 1955; s. Ronald Richard and Joan Beverly DaVerne. BA, U. South Fla., Sarasota, 1980; AS, Tampa Tech. Inst., 1990. Cert. Supervision and Employee Management Fla. Mental Health Inst., 1985, U. So. Fla., 1985. Therapist, behavior analyst Tampa Heights Hosp., 1980—84; behavior analyst, rschr. Fla. Mental Health Inst., Tampa, 1984—88; graphic gesigner, art dir. and illustrator numerous advt. and mktg. cos., 1988—98; creative dir. US West Comms., Denver, 1998—2000; owner, operator DaVerne Creative Group, Denver, 2000—. Cons. Young Authors Conf., Tampa, Fla., 1991, Communique Group Advt., Denver, 2000—01; judge, creative cons. Henry Wurst Press Inc., Denver, 2000—01. Exhibitions include American 76th Nat. Exhbn., Nat. Arts Club, Patrons Internat. Exhbn., others, Represented in permanent collections Carter Presdl. Ctr., Atlanta. Nat. children's cancer soc. nat., 1988—2002; presenter behavioral tng. seminars Fla. Mental Health Inst., Tampa, Fla., 1984—88. Recipient Am. Graphic Design award, Bus. Mktg. Awards, 1999, Internat. Summit Creative award, Summit Awards, 1999, 2000. Mem.: Assn. Behavior Analysis, Art Dirs. Club. Achievements include supr. in the establishment of the first pilot research program for mainstreaming severely emotionally disturbed (SED) children in the Florida education system; development of paintings called the Learning Series which intrepreted and documented the social rsch. experience of (SED) children. Avocations: composing and performing music, skiing, water-skiing, sailing. E-mail: daverne@qwest.net.

DAVES, DON MICHAEL, minister; b. Wichita Falls, Tex., Mar. 4, 1938; s. Floyd Lee and Johnnie Majorie (Dunn) D.; m. Patricia N. McLean, Aug. 29, 1958; children: Paul Lee, Donna Michelle. BA, Midwestern U., 1959; ThM, So. Meth. U., 1963; D. Humanities (hon.), Southwestern Coll., 1971. Ordained to ministry Meth. Ch., 1963. Pastor 1st Meth. Ch., Holliday, Tex., 1963-66, Prarie Heights Meth. Ch., Grand Prairie, Tex., 1966-72; minister to soc. North Tex. Conf. United Meth. Ch., 1972-77; pastor Meml. United Meth. Ch., Dallas, 1977-78; assoc. pastor Preston Hollow United Meth. Ch., Dallas, 1978-81, 1st United Meth. Ch., Duncanville, Tex., 1981-85, pastor Cedar Hill, Tex., 1985-91; assoc. pastor Walnut Hill United Meth. Ch., Dallas, 1992-95; pastor First United Meth. Ch., VanAlstyne, Tex., 1995-99; ret., 1999. Ret. mem. North Tex. Conf.; mem. United Meth. Ch.; trustee Charlton Meth. Hosp., Dallas, 1986-95; mentor pastor Perkins Sch. Theology Intern Program, 1996-97; registrar Sherman-McKinney Bd. Ministry, 1996-99. Author: Devotional Talks for Children, 1961, Famous Hymns & Their Writers, 1962, Sermon Outlines on Romans, 1962, Meditations on Early Christian Symbols, 1963, Come with Faith, 1964, Young Readers Book of Christian Symbolism, 1967, Advent: A Calendar of Devotions, 1971, Joy is Now, 1988. Named Best Children's Book by a Tex. Author, Tex. Inst. Letters, 1968. Mem. Am. Assn. Pastoral Counselors, Dallas Hall Soc. So. Meth. U., Order of St. Luke, Disciplined Order Christ. Home: 5200 Keller Springs Rd Ste 231 Dallas TX 75248-2739

DAVES, DONALD RAE, entertainment industry executive; b. L.A., Dec. 6, 1930; s. Lester Brent and Edwina (Tothill) D.; m. Eleana Farrell, Jan. 26, 1957; children: Victoria Daves Bennett, Antoinette Daves Johnson. BA, U. So. Calif., 1955. Asst. dir. Dirs. Guild Am., L.A., 1957-65; asst. gen. mgr. Samuel Goldwyn Studios, L.A., 1973-80; v.p. Warner Bros. Hollywood Studios, West Hollywood, Calif., 1980-96; pres. Hill-Daves Prodns., 1996—. Dir., prodn. mgr. (TV) Bonanza, 1965-70; assoc. producer (film) Key West, 1972. V.p. West Hollywood Community Alliance, 1988-90; bd. dirs. Warner Bros. Hollywood Studio Fed. Credit Union, 1995—. Sgt. USAF, 1951-52. Mem. Phi Delta Theta. Republican. Episcopalian. Avocations: collecting paper weights, sports, antique smoking pipes.

DAVES, GLENN DOYLE, JR., science educator, chemist, researcher; b. Clayton, N.Mex., Feb. 12, 1936; s. Glenn Doyle and Billye (Parker) D.; m. Pamela Gannarelli, Sept. 5, 1959; children: Laura Lee Daves Schantz, Anne Kathryn Crothers, Glenn Graham BS, Ariz. State U., 1959; PhD, MIT, 1964; PharmD (hon.), U. Uppsala, Sweden, 1987. Rsch. chemist Midwest Rsch. Inst., Kansas City, Mo., 1959-61, Stanford Rsch. Inst., Palo Alto, Calif., 1964-67; asst. prof. chemistry Oreg. Grad. Ctr., Beaverton, 1967-72, assoc. prof., 1972-74, prof., 1974-81, chmn. dept., 1972-79; prof., chmn. dept. chemistry Lehigh U., Bethlehem, Pa., 1981-88; dean provost Rensselaer Poly. Inst., Troy, 1989—2000, dean Project Kaleidoscope, Summer Insts., 2000—, dean provost, 2002—03. Vis. scientist NIH, Bethesda, Md., 1988. Co-editor: Advances in Polyamine Research, Vols. 1-2, 1978, Biologically Active Principals of Natural Products, 1984; contbr. numerous articles to profl. jours. Recipient numerous grants NIH, Am. Cancer Soc., U.S. Forest Svc., 1971—. Mem. Am. Chem. Soc., Internat. Soc. Heterocyclic Chemistry, Coun. for Chem. Rsch. (governing bd. 1985-86, chair manpower and resource com. 1984-87, mem. membership com. 1991). Democrat. Personal E-mail: davesgd@yahoo.com.

DAVES, SANDRA LYNN, poet, lyricist; b. Sacramento, Mar. 14, 1950; d. Willard Glen and Rachel Lucille Humbert; m. Tommy Wilburn Daves, Nov. 16, 1971; children: Todd Eric, Brice Aaron. *Sons Brice Aaron Daves (passed away in 1984) and Todd Eric Daves (passed away in 1994), were the inspiration for her beginning a career in poetry in 1994. She became a public poet in 2002. Todd was a good electric guitarist and has left a legacy of taped songs, which he also wrote. They inspire her as well. The song "Mainstream" is a mother/child love song, which was first written as a poem. This became lyrics for the song, "Flower Power." It was written in tribute to son Todd's life.* Grad., Roseville (Calif.) H.S., 1968; student, Internat. Libr. Poetry, 2003. Sec. McClellan AFB, Sacramento, 1969, Fish and Game Dept., Sacramento, 1970—71; poet, 1994—. *Poems published by the International Library of Poetry can be found also, for a limited time, on its web site (poetry.com). Sandra Lynn Daves' poetry publishings led to her be noticed by Amerecord and also led her to become a lyricist.* Lyricist: songs Songs of Praise, Star of Bethlehem, America At War!, Gospel Millennium Celebration, Home For Christmas, Your Very Special Place, Kingdom of Angels (Four Star award for song Pray Without Ceasing, 2004), lyracist: songs Celebrating Christmas with Jesus, The Joy and Splendor of Christmas, America; author: (poem) An Hour At Sunrise, The Shining Light, Barefoot Afternoons, The Colors of Life. Recipient Poet of Merit, Fla., 2005. Mem.: Internat. Soc. Poets (Editor's Choice award Md. chpt. 2000, 2001, 2002, Poet of Merit Hollywood chpt. 2002, Poet of Merit Fla. chpt. 2003, Poet of Yr. Fla. chpt. 2003, Poem Noble House Pub. 2003, Poet of Merit DC chpt. 2003, Poet of Merit Fla. chpt. 2004, Poet Laureate 2004, Poet of Merit Fla. chpt. 2005). Avocations: reading, writing, walking, crossword puzzles. Home: 6825 Susanna Ct Citrus Heights CA 95621

DAVEY, CHARLES BINGHAM, soil scientist, educator; b. Bklyn., Apr. 7, 1928; s. Francis Joseph and Mary Elizabeth (Bingham) Davey; m. Elizabeth Anne Thompson, July 11, 1952; children: Douglas Alan, Barbara Lynn, Andrew Martin. BS, Syracuse U., 1950; MS, U. Wis., 1952, PhD, 1955. Soil scientist Rsch. Svc. Dept. Agr., Beltsville, Md., 1957-62; assoc. prof. N.C. State U., Raleigh, 1962-65, prof., 1965—, Carl Alwin Schenck Disting. prof., 1978—. Alumni Disting. prof., 1989, head dept., 1970-78. Editor: Tree Growth and Forest Soils, 1970; assoc. editor: Soil Sci. Soc. Am. proc., 1967—72; contbr. articles to profl. jours. With U.S. Army, 1955—57. Fellow: AAAS, Soc. Am. Foresters (Barrington Moore Rsch. award), Soil Sci. Soc. Am. (pres. 1975—78, Disting. Svc. award), Am. Soc. Agronomy; mem.: Internat. Soc. Tropical Foresters, Sigma Xi (Rsch. award), Xi Sigma Pi, Gamma Sigma Delta, Phi Kappa Phi. Achievements include patents in field. Home: 5219 Melbourne Rd Raleigh NC 27606-1619 Office: Forestry Dept 3113 Faucette Dr Raleigh NC 27695-8008 Personal E-mail: char1168@bellsouth.net. Business E-Mail: cdavey@unity.ncsu.edu.

DAVEY, CLARK WILLIAM, newspaper publisher; b. Chatham, Ont., Can., Mar. 3, 1928; s. William and Marguerite (Clark) D.; m. Joyce Gordon, Sept. 13, 1952; children: Richard Gordon, Kevin William, Clark Michael. BA in Journalism, U. Western Ont., 1948, LLD (hon.), 1986. With Chatham Daily News, 1948-51; mng. editor No. Daily News, Kirkland Lake, Can., 1951; hydro. seaway corr. Globe and Mail., 1951-55; mem. Parliamentary Press Gallery, Ottawa, 1956-60; fgn. editor Globe and Mail, 1960-63, mng. editor, 1963-78; pub. Vancouver (B.C., Can.) Sun, 1978-83, Montreal Gazette, 1983-89; pres., chmn. The Canadian Press, 1981-83; pub. Ottawa Citizen, 1989-92; v.p. Southam Inc., 1983-92; dir. Am. Press Inst., 1988-94; commr. Ottawa Hydro, 1999-2000. Pres. Michener Awards Found., 1993-98. Named to Can. News Hall of Fame, 1992. Office: 29 Madawaska Dr Ottawa ON Canada K1S 3G5 E-mail: waldosplace@rogers.com.

DAVEY, DIANE DAVIS, pathologist, educator; b. Sioux Falls, SD, June 23, 1956; d. Donald L. Cara Lee Davis; children: James, Steven. BS with honors, Cornell U., 1978; MD, Washington U., St. Louis, 1981. Diplomate Am. Bd. Pathology, Hematology, Cytopathology, Anatomic and Clin. Pathology. Resident in pathology Ind. U., Indpls., 1981—84; resident U. Iowa, Iowa City, 1984—85, fellow, 1985—86, assoc. pathology, 1986—88; asst. prof. pathology U. Ky., Lexington, 1988—94, assoc. prof. pathology, 1994—2000, prof. pathology, 2000—, dir. Cytopathology Lab., 1988—, vice chair, 2004—. Mem. panel, cons. FDA, Rockville, Md., 1995—; moderator Bethesda 2001 Workshop Nat. Cancer Inst., 2000—04; mem. adv. bd. Nat. Cancer Inst., 2004—; trustee Am. Bd. Pathology, Tampa, 2004—; assembly and task force mem. Am. Bd. Med. Specialists, 2005—. Co-author: The Bethesda System for Reporting Cervical Cytology, 2005; contbr. articles to profl. jours.; mem. editl. bd.: Diagnostic Cytopathology, 1996—, Cancer Cytopathology, 1996—; mem. editl. bd. Archives of Pathology and Laboratory Medicine, 2005—. Mem.: Papanicoloau Soc. Cytopathology (com. chair 1993), Coll. Am. Pathologists (com. chair 1998—2001, William Kuehn Outstanding Communicator award 2001), Am. Soc. Cytopathology (exec. bd. dirs. 1995—2003, v.p. 1999—2000, pres.-elect 2000—01, pres. 2001—02). Office: U Ky Med Ctr MS 117 Pathology 800 Rose St Lexington KY 40536 Office Phone: 859-257-9547. Business E-Mail: diane.davey@uky.edu.

DAVEY, KENNETH GEORGE, biologist, educator, academic administrator; b. Chatham, Ont., Can., Apr. 20, 1932; s. William and Marguerite (Clark) D.; m. Jeannette Isabel Evans, Nov. 28, 1959 (separated); children: Christopher Graham, Megan Jeannette, Katherine Alison. BSc, U. Western Ont., 1954, MSc, 1955, DSc (hon.), 2002; PhD, Cambridge (Eng.) U., 1958. NRC Can. fellow U. Toronto, Ont., 1958-59; Drosier fellow Gonville and Caius Coll., Cambridge U., 1959-63; asso. prof. parasitology McGill U., Montreal, Que., Can., 1963-67, prof. parasitology and biology, 1967-74, dir. Inst. Parasitology, 1964-74; prof., chmn. dept. biology York U., Downsview, Ont., 1974-81, dean of sci., 1982-85, disting. research prof., 1984-2000, disting. rsch. prof. emeritus, 2001—, v.p. acad. affairs, 1986-91. Past pres. Huntsman Marine Lab.; pres. Biol. Coun. Can., 1979-81; mem. animal biology grant selection com. Natural Scis. and Engring. Rsch. Coun. Can., 1980-83, group chmn. life scis., 1983-86, mem. com. grants and scholarships, 1983-86; mem. panel on tropical health NIH, 1978-82; pres. World Exec. Coun., Inst. de la Vie, 1987-2003; coun. Royal Can. Inst., 1996—, v.p., 1998-2000, pres. 2000-02; mem. Nat. Coun. on Ethics in Human Rsch., 1998—, pres., 2002—04. Author: Reproduction in the Insects, 1965; editor Internat. Jour. Invertebrate Reprodn., 1978-86; mem. editl. bd. Internat. Jour. Parasitology, 1973-80, Exptl. Parasitology, 1970-76, Can. Jour. Zoology, 1966-76, editor, 1994—2004; assoc. editor Ency. Reprodn.; contbr. articles to profl. jours. Decorated officer Order of Can.; recipient Queen's Jubilee medal Govt. Can., 1977, 2002, Hitschfeld award Can. Assn. Rsch. Adminstrs., 1997, Wigglesworth medal Royal Entomol. Soc. London. Fellow Royal Soc. Can. (sec. Acad. Sci. 1979-85), Royal Entomol. Soc. Can. (Gold medal 1985); mem. Soc. Exptl. Biology, Internat. Union Biol. Scis. (Can. nat. com. 1977-82), Can. Soc. Zoologists (pres. 1981-82, Fry medal 1987), Can. Com. Univ. Biology Chmn. (chmn. 1975-77, Disting. Biologist medal 1992), Biol. Coun. Can. (Gold medal 1987). Office: York Univ Dept Biology North York ON Canada M3J 1P3 Office Phone: 416-736-2100 33804. Personal E-mail: davey@yorku.ca.

DAVEY, LYCURGUS MICHAEL, neurosurgeon; b. N.Y.C., Feb. 20, 1918; s. Michael Marco and Elizabeth (Delaveris) D.; m. Artemis Diana Pappas, June 7, 1942 (dec. Aug. 2003); children: Michael Dean, Elaine Anne, Elizabeth. BA, Yale U., 1939, MD, 1943. Diplomate Am. Bd. Neurol. Surgery, 1954. Surg. intern New Haven Hosp., 1943-44, asst. resident in surgery, 1946-50, William Harvey Cushing fellow, 1947-48, resident neurosurgeon, 1951-52; asst. resident in neurosurgery Hartford Hosp., 1950-51; clin. clk. Nat. Hosp., London, summer 1954; clin. instr. neurosurgery Yale U., 1952-60, asst. clin. prof., 1960-68, asso. clin. prof., 1968-77, clin. prof., 1977—. Assoc. fellow Trumbull Coll. Yale U., 1959—; cons. practice in neurosurgery New Haven, 1952-2002; emeritus staff Mid State Med. Ctr. (formerly Vets Meml. Med. Ctr.); emeritus Hosp. St. Raphael; hon. staff mem. Yale-New Haven Med. Ctr., 1952-01, pres. med. staff, 1971-72, assoc. sect. chief, 1954-91, emeritus, 1991-2001, hon. staff mem., 2002-; bd. dirs. Tex. Citrus Found. Editl. bd. historian Neurosurgery. Class sec. Yale U. Class of 1939, 1999—. Served to comdr. USNR, 1942-46, 52-54; capt. Res. ret. 1973. Fellow ACS, Internat. Coll. Surgeons; mem. AMA, Naval War Coll. Found., Inc. (life), U.S. Naval Inst. (life), Naval Res. Assn. (life), Navy League of U.S. (life), Conn. Med. Soc. (chmn. sect. on neurosurgery 1971-72), Conn. Soc. Neurol. Surgeons (hon. spkr. 2000), New Haven County Med. Soc. (pres. 1987), New Haven Med. Assn. (pres. 1972), Am. Assn. Neurol. Surgeons, New Eng. Neurosurg. Soc., Congress Neurol. Surgeons (mem. editl. bd., historian Neurosurgery 2001—, Disting. Svc. award 1966), Assn. Rsch. in Nervous and Mental Diseases, Soc. Med. Cons. to Armed Forces, Assn. Yale Alumni in Medicine (pres. 1995-97, Disting. Alumni Svc. award 1997, Peter Parker, M.D. Dean's medal 2003). Home: 1010 Hartford Tpke North Haven CT 06473-3038 Office: 2 Church St S Ste 304 New Haven CT 06510-1717 Office Phone: 203-781-0278. Personal E-mail: lmdavey@hotmail.com. Business E-Mail: lycurgus.davey@yale.edu. *My life has been enriched by treating tasks as a challenge to my resourcefulness, knowledge, originality, inventiveness and faith. The task becomes a game rather than a chore.*

DAVID, CLIVE, hotel executive; b. Manchester, Eng., June 6, 1934; came to U.S., 1957, naturalized, 1962; s. Marcus Wiener and Claire Rose (Levy) Wiener Kattenburg. Student, Blackpool Tech. Coll., 1951-52, Royal Coll. Art, 1955-57. Designer Chippendale's, London, 1955-57; asst. to pres. pub. relations Maybruck Assocs., N.Y.C., 1959; Ea. regional dir. City of Hope, Phila., 1960-62; pres. Clive David Assocs., N.Y.C., Clive David Enterprises div. Party Enterprises Ltd., Beverly Hills, Calif., Party Enterprises, Ltd., Beverly Hills, 1962—. Lectr. Party Planning par excellence, 1966—. Arranger major parties including Miss Universe Coronation Ball, Miami Beach, 1965, State visit of Queen Elizabeth and Prince Philip, Duke of Edinburgh, Bahamas, 1966, An Evening at the Ritz-Carlton, Boston, 1967, 69, Un Ballo in Maschera, Venice, 1967, An Evening over Boston, 1968, M.G.M. Cavalcade of Style, L.A., 1970, Symposium on Fund Raising through Parties, L.A., 1970, Great Midwest Limestone Cave Party, Kansas City, 1972, Une Soiree de Gala, Phila., 1972, 11th Anniv. of the Mike Douglas Show, Phila., 1972, The Mayor's Salute to Volunteers, Los Angeles, 1972, Twenty Fifth Anniv. Salute to Israel, Jerusalem, 1973, The Bicentenary, 1976, The World Affairs Council Silver Ball, Boston, 1977, The Ohio Theatre Jubilee, Columbus, 1978, Mayor's Salute to Vols., 1978, Dedication and Gala Performance, Northwestern U. Performing Arts Ctr., 1980, Metromedia Gala, Los Angeles Bicentennial, 1981, The Albemarle Weekend, Charlottesville, 1985, The La Costa Weekend, Carlsbad, 1987, The Embassy Ball, N.Y.C., 1987, The Lagoon Cycle Premiere, Los Angeles, 1987, State Visit Gala for Her Majesty Queen Elizabeth, Miami, 1991, The Grand Brazilian Clambake, Southampton, 1995, The Democratic Senatorial Campaign Committee Gala, Charlottesville, 1996, DSCC reception for Hillary Rodham Clinton, 1996, Rep. Nat. Conv. Team 100 Reception, San Diego, 1996; mem. Pres.' Summit for Am.'s Future Leadership Roundtable, Phila., 1997, Rep. Govs. Conf. Opening Banquet, 1999; contbr. articles to profl. jours. Served with Royal Arty. Brit. Army, 1953-55. Recipient Freedom Found. award Valley Forge, Pa., 1961, City of Hope award Phila., 1962, Mayor's medal for vol. services Los Angeles, 1972, Shalom award State of Israel, 1974, Mayor's medal City of Columbus; named hon. citizen City of Columbus. Mem. AFTRA Jewish. *I consider myself so fortunate to participate in events that bring joy, employment and funds to diversified causes, and maybe leave a miniscule contribution to history.*

DAVID, DANIEL, musician, social studies educator; b. Detroit, Nov. 23, 1957; s. David Joseph and Liza David. MusB, Wayne State U., 1980, MA, 2004. Leader jazz group Dan David Trio, Detroit, 1978—. Pvt. piano and voice tchr., 1973—; lectr. Am. history, 2003—. Playwright, composer: City Serenade, 1998; playwright: Jefferson Lives, 2004. Del. Dem. Party, Mich., 2003—04; dir., lectr. Ctr. for Peace and Idealism, Dearborn, Mich., 2002—. Mem.: Wayne State Alumni Assn. Avocations: jogging, yoga, golf, hockey, basketball. Office: Ctr for Peace and Idealism PO Box 5203 Dearborn MI 48128

DAVID, DANIELLA, psychiatrist; b. Bucharest, Romania, Dec. 28, 1958; arrived in Israel, 1970, arrived in U.S., 1989; d. Marinel and Beatrice Cotter; m. Gavriel David, Sept. 8, 1981; children: Guy, Adee. MSc, Hadassah Sch. Medicine, Jerusalem, 1985; MD, Hebrew U., Jerusalem, 1988. Diplomate Am. Bd. Psychiatry and Neurology. Resident in psychiatry U. Miami Sch. Medicine, 1989—93, chief resident in psychiatry, 1991—92, clin. rsch. fellow, 1993—94, asst. prof. psychiatry, 1994—99, assoc. prof. psychiatry, 1999—; med. dir., PTSD (Post Traumatic Stress Disorder) Unit Miami VA Med. Ctr., 1994—99, PTSD program dir., 1999—. Mem. com. on PTSD Undersec. of Health, Washington, 2000—. Contbr. articles to profl. jours. Sgt. maj. Israeli Def. Forces, 1977—79. Mem.: Internat. Soc. for Traumatic Stress Studies, South Fla. Psychiatric Soc., Am. Psychiatric Assn. Jewish. Avocations: reading, movies, travel. Office: Dept Vet Affairs Med Ctr 1201 NW 16 St 116A12 Miami FL 33125

DAVID, DARYL D., finance company executive; B in Bus., Whitworth Coll.; MBA, U. St. Thomas, St. Paul. Formerly with human resources dept. AlliedSignal, Inc., Gen. Mills, Inc., Weyerhaeuser Co.; formerly exec. v.p., chief adminstrv. officer, sr. v.p. human resources and adminstrn. MagneTek, Inc.; former v.p. strategic growth and human resources Amazon.com; exec. v.p. human resources Washington Mut., Inc., Seattle, 2000—, mem. exec. team, 2001—. Bd. dirs. Ctr. for Effective Orgns. and Cmtys. in Schs. of State of Wash. Office: Washington Mut Inc 1201 3d Ave Seattle WA 98101

DAVID, EDWARD EMIL, JR., electrical engineer, engineering executive, management consultant; b. Wilmington, N.C., Jan. 25, 1925; s. Edward Emil and Beatrice (Liebman) D.; m. Ann Hirshberg, Dec. 23, 1950; 1 dau., Nancy. BS, Ga. Inst. Tech., 1945; MS, MIT, 1947, Sc.D., 1950; D.Engring. (hon.), Stevens Inst. Tech., 1971, Poly. Inst. Bklyn., 1971, U. Mich., 1971, Carnegie-Mellon, 1972, Lehigh U., 1973, U. Ill.-Chgo., 1973, Rose-Hulman Inst. Tech., 1978, U. Fla., 1982, Rensselaer Poly. Inst., 1982, Rutgers U., 1984, N.J. Inst. Tech., 1985, U. Pa., 1985. Exec. dir. research Bell Telephone Labs., Murray Hill, N.J., 1950-70; sci. adviser to Pres. Nixon; dir. Office Sci. and Tech., Washington, 1970-73; exec. v.p. Gould, Inc., 1973-77; ind. cons., 1977, 86—; v.p. Exxon Corp., N.Y.C., 1978-80; pres. Exxon Research and Engring. Co., Florham Park, N.J., 1977-86, EED, Inc., Bedminster, N.J., 1986—; v.p., prin. Washington Adv. Group, 1997—2004, affiliate, 2004—; founder Bio Avrion, Tecumseh, Mich. Bd. dirs. Spacehab, Inc., Washington, Medjet Inc., Edison, NJ, DeCorp, Nashville, Fraser Rsch., Princeton, NJ, BioAvrion, Tecumseh, Mich., Fraser Rsch., Princeton, NJ; cons. NSC, 1974—77; mem. def. sci. bd. U.S. Dept. Def., 1974—75; mem. tech. adv. bd. Chrysler Corp., 1985—93; chmn. Nat. Task Force on Tech. and Soc.; U.S. rep. to NATO Sci. Com., 1979—95; mem. adv. bd. AMP, Inc., Harrisburg, Pa., Bellcore, Livingston, NJ, Electric Power Rsch. Inst., Palo Alto, Calif., Inst. Def. Analyses, Alexandria, Va., 1993—95, Poly Ventures, Farmingdale, NY, Rowan Coll. N.J., Glassboro; active White House Sci. Coun., 1980—88, N.J. Commn. on Sci. and Tech. Patentee in field. Mem. Bicentennial adv. com. Chgo. Mus. Sci. and Industry, 1974-75; mem. adv. bd. Office of Phys. Scis., NRC, 1976-81; mem. Pres.'s Commn. on Nat. Medal of Sci., 1975-78; mem. vis. com. to div. phys. scis. U. Chgo., 1976—; mem. adv. coun. Humanities Inst., 1976—; trustee Aerospace Corp., 1974-81, chmn. bd. trustees, 1975-81; life mem. corp. MIT, 1974—, also mem. exec. com., energy adv. bd.; bd. dirs. Summit (N.J.) Speech Sch., 1967-70; mem. Marshall Scholarships Adv. Coun.; mem. adv. and resource coun. Princeton U.; mem. cons. sci. com. Chateaubriand Scholarships; trustee Carnegie Instn. of Washington, 20th Century Fund, John Simon Guggenheim Meml. Found. Served with USNR, 1943-46. Recipient Outstanding Young Engr. award Eta Kappa Nu, 1954, George W. McCarty award Ga. Inst. Tech., 1958, award Summit Jr. C. of C., 1959, award of merit ASME, 1971, Harold Pender award Moore Sch., U. Pa., 1972, N.C. award, 1972, award for disting. contbn. Soc. Rsch. Adminstrs., 1980, N.J. Sci. and Tech. medal, 1982, medal Indsl. Rsch. Inst., 1983, Scientist of Yr. award R & D mag., 1984, Fahrney medal Franklin Inst., 1985, Pub. Svc. award Conf. Bd. Math. Csic., 1985, Silver Stein award MIT, 1991; named to Hall of Fame, Ga. Inst. Tech., 1994. Fellow IEEE, AAAS (bd. dirs. 1974-75, 77-82, pres. 1977-78, chmn. bd. dirs. 1979-80), Acoustical Soc. Am., Am. Acad. Arts and Scis., Audio Engring. Soc.; mem. NAS (coun. 1995), NAE (Bueche award 1984), Am. Philos. Soc., Assn. Computing Machinery, Am. Soc. for Engring. Edn. (Hall of Fame 1993), Engring. Soc. Detroit, Nat. Acad. Pub. Adminstrn. Office: EED Inc PO Box 435 Bedminster NJ 07921-0435

DAVID, GEORGE, psychiatrist, economic theory lecturer; b. N.Y.C., Feb. 19, 1940; s. Norman and Jennie (Danziger) D. BA, Yale U., 1961; MD, NYU, 1965. Intern Children's Hosp., San Francisco, 1965; resident in psychiatry Colo. Psychiat. Hosp., Denver, 1965-66; practice medicine specializing in psychiatry San Francisco; staff Calif. Pacific Med. Ctr., San Francisco, 1966-67, San Mateo County (Calif.) Mental Health Svcs., 1968-71; lectr. on application of econ. theory to personal decision making. Mem. San Francisco Clin. Hypnosis (v.p. 1973-74). Libertarian. Office: 399 Laurel St San Francisco CA 94118-1951

DAVID, GEORGE ALFRED LAWRENCE, aerospace transportation executive; b. Bryn Mawr, Pa., Apr. 7, 1942; s. Charles Wendell and Margaret (Simpson) David; m. Barbara Osborn, Sept. 4, 1965; children: Eliza Pell, Hannah Lawrence, Henry Gibb. BA, Harvard U., 1965; MBA, U. Va., 1967. Asst. prof. fin. and acctg. U. Va., Charlottesville, 1967—68; v.p. The Boston Cons. Group, 1968—75; sr. v.p. corp. planning and devel. Otis Elevator Co., N.Y.C., 1975—77, sr. v.p., gen. mgr. Latin Am. ops. West Palm Beach, Fla., 1977—81, pres. N.Am. ops. Farmington, Conn., 1981—85, pres., CEO, 1985—89, chmn., 1989—97; sr. v.p. (parent co.) United Techs. Corp., 1988—89, exec. v.p., pres. comml./indsl., 1989—92, COO, 1992—94, pres., 1992—99, 2002—, CEO, 1994—, chmn., 1997—. Chmn. Greater Hartford chpt. ARC, 1985—87; former chmn. US-ASEAN Coun. Bus. and Tech., Nat. Minority Supplier Devel. Coun.; trustee Wadsworth Atheneum, Hartford, 1984—; bd. dirs. Inst. Internat. Econs., Washington. Republican. Episcopalian. Office: 1 Financial Plz # Ms526 Hartford CT 06103-2608 also: Otis Elevator Co 10 Farm Springs Rd Farmington CT 06032-2526

DAVID, HAL, lyricist; m. Eunice Forester, Sept. 2, 1988; children: Jim, Craig. MusD (hon.), Lincoln Coll., 1991; DHL (hon.), Claremont Grad. U., 2000. Books: What the World Needs Now and Other Love Lyrics, Bacharach and David Songbook; Songs include Raindrops Keep Fallin' On My Head (Acad. award), The Look of Love (Acad. award nomination), What's New Pussycat? (Acad. award nomination), Alfie (Acad. award nomination), Wives and Lovers, Casino Royale, It Was Almost Like a Song (all Grammy award nomination), What the World Needs Now is Love, To Love a Child (written for Foster Grandparents' Program), To All the Girls I've Loved Before (recorded by Julio Iglesias and Willie Nelson), America Is (official song of Liberty Centennial campaign for restoration of Statue of Liberty and Ellis Island); chief collaborator: Burt Bacharach; other collaborators include Henry Mancini, Joe Raposo; Broadway show Promises, Promises (Grammy award, Tony award nomination); films include April Fools; record producer for Dionne Warwick. Elected Songwriters Hall Fame, Nashville Songwriters Hall Fame Internat.; recipient Presdl. award National Association Recording Merchandisers, Creative Achievement award B'nai B'rith, Entertainer of Yr. award Cue Mag. Mem. ASCAP (pres. 1980—), Songwriters Guild Am., Lyricists Guild Am., Dramatist Guild, Authors League. Address: 15 W 53rd St New York NY 10019-5401 *How do you create a hit? I don't know. When I sit down to work, I write what I feel. What happens afterwards is out of my hands. The only thing I'm sure of is you can't write a hit if you don't write a song. Of course, the act of creation, itself, is only one part of being a professional songwriter. To succeed and sustain, you have to have a knowledge of the other parts of the music business. You have to recognize that you are in business for yourself, and as president of your own company, you must be on top of all its aspects.*

DAVID, HERBERT ARON, retired statistician, educator; b. Berlin, Dec. 19, 1925; arrived in U.S., 1957, naturalized, 1964; s. Max and Betty (Goldmann) David; m. Vera Reiss, May 13, 1950 (dec.); 1 child, Alexander John; m. Ruth Finch, Dec. 1, 1992. BSc, Sydney (Australia) U., 1947; PhD, London U., 1953. Rsch. officer Commonwealth Sci. and Indsl. Rsch. Orgn., Sydney, 1953-55; sr. lectr. dept. stats. U. Melbourne, Melbourne, Australia, 1955-57; prof. stats. Va. Poly. Inst., 1957-64; prof. U. N.C., Chapel Hill, 1964-72, Iowa State U., Ames, 1972-96, Disting. prof. liberal arts and scis., 1980-96, disting. prof. emeritus, 1996—, dir. stat. lab., head dept. stats., 1972-84; ret., 1996. Author: (book) The Method of Paired Comparisons, 1963, 2d edit., 1988, Order Statistics, 1970; co-author: 3d edit., 2003, Annotated Readings in the History of Statistics, 2001; co-editor: Advances in Biometry, 1996. Recipient J. Shelton Horsley award, Va. Acad. Scis., 1963, Wilks award, Army Rsch., 1983. Fellow: AAAS, Inst. Math. Stats., Am. Statis. Assn.; mem.: Internat. Statis. Inst., Biometric Soc. (editor Biometrics 1967—72, pres. 1982—83). Jewish. Home: 2334 Hamilton Dr Ames IA 50014-8201 Office Phone: 515-294-7749. Business E-Mail: hadavid@iastate.edu.

DAVID, IVO, artist, poet, real estate broker; b. San Leucio Sannio, Italy, Nov. 22, 1934; came to U.S., 1961; s. Arsudino and Clarice-Olga (Lepore) D.; m. Nancy Pugliese, Sept. 26, 1962 (dec. Nov. 1997). Grad., Lyceum of Sci., Italy; MFA, Acad. Fine Arts, Naples, Italy, 1958; grad., Acad. Fine Arts Paestum Acad., Italy, 1975, Internat. Acad. Micenei, Reggio, Italy, 1976. Lic. real estate broker, N.J. Planning designer Candeub/Fleissig Assoc., Newark, 1963-66; chief architect Design Fed. Warehouses, Newark, 1966-74; archtl. designer Raritan Ctr., Edison, N.J., 1970-75; pres., broker, developer Union (N.J.) Ctr. Realty Corp., 1972—, art advt. cons., 1975—. Illustrator: Divine Comedy, 1970 (Gold medal Acad. Art/Micenei Reggio Cal 1997); exhibited in numerous one man shows in U.S. and Europe, 1960-99; City Hall, Paris France, 1999, Musee d'Unet, France, 2001, Ramapo U., NJ, 2002, Chateau Briand Grandroom, NY, 2003, Biennale Internat. dell'Arte Comtemporanea, Italy, 2004, Merk & co., Inc. author: Manifesto of Fusionism, 1956, Memories of an Artist, 1981; founder new art style Fusinism '56. Mem. Greater Union County Assn. Realtors. Avocation: tennis. Home: 3662 2nd Pl SW Vero Beach FL 32968 E-mail: ivodavid@aol.com.

DAVID, LARRY, television scriptwriter, producer, actor; b. Brooklyn, N.Y., July 2, 1947; m. Laurie David, 1993; 2 children. B.A. in History, Univ. of Maryland, College Park, MD. Staff writer: Fridays, 1980-82, Saturday Night Live, 1984-85; creator, writer: Norman's Corner, 1989; exec. prodr., co-creator TV series The Seinfeld Chronicles, 1989, Seinfeld, 1990-98 (Emmy award outstanding comedy series 1993, Emmy award outstanding writing comedy series 1993); writer/dir. Sour Grapes, 1998; exec. prodr., writer, actor HBO comedy special Larry David: Curb Your Enthusiasm, HBO series Curb Your Enthusiasm, 2000- (AFI award best comedy series, 2001, Emmy nomination best lead actor & best comedy series, 2002, 2003); film appearances include Second Thoughts, 1983, Can She Bank a Cherry Pie?, 1983, Radio Days, 1987, New York Stories, 1989. Office: Endeavor 9701 Wilshire Blvd Beverly Hills CA 90212

DAVID, MARTIN HEIDENHAIN, economics professor; b. Heemstede, The Netherlands, Jan. 21, 1935; s. Hans Theodor and Frances (Heidenhain) D.; m. Elizabeth Jane Likert, Sept. 7, 1957; children— Peter Rensis, Margaret Meigs, Andrew John. AB with honors, Swarthmore Coll., 1955; MA, U. Mich., 1957, PhD, 1960. Study dir. Inst. Social Research, Ann Arbor, Mich., 1959-61; asst. prof. econs. U. Wis., Madison, 1961-63, assoc. prof., 1964-66, prof., 1967—2001; fiscal economist U.S. Treasury, 1961-62; chmn. Social Sci. Reseach Inst., U. Wis., Madison, 1970-71; vis. prof., program dir. Inst. Social Research, U. Mich., 1971-72; vis. prof., sr. fellow Inst. Devel. Studies, U. Nairobi, 1974-76. Mem. Social Sci Rsch. Coun. Com. on Social Indicators, Washington, 1980-83; mem. exec. com. Conf. on Income and Wealth, Nat. Bur. Econ. Research, Cambridge, Mass., 1980-83; mem. com. on stats. on family assistance NRC, Washington, 1980-82, com. on nat. stats., 1988-94; chmn. Social Sci. Rsch. Coun. Com. on Survey of Income and Program Participation, 1982-88; vis. prof. Wirtschafts U. Vienna, 1993; rsch. prof. U. Md., JPSM, 2001-03; sr. assoc. scholar Urban Inst., Washington, 2003—; mem. adv. com. German Socio-econ. Panel, 1990-96. Author: Family Composition and Consumption, 1962, Income and Welfare in the U.S., 1962, Alternative Approaches to Capital Gains Taxation, 1968, Linkage and Retrieval of Micro-Economic Data, 1974; author, editor: Technical, Conceptual and Administrative Lessons of the Income Survey Development Program, 1982, Buying a Better Environment: Cost-Effective Regulation Through Permit Trading, 1983, Horizontal, Equity, Uncertainty, and Economic Well-Being, 1985; contbr. articles to profl. jours. Mem. Tax Reform Commn., State of Wis., 1978-79 Recipient Fred M. Taylor award, 1958; open scholar, 1951-55; doctoral dissertation fellow Ford Found., 1958-59; sr. post-doctoral fellow NSF, 1967-68 Fellow Am. Statis. Assn. (fellowship 1982-83); mem. Am. Econ. Assn. (census adv. com. 1979-84), Internat. Assn. Pub. Fin., Econometric Soc. Unitarian Universalist. Office: Ste 1144 425 8th St NW Washington DC 20004-2115

DAVID, MILES, marketing executive; b. Newark, Mar. 29, 1926; s. Samuel Harry and Estelle Rachel (Sklower) Ginsberg; m. Florence Cotton, Dec. 7, 1952; children: Steven, Amelia, Heidi. BA, NYU, 1946; postgrad., Columbia U., 1946. Assoc. editor Sci. Illustrated mag. McGraw-Hill Co., N.Y.C., 1946-48; editor Sponsor mag., N.Y.C., 1948-58; with Radio Advt. Bur., N.Y.C., 1958-86, formerly v.p. and dir. promotion, exec. v.p., pres., vice chmn., chief exec. officer, bd. dir., adv. bd. dirs.; pres. Am. Values: The Community Action Network; pres. nat. mktg. strategy nat. advertisers Mkt. Soundings subs. TradeOne Mktg. Inc., New York, 1986-88; vice chmn. TradeOne Mktg. Inc., New York, 1988-99; pres. Miles David Assocs., Inc., New York, 1999—. Lectr. Tobe-Coburn Sch. for Fashion Careers; speaker in field to nat., internat. groups.; formerly bd. dirs. Brand Names Found.; bd. dirs. Advt. Coun. Editor: Sponsor mag. (George W. Polk award). Former chmn. Scarsdale Adv. Coun. on Cable TV; mem. nominating com. Scarsdale Village Trustees; mem. procedure com. Non-Partisan Elections, Scarsdale; pres. Am. Values Cmty. Action Network. With AUS, 1943-45, ETO. Recipient Morris Meister award; named Outstanding Alumnus Bronx High Sch., Sci. Man of Yr. Radio Trade Assn., 1975, 76; named to Hall of Fame of Co-op Advt., 1997. Mem. Internat. Radio, TV Soc., Broadcast Pioneers, Perstare et Praestare, Trade Promotion Mgmt. Assn. (bd. dirs. 1998—), Scarsdale Club (N.Y.), Town Club (com. pub. rels. 1970-74). Jewish. Achievements include adminstr. Higbee Study, use of radio for dept. stores, and All-Radio Methodology Study, how to measure radio. Home and Office: 35 Jared Dr White Plains NY 10605-3411 E-mail: mdavid3442@aol.com.

DAVID, PAUL ALLAN, economist, economic historian; b. N.Y.C., May 24, 1935; s. Henry and Evelyn (Levinson) D.; m. Janet M. Williamson, May 24, 1958 (div.); m. Sheila Ryan Johansson, Sept. 19, 1982; children: Rachel, Matthew; step-children: Kenneth, Elizabeth. AB summa cum laude in Econs, Harvard U., 1956, PhD, 1973; postgrad., Pembroke Coll., Cambridge (Eng.) U., 1956-58; MA, Oxford (Eng.) U., 1994; D hon. causa, U. Torino. Asst. prof. econs. Stanford U., 1961-66, assoc. prof., 1966-68, prof., 1969—, prof. history (by courtesy), 1976—, William Robertson Coe prof. Am. econ. history, 1978-94, chmn. dept., 1979-83; sr. rsch. fellow All Souls Coll., Oxford, 1994—2002, emeritus fellow, 2002—; prof. econ. and econ. history U. Oxford, 1997—2002. Sr. fellow Oxford Internet Inst., Stanford Inst. Econ. Policy Research, Stanford U.; vis. prof. Harvard U., 1972-73; vis. professorial fellow Churchill Coll., Cambridge U., 1977-78; prof. Am. history and instns. U. Pitt.; vis. fellow All Souls Coll., Oxford (Eng.) U., 1967-68, 93-94; fellow Center for Advanced Study in Behavioral Scis., 1978-79; vis. prof. U. Paris-Dauphine, U. Maastricht, U. Ancona; cons. in field. Author: Nations and Households in Economic Growth: Essays in Honor of Moses Abramovitz, 1974, Technical Choice, Innovation and Economic Growth: Essays on American and British Experience in the Nineteenth Century, 1975, Reckoning with Slavery: A Critical Study in the Quantitative History of American Negro Slavery, 1976, The Economic Future in Historical Perspective, 2003; founding editor Jour. Econ. of Innovations and New Tech.; contbr. numerous articles to profl. jours. Fulbright scholar, 1956-58; Guggenheim fellow, 1975-76. Fellow Am. Acad. Arts and Scis., Internat. Econometric Soc., Brit. Acad.; mem. Econ. History Assn. (v.p., pres. 1988-89), Am. Phil. Soc. Address: Stanford U Dept Econs Stanford CA 94305-6072 Home: 579 Serra Mall Stanford CA 94305-5007 E-mail: paul.david@economics.ox.ac.uk, pad@stanford.edu.

DAVID, REUBEN, lawyer; b. Baghdad, Iraq, June 12, 1928; arrived in U.S., 1951; s. Isaac Solomon David and Tefaha (Nisan) Solomon D.; m. Nesta Paley David; 1 child, Aram. License in Law, Iraqi Law Coll., Baghdad, 1951; BA, NYU, 1958; JD, N.Y. Law Sch., 1962. Bar: Iraq 1951, N.Y. 1969. Asst. corp. counsel City of N.Y., 1970-76, chief legal unit dept. personnel, 1976-78; dep. dir. for legal affairs N.Y.C. Employees' Retirement System, 1978—2002; pvt. practice law, 2002—. Mem. ABA, N.Y. State Bar Assn. Home: 30 Fifth Ave Apt 12E New York NY 10011-8812

DAVID, STANISLAUS ANTONY, metallurgical engineer; b. Kolar Gold Fields, India, June 3, 1943; naturalized in U.S. married, 1971; 2 children. BSc, Mysore U., 1963; BE, Indian Inst. Sci., 1965, ME, 1967; PhD in Metallurgy Engring., U. Pitts., 1971. Postdoctoral fellow in metallurgy U. Pitts., 1971-72, rsch. assoc. prof. metallurgy engring., 1972-77, adj. prof., 1980—; rsch. staff welding Oak Ridge (Tenn.) Nat. Lab., 1977-83, group leader welding, 1983-92, corp. fellow, group leader materials joining, 1992—. Adj. prof. Colo. Sch. Mines, 1985—, Ohio State U., 1986—. Apptd. editor-in-chief Internat. Jour. Sci. and Tech. of Welding and Joining; editor 6 books; contbr. articles to profl. jours.; patentee in field. Recipient Tech. Achievement awards Martin Marietta Energy Sys., Inc., 1987, 88, 89, Champion H. Mathewson gold medal award Minerals, Metals, and Materials Soc., 1994. Fellow AAAS, ASM Internat. and Am. Welding Soc. (Jacquet Lucas gold medal & award 1987, 88, 90), Metallurgy Soc., Am. Inst. Mining, Metallurgy & Petroleum, Am. Welding Soc. (vice-chmn. r&d com. 1989—, Lincoln Gold medal 1981, Charles H. Jennings award 1990), Am. Soc. Metals (chmn. joining divsn. coun. 1990—, chmn. tech. divsns. bd. 1990—). Achievements include research in welding science and solidification; basic and applied research in joing of materials; promote the advancement of welding science through research publications. Office: Oak Ridge Nat Lab Bldg 4508 MS 6095 PO Box 2008 Oak Ridge TN 37831-2008 Office Phone: 865-574-4804. E-mail: davidsa1@ornl.gov.

DAVID, SUSAN HOLCOMBE, child and family therapist; b. Plainfield, N.J., Aug. 29, 1949; d. Paul Thorne Holcombe and Marilyn Jean Lennon; children: Mark Christian, Jason Esser, Michael John, Karen Marie. BA in Edn., Clemson U., S.C., 1971; MA in Cmty. counseling, U. Phoenix, 2002. Lic. profl. counselor, nat. bd. cert. counselor. Tchr. Cath. Elem. Sch., Tampa, Fla., 1971; cons., internet healthcare Unicity Network, Mesa, Ariz., 1992—; therapist Jewish Family & Childrens Svc., Phoenix, 2002—; therapist, educator E. Valley Family Resource Ctr., Mesa, Ariz., 2002—; therapist Child Crisis Ctr., Mesa, Ariz., 2003—04. Co-chmn., co-founder Morton Plant Hosp. Cruisin' the 60s Ann. Fund-raiser; co-founder Kimberly Home, Kimberly-Brian David Birthing Ctr., Jr. League Clearwater Dunedin, 1986—90. Mem.: Chi Sigma Iota (treas. 2002), Chi Omega. Roman Catholic. Avocations: art, sewing, scrapbooks, theater. Office: Jewish Family & Childrens Svc 1930 S Alma Sch Rd Ste A-104 Mesa AZ 85210 Office Phone: 480-820-0825 247. E-mail: powerperson@cox.net.

DAVID, THEODORE MARTIN, lawyer, educator; b. Passaic, N.J., July 29, 1947; BA, Rutgers U., 1969; JD, N.Y. Law Sch., 1974; LLM in Tax Law, NYU, 1977. Bar: N.J. 1974, U.S. Dist. Ct. N.J. 1974, U.S. Tax Ct. 1975, N.Y. 1980. Trial atty. U.S. Tax Ct., Litigation Divsn., IRS, N.Y.C., 1974-78; pvt. practice law Hackensack, N.J., 1980—. Prof. Fairleigh Dickinson U., Hackensack, 1980—. Author: Dealing With the IRS: Law, Forms & Practice, 2002; contbr. articles to profl. jours. Mem. Bergen County Bar Assn. (chmn. tax com. 1980—), Bergen County Bar Found. (trustee 1991-97). Office: 2 University Plz Hackensack NJ 07601-6202

DAVID, THEOHARIS LAMBROS, architect, educator; b. Farmingdale, NY, June 9, 1938; s. Lambros L. and Thalia (Joaniddes) D.; m. Margarita T. Leptos, July 29, 1967; children: Melissa T., Alexis L. BArch, Pratt Inst., 1961; MArch, Yale U., 1964; studied with Serge Chermayeff and Paul Rudolph. Registered arch., N.Y., N.J., Republic of Cyprus; cert. Nat. Coun. Archtl. Registration Bd. Designer Whittlesy & Conklin Archs./Planners, N.Y.C., 1964-65, William F. Pedersen Assocs., N.Y.C., 1965-66, K. Vafeades, Arch., Nicosia, Cyprus, 1965-66; asst. arch. J & A Philippou, Archs., Nicosia, 1966-67, 72; sr. designer Max O. Urbahn Assocs., N.Y.C., 1968-72; ptnr. David & Dikaios Assocs., Architecture/Planning, Nicosia, N.Y.C., Bahrain, 1973-87; prin. Theo David & Assocs., N.Y.C., 1987—, Theo David Cons. Arch./Planner, Nicosia, 1992—. Founding dir. CAEC Architecture/Engring. Cons., Ltd., Cyprus, 1975; mem. faculty Pratt Inst., Bklyn., 1968-69, asst. prof. arch., 1969-79, assoc. prof., 1979-83, prof. arch., 1983—; nominator Aga Khan Award for Arch., 1984—; disting. juror 1st Presdl. Arch. Awards, Cyprus, 1992; guest lectr. U. Thessaloniki, Greece, 1972, Hellenic Conf. on Tall Bldgs., Athens, Greece, 1975, U. So. Calif., L.A., Archtl. Assn., London, 1982, Cyprus Archs. Assn. and Am. Ctr., Nicosia, 1982, 92, Tex. A&M U., 1984, Cyprus Popular Bank Cultural Ctr., Nicosia, 1987, 91, Hellenic Bank Cultural Ctr., Limassol, Cyprus, 1993, many others; guest critic CCNY, N.Y.C., Archtl. Assn., London, Temple U., Phila., Columbia U., N.Y.C., Yale U., New Haven, U. So. Calif., L.A., others. Author: Housing of a Culture/Cyprus, 1982; exhbns. include Pratt Manhattan Ctr., N.Y.C., 1971, 83, Pratt Inst. Gallery, Bklyn., 1978, Urban Ctr., N.Y.C., 1981, Cyprus House, N.Y.C., 1984, 92, Shafler Gallery Pratt Inst., Bklyn., 1987, Mcpl. Arts Soc., N.Y.C., 1987, Disting. Drawing Gallery, N.Y.C./AIA, 1988, Parson Sch. Design, N.Y.C., 1991, Higgins Hall Gallery, Pratt Inst., 1994, Famagusta Gate Nicosia, Cyprus Cooper Union Gallery, N.Y.C., 2004; contbr. articles to profl. jours. Mem. design adv. com. Pub. Devel. Corp., N.Y.C., 1986; 1st v.p. Am. Cyprus Congress, N.Y.C., 1990-94; appointed mem. adv. com. for New Cultural Ctr., Cyprus Govt., 1992. Served U.S. Army, 1962-63. Grantee N.Y. State Coun. on Arts, 1982, Pratt Rsch. Coun., 1983; recipient Design award Nat. Inst. Archtl. Edn., 1961, Bard Honor award City Club, N.Y., 1992, 1st prize G.S.P. Stadium Competition, Cyprus, 1993. Fellow AIA (N.Y. chpt., mem. overseas practice com. 1980-82, chmn. design awards program 1989-90, honors com. N.Y.C. chpt. 2003, Interior Design award AIA Jour. 1988, Design Excellence citation 1993, Design citation 1993, Archs. Designers & Planners for Social Responsibility Project award 1994, Cyprus State Architecture award 2001), Am. Planning Assn. (chmn. com. on N.Y. Waterfront 1984-86), Inst. Urban Design. Greek Orthodox. Office: Theo David Architects 170 Duane St New York NY 10013 also: PO Box 20319 Nicosia Cyprus also: Pratt Inst Sch Arch Brooklyn NY 11205 Office Phone: 212-226-0788. Personal E-mail: tdanyc@aol.com.

DAVID, TODD R., lawyer; b. NYC, Dec. 3, 1956; BA, Queens Coll., 1982; JD, Northeastern Univ., 1985. Bar: Ga. 1986. Law clk., Hon. Marvin H. Shoob US Dist. Judge (no. dist.), Ga.; ptnr., co-coord. litig. practice Alston & Bird LLP, Atlanta. Contbr. articles to profl. journals. Bd. dir. ALS Soc. Ga., Synchronicity Performance Group. Office: Alston & Bird LLP One Atlantic Ctr 1201 W Peachtree St NW Atlanta GA 30309-3424 Office Phone: 404-881-7357. Office Fax: 404-253-8242. Business E-Mail: tdavid@alston.com.

DAVID, VALENTINA S., physics professor; d. Samuel and Mercy Yohan; m. Sunil Kumar David, June 4, 1971; children: Zerelina Rashmi Mukherjee, Sameer Sunil. PhD, U. Pune, Maharastra, India, 1981. Cert. tchr. U. Indore, 1970. Lectr. Vidya Bhavan Jr. Coll., Pune, India, 1982—91; instr. Bethune-Cookman Coll., Daytona Beach, Fla., 1992—96, asst. prof., 1996—2003, assoc. prof., 2003—. Lead tchr. VISION, Daytona Beach, 1999—2002; lead tchr. MASTT project Bethune-Cookman Coll., Daytona Beach, 2003—04, project mgr. MASTT project, 2004—, project dir. UNCF-FAPT project, 2002—. Author: online course in phys. sci. Recipient Faculty Honors award, Bethune-Cookman Coll., 1999, Provost's award for Outstanding Svc., 1999, award Divsn. Sci. and Math., 2003, Pres.'s award for Faculty Mem. of the Yr., 2003, Best Paper award, CIBER/TLC Conf., Las Vegas, 2004, ABR/TLC Conf., Orlando, 2005, cert. of achievement for completing GLOBE Land Cover, Hydrology, and Soil Protocol, NASA Stennis Space Ctr., 2005. Mem.: Assn. for Advancement of Computing in Edn. (corr.). Office: Bethune-Cookman Coll 621 Dr Mary McLeod Bethune Blvd Daytona Beach FL 32114 Office Phone: 386-481-2667.

DAVID, WARD S., bank officer, retired federal agency executive; b. Bertrand, Nebr., Nov. 29, 1934; s. Stanton S. and Helen M. (Gifford) D.; married Aug. 12, 1956; children: Kim, Teri, Mick, Stan, Rod. BS in Agriculture, U. Nebr., 1956. Conservationist USDA, North Platte, Nebr., 1957-59, work unit conservationist Holdrege, Nebr., 1959-68, dist. conservationist Alma, Nebr., 1968-75, area conservationist Tucumcari, N.Mex., 1975-83, Escondido, Calif., 1983-86, divsn. ops. mgr. Washington, 1986-93, ret., 1993; ops. mgr., v.p. Bank of Am., Fallbrook, Calif., 1994—. Author: Ask Not for Victory, 1991; contbr. articles to various publs. Mem. sch. bd. Alma, 1971-75. With USAFR, 1956-57. Mem. Soc. Conservation Soc. Am. (charter, pres. 1967-69), Am. Assn. Ret. Persons (officer). Republican. Methodist. Avocations: sports, writing, reading, jogging, movies. Home: 4505 108th Street Lubbock TX 79424 Office: Environ Mgmt Solutions LLC PO Box 14586 Des Moines IA 50306 Office Phone: 806-798-2066.

DAVIDEK, STEFAN, artist; b. Flint, Mich., May 15, 1924; s. Stephen Paul and Anna Davidek; m. Angelina Ann Davidek, June 19, 1948; children: Mark, Denise, Debra, Dennis. Commns., Holy Redeemer Cath. Ch., Flint, Mich., 1999, St. Mary's Cath. Ch., 1999, St. Robert Cath. Ch., Flushing, Mich, 2003, Genesee County Courthouse, Flint, 2003. Home: 5391 W Coldwater Rd Flint MI 48504

DAVIDGE, K. GENEVIEVE, clinical social worker; b. Mason, Mich., Apr. 19, 1949; d. John and Margery (Lynk) Lippincott; children: Rebecca, Andrew. BA, U. Iowa, 1970, MSW, 1973. Therapist, program dir. Raintree Svcs., New Orleans, 1974-77, Family & Children's Svc., Tulsa, 1978-84; dir., social worker St. Francis Hosp., Tulsa, 1984-87; program coord., case mgr. Rebound, Inc., Lancaster, S.C., 1987-90; pvt. practice Albuquerque, 1990—. Mem. NASW. Methodist. Avocation: singing. Office: 3150 Carlisle Blvd NE Ste 22 Albuquerque NM 87110-1679 Office Phone: 505-830-6030. Business E-Mail: kgdavidge@earthlink.net.

DAVIDOVSKY, MARIO, composer; b. Medanos, Buenos Aires, Argentina, Mar. 4, 1934; came to U.S., 1960; s. Natalio and Perla (Bulanska) D.; m. Elaine Blaustein, Nov. 19, 1961; children: Matias Gabriel, Adriana. Dir. Electronic Music Center, Princeton and Columbia univs., 1964-94; vis. lectr. Sch. Music, U. Mich., 1964; guest prof. Inst. di Tella, Buenos Aires, 1965; prof. music CCNY, 1968-80, Columbia U., 1981-94, 1989-94; prof. emeritus Harvard U., 1994—2004. Dir. Composer's Conf. Wellesley (Mass.) Coll. Composer chamber music, orchestral works, also works for electronic music.; recs. on, Columbia, Sonnova, C.I.R. Nonesuch, Turnabout, New World, Wergo, Bridge records. Bd. dirs. The Koussevitsky Music Found. in Libr. Congress, Fromm Found., Harvard U.; founder, bd. dirs. Robert Miller Fund for Music. Recipient award Koussevitzky Found., 1964, award Libr. of Congress, 1964, Nat. Inst. Arts and Letters, 1965, Creative Arts award Brandeis U., 1965, Aaron Copeland award Tanglewood, 1966, Naumburg award, 1971, Pulitzer prize in music, 1971, Seamus Nat. award, 1994, Cristoph & Stephan Kaske music prize, Munich, 1997; Guggenheim fellow, 1961-62, 62-63; Rockefeller fellow, 1964, 65. Mem. Am. Acad. Arts and Letters, Am. Acad. Arts and Scis. Home: 490 West End Ave New York NY 10024 E-mail: mario.davidovsky@verizon.net.*

DAVIDOW, CHARLES E., lawyer; b. June 25, 1954; BA magna cum laude, Amherst Coll., 1976; JD magna cum laude, Harvard Univ., 1979. Bar: DC 1980, NY 2000. Law clk. Judge Walter R. Mansfield, US Ct. Appeals (2d cir.), 1979—80; ptnr., co-chmn. Securities Enforcement Litigation group Wilmer Cutler Pickering Hale & Dorr, Washington. Adj. prof. Georgetown Univ. Law Ctr., 1991. Editor (& treas.): Harvard Law Rev. Office: Wilmer Cutler Pickering Hale & Dorr 2445 M St NW Washington DC 20037 Office Phone: 202-663-6241. Office Fax: 202-663-6363. Business E-Mail: charles.davidow@wilmerhale.com.

DAVIDOW, JEFFREY, former ambassador to Mexico; b. Boston, Jan. 26, 1944; m. Joan Labuzoski; 2 children. BA, U. Mass., 1965; MA, U. Minn., 1967; postgrad., Osmania U., Hyderabad, India, 1968-69. Joined Fgn. Svc., Dept. State, 1969; polit. officer Santiago, Chile, 1974-76, Capetown/Pretoria, Republic of South Africa, 1976-78; desk officer Office So. African Affairs, Dept. State, 1978-79; Congl. fellow, 1979-82; head U.S. Liaison Office Am. Embassy, Harare, Zimbabwe, 1982-83; fellow Ctr. for Internat. Affairs, Harvard U., 1983-85; dir. Office Regional Affairs and Office So. African Affairs, Dept. State, 1985-86; dep. chief of mission Am. Embassy, Caracas, Venezuela, 1986-88; U.S. amb. to Republic of Zambia, Lusaka, Republic of Zambia, 1988-90; dep. asst. secy. for African affairs Dept. State, Washington, D.C., 1990-93, U.S. amb. to Venezuela Caracas, 1993-96, asst. sec. state for inter-Am. affairs Washington, 1996-98; amb. to Mex., 1998—2002; pres. Inst. of the Americas, La Jolla, Calif., 2003—. Fellow Ctr. Internat. Affairs, Harvard U., 1982. Fellow Am. Polit. Sci. Assn. (congrl. staff aide). Office: Inst of the Americas 10111 N Torrey Pines Rd La Jolla CA 92037

DAVIDOW, JOEL, lawyer; b. N.J., July 24, 1938; s. Isadore Davidow; m. Katherine Davidow-Lucas (div.); children: Beth, Judy; m. Debra Lynn Miller (div.); children: Abigail, Molly. AB, Princeton U., 1960; LLB, Columbia U., 1963; postdoctoral, U. London, Stanford U. Bar: D.C. 1965, N.Y. 1981. Legal asst. to commr. U.S. Fed. Trade Commn., Washington, 1964-65; assoc. Freeman & Hanley, Chgo., 1969-70; trial atty. Antitrust divsn. U.S. Dept. Justice, Washington, 1966-69, evaluation atty. Antitrust divsn., 1970-73, chief fgn. commerce sect. Antitrust divsn., 1973-77, dir. policy planning antitrust div., 1978-81; ptnr. Mudge, Rose, Guthrie, Alexander & Ferdon, N.Y.C., 1981-87; ptnr., head internat. sect. Dickstein, Shapiro & Morin, Washington, 1987-93; ptnr., vice chmn. Ablondi, Foster, Sobin & Davidow, Washington, 1993-2001; ptnr. Miller & Chevalier, Washington, 2001—03, Kile, Goekjian, Reed & McManus, Washington, 2003—. Del. UN Conf. Restrictive Practice, Geneva, 1974—80; adj. prof. law Columbia U., N.Y.C., 1982—87, Am. U., 1987—91, George Mason U., 1992—2004, Georgetown Law Sch., 2003; mem. U.S.-Can. Free Trade Agreement, Washington and Ottowa, 1991—94; cons. UNCTAD, OECD, 1987, Govt. of Switzerland, 1990, World Bank, 1995. Author: Antitrust Rules for International Business, 1995, 3d edit., 2004; fgn. antitrust editor Antitrust Bull., 1981; adv. bd. Bur. Nat. Affairs Antitrust Bulletin, 1981; contbr. articles to profl. jours. Mem. ABA. Democrat. Avocation: tennis. Home: 4445 Westover Pl NW Washington DC 20016 Office: Kile Goekjian Reed & McManus Ste 520 1200 New Hampshire Ave NW Washington DC 20036 Office Phone: 202-263-0806. Business E-Mail: jdavidow@kgrmlaw.com.

DAVIDS, JODY, information technology executive; BBA, MBA, San Jose State U. Computer programmer Apple Computer, Inc., Cupertino, Calif., 1982, various positions, including Asia Pacific divsn., dir. supply chain reengring.; dir. tech. svcs. Nike, Inc., Beaverton, Oreg., 1997—2000; sr v.p. IT pharm. distbn. bus. unit Cardinal Health, Inc., Dublin, Ohio, 2000—03, exec. v.p., chief info. officer, 2003—. Named one of top tech. innovators, Info. Week mag., 2004. Office: Cardinal Health Inc 7000 Cardinal Pl Dublin OH 43017 Office Phone: 614-757-5000.

DAVIDS, NORMAN, engineering educator, researcher; b. N.Y.C., Mar. 17, 1918; s. Max and Sarah (Flint) Davidowitz; m. Frances White, Mar. 17, 1945; children: Gerald, Laura, Stuart. BS, CCNY, 1937; MS, NYU, 1938, PhD, 1940. Instr. CCNY, 1941; physicist C.E., Cin., 1942; mathematician Carnegie Inst. Tech., Washington, 1943-45; instr. Johns Hopkins U., Balt., 1945-47; assoc. prof. engring. mechanics Pa. State U., University Park, 1947-53, prof., 1953-78, prof. emeritus, 1978—. Mem. Inst. Advanced Study, Princeton, N.Y., 1941-42; project dir. NIH, Bethesda, Md., 1968-78, Ballistics Research Labs., Aberdeen, Md., 1961-66; sr. sci. adviser Army Research Office, Durham, N.C., 1961 Editor: International Symposium on Stress Waves, 1960; contbr. articles to profl. jours. Recipient Naval Ordnance Devel. award Carnegie Inst., 1945; Fulbright scholar Israel Inst. Tech., 1959 Fellow Am. Acad. Mechanics (past treas., dir.); mem. ASME, Soc. Engring. Sci., Phi Beta Kappa, Sigma Xi Democrat. Jewish. Home: 236 E Irvin Ave State College PA 16801-6103 Office: Pa State U Engring Sci and Mechs Dept University Park PA 16802 Office Phone: 814-865-4523. Business E-Mail: nxd2@psu.edu.

DAVIDSON, ABRAHAM ABA, art historian, educator, photographer; b. Dorchester, Mass., June 27, 1935; s. Isaac and Ruth (Feinsilver) D. AB in Archtl. Scis. cum laude, Harvard U., 1957; postgrad., Hebrew U., Jerusalem, 1957-58; AM in Art History, Boston U., 1960; B in Jewish Edn., Hebrew Tchrs. Coll., Boston, 1960; PhD in Art History, Columbia U., 1965. Vis. lectr. art history U. Iowa, 1963-64; instr. Wayne State U., Detroit, 1964-65; asst. prof. Oakland U., Rochester, Mich., 1965-68; mem. faculty Tyler Sch. Art, Temple U., Phila., 1968—, prof. art history, 1975—. Vis. asst. prof. U. Mass., Amherst, summers 1965-67, U. Colo., summer 1968; Thomas P. Johnson disting. vis. scholar Rollins Coll., Winter Park, Fla., 1997; cons. Burlington County C.C., Pemberton, N.J., 1976-77. Author: The Story of American Painting, 1974, 79, Japanese transl., 1976, The Eccentrics and Other American Visionary Painters, 1978, Early American Modernist Painting, 1910-1935, 1981, 3d edit., 1990, Ben Solowey, 1988, Ralph Albert Blakelock, 1996, The Paintings of E.M. Saniga, 2001; also articles; one-man exhbns. of photographs Temple U., 1972, 82, Painted Bride Gallery, Phila., 1974, Burlington County C.C., 1978, Gloucester County (N.J.) Coll., 1979, 92, Villanova U., 1982, Pavilion Galleries Burlington County Hosp., Mt. Holly, N.J., 1987, 1521 Café Gallery, 1997, Phila. C.C., 2001, Northampton County Libr., Richboro, Pa., 2004, 05; represented in permanent collections Bank Leumi, Cigna Corp., Lehigh U., Sch. Pharmacy, Temple U., Villanova U., Sheldon Meml. Art Gallery, U. Nebr., Free Libr. Phila., Newark Pub. Libr., Hudson-United Bank, Jefferson divsn.; numerous TV appearances. Recipient Group 17 prize photography Detroit Inst. Arts, 1969, NEH grantee, 1985 Office: Tyler Sch Art Temple Univ Beech and Penrose Aves Elkins Park PA 19126 Office Phone: 215-204-6933. Business E-Mail: adavidso@temple.edu.

DAVIDSON, ANNE STOWELL, lawyer; b. Rye, N.Y., Feb. 24, 1949; d. Robert Harold and Anne (Breeding) D. BA magna cum laude, Smith Coll., 1971; JD cum laude, George Washington U., 1974. Bar: D.C. 1975, U.S. Dist. Ct. D.C. 1975, U.S. Ct. Appeals (D.C. cir.) 1975, U.S. Supreme Ct. 1980. Asst. chief counsel drugs and enforcement FDA, Rockville, Md., 1974—78; counsel Abbott Labs., North Chicago, Ill., 1978—79, U.S. Pharm. Ops. Schering-Plough Corp., Kenilworth, NJ, 1979—83; sr. counsel Sandoz Pharms. Corp., Inc., East Hanover, NJ, 1983—86, v.p., assoc. gen. counsel, 1987—96; assoc. gen. counsel Novartis Pharms. Corp., East Hanover, NJ, 1997—2000; legal cons. Alamo Pharm., LLC, Parsippany, NJ, 2004—. Contbr. articles to profl. jours. Trustee N.J. Pops Orch.; patron St. Hubert's Giralda Animal Shelter, N.J. Recipient Dawes prize Smith Coll., 1971. Mem. ABA, Pharm. Mfrs. Assn., Food and Drug Law Inst., Healthcare Busisness-women's Assn., Non-prescription Drug Mfrs. Assn. (govt. affairs com.), Smith Coll. Club (pres. 1981-82). Republican. Presbyterian. E-mail: missy224@optonline.net.

DAVIDSON, ANTHONY R., education educator, consultant; b. Southport, Eng., July 31, 1958; s. Benjamin and Janet Davidson; m. Linda B. Steinmetz, Mar. 21, 1988; children: Nechama R., Leah, Binyamin, Yehuda Y. BBA, CUNY, 1982, MBA, 1985; PhD, City U. London, 1998. Electronic Document Profl. Xplor Internat. Cert. Commn., Calif., 2002. Instr. Bernard M. Baruch Coll. CUNY, 1985—90; asst. prof. Adelphi U., Garden City, NY, 1990—2000; prof., asst. dean, dir. grad. programs in mgmt. and sys. NYU, NYC, 2000—. Pres. Perfect Impressions Cons., NYC, 1988—. Author: (article) TQM Mag. (Literati Club award for Excellence: Outstanding Paper of Yr., 2002), Telecomm. Sys. Jour., 2003, IEEE Computer, 2004, (book) Interdisciplinary Research, 2004; rev., contbr. (book) Managing Customer Relationships; contbr. chapters to books. Bd. dirs., exec. adv. bd. of e-learn AACE, Norfolk, Va., 2000; advisor RCCS Cancer Soc., Bklyn., 2002; bd. dirs., bd. trustees Med-Smart, Ann Arbor, Mich., 2002; regional chmn. Child Life Soc. Cystic Fibrosis, 2003; mem. steering com. IPSI, Belgrade, Serbia, 2004; advisor JCSE Ctr. for Spl. Edn., Bklyn., 1993—2004; chmn. QTL Free Lending Libr., Queens, 1990—97. Cecilia S. Cohen scholar, CUNY, 1982. Mem.: Beta Gamma Sigma, Sigma Iota Epsilon (chpt. pres. 1983—84). Avocations: skiing, soccer, football, chess. Office: NYU 11 W 42nd St - Ste 429 New York NY 10036 Office Phone: 212-992-3600. Business E-Mail: anthony.davidson@nyu.edu.

DAVIDSON, BARRY SHELDON, academic administrator, comparative education educator; b. Bklyn., Sept. 18, 1949; s. Jack and Iva Irene Davidson. BS, Pittsburg State U., Pittsburg, KS, 1971, MS, 1973; EDS, Vanderbilt U., Nashville, TN, 1974; EDD, U. Ark., Fayetteville, AR, 1977. Lifetime Teaching Credential NY State, 1973. Vis. prof. East Carolina U., Greenville, NC, 1977—80; assoc. dir. admissions U. Nevada-Reno, Reno, 1980—90; dir. admissions Pittsburg State U., Pittsburg, Kans., 1990—91; acad. historian Am. Cmty. Sch., Athens, Greece, 1991—2000; asst. prof. edn. Lander U., Greenwood, SC, 2000—01, McNeese State U., Lake Charles, La., 2001—02, Troy U., Ala., 2002—. Guest scholar European Humanities U., Minsk, Belarus, 1998, Internat. Solomon U., Kiev, Ukraine, 1999, Ind. U. Tbilisi, Georgia, 1999, Adam Mickiewicz U., Poznan, Poland, 1989; presenter Oxford U. Roundtable, 2005. Editor (assoc.) Nat. Forum Jour.; contbr. articles to profl. jours. Chmn. No. Nev. Soccer League Disciplinary Com., Reno, 1980—84; vol. Probation and Parole, Reno, 1987—90; campaign vol. United Way, Pittsburg, Kans., 1990—91; cross country and track coach ACS Varsity Boys and Girls, Greece, 1991—96. Recipient Part-Time Tchg. Five-Year award, Truckee Meadows CC, 1984, Outstanding Young Alumnus award, Pittsburg State U., 1987. Mem.: Am. Assn. U. Prof. Avocations: travel, gardening, coin and stamp collecting. Home: 1122 Brundidge Boulevard Troy AL 36081 Office: Troy Univ 10 McCartha Hall Troy AL 36082 Office Phone: 334-670-5682.

DAVIDSON, BONNIE JEAN, gymnastics educator, sports management consultant; b. Rockford, Ill., Nov. 19, 1941; d. Edward V. and Pauline Mae (Dubbs) Welliver; m. Glenn Duane Davidson, June 4, 1960 (dec. Oct. 1993); children: Lori Davidson Aamodt, Wendy Davidson Seerup; m. James A. Johnson, Sept. 15, 2001. Student, Rockford Coll., 1965, Rock Valley Coll., Rockford, 1969—77. Founder, owner, dir. Gymnastic Acad. Rockford, 1977-95; pres., dir., owner Springbrook, Ltd., swim and tennis club, Rockford, 1986-95. Rep. trampoline and tumbling com. AAU, 1989-99—; coach nat. and world champion athetes; mgr., judge, head del. U.S.A. gynmastics teams, 1980—; speaker, lectr., clinician in field.; mem. organizing coms. world championships, also others, 1982-99 Contbr. World Book Ency. Bd. dirs. U.S. Olympic Com., 1995—, U.S.A. Gymnastics, 1991—; instr. ARC. Named one of Most Interesting People, Rockford mag., 1987; named to USA Gymnastics Hall of Fame, 2003; recipient YWCA Janet Lynn Sports award, 1996. Mem. Internat. Fedn. Trampoline and Tumbling (internat. judge, mem. tech. com. 1986-99—, del. to congress 1976-86, hon. lifetime mem. 1998), Internat. Fedn. Sport Acrobats (internat. judge), U.S.A. Trampoline and Tumbling Assn. (hon. life; nat. tumbling chairperson 1980-88, advisor 1988-99—, Coach of Yr. award 1980, Outsanding Contbn. to the Sport award 1987, 96, Master of Sport award 1989), U.S. Sports Acrobatics Fedn. (hon. life; v.p. 1984-95), Nat. Judges Assn. (exec. dir.). Republican. Avocations: skiing, boating, bicycling, birding, flying. Personal E-mail: davidsonbj@aol.com. E-mail: davidsonbj11@insightbb.com.

DAVIDSON, CATHY NOTARI, English language educator, writer; b. Chgo., June 21, 1949; d. Paul Celestino Notari and Leona (Behnke) Ripes; m. Arnold E. Davidson (div. 1994); 1 stepchild, Charles Russell. BA, Elmhurst Coll., 1970; MA, SUNY, Binghamton, 1973, PhD, 1974; postdoctoral study, U. Chgo., 1975-76; LHD (hon.), Elmhurst Coll., 1989. Instr. St. Bonaventure U., Olean, N.Y., 1974-75; from asst. to full prof. Mich. State U., East Lansing, 1976-89; prof. dept. English Duke U., Durham, N.C., 1989-96, Ruth F. de Varney prof. English, 1996—, v.p. interdisciplinary studies, 1998—. Vis. prof. Kobe (Japan) Coll., 1980-81, 87-88, Princeton U., 1988-89. Author: The Experimental Fictions of Ambrose Bierce, 1984, Revolution and the Word: The Rise of the Novel in America, 1986, Thirty-Six Views of Mt. Fuji: On Finding Myself in Japan, 1993, Closing: The Life and Death of an American Factory, 1998; editor: The Book of Love: Writers and Their Love Letters, 1992; co-editor: The Lost Tradition: Mothers and Daughters in Literature, 1980, The Art of Margaret Atwood, 1982, The Oxford Book of Women's Writing in the United States, 1994; editor: Reading in America: Literature and Social History, 1989, Charlotte Temple, 1986, The Coquette, 1986; assoc. editor Am. Lit., 1990-91, editor, 1991—; also over 50 articles. Woodrow Wilson fellow, 1970, Woodrow Wilson Dissertation fellowship, 1972, Irving J. Lee Meml. award, 1973, Newberry Libr. Scholar-in-Residence award, 1976, Mich. State Disting. Tchr.-Scholar award, 1979, Mich. State Disting. Faculty award, 1987, Kate B. and Hall James Peterson fellowship, hon. mem. Am. Antiquarian Soc., Worcester, Mass., 1984, Am. Coun. of Learned Socs. grant-in-aid, N.Y., 1986, John Simon Guggenheim Meml. fellowship, N.Y., 1986. Fulbright Sr. fellow, Australia, 1994, Bellagio Ctr. Rockefeller fellow, 1993. Fellow Nat. Humanities Ctr., Am. Coun. Learned Socs.; mem. MLA (exec. com. divsn. late 19th century Am. lit. 1981-86, divsn. early Am. lit. 1987—, mem. del. assembly 1980-86), Am. Studies Assn. (pres. 1993). Office: Duke Univ Dept English 6697 College Station Durham NC 27708

DAVIDSON, CHANDLER, sociologist, educator; b. May 13, 1936; m. Sharon Lavonne Plummer, Nov. 1, 1986. BA, U. Tex., 1961; PhD, Princeton U., 1969. Rsch. prof. sociology Rice U., Houston, 1966—, prof. polit. sci., 1997—2003, prof. emeritus, 2003—, Radoslav Tsanoff prof. pub. affairs, 2000—03, chair dept. sociology, 1979-83, 86-89, 1995—2003, prof. emeritus, 2003—. Co-prin. investigator NSF, 1988-92, Rockefeller Found., 1990. Author: Biracial Politics, 1972, Race and Class in Texas Politics, 1990; editor: Minority Vote Dilution, 1984, (with Bernard Grofman) Controversies in Minority Voting, 1992, (with Grofman) Quiet Revolution in the South, 1994. Fulbright scholar, 1961-62; Woodrow Wilson fellow, 1963-64, rsch. fellow Nat. Endowment for Humanities, 1976-77; recipient Gustavus Myers Ctr. Human Rights award for outstanding book on human rights, 1993, Ally award Ctr. for the Healing of Racism, 1996, Brown award for superior tchg., Rice U., 1997, 99, 2000, 2002, Brown award for excellence in tchg. Rice U., 1998. Mem. Am. Polit. Sci. Assn. (Fenno prize 1995), Philos. Soc. Tex., Phi Beta Kappa. Office: Rice U Dept Sociology 6100 S Main St Houston TX 77005-1892 Office Phone: 713-348-3490. Business E-Mail: fcd@rice.edu.

DAVIDSON, CHARLES D., energy executive; With ARCO AK, Inc., 1972—92, sr. vice-pres., Eastern District, 1993—97; pres., CEO Vastar Resources, Inc., 1997—2000, Noble Energy, 2000—. Office: Noble Energy Ste 100 100 Glenborough Houston TX 77067 Office Phone: 281-872-3100. Office Fax: 281-872-3111.*

DAVIDSON, CLIFFORD MARC, lawyer; b. Yonkers, N.Y., Mar. 7, 1960; s. Maurice and Marilyn (Korb) D.; m. Barbara Branson, July 27, 1991. BS Pharmacy, Rutgers U., Piscataway; JD, Rutgers U., Camden. Assoc. Marmorek, Guttman & Rubenstein, N.Y.C., 1986-87, Hedman, Gibson, Costigan & Hoare, N.Y.C., 1987-88, Kenyon & Kenyon, N.Y.C., 1988-91; ptnr. Steinberg & Raskin, N.Y.C., 1991-94, Steinberg, Raskin & Davidson, P.C., N.Y.C., 1994-97; sr. ptnr. Davidson, Davidson & Kappel, LLC, N.Y.C., 1998—. Mem. Am. Pharm. Assn., Controlled Release Soc., N.J. Intellectual Property Assn., N.Y. Intellectual Property Assn. Avocations: tennis, music. Office: Davidson Davidson & Kappel LLC 485 7th Ave 14th Fl New York NY 10018 Office Phone: 212-736-1940. Business E-Mail: cdavidson@dddkpatent.com.

DAVIDSON, COLIN HENRY, architect, educator; b. Exeter, Eng., Mar. 4, 1928; emigrated to Can., 1968, naturalized, 1975. s. Douglas Nangle and Dulcie Rose (Winter) D.; m. Lucienne Fiant, Jan. 18, 1956; children: Dominique, Philip. Diploma architecture, Brussels Royal Acad., 1951; M.Arch., M.I.T., 1955. Archtl. asst. Luccichenti/Monaco, Rome, 1951-54; asst. architect Architects' Collaborative, Cambridge, Mass., 1954-55, London County Council, 1956-60; pres. C.H. Davidson Cons., London, 1960-68; prof. architecture U. Montreal, 1968—; dean Faculty Environ. Design, 1976-85, ACSA disting. prof., 1997—. Founder Indsl. Forum Rsch. Group, 1969; founder, pres. IF Rsch. Corp.; exec. dir. Cibat-Montreal Internat. Bldg. Ctr.; pres., Organisation canadienne pour la jeunesse et le développement. Prin. works include Cosmos and SB2 industrialized bldg. sys.; author numerous works in field of info. sci. in bldg. including 4 thesauri in bldg. sci. and tech., bldg. procurement, tech. transfer, and post-disaster reconstruction. Mem. Internat. Coun. Rsch. and Innovation in Bldg. and Constrn.-CIB, Order of Archs. Que. Office: U Montreal PO Box 6128 Montreal PQ Canada H3C 3J7 Personal E-mail: colinhdavidson@sympatico.ca. *I have constantly been torn by the dilemma of the Architect: man-of-the-arts or man-of-science. Having opted for the latter (perhaps out of fear of the former), I find I must work in a scientific near-vacuum. For this reason, I dedicate my life to problems of research and its application, to the transfer of information in the building process.*

DAVIDSON, DALE ALAN, secondary school educator, director; b. Canton, Ohio, Apr. 1, 1954; s. Norwood William and Vivian Jane Davidson; m. Karen Kay Ross, Aug. 26, 1959; children: Chad Alan, Amanda Kay. MusB in Music Edn., Kent State U., Kent, Ohio, 1977; M in Music Edn., U. Akron, Akron, Ohio, 1987. Cert. Music, Special, K-12 Profl. Ohio. Student tchr. Rootstown Local Sch. Dist., Rootstown, Ohio, 1977; music tchr. St. Vincent-St. Mary's H.S., Akron, Ohio, 1977—81; head band dir. Springfield Local Schs., Akron, Ohio, 1981—94, Green Local Schs., Green, Ohio, 1994—. Named to Hall of Fame, Nat. H.S. Band Dirs. Hall of Fame, 1992; recipient PTA Outstanding H.S. Tchr., Green PTA, 2005, U. Chgo. Educator Citatin, U. Chgo., 1993, 2004 Honored Educator, Who's Who Among America's Teachers, 2004, Honored Educator, Green H.S. Top 10% Student Recognition, 1998, 2005, Green H.S. Making A difference Award, Green H.S. Prin., 2003, 25 Yr. Recipient Recognition, Ohio Music Educator's Assn., 2003. Mem.: NEA (assoc.), Nat. Band Dirs. Assn. (assoc.), Green Edn. Assn. (assoc.), Ohio Edn. Assn. (assoc.), Music Edn. Nat. Conf. (assoc.), Ohio Music Edn. Assn. (assoc.). Achievements include O.M.E.A. Dist. 6 Chair Jr. H.S. Solo & Ensemble Adjudicated Events, 1982, 1983, 1989, & 1990; O.M.E.A. Dist. 6 Chair Jr. H.S. Large Group Adjudicated Events, 1991; O.M.E.A. Dist. 6 Chair H.S. Large Group Adjudicated Events, 1994. Home: 13213 Carla Ave NW Uniontown OH 44685 Office: Green Local Schs 1474 Boettler Rd Green OH 44685 Office Phone: 330-896-7530.

DAVIDSON, DAN EUGENE, educational association administrator, director, language educator; b. Wichita, Kans., Sept. 18, 1944; s. Clerin D. and Fay E. (Scott) D.; m. Maria D. Lekic, Apr. 20, 1976; children: Michael Scott, Paul Eugene. BA, U. Kans., 1966; MA, Harvard U., 1971, PhD, 1972; DSc (hon.), Russian Acad. Scis., 1995, Almaty State U., Kazakhstan, 1996, U. World Langs., Uzbekistan, 1997. Asst. prof., then assoc. prof. Amherst (Mass.) Coll., 1971-76; from assoc. prof. to prof. Russian Bryn Mawr (Pa.) Coll., 1976—; exec. dir. Am. Coun. Tchrs. of Russian, Washington, 1980—; pres. Am. Couns. for Internat. Edn. ACTR/ACCELS, 1998—. Adj. faculty U. Pa., Columbia U., Harvard U., 1975; cons. UN, N.Y.C., 1987, 88, 91, U.S. Dept. Edn., NEH, Washington; co-chair Internat. Task Force on Ednl. Reform in Russia, Ukraine, Belarus, Kyrgyzstan, Kazakhstan, 1992-94 (Soros Founds.); chmn. Alliance for Internat. Ednl. and Cultural Exch., 1997-99. Series editor: Soviet-American Textbook Series of Russian, 1974—; author, co-author, editor univ. and high sch.-level textbooks on English and Russian; editor, co-editor scholarly collections, jours.; contbr. articles to scholarly publs. Bd. dirs. numerous non-profit ednl. orgns.; mem. leadership com. co-chmn. ann. fund and major gifts, Barrie Sch., 1995-96, trustee, 1997-2000; mem. Fair Share Campaign Sidwell Friends Sch., 1992-97. Recipient Pushkin medal, 1982, Order Internat. Friendship, USSR, 1990; inducted into Russian Acad. Edn., 1995; recipient Disting. Svc. to Profession award, Am. Assn. Tchrs. Slavic Langs., 1995, Disting. Svc. award Assn. Depts. Fgn. Langs./MLA, 1997; hon. fellow Woodrow Wilson Found., 1966. Mem. MLA, Am. Assn. Advancement Slavic Studies, Am. Coun. Tchrs. of Russian (pres. 1975-79), Internat. Assn. Tchrs. Russian Lang. and Lit. (v.p. 1975-80, 91—), Harvard Club, Phi Beta Kappa, Delta Phi Alpha. Democrat. Episcopalian. Avocations: travel, music, swimming. Office: Am Couns Ste 700 1776 Massachusetts Ave NW Washington DC 20036-1904 Office Phone: 202-833-7522. Personal E-mail: ddavidson@ren.net. Business E-Mail: ceo@americancouncils.org.

DAVIDSON, DANIEL IRA, lawyer; b. Bklyn., Sept. 19, 1936; s. Mitchell and Minnie (Needleman) D.; m. Susan Bettina Thomas, Mar. 13, 1966; 1 child, Jill. AB, Columbia Coll., 1957; JD, Columbia U., 1959. Bar: N.Y. 1959, U.S. Ct.Appeals (2d cir.), 1960, U.S. Ct. Appeals (D.C. cir.), 1970, D.C., 1972, U.S. Ct. Appeals (9th cir.), 1975, U.S. Ct. Appeals (5th cir.), 1980, U.S. Ct. Appeals (10th and 11th cirs.), 1981, U.S. Supreme Ct., 1982. Editor Columbia Law Rev., 1958-59; law clk. to Judges Harold R. Medina and Learned Hand U.S. Ct. Appeals 2d Cir., 1960; assoc. Cravath, Swaine & Moore, N.Y.C., 1961-65; spl. asst. to asst. sec. state East Asia and Pacific Affairs, Washington, 1965-67; spl. asst. to ambassador U.S. Dept. State, Washington, 1967-68; U.S. del. to Paris Peace Talks on Vietnam Paris, 1968-69; mem. staff Nat. Security Coun., Washington, 1969; assoc. Wilmer, Cutler & Pickering, Washington, 1969-70; exec. asst. to W. Averell Harriman Washington, 1971-72; assoc. Prather, Levenberg, Seeger, Doolittle, Farmer & Ewing, Washington, 1972-73, Spiegel & McDiarmid, Washington, 1973-74, ptnr., 1974—. Mem. Com. on Internat. Affairs Dem. Policy Coun., Washington, 1971-72; cons. U.S. Dept. State, Washington, 1978-79, pub. mem. fgn. svc. selection bd., 1995; mem. Coun. on Fgn. Rels.; lectr. in polit. sci. CUNY, 1960. Editor: Columbia Law Review; contbr. articles and book revs. to The Economist, NY Times, LA Times, Wash. Post, London Fin. Times, The Atlantic, others; featured in: (documentary) The Trials of Henry Kissinger. 1st lt. USAR, 1960-66. Fellow Salzburg Seminar in Am. Studies, 1959. Mem. Cosmos Club, Phi Beta Kappa. Jewish. Home: 2900 Brandywine St NW Washington DC 20008-2138 Office: Spiegel & McDiarmid 1333 New Hampshire Ave NW Washington DC 20036 Office Phone: 202-879-4060. Business E-Mail: daniel.davidson@spiegelmcd.com.

DAVIDSON, DANIEL MORTON, lawyer; b. Lynbrook, N.Y., July 9, 1950; BA summa cum laude, Williams Coll., 1972; JD magna cum laude, Harvard U., 1975. Bar: D.C. 1975, Calif. 1977, U.S. Tax Ct. 1979, U.S. Supreme Ct. 1992. Law clk. Mass. Supreme Ct., 1975-76; ptnr. Sidley & Austin, Washington, 1985-98, Hogan & Hartson, L.L.P., Washington, 1998—. Contbr. articles to profl. jours. Mem. ABA, D.C. Bar Assn., State Bar Calif., Phi Beta Kappa. Office: Hogan & Hartson LLP 555 13th St NW Ste 900W Washington DC 20004-1109 Office Phone: 202-637-5865. E-mail: dmdavidson@hhlaw.com.

DAVIDSON, DAVID SCOTT, retired architect; b. Great Falls, Mont., Dec. 17, 1925; s. David Adams and Florence Mae (Scott) D.; m. Marjorie Luella Huffman, Sept. 10, 1949; children: Carol M., Marilyn S., Scott L., Bruce F., Craig S. Student, U. Utah, 1943, Pasadena City Coll., 1944; BS in Architecture, Mont. State U., 1950. Registered architect, Mont. Architect in tng. Shanley & Shanley Architects, Great Falls, 1950-52; architect van Teylingen, Knight, van Teylingen, Great Falls, 1952-54; prin. David S. Davidson, Architect, Great Falls, 1954-56; ptnr. Davidson & Kuhr Architects, Great Falls, 1956-75; pres. Davidson & Kuhr Architects, P.C., Great Falls, 1975—2002. Dir., pres. Great Falls Arts Assn., 1980-83; dir., pres. Mont. Inst. Arts, 1981—; mem. state constrn. adv. coun. State of Mont., 1983-84; dir., v.p. Paris Gibson Square, Great Falls, 1982—88. Mem. Great Falls Zoning Bd., 1972-75; mem. rehab. com. Great Falls Housing Task Force, 1975-78; chmn. architecture div. United Way, 1975-78; dir. Great Falls Symphony Assn., 1992-93. Served with U.S. Army, 1943-46. Recipient 1st honor Mont. chpt. AIA, 1973, 75; recipient honor award in architecture Mont. chpt. AIA, 1973, 74, 78, 83, merit in architecture Mont. chpt. AIA, 1965, 2 awards U.S. Dept. Energy, 1986, Interior Design award Arch. Record, 1976, Internat. Union Bricklayers and Allied Crafts award, 1986, 87, 92. Fellow AIA (chpt. pres. 1965-66, dir. 1962-66), Great Falls Soc. Architects (pres. 1958-59), Jr. C. of C. (dir. 1956-60) Home: 1212 Buena Dr Great Falls MT 59404-3750

DAVIDSON, DIANE (MARIE DAVIDSON), publisher; b. L.A., Mar. 6, 1924; d. Charles Casper and Stella Ruth (Bateman) Winnia; divorced, 1953; children: David William, Ronald Mark. AB, U. Calif., Berkeley, 1943; MA, Calif. State U., Sacramento, 1959. cert. secondary tchr., 1944. Tchr. Campbell (Calif.) High Sch., 1944-45; actress Pasadena (Calif.) Playhouse, 1945, U.S.O. Camp Shows, N.Y.C., 1946-47; tchr. El Camino H.S., Sacramento, 1954-85; illustrator, publisher, editor Swan Books, Fair Oaks, Calif., 1979-99. Author: Feversham, 1969, "18 easy-to-read Shakespeare plays without changing the words; editor: History of Trinity Episcopal Church, Folsom, California, 1856-1994, 1996; contbr. articles to Shakespeare mag. Mem. NEA, PEN, Authors Guild, Calif. Writers Club, Calif. Tchrs. Assn., Phi Beta Kappa, Pi Lambda Theta. Democrat. Episcopalian. Avocations: gardening, writing. Home: 8146 Toyon Ave Fair Oaks CA 95628-7633 E-mail: swanbks@aol.com.

DAVIDSON, DONALD WILLIAM, advertising executive; b. Toronto, May 18, 1938; s. John Harvie and Harriet Gertrude Davidson; m. Olive Margaret Somerville, July 28, 1962; children: Scott, Susan. Degree, U. Toronto, York U. Account exec. E.L. Ruddy, Toronto, 1957-68, Foster & Kleiser, Detroit, 1968-70; v.p. Outdoor Advt. Sales, 1971-72, Montreal, 1972-73, v.p. mktg. group, 1973-75; v.p. nat. sales Claude Neon Ltd., Toronto, 1975-77, exec. v.p., 1977-79; pres. Mediacom Inc., Toronto, 1979-80, chmn., pres., 1980-84; exec. v.p., COO, Gannett Outdoor, N.Y.C., 1984-86, pres., CEO, 1986-96; pres. Trading Bay Media, 1996—; ptnr., pres. DCR Media Inc.; with Trading Bay LLC, NYC, 2005—. Past vice chmn. Traffic Audit Bur. Mem. The Advt. Coun. (bd. dirs.), Lambton Golf and Country Club, Bigwin Golf Club. Home: 40 Las Brisas Way Naples FL 34108 Office: Trading Bay LLC 230 Park Ave New York NY 10169-0005

DAVIDSON, DONETTA LEA, state official; b. Liberal, Kans., 1943; County clk. and recorder Bent County, Las Animas, Colo., 1978-86; dir. of elections State of Colo., 1986-94; county clerk & recorder Arapahoe County, Littleton, Colo., 1995—99; sec. of state State of Colo., Denver, 1999—. Mem. Election Assistance Commn., 2005—. Accreditation bd. Nat. Assn. State Election Directors Voting Sys./Ind. Test Authority, 1998—; bd. dirs. Election Ctr., 1998—. Henry Toll Fellowship of Coun. of State Govts., 1993. Mem.: Nat. Assn. Secretaries of State (treas. 2003—04, pres. elect 2004—05, pres. 2005—), Postal Svc. Task Force (chairperson, joint elections officials liaison cmty. 1997—), Fed. Election Commn. Adv. Panel (mem. 1995—), Internat. Assn. Clks., Recorders, Election Officials, and Treasurers (mem. 1995—), Nat. Assn. State Election Dir. (pres. 1994), Colo. State Assn. of County Clk. and Recorders (pres. 1983—84). Republican. Office: Office of Sec of State 1700 Broadway Ste 250 Denver CO 80290 Office Phone: 303-894-2200. Business E-Mail: sos.admin1@sos.state.co.us.

DAVIDSON, DOUGLAS E., lawyer; b. NYC, 1946; BS, Georgetown U., 1968; JD summa cum laude, George Washington U., 1971. Bar: NY 1972. Ptnr. Thelen Reid & Priest LLP, NYC, vice chmn., bus. dept., co-chmn., Latin Am. & Global Fin. & Securities Practice Group, co-chmn., Energy Utilities & Infrastructure Practice Group. Editor-in-chief George Washington Law Rev., 1970—71. Mem.: Assn. Bar City NY (chmn. nuclear tech. & law com. 1982—85), NY State Bar Assn., Fed. Energy Bar Assn., ABA, Order of Coif. Office: Thelen Reid & Priest LLP 875 Third Ave New York NY 10022-6225 Office Phone: 212-603-8977. Office Fax: 212-603-2001. Business E-Mail: ddavidson@thelenreid.com.

DAVIDSON, ERIC HARRIS, molecular and developmental biologist, educator; b. NYC, Apr. 13, 1937; s. Morris and Anne D. BA, U. Pa., 1958; PhD, Rockefeller U., 1963. Research asso. Rockefeller U., 1963-65, asst. prof., 1965-71; asso. prof. devel. molecular biology Calif. Inst. Tech., Pasadena, Calif., 1971-74, prof., 1974—, Norman Chandler prof. cell biology, 1981—. Author: Gene Activity in Early Development, 3d edit, 1986, Genomic Regulatory Systems, 2001. NIH grantee, 1965—, NSF grantee, 1972—. Mem.: Nat. Acad. Scis. Achievements include research, numerous publs. on DNA sequence orgn., gene expression during embryonic devel., gene regulation, evolutionary mechanisms, gene networks. Office: Calif Inst Tech Div Biology Mail Code 156 29 Pasadena CA 91125-0001 Office Phone: 626-395-4937.

DAVIDSON, ERNEST ROY, chemist, educator; b. Terre Haute, Ind., Oct. 12, 1936; s. Roy Emmette and Opal Ruth (Hugunin) D.; m. Reba Faye Minnich, Jan. 27, 1956; children: Michael Collins, John Philip, Mark Ernest, Martha Ruth. BSc, Rose-Hulman Inst. Tech., 1958, DEng (hon.), 1998; PhD, Ind. U., 1961; PhD (hon.), Uppsala U., 2000. NSF Postdoctoral fellow U. Wis.-Madison, 1961-62; asst. prof. chemistry U. Wash., 1962-65, assoc. prof., 1965-68, prof., 1968-84, Ind. U., Bloomington, 1984-86, disting. prof., 1986—2002, chmn. dept. chemistry, 1999—2002; prof. U. Wash., Seattle, 2002—. Disting. vis. prof. Ohio State U., 1974-75; vis. prof. IMS, Japan, 1984, Technion, Israel, 1985; vis. scholar U. N.C., 2002—; Boys-Rahman lectr. Royal Soc. Chemistry, 2002. Editor: Jour. Computational Physics, 1975-98, Internat. Jour. Quantum Chemistry, 1975—, Jour. Chem. Physics, 1976-78, 98—, Chem. Physics Letters, 1977-84, Jour. Am. Chem. Soc., 1978-83, Jour. Phys. Chemistry, 1982-90, Accounts of Chem. Rsch., 1984-92, Theoretica Chimica Acta, 1985-98, Chem. Revs., 1986—; contbr. numerous articles on density matrices and quantum theory of molecular structure to profl. jours. Union Carbide fellow Rose-Hulman Inst. Tech., 1958; NSF fellow Ind. U., 1961; recipient Hirschfelder prize in theoretical chemistry, 1997-98, Schrodinger medal, 2001, Nat. medal of sci., 2002; Sloan fellow, 1967-68; Guggenheim fellow, 1974-75; laureate l'Academie Internationale des Sciences Moleculaires Quantiques, 1971. Fellow Am. Phys. Soc., Sigma Xi; mem. NAS, Am. Chem. Soc. (Computers in Chemistry award 1992, Theoretical Chemistry award 2000), Am. Acad. Arts and Scis., Ind. Acad. Sci. (Chemist of Yr. award 1999), Phi Lambda Upsilon, Tau Beta Pi. Home: 550 Elm Way # 213 Edmonds WA 98020 Office: U Wash Dept Chemistry Bagley 303A Seattle WA 98195-1700

DAVIDSON, EUGENE ABRAHAM, biochemist, educator, academic administrator; b. N.Y.C., May 27, 1930; s. Jack and Sophie Miriam (Deutsch) D. BS, UCLA, 1950; PhD, Columbia U., 1955. Postdoctoral fellow, instr. U. Mich., 1955-58; asst. prof. biochemistry Duke U., 1958-62, assoc. prof., 1962-65, prof., 1965-67; prof., chmn. dept. biol. chemistry M.S. Hershey Med. Center, Pa. State U., 1967-87, assoc. dean for edn., 1975-87; chmn. dept. biochemistry and molecular biology Georgetown U., Washington, 1988—2002, prof., 2003—. Mem. Nat. Bd. Med. Examiners, Part I; cons. in field. Author: Carbohydrate Chemistry, 1967; contbr. numerous articles to profl. publs.; Editorial reviewer for numerous jours. Guggenheim fellow, 1965-66; NIH grantee, 1958— Mem. AAAS, Am. Soc. Biol. Chemists, Assn. Med. Sch. Depts. Biochemistry, Biochem. Soc., Am. Assn. Cancer Research, Soc. Complex Carbohydrates, Glycoconjugate Soc. (pres. 1985-87), Sigma Xi. Home: 5506 Nebraska Ave NW Washington DC 20015-1256 Office: Georgetown U Dept Biochem/Molecular Biology Washington DC 20057 Business E-Mail: davidson@georgetown.edu.

DAVIDSON, EZRA C., JR., obstetrician, gynecologist, educator, academic administrator; b. Water Valley, Miss., Oct. 21, 1933; s. Ezra Cap and Theresa Hattie (Woods) Davidson; children: Pamela, Gwendolyn, Marc, Ezra K. BS cum laude, Morehouse Coll., 1954; MD, Meharry Med. Coll., 1958. Diplomate Am. Bd. Ob-Gyn. (examiner 1973-). Intern San Diego County Gen. Hosp., 1958—59; resident in ob-gyn. Harlem Hosp., N.Y.C., 1963—66, asst. attending ob-gyn, obstet. coordinator maternal and infant care clinics, 1967—68; dir. departmental research, assoc. attending, acting chmn. ob-gyn, co-dir. coagulation research lab. Roosevelt Hosp., N.Y.C., 1968—70; fellow blood coagulation, asst. ob-gyn Columbia U. Coll. Physicians and Surgeons, N.Y.C., 1966—67, instr. dept. ob-gyn, 1967—69, asst. clin. prof., 1970; cons. ob-gyn Office Health Affairs, OEO, Washington, 1970—72; prof. Charles R. Drew U. of Medicine and Sci., L.A., 1971—, acad. v.p., 1982—87, chmn. dept. ob.-gyn., 1971—96, assoc. dean primary care, 1997—; prof. U. So. Calif., Los Angeles, 1971—80, UCLA, 1980—. Chief svc. dept. ob-gyn. King/Drew Med. Ctr., L.A., 1971—96; attending physician dept. ob-gyn. L.A. County-U. So. Calif. Med. Ctr., 1971—80; mem. nat. med. adv. com. nat. found. March of Dimes, 1972—76; bd. cons. Internat. Childbirth Edn. Assn., 1973—81; mem. sec.'s adv. com. population affairs HEW, 1974—77, chmn. svcs. task force, 1975—77; chmn. bd. dirs. L.A. Regional Family Planning Coun., 1975—77; bd. dirs. Nat. Alliance Sch. Age Parents, 1975—79; mem. corp. bd. Blue Shield, Calif., 1989—; chair DHHS Sec.'s Adv. Com. on Infant Mortality, 1990—93; active FDA, 1990—96, chmn. fertility and maternal health drugs adv. com., 1992—96; mem. adv. com. to the dir. NIH, 1995—98, mem. dirs. adv. panel on clin. rsch., 1995—98; mem. roundtable on health care quality Inst. on Medicine, 1995—98; mem. coun. grad. med. edn. HHS, 1997—2000; bd. dirs., chair med. policy com. Blue Shield of Calif., 1998—2002. Bd. dirs. The Calif. Wellness Found., 1995—, chmn., 1996—98; bd. dirs. Children's Bur. So. Calif., 1999—, v.p., 1995—99, pres., 1999—2002; bd. dirs. Jacobs Inst. of Womens Health, 1999—; chmn. bd. trustees Blue Shield Calif. Found., 2004—. Served with USAF, 1959—63. Fellow Johnson Found. Health Policy, Inst. Medicine, NAS, 1979—80. Fellow: ACS, L.A. Ob-Gyn. Soc. (pres. 1982—83), Royal Coll. Ob-Gyn., Am. Coll. Ob-Gyn. (nat. sec. 1983—89, pres.-elect 1989—90, pres. 1990—91); mem.: Calif. Tech. Assessment Forum (chair 2002—), Assn. of Acad. Minority Physicians (pres. 2002—03), Golden State Med. Assn. (pres. 1989—90), Assn. Profs. Ob-Gyn. (pres. 1989—90), Nat. Med. Assn. (chmn. nat. sect. ob-gyn. 1975—77, mem. sci. coun. 1979—88, bd. trustee 1989—95, chmn. bd. trustees 1992—95), Ob-Gyn. Assembly So. Calif. (chmn. 1989—90), Pacific Coast Ob-Gyn. Soc., N.Am. Soc. Pediatric and Adolescent Gynecology (pres.-elect 1993—94, pres. 1994—95), Am. Ob-Gyn. Soc. Office: 12021 Wilmington Ave Los Angeles CA 90059-3019

DAVIDSON, FRANK PAUL, retired macroengineer, retired lawyer; b. N.Y.C., May 20, 1918; s. Maurice Philip and Blanche (Reinheimer) D.; m. Izaline Marguerite Doll, May 19, 1951; children: Roger Conrad, Nicholas Henry, Charles Geoffrey. BS, Harvard U., 1939, JD, 1948; DHL (hon.), Hawthorne Coll., 1987; D in Engring. and Diplomacy (hon.), Roger Williams U., 2003. Bar: NY 1953, U.S. Dist. Ct. (so. dist.) NY 1953. Dir. mil. affairs, gen. counsel Houston C. of C., 1948-50; contract analyst Am. Embassy, Paris, 1950-53; assoc. Carb, Luria, Glassner & Cook, N.Y.C., 1953-54; pvt. practice law N.Y.C., 1955-70; founding pres., counsel, bd. dirs. The Inst. for the Future, 1967-70; rsch. assoc. MIT, Cambridge, Mass., 1970-96, also chmn. system dynamics steering com. Sloan Sch. Mgmt., coord. macro-engring. Sch. Engring. Pres., gen. counsel Tech. Studies Inc., N.Y.C., 1957—96; vice chmn. Inst. for Ednl. Svcs., Bedford, Mass., 1980—84; co-founder Channel Tunnel Study Group, London and Paris, 1957, governing bd., 1957—85; NAS del. Renewable Resources Workshop, Katmandu, Nepal, 1981; mem. adv. bd. Tech. in Soc., Elmont, NY, 1981—, project appraisal, 1986—98; mem. editl. bd. Interdisciplinary Sci. Revs., 1985—; apptd. to exploration task force NASA, Washington, 1989; spl. rectr. Société des Ingénieurs et Scientifiques de France, 1991; mem. internat. sci. and tech. com. Ocean Cities Symposium, Monaco, 1995. *Frank Davidson was awarded the Bronze Star Medal by SHAEF Headquarters. A full account of Frank Davidson's role in the successful 1957 re-launching of the project for construction of a railway tunnel between the United Kingdom and France was published in "The Chunnel" by Drew Fetherston, in 1997. On May 20, 1998, on the occasion of Davidson's 80th birthday, a volume of essays in Honor of Frank Davidson entitled "Macro-Engineering and the Earth" was published in 1998 and edited by Professor Ernst G. Frankel of MIT Ocean Engineering Department and by Uwe Kitzinger, C.B.E., former President of Templeton College, Oxford U.* Author: Macro: A Clear Vision of How Sci. and Tech. Will Shape Our Future, 1983, Macro: Big is Beautiful, 1986; editor: series of AAAS books on macroengring., Tunneling and Underground Transport, 1987; co-editor: Solar Power Satellites, 1978, 1998. Bd. dirs. Internat. Mountain Soc., Boulder, Colo., 1981-2000, Assn. Prospective 2100, Paris, 1997; trustee Norwich (Vt.) Ctr., 1980-83, mem. steering com. Am. Trails Network, 1986-88, bd. dirs. Am. Trails Washington, 1988-90. RCAC, 1941-46, ETO; Troop Leader 10th Cdn., Armoured Rgt. (Fort Garry Horse), Intelligence Officer and Squadron Leader, GSO III (Intelligence) Second Armoured Brigade Group, maj. Tex. State Guard; apptd. to Senate Ft. Garry Horse, 1995, bd. overseers Roger Williams U., 2004. Decorated Bronze Star medal, 1945-46; Chevalier Legion of Honor (France), 1999; named hon. major Fort Garry Horse, 2004; recipient Key to City Osaka, Japan, 1987, Twice the Citizen award Royal Mil. Inst., Man., Can., 1999, William James award Rensselaerville Inst., 2001; elected Mem. Honoraire, Pres. d'Honneur Assn. Louis Armand, Paris, 1996-99; Lewis Mumford fellow Rensselaerville Inst., 1982. Mem. ABA, Internat. Assn. Macro-Engring. Socs. (bd. dirs. 1987—, hon. chmn. 1997-2000), Am. Soc. Macro-Engring. (bd. dirs. 1982—, vice chancellor 1983-97, pres. 1997-98, chmn. 1998), Assn. Bar City N.Y. (internat. law com. 1959-62), Major Projects Assn. (mem. overseas adv. com. U.K. 1995—), Knickerbocker Club, St. Botolph Club, MIT Quarter Century Club. Home: 151 Main St Concord MA 01742-2436

DAVIDSON, GEORGE ALLAN, lawyer; b. N.Y.C., Apr. 6, 1942; s. George Roger and Jean Allan (McKaig) D.; m. Annette L. Richter, Sept. 4, 1965; children: Emily, Charlotte. AB, Brown U., 1964; LLB, Columbia U., 1967. Bar: N.Y. 1967, U.S. Dist. Ct. (so. and ea. dists.) N.Y. 1969, U.S. Ct. Appeals (2d cir.) 1970, U.S. Supreme Ct. 1974, U.S. Tax Ct. 1974, U.S. Ct. Appeals (D.C. cir.) 1976, U.S. Dist. Ct. (no. dist.) Calif. 1980, U.S. Ct. Appeals (9th cir.) 1981, U.S. Ct. Appeals (5th cir.) 1982, U.S. Dist. Ct. (no. dist.) N.Y. 1982, U.S. Ct. Appeals (11th cir.) 1983, U.S. Ct. Appeals (1st cir.) 1986, U.S. Ct. Appeals (7th cir.) 1992. Law clk., 1967-68; assoc. Hughes Hubbard & Reed, N.Y.C., 1968-74, ptnr., 1974—; dir. P.R. Legal Def. and Edn. Fund, Inc., 1980-84. Dir. Legal Aid Soc., 1979-92, pres. 1987-89, N.Y. Lawyers for Pub. Interest, Inc., 1984-86, Columbia Law Sch. Alumni Assn., 1987-91, Practicing Attys. for Law Students, 1989—, VIP Cmty. Svcs., 1994—, Greenwich House, Inc., 2002—, chmn., 2004—; chmn. Fed. Defenders N.Y., Inc., 2005—. Contbr. writings to legal publs. Fellow Am. Coll. Trial Lawyers; mem. ABA, Internat. Bar Assn., Fed. Bar Coun., Am. Law Inst., N.Y. State Bar Assn., Assn. Bar City N.Y., Nat. Assn. Coll. and Univ. Attys., Union Internationale des Avocats, Century Assn. Office: Hughes Hubbard & Reed LLP 1 Battery Park Plz Fl 12 New York NY 10004-1482 Office Phone: 212-837-6585. E-mail: davidson@hugheshubbard.com.

DAVIDSON, GERRY, lawyer; b. Cleve., Dec. 18, 1945; s. William and Charlotte (Bloch) D.; div. Oct., 1974; 1 child, Melanie; div. Jan. 17, 1995; children: Cary, Kimberly, Mandy, Tammy. BBA, Ohio U., 1968; JD, Cleve.-Marshall Coll. Law, 1972. Bar: Ohio 1972, U.S. Dist. Ct. (no. dist.) Ohio 1973. Legal intern Legal Aid Soc., Cleve., 1970-72; pvt. practice Cleve., 1972—. Pres., bd. trustees Crisis Intervention Team, Cleve., 1978-79. Contbr. article to profl. jour. With U.S. Army, 1969-74. Avocations: theater, travel, fishing. Office: 800 Standard Bldg Cleveland OH 44113

DAVIDSON, GLEN HARRIS, federal judge; b. Pontotoc, Miss., Nov. 20, 1941; s. M. Glen and Lora (Harris) D.; m. Bonnie Payne, Apr. 25, 1973; children: Glen III, Gregory P. BA, U. Miss, 1962, JD, 1965. Bar: Miss. 1965, admitted to practice: US Ct. Appeals (5th Cir.) 1965, US Supreme Ct. 1971. Asst. dist. atty. First Jud. Dist., Tupelo, Miss., 1969-74, dist. atty., 1975; US atty. US Dist. Ct. (No. Dist.) Miss., Oxford, 1981-85, US dist. judge Aberdeen, Miss., 1985—2000, chief judge, 2000—, Jud. Conf. U.S., 2004. Atty. Lee County Sch. Bd., Miss., 1974—81. Bd. dirs. Cmty. Devel. Found., Tupelo, 1976-81; exec. bd. Yocona Coun. Boy Scouts Am., 1972—. Maj. USAF, 1966-69. Mem.: Kiwanis (pres. Tupelo 1978), Miss. Prosecutors Assn., ATLA, Lee County Bar Assn. (pres. 1974), Miss. Bar Found., Fed. Bar Assn. (v.p. 1984). Presbyterian. Office: US Dist Courthouse 301 W Commerce St Ste 342 PO Box 767 Aberdeen MS 39730-0767 Office Phone: 662-369-6486. Office Fax: 662-369-8339. E-mail: Glen_Davidson@msnd.uscourts.gov.

DAVIDSON, GORDON, theater producer, theater director; b. Bklyn., May 7, 1933; s. Joseph H. and Alice (Gordon) D.; m. Judith Swiller, Sept. 21, 1958; children: Adam, Rachel. BA, Cornell U.; MA, Case Western Res. U.; L.H.D. (hon.), Bklyn. Coll.; D. Performing Arts (hon.), Calif. Inst. Arts; D.F.A. (hon.), Claremont U. Ctr. Stage mgr. Phoenix Theatre Co., 1958-60, Am. Shakespeare Festival Theatre, 1958-60, Dallas Civic Opera, 1960-61, Martha Graham Dance Co., 1962; mng. dir. Theatre Group at UCLA, 1965-67; artistic dir., producer Center Theatre Group Mark Taper Forum, 1967—; co-founder New Theatre For Now, Mark Taper Forum, 1970. Past mem. theatre panel Nat. Endowment for Arts; past pres. Theatre Communications Group; mem. adv. council Internat. Theatre Inst.; mem. adv. com. Cornell Ctr. for Performing Arts; cons. Denver Center for the Performing Arts; bd. dirs. several arts orgns. including Am. Arts Alliance; producing dir., CTG/Ahmanson Theatre. Producer, dir. over 150 major theatrical prodns. including The Deputy, 1965, Candide, 1966, The Devils, 1967, Who's Happy Now, 1967, In the Matter of J. Robert Oppenheimer, 1968 (N.Y. Drama Desk award), Sew, Murderous Angels, 1970, Rosebloom, 1970, The Trial of the Catonsville Nine, 1971 (Obie award, Tony award nomination), Henry IV, Part I, 1972, Mass, 1973, Hamlet, 1974, Savages, 1974 (Obie award), Too Much Johnson, 1975, The Shadow Box, 1975 (Tony award, Outer Critics Circle Best Dir. award), And Where She Stops Nobody Knows, 1976, Getting Out, 1977, Black Angel, 1978, Terra Nova, 1979, Children of a Lesser God, 1979, The Lady and the Clarinet, 1980, Chekhov in Yalta, 1981, Tales from Hollywood, 1982, The American Clock, 1984, The Hands of Its Enemy, 1984, Traveler in the Dark, 1985, The Real Thing, 1986, Ghetto, 1986, A Lie of the Mind, 1988; dir. operas including Cosi Fan Tutte, Otello, Beatrice and Benedick, Carmen, La Boheme, Il Trovatore, Harriet, A Woman Called Moses, A Midsummer Night's Dream, 1988; TV film The Trial of the Catonsville Nine, 1971; exec. producer Zoot Suit, 1981; producer for TV It's the Willingness, PBS Visions Series, 1979, Who's Happy Now?, NET Theatre in Am. Series; dir. A Little Night Music, 1990. Trustee Ctr. for Music, Drama and Art; past pres. League Resident Theatres; past v.p. Am. Nat. Theatre Acad; advisor Fund for New Am. Plays; mem. adv. bd. Nat. Found. for Jewish Culture. Recipient N.Y. Drama Desk award for direction, 1969; recipient Los Angeles Drama Critics Circle awards for direction, 1971, 74, 75, Margo Jones award New Theatre for Now, 1970, 76, Obie award, 1971, 77, Outer Critics Circle award, 1977, Tony award for direction, 1977, award John Harvard, award Nat. Acad. TV Arts and Scis., award Nosotros Golden Eagle, award N.Y. League for Hard of Hearing, award N.Y. Speech and Hearing Assn., award Am. Theatre Assn., award Los Angeles Human Relations Commn.; Guggenheim fellow, 1983, Pulitzer Prize in Drama for the Kentucky Cycle and Angels in America (Part One- Millennium Approaches). Mem. League Resident Theatres (past pres.), ANTA (v.p. 1975), Nat. Endowment for the Arts. Office: Ctr Theatre Group Mark Taper Forum 135 N Grand Ave Los Angeles CA 90012-3013 Office Phone: 213-972-7353.*

DAVIDSON, GORDON BYRON, lawyer; b. Louisville, June 24, 1926; s. Paul Byron and Elizabeth (Franz) D.; m. Geraldine B. Geiger, Dec. 21, 1948; children: Sally Burgess, Stuart Gordon. AB, Centre Coll., 1949; JD, U. Louisville, 1951; LL.M., Yale U., 1952. Law clk. Supreme Ct. U.S., 1954; of counsel Wyatt, Tarrant & Combs, Louisville, 1955-92, mng. ptnr., 1978-92. Bd. dirs. Norton Healthcare, Inc., Warben, Inc. Pres. Louisville Ctrl. Area, Inc., 1971-73; chmn. River City Mall Com., 1973-74, Louisville Devel. Com.; trustee Louisville Area C. of C., 1986; bd. dirs. The Ky. Ctr.; bd. dirs., chmn. Norton Childrens Hosps., 1973-75, Louisville Fund for Arts, 1987-93; trustee emeritus Centre Coll. Recipient Louisville Citizen of Yr. award, 1973-74, Mayor's Fleur de Lis award, 1974, Louisville Man of Yr. award, 1981, Outstanding Lawyer of Ky. award, 1984, Disting. Alumnus award U. Louisville Law Sch., 1982, Disting. Citizen award City of Louisville, 1987, Man of Vision award, 1991, Ky. Commonwealth award, 1995, Caritas Found. award, 1998; Alumni fellow Brandeis Sch. Law, U. Louisville, 2005; named to Louisville Male High Sch. Hall of Fame, 1989. Mem. Jefferson Club, Louisville Country Club, Dennbarr Club, Lawyers Club, River Valley Club, Gulf Stream Bath and Tennis Club, Gulf Stream Golf Club Democrat. Presbyterian. Home: 435 Lightfoot Rd Louisville KY 40207-1853 also: 1102 Vista Del Mar Dr N Delray Beach FL 33483-7146 Office: Wyatt Tarrant & Combs PNC Plz Louisville KY 40202-2823

DAVIDSON, GORDON K., lawyer; b. Port Chester, N.Y., July 30, 1948; BSEE with great distinction, Stanford U., 1970, MS in Elec. Engring. and Computer Systems, 1971, JD, 1974. Bar: Calif. 1974. Law clk. to Judge Ben C. Duniway U.S. Ct. Appeals, 9th cir., 1974-75; ptnr. Fenwick & West, Palo Alto, Calif. Nathan Abbott scholar Stanford U., 1974. Mem. ABA, State Bar Calif., Order Coif, Phi Beta Kappa, Tau Beta Pi. Office: Fenwick & West Two Palo Alto Sq 8th Fl Palo Alto CA 94306

DAVIDSON, HERBERT ALAN, Near Eastern languages and cultures educator; b. Boston, May 25, 1932; s. Louis Nathan and Ettabelle (Baker) D.; m. Kinneret Bernstein; children: Rachel and Jessica. BA, Harvard U., 1953, MA, 1955, PhD, 1959. Lectr. Harvard U., Cambridge, Mass., 1960-61; asst. prof. UCLA, 1961-66, assoc. prof., 1966-72, prof., 1972-94, prof. emeritus, 1994—, chmn. dept. near eastern langs. and cultures, 1984-91. Author: The Philosophy of Abraham Shalom, 1964, medieval Hebrew transls. of Averroes' Middle Commentary on the Isagoge and Categories, 1969, English transl., 1969, Proofs for Eternity, Creation, and the Existence of God in Medieval Islamic and Jewish Philosophy, 1987, Alfarabi, Avicenna, and Averroes on Intellect, 1992, Maimon: Des Moses Maimoudes, The Man and His Works, 2004; contbr. articles and book revs. to profl. jours. Office: UCLA Dept Near Ea Langs and Cultures 405 Hilgard Ave Los Angeles CA 90095-9000

DAVIDSON, HERBERT M., JR., (TIPPEN DAVIDSON), newspaper owner; b. Chgo., Aug. 10, 1925; s. Herbert Marc and Liliane (Refregier) D.; m. Josephine Field, Dec. 27, 1947 (dec. July 1995); children: Marc, Julia. Student, Juilliard Sch., 1942-43, 45-46; Mus.D. (hon.), Stetson U., 1975. Reporter Chgo. Daily News, 1949-50; city editor Daytona Beach (Fla.) News-Jour., 1951-53, mng. editor, 1953-56, gen. mgr., 1957-85, pub., 1985-98, co-editor, 1985—, pres., CEO, 1998—. Pres. Ctrl. Fla. Cultural Endeavors, Inc., Daytona Beach, 1963—; chmn. Fine Arts Coun. of Fla., 1970-75, 81-82; mem. Fla. Alliance for Arts, 1998—; mem. Fla. Arts Coun., 1998-2000; prodr., artistic dir. Seaside Music Theater, Daytona Beach, 1976—. Cpl. U.S. Army, 1942-44, PTO. Named Ambassador of the Arts, State of Fla., Tallahassee, 1982, Hon. mem. London Symphony Orch., 1989, honoree Daytona Beach Community Coll.'s Tippen and Josephine Field Davidson Endowment for the Arts, 1992; hon. officer Civil divsn. Order of the Brit. Empire, 1998. Mem. Am. Soc. Newspaper Editors Avocations: music, theater, handicraft, stamp collecting/philately. Home: 1608 N Oleander Ave Daytona Beach FL 32118-3415 Office: Daytona Beach News-Jour 901 6th St Daytona Beach FL 32117-3352 Office Phone: 386-252-1511. Business E-Mail: tippen@news-jrnl.com.

DAVIDSON, HUGH MACCULLOUGH, French language and literature educator; b. West Point, Ga., Jan. 21, 1918; s. Robert Calvin Davidson Sr. and Anne Della Stripling; m. Loretta Jane Miller, June 15, 1951; 1 child, Anne Stripling Davidson. AB in Romance Langs., U. Chgo., 1938, PhD in Romance Langs., 1946; MA (hon.), Yale U., 1967. Instr. French U. Chgo., 1946-48, asst. prof. French, 1948-53, asst. dean coll., 1951-53; asst. prof. romance langs. Dartmouth Coll., 1953-56, prof. romance langs., 1956-62, chmn. dept. romance langs., 1957-59; prof. romance langs. Ohio State U., 1962-67, 68-73; prof. French lit. U. Va., 1973-78, commonwealth prof. French lit., 1978, 1978-90, commonwealth prof. French lit. emeritus, 1990—. Vis. prof. French U. Mich., 1967; univ. examiner French and gen. linguistics, humanities U. Chgo., 1946-48; chmn. Coll. French staff U. Chgo., 1948-53; Thomas Jefferson fellow Downing Coll., Cambridge U., Eng., 1979-80; vis. prof. U. Paris Sorbonne, 1982-83; vis. com. humanities and arts Case We. Res. U., 1967; cons. div. edn. programs NEH, 1977; conducts seminars in field. Author: Audience, Words, and Art, 1965, The Origins of Certainty: Means and Meanings in Pascal's Pensées, 1979, Blaise Pascal, 1983, Pascal and the Arts of the Mind, 1993; co-author: A Concordance to the Pensées of Pascal, 1975, A Concordance to Pascal's Les Provinciales, 1980; asst. editor: The Idea and Practice of General Education, 1948; mem. editl. bd. Continuum: Problems in French Literature from the Late Renaissance to the Early Enlightenment, EMF: Studies in Early Modern France; contbr. articles to profl. jours. Capt. USAF, 1942—46. Gen. Edn. fellow Carnegie Found., 1948-49; Fulbright Sr. fellow for rsch. in France, 1959-60; Sr. Rsch. fellow Nat. Found. Arts and Humanities, 1967-68. Mem. MLA (mem. editl. com. publs. 1968-73), Am. Assn. Tchrs. French, Am. Soc. Eighteenth-Century Studies, N. Am. Soc. Seventeenth-Century French Lit., Assn. internat. des études françaises, Soc. internat. d'étude du XVIIe siècle, Soc. internat. d'étude du XVIIIe siècle, Soc. des amis de l'Inst. de littérature française de l'Univ. de Paris Sorbonne, Soc. des amis de Port-Royal, Phi Beta Kappa (mem. nat. Senate 1982-88). Episcopalian. Avocations: history of painting, sculpture, and architecture, history of the liberal arts of grammar, rhetoric, logic, dialectic and their applications in art, science, and philosophy, music. Address: 250 Pantops Mountain Rd Apt 319 Charlottesville VA 22911 Office: U Va Dept French Lit 302 Cabell Hl Charlottesville VA 22908-0001

DAVIDSON, JACK LEROY, academic administrator; b. Indpls., July 14, 1927; s. Lawrence L. and Emma (Jones) D.; m. Ina Stanfill, June 20, 1948; children: William (dec.), Nancy, Evan. BA, Franklin Coll., 1949; MA, Ind. U., 1955, Ed. Adminstrn., 1961, PhD, 1967. Tchr., guidance counselor, coach Mitchell (Ind.) Pub. Schs., 1949-57; elem. prin., supervising prin. Vincennes (Ind.) Pub. Schs., 1957-59; supt. Worthington (Ind.) Pub. Schs., 1959-61, Salem (Ind.) Pub. Schs., 1961-65, Oak Ridge (Tenn.) Pub. Schs., 1965-68, Manatee County (Fla.) Pub. Schs., 1968-70, Austin (Tex.) Pub. Schs., 1970-80, Tyler (Tex.) Public Schs., 1980-91; spl. asst. to pres. U. Tex., Tyler, 1991-96. Vis. prof. U. Tex.; chmn. Tex. Adv. Com. on Ednl. Improvement. Schs.; cons. Tex. Edn. Agy. Author: Effective School Board Meetings, 1970, The Superintendency & Leadership for Effective Schools, 1987; Contbr. articles to ednl. jours. Bd. dirs., pres. Southwest Ednl. Devel. Lab.; charter mem. Tex. Commn. on Inter-Govtl. Rels.; bd. dirs. Austin Jr. Achievement; pres. bd. dirs. Salvation Army, pres. adv. bd., 2005. With USNR, 1945-47. Recipient Super Supt. award Tex. PTA, 1982, award of honor Nat. Sch. Pub. Rels. Assn., 1990, Disting. Svc. award AASA, 1992, Founders award Tyler Ind. Sch. Dist. Found., 2005; named one of 100 Top Exec. Educators Exec. Educator mag., 1984, 89; Dr. Jack L. Davidson Conf. Ctr. named in his honor, 2004. Mem. Am. Assn. Suprs. Curriculum Devel., Am. Assn. Sch. Adminstrs., Tex. Assn. Sch. Adminstrs., Rotary (pres. Tyler club), Phi Delta Kappa (outstanding educator award 1992). Methodist (deacon, dir.). Home: 1807 Picadilly Pl Tyler TX 75703-2409 Office Phone: 903-561-7154. Personal E-mail: davidsonji@coxinternet.com. *The only real profit in life comes from the satisfaction gained in service to others.*

DAVIDSON, JAMES JOSEPH, III, lawyer; b. Lafayette, La., July 27, 1940; s. James Joseph and Virginia Lee (Dunham) D.; m. Kay Cecile Holloway, Aug. 7, 1962; children: Kimberly Kay, James Joseph IV, Lynda Leigh, Virginia Holland. BA, U. SW La., 1963; JD, Tulane U., 1964. Bar: La. 1964, U.S. Dist. Ct. (we. dist.) La. 1965, U.S. Dist. Ct. (ea. dist.) La. 1979, U.S. Dist. Ct. (mid. dist.) La. 1986, U.S. Ct. Appeals (5th cir.) 1972 Us. Supreme Ct. 1975, U.S. Ct. Appeals (11th cir.) 1981. Ptnr. Davidson, Meaux, Sonnier & McElligott, Lafayette, La., 1964—. Mem. exec. bd. Evangeline Area coun. Boy Scouts Am., 1969-80; trustee U. La. Lafayette Found., 1980—, pres., 1988-91. Fellow Am. Bar Found. (life); mem. ABA (ho. of dels. 2002-04), La. State Bar Assn. (del. 1970-96), La. Bar Found., La. State Law Inst. (coun. 2002--), La. Assn. Def. Counsel (dir. 1975-77), Nat. Assn. R.R. Trial Counsel, Am. Bd. Trial Advocates (adv. bd.), Am. Counsel Assn., Internat. Assn. Def. Counsel, Assn. Def. Trial Attys., Assn. Transp. Practitioners. Republican. Baptist. Home: 539 Girard Park Dr Lafayette LA 70503-2601 Office: PO Box 2908 Lafayette LA 70502-2908 Office Phone: 337-237-1660.

DAVIDSON, JAMES WILSON, clinical psychologist; b. Muncie, Ind., Apr. 22, 1950; s. James Wayne and Mary Marguerite (Sanford) D.; m. Nancy Lee Hendershott, Aug. 30, 1969; children: Melissa Ann, Amanda Corynne, Kevin Patrick. BS, Mich. State U., 1972; PhD, Kent State U., 1975; postgrad., Ashland (Ohio) Theol. Sem., 1980-82. Ordained to ministry Assemblies of God, 1988. Coord. Ctr. on Rsch. and Evaluation, Ashtabula, Ohio, 1974-77; pres. The Children's Ctr., Ashtabula, 1978-80, Computech Data Systems, Ashtabula, 1978-82; v.p. Davidson Assocs., Ashtabula, 1977-86; assoc. pastor First Assembly of God, Ashtabula, 1986-88; sr. pastor Metro Ch., Cleve., 1988-94; CEO Heart and Hand Found., Cleve., 1988—, LifeLine Counseling Ctr., 1994—. Dir. Ohio Dist. Coun. Urban Missions Ministries, Columbus, 1990—. Recipient 414th Point of Light award White House, 1991, Health award UNICEF, 1992, 93, Ptnr. Agy. Excellence award CMHA, 1992, 93; Kent State U. fellow, 1973-74. Mem. APA, Am. Assn. Christian Counselors. Republican. Avocations: flying, writing, travel, snorkeling. Home: 2627 Courtland Blvd Cleveland OH 44118-4737

DAVIDSON, JANET G., telecommunications industry executive; b. Short Hills, N.J. B in Physics, Lehigh U.; M in Elec. Engring., Ga. Tech., 1979; M in Computer Sci. Joined Bell Labs., 1978; various positions Bell Labs. & Lucent Techs.; v.p. access product mgmt. Lucent Techs., Murray Hill, NJ, 1996—98, v.p. access, switching and access solutions, 1998, v.p. N.Am. emerging markets, 1999, pres. Access Networks divsn. InterNetworking Sys., 2000, group pres. InterNetworking Sys., 2000, group pres. Network Ops. Software, 2000, group pres. InterNetworking Sys. and Switching Solutions, 2001, pres. Integrated Network Solutions, 2001—. Named one of Top 50 Most Powerful Women in Bus., Fortune 500, 2001; named to Acad. Women Achievers, YWCA, N.Y.C., 1999; recipient Women Enabling Sci. and Tech. award, Working Woman Found., 2001. Office: Lucent Techs 600 Mountain Ave Murray Hill NJ 07974

DAVIDSON, JEANNIE, costume designer; b. San Francisco, Mar. 21, 1938; d. Willis H. and Dorothy J. (Starks) Rich; children from previous marriage: David L. Schultz (dec. Jan. 1996), Mark P. Schultz, Seana Davidson, Michael Davidson; m. Bryan N. St. Germain, June 14, 1980. BA, Stanford (Calif.) U., 1961, postgrad., 1965-68. Resident costume designer Oreg. Shakespearean Festival, Ashland, 1969-91; owner, designer Ravenna Fabric Studio, Inc., Medford, Oreg., 1994—. Mfr. custom ch. vestments and hand-dyed wearable art. Designer over 150 prodns. including all 37 of Shakespeare's plays. Recipient numerous awards for excellence in costume design. Mem. U.S. Inst. for Theatre Tech., Phi Beta Kappa. Avocations: fabric design, painting, writing, quilting. E-mail: jsg@mind.net, jsaintg@earthlink.net.

DAVIDSON, JEFFREY S., lawyer; BS, Columbia U., 1970; AB, Wabash Coll., 1970; JD, Ind. U., 1973. Bar: Ill., Ind. 1973, DC 1980, Calif. 1989. Atty. Kirkland & Ellis LLP, 1973—78, ptnr., mem. firm com., 1978—. Office: Kirkland & Ellis LLP 777 S Figueroa St Los Angeles CA 90017-5800 Office Phone: 213-680-8422. Office Fax: 213-680-8500. Business E-Mail: jdavidson@kirkland.com.

DAVIDSON, JO ANN, political organization executive, retired state legislator; children: Julie, Jenifer. Mem. Ohio Ho. of Reps., Columbus, 1981—2001, minority whip, speaker, 1995—2001; interim dir. Ohio Dept. Jobs and Family Services, 2001; owner JAD & Assoc. Government Cons. Firm, 2001; campaign chmn. OH Bush-Cheney '04, 2004; co-chmn. Rep. Nat. Com., Washington, 2005—. Mem. fin., ethics and stds. and rules coms., house speaker, minority leader, mem. joint com. on mental retardation and devel. disabilities; chmn. OH Ho. Rep. Campaign Com., 1986-2000. Mem. Reynoldsburg (Ohio) City Coun., 1968-77; former vice chmn. Ohio Turnpike Commn.; trustee Franklin U., U. Findlay, Ohio; mem. Columbus Area Women's Polit. Caucus. Named Legislator of Yr., Nat. Rep. Legislators Assn., 1991; named to Ohio Women's Hall of Fame, 1991. Mem. Oho C. of C. (v.p. spl. programs), Rotary. Republican. Office: Rep Nat Com 310 First St SE Washington DC 20003*

DAVIDSON, JOHN HENRY, legal educator; b. Washington, Pa., Dec. 9, 1942; s. John H. and Estous (Lee) D.; m. Cathy F. Beard, Oct. 14, 1967; children: Benjamin, Felix. BA, Wake Forest Coll., 1964; JD, U. Pitts., 1967; LLM, George Washington U., 1971. Bar: Pa. 1967, U.S. Dist. Ct. (we. dist.) Pa. 1967, S.D. 1974, U.S. Dist. Ct. S.D., 1972, U.S. Ct. Appeals (8th cir.) 1974. Sole practice, Pitts., 1967-69; staff atty. Neighborhood Legal Services, Pitts., 1969-71; lectr. in law George Washington U., Washington, 1971-72; prof. of law U. S.D., Vermillion, 1972—. Author: (with Delogu) Federal Environmental Regulations, 1989—; co-author, editor: Agricultural Law Treatise, 1981; Agricultural Law Cases, 1984. Mem. ABA (adv. com. forum on rural lawyers), Western Water Policy Rev. Com., Am. Trial Lawyers Assn., Am. Law Inst., Internat. Coun. Environ. Law, Am. Agrl. Law Assn. (bd. dirs. 1979-82), Dakota Plains Legal Services (bd. dirs. 1977—), Rocky Mountain Mineral Law Found. (trustee 1980-90). Democrat. Home: 31275 Saginaw Ave Vermillion SD 57069-6803 Office: U SD School Law 414 E Clark St Vermillion SD 57069-2307 Office Phone: 605-677-6341. Business E-Mail: jdavidso@usd.edu.

DAVIDSON, JOHN HUNTER, agriculturist; b. Wilmette, Ill., May 16, 1914; s. Joseph and Ruth Louise (Moody) D.; m. Elizabeth Marie Boynton, June 16, 1943 (dec. Feb. 2005); children: Joanne Davidson Hildebrand, Kathryn Davidson Bouwens, Patricia. BS in Horticulture, Mich. State U., 1937, MS in Plant Biochemistry, 1940. Field rschr. agrl. chems. Dow Chem. Co., Midland, Mich., 1936-42, with R&D dept. agrl. products, 1946-72, tech. adviser R&D agrl. products, 1972-80, tech. adviser govt. rels., 1980—86, cons., 1984—. Contbr. articles on plant pathology, horticulture and weed control to profl. jours. Lt. USNR, 1945. Mem. Am. Chem. Soc., Am. Soc. Hort. Sci., Weed Sci. Soc., Am. Pathol. Soc., Exch. Club of Midland, Phi Kappa Phi, Alpha Zeta. Republican. Home: 4319 Andre St Midland MI 48642-3779

DAVIDSON, JOHN KENNETH, SR., sociologist, educator, researcher, writer, consultant; b. Augusta, Ga., Oct. 25, 1939; s. Larcie Charles and Betty (Corley) D.; m. Josephine Frazier, Apr. 11, 1964; children: John Kenneth Jr., Stephen Wood. Student, Augusta Coll., 1956-58; BS in Edn., U. Ga., 1961, MA, 1963; PhD, U. Fla., 1974. Asst. prof. dept. psychology and sociology Armstrong State Coll., Savannah, Ga., 1963-67; asst. prof. sociology Augusta Coll., 1967-74; acting chmn., asst. prof. dept. sociology Ind. U., South Bend, 1974-76; assoc. prof. sociology U. Wis., Eau Claire, Wis., 1976-78, prof., 1978—2004, prof. emeritus, 2004—, chmn. dept. sociology, 1976-80, asst. to dean grad. studies and univ. rsch., 1987-91, coord. family studies, 1990—2004, acting chmn., dept. sociology (summer), 2003—05. Cons. family life edn.; rsch. cons. dept. ob-gyn. Med. Coll. Ga., Augusta, 1969-74, pediatrics, 1972-73, assoc. dir. health care project, 1971-73, rsch. instr., 1971, rsch. assoc., 1972-73, rsch. cons. dept. community dentistry, 1974-79; program coord. Community Devel. in Process Phase II and III, Title I Higher Edn. Act of, 1965, 1970; sociology and anthropology com. Univ. System Ga., 1970-74, chmn. curriculum sub-com., 1970-72; dir. Sex Edn., The Pub. Schs. and You project Ind. Com. on Humanities, 1975 Co-author: Marriage and Family, 1992; co-editor: Speaking of Sexuality: Interdisciplinary Readings, 2001, 2005, Cultural Diversity and Families, 1992, Marriage and Family: Change and Continuity, 1996; editor (assoc.): Jour. Marriage and the Family, 1975—85, Sociol. Inquiry, 1986—92, Sociol. Imagination, 1993—2004; editor: (cons.) Jour. Sex Rsch., 1991—95; editor: (cons) Sociol. Inquiry, 2001—; reviewer: Jour. Deviant Behavior, 1979—90, Sociol. Spectrum, 1985—, Jour. Family Issues, 1995—2004, Jour. Sex Rsch., 1996—2005; contbr. articles to profl. jours. Past state chmn. pub. affairs Ind. Assn. Planned Parenthood Affiliates, 1975-76; past bd. dirs. Planned Parenthood North Cen. Ind., chmn. pub. affairs com., 1975-76; past bd. dirs., 1st v.p., resources allocation com. Wis. Family Planning Coordinating Council; past bd. dirs., exec., info., internat. and edn. coms., chmn. social sci. rsch. com. Assn. for Vol. Sterilization; past pres. citizens adv. bd. Eau Claire and Chippewa Falls Planned Parenthood Clinics; past mem. dirs. Planned Parenthood of Wis., Inc.; past mem. Eau Claire Coord. Coun., Eau Claire County Adv. Health Forum, Eau Claire County Task Force on Family Planning, Eau Claire Task Force on Teen Pregnancy. Fellow Nat. Coun. Family Rels. (past chmn. com. stds. and criteria for cert., former mem. devel. com. and cert. com., Ernest G. Osborne award 2003, 2004); mem. Am. Sociol. Assn., Wis. Sociol. Assn., So. Sociol. Soc., Mid-South Sociol. Assn. (pres.-elect 1998-99, pres. 1999-2000, past pres. 2000-01, hotel negotiator, 2003—), Midwest Sociol. Soc., Groves Conf., Wis. Coun. Family Rels. (bd. dirs., exec. com., past pres.), Soc. Sci. Study Sex., Tex. Coun. Family Rels., Augusta Coll. Alumni Soc., U. Fla. Alumni Soc., U. Ga. Alumni Soc., Pres. Club. U. Wis.-Eau Claire, Kappa Delta Pi, Phi Kappa Phi (chpt. pres. 1991-92, Nat. Forum editl. com. 1992-99), Phi Theta Kappa, Alpha Kappa Delta (editor nat. newsletter 1979-83, nat. v.p. 1992-94, nat. pres.-elect 1994-96, nat. pres. 1996-98, nat. past pres. 1998-2000, exec. coun. 1992-2000) Episcopalian. Home: 1305 Nixon Ave Eau Claire WI 54701-6574

DAVIDSON, JOHN ROBERT, dentist; b. Peru, Ind., Apr. 28, 1947; s. John Howard and Kathryn (Loughran) Davidson; m. Jean-Marie Dobler, Jan. 23, 1965 (div. Oct. 1972); children: James Michael, Jennifer Renee; m. Linda Mary Seasock, Oct. 22, 1977 (dec. Aug. 1997); children: Kathryn Cherise, John Richard. BS, Purdue U., 1969; DDS, UCLA, 1972. Diplomate Am. Bd. Forensic Dentistry, Am. Bd. Forensic Examiners. Gen. practice dentistry, Granada Hills, Calif., 1972-74; prof. clin. and community dentistry, dir. of clinics Ferris State Coll., Big Rapids, Mich., 1974-75; prof. practice dentistry specializing in oral implantology Peru, Ind., 1975—2004; ret., 2003. Chief dental staff Dukes Meml. Hosp., Peru, 1975—96; dep. coroner Miami County, 1987—2003. Recipient Citizen of the Yr. award, Peru, 1978, Pride award, Grissom AFB Cmty. Coun., Peru, 1980. Fellow: Internat. Congress of Oral Implantologists, Am. Coll. Oral Implantaologists (assoc.); mem.: ADA, Ind. Soc. Froensic Odontology (charter), Peru Area C. of C. (bd. dirs. 1976—83, Oustanding Svc. award 1979), Wabash Valley Dental Soc., Ind.

Dental Assn., Am. Coll. Forensic Examiners, Mensa, Scottish Rite, Rotary (chmn. scholarship com. Peru 1975—95), Elks, Masons. Home: 200 Rainbow Dr 10042 Livingston TX 77399 Office Phone: 765-473-4421.

DAVIDSON, JOHN ROBERT (JAY), bank executive; b. L.A., Mar. 30, 1950; s. John Robert Davidson and Carolyn Rose Monson; m. Kristina Maria Jonsson, Dec. 29, 1978; children: Joshua Kingseley, Michelle Maria. BSME, U. ND, 1972; postgrad., AMP Corp. Leadership Coll., 1990. Engr. Dow Chem. Co., Pauls Valley, Okla., 1972-74; real estate investor Mpls., 1974-77; account exec. AMP Inc., Boulder, Colo., 1977-83, mkt. mgr. Harrisburg, Pa., 1983-86, dist. mgr. Denver, 1986-90, nat. mgr., 1990—95; chmn. bd., CEO, pres. 1st Am. State Bank of Colo., 1995—; dir. funds mgmt. com. Am. State Bank, Williston, ND, 1994—, dir. exec. com., 1996—, also bd. dirs.; founder, CEO, chmn. bd. dirs. First Am. State Bank, Denver, 1995—; CEO, chmn. bd. First Am. Bancorp, 1998—. Chmn., bd. dirs. Colo. Housing and Fin. Authority, 1999—; bd. dirs. Step 13, Kenneth King Found.; co-chair FASB Fitness Festival. Supporter Denver Ctr. Performing Arts, F.A.C.E.S., Boy Scouts Am, Children's Hosp., Arthritis Found., Cherry Creek Sch. Found. and Cmty. Asset Program; event co-chmn. Western Fantasy Gala Vols. of Am., 2005; bd. dirs. Kempe Children's Found., 1997—2005, treas., exec. com., chmn. fin. com., chair allocations com., 1998—2002; past bd. dirs., sec., chmn. devel. bd. Am. Heart Assn.; past. bd. dirs. Easter Seals Colo., event co-chmn.; co-chmn. Denver Ctr. Performing Arts New Years Gala, 2000; co-chair First Am. State Bank Fitness Festival, 2001—, Saturday Night Alive Gala; bd. dirs., event co-chmn. Arapahoe House; bd. dirs., sec. Denver Metro Area, 2000—; bd. dirs. Kenneth King Found. Named Pillar of the Cmty., Arapahoe House, 2000; named one of Villagers of Yr., 2005. Mem.: NRA (life), Glenmoore Country Club, Met. Club (bd. dirs. 2002—), Masons (Presdl. Legion of Merit). Avocations: skiing, mountain biking, photography, computers, music. Home: 5780 S Goldsmith Pl Greenwood Village CO 80111-3522 Office: 1st Am State Bank 8390 E Crescent Pkwy Greenwood Village CO 80111-2811 Office Phone: 303-694-6464. Personal E-mail: fasb32@earthlink.net. Business E-Mail: jdavidson@fasbank.com.

DAVIDSON, JOY ELAINE, retired mezzo soprano; b. Ft. Collins, Colo., Aug. 18, 1940; d. Clarence Wayne and Jessie Ellen (Bogue) Ferguson; m. Robert Scott Davidson, Aug. 9, 1959; children: Lisa Beth, Robert Scott II, Jeremy Fergus, Bonnie Kathleen, Jordan Christian. BA, Occidental Coll., Los Angeles, 1959; postgrad., Fla. State U., 1961-64. Dir. vocal/opera dept. New World Sch. Arts Coll./Conservatory Divsn., Miami, Fla., 1992—2002; ret., 2001. Robert A. Carrie Mastronardi endowed prof., 1995—. Debut 1965 with Miami Opera; has performed with Met. Opera, opera cos. throughout U.S. and Can., La Scala, Vienna State Opera, Bayerische State Opera, Lyons (France) Opera, Welsh Opera, Florence (Italy) Opera, Torino (Italy) Opera. (recipient Gold medal Internat. Competition Young Opera Singers, Sofia, Bulgaria 1969), Rio de Janeiro; performed with numerous orchs. including N.Y. Philharm., Los Angeles Philharm., Boston Orch., Pitts. Orch., Columbus (Ohio) Orch.; rec. artist. Named Outstanding Miami Artist at Orange Bowl; recipient Mastronardi endowed chair, 1995, NISOD award for tchg. excellence, 1996, Roberta Rymer Balfe award Fla. Grand Opera. Mem. PEO, United Meth. Women, Sigma Alpha Iota, Zeta Tau Zeta. Methodist. Avocations: swimming, camping, bicycling, church activities. Home: 413 Walnut St #5032 Green Cove Springs FL 32043 Office Phone: 305-510-5131. E-mail: davidsons123@hotmail.com. *Success awaits those who dare to dream big enough. The success achiever is the possibility thinker.*

DAVIDSON, JUDITH LOUISE, foundation administrator; b. Newark, Ohio, Oct. 12, 1944; d. Lester Tibbets and Virginia Louise Russell; m. Arthur Francis Davidson; children: Per, Thomas Anders, Elvira Louise. AB, Cornell U., 1965. Stock and bond advisor in pvt. practice, Orleans, Mass., 1982—; pres. Russell-Davidson Found., Orleans, 1993—. Bd. dirs. Sant Bani Sch., Sanbornton, N.H., 1985—; personal rep. for Cellis Amit Peled. Avocation: amateur chamber musician.

DAVIDSON, JUSTIN, music critic; b. Rome; m. Ariella Budick; 1 child, Milo. BMus, Harvard U.; D of Music, Columbia U. Dir. editl. Sony Classical, N.Y.C., 1995—96; music critic Newsday, Melville, NY, 1996—. Adj. prof. music Columbia U. Contbr. articles to profl. jours. and newspapers. Recipient Pulitzer prize, 1999, award, Press Club of L.I., Deems Taylor award, ASCAP. Office: Newsday 235 Pinelawn Rd Melville NY 11747-4250*

DAVIDSON, KEAY, newswriter; Sci. writer Sentinel Star, Orlando, Fla., 1979—81, L.A. Times San Diego Bur., 1981—85, San Francisco Examiner, 1986—2000, San Francisco Chronicle, 2000—. Author (with George Smoot): Wrinkles in Time, 1993; author: Twister: The Science of Tornadoes and the Making of a Natural Disaster Movie, 1996, Carl Sagan: A Life, 1999; contbg. writer: Scientific American, New Scientist, National Geographic, Sky and Telescope, NY Times. Recipient Westinghouse Sci. Journalism award, 1986, Sci. in Soc. award, Nat. Assn. Sci. Writers. Office: San Francisco Chronicle 901 Mission St San Francisco CA 94103-2988 Office Fax: 415-896-1107. Business E-Mail: kdavidson@sfchronicle.com.

DAVIDSON, KIMBERLY RUSE, music educator; b. Oelwein, Iowa, Oct. 19, 1958; d. Paul Edwin and Myrtle Mae Ruse; m. Daniel Craig Davidson, May 31, 1980; children: Jacob, Noah, Kirsti. BME, Valparaiso U., Ind., 1981. Music tchr. Moline Pub. Schs., Ill., 1981—82, Davenport Pub. Schs., Iowa, 1983—84, Roanoke City Schs., Va., 1984; piano instr. Roanoke Coll. Preparatory Divsn., 1984—87; dir. children's choir Roanoke Coll., 1987—. Home: 704 Maryland Ave Salem VA 24153 Office: Roanoke Coll 221 Coll Ln Olin Hall Salem VA 24153 Office Phone: 540-375-2222. Office Fax: 540-375-2559. E-mail: kdavidso@roanoke.edu.

DAVIDSON, LARRY, psychologist; b. Bklyn., Dec. 31, 1960; s. Bernard and Faye (Bernstein) D.; m. Maryanne Loetterle, Oct. 28, 1990. BA, MA, Emory U., Atlanta, 1982; MA in Psychology, Duquesne U., Pitts., 1983, PhD, 1989. Counseling coord. Duquesne U. Health Svc., Pitts., 1985-86; predoctoral fellow Duquesne U. Psychology Dept., Pitts., 1986-87; predoctoral intern Danbury (Conn.) Hosp., 1987-88; predoctoral fellow Yale U. Med. Sch., New Haven, 1988-89; lectr. Yale U. Nursing Sch., New Haven, 1989; adv. resident Danbury Hosp., 1989-90, clin. cons., 1990; postdoctoral fellow Yale U. Med. Sch., 1990-92, asst. prof. psychiatry, 1992—. Cons. editor Jour. Phenomenological Psychology, Pitts., 1986—. Contbr. articles to profl. jours. Named Disting. Young Investigator, Soc. for Life History Rsch., 1990, Karl Jaspers prize, Assn. for Advancement of Philosophy and Psychiatry, 1991. Mem. APA, Conn. Psychol. Assn., Human Sci. Rsch. Conf., Internat. Soc. for Theoretical Psychology, Am. Assn. Applied and Preventive Psychology, Soc. for Phenomenology and Psychiatry (sec. 1990-94). Democrat. Jewish. Avocations: photography, visual arts, music, family life. Office: Yale Univ Med Sch 34 Park St New Haven CT 06519-1109

DAVIDSON, MARILYN COPELAND, writer, music educator, musician; b. New Castle, Ind., Sept. 2, 1934; d. Clyde Harrison and Hazel Uva Copeland; m. Douglass Albert Davidson, Dec. 28, 1961; children: Jennifer Juntwait, Diana Valencia. BS, Ball State U., 1955; diploma in piano, Juilliard Sch., 1956. Music tchr. Dallas Public Schs., 1956—57, Shortridge H.S., Indpls., 1957—62, Port Washington (NY) Pub. Schs., 1962—66, Troy State U., Troy, Ala., 1966—70, South Lyon (Mich.) Middle Sch., 1970—72, Fairleigh Dickinson U., Teaneck, NJ, 1979—83, Bergenfield (NJ) Pub. Schs., 1972—84, Our Redeemer Luth. Ch., Dumont, NJ, 1973—78, Evangelical Luth. Ch., Hasbrouck Heights, NJ, 1980—82, Pequannock (NJ) Pub. Schs., 1986—90, 1992—95; coord. author MacMillan/McGraw Hill, Inc., NYC, 1984—. Presenter Internat. Reading Assn., NJ, 1995, N.J. Music Supervisors Assn., 1985, Bruno Walter Hall, Lincoln Ctr., NYC, 1994, Carnegie Hall, NYC, 2000, Technology Symposium, Fla. State U., Tallahassee, 2000, Suffolk County Music Educators, 2001, workshops, throughout U.S.; presenter in field. Author: (textbook series) Music and You, 1988, 1991; author: (with Bob McGrath) Music for Fun, 2000; author: (textbook series) Share the Music, 1992, 1995; composer: (orchestrations) Tops in Pops, 1995, An Acoustic Jam, 1996; contbr. articles to profl. newsletters, teacher's guides and other publs.; author: (textbook series) Spotlight on Music, 2005; author: (with Bob McGrath) (profl. training video) Music and the Curriculum; author: Using Music to Help Children Learn, 2004, It's Elementary, 2005. Coun. mem., soloist and accompanist for recitals Bergenfield Coun. for the Arts, 1974—80; accompanist Carley Singers Chamber Choir, Indpls., 1957—61; educational cons. New Jersey Symphony, 1987—92; education com. mem., clinician, tnr. N.J. Symphony Master Tchr. Project; lectr. N.Y. Philharm. Children's Series, 1995; lectr., performer Bergenfield Pub. Libr., 1996; piano soloist Hawthorne Chamber Symphony, 1996, 1997, 1998, North Jersey Symphony, Tenafly, 1996, 2001, Rockland NY Symphony. Named Outstanding Alumnus, Ball State U. Sch. Music, 1993; recipient Young Artists award, Muncie Symphony, 1953, Gov.'s Tchr.'s Recognition award, NJ, 1995. Mem.: NEA, N.J. Edn. Assn., Music Educators Nat. Conf. (music selection com. 1993, nat. assembly, writer for teacher's guides), N.J. Music Educators Assn. (writer "It's Elementary" 1988—96), Northern N.J. Orff Schulwerk Assn. (co-founder, treas., sec., pres., mem-at-large), Am. Orff-Schulwerk Assn. (hon.; life mem., regional rep., chairperson higher edn., nat. v.p., nat. pres., higher edn. post-level III adv. com., AOSA celebrity advocacy panel selection com.), Orgn. Am. Kodaly Educators, Delta Kappa Gamma, Pi Kappa Lambda, Sigma Alpha Iota. Home and Office: 31 Martin St Bergenfield NJ 07621

DAVIDSON, MARK, writer, educator; b. NYC, Sept. 25, 1928; BA in Polit. Sci., UCLA, 1948; MS in Journalism, Columbia U., 1950. Sci. writer U. So. Calif., L.A., 1980-90; prof. comm. Calif. State U., Dominguez Hills, Carson, 1985-99; freelance mag. writer. Faculty adviser Soc. Profl. Journalists, 1993-96; writer Steve Allen Show, 1964, Dinah Shore Show, 1978, CBS Mag. Series with Connie Chung, 1980; spkr. in field. Author: Uncommon Sense (About Systems Science), 1984, Japanese transl., 2000, German transl., 2004, Invisible Chains of Thought Control, 1999, Right, Wrong and Risky: A Dictionary of American English Usage, 2005. Sackett scholar Columbia U.; recipient Nat. Emmy award NATAS, 1978, Best Paper award Internat. Conf. Info. Sci., Pori, Finland, 2003. Mem.: PEN, Soc. Advancement of Edn. (assoc. mass media editor 1997—2001), Calif. Faculty Assn. (v.p. Dominguez Hills chpt. 1992—96), Nat. Writers Union (L.A. steering com. 2002—03), Writers Guild Am., Authors Guild, Am. Med. Writers Assn., Nat. Assn. Sci. Writers, Am. Soc. Journalists and Authors. Personal E-mail: wordwatcher@earthlink.net.

DAVIDSON, MARK EDWARD, lawyer; b. Niskayuna, N.Y., Aug. 18, 1952; s. Robert E. and Mary E. (Morton) D.; m. Mary Helen Woods, June 4, 1977; children: Michael S., Jeffrey P., Kara M. BA, SUNY, Stony Brook, 1974; JD, Georgetown U., 1977. Bar: N.Y. 1978, U.S. Dist. Ct. (so. and ea. dists.) N.Y., U.S. Ct. Appeals (2d and 11th cirs.). Assoc. Shea & Gould, N.Y.C., 1977-85, ptnr., 1986-92; sr. counsel Proskauer Rose LLP, N.Y., 1992—. Author: (with others) Handbook of Auditing and Accounting, 1989, 90; editor jour. Am. Criminal Law Rev., 1976-77. Panelist N.Y. State Surrogate Decision Making Panel, Albany, 1988—; spl. master N.Y. State Supreme Ct., N.Y.C., 1988—. Mem. ABA. Avocations: reading, hiking, canoeing, wine collecting, computers. Office: Proskauer Rose LLC 1585 Broadway Fl 27 New York NY 10036-8299 E-mail: mdavidson@proskauer.com.

DAVIDSON, MARY ANN, information technology executive; BSME, U. Va.; MBA, U. Pa., Wharton Sch. Commd. officer U.S. Navy Civil Engineer Corps; various positions in product devel. and security Oracle Corp., 1988—2001, chief security officer, 2001—. Ed. review bd. Secure Business Quarterly; testified before Congress on info. security four times. Recipient Navy Achievement Medal, U.S. Navy Civil Engr. Corps. Mem.: Info. Tech. Info. Security Analysis Ctr. (bd. dirs.). Avocations: outdoors, surfing, skiing. Office: Oracle Corp 500 Oracle Pkwy Redwood City CA 94065

DAVIDSON, MAYER B., medical educator, endocrinologist, researcher; b. Balt., Apr. 11, 1935; s. David and Esther (Crockin) D.; m. Naomi Berger, Nov. 25, 1961 (div. 1977); children: Elke W., Seth J.; m. Roseann Herman, Aug. 31, 1980. AB, Swarthmore Coll., 1957; MD, Harvard U., 1961. Diplomate Am. Bd. Internal Medicine, Am. Bd. Endocrinology and Metabolism. Intern Bellevue Hosp., N.Y.C., 1961-62, jr. asst. resident, 1962-63; sr. asst. resident U. Wash. Affiliated Hosps., Seattle, 1963-64; rsch. fellow dept. endocrinology and metabolism King County Hosp., U. Wash., Seattle, 1964-66; asst. prof. medicine UCLA Sch. Medicine, 1969-74, from assoc. prof. to prof., 1974-95, clin. prof., 1996—, acting chief div. endocrinology and metabolism, 1973-74. Dir. diabetes program Cedars-Sinai Med. Ctr., L.A., 1979-95; assoc. dir. clin. diabetes City of Hope Nat. Med. Ctr., 1995-98; dir. clin. trials unit Charles R. Drew U.; nat. advisor Diabetes Ctr. Humana Hosp., Phoenix, 1985-91; attending physician diabetic clinic Boston City Hosp., 1966-68; clin. asst. Harvard Med. Sch., 1968-69; cons. AMA Dept. Drugs. Author: Diabetus Mellitus: Diagnosis and Treatment, 4th edit., 1998; contbr. more than 30 chpts. to books; founding editor: Current Diabetes Reports, 2000—02, editor-in-chief: Diabetes Care, 2002—. Co-founder, bd. dirs. free med. facility Venice (Calif.) Family Clinic, 1970. Maj. Med. Svc. Corps U.S . Army, 1966-69. USPHS rsch. fellow Nat. Inst. Arthritis and Metabolic Diseases, 1965-66; recipient Upjohn award for Outstanding Diabetes Educator, 1990, Robert H. Williams/Rachmiel Levine award for sci. contbns. and humanism in tng. young rschrs., 1995, Banting medal for Disting. Svc., 1998; named to Best Doctors in Am., 1992-93, 95-96, 96-97. Fellow ACP; mem. AAAS, Am. Diabetes Assn. (rsch. prizes 1965, 66, R&D award 1974-75, rsch. 1978-81, bd. dirs. 1986-89, 93-99, v.p. 1995-96, pres.-elect 1996-97, pres. 1997-98), Am. Fedn. Clin. Rsch., Western Soc. Clin. Rsch., Endocrine Soc., Am. Soc. Clin. Investigation, Western Assn. Physicians, Am. Assn. Diabetes Educators (editl. bd. jour. 1980-83), Boylston Med. Soc., Am. Diabetes Assn. (pres. 1997-98), Sigma Xi. Democrat. Jewish. E-mail: madavids@cdrewu.edu.

DAVIDSON, MEDORA LEA, dance educator; b. Merriam, Kans., July 2, 1930; d. John Archibald and Mabel Adelaide Davidson; m. Daniel Howe Hoge, Jr., Feb. 6, 1971 (div. June 14, 1984); m. Harry Lee Lydick, June 21, 1953 (div. Nov. 5, 1965); children: Harry Lee Lydick, Jr., Robin Louis Lydick. Grad. h.s., Merriam, 1948. Instr. ballet, tap, jazz, gymnastics, ballroom dance, low-impact aerobics Davidson Dance Studio, Prairie Village, Kans., 1950—89; dance instr. N.A.D.A.A. city chpts., St. Paul, St. Louis, Omaha, Tulsa, Dallas, 1957—59; jazz dance instr. nat. faculty Nat. Assn. Dance and Affiliated Artists, Inc., L.A., Dallas, Chgo., 1957—59; choreographer outdoor mus. shows Johnson County (Kans.) Pks. and Recreation, 1971—73; choreographer Kansas City (Mo.) Royals Banquet shows, 1972—74; tchr. ballet, tap, gymnastics Visitation Parochial Sch., Kansas City, Mo., 1989—91; former owner, instr. ballet, tap, jazz, gymnastics, low-impact aerobics Davidson Dance Studio, Ottawa, Kans., 1991—99; tchr. low-impact aerobics Albuquerque Sr. Ctrs., 1999—2000; tchr. modern dance and children's drama Carnegie Cultural Ctr., Ottawa, 2000—02, tchr. piano, 2002—04, instr. Kindermusik Internat., 2002—04, tchr. yoga, 2002—04. Dance therapist activity dept. Psychiat. Receiving Ctr., Western Mo. Mental Health Ctr., Kansas City, 1969—; taped 65 half-hour ballet class lessons for children Medora and Me, 1970—71; taped 65 half-hour interviews for women The Feminine Touch, 1970—71; dir. Picnic A.C.T. Ottawa!, Ottawa Cmty. Theatre, 1997; writer, dir. 3 plays Fine Arts Singles, Johnson County, Kans., 1990—91; dir. Show Boat Baldwin Cmty. Theater, Baldwin City, Kans., 1999; formed Crackerjack Children's Theatre, Ottawa, 2001; writer, dir. Coventown A.C.T. Ottawa!, Ottawa, 2001, dir. An Old Time Radio Show, 02, dir. Playboy of the Western World, 02; dir. Crackerjack Children's Theatre Christmas Reader's Theatre, 2001, Playboy of the Western World, Ottawa Cmty. Theatre, 2001, Nunsense 2003, Baldwin City Cmty. Theatre, 2003, Another Old Time Radio Show, Ottawa Cmty. Theatre, 2003, Bye, Bye, Bye Birdie, Baldwin City Cmty. Theatre, 2003, One Magical Christmas Eve, Ottawa Cmty. Theatre, 2003, Quilters, Ottawa Cmty. Theatre, 2004. Actor: (plays) Gypsy, 1973, Lady Audley's Secret, 1976, The Farsighted Dragon and the Nearsighted Knight, 1985, Night of January 16th, 1994, Greater Tuna, 1996, The Tempest, 1998, Nunsense, 1999, 2003, Diamonds to Die For, 2000, Cabaret, A Black Tie Affair, 2001, Cabaret, For Ladies Only, 2003, Cabaret, Back & Better, 2004, Driving Miss Daisy, 2005; sculptor, Bas Relief State Line Bridge, Watts Mill, Mo., 1976, Wrought Iron Restoration Winder Bldg, Washington, 1978, Mo., Kans. State Line Bridge, 1976. Vol. dance therapist Johnson County Mental Health Ctr., Overland Park, Kans., 1967—69. Avocations: gardening, painting, sewing, reading. Home: 1103 S Main St Ottawa KS 66067-3523 E-mail: medorad@sbcglobal.net.

DAVIDSON, MICHAEL, lawyer; b. Louisville, July 27, 1954; s. M. and Sonia Davidson; m. Kris Davidson, Dec. 19, 1987; children: Tess, Zachary. Bachelors Degree, U. Ky., 1981, JD, 1986. Bar: Ky. 1986, U.S. Dist. Ct. (ea. dist.) Ky. 1986, U.S. Bankruptcy Ct. 1986. Assoc. Reuff, Alexander & Shriner, Lexington, 1986—87, Summers, Fox, Dixon & McGinty, Lexington, 1987—90, Cleve., 1987—90; prin. Law Offices of Michael Davidson, Lexington, 1990—. Spkr. in field. Editor: Collection Practice in Domestic Relations Matters, 2002. U. Ky. family law plannig com. U. Ky. Law Sch., Lexington, 1997—. With USN, 1972—76. Mem.: ABA (custody com. vice chair 1998—2000), Fayette County Bar Assn. (chair family law 2001—02, Pro Bono award 1995), Ky. Bar Assn. (chair family law 2001—02). Avocations: tennis, swimming, Karate, fishing, golf. Office: 135 W Short St Lexington KY 40507

DAVIDSON, MICHAEL H., cardiologist, researcher; b. Dayton, Ohio, Nov. 22, 1956; MD, Ohio State U., 1981. Med. dir. Caicaco Ctr. for Clin. Rsch., Chgo., 1986—96; assoc. prof. medicine Rush U. Med. Ctr., Chgo., 1986—; pres., CEO Protocare Trials Chgo. Ctr. for Clin. Rsch., 1996—2003, exec. med. dir., 1998—2003; dir. preventive cardiology Rush U. Med. Ctr., Chgo., 2001—; exec. med. dir. Radiant Rsch., Chgo., 2003—. Office: Radiant Research 515 N State St Ste 2700 Chicago IL 60610 Office Fax: 312-494-2217. Business E-Mail: michaeldavidson@radiantresearch.com.

DAVIDSON, MICHAEL RAYMOND, historian, educator; b. Appleton, Wis., Apr. 28, 1972; s. Richard Walter Davidson and Carolyn James Carlson. BS, Bates Coll., 1994; PhD, U. Edinburgh, Scotland, 2003. Lectr. history Bates Coll., Lewiston, Maine, 2001; asst. prof. Newberry (SC) Coll., 2001—04; lectr. So. Ill. U., Carbondale, 2004—. Co-author: Edward the Elder. Participant Newberry Cmty. Players, 2003—04; mem. County Reps., Newberry, SC, 2001—04; lay reader St. Luke's Episcopal Ch., Newberry, 2001—04, St. Andrew's Episcopal Ch., Carbondale, 2004—. Mem.: Scottish Medievalists, Haskins Soc., Am. Hist. Assn., Phi Alpha Theta. Republican. Episcopalian. Avocations: nordic skiing, hiking. Home: 1903 Illinois Ave Murphysboro IL 62966 Office: So Ill U Faner Hall Carbondale IL 62901 E-mail: madmiked@siu.edu.

DAVIDSON, NANCY BRACHMAN, artist, educator; b. Chgo., Nov. 3, 1943; d. Philip and Jane (Blanch) Brachman; m. Donald Davidson, July 15, 1961 (div. 1977); 1 child, Lance A.; m. Greg Drasler, June 15, 1985. BEd, Northeastern Ill. U., 1965; BA, U. Ill., Chgo., 1972; MFA, Sch. Art Inst., Chgo., 1975. Vis. asst. prof. U. Ill., Champaign, 1977-79, Williams Coll., Williamstown, Mass., 1980-84; vis. artist, assoc. prof. SUNY, Purchase, 1984—. One-woman shows include Berkshire Mus., Pittsfield, Mass., 1982, Marianne Deson Gallery, Chgo., 1978, 1981, 1983, 1988, Richard Anderson Gallery, N.Y.C., 1991, 1993, 1995, Shoshana Wayne Gallery, Santa Monica, Calif., 1997, Nova Sin Gallery, Prague, Czech Republic, 1998, Neuberger Mus., Purchase, N.Y., 1998, Dorsky Gallery, N.Y.C., Inst. Contemporary Art, U. Pa., Phila., 1999, Vedanta Gallery, Chgo., 2000, The Contemporary Arts Ctr., Cin., 2001, Robert Miller Gallery, N.Y.C., 2001, Regina Gouger Miller Gallery, Carnegie Mellon U., Pitts., 2002, exhibited in group shows at Albright-Knox Gallery, Buffalo, 1980, Mus. Contemporary Art Chgo., 1984, Art Inst. Chgo., 1974, 1978, 1979, Bad Girls West-UCLA, 1994, Corcoran Biennial, 2002. Fellow NEA, 1978, Mass. Coun. Arts, 1981, Ford Found., 1978; Mass. Coun. Arts grantee, 1984, Anonymous Was a Woman grantee, 1997, Pollock-Krasner grantee, 2001, Creative Capital; Artist grantee, 2004. Home: 137 Duane St Apt 4W New York NY 10013-3892

DAVIDSON, PETER, telecommunications industry executive; b. Minn. m. Kari Davidson; 3 children. Grad., Carleton Coll., 1984; JD, U. Va., 1990. Law clk. to Judge John Porfilio 10th Cir. Ct. Appeals, Denver; atty. advisor Dept. Justice Office Legal Counsel; gen. counsel, policy dir. Ho. Rep. Conf.; gen. counsel, policy dir. majority leader U.S. Ho. Reps. Dick Armey, 1995—99; v.p. congessional affairs Qwest, 1999—2001; gen. counsel U.S. trade rep., 2001—03; sr. v.p. fed. govt. rels. Verizon Comm., Inc., Washington, 2003—. Office: Verizon Comm Inc 1300 I St NW Ste 400 W Washington DC 20005

DAVIDSON, RICHARD J., medical association administrator; b. Phila., 1936; m. Janet Davidson. BA in secondary edn., West Chester (Pa.) State Coll.; EdM in edn., Temple U.; PhD in edn., George Washington U. Dir. edn. Md. Hosp. Assn., pres., 1969—91, Am. Hosp. Assn., Washington, 1991—. Recipient Bd. Dirs. award, Healthcare Fin. Mgmt. Assoc., 2000. Office: 325 7th St NW Ste 700 Washington DC 20004-2801 also: Am Hosp Assn 1 N Franklin Chicago IL 60606

DAVIDSON, RICHARD K., railroad company executive; b. Allen, Kans., Jan. 9, 1942; s. Richard B. and Thelma (Rees) D.; m. Lynne P. Durham, July 11, 1998; children: Richard Byron, Elizabeth Ann. BA in History, Washburn U., 1965, D of Commerce (hon.), 1984. Brakeman, conductor Mo. Pacific R.R., St. Louis, 1960-66, transp. tng. program, 1966, asst. trainmaster, trainmaster, 1966-75, asst. supt. to asst. v.p. ops., 1975-76; v.p. ops. Mo. Pacific Railroad, St. Louis, 1976-85, Union Pacific R.R., Omaha, 1985-89, exec. v.p. ops., 1989-91, chmn., CEO, 1991—; pres. Union Pacific Corp., Omaha, 1994—, COO, 1995-97, chmn., pres., CEO, 1997—. Mem. Nat. Infrastructure Advisory Com., Homeland Nat. Security Coun., US Strategic Command Consultation Com.; mem. bd. dirs. Kroger. Mem. Happy Hollow Club. Office: Union Pacific RR 1400 Douglas St Omaha NE 68179-0002*

DAVIDSON, RICHARD LAURENCE, geneticist, educator; b. Cleve., Feb. 22, 1941; BA, Case Western Res. U., 1963, PhD, 1967. Asst. prof. Harvard Med. Sch., Boston, 1970-73, assoc. prof. microbiology and molecular genetics, 1973-81; research assoc. human genetics Children's Hosp. Med. Ctr., Boston, 1970-81; head dept. molecular genetics U. Ill. Med. Ctr., Chgo., 1981—, Benjamin Goldberg prof. genetics, 1981—. Co-dir. Cell Cult Ctr., MIT, Boston, 1975-81; mem. mammalian genetics study sect. NIH, 1975-81; mem. human cell biology adv. panel NSF, 1973-75. Editor-in-chief: Somatic Cell Genetics. U.S. Air Force Office Research-NRC fellow, 1967-68, Ctr. Molecular Genetics, Paris, 1967-70. Mem. AAAS, Tissue Culture Assn., Cell Biology Assn. Office: U Ill at Chicago Head Dept Mol Gen (M/7 669) 900 S Ashland Ave Ste 669 Chicago IL 60607-4046

DAVIDSON, RICK, staffing company executive; BSEE, Ariz. State U. V.p. global info. svcs. Haworth, Inc.; sr. v.p., CIO CNH Global N.V.; acting global CIO Feld Group; sr. v.p., global CIO Manpower, Inc., Milw., 2003—. Office: Manpower Inc 5301 N Ironwood Rd Milwaukee WI 53217

DAVIDSON, ROBERT BRUCE, lawyer; b. N.Y.C., May 6, 1945; BS in Econs. cum laude, U. Pa., 1967; JD, Columbia U., 1972. Bar: NY 1973, US Dist Ct (so and ea dists) NY 1973, US Ct Appeals (2d cir) 1975, US Ct Appeals (DC cir) 1981, US Supreme Ct 1979, US Tax Ct 1984, US Ct Appeals (fed cir) 1989, US Ct Appeals (3d cir) 1990. Assoc. Baker & McKenzie, N.Y.C., 1972-79, ptnr., 1979—2003; ret., 2003; exec. dir. JAMS Arbitration Practice, N.Y.C., 2003—. Mem. JAMS panel of arbitrators Hong Kong Internat. Arbitration Ctr. Author (with others): Voting Laws and Procedures, 1973; author: International Arbitration Checklists, 2004; contbr. articles to profl jours. Vol US Peace Corps, The Philippines, 1968—70. Master: Fed. Bar Coun. Inn of Ct.; fellow: Am. Bar Found., Coll. Comml. Arbitrators (bd. mem.); mem.: ABA (dispute resolution and internat. law sects.), NASD (panel of arbitrators), Chartered Inst. Arbitrators, Ctr. Pub. Resources (internat. panel), Libr. of Congress Copyright Office, Copyright Arbitration Royalty Panel, Am. Fgn. Law Assn. (v.p.), Assn. Bar City N.Y.

(chair com. arbitration 1982—85, com. internat. law 1986—89, chair com. arbitration 2003—). Office: JAMS 280 Park Ave West Bldg 28th Flr New York NY 10017 Office Phone: 212-607-2752. Business E-Mail: rdavidson@jamsadr.com.

DAVIDSON, ROBERT WAID, lawyer, writer; b. Des Moines, July 26, 1951; s. Waid J. and Judith Ann (Etinger) D.; m. Catherine Spencer, Dec. 6, 1986 (div. Oct., 1995); children: William Spencer, Alice Elizabeth. Student, U. Tex., 1973; BA, U N. Tex., 1977; JD, U. Houston, 1986. Bar: Tex. 1986, U.S. Dist. Ct. (so. dist.) Tex. 1988, U.S. Ct. Appeals (5th cir.) 1992, U.S. Supreme Ct. 1993. Assoc. McLain, Cage, Hill & Niehaus, Houston, 1986-88, Petronella & Bolding, P.C., Houston, 1988-89; sr. atty., staff atty. FDIC, Houston, 1989-94; lawyer pvt. practice, Houston, 1994—; of counsel Petrie & Assocs., Houston, 1994—. Author: Bruised Feelings, 1997. Cub master Cub Scout Pack 30, Boy Scouts Am., Houston, 1997. Mem. Fed. Bar Assn., Houston Bar Assn. Home: 943 Merrill St Houston TX 77009-6005 Office: 1001 West Loop S Ste 100 Houston TX 77027-9085

DAVIDSON, ROBERT WILLIAM, not-for-profit executive; b. Colfax, Wash., Sept. 18, 1949; s. William Martin and Lena (Soli) D.; m. Molly Evoy, Apr. 16, 1977; children: Ford Patrick, Matthew Harpur, Marshall Andrew. AB, Harvard U., 1971; MBA, U. Wash., 2000. Exec. dir. Sabre Found., Cambridge, Mass., 1971-72; adminstrv. asst. Congressman Joel Pritchard, Washington, 1973-79; asst. sec. state State of Wash., Olympia, 1979-80; pres. Frayn Fin. Printing, Seattle, 1982-87, Frayn Printing Co., Seattle, 1985-87; exec. dir. Woodland Park Zool. Soc., Seattle, 1987—94, pres., 1986—87; prin. Alistar Capital Group, Bellevue, Wash., 1994—2001; CEO Seattle Aquarium Soc., Seattle, 2002—. Mem. adv. com. Wash. State Software Ind. Devel. Bd., 1984-85. Chmn. pub. funding com. Mayor's Zoo Commn., Seattle, 1984-85; dir. Discovery Inst., 1992—94, Internat. Snow Leopard Trust, 1994-96; mem. sch. bd. Cath. Archdiocese of Seattle, 1995-98; mem. Seattle U. Exec. Masters in Not-for-Profit Mgmt. vis. com., 1995-96; mem. King County Bond Oversight Com., 1986-93. Mem. N.W. Devel. Officers Assn. (pres. 1994), Downtown Rotary Club (v.p. found. 1997-98, bd. mem. 2005-), Wash. Athletic Club. Republican. Roman Catholic. Avocation: photography. Office: 1415 Western Ave # 505 Seattle WA 98101 Office Phone: 206-838-3910. Business E-Mail: bob@aquariumsociety.org.

DAVIDSON, ROGER H(ARRY), political science professor; b. Washington, July 31, 1936; s. Ross Wallace and Mildred (Younger) D.; m. Nancy Elizabeth Dixon, Sept. 29, 1961; children: Douglas Ross, Christopher Reed. AB magna cum laude, U. Colo., 1958; PhD, Columbia U., 1963. Asst. prof. govt. Dartmouth Coll., Hanover, NH, 1962-68; assoc. prof. polit. sci. U. Calif., Santa Barbara, 1968-71, prof., 1971-83, assoc. dean letters and sci., 1978-80, vis. prof., 1994, 1999—; sr. specialist Congl. Rsch. Svc., Washington, 1980-88; prof. govt., politics U. Md., College Pk., 1981-99. Profl. staff mem. U.S. Ho. of Reps., Washington, 1973—74; rsch. dir. U.S. Senate, Washington, 1976—77; cons. White House, 1970—71, U.S. Com. on Violence, Washington, 1968—69, Ctr. for Civic Edn., 2002—; Leon Sachs vis. scholar Johns Hopkins U., Balt., 1997; John Marshall Disting. Fulbright prof. Debrecen U., Hungary, 2002. Author: The Role of the Congressman, 1969; co-author: A More Perfect Union, 4th edit., 1989, Congress and Its Members, 10th edit., 2005; editor: The Postreform Congress, 1992; co-editor: Masters of the House, 1998, Workways of Governance, 2004, Understanding the Presidency, 3d edit., 2005; contbr. articles to profl. jours. Co-chmn. Upper Valley Human Rights Coun., Hanover, N.H., 1966-68; chmn. Goleta Valley Citizens Planning Group, Santa Barbara, 1974-76; rsch. com. of legis. specialists Internat. Polit. Sci. Assn.; adv. commn. on records of Congress Nat. Archives and Records Adminstrn., 1995-99; bd. dirs. Governance Inst., 1986-, Archtl. Found. of Santa Barbara, 2003-. Woodrow Wilson Nat. Found. fellow, 1958, Gilder fellow Columbia U., 1960, Faculty fellow Dartmouth Coll., 1965-66 Fellow Nat. Acad. Pub. Adminstrn.; mem. Nat. Capital Area Polit. Sci. Assn. (pres. 1985-86), Legis. Studies Group (charter, nat. chmn. 1980-81), Am. Polit. Sci. Assn. (joint com. Project 87-Am. Hist. Assn./Am. Polit. Sci. Assn., chmn. congl. fellowship com. 1990, 93, endowed programs com. 1994-95, chmn. 1995-96, co-chmn. exec. com. Centennial Campaign 1997-2003), Western Polit. Sci. Assn. (bd. editors 1977-78). Baptist. Avocations: music, history. Home: Villa L 400 E Pedregosa St Santa Barbara CA 93103-1970 Office: Dept Polit Sci U Calif Santa Barbara CA 93106 Personal E-mail: publius10@cox.net.

DAVIDSON, RONALD CROSBY, physicist, researcher; b. Norwich, Ont., Can., July 3, 1941; s. William Crosby and Annie Beatrice (Caley) D.; m. Jean Farncombe, May 18, 1963; children: Cynthia Christine, Ronald Crosby Jr. BSc, McMaster U., 1963; PhD, Princeton U., 1966. Faculty dept. physics U. Md., 1968-78; prof. physics MIT, 1978-91; prof. astrophys. scis. Princeton U., 1991—. Vis. scientist Los Alamos Sci. Lab., 1974-75; asst. dir. for applied plasma physics Office of Fusion Energy Dept. Energy, Washington, 1976-78; dir. Plasma Fusion Center MIT, Cambridge, Mass., 1978-88; chmn. magnetic fusion adv. com., 1982-86; dir. Princeton Plasma Physics Lab., 1991-96. Author: Methods in Nonlinear Plasma Theory, 1972, Theory of Nonneutral Plasmas, 1974, 2d edit., 89, Physics of Nonneutral Plasmas, 1990. Recipient Disting. Assoc. award Dept. Energy, 1986, Leadership award Fusion Power Assocs., 1986, Kaul Found. Excellence award, 1993, Particle Accelerator Sci. and Tech. award, 2005; Ford Found. fellow, 1963-64, Imperial Oil fellow, 1963-66, Sloan Rsch. Found. fellow, 1970-72. Fellow AAAS, Am. Phys. Soc. (chmn. div. plasma physics, 1983-84). Office: Princeton U Plasma Physics Lab PO Box 451 Princeton NJ 08543-0451

DAVIDSON, SARAH J., educational consultant, healthcare educator; b. North Little Rock, Ark., Nov. 26, 1947; d. Earnest Jefferson and Alice Sanders D.; 1 child, DeAngelo Kinard. BA in Sociology, Howard U., 1970; MA in Edn., Catholic U., 1971. Elem. sch. tchr. DC Pub. Schs., 1971-72; rsch. assoc. Pres. Nat. Adv. Coun. on Edn., Washington, 1972-74; sr. info. specialist Howard U. Children's Ctr., Washington, 1974-75; head start edn. dir. Wash., DC Parent Child Ctr., Washington, 1975-77; dir. office of field svcs. Child Devel. Assn. Consortium, Washington, 1977-78; child devel. assoc. Enterprise for New Directions, Washington, 1978-79; state coord. children's health DC Dept. of Health Medicaid, Washington, 1979—2000; pres. Nat. Inst. of Family Svcs., 2000—. Child devel. assn. rep. Coun. for Early Childhood Recognition, Wash., 1976—; proposal reader Dept. Edn., 1979; review panelist Dept. Edn., 1986. Assoc. editor: (nat. newsletter) Parent Preschool Press, 1981. Bd. sec. Nat. Fed. Black Women Bus. Owners, 1992—; pub. rels. coord. Coun. of 100 Black Repubs., 1986-91; pres., founder Assn. for the Presevation of N. Little Rock, Ark. Africian Am. History, 2000; bd.mem. Howard Univ. Alumni Assn., 2002-05. Named Outstanding Arkansan Living in DC Arkansas Dem. Gazette, Little Rock, 1993; participant Nat. Security Seminar, U.S. Army War Coll., Carlisle, Pa., 1994. Mem. Nat. Black Child Devel. Inst., Delta Sigma Theta. Republican. Baptist. Avocations: writing, reading, tennis, travel. Personal E-mail: nifamserv@aol.com. Business E-Mail: sdavidson.doh@dcgov.org.

DAVIDSON, SHAE RONALD, historian, researcher; b. Buckhannon, W.Va., Dec. 2, 1973; s. Ronald Davidson and Nancy Waugh. BA in History/Sociology, Marshall U., 1996, MA in History, 1998. Dir. Jenkins Plantation Mus., Lesage, W.Va., 1997—2000; fellow Ohio U. Contemporary History Inst., Athens, 2000—. Rschr. Ohio U. Contemporary History Inst., Athens, 2001—. Exhibit writer (civil war and folk art exhibitions) W.Va. State Mus.; contbr. reviews West Virginia History; author: (political commentaries) Portsmouth Free Press. Fellow, Ohio U. Contemporary History Inst.; John Marshall scholar, Marshall U. Ctr. for Academic Excellence, 1992—96. Mem.: Nat. Coun. on Pub. History, Am. Hist. Assn., Orgn. Am. Historians, Amnesty Internat., Sierra Club. Independent. Achievements include research in in devel. of fed. child nutrition programs, role of lobbyists in edn. Avocations: reading, birdwatching. Office: Ohio U Contemporary History Institute 2 University Terr Athens OH 45701

DAVIDSON, SHEILA KEARNEY, lawyer, insurance company executive; b. Paterson, N.J., Dec. 16, 1961; d. John James and Rita Barbara (Burke) Kearney; m. Anthony H. Davidson, Oct. 5, 1996; children: Andrew John, Patrick Kearney. BA cum laude, Fairfield U., 1983; JD, George Washington U., 1986. Bar: N.Y. 1987, U.S. Dist. Ct. (so. dist.) N.Y. 1987, D.C. 1989. Assoc. Shearson Lehman Bros., Inc., NYC, 1986-87; staff atty. Nat. Assn. Securities Dealers, NYC, 1987-89, regional atty., 1989-90, sr. regional atty., 1990-91; regional counsel N.Y. Life Ins. Co., NYC, 1991-93, assoc. counsel, 1993-94, asst. gen. counsel, 1994-95, v.p., assoc. gen. counsel, 1995-97, sr. v.p. in charge of corp. compliance dept., 1998-00, sr. v.p., gen. counsel, 2000—. Trustee Fairfield U., 2003—. Mem.: D.C. Bar Assn., Phi Delta Phi. Republican. Roman Catholic. Office: NY Life Ins Co 51 Madison Ave New York NY 10010-1603

DAVIDSON, SHIRLEY JEAN, elementary and secondary educator; b. DuQuoin, Ill., June 2, 1946; d. Richard Haley and Doris Jean Gaddis; m. Philip H. Davidson, Aug. 30, 1969; children: Susan Elizabeth, Matthew Philip. BS in Elem. Edn., So. Ill. U., Carbondale, 1969; MAT in Learning Disabilities and Reading, Rockford Coll., 1982; MA in Sch. Adminstrn., Concordia U., River Forest, Ill., 1997. Cert. in sch. adminstrn., learning disabilities, social emotion disorders, educable mentally handicapped, elem. edn., reading, Ill. Thcr. 4th grade Coulterville (Ill.) Elem. Sch., 1968-70; tchr. 2d grade Gifford (Ill.) Grade Sch., 1970-73, Rockton (Ill.) Grade Sch., 1973-85; reading and english/learning disabilities specialist Rockford (Ill.) Area Literacy Coun., 1988-93; spl. edn. tchr. Byron (Ill.) Sch. Dist., 1995-96, Dist. 47, Crystal Lake, Ill., 1993-95, 96—. Ind. reading cons. Elco Industries, Rockford, 1991-92; mem. peacemaking com. Indian Prairie Sch., Crystal Lake, 1998—, mem. tech. com., 1997—, mem. social com., 1996-97, mem. sch. improvement com., 1999—. Active First Presbyn. Ch., Rockford, 1975—. Mem. Crystal Lake Elem. Tchrs. Assn., Pi Lambda Theta, Phi Kappa Phi. Avocations: tennis, reading, cross stitch. Office: Indian Prairie Sch 651 Village Rd Crystal Lake IL 60014-2005 Office Phone: 815-459-2124.

DAVIDSON, SUZANNE MOURON, lawyer; b. Oxford, Miss., Aug. 5, 1963; d. Bertrand D. Jr. and Barbara Jean (Baca) Mouron; m. Garrison H. Davidson III, Dec. 12, 1987; children: Jane Harrington, Catherine Stender. AB in English Lit., U. Calif., 1985, JD, 1988. Assoc. Peterson, Ross, L.A., 1988-89; asst. litigation counsel Ticor Title Ins., Rosemead, Calif., 1989-91; corp. counsel Forest Lawn, Glendale, Calif., 1991—. Deacon San Marino Cmty. Ch., 1995-98, elder, 2000-2003; bd. dirs. San Marino Cmty. Ch. Nursery Sch., 1995-2000; mem. Jr. League, Pasadena, Calif., 1989—, Nat. Charity League Jrs. (San Marino), 2002—, bd. dirs, 2003—. Mem. Calif. State Bar Assn., L.A. County Bar Assn., Pasadena Athletic Club, Salt Air Club, Chi Omega (chmn. nat. area rush info. 1988-95). Presbyterian. Office: Forest Lawn Co Legal Dept 1712 S Glendale Ave Glendale CA 91205-3320

DAVIDSON, THOMAS FERGUSON, retired chemical engineer; b. N.Y.C., Jan. 5, 1930; s. Lorimer Arthur and Elizabeth (Valentine) D.; m. Nancy Lee Selecman, Nov. 10, 1951; children: Thomas Ferguson, Richard Alan, Gwyn Ann. BS in Engring., U. Md., 1951; HHD (hon.), Weber State U., 1998. Sr. project engr. Wright Air Devel. Ctr., Dayton, Ohio, 1951-58; dep. dir. Solid Sys. Divsn., Edwards, Calif., 1959-60; mgr. govt. ops. Thiokol Chem. Corp., Ogden, Utah, 1960-64, dir. aerospace mktg. Bristol, Pa., 1965-67, dir. tech. mgmt. Ogden, 1968-82; v.p. tech. Morton Thiokol Inc., Chgo., 1983-88, Thiokol Corp., Ogden, 1989-90; cons. Ogden, 1990-99. Subcom. lubrications and wear NACA, Washington, 1955-57; chmn. Joint Army, Navy, NASA, Air Force exec. com., 1959-60. Editor: National Rocket Strategic Plan, 1990; contbr. articles to profl. jours. Trustee Family Counseling Svc., Ogden, 1991—98, Weber State U. Found., 1999—, Weber State U., 1999—, Ogden Dinosaur Park, 2000—03; mem. Utah State Bd. Edn., 1992—94; bd. dirs. Habitat for Humanity Internat., 1991—93; chmn. bd. dirs. Wesley Acad., Ogden, 1994—98; bd. dirs. Utah Musical Theatre, 1997—, ARC No. Utah, 1999—2001, Ogden Weber Applied Tech. Coll. Found., 2001—03; mem. athletic bd. Weber State U., 1999—2005. Fellow AIAA (assoc., sect. chmn. 1979-80, chmn. rocket propulsion com. 1987-90, mem. aerospace tech. com. 1987-90, Wyld Propulsion award 1991, WSU Crystal Crest award 2001); mem. Am. Newcomen Soc., Smithsonian Instn., Exch. Club (Book of Golden Deeds award 2001), Ogden Golf and Country Club, Weber State Wildcat Club (bd. dirs. 1996-2000). Republican. Methodist. Home: 4755 Banbury Ln Ogden UT 84403-4484

DAVIDSON, THOMAS MAXWELL, oil industry executive; b. NYC, Dec. 14, 1937; s. Alfred Edward and Claire Helen (Dreyfus) D.; m. Ruth Elizabeth Bovenkerk, Dec. 8, 1962; children: Douglas Edward, Anne Elizabeth. BA, Vanderbilt U., 1959; MBA, Columbia U., 1961. Mgr. Ford Motor Co., Dearborn, Mich., 1963-72; dir. credit ops. White Motor Corp., Eastlake, Ohio, 1972-73, v.p., treas., 1976-77; sr. v.p., COO White Motor Credit Corp., Cleve., 1973-75, pres., CEO, 1975-77, also bd. dirs.; sr. v.p. fin., CFO, dir. Tex. Gas Transmission Corp., Owensboro, Ky., 1977-81; exec. v.p., CFO Arrow Electronics, Inc., N.Y.C., 1981-87, exec. v.p. Greenwich, Conn., 1987-89, also bd. dirs., 1981-94; pres., CEO Global TeleSystems Group, 1989-93, also bd. dirs., 1990-93; pres., CEO Internat. Techs., Inc., Greenwich, 1993—, Med. Info. Internat., 1995-98. Bd. dirs. SOVAM Teleport Russia, Sovintel, Russia, Baltic Comms., Ltd., Russia; bd. dirs., chair CEO XXI Century Hotel Network Ltd., 1998—2000; co-founder, sr. v.p. Vytek Wireless, Inc., 2000—01; mng. dir. Southporter Mgmt. Group, 2002—. Served with U.S. Army, 1959. Mem.: N.Y. Athletic Club. Home: 131 Doubling Rd Greenwich CT 06830-4040 Office: Internat Techs Inc 35 Mason St Greenwich CT 06830-5433 Office Phone: 203-661-4875.

DAVIDSON, THOMAS NOEL, metal products executive; b. Evansville, Ind., Oct. 4, 1939; s. Harry R. and Helen E. Davidson; m. Sally Anne Fries, 1958; children: Thomas N. Jr., John C., James R., Jennifer J. BSc with honors, Mich. State U., 1961. Chmn. bd. dirs. Quarry Hill Group, Nutech Precision Metals Inc., Quarry Hill Ptnrs. Past prin. owner and dir. Am. Brass Co., Ansonia Brass, Atco Controls, Inc., Buffalo Brass Co., Carborundum Abrasives, Inc., Cramco, Inc., Hanson Inc., Jensen Fitting Mfg., Ltd., Jensen Fittings Corp., PCL Industries Ltd., Sandbright & Co., Sklar-Peppler Furniture Inc., Stephenson's Rent-all Inc., Union Drawn Steel Ltd., Volstatic, Inc.; chmn. bd. Azure Dynamics, LP; bd. dirs. TLC Laser Eye Ctrs., MDC Corp., Occulogix Inc., Nutech Precision Metals, TLC Eye Ctr.; past bd. dirs. Am. Mus. Flyfishing; bd. Nat. Marine Sanctuary, Clemmer Industries; past chmn. Ocean Reef Hist. Soc., Ocean Reef Culture Ctr., Ocean Reef Found., Gen. Trust Corp., Henson Chem. With Hugh MacMillan Children's Found., Ocean Reef Cmty. Assn; founding chmn. Ocean Reef Club, Inc., Can. CPGA Golf Championship, Metro Toronto Conv. Ctr.; past bd. dirs. Con. Smythe Rsch. Found., Westhem Corp., USF&G (Can.), Nat. Club, Can. Club, Silcorp Ltd., others; past chmn. and mem. bd. dirs. Ocean Reef Cmty. Found.; chmn. Ocean Reef Cultural Ctr. Recipient Fin. Post Can. award 1979; named Entrepreneur of Yr. by Fin. Post. Mem. Soc. Plastics Engrs. (past dir.), Soc. Plastics Industry (past chmn., Man of Yr. award 1985), Variety Ability Systems Inc. (past dir.), Variety Village (past dir.), Young Pres. Orgn. (internat. pres. 1988-89), World Pres. Orgn. (bd. dirs., internat. pres. 1997), Can. Club (past bd. dirs., N.Y. and Toronto), Nat. Club Toronto (past bd. dirs.), Rosedale Golf Club (Toronto), Card Sound Golf Club (bd. dirs.), English Turn Golf & Country Club (New Orleans), Griffith Island Club (Wiarton, Ont., past chmn.), Ocean Reef Club (past chmn.), The Caledon Mountain Trout Club (Inglewood, Ont.), Tau Beta Pi, Pi Tau Sigma. Home: 7 Sunrise Cay Rd Key Largo FL 33037-5301 Office: Quarry Hill Group PO Box 83 Key Largo FL 33037-0083

DAVIDSON, TOM WILLIAM, lawyer; b. Madison, Wis., Oct. 10, 1952; s. Alvin William and Louise Elizabeth (Zeratsky) D.; m. Linda Mary Greiber, July 27, 1974; children: Jessica, Heather, Thomas. BA, U. Wis., 1977, JD, 1974. Bar: Wis. 1977, U.S. Dist. Ct. (we. dist.) Wis. 1977, U.S. Ct. Appeals (D.C. cir.) 1986, U.S. Supreme Ct. 1986, Va. 2001. Gen. atty. FCC, Washington, 1977-79, trial atty., 1979; assoc. Sidley & Austin, Washington, 1980-84, ptnr., 1985-91, Akin, Gump, Struass, Hauer & Feld, LLP, Washington, 1992—, and chair, comm. practice group. Active Burke (Va.) Ctr. Cmty. Assn., 1977-79; chmn. Bass Pond Cluster Bd., 1977-78. Mem. ABA, FBA, Fed. Comm. Bar Assn., Lowe's Island Club, Tournament Players Club at Avenal, Phi Beta Kappa, Phi Eta Sigma, Phi Kappa Phi. Avocations: golf, softball, soccer, basketball, racquetball. Office: Akin Gump Strauss Hauer & Feld Ste 400 1333 New Hampshire Ave NW Washington DC 20036-1564 Office Phone: 202-887-4011. Business E-Mail: tdavidson@akingump.com.

DAVIDSON, WILLIAM M., manufacturing executive, professional sports team executive; b. Dec. 5, 1922; m. Karen Davidson; children from previous marriage: Ethan, Maria. BBA, U. Mich., 1947; JD, Wayne State U., 1949; LHD (hon.), Jewish Theol. Sem. of Am., 1996; degree (hon.), U. Mich., 2001. Pres., CEO Guardian Glass Co., Northville, Mich., 1957-68; pres., CEO, dir. Guardian Industries Corp., 1968—; mng. ptnr. Detroit Pistons, NBA, 1974—; owner Detroit Shock, WNBA, 1998—, Tampa Bay Lightning, NHL, 1999—; majority owner Palace Sports and Entertainment; former owner Detroit Fury, Arena Football League. Served USN. Office: Guardian Industries Corp 2300 Harmon Rd Auburn Hills MI 48326 also: Detroit Pistons 4 Championship Dr Auburn Hills MI 48326*

DAVIDSON-SHEPARD, GAY, secondary school educator; b. Long Beach, Calif., Dec. 15, 1951; d. Leyton Paul and Ruth Leona (Gritzmaker) Davidson; m. Daniel A. Shepard, June 24, 1983. BA, U. Calif., Irvine, 1972; MA, Columbia Pacific U., 1986. Cert. elem. and secondary edn. tchr. Tchr. mid. sch. Ocean View Sch. Dist., Huntington Beach, Calif., 1973—; team mem. Calif. learning assessment system State Dept. of Edn., Sacramento, 1987—; chief reader Orange County pentathlon and decathlon Orange County Dept. Edn., Costa Mesa, Calif., 1980—; sr. reader new standards State Dept. Edn., Sacramento, 1995—. Lang. arts cons. various sch. dists., Calif., 1976—; chief reader Calif. Learning Assessment System, Sacramento, 1993—; sr. reader New Stds., 1995—; chief reader, asst. chief reader, table leader Golden State Exams, 1997—; item writer Calif. H.S. Exit Exam, 2000—. Author/cons.: Teacher's Guide for Direct Assessment Writing, 1990; test writer Acad. Pentathlon Test, 1984—, Dist. Lang. Art Proficiency Test, 1980—. Mem. NEA, AAUS, AAUW, Nat. Assn. Tchrs. of English, Calif. Reading Assn., Mensa, Calif. Tchrs. Assn., Ocean View Tchrs. Assn. Democrat. Avocations: reading, camping, travel, cooking. Home: 6782 Rook Dr Huntington Beach CA 92647-5641 Office: Mesa View Sch 17601 Avilla Ln Huntington Beach CA 92647-6612 Office Phone: 714-842-6608. Personal E-mail: davshep@earthlink.net.

DAVID-WEILL, MICHEL ALEXANDRE, investment banker; b. France, Nov. 23, 1932; came to US, 1977; s. Pierre Sylvain and Berthe Marie (Haardt) David-W.; m. Hélène Lehideux, July 20, 1956; children: Beatrice David-Weill Stern, Cecile David-Weill, Natalie Merveilleux du Vignaux, Agathe. Ed., Inst. Scis. Politiques, 1953. Ptnr. Lazard Freres & Co., 1961-65; ptnr. Lazard Freres & Cie, 1965—, sr. ptnr., 1975—, Lazard Freres & Co., NYC, 1977-95, chmn., 1995—2005. Bd. dirs. Eurazeo, 1972—, pres., 2003; vice chmn. Groupe Danone, 1970; bd. dirs. Publicis Groupe S.A., 1990. Bd. gov. Soc. of NY Hosp.; trustee Met. Mus. Art, 1985—. Named one of Top 200 Collectors, ARTnews Mag., 2004. Mem. Academie des Beaux-Arts (mem. inst.). Clubs: Brook (NYC), Knickerbocker (NYC). Avocation: collector of 17th to 19th century French paintings. Office: Lazard Freres & Co LLC 30 Rockefeller Plz Fl 59 New York NY 10112-5900

DAVIE, JOSEPH MYRTEN, pathologist, immunologist, educator, science administrator; b. La Porte, Ind., Oct. 14, 1939; s. John James and Dorothy Elizabeth (Hash) Davie; m. Janet Sue Whorwell, Dec. 17, 1960; children: Shelley, Jennifer, Melissa. AB, Ind. U., 1962, MA, 1964, PhD, 1966; MD, Washington U., St. Louis, 1968. Intern Washington U., 1968—69; staff assoc. NIH, 1969—71; resident Nat. Cancer Inst., 1971—72; assoc. prof. pathology Washington U. Sch. Medicine, 1972—75, asst. prof. microbiology, 1972—73, assoc. prof. microbiology, 1973—75, prof., head microbiology and immunology, prof. pathology, 1975—87; sr. v.p. research G.D. Searle and Co., Skokie, Ill., 1987, pres. research and devel., 1987—92, corp. sr. v.p. sci. and tech., 1993; v.p. rsch. Biogen, Inc., Cambridge, Mass., 1993—98, sr. v.p. rsch., 1999—2000; ret., 2000. Assoc. editor Jour. of Immunology, 1975—78, sect. editor, 1978—82. Served with USPHS, 1969—71. Mem.: Inst. Medicine.

DAVIE, MALCOLM HENDERSON, minister, retired municipal official; b. North Bay, Ont., Canada, Oct. 11, 1918; s. William Malcolm and Vera (Henderson) D.; m. Helen Marjorie Marsh, July 1948 (div. Oct. 1954). BA, U. Western Ont., 1945; MA, U. Toronto, 1947; BD, Andover-Newton Theol. Sch., 1950; MA in Psychology, Boston U., 1959. Ordained to ministry Congl. Ch., 1951. Salesman Davie Cheese Co., Idlerton, Ont., 1932-41; with London (Ont.) Provincial Hosp., 1942-44; psychol. counsellor, bus. agt. Gould Farm, Great Barrington, Mass., 1948-51; attendant Hall-Brooke San., Westport, Conn., 1951, Fernald State Sch., Waverly, Mass., 1954-56, acting night supr., 1959-61; minister Congl. chs., Monroe, Conn., 1951-53, Chaplin, Conn., 1953-54, Boston, 1955-58. Appeared as actor with Wellesley (Mass.) Players, Westport (Conn.) Parks and Recreation Commn., 1984-92, one-man show with kilt and bagpipe; sometime lectr. on history of bagpiping in Scotland and Ireland. Mem. Masons (life). Home and Office: PO Box 634 Ridgefield CT 06877-0634

DAVIES, CHARLES R., lawyer; BS, Duquesne U., 1964; JD, Georgetown U., 1967. Bar: D.C. 1968. Asst. v.p., asst. gen. counsel Geico Corp., Washington, 1978, v.p., gen. counsel, 1992—, group v.p., gen. counsel, 1999, sr. v.p., gen. counsel, 2000—. Office: Geico Corp Gelco Plz Washington DC 20076-0001

DAVIES, COLLEEN T., lawyer; b. Sacramento, Calif., Oct. 22, 1958; married; children: Katie, Patrick. BA with honors in English lit., U. Calif., Davis, 1980; JD, Santa Clara U., 1983. Bar: Calif. 1983. With Crosby, Heafey, Roach & May (combined with Reed Smith LLP, 2003), 1983—2003; ptnr., mem. exec. com. Reed Smith LLP, Oakland, Calif., 2003—. Comments editor Santa Clara Law Rev., 1982—83; mem. Product Liability Adv. Coun. Mem.: ABA, Def. Rsch. Inst. (pharm. & med. device sect.), Alameda County Bar Asn., Calif. State Bar, Assn. No. Calif. Def. Counsel, Phi Beta Kappa. Office: Reed Smith LLP 1999 Harrison St Ste 2400 Oakland CA 94612 Office Phone: 510-466-6738. Office Fax: 510-273-8832. Business E-Mail: cdavies@reedsmith.com.

DAVIES, DAVID GEORGE, lawyer, educator; b. Waukesha, Wis., July 19, 1928; s. David Evan and Ella Hilda (Degler) D.; m. Elaine Kowalchik, May 12, 1962; children: Thea Kay, Bryn Ann, Degler Evan. BS, U. Wis., 1950, JD, 1953. Bar: Wis. 1953, Ariz. 1959. Trust rep. First Nat. Bank of Ariz., Phoenix, 1957-58, asst. trust officer, 1958-62, trust officer, head bus. devel. in trust dept., 1962-66, v.p., trust officer, 1966; practice in Phoenix, 1967—; assoc. Wales & Collins, 1967-68; ptnr. Wales, Collins & Davies, 1968-75, Collins, Davies & Cronkhite, Ltd., 1975-85, David G. Davies, Ltd., 1986—. Instr. bus. law local chpt. C.L.U.s, 1965; instr. estate and gift taxation, 1973—; instr. estate planning Phoenix Coll., 1968—; past instr. Maricopa County Jr. Coll. Pres. Central Ariz. Estate Planning Council; pres., bd. dirs. Vis. Nurse Service, United Fund Agy.; chmn. bd. Beatitudes Campus of Care; bd. dirs. Phoenix chpt. Nat. Hemophilia Found.; bd. dirs., treas. trusteeship St. Luke's Hosp. Med. Ctr., Phoenix, 1982—; mem. adv. bd. planned giving com. Salvation Army, 1997—. Served to capt. JAGC, AUS, 1953-57. Mem. Central Assn. Life Underwriters (asso.), ABA, Wis. Bar Assn., State Bar Ariz., Am. Assn. Homes for Aged (legal affairs com., future com.) Congregationalist (chmn. bd. trustees, moderator). Office: 5110 N 40th St Ste 236 Phoenix AZ 85018-2151

DAVIES, DON, education educator; b. Mpls., Dec. 28, 1926; s. Clifford Goetz and Gladys (Herr) D.; m. Mary Joyce Davies; children: Druanne, Donna. BA in Journalism, Stanford U., 1948, MA in Ednl. Adminstrn., 1949; EdD in Curriculum and Tchr. Edn., Columbia U., 1956. Tchr. Beverly Hills (Calif.) H.S., 1949-53; edn. instr. Adelphi Coll., 1953-56; asst. prof. edn. San Francisco State Coll., 1956-57; asst. prof. edn., dir. student teaching U. Minn., 1957-61; exec. sec. Nat. Commn. on Tchr. Edn. and Profl. Stds. NEA, 1961-67; assoc. commr. Dept. Edn., 1968-73; fellow in social sci. Yale U., 1973-74; founder Inst. for Responsive Edn., 1973-94; prof. edn. Boston U., 1974-96, prof. emeritus, 1996—, co-dir. Nat. Rsch. and Devel. Ctr. on

Families, Communities, 1990-96. Bd. dirs. Inst. for Responsive Edn.; vis. lectr. U. Liverpool, U. Cordoba, Argentina, U. Oviedo, Spain, U. Man., U. Lisbon, Portugal; presenter in field. Author: Low Income Parents and the Schools, 1989, Resource Guide on Parent and Citizen Parcipation in Education, 1988, Parents Make a Difference: An Evaluation of New York City's 1987-88 Parent Involvement Program, 1988, Portrait of Schools Reaching Out, 1992, Communities and Their Schools, 1981, Leading the Way, 1980, Schools Where Parents Make a Difference, 1976, Partnerships for Student Success, 1996, Crossing Boundaries: Report on a Multi-National Action Research Study, 1996; editor Jour. of Tchr. Edn., 1961-67; contbr. articles to profl. jours. Trustee life Cambridge Coll.; v.p. Gores' planning com. Ann. Family Reunion Conf., 1999; mem. fair housing com. Marblehead Housing Corp. With USN, 1945-46 Recipient Disting. Svc. medal Dept. Edn., 1971, Internat. Achievement award Nat. Coalition for Parent Involvement in Edn., 1994; grantee John D. and Catherine T. MacArthur Found., Pew Charitable Trusts, Leon Lowenstein Found., Charles Stewart Mott Found Mem. Phi Delta Kappa. Democrat. Avocations: travel, reading. Office: Northeastern Univ Inst for Responsive Edn Boston MA 02115 E-mail: dondav@bu.edu.

DAVIES, GRACE LUCILLE, real estate educator; b. Providence, Apr. 6, 1926; d. Leonard Cerulle and Eleanor De Prete; m. David John Davies, Feb. 8, 1948; children: Mary Ellen, David L., Pamela, Amy. AA, Long Beach City Coll., 1946; BA, U. Calif., Berkeley, 1948; MA, Calif. State U., Long Beach, 1965. Gen. elem. credential Calif., life elem. credential Calif., elem. sch. adminstr. credential Calif., life elem. sch. adminstr. Calif. Elem. educator ABC Unified Sch. Dist., Artesia, Calif., 1956—85, MGM coord., 1960—70, bilingual coord., 1960—70, asst. prin., 1970—80; real estate, bus., investment D. Davies & Assoc., Long Beach, Calif., 1985—. Clk. Long Beach (Calif.) Election Bd., 1990—; mem., vol. Long Beach City Campaign, 1998. Mem.: Calif. Ret. Tchrs. Assn. (legis. chair 1985—, pres. 2000—), Apt. Mgmt. Assn., Delta Kappa Gamma (v.p., pres., Golden Rose award 1996), Pi Lambda Theta (treas., v.p., pres., Outstanding Contbn. Edn. award 1996). Avocations: travel, reading, theater, camping, music. Home: 6215 Parima St Long Beach CA 90803

DAVIES, HUGH MARLAIS, museum director; b. Grahamstown, South Africa, Feb. 12, 1948; came to U.S., 1956; s. Horton Marlais and Brenda M. (Deakin) D.; children: Alexandra, Dorian; m. Lynda Forsha; 1 stepdaughter, Mackenzie Forsha Fuller. AB summa cum laude, Princeton U., 1970, MFA, 1972, PhD, 1976. Dir. Univ. Gallery, U. Mass., Amherst, 1975-83; David C. Copley dir. Mus. Contemporary Art (formerly La Jolla Mus. Contemporary Art), San Diego, 1983—. Vis. prof. fine arts Amherst Coll., 1980-83; mem. adv. coun. dept. art and archeology Princeton U., 1989—, panel mem. fed. adv. com. internat. exhbns., 1990-94; co-curator Whitney Mus. Am. Art Biennial, 2000. Author: (book) Francis Bacon: The Papal Portraits of 1953, 2001, Francis Bacon: The Early and Middle Years, 1928-1958; co-author: Sacred Art in a Secular Century: 20th Century Religious Art, 1978, Francis Bacon (Abbeville), 1986. Nat. Endowment Arts fellow, 1982, 95. Mem. Am. Assn. Mus., Coll. Art Assn., Assn. Art Mus. Dirs. (trustee 1994-2001, pres. 1997-98). Office: Mus Contemporary Art San Diego 700 Prospect St La Jolla CA 92037-4228 Office Phone: 858-454-3541.

DAVIES, J. CLARENCE (TERRY DAVIES), government agency administrator; b. N.Y.C., Nov. 16, 1937; BA cum laude, Dartmouth Coll., 1959; PhD in Am. Govt., Columbia U., 1965. Instr. govt., dir. Bur. Rsch. in Mcpl. Govt. Bowdoin Coll., Brunswick, Maine, 1963-65; chief examiner environ. and consumer protection Bur. of Budget Exec. Office of Pres., Washington, 1965-67, sr. staff mem. Coun. Environ. Quality, 1970-73; asst. prof. politics and pub. affairs Princeton (N.J.) U., 1967-70; fellow, asst. dir. instns. and pub. decisions divsn. Resources for Future, Inc., Washington, 1973-76; exec. v.p. Conservation Found., Washington, 1976-89; asst. adminstr. policy, planning and evaluation U.S. EPA, Washington, 1989-91; exec. dir. Nat. Commn. on Environment, Washington, 1991-92; dir. Ctr. for Risk Mgmt. Resources for Future, Washington, 1992-2000, sr. fellow, 2000—. Cons. U.S. Bur. of Budget, 1967-68, U.S. Dept. Health, Edn. and Welfare, 1968-69, Pres.'s Adv. Coun. on Exec. Orgn., 1969-70, NSF, 1976-79; mem.-at-large exec. com. sci. adv. bd. EPA, 1976-81, chmn. adminstr.'s adv. com. toxic substances, 1977-78, co-chmn. com. on econs. sci. adv. bd., 1979-80, mem. subcom. environ. statis. Nat. Adv. Coun. for Environ. Policy and Tech., 1991-95; mem. sr. steering com. Ctr. Tech. and Adminstrn., Am. U., 1976-79; mem. sci. adv. bd. Internat. Joint Commn. U.S.-Can., 1984-87; mem. adv. bd. Ctr. for Chem. Process Safety, 1985-89; mem. bd. govs. Environ. Health and Safety Inst., Nat. Safety Coun., 1986-89; mem. adv. panel on systems at risk from climate change U.S. Office Tech. Assessment, 1991-92; bd. dirs. Inst. Coop. Environ. Mgmt., 1991-93; chmn. bd. dirs. Resolve, Inc., 1993-2001. Author: Neighborhood Groups and Urban Renewal, 1966, The Politics of Pollution, 2d edit., 1975, Pollution Control in the United States, 1998, (monographs) Risk Assessment and Risk Control, 1985, The Environmental Protection Act: An Integrated Pollution Control Law, 1988; co-author: Training for Environmental Groups, 1984, Determining Unreasonable Risk, 1979, Significant New Use Rules for Existing Chemicals, 1983, Controlling Cross-Media Pollutants, 1984; author: (with others) Growing Against Ourselves: The Energy-Environment Tangle, 1974, Federal Environmental Law, 1974, Environmental Management in the Colorado River Basin, 1974, The Governance of Common Property Resources, 1974, Social Research and Public Policies, 1975, Air Pollution and Administrative Control, 1977, Mechanisms of Toxicity and Hazard Evaluation, 1980, Strategies for Public Health, 1981, TSCA's Impact on Society and the Chemical Industry, 1983, Environmental Policy in the 1980s, 1984, Pollutants in a Multimedia Environment, 1986, Integrated Pollution Control in Europe and North America, 1990, Keeping Pace with Science and Engineering: Case Studies in Environmental Regulation, 1993, Encyclopedia of the Environment, 1994, Pollution Control in the United States, 1998, Reforming Permitting, 2001; co-editor: Business and Environment: Toward Common Ground, 1977, Risk Communication, 1987; mem. editl. bd. Toxic Substances Jour., 1979-89. Mem. bd. dirs. Wildlife Habitat Enhancement Coun., 1987-89. Ford Found. Met. Region fellow. Fellow AAAS; mem. NAS (com. environ. indices 1973-74, com. on environ. decision making 1975-77, com. on prevention significant deterioration under Clean Air Act 1979-81, com. on instl. means for assessment risks to pub. health 1982-83, environ. studies bd. 1983-85, com. on multimedia pollutants 1986-88, chmn. com. on prins. decision making for regulating chemicals in environment 1974-75, com. social and behavioral sci. rsch. priorities for environ. decision making 2003-05), Nat. Inst. for Chem. Studies (nat. adv. bd. 1986-89), NAE (steering com. symposium on environ. regulation 1992-93), Nat. Acad. Pub. Adminstrn. (panel on econ. incentives 1992-93, mem. panel on EPA priorities 1993-95), Phi Beta Kappa. Office: 1616 P St NW Washington DC 20036-1434 Office Phone: 202-328-5080. Personal E-mail: jcd3@verizon.net. E-mail: davies@rff.org.

DAVIES, JOHN ARTHUR, retired physics professor, engineering educator, research scientist; b. Prestatyn, North Wales, Mar. 28, 1927; emigrated to Can., 1940; s. Francis James and Doris Annie (Edkins) D.; m. Florence Smithson, July 29, 1950; children: Susan, Chris, Cathy, Paul, Jim, Anne. BA with honors in Chemistry, St. Michael's Coll., Toronto, 1947; MA in Phys. Chemistry, U. Toronto, 1948, PhD in Phys. Chemistry, 1950; D.Sc. (hon.), Royal Roads Mil. Coll., 1984, Salford U., Eng., 1993. With Atomic Energy of Canada, Chalk River, Ont., 1950-85; prof. engring. and physics McMaster U., Hamilton, 1969-92, prof. emeritus, 1992—. Vis. prof. physics U. Aarhus, Denmark, 1964-65, 69-70; vis. physicist Nobel Inst. Physics, Stockholm, Sweden, 1962, Calif. Inst. Tech., 1969, Osaka U., Japan, 1972. Author: (with J.W. Mayer, L. Eriksson) Ion Implantation, 1970; contbr. over 200 articles to prof. jours. Can. Ramsay Meml. fellow, 1954-56; recipient Noranda medal Chem. Inst. Can., 1965, Callinan award Am. Electrochem. Soc., 1968, W.B. Lewis medal Can. Nuclear Soc., 1998. Fellow Royal Soc. Can., Bohmische Phys. Soc.; mem. Chem. Inst. Can., Can. Assn. Physics, Danish Royal Soc. Roman Catholic. Home and Office: Box 224 7 Wolfe Ave Deep River ON Canada K0J 1P0

DAVIES, LAURA, professional golfer; b. Coventry, Eng., Oct. 5, 1963; Profl. golfer LPGA, 1987—. Mem. European Solheim Cup Team, 1990, 92, 94, 96, 98. 15 career victories, including Circle K LPGA Tucson Open, 1988, Jamie Farr Toledo Classic, 1988, Lady Keystone Open, 1989, Inamori Classic, 1991, McDonald's Championship, 1993, Standard Register Ping, 1994, 95, 96, 97, Sara Lee Classic, 1994, Chick-fil-a Charity Championship, 1995, Star Bank LPGA Classic, 1996, LPGA Tour Championship, 1996, L.A. Womeen's Championship, 2000, The Philips Invitational, 2000; recipient Rolex Player of Yr. award, 1996; named Mem. Brit. Empire, Queen Elizabeth II, 1988. Office: care LPGA 100 International Golf Dr Daytona Beach FL 32124-1082

DAVIES, MATT, cartoonist; b. London; US, 1983; m. Lucy Davies; 2 children. Attended, Savannah Coll. Art and Design, Sch. Visual Arts, N.Y.C. Freelance cartoonist and illustrator; editl. cartoonist Jour. News, White Plains, NY, 1993—; syndicated in 20 newspapers, 1994—. Recipient Robert F. Kennedy Journalism award, 2001, Herbert Block prize for editl. cartooning, 2004, Pulitzer Prize for editl. cartooning, 2004, 4 Deadline Club awards, Soc. Profl. Journalists, NY chpt., 5 time winner, NY AP Editl. Cartooning Competition. Mem.: Assn. Am. Editl. Cartoonists (pres.-elect 2003—). Office: The Jour News One Gannet Dr White Plains NY 10604

DAVIES, MICHAEL A. M., management consultant; b. Papakura, New Zealand, Jan. 17, 1960; arrived in U.S., 1996; s. Graeme John and Florence Isabelle Davies; m. Amy Brewster Bullard, July 21, 2001; children: Charlotte Elizabeth Penniston Bullard Davies, Annabelle Lillian Brewster Bullard Davies. MA in Engring., St. Catharine's Coll., Cambridge, Eng., 1982; MEng, U. Durham, Eng., 1984; MBA with distinction, London Bus. Sch., 1991. Mgr. Boston Consulting Group, Auckland, New Zealand, 1992—94; chief strategy BellSouth Internat./Vodafone NZ, Auckland, 1994—96; prin. GeoPartners Rsch., Cambridge, Mass., 1996—98; chmn. emeritus Mercator Partners, Concord, Mass., 1998—; chmn. Endeavour Ptnrs., Concord, 2004—. Advisor Megisto Sys., Germantown, Md., 2001—04, Ember Corp., Boston, 2002—04, ZonePay, Sterling, Va., 2003—04; chief tech. officer EquuSys, Sudbury, Mass., 2003—. Mem.: Product Devel. Mgmt. Assn., Strategic Mgmt. Soc., Acad. Mgmt., London Bus. Sch. Alumni New Eng. (exec. 1997—2004), Kiwi Expatriates Assn. New Eng. (exec. 2002—04). Achievements include patents for novel applications of wireless technologies; development of 3rd generation wireless technologies; standards for 3rd generation wireless technologies; first PDA with digital cellular. Home: 50 Everett St Concord MA 01742 Office: Endeavour Ptnrs Concord MA 01742 Office Phone: 617-818-0818. Personal E-mail: mail@michael-davies.net. E-mail: michael@endeavourpartners.net.

DAVIES, PAUL LEWIS, JR., retired lawyer; b. San Jose, Calif., July 21, 1930; s. Paul Lewis and Faith (Crummey) D.; m. Barbara Bechtel, Dec. 22, 1955 (dec. June 2001); children: Laura (Mrs. Segundo Mateo), Paul Lewis III. AB, Stanford U., 1952; JD, Harvard U., 1957. Bar: Calif. 1957. Assoc. Pillsbury, Madison & Sutro, San Francisco, 1957—63, ptnr., 1963—89; gen. counsel Chevron Corp., 1984—89. Hon. trustee Calif. Acad. Scis., trustee, 1970-83, chmn., 1973-80; pres. Herbert Hoover Found.; bd. overseers Hoover Instn., chmn., 1976-82, 91-93; hon. regent U. of Pacific, regent, 1959-90. Lt. U.S. Army, 1952-54. Mem. Bohemian Club, Pacific-Union Club, Villa Taverna, Claremont Country Club, Cypress Point Club, Sainte Claire Club, Collectors Club, Explorers Club, Links Club, Met. Club, St. Francis Yacht Club, Palo Alto (Calif.) Club, Phi Beta Kappa, Pi Sigma Alpha. Republican. Office: 3470 Mt Diablo Blvd Ste A210 Lafayette CA 94549-3985 Office Phone: 925-284-8180. E-mail: pauldaviesjr@yahoo.com.

DAVIES, PAUL LEWIS, III, venture capitalist; b. Oakland, Calif., June 29, 1961; s. Paul Lewis Jr. and Barbara Bechtel Davies; m. Pilar Hanigan, Feb. 14, 1963; children: Robert H., Natalie L., Tyler S. BS in Indsl. Engring., Stanford U., 1983, MBA, 1987. With Bechtel Group, Inc., San Francisco, 1987-93; prin. Brentwood Assocs., Menlo Park, Calif., 1993-94, Fremont Group, San Francisco, 1995; mng. prin. Cambria Group, Menlo Park, 1996—. Bd. dirs. Crossbow Tech., Inc., San Jose, Calif., Lakeside Corp., Lafayette, Calif.; chmn. bd. dirs. DSA/Phototech, Inc., L.A. Nat. trustee Boys and Girls Clubs Am., Atlanta; bd. overseers Hoover Instn., Stanford, Calif.; pres., bd. dirs. Llagas Found., Lafayette; bd. dirs. Lakeside Found., Lafayette, Hoover Fedn., Ohio; bd. trustees Menlo Sch., Atherton, Calif. Mem. Inst. Indsl. Engrs., Lincoln Club. Republican. Office: The Cambria Group 1600 El Camino Real Ste 155 Menlo Park CA 94025 Fax: (650) 329-8601. Business E-Mail: davies@cambriagroup.com.

DAVIES, PERCY (PETE) CHARLES, mechanical engineer; b. Pontrilas, Sask., Can., Sept. 18, 1920; s. George Davies, Alice Fanny Wall; m. Nancy Naidee Clark, June 28, 1941 (div. Feb. 1959); children: Denise Diane, Leslie Ann, Joyce Natalie; m. Betty Jean Martin; 1 child, Michael Lane. BSME, U. Wash., 1953. Cert. comml. balloon pilot FAA. Machinist inspector Continental Can Corp., Seattle, 1949—53; gen. mgr. Cert. Mfg., Seattle, 1953—58, Smith-Williston Co., Seattle, 1958—59, Dependable Bldg. Maint., Seattle, 1960—65; owner, gen. mgr. Dictamatic Corp., Portland, 1965—77; owner, chief pilot Rainbow Balloon Flights, Sun City, Ariz., 1983—87; owner Adna Press, Sun City, 1987—. Chmn. bd. Dictamatic Corp., Portland, 1965—77. Author: The Spartan Rebel, 2003, Big Man on Campus, 2003, Kidnapping Susan, 2003, Taser, 2005. With US Merchant Marines, 1945. Mem.: Nat. Assn. Bldg. Svc. Contrs. (nat. bd. dirs. 1965), Tau Beta Pi. Republican. Church Of The Nazarene. Avocations: writing, woodworking, travel, photography, portrait painting. Home and Office: 9206 W Glen Oaks Cir N Sun City AZ 85351 Personal E-mail: iampcd1@aol.com.

DAVIES, PETER JOHN, plant physiology educator, researcher; b. Sudbury, Middlesex, Eng., Mar. 7, 1940; came to U.S., 1966; s. William Bertram and Ivy Doreen (Parmentier) D.; m. Linda Kay DeNoyer, Aug. 2, 1976; children: Kenneth DeNoyer, Caryn Parmentier. BSc with honors, U. Reading, Eng., 1962; MS, U. Calif., Davis, 1964; PhD, U. Reading, 1966. Instr. Yale U., New Haven, 1966-69; asst. prof. plant physiology Cornell U., Ithaca, N.Y., 1969-75, assoc. prof., 1975-83, prof., 1983—, chmn. sect. plant biology, 1992-96. Vis. prof. Cambridge (Eng.) U., 1976-77, Univ. Coll. of Wales, Aberystwyth, 1983-84, U. Minn., 1984, U. Tasmania, Australia, 1996-97. Author: (with others) The Life of the Green Plant, 1980, Control Mechanisms in Plant Development, 1970; editor: Plant Hormones and Their Role in Plant Growth and Redevelopment, 1987, Plant Hormones: Physiology, Biochemistry and Molecular Biology, 1995, Plant Hormones: Biosynthesis Signal Transduction, Action!, 2004; editor-in-chief Plant Growth Regulation, 1987-92. Mem. Am. Soc. Plant Physiology, Internat. Plant Growth Substance Assn. (coun. 1991-98). Office: Cornell U Plant Biology Ithaca NY 14853 Office Phone: 607-255-8237. Business E-Mail: pjd2@cornell.edu.

DAVIES, RICHARD WARREN, lawyer; b. 1946; BA, Salem State Coll., 1967; MA, Purdue U., 1968; JD, Boston U., 1971. Bar: Mass. 1971, Conn. 1972. Law clk. Conn. Supreme Ct., 1971—72; assoc. Hirschberg, Pettengill, Strong & Nagle, 1972—74; asst. gen. counsel Hubbell, Inc., Orange, Conn., 1974—87, asst. sec., 1980—82, sec., 1982—, gen. counsel, 1987—, v.p., 1996—. Mem.: Am. Soc. Corp. Secretaries. Office: Hubbell Inc 584 Derby Milford Rd Orange CT 06477-4024 Office Phone: 203-799-4230. Office Fax: 203-799-4333.

DAVIES, ROBERT ABEL, III, consumer products company executive; b. Englewood, N.J., Sept. 10, 1935; s. Robert Abel Jr. and Lillian Louise (Vila) D.; m. Marilyn Jean Doering, June 16, 1957 (div.); children: Bruce Gregory, Mark Richard, Eric Doering, Nancy Louise; m. Diane M. Church, Sept. 2, 1995, children; Alexander Church, Sophia Catherine. AB, Colgate U., 1957; MBA, Columbia U., 1963. Salesman Proctor & Gamble Co., Cin., 1960-61; product mgr. Colgate Palmolive Co., N.Y.C., 1963-66; group product mgr. Boyle-Midway div. Am. Home Products, N.Y.C., 1966-69; v.p. mktg. Church & Dwight Co. Inc., Princeton, N.J., 1969-76, v.p., gen. mgr., 1976-81, pres., chief oper. officer, 1981-84, also dir., 1981-84; pres., chief exec. officer Calif. Home Brands Inc., Terminal Island, Calif., 1985-89; prin. Gold Coast Calamari Inc., Oxnard, Calif., 1990-94; pres. Church & Dwight Co., Inc., Princeton, NJ, 1995-2001, CEO, 1995—2004, chmn., 2001—, bd. dirs., 1995—. Served to lt. (j.g.) USNR, 1957-60. Office: Church & Dwight Co Inc 469 N Harrison St Princeton NJ 08543-5297

DAVIES, THOMAS MOCKETT, JR., history professor; b. Lincoln, Nebr., May 25, 1940; s. Thomas Mockett and Faith Elizabeth (Arnold) D.; m. Eloisa Carmela Monzón Abate, June 10, 1968 (dec. Jan. 1994); 1 dau., Jennifer Elena; m. Rosemarie Adele Lindsay, Jan. 7, 1995. BA, U. Nebr., 1962, MA, 1964; student, Universidad Nacional Autonóma de México, 1961; PhD, U. N.Mex., 1970; postdoctoral fellow, U. Tex., Austin, 1969-70. Lectr. U. N.Mex. Peace Corps Tng. Center, 1964-66; dir. Ctr. Latin Am. Studies, 1966-68; asst. prof. Latin Am. history San Diego State U., 1968-72, asso. prof., 1972-75, prof. Latin Am. studies, 1979—2001, chmn. Latin Am. studies, 1979—2001, prof. dir. emeritus ctr. Latin Am. studies. Author: (with others) Historia, problema y promesa. Homenaje a Jorge Basadre, 1978, Research Guide to Andean History: Bolivia, Chile, Ecuador and Peru, 1981, The Spanish Civil War: American Hemisphere Perspectives, 1982, EL APRA de la Ideología a la Praxis, 1989, Latin American Military History: An Annotated Bibliography, 1992; author: Indian Integration in Peru: A Half Century of Experience, 1900-48, 1974 (co-winner Hubert Herring Meml. award Pacific Coast Coun. on Latin Am. Studies 1973), (with Victor Villaneuva) 300 Documentos Para la Historia del APRA; Conspiraciones Apristas de 1935 a 1939, 1979, Secretos Electorales del APRA: Correspondencia y Documentos de 1939, 1982; (with Brian Loveman) The Politics of Anti-Politics: The Military in Latin America, 1978, 3d rev. edit., 1997, Che Guevara: Guerrilla Warfare, 1985 (Hubert Herring Meml. award 1985, 3d rev. edit., 1997); mem. editorial bd. Hispanic Am. Hist. Rev., 1985-1990; Contbr. (with Brian Loveman) articles to profl. jours. Recipient Outstanding Faculty award San Diego State U. Alumni Assn., 1981, 97, 1st ann. Internat. Scholar award Phi Beta Delta, 1992, Wiley W. Manuel award Calif. State Bar Assn., 1995, 98; grantee Dept. Edn. for Nat. Resource Ctr. for L.Am. Studies, 1979-2001, San Diego State U. Found., 1971-73, 75, 76, 79, 80, San Diego State U., 1988, 89, 90, William and Flora Hewlett Found., 1997-2001; fellow Henry L. and Grace Doherty Charitable Found., 1966-68 Mem. Latin Am. Studies Assn., Conf. Latin Am. History (exec. sec. 1979-84), Pacific Coast Council Latin Am. (bd. govs. 1989-91, pres. 1996-97), Rocky Mountain Council on Latin Am. Studies (exec. com. 1980—, pres. 1996-97), Am. Hist. Assn., Consortium L.Am. Studies Programs (exec. sec.-treas. 1994-2001). Home: 7524 Maplewood Dr NW Albuquerque NM 87120-3923

DAVIES-JONES, ROBERT PETER, meteorologist; b. Leicester, Eng., Feb. 15, 1943; arrived in U.S., 1964; s. Cyril and Gladys Marjorie Jesse Davies-Jones. BSc with honors, Birmingham (Eng.) U., 1964; PhD, U. Colo., 1969. Postdoctoral fellow Nat. Ctr. for Atmospheric Rsch., Boulder, Colo., 1969—70; meteorologist Nat. Severe Storms Lab., NOAA, Norman, Okla., 1970—. Adj. prof. U. Okla., Norman, 1976—; cons. on tornadoes Nuclear Regulatory Commn., 1973—79; leader tornado intercept project Nat. Severe Storms Lab., Norman, 1975—87. Co-editor: (book) The Tornado: Its Structure, Dynamics, Prediction and Hazards, 1993 (Best New Book in Category, 1994). Recipient Bronze medal, Dept. Commerce, 1985, Outstanding Scientific Paper awards, Nat. Oceanic and Atmospheric Adminstrn., 1983, 1986, 1995—96, 1999, 2002; grantee, NSF, 1994—95, 2000—. Fellow: Am. Meteorol. Soc. (co-chief editor Jour. Atmospheric Scis. 1993—95, Editor's award 1986). Anglican. Achievements include research in dynamics and origins of rotation in tornadoes and their parent supercell thunderstorms. Avocation: soccer. Office: Nat Severe Storms Lab 1313 Halley Cir Norman OK 73069

DAVILA, RAFAEL ANGEL, III, college counselor, educator; b. Rio Piedras, P.R., Nov. 24, 1967; s. Rafael Angel Jr. and Maria Dávila; m. Krista Rae (Schneiderwind) Dávila, July 17, 1993; children: Alexia Irene, Rafael Angel IV. BS, U. Ctrl. Fla., 1990, MA, 1995, postgrad., 1997—. Cert. sch. guidance gounselor, correctional probation officer, Fla.; nat. cert. counselor. Behavior tng. specialist Threshold Inc., Winter Park, Fla., 1990-91, 92-93; probation and parole officer Dept. Corrections, Orlando, Fla., 1991-92; children's svcs. counselor Great Oaks Village, Orlando, 1993-95; sch. counselor Seminole County Pub. Schs., Sanford, Fla., 1995-99; counselor Seminole C.C., Sanford, 1999—, instr. Mem. sch. adv. coun. Winter Springs (Fla.) H.S., 1997-99. With USN, 1985-88. Tchr. edn. Am.'s minorities scholar U. Ctrl. Fla., 1994, scholar Universal Studios, 1999. Democrat. Roman Catholic. Avocations: playing softball and golf, attending sporting events and broadway shows, dance.

DAVILA, SUSAN, guidance counselor; b. Bayaman, P.R., Aug. 11, 1961; came to U.S., 1962; d. Manuel Ramon Valcárcel and Maria Elena Garcia-Meitin; m. Daniel Ricardo Dávila, Dec. 12, 1982; children: Elena Susana, Daniel Antonio, Andrés Daniel. BA in Elem. Edn., St. Thomas U., 1986, MS in Guidance Counseling. Cert. elem. tchr., guidance counselor. Tchr. Sts. Peter and Paul Sch., Miami, Fla., 1986-98; guidance counselor St. Agatha Cath. Sch., Sts. Peter and Paul Cath. Sch., Miami, 1998—. Youth group coord. Sts. Peter and Paul Sch., 1994—, peer tchr., 1994—. Vocations com. Sts. Peter and Paul Ch., Miami, 1997—, festival com., 1990—. Mem. Fla. Counseling Assn., FASERVIC, Nat. Cath. Edn. Assn. Roman Catholic. Avocations: reading, walking.

DAVION, ETHEL JOHNSON, school system administrator, curriculum specialist; b. Raleigh, N.C., July 21, 1948; d. John Arthur and Ethel Mae (Morgan) Johnson; 1 child, Laura Christal. BA, Livingstone Coll., 1971; MA, Glassboro (N.J.) State U., 1983. Cert. tchr., prin., supr., N.J. Sr. English tchr. Camden (N.J.) Bd. Edn., 1977-81; tchr. of English Westfield (N.J.) Bd. Edn., 1982-85, Union County Regional Dist. 1, Berkeley Heights, N.J., 1981-82, Hillside (N.J.) Bd. Edn., 1985-87; supr. English, lang. arts Irvington (N.J.) Bd. Edn., 1987-92; vice prin. Frank H. Morrell H.S., Irvington, NJ, 1992-95, prin., 1996—2000, asst. supt. acad. affairs, 2000—. Writer, researcher Collegiate Rsch. Systems, Camden, 1976-77; participant profl. devel. programs Harvard U., 1989, Notre Dame U., 1990; participate Oxford Univ. Roundtable, Oxford, Eng., 2002. Author: A Tutorial Approach to Teaching English, 1983, Teachers' Resource Manual, 1987; contbr. articles to jours. Bd. dirs., sec. Emmanuel Tabernacle, Linden, N.J., 1988; com. chair Narrowing the Achievement Gap for Kean Univ.'s Diversity, 2000—. Recipient Resolution Town Coun. Irvington, 1992. Fellow N.J. Edn. Assn., Nat. Coun. Tchrs. English; mem. ASCD, NAFE, Am. Assn. Sch. Adminstrs., Linden Scholarship Guild (sec. 1985—), Prin. and Suprs. Assn., Irvington Adminstrs. Assn. (treas.), Internat. Platform Assn., Good Samaritans Club, Obsidian Civic Club (Westfield, historian 1985—), Diversity 2000 Coun. (sec. 1997—). Democrat. Baptist. Office Phone: 973-399-6800. E-mail: ejdavion@irvington.k12.nj.us.

DAVIS, A. DANO, retired retail executive; b. 1945; Student, Stetson U.; MBA, Harvard Bus. Sch.; MS in Economics, Cambridge U. With Winn-Dixie Stores Inc., Jacksonville, Fla., 1968—2004, corp. v.p., mgr. Jacksonville div., 1978-80, sr. v.p. and regional dir. Jacksonville and Orlando (Fla.) and Atlanta divs., 1980-82, pres., 1982-88, CEO, also bd. dirs., 1988-2000, chmn., 1988—2004. Mem. Mayo Foundation Bd. of Trustees, 2001—; Nat. Exec. Bd. Boy Scouts of Am.; mem. bd. dirs. Jacksonville Zoological Gardens, Florida Tax Watch; mem. bd. trustees Jacksonville U.

DAVIS, ALAN JAY, lawyer; b. Phila., Feb. 4, 1937; s. Rudolph Alan and Adele (Saver) Davis; m. Roslyn Kutcher; children: Jennifer C., Michael R. BA, U. Pa., 1957; JSD, Harvard U., 1960. Bar: Pa. 1961, U.S. Dist. Ct. (ea. dist.) Pa. 1961, U.S. Ct. Appeals (3d cir.) 1961, U.S. Supreme Ct. 1979. Law clk. to chief judge U.S. Ct. Appeals (3d cir.), Phila., 1960-61; assoc. Wolf, Block, Schorr & Solis-Cohen, Phila., 1961-66, ptnr., 1968-91, chmn. litig. dept., 1987-91; chief asst. dist. atty. Office Dist. Atty., Phila., 1966-68; sr. litig. ptnr. Ballard Spahr Andrews & Ingersoll, Phila., 1991—. Spl. master to investigate prison sys. and sheriff's dept. Ct. Common Pleas, Phila., 1968—70; lectr. law U. Pa. Sch. Law, Phila., 1973—77; city solicitor City of Phila., 1980—82, chief labor negotiator, 1991—93, Southeastern Pa. Transp. Authority, Phila., 1982, Sch. Dist. Phila., 1984, 96. Chmn. met. adv. bd. Anti-Defamation League B'nai B'rith, Phila., 1986—88; mem. sch. com.

Germantown Friends Sch., Phila., 1986—88; trustee Free Libr. Phila., 1995—98, The Pew Charitable Trusts, 2004—; vice chmn. Third Cir. Lawyers Adv. Com., 2005—; pres. U. Pa. Law Sch. Am. Inns of Ct., 1998—2000. Fellow: Internat. Acad. Trial Lawyers, Am. Coll. Trial Lawyers; mem.: ABA, Am. Law Inst., Phila. Bar Assn., Pa. Bar Assn., Jr. Legal Club, Legal Club. Democrat. Jewish. Office: Ballard Spahr Andrews & Ingersoll 1735 Market St Fl 51 Philadelphia PA 19103-7599 Office Phone: 215-864-8230. Office Fax: 215-864-9516. Business E-Mail: davisa@ballardspahr.com.

DAVIS, ALAN TUCKER, foundation administrator, minister, philanthropist; b. Lubbock, Tex., June 13, 1952; s. Ken W. Davis Jr.; m. Jilynn Elyce Spiers, Jan. 3, 1976; children: Alan, Jeniece. BA in Geology, Tex. Christian U., 1974; BA and M in Speculative Theol.-Philos., U. Metaphysics Internat., 2001, DDiv, 2001; diploma in forensic sci., 2002, diploma in criminal justice, 2003; BS in Psychology, Canyon Coll., 2003. Pres. Mastercraft Printing Co., 1977-79, Unit Rig and Equipment Co., Tulsa, 1982-85, Gt. Western Drilling Co., Midland, Tex., 0985—1995. Author: Texas Mussel Watch, 2000, Advanced Fishwatching, 2001, Reef Coral Identification, 2001, Reef Creature Identification, 2001. Chmn. bd. Riding Unltd., Justin, Tex., 1996-97; master instr. Am. Dragons Tae Kwon Do, N. Richland Hills, Tex., 1989—; SCUBA instr. We B Divin', Hurst, Tex., 1995—; vol. Multiple Sclerosis Soc., Ft. Worth, 1995—, Tarrant County Correctional Facility, Ft. Worth, 1995-96. Named Amateur Biologist of Yr., Tex. Parks and Wildlife Dept., 2000, Herman Smith Man of Yr., Ft. Worth Star Telegram Newspaper, 1995-96. Mem.: Am. Inst. Applied Sci., Coll. Profl. Studies. Avocations: painting, classical guitar, drawing. Office: Gt Western Drilling Co 309 W 7th St Ste 800 Fort Worth TX 76102 Fax: 817-332-4095. E-mail: Tuck52@aol.com.

DAVIS, ALLEN, professional football team executive; b. Brockton, Mass., July 4, 1929; s. Louis and Rose Davis; m. Carol Segall, July 11, 1954; 1 child, Mark. Student, Wittenberg Coll., 1947; AB, Syracuse U., 1950. Asst. football coach Adelphi Coll., 1950—51; head football coach Ft. Belvoir, Va., 1952—53; player-personnel scout Baltimore Colts, 1954; line coach The Citadel, 1955—56, U. So. Calif., 1957—59; asst. coach San Diego Chargers, 1960—62; gen. mgr., head coach Oakland Raiders, 1963—66, owner, mng. gen. ptnr., 1966—82, LA Raiders, 1982—95; now pres., gen. ptnr. Oakland Raiders, 1995—. Former mem. mgmt. council and competition com. NFL. With AUS, 1952—53. Named Profl. Coach of Year, AP, UPI, Sporting News, Pro-Football Illustrated, 1963, Young Man of Yr., Oakland, 1963, only individual in history to be an asst. coach, head coach, gen. mgr., league commr. and owner; named to Pro Football Hall of Fame, 1992. Mem.: Am. Football Coaches Assn. Office: Oakland Raiders 1220 Harbor Bay Pkwy Alameda CA 94502-6570*

DAVIS, ALLEN FREEMAN, history professor, writer; b. Hardwick, Vt., Jan. 9, 1931; s. Harold Freeman and Bernice Susan (Allen) D.; m. Roberta Hazel Green, June 16, 1956 (div.); children: Gregory Freeman, Paul Studley. AB, Dartmouth Coll., 1953; MA, U. Rochester, 1954; PhD, U. Wis., 1959. Instr. history Wayne State U., Detroit, 1959-60; asst. prof. history U. Mo., Columbia, 1960-63, assoc. prof., 1963-68; prof. Temple U., Phila., 1968-99, prof. emeritus, 1999—. Vis. prof. U. Tex., Austin, 1983, U. Amsterdam, 1986-87, John Adams chair. Co-author: March of American Democracy, Vol. V, 1966, Spearheads for Reform, 1967, 84, American Heroine, 1973, 2000, Postcards From Vermont, 2002; (with others) The American People, 1986, 7th edit., 2006; (with Jim Watts) Generations, 1974, 3d edit., 1983; (with Fredric Miller and Morris Vogel) Still Philadelphia, 1983, Philadelphia Stories, 1988; editor: (with Harold D. Woodman) Conflict and Consensus in American History, 1966, 9th edit., 1997; (with Mary Lynn McCree) Eighty Years at Hull House, 1969; (with Mark Haller) The Peoples of Philadelphia, 1973, 2d edit., 1998, Jane Addams on Peace, War and International Understanding, 1974, For Better or Worse, 1980; (with Mary Lynn Bryan) 100 Years at Hull House, 1990, Series in American Civilization, 1978-2000; contbr. articles to profl. jours. Served with AUS, 1954-56. Recipient Friends of Lit. award, 1970, Christopher award, 1974; Danforth Grad. fellow, 1953-59, Am. Council Learned Socs. sr. fellow, 1971-72, NEH fellow, 1975-76, Fulbright fellow, 1986-87; Am. Philos. Soc. grantee, 1962, 65. Mem. Am. Hist. Assn., Orgn. Am. Historians, Am. Studies Assn. (treas. 1971-72, exec. sec. 1972-77, pres. 1989-90, Bode-Pearson award 1996), Soc. Am. Historians. Home: 2032 Waverly St Philadelphia PA 19146-1343 E-mail: davisafd@aol.com.

DAVIS, ANDREA BARBARA, language educator; b. Vienna, Sept. 13, 1960; arrived in U.S., 1981; d. Gerhard Richard Rudolf Wiedermann and Elisabeth Johanna Maria Pichler; m. Adam Brooke Davis, Aug. 26, 1983; children: Naomi, Clement, Paul, August. BA in German and French, U. Mich., 1983; MA in French, U. Mo., 1987. Tchr. German Pioneer H.S., Ann Arbor, Mich., 1983; instr. German and French Truman State U., Kirksville, Mo., 1991—. Tutor English, Freiburg, Germany, 1990—91. Convener, German dept. Truman State U., 2004—05; active Mary Immaculate Ch., Kirksville, 1991—. Mem.: Phi Beta Kappa (treas. 2002—03, resident mem.). Roman Catholic. Avocations: hiking, reading, movies. Home: 804 E Illinois St Kirksville MO 63501 Office: Truman State U MC 311 Normal/Franklin St Kirksville MO 63501

DAVIS, ANGELA YVONNE, political activist, educator, writer; b. Birmingham, Ala., Jan. 26, 1944; D.B. Frank and Sally E. Davis. Studied under Theodor Adorno, Frankfurt Sch., 1960-62; student, U. Paris, 1963-64; BA magna cum laude, Brandeis U., 1965; MA, U. Calif., San Diego, 1968. Mem. faculty San Francisco State U.; tchr. U. Calif., San Diego, 1968; asst. prof. philosophy UCLA, 1969; prof. history of consciousness dept. U. Calif., Santa Cruz, 1991—, presdl. chair in African American and feminist studies, 1995-97. Adv. bd. Prison Activist Resource Ctr., spkr. in field. Removed from teaching position in philosophy dept., UCLA, 1969. On FBI's 10 Most Wanted List, 1970. Captured, tried and acquitted, 1972. Gov. Ronald Reagan vowed she would never teach in Univ. Calif. sys. Candidate for US v.p., Communist Party ticket, 1980. Author: If They Come in the Morning: Voices of Resistance, 1971, Angela Davis: An Autobiography, Women, Race, and Class, 1981, Women, Culture, and Politics, 1989, Violence Against Women and the Ongoing Challenge to Racism, 1992, Resisting State Violence: Radicalism, Gender, and Race in US Culture, 1996, The Angela Y. Davis Reader, 1998, The House That Race Built, 1998, Blues Legacies and Black Feminism: Gertrude "Ma" Rainey, Bessie Smith, and Billie Holiday, 1998, Are Prisons Obsolete?, 2003. Mem. Black Panthers. Mem. Communist Party. Office: History of Consciousness Dept UC Santa Cruz 1156 High St Santa Cruz CA 95064 Office Phone: 831-459-0111.

DAVIS, ANITA YVONNE, small business owner, writer; b. Macon, Ga., Aug. 26, 1948; d. Clarence and Essie Davis. BS in English, Savannah State Coll., 1970; cert. in small bus. devel., Clayton State Coll., 1991; cert. in computer use, Concepts in Automation Tng. Sch., 1992; cert. in reading, Ga. State U., 1998; cert. in working with exceptional children, Ga. Coll. and State U., 1998. Pres., owner Fashion Era Modeling Assn., Macon, 1970—72; English tchr. Ctrl. High Complex, Macon, 1970—72; monitor Learning Found., Macon, 1971—72; flight attendant Delta Airlines, Inc., Atlanta, 1972—78, acct., 1978—2000; pub. rels. mgr. Concepts in Automation, Atlanta, 1992—95; pres., owner A.Y. Davis Enterprises, Inc., Atlanta and Macon. Cmty. in schs. tutor, substitute tchr. Bibb County Bd. Edn., Macon, 2002—03; prodr. ednl. videos and movies A.Y. Davis Reading and Drama Club, Macon, 1998—; singer JOI, Atlanta, 1985—; exec. v.p., COO, exec. mgr. New Sys. Enterprises, Inc.; exec. mgr. New Sys. Rec. Studio and New Sys. Apollo, 2003. Author: Cindé Reader in the Town of Reading Land, 2001; contbr. articles to profl. jours. Pres. Goals 2000 Read Am. Challenge, Macon, 1998—2003; founder A.Y. Davis Health Found. Recipient Goals 2000: Read Am. Challenge award, Pres. Clinton, 1998. Avocations: writing, reading, drawing, singing, dance. Office: AY Davis Enterprises Inc PO Box 5573 Macon GA 31208 Personal E-mail: davisaydavis@aol.com.

DAVIS, ANNA JANE RIPLEY, elementary school educator; b. Uhrichsville, Ohio, Sept. 7, 1931; d. Emmet Frank and Lillie Hazel (Kinsey) Ripley; m. H. Joe Davis, Mar. 16, 1951; children: Alan Joe, Kendal Jay. A, Asbury Coll., 1953; BS with honors, Kent State U., 1962, MEd with honors, 1978, postgrad., 1980—96; student, Richmond Coll., London U., St. Andrews U., Dundee U., Cambridge U., U. Paris, U. Rome, U. Amsterdam, Ohio U. Cert. elem. tchr., Ohio. Tchr. Kenston Schs., Chagrin Falls, Ohio, 1953-55, 58-62, Firestone Rubber Plantation, Harbel, Liberia, West Africa, 1962-64, Newbury (Ohio) Schs., 1964-65, Orange Schs., Pepper Pike, Ohio, 1965-99. Chaperone, counselor Am. Inst. for Fgn. Study, British Isles and Europe, summers 1968-81. Author children's books. Active Kenston PTA, Chagrin Falls and Pepper Pike PTA, Am. Field Svc., Chagrin Falls, Geauga County Personal Growth Com. for workshops; bd. dirs. Friends Geauga County Pub. Libr.; bookmobile project vol. traveling libr. Geauga County Pub. Libr. for Amish Schs., traveling libr., 1994—; elem. sch. tutor, 1998—; vol. ARC, 1955—, Food Pantry and Clothing for Needy, Kiwanis, bookmobile projects Geauga County Pub. Lib. Friends; mem. edn. com., libr., home care, Care Bears com., Prayer Chain, Sunday sch. com., Sunday Sch., membership com., Pepper Pike Garfield Meml. United Meth. Ch. Mem. NEA (life), ASCD, Ohio Edn. Assn., N.E. Ohio Tchrs. Assn., Orange Tchrs. Assn. Avocations: travel, bicycling, hiking, reading, writing.

DAVIS, ARTHUR DAVID, psychology educator, musician; m. Gladys Lesley Joyce, Dec. 29, 1965 (dec.); children: Kimali, Mureithi. Student, Manhattan Sch. Music, 1953-56, Juilliard Sch. Music, 1953-56; BA summa cum laude, CUNY, 1973; MA, City Coll., N.Y.C., 1976, NYU, 1976, PhD with distinction, 1982. Lic. sch. psychologist. Musician various worldwide tours, 1962—, NBC-TV Staff Orch., N.Y.C., 1962-63, Westinghouse TV Staff Orch., N.Y.C., 1964-68, CBS-TV Staff Orch., N.Y.C., 1969-71; prof. Manhattan Community Coll., N.Y.C., 1971-86, U. Bridgeport, Conn., 1978-82; psychologist Lincoln Med. and Mental Health Ctr., Bronx, 1982-85; sch. psychologist, cons. Lakeside Union Free Sch. Dist., Spring Valley, NY, 1985—86; psychologist, tchr. N.Y. Med. Coll., Valhalla, 1982-87; prof. Orange Coast Coll., Costa Mesa, Calif., 1987—, Calif. State U., Fullerton, 1988-90, U. Calif., Irvine, 1993—94; CEO, pres. Arkimu Inc., 1993—; psychologist Cross Cultural Ctr., San Diego, 1986-91; mem. faculty U. Calif., Irvine, 1999—2001. Cons. Head Start, Bklyn., 1981-82, Orange County Minority AIDS, Santa Ana, Calif., 1987-88, Orange County Fair Housing, Costa Mesa, 1988, Sickle Cell Anemia Assn., Santa Ana, Calif., 1987-88, Human Rels. Orange County City, Costa Mesa, 1988-89, William Grant Still Mus., L.A., 1988-90; musician various symphonies Radio City Music Hall Orch. Nat. Symphony, Symphony of the Air N.Y. Philharmonic, Met. Opera Orch., L.A. Philharmonic, 1995; John Coltrane, others, 1960-. Author: The Arthur Davis System for Double Bass, 1976, A Brief History of Jazz, 1995; record composer Interplay, 1980, Art Davis LIFE, 1986, Reemergance, ARKIMU, 1985, Dr. Art Davis, Live, Soulnote, 1987, Art Davis, A Time Remembered, 1995; composer (CD) Puttin on the Ritz, 2002. Composer, condr., mem. coun. Dialogue, Costa Mesa, 1988, Art's Boogie, 1979; mgr. Little League of Cortlandt, N.Y., 1979-82; pack master Cub Scouts Am., Cortlandt and Croton, N.Y., 1979-80, dist. chmn., 1980-81; bd. dirs. Local 47 Musicians' Union, Hollywood, Calif., 1993-97, Orange County Urban League, Inc., 1992-95; chmn. Better Advantages for Students and Soc., Corona del Mar, Calif., 1993; adv. bd. dirs. John W. Cultrane Cultural Soc., Inc. Named World's Foremost Double Bassist, IBA, 1969—; recipient Lion award, Black MBA Assn., 1985, Chancellor's Disting. Lectr.'s award, U. Calif., Irvine, 1991—92, Exemplary Stds. in Music Edn. award, Orange County Urban League, 1993, Congl. award, 2002, Congl. Lifetime Achievement as a jazz legend, Ann. Dr. Art Davis Scholarships established in his honor, Dr. Art Davis Fan Club, Gladys David Scholarship established in honor of his late wife, 1995, Better Advantages for Students and Soc.; grantee, NIMH, 1976—77. Mem. APA, ASCAP, SAG, Am. Soc. Music Arrangers & Composers, Chamber Music Am., N.Y. Acad. Scis., Astron. Soc. of the Pacific (charter), Orange County Psychol. Assn., Assn. of Black Psychologists, Planetary Soc. (charter), Am. Hort. Soc., Nat Trust for Hist. Preservation Soc., Rec. Musicians Assn., Stanford U. Alumni Assn., NYU Alumni Assn., CCNY Alumni Assn., Sierra Club. Avocations: astronomy, gourmet cooking, gardening, photography, dxing. Office: ARKIMU 3535 E Coast Hwy # 50 Corona Del Mar CA 92625-2404 E-mail: drart@artdavis.com.

DAVIS, ARTUR, congressman, lawyer; b. Montgomery, Ala., Apr. 9, 1967; BA in Govt. cum laude, Harvard U., 1990, JD cum laude, 1993. Intern So. Poverty Law Ctr.; law clk. U.S. Dist. Ct. Judge, 1993—94; asst. U.S. atty., 1994—98; pvt. practice Birmingham, Ala., 1998—2002; mem. U.S. Ho. Reps. 7th Dist. Ala., 2003—, mem. budget com. fin. svc. com. Mem. New Dem. Network. Scholar, Harvard U. Democrat. Office: US Ho of Reps 208 Cannon Ho Office Bldg Washington DC 20515-0107 also: Dist Office 2 20th St N Ste 1130 Birmingham AL 35203*

DAVIS, BARBARA SNELL, education educator; b. Painesville, Ohio, Feb. 21, 1929; d. Roy Addison and Mabelle Irene (Denning) Snell; children: Beth Ann Davis Schnorf, James L., Polly Denning Davis Spaeth. BS, Kent State U., 1951; MA, Lake Erie Coll., 1981; postgrad., Cleve. State U., 1982-83. Cert. reading specialist, elem. prin., Ohio. Dir. publicity Lake Erie Coll., Painesville, 1954-59; tchr. Mentor (Ohio) Exempted Village Sch. Dist., 1972-86, prin., 1986-97; prof., field dir. Lake Erie Coll., 1997—. Author: Who Says You Can't Change the World?, 2005; contbr. articles to profl. jours Former trustee Mentor United Meth. Ch. Mem. Delta Kappa Gamma (pres. 1982-84), Phi Delta Kappa (pres. 1992-93), Theta Sigma Phi (charter). Home: 7293 Beechwood Dr Mentor OH 44060-6305 Office: 326 College Hall Lake Erie Coll Painesville OH 44077 Office Phone: 440-375-7159.

DAVIS, BARRY E., energy executive; BA finance, Texas Christian U. V.p., marketing & development Endevco, Inc.; founder Ventana Natural Gas Company (now Crosstex Engergy), 1992; pres., CEO Comstock Natural Gas, Inc., Crosstex Energy, 1996—. Office: c/o Crosstex 2501 Cedar Springs Rd Dallas TX 75201*

DAVIS, BENJAMIN ALANDO, lawyer; s. Carolyn Davis; m. Aysha Khan, July 13, 2004; 1 child, Benjamin Sikander. AS, U. Md., 1991; BS, Columbus U., 1993; JD, U. Ga., 1996. Bar: Ga. 1996. Assoc. Scott, Quarterman and Wells, Athens, Ga., 1995—96; prin. Davis Law Firm, P.C., Atlanta, 1997—. Law clk. to Hon. Steve Jones, Athens, 1994—96. Judge Nat. H.S. Mock Trial, Atlanta, 1996—2004. Cpl. U.S. Army, 1987—91. Scholar, U. Ga. Sch. Law, 1991. Mem.: Ga. Assn. Criminal Def. Lawyers (assoc.). Office: Davis Law Firm PC Ste 200 1201 Peachtree St Atlanta GA 30361 Office Phone: 404-233-0120. Business E-Mail: davislawfirm@msn.com.

DAVIS, BENJAMIN GEORGE, theologian, educator; b. Honesdale, Pa., July 6, 1941; s. Benjamin George and Laura Teneyck (Swingle) D.; m. Janet Marie Gorden, June 21, 1980; children: Leslie Anne, John Nathan. AB, U. Mich., 1967, AM, 1969; MTh, U. Nottingham, England, 1982; DMin, St. Mary's Sem. and Univ., Balt., 1985; MBA, North Ctrl. U., 2004, PhD, 2005. Draftsman, designer Munson Mill Machinery Co., Utica, N.Y., 1961-62; design engr. Gen. Motors Corp., Warren, Mich., 1963-66; devel. coord. City of Ann Arbor, Mich., 1967; research economist Exec. Office of the Pres., Washington, 1970; sr. assoc. RMC Research Corp., Bethesda, Md., 1971-75; dir. Research Svcs., Inc., Clinton, Md., 1975-80; regional dir. World Relief, Landover, Md., 1981-86; dir. Evangelicals for Social Action, Washington, 1987-89; pastor St. John United Ch., Columbia, Md., 1989-90; prof. St. Mary's Sem. and U., Balt., 1986—; assoc. dean Balt. Internat. Coll., 1988-95. Exec. dir. The Religious Coalition, Frederick, Md., 1995-98; dean, campus dir. Potomac Coll., Washington, 1998-2003; dir. acad. affairs U. Phoenix, Columbia, Md., 2003—. Author: A Modern Interpretation of Revelation, 1982, Understanding World Cultures: The United States and Canada, 1990, 2nd edit., 2000, Economics: An Integrated Approach, 1997; editor: The Dictionary of Essential English, 1987. Pres. Fgn.-born Info. and Referral Network, Columbia, 1986-92; chmn. Coalition fo r Refugee Resettlement, Washington, 1985-86; chairperson Md. Refugee Adv. Coun., Balt., 1985-86. Recipient Gov.'s Citation State of Md., 1985, 86; NDEA fellow in economics U. Md., 1969-71, Rickard's fellow in theology U. Nottingham, 1980-81. Mem. Assn. for Psychol. Type, Assn. Overseas Educators, Mensa, Omicron Delta Epsilon. Avocations: jazz, photography, motorcycling. Home: 6580 Madrigal Ter Columbia MD 21045-4628 Office Phone: 410-872-9001. E-mail: benjamin.davis@phoenix.edu. *The search for certainty in life leads only up blind alleys. Accepting the ambiguity and moving forward in faith is all.*

DAVIS, BERTHA, emergency department technician; b. Detroit, Aug. 12, 1958; d. James Otis and Bertha Mae Hardeman; m. Antonio Davis, May 16, 1978; children: Marcia A., Antonio M., Angelo M. Student, Wayne County CC, Detroit. Sec. Allegheny Gen. Hosp., Pitts., 1982—95; emergency dept. tech. DMC Sinai Grace Hosp., Detroit, 1995—. Head tchr., acting dir. Bethel Early Learning Ctr., Detroit, 1996—98; employee appeals adv. Detriot Med. Ctr. Sinai Grace Hosp., Detroit, 1998—99; emergency dept. edn. coun. Sinai Grace Hosp., Detroit, 1999—2001, emergency dept. employee preceptor, 2001—03, emergency dept. employee trauma tng. preceptor, 2001—03; sch. commn. adv. St. Clare of Montefalco Sch., Grosse Pointe Park, Mich., 2001—03. Author: (book) Advance Academics for 4 Year Olds, 1997, The African Princess, The Runaway Pen, Little Red Livin' in the Hood, Little Chocolate Lynn, Chocolate Sister and her Seven Uncles, An Autumn Freeze, The Cardboard Box, A Haunting in the Neighborhood, My Great Grandmother the slave, I Have a New Friend, It's Not For You, Help! I Don't Understand!, God is All Around, You'll Never Know...Until you Try, Money! How Can I Spend It? What Can I Buy?, Brotha's at 15-book of life's expectations, Sista's at 15-book of life's expectations. Recipient Angel of Mercy award, U.S. Senator Carl Levin, 2002, Cert. of Achievement, Congressman John Congers Jr., 2002. Democrat. Roman Catholic. Achievements include invention of over 200 learning games. Avocations: art, antiques, golf, cooking, gardening.

DAVIS, BERTRAM HYLTON, retired literature educator; b. Ozone Park, N.Y., Nov. 30, 1918; s. Hubert Edwin and Gladys (Greenidge) D.; m. Ruth Austin Benedict, Jan. 11, 1946; children: Ralph Paul, Kathryn Davis Kohler, Richard Austin. Grad., Phillips Acad., Andover, Mass., 1933-37; student, Hamilton Coll., Clinton, N.Y., 1937-39; AB, Columbia, 1941, MA, 1948, PhD, 1956; LL.D., Dickinson Coll., 1974. Lectr. English Hunter Coll., 1947-48; instr., then asst. prof. English Dickinson Coll., 1948-57; staff assoc. AAUP, 1957-63, dep. gen. sec., 1963-67, gen. sec., 1967-74; prof. English Fla. State U., Tallahassee, 1974-85, svc. prof., 1985-90, prof. emeritus, 1991—. Author: Johnson Before Boswell, 1960, A Proof of Eminence, 1973, Thomas Percy, 1981, Thomas Percy: A Scholar-Cleric in the Age of Johnson, 1989; editor (Sir John Hawkins): Life of Samuel Johnson LL.D, 1961; editor bull., AAUP, 1960-65; field editor Twayne's English Authors Series, 1977-93; mem. editorial com. Yale Edition of Works of Samuel Johnson, 1979— . Served to capt. AUS, 1941-46. Guggenheim fellow, 1974 Mem. ACLU, MLA, Johnsonians, South Atlantic Modern Lang. Assn., Cosmos Club, Am. Soc. for 18th Century Studies. Home: 2309 Domingo Dr Tallahassee FL 32304-1310

DAVIS, BETTY BOURBONIA, real estate company executive; b. Ft. Bayard, N.Mex., Mar. 12, 1931; d. John Alexander and Ora M. (Caudill) Bourbonia; children: Janice Cox Anderson, Elizabeth Ora Cox. BS in Elem. Edn., U. N.Mex., 1954. Gen. ptnr. BJD Realty Co., Albuquerque, 1977—. Mem. Friends of Little Theatre, 1973—85, Friends of Art, 1978—85, Mus. N.Mex Found.; bd. dirs. Albuquerque Opera Build, 1977—79, 1981—83, 1985—87, membership co-chair, 1977—78; mem. Hodgin Hall preservation com. U. N.Mex. Recipient Matrix award for Journalism, Jr. League. Mem.: N.Mex Hist. Soc., Albuquerque Guild Santa Fe Opera, Mt. Vernon Ladies Assn., Alumni Assn. N.Mex, Jr. League Albuquerque (sustainer), Internat. Platform Assn., Order Rainbow Girls (mem. state exec. com. N.Mex Order 1986—2002, chair pub. rels. com., co-chair gen. arrangemtns com. 1990—97, mem. grand exec. com., past grand worthy advisor N.Mex, past mother advisor Friendship Assembly 50), N.Mex Symphony Guild, Albuquerque Mus. Assn., Las Amapolis Club, Tanoan Country Club, Albuquerque Petroleum Club, Albuquerque Knife and Fork Club, Order Eastern Star, Alpha Chi Omega (chpt. advisor bdlg. corp. 1962—77). Republican. Methodist. Home: 9505 Augusta Ave NE Albuquerque NM 87111-5820

DAVIS, BETTY LOUISE, music educator; b. Alliance, Ohio, June 24, 1930; d. Wehner Charles Kindle and Wehner Dessie (Sproul) May; m. William Howard Davis, Sept. 4, 1949; children: Bruce, Karen, Joan, Mary. MusB in Organ, B in Music Edn., Mount Union Coll., 1965; EdM in Curriculum and Instrn., Ashland U., 1983. Cert. tchr. Ohio. Organist Vine St. United Meth., Alliance, Ohio, 1946—; elem. music tchr. Marlington Local Schs., Alliance, 1965—74, H.S. choral dir., 1974—90. Pres. Alliance Cmty. Concerts Assn., 1990—. Active Friends Alliance City Cemetry, 2002—. Named Educator of Yr., Alliance Area C. of C., 1990; recipient Life Achievement award, Canton (Ohio) Players Guild, 1990. Mem.: Am. Guild Organists (charter mem.), Alliance Music Study Club, Delta Kappa Gamma (Delta Tau chpt., 25 Yr. Mem. award 1999), Mu Phi Epsilon Alumni (treas., 50 Yr. Mem. award 1996). Republican. Methodist. Avocations: travel, gardening, concerts, baseball, grandchildren. Home: 722 Garfield Ave Alliance OH 44601-1632

DAVIS, BETTYE JEAN, school system administrator, state legislator; b. Homer, La., May 17, 1938; d. Dan and Rosylind (Daniel) Ivory; m. Troy J. Davis, Jan. 21, 1959; children: Anthony Benard, Sonja Davis Wade. Cert. nursing, St. Anthony's, 1961; BSW, Grambling State U., 1971; postgrad., U. Alaska, 1972. Psychiat. nurse Alaska Psychiat. Inst., 1967-70; asst. dir. San Bernardino (Calif.) YWCA, 1971-72; child care specialist DFYS Anchorage, 1975-80, soc. worker, 1980-82, foster care coordinator, 1982-87; dir. Alaska Black Leadership Edn. Program, 1979-82; exec. dir. Anchorage Sch. Bd., 1982-89; mem. Alaska Legislature, 1990—2000, Alaska Senate, 2000—. Chair Children's Caucus Alaska Legis., 1992—. Pres. Anchorage Sch. Bd., 1986-87; bd. dirs. Blacks in Govt., 1980-82, March of Dimes, 1983-85, Anchorage chpt. YWCA, 1989-90, Winning with Stronger Edn. Com., 1991, Alaska 2000, Anchorage Ctr. for Families, 1992—, active Anchorage chpt. NAACP, bd. dirs., 1978-82; mem. State Bd. Edn., 1997-2000. Toll fellow Henry Toll Fellowship Program, 1992; named Woman of Yr., Alaska Colored Women's Club, 1981, Child Care Worker of Yr., Alaska Foster Parent Assn., 1983, Social Worker of Yr., Nat. Foster Parents Assn., 1983, Outstanding Bd. Mem, Assn. Alaska Sch. Bds., 1990,; recipient Outstanding Achievement in Edn. award Alaska Colored Women's Club, 1985, Outstanding Women in Edn. award Zeta Phi Beta, 1985, Boardsmanship award Assn. Alaska Sch. Bds., 1989, Woman of Achievement award YWCA, 1991, Outstanding Leadership award Calif. Assembly, 1992. Mem. LWV, Nat. Sch. Bd. Assn., Nat. Caucus of Black Sch. Bd. Mems. (bd. dirs. 1986-87), Alaska Black Caucus (chair 1984—), Alaska Women's Polit. Caucus, Alaska Black Leadership Conf. (pres. 1976-80), Alaska Women Lobby (treas.), Nat. Caucus of Black State Legis. (chair region 12, 1994—), Women Legislators Lobby, Women's Action for New Directions, North to Future Bus. and Prof. Women (pres. 1978-79, 83), Delta Sigma Theta (Alaska chpt. pres. 1978-80). Clubs: North to Future Bus. and Profl. Women (past pres.). Democrat. Baptist. Avocations: cooking, Scrabble, collecting stamps, coins and matches, reading. Home: 2240 Foxhall Dr Anchorage AK 99504-3350 E-mail: bdavis@ak.net.

DAVIS, BEVERLY WATTS, federal agency administrator; b. Cincinnati; BA in Econs., Polit. Sci. and Social Sci., Trinity U., San Antonio; postgrad., Webster U., Jeffersonville, Ind. Statewide coord. Texans' War on Drugs, 1988; cons., then dir. cmty. health Travis County Tex. Health Dept.; exec. dir. San Antonio Fighting Back Anti-Drug Cmty. Coalition; sr. v.p. United Way of San Antonio and Bexar County; dir. Ctr. for Substance Abuse Prevention, Substance Abuse and Mental Health Svcs. Adminstrn., Rockville, Md., 2003—. Mem. Minority-and Women-Owned Bus. Commn. Named Vol. of the Yr., U.S. Atty. Gen., 1997, Advocate of the Yr., Palmer Drug Abuse Program, Yellow Rose of Tex., Gov. of Tex., Outstanding Minority Bus. Owner, Greater Austin C. of C., 1985; named to San Antonio Women's Hall of Fame, 1998; recipient Dir.'s Award for Cmty. Leadership, FBI, Commendation award, U.S. Dept. Justice, Comdr.'s Award for Outstanding Leadership, Dept. Def., Vol. award, Gov. Tex., Award for Neighborhood Action, Tex. Atty. Gen.'s Office, Outstanding Citizen Advocate award, Nat. Crime Prevention Coun. Office: Substance Abuse and Mental Health Svc Adminstrn Rm 4-1057 1 Choke Cherry Rd Rockville MD 20857

DAVIS, BLONDELL GILLIAM, business manager, evangelist, artist, author, poet; b. Ft. Pierce, Fla., Dec. 21, 1942; d. Fred Douglas and Mary Louise Gilliam; m. Levoid Davis, July 15, 1962; 1 child, Sherry Yvonne. AA, Lincoln Jr. Coll., 1962. Ordained to ministry Apostolic (Holiness) House of Prayer. State evangelist House of Prayer, Tampa, Fla., 1980—, mgr. bakery, 1987—. Author: Miracles on the Mind, 1993, Miracles Never Cease; editor Ho. of Prayer Gospel Press. Avocations: writing, cooking, drawing, painting, sewing. Home: 3210 E Lambright St Tampa FL 33610-3609 Office: The House of Prayer 3006 E Ellicott St Tampa FL 33610-2136 Office Phone: 813-238-5221.

DAVIS, BONNIE CHRISTELL, judge; b. Petersburg, Va., July 13, 1949; d. Robert Madison and Margaret Elizabeth (Collier) D. BA, Longwood Coll., 1971; JD, U. Richmond, 1980. Bar: Va. 1980, U.S. Dist. Ct. (ea. dist.) Va. 1980, U.S. Ct. Appeals (4th cir.) 1982. Tchr. Chesterfield County Schs., Chesterfield, Va., 1971-77; pvt. practice Chesterfield, 1980-83; asst. commonwealth atty. Chesterfield County, 1983-93; judge Juvenile and Domestic Rels. Ct. for 12th Jud. Dist. Va., 1993—. Adviser Youth Svcs. Commn., Chesterfield, 1983-93; cons. Task Force on Child Abuse, 1983-93, Met. Richmond Multi-Discipline Team on Spouse Abuse, 1983-93, Va. Dept. of Children for handbook "Step by Step Through the Juvenile Justice System in Virginia, 1988; mem. nat. adv. com. for prodn. on missing and runaway children Theatre IV; mem. adv. group to set stds. and tng. for Guardians Ad Litem, Supreme Ct. Va., 1994; chmn. jud. adminstrn. com. Jud. Conf. Va. for Dist. Cts., 1995-97, 2001-03; mem. state adv. com. for CASA and children's Justice Act, 1998-2002. Co-author: Juvenile Law and Practice in Virginia, 1994. Mem. Chesterfield County Pub. Schs. Task Force on Core Values, 1999. Mem.: Chesterfield-Colonial Heights Bar Assn., Met. Richmond Women's Bar Assn., Va. Trial Lawyers Assn., Va. Bar Assn., Va. State Bar (bd. govs. family law sect. 1997—2001, bd. govs. sr. lawyers conf. 2005—), State-Fed. Jud. Coun. Va. Home: 415 Lyons Ave Colonial Heights VA 23834-3154 Office: Chesterfield Juvenile and Domestic Rels Dist Ct 7000 Lucy Corr Blvd Chesterfield VA 23832-6717 Office Phone: 804-751-4115.

DAVIS, BRIAN MATTHEW, musician; b. Lebanon, NJ, Feb. 6, 1979; s. Walter Raymond and Lucille Davis. BA in jazz guitar performance, Temple U., 2001. Band leader, guitarist Matt Davis' Aerial Photograph, Phila., 2001—; guitar instr. The Cmty Coll. Phila., Phila., 2005—; freelance composer, musician various, 2001—. Clinician U. of the Arts, Phila., 2005. Composer: (recordings) The Music from Matt Davis and Aerial Photograph, 2002. Educator Intercultural Family Svcs., Phila., 2002. Recipient Artist in Residency, The C.E.C. Arts Ctr., 2004, Composer in Residence, Nat. Pks. Svc., 2005; Subito grant, Am. Composers Forum, 2003. Avocations: music, reading, birdwatching. Office: Matt Davis Aerial Photograph 427 W Thompson St Philadelphia PA 19122 E-mail: matt@mattdavisguitar.com.

DAVIS, BRITTON ANTHONY, retired lawyer; b. Highland Park, Ill., Jan. 2, 1936; s. James Archie and Anita (Blanke) D.; m. Lynn Marriott Wegner, 1958 (dec. 1975); children: Hilary, Shepard; m. Peggy M. Swint, 1986; children: Stephen Swint, Thomas Swint. Student, Denison U., 1954-57; BS in Law, Northwestern U., 1959, LLB, 1960. Bar: Ill. 1960. Assoc. Haight & Hofeldt, Chgo., 1959-89; pvt. practice Winnetka, Ill., 1989—96; ret., 1996. Vol. Children's Spl. Edn. Programs, Winnetka. Mem.: ABA, Patent Law Assn. Chgo., Bar Assn. 7th Fed. Cir., Chgo. Curling Club, Indian Hill Club (Winnetka). Home: 4616 Forest Edge Ln Long Grove IL 60047

DAVIS, BRUCE GORDON, retired principal; b. Fulton, Tex., Sept. 2, 1922; s. Arthur Lee and Clara Katherine (Rouquette) D.; B.A., U. Tex., 1950; M.Ed., U. Houston, 1965; m. Mary Virginia Jackson, Aug. 31, 1946; children— Ford Rouquette, Barton Bolling, Katherine Norvell Davis McLendon. Tchr., Edison Jr. High Sch., Houston, 1951; tchr. Sidney Lanier Jr. High Sch., Houston, 1957-60, asst. prin., 1966-74, prin., 1974-83; tchr. Johnston Jr. High Sch., Houston, 1960-66; prin. Sidney Lanier Vanguard Sch., Houston, 1974-82; ret., 1983. Served with USMC, 1942-45; with U.S. Army, 1951-57. Mem. Nat. Assn. Secondary Sch. Prins., Tex. Assn. Secondary Sch. Prins., Houston Profl. Adminstrs., U.S. Army Officers Res. Assn., Tex. Retired Tchrs. Assn., Am. Legion. Republican. Presbyterian. Club: Masons. Home: 7400 Clarewood Dr Apt 624 Houston TX 77036-4339

DAVIS, BUTCH (PAUL HILTON DAVIS), former professional football coach; b. Tahlequah, OK, Nov. 17, 1951; m. Tammy Davis; 1 child, Andrew. BS in Biology & Life Sci., U. Ark., 1974. Head coach Rodgers HS, Tulsa, 1978; asst. Okla. State U. Cowboys, 1979—83; defensive line coach U. Miami Hurricanes, 1984—88, Dallas Cowboys, 1989—93, defensive coord., 1993—94; head coach U. Miami Hurricanes, 1995—2001, Cleve. Browns, 2001—04. Office: Cleve Browns 76 Lou Groza Blvd Berea OH 44017

DAVIS, C. VANLEER, III, lawyer; b. Camden, N.J., 1942; AB summa cum laude, Princeton U., 1964; LLB magna cum laude, Harvard U., 1967. Bar: Pa. 1969. Law clk. to Hon. Abraham L. Freedman U.S. Ct. Appeals (3d cir.), 1967-68; ptnr. Dechert, LLP, Phila. Lectr. Pa. State U. Tax Conf., 1980, mem. planning com., 1986—, chair, 1991-92; lectr. grad. tax program Temple U., 1988-89. Author: (with Jay Zagoren) Pennsylvania Limited Liability Company Forms and Practice Manual, 1996; co-editor (with Patrick Dolan) Securitization Handbook, 2000. Mem. Phi Beta Kappa. Office: Dechert LLP 4000 Bell Atlantic Tower 1717 Arch St Philadelphia PA 19103-2713 Office Phone: 215-994-2528. E-mail: van.davis@dechert.com.

DAVIS, CALVIN DE ARMOND, historian, educator; b. Westport, Ind., Dec. 3, 1927; s. Harry Russell and Abbie Jane (Moncrief) Davis. AB, Franklin Coll., Ind., 1949; MA, Ind. U., 1956, PhD, 1961. Tchr. Wilson Sch., Columbus, Ind., 1949-51, 53-54; asst. prof. history Ind. Central Coll., Indpls., 1956-57; teaching assoc. Ind. U., 1958-59; asst. prof. history U. Denver, 1959-62, Duke U., Durham, N.C., 1962-64, assoc. prof., 1964-76, prof., 1976-96, prof. emeritus, 1996—. Cons. NEH, 1974. Contbr. articles to profl. jours.; author: (essays) Ency. U.S. Fgn. Rels., 1997, Oxford Companion to American Military History, 1999, Scribner's Ency. Am. Fgn. Policy, 2002, The United States and the First Hague Peace Conference, 1962 (Albert J. Beveridge award, 1961), The United States and the Second Hague Peace Conference, 1976; contbg. author: American Statesmen Secretaries of State from John Jay to Colin Powell, 2004; author: Biog. of Elihu Root. With U.S. Army, 1951—53. Mem.: Soc. Historians Am. Fgn. Rels., Orgn. Am. Historians, Am. Hist. Assn. Home: 511 E Nightingale Dr Greensburg IN 47240-8589 Office: Duke U Dept History Durham NC 27708

DAVIS, CAROL, educational association administrator, educator; English tchr.; English curriculum specialist Terrebonne Parish Pub. Sch.; pres. La. Assn. Educators, Baton Rouge, 2000—. Trainer instrn. and profl. devel. La. Assn. Educators; field site coord. Nicholls State U. Mem.: Terrebonne Assn. Educators (pres.), La. Assn. Educators (v.p., bd. dirs., chair program and budget com., co-chair strategic planning com.). Office: Louisiana Association of Educators 8322 One Calais Ave Baton Rouge LA 70809-3412

DAVIS, CARYLON LEE, mortgage company executive, real estate broker; d. Palmus Dupree and Alice Enolia Strickland Dupree; m. Willie Davis, June 2, 1973. AA, L.A. City Coll., 1966; student, L.A. State Coll., 1967—69. Clk.-typist Gold's Furniture and Appliances, L.A., 1960—63, Dept. Def., L.A., 1963—69, sec., 1969—72, adminstrv. asst., 1972—78, exec. sec., 1983—85; office mgr. Dept. Air Force, L.A., 1978—83; bus. owner, pres. Kari's Profl. Svcs., Carson, Calif., 1989—98; real estate agt. Frank Jones Realty, Carson, 1989—98; real estate broker Kari's Enterprises, Carson, 1998—; mortgage broker A Plus Fin., Carson, 1998—. Avocation: piano. Office: A Plus Fin 20715 S Avalon Blvd #300 Carson CA 90746 Office Phone: 310-538-5254. E-mail: carylon@sbcglobal.net.

DAVIS, CATHERINE LUCY, psychologist, diabetes researcher; b. Stamford, Conn., Oct. 28, 1968; d. Flavius Eugene Davis IV and Constance Anne Russell; m. Francisco Ignacio Robles, Nov. 9, 2002. AB in Psychology magna cum laude, Dartmouth Coll., 1990; MS in Clin. Health Psychology, U. Miami, 1995, PhD in Clin. Health Psychology, 1997. Lic. psychologist. Psychology resident Geisinger Med. Ctr., Danville, Pa., 1996—97; postdoctoral fellow U. Miami, Coral Gables, Fla., 1997—2000; asst. prof. pediat. Med. Coll. Ga., Augusta, 2000—. Mem. acad. coun. Med. Coll. Ga., Augusta, 2002—05; investigator Ga. Ctr. for Prevention of Obesity and Related Disorders, Athens/Augusta, 2001—04; ad hoc reviewer Jour. Pediat. Psychology, 2001—, Obesity Rsch., 2001—, Internat. Jour. Obesity, 2002—, Am. Jour. Pub. Health, 2004—; faculty presenter, Motion Explosion exhibit Nat. Sci. Ctrs. Ft. Discovery, Augusta, 2002—02; grant reviewer NIH, Am. Diabetes Assn., 2004—. Contbr. articles to profl. jours. Mem., vol. Cat Network, Miami, 1998—2000. Rufus Choate scholar, Dartmouth Coll., 1990, Benjamin J. Benner '69 Rsch. Support fellow, 1989, Summer Diabetes Student Rsch. Program fellow, Juvenile Diabetes Found., 1992, Maytag fellow, U. Miami, 1992—95, T32 Rsch. fellow, NHLBI/NIH, 1997—2000, Diabetes rsch. grantee, Fraternal Order of Eagles in Augusta, 1999, Summer Inst. on Behavioral Medicine Interventions grantee, NIH, 2001, Summer Inst. on Behavioral Randomized Clin. Trials grantee, NIH, Office Behavioral and Social Sci. Rsch., 2002, NIDDKD/NIH grantee, 2003—. Mem.: APA (divsn. 38 health psychology, divsn. 54 Soc. Pediat. Psychology), Soc. Pediat. Rsch., Soc. Behavioral Medicine, Am. Heart Assn., Am. Diabetes Assn. (chair profl. sect. coun. on behavioral medicine and psychology 2003—05), Vol. Assn. Cultural Hispanoamericana, Phi Beta Kappa, Alpha Theta (pres. 1988—89). Liberal. Unitarian Universalist. Avocation: music. Office: Med Coll Ga Prevention Inst 1499 Walton Way HS 1640 Augusta GA 30912

DAVIS, CATHY, publishing executive; Sr. v.p. mktg. and devel., Ariz. Republic, Phoenix; pres. and CEO Tucson Newspapers, Tucson, 2000—. Office: Tucson Citizen Newspaper 1640 E River Rd Ste 201 Tucson AZ 85718-7645

DAVIS, CHARISSE MARIA, doll maker, artist; b. Peoria, Ill., Aug. 5, 1952; d. Helbert Allen and Donna Jeanne (Davis) Hughes; children: Michael D'Andre, Jermaine LaMont, Joshua Donnidra. Cert., Nat. Sch. Dress Design, Chgo., 1971; AA, Midstate Bus. Coll., Peoria, Ill., 1978. Sec. Urban League, Peoria, Ill., 1967-68, Frank Campbell, Peoria, Ill., 1967—68; seamstress Aubry Tailoring, Peoria, Ill., 1969-70; cashier Cannon's Liquor, Peoria, Ill.; nurses aide Peoria, Ill., 1971-73; supr. Community Workshop & Training, Peoria, Ill., 1974-77; clk. SoFro Fabric House, Peoria, Ill., 1977-78; seamstress McDonald's Tailoring, Peoria, Ill., 1976-78; tailor, owner Cyd's, Inc., 1979-86; Leather Forest seamstress, 1978-79; tailor Sahdrask's Dept. Store, 1979—82, Queen's Way to Fashion, 1982—84; doll maker Cyd's, Inc., Peoria, Ill., 1986-98; owner Cyd's Heritage Dolls and Thangs, Peoria, 1998—, Cyd's Designs Just Black-Women's Clothing, 2005—; ARC telerecruiter, 1998-99. Folk artist Rivereity Art Fair, 2005. Mem. Black Doll Makers Club, Am. Artist, Shad Hill. Avocations: painting, writing short stories about family history. Home: 908 E Republic St Peoria IL 61603-2652

DAVIS, CHARLES MICHAEL, Internet company executive; s. Joel and Carol Davis; m. Jan Leslie Phillips; children: Jared, Jenna. BA in Urban Studies, Brown U., 1982; MBA, Harvard U., 1986. Sr. v.p., mktg. TV Guide Mag., Radnor, Pa., 1992—95; pres., ecommerce Disney Internet Group, Burbank, Calif., 1996—99; pres., CEO Shopzilla, Inc, L.A., 2000—. Dir. Shop.org, Washington, 2002—, Business.com, Santa Monica, 2003—. Dir. Young Pres. Orgn., L.A., 2003—; pres. Huntington Palisades Protective Assn., Pacific Palisades, 2003. Recipient Entrepreneur of Yr. award, Ernst & Young, 2004. Mem.: Harvard Club NY (assoc.). Home: 719 Chapala Dr Pacific Palisades CA 90272 Office: Shopzilla Inc 12200 W Olympic Blvd Ste 300 Los Angeles CA 90064 Office Phone: 310-903-4200. Personal E-mail: cdavis@mba1986.hbs.edu. E-mail: chuck@shopzilla.com.

DAVIS, CHARLES RAYMOND, political scientist, educator; b. Hampton, Va., Jan. 16, 1945; s. Cecil Raymond and Fronda Gail (Bradshaw) D.; m. Terry Lorraine Barr, Oct. 1, 1963 (div. July 1979); children: Kimberly Dawn Ingram, Charles Robert; m. Raymonda Carolyn Mays, Feb. 12, 1982. BA in Polit. Sci., U. Louisville, 1974; MA in Polit. Sci., U. Ky., 1975, PhD of Polit. Sci., 1985. Instr. Jefferson Community Coll., Louisville, 1976; claims rep. Aetna Casualty, Madisonville, Ky., 1977-78; rsch. asst. U. Louisville, 1979-80; rsch. analyst Ky. Health Svcs., Frankfort, 1981-85; asst. prof., masters degree program coord. U. So. Miss., Long Beach, 1986-89, asst. prof. Hattiesburg, 1989, assoc. prof., 1991-99, prof., 1999—. Policy analyst Ky. Gov.'s Coalition on Health Costs, Frankfort, 1982; acting dir. grad. studies, U. So. Miss., Hattiesburg, 1990. Author: Organization Theories and Public Administration, 1996; editl. bd. Internat. Jour. Orgn. Theory & Behavior, 1997; contbr. numerous articles to profl. jours. Mem. AAUP, ASPA, Am. Polit. Sci. Assn., So. Polit. Sci. Assn., Miss. Polit. Sci. Assn., Miss. chpt. ASPA. Mem. Ch. of Christ. Avocations: photography, travel, reading, music, history of old west. Home: 417 Browns Bridge Rd Hattiesburg MS 39401-8703 Office: U So Miss Dept Polit Sci Southern Sta # 5108 Hattiesburg MS 39406 Office Phone: 601-297-9603. Business E-Mail: raymond.davis@usm.edu.

DAVIS, CHARLES S., biostatistician; b. Waterloo, Iowa, Oct. 16, 1952; s. Paul R and Bessie L Davis; m. Ruth E. Spearman, June 7, 1975; children: Michael C., Carrie A., Nathan J. PhD, U. of Mich., Ann Arbor, 1985—87; MS, McMaster U., Hamilton, Ontario, 1975—77; BA, Houghton Coll., NY, 1972—74. Statistician Mayo Clinic, Rochester, Minn., 1977—81; sr. statistician Am. Critical Care, McGaw Park, Ill., 1981—84; prof. U. Iowa, 1987—2001; v.p., biometrics Elan Pharmaceuticals, San Diego, 2001—. Author: (reference book) Statistical Methods for the Analysis of Repeated Measurements; editor: (assoc. editor of profl. journal) The American Statistician, Controlled Clinical Trials, author. Recipient Outstanding Presentation Award, US Bur. of the Census, 1989. Mem.: ASA Biometrics Sect. (chmn. 1999—2001), Internat. Biometric Soc., Am. Statis. Assn. Achievements include research in more than 80 publications in peer-reviewed journals. Office Phone: 858-457-7442. Personal E-mail: chuck-davis@juno.com.

DAVIS, CHERYL K., dean; BA, Cedarville U., 1993; MA, U. Alaska, 1996; PhD, Indiana U. Pa., 2004. Asst. prof., dir. Writing. Ctr. Cedarville (Ohio) U., 1998—2001; dean Alaska Christian Coll., Saldotna, 2001—. Mem. coun. Kenai Peninsula Coll., Soldotna, 2004—. Editor: Real Writing by Real Students, 1995. Recipient Excellence in Tchg. award, Tulda U., 1999; Faculty Incentive grantee, Cedarville U., 2000, Svc. Learning grantee, Kenai Peninsula Coll., 2003. Avocations: hiking, backpacking, running.

DAVIS, CHRISTOPHER, writer, retired writing educator; b. Phila., Oct. 23, 1928; s. Edward and Josephine Blitzstein Davis; (div.); children: Kirby, Katherine, Emily, Sarah; m. Sally Warner. BA, U. Pa., 1955. Writing tchr. U. Pa., Phila., 1958-69, Bryn Mawr (Pa.) Coll., 1977-95. Author: Lost Summer, 1958, First Family, 1959, A Kind of Darkness, 1962, Belmarch, 1964, The Shamir of Dachau, 1966, Sad Adam-Glad Adam, 1966, Ishmael, 1967, A Peep Into the 20th Century, 1971 (Nat. Book Award nominee), The Producer, 1972, The Sun in Mid-Career, 1975, Suicide Note, 1977, Waiting For It, 1980, Dog Horse Rat, 1990, (play) A Peep Into The 20th Century, 1988. Recipient Career award Am. Acad. and Inst. Arts and Letters, N.Y.C., 1991; grantee, NEA, 1967, 74, Guggenheim, 1972. Mem. Authors Guild, PEN West, Pasadena Soc. Artists, Phi Beta Kappa. Avocation: sculpture. Home: 2284 Norwic Pl Altadena CA 91001-2565 E-mail: kitdavis@earthlink.net.

DAVIS, CHRISTOPHER C., diversified financial services company executive; MA, U. St. Andrews. Investment analyst The Davis Funds, Boston, 1989—95, co-portfolio mgr., 1995—. Office: The Davis Funds PO Box 8406 Boston MA 02266-8406

DAVIS, CLARENCE BALDWIN, college dean, historian; b. Berwyn, Ill., Feb. 21, 1944; s. William DeOzro and Selina Grace (Morehouse) D.; m. Barbara Ann Simko, Aug. 3, 1968; children: Elizabeth, Carlton. BA, Yale U., 1966; MA, U. Wis., 1968, PhD, 1972. Instr. Madison (Wis.) Area Tech. Coll., 1970; asst. prof. Stratford Coll., Danville, Va., 1972-73; prof. Coll. Charleston, S.C., 1973-87; dean Lewis and Clark Coll., Portland, Oreg., 1987-90; v.p. acad. affairs Keene (N.H.) State Coll., 1990—. Author: Partners and Rivals, 1987; editor: Proceedings: 13th Consortium on Revolutionary Europe, 1985; contbr. articles to profl. jours. Grantee NEH, 1976, 77-79, Am. Philos. Soc., 1978; Am. Coun. Edn. fellow, 1984-85. Mem. Am. Hist. Assn., So. Hist. Assn., Coun. Fellows, Phi Alpha Theta. Office: Keene State Coll 229 Main St Keene NH 03435-0001

DAVIS, CLARENCE CLINTON, JR., lawyer; b. Alexandria, La., Sept. 24, 1956; s. Clarence Clinton Sr. and Julia Isabel (Pace) D.; m. Lisa Cheryl Russell, Aug. 6, 1977 (div. Aug. 1978). BS with hons., Northwestern State U., 1977; JD cum laude, So. Meth. U., 1980. Bar: Fla. 1980, U.S. Tax Ct. 1981, U.S. Ct. Appeals (5th cir.) 1981, Tex. 1982; cert. tax law Tex. Bd. Legal Specialization; CPA, Tex. Assoc. Trenam, Simmons, Kemker, Scharf, Barkin, Frye & O'Neill, Tampa, Fla., 1980-81, Moore & Peterson, Dallas, 1981-85, mem., 1986-89; ptnr. Krage & Jarvey, LLP, Dallas, 1989—. Author: Partnership Taxation in Theory and Practice, 1991-95, Advanced Problems in Partnership Taxation, 1992—, Fundamentals of LLC and Partnership Taxation, 1996—, Understanding LLC and Partnership Allocations and Basis, 1996—, Real Estate and Tax Deferred Exchanges, 1996-99, Tax Planning for Real Estate and Small Business, 2004—. Mem. ABA (taxation sect.), Tex. Bar Assn. (tax exempt orgn. subcom. taxation sect. 1986-87), Fla. Bar Assn., Dallas Bar Assn., Coll. State Bar Tex., Tex. Soc. CPAs, Order of Coif, Phi Kappa Phi. Republican. Episcopalian. Office Phone: 214-969-7500. Business E-Mail: ccdavis@kjllp.com.

DAVIS, CLARICE MCDONALD, lawyer; b. New Orleans, Jan. 20, 1941; d. James A. and Helen J. (Ross) McDonald. BA cum laude, U. Tex., 1962, MA, 1964; JD magna cum laude, So. Meth. U., 1968. Bar: Tex. 1969, U.S. Dist. Ct. (no. dist.) Tex. 1970, U.S. Ct. Appeals (5th cir.) 1971, U.S. Supreme Ct. 1973. Law clk. to presiding justice U.S. Ct. Appeals (5th cir.), Dallas, 1969-71; ptnr. Akin, Gump, Strauss, Hauer & Feld LLP, Dallas, 1971—, gen. counsel. Comments editor Southwestern Law Jour., 1967-68; instr. Southern Methodist Univ. Sch. of Law, 1968-69. Bd. visitors So. Meth. U., Dallas, 1979-82, v.p. Law Sch. Alumni Adv. Coun., 1992, pres. 1993-94, mem. bd. govs., 1995-98. Avocations: photography, swimming, running, golf. Office: Akin Gump Strauss Hauer & Feld LLP 1700 Pacific Ave Ste 4100 Dallas TX 75201-4675 Office Phone: 214-969-2711. Office Fax: 214-969-4343. Business E-Mail: cdavis@akingump.com.*

DAVIS, CLIVE JAY, record company executive; b. Bklyn., Apr. 4, 1933; s. Herman and Florence (Brooks) Davis; children: Fred, Lauren, Mitchell, Douglas. BA magna cum laude, NYU, 1953; LLB cum laude, Harvard U., 1956. Bar: N.Y. 1957. Assoc. firm Rosenman Colin Freund Lewis & Cohen, N.Y.C., 1958—60; gen. atty. Columbia Records, 1960—65, pres., 1966—73, Arista Records, Inc., N.Y.C., 1974—2000, pres., CEO, 1974—2000; co-founder J Records, 2000—02; chmn., CEO RCA Records, NY, 2002—04, BMG N.Am., 2004—. Author: Clive: Inside the Record Business, 1975. Named Man of Yr., Am. Parkinson Disease, 1972, Record Co. Exec. of Yr., Nat. Assn. TV and Radio Announcers, 1973, Nat. Pop Music Survey, 1974, 1978, 1980, 1984, 1987, 1990—93, Pres. of Yr., Man of Yr., City of Hope, 1978, Man of Yr., Martell Found. for Cancer, Leukemia and AIDS Rsch., 1980, 1985, Humanitarian of Yr., Am. Cancer Soc., 1985; named to, Rock and Roll Hall of Fame, 2000; recipient Humanitarian award, Anti-Defamation League, 1970, Martin Luther King Humanitarian of Yr. award, Congress Racial Equality, 1991, Man of Yr. award, Friars Club Orgn., 1992, Amfar, 1998, Grammy Lifetime Achievement award, 2000. Mem.: Record Industry Assn. Am. (pres., chmn. bd. 1972—73, now dir.). Office: BMG 1540 Broadway New York NY 10036 *Experience has taught me to speak out again and again and, with right on one's side, the voice is eventually heard. Cheers for the reasoned vigilantes in society who prevent those in power from overwhelming the rights of the individual who otherwise cannot surface.*

DAVIS, COLE (COLEMAN DAVIS III), recreational vehicle manufacturing executive; CEO, chmn. Keystone RV, Goshen, Ind. Recipient INC 500 award, INC Mag., 2000. Office: Keystone RV 17400 Hackberry Dr Goshen IN 46526

DAVIS, CONNIE JO, instructional designer; m. Mitchell H. Davis, Feb. 29, 1992. BA, Ea. Ill. U., 2004. Corp. bookkeeper Steak n Shake, Bloomington, Ill., 1977—79; sr. instrnl. designer State Farm Ins. Co., Bloomington, 1979—. Com. chair Eureka Christian Ch., Ill., deacon, 1992—2005. Office Phone: 309-766-0586.

DAVIS, CONNIE WATERS, public relations executive, marketing professional; b. Gainesville, Ga., July 3, 1948; d. Starling Randolph and Evelyn Jeanette (Bonds) Waters; m. John W. Davis Jr., Sept. 24, 1971; 1 child, John Christopher. AA, Gainesville Jr. Coll., 1968; BA in Human Resources Mgmt., Brenau U., 1988; postgrad., Student Evaluation Inst. of Washington, 1988, U. Ga., 1972-73, 85—. Project evaluator Model Cities Program, Gainesville, 1970-74; pers. dir. Lanier Pk. Hosp., Gainesville, 1977-79; asst. dir. Ga. Mountains Ctr., Gainesville, 1979-83; owner, CEO Models by Davis and Davis, Gainesville, 1979—; dir. pub. rels. and sales Ramada Hotel, Gainesville, 1985—; dir. corp. devel. Chestatee Regional Hosp. Dir. Fashion Works, Gainesville; pres. Davis Consulting; owner & pres. Tastefully & Properly Growing Up, 1998—; cons. pub. rels. and mktg., dir. of pub. rels. UP Corp. Devel. Specialty Clinics Ga. Prodr., writer, implementor Gracefully and Properly Growing Up; contbr. articles to mags. and newsletters; writer nat. poulty industry publ., 1990, 95. Publicity chmn. Cancer Soc., 1982, 83, 85; mem. Theatre Wings and Arts Coun.; bd. dirs., mem. mktg. com. Gainesville Jr. Coll., 1985—, trustee, 1995—; bd. dirs. ARC, 1978-79; co-chmn. Flag Com. for Olympics; bd. dirs. Greater-Hall C. of C., 2003—. Recipient Peach award Lions Club, 1979, Vol. award ARC, 1978, various modeling awards So. Models Assn., 1983, 2 Silver Shovel award 1993, 94, state vol. award, 1995; named Best Dressed Woman, Fashion Tour Group, 1984. Mem. Am. Heart Assn. (pres. 1995-96), Am. Lung Assn. (state bd. dirs., Vol. of Yr.), Greater Hall C. of C. (bd. dirs.), Gainesville C. of C., Gainesville Coll. Exec. Coun., Tourism and Conv. Bur. (chmn. 1983-84), N.E. Ga. Advt. Club, Pers. Adminstrs. Group, Ga. Hospitality and Travel Assn., Phoenix Soc., Greater Hall C. of C. (bd. dirs. 2003-), Rotary (cotillion dir. 1998—), Fashion Club (bd. dirs.). Avocations: exercising, skiing, boating, jogging, writing, music, arts. Home: 1214 Chestatee Rd Gainesville GA 30501-2816

DAVIS, CRAIG ANDERSON, secondary school educator; b. St. Augustine, Fla., July 15, 1969; s. Terrell Gene and Cornelia Rosalie Davis; m. Ellen Michelle Burke, Aug. 10, 1996; children: Autumn Leigh, Anderson Phillip. AA, St. John's River Cmty. Coll., 1995; student in English, U. North Fla., 1998, BA in English, 2002; MEd in ednl. leadership, 2002. Police officer St. Augustine, Fla., 1990—91; police officer, dep. sheriff St. John's County Sheriff's Office, St. Augustine, 1989—90, 1991—93; acct. Davis & Davis, St. Augustine, 1998—99; tchr. of English and humanities Palatka HS, Fla., 1999—2003; pre-doctoral fellow U. Fla., Coll. Edn., 2003—. Co-chair for fundraising March of Dimes, 2001—03. Alumni fellowship, U. Fla., 2003. Mem.: Am. Ednl. Rsch. Assn., Phi Delta Kappa. Avocations: reading, exercise. Business E-Mail: cadavis@se.rr.com.

DAVIS, CRAIG WOODS, plastic surgeon; b. Salt Lake City, Nov. 16, 1941; s. Elmer David and Charlene (Woods) Davis; m. Robyn Thorpe Davis; children: Matthew, Michelle, Mark, Monique. BS, U. Utah, 1965, MD, 1969; gen. surgery residency (hon.), Duke U., 1974; plastic surgery residency (hon.), U. Ariz., 1976. Plastic surgeon Pvt. Practice, Salt Lake City, 1974—. Oil and water color, over 150 paintings of wildlife and figures, 1995—. Cleft lip repair team Operation Smile, Philippines, 1990—94; alumni bd. U. Utah, Salt Lake City, 2002—04; missionary LDS Ch., New Zealand, 1960—63. Mjr. USAR, 1965—74. Recipient Gold, Silver and Bronze medals, World Sr. Games Bicycle Racing and Golf, 1991—2004. Mem.: Utah Med. Assn., Am. Bd. Plastic Surgeons. Avocations: golf, tennis, bicycling, art, travel. Home: 6614 S Old Mill Cir Salt Lake City UT 84121 Office Phone: 801-261-2351. Office Fax: 801-265-0425.

DAVIS, CRISPIN, publishing company executive; b. Mar. 19, 1949; Asst. brand mgr. Procter & Gamble, 1970—78, mktg. dir. U.K. ops., v.p. U.S. food ops., 1978—90; mng. dir. European ops. United Distillers, 1990—92, group mng. dir., bd. mem. Guinness (parent co.) Edinburgh (Scotland), London, 1992—94; CEO Aegis Group plc, London, 1994—99; exec. chmn. Reed Elsevier NV, Amsterdam, 1999—2000; co-chmn. Reed Elsevier plc, London, 1999—2000; CEO Reed Elsevier plc, Reed Elsevier NV, Reed Elsevier PLC, 1999—. Office: Reed Elsevier NV 25 Victoria St London SW1H 0EX England E-mail: crispin.davis@reedelsevier.co.uk.*

DAVIS, CYNTHIA JEANNE, academic administrator; b. Wheeling, W.Va., Feb. 27, 1948; d. Albert and Lois (Munn) Shriver; m. Charles B. Davis, Oct. 21, 1969 (dec. Aug. 1989); 1 child, Katya. BS in Biology, U. Ala., 1978. Adminstr. learning mus. program Carnegie Mus. Natural History, Pitts., 1978-79; adminstr. Pitts. NMR Ctr. for biomed. rsch. Carnegie Mellon U., 1979-93, bus. mgr. dept. biol. scis., 1993—. Med. adv. Pitts. Action Against Rape. Mem. Soc. for Rsch. Adminstrs., West Pa. Bot. Soc. Democrat. Avocations: reading, travel. Home: 700 Bellwood Dr Pittsburgh PA 15229-2186 Office: Carnegie Mellon U 4400 5th Ave Pittsburgh PA 15213-2617 Office Phone: 412-268-8086. Business E-Mail: cd25@andrew.cmu.edu.

DAVIS, D. SCOTT, corporate financial executive; b. Oreg. BS in Fin., Portland State U.; advanced mgmt. program, Wharton Sch. Bus., U. Pa. CPA. CEO Overseas Ptnrs., Ltd., 1998—2000; CFO, then CEO, II Morrow UPS, 1986—91, various positions, 1991—98, v.p. fin., 2000—01, sr. v.p., CFO, treas. Atlanta, 2001—. Bd. dir. Honeywell Internat., 2005—; dir. Fed. Res. Bank of Atlanta. Mem. fin. coun. Ga. Coun. Econ. Edn. Office: UPS Corp Hdqrs 55 Glenlake Pkwy NE Atlanta GA 30328

DAVIS, DANNY K., congressman; b. Parkdale, Ark., Sept. 6, 1941; m. Vera Davis; children: Jonathon, Stacey BA, Ark. A. M. & N. Coll., 1961; MA, Chgo. State U., 1968; PhD, Union Inst., 1977. Mem. U.S. Congress from 7th Ill. dist., 1997—; mem. com. on govt. reform and oversight, com. on small bus.; mem. subcom. of census; mem. com. on edn. & workforce. Chgo. alderman, 1979-90; commr. Cook. County, 1990-96; candidate Chgo. mayor, 1991; founder, pres. Westside Assn. for Community Action; pres. Nat. Assn. Community Health Ctrs.; co-chmn. Clinton/Gore/Moseley-Braun Ill. campaigns, 1992; bd. dirs. Nat. Housing Partnership. Democrat. Office: 3333 W Arthington St Ste 130 Chicago IL 60624-4102 also: 1526 Longworth Bldg Washington DC 20515-1307 Office Phone: 202-225-5006.

DAVIS, DARRELL L., retired automotive executive; b. Sharon, Pa., Aug. 8, 1939; s. Paul Darrell and Dorothy Jane (Snyder) D.; m. Jacqueline Donna Pain, July 18, 1986; children: Paul Darrell II, Robert Tod. BS, Youngstown State U., 1963; cert. Stanford Exec. Program, Stanford U., 1987; cert. Global Leadership Program, U. Mich., 1993. Svc. rep., warranty mgr., dist. mgr., asst. zone mgr. Chrysler Motors Corp., Orlando, Fla., 1966-77, zone mgr. Omaha, 1977-78, Troy, Mich., 1978-79, nat. distbn. mgr., regional mgr., gen. mgr. import export ops., gen. sales mgr. Detroit, 1979-88; pres., chief exec. officer Alfa Romeo Distbrs. N. Am., Orlando, 1988-91; gen. sales mgr. Chrysler Corp., Orange, Calif., 1991-93; v.p. Chrysler Internat. Corp., Detroit, 1993-95; gen. mgr. Europe Chrysler Corp., Detroit, 1993-95; pres., COO Chrysler Fin. Corp., Southfield, Mich., 1995-97, chmn., CEO, 1997-98; v.p. Chrysler Corp., 1997—98; sr. v.p. Daimler Chrysler Corp., 1998—2001; bd. mgmt. Daimler Chrysler Svcs. AG, 1999—2000; CEO Daimler Chrysler Fin. Svcs. N.Am., LLC, 1999-2000; sr. v.p., gen. mgr. global svc. and parts divsn. Daimler Chrysler Corp., 2000—01, ret., 2001. Hon. judge Pebble Beach Concours d'Elegance, Meadowbrook Concours d'Elegance; bd. dirs. Boys and Girls Clubs of S.E. Mich., 1998—2001, Walter P. Chrysler Mus., 2001—; bd. advisors Beeghly Coll. of Edn., Youngstown State U., Ohio, 2004—. Lt. U.S. Army, 1963—65. Mem.: Classic Car Club Am. (treas. Fla. region 2001—). Republican. Avocations: auto collecting, American history. Office Phone: 407-330-9100. Personal E-mail: ddavis8839@aol.com.

DAVIS, DAVID BRION, historian, educator; b. Denver, Feb. 16, 1927; s. Clyde Brion and Martha (Wirt) Davis; m. Toni Lisa Hahn, Sept. 9, 1971; children: Adam Jeffrey, Noah Benjamin;children from previous marriage: Jeremiah Jonathan, Martha Elizabeth, Sarah Brion. AB summa cum laude, Dartmouth Coll., 1950, LittD, 1977; AM, Harvard, 1953, PhD, 1956; MA, Oxford U., 1969; LHD, U. New Haven, 1986; LittD, Columbia U., 1999. Scheduler Cessna Aircraft Co., Wichita, Kans., 1950-51; instr. history Dartmouth U., 1953-54; mem. faculty Cornell U., 1955-69, prof., 1963-69, Ernest I. White prof. history, 1964-69; prof. Yale U., 1969—2001, Farnam prof. history, 1972-78, Sterling prof. history, 1978—2001, Sterling prof. emeritus, 2001—, assoc. dir. Nat. Humanities Inst., 1975, dir. Gilder Lehrman Ctr. Study Slavery Resistance Abolition, 1998—2004, dir. emeritus, 2004—. Tchr. summer course Gilder-Lehrman Inst., 1994-2000; John Hope Franklin lectr. Adelphi Coll., 1995; Paley lectr. Hebrew U., Jerusalem, 1995, Taft lectr. U. Cin., 1996, Byrn lectr. Vanderbilt U., 1996, Keynote lectr. U. Chgo., 1997, Wachova lectr. Coll. of Charleston, 1997, Keynote lectr. Rutgers U., 1997, Maisel lectr. Cornell U., 1998, Popkin lectr. UCLA, 1999, Jefferson lectr. U. Cal., Berkeley, 2004; Conferences with Distinguished histoirans U. Houston, 2000, 2001; lectr. Black History Month Coll. Charleston, Commentator on Muslim-Christian mutual enslavement, American Historical Assn., 2001, Tercentennial Symposium Yale U., 2001, Hart lectr. Pomona Coll., 2001, Nathan I. Huggins lectr. Harvard U., 2002, After dinner lectr., Libr. Congress Civil War Sypusium, 2002; keynote lectr. conf. on global slavery Emory U., 2003, N.Y. Pub. Libr., 2003, N.Y. Hist. Assn., 2004, Nantucket Hist. Assn., 2004; Jefferson lectr. U. Calif., Berkeley, 2004. Author: Homicide in American Fiction, 1790-1860, A Study in Social Values, 1957, The Problem of Slavery in Western Culture, 1966, rev. edit., 1988, Italian/Spanish trans., Portuguese trans., 2001, The Slave Power Conspiracy and the Paranoid Style, 1969, The Problem of Slavery in the Age of Revolution, 1770-1823, 1975, rev. edit. 1999, Slavery and Human Progress, 1984, From Homicide to Slavery: Studies in American Culture, 1986, Revolutions: Reflections on American Equality and Foreign Liberations, 1990 (German trans.), In the Image of God: Religion, Moral Values, and Our Heritage of Slavery, 2001, Challenging the Boundaries of Slavery, 2003; co-author: The Great Republic, 1977, 4th edit., 1992, The Antislavery Debate, 1992; editor: Ante-Bellum Reform, 1967, The Fear of Conspiracy, 1971, Ante-Bellum American Culture: An Interpretive Anthology, 1979, 97; contbg. author: The Stature of Theodore Dreiser, edit. Kazin, 1955, The Province of Pose, edit. Keast and Streeter, 1956, Why Man Takes Chances, edit. Klausner, 1968, Surveillance and Espionage in a Free Society, edit. Blum, 1972, Perspectives and Irony in America Slavery, edit. Owens, 1976, The American Family: Dying or Developing, edit. Reiss and Huffman, 1979, Slavery and Freedom in the Age of the American Revolution, edit. Berlin and Hoffman, 1983, British Caplitism and Carribean Slavery, edit. Solow and Eagerman, 1987, Lincoln, the War President, edit. Boritt, 1992; co-editor: The Boisterous Sea of Liberty: A Documentary History of America From Discovery Through the Civil War, 1998; contbg. author Essays in Slavery, Secession, and Southern History, ed., Paquette and Ferlinger, 2000, American Places: Encounters with History: America's Leading Historians Talk about the Sites Where the Past Comes Alive for Them, ed. Leuchtenberg, 2000; contbr. N.Y. Review of Books; co-curator nat. libr. exhibit Free at Last: A History of the Abolition of Slavery in America. Mem. subcom. internal security Dem. Nat. Policy Coun., Pulitzer Prize Com., 1968, Bancroft Prize Com., 1989; co-chair adv. bd. Gilder-Lehrman Inst. Am. History, 1995—. With AUS, 1945-46. Recipient Anisfield Wolf award in race relations, 1967, Pulitzer prize for nonfiction, 1967, Mass Media award NCCJ, 1967, Bancroft prize, 1976, Nat. Book award for history and biography, 1976, Presdl. medal Dartmouth Coll., 1991, Kidger award Improving Tchg. History in New Eng., 2004; Guggenheim fellow, 1958-59; Fulbright grantee, 1980; NEH fellow, 1983-84, Gilder-Lehrman Inaugural fellow, 1996-97. Fellow Am. Acad. Arts and Scis., Brit. Acad. (corr.); mem. Am. Philos. Soc. (adminstrv. bd. Benjamin Franklin papers), Mass. Hist Soc., Am. Hist. Assn. (Albert J. Beveridge award 1975), Inst. Early Am. History and Culture (coun. 1976-79), Am. Antiquarian Soc., Soc. Am. Historians (Bruce Catton prize for lifetime achievement 2004), Orgn. Am. Historians (pres. 1988-89, chair Frederick Jackson Turner award com. 1989, Lincoln prize com. 1992), Milan Group in Early U.S. Hist. Jewish. Home: 733 Lambert Rd Orange CT 06477-1806 Business E-Mail: david.b.davis@yale.edu.

DAVIS, DAVID HOWARD, political science professor; b. Washington, Sept. 14, 1941; s. Dorland J. and Caroline (Baker) D.; m. Laura F. Davis (div.); children: Gregory, Jillian. AB, Cornell U., 1969; MA, Johns Hopkins U., PhD, 1971. Asst. prof. Rutgers U., New Brunswick, N.J., 1971-77; assoc. prof. Cornell U., Ithaca, N.Y., 1977-78; analyst Congl. Rsch. Svc., Libr. Congress, Washington, 1979-80; spl. asst., acting dep. asst. sec. energy and minerals U.S. Dept. Interior, Washington, 1980-81; sr. assoc. cons. Internat. Energy Assocs. Ltd., Washington, 1981-84; assoc. prof. U. Wyo., Laramie, 1984-89; prof. U. Toledo, 1989—, dir. MPA program, 1989-92. Author: How the Bureaucracy Makes Foreign Policy, 1972, Energy Politics, 1992. American Environmental Politics, 1998; editor: Social Sci. Jour., 1986-89. Served to capt. U.S. Army, 1964-67, Vietnam, Korea. Mem.: Am. Soc. Pub. Adminstrn. Episcopalian. Office: U Toledo Dept Polit Sci and Pub Adminstrn Toledo OH 43606 Office Phone: 419-530-2360. Business E-Mail: david.davis@utoledo.edu.

DAVIS, DAVID M., air transportation executive; MBA in fin., BS in aerospace engring., U. Minn. Dir. fin. customer svc. divsn. Delta Airlines; v.p. fin. planning and budget analysis Budget Group Inc., 2000—02; v.p. fin. planning and analysis US Airways Group Inc., 2002—04, exec. v.p. fin., 2004—, CFO, 2004—. Office: US Airways Group Inc 2345 Crystal Dr Arlington VA 22227

DAVIS, DAVID OLIVER, radiologist, educator; b. Danville, Ill., June 25, 1933; s. Oliver and Anna Marie (Collignon) D.; m. Agnes Layden, Dec. 26, 1955; children: Karen, Kathy, Diane, Janet, Nancy. BS, U. Ill., 1954; MD, St. Louis U., 1958. Diplomate Am. Bd. Radiology. Intern Starkloff Meml. Hosp., St. Louis, 1958-59; resident USPHS Hosp., S.I., N.Y., 1959-61, Columbia Presbyn. Med. Ctr., N.Y.C., 1962-63; asst. prof. radiology Washington U., St. Louis, 1966-68, assoc. prof., 1968-70; prof. U. Utah, 1970-72, George Washington U., 1972—, prof. neurology, 1977—, chmn. dept. radiology, 1978-82, 91-96, prof. neurosurgery, 1985—. Vis. prof. U. Calif., San Francisco, 1985; cons. UCLA, 1995-96, UNS; sec.-gen. 12th Internat. Symposium on Neuroradiology. Editor: Principles of Diagnostic Radiology, 1971, Reconstruction Tomography in Diagnostic Radiology and Nuclear Medicine, 1977; mem. editl. bd. Jour. Computer Assisted Tomography, 1977-88, Am. Jour. Neuroradiology, 1979-90, Neuroradiology, 1971-80; mem. editl. exec com. Jour. Investigative Radiology, 1971-80. With USPHS, 1959-64. Recipient Golden Apple award George Washington U., 2000; NIH spl. fellow, 1964-66. Fellow Am. Coll. Radiology (mem. coun. steering com. 1992-94, mem. bd. chancellors 1994-99), Am. Heart Assn. (stroke coun.); mem. AMA, Am. Soc. Neuroradiology (sec. 1971-74, pres. 1979-80, chmn. publs. com. 1988-92, counselor 1992-94, Gold medal 2002), D.C. Med. Soc., D.C. Radiol. Soc. (pres. 1983-84, counselor 1985-91), Assn. Univ. Radiologists, 1973-1990, Soc. Chmn. Acad. Radiology Depts. (sec.-treas. 1981-83), Acad. Radiology Rsch. (bd. dirs. 1994-99), Internat. Microcirculation Soc., Blue Grass Radiology Soc. (hon.), Radiol. Soc. N.Am., Am. Roentgen Ray Soc. (mem. exec. coun. 1992-95, alt. del. to AMA 1995-99, del. 1999-2000), North Pacific Soc. Neurology and Psychiatry (hon.), Am. Head and Neck Radiology, Phila. Roentgen Soc. (hon.), Western Neuroradiology Soc., Am. Soc. Spine Radiology Splty. and Svcs. Soc., Alpha Omega Alpha. Office: George Washington U Med Ctr Dept Radiology 900 23rd St NW Washington DC 20037 Office Phone: 703-508-3200. E-mail: daveandagnes@yahoo.com.

DAVIS, DEMPSIE AUGUSTUS, military officer, educator, financial planner; b. Roebuck, S.C., Oct. 11, 1929; s. Dempsie Augustus and Hontas (Frey) D.; m. Sally Frey, Mar. 5, 1956; children: Elizabeth, Peggy, Dempsie. Student, Primary Armament Sch. Air Tng. Command, Lowry AFB, Colo., 1948; BS, U.S. Mil. Acad., 1955; Edn. with Industry, A.F. Inst. Tech., 1961; MS in Bus. Econ., Clairmont Coll., 1969; diploma in nat. security mgmt., Indsl. Coll., 1973. Small arms tng. instr. USAF, 1946, N.C.O. in charge skeet range and tng. Lakeland AFB, Tex., 1946—48, chief fire control sys. sect. 3525th Aircraft Gunnery Squadron Nellis AFB, Nev., 1948—51, commd. 2d lt., 1955, advanced through grades to col., 1978; served as maintenance officer and test support pilot USAF Spl. Weapons Detachment, Nev., 1967-69; project officer Sci. Advisors Office, Mil. Assistance Command Vietnam, Saigon, Vietnam, 1969-70; systems mgr. USAF Air Logistics Ctr., Warner Robins AFB, Ga., 1970-72; chief F-15 logistics evaluation USAF, Edwards AFB, Calif., 1972-75, dir. flight test evaluation, 1975-77; dir. Joint Acquisition Logistics, Eglin AFB, Fla., 1977-79; ret. USAF, 1979; sr. engring. mgr. Westinghouse, Balt., 1981-82; fin. cons., prof. U. S.C., Spartanburg, S.C., 1982-90; sports shooting, gun safety and exhbn. shooting instr. Spartanburg, 1999—; tchr., video prodr., 1990-99. Decorated Legion of Merit, Bronze Star, Meritorious Service medal, Air medal, Joint Svcs. Commendation medal, Air Force Commendation medal; recipient Leading Skeet award Nat. Skeet Shooting Assn., San Antonio, 1958. Mem. Nat. Sporting Clays Assn. (life), NRA (life, Disting. Expert 1964), Quail Unltd. (charter), Ducks Unltd., Masons (32 degree). Avocations: upland hunting, clay shooting, reading, handball, travel.

DAVIS, DIANE ARLENE (DIANE A. DAVIS), architect, energy and environmental civil engineer, educator, writer; d. George Harry Jr. and Mary Jane (End) Davis. ASID, Art Inst. of Pitts., 1968; BFA, N.Y. Inst. of Tech., N.Y.C., 1982; BArch, Pratt Inst., Bklyn., 1986; MS, N.Y. Inst. of Tech., LI, 2002; post grad. fellow, U. Pa., Phila., 1990—92. Cert. tchr. SUNY Albany, 2001. Prin. profl. Diane Davis & Assoc., N.Y.C., 1979—87; architect Roberta Washington Architects, N.Y.C., 1997—98, URS Engrs./Architects/Planners/Scientists/Constrn. Mgrs, Wayne, NJ, 1999—2000; mgr. tech. rsch. and specifications dept. STV Engrs./Architects/Planners/Scientists/Constrn. Mgrs, 2000—01; prin. profl. CUSTOMDESIGNSPECS, NYC, 1999—. Founder and dir. Inst. for Fusion Energy, N.Y.C., 1989—; founder, exec. dir. Mercy Mission Found. for Children Orphaned by HIV/AIDS; adj. faculty Drake Bus. Sch. Manhattan, 1997—2001; cons. ASTM, Phila., 2000—; guest lectr. Carnegie-Mellon U. Sch. Architecture, Pitts., 2004. Contbr. articles to profl. jours. Vol. emergency room Cabrini Hosp. and Tchg. Ctr., N.Y.C., 1987—88; activist for pub. edn.; founder Mercy Mission Found.; team leader Rep. Party, Oakmont, Pa., 2003—04. Tchg. grant, City of Phila., 1994—95. Mem.: AIA, Am. Concrete Inst., Constrn. Specifications Inst., Am. Soc. of Testing Materials, Assn. of Energy Engrs., Nu Epsilon Tau. Office: Inst for Fusion Energy Edn PO Box 628 Grand Ctrl Sta New York NY 10163 also: Custom Design Specs Ste 1431 250 W 57 St Ste 1431 New York NY 10107 Personal E-mail: archiatrix@yahoo.com. Business E-Mail: customdesignspecs@yahoo.com. E-mail: mercymission@spreadtheword.com.

DAVIS, DIANNE, music educator; b. Cleve. d. Lee Frederick and Mary Kate McQueen; 1 child from previous marriage, Travis. BS in Music Edn., Ky. State U., 1966. Cert. Ohio Bd. Edn. Vocal music tchr., Gary, Ind., 1966—68; vocal instr. Cleve. Music Sch. Settlement, 1977—82; dir. Sanaa Music Sch., Cleve., 1982—, Music Inc., Cleve., 1991—; vocal music tchr. East Cleveland City Schs., 1997—. Bd. dirs. The Cleve. Fine Arts Soc., 1995. Mem.: Ohio Edn. Assn., Music Educators Nat. Conf., Alpha Kappa Alpha. Baptist. Avocations: cooking, designing, home remodeling, gardening, entertaining. Home: 24412 Emery Rd Cleveland OH 44128 Office: East Cleveland City Schs 15320 Euclid Ave East Cleveland OH 44112 Personal E-mail: diannedavis@msn.com.

DAVIS, DON D., III, writer, lawyer; b. Hollywood, Calif., Aug. 14, 1970; s. Donald D. and Miriam S. D. Ba, U. Calif., Santa Barbara, 1992; MA, San Francisco State U., 1995; JD, Tulane U., 1998. Bar: Calif. Author: There Is No Magic, 1995. Avocations: travel, skiing, literature, theater, film. E-mail: threediii@gci.net.

DAVIS, DON H., JR., multi-industry high-technology company executive; Engring. sales trainee Allen-Bradley (aquired by Rockwell 1985), 1963-66, dist. mgr. Birmingham, Ala., 1966-79, gen. mgr. programmable contr. divsn., 1979-80, v.p. programmable contr. divsn., 1980-82, v.p., gen. mgr. indsl. control divsn., 1982-85, sr. v.p., 1985-86, head indsl. control group, 1986-87, sr. v.p., gen. mgr. indsl. computer and comm. group, 1987-89, pres., 1989-93, corp. sr. v.p., pres. automation, 1993-95, pres., COO, 1995-97, pres., CEO, 1997-98; chmn., CEO Rockwell Automation, Inc., 1998—2004, chmn., 2004—. Bd. dirs. Sybron Internat., Ingram Micro, Inc. Nat. trustee Boys and Girls Clubs Am.; chmn. bd. L.A. Mfg. Learning Ctr.; regent Milw. Sch. Engring. Mem. Internat. Soc. for Measurement and Control (hon. chmn.), Nat. Elec. Mfrs. Assn. (past chmn. bd. govs.), Bus. Roundtable, The Conf. Bd. (sr.). Office: Rockwell Internat Corp 777 E Wisconsin Ave Ste 1400 Milwaukee WI 53202-5302

DAVIS, DON LAWRENCE, lawyer; b. San Antonio, Oct. 30, 1939; s. A.F. and Esther Davis; m. Patricia Ann Davis, May 6, 1960; children: Dana Leslie, Derek Lawrence. BS, Abilene Christian Coll., 1962; LLB, U. Tex., 1965. Bar: Tex., Colo., U.S. Dist. Ct. (we. dist.) Tex., U.S. Ct. Appeals (5th, 9th and 11th cirs.), U.S. Supreme Ct. Briefing atty. Supreme Ct. Tex., Austin, 1965—66; ptnr. Byrd, Davis, Eisenberg, Walter & Furman, Austin, 1967—. Editor: legal articles; sculpture, Children's Hosp. of Austin, PGA of Am. Chmn. Austin Smiles, Tex., 1980—85. Fellow: Tex. Bar Found., Am. Bar Found.; mem.: Fed. Bar Assn. Democrat. Mem. Ch. Of Christ. Home: 3917 Balcones Dr Austin TX 78731 Office: Byrd Davis Eisenberg Walter & Furman 707 W 34th Austin TX 78705 E-mail: dondavis@byrddavis.com.

DAVIS, DONALD A., music educator; b. New Brighton, Pa., Nov. 2, 1978; s. Donald and Bonnie Davis; m. Theresa Ann Faltenovich, Nov. 23, 2002. BS in Edn., Ind. U. of Pa., 2001. Cert. tchr. Va. Woodwind instr. New Brighton H.S., 1999—2001; dir. of bands Matoaca H.S., Chesterfield, Va., 2002—. Tenor sax player Matoaca H.S. Show Choir, 2004—. Mem.: Music Educators Nat. Conf., Va. Band and Orch. Dirs. Assn., Phi Mu Alpha. Office: Matoaca HS 17700 Longhouse Ln Chesterfield VA 23838 Office Phone: 804-590-3108. Personal E-mail: donald_davis@ccpsnet.net.

DAVIS, DONALD ALAN, news correspondent, writer, lecturer; b. Savannah, Ga., Oct. 5, 1939; s. Oden Harry and Irma Artice (Gay) Davis; m. Robin Murphy, Mar. 17, 1983 (dec. May 11, 2005); children from previous marriage: Russell Glenn, Randall Scott. BA in Journalism, U. Ga., 1962. Reporter Athens (Ga.) Banner-Herald, 1961-62, Savannah Morning News, 1962; with UPI, 1963-65, 1967-83, Vietnam corr., 1971-73, New Eng. editor, 1977-80, White House corr., 1981-83; reporter, editor St. Petersburg (Fla.) Times, 1965-66; polit. reporter, columnist San Diego Union, 1983-91; pub. Pacific Rim Report newsletter, 1985-88. Instr. journalism Boston U., 1979; instr. writing U. Colo., 1998-99; lectr. U.S. Naval War Coll., 1983, Queen Elizabeth 2, 1991. Author: The Milwaukee Murders, 1991, The Nanny Murder Trial, 1992, Bad Blood, 1994, Death of an Angel, 1994, Fallen Hero, 1994, Appointment with the Squire, 1995, Death Cruise, 1996, A Father's Rage, 1996, The Gris-Gris Man, 1997, Hush, Little Babies, 1997, The Last Man on the Moon, 1999, JonBenet, 2000, Dark Waters, 2002, Lightning Strike, 2005, Shooter, 2005. Fellow Keizai Koho Ctr., Tokyo, 1985, Overseas Press Club, 2000. Unitarian. Home: 2201 S County Rd 23E Berthoud CO 80513 E-mail: tedsalad@mesanetworks.net.

DAVIS, DONALD GORDON, JR., librarian, educator, historian; b. San Marcos, Tex., Aug. 15, 1939; s. Donald Gordon and Ethel Dorothy (Hemmel) D.; m. Avis Jane Higdon, Dec. 6, 1969; children: Lucinda Ellen, Samuel Higdon, Caroline Louise. BA, UCLA, 1961; MA, U. Calif., Berkeley, 1963, MLS, 1964; PhD, U. Ill., 1972; MA in Theol. Studies, Austin Presbyn. Theol. Sem., 1996. Adminstrv. asst. Biola Coll. Libr., La Mirada, Calif., 1961-62; sr. libr. asst. U. Calif., Berkeley, 1961-64; sr. reference libr. Fresno State Coll. Libr., 1964-68, head dept. spl. collections, 1966-68; asst. prof. libr. sci. U. Tex., Austin, 1971-77, assoc. prof., 1977-86, prof., 1986—, assoc. dean Grad. Sch. Libr. and Info. Sci., 2000—02, prof. dept. history, 1998—. Bd. dirs., v.p. Logos Bookstore, Austin, Tex., 1974—80; vis. prin. lectr. Birmingham Poly., England, 1980—81; coord. Libr. History Seminars VI, Austin, Tex., 1980, Ann. Tex. Libr. History Colloquium, 1982—97, Libr. History Seminars VII, Chapel Hill, NC, 1985, Libr. History Seminars VIII, Bloomington, Ind., 1990, Tex. Group Study Books, Print Culture, 1995—; mem. planning com. Libr. History Seminar IX, 1995, Libr. History Seminar X, 2000. Author: The Association of American Library Schools, 1915-68, 1974, Reference Books in the Social Sciences and Humanities, 1977, American Library History: A Bibliography, 1978, ARBA Guide to Library Science Literature, 1970-83, 1987, American Library History: A Comprehensive Guide to the Literature, 1989, Encyclopedia of Library History, 1994, Librarianship and Library Science in India: An Outline of Historical Perspectives, 1994, Library History Research in America, 2000; editor: Librararies and Culture: Proc. of Library History Seminar VI, 1981, Libraries, Books and Culture: Proc. of Library History Seminar VII, 1986, History of Library and Information Science Education: Library Trends, 1986, Reading and Libraries, proc. of Library History Seminar VIII, 1991, Libraries and Philanthropy, Proc. of Libr. History Seminar IX, 1996, Libraries and Culture jour., 1976—, Handbooks of Texas Libraries, 2000, Winsor, Dewey and Putnam: The Boston Experience, 2002, A Bibliography of Texas Library History, 1695-2000, 2002, A Chronology of Texas Library History, 1685-2000, 2002, Dictionary of American Library Biography, supplement, 2003; mem. editl. bd. America: History and Life, 1979—. Annual Bibliography of the History of the Printed Book and Libraries, 1994—, Library History (UK), 1998—; contbr. articles to profl. jours. Pres. PTA Robert E. Lee Sch., Austin, Tex., 1979—80; asst. scoutmaster local troop Boy Scouts Am., 1987—91; mem. adv. bd. Am. History and Life, 1979—, Hertiage Soc., 1987—92; v.p. Hyde Park Neighborhood Assn., 1983—84; active mem. USA, USSR Citizens Dialogue, Austin, Tex., 1985—93. Named Disting. Alumnus, U. Ill., Urbana, 2004; recipient Tex. Excellence Tchg. award, 1991—92; fellow Newberry Libr. fellow, 1974, John P. Commons Tchg. fellow, 1986—87, Am. Inst. Indian Studies fellow, 1988, John P. Commons Tchg. fellow, 1995, 1998—2000, Alumni Tchg. fellow, GSLIS, 2002—03. Fellow: InterVarsity Christian Fellowship (nat. faculty and grad. student adv. bd. 1990—), Christian Librs., Info. Specialists (exec. com. 1978—87, 1997—2001, assoc. christian leadership denmitries 1999—); mem.: Roundtable of Editors of Libr. Jours. (exec. com. 1978—), Internat. Fedn. Libr. Assns. (exec. com. 1987—), World History Assn., Tex. State Hist. Assn. (program com. 1992), Presbyn. Hist. Soc. S.W., Presbyn. Hist. Soc., Soc. Promoting Christian Knowlege, USA (bd. trustees 1999—), Librarians Christian Fellowship (UK, v.p. 1990—), Orgn. Am. Historians, Tex. Libr. Assn. (program com. archives and local history round table 1997—), Libr. Assn. UK, Hymn Soc. (US, Can.), Conf. Faith and History, Am. Antiquarian Soc. (adv. bd. program in history of book 1987—93), Tex. Ctr. for Book (adv. coun. 1987—), Assn. Bibliography History (exec. bd. 1982—85), Assn. Libr. Info., Sci. Edn., Am. Printing History Assn., ALA (chmn. libr. history round table 1978—79, internat. rels. com. 1988—92, exec. com. internat. rels. roundtable 1990—92, Lifetime Achievement award Libr. History Round Table 2003), Am. Hist. Assn., Book Club Tex., Phi Kappa Phi, Beta Phi Mu (Golden Ann. Disting. award 1999). Presbyn. Home: 706 Harris Ave Austin TX 78705-2518 Office: U Tex Sch of Info 1 University Station D7000 Austin TX 78712-0390 Office Phone: 512-471-3806. Business E-Mail: dgdavis@ischool.utexas.edu.

DAVIS, DONALD MARC, lawyer; b. Phila., May 8, 1952; s. Herman S. Davis and Sandra M. (Margolis) Waltzer; m. Noel M. Justic, June 9, 1979; children: Scott, Keith, Cara. BA, U. Pa., 1974; JD, John Marshall Law Sch., 1978. Bar: Ill. 1978, Pa. 1978, U.S. Dist. Ct. (ea. dist.) Pa. 1978, U.S. Ct. Appeals (3d cir.) 1978. Ptnr. Margolis Edelstein, Phila., 1978—. Mem. ABA, Def. Rsch. Inst., Pa. Assn. Def. Counsel, Phila Bar Assn., Phila Assn. Def. Counsel, Pa. Bar Assn., Temple Inn of Ct. Office: Margolis Edelstein The Curtis Ctr 4th Fl Independence Sq W Philadelphia PA 19106 E-mail: ddavis@margolisedelstein.com.

DAVIS, DONALD RAY, entomologist; b. Oklahoma City, Mar. 28, 1934; s. Esker Arnold and Mildred Louise (Fortson) D.; m. Mignon Marie Bush, Sept. 29, 1972; children: Marisa Marie, Steven Ray. BA, U. Kans., 1956; PhD, Cornell U., 1962. With Smithsonian Instn., Washington, 1961—, assoc. curator, then curator entomology, 1961-76, chmn. dept., 1976-81, curator entomology, 1981—. Contbr. articles to profl. jours. Recipient Smithsonian Instn. Rsch. Found. award, 1966-67, 73-74, Scholarly Studies grantee, 1990-2003, Am. Philos. Soc. grantee, 1963; Rsch. Opportunity awardee, various yrs. Mem. Biol. Soc. Washington (pres. 1984-85), Lepidopterists Soc. (Jordan medal 1977, pres. 1985), Assn. Tropical Biology, Entomol. Soc. Am., Hennig Soc., Nat. Speleological Soc., Soc. Systematic Zoology, Entomol. Soc. Washington (pres. 1979), Washington Biologists Field Club. Office: Smithsonian Instn Entomology NHB 127 PO Box 37012 Washington DC 20013-7012 E-mail: davis.don@nmnh.si.edu. *I believe that life's major goal should be to contribute something of lasting value to earth's diverse heritage. Perhaps the most permanent heritage anyone can bequeath lies in the discovery of new knowledge. By thus enriching our common heritage, I feel that I can partially repay, in my own humble way, for the enormous privilege of having once lived on this fascinating planet.*

DAVIS, DONALD ROBERT, nutritionist, researcher, consultant; b. La Jara, Colo., Mar. 19, 1941; s. Robert Cristopher and Ida Mary (Blissard) D.; m. Vera Elaine Wilson, June 27, 1980 (div. Aug. 15, 1989). Ed., Calif. Inst. Tech., 1962; PhD, UCLA, 1965. Postdoctoral fellow, instr. Calif. Inst. Tech., Pasadena, 1965-67; asst. prof. U. Calif., Irvine, 1967-74; rsch. scientist assoc. U. Tex., Austin, 1974-86, rsch. assoc., 1986—. Mem. bd. trustees Internat. Acad. Nutrition and Preventive Medicine, 1983-85, The Wacker Found., 1987—; dir. Roger J. Williams Nutrition Inst., 1987-90; sr. rsch. cons. Ctr. for Improvement of Human Functioning, Wichita, Kans., 1989—. Editor-in-chief Jour. Applied Nutrition, 1986-91; mem. editl. bds. Jour. Applied Nutrition, 1978—, Jour. Internat. Acad. Preventive Medicine, 1983-85, Jour. Advancement in Medicine, 1997—; contbr. over 45 articles to profl. jours; co-developer nutrient content software, NutriCircles, 1985—. Instr. Lifetime Learning, Austin, 1978—. Recipient Rsch. fellowship NSF, Washington, 1965-67; grantee Found. for Nutritional Advancement, Washington, 1986. Mem.: AAAS, Acad. Orthomolecular Medicine, Am. Coll. Nutrition. Office: Univ Tex Biochem Inst Austin TX 78712 E-mail: d.r.davis@mail.utexas.edu.

DAVIS, DONNA, lawyer; b. Scranton, Pa., May 20, 1960; d. A. Robert and Jeanne T. (Mazzatta) D. BS, U. Scranton, 1982; JD, Temple U., 1985. Bar: Pa. 1985, U.S. Dist. Ct. (mid. dist.) Pa. 1985, U.S. Ct. Appeals (3d cir.) 1987, D.C. 1988. Law clk., sr. staff atty. U.S. Ct. Appeals (3d cir.), Phila., 1984-85; law clk., atty. Superior Ct. of Pa., Wilkes Barre, Pa., 1985-86; assoc. Rosenberg & Ufberg, Scranton, Pa., 1986—. Mem. ABA, Lackawanna County Bar Assn., Pa. Bar Assn., Luzerne County Bar Assn. Avocations: piano, voice. Home: 811 Laurel Creek Dr Dickson City PA 18519-1498 Office: Rosenberg & Ufberg PO Box 423 Dunmore PA 18512-0423

DAVIS, DOROTHY SALISBURY, writer; b. Chgo., Apr. 26, 1916; d. Alfred Joseph and Margaret Jane (Greer) Salisbury; m. Harry Davis, Apr. 25, 1946 (dec.). AB, Barat Coll., Lake Forest, Ill., 1938. Mystery and hist. novelist, short story writer. Author: A Gentle Murderer, 1951, A Town of Masks, 1952, Men of No Property, 1956, Death of an Old Sinner, 1957, A Gentleman Called, 1958, The Evening of the Good Samaritan, 1961, Black Sheep, White Lamb, 1963, The Pale Betrayer, 1965, Enemy and Brother, 1967, God Speed The Night, 1968, Where the Dark Streets Go, 1969, Shock Wave, 1972, The Little Brothers, 1973, A Death in the Life, 1976, Scarlet Night, 1980, A Lullaby of Murder, 1984, Tales for a Stormy Night, 1985, The Habit of Fear, 1987, In the Still of the Night, 2000. Recipient Life Achievement award Bouchereon, 1989. Mem. Authors Guild, Mystery Writers of Am. (former pres., recipient Grand Master award 1985), Adams Roundtable. Home: PO Box 595 Palisades NY 10964-0595

DAVIS, DUANE L., music educator, vocalist; b. Sandusky, Ohio, July 13, 1980; s. David L. and Linda K. (Thomas) Davis; m. Jacqueline M. Taylor, July 24, 2004; children: Edison Daniel children: Destiny Jean. MusB in Music Edn. cum laude, Heidelberg Coll., Tiffin, Ohio, 2003. Cert. K-12 Vocal and Instrumental Music Edn. Ohio State Dept. Edn., 2003, Initial Educator License-Vocal Music Edn. Ind. State Dept. Edn., 2005. Dir. choirs (7-12) West Union HS, Ohio, 2003—04; dir. music (k-2) Bradie M. Shrum Lower Elem. (Salem Cmty. Schools), Ind., 2004—. Camp counselor Show Choir Camps Am., Tiffin, Ohio, 2000—01; student asst. dir. Heidelberg Coll. Singing Collegians Show Choir, Tiffin, 2001—03. Singer: (albums) Heidelberg College Concert Choir; actor, asst. dir.: Fremont Cmty. Theater, Playmakers Civic Theater and Washington County Theater, 1996—2005. Recipient Citizenship Educator award, VFW Salem, Ind., 2005; Don Miller Meml. scholar, Clyde-Green Springs Schs., 1999, Margaret Rae Seiler scholar, Heidelberg Coll. Music Dept., 2001-2003. Mem.: Nat. Edn. Assn./Ind. State Teachers Assn. (com. mem. 2004—05), Am. Guild English Handbell Ringers, Music Edn. Nat. Conf., Alpha Phi Omega (com. mem. 2002—03). R-Liberal. Methodist. Office: Bradie M Shrum Lower Elementary Sch 1105 N Shelby St Salem IN 47167 Office Phone: 812-883-3700. E-mail: ddavis@salemschools.com.

DAVIS, DWIGHT, cardiologist, educator; b. Winston-Salem, N.C., Apr. 11, 1948; s. James C. Davis; m. Lorna Jean Enck, July 30, 1988; 1 child, Nathan James. BS, N.C. A&T State U., 1970; MD, U. Rochester, 1975. Rsch. asst. U. Rochester, N.Y., 1970-71; intern in medicine Boston U. Hosp., 1975-76, resident in medicine, 1976-78; cardiology fellow Duke U. Med. Ctr., Durham, N.C., 1978-81; asst. prof. medicine, cardiology divsn. Pa. State U., Hershey, 1981-87, assoc. prof., 1987-92, disting. lectr., 1986, prof. medicine, 1992—, cardiology dir. heart transplantation, artificial organs and preclinical tchg. program, dir. cardiology preclinical tng. program, 1984—, dir., cardiology fellow tng. program, 1984-87, dir. cardiac catheterization lab., 1987—, med. dir. cardiac rehab. program, 1988—, dir. clin. cardiology program, 1991—, asst. dean for admissions, 1994-99, assoc. dean admissions and student affairs, 1999—. Vice chmn. faculty affairs faculty senate Pa. State U., University Park, 1988—; mem. med. alumni coun. U. Rochester Sch. Medicine and Dentistry, 1992—; various disting. lectureships. Contbr. numerous articles to profl. jours.; editorial reviewer Annals Internal Medicine, 1983—; editorial adv. bd. Primary Cardiology, 1985—. Mem. Pa. Coun. on Aging, Harrisburg, 1989—. Recipient Outstanding Physician award Pa. State U. Sch. Medicine, 1984, Disting. Tchg. awards, 1988-89, Tchr. of Yr. award, 1991, Disting. Prof. award for tchg., 1991, Outstanding Tchr. of Yr. award med. sch. class of 1995, 93, Outstanding Tchr. of Yr. award med. sch. class of 1997, 1995, Alumni Excellence award N.C. A&T State U., 1986, Disting. Alumni award Nat. Assn. Equal Opportunity in Higher Edn., 1987. Fellow Am. Coll. Cardiology, Am. Coll. Angiology; mem. AAAS, Am. Heart Assn. (fellow coun. on clin. cardiology, rsch. com. Pa. affiliate 1992—, pres. elect Pa. affiliate 1997, pres. elect Pa./Del affiliate 1998, Disting. Svc. award Pa. Del. affiliate 2000), Am. Fedn. Clin. Rsch., Am. Assn. Med. Colls. (pres. elect North East group on student affairs 1998), Am. Assn. Cardiovasc. and Pulmonary Rehab. (expert panel cardiac rehab. guidelines project 1992—, chair cardiac rehab. criteria devel. panel 1995—), N.Y. Acad. Scis., Alpha Omega Alpha. Mem. United Ch. of Christ. Achievements include discovery that abnormalities of the sympathetic nervous system in patients with heart failure is due to an increase in norepinephrine spillover and a decrease in norepinephrine clearance from the circulation. Office: Pa State U Coll Medicine Divsn Cardiology PO Box 850 Hershey PA 17033-0850

DAVIS, EARL JAMES, chemical engineering professor; b. St. Paul, July 22, 1934; s. Leo Ernest and Mary (Steiner) D.; children: Molly Kathleen, David Leo. BS cum laude, Gonzaga U., 1956; PhD, U. Wash., 1960. Design engr. Union Carbide Chems. Co., South Charleston, W.Va., 1956; from asst. prof. chem. engring. to assoc. prof. Gonzaga U., Spokane, Wash., 1960-68, dir. computing ctr., 1967-68; rsch. fellow Imperial Coll., London U., 1964-65; assoc. prof. chem. engring. Clarkson U., 1968-73, head socio-environ. program, 1972-74, prof., 1973-78, chmn. chem. engring. dept., 1973-74, assoc. dir. Inst. Colloid and Surface Sci., 1974-78; prof., chmn. chem. and nuclear engring. dept. U. N.Mex., 1978-80; dir. engring. divsn., prof. Inst. Paper Chemistry, Appleton, Wis., 1980-83; rsch. fellow in chem. engring. U. Wash., Seattle, 1957-60, prof. chem. engring., 1983—, assoc. vice provost for rsch., 2001—03. Guest prof. Tech. U. of Vienna, Austria, 2000; sr. scientist, cons. Unilever Rsch. Lab., Port Sunlight, Eng., 1974-75; vis. scholar NAS/Chinese Acad. Scis., China, 1989; adj. prof. Sichuan U., Chengdu, China, 2001—. Assoc. editor Aerosol Sci. and Tech., 1993-97; mem. editl. bd. Jour. Colloid and Interface Sci., 1984-86; mem. editl. bd. Jour. Aerosol Sci., 1992-98, editor-in-chief, 1999—; mem. adv. bd. Surface and Colloid Sci., 2000—; regional editor (N.Am. and S.Am.) Colloid and Polymer Sci., 1994-99; contbr. articles to sci. publs. NSF fellow, 1964-65, grantee, 1963-89, 92—2003; recipient Burlington No. award for rsch., 1988; Leeds and Northrup fellow U. Wash., 1960. Fellow AAAS, mem. AIChE (adminstr. Design Inst. Multiphase Processing 1979-87), Am. Chem. Soc., Am. Assn. Aerosol Rsch. (treas. 1990-92, David Sinclair award 1991, v.p. 1996-97, pres. 1997-98), Soc. Applied Spectroscopy, Gesellschaft für Aerosolforschung, Sigma Xi, Phi Lambda Upsilon. Achievements include research in air pollution control, aerosol physical chemistry and colloid science. Office: U Wash Dept Chem Engring PO Box 351750 Seattle WA 98195-1750 Business E-Mail: davis@cheme.washington.edu.

DAVIS, EDGAR GLENN, public health service officer, educator; b. Indpls., May 12, 1931; s. Thomas Carroll and Florence Isabelle (Watson) Davis; m. Margaret Louise Alandt, June 20, 1953; children: Anne-Elizabeth, Amy Alandt, Edgar Glenn Davis Jr. AB, Kenyon Coll., 1953; MBA, Harvard U., 1955. With Eli Lilly & Co., Indpls., 1958—63, mgr. budgeting and profit planning, 1963—66, mgr. econ. studies, 1966—67, mgr. Atlanta sales dist., 1967—68, dir. market rsch. and sales manpower planning, 1968—69, dir. mktg. plans, 1969—74, exec. dir. pharm. mktg. planning, 1974—75, exec. dir. corp. affairs, 1975—76, v.p. corp. affairs, 1976—90, v.p. health care policy, 1990; pres., chmn. bd. dirs. Centre for Health Sci. Info., Boston, 1990—; fellow Ctr. for Bus. and Govt. Kennedy Sch. of Govt. Harvard U., 1991—95; adj. prof. Butler U., Indpls., 1995—. Exec. in residence Butler U. Coll. Bus.; mem. Inst. Ednl. Mgmt., Harvard U. Grad. Sch. Edn., 1987; chmn. staff Bus. Roundtable Task Force on Health, 1981—85; U.S. rep. UN Indsl. Devel. Orgn. Conf., Lisbon, 1980, Casablanca, 81, Budapest, 83, Madrid, 87; participant meeting of experts on pharms UNIDO, 1981; rep. to UN Commn. on Narcotic Drugs, Vienna, 1981, UN Econ. and Social Coun., N.Y.C., 1981, UN Indsl. Devel. Orgn. Conf.; Ctr. for Bus. and Govt. fellow Kennedy Sch. Govt., Harvard U.; co-chmn. Harvard Conf. on Govt. Role in Civilian Tech., 1992, Harvard Conf. Pharmaceutical Rsch., Innovation and Pub. Policy, 1993, Harvard Biotech. Roundtable, 1991—; vis. scholar, advisor Health and Welfare Unit, Inst. for Econ. Affairs, London; vis. scholar Green Coll. Oxford (Eng.) U., 1994—; chmn. Nat. Fund for Med. Edn., 1994—; dir. English Speaking Union, Indpls.; gov. Soc. Indiana Pioneers; lectr. in field. Contbr. articles to profl. jours. Pres. Eli Lilly and Co. Found., 1976—88; pres., chmn. bd. Indpls. Health Inst., 1988—91; trustee Kenyon Coll., Gambier, Ohio, Ind. Hist. Soc.; pres. bd. trustees Boston Biomed. Rsch. Inst., 1991—95, trustee emeritus; chmn. Nat. Fund for Med. Edn., 1996—; bd. dirs. Carnegie Coun. on Ethics and Internat. Affairs, 1985—92; accredited nongovtl. observer rep. to UN Goodwill Found. Ind. Inc., 1987—95; bd. dirs. Sta. WFYI Pub. TV, Indpls., 1983—91, Am. Symphony Orch. League, 1987—92, mem. dirs. coun., 1987—; bd. dirs. Nat. Health Coun., 1984—91, Pub. Affairs Coun., Washington, 1984—92, Nat. Fund for Med. Edn.; bd. advisors Christian Theol. Sem., Bishops Sch., LaJolla, Calif.; chmn. bd. dirs. Ind. Repertory Theatre, 1979—85; vice chmn., exec. com., bd. dirs. Indpls. Symphony Orch. and Ind. State Symphony Soc., 1977—91; chmn. task force on fine arts Commn. for Future of Butler U.; chmn. exec. com. Pan Am. Econ. Leadership Conf. 10th Pan Am. Games, Indpls.; mem. Chgo. Coun. on Fgn. Rels.; bd. govs. Soc. Ind. Pioneers. Mem.: NAM (vice-chmn. health policy com. 1987—91, bd. dirs.), Am. Symphony Orch. League N.Y. (mem. dir. coun.), Inst. Medicine NAS, Ind. Soc. Pioneers (bd. govs.), Univ. Club (Indpls.) (bd. dirs.), Literary Club Indpls., Reform Club London, N.Y. Yacht Club, Edgartown Golf Club, Chappaquiddick Beach Club, Lambs Club, Contemporary Club, Woodstock Club, Naples Yacht Club, Edgartown Yacht Club, Naples (Fla.), Met. Club (Washington). Office: Butler U Coll Bus Adminstrn 4600 Sunset Ave Indianapolis IN 46208-3487 Fax: 317-940-9455.

DAVIS, EDMOND RAY, lawyer; b. Glendale, Calif., Sept. 4, 1928; s. Archie Allen and Eve Mae (Hoover) D.; m. Ruby Evelyn Davis, Oct. 17, 1954; children: Phillip A., Sandra A. Ed., Pepperdine Coll.; JD, U. Calif., San Francisco, 1952. Bar: Calif. 1952, U.S. Dist. Ct. (cen. dist.) Calif. 1952. Assoc. Bailie, Turner & Sprague, 1955-60; trust counsel Security Pacific Nat. Bank, 1960-67; ptnr. Overton, Lyman & Prince, L.A., 1967-87, Brobeck, Phleger & Harrison, L.A., 1987-99, Davis & Whalen, Pasadena, Calif., 1999—. Chmn., pub. adminstr. Pub. Guardian Adv. Commns., Los County Bd. Suprs., 1974-76; bd. dirs. Braille Inst. Am., Inc., 1974—78, Children's Bur. So. Calif., Children's Bur. Found., Fifield Manors, Inc., WM Group of Funds, trustee; bd. dirs. Mut. Funds; pres. Calif. Jaycees, 1962; mem. legal com. Music Ctr. Found., Performing Arts Council, LA county, 1980-85. With U.S. Army, 1952-54. Recipient Alumni award Pepperdine Coll., 1962. Fellow Am. Coll. Trust and Estate Counsel (chmn. Calif. chpt. 1981-86); mem. Internat. Acad. Estate and Trust Law (academician), State Bar of Calif. (chmn. estate planning, trust and probate law sect. 1977-78), L.A. County Bar Assn. (exec. com., probate and trust law sect. 1986-89, Arthur K. Marshall award Probate and Trust Law sect. 1991), Order of Coif, Calif. Club, Chancery Club. Office: Davis & Whalen LLP 553 S Marengo Ave Pasadena CA 91101-3114 Office Phone: 626-564-2880. E-mail: edavis@daviswhalen.com.

DAVIS, EDWARD BERTRAND, retired federal judge, lawyer; b. W. Palm Beach, Fla., Feb. 10, 1933; s. Edward Bertrand and Mattie Mae (Walker) D.; m. Patricia Lee Klein, Apr. 5, 1958; children: Diana Lee Davis, Traci Russell, Edward Bertrand, III. JD, U. Fla., 1960; LLM in Taxation, N.Y. U., 1961. Bar: Fla. 1960. Pvt. practice, Miami, 1961-79; counsel High, Stack, Lazenby & Bender, 1978-79; U.S. dist. judge So. Dist. Fla., 1979-2000; shareholder Ackerman Senterfitt, Miami, 2000, chair state wide litig. practice. Served with AUS, 1953-55. Mem.: Fla. Bar Assn., Dade County Bar Assn. Office: Akerman Senterfitt Suntrust Internat Ctr One SE 3d Ave 28th Fl Miami FL 33131 Fax: 305-374-5095. Office Phone: 305-755-5850. E-mail: edavis@akerman.com.

DAVIS, E(DWARD) MARCUS, lawyer; b. Atlanta, Nov. 24, 1951; s. Edward Martin and Marcine (McConnell) D.; m. Sue Fouquet; children: Edward Clark, Hannah Morgan. AB in Econs., Duke U., 1973; JD, U. Ga., 1976. Bar: U.S. Supreme Ct. 1981. Ptnr. Davis, Zipperman, Kirschenbaum & Lotito, Atlanta, 1983—. Contbr. articles to profl. jours. Mem. ABA, ATLA, Ga. Trial Lawyers Assn., Ga. Criminal Def. Lawyers Assn., Nat. Bd. Trial Advocacy (cert.), Am. Bd. Profl. Liability Attys. (cert.), Lawyers Club of Atlanta. Presbyterian. Avocations: boating, painting, horses, fishing, motorcycling. Office: Davis Zipperman Kirschenbaum & Lotito 918 Ponce De Leon Ave NE Atlanta GA 30306-4212 Office Phone: 404-688-2000. E-mail: marc@dzkl.com.

DAVIS, EDWARD WILSON, business administration educator; b. Thomaston, Ga., Aug. 4, 1935; s. James Royland, Jr. and Hazel (Bass) D.; m. Patricia Gail Forrest, Oct. 20, 1962; children: Matthew Wilson, Edward Royland. BS in Mech. Engring, Ga. Inst. Tech., 1957, MS in Indsl. Engring, 1959; postgrad., Swiss Fed. Inst. Tech., 1957-58; MPhil, Yale U., 1967, PhD, 1968. Project leader Ops. Research, Inc., Washington, 1960-64; asst. prof. Harvard Bus. Sch., Cambridge, Mass., 1968-73; vis. asso. prof. Sloan Sch. Mgmt., M.I.T., Cambridge, 1973-74; assoc. prof., then prof. U. N.C., Chapel Hill, 1974-78; prof. Grad. Sch. Bus. Adminstrn., U. Va., Charlottesville, 1978—, Oliver Wight prof. bus. adminstrn., 1984—, Isidore Horween rsch. prof., 1991-96. Cons. various pvt. and public cos., U.S. and Europe. Author: Case Studies in Material Requirements Planning, 1978; co-author: Project Management with PERT & CPM, 3d edit., 1983, The Extended Enterprise, 2003; editor: Project Management, 1974, 2d edit., 1982. Council mem. Pilgrim Congregation Ch., 1972-74; cub scout and boy scout leader Occoneechee council Boy Scouts Am., 1974-77. IBM faculty fellow in internat. bus., 1976 Mem.: Prodn. Ops. Mgmt. Soc. (v.p. edn. 2003—), Inst. Mgmt. Scis., Am. Inst. Indsl. Engrs., Project Mgmt. Inst., Am. Inst. Decision Scis., Am. Prodn. and Inventory Control Soc. (dir. Ednl. and Research Found., presdl. award 1974, 1989), U. Va. Raven Soc., Westminister Canterbury of the Blue Ridge (bd. dirs. 2000—04). Presbyterian. Office: PO Box 6550 Charlottesville VA 22906-6550 E-mail: ewd@virginia.edu.

DAVIS, EGBERT LAWRENCE, III, lawyer; b. Winston-Salem, NC, Dec. 30, 1937; s. Egbert Lawrence Jr. and Eleanor (Layfield) D.; m. Alexandra Holderness, Aug. 25, 1962; children: Alexandra Davis Hipps, Egbert L. IV, Lucinda Davis, Pamela Davis. AB, Princeton U., 1960; LLB, Duke U., 1963; MBA, George Washington U., 1966. Bar: NC 1963. Assoc. Womble, Carlyle, Sandridge & Rice, Winston-Salem, N.C., 1965-70, ptnr., 1970-82, Raleigh, N.C., 1982-97, of counsel, 1997—. Sec. Wachovia Realty Investments, Winston-Salem, 1969—82. Mem. editl. bd. Duke U. Law Jour., 1963. Chmn. N.W. Environ. Preservation Com., Inc., Winston-Salem, 1980; chmn. bd. trustees N.C. Bapt. Hosp., Winston-Salem, 1981—82; chmn. N.C. Family Bus. Forum, 1993—94; co-chmn. Raleigh Wake Leadership Found., 2002—04; mem. state coun. N.C. Prison Fellowship, 1994—97; bd. dirs. NC Found. for Econ. Edn., 1996—; exec. com. Ea. Ctr. for Regional Devel., 1996—97; bd. dirs. N.C. chpt. Coastal Conservation Assn., 1997—2004; rep. N.C. Ho. of Reps., Raleigh, 1970—74; senator N.C. Senate, Raleigh, 1974—78; chmn. N.C. Dem. Party, 1989—91; bd. dirs. Ctr. for Citizenship, Enterprise and Govt., 2003—. Capt. U.S. Army, 1963—65. Named Citizen of Yr. Winston-Salem Mayor's Com. on Employment of the Handicapped, 1971, Young Man. of Yr. Winston-Salem Jaycees, 1972; recipient Freedom Guard award N.C. Jaycees, 1973, U.S. Jaycees, 1973. Mem. N.C. Bar Assn. (bd. govs. 1979-82), Raleigh Rotary Club (pres. 1986-87). Republican. Presbyterian. Avocations: reading, writing, tennis, biking, fishing. Office: Womble Carlyle Sandridge PO Box 831 Raleigh NC 27602-0831 Office Phone: 919-755-2103. Business E-Mail: ldavis@wcsr.com.

DAVIS, ELISE MILLER (MRS. LEO M. DAVIS), writer, educator; b. Corsicana, Tex., Oct. 12, 1915; d. Moses Myre and Rachelle (Daniels) Miller; m. Jay Albert Davis, June 27, 1937 (dec. June 1973); 1 child, Rayna Miller Davis Loeb; m. Leo M. Davis, Aug. 23, 1974. Student, U. Tex., 1930-31. Freelance writer, 1945—. Merchandiser and dir. Jay Davis, Inc., Amarillo, Tex., 1956-73; instr. mag. writing U. Tex., Dallas, 1978; lectr. creative writing Baylor U., Waco, Tex., 1980, 81, 83. Author: The Answer Is God: The Personal Story of Dale Evans and Roy Rogers, 1955; contbr. articles to periodicals, including Reader's Digest, Woman's Day, Nation's Bus., also others. Mem. Am. Soc. Journalists and Authors (bd. dirs. 1985-91). Home: 5805 Redwood Ct Dallas TX 75209-2439

DAVIS, EMERY STEPHEN, wholesale food company executive; b. Kansas City, Mo., Dec. 31, 1940; s. Vernon Albert and Berneice Marie (Brenner) D.; m. Hildegarde Retzer; children: Angelica, Matthew, Nicholas. Student, Met. Coll., Kansas City, Mo., 1958-59; cert., Stanford U., 1981. Mgr. distbn. Fleming Cos., Kansas City, Mo., 1960-71, Fremont, Calif., 1972-75, dir. warehousing Topeka, 1975-77, dir. distbn. Ea. region, Phila., 1977-79, v.p. distbn., Oklahoma City, 1979-82, sr. v.p. distbn., 1982-85, exec. v.p. distbn., 1985—; exec. v.p. Scrivner Group Fleming Cos., Inc., Oklahoma City, 1994-95, exec. v.p. ops., 1996-97, exec. v.p. food distbn. Okla., 1998—, pres. wholesale, 2000—. Coun. mem. for Continuing Edn. and Pub. Svc. Coun., U. Okla., 1996. Mem. adv. bd. coun. continuing edn. U. Okla., 1996. Served with U.S. Army, 1962-63. Recipient profl. achievement award Traffic Mgmt. Publ., 1980. Mem. Nat. Am. Wholesale Grocers' Assn. (chmn. productivity com., bd. govs. 1995), Nat. Assn. Wholesaler/Distbrs. (bd. dels.), Nat. Coun. Phys. Distbn. Mgmt. Home: 411 W 46th Ter Apt 303 Kansas City MO 64112-1428 Office: Fleming Companies Inc 5701 N Shartel Ave Oklahoma City OK 73118-5924

DAVIS, ERROLL BROWN, JR., utilities executive; b. Pitts., Aug. 5, 1944; s. Erroll Brown and Eleanor Margaret (Boykin) D.; m. Elaine E. Casey, July 13, 1968; children: Christopher, Whitney Diploma in elec. engring., Carnegie-Mellon U., 1965; MBA in Fin., U. Chgo., 1967. Corp. fin. staff Ford Motor Co., Detroit, 1969-73, Xerox Corp., Rochester, 1973-78; v.p. fin. Wis. Power and Light Co., Madison, 1978-82, v.p. fin and pub. affairs, 1982-84, exec. v.p., 1984-87, pres., 1987, pres., CEO, 1988-98; pres. WPH Holdings, 1990—98; pres., CEO Alliant Energy, Madison, 1998—2005, chmn., 2000—. Bd. dirs. BP plc, PPG Industries, Union Pacific Corp.; mem. adv. bd. Fed. Res. Bank Chgo. Conf. Bd. Mem. conf. bd. Selective Svc., Madison, 1982-2001; mem. bd. regents U. Wis., 1987-94; bd. dirs. United Way Dane County, 1984-89, chmn. bd. dirs., 1987; life trustee Carnegie Mellon U., chmn. bd. trustees, 2000-03; bd. dirs. Competitive Wis., 1989—, Ednl. Comm. Bd., 1992-94; chmn. Start Smart of Dane County. Mem. Am. Soc. Corp. Execs., Wis. Mfg. and Commerce (bd. dirs. 1986—, chmn. 1994-95), Am. Gas Assn. (bd. dirs. 1990-95), Electric Power Rsch. Inst. (bd. dirs. 1990—), Assn. Edison Illuminating Cos. (bd. dirs. 1993—), Edison Electric Inst. (bd. dirs. 1995—, chmn. 2002-03, DOE eletcricity adv. bd.), US Olympic Com. (bd. dirs.). Avocations: golf, biking. Office: Alliant Energy 4902 N Biltmore Ln Madison WI 53718

DAVIS, EVAN ANDERSON, lawyer; b. N.Y.C., Jan. 18, 1944; s. Richard T. and Charlotte (Upham) D.; m. Mary Carroll Rothwell; children: Sara Mei-Ping, Charlotte Zhong Xue, Phoebe Ming Ming. BA, Harvard U., 1966; JD, Columbia U., 1969. Bar: N.Y. 1970, U.S. Dist. Ct. (so. dist.) N.Y. 1973, U.S. Ct. Appeals (2d cir.) 1973, U.S. Dist. Ct. (ea. dist.) N.Y., 1978, U.S. Supreme Ct. 1979. Law clk. to judge U.S. Ct. Appeals (D.C. cir.), 1969-70; law clk. to Justice Potter Stewart U.S. Supreme Ct., 1970-71; gen. counsel N.Y.C. Budget Bur., 1971-72; chief consumer protection div. N.Y.C. Law Dept., 1972-74; task force leader, impeachment inquiry staff U.S. Ho. of Reps., 1974; assoc. Cleary, Gottlieb, Steen & Hamilton LLP, N.Y.C., 1975-78, ptnr., 1979—86, 1991—; counsel to gov. of N.Y., 1985-90. Vice chmn. Fund for N.Y.C., 1982-85; trustee Columbia U., 1993-2005, mem. exec. com., 1994-2005, chair bd. Fin. com., 1999-2005, vice chair bd., 2001-2005. Editor-in-chief Columbia Law Rev., 1968-69. Treas. Sch. for Field Studies, 1991-95; dir. Franklin and Eleanor Roosevelt Inst., 1993—, mem. exec. com., 1994-2002; dir. Mus. of Hudson Highlands, 1991-2002, Storm King Sch., 1991-98, Adirondack Coun.; bd. visitors Helen Hayes Hosp., 1992-98, mem. coun. fgn. rels.; chairperson N.Y. Fair Elections Project, 1998—; trustee Spence Sch., 2005— Recipient Hopkins medal St. David's Soc., N.Y., 1988, Bruckner medal Fed. Bar Coun., 1990, Aquarium Environ. award Wildlife Conservation Soc., 1995, Milton Gould award for outstanding advocacy Office Appellate Defender, 1998, award Brennan Ctr., 1999, Law and Soc. award N.Y. Lawyers for the Pub. Interest, 2000, 1844 award New York Correctional Assn, 2001, Aasonl Brookly Legal Svcs., 2004. Mem. ABA (ho. of dels. 1983-85, 91-93, 2000-02, chmn. spl. com. youth edn. for citizenship 1986-88, chmn. standing com. pub. edn.), Assn. Bar City N.Y. (chmn. exec. com. 1982-83, v.p. 1983-84, pres. 2000-02), Legal Aid Soc. (v.p. 1983-85, 97-2000, exec. com. 1992-2000), Am. Law Inst., N.Y. State Bar Assn. (com. on stds. of atty. conduct 1992—, commn. on middle income access to legal svc. 1995-2002, chief judge's commn. jud. election 2003—). Office: Cleary Gottlieb Stern & Hamilton LLP 1 Liberty Plz New York NY 10006-1470 Office Phone: 212-225-2850. Business E-Mail: odavis@cgsh.com.

DAVIS, EVELYN MARGUERITE BAILEY, artist, musician; d. Philip Edward and Della Jane (Morris) Bailey; m. James Harvey Davis, Sept. 22, 1946. Student pub. schs., Springfield; student art, Drury Coll.; piano, organ student of Charles Cordeal. Sec. Shea and Morris Monument Co., before 1946; past mem. sextet, soloist Sta. KGBX. Tchr. Bible, organist, pianist, vocal soloist, dir. youth choir Bible Bapt. Ch., Maplewood, Mo., 1956-69; pvt. instr. piano and organ, voice Croma Harp, Affton, Mo., 1960-71, St. Charles, Mo., 1971-83; Bible instr. 3d Bapt. Ch., St. Louis, 1948-54; pianist, soloist, tchr. Bible Temple Bapt. Ch., Kirkwood, Mo., 1969-71; asst. organist-pianist, vocal soloist, tchr. Bible, Bible Ch., Arnold, Mo., 1969; faculty St. Charles Bible Bapt. Christian Sch., 1976-77; organist for Dr. Jack Van Impe Crusades and Dr. Oliver B. Green Crusades; organist, pianist, soloist, Bible tchr., dir. youth orch., music arranger, floral arranger Bible Bapt. Ch., St. Charles, 1971-78; organist, vocal soloist, floral arranger, Bible tchr. Faith Missionary Bapt. Ch., St. Charles, 1978-82; organist, floral arranger, vocal soloist Belleview Bapt. Ch., Springfield, Mo., 1984-90; tchr. piano, organ, voice, organist, Springfield, 1983—; pianist Golden Agers Pk. Crest Bapt. Ch., Springfield, 1991; interior decorator, floral arranger, organist, vocal soloist for weddings and funerals. Composer: I Will Sing Hallelujah, (cantata) I Am Alpha and Omega, Prelude to Prayer, My Shepherd, O Sing unto the Lord a New Song, O Come Let Us Sing unto the Lord, The King of Glory, The Lord Is My Light and My Salvation, O Worship the Lord in the Beauty of Holiness, The Greatest of These Is Love, Prayer to the Lord Our God, We Will Sing Praises, His Name Is Jesus, From Bethlehem's Manger to the Cross, The King of Kings Is Coming! Alleluia! To the Throne You Go, The Eyes of God, The Most Holy, Dearly Beloved, Precious, Loving Lamb of God, Devine, also numerous hymn arrangements for organ and piano. Past pianist, Sunday sch. tchr., mem. choir East Ave. Bapt. Ch. Fellow Internat. Biog. Assn. (life), Am. Biog. Inst. Rsch. Assn. (life); mem. Nat. Guild Organists, Nat. Guild Piano Tchr. Auditions, Internat. Platform Assn. Home: 5135 E Farm Road 174 Rogersville MO 65742-8220

DAVIS, FERD LEARY, JR., law educator, consultant; b. Zebulon, N.C., Dec. 4, 1941; s. Ferd L. and Selma Ann (Harris) D.; m. Joy Baker Davis, Jan. 25, 1963; children: Ferd Leary III, James Benjamin, Elizabeth Joy. BA, Wake Forest U., 1964, JD, 1967; LLM, Columbia U., 1984. Bar: N.C. 1967. Editor Zebulon (N.C.) Record, 1958; tchr. Davidson County Schs., Wallburg, NC, 1966; ptnr. Davis & Davis and related law firms, Zebulon and Raleigh, NC, 1967—76; asst. pros. Wake County Dist. Ct., Raleigh, 1968—69; town atty. Town of Zebulon, 1969—76; founding dean Campbell U. Sch. Law, Buies Creek, NC, 1975—86, prof. law, 1975—2005; founding dean, prof. law Elon U. Sch. Law, Greensboro, NC, 2005—. Dir. Inst. to Study Practice of Law and Socioecon. Devel., 1985-2005; chmn. The Davis Cons. Group, Inc., Greensboro, 1987-2005; pres. LAWLEAD/NIELLP, 1998—; cons. U. Charleston, W.Va., 1979; vis. scholar Ctr. for Creative Leadership, 1993. Assoc. editor Wake Forest U. Law Rev. Trustee Wake County Pub. Librs., 1971-75, Olivia Raney Trust, 1969-71; mem. N.C. State Dem. Exec. Com., 1970-72, N.C. Gen. Statutes Commn., 1977-79, Commn. on the Future of N.C., 1980-83; dir., Howard Meml. Christian Edn. Fund, Raleigh Bus. and Tech. Ctr., NC BarCares. 1st Lt. USAR, 1959-66. Babcock scholar Wake Forest U., 1963-67; Dayton Hudson fellow Columbia U., 1982-83. Fellow Coll. Law Practice Mgmt.; mem. ABA, N.C. Bar Assn., N.C. State Bar, Rotary, Phi Delta Phi, Delta Theta Phi, Omicron Delta Kappa. Democrat. Office: Elon U Sch Law 201 N Greene St Greensboro NC 27401 Office Phone: 336-278-9201. E-mail: davislaw@elon.edu.

DAVIS, FRANCIS KEITH, civil engineer; b. Bloomington, Wis., Oct. 23, 1928; s. Martin Morris and Anna (Weber) D.; m. Roberta Dean Anderson, May 25, 1957; 1 child, Mark Francis. BSCE, S.D. State U., 1950. Registered profl. engr., Mo., Ind., Nebr., Mich., Colo., Ariz., Oreg. With firm Howard, Needles, Tammen & Bergendoff, Kansas City, Mo., 1950—, asst. chief structural designer, 1960-65, project mgr., sect. chief, 1965-76, dep. chief structural engr., 1976-79, chief engr., 1979—. Mem. bd. advisers N.W. Kans. Area Vocat. Tech. Sch., 1977-80, chmn., 1979-80. With U.S. Army, 1951-53. Fellow ASCE; mem. NSPE, Mo. Soc. Profl. Engrs., Am. Ry. Engring. Assn. (tech. com. 1981—), Homestead Country Club. Home: 5024 Howe Dr Shawnee Mission KS 66205-1465 Office: PO Box 419299 1201 Walnut St Kansas City MO 64106-2117 Business E-Mail: kdavis@hntb.com.

DAVIS, FRANCIS RAYMOND, priest; b. Washington, Feb. 10, 1920; s. Frank Raymond and Ruth Madeline (Donivan) Davis. BA, St. Bernard's Sem., Rochester, NY, 1941; MLS, Cath. U. Am., 1953. Ordained priest Roman Cath. Ch., 1945. Asst. pastor St. Ambrose Ch., Rochester, 1945—50; prof. lit. St. Bernard's Sem., 1950—51, librarian, 1950—69, prof. speech, 1958—67; pastor Our Lady Lourdes Ch., Elmira, NY, 1969—78, St. Mary's Ch., Dansville, NY, 1978—80, St. Patrick's Ch., Corning, NY, 1980—90. Author articles and book revs. Mem. exec. com. Chemung County Coun. Aging, 1973—78; bd. dirs. All Saints' Acad., Corning, 1986—90; founder Ecumentical Preaching Mission; mem. Chemung County gen. edn. bd. Diocese of Rochester, NY, 1971—78; mem. exec. com. Ecumentical Preaching Mission, 1977—78. Fellow: Internat. Biog. Assn.; mem.: Elmira Vicinity Ministerial Assn. (officer 1972—73), Ch. and Synagogue Libr. Assn. (nominating com. 1979), Cath. Libr. Assn. (officer sem. sect. 1958—61), ALA. Address: 155 State St Corning NY 14830-2534

DAVIS, FRANK TRADEWELL, JR., lawyer; b. Atlanta, Feb. 2, 1938; s. Frank T. and Sue (Burnett) D.; m. Winifred Storey, June 23, 1961; children: Frank, Frederick, Gordon. AB, Princeton U., 1960; JD, George Washington U., 1963; LLM, Harvard U., 1964. Bar: Ga. 1963, U.S. Ct. Appeals (5th cir.) 1963, D.C. 1966, U.S. Supreme Ct. 1968, U.S. Ct. Appeals (11th cir.) 1982, U.S. Ct. Appeals (10th cir.) 2003. Assoc. Hansell, Post Brandon & Dorsey, Atlanta, 1964-67; ptnr. Hansell & Post, Atlanta, 1968-77, 79-86, Long, Aldridge & Norman, Atlanta, 1986—2002, McKenna, Long & Aldridge, Atlanta, 2002—. Ptnr., gen. counsel Pres.'s Reorgn. Project Office of Pres., 1977-79; vis. instr. U. Ga. Law Sch., 1964-66, Ga. State U. Law Sch., 1988-90; vis. prof. Emory U. Law Sch., 1992—; dir. Red and Black Newspaper U. Ga., 2005-. Author: Business Acquisitions, 1977, (2d edit.), 1982; contbr. articles to legal jours. Bd. dirs. Nat. Inst. Justice, 1980—81, Westminster Schs., 1969—, chmn. bd. dirs., 1984—89; bd. dirs. Va. Sem., 1980—94, exec. com., 1985—89; mem. Atlanta Charter Commn.; chmn. Atlanta Crime Commn., 1977; mem. bd. councilors Carter Presdl. Ctr., 1988—; chmn. Rotary Ednl. Found. Atlanta; commr. Atlanta Regional Commn., 1999—; sr. warden All Saints' Episcopal Ch., 1982, 2002, vestry, 2000—03. Lt. USNR, 1960—62. Fellow Am. Bar Found. (life); mem. Am. Law Inst. (life), Atlanta C. of C. (bd. dirs. 1975-77), Piedmont Driving Club (Atlanta), Capital City Club (Atlanta), Cedar Creek Racquet Club (Cashiers, N.C.), The Army and Navy Club (Washington), Rotary (pres. Atlanta chpt. 1990-91, bd. dirs., sec. 1988-89, chmn. bd., 1991-92, chmn. Ednl. Found. 1997—). Home: 2525 Peachtree Rd #11 Atlanta GA 30305 Office: 303 Peachtree St NE Ste 5300 Atlanta GA 30308-3264 Office Phone: 404-527-4080. E-mail: ftdjr@earthlink.net.

DAVIS, FRANK WAYNE, lawyer; b. Ada, Okla., Aug. 24, 1936; s. Roscoe Gladstone and Neva Dell (Peck) Davis; m. Kay Diane Higginbotham, Aug. 12, 1961; children: David, Paul. Student, U. Ill., Urbana, 1956-57; BA, East Cen. U., 1958; LLB, U. Okla., Norman, 1959. Bar: Okla. 1959, U.S. Dist. Ct. (we. dist.) Okla. 1965, U.S. Ct. Appeals (10th cir.) 1976. Acting postmaster U.S. Postal Service, Ada, 1959-61; assoc. Denny W. Falkenburg, Medford, Okla., 1961; county atty. Logan County, Guthrie, Okla., 1961-65; sole practice Guthrie, 1965—85, 1988—; ptnr. Davis and Hudson, Guthrie, 1985-88. Mcpl. judge City of Guthrie, 1974—78; rep. State of Okla., Oklahoma City, 1978—2004; vice chmn. judiciary com. Okla. Ho. of Reps., 1981—82, 1989, 1991—2004, minority fl. leader, 1982—86, asst. minority fl. leader, 1986—90. Scoutmaster Troop # 850 Boy Scouts Am., Guthrie, 1961—2000; del. Rep. Nat. Convs., 1984, 1996, alt. del., 2000; chmn. Logan County Reps., Guthrie, 1964—69; del. gen. conf. United Meth. Ch., Portland, Oreg., 1976. Recipient Silver Beaver award, Boy Scouts Am., 1978. Mem.: Logan County Bar Assn. (pres. 1972—73), Okla. Bar Assn., Masons, Lions (v.p. 2004—), Gideons. Methodist. Avocations: fishing, stamp collecting/philately, farming, oil and gas production. Office: 115 N Division St Guthrie OK 73044-3240 also: 509 State Capitol Bldg Oklahoma City OK 73105 Home: 2121 N Walnut Guthrie OK 73044 Office Phone: 405-282-1420. E-mail: repfwdavis@smconnect.com.

DAVIS, FRED, journalist, educator; b. Columbia, S.C., Feb. 14, 1947; s. Nathaniel Lewis Sr. and Arneatha Pearl (Robinson) D.; m. Joan Sineta Walker, Jan. 14, 1967; children: Alex LaMar, Kevin Alexander. BS in English Edn., N.C. A&T State U., 1969. City/coun. reporter WFMY-TV/CBS, Greensboro, N.C., 1969-70; govtl. reporter WJRT-TV/ABC, 1970-74, dir. documentaries and pub. affairs, 1974-75; anchor-reporter WMAL-TV (WJLA-TV/ABC), Washington, 1975; various positions in field to reporter, news editor WRC-TV/NBC News, Washington, 1975; gen. assignment, news program svc. reporter KNBC-TV/NBC News, Burbank, Calif., 1976; writer/reporter KHJ-TV/Ind., Hollywood, Calif., 1976-78; anchor/editor WIS-TV/NBC, Columbia, S.C., 1978-80; asst. news dir., sr. producer WJXT-TV/CBS, Jacksonville, Fla., 1980-81; staff writer Jacksonville Jour./Fla. Pub. Co., 1981; news dir. ABC Direction Radio Network/ABC News, N.Y.C., 1981-88; weekly commentator CBS-owned radio stas., 1992; self-syndicated columnist S.C. newspapers, 1992—; Disting. prof. mass media mgmt. Wash. State U., Pullman, 1995-97; columnist The Seattle Times, The Spokesman-Rev., 1996—98. Adj. prof. Edward R. Murrow Sch. of Comm., Wash. State U., Pullman, 1997—2000; cons./host Sta. KWSU-TV (PBS), 1997—; owner media svcs./broadcast news consultancy, 1989—; vis. lectr. Benedict Coll., Columbia, 1979—80, Columbia, 1990, Coll. Journalism U. S.C., 1987, Coll. Journalism & Mass Comm., U. Nebr., Lincoln, 1997—99; mem. Journalism and Mass Comm. del. to China, Citizens Ambassador Program, 1996, Journalism and Mass Comm. del. to Italy, Switzerland, Austria, Citizens Ambassador Program, 1997, Journalism and Mass Comm. del. to S. Africa, Citizens Ambassador Program, 1999; expert media witness Libel Def. Resource Ctr., San Diego, 1997; del. People to People Internat., Russia, 1998, Finland, 98; cons., host KWSU-TV, KUON-TV, 1997; cons., writer The Gallup Org., Lincoln, Nebr., 1999—; del. News World conf., Barcelona, 1999; lectr. Coll. Journalism & Mass. Comm., U. Nebr., Lincoln, 1997—99, U. Nebr., Lincoln, 1999—; adj. instr. Coll. Journalism & Comm., 2001. Contbr. articles USA Today; provider (news commentaries) CBS-owned radio stas., N.Y., L.A., Chgo., Phila., San Francisco, Detroit, Mpls., columnist (newspaper) The Seattle Times, 1996—97, The Royal Gazette, Bermuda, 1996—97, The Spokesman-Rev., 1996—97, prodr./cons. (global bus. report) Bermuda Broadcasting Co., 2000—01, writer (jour.) Jacksonville Bus. Jour., 2001, prodr./moderator ("Socratic" Roundtables TV series) WJCT-TV (PBS), Jacksonville, Fla., 2001. Bd. visitors, N.C. A&T State U., Greensboro, 1988—; del. Russia and Finland People to People Internat., 1998. Recipient award, Leadership Flint (Mich.), 1973, Internat. Radio Festival of N.Y., 1983—88, Ohio State award, ABC Radio, 1986, award, Nat. Press Club, 1984, 1985, Comm. Excellence to Black Audiences award of distinction, ABC Dir./Radio Network, 1987, b'nai b'rith Edward R. Murrow Brotherhood award, 1986, Disting. Alumni award, Nat. Assn. for Equal Opportunity in Higher Edn., 1988, Disting. Acheivement award, Mass Media Mngmt. Studies, Coll. Liberal Arts, Wash. State U., 1996. Mem.: U.S. Tennis Assn. (USTA), Broadcast Edn. Assn., Assn. for Edn. in Journalism and Mass Comm., S.C. Press Assn., Nat. Assn. Black Journalists, Acad. TV Arts and Scis., Am. Fedn. TV and Radio Artists, Radio-TV News Dirs. Assn., Internat. Platform Assn., PGA Ptnrs., Broadcast Edn. Assn., Assn. for Edn. in Journalism and Mass Comm., Nat. Geog. Soc., Soc. Profl. Journalists, Nat. Assn. Black Journalists, Acad. TV Arts and Scis., Am. Fedn. TV and Radio Artists, Radio-TV News Dirs. Assn., Internat. Platform Assn., PGA Ptnrs. (charter mem., charter), U.S. Tennis Assn., U.S. Golf Assn., The Folio Soc., Planetary Soc., Nat. Geog. Soc., The Folio Soc., S.C. Press Assn., U.S. Golf Assn., Planetary Soc., Alpha Phi Alpha, Alpha Phi Alpha. Baptist. Avocations: gourmet cooking, racquetball, golf, tennis, barbecue judging. Office: Davis Media Svcs & Syndication LLC/ U Fla Coll Journalism & Comm PO Box 56741 Jacksonville FL 32241-6741 E-mail: fdav444@prodigy.net, dms444@mediaone.net.

DAVIS, GARY L., human resources professional; m. Trudie Davis; children: Tisha Ann, Christopher Maurice. BBA, Ohio U., 1964. Various mgmt. positions J.C. Penney Co., Inc., Ohio, Pa., Mich., 1964-84, asst. dir. of corp. personnel to dir. geographic markets, 1984-90, dir. coordination Plano, Tex., 1990-92, pres. Northwest region, 1992-96, sr. v.p., dir. of personnel and adminstrn., 1992-96, exec. v.p., chief human resources/adminstrv. officer, 1996—2005; ret., 2005. Bd. dirs. United Way, 1996-97; vice chmn. bd. trustees Nat. 4-H Coun.; dir. area rels. exec. com. Nat. Jr. Achievement; corp. bd. advisors Nat. Coun. of La Raza; chmn. JC Penney Afterschool Fund; mem. Alumni Adv. Bd. Ohio U.*

DAVIS, GEENA (VIRGINIA DAVIS), actress; b. Wareham, Mass., Jan. 21, 1957; m. Richard Emmolo, 1982 (div. 1983); m. Jeff Goldblum, 1987 (div. 1990); m. Renny Harlin, 1993 (div. 1998); m. Reza Jarrahy, 2001; children Alizeh Keshvar Davis Jarrahy, Kian William and Kaiis Steven. BFA, Boston U., 1979; attended, New England Coll., Henniker, N.H. Founder Genial Pictures; mem. My. Washington (N.H.) Repertory Theatre Co. Actor: motion picture appearances include Tootsie, 1982, Fletch, 1985, Transylvania 6-5000, 1985, The Fly, 1986, Beetlejuice, 1988, The Accidental Tourist, 1988 (Academy award Best Supporting Actress, 1989), Earth Girls Are Easy, 1989, Quick Change, 1990, Thelma and Louise, 1991 (Acad. award nominee Best Actress 1991, British Acad Film and TV Arts award Best Actress in leading role 1991, Golden Globe award nominee Best Actress 1991), A League of Their Own, 1992, Hero, 1992, Princess Scargo and the Birthday Pumpkin (voice), 1993, Angie, 1994, Speechless, 1994 (also prodr.), Cutthroat Island, 1995, The Long Kiss Goodnight, 1996, Stuart Little, 1999, Stuart Little 2, 2002; TV series: Buffalo Bill, 1983-84 (also writer), Sara, 1985, The Geena Davis Show, 2000 (also co-exec. prodr.), Commander-in-Chief, 2005-; appeared in TV film Secret Weapons, 1985; exec. prodr. Mistrial, 1996; guest appearances include Knight Rider, 1983, Fantasy Island, 1984, Family Ties 1984, Remington Steele, 1985, Will & Grace, 2004 and several others.*

DAVIS, GENE, public relations executive, state legislator; b. Salt Lake City, July 2, 1945; s. John Albert and Glenna Rachel (Cameron) D.; m. Penny Lou Hansen, Mar. 9, 1971; children: James, Pamela. Cert. in electronic engring., Radio Operational Engring., Burbank, Calif., 1963; LLB, LaSalle Ext. U., Chgo., 1974. Announcer Radio Sta. KNAK, Salt Lake City, 1965-75; prodn. continuity dir. Radio Sta. KALL AM/FM, Salt Lake City, 1976-86; owner G. Davis Advt., Pub. Rels., Salt Lake City, 1986-91; pub. rels. profl. Valley Mental Health, Salt Lake City, 1990—; mem. Utah Senate, Dist. 3, Minority Whip, Salt Lake City, 1998—. Treas. Comm. Fed. Credit Union, Salt Lake City, 1981-86. Vice-chair East County Recreation Bd., Salt Lake City, 1991—2000; rep. Utah State House of Reps., Salt Lake City, 1986—98; mem. bus. & labor com., retirement com., exec. appropriations com., coun. of state govt.-health capacity task force Utah State Senate, Salt Lake City. Mem. Sugar House Rotary Club (pres. 2003-04), Sugar House Cmty. Coun. (chmn. 1984-85). Democrat. Mem. Lds Ch. Avocations: golf, gardening, politics. Home: 865 Parkway Ave Salt Lake City UT 84106-1704 Office: Valley Mental Health 5965 S 900 E Salt Lake City UT 84121-1794 Business E-Mail: gened@vmh.com.

DAVIS, GENE, retired civil engineer; b. Lower Peach Tree, Ala., Apr. 21, 1935; s. Edgar Thomas and Una (Smith) D.; m. Betty Marie Davidson; children: Jean Marie Davis, Jenifer Davis Cerny, Joanna Davis Palladino, James Andrew Davis. BSCE, U. Ala., 1958; MS in Mgmt., Naval Postgrad. Sch., 1969; cert., Armed Forces Staff Coll., 1974. Commd. ensign USN, 1958, advanced through grades to Capt., 1980; resident engr. Navy Project Office, Cape Canaveral, Fla., 1960-63, Dir. of Constrn. in South East Asia, Bangkok, Thailand, 1963-65; program mgr. Pacific divsn., Naval Civil Engring., Honolulu, 1965-68; exec. officer Naval Constrn. Bat. 121, Gulfport, Miss., 1968-70; dir. constrn. planning Hdqrs., Naval Civil Engring., Washington, 1974-76; comdg. officer Naval Constrn. Bat. 133, Gulfport, 1976-78; chief of staff Naval Constrn. Regiment, Port Hueneme, Calif., 1978-81; comdr. officer Pub. Works Ctr., Great Lake, Ill., 1981-83; vice comdr. Pacific divsn., 1983-86; dir. constrn. Diego Garcia, 1986-87; retired USN, 1987; sr. group engr. Martin Marietta, Orlando, 1987-92; ops. mgr. Brown & Root Inc., Houston, 1992-2001; civil engr. cons., 1997-98; v.p. RSI, Inc., 1997-98; ret., 2001. Author: Analysis of the Imperial Iranian Navy Construction Program, 1974. Mem. Soc. Am. Mil. Engrs. (pres. Diego Garcia post 1992), USN Inst. Republican. Roman Catholic. Home: PO Box 535 Thomasville AL 36784-0535 E-mail: dav3ge@aol.com.

DAVIS, GEOFF, congressman; b. Montreal, Que., Can., Oct. 26, 1958; m. Pat Davis; 6 children. BS, US Mil. Acad., West Point, 1981. Pres. Capstone Inc., 1992—2004; mem. U.S. Ho. Reps., 109th Congress, 4th Dist. Ky., 2005—. Mem. bd. adv. No. Ky. C. of C.; bd. mem. Regional Ct. Appointed Spl. Advocate Assn. Served Rangers, 82d Airborne div. U.S. Army, 1976—87. Mem.: West Pont Assn. Graduates, US Army Ranger Assn., 82d Airborne Assn., NRA (life). Republican. Christian. Office: 1541 Longworth House Office Bldg Washington DC 20515-1704 Office Phone: 202-225-3465.

DAVIS, GEORGE CULLOM, historian; b. Aurora, Ill., May 2, 1935; s. George Cullom and Mary Elizabeth (Scripps) D.; m. Marilyn Louise Whittaker, June 22, 1957 (div. Mar. 1974); children: Catherine, Lesa, Charles; m. Ann Elizabeth Chapman, May 27, 1976. AB, Princeton U., 1957; MA, U. Ill., Urbana, 1961, PhD, 1968; Dr of History (hon.), Lincoln Coll., 1999; Diploma of Honor, Lincoln Meml. U., 1995; DHL (hon.), Knox Coll., 2000. Instr. Punahou Sch., Honolulu, 1957-59, U. Ill., Urbana, 1962-64; asst. prof. Ind. U., Bloomington, 1964-70, assoc. dean, 1967-70; assoc. prof. Sangamon State U., Springfield, Ill., 1970-74, prof., 1974-95; prof. emeritus, 1995—; prof. history U. Ill.-Springfield, 1974—; dir., sr. editor Lincoln Legal Papers Documentary Edit., 1988—. Bd. dirs. Bank One, Springfield; cons. John Nuveen & Co., Chgo., 1989—, Meml. Med. Ctr., Springfield, 1991—. Author: History With a Tape Recorder: An Oral History Handbook, 1972, 4th edit., 1985; co-author: Oral History: From Tape to Tape, 1977, Bench and Bar on the Illinoir Frontier, 1979, The Prairie Bondman, 1996, Memorial Days, 1997; editor: Bicentennial Studies in Sangamon History, 1973-78; co-editor: The Public and the Private Lincoln: Contemporary Perspectives, 1979, Abraham Lincoln Association Papers, 1981-86, The Law Practice of Abraham Lincoln: Complete Documentary Edit. (DVD-ROM), 2000; contbr. numerous articles to profl. jours.; editl. advisor Scholar Book Revs. on CD-ROM, 1991-93. Del. Dem. Nat. Conv., 1972; pres. Springfield Pub. Schs. Found., 1987-88. Recipient Pelzer award Orgn. Am. Historians, 1962, award of Merit Ill. State Hist. Soc., 1975, Writer of Yr. award Friends of Lincoln Libr., 1989; Fulbright Rsch. scholar, 1987-88; fellow Newberry Libr., 1977, NEH/Woodrow Wilson Found. Inst., 1980, NEH Summer Inst. on Pub. History, 1984, Studs Terkel award Ill. Humanities Coun., 2002; grantee Ill. Bicentennial Commn., 1974-75, Ill. State Libr., 1975, 79-81, Ill. Legis. Coun., 1979-87, Ill. Humanities Coun., 1980-82, NEH, 1990-92, 94—, Nat. Hist. Publs. and Records Commn., 1990—, Ill. Bar Found., 1990-91, Ency. Brit., 1991, Shelby C. Davis Found., 1991—, William Nelson Cromwell Found., 1992—. Mem. Manuscript Soc., Assn. for Documentary Editing (chmn. constitution com. 1990-94, pres. 1997-98), Ill. Coalition of Libr. Advocates (bd. dirs. 1982-84), Ill. Humanities Coun. (bd. dirs. 1983-89, vice chair 1985-87, chair 1987-89), Ill. State Hist. Soc. (v.p. 1974-75, 82-83, bd. dirs. 1979-82, exec. com. 1979-82, adv. bd. 1994—), Sangamon County Hist. Soc. (bd. dirs. 1971-74, 79-82, v.p. 1981-82, 90-91, pres. 1991-92), Orgn. Am. Historians (treas. 1984-93), Oral History Assn. (nominating com. 1978-79, 85-87, colloquium program com. 1978, chmn. nat. workshop 1979, nat. coun. 1980-85, v.p. 1982-83, pres. 1983-84), Abraham Lincoln Assn. (bd. dirs. 1977—, chmn. publs. com. 1981-87, v.p. 1984-86, pres. 1995-96). Democrat. Home: 2624 E Lake Shore Dr Springfield IL 62707-5533 Office: Lincoln Legal Papers Old State Capitol Springfield IL 62701

DAVIS, GEORGE DONALD, executive land use policy consultant; b. Oneida, N.Y., Nov. 19, 1942; s. Pearl Floyd and Kathrine Virginia (Connolly) D.; m. Anita Face Riner, June 26, 1976; children: Maria Lisa, Brett Hollis, Sarah Bessie, Lara Emily; stepchildren: Andrea G. Riner, Joel S. Riner. BS in Forestry, SUNY, 1964; postgrad., Cornell U., 1971. Forester, pub. land adminstr. U.S. Forest Svc. Dept. Agr., Colo., 1964-68; ecologist Gov. N.Y. State Temp. Study Commn. on Future of Adirondacks, 1969-71; pvt. land use and natural resources cons. Ithaca, N.Y., 1971; dir. planning Adirondack Park Agy., Ray Brook, N.Y., 1971-76; exec. dir. Wilderness Soc., Washington, 1976-77; spl. asst. U.S. Forest Svc., Washington, 1977-79; dep. forest supr. Idaho Panhandle Nat. Forests, Coeur d'Alene, 1979-82; land use, natural resource cons. Wadhams, N.Y., 1982-94; program dir. Adirondack Coun., 1983-88; exec. dir. Adirondack Land Trust, 1984-88; prin. Davis Assocs., 1988—. Pres. Ecol. Sustainable Devel., Inc., 1994—97; coord. Global Assocs. in Sustainable Devel., 1997—2002; project dir. Land Use Policy and Allocation Program for Lake Baikal Watershed in Russia, 1991—93, Lake Hovsgol/Selenge River Wateshed in Mongolia, 1992—94, Ussuri River Watershed in Russian Far East and China, 1993—97, Altai Rep., Russia, 1994—97; exec. dir. Gov. Commn. on Adirondacks in the 21st Century, 1989—90; mem. environ. task force Rockefeller Bros. Fund; mem. Hudson Basin project task force Rockefeller Found. Co-author: The Unfinished Agenda, 1977, Developing a Land Conservation Strategy, 1987; author: Ecosystem Representative as a Criterion for World Wilderness Designation, 1987, 2020 Vision: Fulfilling the Promise of the Adirondack Park, 1988, Completing the Adirondack Wilderness System, 1990, The Lake Baikal Region in the Twenty-First Century: A Model of Sustainable Development or Continued Degradation?, 1993, A Comprehensive National Program of Sustainable Land Use Policies for the Lake Hovsgol-Selenge River Watershed, 1994, A Sustainable Land Use and Allocation Program for the Ussuri/Wusuli River Watershed and Adjacent Territories, 1996; contbr. to profl. publs. Active Gov. N.Y. State Forest Industry Task Force, 1987-89, N.Y.-New Eng. Gov. Task Force on No. Forest Lands, 1988-90. MacArthur fellow, 1989—. Roman Catholic. Home and Office: 2482 N 32d St Springfield OR 97477-7900 E-mail: davisassoc1@aol.com. *The basic goal of my life has been to promote land and natural resource stewardship, through direct action and example, to help insure that our planet's resources are more equitably distributed among members of the present generation and are sufficient for future generations.*

DAVIS, GEORGE EDWARD, industrial designer; b. Hugo, Okla., July 3, 1928; s. Silas William and Florence Elva (White) D.; m. Betty Sue Walker, July 21, 1951; children: Susan Elizabeth, Laura Ellen. Student, U. Tex., 1946—49; BA, Art Ctr. Coll. Design, LA, 1956. Registered interior designer, Tex. Staff designer Friedrich Refrigeration Co., San Antonio, 1957; design dir. comml. divsn. Woodarts Co., Houston, 1958-59; staff designer Brede, Inc., Houston, 1960-61; designer, co-founder Concept Planners and Designers, Houston, 1962-64; mgr. archtl. dept. Lockheed-Calif. Co., NASA Manned Spacecraft Ctr., Clear Lake, Tex., 1965-66; staff designer office products divsn. Litton Industries, Austin and San Antonio, 1967-68; staff designer Clegg Design Group, San Antonio, 1969-76; ind. design cons. San Antonio, 1977—. Interior designer for USAA, San Antonio, 1991-2001; dir. Systemics, Inc., San Antonio, Christian Bookmark, Inc., San Antonio, 1972-88. Trustee, San Antonio Christian Sch., 1973-82, chmn. bd., 1979-80; bd. elders Christ Presbyn. Ch., San Antonio, 1982-85; mem. Zoning Commn., City of Castle Hills, 1983-93, mem. City Coun., 1993-94, mem. Archtl. Rev. Com., 1995-2001. Served with USAF, 1950-54. Decorated DFC, Air medal with 3 oak leaf clusters. Mem. AIA (profl. affiliate), Tex. Soc. Architects (profl. affiliate, award of merit 1968). Home: 205 Wisteria Dr Castle Hills TX 78213-2109 Office: PO Box 13385 San Antonio TX 78213-0385 E-mail: gdavis22@satx.rr.com.

DAVIS, GEORGE F., food products executive; b. Kittery, Maine; married; 2 children. BS in BioChemistry, U. Conn. With Black & Decker, Avon Products Inc.; dir., corp. info. svcs. JP Foodservice, Inc.; chief info. officer Rocco, Inc.; exec. dir., global infrastructure & fin. sys. Pratt & Whitney; v.p., global infrastructure svcs. Computer Scis. Corp.; v.p., chief info. officer Hershey Foods Corp., Pa., 2000—. With USAF. Office: Hershey Foods Corp PO Box 810 100 Crystal A Dr Hershey PA 17033-0810

DAVIS, GEORGE LINN, banker; b. Des Moines, July 9, 1934; s. James Cox and Elizabeth (Linn) D.; m. Anne Roberts, May 1955 (div. Jan. 1967); children: James, Elliott, George Linn; m. Mary Elizabeth Graham, Apr. 27, 1968; children: Stephen, Thomas. BA, Yale U., 1956; MBA, Harvard U., 1958. Sr. v.p. Citibank NA, N.Y.C., 1958-81; exec. v.p. First Chgo. Corp., Chgo., 1981-87; Citicorp/Citibank group exec. N.Am. Fin. Group, N.Y.C., 1987-90; chmn. Scarborough Ptnrs., Inc., N.Y.C., 1990—; pres., CEO, bd. dirs. 1st Am. Bankshares Inc., Washington, 1990-91. Bd. dirs. Sealy Inc.; CEO Banco de Venezuela Internat., Syscon Inc.; chmn. Emex, Inc. Trustee Central Park Conservancy; chmn. Nat. Stroke Assn. Mem. Robert Morris Assocs., Assn. Equipment Lessors (bd. dirs. 1974-76), Chgo. Club, Glenview Club, Sleepy Hollow Country Club, Univ. Club. Republican. Office: Scarborough Partners Inc 450 Park Ave Fl 6 New York NY 10022-2605 E-mail: GD@JFLPartners.com.

DAVIS, GLENN CRAIG, psychiatrist; b. Columbia, Mo., Apr. 26, 1946; s. Morris S. and Dorothy (Hall) Davis; children: Jason Michael, Galen Brent. BA, Reed Coll., 1968; MD, Duke U., 1972. Diplomate Am. Bd. Psychiatry and Neurology. Intern, then resident Duke U. Med. Ctr., Durham, N.C., 1972-75; clin. assoc. NIMH, Bethesda, Md., 1975-77, chief of drug abuse unit, biological psychiatry br., 1977-79; assoc. prof. U. Tenn. Ctr. Health Scis., Memphis, 1979-81; assoc. prof. then prof. Sch. of Medicine Case Western Reserve U., Cleve., 1981-87; dir. psychiat. rsch. to chief of staff Cleve. VA Med. Ctr., 1981-87; chair psychiatry Henry Ford Med. Ctr., Detroit, 1987-92; v.p. behavioral svcs. Henry Ford Health System, Detroit, 1991-94, v.p. acad. affairs, 1992—2001, chief med. officer suburban regions, 1996-98, assoc. dean Case Western Reserve U., 1993—2001; prof. psychiatry Case Western Reserve U., Cleve., 1994—2001; pres. Am. Bd. Psychiatry & Neurology, Deerfield, IL; dean coll. of human medicine Mich. State U., East Lansing, Mich., 2001—05; sr. client ptnr. Korn Ferry Internat., Phila., 2005—. Clin. prof. U. Mich. Sch. Medicine, Ann Arbor, 1988—2001. Author numerous sci. rsch. papers and book chpts.; contbr. articles to profl. jours. Lt. comdr. USPHS U.S. Army, 1975—79. Fellow: Am. Psychopathological Assn., Am. Psychiat. Assn.; mem.: AMA, AAAS, Am. Bd. Med. Specialties, Am. Bd. Psychiatry and Neurology (dir. 1996—2003, pres. 2000), Alpha Omega Alpha, Sigma Xi. Office: Korn Ferry Internat 1835 Market St Philadelphia PA 19103 Office Phone: 517-656-5356. E-mail: gdavis@kornferry.com.

DAVIS, GORDON J., lawyer; b. Chgo., Aug. 7, 1941; AB, Williams Coll., 1963; JD, Harvard U., 1967; LLM (hon.), Williams Coll., Bard Coll. Bar: Ill. 1968, N.Y. 1973, U.S. Dist. Ct. (so. and ea. dists.) N.Y. 1973. Commr. NYC Dept. Parks and Recreation, 1978-83; ptnr. LeBoeuf Lamb Green & MacRae, LLP. Screening panel fed. magistrates U.S. Dist. Ct. (so. dist.) N.Y., 1983-90; co-founder Ctrl. Partk Conservancy. Mem. N.Y. City Planning Commn., 1973-78; bd. dirs. Harlem Studio Mus., 1981, Lincoln Ctr. Performing Arts, 1983, Mcpl. Art Soc., 1983, Dance Theatre of Harlem, 1984, N.Y. Public Libr., 1993; chmn. Jazz at Lincoln Ctr., 1996; v.p., bd. dirs. N.Y. Shakespeare Festival. Named one of Am.'s Top Black Lawyers, Black Enterprise mag., 2003; recipient Karel Shook Founders Award, Dance Theatre of Harlem, Harlem Sch. Arts Founders Medal, Frederick Law Olmsted Medal, Ctrl. Park Conservancy, Judicial Friends Award for Leadership, Assn. African-Am. Fed., State and City Judges. Mem.: Assn. of Bar of City of N.Y. (com. to enhance profl. opportunities for minorities 1990), N.Y. Chap., Am. Inst. Architects (hon.). Office: LeBoeuf Lamb Green & MacRae 125 W 55th St New York NY 10019-5369 Office Phone: 212-424-8366. E-mail: gdavis@llgm.com.

DAVIS, GORDON RICHARD FUERST, retired biologist, translator; b. Prince Albert, Sask., Can., Apr. 5, 1925; s. Louis James Davis and Nora Sylvia Fuerst; m. Marie Bérengère Pauline Bérubé, May 25, 1949 (sep. 2003); children: Joseph Richard Kevin (dec.), Elyse Bruce, Marie Raymonde Joceline, Marie-Thérèse Danielle. B.Sc. in Zoology with honors, McGill U., 1948, M.Sc., 1949, PhD, 1952. Agrl. scientist biol. control unit Can. Dept. Agr., Que., 1948-52, research officer research br. Saskatoon, Sask., 1952-65, research scientist research br., 1965-85; translator Co-Operators Fin. Svcs. Ltd., Regina, Sask., Can., 1987-90; pres., mng. dir. Triple-D Translation Svcs., Regina, Sask., 1990-95. Mem. Div. III sci. curriculum com. Sask. Dept. Edn., 1974-80 Contbr. articles to profl. jours. Bd. trustees Saskatoon Catholic Bd. Edn., 1974-77; mem. Sask German Council, Inc., rep to Concordia German Language Sch., 1986-87, v.p., 1986-87. Served with Royal Can. Navy Vol. Res., 1944-45. Carpenter Teaching fellow, 1950-51 Mem. Nutrition Soc. Can. (sec. 1973-77, v.p. 1979-80, pres. 1980-81), Can. Fedn. Biol. Socs. (dir. 1973-77, 80-81, hon. sec.-treas. 1980-84), Sask. Geneal. Soc., Can.'s Nat. History Soc. Roman Catholic. Home: Empress Gardens 502-131 Charlotte St Peterborough ON K9J 2T6 Canada Personal E-mail: fuerstdavis@sympatico.ca. *A knowledge of as many areas of learning as possible and a general understanding of related and unrelated fields helps to push back the limitations of our horizons; a dedication to one goal at a time; a desire to improve the environment for the general good and acknowledgement by future inquirers of the value of the contributions that one has made: all provide their own opportunities in a hostile world.*

DAVIS, GRAY (JOSEPH GRAHAM DAVIS), lawyer, former governor; b. N.Y.C., Dec. 26, 1942; m. Sharon Ryer, Feb. 20, 1983. BA cum laude, Stanford U., 1964; JD, Columbia U., 1967. Chief of staff to Gov. Jerry Brown State of Calif., Sacramento, 1975—81, mem. Calif. State Assembly, 1983—87, state contr., 1987—95, lt. gov., 1995-99, gov., 1999—2003; of counsel Loeb & Loeb, LA, 2004—. Chmn. Housing and Community Devel. Com., Calif. Coun. on Criminal Justice, Franchise Tax Bd., State Lands Commn.; mem. Bd. Equalization, State Tchrs. Retirement System, Pub. Employees Retirement System, Nat. Coun. Institutional Investors; U. Calif. Regent, Calif. State U. trustee; mem. intergovtl. policy adv. com. on trade Office of U.S. Trade Rep. Founder Calif. Found. for the Protection of Children. Capt. U.S. Army. Democrat. Office: Loeb & Loeb 1010 Santa Monica Blvd Ste 2200 Los Angeles CA 90067

DAVIS, GUY DONALD, research scientist; b. Newport News, Va., June 15, 1952; s. Donald Arthur and Elinor Wilson (Ware) Davis; m. Norma May Hensler, June 30, 1990; 1 child, Christiana Ashley May. BS in Physics cum laude, Rensselaer Poly. Inst., 1974; MS in Physics, U. Wis., 1975, MS in Materials Sci., 1979, PhD in Materials Sci., 1982. Scientist Martin Marietta Labs., Balt., 1980—85, sr. scientist, 1985—88, staff scientist, group leader, 1988—93, tech. mgr., 1993—95; prin. scientist DACCO SCI., Inc., Columbia, Md., 1995—. Mem. sci. coun. Md. Acad. Sci., 1987—92. Editl. bd. Surface and Interface Analysis, 1987—96, Surface Sci. Spectra, 1991—, Jour. Adhesion Sci. and Tech., 1993—; contbr. articles tech. journals, chpts. to books. Named Disting. Young Scientist, Md. Acad. Scis., 1987; recipient Gov.'s Citation, State of Md., 1987, Citizen's Citation, City of Balt., 1987. Fellow: Am. Vacuum Soc. (chmn. applied surface sci. divsn. 1993—94), ASM Internat.; mem.: ASTM (2d vice-chmn. E-42 com. 1988—93), Soc. Adhesion and Adhesives, Electrochemical Soc. (chmn. Nat. Capital sect. 2001—02, William Blum award 1998), Adhesion Soc. (treas. 1988—95, v.p. 1995—96, pres. 1996—98, Robert L. Patrick fellow), NACE Internat., Soc. for Advancement Material and Process Engrng., Internat. Stds. Orgn. (chmn. TC201 SC2 1993—95), Sigma Xi. Democrat. Methodist. Office: DACCO SCI INC 10260 Old Columbia Rd Columbia MD 21046-1721 Business E-Mail: davis@daccosci.com.

DAVIS, H. CLINTON, retired surgeon; b. Milw., July 4, 1921; Student, Brown U., 1940, U. Chgo., 1941-43; MD, U. Pa., 1946. Diplomate Am. Bd. Surgery. Intern Del. Hosp., Wilmington, 1946-47; resident in surgery U. Pa. Grad. Hosp., Phila., 1948-51; chief gen. surgery Ft. Gordon Hosp., 1953-55; chief dept. of surgery Miami Children's Hosp.; chmn. dept. of surgery Doctors Hosp., Coral Gables; vol. facility U. Miami Sch. of Medicine. Home: 1410 Blue Rd Coral Gables FL 33146-1619

DAVIS, HARLEY CLEO, retired career officer, manufacturing executive; b. Van Buren, Ark., May 7, 1941; s. Aleta (Johnson) D.; m. Patricia Ann White, Mar. 9, 1985. BS, Ark. Tech. U., 1963; MA, Ea. Ky. U., 1972; exec. devel. program, U. N.H., 1987. Commd. 2d lt. U.S. Army, 1963, advanced through grades to maj. gen., 1993; platoon leader 1st Bn., 50th inf., 2d Armored Div., 1963; various assignments, 1963-80; comdr. 3d Bn., 5th Spl. Forces Group, Ft. Bragg, N.C., 1980-82; chief leadership br. Hdqrs. Dept. of the Army, Washington, 1982-84; chief of staff JFK Spl. Warfare Ctr. and Sch., Ft. Bragg, 1985-86; comdt. 5th Spl. Forces Group, Ft. Campbell, Ky., 1987-89; asst. comdt. JFK Spl. Warfare Ctr. and Sch., Ft. Bragg, 1989-91; dep. commdg. gen. U.S. Army Sp. Ops. Command, Ft. Bragg, 1991-92; comdg. gen. U.S. Army Spl. Forces Command (Airborne), Ft. Bragg, 1992-95; dep. commdg. gen. Fifth U.S. Army (west), Ft. Lewis, Wash., 1995-97; sr. v.p. Natec, Inc., Plattsburgh, NY, 2001—. Decorated DSM with oak leaf cluster, Legion of Merit, Soldier's Medal, Bronze Star with two oak leaf clusters, Air medal with with oak leaf cluster. Office: 11 Arkansas St Plattsburgh NY 12903 Office Phone: 518-324-5625.

DAVIS, HARRY REX, political science professor; b. Ozona, Tex., Nov. 9, 1921; s. Rex Otis and Mima (Gowin) D.; m. Ruth Elizabeth Greenlee, Sept. 6, 1947; children: Peter Gowin, Scott Andrew, Martha Greenlee. BA summa cum laude, Tex. Christian U., 1942; AM, U. Chgo., 1949, PhD, 1951; postdoctorate, Union Theol. Sem., 1952-53. Teaching fellow Tex. Christian U., 1945-46; mem. faculty dept. govt. Beloit (Wis.) Coll., 1948-90, assoc. prof., 1956-59, prof., 1959-90, chmn. dept., 1959-84, prof. emeritus, 1990—. Cons. ch. and soc. dept. World Council Chs., 1969. Author: (with others) Small City Government, 1962, Colleges and Commitments, 1971; Editor: (with others) Reinhold Niebuhr on Politics, 1960. Active Beloit City Coun., 1959-60, Beloit Bd. Ethics, 1975-81, Wis. Gov.'s Coun. on Jud. Selection, 1983-86, Beloit Bd. Health, 1996-2002, chmn., 1996-98; chmn. Beloit Dem. Com., 1956, 61-63; local mgr. campaigns congl. candidates. With USAAF, 1942-45. Ford faculty fellow, 1952-53; Social Sci. Research Council grantee; Rockefeller Found. grantee. Mem. Midwest Polit. Sci. Assn. (sec.-treas. 1959-65, mem. exec. coun. 1966-68), Am. Polit. Sci. Assn. (chmn. Burdette award com. 1979), Am. Soc. Polit. and Legal Philosophy, Soc. Christian Ethics. Democrat. Presbyterian (elder, coun. on ch. and society 1965-72, Gen. Assembly commr. 1991). Office: Beloit Coll Dept Government Beloit WI 53511 Home: 2423 Stonehedge Ln Beloit WI 53511-6727

DAVIS, HELEN GORDON, retired state senator; b. N.Y.C., 1926; m. Gene Davis; children: Stephanie, Karen, Gordon. BA, Bklyn. Coll.; postgrad., U. South Fla., 1967—70. Tchr. High Sch. Commerce, N.Y.C., Hillsborough High Sch., Tampa, Fla.; grad. asst. U. South Fla., 1968; mem. Fla. Ho. of Reps. (1st woman to be elected in 1974 from Hills Co., 1st woman to chair the legis. del.), 1974-88; state senator Fla., 1988-92; mem. Fla. Supreme Ct. Commn. on Gender Bias in the Cts., 1988-90, Fla. Supreme Ct. Commn. on Mediation and Arbitration, 1987—. Chmn. senate appropriations subcom. human svcs., mem. rules com., internat. trade and econ. devel. com., health and rehab. svcs. com. Jud. cmn. Local Govt. Study Commn. Hillsborough County (Fla.), 1964; mem. Tampa Commn. on Juvenile Delinquency, 1966-69, Mayor's Citizens Adv. Com., 1966-69, Quality Edn. Commn., 1966-68, Gov.'s Citizen Com. for Ct. Reform, 1972, Hillsborough County Planning commn., 1973-74; mem. Gov.'s Commn. on Jud. Reform, 1976; mem. employment com. Commn. Cmty. Rels., 1966-69; by-laws chmn. Arts Coun. Tampa, 1971-74; 1st v.p. Tampa Symphony Guild, 1974; bd. dirs. U. South Fla. Found., 1968-74, Stop Rape, 1973-74; past pres. PTA; active adv. commn. Nat. Child Care Action Campaign, Nat. Ctr. for Crime and Delinquency; chair Hillsborough Dem. Exec. Com., also pres.; active Fla. Com. on the Status of Women, 2001. Recipient U. South Fla. Young Dems. Humanitarian award, 1974, Diana award NOW, 1975, Woman of Achievement in Arts award Tampa, 1975, Tampa Human Rels. award, 1976, Hannah G. Solomon Citizen of Yr., 1980, St. Petersburg Times/Fla. Civil Liberties award, 1980, Friend of Edn. award, 1981, Fla. Alliance for Responsible Parenting award, 1981, Humanitarian award Judeo-Christian Clinic, 1984, Fla. Network of Runaway Youth award, 1985, Ctr. for Women Leader-adv. Friend award, 1985, Nat. Assn. Juvenile Ct. Judges Appreciation award, 1987, AAUW Leadership award, 1987, Hillsborough County Halfway House appreciation award, 1988, Martin Luther King award City of Tampa, 1988, Appreciation award Nat. Fedn. Dem. Women, 1989, Dept. Legal Affairs appreciation, 1990, Superwoman award Mus. Sci. and Industry, 1990, Nat. Childcare Merit award NASP, 1992, Am. Judicature award Am. Judicature Assn., 1993, Woman of Courage award City of Tampa, 2000, Liberty Bell award, Hillsbrough Bar Assn., 2005; named Fla. Motion Picture and TV Outstanding Legislator, 1990; named to Fla. Women's Hall Fame, 1999. Mem. LWV (pres. Hillsborough County 1966-69, lobbyist, Fla. adminstrn. of justice chmn. 1969-74), Am. Arbitration Assn., Hills County Expy. Authority, Fla. Supreme Ct. Commn. Arbitration. Democrat. Home: 45 Adalia Ave Tampa FL 33606-3301 Home Fax: 813-253-0393.

DAVIS, HENRY BARNARD, JR., lawyer; b. East Grand Rapids, Mich., June 3, 1923; s. Henry Barnard and Ethel Margaret (Turnbull) Davis; m. Margaret Lees Wilson, Aug. 27, 1946; children: Caroline Dellenbusch, Laura Davis, George B. BA, Yale U., 1945; JD, U. Mich., 1950; LLD, Olivet Coll., 1983. Bar: Mich. 1951, U.S. Dist. Ct. (we. dist.) Mich. 1956, U.S. Ct. Appeals (6th cir.) 1971, U.S. Supreme Ct. 1978. Assoc. Allaben, Wiarda, Hayes & Hewitt, 1951-52; ptnr. Hayes, Davis & Dellenbusch PLC, Grand Rapids, Mich., 1952—2002, Davis & Davis Law Office PLC, Grand Rapids, 2002—. Mem. Kent County Bd. Commrs., 1968-72; mem. Cmty. Mental Health Bd., 1970-94, past chmn.; trustee, sec. bd. Olivet Coll., 1965-91, trustee emeritus, 1991—; bd. dirs. Jr. Achievement Grand Rapids, 1960-65; chair Grand Rapids Historic Preservation Com., 1977-79; trustee East Congregational Ch., 1979-81. Served with USAAF, 1943-46, Philippines. Mem. ABA, Mich. Bar Assn., Grand Rapids Round Table (pres. 1969), Masons. Republican. Home: 30 Mayfair Dr NE Grand Rapids MI 49503-3831 Office: 535 Fountain St NE Grand Rapids MI 49503-3421 Office Fax: 616-458-8638. Personal E-mail: hbdavis@mac.com.

DAVIS, HENRY JEFFERSON, JR., former naval officer; b. Quincy, Fla., May 6, 1929; s. Henry and Sara Jewell (Davis) D.; m. Ernestine Hunt Tully, June 8, 1955; children: Frances Cornelia Davis Wallington, Jessica Leigh Davis Coughlin, H.J. Davis V, George Walton Davis II. Student, U. Fla., 1947-48; BS, Fla. State U., 1952; postgrad., U.S. Naval Acad., 1949-51; MS, U.S. Naval Postgrad. Sch., 1962. Commd. ensign U.S. Navy, 1952, advanced through grades to rear adm., 1977; comdg. officer Naval Security Group Activity, Winter Harbor, Maine, 1968-70; asst. chief of staff to comdr. in chief U.S. Pacific Fleet, dir. Naval Security Group Pacific, 1973-76; chief Nat. Security Agy., Pacific, cryptologic adv. to comdr. in chief Pacific, 1976-77; asst. dir. plans and resources Nat. Security Agy., 1977-79, dep. dir. ops., 1979-82; ret., 1982. Mgmt. cons. State of Fla. Info. Resource Commn., 1984-92. Mem. Gadsden County (Fla.) Sch. Bd., 1984—94, chmn., 1988—91, 1993—94; mem. Quincy-Gadsden Airport Authority, 1994—2001; trustee The Bapt. Coll. of Fla., 1994—2001; bd. dirs. Fla. Sch. Bd. Assn., 1990—92, Gadsden Arts Inc., 1996—2002. Decorated Def. Superior Service medal, Bronze star, Def. Meritorious Service medal, others. Baptist.

DAVIS, HENRY VANCE, education educator; s. Iwathia Herman and Ada Lou Davis; m. Diana Lee Davis; children: Makeba, Kelimo, Ada, Henry. BA, Western Mich. U., 1970; MA, U. Mich., 1971, PhD, 1990. Adminstrv. intern to v.p. U. Mich., 1988—90; asst. history prof. Western Mich. U., 1990—93, assoc. history prof., 1993—98; prof. history Ramapo Coll. of N.J., 2002—, dean, 2002—. Pres./founder Nat. Bd. Black Professors, Mahawah, NJ, 2003—; higher edn. commn. Nat. Alliance Bd. Edn., Ann Arbor, Mich., 1972—; cons. NAACP, NYC, 2000—02. Editor: (book) Sankofa, 1990, (bok) Infusing the Dialogue, 2000. Recipient Rsch. award, Gilmore Found., 1996. Mem.: Assn. Fedn. Teachers. Avocations: chess, Karate, music, sports. Office: Ramapo Coll of NJ 505 Ramapo Valley Rd Mahwah NJ 07430 Personal E-mail: henryvdavis@aol.com.

DAVIS, HERBERT OWEN, lawyer; b. Washington, June 11, 1935; s. Owen Stier and Claudie Lea (Pointer) D.; children: Herbert O. Jr., Ann P., Paul B. BA, U. N.C., 1957; JD, Duke U., 1960. Bar: N.C. 1960, U.S. Dist. Ct. (mid. dist.) N.C. 1960. Assoc. Smith Moore Smith Schell & Hunter, Greensboro, NC, 1960—66, ptnr., 1966—86, Smith Helms Mulliss & Moore, Greensboro, 1986—2002, Smith Moore LLP, Greensboro, 2002—. Editor in chief Duke Law Jour., 1959—60. Mem. ABA, N.C. Bar Assn., Greensboro Country Club, Greensboro City Club (bd. dirs.), The Carolina Club, Phi Beta Kappa. Home: 2303 Danbury Rd Greensboro NC 27408-5123 Office: Smith Moore LLP 300 N Greene St Ste 1400 Greensboro NC 27401-2171 Office Phone: 336-378-5275. Business E-Mail: bert.davis@smithmoorelaw.com.

DAVIS, HILLARY, writer, speech professional; b. Bennington, Vt., Jan. 19, 1952; d. Courtney and Blandine Hafela. BA, Columbia U.; MPhil, Cambridge U. Judge New England Writers Awards, NH, 2005. Author: (book) A Million a Minute, 1998, The Two Blondes Restaurant Guide to Southern NH, 2001—, Follow Me: Guide to Lower Manhattan, 2004—05. Mem.: NYC & Co., Publishers Mktg. Assn., Univ. of Oxford and Cambridge Club. Avocations: golf, sailing, skiing, art. Office Phone: 603-321-8359.

DAVIS, HIRAM JOE, public school administrator; b. Spartanburg, S.C., Feb. 13, 1930; s. Flake Revere and Dolorus Jane (Haigler) D.; m. Anna Jane Ripley, Mar. 16, 1951; children: Alan Joe, Kendal Jay. AB, Asbury Coll., 1951; MEd, Kent State U., 1957. Cert. supt., prin., supervisor, tchr. Elem. sch. tchr., Antrim, Ohio, 1951-52; tchr. Auburn Elem. Sch., Chagrin Falls, Ohio, 1952-57; prin. Kenston Elem. Schs., Chagrin Falls, Ohio, 1957-62; prin., dir. of 16 schs. Firestone Rubber Plantation, Harbel, Liberia, West Africa, 1962-64; asst. high sch. prin. Orange Schs., Pepper Pike, Ohio, 1964-66, prin. Brady Mid. Sch., 1966-84; interim prin. Kenston Schs., Chagrin Falls, Ohio, 1984-98. Past bd. mem. Am. Inst. Fgn. Study, Greenwich, Conn., 1968-84, prin. summer sch. groups to Europe, 1968-82; attendee White House Conf. on Edn.; owner JD Mailboxes. Chmn. trustees Garfield Meml. United Meth. Ch., Pepper Pike, mem. p.p.r. com., mission com.; vol. traveling libr. for Geauga County Pub. Libr. to Amish schs.; scoutmaster troop 1 Liberian Boy Scouts and Boy Scouts Am., Harbel, Liberia, 1962-64; summer session missionary svc. Liberia, 1985, Kenya, 1987; founder Chagrin Valley Jr. Athletic Conf. Mid. Schs. Recipient Dedicated Svc. award Chagrin Valley Jr. Athletic Conf., Garfield Meml. award for dedicated svc. in all areas of churchmanship, Harry Denman Evangelism award for lay leader United Meth. Ch. Conf., Cmty. Svc. award Fedn. Orange Cmties. Mem. NEA (life dept. Nat. Elem. Sch. Prin.), Kiwanis (pres. Lander Cir. chpt. 1969-70, 2004—05, George F. Hixon award 2001). Avocation: raising registered belgians. Personal E-mail: farmerhj@webtv.net.

DAVIS, HOWARD TED, engineering educator; b. Hendersonville, NC, Aug. 2, 1937; s. William Howard and Gladys Isabel (Rhodes) D.; m. Eugenia Asimakopoulos, Sept. 15, 1960 (dec. July 1996); children: William Howard II, Maria Katherine; m. Catherine Asimkopoulos, Mar. 9, 2000. BS in Chemistry, Furman U., 1959; PhD in Chem. Physics, U. Chgo., 1962. Postdoctoral fellow Free U. of Brussels, 1962-63; asst. prof. U. Minn., Mpls., 1963-66, assoc. prof., 1966-69, prof., 1969-80, prof., head chem. engrng. and materials sci., 1980-95, dean Inst. Tech., 1995—2004, Regent's prof., 1997—; Humboldt rschr. Cologne U., Germany, 2005. Editor: Springs of Creativity, 1981; author: Statistical Mechanics of Phases, Interfaces and Thin Films, 1995, (with K. Thomson) Linear Algebra and Linear Operators in Engineering, 2000; contbr. over 500 articles to sci. and engrng. jours. Fellow Sloan Found., 1967-69, Guggenheim Found., 1969-70. Mem. AAAS, AIChE (Walker award for excellence in publs. 1990), NAE, Am. Chem. Soc., Soc. Petroleum Engrs., Minn. Fedn. Engrng. Socs. (Disting. Engr. 1998). Democrat. Methodist. Avocations: tennis, golf, reading, movies. Home: 1822 Mount Curve Ave Minneapolis MN 55403-1018 Office: U Minn 421 Washington Ave SE Minneapolis MN 55455-0373 Personal E-mail: htdavismn@yahoo.com. Business E-Mail: davis@cems.umn.edu.

DAVIS, IRVIN, advertising executive, public relations executive, broadcast executive; b. St. Louis, Dec. 18, 1926; s. Julius and Anna (Rosen) D.; m. Adrienne Bronstein, Apr. 25, 1968; 1 child, Jennifer Alison. BSBA, Washington U., 1950; postgrad., St. Louis U., 1952; DHum (hon.), Nat. Coll., 1981, Logan Coll., 2004. Pres. Clayton-Davis & Assoc., Inc., St. Louis, 1953—, Admiral Broadcasting Corp., St. Louis, 1983—. C.p., bd. dirs. Nat. Acad. TV Arts and Scis., 1982—; bd. dirs. Truman Bank; pres. Galtex Broadcasting; pres. Celebrities Prodns. Author: (books) Room for Three, Comprehensive Tng. in Advt. and Pub. Relations; producer (film) Family Album, 1974, Use It in Good Health, Charlie, 1975. Pres. Child Assistance Program, 1986—92; v.p. Boys and Girls Town Mo., St. James, 1976—99, Make Today Count, 1985—86; bd. dirs. Jackie Joyner Kersee Found., 1997—2001, Crusade Against Crime, St. Louis, 1984—; pres. St. Louis Artists Guild. Sgt. USAF, 1945—47, PTO. Recipient Freedom Found. award, 1975, Internat. Film and TV Festival award, 1973-75, Internat. Broadcasting award Hollywood Advt. Club, 1965, 77, 82, 83, Cinegolden Eagle award Coun. on Internat. Non-Theatrical Events, 1975, Nat. Emmy award, 1991; inductee Nat. TV Acad. Silver Cir., 2004. Mem.: AFTRA, Am. Med. Writers Assn., Pub. Rels. Soc. Am. (accredited), St. Louis Club, Press Club, Advt. Club. Office: Clayton-Davis & Assoc Inc 7777 Bonhomme Ave Ste 900 Saint Louis MO 63105-3697

DAVIS, J. ALAN, lawyer, writer; b. N.Y.C., Nov. 7, 1961; Student, Marlborough Coll., Eng., 1979; BA with distinction, So. Meth. U., 1983; JD with honors, U. Tex., 1987. Bar: Calif. 1988. Assoc. O'Melveny & Myers, L.A., 1987-89, Rosenfeld, Meyer & Susman, Beverly Hills, Calif., 1989-90; pvt. practice L.A., 1990-94; ptnr. Davis & Benjamin, L.A., 1995-98, Garvin, Davis & Benjamin, LLP, L.A., 1998-99; pvt. practice L.A., 1999-2000; head legal and bus. affairs Warner Bros. Internat. TV Prodn., Burbank, Calif., 2000—. Mem. Calif. Bar Assn., Beverly Hills Bar Assn. (entertainment law sect. exec. com.), Brit. Acad. Film and TV Arts, L.A. (mng. dir. 1998, bd. dirs.). Avocations: skiing, scuba diving, tennis.

DAVIS, JACK WAYNE, JR., publishing executive; b. Toledo, Ohio, May 21, 1947; s. Jack Wayne and Virginia (Moore) D.; m. Amélie Claiborne Matthews, June 24, 1977; 1 child, Claiborne Levering. Grad., Harvard Coll., 1969. Mng. editor Figaro, New Orleans, 1972-73; reporter, columnist, asst. city editor, city editor The States-Item, New Orleans, 1973—80; metro editor The Times - Picayune, New Orleans, 1980-83; assoc. metro editor, night metro editor, metro editor The Chgo. Tribune, 1983-87; editor, v.p. Daily Press, Newport News, Va., 1987-94, pres., pub., CEO, 1994-98; pres. Tribune Interactive Inc., 1998—99, v.p. planning Tribune Pub., 1999—2000; pres., pub. CEO The Hartford Courant, Hartford, Conn., 2000—. Frank Knox fellow U. Rajasthan, India, 1971, Profl. Journalism fellow Stanford U., 1977-78. Mem. Wadsworth Atheneum Mus. of Art (bd. dirs.), MetroHartford Alliance, The Antiquarian and Landmarks Soc., The Pirate's Alley Faulkner Soc., Hartford Courant Found., Hartford's Camp Courant. Avocations: sculling, reading, squash. Office: Hartford Courant 285 Broad Street Hartford CT 06115-2510

DAVIS, JAMES ALLAN, gerontologist, educator; b. Portland, Oreg., May 20, 1953; m. Louis Carol Lindsay. BS, U. Oreg., 1975, MS, 1976, EdD, 1980. State mental health gerontologist Oreg. Mental Health Div., Salem, 1978-80; project dir. Oreg. Long Term Care Tng. Project, Salem, 1979-80; tng. specialist Nat. Assn. Area Agys. on Aging., Washington, 1981; asst. dir. for internships and vol. svc. exptl. learning programs U. Md., 1981-86, mem. rsch. and instructional faculty, 1982-86; com. adminstr. Oreg. State Human Resources Com., Salem, 1987; exec. dir., legis. dir. Oreg. State Coun. Sr. Citizens, Salem, 1987—2002; program coord. for sr. mental health care Oreg. Sr. and Disabled Svc. Div., Salem, 1989—2001; pres. James A. Davis and Assocs. Inc., Portland, 1991—; state project dir. Oreg. Assn. RSVPs, 1995—. Vis. asst. prof. Ctr. for Gerontology, U. Oreg., 1990-92; co-chair Audio-Visual Program, Internat. Congress Gerontology, 1985; nat. gerontology acad. adv. panel, Nat. Hosp. Satellite Network, 1983-85; lobbyist United Srs. Oreg., Oreg. State Coun. Sr. Citizens, Oreg. State Denturist Assn., Oreg. State Pharmacist Assn., Oreg. Soc. Physician Assts., Oreg. Legal Techs. Assn., Oreg. Dental Lab. Assn., Wash. Denturist Assn., Nat. Denturist Assn.; adj. asst. prof. Urban Studies Inst. on Aging, Portland State U., 2003—; adj. prof. human scis. dept. Marylhurst U., 2005—; presenter in field Co-author: TV's Image of the Elderly, 1985; contbg. editor Retirement Life News, 1988-92; sr. issues editor Sr. News, 1989-96; contbr. articles to profl. jours.; producer, host approximately 400 TV and radio programs. Founding pres. Oreg. Alliance for Progressive Policy, 1988-89; co-chair mental health com., vice chair legis. com., Gov.'s Commn. on Sr. Svcs., 1988-89; exec. coun., media chair Human Svcs. Coalition Oreg., 1988-89; bd. dirs. Oreg. Health Action Campaign, 1988-92; 2d v.p., bd. dirs. Oreg. State Coun. for Sr. Citizens, 1977-80, 90-92, Oreg. Medicaid Com., 1996—2002; co-chair Oreg. Medicare/Medicaid Coalition, 1995—2001, Oreg. Long Term Care Campaign, 1996-98; mem. Gov.'s Task Force for Volunteerism, State of Md., 1983-84, State Legis. Income Tax Task Force, 1990; vice chair Oreg. State Bd. Denture Technology, 1991-96; mem. com. for assessment on needs for volunteerism, Gov.'s Vol. Coun., State of Md., 1984-86; project dir. Oreg. Assn. Ret. and Sr. Vol. Programs, 1995—; mem. exec. bd. dirs. Oreg. Advocacy Coalition of Srs. and People with Disabilities, 1997—; chmn., bd. dirs. Oreg. Campaign for Patient Rights, 1997—2003. Recipient Disting. Svc. award City of Salem, 1980, Spl. Human Rights award, 1981, Svc. award U. Md., 1984, Hometown U.S.A. award Community Cable TV Producers, 1988, Disting. Svc. award Oreg. State Coun. Sr. Citizens, 1991. Mem.: Oreg. State Coun. of Sr. Citizens (Disting. Svc. of Sr. award 2000), Alzheimers Assn. of Oreg. (Pub. Policy award 2000), Nat. Denturist Assn. (exec. dir. 1982—89), Gerontol. Soc. Am.

(mental health task force 1982—84, co-chmn. 1983—84), Nat. Assn. State Mental Health Dir. (nat. exec. com. 1978—80, vice chmn. 1979—80, spl. cons.81 1981—82, mem. aging div., co-chmn. nat. program com. 1984—87, nat. media chair 1985—92), Nat. Gray Panthers (nat. exec. com. 1984—87, nat. bd. dirs. 1984—92, program co-chmn. nat. biennial conv. 1986, nat. health task force 1981—, co-chmn. 1983—84, chmn. mental health subcom. 1981—86, editor Health Watch 1982—84, state program developer Oreg. chpt. 1979—80, 1989, lobbyist 1987—, gov.'s patient protection work group 2000—01). Democrat. Office: James A Davis and Assocs Inc 1020 SW Taylor St Ste 610 Portland OR 97205-2506 E-mail: davisjasr@aol.com.

DAVIS, JAMES HENRY, retired psychology educator; b. Effingham, Ill., Aug. 6, 1932; s. Kenneth E. and Forest (Naylor) D.; m. Elisabeth Bachman, June 27, 1954; children— Stephen J., Kristin E., Leah E. BS, U. Ill., 1954; MA, Mich. State U., 1958, PhD, 1961. Asst. instr. psychology Mich. State U., East Lansing, 1959-60; instr. psychology Miami U., Oxford, Ohio, 1960-61, asst. prof. psychology, 1961-65, assoc. prof. psychology, 1965-66; vis. assoc. prof. psychology Yale U., New Haven, 1966-67, U. Ill., Champaign, 1967-68, assoc. prof., 1968-70, prof. psychology, 1970-97, prof. emeritus psychology, 1997. Fellow Ctr. for Advanced Study in Behavioral Scis., 1987-88. Author: Group Performance, 1969; editor: (with W. Brandstatter and H.C. Schuler) Dynamics of Group Decisions, 1978, (with W. Brandstatter and G. Stocker-Kreichgauer) Group Decision Making, 1982, (with G.M. Stephenson) Progress in Applied Social Psychology, Vol. I, 1981, Vol. II, 1984, (with Erich Witte) Understanding Group Behavior, Vol. 1 and Vol. 2, 1996; contbr. articles to profl. jours. Served with U.S. Army, 1954-56 Fellow AAAS, Am. Psychol. Soc.; mem. Psychonomic Soc., Midwestern Psychol. Assn., Soc. Exptl. Social Psychologists, Soc. for Judgment and Decision Making, Soc. Math. Psychology, Sigma Xi Home: 10 Lake Park Rd Champaign IL 61822-7101 Business E-Mail: j-davis@uiuc.edu.

DAVIS, JAMES LEE, lawyer; b. High Point, NC, May 2, 1940; AB with high honors, Guilford Coll., 1968; JD with honors, U. N.C., 1971. Bar: N.C. 1971. With Ward and Smith P.A., New Bern, N.C. Charles A. Dana scholar. Mem. N.C. State Bar, N.C. Bar Assn. (chmn. real property sect. coun. 1981-82), Craven County Bar Assn. (pres. 1978-79), Order of Coif. Office: Ward and Smith PA PO Box 867 1001 College Ct New Bern NC 28562-4972 Office Phone: 252-672-5404. E-mail: jld@wardandsmith.com.

DAVIS, JAMES NORMAN, neurologist, neurobiology researcher; b. Dallas, Oct. 24, 1939; s. Moses and Ruth (Grossman) D.; m. Frances Isabel Cantor, May 1, 1965; children— Amanda, Adam, Joanna. BA, Cornell U., 1961, MD, 1965. Diplomate Am. Bd. Neurology and Psychiatry. Intern Bellevue Hosp., N.Y.C., 1965-66; rsch. assoc. Lab. Chem. Pharmacology Nat. Heart Inst.-NIH, Bethesda, Md, 1966-68; resident Duke U., 1968-69, asst. prof., 1972-77, assoc. prof. medicine and pharmacology, 1977-80, prof. medicine, 1980-92, prof. pharmacology, 1987-92, prof. neurobiology, 1989-92; prof., chmn. dept. neurology SUNY, Stony Brook, 1992—; resident in neurology Cornell U.-N.Y. Hosp., 1969-72, North Shore Hosp., 1971; instr. neurology Cornell U., 1969-71; Fulbright fellow U. Goteborg, Sweden, 1972. Contbr. articles to profl. jours. Served with USPHS, 1966-68 Mem. Am. Neurol. Assn., Soc. Neurosci., Am. Soc. Pharmacology and Exptl. Therapeutics, Am. Acad. Neurology, N.C. Soc. Neurosci. (pres. local chpt. 1981-82). Democrat. Jewish. Office: SUNY Neurology Dept Hsc T12 020 Stony Brook NY 11794-0001

DAVIS, JAMES ROBERT, cartoonist; b. Marion, Ind., July 28, 1945; s. James William and Anna Catherine (Carter) D.; m. Jill Carol Davis; 1 son, James Alexander. BS, Ball State U., Muncie, Ind., 1967. Artist, Groves & Assocs., advt., Muncie, 1968-69; asst. to cartoonist: Tumbleweeds comic strip, 1969-78; cartoonist: Garfield comic strip, 1978—; TV script Here Comes Garfield, 1982, Garfield on the Town, 1983 (Emmy award 1984), Garfield in the Rough, 1984 (Emmy award 1985), Garfield's Halloween Adventure, 1985 (Emmy award 1986), Garfield in Paradise, 1986, Garfield Goes Hollywood, 1987, The Garfield Christmas Special, 1987; author: Garfield at Large, 1980, Garfield Gains Weight, 1981, Garfield Bigger Than Life, 1981, Garfield Weighs In, 1982, Garfield Takes the Cake, 1982, Garfield Treasury, 1982, Here Comes Garfield, 1982, Garfield Sits Around the House, 1983, Garfield Second Treasury, 1983, Garfield Eats His Heart Out, 1983, Garfield Tips the Scale, 1984, Garfield Loses his Feet, 1984, Garfield: His Nine Lives, 1984, Garfield Makes It Big, 1985, Garfield Rolls On, 1985, Third Garfield Treasury, 1985, Garfield Out to Lunch, 1986, The Unabridged, Uncensored, Unbelieveable Garfield Book, 1986, Garfield Food for Thought, 1987, The 4th Garfield Treasury, 1987, The Garfield Cat Naming Book, 1988, Garfield Chews the Fat, 1989, The 5th Garfield Treasury, 1989, Happy Birthday, Garfield, 1989, Garfield, Tiens Bon La Rampe, 1989, Garfield's Longest Catnap, 1989, Garfield The Big Star, 1989, Garfield in the Park, 1989, Garfield and the Tiger, 1989, Mini-Mysteries featuring Garfield, 1990, Garfield: The Me Book: A Guide to Superiority, How to Get It, Use It, and Keep It, 1990, Garfield's Judgement Day, 1990, Garfield's Feline Fantasies, 1990, Garfield Stories, 1990, Garfield on the Farm, 1990, Garfield Hangs Out, 1990, Garfield Goes to Waist, 1990, The Sixth Garfield Trasury, 1991, Garfield: The Truth About Cats, 1991, Garfield: Seasons Greetings, 1991, Garfield Thanksgiving Special, 1991, Garfield Takes Up Space, 1991, Garfield Says a Mouthful, 1991, Garfield Gets a Life, 1991, Garfield's Ghost Stories, 1992, Garfield Vacation Greetings, 1992, Garfield Learns About Thoughtfulness: Don't Be Late!, 1992, Garfield Learns About Planning: Surprize Party, 1992, Garfield Learns About Money: Money Madness!, 1992, Garfield Learns About Fire Safety: Where's the Fire?, 1992, Garfield Learns About Cooking: Any Cat Can Cook, 1992, Garfield Learns about Conservation: Endangered Odie?, 1992, Garfield Keeps His Chin Up, 1992, Garfield By the Pound, 1992, Garfield Birthday Greetings, 1992, The Seventh Garfield Treasury, 1993, Garfield's Big Fat Hairy Joke Book, 1993, Garfield Takes His Licks, 1993, Garfield Hits the Big Time: His 25th Book, 1993, Garfield's Tales of Mystery, 1994, Garfield's Night Before Christmas, 1994, Garfield's Insults, 1994, Garfield's Haunted House: And Other Spooky Tales, 1994, Garfield's Furry Tales, 1994, Garfield's Big Fat Scary Joke Book, 1994, Garfield's Big Fat Holiday Joke Book, 1994, Garfield Insults, Put-Downs, 1994, Garfield Fat Cat, 1994, Garfield Discovers America, 1994, Garfield's Son of Big, Fat Hairy Jokes, 1994, Big Hairy Garfield, 1994, Garfield, The Easter Bunny?, 1995, Garfield's Stupid Cupid: And Other Silly Stories, 1995, Garfield Fat Cat 3 Pack, 1995, Garfield Dishes It Out, 1995, Mr. Potato Head, 2001. Mktg. Hall of Fame award Am. Mktg. Assn., 1982; recipient Disting. Alumnus award Am. Assn. State Colls. Univs. Mem. Nat. Cartoonists Soc. (Best Humor Strip of 1981, 86, Segar award 1985, Cartoonist of Yr. 1990), Newspaper Comics Council. Protestant. Republican. Achievements include first to Garfield comic strip in 2003 Guiness Book of World Records as most widely distributed comic in the world. Office: Universal Press Syndicate 4520 Main St Ste 700 Kansas City MO 64111-7701

DAVIS, JANE BLEDSOE, music educator; b. Dyersburg, Tenn., July 18, 1945; d. Lynn Hunter and Gladys Louise (McKnight) Bledsoe; m. Patrick James III Flaherty, Oct. 15, 1965 (div. Aug. 1974); children: Della Maureen Flaherty, Amanda Louise Flaherty, Patrick James IV Flaherty; m. Anthony Mathew Davis, July 1, 2001. BMusEdn, Murray State U., Ky., 1976; MA in Edn., S.W. Mo. State U., 1987; MMusEdn, S.E. Mo. State U., 1995. Tchr. music K-6 Lorain City Schs., Ohio, 1967—69; h.s. music, vocal tchr. Portageville H.S., New Medvid, Mo., 1977—79; tchr. music New Medvid Co. R-I, 1979—. Adj. faculty music Dyersburg State C.C., Tenn., 1994—; dir. New Medvid Singers, 1991—. Contbr. articles to profl. jours. Mem., soloist Cmty. Choir, Sikeston, Mo., 1993, Dyersburg Choral Soc., 1997—99. Recipient Excellence in Rsch. award, S.E. Mo. State U., 1996. Mem.: Music Educators Nat. Conf., Mo. Music Educators Assn. (v.p. elem. music 1987—89). Baptist. Avocations: reading, singing, weightlifting. Home: 2352 Hamer Rd Dyersburg TN 38024

DAVIS, JANE G., lawyer; b. Norwich, NY, May 3, 1949; BA in French, Elmira Coll., NY, 1971; MA in French, U. Pitts., 1973; JD, Duquesne U., 1978. Bar: Pa. 1978, US Dist. Ct. We. Dist. Pa. 1978. Assoc. gen. counsel Limbach Co., Pitts., 1978—81; atty. Joy Technologies Inc., Pitts., 1981—88, v.p., gen. counsel, sec., 1988-95, York Internat. Corp., York, Pa., 1995—. Mem. ABA, Pa. Bar Assn. Office: York Internat Corp 631 S Richland Ave York PA 17403

DAVIS, JANET, physician; MA, U. Tex., 1978; BA summa cum laude, Macalester Coll., 1972; MD, Baylor U., 1981. Prof. U. Miami Sch. of Medicine, Miami, Fla., 1989—; fellow vitreoretinal surgery Bascom Palmer Eye Inst., U. Miami Sch. Medicine, 1986—87; sr. staff fellow lab. immunology Nat. Eye Inst., NIH, Bethesda, Md., 1987—89. Recipient Sr. Achievement Award, Am. Acad. of Ophthalmology, 2004. Mem.: Am. Uveitis Soc. (pres. 2005—). Office: Bascom Palmer Eye Inst 900 NW 17th ST Miami FL 33136 Office Phone: 305-326-6377.

DAVIS, JANET R. BEACH, science educator; b. Davenport, Iowa, Jan. 25, 1960; d. James R. and Fern Louise Munday Beach; m. Dennis Kay Davis, Jan. 31, 1978; 1 child, Matthew Glenn. AA, Heartland C.C., Bloomington, Ill., 1995; BA, U. Ill., Springfield, 2004. Sr. sci. lab. tech. Heartland C.C., Bloomington, 1994-99, supr. sci. lab., 1999—. Founder, pres. environ club Heartland C.C., Bloomington, 1993—99; advisor First STEP Environ. Club, 2000—; facilitator Ill. Dept. Natural Resources, 1998—, citizen scientist forest watch, 1999. Author: Earth Science Lab, 1999. Vol. worker Audubon Soc., Bloomington, 1996—; adv. bd. Ecology Action Ctr., Normal, Ill., 1997—, bd. dirs., 2002— Recipient Paul Simon award Ill. C.C. Trustee Assn., 1996; mem. USA Today Ill. Acad. Team, 1995, 96. Mem.: Am. Assn. Women in C.C. (pres.-elect 2001, pres. 2002—04), Bloomington Normal Women Writers Group (founder), Ill. Power Customers United to Save Our Trees (founding mem.), First Step Environ. Club (founder, pres. 1993—), Phi Theta Kappa (founder). Avocations: needlecrafts, reading, mahjong. Office: Heartland CC ICB 1006 1500 W Raab Rd Normal IL 61761 E-mail: janet.beach-davis@heartland.edu.

DAVIS, JANICE, school system administrator; BS, MA in Tchg., PhD in Curriculum and Instruction, U. NC, Chapel Hill. Asst. supt. Granville County, NC, supt., 1994—2000; asst. supt. for curriculum and instruction Durham, NC, 2000—03; dep. state supt. NC Dept. Pub. Instrn., 2003—, interim supt., 2005—. Office: NC Dept Pub Instrn 301 N Wilmington St Raleigh NC 27601 Office Phone: 918-807-3300.*

DAVIS, JEAN E., bank executive; b. Durham, N.C., Dec. 9, 1955; BA in Polit. Sci. and Indsl. Rels., U. N.C.; MBA, Duke U. Joined Wachovia Corp., Charlotte, NC, 1985, regional v.p. Piedmont Triad Region, 1996—98, merger coord. Va. ops., 1998, exec. v.p., dir. human resources, 1998—99, sr. exec. v.p., dir. human resources, 1999—2000, sr. exec. v.p., chief tech. and ops. officer, 2000—01, sr. exec. v.p., divsn. head info. tech., e-commerce and ops., 2001—. Mem. Fin. Svcs. Roundtable; bd. trustees U. N.C., Greensboro, bd. visitors, Chapel Hill. YMCA of Greater Charlotte. Named one of 25 Women to Watch, US Banker Mag., 2003. Office: Wachovia Corp 301 South College St Charlotte NC 28288-0570

DAVIS, JEFFREY BURGESS, writer, educator; s. James Haywood Davis and Sharlette Ray Burgess; m. Cory Hanlon Smith (div.). BA magna cum laude in English, U. Tex., 1988, MA in English, 1992. Author: City Reservoir, 1999, The Journey from the Center to the Page, 2004. Mem.: Am. Acad. Poets.

DAVIS, JENNIE SUE, aerospace engineer; b. Caldwell, Kans., July 18, 1953; d. John Jr. and Anna Mae (Carter) Petrik; m. Terry Lee Davis, Jan. 21, 1972; children: Mistie Rae, Brandon Scott. BS in Engring.- Physics, Colo. State U., Fort Collins, 1984. Radar cross-section engr. Boeing Def. and Space Group, Kent, Wash., 1985—89; aircraft maintenance engr. Boeing Comml. Airplane Group, Seattle, 1989—97; lead engr. payloads, airplane maintenance engr. Boeing Comml. Airplane, 1997—99, sr. svc. engr., 1999—2005, sr. aircraft maintenance engr., 2005—. Mother advisor Issaquah Assembly # 54 Washington & Idaho Internat. Order of Rainbow for Girls, 1991-96, grand dep. Dist. 8, 1996—, dir. comm. grand exec. com., 2002—; troup leader Girl Scouts U.S., 1981-85. Mem. Order of Ea. Star. (Medford, Okla. and Kirkland, Wash. chpts.), Orderof Amaranth (Bellevue Ct.). Avocations: community/service organizations, reading. Home: 1155 Ridgewood Pl SW Issaquah WA 98027-4635 Office: Boeing Comml Airplane Group PO Box 3707 Seattle WA 98124-2207

DAVIS, JEREMY MATTHEW, chemist; b. Bakersfield, Calif., Aug. 5, 1953; s. Joseph Hyman and Mary (Pavetto) D.; m. Bernadette Sobkiewicz, Aug. 28, 1976 (div.); children: Andrew Jeremy, Christopher Peter. BS in Biol. Scis., U. Calif., Irvine, 1974; M in Pub. Adminstrn., Calif. State U., Long Beach, 1983. Chemist I, II, Orange County Water Dist., Fountain Valley, Calif., 1977—84, supervising chemist, 1984—. Papers in field; TV appearance contestant on Jeopardy, 2001. Named Lab. Person of Yr., Calif. Water Environment Assn., Santa Ana River Basin, 1984. Mem. MENSA, Toastmasters Internat. (pres. Watermeisters club 1996, 99, 2003, gov. founder's dist. area C-5, 1999-2001, gov. divsn. C 2001-2002). Office: Orange County Water Dist PO Box 8300 Fountain Valley CA 92728-8300 Office Phone: 714-378-3244. Business E-Mail: jdavis@ocwd.com. E-mail: jermedavis@hotmail.com.

DAVIS, JERRY ARNOLD, judge; b. Waukegan, Ill., July 1, 1946; s. Bobbie and Mary Alice (Trammel) Davis; m. Barbara Purse Beach, June 17, 1972 (div. Sept. 1978); m. Deborah Selph Davis, Dec. 12, 1980; children: Michael Scott, Stuart Sheffield. BA, Miss. State U., Starkville, 1968; JD, U. Va., 1971. Bar: Miss. 1971. Atty.-adviser Dept. of Justice, Washington, 1975-80, asst. U.S. atty. Jackson, Miss., 1980-84; U.S. magistrate judge U.S. Cts., Aberdeen, Miss., 1984—. Criminal investigator USAF, Topeka, 1971-72; magistrate judge's edn. com., Fed. Jud. Ctr. Capt. U.S. Army, 1972-75. Mem. ABA, Fed. Bar Assn. (chpt. v.p. 1986-90), Am. Judicature Soc., Miss. Bar Assn., William Keady Am. Inn of Ct., Ct. Adminstrn. and Case Mgmt. Com. Judicial Conf. of U.S., Judges Edn. Com. (magistrar). Democrat. Episcopalian. Avocations: reading, baseball, fishing, basketball. Office: US Magistrate Judge PO Box 726 Aberdeen MS 39730-0726 Home: 2529 Woodgreen Dr Belden MS 38826-8729

DAVIS, JESSICA G., geneticist; b. Bklyn., Apr. 3, 1934; d. Nathan S. and Sylvia (Teplitz) Grosof; m. Andrew R. Davis, June 17, 1956; children: Jennifer Davis Hall, David. BA, Wellesley Coll., 1955; MD, Columbia U., 1959. Diplomate Am. Bd. Med. Genetics. Intern pediatrics St. Luke's Hosp.-Columbia U.; fellow Albert Einstein Coll. Medicine Yeshiva U., N.Y.C., 1961-68, instr. Albert Einstein Coll. Medicine, 1962, asst. prof. Albert Einstein Coll. Medicine, 1968-74; assoc. prof. clin. pediatric Well Coll. Medicine Cornell U., N.Y.C., 1974—. Cons. March of Dimes, N.Y.C., 1974—, Hastings Inst., Garrison, N.Y., 1979—; mem. sickle cell adv. com. NIH. Contbr. articles to profl. jours. Recipient Antoine Marfan award Nat. Marfan Found., 2005, numerous grants. Fellow: Am. Coll. Med. Genetics (founding fellow, CME officer); mem.: N.Y. Acad. Medicine, Coun. Regional Genetics Network (pres. 1991—94), Am. Soc. Human Genetics. Office: Weill Med Coll Cornell U Presbyn Hosp 525 E 68th St Rm Box 128 New York NY 10021-4870 Office Phone: 212-746-1496. Business E-Mail: jgdavis@mail.med.cornell.edu.

DAVIS, JIM, congressman, lawyer; b. Oct. 11, 1957; m. Peggy Bessent; children: Peter, William. BA, Washington and Lee U., 1979; JD, U. Fla., 1982. Pvt. practice law, Tampa, Fla., 1982-88; ptnr. Bush, Ross, Gardner, Warren and Rudy, Tampa, Fla., 1988; mem. Fla. Ho. of Reps., 1988-97, majority leader; mem. U.S. Congress from 11th Fla. dist., 1997—, mem. budget com., house adminstrn. com., internat. rels. com., mem. energy and commerce com., 2003—, co-chair, New Dem. Coalition. Mem. Brandon Chamber of Commerce, Greater Tampa Chamber of Commerce, Riverview Chamber of Commerce, GTE Awards Commn. for Ed. Initiative; bd. mem. Met. Ministries Shelter for Homeless. Mem.: ABA, Hillsborough County Bar Assn., Fla. Bar Assn. Democrat. Office: US Ho of Reps 409 Cannon Ho Office Bldg Washington DC 20515-0001*

DAVIS, JO, naturopathic physician; b. Pecos, Tex., Jan. 6, 1937; d. Johnnie Rex and Laura (Swann) D.; children: Cassandra Ann, Charles Rex. AA in Nursing, N.Mex. State U., 1992; BSc in Nutrition, Clayton Coll. Naturahealth, 1995, MSc in Nutrition, 1996; DD, Am. Inst. Theology, 1996; PhD in Nutrition, Clayton Coll. Naturahealth, 1997; PhD in Hypnotherapy, Am. Pacific U.; D Naturopathy, Clayton Coll. Natural Health, 1995. Diplomate Am. Psychotherapy Assn.; cert. hypnotherapist; RN, Kans., Mo., Tex., N. Mex. Asst. coord. Carlsbad Hospice, Inc., N. Mex., 1992-98; prin., owner Natural Health Training and Resource Ctr., Carlsbad, N. Mex., 1994-98; dir. New Directions, Inc., Oak Grove, Mo., 1999—. Cons. Westbrooke Chiropractic, Lee's Summit, Mo., 1999—, Chiropractic Physicians, Independence, Mo., 1999—; instr. Continuing Edn. RNs, Tex.; cert. trainer Neuro-Linguistic Programming, Inst. for Time Line Therapy Tng. Contbr. articles to newspapers; newsletter editor, 1994-96. Mem. Internat. Good Neighbor Coun., Mex., U.S.A., 1994-96; pres. Wildlife Rescue, Inc., Carlsbad, 1992-96; ordained minister Reverend Universal Life Ch. Named N. Mex. Woman of Yr. State of N. Mex., 1992. Mem. Internat. Guild Hypnotists, Am. Assn. Univ. Women, Am. Bd. Hypnotherapy, Am. Holistic Health Assn., Nat. Audobon Soc., The Nature Conservancy, Order of Eastern Star. Avocations: raising horses, shaman studies, native american culture. Home and Office: 8311 S Hillside School Rd Oak Grove MO 64075-8245 Office Phone: 816-215-4363. Personal E-mail: doctordavis@micro.com.

DAVIS, JO, nurse, writer, professional speaker, small business owner, photographer; b. St. Louis, Feb. 9, 1947; d. Jesse Marshall Davis and JoAnn (Charlsie Mae) (Skaggs) McCants; children: Jo Alice Gallagher, Andrew W. Lingle, Jr., James M. Lingle, Daniel V. Lingle(dec.), Elizabeth K. Nash. AS in Sci., Forest Park Coll., 1980, AS in Liberal Arts, 1982; studied, State Fair Coll., 1980—81, U. Mo., Columbia, 1980, Kirkwood Coll., 1993; grad., Pacific Inst. Aromatherapy, San Raphael, Calif., Internat. cert., 2000. Lic. practical nurse, Mo., 1981. Columnist Driving Force Mag./Pollard Pub., Ala., 1996—2001; creator, tchr. safe driving course; owner, operator Exterm Pest Control, St. Louis; over-the-road truck driver CRST, Cedar Rapids, Iowa, 1993—97, Henderson Trucking, Salem, Ill., Celadon Trucking, Indpls., USXpress, Chattanooga; census taker Census Bur. U.S. Dept. Commerce. Spkr. in field. Author: (poetry collection) Wings, 1998, Motivational Seven Steps to Assuming Responsibility, 1999; author: (as J. Marshall Davis) The Write to Kill, 1999; author: Tribal Dancer (Hon. Mention); editor: The Scene Newspaper; author: How to Escape Abuse. Leader Girl Scouts Am., Overland, Mo., 1972—73, Boy Scouts Am., Sedalia, Mo., 1981—82. Named Most Valued Leader, Boy Scouts Am., Sedalia, 1982; recipient Presenter's award for serving as a role model, 18th Nat. Women's Tng. Program, New Horizons, St. Louis, 1985, Safety Essay Grand award, T.T.C., Inc., Salem, Ill., 1994, Pres. award for literary excellence, Iliad Press, 1997, 1st, 2nd, 3d Pl. writing contest, State Fair Coll., Cert. of Achievement, Profl. Spkrs. Tng. Program, Wis., 1999. Mem.: Toastmasters, Soc. Children's Book Writers and Illustrators, Truck Writers Nat. Assn., Internat. Women's Writers Guild, Nat. Writers Union, Mo. Women of Today, Mo. Nurses Assn., United Meth. Women (missions coord., membership nurture and outreach 2005), Nat. Geog. Soc., Phi Theta Kappa. Methodist. Achievements include research in a natural cure for HIV as well as studying effects of essential oils on illness and the human body. Avocations: horseback riding, ice skating, free hand climbing, photography, violin. Home: Rt 1 Box 171A Arcadia MO 63621 E-mail: jdavisnow@aol.com.

DAVIS, JO ANN S., congresswoman; b. Rowan County, N.C., June 29, 1950; m. Charles E. Davis II; children: Charloe, Chris. Attended, Hampton Roads Business Coll. Mem. Va. State Legis., 1998-2001, mem. gen. laws com., mem. health welfare & insts., mem. sci, & tech. com., mem. claims com, mem. Chesapeake and its tributaries com.; mem. U.S. Congress from 1st Va. dist., 2001—; mem. armed svcs. com., govt. reform com., internat. rels. com. Republican. Mem. Assembly Of God Ch. Office: 1123 Longworth Ho Office Bldg Washington DC 20515-4601*

DAVIS, JOAN CARROLL, retired museum director; b. Sept. 20, 1931; d. Homer Leslie and Ruby Isabelle (Stone) G.; m. Frederic E. Davis, Aug. 22, 1953; children: Timothy, Terri, Tami, Traci, Todd, Tricia. Student, Bob Jones U., 1949-52. Supr. Day Care Ctr. Bob Jones U., Greenville, S.C., 1953-63; docent Univ. Art Gallery, Greenville, 1964-73, dir., 1974—; ret., 1999. Republican. Baptist. Office: 217 Stadium View Dr Greenville SC 29609

DAVIS, JOANNE FATSE, lawyer; m. Thomas J. Davis, Jr. BS, Boston U., 1977; JD, U. Bridgeport, 1982. Bar: Conn. 1982, N.Y. 1983. Motions law clk. U.S. Ct. Appeals (2d cir.), N.Y.C., 1982-83; assoc. Debevoise & Plimpton, N.Y.C., 1983-89; sr. corp. counsel Uniroyal Chem. Co., Middlebury, Conn., 1989-99; asst. gen. counsel, fin. and adminstrn. Crompton Corp., 1999—. Mem. Am. Corp. Counsel Assn., Conn. Bar Assn., The Corporate Bar, Assn. Bar City of N.Y., Soc. Farsarotul. Eastern Orthodox.

DAVIS, JOE A., lawyer; b. Alexandria, La., Apr. 1, 1960; BS, Univ. Tex., Dallas, 1982; JD, Baylor Univ., Waco, 1985. Ptnr., project devel., fin. leasing Hunton & Williams LLP, Dallas, and mem. exec. com. Mem.: Natural Gas & Electric Power Soc., N. Tex. (past pres.), N. Tex. Chapter, Gas Processors Assn., Texas State Bar. Office: Hunton & Williams LLP 30th Fl Energy Plz 1601 Bryan St Dallas TX 75201-3402 Office Phone: 214-979-3038. Office Fax: 214-979-3201. Business E-Mail: jadavis@hunton.com.

DAVIS, JOEL, publisher; b. Chgo., Apr. 5, 1934; s. Bernard George and Sylvia (Friedman) D.; m. Carol Sue Barnett, Aug. 3, 1958; children: Charles Michael, Andrew Barnett, Jonathan William. BA, Brown U., 1957; student, Columbia U., summer 1953. With Davis Publs., Inc., N.Y.C., 1957-92, exec. v.p., 1959-68, pres., 1969-92, Sylvia Porter's Personal Fin. Mag. Co., 1982-89, Woodworker, Inc., Westport, Conn., 1993-95; ptnr. Davis/Herschbein & Assocs., L.L.C., Westport, 1996—2003; pres. Archtl. Designs, Inc., Wilton, Conn., 1996—. Bd. dirs. Mut. N.Y., Mony Series Fund Inc., 1971-2004. Nat. chmn. univ. fund Brown U., 1965—68; bd. dirs. Brit. Am. Ednl. Found., 1977—80; mem. exec. com. gen. devel. coun. Brown U., 1962—77, Young Pres. Orgn., 1971—83; vice chmn. Brown Devel. Coun., 1968—69; regional dir. Assoc. Alumni Brown U., 1965—67, trustee, mem. corp., 1968—73; mem adv. and exec. com. Brown U., 1971—73, chmn. budget and fin. com., 1971—73, chmn. nat. alumni schs. program, 1982—85; trustee Westport Pub. Libr., 1992—2001; chmn. Westport Libr. Adv. Coun., 2001—; trustee Brookfield Craft Ctr., 1992—94; pres. Westport Pub. Libr., 1997—99. Mem. Am. Arbitration Assn. (mem. nat. panel), Mag. Pubs. Am. (bd. dirs. 1969-94, sec. 1979-81, vice chmn. mktg. com. 1969-73, mem. exec. com. 1971-88, mem. fin. com. 1974-88, chmn. membership com. 1975-91), Brown Club (mem. N.Y.C. bd. govs. 1963-69). Home: 15 Crooked Mile Rd Westport CT 06880-1124 Office: Archtl Designs Inc 57 Danbury Rd Ste 203 Wilton CT 06897 E-mail: prez@architecturaldesigns.com.

DAVIS, JOHN A., film producer; Prodr. (films) Predator, 1987, Three O'Clock High, 1987, Taffin, 1988, License to Drive, 1988, Little Monsters, 1989, The Last of the Finest, 1990, Enid is Sleeping, 1990, Shattered, 1991, Storyville, 1992, The Firm, 1993, The Thing Called Love, 1993, Gunmen, 1994, Grumpy Old Men, 1993, The Hunted, 1994, Waterworld, 1994. Office: Davis Entertainment Ste 2900 2121 Avenue Of The Stars Los Angeles CA 90067-5057

DAVIS, JOHN CHARLES, lawyer; b. Kansas City, Mo., Mar. 4, 1943; s. Ralph B. Jr. and Helen M. (Schneider) D.; m. C. Jane Reusser, June l8, 1966; children: Tracy A., Matthew S. BA, U. Kans., 1965; JD, U. Mich., 1968. Bar: Mo. 1968, Kans. 1983. Ptnr. Stinson Morrison Hecker, LLP, Kansas City, 1968—. Chmn. Fed. Estate Tax Symposium, 1986-87. Chmn. Bacchus Found., Kansas City, 1974; bd. dirs. Crittenten, Kansas City, 1988-94, vice chmn., 1990-92; trustee Schutte Found., Kansas City, 1986—; trustee UMKC, 1989—, treas., 1994-96, counsel, 1996—; trustee Village Presbyn. Ch. Found., chmn., 1991-93; elder Village Presbyn. Ch., 1994-97; bd. dirs. Gamma O Edn. Found., 1991—; bd dirs., Heart of Am. coun. Boy Scouts Am., 1995—, exec. com., 1996—; bd. dirs. John County C.C. Found., 2000—. Fellow Am. Coll. Trust and Estate Counsel (by-laws com. 1987-96, chmn. 1996-99, 2002-05, program com. 1993-96); mem. ABA, Mo. Bar Assn., Kans. Bar Assn., Estate Planning Soc. Kansas City (pres. 1990-91), Nelson-Atkins Mus. Soc. Fellows, Kansas City Club (v.p. 1989-90), Indian Hills Country Club (Mission Hills, Kans.), The River Club (Kansas City, Mo.), Rotary, Gamma Omicron (pres., bd. dirs. 1979-85). Presbyterian. Avocations: squash, Hopi art, Marklin trains, travel, photography. Home: 6421 High Dr Mission Hills KS 66208-1935 Office: Stinson Morrison Hecker LLP 1201 Walnut St Ste 2900 Kansas City MO 64106 Office Phone: 816-691-3252. Business E-Mail: jcdavis@stinsonmoheck.com.

DAVIS, JOHN EDWARD, music educator, musician; b. Omaha, Nebr., July 7, 1954; s. William Edward and Dorothy Ann Davis; m. Susan Lynn Aronovici, June 10, 1990; children: Evan William, Andrew Russell. MusB magna cum laude, San Francisco State U., 1990, MusM, 1991; D in Musical Arts, U. Ariz., 1997. Ordained elder Presbyn. Ch. Saxophonist San Francisco Saxophone Quartet, 1980—87, Nuc. Whales Saxophone Orch., Santa Cruz, Calif., 1987—91; grad. tchg. asst. San Francisco State U., 1990—91, U. Ariz., Tucson, 1991—94, grad. rsch. asst., 1994—95; asst. prof. of music Berry Coll., Mt. Berry, Ga., 1995—2001, assoc. prof. music, 2001—; flutist Rome (Ga.) Symphony Orch., 1995—. Arranger (musical arrangement) Brandenburg Concerto No. 3: For Flute Choir. J. S. Bach, 1998, String Quartet No. 4, K. 157: For Saxophone Quartet. W. A. Mozart, 1999, Three Madrigals: For Flute Quartet or Flute Choir Orlando di Lasso, 1999, Concerto Grosso, Op. 3, No. 8: For Flute Choir. Antonio Vivaldi, 1999, Quartet in C Minor, Op. 18, No. 4: For Saxophone Quartet L. van Beethoven, 1999, Quartet, No. 58, Op. 54, No. 2: For Saxophone Quartet Franz Josef Haydn, 1999, Divertimento, K. 138: For Flute Choir W. A. Mozart, 1999, Lady Radnor's Suite: For Flute Choir. C. Hubert H. Parry, 1999, Sheep May Safely Graze: For Saxophone Sextet, 2000, Intermezzo, Op. 118, No. 2: For Flute Choir Johannes Brahms, 2000, Souvenir de Porto Rico: For Flute Choir. Louis Moreau Gottschalk, 2000, Gloria, from Missa Tu Es Petrus: For Flute Choir. Palestrina, 2000, Trio in G Major, Op. 53, No. 1: For Flute Trio, 2000, Concerto Grosso, Op. 6, No. 3: For Flute Choir. G. F. Handel, 2000, What Wondrous Love: For Flute Choir, 2001, Finale, from Serenade, Op. 22: For Flute Choir Antonin Dvorak, 2001, Allegro, from Sinfonia Concertante: For Flute Choir. J. C. Bach, 2001, Tarentelle Styrienne: For Flute Choir, 2002, I Need Thee Every Hour. Robert Lowry, 2002; arranger: musical arrangement Enigma Variations: For Flute Choir, Edward Elgar, 2003; arranger (musical arrangement) Jig, from St. Paul's Suite: For Flute Choir, 2004, Madrigali di Monteverdi: For Flute Choir, 2004, Menuet, from Tombeau de Couperin: For Flute Choir, 2004, Danza Española: For Flute Choir, 2004, saxophonist (recording) Thar They Blow. Nuclear Whales Saxophone Orchestra. Whaleco Music, Whalin'. Nuclear Whales Saxophone Orchestra, Bach/Mozart. The San Francisco Saxophone Quartet, The San Francisco Saxophone Quartet; contbr. articles to profl. jours. Conducting Fellow, Conductors Inst. SC., 1998. Mem.: ASCAP (Std. award 1999, 2000, 2001, 2002, 2003, 2004), Music Educators Nat. Conf., Nat. Flute Assn., Nat. Assn. Coll. Wind and Percussion Instrs., Coll. Music Soc., Phi Kappa Phi, Pi Kappa Lambda, Phi Mu Alpha. Avocations: photography, bicycling, tennis. Office: Berry College 11 Berry College Mount Berry GA 30149 Home: 121 E Clinton Dr Rome GA 30165 Office Phone: 706-290-2176. Business E-Mail: jdavis@berry.edu.

DAVIS, JOHN EUGENE, restaurant executive, beverage company executive, disc jockey; b. Buffalo, Aug. 27, 1948; s. Stanley and Dorothy (Svennson) D.; m. Carolyn Elizabeth Cummings, June 14, 1969; children: John, Jady. AA, Niagara County C.C., 1968; BA, Oneonta State U., 1970; MS, Russell Sage Coll., 1974. Tchr. Schenectady (N.Y.) City Sch. Dist., 1970-92; pres. PJ's Bar-B-Q, Inc., Saratoga Springs, N.Y., 1986—, Sarasoda, Inc., Saratoga Springs, 1998—. Active Rep. Chairman's Club, Saratoga Springs. Mem. Nat. Restaurant Assn., N.Y. State United Tchrs., Schenectady Fedn. Tchrs., Greater Saratoga C. of C., United Restaurant Hotel Tavern Assn. of N.Y. State, Nat. Rifle Assn., N.Y. State Restaurant Assn., Lions (Lion of the Yr. 1984-85). Methodist. Avocations: physical fitness, boating, fishing, football. Office: PJ's Bar-B-Q Inc RR 9 Saratoga Springs NY 12866-9809 E-mail: pjsbbq@aol.com, sarasodas@loganberry.com.

DAVIS, JOHN F., III, travel company executive; married; 3 children. BSBA, Tex. Christian U., Ft. Worth. Pres. Mid-South Drilling Co.; co-founder 800-FLOWERS; founder ATC Comm.; launched TravelWeb.com, 1994; pres., CEO Dallas-based Pegasus Solutions, Inc., 1989—. Bd. dirs. Dallas Visitors, Convs. Bur., TRX, Inc. Campaign dir., treas. re-election campaign Senator John G. Tower, 1978. Named one of People of Yr., Travel Agt. Mag., 1991, one of bus. travel industry's 25 Most Influential Execs., 1994, 95, 97, 98, 99, Agt. of Change, Computerworld, 1995, one of 25 Most Influential People in Meetings Industry, Meeting News, 1997, Person of Yr. in Interactive Travel, Interactive Travel Report, 1998; named to 1999 list of top 75 execs. in the hotel industry Lodging mag., Travel Industry Hall of Fame, Bus. Travel News, 1999.

DAVIS, JOHN HERSCHEL, retired surgeon, educator; b. Coraopolis, Pa., May 11, 1924; s. John Herschel and Fern (Pew) D.; m. Peggy Lou Seyler, Sept. 7, 1946; children: Karen LaRue, Wendy Sue, Halle Rive'. Student, Allegheny Coll., 1942-43; MD, Western Res. U., 1948. Diplomate: Am. Bd. Surgery. Intern Univ. Hosps., Cleve., 1948-49, resident, 1955-56; asst. prof. surgery Western Res. U., Cleve., 1956-59, assoc. prof. surgery, 1959-64, prof., 1964-69; dir. surgery Cleve. Met. Hosp., 1966-69; prof. dept. surgery U. Vt., Burlington, 1969—; prof. emeritus retired, 1999. Dir. Am. Bd. Surgery, Phila., Am. Bd. Emergency Medicine, East Lansing, Mich., Am. Trauma Soc., Chgo., 1978—; chmn. surgery sect. NIH, Washington, 1982— Editor: Current Concepts of Surgery, 1965, Jour. of Trauma, 1974, Clinical Surgery, 1987, Essentials of Clinical Surgery, 1991; Am. editor: Brit. Jour. Injury; editorial bd.: Medfact; corr. editor: Journal de Traumatologie, Jour. Injury. Mem. Bar. Rev. Com. Vt. Supreme Ct., 1982. Served to capt. U.S. Army, 1950-53. Recipient William Peck Rsch. award Western Res. U., 1961; recipient Surgeon of Year award Nat. Safety Coun., N.Y.C., 1979 Fellow ACS (Scudder Oration award 1979, Disting. Svc. award 1991); mem. AAAS, Am. Assn. for History of Medicine, Am. Surg. Assn., Am. Assn. Surgery Trauma, Am. Burn Assn., Am. Fedn. Clin. Rsch., Am. Heart Assn., Am. Trauma Soc., Central Soc. Clin. Rsch., Central Surg. Soc., Chittenden County Med. Soc., Collegium Internationale Chirurgiae Digestivae, Digestive Disease Found., Eastern Surg. Soc., Halsted Soc., Internat. Soc. for Burn Injuries, Italian Surg. Rsch. Soc., Nat. Rsch. Coun. of Nat. Acad. Scis., New Eng. Soc. for Vascular Surgery, New Eng. Surg. Soc. (Nathan Smith award 1997), N.Y. Acad. Scis., Soc. Internationale de Chirurgie, Soc. Exptl. Biology and Medicine, Soc. Med. Cons. to Armed Forces, Soc. Surgery Alimentary Tract, Soc. Surg. Chairmen, Soc. for Vascular Surgery, Surg. Biology Club II, Vt. State Med. Soc. (Disting. Svc. award 1990), Allen O. Whipple Med. Soc., Sigma Xi, Alpha Omega Alpha Clubs: Ethan Allen (Burlington). Republican. Home: 21 Ridgewood Dr Burlington VT 05401-2625 Personal E-mail: john.davis@adelphia.net.

DAVIS, JOHN JAMES, religion educator; b. Phila., Oct. 13, 1936; s. John James and Cathryn Ann (Nichols) D.; m. Carolyn Ann. BA, Trinity Coll., Dunedin, Fla., 1959, DD (hon.), 1968; MDiv, Grace Coll. & Grace Theol. Sem., Winona Lake, Ind., 1962, ThM, 1964, ThD, 1967. Instr. Grace Coll. & Grace Theol. Sem., 1963-65, prof. of Old Testament, 1965—, exec. v.p., 1976-82, pres., 1986-93; exec. dean Near East Sch. Archaeology, Jerusalem, 1970-71. Area supr. Tekoa Archeol. Expdn., Jordan, 1968, 70, Raddana Expdn., Jordan, 1974, Heshbon Expdn., Jordan, 1976, Abila Archeol. Expdn., Jordan, 1982, 84, Khirbet el-Maqatir Expdn., Israel, 2000. Author: Paradise to Prison, 1975 (Book of Yr.), The Perfect Shepherd, 1979 (Book of Yr.), 16 other books. Chmn., bd. dirs. Kosciusko Comty. Hosp., 1994-2000. Recipient Gold award United Way, 1980, Conservation award Barbee Property Owners Assn., 1983; named Outdoor Writer of Yr., Ind. Dept. Natural Resources, 1986, to the Koscivsko County Rep. Hall of Fame, 1992. Mem. Am. Schs. of Oriental Research, Near East Archeol. Soc., Outdoor Writers Assn., Hoosier Outdoor Writers Assn. (pres. 1984-86). Avocations: fishing, hunting, photography. Home: PO Box 557 Winona Lake IN 46590-0557

DAVIS, JOHN KERR, philosopher, educator, lawyer; b. Bremerton, Wash., June 26, 1956; s. Donald Dewitt and Judith Lee (Moxon) D. BA, Reed Coll., 1981; JD, NYU, 1985; PhD in Philosophy, U. Wash., 2001. Assoc. Elam, Burke & Boyd, Boise, Idaho, 1984-86, Weinstein, Fischer, Riley, Erickson & Wolfe, Seattle, 1988-95; pvt. practice Seattle, 1995-2001; asst. prof. med. humanities Brody Sch. Medicine, East Carolina U., Greenville, NC, 2001—04; asst. prof. philosophy U. Tenn., Knoxville, 2004—. Mem. Phi Beta Kappa. Independent. Office: Univ Tenn Dept Philosophy 816 McClung Tower Knoxville TN 37996-0480

DAVIS, JOHN MACDOUGALL, lawyer; b. Seattle, Feb. 20, 1914; s. David Lyle and Georgina (MacDougall) D.; m. Ruth Anne Van Arsdale, July 1, 1939; children: Jean, John, Bruce, Ann, Margaret, Elizabeth. BA, U. Wash., 1936, LLB, JD, 1940. Bar: Wash. 1940. Assoc. Poe, Falknor, Emory & Howe, Seattle, 1940-45; pvt. practice Seattle, 1945-46; ptnr. Davis & Riese, Seattle, 1946-48, Emory, Howe, Davis & Riese, Seattle, 1948-50, Howe, Davis & Riese, Seattle, 1951-53, Howe, Davis, Riese & Aiken, Seattle, 1953-58, Howe, Davis, Riese & Jones, Seattle, 1958-68, Davis, Wright, Todd, Riese & Jones, Seattle, 1969-85; of counsel Davis, Wright & Jones, Seattle, 1985-89, Davis Wright Tremaine, Seattle, 1990—. Lectr. U. Wash. Law Sch., 1947-52. Bd. dirs. Virginia Mason Hosp., Seattle, 1952-79, pres., 1970-72; bd. dirs. Pacific Sci. Ctr., 1971-90, dir. emeritus, 1990—, past pres., past chmn.; trustee Whitman Coll., 1971-86, chmn., 1983-86; bd. dirs. Blue Cross Wash. and Alaska, 1982-89, Diabetic Trust Fund, 1954—. Wash. Student Loan Guaranty Assn., 1978-83; mem. adv. bd. Chief Seattle council Boy Scouts Am.; mem. Mercer Island Sch. Bd., 1956-66. With USNG, 1931—34. Recipient Disting. Eagle Scout award, 1982 Mem. ABA, Wash. State Bar Assn. (merit award 1965), Seattle-King County Bar Assn. (pres. 1960-61), Order of Coif, Rainier Club (Seattle), The Mountaineers Club (Svc. award, 1974), Phi Delta Phi, Alpha Delta Phi. Clubs: Rainier (Seattle). Presbyterian. Avocation: mountain climbing. Home: 9104 Fortuna Dr #3305 Mercer Island WA 98040-3166 Office: Davis Wright Tremaine 2600 Century Sq 1501 4th Ave Ste 2600 Seattle WA 98101-1688

DAVIS, JOHN MIHRAN, surgeon, educator; b. N.Y.C., Aug. 13, 1946; s. Drought Delaney and Ruth Radcliff (Kalaidjian) D.; m. Marlene Morgan, Oct. 13, 1973; children— Nicholas Mihran, Elisabeth Whitfield. B.A., Columbia Coll., 1968; M.D., Wayne State U., 1972. Diplomate Am. Bd. Surgery. Intern, then resident N.Y. Hosp., N.Y.C., 1972-77; asst. attending surgeon N.Y. Hosp.-Cornell U. Med. Ctr., N.Y.C., 1977—, Jamaica Hosp., N.Y., 1980—; asst. prof. surgery Cornell U. Med. Coll., 1977-84, assoc. prof., 1984-97, prof. surgery Robert Wood Johnson Med. Sch., 1997; program dir. Jersey Shore Med. Ctr.; also assoc. dir. trauma, 1984-97 . Author: Andrew W. Mellon, Teacher-Scientist, 1983. Fellow ACS; mem. Am. Burn Assn., Surg. Infection Soc. (charter), N.Y. County-State Med. Soc., N.Y. Surg. Soc., Soc. Univ. Surgeons. Home: 31 Pitman Ave Ocean Grove NJ 07756-1656 E-mail: jmdavis@meridianhealth.com.

DAVIS, JOHN ROWLAND, academic administrator; b. Mpls., Dec. 19, 1927; s. Roland Owen and Dorothy (Norman) D.; m. Lois Marie Falk, Sept. 4, 1947; children— Joel C., Jacque L., Michele M., Robin E. BS, U. Minn., 1949, MS, 1951; postgrad., Purdue U., 1955-57; PhD, Mich. State U., 1959. Hydraulic engr. U.S. Geol. Survey, Lincoln, Nebr., 1950-51; instr. Mich. State U., 1951-55; asst. prof. Purdue U., 1955-57; lectr. U. Calif., Davis, 1957-62; hydraulic engr. Stanford Rsch. Inst., South Pasadena, Calif., 1962-64; prof. U. Nebr., Lincoln, 1964-65, dean coll. engring. and architecture, 1965-71, faculty rep. intercollegiate athletics; prof., head dept. agrl. engring. Oreg. State U., Corvallis, 1971-75, instl. athletic rep., 1972-87, dir. Agrl. Expt. Sta., assoc. dean Sch. Agr., 1975-85, dir. spl. programs Office of Academic Affairs, assoc. dir. athletics, 1987-89, prof. emeritus, assoc. dir. athletics, 1989—. Governing bd. Water Resources Research Inst., 1975-85; dir. Western Rural Devel. Center, 1975-85, Agrl. Research Found., Jackman Inst.; cons. Stanford Research Inst., Dept. Agr., Consortium for Internat. Devel.; dir. Engrs. Council Profl. Devel., 1966-72; pres. Pacific-10 Conf., 1978-79. Contbr. articles to profl. jours. Mem. budget commn. City of Corvallis, 2003—. With USNR, 1945-46. Fellow Am. Soc. Agrl. Engrs. (dir. 1971-73, Agrl. Engr. Yr. award Pacific N.W. region 1974), NCAA (v.p. 1979-83, sec.-treas. 1983-85, pres. 1985-87), Heartland Humane Soc. (pres. bd. dirs. 2002). Home: 2940 NW Aspen St Corvallis OR 97330-3307 Office: Oreg State U Gill Coliseum Corvallis OR 97331 Personal E-mail: john.r.davis@att.net.

DAVIS (JR.), JOHN V., newswriter, educator; s. Merilyn Albritton and Jerry Audry Strickland (Stepfather); m. Christy Lee Reuter, Aug. 10, 2002. BA, Fla. So. Coll., 1994—98. Part-time reporter The Herald-Advocate, Wauchula, Fla., 1994—98; gen. assignment reporter Highlands Today/The Tampa Tribune, Sebring, Fla., 1998—2000; staff writer/reporter Winter Haven News Chief, Winter Haven, Fla., 2000—03; tchr. Polk County Juvenile Boot Camp, 2003—. Journalism merit badge counselor Boy Scouts of Am. Troop 115, Auburndale, 2002—03. Author: (poetry) Forecasters, 1998 (Wesley Ryals Creative Writing award, 2002), Songs of the Ghost, 2003 (Best of Quill Poetry award, 1997); contbr. literary festival, articles to literary mag. Ch. mem., pub. of Sunday sch. newsletter Faith Bapt. Ch., Winter Haven, Fla., 2002. Recipient Eagle Scout, Boy Scouts of Am., 1994. Mem.: Kappa Alpha Alumni Assn. (So. Gentleman of the Yr. 1998). Christian. Achievements include development of educational lesson plan tying metaphor and mathematical logic together for integrated learning. Avocations: writing, the outdoors, guitar.

DAVIS, JOHN WARREN, real estate broker, contractor; b. York, Pa., Feb. 14, 1946; s. Frank Asbury Jr. and Lillian Margaret (Billings) D. BA in Polit. Sci., Drake U., 1968; AA in Real Estate, San Diego City Coll., 1976; MS in Acquisition and Contract Mgmt., West Coast U., 1987; postgrad., Walden U., 1992—. Real estate sales staff, 1972-79; clk. GS 3 Naval Ocean Sys. Ctr., 1979-80; contract intern, contract adminstr. Office of Naval Rsch., 1980-84; contract specialist, warranted ordering officer Gen. Svc. 1102-11 Naval Weapons Sta., 1984-86; contract specialist Gen Svc. 1102-12 Navy Space Sys. Activity, 1986-88; procurement analyst Gen Svc. 102-12 COMNAVAIR-PAC, 1988-98; def. contract mgr. Def. Contract Mgmt. Command, 1998—2000; sr. v.p. Azan Corp. Group, San Diego, 2001—03; subcontract adminstr. Kellogg,Brown & Root, Houston, 2005—. Del. San Diego State U. to the Nat. Acad. Conf. for Contract Mgmt. Educators, 1991, 92, 93; profl. cons. Computer Applications, Inc., 1992; mem. tech. program com., chairperson for electronic data interchange Soc. of Logistics Engrs., 1995; mem. Golden Hill planning com. City of San Diego; adj. prof. San Diego State U., chmn. curriculum rev. com. for acquisitiion. Author, Paperless Contracting, The EDI Revolution, 1995, contbr. articles to profl. publs. With U.S. Army, Vietnam, 1968-72. Fellow Nat. Contract Mgmt. Assn. (cert. profl. contract mgr.); mem. ABA (mem. sub-com. pub. law sector, sub-com. on intellectual property), SAR (nat., Calif. and San Diego chpts.), Am. Arbitration Assn. (nat. panel mem.), Soc. Govt. Meeting Planners (v.p. San Diego chpt.), Soc. Logistics Engrs., San Diego Athletic Club, San Diego Writers and Editors Guild, Author's Guild (past pres.); rsch. bd. adv. Am. Bio. Inst. Episcopalian. Avocations: swimming, travel. Home: PO Box 620657 San Diego CA 92162-0657 Office: Kellott Brown & Root Govt Ops-LOGCAP III 4100 CLinton Dr Houston TX 77020 also: Kellogg Brown & Root Kaifa Resort APO 09366-5000

DAVIS, JOHN WILLIAM, government science and engineering executive; BSME, U. Tex., 1957; MSME, So. Meth. U., 1962; PhD in Aerospace Engring., Okla. State U., 1972. Aerodynamics design engr., sr. and lead wind tunnel engr. Chance Vought Corp., Grand Prairie, Tex., 1957-61; chief gas dynamics sect. Marshall Space Flight Ctr. NASA, Huntsville, Ala., 1961-75, exptl. investigations br. chief Ames Rsch. Ctr., 1975-80; dir. Propulsion Wind Tunnel Facility Calspan Corp./Arnold Engring. Devel. Ctr. Ops., Arnold AFB, Tenn., 1980-87, v.p., gen. mgr., 1987-1994; vice pres., gen. mgr. Micro Craft Tech./Arnold Engring. Devel. Ctr.Ops., Arnold AFB, Tenn., 1994, chief engr. micro crafttech., 1994-95, AEDC chief scientist, 1995—. Exec. dir. U. Tenn./Calspan Ctr. Aerospace Rsch.; bd. dirs. U. Tenn./Calspan Ctr. Space Transp. and Applied Rsch. Contbr. 38 articles to profl. jours. Bd. dirs. Tenn. Valley Aerospace Region, Hands-On Sci. Ctr., trustee, chmn. fin. com. Recipient Ground Testing award Am. Inst. of Aeronautics and Astronautics, 1994 Fellow AIAA (Ground Testing award 1994, mem. ground testing and simulation tech. com., mem. honors and awards subcom., 1992, liaison officer to thermophysics tech. com.), Arnold Engring. Devel. Ctr., Internat. Test and Evaluation Assn., Air Force Assn., Nat. Mgmt. Assn., Supersonic Tunnel Assn. (past pres., sec., mem.-at-large, exec. bd. dirs.). Office: Arnold Engring Devel Ctr-CN 1099 Avenue C Ste 106 Arnold Afb TN 37389-9010

DAVIS, JOHNNY REGINALD, former professional basketball coach; b. Oct. 21, 1955; m. Lezli Davis; children: Reginald, Austin. Student, U. Dayton. Basketball player Portland (Oreg.) Trail Blazers, 1976-78, Indiana Pacers, 1978-82, Atlanta Hawks, 1982-84, Cleve. Cavaliers, 1984-85; asst. coach Atlanta Hawks, 1990-93, L.A. Clippers, 1993-94, Portland Trail Blazers, 1994-96; head coach Phila. 76ers, 1996-97; asst. coach N.J. Nets, East Rutherford, 1997—99, Orlando Magic, 1999—2003, head coach, 2003—05.

DAVIS, JOLENE BRYANT, magazine publishing executive consultant; b. Lehigh, Iowa, Dec. 11, 1942; d. Joseph Albert and Joyce (Olson) Bryant; m. Richard Alan Alper, Feb. 12, 1967 (dec. July 1975); m. Steven Andrew Davis, Apr. 16, 1979; children: Bryant David, Suzanne Joyce. BA, U. Iowa, 1964; MA, Calif. State U., San Jose, 1972. Registered dietitian, Ind. Home economist The Oregonian, newspaper, Portland, 1965-67; dietitian Ind. U. Sch. Medicine, Indpls., 1973-74; clin. dietitian U. Calif. Hosps. and Clins., San Francisco, 1974-75, chief clin. dietitian, 1975-78, chief rsch. dietitian Clin. Study Ctr., 1979-83; pub., chief exec. officer Our Kids mag. Branford Pub., Inc., San Antonio, 1984-99, v.p., 1988-98; ptnr. Serendipity Video Prodns., 1996—; also bd. dirs., v.p. Branford Pub., Inc., San Antonio, 1983-99; sports nutritionist San Antonio Spurs, 1993—. Sec., bd. govs. Parenting Publs. Am., San Antonio, 1988-89; v.p., bd. dirs. The Magik Theatre, 1995—. Mem. San Antonio Conservation Soc., 1985—; bd. dirs. Jewish Family Svc. Assn., San Antonio, 1986-88, Family Resource Ctr., San Antonio, Children's Bereavement Ctr. South Tex., 1997—; chmn. cultural arts PTA, San Antonio, 1988-94; vol. McNay Art Mus., 1996-98; pres. Alamo Heights Schs. Choir Boosters Club, 1999—. Recipient Life Mem. award PTA, 1994, Supt.'s award N.E. Ind. Sch. Dist., 1995-96. Mem. Women in Comms. (editor Best Mag. Column and Mag. award of Merit 1988, 90), Am. Dietetic Assn., Soc. Nutrition Edn., San Antonio Dist. Dietetic Assn., Soc. Profl. Journalists, Pi Beta Phi. Avocations: volunteer elementary school art history teaching, antiques, rare book collecting, genealogy, travel. Home: 178 Country Ln San Antonio TX 78209-2228 Office: Branford Pub Inc 8400 Blanco Rd Ste 201 San Antonio TX 78216-3055

DAVIS, JON L., engineering executive, consultant; b. Louisiana, Mo., Mar. 1, 1934; s. Lloyd Israel Davis and Mary Isabelle (Cory) Stone; m. Rita Marie Pitts, July 21, 1957; children: Michael Louis, Catherine Faith, Laurie Marie. BSBA magna cum laude, U. Albuquerque, 1977. Cert. profl. logistician. Enlisted USAF, 1956, advanced through grades to col., 1979, ret., 1985; col., dep. comdr. maintenance 479th Tactical Tng. Wing, Holloman AFB, N.Mex., 1979-81, 67 Tactical Reconaissance Wing, Bergstrom AFB, Tex., 1981-83; col., dir. logistics USAF Operational Test & Evaluation Ctr., Kirtland AFB, N.Mex., 1983-85; asst. v.p. Los Alamos Tech. Assocs., Albuquerque, 1985-2000; logistics cons. Albuquerque, 2000—. Author Air Force manuals. Mem. Austin-Bergstrom Community Coun., Austin, Tex., 1981-83, Alamogordo (N.Mex.) Mil. Adv. Com., 1980-81. Decorated Legion of Merit, D.F.C., 12 Air medals. Mem. Intl. Soc. of Logistics (sr. mem., chpt. chmn. 1991), Internat. Test & Evaluation Assn., USAF Logistics Officers Assn., Air Force Assn. (life mem.), Red River Valley Assn. Republican. Home and Office: 9706 Camino Del Sol NE Albuquerque NM 87111-1510 E-mail: jdavis502@comcast.net.

DAVIS, JORDAN S., venture capitalist; BA in econ., State U. NY, Binghamton; MBA, J.L. Kellogg Grad. Sch. Mgmt. Northwestern U. Co-founder Cambridge Heart, Inc., Voxware, Inc.; with Morgan Stanley & Co., Inc.; mng. dir. KBL Healthcare, Inc.; co-founder, v.p., dir. KBL Healthcare Acquisition Corp.; co-founder, mng. ptnr. Radius Ventures, LLC, 1997—. Bd. dirs. CCS Consolidated, Inc., Health Language, Inc., ZettaCore, Inc. Office: Radius Ventures LLC 400 Madison Ave 8th Fl New York NY 10017 Office Phone: 212-897-7778. Office Fax: 212-397-2656.

DAVIS, JOSEPH LLOYD, academic administrator, consultant; b. Crawfordsville, Iowa, May 4, 1927; s. Whitfield and Jane (Lloyd) D.; m. Margaret Florence Cooper, Dec. 28, 1949; children: Stephen Joseph, Thomas Whitfield, Jane Ellen. BSc, Ohio State U., 1949, MA, 1955, PhD, 1967. Reporter Ohio State Jour., 1943-49, 52-53; tchr. Morey Jr. H.S., Denver, 1949-52, Central H.S., Columbus, Ohio, 1953-54; asst. dir. adminstrv. rsch. Columbus Public Schs., 1954-56, dir. publs. and public info., 1956-60, exec. asst. to supt., 1960-64, asst. supt. spl. svcs., 1964-77, supt. of schs., 1977-82; exec. dir. Ohio Coun. Vocat. Edn., 1985-96. Past pres. Columbus Rotary; adj. prof. Ohio State U., 1983—; founder, dir. emeritus Ohio State U. Nat. Acad. for Supt.; cons. and author in field. Mem., bd. trustees Interprofl. Commn. Ohio, 1999—, Kids Voting/Ctrl. Ohio Region, 1999—; mem., past pres. Friends Bd. WOSU AM, FM and TV, Ohio State U., Columbus, 1986—98, 2000—. With USN, 1945—46, with USN, 1950—51. Recipient award for civic leadership Columbus Area C. of C., 1980, Liberty Bell award Columbus Bar Assn., 1980; named to Pub. Schs. Hall of Fame, Columbus, Ohio, 1993. Mem. Am. Assn. Sch. Adminstrs. (disting. svc. award 1989). Nat. Sch. Pub. Rels. Assn. (pres.'s award 1980), Assn. for Career and Tech. Edn., Ohio Assn. for Career and Tech. Edn., Buckeye Assn. Sch. Adminstrs., Nat. Soc. Study Edn., Horace Mann League, Ohio State U. Alumni Assn. (leadership consortium 2003—), Ohio State Advocates, Rotary (Rotarian of Yr. award 1994), Torch Club Columbus, Phi Delta Kappa, Epsilon Pi Tau (laureate 1994, Disting. Svc. award 2000), Kappa Delta Pi, Omicron Tau Theta. Presbyterian. E-mail: jdavis59@columbus.rr.com.

DAVIS, JOSEPH RANDALL, engineer, ergonomist; b. St. Paul, Apr. 3, 1956; s. Arthur Emerson and Carroll Fox Davis; m. Peggy Kay Satterwhite, Nov. 20, 1976 (div. Jan. 3, 1993); m. Heather Dawn Sherrill, Aug. 15, 1995 (div. Jan. 30, 2002); m. Cynthia Anne Baldwin, Sept. 18, 2004; children: Paul Johnson, Austin Emerson, Joseph Vann. BSME, N.C. State U., 1978, MSIE, 1986, PhD in Indsl. Engring. and Ergonomics, 1997. Registered profl. engr., N.C., cert. profl. ergonomist, safety profl. Engr., mgr. IBM, Research Triangle Park, NC, 1978—92; ergonomics rschr. N.C. State U., Raleigh, 1992—, engr. and ergonomist, 1995—. Pres., cons. Ergonomic Engring. Inc., Raleigh, 1992—; pres. Engrs. On Demand, Inc., Raleigh, 2004—. Contbr. articles to profl. jours.; patentee in field. Recipient Best Paper award, IBM, 1990; grantee, State of N.C., 1999. Mem.: Am. Soc. Safety Engrs., Inst. Indsl. Engrs. (pres., v.p. S.E. region 1994—2003, Gold Award for excellence in chpt. leadership 1995), Human Factors and Ergonomics Soc. (pres. N.C. chpt. 2001—03), Phi Kappa Phi, Alpha Pi Mu, Tau Beta Pi. Avocations: nutrition-based ergonomics, scuba diving, tennis. Home: 1524 Delmont Dr Raleigh NC 27606-2610 Office: NC State U Box 7902 Raleigh NC 27695-7902 Office Phone: 919-828-5220. Personal E-mail: dr_joe_davis@att.net. E-mail: joe_davis@ncsu.edu.

DAVIS, JUDY, actress; b. Perth, Australia, Apr. 23, 1955; m. Colin Friels, 1984; children: Jack, Charlotte. Student, Nat. Inst. Dramatic Art, Sydney, Australia. Appearances include: (films) Clean Straw for Nothing, 1976, High Rolling, 1977, My Brilliant Career, 1979 (Best Actress Sammy award Australian Film and TV Awards 1979, Best Actress award Brit. Acad. Film and TV Arts 1981, Best Newcomer Brit. Acad. Film and TV Arts 1981), Hoodwink, 1981 (Best Supporting Actress Sammy award Australian Film and TV Awards 1981), Winter of Our Dreams, 1981 (Best Actress Sammy award Australia Film and TV Awards 1981), Heatwave, 1982, The Final Option, 1983, A Passage to India, 1984 (Acad. award nominee for best actress 1984),

Kangaroo, 1986, High Tide, 1987, Georgia, 1988, Alice, 1990, Impromptu, 1991, Barton Fink, 1991, Naked Lunch, 1991 (Best Supporting Actress award N.Y. Critics Cir. 1991), Where Angels Fear to Tread, 1991, Husbands and Wives, 1992 (Acad. award nominee for best supporting actress 1992), The Ref, 1994, The New Age, 1994, Children of the Revolution, 1996, Absolute Power, 1996, Blood and Wine, 1996, Deconstructing Harry, 1996, Celebrity, 1997, The Echo of Thunder, 1998, Gaudi Afternoon, 2000, The Man Who Sued God, 2001, Swimming Upstream, 2003; (TV movies) Water Under the Bridge, 1980 A Woman Called Golda, 1982 (Emmy award nominee 1982), The Merry Wives of Windsor, 1982, Rocket to the Moon, 1986, One Against the Wind, 1991, Serving in Silence: The Margarethe Cammermeyer Story, 1995 (Emmy award), Echo of Thunder (Emmy nomination), 1997, Dash & Lily, 1997 (Emmy nomination), A Cooler Climate, 1998, Life With Judy Garland: Me and My Shadows, 2000 (Golden Globe award, Am. Screen Actors award, Golden Satellite award, Broadcast Critics Choice award, Am. Film Inst. award, Emmy award), The Reagans, 2003, Coast to Coast, 2004. Office: care Shanahan Mgmt PO Box1509 Darlinghurst NSW 1300 Australia

DAVIS, KAREN, insurance company executive, educator; b. Blackwell, Okla., Nov. 14, 1942; d. Walter Dwight and Thelma Louise (Kohler) Padgett; 1 child, Kelly Denise Collins. BA, Rice U., 1965, PhD, 1969. Asst. prof. econs. Rice U., 1969-70; econ. policy fellow Social Security Adminstrn. Brookings Instn., Washington, 1970-71, rsch. assoc., 1971-74, sr. fellow, 1974-77; dep. asst. sec. for planning and evaluation, health HEW, Washington, 1977-80; adminstr. health resources adminstrn. USPHS, Washington, 1980-81; prof. Johns Hopkins U., Balt., 1981-92; chmn., 1983-92; exec. v.p. Commonwealth Fund, N.Y.C., 1992-94, pres., 1995—. Mem. Physican Payment Rev. Commn., 1986-94; dir. Commonwealth Fund Commn. on Elderly People Living Alone, 1985-91; vis. lectr. Harvard U., 1974-75; nat. adv. com. Agy. for Health Care Rsch. and Quality, 1999-2003; bd. dirs. Geisinger Health Sys. Author: National Health Insurance: Benefits, Costs and Consequences, 1975, Health and the War on Poverty, 1978, Medicare Policy: New Directions for Health and Long-Term Care, 1986, Health Care Cost Containment, 1990. Mem. Inst. Medicine, Phi Beta Kappa. Democrat. Methodist. Home: 1365 York Ave 27K New York NY 10021 Office: The Commonwealth Fund The Harkness House 1 E 75th St New York NY 10021-2692 Office Phone: 212-606-3825. Business E-Mail: kd@cmwf.org.

DAVIS, KAREN S., secondary school educator; b. Indpls., Dec. 13, 1955; d. Monte E. and Helen A. O'Connor; m. William D. Davis, May 21, 1977; children: Katie, Benjamin, Brandon. BSEd, Butler U., 1978, MA in English, 1985. English tchr., phys. edn. tchr., track coach Rushville (Ind.) Consol. Schs., 1978—79; English tchr., tennis coach New Palestine (Ind.) H.S., 1979—84; English tchr., basketball and volleyball coach, chmn. English dept. Center Grove Schs., Greenwood, Ind., 1984—. Mem. profl. devel. com. Ind. Dept. Edn., Indpls., 1993; tchr. Leadership Acad., 2002—04. Co-author: (tng. presentation) Writing Across Curriculum - Teaching Computers, 1993. Active Mt. Olive Luth. Ch., Greenwood. Finalist Tchr. of Yr., Ind. Dept. Edn., 1993; recipient, 2002; grantee, Eli Lily Found., 1992. Mem.: Am. Quilters' Soc., Nat. Coun. Tchrs. English. Avocations: quilting, reading. Office: Center Grove HS 2717 S Morgantown Rd Greenwood IN 46143

DAVIS, KAREN SUE, hospital nursing supervisor; b. Owensboro, Ky., June 5, 1950; d. Robert J. and Mona F. (Urlaub) D. Diploma, Deaconess Sch. Nursing, 1971. RN, Ky.; cert. in pediatric nursing; cert. PALS. Charge nurse pediatrics Daviess County Hosp., 1971-89; clin. supr. pediatrics 11-7 shift Owensboro Med. Health Sys., 1989—. Republican. Lutheran. Avocations: needlecrafts, reading, travel, cooking, decorating. Home: 686 N Fairview Ct Rockport IN 47635

DAVIS, KATHERINE LYON, former lieutenant governor; b. Boston, June 24, 1956; d. Richard Harold and Joy (Hallum) Winer; m. John Marshall Davis, Feb. 22, 1992; 1 child, Madeline Felton. BS, MIT, 1978; MBA, Harvard U., 1982. Engr. Cambridge (Mass.) Collaborative, 1978-80; mfg. mgr. Cummins Engine Co., Columbus, Ind., 1982-87, bus. dir., 1987-89; dep. commr. Ind. Dept. Transp., Indpls., 1989-95; budget dir. State of Ind., Indpls., 1995-97; exec. sec. Ind. Family and Social Svcs. Commn., Indpls., 1997-99; city contr. City of Indpls., 1999—2003; lt. gov. State of Ind., Indpls., 2003—05. Mem. Transp. Rsch. Bd., 1990-93. Recipient commendation Dept. Transp., Fed. Hwy. Adminstrn., 1991. Democrat. Avocations: running, swimming, bicycling, hiking, photography.

DAVIS, KATHRYN WASSERMAN, foundation executive, educator, writer; b. Phila., Feb. 25, 1907; d. Joseph and Edith (Stix) Wasserman; m. Shelby Cullom Davis, Jan. 4, 1932; children: Shelby M. Cullom, Diana Davis Spencer, Priscella Alden (dec.). BA, Wellesley Coll., 1928; MA, Columbia U., 1931; D of Polit. Sci., U. Geneva, 1934; law degree (hon.), Columbia U., 1997. Researcher Coun. on Fgn. Rels., N.Y.C., 1934-36, State of Pa., Phila., 1936-37; writer and lectr. on fgn. affairs N.Y., 1937—; ptnr. Shelby Cullom Davis & Co., N.Y.C., 1985—; pres. The Shelby Cullom Davis Found., N.Y.C., 1985—. Lectr. on fgn. affairs. Author: Soviets at Geneva, 1934. Trustee Wellesley Coll., 1983—2003; v.p. Women's Nat. Rep. Club, 1976—, chmn. internat. affairs com.; bd. govs. Harvard U., mem. vis. com. Russian studies, 1986—; past pres. LWV. Recipient life achievement award Women's Nat. Rep. Club, 1990, gold medal for disting. svc. to humanity Nat. Inst. Social Scis., 1990, Claire Booth Luce medal Heritage Found., 1991, Plymouth Com. award Mayflower Soc., 1992, Life Accomplishment award Internat. House, 1995. Mem. Cosmopolitan Club (N.Y.C., com. fgn. visitors), Sleepy Hollow Club (Scarborough N.Y.), N.Y. Harbor Club, Seal Harbor Club (Maine), Jupiter Island Club (Hobe Sound, Fla.), The Everglades Club, Inc. (Palm Beach, Fla.), Knickerbocker Club, Univ. Club. Avocations: skiing, tennis, swimming, travel. Home: PO Box 689 Hobe Sound FL 33475-0689 Office: Shelby Cullom Davis & Co LP 609 5th Ave New York NY 10017-1021 Office Phone: 800-232-0303. E-mail: k.w.d33455@aol.com.

DAVIS, KEITH EUGENE, psychologist, educator, consultant; b. Clifton, N.C., May 15, 1936; s. Ted Eugene and Mary Flossie (Rol) D.; m. Dorothy Ann Reeves, Feb. 23, 1968; 1 child, Kristin Lee; children from previous marriage: Rachel, Rebecca, Jessica. BA, Duke U., 1958, PhD, 1963. Instr. psychology Princeton U., 1961-62; asst. prof. U. Colo., Boulder, 1962-67, assoc. prof., 1967-70; prof., chmn. dept. psychology Livingston Coll., Rutgers U., New Brunswick, NJ, 1970-73; prof. U. S.C., Columbia, 1973—, adj. prof. health adminstrn., health promotion/edn., 1991—, univ. provost, 1974-78, chair dept. psychology, 1994-96; founder The Paradigm Group, mgmt. cons. Mgmt. cons., mem. population study sect. Nat. Inst. Child Health and Human Devel., 1973-76; mem. mental health rsch. edn. rev. com. NIMH, 1979—, chmn., 1980-83; mem. NSF social psychology grant rev. panel, 2002-03; chmn. State Plan Adv. Com., S.C. State Dept. Mental Health, 1976-78; pres. past participants Greater Columbia Forum, 1975-76. Author: Advances in Experimental Social Psychology, 1963; author, editor: Advanced in Descriptive Psychology, 1981; editor: The Social Construction of the Person, 1985; co-editor: Stalking: Perspectives on Victims and Perpetrators, 2001; contbr. to Theoretical Perspectives on Personal Relationships, 1993; assoc. editor: Personal Relationships, 1993-97; exec. editor Jour. Social Psychology; contbr. over 100 articles to profl. jours. Bd. dirs. Columbia Area Mental Health Ctr., 1976-82, chmn. bd. dirs., 1981. Woodrow Wilson fellow, 1958—59, So. Fellowships Fund fellow, 1958—61. Fellow APA, Am. Psychol. Soc.; mem. Am. Sociol. Assn., Internat. Assn. Relationships Rsch. (program chair 1992), Mind Assn., Nat. Coun. Family Rels., Soc. Descriptive Psychology (1st pres. 1979-81), Phi Beta Kappa, Omicron Delta Kappa. Home: 1808 Catawba St Columbia SC 29205-3010 Office: U SC Dept Psychology Columbia SC 29208-0001 Office Phone: 803-777-4639. E-mail: daviske@sc.edu.

DAVIS, KENNETH BOONE, JR., dean, law educator; b. Louisville, Sept. 1, 1947; s. Kenneth Boone and Doris Edna (Gordon) D. m. Arrietta Evoline Hastings, June 2, 1984; children: Peter Hastings, Mary Elizabeth, Kenneth Boone III. AB, U. Mich., 1969; JD, Case Western Res. U., 1974. Bar: D.C. 1975, Ohio 1974. Law clk. to chief judge U.S. Ct. Appeals (9th cir.), San Francisco, 1974-75; assoc. Covington & Burling, Washington, 1975-78; prof. law U. Wis., Madison, 1978—, dean Law Sch., 1997—. Contbr. articles to profl. jours. Mem. ABA, Am. Fin. Assn., Am. Law Inst., Wis. Bar Assn. (reporter, corp. and bus. law com.). Office: U Wis Law Sch 975 Bascom Mall Madison WI 53706-1399 Office Phone: 608-262-0962. E-mail: kbdavis@wisc.edu.

DAVIS, KENNETH LEON, psychiatrist, pharmacologist, medical educator; b. NYC, Sept. 10, 1947; married, 1972; 2 children. BA, Yale U., 1969; MD, Mt. Sinai Med. Sch., 1973. Diplomate Am. Bd. Psychiatry and Neurology. Intern Stanford U., 1973-74, resident, 1973-76, life sci. rsch. assoc., 1975-76; rsch. assoc. Stanford Psych. Clin., 1974-79; asst. dir. Stanford Psych. Clin. Rsch. Ctr., VA Med. Ctr., 1975-79; clin. psychiat. cons. Santa Clara Valley Med. Ctr., 1976-79; chief dept. psychiat. VA Med. Ctr., 1979-87; assoc. prof. psychiatry and pharmacology Mt. Sinai Sch. Medicine, 1979-84; dir. schizophrenia biol. rsch. ctr., 1981-91; prof. Mt. Sinai Sch. Medicine, 1984—, chair dept. psychiatry, 1987—, Esther and Joseph Klingenstein prof., 1994—2003, dean, 2003—; pres., CEO Mt. Sinai Med. Ctr., 2003—. Editor Alzheimer's Disease and Associated Disorders, Biol. Psychiatry, Clin. Neuropharmacology, Harvard Review of Psychiatry, Internat. Jour. Geriatric Psychiatry, Internat. Jour. Geriatric Psychopharmacology, Jour. Geriatric Psychiatry & Neurology, Jour. Psychiatric Rsch., Jour. Am. Geriatrics Soc., Schizophrenia Rsch., Neuropsychopharmacology, Jour. Exptl. Cognitive and Behavioral Neurosci., Molecular Psychiatry, Sociedade de Psiquiatria Do Rio Grande Do Sul; author, co-author over 500 sci. articles. Recipient A. E. Bennett Clin. Sci. Rsch. award, 1977, Saul Horowitz Jr. Meml. award, 1977-78, Solomon Silver award, 1981, Joel Elkes Internat. award ACNP, 1986, Daniel H. Efron Excellence in Rsch. award, 1990, Rita Hayworth award Alzheimer's Assn., 1991, Lifetime Sci. award Inst. Advanced Sci. in Immunology and Aging, 1992. Mem. NAS, Am. Coll. Neuropsychopharmacology (pres.-elect 2004-05, pres. 05-06), Am. Psychiat. Assn. (APA/KEMPF award 1999), Soc. Biol. Psychiatry (Gold medal award 1999, APA award Rsch. in Psychiatry 2001), Inst. Medicine of NAS. Achievements include research in the biological basis of senile dementia of the Alzheimers' type, and schizophrenia. Office: Mount Sinai Med Ctr - Mount Sinai Sch Medicine Presidents Office One Gustave L Levy Pl Box 1220 New York NY 10029-6574 Business E-Mail: kenneth.davis@mssm.edu.

DAVIS, KENNETH WAYNE, language educator, business communication consultant; b. Chariton, Iowa, June 22, 1945; s. Wayne Pitman and Jeanne Frances (West) Davis; m. Bette Hargrove, Nov. 28, 1970; children: Cassandra Alice, Evan Thomas. BA, Drake U., 1967; MA, Columbia U., 1968; PhD, U. Mich., 1975. From asst. prof. English to assoc. prof. U. Ky., Lexington, 1975-88; assoc. prof. to prof. Ind. U.-Purdue U., Indpls., 1988—, dept. chair, 1998-2001; edn. dir. Am. Cabaret Theatre, 2001—05. Bus. cons., Lexington, 1977-88; pres. Komei, Inc., 1994—. Author: Better Business Writing, 1983, (with others) Business Communication for the Information Age, 1988, Rehearsing the Audience, 1988, (with others) Writing: Process, Product, and Power, 1993, The McGraw-Hill 36-Hour Course in Business Writing and Communication, 2005; prodr.: 2001: Lessons in Leadership videoconf., 1991; numerous other books and articles. Bd. dir. Shepherd's House, Inc., Lexington, 1986-88, Waycross Camp and Conf. Ctr., 1995-2000, World Trade Club Ind., 1998-2001. Sgt. US Army, 1968-71. Woodrow Wilson fellow, 1967; recipient Faculty Service award Nat. Univ. Continuing Edn. Assn., 1987. Mem.: ASTD, Assn. Profl. Comm. Cons. (bd. dirs. 2003—), Assn. Bus. Comm. (bd. dirs. 2003—), Toastmasters Internat., Hon. Order Ky. Col. Episcopalian. Avocations: theater, travel. Office: Ind U-Purdue U Dept English 425 University Blvd Indianapolis IN 46202-5148 Office Phone: 317-274-0084. Business E-Mail: kdavis@iupui.edu.

DAVIS, KEVIN E., law educator; b. 1970; BA in Economics, McGill U., Montreal, 1990; LLB, U. Toronto, 1993; LLM, Columbia U., 1996. Law clk. to Justice John Sopinka Supreme Ct. of Can.; assoc. corp. dept. Torys LLP, Canada; asst. prof. to prof. law U. Toronto; vis. prof. law NYU Sch. Law, 2003, prof., 2004—. Vis. prof. & John M. Olin rsch. fellow U. So. Calif. Law Sch.; vis. fellow Clare Hall, Cambridge U.; vis. lectr. U. West Indies, Barbados. Office: NYU Sch Law Vanderbilt Hall Rm 335 40 Washington Sq S New York NY 10012-1099 Office Phone: 212-992-8843. E-mail: davisk@juris.law.nyu.edu.

DAVIS, KINGSLEY D., investment advisor, consultant; b. Daytona Beach, Fla., Apr. 28, 1972; s. Paulette Davis. BA in Anthropology, BA in Criminal Justice, BA in Sociology, U. Fla., 1996; cert. in Admin. & Mgmt., Harvard U., 2004. Lic. Nat. Assn. Securities Dealers, 2000, N.Am. Securities Adminstrn. Assn., 2002. Counselor Pvt. Industry Coun. Ctrl. Fla., Orlando, Fla., 1991—93; counselor Office Academic Support and Instnl. Svcs. U. Fla., Gainesville, Fla., 1994—95; coord. domestic violence program Fla. Dept. Juvenile Justice, Kissimmee, Fla., 1996—97; therapist Valuemark Behav. Health Care, Orlando, 1997—98; tutor STAR Behav. Cons., Maitland, Fla., 1998; tchr. Orange County Pub. Schs., Orlando, 1999; account exec. Empire Fin., Longwood, Fla., 2000; cons. Westgate Ctrl. Fla. Investments, Orlando, 2001, Vistana Starwood, Orlando, 2001, Hilton Grand, Orlando, 2002—03; prin. commodity trading advisor & commodity pool operator King Davis Ministries, Orlando, 2003—. Vol. rsch. asst. Dept. of Psychology HEALS Project U. Ctrl. Fla., Orlando, 1999—99; dispatcher Am. Automobile Assn. Nat. HQ, Heathrow, Fla., 2000—01; spkr. in field. Candidate U.S. Ho. Reps., Orlando, Fla., 2003—04. Navigator, pilot USAF, 2000. Recipient Excellence in Academics award, USN, 1990. Mem.: Nat. Spkrs. Assn. Avocations: reading, writing, martial arts, theater, musicals. Office Phone: 857-222-2261. Personal E-mail: kingambrosia@yahoo.com.

DAVIS, KRISTIN, actress; b. Boulder, Feb. 23, 1965; d. Keith and Dorothy Davis. BFA, Rutgers U Mason Gross Sch of the Arts, 1987. Actor: (TV series) General Hospital, 1991, "Melrose Place", 1995—96, Sex and the City, 1998—2004 (Women in Film Lucy Award, 1998, Award for Outstanding Ensemble in a Comedy Series, 2001); (TV films) N.Y.P.D. Mounted, 1991, Alien Nation: Body and Soul, 1995, The Ultimate Lie, 1996, Deadly Vision, A., 1997, Atomic Train, 1999, Take Me Home: The John Denver Story, 2000, Sex and the Matrix, 2000, Someone to Love, 2001, Three Days, 2001; (films) "Doom Asylum", 1987, Nine Months, 1995, Sour Grapes, 1998, Traveling Companion, 1998, Blacktop, 2000. Office: HBO 1100 6th Ave New York NY 10036

DAVIS, LARRY MICHAEL, air force officer, healthcare manager, consultant; b. Lodi, Ark., Mar. 30, 1947; s. Harmon Odell and Jeanice (White) D.; m. Linda Ruth Blanchard, Mar. 22, 1969; children: Elizabeth Blanchard, Brooke Alison. BS, U. Ark., 1969; MA, Pepperdine U., 1978; postgrad., USAF Air U., 1975, 83-84. Commd. 2nd lt. USAF, 1969, advanced through grades to col., 1985; navigator, instr. navigator 596th Bombardment Squadron; radar navigator 62d Bombardment Squadron, 1971-75; instr. navigator, asst. curriculum mgr. 450th Flying Tng. Squadron, Mather AFB, Calif., 1975-76; asst. navigator sect. chief Standardization and Evaluation divsn. 323rd Flying Tng. Wing, Mather AFB, Calif., 1976-78; air ops. staff officer Tng. Analysis div. HQ Air Tng. Command, Randolph AFB, Tex., 1978-79; chief navigation tng. HQ Air Tng. Command, Randolph AFB, Tex., 1979-81; air ops. officer 99th Strategic Reconnaissance Squadron Beale AFB, Calif., 1982-83; wing chief of inspection 9th Strategic Reconnaissance Wing, 1983-84; reconnaissance ops. staff officer, reconnaissance emergency war order plans officer, chief reconnaissance plans divsn. HQ Strategic Air Command, Offutt AFB, Nebr., 1984-87; comdr. 3550th USAF Recruiting Squadron, Indpls., 1987-89; comdr. 3555th USAF Recruiting Squadron Milw., 1988; dep. comdr. 3501st USAF Recruiting Group, Hanscom AFB, Mass., 1989-91; health-care cons., customer svc. mgr. Electronic Data Systems, Indpls., 1991-96; mgr. provider rels. Unisys Corp., Frankfort, Ky., 1996-97, mgr. client svcs. Tallahassee, 1997; dir. network devel. and provider rels. Healthplan Southeast, Tallahassee, 1997-99; program adminstr. Medicaid program devel. Agy. for Health Care Adminstrn. State of Fla., Tallahassee, 1999-2000; dir. vet. svcs. Leon. Co., Tallahassee, 2003—. Decorated DFC, Air medal with three oak leaf clusters. Mem. VFW, DAV, Mil. Order World Wars, Mil. Officers Assn., Air Force Assn., Am. Legion, Am. Vets., Vietnam Vets. Am., Rotary (health sharing com. 1989-90), Blue Key, Alpha Zeta, Alpha Gamma Rho. Baptist. Avocations: golf, tennis. Home: 2844 Whittington Dr Tallahassee FL 32309-8214 Office Phone: 850-488-8462. E-mail: davislar@leoncountyfl.gov.

DAVIS, LAURA ARLENE, retired foundation administrator; b. Battle Creek, Mich., Apr. 14, 1935; d. Paul Bennett and Daisy E. (Coston) Borgard; m. John R. Davis, Aug. 7, 1955; children: Scott Judson, Cynthia Ann Davis Welker. BS, Ctrl. Mich. U., 1986. Sec. Mich. Loan Co., Battle Creek, 1952-56; legal sec. Ryan, Sullivan & Hamilton, Battle Creek, 1957-64; exec. sec. W.K. Kellogg Found., Battle Creek, 1965-76, adminstrn./program asst., 1976, fellowship dir., 1977, asst. v.p. adminstrn., asst. corp. sec., 1978-84, v.p. corp. affairs, corp. sec., 1984-95, spl. asst. to pres., CEO, 1996-97. Cons. Mich. State U., 1998—2000. Pres. bd. dirs. Charitable Union, Battle Creek, 1983-85; mem. allocations panel United Way of Battle Creek, 1983, v.p. cmty. rels., 1990-91, 1st v.p., 1994, pres. of bd., 1995-97; bd. dirs. Battle Creek Gas Co., 1988—2004, Riding for the Handicapped Cheff Ctr., 1991-96, sec., 1992; trustee Binder Park Zoo; mem. adv. coun. Argubright Bus. Coll., 1989-90; mem. Visionquest 5000, 1989; mem. selection com. Cmty. Leadership Acad.; bd. dirs. Coun. Mich. Founds., 1994-97; mem. membership com. Recipient Athena award C. of C., Cmty. Svc. award J.C. Penney. Mem. Adminstrv. Mgmt. Soc. (pres. chpt. 1982-83), Am. Mgmt. Assn., Nat. Touring Network (bd. mem. 1997-99, sec. 1998-99), Battle Creek C. of C. Home: 101 Brighton Park Battle Creek MI 49015-9615

DAVIS, LAWRENCE A., JR., academic administrator; BS mathematics, AM&N Coll.; PhD mechanics, Iowa State Univ. Chancellor U. Ark., Pine Bluff, 1991—. Office: U Ark Office of Chancellor PO Box 4982 Pine Bluff AR 71611-4982

DAVIS, LAWRENCE JAMES, editor, writer; b. Seattle, July 2, 1940; s. Maurice Nelson and Eula Jane (Randall) D.; m. Barbara Frances Ball, Sept. 23, 1962 (div. Apr. 1994); children: Jeremy, Gabriel, Barbara, Tina. BA summa cum laude, Stanford U., 1962. Rschr. CBS, N.Y.C., 1963; writing fellow Stanford (Calif.) U., 1963-64; mgr. Sterling Wine & Liquor, Bklyn., 1966-68; program dir. U. Rochester, N.Y., 1972-90; contbg. editor Harper's Mag., N.Y.C., 1981—. Contbg. editor Book World, N.Y.C., 1972-73. Author: Whence All But He Had Fled, 1968, Cowboys Don't Cry, 1969, A Meaningful Life, 1971, Walking Small, 1973, Bad Money, 1979, Onassis, 1986, Billionaire Shell Game, 1998, Fleet Fire, 2003. Recipient Gerald Loeb award Loeb Found., 1983, Champion Tuck award Dartmouth U., 1984, Nat. Mag. award Assn. Am. Mag. Pubs., 1991, William Allen White award U. Kans., 1995. Mem. Century Assn. Democrat. Episcopalian. Avocations: cooking, travel, architecture, gardening. Home and Office: 138A Dean St Brooklyn NY 11217

DAVIS, LAWRENCE WILLIAM, radiation oncologist; b. N. Braddock, Pa., Sept. 5, 1935; s. William Paul Davis and Julia Helen Zukas; children: James G., Karen E. BS, Juniata Coll., Huntington, Pa., 1957; MA, U. Pa., 1969; MBA, Temple U., 1984; MD, Georgetown U., 1961. Diploamte Am. Bd. Radiology (trustee 1981-95, asst. exec. dir. radiation oncology 1994—); lic. physician Pa., Md., N.Y., Ga. Asst. instr. radiology U. Pa., Phila., 1962-66, instr. radiology, 1966, 68-69, asst. prof. radiology, 1969-72, assoc. prof. radiology, 1972-75; prof. radiation therapy Thomas Jefferson Sch. Medicine, 1975-84; prof. and chmn. radiation oncology Albert Einstein Coll. Medicine, Bronx, 1984-91, Emory U., Atlanta, 1991—. Cons. Armed Forces Radiobiology Rsch. Inst., Bethesda, 1968-70; exec. com. of med. staff Montefiore Med. Ctr., 1984-87, 1990-91, div. coun., 1988-89; prof. svc. com. Phila. div. Am. Cancer Soc., 1970-75. Contbr. numerous articles to profl. jours.; assoc. editor Internat. Jour. Radiation Oncology, 1986—; editorial bd. Neuro Oncology, 1989-99, assoc. editor, 1991—; editorial bd Am. Jour. Clin. Oncology, 1991—. Capt. USAF, 1966-68. Fellow Am. Cancer Soc., Phila., 1963-64, NIH, 1964-66, Am. Cancer Soc. traineeship, 1968-71 Fellow Am. Coll. Radiology; mem. AMA, AAAS, Am. Assn. Cancer Rsch., Am. Coll. Radiology (commn. on radiation oncology 1981-90, bd. chancellors 1993-99), Am. Soc. Therapeutic Radiology and Oncology (chmn. bd. 1988-89, pres. 1987-88), Am. Coll. Hosp. Adminstrs., Am. Mgmt. Assn., Am. Radium Soc. (pres. 1992-93), Am. Soc. Clin. Oncology, Med. Assn. Atlanta, N.Y. Acad. Scis., Ga. State Med. Soc., Ga. State Radiol. Soc., Radiation Rsch. Soc., Radiol. Soc. N.Am., Alpha Omega Alpha. Office: Emory Clinic 1365 Clifton Rd NE Atlanta GA 30322-1013 Office Phone: 404-778-5323. Business E-Mail: davis@radonc.emory.org.

DAVIS, LEON, oil industry executive; b. Arkansas City, Kans., Nov. 15, 1918; s. Miriam Kahan; m. Elene Meyer Davis, July 29, 1952; children: Lynn, Lance, Ross, Evan. BA, U. Okla., 1940. Co-owner Davis Bros., Tulsa, Houston, 1945—. Chmn. bd. dirs. Alliance S.B.I. Co., Tulsa. Pres. Urban League, Tulsa, 1964; chmn. Okla. Civil Rights Commn., 1966; co-founder, chmn. Interferon Found., Houston, 1979—90; bd. dirs. M. D. Anderson Hosp. Col. USAAF, 1940—48. Mem.: Kiwanis (pres. 1965). Avocation: tennis. Home: 502 Thamer Ln Houston TX 77024-6920 Office: Davis Bros 1221 Mckinney St Ste 3100 Houston TX 77010-2009 Office Phone: 713-659-3131. Business E-Mail: leondavis@davisbros.com.

DAVIS, LEWIS U., JR., lawyer; b. Pitts., Mar. 25, 1950; s. Lewis Uber and Myrtle Elizabeth (Otte) D.; children: Shannon Lynn, Christin Lynn; m. Laraine Frazzini, May 22, 1993; 1 child, Laura Fitzgerald. BS in Engring. summa cum laude, Lehigh U., 1972; JD summa cum laude, Cornell U., 1975. Bar: Pa. 1975, U.S. Dist Ct. (we. dist.) Pa. 1975, U.S. Ct. Appeals (3d cir.) 1978. Assoc. Buchanan Ingersoll, Pitts., 1975-82, ptnr., shareholder, 1982—, v.p. tech., chief technology officer, 1994—. Contbr. articles to profl. jours. Mem. ABA, Am. Bankruptcy Inst., Pa. Bar Assn. Avocations: computers, tennis, golf. Office: Buchanan Ingersoll One Oxford Centre 301 Grant St Fl 20 Pittsburgh PA 15219-1410

DAVIS, LINCOLN, congressman; b. Sept. 13, 1943; m. Lynda Compton; three children. BS in Agronomy, Tenn. Tech. U. Mem. Tenn. Ho. of Reps. 92nd-93rd Gen. Assemblies, 1980—84, Tenn. Senate 100th Gen. Assembly, 1996—2002, Dem. majority whip, vice-chmn. transp. com., mem. senate environment, conservation, tourism coms., 1996-98, Tenn. Senate 101st Gen. Assembly, 1998—2002; mem. U.S. Ho. of Reps. from 4th Tenn. dist., 2003—. Mayor, Town of Byrdstown, 1978-82; former mem. Upper Cumberland Devel. Dist., Upper Cumberland Human Resource Agy., LBJ&C Devel. Corp. Mem. Tenn. Jaycees (past state pres.). Democrat. Office: 504 Cannon HOB Washington DC 20515-4204 E-mail: sen.lincoln.davis@legislature.state.tn.us.*

DAVIS, LISA CORINNE, artist; b. Balt., Jan. 22, 1958; d. Robert Clarke and Elaine C. (Carsley) D.; children: G. Davis Cathcart, Corinne Davis Cathcart. BFA, Pratt Inst., 1980; MFA, CUNY, 1983. Asst. prof. School of Art, Yale U., New Haven, 1997—2002; critic Yale U., New Haven, 2002—; assoc. prof. Hunter Coll., 2002—. One-man shows include Marlborough Gallery, NYC, June Kelly Gallery, N.Y.C., Print Club, Phila., 1993, 2d St. Gallery, Charlottesville, Va., 1994, Mcpl. Gallery, Atlanta, 1994, Halsey Gallery, Charleston, S.C., 1994, Dell Pryor Galleries, Detroit, 1994, Project Room Bronx Coun. on the Arts, N.Y., 1996; group shows include Inroads Gallery, N.Y.C., 1984, U.S. Capitol Bldg., Washington, 1986, The Schenectady Mus., N.Y., 1986, Ridge St. Gallery, N.Y.C., 1987, 88, Christie's, N.Y.C., 1989, 90, Artist's Space, N.Y.C., 1990, 91, Okeanos Gallery, Berkeley, Calif., 1992, Pyramid Atlantic Workshop, Washington, 1992, Print Club, Phila., 1992, Granary Books, N.Y.C., 1993, Kenkeleba Gallery, N.Y.C., 1993, Orgn. Ind. Artists, N.Y.C., 1993, Art in General, N.Y.C., 1993, 94, The Bronx Mus. Arts, 1993, 96, Butters Gallery, Portland, Oreg., 1993, Barrett House Galleries, Poughkeepsie, N.Y., 1994, Gallery Annext, N.Y.C., 1994, City Without Walls, Newark, 1994, Papermill, N.Y.C., 1995, Ctr. Contemporary Art, Newark, 1996. Regional fellow Mid-Atlantic Arts Found., 1992, fellow NEA, 1995-96, artists' fellow N.Y. Found. for Arts, 1997, 2000, Louis Comfort Tiffany Found. fellow, 2001. Studio: 323 West 39th St New York NY 10018

DAVIS, LISA E., lawyer; b. Flushing, NY, Feb. 6, 1960; BA, Harvard U., 1981; JD, NYU Sch. Law, 1985. Bar: NY 1986. Law clk. to Honorable Constance Baker Motley, US Dist. Ct., So. Dist. NY, 1985—86; assoc. Kramer Levin Naftalis & Frankel LLP; ptnr., entertainment, publ., media Frankfurt Kurnit Klein & Selz, PC, NYC. Contbr. articles to law jour. Named one of Top 50 Black Power Brokers in Entertainment, Black Enterprise Mag., 2002, Am. Top Black Lawyers, 2003; recipient Jacob K. Javits Achievement award, Bedford Stuyvesant Restoration Corp., 2003. Mem.: Black Entertainment and Sports Lawyers Assn., Nat. Bar Assn. (Intellectual Property Sect.), Assn. Bar City of NY. Office: Frankfurt Kurnit Klein & Selz PC 488 Madison Ave New York NY 10022 E-mail: ldavis@fkks.com.

DAVIS, LOIS ANN, computer specialist, educator; b. Thermopolis, Wyo., Nov. 29, 1945; d. Hester Oliver and Ruth Louise (Baker) Davis; m. Harold W. Wright, Dec. 22, 1969 (div. 1988); children: Geraldine Ann, Harold W. III. BS in Bus. Edn. cum laude, U. Wyo., 1968, MS in Bus. Edn., 1988. Cert. office automation profl., Wyo. Instr. Lander (Wyo.) Valley High Sch., 1968-70, Cath. Sch., Chandler, Ariz., 1970-71; part-time instr. Casper (Wyo.) Coll., 1981-83, instr. bus. div., 1983-94, network support specialist, acad. computing, 1994-95, acting dir. acad. computing, 1995-96, dir. acad. computing, 1996—2005, dean ednl. resources, 2005—. Textbook reviewer Prentice-Hall, Englewood, N.J., 1989-91; co-dir. Casper Regional Tech. Ctr., 1999-2000; mem. computer sys. adv. bd. Casper Coll., 1995-2002; chair Casper Coll. Adminstrv. Alliance, 1996-97. Author: Electronic Communications, 2d edit., 1996. Bd. dirs. Murie Audubon Choir Nat. Audubon, 1995—97. Mem. Office Systems Rsch. Assn. (conf. co-chair 1999), Wyo. Bus. Edn. Assn. (sr. rep. 1991-92), Beta Gamma Sigma (life), Phi Kappa Phi (life). Avocations: cross country skiing, hiking, gardening, reading. Home: 1514 Jim Bridger Ave Casper WY 82604-3186 Office: Casper Coll Academic Affairs 125 College Dr Casper WY 82601-4612 Office Phone: 307-268-2703. Business E-Mail: ldavis@caspercollege.edu.

DAVIS, LORI, not-for-profit developer; children: Jacob, Josh, Caitlin, Michael, Eric, Travis. Grad. in acctg., Fresno State C.C., Fresno, Calif. Acctg. position with a cons. co.; acctg. position with a bank; engring. asst. for an ind. oil prodr.; asst. dir. Tread Lightly!, Ogden, Utah, exec. dir. Office: Tread Lightly 298 24th St Ste 325 Ogden UT 84401-1482

DAVIS, LORRAINE JENSEN, writer, editor; b. Omaha, Apr. 2, 1924; d. Theron R. and L. Mildred (Henkel) Jensen; m. Richard Morris Davis, Apr. 4, 1959 (dec.); 1 child, Laura Jensen. BA, U. Denver, 1946. Copywriter Glamour mag., N.Y.C., 1946-54, prodn. editor, 1954-61, Vogue Children mag., N.Y.C., 1963-66. Writer, assoc. features editor, Vogue mag., N.Y.C., 1966-77; mng. editor, writer women's news column, 1977-88; editorial dir. Condé Nast Books, 1988-91; editor: Vogue Living and Food Guide, 1975; editorial cons.: Vogue Beauty and Health Guide, 1979-82; editor: Cooking with Colette (by Colette Rossant), 1975, Fairchild Dictionary of Fashion (by Charlotte Calasibetta), 1975, English translation Paul Bocuse's French Cooking, 1977. Recipient Disting. Citizen award Alpha Gamma Delta, 1981 Mem. NOW, Phi Beta Kappa. Democrat. Episcopalian. Home: 200 Leeder Hill Dr Apt 538 Hamden CT 06517-2729

DAVIS, LOURIE IRENE BELL, computer education and information systems specialist; b. Las Vegas, N.Mex., Apr. 8, 1930; d. Currie Oscar and Minnie I. (Rodgers) Bell; m. Robert Eugene Davis, Aug. 21, 1950; children: Judith Anne, Robert Patrick, (adopted) Jaime Alleyn, (adopted) Flint Christopher. BS, West Tex. U., 1959; student, Ea. N.Mex. U., 1947-49, U. Tulsa, 1980-81. Cert. tchr. Tex., Okla. Programmer/analyst Blue Cross/Blue Shield Okla., Tulsa, 1972-75, Nat. Bank Tulsa, 1968—71; mgr. sys. Blue Cross/Blue Shield Okla., Tulsa, 1977-81, dir. info. sys., 1981-82, mgr. project control, 1983, mgr. info. ctr., 1984-85, mgr. profl. cons. and tng., 1985-87; faculty devel. coord. CAID Okla. State U., Okmulgee, 1987-90; dir. Region 8 Intertel, Inc., Tulsa, 1987—91, adminstrv. officer, 1991-95, pres., CEO, 1995-2000, treas., CFO, 2001—05. Sys. curriculum coord., computer sci. instr. Tulsa Jr. Coll., 1975-76, mem. computer sci. adv. bd., 1976-83, adj. instr., 1977-83, 93-94; computer bus. and edn. cons. Davis Cons., 1991-2002; mem. steering com. US Senate bus. adv. bd., 1981-88; ind. cons., Tulsa, 1987; lectr. computer assisted instr. Success League of Innovation Conf., St. Louis, 1989, Music Users Group Conf., U. Tenn., Chattanooga, 1989, Pres.'s Day Des Moines Area C.C., 1990. Mem. budget panel United Way Tulsa, 1981-87, Allocations Exec. Com. Appreciation award, 1987; mem. US Rep. Presdl. Task Force, 1982-93, Rep. Nat. com., 1983-91; mem. Holy Family Sch. Bd., 1991-95, nominating com. chair, 1993, sec., 1993-95. Recipient Internat. Merit award Assn. Sys. Mgmt., 1980, 84; winner League of Innovation for C.C.S. Competition, IBM, 1989. Mem.: NEA, AAUW, NAFE, Okla. Edn. Assn., Tulsa Classroom Tchrs. Assn., Higher Edn. Acad. Coun. of Okla., Tulsa Area Sys. Edn. Assn. (recorder 1980—81), Intertel (nat. acceptance com. chair 1978, dir. region VIII 1987—91, membership officer 1991—95, pub. Integra, Jour. of Intertel 1992—, pres., chmn. bd. 1995—2000, treas. 2001—04, lifetime mem. and appreciation award 1997, Continuous Outstanding Svc. award 2004, spl. appreciation award 2004), Habitat for Humanity, Arbor Day Found., Sierra Club, Mensa, Alpha Chi. Republican. Mem. Unity Ch. of Christianity. Home and Office: Davis Cons 2403 W Oklahoma St Tulsa OK 74127-3027 Personal E-mail: LourieD@aol.com.

DAVIS, LOWELL LIVINGSTON, cardiovascular surgeon; b. Urbanna, Va. BS in Biology, Morehouse Coll., 1949; MS in Biology, Atlanta U., 1950; MD, Howard U., 1955; postgrad., U. Pa., 1959-60. Diplomate Am. Bd. Surgery, Am. Bd. Thoracic Surgery. Intern Jersey City (N.J.) Med. Ctr., 1955-56; resident Margaret Hague Maternity Hosp., Jersey City, 1956-57; resident ob-gyn. Elmhurst (N.Y.) Gen. Hosp., 1957-58, chief resident ob-gyn., 1958-59; resident in gen. surgery U.S. VA Hosp., Tuskegee, Ala., 1960-61; resident to chief resident in gen. surgery Nassau County Med. Ctr., Hempstead, N.Y., 1961-64; resident in cardiothoracic surgery Cook County Hosp., Chgo., 1967-68, sr. resident, 1968-69; pvt. practice N.Y.C., 1964-65; pvt. practice thoracic and cardiovascular surgery, 1975—; clin. assoc. prof. surgery L.A. County Gen. Hosp., U. So. Calif. Med. Sch., 1988—. Fellow U. Oreg., Portland, 1972, St. Vincent Hosp., Portland, 1972, Med. Coll. Wis., Milw., 1973, Pacific Med. Ctr. Inst. of Med. Scis., San Francisco, 1974, Allen-Bradley Med. Scis. Rsch. Lab. Med. Coll. Wis., 1975, Hosp. for Sick Children, London, 1977-78, Tex. Heart Inst., Houston, 1983, Cardiac Surgery Rsch. Lab.; fellow, vis. prof. Hadassah Med. Sch. and U. Hosp., Jerusalem, 1987; vis. surgeon NYU Med. Sch., 1991, Mayo Clinic, Rochester, Minn., 1991, U. Dusseldorf, Germany, 1991, Deutsches Herzzentrum, Berlin, 1991, Deutsches Herzzentrum, Munich, 1991, Klinik für Thorat-Herz-Und Gefab Chirurgie, Hanover, Germany, 1991, U. Vienna, Austria, 1992; vis. student N.Y. Hosp., Cornell U, 1991; vis. surgeon U. Ala. Med. Ctr., Birmingham, 1991. Contbr. articles to profl. jours. With USN, 1943-46, USNR, 1965-71, comdr., 1965-67, capt. USNR, 1970. Recipient Asiatic Pacific Campaign medal with one Gold Star, Presdl. Unit citation. Fellow ACS, Internat. Coll. Angiology, Am. Coll. Angiology, Internat. Coll. Surgeons, N.Y. Acad. Medicine, Am. Coll. Chest Physicians, Am. Coll. Cardiology; mem. AAAS, Assn. Mil. Surgeons U.S., Am. Assn. for Thoracic Surgery, Soc. Thoracic Surgeons, Albert Starr Cardiac Surg. Soc. (founding), Am. Coll. Emergency Physicians, Lyman Brewer III Internat. Surg. Soc., Royal Soc. Medicine, Denton A. Cooley Cardiovasc. Surgery Soc., L.A. Surg. Soc.

DAVIS, LOYD EVAN, defense industry marketing professional; b. Newark, Ohio, Apr. 10, 1939; s. Paul Edwin and Eleanor Amanda (Loyd) D.; m. Delores Madeline Wells, Nov. 10, 1959 (div. 1975); children: Mark Evan, Geoffrey Scott; m. Judith Ann Lambert, Sept. 15, 1977; 1 child, James Richard. BS in Elec. Engring., Okla. State U., 1963, MS in Elec. Engring., 1968. Commd. 2d lt. USAF, 1964, advanced through grades to maj., 1974; served in various locations, then ret. U.S. Air Force, 1979; mem. sr. profl. staff Dynatrend, Inc., Arlington, Va., 1979-82; mktg. mgr. govt. systems sector Harris Corp., Alexandria, Va., 1982-87; mktg. mgr. E-Systems Melpar Div., Falls Church, Va., 1987-90; mem. sr. profl. staff Adroit Systems, Inc., Alexandria, Va., 1990-95; dir. mktg. comms. L3 Comms. Corp., Salt Lake City, 1996—. Mem.: Armed Forces Comm. Electronics Assn., Air Force Assn., Nat. Def. Indsl. Assn., Assn. U.S. Army, Mt. Vernon Amateur Radio Club (pres. 1987—88), Davis County Amateur Radio Club (v.p. 1997), Woodbridge Wireless Club (pres. 1972—73, 1988—89), Masons (worshipful master 2002, sec. 2003—, grand chaplain 2004, grand orator 2005). Republican. Methodist. Avocation: amateur radio. Home: 1476 Madera Hills Dr Bountiful UT 84010-1523 Office: L3 Comms Corp Comm Systems West 640 North 2200 West Salt Lake City UT 84116-0850 Office Phone: 801-594-2297. E-mail: k8ei@arrl.net.

DAVIS, LUTHER, writer, theater producer, motion picture producer; b. N.Y.C., Aug. 29, 1921; s. Charles Thomas and Henriette (Roesler) D.; m. Dorothy deMilhau, Nov. 3, 1943 (div. 1961); children: Noelle, Laura Duval. BA, Yale U., 1938. Author: (play) Kiss Them for Me, 1945, (libretto with Charles Lederer) Kismet (Tony award 1953); prodr. Timbuktu, 1978 (Tony nomination 1979), (libretto) Grand Hotel, 1989 (Tony nomination 1990, Olivier award London, England, 2005), 15 solo screenplays including The Hucksters, 1946, A Lion Is in the Street, 1950, Across 110th Street, 1972; author, prodr. Lady in a Cage, 1964; numerous TV series, pilots and episodes. Served to maj. USAAF, 1942-45, CBI, ETO. Recipient Tony award, 1953. Mem. Dramatists Guild Am., Writers Guild Am.-West, League Am. Theaters and Prodrs., Acad. Motion Picture Arts and Scis., PEN. Office Phone: 212-288-3870. Personal E-mail: ludavis212@aol.com.

DAVIS, LYDIA, writer, educator; Assoc. prof. lit. Bard Coll., 1986—2001; assoc. prof. of Eng., writer in residence State U. of N.Y., Albany, 2001—. Author: (book) Break it Down, 1986, The End of the Story, 1995, Almost No Memory, 1997, Samuel Johnson Is Indignant, 2001. Fellow N.Y. State writers Inst., U. of Albany, MacArthur Found., 2003. Office: U Albany Humanities 350 1400 Washington A Albany NY 12222

DAVIS, LYNN ETHERIDGE, political scientist, educator; b. Miami, Fla., Sept. 6, 1943; d. Earl DeWitt and Louise (Featherston) Etheridge. BA, Duke U., 1965; MA, Columbia U., 1967, PhD, 1971; DHL (hon.), Va. Theol. Sem., 2000. Lectr. Miles Coll., Birmingham, Ala., 1966-67; asst. prof. polit. sci. Barnard Coll., Columbia U., N.Y.C., 1970-74; rsch. assoc. Internat. Inst. for Strategic Studies, London, 1973; program analysis staff Nat. Security Council, 1974; asst. prof., lectr. dept. polit. sci. Columbia U., 1974-76; prof., staff mem. Senate Select Com. on Intelligence, 1975-76; dep. asst. sec. of def. for policy plans and nat. security affairs Office of the Under Sec. for Policy, Dept. Def., Washington, 1977-79, asst. dep. under sec. for policy planning, 1979-81; rsch. Internat. Inst. Strategic Studies, London, 1981-82; prof. national security affairs National War Coll., Washington, 1982-85; dir. studies Internat. Inst. Strategic Studies, London, 1985-87; hon. sr. rsch. fellow, dept. war studies Kings Coll., London, 1988-90; rsch. fellow John Hopkins Fgn. Policy Inst, Paul H. Nitze Sch. Advanced Internat. Studies, 1988-91; v.p. army rsch. divsn., dir. Arroyo Ctr. RAND, Santa Monica, Calif, 1991-93, sr. fellow Washington, 1997—2001, sr. polit. scientist, 2001—; under sec. for arms control and internat. security affairs Dept. State, Washington, 1993-97. Author: The Cold War Begins, Soviet American Conflict Over Eastern Europe, 1974. Woodrow Wilson fellow, 1965-66, 69-70, 81-82; Columbia U. fellow, 1965-66, 68-69; recipient David D. Lloyd prize Harry S. Truman Library, 1976 Mem.: Coun. on Fgn. Rels., Phi Beta Kappa. Home: 827 S Lee St Alexandria VA 22314-4333 Office: RAND 1200 S Hayes St Arlington VA 22202-5050 Office Phone: 703-413-1100 x5399. E-mail: Lynn_Davis@rand.org.

DAVIS, MAGGIE (MARIE HILL), writer; b. Norfolk, Va. d. George Blair and Dorothy Austin (Mason) Hill; children: Stuart, Richard, David, Cambren. Advt. copywriter Young and Rubicam, N.Y.C.; asst. in rsch. to chmn. dept. psychology Yale U., New Haven. Instr. creative writing courses Yale U.; guest writer/artist Internat. Cultural Ctr., Hammamet, Tunisia. Author: The Far Side of Home, 1992, Daggers of Gold, 1993, Moonlight and Mistletoe, 1993, The Amethyst Crown, 1994, Blood Red Roses, 1991 (named Best Medieval Novel by Romantic Times mag.), A Christmas Romance, 1991 (dramatized as CBS Sunday Night Movie 1994), Eagles, 1980, The Sheik, 1977, Rommel's Gold, 1971, Enraptured, 1999, Masquerade, 1999, Strangers in the Night, 2000, Out of the Blue, 2002, Stage Door Canteen, 2003; feature writer Atlanta Jour. Constn.; contbr. articles and short stories to Ga. Rev., Cosmopolitan, Ladies Home Jour., Good Housekeeping, Holiday, Venture mags. Named Ga. Author of Yr., 1963; recipient Silver Pen award Affaire de Coeur Mag., 1987, Lifetime Achievement award Romantic Times Mag., 1987. Democrat. Mem. Soc. Of Friends. Personal E-mail: madav1@aol.com.

DAVIS, MAMIE (DENISE DAVIS), writer; b. Florence, SC, July 28, 1943; divorced; 1 child, Jacqueline J. Maslin. Cert. IBM data entry, N.Y.C., 1981. From clk grade 2 to prin. admin. assoc. NYC Civil Svc., 1962—86; freelance writer, composer N.Y.C. and, SC, 1986—. Tchg. coord., cons. NYC-DSS/HRA, 1980—86; stock actor Pilgrim Dramatic Playhouse. Author: (plays) So Many Drops of Rain (showcased at NATAS), Sam Blood's Secret, Sibling of Evil, Agency Procedures: Lust and Corruption, 2002, (novel and screenplay) Jessie's Folly, 2000, over 30 short stories; actor: numerous feature films, (Off-Broadway plays) Medea, Damn That Miss Anne, The Nurse, Civil Rights Worker. Mem.: ASCAP. Avocations: fashion design, dressmaking, book cover design. E-mail: bernetha8000@yahoo.com.

DAVIS, MARGARET BRYAN, paleoecology researcher, educator; b. Boston, Oct. 23, 1931; AB, Radcliffe Coll., 1953; PhD in Biology, Harvard U., 1957; DSc (hon.), U. Minn., 2002. NSF fellow dept. biology Harvard U., Cambridge, Mass., 1957-58; dept. geosci. Calif. Inst. Tech., Pasadena, 1959-60; rsch. fellow dept. zoology Yale U., New Haven, 1960-61, prof. biology, 1973-76; rsch. asoc. dept. botany U. Mich., Ann Arbor, 1961-64, assoc. rsch. biologist Gt. Lakes Rsch. divsn., 1964-70, rsch. biologist, assoc. prof. dept. zoology, 1966-70, rsch. biologist, prof. zoology, 1970-73; head dept. ecology and behavioral biology U. Minn., Mpls., 1976-81, prof. dept. ecology, evolution and behavior, 1976-82, Regents prof. ecology, 1983—2000. Vis. prof. Quaternary Rsch. Ctr., U. Wash., 1973; vis. investigator environ. studies program U. Calif., Santa Barbara, 1981-82; adv. panel ecology NSF, 1976-79; sci. adv. com. biology, behavior and social scis., 1989-91; adv. panel geol. record of global change, NRC, 1991-92, planetary biology com., 1981-82, global change com; 1987-90, mem. screening com. in plant scis., internat. exch. of persons com., 1972-75, sci. and tech. edn. com., 1984-86, vis. rsch. scientist scholarly exch. com. NAS/NRC, People's Republic China, mem. grand challenges in environ. sci. com., 1999-2000; U.S. nat. com. internat. Union Quaternary Rsch., 1966-74; bd. trustees Inst. for Ecosys. Studies, 2000—. Mem. editl. bd. Quaternary Rsch., 1969-82, Trends in Ecology and Evolution, 1986-92, Ecosystems, 2000-03. Bd. dir. Ricon Inst., 2005—. Recipient Sci. Achievement award Sci. Mus. Minn., 1988, alumnae Recognition award Radcliffe Coll., 1988, Nevada medal, 1993, Merit award Bot. Soc. Am., 1998, award for Contbn. Grad. Edn., U. Minn., 1999. Fellow: AAAS, Geol. Soc. Am., Am. Acad Arts and Scis.; mem.: NAS, Am. Quaternary Assn. (councillor 1969—70, 1972—76, pres. 1978—80, Dist. Career award 2001), Brit. Ecol. Soc. (hon.), Am. Soc. Naturalists (hon.), Ecol. Soc. Am. (pres. 1987—88, Eminent Ecologist award 1993), Nature Conservancy (bd. dirs. Minn. chpt. 1979—85), Internat. Assn. Gt. Lakes Rsch. (bd. dirs. 1970—73), Sigma Xi, Phi Beta Kappa. Office: U Minn Dept Ecology Evolution & Behavior 100 Ecology Bldg 1987 Upper Buford Cir Saint Paul MN 55108-1051 Business E-Mail: mbdavis@ecology.umn.edu.

DAVIS, MARGARET THACKER, retired critical care, medical and surgical nurse; b. Greensboro, N.C., June 7, 1925; d. Tiller Foltz and Lucy Wright (Spencer) Thacker; m. Joe Southard Davis, Feb. 4, 1961; 1 child, Dana Lee. Diploma in nursing, Baylor U., Dallas, 1947; student, Ea. N.Mex. U., Roswell, 1978. RN, N.Mex., Tex., Fla. Office nurse Drs. Britt & Cafaro, St. Augustine, Fla., 1947-50, Dr. Robert J. Rowe, Dallas, 1950-61, Dr. F.A. English, Roswell, 1964-74; charge nurse post anesthesia care unit Ea. N.Mex. Med. Ctr., Roswell, 1990-91, ret., 1991. Named Employee of Month, Ea. N.Mex. Med. Ctr., 1985. Mem. ANA, Am. Soc. Post Anesthesia Nurses (charter), Post Anesthesia Nurses Assn. N.Mex. (bd. dirs. 1980-86, sec. 1986-87, legis. com. 1989-90), N.Mex. Nurses Assn. (dist. 5 sec. 1983-85, 91-93, pres. 1986-88, bd. dirs. 1988-90, 92-94, 96-98, membership chmn. 1988-90, chmn. nominating com. 1990, Nurse of Yr. award 1989, search for excellence award 1990, dist. 5 honored nurse 1995), Baylor U. Sch. Nursing Alumni Assn. Home: 1301 W Country Club Rd Apt 42 Roswell NM 88201 E-mail: maggied53@aol.com.

DAVIS, MARICA NANCI ELLA RIGGIN, retired artist; b. Phila., Apr. 13, 1934; d. Dale Thomas and Anna (Kudla) Purtle; m. Donald Allen Riggin, Sept. 11, 1954 (dec. Nov. 10, 1970); children: Ralph Allen Riggin, Ronald Dale Riggin, David Wayne Riggin; m. Leonard Nettleton Davis, July 3, 1976; 3 stepchildren. Student, Montgomery Coll., Rockville, Md., 1975—78, student, 1983, student, 1988, student, 1993. Electro-mech. drafter Philco, Phila., 1952—55, Vitro Labs. Automated Industries, Aspen Hill, Md., 1971—73; designer, printer Sears Roebuck, Bethesda, Md., 1970; drafer, illustrator Watkins-Johnson Co. divsn. CEI, Gaithersburg, Md., 1973—86, IDEAS/SAIC, Columbia, Md., 1987—98. Instr. adult edn. craft class Montgomery County, Md.; jury Damascus County Fair Art Show. Juried and award winning shows, Sugar & Frichtle, Kensington, Md., Town Ctr., Ten Oaks, Md., Gurmukh Galleries, Md., Gaithersburg Coun. Arts, Woodlawn Mansion, Md., Kentland Mansion, McCrillus Gardens, Audubon Soc., Unitarian Universalitic Ch., Pyramid Atlantic, Sandy Spring Mus., Visual Sys. Art Ctr., Strathmore Hall, Rockville Arts Pl., Delapaine Visual Arts Ctr., Md., Café Monet, Kensington, Kent Island Federation Art, Md., Sumner Mus., Washington, Saxon Swan Gallery, Del., Dietricks Gallery, Sta. Gallery, Dover (Del.) Art League, one-woman shows include Open Studio Gallery, 2000, 2001, 2002, 2004, Kent Island Fedn. Art, Md., 2003, 2004. Pres. Episcopal Ch. Women, Beathany Beach, Del., 2003. Mem.: Ga. Miniature Art Soc., Miniature Art Soc. Fla. Inc., Cider Painters Am., Printmakers Plus, Olney Art Assn. (pres. 1995, 1996), S. Ea. Del. Artists Studio Tour, Miniature Painters Sculptors and Gravers Soc. (receiver 1989—98), Nat. League Am. Pen Women (membership chair Holly chpt.), Md. Printmakers (assoc.; folio chair 1996), Phi Theta Kappa. Home: 306 Steamboat Ln Dagsboro DE 19939-9226 Personal E-mail: ezdavis306@aol.com.

DAVIS, MARJORIE ANN, program analyst; d. Robert Leo and Juanita Vivienne Davis; 1 child, Carl Levon (dec.). AA, LA Trade Tech. Coll., 1984; BS, U. So. Calif., 1989, MPA, 1990; MA in Edn., OH State U., 1996, PhD, 1997. Correction officer Warren Correctional Instn., Lebanon, Ohio, 1991—92; acad. adv. Ohio State U., Columbus, 1992—97; prof. polit. sci. Sinclair C.C., Dayton, Ohio, 1993—94; project coord. Urban League Pitts., 1998—2000, strategic planning com. mem., 1998—2000; program analyst LA Superior Ct., Van Nuys, Calif., 2000—. Mem. diversity com. Superior Ct. Calif. Mentor El Camino Real HS; commr. pks. and recreation com. Mayor's Office, Carson, Calif., 2000. Recipient Cmty. Svc. award, City of Hope, 1999. Mem.: Toastmasters (vice chair 1985—86). Avocations: reading, bicycling, crossword puzzles, walking, opera.

DAVIS, MARK CAMERON, radiologist; b. Berkeley, Calif., May 9, 1951; s. Lorraine (Lillegard) D.; m. Anh Anh Tran, Sept. 30, 1983; children: Michael, Christopher, Laura. BS in Physics, Stanford U., 1973; MS in Nuclear Engring., U. Mich., 1974, PhD in Nuclear Engring., 1976; MD, Rush U., 1983. Diplomate Am. Bd. Radiology, Am. Bd. Nuclear Medicine. Asst. prof. engring. scis. Tech. Inst., Northwestern U., Evanston, Ill., 1976-79; staff radiologist Lowell (Mass.) Gen. Hosp., 1988-90, Noshoba Cmty. Hosp., Groton, Mass., 1990-91, Shady Grove Adventist Hosp., Gaithersburg, Md., 1991-92, Loudoun Hosp., Leesburg, Va., 1992—; with Profl. Radiology Svcs., P.A., Clinton, Md. Mem. Am. Coll. Radiology, Am. Soc. Neuroradiology, Soc. Magnetic Resonance Imaging, Soc. Nuclear Medicine, Radiol. Soc. N.Am., Sigma Xi. Office: Profl Radiology Svcs PA 7801 Old Branch Ave Ste 300 Clinton MD 20735-1643

DAVIS, MARK HEZEKIAH, JR., electrical engineer; b. Knoxville, Tenn., Oct. 5, 1948; s. Mark Hezekiah and Grace Carson (Owens) D.; m. Susan Nakamura, July 14, 1977; children: Michell Grace, Kelli Michelle, John Micheal. BSEE, U. Tenn., 1972, MS, 1973. Devel. engr. Westinghouse Electric Corp. - U.S. ACE, Pitts. and Oakridge, 1969-76; sr. rsch. engr. N.L. Petroleum Svc., Houston, 1977-79; mgr. rsch. and devel. Advanced Ocean Systems divsn. Hydril Corp., Houston, 1980-81; engring. mgr. Schlumberger Corp., Sugarland, Tex., 1981-82; dir. electronics devel. Tech. for Energy Corp., Knoxville, 1982-84; mgr. digital signal processing N.E.C. Electronics, Mountain View, Calif., 1984-88; dir. comm. Executon Info. Systems, Stamford, Conn., 1988-93; dir., v.p. engring. C.S.I. Telecom, Palm Springs, Calif., 1993—. Pres. N.W. Houston United Civic Assn., 1980-82. Robert Miller scholar, 1971; U. Tenn. Nat. Alumni scholar, 1972; U.S. AEC grantee, 1973. Mem. IEEE (sr.), Am. Soc. Engring. Edn., Optical Soc. Am., Electro-Chem. Soc., Marine Tech. Soc., Soc. Photo-Optical Instrumentation Engrs. Achievements include: current work in fiber optic sensors and comm. systems and high temperature electronics in geosci.; subspecialties: ocean engineering; fiber optics. Home: 15422 Winding Moss Dr Houston TX 77068-3813 Office: CSI Telecom 4505 California Ave Ste 206 Long Beach CA 90807 E-mail: heze@aol.com.

DAVIS, MARK JONATHAN, comedian, writer; b. Plainview, N.Y., Nov. 27, 1965; s. Sol and Beverly Davis. Studied, Ariz. State U., Tempe, 1983—87. Writer, prodr., performer KROQ-FM Radio, L.A., 1992—2004; writer, prodr., announcer NBC-TV, Burbank, Calif., 1996—2002. Writer, designer Walt Disney Imagineering, Glendale, Calif., 1998—. Singer: (albums) Lounge Against The Machine, Tuxicity, I'd Like A Virgin. Activist Revolutioncentral.com, L.A., 2004—05. Avocations: Scrabble, 20th century art, astronomy.

DAVIS, MARK M., microbiologist, educator; b. Paris, Nov. 27, 1952; BA in Molecular Biology, Johns Hopkins U., 1974; PhD in Molecular Biology, Calif. Inst. Tech., 1981. Fellow lab. of immunology NIH, Bethesda, Md., 1980-82, staff fellow lab. of immunology, 1982-83; asst. prof. med. microbiology Stanford (Calif.) U. Sch. Medicine, 1983-86, assoc. prof. microbiology and immunology, 1986-91, prof. microbiology and immunology, 1991—, dir. predoctoral program in immunology, 1994—; assoc. investigator Howard Hughes Med. Inst., Stanford U., 1987-91, faculty coord., 1989—, investigator, 1991—. Instr. Cold Spring Harbor (N.Y.) Lab., 1983; mem. sci. adv. bd. Damon Runyon-Walter Cancer Found., 1985-88; co-organizer UCLA Symposium, 1987; mem. allergy and immunology study sect. divsn. rsch. grants NIH, 1988-92. Recipient Intra-Sci. Rsch. Found. award 1980, Youth Scientist award Passano Found., 1985, Eli Lilly award 1986, Kayden award N.Y. Acad. Scis., 1986, Howard Taylor Ricketts award U. Chgo., 1988, Gairdner Found. award, 1989, King Faisal Internat. prize 1995, Sloan prize Gen. Motors Rsch. Found., 1996; scholar PEW Found. 1985-89. Mem. Nat. Acad. Scis., Inst. Medicine (2004). Office: Stanford U Sch Medicine Fairchild Bldg Rm # D-300 Stanford CA 94305-5124

DAVIS, MARLEEN KAY, architect, educator; b. Pitts., Apr. 24, 1952; d. Edward William and Mary Margaret (Dixon) Kay; m. Thomas Kirby Davis, Apr. 8, 1978; children: Stephen Mabon, Robert Jackson. BArch, Cornell U., 1976; MArch with honors, Harvard U., 1979. Lic. architect, N.Y., Mass. Designer Henry Schadler & Assocs., West Hartford, Conn., 1977-78, Sert Jackson & Assocs., Cambridge, Mass., 1979-80; architect Skidmore, Owings & Merrill, Boston, 1980-81; assoc. prof. architecture Syracuse U., NY, 1981—94; dean Coll. Architecture and Design, U. Tenn., Knoxville, 1994—2003, disting. prof., 2003—. Bd. mem. Nat. Architectural Accreditation Bd. Exhibitor recent faculty competitions, Syracuse U., 1983, 85, 86, portfolios in architecture, N.Y.C., 1983. Recipient Grand Prize award U. Miami Campus Masterplan Design Competition, 1986, Third Prize award Ft. Lauderdale (Fla.) Riverfront Plaza Design Competition, 1982. Mem.: Exec. Women's Assn. of Knoxville. Avocation: travel. Office: U Tenn Coll Architecture and Design 1715 Volunteer Blvd Knoxville TN 37996-2400*

DAVIS, MARTHA FRANCES, lawyer; b. Wichita, Kans., Apr. 4, 1957; d. Robert Louis and Marian (Larson) D. AB in Anthropology, Harvard U., 1979; BA, Trinity Coll., Oxford, Eng., 1981, MA in Jurisprudence, 1987; JD, U. Chgo., 1983. Bar: Ill. 1983, N.Y. 1985, U.S. Supreme Ct. 1988. Law clk. to judge U.S. Dist. Ct. (no. dist.) Ind., Hammond, 1983-85; assoc. Cleary,

Gottlieb, Steen & Hamilton, N.Y.C., 1986-90; staff atty. NOW Legal Def. and Edn. Fund, 1990—. Bd. dirs. Ctr. for Immigrants Rights; Kate Stoneman vis. prof. Albany Law Sch., 2000; adj. prof. NYU Sch. Law. Author: Brutal Need: Lawyers and the Welfare Rights Movement, 1960-73. Bunting Inst. fellow, Radcliffe Coll., 1988-89; Wasserstein fellow, Harvard Law Sch., 1998. Mem. N.Y.C. Bar Assn. (chair adminstrv. law com.). Mem. Soc. Of Friends. Avocations: music, writing. Office: NOW Legal Def & Edn Fund 99 Hudson St Rm 12R New York NY 10013-2815

DAVIS, MARVIN ARNOLD, manufacturing executive; b. St. Louis, Nov. 16, 1937; s. Sam and Pauline (Neuman) D.; m. Trudy Brenda Rein, Aug. 11, 1968; children: Julie, Jeffrey. BS in Chem. Engring., Washington U., St. Louis, 1959; MBA in Fin.and Mktg., Washington U., 1966. Lead engr. Standard Oil Calif., San Francisco, 1962-64; product mgr. Shell Chem. Co., N.Y.C., 1966-69; group controller Pfizer, Inc., N.Y.C., 1969-75; exec. v.p. Good Hope Industries, New Orleans, 1975-77; pres., chief exec. officer Reed Industries, Inc., Stone Mountain, Ga., 1978-79; pres. Sentrex Ltd., Atlanta, 1977-82; v.p. Sentry Ins., 1982-84; chmn., CEO Petrowax PA Inc., 1991-93, Datamax Corp., 1996—; cons., pres. Grisanti Galef Goldress, 1984-97, mng. ptnr., 2001—. Chmn., CEO Petrowax PA, Inc., 1992-94, Signal Apparel Corp., 1993-94; chmn. Folger Adams Corp., Simplicity Pattern Co., Pandick Press; instr. Farleigh Dickinson U., 1968-71; lectr. Washington U., 1966, 77; cons. in field; bd. dirs. Wherehouse Enterntainment Corp., Fairlanes Bowling Corp., Celluland Corp., Northwest Pipe and Casing Co., Z Axis Corp., Crown Crafts Corp., Turn Around Mgmt. Assn., Cherokee Corp.; pres. AMA Fund, Inc. Author: The Profit Prescription, 1985, Turnaround, 1987, The Turnaround Formula, 2002. Served to lt. USNR, 1959-62. Recipient scholarship Washington U., 1959, fellow, 1968. Mem. DeKalb C. of C., Citrus Club, Beta Gamma Sigma, Alpha Chi Sigma. Jewish. Office: Grisanti Galef and Goldress 333 Sandy Springs Cir Ste 106 Atlanta GA 30328 Office Phone: 404-441-3970. Personal E-mail: mdavis2866@aol.com. Business E-Mail: mdavis@gggcrisismanager.com.

DAVIS, MARY BYRD, conservationist, researcher; b. Cardiff, Wales; came to U.S., 1947; d. John Dymond and Joanna Inger (Falconer) Byrd; m. Robert Minard Davis; children: Carol, John. BA, Agnes Scott Coll., 1958; MA, U. Wis., 1968, PhD, 1972; MLS, Simmons Coll., 1974. Acquisitions libr. No. Mich. U., Marquette, 1974—75; asst. libr. Georgetown (Ky.) Coll., 1975—78; libr. U. Ky., Lexington, 1978—83; freelance writer and editor Georgetown, 1983-90, 93—; staff writer, office mgr. Earth First Jour., Canton, NY, 1990; co-founder and pub. Wild Earth, Canton, NY, 1991—92, assoc. editor Richmond, Vt., 1993—98; dir. Yggdrasil Inst., Georgetown, Ky., 1994—. Author: The Military Civilian Nuclear Link, 1988, Guide de L'Industrie Nucleaire Francaise, 1988, The Green Guide to France, 1990, Going Off the Beaten Path: An Untraditional Travel Guide to the U.S., 1991, Old Growth in the East: A Survey, 1993, rev. edit., 2003, La France nucléaire: matières et sites, 1997, 2002, The U.S. Enrichment Establishment 1999, 1999; co-author: Les Déchets nucléaires militaires Français, 1994, Weapons of Mass Destruction, 2005; editor: Eastern Old-Growth Forests: Prospects for Rediscovery and Recovery, 1996, Eastern Old-Growth Notes, 1997-2000. Bd. dirs. Centre de Documentation et de Recherche sur la Paix et les Conflits, Lyon, France, 1989—, Wildlands Ctr. for Preventing Roads, Missoula, Mont., 1996-99. Mem. Nat. Writers Union, Sierra Club (editor energy report 1986-87, exec. com. Cumberland chpt. 1982-84), Phi Beta Kappa. E-mail: yggdrasili@yahoo.com.

DAVIS, MARY ELIZABETH, speech pathologist, educator, counselor; b. Larned, Kans., July 1, 1930; d. LeRoy D. and Katheryn (Herndon) Harris; m. W.G. Davis, Apr. 3, 1969; children: Pamela Koch, Michelle Dalton; 1 stepchild, Wendy Garton. BA, Calif. State U., Fresno, 1959, MA, 1982. Cert. resource specialist, speech pathologist tchr., deaf tchr., counselor, Calif. Dir. recreation and occupl. therapy Wyo. State Hosp., Evanston, 1956-58; tchr. Fresno Unified Sch. Dist., 1960-80, Barton County C.C., Great Bend, Kans., 1990-98. Bd. dirs. Larned Historical Soc., Santa Fe Trail Ctr., Larned, Kans., 2001—04. Mem. Am. Counseling Assn., Nat. Bd. Cert. Counselors. Home: 3100 Nutmeg LN #D Hutchinson KS 67502-2968

DAVIS, MARY ELLEN K., library director; MLS, U. Ill.; MA, Ctrl. Mich. U. Sr. assoc. exec. dir. Assn. Coll. and Rsch. Librs., 1993—2001, exec. dir., 2001—, dir. comm. and systems, publs. program officer; ref. libr., bibliographer Ctrl. Mich. U., now exec. dir. Recipient Girl Scouts Outstanding Vol. award. Mem.: ALA, Am. Soc. Assn. Execs., Soc. Scholarly Publishing, Phi Kappa Phi, Beta Phi Mu. Office: 50 East Huron St Chicago IL 60611 Office Phone: 800-545-2433. E-mail: acrl@ala.org.

DAVIS, MARY HELEN, psychiatrist, educator; b. Kingsville, Tex., Dec. 2, 1949; d. Garnett Stant and Emogene (Campbell) D. BA, U. Tex., 1970; MD, U. Tex., Galveston, 1975; grad. in adult and child psychoanalysis, Inst. for Psychoanalysis, Chgo., 1982-92. Cert. Nat. Bd. Med. Examiners, Am. Bd. Psychiatry and Neurology, Child and Adolescent Psychiatry. Intern, then resident in psychiatry SUNY, Buffalo, 1975-78; fellow in child psychiatry U. Cin., 1978-80; asst. prof. Med. Coll. Wis., Milw., 1980-89, clin. assoc. prof., 1989-93; med. dir. adolescent treatment unit Milw. Psychiat. Hosp., 1981-86, Schroeder Child Ctr., 1986-89; pvt. practice, 1989-93; med. dir. Devereux-Victoria (Tex.) Psych. Residential Treatment Ctr., 1993-94; pvt. practice Lancaster, Pa., 1995—. Cons. Milw. Mental Health Cons., 1980-93, Children's Svc. Soc., Milw., 1982-93, Cath. charities, Harrisburg, Pa., 1996—, Sch. Dist. Lancaster, 1998—. Bd. dirs. Next Generation Theatre, Milw., 1988-90, Next Act Theatre, Milw., 1990-92, Lancaster Guidance Ctr., 2002--. Mem. Am. Psychiat. Assn., Am. Soc. Adolescent Psychiatry, Am. Med. Women's Assn., Assn. for Child Psychoanalysis, Am. Psychoanalytic Assn. Baptist. Avocations: science fiction, music, computers, crochet. Office Phone: 717-392-7062. E-mail: mdsquare@juno.com.

DAVIS, MAYNARD KIRK, accountant; b. Montreal, Aug. 31, 1949; s. Holbrook Reineman and Sarah DeForest (Maynard) D.; m. Joanne Margaret Daugherty, Aug. 5, 1972; children: Tamara Anne, Eric Maynard, Ian Holbrook. BA, U. Pa., 1973; MS, U. Mass., Amherst, 1977; MS in Indsl. Adminstrn., Carnegie Mellon U., 1979. Fin. analyst Corning Inc., Corning, N.Y., 1979-80, plant contr. Solon, Ohio and Danville, Va., 1980-83, ops. analyst Corning, 1983-84, bus. contr., 1984-87, govt. contract adminstrn. mgr., 1987-92, project planner/contr., 1992-95, contr. Corning Glass Ctr., 1995-96; dir. fin. conservation sci. divsn. The Nature Conservancy, Arlington, Va., 1997-00, dir. fin./ops. conservation sci. divsn., 2000—02; dir. fin./ ops. Asia-Pacific and Calif. divsn., 2002—. Trustee youth programs Chemung County YMCA, Elmira, N.Y., 1985-94, bd. dirs., 1986-89; trustee Arthur Vining Davis Founds., Jacksonville, Fla., 1989-98; class D soccer coach USSF. Mem. Inst. Mgmt. Accts., Fairfax (Va.) Audubon Soc. (treas. 1999—). Office: The Nature Conservancy 4245 Fairfax Dr Ste 100 Arlington VA 22203-1650 Home: 101 Woodvalley Ct Danville CA 94506-1411 E-mail: davismk@erols.com.

DAVIS, MELODY DAWN, writer, photographer, art historian; b. Harrisburg, Pa., Sept. 19, 1959; d. Russell Albert and Anna Mae (Smith) D.; m. Shahan Islam, Jan. 29, 1983; children: Ariel Davis Islam, Zachary Davis Islam. BA in English magna cum laude, Columbia U., 1981; MA in Art History, SUNY, Stony Brook, 1989; MPhil in Art History, CUNY, 1997. Adj. prof. Montclair (N.J.) State Coll., 1992, SUNY, Stony Brook, 1993. Author: The Male Nude in Contemporary Photography, 1991, The Center of Distance, 1992; contbr. poems to Poetry, Verse, Westbranch, Poetry New York, Chelsea, others, articles to Art Jour., History of Photography, Millennium Film Jour., others; permanent collections include The Brooklyn (N.Y.) Mus., N.Y. Pub. Libr., N.Y. Hist. Soc., City Mus. N.Y., Canadian Ctr. Architecture, Photo Gallery Internat., Tokyo, Robin Rice Gallery, N.Y., Photocollect, N.Y. Fellow in poetry NEA, 1995, Henry Luce Found. and Am. Coun. of Learned Socs., 1997; recipient First Place nomination Nat. Poetry Series, 1994, Alice Moser Claudel Poetry Contest, La., 1984. Mem. The Coll. Art Assn., Poetry Soc. Am., Perry County Arts Coun. Home: 462 Wildcat Trl Liverpool PA 17045-9135

DAVIS, MERRILL, public relations executive; Various positions including creation of training programs for new policy initiatives within the electric-utility industry, Tex.; formerly with Gov. Office, Tex.; joined Public Strategies, Inc., Austin, 1994—, now mng. dir. Contbr., rsch. project Nat. Sci. Found. Office: Public Strategies Inc Ste 1200 98 San Jacinto Blvd Austin TX 78701*

DAVIS, MICHAEL, medical educator; b. Bronxville, N.Y., Nov. 14, 1942; s. Pearce and Lucia D.; children: Nathaniel, Alexander. BA, Northwestern U., 1965; PhD, Yale U., 1969. Rsch. assoc. Yale U. Sch. Medicine, New Haven, 1969-70, asst. prof., 1970-75, assoc. prof., 1975-84, prof., 1984-98, 1998—; Robert W. Woodruff prof. psychiatry Emory U. Sch. Medicine, Atlanta, 1998—. Contbr. more than 200 articles to profl. jours.;, author 65 book chpts. USPHS Rsch. Scientist award NIMH, 1975-79, 80-85, 85-90, 90-95, 95-99; Sterling fellow Yale U., 1969. Fellow Am. Psychol. Assn., Am. Psychol. Soc., Am. Coll. Neuropsychopharmacology, AAAS; mem. Soc. for Neurosci., Soc. for Psychophysiology, Phi Beta Kappa. Office: Emory U Sch Medicine Dept Psychiatry 1639 Pierce Dr Rm 4311 Atlanta GA 30322-0001 E-mail: mdavis4@emory.edu.

DAVIS, MICHAEL CHASE, retired aerospace engineering executive, retired military officer; b. Fullerton, Calif., Oct. 12, 1931; s. Arthur Elling Davis and Mary Stafford (O'Brien) Greene; m. Jacqueline L. Watkins, Dec. 6, 1976; children from previous marriage: Michael Chase Jr., Mark Stafford. BS, U.S. Naval Acad., 1953; SM, ScD, MIT, 1961. Commd. ensign USN, 1953, advanced through grades to capt., 1971; design supt. Mare Island Naval Shipyard, Calif., 1966-68; sys. analyst Office Asst. Sec. Def., Washington, 1968-70; ship design dir. Trident Submarine and Aegis Warships, Naval Sea Sys. Command, Arlington, Va., 1970-75; comdg. officer David Taylor Naval Ship Rsch. and Devel. Ctr., Bethesda, Md., 1975-77; ret., 1977; program mgr. Sci. Applications, Inc., Arlington, 1977-79; program mgr., dir. Sea Shadow Stealth Ship and other marine programs, Lockheed Martin Missiles and Space Co., Sunnyvale, Calif., 1979-96; pub. Ovarian Cancer Internet Website, 1996-99. Decorated Legion of Merit; recipient DAR award for seamanship, 1953, D.W. Taylor award for sci. achievement, 1963, award for sci. achievement Bur. Ships, 1963, Joint Svc. commendation Sec. Def., 1970. Mem.: IEEE, US Naval Inst. Republican. Address: HC2 Box 2441 Tecumseh MO 65760 E-mail: anchor@townsqr.com.

DAVIS, MICHAEL J., judge; b. 1947; BA, Macalester Coll., 1969; JD, U. Minn., 1972; LLD (hon.), Macalester Coll., 2001. Law clk. Legal Rights Ctr., 1971-73; with Office Gen. Counsel Dept. Health, Edn. and Welfare, Social Security Adminstrn., Balt., 1973; criminal def. atty. Neighborhood Justice Ctr., 1974, Legal Rights Ctr., 1975—78; pub. defender Hennepin County, 1978-83; judge Hennepin County Mcpl. Ct., 1983-84, Hennepin County Dist. Ct. (4th jud. dist.), 1984-94; atty., commr. Mpls. Civil Rights Commn., 1977-82; judge U.S. Dist. Ct. Minn., St. Paul, 1994—. Constnl. law instr. Antioch Mpls. C.C., 1974; criminal def. trial practice instr. Nat. Lawyer's Guild, 1977; trial practice instr. William Mitchell Coll. Law, 1977-81, Bemidji Trial Advocacy Course, 1992, 93; adj. prof. U. Minn. Law Sch., 1982—, Hubert H. Humphrey Sch. Pub. Affairs, 1990; instr. Minn. Inst. Legal Edn., Civil Trial Practice Inst., 1991-92; lectr. FBI Acad., 1991, 92. Mem. Minn. Superior Ct. Racial Bias Task Force, 1990—93, U.S. Dist. Ct.; chmn. Pretrial Release & Bail Evaluation Com., 1997—. Recipient Outstanding Alumni award Macalester Coll., 1989, Good Neighbor award WCCO Radio, 1989, Disting Svc. award William Mitchell Coll. of Law, 2000. Mem. ABA, Nat. Bar Assn., Minn. Minority Lawyers Assn., Am. Inns. of Ct., Fed. Bar Assn., Fed. Judges Assn., Hennepin County Bar Assn., Minn. State Bar Assn., Minn. Lawyers Internat. Human Rights Com. (past mem. bd. dirs.), Internat. Acad. Trial Judges, Nat. Assn. for Pub. Interest Law (bd. dirs.), 8th Cir. Jury Instruction Com., U.S. Assn. Constitutional Law. Office: US Dist Ct Minn 300 S 4th St Ste 14E Minneapolis MN 55415-2251 Office Phone: 612-664-5070. Business E-Mail: mjdavis@mnd.uscourts.gov.

DAVIS, MICHAEL L., assistant principal; b. Lexington, Ky., July 2, 1964; s. William R. and Carol J. Davis; m. Dana R. Turner, June 14, 1986; children: Courtney, Alyssa, Derrick. B in Music Edn., Morehead State U., 1986, MA, 1993. Cert. tchr. Ky., guidance counselor Ky., prin. Ky. Band dir. Tollesboro (Ky.) HS, 1988—94, Lewis County Schs., Vanceburg, Ky., 1994—97; guidance counselor Frankfort (Ky.) HS, 1997—99, prin., 1999—2000, band dir., 2000—02; asst. prin. Gallatin County Mid. Sch., Warsaw, Ky., 2002—05; guidance counselor Gallatin County H.S., 2005—. Mem. adv. bd. Thornhill Learning Ctr., Frankfort, 1998—2001. Named All Acad. Mem., State Jour., 1998. Avocations: tennis, golf, music. Office: Gallatin County Mid Sch 601 E Main St Warsaw KY 41095

DAVIS, MICHAEL RICO, county official; b. Charlotte, NC; s. Lawrence Kenneth and Myrtle Elizabeth (Antrum) D. BA, U. N.C., 1979; MPA, Calif. State U., 1994, MA, 1996. Intern, adminstrv. asst. to majorit floor leader Calif. Assembly, L.A., 1980-81, field rep. assemblywoman Maxine Waters, 1983-86, adminstrv. asst., 1986-89; adminstrv. asst., dist. dir Congresswoman Maxine Waters, L.A., 1990-92; sr. counselor Optimist Homes & Ranch, Inc., L.A., 1981-83; sr. dep. 2nd dist. to Yvonne Burke L.A. County Bd. Suprs., L.A., 1993—. Author: Minorities in Business, 1997. Spl. asst. Jesse Jackson for President, LA, 1984; dir. GOTV Tom Bradley for Mayor, LA, 1989; del. Dem. Nat. Convention, NY, 1992, 2000, regional dir. Bill Clinton for President, LA, 1991-92; bd. dirs. Tng. Rsch./Head Start, LA, 1984—; black adv. com. LA Police Commn., 1984-87; presdl. selection com. Charles Drew Med. U., LA, 1997; nat. steering com. Al Gore for Pres. of U.S., 1999—; active Dem. Nat. Com., 2004—. Named to Outstanding Young Men of Am., 1981, 96, Young Leader, Am. Swiss Found., 1998, Dem. of Yr., LA County Dem. Party, 2004. Mem. Am. Soc. Pub. Adminstrn. mem. nat. coun. 2002—, v.p. LA met. chpt. 2000-02), So. Calif. Mediation Assn., Kappa Alpha Psi (historian 1977-78, regional dir. 1978-79, chmn. social action 1997, bd. dirs. we. province 1982-84, Outstanding Achievement 1978, Man of Yr. 1979), New Frontier Dem. Club (1st v.p. 2004—), Phi Alpha Delta. Democrat. Home: PO Box 19672 Los Angeles CA 90019-0672 Office: LA County Bd Suprs 500 W Temple St Los Angeles CA 90012-2713

DAVIS, MICHAEL STEVEN, lawyer; b. Brookline, Mass., Aug. 1, 1947; s. Ralph and Beatrice (Levy) D.; m. Madelyn O. Davis, Aug. 16, 1970; children: Gregory, Adam, Bethany. AB, U. Rochester, 1969; JD cum laude, Boston U., 1972. Bar: N.Y. 1973, U.S. Dist. Ct. (so. and ea. dists.) N.Y. 1974, U.S. Ct. Appeals (2d cir.) 1974, U.S. Supreme Ct. 1979, U.S. Ct. Claims, 1980. Assoc. Chadbourne & Parke, N.Y.C., 1972-82; sr. counsel corp. litigation Am. Internat. Group, N.Y.C., 1982-88; ptnr. Zalkin, Rodin & Goodman, LLP, N.Y.C., 1988-99, Zeichner, Ellman & Krause, LLP, N.Y.C., 1999—. Asst. adj. prof. C.W. Post Ctr., L.I. U., Glen Cove, NY, 1975—79. Editor: Boston U. Law Rev., 1970—72. Mem. Citizens Ctr. for Children of NY, Inc., 1978—87; trustee The Harvey Sch., Katona, NY, 1994—97; pres. Pelham (NY) Jewish Ctr., 1986—88; v.p. Sinai Free Synagogue, 2003—04. Mem. ABA, Assn. Bar City of N.Y., Am. Arbitration Assn., ARIAS-US AIDA Reinsurance and Ins. Arbitration Soc. (cert. arbitrator), Huguenot Bridge Club. Democrat. Office: Zeichner Ellman & Krause LLP 575 Lexington Ave New York NY 10022-6102 Business E-Mail: mdavis@zeklaw.com.

DAVIS, MICHAEL STUART, philosopher, educator; b. Canton, Ohio, Feb. 6, 1943; s. Albert Meeron and Beatrice (Weinberger) Davis; m. Deborah Jones, June 23, 1975; 1 child, Alexander Davis-Jones. B.A., Western Res. U., Cleveland, Ohio, 1961—65; MA, U.Mich., Ann Arbor, 1968, PhD, 1972. Vis. asst. prof. of philosophy Case Western Res. U., Cleve., 1972—74, vis. asst. prof., law sch., 1974—75. Asst. prof. of philosophy Ill. State U., Normal, Ill., 1977—84; vis. scholar, philosophy dept. U. of Chgo., 1984—85; vis. asst. prof. of philosophy U. of Ill. at Chgo., 1985—86; prof. of philosphy Ill. Inst. of Tech., Chgo, 1986—. Contbr. articles to various publications concerning justice and ethics; author: (books) To Make the Punishment Fit the Crime, 1992, Justice in the Shadow of Death: Rethinking Capital and Lesser Punishments, 1996, Thinking like an Engineer: Essays in the Ethics of a Profession, 1998, Ethics and the University, 1999, Profession, Code, and Ethics, 2002, Actual Social Contract and Political Obligation: A Philospher's History through Locke, 2002; editor: Ethics and the Legal Profession, 1986, AIDS: Crisis an Professional Ethics, 1994, Conflicts of Interest in the Professions, 2001. Fellow Summer Stipend, Nat. Endowment for the Humanities, 1974, Nat. Endowment for the Humanities Fellowship, 1984-85, Nat. Endowment for the Humanities Summer Seminar, 1990, Vis. Fellow, Centre for Applied Philosophy and Pub. Ethics, Charles Sturt University-Canberra, July -August 2001; grantee Ethics Across the Curriculum: Integrating Ethics into Profl. Edn., NSF, 1991-95, The Profl. Autonomy of Engineers, 1994, Ethics Across the Curriculum: Transferring the Tech., 1995—96, Ethics Across the Curriculum: Continuing the Transfer of the Tech., 2000—04, Software Engring. Code of Ethics, 2001—04. Avocations: history, hiking. Home: 5300 S Shore Drive #57 Chicago IL 60615 Office: Illinois Institute of Technology 3241 S Federal St HUB 204 Chicago IL 60616 Office Phone: 312-567-3017. Business E-Mail: davism@iit.edu.

DAVIS, MICHAEL W., lawyer; b. NYC, Nov. 12, 1950; BA magna cum laude, SUNY, Binghamton, 1972; JD cum laude, Northwestern U., 1975. Bar: Ill. 1975, Supreme Ct. Ill. 1975, US Dist. Ct. no. dist. Ill., ea. divsn. 1975, no. dist. Calif. 1981, ctrl. dist. Ill. 2002, US Supreme Ct. 1981, US Ct. of Appeals 2nd cir. 1980, 4th cir. 1986, 6th cir. 1986, 7th cir. 1988. Ptnr. Sidley & Austin, Chgo., and head, product liability and mass tort group, sec. exec. com. Prof. products liability law Chgo. Kent Coll. Law, 1984-88. Mem. drug and med. device steering com. Def. Rsch. Inst. Mem. Internat. Assn. Defense Coun., Legal Club Chgo. Office: Sidley & Austin Bank One Plz 10 S Dearborn Chicago IL 60603 Office Fax: 312-853-7036. Business E-Mail: mdavis@sidley.com.

DAVIS, MULLER, lawyer; b. Chgo., Apr. 23, 1935; s. Benjamin B. and Janice (Muller) D.; m. Jane Lynn Strauss, Dec. 28, 1963 (div. July 1998); children: Melissa Davis Muller, Muller Jr., Joseph Jeffrey; m. Lynn Straus, Jan. 23, 1999. Grad. with honors, Phillips Exeter (N.H.) Acad., 1953; BA magna cum laude, Yale U., 1957; JD, Harvard U., 1960. Bar: Ill. 1960, U.S. Dist. Ct. (no. dist.) Ill. 1961. Practice law, Chgo., 1960—; assoc. Jenner & Block, 1960-67; ptnr. Davis, Friedman, 1967—. Lectr. continuing legal edn., matrimonial law and litig.; legal adviser Michael Reese Med. Rsch. Inst. Coun., 1967-82; co-chair com. to study and recommend a comprehensive rules design for the domestic rels. divsn. Circuit Ct. of Cook County, Ill., 2003—. Author: (with Sherman C. Feinstein) The Parental Couple in a Successful Divorce, 1984; Illinois Practice of Family Law, 1995, (with Jody Meyer Yazici), 6th edit., 2005-; contbg. author Marriage, Health and the Professions, 2002; mem. editl. bd. Equitable Distbn. Jour., 1984—; contbr. articles to law jour. Bd. dirs. Infant Welfare Soc., 1975-96, hon. bd. dirs., 1996—, pres., 1978-82; co-chmn. gen. gifts 40th and 45th reunions Phillips Exeter Acad., chair class capital giving, 1994-98, 50th reunion gift com. Yale Class Coun. 2002—. Capt. U.S. Army, Ill. N.G., 1960-67. Fellow Am. Acad. Matrimonial Lawyers (bd. mgrs. Ill. chpt. 1996-99), Am. Bar Found.; mem. ABA, FBA, Ill. Bar Assn., Chgo. Bar Assn. (matrimonial com. 1968-83, sec. civil practice com. 1979-80, vice chmn. 1980-81, chmn. 1981-82), Am. Soc. Writers on Legal Subjects, Chgo. Estate Planning Coun., Legal Aid Soc. (vice chmn. matrimonial bar 1991-95, vice chmn. 1995-97, chmn. 1997-99), Lawyers Club Chgo., Tavern Club, Lake Shore Country Club, Chgo. Club. Republican. Jewish. Home: 161 E Chicago Ave Apt 34 E Chicago IL 60611-2601 Office: Davis Friedman 135 S LaSalle St 36th Fl Chicago IL 60603 Office Phone: 312-782-2220. Business E-Mail: mdavis@davisfriedman.com.

DAVIS, NATALIE ZEMON, retired history professor; b. Detroit, Nov. 8, 1928; d. Julian Leon and Helen (Lamport) Zemon; m. H. Chandler Davis, Aug. 16, 1948; children: Aaron Bancroft, Hannah Penrose, Simone Weil. BA summa cum laude, Smith Coll., 1949, DHL (hon.), 1977; MA, Radcliffe Coll., 1950; PhD, U. Mich., 1959; D (hon.), U. Lyon II-France, 1983; DHL (hon.), Northwestern U., 1983, U. Rochester, 1986, U. Chgo., 1992, George Washington U., 1987, Reed Coll., 1988, Muhlenberg Coll., 1989, New Sch. for Social Rsch., 1989, Colby Coll., 1990, U. Pa., 1992, U. Chgo., 1992, U. Pa., 1992; LLD (hon.), Tufts U., 1987, Williams Coll., 1987, Goucher Coll., 1989, Muhlenberg Coll., 1989, New Sch. for Social Rsch., 1989, Columbia U., 1990, U. Toronto, 1991. Lectr. to asst. prof. Brown U., 1959-63; asst. prof. to assoc. prof. U. Toronto, 1963-71, Northrop Frye vis. prof. literary theory, 1996—97, adj. prof. history, anthropology, 1997—, prof. medieval studies, 1997—; prof. history U. Calif.-Berkeley, 1971-77, Princeton U., 1978—81, Henry Charles Lea prof. history, 1981—96, Henry Charles Lea prof. history emeritus, 1996—, dir. Shelby Cullom Davis Ctr. for Hist. Studies, 1990—94; Henry Luce vis. prof. humanities Yale U., 1987. Author: Society and Culture in Early Modern France, 1975 (Berkeshire Conf. spl. award 1976), The Return of Martin Guerre, 1983, Fiction in the Archives: Pardon Tales and Their Tellers in Sixteenth-Century France, 1987, Women on the Margins: three Seventeenth-Century Lives, 1995, Slaves on Screen: Film and Historical Vision, 2000, The Gift in Sixteenth-Century France, 2000; co-editor: A History of Women, vol. 3: Renaissance and Enlightenment Paradoxes, 1993; editl. bd. Comparative Studies in Society and History, History and Memory, Yale Journal of Law and Humanities, Literature and History, Historical Reflections; historical cons. (opera) The House of Martine Guerre, 1993, 96, 97. Bd. trustees Ctrl. European U., Budapest, 2000—05. Recipient teaching citation U. Calif.-Berkeley, 1974, Outstanding Achievement award U. Mich., 1975, Disting. Achievement medal, Radcliffe Grad. Soc., 1983, Howard T. Berhman award for Disting. Achievement in Humanities, Princeton U., 1983, New Eng. Hist. Assn. Media award, 1985; decorated Chevalier Ordre des Palmes Academiques France, 1976 Fellow Am. Acad. Arts and Scis.; cooresp. fellow Royal Hist. Soc.; sr. fellow Ctr. Comparative Lit.; cooresponding fellow British Acad.; mem. Internat. Congress Hist. Scis. (bureau mem. 1990-95, first v.p. 1995-2000), John Simon Guggenheim Meml. Found. (selection com. 1988-2003), Can. Inst. Advanced Rsch. (rsch. council 2001-), Renaissance Soc. Am., Soc. French Hist. Studies (pres. 1976-77), Am. Hist. Assn. (council 1972-75, pres. modern history sect. 1980, pres. 1987, Eugene Asher Disting. Tchg. award, 1994), Soc. Reformation Research, Am. Antiquarian Soc. (selected mem. 1987), Phi Beta Kappa Soc. (Sidney Hook Meml. award, 2000). Democrat. Jewish. Home: 78 Alexander St Princeton NJ 08540-5112

DAVIS, NATHANIEL, humanities educator; b. Boston, Apr. 12, 1925; s. Harvey Nathaniel and Alice Marion (Rohde) Davis; m. Elizabeth Kirkbride Creese, Nov. 24, 1956; children: Margaret Morton Davis Mainardi, James Creese, Thomas Rohde; 1 child, Helen Miller Davis Presley. Grad., Phillips Exeter Acad., 1942; AB, Brown U., 1944, LLD, 1970; MA, Fletcher Sch. Law and Diplomacy, 1947, PhD, 1960; postgrad. Russian lang. and area, Columbia, Cornell U., Middlebury Coll., 1953—54, U. Central de Venezuela, 1961—62; postgrad., Norwich U., 1989. Asst. history Tufts Coll., 1947; joined U.S. Fgn. Service, 1947; 3d sec. Prague, Czechoslovakia, 1947-49; vice consul Florence, Italy, 1949-52; 2d sec. Rome, 1952-53, Moscow, USSR, 1954-56; Soviet desk officer State Dept., 1956-60; 1st sec. Caracas, Venezuela, 1960-62; acting Peace Corps dir., Chile, 1962; spl. asst. to dir. Peace Corps, 1962-63, dept. assoc. dir., 1963-65; U.S. minister to Bulgaria, 1965-66; sr. staff Nat. Security Coun. (White House), 1966-68; U.S. amb. Guatemala, 1968-71, Chile, 1971-73; dir. gen. Fgn. Service, 1973-75, asst. sec. of state for African affairs, 1975; U.S. amb. Switzerland, 1975-77; State Dept advisor and Chester Nimitz prof. Naval War Coll., 1977-83; Alexander and Adelaide Hixon prof. humanities Harvey Mudd Coll., Claremont, Calif., 1983—2002, faculty exec. com., 1986-89, acting dean of faculty, 1990, emeritus prof., 2002—. Lectr. in field. Author: The Last Two Years of Salvador Allende, 1985, Equality and Equal Security in Soviet Foreign Policy, 1986, A Long Walk to Church: A Contemporary History of Russian Orthodoxy, 1995, 2d edit., 2003. Mem. ctrl. com. Calif. Dem. Party, 1987—90, 1991—, mem. exec. bd., 1993—, mem. bus. and profl. caucus, 1992—; mem. L.A. County Dem. Ctrl. Com., 1988—90, 1992—, regional vice chmn., 1994—96; del. Dem. Nat. Conv., 1988, 1992, 1996, 2000; del. So. Calif. conf. United Ch. of Christ, 1986—87. Lt. (j.g.) USNR, 1944—46. Recipient Cinco Aguilas Blancas Alpinism award, Venezuelan Andean Club, 1962, Disting. pub. Svc. award, USN, 1983, Elvira Roberti award for outstanding leadership, Los Angeles County Dem. Com., 1995, spl. merit award (as author), So. Calif. Motion Picture Coun., 1998, Prism award for nat., state, county and local svcs., Jerry Voorhis Claremont Dem. Club, 1999; Fulbright scholar, Moscow, 1996—97. Mem.: AAUP (pres. Claremont Coll. chpt. 1992—96, 1998), Am. Acad. Diplomacy, Coun. on Fgn. Rels., Am. Fgn. Svc. Assn. (bd. dirs., vice chmn. 1964), Cosmos Club, Phi Beta Kappa. Home: 1783 Longwood Ave Claremont CA 91711-3129 Office: Harvey Mudd Coll 301 E 12th St Claremont CA 91711-5901

DAVIS, NICHOLAS HOMANS CLARK, finance company executive; b. N.Y.C., Dec. 1, 1938; s. Feltz Cleveland and Loraine Vanderpool (Homans) D.; children from previous marriage: Loraine, Helen, Alexandra, Eleanor; m. Brenda Jean Molen, Dec. 18, 1982; children: Nicholas, Elizabeth. BA in Geology with honors, Princeton U., 1961; MBA in Fin., Stanford U., 1963. Chartered fin. analyst. Research analyst Fahnestock & Co., N.Y.C., 1963-67; mgr. research Andresen & Co., N.Y.C., 1967-71; dir. research Boettcher & Co., Denver, 1971-75; v.p. corp. fin. White Weld & Co., Denver, 1975-78; v.p. asset mgmt. Paine Webber Co., Denver, 1978-92; pres. Mont. Investment Advisors, Inc., Bozeman, 1991—. Trustee, investment officer Thenen Found., Montclair, N.J., 1966—. Mem. Riverside Country Club, Rotary. Avocations: skiing, flyfishing, deepwater voyaging, writing, backpacking. Home: 85 Limestone Meadows Ln Bozeman MT 59715 Office: Mont Investment Advisors Inc 104 E Main St # 416 PO Box 7090 Bozeman MT 59771-7090 Office Phone: 406-586-7711. Personal E-mail: mintnd@aol.com.

DAVIS, NICOLE D., executive secretary, entrepreneur; d. Mace Green and Anna L. Davis; children: Anthony R, David T, Thomas J. AAS in Secretarial Arts, Gibbs Coll., 1992; BTh, MDiv, Christian Life Sch. Theology, 1999; student, Sacred Heart U., 2004—. Min. Shabach Christian Ctr., 2000. Sec. Shabach Ministries, Norwalk, Conn., 1992—; exec. sec. Fairfield County Coun., Boy Scouts Am., Norwalk, 1992—94; adminstrv. sec. Norwalk Pub. Schs., 1994—2000, exec. sec., 2000—. Owner secretarial svcs. AnRay Tobiah, Norwalk, 1998—. Vol. Shabach Christian Ctr., Norwalk, 1992—2000. Scholar, Katharine Gibbs Sch.-Gibbs Coll., 1990. Avocations: dance, reading, writing. Personal E-mail: nicoledd72@yahoo.com.

DAVIS, NIGHTA J., photographer, artist; d. Betty J. Stephens Spratling and Elmer R. Spratling; m. Reuben G. Davis, Sept. 12, 1992; 1 child, Vanessa Alana Flanders-Freuen. AA, GTI, Ga., 1985. Pres./chairwoman Ltd. Signature Edit., Hiawassee, Ga., 1999—. Prin. works include ltd. signature edit. photographic art. Mem. apptd. by the gov. Children and Youth Coordinating Coun. of Ga., Statewide, Ga., 2004—. Mem.: Blue Ridge Art Assn., Ga. Mountain Cultural Alliance, Ga. Assembly Cmty. Arts, Ga. Born Artists Group (founder), North Ga. Arts Guild, Soc. of Children's Book Writers and Illustrators (assoc.), Mountain Arts Assn. (assoc.). Achievements include Her work hangs in the Atlanta Capitol Building in Atlanta, Ga., the Congressional Building in Washington, D.C.as well as many prestigous institutions and homes throughout the world; Some of her finest works hang in the homes and offices of U.S. Senators, Govornors and State Senators. Avocations: travel, collecting various items of interest, classical music, writing, hiking. Office: Ltd Signature Edit 794 Ramey Mountain Rd Hiawassee GA 30546 Office Phone: 706-896-9021. Personal E-mail: nider77777@alltel.net.

DAVIS, O. L., JR., education educator, researcher; b. Amarillo, Tex., Nov. 20, 1928; s. O.L. and Viola Mae (Maxwell) D.; m. Joan Elizabeth King, May 29, 1953; children: Luke III, Matthew Donald. BA with honors, U. North Tex., 1949, MEd, 1950; PhD, George Peabody Coll. Tchrs., 1958. Assoc. sec. Assn. Supervision and Curriculum Devel., Washington; lectr. in edn. U. N.C., Chapel Hill; assoc. prof. edn. Kent (Ohio) State U.; assoc. prof. curriculum and instrn. U. Tex., Austin, 1966-70, prof., 1970—2001, Catherine Mae Parker Centennial prof., 2001—. Author (with others): Religion in the Curriculum, 1987, Schools of the Past, 1976, Perspectives on Curriculum Development: 1776-1976, 1976, Oral History, 1983, Looking at History, 1986, The Social Studies, 1981, Learning from Student Teaching, 1985, Basic Teaching Tasks, 1970, 79, Empathy and Perspective Taking in the Social Studies, 2001, Bending the Future to Their Will; Civic Women, Social Education and Democracy, 1999, Building a Legacy: Women in Social Education, 1784-1984, 2002; (sr. author) textbook series Exploring the Social Sciences, 1970, 73, 75; contbr. articles to profl. jours; editor: Jour. of Curriculum and Supervision, 1993-2005. Capt. USNR, 1948-88. Named Distinguished Alumnus Coll. Edn. U. North Tex., 1983, 1999, Peabody Coll. Vanderbilt U., 2004; recipient Mary Anne Raywid award, Soc. Profs. Edn., 2003. Mem. NEA, ASCD (pres. 1982-83), Am. Ednl. Rsch. Assn. (v.p. 1971-73, Lifetime Achievement award 1996), Soc. Study of Curriculum History (pres. 1979-80), Nat. Coun. for Social Studies (Exemplary Rsch. in Social Studies Edn. citation 1974, Disting. Career Rsch. in Social Studies Edn. award 1996), Kappa Delta Pi (internat. pres. 1980-82, Laureate chpt. 1994), Am. Assn. for Teaching and Curriculum (pres. 1994-95), Midwest History of Edn. Soc.(pres. 2003-04). Home: 6014 Tonkawa Trl Georgetown TX 78628-1224

DAVIS, OTTO ANDERSON, economics professor; b. Florence, S.C., Apr. 4, 1934; s. Otto and Pauline (Anderson) D.; m. Carolyn Quinn, Dec. 26, 1962; children— Craig, Wendy, Ross. AB, Wofford Coll., 1956; MA, U. Va., 1957, PhD, 1960. Asst. prof. econs. Grad Sch. Indsl. Adminstrn., Carnegie-Mellon U., Pitts., 1960-65; assoc. prof. Grad Sch. Indsl. Adminstrn. Carnegie-Mellon U., 1965-67, prof., 1967-68, prof. polit. economy Sch. Urban and Public Affairs, 1968-81, W.W. Cooper univ. prof. econs. and pub. policy, 1981—, assoc. dean, 1968-75, dean, 1975-81; rsch. dir. Pa. Tax Commn., 1979-82. Bd. visitors Air U., Maxwell AFB, 1980-83. Contbr. book revs. and articles to profl. jours. Fellow Econometric Soc.; mem. Public Choice Soc. (pres. 1970-72), Assn. Public Policy Analysis and Mgmt. (policy council, pres. 1982-83), Am. Econ. Assn., Am. Polit. Sci. Assn., Am. Soc. Public Adminstrn. Office: Carnegie-Mellon U Dept Social Decision Scis Porter Hall # 223F Pittsburgh PA 15213-3890 Office Phone: 412-268-8715. Business E-Mail: od0a@andrew.cmu.edu.

DAVIS, OWEN KIDDER, physician, endocrinologist; b. N.Y.C., Aug. 16, 1956; s. Stephen Edward and Joyce Baldwin (Kidder) D.; m. Marianne Alida Gawain, Nov. 19, 1983; children: Zoe Catherine, Alida Ashby. BA, Swarthmore Coll., 1978; MD, Bowman Gray Sch. Medicine, 1982. Diplomate Am. Bd. Ob-gyn., Am. Bd. Reproductive Endocrinology. Intern, resident N.Y. Hosp., Cornell Med. Ctr.; fellow Brigham and Women's Hosp., Boston; instr. Harvard U., Boston, 1986-88; assoc. prof. Cornell U. Med. Coll., N.Y.C., 1988—; assoc. ob-gyn. Brigham & Women's Hosp., Boston, 1986-88; assoc. attending ob-gyn. N.Y. Presbyn. Hosp., 1988—. Acting chief gynecology Cornell Med. Ctr., assoc. dir. In Vitro Fertilization. Contbr. articles to profl. jours. Med. dir. Am. Fertility Assn.; chair instl. rev. bd. N.Y. Presbyn. Hosp.; chief of gynecology Cornell Med. Ctr. John Lockwood Meml. fellow Swarthmore Coll., 1978. Fellow: N.Y. Acad. Medicine (sec. sect. ob-gyn. 1991—92), Am. Coll. Ob-Gyn.; mem.: AMA, Soc. for Reproductive Endocrinologists, Soc. Assisted Reproductive Tech. (pres., exec. coun., past chair membership and practice com.), Am. Soc. for Reproductive Medicine (legis. monitor, practice com., govt. rels. com. 1987—, bd. dirs., mem. editl. bd. of fertility and sterility, editl. bd. on fertility and sterility), Alpha Omega Alpha. Avocations: music, travel, tennis. Office: Weill Med Coll of Cornell U 505 E 70th St New York NY 10021-4872 Home: 165 E 72d St Apt 16A New York NY 10021 Office Phone: 212-746-1765. E-mail: okdavis@med.cornell.edu.

DAVIS, PAIGE (MINDY PAIGE DAVIS), television personality and host; b. Phila., Oct. 15, 1969; m. Patrick Page, 2001. Grad., Meadows Sch. Arts, So. Meth. U., Dallas. Dancer Beach Boys tour; performer: (plays) Company, Pippin, Hello, Dolly, A Chorus Line, (nat. tour) Chicago, Beauty and the Beast, 1995—98, (Off-Broadway plays) The Vagina Monologues, 2003; performer: (lead) (Broadway plays) Chicago: The Musical, 2004; host: (TV series) Trading Spaces, 2001—; author: Paige by Paige: A Year of Trading Spaces, 2003. Office: Trading Spaces Banyan Prodns 530 Walnut St Ste 276 Philadelphia PA 19106

DAVIS, PAMELA BOWES, pediatric pulmonologist; b. Jamaica, N.Y., July 20, 1949; d. Elmer George and Florence (Welsch) Bowes; m. Glenn C. Davis, June 28, 1970 (div. Mar. 1987); children: Jason, Galen. AB, Smith Coll., 1968; PhD, Duke U., 1973, MD, 1974. Cert. Am. Bd. Internal Medicine, 1977, in Pulmonary Diseases 1980, Am. Bd. Pediat., 1996, in Pediatric Pulmonology 2000. Internal medicine intern Duke Hosp., 1973-74, resident in internal medicine, 1974-75; sr. investigator NIAMD/NIH, Bethesda, Md., 1977-79; asst. prof. U. Tenn. Coll. Medicine, Memphis, 1979-81, Case Western Res. U. Sch. Medicine, Cleve., 1981-85, assoc. prof., 1985-89, prof., 1989—, Arline H. and Curtis F. Garvin Rsch. prof., 2002—, sr. assoc. dean for rsch., chief pediatric pulmonary divsn., 1985—, vice chmn. rsch. dept., 1994-96. Pres. Am. Fedn. for Clin. Rsch., Thorofare, NJ, 1989—90; trustee Rsch. Am, Arlington, Va., 1989—90; mem. adv. coun. Nat. Inst. Diabetes, Digestive and Kidney Diseases, 1992—96; mem. bd. sci. counselors NHLBI, 2001—. chmn., 2004—; founding scientist Copernicus Therapeutics, Inc., Cleve. Contbr. articles to profl. jours. Chmn. med. adv. coun. Cystic Fibrosis Found., Bethesda, 1988-90. With USPHS, 1975—79. Named to, Clevel. Med. Hall of Fame, 2001; recipient Samuel Rosenthal award in acad. pediat., 1996, Maurice Saltzman award, Mt. Sinai Health Care Found., 1998, Smith Coll. medal, 2001, Rainmaker of Yr., Edn. Rsch. Northeast Ohio Live Mag., 2002. Fellow ACP; mem. Am. Pediatric Soc., Am. Acad. Pediatrics, Am. Physiol. Soc., Am. Thoracic Soc., Am. Soc. Gene Therapy, Biophys. Soc., Soc. for Pediatric Rsch., Assn. Am. Physicians, Phi Beta Kappa, Sigma Xi, Alpha Omega Alpha. Achievements include 7 patents in field. Office: Rainbow Babies/Child Hosp 2101 Adelbert Rd Cleveland OH 44106-2624 Business E-Mail: pbd@case.edu.

DAVIS, PATRICIA MARGARET ALICE, psychology educator, religion educator; b. Los Angeles, Calif., Mar. 2, 1955; d. Robert Joseph and Sallianne Nissen Davis; m. Daniel Sperling, June 28, 1981; 1 child, Rhiannon Elizabeth Davis Sperling. BA, U.C. San Diego, 1978; MBA, U.C. Berkeley, 1982; MA in theol. studies, San Francisco Theol. Seminay, 2004. Rsch. analyst Calif. Pub. Utilities Commn., San Francisco, 1978—80, So. Pacific RR, San Francisco, 1982—83, asst. mgr., 1984; supr., planning and analysis Am. Pres. Lines, Oakland, Calif., 1985—86, mgr., planning and control, 1987—88; instr., psychology and religion Grad. Theol. Union Summer Session, Berkeley, Calif., 2005—; exec. bd., bd. of directors San Francisco Shakespeare Festival, 2003—. Co-author: (book) Future Drive: Electric Vehicles and Sustainable Transportation; author: (book chapter) Cognition, Conversion and Spiritual Transformation in Soul Psyche Brain edited by Kelly Bulkeley. Mem.: Soc. for the Sci. Study of Religion, Am. Acad. of Religion, APA, Internat. Assn. for the Study of Dreams, Met. Club (mem. com. 2003—05). Office: San Francisco Shakespeare Festival PO Box 460937 San Francisco CA 94146-0937

DAVIS, PATTI, writer; b. L.A., Oct. 22, 1952; d. Ronald Reagan (former U.S. pres., dec. June 2004) and Nancy Davis Reagan; m. Paul Grilley, 1984 (div. 1990). Attended, Northwestern U., U. So. Calif. Hostess, singer Gt. Am. Food and Beverage Co., Santa Monica, Calif. Conducted seminars on dysfunctional families. Appeared in Vega$, Nero Wolfe, Trapper John, M.D.; author: Home Front, 1986, Deadfall, 1989, A House of Secrets, 1992, The Way I See It, 1993, Bondage, 1994, The Long Goodbye, 2004; featured in Playboy Mag., June 1994. Office: Simon & Schuster Ste 383 1230 Avenue Of The Americas Fl Conc1 New York NY 10020-1586

DAVIS, PAUL B., retired mechanical engineer, civil engineer; b. N.Y.C., Jan. 20, 1909; s. Samuel and Esther (Schwartz) D.; m. Sally Vogel (dec.), Nov. 24, 1932; children: Gerald Joseph, Audrey Thea Coll; m. Beatrice Fibus, Aug. 17, 1999. Student, Poly. U. N.Y., 1928. Engring. draftsman Mcpl. Pub. Works, N.Y.C., 1929-41; asst. engr. Bd. Water Supply, N.Y.C., 1941-42; sr. designer to asst. supt. design hydro/nuc./fossil fuel electric generating stas. Ebasco Svcs., Inc., N.Y.C., 1942—66; mgr. Spanish projects Ebasco Overseas Corp., Madrid, 1966-72; project engring. mgr. Burns & Roe, Hempstead, N.Y., 1973-76; ednl. coord. Argonne Nat. Lab., Argonne, Ill., 1977. Dir. Poinciana Condominium Assn., Lake Worth, Fla., 1979-86. Mem. NSPE (life), N.Y. State Soc. Profl. Engrs., Nat. Wildlife Fedn., The Nature Conservancy, Sierra Club, Zionist Orgn. Am., World Jewish Congress, B'nai B'rith. Avocations: spanish culture, painting, bridge, swimming. Home: 3520 Whitehall Dr Apt 303 West Palm Beach FL 33401-1072

DAVIS, PAUL JOSEPH, endocrinologist; b. Chgo., Oct. 28, 1937; s. Paul Albert and Maxine Lydia (Mason) D.; m. Faith Ainsworth Baker, Dec. 8, 1962; children: Matthew, John, Sarah. BA magna cum laude, Westminster Coll., 1959; MD cum laude, Harvard U., 1963. Intern Bronx Mcpl. Hosp. Ctr., 1963-64, resident in medicine, 1964-67; clin. assoc. NIH, Bethesda, Md., 1967-69, sr. staff assoc., 1969-70; head endocrinology div. Balt. City Hosps., 1970-75; prof. medicine, head endocrinology div. SUNY, Buffalo Med. Sch., 1975-90, also vice chmn. dept. medicine; prof., chmn. dept. medicine Albany Med. Coll., Albany Med. Ctr., N.Y., 1990-99, sr. assoc. dean for clin. rsch., 1998—; chief med. svc. VA Med. Ctr., Buffalo, 1980-90. Mem. merit rev. bd. endocrinology, oncology VA; bd. dirs. Am. Bd. Internal Medicine; mem. nat. adv. com. W.Va. U. Health Sci. Ctr.; dir. Ordway Rsch. Inst., Albany, N.Y., 1999—. Trustee Westminster Coll., Fulton, Mo., 2000—; sci. dir. Charitable Leadership Found. Master ACP (gov. Upstate N.Y. region, pres. N.Y. chpt.), Gerontol. Soc.; mem. Am. Fedn. Med. Rsch., Am. Soc. Biochemistry and Molecular Biology, Am. Thyroid Assn. (bd. dirs., pres. 1997-98, Disting. Svc. award 2003), Endocrine Soc., Bd. Sci. Counselors, Nat. Inst. Aging. Achievements include research and publs. on mechanisms of action of thyroid hormone, effects of aging on endocrine function. Home: 35 Old South Rd West Sand Lake NY 12196-2104 Office: Ordway Research Inst Inc 150 New Scotland Ave Albany NY 12208 Office Phone: 518-641-6410. Business E-Mail: pdavis@ordwayresearch.org.

DAVIS, PEGGY COOPER, law educator; b. Hamilton, Ohio, Feb. 19, 1943; d. George Clinton and Margarett (Gillespie) Cooper; m. Gordon Jamison Davis, Aug. 24, 1968; 1 child, Elizabeth Cooper. BA, Western Coll. for Women, 1963; student, Barnard Coll., 1963-64; JD, Harvard U., 1968; student, NY Soc. for Freudian Psychologists, 1972-73. Bar: NY, 1969, US Supreme Ct., 1976. Staff atty. Williamsburg Legal Services, NYC, 1968-69; Reginald Heber Smith Fellow Cmty. Action for Legal Services, 1969-70; assoc. Poletti, Freidin, Prashken, Feldman & Gartner, 1970-72; law clk. to Hon. Robert L. Carter, US Dist. Ct. So. Dist. NY, 1972-73; asst. counsel capital punishment project NAACP Legal Def. Fund, 1973-77; dep. criminal justice coord. City of NY, 1979-80; judge Family Ct. State of NY, 1980-83; assoc. prof. law Rutgers U., Newark, 1977-78, NYU Sch. Law, 1983-86, prof. 1987-, now John S.R. Shad prof. lawyering & ethics, also dir. lawyering program. Author: Neglected Stories: The Constitution and Family Values, 1997. Bd. dirs. Russell Sage Found., 1989-99, chair, 1996-99. Office: NYU Sch Law Vanderbilt Hall Rm 302D 40 Washington Sq S New York NY 10012-1099 Office Phone: 212-998-6465. E-mail: davisp@juris.law.nyu.edu.*

DAVIS, PETER FRANK, filmmaker, writer; b. Santa Monica, Calif., Jan. 2, 1937; s. Frank and Tess (Slesinger) D.; m. Johanna Mankiewicz, Sept. 13, 1959 (dec. July 1974); children: Timothy, Nicholas; m. Karen Zehring, June 10, 1979 (div. Dec., 1995); children: Jesse, Antonia; m. Alicia Anstead, July 4, 2003; stepchild: Kristen Anstead. AB magna cum laude, Harvard U., 1957. Editl. asst. N.Y. Times, N.Y.C., 1958-59; writer, interviewer Sextant Film Prodns., N.Y.C., 1961-64; writer, assoc. prodr. NBC News, N.Y.C., 1964; writer, prodr. CBS News, N.Y.C., 1965-72; freelance filmmaker N.Y.C., 1972-82; freelance writer, 1976—. Vis. lectr. various univs., 1974-75. Documentary cons. Pumping Iron, 1978, Gilda Live, 1980; writer, prodr.: (TV documentaries) The Heritage of Slavery, 1968, The Battle of East St. Louis, 1969, The Selling of the Pentagon, 1971 (Emmy award 1971, Peabody award 1971, Writers Guild Am. award 1971, George Polk award 1971); prodr. The Best Hotel on Skid Row, 1990; writer Age 7 in America, 1991; prodr., writer JACK, 1993; assoc. prodr., writer (documentary) Hunger in America, 1968 (Writers Guild Am. award 1968); dir., prodr.: (films) Hearts and Minds, 1974 (Oscar award 1975), Middletown, 1982; co-writer (TV film) Haywire, 1980; contbg. editor Esquire Mag., 1985-92; author: Hometown, 1982, Where is Nicaragua?, 1987, If You Came This Way, 1995; Iraq correspondent The Nation, 2003; contbr. articles to mags. Served with AUS, 1959-60. Recipient Saturday Rev. award, 1970, 71, Peace and Friendship among Nations medal, 2003; Poynter fellow Yale U., 1971, assoc. fellow, 1972—. Mem. Writers Guild Am., Authors Guild Am., Acad. of Motion Picture Arts and Sci. Democrat. Home and Office: PO Box 357 Castine ME 04421-0357

DAVIS, (CLONNIE) PHILIP, minister, architect; b. Oklahoma City, Jan. 4, 1952; s. Clonnie Levon and Thelma Lorene (Harris) D.; m. Rebecca Irene Taylor; children: Ryan Philip, Jonathan Taylor. BS in Environ. Design with honors, Okla. U., 1974, BArch, 1975, MArch, 1976; MA, Tenn. Bible Coll., 1982. Ordained to ministry Ch. of Christ, 1982. Archtl. draftsman Harwood K. Smith & Assocs., Dallas, 1976-77, EDI-Cape Clement, Hopkins, Dallas, 1977-78; architect The Architects Partnership, Dallas, 1978-79, William Charles Maffett & Assocs., Architects & Engrs., Cookeville, Tenn., 1980-82; min. Athens Ch. of Christ, Sparta, Tenn., 1981-82, South Woodward St. Ch. of Christ, Oklahoma City, 1982-86, Seminole (Okla.) Ch. of Christ, 1986—. Speaker various religious lecture programs, Tex., Tenn., Okla., Miss., Mo., Ind., 1984—. Contbr. articles to profl. jours., various religious anthologies. Former mem., past pres. Rotary; former mem. MENSA. Named one of Outstanding Young Men of Am., 1984, 85, 86, 87, 88. Avocations: horticulture, music, genealogy. Home: 601 Sharondale Dr Tullahoma TN 37388-2855 E-mail: cphilipdavis@netscape.net. *Humanity will make a marvelous stride toward unity when finally people reject subjectivistic pluralism and acknowledge the transcendency, objectivity and unanimity of the God—ordained trinity of ethics, religion and truth.*

DAVIS, PHILIP J., mathematician; b. Lawrence, Mass., Jan. 2, 1923; s. Frank and Annie (Shrager) D.; m. Hadassah Finkelstein, Jan. 2, 1944; children: Abigail, Frank, Ernest, Joseph. BS, Harvard U., 1943, PhD, 1950; PhD honoris causa, Roskilde U., Denmark, 1997. Chief numerical analysis sect. Nat. Bur. Standards, Washington, 1958-63; prof. applied math. Brown U., Providence, 1963-92; prof. emeritus, 1993—. Author: Lore of Large Numbers, 1961, Interpolation and Approximation, 1963, Numerical Integration, 1967, 3.1416 and All That, 1969, The Schwarz Function, 1974, Circulant Matrices, 1979, The Mathematical Experience, 1981 (Am. Book award 1983), The Thread, 1981, Descartes' Dream, 1986, No Way, 1987, Thomas Gray, Philosopher Cat, 1988, The Spiral of Theodorus, 1993, Thomas Gray in Copenhagen, 1995, Mathematical Encounters of the Second Kind, 1996, The Education of a Mathematician, 2000; editor: Royal Soc. Recipient Math. award Washington Acad. Scis., 1960, Chauvenet prize Math. Assn. Am., 1963, Lester R. Ford award, 1983, George Polya award, 1987, Math. Comm. award, 1997. Mem. Math. Assn. Am., Am. Math. Soc. Home: 175 Freeman Pkwy Providence RI 02906-4620 Office: Brown Univ Applied Math Dept Providence RI 02912-0001 E-mail: philip_davis@brown.edu.

DAVIS, PIERRE C. (PETER PATHFINDER DAVIS), priest; b. Jersey City, Mar. 22, 1937; s. Joseph Anthony and Adele Elizabeth (Claveloux) D.; m. Catharine Buenz, 1958 (div. 1979); children: Richard, Robert; m. Wende Elizabeth Young, Dec. 31, 1994. Student, Rutgers U., 1973, U. Okla., 1979, Pacific Luth. U., 1980. Founder, archpriest Aquarian Tabernacle Ch. (Wicca), Seattle, 1979—. Pub. info. officer Covenant of the Goddess, Berkeley, Calif., 1985-86; founding bd. dirs. Wiccan Info. Network, Vancouver, Can.; mem., sec. religious adv. commn. Wash. Dept. Corrections; organizer Pagan Ch. Conf., 1990, other ann. confs. Contbg. author: Witchcraft Today, 1991; editor Panegyria, 1984-97. Councilman, then mayor Andover Twp., N.J., 1960-76; mem. Selective Svc. Bd., Newton, N.J., 1971-76; commr. Sussex County Election Commn., 1973-74; trustee Ctr. for Non-Traditional Religion, Seattle, 1980—, past pres.; regent Woolston Steen Wiccan Theol. Sem., 1998—; creator Spiral Scouts, 1999. With N.J.A.R.N.G., 1956-62. Mem. Interfaith Coun. Wash. (sr. del. 1990—, pres. 1995-97), Am. Soc. for Indsl. Security (cert. protection profl.), Fellowship of Isis. Democrat. Office: Aquarian Tabernacle Ch PO Box 409 Index WA 98256-0409 E-mail: atc@aquatabch.org. *Our whole society is in disarray and our children, in confusion. What is desperately needed is the re-establishment of clear limits of societally acceptable behavior, for both ourselves and our youngsters. Ecology should be considered a sacramental duty. Only by abandonment of today's "maybe" limits in favor of clear, firm, unequivocal yet equitable behavioral limits can we hope to restore moral stability. Teaching of personal responsibility starts at home with each of us, and must be left to the schools or the state where "No" once again needs to mean, simply, "no", and not "maybe.".*

DAVIS, PRESTON LINDNER, lawyer; b. Danville, Pa., Jan. 22, 1936; s. Preston B. and M. Isabelle (Lindner) D.; m. Margaret E. Whitenight, Aug. 30, 1958; children: Kerry P. Davis, Kathy J. Hrenko, Kirk P. Davis, Kelly J. Farquhar. AB, Dartmouth Coll., 1957; LLB, JD, U. Pa., Phila., 1960. Bar: Pa. 1961, U.S. Ct. Appeals (3d cir.) 1961, U.S. Dist. Ct. (mid. dist.) Pa. 1962. Law clk. to Hon. Herbert F. Goodrich U.S. Ct. Appeals (3d cir.), Phila., 1960-61; ptnr. Davis Davis & Kaar, Milton, Pa., 1961—. Solicitor, Northumberland County, 1964-69, Milton Mcpl. Authority, 1980—; chmn. Milton Indsl. Authority, 1985—. Mem. exec. bd. Northumberland Rep. Party, Sunbury, Pa., 1964—. Mem. Northumberland County Bar Assn. (pres. 1984), Milton Rotary, Milton Elks Club, Milton Masons (past master), Moose, Milton Area C. of C. (past pres.). Lutheran. Avocations: sports, golf. Office: Davis Davis & Kaar PO Box 319 Milton PA 17847-0319

DAVIS, R. DUANE, surgeon; b. Charleston, W.Va., Sept. 22, 1958; s. Robert Duane and Loretta Lemay Davis; 1 child, Jackson Mark. MD, UCLA Sch. of Medicine, L.A., Calif., 1984. Cert. General Surgery Am. bd. of Surgery, 1994, Cardiothoracic Surgery Am. Bd. of Thoracic Surgery, 1995. Asst. prof. surgery Duke U. Sch. of Medicine, Durham, NC, 1993—, assoc. prof. surgery, 1999—2004, prof. surgery, 2004—; surg. dir. cardiac and pulmonary transplantation Duke U. Med. Ctr., Durham, NC, 1995—, dir. transplantation, 1994—. Achievements include research in Pulmonary Transplantation, Xenotransplantation. Office: Duke Univ Med Ctr 3543 Duke Hosp S Erwin Rd Durham NC 27514 Office Phone: 919-681-4760. Office Fax: 919-681-4797.

DAVIS, R. STEVEN, lawyer; married; 2 children. BS, JD, U. Kans. Bar: Kans. 1978, Mo. 1981, Tex. 1986. Pvt. practice law, Kans., 1978—81; v.p. law and state govt. affairs AT&T, Basking Ridge, NJ, 1981—2000; sr. v.p. pub. policy Qwest Comm. Internat. Inc., 2000—. Office: Qwest Comm Internat Inc 1801 California St Denver CO 80202 Office Phone: 303-896-4200.

DAVIS, RANDY LEE, soil scientist; b. L.A., Nov. 23, 1950; s. Willie Vernon and Joyce Christine (Manes) D. AA, Yuba Community Coll., 1972; BS in Soils and Plant Nutrition, U. Calif., Berkeley, 1976. Vol. soil scientist U.S. Peace Corps, Maseru, Lesotho, 1976-79; soil scientist Hiawatha Nat. Forest, Sault Saint Marie, Mich., 1979-86; project soil scientist Bridger-Teton Nat. Forest, Jackson, Wyo., 1986-91, forest soil scientist, 1991-97, soil and water program leader, 1997-2001; nat. soils program leader USDA Forest Svc., Washington, 2001—. Detailed soil scientist Boise (Idaho) Nat. Forest, 1989, 92, Mendocino (Calif.) Nat. Forest, 1996, San Bernardino (Calif.) Nat. Forest, 1999; detail assignment Brookings Inst. legis fellow, 2004; Nat. Burned Area Emergency Rehab. program leader, Washington, 2000, 2002-03; acting nat. program leader Wetland and Riparian Program, USDA Forest Svc., 2002—03. Editor Soil Classifiers newsletter; contbr. articles to profl. jours. Pres. Sault Community Theater, Sault Saint Marie, 1984-86. Mem. Am. Chem. Soc., Soil Sci. Soc. Am., Soil and Water Conservation Soc. (bd. dirs. 1991-92, chpt. pres. 1993-97), Am. Water Resources Assn., Internat. Soc. Soil Sci., Soc. for Range Mgmt. Methodist. Home: 208 12th SE Washington DC 20003 Office: USDA Forest Svc 1400 Independence SW Washington DC 20250-0003 Office Phone: 202-205-1082. Personal E-mail: randyd83001@yahoo.com. Business E-Mail: rdavis03@fs.fed.us.

DAVIS, RAY C., energy executive; Chmn., CEO Cornerstone Natural Gas Inc., 1993—96; dir. Crosstex Energy Inc., 1996—2000; v.p. of gen. ptnr. ET Co. 1, 1996—; co-CEO, co-chmn. bd. of gen. ptnr. LaGrange Energy,

2002—; co-CEO of gen. ptnr. LaGrange Acquisition, 2002—; co-CEO, co-chmn. bd. of gen. ptnr. Energy Transfer Partners, Dallas, 2002—. Office: Energy Transfer Partners 2838 Woodside St Dallas TX 75204*

DAVIS, RAYMOND, JR., retired physical chemistry professor; b. Washington, Oct. 14, 1914; s. Raymond D. and Ida Rogers (Younger) D.; m. Anna Marsh Torrey, Dec. 4, 1948; children: Andrew Morgan, Martha Safford Davis Kumler, Nancy Elizabeth Davis Klemm, Roger Warren, Alan Paul. BS, U. Md., 1937, MS, 1939; PhD, Yale U., 1942; DSc, U. Pa., 1990, Laurentian U., 1997, U. Chgo., 2000. Chemist Dow Chem. Co., Midland, Mich., 1937-38, Monsanto Chem. Co., Dayton, Ohio, 1946-48; sr. chemist Brookhaven Nat. Lab., Upton, N.Y., 1948-84; rsch. prof. dept. physics and astronomy U. Pa., Phila., 1984—2005; ret., 2005. Mem., NASA Lunar Sample Review Bd., 1971-73. Contbr. articles to profl. jours. Served with USAAF, 1942-46. Recipient Boris Prejel prize N.Y. Acad. Scis., 1955, award for nuc. applications in chemistry Am. Chem. Soc., 1979, Pontecorvo prize Inst. for Nuclear Rsch., Russia, 2000, Wolf prize for physics Israel, 2000, Nat. Medal of Sci., 2001, Nobel prize for physics, 2002, Benjamin Franklin medal for physics, 2003, Enrico Fermi award, 2003. Mem. AAAS, NAS (Comstock prize 1978), Am. Phys. Soc. (Tom W. Bonner prize 1988, W.K.H. Panofsky prize 1992), Am. Geophys. Union, Am. Astron. Soc. (Beatrice M. Tinsley prize 1994, George Ellory Hale prize 1996).

DAVIS, RAYMOND P., bank executive; b. 1950; Former pres. US Banking Alliance, Atlanta; dir. Umpqua Bank, Portland, Oreg., 1994—, pres., CEO, 1994—2000, CEO, 2002—03, pres., CEO, 2003—, Umpqua Holdings Corp., 1999—. Named Ernst & Young Entrepreneur of the Yr., 2004. Office: Umpqua Holdings Corp Ste 1200 One SW Columbia St Portland OR 97258*

DAVIS, REX DARWIN, business consultant; b. Skiatook, Okla., June 11, 1924; s. Ivan Francis and Ruth Mae (Nabors) D.; m. Amelia Roberts Fry, Apr. 14, 1979; children by previous marriage: Deborah Ruth, Kathleen Marie. LLB, U. Okla., 1949; postgrad., Princeton U., 1966. Exec. asst. to asst. regional commr. Bur. Alcohol Tobacco and Firearms, Cin., 1962-66, asst. regional commr., 1966-70; dir. alcohol tobacco and firearms Dept. of the Treasury, Washington, 1972—78; pres. Nat. Assn. Beverage Importers, Inc., Washington, 1978-85, Delta Cons., Inc., Washington, 1985—2001; pres., chief exec. officer New Europe Wines, Inc., 1991-95; exec. dir. Pres.'s Forum of Beverage Alcohol Industry, 1990—2001. Chmn. Lic. Beverage Info. Coun., exec. dir. Pres.'s Forum of Beverage Alcohol Industry, Washington, 1981—85, Internat. Fedn. Wine & Spirits, Paris, 1982—85; advisor to dir. on history of the bur. Bur. Alcohol, Tobacco, Firearms and Explosives, Dept. Justice, 2004—05. Author: Federal Searches and Seizures, 1964 Vice chmn. Sky Ranch Found., Washington, 1983—85; pres. Treas. Hist. Assn., 1978—79; mem. leadership coun. Brady Ctr. to Prevent Gun Violence. 1st lt. USAAF, 1943—45. Decorated Purple Heart, Air medal with 2 oak leaf clusters; recipient Chevalier de Merite Agricole French Gov., 1983, award for exceptional svc. Dept. Treasury, 1978, Meritorious Svc. award 1977, Lifetime Achievement award Bur. Alcohol, Tobacco, Firearms, 2001; named Fed. Employee of Yr. Cin. chpt. Fed. Bus. Assn., 1965; Meritorious award William A. Jump Found., 1959, Cert. of Appreciation Nat. Law Enforcement Officers Meml. Fund, 2005. Mem. Am. Soc. Assn. Execs., Okla. Bar Assn., Pi Kappa Alpha, Internat. Club, Princeton Club. Avocations: golf, tennis, snorkeling, stamp collecting/philately. Home and Office: Delta Cons Inc 311 10th St SE Washington DC 20003-2130

DAVIS, REX LLOYD, insurance company executive; b. Des Moines, Dec. 29, 1929; s. Leon Mack and Mercedes Johanna (Lamar) D.; m. Sally JoAnne Richard, Apr. 14, 1952; children: Kristine Lynn, Craig Thomas. JD, Drake U., 1952. Bar: Iowa, U.S. Dist. Ct. Iowa, U.S. Supreme Ct.; C.P.C.U. C.L.U. With Employers Mut. Casualty Co., Des Moines, 1954-66, regional v.p. Phila., 1966-72; exec. v.p. Ranger Ins. Co., Houston, 1972-75, pres., 1975-84; pres., chief operating officer Ranger Ins. Mgrs., Ranger Internat. Ins. Ltd., Ranger County Mut.; atty.-in-fact Ranger Lloyds, Houston, 1975-84; pres., chief operating officer Rex L. Davis & Assocs., Inc., 1984—; chmn. United Republic Reins. Co., 1986-92, also bd. dirs. Mem., Houston Bar Assn., Soc. CPCUs, Soc. CLUs, Lakeside Country Club (Houston), Petroleum Club (Houston), Delta Theta Phi. Office: Rex L Davis & Assocs 2537 S Gessner Rd Ste 125 Houston TX 77063 Office Phone: 713-782-1665. Business E-Mail: rexldavis@sbcglobal.net. E-mail: rdavis@ork-hb.com.

DAVIS, RICHARD BRADLEY, pathologist, educator, internist; b. Iowa City, Iowa, Nov. 6, 1926; s. Bradley Nelson and Gladys Mae (Fairbanks) D.; m. Jean Nixeen Anderson, June 22, 1957; children— Janet, Stephen, Catharine. BS, Yale U., 1949; MD, State U. Iowa, 1953; PhD, U. Minn., 1964. Intern Mary Fletcher Hosp., Burlington, Vt., 1953-54, resident, 1954-56; instr. U. Minn., Mpls., 1959-64, asst. prof. medicine, 1964-69; vis. investigator Sir William Dunn Sch. Pathology, Oxford, Eng., 1964-65, MRC Blood Coagulation Research Unit, Churchill Hosp., Oxford, 1965; asso. prof. medicine U. Nebr., Omaha, 1969-73, prof. medicine, 1973-94, acting dir. div. hematology, 1974-76, prof. pathology, 1976-94, dir. hematology div., 1976-79, emeritus prof. internal medicine, 1994—. Contbr. articles to sci. publs. Served with U.S. Army, 1945-46. Borden Undergrad. Med. Research grantee, 1953; USPHS career devel. awardee, 1961-69 Fellow A.C.P., Central Soc. Clin. Research, Am. Fedn. Clin. Research, Am. Soc. Exptl. Pathology, N.Y. Acad. Scis., Am. Assn. History of Medicine Soc. Exptl. Biology and Medicine, Am. Soc. Hematology, Royal Micros. Soc., Internat. Soc. Haemostasis and Thrombosis, Omaha Mid-West Clin. Soc., Sigma Xi, Alpha Omega Alpha, Phi Beta Pi, Theta Kappa Psi. Home: 103 Woodhall Spa Williamsburg VA 23188-9138 Personal E-mail: rbd7@verizon.net.

DAVIS, RICHARD CARLTON, rehabilitation services administrator; b. Salem, Mass., June 10, 1948; s. William Montgomery and Ruth Wiley (Durkee) D.; m. Patricia Lynn Paquette, Apr. 6, 1974; children: Susannah, Amanda, Adam. BA, Concord Coll., 1969; postgrad., U. Iowa. Orientation tchr. Iowa Dept. for the Blind, Des Moines, 1971-73, rehab. tchr., 1973-77, rehab. counselor, 1977-80, sr. svc. specialist, 1980-86; so. area supr. N.Mex. Commn. for the Blind, Alamogordo, 1987-91, orientation ctr. adminstr., 1987-92; asst. commr. State Svcs. for the Blind, Minn. Dept. of Econ. Security, St. Paul, 1992-2000; cons. on blindness and rehab. Circle Pines, Minn., 2000—; asst. dir. BLIND, Inc., Mpls., 2000—. Cons. Nebr. Svcs. for the Visually Impaired, Lincoln, 1980, Am. Printing House for the Blind, Louisville, 1992. Coord./vol. field svc. rep. Job Opportunities for the Blind, Balt., 1979-86; chair, vice chair Mayor's com. for the Handicapped, Alamogordo, 1990-92; bd. dirs. White Sands Press Club (treas., 1998-1990), Alamogordo, 1988-92; mem., treas. White Sands chpg. Nat. Fedn. of the Blind, 1988-92. Recipient Silver award United Way, 1991, over 100% Goal award, 1990, Founders award N.Mex. Commn. for the Blind, 1992, Wayne E. Bonnell award Nat. Fedn. of the Blind, 1982, Gov.'s commendations, 1998, 2000, Cert. of Appreciation, Red Lake Nation's divsn. Rehab. Svcs. Mem. Nat. Coun. of State Agencies for the Blind (bd. dirs. 1994-98, treas. 1999-2000), Coun. of State Adminstrs. of Vocat. Rehab., Nat. Fedn. of the Blind (Des Moines Chpt. award 1983), Alamogordo Rotary Club. Avocations: camping, canoeing, snowshoeing, woodworking. Home: 136 Canterbury Rd Circle Pines MN 55014-1777 Office Phone: 612-872-0100.

DAVIS, RICHARD EARL, lawyer; b. Jackson, Mich., Aug. 13, 1951; s. Richard Allen and Velva Elizabeth (England) Davis; m. Paula Hurst, Dec. 9, 1972; children: Richard Seth, Tessa Rebecca. BA, U. So. Fla., 1973, MA, 1975; JD cum laude, Stetson U., 1977. Bar: Fla. 1978, U.S. Ct. Appeals (11th cir.), U.S. Dist. Ct. (mid. dist.) Fla., bd. cert. city, county and local govt. law: Fla., cert.: (cir. civil mediator). Asst. county atty. Hillsborough County, Fla., 1978-85; assoc. Holland & Knight, Tampa, Fla., 1985-88, ptnr., 1988-96, Richard E. Davis, P.A., Tampa, 1997—. Lectr. in field. Mem.: ABA, Stetson Lawyers Assn., Fla. Bar Assn., Hillsborough County Bar Assn., Tampa Downtown Partnership, Phi Sigma Alpha, Phi Kappa Phi. Office: 220 E Madison St Ste 512 Tampa FL 33602-4826 E-mail: tpaland@earthlink.net.

DAVIS, RICHARD EDMUND, plastic surgeon; b. Washington, Apr. 7, 1958; BS, U. Ga., 1981, MS, 1983; MD, Med. Coll. Ga., 1987. Diplomate Am. Bd. Otolaryngology, Am. Bd. Facial Plastic and Reconstructive Surgery. Intern U. N.C., Chapel Hill, 1987-88, resident in otolaryngology, 1988-92; fellow, instr. Oreg. Health Sci. U., Portland, 1992-93; asst. prof. facial plastic and reconstructive surgery U. Miami (Fla.) Sch. Medicine, 1993-99, assoc. prof., chief divsn. facial & reconstructive surgery, 1999—. Mem. staff VA Med. Ctr., Portland, 1992—93, Miami, 1993—, Jackson Meml. Hosp., Miami, 1993—. Mem.: AMA, Fla. Soc. Facial Plastic and Reconstructive Surgery, Am. Acad. Facial Plastic and Reconstructive Surgery (Sir Harold Gilles award 1993), Am. Acad. Otolaryngology Head and Neck Surgery. Office: U Miami Hosp and Clinic 1475 NW 12th Ave Ste 4035 Miami FL 33136-1002 Office Phone: 305-243-4315.

DAVIS, RICHARD FRANCIS, city government official; b. Providence, Aug. 18, 1936; s. Walter Francis and Mary Elizabeth (Gearin) D.; m. Virginia Catherine Oates, Aug. 27, 1960; children: Walter Douglas, John Richard, Theresa Catherine. BS, U. Ark., Little Rock, 1964; student city and regional planning, MIT, summer, 1964; postgrad., Carnegie Mellon U., 1973. Planner Met. Area Planning Commn., Little Rock, 1964-66; mem. Met. Planning Commn. Kansas City, Mo., 1966-67, dir. econs., 1967-69, dir. ops., 1969-71; exec. dir. Mid-Am. Regional Council, Kansas City, 1972-77; gen. mgr. Kansas City Area Transp. Authority, 1977-2000; instr. city planning U. Mo., Kansas City, 1973-74; Planning commr. City of Gladstone, Mo., 1967—69, 1981—90, 2003—, city councilman, 1969-71, mayor, 1971-72, chmn. park bd., 1972-76, mem. bd. zoning adjustment, 1993—2004; bus. devel. Olsson Assocs., 2002—. Mem. Gladstone Econ. Betterment Coun., 2003-04, chmn., 2004; mem. Clay County (Mo.) Indsl. Devel. Commn., 1972-77, Coun. on Edn., Kansas City, 1974-82, treas., chmn. interdist. rels. com. Mem. coun. advisers, Major League Baseball Players Trust for Children, 2000—; v.p. Brooktree Homeowners Assn., 1979-80; mem. Total Transp. adv. com., MidAmerica Regional Coun., 1977-2000, chmn. transit adv. com., 1997-2000; bd. dirs. Mo. Pub. Transit Assn., 1979-2000, pres., 1987-89, 1999-2000; bd. dirs. Kans. Pub. Transit Assn., 1979-2000; trustee Black Econ. Union, 1984-88; bd. dirs., treas. Heart of Am. United Way Vol. Ctr., 1985-87. With USAF, 1955-59. Recipient Transp. Svc. award Kansas City chpt. Conf. of Minority Transit Officials, 1987. Mem. Am. Soc. Pub. Adminstrn. (pres. Kansas City chpt. 1980, Pub. Adminstr. of Yr. award 1973, L.P. Cookingham award 1991), Am. Planning Assn., Am. Pub. Transit Assn. (bd. dirs. 1980-93, 94-2000, govtl. affairs and legis. steering com., v.p. mgmt. and fin. com. 1984-86, v.p. govt. affairs com. 1991-93, Outstanding Pub. Transp. Mgr. award 2000), Kansas City Royal Lancers (bd. dirs. 2001-04, v.p. 2001-02, pres. 2002-03), Northland Regional C. of C. Home and Office: 5826 N Kensington Ave Kansas City MO 64119

DAVIS, RICHARD HUNT, JR., historian; b. Highland Park, Mich., Sept. 30, 1939; s. Richard Hunt and Helen Grace Davis; m. Jeanne Elizabeth Gruber, May 28, 1939; children: Richard Francis, Jonathan Edward. BA, Grinnell Coll., 1961; MA, U. Wis., 1965, PhD, 1969. Prof. history, now prof. emeritus U. Fla., Gainesville, 1967—, dir. Ctr. for African Studies, 1979—88, dir. internat. studies and programs, 1993—94. Author: Encyclopedia of African History and Culture, Volumes 4&5, 2005, (monograph) Bantu Edn. and the Edn. of Africans in South Africa, 1972; editor: Mandela, Tambo, and the African Nat. Congress, 1991, Apartheid Unravels, 1991. Sec. U. Pk. Neighborhood Assn., Gainesville, 2001—03; troop leader Boy Scouts Am., Gainesville, 1978—88; com. mem. So. Africa Fulbright Rev. Com., Coun. for Internat. Exch. of Scholars, Washington, 2001—03. Sr. Fulbright scholar, Coun. for Internat. Exch. Scholars, 1999, Woodrow Wilson fellow, Woodrow Wilson Found., 1961—62, NDEA Title VI Fgn. Lang. fellow, U.S. Dept. Edn., 1964—66, Younger Humanist fellow, Nat. Endowment for the Humanities, 1973—74. Mem.: United Faculty Fla. (treas., v.p. 1972—78), African Studies Assn. (editor African Studies Rev. 1980—88), Am. Hist. Assn. Presbyterian. Avocations: travel, reading, politics, family. Home: 1812 NW 6th Ave Gainesville FL 32603 Office: Univ Florida History Dept PO Box 117320 Gainesville FL 32611-7320

DAVIS, RICHARD JOEL, former government official, lawyer; b. NYC, Mar. 27, 1946; s. Herbert H. and Sylvia (Ginesin) D.; m. Nancy R. Davis. BA in History, U. Rochester, 1966; JD magna cum laude, Columbia U., 1969. Bar: NY 1970, US Dist. Ct (So. Dist. NY) 1973, DC 1974. Law clk. to Judge Jack B. Weinstein, US Dist. Ct. for Ea. Dist. NY, 1969-70; mem. criminal divsn., asst. chief appellate atty. corruption unit US Atty. Office, So. Dist. NY, 1970-73; task force leader Watergate Spl. Prosecution Force, Washington, 1973-75; asst. sec. of the treasury for enforcement and ops. Dept. Treasury, Washington, 1977-81; assoc. Weil, Gotshal and Manges LLP, NYC, 1976-77, ptnr., gen. counsel adminstrn., litigation, white collar crime, complex settlement negotiations, internal regulatory, and government investigations, 1981—; instr. in trial advocacy Harvard U.; instr. Nat. Inst. Trial Advocacy. Notes and comments editor Columbia U. Law Review, 1968-69; Co-author: American Hostages in Iran, 1988. Mem. Task Force on Ops. of Phila. Police Force, 1986, Citizens Task Force on Use and Security of Central Park (v.p. for development 1987-91), mem. Mayor's Commn. on Police Corruption, 1995—, chmn. 1996—, mem. Mayor's Task Force on Police-Cmty. Rels., Pro Bono Spl. Master for Investment Policy for the Agent Orange Settlement Fund; chmn. Randall's Island Sports Found.; mem., chmn. Citizen's Union, 1994-. Recipient Curtis J. Berger award, The Bridge, Inc., 1999, Whitney North Seymour award, Fed. Bar Coun., 2000, Ari Halberstam award, Jewish Children's Mus., 2000. Mem. ABA, Legal Aid Soc. NYC (v.p. 1987-91, bd. dirs. 1987-92), Citizens Union (bd. dirs. 1991-97, vice chmn. 1993-97), Boys Harbor (bd. dirs. 1993—, co-chmn. lawyers com. on violence 1994-98, bd. dirs. parks coun. 1994—), Assn. Bar City NY., City Bar Assn. (co-chmn. criminal justice coun.). Responsible for overseeing the freeze on Iranian assets and other sanctions imposed as a result of the seizure of hostages during the Carter Adminstration and participated in the development of the US-Iran Hostage Release Agreements in January, 1981. Office: Weil Gotshal & Manges LLP 767 5th Ave New York NY 10153 Office Phone: 212-310-8860. Office Fax: 212-310-8007. Business E-Mail: richard.davis@weil.com.

DAVIS, RICHARD MALONE, economics professor; b. Hamilton, N.Y., June 2, 1918; s. Malone Crowell and Grace Edith (McQuade) Davis. AB, Colgate U., 1939; MA, Cornell U., 1941, PhD, 1949. From instr. to assoc. prof. econs. Lehigh U., Bethlehem, Pa., 1941-54; assoc. prof. econs. U. Oreg., Eugene, 1954-62, prof., 1962-83, prof. emeritus, 1983—. Contbr. articles to profl. jours. Served with U.S. Army, 1942—45, CBI. Mem.: Phi Beta Kappa. Republican. Home: 1040 Ferry St Apt 503 Eugene OR 97401-3332 Office: Univ Oreg Dept Econs Eugene OR 97403 Office Phone: 541-345-1307.

DAVIS, RICHARD RALPH, lawyer; b. Houston, July 28, 1936; s. William Ralph and Virginia (Allison) D.; m. Christina R. Zelkoff, June 1, 1974; 1 child, Virginia Lee Allison. BA, Yale U., 1962, LLB, 1965; MBA, Columbia U., 1965. Bar: N.Y. 1966. Law clk. FAA, Washington, 1964; assoc. Chadbourne & Parke, N.Y.C., 1965-73, ptnr., 1974-83; sr. v.p., gen. counsel Inspiration Resources Corp., N.Y.C., 1983-91; sr. v.p., sec., gen. counsel Bessemer Securities Corp./Bessemer Trust Co., NA, N.Y.C., 1991—. With U.S. Army, 1956-59. Mem. ABA. Home: 1185 Park Ave Apt 6-g New York NY 10128-1309 E-mail: davis@bessemer.com.

DAVIS, ROBERT, police chief; b. 1958; m. Terry Davis; 1 child, Mackenzie. BA in English, San Jose U.; MPA, Golden Gate U.; grad., FBI Nat. Acad.; POST Master Instr. cert., 1993. Patrol officer San Jose Police Dept., 1980—89, sgt., 1989—93, lt., 1993—98, capt., 1998—2001, dep. chief police, 2001—04, chief police, 2004—. Tchr. professionalism and ethics and POST Supervisor's courses San Jose Police Acad. Mem. amb. bd. Santa Clara County Big Brothers and Big Sisters. Avocations: bicycling, tri-athlete events. Office: 201 W Mission St San Jose CA 95110 Office Phone: 408-277-5339.

DAVIS, ROBERT D., rental company executive; BBA, So. Meth. U., 1993. From acct. to treas. Rent A Ctr., Plano, Tex., 1993—97, treas., 1997—, sr. v.p. fin., 1999—, CFO, 1999—. Office: Rent A Center 5700 Tennyson Pkwy Plano TX 75024

DAVIS, ROBERT EDWARD, retired communications educator; b. Wichita, Kans., Apr. 2, 1931; s. Edward Lorenzo and Dorrinda Belle (Packer) D.; m. Jacqueline Peggy Baas, Aug. 22, 1955 (div. 1979); children: Robert J., Sarah J., James E.; m. Martha Toni Merrill, Jan. 8, 1983. BA, U. No. Iowa, 1953; MA, U. Iowa, 1956, PhD, 1965. Instr. Grundy Ctr. (Iowa) High Sch., 1953-54; asst. to dir. radio and TV U. No. Iowa, Cedar Falls, 1954-58; lectr., instr. dept. speech and theatre Hunter Coll., N.Y.C., 1961-63, 65-66; asst. prof. dept. speech U. Mich., Ann Arbor, 1966-69; from assoc. prof. to prof. and chmn. dept. cinema and photography So. Ill. U., Carbondale, 1969-74; prof. and chmn. Dept. Radio-TV-Film, U. Tex., Austin, 1974-87, John T. Jones Jr. Centennial prof. in communication, 1987-89, now emeritus, 1989—. Mem. Pacific Grove Planning Commn., 1999—, chair, 2005-. Author: Response to Innovation, 1976; co-producer, dir. (film) Maple Sugar Farmer, 1973 (7 nat. and internat. awards); writer, performer, dir., producer over 1000 ednl. radio and tv programs; contbr. articles to profl. jours. Mem. Pacific Grove City Coun., 1990-98; mayor pro-tem Pacific Grove, 1994-98; bd. dirs. Heritage Soc. Pacific Grove, 2001-; bd. dirs. Pacific Grove Citizens Police Acad., 2002-. Mem.: Pacific Grove Citizens Police Svc. Acad. Alumni (bd. dirs. 2000—). Republican. Methodist. Avocations: travel, photography. Home: 1212 Del Monte Blvd Pacific Grove CA 93950-2029 Personal E-mail: rtdavis@aol.com.

DAVIS, ROBERT EDWARD, state supreme court justice; b. Topeka, Aug. 28, 1939; s. Thomas Homer and Emma Claire (Hund) D.; m. Jana Jones; children: Edward, Rachel, Patrick, Carolyn, Brian. BA in Polit. Sci., Creighton U., 1961; JD, Georgetown U., 1964. Bar: Kans. 1964, U.S. Dist. Ct. Kans. 1964, U.S. Tax Ct. 1974, U.S. Ct. Mil. Appeals 1965, U.S. Ct. Mil. Review, 1970, U.S. Ct. Appeals (10th cir.) 1974, U.S. Supreme Ct. 1982. Pvt. practice, Leavenworth, Kans., 1967-84; magistrate judge Leavenworth County, 1969-76, county atty., 1980-84, judge dist. ct., 1984-86; judge Kans. Ct. Appeals Jud. Br. Govt., Topeka, 1986-93; justice Kans. Supreme Ct., Topeka, 1993—. Lectr. U. Kans. Law Sch., Lawrence, 1986-95. Capt. JAGC, U.S. Army, 1964-67, Korea. Mem. Am. Judges Assn., Kans. Bar Assn., Leavenworth County Bar Assn. (pres. 1977), Judge Hugh Means Am. Inn of Ct. Charter Orgn. Roman Catholic. Office: Kansas Supreme Ct 301 W 10th Ave Topeka KS 66612

DAVIS, ROBERT G., insurance company executive; degree, MBA, U. Tex. Acct. exec. E.F. Hutton & Co., L.A.; chmn., CEO MBank, Brownville, Tex., MCorp. (acquired by Banc One), San Antonio, 1985-89; chief credit officer Bank One Tex.; pres., CEO Bank One Columbus, 1991-95, Banc One Credit Corp., 1995-96, USAA, San Antonio, 1996—, chmn., 2002—. Served in U.S. Army. Decorated Silver Star, Distinguished Flying Crosses, Air Medals, Bronze Star, Vietnam Cross of Gallantry, Purple Heart. Office: USAA 9800 Fredericksburg RD San Antonio TX 78288*

DAVIS, ROBERT HEATER, chemical engineering educator; b. Paris, Mar. 26, 1957; arrived in US, 1957; s. Richard Malcolm and Helen (Heater) D.; m. Shirley Lynn Giles, Dec. 28, 1982. BS in chem. engring., U. Calif., Davis, 1978; MS in chem. engring., Stanford U., 1979, PhD in chem. engring., 1982. Postdoctoral fellow dept. applied math. and theoretical physics Cambridge U., England, 1982-83; asst. prof. chem. engring. U. Colo., Boulder, 1983-88, assoc. prof., 1988—92, prof., 1992—, chair chem. engring., 1992—2002, Patten Prof., 1997—, dean Coll. Engring. and Applied Sci., 2002—. Vis. prof. MIT, 1990—91, U. Calif., Santa Barbara, 1997—98. Contbr. articles to profl. jours. Bd. dirs. univ. program First. Presbyn. Ch., Boulder, 1985—. Recipient Presdl. Young Investigator Award, NSF, 1985, Jr. Faculty Devel. Award, U. Colo., 1985, Outstanding Undergrad. Tchg. in Chem. Engring. Award, Omega Chi Epsilon, 1989, Outstanding Rsch. Award, U. Colo. Coll. Engring. and Applied Sci., 1993, Outstanding Svc. Award, 1999, Outstanding Tchg. Award, 2000, Outstanding Grad. Tchg. Award, Dept. Chem. Engring., U. Colo., 1996, 2002, Outstanding Rsch. Award, U. Colo. Boulder Faculty Assembly, 2000, Svc. Award, 2003; NATO Postdoctoral Fellowship in Sci., 1982, Guggenheim Fellowship, 1990, U. Colo. Faculty Fellowship, 1997. Mem.: Soc. Indsl. Microbiology, Am. Soc. Engring. Edn. (Rocky Mountain Sec. Dow Outstanding Young Faculty Award 1990), Am. Chem. Soc., Am. Phys. Soc., AIChE (Outstanding Paper Award 1995). Republican. Avocations: hiking, bicycling. Office: Coll Engring and Applied Sci U Colo 422 UCB Boulder CO 80309-0422

DAVIS, ROBERT J., internet company executive; BSc summa cum laude, Northeastern U.; MBA with high distinction, Babson Coll.; D in Comml. Sci. (hon.), Bentley Coll., 1999; D (hon.), Northeastern U., 2000. From mem. staff to pres., CEO Lycos Inc. (merged with Terra Networks), Waltham, Mass., 1995—2000; former CEO Terra Lycos, former vice chmn.; now venture ptnr. Highland Capital, Lexington, Mass. Bd. dirs. Boston Coll. H.S., The Greater Boston C. of C., Mass. Interactive Media Coun., The Man. com. Office: Highland Capital 92 Hayden Ave Lexington MA 02421 Office Phone: 781-861-5500. Business E-Mail: bdavis@hcp.com.

DAVIS, ROBERT LARRY, lawyer; b. Lubbock, Tex., June 6, 1942; s. R. H. and Bernice (Pray) Davis; m. Peggy Saunders, Jan. 23, 1965; children: Lee Michael, Melissa Lynn. BA, Rice U., 1964; LLB (with honors), U. Tex., 1967. Bar: Tex. 1967, U.S. Dist. Ct. (we. dist.) Tex. 1969, U.S. Dist. Ct. (so. dist.) Tex. 1989. Assoc. Royston Rayzor & Cook, Houston, 1967-68; from assoc. to ptnr. Brown McCarroll, Austin, Tex., 1968—. Bus. sect. coord., mem. mgmt. com. Parliamentarian, mem. exec. com. Downtown Revitalization Task Force, Austin, 1978—80; mem., past pres. Boys Club, Austin, Travis County, 1981—; trustee Eanes Ind. Sch. Dist., Austin, 1986—93, pres., 1990—93. Mem.: Assn. Atty. Mediators (pres. Ctrl. Tex. chpt. 1995). Methodist. Avocations: sports, music, reading. Home: 3607-3 Pinnacle Rd Austin TX 78746 Office: Brown McCarroll 1400 One Congress Plz III Congress Austin TX 78701 Office Phone: 512-479-9706. E-mail: rdavis@mailbmc.com.

DAVIS, ROBERT LEACH, retired federal official; b. Torrington, Conn., July 20, 1924; s. Clarence Adelbert and Ruth Mabel (Leach) D.; m. Lorraine Lillian Szabla, Sept. 16, 1950; children: Russell, Cynthia, Vicki, Scott, Gregg. BA in Psychology, U. Mich., 1949. Claims examiner Social Security Adminstrn., Chgo., 1950-52; investigator and personnel specialist U.S. CSC, Chgo., 1952-67; personnel dir. U.S. Post Office Region, Chgo., 1967-71; div. chief, asst. bur. dir. U.S. CSC, Washington, 1971-78; dep. asst. sec. for adminstrn. and mgmt. Dept. Labor, Washington, 1978-82. Served with AUS, 1943-46. Decorated Purple Heart. Democrat. Unitarian-Universalist. Home: 8145 Eilers Rd Montague MI 49437 Office Phone: 734-395-1717. E-mail: rdavis3330@aol.com.

DAVIS, ROBERT NORMAN, hospital administrator; b. July 30, 1938; s. Norman DuBois and Geraldine Elizabeth (Sliker) D.; m. Elizabeth Ann Paine, June 15, 1985; children: Keith Robert, Kathryn Beth, Karl Thomas. BSCE, Pa. State U., 1960; MS in Mgmt., Rensselaer Poly. Inst., 1970. Dir. plant ops. Am. Hosp. Assn., Chgo., 1964-68; dir. mgmt. engring. Hosp. Assn. of N.Y., Albany, 1968-72; assoc. exec. dir. United Hosp., Portchester, N.Y., 1973-75; regional mgr. Arthur Young & Co., N.Y.C., 1975, Medicus Sys. Corp., Nashville, 1976-79; assoc. adminstr. Vanderbilt U. Hosp., Nashville, 1979-81; adminstr. Meml. divsn. Charleston (W.Va.) Area Med. Ctr., 1981-83; pres. Resource Devel. Assocs., Hendersonville, Tenn., 1983—96, 2001—; prin. Ernst & Young Health Care, 1996-2001. Contbr. articles to profl. jours. Bd. dirs., treas. Mid. Tenn. Youth Soccer Inc., 1979-82. With M.S.C., USAF, 1960-63. Fellow Am. Coll. Healthcare Execs., Hosp. Info. Mgmt. Sys. Soc. (dir. 1972-75, hon. fellow 1985). Baptist. Home: 116 Hidden Pt Hendersonville TN 37075-5541 Office Phone: 615-822-0866. E-mail: bobdavis777@comcast.net.

DAVIS, ROBERT TAYLOR, lawyer; b. Chattanooga, Tenn., Mar. 28, 1947; s. Roy and Roberta Davis; m. Kathleen Lynn Pryor, Aug. 26, 1968 (div. May 1980); 1 child, Emilee Michelle Davis Wooten; m. Deborah Jean Davis, Jan. 31, 1985; 1 child, Robert Taylor Davis, II. BS, Memphis State U., 1968, JD, 1973. Bar: Tenn., 1973, D.C., 1974, U.S. Tax Ct., U.S. Supreme Ct. Atty., tax law specialist IRS, Washington, 1973-75, estate & gift tax atty. Birmingham, Ala., 1975-76; pvt. practice Chattanooga, 1976—. Part-time pub. adminstrn., pub. guardian Hamilton County, Tenn., 1980-82; lectr. Dept. Acctg. Chattanooga State Tech. C.C., 1983-93; adv. com. acctg. divsn. Chattanooga C.C.; gen. counsel High Twelve Internat., Inc.; city judge City of Calhoun, Tenn., 2000-2002. Chmn. Hamilton County (Tenn.) Dems., 2003—. Served U.S. Army, 1969—71, Vietnam. Mem. ATLA, Tenn. Bar Assn. (legis. com.), Chattanooga Bar Assn. (legis. com.), D.C. Bar Assn., Greater Chattanooga Memphis State U. Almuni Assn. (pres. 1990-94), Memphis State Nat. Alumni Assn. (bd. dirs. 1990-94), DAV (life), Masons, Order Ea. Star (past worthy patron), Scottish Rite, York Rite, Alhambra Shrine, High 12 Club (past. pres., past chmn. bd., treas.), Downtown Chattanooga Sertoma Club (bd. dirs., pres. 1997-98, v.p. coms., chmn. coms., pres. 1997—, Pres.'s Outstanding Svc. Mankind award 1987), Am. Legion (life), State Assn. High 12 Clubs (pres. Ala., Ky. and Tenn. chpts. 1996-97; apptd. gen. counsel 1997), Fraternal Order Eagles, NRA (life), Vietnam Vets. Am. (life), Alpha Tau Omega. Office: 314 Vine St Chattanooga TN 37403-3414 Office Phone: 423-267-0679. E-mail: RTDavis@prodigy.net.

DAVIS, ROBERT W., computer company executive; BS in Commerce and Acctg., U. Vir.; MBA, Columbia U. Bus. Sch. CPA. Staff acct. Price Waterhouse, sr. mgr., SEC Svcs. Dept.; asst. corp. controller MCI Comm. Corp.; v.p. worldwide fin. and planning, Enterprise Systems Group Dell, Inc., v.p. worldwide corp. planning, 1999—2001, v.p., corp. fin., 2001, chief acctg. officer, 2002; exec. v.p., CFO Computer Assocs. Internat., Inc., Islandia, NY, 2005—. Mem. bus. adv. bd. U. Vir. McIntire Sch. Commerce. Mem.: Fin. Exec. Internat. (mem. com. on corp. reporting, mem. corp. exec. bd. strategy and fin. sects.). Office: Computer Assocs Internat Inc One Computer Associates Plaza Islandia NY 11749*

DAVIS, ROBIN JEAN, state supreme court justice; b. Boone County, W.Va., Apr. 6, 1956; m. Scott Segal; 1 child, Oliver. BS, W.Va. Wesleyan Coll., 1978; MA in Indsl. Rels., JD, W.Va. U., 1982. With Segal & Davis L.C., 1982-96; justice W.Va. Supreme Ct. of Appeals, 1996—, chief justice, 1998, 2002. Mem. W.Va. U. Law Inst., W.Va. Bd. of Law Examiners, 1991-96. Contbr. articles to W.Va. Law Rev.; co-author Litigation Handbook on West Virginia Rules of Civil Procedure. Recipient Dist. West Virginian award, 2000. Mem. ABA, Assn. of Trial Lawyers of Am., Kanawha County Bar Assn., Am. Acad. Matrimonial Lawyers. Office: Supreme Ct of Appeals Bldg 1 Rm E 301 State Capitol Charleston WV 25305 Office Phone: 304-558-4811. Business E-Mail: robindavis@courtswv.org.

DAVIS, ROGER EDWIN, lawyer, retired retail executive; b. Lakewood, Ohio, Dec. 29, 1928; s. Russell G. and Irma (Aboline) D.; m. Eva Grace Keeler, July 25, 1953 (div. Feb. 1980); children: Susan Lee, Lisa Ann, Steven Russell; m. Yvonne L. Berich, June 1, 1980. AB, Harvard U., 1950; LLB, U. Mich., 1953. Bar: Mich. 1953. Pvt. practice, Detroit, 1955-60; assoc. Langs, Molyneaux & Armstrong, 1955-60; counsel Avis Enterprises, 1961-62; with legal dept. S.S. Kresge Co. (now Kmart Corp.), 1963-70, v.p., gen. counsel, sec., 1970-85, sr. v.p., gen. counsel, sec., 1985-91, ret., 1991. Served with AUS, 1953-55. Mem. State Bar Mich., Fla. Bar, Bonita Bay Club. E-mail: roger1498@earthlink.net.

DAVIS, ROGER LEWIS, lawyer; b. New Orleans, Jan. 27, 1946; s. Leon and Anada A. Davis; m. Annette Vucinich; 1 child, Alexandra. BA, Tulane U., 1967; MA, UCLA, 1969, PhD, 1971; JD, Harvard U., 1974. Bar: Calif. 1974. Assoc. Orrick, Herrington & Sutcliffe, L.L.P., San Francisco, 1974-79, ptnr., 1980—, chmn. pub. fin. dept., 1981—, mem. exec. com. Mem. mcpl. fiscal adv. com. Mayor of San Francisco; tech. adv. com. Calif. Debt & Investment Adv. Commn. Fellow: Am. Coll. Bond Counsel (bd. dirs.); mem.: Calif. Pub. Securities Assn. (bd. dirs. 1998—, infrastructure subcom. of state strategic com. on terrorism), Nat. Assn. Bond Lawyers. Office: Orrick Herrington & Sutcliffe LLP The Orrick Building 405 Howard St San Francisco CA 94105 Business E-Mail: rogerdavis@orrick.com.

DAVIS, RONALD, artist, printmaker; b. Santa Monica, Calif., June 29, 1937; Student, U. Wyo., 1955-56, San Francisco Art Inst., 1960-64. Announcer, Sta. KVWO, Cheyenne, Wyo., 1958-59; instr. U. Calif., Irvine, 1966. Represented in permanent collections: Albright-Knox Gallery, Buffalo, Los Angeles County Mus., Mus. Modern Art, N.Y.C., Mus. Contemporary Art, Los Angeles, TateGallery, London, San Antonio Mus. Art, San Francisco Mus. Art, Whitney Mus., N.Y.C., Va. Mus., Richmond, Walker Art Ctr., Minn. and other internat. pub. collections; 57 one-man shows include Leo Castelli, N.Y.C., Nicholas Wilder Gallery, Los Angeles, BlumHelman Los Angeles, Asher/Faure, Los Angeles, John Berggruen, San Francisco, Kasmin Gallery, London, Mirvish Gallery, Toronto, N.Y. Acad. Scis., N.Y.C., Sedona Arts Ctr., Ariz., Oakland (Calif.) Mus., retrospective, 1976, numerous others; also numerous nat. and internat. group shows. Yale-Norfolk Summer Sch. Music and Art grantee, 1962, Nat. Endowment Arts grantee, 1968. Studio: PO Box 293 Arroyo Hondo NM 87513-0293 E-mail: RonDavis@abstract-art.com.

DAVIS, RONALD WAYNE, genetics researcher, biochemistry educator; b. Moroa, Ill., July 17, 1941; s. Lester and Gerzella Mary (Brown) D.; m. Janet L. Dafoe, May 2, 1949; children: Whitney Allen, Ashley Halcyon. BS, Ea. Ill. U., 1964; PhD, Calif. Inst. Tech., 1970. Postdoctoral fellow Harvard U., Cambridge, Mass., 1970-71; asst. prof. biochemistry Stanford (Calif.) U., 1972-77, assoc. prof., 1977-80, prof., 1980—. Mem. sci. adv. bd. Collaborative Rsch., Bedford, Mass., 1978—. Author: Manual for Genetic Engineering, 1980. Recipient Eli Lilly award in microbiology, 1976, U.S. Steel award in molecular biology, 1981, Louis S. Rosensthiel award Brandeis U., 1992. Mem. NAS. Avocation: backpacking. Office: Stanford U Dept Biochemistry 855 California Ave Stanford CA 94305*

DAVIS, RUBY DEE See DEE, RUBY

DAVIS, RUSSELL HADEN, psychotherapist, consultant; b. Washington, Nov. 26, 1940; s. Walter Haden Davis and Virginia (Russell) Edge; m. Iva Lee Crocker, 1964; children: Brandon Denise, Haden Arnold. BA, U. Va., 1962; MDiv, Union Theol. Sem., NYC, 1965, STM, 1978, PhD, 1986; ThM, So. Bapt. Theol. Sem., Louisville, 1966. Ordained to ministry So. Bapt. Ch., 1961, endorsed to chaplaincy Alliance of Baptists in the USA, 2000. Clin. chaplain Ky. State Reformatory, LaGrange, 1966-71, Ctrl. State Hosp., Milledgeville, Ga., 1971-77; assoc. min. The Riverside Ch., NYC, 1977-86; pvt. practice pastoral psychotherapy, 1974-98; asst. prof. psychiatry and religion Union Theol. Sem., NYC, 1986-91; mem. faculty Blanton-Peale Grad. Inst. Pastoral Psychotherapy, NYC, 1989-91; dir. Psy-Law, NYC, 1989-91; asst. prof. U. Va., 1994, assoc. prof., 1994-95; exec. dir. Assn. for Clin. Pastoral Edn., Inc., Decatur, Ga., 1995-98; pres. Legacy Group Internat., 1998—; founder sch. clin. pastoral edn. Sentara Norfolk (Va.) Gen. Hosp., 2001—. Adj. prof. Va. Commonwealth U., 2001—, John Leland Ctr. Theol. Studies, 2004—. Author: Freud's Concept of Passivity, 1993; also articles. Founder Sch. of Clin. Pastoral Edn., Sentara Hosps., Norfolk, 2001; bd. dirs. Tidewater Pastoral Counseling Svcs., Norfolk, 2001—05, Inst. for Relationship Therapy, NY, 1981—88, Counseling Ctr., Riverside Ch., NY, 1978—82. Named Ky. Col., State of Ky., 1970; fellow Union Theol. Sem., 1979-81, rsch. grantee, 1987-90; fellow Oaklawn Found., 1980. Mem.: Assn. Profl. Chaplains (bd. cert. chaplain 1974—99), Assn. Clin. Pastoral Edn. (cert. supr.). Office: Sch Clin Pastoral Edn Sentara Norfolk Gen Hosp 600 Gresham Dr Norfolk VA 23507 E-mail: rhdavis@sentara.com.

DAVIS, RUTH MARGARET (MRS. BENJAMIN FRANKLIN LOHR), information technology executive; b. Sharpsville, Pa., Oct. 19, 1928; d. W. George and Mary Anna (Ackermann) D.; m. Benjamin F. Lohr, Apr. 29, 1961. BA, Am. U., 1950; MA, U. Md., 1952, PhD, 1955; PhD (hon.), CMU, 1978, U. Md., 2000. Statistician FAO, UN, Washington, 1946-49; mathematician Nat. Bur. Standards, 1950-51; head ops. rsch. div. David Taylor Model Basin, 1955-61; staff asst. Office Dir. Def. Rsch. and Engring. Dept. Def., 1961-67; asso. dir. rsch. and devel. Nat. Libr. Medicine, 1967-68; dir. Lister Hill Nat. Center for Biomed. Communications, 1968-70; dir. Inst. for Computer Scis. and Tech. Nat. Bur. Standards, 1970-77; dep. undersec. def. for rsch. and engring., 1977-79; asst. sec. resource applications U.S. Dept. Energy, 1979-81; chmn., pres., CEO Pymatuning Group Inc. FMR, 1981-2000. Chmn. Aerospace Corp., 1994—2001; lectr. U. Md., 1955—57, Am. U., 1957—58; vis. prof. computer sci. U. Pa., 1969—72; adj. prof. U. Pitts.; mem. Md. Gov.'s Sci. Adv. Coun., 1971—77; chmn. nat. adv. coun. Elec. Power Rsch. Inst., 1975—76. Contbr. articles to profl. jours. Recipient Rockefeller Tech. Mgmt. award, 1973, Fed. Woman of the Yr. award, 1973, Systems Profl. of Yr. award, 1979, Disting. Svc. medal, U.S. Dept. Def., 1979, U.S. Dept. Energy, 1981, Gold medal, 1981, Ada A. Lovelace award, 1984, Disting. Alumnus award, U. Md., 1993, Disting. Alumna award, 1995, Alumna of Yr. in Math. and Sci. award, 2003; inducted into Computer News Hall of Fame, 1988. Fellow AIAA, Soc. for Info. Display; mem. AAAS, Am. Math. Soc., Math. Assn. Am., Nat. Acad. Engring. (counselor), Nat. Acad. Pub. Adminstrn., Nat. Acad. Arts and Scis., Washington Philos. Soc., Sigma Pi Sigma, Tau Beta Pi. Office: Pymatuning Group Inc 1500 N Beauregard St Ste 101 Alexandria VA 22311-1878 Office Phone: 703-671-3500. Personal E-mail: rmdavis5@aol.com. *The rapid rate of change in our lives due principally to technology and changing personal values makes adaptability and flexibility key ingredients to success. The one essential invariant of success is integrity, accompanied by compassion.*

DAVIS, RUTH MARIE, retired writer; d. Ralph (Stepfather) and Avalon Tucker; m. Daniel Newton Davis, Jr., Sept. 2000; m. Michael Fox, Sr. (div. 1986); children: Michael Fredric Fox II, Stephanie Marie Fox. Veteran's Rep. Accredidation Calif. Dept. of Veteran's Affairs Nat. Svc. Office, 1994, Veterans Services Rep. Accredidation The Am. Legion, 1994, Completion of Advanced Pay Grade Program USNR, 1993. Veteran's services rep. Yuba-Sutter County Veteran's Services Office, Marysville, Calif., 1979—2000. Bd. of directors Yuba County Employee's Assn., Local Number 1, Yuba City, 1991—92, All Valley Veteran's, Marysville, 1998—2000, Yuba-Sutter Counties Veteran's Meml. Com., Marysville, 1998—2001. Author: (novels) The Reclamation Project, (poem) Family Ties, (short stories) Protecting Your Karma, (poem) A Pl. They Call Vietnam, Mother's Arms, Brother's For All Eternity. With USNR, 1992—96. Recipient Recognition of Disting. Meritorious Svc., VFW, 1999, Cert. of Appreciation, Yuba-Sutter Veteran's Meml. Com., 2000. Mem.: NRA, Soc. for Creative Anachronism. Republican. Mem. Christian Ch. Avocations: creative writing, scuba diving, medieval recreation, garment design. Personal E-mail: rthegreat@yahoo.com.

DAVIS, SAMUEL, hospital administrator, educator, consultant; b. N.Y.C., Sept. 30, 1931; s. Morris and Ethel (Levowitz) D.; m. Ellen Darce Kalker, June 16, 1957; children: Joseph Evan, Thomas Adam, Jonathan Edward, Jessica Ann. BA, CCNY, 1952; MS, Columbia U., 1957. Acct. Roosevelt Hosp., N.Y.C., 1954-55; relief adminstr. Meml. Center Cancer and Allied Diseases, N.Y.C., 1955-56; adminstrv. resident, then adminstrv. asst. to dir. and dir. ambulatory care services Roosevelt Hosp., 1956-59; mem. adminstrv. staff Hillside Hosp., Glen Oaks, N.Y.C., 1959-72, exec. v.p., 1970-72; exec. cons. L.I. Jewish-Hillside Med. Center, New Hyde Park, N.Y., 1972; exec. pres. Mt. Sinai Hosp., Mpls., 1972-75, dir. N.Y.C., 1975-81, pres., 1981-85; sr. v.p. Mt. Sinai Med. Center, N.Y.C., 1975-77, exec. v.p., 1978-84; pres. EcuMed, N.Y.C., 1984-85; prin. Sam Davis & Assocs., Rye, N.Y., 1986—; sr. dir. Delta Cons. Group, N.Y.C., 1990-98; assoc. prof. adminstrv. medicine Mt Sinai Med. Sch., 1975-79, acting chmn., 1977-79, Edmond A. Guggenheim prof. health care mgmt., chmn. health care mgmt., 1979-84, disting. service prof. health care mgmt., 1984—; adj. prof. health care adminstrn. Baruch Coll., CUNY, 1978-87; prof. mgmt., clin. prof. Sch. Pub. Health Columbia U., 1988—; cons. health care strategy and orgnl. change, 1976—; pres. Sam Davis & Assoc., 1999—. Dir. health care research, The Ctr. for Mgmt., CUNY; vice chmn. bd. dirs. Hennepin County (Minn.) Health Coalition, 1973-75; mem. health adv. com. Minn. Met. Health Bd., 1974-75; mem. Hennepin County Health and Social Services Adv. Bd., 1974-75. Author: Decision Analysis in Hospital Administration, 1974; contbr. articles to profl. jours. Trustee Mpls. Fedn. Jewish Service, 1973-75; chmn. health and welfare div. N.Y.C. Fedn. Jewish Philanthropies, 1975-76; trustee, mem. exec. com. Montefiore Med. Ctr., Bronx, N.Y., 1985— . Served with AUS, 1952-54. Recipient Humanitarian award NCCJ, 1984; fellow social studies and humanities CCNY, 1952; WHO fellow, 1970; sr. fellow Wharton Sch. U. Pa., 1986—. Fellow Am. Coll. Hosp. Adminstrs., Am. Pub. Health Assn.; mem. Am. Assn. Hosp. Planning, Am., Am. Acad. Dramatic Arts (bd. dirs., exec. com.), N.Y. State hosp. assns., Am. Mgmt. Assn., Herman Biggs Soc. Office: Sam Davis & Assocs 74 Greenhaven Rd Rye NY 10580-2210

DAVIS, SAMUEL L., lawyer; b. Teaneck, N.J., Sept. 23, 1952; s. Harold Davis and Ruth Kaufman; m. Susan Joan Agner, Dec. 29, 1985; children: Ariel, Alexa, Alana, Joshua. BA, Tufts U., Somerville, Mass., 1973; JD, Rutgers U., Camden, N.J., 1977. Bar: N.J. 1978, D.C. 1980; cert. civil trial lawyer. Law clk. U.S. Dist. Ct., Phila., 1975-76; law sec. Superior Ct. N.J., Hackensack, N.J., 1977-78; assoc. Liebowitz, Kraft, Liebowitz, Engelwood, N.J., 1978-79; pvt. practice Teaneck, 1979-80; founding ptnr. Davis, Saperstein & Salomon, Teaneck and N.Y.C., 1981—. Contbr. chpts. to books. Pres., founder Legal Inst. Med. Edn., Hackensack, N.J., 1988—; chmn. N.J. State Senate Auto Legis. Com., 1992-93. Mem. ABA, Am. Trial Lawyers Assn., Am. Acad. Forensic Sci. Achievements include being the first U.S. attorney to present live testimony via video conferencing; developer of Courtcam communication system. Office: Davis Saperstein & Salomon 375 Cedar Ln Teaneck NJ 07666-3433 E-mail: sam@dsslaw.com.

DAVIS, SAMUEL MARION, dean, law educator, researcher; b. Pascagoula, Miss., Nov. 24, 1944; s. Marion Fuller and Ida Belle (Butler) D.; m. Carolyn Mary Peele, aug. 23, 1964; children: Samantha Carrie, Sarah Ellen. BA, U. So. Miss., 1966; JD, U. Miss., 1969; LLM, U. Va., 1970. Bar: Miss. 1969, U.S. Dist. Ct. (no. dist.) Miss. 1969, U.S. Supreme Ct. 1978, U.S. Ct. Appeals (11th cir.) 1982, U.S. Ct. Appeals (5th cir.) 1992. From asst. prof. to assoc. prof. U. Ga. Law Sch., Athens, 1970-78, asst. dean, 1973-75, prof., 1978-97, assoc. dean, 1986-92, assoc. v.p. for acad., 1994-97; dean U. Miss. Law Sch., Oxford, 1997—, Jamie L. Whitten chair law & govt., 1998—. Vis. assoc. prof. Washington and Lee U. Law Sch., Lexington, Va., 1975-76. Author: Rights of Juveniles, 1974, 2d edit., 1980, 2005; co-author: Children in the Legal System, 1983, 3d edit., 2004, Children's Rights and the Law, 1987. Fellow: Miss. Bar Found.; mem.: ABA, Miss. Bar, Am. Law Inst. Democrat. Methodist. Avocations: sailing, reading, travel. Office: Office of the Dean Univ Miss Law Sch PO Box 1848 University MS 38677 Business E-Mail: smdavis@olemiss.edu.

DAVIS, BISHOP SARAH FRANCES, management consultant, bishop; b. Beaumont, Tex., Feb. 4, 1948; d. Cornelius N. and Thelma (Levy) Taylor; m. Claytie Davis Jr., June 20, 1970; children: Claytie III, Corey Carrington. BA, North Tex. U., 1970; MS, Pace U., 1979; doctorate ministry, So. Methodist Univ. Dist. mgr. Southwestern Bell, Houston, 1970-83; pres. Strategic Mgmt. & Cons. Co., Houston, 1983—. Active awareness program Boy Scouts Am., Houston, 1987—; bd. dirs. south Houston dist. Bible Readers Outreach, 1987—. Mem. Internat. Assn. Fin. Planners (bd. dirs. 1987-88). Methodist. Achievements include third woman in history of African Methodist Episcopal Church elected Bishop. Avocation: bible study. Office: AME Church PO Box 223 nMesaru 100 Lesotho South Africa*

DAVIS, SARAH IRWIN, retired English language educator; b. Louisburg, NC, Nov. 17, 1923; d. M. Stuart and May Amanda (Holmes) Davis; m. Charles B. Goodrich, Nov. 18, 1948 (div. 1953). AB, U. N.C., 1944, AM, 1945; PhD, NYU, 1953. Tchg. asst. English dept. NYU, 1948-51; tchr. English Elizabeth Irwin H.S., N.Y.C., 1951-53; editor coll. texts Henry Holt, N.Y.C., 1953-55; editor coll. texts, encylopedias McGraw-Hill, N.Y.C., Rome, 1955—60; asst. prof. English Louisburg (N.C.) Coll., 1960-63, Randolph-Macon Woman's Coll., Lynchburg, Va., 1963-70, assoc. prof. English, 1970-75, chairperson Am. studies, 1971-87, prof. English and Am. studies, 1975-87, ret., 1987. Contbr. articles to profl. jours. Mem. MLA, Am. Studies Assn., N.C.-Va. Coll. English Assn. (various coms.), Franklin County Hist. Soc. (pres. 1989-94). Address: Carol Woods 139 750 Weaver Dairy Rd Chapel Hill NC 27514

DAVIS, SARAH JANE, health facility administrator; b. Cheyenne, Wyo., Feb. 8, 1949; d. Frederick Eugene and Bernice (Deaver) Fowler; m. David Allen Davis, Dec. 21, 1968 (div. 1973); 1 child, Jacoby. BS in Healthcare, 2003. Key punch operator San Antonio Coll., 1967-70; with personnel dept. Bapt. Meml. Hosp., San Antonio, 1970-71; key punch operator Frost Bank, San Antonio, 1971-72; mgr. Stop and Go, Inc., San Antonio, 1971-72; asst. dir. facilities mgmt. S.W. Tex. Meth. Hosp., San Antonio, 1973—; med. ctr.ops. mgr. Meth. Hosp., San Antonio, Cmty. Hosp. & Meth. Womens & Childrens Hosp., San Antonio. Mem. Nat. Fire Protection Assn. Avocations: needle work, reading, psychology. Office: SW Tex Meth Hosp 7700 Floyd Curl Dr San Antonio TX 78229-3979

DAVIS, SCOTT CHARLES, music educator, political activist; b. Abington, Pa., Oct. 6, 1955; s. Rothmeyer and Diane Davis. BA in History, West Chester U., 1978. Cert. Secondary Sch. Tchr. Pa., 1984. Music tchr., Pa., Md., Va., NJ, NY, Del., 1968—; piano technician Pa., Md., Va., DC, Del., NJ, NY, Conn., 1978—. Polit. cons., Pa., Md., Va., DC, Del., NH, NY, 1982—; real estate investor, Phila., 1991—; broadcaster WGCB-FM, Red Lion, Pa., 1995. Songwriter, performer: US, Europe, Can., 1960—2005; songwriter Hope, 2004, Yes, 2004; editor: New English Revised Sacred Annotated Scriptures, 2004—05. Observer Town Watch, Phila., 1980—; chmn. Solvency Party. Am., 1994—2001; chmn. nat. exec. com. Sovereignty Party Am., 2001—04, Party Am. Revolution, 2004—; founder Christian Assn. Reconciliation, 2004. Reconciliationist. Avocations: languages, geography, history. Office: Party American Revolution PO Box 877 Edgemont PA 19028-0877 Office Phone: 215-233-5369.

DAVIS, SCOTT JONATHAN, lawyer; b. Chgo., Jan. 8, 1952; s. Oscar and Doris (Koller) D.; m. Anne Megan, Jan. 4, 1981; children: William, James, Peter. BA, Yale U., 1972; JD, Harvard U., 1976. Bar: Ill. 1976, U.S. Dist. Ct. (no. dist.) Ill. 1976, U.S. Ct. Appeals (7th cir.) 1977, U.S. Ct. Appeals (8th cir.) 1986. Law clk. to judge U.S. Ct. Appeals (7th cir.), Chgo., 1976—77; assoc. Mayer, Brown, Rowe & Maw LLP, Chgo., 1977—82, ptnr., 1983—. Bd. editors: Harvard Law Rev., 1974—76; contbr. articles to profl. jours. V.p. Chgo. Police Bd. Home: 838 W Belden Ave Chicago IL 60614-3236 Office: Mayer Brown Rowe & Maw 71 S Wacker Dr Chicago IL 60606 Office Phone: 312-701-7311. Business E-Mail: sdavis@mayerbrown.com.

DAVIS, SCOTT MICHAEL, director, music educator; b. Pitts., Apr. 22, 1976; s. James Earl Collins, Jr. and Lynda Sue Quickel. BS in Music Edn., Pa. State U., 1999. Cert. instr. 1 in music edn. Pa. Substitute music tchr. Punxsutawney (Pa.) Area Schs., 1999—2000; band dir. Leisure City K-8 Ctr., Homestead, Fla., 2000—. Mem.: Pa, Music Educators Assn., Fla. Bandmasters Assn., Fla. Music Edn. Assn., Music Educators Nat. Conf., United Tchrs. Dade (bldg. steward 2001—02). Democrat. Avocations: tennis, travel, music. Office: Leisure City K-8 Ctr 14950 SW 288th St Homestead FL 33033 Personal E-mail: scottdavis_76@hotmail.com. E-mail: smdavis100@yahoo.com.

DAVIS, SCOTT WALTER, vocal music educator; b. Portland, Oreg., Oct. 14, 1968; s. Walter and Karen (Hayes) Davis. BA in Vocal Performance, Music Adminstrn, Whitworth Coll., 1991, MAT, 1993. Cert. tchr., Wash., Oreg. Dir. vocal music Clackamas High Sch., Milwaukie, Oreg., 1993—. One of three Americans touring with World Youth Choir, 1990; mem. drug and alcohol team Clackamas High Sch., 1993—. Mem. Music Educators Nat. Conf., Am. Choral Dirs. Assn. (sec. Oreg. exec. bd. 1994—). Avocations: biking, caving, piano, camping, reading. Home: 11855 SE Broyles Ct Clackamas OR 97015-7218

DAVIS, SHELBY MOORE CULLOM, investment company executive, consultant; b. Phila., Mar. 20, 1937; s. Shelby Cullom and Kathryn (Wasserman) D.; m. Wendy Ann Adams, June 20, 1959 (div. 1975); children: Andrew, Christopher, Victoria; m. Gale Abbie Lansing, Apr. 17, 1976; children: Lansing, Alida, Edith. AB with honors, Princeton U., 1958. V.p. in charge equity rsch. Bank of N.Y., N.Y.C., 1958-66; founding ptnr. Davis, Palmer & Biggs, N.Y.C., 1966-78; sr. v.p. Fiduciary Trust Co., N.Y.C., 1978-83, cons., 1983-98; pres. various mut. funds Davis Selected Advisers, Santa Fe, 1983-98, also dir. all mut. funds, 1969-78, 83-98. Contbr. articles to Fin. Analysts Jour. Bd. dirs., trustee Beekman Downtown Hosp., N.Y.C., early 1960s; bd. dirs. Am. Cancer Soc., N.Y.C., early 1970s; trustee United World Coll., 1988—, Teton Sci. Sch., 2001—; mem. adv. bd. Coll. of the Atlantic, 1999—. Mem. N.Y. Soc. Security Analysts (bd. dirs. 1965), Univ. Club, River Club (N.Y.C.), Harbor Club (Seal Harbor, Maine), Tuxedo Club (Tuxedo Park, N.Y.), Jupiter Island Club, Jackson Hole Golf and Tennis Club. Republican. Avocations: skiing, hiking, travel, swimming, tennis. Home: PMB 25185 PO Box 20000 Jackson WY 83001-7000 Office: Davis Advisors PO Box 1688 Santa Fe NM 87504-1688 Business E-Mail: shelby@dsaco.com.

DAVIS, SHELLEY LORRAINE, historian; b. Lincoln, Nebr., Apr. 14, 1956; d. Wallace Carroll and Eunice Vivian (Peterson) Peterson. BA, U. Nebr., 1977, MA, 1979. Historian Office of Air Force History, Washington, 1979, Air Force Communications Command, Belleville, Ill., 1980-82, Air Force Logistics Command, Sacramento, Calif., 1982-83, Air Force Space Communications Div., Colorado Springs, Colo., 1983-84, Tactical Air Command, Austin, Tex., 1984-87, Def. Mapping Agy., Washington, 1987-88, IRS, Washington, 1988—. Grad. exec. leadership deomnstration program U.S. Dept. Def., Washington, 1987-88; IRS historical studies, 1991—. Co-author, designer Air Force Communications Command, I938-8l, History of McClellan AFB, 1983. Equal employment counselor, mem. fed. women's program USAF, Austin, 1985-87. Mem. Soc. for History in Fed. Govt. (treas.). Democrat. Home: 6203 Sierra Ct Manassas VA 20111-2610 Office: IRS 1111 Constitution Ave NW Washington DC 20224-0001

DAVIS, SHIRLEY ROSS See SULLIVAN, SHIRLEY ROSS

DAVIS, SHIRLEY STANCIL, retired elementary education educator; b. Selma, NC, Mar. 11, 1945; d. Needham and Betty (Watson) Stancil; m. William Louis Davis, Nov. 9, 1968; children: Jacqueline, Dana, William Louis Jr. BS, Elizabeth City State U., NC, 1967; EdM, Va. State U., 1983. 4th grade tchr. Surry Elem., Va., 1967-72, 2nd grade, 1983—; 3rd and 7th grade tchr. Lebanon Elem., Surry, 1972-83; media specialist Luther Porter Jackson Mid. Sch., Dendron, Va., 1995-98, ret., 1998. Mem. Surry County Planning Coun., 1988-89; chairperson Self-Study, Surry, 1976; mem. CADRE Adv. Bd., Surry, 1989-97; pres. Bacon's Castle Woman's Club, Surry, 1990-92; bd. dirs. Am. Heart Assn., Surry, 1978, 89; sponsor Saint Jude Bike-A-Thon, Surry, 1991-92; youth dir. Lebanon Bapt. Ch., Surry, 1989—, trustee, 1993-2000, chmn. bd. trustees, 1997-2000, appointed to Chippokes Plantation Farm Found. Bd. of Trustee, 2002. HoneyWell grant Honeywell Edn. Found., 1992; recipient Tchr. of Yr. Daily Press and Hampton Automobile Assn., 1994. Mem. NEA, Va. Edn. Assn., Surry County Edn. Assn., Order of Ea. Stars Grace Union #56. Democrat. Avocations: reading, cooking, sewing, dance. Home: 650 Lebanon Rd Spring Grove VA 23881-7748

DAVIS, STANLEY NELSON, hydrologist, educator; b. Rio de Janeiro, Aug. 6, 1924; s. Nelson Caryl and Mary Faye (Caulkins) D.; m. Barbara Jean Wickham, Apr. 14, 1949 (div.); children: Gerald Nelson, Ruth Ann, Darlene Grace, Randall Wayne, Betty Jean, Nancy Faye.; m. Augusta G. Felty, Feb. 12, 1982; children— Tara Devi, Locana Kamala BS in Geology, U. Nev., 1949; MS, U. Kans., 1951; PhD, Yale, 1955. Geologist U.S. Bur. Reclamation, 1949, Mo. Geol. Survey, 1952, 53, 55; instr. U. Rochester, 1953-54; mem. faculty Stanford, 1954-67, prof. geology, 1965-67, U. Mo., 1967-73, chmn. dept., 1969-72; asso. dean Coll. Arts and Scis., 1972-73; prof. geology Ind. U., Bloomington, 1973-75; prof. hydrology U. Ariz., Tucson, 1975—, head dept. hydrology and water resources, 1975-79. Vis. prof. U. Chile, Santiago, 1960-61; tchr. Bowling Green U., summer 1963, Princeton, summer 1965, U. Hawaii, fall 1966; instr. U. Oriente in Venezuela, summer 1967-68, 72; lectr. Am. Geol. Inst.; mem. East Greenland Expdn., Arctic Inst. N. Am., summer 1959; cons. to govt. and industry, 1955— Author: Hidrogeología,

1961, (with R.M. DeWiest) Hydrogeology, 1966, (with P. Reitan and R. Pestrong) Geology, Our Physical Environment, 1976, (with D.J. Campbell, H.W. Bentley, T.J. Flynn) Ground Water Tracers, 1984; also articles. Served with AUS, 1943-46, PTO. Fellow AAAS, Geol. Soc. Am. (O.E. Meinzer award 1989), Am. Geophys. Union; mem. Assn. Ground Water Scientists and Engrs., Soc. Econ. Paleontologists and Mineralogists, Sigma Xi. Home: 6540 W Box Canyon Dr Tucson AZ 85745-9681 Office: U Ariz Dept Hydrology & Water Resou Tucson AZ 85721-0001 Business E-Mail: sndavis@u.arizona.edu.

DAVIS, STEPHEN, professional football player; b. Mar. 1, 1974; m. Virginia Davis; children: Dentia, Sherrell, Stephen Davis Jr., Stephanie. Degree in vocat. edn., Auburn. Profl. football player Washington Redskins, 1996—2003, Carolina Panthers, Charlotte, 2003—. Founder Rushing for Remembrance. Named to NFC Pro-Bowl Team, 1999, 2003. Achievements include led NFL in rushing touchdowns (17), 1999. Office: Carolina Panthers 800 S Mint St Charlotte NC 28202

DAVIS, STEPHEN ALLEN, lawyer; b. Huntington, W.Va., Jan. 18, 1947; s. Allen Reed and Mary (Richardson) D.; m. Martha Helen Frazier, June 29, 1974; children: Reed Frazier, Andrew Richardson, Jeffrey Allen, Kristin Ann. BA, W.Va. U., 1968, LLD, 1974. Bar: W.Va. 1974, U.S. Dist. Ct. (so. dist.) W.Va. 1974, U.S. Ct. Appeals (4th cir.) 1983. Assoc. Law Office John B. Breckinridge, Summersville, W.Va., 1974-76; ptnr. Breckinridge, Davis, Sproles & Chapman, PLLC, Summersville, 1976—. Mcpl. judge Town of Summersville, 1976-79; chmn. bd. dirs. pub. defender corp. 23d Jud. Cir., Summersville, 1980-89; asst. sec. Strouds Creek & Muddlety R.R., Summersville, 1982-99; past divorce commr., past fiduciary supr. Nicholas County; bd. dirs. Summersville Salvation Army, 1991- Chmn. exec. com. Nicholas County Dems., Summersville, 1980-86; trustee, past chmn. bd. trustees Summersville Meml. Hosp., 1976-83; trustee, chmn. Summersville Libr., 1986-2001; Nicholas County bd. adv. Econ. Devel. Auth., 2001—; former mem. bd. govs. W. Va. State Bar. 1st lt. U.S. Army, 1969-71, Vietnam. Mem. ABA, W.Va. Bar Assn. (bd. govs. 1997-2000), Nicholas County Bar Asssn. (pres. 1978), Am. Assn. Hosp. Lawyers, Summersville Jaycees (pres. 1976). Presbyterian. Home: 211 Main St Summersville WV 26651-1315 Office: Breckinridge Davis Sproles & Chapman PLLC 509 Church St Summersville WV 26651-1493 Office Phone: 304-872-2271.

DAVIS, STEPHEN B., Internet company executive, lawyer; AB, Princeton U., 1979; MA in East Asian studies, U. Wash., 1984; JD, Columbia U., 1988. Atty. Preston, Gates & Ellis, Seattle; pres., CEO Corbis, Seattle, 1993—. Bd. dirs. Lambda Legal Def. Fund, Washington, Wash. Software Alliance, Seattle, Intrepid Learning Solutions; chair Wash. State Tech, Alliance, NPower. Alliance; mem. Gov.'s Competitiveness Coun., President's Coun. Internat. Ctr. Photography. Bd. dirs. United Way of King County, Seattle, 1993—, Prog. Appropriate Tech. in Health (PATH), Alliance for Educ. Office: Corbis 710 Second Ave Suite 200 Seattle WA 98104*

DAVIS, STEPHEN EDWARD FOLWELL, banker; b. Auckland, N.Z., July 12, 1964; s. George Folwell and Elizabeth Ann (Strother) D. BA, Harvard Coll., 1987. Rsch. intern The Brookings Instn., Washington, 1984; sales intern Lotus Devel. Corp., Cambridge, Mass., 1986-87; fin. analyst Salomon Bros. Inc., N.Y.C., 1987-89; interest rate swap trader Kidder Peabody & Co., N.Y.C., 1989-90; derivatives trader Deutsche Bank AG, N.Y.C., 1990-95; proprietary trader Dai-Ichi Kangyo Bank, Ltd., 1995-96; head derivatives trading Hypo Bank AG, N.Y.C., 1996-97; pres. Nuuanu Real Estate Investors, Honolulu, 1997—. Researcher book: The Ultimate Insiders, 1989. Homesteading coord., dir. Crimson Impact Inc., N.Y.C., 1991-95; treas. The Quadrille Soc., N.Y.C., 1991—; vol. Habitat for Humanity, 2002. JFK Sch. Govt. grantee, 1984; Lindsay Exeter Meml. scholar, 1983. Mem. Fgn. Policy Assn., Harvard Club of N.Y. Avocations: foreign policy, golf, running. Address: 1330 Ala Moana Blvd # 2407 Honolulu HI 96814-4231 E-mail: sdavis@post.harvard.edu.

DAVIS, STEPHEN HOWARD, applied mathematics professor; b. N.Y.C., Sept. 7, 1939; s. Harry Carl and Eva Leah (Axelrod) D.; m. Suellen Lewis, Jan. 15, 1966. BEE, Rensselaer Poly. Inst., 1960, MS in Math, 1962, PhD in Math., 1964; BSc honoris causa, U. Western Ont., 2001. Research mathematician Rand Corp., Santa Monica, Calif., 1964-66; lectr. in math. Imperial Coll., London U., 1966-68; asst. prof. mechanics and materials sci. Johns Hopkins U., 1968-70, assoc. prof., 1970-75, prof., 1975-78; prof. engrng. sci. and applied math. Northwestern U., 1979—, Walter P. Murphy prof., 1987—, McCormick Sch. prof., 2000—. Dir. Ctr. for Multiphase Fluid Flow and Transport, 1986-88; cons. in field; vis. prof. math. Monash U., Australia, 1973; vis. prof. chem. engring. U. Ariz., 1977; vis. prof. aerospace and mech. engring., 1981; vis. scientist Institut für Aerodynamik-ETH, Zurich, Switzerland, 1971; vis. scientist Dept. Math. Ecole Polytechnique Federale, Lausanne, Switzerland, 1984, 85, vis. prof. 1987, 88, 91; mem. U.S. Nat. Com. for Theoretical and Applied Mechanics, 1978-87. Asst. editor Jour. Fluid Mechanics, 1969-75, assoc. editor, 1975-89, editor-in-chief, 2000—; contbr. articles to profl. jours. Recipient Alexander von Humboldt award, 1994, Fluid Dynamics prize Am. Phys. Soc., 1994, G.I. Taylor medal Soc. for Engring. Sci., 2001. Fellow Am. Phys. Soc. (chmn. divsn. fluid dynamics 1978-79, 87-88, councillor divsn. fluid dynamics 1980-82); mem. NAS, NAE, Am. Acad. Arts and Scis., Soc. Indsl. and Applied Math. (coun. 1983-87), Sigma Xi, Pi Mu Epsilon. Home: 1199 Edgewood Rd Lake Forest IL 60045-1308 Office: Northwestern U McCormick Sch Engring/Applied Scis Sheridan Rd Evanston IL 60208-0001 Business E-Mail: sdavis@northwestern.edu.

DAVIS, STEPHEN K., engineering and management consultant; b. Irving, Tex., Dec. 6, 1966; s. J. Lee and Mary Ann (Yarborough) Davis; m. Susan M. Stephens, Apr. 14, 1990; children: Garrett, Jeremy, Lindsay, Jennifer. Sr. sys. officer Citicorp, N.Y.C., 1990—95; pres. Park Ave. Tech., Inc., Bedford, Tex., 1990—. Cons. merger, acquisition & divesture info. tech. Park Ave. Tech., Inc., 1990—. Pilot Angel Flight, Addison, Tex., 2000—. Served with aviation, USCG Aux., 2002—04, Grapevine, Tex. Christian. Avocations: networks, travel, aviation. Office: Park Ave Tech Inc 2604 Park Ave Ste 201 Bedford TX 76021 Business E-Mail: mail@ParkAveTech.com.

DAVIS, STERLING EVAN, television executive; b. Mpls., Feb. 10, 1941; s. Lyman Eugene and Ruby Elizabeth (Larson) D.; m. Bonnie S. Taylor, Jan. 15, 1977; children: Evan, Emily, Robin. BA, Taylor U., 1963; postgrad., U. So. Calif., L.A., 1968-70. Chief engr. Metrotape, Hollywood, Calif., 1974-78; v.p. ops. The Vidtronics Co., Hollywood, 1978; chief engr. Telemation Prodns., Seattle, 1978-82; dir. ops. Sta. KTVU, Inc., Oakland, Calif., 1982-98; v.p. engring. Cox Broadcasting, Atlanta, 1998—. Bd. dir. Easter Seals Soc., Advanced TV Sys. Com. Lt. USN, 1963—67, Vietnam. Mem. IEEE, Soc. Motion Picture & TV Engrs., Audio Engring. Soc., Soc. Broadcast Engrs. Office: Cox Broadcasting PO Box 105357 Atlanta GA 30348-5357 E-mail: sterling.davis@cox.com.

DAVIS, STEVEN EUGENE, radiographer, consultant; b. Dillon, S.C., June 8, 1968; s. Willie and Dianne Davis; m. Dian Graham, Dec. 4, 1992; children: Courtney Gibbs, Jenny Gibbs. AS Radiology, Florence Darlington Tech. Coll., 1992. Registered ARRT Am. Registry of Radilogic Tech. Diagnostic and oper. rm. tech. McLeod Regional Med. Ctr., Florence, SC, 1991—96; chief CT and oper. tech. Carolinas Hosp. Sys., Lake City, SC, 1996—99; dir. imaging Clarendon Meml. Hosp., Manning, SC, 1999—. Cons. in field. Contbr. articles pub. to profl. jour. Team mem. Relay for Life, 2002; polit. action com. S.C. Hosp. Assn., 2000—. Sgt. E-5 U.S. Army, 1987—93. Decorated Army Achievement award. Mem.: Soc. for Computer Applications in Radiology, Am. Soc. of Radiology Tech., Am. Health Care Radiology Adminstr., S.C. Soc. Radiologic Tech. Bapt. Achievements include instituted radiology info. sys. and picture arch. and comm. sys; development of customer svc. initiative for hosp. Avocations: hunting, fishing, finance, computing. Office: Claredon Meml Hosp 10 Hosp St Manning SC 29102 Office Phone: 803-435-3121.

DAVIS, SUSAN A., congresswoman; b. Cambridge, Mass., Apr. 13, 1944; m. Steve, 1970; children: Jeffrey, Benjamin. BA in Sociology, U. Calif., Berkeley, 1965; MA in Social Work, U. N.C. Social worker; exec. dir. Aaron Price Fellowship Program, 1990-93; served Calif. State Assembly, 1994-2000; mem. U.S. Congress from 53rd Calif. dist., 2000—, Ho. Com. on Veteran Affairs. Mem. Congressional com. House Armed Svcs., Edn. and Workforce; chaired Women's Caucus for Senate and Assembly, Consumer Protection, Govt. Efficiency, Econ. Devel. com.; created and co-chaired Select com. on Adolescence. Mem. San Diego City Sch. Bd., 1983-1992, pres. and v.p.; pres. League of Women Voters San Diego., Democrat. Office: 1224 Longworth House Office bldg Washington DC 20515

DAVIS, SUSAN ADLER, art educator; b. Balt. d. Harry Adler and Phyllis F. Cahn; children: Andrew Sean, Brian Michael. BFA, Md. Inst. Coll. Art, 1979; MA in Tchg. (hon.), Coll. Notre Dame Md., 2000. Substitute tchr. Gilman Sch., Balt., 1996—2000; tchr. Balt. County Pub. Schs., 2000—. Author: (creative non-fiction book) The Other Sisters, after the Cohns, the Next Generation of Art Collectors in Balitmore, 2000. Mem. Balt. Mus. Art. Democrat. Jewish. Avocations: sailing, swimming, bicycling, textile arts, antiques. E-mail: susalinasail@aol.com.

DAVIS, SUSAN F., human resources specialist; BS, MS, Beloit Coll.; MBA, U. Mich. From strategic planner to corp. mgr. tng. and devel. Hoover Universal Corp., 1983-85; various positions including v.p. orgnl. devel. automotive group Johnson Controls, Inc., Milw., 1983—94, corp. officer, v.p. human resources, 1994—. Bd. dirs. Quanex Corp., Butler Mfg. Co. Mem.: HR Policy Assn. (vice chair). Office: Johnson Controls Inc 5757 N Green Bay Ave Milwaukee WI 53209-4408 Office Phone: 414-228-1200. Office Fax: 414-524-2077.*

DAVIS, SUZANNE SPIEGEL, retired information specialist; b. St. Louis, Sept. 27, 1935; d. Albert Louis Jr. and Dorothy Lydia (Grafeman) Spiegel; m. Glenn Guy Davis Jr., Sept. 23, 1961 (div. Mar. 1986); 1 child, Wendy Sue. BA, U. Okla., 1957; MLS, U. Ill., 1958. Reference asst. Atlanta Pub. Libr., 1958-59, head adult dept. Ida Williams br., 1959-61, head Fulton County dept., 1961-62; pub. svcs. and documents libr. Queens Coll. Libr., Charlotte, 1969-83; info. specialist Pub. Libr. Charlotte and Mecklenburg, NC, 1983—96. Pres. Charlotte Panhellenic Congress, 1965-66, Charlotte Nature Mus. Guild, 1969-70; rec. chmn. ARC, Mecklenburg County Unit, Charlotte, 1968-69, tng. chmn., 1969-70. Mem. Southeastern Libr. Assn., N.C. Libr. Assn., Charity League, Guild of Nature Mus. and Discovery Place, Beta Phi Mu, Phi Alpha Theta, Alpha Phi. (Michaelanean award 1984). Republican. Presbyterian.

DAVIS, TAYLOR, sculptor; Diploma in Fine Arts, Sch. Mus. Fine Arts; BS in Edn., Tufts U.; MFA, Milton Avery Grad. Sch. Arts, Bard Coll. Asst. prof. Mass. Coll. Art, 1999—; faculty mem. Milton Avery Sch. Arts Bard Coll., 2003—. Exhibitions include Whitney Biennial, Whitney Mus. Am. Art, 2004, Triple Candie, NY, Inst. Contemporary Art, Boston, Green Street Gallery, Boston, Chgo. Arts Coun. Recipient Artist Prize, Inst. Contemporary Art, 2001, Assn. Internat. Art Critics Award, 2002; grantee St. Botolph Found. Grant, 2003; Mass. Cultural Coun. Grant, 1999. Mailing: c/o Whitney Museum American Art 945 Madison Ave New York NY 10021 E-mail: dtayd@mindspring.com.*

DAVIS, TERRELL, former professional football player; b. San Diego, Oct. 28, 1972; Student, Long Beach State U., U. Ga. Running back Denver Broncos, 1995—2002; player AFC Championship Game, 1997, Super Bowl, 1997, Pro Bowl, 1996, 1997. Named NFL MVP, 1998, NFL Offensive Player of the Yr., 1998, Super-Bowl XXXII MVP, 1998; named to NFL Pro-Bowl, 1996—98. Achievements include mem. Super Bowl XXXII, XXXIII Champion Denver Bronco's, 1998, 1999; became 4th running back in history to rush for over 2,000 yards in a single season (2,008), 1998; holds NFL record 7 straight playoff 100 yard performances.

DAVIS, TERRY HUNTER, JR., lawyer; b. Charlottesville, Va., Mar. 19, 1931; s. Terry Hunter and Mattie May (Parsons) D.;m. Mary Jane Irwin, Sept. 3, 1960; 1 child, Terry Hunter III. BA, Va. Mil. Inst., 1953; LLB, U. Va., 1958. Bar: Va. 1958, NY 1959, NC 1999, lic.: Va. (instr. in bus. law). Assoc. Thacher, Proffitt, Prizer, NYC, 1958-60; law clk. Chief U.S. Dist. Judge, Norfolk, Va., 1960-61; assoc., ptnr. Taylor, Gustin, Harris, Norfolk, 1961—64; ptnr. Harris, Fears, Davis, Lynch & McDaniel, Norfolk, 1964—. Contbg. author Virginia Lawyer's Basic Practice Handbook, 1964, Federal Special Master, 1964. Chmn. Norfolk Electral Bd., 1971-72. 1st lt. U.S. Army, 1953-55. Mem. ABA, Va. Bar Assn., Va. State Bar (com. mem. 1972-73), Norfolk/Portsmouth Bar (com. chmn. 1962-63), SAR (treas. 1962-64), Jamestown Soc., Kiwanis. Republican. Episcopalian. Avocations: jogging, tennis. Home: 7451 North Shore Rd Norfolk VA 23505-1770 Office: Harris Fears Davis Lynch & McDaniel PO Box 12756 Norfolk VA 23541-0756 Office Phone: 757-461-4100. Personal E-mail: Tdavis5735@aol.com.

DAVIS, THERESA ANN, music educator; b. Ft. Smith, Ark., July 8, 1951; d. Albert Henry and Adeline Alice (Weinzapfel) Ostermann; m. Ben Richard Davis, Nov. 29, 1976; children: Keith, James, Rebecca, Will. Student, U. Dallas, 1971; BA, Benedictine Coll., 1973. Tchr. St. John Sch., Ennis, Tex., 1975-77, St. Joseph Sch., Waxahachie, Tex., 1992-94; music dir. St. Joseph Ch., Waxahachie, 1994-96; pvt. piano tchr. Mem. Am. Coll. Musicians (cert. piano tchr.), Music Tchrs. Nat. Assn., Waxahachie Music Tchrs. Assn. (sec. 1990-93, pres. 1993-95, student affiliate chmn. 1995-00), Sigma Alpha Iota. Roman Catholic. Avocations: cooking, sewing, concerts.

DAVIS, THOMAS M., III, congressman; b. Minot, ND, Jan. 5, 1949; m. Peggy Davis; 3 children. BA in Polit. sci., Amherst Coll., 1971; JD, U. Va., 1975. Legis. asst. Va. House of Delegates, 1964-67; pvt. practice, 1975-79; v.p., gen. counsel Advanced Techs., 1979-90; mem. bd. supervisors Mason Dist., Fairfax, Va., 1980—94; chair bd. supervisors Fairfax County, Va., 1992—94; v.p., gen. counsel then corp. counsel and chair PRC, Inc., McLean, Va., 1990-94; mem. US Congress from 11th Va. dist., 1995—; mem. energy and commerce com., govt. reform com.; chmn. Nat. Rep. Congress. Com., 1998—2002, Govt. Reform Subcom. DC, 1994—2000, Govt. Reform Subcom. on Tech. and Procurement Policy, 2001—; mem., energy and commerce com. Govt. Reform Subcom., 2001, mem. subcom. on telecommunications and the internet, 2001; chair House Government Reform Com. (108th Congress), 2003, House Government Reform Com. (109th Congress), 2005—. Founder, co-chair Info. Tech. Working Group. Advisory bd. Afghanistan-Am. Found.; bd. dir. Boys and Girls Club, Partnership for Pub. Svc.; advisory bd. Women in Governmental Rels. Leader; chair advisory bd. Va. Legal Svcs.; mem. Fairfax County, Va. Tenant-Landlord Assn., Nat. Capitol Planning Commn., No. Va. Transportation Commn., Va. Assn. of Cities, Gen. Govt. Steering Com.; chair, Effective Govtl. Policy Com. Va. Mcpl. League; pres. Washington Metropolitan Coun. of Governments. With U.S. Army, 1971, 1st lt. USAR, with Va. Nat. Guard. Named to Am. Electronics Assn. High Tech Hall of Fame, 2000; recipient Congl. Tech. Policy award, Electronic Industry Alliance, 1999, Friend if the Shareholder award, Am. Shareholders Assn., 2002, Guardian of Small Bus. award, Nat. Fedn. of Independent Bus., 2002, Hero of Taxpayer award, Americans for Tax Reform, 2002, Jefferson award, Citizens for a Sound Economy, 2002, RSA Conf. award for Pub. Policy, RSA Security, 2002, Sr. Guardian Medal of Honor, The Seniors Coalition, 2002, Technology Champion award, Nat. Assn. of State Chief Info. Officers, 2003, Azimuth award, Chief Info. Officers Coun., 2004. Mem.: Baileys Crossroads Rotary Club (charter mem., past pres.). Republican. Office: US House Reps 2348 Rayburn Ho Office Bldg Washington DC 20515-4611 Address: 9878 Main St Fairfax VA 22031 Office Phone: 202-225-1492, 703-277-9635. Office Fax: 202-225-3071, 703-277-9615.*

DAVIS, TINKA GUERGUIEVA, secondary school educator; b. Pazardjik, Bulgaria, Aug. 27, 1969; arrived in U.S., 1995; d. Georgi I. Ventchev and Tonka K. Ventcheva; m. Brent Thomas Davis, Oct. 2, 1998; children: Christopher Lawrence, Catherine Sophia. BS in Math., Sophia U., 1995. Cert. tchr. Wash. Tchr.'s aide Dallas Jr. Acad., Dallas, 1995—96; tchr. math. Ednl. Tutorin and Cons. Acad., Mercer Island, Wash., 1998—2000; dir. math. program Am. Acad., Mercer Island, 2000—. Avocations: horseback riding, reading, hiking. Office: American Academy 7834 SE 32nd St # 204 Mercer Island WA 98040 Office Phone: 206-230-5672. E-mail: tinkadavis@msn.com.

DAVIS, TRAYTON M., lawyer; b. Milwaukee, Wis., 1955; BA, Haverford Coll., 1977; JD, NYU, 1980. Bar: N.Y. 1981. Ptnr. & co-chmn. Global Fin. Group Milbank Tweed Hadley & McCloy, N.Y.C., 1993—. Mem.: ABA (Bus. & Internat. Law sect.), Am. Coll. Investment Counsel. Office: Milbank Tweed Hadley & McCloy 1 Chase Manhattan Plz New York NY 10005-1413 Office Phone: 212-530-5349. Office Fax: 212-530-5219. Business E-Mail: tdavis@milbank.com.

DAVIS, TROY ARNOL, reflexologist, hypnotherapist; b. Quitman, Tex., Apr. 5, 1921; Student, Am. Inst. Reflexology, Am. Inst. Med. Hypnoanalysts. Cert. reflexologist; cert. hypnotherapist. Practice reflexology and hypnotherapy, Karnes City, Tex. Contbr. articles to profl. publs.; songwriter "A Country Stayin' Free," 2002, poet. Served with USN, WWII. Recipient Presdl. medal of merit, Presdl. Task Force. Mem. Internat. Soc. Poets. Home: PO Box 295 Karnes City TX 78118-0295

DAVIS, VANESSA ALTHEA, literature and language educator; d. Roland Jr. and Carolyn M. Dawkins; children: Quiana Lakeisha, Robert Earl III. BA, Converse Coll., Spartanburg, S.C., 1995, EdM, 2005. Tchr. asst. Spartanburg City Sch. Dist. #7, SC, 1985—2001, tchr., 2001—. Mem. Spartanburg Focus on Leadership, 2004—. Mem.: Nat. Coun. Tchrs. English. Democrat. Methodist. Home: 117 Celestial St Spartanburg SC 29306

DAVIS, VIVIAN, English language educator; Tchr. Spanish Prairie View Coll., Tex.; secondary sch. tchr. English; prof. English Eastfield Coll., Mesquite, Tex. Mem. Nat. Coun. Tchrs. English (exec. com., dir. Comm. on Lang., mem. Achievements Awards in Writing adv. com., adv. com. People of Color, com. Status and Role of Women in the Profession, leadership roles Conf. Coll. Compsition and Comm.

DAVIS, W. JEREMY, lawyer, dean; b. Pitts., Apr. 13, 1942; s. Winthrop Neuffer and Eleanor (Power) D.; m. Jacqueline Dvoracek, June 11, 1966; children: Jeremy Michael, Sarah Elizabeth. BSBA, U. Denver, 1964, JD, 1970; LLM, Yale U., 1980. Bar: Colo. 1970, N.D. 1973. Pvt. practice law, Denver, 1970-71; asst. prof. U. N.D., Grand Forks, 1971-74, assoc. prof., 1975-82, dean, prof. law, 1983—2002, gen. counsel, 1993-2000, dir. legal affairs, 2000—02; dean, Sutin prof. law Appalachian Sch. of Law, 2003—. With U.S. Army, 1965-68. Fellow Bush Found., 1979-80. Mem. State Bar Assn. N.D. (bd. govs. 1982-2002), N.D. Trial Lawyers Assn. (bd. govs. 1986-2002), Va. State Bar Assn. (assoc.). Home: PO Box 1008 Grundy VA 24614 Office: Rt 83 Slate Creek Rd PO Box 2825 Grundy VA 24614 Office Phone: 276-935-4349. Business E-Mail: wjd@asl.edu.

DAVIS, WAYNE ALTON, computer science educator; b. Ft. Macleod, Alta., Can., Nov. 16, 1931; s. Frederick and Anna Mary (Barr) D.; m. Audrey M. Zorolow, July 17, 1959 (div. 1989); children: Fredrick M., Peter W., Timothy M.; m. Patricia Ruth Syme, Mar. 24, 1990. BSE, George Washington U., 1960; MSc, U. Ottawa, 1963, PhD, 1967. Sci. officer Def. Resch. Bd., Ottawa, Ont., 1960-68; research scientist Dept. Comms., Ottawa, 1968-69; vis. scientist NRC, Ottawa, 1975-76; assoc. prof. U. Alta., Edmonton, 1969-77, prof. computing sci., 1977-91, prof. emeritus, 1991—, acting chmn. computing sci., 1982-83; acting dir. Alta. Centre for Machine Intelligence and Robotics, 1988-89. Lectr. U. Ottawa, 1965-69; sessional lectr. Carleton U., 1967; cons. Editor: The Barrs of Ardenville, 1978; editor Procs. Graphics Interface, 1994, 95, 96, 97, 98. Grantee NRC, 1970-78; rsch. grantee Natural Scis. and Engring. Rsch. Coun., 1978-92; strategic grantee Natural Scis. and Engring. Rsch. Coun., 1981-83; grantee Def. Rsch. Bd., 1974-76; hon. prof. Harbin Shipbldg. Engring. Inst., China, 1985. Mem. Can. Info. Processing Soc. (pres. 1978-79), Can. Human Computer Comms. Soc. (pres. 1981-96), Can. Soc. Computational Study of Intelligence (treas. 1976-86), Faculty Club. Anglican. Home: Box 817 605-21st St Fort Macleod AB Canada T0L 0Z0 Office: U Alta Dept Computing Sci Edmonton AB Canada T6G 2E8 E-mail: davis@cs.ualberta.ca.

DAVIS, WAYNE PITMAN, public relations executive; b. Phillipsburg, Mo., Sept. 9, 1920; s. William Riley and Alice (Pitman) D.; m. Jeanne Frances West, May 28, 1944 (dec. June 1975); children: Kenneth Wayne, Polly Jeanne Davis Montgomery (dec.); m. Ferne Gater Bonomi, Apr. 20, 1991. BA, The Principia Coll., 1939; B of Journalism, U. Mo., 1941; MS, Iowa State U., 1988. Publisher The Moravia (Iowa) Union, 1942-45; mgr. The Mille Lacs Messenger, Isle, Minn., 1946-47; publisher The Seymour (Iowa) Herald, 1947-77; dir. mktg., pub. rels. and sales Iowa State Ctr., Ames, 1977-87; instr. Iowa State U., Ames, 1988-98. Chmn. Bd. Mcpl. Utilities, Seymour, 1969-75; pres. Genoa & Seymour Farmers Mutual Telephone Co., 1954-61; dir., v.p. Ctrl. Iowa Symphony Bd., Ames, 1989-99. 2d lt. U.S. Army, 1945-46, col. USAR, 46-76 Decorated Meritorious Svc. medal; recipient James W. Schwartz Dist. Svc. to Journalism award Greenlee Sch. Journalism and Comm., Iowa State U., 2005 Mem. Pub. Rels Soc. Am. (accredited, sec. ctrl. Iowa chpt. 1980-8, bd. dirs. 1982-85, newsletter editor 1980-82, 1999-2005), Iowa Newspaper Assn. (Iowa master editor-pub., 1971), Iowa Newspaper Found. (bd. dirs. 1989-93, pres. 1992), Reserve Officers Assn., Soc. Profl. Journalists, Am. Legion, Lions (Seymour 1954-77) Avocation: travel. E-mail: wdavis@iastate.edu.

DAVIS, WENDELL, JR., lawyer; b. N.Y.C., June 22, 1933; m. Penelope Case, May 17, 1969; children: Jennifer C., Virginia W. Hartung, Peter T. AB cum laude, Harvard U., 1954, LL.B. cum laude, 1961. Bar: Conn. 1961, N.Y. 1963, U.S. Dist. Ct. (so. and ea. dist.) N.Y. 1964, U.S. Dist. Ct. Conn. 1966, U.S. Ct. Appeals (2d cir.) 1966, U.S Ct. Appeals (5th cir.) 1972, U.S. Supreme Ct. 1973. Law sec. to Justice Charles D. Breitel, N.Y.C., 1964-65; ptnr. Scheuermann & Davis and predecessor firms, N.Y.C., 1975-78, 92-00, Emmet, Marvin & Martin, N.Y.C., 1978-91. Pres. Carnegie Hill-90th St. Inc., 1977-80 Bd. dirs. United Way Larchmont, 1984-91. Lt. USNR, 1957. Mem. Am. Law Inst., Harvard Club, Univ. Club Larchmont (gov. 1991-94, pres. 1993-94). Home: 35 Village Walk Dr Ponte Vedra Beach FL 32082

DAVIS, WESLEY D., psychologist, educator; b. Shreveport, La., May 13, 1934; s. Homer E. and Fannie G. Davis; m. Lora C. Davis, June 10, 1963 (div. Nov. 10, 1970); children: Evon Michelle, Elizabeth Ann. BA, Hardin-Simmons U., Abilene, Texas, 1956; MA, Baylor U., Waco, Texas, 1957; postgrad., U. Colo., 1958—62; PhD, Fla. State U., Tallahassee, 1985. Cert. tchr. Fla. Asst. prof. psychology Hendrix Coll., Conway, Ark., 1957—59; staff psychologist Colo. State Hosp., 1962—63; staff pschologist Leon County Mental Health Ctr., Tallahassee, 1963—70, Atlantic Mental Health Ctr., Virginia Beach, 1970—75; dir., evaluation services Escambia County Pub. Schools, Pensacola, Fla., 1975—. Adj. prof. ednl. leadership U. West Fla., Pensacola, 1990—93; adj. prof. pschology Troy State U., Pensacola, Fla., 1993—98; psychol. evaluations Divsn. Vocat. Rehab., Tallahassee, also Virginia Beach, Va., 1963—75. Contbr. editls. and articles to various jours. Recipient Pres.'s award, Fla. Ednl. Rsch. Coun., 1999, An Apple from the Tchr. award, Escambia Edn. Assn., 2002. Mem.: Fla. Assn. Test Adminstrs. (bd. dirs. 1992—95), Fla. Ednl. Rsch. Coun. (pres. 1999—2000), Fla. Ednl. Rsch. Assn., Phi Kappa Phi. Democrat-Npl. Southern Baptist. Achievements include research citations in The American Psychologist. Office: Escambia County Public Schools 30 E Texar Drive Pensacola FL 32503-2902 E-mail: wdavis@escambia.k12.fl.us.

DAVIS, WILLIAM ALBERT, parks director; b. New Haven, Sept. 10, 1946; s. Arthur Wilson Davis and Dorothy May (Hellyer) Jordan; m. Rebecca Marsden Haile, Apr. 8, 1965; children: William Albert Jr., Anna Catherine. BA in Profl. Arts, Brooks Inst. Photography, 1971; BSBA, San Diego State U., 1980. Photographer, owner Davis-Hixon Photography, Santa Ana, Calif.,

1971-73; photographer Sea World, Inc., San Diego, 1973, sales rep., 1974-76, sales mgr., 1976-78, mktg. mgr. fast food subs., 1978-80, corp. planning assoc., 1980-81; dir. mktg. Sea World Ohio, Aurora, 1981-85, v.p. mktg., 1985-86, pres., 1986-88, Sea World Fla., Orlando, 1988-97; exec. v.p., gen. mgr. Sea World of Calif., 1997-2001; corp. v.p. guest svcs. Busch Entertainment Corp., St. Louis, 2001—03; mng. dir. Universal Mediterranea, Tarragona, Spain, 2003—04; v.p., gen. mgr. Six Flags Marine World, Vallejo, Calif., 2005—. Bd. dirs. Hubbs-Sea World Rsch. Inst., San Diego, Marine Rsch. Ctr., Sea World, Orlando, Calif. Travel and Tourism Commn. Bd. dirs., exec. com. Conv. and Visitors Bur. Orange County, Orlando, 1988-97, pres.-elect, 1990, pres., 1991, chmn., 1992-93; mem. bd. Efficient Transp. for Community Orlando, 1988-97; mem. adv. coun. Dick Pope Sr. Inst. Tourism Studies, Orlando, 1989-97; commr. Fla. Tourism Commn., 1991—; trustee United Arts of Ctrl. Fla., 1992—; mem. U. Ctrl. Fla. Found., 1994-97; mem. White House Com. on Tourism, 1995, mem. exec. com. San Diego Conv. and Visitors Bur., 1997—, Super Bowl XXXII Host com. Staff sgt. USAF, 1965-69, Vietnam. Fellow Am. Assn. Zool. Parks and Aquariums; mem. San Diego C. of C. Roundtable, Brooks Inst. Alumni Assn., Kiwanis (bd. dirs. Aurora club 1985-87, 1st v.p. 1987—) Avocations: golf, photography, family. Office: Six Flags Marine World 2001 Marine World Vallejo CA 94589 Home: 701 Emerald Bay Dr Fairfield CA 94534 Office Phone: 707-556-5202. Business E-Mail: badavis@sftp.com.

DAVIS, WILLIAM ALLISON, II, retired lawyer; b. High Point, N.C., May 2, 1942; s. Robert Dorsey and Frances Elizabeth (Taylor) D.; m. Elizabeth Gray Heefner, June 18, 1966; children: Sarah Scott, Elizabeth Taylor. AB in Econs., U. N.C., 1964; LLB, Duke U., 1967; LLM in Taxation, NYU, 1968; student, NC State U. Sch. Design, 2004—. Bar: N.C. 1967. Assoc. Womble Carlyle Sandridge & Rice, Winston-Salem, N.C., 1968-72, ptnr., 1972—2005. Trustee NC Sch. Arts, Winston-Salem, vice chmn., 1990, chmn., 1992—96, NC Film Coun., 1994—96, Winston-Salem Piedmont Triad Film Commn., 1993—96; trustee The Penland (NC) Sch., 1998—2005, vice chmn., 2000, chmn., 2001—02; trustee Winston Sch. State Univ. Found., 2001—, NC Audubon, 2003—. Democrat. Avocations: hiking, skiing, travel, fishing. Office: Womble Carlyle Sandridge & Rice PO Drawer 84 Winston Salem NC 27101-3828 Office Phone: 336-721-3624.

DAVIS, WILLIAM E., lawyer; b. Northampton County, NC, Mar. 3, 1943; AB, Univ. N.C., 1965; JD, William and Mary, 1968. Mem. Ross, Marsh & Foster, Washington. Adj. prof., trust and estates George Washington Law Sch., Washington; dir. Coun. for Ct. Excellence. Mem.: DC Bar Assn., Md. State Bar Assn., Am. Bar Assn., NC State Bar, George Washington Am. Inn of Ct. (membership chair), DC Superior Ct. Adv. Com. on Probate and Fiduciary Rules, Bar Assn. DC (pres. 2004, sec.), Phi Delta Phi. Office: Ross Marsh & Foster 2001 L St NW Washington DC 20036

DAVIS, WILLIAM EUGENE, federal judge; b. Winfield, Ala., Aug. 18, 1936; s. A. L. and Addie Lee (Lenahan) Davis; m. Celia Chalaron, Oct. 3, 1963. JD, Tulane U., 1960. Bar: La. 1960. Assoc. Phelps Dunbar Marks Claverie & Sims, New Orleans, 1960—64; ptnr. Caffery Duhe & Davis, New Iberia, La., 1964—76; judge U.S. Dist. Ct., Lafayette, La., 1976—83, U.S. Ct. Appeals (5th Cir.), Lafayette, 1983—. Mem.: ABA, Maritime Assn. U.S., La. Bar Assn. Republican. Office: US Ct Appeals 800 Lafayette St Ste 5100 Lafayette LA 70501-6883 Office Phone: 337-593-5280.

DAVIS, WILLIAM GRENVILLE, lawyer, former Canadian government official; b. Brampton, Ont., Can., July 30, 1929; s. Albert Grenville and Vera M. (Hewetson) D.; m. Helen MacPhee, 1953 (dec. 1962); children— Neil, Nancy, Catherine, Ian; m. Kathleen Mackay, 1963; 1 dau., Meg. BA, U. Toronto, 1951; grad., Osgoode Hall Law Sch., 1954; LLD (hon.), Waterloo Luth. U., 1963, Western Ont. U., 1965, U. Toronto, 1967, McMaster U., 1968, Queen's U., 1968, Windsor U., 1969; DU (hon.), Ottawa U., 1980; LHD (hon.), Yeshiva U., N.Y., Nat. U. of Ireland, U. Tel Aviv. Bar: Ont. 1955. Ptnr. Davis, Webb and Hollinrake, Brampton, 1955-59; mem. Provincial Parliament Ont. from Peel Riding, 1959, 63, Peel North Riding, 1967, 71, Brampton Riding, 1975; 2d vice-chmn. Hydro-Electric Power Commn. of Ont., 1961-62; minister of edn. Province of Ont., 1962-71, also minister of univ. affairs, 1964-71, premier, 1971-85; apptd. spl. envoy on acid rain by prime minister of Can., 1985-86; of counsel Torys LLP, Toronto, 1986—. Apptd. mem. Privy Coun. Queen Elizabeth II, 1982—; bd. dirs. 1st Am. Title Ins. Co., Magellan Aerospace Corp., 1st Am. Title Co., BPO Properties Ltd., Home Capital Group Inc. Author: Education in Ontario, 1965, Building an Educated Society, 1816-1966, 1966, other publs. Leader Progressive Conservative Party, 1975-81. Recipient Order of Ont. award; named Companion, Order of Can. Mem. Can. Bar Assn., Ont. Bar Assn., Albany Club, Kiwanis, Masons. Mem. United Ch. Office: Torys LLP TD/Waterhouse Tower Toronto ON Canada M5K 1N2

DAVIS, WILLIAM L., publishing company executive; BA in Polit. Sci., Princeton U., 1965. With Sears, Roebuck and Co.; pres. Appleton Electric; group v.p. Emerson, 1983—85, pres. skills divsn., 1985—88, exec. v.p., 1988—93, sr. exec. v.p., 1993—95, head process control group, 1995; CEO, chmn. R.R. Donnelley and Sons Co., Chgo., 1997—2004.

DAVIS, WILLIAM MAXIE, JR., lawyer; b. Elizabethtown, N.C., June 7, 1932; s. Willie Maxie and Lucy Victoria (Dowless) D.; m. Shirley Jane Smith, Mar. 24, 1987. B. Gen. Edn., U. Nebr., 1965; MA, U. So. Calif., 1970; JD, N.C. Cen. U., 1986. Bar: N.C. 1986, U.S. Dist. Ct. (we., ea. and mid. dists.) N.C., U.S. Ct. Appeals (4th cir.), U.S. Supreme Ct. 1989. Commd. 2d lt. U.S. Air Force, 1958, advanced through grades to lt. col, 1974, ret., 1975; asst. county mgr., personnel officer, dir. of planning, dir. of emergency mgmt. Bladen County, Elizabethtown, 1976-83; asst. pub. defender N.C. 26th Jud. Dist., Charlotte, 1986—; dir. plans, programs U.K. Comm. Region, Eng., 1967-71; chief systems implementations br. USAF, Hdqrs. SAC, 1971-73, chief career devel., assignments for communications-electronics officers, 1973-75. Pres. Help Every Loving Parent, 1988—; county dir. Boy Scouts Am., Bladen County, N.C., 1976; pres. bd. dirs. Vistana SPA Condo Homeowners Assn., 1992—. Profiled in Champion mag., 1992. Mem. N.C. Bar, N.C. Acad. Trial Lawyers, Elizabethtown-White Lake C. of C. (bd. dirs. 1975-77), Nat. Bd. Trial Advocacy (cert. criminal trial advocacy 1993), Am. Legion, VFW, DAV. Home: PO Box 35006 Charlotte NC 28235-5006 Office: Office Pub Defender 720 E 4th St Charlotte NC 28202-2883

DAVIS, WILLIAM TERRY, software engineer, technology manager; b. Canonsburg, Pa., Apr. 28, 1954; s. William Glen and Dorothy Jane (Bright) D. BS, California (Pa.) State Coll., 1976; postgrad., Pa. State U., 1976; MS, U. Pitts., 1979. Teaching asst. Pa. State U., State College, 1976, U. Pitts., 1977-79; sr. engr. Union Switch & Signal R & D, Pitts., 1978-85; product devel. specialist Dun & Bradstreet, Dunsgate, N.Y.C., 1986-91; mgr. software dept. Casco, Signal Ltd., Shanghai, 1991-92; tech. officer Chem. Bank, Banklink, N.Y.C., 1993-94; product devel. specialist Dun & Bradstreet, N.Y.C., 1986-91, sr. application developer, 1994-97, mgr. voice/fax/email delivery sys., 1997—2002; dir. engring. Direct Revenue, LLC, N.Y.C., 2004—. Discussion panel mem. Transpac Symposium, Balt., 1984; spkr. Assn. Am. Railroads, Toronto, Ont., 1983, and Boston, 1984, Internat. Rail Congress, Brussels, 1985. Contbr. articles to profl. jours. Avocations: bicycling, skiing, playing piano, keeping a journal. Home: 450 Clinton St Apt 3B Brooklyn NY 11231-3413 Office: Direct Revenue LLC 107 Grand St 3d Fl New York NY 10013

DAVIS, WYLIE HERMAN, lawyer, educator; b. Macon, Ga., May 26, 1919; s. Wylie Herman and Florine (Burdick) D.; m. June Marie Patterson, Nov. 9, 1957; children: Ann Marie, Neil, John, Alan; children by previous marriage: Louise, June Elizabeth. AB, Mercer U., 1940, LL.B. magna cum laude, JD, Mercer U., 1947; LL.M., Harvard U., 1948. Bar: Ark. 1953, Ill. 1958, Ga. 1968, U.S. Supreme Ct. 1958, U.S. Ct. Mil. Appeals 1958. Instr. English, Mercer U., 1946; asst. prof. law U. Ark., Fayetteville, 1948-50, assoc. prof., 1950-52, prof., 1952-55, 70-72, disting. prof. law, 1972-89, disting. prof. emeritus, 1989—, dean Law Sch., 1973-78, C.W. Oxford lectr., spring 1985; prof. law U. Tex., 1955-56, U. Ill., 1956-67, U. Ga., 1967-70; of counsel Davis, Cox and Wright, Fayetteville, 1976-88. Pvt. practice cons. comml., ins., maritime law and labor arbitration, 1948—; summer research fellow U. Wis., 1962; chmn. drafting com. on contracts multistate bar exam Nat. Conf. Bar Examiners, 1971-96; Earl F. Nelson vis. prof. law U. Mo., Columbia, 1979-80; vis. summer prof. George Washington U., 1952, 64, U. Mich., 1958, U. Utah, 1960, 90, U. N.C., 1968, U. S.C., 1974, U. Ala., 1982, Tex. Tech U., 1983; vis. prof. law McGeorge Sch. Law, U. Pacific, 1988-93, U. N.C., spring 1990; disting. vis. prof. Tex. Wesleyan U. Sch. Law 1993-2000; faculty mem. Nat. Jud. Coll., Reno, 1989. Contbr. articles to legal jours. Bd. govs. Antaeus Inst., 1973-88. Lt. comdr. USNR, 1940-45, PTO; commd. admiral Tex. Navy, 1995. Recipient cert. of recognition Ark. Bar Assn., 1979 Mem.: Order of Barristers (emeritus), Am. Law Inst., Ret. Officers Assn., Order of Coif, Rotary (pres. 1978—79, Paul Harris fellow), Phi Alpha Delta. Home and Office: 580 N Crest Dr Fayetteville AR 72701-3716 *Says an octagenarian named Wylie, "I enjoy living the full life of Riley. But if you want a big win, Eschew hedonism and sin, And never behave crocodiley.".*

DAVIS, YVONNE D., county official; b. Orange, N.J., Sept. 21, 1947; d. William J. and Alice-Ruth Patterson; m. Royce Davis; children: Shannon K., Sarah K. BA in Spanish, Montclair State Coll., 1975; cert. pub. mgmt., Kean Coll., 1992; cert. equal employment, Rutgers U., 1984. Bilingual family svc. worker dept. citizen svcs. Essex County Divsn. Welfare, Newark, 1971—78, supr. family svc., 1978—81, adminstrv. analyst, 1981—83, prin. pers. technician, 1983—86, pers. mgr., supr. prin. pers. technician, 1984—, adminstrv. dep. dir. welfare, 1992—93, dir. dept., 1994—95, pers. mgr., 1995—99, chief pers. and labor rels., 1999, dep. dir. welfare, 2000—. Mem. exec. bd. Essex County Minority Employees Assn., Newark, 1984-85; mem. employment coun. Tng., Inc., Newark; mem. Essex County Adv. Bd. on Status of Women; mem. Coordinating Coun. for Social Svcs., Essex County, N.J.; mem. Essex County Ins. Commn.; mem. Essex County Juvenile Justice Detention Ctr. Policy Reform Task Force, 1997—; active Epilepsy Found. Am., Trenton; vol. Isaiah Ho. Homeless Shelter, 2000. Recipient Excellence in Personnel Mgmt. award Essex County Minority Employees Assn., 1986, Excellence in Spanish award Nat. Assn. Tchrs. Spanish, 1964, 65, Excellence in French award Nat. Assn. Tchrs. French, 1965, Recognition award United Way, 1984-2000; cert. of appreciation U.S. Dept. Treas., 1984, tng. cert. N.J. Div. Civil Rights, 1988. Mem. NAFE, NAACP, Am. Mgmt. Assn., Am. Assn. Affirmative Action, Nat. Assn. Pub. Sector Equal Opportunity Officers, Nat. Assn. Negro Bus. and Profl. Women Inc., Mcpl. Career Women Newark Inc. Democrat. Baptist. Avocations: photography, theater workshop. Office: Essex County Dept Citizen Svcs Divsn Welfare Admin Offices 18 Rector St 9th Fl Newark NJ 07102-4512

DAVIS GREIVELL, JUDITH ANN, artist; b. Bklyn., Dec. 7, 1977; d. Todd Dempsey and Donna Jean Trefren; m. William Rudolph Davis (div.); 1 child, Richard Alexander Hamrick. AA in Psychology, St. Petersburg Jr. Coll., Fla., 1998. Cert. basic interior design/floristry Fla., 1997, massage therapy Fla., 2002. Gemstone mgr. Gold Coast Promotions, Palm Harbor, Fla., 1997—2000; ind. contractor Galardi Enterprises, Tampa, 2000—04, Ybor Secrets, Tampa, 2004—. Over 50 various ceramic sculptures, 1995—98, 28 various acrylic paintings, 2003—04;, author over 60 various poems. Mentor Largo (Fla.) Mid. Sch., 1998; vol. chair Benefit Victims 9-11, St. Petersburg, Fla., 2002. Republican. Buddhist. Avocations: music, theater.

DAVIS-JEROME, EILEEN GEORGE, educational consultant, principal; b. N.Y.C., Nov. 10, 1946; d. Rennie and Flora May (Compton) George; m. Bruce Davis, Aug. 8, 1970 (div. 1978); m. Frantz Jerome, Sept. 7, 1982; 1 child, Thais Davis. BFA, Pratt Inst., 1968; MA, CUNY, 1971, PD, 1990; EdD, Nova Southeastern U., 1998. Lic. ednl. adminstr., prin., instrn. specialist, NY. Tchr. fine arts Herbert Lehman H.S., Bronx, NY, 1971-75; tchr. English, fine arts Jr. H.S. 131, Bronx, 1975-76; tchr. English Jr. H.S. 22, Bronx, 1976-79; tchr. fine arts Andrew Jackson H.S., Cambria Heights, NY, 1979-83, coord. art dept., 1986-92; admissions counselor Fashion Inst. Tech., SUNY, NYC, 1983-85; coord. Queensborough Coll. Project Prize, Bayside, NY, 1991-92; project dir. Andrew Jackson Magnet H.S., Cambria Heights, 1993—, project dir. Humanities and the Arts, 1994—; ednl. adminstr. Queens High Sch. Office, NYC Pub. High Schs., Corona, NY, 1993-94; prin. Humanities and the Arts Magnet H.S., Cambria Heights, 1994—2003. Coord. internat. studies Friends of Jackson H.S., Cambria Heights, 1986-93, equal opportunity coord., 1989-92; exam asst. NYC Bd. Edn., Bd. Examiners, Bklyn., 1983-87; curriculum/career cons. Fashion Inst., SUNY, Detroit, Washington, Phila., 1983-86. Curriculum writer NY State Project ot Implement Career Edn., 1975, NY State Futuring, 1984; proposal writer Magnet Sch. Funding, 1993; author: Resource Book, 1989. Mem., spkr. Cambria Heights Civic Assn., 1983; mem. NY Urban League, NYC; vol. Mayor's Vol. Action/Alpha Sr. Cr., Cambria Heights, 1984; vol. Black Spectrum Theatre Co., 1983-86; mem. coord. coun. h.s. divsn. NYC Bd. Edn., 1997—; v.p. for edn. Madam C.J. Walker Found., 2001—. Named Educator of Yr., NAACP/ACT-S0, NYC, 1992; recipient Recognition award, Black Spectrum Theatre Co., 1983, Speakers award, NYC Bd. Edn. Open Doors, 1983—84, Black Exec. Exch. Program Nat. Urban League, NYC, 1984, Developer Grant award, Impact II Grant, NYC, 1989, Laurelton Club Prol. award, 1996, Disting. Educator award, L.I. br. Nat. Assn. Univ. Women, 2001, Life Membership award, NAACP, NYC, 2001, Excellence in Edn. award, Omega Psi Phi, 2002, Disting. Educator award, Newsday, 2003, Outstanding Citizen citation, NYC Coun., 2003, Performace award, NYC Dept. Edn., NYC Coun. Suprs. and Adminstrs, 2002—03. Mem. ASCD, UN Assn., NY State Art Tchrs. Assn., NYC Art Tchrs. Assn. (v.p., sec. 1983-85, cert. 1983-86), Cultural Heritage Alliance (assoc., Recognition award 1986), Greater Queens Chpt. The Links, Inc., Delta Sigma Theta (chair arts and letters 1991-97, Golden Life award 1991), Phi Delta Kappa (Disting. cert. 1994). Democrat. Episcopalian. Avocations: painting, travel, dance, writing, theater. Office: Magnet HS Humanities and the Arts 20701 116th Ave Jamaica NY 11411-1038

DAVIS-LEWIS, BETTYE, nursing educator; b. Egypt, Tex., Sept. 19, 1939; d. Henry Sr. and Eliza (Baylock) Davis; divorced; children: Kim Michelle, Roderick Trevor. BS, Prarie View A&M U., 1959; BA in Psychology, U. Houston, 1972; MEd, Tex. Southern U., 1974, EdD, 1982. Dir. edn. Houston Internat. Hosp., 1987—; dir. nurses Mental Health & Mental Retardation Auth. Harris County, Houston, 1982-87, Riverside Gen. Hosp., Houston; CEO, owner Diversified Health Care Systems, Inc., Houston, 1985—; asst. clin. prof. psychiat. nursing U. Tex., 1987-88; asst. prof. allied health sci. Tex. So. U., Houton, 1989—. Adj. prof. Coll. Nursing, Prairie View (Tex.) A&M U., 1986—; lectr. in field; leadership extern. Mem. Harris County Coun. Orgns., 1987—; mem. polit. action com. Coalition 100 Black Women, 1988—; founder, mem. Hattie White Aux. br. NAACP, 1988; mem. grievance com. State Bar Tex., 1988—; chmn. S.W. Regional Nat. Black Leadership Initiative on Cancer, 1988—; grad. Leadership Tex.; bd. dirs. Theatre Under the Stars. Recipient Disting. Rsch. award Internat. Soc. Hypertension, Disting. Crystal award, Impact award Wheeler Ave. Bapt. Ch.; fellow Internat. Leadership Forum, Am. Leadership Forum. Fellow Internat. Soc. Hypertension in Blacks; mem. ANA, Nat. Black Nurses Assn. (past mem. bd. dirs., pres.), Sigma Theta Tau, Chi Eta Phi. Home: 9114 Mcafee Dr Houston TX 77031-1104

DAVISON, CALVIN, retired lawyer; b. Norwood, Ohio, Jan. 9, 1932; s. Emberson and Hazel Hildreth (Jenz) D.; m. Carole Ann Sawyer, Apr. 3, 1971; 1 child, Douglas Sawyer. AB cum laude, Miami U., Oxford, Ohio, 1953; JD cum laude, Harvard U., 1959. Bar: D.C. 1959, U.S. Dist. Ct. D.C. 1959, U.S. Ct. Appeals (D.C. cir.) 1959, U.S. Ct. Appeals (6th cir.) 1973, U.S. Ct. Appeals (2d cir.) 1979, U.S. Ct. Appeals (4th cir.) 1991, U.S. Supreme Ct. 1964. Assoc. Pogue & Neal, Washington, 1959-65, ptnr., 1965-67, Jones, Day, Reavis & Pogue, Washington, 1967-79, Crowell & Moring, Washington, 1979-97. Contbr. articles to profl. jours. Lt. j.g. USN, 1953-56 Mem. ABA, D.C. Bar Assn., Univ. Club. Avocations: swimming, tennis. Home: 4950 Quebec St NW Washington DC 20016-3231

DAVISON, CAROLE SAWYER, retired economist; b. Boston, Aug. 25, 1934; d. Charles Edward and Anna (Gannon) S.; m. Calvin Davison, Apr. 3, 1971; 1 child, Douglas Sawyer Davison. BA magna cum laude, Tufts U., 1956, MA, 1957, MALD, 1962; PhD, Fletcher Sch. Law and Diplomacy, 1965. Sr. economist CIA, Washington, 1957-71; pvt. practice Washington, 1971-78, 80-90; sr. economist Inst. for Energy Analysis, Washington, 1978-80, U.S. Dept. of State, 1990—98; ret., 1998. Author: Communist Trade with Developing Countries, 1966, Italy: Estimates of Future Energy/GDP Relationships, 1979, OECD: Energy Supply and Demand in 2000, 1980. Parent rep. Potomac Sch., McLean, Va., 1977, 82, 84, libr. vol., 1983-85; docent Corcoran Gallery Art, Washington, 1972; mem. Middle East Inst., World Affairs Coun.; mem. Washington Area Women's Found. Mem. Am. Econ. Assn., Nat. Economists Club, City Tavern Club, Rehoboth Beach Country Club (Rehoboth, Del.), Wesley Heights Spring Valley Garden Club (pres.), Phi Beta Kappa. Home: 4950 Quebec St NW Washington DC 20016-3231

DAVISON, EDWARD JOSEPH, electrical engineering educator; b. Toronto, Ont., Can., Sept. 12, 1938; s. Maurice and Agnes (Quinlan) D. Assoc., Royal Conservatory of Music, Toronto, 1957; BA, U. Toronto, 1960, MA, 1961; PhD, Cambridge U., 1964, Sc.D., 1977. Asst. prof. dept. elec. engring. U. Toronto, 1964-66, assoc. prof., 1968-74, prof. dept. elec. engring. and computers, 1974-2000, univ. prof., 2001—04, univ. prof. emeritus, 2004—. Asst. prof. dept. elec. engring. and computer scis. U. Calif., Berkeley, 1966-67; dir. Elec. Engring. Consociates Ltd., Toronto, 1977—; elected Hon. prof. of Beijing Inst. of Aeronautics and Astronautics, 1986; pres. Elec. Engring. Consociates, Ltd., Toronto, 1997-99. Assoc. editor: Jour. Automatica, 1974-87, Jour. Large Scale Systems: Theory and Applications, 1979-90, Jour. Optimal Control and Methods, 1983—; cons. editor IEEE Transactions on Automatic Control, 1985. Contbr. numerous articles infield to profl. jours. Athlone fellow, 1961-63; E.W.R. Steacie Meml. fellow, 1974-77; Killam Rsch. fellow, 1979-80, 81-83; named to U. Toronto Engring. Alumni Hall of Distinction, 2003; recipient Killam Engring. prize Can. Coun., 2003. Fellow Royal Soc. Can., IEEE (v.p. Control Systems Soc. 1979-80, mem. adminstrv. com. 1977-83, dir. Soc. mag. 1980-82, assoc. editor jour. Trans. on Automatic Control 1974-76, editl. adv. bd. IEEE Procs. 1980-81, Centennial medal 1984, elected disting. mem. 1984), Can. Acad. Engring., Internat. Fedn. Automatic Control (vice chmn. theory com. 1978-87, chmn. 87-90, Quazza medal 1993, vice chmn. tech. bd. 1990-93, coun. mem. 1990-96, vice chmn. IFAC policy com. 1996-99, IFAC adminstrv. and fin. com. 1999-2005, IFAC Outstanding Mem. Svc. award 1996); mem. IEEE Control Systems Soc. (pres.-elect 1982-83, pres. 1983-84, Hendrik W. Bode Lectr. prize 1997), Profl. Engrs. Ont. (cons. engr. 1979—),Russian Acad. Nonlinear Scis. Office: U Toronto Dept Elec Engring-Computers Toronto ON Canada M5S 1A4 Business E-Mail: ted@control.utoronto.ca.

DAVISON, ELIZABETH JANE LINTON, education educator; b. Las Cruces, N.Mex., Mar. 9, 1931; d. Melvy Edgar Linton and Clara Virginia Hale; m. Curwood Lyman Davison, Jan. 29, 1954; 1 child, Lawrence. BS, N.Mex. State U., 1957; postgrad., U. N.Mex.; Grad., Norris Sch. Real Estate, Albuquerque, 1984. Cert. tchr., N.Mex., Oreg.; cert. real estate agt., N.Mex., appraiser. Sec., treas. C.L. Davison, Md., Pa., 1975—88, Clovis, N.Mex., 1975—88; ind. real estate contractor Century 21, Las Cruces, 1984—85; ret. Albuquerque Pub. Schs., 1957—60, 1964—68; pres. Sun Dial Enterprises, 1984—95; tchr. Beaverton Pub. Schs., 1960—64. Mem. NEA, Legis. Coun., N.Mex. Albuquerque Classroom Tchrs. Inter-City Coun. (v.p.), AAUW, Phi Delta Kappa (Svc. key). Home: 3013 Cumberland Dr San Angelo TX 76904-6108

DAVISON, HELEN IRENE, secondary school educator, counseling administrator; b. Oskaloosa, Iowa, Dec. 19, 1926; d. Grover C. and Beulah (Williams) Hawk; m. Walter Francis Davison, June 20, 1953 (div.); 1 child, Linda Ellen. BS in Zoology, Iowa State U., 1948; MS in Biol. Sci., U. Chgo., 1951; MA in Ednl. Psychology and Counseling, Calif. State U., Northridge, 1985. Med. rsch. technician U. Chgo. Med. Sch., 1951-53; tchr. sci. Lane High Sch., Charlottesville, Va., 1953-55; med. rsch. asst. U. Va. Med. Sch., Charlottesville, 1955-56, U. Mich., Ann Arbor, 1956-60; tchr. sci. Monroe High Sch., North Hills, Calif., 1966-98, chmn. sci. dept., 1990-91, sch. site coun., 1993-94, ret., 1998. Rsch. technician Los Alamos Sci. Labs., summer 1954; part-time counselor psychotherapy Forte Found., Encino, Calif., 1987-92, Tarzana, Calif., 1993-2000, Northridge, Calif., 2000-04. V.p. San Fernando Valley chpt. Am. Field Svc., 1980-81; vol. counselor Planned Parenthood Am., L.A., 1982-88. NSF fellow, 1985-86. Mem. Calif. Tchrs. Assn., Calif. Assn. Marriage and Family Therapists, Iowa Acad. Sci. (assoc.), AAUW. Avocations: travel, history, cooking.

DAVISON, JOHN S., JR., retired state trooper; b. Springfield, Ill., June 28, 1945; s. John S. Davison Sr. and Stella Davidson; m. Marilyn L. Cook, Nov. 18, 1972; children: Paul Davidson, Nathon Davidson, Melissa Davidson, John C. Davidson, William Davidson, Jeremy Davidson, Chad Davidson, Michel Davidson, Megan Davidson, Melinda Davidson. Degree in electronics, Devry Tech., 1975. State trooper Ill. State Police, Ill., 1968. Pres. Stop Arm Violation Edn. and Enforcement, Springfield, Ill. With USNR, 1965—95. Recipient Salute for Sch. Safety award, Springfield Sch. Bd., 2004. Mem.: Faternal Order of Police, Knights of Columbus. Roman Catholic. Home: 12171 Atlantic Dr Pawnee IL 62558 Office: Stop Arm Violation Edn and Enforcement 12171 Atlantic Dr Pawnee IL 62558 Office Phone: 217-415-6151. E-mail: cop@family-net.net.

DAVISON, KIM M., elementary school educator; b. Buffalo, Dec. 20, 1955; d. George Turpie and Ida Lorraine (Ramsey) D. BS, Daemen Coll., Buffalo, 1978; MA, Mich. State U., 1986. Cert. tchr. Tchr. Calasanctius Sch., Buffalo, 1979-81, coord. enrichment program, 1980-81; tchr., grade level coord. The Am. Sch. Guatemala, 1981-85; tchr. Kalamazoo (Mich.) Pub. Schs., 1986—. Founding mem. Learning to Give. Producer, editor video What I Want to Be When I Grow Up, 1988. Singer St. Augustine's Cathedral, Kalamazoo, 1986—, Kalamazoo Community Chorale, 1988—. Recipient Excellence in Edn. award Kalamazoo County Excellence in Edn. Found., 1989, 92, Presdl. award, 1991; Kalamazoo Pub. Edn. Found. mini-grantee, 1988, 90, 91, Mich. Dept. Edn. mini grantee, 1991. Roman Catholic. Avocations: travel, recycling, video production, photography, singing. Office: Kalamazoo Pub Schs 1220 Howard St Kalamazoo MI 49008-1871

DAVISON, RICHARD, internist, educator; b. Buenos Aires, Nov. 7, 1937; came to U.S., 1966; s. Charles Edward and Matilde (Muller) D.; m. Lisette Glusberg, July 1, 1965; 1 child, Sebastian. MD, U. Buenos Aires, 1963. Diplomate Am. Bd. Internal Medicine, Am. Bd. Cardiovascular Diseases, Am. Bd. Critical Care Medicine. Intern Inst. Med. Rsch., Buenos Aires, 1964; resident Passavant Meml. Hosp., Chgo., 1966-68, chief resident, 1968-69; cardiology fellowship VA Hosp., Chgo., 1969-71; asst. prof. Northwestern U. Sch. Medicine, Chgo., 1973-81, assoc. prof., 1981—, chief sect. critical care medicine, 1982—2003, chief sect. cardiology, 1988-92; dir. med. intensive care area Northwestern Meml. Hosp., Chgo., 1973—2003. Contbr. articles to profl. jours. Recipient Thrombolysis in Myocardial Infarction award NIH. Fellow Am. Coll. Cardiology, Am. Coll. Physicians, Council of Clin. Cardiology (Am. Heart. Assn.), Soc. Critical Care Medicine; mem. Am. Heart Assn., Alpha Omega Alpha. Office: Northwestern Meml Hosp Divsn Critical Care 201 E Huron St Galter 10-240 Chicago IL 60611-2908 Office Phone: 312-695-2745.

DAVISSON, DARRELL DEAN, art educator; b. Long Beach, Calif., July 27, 1937; s. Byron Dale and Edythe L. Walker Davisson; children: Burton, Melissa, Melanie, Tiffany. BA, U. Santa Barbara, 1960; MA, UCLA, 1965; PhD, Johns Hopkins U., 1971. Instr. UCLA, 1965; asst. prof. Colo. Coll., Colorado Springs, 1965—69, U. Ariz., Tucson, 1971—74, U. Tex., Austin, 1974—76, U. Calif. San Diego, La Jolla, 1976—82; assoc. prof. U. Saskatchewan, Saskatoon, Canada, 1970—71; adj. prof. Antelope Valley Coll., Lancaster, Calif., 1998—2005. Author: (book) Art After the Bomb, 2004; contbr. articles to profl. jours. and ency. in field. Recipient Calif. Design award, VHHS, Calif., 1954, Travel award, UCLA Art Coun.; fellowship, Press Found., Johns Hopkins U., 1970. Mem.: ACLU, Amnesty Internat., Sierra Club. Avocations: writing, designing.

DAVLIN, CHRISTINA, education educator; PhD, U. Utah, 2000. Cert. athletic trainer Nat. Athletic Trainers' Assn. Bd. Cert., 1994. Asst. prof. Xavier U., Cin., 2000—. Office: Xavier Univ 3800 Victory Pky Cincinnati OH 45207-6312 Office Phone: 513-745-3430. E-mail: davlin@xavier.edu.

DAVOLI, SUSAN ELIZABETH, music educator; b. Syracuse, N.Y., Nov. 1, 1979; d. Charles William and Jeanine Marie Davoli. BS in Music Edn., Gettysburg Coll., 2001; MusM in Music Edn., SUNY, Potsdam, 2003. Dir. residence hall SUNY, Potsdam, NY, 2001—03; tchr. elem. gen. and vocal music Monticello Ctrl. Sch. dist., 2003—04; tchr. mid. sch. gen. music Utica City Sch. Dist., 2004—. Rec. curriculum summer task force Monticello Ctrl. Sch. Dist., 2004. Alumni rep. Gettysburg Coll. Key Alumni Resource Effort Program, Pa., 2001—. Grantee, Utica Tchr. Ctr., 2004. Mem.: N.Y. Sch. Music Assn., Music Educators Nat. Conf. Avocations: singing, playing musical instruments, hiking, reading. Office: Utica Sch Dist John F Kennedy Mid Sch Deerfield Dr E Utica NY 13502

DAVOREN, STEVEN MICHAEL, marketing professional, psychologist; b. NYC, Nov. 29, 1968; s. Michael Thomas and Helen Adele Davoren. BS in Mktg., Seton Hall U., 1992, MA in Psychol. Studies, 1996; PhD in Natural Health, Clayton Coll., 2004. Cert. crisis counselor Contact We Care, Inc. Asst. project dir. Statis. Rsch., Inc., Westfield, NJ, 1985—93; market rsch. cons. Fortune 500 Corps., N.Y.C., 1993—95; project dir. FRC Rsch. Corp., N.Y.C., 1996—97; primary rsch. mgr. Blue Cross Blue Shield, Newark, 1998—2000; rsch. cons. Blue Cross Blue Shield and JP Morgan, N.Y.C., 2000—. Soup kitchen server St. Joseph's Social Svc. Ctr., Elizabeth, NJ, 1994—95; grant proposal writer Westfield Cmty. Ctr., NJ, 1995—96. Mem.: APA (assoc.), Nat. Campaign for Tolerance (founding mem. 2005), Am. Mktg. Assn. Roman Catholic. Avocations: running, music, comparative religion, animals, nature walks. Home: 641 Maye St Westfield NJ 07090

DAVY, MICHAEL FRANCIS, civil engineer, consultant; b. Springfield, Mo., Mar. 24, 1946; s. Philip Sheridan and Caecilia Magdelen (Thiemann) D.; m. Joyce Kay Young, Aug. 17, 1968; children: Mark Sheridan, Katherine Ann, Jennifer Mary. BS, U. Wis., 1969. Diplomate Am. Acad. Environ. Engrs. Project engr. Davy Engring. Co., La Crosse, Wis., 1969-74, v.p., 1975-88; mgr. Davy Labs., La Crosse, 1975—; pres. Davy Engring. Co., La Crosse, 1989—. Dir. St. Francis Med. Ctr., 1993-95, Wis. Mfrs. and Commerce, 1995-98, Wells Fargo Bank-LaCrosse, 1998—. Mem. Gov.'s Clean Water Task Force, 1988—89; bd. dirs. Gateway Area coun. Boy Scouts Am., La Crosse, 1973—, pres. exec. bd., 1989—91; bd. dirs. La Crosse Family YMCA, 2000—03. Recipient Silver Beaver award Gateway Area Coun. Boys Scouts Am., 1987. Mem. NSPE (nat. bd. dirs. 1987-93), ASCE (Young Engr. Yr. 1980), Wis. Soc. Profl. Engrs. (Engr. Yr. 1987,pres. 1984-85, sec. 1980-82, Young Engr. Yr. 1976), Wis. Assn. Consulting Engrs. (bd. dirs. 1987-90), Profl. Engrs. in Pvt. Practice (vice chmn. 1981-83, Merit award 1990), LaCrosse Country Club (dir. 1993-99, pres. 1997-99). Roman Catholic. Avocations: swimming, boating. Home: 615 23rd St N La Crosse WI 54601-3853 Office: Davy Engring Co 115 6th St S La Crosse WI 54601-4153

DAVY, WILLIAM ALLEN, telecommunciations account executive; b. Montpelier, Vt., July 23, 1955; s. William Allen and Lorraine Mae (Pariezo) D.; m. Katherine Gourdine-Davy, Jan 14. 1999; children: Jordan Katherine, Jaden Gourdine. BBA, Lynn U., Boca Raton, 1978. Technician V.R. Dental Studio, Falls Church, Va., 1983-87; acct. rep. AT&T, Reston, Va., 1987-88, sys. cons. Vienna, Va., 1988-91, design specialist Oakton, Va., 1991-96; sr. design specialist Lucent Tech., Reston, Va., 1996-97, sr. tech. rep., 1997-2000; sr. acct. exec. Expanets, Reston, Va., 2000—01; strategic account mgr. Verizon, Arlington, Va., 2004—. Pres. Jordan Pub., Reston. Va., 1999—. Author: Let Justice Be Done, 1999. Recipient Grand Slam award, AT&T, 1990. Mem. Soc. Profl. Journalists, Nat. Writers Union. Office: # 369 11654 Plaza America Dr Reston VA 20190 E-mail: w.davy@att.net.

DAW, HAROLD JOHN, lawyer, director; b. N.Y.C., July 6, 1926; s. Joseph and Dorothy (Dannenberg) D.; m. Meryl Kann, Sept. 25, 1960. AB, Union Coll., 1950; LL.B., Columbia U., 1954. Bar: N.Y. 1955. Assoc. Shearman & Sterling, N.Y.C., 1954-62, ptnr., 1962-89. Served with USN, 1944-46, ETO. Mem. ABA, N.Y. State Bar Assn., Bar Assn. City N.Y., Phi Beta Kappa Clubs: University. Home: 15 Buena Vista Dr Westport CT 06880-6602

DAW, MURRAY S., physics professor; BS in Physics, U. Florida, 1976; PhD in Physics, Calif. Inst. Tech., 1981. Mem. tech. staff computational materials sci. dept. Sandia Nat. Labs, Livermore, Calif., 1981—89, disting. mem. tech. staff computational materials sci. dept., 1989—94; sr. scientist, section leader computational materials group Motorola, 1998—2000; prof. physics & astronomy dept. Clemson U., 1994—, R. A. Bowen prof. physics, 2003—. Recipient Sustained Outstanding Rsch. award, Dept. of Energy, 1987, Sandia award for excellence, 1990. Fellow: Am. Acad. Arts & Sciences; mem.: Am. Physical Soc. Office: Clemson U Dept Physics & Astronomy 202A Kinard Labs Clemson SC 29634-1911*

DAWDY, DORIS OSTRANDER, writer; d. Archie and Lydia (Matz) Ostrander; m. David R. Dawdy, Feb. 21, 1951; 1 child, Barbara Dahl. Student music, MacPhail Sch. Music, Mpls. Cons. in field of writing. Composer: I Keep Telling Myself, 1947; author: Artists of the American West, vols. I, II, III, reprinted 1987, Congress in its Wisdom: The Bureau of Reclamation and the Public Interest, 1989, George Montague Wheeler: The Man and the Myth, 1993; editor: A Voice in Her Tribe, 1980, 3d edit. 1984, The Wyant Diary/An Artist with the Wheeler Survey, 1980, others. Mem. Mus. Soc. San Francisco, San Francisco Mus. and Hist. Soc., Nat. Mus. Women in Arts

DAWDY, W. DAVID, pediatrician; b. Highland, Ill., Aug. 9, 1940; s. William Dressor and Florine (Kersey) D.; m. Janice Finke; children: Michael, Cathleen. BA in chemistry, Greenville (Ill.) Coll., 1962; MD, U. Ill., Chgo., 1966. Diplomate Am. Bd. Pediatrics. Resident in pediatrics Columbus (Ohio) Children's Hosp., 1969-71; Pvt. practice Westerville, Ohio, 1972—; rotating intern Wayne County HOsp., Eloise, Mich., 1996-97. Cons. Access Health, Broomfield, Colo., 1993—, Physician Continuing Med. Edn., 1990—. Capt. U.S. Army, 1967-69. Mem. Ohio State Med. Assn. (edn. chmn. 1997—), Children's Practicing Pediatricians (pres. 1999, chmn. bd. 2000). Free Methodist. Avocations: tennis, bicycle touring. Office: Associated Pediatrics Inc 801 Eastwind Dr Westerville OH 43081-3303

DAWES, DOMINIQUE, Olympic athlete; b. Silver Spring, Md., Nov. 20, 1976; BS, U. Md., 1999. Mem. U.S. Olympic Team, Barcelona, 1992, Atlanta, 1996. Actor: (TV series) The Jersey; (Broadway plays) Grease. Named U.S.A. Gymnastics Athlete of Yr., 1993, Sportsperson of Yr., USA Gymnastics, 1994, 3d pl. team, Olympic Games, Barcelona, Spain, 1992, 2d pl. all around and floor exercise, 1st in vault and balance beam, 3d uneven bars, Coca Cola Nat. Championships, Salt Lake City, 1993, 2d in uneven bars and balance beam, World Gymnastics Championships, Birmingham, Eng., 1993, 1st pl. in all around, vault, balance beam and floor exercise, McDonald's Am. Cup, Orlando, Fla., 1994, 1st pl. in all around, vault, uneven bars, balance beam and floor exercise, Cola Cola Nat. Championships, Nashville, 1994, 1st pl. in all around, NationsBank World Team Trials, Richmond, Va., 1994, 2d pl. team, World Championships, Dortmund, Germany, 1994, 1st pl. in uneven bars and floor exercise, 3d pl. in balance beam, Coca Cola Nat. Championships, New Orleans, 1995; recipient Arch McDonald award, Touchdown Club Washington, 1995, McDonald's Balancing It All award, 1995, Harry P. Iba Citizen Athlete award, 1995, Gold medal Team Competition, Olympic Games, Atlanta, 1996. Avocations: reading, dance, acting. Office: care USA Gymnastics Pan Am Plz 201 S Capitol Ave Ste 300 Indianapolis IN 46225-1058*

DAWES, ROBERT LEO, mathematician, consultant; b. Big Spring, Tex., Mar. 5, 1945; s. William Robert and Josephine Melloo (Duflot) D.; m. Rosemary Mae Nelson, Oct. 10, 1970; children: Sara Michelle, Karen Melissa. BS in Math., Tex. Tech U., 1966, MS in Math., 1968; PhD in Math., U. Tex., 1977. Mem. tech. staff Tex. Instruments, Inc., Dallas, 1975-81; sr. specialist E-Systems, Inc., Garland, Tex., 1981-85; pres. Martingale Rsch. Corp., Allen, Tex., 1985-94, QED Corp., Bedford, Tex., 1995—; asst. prof. math. Hampton (Va.) U., 2002—04. Founder, chair Metroplex Inst. Neural Dynamics, Dallas, 1986-90. Mem. city coun. City of Parker (Tex.), 1987-99. Lt. USNR, 1968-71. Mem. IEEE (chmn. Dallas chpt. Acoustics, Speech and Signal Processing Soc. 1988), Internat. Neural Network Soc. (chair math. and theory spl. interest group 1990-92). Avocation: quantum mechanics. Home: 2217 Bedford Cir Bedford TX 76021

DAWES, ROBYN MASON, psychology professor; b. Pitts., July 23, 1936; s. Norman H. and Zita (Hill) D.; children by previous marriage: Jennifer, Molly. BA in Philosophy, Harvard U., 1958; MA in Clin. Psychology, U. Mich., 1960, PhD in Math. Psychology, 1963; PhD (hon.), U. Goteborg, Sweden, 1999. Rschr. Ann Arbor (Mich.) VA Hosp., 1962-67; lectr. U. Mich., Ann Arbor, 1963-66, asst. prof., 1966-67; assoc. prof. psychology U. Oreg., Eugene, 1967-71, prof., 1971-85, co-head dept. psychology, 1972-73, acting head, 1979-80, head, 1981-85; prof. psychology Carnegie Mellon U., 1985—, head dept. social and decision scis., 1985-90, 95-96, univ. prof., 1992—, Charles J. Queenan Jr. univ. prof., 1997—. Rsch. scientist Oreg. Rsch. Inst., Eugene, 1967-76, v.p., 1973-74; NATO lectr., The Hague, The Netherlands, 1968; vis. prof. U. Calif., Santa Barbara, 1975-75; cons. numerous insts. and orgns.; Olof Palme vis. prof. U. Stockholm and U. Goteborg, 1999. Author: Fundamentals of Attitude Measurement, 1972, Rational Choice in an Uncertain World, 1988 (William James book award div. gen. psychology Am. Psychol. Assn.), House of Cards: Psychology and Psychotherapy Built on Myth, 1994, paperback edit., 1996, Irrationality in Everyday Life, How Pseudo-Scientists, Lunatics and the Rest of Us Systematically Fail to Think Rationally, 2001, paperback edit., 2003; co-author: (with C.H. Coombs and A. Tversky) Mathematical Psychology: An Elementary Introduction, 1970, (with R. Hastie) Rational Choice in an Uncertain World, (2d edition), 2001; contbr. articles to profl. jours; mem. editl. bds., cons numerous profl. jours. and publs. Rackham Summer fellow, 1961, James McKean Cattell Sabbatical fellow, 1978-79; del. NAS, USA-USSR Acad. Scis. Seminar Decision Making, Moscow-Tblisi, USSR, 1979; fellow Ctr. Advanced Study in Behavioral Scis., 1980-81, Ctr. for Rationality and Interactive Decision Making The Hebrew U. of Jerusalem, 1994. Fellow AAAS, Am. Acad. Arts and Scis., Am. Psychol. Soc., Am. Assn. Applied and Preventive Psychology (exec. bd. 1991—); mem. Oreg. Psychol. Assn. (pres. 1984-85), Am. Statis. Assn., Pub. Choice Soc., Psychometric Soc., West Coast Small Group Rsch. Soc. (pres. 1977-78), Judgement and Decision Making Rsch. Soc. (chmn. exec. bd. 1988, exec. bd. 1994-95), Soc. Advancement of Socio-Econs. (exec. bd. 1991-98—), Sigma Xi, Phi Kappa Phi (sr.). Office: Carnegie Mellon U Dept Social & Decision Scis Pittsburgh PA 15213 Office Phone: 412-268-2055. *It took a while to understand the wisdom of Herodotus to "take good counsel with (ourselves); for even if the event turns out contrary to one's hopes, still one's decision was right"--always drawing support from the knowledge that the future is uncertain.*

DAWISHA, ADEED, political science professor; b. Baghdad, Nov. 2, 1944; m. Karen Hurst, Jan. 1, 1972; children: Nadia, Emile. PhD, London Sch. Econs., 1974. Lectr. Lancaster U., England, 1974—76, Keele U., Stoke-on-Trent, England, 1977—78; sr. rsch. assoc. Internat. Inst. Strategic Studies, London, 1978—79; dep. dir. studies Royal Inst. Internat. Affairs, London, 1979—85; prof. George Mason U., Fairfax, Va., 1985—2000, Miami U., 2000—. Con. Dept. of State, Wash. Author: (book) Arab Nationalism in the Twentieth Century, The Arab Radicals, Syria and the Lebanese Crisis, Egypt in the Arab World; editor: The Making of Foreign Policy in Russia and the New States of Eurasia, Beyond Coercion: The Durability of the Arab State, Islam in Foreign Policy, The Soviet Union in the Middle East. Recipient Fulbright fellow, 1990—91; Fellow, Social Sci. Rsch. Coun., Eng., 1981, Consulting fellow, Coun. Fgn. Rels., 1984—85, fellow, Woodrow Wison Internat. Ctr. Scholars, 1985—86, scholar, Carnegie, 2004—05. Mem.: Mid. East Studies Assn., Mid. East Inst., Am. Hist. Assn., Am. Polit. Sci. Assn. Home: 478 White Oak Dr Oxford OH 45056 Office: Polit Sci Miami U High St Oxford OH 45056 Office Phone: 513-529-2332. Personal E-mail: dawisha@muohio.edu.

DAWKINS, MARVA PHYLLIS, psychologist, educator; b. Jacksonville, Fla., Apr. 12, 1948; d. Ralph and Altamese (Padgett) Dawkins. Student U. Freiburg, Germany, 1969—70; BS Stetson U., 1971, MS Fla. State U., 1972, PhD Fla. State U., 1975. Registered psychologist Ill. Rsch. asst. Fla. State U., Tallahassee, 1970—72; clin. intern dpt. psychology Presbyn.-St. Luke's Med. Ctr., 1973—74; clin. intern dept. mental health Mile Square Health Ctr., Chgo., 1973—74, staff psychologist, dir. aftercare treatment program dept. mental health, 1974—75, staff psychologist, coord. devel. disabilities program, 1976—79; asst. prof. psychology U. N. Fla., Jacksonville, 1975—76, Rush U.-Presbyn. St. Luke's Med. Ctr., Chgo., 1976—; pvt. practice clin. psychology, 1977—. Exec. dir. Inst. Cmty. Mental Health, 1979—89; cons. safety evaluation program Isaac Ray Ctr., 1986—91; dir. Ctr. Applied Psychology and Forensic Studies, 1991—; psychology cons. Disability Policy Br. Social Security Adminstrn., Chgo., 1980—; med. expert Social Security Adminstrn., Chgo., 1995—; cons. in field. Mem.: APA, Assn. Black Psychologists. Office Phone: 312-236-1498.

DAWLEY, DAVID DANIEL, finance educator; b. Detroit, Jan. 31, 1960; m. Tracy Lynn Nicholson, Oct. 5, 1962; children: Allison, Daniel. BS, Clemson U., S.C., 1983; MBA, U. of Ctrl. Fla., 1995; PhD, Fla. State U., 1999. Prof. W.Va. U., Morgantown, 2000—. Contbr. articles to profl. jours. Fellow Tchg. fellow, Fla. State U., 1996—99. Mem.: Delta Gamma Sigma (hon.; faculty advisor 2000—04); mem.: Phi Kappa Phi, Beta Sigma Gamma (life). Home: 3304 Fox Run Ct Morgantown WV 26508 Office: West Virginia University Coll of Business PO Box 6025 Morgantown WV 26506 Personal E-mail: david.dawley@mail.wvu.edu.

DAWN, CLARENCE ERNEST, historian, educator; b. Chattanooga, Dec. 6, 1918; s. Fred Hartman and Hettie Lou (Gibson) D.; m. Pansie Mozelle Dooley, July 8, 1944 (dec.); children: Julia Anne, Carolyn Louise. BA, U. Chattanooga, 1941; MA, Princeton U., 1947, PhD, 1948. Instr. history U. Ill., Urbana, 1949-52, asst. prof., 1952-55, assoc. prof., 1955-60, prof., 1960—, prof. emeritus, 1989—; dir. U. Ill. Tehran Rsch. Unit, Iran, 1972-74. Fellow Inst. Advanced Studies, Hebrew U., Jerusalem, 1981-82 Author: From Ottomanism to Arabism, 1973; contbr. articles to profl. jours. Served with AUS, 1942-46, with U.S. Army, 1951-52. Social Sci. Rsch. Coun. World Area fellow, 1948-49; fellow joint com. on Near and Mid. East Social Sci. Rsch. Coun. and Am. Coun. Learned Socs., 1966-67; Fulbright-Hays fellow, 1966-67. Mem. Mid. East Studies Assn., Mid. East Inst. Home: 1628 72d Ave SE Mercer Island WA 98040

DAWODU, SEGUN TOYIN, sports medicine physician, physiatrist; b. Ilorin, Nigeria, Oct. 13, 1960; arrived in U.S., 1995; s. Michael O. Dawodu and Sarat Dawodu-Bamidele; m. Egbe Monisola Osifo; 1 child, Zainab; m. Florence O. Aigbogun, Oct. 2, 1992 (div. June 23, 1996); children: Osamudiamen, Sarat. MD, U. Ibadan, Nigeria, 1984. Diplomate with subsplty. in pain medicine Am. Bd. Phys. Medicine And Rehab., Am. Bd. Electrodiagnostic Medicine, Royal Coll. Surgeons of Edinburgh, Faculty of Med. Informatics, Am. Bd. Ind. Med. Examiners, cert. Fedn. State Med. Bds.; Ednl. Commn. for Fgn. Med. Grads. Resident physician orthop. surgery and trauma Royal Coll. Surgeons, London, 1992—96; resident physician phys. medicine and rehab. Albany (N.Y.) Med. Ctr., 1996—2000; clin. instr., attending physician traumatic brain injury and stroke rehab. Mt. Sinai Med. Ctr., N.Y.C., 2000—01; med. dir., sole proprietor Pmrehab Pain and Sports Medicine Assocs., Herndon, Va., 2001—. Module tutor, med. informatics Royal Coll. Surgeons Edinburgh, Scotland, 2002—; mem. instn. ethics com. Albany Med. Ctr., 1997, mem. internal rev. com. for urology dept., 99, chief resident dept. phys. medicine and rehab., 1999—2000. Contbr. articles to profl. jours. Asst. sec. Assn. Resident Doctors, U. Benin Tchg. Hosp., Benin-City, Nigeria, 1984—85; pub. rels. officer Nigerian Med. Students Assn., Lagos, 1981—82; Nigerian rep. Internat. Fedn. Med. Students' Assns. Confs., Austria, 1981—83. Named Outstanding Pub. Rels. Officer, Nigerian Med. Students Assn., 1982; scholar Nat. Physical Medicine and Rehab. scholar, Rhone-Poulenc Rhone Pharms., 1999. Fellow: Am. Acad. Electrodiagnostic Medicine, Am. Acad. Phys. Medicine and Rehab.; mem.: AMA, Internat. Spinal Injection Soc., Fairfax County Med. Soc., Internat. Soc. Phys. Medicine and Rehab., Am. Med. Informatics Assn., Rosicrucian Order (Amorc), Am. Mensa. Office: Pmrehab Pain & Sports Medicine Associate 3048 Mitchellville Rd Bowie MD 20716 Office Phone: 301-218-2000. Personal E-mail: segun@dawodu.com. Business E-Mail: drdawodu@pmrehab.com.

DAWOOD, MOHAMED YUSOFF, obstetrician, gynecologist; b. Singapore, Sept. 13, 1943; came to U.S., 1974; s. Sheikh and Fatimah (Hussein) D.; m. Firyal Sultana Khan, July 14, 1978; children: Fatimah Sultana, Fauzia Sultana, Firdaus Sultana, Hassan Yusoff. MB, ChB, U. Sheffield, 1968, MD, 1974; M of Medicine with gold medal, U. Singapore, 1972. Diplomate Am. Bd. Obstetrics and Gynecology, Am. Bd. Reproductive Endocrinology. Lectr. U. Singapore, 1973—74; first asst. ob-gyn. U. Melbourne, Australia, 1974; from instr. to assoc. prof. ob-gyn. Cornell U. Med. Coll., N.Y.C., 1974—79; prof. ob-gyn. U. Ill., Chgo., 1979—90; Berel Held prof. ob-gyn. and reproductive scis. U. Tex. Med. Sch., Houston, 1990—2001; prof., chmn. dept. ob-gyn. Morehouse Sch. Medicine, Atlanta, 2001—03; prof., chmn. dept. ob-gyn, Sanger chair in family planning and reproductive physiology, prof. physiology W. Va. U. Sch. Medicine, 2004—. Mem. study sect. NIH Child Health and Human Devel., 2000—04, chair, 2002—04; coun. mem. Soc. Gynecol. Investigation, 2004—; cons.; editl. cons.; reviewer in field. Author: Green's Gynecology, 1990, Dysmenorrhea, 1981, Premenstrual Syndrome and Dysmenorrhea, 1985, Oxytocin, vol. 2, 1984, Prostaglandin Inhibition in Obstetrics and Gynecology, 1983; mem. editl. bd. Fertility and Sterility, 2000—, Current Obstetrics and Gynecology, 1988-2000; contbr. articles to profl. jours. Recipient Gold medal Jaycee Jr. C. of C. Singapore, 1973. Fellow ACS, ACOG, Internat. Coll. Surgeons, Am. Gynecol. & Obstet. Soc., Royal Coll. Ob-Gyn. (Edgar Gentilli prize 1974, Gold medal 1973); mem. Endocrine Soc. Achievements include research in steroid endocrinology and chemotherapy of trophablastic diseases, prostaglandins in the causation of menstrual cramps and relief by blocking prostaglandins; role of oxytocin in human parturition, bone-depleting effect of GnRH agonists during treatment of endometriosis; presence of neurohypophyseal peptides in primate and human ovaries; regulation of primate corpus luteum. Office: W Va Univ Sch Medicine Dept Ob-Gyn PO Box 9186 Morgantown WV 26506-9186 Office Phone: 304-293-5632. Business E-Mail: ydawood@hsc.wvu.edu.

DAWSON, ANNA MAE HARNE, music educator; b. Ottawa, Ill., Aug. 17, 1931; d. Fletcher Brigham Harne and Ethel Kathrine (Feuerbach) Rupley; m. Donald Gene Dawson, Aug. 11, 1962 (div. 1979); children: Arthur Fletcher (dec.), Michael Gene, David Christopher, Lynne Ann. B in Music Edn., Ill. Wesleyan U., 1953; MusM, So. Ill. U., 1976; studied with, Ruth Slenczynska, St. Louis and N.Y.C., 1974-89; postgrad., Hochshule fur Music, Vienna, Austria, summer 1980, 81. Cert. music tchr., Ill. Pvt. tchr. piano, Moline, Ill., 1953—; tchr. music Silvis (Ill.) Schs., 1953-57; tchr. music and social studies Moline (Ill.) Pub. Schs., 1962—66; prof. piano Blackhawk Coll., Moline, 1977-84; tchr. music St. Mary Cath. Sch., East Moline, 1979-89. Choral dir., mem., Union Congl. Ch., Moline, 1987—; recitalist in field. Mem. Fedn. Tchrs. and Counselors (chmn. student recitals 1987-90), AAUW (arts advisor 1989-90), Ill. Ret. Tchrs. Assn., Fine Arts Club (pres. 1976-78, program chair 1972-76, sec. 2002—), Delta Omicron Alumni Assn. Avocations: travel, reading. Home: 1509 41st St Moline IL 61265-2547

DAWSON, BRANDIE, nurse, nursing consultant; d. Carl and Pamela Smith; m. Richard Scott Dawson, Oct. 23, 1999; children: Seth Ian, Tabitha Joy. ASN, Gloucester County Coll., Sewell, N.J., 1993; BSN, Johns Hopkins U., Balt., 2001. RN NJ Bd. Nursing, 1993. Med. surg. nurse John F. Kennedy Meml. Hosp., Stratford, NJ, 1993—97; labor and delivery nurse Greater Balt. Med. Ctr., Towson, Md., 1997—99; emergency dept. Sinai Hosp., Balt., 1999—2000, emergency dept. agy. nurse, 2000—05; ind. legal nurse cons. Belcamp, 2004. In-ho. legal nurse cons. Cardaro & Peek, LLC, Balt.; presenter to confs. and bar assns. Mem.: Am. Assn. Legal Nurse Cons. (rec. sec. greater Balt. chpt. 2004—05, pres.-elect greater Balt. chpt. 2005), Sigma Theta Tau. Avocations: travel, antiques, reading. Office Phone: 443-695-1003. Personal E-mail: getinsight@comcast.net.

DAWSON, C. BRYAN, mathematician; b. Plainview, Tex., Sept. 16, 1964; s. Jerry and Linda Dawson; m. Martha Dawson, July 18, 1987; children: Matthew, Patricia, Tiffany. BS Math. and Computer Sci., Pittsburg State U., Pitts., Kans, 1986; MS Math, Pitts.State U., Pitts., Kans., 1987; PhD Math, U. North Tex., Denton, Tex., 1992. Tech. analyst Day & Zimmermann, Inc., Parsons, Kans., 1987—88; asst. prof. math. Emporia State U., Emporia, Kans., 1992—98; assoc. prof., math. Union U., Jackson, Tenn., 1998—2004, prof. math., 2004—. Contbr. articles to profl. jour. Tchr. Oakfield Bapt. Ch., Tenn., musician. Mem.: Assn. of Christians in the Math. Sciences (webmaster 2003—), Am. Math. Soc., Math. Assn. of Am., Kappa Mu Epsilon (corr.; editor, The Pentagon, ofcl. jour. 1995—99, regional dir. (se) 2001—05). Conservative. Baptist. Avocations: golf, writing. Office: Union Univ 1050 Union Univ Dr Jackson TN 38305 Office Phone: 731-661-5268. Business E-Mail: bdawson@uu.edu.

DAWSON, CARL, English literature educator; b. Leeds, Yorkshire, Eng., May 2, 1938; came to U.S., 1948, naturalized, 1959; AB magna cum laude, Occidental Coll., 1959; MA with high honors, Columbia U., 1960; postgrad., U. Munich, Fed. Republic of Germany, 1961-62; PhD, Columbia U., 1966. Instr. Dartmouth Coll., Hanover, N.H., 1964-66; asst. prof. U. Calif., Berkeley, 1966-70; assoc. prof. U. N.H., Durham, 1970-76, prof., 1976-89; prof., chmn. dept. U. Del., Newark, Del., 1989—; bd. editors U. Del. Press, Newark, Del., 1989-94. Fulbright lectr. Free U. of Berlin, 1967-68; vis. prof. Shoin U., Kobe, Japan, 1988; lect. U. Wales, 1984, Nat. U. Taiwan, 1989; interviewed for TV and radio, 1990; panelist NEH; mem. Stratford County N.H. Ext. Coun. on Forestry, 1977-80 Author: Thomas Love Peacock, 1968, His Fine Wit: A Study of Thomas Love Peacock, 1970, Matthew Arnold: The Critical Heritage, The Poetry, 1973, (with Hohn Pfordresher) Matthew Arnold: The Critical Heritage, Prose Writings, 1979, Victorian Noon: English Literature in 1850, 1979, Prophets of Past Time: Seven British Autobiographers, 1880-1914, 1988, November 1948, 1990, Lafcadio Hearn and the Vision of Japan, 1992, Living Backwards: A Transatlantic Memoir, 1995, (with Susan Goodman) William Dean Howells: A Writer's Life, 2005; editl. bd. U. Press of New Eng., 1984-89 Fellow Am. Coun. of Learned Socs., 1973-74, John Simon Guggenheim Meml. Fund, 1974-75, NEH, 1980-81, U. Calif., Berkeley, 1967, 69; grantee U. N.H., 1970-86 Mem. Phi Beta Kappa. Office: U Del 132 Memorial Hall Dept English Newark DE 19716

DAWSON, CAROL GENE, former commissioner, writer, consultant; b. Indpls., Sept. 8, 1937; d. Ernest Eugene (dec.) and Hilda Lou (Carroll) D.; m. Robert Edmund Bauman, Nov. 19, 1960 (div. 1982); children: Edward Carroll, Eugenie Marie, Victoria Ann, James Shields; m. Franklin Dean Smith, Aug. 2, 1986. BA, Dunbarton Coll., Washington, 1959, Cath. U., 1960; MA in Internat. Transactions, George Mason U., 1994. Staff asst. Senator Kenneth B. Keating, Washington, 1959; exec. asst. Americans for Constl. Action, Washington, 1959; exec. sec. Youth for Nixon Lodge, Washington, 1959-60; legis. asst. Rep. Donald C. Bruce, Washington, 1961-63; dep. dir., pub. info. Goldwater for Pres. Campaign and Rep. Nat. Com., Washington, 1963-64; editor, assoc. editor The New Guard Mag., Washington, 1965-66; dir. info. Am. Conservative Union, Washington, 1966-67; publs. and news analyst White House, Washington, from 1969; staff reporter Easton (Md.) Star-Democrat, 1971-72; freelance writer Easton, 1972-77; real estate salesperson Latham Realtors, Easton, 1977-80; sr. staff asst. presdl. transition U.S. Office of Personnel Mgmt., Washington, 1980-81; dep. press sec. U.S. Dept. Energy, Washington, 1981-82, dep. spl. asst. to sec., 1982-84; commr. U.S. Consumer Product Safety Commn., Washington, 1984-93. Editor Cath.

Currents newsletter, Washington, 1969-70. Bd. visitors Inst. Polit. Journalism Georgetown U., 1985—89; mem. Nat. Policy Forum, Coun. of Free Individuals in a Free Soc., Coun. on Internat. Trade, 1994—97; bd. dirs. Consumer Alert, 1995—; mem. Commonwealth of Va. Bd. Phys. Therapy, 2000—04; bd. dirs. Nat. Conservative Campaign Fund, Washington, 1999—; chmn. Lancaster County (Va.) Rep. Com., 1996—2002, 99th Legis. Dist. Rep. Com., 2000—; mem. Va. Rep. State Ctrl. Com., 2001—; bd. dirs. Va. Horse Coun., 2004—. Recipient Award of Merit Young Americans for Freedom, 1970. Mem. The Charter 100, Reagan Appointees Alumni, The Fairfax Hunt Club (bd. govs. 1989-91). Roman Catholic.

DAWSON, CHANDLER ROBERT, ophthalmologist, educator; b. Denver, Aug. 24, 1930; married; 3 children. AB, Princeton U., 1952; MD, Yale U., 1956. USPHS epidemiologist Communicable Disease Ctr., 1957-60; resident dept. ophthalmology Sch. Medicine U. Calif., San Francisco, 1960-63; asst. clin. prof. U. Calif., San Francisco, 1963-66, asst. prof. in residence, 1966-69, assoc. prof. opthalmology, 1969-75, prof. ophthalmology, 1975-97, prof. emeritus, assoc. dir. Francis I. Proctor Found., 1970-84, dir., 1984-95. Fellow Middlesex Hosp. Med. Sch., London, 1963-64; co-dir. WHO Collaborating Ctr. for Reference and Rsch. on Trachoma and other Chlamydial Infections, 1970-79, dir. Collaborating Ctr. for Prevention of Blindness and Trachoma, 1979—99. Recipient Knapp award AMA, 1967, 69, Medaille Trachome, 1978. Mem. Am. Soc. Microbiology, Am. Acad. Ophthalmology, Assn. Rsch. Vision & Ophthalmology. Achievements include rsch. in epidemiology of infectious eye diseases and cataracts; prevention of blindness; pathogenesis of virus diseases of the eyes; electron microscopy of eye diseases; clinical trials of treatment for trachoma and for herpes simplex eye infections. Office: U Calif San Francisco Francis I Proctor Found Rsch Ophthalmology San Francisco CA 94143-0412

DAWSON, DAVID SMITH, television executive; b. Chgo., Apr. 25, 1945; s. Thomas H. and Norma (Smith) D.; m. Heidi Caye Henderson; children: Cory Andrew, Ashley Kathleen. AA, San Diego Mesa Coll., 1965; BA, San Diego State U., 1967, MA, 1968. Producer, dir. Sta. KFMB-TV, San Diego, 1963-68; prodn. supr. live ops. CBS-TV, Hollywood, Calif., 1968-72; producer, dir. Sta. KHJ-TV, Hollywood, 1972-75, Sta. KCOP-TV, Hollywood, 1975-81; mgr. broadcast ops. and engring. ABC-TV, Hollywood, 1981-85; v.p. post prodn. ops. Premore, Inc., North Hollywood, 1985-98; broadcast cons., 1998—. Asst. prof. Los Angeles City Coll., 1981-85. Contbr. Los Angeles Childrens Outreach, 1985—. Mem. Acad. TV Arts and Scis. (Emmy award 1969, 71), Soc. Motion Picture and TV Engrs., Nat. Assn. Broadcasters, Dirs. Guild Am., Am. Film Inst. Republican. Avocations: golf, computers. Home: 25139 Amberley Way Valencia CA 91355-3053 Office: 14431 Ventura Blvd Ste 345 Sherman Oaks CA 91423-2606

DAWSON, DENNIS RAY, lawyer, manufacturing executive; b. Alma, Mich., June 19, 1948; s. Maurice L. and Virginia (Baker) D.; m. Marilynn S. Gordon, Nov. 26, 1971; children: Emily Lynn, Brett Thomas. AA, Gulf Coast Coll., 1968; AB, Duke U., 1970; JD, Wayne State U., 1973. Bar: Mich. 1973, U.S. Dist. Ct. (ea. dist.) Mich. 1973, U.S. Dist. Ct. (we. dist.) Mich. 1975. Assoc. Watson, Wunsch & Keidan, Detroit, 1973-75; mem. Coupe, Ophoff & Dawson, Holland, Mich., 1975-77; staff atty. Amway Corp., Ada, Mich., 1977-79; corp. counsel Meijer, Inc., Grand Rapids, Mich., 1979-82; sec., corp. counsel Tecumseh Products Co., 1982-92; corp. counsel, asst. sec. Holnam Inc., Dundee, Mich., 1992-93; v.p., gen. counsel, sec. Denso Internat. Am. Inc., Southfield, Mich., 1993-2000, sr. v.p., gen. counsel, sec., 2000—. Exec. com. Bank of Lenawee, Adrian, Mich., 1984-93, also bd. dirs.; adj. prof. Aquinas Coll., Grand Rapids, 1978-82; govt. regulation and litigation com. Outdoor Power Equipment Inst. Inc., Washington, 1982-92. Trustee Herrick Meml. Hosp., 1988-91, Tecumseh Civic Auditorium, 1986-89; mem. adv. coun. Montessori Children's House and Acad., Adrian, 1987-93; mem. adv. bd. Eastern Mich. U. Coll. Bus., 2004. Mem. ABA, Mich. State Bar Assn., Am. Corp. Counsel Assn., Mich. Mfrs. Assn. (lawyers com. 1987-92), Lenawee C. of C. (bd. dirs. 1988-92). Office: Denso Internat America Inc PO Box 5133 24777 Denso Dr Southfield MI 48034-5244

DAWSON, DONALD ANDREW, mathematics professor, researcher; b. Montreal, Que., Can., June 4, 1937; s. William Norman Cecil and Frances Malcolm (Andrew) D.; m. Elizabeth Jean Hilton, May 9, 1964; children: Michael, Suzanne. BSc, McGill U., Montreal, 1958, MSc, 1959; PhD, MIT, 1963. Sr. engr. Raytheon Corp., Bedford, Mass., 1962—63; assoc. prof. McGill U., 1963—70; prof. Carleton U., Ottawa, Canada, 1970—99; dir. The Fields Inst. for Rsch. in Math. Scis., Toronto, Canada, 1996—2000; prof. emeritus Carleton U., 1999—. Assoc. editor: Electronic Jour. of Probability, 1998; contbr. articles to profl. jours. Fellow Inst. Math Stats. (assoc. editor Annals of Probability jour. 1987-90), Internat. Stats. Inst., Royal Soc. Can.; mem. Can. Math. Soc. (co-editor in chief jour. 1988-93), Can. Statis. Soc., Am. Math. Soc., Bernoulli Soc. (adv. bd. stochastic processes application 1982—, pres. 2003--). Avocations: cross country skiing, walking, music appreciation. Office: Sch Math and Stats Carleton U Ottawa ON Canada K1S 5B6 Business E-Mail: ddawson@math.carleton.ca.

DAWSON, EARL BLISS, medical educator; b. Perry, Fla., Feb. 1, 1930; s. Bliss and Linnie (Calliham) Dawson; m. Winnie Ruth Isbell, Apr. 10, 1951; children: Barbara Gail, Patricia Ann, Robert Earl, Diana Lynn. BA, U. Mo., 1955; postgrad., Bowman Gray Sch. Medicine, 1957—59; MA, U. Mo., 1960; PhD, Tex. A&M U., 1964. Rsch. instr. dept. ob-gyn. U. Tex. Med. Br., Galveston, 1963—65, rsch. asst. prof., 1965—68, rsch. assoc. prof., 1968—89, assoc. prof., 1989—. Cons. Interdeptl. Com. Nutrtion Nat. Def., 1965—68, Nat. Nutrition Survey, 1968—69. Author: Effect of Water Borne Nitrites on the Environment of Man; contbr. articles to profl. jours., chapters to books. Scoutmaster Boy Scouts Am., 1969—. With USNR, 1947—52. Scholar, NSF, 1961—62; Nutrition Rsch. fellow, 1960—61, Rsch. fellow, NIH, 1962—63. Mem.: NY Acad. Scis., Tex. Acad. Scis., Soc. Environ. Geochemistry and Health, Soc. Exptl. Biology and Medicine, Am. Fertility Soc., Am. Coll. Nutrition, Am. Soc. Clin. Nutrition, Am. Inst. Nutrition, Mic-O-Say Club (Kansas City, Mo.), Sigma Xi, Phi Rho Sigma. Baptist. Achievements include research in prenatal nutrition, male fertility, epidemiology of lithium in Texas, biochemical changes associated with pre-menstrual syndrome. Home: Apt 8 3431 S Peach Hollow Cir D Pearland TX 77584-8006 Office: U Tex Med Br Dept Ob-Gyn Galveston TX 77550 Personal E-mail: winniearl@cs.com.

DAWSON, EDWARD C., lawyer; JD, Univ. Tex., 2001. Law clk. U.S. Ct. Appeals (11th cir.); law clk. to Hon. Anthony M. Kennedy U.S. Supreme Ct., 2003—04; assoc. Baker Botts, Houston, 2004—. Editor (in-chief): Tex. Law Rev. Office: Baker Botts One Shell Plz 910 Louisiana St Houston TX 77002-4995

DAWSON, EDWARD JOSEPH, merger and acquisition executive; b. Rochester, Pa., Apr. 1, 1944; s. Ralph Edward and Evelyn May (Riggle) D.; m. Lynda Sue Weir, 1975; 5 children. BS in Indsl. Mgmt., Carnegie Mellon U., 1966; MBA in Fin., U. Chgo., 1968. Lic. security broker/dealer, real estate broker. Computer systems analyst, corp. fin. analyst Tex. Instruments Corp., Dallas, 1968-70, product planning mgr. digital systems divsn., 1970-72, mgr. comml. equipment bus. objective, 1972-74, mgr. mktg. electronic watch divsn., 1975-76, mgr. mktg. home video systems, 1976-77; sr. v.p. ops. and mktg. Capital Alliance Corp., Dallas, 1977-80, exec. v.p. merger ops., 1980-81, chmn. bd., CEO, pres., 1981—. Sec. M&A Internat., 1988, v.p., 89, 96, pres., 90, 97; mem. faculty Bus. Leadership Ctr. So. Meth. U., 1999—; mem. entrepreneurship adv. coun. Carnegie Mellon U., 1998—. Author 4 books. Pres. Marina del Rey Homeowners Assn., 1982-84. Mem. Omicron Delta Kappa, Beta Theta Pi. Mem. Ch. of Christ. Home: 818 Stratford Dr Southlake TX 76092-7109 Office: Capital Alliance Corp 2777 N Stemmons Fwy Ste 1220 Dallas TX 75207-2293 Office Phone: 214-638-8280. Business E-Mail: ed.dawson@cadallas.com.

DAWSON, GERALDINE, medical educator, social worker; b. Huntington, Pa., Oct. 2, 1945; d. Donn and Evelyn Koontz; m. Nathan Maniam. BA, Pa. State U., 1967; MSW, Smith Coll., 1969; MD, Albert Einstein Coll. Medicine, 1988. Fellow Harvard Med. Sch.-Mass. Gen. Hosp., Boston, 1980—82, All India Inst. Med. Sci., New Delhi, 1987—88; med. resident Lenox Hill Hosp., N.Y.C., 1988—89; cons. Dept. of Def., Washington, 1990—92; assoc. prof. Marywood U., Scranton, Pa., 1993—. Contbr. articles to profl. jours. Mem. adv. coun. Regional Health Edn. Ctr. N.E. Pa., Scranton, 2001—; mem. Pa. Health Edn. Interdisciplinary Task Force, Hershey, 2002—. Named N.E. Woman, Scranton Times, 2000, Excellence in Their Field, Johnstown Tribune Democrat, 2000. Mem.: Pa. Nat. Alliance Mentally Ill, Pa. Nat. Assn. Social Workers (chairperson profl. stds. com. 1997—2003), Am. Psychotherapy Assn. (diplomate). Office Phone: 570-348-6282 ext 2390. Business E-Mail: dawson@marywood.edu.

DAWSON, HOWARD ATHALONE, JR., federal judge; b. Okolona, Ark., Oct. 23, 1922; m. Marianne Atherholt, Feb. 2, 1946; children: Amy, Suzanne. BS in Commerce, U. N.C., 1946; JD, George Washington U., 1949. Bar: D.C. 1949, Ga. 1958. Pvt. practice, Washington, 1949-50; atty. civil div. Office Chief Counsel, IRS, 1950-53, asst. regional counsel Atlanta region, 1953-56, regional counsel, 1957, asst. chief counsel adminstrn. Washington, 1958-62; judge U.S. Tax Ct., Washington, 1962—73, 1977—83, chief judge, 1973-77, 83-85, sr. judge, 1990—; prof. law, dir. grad. tax program U. Balt., 1986-89. David Brennan Disting. prof. law U. Akron Sch. Law, spring 1986; Disting. adj. prof. law U. San Diego Sch. Law, spring 1991. Served with AUS, 1943-45, ETO; capt. Res. Mem. ABA, D.C. Bar Assn., Fed. Bar Assn., Chi Psi, Delta Theta Phi. Office: US Tax Court 400 2nd St NW Washington DC 20217-0002

DAWSON, HOWARD W., JR., military officer; b. Ypsilanti, Mich. m. Ellen Carter; children: Maureen, Michael. Grad., U.S. Naval Acad., 1970; MS in Computer Sys., Naval Postgrad. Sch., 1971; MBA, Nat. U., San Diego, 1983. Commd. ensign USN, 1970, advanced through grades to rear adm., 1980, resigned, 1980; v.p. Ea. Ops. Anteon Corp. Active Navy Supply Corps. Found., Southwestern Youth Assn. Va. Rear adm. USNR. Mem. Naval Res. Assn., Naval Acad. Alumni Assn., Army Navy Club.

DAWSON, JAMES CLIFFORD, environmental science educator, geologist; b. Toronto, Ont., Can., Apr. 19, 1941; arrived in US, 1961; s. Clifford and Winifred Mary (Tadman) D.; m. Caroline Weiss, June 12, 1971. AA, Mt. San Antonio Coll., 1963; BA, UCLA, 1965, MS, 1967; PhD, U. Wis., 1970. Asst. prof. geology SUNY, Plattsburgh, 1970-74, assoc. prof., 1974-80, prof. environ sci., 1980-91, univ. disting. svc. prof., 1991—. Pres. Nat. Assn. State Bds. Edn., 1998. Chmn. Adirondack Land Trust, Inc., Elizabethtown, N.Y., 1984-89; bd. dirs. Adirondack Coun., Elizabethtown, 1982-2000; pres. Assn. for Protection of Adirondack, Schenectady, N.Y., 1982-83; mem. exec. coun. Lake Champlain Com., Inc., Burlington, Vt., 1976-98, bd. regents N.Y. State, 1993—. Mem.: AAAS, Am. Assn. Petroleum Geologists, Am. Geophys. Union, Geol. Soc. Am., Sigma Xi. Home: 2 Birchwood Dr Peru NY 12972-2600 E-mail: james.dawson@plattsburgh.edu.

DAWSON, JANIS LOUISE, music educator; b. Ford, Kans., Mar. 26, 1945; d. Vernon and Margaret G. Dawson (Stepmother). B in Music Edn., So. Nazarene U., Bethany, Okla., 1967; M in Music Edn., U. Okla., 1971. Cert. tchr. Okla. Tchr. 3d grade Fla. Bd. Edn., Sarasota, 1968; assoc. prof. So. Nazarene U., Bethany, 1968—71; music tchr. Western Heights Pub. Schs., Oklahoma City, 1971—2000, Heritage Hall Schs., Oklahoma City, 2000—04, Duncan (Okla.) Pub. Schs., 2004—05. Pvt. voice tchr., 1967—. Named Dir. of Distinction, Okla. Choral Dirs., 1982; named to Hall of Fame, Okla. Music Educators Assn., 1996; recipient Outstanding Music Educator award, Okla. Secondary Schs Activities Assn. and Nat. Fedn. High Schs., 1997, Nat. Fedn. High Schs., 1998, Nat. Citation award, 2000. Mem.: Okla. Music Adjudicators' Assn. (assoc.), S.W. Divsn. Am. Choral Dirs. Assn. (life; membership chmn. 2000—04), Okla. Music Educators Assn. (life; vocal v.p. 1988—90, pres. 2003—05, 25 Yrs. Disting. Svc. award 1993), Okla. Choral Dirs. Assn. (life; pres.-elect 1980—82, pres. 1982—84, v.p., editor 1984—86, pres.-elect 1993—95, pres. 1995—97, v.p. 1997—99). Republican. E-mail: janis.dawson@duncanpublicschools.org.

DAWSON, JESSICA, art critic; Writer Washington City Paper; art critic, galleries column Washington Post; art critic Washington Post.com, 2001—. Freelance art critic. Office: Washington Post 1150 15th St NW Washington DC 20071*

DAWSON, JOHN DAVID, academic administrator, religious studies educator; b. Md. m. Ellen Dawson; children: Aaron, Abigail. BA, Towson State U., 1978; MDiv, Duke U., 1982; MA, Yale U., 1983, MPhil, 1986, PhD, 1988. Mem. faculty Haverford (Pa.) Coll., 1987—, Constance and Robert MacCrate prof. in social responsiblity, prof. religion, provost, 2002—. Author: Allegorical Readers and Cultural Revision in Ancient Alexandria, 1992, Literay Theory, 1995, Christian Figural Reading and the Fashioning of Identity, 2001. Named Pa. Prof. of Yr., Carnegie Found. for the Advancement of Tchg., 1994. Avocation: sailing. Office: Office of the Provost Haverford Coll 370 Lancaster Ave Haverford PA 19041-1392

DAWSON, JOHN JOSEPH, lawyer; b. Binghamton, N.Y., Mar. 9, 1947; s. Joseph John and Cecilia (O'Neill) D. BA, Siena Coll., 1968; JD, U. Notre Dame, 1971. Bar: Ariz. 1971, Nev. 1991, Calif. 1993, D.C. 1994, N.Y. 1996. Nat. practice group chair, bankruptcy and creditors rights practice group Quarles & Brady Streich Lang LLP, Phoenix. Reporter local rules ct. U.S. Bankruptcy Ct. for Dist. Ariz.; atty. rep. U.S. Ct. Appeals (9th cir.), 1992-95 Co-author: Advanced Chapter 11 Bankruptcy, 1991. Fellow Ariz. Bar Found.; mem. State Bar Ariz. (chmn. bankruptcy sect. 1976-77, 80-81), Am. Bankruptcy Inst., Comml. Law League Am. Republican. Roman Catholic. Avocations: sports, reading, movies, travel, writing. Office: Quarles & Brady Streich Lang LLP Renaissance One Two North Central Ave Phoenix AZ 85004-2391 Office Phone: 602-229-5414. Business E-Mail: jdawson@quarles.com.

DAWSON, KAREN OLTMANNS, forensic nurse, childbirth educator; b. El Centro, Calif., Mar. 14, 1947; d. Victor Roy and Lois Louise Oltmanns; m. Arthur B. Dawson, Sept. 13, 1970; children: David, Jonathan, Stephen, Matthew, Anna-Lisa. BSN, UCLA, 1969; postgrad., U. Calif., Irvine, 1980; MA, U. Colo., Denver, 1992. Cert. instr. nursing Calif., Colo., pub. health nurse, early childhood spl. edn. instr., lactation cons. Staff nurse, maternal-child Swedish Med. Ctr., Englewood, Colo., 1986-92, parent educator, 1983—; nurse, spl. edn. tchr. Cherry Creek Acad., 1995-97—; adminstr. early intervention ctr. for children with spl. needs, 1997-98; dir., adminstr., v.p. A. Dawson Tutoring, Inc., 1998—; dir. Children's World ARAMARK Ednl. Svcs.; forensic nurse examiner Med. Ctr. of Aurora, 2004—. Clin. instr. Aurora Pub. Schs. Vocat. Ctr., C.C. of Denver, Arapahoe C.C., Littleton, Colo.; spl. edn. tchr. Hope Ctr., Denver, 1992-93. Spl. edn. tchr. United Cerebral Palsy Assn., Denver, 1993-95. Mem. Neonatal ICU Connections Task Force, Swedish Med. Ctr. Colo. Consortium for Preterm Infant Devel. Personal E-mail: doublemint47@earthlink.net.

DAWSON, LEONARD E., college president; b. Augusta, Ga., Feb. 5, 1934; m. Laura Dawson; children: Michael, Lavinia, Stephanie Odom. BA in English, Morris Brown Coll., 1954; MA in Guidance and Pupil Adminstrn., Columbia U.; EdD, George Washington U., 1974. Various to dir. Upward Bound, asst. dean to acad. dean Paine Coll., 1967-70; edn. program specialist U.S. Office of Edn., 1970; exec. v.p. Moton Inst., 1977-80; dir. of spl. projects United Negro Coll. Fund, 1980; pres. Voorhees Coll., Denmark, SC, 1985—2001. Sr. program dir. Moton Inst., 1971-77. Active nat. call to action prompting first nat. conf. Strategies by HBCU's to Prevent Violence in African Am. Communities; capital financing adv. bd. Historically Black Colls. and Univs.; chair Coun. Pres. Eastern Intercollegiate Athletic Conf., 1990-2000. Recipient Disting. Alumni award Morris Brown Coll., 1981, 99. Mem. Am. Mgmt. Assn., Am. Assn. Higher Edn., Am. Coun. on Edn., Assn. Episc. Coll. Bd. of Dirs., Assn. Deans and Registrars, Coun. of Pres.s of Nat. Assn. of Intercollegiate Athletics, Alpha Phi Alpha, others. Office: Booker T Washington Bldg PO Box 678 1411 Voorhees Rd Denmark SC 29042-0678 E-mail: Dawson@voorhees.edu.

DAWSON, LESLIE NARYNE, quality assurance professional; d. Naryne Fowler; children: Donald Bernard Lignore, Jr., Donna Leslie Callaghan, Robert Anthony Lignore, Brian William. B of Journalism, Pub. Rels., U. Ctrl. Fla., 1998. Office mgr. Farber & Halligan, P.C., Media, Pa., 1976—80; computer operator Wing Pubs., Folsom, 1986—88; dept. adminstrv. asst. Martin Marietta Elec. Systems, Orlando, Fla., 1988—90; quality assurance engrng. adminstr. Siemens Westinghouse Power Corp., 1990—. Cons. Jr. Achievement, Orlando, 1999—2002; coord. Orlando UCF Shakespeare Guild, Orlando, 1999—2002; mem. Friends of Winter Pk. Meml. Hosp., Winter Park, 2001—02; participant Ctrl. Fla. Helpline, 1999—2000; coord. Shepherd's Hope, 1999—2001; singer Voices of Valencia, 2000—. Mem.: Phi Theta Kappa (assoc.). Home: 4104 Cleary Way Orlando FL 32828-6401 Office Phone: 407-736-5151. Personal E-mail: leslie.dawson@siemens.com.

DAWSON, MARY E., lawyer; b. Halifax, N.S., Can., June 23, 1942; d. Thomas Paul and Florence Margaret (Thurston) McMillan; m. Peter Dawson, Aug. 30, 1969; children: David, Emily. BA in Philosophy with honors, McGill U., 1963, BCL, 1966; DESD, U. Ottawa, 1968; LLB, Dalhousie U., 1970. Tax rschr. Revenue Can., Ottawa, 1967-68, legal counsel, 1968-69; tchg. fellow Dalhousie U., 1969-70; legis. drafter Dept. of Justice, Ottawa, 1970-79, assoc. chief legis. counsel, 1980-86, asst. dep. minister pub. law, 1986-88, assoc. dep. minister, 1988—2005. Mem. adv. bd. Ctr. Rsch. and Edn. Women and Work, Sch. Bus., Carleton U. Recipient Lyon William Jacobs Q. C. award, 1965, 1978; scholar, McGill U., 1960. Mem.: Ont. Bar, Que. Bar, N.S. Bar, Internat. Bar Assn. (chmn. govt. law com. 1998—2002, mem. coun. 2002—04). Avocations: nordic skiing, swimming, theater, reading, skating. Home: 97 Reid Ave Ottawa ON Canada K1H 1T1 Business E-Mail: mary.dawson@justice.gc.ca.

DAWSON, MARY RUTH, curator, educator; b. Highland Park, Mich., Feb. 27, 1931; d. John Elson and Olga Josephine (Down) D. BS, Mich. State Coll., 1952; postgrad., U. Edinburgh, 1952-53; PhD, U. Kans., 1957; D of Humanities (hon.), Chatham Coll., 1983. Instr. zoology Smith Coll., 1958-61; asst. program dir. NSF, Washington, 1961-62; mem. staff Carnegie Mus., Pitts., 1962—, curator, 1971—, chmn. earth sci. div., 1973-97, acting dir., 1982-83, curator emeritus, 2003. Adj. prof. earth scis. U. Pitts., 1971—. Named Disting. Dau. Pa., 1987; recipient Arnold Guyot award, Nat. Geog. Soc., 1981, Woman in Sci. award, Chatham Coll., 1983, Disting. Alumni award, Mich. State U., 2003, Romer-Simpson medal, Soc. Vertebrate Paleontology; fellow, AAUW, 1958—59; Fulbright scholar, 1952—53; rsch. grantee, NSF, 1961—62, 1965—. Fellow Geol. Soc. Am., Arctic Inst. N.Am.; mem. Soc. Vertebrate Paleontology (hon.; v.p. 1972-73, pres. 1973-74), Paleontol. Soc., Paläontologische Gesellschaft, Bernese Mountain Dog Club Am., Am. Soc. Mammalogists, Phi Beta Kappa. Achievements include research and publication on Tertiary Lagomorpha, 1957—, early Tertiary Holarctic rodents, 1960—, Arctic paleontology, 1975—. Office: Carnegie Mus 4400 Forbes Ave Pittsburgh PA 15213-4080 Business E-Mail: dawsonm@carnegiemnh.org.

DAWSON, MIMI WEYFORTH, public policy consultant; b. St. Louis, Aug. 31, 1944; d. Francis Griffin and Jeanne (Gething) Weyforth; m. Rhett Brewer Dawson, Jan. 15, 1976; 2 children: Elizabeth Stuart, Andrew Brewer. AB, Washington U., St. Louis, 1966. Press sec., legis. asst. to Rep. James Symington, Mo. Dist., 1973; pres. sec., chief staff Sen. Bob Packwood, Oreg., 1973-81; commr. FCC, Washington, 1981-87; dep. Sec. U.S. Dept. Transp., Washington, 1987-89; sr. pub. policy cons. Wiley Rein and Fielding LLP, Washington, 1989—. Apptd. U.S. Holocaust Meml. Coun., 1992-98; adj. fellow Ctr. for Strategic and Internat. Studies. Mem. Atlantic Coun. U.S. (bd. dirs. 1995—). Republican. Roman Catholic. Office: Wiley Rein and Fielding LLP 1776 K St NW Washington DC 20006-2304 Office Phone: 202-719-7034. Business E-Mail: mdawson@wrf.com.

DAWSON, PATRICIA LUCILLE, surgeon; b. Kingston, Jamaica, W.I., Sept. 30, 1949; arrived in U.S., 1950; d. Percival Gordon and Edna Claire (Overton) D.; children: Alexandria Zoe Hiserman, Wesley Gordon Hiserman BA in Sociology, Allegheny Coll., 1971; MD, N.J. Med. Sch., Newark, 1977; MA in Human and Orgn. Devel., The Fielding Inst., 1996, PhD in Human and Orgnl. Sys., 1998. Membership dir. N.J. ACLU, Newark, 1972; resident in surgery U. Medicine and Dentistry N.J. N.J. Med Sch., 1977-79; resident in surgery Virginia Mason Med. Ctr., Seattle, 1979-82; pvt. practice specializing in surgery Arlington, Wash., 1982-83; dir. med. staff diversity Group Health Coop., Seattle, 1993-98, staff surgeon, 1983-98; pvt. practice Seattle, 1998—2003; breast surgeon Swedish Cancer Inst., 2004—. Author: Forged by the Knife—The Experience of Surgical Residency from the Perspective of a Woman of Color, 1999 Fellow ACS, Seattle Surg. Soc.; mem. Physicians for Social Responsibility, Assn. Women Surgeons, Wash. Black Profls. in Health Care, NOW. Avocations: fiction, walking, cooking. Office: Providence Comp Breast Ctr Jefferson Twr 1600 E Jefferson St Ste 300 Seattle WA 98122-5645 Office Phone: 206-320-4880.

DAWSON, ROSARIO, actress, singer; b. NYC, May 9, 1979; Actress (films) Kids, 1995, Girls Night Out, 1995, He Got Game, 1998, Side Streets, 1998, Light It Up, 1999, Down to You, 2000, Josie and the Pussycats, 2001, Sidewalks of New York, 2001, Trigger Happy, 2001, Chelsea Walls, 2001, King of the Jungle, 2001, Love in the Time of Money, 2002, Ash Wednesday, 2002, The First $20 Million Is Always the Hardest, 2002, Men in Black II, 2002, The Adventures of Pluto Nash, 2002, 25th Hour, 2002, This Girl's Life, 2003, Shattered Glass, 2003, The Rundown, 2003, Alexander, 2004, This Revolution, 2005, Sin City, 2005, The Devil's Rejects, 2005, Rent, 2005, guest appearance The Tonight Show with Jay Leno, 2001, 2002, 2005, The Tonight Show With Craig Kilborn, 2002, Punk'd, 2003, Celebrity Poker Showdown, 2004, Live with Regis and Kelly, 2004, 2005, Late Night with Conan O'Brien, 2004, The Tony Danza Show, 2004. Mailing: 1635 N Cahuenga Blvd Los Angeles CA 90028*

DAWSON, STEPHEN EVERETTE, lawyer; b. Detroit, May 14, 1946; s. Everette Ivan and Irene (Dresser) D.; m. Consiglia J. Bellisario, Sept. 20, 1974; children: Stephen Everette Jr., Gina C., Joseph J. BA, Mich. State U., 1968; MA, U. Mich., 1969, JD, 1972. Bar: Mich. 1972, U.S. Dist. Ct. (ea. dist.) Mich. 1972, U.S. Supreme Ct. 1978, U.S. Ct. Appeals (6th cir.) 1980. Assoc. Dickinson, Wright, Moon, Van Dusen & Freeman, Detroit, 1972-79; ptnr. Dickinson, Wright, PLLC, Bloomfield Hills, Mich., 1979—. Adj. prof. law U. Detroit, 1986-88. Mem. ABA, Am. Coll. Real Estate Lawyers, Mich. State Bar Assn. (mem. coun. real property law sect. 1986-93, chair 1992-93, land title stds. com. 1999—), Mich. State Bar Found., Phi Beta Kappa. Republican. Avocations: jogging, reading. Office: Dickinson Wright PLLC 38525 Woodward Ave Ste 2000 Bloomfield Hills MI 48304-5092 Office Phone: 248-433-7200. E-mail: sdawson@dickinsonwright.com.

DAWSON, SUZANNE STOCKUS, lawyer; b. Chgo., Dec. 29, 1941; d. John Charles and Josephine (Zolpe) Stockus; m. Daniel P. Dawson Sr., Sept. 1, 1962; children: Daniel P. Jr., John Charles, Michael Sean. BA, Marquette U., 1963; JD cum laude, Loyola U., Chgo., 1965. Bar: Ill. 1965, U.S. Dist. Ct. (no. dist.) Ill. 1965. Assoc. Kirkland & Ellis, Chgo., 1965-71, ptnr., 1971-82, Arnstein & Lehr, Chgo., 1982-89, Foley & Lardner, Chgo., 1989-94; spl. counsel publicly held corps., 1995-97; corp. counsel Baxter Healthcare Corp., Deerfield, Ill., 1997-98, sr. counsel, 1998—2004, chief transactions counsel, 2004—. Mem. various coms. United Way Chgo.; corp. adv. bd. Sec. State of Ill., 1973; past mem. bd. advisors Loyola of Chgo. Law Sch.; trustee Lawrence Hall Youth Svcs., Chgo., 1983-98, pres., 1991-93, chair 1993-96; mem. adv. bd. Cath. Charities Chgo., 1985—, bd. dirs., 2002—, chair north suburban regional adv. bd., 2002—; mem. exec. com., bd. governance Notre Dame High Sch., Niles, Ill., 1990-97. Recipient Founder's Day award Loyola U., 1980, St. Thomas More award Loyola of Chgo. Law Sch., 1983. Mem.

ABA, Am. Arbitration Assn. (appointed mem. nat. panel of comml. arbitrators 1996—), Ill. Bar Assn. Roman Catholic. Avocations: piano, choir singing, gardening, skiing, gourmet cooking. Home: 2113 Valley Lo Ln Glenview IL 60025-1724 Office: Baxter Healthcare Corp One Baxter Pkwy Deerfield IL 60015-4633 Office Phone: 847-948-3636. E-mail: suzanne_dawson@baxter.com.

DAWSON, VALINA L., science educator; BS in Environ. Toxicology, U. Calif., Davis, 1983; PhD in Pharmacology, U. Utah, 1989. Fellow dept. neurology Hosp. of U. Pa., Phila., 1989—90; fellow Addiction Rsch. Ctr. Nat. Inst. Drug Abuse, Balt., 1990—93; dir. neurobiology of disease program dept. neurology Johns Hopkins U. Sch. Medicine, Balt.; assoc. prof. neurology, neurosci., and physiology Johns Hopkins Hosp., 1994—2001, prof., vice chmn. neurology, prof. neurosci. and physiology, 2001—. Contbr. articles to profl. jours. Named Internat. Soc. for Neurochemistry Young Investigator, 1999, Staglin Music Festival Investigator, 1998; recipient Mary Lou McIlhany scholarship, 1999, Am. Heart Assn. Grant-in-Aid award, 1996, award, Muscular Dystrophy Assn., 1995, Alzheimer's Assn. Scholar award, 1994, Am. Heart Assn. Grant-in-Aid award, 1994, AmFar Scholar award, 1994, ADAMHA Intramural Rsch. Tng. award, 1992, Nat. Inst. Drug Abuse Staff Fellow award, 1992, Winter Conf. on Brain Rsch. fellowship, 1991, NIH PRAT fellowship, 1990. Achievements include research in molecular mechanisms of neurodegeneration and regeneration; experimental models of stroke; gene discovery of novel cell survival pathways; cell based therapies for the treatment of neurologic disorders. Office: Inst for Cell Engring Dept Neurology 733 N Broadway St Ste 711 Baltimore MD 21205 E-mail: vdawson@jhmi.edu.

DAWSON, VIRGINIA SUE, retired editor; b. Concordia, Kans., June 6, 1940; d. John Edward and Wilma Aileen (Thompson) Morgan; m. Neil S. Dawson, Nov. 28, 1964; children: Shelley Diane Dawson Sedwick, Lori Ann Dawson Hughes, Christy Lynn. BS in Home Econs. and Journalism, Kans. State U., 1962. Asst. publs. editor Ohio State U. Coop. Ext. Svc., Columbus, 1962-64; home editor Ohio Farmer mag., Columbus, 1964-78; food editor Columbus Dispatch, 1978—2000, ret. Recipient Commn. award Ohio Poultry Assn., 1980. Mem. Assn. Food Journalists. Avocations: biking, running, reading, cooking. Personal E-mail: ndawson1@cox.net.

DAWSON, WILLIAM B., lawyer; b. Amarillo, Tex., Aug. 24, 1949; BBA, Tex. Tech U., 1972, JD with highest honors, 1975. Bar: Tex. 1975. Atty. Carrington, Coleman, Sloman & Blumenthal LLP, Dallas; ptnr., co-head Litig. Sect. Vinson & Elkins LLP, Dallas. Bd. editors: Tex. Tech Law Rev., 1974-75. Fellow Am. Coll. Trial Lawyers; mem. ABA, Order of Coif, Phi Kappa Phi, Delta Theta Phi. Office: Vinson & Elkins LLP Trammell Crow Ctr 2001 Ross Ave, Ste 3700 Dallas TX 75201 Office Phone: 214-220-7926. E-mail: bdawson@velaw.com.

DAWSON, WILLIAM RYAN, zoology educator; b. Los Angeles, Aug. 24, 1927; s. William Eldon and Mary (Ryan) D.; m. Virginia Louise Berwick, Sept. 9, 1950; children: Deborah, Denise, William. Student, Stanford, 1945-46; BA, UCLA, 1949, MA, 1950, PhD, 1953; DSc, U. Western Australia, 1971. Faculty zoology U. Mich., Ann Arbor, 1953-94, prof., 1962-94, D.E.S. Brown prof. biol. scis., 1981-94, chmn. div. biol. scis., 1974-82, dir. Mus. Zoology, 1982-93, D.E.S. Brown prof. emeritus, 1994—. Lectr. Summer Inst. Desert Biology, Ariz. State U., 1960-71, Maytag prof., 1982; rschr. Australian-Am. Edn. Found., U. Western Australia, 1969-70; Carpenter lectr. San Diego State U., 1996; mem. Speakers Bur., Am. Inst. Biol. Sci., 1960-62; mem. adv. panel NSF environ. biology program, 1967-69; mem. adv. com. for rsch. NSF, 1973-77; adv. panel NSF regulatory biology program, 1979-82; mem. R/V Alpha Helix New Guinea Expdn., 1969; chief scientist R/V Dolphin Gulf of Calif. Expdn., 1976; mem. R/V Alpha Helix Galapagos Expdn., 1978. Editorial bd.: Condor, 1960-63, Auk, 1964-68, Ecology, 1968-70, Ann. Rev. Physiology, 1973-79, Physiol. Zoology, 1976-86; co-editor: Springer-Verlag Zoophysiology and Ecology series, 1968-72; assoc. editor: Biology of the Reptilia, 1972, Birds of N.Am., 1997—. Served with USNR, 1945-46. USPHS postdoc. rsch.fellow, 1953; Guggenheim fellow, 1962-63; recipient Russell award U. Mich., 1959, Disting. Faculty Achievement award, 1976; Wheeler lectr. U. N.D., 1986. Fellow AAAS (council del. 1984-86), Am. Ornithol. Union (Brewster medal 1979); mem. Soc. Integrative Comparative Biology (pres. 1985), Am. Physiol. Soc., Ecol. Soc. Am., Cooper Ornithol. Soc. (hon., Painton award 1963, Miller Rsch. award 1996), Phi Beta Kappa, Sigma Xi, Kappa Sigma. Home: 1376 Bird Rd Ann Arbor MI 48103-2351 E-mail: wrdawson@umich.edu.

DAWSON-HUGHES, BESS, scientist; Grad., Tufts U., 1975. Intern St. Elizabeths's Hosp., Brighton, Mass., chief resident in medicine, 1977; rsch. fellow in medicine Harvard Med. Sch., 1978—81, Peter Bent Brigham Hosp., 1978—81; asst. prof. medicine Tufts U. Sch. Medicine, 1982; asst. med. officer Jean Mayer USDA Human Nutrition Rsch. Ctr. Aging (HNRCA), Tufts U., 1982—86, chief calcium and bone metabolism lab., 1987; prof. medicine Tufts U. Sch. Medicine. Recipient Bolton L. Carson medal Franklin Inst., 1995. Office: USDA Nutrition Rsch Aging Ctr Tufts Univ Boston MA 02111

DAY, ANNETTE J., music educator; d. Edward Leroy and Ada June Shives; m. Mark Stephen Day, June 9, 1984; 1 child, Erin Taylor. BA in Music Edn., Shepherd U., 1981. Tchr. pvt. voice Day Music Studio, Berkely Spring, W.Va., 1976—99, tchr. piano pedagogy Peachtree City, Ga., 1974—. Dir. girl's choir, 2004—. Co-founder Peachtree City Piano Camp; music coord. 1st United Meth. Ch., Berkley Springs, 1974—77, Francis Asbury United Meth. Ch., Berkley Springs, 1977—81; dir. adult and youth choir Christ Our Shepherd Luth. Ch., Peachtree City, 2000—02, girl's choir dir., 2004—. McMurran scholar, Shepherd Coll., 1980. Mem.: Nat. Fedn. Music Clubs, Nat. Guild Piano Tchrs., Music Tchrs. Nat. Assn. (pres.-elect. south metro Atlanta 2000—02, v.p. Cowetta-Fayette 2002—04, pres. 2004—, cert. 2004). Office: Day Music Studio 214 Columns Ln Peachtree City GA 30269 Office Phone: 770-631-2705. Business E-Mail: daystudio@earthlink.net.

DAY, ANTHONY, critic, journalist; b. Miami, Fla., May 12, 1933; s. Price and Alice (Alexander) D.; m. Lynn Ward, June 25, 1960; children— John, Julia (dec.). AB cum laude, Harvard U., 1955, postgrad. (Nieman fellow), 1966-67; L.H.D. (hon.), Pepperdine U., 1974. Reporter Phila. Bull., 1957-60, Washington, 1960-69, chief Washington bur., 1969; chief editorial writer L.A. Times, 1969-71, editor editorial pages, 1971-89, sr. corr., 1989-95; contbg. writer L.A. Times Book Review, 1995—. Mem. Signet Soc. Harvard, Asia Soc., Santa Fe Coun. Internat. Rels.

DAY, ANTHONY, school system administrator; s. Elwin George and Patricia Margaret Day; m. Paulette Butry, May 30, 1966; children: Ryan Michael, Christopher Joseph. BA, SUNY, Buffalo, N.Y., 1988; MSc, Niagara U., 1996. Cert. in sch. administrn. N.Y., 1996. Tchr. social studies Niagara Wheatfield H.S., Sanborn, NY, 1988—96; asst. prin. Niagara Wheatfield Ctrl. Sch. Dist., Sanborn, 1996, prin., 1998—2003; asst. supt. Sweet Home Ctrl. Sch., Amherst, NY, 2003—. Home: Amherst 14228 Office Phone: 716-250-1422. Home Fax: 716-250-1402. Personal E-mail: ghicks@shs.k12.ny.us.

DAY, CECIL LEROY, agricultural engineering educator; b. Dexter, Mo., Oct. 4, 1922; s. Cecil Lawrence and Katherine (Kleffer) D.; m. Peggy Eunice Thrower, Aug. 29, 1948; children: Stanley K., Thomas L. BS in Agrl. Engring., U. Mo., 1945, MS, 1948; PhD, Iowa State U., 1957. Mem. faculty U. Mo. at Columbia, 1945-85, prof. agrl. engring., 1962-85; prof. emeritus, 1985—; chmn. dept., 1969-82. Vis. prof. U. Thessaloniki, Greece, 1972; pres. Penreico, Inc., 1968-79. Author articles, bulls. Chmn. elec. appeals bd., Columbia, 1966-76; elder Ch. of Christ, 1993-98; alumni bd. dirs. U. Mo. Coll. Engring., 1992-2004. Fellow Am. Soc. Agrl. Engrs. (outstanding individual of yr. Mo. sect. 1982); mem. Agrl. Engrs. of Mo. Inc. (pres. 1987-2000), Lakeshore Villa Homes Assn. Inc. (treas. 1985-99, pres. 1996-98), Columbia Golden K Kiwanis Club (pres. 1995-96). Home: 1203 Club Meadows Dr Columbia MO 65203 *"And we know that all things work together for good to them that love God."*.

DAY, CHARLES WILLIAMSON, commentator; b. Chgo., Apr. 30, 1931; s. Lewis Andrew and Isabel Gillette (Williamson) Day; m. Carla Louise Dean, Nov. 30, 1963; children: Spencer Dean children: Charles Williamson Jr., Allison Parker. BA, Yale U., 1954; MS, Columbia U., 1957; MA, U. Chgo., 1958. Accreditation Pub. Rels. Soc. Am., 1981. Mgr. non-product legislation Ford Motor Co., Washington, 1963—79, dir., pub. affairs, 1988—94, with, 1994—98, mgr. Lincoln-Mercury pub. rels. Detroit, 1979—86, mgr. spl. events Dearborn, Mich., 1986—87; classical music host WGMS-FM, 1998—. Chmn. Rd. Gang Washington, 1970—71; pres. Capitol Hill Club, Toastmasters Internat., 1973—73, U.S.Senate Club, Toastmasters Internat., 1974—74; guest lectr. journalism sch. George Wash. U., 1978—79. Author: (column) Roll Call Newspaper, The Toastmaster Magazine; contbr. articles to profl. jours. Advisor Mich. Metro Girl Scouts Coun., Detroit, 1981—87. Capt. USAF, 1954—56. Recipient Sackett prize Libel Law, Columbia U. Grad. Sch. Journalism, 1957, Thoth award Best Radio Promotion, Pub. Rels. Soc. Am., Washington Chpt., 1998, Radio award Best Fill-in Talent, 1999; scholar, C. J. LaRoche, 1957—58. Mem.: Book and Snake Soc., Lowes Island Club, Cosmos Club (life), Beta Theta Pi. Episcopalian. Achievements include first to First transatlantic auto industry TV news conference; Created GreenWire service of Political Hotline, division of National Journal; invention of in-car cell phone (Ford production option); raised funds to complete Martin Luther King, Jr. Center, Atlanta. Avocations: running, art, travel, fine scale modeling. Home: 101 Sinegar Pl Potomac Falls VA 20165 Office: WGMS-FM 3400 Idaho Ave NW Washington DC 20016 Office Phone: 202-895-5000.

DAY, CHRISTOPHER MARK, lawyer; b. Atlantic City, N.J, May 24, 1968; s. Frederick Nicholes and Judith Lee Day. BA in Polit. Sci., Stockton State U., 1990; JD, Widener U., 1994. Bar: N.J. 1994, Pa. 1994, U.S. Dist. Ct. N.J. 1994. Law clk. Hon. Richard J. Williams, Assignment Judge Superior Ct., Atlantic City, 1994-95; assoc. Cooper Perskie Law Firm, Atlantic City, 1995-97; ptnr. Petro Cohen Day Law Firm, Atlantic City, 1998—. Bd. dirs. Chief Arthur Brown Meml. Scholarship Found., 1992—, Chelsea Neighborhood Assn., 1995-97; chmn. Attys. Reaching Others, 1995—. Mem. Atlantic County Bar Assn. (trustee 1998—), N.J. Workers Compensation Am. Inns Ct., Jr. C. of C. Home: 46 S Laclede Pl Atlantic City NJ 08401-5806 Office: Petro Cohen Day Law Firm 2111 New Rd Northfield NJ 08225-1512

DAY, COLIEN, retired secondary school educator; b. Roxboro, N.C., Nov. 3, 1927; d. Luther Davis and Cornelia Lou (Allen) Long; m. Russell Van Buren Day (dec. 1981). AB in English, Trevecca U., Nashville, 1951; MEd, U. N.C., 1955; Sectl. Cert., Elon Coll., 1944-45. With Burlington Ind., Burlington, N.C., 1945-48; tchr. Bartlett-Yancey High Sch., Yanceyville, NC, 1951-53, Sumner High Sch., Greensboro, N.C., 1953-59; tchr. English Asheboro (N.C.) City Schs., 1959-61; librarian Randolph County Schs., Asheboro, 1961-64; tchr. English Marysville (Calif.) Joint Unified Sch. Dist., 1964—91. Tutor in English to Asian immigrants, 1988—. Mem. AAUW, Nat. Geographic Soc., Nat. Edn. Assn., Smithsonian Instn. Democrat. Home and Office: 1739 Glen St Marysville CA 95901-4018

DAY, DELBERT EDWIN, ceramic engineering educator; b. Avon, Ill., Aug. 16, 1936; s. Edwin Raymond and Doris Jennings (Main) D.; m. Shirley Ann Foraker, June 2, 1956; children: Lynne Denise, Thomas Edwin. BS in Ceramic Engring., Mo. Sch. Mines and Metallurgy, 1958; MS in Ceramic Tech., Pa. State U., 1960, PhD in Ceramic Tech., 1961; DSc (hon.), U Mo.-Rolla, 2004. Registered profl. engr., Mo. With U. Mo., Rolla, 1961—, dir. Indsl. Rsch. Ctr., 1965-72, dir. Grad. Ctr. Materials Rsch., 1983-92, Curators' prof. ceramic engring., 1981—; founder, chmn., CEO Mo-Sci Corp., Rolla, Mo., 1985—; dir. State of Mo. Tech. Corp., 1999—2004. Vis. prof. chemistry Miss. Coll., 1963, Eindhoven Tech. U., The Netherlands, 1971; mem. tech. staff Sandia Nat. Labs., Albuquerque, 1981, 91; sr. vis. faculty scientist Battelle Pacific N.W. Labs., Richland, Wash., 1990; asst. dean grad. studies Mo. Sch. Mines and Metallurgy, 1979-81; chmn. acad. coun. U. Mo., Rolla, 1978-79, active numerous other coms.; cons. Los Alamos Nat. Labs., 1983-95, NASA, 1974-88, numerous other glass and refractories cos., 1958—; vice-chmn. Gordon Rsch. Conf. on Glass, 1990-92, chmn., 1992-94; tech. program dir. confs. on glass including Baden-Baden, Germany, 1973, Rolla, 1975, XII Internat. Glass Congress, Albuquerque, 1980, Internat. and 7th U. Conf. Glass Sci., Clausthal-Zellerfeld, Germany, 1983; founder, CEO MO-Sci. Corp., Rolla. Editor: 3 books; contbr. more than 300 articles to profl. jours. Chmn. bd. Wesley Found.; chmn. United Ministries Higher Edn. Bd. Dirs., 1969; adv. Explorer Scout Post 82, 1964-69; bd. dirs. Rolla Cmty. United Fund, 1975-81, Mo. Incutech Found., 1984-87; mem. bd. adjustment City of Rolla, 1973-79; fin. chmn. United Meth. Ch., 1978-80; pres., bd. dirs. Rolla Cmty. Devel. Corp., 1967-71, 82-90. 1st lt. C.E., U.S. Army, 1958-64. Recipient Outstanding Young Man award Clinton (Miss.) Jaycees, 1963, Rolla (Mo.) Jaycees, 1968, Cmty. Builder award Fraternal Order of Eagles, 1971, Pres.'s award for rsch. and creativity U. Mo., 1996, Chancellor medal U. Mo.-Rolla, 2003, Hosler Alumni Scholar medal Pa. State U., 2003. Fellow Am. Ceramic Soc. (v.p. rsch. 1990-91, trustee 1986-98, trustee glass divsn. 1986-89, chmn. glass divsn. 1982-83, fellows com. 1987-92, publs. com. 1980-82, 90-95, v.p. Publs. 1992-93, treas. 1993-94, pres.-elect 1994-95, pres. 1995-96, others, Outstanding Educator award edn. coun. 1991, G.W. Morey Rsch. award 2001, Samuel Geijsbeek award 2001, Harry E. Ebright award for outstanding svc., 2002, W.D. Kingery award 2004), Am. Nat. Inst. Ceramic Engrs., Soc. Glass Tech. (Great Britain); mem. Nat. Acad. Engring., Am. Soc. Engring. Edn. (chmn. mineral engring. div. 1968-69, program chmn. mineral engring. div. 1967-68), Nat. Inst. Ceramic Engrs. (Profl. Achievement in Ceramic Engring. award 1971, Greaves Walker award 2001), Materials Rsch. Soc., Mo. Acad. Sci. (corp. mem. com. 1989-90), Keramos, Blue Key, Tau Beta Pi, Phi Kappa Phi, Sigma Gamma Epsilon, Sigma Xi (treas. U. Mo.-Rolla chpt. 1966-67, sec. 1967-68, v.p. 1968-69, pres. 1969-70). Achievements include 44 U.S. and foreign patents (with others) for Alumina Zircon Bond for Refractory Grains, Chemically Durable Nitrogen Containing Phosphate Glasses Useful for Sealing to Metals; first to include Radioactive Biologically Compatible Glass Microspheres, Radioactive Glass Microspheres, iron phosphate glasses for vitrifying hazardous wastes, others; co-invention of TheraSphere used for treatment of liver cancer. Home: PO Box 357 Rolla MO 65402-0357 Office: U Mo-Rolla Grad Ctr Material Rsch 109 Straumanis Hl Rolla MO 65409-1170 Office Phone: 573-341-4354. Business E-Mail: day@umr.edu.

DAY, DIANE SLAUGHTER, psychologist; b. Atlanta, June 7, 1955; d. Thomas A. and Joyce Williams Slaughter; m. Lawrence J. Lad, May 12, 2004; children: Adrienne, James, Stewart. BBS, U. Ga., 1977; MS, U. Tex., Tyler, Tex., 2000. Mgr. Sears, Pompano Beach, Fla., 1977—78, Jackson, Miss., 1978—80, AT&T, Atlanta, 1980—81, Dallas, 1981—84; intern psychology Oak Forest Psychol. Assn., Longview, Tex., 1999—2000; psychologist Sabine Ind. Sch. Dist., Gladewater, Tex., 2000—04, Decatur Township Schs., Indpls., 2004—. Mem.: Jr. League (bd. dirs. 1990—95), Kappa Delta (pres. alumnae assn. 2000—04). Avocations: reading, golf, tennis, home improvement, travel. Home: 437 E 82nd St Indianapolis IN 46240

DAY, DONALD LEE, retired engineering educator; b. Leedey, Okla., Aug. 14, 1931; m. Sarah F. Day; children: Cheryl, Keith, Dennis. BS in Agrl. Engring., Okla. State U., 1954, PhD in Agrl. Engring., 1962; MS in Agrl. Engring., U. Mo., 1958. Registered profl. engr., Ill. Engr. Allis Chalmers Mfg. Co., Milw., 1954; instr. Tex. Tech U., Lubbock, 1957-58; asst. prof. U. Ill., Urbana, 1962-67, assoc. prof., 1967-71, prof., 1971-97, ret., 1994. Adviser UN/WHO, Romania, 1972-75, U.S. Food Grain Coun., USSR, Poland and Czechoslovakia, 1975; cons. Internat. Exec. Svc. Corps., Mex., summer 1978; leader structures and environ. divsn. agrl. engring. dept. U. Ill., 1989-94. Author: Livestock Manure Management, 1983; inventor elec. conversion of organic matter; contbr. articles to profl. jours. Recipient fellowship Japan Soc. for Promotion of Sci., 1992, USDA, Office Internat. Coop. and Devel., 1993, numerous grants. Fellow: Am. Soc. Agrl. Engrs. (Rsch. Paper award 1966); mem.: Aircraft Owners and Pilots Assn., Ill. Pilots Assn., Coun. Agrl. Sci. and Tech., Agrl. Honor Orgns. Business E-Mail: dld@age.uiuc.edu.

DAY, DONALD SHELDON, lawyer; b. Boston, Nov. 3, 1924; s. Israel and Frances (Goldberg) D.; m. Edythe Greenberg, July 8, 1945; children: Clifford L., Richard J., Halee Beth. BA, Bates Coll., 1946; LLB, Cornell U., 1948. Bar: N.Y. 1948. Past chmn. bd. Saperston and Day P.C., Buffalo, 1979-96; pres. World Union for Progressive Judaism, 1988-95. Bd. dirs. various corps. Gen. chmn. United Jewish Fund Campaign, Buffalo, 1971-73, 75; past co-chmn. Western N.Y. chpt. NCCJ; past pres. United Jewish Fedn. Buffalo; past chmn. bd. Childrens Hosp. Buffalo, Union Am. Hebrew Congregations; trustee Forest Lawn Cemetery and Crematory, Hebrew-Union Coll. With AUS, 1942-45. Mem. Am., N.Y. State, Erie County bar assns., Order of Coif, Phi Kappa Phi. Jewish (past pres. temple). Office: Hiscock & Barclay 3 Fountain Plz Buffalo NY 14203-1486 Business E-Mail: dday@hiscockbarclay.com.

DAY, EDWARD FRANCIS, JR., lawyer; b. Portland, Maine, Nov. 4, 1946; s. Edward Francis and Anne (Rague) D.; m. Claire Ann Nicholson, June 27, 1970; children: Kelley Ann, John Edward. BA, St. Anselm Coll., 1968; JD cum laude, U. Maine, 1973; LLM in Taxation, NYU, 1976. Bar: N.J. 1973, U.S. Dist. Ct. N.J. 1973, U.S. Tax Ct. 1974, N.Y. 1981. Assoc. Hannoch, Weisman, Stern & Besser, Newark, 1973-74, Carpenter, Bennett & Morrissey, Newark, 1974-78, ptnr., 1979-93, sr. ptnr., 1994-98, of counsel, 1999—2004, McElroy, Deutsch, Mulvaney & Carpenter, LLP, Morristown, NJ, 2004—. Instr. employee benefits and comml. law The Am. Coll., Valley Forge, Pa., 1981-82; exec. v.p., gen. counsel Main Steel Polishing Co., Inc., Tinton Falls, N.J., 1999—. Editor Maine Law Rev., 1972-73. Mem., vice-chmn. Allenhurst (N.J) Bd. Adjustment, 1983-85; mem., vice-chmn. Allenhurst Planning Bd., 1985-87; mem. Nat. Ski Patrol, Denver, 1985—; scoutmaster Monmouth coun. Boy Scouts Am., Ocean Twp., 1987-90; mem. 10th Mountain Divsn. Assn., Aspen, Colo., 1996—. Served in U.S. Army, 1968-70. Named One of Outstanding Young Men of Am., 1979; Ford Found. scholar, 1966-68. Mem.: ABA, Appalachian Mountain Club (Boston), Estate Planning Coun. No. N.J., Essex County Bar Assn., N.J. Bar Assn., Forsgate Country Club (Jamesburg, N.J.), Jersey Coast Club of Red Bank (v.p. 1976—77), Deal (N.J.) Golf and Country Club (bd. dirs. 1985—92, sec. 1991—92), Am. Legion. Roman Catholic. Avocations: golf, skiing, piano. Home: 225 Spier Ave Allenhurst NJ 07711-1120 Office: McElroy Deutsch Mulvaney & Carpenter LLP 3 Gateway Ctr Newark NJ 07102-4079 also: Main Steel Polishing Company Inc 2 Hance Ave Eatontown NJ 07724-2726 Office Phone: 732-450-0110. E-mail: edward.day@verizon.net.

DAY, EMERSON, physician; b. Hanover, NH, May 2, 1913; s. Edmund Ezra and Emily Sophia (Emerson) D.; m. Ruth Fairfield, Aug. 7, 1937 (dec. Oct. 1994); children: Edmund Perry, Robert Fairfield, Nancy, Bonnie, Sheryl; m. Germaine Scherman, Sept. 24, 1999. BA, Dartmouth Coll., 1934; MD, Harvard U., 1938. Intern Presbyn. Hosp., N.Y.C., 1938- 40; fellow in cardiology Johns Hopkins U., 1940-42; asst. resident medicine N.Y. Hosp., 1942; med. dir. internat. divsn. Trans World Airline, N.Y.C., 1945-47; asst. prof. preventive medicine and pub. health Cornell U. Med. Coll., 1947-50, assoc. prof. clin. preventive medicine and pub. health, 1950-54, prof. preventive medicine Sloan Kettering divsn., 1954-64; chmn. dept. preventive medicine Meml. Hosp., N.Y.C., 1954-63; dir. Strang Cancer Prevention Clinic, 1950-63; mem., chief divsn. preventive medicine Sloan-Kettering Inst., N.Y.C., 1954-64; cons. in geriat. Cold Spring Inst., Cold Spring-on-Hudson, NY, 1952-57; dir. N.Y.C. Dept. Health Cancer Detection Ctr., 1947-50, Strang Clinic/Meml. Sloan Kettering Cancer Ctr., 1950-63, PMI-Strang Clinic, 1963-69; pres. Preventive Medicine Inst., Strang Cancer Prevention Ctr., 1969—; hon. pres., mem. bd. trustees Preventive Medicine Inst., 1969—; v.p., med. dir. Medequip Corp., 1969-76, sr. med. cons., 1976-82; med. v.p. Health Mgmt. Internat., Inc., 1982-84; med. dir. Physicians for Med. Cost Containment, Inc., 1984-94; prof. medicine Northwestern U. Med. Sch., 1976-81, prof. emeritus, 1981—; assoc. dir. Northwestern U. Cancer Ctr., 1976-81; med. dir. Portes Cancer Prevention Ctr., 1978-79; attending physician Northwestern Meml. Hosp., 1976-81, vis. physician, 1981-99. Lectr. Cook County Grad. Sch. Med., 1977-90; mem. Northwestern U. Med. Assocs., 1980-81; med. dir., chmn. dept. internal medicine Chgo. Splty. Hosp. and Med. Ctr., 1981-84; hon. staff physician Evanston, Glenbrook hosps., 1976-99; attending physician, mem. med. bd. James Ewing Hosp., Meml. Hosp., N.Y.C., 1950-64; founder, sr. mem. PMX Med. Group, N.Y.C., 1956— 70; adj. prof. biology N.Y. U., 1965-70; mem. cancer detection com. Internat. Union Against Cancer, 1954-70; pres. N.Y.C. div. Am. Cancer Soc., 1963-64; med. cons. Medidata Health Svcs., Inc., 1985-90; mem. Dean's Coun. for Future of Dartmouth Med. Sch. Contbr. numerous articles to profl. jours. Dir. Am. Found. for Children and Youth. Served as flight surgeon ATC USAAF, 1942-45. Recipient Bronze medal Am. Cancer Soc., 1956, professorship in early detection Ill. divsn., 1976-79, Lifetime Achievement award Strang Cancer Prevention Ctr., 2003. Fellow ACP, N.Y. Acad. Medicine, N.Y. Acad. Scis. (pres. 1965), APHA, Am. Occupl. Med. Assn., Am. Geriat. Soc., Internat. Acad. Cytology (hon.); mem. AMA, Am. Soc. Cytopathology (founder, pres. 1958, hon., Papanicolaou award 1978), Am. Soc. Preventive Oncology, Internat. Health Evaluation Assn., Soc. for Advanced Med. Sys. (founding dir. 1969-81), Am. Assn. Med. Sys. and Informatics (founding dir. 1981-84), Harvey Soc., Chgo. Clin. Ethics Program (charter), Century Assn., Ill. Med. Soc., Chgo. Med. Soc., Med. Cons. Svcs. Assn., Dartmouth Club (mem. dean's coun., award 1955), Phi Beta Kappa, Alpha Omega Alpha, Zeta Psi. Home and Office: 18 W Rd 216 Orleans MA 02653 E-mail: emerson.day@valley.net.

DAY, GREGORY CHARLES, music educator; b. Mansfield, Mass., Nov. 22, 1960; s. Raymond Warren and Shirley Ann Day; m. Lisa Michelle Oliver; children: Wesley, Nathan, Riley, Tad. B in Music Edn., Furman U., 1984; M in Music Edn., U. So. Miss., 1988. Dir. bands Pickens County Schools, Central, SC, 1984—87, Rowan County Schools, Salisbury, NC, 1988—89, So. Wesleyan U., Central, 2000—. Bd. dirs. Providence Christian Acad., Six Mile, SC, 2000—02. With U.S. Army, 1978—81. Mem.: Music Educators Nat. Conf. Home: 123 Lowery Ln Pickens SC 29671 Office: Southern Wesleyan Univ Wesleyan Dr Central SC 29630 Business E-Mail: gday@swu.edu.

DAY, GREGORY LYNN, music educator; b. Galesburg, Ill., Oct. 18, 1955; s. Harold Edwin and Norma Ferne Day; m. Margaret Marie Dusa, May 19, 1990; 1 child, Ann Marie. MusB Edn., Augustana Coll., 1977; MusM Edn., No. Ill. U., 1979. Cert. tchr. Ill. Music educator/choral dir. Sterling (Ill.) Sch. Dist., 1977—79, Geneseo (Ill.) Sch. Dist., 1979—82, AlWood Sch. Dist., Woodhull, Ill., 1982—84, Flossmoor (Ill.) Sch. Dist., 1984—. Composer 34 original choral pieces. Choir dir. St. Jude Cath. Ch., New Lenox, Ill., 1996. Mem.: NEA, Music Educators Nat. Conf., Flossmoor Edn. Assn., Ill. Edn. Assn., Am. Choral Dirs. Assn., Ill. Music Educators Assn. Roman Catholic. Avocations: astronomy/cosmology, home electronics. Home: 1849 Harvard Ln New Lenox IL 60451 Office: Parker Jr HS 2810 School St Flossmoor IL 60422 E-mail: glday@netscape.com.

DAY, HARRY GILBERT, nutritional biochemist, consultant; b. Lovilla, Iowa, Oct. 8, 1906; s. John Freeman and Minta Emma (Spencer) D.; m. W. Marie Miller, July 10, 1933 (dec. 1968); children: Margaret Day Pruden, Barbara Day Baumann, Robert M.; m. Gertrude Elizabeth Parr, Aug. 14, 1969 (dec. 1991). AB, Cornell Coll., 1930; DS, Johns Hopkins U., 1933; DS (hon.), Cornell Coll., 1967. Assoc. biochem. Johns Hopkins U., Balt., 1936-40; from asst. prof. to prof. chemistry Ind. U., Bloomington, 1940-50, prof. chemistry, 1950-76, retired, 1976, chmn. dept. chemistry, 1951-62, assoc. dean. rsch. & advanced studies, 1967-72. Mem. select com. GRAS Substances, Fedn. Am. Soc. Exptl. Biology, Bethesda, Md., 1973-82. Contbr. numerous articles to profl. jours.; co-developer first successful fluoridized dentifrice. Mem. Bloomington City Coun., 1963-71. Named Outstanding Alumnus in Pub. Health Johns Hopkins U., 1988, Harry G. Day Lectureship named in his honor Ind. U., 1987, Harry G. Day Lecture Hall named in his honor, 1990, Monroe County (Ind.) Hall of Fame, 1995; grantee AMA, 1940-41, others;

postdoctoral fellow Nat. Rsch. Coun., Johns Hopkins U., 1933-34, Rockefeller Found. gen. fellow Yale U., 1934-36. Fellow AAAS, AIN, Ind. Acad. Sci. (pres. 1962-63), Am. Inst. Nutrition (pres. 1971-72); mem. Am. Chem. Soc. (exam. com. 1959-85), Am. Soc. Biol. Chemists, Kiwanis (pres. 1957-58). Republican. Methodist. Office: Ind U Dept Chemistry Bloomington IN 47405

DAY, HOWARD WILMAN, geology educator; b. Burlington, Vt., Nov. 17, 1942; s. Wilman Forrest and Virginia Louise (Morton) D.; children: Kristina, Sarah, Susan; m. Judy Lynn Blevins. AB, Dartmouth Coll., 1964; MS, Brown U., 1968, PhD, 1971. From asst. prof. to assoc. prof. geology U. Okla., Norman, 1970-76; from asst. prof. to prof. geology U. Calif., Davis, 1976—, chmn. dept., 1990-96. Co-editor Jour. Metamorphic Geology, 1985-92; contbr. articles to profl. jours. Fulbright fellow, Norway, 1964, Alexander von Humboldt fellow, Fed. Republic Germany, 1977. Fellow Geol. Soc. Am., Mineral Soc. Am.; mem. Am. Geophys. Union. Office: U Calif Dept Geology Davis CA 95616 Business E-Mail: hwday@ucdavis.edu.

DAY, JAMES, television executive; b. Alameda, Calif., Dec. 22, 1918; s. James Magee and June (Reeve) D.; m. Beverley Anne Hare, Apr. 12, 1943; children: Meredith Johnson, Douglas Craig, Alan Kent, James Ross. BA, U. Calif., Berkeley, 1941; postgrad., Stanford U., 1951; LHD (hon.), Newark State Coll., Newark, N.J., 1972. Dir. pub. svc. NBC, San Francisco, 1946-49; radio specialist Civil Info. & Edn. Sect./Supreme Commdr. Allies/Pacific, Tokyo, 1949-51; dep. dir. Radio Free Asia, San Francisco, 1951-53; pres., gen. mgr. KQED (TV-FM), San Francisco, 1953-69; pres. Nat. Ednl. TV, N.Y.C., 1969-71, WNET-TV, N.Y.C., 1971-73; prof. radio, TV Bklyn. Coll., CUNY, N.Y.C., 1976-89, prof. emeritus, 1989—; pres. Publivision, Inc., N.Y.C., 1973—. Pres. Timely Prodns. for TV, N.Y.C., 1989—; founding dir. Children's TV Workshop, Pub. Broadcasting Svc., Internat. Pub. TV Screening Conf., Comm. Improvement, Inc.; chmn. adv. bd. City Univ. TV. Author: The Vanishing Vision: The Inside Story of Public Television, 1995, interviewer: (TV) Kaleidoscope, 1954-69, Day at Night, 1973-74, Conversations with Eric Hoffer, 1967, Conversations with Arnold Toynbee, 1968; sr. prodr. Black Writers in America. Capt. U.S. Army, 1941-46. Recipient Robert C. Kirkwood award, San Francisco Found., 1966, Golden Plate award, Am. Acad. Achievement, Dallas, 1968, 50th Anniversary Dirs. award, Ohio State U., Columbus, 1986; resident scholar Rockefeller Study Ctr., Bellagio, Italy, 1978. Mem. Internat. Inst. Comm., Soc. Profl. Journalists. Avocations: photography, swimming. Home: 115 E 86th St New York NY 10028-1057 Office: Publivision Inc One Lincoln Pla New York NY 10023 Office Phone: 212-875-6150. Personal E-mail: jdayny@nyc.rr.com.

DAY, JAMES FREDERICK RANSOM, literature educator; b. Pensacola, Fla. s. Howard Malcolm and Elizabeth Ransom Day. BA, Stetson U., DeLand, Fla., 1972, Oxford U., 1977; MA, U. Fla., 1974, Oxford U., 1977; PhD, Duke U., 1985. Prof. Chowan Coll., Murfreesboro, N.C., 1986-87; assoc. prof. English Troy State U., Ala., 1988—2001, prof. English lit., 2001—. Author: Venal Heralds and Mushroom Gentlemen, 1992, The Coat of Arms. Republican. Avocation: early music. Office: Troy State U English Dept Troy AL 36082 E-mail: jday@troy.edu.

DAY, JAMES MCADAM, JR., lawyer; b. Detroit, Aug. 18, 1948; s. James McAdam and Mary Elizabeth (McGibbon); children: Cara McAdam, Brenna Marie, Michael James; m. Kathleen C. Henderson. AB, UCLA, 1970; JD magna cum laude, U. Pacific, 1973. Bar: Calif. 1973, U.S. Dist. Ct. (no. dist.) Calif. 1973, U.S. Ct. Appeals (9th cir.) 1975. Assoc. Downey, Brand, Seymour & Rohwer, Sacramento, 1973-78, ptnr., 1978—, chmn. natural resources dept., 1985—90; mng. ptnr. Downey, Brand, Seymour & Rohmer, Sacramento, 1990—94, chmn. nat. resources dept., 2002—, mng. ptnr., 1997—2001. Contbr. articles to profl. jours. Pres., bd. dirs. Sacramento Soc. for Prevention of Cruelty to Animals, 1976-79, Children's Home Soc. of Calif., Sacramento, 1979-85; bd. dirs. Sta. KXPR/KXJZ, Inc. Pub. Radio, Sacramento, 1984-94, chmn., 1990-93; bd. dirs. Calif. State Libr. Found., 1995-2000, chmn., 1995-2000. Mem. ABA (natural resources sect. 1998), Calif. Bar Assn. (exec. com. 1985-89, chmn. real property law sect. 1988), Rocky Mountain Mineral Law Found., Sacramento Petroleum Assn., Calif. Mining Assn., U. Pacific McGeorge Law Sch. Alumni Assn. (bd. dirs. 1980-83). Avocations: yacht racing and cruising, fishing. Office: Downey Brand Seymour & Rohwer 555 Capitol Mall Fl 10 Sacramento CA 95814-4504

DAY, JANET S., academic administrator; Sr. v.p. Robert Morris Coll., Ill.; pres. Art Inst. Ill., 1998—. Office: Art Institute Atlanta 6600 Peachtree Dunwoody Rd 100 Embassy Row Atlanta GA 30328*

DAY, JOHN ANTHONY, JR., pulmonologist; b. Washington, Sept. 7, 1949; s. John Anthony and Marcia (O'Brien) Day; m. Jane Marie Doyle, July 9, 1983; children: Margaret Eugenie, Nicholas Paul, Helen Elizabeth. AB, Harvard Coll., 1973; MD, Cornell U., 1981. Diplomate Am. Bd. Critical Care Medicine, Am. Bd. Internal Medicine. Intern, resident in internal medicine Vanderbilt U. Hosp., Nashville, 1981-84; instr. medicine Brown U., Providence, 1984-85, fellow in pulmonary medicine, 1985-87; attending physician Carney Hosp., Boston, 1987-93; asst. prof. medicine U. Mass. Med. Sch., Worcester, 1993—. Attending physician Day Kimball Hosp., Putnam, Conn. Fellow: Am. Coll. Chest Physicians; mem.: Am. Thoracic Soc. Home: 270 Old Turnpike Dr Woodstock CT 06282 Office: 346 Pomfret St Putnam CT 06260 Office Phone: 860-928-4344.

DAY, JOHN ARTHUR, lawyer; b. Madison, Wis., Sept. 21, 1956; s. John Donald and Elinor Roletta (Heath) D. BS, U. Wis., Platteville, 1978; JD, U. N.C., 1981. Bar: Tenn. 1981, U.S. Dist. Ct. (mid. dist.) Tenn. 1981, U.S. Ct. Appeals (6th cir.) 1982; civil cert. Nat. Bd. Trial Advocacy 1991. Assoc. Boult Cummings Conners & Berry, Nashville, 1981-86, ptnr., 1987-92; shareholder Branham & Day, P.C., 1993—. Mem. Civil Justice Reform Act adv. group U.S. Dist. Ct. (mid. dist.) Tenn., 1991-95; mem. Tenn. Supreme Ct. Commn. on Continuing Legal Edn. and Specialization, 2001—, Tenn. Judicial Evaluation Commn., 2003-. Co-author: Tennessee Law of Comparative Fault, 1997, 2d edit., 2002; founder, editor Tenn. Tort Law Letter, 1995—; contbr. articles to profl. jours. Com. mem. Cohn Roundtable, Nashville, 1988; assoc. Harry Phillips Inn of Ct., 1990-92, Tenn. John Marshall Inn of Ct., 1999—. Fellow Am. Coll. Trial Lawyers; mem. Tenn. Trial Lawyers Assn. (bd. govs. 1984-85, treas. 1985-89, v.p. 1989-93, pres. 1993-94, chair legal edn. com. 1985-86, chair legis. com. 1987-90, CLE com. 1984-97, pub. rels. com. 1986-88, long range planning com. 1991-93), Assn. Trial Lawyers Am. (Tenn. pub. rels. rep. 1986-87, people's law sch. com. co-chair 1986-88, pub. rels. com. 1986-91, chair 1988-89, edn. com. 1987-88, pub. affairs com. 1987-89, publs. com. 1990-93, vice chmn. 1991-93, co-chair 1992-93, key person com. 1987-89, nursing home litigation group 1985-89, chmn. 1987-89, mem. exec. com. 1994-95, chair pres.'s coun. 1994-95), Nashville Bar Assn. (bd. dirs. 1998-2000, circuit and chancery ct. com. chair 1989, fee disputes com. 1984-85, 87, vice chmn. 1988, chmn. 1989), Lawyers Involved for Tenn. (trustee 1988—), Tenn. Bar Assn. (mem. litigation sect. coun. 1989-90), Nat. Bd. Trial Advocacy (bd. dirs. 1998—, stds. com. 1998-2004, v.p. 2001-02, pres.-elect 2002-03, pres. 2003-04), Tenn. Justice Ctr. (bd. dirs. 1999—, pres. 2003-04). Democrat. Home: 608 Good Springs Rd Brentwood TN 37027-5173 Office: Branham & Day PC PO Box 40592 Nashville TN 37204

DAY, JOHN DENTON, retired company executive, cattle and horse rancher, breeder, trainer, wrangler, actor, educator; b. Salt Lake City, Jan. 20, 1942; s. George W. and Grace (Denton) Jenkins; m. Susan Hansen, June 20, 1971; children: Tammy Denton Wadsworth (dec.), Jeanett B, Barber. Student, U. Utah, 1964-65; BA in Econs. and Bus. Adminstrn. with high honors, Westminster Coll., 1971. Riding instr., wrangler Uinta wilderness area U-Ranch, Neola, Utah, 1955-58; wrangler, riding instr. YMCA Camp Rodger, Kamas, Utah, 1957; stock handler, driver, ruffstock rider Earl Hutchinson Rodeo Contractor, Idaho, 1959; with Mil. Data Cons., Inc., L.A., 1961-62, Carlseon Credit Corp., Salt Lake City, 1962-65; sales mgr. sporting goods Western Enterprises, Salt Lake City, 1965-69; founder Rockin d Ranch, Millcreek, Utah, 1969; ski instr. Brighton (Utah) Ski Sch., 1969-71; Western rep. PBR Co., Cleve., 1969-71; owner, founder, pres. John D. Day, mfrs. reps., 1972—; dist. sales rep. Crown Zellerbach Corp., Seattle and L.A., 1971-73; dist. sales mgr. Surfonics Engrs., Inc., Woods Cross, Utah, 1976-78, Garland Co., Cleve., 1978-81; pres., founder Dapco paper, chem., instl. food and janitorial supplies, Salt Lake City, 1973-79; rancher Heber, Utah, 1976-90, horse tng. facility, horsemanship sch. and ranch, Temecula, Calif., 1984-90, St. George, Utah, 1989-99; pres., founder John D Day Greeting Cards and Art Works, 1990—; horse training Horsemanship Sch., Quarter Horse Breeding Facility, Yerington, Nev., 1999—2004; owner Quarter Horse Breeding Facility, Art Studio, Dammeron Valley, Utah, 2004—. Sec. bd. Acquadyne, 1974, 75. Actor, dir., prodr. (movies) The Big Sky, 1952, Rebel Without a Cause, 1955, Devils Brigade, 1967, Coyote Summer, 1995, (videos) Someday Soon, 1993, A Tour of Snows Canyon, 1993, All For the Love of Horse, 1982-83, Stallion Management, 1985, others; tv spls. and commls., Chev., Palmer, The Osmonds, others; contbr. articles to jours., including Western Artist. Group chmn. Tele-Dex fund raising project Westminster Coll.; founder, supr. vol. group Day's Rangers, 1990-99, 2004—; vol. Dixie Nat. Forest, 1989-94, 2004—, USDA Forest Svc.; 1st U.S. wilderness ranger USDA, US Forest Svc., Dixie Nat. Forest, Pine Valley Ranger Dist., Pine Valley Mountain Wilderness, So. Utah, 1994-99; vol. State of Nev. Ft. Churchill State Hist. Pk. & Pony Express Tr., 1999-2004; vol. Dixie Nat. Forest, 2004—. With AUS, 1963-64. Recipient grand nat. award Internat. Custom Car Show, San Diego, 1962, Award of Excellence Winternationals Nat. Hot Rod Assn., 1962-63, Key to City, Louisville, Ky., 1964, Champion Bareback Riding award, 1957, Vol. award USDA Forest Svc., 1991, 92, 93, nominated U.S. Vol. award, Safety award Dixie Nat. Forest, P.V.R.D., 1992-99; recipient Outstanding Performance award USDA, 1995, 98, Cert. Appreciation, 1997, DNF Outstanding Svc. award, 1997, Pine Valley Mountain Wilderness award, Nev. State Parks, Appreciation cert. Fort Churchill State Historic Park, 1999-2004; Dally team roping heading and heeling champion, 1982. Mem. Internat. Show Car Assn. (co-chmn. 1978-79), Am. Quarter Horse Assn. (life, Horseback Riding Program 5000 Hour award 2002), Profl. Horseman Assn. (high point reining champion 1981, awarded Nat. Reining Horse Assn. Bronze, qualified for world championship, Dodge, Toyota Fall Futurite Circuit Champion Working Cowhorse 1994-95, World Championship Show qualifier and participant Oklahoma City Sr. Cutting 1994, regional championships, region 7, ring steward, 4A horse-testride, 2005), Intermountain Quarter Horse Assn. (sr. reining champion 1981, champion AMAT reining 1979-81), Utah Quarter Horse Assn. (state champion AMAT reining 1979, 80, AMAT barrel racing 1980, working cowhorse champion 1982, trained working cowhorse and rider champion 1992, 98, 2003, trained amateur reining horse and rider champion 1996, 2003, open cutting res. champion 1993-95, 97, open cutting champion 1994, Menlove Dodge Toyota Fall Futurity circuit champion working cowhorse, 1994-95, open working cowhorse champion & broadmare halter champion 1995, Rose cir. working cowhorse champion 1995, 98, Rose Cir. Open working cowhorse champion, showed cir. champion Brodmare at Halter Rose cir. open cutting champion 1996, 97, bd. dirs. 1992-94, trained amateur barrel racing and amateur pole bending horse and rider 1998, State Reserve Champion amateur cutting horse and rider, trained state champion team roping champion roper, herding and heeling, 2003, team roping heeling champion 2004), Profl. Cowhorseman's Assn., Nat. Cutting Horse Assn. (affiliate), Profl. Cowhorseman's Assn. (world champion team roping, heeling 1986, 88, high point rider 1985, world champion stock horse rider 1985-86, 88, world champion working cowhorse 1985, PCA finals open cutting champion, 1985-88, PCA finals 1500 novice champion 1987, PCA finals all-around champion 1985-88, inducted into Hall of Fame 1988, first on record registered Tex. longhorn cutting contest, open champion, PCA founder, editor newsletter 1985-89, pres. 1984-88), World Rodeo Assn. Profls. (v.p. Western territory 1989-98, judge nat. high sch. rodeo, cutting horse and rodeo queen contest, 1990—, hon. life v.p. Western Terr. U.S. 1998—), Future Farmers Am. (horse judge 2003—), Nevada Quarter Horse Assn. (mem. com., Am. Quarter Horse Assn., Ride 2000, "Let Freedom Ride", Fall Circuit 2000 Open Cutting Champion), Nev. Quarter Horse Assn. (Summer Circuit Champion), 2002, Utah Qt. Horse Assn. (mem. com.)

DAY, JOHN N., music educator; b. Jacksonville, Ill., Aug. 2, 1954; s. Neil and Josephine Day; m. Karen Reinette Rowell. M Music Edn., Ea. Ky. U., 1986. Cert. tchr. Ky. Mid. sch. music tchr. Martin County Sch. Sys., Inez, Ky., 1987—98; elem. music tchr. Clarkson (Ky.) Elem. Sch., 1998—. Pvt. piano tchr., Clarkson, 1998—. Co-minister Creative Hearts Ministries, Clarkson, 1994—2005. Home: 220 Franklin Ln Clarkson KY 42726 Office Phone: 270-242-3061. Personal E-mail: johnday4@yahoo.com. E-mail: jday@grayson.k12.ky.us.

DAY, JOHN SIDNEY, management sciences educator; b. Newton, Mass., Oct. 13, 1917; s. Franklin Everett and Marion (Guild) D.; m. Barbara Jane Felch, Nov. 20, 1940; children: John Sidney, Stephen L. Student, Tufts U., 1935-37, Oxford Sch. Bus. Adminstrn., 1939; MBA with distinction, Harvard U., 1950, D.C.S., 1956; D. in Mgmt. (hon.), Purdue U., 1993. Asst. to pres. C. Carlson Co., Boston, 1939-40, 45-46; instr. Oxford Sch. Bus. Adminstrn., Cambridge, Mass., 1946-48; rsch. asst. Harvard Grad. Sch. Bus. Adminstrn., Cambridge, Mass., 1950-51, rsch. assoc., 1951-53, asst. prof., 1953-56; assoc. prof. Purdue U., Lafayette, Ind., 1956-59, prof. indsl. mgmt., 1959-83, dean Krannert Grad. Sch. Mgmt., 1969-78, v.p. for devel., 1978-83, Krannert prof. mgmt., 1983-86, v.p. emeritus, 1986—. Author: (with L. Bollinger) Management of New Enterprises, 1952, Subcontracting Policy in the Airframe Industry, 1956, (with P. Donham) New Enterprise and Small Business Management, 1960. Bd. dirs. Purdue Rsch. Found., 1980-83; mem. Tippecanoe County (Ind.) chpt. ARC, 1968-74, chmn., 1974; treas. Tippecanoe County Easter Seal Soc., 1972-78; mem. West Lafayette Econ. Devel. Commn., chmn., 1975-83; mem. nat. adv. coun. SBA; trustee Joint Coun. on Econ. Edn., 1976-78; pres. Oak Point Cmty. Assn., Inc., 1980-86; bd. dirs. Home Hosp., 1972-78, pres., 1977; bd. dirs. Am. Assemblies Collegiate Schs. Bus., 1974-78, pres., 1977-78. Served to col. USMCR. Decorated Bronze Star (2); Baker scholar; Ford Found. fellow, 1959-60; named Hon. Sec. of State Ind.; receipent Sagamore of the Wabash. Mem. 1st Marine Divsn. Assn., Masons. Home and Office: 25 River Mead Rd Peterborough NH 03458 E-mail: josidday@rivermead.org.

DAY, JOHN T., academic administrator, dean; b. Poughkeepsie, N.Y., Mar. 1, 1948; s. John T. and Catherine M. Day; m. Sharon M. MacFarland, July 4, 1970; children: Caitlin A., Laura E., Nathaniel A. BA summa cum laude, Coll. of the Holy Cross, 1970; MA, Harvard U., 1971, PhD, 1977. Allston Burr sr. tutor Harvard U., Cambridge, Mass., 1976—79; from asst. to full prof. English St. Olaf Coll., Northfield, Minn., 1979—2002, assoc. dean for interdisciplinary studies, 1999—2002, asst. v.p. for acad. affairs, 2000—02; English prof. Roanoke Coll., Salem, Va., 2002, v.p. acad. affairs, dean, 2002—. Trustee Roanoke Higher Edn. Authority, 2002—. Editor: (collection of essays) Word, Church, and State: Tyndale Quincentenary Essays; book reviewer: Sixteenth Century Jour., author essays. Office: Roanoke College 221 College Ln Salem VA 24153 Office Phone: 540-375-2203.

DAY, JONATHAN S., lawyer; b. Houston, 1940; AB, Princeton U., 1962; JD, U Tex., 1965. Bar: Tex. 1965. City atty. City of Houston, 1974—76; ptnr., Pub. Law Andrews Kurth LLP, Houston, mem. mgmt. com. Mem.: ABA, State Bar Tex., Houston Bar Assn., Phi Delta Phi. Office: Andrews Kurth LLP 600 Travis St Ste 4200 Houston TX 77002-3090 Office Phone: 713-220-4715. Office Fax: 713-238-7365. Business E-Mail: jonathanday@andrewskurth.com.

DAY, JULIAN C., retail executive; BA, MA, Oxford U.; MBA, London Bus. Sch. Sr. engagement mgr. McKinsey & Co., 1980-85; v.p., European devel. mgr. Chase Manhattan Bank, 1985-87; exec. mgmt. cons. Kohlberg, Kravis, and Roberts, 1987-93; exec. v.p., CFO Safeway, Inc., 1993-98, Sears, Roebuck and Co., Hoffman Estate, Ill., 1999—2002; pres, COO Kmart Corp., 2002—03, pres, CEO, 2003—04. Bd. dirs. Petco Animal Supplies, Inc., KMart Holding Corp. Office: Kmart Holding Corp 3100 W Big Beaver Rd Troy MI 48084

DAY, KEVIN THOMAS, retired bank executive; b. London, Aug. 24, 1937; came to U.S., 1957; s. William Stanley and Mary Ann (Hook) D.; m. Mary Violet Scheuber, Aug., 1960. BA, Brisbane Tech. Coll., Queensland, Australia, 1957. Pres. Americana Investments, San Francisco, 1960-63; stockbroker Sutro and Co., San Francisco, 1963-66; regional v.p. Am. Express Investment Co., San Francisco, 1966-70; dir. mktg. ITT Fin. Svcs., N.Y.C., 1970-78; pres. Exec. Assocs., Reno, 1978-83, First Interstate Bank Found., Reno, 1983-1991; exec. dir. Cath. Community Svcs., Reno, 1991—2004; ret. Cath. Community Svcs., Reno, 2004. Chmn. Nev. Fgn. Trade Zone, Reno, 1986-91, Desert Rsch. Inst., Reno. Pres. Econ. Devel. Authority, Reno, 1985, Nev. Mus. Art, 1989-91; mem. exec. com. Western Indsl. Nev., Reno, 1985-90; commr. Nev. Commn. on Econ. Devel., Carson City, 1987-90. Named Man of Yr., Reno mag., 1988, Torch of Liberty award, 1989; named to Nev. Order of Silver Spur, 1990. Republican. Roman Catholic. Avocations: adventure travel, wilderness camping, art collecting. Home: 3600 Worthington Way Plano TX 75023 Personal E-mail: kevaday@msn.com.

DAY, LAWRENCE C., auto parts executive; V.p., Auto Express Div. Montgomery Ward; pres., CEO Monro Muffler Brake, Inc., 1995—98; pres. TBC Corp., 1998—, bd. dir., 1998—, CEO, 1999—. Office: c/o TBC Corp 7111 Fairway Dr Palm Beach Gardens FL 33418*

DAY, LAWRENCE ELWOOD, technical manager; b. Columbus, Ohio, Sept. 17, 1947; s. Wilbur Hastings and Gloria Marie (Sega) D.; children: Katherine Ann, James Nelson, Laura Elizabeth; m. Kyung Ae Kim, Apr. 22, 1995. BSEE, Worcester (Mass.) Polytechnic Inst., 1969; MBA in Tech. and Engring. Mgmt., City U., Bellevue, Wash., 1988; ThD, Triune Bibl. U., 2001. Cert. quality analyst, project mgmt. profl.; ordained to ministry, 2000; ordained bishop Ch. of the East, 2000. Software engr. Westinghouse Electric Co., Balt., 1969-73; radar engr. Boeing Aerospace Co., Seattle, 1973-75, software engr., 1975-82, tech. subcontract mgr., 1985-86, software mgr., 1986-87, software devel. mgr., 1987, program mgr., 1987-88, system design mgr., 1988-90; engring. mgr. Boeing Computer Svcs., Seattle, 1990-94; software mgr. Boeing Mil. Airplane Co., Seattle, 1982-85; info. tech. project mgr. Boeing Shared Svcs., Seattle, 1995—; presiding bishop Triune Bibl. Ch., Bellevue, Wash., 2001—. Pres., owner Day Aircraft, Bellevue, Wash., 1981—; charter mem. Boeing Embedded Software Task Team, 1991-92; charter mem. Boeing Software Quality Assurance Coun., 1991—, chmn., 1995-96; IT mgmt. cons., 2000—; internat. conf. spkr., tchr. Quality Assurance Inst., 1998—; real estate investor, 2004—; presenter in field. Rep. precinct committeeman, Renton, 1988-94; deacon Bethel Chapel, Issaquah, Wash., 1976-77; Sunday sch. tchr. Neighborhood Ch., Bellevue, 1979-97; participant Passion Play; group food provider New Horizons Ministry, Seattle, 1989-93; ch. spkr., bd. dirs. Triune Biblical Ch., bd. dirs. Triune Biblical U. Recipient Speaker Recognition award Kiwanis, 1988. Mem. Boeing Employees Flying Assn. (pres. 1987-88, treas. 2000—, high performance check pilot), Boeing Mgmt. Assn., Aircraft Owners and Pilots Assn., Full Gospel Businessmen's Fellowship Internat. (conf., chpt. and luncheon spkr., pres. Bellevue 1979-80, v.p. 1981-82, treas. 1975-78, 79), Internat. Fellowship of Christian Businessmen (pres. 2005, Wash. area dir., 2004-05). Republican. Avocations: pilot, single-engine land multi-engine instrument ground instr., advanced instrument ground instr., open water scuba diver. Home: 17707 SE 60th St Bellevue WA 98006-5915 Office Phone: 425-957-5039. E-mail: lawrence.e.day@boeing.com.

DAY, LINCOLN HUBERT, demographer, educator; b. Ames, Iowa, Jan. 7, 1928; s. John Armstrong and Vera (Hills) Day; m. Alice Taylor, Nov. 26, 1952; children: Thomas Hills, Caroline Day Santesteban. BA, Yale U., 1949; MA, Columbia U., 1951, PhD, 1957. Instr., asst. prof. sociology Mt. Holyoke Coll., South Hadley, Mass., 1955—58; asst. prof. sociology Princeton (NJ) U., 1958—59; rsch. assoc. Bur. Applied Social Rsch. Columbia U., N.Y.C., 1959—62; vis. fellow in demography Australian Nat. U., Canberra, 1962—64, sr. fellow in demography, 1973—94; rsch. assoc. Sch. Pub. Health Harvard U., Boston, 1964—65; assoc. prof. pub. health and sociology Yale U., New Haven, 1965—70; chief demographic and social stats. br. UN, N.Y.C., 1970—73; Hofstee fellow Netherlands Interdisciplinary Demographic Inst., Den Haag, 1994. Vis. prof. sociology Columbia U., 1976. Co-author (with Alice Taylor Day): Too Many Americans, 1964; co-author: (with A.J. Jaffe) Disabled Workers in the Labor Market, 1964; author: Analysing Population Trends, 1983, The Future of Low-Birthrate Populations, 1992; co-editor (with D.T. Rowland): How Many More Australians?, 1988; co-editor: (with Ma Xia) Migration and Urbanization in China, 1994; contbr. numerous articles to profl. jours. Mem. adv. bd. Environ. Film Festival, Washington; bd. dirs. Ctr. for Arms Control and Non-Proliferation, Washington. Cpl. U.S. Army, 1953—55. Fellow, Fulbright Found., 1968; scholar-in-residence, Bellagio (Italy) Study and Conf. Ctr., 1990. Mem.: Am. Sociol. Assn., Sustainable Population Australia, Nature and Soc. Forum, European Assn. for Population Studies, Internat. Union for Sci. Study of Population, Population Assn. Am., Amnesty Internat., Coun. for a Livable World, ACLU, Cosmos Club. Democrat. Avocations: travel, politics, gardening. Home: 2124 Newport Pl NW Washington DC 20037-3001 E-mail: at-lhday@verizon.net.

DAY, LUCILLE LANG, museum administrator, educator, writer; b. Oakland, Calif., Dec. 5, 1947; d. Richard Allen and Evelyn Marietta (Hazard) Lang; m. Frank Lawrence Day, Nov. 6, 1965 (div. 1970); 1 child, Liana Sherrine; m. Theodore Herman Fleischman, June 23, 1974 (div. 1985); 1 child, Tamarind Channah Fleischman; m. Richard Michael Levine, Aug. 25, 2002. AB, U. Calif., Berkeley, 1971, MA, 1973, PhD, 1979; MA, San Francisco State U., 1999, MFA, 2004. Tchg. asst. U. Calif., Berkeley, 1971-72, 75-76, rsch. asst., 1975, 77-78; tchr. sci. Magic Mountain Sch., Berkeley, 1977; specialist math. and sci. Novato (Calif.) Unified Sch. Dist., 1979-81; instr. sci. Project Bridge Laney Coll., Oakland, 1984-86; sci. writer and mgr. precoll. edn. programs Lawrence Berkeley Nat. Lab., 1986-90, life scis. staff coord., 1990-92, mgr. Hall of Health, Children's Hosp. & Rsch. Ctr. at Oakland, 1992—2004, dir. Hall of Health, 2004—. Lectr. St. Mary's Coll. Calif., Moraga, 1997—2000. Author: numerous poems, articles and book reviews; author: (with Joan Skolnick and Carol Langbort) How to Encourage Girls in Math and Science: Strategies for Parents and Educators, 1982; author: (poetry) Self-Portrait with Hand Microscope, 1982, Fire in the Garden, 1997, Wild One, 2000, Lucille Lang Day, Greatest Hits, 1975-2000, 2001, Infinities, 2002, (children's book) Chain Letter, 2005. Recipient Joseph Henry Jackson award in lit., San Francisco Found., 1982; Grad. fellow, NSF, 1972—75. Mem.: Soc. Pub. Health Edn. (No. Calif. chpt.), Math./Sci. Network, Nat. Assn. Sci. Writers, No. Calif. Sci. Writers Assn., Phi Beta Kappa, Iota Sigma Pi. Home: 1057 Walker Ave Oakland CA 94610-1511 Office: Hall of Health 2230 Shattuck Ave Berkeley CA 94704-1416 Office Phone: 510-549-1564. Business E-Mail: lucyday@hallofhealth.org.

DAY, MARLENE E., elementary school educator; b. Biddeford, Maine, July 16, 1955; d. Vincent Louis and Marguerita Marcella Noella Angelosante; widowed; children: Shauna, Chaz; m. Charles E. Day Jr., Oct. 1, 2003. BS, U. Maine, 1977; MS in Reading, U. So. Maine, 1982. Tchr. Old Orchard Beach (Maine) Elem. Sch., 1977—80, Loranger Mid. Sch., Old Orchard Beach, 1980—. Mem. Commn. for Children with Spl. Needs., Augusta, Maine, 1983—84, Gov.'s Commn. Excellence in Edn., Augusta, 1983—85; religious edn. tchr., lectr. St. Margaret Cath. Ch., Old Orchard Beach. Named Maine State Tchr. of Yr., 1983; recipient Project Seed award, 1994. Mem.: Maine Tchrs. Assn., Phi Delta Kappa (past sec.). Roman Catholic. Avocations: reading, gardening, travel. Home: 1 Smith Ave Old Orchard Beach ME 04064 Office: Old Orchard Beach Sch Dept Loranger Mid Sch 148 Saco Ave Old Orchard Beach ME 04064

DAY, MARY, artistic director, ballet company executive; b. Wash. Trained by Lisa Gardinier; ArtsD (hon.), Shenandoah Conservatory; DHL (hon.), Mount Vernon Coll. Co-founder Washington Sch. of Ballet, 1944—; founder Washington Ballet, 1976—. Named Washingtonian of Yr., Washingtonian mag.; recipient Mayor's award, Woman of Achievement award, WETA-TV,

Met. Dance award, Founders award, Cultural Alliance, Excellence in Teaching Chautauqua Dance award, sr. Svcs. Disting. award IONA. Office: Washington Ballet 3515 Wisconsin Ave NW Washington DC 20016-3085

DAY, MARY ANN, medical/surgical nurse; b. Covington, Tenn., Apr. 9, 1944; m. George Day, Jan. 17, 1980; children: Maurice, Michele, Shawn, Corey. AAS, Joliet (Ill.) Jr. Coll., 1989; BSN, Lewis U., 1995; student, U. St. Francis, 1998—. RN, Ill.; cert. emergency nurse pediat. course. Staff nurse Michael Reese Hosp., Chgo., 1989-91, MacNeal Hosp., Berwyn, Ill., 1991-99, Westlake Hosp., Melrose Park, Ill., 1999—; adj. faculty/LPN program Triton Coll., River Grove, Ill., 1996—, instr. RN continuing edn. course, 1998—; asst. patient care mgr. St. Joseph Hosp., Joliet, Ill., 1999—; IV therapist Ctrl. Dupage Hosp., Winfield, Ill., 1999—; nursing supr. St. Anthony's Hosp., Chgo., 2001—. Mem. diversity task force com., Westlake Hosp., 1999; instr. in nursing assistance Waubonsee Coll., 2002; weekend supr. VNA Home Health Nominee Black Profl. Female scholarship, Minority Student of Yr., 1989. Avocations: classical music, classical pianist. Home: 6 Puffin Cir Bolingbrook IL 60440-1236

DAY, MELVIN SHERMAN, information and telecommunications company executive; b. Lewiston, Maine, Jan. 22, 1923; s. Israel and Frances (Goldberg) D.; m. Louisa Walker; children: Cynthia Day Solganick, Wendy Day Young, Robert Marshall. BS, Bates Coll., 1943; postgrad., U. Tenn., 1953—54. Chemist Metal Hydrides Inc., Beverly, Mass., 1943-44, Tenn. Eastman Corp., Oak Ridge, 1944-46; sci. analyst AEC, Oak Ridge, 1946-48, asst. chief tech. info. svc. ext., 1950-56, chief, 1956-58, dir. tech. info. divsn. Washington, 1958-60; dep. dir. Tech. Info. and Ednl. Programs Office, NASA, Washington, 1960-61, dir. Sci. and Tech. Info. divsn., 1961-67, dep. asst. adminstr. tech. utilization, 1967-70; head Office Sci. Info. NSF, Washington, 1970-72; dep. dir. Nat. Libr. Medicine, HEW, Bethesda, Md., 1972-78; dir. Nat. Tech. Info. Svc. Dept. Commerce, 1978-82; v.p. Info. Tech. Group, 1982-84, Rsch. Publs., 1984-86; sr. v.p. Herner & Co., 1986-88; pres. M. Day Cons. Internat., Inc., Arlington, Va., 1988—; exec. v.p. BIIS Corp., Herndon, 1991-94, GlobeNet Holding Corp., 1994-97. Cons. IAEA, 1960; adviser OECD, 1970, 75; U.S. mem. OECD info. policy group; U.S. mem. NATO Tech. Info. Panel, 1960-70, 79-82, chmn., 1970; chmn. com. on sci. and tech. info. Fed. Coun., 1970-72, chmn. com. on intergovtl. sci. rels., 1969-70, chmn. sci. info. exch. adv. bd., 1963-69, mem. chem. abstracts adv. bd., 1964-68; mem. Fed. Libr. Com., 1968-78, chmn. exec. bd., 1973-75; trustee Found. Ctr. 1972-78, trustee emeritus, 1991—; U.S. mem. adv. com. on librs., documentation and archives UNESCO; pres. abstracting bd. Internat. Coun. Sci. Unions, 1977-83; bd. dirs. Internat. Coun. for Sci. and Tech. Info., 1983—, Inst. for Internat. Info. Programs, 1985-88; trustee Engring. Info., Inc., 1981-84, bd. dirs., 1993-98; del. numerous panels; cons., adviser and lectr. in field; mem. adv. com. HHS Health Svcs. Rsch. Dissemination and User Liaison, 1990-92, also mem. dissemination com. Mem. editl. bd. Health Comm. and Informatics, 1977-80, Infomediary, 1990-93, Yearbook of the Database Info. Industry, 1990-91. Bd. visitors U. Pitts. Grad. Sch. Info. Sci., 1977-83. With U.S. Army, 1944-46. Recipient Exceptional Svc. medal NASA, 1971, Superior Svc. award USPHS, 1976. Fellow AAAS, Nat. Fedn. Abstracting and Info. Svcs. (hon. fellow); mem. Am. Soc. Info. Sci. (chmn. internat. rels. com. 1972-75, pres. 1975-76, coun. 1975-77, editl. bd. bull. 1977-80), Am. Chem. Soc., Spl. Libr. Assn., Am. Soc. Cybernetics (bd. dirs. 1975-79), Venezuelan Acad. Scis. (hon. corr.), Internat. Coun. Sci. and Tech. Info. (hon., Disting. Svc. award 1997), Cosmos Club. Home: 4309 Chesapeake St NW Washington DC 20016-4509

DAY, MICHAEL GORDON, information technology executive, educator; b. Madison, Wis., July 30, 1951; s. Lee Monroe and Joan (Meredith) D.; m. Donna Kay Corl, May 26, 1979 (div. Apr. 1986); children: Thomas Lee, Anne Elizabeth; m. Carol Ann Stefanko, Apr. 12, 1997. BA, Pa. State U., 1973; JD, George Washington U., 1976. Bar: Pa. 1976. Assoc. Alan Ellis, Esq., State College, Pa., 1976-77; pvt. practice State College, Pa., 1977-85; with Profl. Planning Cons., State College, Pa., 1985-86, Century Fin. Svcs., State College, Pa., 1986-96; solutions expert Netscape, 1996-99; dir. Info. Tech. Inst./Shepherd Coll., Shepherdstown, W.Va., 1999—. Instr. bus. law Pa. State U., University Park, 1978-79, instr. continuing legal edn., 2002; counsel Boccardo Law Firm, San Jose, Calif., 1983, Rees Law Firm, Washington, 1983; sr. v.p. Century Mortgage Corp., 1991-96. Chmn. Com. to Elect Mel Hodes Senator, Pa., 1982, Dem. Com., State College, 1982-84; active Exec. Com. Centre County, 1982-84, United Pennsylvanians, 1982-83; gen. counsel CLEAN, 1982-85; v.p. Mt. Nittany Conservancy, 2000-02; candidate for Pa. Ho. Reps., 1980; candidate for dist. justice 49th Dist. Pa., 1977, chmn. Potomac Alliance for Kerry, 2004; owner www.4kerry.com, 2004; mem. Md. for Kerry Steering Com.; coord. Washington County Md. for Kerry; founder Free State, 2005—; founder Free State Polit. Action Com., 2005. Mem. Lions Paw Alumni Assn. (pres. 1999-2001), Parmi Nous, Omicron Delta Kappa, Delta Sigma Rho. United Ch. Of Christ. Office: 400 W Stephen St Martinsburg WV 25401 Business E-Mail: michael@michaelday.org.

DAY, PETER RODNEY, geneticist, educator; b. Chingford, Essex, Eng., Dec. 27, 1928; came to U.S., 1963; m. Lois Elizabeth Rhodes, May 26, 1951; children: Susan Catherine, Rupert Peter, William Rodney. BS in Botany, Birkbeck Coll., Eng., 1950; PhD, U. London, 1954. Sr. scientific officer John Innes Inst., Hertford, Eng., 1957-63; assoc. prof. Ohio State U., Columbus, 1963-64; chief, genetics dept. Conn. Agrl. Expt. Sta., New Haven, 1964-79; dir. Plant Breeding Inst., Cambridge, Eng., 1979-87; prof. genetics, dir. Rutgers U., New Brunswick, NJ, 1987—2002, prof. emeritus, 2002—. Sec. Internat. Genetics Fedn., 1984-93; trustee Internat. Ctr. for Maize and Wheat Improvement, Mexico City, 1986-92; chmn. Mng. Global Genetic Resources Bd. on Agrl., NAS, Washington, 1986-93. Author: Genetics of Host-Parasite Interaction, 1974; co-author: (with J.R.S. Fincham) Fungal Genetics, 1963, (with H.H. Prell) Plant-Fungal Pathogen Interaction, 2001. Commonwealth Fund fellow U. Wis., 1954-56; Guggenheim Meml. fellow U. Queensland, 1972. Home: 8200 Tarsier Ave New Port Richey FL 34653 E-mail: day@aesop.rutgers.edu.

DAY, RICHARD ALLEN, chemistry professor; b. Kellogg, Iowa, Apr. 4, 1931; s. Clarence Hodson and Della (Mendenhall) Day; m. Lyn Tibbits, Aug. 19, 1956; children: Eric, Sylvia. Student, William Penn Coll., 1949-50; BS, Iowa State U., 1953; Phd, MIT, 1958. Rsch. assoc. MIT, Cambridge, 1957-59; asst. prof. chemistry U. Cin., 1959-63, assoc. prof. chemistry, 1963-68, prof. chemistry, 1968—, prof. biol. chemistry Coll. of Medicine, 1972—. Faculty rep. to U. Cin. Bd. Trustees, 1990-93; exec. com. Ohio Valley Chromatography Symposium; bd. dirs. DataChem, Inc., Indpls., BioCin Inc., Cin. Patentee in field. Recipient numerous grants. Fellow AAAS; mem. Am. Chem. Soc. (chmn. Cin. sect. 1982-83), Am. Soc. Mass Spectrometry, Am. Soc. Microbiology, Am. Soc. Biochem. & Molecular Biology, Protein Soc. E-mail: richard.day@uc.edu.

DAY, RICHARD PUTNAM, marketing professional, arbitrator, employee benefits consultant; b. Hartford, Conn., Feb. 13, 1930; s. Godfrey Malbone and Sheila (Wilson) D.; m. Patricia Ann Brady, Jan. 26, 1957; children: Richard Jr., Stephen, Thomas (dec.), Gregory, Katharine, Martha, Ward, Emily. Student, The Choate Sch., 1948; AB, Middlebury Coll., 1952. With group field sales Conn. Gen. Life Ins. Co., Hartford, Detroit, Toledo, Phoenix, 1952-61; dir. sales group Bankers Life Nebr. (name changed to Ameritas Life Ins. Corp.), Lincoln, 1961-73, v.p. group, 1973-87, exec. v.p. group, 1987-91, exec. v.p. bus. devel., 1991-93; prin. R.P. Day Consulting, Paradise Valley, Ariz., 1993—. Dir. Nat. Health Care Svcs., Jacksonville, Fla., 1985—95. Trustee, pres. bd. Madonna Profl. Care Ctr., Lincoln, 1970-80, trustee Lincoln Gen. Hosp., 1980. Lt. USN, 1952-56. Mem. VFW, Internat. Soc. Cert. Employee Benefit Specialists (bd. dirs. pres. governing coun., chmn. bd. 1986), Am. Soc. CLUs, Internat. Found. Employee Benefit Plans, Profl. Ins. Mass-Mktg. Assn., Mass-Mktg. Ins. Inst., Nat. Assn. Dental Plans, Am. Legion, Mil. Officers Assn., Country Club of Lincoln, Scottsdale Country Club, Blue Key Honor Soc., Phi Kappa Tau. Republican. Episcopalian. Avocation: golf. Home: 6530 N 61st St Paradise Valley AZ 85253 Office Phone: 480-368-0916. Personal E-mail: daypvaz@aol.com.

DAY, ROBERT ANDROUS, literature and language professor, retired library director, editor, publisher; b. Belvidere, Ill., Jan. 18, 1924; s. Floyd Androus and Mabel May (Dorn) D.; m. Betty Lucy Johnson, Aug. 27, 1949; children— Nancy, Barton, Robin BA, U. Ill., 1949; MS, Columbia U., 1951. Librarian, Sci. and Tech. div. Newark Pub. Library, 1951-53; librarian, editor Inst. Microbiology Rutgers U., 1953-60, dir. Coll. of South Jersey Library, 1960-61; mng. editor Am. Soc. Microbiology, Washington, 1961-80; dir. ISI Press, Phila., 1980-86; v.p. Inst. for Sci. Info., Phila., 1984-86; prof. English, U. Del., Newark, 1986-2000, prof. emeritus, 2000—. Tchr. sci. writing; pub. cons. NSF, NIH, others Author: How to Write and Publish a Scientific Paper, 1979, 5th edit., 1998, Scientific English: A Guide for Scientists and Other Professionals, 1992, 2d edit., 1995. With USAAF, 1943-46. Mem. AAAS, Coun. Science Editors (chmn. 1977-78), Soc. Scholarly Pub. (pres. 1982-84), Am. Med. Writers Assn., Soc. Tech. Comm., European Assn. Sci. Editors, Assn. Tchrs. Tech. Writing. Home: 77 Ritter Ln Newark DE 19711-5174 Business E-Mail: bday@udel.edu.

DAY, ROBERT DWAIN, JR., foundation administrator, lawyer; b. Stockton, Calif., Dec. 14, 1950; s. Robert Dwain and June Rita Day; m. Carol Robin Tyler; children: Leslie Carroll, Ryan Tyler. BS, Va. Tech., 1974; JD, U. S.C., 1977. Bar: S.C. 1977, D.C. 1978. Forester USDA Forest Svc., Washington and Columbia, S.C., 1973-77; dir. resource policy Soc. Am. Foresters, Bethesda, Md., 1977-81; resident fellow Resources for the Future, Washington, 1981-82; exec. dir. Renewable Natural Resources Found., Bethesda, 1982—; corp. sec. RNRF Title Holding Corp., 1997—. Cons. Office of Tech. Assessment U.S. Congress, Washington, 1981-82; mem. nat. task force Soc. Am. Foresters, Bethesda, 1982-83; advisor The Conservation Found., Washington, 1978-79; mem. adv. coun. Coll. Natural Resources, Utah State U., 1992-96, Va. Tech., 1999—; nat. adv. coun. Environ. Careers Orgn., 2004-; mem. nat. awards coun. for environ. sustainability Renew Am. Inc., 1997-98; del. Afghanistan-Am. Summit on Recovery and Reconstn., Washington, 2002; del. White House Conf. on Global Climate Change, Washington, 1997 Author policy analysis column Jour. of Forestry, 1977-81; editor: Renewable Resources Jour., 1982—. Appt. by county exec. to 9/11 Econ. Impact Panel Montgomery County, 2001. Mem. AAAS, D.C. Bar Assn., Soc. Am. Foresters, Soil and Water Conservation Soc., Environ. Law Inst., Coun. Engring. and Sci. Soc. Execs., Montgomery County Soc. for Assns. (exec. com. 1992-94, 98—, vice chmn. 1999-2000, chmn. 2000). Home: 2191 Canterbury Way Potomac MD 20854-6105 Office: Renewable Natural Resources 5430 Grosvenor Ln Ste 220 Bethesda MD 20814-2193 Office Phone: 301-493-9101. Business E-Mail: day@rnrf.org.

DAY, ROBERT EDGAR, retired artist, educator; b. Clinton Falls, Minn., Dec. 27, 1919; s. Judson LeRoy and Blanche Leone (Finch) D.; m. Helen Marie Hanson, Aug. 13, 1944 (dec.); children: Marion Eve, Cynthia Lynn, Brian Louis; m. Kathryn Jean Griswold, June 7, 1969. Student, U. Minn., 1937-39; BA magna cum laude, St. Olaf Coll., 1943; MA, U. Iowa, 1946, PhD, 1958. Instr. art and English, art supr. pub. schs., Owatonna, Minn., 1943-45, Winona, Minn., 1946-49; instr., asst. prof. art edn. and appreciation Kent State U., 1949-56; assoc. prof. art history and sculpture No. Ill. U., 1958-60; prof., chmn. dept. art La. State U., 1960-65; prof. U. Colo., Boulder, 1965-88, prof. emeritus fine arts, 1988—, chmn. dept. fine arts, 1965-68. High sch. wrestling coach, 1943-49; chmn. adv. com. Anglo-Am. Art Mus., 1961-63, dir. art history program in Italy, 1971, 73, 74, 76, 77, 78, 81, 82, 84, 87. Exhibited The Harvester, Regional Sculpture Invitational, Beaumont (Tex.) Art Mus., 1963. Danforth Found. tchr. grantee, 1957; Recipient Purchase award Ohio Printmakers Assn., Purchase award Dayton (Ohio) Mus., 1951 Home: 940 Cypress Ln Louisville CO 80027-9428 *During my career in art and its history, I have come to realize in an ever deeper sense that people are more important than artifacts, and that underlying all values and meaningful human relationships is the working of an infinite and personal God. The great possibilities in any human creative effort can only be understood in this light.*

DAY, ROBERT HUGH, marine ecologist; b. Carrollton, Ohio, June 7, 1952; s. Morris Eugene and Betty Violet (Parsons) D.; m. Karen Anne Stevens Schrader, Apr. 10, 1991; stepchildren: Lloyd, Michael. BA, Antioch Coll., 1974; MS, U. Alaska, 1980, PhD, 1992. Biol. tech. U.S. Fish and Wildlife Svc., Adak, Alaska, 1975-76; teaching asst. U. Alaska, Fairbanks, 1976-79, lab. asst., 1980-83, rsch. asst., 1983-87; ind. cons. Fairbanks, 1987-89; sr. scientist environ. rsch. and svcs. Alaska Biol. Rsch., Inc., Fairbanks, 1989—. Contbr. articles to profl. jours. and books. Named Alfred P. Sloan scholar Alfred P. Sloan Found., Antioch Coll., 1970-74, Angus Gavin fellow Angus Gavin Found., U. Alaska, 1985-86. Mem. Am. Ornithologists' Union (life mem., co-chair annual meeting 1993), Assn. Field Ornithologists (life), British Ornithologists' Union (life), Cooper Ornithol. Soc. (life), Wilson Ornithol. Soc. (life), Colonial Waterbird Soc. (life), Ornithol. Soc. New Zealand (life), Pacific Seabird Group (life, chmn. 2005—), Royal Australian Ornithologists' Union, Soc. Western Field Ornithologists, Sigma Xi (bd. dirs. Alaska chpt. 1988-89). Avocations: music, photography, motorcycling. Home: 798 Gold Mine Trl Fairbanks AK 99712-2069 Office: Alaska Biol Rsch Inc Environl Rsch and Svcs PO Box 81934 Fairbanks AK 99708-1934

DAY, ROBERT MICHAEL, oil company executive; b. Winnfield, La., Jan. 28, 1950; s. Robert Neal and Virginia Ruth (Franklin) D.; m. Noelie Barron, Dec. 20, 1975; children: Robert Michael Jr., Brionne. BS, La. State U., 1976; MBA, U. Houston-Clear Lake, 1989. Roustabout, floorman Global Marine Drilling Co., Houston, 1976-77; sales engr. NL Baroid Petroleum Svcs., Houston, 1977-78; drilling technician East Tex. div. Exxon Co., USA, Houston, 1978-79, sr. drilling technician Southeastern div. New Orleans, 1979-81, drilling supt., 1981-84, drilling supt. hdqrs. Houston, 1984-89, drilling supt. Offshore div. New Orleans, 1989-91; ops. supr. hdqrs. drilling Exxon Co., Internat., Houston, 1991-99; sr. ops. supr. Exxon Mobil Devel. Co. Drilling, Houston, 2000—. Contbr. articles to profl. jours. Ruling elder Clear Lake Presbyn. Ch., Houston, 1987-88. With U.S. Army, 1969-73. Mem.: Soc. Petroleum Engrs., Soc. of 1st Inf. Divsn., Masons. Republican. Home: 20730 Chappell Knoll Dr Cypress TX 77433-5510

DAY, ROBERT WINSOR, preventive medicine physician, researcher; b. Framingham, Mass., Oct. 22, 1930; s. Raymond Albert and Mildred (Doty) Day; m. Jane Alice Boynton, Sept. 6, 1957 (div. Sept. 1977); m. Cynthia Taylor, Dec. 16, 1977; children: Christopher, Nathalia, Natalya, Julia. Student, Harvard U., 1949—51; MD, U. Chgo., 1956; MPH, U. Calif., Berkeley, 1958, PhD, 1962. With USPHS, 1956—57; resident U. Calif., Berkeley, 1958—60; research specialist Calif. Dept. Mental Hygiene, 1960—64; asst. prof. Sch. Pub. Health and Sch. Medicine UCLA, 1962—64; dep. dir. Calif. Dept. Pub. Health, Berkeley, 1965—67; prof., chmn. dept. health services Sch. Pub. Health and Community Medicine, U. Wash., Seattle, 1968—72, dean, 1972—82, prof., 1982—; pres., dir. Fred Hutchinson Cancer Rsch. Ctr., Seattle, 1981—97, pres., dir. emeritus, 1997—, mem. pub. health scis., 1997—. Mem. Nat. Cancer Adv. Bd., 1992—98, Nat. Cancer Policy Bd., 1996—2000; chief med. officer Epigenomics, Inc.; sci. dir. Internat. Consortium Rsch. Health Effects Radiation; chmn. Targeted Growth, Inc.; mgr. Sci. Group DLC Investment Co.; cons. in field. Fellow: APHA, AAAS, Am. Coll. Preventive Medicine; mem.: AMA, King County Med. Soc., Wash. State Med. Assn., Am. Assn. Cancer Insts. (bd. dirs. 1983—87, v.p. 1984—85, pres., chmn. bd. dirs.), Assn. Schs. Pub. Health (pres. 1981—82), Am. Assn. Cancer Rsch., Am. Soc. Preventive Oncology, Am. Soc. Clin. Oncology. Office: 1872 E Hamlin St Seattle WA 98112 Office Phone: 206-954-9922. Personal E-mail: dlcllc@comcast.net.

DAY, ROLAND BERNARD, retired judge; b. Oshkosh, Wis., June 11, 1919; s. Peter Oliver and Joanna King (Wescott) D.; m. Mary Jane Purcell, Dec. 18, 1948; 1 dau., Sarah Jane. BA, U. Wis., 1942, JD, 1947. Bar: Wis. 1947. Trainee Office Wis. Atty. Gen., 1947; assoc. mem. firm Maloney & Wheeler, Madison, Wis., 1947-49; 1st asst. dist. atty. Dane County, Wis., 1949-52; partner firm Day, Goodman, Madison, 1953-57; firm Wheeler, Van Sickle, Day & Anderson, Madison, 1959-74; legal counsel mem. staff Sen. William Proxmire, Washington, 1957-58; justice Wis. Supreme Ct., Madison, 1974-95, chief justice, 1995-96. Mem. Madison Housing Authority, 1960-64, chmn., 1961-63; regent U. Wis. System, 1972-74 Served with AUS, 1943-46. Mem. ABA, State Bar Wis., Am. Trial Lawyers Assn., Ygdrasil Lit. Soc. (pres. 1968), Madison Torske Klubben, Masons (33rd degree). Mem. United Ch. of Christ. Clubs: Madison, Madison Lit.

DAY, RONALD ELWIN, consulting executive; b. Randolph, Vt., Dec. 15, 1933; s. John Ellis and Esther Murle (Tabor) D.; m. Elizabeth Jean McKeage, June 26, 1955; children: Gary Alan, Kathi Ellen, Judy Anne, Jeffrey Evan. AA, Pasadena City Coll., 1958, student, 1958-59; BA, U. Calif., Santa Barbara, 1961; MBA, UCLA, 1962. Internal auditor North Am. Aviation, Downey, Calif., 1962—64; sys. and procedures mgr. Proto Tool Co., L.A., 1964—65; computer programmer First Nat. Bank, Boston, 1966—67, project mgr., 1967—73, sys. analyst, 1974—77, sys. planning com. chmn., trust divsn., 1977—89, trust info. mgmt. sys. adminstr., 1977—89; pres. Edge Sys. Projects, Inc., North Reading, Mass., 1990—2002. With USAF, 1952-56. Mem. Soc. Advancement of Mgmt., U.S. Ski Assn., Nat. Geog. Soc., Boston Computer Soc., Assn. Sys. Mgmt., Alpha Gamma Sigma. Republican. Home and Office: 2 Bigham Rd North Reading MA 01864-2904

DAY, RUSSELL CLOVER, state agency administrator; b. Concord, NH, June 29, 1943; s. Alan C. and Lois M. (Huntington) D.; m. Carol Ann Tasker, July 9, 1965; children: Jennifer Marie, Jeffrey Russell. BA, New England Coll., 1965; postgrad., Fairfield U., 1965, U. N.H., 1965-67; M in Human Svcs. Adminstrn., Antioch U., Keene, N.H., 1978. Examiner State of N.H. Soc. Security Disability Determination Svc., Concord, 1969-73, supr., 1973-81, dep. dir., 1981-85, adminstr., 1985—. Trustee New England Coll., 1987-89; supervisory com. NH Fed. Credit Union, chairperson, 1995-97, bd. dirs., 1997—. Recipient Vol. Achievement award N.H. Credit Union League, Edward Filene award, Social Security Commrs. Citation, 2000, 05, Assoc. Commrs. Citation, 2000, Excellence in Govt. award Greater Boston Fed. Exec. Bd., 2002 Mem. Nat. Coun. Disability Determination Dirs. (exec. com. 1991-94), Masons, Lions Club (pres. 1983-84, chmn. region I, dist. chmn. 1995-96, bd. dirs. 1984—, zone chmn. 1982-83, 94-95, Melvin Jones fellow 2000), New Eng. Coll. Alumni Assn. (chmn. 1987-89). Republican. Congregationalist. Avocations: fishing, boating, stamp collecting/philately, photography. Home: 73 Wallace Rd Goffstown NH 03045 Office: Social Security Disability Determination Svc Ste 30 21 S Fruit St Concord NH 03301 Personal E-mail: rcday2@aol.com.

DAY, SHARON HOELSCHER, family and consumer sciences educator, education program administrator; b. Lima, Ohio, Apr. 7, 1952; d. Oscar William and Ruby Henrietta (Feil) Hoelscher; m. Daniel L. Day, June 27, 1981. BS, Ohio State U., 1973; MA, Mich. State U., 1977; postgrad., U. Ariz., 1975, 80, Bowling Green (Ohio) State U., 1982. Extension educator Ohio State U.-Coop. Extension Svc., Celina, 1973-76, 78-80; extension faculty U. Ariz.-Coop. Extension, Phoenix, 1983—; instr. Bowling Green State U., 1980-83. County coord. Expanded Food and Nutrition Edn. Program, 1983-97; bd. dirs. Ariz. Osteoporosis Coalition, 1998—; mem. Ariz. Food Safety Task Force, 1999-2003. Mem. planning com. Ariz. Hunger Conf., Phoenix, 1986-92; mem. choir United Meth. Ch., 1978—. Recipient Ext. Faculty of Yr. award, U. Ariz., 2004. Mem. Am. Assn. Family and Consumer Svcs. (strategic planning com. 1989, nominating com. 1991—, named New Achiever 1987, Leader 2001), Ariz. Assn. Family and Consumer Svcs. (pres.-elect 1987—, pres. 1988-89, bd. dirs. 1983—), Nat. Extension Assn. Family and Consumer Scis. (long term planning com. 1991-93, western region dir. 1996-98, v.p. pub. affairs 1999-2001, pres, 2003-04, Gen. Foods media grantee 1987, Disting. Svc. award 1990, Excellence in Rsch. award 1990, Frysinger fellow 1991, 99, 2000), Ariz. Extension Assn. Family and Consumer Scis. (pres. 1986, 93, pub. policy chair. 1987—), Ariz. Nutrition Coun., Ariz. Pub. Health Assn., Am. Youth Hostels Orgn., Joint Coun. Ext. Profls. (pres. 2004-05). Democrat. Avocations: music, travel, photography. Office: U Ariz Coop Ext 4341 E Broadway Rd Phoenix AZ 85040-8807 Office Phone: 602-470-8086. Business E-Mail: shday@ag.arizona.edu.

DAY, STACEY BISWAS, physician, medical educator; b. London, Dec. 31, 1927; came to U.S. 1955, naturalized 1977. s. Satis B. and Emma L. (Camp) D.; m. Ivana Podvalova, Oct. 18, 1973; children Kahil Amyn, Selim. MD, Royal Coll. Surgeons, Dublin, Ireland, 1955; PhD, McGill U., 1964; DSc, Cin. U., 1971. Intern King's County Hosp., SUNY Downstate Ctr., 1955-56; resident fellow in surgery U. Minn. Hosp., 1956-60; hon. registrar St. George's Hosp., London, Eng., 1960-61; lectr. exptl. surgery McGill U., Montreal, Que., Can., 1964; asst. prof. exptl. surgery U. Cin. Med. Sch., 1968-70; assoc. dir. basic med. rsch. Shriner's Burn Inst., Cin., 1969-71; from asst. to assoc. prof. pathology, head Bell Mus. Pathobiology U. Minn., Mpls., 1970-74; dir. biomed. comm. and med. edn. Sloan-Kettering Inst., N.Y.C., 1974-80; mem. Sloan-Kettering Inst. for Cancer Rsch., 1974-80; mem. adminstrv. coun., field coordinator, 1974-75; prof. biology Sloan Kettering divsn. Grad. Sch. Med. Sci. Cornell U., 1974-80; clin. prof. medicine divsn. behavioral medicine N.Y. Med. Coll., 1980-92; prof. biopsychosocial medicine, chmn. dept. community health U. Calabar (Nigeria) Sch. Medicine, 1982-85; prof. internat. health, dir. Internat. Ctr. for Health Scis. Meharry Med. Coll., Nashville, 1985-89, dir. WHO Collaborating Ctr. ICHS, 1987-89; founding dir. WHO Collaborating Ctr., Nashville, 1987-89, emeritus dir., 1989; adj. prof. family and cmty. medicine U. Ariz. Coll. Med. Scis., Tucson, 1985-89; univ. prof. internat. health U. Calabar, Nigeria, 1989—; permanent vis. prof. med. edn. Oita Med. Univ., Japan, 1992-99. Arris and Gale lectr. Royal Coll. Surgeons, England, 1972; vis. lectr., Ireland, 72; vis. prof. U. Bologna, 1977, Kyushu, Japan, 90, U. Mauritius, 1991, Bratislava U., 1991, U. Tokyo, Japan, 1992—93, U. Nagasaki, Japan, 1992—93, Beijing, 1993; vis. prof. health comm. U. Santiago, Chile, 1979—80, Colombo, Sri Lanka, 1996; vis. prof. Oncologic Rsch. Inst., Tallinn, Estonia, 1976, All India Insts. Health, 1976, U. Maidugari, 1982, Vellore U., India, 1996, De Quito, Ecuador, 1996; vis. acad. Oxford (Eng.) U., 1993—95; moderator med. cartography and computer health Harvard U., 1978, Acad. Scis., Czech Republic, 1987, Australia, 88; Fulbright prof. Charles U., Czech Republic, 1989; prof. (hon.) Coll. Health Scis. U. San Francisco de Quito (Ecuador), 1996; cons. Pan Am. Health Assn., 1974—90, U.S.-USSR Agreement for Health Cooperation, 1976, WHO Collaborating Ctr. Meharry Med. Coll., Nashville, 1985, NAFEO/USAID, 1986—89; mem. expert com. for health, manpower devel. WHO, 1986—90, cons. divsn. strengthening health care resources, 1987—90, UN-FSSTD, 1987, AID/Joint Memorandum of Understanding Africa, Kenya, 1987—89, West Africa, 1987—89, Sudan, 1985—89; cons. to dean med. coll. faculty med. and health scis. ABHA, Asir, Saudi Arabia, 1981; cons. to dir. High Tatras symposia Post Grad. Med. Inst., Bratislava, 1990—; cons. to rector U. Autónoma Agraria Antonio Narro, Saltillo, Mexico, 1987—89; pres., chmn. Pub. Cultural and Ednl. Prodns., Montreal, Canada, 1966—85; bd. dirs., v.p. Am. Sci. Activities Mario Negri Found., 1975—80; bd. dirs. Internat. Health, African Health Consultancy Svc., Nigeria, Ekologia & Zivot, Slovakia; founding chmn. (hon.), bd. dirs. Lambo Found. U.S.; v.p., trustee Cancer Relief Found., Calabar; pres., exec. dir. Internat. Found. Biosocial Devel. and Human Health, 1978—86, chmn., 1986—; mem. Medzinárodny Poradny Vybor Nadácie Ekológia Zivot, Slovakia, 1995—; cons. Inst. Health, Lyfford Cay, Bahamas, 1981, Govt. Cross River State, Nigeria, Itreto State and H.H. Obong of Calabar, Nat. Bd. Advisors, Am. Biog. Inst., 1982—; cons. cmty. health and health comms. Navaho Nation, Sage Meml. Hosp., Ganado, Ariz., 1984; founder, cons. Primary Self-Health Clinics, Oban, Ikot Oku Okono and Ikot Imo, Nigeria, 1982—84; cons. High Tatras Internat. Health Symposia, Slovakia, 1990—; apptd. ab. Gov. State of Tenn., 1986—; adj. clin. prof. medicine N.Y. Med. Coll.; prof. (hon.) Colegio Ciencias Salud U. San Francisco, Quito, 1965—. Author: (verse) Collected Lines, 1966, (plays) By the Waters of Babylon, 1966, (verse) American Lines, 1967, (plays) The Music Box, 1967, Three Folk Songs Set to Music, 1967, Poems and Etudes, 1968, (novels) Rosalita, 1968, The Idle Thoughts of a Surgical Fellow, 1968, Edward Stevens-Gastric Physiologist, Physician and American Statesman, 1969, Letters to Ivana from Calabar, 2001, (novella) Bellechasse, 1970, A Leaf of the Chaatim, 1970, Ten Poems and a Letter from America for Mr. Sinha, 1971, Curling's Ulcer: An Experiment of Nature, 1972, Tuluak and Amaulik: Dialogues on Death and Mourning with the Innuit Eskimo of Point Barrow and Wainwright, Alaska, 1974, East of the Navel and Afterbirth: Reflections from Rapa Nui, 1976,

Health Communications, 1979, The Biopsychosocial Imperative, 1981, What Is Survival: The Physician's Way and the Biologos, 1981, Developing Health in the West African Bush, 1995; author: (in Czech) Moudrost Samuraju, 1998; author: Selected Poems and Embers of a Medical Life, 1999, In the Shadow of the Bush - Letters from Calabar, 2000, Vitaesophia of Integral Humanism, 2001, The Klacelka in a Slavic Woodland, 2003, The Wisdom of Hagakure, 1996; editor: Death and Attitudes Toward Death, 1972, Membranes, Viruses and Immune Mechanisms in Experimental and Clinical Disease, 1972, Ethics in Medicine in a Changing Society, 1973, Communication of Scientific Information, 1975, Trauma: Clinical and Biological Aspects, 1975, Molecular Pathology, 1975; editor: (with Robert A. Good) (series) Comprehensive Immunology, 9 vols., 1976—80; editor: Cancer Invasion and Metastasis-Biologic Mechanisms and Therapy, 1977, Some Systems of Biological Communication, 1977, Image of Science and Society, 1977, What Is A Scientist?, 1978, Sloan Kettering Inst. Cancer Series, 1974—80; editor: (with K. Inokouchi) Selections from the Chronicle of the Hagakure as Wisdom Literature: The Way of The Samurai of Saga Domain, 1993; editor-in-chief, mem. editl. bd. Health Communications and Informatics, 1974—80, editor in chief The American Biomedical Network: Health Care System in America Present and Past, 1978, A Companion to the Life Sciences, Vol. 1, 1979, A Companion to the Life Sciences, Vol. 2, Integrated Medicine, 1980, A Companion to the Life Sciences, Vol. 3, Life Stress, 1981, Advance to Biopsychosocial Health, 1984, editor in chief, mem. editorial bd. Health Communications and Biopsychosocial Health; editor (with others): Cancer, Stress and Death, 1979, 2nd edit., 1986; editor: Computers for Medical Office and Patient Management, 1981, Readings in Oncology, 1980, Biopsychosocial Health, 1981, Primary Health Care Guidelines: A Training Manual for Community Health, 2nd edit., 1986; editor: (with T.A. Lambo) Contemporary Issues in International Health, 1989; sr. editor, with Salat and others Health and Quality of Life in Changing Europe in the Year 2000, 1992, sr. editor, with H. Koga Hagakure-Spirit of Bushido, 1993, sr. editor, with K. Inokuchi Selections from the Chronicles of the Hagakure as Wisdom Literature: The Way of the Samurai of Saga Domain, 1993, sr. editor, with Salát Health Management, Organization, and Planning in Changing Eastern Europe, 1993, sr. editor, with M. Kobayashi and K. Inokuchi, in Japanese The Medical Student and the Mission of Medicine in the Twenty First Century, 1995, sr. editor Developing Health in the West African Bush, 2 parts, 1995, Letters of Owen Wagensteen to a Surgical Fellow: with a memoir, 1996, Man and Mu: The Cradle of Becoming and Unbecoming, 1997, Czech Caesura: Golden Prague and the Black Years (Notes from Diaries 1970-1990), 1998, Moudrost Samuraju Trigon (in Czech), 1998, Poems and Embers of a Medical Life, 1998, The Surgical Treatment of Ischaemic Heart Disease with An Account of the Coronary and Intercoronary Circulation in Man and Animals, 1999, Introduction-Comprehensive Medicine (Oriental-Occidental Overview), 2000, Letters to Ivana from Calabar, 2001, Purkynje Address and Other Health Care Lectures Czechoslovakia 1989-1999, 2002, Pliskova's Butterflies-When God Says Enough, 2003, mem. editl. bd. Annual Reviews on Stress, Jour. Stress, cons. editl. bd. Comprehensive Medicine (Japan), Wilhelm Von Humboldt Über Die Unter Dem Namen Bhagavad Gita with commentary, 2001, Purkyne Address and Other Healthcare Lectures, 1989-1999; co-editor: various publs.; contbr. articles; prodr.: TV and health edn. programs, 1982—85, (TV film) Onchocerciasis - River Blindness in Africa, 1988; co-author: A Season of Flowers in Death Valley and the California Deserts, 2005. Served with Brit. Army, 1946-49. Recipient Moynihan medal Assn. Surgeons Gt. Britain and Ireland, 1960, Reuben Harvey triennial prize Royal Coll. Physicians, Ireland, 1957, Arris and Gale award Royal Coll. Surgeons, Eng., 1972, disting. scholar award Internat. Communication Assn., 1980, Sama Found. medal, 1982, disting. citation Hagakure Soc., 1992, Nat. Svc. medal Royal Brit. Legion, 1993; named to Hon. Order Ky. Cols., 1968; named Chieftan Ntufam Ajan of Oban Ejagham People, Cross River State, Nigeria, 1983; hon. prof. Del Colegio De Ciencas De La Salud De La Universidad San Francisco De Quito, 1996; recipient Chieftan Obong Nsong Idem Ibibio Nigeria, 1983, Mgbe (Ekpe) honor Nigeria, commendation WHO address Fed. Govt. Nigeria, Calabar, 1983, Leadership in Internat. Med. Health citation Pres. U.S., 1987, WHO medal, 1987, Agromedicine citation Commr. of Agr., State of Tenn., 1987, Assembly citation State of N.Y., 1987, Citation Congl. Record., 1987; Maestro Honorifo, U. Autonoma Agraria, Coahuila, Mex., 1987; presented Key to the City of Nashville, 1987; recipient Vice-Chancellor's Citation and Presentation for Primary Health Care Teaching in Nigeria, U. Calabar, 1988; Pamétni medal Postgrad. Med. Coll., Prague, 1991, Gold medal U. of Bratislava, 1991, Disting. Citation Hagakure Rsch. Soc., Japan, 1992, Nat. Svc. medal Royal Brit. Legion, 1993, Citation Commendation from Pres. Kyoto Prefectural U. Medicine, Japan, 1993, Citation Commendation on Contbn. to Med. Edn. from Pres. Oita Med. U., Japan, 1997; addresses presented by people of Ikot Imo, Nsit Anyang, Oban, 1982-84, Commendation from King of Calabar, 1984; Ciba fellow Can., 1965; Stacey Day Ward named in his honor by Fed. Min. and Gov. of Cross River State, Calabar Med. Ctr., Nigeria, 1986; charter mem. U.S. Normandy Com., 1988; 1st fgn. hon. mem. Hagakure Res. Soc. (Samurai), Kyushu, Japan, 1991. Fellow: African Acad. Med. Scis. (founder), African Acad. Sci., World Acad. Arts and Scis., Japanese Found. for Biopsychosocial Health (internat. hon. fellow and most disting. mem.), Zool. Soc. London Royal Micros. Soc., Royal Soc. Health; mem.: APHA, AMA, AAS, Adelaide Hosp. Soc. (Ireland), Soc. Med. Geographers USSR, Am. Rural Health Assn. (v.p. internat. sci. affairs, bd. dirs.), Am. Anthrop. Assn., Am. Inst. Stress (bd. dirs.), Am. Assn. History Medicine, N.Y. Acad. Scis., Can. Authors Assn., Internat. Burn Assn., Am. Burn Assn. Home: 6 Lomond Ave Chestnut Ridge NY 10977 Home (Summer): Ruzinovska 1228 14200 Prague Czech Republic E-mail: biosocmed@aol.com. *I have tried to assimilate all that is good in many cultures and to bring about a synthesis of these expressions in my own life and writings. It is as if I must find a third eye that can see what is best in all men, to integrate them newly into a changing world, and to be as much a releasing force as to be an absorbing force. This direction, I believe, commits one to an unceasing philosophy to unlearn and to relearn.*

DAY, STEVEN MATTHEW, researcher, consultant; s. Martin Andrew and Loretta Theresa Day; m. Rosario Inciong, Aug. 21, 1999; children: Andrew Joseph Basilio, Ryan Francis Basilio, Samuel Alonzo. PhD, U. Calif., Riverside, 1996—2001. Assoc. prof. math. Riverside C.C., Calif., 1995—2000; prin. rschr. Life Expectancy Project, San Francisco, 1996—. Cons. Strauss and Shavelle Inc., San Francisco, 2001—. Contbr. chapters to books, articles pub. to profl. jour. Recipient Morris J. Garber award, Outstanding Grad. Student in Stats., U. Calif., Riverside, 2001. Mem.: Gerson Lehrman Group's Coun. Healthcare Advisors, Am. Statis. Assn., Phi Beta Kappa (life). Roman Catholic. Avocations: travel, bicycling, walking. Business E-Mail: day@lifeexpectancy.com.

DAY, STOCKWELL BURT, government official; b. Barrie, Ont., Can., Aug. 16, 1950; s. Stockwell and Gwendolyn (Gilbert) D.; m. Valorie Martin Day, Oct. 2, 1971; children: Logan, Luke, Ben. Auctioneer, Alta., Can., 1972-74; dir. Teen Challenge Outreach Ministries, Edmonton, Alta., 1974-75; contractor Comml. Interiors, Alta., 1976-78; sch. adminstr./asst. pastor Bentley (Alta) Christian Centre, 1978-85; mem. Legis. Assembly Alta. Legis., Edmonton, 1986—, govt. caucus whip, 1989-92, govt. house leader, 1994-97, min. of labor, 1992-96, min. of family and social svcs., 1996-97, provincial treas., acting premier, 1997-2000; leader The Can. Alliance, Calgary, 2000—01, sr. critic fgn. affairs, 2002—. Chmn. Alta. Tourism Edn. Coun., Edmonton, 1987-89, Premier's Coun. on Family, Edmonton, 1990-92. Mem. Rotary Club. Avocations: tennis, roller blading, backpacking, reading. Office: Opposition 491 W Block Ho of Commons Ottawa ON Canada K1A 0A6 Office Phone: 613-995-1702.

DAY, WINDLE ALBERT, physician assistant, paramedic; b. Suffolk, Va., Mar. 19, 1968; s. Garret Windle and Allie Elizabeth Day; m. Courtney Leone Day, Oct. 5, 2001; 1 child, Jordan Elizabeth;children from previous marriage: Eric Windle, Emily-Kaye Liaise Day. BS, U. Nebr., 2003. Cert. physician asst. U. Nebr., 2003. Physician asst. Cardiology Clinic, Danville, Va., 2003—. Physician asst., 2lt. U.S. Army Nat. Guard, 1991—. Mem.: Soc. of Army Physician Assts., Am. Acad. of Physician Assts. Office: Cardiology Clinic 1045 Main St Danville VA 24541 Home: 31 Terrace Dr Poquoson VA 23662-2037 E-mail: daywindle@yahoo.com.

DAYA, JACKIE, publishing company executive; Sr. v.p., CFO Cahners Pub. Co., Newton, Mass., 1995—99; sr. v.p., fin. adminstrn. Hasbro Interactive, 1999—2001; sr. v.p. fin. Hasbro Inc., Pawtucket, RI, 2001—. Office: Hasbro Inc 1027 Newport Ave Pawtucket RI 02862-1059

DAYAL, VIJAY SHANKER, medical educator, physician; b. Ranchi, Bihar, India, Sept. 20, 1936; came to U.S., 1986; s. Ram Shanker Dayal and Vindhyachal (Devi) Devi; m. Susheela Sadhu, Oct. 10, 1961; children: Aneeta, Anjali, Amit. MBBS, Patna (India) Med. Coll., 1959; MSc, McGill U., Montreal, Can., 1966. Resident in otolaryngology McGill U., Montreal, 1960-61, 62-64, resident in surgery, 1961-62; clin. tchr. U. Toronto (Can.), 1967-68, asst. prof., 1968-75, assoc. prof., 1975-81, prof., 1981-86, U. Chgo., 1986—. Mem. editl. bd. Am. Jour. Otolaryngology, 1989—, Otolaryngology Head and Neck Surgery, 1990; author: Clinical Otolaryngology, 1981; contbr. over 70 articles to profl. jours. V.p. Am. Neurotology Soc., 1983-84. Fellow Am. Acad. Otolaryngology, Am. Otological Soc., Am. Trilogical Soc., Barany Soc. Achievements include patent (with others) for Artificial Replacement for Larynx. Office: U Chgo Dept Surgery 5841 S Maryland Ave # 412 Chicago IL 60637-1463

DAYES, LLOYD ALBERT, neurosurgeon, minister; b. Kingston, West Indies, Feb. 15, 1929; arrived in U.S., 1953; s. Samuel George Dayes and Legonia Edith Nicholson; m. Thelma Yvonne Goldsmith, 1957; children: Darlene, Albert, Michelle. Ministerial program, West Indies Coll.; BA, Pacific Union Coll., Napa, Calif., 1955; MD, Loma Linda Univ. Sch. of Medicine, L.A., 1959; postgraduate edn., Mt. Sinai Med. Ctr., N.Y., 1985, Oxford Univ., Oxford, Eng., 1993. Lic. Med. Coun. of Can., 1960, cert. Am. Bd. of Neurol. Surgery, 1967. Resident Montreal Neurol. Inst. McGill U., 1960—65, demonstrator in neuropathology, 1962; instr. in neurosurgery Loma Linda Univ., Loma Linda, Calif., 1965—66, asst. prof. neurosurgery, 1966—78, assoc. prof. neurosurgery, 1978—88, prof. of neurosurgery, 1988; attending neurosurgeon Loma Linda Univ. Med. Ctr., Loma Linda, Calif., 1965—, Riverside Gen. Hosp., Riverside, Calif., 1965—, Loma Linda Cmty. Hosp., Loma Linda, Calif., 1978—. Acting chmn. divsn. of neurosurgery Loma Lina Univ. Med. Ctr., Loma Linda, Calif., 1989—89. Contbr. scientific papers to over 27 conf., articles to profl. jour. Ethics com. Loma Linda Univ., 1988—90; welcome com. CNS, 1978; admission com. Loma Linda Univ., 1986—92, cirriculm com., 1975—78, utilization review com., 1988—90; coord.-med. student neurogurgical rotation and electives Loma Linda Univ. Sch. of Medicine, 1995—99. Recipient Univ. Alumnus of the Yr. award, Loma Linda Univ., 2001; Jesse Noyes Found. Fellowship, N.Y., 1955—59. Fellow: The Royal So. of Medicine, Am. Acad. of Neurol. and Orthopedic Surgeons, Am. Coll. of Surgeons, Am. Coll. of Nagiology, Internat. Coll. of Angiology, Internat. Coll. of Surgeons; mem.: Am. Soc. of Forensic Medicine (neurosurgery divsn.), N. Am. Skull Base Soc., The Joint Sec. on Neurtrauma and Critical Care, Am. Soc. of Law and Medicine, Calif. Neurol. Soc., N.Y. Acad. of Sci., Am. Assn. Tissue Banks, AAAS, Am. Chem. Soc., Am. Coll. of Legal Medicine, Congress of Neurol. Surgeons, Canadian Neurol. Soc., L.A. Soc. of Neurology and Psychiarty, Calif. Med. Assn., Pan Am. Med. Assn., San Berardino County Med. Soc., Sigma XI, Alpha Omega Alpha Honor Med. Soc. Achievements include research in magnesuim and its influence on Cerebal Vasospasm; elec. events triggering Cardiac Arrhythmia; Catecholamines and the Cerebrogenci-Cardiac interrelationships; pituitary-Thyroid Dysfunction with Cardiac interface; A search for the killer - Gliob;astoma Multiforme. Avocations: gardening, rosarian. Office: Ch Ogrn 11234 Anderson Loma Linda CA 92354 Home: 1311 Mills Ave Redlands CA 92373

DAY-LEWIS, DANIEL MICHAEL BLAKE, actor; b. London, Apr. 29, 1957; s. Cecil and Jill (Balcon) D.-L; m. Rebecca Miller Nov. 11, 1996; children: Gabriel Kane, Ronan Cal, Cashel Blake. Student, Bedales and Bristol Old Vic Theatre Sch. Appeared in plays Class Enemy, Funny Peculiar, Bristol, Eng., Look Back in Anger, Dracula, Bristol and London, Another Country, London, Futurists, Romeo, Thisbe, R.S.C., Hamlet, 1989; appeared in TV show Insurance Man; films include: Sunday Bloody Sunday, 1971, Ghandi, 1982, The Bounty, 1984, A Room with a View, 1986, My Beautiful Laundrette, 1986, Nanou, 1986, The Unbearable Lightness of Being, 1988, Stars and Bars, 1988, Eversmile, New Jersey, 1989, My Left Foot, 1989 (Academy Award best actor 1989), The Last of the Mohicans, 1992, The Age of Innocence, 1993, In the Name of the Father, 1993 (Academy Award nomination best actor 1993), The Crucible, 1996, The Boxer, 1997, Gangs of New York, 2002 (Best Actor in Leading Role, British Acad. Film Award (BAFTA) 2003), The Ballad of Jack and Rose, 2005. Office: Julian Belfrage Assoc 46 Albemarle St London W1S 4DF England also: Parseghian/Planco Mgmt 23 E 22nd St Ste 3 New York NY 10010*

DAYS, DREW S., III, lawyer, educator; b. 1941; m. Ann Ramsay Langdon, 1966; children: Alison, Elizabeth. Degree in Eng. Lit. with honors, Hamilton Coll., 1963; LLB, Yale U., 1966. Bar: Ill. 1966, NY 1970. Assoc. Cotton, Watt, Jones & King, Chgo., 1966-67; vol. Peace Corps., Honduras, 1967-69; assoc. counsel NAACP Legal Def. Fund, NYC, 1969-73, 75-77; assoc. prof. Temple U., 1973-75; asst. atty. gen. Dept. of Justice, Washington, 1977—80; assoc. prof. Yale U., New Haven, 1981-86, prof., 1986-93, Alfred M. Rankin chair Law Sch., 1992—; solicitor gen. Dept. Justice, Washington, 1993-96; of counsel Morrison & Foerster LLP, 1997—. Founding dir. Orville H. Schell, Jr. Ctr. for Internat. Human Rights Yale U. Law Sch., 1988-93. Bd. dirs. John D. and Catherine T. MacArthur Found., Petra Found., Hamilton Coll. Mem. Am. Law Inst., Am. Bar Found., Am. Acad. Arts and Scis., Am. Acad. Appellate Lawyers, Coun. on Fgn. Rels., Inter-Am. Dialogue. Office: Yale Law Sch PO Box 208215 New Haven CT 06520-8215 Office Phone: 203-432-4948. Business E-Mail: drew.days@yale.edu.

DAYS, MICHAEL, editor; b. Phila., 1953; m. Angela Dodson; 4 children. Grad., Coll. of Holy Cross, Univ. Mo. With Wall St. Jour.; joined as reporter Phila. Daily News, 1986, dep. mng. editor, 1998—2004, mng. editor, 2004—05, editor, exec. v.p., 2005—. Mem.: Nat. Assn. Black Journalists. Office: Phila Daily News 400 N Broad St PO Box 7788 Philadelphia PA 19130 Office Phone: 215-854-5984. Business E-Mail: daysm@phillynews.com.*

DAY-SALVATORE, DEBRA LYNN, medical geneticist; b. Hoboken, N.J., Oct. 23, 1953; m. Francis P. Salvatore, Sr., Dec. 24, 1988. BA in Biology, Harvard U., 1975; MS in Pharmacology, NYU, 1979, PhD in Pharmacology, 1982; MD, Case Western Res. U., 1986. Diplomate Am. Bd. Med. Genetics, Am. Bd. Pediats. Grad. fellow dept. pharmacology NYU Med. Ctr., 1978-79; sr. rsch. asst. dept. medicine Case Western Res. U., Cleve., 1979-82, rsch. assoc. dept. molecular biology and microbiology, 1982-84; pediatric and adolescent medicine resident Cleve. Clinic Found., 1986-89; med. genetics fellow Robert Wood Johnson Med. Sch., New Brunswick, N.J., 1990-91, asst. prof. pediatrics, 1990—, coord. perinatal genetics dept. ob-gyn., 1991-92, dir. divsn. reproductive and perinatal genetics dept. ob-gyn., 1992—, asst. prof. ob-gyn. and reproductive scis. and pediatrics, 1992—, acting chief divsn. clin. genetics, dept. ob-gyn. and reproductive scis., 1993—; physician Robert Wood Johnson Univ. Hosp., New Brunswick, 1990—, St. Peter's Med. Ctr., 1992—, chief divsn. clin. genetics, 1996—. Mem. genetic adv. bd. N.J. State Dept. Health's Parental and Child Adv. Com.; mem. med. adv. bd. Cryo-Cell Internat. Genetics editor Jour. of Perinatology, 1993—; contbr. articles, abstracts to profl. jours. Cons. N.J. Interagency Adoption Coun. Mem. AAAS, AMA, Am. Acad. Pediatrics (mem. N.J. chpt.), Am. Soc. Cell Biology, Am. Soc. Human Genetics, Human Genetics Assn. N.J. (mem. legis. com.), N.Y. Acad. Sci. Office: Saint Peter's Univ Hosp 254 Easton Ave # 4410 New Brunswick NJ 08901-1766 E-mail: Day-Salva@comcast.net.

DAYSON, DIANE HARRIS, parks director, cultural organization administrator; b. N.Y.C., Feb. 14, 1953; d. Robert Gene and Dessie Lee (Osborne) Harris; m. Kevin Maurice Dayson, Sept. 15, 1978; children: Dayna Renee, Kyle Ryan. BA in Early Secondary Edn. and Am. History, SUNY, Cortland, 1975; MS, NYU, 2000; Sr. Exec. Svc. grad., U.S. Dept. Interior, 2000. With Nat. Pk. Svc. U.S. Dept. Interior, 1975—, law enforcement ranger, 1977-79, concessions specialist, 1979-81, site mgr. Nat. Pk. Svc. N.Y.C., 1984-87, supt. Nat. Pk. Svc. Oyster Bay, N.Y., 1987-90, Morristown, N.J., 1990-93, Hyde Park, N.Y., 1993-95; supt. Statue of Liberty Ellis Island, N.Y.C., 1996—. Adj. prof. NYU Wagner Sch. of Pub. Adminstrn.; ambassador to Amsterdam, 1998; ambassador on geneology to Paris, France, 2000, Bremehaven, Germany, 2000, San Marino, Italy, 1997. Active United Way, Dutchess County; exch. steward, Manchester, Eng., 1994; bd. dirs. Christian Ministry in Nat. Parks, 1997—. Mem. NAFE, Oyster Bay C. of C. Republican. Roman Catholic. Avocations: travel, knitting, reading. Office: Statue of Liberty Ellis Island Liberty Is New York NY 10004-1467

DAYTON, MARK, senator; b. Mpls., Jan. 26, 1947; wife, Janice, 2 children: Eric, Andrew. Grad. cum laude, Yale U., 1969. Tchr. gen. sci. N.Y.C. Pub. Sch., 1969-71; counselor, adminstr. Social Svc. agency, Boston, 1972-76; legis. asst. to Minn. Senator Walter Mondale; staff mem. for Govr. Rudy Perpich, Minn., 1977; commr. econ. devel. State of Minn., 1978, commr. energy and econ. devel., 1983—86, state auditor, 1991—95, U.S. senator, 2001—. Mem. Senator Paul Wellstone's re-election campaign, 1995-96; agr., armed svcs., rules, gov. affairs com., state of Minn. Democrat. Office: 123 Russell Senate Office Bldg Washington DC 20510*

DAYTON, SKY, communications company executive; Grad., Delphi Acad., 1988. Mgr. computer graphics dept. Mednick & Assocs., 1988-90; founder Cafe Mocha, L.A., 1990-92; co-founder Dayton Walker Design, 1992-94; founder Earthlink Network, Pasadena, Calif., 1994—, chmn., 1994-99, also bd. dirs. Mem. Assn. Online Profls. (bd. dirs.), Internet Access Coalition.

DCAMP, CHARLES BARTON, music educator; b. Feb. 16, 1932; s. Glenn Franklin and Nina Clarice (Larson) Dc.; m. Ruth Joyce MacDonald, June 27, 1953; children: James Charles, Douglas Kevin, David Michael, Richard Manley, Paul Frederick, Jon Barton; 15 grandchildren. BS, U. Ill., 1956, MS, 1957; PhD, U. Iowa, 1980. Tchr. Watervliet (Mich.) Pub. Sch., 1958-61; tchr. music United Twp. H.S., East Moline, Ill., 1961-63; band dir. Pleasant Valley (Iowa) Schs., 1963-74; prof. music St. Ambrose U., Davenport, Iowa, 1974-97; prof. emeritus, 1997—; dir. bands, chmn. divsn. fine arts, chmn. dept. music St. Ambrose U., Davenport, Iowa. Guest dir., adjudicator festivals, music contests, Iowa, Ill., Minn.; prodr. Quad-City Music Guild, 1973-77, music dir., 1967—; chmn. Iowa All-State Band, 1971-74; instr. woodwinds Bemidji State U. Band Camp, 1967-92. Editor: Iowa Music Educator mag., 1978-80; pub. arrangements for concert band; contbr. articles to profl. jours. Active Riverdale Vol. Fire Co., 1966-75, pres., 1971-73; active Red Cross Constantine; founder, 1st condr. Quad-City Wind Ensemble, 1987—; choirmaster Bettendorf Presbyn. Ch. Choir, 1982-94. With AUS, 1952-55. Recipient Karl King Disting. Svc. award Iowa Bandmasters, 1987, Disting. Svc. to Music Edn. award Iowa Music Educators Assn., 1995; named to Quad City Music Guild Hall of Fame, 1997. Mem. Iowa Bandmasters Assn. (past pres., Karl King Disting. Svc. award 1987), Coll. Band Dirs. Nat. Assn., Music Educators Nat. Conf., Iowa Music Educators (pres., past pres., Disting. Svc. award 1995), Am. Fedn. Musicians, Am. Philatelic Soc., Nat. Band Assn. (Iowa state chmn.), Quad City Stamp Club (editor newsletter 1993-98), Masons (sec. Brubaker Lodge 2000—, Grand Musician Grand Lodge Iowa 2000-01, 04-05), Hi-12 (Davenport chpt., sec. 1999-2005, pres., 2005—), Shriners (Kaaba shrine), Masons (32 degree), Phi Mu Alpha Sinfonia, Phi Delta Kappa, Tau Kappa Epsilon. Republican. Methodist. Home: 803 W Rusholme St Davenport IA 52804-1927 Office: Saint Ambrose U Music Dept Davenport IA 52803

DE, DEVASMITA, research scientist; b. Calcutta, India, Nov. 6, 1966; d. Kamal Chandra and Sheila D.; m. Arijit Das, June 2, 1990. BS, U. Calcutta, 1990; MS in Human Ecology, Vrije U., Brussels, 1994. Aquarist J.G. Shedd Aquarium, Chgo., 2000—; lead rsch. aquarist project seahorse McGill U., Montreal, Can., 2001—. Recipient Internat. Cert. Human Ecology, 1994. Mem. AAAS. Avocations: astronomy, reading, cookery, swimming, classical music. Office: JG Shedd Aquarium 1200 S Lake Shore Dr Chicago IL 60605

DE, SAHADEB, environmentalist, researcher; b. Calcutta, West Bengal, India, Apr. 11, 1966; s. Biswanath and Rita Dey; m. Manidipa Dasgupta, Apr. 22, 1996; 1 child, Sparsho. BS in Geology with honors, U. Calcutta, 1987, MS in Geology, 1990, PhD in Geology, 1998; M Earth and Environ. Resource Mgmt., U. SC, 2000, M Computer Engring., 2001. Project coord. Sch. of Fundamental Rsch., Calcutta, 1991—92; jr. rsch. fellow U. Calcutta, India, 1992—94, sr. rsch. fellow, 1994—95; rsch. fellow Ctr. Study Man and Environment, Calcutta, 1995—98; grad. rsch. asst. Earth Scis. and Resources Inst. U. SC, Columbia, 1998—2001, postdoctoral rsch. assoc. Earth Scics. and Resources Inst., 2001—01, rsch. asst. prof., 2001—, mem. grad. faculty, 2002—. Reviewer divsn. environ. geoscis. Am. Assn. Petroleum Geologists, Tulsa, 2003—. Contbr. articles to profl. jours. Recipient Prof. S. K. Chatterjee Meml. medal for best student in geology, Asutosh Coll., Calcutta, 1987; grantee, USDA, 2003—04; scholar Nat. scholar, Dept. of Edn., Govt. of India, 1982—89, U. Calcutta, 1987—89; Jr. Rsch. fellow and lectr., U. Grant Commn., Govt. of India, 1992—94, Sr. Rsch. fellow, 1994—96. Mem.: Internat. Environ. Modelling and Software Soc., Assn. Computing Machinery, Am. Assn. Petroleum Geologists. Hindu. Achievements include invention of AFOPro, a nutrient management decision support system for the United States; national soil information systems (NASIS) on the Web; AutoRMS, an automated planning of resource management systems. Avocations: photography, philately, music, yoga, calligraphy, stamp collecting/philately. Office: U SC Earth Scis and Resources Inst 901 Sumter St Rm 409 Columbia SC 29208 Office Phone: 1-803-777-5911. E-mail: sde@esri.sc.edu.

DE, SWADES, education educator, consultant; arrived in US, 1999; s. Gopal Chandra and Satya Bala Dey; m. Tamalika Chaira, Dec. 14, 2003; 1 child, Shruti. BS with honors in Physics, U. Calcutta, Calcutta, India, 1989, B Tech., 1992; M Tech, Indian Inst. of Tech. Delhi, New Delhi, India, 1998; PhD, SUNY, Buffalo, N.Y., 2003. Cert. OASIS Tng. program for Software Engrs. Hughes Software Sys., New Delhi, India, 1999; Tng. on Microwave and millimeter waves, U. Calcutta, India, 1993, ALCATEL sys. engring., ALCATEL TELSPACE, Paris, France, 1996. Sys. engr. WEBFIL Ltd., Andrew Yule Group of Co., Calcutta, India, 1993—97; rsch. and tchg. asst. Indian Inst. of Tech. Delhi, New Delhi, 1997—98; software engr. Hughes Software Sys., New Delhi, 1999; project engr. ECE Dept., Indian Inst. of Tech. Kharagpur, Kharagpur, India, 1996—97; rsch. and tchg. asst. U. Tex., Arlington, Tex., 2001—01, SUNY, Buffalo, 1999—2003; asst. prof. of elec. and computer engring. NJ. Inst. of Tech., Newark, 2004—. Supervision of doctoral rsch. students NJ. Inst. of Tech., Newark, 2004—; tech. com. mem. IEEE Wireless Com. and Networking Conf., New Orleans, 2004—05; ofcl. reviewer of rsch. papers, Multiple, 2001—; funded rsch. (specialization: wireless com. networks) NJ. Inst. of Tech., Newark, 1997—. Contbr. scientific papers pub. to profl. jour. (Best departmental wall mag., 1988). Helped enhancing rural edn. facilities Local sch. governing body, Barasat, India, 2004—04. Recipient Acknowledgment for serving the U. hostel governing body, Calcutta U. Hostel, Waliullah Ln., Calcutta, India, 1991-1992, Award of merit, 1989; grantee Start-up rsch. grant, NJ. Inst. of Tech., 2004-2006. Mem.: IEEE (licentiate), IEEE Communication Soc. (licentiate). Hinduism. Achievements include research in ERCIM rsch. fellow (European Rsch. Comsortium for Informatics and Math.), Jan.-July, 2004; Among the best poster papers in ACM MOBIHOC conference, Lausanne, Switzerland, June 2002; design of prototype devel. of asynchronous data card for interfacing with telephony channel cards; development of Prototype 600 MHz 10 channel multiplexer and radio (6RU10) sys. for Indian rural telephony exchanges; first to Contbd. to the poineering iCAR (integrated cellular and ad hoc radio sys.) sys. rsch;

research in Publ. more than 2 dozens of peer reviewed rsch. papers in top conf. and jour. Office: NJ Inst of Tech Univ Heights Newark NJ 07102 Office Phone: +1 973 596 5710. Office Fax: +1 973 596 5680. Personal E-mail: swades.de@njit.edu.

DEA, DAVID YOUNG FONG, electrical engineer, consultant; b. Hong Kong, Mar. 6, 1924; came to U.S., 1937; s. Chun Fong and Teung Heung (Chow) D.; m. Mary Gin, Dec. 17, 1955; 1 child, George Hong. BSEE, U. Calif., Berkeley, 1950; postgrad., U. So. Calif., 1951-54. Mem. tech. staff Hughes Aircraft Co., Culver City, Calif., 1950; sect. mgr. Firestone Missile Div., Southgate, Calif., 1956-57; pres. Dea Electronics Co., L.A., 1957-59; dept. mgr. on missiles Hughes Aircraft Co., Culver City, 1959-63; project mgr. avionics Teledyne Corp., L.A., 1963-65; regional mgr. Bunker Ramo Corp., Canoga Park, Calif., 1965-66; project engr. LTV Corp., Dallas, 1966-73, Lear Siegler Corp., Grand Rapids, Mich., 1973-80; dir. engring. advanced battle tank devel. Nat. Water Lift Corp., Kalamazoo, 1980-82; cons. engr. McDonnell Douglas Corp., St. Louis, 1982-86; project mgr. Simmons Precision Corp., Vergennes, Vt., 1986-87; cons. engr. Control Data Corp., St. Paul, 1987-89; cons. M1 Tank Program Gen. Dynamics Corp., Sterling Heights, Mich., 1990-98; cons. weapon tech. United Defense LP, Mpls., 1998-2000; cons. General Dynamics Corp., Tallahassee, 2001—. Contbr. articles to profl. jours. Violinist Inglewood (Calif.) Symphony. With USAF, 1943-46, Philippines, Japan. Mem. IEEE (sr.), Computer Soc. of IEEE. Republican. Achievements include patents in field. Office: General Dynamics Corp 2930 Commonwealth Rd Tallahassee FL 32303 Home: 29 Santa Bella Rd Rolling Hills Estate CA 90274 E-mail: daviddea@gdls.com.

DEA, FAY SUEY, counselor, history professor; d. William and Jean Dea. AB in History magna cum laude, UCLA, 1972, MA in History, 1973, MA in Edn., 1981. Counselor coll. letters UCLA, L.A., 1975—79; staff aide to dean adminstrn. svcs. L.A. City Colls., 1979—81; dir. outreach cmty. svcs. L.A. Valley Coll., 1981—82; staff asst. to dir. student svcs. L.A. C.C. Dist., 1982—84, budget analyst, 1984—87; dir. C.C. rels. Calif. State U., Long Beach, 1987—88; instr., counselor L.A. Valley, 1988—. Mem. acad. senate L.A. Valley Coll., 1996—. Mem.: Faculty Assn. Calif. C.C.'s, Am. Fedn. Tchrs., Pi Gamma Mu, Phi Lambda Theta, Phi Beta Kappa. Avocations: collecting literary first editions, photography, travel, opera. Office: LA Valley Coll 5800 Fulton Ave Van Nuys CA 91401

DEA, PETER ALLEN, geologist; b. Worcester, Mass., Aug. 28, 1953; s. Allen Pearson and Beverly Jane (Brown) D. B.A. in Geology, Western State Coll., Gunnison, Colo., 1976; M.S. in Geology, U. Mont., 1981. Geologist Novanda Exploration, Missoula, Mont., 1977, WGM, Inc., Anchorage, 1976-77, Converse Cons., Lakewood, Colo., 1980-81; prof. geology Western State Coll., Gunnison, 1980-82; sr. geologist Exxon Co., U.S.A., Corpus Christi, Tex., 1982—; pres., CEO Western Gas Resources. Contbr. articles to profl. jours. Mem. Am. Assn. Petroleum Geologists, Corpus Christi Geol. Soc. Avocations: skiing; sailing; mountain climbing; kayaking; writing. Office: Western Gas Resources Ste 1200 1099 18th St Denver CO 80202*

DE ABREU, SUE, elementary school educator; b. Honolulu, Dec. 29, 1947; d. Lawrence and Mary (Jones-Howard) de Abreu-Morris; 1 child, Steven. AA, Gulf Coast Coll., Panama, 1967; BA, Fla. State U., 1971; BS, Harvard U., 1968; MS, Ga. So. Coll., 1984; MA, U. West Fla., 1985. Cert. art edn. tchr. K-12th, elem. tchr., sci. specialist 5th-6th grades, Fla. Reading specialist Craig Elem. Sch., Vail, Colo., 1980; tchr. sci. 7th-8th grade Ludowic County Schs., Jesup, Ga., 1981-84; tchr. sci. 5th-6th grade Gulf County Pub. Schs., Port St. Joe, Fla., 1985-98. State judge Fla. State Sci. and Engring. U. Fla, instr.; spl. news cons. Time Mag., 2001. Inventor Learning Through Creative Designs series, 2000. Chmn. Gulf County-N.W. Fla. chpt. Nat. Dem. Senatorial Com., 2001; pres. DeAbreu Plantation Nurseries; landscape designer, pres. Abreu Landscaping Design Svcs. Recipient Outstanding Fla. Artist award, Fedn. Fla. Women's Clubs Am., 2000-01. Mem. NEA, ASCD, Nat. Art Edn. Assn., Nat. Middle Sch. Assn., Nat. Wildlife Fedn. (Gulf County dir.), Wewahitchka Fedn. Women's Club (v.p. 1994-96).

DEACON, DAVID EMMERSON, advertising executive; b. Toronto, Ont., Can., July 22, 1949; s. Donald Mac Kay and Florence (Campbell) D.; m. Kathryn Robinson (divorced); m. Mary Cecilia Eberle, July 23, 1982 (divorced). Student, Brock U., St. Catherines, Ont., 1968-70, Casa Sch. Fine Arts, Paris, 1970-71. Chmn. election orgn. Liberal Party Ont., Toronto, 1973-75; chmn., editor polit. alerts F.H. Deacon, Hodgson Inc., Toronto, 1975-79, v.p. retail sales, 1979-84; gen. mgr. Porsche div. VW Can., Toronto, 1984-87; pres. Deacon Day Advt., Toronto, 1988-94; chmn. Lowe SMS, Toronto, 1994-96; mng. dir., COO, CFO Padulo Integrated, Toronto, 1996-2000; ptnr. Investment Profile, Inc., Toronto, 2000—; pres. Azure Dynamics Corp., Toronto, 2001—05, dep. chmn., exec. v.p. bus. devel., 2005—, 2005—. Illustrator: (poetry) Sun Street, 1970; records include Over the Line, 1994, The Iron Clock, 1996, Stranger in the Morning, 1999; narrator Discovery Channel prodn. Frontiers of Construction, 2001, 02, 03. Chmn. campaign tng. Fed. Liberty Party, 1977-79; pres. Ont. Liberal Party, 1983-85; chmn. Ont. campaign John Turner Leadership, 1984. Winner Can. Endurance Racing championship Can. Automobile Sport Club, 1980. Mem.: Toronto Club. Avocations: skiing, tennis, sailing. Personal E-mail: ddeacon@azuredynamics.com.

DEACON, JOHN C., lawyer; b. Newport, Ark., Sept. 26, 1920; BA, U. Ark., 1941, JD, 1948. Bar: Ark. 1948. Ptnr. Barrett & Deacon, Jonesboro, Ark. Commr. from Ark. to Nat. Conf. Commrs. on Uniform State Laws, 1966—, chmn. exec. com., 1977-79, pres. 1979-81. Recipient Ark. Outstanding Lawyer-Citizen award, 1973. Fellow Am. Coll. Trial Lawyers, Internat. Acad. Trial Lawyers (bd. dirs. 1978-84), Southwestern Legal Found. (trustee 1975-95, chmn. Research Fellows 1983-85); mem. Craighead County Bar Assn. (pres. 1968-69), N.E. Ark. Bar Assn. (pres. 1966-68), Ark. Bar Assn. (pres. 1970-71), ABA (chmn. sect. bar activities 1967-68, Ark. del. 1967-79, bd. govs. 1980-83, 92-93, chair sr. lawyers divsn. 1994-95), Am. Counsel Assn. (pres. 1974-75), Am. Bar Found. (pres. 1994-96), Internat. Assn. Def. Counsel, Nat. Assn. R.R. Trial Lawyers, Delta Theta Phi. Office: PO Box 1700 Jonesboro AR 72403-1700 also: Barrett & Deacon PA Union Planters Bank Building 300 S Church St Jonesboro AR 72401-2911 Office Phone: 870-931-1700. E-mail: jdeacon@barrettdeacon.com.

DEACY, THOMAS EDWARD, JR., lawyer; b. Kansas City, Mo., Oct. 14, 1918; s. Thomas Edward and Grace (Scales) D.; m. Jean Freeman, July 10, 1943 (div. 1988); children: Bennette Kay Deacy Kramer, Carolyn G., Margaret Deacy Vickrey, Thomas, Ann Deacy Krause; m. Jean Holmes McDonald, 1988. JD, U. Mo., 1940; MBA, U. Chgo., 1949. Bar: Mo. 1940, Ill. 1946. Practice law, Kansas City, 1940-42; ptnr. Taylor, Miller, Busch & Magner, Chgo., 1946-55, Deacy & Deacy, Kansas City, 1955—. Lectr. Northwestern U., 1949-55, U. Chgo., 1950-55; dir., mem. exec. com. St. L.-S.F. Ry., 1962-80; dir. Burlington No. Inc., 1980-86; mem. U.S. team Anglo-Am. Legal Exchange, 1973, 77. Mem. Juv. Protective Assn. Chgo., 1947-55, pres., bd. dirs., 1950-53; mem. exec. bd. Chgo. coun. Boy Scouts Am., 1952-55; pres. Kansas City Philharmonic Orch., 1961-63, chmn. bd. trustees, 1963-65; trustee Sunset Hill Sch., 1963-73; trustee, mem. exec. com. u. Kansas City, 1963—; trustee Mo. Law Sch. Found., pres., 1973-77, Kans. chpt. The Nature Conservancy, 1994-99. Capt. AUS, 1942-45. Fellow Am. Coll. Trial Lawyers (regent 1968—, treas. 1973-74, pres. 1975-76), Am. Bar Found; mem. Am. Law Inst., Jud. Conf. U.S. (implementation com. on admission of attys. to fed. practice 1979-86), ABA (commn. standards jud. adminstrn. 1972-74, standing com. fed. judiciary 1974-80), Ill. Bar Assn., Chgo. Bar Assn., Mo. Bar, Kansas City Bar Assn., Lawyers Assn. Kansas City, Chgo. Club, La Jolla (Calif.) Country Club, La Jolla Beach and Tennis Club, Kansas City Club, Kansas City Country Club, River Club, Q.E.B.H. Sr. Hon. Soc. of Mo. Univ., Beta Gamma Sigma, Sigma Chi. Home: 2724 Verona Cir Shawnee Mission KS 66208-1265 Office: 920 Main St Ste 1900 Kansas City MO 64105-2010 Business E-Mail: ted@deacylaw.com.

DEAK, ISTVAN, historian, educator; b. Szekesfehervar, Hungary, May 11, 1926; came to U.S., 1956, naturalized, 1962; s. Istvan and Anna (Timar) D.; m. Gloria Gilda Alfano, July 4, 1959; 1 dau., Eva., U. Budapest, 1945-48; student, Sorbonne, 1950-51, U. Md., Munich, W. Ger., 1953-55; MA, Columbia U., 1958, PhD, 1964. Journalist, librarian and bookseller, Budapest, Paris and Munich, 1945-56; instr. history Smith Coll., 1962-63; mem. faculty Columbia U., 1963—, prof. history, 1973-93, Seth Low prof. History N.Y.C., 1993-97, emeritus prof., 1997—. Mem. Inst. Advanced Study, Princeton, N.J., fall 1981; pres. Conf. on Slavic and East European History, 1985. Author: Weimar Germany's Left-Wing Intellectuals: A Political History of the Weltbühne and Its Circle, 1968, The Lawful Revolution: Louis Kossuth and the Hungarians, 1848-1849, 1979, Hungarian edit., 1983, 2d edit., 1994, German edit., 1989, Beyond Nationalism: A Social and Political History of the Habsburg Officer Corps, 1848-1918, 1990, German edit., 1991, 2d edit., 1995, Hungarian edit., 1993, Italian edit., 1994, Essays on Hitler's Europe, 2001, Hungarian edit., 2003; co-editor: Eastern Europe in the 1970's, 1972, Everyman in Europe: Essays in Social History, 2 vols., 2d edit., 1981, 3d edit., 1989, The Politics of Retribution in Europe: World War II and its Aftermath, 2000. Recipient Lionel Trilling Book award Columbia U., 1979 George Washington award Hungarian-Am. Assn., 1999; German Acad. Exch. fellow, 1960-61; Guggenheim fellow, 1970-71; Fulbright-Hays travel fellow, 1973, 84-85; fellow Woodrow Wilson Ctr. for Scholars, Washington, 1985 Mem. Hungarian Acad. Scis., Am. Hist. Assn., Am. Assn. Advancement Slavic Studies (Wayne S. Vuchinich Book prize). Home: 410 Riverside Dr New York NY 10025-7974 Personal E-mail: id1@columbia.edu.

DEAKIN, JAMES, writer; b. St. Louis, Dec. 3, 1929; s. Rogers and Dorothy (Jeffrey) D.; m. Doris Marie Kanter, Apr. 14, 1956; 1 son, David Andrew. AB, Washington U., St. Louis, 1951. Mem. staff St. Louis Post-Dispatch, 1951-81, Washington corr., 1953-80, White House corr., 1955-80; adj. assoc. prof. journalism George Washington U., 1981-87. Fellow Woodrow Wilson Internat. Ctr. for Scholars, 1980-81 Author: The Lobbyists, 1966, Lyndon Johnson's Credibility Gap, 1968, Straight Stuff, 1984, A Grave for Bobby, 1990; co-author: Smiling Through the Apocalypse, 1971, The Presidency and The Press, 1976, The American Presidency, Principles and Problems, vol. II, 1983, The White House Press on the Presidency, 1983; contbr. numerous articles to mags. Recipient Disting. Alumnus citation Washington U., 1973, Merriman Smith award for White House reporting, 1977; Markle Found. grantee, 1981 Mem. White House Corrs. Assn. (pres. 1974-75) Home and Office: 4 Burr Ave Barrington RI 02806-4205

DEAKTOR, DARRYL BARNETT, lawyer; b. Pitts., Feb. 2, 1942; s. Harry and Edith (Barnett) D.; children: Rachael Alexandra, Hallie Sarah. BA, Brandeis U., 1963; LLB, U. Pa., 1966; MBA, Columbia U., 1968. Bar: Pa. 1966, Fla. 1980, N.Y. 1980, Calif. 2003. Assoc. firm Goodis, Greenfield & Mann, Phila., 1968-70, ptnr., 1971; gen. counsel Life of Pa. Fin. Corp., Phila., 1972; asst. prof. U. Fla. Coll. Law, Gainesville, 1972-74, assoc. prof., 1974-80; with Mershon, Sawyer, Johnston, Dunwody & Cole, Miami, Fla., 1980-81, ptnr., 1981-84, Walker Ellis Gragg & Deaktor, Miami, 1984-86, White & Case LLP, Miami, 1987-95, Johannesburg, 1995-2000, Palo Alto, Calif., 2000—01, ret. ptnr., 2002—. Mem. Dist. III (Fla.) Human Rights Advocacy Com. for Mentally Retarded Citizens, 1974-78, chmn., 1978-80; mem. adv. bd. Childbirth Edn. Assn. Alachua County, Fla., 1974-80; mem. resource devel. bd. Mailman Ctr. for Child Devel., 1981-88. Mem. Fla. Bar. Mailing: 1330 Mariposa Ave Boulder CO 80302-7842 Office Phone: 303-544-1811. E-mail: dbd@ionsky.com.

DEAKYNE, WILLIAM JOHN, library director, musician; b. Harrisburg, Pa., June 25, 1936; s. William John and Hazel (Brown) D. MusB, U. Hartford, 1961; MLS, Villanova U., 1962; Diploma in French, Berlitz Sch., Phila., 1967, Berlitz Sch., Stamford, Conn., 1969. Cert. libr., NJ, Mass., NY, Wash. Dir. Meuser Meml. Libr., Easton, Pa., 1962-64, Coyle Free Libr., Chambersburg, Pa., 1964-65, Free Libr. Springfield Twp., Phila., 1965-68, Darien (Conn.) Libr., 1968-78, East Lyme (Conn.) Libr., 1979—, East Lyme Libr. Found., 1991—. Founding mem. Librs.-on-Line, Inc., 1983. Organist, pianist, composer Jeu de Clochette, 1964; contbr. articles to profl. jours. V.p. East Lyme C. of C., Niantic, Conn.; mem. Am. Cathedral of the Holy Trinity, Paris, 1998—; charter mem. Founders Planned Giving Soc., U. Hartford, 1996—. Mem. ALA (del. to Internat. Fedn. Libr. Assn. meetings Chgo., Copenhagen 1969), Les Amis de Vielles Maisons. Democrat. Avocations: restoration of pipe organs in France, promotion of English organs in U.S. Home: Westchester Dr East Lyme CT 06333 Office: East Lyme Pub Libr 39 Society Rd Niantic CT 06357-1100 Office Phone: 860-739-6926.

DEAL, BARBARA NEIGHBORS, literary agent; b. San Pedro, Calif., Oct. 25, 1948; d. Clarance Edwin and Neilya Marsh (Sharon) Neighbors; m. Robert Lewis Deal, Oct. 16, 1976. BA magna cum laude, Calif. Western U., 1970; MA, U.S. Internat. U., 1971; PhD, Columbia Pacific U., 1981. Pres., sr. agt. Barbara Neighbors Deal Literary Assocs., Ojai, Calif., 1978—. Founder, pres. AmaDeus Group Publs. and Found., Walla Walla, Wash., 1985—; admnstr. Nat. Disaster Search Dog Found., Ojai, 1995-98; tng. cons., writer Deal Cons. Svcs., Walla Walla, 1976-80. Advisor Common Ground Mediation, Walla Walla, 1978-83. Named living treasure Calif. State Senate, 1997. Avocations: rose gardening, philosophy, spirituality. Office: PO Box 1174 Ojai CA 93024-1174

DEAL, ERNEST LINWOOD, JR., banker; b. Florence, Ala., Jan. 5, 1929; s. Ernest Linwood, Sr. and Nell W. (Willingham) Deal; m. Mary Cooper, Dec. 27, 1952 (dec. Sept. 2003); children: Theresa Lynn, Sarah Street, Matthew Cooper, Jennifer Willingham. Student, Florence State Coll., 1947-49; BS, U. Ala., 1952; postgrad., Southwestern Grad. Sch. Banking, So. Meth. U., 1961. V.p. Tex. Commerce Bank, Houston, 1956-65; sr. v.p. Capital Nat. Bank, Houston, 1965-71; pres., CEO Fannin Bank, Houston, 1971-82, chmn., CEO, 1982; chmn., chief exec. officer InterFirst Bank, Houston, 1983, First City Nat. Bank (name changed to First City Tex.), Houston, 1984-88; sr. chmn. First City Tex., Dallas, 1988-91, chmn. bd. dirs., pres., CEO Austin, 1991-92; chmn. adv. bd. Frost Nat. Bank-Austin, 1993—. Bd. dirs. Houston Trust Co. Bd. visitors M.D. Anderson Hosp., Houston, 1971-01; bd. dirs. Phi Gamma Delta Ednl. Found., 1996-04; past chmn. Houston Pks. Bd., Houston Aviation Com.; chmn. local organizing com. US Olympic Festival, 1986; Tex. state chmn. US Olympic Com., 1989-93, S.W. regional chmn., 1993-01, nat. fin. com.; past chmn. bd. trustees, life trustee Kinkaid Sch.; trustee Southwestern Grad. Sch. Banking. Lt. USNR, 1952-55. Mem. U. Ala. Alumni Assn., Houston C. of C. (bd. dirs., exec. com.), Am. Bankers Assn. (governing coun., state v.p., govt. rels. coun. 1977-82, v.p. 1978-79), Tex. Bankers Assn. (bd. dirs.), Assn. Res. City Bankers (chmn. golf com.), Houston Country Club, Preston Trail Golf Club (Dallas), Austin Country Club, Phi Gamma Delta (bd. trustees 1990-96), Delta Sigma Pi, Omicron Delta Kappa. Republican. Presbyterian. Office Phone: 512-327-8880. Personal E-mail: eldeal@aol.com.

DEAL, GAYE FOLLMER, writer; b. Omaha, Oct. 22; d. George Crawford and Gladys Mickla Follmer; children: Oliver Evans(dec.), Rebecca Crawford, Peter Crawford, Stuart, Sarah, Kathryn. BPh, U. Chgo., 1945, BA, 1955; cert. TESOL, UCLA, 1968; MA, Calif. State U., Northridge, 1971. Cert. tchr. Calif. Tchr. Eastside Sch., Lancaster, Calif., 1964—67; lectr. Calif. State U., Northridge, 1971. Treas. S.W. Sci. Co., Calif., 1968—72. Author: The Second Best Bed, 1995, Out Takes in the Galaxies, 1999, Fugue, 2004. Calif. coord. Gold Star Parents for Amnesty, 1973—75; sec. Cmty. Consortium, Calif.; pres. Mid-City Neighbors, Santa Monica, Calif., Santa Monica Unitarian Universalist Ch. Avocations: travel, music.

DEAL, JILL B., lawyer; b. Stockton, Calif., Sept. 3, 1942; d. Ronald Emerson and Otilia (MacDonald) Brady; m. Timothy E. Deal, Sept. 5, 1964; children: Christopher, Bartholomew. BA, U. Calif., Berkeley, 1964; JD, Cath. U., 1979. Bar: D.C. 1979. Rsch. asst. FTC, Washington, 1974-78, policy analyst, 1978-79; atty. Arnold & Porter, Washington, 1979-81; Am. legal advisor Gen. Electric Co., p.l.c., London, 1981-85; atty. Rogers & Wells, Paris, 1985-88, of counsel Washington, 1988—96; principal, regulatory group Fish & Richardson, 1996—2000; of counsel, FDA, bioscience and pharmaceuticals Venable LLP, Washington, 2000—. Speaker FDLI Conference on Generic Biologics, 2003, CBI Annual Forum on Generic Drugs, 2003, Biopharmaceutical Comparability Conference, 2004. Contbr. articles to profl. jours.; co-author Biotechnology: Patents, Licensing and FDA Practice, 2001, Liability for Generic Drug Products: Issues to Consider, 2003. Mem. ABA (sects. on antitrust, bus. and internat. law), Club L (Paris). Office: Venable LLP 575 7th St NW Washington DC 20004 Office Phone: 202-344-4713. Office Fax: 202-344-8300. Business E-Mail: jdeal@venable.com.

DEAL, JOANNE BAKER, freelance writer, editor, publicity consultant; b. Long Beach, Calif., July 17, 1955; d. Richard Gene and Grace Lorraine (Thomas) Baker; m. Thomas Everett Deal, Aug. 18, 1979; children: Sarah Joy, Hannah Melody, Stephen Daniel. AA, Long Beach City Coll., 1975; BA Speech Communication and Pub. Relations, U. So. Calif., 1977; postgrad. Calif. State U.-Fullerton, 1978-79, Columbia Biblical Seminary Ext., 1992. Office mgr., research asst. U. So. Calif., Los Angeles, 1975-77; layout typist, copy editor McDonnell Douglas Corp., Long Beach, Calif., 1977-78; creative asst. K. Esterly & Assocs., La Habra, Calif., 1978; grad. asst. Calif. State U., Fullerton, 1978-79; asst. editor, publicity asst. Globe Pequot Press, Chester, Conn., 1980-82; free lance writer, Ivoryton, Conn., 1982—; multi-media cons./asst. Twentyone-hundred Prodns., Madison, Wis., 1977, Karl Karcher Entr., Anaheim, Calif., 1978; research cons., asst. Orange County chpt. Pub. Relations Soc. Am., 1978. Contbr. articles to various publs.; editor: Great New England Churches, 1982; Factory Store Guide to All New England, 1981; The Bluefish Cookbook, 1981. Advisor publicity/fundraising Refugee Resettlement Projects, Interfaith Council Old Saybrook, 1980, Lower Valley chpt. Pro-Life Council Conn., 1980-84; newsletter editor Birthright of Greater Westbrook, Conn., 1988—, mem. exec. bd., 1989—; newsletter editor Shoreline Christian Ministries, 1990—; newsletter editor Clinton Bapt. Ch., Conn., 1983-87; free lance editor Word of Life Clubs, Schroon Lake, N.Y., 1985; co-dir., newsletter editor Shoreline Fellowship Christian Home Educators, 1992—. Mem. Am. Radio Relay League (lic. technician. class amateur radio operator), Women in Communications, Phi Beta Kappa, Phi Kappa Phi. Republican. Mem. Brethren Ch. Address: 68 Mares Hill Rd Ivoryton CT 06442-1257

DEAL, JOSEPH MAURICE, academic administrator, art educator, photographer; b. Topeka, Aug. 12, 1947; s. Percy Harold and Laura Jean (Close) D.; m. Christine Adkin Bertelson, Aug. 8, 1981 (div. 1987); 1 child, Meredith Ivy; m. Betsy Sara Ruppa, July 20, 1991. BFA, Kansas City Art Inst., 1970; MA, U. N.Mex., 1975; MFA, U. N. Mex., 1978. Dir. exhbns. Internat. Mus. Photography at George Eastman House, Rochester, NY, 1975-76; prof. art U. Calif., Riverside, 1976-89, assoc. dean, 1986-89; dean Sch. Art Washington U., St. Louis, 1989-99; provost RI Sch. Design, 1999—2005, prof., 2005—. Mem. overview panel visual arts program Nat. Endowment for Arts, Washington, 1990-93, panel chair, 1992-93. Subject of book: Joe Deal: Southern California Photographs 1976-86, 1992, Between Nature and Culture, Photographs of the Getty Center by Joe Deal, 1999. Fellow Nat. Endowment for the Arts, 1977, 80, John Simon Guggenheim Found., 1983. Mem. Coll. Art Assn. (sec. bd. dirs. 1997—). Office: Rhode Island School Design 2 College St Providence RI 02903-2717 Business E-Mail: jdeal@risd.edu.

DEAL, KEVIN PAUL, furniture designer; b. Chgo., Oct. 3, 1956; s. Paul Sydney Deal and Bernice Lorraine Chowning-Deal; m. Nancy Kaye Ream, Oct. 1, 1988 (div. Jan. 1993); 1 child, Veronica Victoria. AS in fire sci., Crafton Hills Coll., 1997, AS in emergency med. svc., 1998. Owner Wood Dr., San Diego, 1984—90; owner, furniture repair Wood Magic, Riverside, 1990—2003; firefighter, EMT Riverside County Fire Dept., Calif., 1994—99; owner Deal Aviation, Riverside, 2002—03, Kevin Deal Fine Woodworking, 2003—. Scholarship chmn. San Diego Fine Woodworkers, 1987—90. Designer (aviation design) SPAD 13 Drawings, 2002; author: (paper) UR, Home of the Ziggurat, 1997. Mem.: Smithsonian Inst., Nat. Geographic Soc., Exptl. Aircraft Assn., Archeol. Inst. of Am., Valley Coll. Fencing Club, Alpha Gamma Sigma (life). Roman Catholic. Avocations: archaeology, history, archery, sailing, swordsmith. Office: Kevin Deal P O Box 701 Riverside CA 92502 Office Phone: 951-688-7172.

DEAL, LUISA, organizational development/management consultant; b. Naples, Italy, July 15, 1943; came to U.S., 1948; d. Elaine (DeMarino) Bonomo; children: Pamela, Mark, Paula. AA, Muskegon C.C., Mich., 1967; BA, Saginaw Valley State U., 1969; MA, Cen. Mich. U., 1973; Ednl. Specialist, Mich. State U., 1982. Tchr. Saginaw (Mich.) Twp. Cmty. Schs., 1969-72, reading cons., 1972-77, reading specialist, 1977-86; mgmt. devel. trainer Automobile Club of Mich., Dearborn, 1986; assoc. mgr. ops. Gen. Physics Corp., Troy, Mich., 1987; tng. analyst Ball Systems Engring., San Diego, 1988; pres. Tng. Support Network, La Jolla, Calif., 1989—. Spkr. and cons. in field. Active Nine-Nines Internat., Detroit and San Diego, 1988—. Mem. ASTD (Detroit chpt. bd. dirs. 1987-88, San Diego chpt. EFO 1989-90, sec. 1990-91), Am. Soc. for Quality (chmn. 1996-97, chair San Diego sect.), Nat. Speakers Assn., San Diego Orgnl. Devel. Assn., San Diego Coaches Alliance. Avocations: flying (lic. pvt. pilot), tennis, skiing, biking. Home: 537 Piney Way A Morro Bay CA 93442-2353

DEAL, MIKE GARY, art educator; b. Bitburg, Germany, Mar. 21, 1959; arrived in US, 1960; s. Louis Hayes and Maria (Heinz) Deal. AA in speech, Pima Comm. Coll., 1985; BA in German, BA in comm., U. Ariz., 1986; MA in tchg., Sacred heart U., 1993. Cert. educator. Tchr. German Sch. of Conn., Weston, Conn., 1992—2002; supr., tchr. Wide Arts Ctr. fo Handicapped, Bridgeport, Conn., 1992—97; tchr. All Saints Cath. Sch., Norwalk, Conn., 1997—2002, Carden of Tucson, 2002—. Bd. mem. Friends of Ague Caliente, Inc., Tucson, 2003—04. Mem.: Soc. for Ednl. Reconstruction (bd., editor 1991—2001), Phi Kappa Phi. Democrat. Roman Catholic. Avocations: reading, travel, visual and performing arts. Home: 2655 N Conestoga Ave Tucson AZ 85749 Office: Carden of Tucson 5260 N Royal Palm Dr Tucson AZ 85705 Personal E-mail: miguelitodeal@aol.com.

DEAL, NATHAN J., congressman, lawyer; b. Millen, Ga., Aug. 25, 1942; m. Sandra Dunagan; children: Jason, Mary Emily, Carrie, Katie. BA, Mercer U., 1964, JD, 1966. Atty. priv. practice, 1979—82; asst. dist. atty. N.E. cir. Hall County, Ga., 1970—71, judge, juvenile court, 1971-72, atty., 1977—79; mem. Ga. State Senate, 1981—93, pres. pro tempore, 1991—93; mem. U.S. Congress from 10th Ga. Dist., 1993—, dep. whip, mem. energy and commerce com. Mem. Congressional Boating Caucus, Congressional Caucus on Unfunded Mandates, Congressional Travel and Tourism Caucus, Congressional Vietnam-Era Veterans Caucus, Rural Health Care Coalition, Speaker's Immigration Task Force. Capt. JAGC, U.S. Army, 1966-68. Republican. Office: US Ho Reps 2133 Rayburn Ho Office Bldg Washington DC 20515-1009*

DEAL, PAMELA ELLIS, lawyer; b. Panama City, Fla., Feb. 1, 1950; d. Bueford Sanders and Dorothy (Herndon) Ellis; m. Charles T. Deal, Dec. 31, 1970. BA, U. S.C., 1972, MA in Teaching, 1973; JD, U. Ga., 1981. Bar: Ga. 1981, Fla. 1982, S.C. 1982. Clk. Sanders & Deal, Clemson, S.C., 1979-81; bus. law instr. Clemson U., 1981-83; ptnr. Sanders, Deal & Deal, Clemson, 1981-82; mcpl. judge Town of Central, S.C., 1982-83; ptnr. Deal & Deal, P.A., Clemson, 1982—. Chmn. Greater Clemson C. of C., 1985; pres. Assn. Women Profls., Clemson, 1985; bd. dirs. Clemson Child Devel. Ctr., 1991—. Recipient C. Smith Outstanding Svc. award Clemson C. of C., 1988. Mem. Am. Acad. Matrimonial Lawyers, Trial Lawyers Am., S.C. Trial Lawyers Assn., Fla. Bar Assn., Ga. Bar Assn., S.C. Bar Assn., Rotary (pres. Clemson Calhoun chpt. 1993). Avocations: reading, boating, scuba diving. Office: Deal & Deal PA PO Box 1764 600 College Ave Clemson SC 29631-2800

DEAL, TIMOTHY, association executive, former diplomat; b. St. Louis, Sept. 17, 1940; s. Edward F. and Loretta (Fuemuller) D.; m. Jill Brady, Sept. 5, 1964; children; Christopher, Bart. BA, U. Calif., Berkeley, 1962; postgrad., San Francisco State Coll., 1964-65, Am. U., 1972-73. With Am. Embassy, Tegucigalpa, Honduras, 1966-68, Warsaw, Poland, 1969-72, econ. counselor London, 1981-85; various fgn. svcs. assignments Dept. State, Washington,

1972-76; sr. staff mem. NSC, The White House, Washington, 1976-81; dep. U.S. rep. to U.S. Mission to OECD, Paris, 1985-88; dir. office Ea. European/Yugoslav affairs Dept. State, 1988-89; spl. asst. to pres. for nat. security affairs NSC, The White House, 1989-92; minister, dept. chief of mission Am. Embassy, London, 1992-96; ret., 1996; sr. v.p. U.S. Coun. for Internat. Bus., Washington, 1996—. Bd. dirs. Banner Life Ins. Co., William Penn Life Ins. Co., Legal and Gen. Am. Capt. U.S. Army, 1963-65. Avocations: theater, cinema, sports. Home: 5721 Macarthur Blvd NW Washington DC 20016-5304 Office: 1030 15th St NW Ste 800 Washington DC 20005-2633 Office Phone: 202-371-1316. E-mail: tdeal@uscib-dc.org.

DEAL, WILLIAM BROWN, medical school dean, physician, educator; b. Durham, N.C., Oct. 4, 1936; s. Harold Albert and Louise (Brown) D.; m. April Autrey, May 2, 1998; children: Kimberly Deal Wolpert, Kathleen Louise. AA, Mars Hill Coll., 1956; AB, U. N.C., 1958, MD, 1963. Intern in medicine U. Fla. Hosp., Gainesville, 1963-64, asst. resident, 1966-68, fellow in infectious diseases Gainsville, 1968—69, chief resident, instr. dept. medicine Gainesville, 1969-70; asst. prof. dept. medicine U. Fla., 1970-73, assoc. dean Coll. of Medicine, 1973-77, assoc. prof. dept. cmty. health and family medicine, 1973-75, assoc. prof. dept. medicine, 1973-75, prof., 1975-88, acting dean Coll. of Medicine, 1977-78, dean Coll. of Medicine, v.p. clin. affairs, 1978-88, clin. prof. medicine, 1988—; assoc. dean, prof. medicine U. Ala. Sch. of Medicine, 1991-96, sr. assoc. dean, prof. medicine, 1996-97, dean, 1997—; interim CEO UAB Health Sys., 1998-99; v.p. medicine U. Ala., Birmingham, 2000—, sr. v.p., dean emeritus, 2004—. Pres. Maine Med. Ctr. Found., Portland, Maine, 1988—90; asst. to sr. v.p. AMA, 1980; lectr. Northwestern U., 1980; vis. clin. tutor City Hosp. U. Edinburgh, Scotland, 1967; bd. dirs. U. Ala. Health Sys., UAB Health Svcs. Found., Callahan Eye Found. Hosp., UAB Med. West, Children's-Women's Health Sys.; chair nat. adv. com. Sumner Med. Dental Edn. Program. Contbr. articles to numerous profl. jours. Chair R.W. Johnson Found. Fellow: ACP, Royal Soc. Medicine; mem.: AMA (liaison com. on med. edn. 1982—87, chmn. governing coun. sect. on med. schs. 1986—87, exec. com. AAMC 1986—88, disting. svc. mem. AAMC 2005—), Med. Assn. of the State of Ala., Jefferson County Med. Soc., Nat. Rural Health Assn., Ala. Rural Health Assn., Zool. Soc. of Ala., Noble Order of the Flea, Alpha Omega Alpha (bd. dirs. 1986—95, pres. 1993—95), Beta Theta Pi, Phi Chi. Office: Sch of Med FOT 856 UAB Birmingham AL 35294-0001 Office Phone: 205-934-9401. Business E-Mail: wdeal@uab.edu.

DEAL, WILLIAM THOMAS, school psychologist; b. Dec. 18, 1949; s. Richard Lee and Rheta Lucille (Gerber) Deal; m. Paula Nespeca, Aug. 5, 1972. BS, Bowling Green State U., 1972; MA, John Carroll U., 1977; postgrad., Kent State U., 1979—. Sci. tchr. Westlake Schs., 1972-76; intern sch. psychologist Garfield Heights Schs., 1976-77; sch. psychologist, 1977—; pvt. practice Parma Heights, Ohio, 1982—84. Alt. mem. adv. coun. Cuyahoga County Spl. Edn. Svc. Ctr., 1977—. Named Psychologist of the Yr., Cleve. Sch., 1990; recipient cert. of Recognition, Garfield Heights Bd. Edn., 1980, Outstanding Achievement award, Cleve. Assn. Children with Learning Disabilities, Inc., 1980. Mem.: Cleve. Assn. Sch. Psychologists, Ohio Sch. Psychology Assn., United Tchg. Profession, Nat. Assn. Sch. Psychologists, Phi Delta Kappa. Democrat. Methodist. Home: 5290 Kings Hwy Cleveland OH 44126-3059 Office: 12000 Maple Leaf Dr Cleveland OH 44125-2501 Office Phone: 216-475-8105.

DEALBUQUERQUE, JOAN MARIE, conductor, music educator; b. Grosse Pointe, Mich., Feb. 1, 1967; d. Angela May and Anthony Joseph deAlbuquerque. MusB in Edn., Mich. State U., East Lansing, 1993, MusM in Wind Conducting, 1999; DMA, U. North Tex., Denton, 2005. Tchg. fellow U. North Tex., Denton, 2000—03; assoc. dir. of bands Calif. State U., Long Beach, 2003—. Music dir, choir dir., vocal soloist Unity Ch. of Rochester, Mich., 1994; asst. condr. Mich. State U. Concert Band, East Lansing, 1997—99; H.S. band adjudicator No. N.Mex. Dist., 2000; condr. U. North Tex. Concert Band, Denton, 2000—03, H.S. Honor Band, Alamosa, Colo., 2000—00; cantor/vocal soloist Immaculate Conception Cath. Ch., Denton, Tex., 2001—03; rec. prodr. John Wacker, solo trumpet, Denton, Tex., 2002—02; mgr. Conductors Collegium, Denton, Tex., 2002—03; condr. Octet by Stravinsky/Grad. Chamber Group, Denton, Tex., 2003—03. Author: (book) 4 articles in Teaching Music Through Performance in Band. Scholar, Macomb C.C., 1990-1991, Toulouse Grad. Dept., 2000; Tchg. fellowship, U. North Tex., 2000-2003. Mem.: Music Educators Nat. Conf., So. Calif. Sch. Band and Orchestra Assn., Calif. Band Dirs. Assn., Coll. Band Dirs. Nat. Assn., Golden Key Nat. Honor Soc., Pi Kappa Lambda, Phi Kappa Phi. Roman Catholic. Home: 35444 Stillmeadow Ln Clinton Township MI 48035 Office: Calif State Univ 1250 Bellflower Blvd Long Beach CA 90840-7101 Office Phone: 562-985-4533. Personal E-mail: jdealbuq@csulb.edu.

DE ALCUAZ, ANTHONY, lawyer; b. 1950; BA, U. Calif. Santa Cruz, 1972; JD, U. Calif. Hastings Coll. Law, 1975. Dep. dist. atty. Santa Clara County, Calif., 1976—80; ptnr.-in-charge Palo Alto Office McDermott Will & Emery. Mem.: U.S. Supreme Ct., U.S. Ct. Appeals Fed. Cir., Ninth Cir., Calif. State Bar, ABA. Office: McDermott Will & Emery LLP 3150 Porter Dr Palo Alto CA 94304-1212 Office Fax: 650-813-5100, 650-813-5193. Business E-Mail: adealcuaz@mwe.com.

DE ALESSI, ROSS ALAN, lighting designer; b. San Francisco, Apr. 16, 1955; s. August Eugene De Alessi and Angela Maria (Caredio) Leonard; m. Susan Tracey Stearns, Aug. 11, 1990; 1 child, Chase Arthur. BFA, Stephens Coll., 1978. In-house lighting designer GUMP'S, San Francisco, 1981-84; prin. Ross De Alessi & Assoc., San Francisco, 1984-87, Luminae Lighting Design, San Francisco, 1987-93; prin., co-founder Ross De Alessi Lighting Design, Seattle, 1993—. Works include GUMP'S Christmas Windows, San Francisco (award of Distinction Gen. Electric, 1986, Spl. Citation 1989, Edwin F. Guth award Illuminating Engring. Soc. 1989, 90), TAB Products Showroom, L.A. (award of Distinction Gen. Electric 1987), St. Augustine's Ch., Pleasanton, Calif. (Sect. award Illuminating Engring. Soc. 1988), L.A. Quinta (Calif.) Resort Plz. Fountains (award of Excellence Gen. Electric 1988, Paul Waterbury award Illuminating Engring. Soc. 1989), McKesson Bldg. Lobby, San Francisco (award of excellence Gen. Electric 1988, Edwin F. Guth award Illuminating Engring. Soc. 1989), Brown & Bain, Phoenix (Merit award Gen. Electric 1989), Saxe Gallery, San Francisco (Edwin F. Guth award Illuminating Engring. Soc. 1989), Plz. Pk., San Jose, Calif. (Paul Waterbury Spl. Citation Illuminating Engring. Soc. 1990), The Palace Fine Arts, San Francisco (Edison Award Gen. Electric 1990, Paul Waterbury award Illuminating Engring. Soc. 1991, award of Excellence Internat. Assn. Lighting Designers 1991), Le Touessrok, Island of Mauritius (Merit award Gen. Electric 1993, Sect. Award Illuminating Engring. Soc. 1994, Paul Waterbury award 1994), St. Patrick's Sem., Menlo Park, Calif. (Edison award Gen. Electric 1993, Edwin F. Guth award Illuminating Engring. Soc. 1994, Citation Internat. Assn. Lighting Designers 1994), Palace of the Lost City, Republic of Boputhatswana (Award of Merit Gen. Electric 1992, Paul Waterbury award Internat. Assn. Lighting Designers 1993), Wells Fargo Bank-Flagship Bank, San Francisco (award of excellence Gen. Electric 1992, Merit award Illuminating Engring. Soc. 1993, citation Internat. Assn. Lighting Designers 1993), Santa Barbara County Courthouse, Santa Barbara (Paul Waterbury award Illuminating Engring. Soc. 1995, award of excellence Internat. Assn. Lighting Designers 1995), City of Bridges, Cleve. (Edison award 1995, Paul Waterbury award Illuminating Engring. Soc. 1997), MGM Grand Gateway of Entertainment, Las Vegas (award of excellence Gen. Elec. 1998, Edwin F. Guth award Illuminating Engring. Soc. 1999, Merit award Internat. Assn. Lighting Designers 1999), Helsinki Master Plan-Esplanade (Edison award 1999, Award of Distinction, Illuminating Engring. Soc. 2000, Merit award Internat. Assn. Lighting Designers), Space Needle (award of excellence Gen. Electric 2000, Illuminating Engring. Soc. 2001, Merit award Internat. Assn. Lighting Designers 2001), Forth Bridge (award of excellence Internat. Assn. Lighting Designers 2002), Montecasino (Merit award Gen. Electric 2001, Sect. award Internat. Assn. Design awards 2002). Mem. Internat. Assn. Lighting Designers (lighting cert.), Nat. Coun. on the Certification Lighting Profls., Illuminating Engring. Soc., Washington Athletic Club. Avocations: scuba diving, travel. Office: Ross De Alessi Lighting Design 2330 Magnolia Blvd W Seattle WA 98199-3813

DEALEY, LYNN TOWNSEND, artist; b. Smithfield, N.C., July 16, 1954; d. John Sims and Rebecca Barnes Townsend; m. Russell Edward Dealey, May 4, 1985. AS in Advt. Design, Art Inst. Ft. Lauderdale, 1977; BS in Health Edn., U. N.C. Greensboro, 1976. Mem. adv. bd. Artreach, Dallas, 1991—92; spkr. in field. Illustrator: A Coon Creek Chronicle, 1992; mural, tiger exhibit Dallas Zoo, 1998, featured, cover of Philanthropy in Tex. mag., 2002, Texas Women: Trailblazers, Shining Stars and Cowgirls, 2003, Enchanted Galleries, 2004—. Recipient various awards, recognition for charity work, United Way, U. Tex., Austin, others, 1997—. Mem.: Dallas Country Club, Dallas Social Dir. Avocations: science, biology, cartooning, travel, cooking. Office: PO Box 191406 Dallas TX 75219

DEALY, JOHN MICHAEL, chemical engineer, educator; b. Waterloo, Iowa, Mar. 23, 1937; s. Milton David and Ruth Marion (Dorton) D.; m. Jacqueline Dery, Aug. 22, 1964; 1 child, Pamela. BS, U. Kans., 1958; MS, U. Mich., 1959, PhD, 1963; postdoctoral fellow, 1964. Asst. prof. chem. engring. McGill U., Montreal, Que., Can., 1964-67, assoc. prof., 1967-72, prof., 1972—2004, prof. emeritus, 2004, chmn. dept., 1993-94, dean engring., 1994-99. Cons. indsl. rheology and polymer processing Author: 4 books on melt rheology and plastics processing; contbr. articles. Fellow: Can. Acad. Engring., Royal Soc. Can., Soc. Plastics Engrs.; mem.: Soc. Rheology (pres. 1987—89), Sigma Xi, Theta Tau, Tau Beta Pi. Home: 315 Roslyn Ave Montreal PQ Canada H3Z 2L7 Office: McGill U Chem Engring Dept 3610 University St Montreal PQ Canada H3A 2B2 Office Phone: 514-398-4264. E-mail: john.dealy@mcgill.ca.

DEAMER, RICHARD MORRIS, psychiatrist; b. South Bend, Ind., July 1, 1941; s. David Wilson and Zena Morris Deamer; m. Harriet Ann Griffith, July 3, 1965; children: Kelly, Julie. BS, Purdue U., Ind., 1963; MD, Ohio State U., 1967; residency in psychiatry, UCLA, 1971. Med. dir. Vista del Mar Hosp., Ventura, Calif., 1968—71; clin. instr. in medicine Ventura (Calif.) County Med. Ctr., UCLA, 1984—98. Pres., CEO Limbic Sys., Inc., Ventura, Calif., 1994—2003. Pres. Child Abuse & Neglect, Ventura, Calif., 1976—80. Lt. comdr. USN, 1971—73. Grantee Small Bus. Innovative Rsch. Grant, Nat. Inst. Musculoskelatal Diseases, 1993; Fellowship in Child Psychiatry, UCLA, 1974. Fellow: Am. Psychiat. Assn. (Disting. fellow 2003). Democrat. Methodist. Achievements include patents for stoop labor body support; stoop labor assist device. Avocations: classical guitar, scuba diving, private pilot. Office: Richard M Deamer MD Inc 3585 Maple St Ste 297 Ventura CA 93003

DEAMICIS, SUSAN MCNAIR, small business owner; b. Salem, Mass., May 16, 1949; d. Charles Donald and Stacia (Zalewski) McN.; m. John Henry DeAmicis, Dec. 15, 1984; stepchildren: Shawn D., Mary C., Kristen M. Student, U. Mass., 1982-84, Curry Coll., 1986-88. Plan adminstr. Lahey Clinic-Blue Cross Blue Shield Health Maintenance Plan, Burlington, Mass., 1980-86; pres. Mass Mailers Inc., South Boston, 1982—; exec. dir. Metro West Health Plan, Lexington, Mass., 1986-87; asst. regional exec. dir. Med. West Cmty. Health Plan, Hingham, Mass., 1992-94; dir. contract devel. Mass. Blue Cross Blue Shield, Boston, 1992-94; dir. product devel. Small Bus. Svc. Bur., Worcester, Mass., 1995-96. Dir. Plan Credit Union, Boston, 1988-94, pres./chair, 1994; dir. Jaw Joints and Allied Musculo-Skeletal Disorders, Boston, 1995—. Vol. WBUR-Nat. Pub. Radio Sta., Boston, 1993—; allocation vol. United Way of Mass Bay, Boston, 1994—; pheresis donor ARC, Dedham, Mass., 1994—; bone marrow donor Nat. Bone Marrow Registry, 1995. Mem. Group Health Assn. Am. Republican. Roman Catholic. Avocations: reading, gourmet cooking. Home: 101 Emerson Rd Milton MA 02186-5138 Office: Mass Mailers Inc 28 Damrell St Boston MA 02127-2775

DEAN, BEALE, lawyer; b. Ft. Worth, Feb. 26, 1922; s. Ben J. and Helen (Beale) D.; m. Margaret Ann Webster, Sept. 3, 1948; children: Webster Beale, Giselle Liseanne. BA, U. Tex., Austin, 1943, LLB, 1947. Bar: Tex. 1946, U.S. Dist. Ct. (no., we. and ea. dists.), U.S. Cir. Ct. (5th and 11th cirs.) 1952, U.S. Supreme Ct. 1954. Asst. dist. atty., Dallas, 1947-48; assoc. Martin, Moore & Brewster, Ft. Worth, 1948-50; mem. Martin, Moore, Brewster & Dean, 1950-51, Pannell, Dean, Pannell & Kerry (and predecessor firms), 1951-65; ptnr. Brown, Herman, Scott, Young & Dean, Ft. Worth, 1965-71, Brown, Herman, Scott, Dean & Miles, Ft. Worth, 1971-98, Brown, Herman, Dean, Wiseman, Liser & Hart, LLP, Ft. Worth, 1998—2003; sr. counsel Brown, Dean, Wiseman, Liser, Proctor & Hart, LLP, Ft. Worth, 2003—. Spl. asst. Atty. Gen. Tex., 1959-61. Regent Nat. Coll. Dist. Attys., 1985-2003. With AUS, 1942-45, ETO. Named Tex. Super Lawyer, Law and Polit., Tex. Monthly, 2003—04. Mem. ABA, Bar Assn. Fifth Fed. Cir., Ft. Worth-Tarrant County Bar Assn. (past pres. 1971-72, Blackstone award 1991), Am. Coll. Trial Lawyers, State Bar Tex. (dir. 1973-75), Am. Bar Found., Tex. Bar Found. (charter mem.), Ft. Worth Boat Club, Ridglea Country Club, Ft. Worth Club. Presbyterian. Office: 200 Ft Worth Club Bldg 306 W 7th St Fort Worth TX 76102-4905

DEAN, BILL VERLIN, JR., lawyer; b. Oklahoma City, Jan. 11, 1957; s. Bill V. and Mary Lou (Dorman) D.; m. Christine Potter; children: Bill V. III, Mary Megan. BS, Ctrl. State U., 1978; JD, Oklahoma City U., 1991. Bar: Okla. 1982, U.S. Dist. Ct. (we. dist.) Okla. 1983, (no. dist.) Okla. 1986, (ea. dist.) Okla. 1987, Tex. 1990, N.Y. 1992, U.S. Ct. Appeals (10th cir.) 1986; U.S. Supreme Ct., 2002; lic. real estate broker and ins. agt. Second dep. assessor Okla. County Assessor, Oklahoma City, 1978—80; atty. Struthers Oil and Gas Corp., Oklahoma City, 1980—82; cons. Bill Dean & Co., Jones, Okla., 1979—; ptnr. Dean & Assocs. P.C., Jones, 1982—; pres. Dean Ins. Agy. Ltd., 1986—, Casualty Corp. Am., Inc., 1999—; pres., CEO Madewell Holding Corp., 2004—. Bd. dirs. Union Mut. Ins. Co., Madewell & Madewell, Inc., Madewell Holding Corp., 2004—; CEO Casualty Corp. of Am., Inc., 1999—. Mem. Okla. County Bar Assn., Okla. Bar Assn., Tex. Bar Assn., N.Y. Bar Assn., Shriners. Methodist. Home: 200 Cherokee St Jones OK 73049-7709 Office: Dean & Assocs P C PO Box 1060 110 W Main St Jones OK 73049-1060 Office Phone: 405-399-9111. E-mail: bdean@deannet.com.

DEAN, CAROLE LEE, film company executive; b. Dallas, Mar. 23, 1939; d. Roy Webster and Dorothy Lee Dean; children: Richard Dean, Carole Joyce. Student, UCLA. Pres. Studio Film and Tape, L.A., 1969-2000, N.Y.C., 1970-2000, Chgo., 1994—2000, From the Heart Prodn., L.A., 1992—. Spkr. in field. Prodr., host Health Styles, 1994-97; author: Heal Thyself, 1999, The Art of Funding Your Film: Alternative Financing Concepts, 2003, The Art of Manifesting: Create Your Future, 2005. Established Roy W. Dean film, video and writing grants, 1992. Mem. Nat. Arts Club. Republican. Avocations: skiing, equesterian. E-mail: caroleedean@att.net.

DEAN, EDWIN BECTON, entrepreneur; b. Danville, Va., Feb. 7, 1940; s. Edwin Becton and Lois (Campbell) D.; m. Deirdre Anne Jacovides, Aug. 16, 1964; children: Jennifer E., Kristin R., Brian N. BS in Physics, Va. Poly. Inst. and State U., 1963, MS in Math., 1965; postgrad., George Washington U., 1974-77; cert. profl. study engring. mgmt., Old Dominion U., 1998. Technician, assoc. engr. Johns Hopkins U. Applied Physics Lab., Laurel, Md., 1959-64; physicist, mathematician, electronic engr., and ops. rsch. analyst Naval Surface Warfare Ctr., Silver Spring, Md., 1964-79; owner, mgr. Gen. Bus. Svcs. and Beta Systems, Virginia Beach, Va., 1979-84, Virginia Beach Communique Inc., Virginia Beach, Va., 1980-81; registered rep. First Investors Corp., Arlington, Va., 1971-85; dir. Tips Club of Virginia Beach, Inc., 1980-82; computer specialist Naval Supply Systems Command, Norfolk, Va., 1982-83; head cost estimating office NASA Langley Rsch. Ctr., Hampton, Va., 1983-90, tech. resource mgr. Space Exploration Initiative Office, 1990-94, sr. rsch. engr. multidisciplinary optimization br., 1994-98; owner The DFV Group, Virginia Beach, Va., 1996-98; pres. The DFV Group, Inc., Virginia Beach, 1999—2002. Presenter in field; distbr. Shaklee, 1999—. Contbr. articles to profl. jours. NASA fellow, 1963-65. Mem. IEEE, Assn. for Computing Machinery, Internat. Soc. Parametric Analysts (past chmn. bd. dirs.), Am. Soc. for Quality Control, Am. Assn. Cost Engrs., Internat. Neural Network Soc., QFD Inst., Sigma Pi Sigma, Pi Mu Epsilon, Phi Kappa Phi.

DEAN, EDWIN ROBINSON, economist, educator, consultant; b. South Bend, Ind., July 25, 1933; s. William Stover and Eleanor (Hatcher) D.; m. Emily Rebecca Finlay, Feb. 2, 1963; children: Gabrielle N., Natalie R. BA in Philosophy magna cum laude, Yale U., 1955; postgrad., Gokhale Inst. Politics-Econs., Poona, India, 1955—56; PhD in Econs., Columbia U., 1963. Instr., then asst. prof. econs. Columbia U., N.Y.C., 1960-68; assoc. prof. Queens Coll., CUNY, 1968-72; program dir. Am. Friends Svc. Com., N.Y.C., 1970-73; supervisory equal opportunity specialist in econs. U.S. Commn. on Civil Rights, 1973-80; sr. assoc. Nat. Inst. Edn., Washington, 1980-83, acting asst. dir., 1983; supervisory economist Bur. Labor Stats., Washington, 1983-85, chief divsn. productivity rsch., 1985-89, assoc. commr. Office Productivity and Tech., 1989-99, ret., 1999; adj. prof. econs. George Wash. U., Washington, 2000—. Cons. to World Bank, 2001-03; mem. exec. com. Conf. Rsch. Income and Wealth, 1994-2000; chair working party industry stats. OECD, 1998-2000. Author: The Supply Responses of African Farmers: Theory and Measurement in Malawi, 1966, Plan Implementation in Nigeria, 1962-66, 1972; contbg. author: The Challenge Ahead: Equal Opportunity in Referral Unions, 1976, Non-referral Unions and Equal Employment Opportunity, 1982; editor: The Controversy over the Quantity Theory of Money, 1965, Education and Economic Productivity, 1984; contbr. articles to profl. jours. Recipient Julius Shiskin award, Nat. Assn. Bus. Econs., 2000; fellow, NSF, 1961—62; grantee rsch., Columbia U. Coun. for Rsch. in Social Scis., 1964, Rockefeller Found., Ibadan, Nigeria, U.S., 1965—67; scholar, Yale U., 1951—55; Howland travel fellow, 1955, Seager fellow in econs., 1956, 1957, William Bayard Cutting travel fellow, Columbia U., 1958. Mem.: Am. Econ. Assn. Unitarian Universalist.

DEAN, GEOFFREY, book publisher; b. Newcastle-upon-Tyne, Eng., Sept. 18, 1940; s. Thomas Craig and Mildred Catherine (Hoggard) D.; m. Philma Marina Patterson, Aug. 10, 1963; children: Andrea Samantha, Christopher Michael. BA, U. Toronto, 1961. With McGraw-Hill Co. Can. Ltd., 1961-66, coll. editor Scarborough, Ont., 1962-66; sales mgr. Methuen Publs., Toronto, 1966-70; v.p. mktg. Van Nostrand Reinhold Ltd., Toronto, 1970-76; pres., dir. John Wiley & Sons. Can. Ltd., Toronto, 1976-86; cons. Geoffrey Dean Enterprises, 1986—; pres. Tech. Instrnl. Products Inc., 1987-88, Scripto-graphic Communications Ltd., Toronto, 1989-91. Dir. Youth Employment Svc., Toronto, 1995-2000; mem. adv. bd. on sci. pub. Nat. Rsch. Coun. Can., 1982-84; chmn. Book and Periodical Coun., 1988-89; mem. project assessment com. Book Pub. Industry Devel. Program, Govt. Can., 1987-91; internat. cons. Dept. of Edn., Rep. of Philippines, 1996-97. Bd. dirs. Can. Diabetes Assn., 1987-89. Mem. Can. Book Pubs. Coun. (pres. 1983), Ont. Bus. Edn. Assn. (hon. pres. 1982-84), Rotary. Home and Office: 33 Deepglade Cir Toronto ON Canada M2J 1B3 Office Phone: 416-805-1210. E-mail: geoffdean01@hotmail.com.

DEAN, H. CLARK, retired civil engineer, professional genealogist; b. Evanston, Ill., Jan. 22, 1931; s. Herbert Franklin and E(lla) Frances (Clark) D.; m. Mary Margaret McHugh, Aug. 20, 1960; children: Merrick Stephen McHugh, Nancy Lauck Dean Cacioppo. BSCE, Swarthmore Coll., 1953; MBA, U. Chgo., 1964. Registered profl. engr., Pa.; registered structural engr., Ill.; cert. genealogist Bd. for Cert. Genealogists. Engr. Pratt & Whitney, East Hartford, Conn., 1954; jr. engr. Modjeski & Masters, Harrisburg, Pa., 1954, engr., 1956-61, Harza Engring. Co., Chgo., 1961-67, asst. to v.p., 1967-72, asst. project mgr., 1972-74, project mgr., 1974-76, asst. dept. head, 1976-80, dept. head, 1980-97; ret., 1997. Contbr. articles to profl. jours. including Am. Genealogist., Nat. Geneal. Soc. Quar., New Eng. Hist. and Geneal. Register, N.Y. Geneal. and Biog. Record. With C.E., U.S. Army, 1955-56. Mem. ASCE (life), New Eng. Hist. and Geneal. Soc., Nat. Geneal. Soc., Soc. Mayflower Descs. in Ill. (treas. 1967-70, bd. assts., 1990-98, gov. 1998-2001), Order Founders and Patriots Am., Ill. Soc. War of 1812, Assn. Profl. Genealogists, North Suburban Geneal. Soc. (pres. 1976) Home: 422 Kelling Ln Glencoe IL 60022-1113 Personal E-mail: hclarkdean@juno.com.

DEAN, HOWARD BRUSH, III, political organization administrator, former governor; b. N.Y.C., Nov. 17, 1948; s. Howard Brush and Andrea (Maitland) D.; m. Judith Steinberg, 1981; children: Anne, Paul. BA, Yale U., 1971; MD, Albert Einstein Coll. Medicine, 1978. Intern, then resident in internal medicine Med. Ctr. Hosp. Vt., 1978-82; practice medicine specializing in internal medicine Shelburne, Vt.; mem., house edn. com., mcpl. corps. and elections com., rules com. Vt. House of Reps., Montpelier, 1983-86, asst. minority leader, 1985-86; lt. gov. State of Vt., Montpelier, 1986-91, gov., 1991—2003; chmn. Dem. Nat. Com., 2005—. Asst. clin. prof. medicine U. Vt. Coll. Medicine; ran for Democratic nomination in Presdl. election., 2004; established political action com. Democracy for America, 2004; guest host CNBC's Topic A with Tina Brown, 2004. Bd. dirs. Vt. Developmental Capabilities Council, U. Vt. Council, Vt. Adv. Commn. Intergovtl. Affairs, Vt. State Bd. Nat. Forests; founder Vt. Youth Conservation Corps; sponsor Long Trail Preservation Fund. Democrat. Office: Dem Nat Com 430 S Capitol St SE Washington DC 20003

DEAN, JAMES BENWELL, lawyer; b. Dodge City, Kans., May 23, 1941; s. James Harvey and Bess (Benwell) D.; m. Sharon Ann Carver, Sept. 1, 1962 (div. 1991); m. Patricia A. Bostick, Aug. 23, 1993 (div. 1999); children: Cynthia G. Dean Vosburgh, James M.; m. Gail M. Cohen, Sept. 21, 2002. Student, Southwestern Coll., 1959-60, U. Colo., 1961; BA, Kans. State U., 1962; JD, Harvard U., 1965. Bar: Colo. 1965, U.S. Dist. Ct. Colo. 1965, U.S. Tax Ct. 1966, Nebr. 1971, U.S. Ct. Appeals (10th cir.) 1971. From assoc. to ptnr. Tweedy & Mosley, Denver, 1965-71, Kutak Rock Cohen Campbell Garfinkle & Woodward, Omaha, 1971-73; ptnr. Mosley, Wells & Dean, Denver, 1973-77, Kutak Rock & Huie, Denver, 1977-81, James B. Dean, P.C., Denver, 1981-91, Dean, McClure, Eggleston & Husney, Denver, 1991-95, James B. Dean, PC, Denver, 1995-2000, Dean & Stern, LLC, Denver, 2001—05, Dean, Dunn & Phillips LLC, Denver, 2005—. Lectr. U. Ark. Law Sch., Fayetteville, 1982—86, C.C. Aurora, Colo., 1996—97; spl. asst. atty. gen. State of Colo., Denver, 1989—. Co-editor Agricultural Law Jour., 1979-84; contbr. articles to profl. jours. Recipient Erwyn E. Witte Colo. Cooperator award, Colo. Coop. Coun., 1996. Mem.: Am. Agrl. Law Assn. (bd. dirs. 1981—83, pres.-elect 1985—86, pres. 1986—87, strategic planning com. 2000—01, Disting. Svc. award 1989), Denver Bar Assn., Colo. Bar Assn. (bd. dirs. 1989—2001, sec. agrl. law sect. 1991—94, chair, Colo. coop. statute revision com. 1995—), Nebr. Bar Assn., ABA (advisor bd. forum com. on rural lawyers and agrl. bus. 1983—89). Avocations: photography, woodworking, hiking, piano. Office: 4155 E Jewell Ave Ste 703 Denver CO 80222-4511 Office Phone: 303-756-6744. Business E-Mail: jim@lawatddp.com.

DEAN, JANET BLEVINS, psychologist, educator; d. James L. and Helen B. Blevins; m. Kevin L. Dean, Sept. 10, 1994; children: Jonathan F., Rowan R. BA, U. Akron, 1992; MA, MDiv, Asbury Theol. Sem., 1994; MA, Ohio State U., 2001, PhD, 2003. Lic. psychologist Ky., 2004. Intern psychology Fed. Med. Ctr., Lexington, Ky., 2002—03; clin. psychologist Bluegrass Regional Mental Health Mental Retardation Bd., Inc., Nicholasville, Ky., 2003—04; psychologist Asbury Coll., Wilmore, 2004—. Affiliate faculty mem. Asbury Theol. Sem., Wilmore, 2002—; adj. faculty mem. Asbury Coll., Wilmore, 2004—. Contbr. presentations to confs. (hon. mention presentation Ann. Conv. Ohio Psychol. Assn., 2001), articles to profl. jours. Treas. LifeBridge Ch. of Nazarene, Lexington, Ky., 2003—. Nominee Grad. Tchg. Assn. award, Ohio State U., 2002; recipient Golden Key / Peat Marwick award, U. Akron, 1991; fellow, Ohio State U., 1997—98, 1999, Psychology Dept. Ohio State U., 1998—2001; Presdl. scholar, U. Akron, 1989—92, Robert A. Traina English Bible scholar, Asbury Theol. Sem., 1994—95, Myron C. Boyd Free Meth. scholar, Free Meth. Ch., 1994—95. Mem.: APA, Soc. Christian Psychology. Office: Asbury Coll One Macklem Dr Wilmore KY 40390 Office Phone: 859-858-3511. Personal E-mail: janet.dean@asbury.edu.

DEAN, JEAN BEVERLY, artist; b. South Paris, Maine, Aug. 23, 1928; d. Henry Dyer and Doris Filena (Judd) Small; m. Samuel Lester Dean. AS, Becker Coll., Worcester, Mass., 1948; AA, Edison Coll., Ft. Myers, Fla., 1980. Artist, Ft. Myers, 1963—. One-woman shows include Edison C.C. Gallery, Ft. Myers, Joan Ling Gallery, Gainesville, Fla., Berry Coll., Mt. Berry Ga., Gallery 10, Asheville, NC, Sanibel Gallery, Fla., 1993, 1995, Barrier Island Group for the Arts, Sanibel, 1994, 1996, Gallery Mido, Belleview Mido Resort, Belleair, Fla., 1996, No. Trust Bank, Ft. Myers, 1996, Lee County Alliance of the Arts, 1996, Art League of Manatee County, Fla., 1996, Naples Libr., 1997, Sy Zy Gy Gallery, Ft. Myers, 1998, 2000, Barnes and Noble, 2000, Captiva Civic Assn., Fla., 2000, So. County Ctr. for the Arts, Ft. Myers, 2000, Viva Gallery, Captiva, Fla., 2000, Broadway Palm Dinner Theatre, Ft. Myers, 2001, Art House, 2002, Tower Gallery, Sanibel, 2002, Alliance for the Arts, Ft. Myers, 2004, exhibited in group shows at S.E. Painting and Sculpture Exhbn., Jacksonville, Fla., Southeastern Ctr. for Contemporary Art, Ybor City, S.W. Fla. Internat. Airport, 1991, 1995, Ctr. Art Show, St. Petersburg, Fla., 1991, Ridge Juried Art Show, Winter Haven, Fla., 1992, Artists Group, Sarasota, 1992, Women's Caucus for Art, 1993, Polk Mus., Lakeland, Fla., 1993, Daytona Mus., Fla., 1994, Women's Caucus Art Nat. Show, San Antonio, 1995, Capitol Gallery, Tallahassee, 1995, Women's Caucus Art State Show, Sarasota, 1995, Women's Caucus for Art, Miami, 1996, 1998, Fla. Artist Group, Winter Haven, 1996, Jacksonville Art Mus., 1998, Edison Coll., Ft. Myers, 1999, Fla. So. Coll., Lakeland, 1999, Art Ctr., St. Petersburg, 1999, Viva Gallery, Captiva, 2000, Charlotte County Nat., Fla., 2000, Nat. Exhibit, Winter Haven, 2000, The Capitol, Tallahassee, 2001, Venice Art Ctr., 2001, Captiva Art Ctr., 2001, Charlotte County National, Fla., 2002, Alliance of the Arts, Ft. Myers, 2002—03, Barrier Island Group for the Arts, Sanibel, 2002, Gallery on Broadway, Ft. Myers, 2002, Florida Gulf Coast U., 2003, Bonita Arts Ctr., Bonita Springs, Fla., 2003, Crossed Palms Gallery, Bookelia, Fla., 2002—04, Art Serve Gallery, Ft. Lauderdale, 2004, Temple Beth El, Ft. Myers, Fla., 2005, Represented in permanent collections Am. Embassy, Madrid, Edison Coll., Ft. Myers, First Fed. Savs. and Loan, Ft. Myers, Naples, Fla., NCNB Bank, Tampa, Health Park, Ft. Myers, Clara Barton House, Washington, Hirshhorn Collection, Porter Goss Collection. Active Lee County Alliance for Arts, 1994-2004; chair invitational com. Barrier Island Group for Arts, Sanibel, 1994-99; founder Open Doors Lee County Alliance of the Arts, Fla., 1990—. Recipient more than 100 awards. Mem. Nat. Mus. Women in the Arts (charter mem.), Fla. Artists Group, Nat. Soc. Experimental Artists. Democrat. Unitarian Universalist. Home: 17643 Captiva Island Ln Fort Myers FL 33908-6115 Personal E-mail: jeansdean@comcast.net.

DEAN, JOHN F., retired school system administrator; b. Bridgeport, Conn., Nov. 15, 1926; s. James Henry and Mary McKay Dean; m. Katherine Nisbet, Aug. 28, 1949; children: Karol M. Hicks, Brian R. BS in Edn., U. So. Calif., 1950; MA, Calif. State U., 1955; EdD, U. So. Calif., 1966. Tchr. Newport Beach (Calif.) Sch. Dist., 1950-56, elem. sch. prin., 1956-61, dir. curriculum, 1961-69; dean Orange Coast C.C., Costa Mesa, Calif., 1969-70; prof. edn. Whittier (Calif.) Coll., 1970-91; supt. of schs. Orange County Dept. Edn., Costa Mesa, 1991-2001, emeritus, 2001—. Author: Teaching in America, 1978. Bd. dirs. Hoag Meml. Hosp., Newport Beach, Calif., 1972—2003. With USN, 1944—46. Republican. Presbyterian. Avocation: professional writing. Home: 1136 Highland Dr Newport Beach CA 92660-5618

DEAN, JOHN F., federal judge; b. Washington, 1946; BS, Mich. State U., 1970; student, Columbus Sch. Law; JD, Catholic U. Am., 1975; Masters in Laws Taxation, Georgetown U., 1985. Bar: DC 1975, admitted to: US Supreme Ct., Fed. Dist. Ct., No. Dist. Tex., Dist. Md., US Tax Ct. With Office of Chief Counsel, IRS, Dallas Dist. Counsel, 1975—78, Balt. Dist. Counsel, 1978—86, Office of Assoc. Chief Counsel Internat., 1986—94; spl. trial judge US Tax Ct., 1994—. Adj. prof. law Howard U., 1999—. Mem.: Wash. Bar Assn. (vice chair jud. counsel 2002—03). Office: US Tax Ct 400 Second St NW Washington DC 20217

DEAN, JOHN GUNTHER, diplomat; b. Germany, Feb. 24, 1926; came to U.S., 1939, naturalized, 1944; s. Joseph and Lucy (Askenaczy) D.; m. Martine Duphenieux, Dec. 26, 1952; children: Catherine Dean Curtis, Paul, Joseph. BS magna cum laude, Harvard U., 1947, MA, 1950; Doctorate, U. Paris, 1949. With ECA, Am. embassy, Paris, 1950-51, Am. embassy, Brussels, 1951-53, asst. econ. commr. Saigon, 1953-56; polit. officer Am. Embassy, Laos, 1956—58; consul Am. consulate, Togo, 1959-60; chargé d'affaires Am. Embassy, Mali, 1960-61; with Dept. State, Washington, 1961-65; polit. officer Am. Embassy, Paris, 1965—69; regional dir. CORDS in Central Vietnam, 1970-72; dep. chief mission Am. Embassy, Laos, 1972—74, amb. to Cambodia, 1974—75, Denmark, 1975—78, Lebanon, 1978—81, Thailand, 1981—85, India, 1985—88. Adv. U.S. delegation to UN, 1963; now mem. adv. bds. several nat. and internat. cos. and instns. Served to 2d lt. AUS, 1944-46. Fellow Center for Internat. Affairs Harvard, 1969-70 Mem.: Harvard (N.Y.C.); Kenwood Golf and Country (Washington). Office: 29 Blvd Jules Sandeau 75116 Paris France Home: Chalet Crettaz BP 1318 1936 Verbier Valais Switzerland Office Phone: 0033-1-45-04-71-84. E-mail: johnmartinedean@aol.com.

DEAN, JOHN W(ESLEY), III, investment banker, former counsel to President; b. 1938; m. Maureen (Mo) Dean; 1 child from previous marriage. Student, Colgate Univ., Coll. of Wooster; JD, Georgetown Univ., 1965. Counsel to Pres. Richard Nixon White House, 1970—74; private investment banker; writer; lectr.; columnist FindLaw. Author: Blind Ambition, 1976, Lost Honor, 1982, The Rehnquist Choice: The Untold Story of the Nixon Appointment that Redefined the Supreme Court, 2001, Unmasking Deep Throat, 2002, Warren G. Harding (American Presidents Series), 2004; co-author (with Robertson Dean): Worse than Watergate, 2004. Key figure in Watergate scandal; convicted of obstruction of justice, served four months in prison.*

DEAN, K. MATTHEW, elementary school educator; b. Evansville, Ind., Oct. 13, 1952; s. Robert Sheridan and Mae Blanche (Carlisle) D. BS, U. So. Ind., 1974; MS, Ind. U., 1980. Tchr. elem. sch. Bend Gate Sch., Henderson, Ky., 1974-2001. Treas. Tri-State Amateur Radio Soc., Evansville, 1992-95, Friends of Angel Mounds, Evansville, Ind., 1996-98. Fellow Delta Arts Acad.; mem. Ky. Edn. Assn., Kappa Delta Pi. Avocations: amateur radio, woodcarving, photography, history, travel. Home: 1540 S Boeke Rd Evansville IN 47714 E-mail: absolam1@juno.com.

DEAN, LESLIE ALAN (CAP DEAN), international economic and social development consultant; b. Indpls., June 18, 1940; s. Henry Lloyd and Margaret Ann (Pfafman) Dean; m. Jeanne Louise Lambert, Apr. 14, 1962; children: David Richard, Laura Elizabeth. BA, U. Ill., 1963, MA, 1966; postgrad., U. Pitts., 1968-69. Internat. loan analyst Bank Calif., San Francisco, 1970; joined Fgn. Svc., 1970; devel. officer U.S. AID, Washington, 1970, 77-79, Vientiane, Laos, 1971-75, Kathmandu, Nepal, 1975-77, Islamabad, Pakistan, 1979-83, Dar Es Salaam, Tanzania, 1983-85, asst. mission dir. Lusaka, Zambia, 1985-87, mission dir. sr. fgn. svc., 1988-90, office dir. Washington, 1990-92, mission dir. Pretoria, South Africa, 1992-96, dep. asst. adminstr. Africa Bur. Washington, 1996-98; dir. integrated devel. programs sub-Saharan Africa Internat. Found. Edn. and Self Help, Phoenix, 1999—2003, v.p. ops., 2003; regional coord. for Baghdad Coalition Provisional Authority, Baghdad, Iraq, 2004; interim mayor Baghdad, 2004; interim gov. Baghdad Province, 2004. Elder, chair mission com. Pinnacle Presbyn. Ch., 2002—04. Capt. USAF, 1964—68. Mem.: Am. Fgn. Svc. Assn., Beta Gamma Sigma, Phi Eta Sigma. Avocations: swimming, reading, travel. Personal E-mail: cdean5000@aol.com.

DEAN, MARK E., engineer, computer scientist; b. Jefferson City, Tennessee, Mar. 2, 1957; BSEE, U. Tennessee, 1979; MSEE, Florida Atlantic U., 1982; PhD in Electrical Engring., Stanford U., 1992. Former head IBM Austin Rsch. Lab.; IBM fellow & v.p. systems IBM Rsch., 1997—. IEEE sec. U. Tennessee, 1978—89; trustee Huston-Tillotson Coll., 1997; bd. dirs. Inroads, Inc. Named Disting. Sci. Sponsor, NY Hall of Sci., 2001; named one of 50 Most Important African-Americans in Tech., Calif. African-Am. Museum, 2000; named to Nat. Inventors Hall of Fame, Akron, Ohio, 1997; recipient PC Mag. World Class award, 1988, Presidents award, Career Comm. Group, 1997, Ronald H. Brown Am. Innovators award, 1997, Disting. Engr. award, Nat. Soc. of Black Engineers, 1999, Living Legends award, Balt., Maryland, 2000, Black Engr. of the Yr. award, Career Comm. Group, 2000. Fellow: Am. Acad. Arts & Sciences; mem.: Nat. Acad. of Engring., IEEE. Holds over 20 patents for inventions in computing technology including three of the original patents for IBM's PC internal architecture. Office: IBM T J Watson Rsch Ctr PO Box 704 Yorktown Heights NY 10598-0215

DEAN, MARTHA ELIZABETH, music educator; b. Atlanta, Apr. 6, 1976; d. Marcus Gary and Penelope Ann Monk; m. Craig Allan Dean, Mar. 27, 1999. B in Music Edn., Auburn U., 1998. Orch. tchr. Cobb County Schs., Marietta, Ga., 1998—2001, chorus/music/drama tchr., 2001—. Guest dir. McEachern Music Camp, Powder Springs, Ga., 2000, program dir., 2001—02. Camptivity coord. Girl Scouts Am., Mabelton, Ga., 1999—; vol., mem. chamber chorus and chorus Atlanta Symphony Orch., 1999—; advisor Kappa Kappa Gamma, Auburn, 1999—. Recipient Bernstein Tchr. award, Leonard Bernstein Found., 1999—2001, Grammy award, 2002, 2003, Bellsouth Excellence in Edn. Program award, 2003, Grammy award for best choral performance, 2005. Mem.: Am. Choral Dirs. Assn., Music Educators Nat. Conf. Avocations: camping, hiking, swimming, sewing, gardening. Office: Griffin Mid Sch 4010 King Springs Rd Smyrna GA 30082

DEAN, MICHAEL M., lawyer; b. Phila., Jan. 7, 1933; BA, Antioch Coll., 1954; JD cum laude, U. Pa., 1957. Bar: Pa. 1957. Fulbright fellow U. London, 1962-63; ptnr. Wolf, Block, Schorr & Solis-Cohen, Phila., 1966-2000, of counsel, 2000—. Dir. Univ. City. Sci. Ctr., Phila., 1993—, chmn., 2000—02. Bd. dirs. emeritus Ctrl. Phila. Devel. Corp., 1996—, pres., 1987—90, chmn., 1990—95; counsel, bd. dirs., exec. com., chmn. endowment trust Diagnostic and Rehab. Ctr., Phila., 1980—2003; exec. com., bd. dirs., sec. Ctr. City Dist., 1990, solicitor, 1991—. E-mail: mdean@wolf.block.com.

DEAN, NANCY, literature educator, retired playwright; d. Archie Leigh Dean and Ella Cecille Lang; life ptnr. Beatrice Eva Eastman, Sept. 2, 1963. BA with honors, Vassar Coll., 1952; MA in Tchg., Radcliffe Coll., 1953; PhD, NYU, 1963. Tchr. The Madeira Sch., Greenway, Va., 1953—55, Wakefield H.s., Arlington, Va., 1955—56; instr. Robert Coll., Istanbul, Turkey, 1956—59; from instr. to full prof. Hunter Coll., CUNY, N.Y.C., 1963—90; ret. Author, editor (plays) Ophelia's Laughter, 1988, Blood and Water, 1988, Burning Bridges, 1991, Upstairs? In the Afternoon?, 1995, That Ilk, 2000, Crisey de, 2003, Libretts, Crisey de, 2005; author (as Elizabeth Lang): Anna's Country, 1981; author: (screenplays) Ophelia's Rainbows, 2005; co-editor: (short stories) In the Looking Glass, 1977, (plays) Intimate Acts, 1997; translator: Moliere's Misanthrope, 1991. Founder The Astraea Found., N.Y.C., 1977—85; co-founder with Beatrice Eva Eastman Open Meadows Found., N.Y.C. Recipient Significant Achievement As Playwright & Supporter of Other Lesbian Playwrights, Sisters On Stage, 1995; Ford fellow, Vassar Coll., 1953, Louise Hart Van Loon fellow, 1959—60, Woodrow Wilson fellow, NYU, 1962—63, Penfield scholar, 1961, Jay F. Krakauer Meml. grantee, NYU Grad. Sch. Alumni, 1962—63. Mem.: AAUW, Pen and Brush, Washington Sq. Playwrights, Times Sq. Playwrights (chair playwrights 2002—04), Dramatists Guild (assoc.). Democrat. Buddhist. Office: Grimalkyn Ltd 620 King Ave Bronx NY 10464 Personal E-mail: enndean@mindspring.com.

DEAN, NAT, artist, educator; b. Redwood City, Calif., Jan. 13, 1956; d. Richard William and Marianne Ridley (Smith) D.; m. Paul Singdahlsen, May 24, 1987. Student, Calif. Inst. of Arts, 1972-76, Cooper Union Coll., 1975; BFA, San Francisco Art Inst., 1977. Freelance artist, educator, Fla./Calif, 1978-95; annual workshop leader, lectr. Calif. Inst. of Arts, Valencia, 1985—; dir. career planning Calif. Inst. Arts, Valencia, 1986-89; dir. of career ctr. Ringling Sch. of Art and Design, Sarasota, Fla., 1989-92; conf. co-organizer Arts Placment Profls. Groups, 1989, 91, 92, 93; pres., owner Ruta Zinc Fine Arts Agy., San Francisco, NY and L.A., 1980-89; freelance artist, educator N.Mex./Calif., 1995—; owner Ruta Zinc Handmade, San francisco and New Mex., 1999—. Guest lectr. Iowa State U., Ames, 1992; adj. faculty Md. Inst., Balt.; lectr. L.A. Internat. Art Fair, 1988-94; dir., organizer annual Dialogue Among Peers, Santa Fe, 1997—, numerous others. One-person shows and group exhbns. include Valencia C.C., Orlando, Fla., 1995, Durango (Colo.) Art Ctr., 1995, Manatee C.C., Bradenton, Fla., 1994, Ormond Beach (Fla.) Meml. Art Mus., 1994, Oreg. Sch. of Arts & Crafts, Portland, 1993, The Edn. Ctr. Gallery, Longboat Key, Fla., 1993, Nutaalite, Buena Park, Calif., 1993, Sarasota County (Fla.) Arts Coun., 1993, ARTarget, Sarasota, Fla., 1993, Selby Gallery, Sarasota, Fla., 1992, Ctr. Gallaery, Miami-Dade C.C., 1991, NCCA Gallery/New Ctr. for Creative Awareness, Sarasota, 1990, Scottsdale (Ariz.) Ctr. for Arts, 1992, 95, Boca Raton (Fla.) Mus. Art, 1991, Coll. Creative Studies, U. Calif., Santa Barbara, 1990, San Francisco Mus. Modern Art Rental Gallery, 1986, 89, Galerie Anton Meir, Geneva, 1988, Orange County Ctr. Contemporary Art, Santa Ana, Calif., 1990, The Fukuoka Mcpl. Mus., Japan, 1987, Berlin Transit, 2001, San Francisco Ctr. for the Book, 2002, others; co-author: The Visual Artist's Business and Legal Guide, 1995; contbr. Artmaker Mag., 2002. Chmn. visual artists task force Sarasota County Arts Coun., 1991-92; AIDS subcom. Planned Approach to Community Health, Sarasota, 1991-92; visual aids com., Visual Aids: Day Without Art, 1989—; program adv. Regional Occupational Program, Contra Costa Bd. Edn., 1986, numerous others; mem. Mayor's Com. for Concerns of Persons with Disabilities, Santa Fe, 2000-2003. Recipient Residency award The Bemis Project, Omaha, 1986, Profl. Devel. grant Ringling Sch. of Art and Design, Sarasota, 1990, Merit award Calif. Inst. of Arts, Valencia, 1976, others. Mem. Coll. Art Assn. (speaker 1992, 93), Nat. Artists Equity (speaker 1992), Women's Caucus for Art (speaker 1993), Nat. Soc. Exptl. Learning (speaker 1988, 89, 92, 93), Nat. Art Edn. Assn. (speaker 1992), Nat. Assn. Artists Orgns., Coll. Placement Coun., others. Office: 110 Sierra Azul Santa Fe NM 87507-0188

DEAN, PATRICEA LOUISE, lawyer, law educator, small business owner; b. Kansas City, Mo., Sept. 25, 1928; d. Merville Francis Davies and Marie Margaret (Dorsch Davies) Damron; m. Richard Wallace Dean, Mar. 14, 1948 (dec. July 20, 1987); children: Phyllis Carol(dec.), Katherine Ann, Carol Anne. AA, Met. Jr. Coll., Kansas City, 1947; BA, Pepperdine U., 1968, JD, 1971. Bar: Calif. 73, U.S. Supreme Ct. 87, U.S. Tax Ct. 92. Pvt. practice, Anaheim and Sacramento, Calif., 1973—2001; instr. various colls. and law schs., Calif., 1975—2001; continuing edn. instr. N.W. Coll., Powell, Wyo., 2001—04; founder, pres. Office@Home, Inc., 1998—. Legis. coord. Western Manufactured Housing Inst., 1977—83; atty., lobbyist, presenter seminars Golden State Manufactured Home Owners League, 1984—89; dir., pres. telecomms., software and internet businesses, 1990—. Author: Guide to Manufactured Housing, 1980; contbr. articles to profl. publs. Pres. Friends of Cody Libr., 2002—04; precinct worker Dem. Party, Mo. and Calif., 1949—53; campaign mgr. Dist. Atty. race, Iron County, Utah, 1962—63; precinct committeewoman Rep. Party, Park County, Wyo., 2002—03. Achievements include helped draft federal and state laws on building, siting, zoning and taxation of manufactured homes. Office: Office@Home Inc PO Box 836 Powell WY 82435

DEAN, PAUL JOHN, magazine editor; b. Pitts., May 11, 1941; s. John Aloysius and Perle Elizabeth (Thompson) D.; m. Jo-ann Tillman, Aug. 19, 1972 (div. Mar. 1981); children: Jennifer Ann, Michael Paul. Student engring., Pa. State U., 1959-60. Gen. mgr. Civic Ctr. Honda Co., Pitts., 1965-68, Washington-Pitts. Cycle Co., Canonsburg, Pa., 1968-70; nat. svc. mgr. Yankee Motor Co., Schenectady, 1970-73. Competition congressman Am. Motorcyclist Assn., 1971, 72, trustee, sec. bd., 1988-91, chmn., 1991-97; bd. dirs. AMA ProRacing, 1997—; adv. bd., guest speaker L.A. Trade Tech. Coll., 1974-90; trustee Am. Motorcyclist Heritage Found., 1990-91. Engring. editor Cycle Guide mag., Compton, Calif., 1973-74, editor-in-chief, 1974-80, editorial dir., 1980-84; editor-in-chief Cycle World mag., Newport Beach, Calif., 1984-88, editorial dir. Cycle and Cycle World mags., 1988-92; v.p., editorial dir. Cycle World Mag. Group, 1992—; author manuals. Served with AUS, 1964-65. Named to, Nat. Motorcycle Mus. and Hall of Fame, 2002. Home: 5915 Arabella St Lakewood CA 90713-1203 Office: Hachette Filipacchi Media US 1499 Monrovia Ave Newport Beach CA 92663-2752 Office Phone: 949-720-5386. E-mail: CW1Dean@aol.com.

DEAN, PAUL REGIS, retired law educator; b. Leetonia, Ohio, July 12, 1918; s. Edward Joseph and Catherine (Sheets) D.; m. Delores M. Fitch, July 14, 1945 (dec. 1987); children— Mary E., Lawrence E. (dec.), Patricia, John, Paul, William, Delores, Teresa, Brian. Student, DeSales Coll., Toledo, 1936-38; BA, Youngstown State U., 1940; LL.B., Georgetown U., 1946, LL.M., 1952, LL.D., 1969. Bar: D.C. 1946, Va. 1954. Law clk. to presiding judge D.C. Ct. of Appeals, 1946-47; prof. law Georgetown U., 1947-54, 69-88; dean U. Law Ctr., Georgetown U., 1954-69, dean emeritus and prof. emeritus, 1988—. Legal adviser to Pres.'s Com. Govt. Contract Compliance, 1952-53; neutral trustee United Mine Workers Am. Health and Retirment Funds, 1971-94; mem. Pres.'s Commn. Pension Policy, 1979-81, D.C. adv. com. U.S. Civil Rights Commn., 1961-63; trustee, v.p. Loyola Found. Inc., 1957—. Served to lt. USNR, 1942-46. Fellow Am. Coll. Trust and Estate Counsel; mem. Am. Arbitration Assn., Va. Bar Assn., Bar Assn. D.C. (Lawyer of Yr. award 1971), Delta Theta Phi. Office: 600 New Jersey Ave NW Washington DC 20001-2022

DEAN, RICHARD ANTHONY, mechanical engineering executive; b. Bklyn., Dec. 22, 1935; s. Anthony David and Anne Mylod Dean; m. Sheila Elizabeth Grady, Oct. 5, 1957; children: Carolyn Anne, Julie Marie, Richard Drews. BSME, Ga. Inst. Tech., 1957; MSME, U. Pitts., 1963, PhDME, 1970. Registered profl. engr., Calif. From jr. engr. to mgr. thermal and hydraulic engring. Westinghouse Nuclear Energy Sys., 1959-70; v.p., tech. dir. water reactor fuels General Atomics, San Diego, 1970-74, v.p. uranium and light water reactor fuel, 1974-80, sr. v.p., 1980-92; pres. Leading Edge Engring., San Diego, 1993—; pres., CEO Cutting Edge Products, Inc., San Diego, 1997—. Cons. U.S. Congress Office Tech. Assessment. 1st lt. U.S. Army, 1957-59. Mem. AAAS, ASME (former chmn. nuclear fuels tech. com.), Am. Nuclear Soc. (gen. chmn. annual meeting 1993), Global Found. (bd. advisors), Internat. Thermonuclear Experimental Reactor (adv. bd.). Achievements include the develpoment of commercial nuclear power stations; advanced the understanding of boiling heat transfer phenomena; invention of advanced nuclear fuel assembly. Home: 6699 Via Estrada La Jolla CA 92037-6432 Office: Leading Edge Engring # 313 13240 Evening Creek Dr San Diego CA 92128 Office Phone: 858-513-1203. Business E-Mail: dean@leeinc.us.

DEAN, RICHARD N., lawyer; b. Providence, Mar. 5, 1955; BA, Vanderbilt Univ., 1977; MA, JD, Univ. Va., 1980. Bar: NY 1981, DC 1995. Atty. Coudert Bros., NYC, 1980—85, Sydney, Australia, 1985—87, Moscow, 1988—91, ptnr., head Russia, Ukraine & Ctrl. Asia practice Washington, 1991—. Lectr. Univ. Va. Sch. Law, 1993—. Editor (sr.): Va. Jour. Internat. Law; contbr. chapters to books. Office: Coudert Bros LLP 11th Fl 1627 I St NW Washington DC 20006 Office Phone: 202-775-5100. Office Fax: 202-775-1168. Business E-Mail: deanr@coudert.com.

DEAN, ROBERT BRUCE, architect; b. Brockton, Mass., Jan. 15, 1949; s. Robert George and Marjorie Gertrude (O'Donnell) D.; m. Mary Hood Hoskinson, June 18, 1977; children: Robert Maxwell, Anne, Claire. BA, U. Pa., 1971; MArch, Columbia U., 1976. Registered architect, N.Y., Conn. Staff architect Skidmore, Owings & Merrill, Architects, N.Y.C., 1976-77; job capt. Stephen Jacobs & Assn., N.Y.C., 1977-78; staff architect Johnson-Burgee Architects, N.Y.C., 1978-79; pvt. practice architecture N.Y.C. and Syracuse, 1979-85; project architect Robert A.M. Stern Architects, N.Y.C., 1985-86; pres. Dean Design, Inc., New Canaan, Conn., 1986—. Adj. assoc. prof. Columbia U., N.Y.C., 1978-83; asst. prof. Syracuse U., 1980-84. Contbr. articles to profl. jours. Bd. dirs. Redding Hist. Soc.; mem. Planning Commn. Town of Redding, Dem. Town com. Grantee Syracuse U., 1982, grantee Nat. Endowment Arts, 1983-84; William Kinne Fellow, 1976. Mem. AIA, Conn. Soc. Architects. Democrat. Congregationalist. Avocation: american cultural and commercial history. Office: Dean Design Inc 111 Cherry St New Canaan CT 06840-5530 Office Phone: 203-966-8333. E-mail: rdean@deandesign.net.

DEAN, ROBERT FRANKLIN, insurance company executive; b. Houston, Nov. 1, 1942; s. Claude Nathan and Nellie Gladis (Davis) D.; m. Kathy Copeland, Aug. 16, 1963 (div. Jan. 1970); 1 child, Robert Franklin Jr.; m. Betsy Ellen Kniehl, Sept. 20, 1975 (dec. Jan. 1994); children: James, Kyle, Courtney Elizabeth. BBA in Bus. Mgmt., U. Houston, 1968. Cert. safety profl. Safety engr. Gulf Ins. Group, Houston, 1968-69, Indsl. Indemnity Ins., Houston, 1969-75; loss control mgr. Crum & Forester Ins. Group, Houston, 1975-78; sr. mktg. cons. Aetna Ins. Co., Houston, 1978-80; v.p. mktg. div. Stanley Ins., Houston, 1980-81; pres., chief exec. officer Dean & Draper Ins. Agy. Inc., Houston, 1981—. Head football coach Alief Youth Assn., Houston, 1975-81; mem. steering com. Rep. Party, Houston, 1988; bd. trustees Harris County Impact Polit. Action Com., 1991-96; mem. Hartford Prodr. Coun., 2002-03, Tex. Mut. Prodr. Coun., 2001-04. Recipient Cert. of Appreciation, Spring Br. Sch. Dist., 1985, Outstanding Svc. award Tex. Automotive Assn., 1985; named Agt. of the Yr., Travelers Ins. Co., 1999, Travelers Elite Agt, 1999-2004, United Fire Ins. Diamond Agt., 2002-03. Mem. Am. Soc. Safety Engrs. (cert. com. on edn. Houston chpt. 1975-76), Houston Gemini Automation Group (bd. dirs. Houston chpt. 1989-90, pres. 1990-92), Ind. Ins. Agts. of Am. (bd. dirs. Houston chpt. 1991-96), Houston Assn. of Ins. Agts. (legis. com. 1993-94, recreation com., charitable events bd. liaison, bd. dirs. charitable found.), Gemini User of Am. Republican. Episcopalian. Avocations: golf, health, motorcycling, choir, swimming. Office: Dean & Draper Ins Agy 3131 W Alabama 4th Fl Houston TX 77098 E-mail: bdean@deandraper.com.

DEAN, SCOTT P., music educator, director; b. Santa Ana, Calif. s. Frank and Barbara Dean; m. Cynthia Limb; children: Nathan P., Elizabeth L. BA in Music Edn., Calif. State U., 1979, MusM in Conducting. Dir. of music St. Paul's Luth. Ch., Sunny Hills, Calif., 1978—79, Good Shepherd Luth. Ch., Buena Park, Calif., 1979—80, Red Hill Luth. Ch., Tustin, CA, Calif., 1982—89; artisitic dir. and founder South Coast Chamber Singers, Newport Beach, Calif., 1982—89; dir. of music First Presbyn. Ch. of Bellevue, Bellevue, Wash., 1989—. Master class participant, chorus mem. Oreg. Bach Festival, Eugene, Oreg., 1976—91; lectr., adjudicator, clinician Various organizations, We. US, 1985—; chmn., western wash. Am. Choral Dirs. Assn., Wash., 1991—93, nw divsn. chair, music and worship, 1992—2001; music and worship mentor for mdiv candidates Seattle Area Theol. Ext. (Fuller), Seattle, 1995—99; guest condr. Cappella Nymphenburg, Maria Ward Choir, Munich, 2000; nat. chmn. for music in worship Am. Choral Dirs. Assn., Oklahoma City, 2001—. Conductor (recordings) Blessings, Fount of Every Blessing, Songs of the Spirit. Recipient Outstanding Contbn. to the Choral-Vocal Area, Calif. State U. of Fullerton, Music Dept., 1977—78, Outstanding Svc. to the Dept. of Music, Calif. State U., Fullerton, 1978—79. Mem.: Presbyn. Assn. of Musicians, Am. Guild of English Handbell Ringers, Choristers Guild, Am. Choral Dirs. Assn. (assoc.), Phi Mu Alpha Sinfonia (life). Achievements include first to The Company of Heaven-Benjamin Britten (Northwest premiere); Benedicite-Andrew Carter (Western US premiere); Requiem-Mozart, completed by Robert Levin (WA state premiere); Requiem-Brahms, translated Robert Bullock (Western US premiere); International Music Ministry Abroad performances in Austria, Czech Republic, Germany, Hungary, Italy, Slovakia, Slovenia, Switzerland; research in The British Library (London); Biblioteque Nationale (Paris); Various libraries (Rome). Avocations: travel, photography, music. Office: First Presbyn Ch of Bellevue 1717 Bellevue Way NE Bellevue WA 98004 Office Phone: 425-454-3082.

DEAN, SHERRY LYNN, language educator, speech professional; b. New Albany, Ind., July 1, 1960; d. Oscar L. and Betty L. (Jason) Brown; m. A. L. Dean Jr. BA in French, Speech Comm., Secondary Edn., Asbury Coll., 1983; MA in French, U. Tex. Arlington, 1990; Cert. pratique de francais commercial, Chambre de Commerce de d'Industries, Paris, 1990; MA in Interdisciplinary Studies, U. Tex., 1999; PhD in Higher Edn. Adminstrn., U. Tex. Austin, 2003. Mem. adj. French faculty Mountain View Coll., Dallas,

1986—91, mem. French faculty, 1991—, prof. French and speech comm., 1993—. Sponsor French Club, Mountain View Coll., 1989—, chair honors program, 1996—98, sponsor Senegal Studies Club, 1997—98, 1999—2000, coord. Study Abroad Programs, 1998—, mem. study abroad coords., 1998—, chair cultures course com., 1999—, mem. core curriculum cultures course com., 1999—, coord. intercultural spkr. series, 1995, coord. Europe 1992 Conf., 1991—92, mem. numerous other coms.; mem. North Tex. C.C. Consortium for Internat. Edn., 1997—; presenter in field. Compiler AATF Travel Guide, 1996, reviewer Little-known Museums In and Around Paris; author: (book) Discover French-speaking Louisiana: A Brief Guide to Creating An Acadiana Adventure Tour. Dir. DCCC Senegal, West Africa Profl. Devel. Seminar, 2005. Named Outstanding Young Woman of Yr., 1986, Chevalier, Knight of the Acad. Palm, French Govt., 2003; recipient internship, French Cultural Svcs., Washington, 1981; grantee, Dallas County C.C. Dist., 1995—2000; Fulbright/Hays, U.S. Dept. Edn. Mem.: Am. Assn. Tchrs. of French (v.p. North Tex. chpt. 1994—96, com. chair Task Force for Promotion of French in U.S. 1995—97, pres. North Tex. chpt. 1996—98, mem. Commn. for Promotion of French 1999—2000, mem. Nat. French Week Commn. 1998—, co-chair Nat. C.C. Commn. 2000, Coll. Tchr. of Yr. award 1999, Dorothy S. Ludwig Excellence inTchg. award 2000), Tex. Fgn. Lang. Assn. (Coll. Tchr. of Yr. award 1998), l'Alliance Francaise (hon.). Home: 1329 Primrose Ln De Soto TX 75115 Office: Eastfield Coll 3737 Motley Dr Mesquite TX 75150 Office Phone: 972-860-7128. Business E-Mail: sherrydean@dcced.edu.

DEAN, THOMAS EUGENE, music educator, consultant; b. Washington, Nov. 8, 1959; s. Joseph Rober Dean and Joanne Mary Bielefeld, Camille Dean (Stepmother) and Gilbert E. Bielefeld (Stepfather); m. Trisha Ann Ferko, Nov. 5, 1983; children: Heather Marie, Holly Nicole. BS in Music Edn., West Chester (Pa.) U., 1982, MusM in Music Edn., 1993. Cert. tchr. Del., 2002. Music educator The Eisenhower Sch., Levittown, Pa., 1982—83, Twin Spring Farm Day Sch., Ambler, Pa., 1983—84, Dover (Del.) HS, 1984—2004, Mount Pleasant H.S., 2004—. Mem. leadership team for vpac commn. Dept. of Edn., Dover, Del., performance indicator com. mem. Choral dir. Parkersford Bapt. Ch., Pa., 1983—84; choir dir. Wyoming (Del.) United Meth. Ch., 1984—85. Recipient Director's award for Notable Contbn., Fiesta-val Invitational Music Festivals, 1992, 1993, 1996. Mem.: Kent County Music Educators Assn. (assoc.; treas. 1990—94), Music Educators Nat. Conf. (assoc.), Del. Music Educators Assn. (assoc.; chorus chmn. 1988—90, web master 1995—, editor 1995—2002, choir chmn. 2000—02, pres. 2005—), Pi Kappa Lambda. Republican. Roman Catholic. Home: 18 Henderson Hill Rd Newark DE 19711 Office: Mt Pleasant HS 5201 Washington St E Wilmington DE 19809-2156 Office Phone: 302-762-7129. Business E-Mail: thomas.dean@bsd.k12.de.us.

DEAN, WILLIAM EVANS, aerospace transportation executive, consultant; b. Greenville, Miss., July 6, 1930; s. George Thomas Dean and Martha Myrtle (Evans) Carlton; m. Dorothy Sue Hamilton, Oct. 14, 1953; children: Janet Lea, Jody Anne, Justin H. B in Aero. Engring., Ga. Inst. Tech., 1952; MBA, Pepperdine U., 1970; grad., USAF Air Command and Staff Coll., 1970. FAA cert. airplane and instrument flight instr. Commd. officer USAF, 1952, advanced through grades to maj., 1962; divsn. mgr., dir. Rockwell Internat. Corp., L.A., 1962-67, v.p., divsn. gen. mgr., 1967-80; exec. v.p. Acurex Corp., Mountain View, Calif., 1981-82, pres., COO, 1982-83, pres., CEO, 1983-90, vice chmn., 1990-91; assoc. dir. Ames Rsch. Ctr. NASA, Moffett Field, Calif., 1991-93, dep. ctr. dir., 1994-97; v.p., dir. Univs. Space Rsch. Assn., Columbia, Md., 1997—2002; founder, mng. dir. The Dean Group, LLC, Santa Ana, Calif., 2002—. Lectr. Calif. State U., Chico, 1988, Santa Clara U., 1993-98, USAF Acad., 1961, 75. Contbr. articles on gen. mgmt. and aero. engring. to profl. jours. Bd. dirs. NCCJ, San Jose, Calif., 1984-97, co-chmn., 1988-91; bd. dirs. Santa Clara County Mfg. Group, San Jose, 1984-91, vice-chmn., 1988-91; bd. dirs. Saddleback Community Coll., Mission Viejo, Calif., 1976-77, United Fund, Orange County, Calif., 1971; United Way, Santa Clara County, San Jose, 1985-91; vice-chmn., bd. advisors Leavey Sch. Bus., Santa Clara U., 1987-97, vice chmn., 1989-91; tech. com. Orange County Bus. Coun., 1998-2000. Decorated Air Force Commendation medal with oak leaf cluster; recipient Spl. Svc. award United Way, 1986, NASA Astronaut Personal Achievement award, 1972, 84, Outstanding Contbn. to Manned Exploration of the Moon award, 1972, Medal for Outstanding Leadership, 1995, Group Achievement awards, 1995, Disting. Svc. medal, 1997; Silver Knight of Mgmt. award Nat. Mgmt. Assn., 1978, Commendation Cert. Calif. State Assembly, 1986, Pres. award Santa Clara U., 1993, Disting. Alumnus award Woodward Acad., 1999, Acad. Disting. Engring. Alumni award Ga. Inst. Tech., 1995; inducted to Engring. Hall of Fame, Ga. Inst. Tech., 1997. Fellow AIAA (bd. dirs. 1979-86, 91-95, fin. com. 1995—, Space Shuttle award 1984), Internat. Acad. Astronautics (Paris), Am. Astron. Soc., Nat. Space Soc.; mem. Am. Electronics Assn. (edn. found. 1982-88), Aircraft Owners and Pilots Assn. (command pilot), Air Force Assn. Republican. Baptist. Office: The Dean Group 13422 Laurinda Way Santa Ana CA 92705-1926 Office Phone: 714-544-5020. Business E-Mail: wdean1@comcast.net.

DEANE, JAMES GARNER, editor, conservationist; b. Hartford, Conn., Apr. 5, 1923; s. Julian Lowrie and Miriam (Grover) D. BA, Swarthmore Coll., 1943. Mem. editorial staff Washington Star, 1944-60, edn. editor, 1952-57, classical recs. critic, 1952-60; ind. researcher, vol. in conservation activity, 1961-68; assoc. editor Nat. Parks Mag., 1968-69, editor, 1969; asst. editor The Living Wilderness, Washington, 1969-71, exec. editor, 1971-75, editor, 1975-81; editor Defenders mag., Washington, 1981-2001, editor emeritus, 2001; v.p. Defenders of Wildlife, Washington, 1997-2001. Washington corr. Mus. Courier, 1945-55; contbg. editor High Fidelity mag., 1953-55; mem. com. transp. environ. rev. process Transp. Research Bd. NRC, 1974-77; Am. co-chmn. Can. U.S. Environ. Coun., 1975-81. Bd. dirs. Arctic Internat. Wildlife Range Soc., 1979—; trustee Com. of 100 on Federal City, 1967-90, 1st vice chmn., 1967-69; chmn. Potomac Valley Conservation and Recreation Council, 1967. Served with AUS, 1946-47. Recipient award, Edn. Writers Assn., 1956, Public Svc. award, Washington Newspaper Guild, 1956, Charles Carroll Glover award, Nat. Park Svc., 1967. Home: 111 Audubon Rd Leeds MA 01053 Business E-Mail: jdeane111@comcast.net. *Protection of as many as possible of the remaining wild places and, with them, of the marvelous diversity of living species on our crowding planet is one of the imperatives of our time. This need can be met only by developing worldwide understanding of its crucial importance. That is the challenging task of the nature-conservation movement. I find it exhilarating to be making some contribution, however modest, to the accomplishment of that task through the techniques of journalism.*

DEANE, LELAND MARC, plastic surgeon; b. N.Y.C., June 18, 1952; s. Maurice Allen and Barbara Elaine (Ushkow) D.; m. Danielle Anne Sheft, Nov. 21, 1993; children: Ashby Bennett, Galen Ames. BS, Union Coll., 1974; MD, SUNY, Bklyn., 1978. Diplomate Am. Bd. Surgery, Am. Bd. Plastic Surgery. Intern, then resident in surgery New Eng. Med. Ctr., 1978-83; resident in plastic surgery Ea. Va. Grad. Sch. Medicine, 1983-85; fellow in hand surgery Jefferson Med. Coll., 1986; pvt. practice L.I. Plastic Surg. Group P.C., Garden City, N.Y., 1986—. Mem. surg. rev. com. Winthrop U. Hosp., Mineola, N.Y., 1986—, mem. resident edn. com., 1992—; instr. surgery Cornell Med. Coll., 1989—. Contbr. articles to profl. jours. Advisor Mothers of Super Twins, L.I., 1995—. Grantee So. Med. Assn., 1984. Fellow ACS, Am. Acad. Pediat.; mem. Am. Soc. Plastic and Reconstructive Surgeons, Northea. Soc. Plastic Surgeons, N.Y. Regional Soc. Plastic and Reconstructive Surgery, Seawanhaka Corinthian Yacht Club, N.Y. Yacht Club. Office: LI Plastic Surg Group PC 999 Franklin Ave Garden City NY 11530-2913

DEANE, RICHARD HUNTER, JR., former federal judge, lawyer; b. Oct. 18, 1952; BA, U. Ga., 1974, JD, 1977; LLM, U. Mich., 1979. Bar: Ga. 1977. Asst. U.S. atty. No. Dist. Ga., 1980-88; chief gen. crimes sect. U.S. Attys. Office, 1988-91, chief criminal divsn., 1991-94; magistrate judge U.S. Dist. Ct. (no. dist.) Ga., Atlanta, 1994-98; U.S. atty. No. Dist. Ga., Atlanta, 1998—2002; with Jones Day, Atlanta, 2002—. Office: Jones Day 1420 Peachtree St NE Ste 800 Atlanta GA 30309-3053 Office Phone: 404-581-8502. Business E-Mail: rhdeane@jonesday.com.

DEANE, SALLY JAN, health services management, consultant; b. Downey, Calif., Sept. 24, 1948; d. Virgil Eldred and Pearl Jan (Kettell) D. BA, Whittier Coll., 1970; MEd, Boston U., 1971, MPH, 1988. Mgr. community health Peter Bent Brigham Hosp., Boston, 1974-76; coord. WIC program Martha Eliot Health Ctr., 1976-78; dir. S.W. Boston WIC program Shattuck Hosp. Corp., 1978-80; exec. dir. Fenway Community Health Ctr., 1980-84; exec. asst. commr. Boston Dept. Health & Hosps., 1984-86; assoc. dir. spl. projects Health Policy Inst. Boston U., 1986-87; dir. ambulatory reimbursement Mass. Medicaid, 1987-88; assoc. Cambridge (Mass.) Mgmt. Group, 1989; ptnr. Integrated Health Strategies Inc., Cambridge, Mass., 1990-96; adj. asst. clin. prof. Pub. Health Boston U., 1994—; v.p. Chadwick Martin Bailey, Boston, 1996-98; mng. ptnr. Strategic Healthcare Innovations LLC, Boston, 1999—; instr. Boston U., 1999—. Cons. Mass. Dept. Pub. Health, Boston, 1978-80, Citicorp Corp. Hdqrs., N.Y.C., 1986; lectr. Grad. Sch. Mgmt., Boston U., 1999—; bd. visitors Boston U. Sch. Pub. Health, 1999—; innkeeper Charles St. Inn, 1999—. Mem. Mayor's Task Force on AIDS, Boston, 1983—86; v.p. Trustees Charitable Donations, Boston, 1984—88; chair bd. dirs. Boston Women's Health Book Collective, 2000—; chmn. bd. dirs. N.E. Eye Inst. Presbyterian. Personal E-mail: sallydeane@yahoo.com.

DEANGELIS, CATHERINE D., pediatrics educator; b. Scranton, Pa., Jan. 2, 1940; m. James C. Harris. BA, Wilkes Coll., 1965; MD, U. Pitts., 1969; MPH, Harvard U., 1973. Diplomate Nat. Bd. Med. Examiners, Am. Bd. Pediat.; RN Pa., N.Y. Intern in pediat. Children's Hosp., Pitts., 1969—70; resident in pediat. Johns Hopkins Hosp., Balt., 1970—72, teaching fellow pediat. dept. internat. health Sch. Pub. Health, 1972; pediatrician Roxbury Comprehensive Health Clinic, Boston, 1972—73; asst. prof. pediat. Coll. Physicians and Surgeons, asst. prof. health svc. adminstrn. Sch. Pub. Health Columbia U., 1973—75; mem. staff divsn. pediatric ambulatory care, dir. med. edn. Child Care Project Columbia Presbyn. Med. Ctr., 1973—75; asst. prof. pediat. Sch. Medicine U. Wis., 1975—77, assoc. prof. pediat. Sch. Medicine, 1977—78; dir. ambulatory pediatric svcs. U. Wis. Hosps., 1975—78; assoc. prof. pediat. Johns Hopkins Sch. Medicine, 1978—85; dir. pediatric primary care and adolescent medicine Johns Hopkins Hosp., 1978—84, co-dir. adolescent pregnancy program, 1979—82; with dept. health svcs. adminstrn. and dept. internat. health Johns Hopkins Sch. Hygiene and Pub. Health, 1980—90; dir. residency tng. dept. pediat. Johns Hopkins Hosp., 1983—90, dir. divsn. gen. pediat. and adolescent medicine, 1984—90; deputy chmn. dept. pediat. Johns Hopkins Sch. Medicine, 1983—90, prof. pediat., 1986—, assoc. dean acad. affairs, 1990—93, sr. assoc. dean acad. affairs and faculty, 1993—94, vice dean acad. affairs and faculty, 1994—; editor Jour. AMA, 2000—. Mem. Gov.'s Task Force to Evaluate Health Care in Wis. State Prisons, 1975—78; chmn. ambulatory care com. U. Wis. Hosp., 1976—78; mem. med. sch. admissions com. U. Wis. Sch. Medicine, 1976—78, chmn., 1977—78; mem. exec. coun. dept. pediat. and Children's Ctr. Johns Hopkins U. Sch. Medicine, 1982—90, chmn. fin. com. dept. pediat., 1984—85, chmn. assoc. prof.'s promotion com., 1985—88, chmn. com. developing Women's Health Ctr. at Johns Hopkins Med. Instns., 1993—; mem. Md. Gov.'s Task Force on Women's Health, 1993—, chair, 1994—; mem. search com. U. Wis., 1976, Johns Hopkins Sch. Medicine, 1984, 88, 92, 93; mem. nat. rev. com. for accreditation of nurse practitioners Am. Nurses' Assn., 1975—79, co-chmn., 1977; mem. peer rev. com. nurse practitioner programs divsn. nursing Health Resources Agy., Dept. HEW, 1979—81. Author: Basic Pediatrics for the Primary Care, 1984; editor: An Introduction to Clinical Research, 1990; editor: (with others) Principles and Practice of Pediatrics, 1990, 1994; assoc. editor Pediatric Annals, 1990—, editor Archives of Pediatrics and Adolescent Medicine, 1993—. Cons. Robert Wood Johnson Found., 1973—; mem. adv. group on improving outcomes for children Pew Charitable Trusts, 1991—92; mem. adv. panel medicine Pew Health Profn.'s Commn.; mem. nat. adv. com. Robert Wood Johnson Clin. Scholars Program, 1992—; mem. steering com. Rural Health Planning, Wis. Recipient George Armstrong award, Ambulatory Pediatric Assn., scholarship, Acad. Adminstrn. and Health Policy, Assn. Health Ctrs., 1993; fellow NIH, 1973. Fellow: APHA, Am. Acad. Pediat. (govt. affairs com. 1984—88, chpt. III youth com. N.Y. chpt. 1974—75, chmn. adolescent com. Md. chpt. 1981—84); mem.: Inst. Medicine Coun., Soc. Adolescent Medicine, Am. Bd. Pediat. (examiner 1986—, long-range planning com. 1990—91, chmn. long-range planning com. 1992—, bd. dirs. 1990—, fin. com. 1991—, sec., treas. 1993—95, chair-elect 1995—96, chair 1996, search com. 1990), Am. Pediatric Soc. (sec., treas. 1989—), Alpha Omega Alpha. Address: JAMA 515 N State St Chicago IL 60610-4325 Office: Johns Hopkins Sch Medicine 720 Rutland Ave Ste 106 Baltimore MD 21205-2109

DE ANGELIS, JUDY, anchorwoman; b. Passaic, N.J., Oct. 1, 1949; d. Fredrick and Patricia (Zollo) De An.; m. Barry Sheffield, Aug. 28, 1977; children: Alexander, Katelin, Corrine. Student, Hartt Sch. Music, Hartford, Conn., 1968-69; BA in Speech and Drama, U Hartford, 1971; MA in Edn., Montclair State U., 1973. Lic. 3d class operator FCC. Anchor Sta. WALK-AM-FM, Patchogue, N.Y., 1978-79, Sta. WGBB-FM, Freeport, N.Y., 1979-80, Sta. WKJY-FM, Hempstead, N.Y., 1980, Sta. WHLI, Hempstead, 1980, Sta. WCBS-FM, N.Y.C., 1980-81; reporter, anchor Sta. WNBC, N.Y.C., 1981-88; morning anchor Sta. WINS, N.Y.C., 1988—; morning drive anchor WNEW-FM, N.Y.C., 2004—; co-owner Sheffield Studios, Mahwah, N.J. Freelance anchor The Source, 1982-88; freelance anchor NBC Radio Network, 1982-888, host talk-net, 1989-90; news anchor HBO Entertainment, 1988; indsl. voice-over Odyssey Prodns., N.Y.C., 1981-88; comml. voice-over DWJ, Ridgewood, N.J., 1994—, Gourvitz Comm., N.Y.C., 1995—; cons. Media Placement Svcs., Glen Rock, N.J., 1994—. Author: (documentary) Child Abuse: The Darker Side of Growing Up, 1982 (Olive awrd N.Y.C. Coun. of Chs., 1983; appeared on Broadway in Rockabye Hamlet, 1976. Lectr. on broadcasting all ednl. levels, 1985—; dir. religious edn. Christ Episcopal Ch., Ridgewood, 1995—; troop leader Girl Scouts U.S.A., 1994—. Recipient award for pub. svc. N.Y. Deadline Club, 1982, spl. citation Office N.Y.C. Comptr., 1983; name Best Radio Newscaster, N.Y. AIR, 2000, 01. Mem. AFTRA, Actors Equity, Ramapo-Bergen Animal Refuge. Democrat. Avocations: carpentry, swmming, gardening, crossword puzzles, sailing. Office: 1010 WINS Radio 888 7th Ave New York NY 10106-0001

DE ANGELIS, ROSEMARY ELEANOR, actress; b. Bklyn., Apr. 26, 1933; d. Francis and Antoinette (Donofrio) De A.; m. Kenneth Richard Bridges, Sept. 12, 1965 (div. 1983); 1 child, Laurel Ann. BA, Empire State Coll., 1998. Tchr. HB Studio, N.Y.C., 2004—, Uta Hagen Herbert Berghof Studio. Tchr. Practice of Acting HB Studios, N.Y.C. Appeared in plays Spinning into Butter, Over The River and Through the Woods, Queen and the Rebels, High Time, Six Characters in Search of an Author, Mrs. Klein (Barrymore award 1993), The Paradise Kid, In the Summer House, The Transfiguration of Benno Blimpie (Drama Desk award-Best Actress), N.Y. Sharespeare Fest. (with Joseph Papp dir.), numerous others; appeared in movies Frequency, Hit and Runway, Two Family House, The Wanderers, Enormous Changes at the Last Minute, Nothing Lasts Forever, Out of Darkness, Household Saints, Mamma Mia, Angie, Two Bits, The Juror; appeared in TV shows 100 Centre St., Guiding Light, As The World Turns, Monkey, Monkey, The Death of Ivan Ilyich, P.B.S. Theatre in Am., Baker's Dozen, The Equalizer, Law and Order; co-writer (screenplay) Burning Intentions, 1992-99; dir.: Shadow Boxers, 1998; author: The Nightingales; author numerous poems. Recipient residency award, Edna St. Vincent Millay writer's colony, N.Y.C. Mem. AFTRA, SAG, Actors Equity Assn. Avocations: painting, photography. E-mail: redtoes100@aol.com.

DE ANGELUS, DONALD JOHN, lawyer; b. Schenectady, N.Y., Mar. 9, 1940; s. Dominick and Edith (Matarazzo) De A.; m. Marlene C. Viscusi, Aug. 26, 1961; children: Maria L. Buicko, Donald J. II, Sheryl Clark. BBA in Acctg., Siena Coll., 1962; LLB, Albany Law Sch., 1965, JD, 1968. Bar: N.Y. Ptnr. DeAngelus & DeAngelus, Schenectady, 1965-89, Clifton Park, N.Y., 1991—, Englert, DeAngelus, Stillman, McHugh & DeAngelus, Schenectady, 1989-90. Social svcs. atty. County of Schenectady, 1966-68; dep. town atty. Town of Rotterdam, N.Y., 1975-91, town atty., 1992-97. Pub. rels. Sen. Robert Kennedy, Schenectady, 1966-68; dem. com. person Schenectady County Dem. Com., 1962—, town of Rotterdam dem. chmn., 1991-2000. Mem. Italian Am. Bar Assn., Indigent Def. Assn. (law guardian family ct.), N.Y. State Bar Assn., Schenectady County Bar Assn., N.Y. State Defenders Assn., Assn. Town, Elks. Democrat. Roman Catholic. Avocations: golf, collecting movies, watching sports. Home: 334 Dolan Dr Schenectady NY 12306-1013 Office: DeAngelus & DeAngelus Attys 805 Route 146 Clifton Park NY 12065-3817

DEANO, EDWARD JOSEPH, JR., lawyer, retired state legislator; b. New Orleans, Jan. 17, 1952; s. Edward Joseph and Alice Evelyn (Lanusse) D.; m. Susan Kathleen Bailey, Mar. 17, 1990. BS, U. Southwestern La., 1973; JD, La. State U., 1976. Atty. City of Mandeville, La., 1980—83; former prosecutor Mandeville Misdemeanor Ct.; ptnr. Deano & Deano, Mandeville; state rep. La. Ho. of Reps., Baton Rouge, 1984—96; town atty. Town of Abita Springs, 1996—. Mem. civil law com., 1984-88, mcpl. and parochial affairs com., 1984-88, commerce com., 1988-92, ways and means com., 1992—, ins. com., 1992-96; chmn. house sub-com. on recreation, 1984-88, subcom. econ. devel., 1988-92; bd. dir. Area Health Edn. Coun., Mandeville Trail Head. Past pres. St. Tammany Humane Soc., St. Tammany Taxpayer's Assn., Mandeville Horizons; charter mem. Habitat for Humanity; past mem. Mandeville Vol. Fire Dept.; past coord. asst. St. Tammany dist. Boy Scouts Am.; mem. Mandeville City Charter Commn.; founder Krewe of the Emerald Trapazoid. Named Conservationist of Yr. St. Tammany Sportsmen's League, 1985, La. Wildlife Fedn., 1995, Legislator of Yr. La. Preservation Alliance, 1988, Alliance for Good Govt., 1988, 89, La. Alliance for Mentally Ill, 1989, La. Assn. Justices of the Peace and Constables, 1989, 94; named to 25 Mem. Cmty. Hall Fame of Century, St. Tammany News Banner, 1999; recipient Gov.'s award. Mem. La. Bar Assn., Covington Bar Assn., Krewe of the Emerald Trapazoid. Democrat. Roman Catholic. Avocations: historical research, travel, crabbing. Office: Deano & Deano 895 Park Ave Mandeville LA 70448-4920 Office Phone: 985-626-1001. Personal E-mail: deanoanddeano@bellsouth.net.

DE ANTONI, EDWARD PAUL, lab administrator; b. San Francisco, Mar. 7, 1941; s. Attilio Mario and Zita Elizabeth (Lolich) DeA.; m. Karen Dolores Thode, Jan. 22, 1966; children: Marc Edward, Christopher Earl. AB, U. San Francisco, 1962; PhD, Cornell U., 1971. Vol. Peace Corps, Turkey, 1964-66; sr. analyst Planning Bur. State of S.D., Pierre, 1973-76; dir. health planning Dept. Health, 1976-81; asst. dir. Assoc. Sch. Bds. S.D., 1981-84; dir. cancer control program Colo. Dept. Health, 1986-90; rsch. dir. Cancer Ctr., Porter Meml. Hosp., Denver, 1991-92; chair genitourinary cancer control Southwest Oncology Group, 1991-97; rsch. dir. Prostate Cancer Edn. Coun., 1991-97; asst. prof. urology Health Sci. Ctr., U. Colo., Denver, 1992-99, sr. instr., 2000—, sr. instr pathology/urology, 2001—. Woodrow Wilson fellow, 1962-63; ESEA fellow, 1966-69 Business E-Mail: ed.deantoni@uchsc.edu. *The life of the mind, inspired by a classic liberal education and by a faith in truth, has been a major force in my life. I realize, however, that such learning enriches most when it is embedded in a life of practical affairs, when it enlivens my relationships with others, and when it is used to seek a good beyond myself.*

DEAR, RONALD BRUCE, retired social work educator; b. Phila., Sept. 23, 1933; s. John David and Margaret (McDade) D.; 1 child, Bruce. BA, Bucknell U., 1955; honors cert., U. Aberdeen, Scotland, 1955; MSW, U. Pitts., 1957; PhD in Social Work, Columbia U., 1972. Cert. social worker, N.Y., Wash. Chief social worker Mental Hygiene Cons. Svc., Aberdeen Proving Ground, Md., 1958-60; chief Neuropsychiat. Clinic, 7th Inf. Divsn., Korea, 1960-61; residence dir. Horizon House, Inc., Phila., 1961-64; prof. U. Wash., Seattle, 1970—2003, prof. emeritus, 2003—. Vis. prof. U. Bergen, Norway, 1984, U. Trondheim, Norway, 1996; faculty lobbyist U. Wash., 1983-85, 88-91, faculty pres., 1993-95; master tchr. Coun. on Social Work Edn., 1991, 93, 94, 97; mem. adv. bd. Internat. Population and Family Assocs. Author: Social Welfare Policy: Trends and Issues, 6th edit., 2001, Teaching Social Policy in Social Work Education: Model Syllabus, 2003; editor: Poverty in Perspective, 1973; mem. editl. bd. Columns, 2002—, mem. The Social Policy Jour., 2002—; contbr. articles to profl. jours. and encys. Apptd. by gov. to income assistance adv. com., 1987-93, to adv. com. for Dept. Social and Health Svcs., 1980-83, Human Svcs. Policy Ctr., 1996—, adv. com. Wash. State Econ. Svcs., 1996-2004; mem. nat. adv. bd. Influencing State Policy, 1997—; appeared in centennial program of Columbia U. Sch. Social Work, 1998; bd. dirs. U. Wash. Ret. Assn., 2004—. 1st lt. U.S. Army, 1957-61. Mem. NASW (Social Worker of Yr. Wash. chpt. 1981, mem. staff legis. N.Y.C. chpt. 1968-69), Acad. Cert. Social Workers. Avocations: travel in over 50 countries, photography, hiking. Home: 7328 16th Ave NE Seattle WA 98115-5737 Office: U Wash Sch Social Work 4101 15th Ave NE Seattle WA 98105-6250

DE ARAGON, RAGENA CHERI, history educator; b. Boulder, Colo., May 29, 1952; d. Raymond John and M. ErvaGene (Alden) DeA. BA in History, U. Santa Clara, 1974; MA in History, U. Calif., Santa Barbara, 1977, PhD in History, 1982. Vis. asst. prof. history Wichita (Kans.) State U., 1981-83; asst. prof. Gonzaga U., Spokane, 1983-91, assoc. prof., 1991—. Editor: Kings, Saints and Parliaments, 1979; contbr. articles to profl. jours. Grantee NEH, 1978, 85, 89, ACLS, 1996; fellow Newberry Libr./British Acad., 1991. Mem. Am. Hist. Assn., Conf. Brit. Studies, Haskins Soc. Anglo-Saxon, Viking, Anglo-Norman and Angevin History. Democrat. Roman Catholic. Avocations: photography, wine-tasting. Office: Gonzaga U Dept History 502 E Boone Ave Dept History Spokane WA 99258-0001

DEARIE, RAYMOND JOSEPH, federal judge; b. 1944; AB, Fairfield U., 1966; JD, St. John's U., 1969. Pvt. practice law Shearman & Sterling, N.Y.C., 1969-71, Surrey & Morse, N.Y.C., 1977-80; chief Appeals div. U.S. Dept. Justice, 1971-74, chief gen. crimes sect., 1974-76, chief Criminal div., 1976-77; exec. asst. U.S. Atty.'s Office, 1977; asst. U.S. atty. U.S. Dist. Ct. (ea. dist.) N.Y., 1971-77, chief asst. U.S. atty., 1980-82, U.S. atty., 1982-86, judge Bklyn., 1986—. Contbr. articles to profl. jours. Bd. dirs. Daytop Village, L.I. Coll. Hosp. Mem. ABA, N.Y. State Bar Assn., Assn. of Bar of City of N.Y., Fed. Bar Coun. Office: US Dist Ct 225 Cadman Plz E Brooklyn NY 11201-1818*

DEARING, ABHA LATIKA, music educator; b. Dearborn, Mich., Jan. 29, 1975; d. Ramesh and Latika Mangrulkar; m. Steven F. Dearing, Apr. 11, 1998. MusB, Wayne State U., 1997; postgrad., Oakland U., 2005—. Music tchr. Nori (Mich.) HS, 1998—99, Mercy HS, Farmington Hills, Mich., 1999—. Musician: Dearing Concert Duo, 2002, (CD) Take One, 1999, Snapshots of South America, 2001, Romanza!, 2003. Active Met. Organizing Strategy, Enabling Strength, 2000—; choir dir. Birmingham Unitarian Ch., Bloomfield Hills, Mich., 2001—. Named Outstanding Classical Vocalist, Motor City Music Found., 2001—02, Outstanding Small Ensemble award, 2002; recipient Outstanding Classical Recording award, 2004. Mem.: Mich. Sch. Band and Orch. Assn., Music Educators Nat. Conf., Mich. Sch. Vocal Music Assn. Unitarian. Avocations: tennis, hiking, travel. Office: Mercy High Sch 29300 W 11 Mile Farmington Hills MI 48336

DEARING, REINHARD JOSEF, city official; b. Bamberg, Fed. Republic of Germany, May 1, 1947; m. Michele Jack, Feb. 14, 1967 (div. Oct. 1980); 1 child, Lauren; m. Patricia Lee Pollack, Jan. 2, 1982; 1 child, Bradford. AA, La. State U., Baton Rouge, 1968, BA, 1975, MA, 1977, postgrad., 1979; PhD, Northwestern U., 2003. CPM, Tulane U., 1989. Adminstrv. officer La. Nat. Bank, Baton Rouge, 1972-75; teaching asst. La. State U., 1975-79; adj. asst. prof. U. So. Miss., Natchez, 1977-79; chief of staff, chief adminstrv. officer City of Slidell, La., 1979—. Cons. La. Mcpl. Assn., Baton Rouge, 1985-87. Author: The Waffen-SS: A Representative Study, 1977, General James Dearing and the Cause of the Confederacy, 2001, SS General Karl Wolff and his Italian Odyssey, 2003; contbr. articles to profl. jours. Mem. Gov.'s Mcpl. Policy Task Force, PJPHS sch. bd. Officer U.S. Army, 1968-72. Decorated Silver Star, col. La. State Guard; named Hon. State Senator, La. Mem. La. Mcpl. Assn., Nat. League Cities, St. Tammany Mcpl. Assn., Am. Pub. Works Assn., La. State Alumni Assn. (dir. 1985-87), Assn. U.S. Army, Am. Legion, Internat. City Mgrs. Assn., Mil. Order of the Stars and Bars, Sons of

Confederate Vets., Lions, VFW Republican. Avocations: historic research, Civil War reenacting, fencing, racquetball, jogging. Office: City of Slidell PO Box 828 Slidell LA 70459-0828 Office Phone: 985-646-4330. E-mail: RDearing@cityofslidell.org.

DEARING, TERESA ALLISON, librarian; b. Westfield, NY, July 8, 1950; d. Claude Wilbur Dearing and Beulah Berenice Hess; m. Robert James Canuti, Aug. 21, 1971 (div. Apr. 30, 1991); 1 child, Timothy Robert Canuti. BA, SUNY, Geneseo, 1972, MLS, 1975; AS, Genesee C.C., 1994. Pub. libr. profl. cert. NY. Libr. dir. Mt. Morris (NY) Libr., 1973—76, Dansville (NY) Pub. Libr., 1976—. Sec. Dansville Econ. Devel. Corp., 1988—2005. Mem.: NY Libr. Assn., Dansville Rotary Club (sec. 1995—2005, Paul Harris fellow 1998). Methodist. Office: Dansville Pub Libr 200 Main St Dansville NY 14437-1316 Office Phone: 585-335-6720. E-mail: director@dansville.lib.ny.us.

DE ARMAS, FREDERICK ALFRED, foreign language educator; b. Havana, Cuba, Feb. 9, 1945; came to U.S., 1959, naturalized, 1968; s. Alfredo and Ana Maria (Galdos) De A. BA magna cum laude, Stetson U., DeLand, Fla., 1965; PhD (Carnegie fellow 1965-68), U. N.C., 1968. Mem. faculty La. State U., Baton Rouge, 1968-88, prof. Spanish, 1978-88, acting chmn. dept., 1979-80, dir. grad. studies, 1980-85; prof. Spanish and comparative lit. Pa. State U., 1988-91, Disting. prof. Spanish and comparative lit., 1991-98, Edwin Erle Sparks prof. Spanish and Comparative Lit., 1998-2000, fellow Inst. for Arts and Humanities, 1989-2000; prof. Spanish U. Chgo., 2000-01, Andrew W. Mellon prof. of humanities, 2001—05, chmn. dept. romance langs. and lit., 2005—. Vis. assoc. prof. U. Mo., Columbia, summer 1977, vis. prof., fall 1986; vis. prof. Duke U., spring 1994. Author: The Four Interpolated Stories in the Roman Comique, 1971, Paul Scarron, 1972, The Invisible Mistress, 1976, The Return of Astraea, 1986, The Prince in the Tower, 1993, Heavenly Bodies, 1996, A Star-Crossed Golden Age, 1998, Cervantes, Raphael and the Classics, 1998, Writing for the Eyes in the Spanish Golden Age, 2004; editor: Pa. State U. Studies in Romance Literatures, 1991-2001; co-editor: European Literary Careers, 2002; mem. editl. bd. Bull. Comediantes, 1981—, Hispanófila, 1981-88, 2001—, PMLA, 1985-89, South Central Rev., 1987-89, Comparative Literature Studies, 1989-2001, Hispania, 1993-95, Jour. Interdisciplinary Lit. Studies, 1993-2000, South Atlantic Rev., 2003—, Revista Didascalia, 2004—, Revue Romane, 2004—; contbr. articles to profl. jours. NEH grantee, 1979; NEH fellow, 1985, 95, summer inst., 1989, dir. summer inst., 1994, dir. summer seminar, 2003. Mem. MLA, Comparative Lit. Assn., Renaissance Soc. Am., Am. Assn. Tchrs. Spanish and Portuguese, Assn. Internat. Hispanistas, Hispanic Soc. Am. (corr.), Cervantes Soc. Am. (v.p. 2003—). Office: U Chgo Dept Romance Lang 1050 E 59th St Chicago IL 60637 Office Phone: 773-702-8481. Business E-Mail: fdearmas@uchicago.edu.

DEARTH, DENNIS ROBERT, music educator; b. Chickopie Falls, Mass., Mar. 29, 1955; s. Richard Llewlyn and Doris Lucille (Hess) Dearth; m. Mary Dearth, Dec. 29, 0179; children: Erik, Chris. MusB, U. Puget Sound, 1977; M in Music Edn., Ctrl. Wash. U., 1983. Tchr. White Pass (Wash.) HS, 1976—77, Bellamine Prep., Tawnee, Wash., 1977—78, Clover Park HS, Lakewood, Wash., 1978—. Mem.: Music Educators Nat. Conf. Avocation: woodworking. Home: 10908 Meadow Rd SW Lakewood WA 98499

DEASON, DARWIN, information technology executive; b. Ark. With MTech Corp., Dallas, 1968—88, CEO, dir., 1978—88; founder Affiliated Computer Services, Inc., Dallas, 1988, CEO, 1988—99, chmn., 1988—. Office: ACS Inc 2828 North Haskell Dallas TX 75204

DEASON, ELLEN MURIEL See WELLS, KITTY

DEASON, HEROLD MCCLURE, lawyer; b. Alton, Ill., July 24, 1942; s. Ernest Wilburn and Mildred Mary (McClure) D.; m. Wilma Lee Kaemmerle, June 18, 1966; children: Sean, Ian, Whitney. BA, Albion Coll., 1964; JD, Northwestern U., 1967. Bar: Mich. 1968. Assoc. Bodman LLP, Detroit, 1967-74, ptnr., 1975—. City atty. Grosse Pointe Pk., Mich., 1978—. Vice chmn. Detroit, Windsor Freedom Festival, 1978-92; bd. dirs. Spirit of Detroit Assn., 1980-2003. Recipient Spirit of Detroit award, Detroit City Coun., 1986. Mem. ABA, Mich. Assn. Mcpl. Attys. (pres. 1995-97), Detroit Bar Assn., Can.-U.S. Bus. Assn. (pres. 2005), Grosse Pointe Yacht Club (commodore 1992-93), Detroit Racquet Club, Windsor Club, Clinton River Boat Club. Home: 1044 Kensington Ave Grosse Pointe Park MI 48230-1437 Office: Bodman LLP 100 Renaissance Ctr 34th Fl Detroit MI 48243-1001 Office Phone: 313-393-7556. Business E-Mail: hdeason@bodmanllp.com.

DEASON, JONATHAN PIERCE, environmental engineer, federal agency administrator; b. Charleston, S.C., Feb. 8, 1948; married; 3 children. BS in Civil Engring., U.S. Mil. Acad., 1970; MBA in Mgmt., Golden Gate U., 1975; MS in Environ. Engring., Johns Hopkins U., 1978; PhD in Environ. Systems, U. Va., 1984. Registered profl. engr., Va. Commd. U.S. Army, 1970, advanced through grades to capt.; engr. officer U.S. Army Corps of Engrs., 1970-75, civil engr. North Atlantic Divsn., 1975-78; chief water resources program U.S. Bur. Indian Affairs, 1978-82; sr. policy advisor office of water policy U.S. Dept. Interior, 1982-83; spl. asst. Office Asst. Sec. of Army, 1983-86; mgr. Nat. Irrigation Water Quality Program U.S. Dept. of Interior, Washington, 1986-89, dir. Office of Environ. Policy and Compliance, 1989-94; v.p. environ. affairs Am. Rd. and Transp. Builders Assn., Washington, 1994-96; prof. environ. and energy mgmt. program George Washington U., Washington, 1994—. Adj. prof. environ. and energy mgmt. George Wash. U., 1984-94; chmn. fed. liaison group Bd. Environ. Studies and Toxicology Nat. Rsch. Coun./NAS, 1990-91; mem. nat. panel of experts U.S. Com. Irrigation and Drainage, 1987; chmn. Pres.'s Task Force Indian Water Resources Devel., 1978-80. Author: (with others) Risk Based Decision Making in Water Resources, 1989; contbr. over 50 articles to profl. jours. Col. USAR. Recipient Engring. Achievement award Va. Engring. Found., 1993, Founder's medal and Fed. Engr. of Yr. award Nat. Soc. Profl. Engrs., 1992, Arthur S. Flemming award Jr. C. of C., 1984. Mem. Am. Soc. Civil Engrs. (bd. trustees scholarship trust 1992-93, pres. nat. capital sect. 1990-91, Meritorious Svc. award 1988), Am. Water Resources Assn. (dir. Chesapeake region 1989-91). Office: Policy and Compliance Environ Policy and Compliance George Washington U Washington DC 20052-0001 Home: 1331 14th St N Arlington VA 22209-3705

DEASY, CORNELIUS MICHAEL, retired architect; b. Mineral Wells, Tex., July 19, 1918; s. Cornelius and Monetta (Palmo) D.; m. Lucille Laney, Sept. 14, 1941; children: Diana, Carol, Ann. BArch, U. So. Calif., 1941. Practice architecture, LA, 1946—76; ptnr. Robert D. Bolling, 1960—76, ret., 1976. Prin. works include prin. offices student union, Calif. State U., LA; author: Design for Human Affairs, 1974, Designing Places for People, 1985, Gifts From America, 2003. V.p. LA Beautiful; dir. Regional Plan Assn.; commr., LA Bd. Zoning Appeals, 1973-. Recipient numerous design awards, Nat. Endowment Arts award, 1983. Fellow AIA (past pres., dir. So. Calif. chpt., chmn. com. rsch.). Home and Office: Davenport Creek Farm 4979 Davenport Creek Rd San Luis Obispo CA 93401-8109 Office Phone: 805-541-2789.

DEASY, THERESA, finance company executive, accountant; b. N.Y.C., May 19, 1958; d. Thomas Edward Deasy and Dorothy Beatrice Deasy Cox; m. Dennis James Stanton, May 29, 1983. BS in Commerce, DePaul U., 1981; MBA, Keller Grad. Sch. Bus., 1995. Acctg. clk. Kirkland & Ellis, Chgo., 1977-80; acct. Sachnoff Weaver & Rubenstien, Chgo., 1981-83, asst. contr., 1984-86, contr., 1987-88; specialist emerging bus. svcs. Coopers & Lybrand, CPA, Chgo., 1989-91; contr. Seabury-Western Theol. Sem., 1992-93; dir. of adminstrn. AIDS Pastoral Care Network, 1993-95; adminstrv. mgr. grants and contracts Howard Brown Health Ctr., 1995-96, adminstrv. mgr. human resources, 1996-99. Bd. dirs. Voyageur Outward Bound, 1990-91, AIDS Pastoral Care Network, 1992—. Mem. Am. Soc. Women Accts., Chgo. Coun. Fgn. Rels. Avocations: social service, travel, photography. Home: 7526 Turtlebrook Ln New Port Richey FL 34655-0459

DEASY, WILLIAM JOHN, construction, engineering, and mining company executive; b. N.Y.C., June 22, 1937; s. Jeremiah and Margaret (Quinn) D.; m. Carol Ellyn Lemons, Feb. 1, 1963; children: Cameron, Kimberly. BS in Civil Engring, Cooper Union, 1958; LLB, U. Wash., 1963. With Morrison Knudsen Corp., Boise, Idaho, 1964-88, v.p. N.W. region, 1972-75, v.p. mining, 1975-78, group v.p. mining, 1978-83, exec. v.p. mining, shipbuilding and mfg., 1983-84, pres., chief operating officer, 1984-85, pres., chief exec. officer, bd. dirs., 1985-88; vice chair, pres., CEO, bd. dirs. T.L. James & Co., New Orleans, 1991-99; chmn. bd. T.L. James & Co., Inc., 1999—. Mem. adv. bd. Sundt Cos., Inc.; chmn. endowment com., trustee Loyola U., New Orleans. Mem. La. Com. of 100. Mem. Moles. Home: 2427 Camp St Apt C New Orleans LA 70130-5645 Office: T L James & Co LLC PO Box 1260 Ruston LA 71273-1260 E-mail: wjdeasy@bellsouth.net.

DEATHERAGE, WILLIAM VERNON, lawyer; b. Drumright, Okla., Apr. 17, 1927; s. William Johnson and Pearl Mae (Watson) D.; m. Priscilla Ann Campbell, Sept. 16, 1932; children: Thomas William, Andrea Susan. BS, U. Oreg., 1952, LLB with honors, 1954. Bar: Oreg. 1954, U.S. Dist. Ct. Oreg. 1956. Ptnr. Frohnmayer, Deatherage, Pratt, Jamieson & Clarke & Moore, Medford, Oreg., 1954—. Bd. dirs. Oreg. Law Inst., U. Oreg. Found. With USN, 1945-48. Mem. Am. Coll. Trial Lawyers, Internat. Acad. Trial Lawyers, Delta Theta Phi, Rogue Valley Country Club (pres. 1988), Rogue River Valley Univ. Club. Democrat. Episcopalian. Address: 2592 E Barnett Rd Medford OR 97504-8345 Office Phone: 541-779-2333. Personal E-mail: deatherage@fdfirm.com. Business E-Mail: fdfirm@fdfirm.com.

DEATON, BEVERLY JEAN, nursing administrator, educator; b. Plainview, Ill., Oct. 15, 1942; d. Charles Byron Kirby and Wilma Irene Crocker Kirby Novy; m. John H. Deaton, May 18, 1963; children: Mary Kathryn Deaton Lovejoy, Amy Christine Deaton Williams. Diploma, St John's Hosp. Sch. Nursing, Springfield, Ill., 1963; BSN, So. Ill. U., Edwardsville, 1986, MSN, 1994. RN Ill., cert. inpatient obstet. nursing, electronic fetal monitoring. Maternity staff nurse St. Francis Hosp., Litchfield, Ill., 1971-76, maternity supr., 1976-81, dir. maternity, 1981—2001, dir. quality svcs., risk mgmt., 2001—; legal nurse cons., 2000—. Childbirth educator, 1975—2001; presenter at cmty. and profl. orgn. confs.; fetal monitor instr.-trainer Assn. Women's Health, Obstetric and Neonatal Nurses, 1991—. Named Nurse of Yr., March of Dimes, Chgo., 1994, March of Dimes Springfield, Ill. Region, 2002. Mem.: AWHONN (vice chair Ill. sect. 1995—96, dist. VI 1997, nat. bd. dirs. 1999—2002, pres.-elect 2004, pres. 2005), Sigma Theta Tau. Christian. Avocations: travel, photography. Home: PO Box 374 Litchfield IL 62056-0374 Office: St Francis Hosp PO Box 1215 Litchfield IL 62056-0999

DEATON, BRADY J., academic administrator; m. Anne Deaton; children: Tony, Brady Jr., Christina, David. BS in Agrl. Econs., U. Ky., 1966, MA in Diplomacy and Internat. Commerce, 1968; PhD in Agrl. Econs., U. Wis., 1972. Assoc. prof. U. Tenn., 1972—78; dir. Va. Poly. Inst. and State U., 1978—89; prof., Agricultural Econ, dept. chair & social sci. unit leader U. Mo., Columbia, Mo., 1989—98, chief staff, dep. chancellor, provost, 1998—2004, interim chancellor, 2004, chancellor, 2004—. Chair Nat. Assn. State Univs. and Land Grant Colls. Contbr. articles to profl. jours. Office: Office of the Chancellor 114 Jesse Hall Univ Mo Columbia MO 65211

DEATON, CHAD C., oil industry executive; BS, Univ. Wyo. With Schlumberger Oilfield Svcs., 1976—99, exec. v.p., 1988—99, sr. adv., 1999—2001; pres., CEO Hanover Compressor Co., 2002—04; chmn., CEO Baker Hughes, Houston, 2004—. Bd. dir. Carbo Ceramics. Mem.: Petroleum Equip. Suppliers Assn. Office: Baker Hughes 3900 Essex Lane Houston TX 77027 Mailing: Baker Hughes PO Box 4740 Houston TX 77210-4740*

DEATON, CHARLES MILTON, lawyer; b. Hattiesburg, Miss., Jan. 19, 1931; s. Ivanes Dean Deaton and Martha Sarah Elizabeth Fortenberry; m. Mary Dent Dickerson, Aug. 15, 1951; children: Diane Rossi, Dara Rogers, Charles M., Jr. BA, Millsaps Coll., 1949-51, 55-56; JD, U. Miss., 1959. Legis. asst. U.S. Ho. of Reps., Washington, 1957; assoc. Brewer, Deaton & Bowman, Greenwood, Miss., 1958—; mem. Miss. Ho. of Reps., Jackson, 1960—80, appropriations chmn., 1976—80; city atty. City of Greenwood, Miss., 1970-84; adminstrv. asst. to Govs. Wm. Winter, B. Allain State of Miss., Jackson, 1980—88; bd. dirs. Bank of Commerce, Greenwood; mem. Miss. State Bd. of Edn., 2003—. Recipient Miss Conservationist of Yr. award The Nature Conservancy, Jackson, 1991, Nat. Oak Leaf award, Arlington, Va., 1992, Sports Hall of Fame award Millsaps Coll., Jackson, Alumnus of Yr. award, 1995, others. Mem. ABA, The Nature Conservancy, Miss. Wildlife Heritage Commn., others. Avocations: cooking, hunting, fishing, conservation, gardening. Office: Brewer Deaton & Bowman 107 W Market St PO Drawer B Greenwood MS 38935

DEATON, CHRIS HAROLD, lawyer; b. Laurel, Miss., Apr. 15, 1960; s. Harold Eugene and Mary Gwendolyn Deaton; m. Dana Gail Dew, July 17, 1991; children: Sara Kathryn, Eric Chris, Luke Christian;children from previous marriage: Mary Christina, James Robert. BA, Miss. State U., 1982; JD, U. Miss., 1991. Bar: Miss. 1991, U.S. Dist. Ct. (no. and so. dists.) Miss. 1991, U.S. Ct. Appeals (5th cir.) 1991, U.S. Supreme Ct. 1996. Assoc. Holcomb Dunbar Connell Chaffin & Willard, Oxford, Miss., 1991—93, Webb McLaurin & O'Neal, Tupelo, 1993—94; ptnr. Webb, Sanders Deaton Balducci & Smith, Tupelo, 1994—98, Deaton & Deaton, Tupelo, 1998—. Dist. appeals bd. mem. Selective Svc. System, Jackson, 2001—; legis. advisor Miss. Swimming, Inc., 2001—. With U.S. Army, 1984—86. Mem.: Internat. Assn. Arson Investigators, Miss. Fire Investigators Assn. (bd. dirs. 1996—, legal counsel 1997—, instr. 1997—), Am. Legion. Office: PO Box 1726 Tupelo MS 38802-1726 E-mail: chrisd@deatonanddeaton.com.

DEATON, DAVID MATTHEW, lawyer; b. Long Beach, Calif., Mar. 4, 1970; s. Ronald F. and Ellery A. Deaton; m. Shelly Jean Littlejohn, June 15, 1991; children: Lydia, Hannah, Mary, Sarah. BA, U. Calif., Irvine, 1992; JD, So. Meth. U., 1999. Bar: Calif. 1999. Atty. O'Melveny & Myers, LLP, LA, 1999—. Contbr. articles to profl. jours. Mem.: ABA, Health Care Compliance Assn., Am. Health Lawyers Assn. Brethren. Office: O'Melveny & Myers LLP 400 S Hope St 18th Fl Los Angeles CA 90071 Office Phone: 213-430-6191. Office Fax: 213-430-6407. E-mail: ddeaton@omm.com.

DEATON, JANICE ANN, media specialist, elementary school educator; d. Art F and Thelma I Goddard; m. Hank Deaton, Sept. 15, 1967; children: Kenneth F, Mike B. B, East Ctrl. U., 1976—92. Education Okla. State Dept. of Edn., 1992. Media specialist/ tchr. Allen Pub. Schools, Allen, Okla., 1991—. Johnson o'malley dir. Allen Pub. Schools, 2005—, art club sponsor, 1994—; libr. bd. of directors Allen Pub. Libr., 2002—; rec. sec. XI Epsilon Upsilon chpt. of Beta Sigma Phi, Allen, Okla., 2005—. Mem. Allen Pub. Libr., 2002—. Mem.: Holdenville Soc. of Artists, Painters and Sculptors (assoc.). Democrat-Npl. Southern Bapt. Avocations: painting, swimming, reading. Office: Allen Public Schools Lexington & Gilmore St Allen OK 74825 Fax: 580-857-2636. Office Phone: 580-857-2416.

DEATON, RUSSELL JERRY, computer science, computer engineering educator; b. Memphis, Nov. 3, 1958; s. William Jerry and Nancy Jo Deaton; m. Victoria Ann Dixon, Oct. 21, 1959; children: Kathleen Hester, William Duke. BA, U. NC, 1981; BS, Memphis State U., 1984; MS, Duke U., 1988, PhD, 1992. Asst. prof. U. Memphis, 1992—98, assoc. prof., 1998—2000, U. Ark., Fayetteville, 2000—03, prof., 2003—. Mem. tech. staff GE Semiconductor, Research Triangle Park, NC, 1988—95. Contbr. articles to profl. jours. in field. Mem.: ACM, IEEE, Tau Beta Pi, Phi Beta Kappa. Achievements include research in a DNA word design; a DNA-based computation and nanotechnology. Avocations: poetry, basketball. Office: Univ Arkansas Rm 311 ENGR Fayetteville AR 72701 Office Fax: 479-575-5339. Business E-Mail: rdeaton@uark.edu.

DEATS, SUZANNE, writer, editor, artist; b. Abilene, Tex., Nov. 14, 1937; d. Otto and Susan Reynolds Deats; m. Ben Bedford, Aug. 27, 1960 (dec. Jan. 19, 1978); children: Aaron Bedford, John Bedford. BA in Fine Arts, U. N.Mex., 1981. Juror Santa Fe Art Festival, Main St. Show, Ft. Worth, Mus. S.W., Midland, Tex. Exhb. (catalog) Kevin Red Star, Yellowstone Art Mus., Billings, Mont.; contbr. articles to periodicals; author: (book) Evelyne Boren, 1998, Michael Dunbar, 2006; co-author: Santa Fe Design w. Elmo Baca, 1990, Abstract Art w. Stuart Ashman, 2004, Western Traditions w. Michael Duty, 2005, New Mex. Landscape w. Suzan Campbell, 2006; editor: Fresco Fine Art Publ.; exhib. Hill's Gallery, Santa Fe, Happy World Enterprises, Japan. Mem.: Mensa. Avocations: fiction, design, cooking, travel.

DEAVENPORT, EARNEST W., JR., chemical executive; b. Macon, Miss. BS chem. engring., Mississippi State U.; MA in Mgmt., MIT. Chem. engr. Eastman Chem. Co., 1960, pres. Carolina divsn., 1982; asst. gen. mgr. Eastman Chem. Divsn., 1985; v.p. Kodak, 1985, pres. and group v.p., 1989; chmn., CEO Eastman Chem., Kingsport, Tenn., 1994—2002; ret. Chmn. Am. Plastics Coun.; bd. dir. First Am. Corp., AmSouth Bancorporation, Theragenics Corp., King Pharmaceuticals, Inc., Acuity Brands, Inc. Alfred P. Sloan fellow MIT; recipient Exec. Excellence award Chem. Mgmt. and Resources Assn., 1995. Mem. Chem. Mfg. Assn. (bd. dir. 1994—), Soc. Chem. Industry (exec. com. Am. sect., Chem. Industry medal Am. sect. 2002), NAE. Office: Eastman Chem Co PO Box 511 Kingsport TN 37662-5000

DEAVER, JAMES T.H., lawyer; b. Santa Monica, Calif., Feb. 2, 1961; BS, Wharton Sch. Bus. U. Pa., 1985; JD cum laude, Temple U., 1991; LLM, NYU, 1992. Bar: NY 1993. Ptnr. Wilson, Elser, Moskowitz, Edelman & Dicker LLP, NYC. Mem.: ABA, Assn. of the Bar of the City of NY. Office: Wilson Elser Moskowitz Edelman & Dicker LLP 23rd Fl 150 E 42nd St New York NY 10017-5639 Office Phone: 212-490-3000 ext. 2775. Office Fax: 212-490-3038. Business E-Mail: deaverj@wemed.com.

DEAVER, MICHAEL KEITH, public relations consultant; b. Bakersfield, Calif., Apr. 11, 1938; s. Paul Sperling and Marian Mack D.; m. Carolyn Judy, Jan. 17; children— Amanda Judy, Blair Clayton. BA in Public Adminstrn, San Jose State U., 1960. Adminstrv. trainee IBM, 1960-62; with Republican Central Com. of Santa Clara County (Calif.), 1962-66; cabinet sec. State of Calif., 1966-67, asst. to gov., dir. adminstrn., from 1967; partner, pres. Deaver & Hannaford Co., Los Angeles; asst. to pres. of U.S., also dep. chief of staff., 1981-85; owner Deaver and Assocs., pub. relations, Washington, 1985. Author: Behind the Scenes, 1986, A Different Drummer: My 30 Years with Ronald Reagan, 2001; Editor: Why I am a Reagan Conservative, 2005. Served with USAFR, 1961-66. Mem. Am. Coun. Young Polit. Leaders. Republican. Episcopalian. Office: Edelman Pub Rels Worldwide 1420 K St NW Washington DC 20005-2500*

DEAVER, PHILLIP LESTER, lawyer; b. Long Beach, Calif., July 21, 1952; s. Albert Lester and Eva Lucille (Welton) D. Student, USCG Acad., 1970-72; BA, UCLA, 1974; JD, U. So. Calif., 1977. Bar: Hawaii 1977, U.S. Dist. Ct. Hawaii 1977, U.S. Ct. Appeals (9th cir.) 1978, U.S. Supreme Ct. 1981. Assoc. Carlsmith, Wichman, Case, Mukai & Ichiki, Honolulu, 1977-83, ptnr., 1983-86, Bays, Deaver, Lung, Rose & Baba, Honolulu, 1986, mng. ptnr., 1986-95. Contbr. articles to profl. jours. Bd. dirs. Parents and Children Together, 1993—2003, v.p. 2000-2002, chmn. bd., 2003-. Mem. ABA (forum com. on the Constrn. Industry), AIA (affiliate Hawaii chpt.), Am. Arbitration Assn. (arbitrator). Home: 2471 Pacific Heights Rd Honolulu HI 96813-1029 Office: Bays Deaver Lung Rose and Baba PO Box 1760 Honolulu HI 96806-1760 Office Phone: 808-523-9000. E-mail: pdeaver@legalhawaii.com.

DEAVERS, JAMES FREDERICK, optometrist; b. Saint Augustine, Florida, Apr. 23, 1947; s. James Lonnie and Gwen Eula (Fields) D.; m. Janet (Allen), Jan. 1, 1995; children: Samuel, Chris, Marie, Robin, Shea, Christy. BS, So. Coll. of Optometry, Memphis, 1979, OD, 1978. Optometrist Berkeley Eye Care, 1980—95, Cmty. Eye Care Specialists, Moncks Corner, SC, 1995—99, Eyeplus, Lexington, SC, 1997—99, America's Best, North Charleston, SC, 1999—2003, Eyeplus, Summerville, SC, 2004—. Staff sgt. USAF, 1965—69. Republican. Avocations: travel, running. Office: Eyeplus Summerville SC 29483 Office Phone: 843-871-4995. Personal E-mail: doctor4995@hotmail.com.

DEBACKER, MICHAEL L., automotive executive, lawyer; b. 1947; JD, Washburn U. Bar: Kans. 1972, Okla. 1975. Asst. gen. counsel Dana Corp., Toledo, 1986—2001, v.p., 1994—, gen. counsel, sec., 2001—. Office: Dana Corp 4500 Dorr St Toledo OH 43615

DEBAKEY, ERNEST GEORGE, physician, surgeon; b. Lake Charles, La., Feb. 17, 1912; s. Shaker and Raheega DeB.; m. Marsha Lauder, Apr. 8, 1999; 1 child, Elizabeth. BS Pharmacy, Tulane U., 1931, MD, 1939. Diplomate Am. Coll. Surgeons. Intern Charity Hosp., New Orleans, 1939-40, resident, 1941-42, 45-48; resident thoracic surgery Washington U., St. Louis, 1940-41; pvt. practice Mobile, Ala., 1948-93. Prof. emeritus surgery Tulane U., 1949—, U. South Ala., Mobile, 1973—; staff dept. surgery Mobile Infirmary Med. Ctr., Providence Hosp., Springhill Meml. Hosp., USA-Doctors. Chmn. DeBakey Fund Drug Edn. Program, Mobile, 1992—, DeBakey Fund Perioperative Nursing Continuing Edn., 1989—, DeBakey awards excellence perioperative nursing. Major USAF, 1942-45, CBI. Recipient award excellence Mobile Infirmary Med. Ctr., 1993; named Physician of Yr. Mobile County Med. Auxiliary, 1993; dept. surgery Mobile Infirmary Med. Ctr. named DeBakey Surg. Ste. in his honor, 1988, Ernest G. DeBakey Charitable Found., 1997; inducted Ala. Healthcare Hall of Fame, 2001. Fellow Am. Coll. Surgeons; mem. Ala. Thoracic Soc. Republican. Episcopalian. Office: 1729 Springhill Ave Mobile AL 36604-1411 Office Phone: 251-433-2785. E-mail: debakeyfoundation@comcast.net.

DEBAKEY, LOIS, science administrator, educator; b. Lake Charles, La. d. S. M. and Raheeja (Zorba) DeBakey. BA in Math., Tulane U., MA in Lit. and Linguistics, 1959, PhD in Lit. and Linguistics, 1963. Asst. prof. English Tulane U., 1963—64; asst. prof. sci. communication Tulane U. Med. Sch., 1963-65, assoc. prof. sci. communication, 1965-67, prof. sci. comm., 1967-68, lectr., 1968-80, adj. prof., 1981-92; prof. sci. comm. Baylor Coll. Medicine, Houston, 1968—. Mem. biomed. libr. rev. com. Nat. Libr. Medicine, Bethesda, Md., 1973-77, bd. regents, 1981-86, cons., 1986—, co-chmn. permanent paper task force, 1987—, lit. selection tech. rev. com., 1988-93, chmn., 1992-93, outreach planning panel, 1988-89; dir. courses in med. comm. ACS and other orgns.; trustee DeBakey Med. Found., 1995—; mem. exec. coun. Commn. on Colls. So. Assn. Colls. and Schs., 1975-80; mem. nat. adv. coun. U. So. Calif. Ctr. Continuing Med. Edn., 1981; mem. steering com. Plain English Forum, 1984; mem. founding bd. dirs. Friends Nat. Libr. Medicine, 1985—, chmn. med. media award of excellence com., 1992—; mem. adv. com. Soc. for Preservation English Lang. Lit., 1986; mem. nat. adv. bd. John Muir Med. Film Festival, 1990-92; mem. The Internat. Health and Med. Film Festival, Acad. of Judges, 1992-93; mem. adv. bd. U. Tex. at Austin Sch. Nursing Found., 1993—; cons. legal writing com. ABA, 1983—, Ency. Brit. Biomed. and Health Database, 1999—; former cons. Nat. Assn. Std. Med. Vocabulary; pioneered instrn. in sci. comm. in med. sch. Sr. author: The Scientific Journal: Editorial Policies and Practices, 1976; co-author: Medicine: Preserving the Passion, 1987; Medicine: Preserving the Passion in the 21st Century, 2004; mem editl. bd.: Tulane Studies in English, 1966-68, Cardiovasc. Rsch. Ctr. Bull., 1971-83, Health Comms. and Informatics, 1975-80, Forum on Medicine, 1977-80, Grants Mag., 1978-81, Internat. Jour. Cardiology, 1981-86, Excerpta Medica's Core Jours. in Cardiology, 1981—, Health Comm. and Biopsychosocial Health, 1981-82, Internat. Angiology, 1985—, Jour. AMA, 1988-2002. CV Network, 2003—; mem. usage panel Am. Heritage Dictionary, 1980—; cons. Webster's Med. Desk Dictionary, 1986; editl. advisor Ency. Brit.; contbr. articles on biomed. comm. and sci. writing, literacy, also other subjects to profl. jours., books, encys., and pub. press. Active Found. for Advanced Edn. in Sci., 1977—. Recipient Disting. Svc. award, Am. Med. Writers Assn., 1970, Bausch & Lomb Sci. award, 1st John P. McGovern award, Med. Libr. Assn., 1983, Outstanding Alumna award, Newcomb Coll., 1994. Fellow Am. Coll. Med. Informatics, Royal Soc. for Encouragement of Arts, Mfrs., and Commerce; mem. Internat. Soc. Gen. Semantics, Med. Libr. Assn. (hon.), Coun. Biology

Editors (dir. 1973-77, chmn. com. on editl. policy 1971-75), Coun. Basic Edn. (spl. com. writing 1977-79), Assn. Tchrs. Tech. Writing, Dictionary Soc. N.Am., Nat. Assn. Sci. Writers, Soc. for Health and Human Values, Com. of Thousand for Better Health Regulations, Golden Key, Phi Beta Kappa. Office: Baylor Coll Medicine 1 Baylor Plz Houston TX 77030-3411

DEBAKEY, MICHAEL ELLIS, surgeon, educator; b. Lake Charles, La., Sept. 7, 1908; s. Shaker Morris and Raheeja (Zorba) DeBakey; m. Diana Cooper, Oct. 15, 1936; children: Michael Maurice, Ernest Ochsner(dec.), Barry Edward, Denis Alton; m. Katrin Fehlhaber, July 1975; 1 child, Olga Katarina. BS, Tulane U., 1930, MD, 1932, MS, 1935; more than 50 hon. degrees from prestigious univ. throughout the world. Diplomate Nat. Bd. Med. Examiners, Am. Bd. Surgery, Am. Bd. Thoracic Surgery. Intern Charity Hosp., New Orleans, 1932—33, asst. surgery, 1933—35, U. Strasbourg, France, 1935—36, U. Heidelberg, Germany, 1936; instr. surgery Tulane U., New Orleans, 1937—40, asst. prof., 1940—46, assoc. prof., 1946—48; prof., chmn. dept. surgery Baylor Coll. Medicine, 1948—93, Disting. svc. prof., 1968—, v.p. med. affairs, 1968—69, CEO, 1968—69, pres., 1969—79, Olga Keith Wiess prof. of surgery, 1981—, chancellor, 1978—96, chancellor emeritus, 1996—; pres. The DeBakey Med. Found., 1961—; dir. Nat. Heart Blood Vessel Rsch. Demonstration Ctr., Baylor Coll. Medicine, 1974—84; dir. DeBakey Heart Ctr., Baylor Coll. Medicine, 1985—. Surgeon-in-chief Ben Taub Gen. Hosp., 1963—93; sr. attending surgeon Meth. Hosp.; clin. prof. surgery U. Tex. Dental Br.; cons. surgery VA Hosp., U. Tex. M.D. Anderson Cancer Ctr., St. Luke's Hosp., Tex. Children's Hosp., Tex. Inst. Rehab. and Rsch., Houston, Brooke Gen. Hosp., Brooke Army Med. Ctr., Ft. Sam Houston, Tex., Walter Reed Army Hosp., Washington, D.C.; mem. med. adv. com. Office Sec. Def., 1948—50; mem. task force med. svcs. Hoover Commn., 1949; founding bd. dirs. Friends of Nat. Libr. of Medicine, 1985—; mem. bd. regents Nat. Libr. of Medicine, 1956—60, 1994—98, chmn., 1959, 98; past mem. nat. adv. heart coun. NIH; mem. Nat. Adv. Health Coun., 1961—65, Nat. Adv. Coun. Regional Med. Programs, 1965—, Nat. Adv. Gen. Med. Scis. Coun., 1965, Program Planning Com., Com. Tng., Nat. Heart Inst., 1961—; mem. civilian health and med. adv. coun. Office Asst. Sec. Def.; chmn. Pres.'s Commn. Heart Disease, Cancer and Stroke, 1964; mem. adv. coun. Nat. Heart Lung and Blood Inst., 1982—87; chmn. Found. Biomedical Rsch., 1988; trustee, v.p. Baylor Med. Found.; adv. Dag Hammarskjöld Med. Sci. Prize Com.; trustee Baylor Coll. Medicine, 1996; fgn. adj. prof. Karolinska Inst., 1997. Author (with Robert A. Kilduffe): Blood Transfusion, 1942; author: (with Gilbert W. Beebe) Battle Casualties, 1952; author: (with Alton Ochsner) Textbook of Minor Surgery, 1955; author: (with T. Whayne) Cold Injury, Ground Type, 1958; author: A Surgeon's Visit to China, 1974, The Living Heart, 1977, The Living Heart Diet, 1985, The Living Heart Brand Name Shopper's Guide, 1992, The Living Heart Guide to Eating Out, 1993, The New Living Heart Diet, 1996, The New Living Heart, 1997; editor: Yearbook of surgery, 1958—70; chmn. adv. editl. bd.: Medical History of World War II, founding editor: Jour. Vascular Surgery, 1984—88; contbr. over 1600 articles to med. jours. Disting. mem. U.S. Army Med. Dept. Rgt., 1989; cons. to Surgeon Gen., 1946—. Col. Office Surgeon Gen. U.S. Army, 1942—46, now Col. Res. U.S. Army. Decorated Legion of Merit, 1945; named in his honor Michael E. DeBakey Dept. Surgery, Baylor Coll. Medicine, 1999, in his honor Michael E. Debakey Heart Inst. Kan., Hays Med. Ctr., 1999, in his honor Michael E. DeBakey Internat. Surgery Chair, Uniformed Svc. Univ. Health Sci., 2000, in his honor Michael E. DeBakey Inst. Comparative Cardiovascular Sci. and Biomedical Devices, Tex. A&M Univ., 2000, innumerable honors and awards including Leader in Medicine, AMA, 1997, charter mem., Tex. Sci. Hall Fame, 2001, in his honor Michael E. DeBakey Vet. Affairs Med. Ctr., 2004; named an inductee Space Tech. Hall Fame, 1999; named one of 200 Most Influential People in Telemedicine, Ctr. Pub. Svc. Comm., 1996, Top Ten Heroes, Millenium Soc., 1996; named to Health Care Hall of Fame, Modern Healthcare, 1996, Houston Hall Fame, 1999, Sci. in Tex. Hall Fame, 2000; recipient Rudolph Matas award, 1954, Disting. Svc. award, Internat. Soc. Surgery, 1958, Modern Medicine award, 1957, Leriche award, Internat. Soc. Surgery, 1959, Great medallion, U. Ghent, 1961, Grand Cross, Order Leopold, Belgium, 1962, Albert Lasker award for clin. rsch., 1963, Order of Merit Chile, 1964, St. Vincent prize med. scis., U. Turin, 1965, Centennial medal, Albert Einstein Med. Ctr., 1966, Gold Scalpel award, Internat. Cardiology Found., 1966, Eleanor Roosevelt Humanities award, 1969, Meritorious Civilian Svc. medal, Office Sec. Def., 1970, Medal of Freedom with Distinction Presdl. award, 1969, Inst. Med. Nat. Acad. Sci., 1981, Theodore E. Cummings award, 1987, Nat. Med. of Sci. award, 1987, First Issue Michael DeBakey medal, ASME, 1989, Inaugural award, Scripps Clinic and Rsch. Found., 1989, DeBakey-Bard Chair in Surgery, Baylor Coll. of Medicine, 1990, Disting. Svc. award, Am. Legion, 1990, Lifetime Achievement award, Found. for Biomed. Rsch., 1991, Maxwell Finland award, Nat. Found. for Infectious Diseases, 1992, Acad. of Athens award, 1992, Pres. Disting. Svc. award, Baylor Coll. Medicine, 1992, Gibbon award, Am. Soc. Extracorporeal Tech., 1993, named in his honor Michael E. DeBakey Libr. Svc. Outreach award, Friends of the Nat. Libr. Medicine, 1993, Alton Ochsner award relating smoking to health, 1993, Thomas Jefferson award, AIA, 1993, Lifetime Achievement award, Am. Heart Assn., 1994, prize for basic biomed. rsch., Giovanni Lorenzini Med. Fedn., 1994, Disting. Svc. award, Tex. Soc. Biomed. Rsch., 1994, Heart Saver award, Save A Heart Found., Cedars-Sinai Med. Ctr., 1994, Honor award, United Meth. Assn. Health & Welfare Ministries, 1995, Michael E. DeBakey chair in Pharm., Baylor Coll. Medicine, 1995, Nat. Order of Medicine Vasco Nunez de Balboa, Panama, 1995, Pub. Svc. award, AIAA, 1997, Boris Petrovsky Internat. Surgeons award, 1997, Premio Giuseppe Corradi award, Bevagna, Italy, 1997, Rotary Nat. award, 1997, Sesquicentennial medal, Tulane Coll., 1997, Fire of Genius award, So. Utah U., 1997, Commonwealth Trust award for invention and sci., 1997, Michael E. DeBakey Heart Inst. Wis. named in his honor, Kenosha Hosp. and Med. Ctr., 1992, Michael E. DeBakey, M.D. award for Excellence in Visual Edn. named in his honor, 1993, DeBakey Scholar in Cardiovasc. Scis. MD-PhD Program named in his honor, Baylor Coll. Medicine, 1994, Michael E. DeBakey, MD Excellence in Rsch. award named in his honor, 1994, dedication of Northwestern U. Med. Sch. book, 1995, Michael E. DeBakey H.S. Health Professions named in his honor, 1996, Med. Ctr. of LA Found. Inaugural Spirit of Charity award, 1998, Leader in Medicine honor, AMA, 1997, John P. McGovern Lecture award, Cosmos Club Found., 1998, Lifetime Achivement award, Rsch. Am., 1998, Michael E. DeBakey Presdl. Excellence award named in his honor, 1998, Mus. Health and Med. Sci. Lifetime Membership award, 1999, Disting. Svc. award, Soc. Vascular Surgery, 1999, Sci. Achievement award, Am. Assn. Thoracic Surgery, 1999, inaugural Michael E. DeBakey award contbns. to Am.'s Health, AIA, 1999, Bicentennial Living Legends award, Libr. Congress, 2000, Lifetime Achievement Outstanding Alumnus award, Tulane Med. Alumni Assn., 2000, Tall Texan award, Muscular Dystrophy Assn., 2001, Invention Yr., DeBakey Ventricular Assist Device, NASA, 2001, Mendal Medal award, Villanova U., Pa., 2001, Living Legend award, World Artificial-Organ, Immunology, Transplant Soc., Ottawa, Can., 2001, Inspired Leadership award, Am. Bible Soc., 2001, Wall of Honor tribute for lifetime contributions, 2002, Lifetime Achievement award, Internat. Health and Med. Film Festival, 2002, Lindbergh-Carreell Prize, 2002, Michael E. DeBakey Med. Student Poetry award, 2003, Michael E. DeBakey Dept. of Surgery award for excellence in acad. surgery, 2003, award of excellence for tireless work in the field of heart failure, Cleve. Clinic Found. Kaufman Ctr., 2003, Ben Taub Humanitarian award, Harris County Hosp. Dist., 2003, Hon. Alumnus award, Ochsner Clinic Found. Fellows' Alumni Assn., 2003, Millennium Doctor award, People Caring for the Cmty., Inc., 2003, Olaf Acrel Medallion, Swedish Surgical Soc., 2003, Lomonosov Gold medal, Russian Acad. Scis., 2004, David E. Rogers award, Assn. Am. Med. Colls. and Robert Wood Johnson Found., 2004, Lifetime Achievement award, Nat. Arab Am. Med. Assn., 2004, Cert. Congl. Recognition, U.S. Ho. Reps., 2004. Fellow: Internat. Acad. Cardiovascular Scis. (hon.), Am. Coll. Cardiology (hon.), Royal Coll. Physicians and Surgeons of U.S. (hon. disting. fellow 1992), Inst. of Medicine Chgo. (hon.); mem.: AMA (Hektoen Gold medal 1954, Disting. Svc. award 1959, Hektoen Gold medal 1970), AAAS, Uniformed Svc. Alumni Assn. (life hon.), Internat. Soc. Surgery, Soc. Univ. Surgeons, Assn. Internat. Vascular Surgeons (pres. 1983), Internat. Cardiovascular Soc. (pres. 1958, pres. N.Am. chpt. 1964), Am. Assn. Thoracic Surgery (pres. 1959), So. Surg. Assn. (pres. 1989—90, chmn. coun. 1995—), Am. Surg. Assn. (pres. 1989, Disting. Svc. award 1981), Soc. Vascular Surgery Lifeline Found. (pres. 1989), Soc. Vascular Surgery (pres. 1954), Am. Heart Assn. (Nat. Chpt. Lifetime Achievement award 2004), Royal Soc. Medicine, Assn. Française de Chirurgie (hon.), Med. Libr. Assn. (hon.), Hellenic Surg. Soc. (hon.), Mex. Acad. Surgery (hon.), Telemedicine 200 Ctr. for Pub. Svcs., Acad. of Athens, University Club (Washington), Houston Club (hon.), Alpha Omega Alpha, Sigma Xi (William Procter prize for sci. achievement 1995). Episcopalian. Achievements include development of roller pump universally used in heart-lung machine; Dacron artificial arteries and Dacron-velour arteries as surgical replacement of diseased arteries; first successful patch-graft angioplasty; fundamental concept of therapy in arterial disease; left ventricular bypass pump for cardiac assistance and first successful clinical application; first successful resection and graft replacement of fusiform aneurysm; establishment of Meth. DeBakey Heart Ctr., Meth. Hosp., Houston, 2001; establishment of DeBakey USU Brigade, 2001; establishment of Michael E. DeBakey award for Long-life Well-lived in Svc. to Mankind, Huffington Ctr. on Aging, 2001; establishment of Michael E. DeBakey Scholarship in Grad. Sch. Biomedical Sci., Baylor Coll. Medicine, 2001; establishment of Michael E. DeBakey Journalism award, Found. Biomedical Rsch., 2002. Office: Baylor Coll Medicine 1 Baylor Plz Houston TX 77030-3411

DEBAKEY, SELMA, communications educator, writer, editor; b. Lake Charles, La. BA, postgrad., Newcomb Coll., Tulane U., New Orleans. Dir. dept. med. communication Ochsner Clinic and Alton Ochsner Med. Found., New Orleans, 1942-68; prof. sci. communication Baylor Coll. Medicine, Houston, 1968—; editor Cardiovascular Research Ctr. Bull., 1970-84. Mem. panel judges Internat. Health and Med. Film Festival, 1992. Author: (with A. Segaloff and K. Meyer) Current Concepts in Breast Cancer, 1967; past editor Ochsner Clinic Reports, Selected Writings from the Ochsner Clinic; contbr. numerous articles to sci. jours., chpts. to books. Named to Tex. Hall of Fame. Mem. AAAS, Soc. Tech. Communication, Assn. Tchrs. Tech. Writing, Am. Med. Writers Assn. (past bd. dirs.; publ., nominating, fellowship, constn., bylaws, awards, and edn. coms.), Council Biol. Editors (past mem. trn. in sci. writing com.), Soc. Health and Human Values, Modern Med. Monograph Awards Com., Nat. Assn. Standard Med. Vocabulary (former cons.). Office: Baylor Coll Medicine 1 Baylor Plz Houston TX 77030-3411

DE BARBIERI, MARY ANN, not-for-profit developer, management consultant; b. Winston-Salem, N.C., May 1, 1945; d. Robert Carroll and Annie Louise (Neal) Hutcherson; m. Alfredo Emanuelle De B.; children: Maria Luisa, Riccardo Roberto. BA in Theatre Arts, Mary Washington Coll., 1967; student, Herbert Berghof Studio, 1967—69. With J. Walter Thompson, N.Y.C., 1967-68; asst. to prodr. Norman Twain Prodns., N.Y.C., 1968-69, Contemporary Theatre Co., N.Y.C., 1971-74; co. mgr. Folger Theatre Group, Washington, 1974-77, bus. mgr., 1977-80; mng. dir. Shakespeare Theatre at the Folger, Washington, 1980-90; performing arts cons. Alexandria, Va., 1990-92; dir. The Found. Ctr., Washington, 1992-94; pres. De Barbieri and Assocs., 1994—. Adj. prof. arts mgmt. grad. program Am. U., 1994—; treas. League of Washington Theatres, 1983-86; chair selection com. The Washington Post/Washington Coun. Agys. Award for Excellence in Nonprofit Mgmt., 1997, 98, 99, mem. selection com. 1996-99, The Washington Post Grants in the Arts, 1997—; curriculum design cons., core faculty Choral Mgmt. Inst. of Chorus Am., 2002-05; presenter in field. Bd. dirs. Washington Area Lawyers for Arts, 1984-94; bd. dirs. Cultural Alliance Greater Washington, 1986-96, v.p., 1990-96; bd. dirs. Nat. Soc. Fundraising Execs., 1993-96, v.p. edn., 1995, treas., 1996; bd. dirs. Ctr. for Nonprofit Advancement, 2000—, pres., 2004-; chair Performing Arts Coun., Alexandria, Va., 1981-84; founder, first chair Alexandria Commn. for Arts, 1984-88, theatre commr., 1984-94; contbr. to study of downtown stages for new theatre in Washington, 1985; mem. panel Va. Commn. for the Arts, 1990-96, 2005— Recipient Outstanding Svc. to Theatre Cmty. award League of Washington Theatres, 1990. Office: 525 Beauregard Dr SE Leesburg VA 20175 Office Phone: 703-777-3585. E-mail: debarasso@aol.com.

DEBARTOLO, EDWARD JOHN, JR., professional football team owner, real estate developer; b. Youngstown, Ohio, Nov. 6, 1946; s. Edward J. and Marie Patricia DeBartolo; m. Cynthia Ruth Papalia, Sept. 27, 1968; children: Lisa Marie, Tiffanye Lynne, Nicole Anne. Student, U. Notre Dame, 1964—68. With Edward J. DeBartolo Corp., Youngstown, Ohio, 1960—, v.p., 1972—76, exec. v.p., 1976—79, chief adminstrv. officer, 1979—94; pres., CEO, 1995—; owner San Francisco 49ers, 1977—97; chmn. bd. DeBartolo Realty Corp., 1994—; chmn., CEO DeBartolo Entertainment, Inc. Mem. Nat. Cambodia Crisis Com., 1980—; adv. coun. Nat. Assn. People with AIDS, 1992; trustee Youngstown State U., 1974—77; nat. adv. coun. St. Jude Children's Rsch. Hosp., 1978—, local chmn., 1979—80; chmn. local fund drive Am. Cancer Soc., 1975—; chmn. 19th Ann. Victor Warner award, 1985, City of Hope's Spirit of Life Banquet, 1986; apptd. adv. coun. Coll. Bus. Adminstrn. U. Notre Dame, 1988; bd. dirs. Cleve. Clinic Found., 1991; lifetime mem. Italian Scholarship League. With U.S. Army, 1969. Recipient Man of Yr. award, St. Jude Children's Hosp., 1979, Boy's Town of Italy in San Francisco, 1985, Sportsman of Yr. award, Nat. Italian Am. Sports Hall of Fame, 1991, Cert. of Merit, Salvation Army, 1982, Warner award, 1986, Silver Cable Car award, San Francisco Conv. and Visitors Bur., 1988, NFL Man of Yr. award, Football News, 1989, Svc. to Youth award, Cath. Youth Orgn., 1990, Hall of Fame award, Cardinal Mooney High Sch., 1993. Mem.: Internat. Coun. Shopping Ctrs., Dapper Dan Club (bd. dirs. 1980—), Fonderlac Country Club, Tippecanoe Country Club. Office: Debartolo Corp 7620 Market St Youngstown OH 44512-6076 *Personal philosophy: Success in business and sporting competition relies on the same basic ingredients--hire the best qualified people and then provide them with the leadership and best resources to accomplish the task.*

DEBARTOLO, HANSEL MARION, JR., otolaryngologist, plastic surgeon; b. Aurora, Ill., May 13, 1947; s. Hansel Marion and Rosemary (Boetto) Debartolo; m. Susan Elizabeth Debartolo, June 26, 1977; children: Doré, Hansel III, Merrit, Janae, Raquel. BA cum laude, U. Minn., 1969; MD, Loyola U., Chgo., 1972; JD, William Howard Taft U. Diplomate Am. Bd. Otolaryngology, Nat. Bd. Med. Examiners, Am. Acad. Anti-Aging (bd. examiner). Intern, resident Mayo Clinic and Mayo Found., Rochester, Minn.; fellow in surgery Mayo Clinic, Rochester; fellow in otorhinolaryngology Geisinger Clinic, Danville, Pa.; former chief staff AmSurg, Joliet, Ill. Ptnr. Chgo. White Sox, H.M.D., Racing Stables, Chgo. Metro TV, Sportsvision, CETUS Internat., Granada Cosmisky Parks Assocs., Hard Master Recording; CEO H.M.D. Devel.; attending surgeon Mendota (Ill.) Hosp. Contbr. articles to profl. jours. Bd. dirs. Debartolo Rsch. Found. Fellow: Drs. Mayo Soc. Life, Priestly Surg. Soc., Am. Rhinologic Soc., Chgo. Larynigol. and Otological Soc., Am. Acad. Anti-Aging Medicine, Am. Acad. Otorhinolaryngology (legis. key physician Ill., mem. bd. govs.), Deafness Rsch. Assn. (life); mem.: AAAS, Am. Soc. Cosmetic Dermatology, Pa. Acad. Ophthalmology and Otolaryngology, Ill. Soc. Opthalmology and Otolaryngology (mem. exec. coun., sec.-treas., chief editor proceedings), Am. Acad. Advancement Medicine, Aurora Country Club. Roman Catholic. Avocations: tennis, skiing, golf, bicycling, amateur radio. Home: 20 Dorchester Ct Aurora IL 60506-9139 Office: Debartolo Clinic 11 Debartolo Dr Sugar Grove IL 60554-9584 Office Phone: 630-859-1818. Office Fax: 630-859-1830. Business E-Mail: dr@debartoloclinic.com.

DEBARTOLO-YORK, DENISE, sports team executive; m. John C. York II; 4 children. Grad., Notre Dame U. Team pres. Pitts. Penguins; exec. v.p. personnel and corp. mktg./comm. The Edward J. Bartolo Corp., vice chmn., 1994; chmn. The Edward J. DeBartolo Corp., 1994—. Supporter DeBartolo Family Found. Mem. fin. adv. bd. Ursuline Sisters; mem. MADD; recognized for contbn. to St. Charles Elem. Sch., Boardman, Ohio. Named to Italian American Sports Hall of Fame, 2003. Office: care San Francisco 49ers 4949 Centennial Blvd Santa Clara CA 95054-1229

DEBASTIANI, ROBERTA, school psychologist; b. Pitts., Oct. 24, 1956; d. Amedeo Eugene and Asunta (Nuzzo) DeB. BS in Edn., Slippery Rock State Coll., 1978; MS in Edn., Duquesne U., 1984; postgrad., Indiana Univ., Pa., 1992-93; D.Ed., Ind. U. Pa., 1998. Spl. edn. tchr. McKeesport (Pa.) Pre-Sch. for Exceptional Children, 1979-82; tchr. Diocese of Pitts., East Pitts., 1982-85; program coord. McKeesport Pre-Sch. for Exceptional Children, 1985-88; primary resource rm. tchr. Indian River Sch. Dist., Ocean View, Del., 1988-93; primary resource rm. tchr, sch. psychology intern Cape Henlopen Sch. Dist., Lewes, Del., 1993-94, sch. psychologist, 1994—. Mem. Coun. Exceptional Children (div. early childhood), Nat. Assn. Sch. Psychologist. Avocation: reading. Office: Cape Henlopen Sch Dist 1270 Kings Hwy Lewes DE 19958-1783 Office Phone: 302-684-8522. E-mail: BDeBast@aol.com.

DEBAUGE, CHRISTIANE MICHELLE, psychometrician, data analyst; d. Paul Fredrick and Lucia Kathleen (Harcum) DeBauge. BA, Baylor U., Waco, Tex., 1997, MA, 1999; PhD, Ind. U., Bloomington, 2005. Tchr., intern Hillcrest Profl. Devel. Sch., Waco, 1996—97; tchr. Waco Montessori Sch., 1997—98; art coord., tchr. Temple Montessori Sch., Tex., 1998—99; assoc. editor Prufrock Press, Bloomington, 1999—2003; assoc. instr. Ind. U., Bloomington, 1999—2004; test devel. specialist Riverside Publ., Chgo., 2003—04, data analyst, 2004—. Author: Teacher Preparation Guide, 2005. Mem.: Chi Omega (recruiter new mems. 1999—2002, advisor 2004—, reviewer 2004—05). Office Phone: 800-767-8420. Business E-Mail: christy-debauge@hmco.com.

DEBAUN, LINDA LOUISE, performing arts educator; b. L.A., Nov. 11, 1946; d. James Irving and Katherine Adeliade deBaun; life ptnr. Heidi Annette Wilson, June 15, 1996. AA, Mt. San Antonio Jr. Coll., 1966; BA in Writing, Pitzer Coll., 1968; MLitt of English, Clairemont U., 1972; M of Theatre, Calif. State U., 1998. Tchr. Azusa (Calif.) H.S., 1972—73, Vol. State Coll., Gallatin, Tenn., 1973—75; tchr., dir. drama Yucaipa (Calif.) H.S., 1980—. Recipient Tchr. of Yr., San Bernadino County, Calif., 2000. Mem.: Internat. Thespian Soc. (state bd. dirs.). Avocations: writing, music. Home: 11666 Pendelton Rd Yucaipa CA 92399 Office: Yucaipa High Sch 33000 Ycuaipa Blvd Yucaipa CA 92399

DEBEAR, RICHARD STEPHEN, library director; b. N.Y.C., Jan. 18, 1933; s. Arthur A. and Sarah (Morrison) deB.; m. Estelle Carmel Grandon, Apr. 27, 1951; children: Richard, Jr., Diana deBear Fortson, Patricia deBear Talkington, Robert, Christopher, Nancy deBear Naski. BS, Queens Coll., CUNY, 1953. Sales rep. Sperry Rand Corp., Blue Bell, Pa., 1954-76; pres. Libr. Design Assocs., Plymouth, Mich., 1976-97, Am. Libr. Ctr., Plymouth, 1981—. Bldg. cons. to numerous librs., 1965—; mem. interior design program profl. adv. com. Wayne State U. Mem. ALA, Mich. Libr. Assn. (oversight com. Leadership Acad. 1990—). Office: Am Libr Ctr Inc 1149 S Main St Plymouth MI 48170-2213 Office Phone: 734-254-8080. Business E-Mail: ddebear@americanlibrary.com.

DEBEERS, SUE, photographer; b. Tarrytown, NY, Aug. 9, 1973; BFA, Parson Sch. Design, NY, 1995; MFA, Columbia U., 1998. Artist-in-residence Wexner Ctr., Ohio, 1999. One-woman shows include Heidi 2, Deitch Projects, NY, 2000, Photographs / project room: Ghost Stories Mag., Sandroni Rey, LA, 2001, Photographs, Kunstlerhaus Bethanian, Berlin, 2002, Hans & Grete, Kunst Werke, Berlin, 2003, The Dark Hearts, Sandroni Rey at Statements, Basel, Miami, 2004, exhibited in group shows at Imaginary Beings, Exit Art, NY, 1995, Terra Bomba, 1996, 26 Positions, Miriam & Ira D. Wallach Gallery, NY, 1997, Scope 3, Artist's Space, NY, 1998, The Searchers, 1999, Death Race, Threadwaxing Space, NY, 2000, Fresh: The Altoids Curiously Strong Collection, New Mus. Contemporary Art, 2001, Desiring Machines, Dorsky Curatorial Projects, NY, 2002, Internat. Monster League, Derek Eller Gallery, NY, 2003, Working in Bklyn., Bklyn. Mus., 2004, Whitney Biennial, Whitney Mus. Am. Art, 2004, SCREAM, Anton Kern Gallery, NY, 2004. Recipient Franklin Furnace Fund for Performance Art, 1998—99, Joan Sovern Award Excellence in Sculpture, 1999, Philip Morris Emerging Artist Prize, Am. Acad. Berlin, 2001. Mailing: c/o Whitney Museum American Art 945 Madison Ave New York NY 10021 E-mail: sue@sevenseven.com.*

DEBELLEVUE, LUCKY, sculptor; b. Lafayette, La., 1957; BFA, U. Soutwestern La., 1983; MFA, U. New Orleans, 1987. Solo exhibitions at, Feature Gallery, 1997, Realismus Studio, Berlin, 1997, Mus. Contemporary Art, Chgo., 1999, group exhibitions at, Contemporary Arts Ctr., New Orleans, 1986, Dalamas Mus., Falun, Sweden, 1986, Four Walls, Bklyn., 1992, Artists Space, NYC, 1992, The Drawing Ctr., NYC, 1993, Universidad de Buenos Aires, 1995, Bklyn. Mus. Art, 1997, Gasworks, London, 1997, Cornerhouse, Manchester, Eng., 1997, D'Amelio Terras Gallery, NYC, 1998, Galerie Emmanuel Perrotin, Paris, France, 1998, Stephen Friedman Gallery, London, 1999, Grand Arts, Kansas City, 1999, Netherland Gallery Art, Rotterdam, 1999, Museum D'hondt-Dhaenens, Deurl, Belgium, 2000, Galeria d'Arte Moderna, Bologna, Italy, 2002, Wexner Galleries, Columbus, Ohio, 2004, others. Joseph H. Hazen Rome Prize Fellowship in Visual Arts, Am. Acad. in Rome, 2004—05. Mem.: Coll. Art Assn. Office: Feature Inc 530 W 25th St New York NY 10001 Office Phone: 212-675-7772.*

DEBENEDETTI, PABLO GASTON, chemical engineering professor; b. Buenos Aires, Mar. 30, 1953; came to the U.S., 1980; U.S. citizen; s. Sergio Isaias and Francine Fanny (Lehmann) D.; m. Silvia Irene Strauss, July 11, 1987; children: Gabriel Alejandro, Dina Sonia. BS in Chem. Engring., Buenos Aires U., 1978; MS, MIT, 1981, PhD, 1985. Rsch. engr. O de Nora Impianti Elettrochimici, Milan, 1978-80; asst. prof. dept. chem. engring. Princeton (N.J.) U., 1985-90, assoc. prof., 1990-94, prof. chem. engring., 1994—, dept. chair, 1996—2004, Class of 1950 prof., 1998—. Vaughan lectr. Calif. Inst. Tech., 1992; Katz meml. lectr. City Coll. CUNY, 1997; Wohl meml. lectr. U. Del., 1997; Cary lectr. Ga. Inst. Tech., 1998; Berkeley lectr. in chem. engring. U. Calif., Berkeley, 2003; Collaboratus disting. lectr Rutgers U., 2003; Katz lectr. chem. engring. U. Mich., 2005. Author: Matastable Liquids Concepts and Principles, 1996; mem. editl. bd.: Jour. Supercritical Fluids, 1988—, Revs. in Chem. Engring., 1999—, Chem. Engring. Edn., 2000—, Indsl. and Engring. Chem. Rsch., 2001—04, Physica A, 2001—; contbr. articles to profl. jours. including Journ. Chem. Physics, Jour. Phys. Chemistry, Nature, Phys. Rev. Letters, Molecular Physics, Am. Inst. Chem. Engr. Jour., others. Named NSF Presdl. Young Investigator, 1987; European Econ. Cmty. fellow, 1978, Camille and Henry Dreyfus Tchr. scholar, 1989, Guggenheim fellow, 1991, Nat. Acad. Engring., 2000, Prausnitz award 2001. Mem.: AAAS, Am. Phys. Soc., Am. Chem. Soc., Am. Inst. Chem. Engrs. (Profl. Progress award 1997), Sigma Xi. Achievements include protein processing and separations with supercritical fluids; theory of supercritical fluids and mixtures; thermodynamics of supercooled and glassy water; thermodynamics and statistical mechanics of metastable systems; thermodynamics of polyamorphic phase transitions; structure, dynamics, and thermodynamics of glasses. Office: Princeton U Dept Chem Engring Princeton NJ 08544-0001

DEBERARDINE, ROBERT, lawyer; b. Bklyn., June 29, 1958; s. Roger B. and Rose Ann DeBerardine; m. Cara Mia Williams, Nov. 24, 1991; children: Maximilla Williams, Emanuella Williams. BSChemE cum laude, Lafayette Coll., 1980; JD magna cum laude, Cornell U., 1983. Bar: U.S. Patent Office. Assoc. Jones, Day, Reavis & Pogue, L.A., N.Y.C., Dallas, 1983-91; ptnr. Brobeck, Phleger & Harrison, Palo Alto, Calif., 1992—, head litigation Austin. Mem. State Bar N.Y., State Bar Calif., State Bar Tex., Order of the Coif. Avocations: writing, outdoor sports, family. Fax: 512-330-4001. E-mail: rdeberardine@brobeck.com.

DEBERRY, FISHER, college football coach; b. Cheraw, S.C., June 9, 1938; m. LuAnn DeBerry; children: Joe, Michelle BA, Wofford Coll., 1960. Coach, tchr. high schs., S.C., 6 yrs.; asst. football coach Wofford Coll., Spartanburg, S.C., 2 yrs., Appalachian State Coll., Boone, N.C., 9 yrs.; quarterbacks coach Air Force Acad., USAF Acad., Colo., 1980-81, offensive coord., 1981-83, head football coach, 1984—. Led teams in Ind. Bowl, 1984, Blue Bonnnet Bowl, 1985, Freedom Bowl, 1987, Liberty Bowl, 1989-92, Copper Bowl, 1995, Las Vegas Bowl, 1997. Motivational spkr. to religious and corp. groups; fund raiser Easter Seals, March of Dimes, Salvation Army; chmn. Am. Heart

Assn. Named to Wofford Coll. Hall of Fame. Named Western Athletic Conf. Coach of Yr., 1985, 95, Nat. Coach of Yr., 1985. Mem. Fellowship Christian Athletes. Office: Hdqs USAF Acad 2304 Cadet Dr Ste 200 U S A F Academy CO 80840-5099

DE BETHMANN, HEIDI ELIZABETH, architect; b. Mineola, N.Y. d. Daniel René and Carol Ann (King) Luthringshauser; m. Alexandre J. de Bethmann, Oct. 29, 1988; children: Elodie Elizabeth, Elise Anne, Lucas Alexandre. BA, Wellesley Coll., 1984; MArch, MIT, 1988. Registered architect, N.Y. Architect Ellerbe Beckett, N.Y.C., 1988-89; assoc., sr. designer Butler Rogers Baskett, N.Y.C., 1989—. Home: 131 E 81st St New York NY 10028-1450 Office: Butler Rogers Baskett 475 10th Ave Fl 5 New York NY 10018-1139

DEBEVOISE, CHARLES HENRY, lawyer; b. Providence, May 17, 1958; s. Charles Conklin DeBevoise and Dolores Annette (Anderson) Brunt; children: Robert Raymond, Edward Raymond. BA in Polit. Sci., Providence Coll., 1980; JD, Am. U., 1983. Bar: R.I. 1983, Mass. 1984, D.C. 1985, U.S. Dist. Ct. R.I. 1984. Law clk. Supreme Ct. R.I., Providence, 1983—84; assoc. Edwards & Angell, Providence, 1987—92, ptnr. Providence, Boston, 1992—95, Bowditch & Dewey, Framingham, Mass., 1999—2004; shareholder Davis, Malm & D'Agostine, P.C., Boston, 2004—. Bd. dirs. Narragansett Coun. Boy Scouts Am., Providence, 1987-95; sr. warden St. Dunstan's Episcopal Ch., Dover, Mass., 2000-2003. Mem. ABA, R.I. Bar Assn., Mass. Bar Assn., D.C. Bar Assn., Boston Bar Assn., Dedham Country and Polo Club, Pi Sigma Alpha. Republican. Episcopalian. Avocations: reading, tennis, golf, gardening. Home: 10 Cedar Hill Rd Dover MA 02030-1624 Office: Davis Malm & D'Agostine PC One Boston Pl 37th Fl Boston MA 02108 Office Phone: 617-589-3846. E-mail: cdebevoise@davismalm.com.

DEBEVOISE, DICKINSON RICHARDS, federal judge; b. Orange, N.J., Apr. 23, 1924; s. Elliott and Josephine (Richards) D.; m. Katrina Stephenson Leeb, Feb. 24, 1951; children: Kate, Josephine Debevoise Davies, Mary Debevoise Rennie, Abigail D. Boozan. BA, Williams Coll., 1948; LLB, Columbia U., 1951. Bar: N.J. 1953, U.S. Supreme Ct. 1956. Law clk. to Hon. Phillip Forman, chief judge U.S. Dist. Ct. for Dist. N.J., 1952-53; assoc. firm Riker, Emery & Danzig, Newark, 1953-56; ptnr. firm Riker, Danzig, Scherer, Debevoise & Hyland, Newark, 1957-79; judge U.S. Dist. Ct. for N.J., 1979—. Pres. Newark Legal Svcs. Project, 1965-70; chmn. N.J. Gov.'s Workmen's Compensation Study Commn., 1972-73; mem. N.J. Supreme Ct. Adv. Com. on Jud. Conduct, 1974-78; chmn. N.J. Disciplinary Rev. Bd., 1978-79; mem. Lawyers Adv. Com. for 3d Cir., 1975-79, chmn., 1979; chmn. N.J. Legal Svcs. Adv. Coun., 1976-78. Assoc. editor: N.J. Law Jour, 1959-79. Trustee Ramapo Coll., N.J., 1969-73, chmn. bd., 1971-73; trustee Williams Coll., 1969-74, Fund for N.J., 1985—; trustee Hosp. Ctr. at Orange, N.J., v.p., 1975-79; pres. Dems. for Good Govt., 1956-60, active various presdl., senatorial, gubernatorial campaigns; active St. Stephens Episcopal Ch. Sgt. U.S. Army, WWII, 1st lt. Korean War. Decorated Bronze Star. Fellow Am. Bar Found.; mem. ABA, N.J. Bar Assn., Fed. Bar Assn. (v.p. 1976), Assn. Fed. Bar State N.J. (v.p. 1977-79), Essex County Bar Assn. (trustee. 1960-64, trustee 1968-71), Am. Law Inst., Judicature Soc., Columbia Law Sch. Assn. (bd. dirs., pres. 1992-94). Office: US Dist Ct PO Box 999 Newark NJ 07101-0999 Office Phone: 973-645-6121.

DEBEVOISE, ELI WHITNEY, II, lawyer; b. Morristown, N.J., Feb. 8, 1953; BA summa cum laude, Yale Coll., 1974; JD, Harvard U., 1977. Bar: D.C. 1977. Law clk. to William J. Holloway Jr. U.S. Ct. Appeals (10th cir.) Okla., Oklahoma City, 1978-79; ptnr., Internat. Transactions Practice Group Arnold & Porter, Washington, 1979—. Mem. Council on Foreign Rels., ABA (coun. mem. sect. on internat. law and practice), Am. Soc. Internat. Law (exec. coun.), Internat. Bar Assn. Office: Arnold & Porter 555 12th St NW Washington DC 20004-1206 Office Phone: 202-942-5042. Office Fax: 202-942-5999. Business E-Mail: whitney.debevoise@aporter.com.

DE BEVOISE, LEE RAYMOND, editor, writer; b. Paterson, N.J., Aug. 24, 1948; m. Sharon De Bevoise; children: Suzanne, Richard (dec.). Student, Glassboro State Coll., 1968; ASN, Cumberland C.C., Vineland, N.J., 1974; student, Stockton State Coll., 1991; MS in Comm. summa cum laude, La Salle U., 1996. RN, N.J., Nebr. Editor The Artery Millville Hosp., NJ, 1970—73; staff instr. ARC, Phila., 1981—96; v.p. De Bevoise & Assocs., Friend, Nebr., 1993—. Adj. prof. La Salle U., 1996-2003; clin. info. sys. liaison Bryan Home Health Care Svc., Lincoln, 1998—. Columnist Daily Jour., Millville, NJ, 1990-97, The Sentinel, Friend, Nebr., 2005; field editor Disabled Outdoors mag., Grand Marais, Minn., 1994-97; editor South Jersey Angler Mag., Vineland, NJ, 1996-97; editor, webmaster www.ci.friend.ne.us, 2000—, www.fishdreams.com, 1997—, www.computertutor.fishdreams.com, 2004—, www.Isaiah6.fishdreams.com, 2005—; editor, co-webmaster www.f-bcne.org, 2002—, www.Nebraskahomecare.org, 2002—. Asst. advisor Med. Explorer Post, Millville, 1971-72; trustee Millville Day Care Ctr., 1974-77; co-chmn. adv. com. State Assemblyman Salmon, Millville, 1986-89; trustee, deacon, treas. Open Bible Bapt. Ch., Millville, 1986-95; music dir., choir dir., elder, co-youth group leader Friend Berean Ch., Friend, Nebr., 2000—; vol. rep. Dare 2 Share Ministries, 2003—; co-founder Isaiah 6 Ministries, 2004—; dir. pub. rels. Meadowwood Environ. Sanctuary, Millville, 1990-97, S.J. Sportsmen's Jamboree, Maurice River Twp., N.J., 1990-96; chmn., emcee Friend Talent Show, 1999-2000; co-founder South East Nebr. Youth Rally, 2004—. With USN, 1969-70. Recipient 1st pl. award, Bi-centennial Photography, 1976, Nebr. State Svc. award, Nat. Assn. Home Care and Hospice, 2004. Mem. Boat Writers Internat., Boating Writers Internat., Kodak Profl. Network, Internat. Freelance Photographers Orgn., Internat. Webmasters Assn., Mason-Dixon Outdoor Writers Assn. (Gatco Best Mag. column award, Pete Greer Meml. award 1st runner up for best black and white photography), HTML Writers Guild. Avocations: personal computers, fishing, shooting sports, environmental concerns, boating. Home: 607 S Pine St Friend NE 68359-1534 Office: De Bevoise & Assocs 607 S Pine St Friend NE 68359-1534 Office Phone: 402-947-9311. E-mail: lee@fishdreams.com.

DE BLASI, TONY (ANTHONY ARMANDO DE BLASI), artist; b. Alcamo, Italy, Jan. 1, 1933; came to U.S., 1938, naturalized, 1959; s. Frank and Josephine (Frisella) De B.; m. Eva Machauf; children from previous marriage: Keith, Eric. Student, Art Students League, N.Y.C., 1957-59; BA, U. R.I., 1961; MFA, Ind. U., 1963; student of William Leete, Kingston, R.I., 1959-61; student of James McGarrell, Bloomington, Ind., 1961-63; student William Bailey and Dr. Albert Elsen, student of Rudy Pozzatti, Bloomington, 1961-63; also others. Chmn., instr. dept. art Washington and Jefferson Coll., Washington, Pa., 1963-66; prof. painting and drawing Mich. State U., East Lansing, 1966-86; instr. Sch. Visual Arts, N.Y.C., 1988-90. One-man shows of paintings 1963—, including Kresge Art Mus., Mich. State U., East Lansing, 1969, 72, 76, Spectrum Gallery, N.Y.C., 1968, 69, 71, 73, Detroit Art Inst., 1972, Razor Gallery, N.Y.C., 1975, 77, Western Mich. U., Kalamazoo, 1979, Wake Forest U., Winston-Salem, N.C., 1980, Urban Inst. Contemporary Art, Grand Rapids, Mich., 1981, Andrews U., Berrien Springs, Mich., 1983, Louis K. Meisel Gallery, N.Y.C., 1985, 87, 88, 89, 91, 93, 95, Hokin Kaufman Gallery, Chgo., 1988, Hokin Gallery, Bay Harbor Island, Fla., 1990, 92, SUNY Fine Arts Gallery, Oneonta, N.Y., 1998; numerous group shows 1963— including Mus. of Modern Art, Penthouse Gallery, N.Y.C., 1968, Henri Gallery, Washington, 1968, 70, Riverside Mus., N.Y.C., 1970, Spectrum Gallery, 1970, 71, Eastern Mich. U., Ypsilanti, 1972, Corcoran Gallery, Washington, 1973, Razor Gallery, N.Y.C., 1975, 77, 78, 79, Grand Rapids Art Mus., 1980, Neill Gallery, N.Y.C., 1980, Detroit Inst. Arts, 1969, 70, 82, Ball State U. Gallery, Muncie, Ind., 1983, Louis K. Meisel Gallery, N.Y.C., ann. 1984-90, N.J. Ctr. Visual Arts, Summit, 1985, 69th Regement Armory, N.Y.C., 1988, Islip Art Mus., N.Y., 1993, Jaffe Baker Blau Gallery, Boca Raton, Fla., 1995, Dorothy Blau Gallery, Bay Harbor Island, Fla., 1997, Heuser Art Ctr. Gallery, Bradley U., Peoria, Ill., 2001; represented in permanent collections Detroit Art Inst., Ind. U. Mus. Fine Arts, Bloomington, Ulrich Mus. Art, Wichita, Kans., Rose Art Mus., Brandeis U., Waltham, Mass., City Nat. Bank, Detroit, Greenfield Energy Corp., L.A., Best Products Co. Inc., Richmond, Kresge Art Mus., East Lansing, Mich., also numerous pvt. collections; represented by Louis K. Meisel Gallery, N.Y.C., 1984-96, Dorothy Blau Gallery, Bay Harbor Island, Fla., 1997—. Served with USN, 1951-55. Recipient Albert Kahn Assoc. Archs. and Engrs. prize, 1969, Founders Purchase prize (1st prize), Detroit Art Inst., 1970, Mich. Fine Arts Competition award of excellence, Birmingham-Bloomfield Art Ctr., 1982; grantee, Tiffany Found., 1966, Individual Artist grantee, Mich. Coun. for Arts, 1983. Office Phone: 212-226-6475. E-mail: tonydeblasi@verizon.net.

DE BLASIS, JAMES MICHAEL, performing company executive, theater producer; b. N.Y.C., Apr. 12, 1931; s. James and Sarah (de Felice) de B.; m. Ruth Hofreuter, Aug. 25, 1957; 1 child, Blythe. BFA, Carnegie Mellon U., 1959, MFA, 1960. Mem. drama faculty Carnegie Mellon U., 1960-62; head drama dept. Onondaga C.C., Syracuse, N.Y., 1963-72; head Opera Workshop, Syracuse, 1969-70; adv. of opera Corbett Found., Cin., 1971-76; gen. dir. Cin. Opera Assn., 1973-87, artistic dir., 1988-96. Internat. ind. stage dir. of opera, 1962—; pvt. coach, Dramatic Interpretation of Operatic Roles, 1995—. Artistic advisor, Pitts. Opera, Inc., 1979-83. With U.S. Army, 1951-53. Recipient award Omicron Delta Kappa, 1959, Alumni award Bellaire High Sch., 1974, award in arts adminstrn. Gov. Ohio, 1989, Post/Corbett award for performing artist Corbett Found./Cin. Post, 1989. Mem. Actors Equity, Am. Guild Mus. Artists, Drama Alumni Carnegie Mellon U., Beta Theta Pi, Omicron Delta Kappa. Republican. Episcopalian. E-mail: jr45@optonline.net.

DEBO, VINCENT JOSEPH, lawyer, director, manufacturing executive; b. Bklyn., Feb. 14, 1940; s. George and Letitia (Ruggiero) D.; m. Linda Mellucci, June 25, 1966; 1 child, Jennifer Lynn. BS, Fordham U., 1961, JD, 1964. Bar: N.Y. 1965, U.S. Dist. Ct. (so. and ea. dists.) N.Y. 1967, U.S. Tax Ct. 1969, U.S. Ct. Appeals (2d cir.) 1967, U.S. Supreme Ct. 1969. Assoc. various law firms, N.Y.C., 1964-70; corp. counsel Bangor Punta Corp., Greenwich, Conn., 1970-73; from asst. gen. counsel, asst. sec. to v.p., gen. counsel Internat. Rheem Mfg. Co., N.Y.C., 1973—. Dir., officer various corp. subs. and joint ventures. Mem. ABA (subcoms.). Home: 4 Greenlea Ct Westport CT 06883-3016 Office: Rheem Mfg Co 405 Lexington Ave Fl 22D New York NY 10174-0307 Office Phone: 212-916-8100. Business E-Mail: vdebo@rheemny.com.

DEBOCK, RONALD GENE, real estate company executive; b. Buckley, Wash., Sept. 12, 1928; m. Donna J. DeBock, Sept. 24, 1949; children: Beverly J. DeBock Satter, Gary, Janice. BA, N.W. Coll., Kirkland, Wash., 1953; MDiv., Western Evangelical Sem., Portland, Oreg., 1960; AA, Tacoma (Wash.) C.C., 1979; PhD, Calif. Grad. Sch. Theology, Glendale, 1979. Ordained minister Assemblies of God Ch., 1953-96. Commd. ensign USNR, 1957, advanced through grades to lt. comdr., 1971, chaplain, 1958-71; founder, owner Rainier Rentals (now Rainier Rentals & Sales), Puyallup, Wash., 1975—, Fireball Publs., Puyallup, 1993—. Instr. Am. sign lang. Cmty. Ednl. Opportunity, Orting, Wash., 1995-96. Author: Practice What You Preached, 1993. Active Aloha Hotel Chapels Ministry, Honolulu, 1988-96; bd. dirs. Romanian Renewal Internat., 1993-96, v.p., 1995-96; del. Pierce County Rep. Conv.; charter mem. Rep. Presdl. Task Force. Decorated Vietnam Cross of Gallantry with palm; recipient Delta Epsilon Chi award, 1975, Paul Harris award Rotary, 1992. Mem. Wash. Assn Realtors, Inc., Puyallup C. of C., Mil. Chaplains Assn. USA, VFW, DAV. Avocations: deep sea fishing, oriental languages, Scrabble. Office Phone: 253-848-5856. Personal E-mail: rainierron@aol.com.

DE BODO, RICHARD, lawyer; b. NYC, July 19, 1956; s. Richard Charles de Bodo and Kathryn Frances Prescott. BA, Harvard U., 1978; JD, Harvard Law Sch., 1983. Bar: Pa. 1986, Calif. 1987, Cent. Dist. Calif. 1987, No. Dist. Calif. 1987, Ninth Circuit Ct. Appeals 1988, Fed. Ct. Appeals 1989, US Supreme Ct. 1995, SD Calif. 1996, ED Calif. 1996. Law clk. to Honorable James M. Fitzgerald, US Dist. Ct., Anchorage, 1983—84, to Honorable Betty B. Fletcher, Ninth Ct. Appeals, Seattle, 1984—85; staff atty. Ninth Circuit Ct. Appeals, Anchorage, 1985—86; with Irell & Manella LLP, LA, 1986—, ptnr., 1992—. Instr. Nat. Inst. Trial Advocacy, LA, San Francisco, San Diego, 1988—, Hastings Coll. Advocacy Program, San Francisco, 1988—92, Loyola Law Sch. CLE Program, LA, 1990—92. Co-author: (films) Deposition Tactics and Strategy, 1996. Mem.: Fed. Circuit Bar Assn., Am. Intellectual Property Law Assn., ABA Lit. and Intellectual Property Sections. Office: Irell & Manella LLP 1800 Ave Stars Ste 900 Los Angeles CA 90067

DEBOER, ANNABEL, English language educator; b. Toledo, Feb. 7, 1948; d. Stanley Arthur and Shirley Mae (Ackerman) Dolgin; m. Bruce Anthony DeBoer, Aug. 22, 1970; children: Allison Beth DeBoer, Tiffiny Lynn DeBoer. BA, U. Mich., 1970; MA, U. Toledo, 1973, specialist cert., 1976. Summer sch. tchr. Toledo Pub. Schs., 1969-70; tchr. Mt. Clemens (Mich.) Pub. Schs., 1970-71, Bedford Pub. Schs., Temperance, Mich., 1971-96. Lang. arts chairperson, Bedford Pub. Schs., 1976-83, 93-96; dir. Young Authors Conf., U. Toledo, 1974-84. Mem. Toledo Jr. League, Kappa Delta Pi. Avocations: skiing, golf, exercising. Home: 6839 Ridgewood Trail Toledo OH 43617-1181 Office: Bedford Pub Schs 8405 Jackman Rd Temperance MI 48182-9459

DEBOER, JAMES N., lawyer; b. Grand Rapids, Mich. married; 2 children. MBA, Mich. Bus. Sch., 1950; JD, U. Mich. Law Sch., 1950. Assoc. atty. Varnum Riddering Schmidt & Howlett, 1950—. Trustee Davenport U.; former dir. Metropolitan Hospital, Mich., Metropolitan Health Corp., Mich. Served in USN, 1943—45. Named one of Best Lawyers in Am., 1993—. Office: Varnum Riddering Schmidt & Howlett 333 Bridge St NW PO Box 352 Grand Rapids MI 49501-0352

DEBOER, MICHELLE DIANE, secondary school educator, artist; d. Virgil Wayne and Sandra Sue DeBoer. BA, Ea. Ill. U., 1986; MSc, Ill. State U., 2002. Tchr. art Schaumburg (Ill.) H.S., 1986—87, athletic tnr., 1986—87; tchr. art Morton (Ill.) H.S., Ill., 1987—, athletic tnr., 1987—. Bd. dir. Ill. State U., Normal, Ill. Mem.: Internat. Athletic Trainers Assn. (chmn. 2000—), Nat. Art Educators Assn., Nat. Athletic Trainer Assn. (presenter 2003, cert.). Avocation: softball. Office: Morton Unit School Dist 709 350 N Illinois Morton IL 61550

DE BOER, PIETER CORNELIS TOBIAS, mechanical and aerospace engineering educator; b. Leiden, Netherlands, May 21, 1930; s. Pieter and Willemina (Zuydam) deB.; m. Joan Lieshout, June 7, 1956; children: Maarten P., Claire E., Yvette E. MechE degree, Delft U. Tech., 1955; PhD in Physics, U. Md., 1962. Rsch. asst., assoc. Tech. U. Delft, 1954-55; rsch. assoc. U. Md., 1957-62, rsch. asst. prof., 1962-64; asst. prof. Cornell U., 1964-68, assoc. prof., 1968-74; prof. Sibley Sch. Mech. and Aerospace Engring., Cornell U., 1974—2000, assoc. dir., 1982-91; prof. Sibley Sch. Mech. and Aerospace Engring., Cornell U. Grad. Sch., Ithaca, NY, 2000—. Tech. staff Aerospace Corp., 1963, 65, 67, 95, 97, 99, Ford Motor Co., 1971-73, gas turbine div. GE Co., 1978-78, Commissariat Atomic Energy, Grenoble, France, 2000-01; vis. prof. von Karman Inst. for Fluid Dynamics, Belgium, 1968, Cornell Aero. Lab., Buffalo, 1969, Tech. U. Delft, 1985-86; tech. staff; cons. Conelec, Elmira, N.Y., Allied Chem., Inc., Mt. Clemens, Mich., Inst. for Def. Analyses, Arlington, Va., others. Am. editor Applied Sci. Rsch., 1987-98; contbr. articles to profl. jours. With Dutch Army, 1955-57. NATO fellow, 1968. Fellow AIAA (assoc.); mem. ASME, AAUP, Am. Phys. Soc., Am. Soc. Engring. Edn., Royal Inst. Engrs. (The Netherlands), Royal Netherlands Acad. Scis. (corr.), Golden Key, Finger Lakes Cycling Club, Finger Lakes Runners Club, Cayuga Nordic Ski Club, Sigma Xi, Pi Tau Sigma, Sigma Pi Sigma. Office: Cornell U Sibley Sch Mech Aerospace Upson Hall Ithaca NY 14853 Office Phone: 607-255-3583. Business E-Mail: ptdl@cornell.edu.

DE BOER, SIDNEY B., auto dealership executive; Student, Stanford U., U. Oregon. Chmn., CEO Lithia Motors Inc., Medford, Oreg., 1968—. Office: Lithia Motors Inc 360 E Jackson St Medford OR 97501

DEBOER, STEPHEN W., dietician; b. Sioux Falls, SD, Dec. 1, 1954; s. Wendell J. and Marjorie J. DeBoer; m. Gail L. Tischer, Apr. 20, 1991; children: Nathaniel S., Rebecca G. BS, U. Minn., 1978; MPH, U. NC Chapel Hill, 1986. Registered dietician, lic. Nutritionist Migrant Health, Owatonna, Minn., 1981—82; coord. Todd County Pub. Health Dept., Long Prairie, Minn., 1981—82; regional nutritionist SD Dept. health, Mitchell, 1982—84; state nutritionist SD Dept. Health, Pierre, SD, 1986—87; clin. dietician Mayo Clin., Rochester, Minn., 1987—. Nutrition intervention coord. Cardio Vision 2020, Rochester, Minn., 1999—2000. Contbr. articles various profl. jours., chapters to books diet manuals. Deacon Trinity Presbyn. Ch., Rochester, Minn., 1996—, treas., 1997—. Recipient Gamma Sigma Delta award, Agr. Honor Soc., 1976, Joseph Walsh award, Am. Pub. Health Assn., 1985, Delta Omega award, Pub. Health Honor Soc., 1986. Mem.: Rochester Dietetic Assn. (pres.), Minn. Dietetic Assn. (exec. com. 1991—92, Medallion award 2001), Am. Dietetic Assn. Avocations: music, genealogy, long distance running. Office: Mayo Clinic W 18 Nutrition 200 1st St SW Rochester MN 55905 E-mail: deboer.stephen@mayo.edu.

DEBOER-LANGWORTHY, CAROL L., writer, educator; b. Britton, SD, Mar. 18, 1942; d. Harold Theodore DeBoer and Myrtle May Ehnert; m. Anthony A. Rolloff (div.); 1 child, Sylvia Alexi Rolloff; m. Russell L. Langworthy, Dec. 19, 1981. BA, Macalester Coll., 1964; MA, U. Denver, 1980; PhD, Union Inst., 1996. Reporter St. Paul Dispatch & Pioneer Press, 1965—69; grants coord. Macalester Coll., St. Paul, 1976—79; dir. pub. info. Coll. St. Catherine, St. Paul, 1979—81, dir. corp. and fedn. rels., 1985—94; dir. women writers project Brown U., Providence, 1994—98, vis. lectr. English, 1997—. Editor: The Modern World of Neith Boycee: Autobiography and Diaries, 2003. Sr. Fulbright lectr., Ankara, Turkey, 2003—04. Mem.: Authors Guild. Office: Brown U Dept English 70 Brown St Providence RI 02912 E-mail: cdbl@brown.edu.

DE BOLD, ADOLFO J., pathologist, educator, physiologist, researcher; b. Paraná, Argentina, Feb. 14, 1942; arrived in Can., 1968; s. Adolfo E.G. and Ana (Patriarca) deB.; m. Mercedes L. Kuroski; children: Adolfo A., Alejandro J., Cecilia I., Gustavo A., Pablo G. B.Sc. (hon.), Faculty Chem. Sci., Cordoba, Argentina, 1968; M.Sc. in Pathology, Queen's U., Kingston, Ont., 1971, PhD in Pathology, 1973. Cert. clin. chemist. Demonstrator in physics Nat. U. Cordoba, 1961-62, demonstrator normal and path. histology, 1964-67; resident, chief resident Nat. Hosp., Clinicas, Cordoba, 1966-68; asst. prof., lab. scientist Queen's U. and Hotel-Dieu Hosp., Kingston, 1974-82, assoc. prof., 1982-85, prof., 1985-86; prof. pathology and physiology U. Ottawa, Ont., Can., 1986—. Bd. dirs. research U. Ottawa Heart Inst. at Ottawa Civic Hosp., 1986—. Discovered Atrial Natriuretic Hormone, 1981, patented, 1986; contbr. over 100 sci. articles and chpts. to books in field. Bd. dirs. Heart Inst., Ottawa, 1986-93. Decorated officer Order of Can.; recipient Queen Elizabeth II Golden Jubilee medal, Gairdner Internat. award Gairdner Found., Toronto, 1986, Manning Prin. award Manning Found., Alta., Can., 1986, Sci. Achievement award Am. Soc. Hypertension, 1986, rsch. achievement award Can. Cardiovasc. Soc., 1986, CIBA award Am. Heart Assn., 1994; Disting. Rsch. Prof. award Ont. Heart and Stroke Found. Fellow Royal Soc. Can.(McLaughin medal of excellence in rsch. 1988), Royal Coll. Physicians and Surgeons (Can.), AAAS; mem. Can. Hypertension Soc., Am. Soc. for Hypertension, Internat. Soc. Hypertension (Rsch. Achievement award), Internat. Soc. Heart Rsch., Am. Sect. Can. Fedn. Biol. Socs., Histochem. Soc., U.S. Acad. Pathology, Can. Acad. Pathology, Am. Soc. Cell Biology, Can. Soc. Cell Biology, Internat. Acad. Pathology, Am. Assn. Pathology, Fedn. Am. Soc. Exptl. Biology, Microscopial Soc. Can., Soc. Exptl. Biology and Medicine, Can. Soc. Anatomy, N.Y. Acad. Sci. Roman Catholic. Avocation: classical guitar. Office: U Ottawa Heart Inst 40 Ruskin St Ottawa ON Canada K1Y 4W7 Office Phone: 613-761-4265. E-mail: adebold@ottawaheart.ca.

DEBOLD, JOSEPH FRANCIS, psychologist, educator; b. Boston, Nov. 3, 1947; s. Joseph Francis and Patricia (Miltimore) DeB.; m. Carol Lynn Hook, Dec. 20, 1969. AB, UCLA, 1969; PhD, U. Calif., Irvine, 1976. Trainee U. Calif. NICHD Devel. & Reproductive Biology, Irvine, 1971-75; instr., rsch. assoc. Mich. State U., East Lansing, 1975-77; asst. prof. Carnegie-Mellon U., Pitts., 1977-79, Tufts U., Medford, Mass., 1979-83, assoc. prof., 1983-91, chmn. dept. psychology, 1990-93, prof., 1991—, chmn. dept. psychology, 2002—; vis. rsch. assoc. Children's Hosp. Med. Ctr., Boston, 1981-85. Advisor NSF, Washington, 1989-92. Mem. editl. bd. Hormones and Behavior, 1987-92; contbr. articles to profl. jours., chpts. to books. Grantee NSF, 1986-99, Nat. Inst. Alcoholism and Alcohol Abuse, 1980-2002, 03—, Biomed. Rsch. Support Program, 1990-91. Mem. AAAS, Soc. for Neurosci., Nat. Assn. Advisors for Health Professions, N.Y. Acad. Scis., Rsch. Soc. on Alcholism, Sigma Xi, Psi Chi. Avocations: motorcycling, tennis, volleyball. Office: Tufts U Dept Psychology 490 Boston Ave Medford MA 02155 Office Phone: 617-627-5901.

DEBOLD, RICHARD CHARLES, writer; b. N.Y.C., July 20, 1927; s. William John and Emma Anna DeBold; m. Marjorie Warren Warren, Sept. 27, 1957; 1 child, William John. PhD, U. Calif., 1963. Prof. emeritus LI U., Bklyn., 1968—; pub. Higganum Hill Books, Higganum, Conn., 1995—. Author: (novels) The Banana Shooter, (essays) Winter. Trustee The Hartford Art Sch., West Hartford, Conn., 1966—2004. Lt. s.g. USN, 1950—53. James Rowland Angel Rsch. fellow, Yale U., 1957—58. Mem.: Acad. Am. Poets (assoc.). Roman Catholic. Avocation: sailing. Home: 372 Saybrook Rd Higganum CT 06441 Office: Higganum Hill Books PO Box 666 Higganum CT 06441 Office Phone: 860-345-4103.

DEBOLT, PAUL A., lawyer; b. Lorain, Ohio, Sept. 16, 1963; BA, John Carroll U., 1986; JD, Ohio State U., 1989. Bar: Ohio 1989, DC 1997, US Ct. of Military Appeals. Former assoc. Venable LLP, Washington, ptnr., govt. contracts, 2000—. Capt. U.S. Army, 1990—95. Mem.: ABA (mem. public contract law section), Nat. Contract Mgmt. Assn., Bd. of Contract Appeals Bar Assn. Office: Venable LLP 575 7th St NW Washington DC 20004 Office Phone: 202-344-8384. Office Fax: 202-344-8300. Business E-Mail: padebolt@venable.com.

DEBONNEL, CHRISTOPHE, research scientist; s. Henri and Marie-Thérèse Debonnel. MS, U. Calif., Berkeley, 2001. Rschr. assoc. Lawrence Berkeley Nat. Lab., 2001—; lectr. U. Calif., Berkeley, 2005—. Contbr. articles to profl. jours. Mem.: Am. Nuc. Soc. Office: Univ California 4118 Etcheverry Hall Berkeley CA 94720-1730 Office Phone: 510-642-0421. Office Fax: 510-643-9685. Personal E-mail: debonnel@nuc.berkeley.edu.

DE BOOR, CARL-WILHELM R., mathematician; b. Stolp, Germany, Dec. 3, 1937; m. Matilda C. Friedrich, Feb. 6, 1960 (div. Sept. 12, 1984); children: C. Thomas, Elisabeth, Peter, Adam; m. Helen L. Bee, Jan. 2, 1991. Student, Universitaet Hamburg, 1956-59, Harvard U., 1959-60; PhD, U. Mich., 1966; dr. honoris causa in Sci. (hon.), Purdue U., 1993, Technion, 2002. Rsch. mathematician Gen. Motors Research Labs., 1960-64; asst. prof. math., computer sci. Purdue U., 1966-68, assoc. prof., 1968-72; prof. math., computer sci. U. Wis.-Madison, 1972—2003, prof. emeritus, 2003—. Vis. staff mem. Los Alamos Sci. Labs., 1970-95, affiliated prof. U. Wash., 2004-. Author: (with S. Conte) Elementary Numerical Analysis, 1972, 1980, A Practical Guide to Splines, 1978, 2001, (with J.B. Rosser) Pocket Calculator Supplement for Calculus, 1979, Spline Toolbox for Matlab, 1990, (with K. Höllig and S. Riemenschneider) Box Splines, 1993. Named John Von Neumann lectr. Soc. Indsl. and Applied Math., 1996, 2003, recipient Nat. medal of Sci., 2005. Fellow Am. Acad. Arts and Scis.; mem. Nat. Acad. Engring., NAS, Soc. Indsl. and Applied Math., Polish Acad. Sci., Leopoldina, Phi Beta Kappa. Office: PO Box 1076 Eastsound WA 98245

DE BORCHGRAVE, ARNAUD, editor, writer, lecturer; b. Brussels, Oct. 26, 1926; s. Count Baudouin and Audrey (Townshend) de B.; m. Dorothy Solon, Apr. 1950; 1 child, Arnaud; m. Eileen Ritschel, Mar. 31, 1959; 1 child, Trisha; m. Alexandra D. Villard, May 10, 1969. Student, Maredsous, Belgium, 1936-39, King's Sch., Canterbury, Eng., 1940-42. Free-lance writer, Eastern Europe, 1946-47; staff United Press, Western Europe, 1947-51; mgr. Benelux Countries, 1949-51; European Corr. Newsweek, Paris, North Africa, Middle East, Indo-China, 1951-54, fgn. editor, sr. editor, 1955-59, chief fgn. corr., 1959-62, mng. editor internat. edits., 1962-63, chief Newsweek Corr.,

1964-80; columnist, TV host; sr. assoc. Ctr. for Strategic and Internat. Studies, 1981-85; editor in chief The Washington Times and Insight Mag., 1985-91; dir. Transnat. Threats Initiative, sr. advisor Ctr. for Strategic and Internat. Studies, Washington, 1991—; pres., CEO, UPI, Washington, 1999-2001. Editor-at-large, Washington Times and UPI, 2001—. Served with Brit. Royal Navy, 1942-46. Decorated commandeur de l'Ordre de Leopold II, Medaille Maritime Belge; recipient Medal of Honor Def. Council, 1980, Medal of Honor World Bus. Council, 1981, Washington Dateline award Soc. Profl. Journalists, also numerous awards for fgn. reporting. Mem. Am. Soc. Newspaper Editors, Internat. Press Inst., Inter-Am. Press Assn., Coun. on Fgn. Rels., Racquet and Tennis Club, Met. Club, Econ. Club of Washington, Nat. Press Club. Home: 2801 New Mexico Ave NW Washington DC 20007-3921 Office: Ctr for Strategic and Internat Studies 1800 K St NW Washington DC 20006-2202 Office Phone: 202-775-3282. Business E-Mail: adeborchgrave@csis.org.

DE BOTH, TANYA, statistician; b. Green Bay, Wis., Nov. 27, 1972; d. Richard L. and Louise A. De Both. BA in Psychology, U. Wis., 1996; student, Frostburg (Md.) State U., 1996—97; MSc in Exptl. Psychology, U. Wis., 2000. Outcomes specialist Family Svcs., Green Bay, Wis., 2000—01; data rsch. analyst Agnesian Health Care, Fond du Lac, Wis., 2001—. Contbr. articles to profl. jours. Mem.: APA, Am. Civil Liberties Union, Am Assn. U. Women, Nat. Org. Women, Nat. Assn. Female Exec., Planned Parenthood Fedn. Am., Exec. Women's Golf Assn., Phi Kappa Phi. Avocations: walking, volleyball, golf, camping, bicycling.

DEBOW, JAY HOWARD CAMDEN, public relations executive; b. Flushing, N.Y., Sept. 21, 1932; s. Thomas Howard and Dorothea (Camden) DeB.; m. Audrey Ellison, May 4, 1957 (div. 1985); children: Stacy, Carolyn, Jennifer, Hollis; m. Suzanne Hayat, Nov. 12, 1986. AB, U. Ga., 1955. Reporter Athens (Ga.) Banner Herald, 1954; news writer UPI, N.Y.C., 1955; v.p. pub. rels. Merrill Anderson Co., N.Y.C., 1956—60; founder, pres. Jay DeBow & Ptnrs., Inc., N.Y.C., 1960—89; pres. Jay DeBow & Ptnrs. Omnicom Pub. Rels. Network, N.Y.C., 1990—92; founder, mng. prin. The Energy Team, 1993—; mng. ptnr. DeBow Mellow Palmer Group, LLC. Chair Jay DeBow & Ptnrs., Inc., 1992—; chmn. bd. advisors Salvation Army Manhattan. Recipient Ad Week Nat. Mktg. Program award, 1990, Cipra award Inside PR Mag., 1991. Mem. Nat. Investor Rels. Inst. (former chmn. govt. affairs com., ethics com., mem. steering com., sr. Investor Rels. Roundtable), Pub. Rels. Soc. Am. (Silver Anvil award 1991), Internat. Inst. Comms., Counselors Acad., Internat. Pub. Rels. Assn., N.Y. Soc. Security Analysts, Assn. Investment Mgrs., Soc. Profl. Journalists, Nat. Press Club (Washington), Met. Club (N.Y.C.; bd. govs., chmn., mem. com.). Home: 530 Park Ave Apt 6J New York NY 10021-8015 Office Phone: 212-906-9192. E-mail: jay@jaydebow.com.

DEBOW, THOMAS JOSEPH, JR., advertising executive; b. N.Y.C., May 18, 1936; s. Thomas Joseph DeBow and Evelyn Francis (Brooks) Menck; m. Rosalinda Angelini, Sept. 9, 1961; children: Yvette, Thomas J III, Walter Brooks. V.p. McCann Ericson, N.Y.C., 1965—69; dir. Young and Rubicam, N.Y.C., 1969—71; pres. Curry DeBow, N.Y.C., 1971—74; v.p. BBDO, N.Y.C., 1974—76; pres. DeBow Comm. Ltd., N.Y.C., 1976—95, chmn., 1995—; mng. ptnr. Global Card Mktg., LLC, 2001—. Mem. Cystic Fibrosis Found., dir., 1988—; vice chmn. Len Cariou Entreprolebrity Golf Tournament, 1990; vice chmn. children's legacy com. Franciscan Sisters of the Poor Found., 1996—. Mem.: Progresive Era Assn., Friar's Sunshine Com. (chmn. 1987—, Friar of Yr. 1990), N.Y. Athletic Club, Knollwood Country Club. Home: 55 E 86th St New York NY 10028-1059 Office: DeBow Comm Ltd 850 7th Ave Ste 605 New York NY 10019-5230 E-mail: Tom@DeBow.com.

DEBRECZENY, PAUL, Slavic language educator, writer; b. Budapest, Hungary, Feb. 16, 1932; came to U.S., 1960; s. Zsigmond and Margit Ibolya (Csanady) D.; m. Gillian Marjorie Butterworth, Oct. 30, 1959; children: Louise, Martin. BA in Russian Studies, Eotvos U., Budapest, 1953, BA in Hungarian Studies, 1955; PhD in Russian Lit., U. London, 1960. Research assoc. Inst. Lit. Studies, Hungarian Acad. Scis., Budapest, 1955-56; trans. editor Pergamon Press, Oxford, Eng., 1959-60; from asst. to assoc. prof., dept. chmn. Tulane U., New Orleans, 1960-67; assoc. prof. U. N.C., Chapel Hill, 1967-74, prof., chmn., 1974-79, prof. Slavic langs., 1979-83, Alumni disting. prof. Russian and comparative lit., 1983-99, prof. emeritus, 1999—, chmn. humanities divsn., 1984-86; dir. Ctr. for Slavic, Eurasian and East European Studies U. N.C.-Duke U., Chapel Hill, 1991-94. Author: Nickolay Gogol and His Contemporary Critics, 1966, Temptations of the Past, 1982, The Other Pushkin, 1983, 2d rev. edit. in Russian, 1996, Social Functions of Literature: Alexander Pushkin and Russian Culture, 1997; translator: The Captain's Daughter and Other Stories by Alexander Pushkin, 1992; translator, editor: Literature and National Identity, 1970, Alexander Pushkin's Complete Prose Fiction, 1983; editor: Chekhov's Art of Writing: A Collection of Critical Essays, 1977, American Contributions to the Ninth International Congress of Slavists, Vol. 2: Literature, 1983; editor: Russian Visual and Narrative Art: Varieties of Seeing, 1994; mng. editor: The Pushkin Journal, 1993-96, the Pushkin rev., 1997-98. Awarded Golden Key City of New Orleans, 1967; prize for outstanding graduating sr. in his name to be given yearly at U. N.C., Chapel Hill, N.C., 2000—, disting. prof. award in his name to be given as vacancy occurs by U. N.C. Coll. Arts and Scis., 2004—. Mem. AAUP, MLA, Am. Assn. Tchrs. Slavic and East European Langs. (v.p. 1978-79), Am. Assn. for Advancement of Slavic Studies, So. Conf. on Slavic Studies (v.p. 1979, pres. 1980, Sr. Scholar award 1987), N.Am. Pushkin Soc. (pres. 1993). Democrat. Home: 304 Hoot Owl Ln Chapel Hill NC 27514-2743 Office: U NC Dept Slavic Langs Chapel Hill NC 27599-3165 Business E-Mail: pdebrecz@email.unc.edu.

DE BREMAECKER, JEAN-CLAUDE, geophysics educator; b. Antwerp, Belgium, Sept. 2, 1923; came to U.S., 1948, naturalized, 1963; s. Paul J.C. and Berthe (Bouché) De B.; m. Arlene Ann Parker, Nov. 29, 1952, (dec.); m. Ruth F. Baer, July 6, 1998; children— Christine, Suzanne. MS in Mining Engring, U. Louvain, Belgium, 1948; MS in Geology, La. State U., 1950; PhD in Geophysics, U. Cal. at Berkeley, 1952. Research scientist, sr. research scientist Inst. pour la Recherche Sci. en Afrique Centrale, Bukavu, Congo, 1952-58; Boese postdoctoral fellow Columbia, 1955-56; postdoctoral fellow Harvard, 1958-59; faculty Rice U., Houston, 1959—, prof. geophysics, 1965-94, prof. emeritus, 1994. Research asso. U. Calif., Berkeley, 1966; vis. mem. Tex. Inst. for Computational Mechanics, U. Tex., Austin, 1977; vis. prof. U. Paris, 1980-81 Author: Geophysics, the Earth's Interior, 1985. Chmn. Citizens for McCarthy, Houston, 1968. Served with Belgian Army, 1944-45. Mem. AAUP, Am. Geophys. Union, Fedn. Am. Scientists, Internat. Assn. Seismology and Physics of Earth's Interior (assoc. sec. gen. 1963-71, sec. gen. 1971-79). Home: 3115 Broadmead Dr Houston TX 77025-3819 Office: Rice U Dept Earth Sci Box 1892 Houston TX 77251 Office Phone: 713-348-4886. Business E-Mail: deb@rice.edu.

DE BRIER, DONALD PAUL, lawyer; b. Atlantic City, Mar. 20, 1940; s. Daniel and Ethel de B.; m. Nancy Lee McElroy, Aug. 1, 1964; children: Lesley Anne, Rachel Wynne, Danielle Verne. BA in History, Princeton U., 1962; LLB with honors, U. Pa., 1967. Bar: N.Y. 1967, Tex. 1977, Utah 1983, Ohio 1987. Assoc. firm Sullivan & Cromwell, N.Y.C., 1967-70, Patterson, Belknap, Webb & Tyler, N.Y.C., 1970-76; v.p., gen. counsel, dir. Gulf Resources & Chem. Corp., Houston, 1976-82; v.p. law Kennecott Corp. (former subs. BP America Inc.), Salt Lake City, 1983-89; assoc. gen. counsel BP America Inc., Cleve., 1987-89; gen. counsel BP Exploration Co. Ltd., London, 1989-93; exec. v.p., gen. counsel Occidental Petroleum Corp., L.A., 1993—. Bd. dirs. L.A. Philharm., 1995—. Lt. USNR, 1962—64. Mem. Calif. Club, Riviera Tennis Club (chmn. adv. bd. govs. 2002-). Home: 699 Amalfi Dr Pacific Palisades CA 90272-4507 Office: Occidental Petroleum Corp 10889 Wilshire Blvd Los Angeles CA 90024-4201

DE BRIGARD, EMILIE, anthropologist, consultant; b. N.Y.C., Dec. 11, 1943; d. A. Lincoln and Ruth Emilie (Jaeger) Rahman; m. Raul de Brigard, June 11, 1966; 1 child, George. BA, Harvard Coll., 1963; MA, U. Calif., 1972. Guest curator dept. of film Mus. of Modern Art, N.Y.C., 1972-73; asst. to dir. human studies film archives Smithsonian Instn., Washington, 1975-77; prin. programmer Margaret Mead Film Festival Am. Mus. Natural History, N.Y.C., 1977-78; faculty Harvard Summer Sch., Cambridge, Mass., 1980-86; pres. Internat. Film Seminars, Inc., N.Y.C., 1981-83; vis. lectr. dept. anthropology Yale U., New Haven, 1989-91; pres. Soc. for Visual Anthropology, Washington, 1995-97, FilmResearch, Higganum, Conn., 1970—. Cons. Choreometrics Project, N.Y.C., 1970-73; mem. Comité Internat. des Films de l'Homme, Paris, 1977-2004. Author: (books) The History of Ethnographic Film, 1971, Anthropological Cinema, 1973, Cine Antropológico, 1978; producer (film) Margaret Mead: A Portrait by a Friend, 1978. Trustee Wadsworth Atheneum, Hartford, Conn., 2000—; corporator Conn. Inst. for the Blind-Oak Hill, Hartford, Conn., 1996—; pres. Friends of the Ixchel Mus., Guatemala, 2005—. Fellow Am. Anthrop. Assn., Royal Anthrop. Inst.; mem. Soc. Woman Geographers, Harvard Alumni Assn. (dir. 2002-2005, Hiram S. Hunn award 2002), Town and County Club, Harvard Club of So. Conn. (v.p. 1995—), Saturday Morning Club (pres. 2003-05). Avocation: costume and textiles. Home: 285 Riverside Dr Apt 7D New York NY 10025-5227 Office: FilmResearch 8 Christian Hill Rd Higganum CT 06441-4030 E-mail: debrigard@att.net.

DEBROUX, DOUGLAS P., secondary school educator; b. Milw., Dec. 20, 1960; s. Victor William and Ruth Ann (Schmit) D.; m. Cheryl L. Debroux, June 16, 1984. BA, U. Wis., Platteville, 1983, MA, 1988. Grad. asst. U. Wis., Platteville; tchr., cross country coach, asst. track coach Oregon (Wis.) High Sch. Named Dist. Boys Coach of Yr., 1987, Dist. and State Boys Coach of Yr., 1988. Mem. Assn. for Supervision and Curriculum Devel., S.W. Wis. Ednl. Insvc. Orgn., Nat. Fedn. Interscholastic Coaches, Wis. Math. Coun., Wis. Edn. Assn. (coun.). Business E-Mail: dpd@oregon.k12.wi.us.

DEBROVNER, MARTIN, real estate company executive; BA, MA, Columbia U. With J. Weingarten, Inc.; with Manned Spacecraft Ctr. NASA, Houston; from mem. staff to pres. WRI, 1968—92, pres., 1992—97; vice chmn. Weingarten Realty Investors, Houston, 1997—. Mem. Internat. Coun. Shopping Ctrs., Urban Land Inst. Mem.: Nat. Assn. Real Estate Investment Trusts. Office: Weingarten Realty Investors PO Box 924133 Houston TX 77292-4133

DEBRUIN SAMPLE, ANNE, human resources specialist; Formerly with Whirlpool Corp., Benton Harbor, Mich.; numerous human resources positions including mgr. human resources Pepsi-Cola N.Am. PepsiAmericas, Inc., Mpls., 1988—2001, sr. v.p. human resources, 2001—. Office: PepsiAmericas 4000 Dain Rauscher Plz 60 S Sixth St Minneapolis MN 55402 Office Phone: 612-661-4000. Office Fax: 612-661-3737.*

DEBS, BARBARA KNOWLES, former college president, consultant; b. Eastham, Mass., Dec. 24, 1931; d. Stanley F. and Arline (Eugley) Knowles; m. Richard A. Debs, July 19, 1958; children: Elizabeth, Nicholas. BA, Vassar Coll., 1953; PhD, Harvard U., 1967; LLD, N.Y. Law Sch., 1979; LHD, Manhattanville Coll., 1985. Freelance translator editor Ency. of World Art divsn. McGraw-Hill Pub., N.Y.C., 1959-62; from asst. prof. to prof. Manhattanville Coll., Purchase, N.Y., 1968-86, pres., 1975-85; trustee, chmn. collections com. N.Y. Hist. Soc., 1985-87, pres., CEO, 1988-92; cons. non-profit orgns. pvt. practice, 1992—. Contbr. articles on Renaissance and contemporary art to profl. publs. Mem. N.Y. Coun. Humanities, 1978-85; mem. Westchester County Bd. Ethics, 1979-84; trustee N.Y. Law Sch., 1979-89; trustee Geraldine R. Dodge Found., 1985—; bd. dirs. Internat. Found. for Art Rsch., 1985-92; trustee Com. Econ. Devel., 1985-94, Bklyn. Mus. Art, 1996—; mem. Coun. Fgn. Rels., 1983—; mem. exec. bd. Bard Ctr. for Decorative Arts, 1995—; bd. govs. Fgn. Policy Assn., 1996-2002; hon. trustee Manhattanville Coll., 1996—, Midori Found., 1998—. AAUW Nat. fellow and Ann Radcliffe fellow, 1958-59; Am. Council Learned Socs. grantee, 1973; Fulbright fellow, Pisa, Italy, 1953, U. Rome, 1954. Mem. Am. Coun. on Edn. (chmn. commn. acad. affairs 1977-79), Young Audiences (nat. dir. 1977-80), Renaissance Soc. Am., Coll. Art Assn., Phi Beta Kappa. Clubs: Cosmopolitan, Century Assn.

DEBS, RICHARD A., investment banker; b. Providence, Oct. 7, 1930; s. Abraham George and Madge (Fatool) D.; m. Barbara Knowles, July 19, 1958; children: Elizabeth Anderson, Nicholas. BA summa cum laude, Colgate U., 1952; postgrad. (Fulbright scholar), Cairo U., 1952-53; MA, Princeton U., 1956, PhD, 1963; LLB, Harvard U., 1958, grad. Advanced Mgmt. Program, 1973. Bar: N.Y. 1960. Researcher joint project Harvard-Princeton, 1958-59; with Fed. Res. Bank of N.Y., N.Y.C., 1960-76, legal dept., 1960-64, asst. counsel, 1964-69, sec. of bank, 1965-69, v.p. govt. bonds and securities, 1969-72, v.p. loans and credits, 1969-72, v.p. open market ops., 1972, sr. v.p., 1973, 1st v.p., chief adminstrv. officer, 1973-76; alt. mem. Fed. Open Market Com., 1973-76; mng. dir. Morgan Stanley & Co., Inc., 1976-87; pres. Morgan Stanley Internat. Inc., 1976-87; chmn. R.A. Debs & Co., 1987—; adv. dir. Morgan Stanley, 1987—; chmn. The Malaysia Fund Inc., 1987—. Bd. dirs. Gulf Internat. Bank, London, Mizuho Corp. Bank, Mizuho Securities Co.; advisor Bank Julius Baer, 1987—, United Gulf Group (Kuwait), 1987—, Dai-Ichi Mut. Life, Tokyo, 1988—, Nissho Iwai Corp., Tokyo, 1990—; chmn. com. fiscal agy. ops. Fed. Res. System, 1969-76; mem. Fed. Res. Steering Com. on Payments Mechanism, 1973-76, Fed. Res. Steering Com. on Internat. Banking, 1973-76; allied mem. N.Y. Stock Exchange, chmn. adv. com. internat. capital markets; com. multinat. enterprises U.S. coun. Internat. Bus.; mem. internat. capital markets adv. com. Fed. Res. Bank of N.Y.; mem. Nat. Commn. on Pub. Svc. (The Volcker Commn.); mem. Overseas Devel. Coun.; mem. U.S. Office Pers. Mgmt. Task Force on Pay Reform; mem. World Bank Adv. Group on Pvt. Sector Devel.; bus. adv. coun. European Bank for Reconstrn. and Devel., Russian-Am. Banking Forum; mem. Carnegie Commn.; mem. Take Stock in Am. Com., 1973-76; mem. Egypt-U.S. Bus. Coun.; mem. adv. coun. Near Eastern program Princeton U.; mem. N.Y. State Savs. Bond Com., 1973-76; adv. coun. Am. Inst. Banking, 1973-76. Contbr. articles to profl. jours. Chmn. emeritus, trustee Carnegie Hall; bd. dirs. Fedn. Protestant Welfare Agys., Inst. Internat. Edn.; trustee Carnegie Endowment for Internat. Peace, Am. Univs. Field Staff; trustee Am. U., Beirut, vice chmn., 1981-94, chmn., 1994—; bd. dirs. Am. Council on Germany; mem. vis. com. Middle East Center Harvard U., 1976-82, mem. vis. com. Ctr. for Internat. Affairs; mem. Group of 30, Reuters Carnegie Global Pub. Policy Group, 1999—; also mem. exec. com. Bretton Woods Com.; U.S. chmn. U.S.-Saudi Arabia Bus. Coun. Recipient Lifetime Achievement award, Fulbright Assn., Fedn. Protestant Welfare Agencies, Third St Music Sch. Settlement, Nat. Acad. Design, King Abdul Aziz medal, Govt. Saudi Arabia. Mem. ABA (com. Middle Eastern law), Assn. Bar City N.Y., Coun. Fgn. Rels., C. of C. U.S. (internat. policy com., chmn. subcom. on internat. econ. devel. 1979-87), Egyptian Am. C. of C. (chmn.), N.Y. C. of C. and Industry, Japan Soc., Asia Soc., Fgn. Policy Assn. (bd. govs.), Econs. Club, Century Assn. (N.Y.C.), Larchmont Yacht (N.Y.), River Club, Phi Beta Kappa Assocs. Office: Morgan Stanley & Co 1221 Ave of Americas New York NY 10020-1001 Business E-Mail: Richard.Debs@morganstanley.com.

DEBUONO, BARBARA ANN, physician, state official; b. N.Y.C., Apr. 13, 1955; d. Richard Francis and Catherine (Brutto) DeB.; m. David Lavington Farren, June 1, 1980; children: Adam, Douglas. BS, U. Rochester, 1976, MD, 1980; MPH, Harvard U., 1984. Diplomate Am. Bd. Internal Medicine, Nat. Bd. Med. Examiners. Intern in internal medicine New Eng. Deaconess Hosp., Boston, 1980-81, jr. med. resident, 1981-82, sr. med. resident, 1982-83; clin. fellow Brown U., Providence, 1984-86, clin. instr. dept. medicine, 1987-90, clin. asst. prof. medicine, 1990; med. epidemiologist R.I. Dept. Health, Providence, 1986, state epidemiologist, med. dir. Office Disease Control, 1986-91; dir. dept. health State of R.I., 1991—95; commr. NY State Dept. Health, Albany, 1995—98; CEO N.Y. Presbyn. Healthcare Network, 1998—2000; exec. v.p. N.Y. Presbyn. Healthcare System, 1998—2000; sr. med. dir. pub. health Pfizer Inc., 2001—; clin. prof. medicine Columbia U. Coll. Physicians and Surgeons. Lectr. in field; adv. com. to dir. Ctrs. for Disease Control; bd. mem. Ctr. Health Policy Devel.; nat. adv. com. Healthy Steps. Contbr. articles to profl. jours. Robert Wood Johnson Found. Ednl. scholar U. Rochester Sch. Med., 1976-80; recipient James L. Tulis Disting. Study Lectureship award New Eng. Deaconess Hosp., 1992; named Women of Yr. by Bus. and Profl. Women's Club Providence, 1989, Person of Yr. by The Women's Youth League R.I., 1990, Woman of Yr. by R.I. Fedn. Bus. and Profl. Women's Clubs, 1991. Fellow Am. Coll. Internat. Physicians, Am. Coll. Physicians; mem. AMA, APHA, Am. Soc. Microbiology, Infectious Disease Soc. Am., Providence Med. Assn., R.I. Med. Soc., R.I. Med. Women's Assn. (R.I. Women Physician of Yr. 1988), R.I. Environ. Health Assn., Hosp. Assn. R.I., Women Execs. in Govt. Avocations: swimming, tennis, gardening.

DE BURLO, COMEGYS RUSSELL, JR., investment company executive, educator, retired treasurer; b. Phila. s. Comegys Russell and Margaret (Whitehurst) de B.; m. Edith Power Thatcher; children: Jane Thatcher, Charles Russell, John Todd. BS, Swarthmore Coll.; MBA, U. Pa.; DBA, Harvard U. Past CFO Tufts U., v.p., prof., treas., hon. treas. V.p. Ednl. Testing Svc., Princeton, N.J.; dir. UST Corp., NIH, Nat. Cancer Inst., Cancer Program Adv. Com., Cancer Rsch. Ctrs. Rev. Com., Am. Coun. on Edn., Com. on Taxation; pres., prin. The de Burlo Group Inc., 1987—. Past adv. com. No. Calif. Cancer Program; past mem. sci. adv. com. U. N.Mex. Cancer Treatment Ctr., Ohio State U. Comprehensive Cancer Ctr., 1983-97; pres. Mass. Assn. Schs. and Colls.; trustee Cambridge Friends Sch., Belmont Hill Sch., Moses Brown Sch., Lincoln Sch., BB&N Sch.; bd. mgrs. New Eng. Yearly Meeting; trustee Obadiah Brown/Sarah Swift Fund; commr. pub. trust funds. With USNR. Fellow Royal Hort. Soc.; mem. Assn. for Investment, Mgmt. and Rsch., Boston Security Analysts Soc., Internat. Assn. for Comparative Rsch. on Leukemia and Related Diseases (treas.), Am. Rhododendron Soc. (asst. treas. Mass. chpt.), Harvard Club, Green Mountain Club, Appalachian Mountain Club, Tau Beta Pi. Office: 50 Federal St Boston MA 02110-2500 Office Phone: 617-482-0275. E-mail: edith@bloomberg.net.

DEBUS, ALLEN GEORGE, historian, educator; b. Chgo., Ill., Aug. 16, 1926; s. George Walter William and Edna Pauline (Schwenneke) D.; m. Brunilda Lopez-Rodriguez, Aug. 25, 1951; children: Allen Anthony George, Richard William, Karl Edward. BS, Northwestern U., 1947; A.M., Ind. U., 1949; PhD, Harvard U., 1961; postgrad., U. Coll. London, 1959-60; D.Sc. h.c., Cath. U. Louvain, 1985. Research chemist Abbott Labs., North Chicago, Ill., 1951-56; asst. prof. U. Chgo., 1961-65, assoc. prof. history, 1965-68, prof., 1968-78, Morris Fishbein prof. history sci. and medicine, 1978-96, Morris Fishbein prof. emeritus, 1996—; dir. Morris Fishbein Ctr. for Study History Sci. and Medicine, 1971-77. Disting. vis. prof. Ariz. ctr. for medieval and renaissance studies Ariz. State U., 1984; vis. prof. Inst. Chemistry, U. São Paulo, Brazil, 1990; mem. internat. adv. com. Tel-Aviv U. The Cohn Inst. History and Philosophy of Sci. and Ideas, Ctr. for History and Philosophy of Sci. of Hebrew U. of Jerusalem; mem. internat. adv. bd. Annali dell'Istituto e Museo di Storia della Scienza di Firenze; cons. lit. and sci. curriculum Ga. Inst. Tech. Author: The English Paracelsians, 1965, 66, (with Robert P. Multhauf) Alchemy and Chemistry in the 17th Century, 1966, The Chemical Dream of the Renaissance, 1968, 2d edit., 1972, Science and Education in the 17th Century, 1970, (with Brian Rust) The Complete Entertainment Discography, 1973, 2d rev. edit., 1989, The Chemical Philosophy, 2 vols., 1977, 2d edit., 2002, Japanese transl., 1999, Man and Nature in the Renaissance, 1978, 15th rev. edit., 1995, Italian transl., 1982, Spanish transl., 1985, 86, 2d edit., 1995, Japanese transl., 1986, Chinese transl., 1988, 2000, Greek transl., 1997, Portuguese trans., 2002, Robert Fludd and His Philosophical Key, 1979; Science and History: A Chemist's Appraisal, 1984, Chinese transl., 1999, Chemistry, Alchemy and the New Philosophy, 1550-1700, 1987, The French Paracelsians: The Chemical Challenge to Medical and Scientific Tradition in Early Modern France, 1991, 2002, Paracelso e la Tradizione Paracelsiana, 1996, Chemistry and Medical Debate: Van Helmont to Boerhaave, 2001; editor: World Who's Who in Science from Antiquity to the Present, 1968, Science, Medicine and Society in the Renaissance, 2 vols, 1972, Medicine in Seventeenth-Century England, 1974; editor reprint: Theatrum Chemicum Britannicum (1652), 1967, John Dee's Mathematicall Praeface (1570), 1975; editor: (with Ingrid Merkel) Hermeticism and the Renaissance: Intellectual History and the Occult in Early Modern Europe, 1988, (with Michael T. Walton) Reading the Book of Nature: The Other Side of the Scientific Revolution, 1998, Alchemy and Early Modern Chemistry: Papers from Ambix, 2004; essayist: Festschrift: Experiencing Nature: Essays for Allen G. Debus (edited by Paul Theerman and Karen Parshall, 1997); mem. bd. adv. editors Physis Rivista internazionale de storia della scienza, Nuncius, The 16th Century Jour.; adv. editor: History of Science; hon. bd. editors Incognita; programmed 3 records released by Smithsonian Instn. Music of Victor Herbert, 1979; notes to CD releases by Archeophone-Bert Williams, Nora Bayes and Jack Norworth, 2003-04; contbr. articles to profl. jours.; patentee in field. Social Sci. Rsch. Coun. fellow, 1959-60; Fulbright fellow, 1959-60; Fels Found. fellow, 1960-61; Guggenheim fellow, 1966-67; overseas fellow Churchill Coll. Cambridge (Eng.) U., 1966-67, 69; mem. Inst. Advanced Study Princeton, N.J., 1972-73; NEH fellow Newberry Libr., Chgo., 1975-76; fellow Inst. for Rsch. in Humanities U. Wis., Madison, 1981-82, NEH, 1987, Folger Shakespeare Libr., Washington; rsch. grantee Am. Philos. Soc., 1961-62, Wellcome Trust, 1962, NIH, 1962-70, 74-75, 77-78, 92-97, NSF, 1961-63, 71-74, 80-83, Am. Coun. Learned Socs., 1966, 70, 71. Fellow AAAS (mem. electorate nominating com., sect. L 1974-77, chmn. com. 1974); mem. History of Sci. Soc. (council 1962-65, 87-90, program chmn. 1972, Pfizer award 1978, Sarton medal 1994, Disting. lectr. 1996), Soc. Study Alchemy and Early Chemistry (mem. council 1967—), Am. Assn. for History Medicine (program com. 1975), Brit. Soc. for History Sci., Internationale Paracelsus Gesellschaft, Am. Chem. Soc. (assn. mem. history of chemistry div., exec. com. 1969-72, Dexter award 1987), Soc. Med. History of Chgo. (sec.-treas. 1971-72, v.p. 1972-74, pres. 1974-76, mem. council), Académie Internat. d'Histoire de la Medecine, Société Internationale d'Histoire de la Medecine, Academie Internat. d'Histoire des Scis. (corr. 1971, membre effectif 1991), Am. Inst. History of Pharmacy (Edward Kremers award 1978, adv. panel hist. activity 1979-81, awards com. 1981—), Am. Soc. Reformation Research, Assn. Recorded Sound Collections., Midwest Junto for History of Sci. (pres. 1983-84), Academia das Ciencias de Lisboa. Office: U Chgo Dept History Chicago IL 60637 Personal E-mail: adebus@midway.uchicago.edu.

DEBUSK, CHARLES RICHARD, engineer, consultant; s. Charles Malcolm and Margaret DeBusk; m. Mary Elizabeth Roberts, Sept. 5, 1981; stepchildren: Amy Henderson, James Roberts 1 child, Margaret Amelia Monroe. B.S. in Indsl. Engring., Va. Poly. Inst. & State U., 1974—79; M.S. in Indsl. Engring., U. Tenn., 1981—87. Professional Engineer, Tenn., 1984; Certified Six Sigma Master Black Belt GE, 2001. Master black belt/sr. cons. GE Healthcare, Milwaukee, 1991—; sr. mgr. RSM McGladrey, Minneapolis, 1985—91; corp. dir. of cost acctg. The Health Ctrl. Sys., Minneapolis, 1985—86; mgmt. systems cons. HCA, Nashville, 1983—85. Instr. St. Mary's U. of Minn., Minneapolis, Minn., 1986—92. Mem.: Inst. of Indsl. Engring., Am. Soc. for Quality, Alpha Pi Mu. Office: GE Healthcare PO Box 43280 Brooklyn Park MN 55443 Office Phone: 763-561-9230. E-mail: charles.debusk@med.ge.com.

DEBUSK, MANUEL CONRAD, lawyer; b. Grosvenor, Tex., June 13, 1914; s. Elias C. and Ollie (Lewis) DeB. BA, Tex. Technol. Coll., 1933; LL.B., So. Meth. U., 1941. Bar: Tex. 1942. Adminstrv. asst. FHA, Washington, Dallas, 1934-41; spl. agt. FBI, 1941-46; partner DeBusk & DeBusk, Dallas, 1946—. Mem., chmn. coordinating bd. Tex. Colls. and Univs., 1969-70; Chmn. Dallas County Dem. Party, 1967-71; bd. dirs., chmn. bd. regents Tex. Technol. Coll., 1959-65; pres. DeBusk Found., Assn. Small Founds.; mem. Coun. on Founds. Mem. Tex. Bar Assn., Tex., Nat. mortgage bankers assns., Nat. Lefthanded Golf Assn. (past pres.), Cosmopolitan Internat. (past internat. pres.) Home: 7365 Elmridge Dr Dallas TX 75240-3623 Office: 2089 N Collins Blvd Richardson TX 75080-2664 *One's yardstick, whether business or avocation, must be to leave the world a better place that it was before you touched it.*

DECAIRE, JOHN, electronics executive, aerospace engineer; BS in Applied Physics, Mich. Tech. U., 1962; MS in Engring. Space Physics, PhD in Aerospace Engring., Air Force Inst. Tech.; grad. mgt. devel. program, Harvard U. Bus. Sch. Commd. 2d. lt. USAF, 1962, resigned, 1975; mgr. electronic mfg. Wright-Patterson AFB, Dayton, Ohio, 1975-78; program mgr. Bedford engring. labs. Raytheon Co., 1979-80; founder, mgr. Westinghouse

Mfg. Systems and Tech. Ctr., Balt., Md., 1980-84; gen. mgr. design and producibility engring. divsn. Westinghoue Electonics Systems Group, Balt., 1985-88, exec. dir. systems and tech., 1989-91; prin. John Decaire and Assocs., Cons., 1991-93; pres. Nat. Ctr. for Mfg. Scis., Ann Arbor, Mich., 1993—. Bd. dirs. NACFAM and CIMS. Mem. adv. bd. Mich. Tech. U. Coll. Engring., U. Md. MIPS, U. Mich. Tauber Mfg. Inst. Office: Nat Ctr for Mfg Sciences 3025 Boardwalk St Ann Arbor MI 48108-3230

DECAMINADA, JOSEPH PIO, retired insurance company executive; b. Gebo, Wyo., Oct. 17, 1935; s. Pio and Ida (Franch) Decaminada; m. Genevieve Caputo, Aug. 30, 1958; 1 child, Joseph. BA magna cum laude, St. Francis Coll., 1956; JD, St. John's U., 1959; postgrad., Harvard U., 1978-79. CPCU, CLU, chartered fin. cons. From corp. sec. to sr. v.p., sec. Atlantic Mut. Ins. Co., Centennial Ins. Co., N.Y.C., 1971-86, exec. v.p., sec., 1986-96. Past chmn. bd. dirs. CPCU-Harry J. Loman Found., Motor Vehicle Accident Indemnification Corp., N.Y. Property Ins. Underwriting Assn., Ind. Fedn. N.Y. Contbr. articles to profl. jours. Bd. dirs., chmn. bd. Coll. Mt. St. Vincent, Riverdale, NY. Decorated Knight of Malta; named named Ins. Man of Yr., Recovery Forum, 1978; recipient Brotherhood award, NCCJ, 1991; Anglo-Am. fellow, B.D. Cooke & Ptnrs., Ltd., London, 1966. Mem. Soc. CPCU (nat. pres. 1984-85, Disting. Svc. award 1989, Eugene A. Toale Meml. award N.Y. chpt. 1974), Soc. CLU. Home: 3 Ridgecrest N Scarsdale NY 10583-2013

DECAMPLI, WILLIAM MICHAEL, surgeon, researcher; b. Allentown, Pa., Dec. 7, 1951; s. William John and Bernadine Louise (Diehl) DeCampli; m. Kristi Lynn Peterson, May 29, 1989; children: Elissa Cale, William Grant. BS in Physics, MIT, 1973; MA in Astrophysics, PhD in Astrophysics, Harvard U., 1978; MD, U. Miami, 1982; surg. residency, Stanford U., 1982—92. Diplomate Am. Bd. Thoracic Surgery, 1993, Am. Bd. Surgery, 1989, Am. Bd. Med. Examiners, 1983. Attending surgeon Children's Hosp., Oakland, Calif., 1992—95, The Children's Hosp. of Phila., 1996—2004, The Children's Cardiac Ctr., Newark, N.J., 1996—2004; asst. prof. of surgery U. of Pa. Sch. of Medicine, Phila., 1997—2003; co-dir. Ctr. for Adult Congenital Heart Disease, Newark, 1997—2004; rsch. scientist Stokes Rsch. Inst., The Children's Hosp. of Phila., 1998—; assoc. prof. of surgery U. of Pa., Phila., 2003—; attending surgeon The Congenital Heart Inst., Orlando, Fla., 2004—. Mem. strategic planning U.S. space program NASA, Mass., 1982—84, mem. space life sciences strategic planning subcom., 1984—87, mem. radiation biology rev. team, 1987—88; mem. performance subcom. cardiovasc. health adv. panel N.J. Dept. of Health and Sr. Svs., Trenton, 2002—04; guest reviewer Jour. of Thoracic and Cardiovasc. Surgery, Annals of Thoracic Surgery, Circulation, Anesthesia and Analgesia. Author: (peer-reviewed publs.) Journal of Thoracic and Cardiovascular Surgery, Annals of Thoracic Surgery, Circulation, Annals of Surgery, and others, Astrophysical Jour., Icarus, Moon & Planets, and others, (book chpts.) Gardner and Spray's Operative Cardiac Surgery, Current Pediatric Therapy, Pediatric Cardiac Surgery Annual, Yearbook of Medicine 1996, Endovascular Surgery, The Human Quest of Space, and others; contbr. Surgeon internat. vol. med. orgn. Heart to Heart, Inc. Fellow Paul Harris, Rotary Internat., 2000, Carl and Leah McConnell Surg. Rsch. fellow, Stanford U., 1986, Chaim Weismann Rsch. fellow, Calif. Inst. of Tech., 1979-80, ACS, 1996—, Am. Coll. Chest Physicians, 1996—, Am. Coll. Cardiology, 2001—; scholar Lee A. Loomis scholar, Harvard U., 1973. Mem.: Norman E. Shumway Surg. Soc., Internat. Soc. Adult Congenital Cardiac Disease, Soc. Thoracic Surgeons, Am. Assn. Thoracic Surgery. Achievements include patents for #5571127, scalpel handle having retractable blade support and method of use; #5797879 adjustable vascular shunt for control of pulmonary blood flow and method of use; #6053891 apparatus and methods for providing selectively adjustable blood flow through a vascular graft; participation in the greatest distance land-to-sea rescue mission in the history of the U.S. Air Force, 1987; primary authored the first paper analyzing ten year followup of survivors of heart transplantation, reprinted in the 1996 Year Book of Medicine. Home: 314 Salvadore Square Orlando FL 32789 Office: Congenital Heart Institute 50 Sturtevant St Orlando FL 32806 E-mail: wdecampli@orhs.org.

DECANDIA, DONALD ALAN, lawyer; b. Tyrone, Pa., Oct. 10, 1964; s. Nicholas Edward DeCandia and Rita (Prestopino) Newman. BA in English cum laude, U. Notre Dame, 1986; JD, U. Tex., 1989. Bar: N.Mex. 1989, U.S. Dist. Ct. N.Mex. 1990, U.S. Ct. Appeals (10th cir.) 1992, U.S. Supreme Ct. 1994). Shareholder Modrall, Sperling, Roehl, Harris & Sisk, Albuquerque, 1989—. Editor N.Mex. Defense Lawywer Assn. Defense News, 1996-98. Bd. dirs. Animal Humane Assn. N.Mex., 1996-2004. Mem. ABA, State Bar N.Mex. Avocations: golf, travel, writing, tennis. Office: Modrall Sperling Roehl Harris & Sisk PO Box 2168 Albuquerque NM 87103-2168 E-mail: dad@modrall.com.

DE CANDIDO KAMIN, ROSANN THERESE, secondary school educator; b. Englewood, N.J., July 18, 1958; d. Joseph John and Angela (Perrini) De Candido; m. John Russell Kamin, Aug. 24, 1980 (div. Oct. 1994); 1 child, Stefanie Therese. BA with honors, Rutgers U., 1980, MA, 1985, EdD, 2004. English/Spanish tchr. New Milford (N.J.) Bd. Edn., 1980-81; Spanish tchr. Teaneck (N.J.) Bd. Edn., 1981-82; English/Spanish tchr. Maywood (N.J.) Bd. Edn., 1982-83; English tchr. Edison (N.J.) Twp. Bd. Edn., 1983-84; Spanish/ESL tchr. Metuchen (N.J.) Bd. Edn., 1984—; interdisciplinary project coord. Metuchen (N.J.) H.S., 1986—. Brownie and Cadette leader, Older Girl program coord. Girl Scouts USA, Edison, 1993-96. Grantee Geraldine R. Dodge Found., Morristown, N.J., 1995, Playwrights Theatre, N.J., Madison, 1995; recipient best practice in the arts award N.J., 1995-96, Star award Metuchen Cmty., 1998, Appreciation award, Girl Scouts of Del., 2003; named Outstanding Vol. Girl Scouts U.S., 2001-02. Mem. ASCD, Acad. Am. Poets, Am. Ednl. Rsch. Assn., The John Dewey Soc., Fgn. Lang. Educators N.J., N.J. Edn. Assn., Phi Beta Kappa, Phi Sigma Iota, Phi Delta Kappa, Kappa Delta Pi Avocations: travel, dance. Home: 2503 Cricket Cir Edison NJ 08820-4206

DE CANI, JOHN STAPLEY, statistician, educator; b. Canton, Ohio, May 8, 1924; s. John Mustin and Ada Louise (Stapley) deC.; m. Jessie Montrose Farr, Dec. 17, 1955 (dec. Sept. 1969). BS, U. Wis., 1948; MBA, U. Pa., 1951, PhD, 1958. Mem. faculty U. Pa., Phila., 1948—, assoc. prof. stats., 1963-72, prof., 1972-95; prof. emeritus, 1995—; chmn. dept. stats. U. Pa., 1972-78. Cons. USN, 1957—, NAACP., 1967—, EEOC, 1976— Author: (with R. C. Clelland) Basic Statistics, 1973; contbr. articles to profl. jours. Served with USAAF, 1943-45. Recipient Distinguished Teaching award Lindbach Found., 1964; recipient Wharton disting. teaching award, 1978, 95, 97; Fulbright grantee Norway, 1959-60 Fellow: Royal Statis. Soc., Am. Statis. Assn.; mem.: Biometric Soc., Inst. Math. Statistics. Home: 226 W Rittenhouse Sq Apt 1715 Philadelphia PA 19103

DECARO, ANGELO ANTHONY, JR., data processing executive; b. Poughkeepsie, N.Y., June 24, 1951; s. Angelo A. and Carmela (Gasparro) D.; m. Beverly Ann Fulvio, June 25, 1983; children: Francesca, Julianne. BSME, Northeastern U., Boston, 1974; MBA, Pace U., White Plains, N.Y., 1987. Assoc. engr. IBM, Poughkeepsie, 1974-77, sr. assoc. engr., 1977-78, planning/m.e. mgr., 1978-83, sr. engr./mgr., 1983-84, mfg. mgr., 1984-85, mfg. engring. mgr., 1985-86, tech. asst. to v.p. corp. mfg. Armonk, N.Y., 1986-87, asst. plant mgr. Poughkeepsie, 1987-89, plant mgr. Austin, Tex., 1989-93; pres., COO Xetel Corp., Austin, Tex., 1993—. Bd. mem. Austin Quality Coun., dir. Tycom Corp. Active various charitable orgns. in past. Recipient IBM Div. award, 1980. Roman Catholic. Avocations: golf, racquetball. Office: Xetel 2525 Brockton Dr Austin TX 78758-4463 Home: 1014 Eastbourne Ct Frederick MD 21702-5119

DECASTRO, ALFREDO P., physician, consultant; b. Ibaan, Philippines, Apr. 30, 1943; arrived in U.S., 1971; s. Joaquin Guerra and Graciana P. DeCastro; m. Leonora DeCastro, July 21, 1976; 1 child, Elaine. BS, Univ. St. Thomas, Manila, 1964, MD, 1969. Diplomate Am. Bd. Radiology. Cons. Ellenville (NY) Med. Group, 1976—97; med. staff Ellenville Cmty. Hosp., 1976—97, chmn. dept. radiology, 1990—97; pvt. practice Port Jervis, NY. Cons. in field. Home: 11 Tommy Ln Port Jervis NY 12771 Office: 6 Skinner St Port Jervis NY 12771 Office Phone: 845-856-7529.

DE CASTRO, HUGO DANIEL, lawyer; b. Panama City, Panama, Sept. 12, 1935; came to U.S., 1947; s. Mauricio Fidanque and Armida Rebecca (Salas) de C.; m. Isabel Shapiro, July 25, 1958; children: Susan M., Teresa A., Andrea L., Michele L. BSBA in Econs. cum laude, UCLA, 1957, JD summa cum laude, 1960. CPA Calif.; bar: Calif. 61. Prin. de Castro, West, Chodorow, Glickfeld & Nass Inc., L.A., 1961—. Lectr. UCLA, 1962-67, 68, counsel to dean Law Sch., 1963—; commr. tax adv. com. State Bar Calif. Editor UCLA Law Rev., 1959-60, Taxation for Lawyers, 1971-88; contbr. articles to profl. jours. Former trustee Stephen S. Wise Temple, Jewish Fedn. Cmty. Found.; trustee, bd. dirs., chmn. fin. com. UCLA Found.; bd. dirs. Western L.A. Found.; bd. dirs. Hebrew Union Coll.; bd. govs. Trustee Endowment Trusts. Mem. ABA chmn. taxation subcom.), ACLU, L.A. County Bar Assn., Beverly Hills Bar Assn. (bd. dirs. Law Found.), L.A. C. of C. (former chmn., dir.), L.A. World Affairs coun., Am. Jewish Com., Del Rey Yacht Club (Calif., former dir., officer), Founders of Music Ctr., Las Hadas Country Club (Mex.), Pi Lambda Phi. Office: de Castro West Chodorow et al Ste 1400 10960 Wilshire Blvd Los Angeles CA 90024-3702 Office Phone: 310-445-7614.

DECATUR, RAYLENE, former museum director; BA, U. Va.; MA, George Washington U. Various positions Md. Sci. Ctr., Balt., Acad. Natural Scis., Phila., Renwick Gallery; pres., CEO Denver Mus. Nature and Sci. (formerly Denver Mus. Natural History), 1995—2004.

DECAVEL, JEAN-ROBERT, chef; b. Roubaix, France; Exec. chef Le Regence, NYC, 1985—93; chef de cuisine Maisonette, Cin., 1993—2001; owner, chef Jean-Robert at Pigall's, Cin., 2002—. Decorated medal of the Chevalier de Order of Merit France; recipient award, James Beard Found., 2001. Office: Jean-Robert at Pigall's 127 W 4th St Cincinnati OH 45202 Office Phone: 513-721-1345 209. Business E-Mail: info@jean-robertatpigalls.com.

DECECCO, CINDY, art educator, artist; d. Raymond and Bernice (Jones) DeCecco; m. Harv Wardwell, Jan. 1, 1978. BA Art, Portland State U., Oreg., 1977; MA Art, Pittsburg State U., Kans., 1994. Art instr. Portland C.C., Oreg., 1996—2000, Yauapai Coll., Prescott, Ariz., 2000—. Various exhbns., 1982—, Hinge, Alder Brook Park, Prescott, Ariz., 2002. Home: 2960 Garden Ln Prescott AZ 86305

DE CELLES, CHARLES EDOUARD, theologian, educator; b. Holyoke, Mass., May 17, 1942; s. Fernand Pierre and Stella Marie (Shooner) De C. BA, U. Windsor, Ont., Can., 1964; MA in Theology, Marquette U., Milw., 1966; PhD, Fordham U., 1970; MA in Religion, Temple U., Phila., 1979. m. Mildred Manzano Valdez, July 17, 1978; children: Christopher Emanuel, Mark Joshua, Salvador Isaiah. Mem. faculty Dunbarton Coll. of Holy Cross, Washington, 1969-70, Marywood Coll. (became Marywood U., 1997), Scranton, Pa., 1970—, prof. religious studies, 1980—. Mem. bd. examiners U. Calicut, Kerala, India, 1985—86; subject specialist Accrediting Commn. of Distance Edn. and Tng. Coun., 1995; moderator Students Organized to Uphold Life, Marywood Coll., 1982—, co-chmn. Task Force Social Justice and Environment, 1992—93, corrector off-campus degree program, 1977—, dept. scribe, 1995—. Author: Paths of Belief, Vol. 2, 1977, prin. co-author rev. edit., 1987; The Unbound Spirit: God's Universal Sanctifying Work, 1985, Jesus: The Eternally Begotten of the Father as Human Being, 1993; editor Biographical Directory Cath. Acad. Scis. in U.S.A., 1994, Science and Religion in Dialogue, 1999; also pamphlets, articles, book revs., guest editorials, columns, letters, occasional columnist Nat. Cath. Register, 1983-87, The Dunmorean, 1996-97; regular columnist The Catholic Observer, 1996-2005; regular feature writer The Catholic Leader, 2005—; contbr. articles to profl. jours., mags. and newspapers. Mem. Ecumenism and Inter-faith Commn., Diocese of Scranton, 1992—, Ecumenical Leadership Com. (now Christian Cmtys. Gathering of Northeastern Pa.), 1999—; bd. dirs. Scranton UN Assn., 1974-75, chmn. UN Day, 1974; mem. ProLife prep. Commn. Scranton Diocesan Synod, 1984-85; mem. Filipino-Am. Assn. N.E. Pa., 1984-91, pub. rels. officer, 1985-91, editor newsletter, 1988-91; bd. dirs. Scranton chpt. Pennsylvanians for Human Life, 1983—, v.p., 1994—; leader Cath. Charismatic Prayer Group, Scranton, 1970-76; mem. pack com. Boy Scouts, Scranton, 1990-95, Cath. religious emblems counselor, 1993-96; chmn. prolife com. Immaculate Conception parish, 1994—. Recipient cert. of appreciation, U.S. Cath. Conf., 1976, Disting. Svc. award, UN Assn. U.S., 1974, Svc. award, Filipino-Am. Assn. N.E. Pa., 1990, cert. appreciation, Boy Scouts Am., 1991, 1992, 1993, 1994, 1995, Defender of Life cert. of appreciation, Susan B. Anthony List, 2003, several athletic awards for rd. running yearly, 1987—96, multiple awards for speed walking, 1990—96, 2000—02, admitted to the Order Cor Mariae, Marywood Coll., 1990, invested knight, Equestrian Order of the Holy Sepulchre of Jerusalem, 1994, Ronald Reagan Rep. Gold Medal award, Congl. Com., 2004, Cert. Recognition for Commitment and Svc., Marywood U. Distance Learning Program, 2004; Fordham U. Presdl. scholar, 1966—68. Mem. Cath. Acad. Sci. U.S.A. (pub. com. 1991-, chmn. program com. 1993-96, chmn. pub. com. 1997-2001, v.p. 1997-2003), Coll. Theology Soc. Am., Men of the Sacred Heart (Scranton chpt.), Theta Alpha Kappa (chpt. moderator 1982—). Roman Catholic. Home: 923 E Drinker St Dunmore PA 18512-2644 Office: Marywood U Dept Religious Studies Scranton PA 18509-1598 Office Phone: 570-348-6211 2305. Business E-Mail: decelles@es.marywood.edu. *What the world needs is compassion. It needs me to climb out of the confines of my own little ego and embrace humankind: humanity created not in my image but God's - including the senile man, the habitual alcoholic, the AIDS victim, the starving Somalian, the abused woman, the child in the womb.*

DECESARE, DONALD E., broadcast executive; b. Jersey City, Mar. 6, 1947; s. Emilio D. and Anita T. DeCesare; m. Catherine M. Fahey, June 20, 1970; 1 child, Elizabeth Ann. BA, U. Pitts., 1967; MA, U. Conn., 1969. News dir. Sta. WGCH-AM, Greenwich, Conn., 1972—74; reporter Westinghouse Broadcasting Corp., N.Y.C., 1974—76; writer CBS News divsn. CBS Inc., N.Y.C., 1976—78, news editor, 1978—80, fgn. prodr., 1980—83, sr. fgn. prodr., 1983—85, mgr. N.Y./New Eng. bur., 1985—87, fgn. editor, 1987—89, v.p. news coverage, 1989—90, v.p. ops., 1990—96; v.p. CBS News, 1990—96; pres. Crossroads Comm. of Old SaybrookLLC, Norwalk, Conn., 1996—, Crossroads Comm. / Enterprises; owner/operator WMRD-AM, Middletown, Conn., 1996—, WLIS-AM, Old Saybrook, Conn., 1996—. Bd. dirs. Middlesex County United Way, Norwalk Symphony Soc. Recipient Columbia DuPont award Columbia U., 1989; Overseas Press Club award, 1990. Mem.: Conn. Pub. Access Network (bd. dirs., treas.), Conn. Broadcasters Assn. (bd. dirs., 1st vice chmn.), Old Saybrook C. of C. (bd. dirs., pres. 2002—04). Avocations: latin american art, furniture making, computers. Office: Crossroads Comm LLC 157 N Seir Hill Rd Norwalk CT 06850-1333 also: PO Box 1150 777 River Rd Middletown CT 06457-3922 also: PO Box 1420 77 Springbrook Rd Old Saybrook CT 06475-1225 Office Phone: 860-347-9673. E-mail: don@wliswmrd.net.

DECESARE, JOHN, publishing executive; Degree in Bus. Econs., U. Conn.; grad. advanced pub. mgmt. program, Northwestern U. Hotel mgr., Silverthorne, Colo.; began pub. career, 1985; advt. dir. Turnstile Pub. Co.; pub. Travel Directories Group Northstar Travel Media, 2003—04; pub. U.S. edit. Bus. Traveler mag., N.Y.C. Office: Bus Traveler 225 Park Ave S 7th Fl New York NY 10003

DECHAINE, DEAN DENNIS, lawyer; b. Lake Oswego, Oreg., Dec. 12, 1936; s. Bennet Dennis and Hazel Pearl (Vose) DeC.; m. Joan Carolyn Mann, Sept. 29, 1963; children: Michael, Beth, Eve. BS, Portland State U., 1959; LLB, U. Va., 1964. Bar: Va. 1964, Oreg. 1964, Wash. 1986, U.S. Dist. Ct. Oreg. 1964, U.S. Dist. Ct. (we. dist.) Wash. 1986, U.S. Ct. Appeals (9th cir.) 1966, U.S. Ct. Internat. Trade 1996, U.S. Supreme Ct., 2004. Rsch. asst. to U.S. senator from Oreg. Richard L. Neuberger, Washington, 1959-60; legis. asst. to U.S. senator from Oreg. Hall S. Lusk, Washington, 1960; ptnr. Miller Nash LLP, Portland, 1964—. Sec., legal counsel World Forestry Ctr., Portland, 1965—. Contbr. article to profl. jour. Chair Portland State U. Alumni Assn., 1967-68, Portland State U. Alumni Bd., 1986-89; scoutmaster Boy Scouts Am., Lake Oswego, 1983-86; program chair continuing legal edn. Oreg. State Bar, 1971, chair aviation sect. 1989-90, chair admiralty sect., 1983-84, 1997-99; trustee Oreg. Coll. Oriental Medicine, 2004—. With U.S. Army, 1960-61. Mem.: Maritime Law Assn. U.S. (proctor). Home: 443 Country Club Rd Lake Oswego OR 97034-2107 Office: Miller Nash LLP 111 SW 5th Ave Ste 3400 Portland OR 97204-3699 Fax: 503-224-0155. Office Phone: 503-205-2452. E-mail: dean.dechaine@millernash.com.

DECHANCE, YVONNE RENÉ, music educator; b. Mather AFB, Calif., Apr. 6, 1966; d. Richard P. and Gladys A. (Claypool) D.; m. Gary E. Blackburn, June 22, 1996. BA, Whitworth Coll., Spokane, Wash., 1988; MusM, U. Tex., 1991, D of Musical Arts, 1994. Pvt. practice voice instr. YD Studio, Austin, 1989-96; voice instr. U. Tex. Informal Classes, Austin, 1994-96; pvt. instr. Dechance Studios, Redwood City, Calif., 1996-99, ednl. web designer, 1997—, voice instr. Reston, Va., 1999—2002; asst. prof. U. Tampa, Fla., 2002—. Lectr. East Carolina U., Greenville, 1998. Mem. Nat. Assn. Tchrs. of Singing, Nat. Webmaster, U. Tex. Exes, Mu Phi Epsilon. Avocations: costume design, miniatures. Office: Univ Tampa Dept Music 401 W Kennedy Blvd Tampa FL 33606-1490 Home: 306 South Arrawana Ave #1 Tampa FL 33609

DECHANT, VIRGIL C., retired fraternal organization administrator; b. Antonino, Kans., Sept. 24, 1930; s. Cornel J. and Ursula (Legleiter) D.; m. Ann Schafer, Aug. 20, 1951; children: Thomas, Daniel, Karen, Robert. Hon. degree, Pontifical Coll. Josephinum, Columbus, Ohio, St. Anselm's Coll., Manchester, N.H., St. Leo's Coll., Fla., Mt. St. Mary's Coll., Emmitsburg, Md., St. John's U., S.I., N.Y., Providence Coll., Sacred Heart U., Bridgeport, Conn., Pontifical U. Santo Tomas, Manila, Assumption Coll., Worcester, Mass., Albertus Magnus Coll., New Haven; hon. degree, St. Thomas U., St. Paul, Kans. Newman Coll., Wichita, Franciscan U., Steubenville, Ohio, Benedictine Coll., Atchison, Kans., St. Thomas U., Fredericton, N.B., Can., Dallas U. With KC, 1948—63, dir., asst. supreme sec., supreme master 4th degree, 1963, supreme sec., 1967-77, supreme knight, CEO New Haven, 1977—2000. Appointee Pontifical Coun. for the Family, 1982—; consultor, Pontifical Coun. for Social Comm., 1990—; hon. councilor of state, Vatican City State, 2001; mem. Coun. of Superindency, Inst. for Works of Religion (Vatican Bank), 1990—. Past bd. dirs. Nat. Shrine Immaculate Conception, Washington; bd. dirs. Pontifical Coll. Josephinum, Columbus; trustee Cath. U. Am.; commr. Christopher Columbus Quincentenary Commn. for founding of Ams., 1992; apptd. auditor Snyod Am., 1997. Decorated Knight St. Gregory the Great promoted to comdr. with Star elevated to Knight Grand Cross, Knight Grand Cross Equestrian Order Holy Sepulchre, Holy Land Pilgrim Shell, Knight Grand Cross Order Pius IX, Knight Sovereign Mil. Order of Malta; named one of Gentleman of His Holiness, Pope John Paul II, 1987; appointed to Extraordinary Synod of Bishops in Vatican, 1985, Synod of Bishops on Laity, 1987, Synod of Bishops for Am., 1997; recipient Cross of Merit with Golden Star of Holy Sepulchre of Jerusalem, 1990.

DECHAR, PETER HENRY, artist; b. N.Y.C., Apr. 19, 1942; s. Edouard and Diane D.; m. Natasha Gratcheva, Apr. 23, 1999; 1 child, Antonina. Prin. Peter Dechar Inc. Archtl. Furniture. Exhibited one-man shows, Cordier & Ekstrom Gallery, N.Y.C., 1967, 69, 75, Twentieth Century Art from the Rockefeller Collection, N.Y.C., 1969, Mus. Modern Art, N.Y.C., 1969, group shows, Larry Aldrich Mus., Ridgefield, Conn., 1967, Krannert Art Mus., 1967, Whitney Mus. Art, N.Y.C., 1967, 69; represented in permanent collections, Mus. Modern Art, N.Y.C., Whitney Mus. Art, N.Y.C., Larry Aldrich Mus., Ridgefield, Conn., Walker Art Ctr., Fiberglass Tower Art Collection, Julien Levy Collection, Chase Manhatten Collection, Rockefeller Collection. E-mail: pdechar@aol.com.

DE CHASCA, EDMUND, editor, writer; b. Oberlin, Ohio, May 15, 1944; s. Edmund Viella de Chasca and Edith Mae Sexton. BA, U. Iowa, 1966; MA, U. Chgo., 1967, PhD, 1974. Asst. prof. English U. No. Iowa, 1970—72; music critic Hyde Park Herald, Chgo., 1974—77; writer Lawrence Ragan Comms., Chgo., 1975—77; editor Macmillan Inc., Chgo., 1977—79; adj. instr. English St. Louis C.C., 1980—97; writer Christian Hosp., St. Louis, 1980—87; sr. editor Blvd. Mag., 1999—. Author: (lit. criticism) John Gould Fletcher and Imagism, 1978; contbr. short fiction to lit. mags. and anthologies. Mem. Amateur Chamber Music Players, Inc.; pianist St. Stephens Ch., St. Louis, 2002—. Woodrow Wilson fellow, Woodrow Wilson Found., 1966. Mem.: Phi Beta Kappa. Roman Catholic. Avocations: piano, golf. Office: Blvd Mag PMB 325 6614 Clayton Rd Saint Louis MO 63117 Office Phone: 314-367-6082. E-mail: edmunddechasca@yahoo.com.

DE CHASTELAIN, A(LFRED) JOHN G(ARDYNE) D(RUMMOND), Canadian army officer, diplomat; b. Bucharest, Rumania, July 30, 1937; emigrated to Can., 1955, naturalized, 1962; s. Alfred George G. and Marion Elizabeth (Walsh) de C.; m. MaryAnn Laverty, Sept. 9, 1961; children: Duncan John, Amanda Jane. Student, Fettes Coll., Edinburgh, Scotland, 1950-55, Mt. Royal Coll. Calgary, Can., 1956; BA with honors in History, Royal Mil. Coll., Can., 1960; grad., Brit. Army Staff Coll., 1966; D in Mil. Sci. (hon.), Royal Mil. Coll. Can., 1996; LLD in Conflict Resolution (hon.), Royal Rds. U., 2001. Commd. 2d lt. Can. Army, 1960, advanced through grades to gen., 1989; comdg. officer 2d Bn. Princess Patricia's Can. Light Inf., 1970-72; comdr. Can. Forces Base, Montreal, Que., 1974-76; comdr. Can. Contingent UN Force in Cyprus, 1976-77; comdt. Royal Mil. Coll. Can., Kingston, Ont., 1977-80; comdr. 4th Can. Mechanized Brigade Group, Lahr, Fed. Republic Germany, 1980-82; dir. Gen. Land Doctrine Nat. Def. Hdqrs., Ottawa, 1982-83; dep. comdr. Mobile Command, St. Hubert, Que., 1983-86; asst. dep. min. pers. Nat. Def. Hdqrs., Ottawa, Ont., Can., 1986-88, vice chief of Def. Staff, 1988-89, chief of Def. Staff, 1989-93; Can. amb. to U.S. Washington, 1993. Past v.p. Scouts Can.; chief Defence Staff, 1994-95; mem. Internat. Body on Decommissioning of Arms in No. Ireland, 1995-96; mem. ind. chmn. No. Ireland Peace Talks, 1996-98; chmn. Ind. Internat. Commn. on Decommissioning of Arms in No. Ireland, 1997—. Decorated comdr. Order Mil. Merit (Can.), officer Order of Can., comdr. Order St. John of Jerusalem, comdr. Legion of Merit (U.S.), Companion of Honour (U.K.); recipient Hellenic Commendation medal of Merit and Honor (Greece), Vimy award, Conf. Def. Assocs. Mem. Dominion of Can. Rifle Assn. (past pres.), Royal Scottish Country Dance Soc., St. Andrew's Soc., Royal Mil. Coll. Club, Royal Can. Legion, Royal Can. Mil. Inst, Col. of the Regiment, PPCLI, 2000-2003 Home: 170 Acacia Ave Ottawa ON Canada K1M 0R3

DECHENE, JAMES CHARLES, lawyer; b. Petaluma, Calif., May 14, 1953; s. Harry George and Domenica Therese Dechene; m. Teresa Marie Caserza, Aug. 2, 1975; children: Michelle, Mark, Sabrina, Diane. BS summa cum laude, Santa Clara U., 1975; JD magna cum laude, AM in Econs., U. Mich., 1978, PhD in Econs., 1980. Bar: Ill. 1979, U.S. Dist. Ct. (no. dist.) Ill. 1980, U.S. Ct. Appeals (7th cir.) 1993, U.S. Dist. Ct. (ea. dist.) Wis. 1996. Assoc. Sidley & Austin, Chgo., 1980-86; ptnr. Sidley Austin Brown & Wood LLP, Chgo., 1986—. Adj. prof. Health Law Inst. DePaul U. Coll. of Law, 1987—; bd. dirs. Med. Sci. Labs., Wauwatosa, Wis., 1991-95. Author: Establishing a Physician Organization, 1993; author: (with others) Health Law Practice Guide, 1993-2004, Financing and Liability, 1994, Health Law Handbook, 1989, 90, 91, 93, Managed Care, 1996, Telemedicine and E-Health Law, 2004; contbr. articles to profl. jours. Mem. Ill. Bar Assn., Am. Health Lawyers Assn., Am. Econs. Assn. Roman Catholic. Office: Sidley Austin Brown & Wood LLP Bank One Plz 10 S Dearborn St Chicago IL 60603-2000 Office Phone: 312-853-7275. Business E-Mail: jdechene@sidley.com.

DECHERD, ROBERT WILLIAM, newspaper and broadcasting executive; b. Dallas, Apr. 9, 1951; s. Henry Benjamin Jr. and Isabelle Lee (Thomason) D.; m. Maureen Healy, Jan. 25, 1975; children: William Benjamin, Audrey Maureen. AB cum laude, Harvard U., 1973. Exec. v.p. Dallas Morning News, 1980-83, A.H. Belo Corp., Dallas, 1981-84, pres., chief operating officer, 1985-86, chmn., chief exec. officer, 1987-94, chmn., pres. and CEO, 1994—, also bd. dirs. Dir. Kimberly-Clark Corp., 1996—. Pres. Dallas Symphony Assn., 1979-80, Dallas Symphony Found., 1984-86, St. Mark's Sch., Tex., 1988-91; chmn. Dallas Parks Found., 1985-87, Dallas Soc. Profl. Journalists, 1978; trustee Tomas Rivera Policy Inst., 1992—; incorporator, pres. Freedom. of Info. Found. Tex., 1978. Recipient Disting. Svc. award Dallas Jaycees,

1985, Am. Newspaper Exec. of Yr. award Adweek mag., 1985, citation of honor AIA, 1988, Seymour Preston award Nat. Assn. Ind. Schs. Coun. Advancement and Support Edn., 1989, James Madison award Freedom of Info. Found. Tex., 1989, Henry Cohn Humanitarian award Anti-Defamation League, 1992, Freedom of Speech award The Media Inst., 1998; named to the Tex. Bus. Hall of Fame, 1995; recipient St. Mark's Disting. Alumnus award, 1998. Mem. Tex. Soc. Architects (hon.), Newspaper Assn. Am. (mem. exec. bd. 1992-96). Office: A H Belo Corp PO Box 655237 Dallas TX 75265-5237

DE CHERNEY, ALAN HERSH, obstetrics and gynecology educator; b. Phila., Feb. 13, 1942; s. William Aaron and Ruth (Hersh) DeC.; m. Deanna Faith Saver, June 26, 1966; children: Peter, Alexander. BS in Natural Scis., Muhlenberg Coll., 1963; MD, Temple U., 1967; MA (hon.), Yale U., 1985. Diplomate Am. Bd. Ob.-Gyn. (examiner 1984—, bd. dirs. 1995—), Am.Bd. Reproductive Endocrinology (bd. dirs. 1988-94), Nat. Bd. Med. Examiners (examiner 1987-90). Intern in gen. medicine U. Pitts., 1967-68; resident in ob-gyn. U. Pa., Phila., 1968-72, instr. dept. ob-gyn, 1970-72; asst. prof. ob-gyn. Yale U. Sch. Medicine, New Haven, 1974-78, assoc. prof., 1979-84, prof., 1984-91, John Slade Ely prof. ob-gyn, 1987-92, dir. div. reproductive endocrinology, dept. ob-gyn, 1982-92, lectr. dept. biology, 1985-92; Louis E. Phaneuf prof., chmn. dept. ob-gyn. Tufts U. Sch. Medicine, 1992-96; prof. dept. ob-gyn. UCLA, 1996—. Editor (in chief): Fertility and Sterility, 1996—. Maj. U.S. Army, 1972—74. Recipient Disting. Alumni award Temple U., 1989, 2002, Muhlenberg Coll., 1994. Fellow ACOG, IOM, Am. Fertility Soc. (pres. 1994-95), Am. Assn. History of Medicine, Soc. for Assisted Reproductive Tech. (pres. 1987-88), Soc. Reproductive Endocrinologists (pres. 1988), Soc. Reproductive Surgeons (charter, pres. 1991), Endocrine Soc., European Soc. Human Reproductions and Embryology, Soc. Gynecologic Surgeons, Soc. for Study of Reproduction, Soc. Gynecologic Investigation (pres. 1994-95). Office: UCLA Sch Medicine Dept Ob/Gyn 27-177 CHS Mail Code 174017 10833 Le Conte Ave Los Angeles CA 90095-3075 Office Phone: 310-794-1884. Business E-Mail: adecherney@mednet.ucla.edu.

DE CHIARO, JOHN PAUL, music educator; b. Bronx, N.Y., Jan. 19, 1953; s. Arnold and Lucille De Chiaro. BS Music Edn, Kean U., 1975; MA, NYU, 1981. Music tchr. Edgewater (N.J.) Pub. Schs., 1975—76; guitar instr. Delbarton Sch., Morristown, NJ, 1976—81; prof. guitar Coll. St. Elizabeth, Convent Station, NJ, 1976—81, U. So. Miss., Hattiesburg, 1981—. Dir. Hattiesburg Youth Orch., 1981—87, Pine Belt Guitar Symposium, Hattiesburg, 1985—; founder Elmo & Mary Glenn Harrison Guitar Scholarship, U. So. Miss., 1986. Performer: (4 CD set) The Complete Works of Scott Joplin on Guitar, 1999; performer: (CDs) Christmas on Guitar, 1987, Sounds of Christmas on Guitar, 1985, The Guitar on Broadway, 1992, Soundscapes - The Mississippi Guitar Quartet, 2003, The Wedding Album, 2001; author: The Complete Works of Scott Joplin, 2001; performer: for Pope John Paul II, 6 solo recitals, Carnegie Hall, 2 solo recitals, White House; musician: (solo recitals) Carnegie Hall. Recipient Young Artist of Yr. award, Musical Am. Mag., 1982. Mem.: Music Tchrs. Nat. Assn., Lions. Roman Catholic. Avocations: running, model railroad, model airplanes. Office: U So Miss Box 5081 Hattiesburg MS 39406

DECHICK, ELISSA JADE, art educator; b. Md., Vietnam, Oct. 30, 1974; d. Gerald Joseph and Victoria Andres; m. Mark A. DeChick, July 19, 2003; 1 child, Marina Jade. Master's in Art Edn., Nazareth Coll., Rochester, 2001; BS in Fitness and Cardiac Rehab., Ithaca Coll., Ithaca, NY, 1992—96. New York State Teaching Certification NY State. Art tchr. Fairport H.S., Fairport, NY, 2001—, Palmyra Macedon H.S., Palmyra, NY, 1999—2001; exercise specialist in cardiac rehab. Rochester Gen. Hosp. Cardiac Rehab., Rochester, NY, 1996—2000. Internat. baccalaureate visual arts examiner IBO, Rochester Area, NY, 2004—. Mem.: NY State Art Tchrs. Assn. Office: Fairport High Sch 1358 Ayrault Rd Fairport NY 14450 Office Phone: 585-421-2100. Personal E-mail: elissa_dechick@fairport.monroe.edu.

DECI, EDWARD LEWIS, psychologist, educator; b. Clifton Springs, NY, Oct. 14, 1942; s. Charles Henry and Janice Margaret (Upchurch) Deci. AB, Hamilton Coll., 1964; postgrad., London Sch. Econs., 1965; MBA, U. Pa., 1967; PhD, Carnegie-Mellon U., 1970. Postdoctoral fellow Stanford U., 1973-74; mem. faculty U. Rochester, NY, 1970—, prof. psychology, 1978—, chair dept. psychology, 1993—94, Helen F. and Fred H. Gowen prof. social scis., 2005—; pvt. practice psychotherapy, 1975—; pres. Inst. for Rsch. and Reform in Edn., 1995-97, chmn., 1997—. Orgnl. cons., 1970—; lectr., cons., Bulgaria, Canada, Germany, Israel, Japan, Norway, Italy, Poland, Sweden, England, Jordan, Thailand, Australia, Finland, Belgium, Spain. Author: (book) Intrinsic Motovation, 1975, The Psychology of Self-Determination, 1980; co-author: Industrial and Organizational Psychology, 1977, Intrinsic Motivation and Self-Determination in Human Behavior, 1985, Why We Do What We Do, 1995. Pres. Monhegan Mus. Assn., 1984—; trustee Monhegan (Maine) Conservation Assocs., 1982—89, 1992—95, Monhegan Artist Residency Corp., Maine, 1998—, Monhegan Island Sustainable Cmty. Assn., 2001—. Grantee NIMH, 1977—78, 1989—94, NSF, 1981—83, Nat. Inst. Child Health and Human Devel., 1986—89, 1990—96. Fellow: APA, Am. Psychol. Soc. Office: U Rochester Psychology Dept Rochester NY 14627 Business E-Mail: deci@psych.rochester.edu.

DECIUTIIS, ALFRED CHARLES MARIA, oncologist, television producer; b. NYC, Oct. 16, 1945; s. Alfred Ralph and Theresa Elizabeth (Manko) deCiutiis; m. Catherine L. Gohn. BS summa cum laude, Fordham U., 1967; MD, Columbia U., 1971. Diplomate Am. Bd. Internal Medicine, Am. Bd. Med. Oncology. Intern N.Y. Hosp.-Cornell Med. Ctr., N.Y.C., 1971-72, resident, 1972-74; fellow in clin. immunology Meml. Hosp.-Sloan Kettering Cancer Ctr., N.Y.C., 1974-75, fellow in clin. oncology, 1975-76, spl. fellow in immunology, 1974-76; guest investigator, asst. physician exptl. hematology Rockefeller U., N.Y.C., 1975-76; pvt. practice specializing in med. oncology L.A., 1977—. Mem. med. adv. com. Olympics, 1984; co-founder Medtrina Med. Ctr., Torrance, Calif., physician asst. supr., 1984; mem. fgn. policy leadership project Ctr. Internat. Affairs, Harvard, Ill. Host cable TV shows, 1981—, med. editor Cable Health Network, 1983—, Lifetime Network, 1984—; syndicated columnist: Coast Media News, 1980; prodr.: numerous med. TV shows; contbr. articles to profl. jours. Mem. gov. bd. med. coun. Italian-Am. Found.; mem. Italian-Am. Civic Com., L.A., 1983, Cath. League Civil and Rel. Liberty, World Affairs Coun., L.A., Boston Mus. Fine Arts, Met. Mus.; founder Italian-Am. Med. Assn., 1982; co-founder Italian-Am. Legal Alliance, L.A., 1982—; mem. UCLA Chancellor's Assocs. Served to capt. M.C. U.S. Army, 1972—74. Leukemia Soc. Am. fellow, 1974—76. Fellow: ACP, Internat. Coll. Physicians and Surgeons; mem.: AAAS, AMA (Physician's Recognition award 1978—80, 1982—85, 1986—89, 1989—91, 1991—94, 1994—96, 1996—99, 1999—2002, 2002—04), Am. Soc. Hematology (emeritus), Internat. Platform Assn., Drug Info. Assn., Chinese Med. Assn., Am. Geriat. Soc., Am. Pub. Health Assn., N.Y. Acad. Sci. (life), Internat. Health Soc., Am. Union Physicians and Dentists, Los Angeles County Med. Assn., Calif. Med. Assn., Am. Soc. Clin. Oncology, Mensa, Smithsonian Instn., Nat. Geog. Soc. (life), Fondazione Giovanni Agnelli, Nature Conservancy, Nat. Wildlife Fedn., Sigma Xi, Alpha Omega Alpha, Phi Beta Kappa. Achievements include first to 1st comprehensive clinical description of chronic fatigue syndrome as a neuro-immunologic acquired disorder. Office: PO Box 384 Agoura Hills CA 91376-0384

DE CIUTIIS, VINCENT LOUIS, hospital administrator, anesthiology educator; b. N.Y.C., NY, Oct. 11, 1924; s. Alfredo Ralph and Chiara Mary (Giannone) de Ciutiis; m. Claire Adele Ostuni, June 28, 1947 (div. 1976); children: Vilia, Nadine, Vincent, Mario, Elena, Michael, Elisa, Carl; m. Patricia Therese Paulson, June 3, 1976; children: James, Marianna, Michelle, Donald. BA, Columbia U., 1945; MD, NY Med. Coll., 1948; grad., Med. Sch. Walter Reed Army Med. Ctr., 1954; MBA, Pepperdine U., 1976; grad., U.S. Army Command Coll., 1986. Diplomate Am. Bd. Anesthesia. Intern Met. Hosp., N.Y.C., 1948—49, resident in anesthesia, 1952—53; chief anesthesiology U.S. Army Hosp., Ft. Dix, NJ, 1951—52, Misericordia Hosp., Bronx, NY, 1958—62, Torrance (Calif.) Meml. Hosp., 1971—79; chief anesthesiology, assoc. prof. Met. Hosp. NY Med. Coll., N.Y.C., 1956—58; asst. prof. UCLA Med. Sch., L.A., 1958—86, assoc. prof., 1986—; prof. surgery, anesthesiology Coll. Osteo. Medicine U. of the Pacific, Stockton, Calif., 1985; adminstr. Riviera Cmty. Hosp., Torrance, 1963—64; adminstr., med. dir. Surg. Ctr. South Bay, Torrance, 1979—. Cons. U.S. Army Hosp., Ft. MacArthur, Calif., 1965—71; dir. med. edn. Torrance Meml. Hosp., 1972—76. Prodr., dir.: (med. documentary) KNBC, 1972; contbr. articles to profl. jours. Lt. col. U.S. Army, col. Res. Decorated World War II Victory medal, Commendation ribbon. Fellow: Am. Coll. Anesthesiologists; mem.: DAV, AMA, Assn. Mil. Surgeons U.S., Calif. Med. Assn., Res. Officers Assn. (life), Los Angeles County Med. Assn. Republican. Roman Catholic. Achievements include invention of intravenous catheter laryngoscope. Home: PO Box 1684 Bellflower CA 90707-1684 Office: Med Care Internat Surg Ctr of S Bay 23500 Madison St Torrance CA 90505-4702

DECK, GREGORY A., lawyer; b. Fort Wayne, Ind., May 29, 1950; s. Benjamin F. and Carolyn M. (Fackler) D.; m. Elizabeth D. Witheft, May 2, 1981; children: Jonathan M., Kathryn J. BA, Valparaiso U., 1972, JD, 1975. Bar: Ill. 1975. Ptnr. Deck & Baron, Kankakee, Ill., 1975—. Bd. dirs. Prairieview Luth. Home Found., Danforth, Ill., 1985-97, Hospice of Kankakee Valley, 1997—. Mem. ABA, Ill. State Bar Assn., Am. Acad. Healthcare Attys. Office: Deck & Baron PO Box 693 Kankakee IL 60901-0693

DECK, JOANN PASSARIELLO, publishing executive, editor; b. New Haven, Conn., July 18, 1952; d. William Pelligrino and Josephine Lorello Passariello; m. Richard Allen Deck, Nov. 15, 1986. BS in Journalism, Boston U., 1974; postgrad., U. Calif., Berkeley, 1992—93. Rschr. spl. legis. commn. handicapped State Legis Mass., Boston, 1975; freelance journalist, 1974—76; mag. writer, asst. editor Associated Inds. Mass., 1976; pub. rels. specialist ways and means com. N.Y. State Assembly, Albany, 1977—79; credit mgr. Ten Speed Press, Berkeley, Calif., 1980—83, spl. sales mgr., 1984—86, v.p. at large, 1986—; pub. Celestial Arts/Crossing Press, 2001—05. Spkr. in field. Mem. 20 Nation Alliance Reform and Democracy in Asia, Singapore, 2001—05. Mem.: Burmese Am. Dem. Alliance. Democrat. Roman Catholic. Avocations: films, embroidery, cooking. Office: 10 Speed Press/Celestial Arts and Crossing Press PO Box 7123 Berkeley CA 94707

DECK, RICHARD ALLEN, political scientist, consultant, writer, volunteer; b. Concord, NH, May 6, 1953; s. Herbert Heller Jr. and Eleanor DuVall (Deyo) D.; m. Jo Ann Marie Passariello, Nov. 15, 1986. Student, Ripon Coll., 1972—73, Waseda U., Japan, 1974—75; BA in Polit. Sci. and East Asian Studies summa cum laude with honors, Macalester Coll., 1977; cert. in Urban and Regional Planning and Design, Harvard U., 1978; Grad. Cert. in Brit. Fgn. Policy, Oxford (Eng.) U., 1980; MA in Econs., Pub. Policy and Adminstrn., U. Manchester (Eng.), 1982; M in City Planning, U. Calif., Berkeley, 1982; AM in Polit. Sci., Stanford U., 1985, PhD in Polit. Sci., 1997; MALS, Dartmouth Coll., 1994. Internat./intercultural rels. seminar leader Assn. Current English Keio U., Japan, 1975; mag. writer and interviewer English Jour., Japan, 1975; rschr., writer Dem. Farmer Labor Party, Mpls., 1976; survey rschr. and analyst Project on Volunteerism Adelphi U., L.I., 1978; legis. analyst rschr. Assembly Edn. Com. N.Y. State Assembly, Albany, 1979; co-chair external affairs Grad. Assembly U. Calif., Berkeley, 1981—82; fellow internat. peace and security studies Social Sci. Rsch. Coun. and John D. and Catherine T. MacArthur Found., S.E. Asia, 1986—88; vis. joint fellow nat. and internat. security U. So. Calif., UCLA, 1989; rsch. fellow and project coord. Asian Regionalization Asia/Pacific Rsch. Ctr., Stanford U. and The Asia Found. San Francisco, 1991—92; v.p. Catalyst Concepts, Berkeley, 1992—2000, pres., 2001—; founding dir. Asia/Pacific Reg. Policy Rsch. Inst., Berkeley and Emeryville, Calif., 1998—; prodr., dir. Asian Democracy and Human Rights Webcasting Sta. Alliance for Reform and Democracy in Asia, Berkeley and Emeryville, 2001—. Social sys. dir. and bd. dirs. U. Calif. Space Working Group, U. Calif., Berkeley, 1979-80, 81-82; grad. rep. from Berkeley campus for the student body pres. coun. U. Calif. (systemwide), 1981-82; tchg. asst. Stanford (Calif.) U., 1983, 86, mem. grad. studies com., 1983-84, head tchg. asst., 1984, observer Project Peace and Coop. Asia-Pacific Region, 1984, mem. internat. rels. sr. faculty search com., 1985-86, co-instr., 1991; seminar group discussion leader, M.A.L.S. Colloquium on Ctrl. Am., Darmouth Coll., 1984; lectr. and participant World Affairs Coun. No. Calif., study group on the Assn. of So. East Asian Nat., San Francisco, 1985; participant Project Soviet Internat. Behavior, U. Calif., Berkeley and Stanford U., 1985-86; lectr. Inst. S.E. Asian Studies, 1988, Nat. U. Singapore, 1988, Asean Insts. Conf. on U.S.-Asean Rels., Singapore, 1988; conf. participant and delegate 40th Anniv. Commemoration of the Signing of the United Nat. Charter in San Francisco, 1985; ofcl. observer U.S. del. Pacific Econ. Cooperation Coun., PECC Gen. Meeting/Conf., San Francisco, 1992; global media dir. U.S.-S.E. Asian Alliance for a Dem. Asia, Cambridge, Mass., 1998-2000; cons. Def. & Diplomacy, The Newshour with Jim Lehrer, PBS-TV, Washington and Arlington, Va., 2000; panelist and spkr. Good Governance and Dem. Reform in Asia-Ideals in Action, Press Conf. and Staff Briefing, Congl. Human Rights Caucus, Washington, 2001; mem. Nat. Bus. Adv. Coun., Washington, 2002-04; cons. Lawyer's Com. on Human Rights, NYC, 2003, Nat. Dem. Inst. Internat. Affairs, Washington, 2003-04, Sweden-Singapore Initiative for Democracy, Olaf Palme Inst., Swedish Internat. Liberal Ctr., Jarl Hjalmarsson Found., Stockholm, Singapore Dem. Party, 2003—; liason to U.S. Democratic Nat. Convention for Alliance for Reform and Democracy in Asia, Boston, Mass., 2004, ASEAN Sect. leader Burma Pro-Democracy Conf., San Francisco, 2004, organizer, exec. dirs. tour Alliance for Reform and Democracy in Asia, 2004; spkr., lectr. in field. Author: U.S. official delegation "Dialogue Partners" session, First ASEAN Economic Congress, ASEAN Chambers of Commerce and Industry, and the Institute of Strategic and International Studies, 1987, Fourth ASEAN Institutes Conference on the Association of Southeast Asian Nations and the United States, 1988; (with others) Peace, Conflict, and Strategic Cultures in the Asia-Pacific Region, 1999 (nominee Kiriyama Pacific Rim book prize), (with others) The Singapore Puzzle, 1999 (nominee Kiriyama Pacific Rim book prize), Strategic Cultures in the Asia-Pacific Region, 1999 (paper edit., nominee Kiriyama Pacific Rim Book prize); co-author Asia Democracy Index, Singapore, 2005; contbr. to profl. articles; mem. editl. bd., edtl. writer, polit. corr., and polit. feature writer The Stanford Daily, 1982-83; rschr. and writing cons. The Concept of Relationship in International Politics, 1989-90; contbr. papers to various organizations; interview subject (TV) Friday Background, Current Affairs Unit, Singapore Broadcasting Corp., 1987, Berita (Evening news), RTM (Malaysian govt. network), 1987, Official Questionner of Malaysian Prime Minister Mahathir bin Mohamad, Iseas Singapore Lecture, Inst. of Southeast Asian Studies, 1988; (film) co-narrator and co-interviewer The Pennsylvania Underground: The Sanctuary Movement and Illegal Ctrl. Am. Refugees in Philadelphia, 1986; (newspaper) Internat. Herald Tribune, Republic of Singapore, 1987, (radio) The Michael Fay Caning Affair, The World Tonight with Phil Till Show, Radio Can., Vancouver, 1994; spl. contbr. Asiaweek newsmag., Hong Kong, 1998, mem. editl. bd. Asia Democracy Index, Alliance for Reform and Democracy in Asia, Taiwan, 2005; panelist, spkr. Congressional Human Rights Caucus, Washington, DC, 2005; spkr. several confs. and forums. Chmn. NH Govs.' Youth Hwy. Safety Adv. Com., 1972; conf. participant and del. 40th Anniversary Commemoration of the Signing of the UN Charter in San Francisco: Conf. Assessing the UN After 40 Yrs., UN Assn. San Francisco and World Affairs Coun. No. Calif., 1985; spl. fellowship coord. Open Soc. Inst., NYC, 1997—98, 2000; interim chairperson panel of experts and resource persons on Asian democratization Alliance for Reform and Democracy in Asia, Washington, 2000—01; co-dir. Asia Democracy Index Project Alliance for Reform and Democrary in Asia, Osaka, Japan, Berkeley/Emeryville, 2001—05; mem. steering com. Alliance for Reform and Democracy in Asia, Singapore, Washington and Kuala Lumpur, 2004—, liaison ofcl. to US Dem. Nat. Conv. Boston, 2004, West Coast organizer exec. dir.'s tour San Francisco, 2004, mem. editl. bd. Asia Democracy Index Taipei, Taiwan, 2005; co-chair Assn. Scholars and Rschrs. for Asian Dem. Studies, Alliance for Reform and Democracy in Asia, Berkeley, Emeryville, 2001—04, Singapore, Kuala Lumpur, Washington, 2004—05; bd. mem., exec. bd., bd. dirs. Burmese Am. Dem. Alliance, San Francisco, Union City, Calif., 2004—, chair Cmty. and Media Outreach Com., 2005—, chair polit. and collaboration com., 2005—; ASEAN sect. leader Burma Pro-Democracy Conf., San Francisco, 2004; panelist, spkr. on Asia Democracy Index and World Forum for Democratization in Asia Staff Briefing and Press Conf., Congl. Human Rights Caucus, Washington, 2005; del. World Forum for Democratization in Asia, Taipei, 2005; spkr. Burma Freedom Day Rally, San Francisco, 2004, Burma Pro-Democracy Conf., San Francisco, 2004, Tibet Day Cultural Fair, San Francisco, 2004, Burma Human Rights Day, Berkeley, 2005; Del. candidate NH Pres. Preference Primary, Dem. Nat. Conv., Keene, 1972, Calif. Pres. Primary, Stanford, 1984, Berkeley, 1992; candidate NH Constl. Conv., Keene, 1974; city and campus chairperson Calif. Dem. Pres. Primary Campaign, Stanford U. and Palo Alto, 1984, 1992; staff intern Minn. Dem. Farmer Labor Party Hdqs., 1976; bd. dirs. U. Manchester (Eng.) Postgrad. Soc., 1980—81. Recipient World Affairs Coun. Staff award, 1985, Nat. Small-Bus. Legis. Leadership Achievement award Bus. Adv. Coun., Washington, 2002; Nat. Forensics League scholar Ripon Coll., 1972-73; Harry Sherman scholar Macalester Coll., 1976-77; John W. Searle Meml. scholar Macalester Coll., 1976-77, Outstanding Sr. award, Minn. Jaycees, Coll. Ct. of Honor, 1977; NY State Assembly Grad. Scholar fellow, 1979; Roothbert Fund fellow U. Calif., Berkeley, 1979-80, 81-82; Inst. Internat. Edn. scholar Oxford U., 1980; Rotary Internat. Grad. fellow U. Manchester, 1980-81; Lasker scholar U. Calif., Berkeley, 1981-82; Newhouse fellow U. Calif., Berkeley, 1981-82; Eisenhower Meml. Grad. scholar Stanford U., 1982-83; AMVETS scholar Stanford U., 1982-86; Stanford U. Grad. fellow 1982-86; MALS Grad. fellow Dartmouth Coll., 1984, 86; UN Assn. and World Affairs Coun. scholar, 1985; Fgn. Lang. and Area Studies grantee U.S. Dept. Edn., 1985; SSRC/MacArthur found. fellow in Internat. Peace and Security, NYC and Chgo., 1986-88; USC-UCLA Vis. Joint fellowship in Nat. and Internat. Security, LA, 1989; rsch. fellow Asia/Pacific Rsch. Ctr. Stanford U. and the Asia Found., San Francisco, 1991-92; co-nominee (with Dr. Chee Soon Juan, Singapore) Nobel Peace Prize, 1999-2005. Mem. Internat. Studies Assn. (presenter 1998), Assn. Asian Studies, Acad. Polit. Sci., Am. Polit. Sci. Assn., Pi Kappa Delta, Phi Alpha Theta, Pi Sigma Alpha, Phi Beta Kappa. United Ch. of Christ. Avocations: reading novels and screenplays, viewing films. Office: Catalyst Concepts PO Box 8393 Berkeley CA 94707-8393 E-mail: rad-catalyst@webtv.net.

DECKELBAUM, NELSON, lawyer; b. Washington, Apr. 1, 1928; s. Fred and Rose (Egber) D.; m. Louann Jacobs, Oct. 19, 1952; children: David Alan, Todd Stuart. BS, Georgetown U., 1950, JD, 1952. Bar: D.C. 1952, Md. 1957, U.S. Supreme Ct. 1966. Practice law, Washington, 1952—; sr. ptnr. Deckelbaum Ogens & Raftery, Chartered, 1974—. Staff mem. Commn. on Govt. Security, 1956; dir. Independence Savs. Bank. Chmn. Democratic precinct, Montgomery County, Md., 1958. Served with USAF, 1952-54. Named in Best Lawyers in Am. Fellow Am. Coll. of Bankruptcy; mem. Am., Md., D.C. bar assns., Am. Judicature Soc., Georgetown Univ. Alumni Assn., Woodmont Country Club, Univ. Club (pres. 1994-95), D.C. Real Estate Commn. Home: 4200 Massachusetts Ave NW Apt 115 Washington DC 20016 Office: Deckelbaum Ogens & Raftery 3 Bethesda Metro Ctr Bethesda MD 20814-5330 Office Phone: 301-961-9200. E-mail: ndeckelbaum@deckelbaum.com.

DECKELMAN, WILLIAM L., JR., lawyer; b. Crossett, Ark., Aug. 19, 1957; s. William and Marion Deckelman; m. Julie Deckelman. BA, Ark. State U., 1978, MBA, 1979; JD, U. Ark., 1981. Bar: Tex. 1982. Assoc. Winstead Sechrest & Minick, Dallas, 1981—85; with MTech Corp. (acquired by Electronic Data Systems Corp. in 1988), 1985—88; sr. v.p., gen. counsel, sec. Affiliated Computer Services Inc., Dallas, 1989—93, exec. v.p., gen. counsel, sec., 1993—95, 2000—, dir., 2000—03; atty. pvt. practice, 1995—2000; mng. shareholder Munsch Hardt Kopf & Harr PC, Austin, Tex., 1996—2000. Mem.: State Bar Tex. Office: Affiliated Computer Services Inc 2828 N Haskell Bldg 1 Dallas TX 75204

DECKER, CAROL ARNE, magazine publishing executive; b. Rochelle, Ill., Apr. 3, 1946; d. Irvin Norman Arne and Edna (Olsen) Stein; m. Charles Levitt Decker, Feb. 17, 1979; children: Katharine Elizabeth. BA, So. Ill. U., 1969. Advt. sales rep. Travel Agent mag., N.Y.C., 1971-74, Business Week mag., N.Y.C., 1974-80, Reader's Digest Publs., N.Y.C., 1980-82; assoc. pub. The Atlantic Monthly, N.Y.C., 1982-84; pub. Personal Investor, N.Y.C., 1984-86, Lear's Mag., 1992-93; pub. cons. C.A. Decker & Assocs., N.Y.C., 1986-94; founder, CEO Western Interiors and Design Mag., LLC, Jackson, Wyo., 1999—. Office: PO Box 14610 Jackson WY 83002

DECKER, CHARLES RICHARD, investment company executive, educator; b. Murphysboro, Ill., Mar. 13, 1937; s. Ernest George and Joyce Ellen (Gibson) D.; m. Jeanine Ann Cowell, June 6, 1959; children: Ann Marie Britt, Lynn Rochelle Lake, Charles Ernest BBA, U. Miss., 1959; MBA, Ind. U., 1962, EdD, 1968; cert., Harvard U., 1981. Cert. fin. planner, 1990. Asst. prof. Ill. State U., Normal, 1968-70, chmn. dept. bus. adminstrn., 1970-74; dean sch. bus. Millikin U., Decatur, Ill., 1974-80, provost, v.p., 1980-86, Grover M. Hermann prof. bus. policy, 1986-98; ptnr. Black Watch Investment Mgmt., 2002—. Investment mgr., bd. dirs. John Warner Fin. Svcs. Inc., 1996-2002. Contbr. articles to profl. jours. Bd. dirs. Decatur Civic Ctr., 1984-92, vice chmn., 1986-87, chmn., 1987-92; bd. dirs. United Way of Decatur and Macon County, 1984-87, Boys Club, Decatur, 1980-82; mem. exec. bd. Lincoln Trails Coun. Boy Scouts Am., 1988-93, SME chair, 1989-91, v.p., 1990-93. Mem. North Cent. Assn. Acad. Deans (pres. 1984-85), C. of C. (bd. dirs. 1976-79, v.p. 1979), Alpha Lambda Delta, Phi Delta Kappa, Phi Kappa Phi, Omicron Delta Kappa, Sigma Chi. Avocations: photography, tennis, bicycling. Home: 1740 Illini Dr Decatur IL 62521-9169

DECKER, JOHN LOUIS, lawyer; b. Omaha, Jan. 12, 1946; s. Loyal Ernst and Olivia (Buehler) D.; m. Beverly Kaye Shanks, Aug. 17, 1968; children: Elizabeth Ann, John Louis Jr. BS, U. Nebr., Lincoln, 1968, JD, 1971. Bar: Nebr. 1971, Mo. 1988. Atty. Nebr. Dept. Revenue, Lincoln, 1971-76, adminstr. tax policy, 1976-79, dep. tax commr., 1979-82; dir. fin. svcs. Commonwealth Cos., Lincoln, 1982-87; mem. Belz & Beckemeier, P.C., St. Louis, 1987-93; with Stuart, Maue, Mitchell & James, Ltd., St. Louis, 1993—. Pres., adv. Lancaster Office Mental Retardation, Lincoln, 1985-87. Republican. Presbyterian. Home: 705 Villa Capri Ct Saint Louis MO 63132-3604 Office: Stuart Maue Mitchell & James Ltd 3840 McKelvey Rd Saint Louis MO 63044 Office Phone: 314-291-3030. Business E-Mail: johnldecker@charter.net.

DECKER, JOHN WILLIAM, metal products executive; b. Cleve., July 15, 1948; s. James William and Betty Erdmann (Smith) Decker; m. Elaine Marie Metz, Aug. 30, 1971; children: Amanda Elaine, Gregory John. BS, Lincoln Meml. U., 1966-70; MEd, Kent (Ohio) State U., 1970-72. Cert. tchr., adminstr. Ohio. Elem. tchr. Parma (Ohio) City Schs., 1970-78; corp. sec., treas. Decker Steel & Supply, Inc. (formerly Decker Reichert Steel & Supply, Inc.), Cleve., 1978-83, v.p., 1983-85, pres., chmn., CEO, 1985—. Mem. Am. Theater Orgn. Soc., Plahouse Sq. Vol. Group; co-chmn. cmty. fin. com. Parma City Schs., 1994—97; apptd. Parma Bd. Edn., 1997, elected, 1998—2001, v.p., 1999—, pres., 2000—01; ruling elder Parma South Presbyn. Ch., Parma Heights, Ohio, 1979—81, 1983—92, 1996—, clk. of session, 1983—94, chmn. fin. com., 1995—96, chmn. properties coun., 1997—2000, adminstrv. coun. chairperson, 2001. Mem.: Greater Cleve. Growth Assn., Masons. Republican. Avocations: choral group singing, pipe organ playing, repair and building, collecting antique telephones, collecting victorian lighting. Home: 9634 Greenbriar Dr Cleveland OH 44130-4756 Office: 4500 Train Ave Cleveland OH 44102-4515 Office Phone: 216-281-7900.

DECKER, KATE DELANO-CONDAX (KATE DELANO-CONDAX DECKER), marketing and public relations executive; b. Phila., Mar. 23, 1945; d. John Baptiste and Laura Foster (Delano) Condax; m. Arnold Francis Decker. Student, Sweet Briar Coll., 1964—66, U. St. Andrews, Scotland, 1966-67. Legis. aide to Sen. Samuel J. Ervin, Jr. Subcom. Separation of Powers, Com. on Judiciary U.S. Senate, Washington, 1970-73; ptnr. U.S. Trade Trip to People's Republic China, 1973; assoc. producer, asst. dir. KYW-TV, Phila., 1973-74; account exec. Aitkin, Kynett Pub. Rels., Phila., 1975-77, ICPR Pub. Rels., N.Y.C., 1977-79; dir. pub. rels. Am. Heritage Pub. Co., Inc., N.Y.C., 1979-81; account exec. Howard J. Rubenstein Pub. Rels., Inc., N.Y.C., 1981-82; rsch. assoc. Nordeman Grimm Exec. Search Firm, N.Y.C., 1982-84; pres. Kate Delano Condax & Assocs. Mktg., N.Y.C.,

1984-89; nat. dir. mktg. and pub. rels. Allmilmo Corp., Fairfield, N.J., 1989-92; prin. Kate Decker & Assocs., Moorestown, NJ, 1997—. Mktg. and media cons.; exec. dir. Philadelphia 100; pres. Pet Bulls, Inc., bd. dirs. The Eldercare Project, 1998—. Author: Horse Sense: Cause and Correction of Problems, 1979, 2d edit. rev., 1990, Riding: A Guide for New Riders, 1995, 120th edit., 2003, 101 Training Tips for Your Dog, 1994, 13th edit., 2002. Probono housing counselor to elderly, N.Y.C., 1980—; bd. dirs. ex officio, mktg. dir. Interfaith Caregivers; dir. pub. affairs Recording for the Blind & Dyslexic, Princeton, N.J., 1995-97; exec. dir. Elder Project: Creating a Living Environment for the Elderly, 1997—. Mem. Brit. Horse Soc. (instr.), Am. Horse Shows Assn. (judge ex-officio), Soc. Mayflower Descs., Nat. Soc. Colonial Dames Am., Coffee House Club N.Y. Office Phone: 856-231-1245, 609-519-4367.

DECKER, KATE DELANO-CONDAX See DECKER, KATE

DECKER, MICHAEL H., civilian military employee; BBA in Bus. Adminstrn., U. Notre Dame; MA in Govt./Nat. Security Studies, Georgetown U.; MS in Strategic Intelligence, Def. Intelligence Coll. Commd. 2d lt. USMC, advanced through grades, ret., 1991, NBC def. officer, asst. BLT ops. officer, commanding officer Co. G BLT 2/6, security force/marine security guard officer Security br. Washington, asst. ops. officer/liaison officer 26th Marine amphibious unit Honduras, asst. intelligence officer 13th Marine Expeditionary Unit, sr. intelligence analyst 7th MEB and I MEF, asst. dir. intelligence Washington; sr. systems engr. Delfin Systems; dep. program mgr. for long-range info. networked comm. svcs. Sci. Applications Internat. Corp.; dir. intelligence USMC, 2004—. Decorated Bronze Star medal, Navy Commendation medal, Marine Corp Commendation medal, Meritorious Svc. medal. Office: USMC 2511 Jefferson Davis Hwy Arlington VA 22202

DECKER, MICHAEL JOHN, music educator, musician; d. William Spurgeon and Betty Jane Decker. At, Millersville State Coll., Pa., 1968—72, Towson U., Md., 1981—84; MusM, Peabody Conservatory Johns Hopkins U., 1993. Prof. music York Coll. of Pa., 1972—75, Towson U., Md., 1975—. Guitarist Balt. Symphony Orch., 1976—, Kennedy Ctr. Opera Orch., Washington, 1996—; asst. condr. Balt. Opera Co., 1983; artistic prodr. and dir. Md. Arts Festival, Towson, 1987—2001; recording musician. Author: History of Baltimore Musicians Union; translator: Nuevo Metodo Para Bannurvia, 2001. Recipient 2 Grammys, Recording Acad., Gold Record, Recording Industry Assn. Am. Mem.: Music and Entertainers Educators Assn., Guitar Found. Am., Musicians Assn. Met. Balt. Democrat. Home: 3212 Abell Ave Baltimore MD 21218 Office: Towson Univ Music Dept 8000 York Rd Towson MD 21252

DECKER, PETER RANDOLPH, rancher, retired state official; b. N.Y.C., Oct. 1, 1934; s. Frank Randolph and Marjorie (Marony) D.; m. Dorothy Morss, Sept. 24, 1972; children: Karen, Christopher, Hilary. BA, Middlebury Coll., Vt., 1957; MA, Syracuse U., 1961; PhD, Columbia U., 1974. Tchr. Cate Sch., Carpinteria, Calif., 1961-63; sr. writer Congl. Quar., Washington, 1963-64; asst. to pres. Middlebury (Vt.) Coll., 1964-67; staff asst. Sen. Robert Kennedy, Washington, 1967-68; corr. AP, Laos, Vietnam, 1970; instr./lectr. Columbia U., N.Y.C., 1972-74; asst. prof. Duke U., Durham, N.C., 1974-80; owner, operator Double D Ranches, Ridgway, Colo., 1980—; commr. agr. State of Colo., Denver, 1987-89; pres. Decker & Assocs., Denver, Colo., 1989—. Dir. Nat. Western Stock Show, Denver, 1990—; bd. dirs. Fed. Res. Bd. Kansas City, Denver, 1992-98; bd. dirs. Western Colo. Bank, Montrose; pres. Telluride Bancorp, Inc., 1990-97; mem. adv. bd. Crow Canyon Archeol. Ctr., Fulcrum Press. Author: Fortunes and Failures, 1978, Old Fences, New Neighbors, 1998, The Utes Must Go, 2005; contbr. articles to profl. jours. and mags. Trustee Middlebury Coll., 1988-96, Colo. Commn. on Higher Edn., 1985-93; chmn. Ouray County Planning Commn., 1981-85; chmn. Colo. Endowment Humanities, 1982-85; chmn., bd. trustees Ft. Lewis Coll., 2002—. Lt. U.S. Army, 1957-60, capt. Res., 1960-67. English Speaking Union scholar, 1952-53; Nat. Endowment for Humanities fellow Yale U., 1977-78, Rockefeller Found. fellow, 1979-80. Mem. Nat. Cattlemen's Assn., Colo. Livestock Assn., Denver Athletic Club, Elks, Colo. Author's League, Angler's Club (Key Largo, Fla.), Columbia U. Club (N.Y.C.). Democrat. Home: 395 Race St Denver CO 80206-4118

DECKER, PETER WILLIAM, academic administrator; b. Grand Rapids, Mich., Mar. 20, 1919; s. Charles B. and Ruth E. (Thorndill) D.; m. Margaret I. Stainthorpe, June 10, 1944; children: Peter, Marilyn, Christine, Charles. BS, Wheaton Coll., 1941; postgrad., Northwestern U., 1942-43, U. Mich., 1958-60; DSc, London Inst. Applied Rsch., 1973; LLD, 1975; DSTh, Midwestern Baptist Bible Sem., 1995. Withadvtg. dept. Hotels Windermere, Chgo., 1942; with Princess Pat Cosmetics, Chgo., 1943; market rsch. investigator A.C. Nielson Co., Chgo., 1944-48; pres. Peter Decker Constrn. Co., Detroit, 1948-60; sales mgr. Century Chem. Products Co., Detroit, 1961-62, vice pres., 1962-63, pres., 1963-75; sr. ptnr. G & D Advtg. Assocs., 1967-78; vice pres., treas., exec. dir. Christian Edn. Advancement, Inc., 1975-95; registrar, instr. N.T. Greek Missions and Theology Birmingham Bible Inst., MI, 1973-86; prof. Midwestern Baptist Coll., 1984—, dir. student fin. aid, 1984—. Trustee Midwestern Baptist Coll., 1985—, mem. exec. com., 1984—, asst. to pres. 1985-90, treas. 1991-95; bd. dirs., prof., trusteeMidwestern Bapt. Bible Sem., 1995—, vice pres. Midewestern Bapt. Bible Seminary Grad. Sch., 1998—. Author: Gettin to Know New Testament Greek, Christology, The Pauline Epistles. Scoutmaster, Boy Scouts of Am., 1956-61, neighborhood commr., 1961-66, merit badge counselor, emeritus, 1979—; mem. Bd. Rev. Beverly Hills, Mich., 1957-63; chmn. Bd. Rev. Southfield Twp., Mich., 1964-67; past pres., Beverly Hills Civic Assn., 1956, bd. dirs., 1953-57, pres., 1958-59; trustee, deacon, Birmingham Mich. Bible Inst., instr. Bible Inst.; bd. dirs. Mich. Epilepsy Ctr. and Assn., 1957-71, exec. com., 1962-67. Recipient Arrowhead Honor awd. Boy Scouts Am., 1965. Mem. AAAS, ASTM, Mich. Edn. Assocs., Inc. (exec. com. 1994—, treas. 1994-95), Detroit Soc. Model Engrs. (pres. 1958, 62, bd. dirs. 1955-71), Chem. Splty. Mfg. Assn., Nat. Geog. Soc., Internat. Platform Assn., The Heritage Found., Smithsonian Instn. Assocs., Archaeol. Inst. Am., Bibl. Archaeol. Soc., Bible-Sci. Assn., Creation Rsch. Soc., Mich. Student Fin. Aid Assn., Midwest Assn. Student Fin. Aid Adminstrs. Republican. Avocations: biographies, writings of great christians. Office: Midwestern Baptist Coll 825 Golf Dr Pontiac MI 48341-2379 Home: 2304 Northcrest Dr Angola IN 46703-2376

DECKER, RAYMOND FRANK, chemicals executive, metal products executive; b. Afton, N.Y., July 20, 1930; s. Bernett Hurd and Mildred (Bisbee) Decker; life ptnr. Mary Birdsall, Dec. 27, 1951; children: Susan, Elizabeth, Catherine, Laura. BS, U. Mich., 1952, MS, 1955, PhD, 1958. With Inco Ltd., 1958-82, v.p. corp. tech. and diversification ventures, 1978-82; v.p. rsch. and corp. rels. Mich. Technol. U., Houghton, 1982-86; pres., CEO Univ. Sci. Ptnrs., Inc., 1986-98; pres. ASM Internat., 1986-87; founding chmn., pres., CEO Thixomat, Inc., 1988—2004, chair, pres., CEO, 2004—, also bd. dirs.; founding chmn. Wavemat, Inc., 1987-88. Bd. dirs. Spl. Metals Corp., 1990—2003; adj. prof. Poly. Inst. Bklyn., 1962—66, NYU, 1968, U. Mich., 1997—; cons. KMS Fusion, Inc., Howmet turbine Components, Alcoa, GE, GM, 1985—; Van Horn Disting. lectr. Case-Western Res. U., 1975; mem. materials adv. bd. NASA, 1969, Nat. Bur. Stds., 1973, NSF, 1985—86; mem. Nat. Materials Adv. Bd., 1982—88; mem. exec. com. Strategic Hwy. Rsch. Program, 1986—93; long-range planning com. Metall. Soc., 1985—87, State Rsch. Fund Panel Mich., 1983—86; chmn. rsch. & tech. coordinating com. Fed. Hwy. Adminstrn., 1995—98; trustee Foundry Ednl. Found., 1975—77, Welding Rsch. Coun., 1975—80; chmn. bd. trustees Mich. Energy and Resource Rsch. Assn., 1985—86; keynote spkr. on superalloys Seven Springs Conf., 1980, NAE, 1980—. Author: (book) Strengthening Mechanisms in Nickel-Base Superalloys; editor: Maraging Steels. Chmn. alumni com. dept. material sci. and engring. U. Mich., Ann Arbor, chmn. class of 1952 reunion; chmn. Ch. Coun., 2001—03. Recipient IR-100 award, 1964, Sesquicentennial award, U. Mich., 1967, Disting. Grad. award, 1994, Innovation award, Mobile Computing, 1999, Inc 500 award, 1999. Fellow: Am. Soc. Metals Internat. (chmn. materials sys. and design divsn. 1971—73, trustee 1976—79, chmn. diamond decade com. 1980—81, Campbell Meml. lectr. 1985, chmn. organizing com. World Materials Congress 1988, hon. mem. 1991, Alpha Sigma Mu lectr. 2001, Woodside lectr. 2003, Gold medal 1981); mem.: NAE, AAAS, AIME (lectr. Inst. Metals divsn. 1973, R. F. Mehl medal 1973), Afton Ctrl. Sch. Alumni Assn. (v.p. 2004—). Congregationalist. Achievements include co-inventing maraging steels, Thixomolding machine. Home: Apt 204 505 E Huron Ann Arbor MI 48104 Office Phone: 734-995-5550. Business E-Mail: rdecker@thixomat.com.

DECKER, RICHARD JEFFREY, lawyer; b. Manhasset, N.Y., Aug. 26, 1959; s. Alan B. and Shelley T. (Belkin) D.; m. Carrie Ann Gordon, Aug. 13, 1989. BA, Union Coll., Schenectady, N.Y., 1981; JD, Boston U., 1984. Bar: N.Y. 1985, Calif. 1985, Mass. 1985, U.S. Dist. Ct. (cen. dist.) Calif. 1985. Assoc. Turner, Gesterfeld, Wilk & Tigerman, Beverly Hills, Calif., 1985-86, Shapiro, Posell & Close, L.A., 1986-90, Katten, Muchin, Zavis & Weitzman, L.A., 1990-93; ptnr. Stephan, Oringher, Richman & Theodora, L.A., 1993—. Mem. Los Angeles County Bar Assn., Beverly Hills Bar Assn., Century City Bar Assn. Avocations: sports, guitar playing, travel, reading. Office: 2029 Century Park E Ste 600 Los Angeles CA 90067-2907

DECKER, RICHARD KNORE, lawyer; b. Lincoln, Nebr., Sept. 15, 1913; s. Fred William and Georgia (Kilmer) Decker; m. Fern Iona Steinbaugh, June 12, 1938. AB, U. Nebr., 1935, JD, 1938. Bar: Nebr. 1938, U.S. Supreme Ct. 1941, D.C. 1948, Ill. 1952. Trial atty. antitrust div. Dept. Justice, 1938-52; ptnr. Lord, Bissell & Brook, Chgo., 1953-84, of counsel, 1984—2005. Trustee Village of Clarendon Hills (Ill.), 1960-64; chmn. bd. elders Community Presbyn. Ch., Clarendon Hills, 1963-66; mem. Union Ch. of Hinsdale; chmn. bd. Community House, Hinsdale, Ill., 1976, Robert Crown Ctr. for Health Edn., Hinsdale, Ill., 1981-83, also bd. dirs, 1976-2005. With USNR, 1942-45, lt. comdr. ret. Mem. ABA (chmn. antitrust sect. 1971-72), Ill. Bar Assn. (gov. 1969-73, chmn. antitrust sect. 1964-66), Chgo. Bar Assn. (chmn. antitrust law com. 1956-59), The Lawyers Club Chgo., Hinsdale Golf Club (pres. 1968). Republican. Home: 196 Pheasant Hollow Dr Burr Ridge IL 60527-5051 Office: 115 S La Salle St Ste 2900 Chicago IL 60603-3801

DECKER, ROBERT OWEN, history professor, clergyman; b. Lafayette, Ind., Nov. 6, 1927; s. Samuel Owen and Helen Dale (Noble) D.; m. Margaret Ann Harris, May 30, 1948; 1 child, Terry Lynn Decker DeIulis. AB, Butler U., 1953; AM, Ind. U., 1958; PhD, U. Conn., 1970. Ordained to ministry Congregational Ch., 1990. Instr. City of LaPorte (Ind.) Schs., 1956—59, Ctrl. Conn. State U., New Britain, 1959-63, asst. prof., 1963-73, assoc. prof., 1973-77, prof. history, 1977-89, prof. emeritus, 1989—. Editor manuscripts Wesleyan U. Press, 1977-89; advisor NEH, 1977-89, Connecticut River Found. Author: Whaling Industry of New London, 1973, The Whaling City: A History of New London, 1976, A Student Guidebook to American History, 1983, Hartford Immigrants, 1987, The New London Merchants, 1986, Cromwell, Connecticut 1650-1990: The History of A River Port Town, 1991; contbr. articles and book revs. to profl. jours. Mem. Christian Activities Coun., Hartford, 1965—, pres., 1972-74, 76-78, historian, 1983—, life mem., 1996—; bd. dirs. Hartford Inner City Exch., 1971-81, chmn. bd., 1977-80; chmn. state legis. adv. com. Conn. Devel. Disabilities Coun., 1973-75; evaluator programs Conn. Humanities Coun.; historian Rocky Hill (Conn.) Congl. Ch., 1985-89, Conn. 350th Com., 1985-89; justice of peace, Rocky Hill, 1985-89, 2000—, constable, 1986-89, 2002—, apptd. town historian, 1988—; mem. Assn. Conn. Mcpl. Historians, 1988—, membership sec., 1994—, pres., 1996-97; pastor Eagle Rock Congl. Ch., 1989-93, Bozrah Centre Congl. Ch., 1994-95, supply pastor, 1995-2001; pastor Barkhamstead Ctr. Congl. Ch., 2001—; mem. UCC Hist. Com., 1989-92, Rep. Town Comm., Rocky Hill, 2000—; dir. Old Towne Tourism Dist. Com., 1989-90; justice of peace, 1998—. Served with U.S. Army, 1946-52. Asian Studies grantee, 1959; Am. Studies grantee, 1959; Danforth grantee, 1962; Munson Maritime grantee, 1961; Smithsonian Inst. grantee, 1963; recipient Pierport Edwards award Grand Lodge Ct., 2003. Mem. AAUP, Orgn. Am. Historians, Am. Hist. Assn., New Eng. Hist. Assn., Conn. Hist. Assn., Assn. for Study of Conn. History, New London County Hist. Soc., Am. Waldensian Aid Soc. (pres. Hartford chpt. 1986-89), Masons (Master Stepney Lodge 1990, 92, Master's award 1992, Arthur E. Warner award 1996, Master Silas Dean Lodge 2001-02, 2003-2004, Grand Chaplain 1997-2003, High Priest Delta chpt. 1998-99, Knight Mason 1998—, master Philosophic Lodge Rsch., worshipful master 2000-01, Master's award 2001, 2002, eminent comdr. 2001—02, thrice illustrious master Walcott Coun. I 2000-01, high priest 2001—02, assoc. grand prelate, 2002-), Royal Arch Masons (Pierpont Edward Bronze medal 2003), Masonic Vet. Assn. Conn. (Venerable Master 2005-06), Phi Alpha Delta. Republican. Congregationalist (life deacon). Home: 2623 Main St Rocky Hill CT 06067-2507 Office: Barkhamsted Cong Ch 6 Olde Town Hall Rd Pleasant Valley CT 06063 Office Phone: 860-379-5864. Personal E-mail: robertowendecker@worldnet.att.net.

DECKER, SUSAN L., Internet company executive; married; 3 children. BS, Tufts U.; MBA, Harvard U. Cert. Charterd Fin. Analyst. With Donaldson, Lufking & Jenrette (DLJ), 1986—2000, publ. and advtsg. rsch. anlayst, dir. global head rsch., 1998—2000; sr. v.p. fin. & adminstrn. Yahoo! Inc., Sunnyvale, Calif., 2000—02, CFO, 2000—, sr. v.p. fin. and adminstrn., 2002—. Apptd. to acctg. standards adv. coun. Fin. Acctg. Fedn., 2000—04; bd. dirs. Pixar Animation Studios, 2004—. Office: Yahoo! 701 1st Av Sunnyvale CA 04089

DECKER, THEODORE GEORGE, artist; b. Birmingham, Ala., Sept. 10, 1948; s. Francis Decker and Mary Isabell; m. Vaunda Jean Hills, May 22, 1970; children: Melissa Ann, Michelle Lynn. Co-author Morrison-Decker Act, 1983. With U.S. Army, 1968. Democrat. Roman Catholic. Avocations: reading, photography. Home: 821 S Laventure Rd Apt D Mount Vernon WA 98274

DECKER, WALTER JOHNS, toxicologist; b. Tannersville, NY, June 13, 1933; s. H. Russell and Leola May (Coons) D.; m. Barbara Allen Hart, Aug. 19, 1961; children: Karl Hart, Reid Johns, Sam Travis. BA, SUNY, Albany, 1954, MA, 1955; PhD, George Washington U., 1966. Commd. 2d lt. U.S. Army, 1955, advanced through grades to lt. col., 1970, ret., 1975; assoc. prof. U. Tex. Med. Br., Galveston, 1976-83; pres. Toxicology Cons. Svcs., El Paso, Tex., 1984-97. Adj. clin. prof. Tex. Tech. U., El Paso, 1991—. Contbr. articles to jours. Clin. Toxicology, Vet. and Human Toxicology, Toxicology and Applied Pharmacology, others. Mem. sci. rev. panel Nat. Libr. Medicine's Hazardous Substance Data Bank, Bethesda, Md., 1985-2000; chair steering com. West Tex. Poison Ctr., El Paso, 1994-96. Recipient Aesculapius award, Tex. Med. Assn., 1977, Career Achievement award, Am. Acad. Clin. Toxicology, 2001. Fellow: Am. Acad. Clin. Toxicology (Career Achievement award 2001); mem.: Soc. Toxicology. Episcopalian. Achievements include research in toxicology.

DECKER, WAYNE LEROY, meteorologist, educator; b. Patterson, Iowa, Jan. 24, 1922; s. Albert Henry and Effie (Holmes) D.; m. Martha Jane Livingston, Dec. 29, 1943; 1 dau., Susan Jane. BS, Central Coll., Pella, Iowa, 1943; postgrad., UCLA, 1943-44; MS, Iowa State U., 1947, PhD, 1955. Meteorologist U.S. Weather Bur., Washington and Des Moines, 1947-49; mem. faculty U. Mo. at Columbia, 1949—, prof. atmospheric sci., 1958-67, prof., chmn. dept. atmospheric sci., 1967-91; prof. emeritus U. Mo., Columbia, 1992—; dir. coop. inst. applied meteorology U. Mo. at Columbia, 1985-92; cons. climatologist, 1992—. Chmn. com. climatic fluctuations and agrl. prodn. NRC, 1975-76; bd. dirs. Council for Agrl. Sci. and Tech., 1978-85, mem. exec. com., 1981-85; chair organizing com. 16th Internat. Congress Biometeorology. Fellow Am. Meteorol. Soc.; mem. Internat. Soc. Biometeorology (treas. 1990-99, chair, 16th Internat. Congress Biometeorology), Am. Geophys. Union, Am. Agronomy Soc., Sigma Xi, Gamma Sigma Delta. Home: 23 Springer Dr Columbia MO 65201-5424 Office: Univ Mo 302A Anheuser-Busch Natural Resources Bl Columbia MO 65211-7040

DECKERS, PETER JOHN, dean; b. Boston, Feb. 13, 1941; married, 1964; 7 children. BA cum laude, Coll. of the Holy Cross, 1962; MD cum laude, Boston U., 1966. Diplomate Nat. Bd. Med. Examiners, Am. Bd. Surgery. Med. intern Boston City Hosp., 1966—67; jr. asst. resident gen. surgery Boston U. Med. Ctr., Univ. Hosp., 1967—68; clin. assoc. surgery br. Nat. Cancer Inst., NIH, Bethesda, 1968—70; resident gen. surgery Boston U. Med. Ctr., U. Hosp., 1971, UPSHS trainee in acad. surgyer, 1971—72, resident in gen. surgery, 1972—73, chief resident in gen. surgery, 1973—74; staff surgeon Boston City Hosp., 1974—84; asst. to assoc. prof. surgery Boston U. Sch. Medicine, 1974—78; dean U. Conn. Sch. of Medicine, 1995—2000, dean sch. of medicine and exec. v.p. health affairs, 2000—. Attending staff gen. surgery John Dempsey Hosp./U. Conn. Health Ctr., 1984—, VA Med. Ctr., 1984-89; sr. staff dept. surgery Hartford Hosp., 1984—; program dir. Hartford Hosp.-U. Conn. Integrated Surg. Residency Program, 1984-94; dir. divsn. of gen. surgery Hartford Hosp., 1984-87; sr. staff dept. surgery New Britain Gen. Hosp., 1989—, Dept. Surgery, Mt. Sinai Hosp., 1989—, St. Francis Hosp. and Med. Ctr., 1988—; chmn. dept. surgery Hartford Hosp., 1987-94, Murray-Heilig prof., chmn. dept. surgery U. Conn. Sch. of Medicine, 1987-95; surgeon-in-chief John Dempsey Hosp., 1990-94; program dir. U. of Conn. Integrated Gen. Surg. Residency Tng. Program, 1990-94; interim dean, 1992-94; exec. v.p. for clin. affairs U. Conn. Health System, 1994-95; exec. v.p. for physician practice orgn. U. Conn. Health System, 1995—. Editl. bd. Breast Surgery: Index and Reviews, 1993, Surg. Oncology, 1991; contbr. numerous articles to profl. jours. Recipient First Prize James Ewing Resident Rsch. award, 1971; recipient numerous grants. Mem. Transplantation Soc., Am. Assn. for Cancer Rsch., Eastern Coop. Oncology Group, Assn. for Acad. Surgery, Am. Assn. for Cancer Edn., Am. Fedn. for Clin. Rsch., Mass. Med. Soc., Am. Radium Soc. (exec. com. 1989-91), Am. Soc. of Clin. Oncology, Soc. of Surg. Oncology (mem. coms.), Soc. of Univ. Surgeons, New England Cancer Soc. (pres. 1993, pres.-elect 1992, exec. coun. 1991-94), Boston Surg. Soc., Societe Internationale de Chirurgie, Bay State Health Care, Soc. for the Surgery of the Alimentary Tract, New England Surg. Soc. (treas. 1996-98, pres. 1999), Assn. of Program Dirs. in Surgeons (pres.-elect 1990-91, pres. 1991-92), Conn. State Med. Soc. (mem. cancer coordinating com. 1990-91), Am. Cancer Soc. (Hartford chpt.), Connecticare, Hartford County Med. Assn., Soc. of Surg. Chmn. Home: 44 Heritage Dr Avon CT 06001 Office: Univ Conn Health Ctr 263 Farmington Ave Farmington CT 06030-3800 E-mail: deckers@nso.uchc.edu.

DECKO, KENNETH OWEN, trade association administrator; b. New Haven, Aug. 7, 1944; s. Charles C. and Frances D.; m. Marilyn Seaver, Oct. 21, 1972; children: Kurt, Amy. Student, Duke U.; JD, U. Conn., 1969. With Conn. Bus. and Industry Assn., Hartford, 1970—, pres., 1981—. Served with USAR, 1969-70. Office: 350 Church St Hartford CT 06103-1106

DECKROSH, HAZEN DOUGLAS, retired state agency educator and administrator; b. Defiance, Ohio, Apr. 13, 1936; s. Lawrence L. and Martha L. Deckrosh; m. Carol Ann Everett, Nov. 25, 1970; children: Stephanie, Todd, Douglas, Nadia Nicole. BS, Ohio No. U., 1959; MEd, U. Toledo, 1980. Cert. tchr., Ohio. Phys. edn. and history tchr., coach Waynesfield (Ohio)-Goshen Jr. High Sch., 1959-61; coach, history, phys. edn. tchr. Coshocton (Ohio) Sacred Heart High Sch., 1961-63; health-phys. edn. tchr., coach West Holmes Jr. High Sch., Millersburg, Ohio, 1965-70; tchr. history and govt., coach Elida High Sch., 1970-73; occupational work experience tchr.-coord., coach Spencerville (Ohio) High Sch., 1973-77; occupational work edn. tchr., coord. Four County Vocat. Sch., Archbold, Ohio, 1977-82, 99—; vocat. supr. Jefferson County Vocat. Sch., Steubenville, Ohio, 1986-87; occupational work experience tchr., coord. Ohio Dept. of Youth Svcs., Columbus, 1987-94; ret., 1994. Pres. DYS Coordinators, Columbus, 1990-94; ski instr. Swiss Valley, Mich., 1995—; GED instr. Correction Ctr. Northwest Ohio. Editor: Threaded Fasteners, 1987; contbr. articles to profl. publs. Mem. Am. Youth Hostels, Lima, 1972—. Mem. NEA, Ohio Edn. Assn., Am. Vocat. Assn., Ohio Vocat. Assn., Occupl. Work Experience Coords. Assn. (state adv. coun., Lima rep. 1977-80, Columbus rep. 1991-94), Full Gospel Bus. Men's Fellowship Internat., Gideons Internat. (treas., then sec.), 5th Dist. Ofcls. Assn. (v.p., rules interpreter), Capitol West Umpires Assn. (rules interpreter 1991-93), Lima Umpires Assn. (sec.-treas. 1973-77), Ret. Tchrs. Assn. (pres.), Alpha Sigma Phi. Republican. Avocations: sports officiating, high school and college sports, teaching skiing. Home: 12265 County Road 150 Montpelier OH 43543-9613 Personal E-mail: blazinghazen@aol.com.

DECOPPET, LAURA LOUISE, writer, editor; b. N.Y.C., June 21, 1946; d. André and Eileen (Johnston) de C; m. Kenneth Archer LaBarre; 1 child, Susanna Jane. BA, Barnard Coll., N.Y.C., 1968. Asst. Avant Guard Art Gallery, N.Y.C., 1972-76; writer, editor Interview Mag., 2003—. Author, editor: The Art Dealers, 1984, 2d edit., 2002. Mem. Ch. Of Eng. Avocations: backgammon, biking, art collecting, mahjonga, bridge. Home: 50 E 10th St New York NY 10003-6221 Office: Interview Mag 500 Broadway New York NY 10012-4416

DECOSTA, BENJAMIN R., airport executive; BA in Physics, Queens Col.; JD, NY Law Sch., 1975. With Port Authority NY, 1972—78; chief of staff, personnel and labor relations City of NY, 1978—83; gen. mgr. Newark Int. Airport, NJ, 1994—98; gen. mgr. aviation Hartsfield-Jackson Internat. Airport, Atlanta, 1998—. Office: Dept Aviation Hartsfield Jackson Internat Airport 6000 N Terminal Pkwy, PO Box 20509 Atlanta GA 30320

DE COSTER, BARBARA LOU, retired technical services librarian; b. Salt Lake City, Dec. 22, 1932; d. Frederic K. and Lucille (Campbell) Gray; children from previous marriage: Don T. Jr., Carol Ann O'Keefe, Catherine Alvarez. BA, U. Wash., 1965, MLS, 1967; PhD, U. Tex., 1984. Tech. processes libr. Bellevue (Wash.) Community Coll., 1967-95; ret., 1995. Cons. ECNU, Hua Dong Shifan Daxue, Shanghai, People's Republic China, summers, 1987, 88, 90, vis. prof., 1992-93; cons. Nat. Libr. China, Beijing, summers 1987, 90, U. Wash., Seattle, 1967. Subject indexer (book) Texas in Children's Books, 1986. Chair Polit. Action Com. Bellevue Community Coll. Assn. Higher Edn., Bellevue Community Coll., 1987-90. Grad. fellow U. Tex., 1982-83; scholar U. Tex., 1981-82, MIT, 1950. Mem. OnLine Audio-Visual Catalogers (news editor 1985-92), Cmty. Coll. Librs. and Media Specialists (pres. 1985-87), Western Libr. Network-Wash. Users Group (chair 1989-91), Factoria Med. Ctr. Coun. Group Health Cooperate (chair 1989-91), Bellevue Cmty. Coll. Assn. Higher Edn. (pres./pres.-elect 1990-92). Avocations: travel, computers, quilting, photography. Home: 6343 NE 156th St Kenmore WA 98028-4373

DE COURTEN-MYERS, GABRIELLE MARGUERITE, neuropathologist; b. Fribourg, Switzerland, Aug. 8, 1947; came to U.S., 1979; d. Maurice Edmond and Margrit (Wettstein) De Courten; m. Ronald Elwood Myers, Apr. 18, 1981; 1 child, Maximilian. BSBA, Akademikergemeinschaft, Zurich, Switzerland, 1967; MD, U. Zurich, 1974. Resident in psychiatry Hopital Psycho-Geriatrique, Gimel, Switzerland, 1974-75; resident in pediatrics U. Hosp. Zurich, 1977; resident in neuropathology U. Hosp. of Lausanne, Switzerland, 1976-78; rsch. assoc. NIH, Bethesda, Md., 1979-80; fellow in neuropathology Coll. of Medicine U. Cin., 1980-83, asst. prof. neuropathology Coll. of Medicine, 1983-88, assoc. prof. neuropathology Coll. of Medicine, 1988-89, tenured assoc. prof. Coll. of Medicine, 1989—. Cons. Vets. Affairs Med. Ctr., Cin., 1983—, Children's Hosp. Med. Ctr., Cin., 1984—, Good Samaritan Hosp., Cin., 1990—. Grantee VA, 1985—, NIH, 1986-90, 93—, Am. Heart Assn., 1991-94, Am. Diabetes Assn., 1995. Mem. AAAS, Am. Assn. Neuropathologists, Am. Acad. Neurology, AAUP, Soc. Acad. Emergency Medicine, Soc. Exptl. Neuropathology. Office: U Cin Coll of Medicine Dept Pathology PO Box 670529 231 Bethesda Ave Cincinnati OH 45267-0529

DECRANE, ALFRED CHARLES, JR., petroleum company executive; b. Cleve., June 11, 1931; s. Alfred Charles and Verona (Marquard) DeCrane; m. Joan Elizabeth Hoffman, July 3, 1954; children: David, Lisa, Stacie, Stephanie, Sarah, Jennifer. BA, U. Notre Dame, 1953; JD, Georgetown U., 1959; LHD (hon.), Manhattanville Coll., 1990; DJD (hon.), U. Notre Dame, 2002. Cert. Va. Bar, 1959, D.C. Bar, 1959, Tex. Bar, 1961, N.Y. Bar, 1966. Legal dept. Texaco, Inc., Houston, 1959—65, N.Y.C., 1964—66, asst. to vice chmn. bd., 1965—67, asst. to chmn. bd., 1967—68, gen. mgr. producing dept. Eastern hemisphere, 1968—70, v.p., 1970—76, sr. v.p., gen. counsel,

1976—77, sr. v.p., dir., 1977—78, exec. v.p., 1978—83, pres., 1983—86, chmn. bd. dirs., 1987—96, chmn., chief exec. officer, 1993—96. Life trustee U. Notre Dame. 1st lt. USMC, 1954—55. Mem.: ABA (sect. sec. 1964—67). Achievements include co-founder Natural Resources Law Jour. mineral law sect. Office: PO Box 1247 Greenwich CT 06836-1247

DECROSTA, SUSAN ELYSE, graphic designer; b. Cambridge, Mass., Aug. 28, 1956; d. Joseph Mario and Gertrude Ermelinda (Galligani) DeC. BFA, Mass. Coll. Art, 1980. certified art tchr., supr. Graphic artist Nixdorf Computer Corp., Burlington, Mass., 1981—86; artist, illustrator Rivers, Trainor, Doyle, Providence, 1987; lead artist, illustrator Raytheon Co., Andover, Mass., 1986—94; graphic designer Raytheon Svc. Co., Burlington, Mass., 1994—2004; art dir. Raytheon Tech. Svc., Burlington, 2004—. Freelance graphic artist, 1980—; guest spkr. to design and illustration students Northeastern U., 1992. Publ. Graphic Design U.S.A. Mag., 2000 (Am. Graphic Design award, 2000, 2003). Vol. AIDS Action Com., Boston; bd. dirs. Jeannette Neill Dance Scholarship Program, Boston, 1999—. Recipient Excellence award Soc. Tech. Comm. & Art Direction, 1986. Mem.: Women's Initiative Network, Art Alumni Assn. Avocations: dance, painting. Office: Raytheon Svc Co 3 Van DeGraaff Dr Burlington MA 01803-4607 Office Phone: 781-238-3070. Personal E-mail: susandecrosta@rcn.com. Business E-Mail: susan_e_decrosta@raytheon.com.

DECROW, KAREN, lawyer, educator, writer; b. Chgo., Dec. 18, 1937; d. Samuel Meyer and Juliette (Abt) Lipschultz; m. Alexander Allen Kolben, 1960 (div. 1965); m. Roger DeCrow, 1965 (div. 1972, dec. 1989). BS, Northwestern U., 1959; JD, Syracuse U., 1972; DHL (hon.), SUNY, Oswego, 1994. Bar: N.Y., U.S. Dist. Ct. (no. dist.) N.Y. Resorts editor Golf Digest mag., Evanston, Ill., 1959-60; editor Am. Soc. Planning Ofcls., Chgo., 1960-61; writer Ctr. for Study Liberal Edn. for Adults., Chgo., 1961-64; editor Holt, Rinehart, Winston, Inc., N.Y.C., 1965; textbook editor L.W. Singer, Syracuse, N.Y., 1965-66; writer Ea. Regional Inst. for Edn., Syracuse, 1967-69, Pub. Broadcasting System, 1977; tchr. women and law, 1972-74; nat. bd. mem. NOW, 1968-77, nat. pres., 1974-77, also nat. politics task force chair; cons. affirmative action; pvt. practice, Jamesville, N.Y., 1974—. Lectr. topics including law, gender, internat. feminism to corps., polit. groups, colls. and univs., U.S., Can., Mex., Finland, China, Greece, former USSR; nat. coord. Women's Strike for Equality, 1970; moot ct. judge, 1974--; N.Y. State del. Internat. Women's Yr., 1977; originator Schs. for Candidates; participant DeCrow-Schlafly ERA Debates, from 1975; founder (with Robert Seidenberg, MD) World Woman Watch, 1988; gender issues advisor Nat. Congress for Men; mem. Task Force on Gender Bias. Author: (with Roger DeCrow) University Adult Education: A Selected Bibliography, 1967, American Council on Education, 1967, The Young Woman's Guide to Liberation, 1971, Sexist Justice, 1974, First Women's State of the Union Message, 1977, (with Robert Seidenberg) Women Who Marry Houses: Panic and Protest in Agoraphobia, 1983, Turkish edit., 1988, 2d Turkish edit., 1989, United States of America vs. Sex: How the Meese Commission Lied About Pornography, 1988, (with Jack Kammer) Good Will Toward Men: Women Talk Candidly About the Balance of Power Between the Sexes, 1994; editor: The Pregnant Teenager (Howard Osofsky), 1968, Corporate Wives, Corporate Casualties (Robert Seidenberg, MD), 1973; contbr. articles to USA Today, N.Y. Times, N.Y. Times Bus. Sect., L.A. Times, Chgo. Tribune, Nat. Law Jour., Women Boston Globe, Vogue, Mademoiselle, Ingenue, Newsday, Chgo. Sun Times, Penthouse, Washington Post, L.A. Times Mag., Policy Review, Miami Herald, Internat. Herald Tribune, Social Problems, Houston Chronicle, Pitts. Press, Nat. NOW Times, Syracuse U. Mag., San Francisco Chronicle, Civil Rights Quar., Women Lawyers Jour., other newspapers, mags.; regular columnist: Syracuse New Times, 1985—; columnist N.Y. Times Spl. Features; recording: Opening Up Marriage, 1980. Hon. trustee Elizabeth Cady Stanton Found.; active Hon. Com. to Save Alice Paul's Birthplace; Liberal party candidate for Mayor of Syracuse, 1969. Recipient Profl. Recognition award for best newspaper column Syracuse Press Club, 1990, 94, 95, 96, 2000, Best Column award, 1994-95, 99, 2001, 02, Best Column award N.Y. Press Assn., 1991-92, 95, award Barnard Coll., Vet. Feminists of Am. and the Barnard Ctr. for Rsch. on Women, Woman of Achievement/Distinction award Gov. George E. Pataki, 1998; Svc. to Soc. award Northwestern U. Alumni Assn., 2002, Achievement award The Post-Standard, Syracuse, 2003. Mem. NOW (pres.), ACLU (Ralph E. Kharas Disting. Svc. in Civil Liberties award 1985), N.Y. Women's Bar Assn. (ctrl. N.Y. chpt. pres. 1989-90, jud. screening com., Joan L. Ellenbogen Founder's award 2003, Doris Hoffman medal 2005), Women's Bar Assn. State N.Y. (Doris Hoffman medal 2005), N.Y. Bar Assn., Onondaga County Bar Assn. (profl. ethics com.), Elizabeth Cady Stanton Found. (trustee), Working Women's Inst. (bd. advisors), Syracuse Friends Chamber Music, Atlantic States Legal Found., Yale Polit. Union (hon. life), Nat. Congress Men (gender issues advisor), Mariposa Edn. and Rsch. Found., Nat. Coun. Children's Rights (adv. panel), Wilderness Soc., Northwestern U. Alumni Assn., Women's Inst. Freedom Press, Art Inst. Chgo., Nat. Women's Polit. Caucus, Theta Sigma Phi. Address: 7599 Brown Gulf Rd Jamesville NY 13078-9636 Office Phone: 315-682-2563. *I feel especially lucky to be able to participate, as Holmes said, in the passion of our times. The movement to create equality between women and men is the most interesting and exciting during this period in history. My goal is a world where the gender of a baby will have little or no relevance to future pursuits or pleasures - personal, political, economic, social, or professional. It is exhilarating to watch society change in that direction.*

DECRUZ, ADELE GERALDINE, conservator; d. Thomas Cruz and Lucia Gerada Rivecciceo. BA magna cum laude, Marymount Coll. Inst. Fine Arts, 1973; MFA cum laude, Villa Schifanoia, Dominican U., Florence, 1979. Chief conservator NC Mus. Art, Raleigh, 1979—82; prof. collaborator Opificio Pietre Dure, Florence, 2000—05; sr. rsch. conservator, cons. Duke U. Mus. Art, Durham, 2002—05. Cons. conservation Columbia U., NYC, 1986—88; conservator Sarah Campbelle Blaffer, Houston, 1988—89; vis. prof., lectr. U. Pisa, 2002—05. S.H. Kress fellow, S.H. Kress Found. NYC, 1974, 1975, 1980, 1982—84. Mem.: ALC, Salmagundi. Roman Catholic. Achievements include invention of lasers, invention conservation; patents for method cleaning for art work. Office: Duke U Durham NC 27708 Office Phone: 919-660-5670. Business E-Mail: adecruz@duke.edu.

DECTER, MIDGE, writer; b. St. Paul, July 25, 1927; d. Harry and Rose (Calmenson) Rosenthal; m. Norman Podhoretz, Oct. 21, 1956; children: Rachel, Naomi, Ruth, John. Student, U. Minn., 1945-46, Jewish Theol. Sem. Am., 1946-48. Asst. editor Midstream mag., 1956-58; mng. editor Commentary, 1961-62; editor Hudson Inst., 1965-66, CBS Legacy Books, 1966-68; exec. editor Harper's mag., 1969-71; book review editor Saturday Rev./World mag., 1972-74; sr. editor Basic Books, Inc., 1974-80; exec. dir. Com. for Free World, 1980-90; sr. fellow Inst. on Religion and Pub. Life, 1991—95. Author: The Liberated Woman and Other Americans, 1971, Liberal Parents, Radical Children, 1975, The New Chastity and Other Arguments Against Women's Liberation, 1997, An Old Wife's Tale: My Seven Decades in Love and War, 2001, Losing the First Battle, Winning the War, 2002, Rumsfeld: A Personal Portrait, 2003; mem. editl. bd.: First Things. Bd. dirs. Heritage Found., Ctr. for Security Policy, Phila. Soc.; founding mem. Coalition for Dem. Majority; former dir. Nicaraguan Freedom Fund. Recipient Nat. Humanities medal, 2003. Home: 120 E 81st St New York NY 10028-1428

DECUIR, BRYAN JUDE, automotive technician, computer engineer; b. New Rhodes, La., July 6, 1965; s. Eugene Noel DeCuir and Vera Mae Gossarand-DeCuir; m. Stephanie Ruth Baerga; children: Bryanna Joy, Ashley Rhae Grisby, Aralynne Nicole Baerga-Green, Elanni Arabella Baerga-Washington. Cert. master ASE technician ASE, Va., state inspector State of Va., Catepillar cert. Va., GM electronics cert. Va., Ford electronics Va., Bendix cert. Va. Sr. automotive technician II City of Hampton (Va.) Fleet Svcs., 1995—. Computer engr. Q's Autmotive, Newport News, Va., 1992—. Decorated S.W. Asian medal, Good Conduct medal. Mem.: Moose (life; legioneer 2005). Office: City of Hampton Fleet Svcs 413 N Armistead Ave Hampton VA 23669 Office Phone: 757-726-2958. Personal E-mail: bryandecuir@yahoo.com.

DECUIR, WINSTON G., SR., lawyer; b. Baton Rouge, Aug. 17, 1948; s. Maurice and Loffie Decuir; m. Barbara Conant, June 17, 1970; children: Winston Jr., Jason, Brandon. BS, Xavier U., New Orleans, 1970; JD, La. State U., 1975. Bar: La. Asst. atty. gen. La. Dept. Justice, Baton Rouge, 1975—89; ptnr. Decuir & Clark, Baton Rouge, 1989—. Judge ad hoc Baton Rouge City Ct., 1995. Named Practitioner of the Yr., Louis Martenet Soc., 1995; recipient Award of Merit, NAACP-La., 1999. Democrat. Roman Catholic. Home: 961 Castle Kirk Baton Rouge LA 70808 Office: Decuir & Clark 1961 Government St Baton Rouge LA 70806

DE DATTA, SURAJIT KUMAR, soil scientist, agronomist, educator; b. Shwebo, Upper Burma, Burma, Aug. 1, 1936; s. Dinanath and Birahini De Datta; m. Vijayalakshmi L., April 20, 1967; 1 son, Raj Kumar De Datta. BS in Agr., Banaras Hindu U., 1956; MS Soil Sci. and Agrl. Chemistry, Indian Agrl. Rsch. Inst., New Delhi, 1958; PhD in Soil Sci., U. Hawaii, 1962. Postdoctoral agrl. expt. sta. Ohio State U., Columbus, 1962-63; prof. agronomy and soil sci. U. Philippines, Los Banos, Philippines, 1964-91; assoc. agronomist internat. Rice Rsch. Inst., Manila, Philippines, 1964-69, agronomist, 1969-85, radiol. safety officer, 1967-78, acting head dept. soil chemistry, 1975-76, dept. head, agronomy, 1967-89, prin. scientist, 1986-91; assoc. dean internat. agr. Va. Tech., Blacksburg, 1993—2003, dir. office internat. rsch. edn. and devel., 1991—, prof. crop and soil environ. scis., 1991—, chair, 1996-97, assoc. provost internat. affairs, 2003—, assoc. prof. internat. affairs, 2003—. Bd. dirs. S.E. Consrotium for Internat. Devel., Washington; prin. investigator IPM CRSP Project (USAID), Va. Tech., 1993; vis. prof. Purdue U., 1971-72, Kasetsart U., Thailand, 1984-91; vis. scientist U. Calif., Davis, 1978-79; hon. prof. Dniepropetrovsk State Agrarian U., Ukraine, USSR, 1998. Author: Principles and Practices of Rice Production, 1981; consulting editor: Fertilizer Rsch. Jour. 1978-96; contbr. over 366 articles to profl. jours. Recipient Internat. Soil Sci. award Soil Sci. Soc. Am., 1986, Best Paper award Weed Sci. Pest Control Coun. Philippines, 1986, Eminence award Bureau of Plant Industry, Philippines, 1987, Best Paper award Asian-Pacific Weed Sci. Soc., Taiwan, 1987, Second Best Paper award Asian-Pacific Weed Sci. Soc., Korea, 1989, Agronomic Rsch. award Am. Soc. Agronomy, 1990, Norman Borlaug award, New Delhi, India, 1992, Outstanding Alumnus award Coll. Tropical Agr. Human Resources, U. Hawaii, 1998, citation for contribution to the Filipino people, Pres. Rep. Philippines, 2004. Fellow Am. Soc. Agronomy, Soil Sci. Soc. Am., Crop Sci. Soc., Indian Soc. Soil Sci., Internat. Svc. in Agronomy, Internat. Svc. in Crop Sci., Nat. Acad. Agrl. Scis. (India). Hindu. Home: 512 Floyd St Blacksburg VA 24060-5071 Office: Va Tech Office Internat Rsch Edn & Devel 1060 Litton Reaves Hall Blacksburg VA 24061-0334

DEDE, BONNIE AILEEN, librarian, educator; b. Racine, Wis., Mar. 21, 1942; d. Edward Charles and Gracebelle Roeber; children: Suzan A., Ercan M. BA, U. Mich., 1963, MA, 1966, AM in Libr. Sci., 1968; cert., U. Ill., 1970. From mem. staff to head monograph cataloging prodn. U. Mich. Libr., Ann Arbor, 1967—99, head monograph cataloging prodn., 1999—. Mem. part-time faculty libr. and info. sci. program Wayne State U., Detroit, 1993—2000; vis. lectr. Grad. Sch. Libr. and Info. Sci. U. Ill., Urbana-Champaign, 2003—04; cons. Gale Rsch., Detroit, 1993; reviewer Am. Reference Books Ann., 1992—2000; cons. grant projects OCLC, 1991—92, 1994—96; adj. lectr. Law Libr. U. Mich., 2003—04. Mem. editl. bd. MC, Jour. Acad. Media Librarianship, 1992—2002. Grantee Title II-B, U.S. Office Edn., 1970, faculty-libr. coop. rsch. grantee Coun. on Libr. Resources, 1986-88, access grantee NEH, 1990-93. Mem. ALA, Alpha Lambda Delta, Beta Phi Mu (pres. Mu chpt. 1991-96). Office: U Mich 100 Hatcher Libr North Ann Arbor MI 48109-1205

DE DECKERE, DORIS C., retired public relations consultant; b. Grosse Point, Mich., Aug. 21; d. George Joseph and Lillian Anna (Pipper) Clutterbuck; m. Robert D. DeDeckere, Sept. 9, 1950 (dec. Feb. 1992); children: Robert (dec. Dec. 2003), David, James, Adrienne Student, U. Mich. Extension. Exec. sec. Recorder's Court, Detroit, from 1968; vice chmn. Mayor's Narcotics Com., Detroit; chmn. Pub. Health Commn., Detroit, 1970-73; assoc. dir. Mayor's Com. Human Resources Devel., 1973-74; dir. pub. rels. Metro Detroit March of Dimes, 1974-77, 78-81, Detroit Inst. Tech., 1977-78, Island of Boblo, 1981-84; pres. Jade/Assocs., Inc., 1985-90, ret., 1990. Cons. in field; coordinator ethnic classroom project at Wayne State U.; pub. relations cons. to community theatre groups, colls. and businesses; free lance writer, 1965—. Contbr. poetry to various mags. and articles to community publs. and local dailies. Chmn. Housing Poor People's March for Eastside of Detroit, 1967; chmn. Christian Svcs. St. Matthews Ch., 1969-72; pres. bd. trustees Detroit Cmty. Music Sch., 1979-81; bd. dirs. Eastwood Clinic, Greater Mich. Found., Providence Hosp. Found. Recipient Spirit of Detroit medal, 1973, Gov.'s Minute Man award, 1981; certs. of appreciation. Mem. Women in Comm., Women in Advt. Pub. Rels. Soc. Am., Mich. Women's Hall of Fame (ad hoc adv. com.), Univ. Cultural Ctr. Assn. (charter), Detroit Press Club, Econ. Clud of Detroit, Friends of Detroit Libr., Friens of Natural History Mus., Breakfast of Detroit. Roman Catholic. Home: 15061 Ford Rd Apt 110 Dearborn MI 48126-4650

DEDERER, WILLIAM BOWNE, music educator, administrator; b. Poughkeepsie, N.Y., July 15, 1945; s. William Morgan and Marion (Bowne) D.; m. Julia Yvonne Ary; 1 child, William Rockwell. BS in Music Edn., SUNY, Fredonia, 1967; MusM in Edn., U. Mich., 1968, D Mus. Arts in Performance, 1975. Prof. trumpet SUNY, Fredonia, 1969-82; dean Boston Conservatory, 1982-96, v.p. for acad. affairs, 1996-98; dean conservatory of music Capital U., 1998—. Choir dir. 1st United Meth. Ch., Fredonia, 1976-82, 1st Presbyn. Ch., Fredonia, 1969-73, dir. of music, 1st Presbyn. Ch., Haverhill, Mass., 1983-87. Mem. Nashua Symphony, 1986-98; St. Luke Luth. Ch., Gabanna, Ohio, 2002—. Mem. Internat. Trumpet Guild, Pi Kappa Lambda, Phi Mu Alpha (nat. exec. com. 1979-88, nat. pres. 1985-88). Office: Conservatory of Music Capital U Columbus OH 43209 E-mail: wdederer@capital.edu.

DEDERICH-PEJOVICH, SUSAN RUSSELL, harpist; b. Rockville Center, N.Y., Oct. 4, 1951; d. Robert Marwood and Martha Annette (Geffs) D.; m. Svetozar Pejovich; 1 child, Mira Zorina. B. Performing Arts, Cleve. Inst. Music, 1973; student of, Alice Chalifoux. Prin. harpist Oklahoma City Symphony, 1973-74, New Orleans Symphony, 1974-77, Dallas Symphony, 1977—; adj. prof. harp So. Meth. U. Mem. contemporary music ensemble Voices of Change; founder Flute, Viola, Harp Trio Triptych; condr. So. Meth. U. Harp Ensemble; co-dir. Adriatric harp workshop, Krk, Yugoslavia, Summer Festival, Purgatory, Colo., Killington (Vt.) Music Festival. Office: care Dallas Symphony Orch 2301 Flora St Ste 300 Dallas TX 75201-2404

DEDERICK, ROBERT GOGAN, economist; b. Keene, NH, Nov. 18, 1929; s. Frederic Van Dyck and Margaret (Gogan) D.; m. Margarida N. Magalhaes, Aug. 24, 1957; children: Frederic, Laura, Peter. AB, Harvard U., 1951, AM, 1953, PhD, 1958; postgrad., Cornell U., 1953-54. Econ. research mgr. New Eng. Mut. Life Ins. Co., Boston, 1957-64; assoc. economist No. Trust Co., Chgo., 1964, v.p., assoc. economist, 1965-69, v.p., economist, 1969-70, sr. v.p., chief economist, 1970-81, exec. v.p., chief economist, 1983-94, econ. cons., 1994—2003; mem. panel of econ. advisers Congl. Budget Office, 1991—2004; mem. econ. adv. bd. U.S. Commerce Dept., 1968-70, 75-76, 83-85, asst. sec. commerce for econ. affairs, 1981-82, under sec. commerce for econ. affairs, 1982-83; prin. RGD Econs., Hinsdale, 1994—. Fellow: Nat. Assn. Bus. Economists (pres. 1973—74, governing coun. 1969—75); mem.: Internat. Conf. Comml. Bank Economists, Am. Bankers Assn. (alumni coun.), Harvard Discussion Group Indsl. Economists, Conf. Bus. Economists (chmn. 1984—85), Chgo. Coun. on Fgn. Rels., Capitol Hill Club, Hinsdale Golf Club, Harvard Club, Econ. Club. Home: 113 S County Line Rd Hinsdale IL 60521-4722 Office: RGD Economics 113 S County Line Rd Hinsdale IL 60521-4722 Office Phone: 630-325-7183. Personal E-mail: rdederick@aol.com.

DEDMAN, BILL, journalist; b. Chattanooga, Oct. 14, 1960; s. Harold C. and Bobbye (Griswold) Dedman; m. Pamela J. Belluck, Sept. 5, 1993; children: Justin, Arielle, Jillian. Student, Wash. U., St. Louis, 1978—81. Reporter Warrensburg (Mo.) Star-Jour., 1981, Blue Springs (Mo.) Examiner, 1981—82, Chattanooga Free Press, 1983, Chattanooga Times, 1984—86, Knoxville News-Sentinel, 1986—87, Atlanta Journal-Constitution, 1987—89, Washington Post, 1989—91; fellow Freedom Forum Media Studies Ctr. Columbia U., N.Y.C., 1992—93; contbg. writer Mother Jones Mag., 1993—94; dir. computer-assisted reporting AP, 1994—97; writer N.Y. Times, 1997—2001; corr. Boston Globe, 2001—. Hearst vis. fellow U. Md. Coll. Journalism, 1993—94; lectr. Northwestern U. Recipient Pulitzer Prize for investigative reporting, 1989, Robert F. Kennedy Journalism award grand prize, 1989, Worth Bingham prize, 1989, numerous others. Mem.: Investigative Reporters and Editors (bd. dirs. 1990—96, award 1989).

DEDMON, ANGELA MARIE MAXINE, psychologist; b. Oklahoma City, May 25, 1971; d. Hubert Carlton and Patricia Ann Bryan; m. Brian Todd Dedmon, June 15, 1991; children: Caeli Ann Louise, Joshua Todd. BA in Psychology and Sociology magna cum laude, Okla. State U., 1993; MA in Clin. Psychology, Tex. Tech. U., 1997, PhD in Clin. Psychology, 1999. Lic. psychologist Okla. Rsch. asst. Tex. Tech. U., Lubbock, 1995—96; clinic co-dir. Tex. Tech. Psychology Clinic, Lubbock, 1995—97; psychologist in tng. Lubbock County Youth Ctr., 1996—97, Lubbock Ind. Sch. Dist., 1997—98; intern psychology Children's Mercy Hosp., Kansas City, Mo., 1998—99, fellow psychology, 1999—2000; pvt. practice clin. child psychologist Edmond, Okla., 2001—. Clin. child psychologist psychol. evaluations Pauline Meyer Shelter, Oklahoma City, 2001—; spkr. Okla. Foster Care Assn., Oklahoma City, 2002. Contbr. articles to profl. jours. Vol. disaster recovery ARC, Oklahoma City; vol. disaster hotline local TV sta., Oklahoma City, 2001. Mem.: APA, Okla. Psychol. Assn. Avocations: swimming, reading, church activities. Office: 2500 S Broadway #200 Edmond OK 73013 Office Phone: 405-514-1476.

DEDMON, J. CHARLA, elementary school educator, director; b. Walters, Okla., Dec. 1, 1946; d. James E. and Verna Mae Cain; m. Wendall L. Dedmon, Jan. 17, 1970; children: Jimmie, Eric. BA in Vocal, Instrumental and Theory, Southwestern Okla. State U., 1969. Elem. music tchr. Lawton (Okla.) Pub. Schs., 1970—80; Walters choral dir., gen. music educator for mid. sch. and HS Walters Pub. Schs., 1980—. Adv. bd. Okla. Secondary Sch. Activities Assn., 2002—04; bd. dirs. Miss Walters Pageant, Inc., 1970—2005. Named Tchr. of Yr., HS Faculty, 1984, 1993, 2004, Citizen of the Yr., Walters C. of C., 1984, 1995. Mem.: Okla. Music Educators Assn. (chair state chorus 2002—03, vocal v.p. 2004—05), Music Educators Nat. Conf. (bd. dirs.), Okla. Choral Dirs. Assn. (SW rep. 2002—03), MacDowell Club Allied Arts (pres., com. mem.), Delta Kappa Gamma (past music dir.). Methodist. Avocations: golf, art, music. Office: Walters Pub Schs 418 S Broadway Walters OK 73572

DE DUVE, CHRISTIAN RENÉ, chemist, educator; b. Thames-Ditton, Surrey, Eng., Oct. 2, 1917; s. Alphonse and Madeleine (Pungs) de Duve; m. Janine Herman de Duve, Sept. 30, 1943; children: Thierry, Anne, Françoise, Alain. MD, U. Louvain, Belgium, 1941, PhD, 1945; grad., Med. Nobel Inst., Stockholm, 1946—47; MSc, U. Louvain, Belgium, 1946; PhD (hon.), U. Turin, 1969, U. Leiden, 1970, U. Sherbrooke, 1970, U. Lille, 1973, Cath. U. Santiago, Chile, 1974, U. René Descartes, Paris, 1974, State U. Liege, 1975, State U. Ghent, 1975, Gustavus Adolphus Coll., St. Peter, Minn., 1975, U. Rosario, Argentina, 1975, U. Aix-Marseille II, 1979, U. Keele, 1982, Katholieke U. Leuven, 1984, Karolinska Inst., Stockholm, 1986, U. Montreal, 1992, Rockefeller U., 1997. Lectr. physiol. chemistry faculty medicine Cath. U. Louvain, 1947—51, prof., head dept. physiol. chemistry, 1951—85, emeritus prof., 1985—. Prof. biochem. cytology Rockefeller U., NYC, 1962—74, Andrew W. Mellon prof., 1974—88, prof. emeritus, 1988—; vis. prof. Albert Einstein Coll. Medicine, Bronx, NY, 1961—62, Chaire Francqui State U. Ghent, 1962—63, Free U., Brussels, 1963—64, State U., Liège, 1972—73, Facultés U. Notre-Dame de la Paix, Namur, 1990—91; Mayne guest prof. U. Queensland, Brisbane, Australia, 1972; pres. Internat. Inst. Cellular and Molecular Pathology, Brussels, 1974—91. Mem. editl. bd.: Subcellular Biochemistry, 1971—87, Preparative Biochemistry, 1971—80, Molecular and Cellular Biochemistry, 1973—80; author: A Guided Tour of the Living Cell, 1984, Blueprint for a Cell, 1991, Vital Dust, 1995. Conseil d'adminstrn. Fonds Nat. de la Rsch. Sci., 1958—61; conseil de gestion Fonds de la Rsch. Sci. Médicale, 1959—61, commn. sci., 1958—61; com. experts Conseil Nat. de la Politique Sci., 1958—61; adv. bd. Ciba Found., 1960—85; adult devel. and aging rsch. and tng. rev. com. Nat. Inst. Child Health and Devel., NIH, 1970—73; adv. com. for med. rsch. WHO, 1974—79; sci. adv. com. Max Planck-Inst. for Immunbiology, 1975—78, Ludwig Inst. Cancer Rsch., 1985—91, Mary Imogene Bassett Rsch. Inst., 1986—90, Clin. Rsch. Inst. Montreal, 1986—; biology adv. com. N.Y. Hall of Sci., 1986—; adv. sci. com. Basel Inst. for Immunology, 1989—93. Recipient Prix des Alumni, 1949, Prix Pfizer, 1957, Prix Francqui, 1960, Prix Quinquennal Belge des Scis. Médicales, Belgium, 1967, Merit award, Gairdner Found. Internat., Can., 1967, Dr. H.P. Heineken prize, The Netherlands, 1973, Nobel prize for physiology or medicine, 1974, Theobald Smith award, Albany Med. Coll., 1981, Jimenez Diaz award, 1985. Fellow: AAAS; mem.: NAS, Soc. Belge Physiology, N.Y. Acad. Scis., Internat. Soc. Cell Biology, European Cell Biology Orgn., European Molecular Biology Orgn., European Assn. Study Diabetes, Koninklyke Acad. voor Geneeskunde, German Acad. der Naturforscher Leopoldina, Soc. Belge Biochim. (pres. 1962—64), Soc. Chimie Biologique, Am. Soc. Cell Biology (coun. mem. 1966—69, E.B. Wilson award 1989), Pontifical Acad. Sci., Am. Soc. Biol. Chemists, Am. Philos. Soc., Biochem. Soc. (Harden award 1978), Am. Chem. Soc., Royal Acad. Belgium, Royal Acad. Medicine, German Assn. for Cell Biology (assoc.), Acad. Europaea (assoc.), Acad. Scis. d'Athénes (assoc.), Acad. Scis. Paris (assoc.), Royal Soc. Can. (assoc.), Royal Soc. London (assoc.), Am. Acad. Arts and Scis. (assoc.), Sigma Xi. Address: Rockefeller U 1230 York Ave New York NY 10021-6399 Mailing: ICP 75 Ave Hippocrate B-1200 Brussels Belgium*

DEE, FRANCIS X., lawyer; b. N.Y.C., July 13, 1944; BA, Manhattan Coll., 1966; JD, Cath. U. Am., 1969; LLM in Labor Law, NYU, 1975. Bar: N.Y. 1970, N.J. 1972, U.S. Supreme Ct. 1981. Atty. NLRB, 1969-72; labor counsel Litton Industries, 1972-76; sr. ptnr. Carpenter, Bennett & Morrissey, 1976—2004, McElroy, Deutsch, Mulvaney & Carpenter, LLP, Newark, 2004—. Fellow Am. Coll. Trial Lawyers (N.J. state chmn. 1999-01), Internat. Acad. Trial Lawyers, Coll. Labor and Employment Lawyers, Am Bar Found.; mem. ABA (litigation sect., com. on devel. law under nat. labor rels. act labor and employment law sect. 1975—), N.Y. State Bar Assn. (litig., labor and employment law sects.), N.J. State Bar Assn. (litig. sect., del. to gen. coun. 1985-92, exec. bd. 1983-92, mgmt. co-chair com. on practice and procedure under nat. labor rels. act 1980-83, sec. labor employment law sect. 1987-89, vice chmn. 1989-91, chmn. 1991-92), Essex County Bar Assn., Trial Attys. of N.J., Fed. Bar Assn. Office: McElroy Deutsch Mulvaney and Carpenter LLP Three Gateway Ctr 100 Mulberry St Fl 17 Newark NJ 07102-4004 Office Phone: 973-565-2018, 973-425-8708. E-mail: fdee@mdmc-law.com.

DEE, IVAN RICHARD, book publisher; b. Chgo., Mar. 11, 1935; s. Jack Arthur and Jeanette Rose (Melcher) D.; m. Sandra Cohen, June 21, 1959 (div. 1973); m. Phyllis Kirz, Aug. 3, 1977 (div. 1981); m. Barbara Burgess, Apr. 15, 1989; children: Alexander, Sara, Jacob, Gabriel. BJ, U. Mo., 1956, MA, 1957. Pres. Ardivan Press, Macon, Ga., 1960-61; v.p., editor-in-chief Quadrangle Books, Chgo., 1961-72; assoc. editor Chgo. Tribune Book World, Chgo., 1972-73; exec. editor Pubs.-Hall Syndicate, Chgo., 1973-74; editor-in-chief Chicagoan Mag., Chgo., 1974-75; dir. pub. affairs Michael Reese Hosp. and Med. Ctr., Chgo., 1975-89; pres. Ivan R. Dee, Inc., Chgo., 1989—. V.p. South Side Planning Bd., Chgo., 1975-89; commr. Chgo. Baseball League, 1978-00. Lt. (j.g.) USN, 1957-60. Office: Ivan R Dee Inc 1332 N Halsted St Chicago IL 60622-2624 Business E-Mail: ivan@ivanrdee.com.

DEE, JON FACUNDO, financial services executive; b. Borongan, The Philippines, July 6, 1949; arrived in U.S., 1976; s. Facundo Dee and Guadalupe Abordo; m. Tess de Ungria Calma, Oct. 10, 1976; children: Bernadette, Paolo Angelo, Kristina. BSBA in Acctg., Mapua Inst. Tech., The Philippines, 1968; MBA, Ateneo de Manila U., 1983. CPA, The Philippines. Corp. bookkeeper Nat. Irrigation Adminstrn., Quezon City, The Philippines,

1968-70; treas. fgn. exch. Philippine Nat. Bank, Manila, 1970-86; owner Century Fin. Svcs., Daly City, Calif., 1988—. Bd. dirs. Westlake Subdivsn. Improvement Assn., Daly City, 1995—; mem. Dem. Nat. Com., San Mateo County Dem. Com., 1996—. Mem. Nat. Assn. Realtors, Calif. Assn. Realtors, Golden Gate Rose Soc. of San Francisco, Mission Merchants Assn., San Francisco Assn. Realtors, San Francisco C. of C., Commonwealth Club, Sierra Club. Roman Catholic. Avocations: writing, gardening, photography. Home: 9 Lake Vista Ave Daly City CA 94015-1013 Office: Century Fin Svcs 86 88th St Daly City CA 94015-1603

DEE, KELLY G., music educator; s. John J. and Joan F. Dee. BS of Music Edn., Jacksonville State U., 1992. Dir. Kecoughton High Sch, Hampton, Va., 1995—. Pres. SEVA Nat. Bd., Hampton, 2005—. Mem.: Music Educators Nat. Conf. Avocation: rock climbing.

DEE, PAULINE M., artist; b. Concord, N.H., Jan. 9, 1933; d. Arthur Joseph and Anna Marie (Marquis) Champagne; m. Edmond Francis Dee, July 2, 1955; children: James Francis, Diane Mary. Bus. Cert., Burdett Coll., Lynn, Mass. Membership chmn. Danvers (Mass.) Art Assn., 1986-92, v.p., 1990-92; founder Pauline Dee Studio for Oil Painting, 1989; v.p. Lynnfield (Mass.) Art Guild, 1991-93, pres., 1994-96; v.p. Saltbox Gallery, Topsfield, Mass., 1995-2000, pres., 2000—. Demonstrator in field; cons. Kohinor Accent Program, Bloomsbury, N.J., 1995—; founder Pauline Dee Studio, 1989; instituted Lynnfield Art Guild Scholarship Fund, 1993. Exhibited in solo shows at Woman's Club of Boston, 1980, Naval Officers Club, Pearl Harbor, Hawaii, 1994; represented in numerous pvt. collections. Cons. Peabody (Mass.) Internat. Festival, 1995; bd. dirs. North Shore Art Assn., Gloucester, Mass., 1996. Recipient achievement awards, 1985-95; Peabody Arts Lottery grantee, 1996. Mem. Our Lady Guadalupe Sodality (prefect 1966-68). Roman Catholic. Avocations: art, photography. Home: 16 Samoset Rd Peabody MA 01960-3504

DEE, RONDA, poet, photographer, small business owner; b. Bronx, NY, May 6, 1943; d. Maurice Dee and Rachel Hoffer. AA, Manhattan CC, NYC, 1974; BS, NYU, 1976. Sec. Book of Knowledge, NYC, 1962; private tutor City Coll., 1963; tchr. head start Lennox Hill Neighborhood Assoc., NYC, 1970; tchr. k-3 N.W. Harlee Elem. Sch., Dallas, 1977; sec. City of Dallas, 1977; tchr., summer reading prog. Texas Dept. Human Resources, Dallas, 1978; pvt. practice, 1980—83, 2004—; journalist Brookhaven Sch. News, Dallas, 1987, Richland Chronicle, Dallas, 2003—; distributor, dealer Eco-Quest Internat. Co. Living Air Ozone Machines; journalist, photographer Decoy newspaper, Richland Coll., 2004—05, comedy writer, 2004—05. Actress Piquaresque Players, Dallas, 1977; adminstrv. asst. Contact Dallas, 1990; artist Ward Nass Gallery, NYC, 1995; featured reader Barnes & Noble Booksellers, 2000—02; staff photographer Richland Chronicle, 2005. Pupeteer: (plays) Mt. Sinai Hosp. children's ward, 1968; exhibitions include Brookhaven Coll., Dallas, 1988, Mem. D'Art, 1997, Wells Fargo Bldg. Plano, Tex., Richland Coll., 2002—03, 500 X Gallery, Dallas, 2003—04, Richland Coll., 2004; photographer (book) Photograph: Walls of New York City, 2002; author, photographer: Parallex, 2002—05; actor: (documentaries) Homelessness, 1985; extra (films) Veritas, Prince of Truth, 2004; contbr. articles to profl. jours. and newspapers help educate safer environmental practices; author: numerous poems (winning poem Internat. Library of Poetry, 2004). Mem. Concerned Citizens Pesticide Control, Dallas, 2003—; social svc. worker Holy Trinity Ch., 1983—85. Recipient Founders Day award for Scholastic Achievement, NYU, 1976, Juried Art Contest winner for charcoal design collage, Brookhaven Coll., 1986, League Innovation award student lit. competition, Richland Coll., 2002—04. Mem.: Tex. Visual Arts Assn., Internat. Soc. Photographers, Poetry Soc. Am., Sierra Club, Phi Theta Kappa. Achievements include advocate for safer environmental practices; attended The City of Dallas Council meetings with Citizens for Safer Mosquito Control in order to end aerial and ground pesticide spraying and to help educate for safer practices; National Dean's List, 2002-2004. Avocations: camping, theater, films, exercise, drums. Home: PO Box 823478 Dallas TX 75382-3478 Personal E-mail: rondadee2001@yahoo.com.

DEE, RUBY (RUBY DEE DAVIS), actress, writer, director; b. Cleve., Oct. 27, 1924; d. Marshall Edward and Emma (Benson) Wallace; m. Ossie Davis, Dec. 9, 1948; children: Nora, Guy, Hasna. BA, Hunter Coll., 1945; ArtsD (hon.), Fairfield U.; BA (hon. doctorate), Iona Coll., Va. State U.; apprentice, Am. Negro Theatre, 1941-44; LHD (hon.), SUNY, Old Westbury, 1990; DFA, Spelman Coll., 1991. Ind. actress, writer, dir., v.p. Emmslyn II Prodns., 1945—. Author: (poetry) Glowchild, 1972, (musical) Take It from the Top, (collected poetry, humor, short stories) My One Good Nerve; adaptor: (African folk tales) Two Ways to Count to Ten, The Tower to Heaven, (play) Books With Legs, 1993; contbr. column N.Y. Amsterdam News; co-writer (film) Uptight; dir., adaptor (stage prodn.) Zora is my Name!, 1983; stage appearances include Jeb, 1946, Raisin in the Sun, 1959, Purlie Victorious, 1961, The Imaginary Invalid, 1971, Wedding Band, 1972 (Drama Desk award 1972), Boesman and Lena, 1970 (Obie award 1971), Anna Lucasta, Taming of the Shrew, Checkmates, 1988, The Glass Menagerie, 1989, Flyin West, 1994, Two Hah-Hahs and a Homeboy, 1995; actress: (films) Gone are the Days, The Jackie Robinson Story, 1950, Take a Giant Step, St. Louis Blues, A Raisin in the Sun, Purlie Victorious, To Be Young, Gifted and Black, Buck and the Preacher, Countdown at Kusini, Cat People, 1982, Do the Right Thing, 1989 (NAACP Image award as best actress 1989), Jungle Fever, 1991, Cop & 1/2, 1993, Whitewash, 1994, Just Cause, 1995, Simple Wish, A, 1997, Baby Geniuses, 1999, Little Bill, 2001, Feast of All Saints, 2001, Unchained Memories, 2002, Baby of the Family, 2002; narrator: Time to Dance: The Life and Work of Norma Canner, A, 1998, Unfinished Journey, 1999; numerous TV appearances including It's Good to be Alive, 1974, Today Is Ours, 1974, The Defenders, Police Woman, Peyton Place, (TV films) To Be Young, Gifted and Black, All God's Children, The Nurses, Roots: The Next Generation, I Know Why the Caged Bird Sings, Wedding Band, It's Good to be Alive, Decoration Day (Emmy award for Supporting Actress in a Miniseries or Special 1991), The Atlanta Child Murders, (TV spl. with Ossie Davis) Martin Luther King: The Dream and the Drum, The Winds of Change, Windmill of the Gods, TV miniseries Stephen King's The Stand, 1994, Tuesday Morning Ride, 1995, Mr. & Mrs. Loving, 1996, Captive Heart: The James Mink Story, 1996, Porgy and Bess: An American Voice, 1998, Passing Glory, 1999, Having Our Say: The Delany Sisters' First 100 Years, 1999, Finding Buck McHenry, 2000, A Storm in Summer, 2000, Taking Back Our Town, 2001; co-producer: (TV spl.) Today is Ours, The Ernest Green Story, 1993, (radio show) Ossie Davis and Ruby Dee Story Hour, 1974-78, (TV series) With Ossie and Ruby, 1981, (home videotape) Hands Upon The Heart, 1991, Middle Ages, 1992, Hands Upon The Heart II, 1993; rec. artist poems and stories; host (with Ossie Davis) African Heritage Movie Network. Recipient Martin Luther King Jr. award Operation PUSH, 1972, Drama Desk award, 1974, (with Ossie Davis) Frederick Douglass award N.Y. Urban League, 1970, (with Ossie Davis) NAACP Image award Hall of Fame, Master Innovator For Film award Sony, 1991, Nat. Medal of Arts, 1990; Kennedy Ctr. Honors (with Ossie Davis), 2004. Mem. NAACP, CORE, Student Non-Violent Coordinating Com., SCLC. Address: The Artists Agy 10000 Santa Monica Blvd Los Angeles CA 90067-7007

DEEB, MARY-JANE, editor, educator; b. Alexandria, Egypt, Aug. 27, 1946; arrived in U.S., 1973; d. Alix and Stephanie (Klanscek) Anhoury; m. Marius K. Deeb, Sept. 27, 1969; 1 child, Hadi K. BA in Sociology, Am. U., Cairo, 1967, MA in Sociology, 1972; PhD in Internat. Rels., Johns Hopkins U., 1987. Rsch. assoc. Ford Found., Beirut, 1972-73; cons. UN Econ. Commn. for Western Asia, Beirut, 1980, UNICEF, Beirut, 1980-81; project dir. U.S. AID, Beirut, 1982-83; asst. professorial lectr. George Washington U., Washington, 1988-89, 93, 97, Georgetown U., Washington, 1991, 94; asst. prof. Am. U., Washington, 1989-94, adj. assoc. prof., 1994—; editor Mid. East Jour., Washington, 1995-98; Arab world area specialist Libr. of Congress, Washington, 1998—2004, head Near East sect., 2004—. External reviewer for grant proposals U.S. Inst. Peace, Washington, 1991, 92, 97, Woodrow Wilson Ctr. for Scholars, 2003, NEH, 2005; testified on subcom. on Africa fgn. rels. com. U.S. Ho. of Reps., 1991, 92, 98; testified before the select com. on intelligence, U.S. Senate, 1996; testified on fgn. rels. com. U.S. Senate, 1997, UN Monitor of Algerian legislative elections, 1997; dir. Algeria program Corp. Coun. on Africa; leader Libr. of Congress Mission to Iraq, 2003; team mem. Libr. Congress Mission to Iran, 2004. Author: Libya Since the Revolution, 1982, Libya's Foreign Policy, 1991; co-editor: Hasib Sabbagh from Palestinian Refugee to Citizen of the World, 1996, Cocktails and Murder on the Potomac, 2001, (novel) Murder on the Riviera, 2004, A Christmas Mystery in Provence, 2004; rev. editor Internat. Jour. Mid.-East Studies, 1989-94; contbr. articles, revs. to profl. jours. and encys., and chpts. to books; interviewed on numerous TV programs, including CBS Evening News, ABC News, NBC Nightly News, CNN Headline News, Fox Morning News, PBS, and in news publs., including N.Y. Times, Washington Post, Time mag., L.A. Times, The Christian Sci. Monitor, U.S.A. Today, Boston Globe, Tokyo Shimbum, Yomouri, others. Mem. UN Assn., Am. Polit. Sci. Assn., Internat. Studies Assn., Mid. East Studies Assn. N.Am., Women's Caucus for Polit. Sci., Am.-Tunisian Assn. (exec. bd. 1989—), Hannibal Club (founding mem. 1999), World Affairs Coun., Women in Fgn. Policy, Mystery Writers Am., Sisters in Crime, Cosmos Club. Roman Catholic. Office: Libr Congress African and Middle Ea Divsn Jefferson Bldg 101 Independence Ave SE Washington DC 20540-0002 Office Phone: 202-707-1221. Business E-Mail: mdee@loc.gov.

DEEDS, ROBERT CREIGH, lawyer, state legislator; b. Richmond, Va., Jan. 4, 1958; s. Robert Livingston Deeds Jr. and Emma Lewis (Tyree) Hicklin; m. Pamela Kay Miller, Feb. 10, 1981; children: Amanda Jane, Rebecca Lewis, Austin Creigh, Susannah Kemper. BA, Concord Coll., Athens, W.Va., 1980; JD, Wake Forest U., 1984. Bar: Va. 1984, U.S. Dist. Ct. (we. dist.) Va. 1988. Assoc. Carter, Craig & Bass, P.C., Danville, Va., 1984-85, John C. Singleton, Warm Springs, Va., 1985-87; ptnr. Singleton & Deeds, Warm Springs, Va., 1988-99; mem. Va. Ho. of Dels., 1992—2001, Va. Senate, 2001—; sole practice R. Creigh Deeds, P.C., Hot Springs, Va., 2000—. Commonwealth atty. Bath County, Va., 1988-92; chmn. Dem. Caucus, Va. Ho. Dels., 2000-01. Bd. dirs. Va. Mus. Frontier Culture. Mem. Va. State Bar, Allegheny-Bath Bar Assn., Va. Trial Lawyers Assn., Va. Assn. Commonwealth's Attys. (bd. dirs. 1989-91). Democrat. Presbyterian. Avocations: fishing, hunting. Office: R Creigh Deeds PC Drawer D Hot Springs VA 24445 Office Phone: 540-839-2473. E-mail: rcdeeds@tds.net.

DEEGAN, JOHN, JR., academic administrator, educator, researcher; b. Elizabeth, N.J., Nov. 18, 1944; s. John and Margaret (Pignataro) D.; m. Anita Hope Rochelle, Dec. 19, 1964; children: Michael J., Matthew B. Student, Monmouth Coll., West Long Branch, N.J., 1962-64; BS, Evangel Coll., Springfield, Mo., 1967; MA, U. Mich., 1969, PhD, 1972. Asst. prof. Rice U., Houston, 1972-75, U. Rochester, N.Y., 1975-80, assoc. prof., 1980; spl. asst. to dep. adminstr. EPA, Washington, 1980; dir. Love Canal Project, 1980-82; assoc. dean Sch. Pub. Health U. Ill., Chgo., 1982-86, acting dean, 1983-85; prof. U. No. Iowa, Cedar Falls, 1986-89, dean Coll. Social and Behavioral Scis., 1986-89; provost, v.p. acad. affairs, prof. U. So. Maine, Portland, 1989-94; dean coll., v.p. acad. affairs, prof. Westminster Coll., New Wilmington, Pa., 1994—2002; pres., prof. St. Andrews Presbyn. Coll., Laurinburg, NC, 2002—. Cons. EPA, 1983-86; trustee Ill. Cancer Coun., 1983-86; bd. dirs. Leopold Ctr. for Sustainable Agr. State of Iowa, 1987-89. Contbr. articles to sci. jours. Recipient EPA Bronze medal award, 1982; U. Rochester fellow in preventive medicine, 1979, Acad. Adminstrn. fellow Am. Coun. on Edn., 1986-87. Mem. AAAS, APHA, Am. Chem. Soc., Sigma Xi, Delta Omega. Democrat. Presbyterian. Avocations: fishing, golf. Office: Office of the President St Andrews Presbyn Coll Laurinburg NC 28352 Business E-Mail: jdeegan@sapc.edu.

DEEGAN, KATHLEEN LYNN, dietician; b. Houston, Tex., Feb. 20, 1960; d. James Wade and Rebecca Anne Walters; children: Shawn Margaret, Emily Patricia, Carryn Athenia. BS in zoology, Tex. A&M U., 1982; MS in food sci. and human nutrition, U. Fla., 1985. Registered Dietitian Am. Dietetic Assn., 1985, lic. Nutritionist 1989. Nutrition edn. dir., patient care Jacksonville Cardiovascular Clin., Jacksonville, Fla., 1985—90; cons. The Fitness Ctr., Jacksonville, Fla., 1990—92, Mayo Clin. Ponte Vedra Club Internat. Health Spa, Jacksonville, 1993—95; team nutritionist Jacksonville Jauars NFL, 1995; rsch. dietitiona Health Trials 3000, 1996—99. Mem. Mayor's Coun. on Fitness and Well Being, 1992—94, chmn., 1992—94; mem. Soc. Nutrition Educators, 1985—90, Nutrition Com. of Duval County, 1987—88; adv. bd. Am. Heart Assn., 1987—88. Home: 1412 Yukon St Davis CA 95616 E-mail: kathleenwd@aol.com.

DEEGAN, MARY JO, sociology educator; b. Chgo., Nov. 27, 1946; d. William James and Ida May (Scott) Deegan; life ptnr. Michael Ray Hill. AS, Lake Mich. Coll., 1966; BS, We. Mich. U., 1969, MA, 1973; PhD, U. Chgo., 1975. Asst. prof. U. Nebr., Lincoln, 1975—80, assoc. prof., 1980—89, prof., 1989—. Med. trainee U. Chgo. Ctr. for Health Adminstrn., 1972-75; grad. asst. Western Mich. U., 1969-71.; del. Conf. on Directions in Health Econs., New Orleans, 1972. Author: Jane Addams and Men of the Chicago School, 1892-1918, 1988 (Choice award, 1989), American Ritual Dramas, 1989, Race, Hull House, and the University of Chicago, 2002 (Outstanding Scholarly Book, history sociol. sect.ASA, 03, History of Sociology 2nd pl. Racial and Ethnic Oliver C. Cox award); editor: Women in Sociology, 1991, American Ritual Tapestry, 1998, Play, School and Society (by G.H. Mead), 1999, Essays on Social Psychology (by G.H. Mead), 2001, The New Woman of Color (by F.B. Williams), 2002, Women at the Hague, 2003, Social Ethics, 2003; co-editor: Women and Disability, 1985, Women and Symbolic Interaction, 1987, Feminist Ethics in Social Research, 1989, With Her in Ourland, 1997, The Dress of Women (by C.P. Gilman), 2002, On Art, Labor, and Religion by E.G. Starr, 2003, Social Ethics, 2004; series editor Women & Sociological Theory, 2001; contbr. articles to profl. jours. Mem.: Harriet Martineau Sociol. Soc., Internat. Sociol. Assn., Am. Sociol. Assn. (Disting. Scholarly Career award in history of sociology 2002). Office: Dept Sociology 711 Oldfather Hall U Nebraska Lincoln NE 68588-0324

DEEGEAR, JAMES OTIS, III, lawyer; b. Dallas, Oct. 11, 1948; s. James O. Jr. and Madeleine (Couch) D.; m. Pamela Word; children: James O. IV, Frances S., Cynthia S. AA, San Antonio Coll., 1968; BA, U. Tex., 1971, JD, 1974. Bar: Tex. 1974, U.S. Dist. Ct. (we. dist.) Tex. 1980. Assoc. Law Offices of Rudy Rice, San Antonio, 1974-75; ptnr. Collins, DeWall & Deegear, San Antonio, 1975-79, Davis, Smith & Davis, San Antonio, 1979-82; counsel Southers & Lyons, Inc., San Antonio, 1983; pvt. practice law San Antonio, 1983—. Chmn. Leadership San Antonio, 1986-87; pres. Elf Louise, San Antonio, 1987-91. Fellow Tex. Bar Found. (life); mem. State Bar of Tex., San Antonio Bar Assn. (bd. dirs. 1981-83), Assn. Trial Lawyers Am., Tex. Trial Lawyers Assn. (bd. dirs. 1984-89), Tex. Criminal Def. Lawyers Assn., San Antonio Trial Lawyers Assn. (pres. 1980-81). Avocations: community interests, reading, sports. E-mail: jdeegear@aol.com.

DEEL, FRANCES QUINN, retired librarian; b. Pottsville, Pa., Mar. 9, 1939; d. Charles Joseph and Carrie Miriam (Ketner) Q.; m. Ronald Eugene Deel, Feb. 5, 1983. BS, Millersville State Coll., 1960; M.L.S., Rutgers U., 1964; M.P.A., U. West Fla., 1981. Post librarian U.S. Army Armor (Desert Tng. Ctr.), Ft. Irwin, Calif., 1964-66; staff librarian Mil. Dist. of Washington, 1966-67; supervisory librarian 1st Logistical Command, APO San Francisco, 1967-68; tech. process specialist Naval Edn. and Tng. Supervisory Command, Washington, 1968-77, Pensacola, Fla., 1968-77; chief tech. library USAF Armament Lab., Eglin AFB, Fla., 1977-81; dir. command libraries Air Force Systems Command (Andrews AFB), Washington, 1981-92; mem. exec. adv. council Fed. Library and Info. Network, Washington, 1983-86; libr. Air Force Dist. of Washington (Bolling AFB), Washington, 1992-94; dir. Navy Dept. Libr., Washington, 1994; ret., 1994. Mem. ALA (dir.-at-large armed forces libraries sect. Chgo. 1983-86), Spl. Libraries Assn., D.C. Library Assn. Roman Catholic. Home: 99 Country Club Dr W Destin FL 32541-4433

DEELEY, C. CAREY, JR., lawyer; b. Balt., Sept. 30, 1951; BA, U. Va., 1973; JD, U. Balt., 1979. Bar: Md., 1979, US Dist. Ct., Md. Law clerk to Hon. Austin W. Brizendine Circuit Ct. for Balt. County, Md., 1978-79; ptnr. Venable LLP (formerly Venable, Baetjer & Howard), Towson, Md. Former chmn. Pretrial Release Project Advisory Com. Mem. bd. trustees St. Paul's School for Boys; legal advisor Alcoholic Beverage Med. Rsch. Found. Mem. ABA, Md. State Bar Assn. (bd. govs. 1985-86), Balt. County Bar Assn. (mem. exec. council 1987-98, pres. 1996-97), Balt. County Bar Found. (pres. 1997-98); fellow Md. Bar Found. Office: Venable LLP PO Box 5517 210 Allegheny Ave Baltimore MD 21204-4074 Office Phone: 410-494-6259. Office Fax: 410-821-0147. Business E-Mail: ccdeeley@venable.com.

DEELY, MAUREEN CECELIA, community health nurse; b. Washington, Feb. 8, 1960; d. Thomas Michael and Felice R. (Alvarez) Deely. AA, Montgomery Coll., 1984. Staff RN Phi Szabo PG Count/Detention Ctr., Upper Marlboro, Md., 1984-85, Sands Nursing Svcs. Inc., Silver Spring, Md., 1985-86, Windsor HomeCare Inc./Alliance Against AIDS, Washington, 1988-89; community health nurse Montgomery County Health Dept., Silver Spring, 1989—. Mem. adv. com. cmty. programs clin. rsch. Washington Regional AIDS Program, 1990—; chmn. adv. bd. Women's Interagency HIV Study Nat. Cmty., 1997—2000; mem. AIDS adv. com. Montgomery Hospice Soc., 1993; panelist, field reviewer develop treatment improvement protocol Ctr. Substance Abuse Treatment, 1993; mem. cmty. adv. bd. Nat. Women's Interagency HIV Study, 1993; alt. rep. adv. bd. Washington Area Consortium. Nat. WIHS, 1994, nat. rep.; rep., cmty. adv. bd. Nat. Cmty. Adv. Bd. Nat. WIHS; spkr. Bur. NAPWA-Nat. Assn. People with AIDS. Mem. health care and corrections task force and panel Met. Washington Coun. Govts.; mem. nat. adv. bd. rev. and synthesis HIV/AIDS related consumer/client level evaluations Health Resources Svcs. Adminstrn., recuperative care coord. homeless, 1998; co-chair Suburban Md. HIV Care Consortium, 1998; mem. Healthcare for Homeless Montgomery County, Md., 1999; v.p., sec. Suburban Md. HIV/AIDS Alliance, 1996, pres., 1997—98; mem. Suburban Md. HIV Prevention Regional Work Group, 1997, Cmty. Adv. Bd. Food and Friends, 1997, Met. Washington Regional HIV Health Svcs. Planning Coun., 1996—, chair PWA com., 2001—03, mem., 1996—, chair PWA com., 2001—03; bd. dirs. PWA coms. Md., Inc., 1997—98. Recipient Cheryl D. Friedman award, Montgomery County HHS, 1995, Outstanding Svc. award, Montgomery County Dept. Correction and Rehab., 1996, Carol Johnson Meml. Cmty. Svc. award, 2001. Mem.: Am. Pain Soc. E-mail: Maureen.Deely@montgomerycountymd.gov.

DEEM, GEORGE, artist; b. Vincennes, Ind., Aug. 18, 1932; s. George C. and Laura (Bobe) D. Student, Vincennes U., 1951-52; BFA, Sch. Art Inst. Chgo., 1958. Instr. painting Sch. Visual Arts, N.Y.C., 1965-66, Leicester (Eng.) Coll. Art and Design, 1966-67, U. Pa., 1968; artist in residence Mus. Arts and Sci., Evansville, Ind., 1979; vis. artist Ill. State U., Normal, 1982, Branson Sch., Ross, Calif., 1995. Sec. exec. com. MacDowell Colony Fellows, 1982-87. One man shows Allan Stone Gallery, N.Y.C., 1963, 64, 65, 66, 68, 69, 75, 77, Sneed Gallery, Rockford, Ill., 1968, 69, 72, 76, 80, Merida Gallery, Louisville, 1966, 68, 69, 78, 83, Indpls. Mus. Art, 1974, Witte Meml. Mus., San Antonio, 1975, Evansville (Ind.) Mus. Arts and Sci., 1979, Greenberg Gallery, St. Louis, 1979, On View Downtown Gallery, Indpls., 1986, Mus. Arts and Sci., Evansville, Ind., 1993, Harn Mus. Art, U. Fla., Gainesville, 1993, Mitchell Mus. Art, Mt. Vernon, Ill., 1993, Polk Mus. Art, Lakeland, Fla., 1994, Ind. State Mus., Indpls., 1994, Eckert Fine Art Gallery, Indpls., 1994, Capricorn Gallery, Bethesda, Md., 1994, Wichita (Kans.) Ctr. for Arts, 1994, Nancy Hoffman Gallery, N.Y.C., 2000, Mus. Arts and Sci., Evansville, Ind., 2001, Las Vegas Art Mus., 2001, Pavel Zoubok Gallery, N.Y.C., 2002, Yale U. Jonathan Edwards Coll. Masters House, New Haven, 2003, PavelZoubokGallery, N.Y.C., 2004, New Britain (Conn.) Mus. Am. Art, 2005; group shows include Yale U. Art Gallery, 1964, Whitney Mus. Am. Art, N.Y.C., 1978, Pa. Acad. Fine Arts, 1981, Allentown (Pa.) Art Mus., 1983, Ft. Wayne (Ind.) Mus. Art, 1984, Nancy Hoffman Gallery, N.Y.C., 1985, 86, 87, 88, 89, 90, 91, 94, 98, Flint (Mich.) Inst. Arts, 1993, Nassau County Mus. of Art, Roslyn Harbor, N.Y., 1994; Museum of Art, U. of Oregon, Eugene, 1996, Pavel Zoubok/Mary Delahoyd Gallery, N.Y.C., 1998, Nassau County Mus. of Art, Roslyn Harbor, N.Y., 2000, Allan Stone Gallery, N.Y.C., 2000, Miami U. Art Mus., Oxford, Ohio, 2002, Herbert F. Johnson Mus. Art, Ithaca, N.Y., 2002, Musee d'Art moderne et contemporain, Strasbourg, France, 2003; represented in permanent collections Indpls. Mus. Art, Evansville Mus. Arts and Sci., Stiftung Ludwig, Aachen, Germany, Vassar Coll. Art Gallery, Mus. Fine Arts, Houston, Miami U. Art Mus., Oxford, Ohio, Weatherspoon Art Mus. U. N.C., Greensboro, JP Morgan Chase Bank Collection, N.Y.C., Cleary Gottlieb Steen & Hamilton, N.Y.C., Bank of Am. Collection, Fla. Internat. U., Frost Art Mus., Miami, Fla., Ariz. State U. Art Mus., Tempe, Hallmark Cards, Inc., Kansas City, Mo., State Russian Mus., St. Petersburg, Mus. of Modern Art, San Francisco, Am. Gen. Fin., Inc., Evansville, Wellington Mgmt. Co., Boston; commns. Nutter, McLennen & Fish, Boston, 1988, Albrecht-Kemper Mus. Art, St. Joseph, Mo., Seven Bridges Found., Greenwich, Conn., Ogden Mus. So. ARt At U. of New Orleans, Paul, Weiss, Rifkind, N.Y., 1989, Mirage Resorts, 1998; subject (video profiles) Art School: Paintings by George Deem, 1993, How to Paint a Vermeer: A Painter's History of Art, 2004, rev. edit., 2005, Deceptively Real: The Art of Seeing, 2004; contbr. articles to profl. jours. Served with U.S. Army, 1953-55. Home and Office: 10 W 18th St New York NY 10011-4617

DEEM, JASON LEE, music educator; b. Hopkinsville, Ky., June 30, 1977; s. Danny Ray and Beverly Jean Dunn; m. Megan Elizabeth Tyner, Sept. 4, 1980; 1 child, Makinlee Claire. MusB in Music Edn., U. of Tenn., 2000, MS with in Adminstrn. and Supervision, 2005. Educator Tenn., 2000. Band dir. Gibson County Spl. Sch. Dist., Dyer, Tenn., 2001—, Henderson County Sch. Sys., Lexington, 2000—01. Mem.: Phi Mu Alpha Sinfonia (pres. 1998—2000), Music Educator Nat. Conf., Tenn. Music Educators Assn. Achievements include first to Mr. Jason Deem's band programs have consistently received superior awards in marching and concert bands. Home: 1116 South College Trenton TN 38382 Office: Gibson County High Sch Band PO Box 190 Dyer TN 38330 Office Phone: 731-692-3616. Home Fax: 731-692-2123. Personal E-mail: jldeem@gibsoncountyband.com.

DEEN, PAULA H., television personality, restaurant owner, chef; b. Albany, Ga. m. Michael Groover, Mar. 2004; 2 stepchildren;children from previous marriage: Bobby, Jamie. Owner catering bus. The Bag Lady; owner The Lady and Sons restaurant, Savannah, Ga., 1990—. Host (TV series) Paula's Home Cooking, Food Network, 2002—; author: (cookbooks) The Lady and Sons Savannah Country Cookbook, The Lady and Sons Too, The Lady and Sons Just Desserts, 2002; co-author (with Martha Nesbit): Paula Deen & Friends: Living It Up, Southern Style, 2005. Provided sponsorships and donations of money, cookbooks and other services to cmty. groups and causes. Named Most Memorable Meal Yr. at The Lady and Sons restaurant, USA Today, 1999, Small Bus. Person Yr. in Ga., US Small Bus. Adminstrn., 2003; recipient Ga. Women Entrepreneurs (GWEN) award, Ga. Small Bus. Devel. Ctr., 2003. Office: Food Network Studios 604 W 52nd St New York NY 10019 also: Lady & Sons Restaurant 102 W Congress St Savannah GA 31401*

DEENER, LARRY COLBY, lawyer; b. Campbellsville, Ky., Sept. 15, 1950; s. Colby Velmer and Gloria Mae (Reynolds) Deener; m. Martha Jean Strnad, Dec. 28, 1971; 1 child, Elizabeth Anna. BA, U. Ky., 1971; JD, No. Ky. U., 1979. Bar: Ky. 1979, U.S. Dist. Ct. (ea. dist.) Ky. 1980, U.S. Ct. Appeals (6th cir.) 1982, U.S. Supreme Ct. 1987. Law clk. to assoc. justice Supreme Ct. Ky., Frankfort, 1979-80; ptnr. Landrum & Shouse, Attys., Lexington, Ky., 1980—. Capt. USAF, 1972—76, lt. col. USAFR, 1976—99. Mem.: Order of Curiae. Republican. Presbyterian. Office: Landrum & Shouse Attys PO Box 951 106 W Vine St Ste 800 Lexington KY 40507-1688 Office Phone: 859-255-2424. Business E-Mail: ldeener@landrumshouse.com.

DEER, DWAYNE GENE, lawyer; b. Brookhaven, Miss., Apr. 24, 1963; s. Gene Conerly and Charolett Ann Deer; m. Paula Michel Deer, Feb. 20, 1998; children: Jason, Jessica, Zachary, Elisabeth, Eli. BA, Miss. Coll., Clinton, 1992; JD, Miss. Coll., Jackson, 1995. Bar: Miss., U.S. Dist. Ct. (so. and no. dists.) Miss., U.S. Ct. Appeals (5th cir.). Office: PO Box 1361 Mccomb MS 39649

DEER, RICHARD ALAN (ALAN DEER), lawyer; b. Apr. 15, 1963; m. Jill Verdeyen; 2 children. BS in acctg., Auburn U., 1985; JD, U. Ala., 1988. Bar: 1988. Ptnr. Lange, Simpson, Robinson & Somerville LLP, Birmingham, Ala.; joined Regions Fin. Corp., Birmingham, Ala., 1997, chief legal officer, 2003—04, gen. counsel, 2004—, also corp. sec., 2004—. Chmn. banking law com. Ala. Bar Inst. for Continuing Legal Edn. Mem. Ind. Presbyn. Ch. Mem.: Ala. State Bar, Birmingham Bar Assn., ABA (consumer fin. services com. of bus. law sect.). Office: Regions Fin Corp 420 N 20th St Birmingham AL 35202

DEER, RICHARD ELLIOTT, lawyer; b. Indpls., Sept. 8, 1932; s. Leon Leslie and Mary Jane (Ostheimer) Deer; m. Lee Todd, Feb. 22, 1958; children: William K., Laura A., Susannah T., Thomas E. AB, DePauw U., 1954; LLB magna cum laude, Harvard U., 1957. Bar: Ind. 57, U.S. Dist. Ct. (no. and so. dists.) Ind. 57, U.S. Ct. Appeals (7th cir.) 57, U.S. Ct. Appeals (9th cir.) 90, U.S. Supreme Ct. 62. Assoc. Barnes & Thornburg and predecessor firm, Indpls., 1957—65, ptnr., 1965—, chmn. mgmt. com., 1990—93. Author: Indiana Corporation Law and Practice, 1990, Supplement, 1994; co-author: Indiana Limited LIability Company Forms and PRactuce Manual, 1996, Supplement, 1997; bd. editors: Harvard Law Rev., 1956—57; contbr. articles to legal jours.; chief reporter: The Lawyer's Basic Corporate Practice Manual, 3d edit., 1984. Mem. Indpls. Coun. Fgn. Rels., Ind. Corps. Survey Commn., 1983—2000. Fellow: Ind. Bar Found., Am. Bar Found.; mem.: ABA (drafting com., exec. planning group of legal opinion project sect. bus. law, 3d party legal opinion report 1991), Am. Law Inst., Ind. State Bar Assn. (past chmn. corp., banking and bus. law sect.), Indpls. Bar Assn., Columbia Club, Players Club, Hillcrest Country Club. Office: Barnes & Thornburg 11 S Meridian St Ste 1313 Indianapolis IN 46204-3535

DEERING, ALLAN BROOKS, retired soft drink company executive; b. Chappaqua, N.Y., Apr. 1, 1934; s. Clarence and Muriel Deering; m. Carol Ann Werle, Apr. 14, 1957; children: Peter Brooks, Andrew Werle. BA, Columbia U., 1956. Systems analyst IBM Corp., White Plains, N.Y., 1956-58; EDP mgr. R.H. Donnelly Corp., N.Y.C., 1958-68; dir. systems and data processing W.R. Grace & Co., N.Y.C., 1968-76, asst. v.p., 1975; dir. info. systems SCM Corp., N.Y.C., 1976-81; dir. mgmt. info. svcs. Pepsi Co., N.Y.C., 1981-86, v.p. mgmt. info. svcs., 1986—2000. Mem. Mayor's Industry Adv. Bd. for Data Processing, N.Y.C., 1978, adv. bd. Pace U. Sch. Computer Sci., Omicron. Mem. Data Processing Mgmt. Assn., Soc. Mgmt. Info. Systems (bd. dirs.), N.Y. Computer Execs. Roundtable, Grocery Mfrs. Am. (chmn. systems com.), Rocky Point Club, Old Greenwich Yacht Club, Milbrook Club. Home: 3 Perkley Ln Riverside CT 06878-2309 E-mail: abdeering@snet.net.

DEERING, ANTHONY WAYNE MARION, real estate developer; b. Washington, Jan. 28, 1945; s. George Aloysius and Maude Emma (Matheys) D.; m. Kathryn Evelyn Regan, May 31, 1969; children: Heather, Spencer, Maron. BS, Drexel U., Phila., 1968; MBA, Wharton Sch., U. Pa., 1970; postgrad., U. Exeter, Eng. Bus. planner Exxon Co., N.Y.C., 1970-71; cons. Dunuck, Fulton Co., Phila., 1971—; pres., CEO, Rouse Co., Columbia, Md., 1971-98, chmn., CEO, 1998—. Dir. T. Rowe Price Prime Res., T. Rowe Price New Income, T. Rowe Price Mut. Funds, Kleinwort Benson Mcht. Bank, The Rouse Co. Trustee Friends Sch., Balt., Balt. Parks Found., Balt. Mus. Art. Home: 6011 Charlesmead Rd Baltimore MD 21212-2214 Office: The Rouse Company 10275 Little Patuxent Pkwy Columbia MD 21044-3455

DEERING, RONALD FRANKLIN, librarian, minister; b. Paxton, Ill., Oct. 6, 1929; s. Minor Franklin and Grace Gilmour (Perkins) D.; m. Geraldine Gibbons, June 27, 1953 (dec. Jan. 1965); m. Edith Ann Proctor, June 12, 1966; children: Mark David, Daniel Timothy. BA summa cum laude, Georgetown (Ky.) Coll., 1951; MDiv, So. Bapt. Theol. Sem., 1955, PhD, 1962; MLS, Columbia U., 1967. Ordained to ministry So. Bapt. Conv., 1950. Pastor 1st Hilltop Bapt. Ch., North College Hill, Ohio, 1949-50; instr. in Bible Georgetown (Ky.) Coll., 1950-51; pastor Blue River Bapt. Ch., Salem, Ind., 1954-59; instr. Greek, N.T. So. Bapt. Theol. Sem., Louisville, 1958-61, theol. libr., 1962-95, assoc. v.p. for acad. resources, 1995—. Chmn. So. Bapt. Hist. Commn., Nashville, 1987-90; interim pastor 31 chs. in Ind., Ky., 1961-90; del. Bapt. World Alliance, Miami, Fla., Toronto, Ont., Can., L.A., 1965, 80, 85. Contbr. articles to profl. jours. Eli Lilly Theol. Librarianship grantee, 1967. Mem. AAUP, ALA, Southeastern Libr. Assn., Am. Theol. Libr. Assn. (nat. pres. 1984-85), Ky. Libr. Assn., Phi Alpha Theta, Beta Phi Mu, Sigma Tau Delta. Democrat. Home: 3111 Dunlieth Ct Louisville KY 40241-2937 Office Phone: 502-897-4807. E-mail: rondeering@bellsouth.net.

DEERING, THOMAS PHILLIPS, retired lawyer; b. Winfield, Kans., Feb. 15, 1929; s. Frederick Arthur and Lucile (Phillips) D.; m. Marilyn Marie Anderson, Sept. 6, 1952; children: Thomas P. Jr., Robert E., Paul A. BS, U. Colo., 1951, LLB, 1956. Bar: Oreg. 1956, Colo. 1956, U.S. Dist. Ct. Oreg. 1956. Assoc. Hart Spencer McCulloch Rockwood & Davies (now Stoel Rives), Portland, Oreg., 1956-62; ptnr. Stoel Rives LLP, Portland, 1962—99; ret., 1999. Mem. We. Pension and Benefits Conf., 1989-2002; mem. faculty Am. Law Inst.-ABA, 1985-96. Co-author: Tax Reform Act of 1986, 1987. Bd. dirs. Girl Scouts Columbia River Coun., Portland, 1961-70; trustee, moderator First Unitarian Ch., Portland, 1967-70; trustee, pres. Catlin Gabel Sch., Portland, 1970-76; bd. dirs., v.p. ACLU, Portland, 1966-71, 73-80; chmn. Multnomah County Task Force on Edgefield Manor, Portland, 1972-75; bd. dirs., treas. Portland Art Mus., Contemporary Arts Coun., 1986-88; mem. City County Task Fore on Svc. Evaluation, Portland, 1982-85, Citizen's Adv. Com. West Side Corridor Project, Portland, 1988-93; bd. govs. Pacific N.W. Coll. Art, 1991-2000, 2002-, chair, 1996-2000, chair presdl. search com. 2002-2003; mem. collections com. Portland Art Mus., 1992-96; trustee Oreg. Coll. Art and Craft Endowment, Portland, 1991-97. With U.S. Army, 1952-54. Recipient Disting. Mem. award We. Pension and Benefits Conf., 1999. Fellow Am. Coll. Benefits Counsel (emeritus); mem. ABA (tax sect., EB com. 1989-2000), City Club of Portland (bd. govs. 1968-70, 2000-03, rsch bd. 2003—). Democrat. Avocations: hiking, skiing, sailing, reading. Home: 5235 SW Burton Dr Portland OR 97221-2517 Office: Stoel Rives LLP 900 SW 5th Ave Ste 2600 Portland OR 97204-1268 Personal E-mail: tomdeering@comcast.net. Business E-Mail: tpdeering@stoel.com.

DEES, BOWEN CAUSEY, retired institute executive; b. Batesville, Miss., July 20, 1917; s. John Simeon and Ida Lea (Causey) D.; m. Sarah Edna Sanders, Aug. 25, 1937 (dec. 1999); 1 child, Sarah Edna; m. Dorothea Regina Simoneau, Sept. 24, 2001. AB, Miss. Coll., 1937, DSc (hon.), 1963; PhD, NYU, 1942; LLD, Lehigh U., 1976, Phila. Coll. Textiles and Sci., 1979; DSc (hon.), Temple U., 1981. Prof. physics Miss. Coll., 1943-44; instr. elec comms. Radar Sch., MIT, 1944-45; asst. prof. physics Rensselaer Poly. Inst., 1945-47; physicist, then div. chief sci. and tech. div., gen. hdqrs. SCAP, Tokyo, 1947-51; program dir. fellowships NSF, 1951-56, dep. asst. dir. sci. personnel and edn., 1956-59, asst. dir., 1959-63, assoc. dir. for edn., 1963-64, assoc. dir. planning, 1963-66; v.p. U. Ariz., 1966-68, provost acad. affairs, 1968-70; pres. Franklin Inst., Phila., 1970-82, pres. emeritus, 1982—. Adv. com. U.S. Army Command and Gen. Staff Coll., 1967-69; sci. info. coun. NSF, 1970-74; mem. Sci. Manpower Commn., Washington, 1976-79; U.S. co-chmn. U.S.-Japan Com. on Sci. Cooperation, 1981-87. Author: Fundamentals of Physics, 1945, The Allied Occupation and Japan's Economic Miracle, 1997; contbr. articles to profl. jours. Mem. Cosmos (Washington). Personal E-mail: bcdees2@aol.com.

DEES, C. STANLEY, lawyer; b. Tulsa, June 24, 1938; AB, Princeton U., 1960; LLB, U. Va., 1963. Bar: Va. 1963, D.C. 1964. Ptnr. McKenna, Long & Aldridge LLP, Washington. Lectr. U. Va. Law Sch. Contbr. articles to profl. jours. Trustee Legal Aid Soc. D.C., 1970-83, pres., 1978-80; mem. Va. Dem. Ctrl. Com., 1971-74. Fellow Am. Bar Found.; mem. ABA (chmn. fed. cts. com. 1977-78, jud. remedies com. 1978-80, program com. 1980-81, coun. mem. 1981-84, sec. 1984-85, vice-chmn. pub. contract law sect. 1985-86, chmn. pub. contract law sect. 1987-88), U.S. Ct. Fed. Claims Bar, D.C. Bar (vice-chmn. 1974-75, chmn. 1975-77, steering com., govt. contracts and litigation divsn.), Va. State Bar, Coun. Def. and Space Indsl. Assns. (chmn. 1991-93), Nat. Security Indsl. Assn. (v.p. 1983-90, trustee 1990-96), D.C. Bar Found. (adv. com.), Order of Coif. Office: McKenna Long & Aldridge 1900 K St NW Washington DC 20006*

DEES, JULIAN WORTH, retired academic/research administrator; b. Henderson, N.C., Feb. 20, 1933; s. Charles Andrew and Gertrude Elizabeth (Lancaster) D.; m. Bernita June Funk, Aug. 29, 1954; children: Sandra Eileen Dees Anthony, Mark Alan, Gregory Linn. BS in Radio Engring., Tri-State U., Angola, Ind., 1953, BS in Adminstrv. Engring., 1954; MSEE, U. Cin., 1955. Registered profl. engr., Ga. Microwave engr. IT&T Labs., Ft. Wayne, Ind., 1955-60; project mgr., sr. engr. Martin Marietta Corp., Orlando, Fla., 1960-71; dir. electromagnetic lab. Ga. Inst. Tech., Atlanta, 1971-80, assoc. v.p. rsch., dir. office contract adminstrn., prin. rsch. engr., 1980-98; ret., 1998. Asst. sec., asst. treas Ga. Tech. Rsch. Corp., Atlanta, 1980-98; bd. dir. Coun. on Rsch. & Tech., Washington. Contbr. articles to jours. in field; patentee in field. Named Author of Yr., Martin Marietta Corp., 1965. Fellow IEEE (Engr. of Yr. Orlando chpt. 1968); mem. Soc. Rsch. Adminstrs. (sr.), Coun. on Govtl. Rels., Nat. Coun. Univ. Rsch. Adminstrs. Avocations: woodworking, judging barbeque cook-offs. Home: 2128 Rosser Pl Stone Mountain GA 30087-1517

DEES, LAFON CARABO, brokerage house executive; b. Bennettsville, SC, Aug. 13, 1937; s. Willie Ray and Allie Lee Dees; m. Winston Clark, June 15, 1963; 1 child, Kimberly Dees Earle. BBA, Wofford Coll., 1959. Factory rep. Armstrong World Ind., 1962-69; gen. sales mgr. Stewart Co., Dallas, 1969-72; factory rep. Lane Co., Atlanta, 1982; sr. v.p. investments Smith Barney, Atlanta, 1983—. Trustee Charitable Trust. 1st lt. U.S. Army, 1959-62. Mem. Buckhead Club. Republican. Methodist. Avocations: sports, reading, music, travel. Home: 5465 New Wellington Close NW Atlanta GA 30327 Office Phone: 800-688-6002 ext 6551.

DEES, MORRIS SELIGMAN, JR., lawyer; b. Shorter, Ala., Dec. 16, 1936; s. Morris Seligman and Annie Ruth (Frazer) D.; m. Elizabeth Breen; children: Morris Seligman III, John Fuller, Ellie. BS, U. Ala., 1958, LLB, 1960. Bar: Ala. 1960. Chmn. bd. Fuller and Dees Pub., Inc. (merged with Times Mirror), 1960-69; ptnr. Levin and Dees, 1969-71; co-founder (with Joe Levin) and chief trial counsel So. Poverty Law Ctr., Montgomery, Ala., 1971—. Pres. Funding Group, 1983—; instr. criminal law Jones Law Sch., 1960-62; vis. fellow John F. Kennedy Sch. Govt., Harvard U.; elected fellow U. Pa. Law Sch., 1988. Co-author (with Steve Fiffer): A Season for Justice, 1991; author: Hate on Trial: The Case Against America's Most Dangerous Neo-Nazi, 1993, Gathering Storm: America's Militia Threat, 1996. Dir. nat. fund raising McGovern for Pres., 1972; nat. fin. chmn. Carter for Pres., 1976; nat. fin. dir. Kennedy for Pres., 1980; trustee Miles Coll. Named One of 10 Outstanding Young Men Am. U.S. Jaycees, 1967; recipient Outstanding Svc. for Human Rights award Tuskegee Inst., 1976, Trial Lawyer of Yr. award Trial Lawyers for Pub. Justice, 1987, Pub. Svc. Achievement award Common Cause, 1988, Justice award So. Christian Leadership Conf., 1989. Mem. ABA (Young Lawyers Disting. Svc. award 1987), Ala. Bar Assn., Direct Mail Mktg. Assn. (bd. dirs., Showmanship award 1968), Beta Gamma Sigma. Unitarian (pres. ch. 1968). Home: Rolling Hills Rnch Mathews AL 36052 Office: So Poverty Law Ctr 400 Washington St Montgomery AL 36104-4344*

DEES, RICHARD LEE, lawyer; b. Harrisburg, Ill., Jan. 14, 1955; s. David Lee and Joann (Alvey) D.; children: Sarah Elizabeth, Elliott Richard, Spencer Barrett; m. Nora B. Flint, Apr. 21, 2001. AS, Southeastern Ill. Jr. Coll., 1975; BS, So. Ill. U., 1977; JD, U. Ill., 1980. Bar: Ill. 1980, U.S. Tax Ct. 1981. Ptnr. McDermott, Will & Emery, Chgo., 1980—. Invited witness Senate Fin. Com., 1989-90, House Ways and Means Com., 1990. Editor: Agricultural Law and Tax Report, 1984-89; topics editor U. Ill. Law Forum, 1979-80; contbr. articles to profl. jours. Mem. Order of Coif. Presbyterian. Home: 24 S 7th Ave La Grange IL 60525- Office: McDermott Will & Emery 227 W Monroe St Ste 3100 Chicago IL 60606-5096 Office Phone: 312-984-7613. Personal E-mail: rdees@mwe.com.

DEES, SANDRA KAY MARTIN, psychologist, research scientist; b. Omaha, Apr. 18, 1944; d. Leslie B. and Ruth Lillian (May) Martin; m. Doyce B. Dees. BA magna cum laude, Tex. Christian U., 1965, MA, 1972, PhD, 1989. Cert. Montessori Soc., 1977. Adminstrv. asst., rsch. coord. Hosp. Improvement Project, Wichita Falls (Tex.) State Hosp., 1968-69; caseworker adoptions Edna Gladney Home, Ft. Worth, 1970-71; psychologist Mexia (Tex.) State Sch., 1971-72; sch. psychologist Ft. Worth Ind. Sch. Dist., 1971-78, program evaluator, 1978-86; pvt. counselor, 1986-88; rsch. scientist Tex. Christian U., Ft. Worth, 1989—, mem. adj. faculty, 1991-92, mem. grad. faculty, 1994—. Bd. dirs Because We Care, Ft. Worth, 1988-97, Hill Sch., 1994—. Contbr. articles to profl. jours. Dallas TCU Women's Club creative writing scholar, 1962-64, Virginia Alpha scholar, 1963; NASA rsch. asst., 1965-67; USPHS trainee, 1967-68. Mem. APA, Am. Ednl. Rsch. Assn., Mental Health Assn., Mortar Board, Mensa, Sigma Xi, Alpha Chi, Phi Alpha Theta, Psi Chi, Phi Delta Kappa. Home: 29 Bounty Rd W Fort Worth TX 76132-1003 Office: Tex Christian U Dept Psychology Fort Worth TX 76129-0001 E-mail: s.dees@tcu.edu.

DEES, STEPHEN PHILLIP, agricultural products executive, lawyer; b. Tulsa, Feb. 21, 1943; s. Jesse Raymond and Mary Adelia (Ledbetter) D.; m. Mary Louise Porter, June 26, 1966 (div. Oct. 1986); children: Emily Ann, Daniel Ledbetter, Matthew Louis; m. Kristine Ann Odenwald, Oct. 10, 1987 (div. Apr. 1992); 1 child, Charles Jesse; m. Linda Petsch, Sept. 3, 1995. BA, Washington U., 1965, JD, 1967. Bar: Mo. 1967. Assoc. Stinson, Mag, Thomson, McEvers & Fizzell, Kansas City, Mo., 1967-71; ptnr. Stinson, Mag & Fizzell, Kansas City, 1971-84; v.p., gen. counsel Farmland Industries Inc., Kansas City, 1984-87, sec., 1986-91, v.p. law and adminstrn., 1987-93, now exec. v.p. bus. development & internat. mktg., dir. gen., 1993-98; dir. gen. Farmland Industries, S.A. de C.V. of Mex., 1993-95; ptnr. Rochdale Prins., 1998—2000; of counsel Shook, Hardy & Bacon, Kansas City, Mo., 2000—. Officer, bd. dirs. Gt. Am. Basketball League, Shawnee Mission, Kans., 1979-86, commr., 1983-86; mem. Sister Cities Commn., Kansas City, 1982-90; mem. leadership com. Legal Aid Western Mo. Served with USAF, 1967, then with Res. Mem. ABA, Mo. Bar (vice chmn. labor law com. 1977-80, chmn. 1980-81), Lawyers Assn. Kansas City (bd. dirs. 1983-86, treas. 1989-91), Kansas City Met. Bar Assn., Order of Coif. Republican. Jewish. Avocations: stamp collecting/philately, racquetball, travel. Home: 4511 N Mulberry Dr Kansas City MO 64116-4652 Office: Shook Hardy & Bacon PO Box 15607 1010 Grand Blvd Fl 5 Kansas City MO 64106-2220 Office Phone: 816-559-2466.

DEESE, E(THEL) HELEN, retired literature and language professor; b. San Diego, Sept. 15, 1925; d. Clyde Thomas and Ethel (Findlay) Smith; m. Rupert Julian Deese, Mar. 4, 1951; children: Rupert Thomas, Mary Ann, Franklin William, Richard Samuel. BA, U. Calif., Riverside, 1968, MA, 1970, PhD, 1977. Lectr. U. Calif., Riverside, 1977—79, 1992—2005, Calif. State Poly. U., Pomona, 1979-81; assoc. prof. English Mt. St. Mary's Coll., Los Angeles, 1983-89; Fulbright lectr. Hungary, 1989-90, 1990-91; ret., 2005. Critic So. Calif. drama, Shakespeare Bull., N.Y.C., 1985—; author: Robert Lowell: A Reference Guide, 1982; editor: Robert Lowell: New Essays on the Poetry, 1986, Critical Essays on Wallace Stevens, 1988, William Carlos Williams, 1989; contbr. Ency. Am. Poets and Poetry, 2005; contbr. articles to profl. jours. Mem. MLA, Internat. Fedn. for Theatre Rsch., Assn. of Lit. Scholars and Critics, Shakespeare Assn, L.A. World Affairs, Drama League Democrat. Unitarian Universalist. Home and Office: 601 E Baseline Rd Claremont CA 91711-2237 Office Phone: 909-626-6135. Personal E-mail: hsdeese@msn.com.

DEESE, GEORGE E., food products executive; With Flowers Foods, 1964; pres., COO Flowers Bakeries, 1983—2002, Flowers Foods, 2002—04, CEO, 2004. Mem.: Quality Bakers Am. (mem. bd.), Grocery Manufacturers Am. (indus. affairs coun.), Am. Bakers Assn. (former chmn., board exec. com.). Office: Flowers Food 1919 Flowers Circ Thomasville GA 31757*

DEESE, PAMELA MCCARTHY, lawyer; b. Abington, Pa., July 4, 1958; d. John Joseph McC. and Penny Ann (Wells) Knight; m. Charles Michael Deese, May 10, 1986; children: Spencer Michael, Charles Jameson, Kendall Ann. BS, The Am. U., 1980, JD, 1983. Bar: Pa. 1984, DC 1990, US Ct. Appeals (8th cir.) 1989 (4th cir.) 1992, US Supreme Ct. 1995, US Ct. Appeals (DC cir.) 1996. Asst. dir. GSP U.S. Trade Rep., Washington, 1978-83; assoc. atty. Ablondi & Foster, Washington, 1983-86, Robins, Zelle, Larson & Kaplan, Washington, 1986-89; ptnr. Robins, Kaplan, Miller & Ciresi, Washington, 1990—99; ptnr., trademark licensing and advertising Dorsey & Whitney, LLP, 1999—2005; mem. intellectual property practice Arent Fox PLLC, Washington, 2005—. Vol. Offender Aid and Rep., Fairfax, Va., 1983-86; pres. Am. U. Alumni Assn., Washington, 1988-97; elder Lewinsville Presbyn. Ch., McLean, Va., 1989-92; trustee Am. U., 2002—; mem. Circles Bd. Kennedy Ctr., 2001—. Mem. ABA, Am. Intellectual Property Lawyers Assn., Licensing Industry Merchandising Assn. Democrat. Presbyterian. Avocations: skiing, reading, cooking, flower arranging, travel. Office: Arent Fox PLLC 1050 Connecticut Ave NW Washington DC 20036-5339 Office Phone: 202-828-3431. Office Fax: 202-857-6395. Business E-Mail: deese.pamela@arentfox.com.

DEETS, RICHARD M., secondary school educator, consultant; s. Richard M. Deets, Sr. and Mary E. Deets; m. Susan W. May; stepchildren: Kay May, Julie Daniels 1 child, Michelle R. BA, Calif. State U., L.A., 1975; MA, Calif. State U., Northridge, 2000. Cert. resource specialist Calif., 1998, edn. adminstrn. Calif., 2000. Coord. coop. edn. L.A. Unified Sch. Dist., 1982—85, tchr., 1986—96, dean, 1996—2000, title I coord., 2000—01, resource specialist, 2001—. Mentor, tchr. LA Unified Sch. Dist., 2003—05. Author: (poetry) Poetic Divesities. Ednl. programs chair Sierra Madre (Calif.) Search and Rescue Team, 1989—2003; pres. Employment and Tng. Assn. Calif., L.A., 1983—84. Named Coord. of the Yr., Vocat. Industry Clubs Am., 1982; recipient Poetry Grand prize, Internat. Soc. Poets, 2005. Mem.: Educare (assoc.), Phi Delta Kappa (assoc. 20 Yr. Svc. 2003). Republican. Episcopalian. Achievements include research in onsite Soviet Union space program. Avocations: mountain climbing, poetry, reading, mentor for high school students. Office: Los Angeles Unified School District 9229 Haskell Ave North Hills CA 91343 E-mail: rdeets@socal.rr.com.

DEEVER, JANET WILLIAMS, Italian and Spanish educator; b. Oakland, Calif., June 4, 1933; d. John Clarence and Mildred Emelie Williams; children: Mason Lloyd, Nelson Lee, Melissa Lynne Aubert. BA, U. Calif., Berkeley, 1958; degree in bilingual edn., U. Phoenix, 1999. Cert. fgn. lang. tchg. Calif. Grad. asst. U. Calif., Berkeley, 1956—58; Spanish tchr. Ramona H.S., Riverside, Calif.; Italian instr. Mesa (Ariz.) C.C. Spanish club sponsor Tempe (Ariz.) H.S., 1956—. Head trustee Univ. Presbyn. Ch., Tempe, 1994—97. Cesare Barbieri scholar, Middlebury Lang. School-Vermont, 1956. Mem.: Lyric Opera Theater. Avocations: travel, writing. Home: 1127 E Leeward Ln Tempe AZ 85283 Office: Tempe HS 1730 S Mill Ave Tempe AZ 85281 Office Phone: 480-967-1661 x 21110. Personal E-mail: signorad@aol.com.

DEEVY, BEVERLY FERGUSON, artist; b. N.Y.C., Nov. 11, 1953; married. AAS in Interior Design, Chamberlayne Coll., 1982. Solo show at DeHaviland Fine Arts, Boston, 1994; group shows include Salmagundi Club, N.Y.C., 1992, Pastel Soc. Am., N.Y.C., 1992, Am. Artists Profl. League, N.Y.C., 1993, Salon Internat., Jackson, Miss., 1994, Hopper House Gallery, Nyack, N.Y., 1994, 2000, Providence Art Club, 1995, Pastel Soc. West Coast, Sacramento, 1994-95, Attleboro (Mass.) Mus., 1998, Hammond Harkins Gallery, Bexley, Ohio,1999, Fine Furnishings, Providence, Clifton (N.J.) Art Ctr., 2000. Recipient Philip Isenberg award for outstanding portrait, 1991, award Pastel Soc. Am., 1994, Artist's Mag., 1994, Chroma, Inc., 1999, Polaroid Corp., 1997, Winsor Newton award, 2000. Mem. Copley Soc. Boston, Am. Artists Profl. League, Artists' Assn. Nantucket, Oil Pastel Assn./United Pastelists (award 1993).

DEFAZIO, LYNETTE STEVENS, dancer, educator, choreographer, violinist, actress; b. Berkeley, Calif., Sept. 29, 1930; d. Honore and Mabel J. (Estavan) Stevens; children: J.H. Panganiban, Joanna Pang. Student, U. Calif., Berkeley, 1950—55, San Francisco State Coll., 1950—51; studied classical dance tchg. techniques and vocabulary with Gisella Caccialanza and Harold and Lew Christensen, San Francisco Ballet, 1952-56; D in Chiropractic, Life-West Chiropractic Coll., San Lorenzo, Calif., 1983; cert. techniques of tchg., U. Calif., 1985; BA in Humanities, New Coll. Calif., 1986. Lic. chiropracter, Mich.; diplomate Nat. Sci. Bd.; eminence in dance edn., Calif. C.C. dance specialist, std. svcs., childrens ctrs. credentials Calif. Dept. Edn., 1986. Contract child dancer Monogram Movie Studio, Hollywood, Calif., 1938-40; dance instr. San Francisco Ballet, 1953-65; performer San Francisco Opera Ring, 1960-67; performer, choreographer Oakland (Calif.) Civic Light Opera, 1963-70; dir. Ballet Arts Studio, Oakland, 1960; tchg. specialist Oakland Unified Sch. Dist., 1965-80; fgn. exch. dance dir. Academie de Danses-Salle Pleyel, Paris, 1966; instr. Peralta C.C. Dist., Oakland, 1971—, chmn. dance dept., 1985—. Cons., instr. ext. courses UCLA, Dirs. and Suprs. Assn., Pitts. Unified Sch. Dist., 1971-73, Tulare (Calif.) Sch. Dist., 1971-73; rschr. Ednl. Testing Svcs., HEW, Berkeley, 1974; resident choreographer San Francisco Childrens Opera, 1970—, Oakland Civic Theater; ballet mistress Dimensions Dance Theater, Oakland, 1977-80; cons. Gianchetta Sch. Dance, San Francisco, Robicheau Boston Ballet, TV series Patchwork Family, CBS, NYC; choreographer Ravel's Valses Nobles et Sentimentales, 1976. Author: Basic Music Outlines for Dance Classes, 1960, 1965, rev. edit., 1968, Teaching Techniques and Choreography for Advanced Dancers, 1965, Goals and Objectives in Improving Physical Capabilities, 1970, A Teacher's Guide for Ballet Techniques, 1970, Principle Procedures in Basic Curriculum, 1974, Objectives and Standards of Performance for Physical Development, 1975, Techniques of the Ballet School, 1970, rev. edit., 1974, The Opera Ballets: A Choreographic Manual Vols. I-V, 1986; assoc. music arranger: Le Ballet du Cirque, 1964, assoc. composer, lyricist: The Ballet of Mother Goose, 1968; choreographer Valses Nobles Et Sentimentales (Ravel), Transitions (Kashevaroff), 1991, The New Wizard of Oz, 1991, San Francisco Children's Opera (Gingold), Canon in D for Strings and Continuo (Pachelbel), 1979, Oakland Cmty. Orch. excerpts from Swan Lake, Faust, Sleeping Beauty, 1998, Rodeo, Alameda Coll. Cultural Affairs Program, 2000, The Gershwin Dances, 2004, dancer solo dancer Three Stravinsky Etudes, Alameda Coll. Cultural Affairs Program, 1999, appeared in Flower Drum Song, 1993, Gigi, 1994, Fiddler on the Roof, 1996, The Music Man, 1996, Sayonara, 1997, Bye Bye Birdie, 2000, Barnum, the Circus Musical, 2001; musician (violinist): Oakland Cmty. Concert Orch., 1995—; condr. Gil Gleason:. Bd. dirs. Prodrs. Assocs., Inc., Oakland, 1999—. Recipient Foremost Women of 20th Century, 1985, Merit award San Francisco Children's Opera, 1985, 90. Mem. Calif. State Tchrs. Assn., Bay Area Chiropractic Rsch. Soc., Profl. Dance Tchrs. Assn. Home and Office: 4923 Harbord Dr Oakland CA 94618-2506 Office Phone: 510-547-5477. Personal E-mail: lynette.defazio@comcast.net.

DEFAZIO, PETER A., congressman; b. Needham, Mass., May 27, 1947; m. Myrnie Daut. BA in Econs. and Polit. Sci., Tufts U., 1969; postgrad., U. Oreg., 1969-71, MS in Pub. Adminstrn./Gerontology, 1977. Aide to U.S. Rep. Jim Weaver, 1977-82; sr. issues specialist, caseworker, dist. field office U.S. rep. Jim Weaver, 1977-78, legis. asst. Washington office, 1978-80, dir. constituent services, 1980-82; mem. commn. representing Springfield Lane County (Oreg.) Commn., 1982-86; mem. U.S. Congress from 4th Oreg. dist., Washington, 1987—; mem. resources com., water and power subcom.; mem. transp. and infrastructure com., ranking mem. water resources and environ. subcom. Mem. Lane County Econ. Devel. com., Intergovtl. Relations com.; bd. dirs. Eugene-Springfield Met. Partnership; Lane County Dem. precinct person, 1982—. Served with USAFR. Mem. Assn. of Oreg. Counties (legis. com.), Nat. Assn. of Counties (tax and fin. com.). Democrat. Office: US Ho of Reps 2134 Rayburn Ho Office Bldg Washington DC 20515-0001*

DEFEIS, ELIZABETH FRANCES, law educator, lawyer; b. NYC; d. Francis Paul and Lena (Amendola) D. BA, St. John's U., 1956, JD, 1958, JSD (hon.), 1984; LLM, NYU, 1971; postgrad., U. Milan, Italy, 1963-64, Inst. Internat. Human Rights, 1991. Bar: N.Y. 1959, U.S. Dist. Ct. (fed. dist.) 1960, U.S. Dist. Ct. (so. dist.) N.Y. 1961, U.S. Supreme Ct. 1965, U.S. Dist. Ct. (ea.

dist.) N.Y. 1978, N.J. 1983. Asst. U. S. atty. So. Dist. N.Y., Dept. Justice, 1961-62; atty. RCA Corp., 1962-63; assoc. Carter, Ledyard & Milburn, N.Y.C., 1963-69; atty. Bedford Stuyvesant Legal Svcs. Corp., 1969-70; prof. law Seton Hall U., Newark, 1971—, dean Sch. Law, 1983-88. Vis. prof. St. Louis U. Sch. Law, 1988, St. John's U. Sch. Law, 1990, 2001, U. Milan, Italy, 1996; Fulbright-Hays lectr., Iran, India, 1977-79; lectr. Orgn. Security and Cooperation in Europe, Russia, Turkmenistan, Tajikistan, Azerbaijan; vis. scholar Ctr. Study of Human Rights, Columbia U., 1989; project dir. TV series Women and Law, 1974-80; narrator TV series Alternatives to Violence, 1981; mem. com. women and cts. N.J. Supreme Ct., 1982-95; trustee Legal Svcs. N.J., 1983-88; mem. 3rd Cir. Task Force on Equality in the Cts., 1995-98; tech. cons. on Constitution of Armenia, 1992-95; project dir. T.V. series Pub. Internat. Law.; legal expert Armenia election OSCE, 1998; disting. chair fulbright program U. Naples, 2002. Chair Albert Einstein Inst., Boston, 1995—2001. Fulbright-Hays scholar Milan, Italy, 1963-64, Fulbright-Hays, Orgn. for Security and Cooperation in Europe scholar, Armenia, Russia, Italy, 1996; Ford Found. fellow, 1970-71. Mem. ABA, Columbian Lawyers Assn., Assn. of Bar of City of N.Y. (chair, spl. com. United Nations, coun. internat. affairs), N.J. Bar Assn., Nat. Italian Am. Found. Office: Seton Hall U Law Sch One Newark Ctr Newark NJ 07102 Business E-Mail: defeisel@shu.edu.

DEFELICE, EUGENE ANTHONY, internist, educator, magician; b. Beacon, N.Y., Dec. 24, 1927; s. Domenick and Louise (Grippo) DeF. BS, Columbia U., 1951; MD, Boston U., 1956. Ciba fellow, lectr. pharmacology Boston U. Sch. Medicine, 1954-57; intern Newton (Mass.) Wellesley Hosp., 1957; internal medicine/psychosomatic medicine Jackson Meml. Hosp., U. Miami Sch. Medicine, Miami, Fla., 1958-61; asst. dir. clin. rsch. Warner Lambert Rsch. Inst., Morris Plains, NJ, 1961-64; dir. clin. rsch. Bristol Labs. (now Bristol Meyers Squibb), Syracuse, NY, 1965-66, Sandoz Inc. (now Novartis Inc.), East Hanover, NJ, 1967-68, exec. dir. clin. research, 1969-70, dir. sci. affairs and comml. devel., 1970—73, v.p. corp. sci. devel., 1974-77, v.p. internat. med. rsch., med. advisor, 1977-83. Prof. biochemistry, microbiology and pub. health, dir. rsch. New Eng. Coll. Pharmacy, 1956-58; practice in medicine, cons. in medicine and med. rsch., Morristown, N.J., 1961-87, East Schodack and Albany, N.Y., 1988-2003, Niagara Falls, N.Y., 2004—; clin. assoc. prof. medicine Coll. Medicine and Dentistry N.J.-Rutgers Med. Sch., 1977-84; clin. prof. medicine UMD-Robert Wood Johnson Med. Sch., 1985—2003; clin. prof. anesthesiology UCLA, 1978-83. Co-author: Angiotensin Converting Enzyme Inhibitors, 1987, Prostaglandins, Platelets, Lipids: New Developemnts in Atherosclerosis, 1981, Health and Obesity, 1983, Beta Blockers in the Treatment of Cardiovascular Diseases, 1984, The Pharmacological Treatment of Cardiovascular Diseases, 1986; author: Web Health Info. Resource Guide, 2001, Breast Cancer, 2002, Overweight, Obesity and Health, 2002, Nutrition and Health, 2003, Web Health Information Resources, 2004, Prevention of Cardiovascular Disease, 2005; mem. internat. editl. com. Triangle, Sandorama, 1977—81; contbr. numerous articles to profl. jours. Served with U.S. Army, World War II. Named hon. citizen of Italy; named to Notable Italian-Am. Hall of Fame. Fellow Am. Geriat. Soc., Acad. Psychosomatic Medicine; mem. Soc. Am. Magicians, Internat. Brotherhood Magicians; emeritus mem. numerous profl. socs. Home and Office: 600 Spruce Ave Niagara Falls NY 14302 *Success in life comes from constancy of purpose, diligent work, living according to sound moral and religious principles, and having faith and hope in the future. Helping to make the world a better place to live in, autographing one's work in excellence, and doing good by others are the rewards which bring happiness.*

DE FELITTA, FRANK PAUL, film producer, writer; b. N.Y.C. s. Pat and Genevieve (Sibilio) De F.; m. Dorothy Gilbert; children: Eileen Raymond. Student, U. N.C., New Sch. Social Research, 1948. Dir.-writer, CBS, 1950-57, dir. programming, Nat. Telefilms Assos., 1959-61, producer, writer, dir., NBC, from 1962, producer, dir., writer, Universal Studios, 1968-69; film documentaries include Music of the South, 1955; sci. series Conquest, 1957; natural sci. series Adventure, 1953-55; hist. series Odyssey, 1958, The Chosen Child, 1962 (Writers Guild award), Emergency Ward, 1962 (Emmy award), Experiment in Excellence, 1963 (Sch. Bell award), Battle of the Bulge, 1964, The Stately Ghosts of England, 1964, The World of the Teenager, 1966 (Robert J. Flaherty award), Pearl Harbor, 1966 Golden Eagle award; dir., author: films Trapped, 1973, The Two Worlds of Jennie Logan, 1979 (Silver Halo award), Killer in the Mirror, 1986, Scissors, 1990; dir.: film Dark Night of the Scarecrow, 1981; (Brotherhood award of Nat. Conf. Christians and Jews for film Mississippi- A Self Portrait, George Washington Honor medal of Freedoms Found. for film The American Image.); Author: films The First of January, 1970, The Savage Is Loose, 1971, Audrey Rose, 1977, The Entity, 1981; novels Oktoberfest, 1972, Audrey Rose, 1975, The Entity, 1978, Sea Trial, 1980, For Love of Audrey Rose, 1982, Golgotha Falls, 1984, Funeral March of the Marionettes, 1990, A Swift Death to Critics, 2000. Recipient Peabody award, 1954, 63, Thomas Alva Edison award, 1958, 2 Gold Eagle awards Coun. on Internat. Non-Theatrical Events. Mem. Writers Guild Am., Dirs. Guild Am.

DEFENDI, VITTORIO, medical association administrator, pathologist; b. Treviglio, Italy, Nov. 16, 1928; married, 1955; 3 children. MD, U. Pavia, 1951. Instr. pathology dept. U. Pavia, 1951-52; pathologist virus sect. Lederle Labs., N.Y.C., 1956-58; assoc. pathologist Med. Sch., U. Pa., 1958-64, assoc. prof., 1964-68, Wistar prof., 1968-74; prof. pathology, chmn. dept. pathology Sch. NYU Sch. Medicine, N.Y.C., 1974—2002. Brit. Coun. scholar Postgrad. Med. Sch., U. London, 1952-53; Fulbright fellow Med. Sch., U. Vt., 1953-54; rsch. fellow Detroit Inst. Cancer Rsch., 1954-56; assoc. mem. Wistar Inst., 1958-64, mem. staff, 1964-74; rsch. prof. Am. Cancer soc., 1973—. Leukemia Soc. scholar, 1962-66. Mem. Am. Soc. Cell Biology, Am. Soc. Exptl. Pathology, Histochem. Soc., Am. Assn. Immunology, Am. Assn. Cancer Rsch. Achievements include research in viral oncology; tumor biology; mechanism of immunological defense. Office: NYU Sch Medicine Dept Pathology 550 1st Ave New York NY 10016-6402 Business E-Mail: vittorio.defendi@med.nyu.edu.

DEFEO, PHILIP D., brokerage house executive; BA in econ. and internat. fin., Iona Coll. Opers. mgr. Procter and Gamble; sr. v.p. internat. securities divsn. Bankers Trust Co., London; mng. dir. worldwide equities opers. Lehman Bros.; sr. v.p. and mem. oper. com. FMR Corp.; exec. v.p. & dir. mktg. and customer svc. Cedel Internat.; pres. and CEO Van Eck Assocs. Corp.; chmn. and CEO Pacific Exch., San Francisco, 1999—. Bd. dirs. Archipelago Holdings, Inc., 2000—. Office: Pacific Exch 115 Sansome St San Francisco CA 94104

DEFEO, RONALD M., machinery manufacturing executive; B in Econs. and Philosophy, Iona Coll., 1974. Various positions Procter & Gamble, 1974-84; sr. v.p., mng. dir. JI case constrn. equipment Tenneco, Inc., 1984-92; pres. heavy equipment group Terex, 1992, pres., COO, 1993, CEO, 1995, chmn. bd. dir., 1998. Bd. dirs. United Rentals, Inc.; co-chmn. CONEXPO-CON/AGG. Mem. Constrn. Industry Mfrs. Assn. (mem. exec. com.), Young Pres. Orgn. Office: Terex Corp Ste 320 500 Post Rd East Westport CT 06880

DEFFAA, CHIP, jazz critic; b. New Rochelle, N.Y., May 18, 1951; s. Louis Philip and Alberta (Saby) D. AB, Princeton U., 1973. Jazz critic N.Y. Post, N.Y.C., 1986—. Author: Swing Legacy, 1989, Voices of the Jazz Age, 1990, In the Mainstream, 1992, Traditionalists and Revivalists in Jazz, 1993, (with David Cassidy) C'mon Get Happy, 1994, Jazz Veterans, 1995, Blue Rhythms, 1996, (play) George M. Cohan: In His Own Words, 2004; editor F. Scott Fitzgerald: The Princeton Years, 1997; prodr.: Chip Deffaa Invitational Theater Festival, N.Y., 2002. Trustee Princeton Tiger Mag., 1983—. Finalist for Excellence in Recorded Sound Rsch. award Assn. for Recorded Sound Collections, 1991; recipient Deems Taylor award ASCAP, 1993. Mem. Nat. Acad. Recording Arts & Scis., Am. Theatre Critics Assn., The Drama Desk. Avocations: music, theater, hiking, reading. Home: 50 Quartz Ln Paterson NJ 07501-3345 E-mail: watergap18@aol.com.

DEFILIPPI, GEORGE, retired air force officer; b. Mobile, Ala., Sept. 6, 1947; s. George and Margaret Josephine (Lazzari) DeF.; m. Patricia Naismith McAdam, July 21, 1969; children: Jocelyn, Gwendolyn, Geoffrey, James. BS, USAF Acad., Colorado Springs, 1969; MS, Air Force Inst. Technology, Dayton, Ohio, 1977. Enlisted USAF, 1969, advanced through ranks to col., exec. sec., program mgr. Scientific Adv. Bd. HQ USAF, Washington, 1984-86, chief tng. divsn. 602d Tactical Air Control Wing Davis Mountain AFB, Ariz., 1986-88, cmdr. 22d Tactical Air Support Tng. Squadron, 1988-89, cmdr. 23d Tactical Air Support Squadron, 1989-90, cmdr. Air Liaison Office XVIII Airborne Corps Ft. Bragg, N.C., 1991-93, cmdr. Air Liaison Office to 3d Rep. Korea Army Uijongbu, Korea, 1992-93, mil. staff specialist Undersec. Def. Acquisition & Tech. Washington, 1993-96, mil. asst. to dir. strategic tactical systems, 1996-99; ret., 1999; field dir. mil. requirements Carlton Life Support Systems, Inc., Arlington, Va., 1999—. Vol. Arlington Emergency Winter Shelter, 1993-99; mem. Arlington Com. of 100, 1994—; vestryman St. George's Episcopal Ch., 1996-99, Stephen min., leader, 1999—. Mem. Assn. Unmanned Vehicle Sys. (bd. dirs. Capitol chpt. 1993-97), Air Force Assn. (Steele chpt. pres. 2004—, v.p. ops. 2002-04, newsletter editor 1999—). Episcopal. Avocations: jogging, swimming. Office: Carlton Life Support Systems Inc 1215 S Clark St Ste 309 Arlington VA 22202 Office Phone: 703-414-5302. E-mail: gdefilippi@carletonls.com.

DEFIORE, PERRY DENNIS, director, small business owner; b. Allentown, Pa., Dec. 22, 1947; s. Nicholas Samuel and Beatrice Marie (McClellan) D.; m. Leslie Irene Tucker (div. Aug. 1978); children: Perry Jr., Sheryl; m. Blanca Lilia Treviño, Mar. 30, 1980; children: Andrew, Michael, Monica, Franklin. Student, Federated Tax Schs., LaSalle U., Ins. Adjusters Sch., Miami, Fla., Cleve. Inst., Newspaper Inst., Foley-Belsaw Inst., U. Regiomontana, Monterrey, Mex., Stratford Inst., Harcourt Inst. Dept. mgr. C&S Bank, Albany, Ga., 1969-70; supr. Brown Group, various locations, 1970-74, U.S. Shoe, various locations, 1974-85; mgr. Whiddon's, Dallas, 1985-90; jr. high sch. prin. Instituto Columbia S.C., Monterey, 1990—; founder, CEO Soc. Internat. de Cientificos Juveniles. Pres. Math & Sci., Monterrey, 1992—95; mem. Proyecto Jason, Monterrey, 1996—; developer ednl. programs in field. Author textbooks for bilingual schs.; developer ednl. programs in field; author: Escape From Progress, 1986. Staff sgt. USMC, 1965-68. Mem.: Jason Acad. (internat. facilitator), N.Y. Acad. Scis., Soc. Internacional Cientificos Juveniles (founder). Lutheran. Avocations: golf, fishing, astrophysics. Home: Colonia Loma Larga Loma Florida #100 Monterrey Nuevo Leon Mexico Office: Inst Columbia SC Enrique Herrera # 2305 San Pedro Garza García Garza Mexico E-mail: perryblanca@yahoo.com.

DEFLEUR, LOIS B., academic administrator; b. Aurora, Ill., June 25, 1936; d. Ralph Edward and Isabel Anna (Cornils) Begitske; m. Melvin L. DeFleur (div.) AB, Blackburn Coll., 1958; MA, Ind. U., 1961; PhD in Sociology, U. Ill., 1965; HHD (hon.), U. Alaska, 1999. Asst. prof. sociology Transylvania Coll., Lexington, Ky., 1963-67; assoc. prof. Wash. State U., Pullman, 1967-74, prof., 1975-86, dean Coll. Liberal Arts, 1981-86; provost U. Mo., Columbia, 1986-90; pres. Binghamton U., SUNY, 1990—. Disting. vis. prof. USAF Acad., 1976-77; vis. prof. U. Chgo., 1980-81; bd. dirs. Energy East Corp., HealthNow, N.Y. Author: Delinquency in Argentina, 1965; (with others) Sociology: Human Society, 3d edit. 1981, 4th edit., 1984, The Integration of Women into All Male Air Force Units, 1982, The Edward R. Murrow Heritage: A Challenge for the Future, 1986; contbr. articles to profl. jours. Mem. Wash. State Bd. on Correctional Svcs. and Edn., 1974-77, State of N.Y. Edn. Dept. Curriculum and Assessment Coun., 1991-94, Trilateral Task for N.Am. Ednl. Collaboration, USIA, 1993-95. Recipient Disting. Alumni award Blackburn Coll., 1991, Chief Exec. Leadership awrd Coun. for Advancement and Support of Edn., 1999, Civic Leadership award Greater Binghamton C. of C., 2003, Woman of Distinction award Girl Scout Coun., 2002; grantee NIMH, 1969-79, NSF, 1972-75, Air Force Office, 1978-81. Mem. NCAA (pres. commn. 1996, exec. com. 1997-98), Am. Sociol. Assn. (publs. com. 1979-82, nominations com. 1984-86, coun. mem. 1987-90), Pacific Sociol. Assn. (pres. 1980-82), Coun. Colls. of Arts and Scis. (bd. dirs. 1982-84, pres. 1985-87), Aircraft Owners and Pilots Assn., Internat. Comanche Soc., Nat. Assn. State U. and Land-grant Colls. (exec. com. 1990-93, chair coun. of pres. 1994-95, chmn. bd. dirs. 1996-97), Am. Coun. Edn. (bd. dirs. 1994-2000, vp. chair-elect 1997-98, chair bd. dirs. 1998-99), Consortium Social Sci. Assns. (bd. dirs. 1993-96). Office: Binghamton U Office of Pres PO Box 6000 Binghamton NY 13902-6000

DE FOLIART, GENE RAY, retired entomologist, researcher, educator; b. Stillwater, Okla., June 24, 1925; s. Jess Henry and Ruby Marie De Foliart; m. Florence Louise Ball, Jan. 29, 1950 (dec. Feb. 4, 1998); children: David William, Sharon Kay, Linda Suzanne. BS, Okla. State U., 1942—48; PhD, Cornell U., 1948—51. Asst. prof. U. of Wyo., 1951—56, assoc. prof., 1956—59, U. of Wis., 1959—66, prof., 1966—91, prof. emeritus, 1991—. Cons. Ctr. for Disease Control, Atlanta, 1969—69; chair, dept. of entomology U. of Wis., 1968—76; study sect., tropical medicine and parasitology NIH, 1975—79; grant cons. Can. Dept. of Health and Nat. Welfare, Ottawa, 1977—89; chair, dept. of entomology U. of Wis., 1982—83. Contbr. Ensign U.S Naval Aviation, 1943—45, Various Locations. Recipient Hoogstraal Medal for outstanding achievement in med. entomology, Am. Soc. of Tropical Medicine and Hygiene, 1998; Rsch. grants on Mosquitoes/Arboviruses, NIH, 1966—90. Mem.: Entomol. Soc. of Am. (chair, sect. of med. entomology 1971—72). Achievements include helping to pioneer western world interest in insects as a global food resource; contributed to discoveries relative to transovarial transmission of arboviruses by mosquitoes. Avocations: reading, travel. Home: 6 South Kenosha Drive Madison WI 53705 Office: U of Wis 1630 Linden Drive Madison WI 53706

DEFOOR, J. ALLISON, II, lawyer; b. Coral Gables, Fla., Dec. 6, 1953; s. James Allison, Sr. and Marjorie (Keen) DeFoor; m. Terry Ann White, June 24, 1977; children: Melissa Anne, Mary Katherine, James Allison III. BA, U. So. Fla., 1976, MA, 1979; JD, Stetson U., 1979; STD honoris causa, Fla. Ctr. Theol. Studies, 1999, MDiv, 2001, DMin, 2005. Bar: Fla. 1979, U.S. Dist. Ct. (so. dist.) Fla. 1980, U.S. Ct. Appeals (5th cir.) 1981, U.S. Ct. Appeals (11th cir.) 1982. Asst. pub. defender, 1979—80; asst. state's atty. 16th Cir., Key West, Fla., 1980—83, dir. narcotics task force, 1981—83; judge Monroe County, Plantation Key, Fla., 1983—87; assoc. Cunningham, Albritton, Lenzi, Warner, Bragg & Miller, Plantation Key, 1987—89; sheriff Monroe County, 1989—90; sr. v.p., CEO Wackenut Monitoring Systems Inc., Coral Gables, 1991—92; gen. counsel, sec. HEM Pharm. Corp., Phila. and Key Largo, Fla., 1992—93; ptnr. Hershoff, Lupino DeFoor & Gregg, Tavernier, Fla., 1993—99; Everglades policy coord. State of Fla., Office of Gov., Tallahassee, 1999—2000; gen. counsel Tidewater Cons, Inc., Tallahassee, 2000—02; state coord. EarthBalance, Inc., Tallahassee and North Port, 2002—; dir. Beach Restoration, Inc., 2003—, Hydromentia, Inc., 2003—. Adj. faculty St. Leo Coll., Key West, 1980—81, U. So. Fla., Myers, 1981—82, Fla. Internat. U., Miami, 1985, U. Miami Law Sch., 1985—99, Fla. A&M U., 1999—2001; faculty Nat. Jud. Coll., Reno, 1985—86; lectr. Yale U., 2000, U. Pa. Law Sch., 2000. Editor: U. Miami Law Rev., 1985; author: DeFoor & Schultz, Florida Civil Procedure Forms with Practice Commentary, 1989, Odet Philippe, Peninsular Pioneer, 1997. Trustee Fla. Dispute Resolution Consortium, Horizon Cmtys., Collins Ctr. for Pub. Policy, Fla. C. of C., Leroy Collins Inst.; bd. vis. Fla. State U. Law Sch.; del. Rep. Nat. Conv., 1992, 2004; Rep. state committeeman Fla., 2004—; mem. Fla. Rep. Exec. Com., 1995—99, 2002—; Rep. nominee Lt. Gov. of Fla., 1990; chmn. Wakulla County Rep. Exec. Com., 2001—04; vice chmn. Fla. Reps., 2003—. Named one of Five Outstanding Young Men in Fla., Jaycees, 1984, Ten Outstanding Young Men in Am., 1985; recipient Merit award, Fla. Crime Prevention Commn., 1982, Leadership Fla. Class V, Chmn.'s award, Fla. Audubon, 1997. Mem.: ABA, Fla. Bar Assn., Mensa, Key West Yacht Club, Islamorada Fishing Club, Gov.'s Club, Explorer's Club (N.Y.C.), Ocean Reef Club (Key Largo). Episcopalian. Avocations: scuba diving, sailing, golf. Home: 359 River Plantation Rd Crawfordville FL 32327-1517 Office: Earth Balance 200 W College Ave Tallahassee FL 32301 Office Phone: 850-681-6465. Business E-Mail: adefoor@earthbalance.com.

DE FORD, DOUGLAS ATMETLLA, biochemical, biomechanical and industrial engineer; b. San Jose, Costa Rica, Nov. 26, 1945; s. Douglas N. and Enriqueta (Atmetlla) De F.; m. Maria Felicia Zamora, July 9, 1972 (div.); children: Fabiola de Prada, Dougie, Christopher, Steve. Degree in mech. engrng., Monterrey Inst. Tech., 1970; MS in Biotechnology, Teesside U., England, 1985, PhD in Biochem. Engrng., 1988; postgrad., Nat. U., 1990. Chief engr. CCSS Health Svcs., San Jose, Costa Rica, 1975-78; prodn. mgr. Blue Ribbon Meat Processing, Alajuela, Costa Rica, 1978-80; indsl. cons. CCSS Health Svcs., 1980-83; biotech. rschr. North East Biotech. Ctr., Middlesbrough, England, 1983-88; internat. cons. UNIDO, Vienna, Austria, 1988-96; gen. mgr. Pharma Ancla Labs., San Jose, 1988-90; chmn., founder British C. of C., San Jose, 1991-93; dir. rsch. & devel. CCSS Health Svcs., 1990-94; pres. BioBellessa Tropical Biotech., San Jose, 1988—. Author: Industrial Park for Health, 1982, The Concept of Bioreactor Number Applied to Fermentation Scale-Up, ACHEMA, 1985, Frankfurt am Main, Germany, Scale-up of Bioreactors: Physiological Effects on Microorganisms, BIOTECH Asia, Singapore, 1985, Scale-up-down Biotech Operations and Processes, 1988. British Coun. grantee, 1983-88, CCSS Health Svcs. grantee, 1983-87. Mem. Inst. Chem. Engrng., Coll. Engrs. and Architects, CIEME, Biotech. Nat. Coun. Achievements include auto-sledge vehicle for bamboo transportation in bamboo farms; tropical biopharmaceutical active principles from Costa Rica BioDiversity; Anti-Colitis: Juanilamine; Anti-Hypertension and Anti-Hyperglycaemia Agent: Courarine, 1990-95; cibernetic simulation for bioreactor full scale-up-down; novel design multipurpose continuous high retention time algal pond for effluents degradation; novel design/development of a photolysis pretreatment reactor for agricultural and industrial wastewater affluents, 1993. Home: 13714 SW Forest Service Rd #1419 Camp Sherman OR 97730-9716

DEFORD, FRANK, sportswriter, commentator, writer; b. Balt., Dec. 16, 1938; s. Benjamin F. Deford Jr. and Louise (McAdams) Deford; m. Carol Penner, Aug. 28, 1965; children: Christian McAdams, Scarlet Faith. BA, Princeton U., 1962. Writer Sports Illustrated mag., N.Y.C., 1964-89, 98—; editor, pub. The Nat. Sports Daily, N.Y.C., 1989-91; contbg. editor Newsweek, 1991-93, 96-98, Vanity Fair, 1993-96. Commentator Nat. Pub. Radio, Washington, 1980—, Cable News Network, N.Y.C., 1980—86, NBC Sports, N.Y.C., 1986—89, ESPN Radio, N.Y.C., 1991—98, HBO, N.Y.C., 1994—. Author: Five Strides on the Banked Track, 1971, There She Is, 1971, Cut 'n' Run, 1972, The Owner, 1976, Big Bill Tilden: The Triumphs and the Tragedy, 1976, Everybody's All-American, 1982, Alex: The Life of a Child, 1983, The Spy in the Deuce Court, 1986, The World's Tallest Midget, 1987, Casey on the Loose, 1989, Love and Infamy, 1993, The Best of Frank Deford, 2000, The Other Adonis, 2001, An American Summer, 2002, The Old Ball Game, 2005; author: (screenplays) Trading Hearts, 1988, Four Minutes, 2005. Trustee Cystic Fibrosis Found., Washington, 1973—, chmn., 1984—99, chmn. emeritus, 1999—. Named Sportswriter of Yr., Nat. Assn. Sportswriters and Sportscasters, 1982, 1984, 1985, 1986, 1987, 1988, Sportswriter Hall of Fame, 1998, Nat. Mag. Writer of Yr., Wash. Journalism Rev., 1987, 1988, Best U.S. Sportswriter, Am. Journalism Rev., 1992; recipient 1st Winner award for Excellence in Sport Journalism Ctr. for Study of Sport in Soc., Northeastern U., 1985, Disting. Svc. to Journalism award, U. Mo., 1987, Emmy award for TV Writing and Commentary, 1988, George Foster Peabody award for Documentary Writing, 1999, Nat. Mag. Award for Profiles, 1999. Democrat. Episcopalian. Home and Office: PO Box 1109 Greens Farms CT 06838-1109 Office Phone: 203-259-1784. Personal E-mail: frank6de@aol.com.

DE FOREST, SHERWOOD SEARLE, agricultural engineer, agricultural products executive; b. Ames, Iowa, Sept. 20, 1921; s. Frank Ray and Clara Maud (Searle) De F.; m. Virginia Mary Flynn, June 20, 1947; children: David, Debra, Denise, Kimberly. Student, U. Cin., 1939-40; BS, Iowa State U., 1943, MS, 1947. Instr. agrl. engrng. Iowa State U., 1946-47, extension agrl. engr., 1947-52; engrng. editor Successful Farming mag., Des Moines, 1952-59; with USX, Pitts., 1959-77, mgr. agrl. equipment mktg., 1964-70, indsl. rep., 1970-77; v.p., assoc. The Montgomery Group, Inc., Tallahassee, Fla., 1977-96; pollution prevention engr. Fla. Dept. Environ. Protection, Tallahassee, 1996-99; owner De Forest Agri-Serivces, Tallahassee, Fla., 1977-99. Pres. Ginande Corp., 1986-91; tech. transfer project leader No. Agrl. Energy Center, Sci. and Edn. Adminstrn., U.S. Dept. Agr., Peoria, Ill., 1980-81; cons. Pakistan, 1984, Portugal, 1985, 86; mem. indsl. and profl. adv. com. Coll. Engrng. Pa. State U., 1966-71; mem. NE Regional Agrl. Research Planning Com., 1970-72; mem. Fla. Gov.'s Continuing Care Adv. Coun., 1996-2000. Contbg. author: Power to Produce, U.S. Dept. Agr. Yearbook, 1969, Steel in Agriculture, 1966; Pub. TravelHost of Pitts. mag., 1982-83; tech. editor Soc. Automotive Engrs. Internat., 1987-89; numerous articles to Successful Farming Mag. Served to 1st lt. USAAF, 1942-46. Recipient Am. Soc. Agrl. Engrs.-Metal Bldg. Mfrs. Assn. award for disting. work in advancing knowledge and sci. of farm bldgs., 1964 Fellow: Am. Soc. Agrl. Engrs. (pres. 1975—76); mem.: Fla. Life Care Residents Assn., Inc. (chpt. pres. 1999—2003, state bd. dirs. 2001—04, state treas. 2003—04). Presbyterian (ruling elder). Achievements include patents in field. Home and Office: 4173 Covenant Ln Tallahassee FL 32308-5766 E-mail: sdeforesthsd@earthlink.net.

DEFOREST, WALTER PATTISON, III, lawyer; b. Ft. Sill, Okla., Dec. 4, 1944; s. Walter P. Jr. and Mary E. (Miller) DeF.; m. Anna Thun. BA, U. Pitts., 1966; JD, Harvard U., 1969. Bar: Pa. 1970, U.S. Ct. Appeals (2d and 3d cirs.) 1973, U.S. Ct. Appeals (4th, 5th and D.C. cirs.) 1978, U.S. Ct. Appeals (10th cir.) 1981, U.S. Ct. Appeals (11th cir.), U.S. Ct. Appeals (7th cir.) 1986, U.S. Ct. Appeals (fed. cir.) 1995, U.S. Supreme Ct. 1974, W.Va. 1997, Ohio 2001. Assoc. Reed, Smith, Shaw & McClay, Pitts., 1969—77, ptnr., 1978—93, DeForest Koscelnik Yokitis & Kaplan, Pitts., 1994—. Instr. Grad. Sch. Indsl. Adminstrn. Carnegie Mellon U., Pitts., 1974-75. Mem. adv. com. Big Bros. and Big Sisters Western Pa., Pitts., 1984—; bd. dirs. Pa. Small Bus. Advocacy Coun., Harrisburg, 1984-89, 92. Mem. ABA (litigation, labor sects.), Pa. Bar Assn. (litigation, labor sects.), Allegheny County Bar Assn. (litigation sect., fed. ct. sect.). Office: DeForest Koscelnik Yokitis & Kaplan 3000 Koppers Bldg 436 7th Ave Pittsburgh PA 15219-1826

DEFOSSET, DON, manufacturing executive; B in Indsl. Engrng., Purdue U.; MBA, Harvard U. Joined Rockwell Internat., 1971, pres. off-hwy. products and driveline divsn., 1988—89; exec. v.p. ops. Mack Trucks, INc., 1989—92; v.p. planning and bus. devel. Allied Signal Inc., 1992—93, v.p., group exec. turbocharging and truck brake sys., 1993—94; pres. safety restraint divsn. AlliedSignal Inc., 1994—96; corp. exec. v.p., truck group pres. Navistar Internat. Transp. Corp., 1996—99; exec. v.p., COO Dura Automotive Sys., 1999—2000; pres., CEO Walter Industries, Inc., Tampa, Fla., 2000—, chmn., 2002—. Trustee U. Tampa; bd. dirs. Boys and Girls Clubs Tampa Bay, Tampa Bay Performing Arts Ctr., Fla. Coun. on Ecn. Edn. Mem.: Fla. C. of C. (bd. govs.), Greater Tampa C. of C. (bd. govs.). Office: Walter Industries Inc 4211 W Boy Scout Blvd Tampa FL 33607

DEFOSSET, DONALD, diversified financial services company executive; b. Nov. 12, 1921; Exec. vice-pres., CEO Dura Automotive Systems, Inc., 1999—2000; pres., CEO Walter Industries, 2000—, chmn. bd. dir., 2002—. Dir. Terex Corp., Safelight Gas Corp. Office: 4211 W Boyscout Blvd Tampa FL 33607-2551 Office Phone: 813-871-4811. Office Fax: 813-871-4399.*

DEFRAIN, DARREN C., communications educator; b. Fairbanks, Ark., June 15, 1967; s. Dennis Allen and Carol Jean DeFrain; m. Melinda Diane Munzinger-DeFrain, June 20, 1992; children: Madchen Adelle, Ava Jane DeFrain. BA, BS, U. Utah, 1989; MA in English, Kans. State U., 1992; MFA in Creative Writing, Tex. State U., 1995; PhD in Creative Writing, Western Mich. U., 2000. Asst. prof. Waynesburg Coll., Pa., 1999—2000, U. Wis.-Fox Valley, Menasha, 2000—05; dir. writing program Wichita State U., Kans., 2005—. Author: (novel) Salt Palace, 2005, numerous short stories and essays. Mem.: Modern Lang. Assn., Associated Writing Programs. Democrat. Methodist. Office Phone: 316-978-3130. Personal E-mail: dariendefrain@hotmail.com.

DE FRANCESCO, JOHN BLAZE, JR., public relations consultant, writer; b. Stamford, Conn., May 22, 1936; s. John Blaze and Mae (Matyscyk) DeF.; m. Louise C. Terlizzo, Nov. 1, 1958 (div. 1983); children: Daryl, Jay, Dana, Dorian; m. Diana Picchietti, Oct. 20, 1990. BS, U. Conn., 1958. Sr. v.p. Daniel J. Edelman, Inc., Chgo., 1967-77; exec. v.p. Ruder Finn & Rotman,

Inc., Chgo., 1977-85; prin., CEO DeFrancesco/Goodfriend Pub. Relations, 1985-2001; exec. v.p. L.C. Williams & Assoc., Chgo., 2001—03; prin. DeFrancesco Artist and Writer, 2003—. Bd. dirs. Ill. Divsn. Vocat. Rehab., 1976-78; mem. pub. rels. adv. bd. Gov.'s State U., 1994-98. Comdr. USN, 1958-67; comdr. USNR; ret. 1979. Recipient 3 Silver Anvil awards Pub. Rels. Soc. Am., 6 Golden Trumpet awards Publicity Club, Chgo. Mem. Pub. Rels. Soc. Am., Navy League U.S., Mil. Officer Assn. Am. Roman Catholic. Home and Office: 18785 Saint Andrews Dr Monument CO 80132-8824

DEFRANCESCO, MARK STEPHEN, physician; b. New Haven, Conn., Dec. 16, 1949; s. James Joseph and Josephine Elizabeth DeF.; m. Helen Mary Ouellette, May 4, 1984; children: Christopher, Erin, Bethany, Kaitlin. BA, Yale U., 1971; MD, U. Conn., 1980; MBA, U. New Haven, 1997. Diplomate Am. Bd. Ob. Gyn. Pvt. practice physician GYN Ctr. for Women's Health, Waterbury, Conn., 1984—; med. dir. Women's Health Conn., Inc., Avon, Conn., 1997—, chief med. officer, 1999—. Dir. Women's Health Conn., Avon, Conn., 1997—. State rep. Conn. State Legislature, Hartford, 1973-74. Recipient Disting. Grad. award Nat. Cath. Edn. Assn., 1996, Knight of Honor Notre Dame H.S., West Haven, Conn., 1998. Fellow ACOG (officer, vice chair Conn. sect. 1997-99, chair 2000—03, dist. I vice-chair, 2003-), Am. Coll. Surgeons; mem. New England Ob-gyn. Soc. (coun. mem.), Conn. State Med. Soc. (mem. maternal morbidity and mortality com.). Office: GYN Ctr for Women's Health 60 Westwood Ave Waterbury CT 06708-2460 Fax: 203-596-0912. E-mail: markdefran@aol.com, mark.defrancesco@womenshealthusa.com.

DEFRANCIS, SUELLEN MARIA, interior architect; b. Bklyn., Sept. 21, 1946; d. Joseph Agustino and Mary DeF.; m. James D. Block, Apr. 23, 1965 (div. 1983); children: Melissa, Louis, Maximillian. BS, CCNY, 1982; BArch, CUNY, 1982, MS in Urban Design, 1983. Designer John Burgee Architects, N.Y.C., 1985-86; prin., owner Suellen DeFrancis Archtl. Interiors, Scarsdale, 1986—. Real estate investment advisor; lectr. Iona Coll., New Rochelle, N.Y., in field of architecture. Major projects include N.Y. Yacht Club, N.Y.C., Nippon Steel, N.Y.C., Mitsubishi Estate Housing, Ashiya, Japan, Asahi Breweries, Kobe, Japan, Sakikawa residences, Tokyo, Atlanta, and N.Y.C., Okada residences, Iwaki, Japan, N.Y.C., Met. Tower, N.Y.C., Genex Hdqs., N.Y.C., Hilcrest by Hilton, Tarrytown, N.Y., The Castle Restaurant and Inn, Tarrytown, Berkshire Place Hotel, N.Y., IBM Milford (Conn.) Campus, archtl. restoration 1923 Young Apts. Bldg., Scarsdale, N.Y.; works pub. in (book) 100 Designers' Favorite Rooms, 1993, 1st and 3d edits., (mag.) Kukan, Japan, N.Y. Times, Wall St. Jour. Trustee St. Christopher's-Jennie Clarkson Childcare Svcs., Inc. Recipient del Gaudio award N.Y. Soc. Architects, 1982; AIA scholar, 1982. Mem. AIA (assoc., N.Y.C. AIA interiors com.), Internat. Interior Design Assn., Internat. House of Japan, Far East Soc. Architects and Engrs., Nippon Club, Cosmopolitan Club (N.Y.C.). Avocations: travel, tennis.

DEFRANCISCO, JOHN ANTHONY, state legislator, lawyer; b. Syracuse, N.Y., Oct. 16, 1946; s. Frank P. and Clementine J. (Marnell) DeF.; m. Linda M. Malvasi, July 13, 1968; children: John, Jeffrey, Jennifer. BS cum laude, Syracuse U., 1968; JD, Duke U., 1971. Bar: N.Y. 1972, Fla. 1973, U.S. Dist. Ct. (no. dist.) N.Y. 1977, U.S. Ct. Appeals (2d cir.) 1981. Atty. Simpson, Thacher & Bartlett, N.Y.C., 1971-72; asst. dist. atty. Office Dist. Atty. Onondaga County, Syracuse, N.Y., 1975-77; pvt. practice, Syracuse, 1977—; mem. dist. 49 N.Y. State Senate, Albany, 1993—, chmn. tourism, recreation and sports devel. com., mem. judiciary, banking, health, investigations com., taxation and govt. ops. com., local govt. com. Adj. prof. law Coll. Law Syracuse U., 1978-90. Commr. edn. Syracuse Bd. Edn., 1981-84, pres., 1984; mem. Syracuse Common Coun., 1985-88, pres., 1989-92; past v.p. Conf. of Large City Bds. Edn.; past pres. Ctrl. N.Y. Leukemia Soc.; trustee, 1st pres. Ctrl. N.Y. Combined Health Appeal. Capt. USAF, 1972-75. Mem. Onondaga County Bar Assn. Republican. Roman Catholic. Avocations: sports, music. Office: 804 State Office Bldg 333 E Washington St Syracuse NY 13202-1422 also: 903 Legislative Office Bldg Albany NY 12247

DEFRANCO, BONIFACE FERDINAND LEONARD (BUDDY DEFRANCO), clarinetist, bandleader; b. Camden, N.J., Feb. 17, 1923; m. Joyce O. Yount; 1 child, Charles Lee. Student, Mastbaum Music Sch., Phila. Alto saxophonist, solo clarinetist Johnny Scat Davis Band, on tour, 1939, Gene Krupa Orch., on tour, 1941-42, Charlie Barnett Orch., on tour, 1943; solo clarinet Tommy Dorsey Orch., on tour, 1944-48, Count Basie Septet, on tour, 1950; bandleader Buddy DeFranco Orch., 1951; featured clarinetist Jazz at the Philharm. All Star Tours, worldwide, 1952-54; condr. Glenn Miller Orch., 1966-74; leader, guest artist The Buddy DeFranco Group, Panama City, Fla., 1974—. Performer, clinician Yamaha Music Corp., Grand Rapids, Mich., 1973—; clinician, judge various univs., 1950—. Author: Buddy DeFranco Hand in Hand with Hanon, 1996, Buddy DeFranco on Jazz Improvisation, 1973, Mel Bay Presents Modern Jazz Compositions and Studies for the Clarinet, 1983; rec. artist numerous albums including Hark: Buddy DeFranco Meets the Oscar Peterson Quartet, 1994, Chip Off the Old Bop, 1994, You Must Believe in Swing, & Nobody Else But Me, with Metropole Orch., 1997, Flying Fingers of Art Tatum and Buddy DeFranco, Cross Country Suite with Nelson Riddle (Grammy award 1956), Mr. Lucky, Mood Indigo, Chicago Fire with Buddy DeFranco and Terry Gibbs, George Gershwin Songbook with Oscar Peterson, Buddy DeFranco/Dave McKenna: Do Nothing 'Till You Hear From Us, 1999, Buddy DeFranco: Cookin' the Books w/ John Pizzarelli Trio & Butch Miles, 2004 Named #1 Jazz Clarinetist over 45 times Downbeat mag., Metronome mag., Playboy Mag. All Stars-All Stars, Ency. Jazz Musicians poll. Fellow Nat. Assn. Jazz Educators; mem. ClariNetowrk (bd. dirs. 1980—), ASCAP. Home (Summer): 978A Colorado Ave Whitefish MT 59937-3413 Address: 22525 Coral Ave Panama City FL 32413-3047 E-mail: harkii@hotmail.com.

DEFREITAS, DOUGLAS DAVIS, small business owner; b. Summit, NJ, Aug. 10, 1949; s. Horace and Caroline Ruth DeFreitas. AA, DuCret Sch. Art; student, Am. Bartending Sch. Supr. Beckman Grove Originals, Summit, NJ, 1973—74; asst. supr. Berkeley Florist, Berk Heights, NJ, 1974—75; owner, operator, appraiser Centennial Antiques, Somerville and Plainfield, NJ, 1974—. Author: Interviews Along the Road Less Royal, 2002. Mem. steering com. Citywide Neighbors, Plainfield, 1979—80, Woods Assn., Plainfield, 2000—; group liaison Tweed Arts, Plainfield, 1980; mem. com. Plainfield Arts, 1980. Avocations: cooking, gardening, decorating. Home: 1318 Woodland Ave Plainfield NJ 07060 Office Phone: 908-561-9847.

DE FRIESE, GORDON H., health services researcher; b. Trion, Ga., Apr. 25, 1942; BS, Middle Tenn. State U., 1963; MA, U. Ky., 1966, PhD, 1967. Instr. dept. behavioral sci. U. Ky. Med. Ctr., Lexington, 1966—67; asst. prof. sociology and social psychology Cornell U., Ithaca, NY, 1969—71; rsch. assoc. Cecil G. Sheps Ctr. for Health Svcs. Rsch. U. N.C., Chapel Hill, 1971—, asst. prof. sociology, 1971—77, asst. prof. family medicine Sch. Medicine, 1973—75, clin. assoc. prof. dept. epidemiology Sch. Pub. Health, 1978—82, assoc. prof. Sch. Medicine, 1976—82, prof. Sch. Medicine, 1982—, prof. Sch. Pub. Health, 1982—, prof. dept. dental ecology Sch. Dentistry, 1986—, co-dir. Robert Wood Johnson Found. Clin. Scholars Program, 1986—2000. Adj. asst. prof. Sloan Inst. Hosp. Adminstrn.; dir. U.S. Army Armor Sch. Electives Divsn., Fort Knox, Ky., 1967—69; co-dir. Comprehensive Health Planning Tng. Program of the Dept. of Sociology and City and Regional Planning and the Sloan Inst. Hosp. Adminstrn. Cornell U., Ithaca, NY, 1969—71; co-dir. grad. program in med. sociology Dept. Sociology U. N.C., Chapel Hill, 1971—76, dir. Cecil G. Sheps Ctr. for Health Svcs. Rsch., 1973—2000; pres., CEO N.C. Inst. Medicine; cons. and presenter in field; numerous other career related activities. Author (with B.D. Barker): Assessing Dental Manpower Requirements: Alternative Approaches for State and Local Planning, 1982; editor (with J.W. Bawden): Planning for Dental Care on a Statewide Basis: The North Carolina Dental Manpower Project, 1981; editor: (with T.C. Ricketts, J.S. Stein) Methodological Advances in Health Services Research, 1989; editor: Health Svcs. Rsch., 1983—96; co-editor (spl. issue): Jour. Family and Cmty. Health, 1982; assoc. editor: Social Forces, 1971—76, Drugs in Health Care, 1974—76, Jour. Health and Social Behavior, 1985—87, Am. Jour. Health Promotion, 1986—92, mem. editl. bd.: Health Care Mgmt. Rev., 1977—93, Med. Care, 1980—83, Internat. Jour. Health Scis., 1989—, Jour. Gerontology: Med. Scis., 1989—91, Comparative Health Policy: Nations, States, Cmtys., 1993—, book rev. editor: Health Svcs. Rsch., 1979—84; contbr. chapters to books, articles to profl. jours. Fellow: N.Y. Acad. Medicine; mem.: APHA (med. care sect.), Soc. for Gen. Internal Medicine, Found. for Health Svcs. Rsch. (bd. dirs. 1982—94, pres. 1986—87), Assn. for Health Svcs. Rsch. (bd. dirs. 1982—90, pres.-elect 1983—85, pres. 1985—86), Inst. Medicine, Sigma Xi. Office: Dept Social Medicine Med Sch Wing D U NC Campus Box 7240 Chapel Hill NC 27599-7240*

DEGAETANO, ROBERT, composer, pianist; b. N.Y.C., May 31, 1946; s. Dominick and Edith DeGaetano. BA, The Juilliard Sch., 1969, MS, 1970. Musician (pianist): Carnegie Hall, 1999, Lincoln Ctr. for the Performing Arts, numerous performances in all 50 states as well as the major music capitals of Europe and the Far East, (CD) Classical Piano recordings. Achievements include first musician ever to be awarded a rotary internat. scholarship to study in Paris. Avocations: design and decorating, cooking. Home: 9 W 123rd St New York NY 10027-5622 E-mail: rdegaetano@degaetano.com.

DEGARIS, ANNESLEY HODGES, lawyer, educator; b. Birmingham, Ala., June 23, 1963; s. John A. Jr. and Lena Kate (Hodges) DeG.; m. Ashley H. DeGaris, July 1, 1995. BS in Pub. Adminstrn. magna cum laude, Samford U., 1985; JD magna cum laude, Cumberland Sch. Law, 1988; LLM, U. Melbourne, Australia, 1992. Bar: Ala. 1989, U.S. Dist. Ct. (no. dist.) Ala. 1989, U.S. Ct. Appeals (11th cir.) 1992, U.S. Dist. Ct. (mid. dist.) Ala. 1995, U.S. Dist. Ct. (so. dist.) Ala. 1996, U.S. Supreme Ct. 1995. Jud. law clk. U.S. Dist. Ct., Huntsville, Ala., 1988-89; staff atty. U.S. Ct. Appeals 11th Cir., Atlanta, 1991-93; assoc. Johnson & Cory, Birmingham, 1993-95; ptnr. Cory, Watson, Crowder & DeGaris, Birmingham, 1995—. Adj. prof. Emory U. Sch. Law, Atlanta, 1992-93; prof. constnl. law Birmingham Sch. Law, 1993—. Casenote editor Cumberland Law Rev.; contbr. articles to profl. jours. Rotary Found. scholar Rotary Internat., Australia, 1990. Mem. ATLA, ABA, Ala. Trial Lawyers Assn., Vestavia Hills Rotary. Avocations: backpacking, travel. Office: Cory Watson Crowder & DeGaris PC 2131 Magnolia Ave S Birmingham AL 35205-2808

DEGARMO, DENISE KAY, political scientist, educator; b. Syracuse, N.Y., Feb. 16, 1956; d. Arthur V. and Billie L. DeGarmo; children: Carroll Lamar, Casey Johnsen. AS, Monroe C.C., 1990; BS, SUNY, Buffalo, 1992; PhD, U. Mich., 2000. Fellow U. Mich., Ann Arbor, 1992, instr., 1992—2000; asst. prof. polit. sci. So. Ill. U., Edwardsville, 2000—. Facilitator fgn. policy's great decisions program So. Ill. U., Edwardsville, 2001—. Contbr. articles to profl. jours. Active CAN-World Wildlife Fund, Washington, 2000—02; facilitator Fgn. Policy Assn.: Great Decisions Program, Edwardsville, 2001—02; commr. Ann Arbor City Market Commn., 1996—98; v.p. Ann Arbor Artisan Assn., 1996—98; active Slausen Middle Sch. PTO, Ann Arbor, 1992—99; hosts - helping one student to succeed Slausen Middle Sch., Ann Arbor, 1996; pres. Monroe C.C. Activities Club, Rochester, NY, 1989—90. Univ. Honors scholar, SUNY, 1990—92. Mem.: Internat. Studies Assn., Women in Internat. Security, Am. Polit. Sci. Assn., Phi Sigma Alpha, Phi Theta Kappa. Democrat. Office: So Ill Univ Box 1453 3233 Peck Hall Edwardsville IL 62026 Office Phone: 618-650-3375. Business E-Mail: ddegarm@siue.edu.

DEGENERES, ELLEN, actress, comedienne, talk show host; b. Metairie, LA, Jan. 26, 1958; d. Elliott and Betty DeGeneres. Began career as emcee local comedy club, New Orleans; performer various comedy clubs. Comedian (TV spls.) Young Comedians Reunion, HBO, Women of the Night, 1986, Command Performances: One Night Stand, 1989; author: My Point...And I Do Have One, 1995, The Funny Thing Is..., 2003; actor: (films) Coneheads, 1993, Mr. Wrong, 1996, Goodbye Lover, 1998, (voice) Dr. Doolittle, 1998, EDtv, 1999, The Love Letter, 1999, Reaching Normal, 1999, (voice of Dory) Finding Nemo, 2003 (Annie award for Outstanding Voice Acting in Animated Feature Prodn., 2004); writer, dir., actor (films) My Short Film, 2004; actor: (TV films) On the Edge, 2001; (TV series) Open House, 1989, Laurie Hill, 1992; actor, exec. prodr. (TV films) If These Walls Could Talk 2, 2000, (TV series) The Ellen Show, 2001—02, actor, prodr., writer Ellen (originally named These Friends of Mine from 1993-94), 1993—98 (Emmy award for Outstanding Writing for Comedy Series, 1997, Peabody award, 1997), host, exec. prodr. The Ellen DeGeneres Show, 2003— (Best Talk Show, Daytime Emmy award, Acad. TV Arts & Scis, 2005, Best Talk Show Host, Daytime Emmy award, Acad. TV Arts & Scis., 2005), star, exec. prodr. (TV spls.) Ellen DeGeneres: The Beginning, 2000 (Am. Comedy award for Funniest Female Peformer in TV spl., 2001), Ellen DeGeneres: Here and Now, 2003, co-host 46th Annual Primetime Emmy Awards, 1994 (Am. Comedy award for Funniest Female Peformer in TV spl., 1995), host 53rd Annual Primetime Emmy Awards, 2001, 54th Annual Primetime Emmy Awards, 2002, 38th Annual Grammy Awards, 1996, 39th Annual Grammy Awards, 1997, VH1 Fashion Awards, 1998, VH1 Divas Las Vegas, 2002, appeared as herself (documentaries) Wisecracks, 1991. Recipient Funniest Person Am. for videotaped club performances in New Orleans, Showtime, 1982, Am. Comedy award for Funniest Female Stand-Up Comic, 1991, Golden Apple award as Female Discovery Yr., Hollywood Women's Press Club, 1994, Lucy award, 2000, Enduring Spirit award, Amnesty Internat., 2000. Office: c/o Creative Artists Agy 9830 Wilshire Blvd Beverly Hills CA 90212*

DEGENHARDT, ROBERT ALLAN, architectural firm executive, engineering executive; b. Kearney, Nebr., May 29, 1943; s. Robert Franklin and Florence Elizabeth (Spohnheimer) D.; m. Elizabeth Scholl; children: Barry, Christopher, Kathleen. BSME, U. Nebr., 1965, MSME, 1968. Registered profl. engr., D.C. and all states except Alaska and Hawaii. Project engr. Davis & Wilson Architects and Engrs., Lincoln, Nebr., 1964-68, White Sands (N.Mex.) Missile Range, 1968-70, Sundstrand Aviation, Rockford, Ill., 1970-74; dir. engring. Davis, Fenton, Stange, Darling, Architects and Engrs., Lincoln, 1974-77; v.p. mech. engring. Durrant Engrs. Inc., Madison, Wis., 1977-1980; dir. mech. engring . Ellerbe Assocs. Inc., Mpls., 1980-82, dir. archtl./engring. svcs., 1982-83, v.p., dir. ops., 1983-85; sr. v.p., dir. Ellerbe Becket Inc., Washington, 1985-89; exec. v.p., COO Ellerbe Becket Co., Mpls., 1989-93, pres., COO, 1993-94, pres., CEO, 1994-98, CEO, 1998-2001, pres., 2001—; sr. v.p. 3D Internat., Houston. Mem. Ctr. for Ethical Bus. Cultures, 1993—. 1st lt. U.S. Army, 1968—70. Mem. Constrn. Industry Roundtable, U.S. C. of C. (internat. polic com.), Sigma Xi, Pi Tau Sigma. Republican. Lutheran. Avocations: fly fishing, backpacking, fly-fishing.

DE GENNARO, RICHARD, retired library director; b. New Haven, Mar. 2, 1926; s. Ralph and Acquilina (Pedicini) De G.; m. Birgit M. Erikson, June 12, 1953; children: Ralph, George, Christina. BA, Wesleyan U., 1951, MA, 1960; MS in LS, Columbia U., 1956; postgrad., Univs. Paris, Madrid and Perugia, 1951-55; grad. Advanced Mgmt. Program, Harvard U., 1971; DHL (hon.), Wabash Coll., 1991. Jr. acct. Atlas Constructors, Morocco, 1952-53; reference librarian N.Y. Pub. Libr., 1956-58, dir., 1987-90; successively reference librarian, asst. dir., assoc. univ. librarian systems devel., sr. assoc. univ. librarian Harvard U. Libr., 1958-70; dir. librs. U. Pa., 1970-86, adj. prof. English, 1979-86; libr. Harvard Coll., 1990-96. Vis. prof. Grad. Libr. Sch., U. So. Calif., 1968-69; cons. libr. bldgs., tech. and mgmt.; mem. overseers com. to visit libr., Harvard U.; cons. MIT, Johns Hopkins U.; mem. adv. bd. Chem. Abstracts Svc., 1967-70; mem. Palinet bd. Union Libr. Catalogue, 1970—; mem. com. internat. sci. and tech. info. programs NAS-NRC, 1977-79; mem. Mellon Found. JSTOR Bd., 1995—; sr. libr. advisor JSTOR; mem. governing bd. Rsch. Librs. Group, 1979-89, sr. vis. fellow, 1980-81, chmn., 1984-95; Bowker lectr., 1979; Lazerow lectr., 1984. Author: Shifting Gears, Information Technology and the Academic Library, 1984, Libraries, Technology, and the Information Marketplace, Selected Papers, 1987; contbr. articles to profl. jours. Bd. dirs. Ctr. for Rsch. Librs., 1977-81; trustee U. Pa. Press, 1978-82. With USN, 1942-46. Recipient Disting. Alumnus award Wesleyan U., 1991; Hugh Atkinson award, 1993; named Acad. Rsch. Libr. of Yr., 1991; Coun. Libr. Resources fellow, 1971; Rockefeller Found. Ctr. fellow, Bellagio, Italy, 1981; info. tech. fellow U. Edinburgh, 1984. Mem. Assn. Rsch. Librs. (pres. 1975, dir. 1973-76), ALA (pres. info. sci. and automation div. 1975), Am. Soc. Info. Soc. (Melvil Dewey medal 1986), Century Assn. Club, Grolier Club, Harvard Club. Home: Unit 1414 988 Blvd Of The Arts Apt 1414 Sarasota FL 34236-4838

DE GENNES, PIERRE-GILLES, physicist, educator; b. Paris, Oct. 24, 1932; PhD, Ecole Normale Superieure. Rsch. scientist Centre d'Etudes Nucleaires de Saclay, 1955-59; prof. solid state physics U. Paris, Orsay, 1961-71; prof. Coll. de France, Paris, 1971—2004; dir. Ecole de Physique et Chimie, Paris, 1976—2002; sci. adv. for chem. physics Rhodia, France, 1999—. Author: (book) Superconductivity of Metals and Alloys, 1965, The Physics of Liquid Crystals, 1973, Scaling Concepts in Polymer Physics, 1979, Simple Views on Condensed Matter, 1992—2003, Les Objets Fragiles, 1994, Gouttes, Bulles Perles et Ondes, 2002, Petit Point, 2002. Ensign French Navy, 1959—61. Recipient Nobel prize in physics, 1991. Mem.: AAAS, Nat. Acad. Sci., Russian Acad. Sci., Nat. Acad. Scis., Brazilian Acad. Scis., Ukranian Acad. Scis., Royal Soc., Dutch Acad. Scis., Académie des Sciences. Avocations: drawing, hiking. Office: Institut Curie Sect Biophysique 11 Rue P Curie 75005 Paris France Office Phone: (33) 142346497. E-mail: pgg@curie.fr.

DEGENSHEIN, JAN, architect, planner; b. Bklyn., Sept. 15, 1946; s. Harry and Beverly (Oppenheimer) D.; m. Lynne Sheren, Sept. 1, 1968 (div. Mar. 1978); 1 child, Britta; m. Nadja Hoyer-Booth, June 1, 1980 (sep. Sep. 2002); children: Oleg, Anya. BS Archtl. Scis., Washington U., 1967; BArch, MS in Planning, Pratt Inst., 1970; postgrad., CUNY, 1979-84. Registered architect, N.Y., N.J.; cert. Nat. Coun. Archtl. Registration Bds. 1975. Assoc. architect R.C. Weinberg & Assocs., N.Y.C., 1968-70, Seiler Nakrosis Kerner, Liberty, N.Y., 1970-72; v.p. Degan Enterprises Inc., New City, N.Y., 1973-78; pres., prin. Jan Degenshein Architect-Planner, New City, 1975-83; pres. Degenshein Denker Assocs. P.C., Nyack, N.Y., 1983-88, Degenshein Denker Bodnar P.C., Nyack, 1988-91; prin., pres. Jan Degenshein Architects-Planners, Nyack, N.Y., 1991—. Guest critic Pratt Inst. Sch. Architecture, 1982, CCNY Sch. Architecture, 1990. Author: Atlantic-Schermehorn Corridor, 1970. Chmn., com. mem. Rockland County (N.Y.) Art in Pub. Places, 1987-1998; v.p., trustee Blue Rock Sch., West Nyack, 1989-95; mem. bd. advisors Martin Luther King Multi-Purpose Ctr., Spring Valley, N.Y., 1991—; vol., mem. bd. advisors, bd. dirs. Vol. Counseling Svcs., New City, 1994-2002; mem. environ. adv. coun. U.S. Rep. Benjamin Gilman, 1993-96; mem. campaign cabinet Arts Fund for Rockland, Rockland County, 1990-92; mem. N.Y. State Bldg Ofcls. Conf., 1994—, Interfaith Forum on Religious Art and Architecture, 1983-2001, Arts Coun. of Rockland, 1986—; adv. com. Rockland Ctr. Arts, 2004-); nominating com. Rockland County coun. Girl Scouts U.S., 1991-94; mem. Rockland Mcpl. Planning Fedn., 1990—, assoc. dir., 1997—; bd. dirs. Housing Action Coun., 1998-2001, exec. bd., 1999-2001; mem. retention and expansion com. Rockland Econ. Devel. Corp., 1996-2001, cert. recognition, 1999; bd. dirs. Helen Hayes Hosp. Found., 1998-2004, v.p., 2003-04, gala com., 1990—2004, chmn., 2000—04; mem. citizens adv. bd. housing Town Clarkstown, 2002-04. Recipient archtl. excellence award Orange County Bd. Realtors, 1988, 89, Rockland County Execs. Arts award, 1995; winner Arts Coun. of Rockland poetry competition, 2002; named Bus. Man of Yr., Nat. Rep. Congl. Com., 2002, Bus. Leader of Yr., Rockland Jour. News, 2003, Rockland County Execs. Fair Housing award 2004. Mem. AIA (honor award for archtl. excellence Westchester/Mid-Hudson 1987, 88, 92, 94, 96, 2000; cmty.design awards; Rockland County Beautification award. 1992, 94 Rockland County Legislature Cert. of Recognition, 1999, Am. Inst. Cert. Planners, Am. Planning Assn., Rockland County Builders Assn. (Assoc. of Yr. 1978, Builder of Yr. 1980), Leadership Rockland (dir. 1994-2002, 2004—, pres. alumni assn. 1994-96, sec. 1999-2002, mem. selections com., fin. com., chmn. nominations com., recruitment com. coord. econ. devel. day 1995-2000, recruitment com), Rockland Bus. Exch. (v.p., pres. membership com. 1993-97), Rockland Coalition for Democracy and Freedom (dir. 1995), Am. Forum for Global Edn. (advisor 1995-97) Hist. Soc. Rockland, Computer and Telecom. Initiative Rockland (chair nominating com. 1996, bd. dirs. 1997-2001), Rockland Bus. Assn. (mem. svcs. com. 1996, chair amb.'s com. 1996-98, comms. and advocacy com. 1997—, bd. dirs. 1997-2001, 2004—, chmn. affordable housing com. 2001-03, chmn. govt. affairs com. 2004—, exec. com. 2004—), Nyacks C. of C. (v.p. 1988-89), Rotary Internat., Keep Rockland Beautiful, Inc. (nom. com. 2005). Avocations: graphic arts, cooking, golf, writing. Office: 205 S Broadway Nyack NY 10960-4425 Office Phone: 845-358-8400. Business E-Mail: Jan@Degenshein.com.

DE GEORGE, LAWRENCE JOSEPH, diversified financial services company executive; b. N.Y.C., May 6, 1916; s. Frank Phillip and Frances (Cavallo) DeG.; m. Florence A. Efel, Dec. 18, 1943; children: Lawrence F., Peter R. BSEE, Princeton U., 1936; MS, MIT, 1938; PhD in Advanced Math., Columbia U., 1939. Assoc. prof. elec. engring. Columbia U., 1938-39; field engr. Radio Engring. Lab., N.Y.C., 1939-41; pres. Times Wire and Cable Co., Inc., div. Internat. Silver Co., Wallingford, Conn., 1946; also v.p., dir. Times Wire and Cable div., 1958-64, pres., 1964-68; v.p., dir. Insilco Corp., Meridan, Conn., 1968-72, exec. v.p., 1972-77, vice chmn., 1976-77; chmn., pres. Times Fiber Communications, Inc., Meriden, 1977-84, chmn., chief exec. officer, 1985-92, LPL Techs. Inc., Wallingford, Conn., 1985-97, Amphenol Corp., Wallingford, Conn., 1987-97; chmn., CEO DeG Capital Ptnrs. Ltd., Wallingford. Dir. Travelers Equities Fund, Inc., Hartford, Conn. Lt. comdr. USNR, 1941-46. Mem.: Club Collette, Admirals Cove Yacht Club, City Club, Palm Beach Yacht Club. Republican. Home: 176 Spyglass Ln Jupiter FL 33477-4037 Office: DeG Capital Ptnrs Ltd Ste 410 140 Intracoastal Pointe Dr Jupiter FL 33477-5094 Office Phone: 561-745-7000.

DE GERENDAY, Mrs. LACI See CHANDLER, ELISABETH

DEGERSTROM, JAMES MARVIN, retired engineering executive; b. Owosso, Mich., Aug. 9, 1933; s. John Marcellus and Emma Judith (Folkadahl) Degerstrom; m. Ann Blandford, July 3, 1964. BSME, Mich. State U., 1955; MBA, DePaul U., 1966. Cert. plant engr. Adminstrv. asst. Sunbeam Corp., Chgo., 1955-61; mfg. supt. Internat. Register Co., Inc., Chgo., 1961-65; sr. engr. Kitchens of Sara Lee, Inc., Deerfield, Ill., 1965-71; pres. Edmanson Bock Caterers, Chgo., 1972; mgr. bldg. ops. Jewel Cos., Inc., Barrington, Ill., 1972-81; dir. plant ops. Copley Meml. Hosp., Aurora, Ill., 1981-86, Little Co. Mary Hosp., Evergreen Park, Ill., 1986-88; dir. facilities Oak Park Hosp., 1988-89; mgr. plant engring. Honeywell, Inc., Joliet, Ill., 1989-90; dir. facilities mgmt. S. Suburban Hosp. of Adv. Health Care Sys., Hazel Crest, Ill., 1990-98, Oak Brook, Ill., 1990—98; ret., 1998. Bd. dirs., treas. Credit Union Kitchens of Sara Lee, 1966—70. With USAF, 1957—65. Mem.: Am. Inst. Plant Engrs. (sec. 1977—79, pres. chpt. 5 1991), Am. Inst. Indsl. Engrs., Toastmasters (pres. 1981, dist. officer 1982, area gov. 1982, lt. gov. 1983—84, dist. gov. 1984—85). Home: 102 Knollwood Ct Oak Brook IL 60523-1518 E-mail: jaandegerstrom@aol.com.

DE GETTE, DIANA LOUISE, congresswoman, lawyer; b. Tachikawa, Japan, July 29, 1957; came to U.S., 1957; d. Richard Louis and Patricia Anne (Rose) De G.; m. Lino Sigismondo Lipinsky de Orlov, Sept. 15, 1984; children: Raphaela Anne, Francesca Louise. BA magna cum laude, The Colo. Coll., 1979; JD, NYU, 1982. Bar: Colo. 1982, U.S. Dist. Ct. Colo. 1982, U.S. Ct. Appeals (10th cir.) 1984, U.S. Supreme Ct. 1989. Dep. state pub. defender Colo. State Pub. Defender, Denver, 1982-84; assoc. Coghill & Goodspeed, P.C., Denver, 1984-86; sole practice Denver, 1986-93; of counsel McDermott & Hansen, Denver, 1993-96; mem. Colo. Ho. of Reps., 1992-96, asst. minority leader, 1995-96; mem. U.S. Congress from 1st Colo. dist., 1997—; mem. commerce com. Editor: (mag.) Trial Talk, 1989-92. Mem. Mayor's Mgmt. Rev. Com., Denver, 1983-84; resolutions chair Denver Dem. Party, 1986; bd. dirs. Root-Tilden Program, NYU Sch. Law, N.Y.C., 1986-92; bd. trustees, alumni trustee Colo. Coll., Colorado Springs, 1988-94. Recipient Root-Tilden scholar NYU Sch. Law, NYC, 1979, Vanderbilt medal, 1982. Mem. Colo. Bar Assn. (bd. govs. 1989-91), Colo. Trial Lawyers Assn. (bd. dirs., exec. com. 1986-92), Colo. Women's Bar Assn., Denver Bar Assn., Phi Beta Kappa, Pi Gamma Mu. Democrat. Avocations: reading, backpacking, gardening.

DEGHETT, STEPHANIE COYNE, writer, educator, poet; b. Saranac Lake, N.Y., Aug. 31, 1951; d. Ward Robert and Alice Mae (Marshall) C.; m. Victor John DeGhett, Aug. 2, 1980; 1 child, Torie Rose. BA magna cum laude, SUNY, Potsdam, 1976; MA, U. Vt., 1981. Asst. coord. Sch.-within-a-Sch. Potsdam Coll., 1977; manuscript reviewer ABT Assocs., Cambridge, Mass., 1978; cons. Grad. Studies Office/SUNY, Potsdam, 1978; ednl. coord. CETA Title VI Projects, Potsdam, 1978; grad. tchg. fellow U. Vt., Burlington, 1979-81; prof., writing program SUNY, Potsdam, 1981—. Editor: (book) Blueline Anthology, 2004; poetry editor: Blueline mag., 1987—; showed photographs Del Bello Gallery, Toronto, 1991; author (poetry): River of Dreams: American Poems, 1990, New Eng. Rev., 1994, Am. Poets and Poetry, 1999, Potpourri, 2000, The Fiddlehead, 2003, Poem, 2005; author: (story) New Orphic Rev., 2003. Reading vol. Lawrence Ave. Elem. Sch., Potsdam, 1995—; bd. dirs. Environ. Mgmt. Coun., Canton, N.Y., 1984-86. Mem. Nat. Coun. Tchrs. English, Assn. Tchrs. Advanced Composition, SUNY Writers Coun., Assn. Writers and Writing Programs, Soc. Children's Book Writers and Illustrators Democrat. Episcopalian. Avocations: skiing, gardening, photography, birding. Home: 25 Wheeler Rd Potsdam NY 13676-3404 Office: SUNY at Potsdam Pierrepont Ave Potsdam NY 13676 Office Phone: 315-267-2036. Business E-Mail: deghetsc@potsdam.edu.

DEGIOIA, JOHN J., academic administrator; b. Orange, Conn. m. Theresa Miller DeGioia; 1 child, John Thomas. BA in English, Georgetown U., 1979, PhD in Philosophy, 1995. Asst. to the pres. Georgetown U., Washington, 1982—85, dean of student affairs, 1985—92, assoc. v.p., chief adminstrv. officer, 1992—95, v.p., chief adminstrv. officer for main campus, 1995—98, prof. lectr., 1995—, sr. v.p., 1998—2001, pres., 2001—. Mem.: exec. com. Fed. City Coun.; mem. Washington Bd. Trade; trustee Com. for Econ. Devel.; bd. dirs. MedStar Health. Named one of Young Leaders of the Acad., Change mag., 1998; recipient Chmn.'s award, Georgetown Alumni Admissions Program, 1997, Lifetime Achievement award for excellence in academia, Sons of Italy, 2004. Mem.: John Carroll Soc. (bd. govs.), Assn. Jesuit Colls. and Univs. (mem. exec. com., bd. dirs.), Bus.-Higher Edn. Forum, Coun. on Competativeness (mem. exec. com., regional innovation com. and global com.), Assn. Am. Colls. and Univs. (bd. dirs.), Consortium on Financing Higher Edn. (bd. dirs.), Am. Coun. on Edn. (bd. dirs., mem. com. on minorities in higher edn.). Office: Georgetown U Office of the Pres 204 Healy Hall Box 571789, 37th and O Streets, NW Washington DC 20057 Office Phone: 202-687-4134. Business E-Mail: president@georgetown.edu.*

DEGIOVANNI-DONNELLY, ROSALIE FRANCES, biologist, educator; b. Bklyn., Nov. 22, 1926; d. Frank and Rose (Quartuccio) DeGiovanni; m. Edward Francis Donnelly, Sept. 23, 1961; children: Edward F. Jr., Francis M. BA, Bklyn. Coll., 1947, MA, 1953; PhD, Columbia U., 1961. Adj. prof. microbiology, genetics George Washington U., Washington, 1968—; rsch. biologist FDA, Washington, 1968-88. Contbr. articles to profl. jours. Recipient Merit award FDA, 1970. Mem. AAAS, AAUW, Italian Cultural Soc., Environ. Mutagen Soc., NY Acad. Scis., Am. Soc. Microbiology, McLean Indoor Club, Sigma Xi, Sigma Delta Epsilon. Democrat. Roman Catholic. Avocations: theater, swimming, tennis, travel, photography. Home: 1712 Strine Dr Mc Lean VA 22101-4744 E-mail: edndol@earthlink.net.

DEGN, DOUGLAS J., retail executive; BS in Pharmacy, U. Kans., 1981. With Wal-Mart Stores, Inc., 1983—, pharmacy mgr., v.p. and divisional merchandise mgr., v.p. pharmacy merchandising and support, sr. v.p. and gen. merchandise mgr. Wal-Mart Stores div., exec. v.p. food and consumables merchandising, 2001—. Recipient Sam M. Walton Entrepreneur of Yr. award, 1997. Office: Wal-Mart Stores Inc 702 SW Eighth St Bentonville AR 72716*

DEGNAN, JOHN JAMES, III, physicist; b. Phila., Dec. 10, 1945; s. John James Jr. and Ruth Dolores (Vece); m. Adele Susan Henry, June 27, 1969; children: Adam John, Andrew Paul. BS in Physics, Drexel U., 1968; MS in Physics, U. Md., 1970, PhD in Physics, 1979. Student trainee NASA Goddard Space Flight Ctr., Greenbelt, Md., 1964-67, physicist, 1968-72, sr. physicist, 1972-79, sect. head, 1979-89, dep. mgr. crustal dynamics project, 1989-93, head space geodesy and altimetry projects office, 1993-96, head geosci. tech. office, 1996—2003; chief scientist Sigma Space Corp., Lanham, Md., 2003—. Instr. Drexel U., Phila., 1967-68; assoc. mem. Adv. Group on Electron Devices, 1980-85, dep. mem. 1985-89; adj. prof. physics Am. U., Washington, 1988-93; chmn. CSTG SLR/LLR Subcommn., 1992-98, chmn. Internat. Laser Ranging Svc. Governing Bd., 1998-2002; tech. bd. Wegener, 1992-2000, chmn., 2000-03; mem. Am. Geophys. Union Steering Com. for Geodesy, 1998—, CSTG Exec. Bd. Contbr. articles to profl. jours; patentee, microaltimeter, 2002. Mem. Common Cause, Annapolis, Md., 1970—; v.p., treas. Pasadena Theatre Co., Md., 1982-84. Drexel Bd. Trustees scholar, 1963; recipient Marple-Newtown Sch. Dist. Hall of Fame award, Disting. Alumnus, 1989, Moe I. Schneebaum Meml. award for engrng. NASA/GSFC, 1987, Tsiolkovsky medal, 2002, NASA Space Act award, 2003, Cir. of Distinction award Drexel U., 2005. Fellow Internat. Assn. Geodesy; mem. IEEE (sr.), Optical Soc. Am., Am. Phys. Soc., Am. Geophys. Union (steering com. geodesy 1998—), Planetary Soc., Internat. Laser Comm. Soc. (charter), Nat. Space Club, Sierra Club, Sigma Pi Sigma, Sigma Pi. Roman Catholic. Home: 928 Barracuda Cove Ct Annapolis MD 21401-4719 Office: Sigma Space Corp 4801 Forbes Blvd Lanham MD 20706 Office Phone: 301-552-6300. Business E-Mail: john.degnan@sigmaspace.com.

DE GOFF, VICTORIA JOAN, lawyer; b. San Francisco, Mar. 2, 1945; d. Sidney Francis and Jean Frances (Alexander) De G.; m. Peter D. Coppelman, May 2, 1971 (div. Dec. 1978); m. Richard Sherman, June 16, 1980. BA in Math. with great distinction, U. Calif., Berkeley, 1967, JD, 1972. Bar: Calif. 1972, U.S. Dist. Ct. (no. dist.) Calif. 1972, U.S. Ct. Appeals 1972, U.S. Supreme Ct. 1989; cert. appellate law specialist, 1996. Rsch. atty. Calif. Ct. Appeal, San Francisco, 1972-73; Reginald Heber Smith Found. fellow San Francisco Neighborhood Legal Assistance Found., 1973-74; assoc. Field, De Goff, Huppert & McGowan, San Francisco, 1974-77; pvt. practice Berkeley, Calif., 1977-80; ptnr. De Goff and Sherman, Berkeley, 1980—. Lectr. continuing edn. of bar, Calif., 1987, 90-92, U. Calif. Boalt Hall Sch. Law, Berkeley, 1981-85, dir. appellate advocacy, 1992; cons. Calif. Civil Practice Procedure, Bancroft Whitney, 1992; mem. Appellate Law Adv. Commn., 1995; apptd. applicant evaluation and nomination com. for State Bar Ct. by Calif. Supreme Ct., 1995, 2000; presented program for Rutter Group Mastering Appellate Advocacy, 2004; apptd. by Chief Justice Calif. to Supreme Ct. Advisory Com. on publ. of ct. of appeals opinions, 2004-05; pvt. atty., clk. ct. com. Calif. Ct. Appeals, 1997-99; mem. com. on appellate practice ABA, 1997. Author: (with others) Matthew Bender's Treatise on California Torts, 1985. Apptd. to adv. com. Calif. Jud. Coun. on Implementing Proposition 32, 1984—85; mem. adv. bd. Hastings Coll. Trial and Appellate Adv., 1984—91; expert 20/20 vision project, commn. on future cts. Jud. Coun. Calif., 1993, apptd. to appellate standing adv. com., 1993—95; apptd. to Appellate Indigent Def. Oversight Adv. Com. State of Calif., 1995—; com. on appellate stds. of ABA Appellate Judges Conf., 1995—96; com. on appellate practice ABA, 1997; adv. bd. Witkin Legal Inst., West Publishing Co., 1996—; sec. Calif. Supreme Ct. Hist. Soc., 1999—; appointee 9th Jud. Cir. Hist. Soc. Hon. Cecil Poole Biography Project, 1998; v.p. Ctr. for Youth Devel. Through Law, 2004—; chair Roger Traynor State Moot Ct. Com., 1999—; bd. dirs. Calif. Supreme Ct. Hist. Soc., State Bar Calif., 1996—2005; Appellate Law Cons. Group, 1994—95; bd. dirs. Ctr. for Youth Devel. Through Law, 2000—. Fellow Woodrow Wilson Found., 1967-68. Mem. Calif. Trial Lawyers Assn. (bd. govs. 1980-88, amicus-curiae com. 1981-87, editor-in-chief assn. mag. 1980-81, Presdl. award of merit 1980, 81), Calif. Acad. Appellate Lawyers (sec.-treas. 1989-90, 2d v.p. 1990-91, 1st v.p. 1991-92, pres. 1992-93), Am. Acad. Appellate Lawyers, Edward J. McFetridge Am. Inn of Cts. (counsellor 1990-91, edn. chmn. 1991-92, social chmn. 1992-93, v.p. 1993-94, pres. 1994-95), Boalt Hall Sch. Law U. Calif. Alumni Assn. (bd. dirs. 1989-91), Order of Coif. Jewish. Office: 1916 Los Angeles Ave Berkeley CA 94707-2419

DEGRAFFENREIDT, JAMES H., JR., gas company executive; BA, Yale Coll., 1974; MBA, JD, Columbia U., 1978, JD. Pres., COO Washington Gas and Light Co., 1994-97, pres., CEO, 1998, chmn., CEO, 1998—2000, chmn., pres., CEO, 2000—01, chmn., CEO, 2001—. Recipient Pioneers of the Profession award Minority Corp. Counsel Assn., 1997. Office: Washington Gas and Light Co 101 Constitutions Ave NW Washington DC 20080-0002*

DEGRANDIS, RONALD WAYNE, music educator; b. Drexel Hill, Pa., Feb. 6, 1951; m. Janet K. Hardy, July 25, 1998; children: Sarah J. Hardy, Rebekah L. Hardy. MusB in Edn., Temple U., 1973; MusM in Edn., West Chester (Pa.) U., 1978. Cert. tchr. PA, 1973. Band, orch., jazz band dir. Shawnee Mid. Sch., Easton, Pa., 1979—; instrumental music tchr., coord. Tower Hill Sch., Wilmington, Del., 1974—79; instrumental music tchr. Gt. Valley Sr. HS, Malvern, Pa., 1973—74. Prin. viola Allentown (Pa.) Symphony Orch., 1979—; solo violist Assumption B.V.M. Ch. Contemporary Ensemble, Bethlehem, Pa. Composer: (songs) Northampton County 250th Anniversary March, Tracy Sch. Trilogy in 3 movements. Mem.: NEA, Pa. Music Educators Assn. (Nominated Pa. Tchr. of Yr. 2005), Music Educators Nat. Conf., AFM Local 45. Home: 1915 Dartford Road Bethlehem PA 18015 Office: Shawnee Middle School 1010 Echo Trail Easton PA 18040 Office Phone: 610-250-2460 ext. 31204. Personal E-mail: rongovla@east.net.

DE GRASSI, LEONARD, art historian, educator; b. East Orange, NJ, Mar. 2, 1928; s. Romulus-William and Anna Sophia (Sannicolo) DeG.; m. Dolores Marie Welgoss, June 24, 1961; children: Maria Christina, Paul. BA, U. So. Calif., 1950, BFA, 1951, MA, 1956; postgrad., Harvard U., 1953, Istituto Centrale del Restauro di Roma, 1959-60, U. Rome, 1959-60, UCLA, 1970-73. Tchr. art Redlands (Calif.) Jr. High Sch., 1951-53, Toll Jr. High Sch., Glendale, Calif., 1953-61, Wilson Jr. High Sch., Glendale, 1961; mem. faculty Glendale Coll., 1962—, prof. art history, 1974-92, chmn. dept., 1972, 89, prof. emeritus, 1992—. Tchr. Cite U., Paris, 1992, Istituto /Schuola Leonardo da Vinci, Florence, Italy, 1992. Prin. works include: (paintings) high altar at Ch. St. Mary, Cook, Minn., altar screen at Ch. St. Andrew, El Segundo, Calif., 1965-71, 14 Stas. of the Cross Ch. St. Mary, Cook, Minn., altar screen at Ch. of the Descent of the Holy Spirit, Glendale, 14 Stas. of the Cross at Ch. of St. Benedict, Duluth, Minn; research, artwork and dramatic work for Spaceship Earth exhbn. at Disney World, Orlando, Fla., 1980. Decorated Knight Grand Cross Holy Sepluchre, knight St. John of Jerusalem, 1976, knight Order of Merit of Republic of Italy, Cross of Merit; recipient J. Walter Smith Svc. award, 2001; named First Disting. Faculty, 1987, Outstanding Educator of Am., 1971. Mem. Art Educators Assn., Am. Rsch. Ct. Egypt, Tau Kappa Alpha, Kappa Pi, Delta Sigma Rho. Office: 1500 N Verdugo Rd Glendale CA 91208-2809 Office Phone: 818-240-1000 5742. Business E-Mail: degrassi@glendale.edu.

DEGRAVE, DOUGLAS MICHAEL, lawyer; b. Rochester, N.Y., May 23, 1954; s. Gorman Joseph and Elaine (Best) DeG.; m. Deborah Jean Horn, Jan. 11, 1975; children: Jacob Daniel, Jennifer Anne, Joshua Michael. AS in Adminstrn. Justice, U. Hl., 1976; BA in Pol. Sci., Calif. State U., Long Beach, 1978; JD, Loyola U., 1981. Bar: Calif. 1981, U.S. Dist. Ct. (ctrl. dist.) Calif. 1982, U.S. Dist. Ct. (so. dist.) Calif. 1985, U.S. Ct. Appeals (9th cir.) 1986, U.S. Supreme Ct. 1987. Assoc. Stockdale, Peckham & Werner, Santa Ana, Calif., 1981-87; ptnr. Behrens, Recht, Finley & Hanley, Santa Ana, 1986-87; mng. ptnr. Parker.Stanbury, Santa Ana, 1987—. Adj. prof. Western State Univ. Coll. Law, 1993—. Contbr. articles to profl. jours.; speaker in field. Dir., v.p. Orange YMCA, 1986-89, YMCA Indian Guides/Princesses, 1983-96; v.p. Orange Jr. Soccer Club, 1986-87, pres. 1987-88, chmn. bd. 1989-90, coach 1982-90; mgr./coach South Sunrise Little Leage, Orange, 1992—. With U.S. Army, 1973-76. Mem. Assn. Southern Calif. Def. Counsel (chmn. amicus com.), Am. Bd. Trial Adv., Calif. Def. Counsel, Internat. Assn. Def. Counsel, Def. Rsch. Inst., Orange County Bus. Coun., Consumer Attys. Calif., Consumer Attys. Orange County, Orange County Bar Assn. Republican. Roman Catholic. Avocations: little league coach, scuba diving, golf. Home: 369 S Jennifer Ln Orange CA 92869-4628 Office: Parker Stanbury 888 N Main St Fl 7 Santa Ana CA 92701-3518

DEGROAT, WILLIAM CHESNEY, pharmacology educator; b. Trenton, N.J., May 18, 1938; s. William Chesney and Margaret (Welch) deG.; m. Dorothy Marion Albertson, June 13, 1959; children: Allyson L., Cynthia L., Jennifer L. BSc, Phila. Coll. Pharmacy and Sci., 1960, MSc, 1962; PhD, U. Pa., 1965, postgrad., 1965-66, Australian Nat. U., Canberra, 1966-67. Vis. research fellow John Curtin Sch. Med. Research, Canberra, 1967-68; asst. prof. U. Pitts. Med. Sch., 1968-72, assoc. prof., 1972-77, prof. pharmacology, 1977—, acting chmn. dept. pharmacology, 1978-80, adj. prof. pharmacy, 1978-88, prof. psychology, 1982-86, mem. ctr. of neurosci., 1984—, prof. dept. behavioral neurosci., 1986-94, prof. dept. neurosci., 1995-96. Vis. prof. U. Coll., London, 1998; mem. neurobiology study sect. NIH, 1983-88; vis. scientist NIAAA-NIH, 1989-90. Mem. editl. bd. Jour. Pharmacology and Exptl. Therapeutics, 1975—, Jour. Autonomic Nervous Sys., 1979—, assoc. editor, 1985-94, Neurourology and Urodynamics, 1982—, Am. Jour. Physiology, 1983-94, Life Scis., 1993—, Urology, 1996-98, Current Opinion in Central and Peripheral Nervous System Investigational Drugs, 1999—; editl. cons. profl. jours.; contbr. articles to profl. jours., chpts. in books. NSF fellow, 1962-63; pharmacology fellow Riker Pharm. Co., 1966-67; NSF fellow, 1966-67; recipient research Career Devel. award NIH, 1972-77, NIH Merit award, 2000. Fellow: AAAS; mem.: Internat. Soc. for Autonomic Neurosci. (exec. v.p.), Am. Autonomic Soc., Am. Motility Soc., Soc. for Basic Urologic Rsch., Internat. Med. Soc. of Paraplegia, Urodynamics Soc. (Lifetime Achievement award 1995), Am. Gastroent. Assn., Internat. Brain Rsch. Orgn., Soc. for Neurosci. (treas. 1994—95), Am. Soc. Pharmacology and Exptl. Therapeutics (award for exptl. therapeutics 2003), N.Y. Acad. Scis., Am. Urol. Assn. (hon.), Japanese Urol. Assn. (hon.), Rho Chi, Sigma Xi. Republican. Methodist. Home: 6357 Burchfield Ave Pittsburgh PA 15217-2732 Office: U Pitts Med Sch W-1352 Biomed Sci Tower Terrace St Pittsburgh PA 15213 Office Phone: 412-648-9357. Business E-Mail: degroat@server.pharm.pitt.edu.

DEGROOT, LESLIE JACOB, medical educator; b. Ft. Edward, N.Y., Sept. 20, 1928; BS, Union Coll., 1948; MD, Columbia U., 1952. Intern, asst. resident in medicine Presbyn. Hosp., N.Y.C., 1952-54; health physician Nat. Cancer Inst., 1954-55; physician U.S. Mission, Afghanistan, 1955-56; clin. and research fellow medicine Mass. Gen. Hosp., Boston, 1956, 58-60, resident, 1957-58, asst., 1960-64, asst. physician, 1964-66; assoc. prof. exptl. medicine MIT, 1966-68, assoc. dir. dept. nutrition and food sci. Clin. Research Ctr., 1966-68; prof. endocrinology Pritzker Sch. Medicine, U. Chgo., 1968—2005, chief thyroid study unit, 1968—2005, chief endocrinology sect., 1980—87; prof. medicine rsch. Brown U., Providence, 2005—. Nat. Cancer Inst. clin. fellow, 1954-55 Mem. Assn. Am. Physicians, Am. Thyroid Assn., Endocrine Soc., Am. Soc. Clin. Investigation, Am. Fedn. Clin. Research Office: Brown Univ Box G Rm E 308 70 Ship St Providence RI 02912 Home: Po Box P94 South Dartmouth MA 02748-0301 Business E-Mail: leslie_degroot@brown.edu.

DEGROOTE, MICHAEL G., management consulting company executive; Pres., CEO Laidlaw Inc., 1959-90, Republic Industries Inc., 1991-96, also chmn. bd. dirs.; pres. Century Bus. Svcs. Inc., Cleve., 1997-99, CEO, 1999—, also chmn. bd. dirs. Office: Century Bus Svcs Inc 6050 Oak Tree Blvd #500 Cleveland OH 44131-6951

DE GROOTE, ROBERT DAVID, general and vascular surgeon; b. Hackensack, N.J., Aug. 30, 1951; s. Emiel and Filomena Lillian (Candio) De G. BS in Biology, Fordham U., 1973; MD, Autonomous U. Guadalajara, 1978. Diplomate Am. Bd. of Surgery. Resident gen. surgery U. Medicine and Dentistry N.J. Med. Sch., Newark, 1979—84, fellow critical care medicine, 1981—82, fellow vascular surgery, 1984—86; fifth pathway St. Joseph's Hosp., Paterson, NJ, 1978—79; attending surgeon Hackensack Med. Ctr., Hackensack, NJ, 1986—. Contbr. articles to Surgery, Stroke, Archives of Surgery, Annals of Vascular Surgery. Named Man of Yr., Lyndhurst, N.J. chpt. Italian-Am. Nat. Svc. Orgn., 1993, Top Doctor in New York, New York Mag., Top Doctor in N.J., N.J. Monthly. Fellow ACS; mem. AMA, Internat. Soc. for Cardiovascular Surgery, Soc. for Critical Care Medicine, Ea. Vascular Soc. Roman Catholic. Office: 83 Summit Ave Hackensack NJ 07601-1262 Office Phone: 201-646-0010. E-mail: rdegroote@aol.com.

DEGRYSE, BERNARD, cell biologist; s. Claude Degryse and Pierrette Taddei; m. Maddalena de Virgilio, Apr. 23, 2001. PhD in Cell Biology and Microbiology, U. Aix-Marseille II, France, 1993. Head chem. lab. Caleb Brett Co., Port de Bouc, France, 1990—91; postdoctoral fellow Labs. de Biochimie Médicale and U38 INSERM, Marseille, France, 1993—94, Molecular Genetics, Dept. of Cell Biology and Functional Genetics, DIBIT, U. Vita-Salute San Raffaele, Milan, 1996—99; rsch. assoc. Dept. of Genetics and Microorganism Biology, U. of Milan, 1999—2000, Divsn. of Vascular Biology, Dept. of Cell Biology, The Scripps Rsch. Inst., La Jolla, Calif., 2000—. Mem. internat. reviews panel Med. Sci. Monitor Jour., 2002—. Achievements include patents for Inhibitor or antagonist of HMG1 protein used for the cure of vascular disorders; patents pending in field of agonist and antagonistic peptides of the urokinase receptor (UPAR): stimulators and inhibitors of cell migration. Personal E-mail: bdegryse@yahoo.com.

DEGUERIN, DICK, lawyer; b. Austin, Tex., Feb. 16, 1941; s. E. Mack and Marguerite S. DeGuerin; m. Ann DeGuerin; children: Anna Michele, Ann Carlin; m. Janie Mitchell, Apr. 11, 1986. BA, U. Tex., 1963, LLB, 1965. Bar: Tex. 1965, U.S. Dist. Ct. (so. dist.) Tex. 1968, U.S. Ct. Appeals (5th cir.) 1971, U.S. Supreme Ct. 1971, U.S. Dist. Ct. (ea. dist.) Tex. 1973, U.S. Ct. Appeals (8th cir.) 1974, U.S. Dist. Ct. (no. dist.) Tex. 1979, U.S. Ct. Appeals (11th cir.) 1981, U.S. Dist. Ct. (ea. dist.) Mich. 1982, U.S. Ct. Appeals (6th cir.) 1982, U.S. Dist. Ct. (we. dist.) Tex. 1983, U.S. Ct. Appeals (10th cir.) 1984, U.S. Ct. Appeals (4th cir.) 1985; bd. cert. criminal law Tex. Bd. Legal Specialization. Asst. dist. atty. Harris County, Houston, 1965-68; assoc. Butler, Binion, Rice, Cook & Knapp, Houston, 1968-71; ptnr. Foreman & DeGuerin, Houston, 1971-82; sr. ptnr. DeGuerin, Dickson & Szekely, Houston, 1982-84, DeGuerin & Dickson (now DeGuerin Dickson, & Hennessy), Houston, 1984—. Spkr. in field. Contbr. articles to profl. jours. Fellow Am. Coll. Trial Lawyers, Am. Bd. Criminal Lawyers, Am. Bd. Trial Advocates, Internat. Soc. Barristers; mem. Tex. Bar Assn. (various coms.), Houston Bar Assn. (criminal law sect.), Houston Jr. Bar Assn. (coms. on law day, award, criminal law 1965-1976), Tex. Criminal Def. Lawyers Assn. (charter mem., dir. 1973-76), Harris County Criminal Lawyers Assn. (charter mem., dir. 1976-), Tex. Bd. Legal Specialization (cert.), Tex. Trial Lawyers Assn., Houston Trial Lawyers Assn., Nat. Assn. Criminal Def. Lawyers, Delta Theta Phi. Office: DeGuerin Dickson & Hennessy 7th Fl The Republic Bldg 1018 Preston Ave Houston TX 77002-1818 Office Phone: 713-223-5959. Office Fax: 713-223-9231. E-mail: ddeguerin@aol.com.

DEGUILIO, JON E., lawyer; b. Hammond, Ind., June 15, 1955; s. Ernest Michael and Jeanne (Hochis) D.; m. Barbara Jo Wieser, Oct. 3, 1981; 1 child, Suzanne Jeanne. BA, U. Notre Dame, 1977; JD, Valparaiso U., 1981. Bar: Ind. 1981, U.S. Dist. Ct. (so. dist.) Ind. 1981, U.S. Dist. Ct. (no. dist.) Ind. 1981. Pub. defender Lake County Ct., Crown Point, Ind., 1984-87; dep. prosecutor Lake County Prosecutor's Office, Crown Point, 1981-84; 87-94; assoc. James Wieser Law Offices, Highland, Ind., 1981-93; U.S. atty. no. dist. Ind. Dept. Justice, Dyer, 1993-99. Atty. Highland Police Commn., Highland, Ind., 1987— and Highland Water Bd., 1987—; legal advisor, Lake County Sheriff, Crown Point, Ind., 1986-87; atty. Hammond and East Chgo. Fedn. of Tchrs., 1986—. Councilman Hammond City Council, 1984-87; mem. Lake County Med. Ctr. Devel. Agy., 1988—, Greater Hammond Community Services, 1987—; treas. Little Calumet River Basin Com., 1986. Mem. Lake County Bar Assn. (bd. dirs. 1988-90), Justinian Soc. Democrat. Avocations: basketball, bolf, reading. Home: 8944 Liable Rd Hammond IN 46322-2248 Office: US Attorneys Office 5400 Federal Plz #1500 Hammond IN 46320-1843

DEGUTIS, LINDA CHRISTINE, adult education educator, epidemiologist, researcher; b. Chgo., Dec. 16, 1953; d. William Joseph and Genevieve (Karons) D.; m. Robert F. Miller, Aug. 16, 1975 (div. Mar. 1983); m. Bruce Fenton Carmichael, Mar. 26, 1988. BS, DePaul U., 1975; MSN, Yale Sch. of Nursing, 1982; DrPH, Yale Sch. of Medicine, 1994. Cert. RN Conn., Ill. Staff nurse Rush-Presbyn. St. Luke's Med. Ctr., Chgo., 1975-78, Yale-New Haven Hosp., Conn., 1978-81; trauma program coord. Yale Sch. Medicine, New Haven, 1982-91, 92-95; lectr. in surgery Yale Sch. of Medicine, New Haven, 1984-95, asst. prof. sect. of emergency medicine, 1995—2003, assoc. prof. emergency medicine, pub. health, 2003—; trauma coord. Bridgeport (Conn.) Hosp., 1991-92; Robert Wood Johnson Health Policy fellow Office of Senator Paul Wellstone, Washington, 1996-97. Adv. mem. Conn. State com. on trauma; exec. com. mem. Conn. Adv. for Highway Safety, Hartford, Conn., 1995—. Contbr. articles to profl. jours. Founding mem. MADD-New Haven Chpt., 1983; vol. Conn. Spl. Olympic Games, New Haven, 1990-94, Internat. Spl. Olympic Games, New Haven, 1995; pres. Lake Point Condominium Assn. Bd., 1991. Mem. ACS, AAAS, Am. Pub. Health Assn. (exec. bd., chmn. injury control and emergency health svcs. sect.), Am. Trauma Soc., Nat. Assn. for Pub. Health Policy, Soc. Acad. Emergency Medicine. Office: Yale Sch Medicine 464 Congress Ave New Haven CT 06519-1361

DE HAAN, DAVID OWEN, chemistry educator; s. Franklin Peter De Haan. BS, Calvin Coll., 1987—89; PhD, U. of Colo., 1989—94. Asst. prof. of chemistry Lyon Coll., Batesville, Ark., 1997—2001, U. of San Diego. Cottrell Coll. Sci. award, Rsch. Corp., 1999—, Blasker Environ. grant, San Diego Found., 2003—04. Mem.: Am. Geophys. Union, Am. Chem. Soc. Presbyn. Avocation: bicycling. Office: Univ of San Diego 5998 Alcala Park San Diego CA 92110 Office Phone: 619-260-6882.

DE HAAN, PAMELA ROSE, voice educator; b. Sheldon, Iowa, Mar. 28, 1960; d. Lloyd Dale and Rosa Jean Grotenhuis; m. Doug De Haan, Dec. 29, 1981; children: Rosalyn, Rachelle, Jonathan, Rebecca, David. BA, Dordt Coll., 1984; MusM, U. SD, 1986. Voice instr. Dordt Coll., Sioux Center, Iowa, 1985—; saxophone and voice instr. Northwestern Coll., Orange City, Iowa, 1988—90, saxophone instr., 1993—. Choir dir. Orange City Arts Coun., 1997—99, 2001, 2004—05. Mem.: Nat. Assn. Tchrs. Singing (pres. Lewis and Clark chpt. 2004—05). Home: 4244 Kingbird Ave Alton IA 51003 Office: Dordt Coll 498 4th Ave NE Sioux Center IA 51250 Office Phone: 712-722-6206. Business E-Mail: pdehaan@dordt.edu.

DE HAAS, DAVID DANA, emergency physician; b. Hollywood, Calif., May 31, 1956; S. Martin and Norma (Deutsch) De H.; m. Mary Danuta Przybylowski, June 27, 1982; children: Lindsay Alexandra, Heather Brittany, Lance Austin. BS in Biochemistry, UCLA, Westwood, Calif., 1979; MD, Chgo. Med. Sch., 1983. Diplomate Am. Bd. Internal Medicine, Am. Bd. Emergency Medicine, Nat. Bd. Med. Examiners; cert. provider advanced trauma life support, ACLS, Pediatric Advanced Life Support, BCLS, Med. Disaster Response, instr. ACLS, Pediatric Advanced Life Support, Med. Disaster Response. Resident emergency medicine/internal medicine Kern Med. Ctr., Bakersfield, Calif., 1983-87; assoc. med. dir. Family Care Med. Assocs., Huntington Beach, Calif., 1987—; emergency physician Anaheim (Calif.) Meml. Hosp., 1988—; asst. clin. prof. medicine dept. internal medicine U. Calif.-Irvine Med. Ctr., Orange, 1989—; emergency physician St. Bernardine Med. Ctr., San Bernardino, Calif., 1991—; ptnr. Calif. Emergency Physicians Med. Group, San Bernardino, 1991—. Expert reviewer Med. Bd. Calif.; affiliate faculty ACLS, Pediatric Advanced Life Support, Am. Heart Assn.; vice chmn. dept. emergency medicine St. Bernardine Med. Ctr., ACLS dir., dir. quality assurance/continuous quality improvement dept. emergency medicine; mem. edn. com. Med. Disaster Response; ptnr.Calif. Emergency Physician Med. Group. Fellow ACP, Am. Coll. Emergency Physicians; mem. AMA, Calif. Med. Assn., Orange County Med. Soc., Soc. Orange County Emergency Physicians (bd. dirs.), Assn. Clin. Faculty U. Calif., Irvine Coll. Medicine. Avocations: gardening, pin collecting, reading. Home: 26882 Via La Mirada San Juan Capistrano CA 92675-4935 Office: St Bernardine Med Ctr 2101 N Waterman Ave San Bernardino CA 92404-4836

DEHAAS, JOHN NEFF, JR., retired architecture educator; b. Phila., July 4, 1926; s. John Neff and Sadie Lavinia (Hagel) DeH.; m. C. Bernice Wallace, Dec. 27, 1950; children: Kenneth Eric, Jocelyn Hilda. BArch, Tex. A&M U., 1948, MEd, 1950. Registered architect, Mont. Instr. Tex. A&M U., College Station, 1948-50, U. Tex., Austin, 1950-51; successively instr. to prof. Mont.

State U., Bozeman, 1951-80. Supervisory architect Historic Am. Bldgs. Survey, summers San Francisco, 1962, Bozeman, 1963, 65, Milw., 1969; cons. Mont. Historic Preservation Office, Helena, 1977-78, mem. rev. bd., 1968-79. Author: Montana's Historic Structures, Vol. 1, 1864, Vol. 2, 1969, Historic Uptown Butte, 1977; editor quar. newsletter Mont. Ghost Town Preservation Soc., 1972— Bd. dirs. Mont. Assn. for Blind, Butte, 1984-95. Recipient Centennial Preservation award Mont. Historic Preservation Office, 1989, Dorothy Bridgman award for Outstanding Svc. to the Blind Montana Assn. for the Blind, 1990. Fellow AIA (com. on historic resources 1974—); mem. Mont. Hist. Soc. (trustee's award 1989). Republican. Methodist. Home: 2400 Durston Rd 50 Bozeman MT 59718

DEHART, KAREN TRAUTMANN, artist, educator; b. Pitts., Nov. 11, 1953; d. Elmer Martin and Jane Anne (Hesse) T.; m. Shannon Dean DeHart, May 23, 1976; children: Allison Anne, Rebekah Ellen, Rachel Elisabeth. AA, Miami U., 1975; BFA summa cum laude, Wright State U., 1991. Art instr. Troy-Hayner Cultural Ctr., Troy, Ohio, 1991-94; artist Troy, Ohio, 1990—; art tchr., 1991—; drawing tchr. Troy Christian Schs., Troy, Ohio, 1991-92; teaching asst. Wright State Univ., Dayton, Ohio, 1993. Exhibition comm. Troy-Hayner Cultural Ctr., 1991—; chmn. Through Our Eyes Exhibit, 1993-95; adj. instr. Wright State U., 1996. Solo exhbns. include Preble County Fine Arts Ctr., Eaton, Ohio, 1994, The Crandall Gallery Mount Union Coll., Alliance, Ohio, 1995, MacMurray Coll. Art Gallery, Jacksonville, Ill., 2002; exhibited in group shows at Bowery Gallery, N.Y., 1992, Butler Inst., 1994, 95, 96, 97, 98, Margaret Kaulback exhibitor, Trumbull Art Gallery, 1994, Dayton Visual Arts Ctr., 1992, Mus. of Contemporary Art, Wright State U., 1991, 97, Dayton Visual Arts Ctr., 1992, 97, Butler Inst. Am. Art, 1993, 94, 95, 97, 98, Pearl Conard Gallery, 1993, 94, Rosewood Art Ctr. Gallery, Kettering, Ohio, 1993, Olin Fine Arts Ctr. Gallery, Washington and Jeffrson Coll., Washington, Pa., 1994, 97, Books & Co., Kettering, Ohio, 1994, Fine Arts Inst. San Bernardino County Mus., Redlands, Calif., 1994, Evansville (Ind.) Mus. Arts and Sci., 1994, Wichita (Kans.) Ctr. Arts, 1994, Stables Art Gallery, Taos, N. Mex., 1995, Gallery Alexy, Phila., 1996, Hoyt Inst. Fine Arts, New Castle, Pa., 1997, Troy (Ohio)-Hayner Cultural Ctr., 1997, Valdosta State U. Gallery, Valdosta, Ga., 2002; featured in Nexus Mag., 1990, Art Duck, 1989-91, Dayton Daily News, 1992, 98, Alliance Review, 1995. Com. mem. Troy C. of C., 1993; ad hoc mem. Troy-Hayner Cultural Ctr., 1992, chamn. photography exhibit, 1993-95, chmn. sister-city art exchange Troy-Takahashi City, Japan, 1995-96, mem. exhib. com., 1991-96; curriculum com. Troy Christian Schs., 1992-94. Recipient Grumbacher Gold medallion 16th ann. Hoyt Nat., 1997, 26th Nat. Painting Show, 1994, Winsor Newton award Fine Arts Inst., 1994, Evansville Mus. Contemporaries Purchase award, 1994, Jurors Choice award Butler Inst. Am. Art, 1994, Margaret Kaulback award, 1997, Best of Show award Rosewood Art Ctr., 1992, Award of Excellence Edison State C.C., 1989; Spl. Talent scholar Wright State U., 1989-91. Mem. Dayton Visual Arts Ctr., Phi Kappa Phi, Chi Omega. Home and Office: 1498 Cheshire Rd Troy OH 45373-2602

DEHART, ROY LYNCH, physician, educator; b. Grayson, Ky., Jan. 18, 1936; s. Sanford Bomar and Gladys Lillian (Lynch) D.; m. Ella Julia Goodlett, Aug. 8, 1957; children: Evelyn Judith, John Sanford. BS, U. Tenn., Knoxville, 1957; D in Medicine, U. Tenn., Memphis, 1960; MPH, Johns Hopkins U., 1965; MS, George Washington U., 1974. Cert. aerospace medicine, occpl. medicine Am. Bd. Preventive Medicine, Am. Bd. Family Practice. Comdr. Armstrong Aerospace Med. Rsch. Lab., Wright-Patterson AFB, Ohio, 1976-80, USAF Sch. of Aerospace Medicine, Brooks AFB, Texas, 1980-83; pres. Indsl. Medicine Employers Svc., Inc., Tulsa, Okla., 1983-85; dir. divsn. occpl. and environ. medicine U. Okla. Health Sci. Ctr., 1985-94, chmn. dept. of family and preventive medicine, 1993-98; dir. Ctr. for Occupl. and Environ. Medicine Vanderbilt U., 1999—. Bd. dirs., past pres. Am. Coll. Occupational and Environ. Medicine; med. dir. OHA Inc., 2002—; mem. Presdl. Adv. Bd. on Health of Nuclear Workers, 2001—; mem. com. on long duration space flight Nat. Acad. Medicine, 2002—. Author: Fundamentals of Aerospace Medicine, 1986, 3d. edit., 2002; contbr. chpts. to books. Moderator of the bd. Christian Ch., Edmond, Okla., 1997. Col. USAF, 1959-83. Decorated Bronze Star, Air medal, Legion of Merit with two oak leaf clusters. Fellow Am. Coll. Preventive Medicine (pres. 1993-95, Disting. Svc. award 1998), Am. Coll. Occpl. Environ. Medicine (pres. 1992-93, Robert A. Kehos award of merit 1995, William S. Knudson award 1998), Aerospace Med. Assn. (Eric Liljencrantz award 2002, George E. Schafer award 2002), Am. Acad. Family Practice, Internat. Acad. Aviation and Space Medicine; mem. Soc. Tchrs. Family Medicine, USAF Soc. Flight Surgeons. Avocations: recreational travel, theater, religious activities, reading, management information systems. Home: 12 Thorndale Ct Nashville TN 37215-6146 Personal E-mail: rdehart118@aol.com.

DEHART, SUSAN MARIE, music educator; b. Chgo., Aug. 23, 1965; d. Arthur Herman and Jeanne Marie Frank; m. Douglas Wayne Dehart, June 5, 1987; children: Sara Catherine, Amber Elizabeth. MusB, Millikin U., 1987; MMus, U. Nev. LasVegas. Music specialist Desert Christian Schs., Lancaster, Calif., 1987—89, Albuquerque Pub. Schs., 1996—98, Northside Ind. Sch. Dist., San Antonio, 1998—2002, Clark County Sch. Dist., Las Vegas, 2000—. V.p. Ctrl. Tex. Orff Chpt., San Antonio, 1999—2000. Mem.: Music Educators Nat. Conf., Am. Orff Schulwerk Assn. (treas. Nev. Desert Valley chpt. 2002—, v.p. Ctrl. Tex. chpt. 1999—2000). Home: 2024 Spruce Brook Dr Henderson NV 89074

DE HAVILLAND, OLIVIA MARY, actress; b. Tokyo, July 1, 1916; naturalized, 1941; d. Walter Augustus and Lilian Augusta (Ruse) de H. (parents British subjects); m. Marcus Goodrich, Aug. 26, 1946 (div.); 1 child, Benjamin Briggs Goodrich (dec.); m. Pierre Galante, Apr. 2, 1955 (div.); 1 child, Gisele. Student schs. and convent in, Calif.; PhD (hon.), Am. U., Paris, 1994. Made stage debut as Hermia in: Midsummer Night's Dream (Max Reinhardt prodn.), Hollywood Bowl, 1934; 1st motion picture in same role, 1935; actress: (films) including Captain Blood, Anthony Adverse, Robin Hood, Gone With the Wind (nominated for Acad. award 1939), Strawberry Blonde, Hold Back The Dawn (nominated for Acad. award 1941), Princess O'Rourke, To Each His Own (Acad. award for best actress 1946), Dark Mirror, The Snakepit (nominated for Acad. award 1948, N.Y. Critics Award 1948, Laurel Award for best performance 1948-53), The Heiress (Acad. award for best actress 1949, N.Y. critics award), My Cousin Rachel 1952, Not As A Stranger, 1954, Ambassador's Daughter, 1955 (Belgian Critics Prix Femina), Proud Rebel, 1957, Light in the Piazza, 1961, Lady in a Cage, 1963 (British films and filming award), Hush, Hush Sweet Charlotte, 1964, Airport '77, 1976, The Swarm, 1978, The Fifth Musketeer, 1979; TV appearances include Noon Wine, 1966, The Screaming Woman, 1972, Roots: The Next Generations, 1979, Murder is Easy, 1981, Charles and Diana: A Royal Romance, 1982, North and South, II, 1986, Anastasia: The Mystery of Anna, 1986 (Golden Globe award, Emmy nomination), The Woman He Loved, 1988; theatre includes (on Broadway) Romeo and Juliet, 1951, Candida, 1952, A Gift of Time, 1962, (summer stock) What Every Woman Knows, Westport, Conn., Easthampton, Long Island, 1946, Candida, same plus 9 other summer theatres, 1951; (legitimate) Transcontinental Tour Candida 1951-52, (245 Performances); lecture tours, U.S., 1971-80; toured Army and Navy hosps. in U.S., Alaska, Aleutians, South Pacific, 1943-44, Europe, 1957-61; pres. jury Cannes Film Festival, 1965; participant: narration of France's Bicentennial gift to U.S. Son et Lumiere, 1976, Bicentennial Service, Am. Cathedral in Paris, 1976; author: Every Frenchman Has One, 1962. Trustee Am. Coll. in Paris, 1970-71, Am. Libr. in Paris, 1974-81. Recipient Women's Nat. Press Club award for outstanding accomplishment in theater presented by Pres. Truman, 1950; Am. Legion Humanitarian award, 1967; Hon. degree of Doctor of Humane Letters from The Am. U. of Paris, 1994. Mem. Screen Actors Guild, Acad. of Motion Picture Arts and Scis. Democrat. Address: BP 156 75764 Paris Cedex 16 France

DEHAY, JERRY MARVIN, business educator, small business owner; b. Brownwood, Tex., Nov. 21, 1939; s. Marvin Edward and Willie Marie (Daniell) DeHay; m. Dana Lea Laxson, May 29, 1960 (div. June 30, 1973); m. Marilyn Ann Lethco, July 28, 1973; children: Colin, Beva, Sue. BBA, A&M Coll. Tex., 1962; MBA, Tex. A&M U, 1966; PhD, North Tex. State U., 1978. Sales mgr. Procter and Gamble, Corpus Christi, Tex., 1962-65; instr. mktg. Tex. A&M U., College Station, 1966-69; asst. prof. bus. Howard Payne U., Brownwood, Tex., 1969-73; coord. food mktg. Tarrant County Jr. Coll. N.E., Hurst, Tex., 1973-75; instr. math. Brownwood State Sch., 1976-77; asst. prof. mktg. E. Tex. State U., Commerce, 1977-78, prof., 1979-83, dir. Small Bus. Inst., 1979—83; assoc. prof. bus. Hardin Simmons U., Abilene, Tex., 1978-79; dean Coll. Bus. Adminstrn. Tarleton State U., Stephenville, Tex., 1983-94, dir. Small Bus. Inst., 1983—87, dir. Small Bus. Devel. Ctr., 1987—89; CEO JMD Cons., Brownwood, Tex., 1994—; co-owner Recollections Antiques and Collectibles, Brownwood, Tex., 1996—; prof. bus. adminstrn. Howard Payne U., 2001—05, dir. continuing edn., 1971—73. Mem. adv. bd. Small Bus. Devel. Ctr. Co-author: Supervision, 1984; contbr. poems to anthologies; author, presenter (TV series) PBS Business File, 1985. Sec. bd. trustees Brownwood Ind. Sch. Dist., 1972; trustee Mullin (Tex.) Ind. Sch. Dist., 1979; chmn. regional adv. bd. SBA, Dallas; vice chmn. Brownwood Bldg. Stds. Commn., 1997—; bd. dirs. Brown County Hist. Mus., pres., 1999. Named Outstanding Educator of Am., 1973, 1974, 1975, Oustanding Am. of Bi-Centennial Era, 1976. Mem.: Sales and Mktg. Execs. Ft. Worth (educator mem.), Pi Sigma Epsilon (educator v.p. 1984—85, adminstrv. v.p. 1985—86, nat. pres. 1987, Top Faculty Advisor award 1983), Mu Kappa Tau, Delta Sigma Pi. Baptist. Avocations: writing, singing, collecting buttons. Home and Office: 801 Quail Run Brownwood TX 76801-6314 Business E-Mail: dehay@bwoodtx.com. *Do all you can to help others to succeed in whatever endeavour they choose. If you are successful in this, there is no greater success.*

DEHAYES, DANIEL WESLEY, business educator; b. Columbus, Ohio, Sept. 23, 1941; s. Daniel Wesley and June Rosiland (Page) DeH.; children: Sarah Baxter, Benjamin Wesley. BA in Math. and Computer Sci., Ohio State U., 1963, MBA, 1964, PhD in Bus. Adminstrn., 1968. Asst. prof. systems analysis Naval Postgrad. Sch., Monterey, Calif., 1967-69; asst. prof. sch. bus. Ind. U., Bloomington, Ind., 1969-72, assoc. prof.sch. bus., 1972-79, prof. sch. bus., 1979—, dean of acad. computing, 1981-86, asst. v.p. info. tech., 1987-88; dir. Ctr. For Entrepreneurship and Innovation, Ind. U., Bloomington, 1989-98. Exec. dir. Inst. Rsch. on the MIS, 1989-92; cons. in field. Textbook author; contbr. articles to profl. jours. Served to capt. U.S. Army, 1967-69 Recipient fellowships and grants Mem. Decision Scis. Inst. Republican. Methodist. Office: Indiana University Kelley School of Business Bloomington IN 47405 Business E-Mail: dehayes@indiana.edu.

DEHMELT, HANS GEORG, physicist, educator; b. Görlitz, Germany, Sept. 9, 1922; arrived in U.S., 1952, naturalized, 1962; s. Georg Karl and Asta Ella (Klemmt) Dehmelt; m. Diana Elaine Dundore, Nov. 18, 1989; 1 child from previous marriage, Gerd. Grad., Graues Kloster, Berlin, Abitur, 1940; D Rerum Naturalium, U. Goettingen, 1950; D Rerum Naturalium (hon.), Ruprecht Karl-Universitat, Heidelberg, 1986; DSc (hon.), U. Chgo., 1987. Postdoctoral fellow U. Goettingen, Germany, 1950—52, Duke U., Durham, NC, 1952—55; vis. asst. prof. U. Wash., Seattle, 1955, asst. prof. physics, 1956, assoc. prof., 1957—61, prof., rsch. physicist, 1961—. Cons. Varian Assocs., Palo Alto, Calif., 1956—76. Contbr. articles to profl. jours. Sr. pvt. German Army, 1940—45, (captured by US forces, POW to 1946). Recipient Humboldt prize, 1974, award in Basic Rsch., Internat. Soc. Magnetic Resonance, 1980, Rumford prize, Am. Acad. Arts and Scis., 1985, Nobel prize in Physics, 1989, Nat. medal of Sci., 1995; grantee NSF, 1958—. Fellow: Am. Phys. Soc. (Davisson-Germer prize 1970); mem.: NAS, Am. Optical Soc., Am. Acad. Arts and Scis., Sigma Xi. Office: Dept Physics U Wash PO Box 351560 Seattle WA 98195-1560*

DEHMER, GREGORY JOSEPH, cardiologist; b. Milw., Sept. 26, 1949; s. Joseph Anton and Bernadine Elizabeth (Bloom) D.; m. Sue Jane Vencil, Jan. 21, 1977; children: Jeffrey, Laura. BS, Carroll Coll., 1971; MD, U. Wis., 1975. Diplomate Am. Bd. Internal Medicine, Am. Bd. Cardiology. Dir. cardiac catheterization lab. VA Med. Ctr., Dallas, 1984-88; from assoc. prof. to prof. medicine U. N.C., Chapel Hill, 1988—. Asst. prof. medicine U. Tex. Health Sci. Ctr., Dallas, 1984-88; dir. cardiac catheterization lab. U. N.C. Hosps., 1988-96. Editl. bd. Circulation, 1993—, Am. Jour. Cardiology, 1990—. Maj. USAF, 1981-83. Fellow ACP (trustee), Am. Coll. Cardiology, Am. Heart Assn., Soc. Cardiac Angiography and Interventions; mem. AMA (panelist DATTA program 1991—). Mem. Ch. of Christ. Avocation: skiing. Office: U NC Hosps 101 Manning Dr Chapel Hill NC 27514-4220

DEHN, CATHLEEN PATTERSON, pediatrics administrator; b. Akron, Feb. 25, 1958; d. James Edward and Doris Elizabeth (Boyd) P.; m. James Keith Dehn, June 27, 1981; children: Benjamin Jameson and Alexander Hudson (twins). BSN, U. Akron, 1980; MSN, Case Western Res. U., 1988; MA Applied Psychology, NYU, 1995, postgrad., 1995—. RN, N.Y.; cert. PNP, ANCC. Nurse technician Children's Med. Ctr. Akron, 1979-80, staff nurse, 1980-81; pediatric and advanced clin. nurse, asst. head nurse, clin. nurse specialist Rainbow Babies and Children's Hosp., Cleve., 1981-91, edn. coord., 1991-93; PNP, project coord. divsn. nursing, NYU The Child Health Ctr., Brooklyn, 1994-96; PNP dept. pediat. Inst. for Neurology and Neurosurgery Beth Israel Med. Ctr., N.Y.C., 1996-2000; case mgr. dept. pediats. St. Vincent's Hosp. and Med. Ctr., N.Y.C., 2001—. Lectr., clin. instr. Frances Payne Bolton Sch. Nursing, Case Western Res. U., Cleve., 1990-93; mem. adj. faculty divsn. nursing NYU, 1994-96; project coord. Dance Cleve., 1990-91; regional instr. Neonatal Resuscitation Program, Am. Heart Assn., Am. Acad. Pediatrics. Exec. prodr. videos: Getting to Know the Unique Behavioral Capabilities of the Newborn, 1987, One Step at a Time: A Family's Guide to the Neonatal Intensive Care Unit, 1991. Co-founder Sick Kids Need Involved People, Cleve., 1987; team-walk capt. March of Dimes, Cleve., 1989-92 (Edn. grantee 1991); mem. Nat. Mus. Women in Arts. Recipient Samuel E. and Rebecca Elliott award for Cmty. Svc. Case Western Res. U., 1988; named One of Outstanding Young Women of Am., 1988; Fed. Profl. Nurse Trainee scholar, 1986-87. Mem. APA, Am. Ednl. Rsch. Assn., Kappa Delta Pi, Sigma Theta Tau, Pi Lambda Theta. Avocations: health outcomes research, teaching, educational evaluation. Home: 1 University Pl Apt 10L New York NY 10003-4518 Office Phone: 212-604-1021.

DEHN, JAMES KEITH, financial planner; b. Buffalo, Jan. 29, 1957; s. Earl Sylvester and Kathryn Agnes (Pericak) D.; m. Cathleen Patterson, June 27, 1981; children: Benjamin Jameson and Alexander Hudson (twins) BA, Walsh U., 1979; MBA, SUNY, Buffalo, 1981; postgrad., NYU, 1996. Sales rep. Indsl. Metals, Inc., North Canton, Ohio, 1980-97; fin. advisor Prudential Securities, N.Y.C., 1997-2000; fin. advisor pvt. client group UBS PaineWebber, N.Y.C., 2000—04, Wachovia Securities, 2004—. Exec. prodr. (video) Getting to Know the Unique Behavioral Capabilities of the Newborn, 1987. Co-founder Friends of Footpath Footpath Dance Co., Cleve., 1988-90, bd. trustees, 1990-91. Recipient Heritage Home Renovation award Cleve. Heights Cmty. Congress, 1990. Mem. Washing Sq. Assn., Alumni Assn. SUNY Buffalo, Nat. Trust Historic Preservation. Avocations: tennis, sailing, culinary arts, historical preservation. Office: Wachovia Securities 1 Liberty Plz 46th Fl New York NY 10006 Office Phone: 212-978-1103.

DEHN, JOSEPH WILLIAM, JR., chemist; b. Feb. 18, 1928; s. Joseph Williams and Anna Jane (McMahon) D.; m. Mary Baxevanis, June 28, 1953; children: Joseph W. III, George John. BA, Columbia Coll., N.Y.C., 1949; MS, Stevens Inst. Tech., 1953; PhD, Poly. Inst. Bklyn., 1964. Sr. chemist Interchem. Corp., N.Y.C., 1949-63, Clifton, N.J., 1963-64; group leader chemist Wallace & Tiernan Inc., Belleville, N.J., 1964-67; sr. scientist Shulton Inc., Clifton, 1967-70; sr. chemist Process Chem. divsn. Diamond Shamrock Corp., Morristown, N.J., 1971-87; sr. rsch. chemist Atlantic Industries divsn. Jepson Corp., Nutley, N.J., 1988-90, Pall Corp., Glen Cove, N.Y., 1990—. Patentee in field; contbr. articles to sci. jours. Mem. AAAS, Am. Chem. Soc., Am. Inst. Chemists and Colorists, N.Y. Pigment Club, Sigma Xi, Phi Lambda Upsilon. Home: 52 Berkshire Rd Great Neck NY 11023-1416 Office: Pall Corp 25 Harbor Park Dr Port Washington NY 11050-4664

DEHNER, DAVID ANTHONY, music educator, voice educator; b. Middlesboro, Ky., May 8, 1963; m. Ruth Elizabeth Campbell, Mar. 22, 1961. BA, Lee U., 1986; MA, Mid. Tenn. State U., 1993; DMA in Ch. Music and Worship, So. Bapt. Theol. Sem., 2005. Music pastor Coll. Pk. Ch. of God, Huntsville, Ala., 1987—99, Dixie Valley Ch. of God, Louisville, 1999—2002; dir. vocal arts Monte Vista Christian Sch., Watsonville, Calif., 2002—. Singer (soloist) oratorio, opera, and musicals. State music coms. Ch. of God, Birmingham, 1987—99. Mem.: Nat. Assn. Tchrs. Singing (assoc.), Am. Choral Dirs. Assn. (assoc.), Music Educators Nat. Conf. (assoc.), Pi Kappa Lambda. Achievements include research in Life and Work of Delton L. Alford. Home: Two School Way Watsonville CA 95076 Office: Monte Vista Christian School Two School Way Watsonville CA 95076 Office Phone: 831-722-8178 ext. 154. Business E-Mail: tonydehner@mvcs.org.

DEHNER, JOSEPH JULNES, lawyer; b. Cin., Nov. 28, 1948; s. Walter Joseph and Bess (Humphries) Dehner; m. Noel Julnes, Nov. 19, 1983; children: Holly Julnes, Sara Julnes. AB, Princeton U., 1970; JD, Harvard U., 1973. Bar: Ohio 1973, U.S. Dist. Ct. (no. and so. dists.) Ohio 1975, Fla. 1986, U.S. Dist. Ct. (ea. dist.) Ky. 1988, U.S. Ct. Internat. Trade 1992. Law clk. to judge U.S. Ct. Appeals, Cleve., 1973-75; assoc. Kyte, Conlan, Wulsin & Vogeler, Cin., 1975-78, Frost Brown Todd LLC, Cin., 1978—; chmn. Universal Transactions Inc., 1991-95. Co-mgr. Ukraine Investments Ltd., 1995—99. Author: (book) Structured Settlements and Periodic Payment Judgments, 1986, A Guide to Soviet Businesspeople on American Business Law, 1991, Doing Business in Russia, 1992, Dispute Resolution in China, 1994, A Foreign Investors Guide to Ukraine, 1995; contbr. articles to profl. publs. Sec., v.p. Cin. Preservation Assn., 1978—86; mem. Cin. Planning Commn., 1984—85; pres. Charter Com. Greater Cin., 1982—86; chmn. Cin.-Kharkiv Sister City Project, 1988—91; Ohio commodore, 2003—; pres. French-Am. C. of C. of Greater Cin., 2004—; chmn. So. Ohio Dist. Export Coun., 2003—; chancellor Episcopal Diocese So. Ohio, 1997—; trustee Princeton (N.J.) U., 1970—74, Ohio Hist. Soc., 1974—78. Mem.: ABA (vice chair internat. litig. com.), 6th Cir. Jud. Conf., Cin. Bar Assn., Ohio Bar Assn. (chmn. internat. law com. 1989—91), Pub. Investors Arbitration Bar Assn. Avocations: tennis, reading. Home: 822 Yale Ave Terrace Park OH 45174-1258 Office: Frost Brown Todd LLC 2200 PNC Ctr 201 E 5th St Ste 2200 Cincinnati OH 45202-4182 Office Phone: 513-651-6949. Business E-Mail: jdehner@fbtlaw.com.

DEHOPE, EDWARD KIM, lawyer; b. Paterson, N.J., Dec. 4, 1952; s. Edward and Barbara A. (Elsner) DeH.; m. Leanne Heggie; children: Emily Ann, Aimee Elizabeth. AB, Lafayette Coll., Easton, Pa., 1974; JD, U. Va., 1977. Bar: N.J. 1978. Law clk. to assoc. justice Supreme Ct. N.J., Hackensack, 1977-78; assoc. Riker, Danzig, Scherer, Hyland & Perretti, Morristown, N.J., 1978-85, ptnr., 1986—. Mem. Digest Com. N.J. Utilities Assn., 1985—. Author: (with others) Solving the Garbage Disposal Crisis in New Jersey, 1985; contbr. articles to law rev. Mem. pastor nominating com. Presbyn. Ch., Madison, N.J., 1984, elder, 1985-87, 92-94, chmn. nominating com., 1993, chmn. pers. com., 1994; mem. Gov. Whitman's Transition Team on Bd. Regulatory Commrs. and Budget. Mem. ABA, N.J. State Bar Assn. (consultor pub. utility law practice sect. 1990-93, sec. 1994—). Republican. Office: And Perretti 1 Speedwell Ave Morristown NJ 07960-6838

DE HOYOS, DEBORA M., lawyer; b. Monticello, N.Y., Aug. 10, 1953; d. Luis and Marion (Kinney) de Hoyos; m. Walter C. Carlson, June 20, 1981; children: Amanda, Greta, Linnea. BA, Wellesley Coll., 1975; JD, Harvard U., 1978. Bar: Ill. 1978, U.S. Dist. Ct. (no. dist.) Ill. 1980. Assoc. Mayer, Brown & Platt, Chgo., 1978—84, ptnr., 1985—, mng. ptnr., 1991—. Bd. dirs. Evanston Northwestern Healthcare; bd. trustees Providence St. Mel. Sch. Contbr. chpt. to Securitization of Financial Assets, 1991. Trustee Chgo. Symphony Orch. Named one of the Ten Most Influential Women Lawyers in Ill., Am. Lawyer Media, 2000, Fifty Outstanding Women Graduates, Harvard Law Sch., 2003. Office: Mayer Brown Rowe & Maw LLP Ste 3900 190 S La Salle St Chicago IL 60603-3441

DE ICAZA GONZALEZ, CARLOS ALBERTO (CARLOS DE ICAZA), ambassador; Analyst Internat Orgns. desk, Mexico, 1970—71; third sec. Mexican Embassy, Panama, 1971—73; pvt. sec. to undersecretary of fgn rels. Mexico, 1973—77; min., Mexican Permanent Mission to Internat Organs. Geneva, 1979—80; gen. dir. Fgn Svc., Mexico, 1980—83; gen. dir. for Latin Am. and the Caribean Mexico, 1983—86; chief of staff to Mexican sec. of fgn. rels., Mexico, 1988—91; undersecretary for mgmt Mexico, 1991—93; undersecretary for fgn. rels. for Latin Am. and Asia-Pacific, 1998—2000; Mexican amb. to Ecuador, 1986—88, to Argentina, 1995—96, to Belgium and Luxembourg, 1996—98, to Japan, 2001—04, to the U.S., 2004—. Author: (books) La Diplomacia Contemporanea (Contemporary Diplomacy), El Orden Mundial Emergente (Emerging World Order). Office: Embassy of Mexico 1911 Penn Ave NW Washington DC 20006

DEICKEN, RAYMOND FRIEDRICH, psychiatrist, neuroscientist; b. Honolulu, June 28, 1957; s. Raymond T. and Miriam (Ogata) D. AB, MS, Stanford U., 1980; MD, U. Calif., San Francisco, 1984. Diplomate Nat. Bd. Med. Examiners, Am. Bd. Psychiatry and Neurology; lic. physician Med. Bd. Calif. Resident physician U. Calif., San Francisco, 1984-88, rsch. fellow, 1988-91, asst. prof. psychiatry, 1991-97, assoc. prof., 1997—2003, prof., 2003—; staff physician VA Med. Ctr., San Francisco, 1991—, med. dir. Partial Hosp. Program, 2002. Lectr. in field; cons. Exodon Neurosci., 2001, Roche Biosci., 2001, Bristol-Myers Squibb, 2003. Reviewer manuscripts Biol. Psychiatry, 1987—, Psychiatry Rsch., 1992—; contbr. articles to profl. jours; mem. editl. bd. Jour. Integrative Neuroscis. Alumni mentor Stanford U. Student Alumni Mentor Program, 1993—. Recipient Young Investigator award Nat. Alliance for Rsch. on Schizophrenia and Depression, 1992, 94, Ind. Investigator award, 2000, 04, Stanley Found. rsch. award Nat. Alliance for Mentally Ill, 1997, 98, VA Physician Rsch. Assoc. Career Devel. award, 1991-95; Dista fellow Soc. Biol. Psychiatry, 1991. Fellow Collegium Internat. Neuro-psychopharmacologicum; mem. AMA, Soc. for Neuroscience, Soc. Biol. Psychiatry, Internat. Soc. Magnetic Resonance in Medicine, Am. Psychiat. Assn., Internat. Soc. Neuroimaging in Psychiatry, Internat. Soc. for Affective Disorders, N.Y. Acad. Scis. Episcopalian. Home: 197 Carnelian Way San Francisco CA 94131-1780 Office: Dept Veterans Affairs Med Ctr 4150 Clement St San Francisco CA 94121-1545 Office Phone: 415-221-4810. Business E-Mail: deicken@itsa.ucsf.edu.

DEIGHTON, LEN, author; b. London, Feb. 18, 1929; Author: The Ipcress File, 1962 (motion picture U.S., 1963), Horse Under Water, 1963, U.S. edit. 1968, Funeral in Berlin, 1964 (motion picture U.S., 1965), Ou Est le Garlic/Basic French Cooking, 1965, 2d edit., 1979, U.S. edit., 1977, Action Cook Book, 1965, Cookstrip Cook Book, 1966, Billion Dollar Brain, 1966 (motion picture U.S., 1966), An Expensive Place to Die, 1967, Len Deighton's Dossier, 1967, Only When I Larf, 1968 (motion picture U.S., 1968), Bomber, 1970 (radio drama U.S., 1970), U.S. Edit. of Declarations of War, 1971, Close-Up, 1972, Spy Story, 1974 (motion picture U.S., 1974), Eleven Declarations of War, 1975, Yesterday's Spy, 1975, Twinkle, Twinkle, Little Spy, 1976, Catch a Falling Spy, 1976, Fighter, 1977, U.S. edit., 1978, SS-GB, 1978, U.S. edit., 1979, Blitzkreig, 1979, U.S. edit., 1980, XPD, 1981, Goodbye Mickey Mouse, 1982, Berlin Game, 1983, Mexico Set, 1984, London Match, 1985, Winter: A Berlin Family 1899-1945, 1987, U.S. edit., 1988, Spy Hook, 1988, Spy Line, 1989, Spy Sinker, 1990, Basic French Cookery Course, 1990, ABC of French Food, 1989, U.S. edit., 1990, MAMista, 1991, City of Gold, 1992, Violent Ward, 1993, Blood, Tears & Folly, 1993, Faith, 1994, U.S. edit., 1995, Hope, 1995, U.S. edit., 1996, Charity, 1996; co-author: The Assassination of President Kennedy, 1967, Airshipwreck, 1978, U.S. edit., 1979, Battle of Britain, 1980, 2d edit., 1990, U.S. edit., 1980; (13-part TV series) Game, Set & Match, 1985. Office: care Jonathan Clowes Ltd 10 Iron Bridge House London NW1 8BD England E-mail: jonathanclowes@aol.com.

DEIHL, CHARLES L., former college president; b. Chgo., Dec. 12, 1937; s. Elmer Frank and Lois Olive (Waterman) D.; m. Peggy Ann Fleischman, May 1, 1938; children: Geoffrey Charles, Kristen Ann. BA, Ind. U., 1959; MA, Mich. State U., 1963, MFA, 1965. Asst. dir. publs. Ohio U., Athens, 1965-67, head graphic design, 1967-71, Bradley U., Peoria, Ill., 1971-74; head dept. fine arts U. Cin., 1974-79; dean arts and humanities SUNY,

Buffalo, 1979-89; pres. Kendall Coll. Art and Design, Grand Rapids, Mich., 1989-95, Columbus Coll. of Art and Design, 1995—97. Mem. mgmt. devel. program Harvard U., Cambridge, Mass., 1986, seminar for new pres's., 1989; cons. graphic design and illustration in field. Artist to paintings and drawings in field. Sgt. USAF, 1962-63. Ind. U. merit scholar, 1955. Mem. Assn. Governing Bds. Univs. and Colls., Assn. Ind. Colls. and Univs. Mich., Assn. Ind. Colls. Art and Design, Univ. and Coll. Designers Assn. (pres. emeritus 1972—), Rotary Club Grand Rapids. Home: 7245 Sugar Bush Ln Chagrin Falls OH 44022-2667

DEIHL, MICHAEL ALLEN, federal agency administrator; b. Bluffton, Ind., Apr. 22, 1952; s. Robert W. and Betty J. (Miller) D.; m. Deborah Ann Crabb, June 16, 1973; 1 child, Samantha Lynn. BSEE, Colo. State U., 1974. East slope area mgr. ECPO Bur. Reclamation, Loveland, Colo., 1981-85, chief com. and control divsn., ECPO, 1985-87; chief maintenance divsn. Hoover Dam Bur. Reclamation, Boulder City, Nev., 1987-90; project mgr. Alaska Power Adminstrn., Dept. Energy, Juneau, 1990-92, dir. power divsn., 1992, adminstr., 1992-95; adminstr. Dept. Energy Southwestern Power Adminstrn., Tulsa, 1995—. Office: Southwestern Power Admin 1 W 3rd St Tulsa OK 74103-3502

DEIHL, SUSAN GALYEN, historic preservationist; b. Columbus, Miss., May 22, 1973; d. James Bruce Galyen, Jr. and Janice Greear Galyen; m. Joshua John Joseph Deihl; children: Cole children: Grayson. BA, U. Va., 1995; M Hist. Preservation, U. Ga., 1998. Intern Hist. Preservation Soc. Durham, 1997; nat. register asst. Paul Hardin Kapp, AIA, Galax, Va., 1997; preservation planner/grants coord. Mass. Hist. Commn., Boston, 1999—2000; asst. to revolving fund dir. Preservation NC, Raleigh, NC, 2000—01. Mem., vol. Preservation N.C., 2001—04; mem. Capital Area Preservation, Raleigh, NC, 2001—04, Va. Hist. Soc., Richmond, Va., 1995—2004, Colonial Williamsburg Found., Williamsburg, Va., 1993—2004, Nat. Trust for Hist. Preservation, Washington, 1990—2004. Mem.: Student Hist. Preservation Soc. (v.p. 1997—98), Nat. Honor Soc. Hist. Preservation. Home: 605 N Bloodworth St Raleigh NC 27604-1227

DEIKE, KEITH LAWRENCE, lawyer; b. Owatonna, Minn., Aug. 9, 1952; s. Orvin Kenneth and Muriel Felicity Deike; m. Pamela Jean Schubbe, Apr. 8, 1988; children: Jacob Andrew, Maxwell James. BA magna cum laude, Mankato State U., 1979; JD, U. Minn., 1983. Bar: Minn. 1983, U.S. Dist. Ct. Minn. 1985. Sole practitioner Deike Law Offices, Waseca, Minn., 1983—94; assoc. Patton, Hoversten & Berg, P.A., Waseca, 1994—. Third dist. pub. defender State Bd. of Pub. Def., St. Paul, 1990—96; city prosecutor City of Waseca, 1991—94. Dir. Waseca Area C. of C., 1989—91, Waseca Area United Way, 1992—98; chair Sacred Heart Sch., Waseca, Minn., 1995—2001. Named Super Lawyer, Minn. Law & Politics Mag., 2000, Leading Personal Injury Atty., 2001. Mem.: ATLA, Minn. State Bar Assn. Home: 120 4th St NE Waseca MN 56093 Office: Patton Hoversten & Berg PA 215 Elm Ave East Waseca MN 56093-0249 Office Phone: 507-835-5240. Office Fax: 507-835-1827. Personal E-mail: kempa@hickorytech.net. Business E-Mail: keith.deike@phblawoffice.com.

DEILY, LINNET FRAZIER, ambassador; b. Dallas, June 20, 1945; d. William Harold and Ruth (White) Frazier; m. Myron Bonham Deily, Apr. 18, 1981. BA, U. Tex. Austin, 1967; MA, U. Tex. Dallas, 1976. Banking officer, asst. v.p., v.p. Republic Bank, Dallas, 1975—80, sr. v.p., 1980—81; v.p. First Interstate Bancorp, L.A., 1981—83; sr. v.p., divsn. mgr. First Interstate Bank of Calif., L.A., 1983—84, exec. v.p., 1988; chmn., pres., CEO First Interstate Bank of Tex., 1988—96; pres. Schwab Institutional, 1996—98, Schwab Retail Group, 1998—2001; vice chmn. Charles Schwab Corp., 2000—01; dep. U.S. Trade Rep. Exec. Office of the Pres., Washington, 2001—. Bd. dirs. First Interstate Inst., L.A. Mem.: Univ. Club L.A. (fin. com.). Office: World Trade Orgn Centre William Rappard Rue de Lausanne 154 CH-1211 21 Geneva Switzerland

DEINARD, LILE HAMMOND, lawyer; b. Charlottesville, Va., June 26, 1940; d. Lewis Machen and Frances Lile Hammond; m. Ethan Curtis Deinard, June 5, 1962 (div. May 1985); children: Caitlin Lewis Blasdell, Theodore Benedict; m. John Weaver Rosenberger. BA, Smith Coll., Northampton, Mass., 1962; MA, Hofstra U., 1969, JD, 1974. Bar: N.Y. 1975, U.S. Dist. Ct. (so. and ea. dists.) N.Y. 1975, U.S. Ct. Appeals (fed. cir.) 1981. Assoc. Roger, Hoge & Hills, N.Y.C., 1974-82, ptnr., 1982-86, Paskus, Gordon & Mandel, N.Y.C., 1986-87; of counsel White & Case, N.Y.C., 1987-92; ptnr. Schreiber Simmons, N.Y.C., 1992-94; shareholder Greenberg Traurig, N.Y.C., 1994-2000; ptnr., trademark, copyright, brand mgmt. practice group Dorsey & Whitney LLP, N.Y.C., 2000—. Author: Encyclopedia of Chemical Technologies, Professional, Reference and Trade Group, 1993. Mentor Pre-Law Soc., Martin L. King Jr. H.S., N.Y.C., 1994-98. Mem. ABA (intellectual property sect.), Internat. Trademark Assn. (mem. planning com. 1994-96), False Advt. Forum (moderator). Republican. Episcopalian. Avocations: gardening, hiking, cooking. Office: Dorsey & Whitney LLP 250 Park Ave New York NY 10177 Office Phone: 212-735-0778. Office Fax: 212-953-7201. E-mail: deinard.lile@dorseylaw.com.

DEINES, KATRINA, architecture educator; BA in Art History, U. Minn., 1967, MA in Art History, 1974; MArch, U. Wash., 1979. Assoc. prof. dept. arch. U. Wash., Seattle, assoc. dean Coll. Arch. and Urban Planning, 1988—, co-dir. Rome Ctr., 1993—2000, dir. Rome Ctr., 2000—. Guest faculty mem. U. B.C., Sicily, Italy, 2000; mem. coll. exec. com. U. Wash., Seattle, 1988—, faculty senate, 1989—92, chair coll. awards com., 1996—, mem. campus art com., Bothell, 1998—, Wash. State Arts Commn., 1997—; internat. faculty coun., advisor to U. Wash. Pres. and Provost, 1998—. Mem. editl. bd.: Jour. Archtl. Edn., 1995—98, co-founder, mng. editor: N.W. Jour. for Arch. and Design, 1980—85. Soprano, treas., pres. bd. City Contabile Choir, 1986—92; active City of Seattle San Point Design Commn., 1998—99. Recipient Faculty Devel. Rsch. award, U. Wis. Coll. Arch. and Urban Planning, 1998. Office: U Wash Coll Arch and Urban Planning 208N Gould Hall Box 355720 Seattle WA 98195-5726

DEIRO, JUDITH ANNE, chemical dependency educator; d. Guido and Ruby Margaret Deiro. BA, Okla. State U., Stillwater, 1968; MA, U. Fla., 1970; PhD, U. Wash., 1994. Cert. alcohol studies Seattle U., developing capable young people Empowering People Inc., addiction sci. U. of Miami, chem. dependency counselor State of Wash. Vocat. rehab. counselor Dept. of Vocat. Rehab., Gainesville, Fla., 1970—72; rsch. assoc. State of Fla., Office of Drug Abuse, Tallahassee, 1972—73; clin. supr. Whatcom County Alcohol Ctr., Bellingham, Wash., 1974—77; mem. faculty Whatcom C.C., Bellingham, 1977—97; rsch. asst. U. of Wash., Seattle, 1991—94; mem. faculty Western Wash. U., Bellingham, 1997—. Cons. U.S. Office of Edn., Divsn. Addiction Scis., Miami, 1973; cons. to ednl. orgns., Seattle, 1977—; adj. faculty Western Wash. U., Bellingham, 1978—86, Seattle U., 1984—97; advisor Wash. State DSHS Adv. Bd., Olympia, 1980—84. Author: (book) Teachers DO Make a Difference, Teaching with Heart, Handbook for Portfolio Process -ERIC, Handbook for Learning Contracts; contbr. articles to profl. jours., chapters to books. Pres. N.W. Consortium of Chem. Dependency Educators, 1996; mem. statewide steering com. for presdl. candidate Seattle, 2002—04. Named Chem. Dependency Educator of Yr., State of Wash., N.W. Consortium of Chem. Dependency Educators, 1996; recipient Full-time Faculty Excellence award, Whatcom C.C., 1995, Excellence Among Women in Cmty. Colls. award, Assn. of Women in Cmty. and Jr. Colls., 1984; Rachel Royston scholar for Women Leaders in Edn., Rachel Royston Statewide Scholarship Com., 1992, 1993, 1994, James I. Doi Rsch. scholar, U. Wash., 1994, Fund for the Improvement of Postsecondary Edn. grantee, Post-secondary Consortium for Prevention, Prevention Program in Post-Secondary Sch. Mem.: NW Consortium of Chem. Dependency Educators (pres., (2 times) 1996—97). Democrat. Avocations: exercise, skiing, piano, beading, weightlifting.

DEISENHOFER, JOHANN, biochemistry professor, researcher; b. Zusamaltheim, Bavaria, Germany, Sept. 30, 1943; arrived in U.S., 1988, naturalized, 2001; s. Johann and Thekla (Magg) D.; m. Kirsten Fischer-Lindahl, June 19, 1989. Diploma in Physics, Technische U., Munich, 1971, PhD, 1974, Doctor habilis, 1987. Postdoctoral fellow Max-Planck Inst. Biochemie, Martinsried, Fed. Republic of Germany, 1974-76, staff scientist, 1976-88; investigator Howard Hughes Med. Inst., Dallas, 1988—; prof. biochemistry U. Tex., Dallas, 1988—. Contbr. mor than 100 sci. papers to profl. publs. Recipient Nobel prize for chemistry, 1988; co-recipient Biol. Physics prize Am. Phys. Soc., 1986, Otto Bayer prize, 1988; decorated Bavarian Order of Merit, knight comdr.'s cross (badge and star) Order of Merit of Germany, Roentgen-Plakette, 2004. Mem. AAAS, NAS, Am. Crystallographic Assn., German Biophys. Soc., Protein Soc., Biophys. Soc., Academia Europaea, German Acad. Natural Scientists Leopoldina. Office: Howard Hughes Med Inst U Tex Southwestern Med Ctr 6001 Forest Park Rd Dallas TX 75390-9050 E-mail: Johann.Deisenhofer@UTSouthwestern.edu.

DEISLER, PAUL FREDERICK, JR., retired oil company executive; b. El Paso, Tex., Jan. 20, 1926; s. Paul Frederick and Jeanie Donnelly (Monroe) D.; m. Ellen Louise Bardwell, June 15, 1950; children: Jane Ellen, Paul Conrad, Julia Monroe. BS in Chem. Engring, Tex. A&M U., 1948; MS, Princeton U., 1949, PhD, 1952. With Shell Oil Co., 1952—86, v.p. transp. and supplies, 1969-71; dir. supply and refining Compañía Shell de Venezuela, 1971-73; v.p. Chem. Co., Houston, 1973-74; v.p. research and engring. products Shell Oil Co., Houston, 1974-76, v.p. health, safety and environment, 1976-86; dir. Chem. Industry Inst. Toxicology, 1975-86. Chmn. adv. coun. dept. chem. engring. Princeton U., 1978-81; vis. exec. prof. Sch. Bus., U. Houston, 1986-90, mem. curriculum adv. bd. Inst. Corp. Environ. Mgmt., 1992-93; exec. com. sci. adv. bd. EPA, 1986-94, cons., 1994-2000; environ. adv. coun. Rohm and Haas Co., 1989-93; adj. prof. environ. risk assessment U. Tex. Sch. Pub. Health, 1990-94; policy com. Ctr. for Global Studies, Houston Advanced Rsch. Ctr., The Woodlands, Tex., 1992-98; chair policy com. Houston Advanced Rsch. Ctr., The Woodlands, 1995-96; ret. 2003. Editor: Reducing the Carcinogenic Risk in Industry, 1984; area editor for health and environ. risk analysis Risk Analysis: An Internat. Jour., 1997, 98; author articles on environ. health risk assessment and mgmt. Bd. dirs. ARC, Houston, 1975-80; chmn. fin. com. Houston Sci. Fair, 1974-76; alumni councilor, trustee Tex. A&M Research Found., 1977-99, trustee; bd. dirs. Tex. Inst. for Advancement of Chem. Tech., 1988-2000; mem. governing coun. Inst. for Bus., Ethics and Pub. Issues, U. Houston, 1987-90. Served with USN, 1944-46, PTO. Fellow Soc. Risk Analysis (pres. 1986-87); mem. AAAS, AIChE, N.Y. Acad. Scis., U.S. Naval Inst., Assn. Princeton Grad. Alumni (bd. dirs. 1976-79), Am. Petroleum Inst. (chmn. health, environ. and safety gen. com. 1983-84), Am. Chem. Soc., Soc. for Regulatory Toxicology and Pharmacology, Sigma Xi, Tau Beta Pi, Phi Kappa Phi. Address: PO Box 5819 Austin TX 78763-5819 Personal E-mail: sinprisa@earthlink.net.

DEISSLER, MARY ALICE, foundation executive; b. Oneonta, N.Y., Dec. 30, 1957; d. George W. and Carol (Zorda) Baker; m. James N. Deissler, Nov. 24, 1987; children: Benjamin, Eliza. BA, U. Mass., 1978; MBA, Babson Coll., 1982. Fin. analyst Digital Equipment Corporation, Maynard, Mass., 1978-82; devel. dir. Handel & Haydn Soc., Boston, 1984-89, gen. mgr., 1984-89, exec. dir., 1990—. Pres., bd. dirs. Studebaker Movement Theatre Co., Boston, 1986-88. Bd. dirs. Early Music Am., N.Y.C., 1989—, v.p., 1991—, pres., 1994; bd. dirs. Babson Coll., 1990-94, Chorus Am., 1991—, v.p., 1992, pres.-elect, 1996, pres., 1997, pres. bd. dirs., 1997; mem. bd. Arts/Boston, 1994—, pres. bd. dirs., 2003; bd. dirs. Am. Composers Fourm, 2000, chair, 2004—; bd. dirs. Berkshire Choral Soc., 2000—; treas. Handel House of Am. Found. Mem. Am. Symphony Orch. League. Office: Handel & Haydn Soc 300 Massachusetts Ave Boston MA 02115-4544 Office Phone: 617-262-1815. E-mail: mdeissler@handelandhaydn.org.

DEISSLER, ROBERT GEORGE, fluid dynamics researcher; b. Greenville, Pa., Aug. 1, 1921; s. Victor Girard and Helen Stella (Fisher) D.; m. June Marie Gallagher, Oct. 7, 1950; children— Robert Joseph, Mary Beth, Ellen Ann, Anne Marie BS, Carnegie Inst. Tech., 1943; MS, Case Inst. Tech., 1948; PHD, Case Western Res. U., 1989. Researcher Goodyear Aircraft Corp., Akron, OH, 1943-44; aero. rsch. scientist NASA Lewis Rsch. Ctr., Cleve., 1947-52, chief fundamental heat transfer br., 1952-70, staff scientist, sci. cons. fluid physics, 1970-94, disting. rsch. assoc., 1994—. Fellow Lewis Rsch. Acad., 1983—; staff scientist sr. level emeritus, 1994. Author: Turbulent Fluid Motion, Taylor and Francis, 1998; contbr. articles to profl. jours.; areas of rsch. fluid turbulence, turbulent heat transfer, turbulent solutions of equations of fluid motion, nonlinear dynamics and chaos, meteorol. and astrophysical flows, radiative heat transfer in gases, heat transfer in powders. Served as lt. (j.g.) USNR, 1944-46 Recipient NACA/NASA Exceptional Svc. award, 1957, Outstanding Publ. award, 1978, Wisdom Soc. award, 2000; Lewis Rsch. Acad. fellow, 1983—. Fellow AIAA (Best Paper award 1975, Tech. Achievement award 1981), ASME (Heat Transfer Meml. award 1964, Max Jacob Meml. award 1975, Wisdom Hall of Fame 2000); mem. Am. Phys. Soc., Sigma Xi. Roman Catholic. Avocations: violin, reading, walking, natural theology. Home: 4540 W 213th St Fairview Park OH 44126-2106 Office: NASA Glenn Rsch Ctr 21000 Brookpark Rd Cleveland OH 44135-3191 *It is desirable that research be fundamentally based, even when it is undertaken with a view toward an application. Then the research will likely be worthwhile, regardless of whether or not the application materializes.*

DEITCH, LAURENCE B., lawyer; AB, U. Mich., 1969, JD, 1972. Ptnr. Bodman, Longley & Dahling LLP, Detroit. Vice chmn. Mich. Civil Svc. Commn.; bd. regents U. Mich., Ann Arbor, 1992—; treas. Mich. Dem. Party; pres. Temple Beth El, Bloomfield Hills, Mich. Office: Bodman Langley & Dahling LLP 100 Renaissance Ctr 34th Fl Detroit MI 48243

DEITERS, SISTER JOAN ADELE, psychoanalyst, nun, chemistry professor; b. Cincinnati, Apr. 28, 1934; d. Alfred Harry and Rose Catherine (Rusche) Deiters. BA, Coll. Mt. St. Joseph, Cin., 1963; PhD, U. Cin., 1967; M in Christian spirituality, Creighton U., Omaha, 1985. Joined Sisters of Charity, Roman Cath. Ch., 1952; cert. psychoanalyst, Westchester Inst. for Tng. in Psychoanalysis and Psychotherapy, 2000. Prof. chemistry Coll. Mt. St. Joseph, Cin., 1969-78; Matthew Vassar Jr. chair Vassar Coll., Poughkeepsie, NY, 1978-96. Contbr. articles to profl. jours. Mem. Am. Chem. Soc., Sisters of Charity, Sigma Xi; Nat. Assn. for Advancement of Psychoanalysis. Home: 10 Drouilhet Ln Apt 2 Poughkeepsie NY 12603 Office: 39 Collegeview Ave Poughkeepsie NY 12603-2415 Office Phone: 845-485-4920.

DEITRICH, RICHARD ADAM, pharmacology educator; b. Monte Vista, Colo., Apr. 22, 1931; s. Robert Adam and Freda Leona (Scott) D.; m. Mary Margaret Burkholder, Jan. 29, 1954; children: Vivian Gay, Leslie Lynn, Lori Christine. BS, U. Colo., 1953, MS, 1954, PhD, 1959. Postdoctoral fellow, then instr. Johns Hopkins U., Balt., 1959-63; asst. prof., then assoc. prof. U. Colo., Denver, 1963-76, prof. pharmacology, 1976—2005, sci. dir. Alcohol Rsch. Ctr., 1977—2005, prof. emeritus, 2005—. Vis. prof. U. Berne, Switzerland, 1973-74. Editor: Development of Animal Models, 1981, Initial Sensitivity to Alcohol, 1990; contbr. over 100 articles to sci. publs. Pres. Mile High Coun. on Alcoholism, Denver, 1972-73; moderator 1st Universalist Ch., Denver, 1979. With U.S. Army, 1954-56. Grantee Nat. Inst. Alcoholism, 1977—, Nat. Inst. Communicative Disease and Stroke, 1963, numerous others. Mem. Rsch. Soc. on Alcoholism (pres. 1981-83), Internat. Soc. Biomed. Rsch. on Alcoholism (treas. 1986-94), Am. Soc. Pharmacology, Am. Soc. Biol. Chemistry. Avocations: photography, fishing, camping. Office: Univ Colo at Fitzsimmons MS 8303 PO Box 6508 Aurora CO 80045

DEITRICH, WAYNE H., manufacturing executive; Chmn., CEO Schweitzer-Mauduit Internat., Inc., Alpharetta, Ga., 1995—. Office: Schweitzer-Mauduit Internat Inc 100 N Point Ctr E Ste 600 Alpharetta GA 30022-8263

DEITRICK, WILLIAM EDGAR, lawyer; b. N.Y.C., July 30, 1944; s. John English and Dorothy Alice (Geib) D.; m. Emily Jane Posey, June 22, 1968; children: William Jr., Elizabeth, Peter. BA, Johns Hopkins U., 1967; JD, Cornell U., 1971. Bar: Ill. 1972, U.S. Dist. Ct. (no. dist.) Ill. 1972, U.S. Ct. Appeals (7th cir.) 1976, D.C. 1981. Ptnr. Gardner, Carton and Douglas, Chgo., 1972—85; sr. v.p., dep. gen. counsel, mgr. litigation divsn. Continental Bank N.A., 1985—91; ptnr. Mayer, Brown, Rowe & Maw, Chgo., 1991—. Contbr. articles to profl. jours. Trustee North Shore Country Day Sch., 1992-97; gov. mem. Shedd Aquarium; With U.S. Army, 1968-70. Mem. ABA, Ill. Bar Assn., Chgo. Bar Assn., Johns Hopkins U. Alumni Assn. (class agt. 1967-95), Cornell Law Sch. Chgo. Alumni Assn. (chmn. 1985-87), Legal Club, Univ. Club Chgo. (bd. dirs.), Indian Hill Club (Winnetka, Ill.). Home: 1360 N Lake Shore Dr # 1415 Chicago IL 60610 Office: Mayer Brown Rowe & Maw 190 S La Salle St Ste 3100 Chicago IL 60603-3441

DEITZ, LEWIS LEVERING, entomologist, educator, researcher; b. Bel Air, Md., June 22, 1944; s. Charles Phillip and Caroline Edith (Kalbskopf) D. BS in Entomology, U. Md., 1967, MS in Entomology, 1968; PhD in Entomology, N.C. State U., 1973. Rsch. asst. dept. entomology N.C. State U., Raleigh, 1971-73, rsch. assoc., 1973-75, 79-80, asst. prof., 1980-86, assoc. prof., 1986-93, prof., 1993—, curator insect collection, 1980-86, dir. insect collection, 1986—; hemipterist Dept. Sci. and Indsl. Rsch., Auckland, New Zealand, 1975-79. Contbr. articles to profl. jours. Mem. Entomol. Soc. Am., Entomol. Soc. New Zealand, N.C. Entomol. Soc., Entomol. Soc. Washington, Systematics Assn. New Zealand, Sigma Xi, Soc. Systematic Biology, Phi Kappa Phi. Religious Soc. of Friends. Avocation: gardening. Office: NC State U Dept Entomology PO Box 7613 Raleigh NC 27695-0001

DEJAMMET, ALAIN, former diplomat; Perm. rep. of France to UN, NYC, 1995—2000, pres. Security Coun., 1999—. Author: Sleeping at the United Nations, 2000, Supplement with the Voyage in Onusie, 2003.

DEJESUS-RUEFF, MARCIA KAY, mathematics educator, consultant; b. Elkhart, Ind., Nov. 28, 1952; d. Joseph Alvin and Virginia Thorburn Rueff; m. Richard DeJesus, Dec. 20, 1975; children: Virginia Francisca, Vicente Manuel, Joel. AB, Bryn Mawr Coll., 1975; MA, Oberlin (Ohio) Coll., 1981; MS, St. John Fisher Coll., Rochester, NY, 2000. Cert. ednl. adminstrn. NY, 2004, math. tchg. NY, 1998. Math. dept. chair Penfield (NY) H.S., 2001—; lead tchr. Penfield Sch. Dist., U. Rochester. Cons. DeJesus-Rueff Ednl. Consulting, Rochester, 2000—. Vol. Spiritus Christi Ch., Rochester, NY, 1997—2005. Achievements include mathematics education research, specifically on reform-based initiatives and discourse. Home: 139 Parkwood Ave Rochester NY 14620 Office: Penfield H S 25 High School Dr Penfield NY 14526 Office Phone: 585-249-6766.

DE JONG, DAVID SAMUEL, lawyer, educator; b. Washington, Jan. 8, 1951; s. Samuel and Dorothy (Thomas) De J.; m. Tracy Ann Barger, Sept. 23, 1995; children: Jacob Samuel, Franklin Joseph. BA, U. Md., 1972; JD, Washington and Lee U., 1975; LLM in Taxation, Georgetown U., 1979. Bar: Md. 1975, U.S. Dist. Ct. Md. 1977, U.S. Tax Ct. 1977, U.S. Ct. Appeals (4th cir.) 1978, U.S. Supreme Ct. 1979, D.C. 1980, U.S. Dist. Ct. D.C. 1983, U.S. Ct. Claims, U.S. Ct. Appeals (fed. cir.) 1983; CPA, Md.; cert. valuation analyst. Atty. Gen. Bus. Svcs., Inc., Rockville, Md., 1975-80; ptnr. Stein Sperling Bennett De Jong Driscoll & Greenfeig, PC, Rockville, 1980—. Adj. prof. Southeastern U., Washington, 1979-85, Am. U., Washington, 1983-2002; instr. U. Md., College Park, 1986-87, Montgomery Coll., Rockville, 1983; mem. character com. 7th Appeals Cir. Md. Ct. of Appeals. Co-author: (ann. book) J.K. Lasser's Year-Round Tax Strategies, 1989-2004; editor Notes and Comments, Washington and Lee U. Law Rev., 1974-75. V.p. Seneca Whetstone Homeowners Assn., Gaithersburg, Md., 1981-82, pres. 1982-83. Mem. ABA, AICPA, Am. Assn. Atty.-CPAs (bd. dirs. 1998—, sec. 1998-99, treas. 1999-2000, v.p. 2000-02, pres. elect 2002-03, pres. 2003-04), Md. Bar Assn. (mem. tax section coun. 2003—), Montgomery County Bar Assn. (chmn. tax sect. 1991-92, treas. 1996-97), D.C. Bar Assn., Md. Assn. CPAs, D.C. Inst. CPAs, Nat. Assn. Cert. Valuation Analysts v.p. Md. chpt. 2003—), Inst. Bus. Appraisers, Md. Soc. Accts., Estate Planning Coun. Suburban Md. (sec. 2004-05, v.p. 2005—), Phi Alpha Delta. Office: 25 W Middle Ln Rockville MD 20850-2214 Office Phone: 301-838-3204. Business E-Mail: ddejong@steinsperling.com.

DE JONG, GORDON FREDERICK, educational consultant; b. Berea, Ky., Aug. 6, 1935; s. Frederick Henry and Elizabeth (DeVries) De Jong; m. Caroline Jane Miller, July 1, 1961; children: Judith Kristen, Gregory Gordon, Graham Austin. BA, Ctrl. Coll., Pella, Iowa, 1957; MA, Univ. Ky., Lexington, Ky., 1960, PhD, 1963. Instr. Univ. Ky., Lexington, Ky., 1961—63; asst. prof., full prof. Pa. State Univ., Univ. Pk., Pa., 1963—91; sr. fellow East-West Ctr., Honolulu, 1978—79; vis. faculty Netherlands Grad. Sch. in Demography, 1994; disting. prof, dir., grad. program in demography Pa. State Univ., Pa., 1992—. Dir. Population Rsch. Inst., Pa. State Univ., 1974—76, 1982—88; rsch. cons. Govt. Thailand, Philippines, South Africa, 1983—. Editor: (acadmic book) Migration Decision Making, 1981, Social Demography, 1972, (journal) Demography, Population Assn. of Am., 1987—90; contbr. articles to profl. jour. Demographic advisor Exec. officers and Legislators Commonwealth of Pa., 1980—; Task Force on Aging, mem. Atty. Gen. Pa., 1993—2000. Mem.: Faculty Senate, Pa. State Univ., Population Assn. of Am. (chair), Am. Sociol. Assn. (chair). Achievements include research in 27 competitively awarded rsch. grants in demography issues internat; expert scholar on immigration and internal. migration; Founder and dir. of grad. program in demography, Pa. State Univ. Avocations: music, sports. Office: Population Rsch Inst 506 Oswald Tower University Park PA 16802

DE JONG, JAMES EDWARD, conductor; b. Holland, Mich., Nov. 5, 1963; s. Edward De Jong and Kathryn Selles. Worship dir. Harderwyk Ministries, Holland, 1995—; assoc. condr. Holland Chorale, Mich., 2004—. Dir. Revelation, Holland, 2000—02; leader tenor sect. Holland Chorale, Holland, 1998—2001; choir master Holland Mar. Festival, Holland, 1999. Singer: (tenor soloist) Misa Luba, A New Creation. Music coord. Neighbors Plus Celebrate Faith Festival, Holland, 2000—05; centennial music dir. 14th St. Christian Ref. Ch., Holland, 2003. Recipient Spl. Merit award, Holland Christian H.S., 1982, Marvin Baas Choral award, 1982, Music Acad. scholarship, Grand Rapids Jr. Coll., 1982, Calvin Coll., 1983. Republican. Avocations: baseball, travel, live music. Home: 141 W 32nd St Holland MI 49423 Office Phone: 616-399-9190. Personal E-mail: jamesdj@comcast.net.

DE JONGH, JOHN P., JR., real estate company executive; Grad., Antioch Coll. Commr. fin. U.S. V.I., 1987—90, exec. asst. to comr. fin., 1990—92; sr. mng. cons. Pub. Fin. Mgmt., Inc., 1993—96; pres., CEO Lockhart Cos., Inc., St. Thomas, 1996—, also bd. dirs.; chmn. Lockhard Real Estate; pres. Lockhart Ins.; co-head Lockhart Fin. Svcs.; dir. Lockhart Ventures, Inc. Chmn. U.S. V.I. Water and Power Authority, 1987—92; exec. dir. U.S. V.I. Pub. Fin. Authority, 1988—90; chmn. U.S. V.I. Tax Rev. Bd., 1987—90; sec. U.S. V.I. Banking Bd., 1987—90; mem. U.S. V.I. Small Bus. Devel. Agy., 1987—90. Pres. Karen Ingeborg Lockhart Found., Cmty. Found. U.S. V.I., St. Thomas/St. John C. of C. Office: PO Box 7020 St Thomas VI 00801

DEJULIUS, LEON F., JR., lawyer; b. Davenport, Iowa; BSBA magna cum laude, St. Louis Univ., 1998; JD summa cum laude, Univ. Notre Dame, 2002. Bar: Pa. 2003. Law clk. to Hon. Diarmuid F. O'Scannlain U.S. Ct. Appeals (9th cir.), Portland, Oreg., 2002—03; law clk. to Hon. William H. Rehnquist U.S. Supreme Ct., Washington, 2003—04; assoc. Jones Day, Pitts., 2004—. Editor (in chief): Notre Dame Law Rev.; editor: (exec.) Nat. Symposium Editl. Bd., Harvard Jour. Law & Pub. Policy. Office: Jones Day One Mellon Bank Center 31st Fl 500 Grant St Pittsburgh PA 15219-2502 Office Phone: 412-394-9528. Business E-Mail: lfdejulius@jonesday.com.

DEKANICH, STEVEN JOHN, materials scientist, metallurgist; s. Joe Dekanich and Margaret Sluniski; m. Rosa Linda Dobler, Aug. 10, 1974; 1 child, Annette Maria. B of Engring., Youngstown State U., 1974. Mgr. metallurgical svcs. lab. Martin Marietta/Union Carbide, Oak Ridge, Tenn.,

1978—90; mem. sr. devel. staff Martin Marietta Energy Systems, 1990—92; mgr. materials devel. lab. Lockheed Martin/Martin Marietta Energy Sys., 1993—95; sr. ops. mgr. M4 Environ. Mgmt., Inc., 1995—97; sr. materials engr., project mgr. Sci. Applications Internat. Corp., 1997—2001; prin. materials engr. Alstom Power, Knoxville, 2001—02; materials engring. specialist BWXT-Y-12, Oak Ridge, 2002—, larger chamber SEM project lead, 2003—. Chmn., bd. dirs. Tenn. Mountain Writers, Oak Ridge, 1994—; bd. dirs. Hospitality Ho. Meth. Hosp. Found., 1995—; vol., mem. steering com. Am. Cancer Soc., 2004. Mem.: ASM Internat. (mem. exec. com. 1980), Internat. Metallurgical Soc. (bd. dirs. 1995—99, Jacques-Lucas Gold Model award 1979). Achievements include patents in field. Avocations: writing, woodworking, fishing, hiking, travel. Home: 103 Lake Hills Dr Oak Ridge TN 37830 Office: BWXT Y-12 Bear Creek Rd Oak Ridge TN 37831 E-mail: dekanichsj@y12.doc.gov.

DE KANTER, ELLEN ANN, English and foreign language educator; b. Spokane, Wash., Mar. 10, 1926; d. George L. and Alison P. (Christy) Tharp; m. Scipio de Kanter, Feb. 2, 1949 (dec.); children: Scipio, Georgette, Robert, Adriana. BA, Mexico City Coll.-U. of Ams., 1947; MEd, U. Houston, 1972, MA in Spanish, 1974, EdD, 1979. Dir. bilingual edn. U. St. Thomas, Houston, 1979—2005. Editor Tex. Assn. Bilingual Edn. Jour., 2004-05; Contbr. articles to profl. jours. 11 Tchr. Tng. grants undergrad. and grad. students, U. St. Thomas, 1986—. Mem. Nat. Assn. Bilingual Edn. (chmn. 1989 conf., program chair 1993 conf.), Houston Area Assn. Bilingual Edn. (pres. 1987-88), Inst. Hispanic Culture (bd. dirs. 1989-90). Home: 3015 Meadowview Dr Missouri City TX 77459-3308 E-mail: dekanter@stthom.edu.

DEKEN, JEAN MARIE, librarian, archivist; b. St. Louis, Apr. 5, 1953; d. Cornelius John and Loretta Frances (McGuire) D.; m. James Roger Reed, Jan. 2, 1981. BA in English summa cum laude, Washington U., 1974, MA in English, 1976; M in Libr. Info. Sys., San Jose State U., 2002. Cert. archivist Acad. Cert. Archivists. Archivist Mo. Botanical Garden, St. Louis, 1975-78; mgmt. analyst Nat. Archives and Records Svc., St. Louis, 1978-81, supervisory archives specialist, 1981-82; instr. of English St. Louis Community Coll., St. Louis, 1982-83; curator John W. Barriger III collections St. Louis Merc. Libr., 1983-85; libr. Ralston Purina, St. Louis, 1985-86; mgr. libr. svcs. Maritz, Inc., St. Louis, 1986-87; supervisory archivist Nat. Archives and Records Adminstrn., St. Louis, 1987-96; archivist Stanford U. Stanford Linear Accelerator Ctr., 1996—. Author: Henry Shaw: His Life and Legacy, 1977, Stanford Linear Accelerator Center, Celebrating 40 Years: A Photo History, 2002; contbr. articles to profl. jours. Mem.: Soc. Calif. Archivists, Soc. Am. Archivists (webmaster electronic records sect.), Midwest Archives Conf., Stanford Hist. Soc. (webmaster). Avocation: swimming. Office: Stanford U Stanford Linear Accelerator Ctr 2575 Sand Hill Rd MS82 Menlo Park CA 94025

DE KENESSEY, STEFANIA MARIA, composer; b. Budapest, Hungary, Oct. 6, 1956; came to U.S., 1967; d. Zoltan Elek and Stefania Ivanova Kenessey; m. Andrew Henry Chapman, June 20, 1976; children: Dora Rosalia, Jordan Spencer. BA, Yale U., 1976; MFA, Princeton U., 1978, PhD, 1984. Prof. music New Sch. U., N.Y.C., 1980—2000, artist-in-residence, 2001—. Founder, artistic dir. The Derriere Guard, N.Y.C., 1997—. Composer: (Operas) The Monster Bed, The Other Wise Man, (orchestra) Cutting Loose, Manned Flight, Wintersong, Summer Nights, (chamber) Shades of Darkness, Beating Down, Magic Forest Dances, Sunburst, (songs) High Summer, In Memoriam, Autumn Elegy, The Muse Is Not Amused, The Daughters of Odessa, Girl in the Mirror, Jumping Jacks, Mothers and Daughters, Elizabethan Lyrics, (films) Art Under the Radar, The Last Angry Man, The Passing, (albums) Shades of Dark, Shades of Light, Two By three, Sunbursts, Sing for the Cure, An American Sampler, The Orchestra According to the Seven. Meet the Composer grantee, 1990—. Mem. ASCAP (Std. Music award 1990—), Nat. Assn. Composers (sec. East Coast chpt. 1985-92), Internat. Alliance for Women in Music (founding pres. 1993-94), Am. Women Composers (pres. 1990-93). Avocations: novels, poetry, theater, visual and fine arts. Home: 171 W 71st St Apt 2A New York NY 10023 Office: 27 West 67th St Studio 1FW New York NY 10023 E-mail: dekeness@att.net.

DEKIEFFER, DONALD EULETTE, lawyer; b. Newport, R.I., Nov. 8, 1945; s. Robert and Melissa (Hibberd) deKieffer; m. Nancy Kishida, June 27, 1970; 1 child, Nathan Hiroyuki. BA, U. Colo., 1968; JD, Georgetown U., 1971. Bar: U.S. Supreme Ct. 1982, U.S. Ct. Appeals (D.C. cir.) 1971, U.S. Dist. Ct. D.C. 1971, U.S. Ct. Claims 1971, U.S. Ct. Internat. Trade 1971. Mem. profl. staff Senate Rep. Policy Com., Washington, 1969—71; assoc. Collier, Shannon, Rill & Edwards, 1971—74; ptnr. Collier, Shannon, Rill, Edwards & Scott, 1974—80, deKieffer, Berg & Creskoff, 1980; gen. counsel U.S. Trade Rep., 1981—83; ptnr. Plaia, Schaumburg & deKieffer, 1983—84, Pillsbury, Madison & Sutro, 1984—92, deKieffer, Dibble & Horgan, 1992—. Mem. Presdl. Transition Team, 1980—81. Author: How to Lobby Congress, 1981, Doing Bus. with the USA, 1984, Doing Bus. with Romania, 1985, Doing Bus. in the U.S., 1985, Doing Bus. with the New Romania, 1991, Internat. Bus. Traveler's Companion, 1992, How Lawyers Screw Their Clients, 1996, The Citizen's Guide to Lobbying Congress, 1997. Mem.: ABA, Fed. Bar Assn., D.C. Bar Assn., Internat. Antitrust Soc., Am. Soc. Internat. Law. Office: deKieffer & Horgan 729 15th St NW Ste 800 Washington DC 20005-2105 Office Phone: 202-783-6900. Business E-Mail: ddekieffer@dhlaw.com.

DEKKER, EUGENE EARL, biochemistry educator; b. Highland, Ind., July 23, 1927; s. Peter and Anne (Hendrikse) D.; m. Harriet Ella Holwerda, July 5, 1958; children: Gwen E., Paul D., Tom R. AB, Calvin Coll., 1949; MS, U. Ill., 1951, PhD, 1954. Instr. U. Louisville Med. Sch., 1954-56; instr. biol. chemistry U. Mich. Med. Sch., Ann Arbor, 1956-58, asst. prof., 1958-65, assoc. prof., 1965-70, prof., 1970-94, assoc. chmn. dept., 1975-88, emeritus prof., 1994—. Served with USN, 1945—46. Mem. AAAS, Am. Chem. Soc., Am. Soc. Biol. Chemists, Am. Soc. Plant Physiologists, Oxygen Soc., Protein Soc., Sigma Xi, Phi Lambda Upsilon. Mem. Christian Reformed Ch. Home: 4001 Glacier Hills Dr Apt 126 Ann Arbor MI 48105-3655 Office: U Mich Med Sch Dept Biol Chemistry Ann Arbor MI 48109-0606 Business E-Mail: eedekker@umich.edu.

DEKKER, GEORGE GILBERT, literature educator, writer; b. Long Beach, Calif., Sept. 8, 1934; s. Gilbert J. and Laura (Barnes) D.; m. Linda Jo Bartholomew, Aug. 31, 1973; children by previous marriage: Anna Allegra, Clara Joy, Ruth Siobhan, Laura Daye. BA in English, U. Calif.-Santa Barbara, 1955; MA in English, 1958; M.Litt., Cambridge U. (Eng.), 1961; PhD in English, U. Essex (Eng.), 1967. Lectr. U. Wales, Swansea, 1962-64; lectr. in lit. U. Essex, 1964-69, reader in lit., 1969-72, dean Sch. Comparative Studies, 1969-71; assoc. prof. English Stanford (Calif.) U., 1972-74, prof., 1974—2001, prof. emeritus, 2001—, chmn. dept., 1978-81, 84-85, Joseph S. Atha prof. humanities, 1988—, dir. program in Am. Studies, 1988-91, assoc. dean grad. policy, 1993—96, 2000—02. Author: Sailing After Knowledge, 1963, James Fenimore Cooper the Novelist, 1967, Coleridge and the Literature of Sensibility, 1978, The American Historical Romance, 1987, The Fictions of Romantic Tourism, 2005; editor: Donald Davie: The Responsibilities of Literature, 1983 Nat. Endowment Humanities fellow, 1977; Inst. Advanced Studies in Humanities fellow U. Edinburgh (Scotland), 1982; hon. fellow, Clare Hall Cambridge, 1997, Stanford Humanities Ctr., 1997. Mem. Am. Lit. Assn. Democrat. Office: Stanford U Dept English Stanford CA 94305 Office Phone: 650-723-2635. *Over the past forty years I have divided my personal and professional life between the U.S. and Britain; not England alone, but Ireland, Scotland and Wales, too. This experience has given the distinctive stamp to my work as a teacher and writer, making me as much at home with Scott as with Hawthorne, with a British as well as an American university.*

DEKKERS, MARIJN E., electronics executive; b. The Netherlands; PhD in Chem. Engring., U. Eindhoven, The Netherlands. Rsch. scientist R&D Ctr. GE, Schenectady, NY, various operating positions, 1985—95; joined Allied-Signal, 1995; pres. electronics materials divsn. Honeywell Internat. (formerly AlliedSignal), Sunnyvale, Calif.; COO Thermo Electron Corp., Waltham, Mass., 2000—02, pres., CEO, 2002—. Contbr. articles to profl. jours. Achievements include patents in field. Office: Thermo Electron Corp PO Box 9046 81 Wyman St Waltham MA 02454-9046*

DEKMEJIAN, RICHARD HRAIR, political science professor; b. Aleppo, Syria, Aug. 3, 1933; came to U.S., 1950, naturalized, 1955; s. Hrant H. and Vahede V. (Matossian) D.; m. Anoush Hagopian, Sept. 19, 1954; children: Gregory, Armen, Haig. BA, U. Conn., 1959; MA, Boston U., 1960; Middle East Inst. cert., Columbia U., 1964, PhD, 1966. Mem. faculty SUNY, Binghamton, 1964-86; prof., chmn. dept. polit. sci. U. So. Calif., Los Angeles, 1986-90, prof. internat. bus. Marshall Sch. Bus.; also master Hinman Coll., 1971-72. Lectr. Fgn. Svc. Inst., Dept. Def., Dep. State, 1976-87; vis. prof. Columbia U., U. Pa., 1977-78; cons. Dept. State, AID, USIA, UN, Dept. Def. Author: Egypt Under Nasir, 1971, Patterns of Political Leadership, 1975; Islam in Revolution, 1985, 2nd edit., 1995, Ethnic Lobbies in U.S. Foreign Policy, 1997, Troubled Waters: The Geopolitics of the Caspian Region, 2001, The Just Prince: A Manual of Leadership, 2003; contbr. articles to profl. jours. Pres. So. Tier Civic Ballet Co., 1973-76. Served with AUS, 1955-57. Mem. Am. Polit. Sci. Assn., Middle East Inst., Middle East Studies Assn., Internat. Inst. Strategic Studies, Skull and Dagger, Pi Sigma Alpha, Phi Alpha Theta. Office: U So Calif Dept Polit Sci Los Angeles CA 90089-0044 Office Phone: 213-740-3619. Business E-Mail: dekmejia@usc.edu.

DEKOK, DAVID, writer, reporter; b. Holland, Mich., July 17, 1953; s. Paul W. and Olga (Kilian) DeK.; m. Lisa W. Brittingham, Oct. 1, 1988; children: Elizabeth B., Lydia B. BA, Hope Coll., Holland, 1975. Reporter The News-Item, Shamokin, Pa., 1975-87, The Patriot-News, Harrisburg, Pa., 1987—. Cons. PBS documentary Centralia Fire, 1982-83; guest lectr. Bucknell U., Lewisburg, Pa., 1988-97. Author: Unseen Danger: A Tragedy of People, Government and Centralia Mine Fire, 1986, republished, 2000. Del. Mich. Dem. Conv., 1972; mem. St. Stephen's Episcopal Sch. Bd., 1999—, chmn. tech. com. Recipient Keystone Press award Pa. Newspaper Pubs. Assn., 1979, 86, 87, 90, 99, Pub. Svc. award AP Mng. Editors of Pa., 1981, Janus award Mortgage Bankers Am., 1992. Mem. Investigative Reporters and Editors, Nat. Press Club (Freedom of the Press award 1995), Soc. Profl. Journalists (pres. ctrl. Pa. chpt. 1989-91, Spotlight award 1995), Newspaper Guild (pres. local 16 2004—). Episcopalian. Home: 113 Conoy St Harrisburg PA 17104-1608 E-mail: ddekok@mac.com.

DEKOOL, L.M. (THEO), food products executive; With CPC Benelux, B.V., Buhrmann Tetterode; v.p. fin. Household and Pers. Care divsn. Sara Lee/DE, Netherlands, 1990—93, CFO, 1995—96, Blokker retail chain; v.p. Sara Lee Corp., Chgo., 1996—2001, sr. v.p., 2001, exec. v.p., 2002—, chief fin. & adminstr. officer. Office: Sara Lee Corp 10151 Carver Rd Cincinnati OH 45242*

DEKOSKY, STEVEN TRENT, neurologist; b. Camden, N.J., Mar. 23, 1947; s. Aaron and Evelyn (Gorlen) DeK.; m. Beverly Nelson; children: Allison. Lauren. AB in Psychology, Bucknell U., 1968; MD, U. Fla., 1974. Diplomate in neurology Am. Bd. Psychiatry and Neurology. Postdoctoral fellow, instr. neurology U. Va. Sch. Medicine, Charlottesville, 1978-79; asst. prof. neurology, anatomy U. Ky. Coll. Medicine, Lexington, 1979-85, assoc. prof. anatomy and neurology, 1985-90, interim chmn. dept. neurology, 1985-87; grad. faculty U. Ky. Grad. Sch., Lexington, 1981-90; prof. psychiatry U. Pitts. Sch. Medicine, 1990—, prof. neurology, neurobiology, 1990—, grad. faculty, 1991—, interim chair dept. neurology, 2000—01, chair dept. neurology, 2002—. Vis. prof. psychology U. Calif., Irvine, 1983; co-dir. Alzheimer's disease rsch. ctr. U. Pitts. Med. Ctr., 1990-94, dir., 1994—, U. Ky. Med. Ctr., 1985-90; task force on Alzheimer's disease State of Ohio, Columbus, 1986-92; med. sci. adv. bd. Alzheimer's Assn., 1992—; dir. behavioral neurology of aging tng. program U. Pitts., 1990—. Mem. Am. Neurol. Assn. (Presd. award 1988), Am. Acad. Neurology, Am. Soc. Neurochemistry, Am. Heart Assn. (stroke coun.), N.Y. Acad. Scis., Soc. Neurosci., Soc. Exptl. Neuropathology (councillor 1990-92), Behavioral Neurology Soc., Am. Bd. of Psychiatry and Neurology. Office: U Pitts 3471 5th Ave Ste 811 Pittsburgh PA 15213-2593 Office Phone: 412-692-4622. Business E-Mail: dekoskyst@upmc.edu.

DE KRETSER, MICHELLE, writer; b. Colombo, Sri Lanka; arrived in Australia, 1972; Studied French, U. Melbourne, Australia; MA, U. Sorbonne, Paris. Former sr. editor Lonely Planet. Founding editor Australian Women's Book Rev., 1989—92. Author: The Rose Grower, 1999, The Hamilton Case, 2004 (Commonwealth Writers Prize for S.E. Asia and South Pacific Region, 2004, Encore Prize, Brit. Soc. Authors, 2004). Office: Little, Brown & Co 1271 Ave of the Americas New York NY 10020*

DEKU, AFRIKADZATA, Afrikan scholar, writer, lecturer, educator; b. Kadjebi, Ghana, Dec. 13, 1949; m. Yayra Deku; children: Mawunyo, Nukunu Akusika, Mawulolo, Afrikamawuse, Afrikamawuedem, Afrikaworlanyo. BA with honors, U. Cape Coast, Ghana, 1977; MSc, U. Ife, Nigeria, 1981; diploma, Inst. Internat. D'Administrn. Pub., Paris, 1983; MPhil, U. Paris XI, Sorbonne, 1983, PhD, 1985. Lic. mediator, arbitrator, negotiator. Ind. post-doctoral rsch. scholar U. Denver, 1986-87; founder, chief exec., prof. pan-Afrikan studies Afrikan Culture Inst., 1987—; vis. assoc. prof. Afrikan history Clark Atlanta U., 1990-91; vis. assoc. prof. Africana studies Morris Brown Coll., Atlanta, 1990; vis. assoc. prof. Afrikan culture, continuing edn. dept. Ga. State U., 1990; pub. The Afrikan Truth, 1994—, Continental Afrikan Pubs., 1990—. Vis. prof. French and Afrikan lit. Wofford Coll., Spartanburg, S.C., 1988-89, Converse Coll., Spartanburg, 1989; trainer, guest speaker Clemson U. 4-H Operation Pride, 1994—; ACT ESL placement test fairness reviewer and cons., 2000; participant ACT ESL Teleconf., 2000; resident guest artist Kennedy Middle Sch., Aiken, S.C., 1997, Jackson (S.C.) Mid. Sch., 1998, S.C. Writers Ann. Workshop Conf. Faculty, Manuscript Evaluator; poetry judge Pan-Afrikan Poetry Recitals, Myrtle Beach, 1998; founder, bd. chmn. Afrikamawu Miracle Mission made up of: Continental Afrikan Devel. Authority, KADA, Continental Afrikan Govt. Implementation Authority, KAGO, and Continental Afrikan Culture Promotions Authority, KAFO; guest artist Spartanburg Internat. Festival, 1999, Ea. Lit. Fellowship, Clinton, S.C., 1999, Greenville (S.C.) Internat. Festival Cultural Awareness summer jubilee, 2001, Greenville Summer Jubilee Festival for the Arts, 2001; guest author Lee County Young Authors Ann. Conf., Bishopville, S.C., 1999; lectr., spkr. and cons. in field. Author: (poetry) We Are All Continental Afrikans, 1991, Sacred Verses For My Afrikan Queens, 1992, Sacred Afrikan Spiritual Power From Within, 1993, Agbenoxevie Menye, Ablodesafui, Agbedefu (Ewe poetry), Courage, Mere Afrique, Cris de Tonnerre, Coups de Marteau, A Toi le Paradis de Ma Langue (Afrikan Poetry in French); (plays) No Where is Heaven, Breaking the Bloody Sword of Apartheid, (rsch. books) L'Union Continentale Africaine, vols. 1-3, 1986, Continental Afrikan Power Now, 1987, The Afrikan-Centric Perspective of the Afrikan World Crisis, 1988, Continental Afrikan Manifesto, 1999, Continental Afrikan Power in Figures, 1989, 2d edit., 2004, The Afrikan Gospel of Total Happiness Now and Always, 1991, The Power of Afrikan-Centricity, 1992, AFRIKAMAWUNYA or the Holy Afrikan Bible, 1997, Continental Afrika: From Two Hundred Million Seasons to the Present, 1994, The Power and Benefits of Continental Afrikan Culture, 1994, How to Be a Continental Afrikan Again, 1994, Positive Self-Knowledge Technology, 1994, Positive Goal Achievement Technology, 1994, 2d edit., 2005, Positive Problem-Solving Technology, 1996, Positive Decision-Making Technology, 1999, 2d edit., 2005, Continental Afrikan Constitution of the Continental Afrikan Republic, 1998—; Why the World Bank /IMF/UN etc. Are a Curse Rather Than a Blessing to Afrika, 2005, The Afrikan Origin of Humanity, 2005, Behold Your Continental Afrikan Savior Afrikadela Is Born, 2005, Still Slaves in the "Land of the Free," 2005, Passing Our ABC Test of our Afrikan-Centricity, 2005, spkr. in field. Founder Afrikan-Centricity Movement, Continental Afrikan Govt. Orgn., Continental Afrikan Found., Continental Afrikan Devel. Authority. Grantee S.C. Arts Commn., 1990-91; scholar Ghana Govt., 1970-72, 73-77, Commonwealth, 1975, 77, 78, French Govt., 1982-85; recipient OYO State Bursary award, 1980-81, Spartanburg, S.C. Arts Coun. award, 1989-90, S.C. Arts Commn. grant, 1990-91. Mem. ABA, Am. Arbitration Assn., S.C. Coun. for Mediation and Alternative Dispute Resolution, Internat. Biog. Assn., Internat. Platform Assn., French PhD Holders Assn., African Studies Assn., African Heritage Studies Assn., Am. Polit. Sci. Assn. Home: 182 Stribling Cir Spartanburg SC 29301-1651 also: Box 209 Dansoman Accra Ghana Office Phone: 864-576-7992. Personal E-mail: afrikalion@aol.com, afrikafiaga@walla.com.

DE LAAT, GILBERT, automotive executive; b. Paterson, N.J., Apr. 2, 1957; s. Elmer Gilbert and Marjorie Lucille De Laat. BA, Columbia U., 1979; MPP, JD, Harvard U., 1984. Adminstr. legal and regulatory affairs Isuzu Motors Am., City of Industry, Calif., 1985-93; mgr. govt. affairs Nat. Hwy. Traffic Safety Adminstrn. Subaru Am., Inc., Cherry Hill, NJ, 1995—2001; mgr. GM govt. affairs Subaru R&D, Ann Arbor, Mich., 2001—. Congressional aid U.S. Congressman Andrew Maguire, Paramus, N.J., 1977-78. Mem. ABA, UN-USA, World Affairs Coun., Am. Trauma Soc., Am. Polit. Sci. Assn., Sonoma County Wine Growers Assn., N.Am. Riding Handicapped Assn. Republican. Roman Catholic. Avocations: sailing, martial arts, golf. Home: 385 Rolling Meadows Dr Ann Arbor MI 48103 Office: Subaru Rsch and Devel Inc 3995 Rearch Park Dr Ann Arbor MI 48108 E-mail: gdeLaat@subaru.com.

DELACATO, CARL HENRY, education educator; b. Pottstown, Pa., Sept. 10, 1923; s. Ercole S. and Julia (de Bartolomeo) D.; m. Janice E. Fernstrom, June 20, 1951; children— Elizabeth F., Carl Henry, David F. BS in Edn, West Chester State Coll., 1945; MS in Edn, U. Pa., 1948, Ed.D., 1952. Asst. headmaster Chestnut Hill Acad., Phila., 1945-64; founder, dir. Chestnut Hill Reading Clinic, 1948; prof. Avery Postgrad. Inst., Phila., 1963-73; prof., chmn. dept. devel. edn. U. Plano, Tex., 1965-70; asso. dir. inst. Para Le Orgn. Neurologica, Buenos Aires, 1967-70, Insts. Achievement Human Potential, Phila., 1953-73; dir. Inst. Rehab. of Brain Injured, Morton, Pa., 1974-89, Centrao de Rahabilitacao NS de Gloria, Sao Paulo, Brazil, 1976—. Pres. Delacato & Delacato Consultants in Learning, Plymouth Meeting, Pa., 1970—; cons. Asociacion Para Ayuda Lesionados Cerebales, Barcelona, Spain, 1970-89; hon. dir. of The Delacato Center, Holon, Israel, 1974—; dir. of Delacato project at Padagogische Hochschule Rheinland Abteilung fur Heilpadaggogik, Koln, W. Ger., 1975—, Delacato project TIKVA, Haifa, Israel, 1976—; bd. dirs. Delacato and Delacato, Naples, Italy, Delacato Consultation Ctr., Benelux; others. Author: The Treatment and Prevention of Reading Problems, 1959, Diagnosis and Treatment of Speech and Reading Problems, 1963, Elementary School of the Future, 1964, Neurological Organization and Reading, 1966, A New Start for the Child with Reading Problems, 1970, The Ultimate Stranger, The Autistic Child, 1974, contbr. numerous articles on rehab. and edn. to profl. jours.; editor: Am. Lectures in Edn. and Learning, 1969— . Vice pres. U.S. World Orgn. Human Potential, 1968-73; mem. Pa. Commn. Human Potential, 1969-70, Gov. Sergipe (Brazil) Commn. Human Potential, 1968-70; bd. dirs. Centre for Neurol. Rehab., Morton, Pa., 1974— . Recipient Disting. Alumnus award West Chester Coll., 1978, award Greater Long Beach (Calif.) Soc. for Autistic Children, 1977, Diploma Socio-Benmento Porto Allegra, Brazil, 1965, Diploma de Honra Ho Merito Piracioba, Brazil, 1965, Diploma de Reconheciemen, to Sao Paulo, 1965, Diploma e Medalha Comemorative de APAE Rio de Janeiro, 1965, Gold Medal Honor Brazil, 1960, Statuette with Pedestal award Internat. Rehab. Forum, 1966, 1st. Trailblazer award U. Plano, 1966 Mem. NSF. Home: Apt N14 Lincoln Woods 9801 Germantown Pike Lafayette Hill PA 19444

DELACATO, CARL HENRY, lawyer; b. Aug. 18, 1955; BA, Haverford Coll., 1977; JD, Villanova Law Sch., 1980. Bar: Pa. 1980. Ptnr. Hecker Brown Sherry and Johnson, Phila., 1979—. Faculty Dickinson Law Sch. Trial Advocacy Seminar, 1991; fellow, faculty mem. Acad. Advocacy, Pa., 1992—. Mem. ABA (tort ins. practice sect.), Phila. Bar Assn. (chair ins. programs com., mem. civil litigation and real property sects., Chancellor's Spl. Recognition award 1994). Office: Hecker Brown Sherry Johnson 1700 Two Logan Sq 18th and Arch Sts Philadelphia PA 19103

DELACATO, JANICE ELAINE, special education educator, consultant; b. Bklyn., June 6, 1926; d. Frode Siegfried and Vilma Fernstrom; m. Carl Henry Delacato, June 20, 1951; children: Elizabeth Delacato Putnam, Carl Henry, David Fernstrom. AB, Bryn Mawr Coll., 1948. Tchr. Rydal Hall, Ogontz Sch., Pa., 1948-49, The Spence Sch., N.Y.C., 1949-50, Chestnut Hill Acad., Phila., 1950-52; co-dir. The Chestnut Hill Reading Clinic, Phila., 1951-65, Delacato & Delacato Cons. in Learning, Phila., 1972-88; mgr. Morton (Pa.) Book Store, 1972-88; co-dir. The Delacato & Delacato Conf. Autism & Learning Disabilities, 1979-82. Editor newsletter Temple U. Med. Ctr. Women's Aux., Phila., 1953-65; class editor Bryn Mawr Coll. Alumnae Bull., 1966-79. Chmn. fund-raising com. Springside Sch., 1969-71; treas. Main St. Fair Antiques Booth, Chestnut Hill Hosp., 1965-77. Recipient Main St. Fair award Chestnut Hill Hosp., 1972. Mem. AAUW, Phila. Cricket Club. Republican. Unitarian Universalist. Home: Apt 1014 Lincoln Woods 9801 Germantown Pike Lafayette Hill PA 19444

DELACERDA, MELISSA GRINER, lawyer; b. St. Petersburg, Fla., Mar. 17, 1952; d. Joseph Henry and Dorothy Jean (Stephens) G.; m. Fred G. DeLacerda, June 17, 1972. BS, Memphis State U., 1973; JD, U. Tulsa, 1979. Bar: Okla. 1979. Tchr., elem. sch., Crowley, La., 1974-75; sports reporter Daily Advertiser, Lafayette, La., 1974-75; assoc. firm Bird & Hochderffer, Stillwater, Okla., 1979-80; sole practice law, Stillwater, 1980— . Bd. dirs. Alcoholism Council Area Okla., 1981-82, Stillwater Domestic Violence Svcs., 1979—. Mem. Okla. Bar Assn. (pres. elect, 2002-03, pres. 2003-04), Payne County Bar Assn. (sec. 1984), Am. Trial Lawyers Assn., Bus. and Profl. Women Stillwater (pres. 1985), Stillwater C. of C. (ambassador 1982-84). Office: Law Office of Melissa DeLacerda 301 S Duck St PO Box 1252 Stillwater OK 74076

DE LA CRUZ, CARLOS, wholesale distribution executive; b. Havana, Cuba; arrived in Miami, 1975; m. Rosa de la Cruz; 5 children. BS, U. Pa., 1962, MBA in fin., 1963; JD, U. Miami Sch. Law, Fla., 1972. Car dealership exec.; chmn. Eagle Brands, Coca-cola Bottlers, PR. Co-founder Cuba Study Group; co-chmn. Mesa Redonda. Named one of top 200 art collectors, ARTnews Mag., 2004; recipient Silver Medallion Brotherhood Award, Nat. Conf. of Christians & Jews, Distinguished Svc. Award, Fla. Internat. U., Social Responsibility Award, Urban League, Alexis de Tocqueville Award for outstanding philanthropy, United Way, 1997, Simon Weisenthal Ctr. Nat. Cmty. Svc. Award, 1998. Achievements include becoming first hispanic chmn. United Way (1990) & U. Miami Bd. Trustees (1999). Avocation: collector of contemporary art, especially Latin Am. Mailing: 5 Harbor Pl Key Biscayne FL 33149-1715*

DELA CRUZ, JOSE SANTOS, retired state supreme court justice; b. Saipan, Commonwealth No. Mariana Islands, July 18, 1948; s. Thomas Castro and Remedio Sablan (Santos) Dela C.; m. Rita Tenorio Sablan, Nov. 12, 1977; children: Roxanne, Renee, Rica Ann. BA, U. Guam, 1971; JD, U. Calif., Berkeley, 1974; cert., Nat. Jud. Coll., Reno, 1985. Bar: No. Mariana Islands, 1974, U.S. Dist. Ct. No. Mariana Islands 1978. Staff atty. Micro. Legal Svcs. Corp., Saipan, 1974-79; gen. counsel Marianas Pub. Land Corp., Saipan, 1979-81; liaison atty. CNMI Fed. Laws Commn., Saipan, 1981-83; ptnr. Borja & Dela Cruz, Saipan, 1983-85; assoc. judge Commonwealth Trial Ct., Saipan, 1985-89; state supreme ct. chief justice Supreme Ct. No. Mariana Islands, 1989-95; retired, 1995. Mem. Conf. of Chief Justices, 1989-95, Adv. Commn. on Judiciary, Saipan, 1980-82; chmn. Criminal Justice Planning Agy., Saipan, 1985-95. Mem. Coun. for Arts, Saipan, 1982-83; chmn. Bd. of Elections, Saipan, 1977-82; pres. Cath. Social Svcs., Saipan, 1982-85. Mem. No. Marianas Bar Assn. (pres. 1984-85). Roman Catholic. Avocations: golf, reading, walking. E-mail: joedlc@hotmail.com. *There is an inherent goodness in every person, no matter how bad that person may appear. Recognizing that goodness in each gives us hope that the future of mankind will not be destructive.*

DE LA CRUZ, ROSA, art collector; b. Havana, Cuba; m. Carlos de la Cruz; 5 children. Co-founder Moore Space, Fla., 2001. Curator (exhibitions) THAT PLACE, Moore Space, 2002. Named one of top 200 collectors, ARTnews Mag., 2004; recipient Alexis de Tocqueville Award for outstanding philanthropy, United Way, 1997, Simon Weisenthal Ctr. Nat. Cmty. Svc. Award, 1998. Mem.: Mus. Contemporary Art N. Miami, Miami Art Mus. (aquisition com.), Mus. Contemporary Art Chgo. (exhibitor com.). Avocation: collector of contemporary art, especially Latin Am. Mailing: 5 Harbor Pl Key Biscayne FL 33149-1715 E-mail: rdelacr@aol.com.*

DELA CRUZ HALSTEAD, ELSIE LYNN MANGLONA, human resources specialist; b. Majuro, Marshall Islands, Federated States of Micronesia, Oct. 5, 1969; d. Edward Tamaoki and Florida Manglona Dela Cruz; m. Mark Esteves Halstead, Oct. 16, 2004; children: Travis Thomas Dela Cruz Diaz, Tomiko Florilyn Dela Cruz Diaz. MBA, Hawaii Pacific U., BS in bus. adminstrn., 1992, M in bus. adminstrn., 1997. Cert. human resource concepts BRAINBENCH, 2003, recruiting concepts BRAINBENCH, 2003, sexual harassment awareness BRAINBENCH. Pers. officer No. Marianas Coll., Saipan, 1997—2003, dir. human resources office, 2003—. Mem. Cir. K Club, Honolulu, 1989—89. Mem.: Soc. Human Resources Mgmt. (dir. 2005—), Napu Outrigger Canoe Club. Avocations: paddling, travel, wine tasting, reading, walking. Home: 504132 Chalan Kanoa Saipan MP 96950 Office: Northern Marianas College Po Box 501250 Saipan MP 96950 Office Phone: 670-234-5498. Office Fax: 670-235-3696. Personal E-mail: elsieh@nmcnet.edu.

DE LA FUENTE RAMIREZ, JUAN RAMON, academic administrator; b. Mexico City, Sept. 5, 1951; married; 3 children. MSc, U. Minn.; postgrad. psychiatry, Mayo Clinic. Prof. Nat. Nutrition Inst.; rschr. Mex. Inst. Psychiatry; dir. health rsch. program U.N.A.M., mem., 1980, dir. med. faculty, 1991—94, health sec., 1994; sec. health Govt. of Mex., Washington, 1995—99; served in Cabinet as rector U.N.A.M., 1999; rector Nat. Autonomous U. Mex., 2002—; chief resident U. Minn. Vis. prof. several fgn. univs; v.p. Internat. Assn. Univs. Author books on health rsch. Vol. internat. health orgns.; investigator Nat. Inst. Nutrition, Mex. Inst. Psychiatry, Mexico City. Recipient Eduardo Liceaga prize, Nat. Acad. Medicine. Office: U Nat Autonoma Mex DGSCA Circuito Exterior Ciudad U Delegacion Coyoacan Distrito Federal CP 04510 Mexico

DE LA GARZA, LUIS ADOLFO, lawyer; b. Mission, Tex., Nov. 22, 1943; s. Adolfo and Carmen (Barrera) de la G.; m. Sherry Lynn Hatcher, Apr. 12, 1974; children: Miguel, Gabriel, Lucas. BBA, U. Tex., 1966; MBA, U. Hawaii, 1972; JD, U. Tex., 1975. Bar: Tex. 1975. Counsel El Paso Natural Gas Co., Tex., 1975-78; sr. counsel El Paso Co., Houston, 1978-81; sr. atty., asst. sec. Valero Energy Corp., San Antonio, 1981-87, v.p. corp. rels., 1987-97, PG&E Gas Transmission-Tex. Corp., San Antonio, 1997-2000; ptnr. Holland & Knight, LLP, San Antonio, 2001—03. Co-founder, pres., CEO Texen Power Co., 2000. Chmn. March of Dimes San Antonio Walk Am., 1996, 97; bd. dirs., chmn. Latino leadership for the libr. campaign San Antonio Pub. Libr. Found.; bd. dirs. Tex. Equal Access to Justice Found., comms. com., 1994-2003; bd. dirs. Valero Polit. Action Com., San Antonio, 1984-97, chmn., 1987-97; bd. dirs. Valero Fed. Credit Union, 1987-88; bd. dirs. World Affairs Coun., San Antonio, 1987, exec. com., 1988-90; scout leader Boy Scouts Am., San Antonio, 1984-2005; mem. Witte Coun., Witte Com., San Antonio Mus. Assn., 1985-90; bd. dirs., chmn. United Way Tex., mem. pub. policy com., 2000-03; bd. dirs. Tex. Civil Justice League; mem. bus. adv. coun. U. Tex., San Antonio; commr. Tex. Equal Access Justice Commn., 2001-2003. Capt. USMC, 1966-72, Vietnam. Decorated Air medal with 15 oak leaf clusters; named One of the Hundred Most Influential Hispanics in Am. Hispanic Bus. Mag., 1990, One of the Corp. Elite in Am. Hispanic Mag., 1990-2000; recipient Breaking Barriers award Nat. Hispanic Employees Assn., 1993, Vol. of Yr. March of Dimes 1998. Fellow Tex. Bar Found.; mem. Tex. Bar Assn., San Antonio Bar Assn. (chmn. corp. counsel sect. 1986-88), Greater San Antonio C. of C. (govtl. affairs, edn. coun. steering com., bd. dirs. 1987-90), Southside C. of C. (bd. dirs. 1989-90, 05), San Antonio Hispanic C. of C. (bd. dirs. 1989-91). Methodist. Office: Tex Power Co LLC 8940 Wurzbach Rd San Antonio TX 78240 Office Phone: 210-949-1846. Business E-Mail: ldelagarza@texenpower.com.

DELAHANTY, CARLOS ANTHONY, industrial engineer; b. Scottsdale, Ariz., May 3, 1965; s. Carlos Victor and Mary Martha (Santa Marina) D. BS in Indsl. Engring., Ariz. State U., 1991. Indsl. engr. Intel Corp., Chandler, Ariz., 1993, Gaylord Container Corp., Glendale, Ariz., 1994; project scheduling engr., planning cons. Lockwood Greene Engrs., Phoenix, 1994-95; project scheduling engr. Honeywell Air Transp. Sys., Phoenix, 1996; indsl. engring. cons. Knight Architects Engrs. Planners, Inc., Phoenix, 1997; project and cost control engr. Honeywell Indsl. Automation and Control, Phoenix and Houston, 1997-99; project controls engring. dept. mgr. Goss Graphic Sys., Westmont, Ill., 1999-2000; indsl. engr., master scheduler Intel Corp., Albuquerque, 2000—. Mem. Inst. Indsl. Engrs., Project Mgmt. Inst., Alpha Pi Mu. Roman Catholic. Avocation: amateur bowling. Office: Intel Corp 4100 Sara Rd Rio Rancho NM 87124 Home: 1701 E Meadowbrook Ave #131 Phoenix AZ 85016 Office Phone: 602-222-5349. E-mail: Anthony.Delahanty@Intel.com, anthonydelahanty@aol.com, adelahanty@kitchell.com.

DELAHANTY, REBECCA ANN, school system administrator; b. South Bend, Ind., Oct. 18, 1941; d. Raymond F. and Ann Marie (Batsleer) Paczesny; m. Edward Delahanty, June 22, 1963; children: David, Debbie. BA, Coll. of St. Catherine, Minn., 1977; MA, Coll. St. Thomas, Minn., 1983; PhD, Ga. State U., 1994. Cert. in adminstrn. and supervision Ga. Initiator, tchr. gifted kindergarten Dist. 284 Sch., Wayzata, Minn., 1977-83; gifted kindergarten coord. St. Barts Sch., Wayzata, 1983-85; prin. Dabbs Loomis Sch., Dunwoody, Ga., 1987-91; asst. to supt. Buford (Ga.) City Schs., 1993-98, supt., 1998-99; prof. Ga. State U., 1999-2000; ednl. cons., 2000—; adv. bd. U. Saint Thomas, Coll. Edu., 2001—. Staff devel. adv. coun. Ga. Contbr. Mem. adv. bd. Coll. Edn. U. St. Thomas, 2001—. Mem.: ASCD, Minn. Coun. Gifted and Talented, Minn. Assn. Gifted Children, Nat. Assn. Gifted Children, Am. Ednl. Rsch. Assn., Omicron Gamma, Phi Delta Kappa. E-mail: beckydelah@aol.com.

DE LA HOYA, OSCAR, Olympic athlete, professional boxer; b. Bel Air, Calif., Feb. 4, 1973; Olympic boxer, lightweight divsn., Barcelona, Spain, 1992; champion jr. lightweight divsn. World Boxing Orgn., 1994, former champion lightweight divsn., 1994—, Internat. Boxing Fedn., 1995—; champion lightweight divsn World Boxing Council, 1996—. Recipient Gold medal lightweight boxing divsn. Olympics, Barcelona, 1992; winner 4 championship titles in 4 different weight classes. Office: care Top Rank Boxing 3980 Howard Hughes Pkwy Ste 580 Las Vegas NV 89109-0995

DELAHUNT, WILLIAM D., congressman; b. Quincy, Mass., July 18, 1941; s. Bill Sr. and Ruth Delahunt; children: Kirstin, Kara. BA, Middlebury Coll., 1963; JD, Boston Coll., 1967. Asst. clk. Norfolk Superior Ct., 1968—70; legal counsel Quincy Police Dept., 1970; pvt. practice law, 1971-75; dist. atty. State of Mass., 1975—96; mem. 105-108th Congresses from 10th Mass. dist., 1997—; mem. judiciary resources com. 105th Congress from 10th Mass. dist. Mem. Quincy City Coun., 1971; mem. Mass. Ho. of Reps., 1973-75, asst. majority leader. With USCGR, 1963-71. Democrat. Office: 1317 Longworth House Washington DC 20515-2110*

DELAMOTHE, CASSANDRA MACON, lawyer; b. Trenton, NJ, Mar. 8, 1958; d. Mary Harris and Paul Macon; children: Danielle C., Phillipe A., Rachelle M., Justin D. BA, The Coll. of NJ., Trenton, New Jersey, 1980; JD, Fordham U. Sch. of Law, N.Y.C., 1996. Bar: NY 1997, NJ 1997, U.S. Dist. Ct. (so. dist. NY) 1999. Pvt. practice atty., Cortlandt Manor, NY, 1997—. Contbr. articles to profl. jours. Mem.: ABA, Westchester County Bar Assn., NY State Bar Assn. Office: Law Office of Cassandra M DeLaMothe 2117 Crompond Road Suite 25 Cortlandt Manor NY 10567 Office Phone: 914-737-4909. Business E-Mail: delamothelaw@aol.com.

DELAND, MICHAEL REEVES, energy executive; b. Boston, Dec. 13, 1941; s. Frank Stanton and Susan Robertson (Reeves) D.; m. Jane Slocum, Aug. 18, 1973; children: Stanton, Melissa, Holly. AB, Harvard U., 1963; JD, Boston Coll., Newton, Mass., 1969; PhD (hon.), Taegu (South Korea) U., 1998. Bar: Mass. 1970, U.S. Supreme Ct. 2000. Mgr. U.S. Congl. campaign, Concord, Mass., 1970; staff asst. to pres. U. Mass., Boston, 1971; chief enforcement br. EPA, Boston, 1971-76, regional adminstr., 1983-89; environ. counsel Environ. Rsch. Tech., Concord, 1976-83; chmn. Pres. Coun. on Environ. Quality, Washington, 1989-93; vice chmn. Am. Flywheel Systems Inc., Washington, 1993-2000. Bd. adv. HYDRO Que., 1993-96. Chmn. bd. Nat. Orgn. on Disability, 1990—; vice-chmn. World Com. on Disability, 1996—; bd. dirs. Assoc. Harvard Alumni, 1977-79, Mgmt. Inst. Environ and Bus., 1990-96, World Resources Inst., 1997—, Boston Globe Newspaper Co., 1998-2003; mem. corp. Woods Hole Oceanographic Instn., 1993-2002; trustee Noble and Greenough Sch., Dedham, Mass., 1976-82; vestryman Trinity Episcopal Ch., Boston, 1976-78, St. John's Ch. Lafayette Sq., Washington, 1998-2002. Lt. (j.g.) USN, 1963-65. Recipient award Mass. Audubon Soc., 1986, Spl. Achievement award Nat. Wildlife Fedn., 1989. Mem. The Country Club (Brookline, Mass.), Beverly Yacht Club, Met. Club, Chevy Chase Club, Phi Beta Kappa (hon.). Republican. Avocation: sailing. Home: 4901 Loughboro Rd NW Washington DC 20016-3456 Office: 910 16th St NW Ste 500 Washington DC 20006-2903 Fax: 202-833-4174.

DELANEY, EUGENE A., electronics executive; BS, So. Ill. U.; MBA, DePaul U. Chmn. Motorola China Electronics Ltd. Motorola, Inc., 2002—, joined, 1978, fin. analyst comm. sector, 1978, contr. Motorola Credit Corp., 1986, ops. mgr. ctrl. region cellular bus., 1989—94, v.p., dir. ops. ctrl. and N.E. region Pan Am. wireless infrastructure group, 1994—95, v.p., gen. mgr. Japan cellular infrastructure divsn., 1995—97, corp. v.p. cellular infrastructure group, 1997—98, exec. v.p., pres. global rels. and resources orgn., 2002—05, sr. v.p. Europe, Middle East, Africa and Asia/Pacific Govt. Enterprise Mobility Solutions Schaumburg, Ill., 2005—. Office: Motorola Inc 1303 E Algonquin Rd Schaumburg IL 60196*

DELANEY, JEFFREY J., lawyer; b. Queens, NY, Aug. 17, 1967; BA summa cum laude, Pace Univ., 1989, JD summa cum laude, 1992. Bar: Conn. 1992, NY 1993. Ptnr. Corp. & Securities practice, co-chmn. Global Energy industry team Pillsbury Winthrop Shaw Pittman, NYC. Editor (rsch. & writing): Pace Law Rev. Office: Pillsbury Winthrop Shaw Pittman 1540 Broadway New York NY 10036 Office Phone: 212-858-1292. Office Fax: 212-858-1500. Business E-Mail: jeffrey.delaney@pillsburylaw.com.

DELANEY, JOHN, protective services official; s. John Paul and Ellen Lee Delaney; m. Abigail Arellano Camargo, Oct. 10, 1978; children: Patricia, Kathleen, Stephanie, John Michael Jr. PhD in Bus. Adminstrn., Calif. Coast U., Santa Ana, 1998. Police officer, Blythe, Calif., 1986—90; pub. safety mgr. Cmty. Hosp. of San Bernardino, 1990—. Cons. Peace Offering Solutions, Colton, Calif., 1992—. Author: (novels) Lights Out, Gangz, Behind the Badge, The Green Shadow, The Zenith Resolution, The Ring Killer. Named Police Officer of Yr., City of Blythe, 1987; recipient City commendations, 1987, 1988. Democrat-Npl. Roman Catholic.

DELANEY, JOHN ADRIAN, academic administrator; b. Lansing, Mich., June 29, 1956; s. James Edward and Mary Ann (Langius) D.; m. Gena Barrett, Sept. 6, 1980; children: William Langius, Adrian Anne, Marye Margaret, James Barrett. BA in History, U. Fla., 1977, JD, 1981. Bar: Fla. 1981. With State Atty.'s Office, Jacksonville, Fla., 1981-91; chief asst. state atty. Jacksonville, Fla., 1986-91; gen. counsel City of Jacksonville, 1991-92, 94-95, chief of staff, mayor, 1992-94, mayor, 1995—2003; pres. U. North Fla., Jacksonville, 2003—. Mem. Leadership Jacksonville, 1986, Leadership Fla.-13; chmn. bd. St. Paul's Episcopal Sch. Mem. Inns of Ct., Fla. Blue Key (pres. 1980), Rotary, Delta Upsilon. Roman Catholic. Avocation: camping. Home: 110 Bowles St Jacksonville FL 32266-4917 Office: Office of the Pres U North Fla Jacksonville FL 32224-2648 Office Phone: 904-620-2500. Business E-Mail: jdelaney@unf.edu.

DELANEY, JOHN WHITE, lawyer; b. Springfield, Mass., Feb. 28, 1943; s. Frank T. and Emily (White) D.; m. Betsey Secor; children: Erin, Elizabeth. AB, Harvard U., 1964, JD, 1967. Bar: Mass. 1967, U.S. Dist. Ct. Mass. 1968. Staff asst. to U.S. senator Leverett Saltonstall, Washington, 1966; law clk. Mass. Superior Ct., Boston, 1967-68; asst. atty. gen. State of Mass., Boston, 1968-69; legis. asst. Gov. Commonwealth of Mass., Boston, 1969-73; asst. sec. consumer affairs and bus. regulation Commonwealth of Mass., 1973-76; exec. dir. Boston Mcpl. Rsch. Bur., 1976-80; dir. govt. and community affairs Bank of Boston, 1980-89; sr. ptnr. Hale and Dorr, Boston, 1989—2004; ptnr. Wilmer Cutler Pickering Hale and Dorr LLP, Boston, 2004—. Dir. New England Legal Found., Boston, 1986—. Dir. Robert F. Kennedy Action Corps, Boston, 1973-92; sec. Coordinating Com., Boston, 1984-87; trustee, mem. exec. com. Mass. Taxpayers Found., Boston, 1986—; trustee Boston Mcpl. Rsch. Bur., 1991—; mem. adv. coun. The Trustees of Reservations, 1993-99, 2000—; dir. Greater Boston C. of C., 1992—; pres. Friends of RFK Children's Action Corps, Inc., 1996—2003; dist. rep. Dedham (Mass.) Town Meeting, 1986—; mem. Mass. IOLTA Com., 2004—. Fellow Mass. Hist. Soc.; mem. Boston Bar Assn. (mem. coun. 2003—), Clover Club Boston. Office: Wilmer Cutler Pickering Hale and Dorr LLP 60 State St Boston MA 02109-1800 Office Phone: 617-526-6939. Business E-Mail: john.delaney@wilmerhale.com.

DELANEY, KEVIN FRANCIS, retired military officer, health facility administrator; b. Wolcott, Conn., Sept. 23, 1946; s. John and Mildred Delaney; m. Patricia Delaney, June 8, 1968; children: Kelly, Diana, Seana. BS in Engring., U.S. Naval Acad., Annapolis, Md., 1968; M in Bus., George Washington U., 1977; postgrad., MIT, 1984, Harvard U., 1993. Commd. USN, 1968, advanced through grades to rear admiral, 1991, ret., 1998; commdg. officer Heli Anti-Sub Squadron 32, Norfolk, Va., 1980-82, 82-84; air boss USS Guadalcanal, 1984-86; commdg. officer HSL-31, wing comdr. Helo Sea Control Wing 3, Mayport, 1987; commdg. officer Naval Air Sta., Jacksonville, Fla., 1989-91; comdr. shore activities U.S. Atlantic Fleet, Norfolk, Va., 1993-94; dir. shore installation mgmt. Chief Naval Ops., Washington, 1994-95; comdr. Navy Region S.E. Jacksonville, 1995-98; exec. v.p. Coggin Automotive Group, Jacksonville, Fla., 1998-2000; exec. v.p., COO HealthScreen Am., Jacksonville, Fla., 2000—02; pres., CEO Delaney & Assocs. Consulting, Mil. Reunions Inc.; pres. Futura Sales Inc. Bd. mem. 12 Who Care, Jacksonville, 1995-, Vol. Jax, Inc., Jacksonville, 1995-98, Childrens' Haven, Orange Park, Fla., 1995-98; chmn. Navy/Marine Corp. Relief Soc., Jacksonville, 1995-98; bd. dirs. Salvation Army, United Way, USO, YMCA, Jr. Achievement, N.E. Fla. Safety Coun., World Affairs Coun., Freedoms Found.; vice chmn. Toyota Gator Bowl; past chair United Way Campaign N.E. Fla.; pres. Ronald McDonald House; bd. govs., pres. Fla. C.C. Jacksonville Found; bd. trustees Jacksonville U.; bd. dirs. Jacksonville C. of C.; chmn. Jacksonville Beaches C. of C. Mem. Fla. C. of C. (bd. dirs.), Rotary (pres. 2000), N.E. Fla. Safety Coun. (pres.). Home: 4551 Swilcan Bridge Ln N Jacksonville FL 32224-5618 Office: Delaney and Assocs 8505 Baycenter Rd Ste 300 Jacksonville FL 32256 Office Phone: 904-733-7336. E-mail: kdelaney@military-reunions.com.

DELANEY, KIM, actress; b. Phila., Nov. 29, 1961; 1 child, Jack. Appeared in (TV series) All My Children, 1981-84, 94, Tour of Duty, 1987, The Fifth Corner, 1992, NYPD Blue, 1995-2001 (Emmy award 1997), Philly, 2001, CSI: Miami, 2002, 10.5: Apocalypse, 2005 (TV movies) First Affair, 1983, Perry Mason: The Case of the Sinister Spirit, 1987, Cracked Up, 1987, Christmas Comes to Willow Creek, 1987, All My Darling Daughters, Please Take My Daughters, 1988, Something Is Out There, 1988, The Broken Cord, 1992, Lady Boss, 1992, Closer and Closer, The Disappearance of Christina, 1993, Tall, Dark, and Deadly, 1995, Tall Dark and Deadly, 1995, All Lies End in Murder, 1997, The Devil's Child, 1997, Love and Treason, 2001, (films) That Was Then...This Is Now, 1985, The Delta Force, 1986, Hunter's Blood, 1987, Campus Man, 1987, The Drifter, 1988, Hangfire, 1991, Body Parts, 1991, The Force, 1994, Inferno, Darkman II: The Return of Durant, 1994, Dark Goddess, 1994, Serial Killer, 1995, Project: Metalbeast, 1995, Closer and Closer, 1995., Mission to Mars, 2000. Avocations: biking, swimming, working out, watching films. Office: care The Gersh Agy attn Bob Gersh 232 N Canon Dr Beverly Hills CA 90210-5302 also: care Melissa Prophet Mgmt 1041 N Formosa Ave Los Angeles CA 90046 also: CSI Miami Prodn Office El Segundo Studios 2265 E El Segundo Blvd El Segundo CA 90245*

DELANEY, MARGARET L., academic administrator; BS in Chemistry summa cum laude, Yale U., 1977; PhD, MIT, 1983. Rsch. scientist Scripps Instn. Oceanography, LaJolla, Calif., 1983—84; asst. prof. marine scis. U. Calif., Santa Cruz, 1983—90, assoc. prof. marine scis., 1990—96, prof. ocean scis., 1996—, interim exec. vice chancellor, provost, 2004—. Mem. U.S. Adv. Com. to the Ocean Drilling Program, 1996—, mem. exec. com., 1998—. Editor: Paleoceanography, 1996; mem. editl. rev. bd.: Marine Geology, 1991—. Fellow: Am. Geophysical Union (mem. com. on paleoceanography 1990—94, 1996—); mem.: Soc. for Sedimentary Geology, Oceanography Soc., Geochemical Soc., Assn. for Women Geoscientists (Outstanding Educator award 1993), Sigma Xi. Office: Interim Campus Provost and Exec Vice Chancellor 280 McHenry Libr Univ Calif Santa Cruz CA 95064

DELANEY, MARTIN, not-for-profit developer; Founding dir. Project Inform, San Francisco, 1985—. Spkr. on AIDS treatment and rsch.; mem. Coun. Nat. Inst. Allergy and Infectious Diseases NIH; mem. bd. adv. Inst. Human Virology, U. Md., Baltimore. Co-author: Strategies for Survival: A Gay Men's Health Manual for the Age of AIDS, 1987; editor: Project Inform's HIV Drug Book, 1995; contbr. writings to med. pubs. and nat. mags. Recipient Stonewall award, Anderson Prize Found., 1991, Award of Courage, Found. AIDS Rsch., 2001. Mem.: Am. Assn. Med. Coll. (mem. task force on fin. conflicts of interest in clin. rsch. 2001—). Office: Project Inform 205 13th St # 2001 San Francisco CA 94103

DELANEY, MARY ANNE, retired theology studies educator; b. Waltham, Mass., Feb. 15, 1926; d. Thomas Joseph and Mary Teresa (Berry) D. BA, Regis Coll., 1953; MEd, U. Mass., Boston, 1973; MDiv, Andover Newton Theol. Sch., Newton Ctr., Mass., 1978. Tchr. various schs., Mass., 1953-73; pastoral counselor Boston City Hosp., 1974-76; dir. pastoral care Cape Breton Hosp., Sydney River, Canada, 1978-81, Nova Scotia Hosp., Dartmouth, 1981-86, Misericordia Hosp., Edmonton, Canada, 1986-91; pastoral counselor Assn. Pastoral Edn., Waltham, Mass., 1992-96, Emmanuel Coll., Boston, 1996—2001; supr. pastoral edn. Leland Retirement Home, Waltham, 1992—2001; ret., 2001. Vice chair bioethics consultative svc. Misericordia Hosp., Edmonton, 1987-91; vis. scholar Andover Newton Theol. Sch., 1991-92. Trustee Pastoral Inst., Halifax, N.S., Can., 1981-86; mem. commn. on ecumenism Archdiocese of Halifax, 1982-86; mem. of the Congregation of Sisters of St. Joseph, Boston, 1945—. Mem. Can. Assn. Pastoral Edn. (cert. com. 1987-91), Assn. for Clin. Pastoral Edn. (cert. supr., accreditation com. 1993-98, cert. com. 1998-2001). Roman Catholic. Avocations: international travel, classical music, art. Home and Office: 637 Cambridge St Waltham MA 02453-5911 E-mail: sr.marydelaney@mediaone.net.

DELANEY, MATTHEW SYLVESTER, mathematics professor, academic administrator; b. Ireland, Nov. 26, 1927; arrived in U.S., 1947, naturalized, 1952; s. Joseph C. and Elizabeth M. (Bergin) Delaney. Student, St. John's Coll., 1947—51; BA, Immaculate Heart Coll., L.A., 1958; MS, Notre Dame U., 1960; PhD, Ohio State U., 1971. Ordained priest Roman Cath. Ch., 1951. Assoc. pastor L.A. Cath. Diocese, 1951—55; instr. math., physics Pius X H.S., Downey, Calif., 1955—58, vice prin., 1960—62; instr. math. Immaculate Heart Coll., 1962—65, asst. prof., 1972—76, prof., 1976—, asst. acad. dean., 1973—78; dean acad. devel. Mt. St. Mary's Coll., L.A., 1978—82, acad. dean, 1978—91, prof. math., 1991—96, prof. emeritus, 1996—. Contbr. articles to math. publs., profl. jours. Grantee, NSF, 1959—60, 1961. Mem.: NY Acad. Scis., Math. Assn. Am., Am. Math. Soc., Internat. Union Crystallography. Democrat. Achievements include Formal recognition of the eponyms, "Delaney Sets" and "The Delaney Symbol" in the disciplines of discrete geometry and math. crystallography. Home: Apt 32C 13700 El Dorado Dr Seal Beach CA 90740-3843 Office: Mount Saint Mary's Coll 12001 Chalon Rd Los Angeles CA 90049-1526 E-mail: mdel2611@adelphia.net.

DELANEY, ROBERT FINLEY, columnist, political sociologist, lecturer; b. Fall River, Mass., Aug. 2, 1925; s. Joseph Patrick and Mary Gertrude (Finigen) D.; m. Mary Elizabeth Flynn, Jan. 21, 1950; children: Mary Ellen, Flynn, Nancy, Carrie, Deirdhre, Sarah; m. Patricia Ann Riley, Jan. 21, 1984. Student, Dartmouth Coll., 1943; B.N.S., Holy Cross Coll., 1946; postgrad., Harvard U., 1946, U. Vienna, 1956; MA, Boston U., 1948; BSL.S., Cath. U. Am., 1955; D.H.L. (hon.), U. Mass., 1981. Fgn. service info. officer Dept. of State, 1950—69; asst. dir. USIA, Washington, 1968-69; dir. Edward R. Murrow Center Public Diplomacy Fletcher Sch., Tufts U., Boston, 1969-70; pres. Thunderbird Grad. Sch. Internat. Mgmt., Phoenix, 1970-71; Milton Miles prof. internat. relations U.S. Naval War Coll., Newport, RI, 1971—81; pres. Michael W. Moynihan Public Affairs, Washington and N.Y., 1981—83; chmn. RFD, Inc., Newport, 1983-91; sr. policy advisor U.S. Space Sta., NASA, 1994-97; adj. prof. internat. mgmt. Salve Regina U., Newport, 1972-78; pres. Global Scis., Ltd., 1985-89; pub. affairs cons. Esso S.A.; editor Newport This Weekly, 2003. Author: Your Career in Foreign Service, 1957, Literature of Communism in America, 1958, The Psychology of Terror, 1980, Terror as a Tactic, 1988; editor: This is Communist Hungary, 1959, First Fifty Years of American Public Diplomacy, 1969, International Communications and the New Diplomacy, 1970, The Fourth Estate: The Impact of the Media on National Security Decision-Making, 2002. Incorporator Newport Hosp., 1979-82; mem. Rochambeau Bicentennial Commn., 1979-80; bd. advisors Salve Regina Coll., 1973-77; naval aide to Gov. of R.I., 1976-81; R.I. press sec. Edward Kennedy primary campaign, 1980. Served to capt. USNR, 1943-81, PTO, Vietnam. Decorated Air medal (U.S.), Medal of Merit (Vietnam); Knight (Chev.) of St. Lazarus (KSL), Mil. and Hospitaller Order of Jerusalem; recipient citation for Inter-am. Cooperation Orgn. Am. States, 1965, Volker Found. award, 1954-55, Superior Service award Dept. State, 1962, Disting. Service award, 1965. Mem. Pub. Rels. Soc. Am., Am. Fgn. Service Assn., Pres.' Assn., Am. Mgmt. Assn., Navy League, Naval War Coll. Found., Inter Univ. Seminar on Armed Forces, Delta Phi Epsilon, Alpha Sigma Nu. Clubs: N.Y. Yacht (N.Y.C.), Reading Room (Newport), Dacor House, Met., Nat. Press (Washington). Roman Catholic. Home: 4265 Via del Villett Venice FL 34293-7060

DELANEY, ROBERT PATRICK, librarian, writer; b. Miles City, Mont., Mar. 16, 1961; s. Alfred John and Ann Lois (D'Ambrosia) D. AAS in Broadcast Comm., Suffolk County C.C., 1982; BA in English magna cum laude, Dowling Coll., 1985; MSLS, L.I. U., 1987. Grad. asst. Southampton (N.Y.) Campus Libr., L.I. U., 1986-87, libr., 1987—. Babylon (N.Y.) Pub. Libr., 1987-88; librarian Farmingdale (N.Y.) Campus Libr., Poly. U., 1988, C.W. Post Campus Libr., L.I. U., Brookville, N.Y., 1989—. Author: Dreamfinder, 1986, Nightfawn and the Gleam, 1989, Brightblossom and the Gleam, 1990, The Sinking Star, 1990, Sex and the Single Elf, 1993, The Quiet and Fertile Plain, 1995, There Goes the Neighborhood, 1997, Back to Camelot, 2001. Mem. Suffolk County Libr. Assn., Film Music Soc., Internat. Arthurian Soc. Avocation: Shakespeare, poetry, filmscores, Athurian legends, mythology. Home: 34 University Dr Lake Ronkonkoma NY 11779-1905

DELANEY, TERENCE (TERRY) P., gas industry executive; b. Jan. 1956; Internal auditor Sunoco Inc., 1979, mgr. investor rels., 1995—2000, dir. investor rels. and strategic planning, 2000—03, v.p. investor rels. and planning Phila., 2003—. Office: Sunoco Inc Ten Penn Ctr 1801 Market St Philadelphia PA 19103-1699*

DELANEY, TIM, sociologist, educator; s. Thomas James and Mary Elizabeth (Ryan) Delaney. AAS, Cayuga CC, Auburn, NY, 1977; BS, SUNY, Brockport, 1979; MA, Calif. State U.-Dominguez Hills, Carson, CA, 1990; PhD, U. Nev., Las Vegas, 1994. Asst. prof. Suny-Oswego Coll., 2003—. Editl. adv. bd. Collegiate Press, San Diego, 2001. Author: Community, Sport and Leisure, 2001, Classical Social Theory: Investigation and Application, 2004; editor: Values, Society & Evolution, 2002, Mafia, Terrorism and Totalitarianism, 2004; author: Contemporary Social Theory: Investigation and

Application, 2005, American Street Gangs, 2006. Media expert Pub. Rels., Suny-Oswego, Oswego, 2002—. Recipient Cert. of Appreciation, Russian Acad. of Scis., 1999, Moscow State U., 2001. Mem.: State Sociological Assn. NY (pres. 2001—04), North Am. Soc. for Sociology of Sport (pres. 2000—01, 2003—04), Pacific Sociol. Assn., Phi Kappa Phi, Alpha Kappa Delta. Avocations: running, weightlifting, writing, travel, improving social awareness. Home: 29 Birch Ln Apt 240 Oswego NY 13126-4309 Office: Suny-Oswego Dept Sociology Oswego NY 13126 Business E-Mail: tdelaney@oswego.edu. E-mail: delanyt@osweed.edu.

DELANEY-LAWRENCE, AVA PATRICE, secondary school educator; b. Knoxville, Tenn., Apr. 12, 1960; d. William J. and Lena (Guilford) Delaney; 1 child, Brian. BS, U. Tenn., 1982; MA, Clark Atlanta U., 1994. Cert. English tchr. grades 7-12, Ga., Tenn.; Leadership cert., 2000. Substitute tchr. Knoxville City Schs., 1982; English tchr. Chattanooga (Tenn.) City Schs., 1982-85, Atlanta Pub. Schs., Therrell H.S., 1985-99, Booker T. Washington H.S., 1999—; instr. edn. curriculum Clark Atlanta U., 1997—2002. Testing cons. R&R Evaluations, Decatur, Ga., 1985-87; ednl. cons. Harris Learning Sys., Atlanta, 1988-2000. Mem. Nat. Assn. Educators, Nat. Coun. Tchrs. English, Zeta Phi Beta. Home: PO Box 724373 Atlanta GA 31139-1373

DE LANGE, TITIA, research scientist; BA, MS, PhD in biochemistry, U. Amsterdam; MS, Nat. Inst. Med. Rsch.; PhD in biochemistry, Netherlands Cancer Inst.; postdoctoral fellow, U. Calif., San Francisco, 1989; doctorate (hon.), U. Utreecht. With Rockefeller U., NY, 1990—, asst. prof., 1990, assoc. prof., 1994, prof., 1997, Leon Hess prof. and head lab. cell biology and genetics, 1999. Recipient Rita Allen award, 1995, Burroughs Wellcome Fund Toxicology Scholar award, 1997, Cancer Rsch. award, NY Cmty. Trust, 1997, Sr. Scholar award, Ellison Med. Found., 2000, Paul Marks Prize, Meml. Sloan Kettering Cancer Ctr., 2001, AACR Women in Cancer Rsch. Charlotte Friend Meml. Lectureship, 2004. Mem.: Dutch Royal Acad. Sci. Office: Rockefeller Univ 1230 York Ave New York NY 10021

DELANO, DANNAE L., lawyer; b. Hays, Kans., July 5, 1975; d. Danny Delgado and Vicki L. Barrett-Delgado; m. Aaron R. Delano, Oct. 4, 2003; 1 child, Will O. BA, So. Ill. U., 1997, JD, 2000. Bar: Mo. 2000, Ill. 2001. Assoc. Suelthaus & Walsh, P.C., St. Louis, 1999—2004, Thompson Coburn LLP, St. Louis, 2004—. Dir. Family Support Coun., St. Louis. Named one of 30 Under Thirty, St. Louis Bus. Jour., 2004. Mem.: Profl. Women's Assn., Employee Benefits Assn. St. Louis, WEB Network Benefits Profls., Bar Assn. Met. St. Louis, Nat. Hispanic Bar Assn. Office: Thompson Coburn LLP One US Bank Plaza Saint Louis MO 63101 Office Phone: 314-552-6344. Office Fax: 314-552-7344. Business E-Mail: ddelano@thompsoncoburn.com.

DELANO, JONATHAN WILLIAM, lawyer, journalist; b. New Haven, Apr. 8, 1949; s. Hubert William and June Elizabeth (Sprague) Delano; m. Jane Marie Lahey. BA, Haverford Coll., 1971; JD, U. Pa., 1974; student, U. Edinburgh, Scotland, 1969-70. Bar: Pa. 1974, U.S. Dist. Ct. (we. dist.) Pa. 1974, U.S. Ct. Appeals (3d cir.) 1974, U.S. Supreme Ct. 1985. Assoc. Reed Smith Shaw & McClay, Pitts., 1974-77; chief staff U.S. Rep. Doug Walgren, Pitts., Washington, 1977-91; ptnr. Eckert Seamans Cherin & Mellott, Pitts., 1991-93; mng. dir. Meyer Darragh, 1998—2001; money & politics editor Sta. KDKA-TV, 2001—. Weekly columnist Pitts. Bus. Times, 1995—; adj. prof. pub. policy Carnegie Mellon U., 1995—. Bd. dirs. Magee Women's Health Found., Family Health Coun.; Dem. candidate Pa. Senate, 1984, U.S. Congress, 1994. Mem.: Allegheny County Bar Assn., Phi Beta Kappa. Episcopalian. Home: 90 Longuevue Pittsburgh PA 15228-1539

DELANO, LESTER ALMY, JR., advertising executive; b. New Bedford, Mass., Nov. 28, 1928; s. Lester A. and Beatrice (Thomas) D.; m. Margaret Dent (div.); 1 child, Leslie Ann; m. Helaine Shipper; children: Oliver Evan, Peter Franklin. Student, Amherst Coll., Brown U.; MA, U. Chgo. Mktg. cons., Chgo., 1950-54; v.p. North Advt., Inc., Chgo., 1955-60; pres. Dodge & Delano, Inc., N.Y.C., 1961-71, Tinker, Dodge & Delano, Inc., 1971-76; chmn., chief exec. officer Tinker, Campbell-Ewald Inc., N.Y.C., 1976-77; pres. Campbell-Ewald Internat., London, Eng., 1977-80, Marschalk Campbell-Ewald Worldwide, N.Y.C., 1980-85; chmn. exec. com. Lowe Marschalk Worldwide, 1986-87; exec. dir. The Lowe Group PLC, N.Y.C., 1987—2002; CEO Octagon Worldwide, 2001—02. Author: Creative Advertising Planning. Served with USN, 1945-48. Home: 115 Central Park W New York NY 10023-4153 E-mail: delano@speakeasy.net.

DELANO, VICTOR, retired naval officer; b. Washington, Dec. 20, 1919; s. Harvey and Marcia (Murdock) D.; m. Jacqueline Stinson (dec. 1990); children: Katherine Delano Jahnig, Harvey II. BSEE with distinction, U.S. Naval Acad., 1941; MS in Physics, MIT, 1949; postgrad., Indsl. Coll. Armed Forces, 1961-62. Ensign USN, 1941, advanced through grades to capt., 1959; staff comdr. 2d Fleet, 1956-58, Atlantic Fleet, 1963-65; chief of staff Atlantic Amphibious Force, 1966-67; with Office Chief of Naval Ops., 1967-69; ret., 1969; pres. Wichita Eagle-Beacon Pub., 1970-71. V.p., treas. Naval Hist. Found., Washington, 1980-99; trustee Naval Acad. Found.; trustee, bd. dirs. Avon (Conn.) Old Farms Sch., 1980-92, 95—; bd. dirs. Friends Nat. Zoo, Washington, 1971-80, Episc. Ctr. for Children, Washington, 1975-84, 88-94, Kingsbury Ctr., Washington, 1986-95. Decorated Legion of Merit (2), Bronze Star, Purple Heart. Mem. Naval Inst., Naval Acad. Alumni Assn., Mil. Order Carabao, Pearl Harbor Survivors Assn., Chevalier du Tastevin, Commanderie de Bordeaux (Naples), Chevy Chase Club, Metropolitan Club (Washington), Army-Navy Club, Eagle Creek Golf and Country Club (Naples, Fla.), Burning Tree Club. Avocation: golf. Home: 5610 Wisconsin Ave Apt 1409 Chevy Chase MD 20815-4439

DE LANOY, CHARLES JAMES, accountant; b. Detroit, May 26, 1956; s. Robert Le Roy and Helen Marie (Maciag) D.L. BA, Mich. State U., 1979. CPA, Mich. Fin. analyst Control Data Corp., Rochester, Mich., 1979-81; sr. mgr. nat. tax office BDO Seidman, Washington, 1981—95; v.p. fin. and CFO Klockner Pentaplast of Am., Gordonsville, Va., 1995—. V.p. Checker Drugs, Westland, Mich., 1981—, bd. dirs. Columnist for newspapers and mags. Mem. Am. Inst. CPA's, Mich. Assn. CPA's.

DELAP, MIRIAM ANNE, music educator; b. Wichita, Kans., Jan. 9, 1944; d. Ewald William and Norine Bertha (Scar) Nath; m. David Frank, Jr. DeLap, Dec. 21, 1968; children: David William, Lora Colleen. BA, MA, Wichita (Kans.) State U., 1966. Cert. elem. tchr. Kans., 1968. Tchr. Wichita (Kans.) Sch. Dist. McLean Elem., 1966—68; 6th grade tchr. Anchorage (Alaska) Sch. Dist. Nunaka Valley, 1969—71; 5th and 6th grade tchr. Lake Otis Elem., Anchorage, 1971—73, music tchr., 1983—. Prin. bassist Anchorage Symphony Orch., 1969—; adj. faculty bass tchr. U. of Alaska, Anchorage, 1996—; instr. record for Anchorage (Alaska) Sch. Dist., 1997—; adj. faculty music edn. Alaska Pacific U., 2004—. Recipient Oustanding Alaska Music Educators, Alaska Music Educators Assn., 2000, Tchr. of Excellence award, Brit. Petroleum Exploration Inc., 2000. Mem.: Alaska Orff Schulwerk (v.p. 1997—99), Am. Orff Schulwerk Assn., Music Educators Nat. Conf. Achievements include Created Miss Mimi's Music Room, thirty minute music program for preschool children, for sch. dist. TV channel in Anchorage. Office: Lake Otis Elem Sch 3331 Lake Otis Pkwy Anchorage AK 99508 E-mail: delap_miriam@asdk12.org.

DELAP, TONY, artist; b. Oakland, Calif., Nov. 4, 1927; s. Truman Henry and Catherine (Yontz) D.; m. Kathleen Rose Campbell, Dec. 27, 1964; children— Kelly Rose, Jack Henry. AA, Menlo Jr. Coll., 1947; student, Claremont Grad. Sch., 1947-49. Prof. U. Calif. at Irvine, 1965-91. Exhibited group shows, San Francisco Mus., Oakland Mus., Whitney Mus., U. Ill., Mus. Modern Art N.Y., L.A. County Mus., Pasadena Mus., one man shows, Dilexi Gallery, San Francisco, 1963, 67, Robert Elkon Gallery, N.Y.C., Felix Landau Gallery, L.A., 1966, 68, U. Calif. at Irvine, Nicholas Wilder Gallery, L.A., 1972, 74, 76, Calif. Inst. Tech., 1974, Calif. State U., Long Beach, 1974, John Berggruen Gallery, San Francisco, 1972, 76, Jan Turner Gallery, L.A., 1987, 89, 91, Modernism Gallery, San Francisco, 1986, 89, 92, 96, Klein Gallery, Chgo., 1985, Beatrix Wilhelm Gallery, Stuttgart, Germany, 1992, Gudrun Spielvogel Gallery, Munich, 1993, Works Gallery, Santa Ana, Calif., 1992, Allene Lapides Gallery, Santa Fe, N.Mex., 1992, Mark Moore Gallery, Santa Monica, Calif., 1994-95, 98, Calif. State U., Fullerton, 1994, Peter Blake Gallery, Laguna Beach, 2000, 2002, 2004, Patricia Faure Gallery, Santa Monica, Calif., 2004, Tony DeLap Retrospective Ex. at OCMA, Newport Beach, 2000, San Jose Mus. of Art, 2001; represented in permanent collections: Whitney Mus., Mus. Modern Art N.Y.C., Walker Art Inst., Tate Gallery, London, Long Beach Mus. Art, Los Angeles County Mus. Art, Santa Barbara (Calif.) Mus. Art, Newport Harbor Art Mus., Newport Beach, Calif., Guggenheim Mus., N.Y.C. Address: 225 Jasmine St Corona Del Mar CA 92625-3035

DELAPA, JUDITH ANNE, business owner; b. Bad Axe, Mich., Feb. 1, 1938; d. John Vincent and Ellen Agatha (Peters) McCormick; m. James Patrick DeLapa, Jan. 10, 1959; children: Joseph Anthony, James P. II, John M., Gina M. BS, Mich. State U., 1959, MA, 1985. Tchr. various schs., Mich., 1959-64; co-founder Saluto Foods Corp., Benton Harbor, Mich., 1963-76; founder Earthtone Interiors, St. Joseph, Mich., 1977-82, High Impact Coaching and Cons. Inc., Grand Rapids, Mich., 1987—. Mktg. rsch. and mgt. cons., writer various clients, nationwide. Author: High-Impact Business Strategies, 1993, The McCormick-DeLapa Family Cookbook, 1997, A Place Called Ireland, 2000, Was That Really Us God?, 2001. Past vice chair exec. bd. Grand Rapids Symphony Orch.; bd. dirs., pres. The Samaritan Found.; bd. dirs. Grand Rapids Art Mus. Judith A. DeLapa Perennial Garden named in her honor Mich. State U. Avocations: reading, travel, theater. Office: High Impact Coaching & Cons Inc 2505 E Paris Ave SE Ste 195 Grand Rapids MI 49546 E-mail: jdelapa@high-impact.com.

DE LA PENA, CORDELL AMADO, pathologist; b. Honolulu, Apr. 30, 1934; s. Eusebio de Guzman Awanan and Virginia Uyeno de Costa; m. Linda Laron Lapuz, Apr. 1, 1957; children: Leslie, Nina, Cordell Amado. MD, U. Santo Tomas, Manila, 1958. Diplomate Am. Bd. Anatomy and Clin. Pathology (subcert. in hematology), Am. Bd. Infection Control. Intern St. John's Hosp., Lowell, Mass., 1960-61; resident New Britain (Conn.) Gen. Hosp., 1963-67; pathologist St. Mary's Hosp., Clarksburg, W.Va., 1967, Union Protestant Hosp., Clarksburg, 1967, United Hosp. Inc., Clarksburg, 1967-78, pres. med. staff, 1974—, bd. dirs., chief pathologist, dir. lab. and blood bank, 1978—; dir. lab. Stonewall Jackson Meml. Hosp., 1998—, Webster Spring Meml. Hosp., 1998—. Cons. VA, St. Joseph's Stonewall Jackson Meml. hosps.; asst. prof. pathology W. Va. Sch. Medicine, 1980-81, dir. 1997—, clin. prof. pathology Sch. Medicine and Osteo. Sch. Medicine; clin. prof. med. tech. Fairmont State Coll.; pres. Harrison County Cancer Soc., 1974-76; bd. dirs. W.Va. United Health Sys. Fellow Coll. Am. Pathologists (ho. of dels. 1982-86. 88--), Am. Soc. Clin. Pathologists, Am. Soc. Hematology; mem. Internat. Acad. Pathology, Am., W.Va. (state councillor 1981-85, pres. 1987-88), med. assns., W.Va. Pathol. Soc. (treas. 1975-77, pres.-elect 1977-80, pres. 1980-81), Harrison County Med. Soc. (treas. 1977-78, pres. 1980-81), W.Va. State Soc. Hematology (pres. 1980-81), W.Va. Assn. Blood Banks (pres. 1982—), Assn. Philippine-Am. Pathologists (pres. 1981-83), Nat. Skeet Shooting Assn., W.Va. Bird Dog Club (pres. 1972), W.Va. Assn. Blood Banks (pres. 1982-83), Oreg. State Med. Assns., Orgn. State Med. Assn., Masons (pres.). Home: 209 Candlelight Dr Clarksburg WV 26301-9725 Office: United Hosp Clarksburg WV 26301

DE LA PENA-ALMAGUER, ERASMO, cardiologist, researcher; b. Saltillo, Coahuila, Mexico, Dec. 18, 1969; s. Erasmo and Rosalina (Almaguer-Vega); m. Maria del Socorro Tamez, Oct. 11, 1997; 1 child, Miranda De La Pena-Tamez. MD, Coahuila U., Mexico, 1992. Diplomate Bd. Cardiology, Bd. Internal Medicine. Clin. rsch. fellow nuc. cardiology Harvard Med. Sch., Brigham Women's Hosp., Boston, 1999—2000; clin. rsch. fellow cardiovasc. MRI and CT Stanford U., Calif., 2000—02; dir., founder, cardiovasc. imaging Christus-Muguerza Med. Ctr., Mexico. Instr., core radiology clerkship Harvard Med. Sch., Boston, 1999—2000. Contbr. articles to profl. jours. Dep. Mexican Bd. of Cardiology, Mexico City, Mexico, 2004—05. Scholar, Mexican Soc. of Cardiology. Fellow: Mexican Soc. of Cardiology. Achievements include research in non-invasive cardiovascular imaging. Avocations: computers, golf. Home: 2010 Madero Dr Brownsville TX 78526 Office: Hidalgo 2525 pte Col Obispado Nuevo Leon Monterrey 64040 Mexico Office Phone: 52-8183993470. Personal E-mail: edelapena@cvmed.stanford.edu.

DELAPP, TINA DAVIS, retired nursing educator; b. L.A., Dec. 18, 1946; d. John George and Margaret Mary (Clark) Davis; m. John Robert DeLapp, May 31, 1969; children: Julia Ann, Scott Michael. Diploma, Good Samaritan Hosp., Phoenix, 1967; BSN, Ariz. State U., 1969; MS, U. Colo., Denver, 1972; EdD, U. So. Calif., 1986. Health aide instr. Yukon-Kuskokwim Health Corp., Bethel, Alaska, 1970-71; asst. prof. nursing Bacone Coll., Muskogee, Okla., 1972-74; instr. nursing Alaska Meth. U., Anchorage, 1975-76; asst. prof. U. Alaska, Anchorage, 1976—2004, assoc. dean for nursing, 1986—96, dir. Sch. Nursing, 1996—2004, emeritus prof., 2004—. Mem. Alaska Bd. Nursing, 1989-92. Mem. editl. adv. bd. Jour. Nursing Edn., 2004—; contbr. articles to profl. jours. Treas. Atlanta Nurses Found., 2004—. Named Legend of Nursing, Alaska March of Dimes, 2004. Fellow: We. Acad. Nursing; mem.: Alaska Nurses Found. (treas. 2004—), Am. Assn. Coll. Nursing (mem. nominating com. 2003), Nat. League for Nursing Accreditation Comn. (program evaluator 1986—, eval. review panel mem. 2000—05), We. Inst. Nursing (chair program com. 1994—95, sec.-treas. 1995—2005, gov.-at-large 2005—, Jo Elinor Elliott Leadership award 2002), Sigma Theta Tau (pres. chpt. 1986—88, v.p. 1988—93, counselor 1995—2000). Personal E-mail: tdelapp@ak.net.

DE LA RENTA, OSCAR, fashion designer; b. Santo Domingo, Dominican Republic, July 22, 1936; s. Oscar and Maria Antonia (deFiallo) de LaR.; m. Francoise de Langlade, Oct. 31, 1967 (dec. 1983); 1 adopted child, Moises; m. Anne E. de la Renta, Dec. 26, 1989. Student, Santo Domingo U., Academia de San Fernando, Madrid. Launched signature fragrance Oscar de la Renta, 1977, fragrance for men, Pour Lui, 1980, Oscar for men, 1995, Intrusion, 2002. Mem. staff Balenciaga's AISA, Madrid; asst. to Antonio Castillo at Lanvin, Paris, 1961-63; chief designer Elizabeth Arden, NYC, 1963-65; chief designer, chmn. bd. dirs. Oscar de la Renta, Ltd., NYC, 1965—; designer Pierre Balmain, Paris, 1993—. Bd. dirs. La Casa del Nino Orphanage and Sch., Santo Domingo, Met. Opera, Carnegie Hall, Thirteen/WNET, Hispanic Designers, Spanish Inst., The Americas Soc., New Yorkers for Children, UNICEF. Decorated Order Juan Pablo Duarte, Order Cristobal Colon (Dominican Republic); recipient Coty awards, 1967, 68, Golden Tiberius award, 1968, Neiman-Marcus award, 1968, Perennial Success award, Fragrance Found. 1991, French Legion d'Honneur as Comdr., 1993, Living Legend award Am. Soc. Perfumers, 1995, Lifetime Achievement award Hispanic Heritage Soc., 1996, Gold Medal of Bellas Artes, King of Spain, 2000, Lifetime Achievement award, 1990, Womenswear Designer of Yr., award, 2000, Coun. of Fashion Designers of Am.; named to Coty Hall of Fame, 1973, Grand Marshall of NY Hispanic Day Parade, 2000. Mem.: Coun. Fashion Designers Am. (bd. dirs., pres. 1973—76, 1986—88, Womenswear Designer of Yr. award 2000, Lifetime Achievement award 1990). Achievements include helped build two schools incorporating orphanages and day-care centers in La Romana and Punta Cana, Dominican Republic. Office: Oscar de la Renta Ltd 550 7th Ave Fl 8 New York NY 10018-3207

DE LARES, ESTEBAN See PÈREZ-RODRIGUEZ, JUAN II

DE LARIOS, DORA, artist; b. L.A., Oct. 13, 1933; d. Elpidio and Concha (Martinez) De L.; 1 child, Sabrina. BFA, U. So. Calif., 1957. Tchr. ceramics UCLA, 1979, U. So. Calif., L.A., 1959; curator 1st internat. ceramic exhbn., L.A., 1988. Ceramic artist, commd. work for site specific areas, including Montage Resort and Spa, Laguna Beach, Calif., 2003; over 40 major works located in Tahiti, Hawaii, Japan, N.J., Fla., pvt. residential projects. Democrat. Avocations: reading, collecting cook books, cooking, drawing edwin the rabbit. Studio: 8560 Venice Blvd Los Angeles CA 90034-2549 Office Phone: 310-839-8305.

DE LA RIVA, MYRIAM ANN, artist; b. Mexico City, Mex., Oct. 8, 1940; arrived in U.S., 1989; d. Adolfo De La Riva and Marianne Kayser; m. Conrado Gallegos, Feb. 26, 1961; children: Conrado Bernardo, Aileen, Eugenio Eduardo. Grad. in Fine Arts, IberoAm. U.; student, Kent State, U. Femenina Mex., Master Carlos Orozco Romero Studio, Master Gilberto Aceves Navarro Studio. V.p. World Coun. Visual Artists, Mexico City, 1994—96; bd. dirs. Mus. Americas; coord. Artists Libr. European Cmty., 2003; coord. Mexican cultural month Latin Am. Art Mus., Miami, 2004; coord., creator World Trade Ctr., Veracruz, 2004; bd. dirs. Mus. of the Am. One-woman shows include include over 40 internat. shows, 1988—, exhibited in group shows at including over 500 internat. shows, 1988—, prin. works include mural Today XXist Century. Vol. Tamayo Comtemporary Art Mus., Mexico City, 2000—04, Munal Mus., San Carlos, 2000—02; mem. Miami Art Mus., 1991—2004, Nat. Mus. Women in Arts, 1991—2004, Global Culture Ctr., 1991—98. Named Hon. Mention Women in the Arts, Latinam. Art Mus., Fla., 1994; recipient 1st prize, Sor Juana Found. Mex.-Lebanon Inst. Cultural, 1998, 3d prize, Francisco Goitia prize, 1994, Francisco Goitia prize, Ateneo del Anahuac, 1991, 1992. Mem.: Assn. Artac Aiap-Unesco, Soc. Mex. de Artistas Plasticos. Home: 99 Abram Cir The Woodlands TX 77382 Office: Delariva Bosque de Guayacanes #57 11700 Mexico City Mexico Personal E-mail: delarivamyriam@hotmail.com.

DE LA ROCHA, CARLOS A., retired physician; b. Santo Domingo, Dominican Republican, Aug. 12, 1934; s. Carlos A. and Germania (Contin) de la R.; m. Penelope Lynn Lansing, May 20, 1961; children: C. Andrew, Maria L., Michael J., David L., Alicia M., Juan A. MD, Univ. de Santo Domingo, 1958. Diplomate Am. Bd. Surgery. Rotating intern City Hosp. at Elmhurst, Queens, N.Y., 1958-59; asst. resident surgery Albert Einstein Med. Ctr., Phila., 1959-60, Ellis Hosp., Schenectady, N.Y., 1960-62, chief resident surgery, 1962-63; tchg. fellow surgery St. Clares Hosp., Schenectady, 1963-65; asst. attending surgeon St. Clares and Ellis Hosp., 1965-69, attending surgeon, 1969-98; ret., 1998. Chmn. tissue unit Ellis Hosp., 1985-90; mem. Ellis Hosp. Found. Bd., 1988-94. Fellow Am. Coll. Surgeons; mem. Am. Soc. Gen. Surgeons, N.Y. State Soc. Surgeons, N.Y. State and County Med. Soc. Republican. Roman Catholic. Avocations: travel, classical music. Home: 44 Van Voast Ln Scotia NY 12302-9621 also: PO Box 1397 Schenectady NY 12301-1397 E-mail: delarochac@hotmail.com.

DE LASA, JOSÉ M., lawyer; b. Havana, Cuba, Nov. 28, 1941; came to U.S., 1961; s. Miguel and Conchita de Lasa; m. Maria Teresa Figueroa, Nov. 23, 1963; children: Maria Teresa, José, Andrés, Carlos. BA, Yale U., 1968, JD, 1971. Bar: N.Y. 1973. Assoc. Cleary, Gottlieb, Steen & Hamilton, N.Y.C., 1971-76; legal dept. Bristol-Myers Squibb Co., N.Y.C., 1976-94; exec. v.p., gen. counsel Abbott Labs., 1994—2005; ptnr. Baker & McKenzie, Chgo., 2005—. Lectr. internat. law, various locations. Bd. dirs. Am. Arbitration Assn., The Resource Found., Coun. Fgn. Rels., The Stovir Found. Mem. ABA, Assn. of Bar of City of N.Y., Assn. Gen. Counsel, North Shore Gen. Counsel Assn., Ill. State Bar Assn. Roman Catholic. Office: Baker & McKenzie 1 Prudential Plz 130 E Randolph Dr Ste 3500 Chicago IL 60601 Business E-Mail: jose.delasa@bakernet.com.

DE LA SABLIERE, JEAN-MARC, international organization administrator; b. Athens, Greece, Nov. 8, 1946; married; 3 children. Student, Nat. Sch. Adminstrn., 1971—73. Appointed secrétaire des affaires etrangères French Ministry Foreign Affairs, 1973, with, 1973—75; private office French Min. of Foreign Affairs, 1975—77, tech. advisor in private office, 1977—78, dep. dir. of African and Malagasy Affairs, 1985—86, dep. dir., UN and Internat. Orgns. Directorate, 1986—89, dir. of African and Malagasy Affairs, 1992—96; chargé de mission in the private office of Prime Min., 1978—81; second counsellor Permanent Mission of France to the UN, NY, 1981—84; dep. permanent rep. for France UN, NY, 1989—92; French amb. Arab Republic of Egypt, 1996—2000; diplomatic advisor and sherpa Pres. of the French Republic, 2000—02; amb. extraordinary and plenipotentiary, permanent rep. of France to the Security Coun., head of French Mission to the UN, 2002—. Office: 350 E 35th St New York NY 10016 also: UN Hdqs First Ave at 46th St New York NY 10017 Office Phone: 212-655-6100. Office Fax: 212-634-7626.

DELASHAW, JOHNNY BILL, JR., neurosurgeon; s. Johnny Bill, Sr. and Treasure Delashaw; m. Mary Frances Patrick, July 10, 1982; children: Johnny Bill III, Patrick Paul. BS in Biology, Stanford U.; MD, U. Wash., Seattle, 1979—83. Resident, neurol. surgery U. Va., Charlottesville, 1983—90; asst. prof., neurol. surgery U. Fla., Gainesville, 1990—92; prof., vice-chmn. neurol. surgery Oreg. Health & Sci. U., Portland, 1992—. Recipient Leadership Award, Rep. Congl. Com., 2001, award, Crutchfield, Gage, Thompson, 1988, 1990, Bigger - Lehman, 1988. Mem.: Soc. U. Neurosurgeons (life), Neurosurgical Soc. Am. (life), Southwestern Oncology Group (life), Am. Assn. Neurol. Surgeons (life), Western Neurol. Soc. (life), Oreg. Neurosurgical Soc. (life), N.Am. Skull Base Soc. (life; bd. dirs.), Congress Neurol. Surgeons (life), Am. Acad. Neurol. Surgery (life), Sr. Soc. Neurol. Surgeons (life), Am. Bd. Neurol. Surgery (life). Conservative. Avocations: fishing, golf. Office: Oreg Health & Sci Univ 3181 SW Sam Jackson Park Rd MC: L-472 Portland OR 97239 Office Phone: 503-494-7737.

DELATEUR, BARBARA JANE, medical educator; b. Hoquiam, Wash., Nov. 17, 1936; Student, Marylhurst (Oreg.) Coll., 1954-56; BS in Philosophy, St. Louis U., 1959; MD, U. Wash., 1963, MSc, 1968. Cert. Am. Bd. Phys. Medicine and Rehab.; lic. physiatrist, Wash., Md. Rotating intern U. Hosp., U. Wash., 1963-64; resident dept. phys. medicine and rehab. U. Hosp., 1964-67; instr. dept. phys. medicine and rehab. U. Wash. Sch. Medicine, 1967-68, asst. prof., 1968-71, assoc. prof., 1971-76, prof. dept. rehab. medicine, 1976-93; prof., dir. dept. phys. medicine and rehab. Johns Hopkins U. Sch. Medicine, Balt., 1993—, Lawrence Cardinal Shehan chair phys. medicine and rehab., 1993—, joint prof. health policy & mgmt. Sch. Hygiene & Pub. Health, 1994—; acting physiatrist-in-chief Rehab. Medicine Svc. Harborview Med. Ctr., Seattle, 1970-72, physiatrist-in-chief, 1972-93; dir. Muscular Dystrophy Clinic Meml. Hosp., Yakima, Wash., 1979-88; dir. dept. phys. medicine and rehab. Johns Hopkins Hosp., Balt., 1993—; med. dir. dept. rehab. medicine Good Samaritan Hosp., Balt., 1993—. Vis. prof. dept. rehab. medicine and dept. internal medicine SUNY, Syracuse, 1988; cons. physiatrist Johns Hopkins Geriatrics Ctr., Johns Hopkins Bayview Med. Ctr., Balt., 1994—; vis. lectr. dept. phys. medicine Coll. Medicine, Ohio State U., 1985; Arthur Grant lectr. U. Tex., San Antonio, 1992; Marquette lectr. Jefferson Med. Coll., Phila., 1993; spkr. various univs. and orgns.; pres. Phys.Medicine and Rehab./Edn. and Rsch. Found., 1990-94; mem. governing coun. sect. rehab. hosps. and programs Am. Hosp. Assn., 1993—; mem. adv. bd. Wash. State Divsn. Vocat. Rehab., 1979-84. Contbr. articles to profl. jours.; mem. editl. bd. Archives Phys. Medicine and Rehab., 1978-84, Health After 50, Johns Hopkins Hosp., 1994—; reviewer Jour. Am. Geriatrics Soc., 1994—. Recipient Elizabeth and Sidney Licht award for sci. writing, 1990, Excellence in Tchg. award N.J. Med. Sch., 1992, Excellence in Rsch. Writing award Assn. Acad. Physiatrists and Am. Jour. Phys. Medicine and Rehab., 1992, Golden Goniometer award Phys. Medicine and Rehab. Residents, 1995, Labe Scheinberg award, Meeting of Consortium of MS Ctrs., Portland, Oreg., 1995. Fellow Am. Acad. Phys. Medicine; mem. AMA, Am. Acad. Phys. Medicine and Rehab. (bd. govs. 1983-90, v.p. 1986-887, pres-elect 1987-88, pres. 1988-89, past-pres. 1989-90, Disting. Clinician award 1998), NAS, Am. Burn Assn., Am. Congress Rehab. Medicine, Assn. Acad. Physiatrists (Disting. Academician award 1998), Internat. Assn. for Study of Pain, King County Med. Assn., Northwest Assn. Phys. Medicine and Rehab. (pres. 1974-76), Gerontol. Soc. Am. (clin. medicine sect.), Wash. State Med. Assn. Office: JHPM & R Good Samaritan Profl Bldg 5601 Loch Raven Blvd Ste 406 Baltimore MD 21239-2905

DE LA TORRE, JACK CARLOS, clinical neuroscientist; b. Paris, Dec. 2, 1942; s. Rafael de la Torre, Maria de la Torre; m. Helene de Socarraz; 1 child, Lauren Nicole. BS in Biology, Am. U., 1961; MD, U. Madrid, 1979; PhD, U. Geneva, Switzerland, 1969. Asst. prof. neurosurgery and psychiatry U. Chgo., 1969—75, assoc. prof. neurosurgery and psychiatry, 1975—77; assoc. prof neurosurgery U. Miami, Fla., 1979—82; prof. neurosurgery, anatomy and pharmacology U. Ottawa, Canada, 1983—94; prof. neurosurgery and neurosci. U. N.Mex., Albuquerque, 1994—99; vis. prof. pathology U. Calif., San Diego, 1999—. Adj. prof. pathology Case Western Re's. U., Cleve., 2001—. Author: Dynamics of Brain Monoamines, 1972; translator: The Neuron and the Glial Cell, 1984; editor: Cerebrovascular Pathology in Alzheimer's Disease, 1997, Vascular Pathophysiology in Alzheimer's Disease, 2000, Pathology of the Aging Human Nervous System, 2001, Alzheimer's Disease: Vascular Etiology and Pathology, 2002, Vascular Dynamics in Alzheimer and Vascular Dementia, 2004; contbr. articles to profl. jours. Grantee Head Injury Ctr., NIH, 1970—80, Can. Heart Assn., 1983—88, Heart & Stroke Found. Ont., 1986—91, Internat. Spinal Rsch. Trust, 1989—94, Alzheimer's Assn., 2000—. Fellow: Am. Heart Assn. (stroke coun.); mem.: Interam. Coll. Physicians and Surgeons, Coll. Physicians and Surgeons Ont., N.Y. Acad. Sci., Soc. Neurosci. Avocations: photography, chess, tennis. Office: Inst Pathology 2085 Adelbert Rd Cleveland OH 44106 Office Phone: 216-368-6686.

DELATORRE, PHILLIP EUGENE, law educator; b. Chanute, Kans., July 6, 1953; s. Jose Crespin and Margaret (Alonzo) DeL.; m. Patrice Ann Kutz, Sept. 19, 1981; children: Edward Phillip, Daniel Patrick, Ryan Andrew. BA, U. Kans., 1975; JD, Harvard U., 1978. Bar: Mo. 1978, Kans. 1979. Assoc. Watson, Ess, Marshall & Enggas, Kansas City, Mo., 1978-80; prof. law U. Kans., Lawrence, 1980—. Commr. Kans. Human Rights Commn., 1991—. Contbr. articles to profl. jours. (recipient Best Article award 1985). Mem. ABA, Kans. Bar Assn., Mo. Bar Assn. Office Phone: 785-864-9240, 785-864-9240. E-mail: ped@ku.edu.

DELATY, SIMONE, retired language educator; b. Valenciennes, France, Jan. 17, 1939; came to U.S., 1963; d. Georges and Hélène (Lagarde) D.; m. Joseph Szertics, Dec. 8, 1962 (div. 1978); 1 child, Claire Szertics. Lic. ès-Lettres, U. Grenoble, France, 1962; D in Comparative Lit., U. Bordeaux, 1970. Instr. French Bowling Green U., Bowling Green, Ohio, 1964-67, U. Iowa, Iowa City, 1968-69, asst. prof. French, 1969-76, assoc. prof. French, 1976-86, prof. French, 1986—96; ret., 1996; owner, operator of Simone's Plain and Simple-Artisan Bread and Farm Fresh Products, Wellman, Iowa, 1996—. Author: L'héritage espagnol de José-Maria de Heredia, 1975, Oeuvres poétiques complètes de J.M. de Heredia, 1984. Grantee Am. Philos. Soc., 1976, Am. Coun. Learned Socs., 1976. Mem.: MLA.

DELAUGHTER, THOMAS GLENN, business administration educator, consultant; b. New Orleans, La., Apr. 3, 1948; s. Thomas Jefferson and Lurlean Waldrup DeLaughter; m. Grace Noel Tatum, June 20, 1998; 1 child, Madeline Elizabeth Costa. PhD in Bus. Adminstrn., Fla. State U., 1995; MBA, Miss. Coll., 1989, BA, 1971. Vis. asst. prof. U. Fla., Gainesville, 1996—; asst. prof. bus. adminstrn. Flagler Coll., St. Augustine, Fla., 1998—. Author: (book) Gator Marketing, management.org. Elder Presbyn. Ch., Hernando, Miss., 1979—81. Recipient Tchr. of Yr., BACC U. Fla., 1997. Mem.: Acad. Mgmt. Episcopalian. Avocation: golf. Office: Flagler Coll 74 King St Saint Augustine FL 32084 Office Phone: 904-819-6295. Business E-Mail: doc@flagler.edu.

DELAURENTI MCCLURE, TRACY, elementary school educator; b. Walnut Creek, Calif., May 8, 1966; d. Loren Joseph and Vicki Lee DeLaurenti; m. Robert Kreger McClure, July 8, 2000. BA, Sonoma State U., 1987. Tchr. Rio Vista Elem. Sch., West Pittsburg, Calif., 1988—94, Highlands Elem. Sch., Concord, Calif., 1994—95, Bernard Eldredge Elem. Sch., Petaluma, Calif., 1995—2000, Old Adobe Elem., Petaluma, 2000—. 2 grants, Petaluma Edn. Found., 2004—05. Mem.: Old Adobe Tchrs. Assn. (sec. 2004—), Calif. Reading Assn. Home: 709 East D Street Petaluma CA 94952 Office: Old Adobe Elementary School 2856 Adobe Road Petaluma CA 94954 Office Phone: 707-765-4301. Personal E-mail: miss-d@comcast.net. Business E-Mail: tmcclure@oldadobe.org.

DELAURENTIS, LOUISE BUDDE, writer; b. Stafford, Kans., Oct. 5, 1920; d. Louis and Mary (Lichte) Budde; m. Mariano Anthony DeLaurentis, Mar. 26, 1948 (dec. Oct. 1991); 1 child, Delbert Louis. BA, Ottawa (Kans.) U., 1942. Airport traffic contr. FAA, various cities, 1943-55. Author: Etta Chipmunk, 1962, A Peculiarity of Direction, 1975, Traveling to the Goddess, 1994; editor: Gentle Sorcery by Bessie Jeffery, 1972; author numerous poems various periodicals; contbr. articles to profl. jours. Chairperson Tompkins County Liberal Party, Ithaca, N.Y., 1969-72; mem. local women's spirituality groups. Mem. LWV, AAUW, Writers Assn. of Ithaca Area (pres. 1964-65, co-editor anthology 1967, 95). Avocations: swimming, camping, backpacking, making lunar calendars. Home: 983 Cayuga Heights Rd Ithaca NY 14850-1044

DELAURO, ROSA L., congresswoman; b. New Haven, Conn., Mar. 2, 1943; m. Stanley Greenberg; 3 children. Student, London Sch. Econs. & Polit. Sci., 1962-63; BA in History and Polit Sci. cum laude, Marymount Coll., 1964; MA in Internat. Politics, Columbia U., 1966. Tng. assoc. Community Progress Inc., New Haven, 1967-69; instr. in internat. rels. Albertus Magnus Coll., 1967-68; adminstrv. asst. Nat. Urban Fellows, 1969-72, asst. dir., dir., 1972-75; city coord. Carter-Mondale Presdl. Campaign, New Haven, 1976; exec. asst. Mayor Frank Logue, New Haven, 1976-77, campaign mgr., 1977; exec. asst., devel. adminstr. City of New Haven, 1977-79; campaign mgr. Chris Dodd for U.S. Senate, 1979-80, 86; adminstrv. asst. U.S. Senator Christopher J. Dodd, Washington, 1981-87; state dir. Mondale-Ferraro Presdl. Campaign, NJ, 1986; ptnr. DeLauro-Geller, 1987-88; regional dir. Dukakis for Pres. Campaign, NY, NJ, Conn., 1988; exec. dir. EMILY's List, 1989; mem. U.S. Congress from 3rd Conn. dist., 1991—; mem. house appropriations com. and budget com. Del. to Dem. Nat. Conv., 1984; bd. dirs. Pax Ams. Past pres. New Haven Arts Coun. Assoc. fellow Timothy Dwight Coll., Yale U.; recipient Leadership award Am. Com. on Italian Migration. Mem. Nat. Italian-Am. Found., Dem. Women for Progress. Democrat. Roman Cath. Office: US House of Reps 2262 Rayburn Ho Office Bldg Washington DC 20515-0703 also: District Office 59 Elm Street New Haven CT 06510

DE LA VIÑA-SIERRA, DIANA MARIA, music educator; b. Holguin, Cuba, Apr. 22, 1956; arrived in U.S., 1962; d. Santos Rafael de la Viña and Ana Julia Viamonte-de la Viña; 1 child, Michael Arles. BS, Kean Coll., 1980; cert., Villa Walsh Acad., 2005. Cert. piano tchr. Nat. Guild Piano Tchrs., 2003. Tchr. music Uruguay USA Sch., Elizabeth, NJ, 1983—86; tchr. voice, piano Newark Cmty. Sch. Arts, 1983—94, chmn. music dept., 1993—; head Dept. Music St. Hegwig's Sch., Elizabeth, NJ, 1997—2002; chmn. Music Dept. Blessed Sacrament Sch., Elizabeth, 2003—04; chmn. Dept. Music and Spanish St. Mary's Sch., Elizabeth, 2004—. Author: (song) Danza Cubana. Head cultural affairs Pro Cuba Orgn., Elizabethtown, 1990—94. Recipient Piano Competition First prize, Cath. Youth Orgn., 1969, Excellence in Tchg. award, Newark (N.J.) Cmty. Sch. Arts, 1993, Don Galaor award, La Tribuna newspaper; scholar, Villa Walsh Acad., 1971. Home: 151 Morristown Rd Elizabeth NJ 07208-1315

DELAWARE, RICHARD RAYMOND, mathematician, educator; b. Woonsocket, RI, Dec. 30, 1951; s. Raymond Rene and Lucille Hattie Delaware. BS cum laude, Santa Clara U., Calif., 1974; MA, U. Kans., Lawrence, 1977; PhD, U. Mo., Kans. City, 2000. Tchr. math. 9-12 Mo., 2002, tchr. gifted and talented tchr. K-12 Mo., 2003. Grad. asst. U. Kans., Lawrence, 1974—77; lectr. U. Mo., Kans. City, 1981—84, tchg. asst. Physics dept., 1983—84, math. coord. Math. and Physics Inst., 1984—2003, vis. instr., 1984—2003, assoc. clin. prof., 2004—. Assoc. dir., Math. and Physics Inst. U. Mo., Kans. City, 1998—2003; spkr. in field. Author: (videotape course) VSI Coll. Algebra; contbg. editor: (newsletter) Math. and Physics Newsletter; contbr. scientific papers to profl. jours. Recipient Superior Tchg. Award, Sch. of Grad. Studies U. Mo. Kans. City, 1984, Ednl. Ptnrs. award, INROADS, Inc., 1989, Dean's award Outstanding Tchg., Sch. of Arts and Sciences U. Mo. Kans. City, 1995, Founding Faculty Mem. award, Math. and Physics Inst., 2003; U.G. Mitchell scholar, Dept. Math. U. Kans., 1975—77. Mem.: Gifted Assn. of Mo., Kans. City Area Tchrs. of Math., Mo. Coun. Tchrs. of Math., Nat. Coun. Tchrs. of Math., Math. Assn. of Am., Am. Math. Soc., Am.-French Geneal. Soc. (life), Alpha Sigma Nu SJ, Pi Mu Epsilon. Avocations: paleoanthropology, family genealogy, technical theatre. Office: U MO Kans City 5100 Rockhill Road Kansas City MO 64110 Business E-Mail: delawarer@umkc.edu.

DELAWIE, HOMER TORRENCE, retired architect; b. Santa Barbara, Calif., Sept. 24, 1927; s. Fred Ely and Gertrude (Torrence) D.; m. Billie Carol Sparlin (div. 1969); m. Ethel Ann Mallinger, Sept. 3, 1973; children: Gregory, Claire, Shandell, Tracy, Stephanie, Scott. BS in Archtl. Engring., Calif. Poly. State U., San Luis Obispo, 1951. Registered architect, Calif. Pvt. practice architecture, San Diego, 1958-61; founder, CEO Delawie Wilkes Rodrigues Barker & Bretton Assocs., San Diego, 1961—98, ret., 1998, ptnr. emeritus, 1998—. Mem. Planning Commn., City of San Diego, 1969-82; adv. bd. KPBS Pub. TV. Recipient Award of Merit Calif. chpt. Am. Inst. Planners, Lay Citizens award Phi Delta Kappa, 1975, award Calif chpt. Am. Planning Assn., 1982; named Disting. Alumnus, Calif. Poly. State U., 1972. Fellow AIA (over 60 design awards 1973—, Architects Svc. award Calif. coun. 1973, spl. award San Diego chpt. 1978, Pub. Svc. award Calif. coun. 1981, Outstanding Firm award San Diego chpt. 1986, Calif. Coun. Lifetime Achievement award 1998). Democrat. Home: 2749 Azalea Dr San Diego CA 92106-1132 Office: Delawie Wilkes Rodriques Barker & Bretton Assocs 2265 India St San Diego CA 92101-1725

DELAY, EUGENE RAYMOND, psychologist, educator, researcher; b. Coeur d'Alene, Idaho, Dec. 24, 1948; s. Raymond Joseph and Fairy Louise (Fisher) D.; m. Rona Jane Moore, Sept. 12, 1971; 1 child, Shawn Patrick. BS in Psychology, U. Idaho, 1972; MS in Biopsychology, U. Ga., 1977, PhD in Biopsychology, 1979. Asst. prof. Regis U., Denver, 1979-84, assoc. prof., 1984-90, prof., 1990—2005, dir. neurosci. program, 1997—2005, prof. emeritus, 2005—; assoc. prof. U. Vt., Burlington, 2005—. Provisional clin. cons. Denver VA Hosp., 1981-87; rsch. cons. Brenau Coll., Gainesville, Ga., 1978, Colo. State U., Ft. Collins, 1987-94, rsch. assoc. U. Miami, 1993-94, 97-2003; vis. scientist Brown U., Providence, 1995-96. Contbr. articles to profl. jours. Served with U.S. Army, 1973-75. NSF grantee, 1989, 2000, 05, NIH, 2000, 2003, 05; NIH sr. fellow, 1995. Mem. APA, N.Y. Acad. Sci., Rocky Mountain Neurosci. Group, Soc. Neurosci., Am. Psychol. Soc., Internat. Behavioral Neurosci. Soc., Assn. for Chemoreception Scis. Achievements include research in cross-modality transfer processes after damage to brain, particularly cortex with emphasis on potential for rehabilitation, recovery of function after brain damage, neuropsychological effects of brain damage and taste transduction of monosodium glutamate and amino acids. Home: 5786 W 81st Pl Arvada CO 80003-1834 Office: Univ Vt Dept Biology Marsh Life Scis Burlington VT 05405 E-mail: edelay@regis.edu.

DELAY, THOMAS DALE (TOM DELAY), congressman; b. Laredo, Tex., Apr. 8, 1947; s. Charles Ray and Maxine (Wimbish) DeL.; m. Christine Ann Furrh, Aug. 26, 1967; 1 child, Danielle BS, U. Houston, 1970. Gen mgr. Redwood Chem., Houston, 1970-73; owner, operator Albo Pest Control, Stafford, Tex., 1973-84, pres., 1984—; mem., appropriations com. vice chmn. adminstrn. com., chmn. budget and oversight of transp. com. Tex. Ho. of Reps., Austin, 1979-84; mem. 99th-108th Congresses from 22d Tex. dist., 1985—; mem. HUD com. 99th-106th Congresses from 22d Tex. dist., mem. appropriations com., Ho. majority whip, 1995—2002; Ho. majority leader 108th Congress, 2002—. Mem. appropriations and pub. health coms. Tex. Ho. of Reps.; mem. Grace Caucus, Washington, 1985—; mem. U.S.-Mexico Interparliamentary Del., Washington, 1985-86; mem. Republican study com. Sci. and Tech. Task Force, 1985-86; mem. Rep. research com. Regulatory Reform Caucus, 1985-86. Bd. dirs. Youth Opportunities Unltd., Houston; precinct chmn. Republican Party, Simonton, Tex., 1974-78; Gala chmn. Ft. Bend County "War on Drugs" Coalition, 1987; adv. bd. CloseUp Found.; active drug abuse and rehab. ctr. Odyssey House, Tex; adv. bd. Joint Ctr. for Urban Mobility Research, Houston; mem. Ft. Bend Arts Adv. Council. Recipient Legislator of Yr. award Tex. Assn. to Improve Distbn., 1983; ABC's Outstanding Legislator for the 67th Session Leadership award Young Conservatives of Tex., 1984; Nat. Security Leadership award Coalition Peace Through Strength, Washington, 1985-90; Freshman Class Rep., U.S. House GOP Com. on Coms., Washington, 1985-86; Golden Bulldog award Watchdog of the Treasury, 1985-90. Mem. Congl. Leaders for a Balanced Budget, Greater Houston Pest Control Assn. (former pres.), Tex. Pest Control Assn. (bd. dirs.), Southwest Energy Council, Am. Legis. Exchange Council, Nat. Conf. State Legislators, Fort Bend County Fair Assn. (life) Clubs: Sweetwater Country (Sugar Land, Tex.); Fort Bend 100. Lodges: Rotary. Republican. Baptist. Avocations: hunting, skiing, golf. Office: US Ho of Reps 242 Cannon House Office Bldg Washington DC 20515-4322*

DELBANCO, NICHOLAS FRANKLIN, language educator, writer; b. London, Aug. 27, 1942; came to U.S., 1948; s. Kurt and Barbara Gabriele Delbanco; m. Elena Greenhouse, Sept. 12, 1970; children: Francesca Barbara, Andrea Katherine. AB, Harvard U., 1963; MA, Columbia U., 1966. Mem. faculty Bennington (Vt.) Coll., 1966-85; prof. English Williams Coll., Williamstown, Mass., 1983, Skidmore Coll., Saratoga Springs, N.Y., 1984; Robert Frost Collegiate prof. English U. Mich., Ann Arbor, 1985—. Dir. MFA in writing program U. Mich., 1985—; vis. prof. Iowa U. Writer's Workshop, Iowa City, 1980; vis. adj. prof. Columbia U., N.Y.C., 1981, 96-98; founding dir. Bennington Writing Workshops, 1978-85; chair fiction panel Nat. Book Awards, N.Y.C., 1997; vis. fellow Woodrow Wilson Nat. Found., Princeton, N.J., 1981—. Author: Group Portrait: Conrad, Crane, Ford, James & Wells, 1983, The Writer's Trade, 1990, Running in Place: Scenes from the South of France, 1991, In the Name of Mercy, 1995, Old Scores, 1997, What Remains, 2000, Sincerest Form, 2003, Vagabonds, 2004, others; editor: Stillness and Shadows, 1985, Speaking of Writing, 1990, Bernard Malamud on Life and Art, 1996, others. Mem. ant. adv. bd. Share Our Strength, Writers Harvest, Washington, 1994—; mem. governing bd. Mich. Journalism Fellows Program, 1990—; mem. Arts Am. U.S. Info. Agy., Washington, 1992. Fellow Nat. Endowment for Arts, 1973, 82, J.S. Guggenheim Meml. Found., 1980; nominee Mich. Author of the Yr., Mich. Assn. Librs., 2002. Fellow Internat. Am. Studies and Lang. Faculty Salzburg; mem. Authors Guild, Authors League, PEN, Century Assn., Signet Soc., Phi Beta Kappa. Office: U Mich Hopwood Rm Angell Hall Ann Arbor MI 48109 Office Phone: 734-764-6296. E-mail: delbanco@umich.edu.

DELBANCO, SUZANNE F., human services administrator; MPH, U. Calif., Berkeley; PhD in Pub. Policy, Goldman Sch. Pub. Policy. With Henry J. Kaiser Family Found.; sr. mgr. Pacific Bus. Group on Health; exec. dir. The Leapfrog Group, Washington, 2000—. Office: Leapfrog Group 1801 K St NW Ste 701L Washington DC 20006

DELBANCO, THOMAS LEWIS, medical educator, researcher; b. London, Dec. 7, 1939; came to U.S., 1948; s. Kurt and Barbara Gabriele (Bernstein) D.; m. Jill Martin Behrens, Dec. 13, 1964; children: Steven, Suzanne, Jennifer. BA, Harvard U., 1961; MD, Columbia U., 1965. Diplomate Am. Bd. Internal Medicine. Intern in medicine Bellevue Hosp., N.Y.C., 1965-66, resident, 1967-68, Presbyn. Hosp., N.Y.C., 1966-67; chief resident Harlem Hosp. Ctr., N.Y.C., 1968-69; mem. staff, dir. div. gen. medicine and primary care Beth Israel Hosp., Boston, 1971—2002; Richard and Florence Koplow - James Tullis prof. gen. medicine and primary care Harvard Med. Sch., 2000—. Dir. Picker/Commonwealth Program Patient-Centered Care, 1987-94; chmn. Picker Inst., 1994-2000; mem. coun. APHA, 1983-85; mem. program com. Inst. Medicine, NAS, 1991-94. Editor: 4 books; contbr. numerous articles to profl. jours. Vice chmn. United Way Mass. Bay, Boston, 1987-91; co-dir. Learning Through Drama Program, Lexington, Mass., 1982-90; bd. dirs. Health Commons Inst., 1994-2001. Maj. U.S. Army, 1969-71. Robert Wood Johnson Health Policy fellow Inst. Medicine, 1977-78. Master ACP; mem. Am. Fedn. Clin. Rsch., Soc. Gen. Internal Medicine (pres. 1986-87, councillor), Nat. Pub. Health and Hosps. Inst. (bd. dirs.). Jewish. Avocation: violin. Office: Beth Israel Deaconess Med Ctr 330 Brookline Ave Boston MA 02215-5400 Office Phone: 617-667-3992. Business E-Mail: tdelbanc@bidmc.harvard.edu.

DELBOURGO, JOËLLE LILY, publishing executive; b. Alexandria, Egypt, Sept. 10, 1953; arrived in US, 1960; d. Edward Daniel and J. Andrée (Domergue) D.; m. Lewis Foster Patton, May 16, 1976 (div. May 1996); children: Caroline Emily, Andrew David. Student, Vassar Coll., 1970-72; BA, Williams Coll., 1974; MA, Columbia U., 1975. Editorial asst. Bantam Books, N.Y.C., 1975-76, asst. editor, 1976-78, assoc. editor, 1978-80; sr. editor Ballantine Del Rey Fawcett Ivy Books div. Random House Inc., N.Y.C., 1980-81, exec. editor, 1981-83, editor-in-chief, 1983-86, v.p., editor-in-chief trade books, 1986-89, editor-in-chief hard cover books and trade paperback, 1990-95; v.p., editl. dir. HarperCollins, N.Y.C., 1996, sr. v.p., assoc. publ., editor-in-chief, 1997-99; CEO, pres. Joëlle Delbourgo Assocs. Inc. Lit. Mgmt., Pub. Cons., 1999—. Columbia faculty fellow, 1974—75. Mem.: Women's Media Group (bd. dirs., treas.), Phi Beta Kappa. Office: 516 Bloomfield Ave Ste 5 Montclair NJ 07042 Office Phone: 973-783-6800. Business E-Mail: info@delbourgo.com.

DELBRIDGE, CECELIA BELL, librarian; b. New Orleans, July 10, 1959; d. Thomas Alvin and Barbara Jean (Trapp) B.; m. Richard Lane Delbridge, Aug. 21, 1993. B.S., Miss. State U., 1981; M.L.S., U. So. Miss., 1982. Asst. librarian Univs. Ctr. Library, Jackson, Miss., 1982-87; health scis. librarian Miss. Baptist Med. Ctr., Jackson, 1987-2001; program coord. divsn. digestive diseases U. Miss. Med. Ctr., Jackson, 2001—; summer intern Miss. Library Commn., 1980; grad. asst. Sch. Library Sci., U. So. Miss., 1981-82. Miss. State U. pres.'s scholar, 1980-81. Mem. ALA, Miss. Library Assn., Miss. Biomed. Library Assn., Med. Library Assn. Presbyterian. Home: 4305 Lakeshore Dr Pearl MS 39208-9319 Office: Univ Miss Med Ctr Divsn Digestive Diseases 2500 N State St Jackson MS 39216 Office Phone: 601-815-1770. E-mail: ceceliadelb@att.net.

DEL CALVO, JORGE A., lawyer; b. Havana, Cuba, Oct. 13, 1955; BA with distinction, Stanford Univ., 1977; MA Latin Am. history, UCLA, 1978; MA pub. policy, JD cum laude, Harvard Univ., 1981; ND, Univ. Philippines, 1982. Bar: Calif. 1982. Assoc. Pillsbury Winthrop Shaw Pittman, Palo Alto, Calif., 1982—90, ptnr., 1990—, co-chmn. Silicon Valley Bus. group. Bd. dir. Riverstone Networks, Berkeley Process Control, Deepa Textiles; mem. adv. bd. Linklore LLC; vis. lectr. Stanford Univ. Law Sch. Editor (coord.): Venture Capital & Pub. Offering Negotiation. Mem.: ABA, HispanicNet, Asian Multicultural Assn., Indus Entrepreneurs, Phi Beta Kappa. Office: Pillsbury Winthrop Shaw Pittman 2475 Hanover St Palo Alto CA 94304-1114 Office Phone: 650-233-4537. Office Fax: 650-233-4545. Business E-Mail: jorge@pillsburylaw.com.

DEL CAMPO, MARTIN BERNARDELLI, architect; b. Guadalajara, Mex., Nov. 27, 1922; came to U.S., 1949; s. Salvador and Margarita (Bernardelli) Del C.; m. Laura Zaikowska, May 25, 1945; children: Felicia (dec.), Margarita, Mario. BA, Colegio Frances Morelos, Mexico City, 1941; archtl. degree, Univ. Nat. Autonoma de Mexico, Mexico City, 1948. Ptnr. Del Campo & Fruiht, architects, Santa Rosa, Calif., 1955-56, Del Campo & Clark, San Francisco, 1957-63; mgr. Hotel Victoria, Oaxaca, Mex., 1964-67; pres. Gulli-Del Campo, architects, San Francisco, 1968-70; ptnr. Del Campo Assocs., San Francisco, 1977-81. Lectr. archtl. design Coll. Environmental Design, U. Calif., Berkeley, 1973-74. Archtl. works include: Calif. Med. Facility South, Vacaville, Phillip Burton Fed. Bldg. remodeling, San Francisco, Hall of Justice, San Francisco, San Francisco Airport Internat. Terminal, Mex. Heritage Gardens, San Jose, Four Seasons Tower, San Francisco. Mem. AIA. Address: Del Campo & Maru Architects Inc 45 Lansing St San Francisco CA 94105-2611 Office Phone: 415-777-4025. Business E-Mail: martin@dcmsf.com.

DEL CERRO, GERARDO, sociologist, researcher; b. Burgos, Spain, Feb. 22, 1966; s. Gerardo del Cerro-Rueda and Herminia Santamaria. BA, Logic and Philosophy of Sci., U. Autonoma, Madrid, 1989; MA, Sociology, New School for Social Research, New York City, 1992—94; MA, Music Theory and Piano Performance, Real Conservatory of Music, Madrid, 1996; PhD, Urban Planning, New School for Social Research, New York, 1992—97. Assoc. rschr. Spanish Ministry of Edn., Madrid, 1990—92; project area leader National Sci. Found. Gateway Program, N.Y.C., 1997—2002; dir. assessment and innovation The Cooper Union for Advancement of Sci. and Art, N.Y.C., 1999—. Prof. of Sociology U. Madrid, 1995—96; social sci. analyst PREMDAM, Madrid, Spain, 1994—96; rsch. cons. Burgos City Hall, Burgos, Burgos, Spain, 2001—02. Contbr. articles to profl. jours., 1999. Pres. Music Soc. Coll. Mayor Ximenez de Cisneros, Madrid, 1986—89. Recipient Alumni Assn. award, Coll. Mayor Ximenez de Cisneros, 1991, Vis. Scholarship, Skidmore Coll., 1989-90; fellow, New Sch. for Social Rsch., 1993, Univ. Autonoma de Madrid, 1984 through 1989. Mem.: New York Acad. of Scis., Soc. for Social Implications of Tech., Am. Soc.of Engring. Edn., World Future Soc. Avocation: languages. Office: The Cooper Union 51 Astor Place New York NY 10003 Office Phone: 212-353-4321.

DEL CHIARO, MARIO ALDO, art historian, archaeologist, etruscologist, educator; b. San Francisco, Apr. 22, 1925; s. Casimiro and Elisa (Bianchi) A.; m. Christina Falkman, Sept. 13, 1958; children: Kari Louise, Marco Claudio, Paola Christina. AB, U. Calif.-Berkeley, 1950, MA, 1951, PhD, 1956. Teaching asst. art history U. Calif. at Berkeley, 1950-51, 55, Univ. fellow in art, 1951-52; John Wesley Britton traveling fellow in classics, 1952-53; Met. Mus. Art fellow N.Y.C., 1953-54; grantee Am. Numismatic Soc. Seminar, 1954; faculty U. Calif., Santa Barbara, 1956—, prof. art history, 1966-94, prof. emeritus, 1994; chmn. dept. U. Calif.-Santa Barbara, 1969-72; Mem. archeol. staff for excavations in Turkey, Yugoslavia, Egypt, Sicily and Italy; dir. U. Calif.-Santa Barbara archeol. expdns. to, Tuscany, Italy. Author: The Genucilia Group: A Class of Etruscan Red-Figured Plates, 1957, Etruscan Red-Figured Vase-Painting at Caere, 1974, The Etruscan Funnel Group: A Tarquinian Red-Figured Fabric, 1974; exhbn. catalogues Greek Art in Private Collections of Southern California, 1963, Etruscan Art from West Coast Collections, 1967, Roman Art in West Collections, 1973, Etruscan Ghiaccio Forte, 1976, Re-exhumed Etruscan Bronzes, 1981; Classical Art, Sculpture in the Santa Barbara Mus. Art, 1984; editor: Corinthiaca, Studies in Honor of Darrell A. Amyx, 1986; contbr. book revs. and articles to profl. jours. Decorated Cavaliere Ufficiale Order of Merit (Italy); recipient Internat. award in archaeology, Tutto Maremma, Italy, 1990; grantee, Am. Philos. Soc., 1957, 1975, NEH, 1977; Prix de Rome fellow, Am. Acad. in Rome, 1958—60, Sr. Faculty fellow, Humanities Inst. U. Calif. at Berkeley, 1967—68. Mem. Archeol. Inst. Am., Explorers Club, Istituto Studi Etruschi ed Italici, Florence, Deutsches Archäologisches Inst., Istituto Archeologico Rome, European Acad. Scis. and Art, Salzburg, Phi Beta Kappa. Home: Hope Ranch 1376 Estrella Dr Santa Barbara CA 93110-2418

DEL COLLE, PAUL LAWRENCE, communications administrator, educator; b. Lynn, Mass., Dec. 16, 1950; s. Alfiero Luigi and Doris Claire (Rich) D.; m. Ellen Mary Ambrose, May 26, 1979 (div. 2001). BA, Holy Cross Coll., 1972; MS, Boston U., 1975; PhD, NYU, 1990. News dir. Sta. WGNG, Providence, 1972-73; writer, assoc. prodr. Boston U. Prodns., 1974-76; instr. comms. Iona Coll., New Rochelle, N.Y., 1976-80; asst. prof. comms. William Paterson Coll., Wayne, N.J., 1980-83, Marist Coll., Poughkeepsie, N.Y., 1983-90; pres., owner D.C. Media Cons., 1981-93; asst. prof. comms. Coll. of Mt. St. Vincent, Riverdale, N.Y., 1991-95; journalism lectr. NYU, 1995; sr. media analyst Forbes for Pres., Inc., 1995-96; media analyst John McLaughlin and Assocs., 1996-97; pres. sec. Yonkers (N.Y.) Pub. Schs., 1997-98; comm. project mgr. Integrated Supply Chain, IBM, Somers, N.Y., 1998-99; assoc., media rels exec. fin. rels. bd. BSMG Worldwide, 1999—. Judge news/documentary divsn. Emmy awards NATAS, 1988—; sr. media splst. Bliss Gouverneur & Assocs., N.Y.C.; cons. in field. Writer TV show The Pennant Chase, 1988; writer, announcer (radio spots) Thanks to You, 1986, (video news releases) Positalker/Grand Union, 1982; writer (book review) Review of Broadcasting: An Introduction, 1981, Review of Writing News for Broadcast, 1981, (mag. article) Bicentennial Burger Boutique, 1975; contbg. book reviewer Bookscapes, 1994-96. Cons. United Way of Dutchess County, Poughkeepsie, 1984-92; vol. Mental Health Assn., 1983-97, Am. Heart Assn., Poughkeepsie, 1989—, Am. Diabetes Assn., 1998—. Recipient Scholarship Internat. Radio/TV Found., 1988, 90, 94, Grad. Assistantship Boston U.,

1973-74; named Outstanding Young Men in Am., 1981; tchg. fellow Poynter Inst. for Media Studies, St. Petersburg, Fla., 1993. Roman Catholic. Avocations: gardening, baseball memorabilia. Home: 13 Oxford Rd # 1 Hastings On Hudson NY 10706 E-mail: paul@blisspr.com.

DELCOMYN, FRED, physiology and neurobiology educator; b. Copenhagen, June 4, 1939; came to U.S., 1947, naturalized, 1960; s. Niels Theodor and Erna A. Delcomyn; m. Nancy Ann Nigg, Dec. 14, 1969; children— Julia C. M., Michael T.W., Erik A.W. B.S., Wayne State U., 1962; M.S., Northwestern U., 1964; Ph.D., U. Oreg., 1969. Research assoc. dept. zoology U. Glasgow (Scotland), 1969-71, lectr. inst. physiology, 1971-72; asst. prof. dept. entomology U. Ill.-Urbana, 1972-77, assoc. prof., 1977-95, prof., 1995—, dir. Sch. Integrative Biology, 2000—. Contbr. articles to profl. jours., chpts. to books. Fellow U. Ill., 1973; Sr. Fulbright scholar U. Kaiserslautern, Germany, 1987-88; grantee NIH, NSF, Whitehall Found. Fellow AAAS; mem. Soc. Exptl. Biology, Soc. Neurosci. Office: U Ill Dept Entomology 505 S Goodwin Ave Urbana IL 61801-3707 Office Phone: 217-333-8793. E-mail: delcomyn@life.uiuc.edu.

DEL CONTE, L. CATHERINE, special education educator; b. Montour Falls, N.Y., June 8, 1955; d. Leon Clarence and Dorothy Louise May; m. Douglas Kelsey, Aug. 2, 1973; children: Henry Lee Kelsey, Bryon Douglas Kelsey; m. Richard Ralph Del Conte, Apr. 8, 1995. AA in Human Svcs., Genesee C.C., Batavia, N.Y., 1981; BSW, SUNY-Brockport, 1983, MPA in Geriatrics, 1986; M.Spl. Edn., George Mason U., Fairfax, Va., 2000. Case mgr. We Care, Inc., Washington, 1991—92, Brice Warren Corp., Washington, 1992—94, State of Md./Great Oaks MR Ctr., 1994—95, Jewish Social Svcs., Rockville, Md., 1995—97; learning disabilities/ED tchr. Fairfax County Pub. Schs., Annandale, Va., 1998—2004, Robinson HS, Fairfax, Va., 2004—. Historian Phi Delta Kappa/George Mason U., 1998—2000; ct. apptd. specialist Fairfax County, Fairfax, Va., 1991—93; lead tchr. remediation program Annandale H.S., 1999—2002, mem. attendance adv. com., 2003—04. Avocations: hiking, reading, working out, poetry. Home: 6006 Scarborough Commons Ln Burke VA 22015 Office: Fairfax County Pub Sch 5035 Sideburn Rd Fairfax VA 22032 E-mail: lcdelconte@cox.net.

DELEHANTY, MARTHA, human services administrator; B in Psychology, Mount Holyoke Coll.; M in Bus., U. Tex. With GTE, 1991—2000; field dir. Midwest Area GTE Wireless; joined Verizon Wireless, 2000; exec. dir. employee rels. Verizon Wireless LLC, Bedminster, NJ, 2000—04, v.p. human resources, 2004—. Office: Verizon Wireless LLC 180 Washington Valley Rd Bedminster NJ 07921

DELEHANTY, SUZANNE, museum director; b. Worcester, Mass., July 18, 1944; d. George B. and Catherine (Powers) D. BA with honors, Skidmore Coll., 1965; student, U. Pa., 1966-68. Curatorial asst. Inst. Contemporary Art, Phila., 1968-71, dir., 1971-78, Neuberger Mus., Purchase, N.Y., 1978-88, Contemporary Arts Mus., Houston, 1989—93; ind. curator and cons. NYC, 1994—95; dir. Miami Art Mus., 1995—. Mem. adv. coun. The Art Mus. at Princeton U., 1984—. Author: Agnes Martin, 1973, Cy Twombly and Video Art, 1975, George Segal/Environments, 1976, Fred Sandback/Sculpture, 1991. Mem. visual arts panel Tex. Commn. on Arts, 1990-91. Mem. Assn. Art Mus. Dirs., Urban League of Greater Miami. Office: Miami Art Mus 101 W Flagler St Miami FL 33130-1504 E-mail: sdeleha@miamidade.gov.*

DE LEON, LIDIA MARIA, magazine editor; b. Havana, Cuba, Sept. 10, 1957; d. Leon J. and Lydia (Diaz Cruz) de L. BA in Communications cum laude, U. Miami, Coral Gables, Fla., 1979. Staff writer Miami Herald, Fla., 1978-79; editorial asst. Halsey Pub. Co., Miami, 1980-81, assoc. editor, 1981, editor, 1981—, editor Delta Sky mag., 1983-95. Mem. Am. Soc. Mag. Editors, Am. Assn. Travel Editors, Golden Key, Sigma Delta Chi. Roman Catholic. Avocation: tennis. Office: 12550 Biscayne Blvd # 212 Miami FL 33181

DE LEON, RUDY, aerospace transportation executive; b. Pasadena, Calif., Aug. 28, 1952; BA in History, Loyola U., L.A., 1974; grad. exec. program, Harvard U., 1984; grad. seminar XXI program in fgn. politics, MIT, 1987. Legis. asst. U.S. Senate, Washington, 1975-77, U.S. Ho. of Reps., Washington, 1977-80, legis. asst., adminstrv. asst., 1980-85, profl. staff mem., Com. on Armed Svcs., 1985-89, staff dir., Com. on Armed Svcs., 1989-93; spl. asst. to sec. and dep. sec. of def. Dept. Def., Washington, 1993-94; under sec. of Air Force Dept. of Air Force, Washington, 1994-97; under sec. def. pers. and readiness Dept. of Def., 1997-2000, dep. sec. def., 2000-2001; sr. v.p. Boeing Co., 2001—, sr. v.p. Washington ops., 2001—. Recipient Defense Civilian Dist. Service award, 1994, 1995, Air Force Assoc. Special award, 1996, Air Force Meritorious Civilian Service award, 1997, Defense Civilian Dist. Service award, 2001, Nat. Intelligence Dist. Service Medal, 2001. Office: Boeing Co 100 No Riverside Chicago IL 60606 Office Phone: 312-544-2000.

DE LEON, SYLVIA A., lawyer; b. Corpus Christi, Tex., Mar. 2, 1950; m. Lynn R. Coleman; 3 children. BA, Briarcliff Coll., 1972; JD, U. Tex., 1976. Bar: Tex. 1976, DC 1977. Ptnr., founding mem. public law and policy practice group and mem. mgmt. com. Akin, Gump, Strauss, Hauer & Feld LLP, Washington. Adj. prof. law Georgetown U. Law Ctr., 1988-90; bd. dirs. (pres. apptd. senate confirmed) Amtrak, Nat. Railroad Passenger Corp., 1994—, vice chmn. 2003-, chair corp. strategy com. Bd. trustees U. Tex. Law Sch. Found. 2002-, U. Tex. Law Assn., 1985-89, 92-96, 2000-03, U. Tex. Devel. Bd., 1996—, bd. dirs. exec. com. Washington Ballet, 2001-; coord. issues transp. Clinton-Gore Presdl. Transition Team, 1992; presdl. appointee Nat. Commn. Ensure Strong Competitive Airline Industry, 1993, White House Conf. on Travel and Tourism. Mem. Bar Assn. DC, State Bar Tex. (chmn. fed. law and regulations com. 1984-87), Nat. Civil Aviation Rev. Commn. Office: Akin Gump Strauss Hauer & Feld Rm 1214 1333 New Hampshire Ave NW Washington DC 20036-1564 Business E-Mail: sdeleon@akingump.com.

DELFASSY, GILLES, semiconductor company executive; B in math. and physics with honors, Ecole Nat. Superieure d'Electronique, 1972, diploma in engring., 1977; cert. d'Aptitude Adminstrn. des Entreprises, Inst. Adminstrn. des Entreprises, 1978. Product line mgr. microprocessor and microcontroller divsn., semiconductor group Tex. Instruments, Dallas, 1978—89; dept. mgr. European DSP dept. Tex. Instruments Inc., 1989—94, sr. v.p., mgr. Worldwide Wireless Terminals Bus. Unit, 1994—. Office: Tex Instruments Inc 12500 TI Blvd Dallas TX 75243 Office Phone: 972-995-2011. Office Fax: 972-995-4360.

DELFFS, DUDLEY J., writer, educator; b. Sewanee, Tenn., Nov. 27, 1964; s. Dudley Julian and Norma (Thompson) D.; m. Dorothy Kilpatrick Scruggs, May 14, 1989; children: Mary Elise, Annie Kilpatrick. BA in English, U. Tenn., 1987, MA in English, 1989; MA in Counseling, Colo. Christian U., 1992. Tech. writer, rschr. Energy, Environ. Resource Ctr., Knoxville, Tenn., 1990-91; instr. English U. Tenn., Knoxville, Tenn., 1988-91, Colo U., Lakewood, 1991-96; counseling intern Colo. Christian U., Morrison, 1993-94, asst. prof. English, 1996—; fiction editor WaterBrook Press (divsn. of Random House), Colorado Springs, Colo., v.p. and editor-in-chief, 2005—. Author: (novels) Forgiving August, 1993, The Martyr's Chapel, 1998, The Judas Tree, 1999; (non-fiction) Repentant Heart, 1995, Prayer Centered Life, 1997, Mastering Money: A Pilgrimage Small Group Guide, 1998, Seeking God's Will, 1998, Balm in Gilead: Healing for the Repentent Heart, 2002; contbr. poetry and short stories to lit. mags. Recipient Scholastic Press Poetry award Columbia U., 1986, award Fiction Editor, Mars Hill review. Mem. Nat. Coun. Tchrs. English, Am. Counseling Assn., Assembly on Lit. for Adolescents, Colo. Lang. Arts Soc., Colo. Authors' League. Avocations: mountain biking, hiking, fishing, movies and film, travel. Office: WaterBrook Press Ste 200 5446 North Academy Colorado Springs CO 80918 Office Phone: 719-590-4999. Office Fax: 719-590-8977.*

DELFIN, DONNA K., writer, web programmer; b. Whittier, Calif. Attended, U. Denver; BA, Calif. State U., Fullerton. Former software developer Metafuse, Inc.; former senior contbr./editor Progressivetimes.com; former youth contbr./editor Asian Am. Register; former staff accountant/MIS specialist Contiki Holidays; former account repr. Triumph Bus. Sys.; former writer Asian Journal; freelance writer Filipinas Mag., San Francisco; web coord. Calif. State U., Dominguez Hills. Founder, exec. dir. Katipunan-USA, 2000—. Mem.: Asian Am. Journalists Assn. Office: Calif State U Dominguez Hills 1000 E Victoria St Carson CA 90747*

DELFINO, JOSEPH JOHN, environmental engineering sciences educator; b. Port Chester, N.Y., 1941; s. John J. and Frances C. Delfino; m. Dorothy Delfino; children: Janelle, Justin. BS in Chemistry, Holy Cross Coll., 1963; MS in Chemistry, U. Idaho, 1965; PhD in Civil and Environ. Engring. & Water Chemistry, U. Wis., 1968. From instr. to assoc. prof. chemistry USAF Acad., Colorado Springs, Colo., 1968-72; sect. head, tech. mgr. IBT & Nalco Environ. Sci., Northbrook, Ill., 1972-74; sect. head environ. scis. Wis. State Lab. Hygiene, Madison, 1974-82; from asst. prof. to assoc. prof. U. Wis., Madison, 1974-80, assoc. dir. water resources ctr., 1977-78, prof. civil and environ. engring., 1980-82; prof. environ. engring. sci. U. Fla., Gainesville, 1982—, affiliate prof. chemistry, 1990—, chmn. dept. environ. engring. sci., 1990—99, interim chmn., 2002—03, affiliate prof. natural resources and environment, 1994—, interim dir. Ctr. for Wetlands and Water Resources, 1995. Writer, co-originator, chief tech. advisor documentary Fla. Water Story, Sta. WEDU-TV, Tampa, Fla.; assoc. editor Jour. Am. Water Resources Assn., 2004—; contbr. articles on water chemistry, environ. scis. and engring. to profl. publs. Mem. Citizens Environ. Quality Coun., Northbrook, Ill., 1972-74; mem. Mercury Tech. Adv. Com., State of Fla., 1991-93; mem. Alachua County Air Quality Commn., Fla., 1999; mem. T.M.D.L. tech. adv. com. Fla. Dept. Environ. Protection, 1999-2000. Capt. USAF, 1968-72. Recipient Pub. Svc. award Univs. Coun. on Water Resources, 1990. Fellow AAAS; mem. Am. Chem. Soc. (exec. com. environ. chem. divsn. 1973-76, editor Envirofacs environ. chem. divsn. 1973-76, student awards com. environ. chem. divsn. 1995-97, com. on environ. improvement 1998-2001, Cert. of Merit environ. chem. divsn. 1991), Am. Soc. Civil Engring., Nat. Assn. State U. and Land Grant Colls. (ecology sect., exec. com. 1998-2001), Assn. Environ. Engrs. and Sci. Profs. Office: U Fla Dept Environ Engring Scis PO Box 116450 310 Black Hall Gainesville FL 32611-6450

DELFS, ANDREAS, conductor, musical director; b. Flensburg, Germany; Grad., Hamburg Conservatory, 1981; MA, Juilliard Sch., 1984. Staff conductor Lüneburg Stadttheater; music dir. Hamburg U. Orch.; musical asst. Hamburg State Opera; guest conductor Bremen State Theater, 1981; dir. Pitts. Youth Symphony; resident conductor Pitts. Symphony, 1986-90; music dir. Orch. Suisse Jeunes, 1984-95, Bern Opera, 1991-94; conductor N.Y. City Opera, 1995-96; music dir. Milw. Symphony Orch., 1997—; gen. music dir. Hannover State Opera and Orch. Guest condr. Phila. Orch. at Carnegie Hall, 1998, London Philharm., 1997, Dallas Symphony Orch., 1997, Houston Symphony, 1996—98, Junge Deutsche Philharmoni, Germany, 1995—98, Bern Symphony Orch., Minn. Orch., Detroit Symphony, Rochester Philharm. Bruno Walter scholar, Juilliard Sch., Steinburg fellow, Pitts. Symphony. Office: Milwaukee Symphony 700 N Water St #700 Milwaukee WI 53202-4239

DELFYETT, PETER, engineering educator; PhD, Grad. Sch. & U. Ctr. CUNY, 1988. Mem. tech. staff Bell Comm. Rsch.; joined Sch. of Optics and Ctr. for Rsch. and Edn. in Optics and Lasers (CREOL), U. Ctrl. Fla., 1993—; trustee chair prof. optics, electrical and computer engring. and physics U. Ctrl. Fla. Editor-in-chief IEEE Jour. of Selected Topics in Quantum Electronics, assoc. editor IEEE Photonics Technology Letters; contbr. articles for profl. jours. and conf. proceedings. Recipient Bellcore Synergy award, Bellcore award for Appreciation, Presdl. Early Career award for Scientists and Engrs., Nat. Sci. Found., Researcher of Yr., U. Ctrl. Fla., 1999, Black Engr. of Yr. award, 2000, Pegasus Prof. award, 2001. Fellow: IEEE/LEOS (fmr. mem. bd. gov.), Optical Soc. Am. Achievements include 12 US Patents. Office: Coll Optics & Photonics: CREOL & FPCE U Ctrl Fla PO Box 162700 Office CREOL 272 Orlando FL 32816-2700 Office Phone: 407-823-6812. Business E-Mail: delfyett@creol.ucf.edu.

DELGADILLO, ROCKARD J. (ROCKY DELGADILLO), lawyer; b. L.A., July 15, 1960; m. Michelle Delgadillo; children: Christian, Preston. BA with honors, Harvard U.; JD, Columbia U. Tchr., coach L.A. Unified Sch. Dist.; sr. atty. O'Melveny and Myers, L.A.; dir. bus. devel. Rebuild L.A.; dep. mayor econ. devel. City of L.A., city atty., 2001—. City Atty., L.A., 2001—. Bd. dirs. Arnold's All-Stars, Para Los Niños, Cath. Big Bros., 1st AME Ch. Renaissance Program, Franklin HS Scholarship Found., Friends Jordan HS, Workforce L.A.; leader L.A. ann. salute to Latino Heritage Month, 1993—. Named Disting. Young Alumnus, Columbia U., 1998, Alumnus of the Yr., 2002; named an All-Am. Football Player; recipient medal of excellence, Columbia U., John F. Kennedy Award, LA County Dem. Party, 2002. Office: City Hall E 200 N Main St Rm 1800 Los Angeles CA 90012-4131 Office Phone: 213-978-8100.*

DELGADO, CARLOS JUAN, professional baseball player; b. Aguadilla, Mayaguez, P.R., June 25, 1972; Player St. Catharines/N.Y.-Penn League, 1989-91, Toronto Blue Jays, 1993—2004, Florida Marlins, 2005—. Named to Am. League All-Star Team, 2000, 2003. Achievements include led Am. League in RBI's (145), 2003. Office: c/o Florida Marlins 2269 Dan Marino Blvd Hollywood FL 33028*

DELGADO, DWIGHD D(UBIED), electric power industry executive; b. Mayaguez, P.R., June 5, 1950; s. Ramon T. Delgado-Murphy and Rosalina (Ortiz) Delgado; m. Laurel Lee Waters, Feb. 1986; stepchildren: Jennifer Leigh, Sarah Noel. B in Inds. and Sys. Engring., Ga. Inst. Tech., 1977; M in Engring. Mgmt., George Washington U., 1997. From specialist in materials and prodn. control to mgr. shop ops. Lighting Bus. Group, Gen. Electric Co., Cleve., 1977—83, mgr. shop ops. splty. unit, 1983—84; mgr. spl. projects GE Ceramics, Gen. Electric Co., Pepper Pike, Ohio, 1984; ops. mgr. ECOM de Mex., SA de CV (Gen. Electric Tech. Svcs. Co.), Ciudad Juarez, Chihuahua, Mex., 1984-86; from mgr. new processes and equipment programs prodn. divsn. to tech. leader GE Lighting, Gen. Electric Co., 1987—90, tech. leader, 1990-91; dir. fabrication Fusion Sys. Corp., Rockville, Md., 1991-94, dir. mfg., 1994-96, Fusion UV Sys., Spectris, plc, Gaithersburg, Md., 1996-99, v.p. mfg., 2001—03, v.p. ops., 2003—04, project mgr., cons., 2003—04, Brüel & Kjaer Vibro GmbH Spectris, PLC, Darmstadt, Germany, 2004—; v.p. ops. NDC Infrared Engring. Spectris, PLC, Irwindale, Calif., 2004—. Founder, sole mem. Strategic Ops. Solutions, LLC, 2000—; pres., bd. dirs. Strategic Path and Engring., Inc., 2001—. Mem. U.S. Chess Fedn. Mem. Am. Inst. Indsl. Engrs. (sr.; bd. dirs. 1980-83, v.p. student and external affairs 1983-84, pres.-elect 1984-85, Chpt. Devel. Excellence award 1980), Am. Soc. for Quality Control (sr.; cert. quality engr. 1986), Aircraft Owners and Pilots Assn. (pvt. pilot lic. 1998), Angel Flight, Sports Car Club Am. (autocross, pit crew), U.S. Sailing Club (basic keelboat cert., basic cruising cert., bareboat cruising cert.). Roman Catholic. Avocations: flying, sailing, auto racing, chess. Home: 9443 Hickory View Pl Gaithersburg MD 20886-1409 Personal E-mail: dwighd@aol.com. Business E-Mail: ddelgado@fusionuv.com.

DELGADO, JANE, health policy executive, writer, psychologist; b. Havana, Cuba, June 17, 1953; d. Juan Lorenzo Delgado Borges and Lucila Aurora Navarro Delgado; m. Mark A. Steo, May 15, 1999; 1 child, Elizabeth A. Steo. BA, SUNY, New Paltz, 1973; MA, NYU, 1975; MS, W. Averell Harrimann Sch., 1981; PhD in Clin. Psychology, SUNY, Stony Brook, 1981. Children's talent coord. Children's TV Workshop, 1973-75; rsch. asst. SUNY, Stony Brook, 1975-79; social sci. analyst U.S. Dept. HHS, 1979-83, health policy advisor, 1983-85; pres., CEO Nat. Alliance for Hispanic Health, 1985—; pvt. practice in psychology, 1979—. Bd. dirs. Nat. Health Coun., 1986—97, Carter Ctr. Mental Health Taskforce, 1991—2000, Patient Safety Inst., 2001—; trustee The Kresge Found, 1997—, Found. Child Devel., 1989—97. Author: Salud! A Latina's Guide to Total Health, 1997, 2d edit., 2002. Bd. dirs. Lovelace Respiratory Rsch. Inst., 2002—. ABC Coalition, 2003—, Health Found. Am., 2003—. W.K. Kellogg Found. Nat. fellow, 1988, NIMH fellow, 1975-79; recipient Surgeon Gen.'s award, 1992, Florence Kelley award, 2002, Health and Sci. Latina Excellence award, 1995, FDA Commr.'s Citation award, 2005; named SUNY Alumna of Yr., 1993 Office: Nat Alliance for Hispanic Health 1501 16th St NW Washington DC 20036-1401 Office Phone: 202-797-4321. Business E-Mail: jdelgado@hispanichealth.org.

DELGADO, MARICA LADONNE, librarian, educator; b. Murray, Ky., Nov. 28, 1959; d. Billie Ray Roberts and Ada Sue Ross Roberts; m. Jon E. Delgado; children: Maurya, Jessamyn, Ian. BS, Murray State U., 1981; ML, Vanderbilt U., 1982. Libr. spl. projects Tenn. Tech. U., Cookeville, 1982, libr. collection develop./spl. projects, 1983—88, exch. libr. head periodicals and gifts, 1986—88; libr. gifts and exch., instr. Miss. State U., Starkville, 1988—92, libr. govt. documents, asst. prof., 1992—97, coord. govt. documents and microforms, assoc. prof., 1997—2005, prof., 2005—. Contbr. articles to profl. jours. Mem.: ALA (poster sessions rev. panel 1992—2002, 2005), MSU Robert Holland Faculty Senate (sec. 1999—2005), Miss. Libr. Assn. (GODORT sec. 1996—97, chair 2004), Southeastern Libr. Assn. (SELA poster sessions coord. 1992—94, 1998—2000). Avocations: boating, travel, camping, hiking. Home: 507 Sycamore St Starkville MS 39759 Office: Miss State U Libr Hardy Rd Mississippi State MS 39762 Office Phone: 662-325-7660. Office Fax: 662-325-3560. Business E-Mail: Ldelgado@library.msstate.edu.

DELGADO, MARY LOUISE, elementary school educator, secondary school educator, consultant, Internet company executive; b. Manitowoc, Wis., June 6, 1943; d. Walter Anthony and Jane Mary Jagodensky; 1 child, Daniel David. BA in English, Edn., Silver Lake Coll., 1971; MA, Govs. State U., Park Forest, Ill., 1983. Cert. tchr. Wis., Ill. Tchr. Colegio San Antonio Abad, Humacao, PR, 1973—75, Chgo. Pub. Schs., 1984—88, Milw. Pub. Schs., 1988—; pres., cons. Quality Online Connections, Milw., 2000—. Presenter in field. Pres. Lenox Heights Neighborhood Assn., Milw., 1999—2002. Fellow, Am. Coun. Learned Socs., 1994, 1995; grantee, Coun. Basic Edn. Ind. Study, 1994, NEH, 2000; Eleanor Roosevelt Tchr. scholar, 1999. Mem.: ASCD, AAUW, Wis. Tchrs. English to Students Second Langs. Democrat. Avocations: bicycling, reading, weaving. Office: Quality Online Connections 6333 W Chambers St Milwaukee WI 53210 Personal E-mail: mdelgado1@wi.rr.com.

DELGADO, RAMON LOUIS, theater educator, author, director, playwright, lyricist; b. Dec. 16, 1937; s. Eloy Vincent and Hildegard (Chapman) D. BA, Stetson U., 1959; MA, Baylor U., 1960; MFA, YAle U., 1967; PhD, So. Ill. U., 1976. Tchr. Lyman H.S., Longwood, Fla., 1960-62; mem. faculty Chipola Jr. Coll., Marianna, Fla., 1962-64, Ky. Wesleyan Coll., 1967-72, Hardin-Simmons U., 1972-74, So. Ill. U., 1974-76, St. Cloud (Minn.) State U., 1976-78; prof. speech and theater Montclair State U., Upper Montclair, NJ, 1978—2003, prof. emeritus, 2004—. Evaluator N.J. Teen Arts Festival, 1980, 81; judge Am. Theatre Assn. Coll. Theater Festival, 1980, 82, 83, 84, 85, N.J. Teen Galaxy Competition, 1984. Playwright: Waiting for the Bus, 1968, Once Below a Lighthouse, 1972, The Jerusalem Thorn, 1979, A Little Holy Water, 1983, Stones, 1983, The Flight of the Dodo, 1990, Remembering Booth, 1997, The Iron Corset, 1999, Consider the Phoenix, 2000; editor: The Best Short Plays, 1981-89; author: Acting with Both Sides of Your Brain, 1986; contbr. articles to profl. jours. Sec. Forest St. Manor Condo Assn., 1997-99; bd. dirs. 12 Miles West Theatre, 2000-2002. Recipient Samuel French Play award, 1966, U. Mo. Play award, 1971, 75, playwriting awards Am. Coll. Theatre Festival, 1976, 77, 78, Grand prize Music City Song Festival contest, 1988, 7 hon. mentions, 1989; Midwest Profl. Playwrights fellow, 1978; Ford Found. grantee, 1961; playwright-in-residence INTAR, 1980 Mem. Dramatists Guild, Assn. for Theatre in Higher Edn., Nat. Theatre Conf., Theta Alpha Phi, Phi Kappa Phi. Democrat. Home: 16 Forest St Apt 107 Montclair NJ 07042-3519

DELGADO, ROGER RODRIGUEZ, surgeon, educator; b. El Paso, Jan. 11, 1946; s. Roger R. and Eva (West) D.; m. Linda Susan Ferguson, Dec. 27, 1968; children: Jessica Lorraine, Nathan Roger. BA, U. Tex. El Paso, 1966; MD, U. Tex. Galveston, 1970. Diplomate Am. Bd. Surgery. Intern R.E. Thomason Horst, El Paso, 1970-71; resident surgery Naval Regional Med. Ctr., Portsmouth, Va., 1971-75, staff surgeon lt. comndr. Camp Pendleton, Calif., 1975-78; pvt. practice surgeon Sebastopol, Santa Rosa, Calif., 1978—. Assoc. clin. prof. U. Cal. San Francisco, 1978—; chief staff Palm Dr. Hosp., Sebastopol, 1980-81, bd. trustees, 1980-83, 90-94, dir. surg. svcs., 1996—. Contbr. articles to profl. jours. Master: ACS; mem.: Southwest Surgical Congress and Am. Soc. of Breast Surgeons, Soc. Am. Gastrointestinal Endoscopic Surgeons, Soc. Clin. Vascular Surgery, Beta Beta Beta. Roman Catholic. Avocations: skiing, biking. Office: Santa Rosa Sebastopol Hosp 6800 Palm Ave Ste C-1 Sebastopol CA 95472-4251

DEL GUERCIO, LOUIS RICHARD MAURICE, surgeon, educator; b. N.Y.C., Jan. 15, 1929; s. Louis and Hortense (Ardengo) Del G.; m. Paula Marie Helene de Vautibault, May 18, 1957; children: Louis, Francsca, Paul, Catherine, Maria, Michelle, Christopher, Anthony. BS, Fordham U., 1949; MD, Yale U., 1953. Diplomate Am. Bd. Surgery, Am. Bd. Thoracic Surgery. Intern Columbia-Presbyn. Med. Ctr., N.Y.C., 1953-54; resident St Vincent's Hosp., N.Y.C., 1954-58, Cleve. City Hosp., 1958-60; practice medicine specializing in thoracic surgery, 1960—; mem. faculty Albert Einstein Coll. Medicine, N.Y.C., 1960-71, assoc. prof., 1966-70, prof. surgery, 1970-71, dir. Clin. Rsch. Ctr.-Acute, 1967-71; clin. prof. surgery N.J. Coll. Medicine, Newark, 1971-76; prof. surgery N.Y. Med. Coll., N.Y.C., 1976—, chmn. dept., 1976—2001, emeritus prof. surgery, 2001—; chief surgery Westchester County Med. Ctr., 1976—. Cons. surgeon other hosps.; mem. surg. study sect. NIH, 1970-74; mem. com. on shock NRC-NAS, 1969-71; mem. merit rev. bd. VA, 1971-74; mem. health care tech. study sect. Dept. HHS, 1980-84; cons. Nat. Ctr. Health Svcs. Rsch., 1980-84; chmn. bd. dirs. Daltex Med. Scis., Inc. Author: (with B.G. Clarke) Urology, 1956, The Multilingual Manual for Medical History Taking, 1972, (with S.G. Hershey, R. McConn) Septic Shock in Man, 1971; editor-in-chief Critical Care Monitor, 1980-85, Complications in Surgery, 1990—; contbr. articles to med. jours.; patentee in field. With Mcht. Marine, 1946-47; with AUS, 1949-51; col. med. dept. USAR, 1990—. Recipient award in medicine Fordham U. Alumni Assn., 1974, Gold award Am. Acad. Pediat., 1973, Humanitarian award Boys' Towns of Italy, 1994; grantee Health Rsch. Coun. N.Y., 1965-71, NIH, 1962-71. Fellow ACS, Coll. of Critical Care Medicine, Am. Thoracic Soc.; mem. Am. Trauma Soc. (founding mem.), Soc. Critical Care Medicine (founding mem., pres. 1976), Am. Surg. Assn., Am. Physiol. Soc., Soc. Univ. Surgeons, French Nat. Acad. of Surgery, Equestrian Order of Holy Sepulchre of Jerusalem; hon. police surgeon City of NY. Home: 14 Pryer Ln Larchmont NY 10538-4021 Office: NY Med Coll Dept Surgery Valhalla NY 10595 Office Phone: 914-834-8265. E-mail: lou@delguercio.com. *Adaptability and the determination of what is possible are the keys to personal success and contentment.*

DELGYER, LESLIE AMELIA, artist; b. Plainfield, N.J., Sept. 11, 1946; d. Frederick Theodore Delgyer and Doris Marie Moore; m. Kenneth S. Roe, Mar. 24, 1968; 1 child, James F. Roe. Grad., duCret Sch. Arts, Plainfield, N.J.; studied under, Marjorie Van Emburgh and Dudley V. duCret, 1965—68. V.p., bd. trustees duCret Sch. Arts, Plainfield, NJ, 1987—. One-woman shows include The Ark III, Lahaska, Pa., 1977, The Inn Gallery, Shaftsbury, Vt., 1983, The Ark II, Flemington, N.J., 1976, 1978, 1983, 1989, Swain Galleries, Plainfield, N.J., 1975, 1979, 1983, 1985, 1989, 1996, 2003, Hiram Blauvelt Art Mus., Oradell, N.J., 2003, Represented in permanent collections The Ronald Reagan Presdl. Libr. & Mus., Simi Valley, Calif., Leigh Yawkey Woodson Art Mus., Wausau, Wis., Hunterdon Med. Ctr., Flemington, N.J., Hiram Blauvelt Art Mus., Oradell, N.J., numerous group shows including most recently, exhibited in group shows at The Pen and Brush Club, N.Y., 1983 (Philip Isenberg award, 1983), 1991 (Margaret Sussman award, 1991, Philip Isenberg award, 1991), Catherine Lorillard Wolfe Art Club, 1983 (Katherine A. Lovell Meml. award, 1983), Norton Art Mus., Shreveport, La., 2000, North Mus. Natural History and Sci., Lancaster, Pa., 2000, West Valley Art Mus., Surprise, Ariz., 2001, 2004, 2005, Sam Noble Okla. Mus. Natural HIstory, Norman, 2002, 2005, Nat. Geographic Soc., Washington, D.C., 2002, Cleve. Mus. Natural History, 2005, Lakeview Mus. Arts and Scis., Peoria, Ill., 2005, U. Nebr. State Mus., Lincoln, Nebr., 2005, Ariz.-Sonora Desert Mus., Tucson, Ariz., 2005; contbr. chapters to books; Exhibited in group shows at

Lakeview Mus. Arts & Scis., Peoria, Ill., 2005, U. Nebr. State Mus., Lincoln, 2005, Nev. State Mus., Carson City, 2005. Recipient Patricia Bott Meml. award, Catherine Lorillard Wolfe Art Club, N.Y., 1996. Mem.: Pastel Soc. Am. (Artists Mag. award 1996), Nat. Mus. Women in the Arts, Soc. Animal Artists (pres. 2004—, asst. sec. 1989, sec. 1994), Salmagundi Club (v.p., admissions com. 1998—2000, Ogden Pleissner Meml. award 1995, George Innes Jr. Meml. award 1994, Forbes Mag. award 1994, A.Henry Nordhausen award 1995, William Alfred White Meml. award 1996). Home: 168 Wester-velt Ave North Plainfield NJ 07060

DELHOMME, JAKE CHRISTOPHER, professional football player; b. Jan. 10, 1975; m. Keri Delhomme; 1 child. Grad., U. Louisiana-Lafayette. Quarterback Frankfurt Galaxy (NFL Europe), 1999, New Orleans Saints, 1999—2002, Carolina Panthers, 2003—. Achievements include mem. World Bowl Champion Frankfurt Galaxy, 1999; led Carolina Panthers to first ever Super Bowl Appearance, Super Bowl XXXVIII, 2004. Office: c/o Carolina Panthers 800 South Mint Street Charlotte NC 28202

DELI, ANNE TYNION, retail executive; b. Milw., Apr. 18, 1956; m. Steven F. Deli; 2 children. BA in History and French, Georgetown U., 1978. Acct. exec. Dancer Fitzgerald Sample, N.Y.C., 1978—80; acct. supr. Grey Advt., N.Y.C., 1980—82; v.p. Wells Rich Greene, N.Y.C., 1982—84; sr. v.p. Lawrence Charles Free, N.Y.C., 1984—86; prin. Anspach Grossman Portugal, N.Y.C., 1986—88; sr. v.p. Siegel & Gale, N.Y.C., 1988—93; v.p., global mktg. Harley-Davidson, Inc., Milw., 1993—95; pres., founder North River Strategies, Milw./Chgo., 1995—2000; pres. HD Am. Rd. LLC/Orlando Harley-Davidson, 2000—. Dir. Milw. Zool. Soc.; bd. dir. Chgo. Shakespeare Theatre, 2001—02, Orlando Mus. Art, 2002—05, Orlando and Orange County Convention and Visitor's Bur. Named Bus. Woman of Yr., Orlando Bus. Jour., 2005. Mem.: Orlando Regional C. of C. (vice chmn. 2003—), Orlando Women Who Mean Bus. Republican. Avocations: world travel, tennis, theater, art. Office: H-D Am Rd LLC Ste 2144 875 N Michigan Ave Chicago IL 60611 Office Phone: 312-280-6001. Personal E-mail: annetdeli@aol.com.

DELI, STEVEN FRANK, business investment and development executive; married; 1 child. BA in Econs., Northwestern U., 1973; MBA, Harvard U., 1977. Staff mem. comml. and real estate banking dept. Continental Ill. Nat. Bank, Chgo., 1973-75; investment banker Warburg Paribas Becker Inc., Chgo., 1977-84; mng. dir., head corp. fin. Dean Witter Reynolds, Inc., Chgo., 1984-92; founder, chmn., CEO Harley-Davidson Fin. Svcs., Inc., 1992-99; founder, chmn. Unicorn Fin. Svcs., Inc., 1997-2000; CEO H-D Am. Rd. LLC, Orlando, Fla., 2000—; founder, CEO Am. Rd. Retail, LLC, Orlando, 2005—. Mem. fin. com. and gov. mem. Chgo. Symphony Orch.; mem. Chgo. Com. of the Chgo. Coun. on Fgn. Rels. and Mid-Am. Com.; past sr. warden, vestryman Christ Ch., Winnetka, Ill. Mem. Chgo. Club (past bd. dirs.), Econ. Club Chgo., Indian Hill Club, Commonwealth Club, Eldorado Country Club, Country Club of Orlando, The Casino. also: 3770 37th St Orlando FL 32805

D'ELIA, CHRISTOPHER FRANCIS, marine biologist, educator, academic administrator; b. Bridgeport, Conn., Aug. 7, 1946; s. Francis G. and Marian Frances (Wakeman) D'Elia; m. Jennifer Anne Hunnicutt, June 10, 1973; 1 child, Tallmadge Wakeman. AB, Middlebury Coll., 1968; PhD, U. Ga., 1974. Postdoctoral scholar UCLA, 1974; vis. asst. prof. U. So. Calif., L.A., 1975; Noyes postdoctoral fellow Woods Hole (Mass.) Oceanog. Inst., 1975-77; from asst. prof. to assoc. prof. Chesapeake Biol. Lab. U. Md., Solomons, 1977—88, prof., 1988-99, SUNY, Albany, 1999—2004; dir. biol. oceanog. program NSF, Washington, 1987—89; dir. Md. Sea Grant Coll., 1989—98; v.p. rsch. SUNY, Albany, 1999—2002, prof. biology and pub. adminstrn. and policy, 2002—04; regional assoc. vice chancellor for rsch. and grad. studies, prof. environ. sci. and policy U. South Fla., St. Petersburg, 2004—. Chair tech. adv. group Patuxent 208 Basin Plan, 1980—82; mem. adv. panel ocean scis. divsn. NSF, Washington, 1982—84, mem. fleet rev. com., 1999; chmn. Mid-Atlantic Regional Marine Rsch. Bd., 1991—96; mem. rsch. planning adv. group, priorities workgroup Chesapeake Bay Program, 1989—91, mem. sci. and tech. adv. com., 1993—98; cons. to govt. and industry, 1976—; regional rep. coastal resources adv. com., Md., 1982—83; mem. adv. com. Md. Sea Grant program, 1980—86; mem. Future Am. Soc. Limnology and Oceanography, 1988; mem. sci. adv. bd. ecol. processes and effects com., marine monitoring com. EPA, 1991; mem. Leadership Md., 1997; mem. sea grant program assessment team NOAA, 2004; mem. Leadership St. Petersburg, 2005, Nat. Ctr. for Environ. Rsch. panel, 2004. Mem. editl. bd. Limnology and Oceanography, 1983—86; contbr. over 60 articles in profl. jours. and books. Bd. dirs. Hudson River Found., 1998—; acad. adv. com. Indsl. Rsch. Inst., 2001—; mem. exec. inst. Albany-Colonie C. of C., 2000; bd. dirs. Astrolabe, Inc., 1991—99, v.p., 1994—99; bd. dirs. Sci. Ctr. of Pinellas, 2004—. Recipient Outstanding Service cert., Tri-County Coun., Meritorious Svc. award, Chesapeake Bay Program, Gov.'s Salute to Excellence award; grantee, ERDA, 1976, EPA, 1978—82, Dept. Energy, 1979, NOAA, 1989—98, NSF, 1979—; Disting. Patrick scholar, Acad. Natural Scis., 1982—83. Fellow: AAAS; mem.: Great Lakes Rsch. Consortium (bd. gov. 1999—2004), Indsl. Rsch. Inst. (mem. acad. advancment com. 2001—04), Coun. Soc. Pres. (sec. 1993—96, treas. 1997, chmn.-elect 1998, chmn. 1999, past chmn. 2000, chmn. emeritus 2001—), Coun. Sea Grant Dirs. (chmn.-elect, chmn. budget com. 1994), Sea Grant Assn. (pres. 1991—92, chmn. fed. rels. com. 1992—93, pres. 1999, President's award), N.Y. Acad. Sci., Nat. Assn. State Univs. and Land Grant Colls. (co-chmn. bd. dirs. 1994—95, coun. grad. rsch. and grad. edn. exec. com. 2000—01, bd. oceans and atmosphere, mem. exec. com., chmn. edn. com., chmn. spl. task force reorganization), Nat. Assn. Environ. Profs. (bd. dirs. Md. 1985—86), Internat. Soc. Reef Studies, Estuarine Rsch. Fedn. (v.p. 1989—91, pres. 1991—93, past pres. 1993—95), Ecol. Soc. Am. (chmn. pub. affairs com. 1989—91, vice chmn. 1991—92), Am. Soc. Limnology and Oceanography, Am. Chem. Soc., Oceanog. Soc. (life), Vinoy Club, Cosmos Club, Sigma Xi. Avocations: sailing, skiing, private pilot. Office: Office Academic Affairs U South Fla St Petersburg 140 7th Ave S Saint Petersburg FL 33701-5016 Office Phone: 727-553-4812. Business E-Mail: cdelia@spadmin.usf.edu.

DELIA, CLAUDE WILLIAM, retired physician, pathologist; b. Medford, Mass., July 24, 1924; s. T. P. and Rose (Daiute) D.; m. Jeanne Wetmore, Aug. 2, 1949 (dec. Sept. 2002); children: Nancy Ann Delia, Deborah Delia Webster, Pamela Egan, Patricia J. Campbell; m. DeAnna B. Stein, Dec. 11, 2003. Student, Harvard U., 1946; MD, Yale U., 1950. Diplomate Am. Bd. Pathology. Dir. lab. Conway Hosp., S.C., 1960-97; ret., 1998. Mem. adv. bd. First Citizens Bank, Conway. Served U.S. Army, 1943—46, WWII, maj. U.S. Army, 1950—60, Korean Conflict. Fellow Coll. Am. Pathologists, Am. Soc. Clin. Pathologists; mem. AMA, Japanese-Am. Soc. Pathologists, S.C. Med. Assn., N.Y. Acad. Scis., Conway Hosp. Found. (mem. ethics com. 2001—, investment com.), Conway Med. Ctr. Republican. Avocations: reading, writing. Home: River Bend 407 Sasser Ln Conway SC 29527-7659 Personal E-mail: clodsez@aol.com.

D'ELIA, NICHOLAS, secondary school educator; b. NY, Sept. 22, 1959; s. Mario John and Angela Rose (Puma) D'Elia; m. Carolyne Gilroy, Aug. 24, 1984; children: Nicole, Michael, Philip. *Father Mario D'Elia has been a pioneer in the field of dental prosthetics since 1953. Conducting his work at Memorial Sloan Kettering Hospital in New York City he has contributed to the recovery of countless cancer patients. Parents Mario and Angela D'Elia have celebrated 49 years of marriage. Wife Carolyne has continued her endeavors in finance and insurance.* BA, CUNY, 1981; MS, Coll. S.I., 2004. V.p. prodn. Flying Tiger Comm., N.Y.C., 1981-84; prodr., dir. Merrill Lynch Video Network, N.Y.C., 1985-89; freelance dir. N.Y.C., 1980-90; prodr., dir. Rainbow TV Prodns., Inc., N.Y.C., 1990—94; tchr. Holy Name Sch., Bklyn., 1995—2001, New Utrecht HS, Bklyn., 2001—. Freelance dir. TV Generation, 1982 (U.S.A. Cable Video of the Week, 1983); freelance video engr. ABC Sports, 1981-85, ABC DayTime, N.Y.C. and remote locations, 1983-85, MacNeil-Lehrer News Hour, N.Y.C., 1983-85, CBS News, N.Y.C. and remote locations, 1983-84. Writer, producer (corp. mktg. tape) You Must Remember This..., 1989 (AVCA Bronze award, 1989). Mem. NATAS, Internat. TV Assn. Roman Catholic. Avocations: performing and fine arts, scuba diving, auto racing. Office: New Utrecht HS 1601 80th St Brooklyn NY 11214

DELIENNE, JACQUELYN E., e-commerce consultant, publisher; b. Little Rock, Ark., Aug. 3, 1947; d. John Henry and Blanche Evon (Green) E.; m. Dennery Delienne; 1 child, Christopher Malik. Student, Harvard U., 1964-66; BSBA, SUNY, Albany, 1980; postgrad., Golden Gate U. and Columbia Pacific U. CPA, Calif., S.C. Assoc. acct. Deloitte Haskins & Sells CPAs, San Francisco, 1979-82, Friedlander & Daiker CPAs, San Francisco, 1982-83; pvt. practice acctg. San Francisco, 1983-84; contr. Sheriar Press Inc., Myrtle Beach, S.C., 1984-86; pvt. practice acctg. North Myrtle Beach, S.C., 1987-91; pub. Windy Hill Publs., North Myrtle Beach, 1987-93; pvt. practice therapeutic edn., performance enhancement Mrytle Beach, 1988-91; CFO Health Care Ptnrs., Inc., Conway, S.C., 1993-96; bus. process and strategy cons., mgr. Qualcomm., Inc., San Diego, 1997-99; pub. Renaissance 9, 1998—. Bd. dirs. Internat. Coun. on Sys. Engring., San Diego; electronic commerce cons. eForce Inc., Hayward, Calif., 1999-2001; prin. Digizine Creative LLC, Oceanside, Calif., 1999—. Mem. Oceanside Bahá'í Spiritual Assembly. Mem. Company of Friends, Incose, San Diego Software Industry Coun., Soc. Tech. Comm., Stellcommunicators Toastmasters (pres. 1998-99). Avocations: dance, volunteer work. Office: 3584 Windrift Way Ste 293 Oceanside CA 92056-5232 E-mail: renaissance9@att.net.

DELIGNE, PIERRE RENÉ, mathematician; b. Brussels, Oct. 3, 1944; s. Albert and Renée (Bodart) D.; m. Elena Vladimirovna Alexeeva, Sept. 9, 1980; children: Natalia, Alexis. Licence en mathématiques, ULB (Université Libre de Bruxelles), Brussel, 1966, PhD in Mathematics, 1968. Jr. scientist Fond National de la Recherche Scientifique Belgium, Brussel, 1967-68; vis. mem. Institut des Hautes Etudes Scientifiques, Bures sur Yvette, France, 1968-70; permanent mem. Inst. des Hautes Etudes Scientifiques, Bures sur Yvette, France, 1970-84; prof. Inst. for Advanced Study, Princeton, NJ, 1984—. Editor Pub. Math. Institut des Hautes Etudes Scientifiques, 1970; contbr. articles to profl. jours. Recipient Francois Deruyts prize, 1974, Henri Poincare Medal, Acad. Scis., Paris, 1974, Fields medal Internat. Math. Union, 1978, Crafoord prize, 1988, Balzan prize in Mathematics, 2004. Mem. Associé Etranger Academie des Sciences, AAAS (fgn. hon.), Royal Belgian Acad. Office: Inst for Advanced Study Sch Mathematics Einstein Dr Fuld Hall 210 Princeton NJ 08540 Business E-Mail: deligne@ias.edu.

DELIKAT, MICHAEL, lawyer; b. NYC, Apr. 3, 1952; s. Otto and Pearl (Soffer) D.; m. Alice Baron; children: Stacey, Jonathan. BS in Indsl. and Labor Rels., Cornell U., 1974; JD, Harvard U., 1977. Bar: N.Y. 1978, U.S. Dist. Ct. (so., ea. and we. dists.) N.Y. 1978, U.S Ct. Appeals (9th cir.) 1991, U.S. Supreme Ct. 1992. Ptnr. Baer Marks & Upham, N.Y.C., 1977-91, Orrick Herrington & Sutcliffe LLP, N.Y.C., 1991—, mng. dir. litigation divsn., chair employment law practice group NYC. Author: Summary Judgement Motion Practice, 1995, Legal Dangers in Diversity, 1995, Am. with Disabilities Act: New Fed. Rights for Disabled Employees, 1993, Protection Trade Secrets & Confidential Bus. Info.: Employer's Guide, 1993, Whistleblowing Claims, 2005. Arbitrator U.S. Dist. Ct. (ea. dist.) N.Y., Bklyn., 1987. Mem. NY Univ. Ctr. for Labor and Employment Law, Cornell Club, NY State Bar (Comml. & Fed. Litig. Sect., Com. Practice & Procedure Before the NLRB), ABA (equal employment opportunity com.). Office: Orrick Herrington & Sutcliffe 666 5th Ave New York NY 10103-1798 Office Phone: 212-506-5230. Office Fax: 212-506-5151. Business E-Mail: mdelikat@orrick.com.

DELIMAN, ROBERT MICHAEL, surgeon; b. Braddock, Pa., Mar. 11, 1928; m. Renate Marie; children: Belle, Darwin, Michael. MD, George Washington U., 1953. Diplomate Am. Bd. Surgery. Intern Highland (Calif.) Alameda County Hosp., 1953-54; resident Kaiser Found. Hosp., Oakland, Calif., 1954-55, City Hope Med. Ctr., Duarte, Calif., 1958-59, Long Beach (Calif.) VA Hosp., 1959-62; surgeon So. Calif. Surg. Med. Group Inc., Arcadia, 1962-98. Surgeon Meth. Hosp., Arcadia, 1962-98, City Hope Med. Ctr., Duarte, Santa Teresita Hosp.(v.p. med. affairs, bd. dirs. 1995-99); pres. So. Calif. Physicians Coun.; former bd. dirs. L.A. County Found. Medical Care; former med. dir. Mid Valley Physicians, Greater Pacific HMO. Recipient commendation for exemplary record of civic leadership, Calif. Senate, 2001. Fellow ACS, Am. Coll. Physician Execs., Am. Coll. Angiology; mem. Soc. Clin. Vascular Surgery, L.A. Surg. Soc. Office: 324 W Walnut Ave Monrovia CA 91016-3346 Office Phone: 626-359-3594.

DE LINE, DONALD, former film company executive; b. L.A. BA, UCLA. Casting and drama devel. exec. ABC Entertainment; dir. for prodn. filmed entertainment divsn. The Walt Disney Studios, 1985—86; v.p. prodn. The Disney Sunday Movie, 1986, pres. prodn., 1986, Snowback Prodns., 1987; v.p. prodn. Walt Disney Pictures, 1988; sr. v.p. Touchstone Pictures, 1990—91, exec. v.p., 1991—93, pres., 1993—98; with Paramount Pictures, Hollywood, Calif., 1998—2003, vice chmn. motion picture group, pres., 2004—05. Prodr.: (films) Domestic Disturbance, 2001, The Italian Job, 2003, The New Foon, 2004, Without a Paddle, 2004, The Stepford Wives (Remake), 2004.*

DE LISA, JOEL ALAN, rehabilitation physician, research executive; b. Seattle, Mar. 18, 1942; s. Joseph Phillip and Alice Georgia (Jensen) DeL.; m. Janet Hopper, July 25, 1971. BS in Zoology, Wash. State U., 1964; MD, U. Wash., 1968, MS, 1976. Diplomate Am. Bd. Phys. Medicine and Rehab. (chmn. 1993-98); diplomate spinal cord injury medicine. Intern St. Josephs Hosp., Phoenix, 1968-69; resident in phys. medicine and rehab. U. Wash., Seattle, 1972-75; med. dir., chief med. officer Kessler Inst. Rehab., West Orange, N.J., 1987-93; sr. v.p., chief med. officer Kessler Rehab. Corp., West Orange, 1994-2000; pres., CEO Kessler Med. Rehab. Rsch. and Edn. Corp., West Orange, 1998—. Prof., chmn. dept. phys. medicine and rehab. Univ. Medicine and Dentistry N.J., Newark, 1987—, interim dean, 2000; chmn. dept. phys. medicine and rehab. St. Barnabas Med. Ctr., Livingston, N.J., 1990-98; spkr. Taiwan Nat. U. Hosp., 1995, 23d ann. meeting Korea Acad. Rehab. Medicine, 2004. Author: Principles and Practice of Physical Medicine and Rehabilitation, 2004, Manual of Nerve Conduction Study and Surface Anatomy and Needle Electromyography, 2004. Mem. AMA, Assn. Acad. Physiatrists, Am. Acad. Phys. Medicine and Rehab., Am. Congress Rehab. Medicine, Am. Paraplegic Soc. (hon., pres. Jackson Heights chpt. 1989-91, Excellence award 1995). Office: Kessler Med Rehab Rsch and Edn Corp 1199 Pleasant Valley Way West Orange NJ 07052-1424 Office Phone: 973-243-6805. Business E-Mail: delisaja@umdnj.edu.

DE LISIO, STEPHEN SCOTT, lawyer, director, pastor; b. San Diego, Dec. 30, 1937; s. Anthony J. and Emma Irving (Cheney) DeL.; m. Margaret Irene Winter, June 26, 1964; children: Anthony W., Stephen Scott, Heather E. Student, Am. U., 1958-59; BA, Emory U., 1959; LLB, Albany Law Sch., 1962; LLM, Georgetown U., 1963. Bar: N.Y. 1963, D.C. 1963, Alaska 1964. Practice law, Fairbanks, Alaska, 1963-71, Anchorage, 1972-96; asst. dist. atty. Fairbanks, 1963-65; assoc. McNealy & Merdes, 1965-66; lectr. U. Alaska, 1965-67; ptnr. Staley, DeLisio & Cook, 1966-93, DeLisio, Moran, Geraghty & Zobel, Inc., 1994—2003; pastor Anchorage Bible Fellowship. Bd. dirs. Woodstock Property Co., Inc., Pasit Inc., Challenger Films Inc.; vice chmn. Crosstown CBMC, 1986—87, chmn., 1987—88, 1990—91, area coord., 1987—92; city atty., Fairbanks, 1967—70, Barrow, 1969—72, Ft. Yukon and North Pole, 1970—72; past sec. U. Alaska Heating Corp., Inc.; past sec.-treas. Trans-Alaska Electronics, Inc., Baker Aviation, Inc.; former arbitrator, mem. Alaska regional coun. Am. Arbitration Assn. Author: (with others) Law and Tactics in Federal Criminal Cases, 1964. Past pres. Tanana Valley State Fair Assn.; past v.p. Fairbanks Mental Health Assn., Fairbanks United Good Neighbors Fund; bd. dirs. Anchorage Cmty. Chorus, 1975—77, Common Sense for Alaska, 1987—94, Alaska chpt. Lupus Found., 1989—96; chmn. bd. Alaska Voluntary Health Assn., 1993—96; former bd. dirs. Greater Fairbanks Cmty. Hosp. Found.; met. dir. Christian Businessmen's Outreach, 1993—94, bd. dirs. Anchorage, 1985—92; met. dir. Alaska Christian Businessmen's Com. U.S.A., 1994—2000; rep. precinct committeeman, 1970—76; chmn. Alaska Rep. Rules Com. Anchorage Rep. Com, 1973; v.p. We the People, 1977—79; vice chmn. Alaska Libertarian Party, 1983—84; mem. nat. com. Libertarian Party, 1982—85; deacon Anchorage Bible Fellowship, 1986—90, elder, pastor, 1990—; Alaska coord. Crown Ministries, 1991—93. Recipient Jaycee Disting. Service award, 1968 Mem. Am. Trial Lawyers Assn., Am. Judicature Soc., Alaska Bar Assn., D.C. Bar Assn., Anchorage Bar Assn., Spenard Bar Assn. (pres. 1975-77), U.S. Jaycees (past dir.), Alaska Jaycees (past pres.), Fairbanks Jaycees (past pres.), Chi Phi, Pi Sigma Phi, Woodstock Golf Inc. Club (pres. 1984—). Home: 5102 Shorecrest Dr Anchorage AK 99502-1329 Office: Anchorage Bible Fellowship 7348 Abbott Loop Rd Anchorage AK 99507 Personal E-mail: cbmcak@alaska.net. *A well-defined sense of values and the courage and determination to adhere to it is as essential to a life of purpose and fulfillment, as the rising of the sun is to life on this planet. The challenge is to develop values that are as relevant to the changes of tomorrow as to the reality of the now and the past. The "situation ethics" approach is as disastrous as a smashed rudder on a storm tossed vessel. The Way, the Truth and the Life is found only in Christ Jesus.*

DELISLE, JACQUES, law educator; AB, Princeton U., 1982; JD, Harvard U., 1990. Law clk. to Chief Judge Stephen G. Breyer US Ct. Appeals (1st Cir.), 1991—92; atty. / adv. Office of Legal Counsel, US Dept. Justice, 1992—94; asst. prof. U. Pa. Law Sch., Phila., 1994—99, faculty mem. Ctr. for East Asian Studies, 1996—, prof., 1999—; dir. Asian Programs Foreign Policy Rsch. Inst. Contbr. articles to law jours. Office: U Pa Law Sch 3400 Chestnut St Philadelphia PA 19104 Office Phone: 215-898-5781. Office Fax: 215-573-2025. E-mail: jdelisle@law.upenn.edu.*

DELL, DIANA JEAN, writer; b. East Vandergrift, Pa., Feb. 11, 1946; d. James Albert Dell and Clara Dorothy Masgay; 1 child, Mark Clark. BS, W.Va. U., 1967. Dir. USO, Washington, 1970—75; instr. Tampa (Fla.) Coll., 1995—96; pres. VietnamWar.net, Boston, 1996—. Freelance writer, Boston, 1976—. Author: (book) A Saigon Party: And Other Vietnam War Short Stories, 1999, Memories Are Like Clouds, 2000; editor: Memorable Quotations: American Women Writers of the Past, 2000, Memorable Quotations: Famous Teachers of the Past, 2001, Memorable Quotations: Humorists, Wits, and Satirists of the Past, 2000, (web site) IntelligentsiaNetwork.com, 1997, MemorableQuotations.com, 2000, VietnamWar.net, 1996. Recipient Outstanding Civilian Svc. medal, U.S. Dept. of Army, 1972. Home and Office: 21 Elm St #2 Malden MA 02148 Personal E-mail: dianajdell@aol.com.

DELL, MICHAEL S., computer company executive; b. Houston, Feb. 23, 1965; s. Alexander and Lorraine D.; m. Susan Lieberman, Oct. 23, 1989. Student, U. Tex., 1983-84. Founder, chmn. Dell Computer Corp. (formerly PC's Ltd.), Austin, 1984—; CEO Dell Computer Corp., 1984—2004. IT Governor World Econ. Forum; Mem. Internat. Bus. Coun., US Bus. Coun. Author: Direct From Dell: Strategies that Revolutionized an Industry, 1999. Recipient Entrepreneur of Yr. award Inc. Mag., 1990, Customer Satisfaction award JD Power, 1991, 93; named CEO of Yr. Fin. World Mag., 1993, Chief Exec. of Yr. Chief Exec. Mag., 2001, One of Top-Ten Most Powerful People in Bus. Fortune Mag., 2003, 2004. Office: Dell Computer Corp 1 Dell Way Round Rock TX 78682-0001

DELL, RALPH BISHOP, retired pediatrician, researcher; b. Mt. Village, Alaska, July 31, 1935; s. Elwin B. and Elizabeth B. (Bishop) D.; m. Kathryn M. Bownass, June 17, 1957 (div. Dec. 1982); children: Laura, Kenneth; m. Karen K. Hein, Aug. 28, 1983; stepchildren: Ethan Hein, Molly Hein. BA, Pomona Coll., 1957; MD, U. Pa., 1961. Diplomate Am. Bd. Pediat. Intern and resident Children's Hosp. Med. Ctr., Boston, 1961-63; NIH postdoctoral fellow Coll. Physicians and Surgeons, Columbia U., N.Y.C., 1963-66, assoc., 1966-67, asst. prof. pediat., 1967-72, assoc. prof., 1972-78, prof., 1978-97; dir. Inst. for Lab. Animal Rsch. NRC, Washington, 1997-2000, ret., 2000. Author 3 books, 100 rsch. papers; co-inventor amino acid solution. Recipient Rsch. Career Devel. award NIH, 1966-71, Career Scientist award Health Rsch. Coun. N.Y., 1972-75; Fogarty Sr. Internat. fellow NIH, 1975-76. Mem. Am. Pediat. Soc., Am. Physiologic Soc., Am. Soc. Clin. Investigation, Soc. for Pediat. Rsch., Assn. for Computing Machinery, Am. Assn. Accreditation Lab. Animal Care (coun. on accreditation). Democrat. Home: PO Box 607 Jacksonville VT 05342 Personal E-mail: rbdell@direcway.com.

DELL, ROBERT CHRISTOPHER, sculptor, art educator; b. Nyack, N.Y., Feb. 22, 1950; s. Edward John and Laurel Jean (McGrath) D.; children: Robert Carroll, Malcolm Vincent, Terrence Edward; m. Siena Gillan Porta, May 30, 1986. BS in Edn., SUNY, Oneonta, 1972; MFA in Sculpture, SUNY, New Paltz, 1975. Mem. arch. and cmty. appearance bd. rev. Orangetown, N.Y., 1979-2001, vice-chmn., 1987-2001, mem. planning bd., 2001—; dir. visual arts Vriesland W. Hudson Art Ctr., Pearl River, N.Y., 1978-80, artist-in-residence, 1980; vis. artist Akureyri Sch. Visual Art, 1999, Am. Scandinavian Found. fellow, 1999-2000; adj. prof. Sch. Engring. The Cooper Union, 2003—, Westchester C.C., Valhalla, N.Y., 2003-04; spkr. in field; lectr. in field. One-man shows include Vorpal Gallery, Chgo., 1978, N.Y.C., 1981, 88, San Francisco, 1985, New Acquisitions Gallery, Syracuse, 1983, Blue Hill Cultural Ctr., Pearl River, N.Y., 1987, 98-99, Am. Embassy, Am. Cultural Ctr., Reykjavik, Iceland, 1988, geothermal sculpture installation, Country Park Reykjanesfolkvangur, Iceland, 1988, Perlan, Reykjavik (permanent geothermal sculpture installation) 1991, Mid-Hudson Arts and Sci. Ctr., Poughkeepsie, N.Y., 1992, Castle and Old Faithful, Grotto Geyser Groups Yellowstone Nat. Park, Wyo., 1996, Kresge oval MIT, 1997, Kresge Oval MIT, 1997, Akureyri Art Mus., Iceland, 1999, The Great Geysir, Geysir Nature Conservation Area Haukadalur, Iceland, 1999, Akureyri Art Mus., Iceland, 1999, Geysir, Haukadal, Iceland, 1999, Reykjavik Mcpl. Art Mus. Harbour House, 2001, Albert Neikon Sch. Engring., Cooper Union, N.Y.C., 2004; numerous group shows including most recently Noho Gallery N.Y.C., 2002, Hafnarborg Inst. Culture and Fine Art, Hafnarborg Museum, Hrafnarfurdor, Iceland, 2002, Museum House at Húsavík, Húsavík, Iceland, 2003, Regional Museum of Hornafjordur, Hofn, Iceland, 2003, McLevy Pk., Bridgeport, Conn., 2004-05; permanent collections include U.S. Embassy, Am. Cultural Ctr., Iceland MIT, Fulbright Commn., Reykjavik, Syracuse U., Mus. Fine Art, Springfield, Mass., MacDowell Colony, Peterborough, N.H., SUNY, Town of Orangetown (N.Y.), Hafamborg inst. Art and Culture, Iceland; subject of video Hitavaetur MIT, Circumstantial Prodns., 1991, News Story, Frettir, geothermal sculpture State TV Iceland, 1993-96; scenic artist motion pictures, TV shows; master scenic artist One Life to Live ABC, 1988-99 (Daytime Emmy honoree 1995); author: Hitavaettur and The Implications of Geothermal Sculpture, 2000; several articles in field. Fellow MacDowell Colony, 1980, Am. Scandinavian Found., 1999-00, Fulbright Found., 1988, The Cooper Union Rsch. Found., N.Y.C., 2004—; Collaboration Art, Sci. and Tech. grantee Syracuse U., 1978, grantee NYSCA, 1986, Ptnrs. of Ams., 1993, Robert E. Brennan Found., 1993, Waterloo Found. Arts, 1994, Coun. Arts at MIT, 1997, N.Y. Found. for the Arts, 2001. Home: 421 Washington St Tappan NY 10983-2703

DELL, ROBERT MICHAEL, lawyer; b. Chgo., Oct. 4, 1952; s. Michael A. and Bertha Dell; m. Ruth Celia Schiffman, May 29, 1976; children: David, Michael, Jessica. BGS, U. Mich., 1974; JD, U. Ill., 1977. Bar: U.S. Dist. Ct. (no. dist.) Ill. 1977, U.S. Ct. Appeals (7th cir.) 1977, U.S. Dist. Ct. (no. dist.) Calif. 1990. Law clk. to justice U.S. Ct. Appeals (7th cir.), Chgo., 1977—79; assoc. Latham & Watkins, Chgo., 1982—85, ptnr., 1985—, mng. ptnr. San Francisco office, 1990—94, firm chmn. and mng. ptnr., 1995—. Home: 19 Tamal Vista Ln Kentfield CA 94904-1005 Office: Latham & Watkins LLP 505 Montgomery St Ste 2000 San Francisco CA 94111-2552

DELL, WARREN FRANK, II, management consultant; b. Louisville, Aug. 8, 1945; s. George Justus and Opal Lee (Roberts) D.; m. Theresa LoParco, July 11, 1970; child, Stacy Lee. BS, Northeastern U., 1968; MBA, Iona Coll., 1973. Cert. mgmt. cons. Systems analyst Am. Can Co., Greenwich, Conn., 1968-69; cons. Info. Techniques, Inc., Norwalk, Conn., 1969-70; systems analyst Colgate Palmolive, N.Y.C., 1970-72, supr. mktg. stats., 1972-73, mgr. forecast and adminstrn., 1973-77; cons. Case and Co., Stamford, Conn., 1977-80, prin., 1980-83, sr. ptnr., dir., 1983-85; prin. Cresap, a Towers Perrin Co., N.Y.C., 1985-86, v.p., 1986-90; pres. Dellmart & Co., Stamford, Conn., 1989—. Bd. dirs. JSL Perekriosrok, TDS Logistics. Contbr. articles to profl. jours. Mem. Republican Town Com.; bd. dirs. Stamford Hist. Soc. Mem.

Coun. Logistics Mgmt., Warehouse Edn. Rsch. Coun., Food Distbn. Rsch. Soc., Am. Philatelic Soc., Inst. Mgmt. Cons. Avocations: stamp collecting/philately, golf, travel. Office: Dellmart & Co 125 Hardesty Rd Stamford CT 06903-4327 Business E-Mail: Frank@Dellmart.com.

DELLACORTE, CHRISTOPHER, engineer; b. Port Jefferson, N.Y., Dec. 10, 1963; s. Franklin Alfred and Suzanne DellaCorte; m. Patricia DellaCorte. BS, Case Western Res. U., 1986, MS, PhD, Case Western Res. U., 1987. Rsch. engr. Case Western Res. U., Cleve., 1986-87, NASA, Cleve., 1987—. Contbr. over 50 articles to profl. jours. Bd. dirs. Medina (Ohio) County Bd. Mental Retardation and Devel. Disabilities, 1992-96. Mem. ASME (Burt L. Newkirk award 1996, conf. planning com. 1995—), Soc. Tribologists and Lubrication (assoc. editor, solid lubricants com. chair 1989-92). Avocations: mechanical devices, technical history, natural history. Office: NASA Glenn Rsch Ctr MS 23-2 21000 Brookpark Rd Cleveland OH 44135-3191

DELL'ACQUA-BELLAVITIS, LUDOVICO MATTEO, research scientist; b. Milan, July 24, 1977; arrived in U.S., 2001; s. Arturo Enrico Dell'Acqua-Bellavitis and Grazia Francesca Reggio. BSc, U. Coll. London, 2000; MS, Rensselear Polytech. Inst., 2003; MBA, Rensselear Polytech. Inst., 2004. Rsch. asst. cognitive neuropsychology lab. Harvard U., Cambridge, Mass., 1998; rsch. asst. cognitive neurology Wellcome, London, 2000; rsch. asst. Rensselaer Nanotech. Ctr., Troy, NY, 2001—05; pres., CEO Hytwo, LLC, Watervliet, NY, 2005—. Cons. Grizoni Svc. SRL, Milan, 2001—03; rsch. asst. Cornell Nanofabrication Facility, Ithaca, NY, 2004; cons. hydrogen divsn. Gen. Electric, Niskayuna, NY, 2003. Author: Kinetics for the Synthesis Reaction of Aligned Carbon Nanotubes, 2003. Fellow, Philip Morris U.S.A., 2001—05; Socrates Erasmus fellow, European Commn., Italian Ministry of U., Sci. and Tech. Rsch., London, 1999—2000. Fellow: London Geoxnough Trust, Materials Rsch. Soc.; mem.: Soc. Biomaterials, Am. Chem. Soc. Achievements include invention of location and timing in face processing. Avocations: photography, bicycling, skiing. Home: 277 Pawling Ave Troy NY 12180-4842 Office: Hytwo LLC 877 25th St Watervliet NY 12189-1960

DELLA-GIUSTINA, JO-ANN SUBOTIN, lawyer; b. Springfield, Mass., Sept. 6, 1951; d. Joseph Augustus and Jennie Delores (Subotin) Della-G. BA, Clark U., 1972; MA, Columbia Coll., Chgo., 1983; JD, Chgo.-Kent Coll. Law, 1987; PhD in Criminal Justice, CUNY, 2005. Bar: Ill. 1987, Mass. 1996, N.Y. 1998, U.S. Dist. Ct. (no. dist.) Ill. 1987, N.Y. 1998. Tchr. S.W. Ind. Sch. Dist., San Antonio, 1976-78, Malcolm X Coll., Chgo., 1978-80; dir. pub. rels. H&R Block, Chgo., 1983-85; asst. corp. counsel City of Chgo., 1987-89; sr. atty. Office of Cook County Pub. Defender, Chgo., 1989-90; judicial law clk. to Justice David Cerda Ill. Appellate Ct., Chgo., 1990-98; asst. prof. Bridgewater State Coll., Bridgewater, Mass., 2005—. Cons. Am. Planning Assn., Chgo., 1990—98; bd. dir. loan repayment and assistance program ITT Chgo., 1995—97, mem. exec. com. criminal justice PhD program, 2001—02; mem. curriculum com. criminal justice PhD program CUNY, 1999—2001, graduate tchg. fellow, 2001—04, mem. exec. com. PhD program, 2001—02; adj. asst. prof. John Jay Coll., 2001—05; presenter in field; mem. exec. com., PhD program CUNY, 2002—03; asst. prof. dept. criminal justice Bridgewater State Coll., Mass. Author: Blossom of the Flower, 1990; author (legal jour.) Land Use Law and Zoning Digest, 1990-98; contbr. articles to profl. jours. Pres. Greenwood Ct. Condominium Assn., Chgo., 1989-98. Mem. Justinian Soc. Lawyers, Nat. Assn. Women Lawyers (named Outstanding Law Grad. 1987), Women in Film (programs com. 1992-94), Acad. Criminal Justice Scis., Nat. Women's Studies Assn., Am. Soc. Criminology, Nat. Italian-Am. Bar Assn., Order of Coif, Homicide Rsch. Working Group, Justice Studies Assn. Avocations: travel, reading. Home and Office: 84 Fairway Dr Plymouth MA 02360 E-mail: jdgiustina@hotmail.com.

DELLAGLORIA, JOHN CASTLE, lawyer, educator; b. NYC, June 29, 1952; s. Arthur A. and Marianne Dellagloria; divorced; 1 child, Rebecca; m. Marilyn Castle Dellagloria, Sept. 25, 1988; 1 child, Caitlin. BA in English Lit., SUNY, Binghamton, 1976; JD, U. Miami, 1979. Bar: Fla. 1979, N.Y. 1986, U.S. Ct. Appeals (11th cir.) 1981, U.S. Dist. Ct. (so. dist.) Fla. 1980, U.S. Supreme Ct. Rsch. asst. 3rd Dist. Ct. Appeal, Miami, Fla., 1980-81; assoc. Cassel & Cassel PA, Miami, 1981-82; dep. city atty. City North Miami Beach, Fla., 1983-86; city atty. City South Miami, Fla., 1986-90; chief dep. city atty. City Miami Beach, Fla., 1990-96; city atty. City North Miami, Fla., 1995—2004; gen. counsel Miami Beach Housing Authority, 1997-2000, South Miami Cmty. Redevel. Agy., 1998—2002; spl. counsel City of Palm Bay, Fla., 2004—. Lectr. Sch. Profl. Devel., U. Miami, 1982-88, dir. paralegal program, 1984-86, lectr. Sch. Bus., 1989—, lectr. real property program; lectr. govt. law sect. Fla. Bar; moderator Rachlin, Cohen & Holtz, Ann. Govt. Law Symposium, 1996—. Com. person Parrot Jungle Com., Pinecrest, Fla., 1998. Recipient Excellence in Tchg. award, U. Miami, 2004. Mem. Eugene P. Spellman Am. Inn of Ct. (alumnus). Democrat. Jewish. Avocation: long distance running. Office: 11200 NW 25th St Miami FL 33172-1807 Office Phone: 305-392-4772. Personal E-mail: catdel@hotmail.com. E-mail: johndellagloria@dellaglorialaw.com.

DELLAGNENA, GAIL LYNN, computer programmer, analyst, consultant; b. Akron, Ohio, Oct. 19, 1956; d. George McInnes Massie and Iva Gena Ridgeway. BA in Polit. Sci., Kent State U., 1977. Programmer PACCAR, Seattle, 1990, Boeing, Seattle, 1991-92; cons. Computer People, Portland, 1992-94; programmer Fred Meyer, Portland, Oreg., 1994-98, Oreg. Dental Svcs. Health Plan, Portland, 1998-99; cons. E-Core Tech., Portland, 2000, ADECCO, Portland, 0200—2002, State of Oreg., Salem, 2003, Oat Tech. Solutions, Portland, 2004—05, Comsts, Salem, 2005—. Democrat. Presbyterian. Avocations: biking, aerobics, hiking, reading. E-mail: g.dellagnena@att.net.

DELLAPENNA, JOSEPH WILLIAM, former lawyer, educator; b. Detroit, Dec. 28, 1942; s. William and Elizabeth Julia (Fabian) D.; m. Mary Ann Lang, 1964 (div. 1974); children: Diane Marie, Joseph William II, Thomas Joseph; m. Caroline Gu, June 4, 1979; children: Elizabeth Gu, Eugenia Gu. BBA, U. Mich., 1965; JD, Detroit Coll. Law, 1968; LLM, George Washington U., 1969, Columbia U., 1974. Bar: Mich. 1968. Instr. acctg. Detroit Inst. Tech., 1966-68; of counsel NASA, Washington, 1969; instr. law George Washington U., Washington, 1968-70; asst. prof. Willamette U., Salem, Oreg., 1970-73; assoc. prof. U. Cin., 1974-76; Fulbright prof. Nat. Chengchi U., Republic of China, 1978-79, Jilin U., Peoples Republic of China, 1987-88; prof. law Villanova (Pa.) U., 1976—. Vis. prof. Ohio State U., 1989. Author: Suing Foreign Governments and Their Corporations, 1988; co-author: Waters and Water Rights, 1991; contbr. numerous articles to profl. jours. Democratic committeeman Marion County, Oreg., 1972-73, Montgomery County, Pa., 1983-87; bd. dirs. Lawyers' Alliance for Nuclear Arms Control, Phila., 1985-87, First Unitarian Ch., Phila., 1980-82. Mem. ABA, Am. Law Inst., Am. Soc. Internat. Law, Am. Assn. Chinese Studies, Phi Kappa Phi (life). Avocations: travel, stamp collecting/philately. Office: Villanova U Sch Law Villanova PA 19085

DELLA PENTA, DAVID T., medical products executive; Pres. Nalge Nunc Internat., 1994—98; pres., COO Fisher Sci., Hampton, NH, 1998—. Recipient Disting. Alumni award, Rochester Inst. Tech., 1996. Office: Fisher Sci Internat Liberty Ln Hampton NH 03842

DELLAPOSTA-BEDOYA, JO-ANN, art educator; b. Jamaica, N.Y., July 12, 1964; MFA in Imaging Arts, Rochester Inst. Tech., N.Y., 1989. Cert. tchr./permanent N.Y. State, 1999. Asst. prof. LI U., Southampton, NY, 1990—95, Suffolk County C.C., Riverhead/Brentwood, 1991—97; art educator Riverhead H.S., Riverhead, NY, 1997—. Adjudicator LI Media Arts Show, 1995—96. Photography, A Child's Fancy (hon. mention, 1993), Roots (hon. mention, 1990), Untitled (hon. mention, 1986); author: Considering A Career In Education. Office: Riverhead HS 700 Harrison Ave Riverhead NY 11901-2787 Office Phone: 631-369-6727. E-mail: giovannadb@aol.com.

DELLAR, MICHAEL D., restaurant owner, hospitality industry consultant; BS magna cum laude, U. So. Calif., 1969, MBA with honors, 1970. Dir. mktg. restaurant ops. divsn., assoc. advt. mgr. new products, brand mgr. various products The Clorox Co., Oakland, Calif., 1970—84; v.p., ptnr. Spectrum Foods, Inc., San Francisco, 1984—88; co-owner The Lark Creek Inn, Larkspur, Calif., 1989—, One Market Restaurant, Yankee Pier, Larkspur, Birch Creek, Roseville, Calif., Lark Creek Cafe, Walnut Creek, Calif., 1995—, San Mateo, Calif., 1995—. Pres. Dellar Restaurant Enterprises, Inc., 1988—; bd. dirs. Calif. Restaurant Assn., Ginger Club, Inc., Red Tractor Cafe, Inc.; mem. Am. Airlines Chef's Conclave; lectr. Sch. Restaurant and Hotel Mgmt. U. San Francisco; spkr. Hotel Forum Restaurant Hospitality mag.; spkr. Hospitality Industry Assn., San Francisco; spkr. Soc. Foodsvc. Mgmt., Young Presidents' Orgn., San Francisco; commencement spkr. Calif. Culinary Acad., 1992; mem. tasting panel Connoisseurs' Guide to Calif. Wine; mem. wine tasting panel Bon Appetit mag.; judge San Francisco Fair Wine Competition. Bd. dirs., v.p. Oakland Symphony; advisor Assn. Retarded Citizens; mem. exec. com. bd. dirs. Anti-Defamation League; creator restaurant assistance program San Francisco Unified Sch. Dist. lunch program; bd. dirs. No. Calif. chpt. Am. Inst. Wine and Food; bd. dirs. The Film Inst. of No. Calif. (Mill Valley Film Festival). Recipient Restaurant Industry Achievement award, Ctrl. Pacific Region Anti-Defamation League, 1994. Office: The Lark Creek Inn 234 Magnolia Ave Larkspur CA 94939-2099

DELLA ROCCA, STEVEN, lawyer; BS cum laude, Univ. Pa., 1977; JD, NYU, 1980. Bar: Calif. 1980, NY 1998. Chmn., corp. dept. Latham & Watkins, NYC, 1991—2001, ptnr., 2001—. Mem., exec. com. Latham & Watkins, NYC. Mem.: ABA. Office: Latham & Watkins Ste 1000 885 Third Ave New York NY 10022-4834

DELLAS, ROBERT DENNIS, investment banker; b. Detroit, July 4, 1944; s. Eugene D. and Maxine (Rudell) D.; m. Shila L. Clement, Mar. 27, 1976; children: Emily Allison, Lindsay Michelle BA in Econs., U. Mich., Ann Arbor, 1966; MBA, Harvard U., Cambridge, 1970. Analyst Burroughs Corp., Detroit, 1966-67, Pasadena, Calif., 1967-68; mgr. U.S. Leasing, San Francisco, 1970-76; pres., dir. Energetics Mktg. & Mgmt. Assn., San Francisco, 1978-80; sr. v.p. E.F. Hutton & Co., San Francisco, 1981-85; prin. founder Capital Exchange Internat., San Francisco, 1976—. Gen. ptnr. Kanland Assocs., Tex., 1982, Claremont Assocs., Calif., 1983, Lakeland Assocs., Ga., 1983, Americal Assocs., Calif., 1983, Chatsworth Assocs., Calif., 1983, Walnut Grove Assocs., Calif., 1983, Somerset Assocs., N.J., 1983, One San Diego Assocs., Calif., 1984, Big Top Prodns., L.P., Calif., 1994. Bd. dirs. Found. San Francisco's Archtl. Heritage. Mem. U.S. Trotting Assn., Calif. Harness Horse Breeders Assn. (Breeders award for Filly of Yr. 1986, Aged Pacing Mare, 1987, 88, Colt of Yr. 1990), Calif. Golf Club San Francisco (bd. dirs.). Office: Capital Exch Internat 1911 Sacramento St San Francisco CA 94109-3419 Office Phone: 415-928-3062. Personal E-mail: bobdellas@earthlink.net.

DELLASEGA, CHERYL, humanities educator; b. Patuxant River, Md., Dec. 12, 1953; d. James Robert and Lillian Margaret (Diehl) Miller; m. Paul Dellasega, Aug. 1984; children: Matthew, Ellen, Joe. BSN, Millersville U., 1981; MS in Nursing, C.R.N.P., U. Del., 1982; PhD in Health Edn., Temple U., 1988. RN; cert. gerontologic nurse practitioner. Clin. instr. nursing care of the elderly Sch. Nursing Lancaster (Pa.) Gen. Hosp., 1982; instr. dept. nursing Millersville (Pa.) U., 1982-84, Messiah Coll., Grantham, Pa., 1984-85; asst. prof. Sch. Nursing Pa. State U., University Park, Pa., 1986—; staff nurse PRN Medox Nursing Pool, Phila., 1975-76; staff nurse CCU Lancaster (Pa.) Gen. Hosp., 1976, Muhlenburg Hosp., South Plainfield, NJ, 1977; vis. nurse, team coord. Centre Community Home Health Agy., Bellefonte, Pa., 1977-78; charge nurse infirmary St. Joseph's Hosp. and Health Care Ctr., Lancaster, Pa., 1978-80; staff nurse recovery room Lancaster Gen. Hosp., 1980-81; assoc. prof. medicine, dept. of humanities Pa. State Univ. Coll. Medicine, Hershey, Pa. Nurse practitioner, cons. Dr. B. Eggler, Reedsville, Pa., 1989—, Susquehanna Nursing Svcs., Harrisburg, Pa., 1985; nurse practitioner So. Huntingdon County Family Health Ctr., Orbisonia, Pa., 1988, Rehab Hosp. for Spl. Svcs., Bellefonte, Pa., 1987; cons. devel. of geriatric assessment team Carlisle (Pa.) Hosp., 1985, Mifflin County Area Agy. on Aging, Lewistown, Pa. Author: Surviving Ophelia: Mothers Share Their Wisdom in Navigating the Tumultuous Teenage Years, 2001, Girl Wars, 2003, Mean Girls Grown Up: Adult Women Who are Still Queen Bees, Middle Bees and Afraid to Bees, 2005, contbr. articles to profl. jours. GSA Postdoctoral fellow. Mem. ANA, Pa. Nurses Assn., Am. Pub. Health Assn., Nat. League Nursing (researcher coun.), Am. Soc. Aging, Pa. Long Term Care Coun. (system orgn. subcom. 1988), AAUW (legal advocacy fund rep.), Gerontological Soc. Am., Sigma Theta Tau, Phi Delta Kappa. Office: Pa State Univ Coll Med Dept Humanities 500 University Dr Hershey PA 17033*

DELLA TORRE, EDWARD, electrical engineer, educator; b. Milan, Italy, Mar. 31, 1934; came to U.S., 1940, naturalized, 1945; s. Rene and Anna (Rosner) Della Torre; m. Sonia Viola Peltz, Jan. 1, 1956; children— Neal, Marc, Cynthia. B.S.E.E., Bklyn. Poly. Inst., 1954; M.S.E.E., Princeton U., 1956; M.S. in Physics, Rutgers U., 1961; E.Sc.D., Columbia U., 1964. With elec. engring dept. Rutgers U., New Brunswick, N.J., 1956-67; with solid state physics lab. Bell Telephone Labs., 1967-68, with McMaster U., 1968-79, Wayne State U., 1979-82; George Washington U., Washington, 1982—. Author: Electromagnetic Field, 1969; Magnetic Bubbles, 1975; contbr. articles to profl. jours.; patentee in field. Recipient numerous grants, 1968—. Fellow IEEE (v.p. Magnetic Soc. 1997—); mem. Am. Phys. Soc., Assn. for Computing Machinery, Sigma Xi, Eta Kappa Nu, Tau Beta Pi. Office: George Washington U Elec Engring & Computer Sci Dept Washington DC 20052-0001

DELLA TORRE O'KEEFE, KATHY JANET, elementary school educator, writer, adult education educator; b. Teaneck, N.J., Jan. 6, 1952; d. Charles Della Torre and Virginia Marie Gardner; m. Michael F. O'Keefe, Sept. 28, 1986; 1 child, Ryan. BS in Journalism, W.Va. U., 1973. Copywriter, editor Prentice Hall, Inc., Englewood, Clifton, NJ, 1973—78, mgr. book club, 1978—84, merchandiser, customer svc., 1984—88; apparel designer Kathy's Cut Ups, Columbus, Ohio, 1994—2000; freelance writer Bergen County, NJ, 1988—; educator elem. schs., 1999—, adult schs., 1999—. Individual instr. Careers in Writing, Elmwood Park, NJ, 2003—04; cons. in field. Contbr. articles to mags.; actor: (of poems);, editor newsletters. Pub. rels. liaison Valley Hosp., Ridgewood, NJ, 1988—89; participant Cmty. Food Drs., Elmwood Park, 1996—99; sec. Elmwood Park Soccer, 1999—2001; participant Breast Cancer Walkathon, Ridgewood, 2003. Mem.: St. Leo's Rosary Soc., Soc. Children's Book Writers & Illustrators. Avocations: art, crafts, ping pong/table tennis, computers, bowling.

DELLEUR, JACQUES WILLIAM, retired engineering educator; b. Paris, Dec. 30, 1924; came to U.S., 1952, naturalized, 1957; s. Georges Leon and Simone (Rossum) D.; m. DeLores Ann Horne, June 18, 1957; children: James Robert, Ann Marie. Civil and Mining Engr., Nat. U. Colombia, 1949; MS in Civil Engring., Rensselaer Poly. Inst., 1950; D.Engring. Sci., Columbia U., 1955. Civil engr. R.J. Tipton and Assocs., 1950—52; from research asst. to instr. civil engring. and engring. mechanics Columbia U., 1952—55; mem. faculty Purdue U., 1955—95, prof. hydraulic engring. and hydrology, 1963—95, prof. emeritus hydraulic engring., 1995—, head hydromechanics and water resources area, 1965—76, head hydraulic and systems engring. area, 1981—90, 1991—92; assoc. dir. Purdue U. Water Resources Rsch. Ctr., 1971—89, acting dir., 1983. Rschr. fluid mechanics U. Grenoble, Fance, 1961-62, hydrology and environ. fluid mechanics French Nat. Hydraulics Lab., Chatou, France, 1968-69, 76-77, statis. hydrology U. Brussels, Belgium, 1991; NSF sr. exch. scientist U. Grenoble, France, 1983-84; vis. prof. U. Quebec, Canada, 1996—, Vrije U., Brussels, 1991—2005; mem. sci. coun. Revue des Sciences de L'eau/Water Scis. Sci. Interest Group/Nat. Inst. Sci. Rsch., Quebec, 1988—; vis. lectr. Ecole Polytechnique Federale de Lausanne, Switzerland, 1991, 93, 95, 97; coord. Consortium of U.S. and European Cmty. Univs. for Scholar and Multimedia Exchs. in Environ. and Water Resources Engring. and Scis., 1998-2003. Author and co-author 2 books on statis. hydrology; co-author book on urban hydorlogy; editor: Handbook of Groundwater Engineering, 1999; assoc. editor: Handbook of Civil Engineering, 1995, 2d edit., 2002; assoc. editor Jour. Hydraulic Engring., 2003-, also articles, reports in field. Fellow Ind. Acad. Sci.; mem. ASCE (Freeman fellow 1961-62, chmn. fluid dynamics com. 1964-66, task com. mechanics of turbulence 1964-69, task com. hydraulics of bridges 1963-68, task com. on rehab. urban drainage infrastructure 1988-90, co-chmn. task com. on urban drainage rehab. & techniques 1990-94, chmn. com. urban water resources 1994-95, chmn. com. sediment movement in urban drainage sys. 1998-2003, internat. bd. advisors Jour. Hydrologic Engring. 1996—, Svc. to the Profession award 2000, Ven Te Chow Hydrology award 2002, Type 2 award, Environ. and Water Resources Inst., 2003), Am. Geophys. Union (chmn. urban hydrology com. 1978-83), Am. Water Resources Assn., Am. Soc. Engring. Edn., Internat. Assn. Hydraulic Rsch. (U.S. del. joint com. on urban storm drainage with Internat. Assn. Water Quality 1987-93), Internat. Assn. Sci. Hydrology, Ind. Water Resources Assn. (Charles Harold Bechert award 1992). Home: 124 Mohican Pl West Lafayette IN 47906-2159 Office: Purdue U Sch Civil Engring 550 Stadium Mall Dr West Lafayette IN 47907-2051

DELLIBOVI, ALFRED A., bank executive; b. Queens, N.Y., Feb. 1, 1946; m. Elizabeth Power; children: Robert, Christine. BA, Fordham Coll., 1967; MPA, Baruch Coll., 1973. High sch. tchr.; mem. N.Y. State Assembly, Albany; adminstr. N.Y. region Urban Mass Transp. Adminstrn., U.S. Dept. Transp., N.Y.C., 1981-84, dep. adminstr. Washington, 1984-87, adminstr., 1987-89; deputy sec. HUD, Washington, 1989-92. Roman Catholic. Office: Federal Home Loan Bank 101 Park Ave New York NY 10178-0500

DELLINGER, WALTER ESTES, III, lawyer, law educator; b. Charlotte, N.C., May 15, 1941; s. Walter Estes and Grace Phelan (Lawing) D.; m. Anne Elizabeth Maxwell, June 12, 1965; children— Hampton, Andrew. AB with honors, U. N.C., at Chapel Hill, 1963; LLB, Yale U., 1966. Bar: N.C. 1970, DC, 1998. Assoc. prof. law U. Miss., 1966-68; law clk. to Justice Hugo L. Black, U.S. Supreme Ct., 1968-69; assoc. prof. law Duke U., 1969-72, Douglas B. Maggs prof., 1972-93, 98—; assoc. dean Duke U. Law Sch., 1974-76, acting dean, 1976-78; vis. prof. U. So. Calif. Law Ctr., 1973-74, U. Mich. Law Sch., 1977, Cath. U. Leuven, Belgium, 1985; prof. in residence U.S. Dept. Justice, Washington, 1980-81, advisor to the President, 1993; asst. atty. gen., head legal counsel U.S. Justice Dept., Washington, 1993-96; acting Solicitor Gen. U.S. Supreme Ct., 1996-97; chair, head appellate practice O'Melveny & Myers, Washington, ptnr. Cons., draftsman N.C. Criminal Code Commn., 1970-78; lectr. in the field. Mem. bd. editors Yale Law Jour., 1965-66, Am. Prospect; contbr. articles to profl. jours. Rockefeller Found. Humanities fellow, 1981-82; Nat. Humanities Ctr. Fellow, 1988-89. Mem. ABA, N.C. State Bar.; mem. exec. com. Yale Law Sch. Assn. Democrat. Home: 604 E Franklin St Chapel Hill NC 27514-3822 Office: Duke U Sch Law Box 90389 Science Dr & Towerview Rd Durham NC 27708

DELLO JOIO, JUSTIN NORMAN, music educator; b. N.Y.C., Oct. 18, 1960; s. Norman Joseph and Grayce Baumgold Dello Joio; m. Marianne Bachman Dello Joio, Dec. 22, 1986; 1 child, Chiara. MusB, Juillard Sch., 1981; MusM, Juilliard Sch., 1952, MusD, 1986. Faculty composer in residence, assoc. prof. NYU, N.Y.C., 2000—. Composer: (chamber music) Sonate for Piano, 2000, (orch.) Two Concert Etuder Musica Humana, Symphic Poem, 2001, (chamber music) Music for Piano Trio, 2004. Recipient Lado award, Am. Acad. of Arts and Letters, 1996, Acad. award in music, 2004; grant, NY Found. for the Arts, NEA, NY State Coun. on the Arts, Presser Found., John S. Guggenheim fellowship, JS Guggenheim Found., 1998. Mem. ASCAP. Democrat. Home: 400 E 89th St Apt 3J New York NY 10128-6728 E-mail: jnd12@nyu.edu.

DELLO JOIO, NORMAN, composer; b. N.Y.C., Jan. 24, 1913; s. Casimir and Antoinette (Garramone) Dello J.; m. Barbara Bolton, 1974; children: Victoria, Justin, Norman. Student, All Hallows Inst., 1926-30, Coll. City N.Y., 1932-34, Inst. Mus. Art, 1936, Juilliard Grad. Sch., 1939-41, Yale Sch. Music, 1941; Mus.D. (hon.), Colby Coll., Lawrence Coll., U. Cin., 1967, St. Mary's Coll., 1969, Susquehanna U., 1980. Tchr. composition Sarah Lawrence Coll., 1945-50, Mannes Coll. Music, 1952—; commentator Met. Opera broadcasts; dean Sch. for the Arts, Boston U., 1972-78. Mem. rsch. adv. coun. U.S. Office Edn.; adv. coun. State U. N.Y., Potsdam; chmn. policy com. contemporary music Ford Found. Composer: Ballet On Stage, 1944; piano and chorus Jubilant Song, 1945, Piano Sketchers, 2000, A Dream, 2000, Ricercari; for piano and orch., 1946, Variations- Chaccone-Finale, 1947, Diversion of Angels; dance, 1948, Concertante for Clarinet and Orch, 1949, New York Profiles; for orch., 1949, The Triumph of St. Joan; opera, 1950, Psalm of David; chorus and strings and brass orch., 1950, Song of Affirmation; soprano, chorus strings and brass, narrator, orch., 1950, Somebody's Coming; chorus and piano, The Tall Kentuckian; score for musical play, 1952, Song of the Open Road; chorus, 1952, (opera) The Ruby, 1953, The Lamentation of Saul, Baritone solo orch., 1954, The Trial at Rouen, 1955, Mediations on Ecclesiastes, 1956 (Pulitzer prize 1958), Air Power, symphonic suite, 1956, Ballad of the 7 Lively Arts, 1957, To St. Cecilia mixed chorus and brass, 1958, (opera) Blood Moon; also: Variations and Fantasy for Piano and Orchestra, 1961; (love songs) There is a Lady Sweet and Kind, Why So Wan, Pale Lover, Let Me Count the Ways, Meeting at Night; score Songs of Adieu, The Orch. Louvre, NBC TV, 1965 (Emmy award), Beyond Every Horizon; for Symphonic band Antiphonal Fantasy; organ, brass, strings, 1965, Songs of Walt Whitman for Orch. and Chorus, 1966, Capriccio; for piano, 1968, Fantasies on Theme of Haydn (orchestra), 1968, Time of Snow; ballet, 1968, Proud Music of the Storm; chorus, brass, organ, 1967, Days of the Modern; chorus, brass, percussion, 1968, Evocations; Variants on Medieval Tunel Band, 1965, chorus, orch., 1970, Psalm of Peace; chorus, organ, french horn, trumpet, 1971, Mass; chorus, organ, brass Concertante for Wind Instruments, 1972, Of Crows and Clusters; chorus and piano, 1972, Suite for Flute and Piano, 1973, Suite for Clarinet and Piano, 1973, Suite for Organ, 1973, Folio for Piano, 1973, Lyric Fantasies for Viola and Strings, 1973, The Poet's Song, 1973, Leisure, 1973, Songs of Abelard (band and voice) Mass to the Blessed Virgin; organ and chorus, 1974, Satiric Dances; band, 1974, Stage Parodies; piano 4 hands, 1974, Mass of the Eucharist in honour of Pope John XXIII; organ, brass, strings and chorus, 1975, Notes from Tom Paine; chorus and piano, 1975, Colonial Variants; orch., 1976, Southern Echoes, 1976, Colonial Ballads; band, 1977, As of a Dream; orch., soloists, chorus, narrator and dancers, 1978, Sonata for Trumpet and Piano, 1978, Songs of Remembrance; voice solo and orch., 1978, Salute to Scarlatti; piano, 1978, The Psalmist's Meditation; chorus and piano, 1978, Variations; piano, 1980, Hymns Without Words; chorus and piano, 1979, Ballabili; dances for orch., 1981; chorus and piano Love Songs at Parting, 1982; string orch. East Hampton Sketches, 1983; piano and 4 hands Song at Springtide, 1984; concert band Aria and Roulade, 1983; chorus and concert band Let Us Sing a New Song, 1984, concert band Metaphrase, 1985, orch. Variants on a Bach Chorale, 1985, piano Introduction and Fantasies, 1985, Short Intervallic Etudes for Piano, 1986, Sing a Song Universal for chorus and piano, 1987, Nativity for chorus, soloists and orch., 1987, The Quest, 1990, mixed chorus and piano, A Memory: Men's Chorus and Piano, 1991, Songs of Memory, 1991, Variants on a Medieval Tune, 1993, Reflections on an Ancient Hymn for chamber orch., 1996, Salute to the Orch. Chamber Orch. Player, 1997, chamber orchestra Divertimento, 1997, Reflections on an Ancient Tune, 1997, piano 2 Songs Without Words, 1997, String Quartet, "Lyrical Interludes," 1998, concert band Fantasies, The Vigil for Mixed Chorus and Brass Instruments, band arrangement Jubilant Song, (music for TV series) Air Power, Directimento for Chamber Orch., 1997, mixed chorus and piano Passing Strangers, 2002; Lyrical Movement for string orch., 1995; Lyrical Interludes-string quartet Simple Sketches for piano, 2000, chorus and piano Dreamers, 2000, chorus and piano Passing Strangers, 2002, concert band City Scenes, 2003. Chmn. planning com. Ford Found.; Bd. dirs. Am. Music Center. Recipient Elizabeth Sprague Coolidge award, 1937; recipient Town Hall Composition award, 1941, N.Y. Music Critics Circle award, 1949, 58, Pulitzer prize for music, 1957, Emmy award for TV Score, Lifes Achievement award, Nat. Band Dirs. Assn., 2003; Grants and Scholarships in name of Norman Dello Joio awarded to Choral Soc. East Hampton students, 2003; Guggenheim fellow, 1943-44; Am. Acad. Arts and Letters grantee, 1945. Mem. Nat. Acad. Arts and Letters (coun.), Broadcast Music, Devon Yacht Club. Home: PO Box

154 East Hampton NY 11937-0154 *Whatever recognition I have received for my creative work, I owe for the most part, to an understanding mother and disciplinarian father. In this, my 70th year, I give thanks for a loving wife, a composer son whose music I feel will be an extension of myself into the future, and a son who is an Olympic equestrian of whom I am proud.*

DELL'OSSO, LOUIS FRANK, neuroscience educator; b. Bklyn., Mar. 16, 1941; s. Frank and Rose (Perrone) Dell'O.; m. Aquilina Marie Ferlo, May 22, 1965 (div. 1976); single ptnr. Charlene Hale Morse, Sept. 30, 1977. BEE, Bklyn. Poly. Inst., 1961, postgrad., 1961-63; PhD, U. Wyo., 1968. Co-dir. Ocular Motor Neurophysiology Lab. VA. Med. Ctr., Miami, Fla., 1972-80; asst. prof. biomed. engring. and surgery U. Miami, 1970-72, asst. prof. neurology, 1972-75, assoc. prof. neurology, 1975-79, prof. neurology, 1979-80; dir. Ocular Motor Neurophysiology Lab. VA Med. Ctr., Cleve., 1980—2004; prof. neurology and biomed. engring. Case Western Res. U., Cleve., 1980—, dir. Daroff-Dell Osse Ocular Military Lab., 2004—. Cons. Westinghouse Research Lab, Pitts, 1966-67, 70-71, Mt. Sinai Hosp., Miami, Fla., 1972-75. Bd. dirs. Vineland Galloway Civic Assn., Miami, 1973-76. Grantee NIH, 1971-77, VA Med. Ctr., 1972—, NSF, 1970. Fellow N.Am. NeuroOphthalmology Soc.; mem. IEEE, Engring. in Medicine and Biology Soc. (sr., chpt. chmn. 1977-78), Assn. Rsch. in Vision and Ophthalmology, Soc. Neurosci., NY Acad. Scis., Train Collectors Assn., CCCC Rod & Gun Club. Democrat. Home: 2356 Tudor Dr Cleveland OH 44106-3212 Office Phone: 216-421-3224. Business E-Mail: lfd@cwru.edu.

DELMAN, MICHAEL ROBERT, physician; b. N.Y.C., Oct. 28, 1942; s. Alex and Dorothy (Scher) D.; m. Joan Ellen Dubin, July 9, 1967; children: Keith Andrew, Danna Lee. BA, Alfred U., 1963; MD, N.Y. Med. Coll., 1968. Diplomate Am. Bd. Gastroenterology, Am. Bd. Quality Assurance and Utilization Rev. Physicians, Am. Bd. Internal Medicine. Intern N.Y. Med. Coll.-Met. Hosp. Ctr., 1968-69, resident in internal medicine, 1969-70, chief resident in internal medicine, 1970-71; resident in gastroenterology, 1971-72; fellow gastroenterology N.Y. Med. Coll.-Met. Hosp. Ctr., 1972-73; asst. clin. prof. medicine SUNY, Stony Brook, 1974—; chief chem. dependency svcs. Southside Hosp., Bay Shore, N.Y., 1989—, chmn. med. staff quality assurance, 1992-97, pres. med. staff, 1997-98, sr. v.p. for med. affairs, 1999—, chief dept. medicine, 1999—. Surgeon, vol. fireman East Islip (N.Y.) Fire Dept., 1978—. Recipient McAulay award East Islip Soccer Club, 1984, citation Town of Islip, 1992. Fellow ACP, Am. Coll. Gastroenterology; mem. Am. Gastroenterology Assn., Am. Soc. Addiction Medicine (cert.), N.Y. State Med. Soc. Avocations: golf, fishing, reading, guitar, music. Office: Southside Hosp 301 E Main St Bay Shore NY 11706-8458 E-mail: mdmd13@optonline.net.

DELMAR, EUGENE ANTHONY, architect; b. Gallitzin, Pa., June 8, 1928; s. Frank and Viola (Bocci) DiMaria; m. Bettie Hardin, Apr. 7, 1951; children: Diana, Daniel, David. B.Arch., Columbia U., 1954; M.Arch. in Urban Design, Catholic U. Am., 1971. Architect Ronald S. Senseman, FAIA, Washington, 1954-59; pres. Eugene A. Delmar, Silver Spring, Md., 1959-93, Delmar Architects, P.A., Olney, Md., 1993—. Mem. vis. com. Sch. Architecture U. Md., 1975. Important works include Electrophysics Lab., Columbia, Md., Montgomery County Jud. Ctr., Natatorium, Washington, Charlotte Hall Vets. Retirement Home, Denton Courthouse/Multi-Svc. Ctr., Brooke Grove Elem. Sch., F. Douglass H.S., Springbrook H.S., Rocky Hill Mid. Sch., Blake H.S., Francis Scott Key Elem. Sch., Rockville Nursing Home, Treatment and Learning Ctr., G. James Gholson Midl Sch., Cora L. Rice Elem. Sch. Ednl. Complex, Huntingtown H.S. Mem. code enforcement bd. Dept. Econ. and Community Devel. Md., 1973-76; mem. Montgomery County Beautification Com., 1965, Montgomery County Sign Rev. Bd., 1968-71; bd. dirs. Rockville Nursing Home. Served to 2d lt. C.E., U.S. Army, 1946-48. Recipient Disting. Service award U.S. Jaycees, 1964, E.B. Morris Disting. Service award, 1976 Fellow AIA (First award design 1966, award of merit for design Potomac Valley chpt. 1966, bd. dirs. Potomac Valley chpt. 1992-97); mem. Md. Soc. Architects (pres. 1972-73), Sigma Chi. Clubs: Silver Spring Lions (pres. 1978-79), Columbia University. Office: Delmar Architects PA 3411 Olandwood Ct Ste 205 Olney MD 20832-1488

DEL MONTE, MONTE ANTHONY, medical educator; s. Anthony and Joyce Del Monte; m. Kristen De Pree, Oct. 16, 1976; children: Derek, Marcy. BA, Johns Hopkins U., 1969—74. Bd. cert. Am. Bd. of Ophthalmology, 1982. Skillman prof. of pediatric ophthalmology U. of Mich., 1985—. Pres. Am. Orthopedic Coun., Madison, Wis., 1992—96; dir. at large Am. Assn. for Pediatric Ophthalmology and Strabismus, San Francisco, 1994—97. Dir. Delta Gamma Med. Found., St Louis, Mo., 1982—87. Recipient Honor award, Am. Assn. of Pediatric Ophthalmology and Strabismus, 1996, Sr. Achievement award, Am. Acad. of Ophthalmology, 2001, Best Doctors in Am., Woodward/White, Inc, Aiken, SC., 1998—. Achievements include patents pending for new treatment for Graves Eye Disease. Office: University of Michigan 1000 Wall St Ann Arbor MI 48105

DEL NEGRO, JOHN THOMAS, lawyer; b. Springfield, Mass., Oct. 2, 1948; s. Angelo Antonio and Marguerite (Garofalo) Del N.; m. Linda Anne Mayberry, July 6, 1973. BA, George Washington U., 1970; JD, Cornell U., 1975. Bar: Conn. 1975, U.S. Dist. Ct. Conn. 1978, U.S. Tax Ct. 1981. Assoc. Murtha, Cullina, Richter & Pinney, Hartford, Conn., 1975-81, ptnr., 1982-95, Del Negro & Feldman, LLC, Hartford, 1995—. Author: (with Levenson) Depreciation and Investment Tax Credits, 1983. Bd. dirs. Conn. Opera Assn., 1990-2003, Watkinson Sch., 1992-2000. Mem. ABA, Conn. Bar Assn. (tax exec. com. 1992-2002). Office: Del Negro & Feldman LLC Goodwin Sq 225 Asylum St Hartford CT 06103-1524 E-mail: jdelnegro@dfctlaw.com.

DELNIK, ALEXANDER, business development executive, consultant; b. Zhitomir, Ukraine, Nov. 10, 1961; came to U.S., 1991; s. Yefim and Bera (Nevelskaya) D. MS, Civil Engring. Inst., Kiev, Ukraine, 1983, PhD, 1987; MBA, UCLA, 1997. Registered profl. engr., Calif. Engr. Civil Engring. Inst., Kiev, 1987-88, sr. rschr./lectr., 1988-91; engr./lab. supr. Soil Tech, Inc., Temecula, Calif., 1991-93; project mgr. Dames & Moore, Inc., L.A., 1993-98; mgr. strategic planning and new bus. devel. Edison Internat., Rosemead, Calif., 1998—; prin. Del Mar Tech. Solutions, Inc., Studio City, Calif., 2003—. Editor: English-Russian-Ukrainian Geotechnical Dictionary, 1992; contbr. articles to profl. jours.; editl. bd. Ukrainian Jour. of Found. Engring., 1990-92. Recipient Diploma of Sr. Rschr., Coun. Ministers of USSR, 1990; Ministry of Higher Edn. Lenin's scholar, 1982-83, grantee, 1989-91. Achievements include research and development of numerical techniques to simulate soil-structure interaction; major design and construction projects worldwide; risk management, strategic planning and development of major business opportunities for a leading energy company. Home: 12745 Sarah St Studio City CA 91604 E-mail: alex.delnik@usa.net.

DELO, ELLEN SANDERSON, retired lawyer; b. Nassawadox, Va., Nov. 29, 1944; d. Robert G. and Daisy B. (Hitchens) Sanderson; m. Arthur C. Delo Jr., Mar. 20, 1971; 1 child, Marjorie Cotton Delo. BA, U. Richmond, 1966; JD, Rutgers U., 1977; LLM, NYU, 1985. Bar: N.J., 1977, U.S. Dist. Ct. N.J., 1977, U.S. Tax Ct., 1987, U.S. Ct. Appeals (2nd cir.) 1997, D.C. 1999, N.Y. 1999. Law clk. to Hon. John J. Geronimo N.J. Superior Ct., 1977-78; assoc. Lamb Hutchinson Chappell Ryan & Hartung, Jersey City, 1978-80, Chasan Leyner Holland & Tarrant, Jersey City, 1980-84, Stryker Tams & Dill, Newark, 1985-92, ptnr., 1993-98; exec. compensation assoc. Bachelder Law Offices, N.Y.C., 1998—2002, of counsel, 2002—05; ret., 2005—. Lectr. on tax issues. Contbr. articles to profl. jours. Lay reader Ch. St. Andrew and Holy Communion, South Orange, N.J. Democrat. Episcopalian. Avocation: animal welfare organizations and activities. Home and Office: 340 Montrose Ave South Orange NJ 07079-2439 Office Phone: 973-763-3617. Personal E-mail: esdelo@msn.com.

DE LOACH, BERNARD COLLINS, JR., retired physicist; b. Birmingham, Ala., Feb. 19, 1930; s. Bernard Collins and Ada Blanche (Moore) De L.; m. Annie Ruth Wilson, Aug. 24, 1951; children: Linda Louise, Bernard Collins III. BS in Physics, Auburn U., 1951, MS in Physics, 1952; PhD in Physics, Ohio State U., 1956. Mem. tech. staff AT&T Bell Labs., Holmdel, N.J., 1956-63, supr. Murray Hill, N.J., 1963-66, dept. head, 1966-89, ret., 1989. Courtesy prof. engring. sci. U. Ctrl. Fla., Orlando, 1993—. Author tech. papers and lectures; patentee in field. Recipient Stuart Ballantine medal Franklin Soc., 1975, Vladimir Karapetoff award Eta Kappa Nu, 2003. Fellow IEEE (David Sarnoff medal 1975, co-recipient Engring. Excellence medal, 1993). Avocations: gardening, jogging, fishing.

DELOACH, DINA C., secondary school educator; b. Savannah, Ga., Aug. 16, 1971; d. Michael Cameron and Ann (DeLoach) Crummey; m. Keith Lawrence DeLoach, Dec. 12, 1992; 1 child, Lawson P. J. BBA in Acctg., Ga. So. U., 1992, MEd in Bus. Edn., 1999. Staff acct. Golden & Assocs., CPA, Hinesville, Ga., 1993—95, Dennis B. Stanfield, CPA, Glennville, Ga., 1995—96; bus. tchr. Long County HS, Ludowici, Ga., 1996—2002, Tatthall County HS, Reidsville, Ga., 2002—. Advisor Future Bus. Leaders Am., Future Educators Am.; T-ball coach; pre-sch. Sunday sch. tchr. Named STAR Tchr., Long County HS, 2001. Mem.: Nat. Bus. Edn. Assn., Ga. Bus. Educators Assn., Assn. Career and Tech. Edn. Baptist.

DELOACH, HARRIS E(UGENE), JR., lawyer, manufacturing executive; b. Aug. 7, 1944; s. Harris Eugene and Julia (Murdock) Del; m. Louise Hawes, June 12, 1969; children: Harris Eigene III, John Wilson Malloy, Jeanette Hawes. BBA, U.S.C., 1966; JD, 1969. Bar: S.C. 1969, U.S. Dist. Ct. S.C. 1969, U.S. Ct. Appeals (4th cir.) 1974. Ptnr. Wilmeth & DeLoach, Hartsville, S.C., 1972-85; v.p., gen. counsel Sonoco Products Co., Hartsville, S.C., 1986-90; exec. v.p., 1966-98; sr. exec. v.p., 2000; pres., CEO, 2000—. V.p. HDFP, 1990-92; bd. dirsBank of Hartsville, Coker's Pedigreed Seed Co., Har tsville, Sonoco Products Co. Trustee Coker Coll., Hartsville, 1974-79, vice chmn., 1979; chmn. bd. trustees Byerly Hosp., Hartsville, 1976-79, chmn. 1997; chmn. bd. dirs. Thomas Hart Acad., Hartsville, 1984. Served to capt. USAF, 1969-72. Recipient Algernon Sydney Sullivan award Coker Coll., 1985, Disting. Alumnus award U. S.C., 1998. Mem. ABA, S.C. Bar Assn., 4th Jud. Cir. Assn., S.C. (v.p. 1974-78), Darlington County Bar Assn. (pres. 1984), Hartsville C. of C. (pres. 1977), Rotary (pres. Hartsville club 1977, Citizen of Yr. Hartsville club 1980). Presbyterian. Home: 620 W Home Ave Hartsville SC 29550-4430 Office: Sonoco Products Co North Second St Hartsville SC 29550-3305

DELOACH, ROBERT EDGAR, electronics executive; b. Daytona Beach, Fla., Jan. 6, 1939; s. Ollie Newman and Sally Gertrude (Schrowder) DeL. Student, U. Alaska-Anchorage, 1967-69, Alaska Meth. U., 1970, Pacific Luth. U., 1972. Lic. elec. engr. and adminstrs., Alaska, 1979; lic. pvt. pilot, real estate broker, ins. agt. Former chmn. bd. Alaska Stagecraft, Inc., Anchorage; pres. BG Systems Co., BG Tax & Acctg., Inc., The Electric Doctor, Inc., Apollo Travel, Inc.; former pres. Coastal Electronics, Inc.; former owner-mgr. Bargain Towne, Anchorage. Active Anchorage Cmty. Theatre, Anchorage Theater Guild. Mem. Assn. Ind. Accts., Internat. Assn. Theatrical Stage Employees and Moving Picture Machine Operators U.S. (past pres. local 770), Ind. Elec. Contractors Assn., Internat. Assn. Elec. Insps. Home: PO Box 520569 Big Lake AK 54481-8469

DELONG, DAVID G., architect, urban planner, educator; Bachelors, U. Kans.; M in Architecture, U. Pa., 1963; PhD in Arch. History, Columbia U., 1976. With Conklin & Rossant, N.Y.C.; restoration arch. Harvard-Cornell Archeol. Expn., Sardis, Turkey, 1967—68; sr. designer, then assoc. John Carl Warnecke & Assocs., N.Y.C., 1969—74; prof., chair grad. program hist. preservation Columbia U., N.Y.C., U. Pa., Phila., 1984—96. Bd. dirs. Frank Lloyd Wright Bldg. Conservancy, Phila. Hist. Preservation Corp., Nat. Coun. Preservation Edn.; dir. Preservation Alliance Greater Phila.; J.M. Fitch resident in hist. preservation Am. Acad., Rome, 1997; cons. in field. Author: Bruce Goff: Toward Absolute Architecture, Historic American Buildings: Texas, 2 vols., Calif., 4 vils., New York, 8 vols., The Architecture of Bruce Goff: Buildings and Projects, 1916-74; co-author: Frank Lloyd Wright: Designs for an American Landscape, Louis I. Kahn: In the Realm of Architecture (AIA Internat. Frank Lloyd Wright and the Living City Book award); editor: Working with Mr. Wright: What It Was Like, Wright in Hollywood: Visions of a New Architecture; co-editor: American Architecture: Innovation and Tradition; co-author: Out of the Ordinary: Robert Venturi, Denise Scott Brown and Associates. Fellows Fulbright, 1967—68, Chettle Vis., U. Sydney, 1992, Guggenheim, 1997—98; scholar vis., Getty Ctr. History Art and Humanities, 1989. Mem.: Soc. Arch. Historians (dir.). Office: U Pa Grad Program Hist Pres 115 Meyerson Hall Philadelphia PA 19104-6311

DELONG, DAVID STEPHAN, mathematician, educator; s. David and Bonnie DeLong; m. Debbie P. Mayer, Mar. 4, 1969. Degree summa cum laude, No. Ill. U., 1989; MS, Lehigh U., 1992. Prof. math. Tidewater C.C., Virginia Beach, Va., 1993—2004, Front Range C.C., Longmont, Colo., 2004—. Decorated mem. peacekeeping taskforce USN; recipient Chairman's award for acad. excellence, No. Ill. U., 1989; scholar, Colo. State U., 2005. Mem.: Am. Math. Assn. Two Yr. Colls., Math. Assn. Am., Phi Kappa Phi. Roman Catholic. Office: Front Range C C 2121 Miller Dr Longmont CO 80501 Home: 5613 Hummel Ln Fort Collins CO 80525 Office Phone: 303-678-3808. Personal E-mail: profsd@hotmail.com.

DE LONG, JACOB EDWARD, real estate broker; b. Syracuse, N.Y., Oct. 5, 1939; s. Jacob Edward (dec.) and Eva Ann (Sposato) D. (dec.); children: Edward Andrew, Michael Anthony, Sean Michael (dec.). Grad. H.S., Fayetteville, NY. Sales rep. Ill. Shade Divsn., Slick Airways, Chgo., 1963-67; dir. mktg. Bean Bros. Inc., Walton, NY, 1967-71; real estate sales Longley Jones Assoc., Syracuse, 1971-73, Radclif Real Estate, Syracuse, 1973-76; comml. real estate J. Edward De Long Real Estate, Syracuse, 1976-80, Eagan Real Estate Inc., Syracuse, 1980—. Pres. bd. dirs. The Andrew Nelson Self Help Ctr., Syracuse. Fund raiser, Friends of the Burnet Park Z00, Syracuse, 1986. Sgt. USAF, 1957-62. Mem. NY State Bd. Realtors, Onandaga Bd. Realtors, Onondaga Ski Club, Syracuse Ski Hawks, Am. Legion, Rotary. Republican. Roman Catholic. Office: Eagan Real Estate Inc 1208 James St Syracuse NY 13203-1324 Office Phone: 315-474-7411 210. Business E-Mail: edelong@eaganrealestate.net.

DELONG, RAY, editor; Copy editor Dayton (Ohio) Jour. Herald, 1972-73; editor, reporter Chgo. Daily News, 1973-78; city editor Columbia Missourian, summer 1980; freelance writer, 1978—; editor Bus. Law Today ABA Pub., Chgo., 1986—. Asst. prof. journalism U. Ill., 1978-84; asst. prof. Medill Sch. Journalism, Northwestern U., 1984-86; lectr. Univ. Coll., Northwestern U., 1985-2001. Office: ABA Publishing 321 N Clark St Chicago IL 60610-4403*

DELONG, RONALD, artist, educator; b. Bethlehem, Pa., Nov. 18, 1949; s. Kermit and Mary Jane Delong. BS in Art Edn., Kutztown U., 1972, MEd in Art Edn., 1988. Tchr. Northwestern Lehigh S. Dist., New Trifoll, Pa., 1972-95, Palisades Sch. Dist., Kintnersville, Pa., 1979-83; mgr. art edn. Binney & Smith, Inc., Easton, Pa., 1995—; prof. Moravian Coll., Bethlehem, Pa., 1996—. Author, editor: Teacher Resource Guide, 1985-97, Crayola Dream Makers, 1995-00. Pres. Lehigh Art Alliance, 1976-79; bd. dirs. Allentown (Pa.) Art Mus., 1997-00, Mayfair Art Festival, Allentown, 1997-00. Mem. Pa. Art Edn. Assn. (pub. chair 1985-97, pres.-elect 1998-00). Home: 2908 Rockdale Rd Slatington PA 18080-4013 Office: Binney and Smith Inc 1100 Church Ln Easton PA 18040-6638

DELORENZO, DAVID JOSEPH, retired public relations executive; b. Auburn, NY, Nov. 25, 1932; s. Joseph Robert and Marie (Hahn) DeL.; m. Margaret Mae Pinckney, July 21, 1956; children: David William, Mary Beth DeLorenzo Waldo. Student public schs., Auburn. With lab. Gen. Electric Co., Auburn, 1951, 54-57; asst. bur. chief Elmira Star Gazette, 1957-58; bur. chief Syracuse (N.Y.) Post Standard, 1958-66; polit. writer, city hall reporter Auburn Citizen-Advertiser, 1966-71, asst. sports editor, 1971-77; editor Bowling mag. Am. Bowling Congress, Greendale, Wis., 1977-81, asst. mgr. pub. relations dept., 1981-82, mgr. pub. relations dept., 1982-96; ret., 1996. Sports chmn. Cayuga County (N.Y.) March of Dimes, 1965-77. Served with USCG, 1951-54. Recipient writing awards including 5 1st place awards Cayuga County Fire-Police Assn., 1960-65; Journalism award Auburn Police Benevolent Assn., 1974; First place writing award Profl. Bowlers Assn., 1982; Bowling Mag. writing awards. Mem. Bowling Writers Assn. Am. (pres. 1974-75, meritorious service award 1976, exec. dir. 1997-98), Mid-Am. Bowling Writers (pres. 1986-88). Democrat. Roman Catholic. Home: Apt 208 4900 Brittany Dr S Saint Petersburg FL 33715-1644 E-mail: pegdadelo@aol.com. *Fortunate most aptly describes my life. With little background, I first was accepted as a newspaperman which led to being editor of a national publication and eventually to my former position of public relations manager of the world's largest sports membership organization. I sincerely appreciate the confidence so many others had in me through the years.*

DELORENZO, DOMINICK, academic administrator; s. Dominic and Anna Maria DeLorenzo; m. Jane DeLorenzo; children: Ryan, Nicholas. BBA in Acctg., Tenn. State U., 1983; MBA, Cumberland U., 1999. Territorial underwriting mgr. Allstate Ins. Co., Nashville, 1987—92; agy. sales mgr. USF&G, Richmond, Va., 1992—97; sr. product mktg. mgr. Nortel Networks, Nashville, 1997—2001; campus coll. chair U. Phoenix, Little Rock, 2002—04. Bus. cons. USF&G, Balt., 1994—96. Deacon Bellevue Bapt. Ch., Nashville, 2001—04. Home: 112 Limoges Ct Maumelle AR 72113 Office: U Phoenix 10800 Financial Ctr Pky Little Rock AR 72211 Office Phone: 501-225-9337. Office Fax: 501-225-1177. Personal E-mail: ddlorenzo@email.uophx.edu. E-mail: dominick.delorenzo@phoenix.edu.

DE LORENZO, WILLIAM E., retired foreign language educator; BA in Spanish and Speech, Montclair State Coll., 1959, MA in Speech and Drama, 1964; PhD in Fgn. Lang. Edn. and Tchr. Edn., Ohio State U., 1971. Tchr. Spanish various locations, N.J.; asst. prof. Spanish, Montclair State Coll.; assoc. prof. emeritus, coord. fgn. lang. edn./2d lang. edn. U. Md., College Park; ret. Organizer, co-dir. symposium for fgn. lang. tchr. candidates. Recipient Florence Steiner award, 1992. Mem. Am. Coun. on Tchg. Fgn. Langs. (charter).

DELOREY, JOHN ALFRED, printing company executive; b. Malden, Mass., July 13, 1924; s. John Alfred and Alice Gertrude (Collins) D.; m. Ann M. Abbott, Dec. 27, 1952; children— Debra Ann, Michael John, David Abbott BS in Econs., Boston Coll., 1950; MBA, Harvard U., 1953. Plant mgr. Container Corp. Am., Renton, Wash., 1965-69, mgf. mgr. Carol Stream, Ill., 1969-73, gen. mgr. St. Louis, 1973-77, Carol Stream, 1977-81, v.p., divsn. gen. mgr. St. Louis, 1981-82; exec. v.p. W.F. Hall Printing Co., Chgo., 1982-87; v.p. Container Corp. Am., 1987-93; pres. DeLorey & Assocs., Oak Brook, Ill., 1993—. Dir. Container Corp. Am. Polit. Action Com., Chgo., 1981-86. Author: (with others) Consumer Packaging, 1953 Served to maj. USAF, 1942-53, ETO. Decorated DFC, Air medal with 3 oak leaf clusters, European Theater medal with 3 battle stars. Mem.: Paperboard Packaging Assn. (dir. midwest region 1977—81), Boston Coll. Club (Naples, Fla.), Kensington Country Club, Harvard Bus. Club, Butterfield Country Club. Avocations: golf, swimming, skiing, bridge, reading. Home and Office: DeLorey & Assocs 194 Briarwood Loop Oak Brook IL 60523-8714

DELOREY, JOHN FRANCIS, music educator; b. Weymouth, Mass., Aug. 24, 1959; s. John Francis and Janet Ireland Delorey. BA in Music History, Vassar Coll., N.Y., 1981; MusM in Choral Conducting, The Boston Conservatory, 2003. Singer Scholar Cantorum of Boston, 1993—, Schola Discantus of San Francisco, 1993—, Boston Camarata, 1995—; dir. The Ethos Ensemble, 1996—, Choral Arts Soc., 1996—, Convivium, 1998—2000, 2004—; interim music dir. St. Mark's Sch., Southboro, Mass., 1998—99; prof., condr. Clark Univ., Worcester, Mass., 1999—2000, Worcester (Mass.) Polytechnic, 2001—; dir. Vox Futurae, 2001—; interim music dir. Holy Cross Coll., 2003—; choral condr. The Boston Conservatory, 2003—. Clinician Ethos Prodns., Shrewsbury, Mass., 1996—; adjudicator World Music Festivals, Mass., 2000—; bd. dirs. Arts Worcester, 2000—02; R&S chair Am. Choral Dirs. Assn., 2002—. Mem.: Am. Choral Dirs. Assn. (ea. divsn. tech. chair 2005—). Home: 496 Main St Shrewsbury MA 01545 Office: Worcester Polytechnic Inst 100 Inst Rd Worcester MA 01609 Office Phone: 508-831-5051. E-mail: jfd@wpi.edu.

DE LORIMIER, ALFRED ALEXANDRE, retired pediatric surgeon; b. Washington, May 30, 1931; s. Alfred Alexandre and Emilie Blanche (Kidder) de L.; m. Sandra Marie Veano, Nov. 21, 1953; children: Robert Maurice, Sally Renee, Nancy Denise. BS, U. Calif., Berkeley, 1953; MD, U. Calif., San Francisco, 1956. Diplomate Am. Bd. Surgery. Intern San Joaquin Gen. Hosp., Stockton, Calif., 1956-57; resident in gen. surgery U. Calif., San Francisco, 1957-62; fellow in pediat. surgery Ohio State U., Columbus, 1962-64; asst. prof. surgery U. Calif., San Francisco, 1964-71, assoc. prof. surgery, 1971-80, prof. surgery, 1980-96, chief pediat. surg. divsn., 1965-88, Calif. Pacific Med. Ctr., San Francisco, 1994-96; ret., 1996. Owner de Lorimier Winery, Geyserville, Calif., 1986-2005 Maj. USAFR, 1966-71. Avocations: sailing, growing winery grapes.

DELORME, ARNOLD, research scientist, consultant; b. Tunis, Tunisia, Feb. 26, 1974; arrived in U.S., 2000; s. Guy Alfred and Jocelyne Delorme; m. Setareh Moghaddam, Sept. 25, 1999; 1 child, Leili. B of Math., U. Paris, 1994, M of Cell Biotech., 1995, M of Computer Sci., 1996; PhD in Cognitive Sci., U. Paul Sabatier, 2000. Project scientist U. San Diego, La Jolla, 2004—. Cons. Lilly Pharms., Brussels, 2003—05; panel mem., reviewer European Union, 2005—; cons. USN, San Diego, 2005. Author: Encyclopedia of Medical Device, 2005, (software) SPIKENET, 1997, EEGLAB, 2000. Recipient Young Investigator award, Bretencourt-Shuller Found., Paris, 2001; fellow, Salk Inst., La Jolla, 2000—02, U. San Diego, 2002—04; grantee, NIH, 2004, Mind & Life, Boston, 2005. Mem.: Assn. Study Consciousness, Neurosci. Soc., Cognitive Neurosci. Soc. Avocations: meditation, metaphysics. Office: Swartz Ctr Computational Neurosci U Calid 9500 Gilman Dr La Jolla CA 92093

DELORME, MICHAEL, toxicologist, researcher; b. Detroit, Mich., Dec. 18, 1966; s. Lawrence and Carolyn DeLorme; m. Holly Hodgins, June 18, 1994; 1 child, Evan. BS, Wayne State U., 1985—89, MS, 1991—94, PhD, 1994—99. Registered Medical Technologist Am. Soc. for Clin. Pathology, Ill., 1989. Med. technologist Damon Clin. Laboratories at the Detroit Med. Ctr., 1989—90, Cottage Hosp., Grosse Point Farms, Mich., 1990—94; grad. rsch. asst. II Wayne State U., Detroit, 1994—99; postdoctoral fellow CIIT Centers for Health Rsch., Rsch. Triangle Pk., NC, 1999—2002; rsch. toxicologist - inhalation group DuPont Haskell Lab., Newark, Del., 2002—. Contbr. articles to profl. jours. AIHA Found. scholarship, Am. Indsl. Hygiene Assn., 1996. Mem.: Soc. of Toxicology, Am. Indsl. Hygiene Assn. Office: DuPont Haskell Lab PO Box 50 Newark DE 19714 E-mail: michael.p.delorme@usa.dupont.com.

DELOSH, JOAN MARIE, retired Spanish language educator; b. Hudson, N.Y., Feb. 6, 1947; d. Phillip Spencer and Barbara (Wickham) D.; m. Douglas Eugene Delosh, June 25, 1947. BA, SUNY, Potsdam, 1969. Tchr. of French Mater Dei Coll., Ogdensburg, N.Y., 1980s; tchr. French border patrol, custom ofcls., others, 1980s; tchr. girl's sch., Guayaqui, Ecuador, summer 1996. Sponsor for exch. program Ednl. Found. for Fgn. Study; rep. Internat. Fellowship/Spanish and French Clubs; active with fgn. exch. students. Vol. Ogdensburg Correctional Facility, 1980s, tchr. Spanish to non-hispanic inmates Hudson City Sch., 1970; missionary CEDEPCA office, Guatemala City, 1997; deacon Hammond Presbyn. Ch., N.Y., lay preacher, Sunday Sch. tchr. Recipient Dewitt Clinton award for Cmty. Svc., Masonic Lodge, Hammond, 1995. Mem. Delta Kappa Gamma. Avocations: travel, swimming, reading, skating, camping.

DELOUISE, TIA CAPUTI, university executive; b. Jersey City, Sept. 13, 1949; d. Lawrence and Mildred (De Riso) Caputi; m. Patrick Anthony DeLouise, Nov. 5, 1983. BA, Montclair State U., 1971; MA, NYU, 1983. Tchr. bus. edn. Berkeley Sch., White Plains, N.Y., 1976-81, dept. chair bus.

edn. West Paterson, N.J., 1981-86, acad. dean Woodbridge, N.J., 1986-87; v.p., dean Berkeley Coll., N.Y.C., 1987-93, v.p. acad. support svcs. West Paterson, 1993-94, sr. v.p. academics, 1994-98, v.p., registrar, 1998—. Recipient Outstanding Tchr. award Assn. Ind. Colls., 1985. Mem. Am. Assn. Collegiate Registrars and Admissions Officers, Nat. Bus. Edn. Assn., N.J. Bus. Edn. Assn. (exec. bd. 1985-86), Ea. Bus. Edn. Assn., Am. Mgmt. Assn., Phi Delta Kappa. Home: 154 Eagle St North Arlington NJ 07031-5819 Office: Berkeley Coll 44 Rifle Camp Rd West Paterson NJ 07424-3353

DELOZIER, DORIS M., retired secondary school educator; b. Hartford, Vt., June 11, 1933; d. Arthur James and Lena Anne Moffitt; m. A. John Lacaillade, Aug. 19, 1958 (div. Sept. 6, 1964); m. Dean K. Delozier, July 9, 1969; 1 child, Tracy. BA, Plymouth State Coll., 1957; MEd, Boston U., 1968; advanced grad. studies, Harvard U., 1987. Lic. tchr. N.H., Mass. Tchr. English Laconia (N.H.) Sch. Dist., 1958—68, reading specialist, 1969—96; ESL specialist Harvard U., Cambridge, Mass., 1984—87; reading cons. Coll. Park Elem. Sch., Ocala, Fla., 1999—2001; ret., 2001. Head Right to Read program Supervisory Assn. Union # 30, Laconia, 1970—80; mem. adv. bd. N.H. Edn. Assn., Concord, 1975—85; literacy chmn. Delta Kappa Gamma, Laconia, 1970—80; reading curriculum devel. Laconia Sch. Sys., 1979; literacy sec. AAUW, Laconia, 1967—77; literacy chmn. Zonta Internat., Laconia, 1990—. Co-author: (booklet) Sign Posts in Reading, 1975; author: (study skills book) Fishing for Success, 1992, (guide booklet) Keep It Simple, 2001 (Am. Assn. Ret. Persons award, 2001). Recipient tchg. fellowship, Harvard U., 1984. Republican. Episcopalian. Avocations: golf, bridge, reading, antiques. Home: 11558 SW 72 Cir Ocala FL 34476-9487

DELP, WILBUR CHARLES, JR., lawyer; b. Cedar Rapids, Iowa, Oct. 26, 1934; s. Wilbur Charles and Irene Frances (Flynn) D.; m. Patricia Lynn Vesely, June 22, 1963; children: Marci Lynn, Melissa Kathryn, Derek Charles. BA, Coe Coll., 1956; LL.B., NYU, 1959. Bar: Ill. 1960, U.S. Supreme Ct. 1962. Assoc. Sidley Austin Brown & Wood, Chgo., 1959—68, ptnr., 1968—2000, sr. counsel, 2000—. Lectr. securities law seminars With USAF, 1959-65. Mem. ABA (securities com.), Chgo. Bar Assn., Lawyers Club (Chgo.), Mid-Day Club (Chgo.), Phi Beta Kappa, Phi Kappa Phi. Home: PO Box 97 Wayne IL 60184-0097 Office: Sidley Austin Brown & Wood Bank One Plz Chicago IL 60603-0001 Office Phone: 312-853-7416. Personal E-mail: retlaw1934@aol.com. Business E-Mail: wdelp@sidley.com.

DELPARIGI, ANGELO, research scientist; b. Matera, Italy, Nov. 7, 1961; arrived in U.S., 1999; s. Mario and Antonietta DelParigi. Degree in medicine and surgery, U. of Bari, Italy, 1993; degree in nutrition, U. of Bari, 1996. Resident Sch. Geriatrics U. Bari, Italy, 1996—99; rsch. fellow NIH, Phoenix, 1999—. Contbr. articles to profl. jours. Vol. various causes and orgns. Recipient award, Am. Coll. of Nutrition, 2000, Internat. Assn. for Study of Obesity, 2002, Natl. Inst. Health, 2002—04. Mem.: Endocrine Soc. (assoc.), Am. Soc. Nutritional Scis. (assoc.). Achievements include research in Brain activity in humans in hunger, taste, and satiation; Gene expression in human brain of obese and lean donors. Home: 35 Union St Apt 205 New London CT 06320 Business E-Mail: adelpari@mail.nih.gov.

DELPH, DONNA JEAN (DONNA MAROC), education educator, consultant, academic administrator; b. Hammond, Ind., Mar. 7, 1931; d. Edward Joseph and Beatrice Catherine (Ethier) Maroc; m. Billy Keith Delph, May 30, 1953 (div. 1967); 1 child, James Eric. BS, Ball State U., 1953, MA, 1963, EdD, 1970. Cert. in ednl. adminstrn./supervision, reading specialist, Ind.; cert. elem. sch. tchr., Ind., Calif. Elem. tchr. Long Beach (Calif.) Community Schs., 1953-54; elem. tchr., reading specialist, asst. dir. elem. edn. Hammond Pub. Schs., 1954-70; prof. edn. Purdue U. Calumet, Hammond, 1970-84, 88-90, prof. emeritus, 1990—, head dept. edn., dir. tchr. edn., 1984-88. Cons. pub. schs., Highland, Ind., 1970-88, Gary, Ind., 1983-88, East Chicago, Ind., 1987-88, Hammond, 1970-88; speaker/workshop presenter numerous profl. orgns., Hammond, 1964—; mem. exec. coun. Nat. Coun. Accreditation Tchr. Edn., 1991-97. Author: (with others) Individualized Reading, 1967; contbr. articles, monographs to profl. jours. Bd. dirs. Bethany Child Care and Devel. Ctr., Hammond, 1972-77. Recipient Outstanding Teaching award Purdue U. Calumet, 1981. Mem. Assn. Tchr. Educators, Assn. for Supervision and Curriculum Devel. (rev. coun. 1987-91, bd. dirs. 1974-85), Internat. Reading Assn., Ind. Reading Profs. (pres. 1985-86), Pi Lambda Theta. Office: Purdue Univ Calumet Dept Education Hammond IN 46323 Personal E-mail: delnjohn@otherside.com.

DELPH, KATHLEEN ANNE, foundation administrator; b. L.A., May 30, 1956; d. Joseph Michael and Edna Mae (Salem) Nassany; m. Stephen Alan Delph, Aug. 29, 1981; children: Brittany, Taylor. BA, U. Calif., Irvine, 1980. Dir. found. and corp. devel. Internat. Bible Soc., Colorado Springs, Colo., 1995-98; devel. dir. Commn. Internat., Colo. Springs, 1999—2001; assoc. v.p. Advancement Ptnrs. Internat., Spokane, Wash., 2002—. Cons. in field. Participant Nat. Prayer Breakfast, Washington, 2000, 2001; presenter, participant The Leadership Luncheon, Colorado Springs, 2000, The Grant Seekers Foru, Colorado Springs, 1996-99; adv. com. Colorado Springs Pregnancy Ctr., 2001; mem., presenter Evang. Devel. Ministries, 1998-99. Mem.: AFP Colo. Springs (bd. mem.), Hi Kidz Internat. (bd. mem.), Devel. Assoc. Internat. (bd. mem.), Assn. of Fund Raising Profl. (bd. mem.). Avocations: skiing, reading, cooking.

DELPHA, KATHLEEN SHARKEY, accountant; b. Phila., Jan. 25, 1951; d. Joseph Philip and Florence Veronica (Noykoff) Sharkey; m. Joel David Delpha, Sept. 24, 1977; children: Daniel Joseph, Madeleine Day. BA, John Carroll U., 1973. Tchr. St. Michael's Sch., St. Louis, 1976-79; acct. Citicorp Acceptance, St. Louis, 1986-89; fin. dir., adminstr. Women's Support and Cmty. Svcs., St. Louis, 1989—. Bd. dirs. Mo. Religious Coalition for Reproductive Choice, St. Louis, 1992—; co-chair St. Louis Caths. for a Free Choice, 1992—; treas. Shaw Neighborhood Improvement Assn., 1994-97, Mo. Coalition Against Domestic Violence, 1995-97; coun. mem. St. Margaret of Scotland Parish, 2000-03, pres., 2002-03. Democrat. Roman Catholic. Home: 4047 Magnolia Pl Saint Louis MO 63110-3914 Office: Women's Support and Cmty Svcs 2165 Hampton Ave Saint Louis MO 63139 Office Phone: 314-646-7500. E-mail: kathleen@womenssupport.org.

DEL PRADO, SERGIO, professional soccer team executive; b. Havana, Cuba; arrived in U.S., 1962; m. Leslie Del Prado; children: Monica, Eric. BS in Bus. Adminstrn., Calif. State U., Long Beach. Formerly with L.A. Kings/Nat. Hockey League, dir. mktg., corp. acct. mgr., 1997-92, Hispanic broadcast mgr., 1992-94, corp. account mgr., dir. mktg.; gen. mgr. L.A. Galaxy, 1999—. Office: LA Galaxy 18400 Avalon Blvd #200 Carson CA 90746-2172

DEL PRIORE, LUCIAN V., ophthalmologist, educator; b. Italy, Dec. 13, 1953; m. Susan Panzarine, Oct. 16, 1981; children: Lia, Eric. BS in Physics summa cum laude, Cooper Union for Advancement of Sci. and Art, N.Y.C., 1975; MS in Physics, Cornell U., 1977, PhD in Physics, 1984; MD with distinction in rsch., U. Rochester, 1982. Diplomate Am. Bd. Ophthalmology, Nat. Bd. Med. Examiners. Intern in internal medicine Greater Balt. Med. Ctr., 1983-84; resident in ophthalmology Wilmer Ophthalmol. Inst., 1984-87, fellow in glaucoma, 1987-88; fellow in vitreoretinal surgery, asst. surgeon Wilmer Ophthalmol. Inst.-Johns Hopkins Hosp., Balt., 1988-89; attending ophthalmologist Washington Eye Physicians and Surgeons, Chevy Chase, Md., 1989-91; attending surgeon Washington Hosp. Ctr., 1989-91, Wilmer Opthalmol. Inst.-Johns Hopkins Hosp., Balt., 1988-91; attending surgeon in ophthalmology Ctr. for Sight Georgetown U. Hosp., Washington, 1990-91, clin. asst. prof. ophthalmology Ctr. for Sight, 1990-91; asst. surgeon in ophthalmology Jewish Hosp., St. Louis, 1991—98, St. Louis Children's Hosp., 1991—98; asst. ophthalmologist Barnes West County Hosp., St. Louis, 1991—98, Barnes Hosp. at Washington U. Med. Ctr., St. Louis, 1991—98; asst. prof. ophthalmology and visual scis., asst. prof. biochemistry and molecular biophysics, co-dir. vitreoretinal surgery fellowship prog. Washington U. Sch. Medicine, St. Louis, 1991—98, mem. exec. clinical faculty, 1997—98; chief vitreoretinal surgery, assoc. prof. ophthalmology & neurosciences UMDNJ, Newark, 1998—2000; ophthalmologist U. Hospital, Newark, 1998—2001; Robert L. Burch III scholar, assoc. prof. ophthalmology Columbia U. Coll. of Physicians and Surgeons, NYC, 2000—; ophthalmologist Columbia Presbyterian Hosp., NYC, 2000—. Ophthalmology surgery cons. Loch Raven VA Hosp., Balt., 1987-91; physician cons. in ophthalmology VA Hosp., St. Louis, 1991—. Contbr. articles to profl. jours.; presenter in field. Heed Found. fellow, 1987-88, Heed/Knapp Found. fellow, 1988-89. Mem. AAAS, AMA, Am. Acad. Ophthalmology, Assn. for Rsch. in Vision and Ophthalmology, Am. Diabetes Assn. (rsch. award 1995), Internat. Soc. for Eye Rsch., Retina Soc., Vitreous Soc., Rsch. to Prevent Blindness.

DELPY, JULIE, actress; b. Paris, Dec. 21, 1969; Appeared in films Détective, 1985, Mauvais sang, 1987, Beatrice, 1987, Europa, Europa, 1991, Voyager, 1991, Blue, 1993, The Three Musketeers, 1993, Killing Zoe, 1994, White, 1994, Red, 1994, Trzy kolory:Bialy, 1994, Before Sunrise, 1995, Tykho Moon, 1996, An American Wolf in Paris, 1997, Alleys and Motorways (video), 1997, LA Without a Map, 1998, The Treat, 1998, (TV) Crime and Punishment, 1998, The Passion of Ayn Rand, 1999, Sand, 2000, MacArthur Park, 2001, (voice) Waking Life, 2001, Beginner's Luck, 2001, Villa des roses, 2002, Cinemagique, 2002, Notting Hill Anxiety Festival, 2003, Before Sunset, 2004 (also writer, composer), Frankenstein, 2004, Broken Flowers, 2005 and others; actress, dir. short film Blah, Blah, Blah, 1995; dir., casting dir., writer, prodr., editor Looking for Jimmy, 2002; guest appearances ER, 2001, Graham Norton Effect, 2004, Real Time with Bill Maher, 2004 and others. Address: Pippa Markham Markham & Froggatt Ltd 4 Windmill St London W1T 2HZ England*

DEL RASO, JOSEPH VINCENT, lawyer; b. Phila., Dec. 21, 1952; s. Vincent and Dolores Ann (D'Adamo) Del R.; m. Anne Marie McGloin, Apr. 17, 1982; children: Joseph Vincent Jr., Katherine Anne, Marianna. BS in Acctg., Villanova U., 1974, JD, 1983. Bar: Pa., 1983, Fla. 1988. Exec. v.p. Belgrade Constrn., Inc., Wayne, Pa., 1974-80; atty. SEC, Washington, 1983-85; assoc. Dechert, Price & Rhoads, Washington, 1986-88; ptnr. Holland & Knight, Ft. Lauderdale, Fla., 1988-92, Stradley, Ronon, Stevens & Young, Phila., 1992-98, Pepper Hamilton LLP, Phila., 1998—. Exec. v.p., bd. dirs. Nat. Italian-Am. Found.; chair bd. trustees Am. Univ., Rome. Co-editor-in-chief Villanova Jour. Law and Investment Mgmt. Mem. Columbus Citizens Found.; bd. dirs. Justinian Found., World Affairs Coun. Phila.; vice-chair bd. counsultors Villanova U. Sch. Law; co-chair Ctr. for Mktg. and Pub. Policy Rsch. Villanova U. Decorated knight Constantinian Order. Mem. ABA, Aronimink Golf Club. Republican. Roman Catholic. Office: Pepper Hamilton LLP 18th & Arch Sts 3000 Two Logan Sq Philadelphia PA 19103

DEL RIEGO, RUTILIO J., bishop; b. Valdesandinas, Spain, Sept. 21, 1940; arrived in US, 1964, naturalized, 1981; Grad., Sem. of Diocesan Labor Priests, Salamanca, Spain; ThL, M in Spanish, Cath. U. of Am. Ordained priest, 1965; Spanish language instr. St. Vincent Coll., Latrobe, Pa., 1966—69; dir. Spanish Cath. Apostolate Archdiocese of Washington, DC, 1969—73; dir. Office of Vocations Archdiocese of San Antonio, Tex., 1975—78; dir. Office for Hispanics N.E. Pastoral Ctr., NY, 1978—92; pastor Santa Lucia Parish, El Paso, Tex., 1983—93, San Antonio Parish, El Paso, 1993—94; dir. Diocesan Laborer Priests House of Formation, Washington, 1994—99; vice rector Serra House Diocese of San Bernardino, Calif., 1999—2000; pastor Our Lady of Perpetual Help, Riverside, Calif., 2000—05; ordained bishop, 2005; aux. bishop Diocese of San Bernardino, 2005—. Office: Diocese of San Bernardino 1201 E Highland Ave San Bernardino CA 92404-4641*

DEL RIO, JACK, professional football coach, former professional football player; b. Castro Valley, Calif., Apr. 4, 1963; m. Linda Del Rio; children: Lauren, Hope, Aubrey, Luke. Student, U. So. Calif., 1985. Linebacker New Orleans Saints, 1985—86, Kansas City Chiefs, 1987—88, Dallas Cowboys, 1989—91, Minn. Vikings, Eden Prairie, 1992-95; asst. strength coach New Orleans Saints, 1997, linebackers coach, 1998, Balt. Ravens, 1999—2001; def. coord. Carolina Panthers, 2002; head coach Jacksonville Jaguars, 2003—. Selected to Pro Bowl, 1994. Office: 1 ALLTEL Stadium Pl Jacksonville FL 32202*

DEL ROSARIO, ALBERT F., Philippine ambassador to US; b. Manila, Philippines, 1939; m. Gretchen de Venecia; 5 children. BS in Econs., NYU. Top level positions Metro Pacific Corp., Philippine Indocoil Corp., Fort Bonifacio Devel. Corp., Philippine Long Distance Telephone Co.; amb. Philippine Embassy, Washington, 2001—. Joined official delegations state visits pres. Corazon Aquino, United States, State Visit pres. Fidel V. Ramos, Indonesia. Chmn. Philippine Cancer Soc. Nat. Fund Drive, Free Rural Eye Clinic, Makati Found. Edn. Mem.: Korean Hwa Rang Do Martial Arts Assn. Philippines (incumbent chmn., 1st degree Black Belt). Office: Emb Philippines 1600 Massachusetts Ave NW Washington DC 20036

DEL ROSSO, JEANA MARIE, literature educator; b. Binghamton, N.Y., Dec. 21, 1970; d. Paul Joseph and Roseann A. Del Rosso; m. David M. Freeman, June 18, 1994. BA in English, Binghamton U., 1992; MA in English, U. Md., 1993, women's studies cert., 1998, PhD in English, 2000. Tchg. asst. U. Md., College Park, 1994—2000; asst. prof. Coll. Notre Dame of Md., Balt., 2001—. Adj. faculty UMBC, Balt., 2000—01, Trinity Coll., Washington, 2000—01. Contbr. articles to jours. Mem.: MLA, Nat. Women's Studies Assn., Nat. Assn. Univ. Women, Golden Key, Phi Kappa Phi, Sigma Tau Delta (sponsor), Phi Beta Kappa. Office: Coll Notre Dame Md Dept English 4701 N Charles St Baltimore MD 21210

DEL SESTO, JANICE MANCINI, opera company executive; Grad., New England Conservatory. Dir. development and comm. New England Foundation for the Arts, 1983—89; dir. development and public relations Computer Museum, 1989—92; gen. dir. Boston Lyric Opera Co, Boston, 1992—. Office: Boston Lyric Opera Co 45 Franklin St Boston MA 02110-1301

DELSON, SIDNEY LEON, architect; b. Chgo., Apr. 10, 1932; s. Robert and Evelyn (Fistel) D.; m. Elizabeth Pfannmuller, Sept. 10, 1955; children: Karen Lee, Sara Jeanne, Matthew Robert. BArch, Pratt Inst., 1959. Registered architect, N.Y. Archtl. draftsman Irving G. Kay, N.Y.C., 1957-59; project architect William B. Tabler Assocs., N.Y.C., 1959-62; architect-designer Union Carbide Corp., Tarrytown, N.Y., 1962-64; archtl. dept. head Metcalf and Eddy Engrs., N.Y.C., 1965-66; devel. administr. N.Y. State Facilities Devel. Corp., N.Y.C., 1966-80, dir. design, 1980-91; pvt. practice architecture Bklyn., 1991-99, East Hampton, N.Y., 1999—. Editor: Design Procedure Manual, 1986, 2d edit., 1988, 3d edit., 1991. Mem. Community Planning Bd. Bklyn., 1968-71, vice chmn., 1971; chmn. adv. com. Bklyn. Mus. Community Gallery, 1970-73. Served as sgt. U.S. Army, 1951-53. Fellow AIA; mem. N.Y. State Assn. Architects (bd. dirs. 1982-85, 89, sec.-treas. 1988, Matthew W. DelGaudio award 1992), Am. Cons. Engrs. Coun. (peer rev. 1987—), Am. Arbitration Assn. (panelist 1971—). Home and Office: 29 Orkney Rd East Hampton NY 11937-1313

DEL TIEMPO, SANDRA KAY, sales executive; b. Willoughby, Ohio, Nov. 21, 1962; d. Charles Soloman and Lacey Marie (Webb) Eggers; m. Robert Joseph Craig, June 28, 1986 (div. Jan. 1993); 1 child, Misty Marie Mangus; m. Robert David Del Tiempo, Feb. 14, 1995; stepchildren: Jaime Brandon, Joseph David Del Tiempo. AAB cum laude, Shawnee State U., 1985; BBA summa cum laude, Ohio U., 1987; postgrad., Pepperdine U., 1998—2000. From ter. mgr. to sales mgr. ARA Cory, San Diego, 1988—90; sales rep. Rsch. Inst. Am., Riverside, Calif., 1990—92, 1996—2000, regional sales mgr. So. Calif., L.A., 1992—95, leader's coun. Culver City, 1996—2000, pres. bd. dirs., 1996—97, asst. mgr., 1997, 1999—2000, corp. acct. mgr., 1997—2000; mem. sales adv. bd. RIA/CLR Group (formerly Rsch. Inst. Am.), Culver City, 1998—2000; sr. v.p. Media Strategy Lawnmower Media, Culver City, 2000; sr. account exec. SAP Am., Irvine, Calif., 2000—03; acct. mgr. CCH, Inc., 2003—04; cons. internet mktg. LexisNexis, New Providence, NJ, 2004—. Cons. Video Ave., Paradise Pizza, Chillicothe, Ohio, 1987-88; sales rep. to corp. acct. mgr. Rsch. Inst. Am. Orange County, L.A., 1990-2000 Active Girl Scouts U.S., Menifee, 1988—92, Jr. All Am. Football. Mem. NAFE, NOW, Phi Kappa Phi, Phi Theta Kappa, Delta Mu Delta. Democrat. Avocations: travel, reading, jazz. Home: 6732 E Ashler Hills Cave Creek AZ 85331-3130 Office: Martindale Hubbell 123 Chanlon Rd New Providence NJ 07974 Office Phone: 480-575-0050. Personal E-mail: sdeltiempo@yahoo.com. Business E-Mail: sandra.deltiempo@martindale.com.

DEL TORO, BENICIO, actor; b. Santurce, P.R., Feb. 19, 1967; Actor: (films) Licence To Kill, 1989, China Moon, 1994, The Usual Suspects, 1995, The Funeral, 1996, The Fan, 1996, Joy Ride, 1996, Cannes Man, 1996, Basquiat, 1996, Excess Baggage, 1997, Fear and Loathing in Las Vegas, 1998, Snatch, 2000, The Way of the Gun, 2000, Traffic, 2000 (Acad. award best sup. actor, 2001, BAFTA award best sup. actor, 2001, Golden Globe award best sup. actor, 2001), The Pledge, 2001, The Hunted, 2003, 21 Grams, 2003 (Acad. Award nomination for best supporting actor, 2004, Screen Actors Guild Award nomination for best supporting actor, 2004), Sin City, 2005; prodr., writer: (films) Submission, 1995. TV appearances include Miami Vice, 1987, Private Eye, 1987, Tales from the Crypt, 1994, Fallen Angels, 1995, T4, 2004. Office: IFA Talent Agy 8730 W Sunset Blvd Ste 490 Los Angeles CA 90069-2248*

DEL TUFO, ROBERT J., lawyer, retired state attorney general; b. Newark, Nov. 18, 1933; s. Raymond and Mary (Pellecchia) Del T.; m. Katherine Nouri Hughes; children: Barbara, Ann, Robert, David. BA cum laude in English, Princeton U., 1955; JD, Yale U., 1958. Bar: NJ 1959. Law sec. to chief justice N.J. Supreme Ct., 1958-60; assoc. firm Dillon, Bitar & Luther, Morristown, N.J., 1960-62, ptnr., 1962-74; asst. prosecutor Morris County, N.J., 1963-65; 1st asst. prosecutor, 1965-67; 1st asst. atty. gen., 1974-77; dir. criminal justice, 1976-77; U.S. atty. Dist. of N.J., Newark, 1977-80; prof. Rutgers U. Sch. Criminal Justice, 1979-81; ptnr. firm Stryker, Tams & Dill, 1980-86, Hannoch Weisman, 1986-90; atty. gen. State of N.J., 1990-93; ptnr. Skadden, Arps, Slate, Meagher & Flom, N.Y.C. and Newark, 1993—; commr. N.J. State Commn. of Investigation, 1981-84. Instr. bus. law Fairleigh-Dickinson U., 1964; mem. N.J. State Bd. Bar Examiners, 1967-74; mem. criminal law drafting com. Nat. Conf. Bar Examiners, 1972-2002; bd. dirs. Nat. Ctr. for Victims of Crime, 1995-2003, Nat. Italian Am. Found., 1995-2003, Integrity Inc., 1995—, John Cabot U. in Rome, 1997—, Legal Svcs. N.J., 2000—; adv. bd. Yale Law Jour., 2003-, IOLTA, 1994-99, N.J. Pub. Interest Law Ctr., 1996-99, Daytop Village Found., 1998—, Planned Parenthood, 1998-99; mem. com. on character N.J. Supreme Ct., 1982-84; mem. lawyers' adv. com. NJ Fed. Dist. Ct., 1998—; mem. adv. com. of former attys. gen. NJ Atty. Gen.; spl. master, fed. jail overcrowding litigation, Essex County, 1989-90; trustee Boys and Girls Clubs of Am., 2000—, Lawyers' Fund for Client Security, N.J., 2000-05; mem. bd. regents Nat. Coll. Dist. Attys., 2003— Bd. editors Yale U. Law Jour.; contbr. articles to profl. jours. Mem. law enforcement adv. com. County Coll. of Morris, 1970-85; mem. Morris County Ethics Com., 1968-71, Morris County Jud. Selection Com., 1970-72, Essex County Jud. Selection Com., 1982-84; v.p., mem. exec. com. United Fund of Morris County, 1966-70; chmn. Morris Twp. Juvenile Conf. Com., 1963-74; bd. dirs. Nat. Found. March of Dimes, 1966-68, Vis. Nurse Assn. Morris County, 1963-70, Morristown YMCA, 1970-74; trustee Boys & Girls Club Am., 1999—, Atty.'s Fund for Client Protection, 1999-2005; trustee Newark Acad., 1976-95, 97—2002, pres. bd. dirs. 1983-87; bd. regents St. Peter's Coll., 1979-85. Fellow Am. Bar Found.; mem. Am., N.J., Morris County bar assns., Nat. Dist. Attys. Assn., Soc. Former Attys. Gen., Nat. Assn. Former U.S. Attys., Yale Law Sch. Assn. (exec. com. 1978-84), Order of Coif. Home: 13 Ober Rd Princeton NJ 08540-4917 Office: Skadden Arps Slate Meagher& Flom 4 Times Sq New York NY 10036-6522 Office Phone: 212-735-3880. Business E-Mail: rdeltufo@skadden.com.

DELUCA, ANNETTE, professional golfer; b. North Bergen, N.J., May 13, 1968; Golfer LPGA, 1989—; mem. Asian Tour, 1993; mem. Gold Coast Tour, 1994, 95; 3 Gold Coast victories, 1995; qualifier U.S. Women's Open, 1994, 95. Avocations: fishing, water sports, harley davidson motorcycles, movies, working out. Office: c/o LPGA 100 International Golf Dr Daytona Beach FL 32124-1082

DELUCA, ANTHONY J., civilian military employee; b. N.Y.C., Apr. 29, 1946; s. Joseph Anthony and Jean (Trentalange) DeL.; m. Mary Alaimo, June 18, 1967; children: Renee, Joseph, Regina. B in Econs., Fordham U., 1967; M in Pub. Adminstrn., Troy State U., 1976. Cert. Acquisition Profl. Level III. USAF procurement officer Eglin AFB, Fla., 1967-72, civil svc. various positions with the deputy for procurement and mfg., 1972-78; procurement analyst, USAF mem. Fed. Acquistion Regulation Project Office, 1978-79; supervisory procurement analyst Hdqs. Air Force Syss. Command, Andrews AFB, Md., 1979-82, advanced from first command competition advocate to deputy Air Force competition advocate gen., 1984-87; first civilian competition advocate gen. Office of the Asst. Sec. of the Air Force (Acquistion), Washington, 1987; dir. Air Force Office Small and Disadvantaged Bus. Utilization, Washington, 1990-2001; pres. INTECS Internat., Alexandria, Va., 2001—. Ira Eaker fellow Air Force Assn.; recipient Meritorious Civilian Svc. award, Exceptional Civilian Svc. award, Presdl. Disting. Rank award, Presdl. Meritorious Rank award, Minority Participation Program award Latin Am. Mgmt. Assn., Fed. Advocate award SBA, Frances Perkins award, Applause award; named Advocate of Yr., Small Disadvantaged Bus. Mem. Sr. Exec. Assn., Air Force Assn. Roman Catholic. Avocations: biking, music. Office: INTECS International Inc 5252 Cherokee Ave Ste 220 Alexandria VA 22312-2000

DE LUCA, CARLO JOHN, biomedical engineer, educator; b. Bagnoli del Trigno, Italy, Oct. 12, 1943; came to the U.S., 1973; s. John and Josephine (De Blasio) DeL.; m. Christine M. Rafferty. B in Applied Sci., U. B.C., Can., 1966; MS, U. N.B., Can., 1968; PhD, Queen's U., 1972. Lectr. U. N.B. Computing Ctr., Fredericton, 1968; lectr. biomed. engring. unit Queen's U., Kingston, Ont., Can., 1969-70, lab. instr. dept. anatomy, 1970-71, lectr. dept. anatomy, 1971-72, asst. prof. dept. anatomy, 1972-73; lectr. MIT, Cambridge, Mass., 1973—. Rsch. assoc. in orthopaedic surgery Children's Hosp. Med. Ctr., Harvard U. Med. Sch., Boston, 1973-79, prin. rsch. assoc. in orthopaedic surgery, 1979-84, dir. Neuromuscular Rsch. Lab., 1980-84; adj. assoc. prof. biomed. engring. Boston U., 1977-84, prof. biomed. engring., 1984—, rsch. prof. neurology, 1985—, dir. NeuroMuscular Rsch. Ctr., 1984—, chmn. dept. biomed. engring., 1986; dean Coll. Engring., Boston U., 1986-89; founder, pres. DelSys, Inc., 1993—; cons. Liberty Mut. Rsch. Ctr., Hopkinton, Mass., 1973-94; rsch. mem. Harvard-MIT divsn. health sci. and tech., 1978-84; affiliated scientist New Eng. Regional Primate Ctr., 1977-87; mem. nat. and internat. coms.; apptd. dir. Inst. for Disability Prevention and Wellness, U. Medicine and Dentistry of N.J., 1999; mem. nat. adv. coun. Nat. Inst. Biomed. Imaging and Engring., NIH, 2002 Founding editor-in-chief Jour. Electromyography and Kinesiology, 1990; mem. editl. bds. sci. jours.; co-author: Muscles Alive; contbr. articles on biomed. engring. and neurophysiology to sci. publs. Founder, pres. Neuromuscular Rsch. Found., 1985—. Recipient Volvo award Internat. Soc. for Study of Lumbar Spine, 1989, Wartenweiler Lecture award Internat. Soc. Biomechanics, 1993, Stuart Reiner Meml. Lectr. award Am. Assn. Electrodiagnostic Medicine, 1994, United Cerebral Palsy Found. Tech. award, 1999; named to Italian Cultural Ctr. Hall of Fame, Vancouver, Can., 1991; Ont. Govt. fellow, 1969-70; grantee RSA, VA, NIH, NASA, U.S. Army, USAF. Fellow IEEE, Am. Inst. Med. and Biol. Engring. (founding fellow 1993, Basmajian Lectr. award 1998); mem. AAAS, Biomed. Engring. Soc., Internat. Soc. Electrophysiol. Kinesiology (sec. gen. 1976-80, sec. 1980-84, v.p. 1985-88, pres. 1988-92), Can. Med. and Biol. Engring. Soc., Soc. Neuro-Sci., Orthopaedics Rsch. Soc., Nat. Inst. Biomedical Imaging Bioengring (adv. coun.), Dante Alighieri Soc. (bd. govs. 1986-88), Mass. Tech. Park Corp. (bd. govs. 1987-90), Harvard Club Boston, Sigma Xi. Home: 107 Livingston Rd Wellesley MA 02482-7308 Office: Boston U NeuroMuscular Rsch Ctr 19 Deerfield St Boston MA 02215-1904 Business E-Mail: cjd@bu.edu.

DELUCA, DOMINICK, medical educator, researcher; BA in Bacteriology, UCLA, 1969, PhD in Microbiology, 1974. Predoctoral fellow NIH dept. bacteriology UCLA, 1970—74, rsch. asst. dept. bacteriology, 1974; postdoctoral fellow Leukemia Soc. Am., Walter and Eliza Hall Inst., Parkville, Australia, 1974—77; scientist cancer biology program Frederick (Md.) Cancer Rsch. Ctr., 1977—80; asst. prof. biochemistry Med. U. SC, Charleston, 1980—85, assoc. prof. biochemistry, 1985—90; assoc. prof. microbiology and immunology U. Ariz., 1990—. Mem. pub. policy com. Ariz. Diabetes Control Coun., 1997—2001, chmn., 1999—2001; mem. AIDS rsch. program basic scis. rev. panel U. Calif., 1996—99; mem. brain disorders and clin. neuroscis. study sect. NIH, 1999—. Mem. editl. adv. bd.: Devel. and Comparative Immunology, 1995—2002; contbr. articles to profl. jours., chapters to books. Recipient Developing Scholar award, Health Scis. Found. Med. U. S.C., 1987, Rsch. award, NIH, 1983, 1986, 1989, 2002, 2003, NASA, 1999, 2004, Juvenile Diabetes Rsch. Found., 1988, 1998, 2001, 2003, Ariz. Disease Control Rsch. Commn., 1992, 1996, 1998, 2000, 2003, Am. Diabetes Assn., 1995, 2002. Mem.: Ariz. Cancer Ctr., Southeastern Immunology Conf. (pres.-elect 1982—83, pres. 1983—84, bd. dirs. 1985). Office: U Ariz Dept Micro Immuno PO Box 245049 Tucson AZ 85724-5049

DE LUCA, EVA, vocalist, writer, composer, entrepreneur, set designer; d. John Adolph De Luca and Rosa Maria Litrenta; m. Alfred A. Sima, May 11, 1975 (dec. Dec. 1984); m. Russell Frederick Du Laux, Dec. 24, 1985. Student, Peabody Conservatory, 1936—37, Juilliard Sch., 1943—44, Marymount Coll., 1985; D (hon.), Dewey Internat. Consortium, 1999. Pres. Eva De Luca Co., N.Y.C., 1950, Greeting Scrolls, Ltd., N.Y.C., 1960; mem. adv. bd. Humanity Against Hatred, N.Y.C., 1992—96; cons. Creative Consultations, N.Y.C., 1994; CEO, dir. creative ideas Unlimited U.S.A., 2001. Singer: (Operas) (profl. operatic debut) Phila. La Scala Opera Co., (European debut) La Boheme, Madama Butterfly; singer: (starred in 1st recording) (albums) (for Columbia Records) La Rondine (Puccini), 1955; author: poetry; design patent Mirror-View Measuring Stick, 1972, personal dental aid. Active Italian Welfare League, N.Y.C., 1978, Met. Opera Guild, N.Y.C., 1979; mem. Women's Nat. Rep. Club, N.Y.C., 1978—85. Recipient Editor's Choice award for Outstanding Achievement in Poetry, Nat. Libr. Poetry, 1997. Mem.: Famous Poets Soc., Russian Nobility Assn. Am., Inc. (mem. benefit com.), Sovereign Order Orthodox Knights Hospitalier St. John of Jersusalem (dame comdr.), Nat. Orgn. Italian-Am. Women. Roman Catholic. Achievements include patents for mirror-view measuring stick, personal dental aid; inventor in field; patents for personal dental aid. Avocations: reading, politics, theater, opera. Home: Apt 2F 3510 Bainbridge Ave Woodtown NY 10467-1419 Office Phone: 718-653-4095.

DELUCA, JENNIE M., literature and language educator; b. Scranton, Pa., Dec. 12, 1964; d. Russell Michael and Mary Ann Nowalk; m. Robert Anthony DeLuca, Sept. 23, 1989; 1 child, Nicole Marie. BS in Secondary Edn., Pa. State U., 1988, MEd in Instructional Sys., 1995; EdD in Ednl. Leadership, Immaculate U., 2000. Tchr. lang. arts Penn Wood West Jr. High Sch., Darby, Pa., 1988—89, Penn Wood East Jr. High Sch., Readen, 1989—91, Marple Newton Sr. High Sch., New Townsquare, 1993—. Mem.: ASCD, Am. Ednl. Rsch. Assn., Phi Delta Kappa. Avocations: theater, music, art, travel, tennis. Home: 11 Smedley Dr Newtown Square PA 19073 Office: Marple Newtown Sr High Sch 120 Media Line Rd Newtown Square PA 19073

DELUCA, MICHAEL, film company executive; b. 1965; Attended, NYU. Pres. prodn. and devel. New Line Cinema, L.A., pres., COO of prodn.; pres. prodn. DreamWorks Pictures, 2001—. Named to Power 100, Premiere mag., 2002, 2003. Office: Dreamworks LLC 1000 Flower St Glendale CA 91201

DELUCA, PATRICK PHILLIP, pharmacist, educator, medical association administrator; b. Scranton, Pa., Sept. 7, 1935; m. Judy Beitzel, June 16, 1956; children: Paul, Thomas, Patrick, Donald, Michelle, Michael. BS in Pharmacy, Temple U., 1957, MS in Pharmacy, 1960, PhD in Pharmacy (SKF W.G. Karr fellow), 1963. Analytical chemist SKF Co., 1957-59; instr., rsch. assoc. Temple U., 1959-62; sr. rsch. pharmacist CIBA Co., Summit, N.J., 1963-66, plant mgr., 1966-69, dir., 1969-70, Cormedics Corp., Somerville, N.J.; faculty U. Ky., 1970—; prof., assoc. dean U. Ky. Coll. Pharmacy, 1972-87, dir. ctr. for pharmaceutical sci. and tech., 1987-88, chmn. faculty pharm. scis., 1998-2000. Pharm. sci. adv. com. FDA; cons. to pharm. industry and FDA. Editor-in-chief: Jour. Pharm. Devel. and Tech., 1995—99; contbr. more than 200 articles to sci. and profl. jours. Mem., pres. parish pastoral coun. Christ the King Cathedral, 1996—99. Recipient Leo G. Penn award Temple U., 1957, Lunsford-Richardson Pharmacy Rsch. award Richardson Merrell Co., 1960, 62, Best Paper Toward Advancement Indsl. Pharmacy award N.J. Pharmacy Discussion Group, 1965, Disting. Alumni award Temple U., 1989, Outstanding Educator award in U.S., 1974, Sturgill Rsch. award U. Ky., 1995; also numerous grants. Fellow: Am. Assn. Indian Pharm. Scientists, Acad. Pharm. Sci. (pres. 1979—80), Am. Assn. Pharm. Scientists (bd. dirs. 1986—88, editor-in-chief PharmSciTech electronic jour. 1999—, bd. dirs. 2005—07, Rsch. Achievement award 1988, Outstanding Manuscript award in pharm. devel. and technology 1998, Outstanding Educator award 2000, Sullivan medalist at UK 2001, Ky Pharmacist of Yr. 2002, Outstanding Manuscript award in pharm. tech. 2002, Swintosky Disting. lectr. 2003), Inst. for Advanced Biotech. (sr.); mem.: Am. Soc. Enteral and Parental Nutrition, N.Y. Acad. Sci., Am. Soc. Hosp. Pharmacists (Rsch. award 1975), Parenteral Drug Assn. (Rsch. Achievement award 1975), Am. Pharm. Assn., Rho Chi, Sigma Chi. Achievements include research in pharmaceutical technology and novel drug delivery; co-founder Faith Pharmacy. Home: 3292 Nantucket Dr Lexington KY 40502-3269 Office: U Ky Coll Pharmacy Rose St Lexington KY 40536-0001 Office Phone: 859-257-1831. Business E-Mail: ppdelu1@uky.edu.

DELUCA, RONALD, former advertising agency executive, consultant; b. Reading, Pa., Oct. 28, 1924; s. Nicola and Grace (Carabello) DeL.; m. Lois Ann Hall, Nov. 27, 1952; children: Christine, Diane, Patricia, Maria, Lisa, Nicholas. Certificate comml. art, Pratt Inst., 1949; B.F.A., Syracuse U., 1951; BA, New Sch. Social Research, 1966. Artist J.C. Penney, N.Y.C., 1951-52; designer Remington Rand, N.Y.C., 1952-53; art dir. Roy S. Durstine (advt.), N.Y.C., 1954-56, Kenyon & Eckhardt (advt.), N.Y.C., 1956-66; head creative group Grey Advt., N.Y.C., 1966-67; with Kenyon & Eckhardt Advt., N.Y.C., 1967-85, exec. v.p., vice chmn., 1976-85; pres. Bozell Jacobs, Kenyon & Eckhardt, N.Y.C., 1986-89, vice chmn., 1989-91; cons., 1991—. Founder, v.p. Hancock Cmty. Edn. Found., 1998—. Home and Office: PO Box 551 Hancock NY 13783-0551

DELUCCIA, PAULA, artist; b. Paterson, N.J., Sept. 9, 1953; d. Ralph Lincoln and Isabel Miriam (Santucci) DeLuccia; m. Larry Poons, Dec. 18, 1981. Student, Ridgewood (N.J.) Sch. Art, 1971-73, Kansas City (Mo.) Art Inst., 1973-74. Exhibited in group shows at Nelson Atkins Mus., Kansas City, 1974, Ridgewood Sch. Art, 1978, Soghor Leonard & Assocs., N.Y.C., 1985, Art & Design, Phila., 1985, Jerusalem Gallery, N.Y.C., 1986, Helander Gallery, Palm Beach, Fla., 1990, 91, 92, 93, Wetherholt Gallery, Washington, 1991, Perspectives, Ghent, N.Y., 1991, Schulte Galleries, South Orange, N.J., 1992, Greene County Coun. on the Arts, Catskill, N.Y., 1992-93, Lorraine Kessler Gallery, Poughkeepsie, N.Y., 1992-93, Philharmonic Ctr. for the Arts, Naples, Fla., 1993, Farah Damji Fine Art, N.Y.C., 1993, Mountaintop Gallery, Windham, N.Y., 1994, 95, Roger Smith Gallery, N.Y.C., 1994, Art/Omi Studios, Omi, N.Y., 1994, Planet Thailand, Bklyn., 1995, Mountain Top Gallery, Windham, N.Y., 1995, 98, Tribes Gallery, N.Y.C., 1996, Planet Thailand, Bklyn., 1997, 98, Sideshow, Bklyn., 1998, Claudia Carr Gallery, N.Y.C., 1998, Steinbourn Kraus Gallery, N.Y.C., 1999, Greene City Coun. on Art Small Works, Catskill, N.Y., 2000, 01, Side Show Gallery, 2001, Greene County Coun on Arts, 2002, Phoenix Gallery, 2002, Perrella Gallery, Johnstown, NY, 2003, Side Show Gallery, 2004, Hudson (N.Y.) Opera House, 2004, McIninch Art Gallery, Manchester, N.H., 2004, Side Show Gallery, 2004, Greene County Coun. on the Arts, Windham, N.Y., 2004, AIR Gallery, N.Y.C., others; two-person exhbns. include Farah Damji Fine Art, 1993, LaCappelli, Cambridge, Mass., 1995; one-woman shows include The Bentley Inn, Bay Head, N.J., 1993, Hair Gallery, N.Y.C., 1995, Side Show Gallery, Bklyn., 2001, 02, C.W. White Gallery, Portland, 2003, Side Show Gallery, 2003, Phoenix Gallery, 2003, Richard Sena Gallery, Hudson, N.Y., 2003, Deborah Davis Fine Art, Hudson, 2004, AAWAA Gallery, Bklyn., 2004, Studio 18, N.Y., 2004, 05; represented in permanent collections of City of Barcelona, Art Omi, Leshanski, O'Sullivan & Maybaum, N.Y.C., Pondside Press, Ghant, N.Y., and numerous private collections; drawing reproduced in Cover Mag., 1982; paintings reproduced in Long Shot, 1993. Recipient Art Triangle Barcelona, Spain, 1987, Inaugural Yr. award Art/Omi, 1992. Home: 831 Broadway New York NY 10003-4706 E-mail: sixthkid9@yahoo.com.

DELUCE, RICHARD DAVID, lawyer; b. Nanaimo, B.C., Can., Oct. 3, 1928; came to U.S., 1929; s. Robert and Myrtle (Hickey) DeL; m. Joanne Strang, Sept. 10, 1955; children: David S., Amy Jane Eigner, Daniel R. AB, UCLA, 1950; JD, Stanford U., Palo Alto, Calif., 1955. Bar: Calif., 1955, U.S. Dist. Ct. (no. dist.) Calif. 1955, U.S. Ct. Appeals (9th cir.) 1955, U.S. Dist. Ct. (cen. dist.) Calif. 1956, U.S. Supreme Ct. 1963, U.S. Dist. Ct. (so. dist.) Calif. 1972. Rsch. atty. Calif. Supreme Ct., San Francisco, 1955-56; assoc. Lawler, Felix & Hall, L.A., 1956-62, ptnr., 1962-90, Arter, Hadden, Lawler, Felix & Hall, L.A., 1990—2000. Co-author: California Civil Writ Practice, 2d edit., 1987. Capt. U.S. Army, 1951-53, Korea. Fellow Am. Coll. Trial Lawyers, Am. Bar Found.; mem. Calif. Club. Home: 3617 Paseo Del Campo Palos Verdes Estates CA 90274-1161

DE LUCIA, FRANK CHARLES, physicist, researcher; b. St. Paul, June 21, 1943; s. Frank Charles and Muriel Ruth (Rinehart) D.; m. Shirley Ann Wood, June 25, 1966; children: Frank Charles, Elizabeth Ann. BS, Iowa Wesleyan Coll., 1964; PhD, Duke U., 1969. Instr, research assoc. Duke U., Durham, N.C., asst. prof., assoc. prof.; program mgr. Army Research Office, Research Triangle Park, N.C.; prof. Duke U., Durham, chmn. physics dept.; prof., chmn. dept. physics Ohio State U., Columbus, 1990-98, prof., 1998—. Recipient Max Planck Rsch. prize, 1992, William F. Meggers award, 2001; named Disting. rsch. scholar, 1999, Disting. Univ. prof., 2000. Mem. Am. Phys. Soc., IEEE, Optical Soc. Am., Phi Beta Kappa. Office: Ohio State U Dept Of Physics Columbus OH 43210 Office Phone: 614-688-4774. Business E-Mail: fed@mps.ohio-state.edu.

DELUE, STEVEN MULLER, political scientist, educator; b. Chgo., Mar. 6, 1945; s. William DeLue and Dorothy Pokedoff; m. Karen Doering, Aug. 3, 1968; children: Erik Nathaniel, Dana Daniel, Anna Renee. BA, U. Ill., 1967; MA, U. Wash., 1969, PhD, 1971. Instr. polit. sci. U. Wash., Seattle, 1971—72; asst. prof. U. North Fla., Jacksonville, 1972—77, assoc. prof., 1977—83, prof., 1983—, chair polit. sci., 1977—83; prof., chair dept. polit. sci. Miami U., Oxford, Ohio, 1983—94, assoc. dean Coll. Arts and Sci., 1994—2003, sr. assoc. dean, 2003—04, acting dean, 2004—05, interim dean, 2005—. Author: Political Obligation in a Liberal State, 1989, Political Thinking, Political Theory and Civil Society, 1997, 2002, 2d Edit., transl. into Arabic; contbr. articles to numerous profl. jours. Campaign worker Dem. candidates. Recipient NEH award, 1976, 79, 81, 82, 87. Mem. Am. Polit. Sci. Assn., Assn. Am. Colls. and Univs. (campus rep.), Phi Kappa Phi. Jewish. Avocations: running, reading, travel. Home: 714 Melissa Dr Oxford OH 45056 Office: Miami U 143 Upham Hall Oxford OH 45056 Business E-Mail: deluesm@muohio.edu.

DELUGACH, ALBERT LAWRENCE, journalist; b. Memphis, Oct. 27, 1925; s. Gilbert and Edna (Short) D.; m. Bernice Goldstein, June 11, 1950; children: Joy, David, Daniel, Sharon. B.J., U. Mo., 1951. Reporter Kansas City (Mo.) Star, 1951-60, St. Louis Globe Democrat, 1960-69, St. Louis Post Dispatch, 1969-70; investigative reporter Los Angeles Times, 1970-89. Served with USNR, 1943-46. Recipient Pulitzer prize for spl. local reporting, 1969, Gerald Loeb award for disting. bus. and fin. journalism, 1984 Home: 4313 Price St Los Angeles CA 90027-2815

DELUGO, ERNEST MARIO, JR., electrical engineer; b. N.Y.C., Sept. 25, 1950; s. Ernest M. and Irma (Maisonett) DeL.; m. Yolanda Garcia, Oct. 17, 1971; children: Jessica, Lisa, David. BSEE, Polytech. U. N.Y., 1971; MBA in Fin., U. Conn., 1995; postgrad. tech. and product strategy, MIT/Sloan, 1999; MSc in Info. Sys. Engring., Poly. U., 2002. Cert. cogeneration engr., project mgr. Field engr. General Elec. Co., N.Y.C., 1971-75, elec. engr. Schenectady, N.Y., 1975-81; constrn. engr. Burns & Roe, Oradell, N.J., 1977; sr. control sys. engr. Bechtel Power, Ann Arbor, Mich., 1981-84; sr. elec. engr. General Elec. Co., Schenectady, 1984-86, prin. engr., 1986-88, v.p. Stamford, Conn., 1988-92; sr. v.p., dir. projects and bus. devel. Ridgewood (N.J.) Power Corp., 1992-94; pres., mng. dir., project mgr. DeLugo Tech. LLC, Bethel, Conn., 1994—. Author: Project Management: Managing the Investors' Perspective, 1995; contbr. articles to profl. jours. Recipient Project Mgmt. award, Gov. of South Korea, 1979. Mem.: IEEE, Assn. Energy Engrs., Am. Mgmt. Assn., Project Mgmt. Inst., Computer Soc., Assn. of Computing Machinery. Avocation: model railroading. Home: 18 Payne Rd Bethel CT 06801-1239 Office: Delugo Techs LLC 18 Payne Rd Bethel CT 06801-1239 Fax: 203-792-5496. Office Phone: 203-792-8789. E-mail: erniedelu1@aol.com.

DELUHERY, PATRICK JOHN, state official; b. Birmingham, Ala., Jan. 31, 1942; s. Frank B. and Lucille (Donovan) D.; m. Margaret Morris, 1973; children: Allison, Norah, Rose. BA with honors, U. Notre Dame, 1964; BSc in Econs. with honors, London Sch. Econs., 1967. Legis. asst. U.S. Senator Harold Hughes, Washington, 1969-74, U.S. Senator John Culver, Washington, 1975; asst. prof. econs. and fin. St. Ambrose U., Davenport, Iowa, 1975—; COO Gen. Svcs. Enterprise Iowa Dept. Adminstrv. Svcs., Des Moines, 2002—05; dir. strategic partnerships Dept. Adminstrv. Svcs., Des Moines, 2005—. Mem. Iowa State Senate, 1979-2002. Democrat. Roman Catholic. Home: 629 Foster Dr Des Moines IA 50312-2517 Office: Dept Adminstv Svcs Hoover Bldg Level A Des Moines IA 50319-0001 Business E-Mail: patrick.deluhery@iowa.gov.

DELUISE, MICHAEL BRADFORD, academic administrator; b. Bklyn., Jan. 14, 1950; s. Charles DeLuise and Nancy Bradbury; m. Victoria H. Kane, May 29, 1971; children: Danielle DeLuise Fix, Nicole. BA, NYU, 1971. Acct. supr. BLaine Thompson Co., NYC, 1970—77; pres. DeLuise Hirshman & Holley, 1977—86; v.p. univ. rels. Hofstra U., Hempstead, 1986—2003; v.p. devel., external affairs Dowling Coll., Oakdale, 2003—. Chmn. L.I. Visitors and Conv. Bur., 2001—04; dir. Melville Farmingdale Chamber. Mem. Rep. Com., Huntington, 2002—; bd. dirs. Vanderbilt Mus., Huntington, NY, 2004—, Friends L.I. Heirtage, 2001—04, L.I. Econ. Devel. Commn., 2001—. Recipient Lifetime Achievement award, Pub. Rels. Profls. L.I., 2002. Mem.: L.I. Advt. Club (pres. 2001—04, bd. dirs.). Office: Dowling Coll Idle Hour Blvd Oakdale NY 11769

DELUKE, DEAN M., oral surgeon; b. Schenectady, N.Y., Jan. 16, 1952; s. Dominick J. and Virginia D. (Anderson) DeLuke; m. Theresa S. Slowey, Oct. 6, 1984; 1 child, Deanna Marie. BA, St. Michaels Coll., Burlington, Vt., 1974; DDS, Columbia U., 1978. Diplomate Am. Bd. Oral and Maxillofacial Surgery. Pvt. practice oral and maxillofacial surgery, Schenectady, 1982—; chief dept. dentistry St. Clare's Hosp., 1989—93. Cons. Sunnyview Hosp., Schenectady, 1982—2000, VA Med. Ctr., Albany, NY, 1988—2001; pres. N.Y. State Soc. Oral and Maxillofacial Surgeons, 1994; mem. nat. adv. bd. OMS Nat. Ins. Co., 1994—. Contbr. articles to profl. jours. Trustee Albany (N.Y.) Acad. for Girls, 1996—; bd. dirs. St. Clares Hosp. Found., Schenectady, NY, 1987—93, Oral and Maxillofacial Surgery Polit. Action Com., 1996—98. Fellow: Internat. Assn. Oral and Maxillofacial Surgeons, Am. Assn. Oral and Maxillofacial Surgeons (del. 1992—96), Am. Coll. Dentists; mem.: Am. Assn. Dental Cons., Am. Med. Writers Assn., Am. Cleft Palate-Craniofacial Assn. Avocations: skiing, boating. Home: 25 Robinwood Dr Clifton Park NY 12065 Office: 1070 Nott St Schenectady NY 12308

DE LUNA-GONZALEZ, ELMA, accountant; b. Edinburg, Tex., June 22, 1950; d. Emilio De Luna and Julia Andaverde; m. Antonio Gonzalez, Oct. 10, 1975; 1 child, Julissa Priscilla Gonzalez. AA, Houston C.C., 1986; BA, Houston Internat. U., 1990, U. Houston, 1997; MA, Prairie View A&M U., 1999. Bookkeeper Aluminum Industries, McAllen, Tex., 1973—75; estimator Clow Corp., Tarrant City, Ala., 1975—79; acct. Freeman Design and Display Co., Houston, 1980—86, Forrest Mfg. Co., Houston, 1988, Hispanic Bus. and Acctg. Svcs., Houston, 1988—2001; asst. to dean Prairie View (Tex.) A&M U., 2001—. Musician, vocalist De Luna Band, Dekalb, Ill., 1968—88. Composer: Impossible Love, 1987. Chair, treas. Gonzalez for Tex. Ho. Reps. Campaign, Houston, 1994. Named Women of the Yr., Ala. Women Soc., 1988; recipient Mayors award, City Kendelton, Tex., 2002. Mem.: ACA, AAUW, Tex. Counseling Assn., Nat. Soc. Pub. Accts., League United L.Am. Citizens, No. Ill. U. Women Club, Phi Delta Kappa, Chi Sigma Iota. Avocations: writing, music, reading. Home: 16614 Dounreay Dr Houston TX 77084 Office: Prairie View A&M U PO Box 4207 Prairie View TX 77446 Office Phone: 936-857-2014. Personal E-mail: elma_gonzalez@aol.com. Business E-Mail: elmagonzalez@pvamu.edu.

DE LUNG, JANE SOLBERGER, independent sector executive; b. Anniston, Ala., July 9, 1944; d. Samuel and Margaret Polk (Oldham) S.; m. Harry Leonard De Lung, Apr. 23, 1965 (div. 1972); m. Charles F. Westoff, May 2, 1997. BA in History, Emory U., 1966; MA in Urban Planning, Roosevelt U., Chgo., 1972. Exec. asst. Cook County Legal Assistance, Chgo., 1967-69; asst. dir. family planning Am. Coll. Ob-gyn., Chgo., 1969-71; v.p. Ill. Family Planning Coun., Chgo., 1971-80; asst. commr. Chgo. Dept. Pub. Health, 1981-82; pres. Pub. Solutions, Princeton, NJ, 1982-88, Population Resource Ctr., N.Y.C., 1988—. Bd. dirs. Planned Parenthood Mercer County, Trenton, NJ, 1986-96, Population Resource Ctr., 1989—, Trenton Head Start, 1993-98; adv. bd. dept. sociology Princeton U., 1991— Mem. APHA, AAUW, LWV, Internat. Union Sci. Study of Population, Population Assn. Am., UN Assn. of U.S.A. (nat. adv. com. 1998-). Democrat. Episcopalian. Office: Population Resource Ctr 15 Roszel Rd Princeton NJ 08540-6248 Office Phone: 609-452-2822. Business E-Mail: jdelung@prcnj.org.

DELURY, BERNARD EDWARD, JR., lawyer; b. NYC, Aug. 30, 1960; s. Bernard Edward and Jane Frances (Sheldon) DeL.; m. Margaret Louise Hollings, Sept. 27, 1986; children: Bernard Edward III, Frank William, Emma Jane. BA, St. Charles Borromeo Sem., Phila., 1982; JD, Rutgers U., 1986. Bar: Pa. 1986, D.C. 1989, N.J. 1987, U.S. Dist. Ct. (ea. dist.) Pa. 1986, U.S. Dist. Ct. N.J. 1987, U.S. Ct. Mil. Appeals 1987, U.S. Ct. Appeals (3d cir.) 1987, U.S. Supreme Ct. 1990. Staff atty. Bally's Park Pl., Atlantic City, 1990-92, corp. counsel, 1992-96, asst. v.p., corp. counsel, 1996-98, v.p., gen. counsel, 1998-2000; sr. v.p., gen. counsel east region Park Place Entertainment Corp., Atlantic City, 2000—03, sr. v.p., sec., gen. counsel, 2003; exec. v.p., gen. counsel Caesar's Entertainment, Inc., Las Vegas, 2003—. Translator: Constitutions of Italy, 1987, Constitutions of Dependencies and Special Sovereignties, 1994. Active Brigantine (NJ) Sch. Bd., 1997—. Lt. comdr. JAG, USN, 1986-90, comdr. USNR, 1986-90. Mem. N.J. State Bar Assn. (chmn. casino law sect. 1997—, mem. spl. com. on mil. law VA 1990—), Elks. Republican. Roman Catholic. Office: Caesars Entertainment Inc 3930 Howard Hughes Pkwy Las Vegas NV 89109-0943 Office Fax: 702-699-5121, 702-699-5000.

DE LUTIS, DONALD CONSE, investment advisor, consultant; b. Rome, N.Y., Apr. 25, 1934; s. Conse R. and Mary D.; m. Ruth L.; 1 child, Dante. BS in Econs., Niagara U., 1956; MBA, Boston Coll., 1962. V.p. John Nuveen & Co., Inc., San Francisco, 1968-74; acct. exec. Dean Witter & Co., London, 1975-77; sr. investment officer Buffalo Savs. Bank, N.Y., 1978-80; exec. v.p. Robert Brown & Co., Inc., San Francisco, 1980-89, Capitol Corp. Asset mgmt., 1989-91; exec. v.p., dir. Pacific Securities, Inc., San Francisco, 1980-91; mng. dir. Coast Ptnrs. Securities, Inc., 1998-99; chmn. Orrell Capital Mgmt., Inc., 1991-98, 2000—. Commr. San Francisco Bay Conservation and Devel. Commn., 1983-93, State of Calif. Commn. Housing and Community Devel., 1974-77. Served with USAF, 1957-58. Mem.: San Francisco Bond Club. Republican. Roman Catholic. Office Phone: 415-274-1896.

DELVA, PAUL D., lawyer; b. 1962; BA, Concordia Coll.; MA Purdue U.; JD, Temple U. Bar: 1996. Former reporter Montreal Gazette; atty. Dechert, Price & Rhoads (now Dechert LLP), Phila., 1995—99; asst. gen. counsel Fairchild Semiconductor Internat., Inc., South Portland, Maine, 1999—2003, v.p., gen. counsel, 2003—05, corp. sec., 2005—. Mem.: ABA, Soc. Corp. Sec. Gov. Profl., Assn. Corp. Counsel., Maine Bar Assn. Office: Fairchild Semiconductor Internat Inc 82 Running Hill Rd South Portland ME 04106 Office Phone: 207-775-8100.

DEL VALLE, TERESA JONES, lawyer; b. Dayton, Ohio, July 20, 1965; BS, Ariz. State U., 1988; JD, U. Houston, 1993. Bar: Tex. 1993, US Dist. Ct. (so. and ea. dists.) Tex. 1994. Underwriter Prudential Property and Casualty Ins. Co., Scottsdale, Ariz., 1988-90; assoc. Doyle, Rider, Restrepo, Harvin & Robbins, LLP, Houston, 1993-97, Cash, Jones & Springhetti, LLP, Houston, 1997—99, Rios & Bain, P.C., 1999—2002; atty. Del Valle Law Firm, P.C., Houston, 2002—. Office: Del Valle Law Firm PC 3200 SW Fwy # 3300 Houston TX 77027 Office Phone: 713-402-6195. Business E-Mail: teresa@delvallelawfirm.com.

DEL VECCHIO, ANTIMO A., lawyer; b. Paterson, N.J., Oct. 24, 1964; s. Pacifico and Mary (Diminni) Del V.; m. Sandra Tafuri, Aug. 21, 1994. BA, Rugers U., 1986; JD, Seton Hall U., 1989. Bar: N.J., N.Y., D.C., U.S. Dist. Ct. (so. and ea. dists.) N.Y. 1992, U.S. Dist. Ct. N.J. 1989, U.S. Ct. Appeals (3d cir.) 1990, U.S. Claims Ct. 1991, U.S. Supreme Ct. 1995. Mem. Beattie Padovano, Montvale, N.J., 1989—. Office: Beattie Padovano PO Box 244 50 Chestnut Ridge Rd Montvale NJ 07645-1830

DEL VECCHIO, DANIEL ALEXANDER, plastic surgeon, investment advisor; b. Attleboro, Mass., Apr. 10, 1958; s. Daniel and Anne Angela Del Vecchio; children: Sharon Juliet, Lana Alessandra. BA, Yale, New Haven, 1980; MD, Harvard Med. Sch., Boston, 1984; MBA, Columbia Bus. Sch., N.Y.C., 1998. Diplomate Am. Bd. Plastic Surgery, 1995. Investment profl. Ferrer Freeman and Co., Greenwich, Conn., 1996—; med. dir. Back Bay Plastic Surgery, Boston, 2000—. Author: Role of Micro Fixation in Fetal Bone Repair (Am. Soc. Maxillofacial Surgeons Rsch. award, 1991). Mem.: Union Boat Club, Harvard Club (N.Y.C. chpt.), Phi Beta Kappa, Phelps Assn. Achievements include patents pending in field. Home: 15 Ray Rd Wrentham MA 02093 Office: Back Bay Plastic Surgery 38 Newbury St Boston MA 02116 Office Phone: 617-262-8528. Home Fax: 617-262-2256; Office Fax: 627-262-2256. Personal E-mail: dandelvecchio@aol.com.

DEL VECCHIO, ELIZABETH ANN, secondary school educator; b. Newark, Feb. 1, 1961; d. Donald Del V. and Dolores (Coppola) PeKaar. BS, Trenton State Coll., 1983; MA in Physical Edn., NYU, 1987; MA in Adminstrn., Montclair U., 2003. Tchr. spl. edn. Benway Sch., Mahwah, N.J., 1985-87; tchr. dir. athletics Paramus (N.J.) Cath. High Sch., 1987-99; activity/athletic dir., area supr. Cresskill (N.J.) High Sch., 1999. Home: 798 Saddle River Rd Saddle Brook NJ 07663-4447 Office: Creskill High Sch 1 Lincoln Dr Cresskill NJ 17626 E-mail: bdelvecchio@cresskillboe.k12.nj.us.

DELY, STEVEN, retired aerospace company executive; b. N.Y.C., July 16, 1943; m. Kristine Jon Kolbe, June 7, 1975; 1 child, Jonathan Laurence. BBA, CCNY, 1966; JD, Bklyn. Law Sch., 1968; postgrad. program mgmt. devel., Harvard U., 1979. Bar: N.Y. 1972, U.S. Supreme Ct. 1983. Corp. counsel, dir. pers. svcs. Grumman Allied Industries Inc., Garden City, NY, 1971-75, gen. counsel, sec., 1976-78; v.p. human resources Melville, NY, 1979-82; dir. human resources Grumman Corp., Bethpage, NY, 1982-85; v.p. resources and adminstrn. Grumman Electronics Systems divsn., Bethpage, 1985-86; v.p., asst. to chmn. bd. Grumman Corp., Bethpage, 1986-91, v.p. exec. staff, 1991-92, sr. v.p. exec. staff, corp. sec., 1993-94; co-founder Dispute Resolutions Inc., Huntington, NY, 1998—. Bd. dirs. Family Svc. League, Huntington. Capt. U.S. Army, 1969—71.

DELZELL, JOHN E., JR., medical educator; b. Springfield, Mo, Sept. 28, 1967; married. BA, Baylor U., 1989; MD, U. Mo., Columbia, 1993, MSPH, 2000. Diplomate Am. Bd.Family Practice. Asst. prof. U. Mo., Columbia, 1996—2001; assoc. prof. U. Tenn., Memphis, 2001—. Dir. residency program St. Francis, Memphis, 2001—. Mem.: Am. Acad. Family Physicians. Office: U Tenn Saint Francis FP Residency Program 1301 Primacy Parkway Memphis TN 38119 Office Phone: 901-761-2997.

DEMAIN, ARNOLD LESTER, microbiologist, educator; b. N.Y.C., Apr. 26, 1927; s. Henry and Gussie (Katz) D.; m. Joanna Kaye, Aug. 2, 1952; children: Pamela Robin Demain McCloskey, Jeffrey Brian. BS, Mich. State U., 1949, MS, 1950; PhD, U. Calif., Berkeley, 1954; Doctorate (hon.), U. Leon, Spain, 1997, Ghent (Belgium) U., 1999, Technion-Israeli Inst. Tech., 2000, Mich. State U., 2000, U. Muenster, Germany, 2003. Rsch. asst. U. Calif., Davis, 1952-54; rsch. microbiologist Merck & Co., Inc., Danville, Pa., 1954-56, Rahway, N.J., 1956-65, founder, head of dept. ferm. microbiology, 1965-69; prof. of ind. microbiology MIT, Cambridge, 1969—2001; fellow Charles A. Dana Rsch. Inst., Drew U., Madison, NJ, 2001—. Author or editor 10 books; contbr. more than 490 articles to profl. jours. With USN, 1945—47. Recipient Hotpack award Can. Soc. Microbiology, 1978, Rubro award Australian Soc. Microbiology, 1978, Indsl. Microbiology award Italian Pharm. Assn., 1989, Hans Knoll meml. award, Germany, 1990, G. Mendel award Czech Acad. Sci., 1998, Andrew Jackson Moyer award USDA, 1998. Mem.: NAS, Am. Chem. Soc. (Marvin Johnson biotech. award), Am. Soc. Microbiology (Waksman award N.J. br. 1975, Biotech. award 1990, Disting. Svc. award 1994, Alice C. Evans award 1998, hon. mem. N.E. br. 1999), Soc. Indsl. Microbiology (pres. 1990, Charles Thom award 1978, Waksman Tchg. award 1995), Hungarian Acad. Sci., Mex. Acad. Sci., Croatian Soc. Biotech. (hon.), Czech Soc. Microbiology (hon.), Soc. Actinomycetes Japan (hon.), French Soc. Microbiology (hon.). Achievements include 21 patents; elucidation of biosynthetic pathway to penicillins and cephalosporins; recognition of phenomenon of biochemical regulation of secondary metabolism; discovery of role of lysine and amino adipic acid in penicillin biosynthesis. Office: Drew Univ RISE HS-330 Madison NJ 07940 Office Phone: 973-408-3937. Business E-Mail: ademain@drew.edu.

DE MAIN, JOHN, opera company director; b. Youngstown, Ohio, Jan. 11, 1944; m. Barbara De Main; 1 child, Jennifer. BMus, Juilliard Sch. Music, 1966, MusM, 1968; studies in conducting with, Leonard Bernstein, Peter Adler. Assoc. condr. St. Paul Chamber Orch., 1972-74; music dir. Tex. Opera Theater, 1974-76; former music dir. Houston Grand Opera, Opera Omaha; music dir. Madison Symphony Orch., Wis., 1994—; artistic adv. Madison Opera, Wis., 1994—; artistic dir. & prin. condr. Opera Pacific, Calif., 1998—. Prin. guest condr. Chautauqua Opera Inst., 1985. Rec. performances: Piano Concerto (Frances Thorne), 1975, Porgy and Bess, 1976, Nocturnes (Miriam Gideon), 1978. Finalist Grand Prix, 1977; recipient Julius Rudel award, 1971, Grammy award, 1977; Juilliard Sch. Music scholar, 1964—68. Office: Madison Symphony Orch 6314 Odana Rd Madison WI 53719 Home: 52 White Oaks Ln Madison WI 53711-6216 E-mail: jldemain@operapacific.org.*

DEMANT, HANS HENRICH, automotive executive; b. Wiesbaden, Germany, Sept. 21, 1950; MME, Tech. U., 1979. Product devel. engr. GM Opel, Germany, 1979; with GM Fellowship Program, 1981; project engr. GM Opel, Germany, 1982; staff engr. GM Corp., 1985; with GM Opel Chassis Dept., Russelsheim, Germany, 1987; project mgr. GM Corsa Series; staff engr. GM Concept Devel. Advanced Engring., 1992; exec. vehicle line GM Corp., 1997; v.p. engring. GM Europe, 2001—.

DEMAPAN, MIGUEL S., commonwealth supreme court justice; b. Saipan, Northern Marianas; m. Frances Tenorio; 5 children. BS in Chemistry, Seattle U., 1975; MBA with honors, Golden Gate U., 1983; JD, Santa Clara U., 1985. Gen. counsel J. C. Tenorio Enterprises, Inc.; pvt. practice; ptnr. Demapan and Atalig; assoc. judge Commonwealth Northern Mariana Islands Superior Ct., 1992—98; assoc. justice Commonwealth Northern Mariana Islands Supreme Ct., 1998—99, chief justice, 1999—. Judge pro tem Superior Ct. Guam, Supreme Ct. Guam; mem. Pacific Jud. Coun., 1998—, pres., 2000—02; chmn. Commonwealth Law Revision Commn.; bd. mem. U.S. Conference of Chief Justices, 2002—03; mem. Asia Pacific Conference of Chief Justices, Commonwealth Northern Mariana Islands Federal Bench Council. Chmn. Commonwealth Law Revision Commn.; mem. CNMI Tax Task Force. Trust Ter. scholar, Seattle U. Mem.: World Jurist Assn. Office: Supreme Ct Commonwealth Northern Mariana Islands PO Box 502179 Saipan MP 96950-2165

DEMARA, RONALD F., computer engineer, educator; PhD, U. So. Calif., 1992. Registered profl. engr., Calif., 1992. Assoc. engr. IBM Corp., Manassas, Va., 1986—89; assoc. prof. U. Ctrl. Fla., Orlando, Fla., 1992—. Contbr. articles to profl. jours. Mem.: IEEE. Office: University of Central Florida 4000 Central Florida Blvd Orlando FL 32816-2450 Office Phone: 407-823-5916. Business E-Mail: demara@mail.ucf.edu.

DEMARCO, ANITA JOYCE, elementary school educator; b. New Castle, Pa., Feb. 9, 1933; d. Alex Durgam and Emma (Hasson) Durgam; m. Pat S. DeMarco, Oct. 18, 1952; children: Donald, Gerald, David. BS in Edn., Slippery Rock U., 1972, M.Ed, 1975, MEd in Supervision of Reading, 1978. Cluster II tchr. Franklin (Pa.) Schs.-Polk, 1973-75; tchr. 2d grade Victory Elem. Sch. Franklin Sch. Dist., Harrisville, 1982-92; reading specialist Title I ESEA, 1975-82. Tchr. grad. courses I.U. IV Grove City, 1980—. Author: Title I Helpbook, Helping Energetic Learning Parents in Readiness, 1979. V.p. Grove City Area Historical Soc. Mem. AAUW, Nat. Assn. for Preservation and Perpetuation of Storytelling, Delta Kappa Gamma (2d v.p. 1990, pres. Alpha Tau chpt. 1992—). Avocations: teaching and playing bridge, book compiler. Home: 508 Oakland Ave Grove City PA 16127-1814 Personal E-mail: ajdemarco@zoominternet.net.

DEMARCUS, JAY (STANLEY DEMARCUS), country musician, songwriter; b. Columbus, Ohio, Apr. 26, 1971; s. Wayne and Caron; m. Allison Alderson, May 15, 2004. Performer Printers Alley, Nashville, Chely Wright Band; founder, guitarist, bass, keyboard, songwriter Rascal Flatts, Nashville, 2000—. Musician: (albums) East to West, 1993; engineer, prodr., rhythm and vocal arrangements: (albums) Gospel, 1998; musician (bass) "It's Not Just Me", Rascall Flatts, 2000; songwriter: albums "It's Not Just Me", Rascal Flatts, 2000; musician Rascal Flatts, 2000, Melt, 2002, Feels Like Today, 2004 (Group/Duo Video of Yr., Country Music Television Music awards, 2005); performer: (songs) "Walk the Llama Llama", Emperor's New Groove (Original Soundtrack), 2000; musician: (singles) Praying for Daylight/Long Slow Beautiful Dance, 2000. Recipient Vocal Group Yr., Country Music Assn., 2002, 2004, Song Yr. for "I'm Movin On", Acad. Country Music Awards, 2002, Top Vocal Group, 2003, 2005.

DEMAREST, DAVID FRANKLIN, JR., banker, retired government official; b. Glen Ridge, N.J., Oct. 8, 1951; s. David Franklin Demarest and Alison (Clark) Fahrer; m. Leigh Ann Wisniewski, Feb. 5, 1977 (div. 1981); m. Sarah Tinsley, July 16, 1983; 2 children. BA, Upsala Coll., 1973. Dep. dir. local elections Republican Nat. Com., Washington, 1977-80; dir. pub. and intergovtl. affairs U.S. Trade Rep., Washington, 1981-84; asst. U.S. Trade Rep. Exec. Office of Pres., Washington, 1984; dep. undersec. U.S. Labor Dept., Washington, 1985-87, asst. sec. labor, 1987-88; dir. comm. George Bush for Pres. Com., 1988; dir. pub. affairs Presdl. Transition Office, 1988-89; asst. to pres. for comm. White House, Washington, 1989-92; sr. cons. Internat. Mgmt. and Devel. Group, Ltd., Alexandria, Va., 1993; dir. corp. comms., exec. v.p. Bank of Am., San Francisco, 1993-99; exec. v.p. global corp. rels. Visa Internat., San Francisco, 1999—. Presbyterian. Office: Visa Internat PO Box 8999 San Francisco CA 94128-8999

DEMAREST, SYLVIA M., lawyer; b. Lake Charles, La., Aug. 16, 1944; d. Edmand and Emily Demarest; m. James A. Johnston, Jr., Oct. 31, 1975 (div. Dec. 1979). Student, U. S.W. La., 1963-66; JD, U. Tex., 1969. Bar: Tex. 1969, U.S. Supreme Ct. 1973, U.S. Ct. Appeals (5th cir.) 1970, U.S. Ct. Appeals (7th cir.) 1979, U.S. Ct. Appeals (11th cir.) 1980, U.S. Dist. Ct. (no. dist.) Tex. 1970, U.S. Dist. Ct. (ea. dist.) Tex. 1970, U.S. Dist. Ct. (so. dist.) Tex. 1972. Reginald H. Smith Cmty. Lawyer fellow, Corpus Christi and Dallas, 1969-71; house counsel Tex. Inst. Ednl. Devel., San Antonio, 1972-73; staff atty. Dallas Legal Svsc. Found., Inc., 1973, exec. dir., 1973-76; sole practice Dallas, 1977-78; mgr. product litig., dir. Windle Turley, P.C., Dallas, 1978-83; sole practice Dallas, 1983-85; ptnr. Demarest & Smith, Dallas, 1985—. Mem. faculty trial advocacy program So. Meth. U. Law Sch., 1984; lectr. Contbr. articles to profl. jours. Mem. ABA, State Bar Tex., ATLA, Dallas Bar Assn., Dallas Trial Lawyers Assn. (past pres.), Dallas Inn of Ct. (master of the bar 1989—). Democrat. Home: 1812 Atlantic St Dallas TX 75208-3002 Office: 10440 N Central Expy Ste 1100 Dallas TX 75231

DE MARGITAY, GEDEON, acquisitions and management consultant; b. Budapest, Hungary, Mar. 6, 1924; came to U.S., 1953, naturalized, 1958; s. Joseph and Anne (de Bessenyei) de M.; m. Virginia Varet Martin, Dec. 30, 1963. Student, U. Budapest Grad. Sch. Econs., 1941-44, Ecole des Scis. Politiques, Paris, 1946-48. With N.Y. Times, 1947-50, 54-61; with European info. divsn. Mut. Security Agy., 1950-53; chief exec. Magnum Photos, Inc., N.Y.C., 1961-63; with Time Inc., 1964-75, dir. mktg. svcs. Time/Life TV, 1975; dir. broadcast and corp. planning NBC, 1975-78; acquistions and mgmt. cons. N.Y.C., 1978—. Co-author: Broadcasting: The Next Ten Years, 1977. Mem. Internat. Radio-TV Soc., Am. Acad. Polit. and Social Sci. Republican. Presbyterian.

DE MARIA, ALFRED ANTHONY, neurologist; b. Sewickley, Pa., Mar. 27, 1952; s. Alfred Anthony and Helen Josephine (Goray) De M.; m. Katherine Grace Bridge, June 25, 1977; children: Genevieve Camille, Gabrielle Christine. BA, Johns Hopkins U., 1973; MD, Ohio State U., 1976. Diplomate Am. Bd. Psychiatry and Neurology. Intern N.C. Baptist Hosp., Winston-Salem, 1976-77; resident in neurology N.C. Meml. Hosp., Chapel Hill, 1977-80; fellow in EEG Mayo Clinic, Rochester, Minn., 1980-81; attending physician Neurol. Assocs., Columbus, Ohio, 1981-92, Wilmington (N.C.) Health Assocs., 1993—. Med. dir. EEG lab. Riverside Meth. Hosp., Columbus, Ohio, 1981-92; med. dir. sleep lab. Cape Fear Meml. Hosp., Wilmington, 1993—. Host (TV show) Second Opinion, 1996—. Mem. Am. Acad. Neurology, Am. Sleep Disorders Assn., Am. EEG Soc., Am. Epilepsy Soc., Nat. Stroke Assn., Nat. Headache Found., Nat. Assn. Physician Broadcasters. Avocations: music, skiing. Office: Wilmington Health Assocs 1202 Medical Center Dr Wilmington NC 28401-7307 Office Phone: 910-341-3358. E-mail: ademaria@wilmingtonhealth.com.

DE MARIA, ANTHONY JOHN, electrical engineer; b. Santa Croce, Italy, Oct. 30, 1931; came to U.S., 1935; s. Joseph and Nicolina (Daddona) De M.; m. Katherine M. Waybright, Aug. 29, 1953; 1 dau., Karla Kay. BS in Elec. Engring., U. Conn., 1956, PhD in Elec. Engring., 1965; MS, Rensselaer Poly. Inst., 1960. Acoustic research engr. Andersen Lab., West Hartford, Conn., 1956-57; magnetic research engr. Hamilton Standard Div. United Techs. Corp., Windsor Locks, Conn., 1957-58; asst. dir. rsch. electronics and photonics United Techs. Rsch. Ctr., East Hartford, Conn., 1958-94; founder, chmn., CEO DeMaria ElectroOptics Sys., Inc., Bloomfield, Conn., 1994-2001, chief scientist Coherent Laser divsn., 2001—; rsch. prof. Photonics Rsch. Ctr. U. Conn., Storrs, 1994-98; pres. TeraBit Commns., LLC, 2001—; prof.-in-residence elec. and computer engring. U. Conn., Storrs, Conn., 2004—. Instr. electronics U. Hartford, 1957-60; adj. prof. physics Rensselaer Poly. Inst. Grad. Ctr., Hartford, 1970-77; lectr. in lasers UCLA, 1974-82; mem. adv. group on electronic devices Dept. Def., 1977-86, chmn., 1980-85; mem. evaluation com. on electromagnetic tech. Nat. Bur. Standards, 1977-79; mem. Ctr. Elec. and Electronic Engring., 1979-83; mem. LANL Adv. Com. for Chemistry and Laser Sci., 1985-92. Author: Lasers, Vol. III, 1972, Vol. IV, 1976; Contbr. articles to profl. jours. Mem. Air Force Sci. Adv. Bd., 1981-86. Recipient Disting. Alumnus award U. Conn., 1978, Disting. Engring. award, U. Conn., 1983, Davies medal and award Rensselaer Poly. Inst., 1980, Air Force Meritorious medal for civilian svc., 1986. Fellow IEEE (editor Jour. Quantum Electronics, Morris N. Liebman meml. award 1980), SPIE (bd. dirs. 1995—, v.p. 2002, pres. 2003), Optical Soc. Am. (v.p. 1979, pres. 1981, chmn. bd. editors 1986-89, Frederic Ives medal 1988), Am. Phys. Soc.; mem. NAE (Farichild Disting. scholar 1982-83, Calif. Inst. Tech.), NAS, Conn. Acad. Scis. and Engring. (pres. 1994-99). Address: Coherent DEOS LLC 1280 Blue Hills Ave Bloomfield CT 06002-5304 Office Phone: 860-769-3313.

DEMARIA, ANTHONY NICHOLAS, cardiologist, educator; b. Elizabeth, N.J., Jan. 12, 1943; s. Anthony and Charlotte DeMaria; m. Delores Horn; children: Christine, Anthony, Jonathon. BA, Coll. Holy Cross, 1964; MD, N.J. Coll. Medicine, 1968; hon. degree, Kagawa Med. U., Japan, U. Bordeaux, France. Diplomate Am. Bd. Internal Medicine, Am. Bd. Cardiovascular Disease, Am. Bd. Cardiovascular Medicine. Intern St. Vincent Hosp., Worcester, Mass., 1968-69; resident USPHS Hosp., Staten Island, N.Y., 1969-71; fellow cardiology U. Calif., Davis, 1969-73, asst. prof. medicine, 1972-77, assoc. prof. medicine, 1977-81, prof. medicine, 1977-81; prof. medicine, chief cardiology div. U. Ky., Lexington, 1981-92; dir. Ky. Heart Inst., Lexington, 1989—; prof. medicine, chief cardiology U. Calif. Sch. Medicine, San Diego, 1992—2994, vice chmn. internal medicine, 1998—2001, med. dir. Cardiovasc. Ctr., Judith and Jack White chair cardiovasc. medicine, dir. Cardiovasc. Ctr., 2004—. Mem. rev. bds. Vets. Adminstrn. Med. Research Merit in Cardiovascular Studies, Nat. Inst. Health, NSF, NIH, NHLBI, U. Calif., U.S. FDA; chmn. Diagnostic Radiology Study Sect. NIH; vice-chmn. dept. medicine U. Calif., San Diego, 1998-2001. Mem. editl. bd. Am. Heart Jour., Am. Jour. Cardiac Imaging, Circulation, Am. Jour. Cardiology, Jour. Am. Coll. Cardiology, Health News from New Eng. Jour. Medicine; editor-in-chief Jour. Am. Coll. Cardiology, 2001—; assoc. editor Jour. Am. Coll. Cardiology; editl. cons. Am. Jour. Physiology, Annals Internal Medicine, Archives Phys. Medicine and Rehab., Catheterization and Cardiovascular Diagnosis, Jour. Clin. Investigation, New Eng. Jour. Medicine; contbr. numerous articles to profl. jours.; host Cardiology Update, Lifetime Med. TV. Recipient Humanitarian award Theodore and Susan Cummings, 1978, Disting. Alumnus award Coll. Medicine and Dentistry of N.J., 1988, Echocardiography award Tufts U., 1988, award of excellence Am. Acad. Med. Adminstrs., 1994, William Harvey award Am. Med. Writers Assn., 1996; named one of Best Doctors in Am., Best Heart Specialist in U.S. Good Housekeeping mag., 1996; Golden Empire Heart Assn. grantee, Am. Heart Assn. grantee, Ky. Heart Assn. grantee, Vet. Adminstrn. grantee, Nat. Heart, Lung and Blood Inst. grantee; teaching scholar Am. Heart Assn. Fellow ACP, Am. Coll. Cardiology (chmn. 27th ann. scientific session 1978, cardiovascular procedures com., govt. rels. com., v.p. elect 1986, pres. elect 1987-88, pres. 1988—, active various coms., Young Investigator award 1976), Am. Coll. Chest Physicians; mem. Am. Heart Assn. (bd. dirs. work evaluation unit Yolo Sierra chpt., Ky. chapter, active various coms., Teaching scholar 1979-82), Am. Fedn. Clin. Rsch., Yolo County Med. Socs., Am. Inst. Ultrasound in Medicine (bd. dirs.), Am. Soc. Echocardiography (bd. dirs. 1975-87, v.p. 1983-85, pres. 1985-87, assoc. editor), N.Am. Soc. for Cardiac Radiology, Assn. U. Cardiologists. Roman Catholic. Office: U Calif Med Ctr 225 Dickinson St Ste 360 San Diego CA 92103-1910

DE MARINO, DONALD NICHOLSON, federal agency administrator, diversified financial services company executive; b. Greensburg, Pa., Sept. 28, 1945; s. Thomas C. and Sue Eleanor (Nicholson) De M.; m. Caroline Mack, Dec. 27, 1967 (div. 1981); children: Christopher Tyson, Benjamin Nicholson; m. Betsy Reiver, July 18, 1981; children: Alexander Reiver, William McCurdy. BA, U. Pa., 1967. Dir. Mack & Nicholson, West Chester, Pa., 1972-76; bus. cons. The Nicholson Group, Inc., NYC, 1976-81; sr. project officer U.S.-Saudi Arabian Joint Commn. on Econ. Cooperation, Riyadh, Saudi Arabia, 1981-84, dir., 1985-87; mgr. Litton Industries Offset Investment Programs, Riyadh, 1984-85; sr. project adviser The Arab Investment Co., Riyadh, 1985; internat. bus. cons., prin. De Marino Assocs., Coatesville, Pa., 1987-88; dep. asst. sec. Africa, Near East and South Asia U.S. Dept. Commerce, Washington, 1989-90; U.S. advisor Tata Group of India, 1991—; chmn. Nat. U.S.-Arab C. of C., 1991—; prin. De Marino Ptnrs., LLC, 2004—. Lectr. Wharton Sch. Advanced Mgmt. Program, 1994-96; nat. adv. bd. Mid. East Policy Coun.; bd. dir. Mcht. Bridge & Co., Ltd.; mem. Iraq pers. evaluation team U.S. Dept. Def., 2004. Recipient Disting. Svc. award Govt. of Saudi Arabia, 1987. Mem. Sovereign Mil. Order Temple of Jerusalem (decorated Chevalier Templars), Arab-Fgn. C. of C. (chmn. 1999-2000), Racquet Club, Mask and Wig Club. Republican. Presbyterian. Home: 43 Longview Rd Coatesville PA 19320-4311 Office: PO Box 791 Unionville PA 19375-0791 Office Phone: 610-347-0701. Personal E-mail: dndemarind@aol.com.

DE MARNEFFE, BARBARA ROWE, historic preservationist; b. Boston, June 2, 1929; d. H S Payson and Florence Van Arnhem (Cassard) Rowe; m. James Hopkins, Oct. 9, 1954 (div. 1969); m. Francis de Marneffe, 1969; stepchildren: Peter, Daphne, Colette. BA, Vassar Coll., 1952. Tchr. Chapin Sch., NYC, 1952-54; adminstrv. asst. to dean Sch. of Indsl. Mgmt., MIT, Cambridge, 1959-60; asst. pub. rels. dir. Peter Bent Brigham Hosp., Boston, 1960-61, pub. rels. dir., 1961-63; pub. rels. cons. Diabetes Found. and Joslin Clinic, Boston, 1963-64; pub. rels. dir. McLean Hosp., Belmont, Mass., 1964-68; mgr. pub. affairs Cambridge (Mass.) C. of C., 1975-78; pres. de Marneffe Selections, Cambridge, 1978-90. Trustee Edith Wharton Restoration, Inc, 1999; chair Edith Wharton Restoration, Inc., 2002—03, co-chair, 2003—; corporator Brookline (Mass.) Savs. Bank, 1995—. Contbr. articles to profl. jours. Trustee Archives Am. Art Smithsonian Inst., Washington, 1983—99, trustee coun., 1999—2000; officer, bd. dirs. Family Counseling Svcs. Cambridge, 1969—78; trustee Peterborough (NH) Players, 1983—89; docent NC Mus. Art, Raleigh, 1992—93; chair Friends of Pain Ctr. Mass. Gen. Hosp., Boston, 1995—99; mem. adv. coun. Farnsworth Art Mus., Rockland, Maine, 1995—98; state comitteewoman Mass. Rep., 1977—80; exec. sec. Cambridge Rep. City Com., 1956—57; pub. rels. dir. Peabody for Congress Campaign, Newton, Mass., 1968; vestry Emmanuel Episcopal Ch., Dublin, NH, 1995—; com. mem. Ellis Mem. Settlement House Antiques Show, 1968—89; bd. dirs. Friends McLean Hosp, Belmont, Mass., 1967—89, Friends Frances Lehman Loeb Art Ctr., Vassar Coll., 2001—05, Nat. Com. Treatment Intractable Pain, Washington, 1980—90. Mem.: Jewelers Am. Inc., Vassar Club (pres. Boston chpt. 1989). Avocations: medicine, business, politics, historic preservation, decorative arts. Home: 126 Coolidge Hl Cambridge MA 02138-5522

DE MARNEFFE, FRANCIS, psychiatrist, hospital administrator; b. Brussels, May 7, 1924; arrived in Eng., 1940; came to US, 1950; s. Armand Gustave and Esther Magdalen (Loveday) de M.; m. Nancy Marie Edmonds, Aug. 5, 1955 (div. Sept. 1967); children: Peter Loveday, Daphne Elizabeth, Colette; m. Barbara Rowe Hopkins, Dec. 5, 1969. MB, BS, U. London, 1950. Diplomate Am. Bd. Psychiatry Neurology. Intern Muhlenberg Hosp., Plainfield, NJ, 1950-51; asst. resident psychiatry Mass. Gen. Hosp., Boston, 1952; tchg. fellow psychiatry Med. Sch. Harvard U., Boston, 1955-56, rsch. fellow, 1955-56; resident psychiatry McLean Hosp., Belmont, Mass., 1953-54, staff psychiatrist, 1955-90, cons. psychiatrist, 1990—, gen. dir., 1962-87, gen. dir. emeritus, 1987—, pres., CEO McLean Health Svcs., Inc., 1986-89; med. dir. Holly Hill Mental Health Svcs., Raleigh, NC, 1990-93. Instr. psychiatry Med. Sch. Harvard U., 1961-66, lectr. 1966—; mem. accreditation coun. psychiat. facilitities Joint Commn. Accreditation Hosps., Chgo., 1979-84, mem. tech. adv. com., 1979-84, chmn. accreditation, 1970-72, mem. coun., 1970-79; adminstr. McLean divsn. Hall-Mercer Hosp., Phila., 1969-87; v.p. Hall-Mercer Hosp., 1980-87; exec. v.p. Belmont programs Mass. Gen. Hosp., Boston, 1986-87; clin. prof. psychiatry U. NC, Chapel Hill, 1991-93; assoc. cons. prof. psychiatry Duke U. Med. Sch., 1991-93, v.p. Wake County Mental Health Assn., 1992-93, med. staff Rex Hosp., Raleigh, NC, 1993; mem. Corp. Ptnrs. Health Care Inc., Boston, 1994—; trustee working group McLean Hosp., 1996, co-chair com. expanding svcs. revs.; cons. Exec. Svcs. Corps., Boston, 1996—; cons. Mass. Soc. Prevention of Cruelty to Children, 2004-. Author: (non-fiction) Introduction to Adolescent Patients in Transition, 1974; author: (contbg.) The Changing Mental Health Scene, 1976; author: Last Boat From Bordeaux, 2001; mem. editl. bd. (jour.) McLean (Hosp.) Jour., 1976—90. Trustee Guidance Camps, Inc., Boston, 1968-90, Preschool, Inc., Cambridge, Mass., 1961-62, Concord Acad. Mass., 1975-78, Nat. Assn. Pvt. Psychiat. Hosps., Washington, 1982-85, 93-94, McLean Hosp. Corp., Belmont, 1985-87; mem. Corp. Family Svc. Assn. Greater Boston, 1978-81; hon. trustee Concord Acad., 1978—; bd. dirs. Mass. chpt. Nat. Com. Prevention Child Abuse, Boston, 1979-81, Health Planning Coun. Greater Boston, 1972-76; chmn. med. divsn. United Way, 1986; mem. Mass. Gen. Hosp. Corp., 1988-94, coll. Des Conseillers French Libr. & Cultural Ctr., Boston, 1995-99; bd. dirs. Friends McLean, 1995—, 1st v.p., 1997-99, pres., 1999—; chmn. Boston chpt. French Heritage Soc. (formerly Friends of Vieilles Maisons Françaises), 2000—; cons. Mass. Soc. Prevention of Cruelty to Children, 2004-. Served as flying officer RAF, 1943-46. Recipient Presdl. award Nat. Assn. Pvt. Psychiat. Hosps., 1991. Fellow: Am. Coll. Mental Health Adminstrn., Mass. Med. Soc., Royal Coll. Psychiatrists, Am. Coll. Psychiatrists, Am. Psychiat. Assn. (life), Royal Coll. Physicians (licentiate); mem.: Ctrl. Neuropsychiat. Hosp. Assn. (pres. 1986—87), Royal Coll. Surgeons, The Royal Air Force Club (London), Lake (Dublin, N.H.) Club, Thames Rowing Club (London), Cambridge Boat Club, Leander (Henley-on-Thames, Eng.) Club, Somerset (Boston) Club, The Country Club (Brookline). Home: 126 Coolidge Hl Cambridge MA 02138-5522 Office: McLean Hosp 115 Mill St Belmont MA 02478-9106 Office Phone: 617-855-3802.

DEMARR, BEVERLY J., management educator; b. Muskegon, Mich., Apr. 4, 1959; d. Arthur and Hazel B. DeMarr; children: Melita M. Cioe, Eric S. Cioe. BSBA, Aquinas Coll., 1982; MBA, Grand Valley State U., 1988; PhD, Mich. State U., 1996. Cert. cmty. mediator Mich. State Ct. Adminstrv. Office, 2004. Vis. instr. mgmt. Grand Valley State U., Allendale, Mich., 1988—92; assoc. prof. mgmt. Davenport Coll., Grand Rapids, 1992—2000; prof. mgmt. Ferris State U., Big Rapids, 2000—. Vol. mediator West Mich. Dispute Resolution Ctr., Grand Rapids, 2004. Mem.: Soc. Human Resource Mgmt., Acad. Mgmt. Office: Ferris State U Bus 345 119 South St Big Rapids MI 49307 Office Phone: 231-591-3756. Business E-Mail: demarrb@ferris.edu.

DE MARR, MARY JEAN, English language educator; b. Champaign, Ill., Sept. 20, 1932; d. William Fleming and Laura Alice (Shauman) Bailey. BA, Lawrence Coll., 1954; MA, U. Ill., 1957, PhD, 1963; postgrad., U. Tuebingen, 1954-55, Moscow State U., 1961-62. Asst. prof. English Willamette U., 1964-65; asst. prof. English Ind. State U., 1965-70, assoc. prof., 1970-75, prof., 1975-95, prof. emerita English and women's studies, 1996—. Author: Colleen McCullough: A Critical Companion, 1996, Barbara Kingsolver: A Critical Companion, 1999, Kaye Gibbons: A Critical Companion, 2003; co-author: Adolescent Female Portraits in the American Novel, 1961-81: An Annotated Bibliography, 1983, The Adolescent in The American Novel Since 1960, 1986; Am. editor: Annual Bibliography of English Language and Literature, 1979-90; editor, contbr. In the Beginning: First Novels in Mystery Series, 1995. Recipient Fulbright assistantship, 1954—55, Dove award, Popular Culture Assn., 1996, Midam. award, Soc. for the Study of Midwestern Lit., 2000. Mem.: ACLU, AAUP, MLA, Modern Humanities Rsch. Assn., Phi Kappa Phi, Phi Beta Kappa. Home: 594 Woodbine Terre Haute IN 47803-1760 E-mail: mjd594@msn.com.

DEMARTINI, RICHARD MICHAEL, retired bank executive; b. San Francisco, Oct. 12, 1952; s. James G.B. and Mary (Nehls) D.; m. Jennifer Brorsen; children: Chad, Susan, Jake. BS in Mktg., San Diego State U., 1974. Account exec. Dean Witter, San Mateo, Calif., 1975-78, br. mgr. Bakersfield, Calif., 1978-80, 1st v.p. and br. mgr. Chgo., 1980-83, sr. v.p., regional dir., 1983-84, exec. v.p., nat. sales dir. NYC, 1984-85; pres., COO Dean Witter Consumer Markets Dean Witter Fin. Svcs. Group, NYC, 1985-88, pres., COO Sears Consumer Fin. Corp. Lincolnshire, Ill., 1988-89, pres., COO Dean Witter Capital NYC, 1989—98; chmn., CEO, internat. private client group Morgan Stanley Dean Witter, NYC, 1998—2001; pres., asset mgmt. group Bank Am., 2001—04. Chmn. Nasdaq, 1996—97; former vice chmn. Nat. Assoc. Securities Dealers. Trustee Cancer Rsch. Inst.; bd. dirs. Graham Windham, NYC.

DEMARTINO, ANTHONY GABRIEL, cardiologist, internist; b. Bronx, N.Y., Oct. 7, 1931; s. Agostino and Vincenzina (Clarizia) DeM.; m. Marlene Mignone, Aug. 8, 1964; children: Anthony Augustin, Laura Jean. BS cum laude, Iona Coll., 1953; MD, SUNY, 1957. Diplomate Nat. Bd. Med. Examiners, Am. Bd. Internal Medicine (cardiovascular disease). Intern U. divsn. Kings County Med. Ctr., Bklyn., 1957-58, med. resident, 1960-62;

fellow cardiopulmonary Cornell U., N.Y. Hosp., 1962-64; acting chief medicine Fordham divsn. Misericordia Fordham Affiliation, Bronx, 1964-65; physician in charge cardiac lab. Misericordia-Fordham Affiliation, 1965-69; attending physician dept. medicine and cardiology Our Lady of Mercy Med. Ctr., Bronx, 1967-95, sr. physician, 1995—, mem. med. bd., 1985-93; asst. attending The Presbyn. Hosp., N.Y.C., 1998—. Attending physician dept. medicine and cardiology Lawrence Hosp., Bronxville, N.Y., 1977-97, sr. attending physician, 1997—, mem. med. bd., 1989-94, sec., treas. med. bd., 1996-97, assoc. dir. dept. medicine, 1993-97; practice medicine, specializing in cardiology and internal medicine, Bronxville, 1964—; v.p. med. bd. Misericordia Hosp. Med. Ctr., Bronx, 1973-75, pres., 1975-77; clin. asst. prof. medicine N.Y. Med. Coll., 1971—; hon. police surgeon N.Y.C., 1978—; asst. attending physician Presbyn. Hosp., N.Y., 1996—; asst. in medicine Columbia U., N.Y.C., 1996—. Mem. editl. bd. N.Y. Med. Quar., 1980-84; contbr. articles to profl. jours. Trustee Misericordia Hosp., 1977-83; sec., treas. med. bd. Lawrence Hosp., 1996-97. Served to capt., M.C., U.S. Army, 1958-60. Nat. Heart Inst. fellow, 1962-64. Fellow ACP/Am. Soc. Internal Medicine, Am. Coll. Cardiology, Coun. Clin. Cardiology of Am. Heart Assn., Am. Coll. Chest Physicians, N.Y. Cardiol. Assn.; mem. AMA, Westchester County, N.Y. County Med. Soc., Am. Coll. of Med. Roman Catholic. Office: 77 Pondfield Rd Bronxville NY 10708-3809 Office Phone: 914-337-2033.

DEMARY, JO LYNNE, school system administrator, elementary school educator; BEd, DEd, Coll. of William and Mary; MS in Spl. Edn., U. Va. Commonwealth. Tchr. Fairfax County Schs., Va., Henrico County Schs., Va., from tchr. to asst. supt.; asst. supt. pub. instruction Commonwealth of Va., 1994—99, acting supt. pub. instruction, 1999—2000, supt. of pub. instruction, 2000—. Office: Va Dept Edn PO Box 2120 Richmond VA 23218*

DEMASI, KARIN A., lawyer; b. San Francisco, July 20, 1971; BS, Northwestern Univ., 1993; JD, Univ. Pa., 1996. Bar: Pa. 1996, NY 1997. Law clk., Hon. D. Brock Hornby US Dist. Ct., Dist. of Maine; assoc. Cravath Swaine & Moore LLP, NYC, 1997—2005, ptnr., litig., 2005—. Editor: Univ. Pa. Law Rev. Office: Cravath Swaine & Moore LLP Worldwide Plz 825 Eighth Ave New York NY 10019-7475 Office Phone: 212-474-1059. Office Fax: 212-474-3700. Business E-Mail: kdemasi@cravath.com.

DE MASI, KENNETH FORREST, secondary school educator; b. Phoenix, May 11, 1950; s. Charles Armand and Delphine Edna (Fuller) de Masi; m. Josephine MacLaren Shepard (div.); children: Chauncey Adin Fuller, Michael Orlando Sage; m. Linda Ann Redburn, Dec. 13, 1943; stepchildren: Scott Aaron, Peter M., Matthew Jon, Kristen Madeleine Gundersen. BA in Edn., Ariz. State U., 1974, MEd, 2000. Std. secondary tchg. cert. Ariz., 1974. Tchr. South Mountain H.S., Phoenix, 1974—78, social studies dept. chmn., 1975—78; tchr. Mesa (Ariz.) Vista H.S., 1983—, social studies dept. chmn., 1983—. Tchr. cons. Ariz. Geog. Alliance, Tempe, 2001—05. Author: (curriculum materials-CD) Making Sense of Place: Phoenix-the Urban Desert, 2004; co-author: (curriculum package) The Panama Canal: Building the 8th Wonder of the World, 2003. Chmn. investment com. Mesa United Way, 1991—2000, chmn. neighborhood small grants, 1995—2000; com. mem. Mesa Mayor's Alliance Against Drugs. With U.S. Army, 1970—71. Named Betty Kerr Vol. of Yr., Mesa United Way, 1998; recipient Tribune Newspapers' Ednl. Leadership award, Mesa Tribune, 1992, ambassadorship, Motorola/Mesa Pub. Schs./Industry, 1993—94; Nat. Security Coun. Tchr. fellow, 1975—76, sr. fellow, James Madison Meml. Found., 1998. Mem.: ASCD, Nat. Coun. for Geog. Edn., Nat. Coun. for the Social Studies (curriculum com. 2005—), Ariz. Coun. for the Social Studies (v.p. 2003—04, pres. 2004—05). Democrat. Avocations: hiking, fishing, backpacking, woodworking, birdwatching. Office: Mesa Vista HS 1731 N Country Club Dr Mesa AZ 85201 Office Phone: 480-472-5366. E-mail: kfdemasi@mpsaz.org.

DEMASO, DAVID RAY, psychiatrist; b. Battle Creek, Mich. BS with distinction, U. Mich., 1971, MD cum laude, 1975. Diplomate Am. Bd. Psychiatry and Neurology, also sub.-bd. Child and Adolescent Psychiatry. Resident in pediatrics Mass. Gen. Hosp., Boston, 1975-76; resident in psychiatry Duke U. Med. Ctr., Durham, N.C., 1976-78; fellow in child psychiatry Judge Baker Children's Ctr. and Children's Hosp., Boston, 1980-81; cons.-liaison fellow Children's Hosp., Boston, 1980-81, sr. assoc. in psychiatry and cardiology, 1983—. Psychiatrist-in-chief Childrend's Hosp., Boston, 2004—, 1995—; prof. psychiatry Harvard Med. Sch., Boston. Mem. Alpha Omega Alpha. Office: Children's Hosp 300 Longwood Ave Boston MA 02115-5737

DE MATTEO, DREA, actress; b. Queens, NY, Jan. 19, 1973; BFA in film prodn., NYU, Tish Sch. Arts. Owner Filth Mart Clothing, NY. Actor: (TV series) The Sopranos, 1999—2004 (Emmy award Outstanding Supporting Actress in a Drama Series, 2004), Joey, 2004—; (films) Meet Prince Charming, 1999, Sleepwalk, 2000, Swordfish, 2001, The Perfect You, 2002, Deuces Wild, 2002, Love Rome, 2002, Prey for Rock & Roll, 2003, Beacon Hill, 2003, Assault on Precinct 13, 2005.*

DEMAUSE, LLOYD, psychologist; b. Detroit, Sept. 19, 1931; s. Leon and Martha (Koren) DeM.; m. Susan Hein; children: Neil, Jennifer, Jonathan. Student, GM Inst., 1948-52; AB, Columbia U., 1957, postgrad., 1957-61, Nat. Psychol. Assn. for Psychoanalysis, 1959-60. Founder Atcom Inc. (pub.), 1959; chmn. bd., dir. Inst. for Psychohistory; pub. Psychohistory Press; mem. faculty N.Y. Center for Psychoanalytic Tng. Editor, author: Jimmy Carter and American Fantasy, The History of Childhood, The New Psychohistory, A Bibliography of Psychohistory, Foundations of Psychohistory, Reagan's America: The Emotional Life of Nations; editor: Jour. Psychohistory. With AUS, 1952-54. Mem. Internat. Psychohist. Assn. (pres.). Home and Office: Inst for Psychohistory 140 Riverside Dr New York NY 10024-2605 Office Phone: 212-799-2294. E-mail: psychhst@tiac.net.

DEMB, HOWARD BERTRAM, psychiatry educator, pediatrics educator; b. NYC, Oct. 30, 1931; BS, CCNY, 1953, MA, 1957; MD, SUNY, Syracuse, 1962. Asst. clin. prof. psychiatry and pediatrics Albert Einstein Coll. Medicine, N.Y.C., 1972-86, asst. prof. psychiatry, 1986—, asst. prof. pediatrics, 1986-90, assoc. prof. pediatrics, 1990—2000, prof. clinical pediat., 2000—. Office: Albert Einstein Coll Medicine 1410 Pelham Pky S Bronx NY 10461-1101

DEMBER, WILLIAM NORTON, retired psychologist, educator; b. Waterbury, Conn., Aug. 8, 1928; s. David and Henrietta Dember; m. Cynthia Fox, Dec. 21, 1958; children: Joanna, Laura, Gregory. AB, Yale U., 1950; MA, U. Mich., 1951, PhD, 1955. Instr. dept. psychology U. Mich., 1954-56; asst. prof. Yale U., 1956-59; faculty U. Cin., 1959-98, prof. psychology, 1965-98, asst. dean, grad. sch., 1965-67, head dept. psychology, 1968-76, 79-81, dean Coll. Arts and Scis., 1981-86, disting. rsch. prof., 1989, prof., dean emeritus, 1998; ret. Author: Psychology of Perception, 1960, 2d edit., 1979, Visual Perception, 1964, General Psychology, 1970, 2d edit., 1984, Exploring Behavior and Experience, 1971, Spontaneous Alternation Behavior, 1989; contbr. articles to profl. jours. Fellow APA, Am. Psychol. Soc.; mem. Midwest Psychol. Assn. (pres. 1976). Achievements include developing and testing theory of motivation applying to behavior of human beings and animals; rsch. in visual metacontrast, optimism/pessimism, and sustained attention. Home: 920 Oregon Trl Cincinnati OH 45215-2536 Personal E-mail: Drsdember@aol.com.

DEMBLING, PAUL GERALD, lawyer, former government official; b. Rahway, NJ, Jan. 11, 1920; s. Simon and Fannie (Ellenbogen) D.; m. Florence Brotman, Nov. 22, 1947; children: Ross Wayne, Douglas Evan, Donna Stacy. BA, Rutgers U., 1940, MA, 1942; JD, George Washington U., 1951. Bar: D.C. 1952. Grad. asst., teaching fellow Rutgers U., 1940-42; economist Office Chief Transp., Dept. Army, 1942-45; since practiced in Washington; indsl. relations NACA, 1945-51, spl. counsel, legal adviser, gen. counsel, 1951-58; asst. gen. counsel NASA, 1958-61, dir. legis. affairs, 1961-63, dep. gen. counsel, 1963-67, gen. counsel, 1967-69, chmn. bd. contract appeals, 1958-61, vice chmn. inventions and contbns. bd., 1959-67; mem. and alt. rep. U.S. del. UN Legal Subcom. Com. on Outer Space, 1964-69; gen. counsel GAO, 1969-78; partner Schnader, Harrison, Segal & Lewis, Washington, 1978-93, sr. counsel, 1994—2002. Prin. author NASA Act, 1958; professorial lectr. George Washington U. Law Sch., 1965-86; lectr. Am. Grad. U., 1978-2000. Co-author: Federal Contract Management, 1988, Essentials of Grant Law Practice, 1991; editor in chief Fed. Bar Jour., 1962-69; contbr. articles to profl. jours. Recipient Meritorious Civilian Service award War Dept., 1945, Disting. Service medal NASA, 1968, Nat. Civil Service League award, 1973, Earl W. Kintner award FBA, 2003, Newton award Nat. Grants Mgmt. Assn., 2005. Fellow: AIAA (chmn. com. law and sociology 1969—71), FBA (life; nat. coun. 1963—, pres. Capitol Hill chpt. 1977—78, nat. sec. 1978—79, pres.-elect 1981—82, nat. pres. 1983—84, bd. dirs. bldg. corp. 1989—, Earl W. Kintner Disting. award 2003), Nat. Acad. Pub. Adminstrn., Nat. Contract Mgmt. Assn. (bd. advisers 1973—98), Fed. Bar Found. (life); mem.: ABA (coun., pub. contract law sec. 1983—84, vice chmn. 1984—85, chmn. elect 1985—86, chmn. 1986—87), Internat. Inst. Space Law (pres. Am. assn. 1970—72, Internat. Astronaut. Fedn. award 1992), Procurement Roundtable (bd. dirs. 1984—, vice chmn. 1988—), D.C. Bar (mem. steering com. govt. contracts and litigation sect. 1989—95), Cosmos Club, Phi Delta Phi. Home: 11625 Pamplona Blvd Boynton Beach FL 33437-4077 Office: Schnader Harrison Segal & Lewis 2001 Pennsylvania Ave NW Washington DC 20006 E-mail: pfdemb@webtv.net.

DEMBOWSKI, PETER FLORIAN, foreign language educator; b. Warsaw, Dec. 23, 1925; arrived in U.S., 1966, naturalized, 1974; s. Wlodzimierz and Henryka (Sokolowski) D.; m. Yolande Jessop, June 29, 1954; children: Anne, Eve, Paul. BA with honors, U. B.C., 1952; Doctorat d'Universite, U. Paris, France, 1954; PhD, U. Calif. at Berkeley, 1960. Instr. French U. B.C., 1954-56; asst. prof. French U. Toronto, 1960-63, assoc. prof., 1963-66; mem. faculty U. Chgo., 1966-95, prof. French, 1970-95, Disting. Svc. prof., 1989-95, prof. emeritus, 1995—, dean students div. humanities, 1968-70, chmn. dept. Romance langs. and lits., 1976-83, resident master Snell-Hitchcock halls, 1973-79; vis. mem. Sch. Hist. Studies, Inst. Advanced Study, Princeton, N.J., 1979-80. Author: La Chronique de Robert de Clari, 1963, Jourdain de Blaye, 1969, Ami et Amile, 1969, La Vie de sainte Marie l'Egyptienne, 1977, Jean Froissart and his Meliador, 1983, Jean Froissart, Le Paradis d'Amour et l'Orloge Amoureus, 1986, Erec et Enide, 1994, L'Estrif de Fortune et Vertu, 1999. Served with Polish Army, 1944-46. Decorated Cross of Valor, Cross of Service with swords (Poland), Chevalier des Palmes Academiques (France); Guggenheim fellow, 1970-71; Danforth Found. assoc., 1976-84 Fellow Am. Acad. Arts and Scis.; mem. Société de Linguistique Romane (councillor 1995-99), Medieval Acad. Am. (councillor 1980-82). Office: U Chgo Dept Romance Langs and Lit 1050 E 59th St Rm 205B Chicago IL 60637-1559

DEMCHAK, WILLIAM S., corporate financial executive; b. 1962; BA, Allegheny Coll.; MBA, U. Mich. Global head, structured fin. and credit portfolio JP Morgan Chase, 1997—2002; vice chmn., CFO PNC Fin. Svcs. Group, Inc., Pitts., 2002—. Bd. mem. Black Rock, Inc. Office: PNC Fin Svcs Group Inc One PNC Plaza 249 5th Ave Pittsburgh PA 15222-2707

DEMELFI, (RONALD) DANIEL, music educator, director, financial consultant; b. Hazleton, Pa., Feb. 16, 1954; s. Daniel Donald and Gertrude Marie (Boyle) DeMelfi; m. Esme Theresa Mary Risboskin, Dec. 15, 1996; children: Chiara Maria, Gabriella Elise, Daniel Joseph. Lic. ins. representative Pa., securities broker Nat. Assn. Securities Dealers. Dir. music Moratto and Lesante Musical Enterprises, Hazleton, 1975—91; prin, owner DeMelfi Sch. Music, Hazleton, 1991—. Fin. cons. Primerica Fin. Svcs., Hazleton, 2002—. Composer: numerous songs. Bd. dirs. Silent Santa, Hazleton, 2003—. Mem.: Nat. Guild Piano Tchrs. (named to Piano Tchrs. Hall Fame), Pa. Music Tchrs. Assn. (host Carnegie Hall student recital 2003, 2005), Music Tchrs. Nat. Assn., Nat. Acad. Recording Arts & Scis. (assoc.), Hazleton (Pa.) Area Landlord's Orgn. (co-founder, pres.). Office: DeMelfi School Music PO Box 276 Hazleton PA 18201

DEMENCHONOK, EDWARD VASILEVICH, philosopher, linguist, researcher, educator; b. Vitebsk, Belarus, Jan. 1, 1942; came to U.S., 1992; s. Vasiliy Ivanovich Demenchonok and Olga Stanislavovna Plovinskaya; m. Sondra Marisa Franceil, July 1, 1993; children: Anna, Leonid. BA in Music, Mus. Coll., Minsk, Belarus, 1961; MA in Russian and Spanish, Moscow State U. Lomonosov, 1969; PhD, Russian Acad. Scis., Moscow, 1977. Rschr., then sr. rschr. Inst. Philosophy Russian Acad. Scis., 1970-95; assoc. prof. Moscow State U. Lomonosov, 1982-84; prof. Moscow State Pedagogic U., 1991-92; prof. Spanish Am. dept. Acad. Slavic Culture, Moscow, 1991-92; assoc. prof. Spanish Brewton-Parker Coll., Mt. Vernon, Ga., 1994-95; assoc. prof. fgn. langs. Ft. Valley (Ga.) State U., 1995—. Vis. rschr. Acad. Scis. Cuba, 1978, 79, 83; vis. prof. U. INCCA Colombia, Bogota, 1988-90, Spanish U. Ga., Athens, 1992-93; lectr. in field. Author: Contemporary Technocratic Thought in the U.S.A., 1984; (in Spanish) América Latina en la Época de la Revolución Científico-Téchnica, 1990, Filosofía en el Mundo Contemporaneo, 1990, Filosofía Latinoamericana: Problemas y Tendencias, 1990; editor: Problems of Philosophy and Culture in Latin America, 1983, Contemporary Catholic Philosophy, 1985, New Tendencies in Western Social Philosophy, 1988; contbr. articles to profl. jours., chpts. to books. Mem. MLA (participant convs. 1992, 93, 99), L.Am. Studies Assn. (participant XVIII congress 1994), Am. Philos. Assn., Internat. Soc. Universal Dialogue, Russian Philosophical Soc., Assn. Cultural Rschrs. Russia, Assn. for Philosophy and Liberation, Southeastern Coun. Latin Am. Studies, Soc. for Iberian and L.Am. Thought. Russian Orthodox. Avocation: music. E-mail: demenche@usa.net.

DE MENIL, LOIS PATTISON, historian, philanthropist; b. NYC, May 15, 1938; d. Charles Krone and Julia Anne (Hasson) Pattison; m. Georges Francois Conrad de Menil, Aug. 3, 1968; children: John-Charles, Joy-Alexandra, Benjamin, Victoria. AB, Wellesley Coll., 1960; diploma, Inst. d'Etudes Politiques, Paris, 1962; Lic. in Law, U. Paris, 1962; PhD, Harvard U., 1972. Pres. D. M. Found., N.Y.C., 1986—2001, Ctr. Khiner Studies, Cambodia, 2001—. Bd. dirs. AXA Art Ins. Corp., 1998—; counsellor to Ministry of Culture, Romania, 1997—2001; mem. Coun. Fgn. Rels., 1976—, Inst. for Strategic Studies, London, 1978—, French Inst. Internat. Rels., Paris, 1980—, U.S. Coun. on Germany, N.Y.C., 1978—, Festival d'Automne, Paris, 1997—. Author: Who Speaks for Europe?, 1978; editor, translator: The African Unity Movement, 1965, French Foreign Policy under De Gaulle, 1967. Internat. coun. Mus. Modern Art, NYC, 1975—; vis. com. to art mus. Harvard U., Cambridge, Mass., 1977—; vice-chair bd. dirs. Dia Ctr. for Arts, N.Y.C., 1985—96; vice-chair trustees coun. Nat. Gallery Art, Washington, 1988—96; bd. dirs. World Monuments Fund, N.Y.C., 1990—, Groton Sch., 1991—2004, NASDAQ Found., 2000—04, Coun. Am. Overseas Rsch. Ctrs., 2003—. Fulbright scholar, France, 1960-62; Ford Found. fellow, 1966-68. Mem. Century Assn., Univ. Club, River Club, Harvard Club, Fishers Island Country Club, Phi Beta Kappa. Episcopalian. Avocations: art, skiing, tennis, adventure travel. Office: D M Found 149 E 63rd St New York NY 10021-7405 Office Phone: 212-744-5374.

DEMENT, JAMES ALDERSON, JR., lawyer; b. Clinton, Okla., Sept. 11, 1947; s. James Alderson and Ruby (Weaver) DeM.; m. Sally Anne Wylder, June 6, 1970; children: Stephen, Suzanne, Jonathan. BA summa cum laude, Tex. Christian U., 1969; JD in Internat. Affairs, Cornell U., 1972. Bar: N.Y. 1973, Tex. 1974. Assoc. Alexander & Green, N.Y.C., 1972-73, Baker Botts, LLP, Houston, 1977-85, ptnr., 1998—; ptnr., chmn. corp. tax and internat. sect. Butler & Binion, LLP, Houston, 1985-97. Adj. prof. U. Houston, 1987-88; dir. Houston World Affairs Coun. 2002—. Mem. edtl. rev. bd. The Internat. Lawyer, 1987-94. Trustee Houston Ballet Found., 1989-96, Brazos Presbyn. Homes, Inc., 1990-96. Capt. USAF, 1973-77. Fellow Tex. Bar Found.; mem. State Bar Tex. (internat. law sect., chmn. 1989-90), Internat. and Comparative Law Ctr. Southwestern Legal Found. (adv. coun. 1986—), Houston Bar Assn. (internat. law sect., pres. 1989-90). Presbyn. Office: Baker Botts LLP 910 Louisiana St Houston TX 77002-4995 Office Phone: 713-229-1816. Business E-Mail: jdement@bakerbotts.com.

DEMENT, WILLIAM CHARLES, medical researcher, educator; b. Wenatchee, Wash., July 29, 1928; s. Charles Frederick and Kathryn (Severyns) Dement; m. Eleanor Weber, Mar. 23, 1956; children: Catherine Lynn, Elizabeth Anne, John Nicholas. BS, U. Wash., 1951; MD, U. Chgo., 1955, PhD, 1957. Bd. cert. in clin. polysomography. Intern Mt. Sinai Hosp., N.Y.C., 1957—58, rsch. fellow dept. psychiatry, 1958—63; assoc. prof. dept. psychiatry and behavioral scis. Stanford U., 1963—67, prof., 1967—; dir. Stanford Sleep Disorders Clinic and Lab., 1970—, Sleep Rsch. Lab., Stanford, Calif., 1963—. Chmn. U.S. Surgeon Gen.'s Joint Coord. Coun., Project Sleep, 1979—, Nat. Commn. on Sleep Disorders Rsch., 1990—92. Author: Some Must Watch While Some Must Sleep, 1972, The Sleep Watchers, 1992; editor-in-chief: Sleep, 1977—, mem. editl. bd.: Neurobiology of Aging, 1982—. Recipient medal, Intra-Sci. Rsch. Found., 1981, Disting. Svc. award, U. Chgo. Med. Alumni Assn., 1978. Mem.: Am. Physiol. Soc., Am. EEG Soc., Western EEG Soc., Soc. Neuroscience, Psychiat. Rsch. Found., Inst. Medicine of NAS, Assn. Sleep Disorders Ctrs. (pres. 1982, Nathaniel Kleitman prize), Sleep Rsch. Soc. (founder). Office: Stanford Sleep Disorders Ctr 701 Welch Rd Ste 2226 Palo Alto CA 94304-1711

DEMENTIEVA, ELENA, professional tennis player; b. Moscow, Oct. 15, 1981; d. Viatcheslav and Vera Dementieva. Profl. tennis player WTA Tour, 1998—. Named WTA Tour Most Improved Player, 2000; recipient Female of Yr. Award, Russia, 2001. Achievements include Winner 4 WTA Tour singles titles: Amelia Island, 2003, Bali, 2003, Shanghai, 2003, Hasselt, 2004; Winner 5 WTA Tour doubles titles: (with Husarova) Moscow, 2002, San Diego, 2002, Berlin, 2002, Season-Ending Championships, 2002, (with Krasnoroutskaya) Hertogenbosch, 2003; Member Russian Olympic Team, 2000, 2004. Office: c/o WTA Tour Corp Hdqs One Progress Plz Ste 1500 Saint Petersburg FL 33701

DEMENY, PAUL GEORGE, demographer, researcher; b. Nyiregyháza, Hungary, Dec. 24, 1932; s. József Demény and Margit Iványi; m. Lynn Hall, Sept. 7, 1962; children: Lylla Carter, John. BA, U. Budapest, Hungary, 1955; PhD, Princeton U., 1961. Asst. prof., economics and rsch. assoc. Princeton U., NJ, 1961—66; assoc. to full prof. econs. U. of Mich., Ann Arbor, 1966—69; prof. econs. U. of Hawaii, Honolulu, 1969—73; dir. east-west population inst. East-West Ctr., Honolulu, 1969—73; v.p. The Population Coun., N.Y.C., 1973—88, disting. scholar New York, 1989—. Founding editor Population and Devel. Rev., N.Y.C., 1975—. Co-author: (book) Regional Model Life Tables and Stable Populations; co-editor: Population and Development, Encyclopedia of Population. Pres. Population Assn. of Am., Washington, 1986. Recipient External Mem., Hungarian Acad. of Scis., 2001, Laureate, Internat. Union for the Sci. Study of Population, Paris, 2003. Mem.: Princeton Club of N.Y. (assoc.). Home: 4 Alden Rd Greenwich CT 06831 Office: The Population Coun One Dag Hammarskjold Pl New York NY 10017 Office Phone: 212-339-0691. Personal E-mail: pauldemeny@hotmail.com. E-mail: pdemeny@popcouncil.org.

DEMERDASH, NABEEL ALY OMAR, electrical engineer; b. Cairo, Apr. 26, 1943; came to U.S., 1966; s. Aly Omar and Aziza D.; m. Esther Adel Feher, Feb. 22, 1969; children: Yvonne, Omar, Nancy. BScEE with 1st class honors, Cairo U., 1964; MSEE, U. Pitts., 1967, PhD, 1971. Tchg. asst. in elec. engring. Cairo U., 1964-66, U. Pitts., 1966-68; engr. Westinghouse Electric Corp., Pitts., 1968-72; asst. prof. elec. engring. Va. Poly. Tech. Inst. and State U., Blacksburg, 1972-77, assoc. prof. elec. engring., 1977-81, prof., 1981-83; prof. dept. elec. and computer engring. Clarkson U., Potsdam, N.Y., 1983-94; prof., chmn. dept. elec. and computer engring. Marquette U., Milw., 1994-97, prof. dept. elec. and computer engring., 1994—. Cons. Sundstrand Corp., Rockford, Ill., 1985-98. Contbr. articles to profl. jours. Recipient Cert. of Recognition, NASA, 1979, Cert. of Tchg. Excellence, Va. Poly. Inst. and State U., 1980, Tchr. of Yr. award, Beta Omicron chpt. Eta Kappa Nu, Marquette Univ., 2003, Outstanding Rsch. award Coll. Engring, Marquette U., 2004. Fellow IEEE (subcom. chmn. 1988-92, 94-97, Nikola Tesla award 1999); mem. IEEE Power Engring. Soc. (disting. lectr. 1987—, Elec. Machinery Com. prize paper award 1993, working group award 1994, PES prize paper award 1993, working group award 1994), Indsl. Electronics Soc. (Disting. Spkr. program 1990—), Electromagnetics Acad. Achievements include development of three dimensional finite element vector potential and coupled 3D vector potential-scalar potential methods of solution of electromagnetic fields in electric devices; time-stepping coupled finite element-state space computer simulation models and design of electronically operated/controlled AC and DC motor drives. Office: Marquette Univ Elec Computer Engring Dept PO Box 1881 Milwaukee WI 53201-1881 Office Phone: 414-288-5680. Business E-Mail: nabeel.demerdash@marquette.edu.

DEMERI, MAHMOUD Y., materials engineer, educator; b. Jerusalem, Palestine, Jan. 9, 1945; s. Yehia and Raisa Demeri; m. Faten El-Said, Apr. 24, 1975; 1 child, Nader M. BS, Am. U., Cairo, 1970, MS, 1973; PhD, U. Ky., 1976; MS, Wayne State U., Detroit, 1986. Sr. tech. specialist Ford Motor Co., Dearborn, Mich., 1977—2002; dir. FormSys Inc., Northville, Mich., 2002—. Symposium organizer Minerals, Metals, Materials Soc., Warrendale, Pa., 1990—2001, chair shaping and forming com., 1998—2000; chair automotive metals divsn. USCAR Consortium, Southfield, Mich., 2001—02; panelist NSF, Washington, 2004. Editor: (tech. procs.) Innovations in Processing & Manufacturing of Sheet Materials, Sheet Metal Forming Technology, Computer Applications in Shaping & Forming of Materials, 48 tech. publ. Recipient Best Paper award, Soc. Automotive Engrs., 2000. Mem.: Minerals, Metal, Materials Soc. (com. chair 1998—2000, Recognition award 2000), ASM Internat. Independent. Moslem. Avocation: travel. Office: FormSys Inc 40180 Woodside Dr S Northville MI 48167 Office Phone: 734-462-2742. E-mail: mdemeri@formsysinc.com.

DEMERS, ELIZABETH ANNE, education educator; b. Windsor, Ontario, Canada, July 13; d. Roland Joseph and Annie Hamilton (Drummond) Demers. BA in Acctg., U. of Waterloo, 1989; M in Acctg., U. Waterloo, 1990; PhD Bus. Admin., Stanford U., 2000, M.S. Stats., 1997. Asst. mgr. fin. adv. Price Waterhouse, Toronto, Canada, 1992—93; rsch. asst. grad. sch. of bus. Stanford U., 1994—99; asst. prof. Simon Sch. of Bus. U. of Rochester, 1999—. Author: (research article) Jour. of Fin. Econ., 2002, Review of Acctg. studies, 2000, Jour. of Acctg. Rsch., 2001. Grantee Rsch. Grant, CIMA, 2001, Fellowship, Soc. of Mgmt. Acctg. of Can., 1994—98. Mem.: Am. Fin. Assn., Am. Academic Acctg. Assoc. Office: Simon Sch Bus U Rochester Rochester NY 14627 Office Phone: 585-273-1650. Business E-Mail: lizdemers@simon.rochester.edu.

DEMERS, LAURENCE MAURICE, medical educator, editor, biochemist; b. Lawrence, Mass., May 9, 1938; s. Laurence Onezime and Doris Corrine (Goulet) D.; m. Susan Ruth Bernard, Sept. 29, 1962; children: Laurence H., Michele L., Marc B., Christpher J., Andrew U. AB, Merrimack Coll., 1960; PhD, SUNY Upstate Med. Ctr., Syracuse, 1970. Postdoctoral fellow Med. Sch. Harvard U., Boston, 1970-72, instr., 1972-73; asst. prof. M.S. Hershey Med. Ctr. Pa. State U., Hershey, 1973-76, assoc. prof., 1976-80, prof., 1980—, disting. prof., 1997—. Cons. Robert Wood Johnson Pharm Rsch. Inst., Raritan, N.J., 1978—; bd. dirs. dBi Labs. Inc., Harrisburg, Pa.; vis. prof. U. Oxford, Eng., 1981-82. Editor: Liver Function Testing, 1978, Premenstrual Syndrome, 1985, Premenstrual Syndrome and Menopausal Mood Disorders, 1989, Biomarkers of Disease, 2002; editl. editor Clin. Chemistry Jour., 1990-2000. Eucharistic min. St. Joan of Arc Cath. Ch., Hershey, 1981—, mem. Knights of Malta, 1990—; trustee Merrimack Coll., 2000. Capt. Med. Svc. Corps U.S. Army, 1961—65. Recipient Lalor award Lalor Found., 1973, Fogarty Internat. award Fogarty Ctr., NIH, 1981, Pharm. Mfrs. Assn. award, 1974. Fellow Nat. Acad. Clin. Biochemistry (pres. 1984-85, Dubin award 1991); mem. Endocrine Soc., Am. Assn. Clin. Chemistry (pres. 1997, Ames award 1986), Am. Soc. Clin. Pathology, N.Y. Acad. Scis., Assn. Clin. Scientists, Acad. Clin. Lab. Physicians and Scientists, Knights of Malta, Country Club of Hershey (bd. govs. 2000—). Avocations: golf, tennis. Home: 1175 Stonegate Rd Hummelstown PA 17036-9776 Office: Pa State U MS Hershey Med Ctr University Dr Hershey PA 17033 Office Phone: 717-531-8316. Business E-Mail: imd4@psu.edu.

DEMERS, NANCY KAE, nursing educator; b. Manchester, NH, Oct. 18, 1938; d. Paul E. and Nellie (Matijas) Watts; m. Raymond Joseph Demers, Feb. 13, 1960; children: Paula, John, Diane. RN, Elliot Hosp. Sch. Nursing, Manchester, N.H., 1959; BSN, St. Anselm Coll., 1969; MSN, Boston U., 1978; postgrad., Nova U., 1994—. Social and health educator NH Youth Devel. Ctr., Manchester, 1969—74; dir. nursing svcs. Hanover Hill Nursing Home, Manchester, 1974—75; asst. prof. St. Anselm Coll., Manchester, 1974-82; maternal and child health coord. Concord (N.H.) Hosp., 1982-83; assoc. prof. NH Tech. Coll., Manchester, 1983—88; prof. nursing NH Cmty. Tech. Coll., Manchester, 1988—2000; adminstr. Regency Nursing Care, LLC, Bedford, NH, 2000—. Panel item writer Nat. Coun. Licensure Exam, 1993; developer evaluation component for an ongoing AIDS edn./prevention program for youths between the ages of 14 and 19, Claremont Coll. and Fed. U. Ceara, Brazil. Recipient Ptnrs. of the Ams. award W.K. Kellogg Found., 1996. Mem. N.H. Am. Diabetes Assn. (bd. mem. 1988-93, Disting. Svc. award 1993), N.H. Nurse Educators, N.H. Ptnrs. of Americas (corr. sec. 1992-2005, travel awards 1991, 93, 95, Internat. award 1996), Transcultural Nursing, Sigma Theta Tau. Home and Office: 501 Route 101 Bedford NH 03110-4710 Personal E-mail: ndemers501@aol.com.

DEMERTZOGLOU, PINDARO EPAMINONDA, systems administrator, education educator; s. Epaminodas Pindaros and Gesthimani Prodromos Demertzoglou. BS, Am. Coll. of Thessaloniki, Greece, 1995; MBA, Rensselaer Poly. Inst., N.Y., 1998, MS, 2001; postgrad. in Info. Sci., SUNY, 2001—. Network database adminstr. Am. Coll. of Thessaloniki, Greece, 1995—96; database developer Aristotelian U., Thessaloniki, Greece, 1996; bus. mgr. The Design Works, Troy, NY, 1997; database developer Rensselaer Poly. Inst., Troy, NY, 1997—98, database specialist, 1999—2001, sr. sys. adminstr., 2001—. Adj. mis faculty Rensselaer Poly. Inst., Troy, NY, 2000—, Union Coll., Schenectady, NY, 2003—. Scholar Tuition Scholarship, Am. Coll. of Thessaloniki, 1994—95, Rensselar Poly. Inst., 1997—98. Mem.: Am. Mgmt. Assn., AAUP, N.Y. State Sheriffs' Assn. Inst., Inc. (hon.). Home: 16 Ann Lee Ct Latham NY 12110 Office: Rensselaer Polytechnic Inst 110 8th St Pitts 4106 Troy NY 12180 Office Phone: 518-276-2753. Personal E-mail: demerp@hotmail.com. E-mail: demerp@rpi.edu.

DEMESA, PRAXEDES SEDY, health facility administrator; b. Manila, Philippines, Oct. 11, 1953; d. Gaudenicio Ramos Demesa and Jovita Ymasa Bernardo; m. Emmanuel Ilagan Bernabe, Oct. 11, 1990; children: Emma Nuelle, Emmanuel. A in nursing home adminstrn., McClennan C.C., 1989; BS in med. tech., U. Santo Tomas, Philippines, 1972, M in pub. adminstrn., 1978, MS in psychology, 1982. Lic. nursing home adminstrn., med. tech. Calif., Tex., Nevada. Chief planning and rsch. Civil Svc. Commn., 1975—88; nursing home adminstrn. Pleasant Care Corp., 1989—, exec. v.p., 1990—. Chmn. of bd. Willis Mgmt. Group, Inc., Calif., 2002—; exec. v.p., owner Stockton Edison Healthcare Corp., Calif., 1990—; operator Good Samaritan Rehab and Care Ctr., Stockton, Calif., 1988—. Contbr. articles various profl. jours. Vol. Martha's Kitchen, Stockton, Calif., 1990—; mem. Rep. Party Northern Calif., 2004; vol. Cath. Charities, 1980—. Named Most Outstanding Filipino, 2004, Most Outstanding Jaycee Organizer, Internat. Coll., Embassies of Asian Countries, 1989; recipient Philippine Ambassador award, 2004. Fellow: Am. Health Care Assn.; mem.: Nat. Assn. of Female Exec., Jaycees Internat. Republican. Cath. Avocations: reading, writing, guitar, piano, skiing. Office: Pleasant Care Corp 1111 W Robinhood Dr Stockton CA 95212 Office Phone: 209-956-9606. Office Fax: 209-931-4316. E-mail: sedy@pleasantcare.com.

DEMETRESCU, MIHAI CONSTANTIN, research scientist, educator, computer company executive; b. Bucharest, Romania, May 23, 1929; came to U.S., 1966; s. Dan and Alina (Dragosescu) D.; m. Agnes Halas, May 25, 1969; 1 child, Stefan. M.E.E., Poly. Inst. of U. Bucharest, 1954; PhD, Romanian Acad. Sci., 1957. Prin. investigator Rsch. Inst. Endocrinology Romanian Acad. Sci., Bucharest, 1958-66; rsch. fellow dept. anatomy UCLA, 1966-67; faculty U. Calif.-Irvine, 1967-83, asst. prof. dept. physiology, 1971-78, assoc. rschr., 1978-79, assoc. clin. prof., 1979-83; v.p. Resonance Motors, Inc., Monrovia, Calif., 1972-85; pres. Neurometrics, Inc., Irvine, 1978-82, Lasergraphics Inc., Irvine, 1982-84, chmn., CEO, 1984—. Mem. com. on honor degrees U. Calif.-Irvine, 1970-72. Contbr. articles to profl. jours.; patentee in field. Postdoctoral fellow UCLA, 1966. Mem. IEEE (sr.), Am. Physiol. Soc. Republican. Home: 8 Sunset Hbr Newport Coast CA 92657-1706 Office: 20 Ada Irvine CA 92618-2303 Business E-Mail: dr.d@lasergraphics.com.

DEMETRION, JAMES THOMAS, retired museum director, consultant; b. Middletown, Ohio, July 10, 1930; s. Tom and Susie (Tsifiklis) D.; m. Barbara Parrish, 1954; 1 child, Elaine. BS in Edn., Miami U., 1952; hon. doctorate, Simpson Coll., 1984. Curator Pasadena Art Mus., Calif., 1964-66, dir., 1966-69, Des Moines Art Ctr., 1969-84, Hirshhorn Mus. & Sculpture Garden, Washington, 1984—2001; interm dir. Menil Collection, Houston, 2002—03; ret., 2003. Mem. bd. trustees Noguchi Found., 2002-03; mus. adv. panel Nat. Endowment for Arts, 1973-76, co-chmn., 1974-76; art adv. panel IRS, 1983-86; cons. in field. Mem. Assn. Art Mus. Dirs. (treas. 1976-77, pres. 1979-80). Home: 1276 N Wayne Apt 1207 Arlington VA 22201-5856

DEMETRIOS, (DEMETRIOS TRAKATELLIS), archbishop; b. Thessaloniki, Greece, Feb. 1, 1928; Degree with honors, U. Athens, 1950, ThD in Theology, 1977; PhD in Philosophy with distinction, Harvard U., 1972. Ordained deacon, 1960, priest Greek Orthodox Ch., 1964. Elected titular bishop, aux. bishop to Archbishop of Athens, Vresthena, Greece, 1967; disting. prof. Biblical studies and Christian origins Holy Cross Greek Orthodox Sch. of Theology, Brookline, Mass., 1983-93; elected Archbishop of Am., Exarch of Atlantic & Pacific Oceans Greek Orthodox Ch. in Am., 1999—. Vis. prof. New Testament Harvard Divinity Sch., 1984-85, 1988-89; abroad-residing mem. in theol., Acad. of Athens, 2003-; mem. Holy & Sacred Synod of Ecumenical Patriarchate, 2004-. Author: Authority and Passion, 1987, The Transcendent God of Eugonostos, 1991, Christ, the Pre-Existing God, 1992, The Fathers Interpret, 1996. Office: Greek Orthodox Archdiocese of Am 8-10 E 79th St New York NY 10021*

DEMETS, DAVID L., medical educator, biomedical researcher; b. Austin, Minn., Nov. 27, 1944; married; 2 children. BA in Math., Gustavus Adolphus Coll., St. Peter, Minn., 1966; MS in Biostats., U. Minn., 1968, PhD in Biostats., 1970. Statistician, divsn. computer rsch. and tech. NIH, Bethesda, Md., 1970-72, math. statistician, Nat. Heart, Lung and Blood Inst., 1973-79, chief, mathematical and applied statistics br., 1979-82; dir. biostats. Ctr., prof. stats. and biostats. U. Wis., Madison, 1982-91, assoc. dir. Clin. Cancer Ctr., 1982-91, chair dept. biostats., prof. stats. and biostats., 1991—, assoc. dir. Comprehensive Cancer Ctr., 1991—. Lectr., cons. in field; bd. scientific counselors Nat. Cancer Inst., 1993-96. Co-author: Fundamentals of Clinical Trials, 1981, 2d edit. 1985, 3d edit. 1995; contbr. numerous articles to profl. jours., chpts. to books; presenter in field; mem. adv. bd. jour. Controlled Clin. Trials, 1993—, editl. bd. 1994—; assoc. editor Jour. Clin. Rsch. and Drug Devel., 1987-90. Recipient Disting. Alumni award Gustavus Adolphus Coll., 1990, Gaylord Anderson Leadership award U. Minn. Sch. Pub. Health Alumni Soc., 1993. Fellow Am. Statis. Assn. (bd. dirs. 1987-89), Internat. Statis. Inst.; mem. Biometrics Soc. (regional adv. bd. 1975-77, 80-82, exec. com. Ea. N.Am. region 1992-94, pres. 1993), Soc. for Controlled Clin. Trials (bd. dirs. 1983-87, program com. 1984, 85, program chmn. 1988, v.p. 1988-89, pres. 1989-90, joint program com. with Internat. Soc. Clin. Biostats., Brussels, 1991, policy com. 1993—), Internat. Soc. Clin. Biostats. Office: U Wis Clin Science Ctr Dept Biostatistics & Med In 600 Highland Ave K61446 Madison WI 53792-0001

DEMETZ, KATHLEEN SUSAN, lawyer; b. Mishawaka, Ind., Nov. 1, 1952; d. Achille and Adrienne Marie Christine (DeKesel) D.; children: Carrie Kathleen, Marc Lawrence. BA cum laude, Brandeis U., 1974; JD, U. Notre Dame, 1977. Bar: Ohio 1977. Atty. Legal Aid-Civil, Cleve., 1977-80, Legal Aid-Criminal, Cleve., 1980—. Vol. Ambassador Nursing Ctr., East Cleveland, Ohio, 1985-88, Valley Save-A-Pet, 1985—, St. Gregory the Great Parish, 1989—; active Animal Legal Defense Fund, 1986—; fund com. U. Sch., 2003— Mem. Bar Assn. Greater Cleve. (adopt-a-class 1978—), Notre Dame U., Brandeis U. Alumni Assn. Roman Catholic. Avocations: animal welfare, sports, walking, reading, dogs. Home: 3574 St Albans Rd Cleveland OH 44121-1552 Office: Pub Def Office 100 Lakeside Pl 1200 W Third St NW Cleveland OH 44113 Office Phone: 216-443-7579.

DE MICHELE, O. MARK, real estate company executive; b. Syracuse, N.Y., Mar. 23, 1934; s. Aldo and Dora (Carno) De M.; m. Faye Ann Venturin, Nov. 8, 1957; children: Mark A., Christopher C., Michele M., Julianne; m. Barbara Joan Stanley, May 22, 1982; 1 child, Angela Marie. BS, Syracuse U., 1955; doctorate (hon.), No. Ariz. U., 1997. Mgr. Seal Right Co., Inc., Fulton, NY, 1955-58; v.p., gen. mgr. L.M. Harvey Co. Inc., Syracuse, 1958-62; v.p. Niagara Mohawk Power, Syracuse, 1962-78, Ariz. Pub. Svc., Phoenix, 1978-81, exec. v.p., 1981-82, pres., CEO, 1982-97, also bd. dirs.; pres., CEO Greater Phoenix Econ. Coun., 1997-98; chmn., CEO Urban Realty Ptnrs. LLC, 1998—. Bd. dirs. Ont. Power Generation. Pres. Jr. Achievement, Syracuse, 1974-75, Phoenix, 1982-83, United Way Ctrl. N.Y., Syracuse, 1978, Ariz. Opera Co., Phoenix, 1981-83, Phoenix Symphony, 1984-86, United Way Phoenix, 1985-86, Ariz. Mus. Sci. and Tech., 1988-90; pres. Children's Action Alliance, 1989-92; chmn. Valley Sun United Way, 1984-86, Phoenix Econ. Coun., 1991-94; chmn. Morrison Inst. Pub. Policy at Ariz. State U.; chmn. Ariz. Cities in Schs., 1994-97, Nat. Environ. Edn. Found., 1997—; pres. Episcopal Cmty. Svc. Found. Named Outstanding Young Man of Yr., Syracuse Jaycees, 1968, Phoenix Man of Yr., Phoenix Ad Club, 1992; recipient Humanitarian award Nat. Conf., 1995. Mem. Phoenix C. of C. (chmn. bd. 1986-87), Phoenix Country Club, Ariz. Club (Phoenix). Republican. Home: 1536 Glorietta Blvd Coronado CA 92118-2306 Office: Urban Realty Ptnrs LLC 2415 E Camelback Rd Ste 700 Phoenix AZ 85016-4245 E-mail: mdemichele@aol.com.

DEMIERI, JOSEPH L., retired bank executive; b. N.Y.C., Aug. 31, 1940; s. Leo A. and Frances (Garone) DeM.; m. Anne Patricia McCue, May 15, 1965. BBA, Tex. A&M U., 1962. C.P.A., N.Y. With Peat, Marwick, Mitchell & Co., N.Y.C., 1962-68; v.p., controller City Investing Co., N.Y.C. and Beverly Hills, Calif., 1968-82; exec. v.p. Motown Industries, Los Angeles, 1982-84; chmn., CEO Calif. Millworks Corp., Valencia, 1985-95; sr. v.p., CFO Western Security Bank, Burbank, Calif., 1995—2002. Home: 6259 Ebbtide Way Malibu CA 90265-3608

DEMIERO, CARMELYN YVONNE, primary school educator; b. Seattle, Wash., Sept. 21, 1967; d. Francis Gene and Yvonne Evelyn DeMiero. Grad., Wash. State U., 1999. Elem. tchr. Edmonds Sch. Dist., Lynnwood, Wash., 2000—. Organizer Orion Ctr. Holy Rosary Parish, Edmonds, Wash., 2000—03. Mem.: NEA, Wash. Edn. Assn. Office: Madrona Sch 9300 236th St SW Edmonds WA 98020 Home Fax: 425-771-7562. E-mail: TchrCamra@aol.com.

D'EMILIO, JOHN, humanities educator, writer; BA cum laude, Columbia, 1970, MA, 1972, PhD, 1982. Asst. prof. U. N.C., Dept. History, 1983—88, dir. grad. studies, 1988—93, assoc. prof., 1988—92, prof., 1992—98; vis. scholar George Wash. U., Grad. Program in Pub. Policy, 1998—99; dir. and prof. U. Ill. at Chgo., 1999—; prof. Gender and Women's Studies Program, Dept. History, U. Ill. at Chgo., 1999—. Author: (book) The Universities and the Gay Experience: Proceedings of a Conference Sponsored by the Women and Men of the Gay Academic Union, 1974, The Civil Rights Struggle: Leaders in Profile, 1979, Making Trouble: Essays on Gay History, Politics and the University, 1992, Intimate Matters: A History of Sexuality in America, 1998, Creating Change: Sexuality, Public Plicy and Civil Rights, 2000, The World Turned: Essays on Gay History, Politics and Culture, 2002, Lost Prophet: The Life and Times of Bayard Rustin, 2003 (Nat. Book award nominee, 2003); contbr. articles to jours. Mem. Chancellor's Com. on Lesbian, Gay, Bisexual and Transgender Concerns, 2000—; co-chair Women's Studies Program Dir. Search, 1999—2000; mem. Gender and Women's Studies Program Com., 1999—; mem. adv. bd. Between Men, Between Women series, Columbia U. Press, 1995—. Nominee U. of Chgo. Press for Pulitzer prize in U.S. History, 1983; Rsch. grant, Lyndon Baines Johnson Libr. Found., 1999, fellowship, John Simon Guggenheim Meml. Found., 1998—99, Nat. Endowment for the Humanities, 1997—98, Rsch. grant, Am. Philosophical Soc., 1994, John F. Kennedy Libr., 1993. Mem.: Phi Beta Kappa. Office: U Ill at Chgo Dept History 913 University Hall 601 S Morgan St Chicago IL 60607-2502

DEMILLE, DALE ESTHER, medical/surgical nurse, educator; b. New Britain, Conn., Nov. 3, 1953; d. Jared Armand Tofani and Esther Constance Tofano; m. Richard Kenneth DeMille, July 24, 1993 (div.); m. Robert John Zdankiewicz, June 8, 1974 (div.); children: Kristen Leigh Zdankiewicz Martin, Eric Robert Zdankiewicz. Assocs. degree, Greater Hartford C.C., 1990; BS in Nursing, Cen. Conn. State U., 1993; MS in Nursing, U. of Hartford, 2001. RN Conn., cert. CCRN. Nurse critical care New Britain Gen. Hosp., 1990—99, cardiovasc. angiographic radiology nurse, 1999—2003, nurse med. telemetry, 2002—. Std. setting Exelsior Coll., Albany, NY, 2002—, exam item writer, 2002—; manuscript reviewer Prentice-Hall, Pearson Edn., Livonia, Mich., 2002—; adj. faculty U. Conn., Storrs, 2001—02, Quinnipiac U., Hamden, Conn., 2001—02. Topical spkr. New Britain Gen. Hosp.'s Instl. Ethics Com.'s Pub. Ethics Com. Meeting, New Britain, 2001. Scholar, Greater Hartford Region Soroptimist Internat., 1989, Arthur C. Banks, Jr. Found., 1990, AAUW, 1990. Mem.: Sigma Theta Tau. Conservative. Avocations: antiques and collectibles, singing, furniture restoration, hot-air ballooning, travel. Personal E-mail: ddemille53@yahoo.com.

DEMILLE, DIANNE LYNNE, mathematics professor, academic administrator; b. Dundas, Ont., Can., Mar. 21, 1948; d. Leslie Benjamin and Helen Isobel (Don) DeMille; m. Tate Stanley Casey, June 16, 1971 (div. June, 1975); 1 child, Marie Anne; m. Thomas John Camacho, Aug. 30, 1980 (div. June, 1999); children: Patricia Suzanne, Tara Lynne. BA in Math., Whittier Coll., 1970, secondary tchg. credential, 1972; PhD, Walden U., 2000. Math. tchr. Mater Dei H.S., Santa Ana, Calif., 1972-79, Santa Ana (Calif.) H.S., 1979; instr. math. Coast C.C., Costa Mesa, Calif., 1979-81; math. tchr., mentor tchr. Downey (Calif.) Unified, 1979-93; specialist Orange County Dept. Edn., Costa Mesa, 1993—2002, coord. math. and assessment NSF CO-PI project, 2002—. Coord. assessment/Golden State exams, devel. algebra/Geometry/h.s. math., 1983—; cons., presenter confs., Orange County Dept. Edn., Costa Mesa, 1986—, Calif. State Dept. of Edn., Sacramento, 1989—; chief math devel. team Calif. Learning Assessment Sys.; chief reader, table leader Golden State Math. Exam.; mem. devel. team, chief reader Calif. State Regional Lead Assessment, coord. devel. team, 1996—; reviewer Am. Coll. Testing. Author: Batch Basic, 1973; author and project specialsit (series of books and workshops) So. Calif. Regional Algebra Project Focus on Algebra, Focus on Geometry, 1989—, (units in book) Math A, Investigating Mathematics, 1989. Recipient Wright Bros. Innovative Tchrs. award, Rockwell Co., L.A., 1991; grantee Rockwell Co., 1992. Mem. ASCD, Am. Sch. Counselors Assn., Nat. Coun. Tchrs. Math., Nat. Coun. Suprs. Math., Calif. Math. Coun., Assn. Calif. Sch. Adminstrs., Phi Delta Kappa. Home: #101 1700 W Cerritos Ave Anaheim CA 92804 Office: Orange County Dept Edn 200 Kalmus Dr Costa Mesa CA 92626-5922 E-mail: drdianne@adelphia.net.

DE MILLE, NELSON RICHARD, writer; b. NYC, Aug. 23, 1943; s. Huron and Antonia (Panzera) DeM.; children: Lauren, Alex. BA in Polit. Sci. and History, Hofstra U., 1970, LHD (hon.), 1989; DLitt (hon.), L.I. U., 1993; LDH (hon.), Dowling Coll., 1997. Freelance writer, 1973—. Judge Book-of-the-Month Club. Author: By the Rivers of Babylon, 1978, Cathedral, 1981, The Talbot Odyssey, 1984, Word of Honor, 1985, The Charm School, 1988, The Gold Coast, 1990, The General's Daughter, 1992, Spencerville, 1994, Plum Island, 1997, The Lion's Game, 2000, Up Country, 2002, Night Fall, 2004 (Publishers Weekly bestseller list); co-author: Mayday, 1998; contbr. short stories to mags. 1st lt. U.S. Army, 1966-69. Decorated Air medal, Bronze Star, Vietnamese Cross of Gallantry; recipient Estabrook award Hofstra U. Mem. Mystery Writers Am., Author's Guild, Mensa. Roman Catholic.

DEMING, ANNE LOUISE, university administrator; b. Pottsville, Pa., Feb. 23, 1939; d. James J. and Anne V. (Kelly) Bruggy; m. Robert H. Deming, Mar. 3, 1962; children: Michael, Maura, Sean. AB in French, Coll. Notre Dame of Md., 1961; MA in French, Miami U., Oxford, Ohio, 1969; MEd in Counseling, SUNY, Buffalo, 1974, PhD in Counseling Psychology, 1977. Asst. prof. psychology SUNY, Fredonia, 1977-79, counseling psychologist, 1978-83, asst. to pres. devel./alumni affairs, exec. dir. Found., 1983-88; v.p. advancement West Chester (Pa.) U., 1988-91; v.p. devel. & univ. rels. Middle Tenn. State U., Murfreesboro, 1991—. Mem. adj. faculty, mentor Empire State Coll., Fredonia, 1978-88; cons. employee assistance program J.N. Adam Devel. Ctr., Perrysburg, N.Y., 1979-82, Inmate Coll. Adv. Project, Albany, N.Y., 1977-78. Contbr. articles to profl. jours., translator articles from Frech, review books Choice mag. Exec. com., adv. bd. Chester County Coun. Aging, West Chester, 1989-91; pres. Fredonia Citizens Adv. Com., 1986-87; chmn. Chautauqua County Community Svcs. Bd., Mayville, N.Y., 1983-85. Fulbright fellow, 1991-92; recipient Calista Jones award for advancing rights women Lakeshore Women's Svcs. Coalition, Chautauqua County, N.Y., 1988. Mem. Am. Assn. Profl. Hypnotherapists, Nat. Soc. Fund Raising Execs., Coun. Advancement and Support of Edn., Western N.Y. Com. Am. Coun. Edn's. Nat. Identification Program for Advancement Women in Higher Edn. Adminstrn., Pi Delta Phi, Phi Lambda Theta, Phi Kappa Phi. Avocations: collecting antiques, travel, reading, hypnosis. Office: Middle Tenn State U Cope Admin Bldg Murfreesboro TN 37132-0001

DEMING, BRUCE ROBERT, lawyer; b. July 27, 1964; BS, U. Colo., 1986; JD, Harvard U., 1992. Bar: Calif. 1996, U.S. Dist. Ct. (no. and so. dists.) 1996. Sr. acct. Price Waterhouse, Denver, 1986-89; law clk. to Judge Skinner U.S. Dist. Ct., Boston, 1992-93; assoc. Farella, Braun & Martel LLP, San Francisco, 1993-98, ptnr., 2002—05; v.p., gen. counsel Tier Tech., Inc., Walnut Creek, Calif., 1998-99; exec. v.p. Workspeed, Inc., San Francisco, 2000—02; ptnr. Covington & Burling, San Francisco, 2005—. Co-founder, bd. dirs. Computer Repeats, Inc., Boulder, Colo., 1986-89. Office: Covington & Burling One Front St San Francisco CA 94111 Office Phone: 415-591-6000.

DEMING, CLAIBORNE PAYNE, oil industry executive; Positions in law, prodn., exploration, mktg., land depts. Murphy Oil, El Dorado, Ark., 1979; v.p., 1988; v.p. petroleum ops., 1988; exec. v.p., COO, 1992; mem. exec. com.; also bd. dirs.; mgr. land and contracts Murphy Oil USA Inc., 1988-92; pres., 1992-93. On assignment Ocean Drilling and Exploration Co. (ODECO, now Murphy Exploration & Production Co.), New Orleans. Office: Murphy Oil 200 Peach St El Dorado AR 71730 E-mail: claiborne.deming@murphyoilcorp.com.

DEMING, DAVID LAWSON, art educator; b. Cleve., May 26, 1943; s. Lawson Joseph and Mary Rita (Basile) D.; m. Ann Elizabeth Haldeman, Sept. 4, 1965; children: Matthew Lawson, Lisa Ann, Michael David. BFA, Cleve. Inst. Art, 1967; MFA, Cranbrook Acad. Art, Bloomfield Hills, Mich., 1970. Instr. Boston U., 1967-68, U. Tex., El Paso, 1970-72, asst. prof., assoc. prof. art Austin, 1972, prof., 1985, chmn. art dept., Marguerite Fairchild prof. art, 1991-96; interim dean Coll. of Fine Arts U. Tex., Austin, 1996-97, dean, 1997-98; pres. Cleve. Inst. Art, 1998—. Sculptures represented in permanent collection Columbus (Ohio) Mus. Art, Ark. Art Ctr., Little Rock, U. Tex. Southwestern Regional Med. Ctr. Dallas; included in White House Garden Exhbn. of Am. Sculptors, 1995. Recipient award of honor Austin chpt. AIA, 1983. Mem. Internat. Sculpture Assn. Roman Catholic. Office: Cleveland Inst of Art 11141 East Blvd Cleveland OH 44106-1700 Office Phone: 216-421-7410. E-mail: ddeming@gate.cia.edu.*

DEMING, FRANK STOUT, lawyer; b. Oswego, Kans., Aug. 12, 1927; s. Robert Orin Jr. and Helen Josephine (Stout) D.; m. Carolyn Ruth Kauffman, June 24, 1950; children: Frank S. Jr., Christiana Deming Jacobsen, David M., Robert W. BS in Econs., U. Pa., 1949, LLB, 1952. Bar: Pa. 1953, U.S. Dist. Ct. (ea. dist.) Pa. 1953, U.S. Ct. Appeals (3d cir.) 1953, U.S. Ct. Appeals (9th cir.) 1965. Assoc., then ptnr., now of counsel Montgomery, McCracken, Walker & Rhoads, Phila., 1952—. Bd. dirs. New Covenant Trust co. Contbr. articles to profl. jours. Trustee Bricker Found., Phila., 1980—, Presbyn. Ch. (U.S.A.) Found., Jeffersonville, Ind., 1989-94, chmn., 1993, mem. gen. assembly coun., Louisville, 1990-91; dir. Presbyn. Children's Village, 1992-94. Sgt. U.S. Army, 1946-47. Fellow Am. Coll. Trust and Estate Counsel; mem. ABA, Pa. Bar Assn., Phila. Bar Assn., Mil. Figure Collectors Am., Phi Delta Theta, Beta Alpha Psi, Beta Gamma Sigma. Republican. Avocation: travel. Home: Riddle Village 410 Hampton Media PA 19063-6009 Office: Montgomery McCracken Walker & Rhoads 123 S Broad St Fl 25 Philadelphia PA 19109-1029 Fax: 215-772-7620. E-mail: frankdeming@WebTV.net.

DEMING, FREDERICK WILSON, retired economist, banker; b. St. Louis, Dec. 29, 1935; s. Frederick Lewis and Corinne Inez (Wilson) D.; m. Lynne Eve Anken, Mar. 24, 1960; children: Susanne Lyn, Frederick Lawrence. BA, Princeton U., 1957; MA, Yale U., 1958. With Fed. Res. Bank of N.Y., 1961-71; sr. staff economist Council Econ. Advisers, 1968; exec. dir. Commn. Mortgage Interest Rates, 1969; spl. asst. to Sec. of HUD, 1970-71; sr. v.p., economist Chem. Bank, N.Y.C., 1971—89; exec. asst. to chmn. Chem. Bank/Chase Manhattan Bank, N.Y.C., 1989—99; ret., 2000. Home: 24 Colt Rd Summit NJ 07901-3040

DEMING, JOAN, clergy; b. Milw., Nov. 7, 1949; d. Jarvis Roy and Mirabel Fay (Hansen) Deming; m. Kirk Michael Cavallo, Dec. 21, 1974 (div. June 1987); children: Kathryn Joan Cavallo, Anna Lee Cavallo; m. Donald F. Schultz, July 7, 1989. BA, Carroll Coll., Waukesha, Wis., 1972; student, U. Nairobi, Kenya, 1970-71; MDiv, Pacific Sch. Religion, Berkeley, Calif., 1976. Ordained deacon United Meth. Ch., 1974, elder, 1977. Pastor First United Meth. Ch., Milton, Wis., 1976-80, Sherman Ave United Meth. Ch., Madison, Wis., 1981-82; interim campus min. Madison Campus Ministry, 1985-87; pastor of visitation First United Meth. Ch., Madison, 1985-88; pastor Trinity United Meth. Ch., Montello, Wis., 1988-90, First United Meth. Ch., Waukesha, 1990-94, Madison, 1994—2002; fund devel. dir. United Meth. Childrens Svcs. Wis., Inc., 2002—. Bd. dirs. United Meth. Children's Svcs., Milw., 1993-97, chair, 1997—; chair bd. global ministries Wis. Conf. United Meth. Ch., Sun Prairie, Wis., 1984-92, chair commn. status and role of women, 1979-84. Mem. AAUW, Wis. Ctr. for Academically Talented Youth. Democrat. Avocations: gardening, yardwork, playing pipe organ and piano. Home: 1541 Comanche Gln Madison WI 53704-1012 E-mail: jdeming7@charter.net.

DEMING, JODY WHEELER, oceanography educator; b. Houston, July 2, 1952; d. Samuel Henry Wheeler and Laverne (Lewis) Kraft. BA in Biol. Scis., Smith Coll., 1974; PhD in Microbiology, U. Md., 1981. Rsch. asst. biology Sloan Found. Rsch. Smith Coll., Northampton, Mass., 1973; field biologist Water Quality Div. Md. State Dept. Natural Resources, Annapolis, 1974; rsch. technician Div. Infectious Diseases Tufts/New Eng. Med. Ctr. Hosp., Boston, 1974-75; rsch. assoc. Bioluminescence Lab. NASA/Goddard Space Flight Ctr., Greenbelt, Md., 1975-77; grad. teaching and rsch. asst. microbiology U. Md., College Park, 1977-81; NSF postdoctoral fellow Marine Biology Rsch. Div. Scripps Inst. Oceanography, La Jolla, Calif., 1981-82; NOAA postdoctoral fellow Office of Marine Pollution and Assessment, Rockville, Md., 1982-83; assoc. rsch. scientist Chesapeake Bay Inst. Johns Hopkins U., Shady Side, Md., 1981-86, rsch. scientist Chesapeake Bay Inst., 1986-88, asst. prof. biology, 1983-86; scientist Ctr. Marine Biotech., U. Md., Balt., 1986-88; dir., Marine Bioremediation Program U. Wash., Seattle, 1993—99; assoc. prof. U. Wash. Sch. Oceanography, Seattle, 1988—95, prof., 1995—, U. Wash. Astrobiology Program, 1998—. Mem. nat. com. ALVIN Rev. Com., 1984-87, internat. Arctic projects and steering coms., numerous proposal review panels for NOAA, NSF and others. Contbr. numerous chpts. to books and articles to profl. jours. Recipient award for Sci. Achievement in the Biol. Scis., Wash. Acad. Scis., 1987, Presdl. Young Investigator NSF award, 1989-94. Mem. AAAS, Am. Soc. for Microbiology, Am. Acad. of Microbiology, Am. Soc. of Limnology and Oceanography, Am. Geophys. Union, The Oceanography Soc., Sigma Xi. Achievements include patents for rapid quantitive determination of bacteria and their antibiotic susceptibilities in a variety of fluid samples. Office: U Wash Sch Oceanography Box 357940 Seattle WA 98195-0001 E-mail: jdeming@u.washington.edu.

DEMING, N. KAREN, lawyer; b. Valdosta, Ga., Sept. 7, 1953; BA magna cum laude, Valdosta State Coll., 1975; JD cum laude, U. Ga., 1978. Bar: Ga. 1978, U.S. Ct. Appeals (4th, 5th and 11th cirs.), U.S. Dist. Ct. (no., mid. and so. dists.) Ga. Assoc. Troutman Sanders LLP, Atlanta, 1978—85, ptnr., 1986—, practice group leader, product liability, mem. exec. com. Mem. editorial bd. Ga. Law Rev., 1976-77, rsch. editor, 1977-78. Named a Super Lawyer, Atlanta Mag., 2004, Legal Elite in personal injury, Ga. Trends Mag., 2004. Mem. ABA, Def. Rsch. Inst., State Bar Ga., Ga. Def. Lawyers Assn., Atlanta Bar Assn., Atlanta Coun. Young Lawyers (bd. dirs. 1983-85), Lawyers Club Atlanta, Order of Coif., Phi Kappa Phi. Office: Troutman Sanders LLP 600 Peachtree St NE Ste 5200 Atlanta GA 30308-2216 Office Phone: 404-885-3124. Office Fax: 404-962-6543. Business E-Mail: karen.deming@troutmansanders.com.

DEMING, RUST M., ambassador; b. Oct. 1941; m. Kristen Deming; 3 children. Diploma, Rollins Coll., 1964; Postgrad. Diploma, Stanford U., 1981. Former polit. officer U.S. Embassy, Tunisia, 1966; dir. Office of Japanese Affairs, Washington, 1991—93; dep. chief of mission Japan, 1993—96; Charge d'Affaires, ad interim, 1996—97; prin. dep. asst. sec. for East Asian and Pacific Affairs U.S. Embassy, Tunisia, 1998—2000; U.S. amb. to Rep. of Tunisia, 2001—. Recipient Civilian Meritorious awards, U.S. Def. Dept., 1995—97. Office: DOS Amb 6360 Tunis Pl Washington DC 20521

DEMING, THOMAS EDWARD, publishing executive; b. Chgo., May 5, 1954; s. Anthony A. and Josephine (Andracki) Dziurdzik; m. Mary Ann Jadowic, May 15, 1976; children: Mark Thomas, Emily Marie, William Joseph. BS in Acctg., De Paul U., 1976, MBA, 1986. CPA, Ill. Acct. Arthur Andersen & Co., Chgo., 1975-81; asst. contr. Scott, Foresman & Co., Glenview, Ill., 1981-83, v.p., contr., 1983-88, v.p. fin., 1988-89, v.p. fin. and adminstrn., 1990; treas. Macmillan/McGraw-Hill Sch. Pub. Co., Lake Forest, Ill., 1990-91, v.p., treas., 1991-92, Harper Collins Pubs., N.Y.C., 1992-95; v.p. fin. Harper Collins Pubs., Inc., N.Y.C., 1995-96; v.p. fin. planning & ops. McDougal Littell Pub., Inc., Evanston, Ill., 1996—; corp. v.p. McDougal Littell parent co. Houghton Mifflin, 1996—. Mem. Fin. Execs. Inst., Am. Inst. CPA's, Ill. Soc. CPA's, DePaul U.'s Ledger & Quill, Beta Alpha Psi, Delta Mu Delta, Beta Gamma Sigma. Avocations: golf, skiing. Office: McDougal Littell Inc 909 Davis St Evanston IL 60201 Business E-Mail: tom_deming@hmco.com.

DEMING, WILLIS RILEY, lawyer; b. Ada, Ohio, Nov. 28, 1914; s. Cliffe and Okla (Riley) D.; m. Dorothy Arline Hill, 1950 (div. 1971); children: Susan Elizabeth, Deborah Anne Gunst, David Riley; m. Constance S. Mori, 1971 (div. 1986); m. Olive Plunkett Rose, 1994 (dec. 1999). BA, Ohio State U., 1935, JD, 1938. Bar: Ohio 1938, Calif. 1947, D.C. 1957. Pvt. practice, Columbus, Ohio, 1938-39; casualty claim examiner Am. Surety Co., N.Y.C., 1939-41; chief bds. and claims rev. br. San Francisco Port of Embarkation, 1946-47; atty. Treadwell and Laughlin, San Francisco, 1947-54, Brobeck, Phleger & Harrison, San Francisco, 1954-56, Washington, 1956-60; pvt. practice Washington, 1961-62; sr. v.p., gen. counsel Matson Nav. Co., San Francisco, 1962—71, 1974—92; v.p., sec., gen. counsel Alexander & Baldwin, Inc., Honolulu, 1968—74. Served to lt. col. AUS, 1941-46; col. U.S. Army, ret. Mem. ABA, State Bar Calif., Soc. for Asian Art (pres. 1995-97), Assn. for Preservation of the Presdl. Yacht Potomac (bd. govs., sec. 2005-), Claremont Country Club (Oakland). Home: 5649 Country Club Dr Oakland CA 94618-1715 E-mail: wrdeming@hotmail.com.

DEMINT, JIM (JAMES WARREN DEMINT), senator, former congressman; b. Greenville, SC, Sept. 2, 1951; s. Thomas Eugene and Betty (Rawlings) Batson; m. Deborah Henderson, Nov. 6, 1951; children: Jake, Ginger, Timothy, Donna. BS in Comm., U. Tenn., 1973; MBA, Clemson (S.C.) U., 1979. Sr. sales rep. Scott Paper Co., Greensboro, NC, 1973-75; writer Henderson Advt., Greenville, 1975-81; v.p. Leslie Advt., Greenville, 1981-83; CEO, pres. The DeMint Mktg. Group, Greenville, 1983—; mem. US Congress from 4th SC dist., 1999—2005; mem. edn. and workforce com., small bus. com., transp. and infrastructure com.; U.S. senator from SC, 2005—. Speaker, workshop leader, Success 88 Small Bus. Admin. and So. Bell 1988. Chmn. bd. Greenville Vocat. Rehab. Ctr. 1986, Christian Bus. Men's Com., 1983, Mitchell Rd. Christian Acad., 1988, 1st v.p. Speech, Hear and Learning Ctr., 1986. Mem. Greenville C. of C., S.C. C. of C., Rotary. Republican. Presbyterian. Avocations: sailing, running, biking, tennis, music. Office: US Senate 105 N Spring St Ste109 Greenville SC 29601 also: US Senate Dist Ofc 112 Customs House 200 E Bay St Charleston SC 29401 also: US Senate 340 Russell Senate Office Bldg Washington DC 20510

DEMIRO, DIANE MOLLIE, parochial school educator; b. Montclair, N.J., Aug. 29, 1946; d. William Michael and Marie Barbara DeMiro; 1 child, Gregory William. BA, Trenton State Coll., 1968. Pre-sch. Chambers Child Devel. Ctr., N.Y.C., 1968—69; third grade tchr. Chancellor Ave. Sch., Newark, 1970—71; substitute tchr. Jefferson County (Colo.) Pub. Schs., 1992—2002, Denver Pub. Schs., 1992—2002; first and second grade tchr. Westland Christian Acad., Lakewood, Colo., 2002—03, Grace Christian Sch., Evergreen, Colo., 2003—. Author: Too High A Price for Harmony: A Perspective on School Shootings, 2002. Active LBJ First Head Start, East Orange, NJ, 1965, The Experiment in Internat. Living, Berlin, 1967. Avocations: art, painting, pottery. Home: PO Box 171 Morrison CO 80465

DE MITA, FRANCIS ANTHONY, mathematics professor; b. N.Y.C., Oct. 13, 1927; s. Michael Joseph and Rachel Catherine (Prudente) DeM.; m. Lois Marie Smith, Mar. 22, 1934; children: Francis Anthony Jr., Michael Spencer. BS, NYU, 1950, MA, 1951; diploma in mgmt., Cornell U., 1988. Tchr. math. Bedford Park Acad., N.Y.C., 1951-53, Valley Stream (N.Y.) Cen. High Sch., 1953-90; chmn. dept. math. Valley Stream (N.Y.) Central High Sch., 1981-90, ret., 1990. Asst. prof. math. Queensborough C.C., N.Y.C., 1964-96; pres., chmn. bd. Nassau Educators Fed. Credit Union, Valley Stream, 1967-2002. Contbr. articles to mags. Founder, pres. East Central Civic Assn., Valley Stream, 1967-69, 79-89; bd. dirs. Friends of Arts, V.S. C. of C.; Nat. Assn. Fed. Credit Unions; adv. coun. WLIW21-PBS TV, L.I.; bus. adv. com. B.O.C.E.S., L.I.; trustee North Shore-L.I. Jewish Health Sys. Cpl. U.S. Army, 1946-48. Recipient Humanitarian award Nat. Fedn. Italian-Am. Socs., 2002, Congl. citation U.S. Congress, 1982; named Vol. of Yr., Nat. Assn. Fed. Credit Unions, Denver, 1981, Dir. of Yr. Credit Union Execs. Soc., Honolulu, 1989, Businessman of Yr., Valley Stream C. of C., 1998, Nassau Coun. Chambers, 1999; NSF grantee, 1958-65. Mem. Nat. Assn. Credit Union Pres., Elks, Lions (pres. 1973-74), Nat. Italian-Am. Found. Republican. Roman Catholic. Avocations: photography, golf, opera, computers, travel. Home: 108 E Euclid St Valley Stream NY 11580-4145 also: 55 Forest Dr Palmyra VA 22963-2116 E-mail: fdemita@cs.com.

DEMITCHELL, TODD ALLAN, education educator; b. Portsmouth, Va., Aug. 9, 1947; s. Wilfred E. and Mary Anna DeM.; m. Terri A. Wheeler, Aug. 14, 1982. BA, U. La Verne, 1969, MA, 1973; EdD, U. So. Calif., 1979; MA, U. Calif., Davis, 1990. Tchr. Pomona (Calif.) Unified Sch. Dist., 1969-71, South Bay Union Elem. Sch. Dist., Imperial Beach, Calif., 1974-75, lead tchr., 1975-78; asst. prin. Fallbrook (Calif.) Union Elem. Sch. Dist., 1978-80, prin., 1980-83; supt., prin. Pauma (Calif.) Sch. Dist., 1983-86; dir. pers. and labor rels. Travis (Calif.) Unified Sch. Dist., 1986-89; postdoctoral vis. scholar, rsch. asst. Nat. Ctr. Ednl. Leadership Harvard U., Cambridge, Mass., 1989-90; asst. prof. U. N.H., Durham, 1990-96, coord. grad. studies, 1993-95, assoc. chair dept. edn., 1995-98, assoc. prof., 1996—99, prof., chair dept. edn., 2001—04; assoc. prof., chair dept. ednl. leadership/spl. edn., coord. grad. studies, justice studies program Sonoma State U., 2004—. Design team Sch. Leaders Acad., N.H., 1991-93. Co-author: Teacher Unions and TQE: Building Quality Labor Relations, 1994, The Limits of Law-Based School Reform: Vain Hopes and False Promises, 1997; mem. authors com. Education Law Reporter; contbr. more than 100 articles to profl. jours., chpts. to books. Recipient Jim Rubovitz award, New Eng. Ednl. Rsch. Orgn., 2003. Mem. ASCD, Am. Ednl. Rsch. Assn., Edn. Law Assn. Office: U NH Morrill Hall Durham NH 03824 Office Phone: 603-862-5043. E-mail: tad@unh.edu.

DEMITRA, PAVOL, professional hockey player; b. Dubnica, Slovakia, Nov. 29, 1974; Drafted left wing/ctr., 1993—96; traded left wing/ctr. St. Louis Blues, 1996—2005; with L.A. Kings, 2005—. Mem. Slovia Hockey Team Winter Olympics, Nagano, Japan, 1998. Office: c/o St Louis Blues 1401 Clark Ave Saint Louis MO 63103-2700*

DEMITRACK, THOMAS, lawyer; b. Denville, NJ, 1954; MusB, Univ. Hartford, 1976; JD summa cum laude, Ohio State Univ., 1979. Bar: Ohio 1979. Profl. responsibilities ptnr. and coord. of antitrust practice Jones Day, Cleve., and mem. profl. services com. Mem., profl. services com. Jones Day. Author: numerous articles in profl. publications. Named a leading lawyer in antitrust, N.E. Ohio Inside Bus. mag. and Ohio Super Lawyers. Mem.: Order of Coif. Office: Jones Day North Point 901 Lakeside Ave Cleveland OH 44114-1190 Office Fax: 216-579-0212.

DEMITRY, ELPIS HOPE, music educator; b. Trenton, NJ, Apr. 4, 1947; d. Lillian and James Demitry. MusB, Trenton State Coll., 1970, MA in Music Edn., 1976. Teacher of Music Mercer County/State of NJ., 1970, Supervisor/Principal Certification Mercer County/State of NJ., 1983, Nursery/Kindergarten Certification Mercer County/State of NJ., 1983. Internal coach,facilitator for the accelerated sch. plus program, our whole sch. reform Trenton Bd. of Edn. - Wash. Elem. Sch., NJ, 1999—; vocal/gen. elem. music tchr. Trenton Bd. of Edn., 1970—2003; pvt. piano tchr. Trenton Conservatory of Music and Home Instrn., 1966—2003; coord. of elem. music faculty meetings Trenton Pub. Schs., 1993—, coord. all city elem. music festivals. Coord. of the all city elem. music festivals Trenton Pub. Schs., Trenton, NJ, 1971—86, coord. of elem. music faculty meetings, 1993—98; acting prin. in principals absence Wash. Elem. Sch., Trenton, NJ, 1998—, profl. devel. coord., 1999—, trainor of staff, 1999—. Nat. grand gov. zone i Daughters of Penelope, 1993—95, dist. gov., 1982—83; organist St. George Greek Orthodox Ch., Trenton, NJ, 1960—2005; treas. - diocesan svc. Ea. Fedn. of Greek Orthodox Choirs and Musicians, NJ, 1993—2005. Recipient Patriarch Athenagoras I Medal for Ch. Musicians, Diocesan Svc. Award- Ea. Fedn. of Greek Orthodox Ch. Choirs and Musicians, 1999. Mem.: NEA, Assn. Supr. and Curriculum Devel. (assoc.), Am. Choral Dirs. Assn. (assoc.), Trenton Edn. Assn. (assoc.), Music Educators Nat. Conf., NJ. Music Educators Assn. (assoc.), Nat. Forum of Ch. Musicians (life). Greek Orthodox. Avocations: swimming, travel, needlecrafts. Home: 95 Beechwood Ave Trenton NJ 08618 Office: Washington Elem Sch 331 Emory Ave Trenton NJ 08611 Office Phone: 609-656-4960 3714. Personal E-mail: ehoped@comcast.net. E-mail: hdemitry@trenton.k12.nj.us.

DEMKO, CATHY, artist, art educator; b. Chgo., July 8, 1944; d. Jean S. Badiaco; m. E. Ramon Nelson; 1 child, Patricia Ann Jedike. Student, Art Inst., Chgo., Cape Cod Sch. of Art, Scottsdale Artist Sch., Design Masters of Calif.; BBA, Tempe Bus. Coll., 1983. Artist Marion Helpers, Stockbridge, Mass., 1992—. USCG, Washington. Tchr. Mesa (Ariz.) Parks and Recreation, 1983—85, Collier County Recreational Bd., Naples, Fla., 1985—92, Snowflake Gallery, Wilmington, Vt., 1992—96, Collier County Pub. Schools, Naples, 1996—98, Marco Island Art League, Marco Island, Fla., 1997—. Exhibitions include Studio Art Gallery, Marco Island, Fla., 1986—2001, Nat. Wildlife Gallery Am., Carmel, Calif., 1986—90, Panache Art Gallery, 1990—92, Mendocino Gallery in Calif., 1990—92, Galerie Internat., Marco Island & Naples, Fla., 1991—2002, Mangrove Art Gallery, Marco Island, Fla., 1993—98, Lucky's Wave (So. Waters award, 2000), scratch board, Preening Egret, 1999 (Audubon award, 2001), exhibitions include Orange Blossom Express, 2000 (R.R. Excellency award, 2000), one-woman shows include Golden Gecko Art Gallery, Sedona, Ariz., 2003, Rookery Bay Field Guide, 1998. Tchr. Sr. Citizens Recreational Activities, Naples, 1982—2002; artist Christian Womens Assn., Marco Island, 1982—2002. Mem.: Am. Soc. Marine Artists (assoc.), Plein Air Painters (assoc.), Art League of Marco Island (assoc.), Am. Women Artists (assoc.). Avocations: travel, writing, nature. Home: 1225 Skyline Dr Naples FL 34114-8290 Office: Snowflake Gallery 1225 Skyline Dr Naples FL 34114

DEMKO, GEORGE JOSEPH, geographer; b. Catasauqua, Pa., Apr. 10, 1933; s. George and Anna (Scarba) D.; m. Jeanette Edwina Small, Aug. 29, 1959; children: Megan, Kerstin. BS, West Chester U., 1958; MS, So. Ill. U., 1959; PhD, Pa. State U., 1964; postgrad., Moscow State U., USSR; DSc (hon.), Shawnee State U. of Ohio, 1995. Instr. Pa. State U, State College, 1963-64; asst. prof. Ind. U., Bloomington, 1964-65; prof. Ohio State U., Columbus, 1965-83; program dir. Geography and Regional Sci., NSF, Washington, 1983-84; The Geographer, dir. Office of The Geographer, State Dept., Washington, 1984-89; dir. Rockefeller Ctr. for Social Scis., Dartmouth Coll., Hanover, N.H., 1989-95, prof. geography, 1989—. Cons. Internat. Research and Exchanges Bd., Princeton, N.J., 1970-95, NASA, 1979-80, Microsoft Corp., 1992—; head subcommn. on geography, US/USSR, Princeton, 1980-91; adj. prof. Charles U., Prague, Czech Republic. Author: The Russian Colonization of Kazakhstan, 1966, Kazakh transl., 1998, Discovery in Geography, 1980, Regional Development in East and West Europe, 1986, Perspectives on Soviet Geography, 1980, Geography in the USSR and U.S.: A Spectrum of Views, 1992, Why In The World: Adventures in Geography, 1993, Populations at Risk in America, 1995, Reordering the World: Geopolitical Perspectives on the 21st Century, 1995; contbr. numerous articles to profl. jours. Sgt. USMC, 1951-54, Korea. Named Outstanding Alumnus, W. Chester (Pa.) U., 1980, University Fellow, Pa. State U., State College, 1986; recipient numerous grants and awards for research and teaching from the Nat. Sci. Found., Rockefeller Found., Gold Medal award for scholarly contbns. Charles U., Prague, Czech Republic, 1998, others. Mem. Assn. Am. Geographers (pres. 1986-88), Am. Assn. for Advancement of Slavic Studies (exec. dir. 1969-74), Kennan Inst. for Advanced Russian Studies (acad. advisor 1982-86), Russian Geog. Soc. (hon.). Avocations: sailing, squash, piano. Office: Dartmouth Coll Dept Geography Hanover NH 03755 E-mail: george.demko@dartmouth.edu.

DEMKOVITZ, RUSSELL BERNARD, deacon, ceremetary director; b. Elizabeth, NJ, May 21, 1949; s. Russell and Hedwig Demkovitz; m. Monica Patricia Michalski, May 8, 1976; 1 child, Abigail. BA, Rutgers U., 1967—71, MPA, 1972—74. Inside auditor Southland Corp., Parsippany, NJ, 1974—79; inside sales Naporano Iron and Metal, Newark, 1977—79; sales engr. Otis Elevator, Mahwah, NJ, 1979—84; regional mgr. Gen. Elevator, Springfield, NJ, 1984—89; v.p. sales and admin. Advance Elevator, New Brunswick, NJ, 1989—96; territory rep. Dover Elevator, Secaucus, 1996—98; dir. of cemeteries Diocese of Metuchen, Piscataway, NJ, 1998—; cemetary dir., pres. NJ. Cemetary Assn., 2004—. Mem. adv. bd. St. Peter's Cemetery Assn., New Brunswick, NJ, 1999—, NJ Allied Meml. Coun., Flemington, NJ, 2001—, NJ Legislative Commn., Westfield, NJ, 1999—. Councilman at large Franklin Township, Somerset, NJ, 1987—95, dep. mayor, 1987—90, mayor, 1990—91. Mem.: NJ Cemetery Assn. (pres.). Republican. Roman Cath. Avocations: golf, travel, automobilia collecting. Home: 15 Liberty Lane Somerset NJ 08873 Office: Diocese of Metuchen P O Box 191 Metuchen NJ 08840 Office Fax: 732-562-9650. Personal E-mail: rdemkovitz@aol.com.

DEMLOW, DANIEL J., lawyer; b. Ludington, Mich., Oct. 16, 1944; s. Richard M. and Nan (Jager) D.; m. Catherine M. Jerzak, Aug. 7, 1982; children: Sara Beth, Michelle Catherine. BA, Mich. State U., 1966; JD, U. Mich., 1969. Atty. Fraser Trebilock Davis & Foster, Lansing, Mich., 1969-70, Securities Bur., Lansing, State of Mich., 1970-71; dep. dir. Mich. Dept. Commerce, Lansing, 1971-73; commr. ins. Ins. Bur., Lansing, 1973-75; chmn. Mich. Pub. Svc. Commn., Lansing, 1975-81; assoc. Honigman Miller Schwartz & Cohn LLP, Lansing, 1985—. Fellow Mich. State Bar Found. Republican. Presbyterian. Avocations: tennis, boating, grouse hunting. Home: 3773 Yosemite Dr Okemos MI 48864-3838 Office: Honigman Miller Schwartz & Cohn LLP 222 N Washington Sq Ste 400 Lansing MI 48933-1800 Office Phone: 517-377-0700. Business E-Mail: ddemlow@honigman.com.

DEMME, JONATHAN, director, producer, writer; b. Baldwin, LI, NY, Feb. 22, 1944; m. Evelyn Purcell (div.); m. Joanne Howard; children: Ramona Castle, Brooklyn James. Student, U. Fla.; degree (hon.), Wesleyan U., 1990. With Avco Embassy Films, 1966, Pathe Films, 1966-67; with publicity dept. United Artists, 1968-69; writer Film Daily, 1966-68. Actor: (films) The Incredible Melting Man, 1977, Into the Night, 1985; dir.: Crazy Mama, 1975, Handle with Care, 1977, Last Embrace, 1979, Melvin and Howard, 1980, Swing Shift, 1984, Swimming to Cambodia, 1987, Married to the Mob, 1988, Famous All Over Town, 1988, The Silence of the Lambs, 1991 (Acad. Award for best dir., 1992, Dir.'s Guild of Am. Award for Outstanding Directorial Achievement in Motion Pictures, 1992), Cousin Bobby, 1992, The Complex Sessions, 1994, Storefront Hitchcock, 1998; (TV films) Columbo: Murder Under Glass, 1978, Who Am I This Time?, 1982; (TV series) Alive From Off Center, 1984—87, Trying Times, 1987; exec. prodr.: (films) Amos & Andrew, 1993, Household Saints, 1993, Ray Cohn/Jack Smith, 1994, Devil in a Blue Dress, 1995, Shadrach, 1998, The Opportunists, 2000, Maangamizi: The Ancient One, 2001; prodr.: Miami Blues, 1990, One Foot On a Banana Peel, the Other Foot in the Grave: Secrets From the Dolly Madison Room, 1994, That Thing You Do! (also actor), 1996, Mandela, 1996, Into the Rope, 1996, Courage and Pain, 1996, The Uttmost, 1998, Adaptation, 2002, Beah: A Black Woman Speaks, 2003; (TV films) Women & Men 2: In Love There Are No Rules, 1991; writer (films) Black Mama, White Mama, 1972, Ladies and Gentlemen, the Fabulous Stains, 1981, cinematographer, dir., prodr. The Agronomist, 2003, dir., exec. prodr. (TV films) Subway Stories: Tales from the Underground, 1997, dir., prodr. (films) Something Wild, 1986, Philadelphia, 1993, Beloved, 1998, The Manchurian Candidate, 2004, dir., writer Caged Heat, 1974, Fighting Mad, 1976, Stop Making Sense, 1984, dir., prodr., writer The Truth About Charlie, 2002, prodr., writer Angels Hard as They Come, 1971, The Hot Box, 1972; dir.: (Bruce Springsteen music video) Murder, Inc., 1995; co-dir.: Streets of Philadelphia. Mem.: Dirs. Guild Am. Office: c/o Robert Newman Internat Creative Management 8942 Wilshire Blvd Beverly Hills CA 90211

DEMMLER, JOHN HENRY, retired lawyer; b. Pitts., June 20, 1932; s. Ralph Henry and Catherine (Hollinger) D.; m. Janet Rice, July 20, 1957; children: Richard H., Ralph W., Carol L. BA, Princeton U., 1954; LLB cum laude, Harvard U., 1959. Bar: Pa. 1960, U.S. Dist. Ct. (we. dist.) Pa. 1960. Assoc. Reed Smith Shaw & McClay, Pitts., 1959-65, ptnr., 1966-93, of counsel, 1994—. Dir. Duquesne Light Co., Pitts., 1977-90. Trustee Shady Side Acad., Pitts., 1969-75, 77—, vice chmn., 1980-84, chmn., 1984-87; chmn. Fox Chapel Borough Zoning Hearing Bd., 1993-2005. Mem. Pa. Bar Assn. (pub. utility law sect. 1976-05), Fox Chapel Golf Club, Allegheny-HYP Club. Republican. Episcopalian. Office: Reed Smith LLP 435 6th Ave Pittsburgh PA 15219-1886 Home: Two Winding Way Verona PA 15147

DEMOFF, MARVIN ALAN, lawyer; b. L.A., Oct. 28, 1942; s. Max and Mildred (Tweer) D.; m. Patricia Caryn Abelov, June 16, 1968; children: Allison Leigh, Kevin Andrew. BA, UCLA, 1964; JD, Loyola U., L.A., 1967. Bar: Calif. 1969. Asst. pub. defender Los Angeles County, 1968-72; ptnr. Steinberg & Demoff, L.A., 1973-83, Craighill, Fentress & Demoff, L.A. and Washington, 1983-86; of counsel Mitchell, Silberberg & Knupp, L.A., 1987—2002; mng. dir. Neuberger Berman LLC, L.A., 2002—. Mem. citizens adv. bd. Olympic Organizing Com., L.A., 1982-84; bd. trustees Curtis Sch., L.A., 1985-94, chmn. bd. trustees, 1988-93; sports adv. bd. Constitution Rights Found., L.A., 1986—. Mem. ABA (mem. forum com. on entertainment and sports), Calif. Bar Assn., UCLA Alumni Assn., Phi Delta Phi. Avocations: sports, music, art. Office: Neuberger Berman LLC 1999 Ave of the Stars Los Angeles CA 90067 Office Phone: 310-556-4270. Business E-Mail: MDemoff@nb.com.

DEMOND, JEFFREY STUART, cable television and telecommunications executive; b. Morristown, N.J., June 27, 1955; s. Marvin Harry DeMond and Lois Ann (Worrell) Kramer; m. Helene Regina Sullivan, Dec. 24, 1987; children: Brendan, Christopher. BS, U. Ala., 1978. CPA, N.Y. Sr. mgr. Peat, Marwick, Mitchell & Co., N.Y.C., 1978-85; exec. v.p., CFO Bresnan Comm. Inc., Purchase, NY, 1985—. Lectr., adj. prof. Hunter Coll., N.Y., 1984-85. Composer various popular music, 1974—; performer Sailcat record album Cathouse, 1976. Named an Outstanding Musician, Nat. Assn. Jazz Educators, 1978, Outstanding Jazz Soloist, Stan Kenton Coll. All-Star Orch., 1978. Mem. AICPA, Nat. Cable and Telecomm. Assn. (fin. com.), N.Y. State Soc. CPA, Beta Gamma Sigma. Avocations: guitar, performing, composing music. Office: Bresnan Comm Inc 1 Manhattanville Rd Purchase NY 10577-2596 E-mail: jdemond@bresnan.com, jdemond@optonline.net.

DEMOND, WALTER EUGENE, lawyer; b. Sacramento, Oct. 15, 1947; s. Walter G. and Laura (Bartlett) D.; m. Kari Demond; 1 child, William. BA, U. Tex., 1969, JD with honors, 1976. Bar: Tex. 1976, Nebr. 2004. With Clark, Thomas & Winters, Austin, 1976—, CFO, 1984—, sr. ptnr. energy and telecomm. sect. Mem. mgmt. com. Clark, Thomas & Winters, 1984-94, 97-99, 2002-04. Capt. USAF, 1970-74. Fellow: Am. Bar Found., Astin Bar Found. (life; founding mem.), Tex. Bar Found. (life); mem.: ABA (vice chmn. gas com. pub. utility, comm. and transp. law sect. 1986—91, chmn. gas com. 1991—93, long-range planning com. 1995—, vice chmn. gas com. pub. utility, comm. and transp. law sect. 1997—2003, vice chair corp. governance com. 2003—, pub. utility comm. and transp. law sect.), State Bar of Tex. (adminstrv. law com. 1984—87). Office: Clark Thomas & Winters Box 1148 Austin TX 78767 Office Phone: 512-472-8800. Business E-Mail: wed@ctw.com.

DEMONG, RICHARD FRANCIS, finance and investments educator; b. Freeport, Ill., May 2, 1944; s. Maurice Dale and Ruth Jane (Kidwell) DeM.; m. Sue Ann Liddle, June 17, 1967 (div. Dec. 1983); children: Cheryl Ann, Lynn Ann; m. Linda H. Krongaard, May 15, 1988. AA, Orange Coast Coll., Costa Mesa, Calif., 1964; BA, Calif. State U., 1966; MBA, Coll. of William & Mary, 1974; PhD, U. Colo., 1977. Cert. cost analyst; chartered fin. analyst. Time keeper Douglas Aircraft Co., Long Beach, Calif., 1966; instr. U. Colo., Boulder, 1974-77; Va. Bankers prof. bank mgmt. U. Va., Charlottesville, 1977—, dir. Ctr. for Fin. Studies, 1991—97; rsch. dir. Fin. Analyst Rsch. Found., Charlottesville, 1982-85; registered investment adv. Va., 1996—. Cons. Fin. Forecasting & Svc., 1978—; fin. coord. Dalkon Shield Claimants Trust, 1989-1999. Author: (with others) (monograph) New Financial Instruments: A Descriptive Guide, 1985, 1998 Home Equity Loan Study, 1998, (with others) Principles of Financial Management, 2d edit., 1988; editor (with others) (monograph) Takeovers and Shareholders: The Mounting Controversy, 1985 (monograph, with others) Investing Worldwide III, 1992, The Technology Industry: The Impact of the Internet, 2002. Mem. Va. Small Bus. Coun., Richmond, 1981-82; chmn. U. Va. ROTC com., Charlottesville, 1981-84, 2001—; co-chmn. Central Va. Score and Ace chpt., Charlottesville, 1981; dir. McIntire Small Bus. Inst., Charlottesville, 1978-82, Innisfree Village, 1995-98, 2002—, Charlottesville Cath. Sch. Bd., 2002-05. Capt. USAF, 1966-72, Vietnam, col. USAFR, ret. Decorated DFC; named outstanding Air Force Mobilization Augmentee (reservist), Air Tng. Command, 1980. Mem. Fin. Mgmt. Assn., Am. Fin. Assn., So. Fin. Assn., CFA Inst. Roman Catholic. Avocation: gardening. Office: U Va McIntire Sch of Commerce PO Box 400173 Charlottesville VA 22904 Business E-Mail: rfd@virginia.edu.

DEMONIC, BETTY L., music educator; d. Oscar Lee Gray and Alice Elizabeth Parker; m. James R. DeMonic, Aug. 3, 1984. BS in Music Edn., Concord Coll., 1971; MusM in Edn., W.Va. U., 1973. Tchr. vocal music Morgantown (W.Va.) Jr. H.S., 1972—74, Sabraton Jr. H.S., Morgantown, W.Va., 1974—75; tchr. vocal music, drama John Dickinson H.S., Wilmington, Del., 1975—83; tchr. vocal prodn. Am. Acad. Dramatic Arts, N.Y., 1988—95; tchr. vocal music, musical theater Franklin H.S., Somerset, NJ, 1984—. Dir. Madrigal Singers Franklin H.S. Nominee Disting. Educator award, Princeton U., 1997. Mem.: NEA, Am. Choral Dirs. Assn., Music Educators Nat. Conv., N.J. Educators Assn. Office: Franklin High School 415 Francis Street Somerset NJ 08873 Office Phone: 732-249-6410 477. E-mail: bdemonic@franklinboe.org.

DEMONTE, CLAUDIA ANN, artist, educator; b. Astoria, N.Y., Aug. 25, 1947; d. Joseph James and Ammeda Ellen (Heiss) DeM.; m. William Edward McGowin, May 28, 1977. BA, Coll. Notre Dame, 1969; MFA, Cath. U., 1971. Instr. Bowie State Coll., Md., 1971-72, Prince Georges C.C., Largo, Md., 1972; prof. dept. art U. Md., College Park, 1972—2005. Dir. Art Workshops, New Sch. Social Rsch., N.Y.C., 1980-94; USIA artist in residene (Sofia) Bulgaria, 1982; mem. art bd. Queens Coll., N.Y. Selected exhbns.: Corcoran Gallery Art, 1976, Contemporary Arts Ctr., New Orleans, Cranbrook Acad., 1978, Marianne-Deson Gallery, 1979, Miss. Mus., Fort Worth Mus., Washington Project for Arts, 1980, Marion Locks Gallery, Miami Dade Gallery, Xochipilli, 1981, 86, 95, New Sch. Social Rsch., 1982, Queens Mus., N.Y., Stamford Mus., Conn., Gallery 121, Antwerp, Belgium, 1985, Gracie Mansion Gallery, N.Y., 1987, Brentwood Art Gallery, St. Louis, 1987, Nina Freunenheim Gallery, Buffalo, 1987, 92, 94, Internat. Rev. of Arts Arsenal, Amalfi, Italy, 1987, Esbo Mus., Helsinki, Finland, 1988, Evanston (Ill.) Art Ctr., 1989, Barbara Gillman Gallery, Miami, 1991, 92, 94, Gallery 86, Lodz, Poland, Slow Art, Painting in N.Y. Now, P.S. 1 Mus., N.Y., 1991, Haggerty Mus., Wis., 1993, Nina Freudenheim Gallery, Buffalo, 1994, Leedy Voulkos Gallery, Kansas City, Mo., 1996, Panaroma Gallery, Barcelona, Spain, Silpakorn U., Bangkok, 1997, Retrospective, Choklalfabuken, Malmo, Sweden, 1998, Liesbeth Lip Gallery, Rotterdam, The Netherlands, 1999, Retrospective Rosemont Coll., Pa., 2000, U. New Eng., Tucson Mus., 2001, Mus. of S.W., Midland, Tex., 2002, Internat. Mus. of Women, San Francisco, 2003, Tallinn Kunsit House, Estonia, Gerdubery Cultural Ctr., Iceland, 2004, Contemporary Art Ctr., New Orleans, 2005; pub. collections include Indpls. Mus., Stamford Mus., Miss. Mus., Prudential Life Ins., Hyatt-Regency, Chem. Bank, Best Products, U. Md., Mus. Modern Art, New Orleans Mus., Minn. Mus., Grand Rapids Mus., Mich., UCLA, Corcoran Gallery of Art, Bklyn. Mus., Mus., Bass Mus., Tucson Mus., Boca Raton Mus.; author: (with Judy Bachrach) The Height Report, 1983, (pomegranate) Women of the World: A Global Collection of Art, 2000; commd. works include: U. No.Iowa, 2003. Mem. art bd. Queens (N.Y.) Coll. Recipient award Am.-Italian Assn., 1971, Head Balt. Bus., 1972, Creative award Me., 1974, 77, 83, 87; N.Y. Found. for the Arts fellow, 1989—, N.Y.C. Dept. Cultural Affairs Art in Pub. Places Sculpture Commn., 1991, N.Y.C. Dept. Cultural Affairs Mural Commn. fellow 1993, sculpture commn. N.Y.C. Dept. Cultural Affairs, 1997, N.Mex. State Art Commn., Sculpture Commn., Socorro, 1998, U. No. Iowa Commn., 2003, N.Mex. State Hwy. Rte. 66 Commn., 2004, Gund Found. grant, 1998, Ancohrage Found. of Tex. grant, 1999, Cantor Found. grantee, 2004. Democrat. Home: 96 Grand St New York NY 10013-2633 Office Phone: 212-966-4496. Business E-Mail: demonte@umd.edu.

DE MONTEBELLO, PHILIPPE LANNES, museum director; b. Paris, May 16, 1936; came to U.S., 1951, naturalized, 1955; s. Roger L. and Germaine (de Croisset) de M.; m. Edith Bradford Myles, June 24, 1961; children: Marc, Laure, Charles. BA magna cum laude, Harvard U., 1958; MA, NYU Inst. Fine Arts, 1963; LLD (hon.), Lafayette Coll., 1979; DHL (hon.), Bard Coll., 1981; DFA (hon.), Iona Coll., 1982; LLD (hon.), Dartmouth Coll., 2004. Assoc. curator European paintings Met. Mus. Art, N.Y.C., 1963-69; dir. Mus. Fine Arts, Houston, 1969—74; vice dir. for curatorial and ednl. affairs Met. Mus. Art, 1974-77, acting dir., 1977-78, dir. N.Y.C., 1978-99, dir., CEO, 1999—. Mem. adv. coun. depts. art and archaeology Columbia U.; fellow, Fogg Mus., Harvard U. Author: Peter Paul Rubens, 1968; mem. editorial bd. Internat. Jour. of Mus. Mgmt. and Curatorship. Trustee, NYU Inst. Fine Arts. Served to 2d lt. AUS, 1956-58. Decorated chevalier Legion d'Honneur (France), Encomienda de Numero de la Orden Isabel la Catholica (Spain), officier Ordre de Leopold (Belgium), Knight Commdr. Pontifical Order of St. Gregory the Great, Comdr. Order of Arts and Letters, 2001; recipient NYU Grad. Sch. Alumni Achievement award, 1978, gold medal Nat. Inst. Soc. Sci., 1989, The Spanish Inst., 1992, Rebekah Kohut award Nat. Coun. Jewish Women, 1993, NYU Alumni Assn. Disting. Alumni award, 1998, Living Landmark award NY Landmarks Conservancy, 2001, Mayoral Proclamation, 2002, Nat. Endowment for the Arts, Nat. Medal of Arts, 2003; Woodrow Wilson fellow, 1961-62; Gallatin fellow, 1981. Mem. Assn. Art Mus. Dirs. (works of art com.), Mus. Coun. N.Y.C., Am. Fedn. of the Arts (trustee, exec. com.), Am. Assn. Mus. Avocations: collecting old master drawings, chess, tennis. Office: Met Mus of Art 1000 5th Ave New York NY 10028-0113 Home: 25 E 86th St New York NY 10028

DE MONTEIRO, NADSA, chef; b. Cambodia; d. Longteine de Monteiro; m. Bob Perry, Dec. 1986. Travel agt., Boston, 1986—92; owner, sous chef The Elephant Walk, Somerville, Mass., 1992—94, owner, exec. chef Boston, 1994—; owner, chef Carambola, Waltham, Mass., 1997—. Office: The Elephant Walk 2067 Massachusetts Ave Cambridge MA 02140

DEMOREST, ALLAN FREDERICK, retired psychologist; b. Omaha, Dec. 20, 1931; 1 child, Steven M. BA, U. Omaha, 1957; MA, U. Mich., 1959, postgrad., 1960. Lic. psychologist, Iowa, Nat. Register Health Svc. Providers. Counselor Mayor's Com. on Skid Row Problems, Detroit, 1959-61; psychologist Macomb County Schs., Mt. Clemens, Mich., 1961-64; chief psychologist Jasper County Mental Health Ctr., Newton, Iowa, 1964-68; exec. dir. North Cen. Iowa Mental Health Ctr., Ft. Dodge, 1968-75; pvt. practice Ft. Dodge, 1968-85; psychologist Iowa Luth. Hosp., Des Moines, 1985-87; clin. dir. United Behavioral Systems, Des Moines, 1987-94, sr. psychologist, 1994-96; cons. pvt. practice, Des Moines, 1996—. Adj. prof. psychology Buena Vista U., Ft. Dodge, 1974-2002; substitute tchr. Des Moines Pub. Schs., 1999—; chief trainer AARP Iowa Safe Driving Instrs., 2005—. Contbr. articles on rational therapy to profl. jours. Founding bd. dirs. Rape and Sexual Assault Victim Program, Ft. Dodge, 1976-85, Family Violence Ctr., Ft. Dodge, 1976-85, Youth Shelter Svcs., Ft. Dodge, 1979. With U.S. Army, 1952-54, Korea. Recipient appreciation award Community Mental Health Ctrs. Assn., 1968, community svc. award Iowa Dept. Human Svcs., 1985. Fellow Albert Ellis Inst.; mem. APA., Iowa Psychol. Assn., Adminstrv. Mgmt. Soc. (pres. Ft. Dodge 1979-80, 84-85), Iowa Assn. for Advancement Psychology (pres. 1984, appreciation award 1988), Elks (exalted ruler 1979, trustee 2002, Elk of Yr. 2004). Home and Office: 4225 Hickman Rd Des Moines IA 50310-3334 Personal E-mail: ademorest@aol.com. *Honesty and integrity are the greatest personal assets of a human being.*

DE MORNAY, REBECCA, actress; b. Santa Rosa, Calif., Aug. 29, 1962; d. Richard and Julie De Mornay; m. Bruce Wagner, 1989 (div. 1990); m. Patrick O'Neal; 2 children. Student, Lee Strasberg Theatre Inst., Los Angeles; also studied with Kristin Linklater. Apprentice with Francis Coppola's Zoetrope Studio, 1981. Actress: (films) Risky Business, 1983, Testament, 1983, The Slugger's Wife, 1985, The Trip to Bountiful, 1985, Runaway Train, 1985, Cannon Movie Tales: Beauty and the Beast, 1987, And God Created Woman, 1988, Feds, 1988, Dealers, 1989, Backdraft, 1991, The Hand That Rocks the Cradle, 1992, Guilty as Sin, 1993, The Three Musketeers, 1993, Thick as Thieves, 1998, The Right Temptation, 2000, Identity, 2003, Raise Your Voice, 2004, Lords of Dogtown, 2005; (TV films) The Murders in the Rue Morgue, 1986, By Dawn's Early Light, 1990, An Inconvenient Woman, 1991, Blind Side, 1993, Getting Out, 1994, The Con, 1998, Night Ride Home, 1999, Range of Motion, 2000; (TV miniseries) The Shining, 1996, A Girl Thing, 2001; (plays) Born Yesterday, 1988, Marat/Sade, 1990; actor, exec. prodr.: (films) Never Talk to Strangers, 1995, The Winner, 1996; actor, co-exec. prodr.: (films) A Table for One, 1999; TV appearances include The Outer Limits, 1995. ER, 1999, Boomtown, 2003, The Practice, 2004.*

DEMOS, DAVE, marketing executive; V.p. sales, mktg. Am. Axle & Mfg., Detroit, v.p. sales and bus. devel., 1997-99, v.p. strategic planning, 1999—. Office: Am Axle & Mfg 1840 Holbrook Ave Detroit MI 48212-3442

DEMOS, NICHOLAS JOHN, physician, surgeon, researcher; b. Tripolis, Greece, Apr. 5, 1930; came to U.S., 1949; s. John Nicholas and Vakoula (Haritopoulos) D.; chilcren: Victoria N., Stephanie N. BS, Northwestern U., 1952, MS in Pathology, 1954, MD, 1955. Cert. Gen. Surgery, thoracic Surgery, Gen. Vascular Surgery. Resident in surgery Northwestern U. Med. Sch., Chgo., 1955-58, 60-63; internship Passavant Hosp., Chgo., 1955-56; lt. commdr. USN, 1958-60; resident in thoracic surgery Seton Hall U. Med. Sch., Jersey City, N.J., 1960-63, NIH fellow surgical cardiology, 1963-64; chief cardiovascular surgery Christ Hosp., Jersey City, N.J., 1977—; chief dept. surgery St. Francis Hosp., Jersey City, N.J., 1979-84; chief thoracic surgery Meadowlands Hosp., Secaucus, N.J., 1994—; clin. prof. surgery Newark Med. Sch., 1998—. Past pres. Med. Staff Christ Hosp., Jersey City, N.J., 1980, N.J. Soc. Thoracic Surgeons, 1980, N.J. Soc. Vascular Surgery, 1980; liaison officer ACS, 1980—. Author: Stapled Gastroplasty, 1974, Surgery of Esophogus (movies), 1970—, Thorascopic Surgery of Esophogus; patentee of surgical instrument, 1987; contbr. over 100 articles to profl. jours. Fellow Am. Coll. Cardiology, ACS; mem. Soc. Thoracic Surgeons, N.J. Soc. Vascular Surgery, Am. Gastroenterological Assn. Greek Orthodox. Avocations: photography, painting. Office: 142 Palisade Ave Jersey City NJ 07306-1108

DEMOSS, HAROLD RAYMOND, JR., federal judge; b. Houston, Tex., Dec. 30, 1930; s. Harold R. and Jessy May (Cox) DeMoss; m. Judith Phelps; children: Harold R. III, Louise Holland. BA, Rice U., 1952; LLB, U. Tex., 1955. Bar: Tex. Assoc. Bracewell & Patterson, Houston, 1957—61, ptnr., 1961—91; judge U.S. Ct. of Appeals (5th cir.), Houston, 1991—. Dir. Panama Canal Co., 1976—77; coun. mem. Admin. Conference of US, 1990—91. Chmn. bd. Tex. Bill of Rights Found., Houston, 1969—70; pres. Tanglewood Homeowners Assn., 1987; area chmn. Bush Congl. Campaign, 1968; mem. platform group Bush for Pres., Washington, 1988; rsch. analyst Bush/Quayle campaign, 1988; dist. del.-at-large Rep. Nat. Conv., Houston, 1980, alt. del.-at-large, 1984, 1988; Harris County vice chmn. Tower Senate campaign, Houston, 1972, Ford/Dale campaign, 1976; Harris County chmn. Loeffler for Gov. Primary, 1986; Harris County co-chair Regan/Bush campaign, 1980, 1984; Tex. state chmn. Bush for Pres. Primary, 1979—80, Tex. vice chmn., 1988; del. Rep. State Conv., Houston, 1968; vestryman St. Martin's Episcopal Ch., Houston, 1968—72; mem. exec. bd. Episcopal Diocese Tex., 1983—86, chmn. planning com., 1985—88, del. Diocesan Conv., 1976—88; bd. dirs. Amigos de las Americas, 1974—76. Sgt. U.S. Army, 1955—57. Fellow: Tex. Bar Assn. (life); mem.: ABA, N.Mex. Trial Lawyers Assn., Tex. Assn. Def. Counsel (bd. dirs. 1972—74), Houston Bar Assn. (bd. dirs. 1969—71, 1st v.p. 1972—73), Maritime Law Assn. U.S., Am. Judicature Soc., Internat. Bar Assn., The Houston Club. Avocations: fishing, waterskiing. Office: Bob Casey US Courthouse 515 Rusk St Ste 12015 Houston TX 77002-2605*

DEMOSS, JON W., insurance company executive, lawyer; b. Kewanee, Ill., Aug. 9, 1947; s. Wendell and Virginia Beth DeMoss; m. Eleanor T. Thornley, Aug. 9, 1969; 1 child, Marc Alain. BS, U. Ill., 1969, JD, 1972. Bar: Ill. 1972, U.S. Dist. Ct. (cen. dist.) Ill. 1977, U.S. Supreme Ct. 1978, U.S. dist. Ct. (no. dist., trial bar) Ill. 1983. In house counsel Assn. Ill. Electric Coop., Springfield, 1972-74; registered lobbyist Ill. Gen. Assembly, Springfield, 1972-74; asst. dir. Ill. Inst. for CLE, Springfield, 1974-85; exec. dir. Ill. State Bar Assn., 1986-94; pres., CEO ISBA Mut. Ins. Co., Chgo., 1994—. Bd. dirs. Bar Plan Surety & Fidelity Co., St. Louis, 1999-2005 Bd. dirs. Springfield Symphony Orch., 1982-87, Ill. Inst. for CLE, 1986-89, Nat. Assn. of Bar Related Ins. Cos., 1989, pres., elect., 1998-99, pres. 1999-2000; bd. dirs. Lawyers Reins. Co., 1997—; bd. visitors John Marshall Law Sch., 1990—. Capt. U.S. Army, 1972. Fellow Am. Bar Found. (life, co-chmn. projects to prepare Appellate Handbook 1978, 90), Ill. Bar Found. (life, bd. dirs. 1983-85); mem. ABA (ho. of dels. 1979-85, 89, 91, 93-94), Nat. Conf. Bar Pres., Am. Judicature Soc. (bd. dirs. Ill. state chpt., treas. 2002-04), Ill. State Bar Assn. (pres. 1984-85, bd. govs. 1975-85, chmn. com. on scope and correlation of work 1982-83, chmn. budget com. 1983-85, chmn. legis. com. 1983-84, 85, chmn. com. on merit selection of judges 1977, del. long-range planning conf. 1972, 78, liaison to numerous coms. and sects.), Chgo. Bar Assn., Lake County Bar Assn., U. Ill. Coll. Dean's Club, La Chaine des Rotisseurs (Chgo.), Ordre Mondial des Gourmet Degustateurs (Chgo.). Home: 180 Norwich Ct Lake Bluff IL 60044-1914 Office: ISBA Mutual Ins Co 223 W Ohio St Chicago IL 60610-4101 Office Phone: 312-379-2000. Business E-Mail: jon.demoss@isbamic.com.

DE MOTT, BENJAMIN HAILE, literature educator, writer; b. Rockville Centre, N.Y., June 2, 1924; s. D. Gerard and Janet (Sanders) DeM.; m. Margaret Jane Craig, June 22, 1946; children— Joel, Thomas, Benjamin, Megan. BA, George Washington U., 1949; PhD, Harvard, 1953; MA, Amherst Coll., 1960; D.Litt., Franklin and Marshall Coll., 1970; LLB, Union Coll., 1975. Tchg. fellow Harvard U., 1950; from instr. to Mellon prof. humanities Amherst (Mass.) Coll., 1951—; columnist Harper's, 1962—64, 1990—, Am. Scholar, 1962-64, Atlantic Monthly, 1973-80. Prof. MIT, 1962; Fulbright prof. Birmingham (Eng.) U., 1965; vis. prof. Utah U., 1966, Yale, 1968-70; writer Nat. Ednl. TV, 1964; also cons.; mem. Columbia Seminar Am. Civilization; cons. Dept. Edn., Carnegie Commn. on Future Pub. Broadcasting; cons. Soc. Mag. Writers, Nat. Inst. Edn., N.Y. State Arts Coun., Nat. Endowment for Arts, Am. Coun. Learned Socs., Coun. Grad. Schs., Danforth, Rockefeller founds; Aspen Inst. Edn. dept. Amalgamated Clothing Workers Union, AFL-CIO; exec. com. Tchrs. and Writers Collaborative, N.Y.C.; seminar dir. Nat. Endowment for Humanities, 1973-74, 76-77, 78-79 Author: novels The Body's Cage, 1959, A Married Man, 1968; essays Hells & Benefits, 1962, You Don't Say, 1966, Supergrow, 1969, Surviving the Seventies, 1971, Scholarship for Society, 1974, America in Literature, 1977, Close Imagining, 1982, The Imperial Middle, 1990, The Trouble with Friendship, 1996, Killer Woman Blues, 2000, Junk Politics, 2004; mem. bd. editors: essays College English, 1964-70; contbg. editor: essays Sat. Rev., 1972-73, Atlantic Monthly, 1977—; contbr. articles to profl. jours. Bd. acad. advisers Marlboro Coll., 1963-65; mem. Presdl. Adv. Council Women's Ednl. Programs, 1975-76, Gov.'s Council Arts and Humanities, 1974-77; bd. dirs. Mass. Found. Humanities in Pub. Affairs, 1974—; mem. exec. bd. Fedn. Humanities Programs, 1979—; trustee Nat. Humanities Faculty; mem. selection com. Guggenheim Found., 1975—89. Recipient Harbison award for distinguished teaching Danforth Found., 1969; Guggenheim fellow, 1964, 69 Mem. PEN, Nat. Book Critics Circle, Modern Lang. Assn., Phi Beta Kappa. Clubs: Century. Home: PO Box 356 Worthington MA 01098-0356

DEMOTT, DEBORAH ANN, law educator; b. Collingswood, N.J., July 21, 1948; d. Lyle J. and Frances F. (Cummings) DeM. BA, Swarthmore Coll., 1970; JD, NYU, 1973. Bar: N.Y. 1974. Law clk. U.S. Dist. Ct. (so. dist.) N.Y., 1973; assoc. Simpson, Thacher & Bartlett, N.Y.C., 1974-75; from asst. prof. to assoc. prof. Duke U., Durham, N.C., 1975-80, prof. law, 1980—, David F. Cavers prof. law, 2000—. Vis. asst. prof. U. Tex., Austin, 1977-78; Bost rsch. prof. law, 1981; vis. prof. U. Calif. Hastings Coll. Law, 1986, U. Colo., 1989, U. San Diego, 1991; James L. Lewtas vis. prof. law Osgoode Hall Law Sch., Toronto, Ont., Can., 1991; vis. fellow U. Melbourne, 1993, 95, 98; Huber C. Hurst Eminent vis. scholar U. Fla. Coll. Law, 1996; Frances Lewis Scholar-in-Residence Washington and Lee Law Sch., 1998; centennial vis. prof. law dept. London Sch. Econs., 2000-02; vis. prof. internat. faculty U. Sydney Faculty of Law, 2004. Author: Shareholder Derivative Actions, 1987, Fiduciary Obligation Agency and Partnership, 1991; editor: Corporations at the Crossroads: Governance and Reform; contbr. articles to profl. jours.; bd. advisors Jour. Legal Edn., 1983-86. Trustee Law Sch. Admission Coun., 1984-88; mem. N.C. Gen. Statutes Commn., 1990-98; mem. selection com. Coif Book Award, 1988-90. Recipient Pomeroy prize NYU Sch. Law, 1971-73; AAUW fellow, 1972-73; Fulbright Sr. scholar Sydney U. and Monash (Australia) U., 1986. Mem. ABA, Am. Law Inst. (reporter restatement of agy. 1995—). Office: Duke U Law Sch PO Box 90360 Durham NC 27708-0360 Office Phone: 919-613-7082. Business E-Mail: demott@law.duke.edu.

DEMOURA, KRIS SAMUEL, music educator; s. Samuel Jauquin and Jean Theresa DeMoura; m. Jennifer Esther Bolivar, July 30, 2000; 1 child, Creighton Joseph. MusB Edn. with honors, MusM, U. Mass., Lowell, 2000. Tchg. cert. Mass., 2004. Music dir. Oakmont Regional H.S., Ashburnham, Mass., 2000—. Brass coord. Reading Mass. H.S. Band, 1999—2000. Office Phone: 978-827-5907 2168. Personal E-mail: kdemoura@awrsd.org.

DEMPSEY, CECELIA **See BYRNE-DEMPSEY, CECELIA**

DEMPSEY, CLAIRE WOODFORD, humanities educator, consultant; b. Neptune, NJ, Apr. 24, 1952; d. Joseph N. and Sarah W. Dempsey. BA, Wheaton Coll., 1974; MA, Boston U., 1980. Archtl. historian Mass. Hist. Commn., Boston, 1983—88; faculty Am. and New Eng. studies Boston U., 1991—, assoc. prof., dir. ad interim preservation studies, 2004—. Mem. archvist bd. Vernacular Arch. Forum, pres. New Eng. chpt.; cons. in field. Author: Building Handbook, 1991; co-author: Building Portsmouth, 1993, Early Architecture and Landscapes of the Narrogansit Basin, 2001. Unitarian. Office: Boston U Am & New Eng Studies Program 226 Bay State Rd Boston MA 02297

DEMPSEY, DONALD CHANDLER, stockbroker, financial planner; b. Detroit, Nov. 13, 1951; s. Donald Chandler Sr. and Phillippa E. D.; m. Karen Lynn Petroskey, Apr. 19, 1980; 1 child, Michael Patrick. B of Bus., Cleary Coll., 1975. CFP, Coll. Fin. Planning Denver. Sr. v.p. investments E.F. Hutton, Detroit, 1977-94, Wachovia Securities, Detroit, 1994—. Roman Catholic. Home: 18134 Shelley Pond Ct Northville MI 48167-3543 Office Phone: 248-737-8468. Personal E-mail: ddempsey@ameritech.net.

DEMPSEY, EDWARD JOSEPH, lawyer; b. Lynn, Mass., Mar. 13, 1943; s. Timothy Finbar and Christine Margaret (Callahan) D.; m. Eileen Margaret McManus, Apr. 15, 1967; children: Kristen A. Stolfi, Katherine B. Aydin, Shelagh E., James P. AB, Boston Coll., 1964; JD, Cath. U. Am., 1970. Bar: D.C. 1970, Conn. 1982. Assoc. Arent, Fox, Kintner, Plotkin & Kahn, Washington, 1970-72, Akin, Gump, Strauss, Hauer & Feld, Washington, 1972-75; supervisory trial atty. EEOC, Washington, 1975-79; assoc. Whitman & Ransom, Washington, 1979-81, Farmer, Wells, McGuinn & Sibal, Washington, 1981-82; ptnr. Farmer, Wells, Sibal & Dempsey, Washington, Hartford, Conn., 1983-84; dir. indsl. rels. and labor counsel United Technologies Corp., Hartford, 1985—. Editor-in-chief: Cath. U. Law Rev. Capt. USNR (ret.). Fellow Coll. Labor and Employment Lawyers; mem. ABA. Office: United Techs Bldg Hartford CT 06101

DEMPSEY, JAMES RAYMON, manufacturing executive; b. Red Bay, Ala., Oct. 4, 1921; s. Newman W. and Maude (Berry) D.; m. Dolores Barnes, Jan. 19, 1943 (dec. Sept. 1997); children: Susan, David Barnes, Anne. Student, U. Ala., 1937-39; BS, U.S. Mil. Acad., 1943; MS, U. Mich., 1947, D of Engring. (hon.), 1964. Commd. 2d lt. U.S. Army, 1943; advanced through grades to lt. col. USAF, 1951; with photo reconnaissance squadron Eng., France, World War II; squadron comdr., 1945; guided missiles project officer, then chief guided missile projects (Research and Devel. Directorate, Air Force Hdqrs.), 1948- 49; exec. officer to (Dep. Chief Staff for Devel.), 1950-51; chief project sect. (Air Force Missile Test Center), Patrick AFB, Fla., then operations officer missile test range, 1951-53, resigned, 1953; asst. to v.p. planning Convair div. Gen. Dynamics Corp., 1953-54; dir. Gen. Dynamics Corp. (Atlas program), 1954-57; mgr. Gen. Dynamics Corp. (Convair-Astronautics div.), 1957-58; v.p. Gen. Dynamics Corp. (Convair div.), 1958-61; sr. v.p. Gen. Dynamics Corp.; pres. Gen. Dynamics Astronautics, 1961-65, Gen. Dynamics Convair, 1965-66; v.p. missiles, space and electronics group Avco Corp., 1966-68, v.p., group exec. govt. products group, 1968-75; pres. Digital Broadcasting Corp., 1978-79; mng. partner J.J. Finnigan Industries, Duluth, Ga., 1978-85; pres. Southeastern Rail Car Co., 1986-89; pvt. investor, 1990—. Trustee Phoenix Series Fund, 1968-91, Big Edge Series Fund, 1985-91, Phoenix Multi-Portfolio Fund, 1989-91, Precious Metal Holdings, 1980-93, Keystone Internat., 1987-93; chmn. bd. Transatlantic Capital Corp., Transatlantic Investment Corp., 1984-86; mem. spl. com. on space tech. NASA. Decorated Air medal with clusters, D.F.C.; Croix de Guerre (France); Disting. Grad. award U.S. Mil. Acad., 2002. Fellow AIAA, Am. Astronaut. Soc.; mem. Air Force Assn. (bd. dirs. 1958-59), Burning Tree Club, Congl. Country Club. Home and Office: 4081 Ridgeview Cir Mc Lean VA 22101-5809

DEMPSEY, JERRY EDWARD, retired service company executive; b. Landrum, S.C., Oct. 1, 1932; s. Adolphus Gerald and Willie Ceyattie (Lee) D.; m. Harriet Coan Calvert; children: Jerrie E., Harriet R., Margaret. BS, Clemson U., 1954, LLD (hon.), 2001; MBA, Ga. State Coll., 1968. With Borg-Warner Corp., Chgo., 1956-84, gen. mgr. York divsn., 1972-77, exec. v.p., 1977-79, pres., COO, 1979-84; sr. v.p. Waste Mgmt. Inc., Oak Brook, Ill., 1984-93; chmn., CEO PPG Industries, Inc., Pitts., 1993-97, chmn., 1997. Bd. dirs. Navistar, Eastman Chem. Co. Dean's adv. coun. Sch. Engring. Clemson U., chmn. pres.'s adv. coun.; bd. dirs. Pitts. Theol. Sem., Greenville Symphony, Greater Greenville Forum. Named Bus. Leader of Yr., Oak Brook (Ill.) Jaycees, 1989; recipient Bronze award Fin. World, 1989, 90, Pres.'s award Clemson U., 1990, Disting. Svc. award, 1992, Horatio Alger award, 1995, Am. Heritage award Anti-Defamation League, 1995, Disting. Alumni award Ga. State U., 1999, Lifetime Achievement award Ga. State U., 2004. Mem. ASHRAE, Melrose Club, Duquesne Club (dir.), Thornblade Country Club, Greenville Country Club, Fox Chapel Golf Club. Office: PPG Industries Inc 1 Ppg Pl Pittsburgh PA 15272-0001

DEMPSEY, JOAN, federal agency administrator; BA Polit. Sci., So. Ark. U.; MA Pub. Adminstrn., U. Ark. Deputy dir. Gen. Defense Intelligence Program Staff; dir. Mil. Intelligence Staff, Nat. Mil. Intelligence Prodn. Ctr.; acting asst. sec. defense Command, Control, Comm. and Intelligence; deputy asst. sec. Defense for Intelligence and Security; deputy dir. cmty. mgmt. CIA, Washington, 1997—; exec. dir. Fgn. Intelligence Adv. Bd., Office of Pres., Washington, 2003—. With USN. Mailing: c/oj President's Foreign Int Adv Board 1600 Pennsylvania Ave Washington DC 20500

DEMPSEY, MARY A., commissioner, lawyer; m. Philip Corboy, Sept. 4, 1992. BA (hon.), St. Mary's Coll., Winona, Minn., 1975; MLS, U. Ill., 1976; JD, De Paul U., 1982. Bar: Ill. 1982. Libr. Hillside Pub. Libr., Ill., 1976-78; assoc. Reuben and Proctor, Chgo., 1982-85; assoc. gen. counsel Michael Reese Hosp. and Med. Ctr., Chgo., 1985-86; pvt. practice Chgo., 1987-89; counsel Sidley and Austin, Chgo., 1990-93; commr. Chgo. Pub. Libr., 1994—. Adj. prof. law DePaul U. Coll. Law and Health Inst., Chgo., 1986-90; spl. counsel Chgo. Bd. Edn., 1987-89; mem. adv. bd. Dominican U. Grad. Sch. Libr. and Info. Sci., River Forest, Ill. Mem. State Street Commn., Chgo.; bd. dir. Big Shoulders Fund (for inner city Cath. sch.), Urban Libr. Coun.; trustee DePaul U., Chgo.; mem. Ill. State Libr. Adv. Coun. State libr. scholar in Ill. Mem. Chgo. Bar Assn., Chgo. Network. Office: Chgo Pub Libr 400 S State St Chicago IL 60605-1203

DEMPSEY, RAYMOND LEO, JR., radio and television producer, moderator, writer; b. Providence, June 18, 1949; s. Raymond Leo Sr. and Louise Veronica (Gambuto) D.; m. Patricia Batchelder (div. 1984); children: Joab, Jahdeam, Deezsha, Nathaniel, Talitha. BA in Liberal Arts, R.I. Coll., 1973; cert., Blake Computer Programming Inst., 1977; cert. in Bus., U. R.I., 1979; cert., Billy Graham Sch. Evangelism, Ashville, N.C., 1989; postgrad., Harvard U., Roger Williams U., Bryant U., Bristol C.C., C.C. R.I., Providence Coll. Lic. real estate agt., R.I.; lic. radio sta. operator FCC; cert. secondary tchr., videographer, contractor, R.I. Writer local and nat. publs., 1980—88; producer, moderator Chapter & Verse TV, Sta. RICA-TV, Providence, 1983—; tchr. R.I. Pub. High Schs., Providence and Cranston, 1988; producer, moderator radio programs Ch. Focus and People, Sta. WRIB, East Providence, 1989—97. Bd. dirs. Blessing, Inc., Providence; spl. corr. Songtime U.S.A. Radio Network, 1988—96, spl. reporter, spl. contbr., 1991; host Straight Talk, Sta. WKRI, 1989, dir. World Exch., 1991-93; co-host The Bible Answer Program, Sta. WARV, 1986; judge The Ace Awards, 1992, Cable Ace Awards, 1992; interviewer Gallup Poll, 1987; trainee N.E. Law Enforcement Officers Assn., 1991; elector Radio Hall of Fame, 1993, Stellar Awards, 1993; nursing asst. nursing homes, R.I., 1979; pvt. nurse's asst. R.I. Hosp., 1979; patient attendant R.I. Mental Hosp.; papers placed in permanent reference res. Brit. Libr., London, N.Y.C. Pub. Libr., Libr. Congress, Washington; preliminary judge Audio Pub. Assn. awards, 1996—. Dancer R.I. Coll. Dance Co., 1969; actor: The Wig and Mask Society of La Salle Acad., 1965. Bd. dirs. R.I. Right to Life, Cranston, 1973—95; witness R.I. Gen. Assembly, 1973—75, R.I. Bd. Health, 1973—; vol. ARC, R.I. Hosp.; registrar voters State of R.I., 1980, 91-92; del. Rep. Nat. Conv. 1980; sponsor World Vision, Pasadena, Calif., 1981—, Compassion Internat., Colo. Springs, Colo., 1989—; chief boys instr. karate Mattson Acad., Providence, 1968-71; mem. Providence Sci. Outreach of Brown U.; del. Gov.'s Conf. on Libr. and Info. Svcs., 1991; elector White House Conf. on Libr. and Info. Svcs.; Justice of Peace, 1991;

regional rep. Students Against Vietnam War, 1971, Taxpayers Action Network, 1991; ptnr. Food for the Hungry, 1984—; del. Ellen McCormack for Pres., 1976; vol. U.S. Fish and Wildlife Svc., R.I. Hosp., Providence, 1975, Providence Amb. Clinic, 1975; elected Rep. City Com. and Rep. State Ctrl. Com.; chmn. Issues and Rsch. Com. Rep. party Providence; collection donations to Holy Name Sch. Libr., Archdiocese of NY; ret. dir. Ground Zero, Citizens Against Govt. Waste; donator Vt. Hist. Soc., Brattleboro, 1975, Dominican Phillips Meml. Libr., Providence Coll., 1975, U. Steubenville, Ohio, 1995, Brown U. Libr., 2001, Cranston (RI) Pub. Libr., 2001, The Master's Sem., Calif., 2001, Joseph Stanton Meml. Libr., NYC, 2001. Named One of Top 4 Local Cable TV Prodrs. in Nation, Nat. Assn. Local Cable Programming, 1987, ofcl. Jerusalem Pilgrim, State of Israel, 1990, Ptnr. in Philanthropy, 1995; recipient 2 Internat. Angel awards for excellence in Cable TV presentations, 1991, cert. U.S. SBA, 1990, Diamond award, 1992, 1st prize for excellence in pub. affairs in R.I. and Mass., 1992, Achievement award Dale Carnegie Orgn., 1992, 1st pl. award Mastermedia: The Spotlight award, 1993. Mem. AAAS, ASCD, NRA, Am. Math. Soc., Coll. Sci. Tchrs., Sons Union Vets., Nat. Assn. H.S. Tchrs. English, Evangel. Theol. Soc., Soc. for Coll. Tchrs., Nat. Assn. Edn. of Young Children, Nat. Assn. Tchg. Sci., Modern Poetry Assn., Am. Soc. Oriental Rsch., Archaeol. Inst. Am., R.I. Assn. for Edn. Young Children, R.I. Assn. for Supervision and Curriculum Devel., Mental Health Assn. R.I., N.Y. Acad. Scis., Internat. Press Assn. (founding mem.), Nat. Geog. Soc., Nat. Assn. Broadcasters, Modern Poetry Assn., Nat. Assn. Radio Talk Show Hosts, Nat. Acad. Cable Programming, Near East Archaeol. Soc., Internat. Platform Assn., Nat. Assn. Tchrs. Sci., Jewish TV Inst. (charter), Smithsonian Air and Space Mus., Smithsonian Instn. (assoc.), Royal Inst. Pub. Health and Hygiene London (affiliate), Bread for the World, Evangs. for Social Action, Mus. Heritage Soc., Interscholastic Inst., Libr. Co. Phila., John Russell Bartlett Soc. (Brown U.), Intertel, Mensa, USCG Aux., Golden Key, Abraham Lincoln Soc., Internet Soc., Rel. Heritage Am., Providence Athenaeum, Toastmasters Internat., R.I. Pilots Assn., Phi Theta Kappa. Avocations: scuba diving, marksmanship, archaeology. Home and Office: PO Box 41000 Providence RI 02940-1000 *Orthodoxy presumes orthopraxy, and correct knowledge must precede correct action; yet anything minus love equals zero.*

DEMPSEY, RYAN GREGORY, music educator; b. Cortland, NY, Oct. 30, 1977; s. Shane Tyler Smith and Susan (Dempsey) Dempsey; m. Kimberly Irene Alexander, Dec. 21, 2002. MusB, James Madison U., 1999. Dir. of bands Rockbridge County Mid. Sch., Fairfield, Va., 2000—02, Rockbridge County H.S., Lexington, Va., 2002—04, Sherando H.S., Stephens City, Va., 2004—. Mem.: NEA, Music Educators Nat. Conf. Home: 110 Timberlake Terr # 4 Stephens City VA 22655 Office: Sherando HS 185 South Warrior Dr Stephens City VA 22655 Office Phone: 540-869-3995. Personal E-mail: jmubrass@yahoo.com. E-mail: dempseyr@frederick.k12.va.us.

DEMPSEY, STANLEY (HOWARD STANLEY DEMPSEY), lawyer, mining executive, investment company executive; b. LaPorte, Ind., Aug. 12, 1939; s. Howard Taft and Katheryn Alice (Prichard) D.; m. Judith Rose Enyart, Aug. 20, 1960; children: Howard Stanley, Whitney Owen, Bradford Evan, Matthew Charles. Student, Colo. Sch. Mines, 1956-57; AB, U. Colo., 1960, JD, 1964; cert., Harvard Sch. Bus., 1969. Bar: Colo. 1964. Ind. mine operator, Colo. and Mont., 1957—60; from indsl. engr. to divsn. atty. western ops. Climax (Colo.) Molybdenum Co., 1960—70; gen. atty. law dept. western area, dir. environ. affairs AMAX Inc., Denver, 1970—81, v.p., 1977-83; ptnr. Arnold & Porter, Denver, 1983—86; pres. Denver Mining Fin. Co., 1987—; chmn., CEO Royal Gold, Inc., Denver, 1984—, also bd. dirs.; pres. Environ. Strategies, Inc., 1991—. Chmn. AMAX Australia Ltd., 1981-83; chmn., exec. com. AMAX Iron Ore, 1981-83; dep. chmn., exec. com. Australian Consol. Mines Ltd., 1981-83; bd. dirs. Mineral Info. Inst., World Gold Coun. Author: Mining the Summit, 1978, 2d edit., 1986; contbr. articles to profl. jours. Legal rsch. asst. Rocky Mountain Mineral Law Found., Boulder, Colo., 1962-64, trustee, pres., 1979-80; pres. Colo. Mining Assn., 1979-1980; bd. dirs. Colo. Hist. Found., 1997—, Gov. Nat. Mining Hall of Fame, 1997— Mem. Nat. Mining Assn. (chmn. public lands com. 1994-2000, 04, chmn. MINEPAC 2000-02), ABA (chmn. hard minerals com. 1975-77), Colo. Bar Assn. (coun. mem. mineral law sect. 1975-79), Colo. Natural Resources Law Ctr. (bd. dirs. 1998-2000), Continental Divide Bar Assn. (sec.-treas. 1967-68), Colo. Hist. Soc. (bd. dirs., chmn. 1991-94), Soc. Mining Law Antiquarians (co-founder), Mining and Metall. Soc. Am., Mining History Assn. (pres. 1992-94), Mountain States Employers Coun. (bd. dirs. 1990—), Rotary, Rollings Hills Country Club(Golden), Am. Alpine Club, Univ. Club, Harvard Club (NYC). Presbyterian. Office: Royal Gold Inc 1660 Wynkoop St Ste 1000 Denver CO 80202-1161 Office Phone: 303-573-1660.

DEMPSEY, WILLIAM G., pharmaceutical executive; b. Evergreen Park, Ill., Nov. 17, 1951; B of Acctg., DePaul U. With Abbott Labs., Abbott Park, Ill., 1982—, gen. mgr. home infusion svcs., civisional v.p. critical care systems, divisional v.p. hosp. bus. sector sales, 1995—96, v.p. hosp. products bus. sector, 1996—98, sr. v.p. chem. and agrl. products, 1998—99, sr. v.p. internat. ops., 1999—2003, sr. v.p. pharm. ops., 2003—. Chmn. internat. sect. exec. com. PhRMA; mem. governing coun. Adv. Good Shepherd Hosp.; chmn. supervisory bd. Knoll GmBH, Germany; bd. dirs. TAP, Dainabot. Office: Abbott Labs 100 Abbott Park Rd Abbott Park IL 60064-6400

DEMPSTER, BARRY (EDWARD), poet; b. Toronto, Ont., Can., Jan. 17, 1952; s. Albert Edward and Helen Florence (Robinette) D.; m. Karen Ruttan, Sept. 26, 1981. Student, Centennial Coll., 1972-75. Lectr. poetry workshops League Can. Poets and Writers Union Can. Author: Fables for Isolated Men, 1982, Globe Doubis, 1983, Real Places and Imaginary Men, 1984, David and the Daydreams, 1985, Writing Home, 1989, Positions To Pray In, 1989, The Unavoidable Man, 1990, Letters From a Long Illness With the World, The D.H. Lawrence Poems, 1993, The Ascension of Jesse Rapture, 1993, Fire and Brimstone, 1997, The Salavation of Desire, 2000, The Words Wanting Out, New and Selected Poems, 2003, The Burning Alphabet, 2005; co-author: Best Canadian Stories, 1980, Third Impressions, 1982; editor: Tributaries, An Anthology: Writer to Writer, 1978; contbr. to anthologies; book rev. and poetry editor. Recipient Confedn. Poets prize, 1995, Scarborough Bicentennial award of merit, 1996, Petra Kerney Poetry prize, 2002. Mem. League Can. Poets, Writers' Union Can. Avocations: writing film criticism, travel, music, gardening, bicycling. Address: 45 French Cres Holland Landing ON Canada L9N 1J8 E-mail: dempster@passport.ca.

DEMSETZ, HAROLD, economist, educator; b. Chgo., 1930; BA, U. Ill., 1953; MBA, Northwestern U., 1954, PhD in Econs., 1959. Prof. econs. U. Chgo., 1963-71; sr. rsch. fellow Hoover Instn., Stanford, Calif., 1971-77; prof. econs. UCLA, 1971—, Arthur Anderson Alumni prof. bus. econs, 1988-95, emeritus, 1995—. Author: Economic, Legal, and Political Dimensions of Competition, 1982, The Organization of Economic Activity, Vol. I, 1988, Vol. II, 1989, The Economics of the Firm, 1995; contbr. numerous articles, book chpts. Fellow AAAS; mem. Mont Pelerin Soc., Am. Econs. Assn., WEA Internat. (pres. 1996). Office: UCLA Dept Econs 405 Hilgard Ave Los Angeles CA 90095-9000 Office Phone: 310-825-3651. Business E-Mail: hdemsetz@ucla.edu.

DEMSEY, RICHARD L., lawyer, educator; b. Cleve., Nov. 27, 1953; s. Delbert and Ruth Demsey; m. Cynthia S. Demsey, Sept. 29, 1985; 3 children. BFA, Ohio U., 1976; BA, Cleve. State U., 1979; JD, Case We. Res. U., 1982. Bar: Ohio, U.S. Supreme Ct. Ptnr. Nurenberg, Plevin, Heller & McCarthy LPA, Cleve., 1982—. Adj. prof. law Case We. Res. U., Cleve., 1996—, Cleve. Marshall Coll. Law, 1997—. Office: Nurenberg Plevin Heller & McCarty 1370 Ontario St 1st Fl Cleveland OH 44113 E-mail: rdemsey@nphm.com.

DEMSTER, DAWNA KAY, orchestra director; d. Sharon Kay Sager. MusB, Columbus State U., Ga., 1984—89. Cert. tchg. SACS, 1989. Orch. dir. Youth Orch. of Greater Columbus, Ga., 1993—96, M. D. Roberts Mid. Sch., Jonesboro, Ga., 1999—. Orch. dir. Clayton County Honor Orch., Jonesboro, 1998—2002. Oil painting, Eminations (Beaux Art Festival Award of Merit, 2000). Recipient Tchr. of the Yr., Clayton County Bd. of Edn., 2002-2003, Page One Headling Award for Excellence, Columbus Ledger-Enquirer, 1995, Outstanding Instrumental Music Edn. Award, Phi Beta Mu, Zeta Chpt., 1989, Cert. of Commendation, Clayton County Bd. of Edn., 1999, Cert. of Achievement, 2002, Who's Who Among America's Teachers, Parke Davis, Pub., 2002. Mem.: Ga. Music Educator's Assn. (dist. 6 orch. divsn. chair 2000—01). Achievements include invention of beginning string student training bow. Avocations: motorcycling, painting, sculpting, collecting art glass, practicing violin. Office: M D Roberts Millde School 1905 Walt Stephens Road Jonesboro GA 30236 Personal E-mail: ddemster@mdrms.ccps.ga.net.

DEMUELLER, LUCIA, investment consultant; b. Manizales, Caldas, Colombia, Aug. 14, 1937; came to U.S., 1960; d. Ricardo Aristizabal and Soledad Villegas; m. Harold Charles Mueller, Feb. 26, 1966; children: Christine and Anne Marie (twins). Degree in journalism, U. Caldas, 1960; degree in bus. and fin., NYU, 1965; cert. in gerontology, Marymount Manhattan Coll., 1991; grad., Nat. Def. U., Washington, 2000. Editor Young Women's Mag., Bogota, Colombia, 1959-60; asst. export mgr. M & T Chems. Inc., N.Y.C., 1963-66; mgr. banker acceptances Mitsui & Co., N.Y., N.Y.C., 1970-73; acct. exec. Conn. Mut., N.Y.C., 1976-83; assoc. Cowan Agy., Mass. Fin., N.Y.C., 1983-86; investment cons. Chem. Investment Svcs., N.Y.C., 1993-94; internat. bus. cons., 1994—. Contbr. articles to profl. publs. Mgr. disaster assistance ctr. Fed. Emergency Mgmt., N.Y., 1985, 91. Mem. Nat. Def. Exec. Res. (mgr. various disaster sites), L.Am. Progressive Group (pres. 1990—, founder). Home: 4 Sutherland Dr Monroe NY 10950-4116

DEMUNBRUN-HARMON, DONNE O'DONNELL, retired family physician; b. St. Paul, Aug. 26, 1926; d. Francis Joseph and Julia (Hoffmann) O'Donnell; m. Truman Weldon DeMunbrun, Mar. 17, 1948 (dec. Aug. 1996); children: Michael J., Steven M., Julie F., Suzanne B.; m. Donald Laurance Harmon, Aug. 26, 1997. BS, U. Ky., 1948, MS, 1949; MD, U. Louisville, 1954. Diplomate Am. Bd. Family Practice. Rotating intern St. Anthony Hosp., Louisville, 1955—56; pvt. practice Louisville, 1956—85; med. dir. St. Mary and Elizabeth Hosp., Louisville, 1971—76, Parkway Med. Ctr., Louisville, 1976—99, Family Health Ctrs., Louisville, 1985—90; ret., 1999. Case reviewer Health Care Rev., Louisville, 1995-96; criteria writer Nat. Health Svc., Louisville, 1995-96; asst. clin. prof. family practice, U. Louisville Med. Sch., 1987-90. Pres. Jacques Timothe Boucher Sieur de Montburn Heritage Soc., Nashville, 1996-97. Recipient mayor's citation Cify of Louisville, 1990, proclamation of tribute Jefferson County, Ky., 1990. Mem.: Jefferson County Med. Soc. (life; v.p. 1976—77), Ky. Acad. Family Practice (life), Ky. Med. Assn. (life; del.), Am. Acad. Family Practice (life), Frazier Arms Mus., Filson Club, Execs. Club, Univ. Club, Sigma Pi Sigma, Pi Mu Epsilon, Alpha Lambda Delta. Avocations: gardening, reading, travel, family, dogs. Home: 3004 Beals Branch Dr Louisville KY 40206-2902 E-mail: d2d.harmon@att.net. *Wants change in enhanced listing.*

DE MUNIZ, PAUL J., state supreme court justice; BS, Portland State U., 1972; JD, Willamette U., 1975. Bar: (Oreg. State Bar) 1975, (U.S. Dist. Ct.) 1977, (U.S. Ct. of Appeals, Ninth Circuit) 1980, (U.S. Supreme Ct.) 1981. Judge Oreg. Ct. Appeals, 1990—2001, presiding judge dept. one, 1997—2000; justice Oreg. Supreme Ct., 2001—. Mem. Jud. Fitness & Disability Commn., Supreme Ct. Access to Justice for All Com.; chair Com. to Implement Recommendations; mem. Oreg. Supreme Ct. Task Force on Racial/Ethnic Issues in Jud. System, Defense Advisory Com. on Women in Services, 1998—2001; former prof. Nat. Jud. Coll.; former mem., chair Oreg. Criminal Justice Council. Author (with others): Immigrants in Courts, 1999. Mem.: ABA. Office: Supreme Ct 1163 State St Salem OR 97301

DEMURO, PAUL ROBERT, lawyer; b. Aberdeen, Md., Mar. 21, 1954; s. Paul Robert and Amelia C. DeMuro; m. Susan Taylor, May 26, 1990; children: Melissa Taylor, Natalie Lauren, Alanna Leigh. BA summa cum laude, U. Md., 1976; JD, Washington U., 1979; MBA, U. Calif., Berkeley, 1986. CPA Md.; bar: Md. 1979, U.S. Dist. Ct. Md. 1979, DC 1980, U.S. Dist. Ct. DC 1980, U.S. Tax Ct. 1981, U.S. Ct. Appeals (4th cir.) 1981, Calif. 1982, U.S. Dist. Ct. (no. dist.) Calif. 1982, U.S. Dist. Ct. (ea. dist.) Calif. 1986. Assoc. Ober, Grimes & Shriver, Balt., 1979-82; ptnr. Carpenter et al, San Francisco, 1982-89, McCutchen, Doyle, Brown & Enerson, San Francisco, 1989-93, Latham & Watkins, San Francisco, 1993—. Author: The Financial Managers Guide to Managed Care and Integrated Delivery Systems, 1995, The Fundamentals of Managed Care and Network Development, 1999; co-author: Health Care Mergers and Acquisitions: The Transactional Perspective, 1996, Health Care Executives' Guide to Fraud and Abuse, 1998; editor, contbg. author: Integrated Delivery Systems, 1994, article and rev. editor: Washington U. Law Quar., 1975—76. Mem. San Francisco Mus. Art, 1985—. Fellow: Am. Coll. Med. Practice Execs., Med. Group Mgmt. Assn. (cert. med. practice exec.), Healthcare Fin. Mgmt. Assn. (bd. dirs. No. Calif. chpt. 1990—93, nat. principles and practices bd. 1992—95, vice chair 1993—95, nat. bd. dirs. 1995—97, mem. exec. com. 1996—97, chair compliance officers forum adv. coun. 1998—2000, sec. 1999—2001, bd. dirs. No. Calif. chpt. 1999—2005, mem. nominating com. 2001—02, pres.-elect 2001—02, pres. 2002—03, mem. governance com. 2002—03); mem.: AICPA, ABA (chair transactional and bus. health care interest group 1998—2000, chair programs com. 2000—02, governing coun. 2000—, chmn. mem. and mktg. com. 2002—04, vice chair coord. com. diversity 2002—, budget officer 2003—05, health law sect., chair elect 2005—), Md. Assn. CPAs, San Francisco Bar Assn., Healthcare Compliance Assn. (cert. in health care compliance), Am. Coll. Healthcare Execs., Am. Health Lawyers Assn. (task force best practices in advising clients 1998—99, fraud and abuse and self-referral substantive law com. 1998—, task force on ENRON 2002), Calif. Bar Assn., LA County Bar Assn. (health law sect.). Republican. Office: Latham & Watkins LLP 505 Montgomery St Ste 2000 San Francisco CA 94111-2552 Office Phone: 415-395-8180. Business E-Mail: paul.demuro@lw.com.

DEMUTH, ALAN CORNELIUS, lawyer; b. Boulder, Colo., Apr. 29, 1935; s. Laurence Wheeler and Eugenia Augusta (Roach) DeM.; m. Susan McDermott; children: Scott Lewis, Evan Dale, Joel Millard. BA magna cum laude in Econs., U. Colo., 1958, LLB cum laude in Gen. Studies, 1961. Bar: Colo. 1961, U.S. Dist. Ct. Colo. 1961, U.S. Ct. Appeals (10th cir.) 1962. Assoc. Akolt, Turnquist, Shepherd & Dick, Denver, 1961-68; ptnr. DeMuth & DeMuth, Denver, 1968—. Conf. atty. Rocky Mountain Conf. United Ch. of Christ, 1970-95; bd. dirs. Friends of U. Colo. Libr., 1978-86; bd. dirs., sponsor Denver Boys Inc., 1987-93, sec., 1988-89, v.p., 1989-90, pres., 1992-93; bd. dirs. Denver Kids, Inc., 1993—, Children's Ctr. for Arts and Learning, 1995—; mem. bd. advisors Lambuth Family Ctr. of Salvation Army, 1994—, chmn., 1994—; bd. advisors Metro Denver Salvation Army, 1988—, vice chmn. 1994-96. Mem. ABA, Colo. Bar Assn., Denver Bar Assn., Denver Rotary (bd. dirs. 1996-98), Phi Beta Kappa, Sigma Alpha Epsilon, Phi Delta Phi. Republican. Mem. United Ch. of Christ. Home: 1900 E Girard Apt 1007 Englewood CO 80111

DEMUTH, C. JEANNE, lawyer; JD, Kans. U., 1983. Bar: Kans. 1983, Calif. 1985, Tex. 1989; CPA, Kans. Home: Ste B-2 3503 Cedar Knolls Dr Kingwood TX 77339-2468

DEMUTH, CHRISTOPHER CLAY, think-tank executive; b. Evanston, Ill., Aug. 5, 1946; s. Harry Clay and Ethel Marie (Schaiell) DeM.; m. Susan Ann Shultis, June 9, 1973; children: Christopher Clay, Elizabeth Ann, Catherine Leas. AB, Harvard Coll., 1968; JD, U. Chgo., 1973. Bar: Ill. 1973, D.C. 1984. Staff asst. to Pres. Richard Nixon, Washington, 1969-70; assoc. Sidley & Austin, Chgo., 1973-76; assoc. gen. counsel Consol. Rail Corp., Phila., 1976-77; lectr., dir. regulatory studies Harvard Sch. Govt., Cambridge, Mass., 1977-81; adminstr. info. and regulatory affairs U.S. Office Mgmt. and Budget, Washington, 1981-84, exec. dir. Presdl. Task Force on Regulatory Relief, 1981-83; mng. dir. Lexecon Inc., Washington, 1984-86; editor-in-chief, pub. Regulation mag., 1986; pres. Am. Enterprise Inst. for Pub. Policy Research, Washington, 1986—. Chmn. bd. DeMuth Steel Products, 1993—, Clean Burn, Inc., 1993—. Mem. Am. Econ. Assn., Am. Law Econ. Assn. Republican. Episcopalian. Office: Am Enterprise Inst Pub Policy Rsch 1150 17th St NW Washington DC 20036-4603

DEMUTH, LAURENCE WHEELER, JR., lawyer, utilities executive; b. Boulder, Colo., Nov. 22; s. Laurence Wheeler and Eugenia Augusta (Roach) DeM.; m. Paula Phipps, Mar. 7, 1987; children: Debra Lynn, Laurence Wheeler III, Brant Hill. AB, U. Colo., 1951, LLB, 1953. Gen. atty. Mountain State Telephone and Telegraph Co., Denver, 1968, v.p., gen. counsel, 1968-84, sec., 1974-84; exec. v.p., gen. counsel, sec. U.S. West, Inc., Englewood, Colo., 1984-92, ret., 1992. Dist. capt. Rep. Precinct Com., 1957-70' trustee Lakewood (Colo.) Presbyn. Ch., 1965-68; bd. dirs. Colo. Epilepsy Assn., 1973-79; bd. litigation Mountain States Legal Found., 1980-89; Colo. Commr. on Uniform State of Laws, 1997—. Mem. ABA, Colo. Bar Assn. (chmn. ethics com. 1973-74, bd. govs., fellow found.), Denver Bar Assn., Am. Judicature Soc., Colo. Assn. Corp. Counsel (pres.), Order of Coif, Phi Beta Kappa, Pi Gamma Mu. Clubs: University, Metropolitan. Office: AT&T Broadband 188 Inverness Dr W Englewood CO 80112-5202

DEMY, TIMOTHY JAMES, military chaplain; b. Brownsville, Tex., Dec. 6, 1954; s. Millard Nile and Pauline Juanita (Owen) D.; m. Lyn Elizabeth Evans, Aug. 26, 1978. BA, Tex. Christian U., 1977; ThM, Dallas Theol. Sem., 1981, ThD, 1990; MA, U. Tex. at Arlington, 1994, Salve Regina U., 1990, PhD, 2004; MA, Naval War Coll., 1999. Commd. lt. jr. grade USN, 1981, advanced through grades to cmdr., 1993. Adj. instr. Naval War Coll., Newport, R.I., 1996—; co-dir. Ctr. for the Am. Family, Springfield, Va., 1995—. Co-author: When the Trumpet Sounds, 1995, The Coming Cashless Soc., 1996, Suicide: A Christian Response, 1998, Winning the Marriage Marathon, 1999, Genetic Engineering: A Christian Response, 1999, The Return, 1999, Politics and Public Policy: A Christian Response, 2000, In the Name of God, 2002; contbr. articles to profl. jours. Mem. Nat. Assn. Evangelicals, Evangelical Theol. Soc., Soc. Biblical Lit., Ctr. for Bioethics and Human Dignity, Orgn. Am. Historians, Naval Order U.S. Avocations: reading, cartography, animals. Office: 7 Ellen Rd Middletown RI 02842-5504 E-mail: lynd1@mindspring.com.

DEMYANOVICH, KAREN LEE, language educator; b. Oil City, Pa., July 5, 1949; d. Clemens Lee and Esther Louise Berlin; m. Mark Edward Demyanovich, Aug. 11, 1973; children: John, Mark. BS in English, Ind. U. Pa., 1971; M in Reading, Clarion U., 1973. Tchr. reading Cameron County Sch. Dist., 1971—80, San Antonio Sch. Dist., 1980—81; tchr. English Hudson Sch. Dist., NH, 1973—2000; reading specialist Merimack Sch. Dist., 2001—. Avocations: reading, animals.

DENACO, PARKER ALDEN, state official, lawyer, arbitrator; b. Bangor, Maine, Apr. 19, 1943; s. Alden F. and Pauline N. Denaco; m. Gayle Gernert Denaco, May 23, 1989. BA in History and Govt., U. Maine, 1965, MBA, 1975; JD, Washington and Lee U., 1968; postgrad., Air Command and Staff Coll., 1981. Bar: Maine 1968, U.S. Dist. Ct. Maine 1968, U.S. Ct. Mil. Appeals. Assoc. Eaton & Peabody, Bangor, Maine, 1968—69; exec. officer and adj. 100 MP Bn, Ft. Bragg, NC, 1969—70; provost marshal US Army, Inchon, Republic of Korea, 1970—71; exec. dir. Maine Labor Rels. Bd., Augusta, 1972—88; adj. grad. instr. Thomas Coll., Waterville, Maine, 1977—80; state staff judge adv. Maine Air N.G., Augusta, Maine, 1973—86; vis. prof. in constl. law U. Maine, 1990—91; hon. faculty mem. USAF Judge Adv. Gen. Sch., Maxwell AFB, Ala.; exec. dir. N.H. Pub. Employee Labor Rels. Bd., 1991—2003. Contbr. articles to profl. jours. Bd. dirs. Acad. Collective Bargaining Info. Svc., 1979-82; bd. dirs. Pub. Employment Rels. Svcs., 1978-81; founding mem. and dir. New Eng. Consortium of State Labor Rels. Agys., 1978-2003; neutral pub. mem. Com. on Pub. Sector Bargaining, ABA, 1974—; neutral chair, 1987-01, mem. Alternate Dispute Resolution Section, ABA, 1998—; mem. Boston Adv. Coun., Am. Arbitration Assn., 1978—; elected Nat. Acad. Arbitrators, 1987; Judicial Divsn., ABA, 1998—, Nat. Conf. of Admin. Law Judges; corporator Maine Savs. Bank, 1982-84; mem. law coun. Washington and Lee U., 1988-92. Served to capt. U.S. Army, 1969-73, to col. Air NG and USAFR, 1973-95. Recipient Harmon award USAF, 1986, Legion of Merit, 1990, Disting. Svc. award ABA, 2001, Inchon City medal Republic of Korea, 1970, Dirigo award State of Maine Air N.G., 1990. Fellow Coll. Labor and Employment Lawyers (chmn. First Circuit Com., 2003); mem. ABA (Disting. Svc. award 2001), Assn. Labor Rels. Agys. (pres. 1978-79), Maine Bar Assn. (labor sect. co-chmn. 1980-85), N.H. Bar Assn. (chmn. labor and employment law sect. 2002-03) Soc. Profls. in Dispute Resolution (charter), Indsl. Rels. Rsch. Assn., Nat. Acad. Arbitrators, Res. Ofcrs. Assn. (life), N.G. Assn. of U.S. (life), Phi Delta Phi, Beta Gamma Sigma. also: PO Box 227 Lincolnville ME 04849-0227 Mailing: 48 Augusta Way Dover NH 03820 Office Phone: 603-343-5166. Personal E-mail: denaco4adr@yahoo.com.

DEN ADEL, RAYMOND LEE, classics educator; b. Pella, Iowa, Apr. 23, 1932; s. John J. and Nellie (DeGeus) D. BA, Ctrl. Coll., 1954; MA, U. Iowa, 1959; PhD, U. Ill., 1971. Latin tchr. Pella H.S., 1954-55; grad. student Am. Acad., Rome, 1960, Vergilian Sch., Cumae, Italy, 1960, 73; fellow U. Iowa, Iowa City, 1957-58, tchg. asst., 1962-63; Latin and English tchr. Proviso West H.S., Hillside, Ill., 1958-62; v.p. Proviso Ednl. Assn., 1960-61; grad. student Am. Sch. Classical Studies, Athens, 1961, on-site participant, 1989, 1990; fellow, asst. and instr. in classics U. Ill., Urbana, 1963-67; dir. Ill. H.S. Latin Conf., 1967; faculty, chair classics dept. Rockford (Ill.) Coll., 1967—97, chair div. lang. and lit., 1971—74, prof., 1975—97, prof. emeritus, 1997—. Lectr. Ctr. for Learning in Retirement Rock Valley Coll., 2001—03; lectr. Beloit Coll., 1985. Bd. dirs. Rockford Cmty. Concert Assn., 1979-85; mem. Burpee Museum of Natural Hist. (life) mem. exec. com. Archaeol. Inst. Am., 1976-82, governing bd., 1990-96, trustee, 1990-94, v.p., 1994-96, Disting. Svc. award, 1997. With CIC, U.S. Army, 1955-57. Fulbright grant, Italy, 1960; named Vol. of Yr., Source Program in Rockford, 1983, Outstanding Coll. Latin Tchr. in Ill., 1987, Outstanding Fgn. Lang. Tchr. in Ill., 1989; recipient AIA Colloquium of Honor, 1997. Mem.: AAUP (pres. Rockford chpt. 1974—76, Ill. coun. 1977—80, sec. 1984—86, v.p. 1988—89), AIA (Ctrl. Ill. Soc. sec.-treas. 1966—67, mem. nat. coun. 1966—98, Rockford Soc. pres. 1968—70, 1972—74, 1991—93, sec. Rockford chpt. 1993—94, v.p. 1998—99), Classical Soc. Am. Acad. Rome (sec. 1990—93), Ill. Coun. Tchg. Fgn. Langs., Biblical Archaeol. Soc., Am. Assn. Dutch-Am. Studies, Vergilian Soc. Am. (life; sec. 1978—80), Classical Assn. Mid. West and South (life; 1st v.p. 1980—81), Fulbright Alumni Assn. (life), Ill. Classical Conf. (life; v.p. 1968—69, pres. 1969—70), Am. Philol. Assn. (life Field Scholarship award 1961), Am. Classical League (life; nat. coun. 1969—82, Scholarship award 1960), Pella Hist. Soc., Chgo. Classical Club (life; v.p. 1975—77, pres. 1977—79), Rotary (bd. dirs. Rockford chpt. 1987—89, dist. gov. rep. 1989—91, bd. dirs. Rockford chpt. 1991—95, v.p. 1992—93, pres. 1993—94, dist. gov. rep. 1994—97, gov. dist. 6420 1997—98, chmn. past dist. gov. coun. 2001, Paul Harris 711 Club, bd. dirs. 2002—, Svc. Above Self award Rockford Club and Dist. 6420 1989, Paul Harris fellow, benefactor 1982), Chi Gamma Iota, Phi Sigma Iota, Eta Sigma Phi (nat. exec. sec. 1974—78), Phi Beta Kappa (life; v.p. 1988—89, triennial coun. 1988—2003, pres. Eta Ill. chpt. 1989—92), Sigma Tau Delta. Presbyterian. Avocations: photography, travel, reading, stamp collecting/philately, music. Home: 701 Broadway St Pella IA 50219

DENARO, ANTHONY THOMAS, psychiatrist; b. N.Y.C., Aug. 9, 1929; s. Joseph and Maria (DeGennaro) Denaro; m. Mitsuru Suzuki, Nov. 23, 1963. BS, CCNY, 1960; MD, U. Okla., 1969; MPA, U. Hartford, 1981. Diplomate Nat. Bd. Med. Examiners, Am. Bd. Psychiatry, Am. Bd. Gen. Psychiatry and Child Psychiatry, Adminstrv. Psychiatry. Intern Nassau County Med. Ctr., East Meadow, N.Y., 1969-70; resident in child psychiatry U. Pa., Phila., 1970-72; resident in gen. psychiatry, 1972-74; dir. child psychiatry U. Conn. Health Ctr., Farmington, 1974-78; dir. adolescent unit Natchaug Psychiat. Hosp., Willamantic, Conn., 1978-80; assoc. dir. child and adolescent service Mt. Sinai Hosp., Hartford, Conn., 1980-82; assoc. dir. child and adolescent psychiatry Elmcrest Psychiat. Inst., Portland, Conn., 1982-84; dir. outpatient psychiatry Woodhull Med. and Mental Health Ctr., N.Y.C., 1984-85; dir. child and adolescent psychiatry First Hosp. Wyoming Valley, Kingston, Pa., 1985-98; child and adolescent behavioral health svcs. Child Devel. Clinic, Scranton, Pa., 1998—2001; dir. child and adolescent svcs. First Hosp. Wyoming Valley, Kingston, 2001—04; with KidsPeace Nat. Ctrs., Temple,

Pa., 2004—. Asst. prof. dept. psychiatry U. Conn. Sch. Medicine, Farmington, 1974-83. With U.S. Army, 1947-49. Fellow Am. Acad. Child and Adolescent Psychiatry; mem. AMA, Am. Psychiat. Assn., Am. Assn. Psychiat. Adminstrs., Northeastern Pa. Psychiat. Soc. (pres. 1990-91), Phi Beta Kappa. Republican. Office: KidsPeace Nat Ctrs 8th Ave and May Rd Temple PA 19560

DE NATALE, ANDREW PETER, lawyer; b. Bklyn., July 7, 1950; s. Peter E. and Mary (Tamberino) DeN.; m. Lynn Susan Kennedy, July 28, 1973; children: Andrew, Christopher. BS in Econs., U. Pa., 1972; JD, Fordham U., 1975. Bar: N.Y. 1976, U.S. Dist. Ct. (so. dist.) N.Y. 1976, U.S. Dist. Ct. (ea. dist.) N.Y. 1977, U.S. Ct. Appeals (2d cir.) 1978, U.S. Supreme Ct. 1979, U.S. Dist. Ct. (no. dist.) N.Y. 1982. Assoc. Krause, Hirsch & Gross, N.Y.C., 1975-79, Stroock & Stroock & Lavan, N.Y.C., 1980-83, ptnr., 1984-91, White & Case, N.Y.C., 1991—. Contbr. numerous articles to newspapers and profl. jours. Mem.: ABA, Insol Internat., Am. Bankruptcy Inst., N.Y. Yacht Club, Seawanhaka Corinthian Yacht Club. Office: White & Case LLP 1155 Avenue Of The Americas New York NY 10036-2787 Office Phone: 212-819-8303. Business E-Mail: adenatale@whitecase.com.

DENAVAEZ, DENNY, health facility administrator; b. Canada; m. Oscar DeNavaez; 2 children. B in Acctg. magna cum laude, Drake U. CPA. Acct. Coopers & Lybrand, Fla.; dir. fin. Internat. Media Ctrs., Miami, 1983—89; assoc. admin. fin. svcs. Fla. Med. Ctr., Fort Lauderdale, Fla., 1989—91, CFO, 1991—93, CEO, 1993—98; dir. contracting Medica, Allina Health Sys., Minn., 1998—2000; interim sr. v.p., lead adminstr. and ops. v.p. cardiovasc. svcs. Abbott Northwestern and Mpls. Heart Inst., Mpls., 2000—01; interim chief ops. officer Abbott Northwestern Hosp., Mpls., 2001—02. Office: Abbott Northwestern Hosp 800 E 28th St Minneapolis MN 55407

DENAVIT, JACQUES, retired physicist; b. Paris, Oct. 1, 1930; came to U.S., 1952; s. Georges and Marie (Arnould) D.; m. Catherine Dahlinger, Aug. 6, 1954; children: George, Paul, Mary. Degree in Gen. Math./Physics, U. Paris, 1952; MSEE, Northwestern U., 1953, PhD in Mech. Engring., 1956. From asst. prof. to prof. mech. and nuclear engring. Northwestern U., Evanston, Ill., 1958—82; rsch. physicist plasma physics divsn. Naval Rsch. Lab., Washington, 1969-71; rsch. physicist Lawrence Livermore Nat. Lab., Livermore, Calif., 1982-93; ret., 1993. Author: (with R.S. Hartenberg) Kinematic Synthesis of Linkages, 1964; contbr. numerous articles on plasma physics and computer simulation to profl. jours. Fellow Am. Phys. Soc. Home: 3536 Gresham Ct Pleasanton CA 94588-3431 Personal E-mail: jacdenavit@comcast.net.

DENCE, EDWARD WILLIAM, JR., lawyer, bank executive; b. Newport, R.I., Feb. 25, 1938; s. Edward William and Dorothea Margaret (Conway) D.; m. Claire A. Guertin, Nov. 14, 1970; children: Suzanne Lynn, Christine Anne. AB summa cum laude, Providence Coll., 1959; LL.B., Harvard U., 1963. Bar: Mass. 1963, R.I. 1965. Atty. New Eng. Electric System, 1963-68; sec., gen. counsel, v.p., mem. mgmt. com. Fleet Boston Fin. Corp. (now Bank of Am. Corp.), Providence, 1969—85; v.p., mem. mgmt. com. Edwards & Angell, Providence, 1992—. Mem. stockholders' adv. com. Fed. Res. Bank, Boston. Trustee, chmn. audit com., chmn. compensation com. St. Joseph Hosp.; trustee So. New Eng. Rehab. Ctr. Named One of Outstanding Young Men in Am., 1972 Mem. R.I. Bar Found., R.I. Bar Assn., Boston Bar Assn. Home: 1485 High Hawk Rd East Greenwich RI 02818-1364 Office Phone: 401-274-9200. E-mail: edence@ealaw.com.

DENCH, JUDI, actress; b. York, Eng., Dec. 9, 1934; d. Reginald Arthur and Eleanora Olave (Jones) D.; m. Michael Williams, Feb. 5, 1971; 1 child, Tara Cressida Frances. Student, Ctrl. Sch. Speech Tng.; LittD (hon.), Warwick U., 1978, York U., 1983. Theatrical appearances include: (Old Vic) Hamlet, Midsummer Night's Dream, Twelfth Night, 1957-58, The Importance of Being Earnest, As You Like It, Romeo and Juliet, 1959-61; (Venice Festival) Romeo and Juliet (Paladino d'Argentino), 1961; (Royal Shakespeare Co., Stratford) The Cherry Orchard, Measure for Measure, Midsummer Night's Dream, A Penny for a Song, 1961-62; (Oxford Playhouse) The Alchemist, The Three Sisters, Romeo and Jeanette, 1964; (Oxford and London) The Promise, 1966-67; (London) Sally Bowles in Cabaret, 1968; (Royal Shakespeare Co., London) Twelfth Night, A Winter's Tale, London Assurance, 1970; (Royal Shakespeare Co., Stratford) The Merchant of Venice, The Duchess of Malfi, 1971; tour of Japan with Twelfth Night, 1972; (London) London Assurance, 1973; (Oxford and London) The Wolf, 1974; (London) The Good Companions, 1974-75, The Gay Lord Quex, 1975; (Royal Shakespeare Co., Stratford) Much Ado About Nothing, The Comedy of Errors, Macbeth (SWET Best Actress award for Lady Macbeth), King Lear, 1976-77; Cymbeline, 1979; (Royal Shakespeare Co., London) Pillars of the Community, The Way of the World, 1977-78, (Aldwych) Juno and the Paycock (SWET Best Actress award, Evening Std. Drama award for best actress, Plays and Players award for Best Actress, Variety Club award Actress of Yr.), 1981, A Kind of Alaska, The Importance of Being Earnest (Std. Best Actress award, Plays and Players award for best actress), Pack of Lies (Plays and Players award, SWET Best Actress award), Mr. and Mrs. Nobody, 1988, Antony and Cleopatra (Olivier award, Evening Std. Drama award, Drama mag. award), Gertrude in Hamlet, The Cherry Orchard, 1989, 90, The Blough and the Stars, The Sea, Coriolanus, 1992, The Gift of the Gorgon, 1992-93, The Seagull, 1994, Filumena in London, 1998, Amy's View in New York, 1999, The Royal Family, 2001, The Breath of Life, 2002, All's Well That Ends Well, London and Stratford-upon-Avon, 2003-04; dir. plays Much Ado About Nothing, Look Back in Anger, The Boys from Syracuse, Romeo and Juliet; TV appearances include: Major Barbara, Talking to a Stranger (Best TV Actress of Yr. award 1967), Jackanory, Luther, Nieghbours, Marching Song, Days to Come, The Comedy of Errors, Macbeth, Village Wooing, Love in a Cold Climate, A Fine Romance, The Cherry Orchard, Going Gently, Saigon, Mr. and Mrs. Edgehill, 1988 (ACE award), Ghosts, Make and Break, Behaving Badly, Can You Hear Me Thinking, Torch, Absolute Hell (Oliver award Best Actress 1996), As Time Goes By; (films): He Who Rides a Tiger, A Study in Terror, Four in the Morning (Brit. Film Acad. Most Promising Newcomer award 1965), A Midsummer Night's Dream, The Third Secret, Dead Cert, Wetherby, 1985, A Room with a View, 84 Charing Cross Road, A Handful of Dust (Brit. Acad. Film and TV Arts award 1989), Henry V, 1989, Jack & Sarah, 1994, Golden Eye, 1995, A Little Night Music, 1995 (Oliver award Best Actress in a Musical 1996), Mrs. Brown (Brit. Acad. Film and TV Arts Scotland award 1997, Critics Circle Film award 1997, Golden Globe award for best actress 1997, Acad. award nomination 1997), Amy's View, 1997 (Critics Circle Drama award 1997), Tomorrow Never Dies, 1997, Shakespeare in Love, 1998 (Acad. award Best Supporting Actress 1998), Tea With Mussolini, 1999, The World is Not Enough, 1999, The Last of the Blond Bombshells, 2000, Chocolat, 2000, Iris, 2002 (BAFTA award best actress), The Shipping News, 2002, The Importance of Being Ernest, 2002, Die Another Day, 2002, Home on the Range (voice), 2004, The Chronicles of Riddick, 2004, Ladies In Lavender, 2004, Pride & Prejudice Mrs. Henderson Presents, 2005. Recipient Rothermore award for lifetime achievement, 1997, Critics Circle award for outstanding svc. to the arts, Acad. Award for Best Supporting Actress for Shakespeare in Love, 1999, Tony Award for Best Actress in Amy's View; decorated Order Brit. Empire, Dame Comdr. Brit. Empire, Order Companion of Honour, 2005; named UK Entertainment Personality of Yr. Variety, 1999, Walpole medal, NY, 2000, Benjamin Franklin medal, Royal Soc. Arts, London, 2000, Golden Globe award for best supporting actress in Chocolat, 2000, Olivier award lifetime achievement, 2004, Evening Standard Theater award, 2004; BAFTA fellow, 2001, Lucy Cavendish Coll. fellow, Cambridge, Eng., 2005. Mem. Religious Soc. Friends.

DENDINGER, WILLIAM J., career officer, chaplain; BA in Philosophy and English, Immaculate Conception Sem., 1961; MA in Theology, Aquinas Inst., 1964; MS in Counseling, Creighton U., 1969; student, Squadron Officer Sch., 1973; postgrad., Sch. Applied Theology, 1978; student, Air War Coll., 1987. Commd. capt. USAF, 1970, advanced through grades to maj. gen., 1997; base chaplain Maxwell AFB, Ala., 1970-72, Yokota Air Base, Japan, 1972-74; cadet wing chaplain USAF Acad., Colorado Springs, Colo., 1974-78; base chaplain Osan Air Base, S. Korea, 1979-80, Mather AFB, Calif., 1980-82; mem. chaplain resource bd. USAF Chaplain Svc. Inst., Maxwell AFB, 1982-85; base chaplain Hahn Air Base, W. Germany, 1985-88; plans and programs officer then chief plans/programs div. Office Air Force Chief Chaplains, Bolling AFB, D.C., 1988-93; command chaplain Hdqs. Air Combat Command, Langley AFB, Va., 1993-95; dep. chief Air Force Chaplain Svc. Hdqs. USAF, Washington, 1995-97, chief Air Force Chaplain Svc., 1997—. Decorated Legion of Merit with oak leaf cluster. Named Prelate of Honor with title of Rev. Monsignor, His Holiness Pope John Paul II, 1994. Office: HQ USAF/HC 112 Luke Ave SW Ste 316 Bolling Afb DC 20332-5113

DENEGRE, GEORGE, lawyer; b. New Orleans, Oct. 10, 1923; s. Thomas Bayne and Alma (Baldwin) D.; m. Gayle Stocker, Oct. 4, 1950; children: Stanhope Bayne-Jones, Gayle Denegre Felchlin, George, John Gayle. BA, Yale U., 1943; LLB, Tulane U., 1948. Bar: La. 1948. With firm Chaffe, McCall, Toler & Philips, 1948-49; assoc. Jones, Walker Waechter, Poitevent, Carrère & Denègre, New Orleans, 1949-52; ptnr. Jones, Walker, Waechter, Poitevent, Carrère & Denègre, 1952—. Sec., dir. Canal Barge Co., Inc., 1951-2002; sec., dir. Cen. Gulf Lines, Inc., 1958-99; sec. Internat. Shipholding Corp., 1978-99; dir. Dr. G.H. Tichenor Antiseptic Co., 1966-2002. Bd. dirs. Met. Crime Commn., 1966-02, Eugenie and Joseph Jones Family Found., 1963-93, Bus. Task Force for Edn., New Orleans Neighborhood Devel. Found., 1989-90, New Orleans Regional Med. Ctr., La. Assn. Mental Health, 1953-77, pres., 1960-61; bd. dirs., sec., exec. com., pres. World Trade Ctr.; bd. govs. Tulane Med. Ctr., 1969-83, vice-chmn., 1977-82, chmn., 1983; vice-chmn., bd. adminstrs. Tulane U., 1980-93; bd. dirs. Chamber New Orleans and River Region, chmn., 1991-2002; vice-chmn. bd. dirs. Met. Arts Fund, 1989-90, New Orleans Coun.-Navy League U.S.; bd. dirs., sec. Bus. Coun., 1986-2001; mem. bd., exec. com. Pub. Affairs Rsch. Coun., 1998-2004; sec. La. Coun. for Fiscal Reform, 1987-96; bd. commrs. Downtown Devel. Dist., 1989-95, chmn., 1992; co-chmn. Mayor's Found. for Edn., 1987-91; chmn. Mayor's Com. for Charity Hosp.; founding mem. La. Partnership for Innovation and Tech. Metrovision Partnership, 1990-2002; sec. bd. dirs. Orleans Intercmty. Coun.; vice-dean Consular Corps, 1988-91; Com. 100, 1993-95, Select Com. on Revenues and Expenditures in La. Future (SECURE), 1993-95; adv. bd. Coll. Bus. Adminstrn., U. New Orleans, 1994-96; mem. Com. for Better New Orleans, 2000-04. Lt. USNR, 1943-46. Hon. Consul of India, 1977-2002; Rex, King of Carnival, 1986. Mem. La. Bar Assn., New Orleans Bar Assn., Maritime Bar Assn., Boston Club of New Orleans, Pickwick Club, La. Club, Stratford Club. Office: Jones Walker Waechter Poitevent Carrere Denegre 201 Saint Charles Ave New Orleans LA 70170-5100 Address: c/o 2945 Danbury Dr New Orleans LA 70131-3851 E-mail: gdenegre@joneswalker.com.

DENENBERG, HERBERT SIDNEY, journalist, lawyer, educator, retired state official; b. Omaha, Nov. 20, 1929; s. David Aaron and Fannie (Rothenberg) Denenberg; m. Naomi N. Glushakow, June 22, 1958. BS, Johns Hopkins U., 1958; JD, Creighton U., 1954; LLM, Harvard U., 1959; PhD, U. Pa., 1962; LLD, Allentown Coll. St. Francis de Sales, 1989; LHD, Spring Garden Coll., 1992. CLU, CPCU. Mem. firm Denenberg & Denenberg, Omaha, 1954—55; asst. prof. ins. U. Iowa, Iowa City, 1962, Wharton Sch. Fin. and Commerce, U. Pa., 1962—65, assoc. prof., 1965—68, Harry J. Loman prof. ins., 1968—73; commr. ins. State of Pa., 1971—74; commr. Pa. Pub. Utility Commn., 1975; columnist Phila. Bull., 1975—79; consumer columnist Phila. Daily News, 1979—81, Phila. Jour., 1981—82, Del. County Daily and Sunday Times, 1987—90, Bucks County Courier Times, 1987—90, Pottstown Mercury, 1988—94, Burlington County Daily Times, 1987—90, Reading Eagle, 1989—, Doylestown Patriot, 1991—, Citizen's Choice of Wilkes-Barre, Pa., 1992—, Mainliner, 1992—94, Auto Insider, 1992—93, Collector's Guide, 1992—93, New Chester Jour., 1992—94, Del. County Bus. Monthly, 1993—96, Hellenic News, 1993—, 1994, Phoenixville, Phoenix, 1994—96, Eastern Poconos Cmty. News, 1999—; editor The Denenberg Report Orgn., 1999—; consumer and investigative reporter Adelphia Cable Update Cable Sys., 1999—2000, Sta. WCAU-TV (NBC), Phila., 1975—98; talk show host Sta. WCAU-AM CBS, Phila., 1976—80; consumer reporter WLVT-TV (PBS), 2001—. Columnist Sales and Mktg. Mag., 1976—80, Ins. Monitor, Hyderalnd, India; regular on Real People NBC-TV, 1979—80; consumer reporter Nat. Pub. Radio, 1979; spl. counsel, rsch. dir. Pres.'s Nat. Adv. Panel on Ins. in Riot-Affected Areas., 1967—68; spl. adviser to Gov. Pa. on consumer affairs, 1974—75; assoc. dir. Wis. Ins. Laws Rev. Project, 1966—71; cons. Dept. Labor, 1965—68, Coop. Devel. Adminstrn., PR, 1967—68, John F. Kennedy Ctr., Washington, 1966—71, Small Bus. Adminstrn., 1968—71, Dept. Justice, 1969, FTC, 1968, Dept. Transp., 1969—70, State of Nev., 1969—71, Alaska Legislature, 1976, U.S. Commn. Civil Rights, 1977—78, Concerned Physicians for Patient Care; spl. cons. to Mayor Washington, 1968—69; mem. Bd. of Health Promotion and Disease Prevention of Inst. Medicine NAS, 1973—74, mem., 1973—; vis. prof. law Temple U.; adj. prof. ins., info. sci. and tech. Cabrini Coll., 1999—; rsch. fellow Sapio Inst. Interactive Learning, 1999—. Author (with others): (book) Risk and Insurance, 2d edit., 1973; author: (with Spencer L. Kimball) Insurance Government and Social Policy, 1969; author: (with J.R. Ferrari) Life Insurance and/or Mutual Funds, 1967; author: (with S.L. Kimball) Mass Marketing of Property and Liability Insurance, 1970; author: The Insurance Trap, 1972, Shopper's guide to Surgery, 1972, Shopper's Guide to Dentistry, 1973, Shopper's Guide to Insurance on Mobile Homes, 1973, A Citizens Bill of Hospital Rights, 1973, Shopper's guide to Bankruptcy, 1974, Shopper's guide Book, 1974, Herb Denenberg's Smart Shopper's Guide, 1980, Shopper's guide to Medical Equipment, 1990, A Consumer's Guide to Herbal Medicines, 1999, Guide to Selecting a Pharmacist, 1999; columnist, mem. editl. bd. Caveat Emptor, 1971—79, mem. adv. bd. medicine and health newsletter The Dr.'s People, 1989—93. Mem. adminstrv. bd. S.S. Huebner Found., 1968—71; pres. Am. Risk and Ins. Assn., 1969—70; Dem. candidate U.S. Senate, 1974; bd. dirs. Consumers Union, 1973—76; bd. trustees Ctr. for Proper Medication Use, 1994—. 1st lt. JAGC U.S. Army, 1955—58. Named to Phila. Press Club Hall of Fame, 1995; recipient awards for articles, Jour. Risk and Ins., Lambert award, 1972, Nat. Press Club award, 1976, 1977, 1980, 1984, 1988, Journalism award, Am. Osteo. Assn., 1976, Am. Chiropractors Assn., 1977—80, 1988, citation, Columbia U., Media award, ATLA, 1986, Enterprise Reporting award, Phila. Press Club, 1986, 1987, 1999, Pub. Svc. award, 1987, 1989, 1996, 1997, 1999, Best Feature award, 1995, 1996, 1997, Spot News award, 1999, award for lifetime achievement, 1998, Gov.'s Hwy. Safety award, State of Pa., 1997, Enterprise Reporting award, Pa. AP, 1988, Nat. Headliner award, 1987—88, 1990, 1992, 40 Emmy awards, Best TV Pub. Svc. award, Soc. Profl. Journalists, 1987, 1988, 1990, 1992, 1993, 1994, 1998, 1999, TV Feature award, 1989, 1994, 1995, 1996, 1997, 1998, TV Mag. Feature award, 1989, 1992, Best Media Criticism, 1990, 1993, Best Investigation, 1990, 1992, 1993, 1994, 1995, 1996, 1997, 1998, 1999, Best Health and Sci. Report, 1995—99, Breaking News award, 1998, Outstanding Media Consumer Svc. award, Consumer Fedn. Am., 1990, Sam Beber Disting. AZA Alumnus award, B'nai B'rith, 1990, Outstanding Citizen award, Firemen's Assn. Pa., 1991, Consumer of Yr. award, Pa. Assn. Weights and Measures, 1991, Phila. award integrity in journalism, 1988, Award of Excellence in legal reporting and analysis, Am. Bd. Trial Advocates, 1996, Award of Lifetime Achievement, Phila. Press Club, 1998, Award for Excellence in Legal Reporting and Analysis, Am. Bd. Trial Advocates, 1996, Phila. Press Club award for lifetime achievement, 1998, others, Am. Bd. Trial Advocates award, 1996. Mem.: ABA (life), Internat. Assn. Ins. Law (v.p. sci. sect. Am. chpt. 1967—71), Med. Soc. Access to Physicians (blue ribbon panel Phila. County 1998—), Am. Risk and Ins. Assn. (2nd v.p. 1967—68, bd. dirs. 1967—71, pres. 1969—70), Montgomery County Bar Assn., Pa. Bar Assn., Old Clunker Club (founder, pres. 1982—). Home: PO Box 7301 Saint Davids PA 19087-7301 Office Phone: 610-687-0293. Personal E-mail: hdenenberg@aol.com. *Our governmental system is designed to make politicians fat and special interests groups rich. Government has become our number "one" consumer fraud. As a government official, educator, and author I have attempted to make government work for people instead of for special interests and politicians only. I have been willing to make waves and rock boats. I have tried to show that government can help people.*

DENENBERG, KATHARINE W. HORNBERGER (TINKA DENENBERG), artist, educator; b. Ann Arbor, Mich., Nov. 2, 1932; d. Theodore Roosevelt and Marian Louise (Welles) Hornberger; m. Allan Neal Denenberg; children: Peter David, Thomas Andrew. Student, Brown U., 1950-51; BA, U. Minn., 1953; MAT, Harvard U., 1954. Intern tchr. art Concord (Mass.) H.S., 1954-55; tchr. art Bedford and Pound Ridge (N.Y.) Schs., 1955-56, New Lincoln Sch., N.Y.C., 1956-62, Mus. Modern Art, N.Y.C., 1964-71, Children's Art Workshop, Mamaroneck, N.Y., 1971-81, Pelham (N.Y.) Art Ctr., 1981. One-woman shows include Manhattanville Coll., Purchase, N.Y., 1975, Rye (N.Y.) Libr., 1975, 85, West Cornwall (Conn.) Gallery, 1978, 79, West Cornwall Libr., 1979, 84, Condeso Lawler Gallery, N.Y., 1982, 84, Moviehouse Gallery, Millerton, N.Y., 1987, Larchmont Libr., 1988, St. Peter's Ch., N.Y., 1990; exhibited in group shows at Duffy-Gibbs Gallery, N.Y., Nat. Mus. of Taiwan, Bridge Gallery, White Plains, N.Y., Westport-Weston Arts Coun., Greenwich (Conn.) Libr., Manhattanville Coll., New Britain (Conn.) Mus., Sarah Rentzler Gallery, Condeso-Lawler Gallery, Silvermine Gallery, The Castle Gallery, Coll. New Rochelle, N.Y.; represented in permanent collections at Credit Lyonais, Bank of Boston, Chermayeff and Geismar, Great Lakes Corp., Tex. Comml. Bank, Sohio Petroleum, Cleary Gottlieb, Chemical Bank, Mobil. N.Y.State Coun. for the Arts grantee, 1975. Mem. Phi Beta Kappa.

DENERY, DALLAS G., aeronautical engineer, researcher; b. Detroit, May 10, 1939; s. Herman and W. L. (Dallas) Denery; m. Sharon K. Keegan, July 13, 1963; children: Dallas G. II, Celia A., John P. BS in Engring., U. Mich., 1962; MS in Engring., U. Washington, 1965; PhD, Stanford U., 1971. Aerospace engr. Boeing Co., Seattle, 1962—66, NASA Ames Rsch. Ctr., Moffett Field, Calif., 1966—81, chief guidance and naval br., 1981—95, dep. chief aviation sys. divsn., 1995—. Dr. Hugh L. Dryden Meml. fellow, Nat. Space Club, 1979. Fellow: AIAA; mem.: Sigma Xi. Achievements include development of avionics for two-segment noise abatement approaches, method for extracting parameter estimates from dynamic sys. that is insensitive to initial parameter estimates and air traffic control automation. Home: 12611 Larchmont Ave Saratoga CA 95070 Office: NASA Ames Rsch Ctr MS 210-4 Moffett Field CA 94035 Office Phone: 650-604-5427. Personal E-mail: denery@msn.com. Business E-Mail: dallas.g.denery@nasa.gov.

DE NEUFVILLE, RICHARD LAWRENCE, engineering educator; b. N.Y.C., May 6, 1939; s. Lawrence Eustace and Adeline de N.; m. Virginia Lyons; children: Robert, Julie. SB, SM, MIT, 1961, PhD, 1965; Dr. h.c (hon.), Tech U., Delft, 2002. Asst. prof. to assoc. prof. dept. civil engring. MIT, Cambridge, Mass., 1965-75, prof., chmn. Tech. and Policy Program, 1975-2000, prof. engring sys., 2000—. Vis. prof. U. Calif., Berkeley, 1974—76, London Grad. Sch. Bus., 1973, Ecole Centrale de Paris, 1981—82; mem. vis. com. U. Va., Charlottesville, 1987; adj. prof. Ecole Nationale des Ponts et Chausees of Paris, 1988—, U. Bristol, England, 1992—99; vis. prof. Australian Bur. Transport and Comml. Econs., 1995; mem. vis. com. Tech. U., Delft, Eindhoven and Utrecht, The Netherlands, 1996—97, Instituto Superior Tecnico, Portugal, 2004, U.S. Army Engring. Ctr., 2005; vis. prof. Harvard U., 2000—; advisor Alta. Heritage Fund for Sci. and Engring. Rsch., 2000—, B.C. Leading Edge Found., 2003, Laing O'Rourke, PLC; adj. prof. Ecole Hassania des Travaux Publics of Casablanca, 2000—01, MBA des Ponts, 2000—; vis. prof. Balliol Coll., Oxford U., 2001; life mem. Clare Hall Coll., Cambridge U., 2002—; mem. Netherlands Rev. on Engring. Sys., 2002—03; sr. rsch. assoc. Judge Inst. Author: Airport Systems Planning, Design and Management, 2003, Applied Systems Analysis, 1990, Airport Systems Planning, 1976, Systems Planning and Design, 1979, Systems Analysis for Engineers and Managers, 1971; editor Jour. Transp. Rsch., 1975-86, Jour. Air Transport Mgmt., 1993—, Internat. Jour. Tech. Policy and Mgmt., 1999—. Bd. dirs. Geographic Data Tech., 1982-90, Urban Data Processing, 1970-80, Ecole Bilingue, French-Am. Internat. Sch. of Boston, 1992-97; trustee Kennedy Meml. Trust (U.K.), 1993-98; Consejo del Rector, Universidad Anahuac del Sur, Mexico, 1999. 1st lt. C.E., U.S. Army, 1961-62. Decorated chevalier Ordre des Palmes Academiques (France); White House fellow, 1964-65, Guggenheim fellow, 1973, U.S.-Japan Leadership fellow, 1990, Class of 1960 fellow, 2000; recipient Sys. Sci. prize NATO, 1974, Risk and Ins. prize Risk and Ins. Soc., 1976, Alpha Kappa Psi award, 1985, Engring. Excellence award Australia Instn. Engrs., 1986, Irwin Sizer award, 1988, FAA prize for tchg. excellence, 1990, Martore prize for tchg. excellence, 2004. Mem. ASCE (life), AAAS, Ops. Rsch. Soc. Am., Brit.-N.Am. Com., Am. Alpine Club, Cambridge Boat Club, Cambridge Skating Club, Cambridge Tennis Club, Internat. House of Japan. Office: MIT Rm E40-245 Cambridge MA 02139 Business E-Mail: ardent@mit.edu.

DENEUVE, CATHERINE (CATHERINE DORLEAC), actress; b. Paris, Oct. 22, 1943; d. Maurice Dorleac and Renee Deneuve; m. David Bailey, 1965 (div. 1970); children: Christian Vadim, Chiara Mastroianni. Ed., Lycée La Fontaine, Paris. Co-chair UNESCO campaign to protect World's Film Heritage, 1994—. Films include Les Petits Chats, 1956, Les Collegiennes, 1956, Les portes claquent, 1960, Les Parisiennes, 1961, Et Satan conduit le bal, 1962, Vacances portugaises, 1963, Le Vice et la Vertu, 1963, Les Parapluies de Cherbourg, 1964 (Golden Palm of Cannes Festival), La Chasse à l'homme, 1964, Les Plus belles escroqueries du monde, 1964, Un Monsieur de compagnie, 1964, Repulsion, 1965, Coeur à la gorge, 1965, Le Chant de Ronde, 1965, La Vie de Chateau, 1965, Les créatures, 1966, Les Demoiselles de Rochefort, 1966, Benjamin, 1967, Manon 70, 1967, Belle de Jour, 1967 (Golden Lion of Venice Festival), Meyerling, 1967, La Chamade, 1968, The April Fools, 1968, La Sirène du Mississippi, 1968, Tristana, 1969, It Only Happens to Others, 1971, Dirty Money, Hustle, 1975, Lovers Like Us, 1975, Act of Aggression, 1976, March or Die, 1977, La Grande Bourgeoise, 1977, The Last Metro, 1980, A Second Chance, 1981, Reporters, 1982, The Hunger, 1983, Fort Saganne, Scene of the Crime, Agent Trouble, 1987, FM-Frequency Murder, 1988, Drole d'endroit Pour Une Rencontre, 1988, Helmut Newton: Frames from the Edge, 1989, Indochine, 1992 (César award Best Actress, Acad. award nominee for Best Actress), Ma Saison Preferee, 1993, La Partie d'Echecs, 1994, Les Cent et Une Nuits, 1995, Les Voleurs, 1996, Place Vendome, 1997, Généalogies d'un Crime, 1997, Pola X, 1998, Le Temps retrouvé, La Princesse de Clèves, 1999, The Last Napoleon, 1999, Est, ouest, 1999, Le Vent de la nuit, 1999, Belle Maman, 1999, Dancer in the Dark, 2000, Je rentre à la maison, 2001, Absolument fabuleux, 2001, The Musketeer, 2001, Le Petit poucet, 2001, 8 femmes, 2002 (Berlin Film Festival Silver Bear for Individual Artistic Contbn.), Au plus près du paradis, 2002, Um Filme Falado, 2003; TV movies include Les Liaisons dangereuses, 2003, Princesse Marie, 2004; prodr. A Strange Place to Meet, 1988. Recipient Berlin Film Festival Golden Bear for Lifetime Achievement, 1998, Venice Film Vestival Silver Lion for Best Actress, 1998. Office: 76 Rue Bonaparte 75006 Paris France

DENEVAN, WILLIAM MAXFIELD, geographer, educator, historical ecologist; b. San Diego, Oct. 16, 1931; s. Lester W. and Wilda M. D.; m. Patricia Sue French, June 21, 1958; children: Curtis, Victoria. BA, U. Calif., Berkeley, 1953, MA, 1958, PhD, 1963. Faculty dept. geography U. Wis., Madison, 1963-94, prof., 1972-94, chmn. dept., 1980-83, dir. L.Am. Ctr., 1975-77, prof. emeritus, 1994—. Author/co-author: The Upland Pine Forests of Nicaragua, 1961, The Aboriginal Cultural Geography of the Llanos de Mojos of Bolivia, 1966, The Biogeography of a Savanna Landscape, 1970, Adaptive Strategies in Karinya Subsistance, Venezuelan Llanos, 1978, Campos Elevados en los Llanos Occidentales de Venezuela, 1979, Cultivated Landscapes of Native Amazonia and the Andes, 2001; editor/co-editor: The Native Population of the Americas in 1492, 1976, Pre-Hispanic Agricultural Fields in the Andean Region, 1987, Swidden-Fallow Agroforestry in the Peruvian Amazon, 1988, Hispanic Lands and Peoples, 1989, Las Chacras de Coporaque, 1994; contbr. 70 articles to profl. jours., chptrs. to books. With USNR, 1950—55. Fulbright grantee, 1957; grantee NRC, 1961-62, Ford Found., 1965-66, NSF, 1972-73, 84-86, Nat. Geog. Soc., 1985-86, NEH, 1989-90; Guggenheim fellow, 1977-78. Mem. Assn. Am. Geographers (Honors award 1987), Am. Geog. Soc., Am. Anthrop. Assn., Soc. for Am. Archaeology, Am. Acad. Arts and Scis. E-mail: sbden@saber.net.

DENG, CHANGCHUN, medical geneticist, physician; MB, Suzhou Med. Coll., 1990; PhD, U. Pitts., 2001. Resident physician Suzhou Children's Hosp., China, 1990—93, hematology fellow, 1993—94; postdoctoral rsch. fellow Stanford U., Calif., 2001—04; resident physician Lincoln Med. Mental Health Ctr., Bronx, NY, 2004—. Contbr. articles to jours. in field. Mem.: Radiation Rsch. Soc. (Travel award 2004), Am. Soc. Cell Biology, Am. Assn. for Cancer Rsch. Achievements include discovery of the genes involved in the cytotoxicity of the promising anticancer drug Tirapazamine; new mechanisms of Tirapazamine anticancer activity; new ways of increasing the cytotoxicity of tirapazamine; genes involved in the metabolism of the anticancer drug Arsenic Trioxide; new genes involved in the unfolded protein response pathway; a new gene that switches cell from mitosis to meiosis; a new gene that is essential for the completion of meiosis; mechanisms of the molecular motor KAR3. Home: 68 22 Clyde St Apt 2 Forest Hills NY 11375 Office: Lincoln Med Mental Health Ctr 239 149th St Bronx NY Office Phone: 718-579-5000. Personal E-mail: chdstpt@yahoo.com.

DENG, HEPING, research scientist; s. Shijun Deng and Youlin Shan. BA, Anhui Normal U., 1987; MA, Jinan U., 1989; EdD, East Tenn. State U., 2000. Asst. rschr. Alfred State Coll., Alfred, 2000—02; rschr. Borough of Manhattan CC, NYC, 2002—. Paper com. mem. So. Assn. for Instl. Rsch., Charleston, SC; paper reviewer Jour. of Computer-Enhanced Learning, Winston-Salem, NC, 2005—; instl. rsch. bd. Borough of Manhattan CC, NYC, 2002—. Contbr. articles to profl. jours. Recipient Outatanding Acad. Acheievement, East Tenn. State U., 1984—86, Outstanding Acad. Achievement, 1995; Doctoral fellow, 1994—99. Mem.: Mid South Ednl. Rsch. Assn. (assoc.), Ea. Edn. Rsch. Assn. (assoc.), Am. Assn. for Higher Edn. (assoc.), Am. Ednl. Rsch. Assn. (assoc.), Overseas Chinese Assn. for Instl. Rsch. (assoc.), Assn. for Instl. Rsch. (assoc.). Freedom. Office Phone: 212-220-8332. E-mail: yedeng@yahoo.com.

DENGER, MICHAEL LOUIS, lawyer; b. Davenport, Iowa, Sept. 8, 1945; s. Ralph Henry and Bernice Marie (Cederberg) D.; m. Mary Elizabeth Colbert, Aug. 30, 1969; children: Lorna Marie, Mary Catherine, Rachel Anne. BS with highest distinction, Northwestern U., 1967; JD cum laude, Harvard U., 1970. Bar: D.C. 1970, U.S. Ct. Appeals (D.C. cir.) 1971, U.S. Supreme Ct. 1978. Assoc. atty. Sutherland, Asbill & Brennan, Washington, 1970-76, ptnr., 1976-92, Gibson, Dunn & Crutcher LLP, Washington, 1992—. Adj. prof. law Washington and Lee U., 2000—; speaker on antitrust, trade regulation numerous groups. Bd. editors Antitrust Report, 1992—; contbr. articles to profl. jours. Mem. nat. adv. coun. Northwestern U. Sch. Comm., Evanston, Ill., 1990—. 2nd lt. USAR, 1970. Mem. ABA (vice chair antitrust law sect. 1985-86, sec. antitrust law sect. 1988-91, chair-elect antitrust law sect. 1991-92, chair antitrust law sect. 1992-93, chair edit. bd. antitrust sect. Federal and State Price Discrimination Law 1991, co-editor in chief antitrust sect. State Antitrust Practice and Statutes 3 vols. 1990, vice chair edit. bd. antitrust sect. Antitrust Law Devels. 2d edit. 1984), Columbia Country Club (Chevy Chase, Md.). Republican. Roman Catholic. Avocations: tennis, collecting military miniatures, military history, bridge. Home: 5802 Kirkside Dr Chevy Chase MD 20815-7118 Office: Gibson Dunn & Crutcher LLP 1050 Connecticut Ave NW Ste 900 Washington DC 20036-5306 E-mail: mdenger@gibsondunn.com.

DENGLER, DOROTHY DENISE, artist; b. Meridian, Miss., July 6, 1956; BFA, Miss. U. for Women, 1970; MA, Syracuse U., 1992. Assoc. prof. U. of W. Ala., Livingston, 1994—96; adj. art instr. Miss. State U., Meridian, 1996, E. Miss. Cmty. Coll., 1999—2001. Home: 8470 Club Dr Lauderdale MS 39335

DENGLER, ROBERT ANTHONY, professional association executive, educator; b. Upper Darby, Pa., Aug. 23, 1947; s. Anthony William and Harriet Josephine (Schneider) D.; m. Renee Faith Aird, Oct. 26, 1985. BS, Drexel U., 1970, MBA, 1972; MS in MIS, Benedictine U., 2000, postgrad., 2000—. Cert. assn. exec., mtg. profl. Cons. orgn devel. Abinton Hosp., Abington, 1970—73; dir. tng. & edn. Parkview Meml. Hosp., Ft. Wayne, Ind., 1973-76; dir. human resource mgmt. Americana Healthcare Corp., Chgo., 1976-82; corp. mgr. Human Resource Tng. and Devel. Means Svc. Inc., Chgo., 1982-83; dir. physician services West Suburban Hosp. Med. Ctr., Oak Park, Ill., 1983-85; assoc. dir. Assoc. Equipment Distributors, Oak Brook, Ill., 1985-88; exec. v.p. Internat. Reprographic Assn., Oak Brook, 1988-92; exec. dir. Data Processing Mgmt. Assn., Park Ridge, Ill., 1993-94; pres. R.A. Dengler & Assocs., 1994—; exec. dir. Nat. Assn. Med. Staff Svcs., Lombard, Ill., 1996-98; engring. leadership devel. adminstr. Commonwealth Edison/Exelon Corp., 2001—03. Adj. instr. orgn. behavior Aurora (Ill.) U.; adj. instr. mgmt. info. sys., orgn. devel. change Hawaii Pacific U., Honolulu; instr. creative mgmt. Phoenix U. Capt. USAR, 1972-80. Mem. Inst. Mgmt. Cons., Project Mgmt. Inst., Am. Soc. Assn. Execs., Acad. of Mgmt., Midwest Acad. Mgmt., Orgn. Devel. Network, Orgn. Devel. Inst., Mensa. Home and Office: 294 Lionel Rd Riverside IL 60546-2204

DENHAM, BRYAN ERROL, communications educator; b. Belleville, Ill., Feb. 8, 1967; s. Charles William Denham Jr. and Deanna Mary Gregory. BA, Ind. U., 1989; MA, Calif. State U., Fullerton, 1993; PhD, U. Tenn., 1996. Asst. prof. S.W. Mo. State U., Springfield, 1997-99; Charles Campbell assoc. prof. sports comm. Clemson (S.C.) U., 1999—. Co-author: Introduction to Journalism, 2001; contbr. articles to profl. jours. Mem. Assn. for Edn. in Journalism and Mass Comm., Am. Polit. Sci. Assn., Am. Assn. for Pub. Opinion Rsch., Nat. Comm. Assn., N.Am. Soc. for the Sociology of Sport, Midwest Assn. for Pub. Opinion Rsch. Avocations: Americana, films. Home: 854 Issaqueena Trail #1007 Central SC 29630 Office: Clemson Univ 412 Strode Tower Clemson SC 29634 E-mail: bdenham@clemson.edu.

DENHAM, ROBERT EDWIN, lawyer, investment company executive; b. Dallas, Aug. 27, 1945; s. Wilburn H. and Anna Maria (Hughes) Denham; m. Carolyn Hunter, June 3, 1966; children: Jeffrey Hunter, Laura Maria. BA, U. Tex., 1966; MA, Harvard U., 1968, JD, 1971. Bar: Calif. 1972. Assoc. Munger Tolles and Olson, L.A., 1971—73; ptnr. Munger Tolles Olson, L.A., 1973—85, 1992—93; mng. ptnr. Munger Tolles and Olson, L.A., 1985—91; chmn., chief exec. officer Salomon Inc, N.Y.C., 1992—97; ptnr. Munger Tolles and Olson, L.A., 1998—. Pres. Pasadena (Calif.) Ednl. Found., 1977—79; trustee Poly. Sch. Pasadena, 1989—93, v.p. bd. trustees, 1991—93; trustee New Sch. U., 1995—, Natural Resources Def. Coun., 1992—2002; adv. bd. of the pres. Calif. State U., Sonoma, 1993—; trustee The Conf. Bd., 1994—2003, Russell Sage Found., 1997—; pub. mem. Ind. Stds. Bd., 1997—2000; former co-chmn. Subcoun. on Capital Allocation of the Competitiveness Policy Coun.; former mem. Bipartisan Commn. on Entitlement and Tax Reform; former U.S. rep. to the Asia Pacific Econ. Coun. Bus. Adv. Coun.; mem. bus. sector adv. group on corp. governance OECD; trustee Cathedral Corp. Diocese of L.A., 1986—92; bd. dirs. Pub. Counsel, L.A., 1981—84, United Way, N.Y.C., 1994—97, U.S. Trust Co., AMKOR Tech., Inc., 1998—99. Mem.: ABA, L.A. County Bar (bus. and corps. exec. com. 1985—), State Bar Calif. Democrat. Episcopalian. Avocations: soccer, cooking, running. Office: Munger Tolles and Olson 355 S Grand Ave # 3500 Los Angeles CA 90071-1560

DENHARDT, DAVID TILTON, molecular and cell biology educator; b. Sacramento, Feb. 25, 1939; s. David Burton and Edith (Tilton) D.; m. Georgetta Louise Harrar, July 1, 1961; children: Laura Jean, Kristin Ann, David Harrar. BA in Chemistry with high honors, Swarthmore Coll., 1960; PhD in Biophysics, Calif. Inst. Tech., 1965. Instr. biol. labs Harvard U., 1964-66, asst. prof., 1966-70; assoc. prof. biochemistry McGill U., Montreal, Que., Can., 1970-77, prof., 1977-80; prof. biochemistry, microbiology and immunology, dir. Cancer Research Lab., U. Western Ont., London, 1980-88; prof. biol. scis. Rutgers U., New Brunswick, N.J., 1988—, chmn., 1988-95, dir. Bur. Biol. Rsch., 1988-95, dir. cell devel. biology grad. program, 1991-94. Mem. sci. adv. bd. Ctr. for Advanced Biotech. and Medicine, Piscataway, N.J., 1988-91, 1988-91. Editor: Jour. Virology, 1977-87, Gene, 1985-93, Exptl. Cell Rsch., 1994—; assoc. editor: Jour. Cellular Biochemistry, 1994—; mem. editorial bd. Jour. Cancer Rsch. Methods and Clin. Oncology, In Vivo Internat. Jour. Fellow AAAS, Am. Acad. Microbiology, Royal Soc. Can.; mem. Am. Cancer Soc., Am. Soc. Biol. Chemists, Am. Microbiol. Soc., N.Y. Acad. Scis., Am. Soc. Cell Biology, Phi Beta Kappa. Office: Rutgers U Nelson Biol Labs 604 Allison Rd Piscataway NJ 08854-8000 Office Phone: 732-445-4569. Business E-Mail: denhardt@biology.rutgers.edu.

DEN HARTOG, GRACE ROBINSON, lawyer; b. Richmond, Va., Jan. 19, 1952; d. Eldred Hiter and Jane Haddon (Pitt) Robinson; m. Wilhelm H. King, June 14, 1997; children: Jonathan Wilhelm, Mary Douglas. BA, U. Richmond, 1974; JD, U. Va., 1980. Bar: Va. 1980, US Dist. Ct. Ea. and We. Districts Va. 1984, US Ct. Appeals 4th Cir. 1983, Tex. 1993. Assoc. Tremblay & Smith, Charlottesville, Va., 1980-83, McGuire, Woods, Battle & Boothe LLP (McGuire Woods LLP as of 2000), Richmond, Va., 1984—90, ptnr., 1990—2003, chmn., product liability litig. mgmt. group, 1994-97, mem. associates com., 1992-97; sr. v.p., gen. counsel Owens & Minor Inc., Glen Allen, Va., 2003—. Mem. allocations com. United Way, Charlottesville, 1980-83; mem. Jefferson Area Cmty. Corrections Resources Bd., 1983-84. Named one of Nation's Top 50 Women Litigators, Nat. Law Jour., 2001. Mem. Va. Bar Assn., Va. State Bar (bd. governors young lawyers com. 1983-87, chmn. cir. representatives com. 1985-87; chmn. membership com. 1983-85). Office: Owens & Minor Inc 4800 Cox Rd Glen Allen VA 23060-6292

DENICE, MARCELLA L., counselor; b. 1934; BA in English, Our Lady of the Lake U., 1973, MA in Counseling, 1990. English tchr., volleyball/basketball coach Anson Jones Mid. Sch., San Antonio, 1974—80; head basketball coach Alamo Heights H.S., 1978—80; English tchr., cross-country track coach Burbank H.S., San Antonio, 1983—90; guidance counselor Highland Park Elem. Sch., San Antonio, 1990—. Bd. dirs. Nat. Bd. for Profl. Tchg. Stds.; mem. adv. com. for counselors San Antonio Ind. Sch. Dist., mem. dist. leadership team, 2002—. Mem. spkrs. bur. Am. Cancer Soc. Nominee H.E. Butt Grocery Chain Excellence in Tchg. award, 2005; named Outstanding Counselor of Yr., Tex. Counseling Assn., 1991, Tex. Tchr. of Yr., Peer Assistance Leadership Skills, 2002, Counselor of Yr., So. Tex. Counseling Assn., 2004; recipient Remarkable Woman award, Our Lady of the Lake, 1995. Mem.: So. Tax Counseling Assn. (named counselor of yr. 2004). Office: Highland Park Elem 635 Rigsby San Antonio TX 78210 Business E-Mail: marcella@fittingadventures.com.

DE NICOLA, ANTHONY J., investment company executive; m. Christie de Nicola, 1987; 3 children. BA in Econ. summa cum laude, DePauw Univ., 1986; MBA with distinction, Harvard Univ., 1990. Fin. analyst, mergers, acquisitions Goldman, Sachs; assoc. William Blair & Co., Chgo.; several positions to gen. ptnr. Welsh, Carson, Anderson & Stowe equity investments, NYC; and non-exec. co-chmn. Dex Media Inc. (acquired by Welsh, Carson, Anderson & Stowe), Englewood, Colo., 2002—. Alumni bd. pres. DePauw Univ., 1995—97, bd. trustees, 1997—2001. Recipient Young Alumni award, DePauw Univ., 2002. Mem.: Phi Beta Kappa. Roman Catholic. Office: Welsh Carson Anderson & Stowe Ste 2500 320 Park Ave New York NY 10022-6815 Office Phone: 212-893-9500. Office Fax: 212-893-9575.*

DENICOLA, T. KEVIN, chemicals executive; Grad. in chem. engring., U. Va., 1979. Ethylene products mgr. Lyondell Chem., Houston, 1993—96, dir., investor relations, 1996—98, v.p., corp. devel., 1998—2002, sr. v.p., CFO, 2002—. Mem.: Parnership Governance Com. of Equistar and LCR. Office: Lyondell Chem 1221 McKinney St Ste 1600 Houston TX 77253-3646

DENICUOLO, RITA MARIE, retired vice principal; b. Phila., Aug. 19, 1931; d. Anthony and Maria Domenica DeNicuolo. BS in Edn., Temple U., 1955, EdM, 1965. Tchr. Spanish Thomas Jr. High Sch., Phila., 1957, Northeast High Sch., 1957—69; head dept. fgn. lang. Olney High Sch, 1969—82; vice prin. Gillespie Jr. High Sch., 1982—86, Olney High Sch., 1988—93; ret., 1993. Acting prin. Gillespie Jr. High Sch., 1982, 1983—84; chmn. mid. states Olney High Sch., 1990—91. Recipient Italian Lang. Study medal, Sons Italy, 1949. Mem.: Pa. Assn. Sch. Retirees.

DENIG, STEPHEN JOSEPH, education educator; b. N.Y.C., June 14, 1948; s. Joseph Anthony and Marie Katherine (Smith) D. BA in Philosophy, Niagara U., 1971; MDiv, Mary Immaculate, Northampton, Pa., 1974, ThM, 1980; MA in Ednl. Adminstrn., Rider Coll., 1990; EdD, Rutgers U., 1994. Asst. pastor Queen of Miraculous Medal, Jackson, Mich., 1975-76; tchr. Archbishop Wood H.S., Warminster, Pa., 1976-85; headmaster St. Joseph's Seminary, Princeton, N.J., 1985-92; asst. prof. St. Johns U., Jamaica, NY, 1996—2002, Niagara U., NY, 2002—. Trustee United Way, Princeton, 1986-89, Bucks County coun. Boy Scouts Am., Doylestown, Pa., 1978-85, George Washington coun., Pennington, N.J., 1985-93, advisor Suanacky Lodge, 1993—. Mem. ASCD, Am. Edn. Rsch. Assn., Cath. Bibl. Assn. (assoc.), Phi Delta Kappa. Republican. Roman Catholic. Home and Office: Meade Hall Niagara Univ Niagara University NY 14109 Office Phone: 716-286-8213.

DENIGAN, SUSAN MARIE, lawyer; b. St. Louis, Nov. 1, 1957; d. Joseph J. and Albert (Kroner) S.; m. James Bernard Denigan, Oct. 6, 1989. BA, St. Louis U., 1980, JD, 1983. Bar: Mo. 1983, U.S. Dist. Ct. (ea. dist.) Mo. 1983, U.S. Ct. Appeals (8th cir.) 1983, Ill. 1984, Minn. 1990. Assoc. Ziercher & Hocker, St. Louis, 1983-86; assoc. counsel Eveready Battery Co. Inc., St. Louis, 1987-90, Protection Svcs. divsn. Honeywell Corp., Mpls., 1991; assoc. counsel litigation Ralston Purina Co., St. Louis, 1992-95, sr. counsel, 1995—, assoc. gen. counsel, 1996—; v.p., gen. counsel Nestlé Purina PetCare Co. (formerly Ralston Purina Co.), 2002—. Mem. ABA, Mo. Bar Assn., Ill. Bar Assn., Bar Assn. St. Louis. Office: Nestlé Purina PetCare Co Saint Louis MO 63164-0001 Office Phone: 314-982-1000.

DENINNO, DAVID L., lawyer; b. Pitts., Dec. 28, 1955; BA, U. Va., 1977; JD with honors, George Washington U., 1981. Bar: Pa. 1981. Law clerk to Judge Roger Robb US Ct. Appeals for DC Cir., 1981—82; with Reed Smith LLP, Pitts., 1981—; now ptnr., mem. exec. com., chair bus. & regulatory dept. Office: Reed Smith LLP PO Box 2009 Pittsburgh PA 15230-2009 Office Phone: 412-288-3214. Office Fax: 412-288-3063. Business E-Mail: ddeninno@reedsmith.com.

DENIOUS, SHARON MARIE, retired publishing executive; b. Rulo, Nebr., Jan. 27, 1941; d. Thomas Wayne and Alma (Murphy) Fee; m. Jon Parks Denious, June 17, 1963; children: Timothy Scot, Elizabeth Denious Cessna. Grad. high sch. Operator N.W. Pipeline co., Ignacio, Colo., 1975-90; pub. The Silverton Standard & The Miner, Colo., 1990-99. Avocations: reading, hiking. E-mail: denious@frontier.net.

DENIRO, MARY LYN S., lawyer; b. Salt Lake City, Feb. 15, 1959; d. Ted Gordon and Marilyn Valoe (Butcher) Symes; m. Dan DeNiro. BS magna cum laude, U. Utah, 1980; JD magna cum laude, Fordham U., 1992. Bar: N.Y. 1993. Exec. asst. to chmn. ASARCO Inc., NYC, 1983-91, legal asst., 1991-92; jud. clk. US Dist. Ct. (ea. dist.), Bklyn., 1992-93; assoc. Davis Polk & Wardwell, NYC, 1993-99; v.p., legal counsel Zurich Centre Group, NYC, 1999—2003; v.p. Counsel Ace Capital Re Inc., 2003. Mem. Order of Coif, Phi Kappa Phi, Phi Eta Sigma. Office: Ace Fin Svc 1325 Ave of the Americas New York NY 10019

DE NIRO, ROBERT, actor, film producer, film director, restaurant owner; b. NYC, Aug. 17, 1943; s. Robert and Virginia De Niro; m. Diahnne Abbott, 1976 (div. 1988); 1 child, Raphael Eugene, 1 stepchild, Drina; m. Grace Hightower, June 17, 1997; 1 child, Elliot; 2 children, Aaron Kendric DeNiro, Julian Henry De Niro (with Toukie Smith). Studied acting with, Stella Adler, Lee Strasberg. Co-founder Tribeca Productions, 1988, Tribeca Film Festival, 2002; co-owner Tribeca Grill, 1990, Nobu, NYC, 1994, Rubicon, San Francisco, 1994. Actor: (films) The Wedding Party, 1969, Hi, Mom!, 1970, Bloody Mama, 1970, Jennifer On My Mind, 1971, Born to Win, 1971, The Gang That Couldn't Shoot Straight, 1971, Bang the Drum Slowly, 1973, Mean Streets, 1973, The Godfather, Part II, 1974 (Acad. award best supporting actor), The Last Tycoon, 1976, 1900, 1976, Taxi Driver, 1976, New York, New York, 1977, The Deer Hunter, 1978, Raging Bull, 1980 (Acad. award best actor), True Confessions, 1981, The King of Comedy, 1982, Once Upon a Time in America, 1984, Falling in Love, 1984, Brazil, 1984, The Mission, 1985, Angel Heart, 1987, The Untouchables, 1987, Midnight Run, 1988, Jacknife, 1989, Stanley & Iris, 1990, Goodfellas, 1990, Awakenings, 1991 (Acad. award nom.), Backdraft, 1991, Cape Fear, 1991, Guilty By Suspicion, 1991, Mistress, 1992, Night and the City, 1992, Mad Dog and Glory, 1993, This Boy's Life, 1993, Mary Shelley's Frankenstein, 1994, Casino, 1995, Heat, 1995, The Fan, 1996, Marvin's Room, 1996, Sleepers, 1996, Copland, 1997, Great Expectations, 1998, 15 Minutes, 1999, Analyze This, 1999, Flawless, 1999, The Score, 2001, Showtime, 2002, Analyze That, 2002, Godsend, 2004, (voice) Shark Tale, 2004, Hide and Seek, 2005; actor, exec. prodr.: (films) We're No Angels, 1989, Meet the Parents, 2000; actor, prodr.: (films) Wag the Dog, 1997, Lenny Bruce: Swear to Tell the Truth, 1998, The Adventures of Rocky and Bullwinkle, 1999, Meet the Fockers, 2004; actor, dir.: (films) A Bronx Tale, 1993; dir., actor: (films) City by the Sea, 2002; (plays) Strange Show, 1982; (documentaries) Dear America: Letters Home From Vietnam, 1987; prodr.: (films) Entropy, 1999, About a Boy, 2002, Stage Beauty, 2004; co-prodr.: Thunderheart, 1992; exec. prodr.: (TV films) Tribeca, 1993, Holiday Heart, 2000; (films) Faithful, 1996, Navy Driver, 2000, Conjugating Niki, 2000. Named Greatest Living Movie Star, Empire Mag., 2004; recipient Hasty Pudding award, Harvard U., 1979, D.W. Griffith award for best actor, 1990. Office: Creative Artists Agy 9830 Wilshire Blvd Beverly Hills CA 90212-1825*

DENISE, THEODORE CULLOM, philosophy educator; b. Whitewater, Wis., Mar. 9, 1919; s. Malcolm F. and Margaret E. (Lawrence) D.; m. Kathleen W. Cowles, Oct. 4, 1942; children: Patricia Denise White, Theodore Cullom (dec.). BA, U. Mich., 1942, MA, 1947, PhD, 1955. Teaching fellow U. Mich., 1946-48; mem. faculty Syracuse U., 1948—, assoc. prof. philosophy, 1959-64, prof. philosophy, 1964-89, prof. emeritus philosophy, 1989—, chmn. dept., 1959-72, chmn. humanities depts., 1973-76; dir. liberal studies Inst. Univ. Adminstrs., 1961-63; dir. of semester in Italy, 1967-68, 76-77; dir. grad. studies in philosophy, 1976-84; mem. editl. com. Univ. Press, 1972-78. Co-author (editor): Great Traditions in Ethics, 1953, 2d edit., 2005; author: The Social Writings of Bertrand Russell, 1955, Contemporary Philosophy and Its Origins, 1967, Retrospect and Prospect, 1956; contbr. articles to philos. jours. Served with AUS, 1942-46. Mem. Assn. Symbolic Logic, Am. Philos. Assn., Alpha Kappa Lambda. Home: 8 Cranberry Ln Easthampton MA 01027 Office: Syracuse U Dept Philosophy Syracuse NY 13244-0001 Personal E-mail: teddenise@juno.com.

DENISH, DIANE D., lieutenant governor; d. Libby Donley and Jack Daniels; m. Herb Denish; 3 children. Assoc. pub., bus. devel. and advt. sales Starlight Pub. Ltd., Albuquerque Living and NMex. Monthly, Albuquerque; state chmn. N.Mex Dem. Party, 1999—2001; former owner Target Group; lt. gov. State of Nev., 2003—. Chair Children's Cabinet, Mortgage Fin. Authority, Mil. Base Planning Commn., Ind. Devel. Account Adv. Coun.; active Equal Pay Task Force, Spaceport Commn., Border Authority, Fin. Independence Task Force, Workforce Devel. Bd., Commn. on Volunteerism; trustee N.Mex. Mil. Inst. Found. Bd.; former chair N.Mex. First, N.Mex. Cmty. Found., N.Mex. Tech. Bd. Regents; former mem. N.Mex. Commn. on the Status of Women; former mem. nat. adv. bd. Small Bus. Adminstrn.; pres. N.Mex. State Senate; bd. mem. Daniels Fund. Named 2003 YWCA New Mexican of Vision; named one of Top 100 New Mexicans in honor of her cmty. leadership. Democrat. Address: 1301 San Pedro Albuquerque NM 87110 Office: State Capitol, Ste 417 Santa Fe NM 87501*

DENISON, CYNTHIA LEE, accountant, tax specialist; b. Hyannis, Mass., Feb. 1, 1956; d. Gordon Avery Denison, Elizabeth Theresa Bourque-Denison; children: Randall Wayne Brown, Shaun Avery Brown, Kelly Joseph Brown. BS in Bus. Adminstrn., Hawaii Pacific U., 1990. Office mgr., tax preparer H&R Block, Fayetteville, NC, 1979—83; asst. acct., acctg. supr. Dept. of Def. Acctg. and Fin., Germany, 1984—86; revenue agt. IRS, Bailey's Crossroads, Va., 1990—91, taxpayer rep., 1991—97, lead tax specialist, 1997—2000, sr. tax specialist, taxpayer rep., 2000—. Electronic filing No. Va. coord. IRS, Bailey's Crossroads, 1998—. Unoffical scoutmaster and cubmaster, den mother, com. mem., counselor Boy Scouts Am., Honolulu, 1986—90; football, baseball, soccer coach Moral, Recreation & Welfare, Honolulu, 1986—90; baseball coach Youth Sports, Spring Lake, NC, 1981—83. Mem.: AAUW, Statue of Liberty/Ellis Island Soc., Smithsonian Instn., Nat. Preservation Soc., Nat. Geog. Soc., Denison Soc., Nat. Geneal. Soc., New Eng. Hist. and Geneal. Soc. Avocations: genealogy, historic preservation, animal preservation, reading, crafts. Home: 2909 Marsala Ct Woodbridge VA 22192 Personal E-mail: cdenison88@comcast.net.

DENISON, JAMES DICKEY, retired broadcasting executive; b. Clarendon, Tex., July 1, 1926; s. Dallas D. and Gladys (Condron) D.; m. Jo Beth Huser, June 27, 1965; children: Jack D., P. Dianne, Robert Ladd, Kathryn Anne Denison (Kit). Student, McMurry Coll., 1943, student, 1946, U. Tex., 1947—49; BArch, U. Houston, 1952. Contracting engr. Am. Bridge divsn. U.S. Steel, Houston, 1952-60; co-owner, v.p. Globe Equipment Rental, Houston, 1961-67; owner, operator B & B Steel, Hobbs, N.Mex., 1967-73; co-owner, CEO VLA Fabrication divsn. Structures, Inc., Hobbs, 1973-79; owner, operator Denison's Photography, Kingwood, Tex., 1979-82, Sta. KKTC-FM, Brownfield, Tex., 1985-96; ret., 1996. Chmn. N.Mex. State Hwy. Commn., 1974-79; congl. aide U.S. Congressman Harold Runnels, N.Mex., 1971-72. Served with USN, 1944-46, PTO. Mem. Brownfield C. of C., Rotary (v.p. Hobbs club 1971-72). Democrat. Methodist. Avocations: photography, fishing. Home: 1002 E Cardwell Brownfield TX 79316-4608 Office Phone: 806-637-3777. E-mail: jden140847@aol.com.

DENISON, JULIAN RAIN, lighting designer, writer; b. Flemington, NJ, Aug. 29, 1971; s. Vernon Brian Anderson and Meredith Vivian Walling. Ordained min. Ch. of Spiritual Humanism, 2003. Tech. adminstr. Nelson Enterprises, Frenchtown, NJ, 1994—2002; mgmt. Circuit Lighting, Inc., Green Brook, NJ, 1992—94; cons., designer, author Oldwick, NJ, 2002—. Mem.: Tewksbury Rep. Club. R-Liberal. Avocations: reading, travel, stained glass art, gothic culture, gay culture. Personal E-mail: designcolour@aol.com.

DENISON, MARY BONEY, lawyer; b. Wilmington, N.C., June 8, 1956; d. Leslie Norwood Jr. and Lillian (Bellamy) Boney; m. John R. Clark III; children: Mary Catesby Bellamy, James Wholley IV. AB, Duke U., 1978; JD, U. N.C., 1981. Bar: N.Y. 1982, U.S. Dist. Ct. (so. and ea. dists.) N.Y. 1983, U.S. Ct. Appeals (2d cir.) 1984, DC 1988, U.S. Dist. Ct. DC 1988, U.S. Ct. Appeals (DC cir.) 1988. Assoc. Law Office William G. Kaelin, N.Y.C., 1981-82, Smith, Steibel, Alexander & Saskor, N.Y.C., 1982-86, Graham & James, Washington, 1986-91, ptnr., 1992-96, Farkas & Manelli PLLC, Washington, 1996-2000, Manelli, Denison & Selter, PLLC, Washington, 2001—. Vol. Legal Aid Soc., N.Y.C., 1983—86. Mem.: ABA, Internat. Trademark Assn. (vice chair treaty analysis com. 2000—01, chair treaty analysis com. 2001—03, bd. dirs. 2003—), French Am. C. of C. Washington (treas. 1991—97). Democrat. Episcopalian. Office: Manelli Denison & Selter PLLC 2000 M St NW Ste 700 Washington DC 20036-3364 Office Phone: 202-261-1000. Business E-Mail: mdenison@mdslaw.com.

DENISOV, ANDREY I., international organization administrator; b. Kharkov, USSR, Oct. 3, 1952; married; 1 child. Grad., Moscow State Inst. Internat. Rels., 1974; post-grad. student, Inst. Internat. Polit. and Econ. Studies, 1974—77; PhD in Econ. Hold diplomatic rank of Amb. Extraordinary and Plenipotentiary. Interpreter Trade Representation of the USSR in the People's Republic of China, 1973—74, economist, 1978—81; expert, dep. head, head of sect. of People's Republic of China CPSU Central Com., 1981—91; counselor, sr. counselor, min.-counselor Embassy of the Russian Fedn. in People's Republic of China, 1992—97; dir., dept. econ. cooperation Ministry Foreign Affairs of the Russianh Fedn., 1997—2000; mem. Ministry Foreign Affairs Collegium, 1998; amb. Russian Fedn. to the Arab Republic of Egypt, 2000—01; dep. min. Foreign Affairs of the Russian Fedn., 2001—04; permanent rep. of Russian Fedn. UN, 2004—. Office: 136 E 67th St New York NY 10021 Business E-Mail: rusun@un.int.

DENITTIS, ALBERT STEPHEN, oncologist; b. Phila., Mar. 22, 1965; s. Albert Peter and Theresa DeNittis; m. Lisa Bassano, Oct. 14, 1995; children: Andrew Stephen, Julianna Lisa. MS, Rutgers U., 1990; MD, Robert Wood Johnson Med. Sch., 1995. Diplomate Am. Bd. Radiology, 2000. Med. intern Cooper Hosp., Camden, NJ, 1996; resident U. Pa., Phila., 1998—2000; chief dept. radiation oncology Lankenau Hosp., Wynnewood, Pa., 2001—. Prin. investigator Radiation Therapy Oncology Group, Wynnewood, Pa., 2002—; co-dir. Man to Man, 2003—. Contbr. chapters to books, more than 35 articles to profl. jours. Mem.: AMA, Am. Coll. Radiology, Am. Soc. Clin. Oncology, Am. Soc. Therapeutic Radiation Oncology. Achievements include research in recipiant of Sharp grant for prostate research. Office: Lankenau Hosp 100 Lancaster Ave Wynnewood PA 19106 Office Phone: 610-645-2433. E-mail: denittisa@mlhs.org.

DENIZMAN, CAN, geologist, educator; b. Ankara, Turkey, Feb. 13, 1962; arrived in US, 1991; s. Ali and Neside Denizman; m. Isik Akyollu, Dec. 25, 1994; 1 child, Oya. PhD, U. Fla., 1998. Hydrogeologist and GIS analyst Jones & Edmunds Assocs., Gainesville, Fla., 2001; faculty Valdosta (Ga.) State U., 2001—. Contbr. articles to profl. jours. Mem.: Geol. Soc. Am. Office Phone: 229-249-2745. Personal E-mail: denizman@earthlink.net.

DENKE, CONRAD WILLIAM, motion picture producer; b. Cottonwood, Ariz., July 23, 1947; s. Lee Ernest and Barbara Ann (Russell) D.; m. Laura Lee Nielson; children: Alexander, Elisabeth. BA in Radio-TV Communications and Psychology, U. Wash., 1969. Dir. Sta. KCTS-TV, Seattle, 1967-69; dir. prodr. Cinema Assocs., Seattle, 1973-78; pres. Am. Motion Pictures, Seattle, 1978—2002; CEO Victory Studios, Seattle, 2002—. Bd. dirs. Am. Cinema Found., Whidbey Island Films; ptnr. Post Solutions, L.A., 2003—; publ., founder Highdef Mag., 2002—. Dir., producer: (indsl. documentary) Tunnels Under Chicago, 1981 (Chris award 1981, Gold award, Silver award, Cine Golden Eagle award, 1981); dir. (ednl. documentary) More Than Bows and Arrows, 1978 (Best Western Documentary 1978); producer: (TV series) Adventures on Sinclair Island, 1986, (talk show series) Teens Talk, (PBS documentary) Educations Wars, 1996, National Desk, 1997, 99. Mormon bishop, stake presidency. With USAF, 1969-73. Recipient Cine Golden Eagle award Council on Internat. Nontheatrical Events, 1977, 79, 89, 95, Silver Cindy award Info. Film Producers Am., 1977, 98, Gold Camera award U.S. Indsl. Film Festival, 1978, Telly award, 1989, 95, 97, 2 Telly's, 1998, 3 Gold awards Emerald City awards, 1997, 2000, World medal N.Y. Film Festival, 1998, 2 Aegis awards, 1998, 2 Aurora awards, 1998, Nat. ITVA award, 2000, Silver Screen award 2000. Mem. Internat. TV Assn. (dir. Seattle chpt. 1980-90, chpt. pres. 1983-84, chmn. HD Consortium for Nat. Assn. TV Program Execs., Silver Reel, 1986, Gold Reel 1997), Wash. Motion Picture Coun. (pres. 1992-96), Assn. Ind. Comml. Prodrs. (v.p. N.W. chpt. 1985-87, pres. 1987-90), Am. Cinema Found. in L.A. (bd. dirs., v.p. 1994—), Prodrs. Guild Am. Republican. Formed E Pluribus Unum Films in 2000. Office: Victory Studios 2247 15th Ave W Seattle WA 98119-2417 Office Phone: 206-282-1776. Business E-Mail: conrad@victorystudios.com.

DENKE, PAUL HERMAN, retired aircraft engineer; b. San Francisco, Feb. 7, 1916; s. Edmund Herman and Ella Hermine (Riehl) D.; m. Beryl Ann Lincoln, Feb. 10, 1940; children: Karen Denke Mottaz, Claudia Denke Tesche, Marilyn Denke Oliver. BCE, U. Calif.-Berkeley, 1937, MCE, 1939. Registered profl. engr., Calif. Stress engr. Douglas Aircraft Co., Santa Monica, Calif., 1940-62, mgr. structural mechanics Long Beach, Calif., 1962-65, chief sci. computing, 1965-71, chief structures engr. methods and devel., 1972-78, chief scientist structural mechanics, 1979-84, staff mgr. Boeing fellow, 1985-2000; ret., 2000. Mem. faculty dept. engring. UCLA, 1941-50. Author numerous tech. papers. Assoc. fellow AIAA; mem. Soc. Automotive Engrs. (Arch T. Colwell merit award 1966, IAE Outstanding Engr. merit award 1985), Sigma Xi, Chi Epsilon, Tau Beta Pi. Democrat. Achievements include pioneering and developing finite element method of structural analysis. Home: 1800 Via Estudillo Palos Verdes Peninsula CA 90274-1908 Personal E-mail: pauldenke@earthlink.net.

DENKER, HENRY, playwright, author, director; b. N.Y.C., Nov. 25, 1912; s. Max and Jennie (Geller) D.; m. Edith Rose Heckman, Dec. 5, 1942. LL.B., N.Y. Law Sch., 1934. Bar: N.Y. 1935. Practiced law, N.Y.C., 1935-38; exec. Research Inst. Am., N.Y.C., 1936-37; tax cons. Standard Stats. subs. Standard and Poor, N.Y.C., 1937-39. Lectr. dramatic writing Am. Theatre Wing, 1961-63, Coll. of the Desert. Writer, dir., prodr.: (radio series) The Greatest Story Ever Told, N.Y.C., 1947-57; author: (Broadway plays) Time Limit, 1956, A Far Country, 1961, Venus at Large, 1962, A Case of Libel, 1964, What Did We Do Wrong, 1968, Something Old, Something New, 1976, Horowitz and Mrs. Washington, 1979; (off-Broadway) The Name of the Game, 1967, A Sound of Distant Thunder, 1969, The Headhunters, 1974, CurtainCall, 1999; (screenplays) The Heartfarm, 1970, The Hook, Twilight of Honor, Time Limit, A Time for Miracles, 1980, Outrage, 1984; writer, dir., prodr. numerous TV dramas, 1950-66; TV spls. include Give Us Barrabas, 1964, Neither Are We Enemies, 1971, The Choice, The Court Martial of Lietenant Calley, Mother Seton, 1980, Love Leads the Way, 1985, Outrage, 1986, Case of Libel, 1986; author: I'll be Right Home Ma, 1949, My Son, The Lawyer, 1950, Salome, Princess of Galilee, 1954, That First Easter, 1956, The Director, 1970, The Kingmaker, 1972, A Place for the Mighty, 1973, The Physicians, 1975, The Experiment, 1976, The Starmaker, 1977, The Scofield Diagnosis, 1977, The Actress, 1978, The Error Judgement, 1979, Horowitz and Mrs. Washington, 1979, The Warfield Syndrome, 1981, Outrage!, 1982, The Healers, 1983, Kincaid, 1984, Love Leads the Way, 1985, A Case of Libel, 1985, Robert, My Son, 1985, Judge Spencer Dissents, 1986, The Choice, 1987, The Retreat, 1988, A Gift of Life, 1989, Payment in Full, 1990, Doctor on Trial, 1991, Labyrinth, 1994, This Child is Mine, 1995, To Marcy, With Love, 1996, A Place for Kathy, 1997, The Third Day, 1999, Benjie, 1999, Class Action, 2000, Clarence, 2002, Final Shooting Script, 2004. Recipient Peabody award, 1949; Christopher award, 1953; Emmy award, 1948 Mem. Acad. TV Arts and Scis. (coun.), Authors League (coun.), Dramatists Guild (coun. 1967-69), Authors Guild, Writers' Guild. Jewish. Address: 241 Central Park W New York NY 10024-4530 Office Phone: 212-873-5821. E-mail: hwdenker@aol.com.

DENLINGER, ANN T., school system administrator; b. Waynesville, N.C., July 15, 1944; m. Robert Denlinger; 1 child. B in Elem. Edn., Campbell Coll., 1966; M in Ednl. Adminstrn., Campbell U., 1982, D in Ednl. Adminstrn., 1992. Tchr. Harnett County Schs., 1966—68, Wake County Schs. and Raleigh (N.C.) City Schs., 1968—80; prin. A.V. Baucom Elem. Sch., 1980—82, Lynn Rd. Elem. Sch., 1982—85, Fuquay-Varina Mid. Sch., 1985—87; asst. supt. for elem. curriculum and instrn. Wake County Schs., 1990—92; supt. Wilson County Schs., 1992—97, Durham (N.C.) Pub. Schs., 1997—. Named Supt. of Yr., N.C. Assn. Sch. Adminstrs., 2000; recipient Disting. Alumna award, Campbell U., Reading Recovery Tchr. Leader award, Boston Tchr. Leader Inst., 2002. Avocations: following U. N.C. basketball and football, reading, landscaping, gardening. Office: Durham Pub Schs 511 Cleveland St PO Box 30002 Durham NC 27701

DENLINGER, EDGAR JACOB, electronics engineering executive, researcher; b. Lancaster, Pa., June 17, 1939; s. Victor Jacob and Marian Alice (Shoemaker) D.; m. Cynthia Della Wilson, June 24, 1967; children— Crystal Shereen, Craig Wesley BS in Engring. Sci., Pa. State U., 1961; MSE.E., U. Pa., 1964, PhD in E.E., 1969. Research engr. Applied Research RCA, Camden, NJ, 1961—65; research assoc. Moore Sch. U. Pa., Phila., 1965—67; mem. tech. staff MIT Lincoln Lab., Lexington, Mass., 1967—73, RCA Labs, Princeton, NJ, 1973—83, group head signal conversion systems research, 1983—87; group head microwave systems rsch. David Sarnoff Research Ctr., Princeton, NJ, 1987—92, sr. mem. tech. staff, 1992—2003; ret., 2003—. Adj. prof. dept. elec. engring. Drexel U., Phila., 1982-88. Contbr. articles to profl. jours. Patentee microwave devices and circuits Mem. Hickory Acres Civic Assn., East Windsor, N.J., 1973-81 Recipient Achievement award David Sarnoff Rsch. Ctr., Princeton, 1979, 94. Fellow IEEE (treas. sect. 1980-83, vice chmn. 1984, chmn. 1985) Lodges: Mason, Tall Cedars, Shriners. Republican. Presbyterian. Avocations: music, swimming. Home: 7 Wheatston Ct Princeton Junction NJ 08550-1936 Personal E-mail: edenlinger@msn.com.

DENLINGER, JOHN KENNETH, journalist; b. Lancaster, Pa., Mar. 25, 1942; s. John Emory and Elizabeth (Smith) D.; m. Nancy Dodson, July 29, 1995; children: Lauri, Scott. BS in Econs, Pa. State U., 1964. Mem. staff Pitts. Press, 1964-66; mem. staff Washington Post, 1995—2005; sports columnist, 1975-90. Author: For the Glory, 1994; co-author: Athletes for Sale, 1975, Redskin Country: From Baugh to the Super Bowl, 1983, Golf: The Mind Game, 1990, Tennis: The Mind Game, 1991, Skiing: The Mind Game, 1993. Named to U.S. Basketball Writers Assn. Hall of Fame, 2001.

DENMARK, BERNHARDT, manufacturing executive; b. Bklyn., June 6, 1917; s. William M. and Kate (Lazarus) D.; m. Muriel Schechter, Sept. 22, 1943; children: Richard J., Karen. AB, NYU, 1941; postgrad., Am. U., 1941-42, Nat. Inst. Pub. Affairs, 1941-42. Vice pres. sales Telecoin Corp., N.Y.C., 1946-49; v.p. sales Internat. Latex Corp., N.Y.C., 1949-55; mgr. mktg. Playtex Co., N.Y.C., 1955-59, v.p., gen. mgr. family products div., 1959-63, v.p. mktg., 1963-65; pres. Playtex Co. Playtex div., 1965-67, Internat. Playtex Corp., N.Y.C., 1968-69, chmn. bd., 1969; exec. v.p., dir., mem. exec. com. Glen Alden Corp., N.Y.C., 1969-72; pres. Bevis Industries, Inc., White Plains, N.Y., 1972-76, Bus. Mktg. Corp. for N.Y.C., 1977-78; chmn. Denmark, Donovan & Oppel Inc., N.Y.C., 1978-85; chmn. bd. dirs. Advanced Photonix, Inc., Camarillo, Calif., 1992—, Xsirius, Inc., Camarillo, 1992—. Bd. dirs. Stanley Warner Corp., Schenley Industries, BVD Corp., Kleinerts Inc., Advanced Photonics Inc. Served to capt. AUS, 1942-46. Mem.: Fairview Country (Greenwich, Conn.). Home: 870 United Nations Plz Apt 34B New York NY 10017-1820

DENMARK, DARRON B., academic administrator; b. Hollywood, Fla., May 7, 1968; s. Ellen D and Henry R Taylor (Stepfather). BA in Pub. Adminstrn., Fla. Meml. Coll., Miami, 1999; MA in Orgnl. Mgmt., U. of Phoenix, Ft. Lauderdale, Fla., 2001; MPA in Pub. Adminstrn. (Pub. Policy), Clark Atlanta U., Atlanta, 2003. Appeals analyst United Healthcare of Ga., Atlanta, 1997—2001; compliance specialist Emory U., Atlanta, 2001—. With USAR, 1987—95. Mem.: Nat. Forum for Black Pub. Adminstrs. (assoc.). Democrat. Home: 305 Avery Glen Decatur GA 30030 Office: Emory University 1256 Briarcliff Rd 4th Flr Atlanta GA 30306 Personal E-mail: dbdenm@aol.com.

DENMARK, STANLEY JAY, orthodontist; b. Queens, N.Y., May 26, 1927; s. Jack and Frieda (Kirschenbaum) D.; m. Florence Levin, June 7, 1953 (div. June 1973); children: Valerie, Pamela (dec.) and Richard (twins); m. Anita Goodman, Jan. 2, 1983. BS, Queens Coll., 1950; MSc, NYU, 1955; DDS, U. Pa., 1955, orthodontics cert., 1957. Diplomate Am. Bd. Orthodontics. Practice dentistry specializing in orthodontics, Westbury, N.Y., 1955-91; asst. prof. orthodontics Fairleigh Dickinson U., Hackensack, N.J., 1974-79; clin. assoc. prof. growth and devel. scis. (orthodontics) Sch. Dentistry NYU, 1991—. With USN, 1945-47. Mem. ADA, Am. Assn. Orthodontists, Northeastern Soc. Orthodontists, Coll. Diplomates of Am. Bd. Orthodontists, Sigma Xi. Jewish. Avocations: painting, woodcuts, tennis, cross country skiing. Office: NYU Coll Dentistry 345 E 24th St New York NY 10010-4086 Home: 351 E 54th St #6B New York NY 10022-4943 Office Phone: 212-759-2209.

DENN, CYRIL JOSEPH, retired financial advisor; b. Mankato, Minn., Jan. 23, 1948; s. Bertram Henry and Hildegard M. (Drummer) D.; m. Sandra Lee Jones, Oct. 22, 1966 (div. 1970); m. Darlene Kay Wittrock, Apr. 19, 1974; children: Darcy Ann, Amanda Kay, Cassandra Jo. BS, Mankato State U., 1977; ChFC, Am. Coll., 1985. Chartered Life Underwriter, Chartered Financial Cons. Factory laborer Kato Engring. Co., Mankato, 1971—74; sales rep. Met. Life, Mankato, 1974—76, sales mgr., 1976—79, sales rep., 1979—82, mktg. specialist Aurora, Ill., 1982—83, br. mgr. Sioux Falls, SD, 1983—84, sales rep., 1984—86; regional mgr. Cath. Aid Assn., St. Paul, 1986—89; mgr. Prudential Ins. Co., Sioux Falls, 1989—91, Aberdeen, SD, 1992—94; asst. mgr. Farm Bur. Fin. Svcs., Aberdeen, 1995—96; fin. advisor Bus., Estate, Retirement & Ins. Planning, Mankato, 1996—2000; fin. svcs. rep. Denn Ins. & Fin. Svcs., 1996—2000; fin. svcs. exec., fin. planner MetLife Fin. Svcs., Mankato, 1997—2000; ret., 2001. Mem. St. Clair (Minn.) Pub. Sch. Bd., 1981-83. With U.S. Army, 1968-71. Fellow: Life Underwriters Tng. Coun.; mem.: So. Minn. Soc. Fin. Svc. Profls., Farmamerica (devel. com., mktg. com., programs com., amb. program 2003—), Ea. S.D. Soc. Fin. Svc. Profls. (pres. 1992—93, video teleconf. coord. 1992—96), Greater Mankato Area C. of C. (bus. devel. com. 1996—2001, bus. devel. chair 2000—01), Am. Legion (post 475), Leave-A-Legacy (Mankato Chpt.) (chmn. mem. com. 1997—), S.D. Planned Giving Coun. (steering com. 1994—95, chair 1995—2001, v.p. programs), Soc. Fin. Svc. Profls. (profl. achievement in cont. edn. com. 1991—94, midwest liaison team 1992—2000, mem. devel. com. 1994—97), NAIFA (bd. dirs. Aberdeen chpt. 1992—96, chmn. life underwriters tng. coun. S.D. chpt. 1993—96, sec.-treas. Aberdeen chpt. 1994—95, pres. elect Aberdeen chpt. 1995—96, bd. dirs. Sioux Falls chpt. 1991—92, edn. chmn. Sioux Falls chpt., co-chmn. life underwriting tng. coun. Sioux Falls chpt.), Gen. Agy. Mgrs. Assn. (career devel. award 1994), Midwest Pony of Americas Club (pres. 1988—91, horse show chmn. 1989), S.D. Ponies of Americas Club (bd. dirs. 1986—97, pres. 1987—89). Independent. Roman Catholic. Avocations: horses, reading. Personal E-mail: cydenn@gotocrystal.net. Business E-Mail: cydenn@hickorytech.net.

DENNARD, ROBERT HEATH, engineering executive, scientist; b. Terrell, Tex., Sept. 5, 1932; s. Buford Leon and Loma (Heath) Dennard; m. Jane Bridges; children: Robert(dec.), Amy, Holly. BSEE, So. Methodist U., 1954, MSEE, 1956; PhD, Carnegie Inst. Tech., 1958. Staff engr. IBM, Yorktown Heights, NY, 1958—63; rsch. staff mem. IBM Rsch. Ctr., Yorktown Heights, NY, 1963—71, group mgr., 1971—79, fellow, 1979—. Contbr. articles to profl. jours.; patentee (scientific works) in field, including basic dynamic RAM memory cell. Named Inventor of Yr., N.Y. Intellectual Property Law Assn., 1995; named to Nat. Inventors Hall of Fame, 1997; recipient Nat. medal of Tech., Pres. U.S., 1988, Harvey prize, Technion-Israel Inst. Tech., 1990, Aachener and Munchener prize for tech. and applied sci., 2001, Lifetime Achievement award, Lemelson MIT, 2005. Fellow: IEEE (Edison medal 2001); mem.: Am. Philos. Soc., NAE. Avocation: Scottish country dancing. Office: IBM Rsch Ctr PO Box 218 Yorktown Heights NY 10598-0218

DENNEE, PETER DANIEL, music educator, conductor; b. Neenah, Wis., Jan. 10, 1964; s. Lawrence Peter and Yvonne Anne Dennee; m. Eliza Carpenter Dennee, Apr. 14, 1990; 1 child, Isaiah Richard. MusD Arts, Ariz. State U., 1996. Vis. asst. prof. of music U. Mich., Ann Arbor, 1995—96, U. Colo., Boulder, 1996—97; music dept. chair, coord. of music edn. Susquehanna U., Selinsgrove, Pa., 1997—2001; asst. prof. of music W.Va. U., Morgantown, 2001—; dir. of music First Presbyn. Ch., Morgantown, 2001—. Mem.: Soc. for Edn., Music, and Psychology Rsch., Am. Choral Directors Assn., Coll. Music Soc., Nat. Assn. of Music Educators (state rsch. and grants chair 2001—05). Office: WVa Univ CAC-Music Evansdale Drive Morgantown WV 26506-6111 Office Phone: 304-293-4617 ext. 3172. E-mail: peter.dennee@mail.wvu.edu.

DENNEEN, JOHN PAUL, lawyer; b. N.Y.C., Aug. 18, 1940; s. John Thomas Denneen and Pauline Jane Ludlow; m. Mary Veronica Murphy, July 3, 1965 (dec. Dec. 2000); children: John Edward, Thomas Michael, James Patrick, Robert Andrew, Daniel Joseph, Mary Elizabeth; m. Ginger O'Brien, Feb. 21, 2004. BS, Fordham U., 1963; JD, Columbia U., 1966. Bar: N.Y. 1966, U.S. Ct. Appeals (2d cir.) 1974, U.S. Dist. Ct. (so. and ea. dists.) N.Y. 1975, Mo. 1987. Assoc. Seward & Kissel, N.Y.C., 1966-75; sr. v.p., gen counsel, sec. GK Techs., Inc., Greenwich, Conn., 1975-83; exec. v.p., gen. counsel, sec. Chromalloy Am. Corp., St. Louis, 1983-87; ptnr. Bryan Cave LLP, St. Louis, 1987-99; exec. v.p. corp. devel. and legal affairs, sec. NuVox, Inc., St. Louis, 1999—. Mem. ABA, Internat. Bar Assn., N.Y. State Bar Assn., N.Y.C. Bar Assn., Bar Assn. Met. St. Louis. Office: NuVox Inc Ste 500 16090 Swingley Ridge Rd Chesterfield MO 63017-6029 Office Phone: 636-537-7356.

DENNEHY, BRIAN, actor; b. Bridgeport, Conn., July 9, 1938; m. Judith Scheff, 1959 (div. 1974); 3 children; m. Jennifer Arnott, 1988; 1 adopted child. Grad., Columbia U.; postgrad., Yale U. Appeared in motion pictures Semi-Tough, 1977, F.I.S.T., 1978, Foul Play, 1978, Butch and Sundance: The Early Days, 1979, 10, 1979, Little Miss Marker, 1980, Split Image, 1982, First Blood, 1982, Never Cry Wolf, 1983, Gorky Park, 1983, Twice in a Lifetime, 1985, Silverado, 1985, Cocoon, 1985, F/X, 1986, Legal Eagles, 1986, Best Seller, 1987, The Belly of an Architect, 1987, Return to Snowy River, 1988, Miles from Home, 1988, Cocoon: The Return, 1988, The Last of the Finest, Seven Minutes, Presumed Innocent, 1990, F/X 2, 1991, Gladiators, 1991, Midnight Movie, 1993, Gilligan's Island: The Movie, 1997, Tommy Boy, 1995, The Stars Fell on Henrietta, 1995, Romeo and Juliet, 1996, Dish Dogs, 1998, Out of the Cold, 1999, Deep River, Finders, Keepers, Looking for Mr. Goodbar, Summer Catch, 2001, Stolen Summer, 2002, She Hate Me, 2004, Assault on Precinct 13, 2005; theatre appearances include Streamers, off-Broadway, 1976, The Rat in the Skull, Death of a Salesman (Tony award 1999), Wisdom Bridge Theatre, Chgo., 1985, The Cherry Orchard, Bklyn. Acad. Music, 1988, The Iceman Cometh, Goodman Theatre, Chgo., 1990, Says I, Says He, Sea Plays, Bus Stop, Julius Caesar, Ivanov, The Front Page, Translations, Galileo, A Touch of the Poet, Goodman Theatre, Chgo., MacBeth, Romeo & Juliet, 1996, Long Days Journey into Night (Tony award winner for best actor), 2003); appeared in TV series Big Shamus, Little Shamus, 1979, Star of the Family, 1982-83, Birdland, 1993-94, (BBC series) Nostromo, 1995, A Season in Purgatory, 1996, Undue Influence, 1996, Larry McMurty's Dean Man Walk, 1996; numerous movies for TV including Annie Oakley, Showtime Cable TV Tall Tales and Legends series, 1985, Acceptable Risk, 1986, HBO prodn. The Lion of Africa, 1987, Perfect Witness, 1989 (Cable Ace nominee), The Last of the Finest, 1990, Shattered Vows, 1993, Murder in the Heartland, 1993 (Emmy nomination, Supporting Actor - Miniseries or Special, 1993), Prophet of Evil, 1993, Foreign Affair, 1993 (CableAce award, Best Actor in a movie or miniseries), Rising Son, Bloodfeud, Evergreen, Acceptable Risks, The Terrorist, A Rumor of War, In Broad Daylight, The Last Place on Earth, Teamster Boss: The Jackie Presser Story, Birdland, Leave of Absence, Jack Reed: An Honest Cop, Final Appeal, Pride and Extreme Prejudice, (miniseries) A Killing in a Small Town, 1990 (Emmy nominee for Outstanding Supporting Actor), To Catch a Killer, 1991 (Emmy nominee, Am TV awards nominee), The Burden of Proof, 1992 (Emmy nominee for Outstanding Supporting Actor), A Season in Purgatory, 1996, Nostromo, 1996, Dead Man's Walk, 1996, Day One, Undue Influence, 1996; dir., co-writer, actor, co-exec. prodr.: (TV movies) Jack Reed: Champion of the Cheap Homicide, Jack Reed: A Killer Amoungst Us, Jack Reed: One of Our Own, Shadow of A Doubt, Jack Reed: A Search for Justice, Jack Reed: Death and Vengeance, 1996, Netforce, 1999, Too Rich: The Secret Life of Doris Duke, Fail Safe, 2000, A Season on the Brink, 2002, Our Fathers, 2005; exec. prodr. (TV films) Three Blind Mice, 2001, Warden of Red Rock, 2001, Death of a Salesman, 2000. Served with USMC, Vietnam Mem.: Sigma Chi. Office: c/o Susan Smith & Assocs 121 N San Vicente Blvd Beverly Hills CA 90211-2303*

DENNEHY, RAYMOND LEO, philosopher, educator; b. San Francisco, Aug. 31, 1934; s. Joseph Patrick and Mary Agnes Dennehy; m. Maryann Dennehy, Aug. 4, 1990; children: Mark, Bridget, Andrea, Rosalind. BA, in Philosophy, U. San Francisco, 1962; postgrad., U. Calif., Berkeley, 1962—64; PhD in Philosophy, U. Toronto, 1973. Asst. prof. philosophy U. Santa Clara, Calif., 1966—72; instr. philosophy West Valley C.C., Saratoga, Calif., 1972—74; asst. dean, lectr. philosophy U. San Francisco, 1974—79, assoc. prof. philosophy, 1979—85, prof. philosophy, 1985—. Founding mem., tchr. St. Ignatius Inst., U. San Francisco, 1976—2001, Campion Coll., San Francisco, 2002—. Author: Reason & Dignity, 1981, Anti-Abortionist at Large, 2002; editor: Christian Married Love, 1981. With USN, 1954—58, PTO. Recipient Human Life award, San Francisco United for Life, 1999, St. Luke's award, San Francisco Guild of the Cath. Med. Assn., 2004, 1st ann. St. Luke's award, San Francisco Guild Cath. Med. Assn., 2004. Mem.: Cath. Acad. Scis. U.S.A., Nat. Assn. Scholars, Am. Soc. for Bioethics and Humanities, Fellowship of Cath. Scholars (bd. dirs. 1984—87), Am. Cath. Philos. Assn. (exec. com. 1983—86), Am. Maritain Assn. (pres. 1986—94, Humanitarian award 2003). Republican. Roman Catholic. Office: Univ San Francisco Philosophy Dept 2130 Fulton St San Francisco CA 94117 Office Phone: 415-422-6456.

DENNERY, LINDA, newspaper publishing executive; b. Phila., July 7, 1947; V.p., gen. mgr. Times-Picayune, New Orleans, 1987—97, pres., mem. of advisory bd., 1997—99; pub. Star-Ledger, Newark, 1999—2004; exec. v.p. benefits Advance Newspaper Group, 2004—. Bd. dirs. Kingsley House, Touro Infirmary, Bur. Govtl. Rsch., So. Newspaper Pub. Assn., Internat. Women's Forum. Mem.: bd. of dir. of Kingsley House, Touro Infirmary, Bureau of Governmental Research, Southern Newspaper Pub. Assoc., International Women's Forum. Office: Exec VP Benefits Advance Publications Inc 950 Fingerboard Rd Staten Island NY 10305 Office Phone: 212-286-2860.*

DENNEY, ARTHUR HUGH, management consultant; b. Rosendale, Mo., Sept. 25, 1916; s. Frank M. and Cora L. (Beatie) D.; m. A. Ilene Tucker, Aug. 5, 1939 (dec. Jan. 1995); children: Charles Hugh, Jo Ann (Mrs. Raymond Fisher); m. Dorothy May Stammerjohn Cline, July 10, 1998. BS, U. Mo., 1938, MA in Econs., 1950; Diploma in Cmty. Devel., U. London, 1969. Technician U.S. Forest Service, Mo., 1938; state coordinator Mo. Conservation Commn., Jefferson City, 1938-44; recreation dir. Mo. Dept. Resources and Devel., Jefferson City, 1944-45, dir., 1945-48; owner, operator Blue Springs (Mo.) Lodge Resort, 1948-50, 54-57; adminstrv. asst. McDonnell Aircraft, St. Louis, 1950-54; instr. regional and community affairs U. Mo., Columbia, 1958-67, asso. prof., 1967-70, prof., 1970-79, prof. emeritus, 1980, chmn. dept., 1968, 73-75; dir. rural planning and devel. Black and Veatch Internat., 1979-82; pvt. cons., 1982—. Cons. USDA, U.S. Dept. Labor, U.S. Dept. Commerce, Purdue U., U. Ark., Govt. of Indonesia, Govt. of Thailand; rsch. cons. for local history and genealogy in field. Author: Decongesting Metropolitan America, 1972, Growth Centers in America 1950-1990, 1993, 20 vols. Regional Profiles of Missouri, 1973-76; contbr. articles to profl. jours. Chmn. civic improvement com. Columbia Indsl. Commn., 1966-68; chmn. Greater Columbia Planning Com., 1960-62. Danforth fellow, 1937 Mem. AAAS, SAR, Comty. Devel. Soc. N.Am. (dir. 1973—, pres. 1976-77), Nat. Univ. Ext. Assn. (adminstrv. bd. 1975-76), Am. Assn. Ret. Persons, Masons, Alpha Gamma Rho, Alpha Zeta. Home: 208 Westridge Dr Columbia MO 65203-1768

DENNEY, KEVIN SCOTT, secondary school educator; b. Jacksonville, Fla., Mar. 4, 1960; s. George Scott and Madelyn Cottle Denney; m. Lisa Voigt, June 22, 1990; children: Patrick, Hannah. BA in History, Presbyn. Coll.; MEdn, Kennesaw State U., 1998. Cert. tchr. secondary history 7-12 Ga., 1989, tchg. add on, gifted in-field Ga., 1997, tchg. add-on, middle grades social studies and sci. Ga., 1990. Tchr. South Ctrl. Mid. Sch., Emerson, Ga., 1989—98, South Forsyth Mid. Sch., Cumming, Ga., 1999—2004, South Forsyth H.S., Cumming, 2004—. Track coach South Ctrl. Mid. Sch., Emerson, 1989—96, pres. of shared governance coun., 1990—94, team leader, 1993—96, soccer coach, 1994—98, sponsor for Jr. C. of C., 1994—98, fastpitch softball coach, 1997—98; team leader South Forsyth Mid. Sch., Cumming, 1999—2003, leadership team, 1999—2003, gifted testing coord., 2001—04; grant writer CSRD, Ga., 1999. Grantee, Etowah Found., 1994. Mem.: Gifted Children Ga. (assoc.). Office: South Forsyth High School 585 Peachtree Parkway Cumming GA 30041 Office Phone: 770-781-2264.

DENNEY, PATRICK BRENNEN, music educator, conductor; b. Chattanooga, Tenn., Apr. 30, 1970; s. Floyd Dearing and Carol Colette Denney; m. Renee Beth Sanders. MusB, Berry Coll., Rome, Ga., 1993. Cert. tchr. Ga., 1993. Dir. of instrumental music Darlington Sch., Rome, Ga., 1993—97,

South Forsyth H.S., Cumming, Ga., 1997—2002, Pinecrest Acad., Cumming, Ga., 2002—. Condr. and music dir. Atlanta Lawyer's Orch., Atlanta, 1999—; assoc. condr. Sounds of Sawnee Cmty. Band, Cumming, Ga., 1997—2000. Named State rep. for Fifty Directors Who Make a Difference, Sch. Band and Orch. Mag., 2000. Mem.: Condrs. Guild, Music Educator's Nat. Conf., Phi Mu Alpha Sinfonia. Home: 4120 Longmont Dr Cumming GA 30040

DENNIES, SANDRA LEE, city official; b. Buffalo, Dec. 26, 1951; d. Norman John and Shirley Edith (Dils) D.; m. Robert Francis Gilbane, Sept. 21, 1974 (div. Apr. 1987); children: Brandon Michael, Gianpatrick. AS in Dental Hygiene, U. Bridgeport, Conn., 1972, BS in Dental Hygiene Edn., 1973; MS in Health Scis., So. Conn. State U., 1979. Dental hygienist various orgns., New Haven, 1972-73, Leonard B. Zaslow, DDS, Westport, Conn., 1973-81; lectr. U. Bridgeport, 1973-76; planner City of Bridgeport, 1977-79, planning asst., 1979-81; grants dir. City of Stamford, Conn., 1981—. Sec. Com. Emergency Med. Disaster Planning, Bridgeport, 1978-79; dir., dep. dir. Stamford Coliseum Authority, 1982-91; dep. dir. Stamford Film Commn., 1986-88. Editor, chief Hy-Light Jour., 1973-76. Mem. Stamford Youth Planning Adv. Bd., 1981-91, Stamford Youth Svc. Bur., 1991-95, United Way Corp., Stamford, 1986-93; pres., sec. Alcohol Drug Abuse Coun., 1987-92; mem. bd. Christian Outreach North Stamford Congl. Ch., 1988-92, 1995-2000, mem. pastoral rels. com., 1995—; mem. Coun. Chs. Synagogues Assembly, Stamford, 1989; pres. Stamford Mcpl. Supervisory Employees Union, 1991-99, mem. 1981—; v.p., sec. Stamford Sch. Readiness Found., 1998—; advisor Stamford Sr. Ctr, 2004—. Democrat. Avocations: piano, clarinet, guitar, skiing. Home: 171 Shadow Ridge Rd Stamford CT 06905-1813 Office: City of Stamford 888 Washington Blvd PO Box 10152 Stamford CT 06904-2152 Personal E-mail: sandra171@aol.com.

DENNIN, JOSEPH FRANCIS, former government official, lawyer; b. N.Y.C., June 9, 1943; s. William Wilfred and Kathryn L (Sever) D.; m. Sandra Earl Peek, Dec. 28, 1968; children: Theresa Michel, Allison Kathleen, James Joseph. AB with great distinction, Stanford U., 1965, JD, 1968; postgrad., U. Helsinki, Finland, 1968-69. Bar: Calif. 1969, N.Y. 1970, D.C. 1986, U.S. Supreme Ct. 1985, U.S. Ct. Appeals (fed. cir.) 1987, Ct. Internat. Trade 1987. Assoc. Simpson, Thacher & Bartlett, N.Y.C., 1969-75; counsel U.S. Senate Intelligence Com., Washington, 1975-76; staff asst. to Pres. White House, Washington, 1976-78; dir. ops. U.S. Internat. Trade Commn., Washington, 1978-79; dep. assoc. atty. gen. Dept. Justice, Washington, 1979-81; dep. asst. sec. for fin., investment and svcs. Dept. Commerce, Washington, 1981-82, dep. asst. sec. for Africa, the Near East and South Asia, 1982-84, asst. sec. for internat. econ. policy, 1984-86; ptnr. internat. dept. McKenna Long & Aldridge LLP, Washington, 1986—. Bd. dirs. U.S.-Taiwan Bus. Coun.; mem. bd. advisors N.Am. Free Trade and Investment Report; mem. N.Am. Free Trade Agreement Article 19 Panel. Gen. editor Law and Practice of the World Trade Orgn. Fulbright grantee Inst. Internat. Edn., 1968 Mem. ABA. Home: 5108 Nahant St Bethesda MD 20816-2336

DENNING, KAREN CRAFT, finance educator; b. Pitts., Mar. 23, 1952; d. Edward Harvey and Esther Naomi Craft; m. John Thomas Denning; children: Naomi Liza, Chloe, Lacey. AB, Cornell U., 1974; PhD, U. Pitts., 1986. Lectr., asst. prof. Case Western Res. U., Cleve., 1985—88; prof. W.Va. U., Morgantown, 1988—2003, Fairleigh Dickinson U., 2003—. Editor: e-Jour. Social Studies, 2002—; contbr. articles to profl. jours. Bd. dirs. Katz Grad. Sch. Bus. Ph.D. Alumni Bd., Pitts. Grantee Internat. Programs Instrnl. Tech. grantee, W.Va. U., 1998—99. Mem.: Am. Fin. Assn., So. Fin. Assn., Midwestern Fin. Assn., Ea. Fin. Assn., Fin. Mgmt. Assn., 20th Century Club, Beta Gamma Sigma (pres. 1998). Presbyterian. Avocations: travel, piano, reading, skiing.

DENNING, PETER JAMES, computer scientist, engineer; b. N.Y.C., Jan. 6, 1942; s. James Edwin and Catherine M. (Manton) D.; m. Dorothy Elizabeth Robling, Jan. 24, 1974; children— Anne, Diana. BEE, Manhattan Coll., 1964, ScD (hon.), 1985; MS in Elec. Engring., MIT, 1965, PhD, 1968; LLD (hon.), Concordia U., 1984; PhD (hon.), Pace U., 2002. Asst. prof. elec. engring. Princeton U., 1968-72; assoc. prof. computer scis. Purdue U., 1972-75, prof., 1975-84, head dept., 1979-83; dir. Rsch. Inst. Advanced Computer Sci. NASA Ames Rsch. Ctr., Mountain View, Calif., 1983-90, rsch. fellow, 1990-91; assoc. dean, chair of computer sci. dept. George Mason U., 1991-97, dir. Ctr. for New Engr., 1993-98, vice provost for continuing profl. edn., 1997-98, univ. coord. for process reengring., 1998-2000, spl. asst. to v.p. for info. tech., 2000—02, chair of technology coun., 2001—02; prof., chmn. computer sci. dept. Naval Postgrad. Sch., 2002—, dir. Cebrowski Inst. Info. Superiority and Innovation, 2003—. Co-founder CSNET, 1981; bd. dirs. Charles Babbage Inst., 2000-04, trustee, 1997—; bd. dirs. Ctr. for Nat. Software Studies, 1996—; mem. tech. adv. bd. Sequent Computer Corp., 1985-91, Hewlett-Packard Labs., 1989-93. Author: Professional Development Seminars, 1968—, also textbooks and numerous rsch. papers; columnist Am. Scientist mag., 1985-93. Recipient Outstanding Faculty award Princeton U. Engring. Assn., 1971, Best Paper award Am. Fedn. Info. Processing Socs., 1972, Disting. Svc. to Computing Rsch. award Computing Rsch. Assn., 1989, Centennial Engring. award Manhattan Coll., 1992, Commonwealth Va. Outstanding Educator award, 2003, Engring. Best Tchr. award George Mason U., 2002, Univ. Outstanding Faculty award 2002; NSF fellow, 1964-67. Fellow IEEE, AAAS, Assn. for Computing Machinery (pres. 1980-82, Karl Karlstrom Outstanding Educator award 1996, Outstanding Contbn. award 1998, Outstanding Computer Sci. Educator award 1999), Am. Soc. for Engring. Edn., Assn. for Computing Machinery (chmn. publs. bd. 1992-98, chmn. edn. bd. 1998—2003, dir. info. tech. profession initiative 1999-2001, editor-in-chief Computing Surveys 1977-79, Comm. ACM 1983-92, Best Paper award 1968, Recognition of Svc. award 1974, Disting. Svc. award 1989), N.Y. Acad. Scis.; mem. Sigma Xi, Eta Kappa Nu, Tau Beta Pi. Office: Naval Postgrad Sch Code CS Monterey CA 93943 Office Phone: 831-656-3603. Business E-Mail: pjd@nps.edu.

DENNIS, ANDRE L., lawyer; b. Burton-on-Trent, Eng., May 15, 1943; came to U.S., 1946; m. Julie B. Carpenter; 1 child, Matthew A. BA, Cheyney U., 1966; JD, Howard U., 1969. Bar: Pa. 1970, D.C. 1969, U.S. Dist. Ct. (ea. dist.) Pa. 1970, U.S. Ct. Appeals (3d cir.) 1977, U.S. Supreme Ct. 1990. Ptnr. Stradley, Ronon, Stevens & Young LLP, Phila., 1969—. Vols. for the Indigent Program, Phila., 1988-95. Recipient Judge William H. Hastie award NAACP Legal Def. and Ednl. Fund, Inc., 1995, Martin Luther King Jr. Humanities award Salem Bapt. Ch., 1993; Hon. fellow U. Pa. Law Sch., 1999. Mem. ABA (co-dir. divsn. IV litigation, Pro Bono Publico award 1994), Pa. Bar Assn. (ho. of dels. 1988—), Am. Coll. Trial Lawyers, Am. Law Inst., Nat. Bar Assn., Phila. Bar Assn. (chancellor 1993), Am. Inns of Ct. Office: 2600 One Commerce St 2005 Market St Philadelphia PA 19103-7098

DENNIS, DIANE JOY MILAM, retired architect; b. Jacksonville, Fla., Oct. 8, 1925; d. Robert Richerson Milam, Meriel Lapham Wilson; m. Thomas Gordon Dennis, Nov. 9, 1974 (dec. Apr. 1999). Grad., Bennington Coll., 1943—47, MArch, Columbia U., 1949—55; studied landscape arch., Harvard U., 1998. With several archtl. firms, N.Y.C.; with Edward Durell Stone on Kennedy Ctr. Mem.: AIA. Home: 47 E 64th St Apt 10A New York NY 10021

DENNIS, DONNA FRANCES, sculptor, art educator; b. Springfield, Ohio, Oct. 16, 1942; d. Donald Phillips and Helen Frances (Hogue) D. BA in Art, Carleton Coll., 1964; student, Coll. Art Studies Abroad, Paris, 1964-65, Art Students League, N.Y.C., 1965-66. Instr. Skowhegan Sch. Painting and Sculpture, Maine, 1982, Sch. Visual Arts, N.Y.C., 1983-90, SUNY, Purchase, 1984-85, 87, Princeton U., N.J., 1984; assoc. prof. SUNY Purchase Coll., 1990-96; prof. SUNY, 1996—, Doris and Karl Kempner disting. prof., 2001—03. One-woman shows include Holly Solomon Gallery, N.Y.C., 1976, 80, 83, 98, Contemporary Arts Ctr., Cin., 1979, Neuberger Mus. of SUNY-Purchase, 1985, Univ. Gallery, U. Mass., Amherst, 1985, Bklyn. Mus., 1987, Del. Art Mus., Wilmington, 1988, Indpls. Mus. Art, 1991-98, Sculpture Ctr., N.Y.C., 1993, Dayton Art Inst., 2003, Five Myles, 2005; exhibited in group shows Venice Biennale, Italy, 1982, 84, Whitney Mus., N.Y.C., 1979, 81, Tate Gallery, London, 1983, Hirshhorn Mus., Washington, 1979, 84, Biennial of Pub. Art, Neuberger Mus., 1997, Asheville (N.C.) Mus. Art, 1998, Palazzo Ducale, Genoa, Italy, 2004, Ctr. for Arch., N.Y., 2005, Margulies Collection at the Warehouse, Miami; commd. decorative fence P.S. 234, N.Y.C., I.S. 5, Queens, N.Y.; represented in permanent collections at Wonderland Sta., MBTA, Boston, North Plaza, Klapper Hall, Queens Coll., Queens, N.Y., Am. Airlines Terminal, Terminal One, Kennedy Airport, N.Y.C. Recipient Art award for excellence in design N.Y.C. Art Commn., 1987, Art award Am. Acad. and Inst. of Arts and Letters, 1984, Bessie Set Design award, 1992; grantee N.Y. State Creative Artists, 1975, 81, N.Y. Found. for Arts, 1985, 92; fiscal sponsorship, N.Y. Found. for Arts, 2002-; fellow Guggenheim Found., 1979, NEA, 1977, 80, 86, 94, Pollock-Krasner award, 2001, 05; Doris and Karl Kempner Dist. Prof. award Purchase Coll. SUNY, 2001-03. Democrat. Home: 131 Duane St New York NY 10013-3850 E-mail: tunnelsandtowers@att.net.

DENNIS, EDWARD ALAN, chemistry and biochemistry educator; b. Chgo., Aug. 10, 1941; s. Sol E. and Ruth (Marks) D.; m. Martha S. Greenberg; Mar. 30, 1969; children: Jennifer, Evan, Andrew. BA, Yale U., 1963; MA, Harvard U., 1965, PhD, 1968. Research fellow Harvard Med. Sch., Boston, 1967-69, vis. prof., 1983-84; asst. prof. chemistry U. Calif.-San Diego, La Jolla, 1970-75, assoc. prof., 1975-81, prof., 1981—, vice chmn. dept. chemistry, 1984—87, 1992—99, chair dept. chemistry and biochemistry, 1999—2002, prof. dept. pharmacology, 1999—. Mem. NSF adv. panels, 1981-85; chmn. Faculty Acad. Senate U. Calif., 1987-88, mem. bd. overseers, 1988—; vis. scientist Brandeis U., 1984; cons. to pharm. industry; adj. prof. Scripps Rsch. Inst., 1999—. Editor: Methods in Enzymology Cumulative Indexes, 1975-85, Phospholipases, 1991, Phospholipid Biosynthesis, 1992, Lipases, 1996, Handbook of Cell Signaling, 2003, Jour. Lipid Rsch., 2003—; mem. editl. bd. Jour. Biol. Chemistry, 1988-93, Jour. Cellular Biochemistry, 1986—; contbr. over 250 articles to profl. jours.; patentee in field. Recipient Avanti award in lipid enzymology, 2000; Guggenheim fellow, 1983-84; grantee NSF, 1970—, NIH, 1970—. Fellow AAAS; mem. Biophys. Soc. (chmn. biopolymers subgroup 1981-82), Am. Chem. Soc., Am. Soc. Biol. Chemists (membership com. 1979-81, program chair 1996, coun. 1995-96, publs. com. 1996—, edn. com. 1996—), Am. Assn. Med. Grad. Depts. Biochemistry (bd. dirs., pres.), N.Y. Acad. Sci., Sigma Xi, Alpha Chi Sigma Chem. Home: 1921 Hypatia Way La Jolla CA 92037-3322 Office: U Calif Dept Chemistry and Biochemistry 9500 Gilman Drive La Jolla CA 92093-0601 Office Phone: 858-534-3055. E-mail: edennis@ucsd.edu.

DENNIS, EDWARD S(PENCER) G(ALE), JR., lawyer; b. Salisbury, Md., Jan. 24, 1945; s. Edward Spencer and Virginia (Monroe) D.; m. Lois Juliette Young, Dec. 27, 1969; 1 son, Edward Brookfield. BS, U.S. Mcht. Marine Acad., 1967; LLD, U. Pa., 1973. Bar: Pa. 1973. Law clk. Hon. A. Leon Higginbotham, Jr., U.S. Dist. Ct., Phila., 1973-75; asst. U.S. atty. U.S. Atty. Office, Phila., 1975-80, dep. chief. criminal div., 1978-80; chief narcotic and dangerous drug sect. U.S. Dept. Justice, Washington, 1980-83, asst. atty. gen. criminal div., 1988-90, acting dep. atty. gen., 1989; U.S. atty. Ea. Dist. Pa., Phila., 1983-88; ptnr., co-chair corp. investigations, criminal def. practice Morgan, Lewis & Bockius, Phila., 1990—. Adj. prof. Law Sch. U. Pa. Fellow Am. Coll. Trial Lawyers; mem. ABA, Nat. Bar Assn., Phila. Bar Assn., Internat. Soc. Barristers. Office: Morgan Lewis & Bockius 1701 Market St Philadelphia PA 19103-2903 also: 1800 M St NW Washington DC 20036-5802

DENNIS, EVERETTE EUGENE, JR., foundation executive, educator, writer; b. Seattle, Aug. 15, 1942; s. Everette Eugene and Kathryn Marie (Platt) D.; m. Emily Thompson Smith, 1987. BS, U. Oreg., 1964; MA, Syracuse U., 1966; PhD, U. Minn., 1974; postdoc., Harvard U., 1978-79. Info. officer dept. mental health State of Ill., Chgo., 1966-68; asst. prof. Kans. State U., Manhattan, 1968-72; asst. prof., assoc. prof. then prof. U. Minn., Mpls., 1972-81, dir. grad. program. Sch. Journalism and Mass Communication, 1978-81; prof., dean Sch. Journalism U. Oreg., Eugene, 1981-84; founding exec. dir. Freedom Forum Media Studies Ctr. Columbia U., N.Y.C., 1984-96; also v.p., 1989-94; sr. v.p., 1994-97; exec. dir. Internat. Consortiums Univs., 1996-97; founding pres. Am. Acad. in Berlin, 1996-2000; Felix E. Larkin disting. prof. Grad. Sch. of Bus., Fordham U., 1997—; COO Internat. Longevity Ctr., 1999—. Head Project on Future of Journalism and Mass Communication Edn.; former trustee Internat. Mus. Photography at Eastman House, Rochester, N.Y., Internat. Inst. Communications, London, Ctr. Internat. Journalists. Reston, Va.; councillor Am. Antiquarian Soc., Worcester, Mass.; mem. adv. bd. Fred Rogers Ctr., Latrobe, Pa.; mem. Annenberg Found. Commn. on the Press, 2005. Author, editor 42 books including: The Magic Writing Machine, 1971, Other Voices: The New Journalism in America, 1973, Justice Hugh Black and the First Amendment, 1978, Enduring Issues in Mass Communication, 1978, The Media Society, 1978, Reporting Processes and Practices, 1981, New Strategies for Public Affairs Reporting, 1983, Basic Issues in Mass Communication, 1984, Reshaping the Media, 1989, Media Freedom and Accountability, 1989, The Cost of Libel, 1989, Media Debates, 1991, 5th edit., 2002, Understanding Mass Communication, 7th edit. 2002, Media and the Environment, 1991, Beyond the Cold War, 1991, Of Media and People, 1992, Demystifying Media Technology, 1993, Higher Education in the Information Age, 1993, America's Schools and the Mass Media, 1993, Radio-The Forgotten Medium, 1995, The Culture of Crime, 1995, American Communication Research, 1996, Publishing Books, 1997, Media and Public Life, 1997, Media and Children, 1996, Media-Black and White, 1996, Media and Congress, 1997, Media and Democracy, 1998; editor-in-chief Media Studies Jour. 1987-96; contbr. articles to profl. jours. Summer fellow Stanford U., 1969, East-West Communication Inst., Hawaii, 1976; liberal arts fellow in law, Harvard U., 1978-79, vis. Nieman fellow, 1980, John F. Kennedy Sch. Govt. rsch. fellow, 1981, John Henry Newman fellow Fordham U., 2002-03, fellow Ctr. for Journalism and Democracy, U. So. Calif.; recipient H. Kreighbaum Under 40 award for nation's outstanding journalism educator, 1982, U. Oreg. Webfoot award, 1985, Disting. Svc. award U. Oreg., 2002, Global Media Rsch. award Ctr. Global Media, 2002, Eleanor Blum award for rsch. and rsch., 2004; inducted to Oreg. Journalism Hall of Fame, 2001. Fellow Am. Orthopsychiat. Assn.; mem. Assn. Edn. in Journalism and Mass Comms. (pres. 1983-84, Eleanor Blum award for svc. to rsch. 2004), Am. Polit. Sci. Assn., Internat. Comm. Assn., Soc. Profl. Journalists, Internat. Mass Comm. Rsch. Soc., Internat. Inst. Comm., Coun. Fgn. Rels., Century Assn. (N.Y.), Harvard Club (N.Y.). Office: ILC-USA 60 E 86th St New York NY 10028-1009 also: Fordham U 113 W 60th St New York NY 10023-7404 Office Phone: 212-517-1317. Business E-Mail: dennis@fordham.edu.

DENNIS, FRANK GEORGE, JR., retired horticulture educator; b. Lyons, N.Y., Apr. 12, 1932; s. Frank George and Corinne Isabel (Smith) D.; m. Katharine Ann Merrell, June 5, 1954. BS in Agriculture, Cornell U., 1955, PhD in Pomology, 1961. Postdoctoral fellow NSF, Gif-sur-Yvette, France, 1961-62; asst. prof. Cornell U., Geneva, N.Y., 1962-68, assoc. prof., 1968—, Mich. State U., East Lansing, 1968-72, prof., 1972-96; ret., 1996. Fulbright fellow, Morocco, 1990. Fellow Am. Soc. for Hort. Sci. (v.p. 1985-86, Gourley award 1985, sci. editor HortScience 1997-2000); mem. Internat. Soc. Hort. Sci. (chmn. working group 1984-90), Sigma Xi. Home: 1600 Ridgewood Dr East Lansing MI 48823-2936 Business E-Mail: fgdennis@msu.edu.

DENNIS, GARY C., neurosurgeon, educator; b. Washington, Dec. 27, 1950; s. Creed and Yvonne (Bush) C.; children: Gary Jr., Gina, Gregory. BA, Boston U., 1972; MD, Howard U., 1976. Intern Johns Hopkins Hosp., Balt., 1976-77; resident Baylor Coll. Medicine Affiliated Hosp., Houston, 1977-81; chief of neurosurgery Kern Med. Ctr., Bakersfield, Calif., 1981-83; clin. assoc. prof. U. Calif., San Diego, 1981-85; chief of neurosurgery Howard U., Washington, 1984—, asst. prof. surgery, 1984-90, assoc. prof., 1990—; attending physician DC Gen. Hosp., Washington, 1990—. Vis. lectr. neurosurgery Johns Hopkins Sch. Med., 1980-98; surg. cons. DC Gen. Hosp., 1986-89; mem. Mayors Commn. to oversee Med. Examiners Office, Washington, 1990, Mayors Transition Team for Health, Washington, 1990; mem. DC Commn. on Jud. Disabilities and Tenure, 2000—; mem. Sec.'s Adv. Com. on Regulatory Reform, 2001-02; chmn. bd. Delmarva Found. DC; mem. Bd. Med. Edn. for South African Blacks, 2002-. Mem. Practicing Physicians Adv. Coun., Health Care Fin. Agy., Washington, 1991-99, Com. on Health Care Reform, Congl. Black Caucus, Washington, 1994—; bd. dirs. Am. Liver Found., 1999-2002; mem. DC Health Care Reform Commn. Named One of Top Drs. S.E. Area, Washingtonian Mag., 1995. Fellow ACS; mem. Med. Soc. DC (pres. 1996-98, chmn. bd. dirs. 1998-99, alt. del. to AMA 2001), Nat. Med. Assn. (treas. 1992-97, 98-, pres.-elect 1997, pres. 1998-99), Am. Assn. Neurol. Surgeons (mem. chair 1994-95), Howard U. Med. Alumni Assn. (pres. 2002-04). Avocations: music, outdoor cooking, fishing. Office: Howard U Hosp 2041 Georgia Ave NW Washington DC 20060-0001 E-mail: gcdennis@pol.net.

DENNIS, JACK BONNELL, computer scientist, educator; b. Elizabeth, N.J., Oct. 13, 1931; SB, SM, MIT, 1954, ScD in Elec. Engring., 1958. Asst. prof. elec. engring. MIT, Cambridge, 1959-65, assoc. prof., 1965-69, prof. computer sci. and engring., 1969-87; prof. computer sci. and engring. emeritus, 1987—; pres. Dataflow Computer Corp., 1987-2000. Chief scientist Acorn Networks, 1996-2001. Recipient Eckert-Mauchly award IEEE Assn. for Computing Machinery, 1984 Fellow IEEE, Assn. for Computing Machinery. Office: Computer Sci and Artificial Intelligence Lab MIT Rm 32-G864 Cambridge MA 02139

DENNIS, JAMES LEON, federal judge; b. Monroe, La., Jan. 9, 1936; s. Jenner Leon and Hope (Taylo) Dennis; children: Stephen James, Gregory Leon, Mark Taylo, John Timothy. BS in Bus. Adminstrn, La. Tech. U., Ruston, 1959; JD, La. State U., 1962; LLM, U. Va., 1984. Bar: La. 1962. Assoc. firm Hudson, Potts & Bernstein, Monroe, 1962—65, ptnr., 1965—72; judge 4th Dist. Ct. La. for Morehouse and Ouachita Parishes, 1972—74, La. 2d Circuit Ct. Appeals, 1974—75; assoc. justice La. Supreme Ct., 1975—95; coord. La. Constnl. Revision Commn., 1970—72; del., chmn. judiciary com. La. Constnl. Conv., 1973; judge U.S. Ct. Appeals Fifth Cir., New Orleans, 1995—; visiting prof. Tulane Law School, 2003. Chmn. La. Commn. on Bicentennial U.S. Constn.; mem. La. Ho. of Reps., 1968—72. With U.S. Army, 1955—57. Mem.: ABA (com. on appellate practice), 4th Jud. Bar Assn., La. Bar Assn., Rotary. Methodist. Office: US Courthouse 600 Camp StRm 219 New Orleans LA 70130-3425*

DENNIS, JOHN DAVISON, minister; b. Pitts., Sept. 18, 1937; s. John Wellington and Helen Isabella (Davison) D.; m. Nancy Schumacher, Jan. 7, 1967; children: Michael, Andrew. AB, Wesleyan U., 1959; BD, Princeton Theol. Sem., 1962, ThM, 1965. Ordained to ministry United Presbyn. Ch. (USA), 1962. Asst. pastor First Presbyn. Ch., Germantown, Pa., 1962—69, sr. pastor Corvallis, Oreg., 1969—. Exch. min. St. Columba's Presbyn. Ch., Johannesburg, Republic of South Africa, 1978. Chaplain Germantown Hosp., 1965-69; west coast dean Presbyn. Young Pastors Seminars, 1983-85; pres. Madison Ave. Task Force, 1975-77, pres. Corvallis Community Improvement, Inc., pres. USSR Sister City Assn., 1989-90; founder Corvallis Fish Emergency Aid Svc., 1969-76; trustee Ecumenical Ministries of Oreg., 1989-98, chmn. bd. dirs. 1996-98; bd. dirs. United Way of Benton County, 1986-90; candidate U.S. Congress from Oreg. 5th dist., 1988; asst. squash coach Princeton U., 1959-62; fundraiser for humanitarian orgns. working with landmine victims in Cambodia, 1994—. Recipient Spl. Achievment award City of Corvallis, 2002; fellow Aspen Inst., 1987; Pacific coast doubles squash champion, 1972-73. Mem. Rotary (charter mem., dir. local club, Rotarian of Yr. 1998). Home: 2760 NW Skyline Dr Corvallis OR 97330-3168 Office: 114 SW 8th St Corvallis OR 97333-4546 Office Phone: 541-753-2228. E-mail: church@1stpres.org.

DENNIS, KEVIN M., lawyer; BA cum laude, Middlebury Coll., 1976; JD, Boston Coll., 1983. Bar: Mass. 1983. Assoc. Goodwin Procter LLP, Boston, 1983—90, ptnr., bus. law dept., 1990—, mem., private equity group, ptnr. in charge, profl. develop., training. Staff Boston Coll. Law Rev. Mem.: ABA, Mass. Bar Assn., Boston Bar Assn. Office: Goodwin Procter LLP Exchange Pl 53 State St Boston MA 02109 Office Phone: 617-570-1528. Office Fax: 617-523-1231. Business E-Mail: kdennis@goodwinprocter.com.

DENNIS, PATRICIA DIAZ, lawyer; b. Santa Rita, N.Mex., 1947; d. Porfirio Madrid and Mary (Romero) Diaz; m. Michael John Dennis, Aug. 3, 1968; children: Ashley Elizabeth, Geoffrey Diaz, Alicia Sarah Diaz. BA in English, UCLA, 1970; JD, Loyola U. LA Sch. Law, 1973. Bar: Calif. 1973, DC 1984, Tex. Law clk. Calif. Rural Legal Asst., McFarland, 1971; assoc. Paul, Hastings, Janofsky & Walker, LA, 1973-76; atty. Pacific Lighting Corp., LA, 1976-78; atty., asst. gen. atty. ABC, Hollywood, 1978-83; commr. FCC, Washington, 1986-89; ptnr., head comm. Jones, Day, Reavis & Pogue, Washington, 1989-91; v.p. govt. affairs US Sprint/United Telecom, Washington, 1991-92; asst. sec. State for Human Rights and Humanitarian Affairs Dept. State, Washington, 1992; special coun. comm. Sullivan & Cromwell, Washington, 1991—98; sr. v.p. regulatory and pub. affairs SBC Comm., San Antonio, 1998—2002; mem. bd. dirs. Entravision Comm. Corp., 2001—, 2001—. Chmn. US del. Internat. Telecomm. Union Region 2 Broadcasting Conf., Rio de Janeiro, 1988; bd. dirs. Telemundo Group Inc., 1989-92, Conn. Mut. Life Ins. Co., Nat. Pub. Radio, 1992, PR Legal Def. and Edn. Fund, 1991-92, Nat. Labor Rels. Bd., Regan adminstrn.; mem. adv. bd. Ctr. for Telecomm. and Info. Studies, Columbia U., 1991-92, Latin Am. Inst., Loyola U. (LA Sch. Law), 1991-92, Bur. Nat. Affairs, Media Law Reporter, 1990-92; mem. Nat. Adv. Com. (Women Judges' Fund for Justice), 1990-92. Exec. editor: Loyola Law Rev., 1972-73. Com. mem. Hispanic leadership program Coro Found., LA, 1981-82; US del. UN Commn. on Status of Women, 30th session Econ. and Social Coun., Vienna, Austria, 1984, World Conf. UN Decade for Women, Nairobi, Kenya, 1985; bd. dirs. Resources for Infant Educators, 1981-83, Nat. Network Hispanic Women, LA, 1983-92, Reading is Fundamental, 1991—; mem. exec. com., nat. adv. bd. Leadership Am., Found. for Women's Resources, 1987—, bd. mem., trustee; bd. visitors Pepperdine U. Sch. Law, 1988-92; mem. adv. coun. Ctr. for Pub. Utilities, N.Mex. State U., 1988-92; bd. mem. and trustee Thomas Rivera Policy Inst., 1991—, Radio and Television News Dirs. Found., 1992—, Women's Mus., Bexar County Women's Bar Assn., Tex. State U. Sys. Bd. Regents, Hispanic Scholarship Fund, Mex. Am. Legal Defense and Ednl. Fund, Mass. Mutual Life Ins. Recipient cert. achievement YWCA, LA, 1979, Woman Yr. award merit Mex. Am. Opportunity Found., 1984, Recognition Outstanding Achievements award Nat. Coun. Hispanic Women, 1986, Woman Achievement award City Club Cleve., 1986, Friend Family award The Family Place, 1987, Woman Yr. award Hispanic Women's Coun., Inc., 1989, Belva Lockwood Outstanding Lawyer award, Bexar County Women's Bar Assn., 2000, Pub. Endeavor award, Assn. Women in Comm., 2001; named one of 100 Influentials, Hispanic Bus. mag., 1987, 88, 90, 96; named Hispanic Woman Yr., Houston YMCA, 1992, Alumna Yr., UCLA Latino Alumni Assn., 1999, Corp. Exec. Yr., San Antonio Women's C. of C., 1999. Mem. Mex.-Am. Bar Assn. (sec. 1980-81, trustee 1979-80, 81-82), LA County Bar Assn. (child abuse subcom. chmn. barristers sect. 1980-81, exec. com. barristers sect. 1980-82), Hispanic Bar Assn. DC, ABA (com. labor arbitration and law of collective bargaining agreements, labor law sect. 1979-82), Women's Forum Wash., Am. Bar Assn. Commn. (on opportunities for minorities in the profession 1991-92, mem. nominations com., 1991-92, co-chmn. common carrier com., 1990-91), Fed. Comm. Bar Assn. Democrat. Roman Cath. Office Phone: 925-806-4090. Office Fax: 925-866-2030.

DENNIS, RALPH EMERSON, JR., lawyer; b. Marion, Ind., Dec. 19, 1925; s. Ralph Emerson Sr. and Martha Elnora (Bahr) D.; m. Virginia Lea Harter, June 19, 1949 (dec. Oct. 1981); children: Nancy J. Barefoot, Kathleen Ann Polk, Amel Joseph, Mary Elizabeth Saler, Ralph E. III; m. Barbara Grose, May 31, 1985. BS, Dartmouth Coll., 1946; JD, Ind. U., 1950. Bar: Ind. 1950, U.S. Supreme Ct. 1971. Sr. ptnr. Dennis, Cross, Raisor, Jordan & Marshall, P.C., Muncie, Ind., 1956-80, Dennis, Raisor, Wenger & Haynes, P.C., Muncie, 1980-85, Dennis & Wenger, P.C., Muncie, 1985-86, Dennis, Wenger & Abrell, P.C., Muncie, 1986—. Chmn. bd. dirs. Lift-A-Loft Corp., Muncie. City judge, Muncie, 1951-59, city atty., 1964-67; trustee Muncie Community Schs., 1960-63. With USN, 1944-46. Recipient Disting. Service award, Muncie Jaycees, 1959, Good Govt. award, Muncie Jaycees, 1959. Mem. ABA, Ind. Bar Assn. Clubs: Del. Country (Muncie). Lodges: Elks, Masons. Republican. Lutheran. Home: 411 N Greenbriar Rd Muncie IN 47304-3717 Office: Dennis Wenger & Abrell PC 324 W Jackson St Muncie IN 47305-1625

DENNIS, RUTLEDGE M., sociologist, educator; b. Charleston, S.C., Aug. 16, 1939; s. David and Ora Jane (Porcher) D.; children: Shay Tchaka, Imaro Marlin Aki, Kimya Nuru, Zuri Sanyika. BS, S.C. State U., 1966; MA, Wash. State U., 1969, PhD, 1975. Dir. Black studies program Va. Commonwealth U., Richmond, 1971—78, assoc. prof. dept. sociology, 1978—89; Commonwealth prof. dept. sociology George Mason U., Fairfax, Va., 1989—, prof. dept. sociology, 1992—. Co.-dir. sociology grad. program George Mason U., 1993—2001; coord. Southeastern Regional African Seminar, Richmond-Charlottesville, 1973—76; del. Ea. Va. Internat. Consortium, 1972—77; pres. Assn. Black Sociologists, 1981—83; founder Rutledge Dennis Found. for Human Devel., Ctr. for African Am. Culture and Leadership; co-founder African-Am. Acad.; creator of Dennis-Weathers award for intergroup rels. George Mason U., 2004, mem. exec. com. African Am. Studies Program, 2004—. Co-author: The Politics of Annexation, 1982; editor: Elsevier Sci. Ltd. Series in Race and Ethnic Rels., 1990—, Racial and Ethnic Politics, 1994, The Black Middle Class, 1995, W.E.B. Du Bois: The Scholar as Activist, 1996, Black Intellectuals, 1997, Marginality, Power and Social Structure: Issues in Race, Class and Gender Analysis, 2005; series editor: Oliver C. Cox, 2000; co-editor: The Afro-Americans, 1976, Race and Ethnicity in Rsch. Methods, 1993, Race and Ethnicity: Comparative and Theoretical Approaches, 2003, Booker T. Washington: The Leader as Pragmatist and Decommissionist. Housing commr. Richmond Redevel. and Housing Authority, 1977-80; bd. dirs. Housing Opportunities Made Equal, Richmond, 1976-80. With U.S. Army, 1960-63. Fellow Fgn. Affairs scholar, 1965; recipient Cmty. Svc. award Boys Clubs Am., 1976; named Outstanding Educator of Am., 1975; Fenwick fellow George Mason U., 2005—; recipient Reise-Melton Cultural award, 1980, Disting. Leadership award Afro-Am. Studies Program, 1991, Nat. Black Monitor Family and Cmty. award 1985, Va. Commonwealth U., 1991, Pres.'s award S.C. State U., 1966, Jewish Educators award, 1998, Joseph Himes award for Disting. scholar, 2001, Ba'Alay Keriyah Soc., 2003, others; grantee Ford Found., 1970, NEH, 1978, NIMH, 1980-81; 25th Ann. lectr. African-Am. studies program Va. Commonwealth U., 1996, others. Mem. AAUP (v.p. George Mason U. chpt. 2005—), NAACP (life), Am. Sociol. Assn., Soc. Study Social Problems, So. Sociol. Soc., Ea. Sociol. Soc. (chmn. minorities com. 1992-96, mem. editl. bd. Race and Soc. 1998-2005), Assn. Black Sociologists (pres. 1981-82, 82-83, chmn. hist. and archives com., 2002—, Leadership award 1995), African Heritage Soc., Sigma Xi, Omicron Delta Kappa, Alpha Phi Alpha (Acad. Excellence award 1985), Alpha Kappa Mu, Alpha Kappa Delta. Office: George Mason U Dept Sociology Anthrop Fairfax VA 22030 Office Phone: 703-993-1431. Business E-Mail: rdenni1@gmu.edu.

DENNIS, WILLIE E., lawyer; b. Queens, NY, Mar. 30, 1962; BA in English, Columbia U., 1984, JD, 1988. Bar: NJ 1988, NY 1990, DC 1992. Assoc. Orrick, Herrington & Sutcliffe, 1988—91, Mudge Rose Guthrie Alexander & Ferdon, 1991—95; ptnr. Thelen Reid & Priest LLP, NYC, and co-chair, private equity and venture capital practice. Bd. dirs. Upper Manhattan Empowerment Zone Devel. Corp., Harlem YMCA, Thurgood Marshall Scholarship Fund. Named one of Am. Top Black Atty., Black Enterprise, 2003. Office: Thelen Reid & Priest LLP 875 Third Ave New York NY 10022-6225 Office Phone: 212-603-2365. Office Fax: 212-603-2001. Business E-Mail: wdennis@thelenreid.com.

DENNISON, DONALD LEE, lawyer; b. Dec. 5, 1932; s. Robert Irving and Hannah W. Dennison; m. Tina L. Dennison, Feb. 12, 1955; children: Scott A., Carol R., David R. BSME, Carnegie Inst. Tech., Pitts., 1955; JD, George Washington U., 1961. Bar: Va. 1969, U.S. Supreme Ct. 1965, U.S. Ct. Appeals (fed. cir.) 1969, Md. 1968, D.C. 1962, U.S. Ct. Appeals (4th cir.) 1970. Examiner U.S. Patent Office, Washington, 1957-60; ptnr. Dennison & Dennison, Washington, 1960-66, Dennison, Meserole, Pollack & Scheiner, Arlington, Va., 1966-98, Dennison, Meserole, Scheiner & Schultz, 1999-2000, Dennison, Scheiner, Schultz and Wakeman, 2000—01, Dennison, Schultz, Dougherty and MacDonald, 2002—. Past pres. Met. Washington Soccer Referees Assn., 1980-83; v.p. Mid-Atlantic D.O.G.S., Inc. Search and Rescue Unit. 1st lt. U.S. Army, 1954-57. Mem. Internat. Trademark Assn., European Cmty. Trademark Assn., Internat. Assoc. Intellectual Property. Republican. Home: 11209 Farmland Dr North Bethesda MD 20852-4521 Office: Dennison Schultz Doughterty & MacDonald 1727 King St Alexandria VA 22314 Office Phone: 703-837-9600. Business E-Mail: ddennison@dennisonlaw.com.

DENNISON, GEORGE MARSHEL, academic administrator; b. Buffalo, Ill., Aug. 11, 1935; s. Earl Fredrick and Irene Gladys (McWhorter) D.; m. Jane Irene Schroeder, Dec. 26, 1954; children: Robert Gene, Rick Steven. AA, Custer County (Mont.) Jr. Coll., 1960; BA, U. Mont., 1962, MA, 1963; PhD, U. Wash., 1967. Asst. prof. U. Ark., Fayetteville, 1967-68; vis. asst. prof. U. Wash., Seattle, 1968-69; asst. prof. Colo. State U., Fort Collins, 1969-73, assoc. prof., 1973-77, assoc. dean Coll. Arts, Humanities and Social Sci., 1976-80, prof., 1977-87, acting acad. v.p., 1980-82, acting assoc. acad. v.p., 1982-86, assoc. acad. v.p., 1987; provost, v.p. acad. affairs Western Mich. U., Kalamazoo, 1987-90; pres. U. Mont., Missoula, 1990—. Cons. U.S. Dept. Justice, 1976-84; bd. dirs. Inst. Medicine and Humanities, Missoula, Internat. Heart Inst. Mont., Missoula. Author: The Dorr War, 1976; contbr. articles to jours. in field. Bd. dirs. Kalamazoo Ctr. for Med. Studies, 1989-90, Missoula Rocky Mountain Coll., Billings, Mont. Campus Compact, Internat; Maureen & Mike Mansfield Found.; bd. dirs., chair Student Exchange Program; chair Mont. Commn. Cmty. Svc.; presdl. appointee Nat. Security Edn. Bd. With USN, 1953-57. ABA grantee, 1969-70; Colo. State U. grantee, 1970-75, Nat. Trust for Hist. Preservation grantee, 1976-78; U.S. Agy. for Internat. Devel. grantee, 1979—; Colo. Commn. on Higher Edn. devel. grantee, 1985. Mem. Am. Hist. Assn., Orgn. Am. Historians, Am. Assn. Higher Edn., Am. Soc. for Legal History. Avocations: handball, cross country skiing. Office: U Montana Office of The Pres Univ UH 109 Missoula MT 59812-0001 Business E-Mail: dennisongm@mso.umt.edu.

DENNISON, GERARD FRANCIS, economic analyst; b. Lewiston, Maine, Aug. 3, 1948; s. Alfred Alexandre Jr. and Regina Violet (Routhier) D.; m. Patricia Elaine Potter, June 24, 1989; stepchildren: Rochelle Elizabeth Riordan, Melanie Lois Wentworth. BS BA, Thomas Coll., 1970, MBA, 1986. Lic. stockbroker, Maine. Sr. econ. analyst Maine Dept. Labor, Lewiston, 1971—. Mem. confs. in field. City councilor City of Auburn, Maine, 1994—2000; corporator, bd. dirs., mem. various coms. Auburn-Lewiston Boys/Girls Club; corporator Auburn Pub. Libr; mem. cmty. bldg. com. United Way; mem. mem. Kittyhawk Indsl. Park Com.; chair Enhanced Cmty. Policing Com.; mem. adv. coun., planning com. Lewiston-Auburn Coll.; chair Auburn Indsl. Park Site Selection Com.; mayor's rep. Auburn Sch. Com., Lewiston Auburn Edn. Coalition; dir. Auburn Exch. Club; dir. exec. com. Androscoggin Valley Coun. of Govts.; coord. Androscoggin County campaign for Gov. Angus S. King Jr., 1998; mentor Togolese Refugee Family Resettlement Program; mem. long range planning task force Auburn Pub. Libr.; mem. Androscoggin County Budget Rev. Com.; bd. dirs. Franco-Am. Heritage Ctr.; mem. John Baldacci Gubernatorial Campaign, 2001—02, Auburn Charter Commn., 2004—05; bd. dirs. Lewiston-Auburn Econ. Growth Coun., Lewiston-Auburn R.R. Mem. USA Forum Francophone des Affaires, Auburn Exch. Club, Auburn Bus. Devl. Corp., Am. Legion, Poland Spring Country Club. Roman Catholic. Avocations: golf, reading. Home: 28 7th St Auburn ME 04210-5633 Office: Maine Dept Labor 5 Mollison Way Lewiston ME 04240-5805 Personal E-mail: gerry.dennison@verizon.net. Business E-Mail: gerard.dennison@maine.gov.

DENNISON, RONALD WALTON, engineer; b. Oct. 23, 1944; s. S. Mason and Elizabeth Louise (Hatcher) D.; m. Deborah Ann Rutter, Aug. 10, 1991; children: Ronald, Frederick. BS in Physics and Math., San Jose State U., 1970, MS in Physics, 1972. Physicist Memorex, Santa Clara, 1970—71; sr. engr. AVCO, San Jose, Calif., 1972—73; advanced devel. engr. Perkin Elmer, Palo Alto, Calif., 1973—75; staff engr. Hewlett-Packard, Santa Rosa, Calif., 1975—79; program gen. mgr. Burroughs, Westlake Village, Calif., 1979—82; dir. engring., founder EIKON, Simi Valley, Calif., 1982—85; sr. staff technologist Maxtor Corp., San Jose, 1987—90; dir. engring. Toshiba Am. Info. Sys., 1990—93, cons. engr., 1994—. Author: tech. publs. Sgt. USAF, 1963—67. Mem.: IEEE, Internat. Comanche Soc., Aircraft Owners and Pilots Assn., Internat. Disk Drive Equipment and Materials Assn., Internat. Soc. Hybrid Microelectronics, Am. Vacuum Soc. Republican. Methodist. Home: 4050 Soelro Ct San Jose CA 95127-2711 Office Phone: 408-929-7023. E-mail: ron@rondennison.com.

DENNISON, RUSSELL FRANCIS, school librarian, educator; b. Cedar Rapids, Iowa, Jan. 28, 1954; s. Lorren Hatch and Frances Myrtle Dennison; m. Mary Elizabeth Ito, Feb. 15, 1992; children: April Kyoko, Brandon Michael, Keary Francis, Rory Allen; m. Terese Ann Evert (div.). BA in Philosophy, Ctrl. Coll., Pella, Iowa, 1976; MA in Libr. Sci., U. Wis., 1980. Libr. journalism U. Wis., Madison, Wis., 1979—80; prof. Winona (Minn.) State U., 1980—. Cons. in field; presenter in field. Co-author: (cd-rom) Technology Tools for Today's Campuses, 1997; contbr. articles to profl. jours. Adult leader Cub Scouts, Winona, 1986—89; tchr. Coll. for Kids, Winona, 1989—93, Elderhostel, Winona, 1993—95; bd. dirs. South East Librs. Cooperating, Rochester, Minn., 2005. H. W. Wilson fellowship, Ind. U., 1994. Mem.: ALA (mem. com. quantitative measures collection mgmt. 1998—2002), Minn. Libr. Assn. (mem. com. newsletter and pubs. 1997—99), Am. Soc. Info. Sci. and Tech., Libr. Rsch. Round Table (nominating com. 2003—04). Avocation: fencing. Home: 2440 60th St NW Rochester MN 55901 Office: Winona State University Winona MN 55987 Office Phone: 507-457-5143. Office Fax: 507-457-5595. E-mail: rdennison@winona.edu.

DENNISON, STANLEY SCOTT, retired forest products company executive, consultant; b. Mitchelville, Md., Sept. 1, 1920; s. Ralph Stanford and Cora Adeline (Scott) D.; m. Sharon Lee Johnson, June 1, 1983; 1 stepchild, Whitney C. Maddox; children by previous marriage: Judith Dennison Tucci (dec.), Joan Dennison Daffron, Joyce Dennison Bischoff. Ed., Columbia Union Coll., 1938; BS, Calif. We. U., 1976, MS, 1979, PhD, 1983. Operative builder Dennison Co., 1939-43; traffic rep. U.P. R.R., 1943-49; v.p. Arlington Millwork, Va., 1949-52, Internat. Filling Machine Co., Petersburg, Va., 1952-57, Atlanta Oak Flooring Co., 1957-62; regional mgr. Ga.-Pacific Corp., Portland, Oreg., 1962-70, v.p., 1970-78, sr. v.p., 1978-82, exec. v.p., 1982-85; exec. mgmt. cons., 1985—. Past trustee Stonehill Coll., U. Portland, Calif. Western U.; bd. dirs. Aquinas Ctr. Theology at Emory U., Atlanta. Mem. Capital City Club (Atlanta), Commerce Club (Atlanta), Alpha Kappa Psi. Democrat. Roman Catholic. Home: 100 E Ocean View Ave Apt 806 Norfolk VA 23503-1633 E-mail: drssd@atl.mediaone.net.

DENNISTON, BRACKETT BADGER, III, lawyer; b. Oak Park, Ill., July 23, 1947; s. Brackett Badger Jr. and Frances Ann (Jones) D.; m. Kathleen Foley, Aug. 2, 1975; children: Alexandra, Brackett Badger IV, Elizabeth. AB, Kenyon Coll., 1969; JD, Harvard U., 1973. Bar: Mass. 1974, U.S. Dist. Ct. Mass. 1975, U.S. Dist. Ct. (we. dist.) Tex. 1987, U.S. Ct. Appeals (1st cir.) 1975, U.S. Ct. Appeals (D.C. cir.) 1976, U.S. Ct. Appeals (7th cir.) 1978, U.S. Ct. Appeals (10th cir.) 1981, U.S. Supreme Ct. 1981. Law clk. to judge U.S. Ct. Appeals for 9th Cir., Honolulu, 1973-74; assoc. Goodwin, Procter & Hoar, Boston, 1974-81, ptnr., 1981-82, 86-93, mem. exec. com., 1990-93; chief major frauds unit U.S. Atty.'s Office, Boston, 1982-86; chief legal counsel Gov. of Mass., Boston, 1993-96; v.p., sr. counsel litigation GE, Fairfield, Conn., 1996—2004, v.p., gen. counsel, 2004—. Chair, compliance review bd. GE, 1999—. Class chmn. Kenyon Coll., Gambier, Ohio, 1979-90, trustee, 2000-04, sec., 2005-; mem. Duxbury (Mass.) Zoning Bd. Appeals, 1980-92, chmn., 1984-90, dir. New England Legal Found., 1998- (vice-chair 2003-). Recipient Dir.'s award for superior achievement U.S. Dept. Justice, 1986. Mem. Am. Arbitration Assn. (bd. dirs. 2004—), Mass. Bar Assn. (chmn. coun. jud. adminstrn. sect. 1989-90, jud. adminstrv. coun. 1987-90, Boston Bar Found. (trustee 2002-04). Office: GE Corp 3137 Easton Tpke Fairfield CT 06432-1008 Office Phone: 203-373-2453. Business E-Mail: brackett.denniston@corporate.ge.com.

DENNY, BREWSTER CASTBERG, retired university dean; b. Seattle, Sept. 5, 1924; s. Merle Wilson and Margaraith (Castberg) D.; m. Patricia Virginia Sollitt, June 14, 1950; 1 child, Maria Janet. AB, U. Wash., 1945; MA in Law and Diplomacy, Tufts U., 1948, PhD, 1959. Instr. Mass. Inst. Tech., 1948-52; with Office of Sec. of Def., 1952-60; profl. staff mem. Sub-Com. on Nat. Policy Machinery, US Senate, 1960-61; asso. prof. pub. affairs U. Wash., 1961-64, prof. pub. affairs, 1964—, 1st dir. Grad. Sch. Pub. Affairs, 1962-68, 1st dean, 1968-80, dean emeritus, 1980—, chmn. marine affairs bd., 1972-79, prof. Am. diplomatic history, 1991—. US rep. to 23d Gen. Assembly UN, 1968; cons. RAND Corp., 1961-68; mem. vis. com. dept. govt. Harvard U., 1967-72; mem. Presdl. Adv. Coun. on Intergovtl. Pers. Policy, 1971-74; chmn. Gov. Task Force on Exec. Orgn., 1968-72; presdl. mem. US-PR Commn. on Status of PR, 1964-66; mem. bd. sci. and tech. in devel. NAS, 1976-81, co-chmn. Korean com. on sci. and tech., 1977-82; mem. Rsch. and Edn. Adv. Panel to Compt. Gen. US, 1979-2000. Author: Seeing American Policy Whole, 1985; contbr. to Am. Polit. Sci. Rev., Sci., Pub. Adminstrn. Rev.; author, co-author, editor articles, books, chpt., and reports. Trustee Century Fund, 1975—, vice chmn., 1982-86, chmn., 1986-94; co-chair Children's Budget Coalition, 1991—. Mem. AAAS (com. on new directions 1975-78, charter mem. com. on sci. and pub. policy 1968-72, com. on arms control 1980-88), ASPA, UN Assn. USA (nat. policy panel on UN capabilities in the 1970s 1970-71), Nat. Acad. Pub. Adminstrn., Am. Hist. Assn., Coun. Fgn. rels., Nat. Assn. Sch. Pub. Affairs and Adminstrn. (pres. 1968-69). Home: 2021 1st Ave Apt F12 Seattle WA 98121-3113 Office Phone: 206-441-0222.

DENNY, COLLINS, III, lawyer; b. Richmond, Va., Dec. 5, 1933; s. Collins Jr. and Rebecca (Miller) Denny; m. Anne Carples, June 28, 1957; children: Collins IV, William R., Katharine D. Joyce. AB, Princeton U., 1956; LLB, U. Va., 1961. Bar: Va. 1961, U.S. Dist. Ct. (ea. dist.) Va. 1962, U.S. Ct. Appeals (4th cir.) 1962, U.S. Tax Ct. 1971, U.S. Ct. Claims 1976. Assoc. Denny, Valentine & Davenport, Richmond, 1961-67; ptnr. Mays & Valentine LLP, Richmond, 1967-2000, mng. ptnr., 1992-93; gen. counsel, corp. sec. Coastal Lumber Co., Weldon, NC, 1980—2003; ptnr. Troutman, Sanders, Mays & Valentine LLP, Richmond, 2001. Gen. counsel Bear Island Timberlands Co., LLC, Ashland, Va., 1985—99, Bear Island Paper Co., LLC, 1989—2000. Contbr. chapters to books, articles to profl. jours. Lt. USNR, 1956—66. Mem.: ABA (chmn. exempt orgns. subcom., tax. sect. 1971—86), Richmond Feeder Cattle Assn. (pres. 1972—77), Va. Forestry Assn., Va. Tax Rev. (adv. bd. 1978—2002), Va. State Bar (com. chmn. 1981—83), Va. Bar Assn. (chmn. jr. bar 1965—66), Princeton Alumni Assn. Va. (pres. 1974—78), Country Club Va., Deep Run Hunt Club (pres. 1987—88), Richmond-First Club (pres. 1969—70). Episcoplian. Avocations: horse sports, tree farming, agriculture. Office: Troutman Sanders LLP 1111 E Main St PO Box 1122 Richmond VA 23218-1122

DENNY, JAMES M., health care services company executive; Chmn. Pearle Heath Svcs. Inc., Dallas, Gilead Sci. Address: Pearl Health Svcs Inc 2534 Royal Ln Dallas TX 75229-3417 Office: Gilead Sciences Inc 333 Lakeside Dr Foster City CA 94404*

DENNY, MARY CRAVER, state legislator, business owner; b. Houston, July 9, 1948; d. Kenneth and Lois (Skiles) Craver; m. Henry William Denny, Jan. 26, 1969 (div. Aug. 1990); 1 child, Bryan William; m. Norman C. Tolpo, May 6, 2005. Student, U. Tex., 1966—70; BS in Elem. Edn. magna cum laude, U. North Tex., 1973. Cert. tchr. Tex. Mem. Tex. Ho. of Reps., Austin, 1993—, chair ho. com. on elections. Mem. numerous other civic orgns.; del. state and nat. Rep. convs., 1972—; chmn. Denton (Tex.) County Rep. Com., 1983—91; bd. dirs. Tex. Fedn. Rep. Women, 1988—2003, Tex. Com. Humanities, 1990, YMCA, Denton, 1985—; life mem. pres.'s coun. U. N. Tex., Denton, 1974—, chmn., 1983; mem. Denton Benefit League, 1976—, Denton Arts Coun., 1986—. Named Outstanding Rep. Vol., Denton County Rep. Com., 1985, Outstanding Alumna in Edn., U. N. Tex. Coll. Edn., 1993; named one of 10 Outstanding Rep. Women, Tex. Fedn. Rep. Women, 1991. Mem.: Nat. Conf. State Legislature, Am. Legis. Exch. Coun., Ariel Club, Delta Zeta. Episcopalian. Avocations: swimming, bridge. Address: 8684 FM 2153 Aubrey TX 76227-3029 Office: PO Box 2910 Austin TX 78768-2910 also: 1001 Cross Timbers Rd Flower Mound TX 75028 Office Phone: 972-724-8477, 800-371-6179, 512-463-0688. E-mail: mary.denny@house.state.tx.us.

DENNY, RICHARD ALDEN, JR., retired lawyer; b. Atlanta, Oct. 13, 1931; s. Richard Alden and Maybeth Sullivan (Graham) D.; m. Margaret Hunt, Aug. 1954; children: Margaret Denny Dozier, Richard Alden III, Dallas Hunt, Lee Denny Griffith. BA, Washington and Lee U., 1952; LLB, Emory U., 1954. Bar: Ga. 1954. Assoc. King & Spalding, Atlanta, 1954-60, ptnr., 1960-92. Chmn. bd. Met. Atlanta Crime Commn., 1972-73; bd. dirs. Woodruff Arts Ctr., 1991-97, life trustee, 1997—; bd. dirs. High Mus. Art, Atlanta, 1971—, chmn., 1991-94; bd. dirs. Lovett Sch., Atlanta, 1969—, chmn., 1980-83, emeritus trustee, 1999—; founder High Mus. Atlanta Wine Auction, 1993, chief taster, 1998—. Mem. Lawyers Club Atlanta (pres. 1972-73), Atlanta Lawyers Found. (chmn. 1976-77), Washington and Lee Alumni Assn. (pres. 1980-81), Piedmont Driving Club (pres. 1982-84), Peachtree Golf Club, Omicron Delta Kappa. Episcoplaian. Office: King & Spalding Ste 4900 191 Peachtree St NE Atlanta GA 30303-1740

DENNY, WILLIAM MURDOCH, JR., investment management executive; b. Schenectady, NY, June 10, 1934; s. William Murdock and Ione Elizabeth (Lundy) D.; m. Delores Gay Shillady, June 11, 1966; children: Ellen Gay, Nancy Beth, Linda Ann. ScB in Chemistry, Brown U., 1958; MBA in Fin., Drexel U., 1974. Mem. mgmt. staff chem. spltys. divsn. Pennwalt Corp., Phila., 1961-73; pres. Denny Fin. Enterprises, Paoli, Pa., 1974—. Chmn. mgmt. com. Houston-Leon County Coal Co. Interests, Crockett, Tex., 1987-2002; winegrower Clover Mill Farm Vineyards, LLC, Chester Springs, Pa., 1998—. Bd. dirs. United Way North Central Chester County, 1980—83. Lt. comdr. USN, 1959—61. Mem. Fin. Analysts Fedn., Fin. Analysts Phila., Navy League U.S., Corinthians Assn. (Phila. fleet capt. 1996-97, corp. sec. 2002-05), Phi Kappa Psi, Brown U. Club (pres. 1979-81, Phila.), Aronimink Golf Club (Newtown Square, Pa.), Yacht Club of Hilton Head Island (S.C.), Sea Pines Club. Home: Clover Mill Farm Chester Springs PA 19425 Office: PO Box 458 Paoli PA 19301-0458

DENOMMÉ, ROBERT THOMAS, foreign language educator; b. Fitchburg, Mass., May 17, 1930; s. George Edward and Sara (Richards) D. BA, Assumption Coll., Worcester, Mass., 1952; MA, Boston U., 1953; Grad. Diploma, Sorbonne, U. Paris, 1959; PhD, Columbia U., 1962; LHD, Assumption Coll., 2001. Instr. in French St. Joseph's Coll., Phila., 1956-60; asst. prof. French U. Va., Charlottesville, 1962-64, U. Chgo., 1964-66; assoc. prof. French U. Va., Charlottesville, 1966-70, prof. French, 1970—, Douglas Huntly Gordon prof. French lit., 1991—, prof. and chmn. French dept., 1977-89. Vis. prof. French U., Orléans, France, 1978. Author: The Naturalism of G. Geffroy, 1963, Nineteenth Century French Romantic Poets, 1969, French Parnassian Poets, 1972, Le Conte de Lisle, 1973, Alfred de Vigny, 1985. Decorated officier Order de Palmes Académiques (France); recipient All-Univ. Tchg. award U. Va. Bd. Visitors, 1994; Fulbright scholar, France, 1959. Mem. MLA (sec., chmn. 1971-72), Am. Assn. Tchrs. French, South Atlantic MLA (pres., past pres.), Assn. Internationale Ètudes Françaises (Paris), Société des Amis d'Alfred de Vigny (Paris), Colonnade Club (Charlottesville), Phi Beta Kappa (hon., Beta Va. chpt.). Roman Catholic. Avocations: reading, classical music. Home: 119 Cameron Ln Charlottesville VA 22903-1707 Office: Univ Va Dept French 302 Cabell Hall Charlottesville VA 22903-3196

DENSEN, PAUL MAXIMILLIAN, retired health facility administrator; b. NYC, Aug. 1, 1913; s. Charles Edwin and Carrie (Weinberg) Densen; m. Elizabeth A. Reed, Dec. 19, 1939; children: Rebecca E., Peter. AB, Bklyn-.Coll., 1934; D.Sc., Johns Hopkins U., 1939; MA (hon.), Harvard U., 1968. From instr. to assoc. prof. preventive medicine Vanderbilt U. Med. Sch., 1939—46; chief div. med. research statistics VA, Washington, 1946—49; assoc. prof., then prof. biometry Grad. Sch. Pub. Health, U. Pitts., 1949—54; dir. div. research and statistics Health Ins. Plan Greater N.Y., 1954—59; dept. commr. N.Y.C. Dept. Health, 1959—66; dept. adminstr. N.Y.C. Health Services Adminstrn., 1966—69; dir. Harvard Center Community Health and Med. Care, 1968—85; prof. community health Harvard Sch. Pub. Health, 1968—85, prof. emeritus, 1985—. Fellow: AAAS, APHA, Am. Statis. Assn.; mem.: Inst. Medicine of NAS, Am. Epidemiol. Soc. Home: PO Box 405 165 Fremont Rd Sandown NH 03873-2204

DENSLEY, COLLEEN T., principal; b. Provo, Utah, Apr. 12, 1950; d. Floyd and Mary Lou (Dixon) Taylor; m. Steven T. Densley, July 23, 1968; children: Steven, Tiffany, Landon, Marianne, Wendy, Logan. BS in Elem. Edn., Brigham Young U., 1986, MEd in Tchg. and Learning, 1998. Cert. in elem. edn., K-12 adminstrn. Utah. Substitute tchr. Provo Sch. Dist., 1972-85, curriculum specialist, 1999-2001; tchr. 6th grade, mainstreaming program Canyon Crest Elem. Sch., Provo, 1985—94; instructional facilitator Campus Crest Elem., 1994—99; prin. Wasatch Elem. Sch., Provo, 2001—. Tchr. asst., math. tutor Brigham Young U., 1968—69; attendee World Gifted and Talented Conf., Salt Lake City, 1987, Tchr. Expectations and Student Achievement, 1988—89, Space Acad. for Educators, Huntsville, Ala., 1992; supr. coop. tchr. for practicum tchrs., 1987—90; co-chmn. accelerated learning and devel. com.; trainee working with handicapped students in mainstream classroom, 1989; mem. elem. sch. lang. arts curriculum devel. com., 90; mem. task force Thinking Strategies Curriculum, 1990—91; extensions specialist gifted and talented, 1990—91; math, 1991—; master tchr. Nat. Tchr. Tng. Inst., 1993. Co-author: (curricula) Provo Sch. Dist.'s Microorganism Sci. Kit, 1988, Arthropod Sci. Kit, 1988, Tchg. for Thinking, 1990—, PAWS Presents the Internet and the World Wide Web, 1997. Named Utah State Tchr. of the Yr., 1992; recipient Honor Young Mother of Yr. award, State of Utah, 1981, Mayor's award of Excellence, Provo, Utah, 2003. Mem.: NEA, Provo Edn. Assn. (Tchr. of the Yr. 1991—92), Internat. Space Edn. Initiative (adv. bd.), Utah Coun. Tchrs. Math., Utah Edn. Assn., Nat. Coun. Tchrs. Math. Republican. Mem. Lds Ch. Office: Wasatch Elem Sch 1080 N 900 E Provo UT 84604 Office Phone: 801-374-4910. E-mail: colleend@provo.edu.

DENSLOW, DEBORAH PIERSON, primary school educator; b. Phila., May 2, 1947; d. Merrill Tracy Jr. and Margaret (Aiman) D.; m. James Tracy Grey III, Nov. 24, 1972 (div. Dec. 1980); 1 child, Sarah Elizabeth. BS, Gwynedd Mercy Coll., 1971; MA, Marygrove Coll., Detroit, 2000; M in Ednl. Adminstrn., Gwynedd Mercy Coll., Gwynedd, Pa., 2005. Tchr. Willingboro (N.J.) Bd. Edn., 1971—. Union rep. Burlington County Edn. Assn., Willingboro, 1981-82, ednl. adv. Nat. Constitution Ctr., Phila., 2002-.; mem. task force for reoganization Morrisville Sch. Dist., 1991-92. Mem. Borough Coun., Morrisville, 1988—94, pres., 1992—94, rep. candidate, 1986; borough chmn. Am. Cancer Soc., 1986—87; sec. bd. dirs. Morrisville Free Libr., 1988—90, bd. dirs., 1988—2001; mem. Morrisville Mcpl. Authority, chmn., 1994—95, 1996—2000, asst. sec., treas., 1995—96, 2001; judge City Gardens Contest The Pa. Horticultural Soc., Phila., 2002; committeewoman 1st ward Morrisville (Pa.) Rep. Com., 1986—98. Mem. NEA, N.J. Edn. Assn., Willingboro Edn. Assn. (union rep. 1981-82, alt. union rep. 1988-89), Parents without Ptnrs. (bd. dirs. Mercer County chpt. 1981-82, sec. 1982-84), Bucks County Boroughs Assn. (bd. dirs. 1989—, v.p. 1990-92, pres. 1992-93), Pa. Mcpl. Authorities Assn. (profl. devel. com. 2000-2001). Presbyterian. Avocations: swimming, sailing. Home: 1 Garrett Lane Willingboro NJ 08046

DENSMORE, ANN, speech pathology/audiology services professional, audiologist, writer; b. LA, Nov. 24, 1941; d. Ray B. and Margaret M. (Walsh) D.; children: Kristin Ann, Jennifer Ann. BS cum laude, UCLA, 1963; MA in Communicative Disorders, Calif. State U., 1975; postgrad., Cape Cod Conservatory Arts, 1977—79; EdM in Human Devel. and Psychology, Harvard U., 1991; EdD, Clark U., 1997. Cert. in speech-lang. pathology and audiology, in clin. competence speech lang. pathology and audiology. Cons., owner Child Talk. AAUW fellow Harvard U., 1990-91, Clark U., 1992-94. Clark U. fellow, 1992-94. Office: 4 Militia Dr Ste 15 Lexington MA 02420 Office Phone: 617-497-9222. Business E-Mail: ann_densmore@post.harvard.edu.

DENSMORE, VIRGINIA LEE, music educator; b. Chattanooga, Aug. 18, 1939; d. DeWayne Edward and Sadie (Schneider) Nolting; m. Gene Densmore, Aug. 31, 1968. B in Music Edn., Fla. State U., 1961, M in Music Edn., 1967. Cert. tchr. Fla. Tchr. elem. music Sabal Palm Elem. Sch., Tallahassee, 1962-67; prof. Fla. State U. Sch., Tallahassee, 1967-92, ret., 1992. Mem. Capital City Band, Tallahassee, 1966—; co-founder, mem. Big Bend Cmty. Orchestra, 1994—; mem. The Tallahassee Winds, 1997—. Mem. Am. Orff Schulwerk Assn., Music Educators Nat. Conv., Fla. Music Educators Assn., Fla. Elem. Music Educators Assn. (pres. 1973-75), Tallahassee Orff Ch. (pres. 1984-85), Tallahassee Music Guild (pres. 2000-02), Delta Kappa Gamma of Alpha Kappa (pres. 1983-85), Artist Series (bd. dirs. 1995—), Tallahassee Symphony Soc. Personal E-mail: ginnyden@comcast.net.

DENSON, J. RUSSELL, publishing executive; b. Houston, Texas; m. Carolyn Denson; 3 children. BBA in Accounting, U. Houston. CPA. Exec. v.p. HEI Corp., 1981—87, CFO, 1983; COO Hippocrates Partners; mng. partner Denson Pub. Group, 1987—92; pres., CEO Houston Biotechnology Inc., 1992—97; exec. v.p., CFO DSI Toys Inc., 1997—99; chmn., dir. ICELEBRATE.com, 1999—2000; COO, CFO Weider Publications, 2000—01, pres., CEO, dir., 2001—03; pres., CEO Reiman Media Group, Greendale, Wis., 2003—04, Gruner + Jahr USA Pub., NYC, 2004—. Office: Gruner + Jahr Pub 375 Lexington Ave New York NY 10017-5514

DENSON, WILLIAM FRANK, III, lawyer; b. Birmingham, Ala., Aug. 1, 1943; s. William Frank Jr. and Martha Jane (Wilson) D.; m. Deborah Lynn Davis, July 6, 1974; 1 child, Patricia Lynn Pyle. BA, U. Montevallo, 1965; JD, Emory U., 1968. Bar: Ala. 1968. Atty. Spain, Gillon, Riley, Tate & Ansley, Birmingham, 1969-73; atty., asst. sec., sec. Vulcan Materials Co., Birmingham, 1973-88, sec., asst. gen. counsel, 1988-92, v.p., sec., asst. gen. counsel, 1992-94, v.p. law, sec., 1994-98, sr. v.p. law, sec., 1998-99, sr. v.p., gen. counsel, sec., 1999—. Trustee U. Montevallo, 1987-99; bd. dirs. Glenwood Mental Health Svcs., 1990-96. Mem. ABA, Ala. State Bar, Country Club of Birmingham, Willow Point Country Club (Alexander City, Ala.), Kiwanis Club Birmingham. Republican. Episcopalian. Avocations: golf, reading, travel. Home: 3215 E Briarcliff Rd Birmingham AL 35223-1304 Office: Vulcan Materials Co 1200 Urban Center Dr Birmingham AL 35242-2545

DENT, CATHERINE GALE, secondary school educator; b. Salem, Mo., Apr. 20, 1953; d. James Ferguson and Virgina Gale (Martin) Dent; 1 son from previous marriage, M. Cole Schafer; m. Hobart E. Porter, Dec. 29, 1997. Student, U. Mo., 1971-74, 91—, Longview Commun. Coll., Lee's Summit, Mo., 1975, S.W. Bapt. U., Bolivar, Mo., 1985; BA in Liberal studies, Thomas Edison State Coll.; MS in Ednl. Counseling, PhD in Ednl. Adminstrn., Columbia State U., 1997; MA in Edn., Univ. of Phoenix, 2003. Lic. funeral dir.; cert. secondary tchr., Mo. Feature writer, reporter Dent County Headliner, 1972-74; acctg. clk. Assn. of Unity Chs., Unity Village, Mo., 1974-77; graphic artist The Salem News, 1979; adminstrv. asst. Ozark Lead Co.-Kennecott Corp., Sweetwater, Mo., 1979-82; ch. organist United Meth. Ch., Salem, 1977-97; music tchr. Salem, 1983—; substitute tchr. Salem R-80 Sch. Dist., 1991—99, contracted tchr., 1999—; owner Dent LLC. Bd. dirs. Salem Arts Coun., 1984—; mgr. Salem Community Jazz Band, 1985—; accompanist Salem Community Choir, 1984—, Salem R-80 Sch. Sys. Music Dept., 1990—; dir. Temple Carillons Handbell Choir, Salem, 1985-94; sec. Vocat. Edn. Adv. Com., 1996-99, 2000—. Recipient Children's award Cosmopolitan Club; named to Outstanding Young Women in Am., 1985. Mem. Salem Computer Club, Dent County Hist. Soc., Order Ea. Star, Order of Amaranth, Salem Rebekah Lodge, Fraternal Order of Eagles Ladies Aux., Internat. Order Rainbow for Girls (Grand Cross of Color 1968, supreme dep. 1998), Sorosis Club (pres. 1992-93), Cosmopolitan Club (sec. 1994-98, pres. 1998—), Phi Beta Mu. Democrat. Methodist. Avocations: playing piano, travel. Home: 1300 W Rolla Rd Salem MO 65560-2736

DENT, CHARLES WIEDER, congressman; b. Allentown, Pa., May 24, 1960; s. Walter and Marjorie (Wieder) D.; m. Pamela J. Serfass, Aug. 17, 1991; children: Kathryn, William, C. John. BA, Pa. State U., 1982; MPA, Lehigh U., 1993. Sales rep. P.A. Peters, Inc., Allentown, to 1986; devel. officer Lehigh U., Bethlehem, Pa., 1986-90; mem. Pa. Ho. of Reps., Dist. 132, Harrisburg, 1991-98, Pa. Senate, Dist. 16, Harrisburg, 1998—2004, U.S. Ho. Reps., 109th Congress, 15th Dist Pa., 2005—. Bd. dirs. Ben Franklin Partnership, Pa. Coun. Arts, Pa. Commn. on Crime and Delinquency; chair bd. dirs. task force Jt. State Govt. Commn. Studying Children and Youth Svcs. Delivery Sys. Mem. pres.' adv. bd. Good Shepherd Rehab. Hosp.; mem. bd. ambs. Lehigh Carbon C.C., Cedar Crest Coll., Allentown; active Cmty. Svcs. for Children, N.E. chpt. Pa. Cystic Fibrosis Found., Crime Victims Coun. Lehigh Valley, Program for Women and Families, Minsi Trails Coun. Boy Scouts Am. Republican. Protestant. Office: 502 Cannon House Office Bldg Washington DC 20515-3815 Office Phone: 202-225-6411.*

DENT, EDWARD DWAIN, lawyer; b. Ft. Worth, Dec. 23, 1950; BA, Tex. Christian U., 1973; JD, St. Mary's U., Tex., 1976. Bar: Tex., U.S. Dist. Ct. (no. and so. dists.) Tex., U.S. Supreme Ct. Atty., ptnr. Kugle, Stewart, Dent, Frederick, Ft. Worth, 1979-89; founder Dent Law Firm, Ft. Worth, Dallas, 1990—. Bd. dirs. West Side Little League. Recipient Hist. Preservation Award, Tarrant County Hist. Soc., 1992. Mem. ATLA, Pres.'s Club (life), U.S. Supreme Ct. Hist. Soc., Tex. Trial Lawyers (bd. dirs. 1989-2002, Tarrant County Trial Lawyers (bd. dirs. 1988-89, officer 1989), Trial Lawyers for Pub. Justice, Ft. Worth Club, Colonial Country Club, Million Dollar Advocacy Soc. (life). Democrat. Office: Dent Law Firm 1120 Penn St Fort Worth TX 76102-3417

DENT, FREDERICK BAILY, textiles executive, retired ambassador; b. Cape May, N.J., Aug. 17, 1922; s. Magruder and Edith (Baily) D.; m. Mildred C. Harrison, Mar. 11, 1944 (dec.); children: Frederick Baily, Mildred Hutcheson, Pauline Harrison, Diana Gwynn, Magruder Harrison. BA, Yale U., 1944. With Joshua L. Baily & Co., Inc., N.Y.C., 1946-47; with Mayfair Mills, Arcadia, SC, 1947—, 2003, pres., 1958-88, treas., 1977—2001, chmn., 1998—2001, bd. dirs. Sec. Dept. Commerce, Washington, 1973-75; amb., spl. rep. for trade negotiations, 1975-77; bd. dirs. Joshua L. Baily & Co. Chmn. Spartanburg County Planning and Devel. Commn., 1960-72; trustee Spartanburg Day Sch., Brevard Music Ctr.; past mem. corp. Yale U.; mem. Pres.'s Commn. on an All-Vol. Army, 1969-70; mem. Pres.'s Commn. on Indsl. Competitiveness, 1982. Lt. USNR, 1943-46, PTO. Named Laureate, S.C.; named to S.C. Bus. Hall of Fame, Textile Hall of Fame. Mem. Spartanburg Area C. of C. (chmn. 1991). Episcopalian. Home: 221 Montgomery Dr Spartanburg SC 29302-3443 E-mail: dentf@bellsouth.net.

DENT, JULIE, executive director; d. Ernest and Elaine (King) Dent; m. Barry Morrow; 1 child, Christopher Dent Morrow. AAS, Borough Manhattan CC, 1988; BS in Edn., Empire State Coll.; MS with honors in Edn., CUNY, 1995. Tchr. Horace E. Greene Day Care Ctr., Bklyn., 1983—88, adminstrv. dir., 1988—97; exec. dir. Audrey Johnson Day Care, Bklyn., 1997—. Domestic violence prevention counselor Women Working for a Better Cmty., 1996—; exec. bd. 1st vice chair Woodhull Hosp., Bklyn., 1999—; exec. vice chair Cmty. Sch. Bd. Dist. # 32, Bklyn., 2002—; dir. universal pre-K program dept. of edn. Long Island U., 1994—. Recipient award for excellence in early childhood edn., Profl. Assn. Day Care Dirs. Inc., 1989, award for outstanding cmty. svc., City Coun. N.Y., 1996, Key Stone award, Fedn. Protestant Welfare Agy. Inc., 2000, Citation of Honor, Charles J. Hynes, Dist. Atty., 2002, award for dedicated svc. to children, State Senator Martin M. Dilan, 2003, Citizenship award, Assemblyman Vito Lopez, Cmty Svc. award, Hon. D. Towns, 2004, Congressional Recognition award, Hon. E. Towns, 2004. Mem.: Nat. Assn. for Female Exec., Nat. Assn. For the Edn. of Young Children, Phi Delta Kappa (mem. Beta Omicron chpt.). Avocations: reading, dance. Office Phone: 718-574-0130. Personal E-mail: julieeduc@aol.com. Business E-Mail: audreyjo272@aol.com.

DENT, TAYLOR, professional tennis player; b. Newport Beach, CA, Apr. 24, 1981; s. Phil Dent, Betty Ann Stuart. Profl. tennis player ATP Tour, 1998—. Mem. US Davis Cup Team, 2003. Achievements include winner, Bangkok, Memphis, Moscow, 2003, Newport, 2002. Office: c/o ATP Tour 201 ATP Boulevard Ponte Vedra Beach FL 32082*

DENTINGER, RONALD LEE, comedian, speaker, freelance writer; b. Milw., Feb. 14, 1941; s. William Cassel and Kathryn Faye (Ritzman) D.; m. Kaylee Ann Kasten, Aug. 28, 1965; children: Ronald Lee Jr., Joann Jean. Officer Milw. Police Dept., 1962-67; dist. mgr. Am. Automobile Assn., Madison, Wis., 1967-71; gen. mgr. Don Q Inn, Dodgeville, Wis., 1971-85; comedian, spkr. Dodgeville, 1976—. Humorist quoted in comedy mags., books; jokes sold to Rodney Dangerfield Joan Rivers, The Tonight Show, Saturday Night Live, 20/20 Show, Time Mag.; author: (with others) The Art of Communication, The Great Communicators II, (joke books) Down Time, How to Argue with Your Spouse. Pres. Hidden Valley Tourism Region, Wis., 1984. Named Funniest Person in Wis., Showtime-TV Network, 1985. Mem. Nat. Spkrs. Assn., Wis. Profl. Spkrs. Assn., Wis. Soc. Assn. Execs., Dodgeville C. of C. (pres. 1984), Internat. Assn. Profl. Pranksters (founding mem. 2005). Home and Office: PO Box 151 Dodgeville WI 53533-0151 Office Phone: 608-935-2417.

DENTLER, ROBERT ARNOLD, sociologist, educator; b. Chgo., Nov. 26, 1928; s. Arnold E. and Jennie (Munsen) D.; m. Helen Hosmer, Sept. 7, 1950; children: Deborah, Eric, Robin. BS, Northwestern U., 1949, MA, 1950, Am. U., 1954; PhD, U. Chgo., 1960. Reporter Chgo. City News Bur., 1949; tchr. Pomfret Sch., 1950-52; intelligence officer U.S. Govt., 1952-54; instr. Dickinson Coll., 1954-57; fellow U. Chgo., 1957-59; rschr. U. Kans., 1959-61; asst. prof. Dartmouth Coll., 1961-62; mem. faculty Tchrs. Coll., Columbia U., N.Y.C., 1962-72, prof. sociology, dep. dir. to dir. Ctr. for Urban Edn., 1966-72; dean Sch. Edn., Boston U., 1972-79; sr. sociologist Abt Assocs., Cambridge, Mass., 1979-83; prof. sociology U. Mass., Boston, 1983-92; sr. fellow McCormack Inst. Pub. Affairs, 1993-94; faculty assoc. Trotter Inst., 1994—2001; dir. Inst. for Learning and Teaching U. Mass., Boston, 1987, acting dean Coll. Edn., 1988. Author: (with Peter Rossi) The Politics of Urban Renewal, 1961, (with Nelson W. Polsby and Paul A. Smith) Politics and Social Life, 1963, (with Phillips Cutright) Hostage America, 1963, (with B. Mackler and M.E. Warshauer) The Urban R's: Race Relations as the Problem in Urban Education, 1967, Major American Social Problems, 1967, (with M.E. Warshauer) Big City Dropouts and Illiterates, 1967, American Community Problems, 1967, Major Social Problems, 1973, Urban Problems, 1977, (with M.B. Scott) Schools on Trial: An Inside Account of the Boston School Desegregation Case, 1981, (with D.C. Baltzell and D.J. Sullivan) University on Trial, 1983, (with A.L. Hafner) Hosting Newcomers, 1997, Practicing Sociology, 2001, The Looking-Glass Self: A Memoir, 2002; editor Sociol. Practice Rev., 1989-92. Home: 11 Childs Rd Lexington MA 02421-4517 Office: U Mass Dept Sociology Boston MA 02125-3393

DENTON, CHARLES MANDAVILLE, corporate communications specialist, journalist; b. Glendale, Calif., June 22, 1924; s. Horace Bruce and Marguerite (Mandaville) D.; m. Jean Margaret Brady, Dec. 3, 1955; children— Charles Mandaville II, Margot Elizabeth. Student, U. Calif., 1942, Okla. A. and M. Coll., 1943; BA in Journalism, U. So. Calif., 1949. Reporter San Fernando Valley Times, N. Hollywood, Calif., 1949-50, U.P., Los Angeles, 1950-52; reporter, sportswriter, columnist I.N.S., Los Angeles, 1952-59; reporter, feature writer, TV editor-columnist Los Angeles Examiner, 1959-62; free-lance TV and mag. writer, 1962-63; reporter Los Angeles Times, 1963; columnist San Francisco Examiner, 1963-68; communications dir. Leslie Salt Co., San Francisco, 1968-73. Comm. dir. Crown Zellerbach Corp., San Francisco, 1973-83; v.p. Hilland Knowlton Inc., 1983-90. Author: (with Dr. W. Coda Martin) A Matter of Life, 1964. Pres. Greater Los Angeles Press Club Welfare Found., 1961. Served with USNR, 1943-46. Mem. Phi Beta Kappa, Phi Kappa Phi, Sigma Delta Chi, Blue Key. Clubs: Greater Los Angeles Press (pres. 1955-57), Tiburon Peninsula, Bohemian. Home and Office: 40 Seafirth Rd Belvedere Tiburon CA 94920-1125 Fax: (415) 435-0454. E-mail: chzdenton@aol.com.

DENTON, D. KEITH, finance educator; b. Paducah, Ky., June 28, 1948; s. Derward and Bonnie Denton; children: Shane, Taylor. BS, Murray State U., 1971; M in Pub. Adminstrn., Memphis State U., 1974; PhD, So. Ill. U., 1981. Supr. Shelby Pre-Casting, Memphis, 1971-72; safety engr. Md. Casualty Corp., Memphis, 1972-76; instr. Draughn's Bus. Coll., Paducah, 1977; safety trainer Union Carbide Corp., Paducah, 1977-78; prof. So. Ill. U., Carbondale, 1978-83, S.W. Mo. State U., Springfield, 1983—. Cons. Small Bus. Research Ctr., Springfield, 1985—, Springfield Remfg. Corp., 1986. Author: Safety Management, 1982; (with others) Safety Performance, 1985, Quality Service in America, 1989, The Production Game, 1990, Handling Employee Complaints, 1990, Horizontal Management, 1991, The Service Trainer, 1992, Recruitment Retention and Employee Relations, 1992, Did You Know?, Fascinating Facts and Fallacies, 1994, Enviro-Management: How Companies Turn Pollution Cost into Profits, 1994, The Toolbox for the Mind, 1999, Empowering Intranets, 2002; contbr. over 150 articles to profl. jours. Mem. Acad. Mgmt., Nat. Assn. Purchasing, Am. Soc. Prodn. and Inventory Control, Inst. Indsl. Engrs. Office: SW Mo State U 901 S National Ave Springfield MO 65804-0088 Office Phone: 417-836-5573. Business E-Mail: dkd848f@smsu.edu.

DENTON, DENICE D., academic administrator, engineering educator; b. El Campo, Tex. d. Carolyn Mabee. BSEE, MIT, MSEE, 1982, PhD in elec. engring., 1987. Asst. prof. dept. elec. & computer engring. U. Wis., Madison, 1987—92, assoc. prof., 1992—95, prof., 1995—96, prof. dept. chemistry, 1995—96, co-dir. NSF Inst. for Sci. Edn., 1995—96; prof. dept. elec. engring. U. Wash., Seattle, 1996—2005, dean Coll. Engring., 1996—2005; vis. scientist Inst. Quantum Electronics, Swiss Fed. Inst. Tech., Zurich, 1991, vis. prof., 1993; chancellor U. Calif., Santa Cruz, 2005—. Mem. NAS/NRC Bd. on Engring. Edn., 1991—96, chair, 1997—; mem. adv.bd. Initiatives to Diversify the Professoriate MIT, 1995—; mem. nat. vis. com. NSF Modular Chemistry Consortium U. Calif., Berkeley, 1995—; mem. adv. com. Directorate of Edn. and Human Resources NSF, 1996—; mem. nat. adv. com. Mathlinks Consortium Rensselaer Poly. Inst., 1996—; mem. planning com. Nat. Libr. for SME&T Edn. NRC, 1997—; mem. steering com. Celebration of Women in Engring. NAE, 1997—; mem. exec. bd. Engring. Deans Coun., 1997—. Recipient Presdl. Young Investigator Award, NSF, 1987, Elec. and Computer Engring. Prof Yr. Award, U. Wis. Madison, 1988, Polygon Outstanding Instructor Award, 1989, Kiekhofer Disting. Tchg. Award, 1990, C.H. MacDonald Dist. Young Elec. Engr. Nat. Tchg. Award, Eta Kappa Nu, 1993, Engring. Tchg. Excellence Award, W.M. Keck Found., 1994, Benjamin Smith Reynolds Tchg. Award, U. Wis. Madison Coll. Engring., 1994; Hertz Fellow, 1984—87. Fellow: IEEE (Prof. of Yr. 1993, Harriet B. Rigas Award 1995); mem.: Am. Soc. Engring. Edn. (George Westinghouse Award 1995). Office: U Calif, Santa Cruz 1156 High St Santa Cruz CA 95064*

DENTON, DEREK ASHWORTH, medical researcher, foundation administrator; b. Launceston, Tasmania, Australia, May 27, 1924; s. Arthur A. and Catherine (Edwards) D.; m. Margaret Catherine Scott, Mar. 13, 1953; children: Matthew, Angus. MBBS, Melbourne U., 1947. Haley Rsch. Fellow Walter and Eliza Hall Inst., Melbourne, 1948; med. rsch. fellow, sr. med. rsch. fellow Nat. Health and Med. Rsch. Coun., Melbourne, 1948—, prin. med. rsch. fellow, 1970; founding dir. Howard Florey Inst. Exptl. Physiology and Medicine, Melbourne, 1971-89, emeritus dir., 1990—; pres. Howard Florey Biomed. Found., Melbourne, 1997—. Bd. dirs. David Syme Ltd. Pubs. The Age, 1984-93; invited OECD examiner of sci. and tech. policy Govt. Sweden, 1985-86; 1st v.p. Internat. Union of Physiol. Scis., 1983-89 (chmn. nominating com. and com. on commns. 1986-93), jury Albert and Mary Lasker Found. awards in med. sci., 1979-90; fgn. assoc. NAS of U.S., 1995; adj. scientist Southwest Found. Biomed. Rsch., San Antonio, 1994—; fgn. assoc. Inst. France Acad. Scis., 2000. Author: The Hunger for Salt, 1982, The Pinnacle of Life: Consciousness in Animals and Humans; editor: Olfaction and Taste, 1985. Decorated companion Order of Australia. Fellow Royal Soc. (London), Royal Coll. Physicians (hon., London and Australia), Am. Physiol. Soc. (hon.), Am. Acad. Arts and Scis. (fgn.); mem. Royal Swedish Acad. Scis. (fgn. med. mem.). Avocations: wine, tennis, fly fishing. Home: 816 Orrong Rd Toorak 3142 Melbourne Australia Office: Univ Melbourne Dept Physiology Parkville 3010 Australia Office Phone: 61 3 8344 5639. Business E-Mail: ddenton@unimelb.edu.au.

DENTON, FRANK M., newspaper editor; b. Tulsa, Mar. 30, 1945; s. Frank McCray and Eydith (Langley) D.; m. April Murphy, June 18, 1983 (div. 2000); children: Langley Sara, Allegra Murphy. BA, U. Tex., 1968; MS, Columbia U., 1970; MBA, U. Wis., 1994, PhD, 1996. Sportswriter Austin Am. Statesman, 1964-66; reporter Stuart Long News Svc., Austin, Tex., 1966-69, Anniston (Ala.) Star, 1970-72, Cin. Enquirer, 1972-75; asst. lifestyle editor Detroit Free Press, 1976-78, lifestyle editor, 1978-81, asst. mng. editor, 1981-86; editor Wis. State Journal, Madison, 1986—2004, The Tampa Tribune, Fla., 2004—. Bd. dirs. Mid-Am. Press Inst. Mem. Am. Soc. Newspaper Editors (bd. dirs.), Phi Kappa Phi. Office: The Tampa Tribune 200 S Parker St Tampa FL 33606 Office Phone: 813-259-7591. Business E-Mail: fdenton@tampatrib.com.

DENTON, LAWRENCE A., automotive executive; Formerly with Ford Motor Co.; pres. Dow Automotive, 1996—2002; pres., CEO DURA Automotive Systems, Rochester Hills, Mich., 2003—. Bd. dirs. Autotemp Co. Bd. dirs. Kettering U. Mem.: Motor & Equipment Mfrs. Assn. (bd. dirs.), Original Equipment Suppliers Assn. (bd. dirs.). Office: DURA Automotive Systems 2791 Research Dr Rochester Hills MI 48309-3575

DENTON, RAY DOUGLAS, insurance company executive; b. Lake City, Ark., May 16, 1937; s. Ray Dudney and Edna Lorraine (Roe) Denton; m. Cheryl Emma Borchardt, Mar. 9, 1964; children: Ray D., Derek St. Clair, Carter Lee(dec.). BA, U. Mich., 1964, postgrad., 1969—70, Wayne State U., 1964—65, JD, 1969. Claims rep. Hartford Ins. Co. Crum & Forster, Detroit, Am. Claims, Chgo., 1962-73; ptnr. Chgo. Metro Claims, Oak Park, Ill., 1974-75; founder, pres. Ray D. Denton & Assocs., Inc., Hinsdale, Ill., 1975—. Mem.: Phi Alpha Delta, Pi Kappa Alpha. Office: Ray D Denton and Assoc Inc 930 N York Rd Ste 14 Hinsdale IL 60521-2993 Personal E-mail: cherayden@sbcglobal.net.

D'ENTREMONT, EDWARD JOSEPH, application developer, educator; b. Lynn, Mass., June 25, 1954; s. Joseph Albenie and Gertrude Grace (Flattery) D'E. BA in Math., Salem State Coll., 1976; MS in Applied Math., Northeastern U., 1982. Floor supr. Jordan Marsh Co., Peabody, Mass., 1972—76; sci. programmer Electronics Corp. Am., Cambridge, Mass., 1977, Sulivan and Cogliano, Waltham, Mass., 1977; software engr. Raytheon Svc. Co., Burlington, Mass., 1977—86, Baytheon Missile Sys. divsn., Bedford, Mass., 1986—96, Desktop Data Inc., Burlington, Mass., 1995—98; prin. software engr. Newsedge Corp., Burlington, 1998—2002, Dialog Corp., Burlington, 2002—. Instr. Fitchburg State Raytheon Inst., Tewksbury, Mass, 1986-96, U. Lowell, Mass., 1991-2001; sr. software engr. Raytheon Co.; instr. continuing edn. Salem State Coll., 1993-95. Campaign worker presdl. campaigns, 1968-72, city coun., state rep., Lynn, 1976, Dukakis for Gov., Lynn, 1982; vol. tech. com. Aborn Elem. Sch. Mem. IEEE, Am. Math. Soc., Math. Assn. Am., Soc. for Indsl. and Applied Math., IEEE Computer Soc., N.Y. Acad. Scis., Assn. Computing Machinery, St. Mary's H.S. Alumni Assn., Salem State Coll. Alumni Assn., Northeastern U. Alumni Assn., Lexington Racquet and Swim Club. Democrat. Roman Catholic. Home: 50 York Rd Lynn MA 01904-1130

DENUZZO, RINALDO VINCENT, pharmacy educator; b. Cleve., Oct. 21, 1922; s. Luigi and Domenica Mary (Razzano) DiNuzzo; m. Lucy Bernadine Sneed, June 29, 1946; 1 child, Lisa Ann. BS, Albany Coll. Pharmacy, 1952; MS in Edn., SUNY-Albany, 1956; LHD, Union U., 2003. Registered pharmacist, N.Y., Fla., Vt. Prof. pharmacy N.Y. Coll. Pharmacy, Albany, 1952—, adminstrv. asst., 1963-80. Pharmacist N.Y., Fla., Vt., 1968-95; sr. pharmacist inspector N.Y. State Dept. Health, 1966-95; field dir. Market Measures, Inc.; chmn. tech. pharmacy adv. com., 1977-95; lectr. drug product substitution and generic drugs; notary public. Author: Ann. Albany Coll. Pharmacy Prescription Survey, 1956—84, Substitution, The New York State Experience, 1980, RX Services, XIII Winter Olympic Games, 1980, Ann. DeNuzzo Prescription Survey, 1985—96, Imapct of One-Line Prescription Form on Generic Drug Use, 1987, Cipro, Vasotec, Volatren Post Biggest Gains, 1987, Using the Right Tools to Achieve Personal Success, 1990, Personal Selling, 1991, Annual Survey Tracks Drug Prescribing Trends, 1990, Consumer Prescription Prices Increase, 1991, Changes in Dental Prescribing, 1991, How to Reduce Prescription Medical Costs, 1992, Are Dental Prescriptions a Viable Target for RPhs?, 1992, Financial Success: A Challenge for the Future, 1996, A National Drug Expert Is Needed, 1999, Down Memory Lane, 1999, 2002, What Graduates Need to Know: A Prescription for the Future Financial Success: ACP's Reflection of Progress 1881-2001; A Brief Written and Pictorial History, 2001; editor: Albany Coll. Pharmacy Alumni News, 1961—81; mem. editl. bd. MMM, 1977—80. Instr. first aid, responding to emergencies CPR ARC; mem. East Greenbush Ctrl. Sch. Dist. Bd. Edn., 1974—92, v.p., 1975—76, pres., 1976—78, 1991—92, East Greenbush Edn. Found.; chmn. Albany Coll. Pharmacy Faculty, 1987—89, com. on coms., 1984—87, promotions com., 1989—92, exec. com., grievance com., chair strategic planning steering com., 1995—96; faculty affairs chmn. and rev. Albany Coll. Pharmacy, 1990—94; sr. student status com., faculty ombudsman Albany Coll. Pharmacy Faculty, 1991—2002, mission statement com., 1995; mem. adv. bd. Merrell-Dow Hosp., 1987; sec.-treas. Union U. Pharmacy Coll. Coun., 1970—80; com. on coms. Albany Coll. Pharmacy Faculty, 1996—97; mem. profl. adv. com. Albany Vis. Nurses Assn.; mem. rev. panel on prescription payment rev. commn. Office Tech. Assessment U. S. Congress, 1988; mem. ethics panel Siena Coll., 1992; mem., dir. Rensselaer County Taxpayers Assn.; cons. pharmacist, coord. pharm. svcs. XIII Olympic Winter Games, Lake Placid, NY, 1980; liaison Health Sys. Mgmt. degree Joint MS with Union Coll. With U.S. Army, 1941—46, with USAF, 1946—47, capt. M.C., pharm. officer USAFR, 1948—63, ret. USAFR, 1982. Named Francis J. O'Brien Pharmacy Man of Yr., 1979, 2002; recipient 25 Yr. Svc. citation, ARC, 30 Yr. Svc. citation, Svc. plaque, East Greenbush Ctrl. Sch. Dist., 25 Yr. Svc. award, N.Y. State Dept. Health, Disting. Svc. citation, Rensselaer County Taxpayers Assn., established L. Sneed DeNuzzo Sch., Concord Coll., W.V. Mem.: AAUP (pres. 1978—), AARP, Albany Coll. Pharmacy Alumni Assn. (exec. dir. 1965—86, disting. svc. medal 1975), N.Y. State Pub. Employees Fedn., N.Y. Sch. Bd. Assn., N.Y. State Pharm. Soc., Am. Pharm. Assn., Am. Assn. Colls. Pharmacy (sec.-treas., coun. faculties 1979—80, chmn. elect 1982—83, chmn. 1984—87, dir. 1984—89, roundtable presentation ann. meeting 1996, del. ann. meeting 1997), USA Air Muse, 46th and 72nd Recon. Assn., Nat. Italian-Am. Found. (coun.), Officers Club (West Point, N.Y.), Albany Coll. Pharmacy Pres.'s Club (chmn. bd. 1962—87), Kappa Psi (dep. grand coun. Beta Delta chpt., sec.-treas., Albany grad.), Army Five Star, Beta Delta (ann. Rinaldo V. DeNuzzo lucnheon 1988—). Republican. Roman Catholic. Home: 19 Alva St East Greenbush NY 12061-2027 Office: 106 New Scotland Ave Albany NY 12208-3425 E-mail: reutterd@acp.com.

DENVER, EILEEN ANN, retired editor; b. N.Y.C., Nov. 16, 1942; d. Daniel Joseph and Katherine Agnes (Boland) D.; m. Duncan C. Stephens, July 2, 1988. BA, Coll. New Rochelle, 1964; certificate, Radcliffe Sch. Pub., 1964; MA, Ind. U., 1967. Editorial asst. Mass. Inst. Tech. Tech. Review, Boston, 1965-66; instr. English St. Peter's Coll., Jersey City, 1967-70; assoc. editor, writer Am. Home mag., N.Y.C., 1971-75; asst. editor Consumer Reports, Mt. Vernon, NY, 1975-77, asst. mng. editor, 1977-79, mng. editor, 1979-91, exec. editor, 1991-96, dir. editl. ops., 1997-2000, assoc. editl. dir./exec. editor, 2000—04, ret. Office: Consumer Reports 101 Truman Ave Yonkers NY 10703-1044

DENVER, THOMAS HR, lawyer; b. NYC, Oct. 29, 1944; s. Thomas H. Rorke and Eileen Ann Boland; m. Barbara Ann Denver, Dec. 19, 1987; children: Rorke, Nate. BS, Syracruse U., 1966; MS, U. Wash., 1967; JD, U. Calif., San Francisco, 1973. Bar: Calif. 1973, U.S. Dist. Ct. (no. dist.) Calif. 1973. From assoc. to mng. ptnr. Hoge, Fenton, Jones & Appel, Inc., San Jose, Calif., 1973—99. Judge pro tem Santa Clara County Superior Ct., San Jose, 1980—; instr. Stanford U. Law Sch. Advocacy Program; mem. faculty Hastings Coll. of Advocacy; mediator, arbitrator. Contbr. articles to profl. jours. Fellow Am. Coll. Trial Lawyers; mem. Am. Bd. Trial Advocates, Santa Clara County Civil Litigation Com., Santa Clara County Bar Assn. (chmn. fast track com.). Avocations: running, fishing, reading. Office: Mediation Masters 96 N Third St # 300 San Jose CA 95112 Office Phone: 408-535-3298. Business E-Mail: tdenver@mediatimmasters.com.

DENVIR, ROBERT F., lawyer; b. Chgo., Sept. 24, 1945; BBA, U. Notre Dame, 1967; JD, DePaul U., 1971. Bar: Ill. 1971, U.S. Dist. Ct. Ill. (No. dist.), U.S. Ct. Appeals (Fed. cir.); CPA, Ill. Assoc. to ptnr. Winston & Strawn LLP, Chgo., 1976—, chmn. tax dept., mem. exec. com. Bd. trustees Goodman Theatre. Mem. ABA (mem. fed. taxation sect.),Chgo. Bar Assn. Office: Winston & Strawn 35 W Wacker Dr Ste 4200 Chicago IL 60601-1695 Office Phone: 312-558-5765. Office Fax: 312-558-5700. E-mail: rdenvir@winston.com.

DENYSYK, BOHDAN, marketing professional, consultant; b. Kornberg, Germany, Feb. 13, 1947; came to U.S., 1949; s. John and Maria (Zelenewich) D.; m. Halina Bubela, June 28, 1969; children: Maria H., Danya L., Adrienne Y., Alexis M. BS, Manhattan Coll., 1968; MS, Cath. U. Am., 1971; PhD, Union Inst. (formerly Union for Experimenting Colls. and Univs.), Cin., 1981. Project mgr. Naval Weapons Lab., Bethesda, Md., 1968-72, analyst and ops., 1972-75; program mgr. Naval Surface Weapons Ctr., 1975-78; dept. head E.G. & G. Inc., Rockville, Md., 1978-81; dep. asst. sec. U.S. Dept. Commerce, Washington, 1981—84; dir. civil programs IBM Corp., 1984—86; pres. DLR Assocs., Arlington, Va., 1972-80, 83—, Global U.S.A., 1987—, also owner, bd. dirs. Mem. Congl. Adv. Panel on China, 1985—; bd. dirs. Mazak Corp.; mem. Def. Sci. Bd., 1990—. Contbr. articles to profl. jours. Mem. Presdl. Transition Team, Washington, 1980; regional dir. Rep. Nat. Com., 1980; dir. pub. rels. Ukrainian Nat. Info. Svc., 1976-80; mem. Pres.'s Export Coun., 1981—, Presdl. Awards Commn., 1986-87, 2005; exec. dir. Md. Reagan-Bush Campaign, 1984, Bush-Quayle Campaign, 1992; mem. nat. policy forum Fgn. Affairs Coun., 1995—; pres. Phi Mu Alpha Sinfonia, 1967-68; nat. dir. for coalitions Dole for U.S. Pres. Campaign, 1987-88; dep. polit. dir. Dole for Pres., 1995-96; regional polit. dir. Gov. Bush for Pres. 2000, 1999—; mem. Bush-Cheney Transition Team, 2001; mem. sr. commn. on nat. security CSIS, 2000-2001; mem. Md. State Info. Tech. Bd., 2003—. Navy fellow, 1969-72; Regents scholar, 1964-68 Fellow N.Y. Acad. Sci.; mem. AIAA, AAAS, Am. Def. Preparedness Assn., Am. Phys. Soc. Republican. Roman Catholic. Avocations: scuba, skiing, running. Office: Global USA Inc 2121 K St NW Ste 650 Washington DC 20037-1825 Office Phone: 202-296-2400.

DENZEL, NORA, information technology executive; Graduate, SUNY, Plattsburgh; MS in bus. admin., Santa Clara U., Calif. Various tech. and bus. roles to dir. storage-mgmt. products IBM; sr. v.p. product operations Legato Systems, 1997—2000; v.p. storage Hewlett Packard Co., 2000—03, sr. v.p. adaptive enterprise and software group, 2003—. Named one of the 50 Most Powerful People in Networking, Network World mag., 2003. Office: Hewlett-Packard Co 3000 Hanover St Palo Alto CA 94304

DENZLER, JAMES WYATT, pharmacist; b. Marion, Va., Jan. 30, 1958; s. Roger Vincent Denzler and Helen Margaret Lambert Williams. BS in Biology, East Tenn. U., 1981, U. Minn., 1988. Registered pharmacist, Va., Calif., N.Y. Pharmacist Longs Drugs, Santa Barbara, Calif., 1988-90, Thrifty Drugs, Santa Barbara, 1990-91, Eckerd/Revco, Virginia Beach, Va., 1991-2000, Norfolk (Va.) Gen. Hosp., 1998—; pharmacist mgr. Rite Aid, Virginia Beach, Va., 2000—. Pres., owner Denzler Corp., Norfolk, 1996—; diabetes educator, mem. AADE, 2000—; adj. faculty Hampton U., 2001. Mem. Am. Pharm. Assn., Aubudon Soc., U.S. Table Tennis Assn., Pi Kappa Alpha (chpt. pres.), Phi Delta Chi (chpt. pres.). Avocations: birding, ping pong/table tennis, weightlifting, photography. Office: Rite Aid 5795 Princess Anne Rd Virginia Beach VA 23462 E-mail: jamz9260@aol.com.

DENZLER, NANCY J., artist; b. Newport, Ark., Apr. 17, 1936; d. Walter and Eathel (Faulkner) Blanchard; m. Ronald Ray Hopkins, Dec. 10, 1956; m. Arthur Henry Denzler, Dec. 31, 1969; m. Timothy Joseph Riordan, Apr. 10, 1989; children: Ronald Ray Hopkins Jr., Carrie Jayne Tel-Oren. BFA magna cum laude, SUNY, Buffalo, 1976, MFA, 1978. Instr. sculpture, watercolor, acrylic, pastel and drawing, pvt. groups, 1971—. Works exhibited at Albright-Knox Gallery, Buffalo, 1976, 77, 79, Mainstreams, Marietta, Ohio, 1976, Erie (Pa.) Art Ctr., 1976, AAO Gallery and AC Gallery, Buffalo, 1977, 78, 79, Niagara Falls (N.Y.) Art Ctr., 1977, Patterson Art Gallery, Westfield, N.Y., 1979, Barn Workshop Gallery, Danvers, Mass., 1980, Union Gallery, Boston, 1982, Montserrat Gallery, Beverly, Mass., 1983, Copley Soc., 1997, others. Artists fellow Creative Artists Pub. Svc. Program, N.Y.C., 1980. Mem. Boston Visual Artists Union, The Copley Soc. of Boston. Address: 9685 N Linda Vista Pl Tucson AZ 85742-8576

DEO, NARSINGH, computer scientist, educator; b. Raniganj, Bihar, India, Jan. 2, 1936; s. Bihari Lal and Durga (Modi) Jee; m. Karen Ruth Baier, June 29, 1968. BS, Patna U., India, 1956; Dip. I.I.Sc., Indian Inst. Sci., 1959; MS, Calif. Inst. Tech., 1960; PhD, Northwestern U., 1965. Assoc. electronic engr. Burroughs Electro Data divsn., 1960-62; sr. engr. Jet Propulsion Lab., Pasadena, 1966-69, mem. tech. staff, 1969-71; v.p. Britt Electronics Corp., Santa Monica, Calif., 1968-69; asst. prof. elec. engring. Calif. State Coll., 1971; assoc. prof. elec. engring. Indian Inst. Tech., Kanpur, 1971-74, prof., head computer ctr., 1975-77; prof. Wash. State U., Pullman, 1977-87, chmn. dept. computer sci., 1980-84; Millican chair prof. U. Ctrl. Fla., Orlando, 1986—; dir. Ctr. Parallel Computation, 1989—. Electronics design cons. Ctr. Behavior Therapy, Beverly Hills, Calif., 1967—71; mem. faculty engring. ext. UCLA, 1965—68; vis. assoc. prof. U. Ill., Urbana; vis. prof. Wash. State U., Pullman, 1974—75, ETH, Zurich, Switzerland, 1993, Australian Nat. U., Canberra, 1996, Chuo U., Tokyo, 2002; vis. faculty IBM Thomas J. Watson Rsch., Yorktown Heights, NY, 1984, Oak Ridge Nat. Lab., 1994. Author: 4 textbooks; contbr. scientific papers to profl. jours. Recipient Fla. Gov.'s award, 1989; grantee, NSF, U.S. Dept. Transp., Army Rsch. Office, U.S. Army's PM-TRADE, Fla. High Tech. and Industry Coun. Fellow: IEEE, Assn. Computing Machinery. Achievements include patents in field. Home: 3901 Orange Lake Dr Orlando FL 32817-1637 Business E-Mail: deo@cs.ucf.edu.

DEONES, JACK E., lawyer, broadcast executive; b. Mankato, Minn., Sept. 21, 1931; s. Nicholas H. and Beatrice R. (Viste) D.; m. Cleo Pat Peters, May 29, 1955; children— Gregg N., Alexa M. BSS, St. Mary's Coll., 1953; JD, Yale U., 1956. Bar: Minn. 1956, N.J. 1974. Spl. agt. FBI, 1960-62; atty. Pfizer, Inc., 1962-65; div. counsel Honeywell, Inc., 1965-69; asst. gen. counsel Foster Wheeler Corp., Livingston, N.J., 1969-77, corp. sec., 1977-96, v.p., 1984-96; chmn., pres. Castlerock Assocs., Parsippany, N.J., 1996—. Dir. Briarcliff Assocs., Inc. Served with USN, 1956-60. Mem. ABA, N.J. Bar Assn., Minn. Bar Assn. Home: 59 Briarcliff Rd Mountain Lakes NJ 07046-1304 Office: Castlerock Assocs PO Box 6133 Parsippany NJ 07054-7133 Office Phone: 973-402-1866.

DEORCHIS, FRANKIE JUANITA, forester, writer; b. Hawkins, Tex., Dec. 10, 1920; d. E. Whitney and Bura Moseley Moore; m. M. E. DeOrchis, June 27, 1948; children: Vincent Moore, Diane Frances Vogth-Eriksen, Douglas F. BS, Columbia U., 1948. Bookkeeper Civil Svc., Washington, 1942—44; law office mgr. DeOrchis & Ptnrs., N.Y.C.; mgr. hardwood forest The Timbers, Killingworth, Conn., 1967—. Author: Breaking Bread with Friends Around the World, 2000. Republican. Avocations: travel, reading, cooking, entertaining, charity work. Home: 50 Shore Rd Old Greenwich CT 06870 E-mail: medeorchis@aol.com.

DEOTTE, MICHAEL J., marketing professional; b. Putnam, Conn., June 9, 1971; s. Anne M. and Armand Deotte; life ptnr. Jonathan M. Wyse. BS, Bryant U., Smithfield, RI, 1993; MBA, U. Conn., Storrs, 1998. Mktg. mgr. U. Conn. Sch. Bus., Storrs, 1998—99, dir. mktg., 2000—; dir. mktg. for enrollment planning Sacred Heart U., Fairfield, Conn., 1999—2000. Sec. Hartford Gay & Lesbian Health Collective, Conn., 2003—. Recipient Admissions Mktg. Award, Admissions Mktg. Report, 2003, 2004, 2005. Mem.: Am. Mktg. Assn. Office: Univ Conn Sch Bus 2100 Hillside Rd Unit 1041 Storrs Mansfield CT 06269-1041 Office Phone: 860-486-4478. Office Fax: 860-486-5222. E-mail: mdeotte@business.uconn.edu.

DEOUL, KATHLEEN BOARDSEN, publishing executive; b. New London, Conn., May 5, 1944; d. Harry Kostrope Boardsen and Elizabeth (Conti) Dunham; m. Neal Deoul, June 20, 1982; 1 child, Shannon Rae. Grad. high sch., New London. Br. mgr. Qwip Sys. divsn. Exxon, Balt.; br. ops. mgr. Exxon Office Sys., Pitts., 1977-82; owner, pres. Bus. Quars., Crystal City, Va., 1983-95, Wellness Alternatives, Balt., 1993—2005, Cassandra Books, LLC, Balt., 2001; pres., dir. Bio Pro Tech., 2005—. Author: Cancer Cover-up, 2001. Active Team Diamond; co-chair Found. Alternative and Complementary Therapies. Mem.: Pres.'s Club Nikken, Inc. (Distbr. of Yr. 1999), Pres.'s Club Exxon. Avocations: venture capitalist, travel, writing, interior decorating, public speaking. E-mail: kathleendeoul@comcast.net.

DEPACE, NICHOLAS LOUIS, physician; b. Nutley, N.J., Oct. 18, 1953; s. Nicholas Frank and Rose (Piro) DeP.; m. Marilyn Tomaro, Jan. 17, 1981. BS, Seton Hall U.; MD, N.J. Sch. Medicine, Mt. Sinai, N.Y.C.; internal medicine cardiology, Hahnemann U., Phila. Diplomate Am. Bd. Internal Medicine and Cardiology. Intern in internal medicine Overlook Hosp., Summit, N.J., Columbia U., N.Y.C., 1978-79; resident internal medicine, fellow in cardiology Hahnemann Med. Coll. and Hosp., Phila., 1979—83; practice medicine specializing in internal and cardiology medicine Phila., 1982—; with radio Sta. WPEN, Phila., 1990—2001; clin. prof. medicine Thomas Jefferson U. Hosp., 1997—; chief divsn. preventive cardiology Grad. Hosp., 1996-97; dir. heart repair program Phila. Heart Inst., Presbyn. Med. Ctr., Phila., 1993-95; dir. Jefferson Heart Ctr. South, 1997—. Co-author: The Heart Repair Manual; mem. editl. bd. Am. Jour. Cardiology. Fellow Am. Coll. Cardiology, Am. Coll. Chest Physicians; mem. Phila. Coll. Physicians. Republican. Roman Catholic. Avocations: reading, writing, travel, sports. Office: 188 Fries Mill Rd Ste N2 Turnersville NJ 08012-2055 also: 2422 24 S Broad St Philadelphia PA 19145

DE PALMA, BRIAN RUSSELL, film director, writer; b. Newark, Sept. 11, 1940; s. Anthony Fredrick and Vivenne (Muti) DeP.; m. Gale Anne Hurd, July 21, 1991; daughter, Lolita. BA, Columbia Coll., 1962; MA, Sarah Lawrence Coll., 1964. Dir. and writer: short film Woton's Wake, 1963 (Rosenthal Found. award 1963); documentary films Dionysus in '69, 1970, The Responsive Eye, 1966; feature films include Murder a la Mod, 1968, Greetings, 1968 (Silver Bear Berlin Film Festival award 1969), The Wedding Party, 1969, Hi Mom, 1970, Get to Know Your Rabbit, 1972, Sisters, 1973, Phantom of the Paradise, 1974 (Grand prize 1975), Obsession, 1976, Carrie, 1976 (Avoriaz prize 1977), The Fury, 1978, Home Movies, 1979, Dressed to Kill, 1980, Blow Out, 1981, Scarface, 1983, Body Double, 1984, Wise Guys, 1986, The Untouchables, 1987, Casualties of War, 1989, Bonfire of the Vanities, 1990, Raising Cain, 1992, Carlito's Way, 1993, Mission Impossible, 1996, Snake Eyes, 1998, Mission to Mars, 2000, Femme Fatale, 2002

DEPALMA, RALPH GEORGE, surgeon, educator; b. N.Y.C., Oct. 29, 1931; s. Frank and Maria (Sibilio) deP.; m. Maleva Tankard, Sept. 17, 1955; children: Ralph L., Edward F., Maleva B., Malinda G. AB, Columbia U, 1953; MD, NYU, 1956. Diplomate Am. Bd. Surgery, Am. Bd. Vascular Surgery. Resident in surgery Univ. Hosps., Cleve., 1962-64; from instr. to prof. surgery Case Western Res. U., Cleve., 1964-80; prof., chmn. surgery U. Nev., Reno, 1980-82, George Washington U. Sch. Medicine, Washington, 1982-92; Lewis B. Saltz prof. of surgery George Washington U. Med. Ctr., Washington, 1992-94; prof. surgery, vice-chmn. dept. surgery, assoc. dean U. Nev., Reno, 1994-2000; nat. dir. surgery Dept. Vets. Affairs, Washington, 2000—; prof. surgery Uniformed Svsc. U. Health Scis., Bethesda, Md., 2000—. Editor: (with J.M. Giordano) Reoperative Vascular Surgery, 1987, Basic Science of Vascular Surgery, 1988, Practicing and Other Stories XLibris, 2005; assoc. editor: Haimovici Vascular Surgery: Principles and Techniques, 1989; co-editor: Basic Science in Vascular Disease, 1997, Vascular Surgery, Internat. Jour. Impotence Rsch.; mem. editl. bd. Vascular and Endovascular Surgery, 2003; contbr. articles to profl. jours. Stroke liaison nat. chpt. Am. Heart Assn., 1992-94; bd. dirs. Reno Chamber Orch., 1999-2000. Capt. USAF, 1958-61. Grantee USPHS, 1974-82. Fellow ACS; mem. Cleve. Vascular Soc. (pres. 1977-78), Rocky Mt. Vascular Soc. (pres. 1981-82), Am. Surg. Assn., Soc. Vascular Surgery, Washington Acad. Surgery (sec. 1991-92, v.p. 1992-93, pres. 1993-94), Am. Venous Forum (sec. 1991-94, bd. dirs. found. 1992-95), Am. Coll. Healthcare Execs. (assoc.), 1996, Cosmos Club (admissions com. 1992-94, awards com. 2001, chair 2003—), Western Vascular Soc., Prospectors Club Reno. Office Phone: 202-273-8505. Business E-Mail: rgdepalma@mail.va.gov.

DEPAOLA, DOMINICK PHILIP, academic administrator; b. Bklyn., Dec. 29, 1942; s. Dominick and Marie (DeStefano) DeP.; m. Rosemary Elizabeth Femiano, Aug. 2, 1969; 1 child, Alexis Jane. BS, St. Francis Coll., 1964; DDS, NYU, 1969; PhD, MIT, 1974; ScD (hon.), Baylor U., 1995; PharmD (hon.), Mass. Coll. Pharmacy and Health Scis., 2002. Assoc. prof. Va. Commonwealth U., Med. Coll. Va., Richmond, 1974-78; dean Dental Sch. U. Tex. Health Sci. Ctr., San Antonio, 1983-87, interim dean Grad. Sch. Biomed. Scis., 1986-87; dean Dental Sch. U. Medicine and Dentistry N.J., Newark, 1988-90; pres., dean Baylor Coll. Dentistry, Dallas, 1990-96; pres. Tex. A&M Univ. Sys.-Baylor Coll. Dentistry, Dallas, 1996-97; pres., CEO Forsyth Inst., Boston, 1998—; prof. Harvard U. Sch. Dental Medicine, Boston, 1999—. Mem. Nat. Adv. Dental Rsch. Coun. for Nat. Inst. Dental Rsch., 1996-2000; mem. dental adv. com. Pew Commn. for Health Professions, 1991; chair, bd. dirs. Oral Health Am., 1999-2000; bd. dirs. Block Drug Co.; mem. Commn. on Dental Accreditation, 1992-97. Recipient Presdl. award San Antonio Dist. Dental Soc., 1987, Alumni Achievement award NYU Coll. Dentistry, 1993, Kriser medal NYU Coll. Dentistry, 2003, Dising. Svc. award Am. Dental Edn. Assn., 2005. Fellow Am. Acad. Oral Medicine (hon.); mem. ADA, Am. Inst. Nutrition, Am. Assn. Dental Schs. (past pres. 1989-91), Am. Soc. for Clin. Nutrition (chair pub. info. com. 1995-2002), Am. Soc. Nutritional Scis. (chair pub. info. com. 1995-2002), Am. Assn. Dental Rsch. (pres. 2004), Internat. Assn. Dental Rsch., Hispanic Dental Assn. (hon.), Am. Dietetic Assn. (hon.), Rsch. Am (bd. dirs.). Avocations: skiing, racquetball, tennis, golf, reading. Office: Forsyth Inst 140 Fenway Boston MA 02115-3799 Office Phone: ddepaola@forsyth.org.

DEPAOLI, GERI M. (JOAN DEPAOLI), artist, art historian; b. June 8, 1941; m. Alexander DePaoli, July 4, 1961; children: Alexander Mark, Michael Alexander. BA, U. Md., 1974, MA, 1978; student, U. Calif., Davis, 1965-68. Art history educator, artist, curator slides and photos Nat. Mus., Bangkok, Thailand, 1968-71; art prof. Montgomery Coll., Rockville, Md., 1978-82; cons. oriental slide and photo collection Princeton U., 1983-84; lectr. Princeton Sch. Visual Arts, 1986-90; curator The Mus. Art, Ft. Lauderdale, Fla., 1986; dir. Coun. for Creative Projects, N.Y.C., 1989-91; faculty artworks Princeton Sch. Visual Arts, 1984-91; exec. dir. EducArt Projects Inc., Davis, Calif., 1991—. Cons. in field. Author: Emmy Lou Packard: A Woman and a Century, 1998, Barbara Spring, Populations from the Collective Unconscious, 1998, Donna Billick: Making Art out of Stone, 1999, Clayton Bailey: Happenings in the Circus of Life, 2000; editor (exhbn. catalog): Elvis & Marilyn: 2 X Immortal, Rizzoli, 1994; author (ednl. resource guide) Elvis & Marilyn: 2 X Immortal, 1994, (ednl. program) Images of Power, 1994, video prodr. Images of Power: Balinese Paintings made for Gregory Bateson and Margaret Mead, 1994, editor/co-curator (exhbn. catalog) Transcending Abstraction, 1986, reviewer ArtMatters Newspaper, Phila., 1987—90, author-curator The Trans Parent Thread: Asian Philosophy in Recent Am. Art, 1990, contbg. author Art of Calif. Mag.; one-woman shows include E.W. Gallery, Bethesda, Md., 1978, Upstairs Gallery, Kingston, N.J., 1982, Gallery at the Purple Barge, N.Y.C., 1984, The Art Gallery, Kingston, 1985, Back Door Gallery, Princeton, 1986, Campion Gallery of Art, 1987, AT&T Corp. Gallery, Princeton, 1989, Rider Coll. Gallery, Lawrenceville, N.J., 1990; also numerous group shows. Councilor Nat. Abortion Rights Action League, 1989—. Recipient award for excellence in pub., Office of Pres. of U.S., 1969. Fellow Soc. for Arts Religion and Contemporary Culture; mem. Assn. Ind. Historians of Art (v.p. 1988—), Coll. Art Assn., Princeton Rsch. Forum, Nat. Coalition of Ind. Scholars, Sierra Club, Greenpeace. Buddhist. Avocations: skiing, philosophy discussion groups, intellectual history. Office: EducArt Projects Inc PO Box 267 Davis CA 95617-0267

DEPAOLIS, PETER CANDITO, lawyer; b. Hartford, Conn., Apr. 20, 1949; s. Salvatore V. and Louise (Vona) DeP.; children: Peter, Diana, Stephanie, Katie. BA, Lafayette Coll., 1971; LLB, George Washington U., 1976. Bar: Va. 1976, D.C. 1977, U.S. Dist. Ct. Va. 1977, U.S. Ct. Appeals (4th cir.) 1977, U.S. Ct. Appeals (D.C. cir.) 1977, U.S. Supreme Ct. 1981. Jud. law clk. Superior Ct. D.C., Washington, 1976-77; asst. U.S. atty. Washington, 1977-80; assoc., ptnr. Koonz, McKenney, Johnson & DePaolis, Washington, 1980—. 1st lt. U.S. Army, 1971-73. Mem. Order of Coif, Phi Beta Kappa. Office: Koonz McKenney Johnson & DePaolis 10300 Eaton Pl Fairfax VA 22030 Office Phone: 703-218-4410.

DEPAOLIS, POTITO UMBERTO, food company executive; b. Mignano, Italy, Aug. 28, 1925; arrived in U.S., 1966, naturalized, 1970; s. Giuseppe A. and Filomena (Macchiaverna) DePaolis; m. Marie A. Caronna, Apr. 10, 1965. Vet Dr, U. Naples, 1948; Libera Docenza, Ministero Pub. Istruzione, Rome, 1955. Prof. food svc. Vet. Sch., U. Naples, Italy, 1948—66; asst. prof. A Titre Benevole Ecole Veterinaire Alfort, Paris, 1956; vet. inspector U.S. Dept. Agr., Omaha, 1966—67; sr. rsch. chemist Grain Processing Corp., Muscatine, Iowa, 1967—68; v.p., dir. prod. devel. Reddi Wip, Inc., L.A., 1968—72; with Kubro Foods, L.A., 1972—73, Shade Foods, Inc., 1975—; pres. Vegetable Protein Co., Riverside, Calif., 1973—, Tima Brand Food Co., 1975—, Dr. Tima Natural Foods, 1977—. Contbr. articles in field to profl. jours. Fulbright scholar, Cornell U., Ithaca, N.Y., 1954, British Coun. scholar, U. Reading, Eng., 1959—60, postdoctoral rsch. fellow, NIH, Cornell U., 1963—64. Mem.: AAAS, Greater L.A. Press Club, Italian Press Assn., Biol. Sci. Assn. Italy, Vet. Med. Assn., Italian Assn. Advancement Sci., Inst. Food Technologists ("Seminatore D'oro" as best soccer referee for all Italy). Achievements include patents in field. Home: Bel Air 131 Groverton Pl Los Angeles CA 90077-3732 Personal E-mail: drtima@aol.com.

DEPAOLO, RONALD FRANCIS, editor-in-chief, writer; b. Jamaica, N.Y., July 12, 1938; s. Francis Edward and Evelyn Helen (Turck) deP.; m. Meredith Nell Mass, Aug. 12, 1967; children— Britton, Damon, Baird. BA cum laude, Moravian Coll., Bethlehem, Pa., 1964; MS, Northwestern U., 1965. Reporter, corr., writer Life mag., 1965-70; news editor, corr. Business Week mag., 1970-72; freelance writer and editor, 1972-76; editor-in-chief, asso. pub. I-AM mag., N.Y.C., 1976-78; sr. editor Boardroom Reports, N.Y.C., 1978-80; editor-in-chief M.D. Mag., N.Y.C., 1980-84; editor, pub. Kirkus Revs., N.Y.C., 1984-87. Pres. Rock Lodge Devel. Corp., 1987—; adj. prof. communications Ramapo Coll., Mahwah, N.J., 1974-75 Author: Russia and the Independent States, 1992, The Presidency from A to Z, 1998, Elections from A to Z, 1998, Guide to Congress, 1999; contbr.: Encyclopedia of American Political History, 2001. Served with AUS, 1957-59, 60-61. Home: Box 255A Route 177 Penobscot ME 04476 E-mail: rondep@direcway.com.

DEPARLE, NANCY-ANN MIN, former federal agency administrator, lawyer; b. Rockwood, Tenn., Dec. 17, 1956; m. Jason DeParle. BA, U. Tenn., 1978; JD, Harvard U., 1983; BA, MA, Balliol Coll., Oxford U., Eng., 1981. Past pvt. practice in law; commr. human svcs. Gov. Ned McWherter State of Tenn., 1987-89; past assoc. dir. health and pers. White House OMB, Washington; administr. Health Care Financing Adminstrn. HHS, Washington, 1997—2000; mem. board of dir. Cerner Corp., Kansas City, Mo., 2001—. Rhodes scholar, 1979-81.

DEPASCALE, DIANE KAPPELER, lawyer; b. Dayton, Ohio, July 1, 1957; d. Robert L. and L. Ann Kappeler; m. Vincent N. DePascale, July 11, 1992. BA in Pol. Sci., U. Dayton, 1978, JD, 1981. Bar: Ohio 1981, U.S. Dist. Ct. (so. dist.) Ohio 1981, U.S. Ct. Appeals (6th cir.) 1986, U.S. Supreme Ct. 1986, U.S. Dist. Ct. (no. dist.) Ohio 1996. Law clk. to Judge Michael Merz, Mcpl. Ct., Dayton, 1980; assoc. Biegel, Kirkland & Berger, Dayton, 1981-84; pvt. practice, Dayton, 1984-92; ptnr. DePascale Law Offices, Columbus, Dayton, Ohio, 1992—. Facilitator 1991 Bench-Bar Conf.; mem. Ohio Supreme Ct. Task Force on Ct. Costs & Indigent Defense, 1991-92, Dayton Bar Assn. Vol. Lawyer's Project, 1990-92, Ohio Supreme Ct. Com. Study Impact of Substance Abuse on the Cts., 1989-90; adj. prof. U. Dayton, 1986—; visiting referee Montgomery County Domestic Ct., 1986. Named Outstanding Lawyer Greater Dayton Vol. Lawyer's Project, 1992. Mem. Dayton Bar Assn., Columbus Bar Assn. (family law com.), Ohio Bar Assn. (chmn. criminal justice com., 1991-93, family law com.), Ohio Assn. Criminal Def. Lawyers. Republican. Roman Catholic. Avocations: model railroads, toy poodle. Office: DePascale Law Offices 786 Northwest Blvd Columbus OH 43212-3832 also: 120 W 2d St Dayton OH 45402-1604 Office Phone: 614-298-8200.

DEPAUL, CHRISTINA, dean, artist; b. Pitts., 1959; BFA, Carnegie-Mellon U., 1981; MFA, Temple U., 1984. Assoc. prof. art in metals U. Akron, Ohio, 1986—2002, dir. Mary Schiller Myers Sch. Art, 1995—2002; dean Corcoran Coll. Art and Design, Washington, DC, 2002—. Office: Corcoran Coll Art and Design 500 Seventeenth St, NW Washington DC 20006-4804 Office Phone: 202-639-1801.*

DE PAULI, FRANK EDWARD, lawyer; b. St. Louis, Nov. 20, 1927; s. Edward and Frieda Julia (Fritz) De P.; m. Wanda Jean De Pauli, Oct. 11, 1952; 1 child, Susan Jean De Pauli Garnett. AA, Harris Tchrs. Coll., St. Louis, 1947; BSBA, Washington U., St. Louis, 1950; JD, St. Louis U., 1960. Bar: Mo. 1960, Ill. 1965, U.S. Supreme Ct. 1976. Atty. U.S.F.&G., St. Louis, 1960—65; mem. firm Keefe & DePauli, P.C., Fairview Heights, Ill., 1965—96; ret., 1996. Mem. Mo. Bar Assn., Ill. Bar Assn. Home and Office: 2 Doubletree Ln Saint Louis MO 63131-3908

DE PAULO, CRAIG J. N., philosopher, educator; b. Phila., Jan. 1, 1968; s. Michael Alexander, Jr. and Maria Margaret (Florio) de Paulo; m. Catherine Conroy, Aug. 28, 1999; 1 child, Christian. BA in Philosophy, La Salle U., 1989; MA in Philosophy, Villanova U., 1991; PhL in Philosophy, Pontificia Universitá Gregoriana, Vatican City, 1994, PhD in Philosophy, 1995. Asst. prof. Temple U., Phila., 2000—. Author: Being and Conversion, 2002. Decorated knight Order of Malta, Equestrian Order of Holy Sepulchre, Order of Merit. Mem.: Am. Philos. Assn., Am. Cath. Philos Assn. Roman Catholic. Office: Temple U 213E Anderson Hall Philadelphia PA 19122-6090

DEPAULO, J RAYMOND, JR., psychiatrist, researcher; b. Charleston, W.Va., May 21, 1946; s J Raymond and Mary Catherine DePaulo; m. Joanne M. Althoff, May 17, 1997; children: Marianne DePaulo Plant, Margaret DePaulo Kottke. MD, Johns Hopkins U. Sch. Medicine, 1972. Cert. Am. Bd. Psychiatry and Neurology, 1977. Asst. prof. to assoc. prof., psychiatry and behavioral scis. Johns Hopkins U. Sch. Medicine, Balt., 1977—2002, Henry Phipps prof. & dir. dept. psychiatry and behavioral sci., 2002—. Dir., affective disorders clinic Johns Hopkins Hosp., Balt., 1977—. Author (teacher, lectr.): (books about depression) How To Cope with Depression, Understanding Depression (Nat. Edn. Award, Depression Awareness Recognition and Treatment, NIMH, 1992); editl. bd. Am. Jour. Psychiatry, Biol. Psychiatry, Bipolar Disorder, Psychiatric Genetics, Jour. Nervous and Mental Disease. Recipient Selo Prize, Nat. Assn. Rsch. on Schizophrenia and Depression, 1996, Disting. Investigator award, 1998, 2003; grantee R0-1 Grants on Genetics of Bipolar and Depressive Disorders, NIH, 1988-2005. Fellow: Am. Psychopathological Assn. (v.p. 2004—05), Am. Psychiat. Assn. (life); mem.: Internat. Soc. for Psychiat. Genetics, Am. Coll. Psychiatrists. Roman Catholic. Achievements include principal investigator of several studies into the genetics of bipolar disorder and unipolar depression; founded Affective Disorders Clinic, Johns Hopkins Hospital, 1977; co-founder Depression and Related Affective Disorders Assn., 1986; patents pending for 2 genes contributing to bipolar disorder. Office: Dept of Psychiatry Johns Hopkins Hosp Meyer 4-113 601 N Wolfe St Baltimore MD 21287-7413 Home Fax: none; Office Fax: 410-955-0946. E-mail: psychchair@jhmi.edu.

DE PAUW, GOMMAR ALBERT, priest, educator; b. Stekene, Belgium, Oct. 11, 1918; came to U.S., 1949, naturalized, 1955; s. Desiré and Anna (Van Overloop) De P. Diplomate Classical Humanities, Coll. St. Nicholas, Belgium, 1936; JCB, U. Louvain, 1943, JCL, 1945; Juris Canonici Dr., Catholic U. Am., 1953. Ordained priest Roman Cath. Ch., 1942. Parish priest, chaplain Cath. Social Action, Ghent, Belgium, 1945-49, N.Y.C., 1949-52; successively prof. moral and fundamental dogmatic theology and canon law sem. div., assoc. prof. philosophy coll. div. Mt. St. Mary's Coll., Emmitsburg, Md., 1952-65, dean studies maj. sem. div., 1954-64, mem. council adminstrn., 1957-65. Theol. adviser II Vatican Ecumenical Council, 1962-65; founder-pres. Cath. Traditionalist Movement, Inc., 1964—. Author: The Educational Rights of the Church, 1953, The Rebel Priest, 1965, The Traditional Roman Catholic Mass, 1977, Bishops on War and Peace, 1983, The Traditional Requiem Mass, 1989, The Challenge of Peace Through Strength, 1989, Keep The Faith-Reagan Dicta, 2000, The Tallest of All Marines, 2002, The Passion of Christ, 2004; co-author: New Catholic Ency.; Dictionary of the Bible, Ephemerides Theologicae Lovanienses; editor: Sounds of Truth and Tradition, Quote... Unquote; producer Latin weekly radio mass, daily internet mass, various religious phonograph records, audio and video cassettes. Combat medic and chaplain Belgian Army inf. M.C., 1939-45, World War II Resistance and Free Polish Forces. Decorated Honor Cross (Free Polish Forces); recipient Achievement Citation, U.S. Army. Mem. AAUP, Internat. Platform Assn., Cath. Theol. Soc., Am. Canon Law Soc. Am., Am. Security Coun., Am. Cath. Philos. Assn., Nat. Cath. Ednl. Assn., Univ. Prof. for Acad. Order. *Especially since my founding of the Catholic Traditionalist Movement in 1964 has made me somewhat "controversial," I draw great inspiration from two sayings adorning the walls of my office. One, attributed to Davy Crockett: "Be sure you're right. Then go ahead!" The other, quoting Saint Athanasius: "If the whole world goes against the truth, then Athanasius must go against the whole world!" And when living by those axioms becomes heavy at times, I just brace myself and coin another one of my own: "It's better to be right alone, than to be wrong with a thousand others!".* Died May 6, 2005.

DE PAUW, LINDA GRANT, historian, educator, writer; b. N.Y.C., Jan. 19, 1940; d. Phillip and Ruth (Marks) Grant. BA, Swarthmore Coll., 1961; PhD, Johns Hopkins U., 1964. Asst. prof. history George Mason Coll.-U. Va., Fairfax, 1964-65; spl. asst. to archivist U.S. Nat. Archives, Washington, 1965-66; asst. prof. history George Washington U., Washington, 1966-69, assoc. prof., 1969-75, prof. Am. history, 1975-98, prof. emeritus, 1999—. Editor-in-chief, project dir. Documentary History of the First Fed. Congress, 1966-84; author: The Eleventh Pillar: New York State and the Federal Constitution, 1966, Founding Mothers: Women of America in the Revolutionary Era, 1975, Remember the Ladies, 1976, Seafaring Women, 1982; Baptism of Fire, 1993, Battle Cries and Lullabies, 1998, Sea Changes, 2003; editor, pub. Minerva: Quar. Report on Women and the Mil., 1983-2002, Minerva's Bulletin Bd., 1988-98; writer/producer Minerva on the Air (armed forces radio), 1987-89; editor H-Minerva, 1995—. Founder, pres. The Minerva Ctr., 1983-2004. Woodrow Wilson fellow, 1961 Mem. Am. Hist. Assn. (Beveridge award 1964). Home: 20 Granada Rd Pasadena MD 21122-2708 Office Phone: 410-437-5379. E-mail: minervacen@aol.com.

DEPERSIO, RICHARD JOHN, otolaryngologist, plastic surgeon; b. Oak Ridge, Tenn., July 10, 1949; s. John Dominick DePersio and Genevieve (Kellerman) Weinberg; m. Melissa Eddlemon, Nov. 23, 1994; children: Lauren Elizabeth, Katherine Genevieve, Gerard Edward, Richard John, Robert James, Elizabeth Genevieve. BS with honors, U. Tenn., Knoxville, 1971; MD, U. Tenn., Memphis, 1974. Diplomate Am. Bd. Facial, Plastic and Reconstructive Surgery, Am. Bd. Otolaryngology. Intern City of Memphis Hosps., 1975; surgery resident Meth. Hosp., Memphis, 1976-77; otolaryngology resident U. Tenn., Memphis, 1977-80; pvt. practice Knoxville Otolaryngology Facial Surgery Clinic, 1980—, Ear, Nose and Throat, Greater Knoxville. Clin. assoc. prof., U. Tenn. Dept. Surgery, Knoxville, 1980—; chmn. surgery, St. Mary's Med. Ctr., 2003-05. Pres. Knoxville Acad. Medicine Found., 2002—. Fellow: ACS, Am. Head and Neck Soc., Am. Soc. Laser Medicine and Surgery, Am. Acad. Aesthetic and Restorative Surgery, Am. Rhinologic Soc., Am. Soc. TMJ Surgeons, Am. Acad. Otolaryngology-Head and Neck Surgery, Am. Acad. Cosmetic Surgery, Am. Acad. Facial, Plastic and Reconstructive Surgery; mem.: AMA (del. to ho. dels.), Trustee Tennesee Med. Assoc. (assoc. 2002—05), Knoxville Acad. Medicine Found.; Knoxville Acad. Medicine (pres.-elect 1998, pres. 1999, 2002), Tenn. Med. Assn. (v.p. 2000, bd. trustees 2002—05, del. AMA 2005). Roman Catholic. Avocations: tennis, golf, basketball. Home: 6805 Shadow Ridge Dr Knoxville TN 37918-9530 Office: Greater Knoxville ENT Assocs Ste 200 1515 St Mary's St Knoxville TN 37917-4540 Office Phone: 865-521-8050. E-mail: missdepersio@aol.com.

DEPEW, HARRY LUTHER, lawyer; b. Neodesha, Kans., Nov. 18, 1923; s. Clarence William and Dorothy J. (Bushaway) Depew; m. Frances Allene Crisp, Mar. 27, 1951; children: Douglas D., Dennis D. BS in Bus., Kans. U., 1948, LLB, 1951. Bar: Kans. 1951. County atty. County of Wilson, Kans., 1955—58; ptnr. Depew Law Firm, Neodesha, 1952—2003; ret., 2003. With U.S. Army, 1942—45, with U.S. Army, 1951—52, Korea. Mem.: Kans. Bar Assn. (various coms.), Wilson County Bar Assn. (past pres.), SE Kans. Bar Assn. (past pres.), C. of C., Lions. Republican. Home: PO Box 313 Neodesha KS 66757-0313 Office: 620 Main St Neodesha KS 66757-0313 Office Phone: 620-325-2026. E-mail: hld@terraworld.net.

DEPEW, SPENCER LONG, lawyer; b. Wichita, Kans., June 6, 1933; s. Claude I. and Frances Ann (Bell) D.; m. Donna Wolever, Dec. 28, 1957; children: Clifford S., Sally F. AB, U. Wichita, 1955; LLB, U. Mich., 1960. Bar: Kans.; U.S. Dist. Ct. Kans.; U.S. Supreme Ct. Lawyer Depew, Gillen Rathbun & McInteer, LC. Mem. Interstate Oil and Gas Compact Commn., Oklahoma City. With U.S. Army, 1955-57, Germany. Mem. IPAA, Kans. Ind. Oil and Gas Assn., Kans. Energy Coun. Home: 6322 E English St Wichita KS 67218-1802 Office: Depew Gillen Rathbun & McInteer LC 8301 E 21st N #450 Wichita KS 67206 Office Phone: 316-265-9261. Business E-Mail: spencer@depewgillen.com.

DEPIANO, RICHARD JOHN, medical products executive; b. Phila., July 19, 1941; BS in Acctg., Drexel U., 1964. CPA. Ptnr. Touche Ross, Phila., 1966-86; pres. D.P. Assocs. Inc., Wayne, Pa., 1986-97; chmn., CEO Escalon Med. Corp., Wayne, 1997—. Bd. dirs. Photomedex, Montgomeryville, Pa., LaFrance Corp., Concordville, Pa. Mem. AICPA. Office: 565 E Swedesford Rd Ste 200 Wayne PA 19087-1625 E-mail: rdepiano@escalonmed.com.

DE PIERNE, OTTO S., chemist, researcher; b. Norwalk, Conn., June 16, 1948; s. Armand L. de Pierne and Margaret Barbara de Pierne-Wibben; m. Barbara R. de Pierne (dec.). BA, Sacred Heart U., Fairfield, Conn., 1987, BS in Chemistry, 1988. Chemist, safety dir. composite divsn. Ferro Corp., Norwalk, 1978—85; rsch. chemist Cytek Industries, Stamford, Conn., 1988—2000; dir. De Pierne Rsch. Group, East Norwalk, 2002—. Asst. organist St. Philip Roman Cath. Ch., Norwalk. Recipient Sci. Achievement award, Am. Cyanamid Co., 1992. Mem.: Wilton Hist. Soc. Achievements include patents in field.

DEPINHO, RONALD, research scientist; MD, Albert Einstein Med. Coll., 1981; postgraduate rsch., Columbia Presbyn. Hosp. Prof. medicine (genetics) Harvard Med. Sch., 1998—; Feinberg scholar Albert Einstein Med. Coll. Bd. dirs. Am. Assn. Cancer Rsch., 2001. Recipient Rsch. Prof., Am. Cancer Soc., 1998, Am. Soc. Clin. Investigation award, 2000, Steven and Michele Kirsch Found. Investigator award, 2000, AACR-GHA Clowes award, 2003. Mem.: Inst. Medicine. Office: 44 Binney St Mayer 413 Boston MA 02115

DEPINTO, DAVID J., public relations executive; BA in Polit. Sci., Brown U.; MBA, U. So. Calif. Dir. mktg., pub. rels., pub. affairs Coca-Cola Bottling Co., L.A.; exec. v.p. Pacific/West Comm. Group, L.A.; pres., CEO Stoorza Comm., Inc., San Diego. Mem. bd. dirs. L.A. Ednl. Partnership, Adopt-A-School-Coun. L.A. Unified Sch. Dist., Crescenta Youth Sports Assn.

DE PLANQUE, E. GAIL, physicist; b. Orange, N.J., Jan. 15, 1945; d. Martin William and Edna de Planque. AB, Immaculata Coll., 1967; MS in Physics, N.J. Inst. Tech., 1973; PhD in Environ. Health Scis., NYU, 1983. Physicist U.S. AEC, U.S. Dept. Energy, N.Y.C., 1967-82; dep. dir. environ. measurement lab. U.S. Dept. Energy, N.Y.C., 1982-87, dir. environ. measurement lab., 1987-91; commr. U.S. Nuclear Regulatory Commn., 1991—95; pres. Strategy Matters, Inc., 1998—; dir. Energy Strategists Consultancy, Ltd., 2000—. Adj. prof. NYU, N.Y.C., 1986—; pres. Pacific Nuclear Coun., 1989-91; mem. engring. sci. dept. adv. com., bd. trustees N.J. Inst. Tech., Newark, 1985-91; bd. dirs. TXU Corp. Landauer, Inc.; mem. visiting com. dept. nuclear engring. MIT, Diablo Canyon Ind. Safety Commn.; mem. TU Electric Ops. Rev. Com.; cons. in field. Contbr. articles to profl. jours. Commr. U.S. Nuclear Regulatory Commn., 1991-95; bd. trustees Northeast Utilities, 1995—; bd. dirs. British Nuclear Fuels, Inc., 1996—; Tex. Utilities Elec. Ops. Review Com., 1996—; cons. United Nation's Internat. Atomic Energy Agy., 1996—; mem. external adv. com., Amarillo Nat. Resource Ctr. for Plutonium, 1996—. Named to Hall of Fame, Women in Tech. Internat., 2004. Fellow Am. Nuclear Soc. (bd. dirs. 1977-80, 84-91, v.p. 1987-88, pres. 1988-89), Health Physics Soc., AAAS, Am. Phys. Soc., Assn. for Women in Sci. (v.p. N.Y. met. sect. 1980-82), Internat. Nuclear Energy Acad., (sec. 1996—); mem. NAE. Achievements include research in environmental radiation, radiation protection, solid state dosimetry, thermoluminescence. Office: Energy Strategists Consultancy Ltd Ste 114 9812 Falls Rd Potomac MD 20854

DE POUZILHAC, ALAIN DUPLESSIS, advertising executive; b. Sete, Herault, France, June 11, 1945; s. Pierre and Jeanine (Caffarel) de P.; m. Carole de Pouzilhac, Sept. 6, 1969; children: Edouard, Cedric, Philippine. Asst. advt. mgr. Publicis, Paris, 1968; advt mgr. DDB, Paris, 1968-75; exec. v.p. Havas Conseil, Neuilly, France, 1976-82, chmn., CEO, 1982-87, HDM, Neuilly and Puteaux, France, 1987-89, Eurocom, Neuilly, 1989—, EURO RSCG Worldwide, Neuilly, France, 1991, Havas Advt., 1996—2005, Havas, 2001—05, advisor, 2005—. Avocations: soccer, rugby. Home: 21 rue de Miromesnil 75008 Paris France Office: Havas 2 Allee De Longchamp 92150 Suresnes France Office Phone: 33 1 58 47 9001. E-mail: alain.depouzilhac@havas.com.

DEPP, JOHNNY, actor; b. Owensboro, Ky., June 9, 1963; s. John and Betty Sue D.; m. Lori Anne Allison Dec. 20, 1983 (div. 1985); 2 children. Guitarist; ex-member bands the Flame, the Kids, Rock City Angels, 1985; actor TV series 21 Jump Street, 1987-90; actor (films) A Nightmare on Elm Street, 1984, Private Resort, 1985, Platoon, 1986, Cry-Baby, 1990, Edward Scissorhands, 1990, Freddy's Dead: The Final Nightmare, 1991, American Dreamers, 1992, Benny & Joon, 1993, What's Eating Gilbert Grape, 1993, Ed Wood, 1994, Arizona Dreamer, Don Juan DeMarco, 1995, Dead Man, 1995, Nick of Time, 1996, Donnie Brasco, 1997, The Astronaut's Wife, 1998, L.A. Without a Map, 1998, Fear and Loathing in Las Vegas, 1998, The Source, 1999, The Ninth Gate, 1999, Just to Be Together, 1999, The Astronaut's Wife, 1999, Sleepy Hollow, 1999, The Source, 1999, The Man Who Cried, 2000, Chocolat, 2000, Blow, 2001, From Hell, 2001, Pirates of the Caribbean: The Curse of the Black Pearl, 2003 (Screen Actors Guild Award for best actor, 2004, Acad. Award nomination for best actor, 2004, Golden Globe nomination for best actor in a musical or comedy, 2004), Once Upon A Time in Mexico, 2003, Secret Window, 2004, Ils se marièrent et eurent beaucoup d'enfants, 2004, Finding Neverland, 2004, The Libertine, 2004, Charlie and the Chocolate Factory, 2005, (voice) Corpse Bride, 2005; writer, dir., actor: The Brave, 1997; TV movies include Slow Burn, 1986; TV guest appearances include Lady Blue, 1985, Hotel, 1987, The Vicar of Dibley, 1999, (voice) King of the Hill, 2004. Named one of Time Mag. 100 Most Influential People, 2005, 50 Most Powerful People in Hollywood, Premiere mag., 2004, 2005. Office: 9100 Wilshire Blvd Ste 725E Beverly Hills CA 90212-3441*

DEPPERSCHMIDT, THOMAS ORLANDO, economist, consultant; b. St. Louis, Dec. 3, 1935; s. Robert O. and Marcella C. (Meier) D.; m. Bertha Marie Waldman, Nov. 28, 1957; children: M. Susan, Mark, Joel, Andrew, Amy, Joan. AB, Ft. Hays (Kans.) State U., 1958; PhD, U. Tex., 1965. Asst. prof., then asso. prof. W. Tex. State U., Canyon, 1961-66; prof. econs. Memphis State U., 1966—2001, prof. emeritus, 2001—, chmn. dept., 1977-83. Research assoc. study N.Y.C. elevator industry, 1996, 2004. Co-author: Encyclopedia of Economics, 1974, Assessing Family Loss in Wrongful Death Litigation, 1999; editor: Financial Policies in Transition, 1968; author over 40 tech. treatises. With AUS, 1954-56. Mem.: Am. Acad. Econ. and Fin. Experts, Nat. Assn. Forensic Economists, Am. Econ. Assn. Home and Office: 1957 Mt Repose Germantown TN 38139-3443 E-mail: tdpprsch@memphis.edu.

DEPPMAN, JOHN C., lawyer; b. Evanston, Ill., Sept. 25, 1943; s. George and Elsie Jane (Erickson) D.; children: Ann, Jed, Benj; m. Clara. BS, Middlebury Coll., 1965; JD, Georgetown U., 1969. Bar: Vt. 1969. State's atty. Addison County, 1972-74; pvt. practice Middlebury, Vt., 1974-90; ptnr. Deppman & Foley, P.C., Middlebury, 1990-2000. Pres. Am. Land Title, Inc., Middlebury, 1984—. Selectman Town of Middlebury, 1970-72. Mem. Vt. Bar Assn., Addison County Bar Assn. (past pres.). Avocation: birding. Home: 8 Northshore Dr Burlington VT 05401-1255 Office: PO Box 688 Middlebury VT 05753-0688

DEPRA, ALAN JAY, mechanical engineer; b. Johnstown, Pa., Dec. 30, 1959; s. Alfred Dominic and Janet Lou Depra. BSME, U. Pitts., 1981, MS in Mfg. Engring., 1998, MS in Indsl. Engring., 2001; MBA, St. Francis U., 2003. Registered profl. engr., DC, Ga., Md., N.J., N.Y., N.C., Ohio, Pa., Va., W.Va., Del. Mech. cons. H. F. Lenz Cons. Engrs., Johnstown, 1981—84; sr. engr. Gen. Pub. Utilities, Inc., Johnstown, 1994—2000, Reliant Energy Inc., Johnstown, 2000—03, Johnstown Engring. Assocs. Inc., 2003—. Mem.: ASME, Assn. Facilities Engring. (cert. plant engr.), Am. Soc. Metals, Soc. Mfg. Engrs. (cert. mfg. engr., cert. enterprise integrator, cert. engring. mgr.). Achievements include development of computer assisted furthest neighbor, nearest neighbor clustering heuristic for optimization of classical vehicle routing problems; computer simulations to optimize classical uncapacitated facility location problems; computer simulations to optimize equipment placement and relocation during heat exchanger tube welding and rolling processes; an advanced product design process model that effectively combines the use of quality function deployments with design for manufacturing and design for assembly techniques. Avocation: motorcycle touring. Home: 131 Breck Ln Johnstown PA 15904-2818 Office: Johnstown Engring Assocs Inc 319 Belmont St Ste 2 Johnstown PA 15904

DEPREIST, JAMES ANDERSON, conductor; b. Phila., Nov. 21, 1936; s. James Henry and Ethel (Anderson) DePriest; m. Betty Louise Childress, Aug. 10, 1963; children: Tracy Elisabeth DePriest, Jennifer Anne DePriest; m. Ginette Grenier, July 19, 1980. BS, U. Pa., 1958, MA, 1961, LHD (hon.), 1976; student, Phila. Conservatory Music, 1959—61; LHD (hon.), Reed Coll., 1990, Portland State U., 1993; MusD (hon.), Laval U., Quebec City, Can., 1980, Linfield Coll., 1986, Juilliard, 1993; DFA (hon.), U. Portland, 1983, Pacific U., 1985, Willamette U., 1987, Drexel U., 1989, Oreg. State U., 1990; D of Arts and Letters (hon.), St. Mary's Coll., Moraga, Calif., 1985; HHD (hon.), Lewis and Clark U., 1986. Am. specialist music for State Dept., 1962—63; condr.-in-residence Bangkok, 1963—64; condr. various symphonies and orchs., 1964—; condr., music dir. Oreg. Symphony, Portland, 1980, laureate music dir.; now permanent condr. Tokyo Met. Symphony Orchestra; and dir. of conducting and orchestral studies the Julliard Sch., NYC. Prin. artistic adv. Phoenix Symphony. Condr.: Am. debut with N.Y. Philharm., 1964, asst. condr. to Leonard Bernstein N.Y. Philharm. Orch., 1965—66, prin. guest condr. Symphony of New World, 1968—70, European debut with Rotterdam Philharm., 1969, Helsinki Philharm., 1993, assoc. condr. Nat. Symphony Orch., Washington, 1971—75, prin. guest condr., 1975—76, music dir. L'Orch. Symphonique de Que., 1976—83, Oreg. Symphony, 1980—, prin. guest condr. Helsinki Philharm., 1993, music dir. Monte Carlo Philharm., 1994, appeared with Phila. Orch., 1972, 1976, 1984—85, 1987, 1990, 1992—94, Chgo. Symphony, 1973, 1990, 1992, 1994, Boston Symphony, 1973, 1997—99, Cleve. Orch., 1974, condr. Am. premiere of Dvorak's First Symphony, N.Y. Philharm., 1972, London Symphony, Barbican, 2005, chief condr. Malmö Symphony, 1991—94; author: (poems) This Precipice Garden, 1987, The Distant Siren, 1989. Trustee Lewis and Clark Coll., 1983—. Decorated Insignia of Comdr. of Order of Lion of Finland; recipient 1st prize gold medal, Dimitri Mitropoulos Internat. Music Competition for Condrs., 1964, Merit citation, City of Phila., 1969, medal, City of Que., 1983, Officer of the Order of Cultural Merit of Monaco; grantee, Martha Baird Rockefeller Fund for Music, 1969. Fellow: Am. Acad. Arts and Scis.; mem.: Royal Swedish Acad. Music. Office: Oreg Symphony 921 SW Washington St Ste 200 Portland OR 97205-2800*

DEPREZ, GENE EDWARD, management consultant; b. Rochester, N.Y., Jan. 31, 1940; s. Jean Victor and Eleanor (Winnek) DeP.; m. Patricia Louise Donahue, June 23, 1962; children: Michel Jean, Therèsé Marie. BFA in Communications, Rochester Inst. Tech., 1962, MFA in Communications, 1968; postgrad. in community devel., pub. policy formation, Syracuse U., 1972-74. Head instl. resources Rochester (N.Y.) Inst. Tech., 1962-65, dir. communications, 1971-78; producer/dir., asst. to gen. mgr. Eastman Kodak Co. Market Edn. Ctr., Rochester, 1965-70; dir. communications Rochester Mus. and Sci. Ctr., 1970-71; pres., chief exec. officer Urbanarium, Inc., Rochester, 1978-82; mng. ptnr. Concept Ventures, Rochester, 1982-84; pres., chief exec. officer Partnerships Data Net, Inc., Washington, 1984-87; v.p. PHH Fantus Corp., N.Y.C., 1987-90, v.p., prin., mem. exec. com., 1990—93; founding ptnrr. Location Adv. Svcs., Inc., Morristown, N.J., 1993-94; prin. Fluor Daniel Consulting Global Location Strategies, Florham Park, N.J., 1995-97; nat. dir. Global Location Strategies Pricewaterhouse Coopers LLP, N.Y.C., 1997—2002; assoc. ptnr. and Am. leader Global Location Strategies IBM Bus. Cons., N.Y.C., 2003—. Chmn. strategic planning HMO, 1981-82; chair adv. com. Coll. of Imaging Arts and Scis. Rochester (N.Y.) Inst. Tech., 2002—; vis. lectr. grad. comm. program Rochester Ins. Tech., 1983-84; mem. cmty. and pub. issues coun. Conf. Bd.; mem. adv. bd. NJ Transit, NYU, Rutgers U., Real Estate Ctr.; mem. internat. adv. bd. Contact Carter Summit Co-host Real to Reel TV News mag., 1981-82; mem. editl. bd. CoreNet, Internat. Corp Real Estate Exec. Mem. exec. com. Arts for Greater Rochester, 1980-84, econ. devel. commn. Sparta (N.J.) Township, 2001—; chmn., dir. Rochester Internat. Film Festival, 1972; chmn. exec. com. Rochester City Charter Commn., 1974-77; bd. dirs., sec. Genesee Hosp. Health Svc., Rochester, 1975-80; bd. dirs. Internat. Econ. Devel. Coun., 2002—; chmn. Monroe County Cultural Resources Commn.; bd. govs. Park Avenue Found. and Club, Florham Park, 1993—; trustee Ptnrs. for Livable Cmtys Recipient gold award N.Y.C. Internat. Film and TV Festival. Mem. Internat. Sci. Devle. Coun. (bd. dirs. 1996—, exec. com. 2001—), Am. Soc. Assn. Execs., Pub. Rels. Soc. Am. (exec. com. Rochester 1980-84), Rochester-Monroe County Bar Assn. (chmn. long-range planning retreat 1982-83), Urban Land Ins., Nat. Civic League (all-Am. city selection com.), Internat. Assn. Mgmt. Cons., Internat. Strategic Leadership Forum, Internat. Assn. Corp. Real Estate Execs. (chpt. v.p. 1997—), Rochester Inst. Tech., Lake Mohawk (N.J.) Country Club (trustee 1990—, pres. 1997-99), Rotary (bd. dirs. Rochester 1978-80). Democrat. Roman Catholic. Avocations: travel, photography, bicycling, cross country skiing. Home: 14 Oakwood Trl Sparta NJ 07871-1502 Office: IBM Business Consulting Services 11 Madison Avenue New York NY 10010

DEPRIEST, C(HARLES) DAVID, engineering executive, retired military officer; b. Mount Pleasant, Pa., Oct. 18, 1938; s. Charles Leonard and Elizabeth Carolyn (Hoover) DeP.; m. Blanca Reinoso Rivas, July 1, 1960 (div.); children: Lisa Lynn Nees, Diane Cokerdem DePriest, David Eric; m. Marlena J. Brechtel, Aug. 1, 2001 (dec.). BSEE with distinction, Air Force Inst. Tech., 1974, MS in Electro-Optics, 1975. Cert. profl. logistician Soc. Logistics Engrs. Enlisted USAF, 1959, advanced through grades to col., 1984, squadron navigator Beale AFB, Calif., 1964-68, squadron radar navigator, wing flight examiner Wright-Patterson AFB, Ohio, 1968-72; chief missile guidance br. USAF armament lab., Eglin AFB, Fla., 1975-79; program element monitor, dep. chief, avionics & armament divsn. air staff HQ USAF, Washington, 1979-83; chief engring. divsn. matérial mgmt. directorate Warner-Robins ALC, Ga., 1984-86; dir. intercommand electronic warfare aero. systems divsn. Wright-Patterson AFB, 1986-88; dir. plans and ops. AF electronic combat office USAF, Wright-Patterson AFB, 1988-91; ret., 1991; mgr. Warner Robins applications dept. The Analytic Scis. Corp., Inc., Warner Robins, Ga., 1992-97; pres. DePriest Assocs., Inc., Warner Robins, 1997—. Decorated Legion of Merit, DFC, Air medal with silver oak leaf cluster, Meritorious Svc. medal with two bronze oak leaf clusters. Mem.: IEEE (sr.), Soc. Logistics Engrs., Air Force Assn., Mensa, Rotary, Assn. Old Crows, Tau Beta Pi. Office: DePriest Assocs Inc 110 Park Dr Warner Robins GA 31088-5167 Office Phone: 478-329-9258. Personal E-mail: cddeprie@ix.netcom.com. Business E-Mail: dave@depriest-associates.com.

DEPRIEST, JON, academic administrator, department chairman; b. San Diego, Calif., June 1, 1958; s. Luella A. DePriest; m. Debbie F. Bonebright, Aug. 21, 1982; children: Richelle R., Heather A., Kelsey R. PhD History, Claremont Grad. U., 2001; MA History, San Diego State U., 1990; BA History/Social Sci., Christian Heritage Coll., El Cajon, 1984. Academic v.p. Christian Heritage Coll., El Cajon, Calif., 2003—, chair, history/social sci. dept., 1992—; prin. Fellowship Christian Sch., National City, Calif., 1986—91. Strategic planning dir. Christian Heritage Coll., El Cajon, Calif., 1994—2001. Mem.: Am. Hist. Assn. (assoc.), Am. Soc. of Ch. History (assoc.), Orgn. of Am. Historians (assoc.).

DEPUE, TRACY L., music educator; d. L Dale and Barbara J DePue. MusB, Maryville Coll., 1980—84; MusM, U. of Houston, 1989—91. Music ministry assn. Meml. Dr. Presbyn. Ch., Houston, 1989—91; dir. of music ministry Grace Presbyn. Ch., Plano, Tex., 1991—. Freelance clinician, Tex., 1994—. Dir.: (CD) Vessel in Your Hands; prodr.: Midnight Clear; contbr. articles to profl. jours. Singer Houston Oratorio Soc., 1985—88; handbell ringer Houston Bronze Ensemble, 1987—91, Dallas Handbell Ensemble, 1991—2000; singer Dallas Symphony Chorus, 1995—2005; newsletter editor and publicity chair Area IX, Am. Guild of English Handbell Ringers, Dayton, Ohio, 1992—94; mem. at large Youth Cue, Inc., Shreveport, La., 1999—2001; regional representatives coord. Presbyn. Assn. of Musicians, Louisville, 2003—; historian, publicity chair, program chair, midwinter chair Dallas Chpt. Choristers Guild, 1992—95; director's seminar chair Greater Dallas Handbell Assn., 1999—2001; 2006 midwinter chair Dallas Chpt. Choristers Guild, 2004—. Mem.: Youth Cue, Inc. (assoc.), Presbyn. Assn. of Musicians (assoc.; regional rep. coord. 2004—), Choristers Guild (assoc.), Am. Guild of English Handbell Ringers (assoc.), Am. Choral Directors Assn. (assoc.). Conservative-R. Christian - Presbyn. Avocations: reading, travel. Office: Grace Presbyn Ch 4300 W Park Blvd Plano TX 75093 Office Phone: 972-596-6233 114.

DE PUGET, ALBERT BORG OLIVIER, magistrate judge; b. Valletta, Malta, Apr. 15, 1932; s. Joseph and Helen Lowell. Diploma of Legal Procurator, Royal U. Malta, Valletta, 1954, LLD, 1958. M.P. Ho. of Reps., Malta, 1966-81; mem. Parliamentary Assembly Coun. Europe, Strasbourg, France, 1966-75; magistrate Cts. of Justice, Malta, 1983-87; amb. to France, Spain, Portugal, Switzerland and UNESCO, 1987-91, U.S., Washington, 1991-97; high commr. to Can., 1992-97; amb. designate to Mex., 1996; amb.-in-residence Ctr. for Global Edn., George Mason U., 1997—2002; lectr. multilateral diplomacy Elliott Sch. Internat. Affairs, George Washington U., 1998; apptd. amb. of Malta to Brazil, 2002, to Mexico, 2003. Pvt. law practice, 1958-83; vice chmn., sr. ptnr. Washington World Group Ltd., 1998;

sr. counsel Zammit Dimech and Bausuttil, Advs., Malta; dir. Assn. on Third World Affairs, Inc., Washington, DC. Editor: Studenti; mem. edit. bds. (newspapers) Patria, Il-Poplu, Malta Taghna, Encounter, In-Nazzjon Taghna; contbr. articles to profl. jours. V.p. Christian Dem. Group; mem. Bur. European Union Christian Dems.; hon. v.p. Malta Coun. European Movement; internat. sec. Nationalist Party, Malta, 1975-77; bd. gov. Internat. Student Ho., Washington, DC, mem. embassy liaison com; bd. trustees Elsie Whitlow Stokes Cmty. Freedom Pub. Charter Sch., Washington, DC. Mem. La Valette Phil. Soc., The Casino (1852), Cercle de L'Union Interalliée, Internat. Club, Univ. Club, Hannibal Club of Washington (founding mem.). Roman Catholic. Avocations: reading, music, walking. Home and Office: 1673 Columbia Rd NW Apt 309 Washington DC 20009-3604 Office Phone: 202-387-5435. E-mail: abodepuget@aol.com.

DEPUY, CHARLES HERBERT, chemist, educator; b. Detroit, Sept. 10, 1927; s. Carroll E. and Helen (Plehn) DeP.; m. Eleanor Burch, Dec. 21, 1949; children: David Gareth, Nancy Ellen, Stephen Baylie, Katherine Louise. BS, U. Calif., Berkeley, 1948; A.M., Columbia U., 1952; PhD, Yale U., 1953. Asst. prof. chemistry Iowa State U., 1953-59, asso. prof., 1959-62, prof., 1962-63; prof. chemistry U. Colo., Boulder, 1963-92, prof. emeritus, 1992—. Vis. prof. U. Ill., summer 1954, U. Calif., Berkeley, summer 1960; NIH sr. postdoctoral fellow U. Basel, Switzerland, 1969-70; cons. A.E. Staley Co., 1956-80, Marathon Oil Co., 1964-89. Author: (with Kenneth L. Rinehart) Introduction to Organic Chemistry, 1967, rev. edit., 1975, (with Orville L. Chapman) Molecular Reactions and Photochemistry, 1970, (with Robert H. Shapiro) Exercises in Organic Spectroscopy; contbr. articles profl. jours. Served wih AUS, 1946-47. John Simon Guggenheim fellow, 1977-78, 86-87; Alexander von Humboldt fellow, 1988-89, James Flack Norris Award, Am. Chem. Soc., 2001. Fellow AAAS; mem. Am. Chem. Soc. (exec. com. organic div., chmn. Colo. sect., mem. adv. bd. jour. 1987-92, gold medal), Sigma Xi, Nat. Acad of Sci., 1999, Am. Acad. of Arts and Sci., 2003. Home: 1509 Cascade Ave Boulder CO 80302-7631 Office: U Colo Boulder Dept Chemistry & Biochemistry PO Box 215 Boulder CO 80309-0215 Office Phone: 303-492-7652. Business E-Mail: charles.depuy@colorado.edu.

DERAMUS, BETTY JEAN, columnist; b. Tuscaloosa, Ala., Mar. 29, 1941; s. Jim Louis and Lucille (Richardson) DeR. B.A., Wayne State U., 1963, M.A., 1977. Reporter, copy editor Mich. Chronicle, Detroit, 1963-67; writer Detroit Bd. Edn., 1967-71; reporter Detroit Free Press, 1972-75, instr. English Wayne State U., 1976-78; editorial writer, columnist, from 1978; now columnist Detroit News. Contbr. Essence mag., N.Y.C.; author: The Constant Search, 1969, Forbidden Fruit: Love Stories from the Underground Railroad and Beyond, 2005; contbr. anthologies Sturdy Black Bridges, 1979, The Third Coast, 1982. Recipient 1st prize commentary Edn. Writers Assn., 1981; Ernie Pyle award spl. citation Scripps-Howard Found., 1981; Best Editorial Series award Overseas Press Club Am., 1982; finalist Pulitzer Prize for Commentary, 1993; Gen. Excellence award ASCAP, 1983, finalist, Pulitzer prize for commentary. Mem. Nat. Conf. Editorial Writers, Nat. Assn. Black Journalists (2d v.p. 1982). Office: Detroit News 615 W Lafayette Blvd Detroit MI 48226-3197 Office Phone: 313-222-2296. Business E-Mail: bderamus@detnews.com.*

DERBES, DANIEL WILLIAM, manufacturing executive; b. Cin., Mar. 30, 1930; s. Earl Milton and Ruth Irene (Grauten) D.; m. Patricia Maloney, June 4, 1952; children: Donna Ann, Nancy Lynn (dec.), Stephen Paul. BS, U.S. Mil. Acad., 1952; MBA, Xavier U., Cin., 1963. Devel. engr. AiResearch Mfg. Co., Phoenix, 1956-58; with Garrett Corp., L.A., 1958-80, v.p., gen. mgr., then exec. v.p., 1975-80, dir., 1976-87; pres. Signal Cos., Inc., La Jolla, Calif., 1980—82, Signal Advanced Tech Group, 1982—85, Allied-Signal Internat. Inc., 1985-88; exec. v.p. Allied-Signal, Inc., Morristown, N.J., 1985-88; pres. Signal Ventures, Solana Beach, Calif., 1990—2004. Chmn. bd. dirs. WD-40 Co.; bd. dirs. Sempra Energy. Exec. bd. nat. coun. Boy Scouts Am., 1981-95; trustee U. San Diego, 1981—, vice-chmn., bd. trustees, 1990-93, chmn., 1993-96. With AUS, 1952-56. Republican. Roman Catholic. Office: PO Box 8185 Rancho Santa Fe CA 92067-8184 Personal E-mail: dwderbes@aol.com.

DERBY, DEBORAH, retail executive; BA in Econs., Harvard U.; MBA, JD, U. Notre Dame. Fin. analyst Goldman Sachs; atty. Miller, Canfield, Paddock and Stone; various human resources positions Whirlpool Corp., 1992—2000; from v.p. human resources Babies "R" Us Divsn. to exec. v.p. human resources Toys "R" Us, Inc., Wayne, NJ, 2000—03, exec. v.p. human resources, 2003—. Bd. dirs. Jobs for America's Graduates, Inc. (JAG). Mem.: ABA, Soc. Human Resource Profls., Mich. Bar Assn. Office: Toys R Us Inc 1 Geoffrey Way Wayne NJ 07470-2030 Office Phone: 973-617-3500.*

DERBY, ERNEST STEPHEN, federal judge; b. Boston, July 10, 1938; s. Elmer Goodrich and Lucy (Davis) D.; m. Gretel Hanauer, June 10, 1961 (dec. Oct. 2000); children: Anne Gray, Michael Stephen; m. Carolyn Schwenk, May 11, 2002. AB with distinction, Wesleyan U., 1960; LLB cum laude, Harvard U., 1965. Bar: Md. Ct. Appeals 1965, U.S. Dist. Ct. Md. 1966, U.S. Ct. Appeals (4th cir.) 1968, U.S. Supreme Ct. 1973. Law clk. to presiding justice U.S. Dist. Ct. Md. and U.S. Ct. of Appeals 4th cir., 1965-66; assoc. Piper & Marbury, Balt., 1966-71, ptnr., 1973-87; asst. atty. gen. Atty. Gen. Md., 1971-73; judge U.S. Bankruptcy Ct., Balt., 1987—2004, recalled, 2004—, chief, 2005. Adj. faculty U. Md. Sch. Law, 1987, 90-99. Pres. Dismas Ho., Balt. Inc., 1969—; trustee Enoch Pratt Free Libr., Balt., 1977-93. Fellow Am. Coll. Bankruptcy, Md. Bar Found.; mem. Md. State Bar Assn., Anne Arundel County Bar Assn., Paca/Brent Am. Inn of Ct. (pres. 1993-94). Office: US District Court US Courthouse 101 W Lombard St Ste 9442 Baltimore MD 21201-2906 Office Phone: 410-962-7801.

DERBYSHIRE, WILLIAM WADLEIGH, language educator, translator; b. Phila., Dec. 30, 1936; s. Roger S. and Arline (Wadleigh) Derbyshire; m. Kathleen Derbyshire (div. 1981); children: Ann, Wesley, Lee. BA, U. Pa., 1958, MA, 1959, PhD, 1964. Cert. Russian-English translator. Instr. U. Pa., Phila., 1959-61; asst. prof. Lycoming Coll., Williamsport, Pa., 1961-63, SUNY-Binghamton, Vestal, NY, 1964-69; assoc. prof. Rutgers U., New Brunswick, NJ, 1969-76, prof., 1976-94; freelance translator, 1994—. Cons. Thomas Edison Coll., Trenton, NJ, 1981—94. Author: (book) Reference Grammar of Slovene, 1993, A Learner's Dictionary of Slovene, 2002; contbr. articles to profl. jours. Active Gov.'s Coun. Ethnic Affairs, NJ, 1992—94. Fulbright fellow, 1972—73, N.J. Dept. Higher Edn. fellow, 1984—85, Rsch. grantee, Dept. Edn., Washington, 1989—90, 1995—96. Mem.: Am. Translators Assn., Soc. Slovene Studies (treas. 1982—86, sec. 2002—), Am. Assn. Tchrs. Slavic and Eastern European Langs. (pres. 1985—86), Am. Assn. Advancement Slavic Studies (bd. dirs. 1986—89). Avocation: opera. Personal E-mail: wwdslovene@aol.com.

DERCHIN, DARY BRET INGHAM, writer; b. Camden, N.J., Sept. 15, 1941; d. Charles and Dorothy Roberta (Ingham) Lambiase; m. Michael Wayne Derchin, Dec. 29, 1970; children: Taylor-Leigh, Danielle Ashlin Lacey. BA, Montclair State Coll., 1962; postgrad., NYU, 1965, New Sch., 1966. Tchr., Randolph, N.J., 1962-64; rsch. asst. NYU, N.Y.C., 1965-67, Bolivian Peace Corps Project, N.Y.C., 1966; co-head rsch. Derchin Enterprises, N.Y.C., 1970-75. Author: Real Talk, 1992; playwright Blue No More; contbr. articles to the N.Y. Times, Harper's and book the Big Picture, others; talk show host: The Better Sex with Danna Day, Sta. WALE, 1999—, KFNY, WEVD; spkr., guest talk shows. Mem. Drama League, Lincoln Ctr. Film Soc., Am. Film Inst., Friends of Poets and Writers, Univ. Club, Nat. Art Club (lit. com., film com., Joseph Kesselring Playwright award com.). Home: Laurel Cove PO Box 200 Fair Haven NJ 07704-0200

DERCHIN, MICHAEL WAYNE, portfolio manager and financial analyst; b. N.Y.C., Aug. 17, 1942; s. James and Rose (Minenberg) D.; m. Dary Bret Ingham, Dec. 29, 1970; children: Taylor-Leigh, Danielle-Ashlin Lacey. BA, Bklyn. Coll., 1964; MBA, CCNY, 1966; postgrad., Syracuse U., 1966-69. Sr. analyst Am. Airlines, N.Y.C., 1969-70; dir. mktg. Pan Am. World Airways, N.Y.C., 1970-74, Am. Airlines, N.Y.C., 1974-79; v.p. Oppenheimer & Co., Inc., N.Y.C., 1979-82, First Boston Corp., N.Y.C., 1982-88; mng. dir. Drexel Burnham Lambert, N.Y.C., 1988-90; sr. v.p., dir. rsch., chmn. stock selection com. Nat. West Securities, N.Y.C., 1990-95; mng. dir. Tiger Mgmt., 1995-2000; founder, pres. JetCap, Fair Haven, N.J., 2000—, Derchin Mgmt., N.Y.C., 2002—. Columnist Travel Weekly, N.Y.C., 1984-90; spl. guest Wall St. Week, Owings Mills, Md., 1982-90, guest MacNeil Lehrer Newshour, N.Y., 1985; expert witness U.S. Senate Aviation subcom., 1984; lectr. Travel Research Assn., N.Y.C., 1981-84. Named to first team All Am. Analysts Instnl. Investor mag., 1983, 90, stock picker, 1995. Mem. N.Y. Soc. Security Analysts, N.Y. Airline Analysts Soc. (chmn. mem. com. 1985, pres. 1986-87), Wings Club, Travel Tourism Rsch. Assn., Nat. Arts U. Club (N.Y.C.), Union League Club (N.Y.C.), Navesink Country Club (Rumson, N.J.). E-mail: michael@derchin.com.

DERDENGER, PATRICK, lawyer; b. LA, June 29, 1946; s. Charles Patrick and Drucilla Marguerite (Lange) D.; m. Jo Lynn Dickins, Aug. 24, 1968; children: Kristin Lynn, Bryan Patrick, Timothy Patrick. BA, Loyola U., L.A., 1968; MBA, U. So. Calif., 1971, JD, 1974; LLM in Taxation, George Washington U., 1977. Bar: Calif. 1974, U.S. Ct. Claims 1975, Ariz. 1979, U.S. Ct. Appeals (9th cir.) 1979, U.S. Dist. Ct. Ariz. 1979, U.S. Tax Ct. 1979, U.S. Supreme Ct. 1979; cert. specialist in tax law. Trial atty. honors program U.S. Dept. Justice, Washington, 1974-78; ptnr. Lewis and Roca, Phoenix, 1978—. Adj. prof. taxation Golden Gate U., Phoenix, 1983-87; mem. Ariz. State Tax Ct. Legis. Study Commn., Tax Law Specialist Commn., Ariz. Property Tax Oversight Commn.; appt. Ariz. Property Tax Oversight Commn., 1997—. Author: Arizona State and Local Taxation, Cases and Materials, 1983, Arizona Sales and Use Tax Guide, 1990, Advanced Arizona Sales and Use Tax, 1987-96, Arizona State and Local Taxation, 1989, 93, 96, Arizona Sales and Use Tax, 1988-96. Arizona Property Taxation, 1993-96, ABA Sales and Use Tax Deskbook, Property Tax Deskbook. Past pres., bd. dirs. North Scottsdale Little League; apptd. Ariz. Property Tax Oversight Commn. Served to capt. USAF, 1968-71. Recipient U.S. Law Week award Bur. Nat. Affairs, 1974. Mem. ABA (taxation sect., various coms.), Ariz. Bar Assn. (taxation sect., former chair sect. taxation, former treas., chmn. state and local tax com., chmn. continuing legal edn. com., tax adv. com., others, mem. tax law specialist commn.), Maricopa County Bar Assn., Inst. Sales Taxation, Nat. Tax Assn., Inst. Property Taxation Met. C. of C., Ariz. C. of C. (chair tax com.), U. So. Calif. Alumni Club (past pres., bd. dirs.), Phi Delta Phi. Home: 10040 E Happy Valley Rd Scottsdale AZ 85255-2395 Office: Steptoe & Johnson LLP 201 E Washington St Fl 16 Phoenix AZ 85004-4453 Office Phone: 602-257-5209. Business E-Mail: pderdenger@steptoe.com.

DEREMEE, RICHARD ARTHUR, internist, educator, researcher; b. Red Wing, Minn., July 4, 1933; s. Arthur Eugene and Anna Helen (Vinquist) DeR.; m. E. Lucille Fogelstrom, Mar. 17, 1956; children: Lisa C., Brita L., Bo A. BA, Gustavus Adolphus Coll., 1955; BS, MD, U. Minn., 1959. Diplomate Am. Bd. Internal Medicine. Intern William Beaumont Gen. Hosp., El Paso, 1959-60; resident Mayo Clinic, Rochester, Minn., 1962-66, fellow in internal medicine and pulmonary disease, 1962-66, cons. in internal medicine and pulmonary disease, 1966—; assoc. prof. medicine Mayo Med. Sch., Rochester, 1977-83, prof. medicine, 1983-96; ret., 1996. Friedrich Wegener Meml. lectr. Lübeck, Germany, 1992. Author: (book) Time and the Mystery of Consciousness, 2003; contbr. articles to profl. jours. Served as capt. M.C., U.S. Army, 1959-62 Recipient cert. of achievement U.S. Army, 1962; Judson Daland travel award Mayo Found., 1966; Alumni citation Gustavus Adolphus Coll., 1982; named to Red Wing H.S. Wall of Honor, 2000. Fellow ACP, Am. Coll. Chest Physicians; mem. Am. Thoracic Soc. Republican. Lutheran. Home: 2209 5th Ave NE Rochester MN 55906-4017 Personal E-mail: radrst@aol.com.

DERENIAK, EUSTACE L., engineering educator, researcher; b. Standish, Mich., Dec. 29, 1941; s. Peter and Julia D.; m. Barbara C., Sept. 31, 1968; children: Teresa, Andreana. BS, Mich. Tech., 1963; MS, U. Mich., 1965; PhD, U. Ariz., 1976. Engr. Raytheon, Boston, 1963-65, Rockwell, Anaheim, Calif., 1965-72, Ball Corp., Boulder, Colo., 1973-74; researcher U. Ariz., Tucson, 1975—. Author: Optical Detectors, 1984, Infrared Detector and Systems, 1996. Fellow SPIE, Optical Soc. Am. Office: Optical Scis Ctr PO Box 210094 Tucson AZ 85721-0094

DERENZO, STEPHEN E., electrical engineering and computer science educator, researcher; b. Chgo., Dec. 31, 1941; married, 1966; 2 children. BS in Physics, U. Chgo., 1963, MS in Physics, 1965, PhD in Physics, 1968. Rsch. asst. Enrico Fermi Inst. U. Chgo., 1964-68; physicist Lawrence Berkeley Lab. U. Calif., Berkeley, 1968-82, lectr. dept. physics, 1969-70, lectr. dept. elec. engring. and computer sci., 1979-87, sr. scientist Lawrence Berkeley Lab., 1982—, prof., 1988—. Grant application reviewer U.S. Dept. Energy, U.S. Nat. Insts. Health; co-chmn. Internat. Workshop on Bismuth Germanate, Princeton U., 1982; active numerous coms. Lawrence Berkeley Lab., U. Calif., mem. recreation adv. panel, 1984-87, mem. computer svc. adv. panel, 1985-88, quality assurance coord. bio-med divsn., 1986-88, asst. dir. rsch. medicine and radiation biophysics divsn., 1990-92, safety coord. rsch. medicine and radiation biophysics divsn., 1991-92, mem. mgmt. integration group, 1990—, authorized reviewer, quality assurance rep., environ. safety and health coord., and asst. dep. life scis. divsn., 1992—. Reviewer Jour. Cerebral Blood Flow and Metabolism, Physics in Medicine and Biology, Jour. Computer Assisted Tomography. Recipient Tech. Brief award NASA, 1973; grantee NIH, 1973—, IBM, 1986, U.S. Nat. Insts. Health, 1989—; ANL fellow Associated Midwest Univs., 1965-66, Shell Found. fellow, 1967-68; Ill. State scholar, 1959-62, U. Chgo. scholar, 1961-63. Mem. IEEE (sr., reviewer Transactions on Nuclear Sci., guest editor 1989, chair med. imaging conf. 1991, fellow award, radiation intrumentation achievement award, 01), Nuclear and Plasma Scis. Soc. of IEEE (mem. tech. com. on nuclear med. sci. 1983—, chair 1988-91, mem. adminstrv. com. 1988-91, Merit award 1992), Am. Phys. Soc., Materials Rsch. Soc. Avocations: long distance running, photography, astronomy. Office: U Calif Lawrence Berkeley Lab Berkeley CA 94720-0001

DERESIEWICZ, HERBERT, retired mechanical engineering educator, retired academic administrator; b. Brno, Czechoslovakia, Nov. 5, 1925; s. William and Lotte (Rappaport) D.; m. Evelyn Altman, Mar. 12, 1955; children: Ellen, Robert, William. BME, CCNY, 1946; MS, Columbia U., 1948, PhD, 1952. Sr. staff engr. Applied Physics Lab., Johns Hopkins U., 1950-51; mem. faculty Columbia U., N.Y.C., 1951—, prof. mech. engring., 1962-94, chmn. dept. mech. engring., 1981-87, 90-93, emeritus, 1994—; ret., 1994. Cons. stress analysis, vibrations, elastic contact, wave propagation, mechanics of granular and porous media., Fulbright sr. research scholar, Italy, 1960-61, Fulbright lectr., Israel, 1966-67; vis. prof., Israel, 1973-74. Editor Columbia Engring. Rsch., 1975-92; contbr. articles to profl. jours. Served with AUS, 1946-47. Univ. fellow, Columbia U., 1949—50. Home: 240 E Palisade Ave Apt H3 Englewood NJ 07631

DERETICH, GEORGE, lawyer; b. Carson Lake, Minn., June 19, 1933; s. Thomas Simeon and Bosilka (Samardzich) D.; m. Shirley Renee Stark, Nov. 14, 1959; children: Thomas Stark Deretich, Christin Dana Deretich. AA, Hibbing (Minn.) C.C., 1953; BS, U. Minn., 1955, MA, 1957, JD, 1965. Bar: Minn. 1965, U.S. Dist. Ct. Minn. 1965, U.S. Ct. Appeals (8th cir.) 1987, U.S. Supreme Ct. 1988. Rsch. assoc. Employers Assn., Mpls., 1960-62; labor rels. dir. Lind, Olson & McCabe, Mpls., 1962-65; ptnr. Lind, Olson, McCabe & Deretich, Mpls., 1965-66; pvt. practice Mpls., 1966-75; adminstrv. law judge State of Minn., St. Paul, 1975-82; ptnr. Deretich & Sarazin, St. Paul, 1982—. Mem. Orthodox Christian Ch. Office: Deretich and Sarazin PO Box 1662 # 136 Saint Paul MN 55101-0662 Office Phone: 651-228-0986.

DE REVERE, DAVID WILSEN, retired professional society administrator; b. Englewood, N.J., Nov. 13, 1937; s. Wilbur L. and Ethel M. (Gilchrist) De R.; m. Ellen B. Tompkins, June 7, 1958; children: Mark S., Roger T. BA, Colgate U., 1959; MDiv, Yale U., 1963. Cert. master chaplain Internat. Conf. Police Chaplains. Sr. pastor 1st Ch. of Christ in Saybrook, Old Saybrook, Conn., 1963-85; exec. dir. Internat. Conf. Police Chaplains, Destin, Fla., 1985—2003. Author, editor: Chaplaincy in Law Enforcement, 1989. Chaplain Old Saybrook (Conn.) Dept. Police Svcs., 1964-85, FBI, 1991—. Home: 408 Spanish Moss Tr Destin FL 32541 Personal E-mail: davede@cox.net.

DERGALIS, GEORGE, artist, educator; b. Athens, Greece, 1928; s. Demetrios and Zina Dergalis; m. Margaret Murphey; 1 child by previous marriage, Alexis. MFA, Acad. Belle Arti, Rome, 1951; diploma, Boston Museum Sch., 1956-59. Instr. Boston Mus. Sch., 1961-69, De Cordova Mus., Lincoln, Mass., 1961-94; pvt. instrn. Wayland, Mass., 1969—; chmn., curator Festival Bostonians for Art and Humanity, 1976; chmn. curator prisom art Inst. Contemporary Art Boston, 1975-76; artist-in-residence Ptnrs. of Ams., Colombia, 1979; lectr. Helicon, Harvard U., 1981 One-man shows include Woodstock Gallery, London, 1974, Cámera de Comercio de Medellin, Colombia, 1980, Galesburg (Ill) Civic Art Ctr., 1985, Hotel Meridien, Boston, 1987, Wayland Art/Space, 1994; exhibited in group shows at Danforth Mus., Framingham, Mass., 1988-90, Mus. Fine Arts, Boston, 1989 (Merit award), Boston Pub. Libr., 1994-95, Boston Corp. Art, 1995-, Indpls. Art Ctr., 2000-01, Mass. State House and Commonwealth Mus., Boston, 2000, Springfield Art Mus., 2002, Foothills Art Ctr., 2003, De Cordova Mus., 2003-04, No. Ky. U., 2004, others; designer Wayland Vets. Meml.; represented in permanent collections Loomis and Sayles, Boston, Scudder, Stevens and Clark, Boston, Novartis, Hale & Dorr, Boston, Decordova Mus. Lincoln, Mass., Alliance Capital Mgmt., NY, Museo de Zea, Colombia, U.S. Army Ctr. Mil. History, Washington, also pvt. collections; contbr. It's All in Your Head, 1991, Art of War, 2002. Trustee, Graham Jr. Coll., 1971; hon. dir. Boston Ballet, 1971; mem. Attleboro Mus. With USAF, 1951-54. William Paige scholar, 1959; recipient Prix de Rome, 1951, Civilian Merit award U.S. Army Hist. Soc., 1969, Gold medal Acad. Italia delle Arte, 1980, Best of Show award Commonwealth of Mass., 2000, Juror's award Watercolor USA, 2002, Juror's Choice award Attleboro Mus., 2004. Mem.: Attleboro Mus., Copley Soc. Boston (v.p., art chmn. 1978, Excellence in Technique award 1978), Alumni Assn. Boston Mus. Sch. (pres. 1966—67). Home: 72 Oxbow Rd Wayland MA 01778-1009

DERGARABEDIAN, PAUL, environmental services administrator, consultant; b. Racine, Wis., Jan. 19, 1922; s. John and Mary (Hirmizian) D.; m. Mary A. Jansouzian, Dec. 27, 1947; children— Celeste, Claudia, Clarice, Paul. BS, U. Wis., 1948, MS, 1949; PhD (Shell Oil fellow), Caltech, 1952. Br. head U.S. Naval Weapons Center, Pasadena, Calif., 1952-55; lab. dir. TRW Systems, Redondo Beach, Calif., 1955-72; staff dir. TRW Systems (Energy Systems group), 1974-80; dir. The Aerospace Corp., El Segundo, Calif., 1972-74, 80-89, tech. cons., 1989—. Vis. prof. aeros. Caltech, 1971-72; founder, dir. Frontier Savs. & Loan; cons. in field. Served with USAAF, 1943-46. Fellow Inst. Advancement of Engring., Am. Astron. Soc. (dir. 1971—, nat. pres. 1969-71); mem. Phi Beta Kappa, Sigma Xi. Democrat. Armenian Apostolic. Club: Stereophonic of So. Calif. (pres. 1967-69). Office Phone: 949-713-6551. E-mail: sysanalcon@compuserve.com. *As a scientist I have been moderately successful - and lucky - in doing what people in my field would consider creative work. The greatest contribution to this success, I feel, has been methodology which was gleaned from certain teachers and associates. If I have done the same for someone else, that would be the greater success.*

DE RHAM, CASIMIR, JR., lawyer; b. N.Y.C., Sept. 5, 1924; s. Casimir and Lucy Lathrop (Patterson) de Rham; m. Elizabeth Moran Evarts, June 9, 1945; children: Elizabeth Morgan, Henry Casimir, Rufus Patterson, Jeremiah Evarts. Student, Yale U., 1943-44; AB, Harvard U., 1946, JD, 1949. Bar: Mass. 1949, U.S. Dist. Ct. Mass. 1949. Assoc. Palmer & Dodge, Boston, 1949-51, 52-55, ptnr., 1956-94, of counsel, 1994—. Dir. Cambridge Trust Co., Cambridge Bancorp, 1967-99, hon. dir., 1999-2002. Trustee Mount Auburn Hosp., Cambridge, Mass., 1962-93, pres., 1966-77, chmn. bd. dirs., 1977-80, treas., 1993-, The Mount Auburn Found., Inc., 1985-91, 93-96, Commonwealth Sch., Boston, 1958-2002, chmn. bd. dirs., 1966-87, sr. adv. com., 2002-, St. Mark's Sch., Southborough, Mass., 1962-74, Cambridge Cmty. Found., 1985-; overseer, dir. Boys and Girls Clubs of Boston Inc., 1956-93, sec., 1973-93, sr. adv. bd., 1993—; dir. Ctr. Blood Rsch. Inst. Boston, 1964-90, clk., 1964-84, hon. trustee, 1990—; trustee, sec. Sterling and Francine Clark Art Inst., Williamstown, Mass., 1973-95, hon. trustee, 1995-; dir. The Women's Union, Boston, 1975-98; dir., treas. Florence Evans Bushee Found., Boston, 1982-94; trustee Campbell & Hall Charity Fund, Boston, 1981-; dir. Dino Olivetti Found. Inc., Boston, 1960-, treas., 1983-94, clk., 1960-94; trustee Little Harbor Chapel, Portsmouth, N.H., 1959-; fin. adv. com. Cambridge Hist. Soc., 1980-91, chmn., 1988-90; chmn. Cambridge Rep. City Com., 1954-58; mem. Mass. Rep. State Com., 1960-69; alt. del. Rep. Nat. Conv., 1964, 68; mem. exec. com. Permanent Fund Soc., The Boston Found., 1993-94. Capt. USMCR, 1943-46, 51-52. Mem. ABA, Mass. Bar Assn., Boston Bar Assn., Cambridge-Arlington-Belmont Bar Assn. (pres. 1982-83), Am. Bar Found., St. Botolph Club (Boston), The Country Club (Brookline, Mass.), Masons (Harvard Lodge), Am. Legion. Episcopalian. Avocations: reading, tennis, politics. Home: 47 Lakeview Ave Cambridge MA 02138-3255 Office: Palmer & Dodge Prudential Ctr 111 Huntington Ave Boston MA 02199-7613 Office Phone: 617-239-0124. Business E-Mail: cderham@palmerdodge.com.

DER-HOUSSIKIAN, HAIG, linguistics educator; b. Cairo, Aug. 16, 1938; s. Vagharsh and Adrine (Karalian) Der-H.; m. Gaylynne Hall, Aug. 27, 1961. Student, Am. U., Cairo, 1957-59; BA, Am. U., Beirut, 1961, MA, 1962; PhD, U. Tex., 1969. Research assoc. U. Dar-es-Salaam, Tanzania, 1966-67; asst. prof. linguistics U. Fla., Gainesville, 1967-72; dir. linguistics, 1971-72, 84-85; assoc. prof. U. Fla., Gainesville, 1972-77, dir. Ctr. for African Studies, 1973-79, prof., 1977—2003, chmn. dept. African and Asian langs. and lits., 1982-91, prof. emeritus, 2003—. Mem. grad. council U. Fla., 1988-91; sr. Fulbright lectr. Universidade de Luanda, Angola, 1972-73, Universite du Benin, Lome, Togo, 1979-81; vis. prof. African linguistics U. Zimbabwe, Harare, 1989; panelist, grant proposal reviewer U.S. Dept. Edn., Washington, 1976—; USIA Acad. Specialist Grant cons. to U. De Ouagadougou, Burkina Faso, 1981; USIA Acad. Specialist Grant lectr. U. Marien Ngouabi, Brazzaville, Congo, May-Aug. 1988; occasional grant proposal evaluator Social Sci. and Humanities Coun. Can. Author: TEM, Grammar Handbook, 1980, TEM, Communication and Culture, 1980, TEM, Special Skills, 1980; contbr. chapters to books; co-editor: Language and Linguistics Problems in Africa, 1977; compiler: A Bibliography of African Linguistics, 1972, reviewer: African Book Publ. Rev., 1996—. ACTION grantee, 1980-81. Mem. MLA (African Linguistics bibliographer 1967-74), Linguistics Soc. Am., African Studies Assn., Southeastern Conf. on Linguistics, Phi Kappa Phi. Armenian Apostolic. Avocations: reading, hiking, travel. E-mail: haig@ufl.edu.

DERICCO, LAWRENCE ALBERT, college president emeritus; b. Stockton, Calif., Jan. 28, 1923; s. Giulio and Agnes (Giovacchini) DeR.; m. Alma Mezzetta, June 19, 1949; 1 child, Lawrence Paul. BA, U. Pacific, 1949, MA, 1971, LLD (hon.), 1987. Bank clk. Bank of Am., Stockton, 1942-43; prin. Castle Sch. Dist., San Joaquin County, Calif., 1950-53; dist. supt., prin. Waverly Sch. Dist., Stockton, 1953-63; bus. mgr. San Joaquin Delta Jr. Coll. Dist., Stockton, 1963-65, asst. supt., bus. mgr., 1965-77, v.p. mgmt. services, 1977-81; pres., supt. San Joaquin Delta Coll., 1981-87, pres. emeritus, 1988—. Mem. Workforce Investment Bd. With AUS, 1943-46, PTO. Mem. NEA, Calif. Tchrs. Assn., Native Sons of Golden West (past pres.), Phi Delta Kappa. Office: 6847 N Pershing Ave Stockton CA 95207-2524 Personal E-mail: ldericco@softcom.net.

DERISI, JOSEPH L., science educator, biochemist; BA Biochemistry, U. Calif., Santa Cruz, 1992; PhD Biochemistry, Stanford U., 1999. Asst. prof. biochemistry, biophysics U. Calif., San Francisco, 2000—04, assoc. prof. biochemistry, biophysics, 2004—. Named a MacArthur Fellow, 2004; recipient JPMorgan Chase Health award. Fellow: The David & Lucille Packard Found., 2003. Achievements include invention of microarray known as the virus chip, a glass slide embedded with 12,096 snippets of viral DNA which has advanced the diagnosis and treatment of disease; along with colleagues, identified and characterized a novel coronavirus responsible for the outbreak of Severe Acute Respiratory Syndrome (SARS) in early 2003. Office: 513 Parnassus Ave Box 0448 San Francisco CA 94143 Business E-Mail: joe@desrilab.ucsf.edu.

DERITA, PEGGY ANN, business owner, writer; b. Easton, Md., May 20, 1968; d. Howard Albert and Jenevieve Ann Wille; m. Michael Anthony DeRita, May 22, 2004; children: Michael, Salvatore stepchildren: John, Nicole, Renee. AA, Essex CC, Balto, Md., 1994; BA in Psychology, U. Balto, Md., 1996, MA in Psychology, 1998, student in Law, 2001—. Vol. Family Crisis Ctr., Balto, Md., 1994—96; child behavioral counselor Kennedy Kreiger Inst., Balto, Md., 1996; program specialist Sheppart Prat Hosp., Balto, Md., 1996—2001; bus. owner Heating and Air Conditioning Bus., Balto, Md., 2001—. Recipient 3rd Place award, Md. Psychological Assn. Home: 614 Priestford Rd Churchville MD 21028

DE RIVAS, CARMELA FODERARO, retired psychiatrist, retired health facility administrator; b. Cortale, Italy, Nov. 25, 1920; arrived in U.S., 1935, naturalized, 1942; d. Salvatore and Mary (Vaiti) Foderaro; m. Aureliano Rivas, Oct. 30, 1948; children: Carmen, Norma, Sandra, David. Student, U. Pa., 1940-42; MD, Women's Med. Coll. Pa., 1946. Diplomate Am. Bd. Psychiatry and Neurology. Intern women's Med. Coll. Pa. Hosp., 1946-47; gen. med. resident Chestnut Hill Hosp., Phila., 1947-48; gen. practice Tex., 1948-49; mem. staff Norristown (Pa.) State Hosp., 1949-63, supt., 1963-70, dir. family planning, 1979-87, clin. dir. spl. assignments, 1979-82; assoc. psychiatry U. Pa., 1963-75. Psychiatrist Penn Found. Mental Health, Sellersville, Pa., 1970—72; dir. intake coping svcs. Ctrl. Montgomery Mental Health/ Mental Retardation Ctr., Norristown, Pa., 1972—77, med. dir., 1977—82, psychiatrist, 1980—82; cons. surveyor Health Care Fin. Adminstrn., 1987—2001; dir. program evaluation Norristown State Hosp., 1979—82, med. dir., 1982—87. Named to Hall of Fame S. Phila. H.S., 1968; recipient citation Women's Med. Coll. Pa., 1968, Amita achievement award, 1976, achievement award Grad. Club Phila., 1976; named Woman of Yr. Pa. Fedn. Bus. and Profl. Women, 1979. Disting. life fellow Am. Psychiat. Assn., Pa. Psychiat. Soc. (rep. assembly of dist. brs. 1979-88); mem. AMA, Phila. Psychiat. Soc. (councilor), Montgomery County Med. Soc. (bd. dir., past pres.), Pa. Med. Soc. (chmn. adv. com. to aux. 1981-88, mem. ho. of dels., mem. commn. on med. edn. 1991-94, mem. com. on continuing med. edn. 1994-98). Home: Dunwoody Village-CH 112 3500 W Chester Pike Newtown Square PA 19073-4101

DERKSEN, CHARLOTTE RUTH MEYNINK, librarian; b. Newberg, Oreg., Mar. 15, 1944; BS in Geology, Wheaton (Ill.) Coll., 1966; MA in Geology, U. Oreg., 1968, MLS, 1973. Faculty and libr. Moeding Coll., Ootse, Botswana, 1968—71, head history dept., 1970-71; tchr. Jackson (Minn.) Pub. High Sch., 1975-77; sci. libr. U. Wis., Oshkosh, 1977-80; libr. and bibliographer Stanford (Calif.) U., 1980—2004. Acting chief scis., 1985-86, head Sci. and Engring. Librs., 1992-97. Contbg. author: Union List of Geologic Field Trip Guidebooks of North America; contbr. articles to profl. jours. Mem. ALA, Western Assn. Map Librs., Geosci. Info. Soc. (v.p. 1997-98, pres. 1998-99), Am. Geol. Inst. (mem. soc. coun. 2000-02), Geol. Soc. Am. (publ. com. 2002-05), Cartographic Users Adv. Coun. (chair 1988-90), GeoRef Adv. Bd. (chair 1998-2004), Geoscience World (libr. adv. com., chair 2005—). Republican. Lutheran. Office: Stanford U Branner Earth Scis Library Stanford CA 94305 Home: 12522C 26th Ave NE Seattle WA 98125-8803 E-mail: cderksen@stanford.edu.

DERKSEN, MARY LOU, writer, retired secondary school educator; b. Colorado Springs, Colo., June 12, 1937; d. George David and Frances Amelia (Bradley) Doty; m. Donald Earl Derksen, Aug. 31, 1956 (div. 1988), remarried, 1996; children: Paul, Deborah, Peter, Philip. BA in Anthropology, Wheaton (Ill.) Coll., 1957; MS in Counseling and Human Resource, S.D. State U., 1990. Cert. med. transcription Med. Transcription Advantage Career Ctr. Tchr. Head Start, Rapid City, S.D., 1987-88; youth coordinator First Presbyn. Ch., Rapid City, 1988-89; counselor Community Coll. of the Air Force, Ellsworth AFB, S.D., 1989-90; rsch. asst. Black Hills Coop. S.D. State U., 1989-90; psychotherapist in cmty. mental health ctr. Sturgis and Spearfish, 1990-95; customer svc. rep. Conseco Ins. Group, 2002—03; collections agt. and underwriter GE Consumer Credit Card Co., 2002—. Descriptive linguist-Bible tchr. Summer Inst. Linguistics/Wycliffe Bible Translators, Santa Ana, Calif., 1959-65; tchr., librarian, bookkeeper Rapid City Christian Acad., 1978-86. Author: AD/HD, What We Know, What We Think We Know, What We Don't Know, What We Should Know, 2002, Path to Destruction, 2002, Parenting Tales, 2002, monthly internet column. Mem. soloist Black Hills Voices in Concert, Rapid City, 1986-90; mem. Rapid City Symphony Concert Choir, 1986-90. Republican.

DERMAN, CYRUS, mathematical statistician; b. Phila., July 16, 1925; s. Samuel and Bessie (Segal) D.; Martha Winn, Feb. 24, 1961; children: Adam Jason Winn (dec.), Hester Beth Rebecca. AB, U. Penn., 1948, A.M., 1949; PhD, Columbia U., NYC., 1954. Instr. Syracuse U., Syracuse, NY, 1954-55; faculty Columbia U., NYC, 1955—, prof. ops. rsch. NYC., 1965-94; prof. emeritus, 1994. Vis. prof. Israel Inst. Tech., Haifa, 1961-62, Stanford, 1965-66; vis. prof. U. Calf., Davis, 1975-76, U. Calif., Berkeley, 1979 Author: (with Morton Klein) Probability and Statistical Inference for Engineers, 1959, Finite State Markovian Decision Processes, 1970, (with Leon Gleser and Ingram Olkin) A Guide to Probability Theory and Application, 1973, Probability Models and Applications, 1980, 2d edit., 1994, (with Sheldon Ross) Statistical Aspects of Quality Control, 1996. With U.S. Navy, 1943-46. Recipient John von Neumann Theory prize, INFORMS, 2002. Fellow Inst. Math. Statistics, Am. Statis. Assn. Achievements include research and publs. on theory of Markov chains, Brownian motion, statis. inference, mgmt. sci. and ops. research. Home: 15 Pond Hill Rd Chappaqua NY 10514-2531 Office: Columbia U Mudd Bldg New York NY 10027 Personal E-mail: dermancyrus@hotmail.com.

DERMANIS, PAUL RAYMOND, architect; b. Jelgava, Latvia, Aug. 2, 1932; came to U.S., 1949; s. Pauls and Milda (Argals) D. BArch, U. Wash., 1955; MArch, MIT, 1959. Registered arch., Wash. Arch. John Morse & Assocs., Seattle, 1961-62; assoc. Fred Bassetti & Co., Seattle, 1963-70; arch. Ibsen Nelsen & Assocs., Seattle, 1970-71; ptnr. Streeter/Dermanis & Assocs., Seattle, 1973-97; owner Paul Dermanis Archs., 1997—. Designs include Sunset house (citation 1984), treatment plant, 1992. Mem. Phinney Ridge Neighborhood Assn., Seattle, 1985—. With USN, 1955-57. Mem. AIA, Apt. Assn. Seattle and King County, U. Wash. Alumni Assn., MIT Club of Puget Sound, Phi Beta Kappa, Tau Sigma Delta. Democrat. Lutheran. Avocations: skiing, painting, photography. Office Phone: 206-783-0266. E-mail: pdermanis@comcast.net.

DERMODY, DIANA DOROTHY, elementary school educator; b. Dayton, Ohio, Nov. 27, 1944; d. Jack Thomas and Ethel Frances Edwards; 1 child, Kristina McBride Purnhagen. BS in Edn., Ind. U., 1968; MS in Edn., U. Dayton, 1984; student in piano, 1998—2003; courses, Wright State U., 1999, courses, 2003—04. Cert. profl. std. elem. edn. grades 1-8 2000, profl. std.-reading grades K-12 2000, edn. handicapped 2002, specific learning disabled 2002, severe behavioral handicapped 2002, lic. tchr. Dept. Edn., Ohio, 2000. Elem. tchr. grades 1-2 Indpls. (Ind.) Pub. Schs., 1968—69; elem. tchr. grade 1 North Lawrence (Ind.) Cmty. Schs., 1969—70; elem. tchr. grade 4 Richard Bean Blosson Schs., Elletsville, Ind., 1970—71; elem. tchr. grades 1-4 Tipp City (Ohio) Schs., 1971—73; tutor learning disabled Dayton (Ohio) Pub. Schs., 1979—88, reading tchr., 1988—90, tchr. Am. history, 1990—2004; Dayton pub. tchr. grades 7-8 in lang. arts, reading, social studies Kiser Mid. Sch., 2004—. Mem. programatic change process com. Dayton (Ohio) Pub. Schs., 1997, social studies liaison Kiser Mid. Sch., 1997—2002, mem. intervention com., 1998—99; workshops Wright State U., U. Dayton, 1999; mem. faculty coun. Kiser Mid. Sch. Dayton (Ohio) Pub. Schs., 2000—02, mem. discipline com. Kiser Mid. Sch., 2003—04; presenter Sinclair Cmty. Coll. Western Ohio Ednl. Assn. Day, 2004. Artist (mixed media) Dreamscapes (1st pl., 1998), (watercolor) Ladies in Waiting (Hon. Mention, 1998), photographer consigment original photography (contemporary and modern art) Jade Gallery, 2000, artist (contemporary and modern art exhibitions), Dayton, Ohio (1st pl., Hon. Mention award, 1998), (exhibitions) Cox Arboretun, Gardens Metro Park, 1999. With Smart Retreat Dayton Pub. Schs. Fellow Am. history, Wright State U., 2003—04. Mem.: Orgn. Am. Historians, Nat. Hon. Soc., Alpha Delta Kappa, Delta Delta Delta (news editor alumnae soc. 1973). Independent. Unitarian Universalist. Avocations: art, photography, travel, bicycling, hiking. Home: 9805 Mandel Dr Centerville OH 45458 Office: Dayton Pub Schs 115 South Ludlow Dayton OH 45402 Personal E-mail: ddermody@woh.rr.com.

DERMODY, WILLIAM CHRISTIAN, biomedical consultant; b. Lompoc, Calif., Sept. 22, 1941; s. William Frederick and Ann Drusilla Dermody; m. Lynne Heringer, Sept. 19, 1964; 1 child, Christina. BS, Calif. State Polytechnic U., 1964; MS, Utah State U., 1968, PhD, 1970. Postdoctoral fellow Cornell U., Ithaca, N.Y., 1969-70; sr. rsch. physiologist Parke-Davis & Co., Ann Arbor, Mich., 1970-76; sect. head cancer markers Frederick (Md.) Cancer Rsch. Ctr., 1976-81; dir. biotech. Am. Dade, Miami, Fla., 1981-84; mktg. mgr. ICN Biomed./Miles Sci., Lyle, Ill., 1984-86; mgr. tech. resources Difco Labs., Ann Arbor, 1986-88; assoc. dir. sci. Am. Type Culture Collection, Rockville, Md., 1988-90; pres. Bio World Assoc., Gaithersburg, Md., 1990—. Adj. prof. U.Miami Cancer Ctr., 1982-84, Fla. Internat. U., Miami, 1982-84; proposal reviewer Advanced Tech. Program, NIST, Gaithersburg, 1995—; mem. steering com. Molecular Biology Ctr., Wayne State U., Detroit, 1987-88; pub. spokesperson to civic and sci. orgns. Pres. Homeowners Assn., North Potomac, Md., 1990-92; bd. dirs. Hyde Park Condominium Assn. Grantee NSF, 1967-70. Mem. Alpha Zeta. Avocation: antiques. Home and Office: 405 Christopher Ave Apt 34 Gaithersburg MD 20879-3539 Office Phone: 301-947-6914. E-mail: cldermody@comcast.net.

DERN, BRUCE MACLEISH, actor; b. Chgo., June 4, 1936; s. John and Jean (MacLeish) D.; m. Diane Ladd, 1960 (div.); 2 children; m. Andrea Beckett, Oct. 20, 1969 Student, U. Pa., 1954-57. Appeared in numerous motion pictures, 1960—; films include Wild River, 1960, Hush, Hush Sweet Charlotte, 1964, Marnie, 1964, Wild Angels, 1966, The Trip, 1967, War Wagon, 1967, Support Your Local Sheriff, 1968, Waterhole 3, 1967, Will Penny, 1968, Number One, 1969, Castle Keep, 1969, Bloody Mama, 1970, They Shoot Horses, Don't They?, 1970, Silent Running, 1972, Drive He Said, 1971 (Nat. Soc. Film Critics award), The Cowboys, 1972, King of Marvin Gardens, 1972, Laughing Policeman, 1973, The Great Gatsby, 1974, Smile, 1975, Posse, 1975, Family Plot, 1976, Won Ton Ton, 1976, Black Sunday, 1977, Coming Home (nominated Best Supporting Actor, Academy Motion Picture Arts and Scis., 1978), Driver, 1978, Middle Age Crazy, 1980, Tattoo, 1981, That Championship Season, 1982, Harry Tracy, 1983, On the Edge, 1986, The Big Town, 1987, World Gone Wild, 1988, The 'Burbs, 1989, After Dark My Sweet, 1990, Diggstown, 1992, Wild Bill, 1995, Mrs. Munck, 1995, Mullholland Falls, 1996, Last Man Standing, 1996, Down Periscope, 1996, The Haunting, 1999, If...Dog...Rabbit, 1999, Madison, 2000, The Glass House, 2000, All The Pretty Horses, 2000, Masked and Anonymous, 2003, Milwaukee, Minnesota, 2003, Monster, 2003; N.Y. stage debut in Shadow of a Gunman, 1959; appeared in Broadway play Strangers, 1979; other appearances include Sweet Bird of Youth; appeared in (TV movie) Toughlove, 1985, A Mother's Prayer, 1995, Comfort Texas, 1996, Hard Time: The Premonition, 1999; (TV miniseries) Space, 1985, Roses Are For The Rich, 1987, Trenchcoat in Paradise, 1989, The Court-Martial of Jackie Robinson, 1990, Into the Badlands, 1991, Carolina Skeletons, 1991, It's Nothing Personal, 1993, A Mother's Prayer, 1995, Comfort Texas, 1997, series Stoney Burke, 1962-63. Named Actor of Yr., Pacific Archives, Berkeley, Calif. 1972. Mem. Santa Monica Track Club. Office: care Creative Artists Agy 9830 Wilshire Blvd Beverly Hills CA 90212-1804

DERN, JOHN ANDREW, language educator; b. Phila., May 19, 1965; s. Charles Henry and Germaine Elizabeth Dern; m. Patricia Ann Yerkes, Oct. 10, 1992; 1 child, John Robert. BA, Temple U., 1988, M in Liberal Arts, 1992; PhD, Lehigh U., 1998; cert. completion, U. London, 1992. Bus. writer Bucks County Courier Times, Levittown, Pa., 1989—90; instr. English Temple U., Phila., 1991—99; lectr. English Gwynedd-Mercy Coll., Gwynedd Valley, Pa., 1999—. Lectr. English Pa. State U., Abington, 1997—98. Author: Martians, Monsters and Madonna: Fiction and Form in the World of Martin Amis, 2000; contbr. articles to profl. jours. Mem.: Pa. Coll. English Assn., Nat. Coun. Tchrs. English, Coll. English Assn., Poe Studies Assn., Modern Lang. Assn. Avocations: writing, play Highland bagpipes, movies, old time radio shows. Office: Gwynedd-Mercy College Gwynedd Valley PA 19437 Office Phone: 215-646-7300.

DERN, LAURA, actress; b. LA, Feb. 10, 1967; d. Bruce Dern and Diane Ladd; children: Ellery Walker, Jaya. Student, Lee Strasberg Inst., Royal Acad. Dramatic Art, London. Appeared in films Alice Doesn't Live Here Anymore, 1975, Foxes, 1980, Ladies and Gentlemen, The Fabulous Stains, 1982, Teachers, 1984, Mask, 1985, Smooth Talk, 1985, Blue Velvet, 1986, Haunted Summer, 1988, Fat Man & Little Boy, 1989, Wild At Heart, 1990, Rambling Rose, 1991 (Acad. award nomination for best actress, Golden Globe nomination for best actress in a drama), Jurassic Park, 1993, A Perfect World, 1993, Citizen Ruth, 1996, Bastard Out of Carolina, 1996, October Sky, 1999, Daddy and Them, 2001, Jurassic Park III, 2001, Novocaine, 2001, I Am Sam, 2001, We Don't Live Here Anymore, 2004, Happy Endings, 2005; TV appearances include: Afterburn, 1992 (Golden Globe award for best actress in TV movie or mini series), Fallen Angels (Murder, Obliquely), 1993 (Emmy nomination, Best Actress - Drama, 1994), Ruby Ridge, 1996, The Baby Dance, 1998, Damaged Care, 2002 (also co-prodr.); exec. prodr.: (TV film) Down Came a Blackbird, 1995; dir.: (TV film) The Gift, 1994; TV guest appearances include Shannon, 1981, Fallen Angels, 1993, Frasier, 1995, Ellen, 1997, The West Wing, 2002, (voice) King of the Hill, 2003; stage appearances include The Palace of Amateurs (N.Y.), 1988, Brooklyn Laundry (L.A.).*

DERNER, CAROL A., retired librarian; b. Evansville, Ind., May 12, 1934; d. Jacob Christopher and Catherine Loretta (Grant) Niedhammer; m. George Bendix Derner, May 4, 1957. BA in Am. Lit., Ind. U., 1956, MA in Libr. Sci., 1958. Children's libr. Monroe County Pub. Libr., Bloomington, Ind., 1958-59, Pub. Librs. of Lake County, Merrillville, Ind., 1959-60; sch. libr. Valparaiso (Ind.) Cmty. Schs., 1960-63; head popular libr. Gary (Ind.) Pub. Libr., 1963-64, head extension dept., 1964-67; head libr. Elmwood Park (Ill.) Pub. Libr., 1968-76; asst. dir. Lake County Pub. Libr., Merrillville, 1976-85, dir., 1985-99. Adj. faculty Ind. U. Sch. Libr. and Info. Sci., Bloomington, 1982—94. Contbr. articles to profl. jours. Mem. edn. com. N.W. Ind. Forum, Portage, 1992-99; mem., sec. Ednl. Referral Ctr., Highland, Ind., 1996-99. Named Woman of Yr., Merrillville Bus. and Profl. women, 1990. Mem. ALA (coun. 1983-87), Ind. Libr. Fedn. (Libr. of Yr. 1997), Exec. Coun., Altrusa Club of Ind. Dunes (pres. 1998-99), Sun City Anthem Book Club (pres. 2004). Avocations: reading, travel, antiques. Home: 2558 Shellsburg Ave Henderson NV 89052-6442 E-mail: caderner@aol.com.

DEROBERTIS, EUGENE MARIO, psychology professor; b. Hoboken, N.J., Sept. 2, 1970; s. Eugene P. and Arlene DeRobertis. BA in Philosophy, St. Peter's Coll., 1992; MA in Psychology, Duquesne U., 1993, PhD in Psychology, 2000. Psychotherapist Duquesne Counseling Ctr., 1993—95; counselor drug and alcohol WINCO Med. Facility, 1996; adj. faculty Bergen C.C., 1996—2001; instr. Brookdale C.C., 2001—. Counselor drug and alcohol Straight & Narrow, Inc., 2000—01; presenter in field. Author: Phenomenological Psychology: A Text for Beginners, 1996; contbg. editor: The Quest for Personality Integration: reimaginizing our lives, 2001; contbr., articles to profl. jours. Recipient Rankin medal, St. Peter's Coll., 1992. Mem.: APA, Nat. Orgn. Human Svcs. Edn., Mid-Atlantic Consortium Human Svcs., Phi Theta Kappa (mem. panel discussion 2002), Psi Beta (presenter). Independent. Roman Catholic. Avocation: philosophy. Office: Brookdale College 765 Newman Springs Rd Lincroft NJ 07738

DE ROCCO, ANDREW GABRIEL, physicist, educator; b. Westerly, R.I., July 31, 1929; s. Joachim and Ida Lovat De R.; 1 son, J. Lovat. BS (Merit scholar), Purdue U., 1951; MS, U. Mich., 1953, PhD (Du Pont fellow), 1956; postdoctoral fellow, NRC, 1956-57. Mem. faculty U. Mich., Ann Arbor, 1957-62; vis. prof. U. Colo., Boulder, 1962-63; prof. molecular physics U. Md., College Park, 1963-79; First Disting. vis. prof. USAF Acad., 1975-76; vis. prof. Tufts U., 1968, 69; dean of faculty and Coll. prof. natural scis. Trinity Coll., Hartford, Conn., 1979-84; pres. Denison U., Granville, Ohio, 1984-89; dir. ind. coll. challenge program Ohio Bd. Regents, Columbus, 1988-89; cons. Ohio Found. Ind. Colls., 1989-91; commr. higher edn. State of Conn., Hartford, 1991-99; sr. fellow New England Bd. of Higher Edn., 1999—, sr. moderator ednl. leadership program. Mem. staff phys. scis. lab., div. computer research and tech. NIH, 1969-79; cons. Bendix Corp., Office of Sec. Def., Inst. for Def. Analysis, IBM, Dana Found., NIH, C.A. Johnson Found., Alfred E. Sloan Found., Am. Coun. on Edn., Assn. Am. Colls., Nat. Sci. Found., North Cent. Assn. Colls. and Secondary Schs.; pres. Nat. Collegiate Honors Coun., 1977-78. Contbr. numerous articles to profl. jours., chpts. to books; editorial cons., Acad. Press, Cambridge Univ. Press, Harper & Row, Holt, Rinehart & Winston, others. Bd. dirs. Greater Washington Coun. for Clean Air, 1967-71; mem. village coun. Friendship Heights, Chevy Chase, Md., 1974-76; bd. dirs. World Affairs Ctr., Conn., Innovations, Inc., CHESLA, Conn. Student Loan Found., Edn. Commn. of the States, Ednl. Leadership Program; chmn. bd. New Eng. Bd. Higher Edn., Shaliko Theatre Co., N.Y.C.; bd. dirs. MetaArts, Sci. Ctr. Conn.; pres. North Coast Athletic Conf., 1986-88; bd govs. Rackham Sch. Grad. Studies, U. Mich.; mem. dean's adv. coun. Sch. Sci., Purdue U.; pres. bd. dirs. Chamber Music Plus, 2001-03; chmn. bd. Conn. Acad. for Edn. in Sci., Math., Tech., 2002--; bd. incorporators Hartford Sch. Art, 2003—; trustee Barbieri Endowment Italian Studies, Conn. Early Music Soc. Recipient William Raney Harper medal, 1988, Disting. Alumnus award Purdue U., 1999, Disting. Svc. award Conn. Innovations, 1999; NRC fellow, 1956-57; Am. Cancer Soc. fellow, 1956-57; NATO sr. fellow, 1964. Fellow: AAAS, Random Soc.; mem.: Conn. Acad. Sci. and Engring., State Higher Edn. Exec. Officers (exec. com.), Engring. Acad. So. New Eng. (bd. govs.), Md. Acad. Scis. (sci. coun. 1970—79), Am. Assn. Physics Tchrs. (com. internat. edn.), Biophys. Soc., Am. Phys. Soc., Am. Chem. Soc., Ohio Found. Ind. Colls. (exec. com.), The Compact for Faculty Diversity (nat. adv. com.), Omicron Delta Kappa, Sigma Pi Sigma, Delta Rho Kappa, Phi Lambda Upsilon, Sigma Xi. Office: Conn Acad for Edn in Sci Math and Tech 211 S Main St Middletown CT 06457 Fax: 860-346-2157. Office Phone: 860-346-1177. E-mail: agdr731@aol.com.

DEROMEDI, ROGER K., food products executive; BA in Econs. and Math., Vanderbilt U.; MBA, Stanford U. V.p. corp. devel. Kraft, 1988; v.p. mktg. Kraft USA's Grocery Products Divsn. and Retail Cheese Divsn.; exec. v.p., gen. mgr. splty. products divsn. Kraft Foods, exec. v.p., gen. mgr. cheese divsn., exec. v.p., area dir. Paris; group v.p. Kraft Foods Internat; pres. Kraft Foods Asia Pacific; Co-CEO Kraft Foods, Inc., 1999—2001; pres., CEO Kraft Food Internat., 2001—03; CEO Kraft Foods Inc., 2003—. Office: Altria Group Inc 120 Park Ave New York NY 10017-5592

DERONDE, JOHN ALLEN, JR., lawyer, author; b. Albany, N.Y., July 22, 1947; s. John Allen and Kathleen (Doran) DeR.; m. Marianne E. Karlsson, Mar. 19, 1983 BA, U. Calif., Davis, 1969; JD, U. Pacific, 1972. Bar: Calif. 1974, U.S. Dist. Ct. (ea. and no. dists.) Calif. 1978, U.S. Tax Ct. 1984, U.S. Supreme Ct. 1981. Trial counsel State Dept. Motor Vehicles, Sacramento, 1973-74; ptnr. DeRonde & DeRonde, Fairfield, Caif., 1974—. Bd. dirs. Calif.-Hawaii Corp., Pietro's Pizza Parlors, Inc. Contbr. numerous articles to profl. jours. Active Vacaville, Fairfield, Calif. chambers of commerce; pres. North Bay Opera; bd. dirs. Solano Ballet Assn. Recipient Highest Score Jessup Internat. Moot Ct. Competition, Seattle, 1972. Mem. Calif. State Bar Assn. (family law sect.), Calif. Trial Lawyers Assn., Assn. Cert. Family Law Specialists, Calif. Assn. Realtors, Nat. Fedn. Ind. Bus., Comonwealth Club Calif. Republican. Roman Catholic. Home: 416 Mergansed Pl Davis CA 95616 Office: DeRonde & DeRonde 460 Union Ave Ste B Fairfield CA 94533-6320 E-mail: derondelaw@aol.com.

DE ROSA, CHRIS THOMAS, biomedical researcher; b. Cin., June 18, 1949; s. Frank P. and Mary Lorean De Rosa; m. Yolan Susan De Rosa, Aug. 25, 1979; children: Brian, Erin, Phillip, Joel. BA, Ohio Weslyan U., 1971; MS in Ecology, Miami U., Oxford, Ohio, 1974, PhD in Biology, 1977. From instr. to asst. prof. biology U. Va., Charlottesville, 1976—80; sr. scientist U.S. EPA, Cin., 1980—82, br. chief, 1984—88, dir. Nat. Ctr. Environ. Assessment, 1988—91; asst. prof. botany and zoology U. Maine, Orono, 1982—84; dep. assoc. adminstr. sci. Ctr. Disease Control, Atlanta, 1991—92, dir. divsn. toxicology, 1991—2005, dir. divsn. toxicology and environ. medicine, 2005—. Tchr. St. Bernard's Parish Sch., Cin., 1986—88; mem. steering com. risk assessment WHO, Geneva, 1992—, cons., State Dept., NASA, Dept. Energy, Dept. Def., NATO, Pan Am. Health Orgn.; reader, contbr. Ednl. Testing Svc., Princeton, NJ, mem. test devel. com.; presenter in field. Editor: Toxicology Letters, 1995; reviewer: Jour. Ambulatory Pediat., Quar. Rev. Biology, Oxford (Eng.) U. Press.; contbr. articles to profl. jours.; mem. editl. bd. Animal Behavior, Copeia, Toxicology and Indsl. Health, Environ. Rsch., others. Mem. bd. edn. Hampden (Maine) Sch. Dist., 1982—84. Recipient Bronze medal, U.S. EPA, 1981, 1986, 1988, 1998, Publ. award, Ctr. Disease Control, 1998, Hammer award, U.S. Vice President Al Gore, 2000, others; fellow, NSF, 1975; grantee, Sigma Xi, 1975, Am. Philos. Soc., 1977, Exxon Found., 1983, U.S. EPA, 1989, NSF, 1975, 1978; Faculty Rsch. grantee, U. Maine, 1982, Faculty Equipment grantee, 1983. Fellow: Collegium Ramazzini; mem.: AAAS, Soc. Occupl. and Environ. Health, N.Y. Acad. Scis., Animal Behavior Soc., Rsch. Soc. N.Am., Soc. Integrative and Comparative Biology, Ecol. Soc. Am., Soc. Risk Analysis, Am. Coll. Toxicology, Sigma Xi. Avocations: landscape design, fly fishing, natural history. Office: CDC F32 Divsn Toxicology and Environ Medicine 1600 Clifton Rd Atlanta GA 30333 Home: 5305 Burdock Creek Acworth GA 30101

DEROSA, FRANCIS DOMINIC, chemical company executive; b. Seneca Falls, NY, Feb. 26, 1936; s. Frank and Frances (Bruno) DeR.; m. Vivian DeRosa, Oct. 24, 1959; children: Kevin, Marc, Terri. Student, Rochester Inst. Tech., 1959—61; BS, MBA, Chadwick U.; PhD, City U. L.A. Cert. med. photographer. CEO Advance Paper & Equipment Supply Inc., Mesa, Ariz., 1974—, Pottery Plus Ltd., Mesa, 1984—, Advance Tool Supply Inc., Mesa, 1993—94. Vice chmn. bd. adjustments City of Mesa, 1983-89, bd. dirs. dept. parks and recreation, 1983-86; pres. Christ the King Mens Club, 1983-84; bd. dirs. Mesa C. of C., 1983-88. Mem. Ariz. Sanitary Supply Assn. (pres. 1983-84), Internat. Sanitary Supply Assn. (coord. Ariz. chpt. 1994-96, sec. bd. 1994-96), Gilbert, Ariz. C. of C. (bd. dirs., v.p. 1992-96, pres. 1996-97, sec. internat. bd. 1994-96), Gilbert Heights Owners Assn. (pres. 1992-93), Mesa Country Club, Calif. Yacht Club, Santa Monica (Calif.) Yacht Club, Rotary (pres. Mesa Sunrise chpt. 1987-88, Paul Harris fellow 1988), Masons (32 degree, pres. 1973), Sons of Italy (pres. 1983-84), Shriners. Avocations: music, physical fitness, sailing, golf. Home: 1325 E Treasure Cove Dr Gilbert AZ 85234 Office: Advance Paper & Maintenance Supply Inc 33 W Broadway Mesa AZ 85210-1505 Office Phone: 480-964-6108. Business E-Mail: frank@advancepaper.com.

DE ROSA, GUY PAUL, orthopedic surgery educator; b. Napoleon, Ohio, Oct. 25, 1939; married. BS, Notre Dame U., 1961; MD, Ind. U., 1965. Diplomate Am. Bd. Orthopedic Surgery. Resident in gen. surgery Sch. Medicine, Ind. U., Indpls., 1965—66, resident in orthopedic surgery, 1966—70; fellow in pediat. orthopedics Hosp. for Sick Children, London, 1969—70; asst. prof. orthopedic surgery Sch. Medicine, Ind. U., Indpls., 1970—76, assoc. prof., 1976—82, dir. undergrad. edn. dept. orthopedic surgery, 1972—, chief neuromuscular disease, 1972—, coord. Garceau-Wayu Lectureships dept. orthopedic surgery, 1975—, dir. Cerebral Palsy Clinic, 1978—88, orthopedic cons. Hemophilia Clinic, 1978—91, prof. orthopedic surgery, 1981—, orthopedic cons. Rheumato-Orthopedic Clinic, 1984—, chmn. dept. orthopedic surgery, 1986—95; exec. dir. Am. Bd. Orthopaedic Surgery, Chapel Hill. Attending physician Wishard Meml. Hosp., Indpls., 1970—95, Ind. U. Med. Ctr., Indpls., 1970—95, James Whitcomb Riley Hosp. for Children, Indpls., 1970—95; coord. Ctrl. Ind. and So. Ind. State Bd. Health Programs, Scoliosis and Sch. Screening, 1977; mem. orthop. surgery steering com. Children's Cancer Study Group, 1990; mem. residency rev. com. for orthop. surgery Accreditation Coun. for Grad. Med. Edn., 1990—;

vis. prof. Children's Hosp., Columbus, Ohio, 1977, St. Joseph Hosp., Ft. Wayne, Ind., 1977, Miami Valley Hosp., Dayton, Ohio, 1978, Dayton, 82, Dayton, 85, Dayton, 86, Deaconess Hosp., Evansville, Ind., 1980, Bloomington (Ind.) Hosp., 1982, U. Tex., Galveston, 1982, U. Mo. Med. Ctr., Columbia, 1983, Southwestern Mich. Area Health Edn. Ctr., Kalamazoo, 1985, Newington (Conn.) Children's Hosp., 1988, Children's Hosp. Med. Ctr., Akron, Ohio, 1992; and numerous others; active Hemophilia Med. Adv. Coun., 1978—; presenter in field. Contbr. articles to profl. jours. Bd. dirs. United Cerebral Palsy, 1973—85, Hemophilia Found., 1978—, New Hope of Ind., 1984—86, mem. long range planning com., 1984—85, mem. task force on serving brain injured, 1988; bd. dirs. Ind. Found. Hand Surg. Rsch. and Edn., 1989—95; mem. adv. bd. Head Injury Found., 1995, Children's Limb Found., 1992—; mem. pub. rels. and promotion com. Ind. Gov.'s Coun. on Phys. Fitness and Sports Medicine, 1986—92, mem. promotion com., 1988—92; dir. State of Ind. Orthop. Rsch. and Edn. Found., 1993, bd. trustees, 1994. Maj. USAF, 1970—72. Recipient Ensminger award for rsch. in trauma, 1967, Willis Gatch award, 1968; grantee grantee in field. Mem.: 20th Century Orthop. Assn., Internat. Soc. Orthop. Surgery and Traumatology, Scoliosis Rsch. Soc. (mem. edn. com. 1985—), Russell Hibbs Soc., Pediat. Orthop. Soc. N.Am. (mem. com. on fellowships 1986—92, bd. dirs. 1990—92, 2d v.p. 1994, 1st v.p. 1995, pres. 1996), Mid-Am. Orthop. Assn. (chmn. program com. 1986—87, bd. dirs. 1986—, sec. 1990—93, 2d v.p. 1993—94, 1st v.p. 1994—), Marion County Med. Soc., Acad. Orthop. Soc. (mem. undergrad. edn. com. 1983—87), Clin. Orthop. Soc., Assn. Orthop. Chmn., Ind. State Med. Soc., Ind. Orthop. Soc. (mem. exec. com. 1986—95), Am. Orthop. Foot and Ankle Soc. (mem. com. biomechanics 1982—84, mem. program com. 1985—), Am. Acad. Cerebral Palsy and Devel. Medicine, Am. Acad. Orthop. Surgeons (mem. com. undergrad. edn. 1976—83, chmn. 1979—83, mem. com. pediat. orthopedics 1988—94, mem. subcom. on spine 1990, mem. subcom. on pediats. program com. 1992, mem. coun. clin. resources 1993—94), Am. Acad. Pediats., Am. Fracture Assn. (Wellmerling award 1982), Am. Orthop. Assn. (mem. nominating com. 1988—89, del.-at-large exec. com. 1988—89, mem. com. on N.Am. traveling fellowship 1989—93, mem. com. planning and devel. 1991—, 2d pres.-elect 1994—), AMA, Am. Bd. Orthopedic Surgery (oral examiner 1983—, site investigator residency rev. com. 1983—, mem. credentials com. 1990—93, bd. dirs. 1990—, mem. oral examinations com. 1990—, mem. grad. edn. com. 1990—, mem. oral recert. examination com. 1992—93, mem. practice audit com. 1992—93, rep. alt. 1992—93, ACS adv. coun. 1992—94, sec. 1993—94, mem. cert. renewal com. 1993—94, mem. fin. com. 1993—94, mem. exec. com. 1993—94, vice chmn. residency rev. com. 1994—, chmn. 1995—97), Spectators Orthop. Letters Club, Little Orthop. Club, Orthop. Letters Club, Alpha Epsilon Delta, Alpha Omega Alpha. Office: Am Bd Orthopedic Surgery 400 Silver Cedar Ct Chapel Hill NC 27514-1585

DEROSA, MICHAEL L., elementary school educator, artist; b. Bartlesville, Okla., July 6, 1965; s. Louis Robert and Ema Jane DeRosa; 1 child, Joshua Michael. BFA, Okla. State U., 1987; MA, Ill. State U., 1990, MFA, 1992. Instr. Tulsa (Okla.) Pub. Sch. Sys., 1996—. Dir. houses retreat Coffeyville (Kans.) C.C., 1996—2000, instr. field biology, 1998—2004; photographer Kramanca Photography, St. Louis, 1997—. Mem. restoration city morals com. City Coffeyville, 1999—. Named Outstanding C.C. Instr., U. Kans., 1998, 1999; recipient Outstanding Prof. of Yr. award, Coffeyville (Kans.) C.C., 1998. Mem.: Kans. City Artists Coalition, Coll. Art Assn. Avocation: camping. Home: 601 Norwood Coffeyville KS 67337 Office: Coffeyville Cmty Coll 400 West 11th St Coffeyville KS 67337

DEROSA, RICHARD JEROME, composer, musician, educator; b. Huntington, N.Y., 1955; s. Clement Richard and Shirley Ramsdell DeRosa; m. Julie Mary Geiger (div.); 1 child, Martina. MusB, Jersey City State Coll., 1977; MusM, Manhattan (N.Y.) Sch. Music, 1985. Drummer Gerry Mulligan, Darien, Conn., 1979—90, JackieCain and Roy Kral, Montclair, NJ, 1987—2001; prin., owner Blane & DeRosa Prodn., N.Y., 1985—. Arranger, performer Concord (Calif.) Records, 1992—99; composer various soap operas, N.Y., 1990; arranger for Wynton Marsalis Lincoln Ctr. Jazz Orch., N.Y., 2002—; composer Artspower Theater Co., Montclair, 1990—; adj. prof. Jersey City (N.J.) State Coll., 1980—82, Manhattan (N.Y.) Sch. Music, N.Y., 1982—98; assoc. prof. William Paterson U., Wayne, NJ, 1999—. Author: Concepts For Improvisation, 1997; composer: (songs) (suite f9r percussion) Millennium, 1999. Mem.: Am. Fedn. Musicians, Internat. Assn. Jazz Educators, Broadcast Music Inc. Office: William Paterson Univ Shea Ctr Arts 300 Pompton Rd Wayne NJ 07470 Office Phone: 973-720-3802.

DEROSA, THOMAS J., investment banker, investment company executive; b. N.Y.C., 1958; m. Leslie Gorman; 4 children. BS, Georgetown U., 1980; MBA, Columbia U., 1988. V.p. Real Estate Investment Banking Group Alex Brown & Sons, Balt., 1992—96, mng. dir., 1996; global co-head Investment Banking Group Deutsche Bank, London, 1996—2002; vice chmn. The Rouse Co., Columbia, Md., 2002—, CFO, 2002—. Bd. visitors Med. Sch. Georgetown U. Office: The Rouse Company 10275 Little Patuxent Pkwy Columbia MD 21044

DE ROSA, WILLIAM THOMAS, internist, hematologist, oncologist; b. Newark, Nov. 1, 1953; DO, Kirksville Coll. Osteo., 1980. Diplomate Am. Bd. Internal Medicine, Am. Bd. Hematology, Am. Bd. Oncology. Intern USPHS Hosp., Staten Island, N.Y., 1980-81; resident in internal medicine Morristown (N.J.) Meml. Hosp., 1983-85; fellow in hematol. oncology Yale U. Sch. Medicine, New Haven, 1985-88; pvt. practice Morristown, 1988—. Staff Morristown Meml. Hosp. Fellow Am. Coll. Physicians; mem. Am. Soc. Hematology, Am. Soc. Clin. Oncology. Office: Carol G Simon Cancer Ctr PO Box 1089 100 Madison Ave Morristown NJ 07960-6136 Office Phone: 973-538-5210. Business E-Mail: william.derosa@ahsys.org.

DEROSE, KATHRYN PITKIN, medical researcher, minister; d. Roy MacBeth and Marcia Jenkins Pitkin; m. Stephen Francis Derose, Apr. 10, 1999; children: Leander Pitkin children: Nathanael Pitkin. BA, Duke U., 1985; MPH, UCLA, 1992, PhD, 2003. Program officer MAP Internat., Quito, Ecuador, 1986—90; project coord. Harbor UCLA Rsch. and Edn. Inst., Torrance, Calif., 1992—94; project dir. RAND Corp., Santa Monica, Calif., 1994—99, soc. rsch. analyst, 1999—2003, assoc. social sci., 2003—05, social scientist, 2005—. Cons. UCLA Ctr. Health Policy Rsch., 2001—02. Contbr. articles to profl. jours. Deacon Episc. Diocese of L.A., 1998. Recipient Beverlee Myers award, UCLA Sch. Pub. Health, 2000-2001; Celia and Joseph Blann fellow, 2000-2001, Maternal and Child Health Econs. Tng. grantee, UCLA Child and Family Health Program, 1999-2000, Cmty. Health Promotion grantee, UCLA Cmty. Health Promotion Program, 1998-1999. Health Svcs. Rsch. predoc. trainee, Agy. Health Care Rsch. and Policy, 1996-1998, Learning fellow on Social Change, Inter-Am. Found., 1991, Unrestricted Grad. fellow, UCLA Sch. Pub. Health. Mem.: APHA, N.Am. Assn. for Diaconate, Acad. Health. Office: RAND Health 1776 Main St PO Box 2138 Santa Monica CA 90407-2138 E-mail: pitkin@rand.org.

DE ROSE, PETER LOUIS, lawyer; b. N.Y.C., June 3, 1947; s. Peter and Florence (Brigiotti) De R. BA, Fordham U., 1969; PhD, Ind. U., 1974; JD, U. Tex., 1984. Bar: Tex., 1986, U.S. Dist. Ct. (no. dist.) Tex. 1986. Asst. prof. English Lamar U., Beaumont, Tex., 1975-85; assoc. Eakins, Kraft, & Johnson, Dallas, 1986, Law Offices of Melvin D. Morgan, MD, JD, Dallas, 1987-88, Gould & Assocs., Ft. Worth, 1989, Dallas, 1990, Austin, Tex., 1991—. Author: Jane Austen and Samuel Johnson, 1980; editor: A Concordance to the Works of Jane Austen, 1982; contbr. articles to profl. jours. Dir. bd. advocates U. Tex. Sch. Law, 1983-84. N.Y. State Regents scholar, 1965-70, grad. fellow Ind. U., 1969, 72; recipient Regents' Merit award for Disting. Teaching, 1981. Mem. ABA, Assn. Trial Lawyers Am., Fed. Bar Assn., Tex. Trial Lawyers Assn., Coll. of the State Bar of Tex., Phi Beta Kappa. Roman Catholic. Home and Office: 11811 Knights Brg Austin TX 78759-3610

DE ROSE, SANDRA MICHELE, psychotherapist, educator, administrator; b. Beacon, NY; d. Michael Joseph Borrell and Mabel Adelaide Edic Sloane; m. James Joseph De Rose, June 28, 1964 (div. 1977); children: Stacey Marie, Harrison Marquisa. Diploma in nursing, St. Luke's Hosp., 1964; BA in Child and Cmty. Psychology, Albertus Magnus Coll., 1983; MS in Counseling Psychology with honors, Century U., 1986, PhD in Counseling Psychology with honors, 1987. Gen. duty float nurse St. Luke's Hosp., Newburgh, N.Y., 1964-65; pvt. practice New Haven, 1975—; supr. nurses Craig House Hosp., Beacon, NY, 1965—70; dir. staff devel., team dir. divsn. outpatient treatment svc. Conn. Mental Health Ctr., New Haven, 1986-94; dir. edn., 1994-95; clin. instr. Sch. Nursing Yale U., New Haven, 1979-84, clin. instr. dept. psychiatry, 1989-96; dir. edn. outpatient divsn. Conn. Mental Health Ctr., New Haven, 1994-95. Clin. dir. Comprehensive Psychiat. Care, Norwich, Colchester and Willimantic, Conn., 1994-96; group practice Comprehensive Psychiat. Care, Norwich, Conn., 1995-2003, Alternative Paths, Yalesville, Conn., 1995-97. Mem. AAUW, ANA (cert.), Conn. Nurses Assn., Conn. Nurse Psychotherapists Assn., Western New Eng. Psychiat. and Psychologists Assn., Psychoanalytic Psychologists Soc., New Haven C. of C., Sigma Theta Tau, Delta Mu, Alpha Sigma Lambda. Avocations: music, theater, antiques, interior design/architecture, travel. Office: 100 Crown St Ste 2 New Haven CT 06510 Office Phone: 203-787-5381.

DE ROSSI, PORTIA, actress; b. Melbourne, Victoria, Australia, Jan. 31, 1973; d. Barry and Margaret Rogers; m. Metcalf Mel de Rossi (div.). Grad., Melbourne U. Actor: (films) Sirens, 1994, Scream 2, 1997, The Invisibles, 1999, American Intellectuals, 1999, Stigmata, 1999, Women in Film, 2001, Who is Cletis Tout?, 2001, I Witness, 2003, The Night We Called It a Day, 2003, Dead & Breakfast, 2004, Cursed, 2004; (TV series) Too Something, 1995—96, Nick Freno: Licensed Teacher, 1996—97, Ally McBeal, 1998—2002, Arrested Development, 2003—; (TV films) Perfect Assassins, 1998, Astoria, 1998, The Glow, 2002, America's Prince:The John F. Kennedy Jr. Story, 2003; TV appearances include Veronica's Closet, 1997, (TV series) Mad TV, 1997, The Twilight Zone, 2002, Mister Sterling, 2003. Office: c/o Internat Creative Mgmt 8942 Wilshire Blvd Beverly Hills CA 90211*

DEROUCHEY, BEVERLY JEAN, investment company executive; b. Kenosha, Wis., Sept. 3, 1958; d. Dean Rodney and Doris May (Rasch) DeR. BS in Bus. Mgmt., U. Wis., 1982; MBA in Fin., Cornell U., 1984. Chartered fin. analyst, 1993; lic. NASD-series 2-7-63-65. Acctg. asst. Kenosha (Wis.)-News Pub. Corp., 1979—81; polit. intern Office of Congressman Les Aspin, Racine, Wis., 1982; teaching asst. Cornell U., Ithaca, NY, 1983; audit intern Coopers and Lybrand, Syracuse, NY, 1983; staff cons. Peterson & Co., N.Y.C., 1984—86; assoc. Salomon Bros., N.Y.C., 1986—90, v.p., 1991; assoc. investment officer Dartmouth Coll., Hanover, NH, 1992—94; v.p., dir. asset allocation CTC Consulting, Portland, Oreg., 1995; investment mgr. Constellation Investments, Inc., Balt., 1996—97; dir. rsch. Paradigm Cons. Svcs. LLC, Quechee VT. and Clifton NJ., 1998—2000; founder, mng. dir. Long Trail Capital LLC, Quechee, Vt., 2000—; registered rep. IIG Horizons Securities, LLC, N.Y.C., 2000—04, APB Fin. Group, Inc., N.Y.C., 2004—. Alumni phonathons Cornell U., Ithaca, N.Y. and N.Y.C., 1982-87, co-chair new donor com., 1985-87; active Rep. Senatorial Inner Circle. Cornell U. scholar, 1982-84, BPW scholar, 1977, 82-83, AAUW scholar, 1981. Mem. Am. Film Inst., N.Y. Soc. of Security Analysts, CFA Inst., Bus. and Profl. Women (bd. dirs. 1991-92), Film Soc. Lincoln Ctr., Quechee (Vt.)-Lakes Landowners' Assn. Republican. Lutheran. Avocations: tennis, golf, travel, writing. Home: PO Box 1309 Quechee VT 05059-1309

DEROUIN, JAMES GILBERT, lawyer; b. Eau Claire, Wis., July 11, 1944; BA cum laude, U. Wis., 1967, JD, 1968. Bar: Wis. 1968, Ariz. 1986. Ptnr. Steptoe & Johnson LLC, Phoenix, Ariz.; atty. Meyer, Hendricks, Victor, Osbonn & Maledon, Phoenix, Ariz.; ptnr. Dewitt, Ross & Stevens, Madison, Wis. Mem. bd. sci. counselors Agy. for Toxic Substances and Disease Registry, 2003—; mem. profl. task force Ariz. State Bar. Polychlorinated-byphenol chair Wis. Dept. Natural Resources, 1976-78; mem. spl. com. on solid waste mgmt. Wis. Legis. Coun., 1976-79, ad hoc com. on hazardous waste mgmt., 1980-82, spl. com. on groundwater mgmt.; mem. Wis. Dept. Nat. Resources Metallic Mining Coun., 1978-85; chair Phoenix Environ. Quality Commn., 1986, Phoenix Environ. Quality Com., 1989-92; mem. Ariz. Govs. Regulatory Review Coun. 1986—; co-chair Ariz. Dept. Environ. Quality/Ariz. Dept. Water Resources Groundwater Task Force, 1996-97; mem. nat. adv. coun. superfun subcom. EPA. Chair. State Bar Ariz. (environ. and nat. resources law sect. 1989-90). Office: 201 E Washington St # 1600 Phoenix AZ 85004-2382

DEROUSIE, CHARLES STUART, lawyer; b. Adrian, Mich., May 24, 1947; s. Stuart J. and Helia I. (Juntunen) DeR.; m. Patricia Jean Fetzer, May 31, 1969; children: Jennifer, Jason. BA magna cum laude, Oakland U., 1969; JD magna cum laude, U. Mich., 1973. Bar: Ohio, 1973, U.S. Dist. Ct. (so. dist.) Ohio 1974. Ptnr. Vorys, Sater, Seymour and Pease, LLP, Columbus, Ohio, 1973—. Trustee Ballet Met., Inc., Columbus, 1978-90, pres., 1986-88; trustee Gladden Community House, Columbus, 1975-81, pres., 1979-81; mem. Children's Hosp. Devel. Bd., Columbus, 1987—, pres. 1995-96; trustee Elder Choices of Ctrl. Ohio, Columbus, 1989-95, Heritage Day Health Ctrs., Columbus, 1992-98. Fellow Columbus Bar Found.; mem. ABA, Am. Health Lawyers Assn., Columbus Bar Assn., Ohio Bar Assn., Order of Coif. Office: Vorys Sater Seymour and Pease LLP PO Box 1008 52 E Gay St Columbus OH 43215-3161

DEROW, JONATHAN PAUL, conservator; s. Peter A. and Ruth J. Derow; m. Janice Catherine Brodie, Aug. 18, 1991; 1 child, Jaxon Quinn. BA, Harvard U., 1988; M in Conservation of Art, U. Northumbria, Newcastle-upon-Tyne, Eng., 1991. NEA master apprenticeship intern Bklyn. Mus., 1991—92, Getty Grant Program intern, 1992—93; pres. J. D. Conservation, Inc., Bklyn., 1994—2005. Mem.: Am. Inst. for Conservation (assoc.). Office: J D Conservation Inc 790 Union St Brooklyn NY 11215 Office Phone: 718-789-1270. Office Fax: 718-789-1270.

DEROW, PETER ALFRED, publishing company executive; b. Boston, Apr. 18, 1940; s. Harry A. and Ruth D. (Dimond) Derow; m. Ruth C. Joffe, June 13, 1965; children: Jonathan, Polly, James. BA cum laude, Harvard U., 1963, MBA, 1965. Pres. Newsweek, Inc., N.Y.C., 1976-77; sr. v.p., dir. CBS, Inc., N.Y.C., 1977-78; v.p., dir. The Washington Post, 1978-81; chmn. Newsweek, Inc., N.Y.C., 1978-81; pres. CBS Pub. Group, N.Y.C., 1981-86; v.p. CBS, Inc., N.Y.C., 1981-86; pres. Goldmark Industries, N.Y.C., 1987-88; sr. v.p. Reed Pub. USA, Stamford, Conn. and Newton, Mass., 1988; pres. Instl. Investor, Inc., N.Y.C., 1988-97; dir. Publishers Clearing House, Port Washington, NY, 1998—, 101 Comm., LLC, Chatsworth, Calif., 1999—, GlobalSpec, Troy, NY, 1999—, CACI, Inc., Arlington, Va., 2000—, The Motley Fool, Alexandria, Va., 2003—, Money Media, N.Y.C., 2004—, Asare Media Inc., Loveland, Colo., 2005—. Author: Successful Publishing on Campus, 1966; mem. edit. bd. Harvard Bus. Rev., 1981-95. Avocations: tennis, sculling, reading, bicycling. Home: PO Box 534 Bedford NY 10506-0534 Office: 19th Fl 6 E 43rd St New York NY 10017 Fax: 212-286-8046.

DEROY, CRAIG I., lawyer; b. 1953; BA, U. So. Calif.; MA, U. San Diego; JD, Loyola U. Dep. chief, asst. atty., L.A.; gen. counsel 1st Am. Corp., Santa Ana, 1993—2004, sr. v.p., 2002—. Office: First Am 1 First Am Way Santa Ana CA 92707

DERR, KENNETH T., retired oil company executive; b. 1936; m. Donna Mettler, Sept. 12, 1959; 3 children. BME, Cornell U., 1959, MBA, 1960. With Chevron Corp. (formerly Standard Oil Co. of Calif.), San Francisco, 1960—, v.p., 1972—85; pres. Chevron U.S.A., Inc. subs. Chevron Corp., San Francisco, 1978—84; head merger program Chevron Corp. and Gulf Oil Corp., San Francisco, 1984—85; vice-chmn. Chevron Corp., San Francisco, 1985—88, chmn., CEO, 1989—99; ret., 1999. Bd. dirs. AT&T, Am. Productivity and Quality Ctr., Citigroup, Potlatch Corp. Trustee emeritus Cornell U. Mem.: The Bus. Coun., Pacific Union Club, Orinda Country Club, San Francisco Golf Club. Office: Chevron Texaco 6001 Bollinger Canyon Rd San Ramon CA 94583-2324

DERR, THOMAS SIEGER, religion educator; b. Boston, June 18, 1931; s. Thomas Sieger and Mary Ferguson (Sebring) D.; children: Peter Bulkeley, Laura Seely, Mary Williams, Erin Vincent, Philip Henry; m. Linda Vincent, Feb. 14, 1986. AB, Harvard U., 1953; MDiv, Union Theol. Sem., 1956; PhD, Columbia U., 1972. Ordained to ministry, United Ch. of Christ, 1956. Researcher World Council Chs., Geneva, 1961-62; asst. chaplain Stanford U., Calif., 1956-59, Smith Coll., Northampton, Mass., 1963-65, asst. prof. religion, 1965-71, assoc. prof., 1972-77, prof., 1977—. Cons. World Coun. Chs., 1965—; dir. Inst. on Religion in Pub. Life, N.Y.C.; mem. complemental faculty Rush Med. Coll., Chgo., 1979-84. Author: The Political Thought of the Ecumenical Movement, 1972, Ecology and Human Need, 1975, Church, State and Politics, 1981, Barriers to Ecumenism: The Holy See and the World Council of Churches on Social Questions, 1983, Believable Futures of American Protestantism, 1988, Creation at Risk? Religion, Science, and Environmentalism, 1995, Environmental Ethics and Christian Humanism, 1996; contbr. articles to profl. jours. Danforth Found. grantee, 1959-60, 65-66; Inst. for Advanced Study of Religion U. Chgo. fellow, 1981. Soc. for Christian Ethics. Home: 60 Harrison Ave Northampton MA 01060-2911 Office: Smith Coll Dept Religion Northampton MA 01063-0001 Business E-Mail: tderr@smith.edu.

DERR, WILLIAM JAMES, retired non-commissioned officer; b. Catawissa, Pa., Oct. 24, 1934; s. Cyrus Sylvester and Dorothy Mae Derr; m. Marie Louise Parise, Oct. 27, 1956; children: Tina Marie, Theresa Ann. Grad. with GED, 1957. Enlisted U.S. Army, 1951, served with Korea, Germany, Vietnam, Alaska, 1951—72, ret., 1972; warehouse supt. Pa. Liquor Control Bd., Harrisburg, Pa., 1972—94, ret., 1994. Author: Righteousness or Iniquity, 2001. Mem. retiree coun. U.S. Army, Carlisle Barracks, Pa., 1984—; vol. ombudsman Dept. of Aging, Carlisle, Pa., 1999—2000. Decorated Army meritorious Unit Commendation, Vietnam Gallantry Cross with bronze palm., Vietnam Civil Action medal with Silver Star, Army Commendation Medal with Oak Leaf Cluster, Nat. Defense Svc. Medal with Bronze Star, Korean Svc. Medal, Vietnam Service Medal with Silver Star, UN Svc. Medal (Korea), Republic of Vietnam Campaign Medal, Korean Def. Svc. medal. Mem.: AARP, VFW (life), Disabled Am. Vet. (life), Nat. Assn. for Uniformed Svc. (life), Mechanicsburg Lions Club (pres. 2000—01, 2005—, Lion of Yr. 2001—02), Am. Legion (life). Avocations: world travel, hunting, fishing, reading, gardening. Home: 8 Cumberland Dr Mechanicsburg PA 17050

DERRICK, BUTLER CARSON, JR., lawyer, retired congressman; b. Springfield, Mass., Sept. 30, 1936; s. Butler Carson and Mary English (Scott) D.; m. Beverly Davis; children: Lydia Gile, Butler Carson III, Charlotte Grantham, George Grantham. Student, U. S.C., 1954-58; LLB, U. Ga., 1965; hon. degree, Lander Coll., 1978, Erskine Coll., 1978; LLD (hon.), U. S.C., 1986; LHD (hon.), Med. U. S.C., 1988. Bar: S.C. 1965, D.C. 1988. Ptnr. Derrick & Byrd, Edgefield, S.C., 1970-75; mem. S.C. Ho. of Reps., 1969-74, 94th-103rd Congresses from 3rd S.C. dist., Washington, D.C., 1975-95; Dem. steering and policy com.; house adminstrn. com.; rules com.; chief majority dep. whip; ptnr. Williams & Jensen, PC, Washington, 1995—98, Powell, Goldstein, Frazer & Murphy, Washington, 1998—2004, Nelson, Mullins, Riley & Scarborough, LLP, Washington, 2004—. Adv. bd. Sec. of Energy. Named Conservationist of Yr. S.C. Wildlife Fedn., 1977; Conservationist of Yr. Nat. Wildlife Fedn., 1977; one of Our Ten Best Friends in Congress Outdoor life mag.; recipient Disting. River Conservation award Am. Rivers Conservation Council, 1977 Mem. S.C. Bar Assn., ABA, D.C. Bar Assn., Edgefield County Bar Assn. (past pres.), Spl. Forces Assn. (hon., mem. Green Berets), Phi Beta Kappa; bd. dirs, Entrust, 1999-. Democrat. Episcopalian. Office: Nelson Mullins Riley & Scarborough LLP 101 Constitution Ave NW Ste 900 Washington DC 20010 Office Phone: 202-712-2802. E-mail: hderrick@nmrs.com.

DERRICK, C. WARREN, JR., medical educator; b. Mullins, S.C., Nov. 12, 1935; s. Charles Warren Derrick and Helen Slaughter; m. Ann Berry Derrick, Aug. 15, 1959; children: Andrea, Hope, Scott. AB, Wofford Coll., 1958; MD, Med. Coll. S.C., 1962. Diplomate Am. Bd. Pediats. Intern Greenville (S.C.) Gen. Hosp., 1962—63; resident in pediats. U. Ala., Birmingham, 1966—68, fellow, 1968—71, asst. prof. pediats., 1971—75, assoc. prof. pediats., 1975—76; prof. pediats. U. S.C., Columbia, 1977—; pvt. practice Sumter, SC, 1976—77; William Weston endowed chair U. S.C., Columbia, 1986—. Dir. edn. pediats. Palmetto Health Children's Hosp., Columbia, 1977—. Contbr. articles to med. jours. Capt. U.S. Army, 1963—65. Fellow, NIH/NIAID, 1969—71, Am. Heart Assn. Mem.: Alpha Omega Alpha. Methodist. Office: U SC Sch Medicine Dept Pediats 4 Medical Park Ste 301 Columbia SC 29223

DERRICK, FOX A., music educator, singer; s. Johnnie M. Williams. MusB in Edn., Ark. State U., 2001. Cert. music tchr. Ark. Dept. Edn., 2001. Dir. choral music MacArthur Jr. H.S., Jonesboro, Ark., 2001—. Dir., guest clinician N.E. Ark. Female Chorus; supr. concert office Interlochen Arts Camp. Actor: (plays) Bye, Bye Birdie, (singer): State Fair; (plays) Anything Goes, Dracula, Ragtime. Mem.: Tex. Choral Dirs. Assn., North Ctrl. Accreditation Assn., Am. Choral Dirs. Assn., Ark. Choral Dirs. Assn. (chmn. jr. events N.E. region), Kappa Kappa Psi. Personal E-mail: derrickfox@hotmail.com.

DERRICK, GARY WAYNE, lawyer; b. Enid, Okla., Nov. 3, 1953; s. John Henry and Leota Elaine (Glenn) D.; m. Susan Adele Goodwin, Dec. 22, 1979 (div. June 1981); m. Francys Hollis Johnson, May 3, 1986; children: Meghan, Drew, Jane. BA in History, English, Okla. State U., 1976; JD, U. Okla., 1979. Bar: Okla. 1979. Assoc. Andrews, Davis, Legg, Bixler, Milsten & Price, Oklahoma City, 1979-84, ptnr., 1985-90; of counsel McKinney, Stringer & Webster, P.C., Oklahoma City, 1990-93; ptnr. Derrick & Briggs, LLP, Oklahoma City, 1994—. Active Securities Law and Acctg. Group, Oklahoma City, 1979—; chmn. Gen. Corp. Act Commn., Okla., 1984—, chmn. Securities Liaison Com., Okla., 1985-86; lectr. sem. Okla. Corp. Act, 1986—. Contbg. author Oklahoma Business Organizations. Mem. Okla. State U. Found., Stillwater, 1983—89, Univ. Found., Norman, 1982—; mem. condr.'s cir. Okla. Symphony Orch., 1981—88; mem. conductor's cir. Okla. Philharmonic, 2001—; chmn. constn. and canons com. Episcopal Diocese of Okla., 1999—; bd. dirs. Historic Preservation, Inc., 1990—. Mem.: ABA (taxation and corp. sect., banking and bus. law sect.), Am. Soc. Corp. Secs. (pres. Okla.-Ark. chpt. 1994—95), Oklahoma County Bar Assn. (bd. govs. young lawyers divsn. 1981—82), Okla. Bar Assn. (chmn. bus. assn. sect. 1985—87, 2004—, outstanding contbn. to continuing legal edn., Earl Sneed award 1997), Oklahoma City Boat Club, Oklahoma City Golf and Country Club. Republican. Episcopalian. Avocations: sailing, violin. Home: 500 NW 15th St Oklahoma City OK 73103-2102 Office: Derrick & Briggs LLP Bank One Ctr 28th Fl 100 N Broadway Ave Oklahoma City OK 73102-8819 Office Phone: 405-235-1900. Business E-Mail: derrick@derrickandbriggs.com.

DERRICK, MALCOLM, physicist; b. Hull, Eng., Feb. 15, 1933; came to U.S., 1963, naturalized, 1976; s. Arthur Henry and Gladys (Hopkinson) D.; m. Kathleen Allen, 1957; 1 child, Matthew; m. Christa Zars Baumgardner; 1966; m. Eva Krebbers, 1995. B.Sc. with 1st class honours, U. Birmingham, 1954, PhD, 1959; MA, Oxford U., 1961. Instr. Carnegie Inst. Tech., 1957-60; asst. prof. Oxford U., 1960-63; asst. physicist Argonne (Ill.) Nat. Lab., 1963-67, sr. physicist, 1967—, dir. high energy physics div., 1974-81. Vis. prof. U. Minn., 1969-70, Univ. Coll., London, 1972-73; adv. com. Stanford U. Accelerator Center, Fermi Nat. Accelerator Lab.; mem. high energy physics adv. panel Dept. Energy. Author numerous research papers on high energy physics. Fellow Am. Phys. Soc. Home: 20 Equestrian Way Lemont IL 60439-9785 Office: Argonne Nat Lab Bldg 362 Argonne IL 60439 Office Phone: 630-252-6272. Business E-Mail: mxd@hep.anl.gov. *The opportunity to spend a lifetime's career investigating the Fundamental physical basis of matter is one that has been given to relatively few people. Such research requires large and expensive accelerators and particle detectors and so can only be funded by government agencies. It is to the credit of the United States that such support has been generously given, and the resulting revolution in our understanding of nature is the outstanding intellectual achievement of our times.*

DERRICK, WILLIAM DENNIS, retired physical plant administrator, consultant; b. San Diego, Feb. 7, 1946; s. Charles Woodrow and Catherine Elizabeth (McCormick) D.; m. Lynda Ray Adams, June 15, 1964 (div. 1971); children: Tod Sean, Shannon Kay, Nicole Dione, Johnathon Robert; m. Frances C. Bouck, Nov. 19, 1979; children: Kaila June Warner, Bryan Charles. Student, U. Nebr., 1971-72, 73-74, U. Mont., 1974-77, 98-99, Internat. Corr., 1966-67, 81, Battelle Meml. Inst., 1985, Project Mgmt. Inst., 1986-95, 98—. Elec. draftsman City of Lincoln (Nebr.) Light Dept., 1964-65; asst. engr. to adjutant gen. Nebr. N.G. State of Nebr., Lincoln, 1965-66; owner, mgr., archtl. draftsman Lumberman's Plan Svc., Inc., Lincoln, 1966-70; owner, mgr. Lenny's Lounge, Missoula, Mont., 1978-80; engring. technician, constrn. insp., adminstr. USDA/Helena (Mont.) Nat. Forest, 1980-83; facilities project mgr. pub. office bldgs. div. City and County of Denver, 1984-86; supt. bldgs. and grounds Denver Pub. Libr., 1986-91; dir. phys. plant Red Rocks C.C., Lakewood, Colo., 1991-94; CEO Derrick, Inc., Stevensville, Mont. Mem. Local Govt. Study Commn., Stevensville, Mont., 1974; bd. dirs. Lewis and Clark County Fair Bd., Helena, Mont., 1979-83; candidate U.S. Ho. of Reps., 1999—. Mem. Project Mgmt. Inst. (cert. project mgr. profl. #619, v.p. programs Denver chpt. 1986-89, pres. 1990-91, v.p. pub. rels. 1992-93, bd. dirs., ex-officio). Avocations: computers, videography, photo journalism, golf. Home: PO Box 401 Stevensville MT 59870-0401 E-mail: wder789456@msn.com.

DERRICKSON, KEITH WAYNE, musician, educator; s. Arthur Andrew and Ruth Lorraine Derrickson. BS in Music Edn., Towson U., 1978; MS in Music Edn., Johns Hopkins U., 1996. Music tchr., dept. chair Hereford HS, Parkton, Md., 1978—86; music dept. chair Parkville HS, Md., 1986—98; music dir. St. Andrew's Luth. Ch., Parkville, Md., 1988—95, St. John's Luth. Ch., Parkville, Md., 1996—; choir dir. Essex CC, Essex, Md., 1995—97; arts chmn. Overlea HS, Overlea, Md., 1998—2001; music tchr. Pleasant Plains Elem., Towson, Md., 2001—. Composer: (sheet music) We Are the Chorus, 1985, Child of Winter, 1987, This is Christmas, 1989. Recipient Tchr. of Yr. award, Parkville HS PTA, 1997, Loch Raven Kawanis Club, 2004. Mem.: Tchrs. Assn. Balto County (rep. 2003—04), Md. Music Educators Assn. (pres. north-ctrl. region 1993—95), Parkville HS Sch. Alumni Assn. (founding pres. 1997—2004). Republican. Lutheran. Achievements include having church choir featured in Voices Magazine after organizing trip to mission congregation and composing 4 children's musicals that raised over $15,000 for Pleasant Plains Elementary School.

DERRICKSON, WILLIAM BORDEN, manufacturing executive; b. Milford, Del., May 30, 1940; m. Patricia Jean Hayes, Feb. 1, 1964; children: Stephen Russel, Michael Scot BSEE, U. Del., 1964; diploma, Harvard Bus. Sch., 1979. Registered profl. engr. Supr. elec. maintenance Delmarva Power, Salisbury, Md., 1964-68; instrumentation engr. Hercules, Inc., Wilmington, Del., 1968-69, Sun Shipbldg., Chester, Pa., 1969-70; dir. project Fla. Power & Light Co., Juno Beach, Fla., 1970-84; sr. v.p. Pub. Svc. Co. N.H., Manchester, 1984-85; pres. New Hampshire Yankee Electric Co., Seabrook, 1985-87; pres., COO WPD Assocs., Inc., 1986-88, Quadrex Corp., Campbell, Calif., 1988-89, chmn. bd., CEO, 1989-93; also chmn. bd. dirs.; chmn. bd., CEO QES Inc., Palm City, Fla., 1994—, IBEX Engring. Svcs., Palm City, 1995—2002. Nuclear advisor Tenn. Valley Authority Bd. Dirs., 1987. Contbr. articles to profl. publs. Named Constrn. Man of Yr. ENR/McGraw-Hill Publs., 1984 Mem. NSPE, Am. Nuclear Soc., Project Mgmt. Inst., N.H. Soc. Profl. Engrs., Internat. Platform Assn., Rep. Senatorial Inner Circle. Republican. Avocations: golf, travel, coin collecting/numismatics, piano. Office: IBEX Engring Svcs PO Box 948 Palm City FL 34991-0948 Home: 316 SW Atlanta Ave Stuart FL 34994 Office Phone: 772-781-1894. E-mail: bderricksn@aol.com.

DERRICO, GEORGIA SANTANGELO, banker; b. N.Y.C., Oct. 6, 1944; d. George M. Derrico and Rose Mary (Rao) Santangelo; m. R. Roderick Porter, Feb. 6, 1982. BA, St. Mary's Coll., Notre Dame, Ind., 1966; deg. Internat. Affairs, Johns Hopkins U., Bologna, Italy, 1969; M Internat. Affairs, Columbia U., 1970; postgrad. exec. seminar, Harvard U., 1977. Various positions including lending officer, dist. head corp. divsn., chief adminstrv. and credit officer multinat. divsn. Chem. Bank, N.Y.C., 1971—, sr. v.p., 1982—84, dir. corp. affairs, 1982—84; chmn. So. Fin. Fed. Savs. Bank, N.Y.C., 1985—. Bd. dirs. Oneida, Ltd. Contbr. articles to profl. jours. Bd. dirs. Nat. Dance Inst. Mem.: Assn. MBA Execs.

DERRO, ROBERT ARTHUR, retired physician; b. Winchester, Mass., Nov. 10, 1935; s. Joseph John and Concetta (Ferrina) D.; m. Lieselotte Marie Derro, Sept. 8, 1967; children: Brian, David, Yvonne, Roger. BA, Harvard U., 1957; MD, George Washington U., 1961. Diplomate Am. Bd. Internal Medicine. Intern D.C. Gen. Hosp., 1961—62; resident in internal medicine Lemuel Shattuck Hosp., Jamaica Plain, Mass., 1962—63; resident in internal medicine, fellow in cardiology Boston City Hosp., 1963—64; staff physician Matthew Walker Health Ctr., Nashville, 1969—72; assoc. dir. U. Minn. affil. family practice residency program St. Paul-Ramsey Med. Ctr., 1972—83; staff physician Kaiser Permanent, Atlanta, 1983—2001; ret., 2001. Contbr. articles. Capt U.S. Army, 1965—67. Recipient Cert. of Achievement for initiating program of rheumatic fever prophylaxis, 1966. Mem.: Am. Coll. Physicians. Roman Catholic. Avocations: Indigenous forms of American music, gardening. Home: 3662 Howell Wood Tr Duluth GA 30096

DERRY, JENNIFER ANNE, academic administrator; b. Muncy, Pa., Mar. 13, 1979; d. Edward E. and Mary L. Goodwillie; m. Anthony P. Derry, Dec. 27, 2003. BA, U. Notre Dame, 2001; MEd, Millersville (Pa.) U., 2003. Coord. residence mgmt. Office for Residence Life Villanova (Pa.) U., 2003—04, asst. dir. staff tng. and devel. Office Residence Life, 2004—. Facilitator Svc. Learning Cmty., Villanova, 2004—, Villanova (Pa.) Experience, 2003—04. Vol. Hugh O'Brien Youth Leadership Seminars, Phila., 2004—05; dir. CLEW Ctrl. Pa. Leadership Seminars, Inc., Malvern, Pa., 2004—05. Mem.: Assn. Coll. & Univ. Housing Officers Internat., Am. Coll. Personnel Assn., Notre Dame Club. Roman Catholic. Home: 412 Bill Smith Boulevard King of Prussia PA 19406 Office: Villanova University 800 Lancaster Avenue Villanova PA 19406 Office Phone: 610-519-7229.

DERRY, WILLIAM R., JR., lawyer; b. Cleve., Jan. 21, 1946; BA, Yale U., 1967; JD, U. Va., 1974. Bar: Va. 1974. Atty. Mays & Valentine (merged with Troutman Sanders), Richmond, Va.; ptnr., public fin. group leader Troutman Sanders LLP, Richmond, Va., 2001—. 1st lt. U.S. Army, 1969-71. Mem. ABA, Nat. Assn. Bond Lawyers, Va. Bar Assn., Richmond Bar Assn. Office: Troutman Sanders LLP 1111 E Main St PO Box 1122 Richmond VA 23218-1122 Office Phone: 804-697-1375. Office Fax: 804-697-1339. Business E-Mail: bill.derry@troutmansanders.com.

DERSH, RHODA E., management consultant, business executive; b. Phila., Sept. 10, 1934; civ; d. Maurice S. and Kay (Wiener) Eisman; m. Jerome Dersh, Dec. 23, 1956; children: Debra Lori, Jeffrey Jonathan. BA, U. Pa., 1955; MA, Tufts U., 1956; MBA, Manhattan Coll., 1980. Interpreter Consul of Chile, 1954-57; various teaching and staff positions Albright Coll., Mt. Holyoke Coll., Amherst Coll., Marple Newtown Sch., 1957-58; pres., chief exec. officer Profl. Practice Mgmt. Assocs., Reading, 1976—, Pace Inst., Reading, 1981—, Pace Mgmt., Inc., 1983—;, 1984-90. Mem. regional adv. bd. First Union Bank, 1998—. Author: The School Budget is Your Business, 1976, Business Management for Professional Offices, 1977, The School Budget: It's Your Money, It's Your Business, 1979, Improving Public School Management Practices, 1979, Part-Time Professional and Managerial Personnel: The Employers View, 1979; contbr. articles to profl. jours. Bd. dirs. Pa. State Bd. Pvt. Lic. Schs., 1987-93; cons. dir. pub. sch. budget study project City of Reading, 1967-78, chmn. comprehensive community plan task force, 1973-75; chmn. pub. svc. cons. project 1980-90; panel chmn. budget allocations United Way, 1974-76; del. White House Conf. on Children Youth, 1970; co-founder World Affairs Coun., Reading and Berks County, 1963-65; chmn. Berks County Com. for Children Youth, 1968-72; commr. Trial Ct. Nominating Commn. of Berks County (Pa.), 1982-84; bd. dirs. United Way of Berks County, 1984-89; chmn. programs Leadership Berks, 1986-87; bd. dirs. Reading Ctr. City Devel. Corp., Berks Bus.-Edn. Coalition Corp., 1991—; mem. Greater Berks Devel. Bd., 1998—. Recipient Trendsetter award YWCA, 1985. Mem. AAUW (ednl. found. grant.), LWV, Pa. Assn. Pvt. Sch. Bus. Adminstrs. (bd. dirs. 1985-89), Berks County C. of C. (bd. dirs. 1983-86, chmn. edn. com. 1983-85), Am. Acad. Ind. Cons. (pres. 1978-80), Reading and Berks C. of C (Entrepreneur of Yr. 1985), Rotary (bd. dirs. Reading, Pa., chpt. 1989-90). Office: 606 Court St Reading PA 19601-3542

DERSHOWITZ, ALAN MORTON, law educator; b. Bklyn., Sept. 1, 1938; s. Harry and Claire Dershowitz; m. Carolyn Cohen; children: Elon Marc, Jamin Seth, Ella Kaille Cohen Dershowitz. BA magna cum laude, Bklyn. Coll., 1959, LLD (hon.), 2001; LLB magna cum laude, Yale U., 1962; MA (hon.), Harvard Coll., 1967; LLD (hon.), Yeshiva U., 1989; PhD (hon.), Haifa U., 1993; LLD (hon.), Hebrew Union Coll., 1993, Syracuse U., 1997, Monmouth Coll. Bar: DC 1963, Mass. 1968, US Supreme Ct. 1968. Law clk. to Hon. David L. Bazelon US Ct. Appeals DC Cir., 1962—63; law clk. to Hon. Arthur J. Goldberg US Supreme Ct., 1963—64; asst. prof. law Harvard Law Sch., 1964—67, prof. law, 1967—, Felix Frankfurter Prof. Law, 1993—; fellow Ctr. for Advanced Study of Behavioral Sciences, 1971—72. Cons. to dir. NIMH, 1967—69, Pres.'s Commn. Civil Disorders, 1967, Pres.'s Com. Causes Violence, 1968, NAACP Legal Def. Fund, 1967—68, NIMH's Pres.'s Commn. Marijuana and Drug Abuse, 1972—73, Coun. on Drug Abuse, 1972—, Ford Found. Study on Law and Justice, 1973—76; rapporteur Twentieth Century Fund Study on Sentencing, 1975—76. Co-author: Psychoanalysis, Psychiatry and the Law, 1967, Criminal Law: Theory and Process, 1974; author: The Best Defense, 1982, Reversal of Fortune: Inside the von Bulow Case, 1986, Taking Liberties: a Decade of Hard Cases, Bad Laws and Bum Raps, 1988, Chutzpah, 1991, Contrary to Public Opinion, 1992, The Abuse Excuse, 1994, The Advocate's Devil, 1994, Reasonable Doubts: The O.J. Simpson Case and the Criminal Justice System, 1996, The Vanishing American Jew: In Search of Jewish Identity for the Next Century, 1997, Sexual McCarthyism: Clinton, Starr and the Emerging Constitutional Crisis, 1998, Just Revenge, 1999, The Genesis of Justice: Ten Stories of Biblical Injustice That Led to the Ten Commandments and Modern Law, 2000, Supreme Injustice: How the High Court Hijacked Election 2000, 2001, Letters to a Young Lawyer, 2001, Why Terrorism Works: Understanding the Threat, Responding to the Challenge, 2002, Shouting Fire: Civil Liberties in a Turbulent Age, 2002, America Declares Independence, 2003, The Case for Israel, 2003, America on Trial, 2004, Rights from Wrongs: The Origins of Human Rights in the Experience of Injustice, 2004, The Case for Peace: How the Arab-Israeli Conflict Can Be Resolved, 2005; contbr. articles to profl. jounals; editor-in-chief: Yale Law Jour., 1961—62. Chmn. civil rights com. New England region Anti-Defamation League, B'nai B'rith, 1980—85; bd. dirs. ACLU, 1968—71, 1972—75, Assembly Behavioral and Social Scis. at NAS, 1973—76. Fellow Guggenheim, 1978—79. Mem.: Order of Coif, Phi Beta Kappa. Jewish. Office: Harvard Law Sch 1563 Massachusetts Ave Cambridge MA 02138 Office Phone: 617-495-4617. Office Fax: 617-495-7855. Business E-Mail: dersh@law.harvard.edu.

DERSTADT, RONALD THEODORE, health facility administrator; b. Detroit, June 9, 1950; s. Theodore Edward and Dorothy J. (Semko) D.; m. J. Gail Adamson, June 9, 1990. BA, U. Detroit, 1971; M of Hosp. Healthcare Adminstn., Xavier U., 1975. Mgr. shared svcs. Bethesda Hosp. North, Cin., 1975-76; asst. adminstr. McCullough-Hyde Meml. Hosp., Oxford, Ohio, 1977-79; pres. Hospice of Cin., Inc., 1979-82; dir. strategic planning St. Francis-St. George Hosp., Cin., 1982-84; v.p. Mgmt. Dynamics, Inc., Cin., 1984-85; sr. v.p. St. Francis-St. George Mgmt. Co., Cin., 1986-88; v.p. Franciscan Health System of Cin., 1988-91; dir. hosp. affairs ChoiceCare, Cin., 1991-95; CEO Medquest, Owensboro, Ky., 1995-98; COO Ctr. for Chem. Addictions Treatment, Cin., 1998—. Vice-chmn., bd. dirs. Franciscan Health Network, Cin., Franciscan Health Ventures, Cin. Treas., bd. dirs. Ohio Easter Seals Soc., Columbus, 1987-93; bd. dirs. S.W. Ohio Easter Seal Soc., Cin., 1986-92; adv. bd. Dater Jr. H.S., Cin., 1984-88. Fellow Am. Coll. Healthcare Execs.; mem. Healthcare Fin. Mgmt. Assn., Am. Hosp. Assn., Ohio Hosp. Assn. Avocations: boating, golf, radio control model building. Home: 7363 Dogtrot Rd Cincinnati OH 45248 Office: 830 Ezzard Charles Dr Cincinnati OH 45214-2525

DERTHICK, ALAN WENDELL, architect, architectural firm executive; b. Johnson City, Tenn., July 6, 1931; s. Lawrence Gridley and Helda Lee (Hannah) Derthick; m. Jane Bailey, Dec. 22, 1958; children: Mark Alan, Steven John. BArch, Auburn U., 1954. Registered arch., Tenn., Ga., Ala. Ptnr. Derthick, Henley & Wilkerson Archs., Chattanooga, 1960—. Prin. works include Miller Pl., 1989 (Honor award), Hunter Mus. Art, 1977 (Honor awards), 1994, 2004, 2005, Chattanooga Pub. Libr., 1977 (Honor award), 1992, Hamilton County Cts. Bldg., 1992, Alexian Village, 1993, 2003, 2005, Covenant Transport Nat. Hdqrs., 1997, 2000, 2005, Chattanoooga Conv. Ctr., 2003, EPB Garage, 2003, 2005, TVPPA, 2002, Hardy Sch., 2001. Chmn. Chattanooga Codes Rev. Bd., 1975—95, Mayor's Better Schs. Task Force, Chattanooga, 1984—85, Hamilton County Codes Appeals Bd., 1999—2005; pres. 1st Christian Ch., 1978, 1984, 1998, 1999, 2000. With USAF, 1954—56. Recipient Honor award, Nat. Concrete Reinforcing Steel Inst., 1977. Mem.: AIA (pres. Chattanooga chpt. 1966, 1972, Gulf States Regional and Nat. Honor award 1961, 1977, 1978, 1989), Tenn. Soc. Archs. (pres. 1991), Mountain City Club. Home: 602 Marr Dr Signal Mountain TN 37377-2228 Office: Derthick Henley Wilkerson 1001 Carter St Chattanooga TN 37402-5014 Office Phone: 423-266-4816.

DERTIEN, JAMES LEROY, librarian; b. Kearney, Nebr., Dec. 14, 1942; s. John Ludwig and Muriel May (Cooley) D.; m. Elaine Paulette Mohror, Dec. 26, 1966; children— David Dalton, Channing Lee AB, U. S.D., 1965; MLS, U. Pitts., 1966; MPA, U. S.D., 1995. Head librarian Mitchell Pub. Library, S.D., 1966-67; head librarian Sioux Falls Coll., S.D., 1967-69; acting dir. libraries U. S.D., Vermillion, 1969-70; head librarian Vets. Meml. Pub. Library, Bismarck, N.D., 1970-75, Bellevue Pub. Library, Nebr., 1975-81; libr. dir. Siouxland Librs., S.D., 1981—. Pres., bd. dirs. Vol. and Info. Ctr., Sioux Falls, 1991-93. Mem. ALA, Mountain Plains Library Assn. (pres. 1978-79, editor newsletter 1982—), S.D. Library Assn. (pres. 1986-87). Lodges: Rotary. Unitarian Universalist. Avocations: backpacking, reading, fishing. Office: Siouxland Librs 201 N Main Ave Sioux Falls SD 57104-6002 Home: 21635 Gold Dust Trl Nemo SD 57759-7611 E-mail: jimd@siouxland.lib.sd.us.

DER TOROSSIAN, PAPKEN, engineering executive; B of Mech. engring., MIT; M, Stanford U. Pres., CEO EVS Microsystems, Inc.; pres. Santa Cruz divsn., v.p. telephone products group Plantronics; pres. Silicon Valley Group, San Jose, Calif., 1984—, CEO, 1986—, chmn. bd. dirs., 1991—. Spkr. in field. Office: 541 E Trimble RD San Jose CA 95131-1284

DERUBERTIS, PATRICIA UHL, software company executive; b. Bayonne, N.J., July 10, 1950; d. George Joseph and Veronica (Lukaszewich) Uhl; m. John Stryker, 1975; m. Michael DeRubertis, 1986. BS in Bus. Adminstrn., U. Md., 1972. Account rep. GE, San Francisco, 1975-77; tech. rep. Computer Scis. Corp., San Francisco, 1977-78; cons., pres. Uhl Assocs., Tiburon, Calif., 1978-81; cons. mgr. Ross Sys., Palo Alto, Calif., 1981-83; COO, exec. v.p. Distributed Planning Sys., Calabasas, Calif., 1983-92; pres. DeRubertis & Assocs., Thousand Oaks, Calif., 1992-94, DeRubertis Software Sys., Inc., Windermere, Fla., 1995—. Author: Rose Gardening By Color, 1994. Troop leader San Francisco coun. Girl Scouts Am., 1974; participant Woman On Water, Marina Del Rey, Calif., 1983; vol. Martin County Coun. for the Arts, 1995, Habitat for Humanity, 2002, Windermere Preparatory Sch., 2003—; sec./tread. Windermere Tree Bd., 2005—; vol. Gayle Harrell campaign for state legis., 2000. Mem. AAUW, NAFE, Windermere Garden Club, Lake Eustis Sailing Club, Delta Delta Delta. Democrat. Office: 109 Main St Windermere FL 34786 Office Phone: 800-411-7213. Office Fax: 407-909-0863. E-mail: dssincpd@aol.com.

DERVAN, PETER BRENDAN, chemistry professor; b. Boston, July 28, 1945; s. Peter Brendan and Ellen (Comer) D.; m. Jackqueline K. Barton; children: Andrew, Elizabeth. BS, Boston Coll., 1967; PhD, Yale U., 1972. Asst. prof. Calif. Inst. Tech., Pasadena, 1973-79, assoc. prof., 1979-82, prof. chemistry, 1982-88, Bren prof. chemistry, 1988—; chmn. div. chemistry & chem. engring., 1994—. Adv. bd. ACS Monographs, Washington, 1979-81 Mem. adv. bd. Jour. Organic Chemistry, Washington, 1981—; mem. editorial bd. Bioorganic Chemistry, 1983—, Chem. Rev. Jour., 1984—, Nucleic Acids Res., 1986—, Jour. Am. Chem. Soc., 1986—, Acct. Chem. Res., 1988—, Bioorganic Chem. Rev., 1988—, Bioconjugate Chemistry, 1989—, Jour. Med. Chemistry, 1991—, Tetrahedron, 1992—, Bioorganic and Med. Chemistry, 1993—, Chemical and Engineering News, 1992—; contbr. articles to profl. jours. A.P. Sloan Rsch. fellow, 1977; Camille and Henry Dreyfus scholar, 1978; Guggenheim fellow, 1983; recipient Arthur C. Cope Scholar award 1986, Maison de la Chimie Found. prize, 1996. Fellow Am. Acad. Scis.; mem. NAS, Am. Chem. Soc. (Nobel Laureate Signature award 1985, Harrison Howe award 1988, Arthur C. Cope award, 1993, Willard Gibbs medal, 1993, Rolf Sammet prize, 1993, William H. Nichols medal 1994, Kirkwood medal 1998, Alfred Bader award 1999, award Achievement in Biometric Chemistry, 2005), Inst. Medicine (Remsen award 1998, Linus Pauling medal 1999, Richard Tolman medal 1999), French Acad. Scis. (fgn., Tetrahedron prize 2000); mem. Am. Philos. Soc. (Harvey prize 2002), German Acad. Natural Scientists. Office: Calif Inst Tech Leopoldin 1201 E California Blvd Pasadena CA 91125-0001

DERWENSKUS, MARILYNN, artist, educator; b. Detroit, Dec. 23, 1937; BFA, Wayne State U., 1960, MA, 1962; MFA, U. Chgo., 1988. Assoc. prof. Ball State U., Muncie, Ind., 1988—. Co-dir. Art in Italy Ball State U., Muncie, 1994-97. Represented by Cary Gallery, Rochester, Mich. Lilly fellow, 1995-96. Mem. Nat. Watercolor Soc., Watercolor Soc. Ind., N.W. Watercolor Soc., Ala. Watercolor Soc., Ga. Watercolor Soc., Pa. Watercolor Soc., Mich. Watercolor Soc., Soc. Exptl. Artists, Ptnrs. of Ams., Penwomen. Home: 3716 N Lakeside Dr Muncie IN 47304-5266 Office: Ball State U Dept Of Art Muncie IN 47306-0001

DERYUGA, VYACHESLAV O., nuclear physicist; b. Krasny Liman, Ukraine, Mar. 9, 1955; s. Oleksiy D. and Polina P. Deryuga; m. Larisa P. Kolomiets, July 28, 1978 (div. Nov. 1984); 1 child, Anna Dotsenko; m. Vera B. Smirnova, Apr. 18, 1986; 1 child, Polina. BSc, Kharkov (Ukraine) State U., 1978; MSc, Kharkov State U., 1978; PhD, Kharkov (Ukraine) State U., 1982. Vis. rschr. Joint Inst. for Nucler Rsch., Dubna, Russia, 1978-81; sr. rsch. scis. Kharkov State U., 1981-86, assoc. prof., sr. rsch. scientist, 1992—97; assoc. prof., head dept. Kharkov Inst. Zootechniques and Vet. Medicine, 1986-92; cons. Computer Tech., Inc., NYC, 1997—2002; project leader Morgan Stanley, NYC, 2002—. Mem. coun. Soc. for Sci. Edn. Knowledge, Kharkov, 1986-91; docent USSR Bd. Edn., 1991; fellow James Beard Found. Author: Physics, 1993; contbr. articles to profl. jours. including Instruments and Exptl. Techniques, Nuclear Physics, Jour. Physics, Hyperfine Interactions. Mem. IEEE (sr.), IEEE Computer Soc. (sr.), Ukrainian Phys. Soc. Inventor of electro-hydraulic desintegrator of microorganisms; research on acoustic effects of high-current electron beams; pioneering work in design computer programs for automated spectra processing; design of automated customer account transfer service. Business E-Mail: deryuga@computer.org.

DERZON, GORDON M., hospital administrator; b. Milw., Dec. 28, 1934; married. BA, Dartmouth Coll., 1957; MHA, U. Mich., 1961. Adminstrv. resident Bklyn. Hosp., 1960-61, adminstrv. asst., 1961-63, asst. exec. dir., 1963-65, exec. dir., 1966-67, State U. Hosp., Bklyn., 1967-68, Kings County Hosp. Center, Bklyn., 1968-74; CEO U. Wis. Hosps. and Clinics, Madison, 1974-2000; assoc. prof. SUNY, 1967-74; clin. prof. U. Wis., now emeritus prof. Bd. dirs. Ind. Living, MATC Found., Madison Cmty. Health Ctr. Hospice, Combat Blindness Found., Ctr. Health Emotions. Contbr. articles to profl. jours. Mem. Am. Hosp. Assn. (past chmn. pub. gen. hosp. sect.). Home: 3440 Topping Rd Madison WI 53705-1439 Office Phone: 608-238-9407. Business E-Mail: gm.derzon@hosp.wisc.edu.

DESA, JUANITA M., dentist; BS, Cornell U., 1995, DDS, 2000. Gen. dentist N.Y. Hotel and Trades Assn., N.Y.C., 2002—03, Batavia Esthetic Dentistry, Batavia, NY, 2003—. Asst. instr. Columbia U., N.Y.C., 2001—02. Recipient grant, Am. Coll. of Rasthodonists, 2001. Mem.: Am. Dental Assn. Office Phone: 585-343-1958.

DE SA E SILVA, ELIZABETH ANNE, secondary school educator; b. Edmonds, Wash., Mar. 17, 1931; d. Sven Yngve and Anna Laura Elizabeth (Dahlin) Erlandson; m. Claudio de Sá e Silva, Sept. 12, 1955 (div. July 1977); children: Lydia, Marco, Nelson. BA, U. Oreg., 1953; postgrad., Columbia U., 1954—56, Calif. State U., Fresno, 1990, U. No. Iowa, 1983; MEd, Mont. State U., 1978. Med. sec., 1947—49; sec. Merced Sch. Dist., Calif., 1950—51; sec., asst. Simon and Schuster, Inc., N.Y.C., 1954—56; tchr. Casa Roosevelt-União Cultural, São Paulo, Brazil, 1957—59, Coquille Sch. Dist., Oreg., 1978—96; tchr. music Cartwheels Pre-sch., North Bend, Oreg., 1997—99, 2001. Tchr. piano, 1967—78; instr. Spanish Southwestern Oreg. C.C., Coos Bay, 1991—94; pianist/organist Faith Luth. Ch., North Bend, Oreg., 1995—2002, New Life Luth. Ch., Florence, Oreg., 2002—04; vocal soloist, 1996—; voice tchr., 1997—99. Chmn. publicity Music in Our Schs. Month, Oreg. Dist. VII, 1980-85; sec. Newcomer's Club, Bozeman, Mont., 1971. Quincentennial fellow U. Minn. and Found. José Ortega y Gasset, Madrid, 1991, Berkshire Choral Festival, Sheffield, Mass., 2004-05. Mem. AAUW (sec., scholarship chmn., co-pres., pres., treas., editor newsletter), Nat. Trust Hist. Preservation, Am. Coun. on Tchg. Fgn. Langs., Am. Assn. Tchrs. Spanish and Portuguese, Nat. Coun. Tchrs. English, Music Educators Nat. Conf., Oreg. Music Educators Assn., Oreg. Coun. Tchrs. English, Confedn. Oreg. Fgn. Lang. Tchrs., VoiceCare Network, Am. Guild Organists, Berkshire Choral Festival. Democrat. Avocations: swimming, walking, travel, drama. Home: 14425 SW Arabian Dr Beaverton OR 97008 Personal E-mail: edesaesilva@gbronline.com.

DESAI, NIRANJAN A., chemical engineer; b. Pune, Maharashtra, India, Feb. 20, 1978; s. Anil M. and Snehal A. Desai. B of Engring., U. Pune (India), 1999; MS, Pa. State U., University Park, 2001; postgrad., Carnegie Mellon U., Pitts., 2003—. Engr. Carrier Corp., United Technologies Corp., Syracuse, NY, 2001; advanced engr. Siemens Westinghouse Power Corp., Pitts., 2002—. Grad. rsch. asst. Pa. State U., University Park, 2000—01, grad. tchg. asst., 2000. Nat. Talent Search scholar, Nat. Coun. of Ednl. Rsch. and Tng., 1993. Mem.: SAE Internat., Mensa, Tau Beta Pi. Office: Siemens Westinghouse Power Corp 1310 Beulah Road Pittsburgh PA 15235 E-mail: niradesai@yahoo.com.

DESAI, NITIN DAYALJI, international organization official; b. Bombay, July 5, 1941; s. Dayalji M. and Shantaben Desai; m. Aditi Gupta, Apr. 28, 1979; children: Kartikeya, Nandan. BA with honors, U. Bombay, 1962; MSc in Econs., London Sch. Econs., 1965. Econs. lectr. Liverpool (Eng.) U., 1965-67, Southampton (Eng.) U., 1967-70; cons. Tata (India) Econ. Consultancy Svcs., 1970-73; cons., adviser Planning Commn. Govt. of India, 1973-85, sr. adviser Brundtland Commn., 1985-87, spl. sec. Planning Commn., 1987-88, sec., chief econs. adviser Min. of Fin., 1988-90; dep. sec. gen. UNCED UN, Geneva, 1990-92, undersec. gen. for policy coordination and sustainable devel. NYC, 1993-97, undersec. gen. for econ. and social affairs, 1992—2003, spl. adviser to U.N. Sec.-Gen. on the World Summit on the Info. Soc., 2003—; disting. vis. fellow London Sch. of Econs. and Polit. Scis., 2003—. Office: London School of Economics Houghton Street London WC2A 2AE England

DESAI, SAMIR T., electronics executive; BS in Physics and Elec. Engring., U. India; MSEE, Ill. Inst. Tech.; MBA, Loyola U., Chgo. Joined Motorola, Inc., Schaumburg, Ill., 1973, gen. mgr. iDEN Subscriber Group Plantation, Fla., 1993—99, sr. v.p., gen. mgr., 1999—2000, sr. v.p., dir. office of e-bus. and bus. transformation Comm. Enterprise, 2000—01, sr. v.p., dep. to the pres. of personal comm. sector, 2001—02, sr. v.p., chief info. officer, 2002—04, sr. v.p., gen. mgr. iDEN Networks and Devices, 2004—. Office: Motorola Inc 1303 E Algonquin Rd Schaumburg IL 60196*

DESAI, SHIV RAJ, researcher; s. Satish and Gita Desai; m. Sharina Garcia, June 6, 2005. B, Rutgers U., 1998; EdM, Columbia U., 2003. Cert. tchr. multiple subjects Calif. Tchr. 99th St. Elem. Sch., L.A., 1998—2001; univ. field supr. UCLA, 2003—04, grad. student rschr., 2004—. Presenter in field. Educator Bert Corona Charter Sch., Pacoima, Calif., 2004. Edn. fellow, UCLA, 2003—05. Mem.: AERA. Avocations: travel, activism.

DESAI, VEENA BALVANTRAI, obstetrician, gynecologist, educator; b. Karvan, Gujarat, India, Oct. 5, 1931; came to U.S., 1973; d. Balvantrai P. and Maniben (Vashi) Desai; m. Vinay D. Gandevia, Sept. 19, 1964. MBBS, Seth G.S. Med. Coll., Bombay, 1957, MD, 1961. Jr. resident Bombay U., 1957-59; house officer gyn. Chalmer's Hosp., Edinburgh, Scotland, 1962-63; registrar ob-gyn. Neath (U.K.) Gen. Hosp., 1963-64, Scunthorpe (U.K.) Gen. Hosp., 1964-66; chief resident ob-gyn. St. John (Can.) Gen. Hosp., 1973-74; attending ob-gyn. Portsmouth (N.H.) Hosp., 1975-84; assoc. prof. Boston U., 1985-86; sr. staff ob-gyn. Santa Clara (Calif.) Valley Med. Ctr., 1986-87; mem. staff ob-gyn. West Anaheim (Calif.) Med. Ctr., 1988-98, chief dept. ob-gyn., 1992-93, vice chief of gen. med. staff, 1994—95; ob/gyn Bay State Med. Ctr., Springfield, Mass., 1998—; chief ob-gyn. Mercy Med. Ctr., Springfield, 2002—03. Assoc. clin. prof. ob-gyn. U. Calif., Irvine, 1990-98; pres. Desai Med. Corp., Anaheim, 1989—. Chmn.'s advisor Nat. Security Coun.; charter mem. Presdl. Task Force; mem. Rep. Party Inner Cir., 1984-2003. Recipient Presdl. Medal of Merit, 1982, award Spl. Congl. Adv. Bd., 1984, Order of Liberty, U.S. Congress, 1995, Medal of Freedom, U.S. Senate, 1994, medal Ronald Wilson Reagan Eternal Flame of Freedom, 1996, Millennium Medal of Freedom, Rep. Senate, 1999, Internat. Peace prize United Cultural Conv., 2003, Congl. Order of Merit, 2004; named Pioneer of Healthcare Reform, Nat. Repl. Congl. Com., 2004. Fellow ACS, Internat. Coll. Surgeons, Am. Coll. Ob-Gyn., Western Mass. Ob-Gyn. Soc. (pres. 2002—), Royal Coll. Ob-Gyn. (chmn. Am. rep. com. 1997-2002); mem. Buena Park Rotary (pres. 1994, chair internat. svc. 1992-93). Avocations: latchhook work, international politics, travel. Home: 35 Sean Louis Cir West Springfield MA 01089-4547 Personal E-mail: veenadesai@comcast.net.

DESAI, VISHAKHA N., museum director, professional society administrator; b. Ahmedabad, Gujarat, India, May 1, 1949; came to U.S., 1966; m. Robert B. Oxnam, 1993. BA, Bombay U., Elphinstone Coll., 1970; MA in History of Art, U. Mich., 1975, PhD in History of Art, 1984. With edn. div. Bklyn. Mus., N.Y.C., 1972-74; head exhibit resource Mus. sect. edn. dept. Fine Arts, Boston, 1977-80; acting dir. edn. dept. Mus. Fine Arts, Boston, 1980-81, coord. acad. program, 1981-88, asst. curator, 1981-90, mus. pres.; dir. Asia Soc. Galleries, N.Y.C., 1990—; v.p. Asia Soc., 1993—. Adj. asst. prof. Boston U., 1982-87; assoc. prof. U. Mass., Boston, 1986-90; adj. prof. Columbia U., 1995-96, 97; bd. dirs. Am. Com. South/S.E. Asia Art; reviewer Bunting Inst., Radcliffe Coll., Boston, 1990—; bd. dirs. Art Table, N.Y.C., 1991-94. Contbr. articles to profl. jours. Pres. Mass. Found. for Humanities, 1989-91. Outstanding Teaching fellow U. Mich., 1977, Am. Inst. of Indian Studies fellow, 1978; grantee, Nat. Endowment for the Arts, NEM, 1979—, Mus. Sabbaticatal grantee Nat. Endowment for the Arts, 1982. Mem. Coll. Art Assn. (bd. dirs. 1995—), Am. Assn. Art Mus. Dirs. (bd. dirs. 1995—. pres. 1998—). Office: Asia Soc and Mus 725 Park Ave New York NY 10021-5025

DE SAINT PHALLE, THIBAUT, investment banker, consultant; b. Tuxedo Park, New York, July 23, 1918; s. Fal and Marie (Duryee) de Saint P.; m. Rosamond (Frame), Jan. 12, 1946 (dec. 1960); children: Fal, Pierre, Thérèse; m. Elene Canrobert (Isles), June 21, 1965 (div. 1983); children: Marc, Diane; m. Mariana M. (Smith), April 24, 1983. Student, Harvard U., 1935—37; BA, Columbia U., 1939, JD, 1941. Bar: N.Y. 1942, U.S. Supreme Ct., 1945, D.C. 1984. Assoc. Chadbourne, Wallace, Parke, and Whiteside, N.Y.C., 1941—50; ptnr., head corp. law dept. Lewis 1950and McDonald, N.Y.C., 1950—58; v.p., treas. Becton, Dickinson, and Co., Rutherford, NJ, 1958—62, dir., 1958—67; sr. ptnr. Coudert Bros., N.Y.C., 1962—66, counsel, 1966—77; of counsel Vorys, Sater, Seymour, and Pease, Washington, 1983—86. Ltd. ptnr. Dean Witter and Co., pres. Dean Witter Overseas Fin. Corp., N.Y.C., 1967-68; investment banker Stralem, Saint Phalle and Co., Inc., N.Y.C., 1968-70, vice chmn. bd. dir., 1968-70; mem. faculty, prof. internat. fin. and law Ctr. d'Etudes Industrielles, Geneva, 1971-76; dir. Export Import Bank U.S., Washington, 1977-81; Scholl chair internat. bus. Georgetown U. Ctr. Strategic and Internat. Studies, 1981-83; chmn. Saint Phalle Internat. Group, 1985—. Author: The Dollar Crisis, 1963; Multi Nat. Corporations, 1976; U.S. Productivity and Competitiveness in Internat. Trade, 1980; Trade Inflation and the Dollar, 1981, (rev. edit., 1984), The Federal Reserve, an Intentional Mystery, 1985; Saints, Sinners and Scalawags, 2004; contbg. numerous articles on internat. fin. and trade to profl. journals. Lt. USNR, 1942—46. Decorated Navy Commendation medal, Bronze Star, Legion of Honor, (France). Mem.: ABA, Jockey Club, Met. Club. Roman Catholic. Home and Office: Saint Phalle Internat Group PO Box 2038 Boca Grande FL 33921 Office Phone: 941-964-4416. Home Fax: 941-964-4436. Personal E-mail: thibaut@comcast.net.

DE SALME, JOHN W., retired music educator, music association administrator; b. Corpus Christi, Tex., May 12, 1935; s. Orrin Richard and Martha Frances de Salme; m. Margaret Clare Brown, Nov. 27, 1983; children: John W., Robert E., Suzanne E. de Salme-Kaiser. MusB, U. Iowa, 1957, MA, 1960, MFA, 1967. Iowa permanent profl. cert. Dir. of bands Orange Grove (Tex.) H.S., 1957—59, Iowa Valley Cmty. Schs., Marengo, 1960—62; music dept. chair, dir. of bands West H.S., Iowa City, 1968—93; music dir., prin. condr. Ea. Iowa Brass Band, Mt. Vernon, 1992—2001; v.p., contest contr. N.Am. Brass Band Assn., 2000—. Music adjudicator Iowa H.S. Music Assn., Boone, 1960—; trombonist Corpus Christi Symphony Orch., 1955—59; guest condr. Iowa City Cmty. Band, 1966—76. Mem.: NEA, Iowa Bandmasters Assn., Music Educators Nat. Conf., N.Am. Brass Band Assn., Am. Sch. Band Dirs. Assn. Avocations: bicycling, outdoor sports, archery, stamp collecting/philately, photography. Home: 3718 Cottage Res Rd NE Solon IA 52333 Office: NAm Brass Band Assn 3718 Cottage Res Rd NE Solon IA 52333 E-mail: jwdesalme@aol.com, jwdesalme@southslope.net.

DE SALVA, CHRISTOPHER JOSEPH, lawyer, consultant; b. Milw., June 16, 1950; s. Salvatore Joseph and Elaine Mae De S.; m. Erika Marie De Salva, May 24, 1975; 1 child, Jessica Anne. BA in Polit. Sci., St. Vincent Coll., 1972; JD summa cum laude, Am. Coll. Law, 1987; MBA, Calif. Coast U., 1993, postgrad., 1994. Bar: Calif. 1994, U.S. Dist. Ct. (ctrl. dist., so. dist.) Calif. 1995, U.S. Ct. Fed. Claims 1995, U.S. Tax Ct. 1995, U.S. Supreme Ct., 2000. Founder, owner C.J. De Salva & Assocs. Investment and Mktg. Svcs. of La Quinta (now C.J. De Salva & Assocs., La Quinta, 1979—; pvt. practice La Quinta, Calif., 1994-98, Indio, Calif., 1994—, San Diego, 1996-98. CEO, pres. The Kings Vault Gallery, Inc., 1985; adj. faculty property law Am. Coll. Law, Brea, Calif., 1989-90, 92-95; life and disability ins. agent C.J. De Salva Ins. Agency 1978—; real estate broker De Salva Realty Calif., 1980—, realtor, 1985-94; tax cons., preparer Christopher De Salva Tax Cons.; cons. Christopher De Salva Bus. and Mgmt. Cons.; lectr. property law. Am. Coll. Law. Author: NAFTA, The Hidden Agenda, 1995. 1st lt. USMC, 1974-77. Recipient Am. Jurisprudence scholarship award Am. Coll. Law. Mem. ABA, Assn. Trial Lawyers, Vietnam Era Vet., Vet. of Latin Am., Nat. Soc. Pub. Accts (cert. 1984), Calif. Bar Assn. Avocations: music, sports, writing songs, flying. Office: 45-902 Oasis St Ste D Indio CA 92201

DE SALVA, SALVATORE JOSEPH, retired pharmacologist, toxicologist; b. NYC, Jan. 14, 1924; s. Nicola Carlo and Frances Agnes (Caldarella) De S.; m. Elaine Mae Radloff, June 14, 1948; children: Salaine Claire De Salva Bonanne, Christopher Joseph, Stephanie De Salva Farrelly, Steven William, Gregory Vincent, Peter Nicholas, Philip Anthony, Deidre De Salva Berry. BS, Marquette U., 1947, MS, 1949; postgrad., U. Ill., Chgo., 1951-53; PhD, Stritch Sch. Medicine, Loyola U., Chgo., 1958. Research and teaching asst. Marquette U., Milw., 1947-49; research biochemist Milw. County Gen. Hosp., 1954; instr. U. Ill., Chgo., 1951-52; asst. prof. Chgo. Coll. Optometry, 1951-53; pharmacologist Armour Pharm. Lab., Chgo, 1953-59; sect. head Colgate Palmolive Co., Piscataway, N.J., 1959-66, sr. research assoc., 1966-72, mgr., 1972-76, assoc. dir. research for pharmacology and toxicology, 1976-83, dir. research pharmacology and toxicology, 1983-88, worldwide ops. dir., 1988-90, corp. dir. human and environ. safety worldwide, 1990-92; pres. Salva Cons. Svcs., Somerset, N.J., 1992-99; ret., 1999. Lectr. Loyola U., 1957-59; mem. technician tng. N.J. Council for Research and Devel., Rutgers U., 1969-72. Editor: Symposium for Biomedical Electronic Instrumentation, 1965; contbr. articles to profl. jours.; patentee in field; current work in pharmaco-toxicology of flourides, sequestering agts. and surfactants, nitrosamine risk assessment, alternative safety testing method devel., safety of triclosan and use in dental therapeutic products. Mem. Park Forest (Ill.) Mosquito Abatement Program, 1952-55, Franklin Twp. (N.J.) Sch. Bd., 1969-70, Somerset (N.J.) Bd. Health, 1965-67, Cath. Youth Orgn., Somerset; v.p. Cedar Hill Swim Club, Somerset; active Boy Scouts Am., Somerset, 1965-67; trustee Franklin Twp. Day Care Ctr., 1969. Served with USN, 1942-46. Mem. AAAS, Soc. Exptl. Biology and Medicine, Am. Soc. Pharmacology and Exptl. Therapeutics, Soc. Toxicology, Internat. Union Pharmacology (toxicology sect.), N.Y. Acad. Scis., Internat. Soc. Regulatory Pharmacology and Toxicology, Internat. Soc. Study of Xenobiotics, Sigma Xi. Roman Catholic. Home: 83 Demott Ln Somerset NJ 08873-1604 Personal E-mail: saldesalvasafety@aol.com.

DESAN, CHRISTINE, law educator; b. Washington, Mar. 20, 1959; AB in Religion, Princeton U., 1981; MALD Fletcher Sch. Law & Diplomacy, Tufts U., 1987; JD, Yale U., 1987. Bar: Mass. 1987, DC 1989. Law clk. to Judge Stephen Breyer US Ct. Appeals 11th Cir.; asst. to Solicitor Gen. Charles Fried; asst. prof. law Harvard Law Sch., Cambridge, Mass., 1992—98, prof., 1998—. Office: Harvard Law Sch 1563 Massachusetts Ave Cambridge MA 02138 Office Phone: 617-495-4613, 617-495-5156. Business E-Mail: desan@law.harvard.edu.

DESANCTIS, ROMAN WILLIAM, cardiologist, educator; b. Cambridge Springs, Pa., Oct. 30, 1930; s. Vincent and Margherita (Marini) DeSanctis; m. Ruth Ann Foley, May 7, 1955; children: Ellen Ruth, Lydia Marie, Andrea Jean, Marcia Louise. BS summa cum laude, U. Ariz., 1951, DSc (hon.), 1999; MD magna cum laude, Harvard U., 1955; DSc (hon.), Wilkes Coll., 1984, U. Ariz., 1998. Diplomate Am. Bd. Internal Medicine, Sub Bd. Cardiovasc. Diseases. Successively intern, asst. resident, sr. resident medicine Mass. Gen. Hosp., Boston, 1955—56, successively intern, asst. resident, sr. resident medicine, 1958—60, fellow cardiology, 1960—62; dir. CCU, 1967—80, dir. clin. cardiology, 1980—98, emeritus, 1998—, physician, 1970—. Mem. faculty Harvard U. Med. Sch., 1964—, Evelyn and James Jenks and Paul Dudley White prof. medicine, 1998—. Co-author: Cardiac Clinico-Pathological Conferences of the Massachusetts General Hospital, 1972, The Practice of Cardiology, 1989; contbr. articles to med. jours. Officer M.C. USNR, 1956—58. Decorated Order of Dynasty of Alouite Morocco; recipient Excellence in Clin. Tchg. award, Harvard U. Med. Sch., 1990, Centennial Achievement award, U. Ariz., 1989, Alumni Achievement award, US Army, 2001, Glorney-Raisbeck award, NY Acad. Medicine, 2003. Fellow: ACP (master coll. 1994), Am. Coll. Cardiology (Gifted Tchr. award 1991, Disting. Fellow award 1999); mem.: N.Y. Acad. Medicine (Glorney-Raisbeck award 2003), Am. Clin. Climatol. Soc., New Eng. Cardiovasc. Soc. (pres. 1979—80), Inst. Medicine, Assn. Am. Physicians, Am. Heart Assn. (David Littmann award 1996, Paul Dudley White award 1999, Master Clinician award 2003), Knights of Malta, Aesculapian Club, Winchester Country Club. Roman Catholic. Home: 5 Thoreau Cir Winchester MA 01890-3340 Office: Mass Gen Hosp Yaw Key Bldg 55 Fruit St Ste 5800 Boston MA 02114 Office Phone: 617-726-2889.

DE SA NOGUEIRA, JOAO, recreational facility executive; Grad., Carlton Inst. Hospitality Mgmt., 1984. With Imperial Ocean Svcs., 1984—91; gen. mgr. Vilar do Golfo Resort, Quinta do Lago, Portugal, 1991—92, 1998—2001, food and beverage mgr., 1993—98; pres., COO Regal Enterprises, 2001—03; co-founder, pres. Marine Ctr. LLC, 2003—. Home: 2915 Barnard Rd Bradenton FL 34207

DESANTIS, SHEROLYN SMITH, foundation executive; b. Ontario, Oreg., Feb. 7, 1949; d. Ronald Duane Smith and Dorothy Lorene Hergert Smith; divorced; children: Louie Duane, Rhonda Marie, Paul Nunzio. BA, Idaho State U., 1971. Chmn., founder, exec. dir. Diagnostek Charitable Found., Albuquerque, 1990-95, Joshua Chariable Found., Albuquerque, 1995—; chmn., founder, ex-dir. Albuquerque Women's Resource Ctr., 1998—. Bd. dirs. Caballero Norte Neighborhood Assn., Albuquerque, 1985-87; mem. fundraising Albuquerque Pregnancy Ctr., 1984-99, bd. dirs., 1996-98, sec. bd. dirs., 1997-98; mem., del. Rep. State Ctrl. Com., Albuquerque, 1998—; mem. Rep. Assembly, Albuquerque, 1998—, Rep. Ward vice-hmn.; mentor Wise Men & Women, Albuquerque, 1998-99; mem. nat. adv. com. on violence against women U.S. Dept. Justice and U.S. Dept. Health and Human Svcs., 2002—; mem. N.Mex. Crime Victims Reparation Commn., 2004; N.Mex. alt. del. to Rep. Nat. Conv., 2000, 2004; N.Mex. state chmn. W Stands for Women, 2004; mem. Gov.'s Met. Judge Nominating Commn., 2002; elected 2d vice chmn. N.Mex. State Rep. Party, 2001-2003. Mem. N.Mex. Soc. Fundraising Execs. Baptist. Avocations: reading, cooking, entertaining, politics, fundraising. Office Phone: 505-350-2305.

DE SANTIS, SYLVIA, retired library director; b. Palmer, Mass., Mar. 27, 1920; d. Ezio DeS. and Josephine Alonzo. BA in Chemistry, Mt. Holyoke Coll., 1942. Chem. rsch. libr. Jackson Lab., E.I. DuPont, Wilmington, Del., 1942-43, Naugatuck (Conn.) Chem., 1944-45, libr. dir., 1944—49, Monson (Mass.) Free Libr. & Reading Room Assoc., 1949-97; retired, 1997. Cons. in field. Mem. Monson Arts Coun. Mem.: Monson Hist. Soc., Western Mass. Libr. Club. Avocations: collecting art, books, photography, gardening. Home: PO Box 358 Monson MA 01057-0358

DE SANTO, DONALD JAMES, psychologist, educational association administrator; b. Bklyn., July 5, 1942; s. Vincent James and Rose Ann (Dowd) DeS.; m. Loretta DePippo, Aug. 25, 1962; children: Dolores, Jennifer, Marisa. BA cum laude, St. Francis Coll., N.Y., 1964; MA in Clin./Child Psychology, St. John's U., 1966; profl. diploma, 1976; hon. degree, Oglala Lakota Coll., 1999. Asst. law libr. rsch. asst. Dewey, Ballantine, Bushby, Palmer & Wood, N.Y.C., 1960-64; rsch. asst. St. John's U., N.Y.C., 1964-65, tchg. fellow, 1965-66; project dir. 2 federally funded grants, 1975-76; dir. The Rugby Sch., Freehold, N.J., 1977—. People to People amb. to Cuba, 2001. Contbg. editor Channels jour. spl. educators, 1986-90, 96—. Mem. Youth Guidance; mem. Youth Guidance Com., Freehold, 1983—, chmn. econ. devel. com., 1984-86; mem. Econ. Devel. Com., Freehold, 1983-87; mem. Zoning Bd Adjustment, Freehold, 1985-86; commr. Lake Topanemus Commn., 1990-94; Rep. campaign chmn., Freehold, 1990, 91; bd. dirs. Monmouth County Transp. Assn., 1990, 91-92; mem. U.S. Selective Svc. Bd., 1991-2004; apptd. Selective Svc. Commn., 1992; v.p. Freehold Rep. Club, 1991-92; mem. adv. bd. Congl. Awards Com., 1994-98; mcpl. chmn. Freehold Borough Rep. Party, 1995; appt. Rep. Nat. Com., 1995; mem. exec. bd. Monmouth County Mental Health Assn. Recipient Fire Prevention medal, N.Y.C., 1954, citation for outstanding contbn. to arts in edn. N.J. Commr. Edn., 1981, Pres. award Assn. Schs. and Agys. for the Handicapped, 1995-96, N.J. Very Spl. Arts award, 1996, N.J. Gov's. Arts in Edn. award, 1996; Title VIb Fed. grantee, 1972-78. Mem. NRA (life), APA (pub. rels. com. div. 16), Nat. Assn. Pvt. Schs. Exceptional Children, Coun. Exceptional Children, N.J. Assn. Schs. and Agys. for Handicapped (sec., conf. chmn. 1983-84, pub. rels. chmn. 1984-86, Pres. award 1995-96, Legacy of Caring award 2002), Nat. Soc. Psychologists in Mgmt., Assn. for Help Retarded Children, Monmouth County Hist. Assn., N.J. Assn. Children With Learning Disabilities, Nat. Assn. Pvt. Schs. Exceptional Children, Optimists, Monmouth County Mental Health Assn. (bd. dirs.), Elks, Nat. Assn. Sch. Psychologists, Psi Chi, Phi Delta Kappa. Roman Catholic. Office: care Rugby Sch at Woodfield PO Box 1403 Belmar NJ 07719-1403 Personal E-mail: Poppled@aol.com.

DESAPRIYA, EDIRIWEERA B.R., public health service officer, researcher; b. Kandy, Sri Lanka, June 6, 1963; s. Ediriweera Bandarage Robert and Jenat Robert Munasinghe; m. Mahendra G.J. Jayasooriya; children: Akalanka Dinidu Wijesinghe, Aki E.B. Nilanga. PhD, U. Tsukuba, Japan, 1998. Sr. lectr. U. Sri Jayewardanapura, Nugegoda, Sri Lanka, 1998—2000; vis. prof. Inst. Social Scis. U. Tsukuba, Japan, 2001—. Cons. NIMH, Japan, 1995—98. Nat. coord. Medineed Sri Lanka, Maharagama, 1991—2002. Fellow Japan Soc. for Promotion of Scis., Ministry of Edn. Japan, 2000—. Mem.: Can. Assn. Rd. Safety Profls., Japan Sociol. Assn., Med. Soc. for Alcohol and Drug Problems in Japan (assoc.). Buddhist. Avocations: bird-watching, football, travel, camping, boating. Office: BC Injury Rsch and Prevention Ctr for Cmty Child Health Rsch 4480 Oak St L 408 Vancouver BC Canada V6H 3V4 Office Fax: 604-875-3252. Personal E-mail: desapriya@hotmail.com. E-mail: edesap@cw.bc.ca.

DE SAVORGNANI, ADRIANE ALDRICH, healthcare administrator, nurse; b. Boston, Dec. 17, 1940; d. Merritt James Aldrich and Edith Carolyn (Borrebach); m. Luciano de Savorgnani, Aug. 1, 1979 (dec. Aug. 2002); children: Andrew, Alexia, Miranda. AB, Radcliffe Coll., 1962; diploma in nursing coord. program, Radcliffe Coll./Mass. Gen Hosp, 1965; MPH, U. Hawaii, 1974; DBA, Nova U., 1992. RN, Hawaii; cert. nursing adminstrn. advanced. Clin. nurse Dept. Public Health, Washington, 1966-67; staff nurse pediat., obstetrics, nursery, med.-surg. US Naval Hosp., Naples, Italy, 1967-69; pub. health nurse Dept. Human Resources, Washington, 1969-72; staff nurse, ob-gyn., nursery, recovery rm. Kapiolani Hosp., Honolulu, 1972-75; rsch. nurse U. Hawaii Newborn Psychology Rsch. Lab, Honolulu, 1974-75; staff nurse, med. and gynecol. oncology Naval Regional Med. Ctr., San Diego, 1975-78; staff nurse emergency rm. Naval Aerospace Reg. Med. Ctr., Pensacola, Fla., 1978-79; charge nurse, emergency rm. outpatient-inpatient care coord. US Naval Hosp., Naples, Italy, 1979-83; charge nurse military med. dept., utilization rev., discharge planning Naval Hosp., Newport, RI, 1983-86; head, Reg./Fleet Support, Naval Med. Command N.E. Region, Great Lakes, Ill., 1986-89; head health care plans spl. projects, head preventive med. health promotion br. Bur. Medicine and Surgery, Washington, 1989—92; exec. officer Naval Med. Clinic, Key West, Fla., 1993—. Asst. dir. nursing svcs. Jacksonville Naval Hosp., Fla., 1992—95; exec. officer Lemoore Naval Hosp., Calif., 1995—98; comdg. officer US Naval Med. Clinics, UK, 1998—2001; head clin. plans and mgmt., acting asst. dep. chief med. ops. support Bur. Medicine and Surgery, Washington, 2001—03; adminstrv. asst. to Def. Attaché Office Am. Embassy, London, 2003—. Contbr. articles to profl. jours. Lector, lay eucharistic minister, choir accompanist; vol. local sch.; vol. tchr. ESL; vol. women's homeless shelter. Capt., Nurse Corps, US Navy, 1975-2003. Decorated Legion of Merit, Meritorious Svc. medal (5), Navy and Marine Corps Commendation medal (2), Nat. Def. medal (2), Global War on Terrorism Svc. medal, Navy and Marine Corps Overseas Svc. Ribbon (7 stars), Global War on Terrorism Svc. medal; recipient Clara Barton award, ARC, Naples, 1983, cert. of appreciation, Operation Desert Storm, Washington, 1991, Jane A. Delano award, ARC London, 2001, dir.'s award, Human Resources Svc. Ctr., Europe, 2001. Fellow Am. Coll. Healthcare Execs.; mem. ANA, APHA, Assn. Mil. Surgeons US (life), Acad. Mgmt., Internat. Tng. in Comm., ARC (instr.), Navy Nurse Corps. Assn., Coll. Alumnae Assns., Sigma Theta Tau. Republican. Roman Catholic. Avocations: piano, theater, art, travel, physical fitness. Home: 14 Bardsley Ln London SE10 9RF England

DESBARATS, PETER HULLETT, journalist, educator, academic administrator; b. Montreal, Que., Can., July 2, 1933; s. Hullett John and Margaret Ogston (Rettie) D. Student, Loyola Coll., Montreal, 1951. Feature writer The Gazette, Montreal, 1953-55; local reporter Reuters, London, Canada, 1955; feature writer The Winnipeg (Can.) Tribune, 1956, legis. reporter, 1957-60; polit. reporter, feature writer The Montreal Star, 1960-65; editor Parallel Mag., Montreal, 1965; host nightly news and pub. affairs show Sta. CBC-TV, Montreal, 1966-70; Ottawa editor Toronto Star, 1970-72; Ottawa bur. chief Global TV, 1973-80; sr. cons. Royal Commn. on Newspapers, Ottawa, 1980-81; dean Sch. Journalism U. Western Ont., London, Canada, 1981-96, assoc. prof. journalism, 1981-86, prof., 1986-96, dir. Univ. Club, 1987, adj. prof., 2005—. MacLean Hunter chair comm. ethics U. Toronto, 2000—01; mem. comms. adv. com. Can. commn. UNESCO; cons. Task Force on Broadcasting Policy, 1985, Royal Commn. Electoral Reform, 1991, House of Commons Broadcasting com., Ottawa, 2002, others; mem. selection com. Can. News Hall of Fame, 1986—; spkr. on journalism and the role of the media numerous sites throughout the U.S., Can., overseas; mem. Ont. Task Force Cardiovasc. Scis., 1991, Can. Observers' Mission to Romania, 1992; commr. Commn. on Inquiry into Deployment of Can. Forces to Somalia, 1995—96; columnist The Globe and Mail, Toronto, 1997—2002, The Free Press, London, 1998—2002; former Can. corr. The Nat. Observer, Washington; mem. social scis. and humanities rsch. coun. Can. adjudication com. Std. Rsch. Grants Program, 2005—. Author: The State of Quebec, 1965, Gabrielle and Selena, 1966, René: A Canadian in Search of a Country, 1976; author: (book of poetry) The Night the City Sang, 1977; author: The Hecklers, 1979, Canada Lost/Canada Found: The Search for a New Nation, 1981, Colin and the Computer, 1985, Guide to Canadian News Media, 1990, rev. edit., 1996, Somalia Cover-up: A Commissioner's Journal, 1997, (plays) The Great White Computer, 1966, Her Worship, 2002, Lucretia, 2003, The Practical Joke, 2005; editor: What They Used to Tell About Indian Legends from Labrador, 1969, Freedom of Expression and New Communication Technologies, 1998; mem. editl. bd. Can. Jour. Comm., 1987—, co-host PBS series The Editors, 1987—91. Bd. dirs. Performing Arts Ctr. for Today, London, 1993-95, Orch. London, 1993-99; bd. dirs. London Mus. Archaeology, 1993—, v.p., 2001-2003, pres., 2003—. Recipient Best News Broadcaster award Assn. Can. TV and Radio Artists, 1977, Best TV Interviewer award Assn. Can. TV and Radio Artists, 1980, 125th Anniversary Confedn. Can. medal, 1992. Mem. Can. Assn. Journalists, Can. Civil Liberties Assn. (bd. dirs. 1998—), Can. Journalism Found. (bd. dirs. 1997-2005, chmn. Excellence award 2005—), Soc. Environ. Journalists (mem. adv. bd. 1995—). E-mail: pdesbarats@sympatico.ca.

DESBIENS, NORMAN A., medical educator; b. Fall River, Mass., Nov. 24, 1946; s. J. Arthur and Cecile R. D.; m. Sarah F. Desbiens; children: Meaghan, Nicholas. BA, Providence Coll., 1968; MBS, Dartmouth Med. Coll., 1970; MD, Harvard Med. Sch., 1972. With Nat. Health Svc. Corps., Ladysmith, Wis., 1975-77; staff physician, internal medicine residency Marshfield (Wis.) Clinic, 1991-97, transitional residency, program dir., 1995-97; chmn. of medicine U. Tenn., Chattanooga, 1997—; acting med. dir. Hamilton County NH, Chattanooga, 1998; med. dir. Program of All-Inclusive Care of the Elderly, Chattanooga, 1998—. Contbg. author: Critica Cre Symposium, 1996; contbr. articles to profl. jours. Mem. Chattanooga Coalition for Improving End of Life Care, 1998—; bd. dirs. Met. Coun. for Cmty. Svcs., 1999—. Lt. comdr. USPHS, 1975-77. Recipient Gwen Sebold Rsch. award Marshfield Clinic, 195, Disting. Tchg. award U. Wis., Madison, 1993, George Magnin Tchg. award Marshfield Clinic, 1992, 84. Fellow ACP; mem. soc. Gen. Internal Medicine, Assn. of Program Dirs. in Internal Medicine, Soc. of Med. Decision Making, Soc. Crit. Care Medicine. Office: Univ Tenn Coll of Medicine 975 E 3rd St # 94 Chattanooga TN 37403-2103

DESCALZO DE BLAS, ALBERTO, humanities professor; b. Madrid, Jan. 20, 1964; s. Julian Descalzo Maceira and Victoria De Blas Prieto; m. Sherri Kurz, Mar. 5, 2005. BA in Theology, Pontifical U. Salamanca, 1990; MA in Spanish Philology, U. Salamanca, 1995, PhD in Spanish Philology, 2003. Prof. U. Salamanca, Spain, 1993—2002, U. Porto, Portugal, 2003, Georgetown U., 2003—. Acad. coord. U. Salamanca, 2000—02; acad. advisor Georgetown U.-Salamanca, 2002—03. Contbr. articles to profl. jours. Advisor Scouts Castilla-Leon, Salamanca, 2000—02, chief campings, 1983—2000. Mem.: Modern Lang. Assn. Catholic. Avocations: theater, movies, bicycling, cooking, mountain climbing.

DESCH, THEODORE EDWARD, retired insurance company executive, lawyer; b. Chgo., Oct. 1, 1931; s. Louis G. and Dorothy (Prieb) D.; m. Donna K. Thorsell, Feb. 3, 1951; children: Theodore M. (dec. 1968), Steven R., Katherine S. Collins, Gregory S. AB, U. Ill., 1952, LLB, 1954. Bar: Ill. 1954; cert. employee benefits specialist, CLU, ChFC. Asst. gen. atty. C.,R.I.&P. R.R., 1956-59, gen. atty., 1959-65, gen. counsel, 1965-68, v.p. and gen. counsel, 1968-70, vice chmn. bd., 1970-73, chmn. bd., 1973-74, chief exec. officer, 1970-74, dir., 1970-75; ptnr. Kirkland & Ellis, Chgo., 1975-77; sr. v.p. law and pub. affairs Health Care Svc. Corp., a Mut. Legal Res. Co., Blue Cross and Blue Shield Ill., Chgo., 1977-86, sr. v.p. law and corp. affairs,

1986-97; sr. v.p. govt. contracts Chgo., 1997-98; ret., 1998; acting deputy gen. counsel Blue Cross and Blue Shield Assoc., Chgo., 2001—02. Chmn. Preferred Fin. Corp., Denver, 1995-98; bd. dirs. Walker Parking Cons., Inc., Elgin, Ill., Isaac Ray Ctr., Inc., Chgo. Trustee North Cen. Coll., Naperville; bd. dirs., pres. Naperville Elderly Homes, Inc.; mem. adv. bd. dirs. Salvation Army, Chgo. 1st lt., inf. U.S. Army, 1954-56. Mem. ABA, Ill. Bar Assn., Chgo. Bar Assn., Union League, Sky-Line Club, Cress Creek Country Club, Delta Sigma Phi (found. bd. trustees), Phi Alpha Delta. Home: 129 Springwood Dr Naperville IL 60540-7331

DESCHAINE, BARBARA RALPH, retired real estate broker; b. Syracuse, N.Y., Feb. 16, 1930; d. George John and Dora Belle (Manchester) Ralph; children by previous marriage: Olav Bernt Kollevoll Jr., Kristan George Kollevoll, Eric John Kollevoll; m. Bernard Richard Deschaine May 23, 1981 (dec. 1994). BA, St. Lawrence U., 1952; postgrad., Pa. State U., 1969-72; grad., Pa. Realtors Inst., 1973; student, Realtors Nat. Mktg. Inst., 1974-75. Salesman Brose Realty, Easton, Pa., 1967—71, assoc. broker/mgr., 1972—73, broker, owner, 1974-85; broker, mgr. John W. Monaghan Corp. Realtors, 1985-91; assoc. broker The Prudential/Paul Ford Realtors, Easton, 1991-99. Mem. Pa. Real Estate Polit. Edn. Com. Bd. dirs. Easton Area C. of C., 1973-79, v.p. organizational improvement, 1975-76, v.p. econ. devel., 1976-77, pres., 1977-78; mem. Greater Easton Corp. Strategy Group, 1977-78; mem. Northampton County Revenue Appeals Bd., 1982-98, co-chmn., 1994-98; trustee Easton area YMCA, 1984-91; bd. dirs. State Theatre for the Arts, 1994-2002. Mem.: NAFE, Sales and Mktg. Execs. (bd. dirs. Easton area chpt. 1976—91, Disting. Sales award 1982), Homes for Living Network (state chmn. 1980), Ea. Northampton County Multiple Listing Svc. (bd. dirs. 1987—91, pres. 1986), Easton Area Bd. Realtors (bd. dirs. 1973—87, sec. 1977, v.p. 1980—81, pres. 1972, Realtor of Yr. 1978), Pa. Assn. Realtors, Nat. Assn. Realtors, Phi Beta Kappa. Republican. Presbyterian. Address: 384 Hobson Place Blue Bell PA 19422

DESCHANEL, CALEB, cinematographer, film director; b. Phila., Sept. 21, 1944; m. Mary Jo Deschanel; children: Zooey, Emily. Student, Johns Hopkins U.; grad., Univ. So. Calif. Sch. Cinema-TV, 1968; attended, Am. Film Inst. Camera operator Wakefield Orloff and Paisley Prodns.; co-founder Dark Light Pictures, West Hollywood, Calif., 1994—. Cinematographer for films including: Trains, 1976 (also dir.), More American Graffiti, 1979, The Black Stallion, 1979, Being There, 1979, Let's Spend the Night Together, 1982, The Right Stuff, 1983, The Natural, 1984, The Slugger's Wife, 1985, 50 Years of Action!, 1986, It Could Happen to You, 1994, Fly Away Home, 1996, Hope Floats, 1998, Message in a Bottle, 1999, Anna and the King, 1999, The Patriot, 2000, The Hunted, 2003, The Passion of the Christ, 2004, National Treasure, 2004; camera operator, dir. photography, Titanic, 1997; dir. photography, Apocalypse Now, 1979; dir. films The Escape Artist, 1982, Crusoe, 1989; dir. 3 episodes (TV series) Twin Peaks, 1989-90; additional photographer A Women Under the Influence, 1974, Black Stallion Returns, 1983; provided footage (video) for T-20 Years and Counting, 2003; dir., photographer (commercials) for Microsoft, UPS, Nestle, Perrier, Carnation, Max Factor, McDonald's, Callaway, Vidal Sassoon, and Sprint. Office: Dark Light Pictures 812 N Highland Ave West Hollywood CA 90038 Office Phone: 323-460-2077. Fax: 323-460-7097.*

DESCY, DON EDMOND, educational technology educator, writer, editor; b. Hartford, Conn., Jan. 11, 1944; s. Henry Julian and Lillian D.V. (Svenson) D. BS in Biology Edn., Ctrl. Conn. State U., 1967, MS in Biology Edn., 1970; cert. in instrnl. media, U. Conn., 1981, PhD in Media and Tech., 1987. Tchg. asst. Ctrl. Conn. State U., New Britain, 1967-68; rsch. asst. Coll. Edn. U. Conn., Storrs, 1985-87; asst. adminstrv. dir. Conn. State Bar Examining Com., Hartford, 1987-89; adj. prof. Ea. Conn. State U., Willimantic, 1987-89, Ctrl. Conn. State U., New Britain, 1988-89; prof. Minn. State U., Mankato, 1989—, tech. coord., 1994—2004, program dir., 1998—2004. Numerous presentations in field in 5 countries. Author: Computer as an Educational Tool; mem. editl. bd. Internat. Jour. Instrnl. Media, 1991—, Quar. Jour. Distance Edn., 1999—, Techtrends, 1994—; columnist, Techtrends, 1993—, editor-in-chief, 1993-2003; contbr. articles to profl. jours., 5 chpts. to books, 1 textbook. Scholar Conn. Ednl. Media Assn., 1984, rsch. scholar Japan, 1996, China, 2001. Mem. Internat. Soc. Tech. in Edn., Assn. Ednl. Comm. and Tech. (pres. Twin Cities chpt., Disting. Svc. award 2000), Minn. Ednl. Media Orgn. Office: Minn State U Mankato 313 Armstrong Hall Mankato MN 56001-6042 Business E-Mail: don.desc4@mnsu.edu.

DE SEAR, EDWARD MARSHALL, lawyer; b. Bradenton, Fla, Oct. 27, 1946; s. Robert Ashland and Shirley Ethelwyne (Griffin) De S.; m. Patricia Gail Healy, Aug. 8, 1970; children: Emily, Andrew. AB, Columbia Coll., 1968; JD, U. Va., 1973. Bar: NY 1974. Ptnr. Brown & Wood, NYC, 1973-82; v.p. Salomon Bros., Inc., NYC, 1982-88; ptnr. Milbank, Tweed Hadley & McCloy, NYC, 1988-93, Orrick, Herrington & Sutcliffe, LLP, NYC, 1993—2003, head structured fin. group, 1998—2003; ptnr. McKee Nelson LLP, NYC, 2003—. Mem. editl. bd.: Jour. Structured Fin., 2004—. Mem. Alumni Recruiting Comm., Columbia U., NYC, 1984—. Mem. ABA, Columbia Club (bd. govs. 2004—), Phi Gamma Delta. Republican. Episcopalian. Office: McKee Nelson LLP One Battery Park Plaza 33d Fl New York NY 10004 Office Phone: 917-777-4565. Business E-Mail: edesear@mckeenelson.com.

DE SELDING, EDWARD BERTRAND, retired bank executive; b. Summit, N.J., June 15, 1926; s. Edward Fitzgerald and Alene (Rockwell) deS.; m. Joan Bulkley, Oct. 21, 1950; children— Peter, Ann, Edward Bertrand. BA, Yale, 1950. With Spencer Trask & Co., Inc., N.Y.C., 1950-77, ptnr., 1962-68, sr. v.p., dir., 1968-77, Hornblower, Weeks, Noyes & Trask, Inc., N.Y.C., 1977-78; 1st v.p. Loeb Rhoades, Hornblower & Co., 1978-79; v.p. Bruns, Nordeman, Rea & Co., N.Y.C., 1979-81, Bache Halsey Stuart, Inc., 1981-82, Conn. Nat. Bank, 1982-91, ret. Served with USAAF, 1944-46. Mem.: NASD (chmn. dist. 12 com. 1971, gov. 1972), Tokeneke Club (pres. 1974—75), Sawgrass Country Club (gov., pres. 2001). Republican. Episcopalian (vestryman 1961-63, 67-69, 77-79, warden 1984-87). Home: 9003 Lake Kathryn Dr Ponte Vedra Beach FL 32082-2919

DE SENA, FERDINANDO, composer, educator; b. N.Y.C., July 12, 1950; s. Carlo and Michelina De Sena; m. Laura Norkin, Jan. 26, 1994; children: Johan Gilbert, Samuel Gilbert. BA, Ithaca Coll., 1987; MusM, U. Miami, 1989, Dr. in Mus. Arts, 1994. Asst. prof., music theory and composition U. Miami, Coral Gables, 2002—, dir. electronic and computer music, 2003—. Composer: (computer music and chorus) Requiem for the Living, (computer music and flute) Elegy, (clarinet choir) Increase (n.), (chorus and string quartet) On These Restive Shores, (woodwind quintet) Midsummer Quintet. Mem.: Soc. Electroacoustic Music US, Internat. Computer Music Assn., Coll. Music Soc., Soc. Composers. Office: Frost Sch U Miami PO Box 248165 Coral Gables FL 33124-7610 Office Phone: 305-284-3110. E-mail: fdesena@miami.edu.

DESER, STANLEY, physicist, researcher; b. Rovno, Poland, Mar. 19, 1931; BS summa cum laude, Bklyn. Coll., 1949; MA, Harvard U., 1950, PhD, 1953; DPhil (hon.), Stockholm U., 1978; DTech (hon.), Chalmers Tech. U., 2001. Mem. Inst. Advanced Study, Princeton, 1953-55, 93-94, Parker fellow, 1953-54; Jewett fellow Inst. for Advanced Study, Princeton, 1954-55; NSF postdoctoral fellow, mem. Inst. Theoretical Physics, Copenhagen, 1955-57; lectr. Harvard U., 1957-58; mem. faculty Brandeis U., Waltham, Mass., 1958—, prof. physics, 1965—, chmn. dept., 1969-71, 76-77, Ancell prof. physics, 1979—; E. Schrödinger prof. U. Vienna, 1996. Vis. scientist European Ctr. Nuclear Rsch., Geneva, 1962-63, 76, 80-81, 94; mem. physics adv. com. NSF, 1982-86; Fulbright and Guggenheim fellow, vis. prof. Sorbonne, Paris, 1966-67, 71-72; Loeb lectr. Harvard U., 1975; S.R.C. sr. fellow Imperial Coll., 1976; vis. prof. College de France, Paris, 1976, 84; vis. fellow All Souls' Coll., Oxford (Eng.) U., 1977; investigator titular ad honorem CIDA (Venezuela); Fulbright prof. U. of the Republic Montevideo Uruguay, 1970. Mem. editl. bd. Jour. Geometry and Physics, Jour. Math Physics, Jour. High Energy Physics, mem. sci. bd. I.H.E.S., France, 1991—97, Inst. Theoretical Physics, Santa Barbara, 1989—93, chmn. sci. bd., 1992—93. Recipient Dannie Heineman prize, Am. Inst. Physics, 1994. Fellow: NAS, Am. Acad. Arts and Scis., Am. Phys. Soc.; mem.: Turin (Italy) Acad. Sci. (hon.; fgn.). Office: Brandeis U Physics Dept MS057 Waltham MA 02454

DESFORGES, JANE FAY, retired internist, hematologist, educator; b. Melrose, Mass., Dec. 18, 1921; d. Joseph Henry and Alics Maher (Fay) Desforges; m. Gerard Desforges, Sept. 11, 1948; children: Gerard Joseph, Jane Alice. BA cum laude (Durant scholar), Wellesley Coll., 1942; MD cum laude, Tufts U., 1945; ScD (hon.), Holy Cross Coll., 1990. Diplomate Am. Bd. Internal Medicine, Am. Bd. Hematology. Intern in pathology Mt. Auburn Hosp., Cambridge, Mass., 1945—46; intern in medicine Boston City Hosp., 1946—47, resident in medicine, then chief resident, 1948—50; USPHS rsch. fellow in hematology Salt Lake Gen. Hosp., Salt Lake City, 1946—47; rsch. fellow in hematology hosp. Thorndike Lab., 1950—52; physician-in-charge RH lab., 1952—53; faculty Tufts U. Med. Sch., 1952—72, prof. medicine, 1972—92, disting. prof., 1992—94, prof. emerita, 1994—; asst. dir. Tufts Med. Svc., Boston City Hosp., 1952—67; assoc. dir. Tufts Med. Svc., 1967—68, acting dir., physician in charge, 1968—73, dir., 1968—69; ret., 1999. Sr. physician in hematology New Eng. Med. Ctr. Hosp., Boston, 1973—, rsch. assoc. blood resch. lab, 1973—92; attending physician VA Hosp., Jamaica Plain; cons. in hematology to various area hosps., 1955—72. Contbr. numerous articles to med. jours. Bd. dirs. Med. Found., Inc., 1976—82; bd. trustees Boston Med. Libr., 1977—81; chmn. automation in med. lab. scis. rev. com. Nat. Inst. Gen. Med. Scis., 1974—76; chmn. consensus com. of infectious disease testing for blood transfusions NIH, 1995—96; mem. subcom. on hematology Am. Bd. Internal Medicine, 1976—82, bd. dirs., 1980—88, exec. com., 1984—88; chmn. blood diseases and resources adv. com. Nat. Heart, Lung and Blood Inst., 1978—81. Named to Internat. Women in Medicine Hall of Fame, Am. Med. Women's Assn., 2003; recipient Disting. Alumna award, Wellesley Coll., 1981; grantee NIH, 1955—88. Fellow: AAAS; mem.: Inst. Medicine, Am. Assn. Physicians, N.Y. Acad. Scis., Mass. Med. Soc. (mem. publs. com. 1995—99, Lifetime Achievement award 2001), Internat. Soc. Hematology, Am. Soc. Hematology (exec. com. 1975—78, adv. bd. 1980—82, v.p. 1982—83, pres. 1984—85), Am. Soc. Clin. Pathology, Am. Fedn. Clin. Rsch., ACP (chmn. med. knowledge self assessment program IX 1989—92, Master 1983, Disting. Tchr. award 1987), Alpha Omega Alpha (Outstanding Tchr. award 1994), Phi Beta Kappa. Home: 49 Lake Ave Melrose MA 02176-2701

DESHAZER, JAMES ARTHUR, biological engineer, educator, administrator; b. Washington, July 18, 1938; s. Grant Arthur and Velma DeShazer; m. Alice Marie DeShazer, Apr. 5, 1969; children: Jean Marie, David James. BS in Agr., U. Md., 1960, BSME, 1961; MS, Rutgers U., 1963; PhD, N.C. State U., 1967. Profl. engr., Idaho, Nebr. Assoc. prof. U. Nebr., Lincoln, 1967-75, prof., 1975-91, asst. dean, 1988-89; head agrl. engring. dept. U. Idaho, Moscow, 1991-95, head biol. and agrl. engring. dept., 1995—2001. Chair animal care and use com. U. Nebr., 1989—90; program coord. North Cen. Sustainable Agrl., Washington, 1988—89; nat. chair Modeling Responses of Swine CSRS, Washington, 1989-90, Sys. Approach to Poultry Prodn.-CSRS, Washington, 1990-91; dir. Idaho Rsch. Found., 1996—2001. Editor procs. Optics in Agr., 1990, Optics in Agr. & Forestry, 1992, Optics in Agr., Forestry & Biol. Processing, 1994, Optics in Agr., Forestry & Biol. Processing II, 1996, Precision Agriculture and Biological Quality, 1998, vol. II, 2000; contbr. chpt. in book. Trustee ASAE Found., 1996—2002; biol. and agr. engring. adv. bd. N.C. State U., 2002—04. Recipient Livestock Svc. award Walnut Grove, Iowa, 1988. Fellow: Am. Soc. Agrl. Engrs. (chair 1984—94, nat. medal 1979); mem.: NSPE (chpt. chair 1986-87, 93-94, bd. dirs. 1994-2001, state pres. 1998-99, Young Engring. award 1974), Internat. Soc. Biometeorology, Am. Soc. Engring. Edn. (chair 1993—94), Lions (chpt. dir. 1995—97, 2002—04, Lion of Yr. 2004—05), Alpha Gamma Rho (alumni bd. dirs. 1993—99). Home: 819 Nylarol St Moscow ID 83843-9313 Office: Biol & Agr Engring Dept Univ Idaho Moscow ID 83844-0904 Office Phone: 208-885-6182. Business E-Mail: Jades@uidaho.edu.

DE-SHAZO, RICHARD DENSON, medical educator, academic administrator; b. Birmingham, Ala., Apr. 4, 1945; s. Hyman Denson and Agnes L. (Carr) de S.; m. Gloria L. Jenkins, June 4, 1967; children: Melanie, Mollie, Matthew. BA in Chemistry, Religion, Birmingham So. Coll., 1967; MD, U. Ala., 1971. Diplomate Am. Bd. Internal Medicine, Am. Bd. Allergy and Immunology, Am. Bd. Rheumatology, Am. Bd. Geriatrics, Nat. Bd. Med. Examiners. Lt. col. U.S. Army Med. Corp., 1972-80; intern in pediat. Children's and Univ. Hosp., Birmingham, 1971-72; resident in internal medicine Walter Reed Army Med. Ctr., Washington, 1972-74, fellow in immunology, microbiology, 1974-75, fellow in clin. immunology, 1975-77; clin. asst. prof. medicine U. Colo. Sch. Med., Denver, 1977-78; asst. prof. medicine and pediatrics Uniformed Svcs. Univ. Health Scis., Bethesda, Md., 1978-80; assoc. prof. medicine and pediat. Tulane U. Sch. Medicine, New Orleans, 1980-85, prof. medicine and pediat., 1985-89; prof., chmn. dept. medicine U. South Ala. Coll. Medicine, Mobile, 1989-97; prof. medicine and pediat., chmn. dept. medicine U. Miss. Med. Ctr., Jackson, 1997—, Billy Guyton disting. prof. medicine and pediat., 2004—. Clin. immunologist Fitzsimmons Army Med. Ctr., Denver, 1977-78; staff attending internal medicine, asst. chief, clin. immunologist, dir. lab. exptl. immunology, allergy, clin. immunology Svc. Walter Reed Army Med. Ctr., Washington, 1978-80; staff internist S.E. Cmty. Hosp., Washington, 1978-80; chief allergy and rheumatology dept. pediat. Tulane U. Sch. Med., New Orleans, 1980-85, adj. assoc. prof. microbiology, 1983-85, dir. rsch. and clin. ops. dept. medicine, 1985-89, dir. immunology program AIDS clin. trials unit, 1987-89; attending physician VA and U. Hosps., New Orleans, 1980-89, St. Jude Hosp., Kenner, La., 1987-89; mem. Nat. Sci. Adv. Com. on AIDS, NIH, 1987-91, study sect. on epidemiology of AIDS, 1987-91, AIDS clin. trials group, 1987-89, reviewers res., 1990-94; chief clin. immunology and allergy VA med. Ctr. New Orleans, 1985-89, assoc. chief staff edn., 1988-89; dir. tng. program internal medicine, v.p. health svcs. found., chief divsn. allergy depts. medicine and pediat., mem. various com. U. South Ala. Hosps. and Clinics, Mobile, 1989-97; chief clin. immunology, allergy and rheumatology dept. medicine VA Med. Ctr., Biloxi, Miss., 1989-97; mem. expert panel allergenic products FDA, 1991-96; asst. clin. coord. Health Care Financing Agy. coop. cardiovasc. project Ala. Quality Assurance Found, Birmingham, 1993-94, bd. dirs., 1994-95, fin. and planning com., 1995-96; pres. UMC Faculty Practice Plan, 2001-; guest profs. Children's Hosp. Kansas City, St. Louis U. Med. Sch., Brooke Army Med. Ctr., Nat. Jewish Hosp., U. South Fla., U. Tex. Med. Br. at Galveston, Houston, others; presenter in field. Assoc. editor, editl. bd. So. Med. Jour., 1995—, Am. J. Med., 2005-; mem. editl. bd. Jour. Allergy and Clin. Immunology, 1986-89, Postgrad. Medicine, 1986-94, Jour. Investigational Allergology and Clin. Immunology, 1987-93, Am. Jour. Med. Scis., 1989—, Annals of Allergy, 1991-96, Clin. Immunotherapeutics, 1993-99; contbr. 25 chpts. to books, over 110 articles to profl. jours. Elder Cumberland Presbyn. Ch., 1986-89; mem. adminstrv. bd. Christ United Meth. Ch., Mobile, 1990-97, chmn., 1993-96, chmn. coun. on ministries 1993-95; bd. dirs. Leadership Mobile, 1994-97; bd. stewards Galloway United Meth. Ch., 1999-2002. Optimist Club scholar, 1963-67; Caduceus Club Travel fellow St. George Hosp. Med. Sch., London, 1970; grantee NIH, 1981-89, NIAID, 1985-88, Cancer Assn. New Orleans, 1982, 83, La. Lung Trust, 1982, 83, others; recipient Armed Forces Meritorious Svc. medal, 1980, Cert. Merit Cmty. Svc., City New Orleans, 1983. Fellow ACP (program com. 1993-95), Am. Coll. Rheumatology, Am. Coll. Chest Physicians, Am. Coll. Allergy and Immunology, Am. Acad. Allergy and Immunology (program and workshop com. 1985, chmn. 1986, grad. edn. com. 1988-89, allergy and immunology program dirs. assn. 1989—, standing com. fellowship programs 1990-97, standing com. immunology in med. schs. 1993, chmn. primer adv. com. 1992-93, co-chair com. on allergy in VA Med. Ctr. 1995-96, chair com. med. sch. 1994, Young Investigators award, 1979, Special Svc. award, 1993, 1996), Am. Coll. Allergy, Asthma, Immunology (editl. bd. 1995, Bernard Burman Lecturship 2002), Am. Thoracic Soc. (program and workshop com. 1986-87, sec.-treas. 1987, nat. program com. 1988-90, vice-chmn. 1989, chmn. 1989, chair sect. immunology 1992); mem. AMA (editor Primer on Allergy 1994), Am. Assn. Immunology, Am. Coll. Physician Execs., Clin. Immunology Soc. So. Med. Assn., Ala. Soc. Allergy and Immunology, Am. Assn. Med. Colls. (coun. acad. socs. 1994—), Am. Fedn. Clin. Rsch. (coun. so. sect. 1984-87, 93), Assn. Profs. Medicine (bd. dirs. 1995—2004, nat. manpower com. 1994-96, pres. 2001), Am. Bd. Med. Specialists (coun. bd. reps. and adminstrn. 1996-99), 2 Carnival Orgns., Am. Bd. Internal Medicine (bd. dirs. 2000—), So. Soc. Clin. Investigation (pres. 2001, Founder's medal 2004), Am. Bd. Allergy-Immunology (bd. dirs. 1995-2004). Avocations: gardening, swimming, youth work, writing. Office: U Miss Med Ctr Dept Internal Medicine 2500 N State St CSB6 Jackson MS 39216-4105 Office Phone: 601-984-5600. Business E-Mail: Rdeshazo@medicine.umsmed.edu.

DESHEFY, GREGORY SCOTT, ecologist, environmentalist; b. Fortress Monroe Hampton Rds, Va., Mar. 8, 1952; s. Eugene Ernest Jr. and Barbara Ruth (Retoske) Deshefy; m. Nancy Jean Izbicki, Aug. 7, 1976; 1 child, Aleandra Kit. BS Biology, Rensselaer Polytech. Inst., Troy, N.Y., 1974; MS Zoology, Clemson U., S.C., 1978, PhD study in Zoology/Behavioral Ecology, 1982. Lectr. Clemson U., SC, 1976—82; prof., lectr. Middlesex C.C., Middletown, Conn., 1982—88; scientist environ. protection dept. State of Conn., Hartford, 1982—. Mem. New Eng. Interstate Water Pollution Control Commn., Lowell, Mass., 1984—, chair com. on impact of Ethanol in motor fuel, 2002; lectr. on animal rights and environ. ethics. Author (editor): (poetry book) Touch the Earth, 1995; author: Houyhnhnms All, 1998, Shadow Stones, 2004; contbr. articles to profl. jours., poems to anthologies and mags., essays to literary publs. Presenter S.C. Acad. Sci., 1998; local leader Conn. Green Party, Windham, 1997—; chmn. Bd. Edn., Montville, Conn., 1982—87; radio host WWUH. Nominee Conn. Poet Laureate, Hartford, 2002; named Best Supporting Actor, Clemson (SC) Theatre, 1978; recipient Poetry award, Hartford Advocate Mag., 1997, Environ. Edn. award, Briarwood Coll., Conn., 2002. Green Party. Avocations: baseball, fencing, golf, antique cars, book collecting.

DE SHIELDS-MINNIS, TARRA RAMIT, lawyer; b. Balt. d. Lawrence Franklin DeShields and Ramona Fleurette Brown. BA, U. Md., 1984; JD, U. Balt., 1987. Bar: Md. 1988, U.S. Dist. Ct. Md. 1990, U.S. Ct. Appeals (4th cir.), U.S. Supreme Ct. 1993. Jud. clk. Md. Ct. of Spl. Appeals, 1987-88; asst. state's atty. Office of the State's Atty., Montgomery County, 1988-90; asst. atty. gen. Office of the Atty. Gen., Balt., 1990-96; asst. U.S. atty. U.S. Atty.'s Office, Balt., 1996—. Recipient Am. Jurisprudence award Lawyer's Cooperative Pub. Co., 1988; Supreme Ct. fellow Nat. Assn. of Attys. Gens., 1993. Mem. Md. State Bar Assn., Nat. Bar Assn. Roman Catholic. Avocations: reading, antique shopping, racquetball. Office: US Attys Office 36 S Charles St Baltimore MD 21201

DESHPANDE, NILENDRA GANESH, physics professor; b. Karachi, Pakistan, Apr. 18, 1938; came to U.S., 1961; s. Ganesh V. and Myna G. (Junnarkar) D.; m. Kanchan S. Karnik, May 15, 1960; children: Pranay N., Rahul N. BS with honors, U. Madras, India, 1959, MA in Physics, 1960, MS in Physics, 1961; PhD, U. Pa., 1965. Asst. prof. physics Northwestern U., Evanston, Ill., 1967-73; assoc. prof U. Tex., Austin, 1973-75, U. Oreg., Eugene, 1975-83, prof., 1983—, head dept. physics, 1992-98, dir. Inst. Theoretical Sci., 1987-92, assoc. dean scis., 1998—2001. Contbr. articles to profl. jours. Named Outstanding Jr. Investigator, U.S. Dept. Energy, 1981-86; prin. investigator High Energy Physics Grant, U.S. Dept. Energy, 1981—. Fellow Am. Phys. Soc. (organizer annual meeting div. particles and fields 1985), Sigma Xi. Office: U Oreg Inst Theoretical Sci Eugene OR 97403 Office Phone: 541-346-5204. Business E-Mail: desh@uoregon.edu.

DESHPANDÉ, ROHIT, business educator; b. Bombay, Dec. 7, 1951; came to U.S., 1973; s. Prabhakar and Vimala (Waglé) D.; m. Rebecca Schorin, Dec. 29, 1979; children: Jay Alexander, Neil Benjamin. BSc, U. Bombay, 1971, MMS, 1973; MBA, Northwestern U., Evanston, 1975; PhD, U. Pitts., 1979; MA (hon.), Dartmouth Coll., 1993, Harvard U., 2000. Asst. and assoc. prof. mktg. U. Tex., Austin, 1979-87; assoc. prof. mktg. Dartmouth Coll., Hanover, 1987-89, prof., 1989-93, E.B. Osborn prof. mktg., 1993-97; prof. Harvard Bus. Sch., Cambridge, Mass., 1997-98, Sebastian S. Kresge prof. mktg., 1998—. Thomas Henry Carroll Ford Found. vis. prof. bus. adminstrn. Harvard Bus. Sch., 1993, chmn. strategic mktg. mgmt. program, 2001—; vis. scholar and vis. prof. Stanford Bus. Sch., 1994, 96; exec. dir. Mktg. Sci. Inst., 1997-99, mem. exec. dirs. coun., 1999—; mem. adv. coun. David Rockefeller Ctr. for L.Am. Studies, Harvard U., 2000—. Author/editor: Developing a Market Orientation, 1999, Using Market Knowledge, 2001, The Global Market, 2004; mem. editl. bd. Jour. Mktg., Jour. Mktg. Rsch., Jour. Bus. Rsch., Internat. Jour. Rsch. Mktg., Asian Jour. Mktg., Jour. Internat. Mktg.; contbr. articles to profl. jours. Recipient Jack Taylor Teaching Excellence award. Fellow (consortium) Am. Mktg. Assn. (fin. com., ethics com., progressive learning com.); mem. Assn. for Consumer Rsch., Am. Sociol. Assn., Omicron Delta Kappa, Beta Alpha Phi. Office: Harvard Bus Sch Boston MA 02163

DESIATO, MICHAEL, editor-in-chief; b. Rochester, N.Y., Dec. 9, 1955; s. Nicholas and Jenny Desiato; m. Lauren Desiato, Nov. 5, 1983; 1 child, Anthony. BSJ, Ohio U., 1977; postgrad., NYU. With Real Estate Forum, N.Y.C., 1978—, editor-in-chief, now group mng dir; also pub. dir. Real Estate N.Y.; editl. dir. Globest.com. Mem. Nat. Assn. Real Estate Editors (bd. dirs., pres.). Office: Real Estate Forum 520 Eighth Ave 17th Fl New York NY 10018 Office Phone: 212-929-6900. E-mail: mgd@remediainc.com.

DESIDERI, LAWRENCE R., lawyer; b. Chgo., June 6, 1958; BS summa cum laude, No. Ill. U., 1980; JD summa cum laude, U. Ill., 1983. Bar: Ill. 1983, U.S. Dist. Ct. Ill. (No. dist.), U.S. Ct. Appeals (7th cir.). Assoc. to ptnr. Winston & Strawn LLP, Chgo., 1983—, mem. exec. com. Topics editor: U. Ill. Law Rev., 1982—83. Mem.: ABA, Chgo. Bar Assn., Order of Coif. Office: Winston & Strawn LLP 35 W Wacker Dr Chicago IL 60601 Office Phone: 312-558-5960. Office Fax: 312-558-5700. E-mail: ldesideri@winston.com.

DESIDERIO, DOMINIC MORSE, JR., chemistry and neurochemistry professor; b. McKees Rocks, Pa., Jan. 11, 1941; s. Dominic Morse and Jewell Aline (Hull) D.; m. Julie Marie Thomas, Oct. 9, 1965; children— Annette Marie, Dominic Michael. BA, U. Pitts., 1961; MS, MIT, 1964, PhD, 1965. Organic control chemist Pitts. Coke and Chem. Co., 1958-60; research chemist U. Pitts., 1960-61; teaching asst. MIT, Cambridge, 1961-62, research asst., 1962-65; research chemist Am. Cyanamid Co., Stamford, Conn., 1966-67; asst. prof. chemistry Baylor Coll. Medicine, Houston, 1967-71, assoc. prof. chemistry and biochemistry, 1971-78; prof. neurology (chemistry) and moleclar scis., dir. U. Tenn., Memphis, 1978—. Exch. student Internat. Assn. Exch. Students for Tech. Experience; polymer chemist Badische Anilin and Sodafabrik, Germany, summer 1962. Author and editor of books, chpts. in books and articles including Analysis of Neuropeptides by Liquid Chromatography and Mass Spectrometry, 1984, Mass Spectrometry of Peptides, 1990, Mass Spectrometry: Clinical and Biomedical Applications, vol. I, 1992, vol. II, 1994; co-editor (book series) Mass Spectrometry, 1997—; editor Mass. Spectrometry Rev., 1993—. Recipient 1st Ann. Internat. award Mass Spectrometry in Biochemistry and Medicine, Alghero, Italy, 1975; Intra-Sci. Research Found. fellow, 1971-75 Mem. Am. Soc. Biol. Chemistry, Am. Chem. Soc., Am. Soc. Mass Spectrometry, AAAS, Soc. for Neurosci., Memphis Neurosci. Soc. (pres. 1984-85), NIH (Metallobiochemistry study sect. 1985-89). Avocations: reading, amateur radio, fishing, travel. Office: U Tenn Health Sci Ctr Stout Neurosci Mass Spectrom Lab 847 Madison Ave Rm 117 Memphis TN 38163-0001 Business E-Mail: ddesiderio@utmem.edu.

DESIDERIO, MIKE FRANCIS, education educator; b. Russellville, Ark., Feb. 8, 1957; s. Frank and Joyce (Johnson) D.; m. Nidia Alicia Farias, Nov. 1, 1986; 1 child, Catherine Inez. BS in Edn., John Brown U., 1985; MEd, Sul Ross State U., 1990; PhD, Tex. A&M U., 1997. Cert. tchr., supt., Tex. Asst. prof. edn. Tex. A & M Internat. U., Laredo, 1998—. Sgt. U.S. Army N.G., 1979-85. Mem. Nat. Mid. Sch. Assn., Nat. Soc. for Study of Edn., Assn. of Tchr. Educators, Kappa Delta Pi. Avocations: golf, woodworking, golf trading cards, making golf clubs. Office: Tex A & M Internat U Coll of Edn 5201 University Blvd Laredo TX 78041-1920

DESILVA, ALAN W., physics professor, researcher; b. L.A., Feb. 8, 1932; s. Woodruff and Dorothy Belle (Cole) DeS.; m. Mochiko Yokoyama, July 27, 1959; children: Audrey Hope, Eric Woodruff, Eliot Gen. MS, UCLA, 1954; PhD, U. Calif., Berkeley, 1961. NSF postdoctoral rsch. fellow The Culham Lab., Abingdon, Berkshire, Eng., 1962-64; asst. prof. physics U. Md., College Park, 1964-68, assoc. prof., 1968-74, prof., 1974-97, prof. emeritus, 1997—. Cons. Los Alamos Nat. Lab., 1963-81, U.S. Naval Rsch. Lab., Washington, 1973-90. Contbr. over 30 articles to sci. jours. With U.S. Army, 1954-56. Recipient sr. U.S. scientist award Alexander von Humboldt Found., Ruhr U., Bochum, Fed. Republic Germany, 1984-85. Fellow Am. Phys. Soc. Achievements include devel. of light scattering as a plasma diagnostic, light scattering observations of plasmas; rsch. on shock waves in plasmas and transport in strongly coupled plasmas. Office: U Md Inst Rsch Electronics/Applied Physics College Park MD 20742-0001 Office Phone: 301-405-4958.

DE SILVA, EUGENE LAKSHMAN, academic administrator, educator; b. Colombo, Sri Lanka, Jan. 6, 1964; s. Angelo Lakshman and Latha (Nissanka) de Silva; m. Cheryl Lowe, May 21, 1994; 1 child, Eugenie. Grad., Royal Soc. Chemistry, London, 1989; MSc, Manchester Met. U., 1997; PhD of Chemistry, U. Herts/Knightsbridge U., 1997; PhD of Plasma Physics/Materials Engring., Manchester Met. U., 2001. Chartered chemist, engr., mgmt., mfg. mgmt. systems. Prodn. supr. Exchemie Ltd., Sri Lanka, 1982—83; tech. rep. Chemanex Ltd., Sri Lanka, 1983—85; plant mgr. Ceylon Pencil Co., Sri Lanka, 1985—86; stringer journalist The Island/Sunday Times, Sri Lanka, 1986—89; mktg. dir. HE Sequence Suppliers, Sri Lanka, 1986—89; pres., founder Soc. Martial Arts, Manchester, England, 1994—; quality mgr. H. Marcel Guest Ltd., Manchester, 1997—99; dir. IISER, England, 2000—. Cons. He Sequence Suppliers, Sri Lanka, 1989—; dean faculty of rsch. Knightsbridge U., 1999—; prof. Mont. State U., 2001—; rsch. fellow Ctr. for Def. and Internat. Security Studies U. Lancaster, 2000—. Author: Lecture Notes on Chemistry (25 books), 1998, In Recognition of Wisdom-A Degree in Martial Arms, 1998, Lecture Notes on Physics (25 books), 1998; organizer, editor Procs. Internat. Conf. Martial Arts and Internat. Jour. Martial Arts Rsch., 1998; patentee in field. Fellow Bus. and Tech. Inst., 1989, Inst. Mfg., 1989, Inst. Mgmt. Systems, 1989, Soc. Martial Arts, 1994; inducted into Internat. Hall of Fame of Martial Arts, 2000. Fellow: Royal Soc. Arts; mem.: Soc. Martial Arts (pres. 1994—, editor jour. 1998—). Avocations: martial arts, reading, journalism, cinema. Achievements include being the first to design a university degree in martial arts, 1994. Office: IISER 69 Piccadilly Manchester M12BS England Home: Apt 203 40 Smokewood Ct Stafford VA 22556 Office Phone: 540-841-1264. E-mail: e.desilva@adelphia.net.

DESILVEY, DENNIS LEE, cardiologist, educator, academic administrator; b. May 17, 1942; m. Kathleen Selkirk, Aug. 28, 1965; children: Ethan Selkirk, Caitlin O'Brian, Sarah Candace Shaw. BA in History and Religion magna cum laude, Yale U., 1964; MD, Columbia U., 1968. Lic. Vt., Va.; cert. Advanced Trauma Life Support instr. Intern medicine Cornell Med. Ctr., N.Y.C., 1968-69, resident medicine, 1969-71, resident medicine, cardiology, 1971; chief med. resident medicine North Shore U. Hosp., Manhasset, N.Y., 1972-73, instr. medicine, 1972-73; mem. staff Rancocas Valley Hosp., Willingboro, N.J., 1973-75; cardiologist Brachfeld Med. Assocs., Willingboro, N.J., 1974-75, Castleton (Vt.) Med. Assocs., 1975-77; attending physician Rutland Regional Med. Ctr., Rutland, Vt., 1975-92; pvt. practice Rutland, Vt., 1977-92; adj. asst. prof. clin. medicine Dartmouth Hitchcock Med. Ctr., Hanover, N.H., 1979-92; asst. prof. medicine U. Vt., Burlington, 1983-92; mem. staff Dwight David Eisenhower Med. Ctr., Ft. Gordon, Ga., 1991; dir. ambulatory cardiology, dir. cardiology consult svc., mem. clin. faculty cardiovascular divsn., dept. medicine Health Scis. Ctr. U. Va., Charlottesville, 1992—2001, assoc. prof. medicine Health Scis. Ctr., 1992—. Cons. Southwestern Vt. Med. Ctr., Bennington, 1986—, Keller U.S. Army Hosp., West Point, N.Y., 1985—, internal medicine Veteran Affairs Med. Ctr., Salem, Va., 1993—; mem. critical care com. Rutland Regional Med. Ctr., pharmacy and therapeutics com., investigational review bd., ethics com.; mem. pharmacy and therapeutics com. Health Scis. Ctr. U. Va., nutrition com., health care evaluation com., ambulatory policy com.; bd. dirs., mem. profl. affairs com., mem. bylaws com. Blue Cross/Blue Shield Vt.; bd. dirs., founding mem. Vt. Cardiac Network; presenter New Eng. regional meeting Am. Coll. Physicians, Hanover, N.H., 1976, Advanced Concepts Shock and Trauma, Woodstock (Vt.) Inn, 1982; dir. ACLS Tng. Ctr.; chmn/. Resolution Com. Contbr. articles to profl. jours. Med. advisor skiing svcs. Killington Ski Area, 1975-92, Smokey House Found., 1975-80, Farm and Wilderness Camps, 1975-85; mem. steering com. Vt. Med. Practice Variation Assessment Program, 1988; mem. cardiology study sect. Vt. Program Quality Care, 1988-92, Vt. Gov.'s Coun. Phys. Fitness, 1985-88; vestry Trinity Episcopal Ch., 1986-89; bd. dirs. Vermont Diabetes Assn., 1975-79, Rutland Mental Health Svc., 1975-82, Rutland Area Vis. Nurses Assn., 1975-77, chmn. profl. affairs com., mem. utilization review com.; bd. dirs. Barstow Sch., 1986-90; town health officer Wallingford, Vt., 1975-80. Maj. U.S. Army, 1973-75; col. USAR, 1985—. Decorated Nat. Def. Svc. medal, Reserve Achievement medal, Army Commendation medal; recipient Physician Recognition award Am. Med. Assn., Exceptional Svc. award, Spiritual Aims award Kiwanis Club Am., 1983, U. Va. Pres.'s Report award, 1992. Fellow Am. Coll. Physicians, Am. Coll. Cardiology, N.Am. Soc. Pacing and Electrophysiology; mem. Am. Heart Assn. (ACLS instr., BCLS instr., nat. faculty ACLS Vt., mem. mil. tng. network ACLS, Advanced Trauma Life Support; bd. dirs. 1978-80, bd. dirs., at large appointee 1988-93, agenda planning com. 1986-89, affiliate relations com. 1986-88, sci. pub. com. 1989-93, "heart and stroke" planning com. 1989-90, participant edn. and inf. group heart guide consumer health and info. program, 1989-91, chmn. task force mission to elderly 1989-90; v.p.-elect New Eng. region 1986-87, regional v.p. 1987-88, fellow coun. clin. cardiology, bd. dirs. Charlottesville divsn. 1992—, bd. dirs. Va. affiliate 1992—, bd. dirs. Rutland, Vt. divsn. 1986-92, program coun. 1986-92, bd. dirs. Vt. affiliate 1975-92, exec. com. 1978-92, pres.-elect 1982-83, pres. 1983-85, co-chair capital campaign 1988-90, nominating com. 1984-86, cardiac rehab. com. 1982-85, program coun. 1978-90, ACLS com. 1978-90, cardiac critical care com. 1978-82, hypertension com. 1975-82, chmn. emergency cardiac care com. region V 1976-80, bd. dirs. N.J. affiliate 1973-75, BCLS com. 1973-75, mem. greater N.Y. affiliate 1966-72, BCLS instr. 1968-72, del. N.E. regional heart com. 1985-91, reaffiliation com. 1987-89, nominating com. 1987-88, Pysician of Yr. award 1992), Am. Soc. Echocardiology, N.Y. Acad. Scis., Vt. Cardiac Network (vice chmn. 1982-86), Phi Beta Kappa. Avocations: bicycling, running, cross country skiing, hiking, mountain climbing, theology. Office: Consultiants in Cardiology 108 Houston St Ste B Lexington VA 24450 Home: 308 S Jefferson St Lexington VA 24450 Office Phone: 540-463-2227. Business E-Mail: dld3a@virginia.edu.

DESIMONE, JOSEPH M., chemist, educator; b. May 16, 1964; m. Suzanne, 1986; children: Philip, Emily. BS in Chemistry, Ursinus Coll., 1986, doctorate (hon.) in Sci., 1999; PhD in Chemistry, Va. Poly. State U., 1990. Rsch. tech. Pennwalt Corp., King of Prussia, Pa., 1986; asst. prof. chemistry U. N.C., Chapel Hill, 1990-94, Mary Ann Smith assoc. prof., 1995—, Mary Ann Smith prof., 1996—99, William R. Kenan Jr. disting. prof. chemistry, 1999—, dir. inst. advanced materials, 2003—; William R. Kenan Jr. disting. prof. chem. engring. NCSU, 1999—. Co-dir. Kenan Ctr. Utilization of CO2 in Mfg., 1997—99; dir. sci. and tech ctr. environmentally responsible solvents and processes NSF, 1999—; co-founder, mem. sci. advisory bd. BioStent; co-founder, chmn. MICELL Technologies, Inc.; mem. bd. trustees Ursinus Coll., 2001—; mem. adv. coun. dept. chemistry Va. Tech., 2001—; mem. nat. rsch. coun. bd. chem. scis. and tech., 2000—. Editl. bd. Jour. Applied Polymer Sci., 1992-99, Trends in Polymer Sci., 1993-94, High Performance Polymers, 1994-99, Jour. Polymer Sci, 1999-, Macromolecules, 2001-03, Indsl. and Engring. Chemistry Rsch., 2000-03; contbr. articles to profl. jours. Recipient Charles H. Stone award 1995, Entrepreneur of Yr. in Technology award Ernst & Young, 2001, Engring. Excellence award DuPont, 2002, John Scott award City Trusts Phila., 2002; NSF young investigator, 1992; fellow Bell Comms., 1989-90, Lord Corp., 1988-89. Mem. AAAS, Am. Chem. Soc. (Wallace H. Carothers award 2002, award Creative Invention 2005), Soc. Advancement of Material and Process Engring., Sigma Xi., Phi Lambda Upsilon. Achievements include patents in field. Office: U NC Dept Chemistry Venable Hall 300 Chapel Hill NC 27599-0001 Fax: 919-962-5467. Business E-Mail: desimone@unc.edu.

DESIMONE, SAMUEL RICHARD, lawyer; JD, NYU, 1984; BA, Amherst Coll., 1981. Assoc. Testa, Hurwitz & Thibeault, Boston; ptnr. Lane Powell Spears Lubersky, Portland, Oreg.; v.p. corp. devel. Merix Corp., Forest Grove, Oreg.; exec. v.p., gen. counsel Earthlink, Inc., Atlanta, 1998—. Mem. Oreg. Young Entrepreneurs Assn. (co-founder), Oreg. Entrepreneurs Forum (former dir.), Phi Beta Kappa. Office: Earthlink Enterprises Inc 1375 Peachtree St NW Atlanta GA 30309

DESIO, DELORES JEAN, writer, artist, retired elementary school educator; b. Detroit, May 20, 1933; d. Thomas Matthew Lannie and Anne Charlotte Zambon; m. Anthony William Desio, June 27, 1959; children: Douglas Anthony, Darcy Desio Rouse. BS in Fine Arts and Art Edn., Wayne State U., Detroit, 1955. Life credential tchg. Calif. Art educator Clawson (Mich.) City Schs., 1955—56; elem. tchr. Redondo Beach (Calif.) Schs., 1956—57; tchr. Inglewood (Calif.) Schs., 1957—59, Palo Alto (Calif.) Unified Schs., 1959—63, Cupertino Schs., Los Altos, 1963—65, St. John's Sch., Encinitas, 1979—85; art tchr. St. Patrick's Sch., Carlsbad, 1986—87; owner, writer, illustrator Primo Publs. Bd. trustees Interfaith Shelter Network Homeless, San Diego, 1992—, Nev. Mus. Art, Reno, 2000—. Author: Rescue of the Gem Children, 1999; Distinctly Duck, 2003, periodicals. Prin. Anthony and Delores J. Desio Found., 1998—. Recipient Christian Unity award, Ecumenical Coun. of San Diego, 1995. Office Phone: 775-849-1429, 760-806-8070. Business E-Mail: adesio2210@aol.com.

DESIREE, LAURA, dancer; Studied with, Natalia Clare; student, Joffrey Ballet Sch. Former mem. Joffrey Ballet Concert Group; mem. Pitts. Ballet Theatre, 1982—, 1st soloist, 1986, prin. dancer, 1990. Originated role of Jordan Baker in Prokovksy's The Great Gatsby. Office: Pitts Ballet Theatre 2900 Liberty Ave Pittsburgh PA 15201-1511

DESJARDINS, CLAUDE, physiologist, dean; b. Fall River, Mass., June 13, 1938; s. Armand Louis and Marguerite Jean (Mercier) D.; m. Jane Elizabeth Campbell, June 30, 1962; children: Douglas, Mark, Anne. BS, U. R.I., 1960; MS, Mich. State U., 1964, PhD, 1967. Asst. prof. dept. physiology Okla. State U., Stillwater, 1968-69, assoc. prof., 1969-72; assoc. prof. physiology U. Tex., Austin, 1970-75; prof. physiology Inst. Reproductive Biology, Patterson Labs., 1975-86, U. Va. Med. Sch., Charlottesville, 1987-96, dir. Ctr. Rsch. Reprodn., 1990-96; prof. physiology & biophysics, sr. assoc. dean med. coll. U. Ill., Chgo., 1996—. Mem. Ctr. for Advanced Studies, 1986; cons. NIH, ASA, VA, FDA. Author: Cell and Molecular Biology of the Testis, 1993, Molecular Physiology of Testicular Cells, 1996; editor-in-chief Am. Jour. physiology: Endocrinology and Metabolism, 1991-95; editor-in-chief Jour. Andrology, 1989-91, Ency. of Reprodn., 1997-98; mem. editl. bd. Biology Reprodn., Endocrinology; contbr. articles to profl. jours.; patentee techs. for male contraception, mechanisms of peptide hormone transport in the microcirculation and ligand-dependent and ligand ind. action of steroid hormones in peripheral vasculature. Fellow The Jackson Lab., Bar Harbor, Maine, 1967, NIH Sr. fellow U. Va. Med. Sch., 1983-84, Danforth Found. fellow, 1960; C.F. Wilcox Found. scholar, 1958. Mem. Am. Physiol. Soc., Soc. Neurosci., Soc. Study Reprodn. (pres. 1982-83), Endocrine Soc., Am. Soc. Cell Biology, The Microcirculatory Soc. Office: U Ill at Chgo Office of Dean M/C 784 1853 W Polk St Chicago IL 60612-4316 Office Phone: 312-966-5392. Business E-Mail: clauded@uic.edu.

DESJARDINS, RAOUL, medical association administrator, financial consultant; b. Montreal, Quebec, Can., Oct. 8, 1933; came to U.S., 1962; s. Elso and Blanche (Lemieux) D.; m. Regina Turgeon, Oct. 10, 1961; children: Bryan-Claude, John Andrew. BA, U. Montreal, 1953, MD, 1958; MS, Baylor U., 1964, PhD, 1966; MBA, Rutgers U., 1990. Diplomate Am. Bd. Medicine. Chief intern, resident St. Joan of Arc Hosp., Montreal, 1958-59; med. dir. Candiac (Can.) Med. Clinic, 1953-62, Ortho Research Found., Raritan, N.J., 1966-72; pres. Raoul Desjardins Assocs. Inc., Mendham, N.J., 1972-83, Research Cons. Inc., Mendham, 1983—, APG Internat., Inc., 1991—. Med. dirs. Iroquois Class Co., Candiac, 1959-62; asst. prof. Hahnemann Hosp. and U., Phila., 1976-80; bd. govs. Internat. Medicines Exch. and Devel., Georgetown, Ga., 1986—; chmn. bd. advisors Fed. Inst. Health, 1991—; chmn. bd. govs. Grand Masters Found., 1989—. Prodr. video: The Apgram: A New Tool to Measure Cardiovascular Performance, 1995. Recipient physician's recognition award AMA, 1969. Fellow: N.Y. Acad. Medicine, Am. Coll. Clin. Pharmacology, The Royal Soc. Health, Am. Coll. Angiology; mem.: Petroleum Club Houston, Doctors Club, Met. Club (membership com. 1991—), Med. Execs. Club, Beta Gamma Omega, Sigma Xi. Roman Catholic. Avocations: safaris, medieval history, economic theory, anti-aging. Office: Fed Inst Health 35 Stonecroft Pl The Woodlands TX 77381-5226 E-mail: doctord@fih.ky.

DES JARDINS, TRACI, chef, restaurant owner; b. Calif. Student, U. Calif., Santa Cruz. Formerly mem. staff 7th St. Bistro, L.A.; former apprentice Michel and Pierre Troisgros, Lucas Carton, Alain Ducasse, Alain Passard, France; former mem. staff Montrachet, N.Y.C.; former chef de cuisine Patina, Calif.; former chef Aqua, San Francisco, Elka, San Francisco; exec. chef Rubicon, San Francisco, 1993—97; ptnr., chef Jardiniere, San Francisco, 1997—. Environ. activist. Named a Rising Star Chef of Yr., James Beard Found.; named Chef of Yr., San Francisco Mag.; named one of Best New Chefs, Food & Wine Mag., Top 3 Chefs in Bay Area, San Francisco Chronicle. Office: Jardiniere 300 Grove St San Francisco CA 94102

DESKIN, WILLIAM C., healthcare educator; b. Des Moines, Iowa, Sept. 9, 1947; s. Jack L. and Iris E. Deskin; m. Patricia L. Snyder, Feb. 2, 1970; children: William C. Jr., Catherine D. Deskin-Constantine. BS in Health Planning, U. of Minn., 1976; MS in Health Svcs. Adminstrn., U. of St. Francis, Joliet, Ill, 1989; Exec. MBA, U. of Iowa, 1992; PhD, Walden U., Mpls., 2001. V.p. Ottumwa (Iowa) Regional Health Ctr., 1989—96; dir. quality mgmt., utilization and planning Bay Med. Ctr., Bay City, Mich., 1997—2001; educator Cen. Mich. U. Coll. of Extended Learning, Lansing, Mich., 1998—, Delta Coll., University Center, Mich., 1998—, Bay City, 1998—, Spring Arbor U., Flint, Mich., 2001—. Sculptures in stone and hard wood, various. Long range planning YMCA, Bay City, 1998—2002. Sgt. USMC, 1966—70. Fellow: Am. Coll. of Healthcare Execs. (profl. exam. com. 2000—04, product planning com. 2004—); mem.: Nat. Coun. Quality Assurance (cert. profl. healthcare quality, cert. profl. in healthcare). Methodist. Avocations: racquetball, guitar, sculpting. Office: 408 Deerhaven Ln Hendersonville NC 28791-8613

DESKINS, WILBUR EUGENE, mathematician, educator; b. Morgantown, W.Va., Feb. 20, 1927; s. Wilbur Lawrence and Avis (Creasy) D.; m. Barbara Brown, Apr. 18, 1953 (dec.); children— Lucinda Eugenie, Samantha Eugenie. BS, U. Ky., 1949; MS, U. Wis., 1950, PhD, 1953. Teaching asst. U. Wis., 1949-51, fellow, 1951-52, teaching asst., 1952-53, instr., 1953, Ohio State U., 1953-55, asst. prof., 1955-56, Mich. State U., East Lansing, 1956-59, assoc. prof., 1959-63, prof. math., 1963-71, U. Pitts., 1971-96, chmn. dept. math, 1971-87, assoc. dean Coll. Arts and Scis., 1988-96, prof. emeritus, 1996—. Author: Abstract Algebra, 1964. Mem. steering com. Pitts. Math. Collaborative, 1985-91; mem. exec. bd. Pitt. Sci. Inst., 1989-93. Mem. Math. Assn. Am. Achievements include research and articles on algebra and group theory. Office: Univ Pitts Pittsburgh PA 15260

DESLAURIERS, SUZANNE DAWSEY, secondary school educator, artist; b. Wilmington, N.C., Sept. 13, 1950; d. Cyrus Bassett and Marshlea (Cottingham) Dawsey; m. Cecil Hörger Knight, Dec. 28, 1972 (dec. Nov. 25, 1995); 1 child, Jesse Hörger Knight; m. E. Joseph Deslauriers, Dec. 16, 1996. BA in Fine Arts, Fla. So. Coll., Lakeland, Fla., 1972; MA in Art Edn., U. S.C., Columbia, S.C., 1985. Cert. Nat. Bd. Cert. Tchr., 99. Child care program dir. Appalachia State Wesley Found., Boone, NC, 1977—78; supr. aftercare sch. program Hardin Park Elem., Boone, 1977—78; art tchr., asst. soccer coach Holly Hill-Roberts High Sch., Holly Hill, SC, 1979—88; art tchr., social studies tchr. Hiwassee Dam Sch., Murphy, NC, 1988—, A+ Schs. coord., 1994—. Presenter, cons. on integrated instrn. Cherokee County Schs., Murphy, 1994—; mentor for nat. bd. tchr. cert. NEA, Western, NC, 2000—; adj. prof. West Carolina U., Cullowhee, NC, 2002; painting and drawing tchr. John C. Campbell Folk Sch., Brasstown, NC, 1995—. Recipient Creative Tchr. of the Yr., Western North Carolina, 1996. Mem.: North Carolina Art Educator Assn. (Secondary Art Educator of the Yr. 1999—2000). Home: 24 Lady Slipper Ln Brasstown NC 28902-8073

DESLER, PETER M., lawyer; b. Troy, N.Y., Oct. 2, 1947; s. Joseph Francis and Helen (Meagher) D.; m. Cynthia Lee Hymes, Sept. 20, 1980; children: Frances Lauren, Audrey Rose, Emily Helen. BA, Providence Coll., 1969; JD, Coll. William and Mary, 1972. Bar: Va. 1972, Calif. 1975, Idaho 1992, U.S. Dist. Ct. (ea. dist.) Va. 1972, U.S. Dist. Ct. (no. dist.) Calif. 1975, U.S. Dist. Ct. (ea. dist.) Calif. 1982, U.S. Dist. Ct. Idaho 1992, U.S. Mil. Appeals 1972, U.S. Ct. Appeals (4th cir.) 1974, U.S. Ct. Appeals (9th cir.) 1975. Atty. litigation dept. The Pentagon, U.S. Army, Washington, 1972-74; atty. Presidio of San Francisco, 1974—76; assoc. Law Offices of Yanello & Flippen, San Francisco, 1979-81, Law Offices of Berger & Taggart, San Francisco, 1981-86; pvt. practice San Rafael, Calif., 1986-92, Boise Arbitration/Mediation Svcs., Boise, Idaho, 1992—, Law Offices of Peter Desler, Boise, Idaho, 1992—. Faculty Dominican U., San Rafael, Calif., 1980-88, U. San Francisco, 1989-92, Boise State U., 1992—; judge pro tempore Marin County Superior Ct., 1985-92, Marin County Mcpl. Ct. 1983-92. Capt. U.S. Army, 1972-76. Mem. Bar Assn. San Francisco (arbitrator 1986-92), Marin County Bar Assn. (arbitrator1986-92), Am. Arbitration Assn. (arbitrator/mediator 1986—), Idaho Bar Assn., alt. dispute resolution sect. gov. council mem.), Idaho Mediation Assn., Nat. Arbitration forum, 2003, World Intellectual Property Organ., 2003. Avocations: motorcycling, golf, skiing, music, mountain biking, fishing. Office: Law Offices of Peter Desler PC 623 W Hays St Boise ID 83702 Office Phone: 208-344-0654. Personal E-mail: bams1@mindspring.com.

DESLOGE, CHRISTOPHER DAVIS, SR., real estate company executive, merchant banking executive; b. St. Louis, July 23, 1958; s. William Livingston and Loriel Martens (Johnson) D.; m. Mary Roberta Dubuque, May 22, 1981; children: William Livingston II, Christopher Davis Jr., Raymond Amadee Dubuque. Student, Drake U., 1977-79, Maryville Coll., 1979-80. V.p. Follman Properties, St. Louis, 1982-85; leasing mgr. Paragon Group, St. Louis, 1985-86; pres. Desloge Co., St. Louis, 1986-90; v.p. Hilliker Corp., St. Louis, 1990-92; pres. Braeburn Ptnrs., St. Louis, 1992-96; account mgr. Maritz, Stamford, Conn., 1996-98; owner Desloge Oak Tree Real Estate and Mcht. Banking, 2001—; pres. Desloge Consolidated Lead Co., 2004—; CEO Desloge Consolidated Pvt. Investment Co., 2004—. Arbitrator BBB, St. Louis, 1991—. Author: Tenant's Guerilla Guide to Office Leasing, 2004; contbg. editor: St. Louis Bus. Jour., 1986—94. Mem. Real Estate Bd. Met. St. Louis, 1982—93; bd. dirs. St. Louis Psychoanalytic Inst., 1988—91, Internat. Tenant Representation Alliance, St. Louis, 1992—94, Ctr. Head Injury Svcs., 1994—96; co-chmn. disaster svcs. ARC-Bi State Chpt., St. Louis, 1992—94; pres. bd. dirs. Desloge Found., St. Louis, 1993—; founder, bd. dirs. President's Coun., St. Louis, 2004—; elected. to bd. Tax Assessment Appeals, Darien, Conn., 1999—. Recipient Recognition award for effort St. Louis Psychoanalytic Inst., 1992, Honor award Red Cross-Bi State Chpt., St. Louis, 1994. Mem. Nat. Coun. Consumer Arbitrators, Barnes Road Luncheon Group, Noonday Club, Veiled Prophet, St. Louis Country Club, Landmark Club, Darien Boat Club (bd. dirs., fin. sec. 1998-2002), Racquet Club. Republican. Roman Catholic. Avocations: boating, shooting, golf, tennis, automobiles. Home and Office: Sunny Hills Farm PO Box 127 Gray Summit MO 63039

DESLOGE, ROSEMARY BYRNE, otolaryngologist, educator; b. Tallahassee, Fla., Feb. 25, 1962; d. Edward Augustine and Moira Dunne Desloge. BS in Biology, U. Notre Dame, 1984; MD, U. Miami, 1989. Diplomate Am. Bd. Otolaryngology, Nat. Bd. Med. Examiners. Gen. surgery resident U. S.C., Columbia, 1989—91; internal medicine resident NYU/Bellevue Hosps., N.Y.C., 1992—93; ENT resident/fellow Manhattan Eye/Ear/Throat Hosp., N.Y.C., 1993—98; laryngology fellow Harvard U., Boston, 1993—99; asst. prof. dept. otorhinolaryngology Weill Med. Coll., Cornell U., N.Y.C., 1999—. Contbr. articles to profl. jours. Fellow: ACS; mem.: AMA, Am. Acad. Otolaryngology Head and Neck Surgery. Office: Dept Otorhinolaryngology Ste 541 520 E 70th St New York NY 10021

DESLONGCHAMPS, PIERRE, chemistry professor; b. St.-Lin, Que., Can., May 8, 1938; s. Rodolphe and Madeleine D.; 3d m. Marie-Marthe Leroux; children: Patrice, Ghyslain. BS., U. Montreal, Que., Can., 1959; PhD (hon.), U. Montreal, 1984; PhD, U. N.B., 1964, PhD (hon.), 1985, U. Pierre et Marie, 1983, Bishop's U., 1984, Laval U., 1984; DSc, U. Moncton, N.B., Can., 1995. Research fellow Harvard U., 1964, postdoctoral fellow, 1965; asst. prof. chemistry U. Montreal, 1966-67; asst. prof. U. Sherbrooke, Que., 1967-68, assoc. prof., 1968-72, prof., 1972—. Author: Stereoelectronic Effects in Organic Chemistry, 1983; contbr. over 225 articles to profl. jours.; holder 9 patents in field; inventor in field. Decorated Officer Order of Can., 1989; recipient E.W.R. Steacie prize Nat. Rsch. Coun. Can., 1974, Can. Gold medal for sci. and engring. Nat. Scis. and Engring. Rsch. Coun. Can., 1993, Sci. prize Province Que., 1971-72, Marie-Victorian prize, 1987, Alfred Bader award Can. Soc. Chemistry, 1991, R.U. Lemieux award Chem. Soc. of Chemistry, 1994; fellow A.P. Sloan, 1970-72, E.W.R. Steacie, 1971-74, John Simon Guggenheim Meml. Found., 1979; Izaak Walton Killam scholar Can. Coun., 1976-77. Fellow AAAS, Chem. Inst. Can. (Merck, Sharp and Dohme Lectrs. award 1976), Royal Soc. Can., Royal Soc. London, World Innovation Found.; mem. Corp. Profl. Chemists Que., Am. Chem. Soc., Assn. Canadienne-Francaise pour l'Advancement des Sciences (medaille Vincent 1975, medaille Pariseau 1979), Acad. des Scis. de Paris (foreign asst.). Address: Univ Sherbrooke Inst Pharm 3001 12 North Ave Sherbrooke Canada J1H 5N4 Home: 161 de Vimy Sherbrooke PQ Canada J1J 3M6 Business E-Mail: pierre.deslongchamps@usherbrooke.ca.

DESMARAIS, CHARLES JOSEPH, museum director, writer; b. NYC, Apr. 21, 1949; s. Charles Emil and Helen Barbara (Young) D.; m. Sharon McLeod, May 1, 1970; m. Patricia Jon Carroll, June 15, 1979; m. Katherine Ann Morgan, Dec. 31, 1985 Student, Western Conn. State Coll., Danbury, 1967-71; BS, SUNY-Rochester, 1975; MFA, SUNY-Buffalo, 1977. Curator Friends of Photography, Carmel, Calif., 1973-74; asst. editor Afterimage, Rochester, 1975-77; editor Exposure, Chgo., 1977-81; dir. Art Gallery, Columbia Coll., Chgo., 1977-79, Calif. Mus. Photography, U. Calif.-Riverside, 1981-88, Laguna Art Mus., Laguna Beach, Calif., 1988-94, Contemporary Arts Ctr., Cin., 1995—2004; dep. dir. for art Bklyn. Mus., 2005—. Guest curator Mus. Contemporary Art, Chgo., 1980, L.A. Ctr. Photog. Studies, 1981; arts adv. com. Riverside County Bd. Suprs., 1981-86; chair Orange County Arts Coun., 1989-91; bd. dirs. Regional Cultural Alliance, 2000—03. Author, editor: Roger Mertin: Records 1976-1978, 1978, Michael Bishop, 1979, The Portrait Extended, 1980, Why I Got Into TV and Other Stories: The Art of Ilene Segalove, 1990, Proof: Los Angeles Art and the Photograph, 1960-1980, 1992, Humongolous: Sculpture and Other Works by Tim Hawkinson, 1996, Jim Dine Photographs, 1999, Stephan Balkenhol, 2000; arts columnist Riverside Press Enterprise, 1987-88. Art Critic's fellow Nat. Endowment Arts, 1979 Mem. Assn. Art Mus. Dirs., Soc. Photog. Edn. (dir. 1979-83), Am. Assn. Museums, Coll. Art Assn. Office: Bklyn Museum 200 Eastern Pkwy Brooklyn NY 11238-6052 Business E-Mail: charles.desmarais@brooklynmuseum.org.

DESMARAIS, GERALD WAYNE, social studies educator, department chairman; b. Nashua, NH, Nov. 26, 1957; s. Raymond Lucien and Leora Ella (Haight) Desmarais. BA, U. NH, Durham, 1979; MAT, U. NH, 1982. Cert. social studies educator Vt., 2001. History dept. chair Spaulding HS, Barre, Vt., 1987—. Advanced Placement consulting tchr. The Coll. Bd., Waltham, Mass., 2000—. Democrat. Home: 27 School St Montpelier VT 05602 Office: Spaulding HS 155 Ayers St Barre VT 05641

DESMARAIS, JOHN M., lawyer; BS in Chem. Engring., Manhattan Coll., 1985; JD, NYU, 1988. Bar: NY 1989, DC 1989, U.S. Dist. Ct. (So. and ea. dist. NY) 1989, U.S. Ct. Appeals (2d and Fed. cir.) 1989, U.S. Supreme Ct., registered: U.S. Patent and Trademark Office. Atty. Fish & Neave, 1988—92; asst. U.S. atty. criminal divsn. U.S. Atty.'s Office So. dist., NY, 1992—95; ptnr., mem. firm com. Kirkland & Ellis, N.Y.C. Mem. judge's intellectual property adv. com. Del. Dist. Ct., 1999—. Named one of America's Leading Bus. Lawyers in Intellectual Poperty, Chambers & Partners, 2004, 45 Under Forty-Five, Am. Lawyer, 2003, 40 Under 40, Nat. Law Jour., 2002. Mem.: AIChE, ABA, Del. Dist. Ct. Judges' Intellectual Property Adv. Com., Internat. Trademark Assn., Bar Assn. City of NY, NY Intellectual Property Owners Assn., NY County Lawyer's Assn., Fed. Bar Coun., NY Bar Assn. Office: Kirkland & Ellis LLP Citigroup Ctr 153 E 53rd St New York NY 10022-4675 Office Phone: 212-446-4739. Office Fax: 212-446-4900. E-mail: jdesmarais@kirkland.com.

DESMARAIS, PAUL, diversified financial services company executive; b. Sudbury, Ont., Can., Jan. 4, 1927; s. Jean-Noël and Lébéa Desmarais; m. Jacqueline Maranger, Sept. 8, 1953; children: Paul, André, Louise, Sophie. BComm, U. Ottawa, Canada, 1949. Chmn., CEO, Power Corp. Can., Montreal, 1968—96, chmn. exec. com., 1996—, also. bd. dirs. Dir. emeritus Great-West Lifeco Inc.; bd. dirs. Gesca Ltée, Groupe Bruxelles Lambert S.A., Power Corp. Can., Power Fin. Corp., La Presse Ltée, Power Tex. Investment Corp., Canada Life Capital Corp. Inc.; mem. internat. adv. bd. Barrick Gold Corp. Can.; chmn., mng. dir. Pargesa Holding S.A. Mem. Queen's Privy Coun., Canada. Decorated companion Order of Can., officer Nat. Order of Que., Legion of Honor France, Ordre de Léopold II Belgium. Office: Power Corp Can 751 Victoria Sq Montreal PQ Canada H2Y 2J3

DESMARTEAU, DARRYL DWAYNE, chemistry professor, geology educator; b. Garden City, Kans., May 25, 1940; s. Arthur L. and Esther P. (Deines) DesM.; m. Genie L. Hardy, Sept. 16, 1962; children: Scott (dec.), Noel, Chad. BS in Chemistry, Wash. State U., Pullman, 1963; PhD, U. Wash, 1966. Acting asst. prof. U. Wash., 1966-67; asst. prof. Northeastern U., Boston, 1967-71, Kans. State U., Manhattan, 1971-73, assoc. prof., 1973-77, prof., 1977-82; prof., chmn. dept. chemistry and geology Clemson U., S.C., 1982-89, Tobey-Beaudrot prof. chemistry, 1989—; cons. Monsanto Chem. Co., St. Louis, 1976-78, Hooker Chem. Co., Grand Island, N.Y., 1978-80, Ausimont, Milan, Italy, 1985—, DuPont Co., Wilmington, Del., 1986-93. Bd. editors: Jour. Flourine Chemistry, 1981—; contbr. articles on fluorine chemistry to profl. jours. Served with USMCR, 1960-66. Recipient award for outstanding research Clemson U. Alumni Assn., 1985, award for Contbrn. to Sci. in S.C. Drug Sci. Found., 1988, Wash. State U. Alumni Achievement award, 1995, Sr. U.S. Scientist award (Humboldt-Preis) Alexander von Humboldt Found., 1988—; Sloan Found fellow, 1975-77, Alexander von Humboldt Found. Research fellow Bonn., W.Ger., 1979-80; numerous research grants Mem. Am. Chem. Soc. (chmn. div. fluorine chemistry 1979, sec.-treas. 1976-78, exec. council 1973-80, award for Creative Work in Fluorine Chemistry 1983, Charles H. Stone award 1994), Sigma Xi, Phi Lambda Upsilon, Alpha Chi Sigma Republican. Roman Catholic. Home: 1007 Berkeley Dr Clemson SC 29631-2301 Office: Clemson Univ Dept Chemistry Clemson SC 29634-0001 E-mail: fluorin@clemson.edu.

DESMOND, J. CHRISTOPHER, lawyer; b. Amityville, N.Y., July 9, 1955; s. John and Mary Desmond. BA, Binghamton U., Binghamton, 1980; JD cum laude, U. Buffalo, Buffalo, 1983. Bar: Ga. 1983, U.S. Ct. Appeals (5th crct.) 1986, U.S. Dist. Ct. (no. dist.) Ga. 1987, U.S. Ct. Appeals (11th crct.) 1989. Law clk. Hon. B. Avant Edenfield, U.S. Dist. Ct. (so. dist.) Ga., Savannah, 1983-85, 95—; staff atty. U.S. Ct. Appeals (5th cir.), New Orleans, 1985-87; assoc. Kilpatrick & Cody, Atlanta, 1987-88, Schreeder, Wheeler & Flint, Atlanta, 1988-94. Mng. editor Buffalo Law Rev., 1982-83. Mem. Phi Beta Kappa. Home: 26 Oak Park Pt Savannah GA 31405-1019 E-mail: chris_desmond@juno.com.

DESMOND, NED, editor, writer; Student, Amherst Coll., 1980; MA, Tufts U.; Reuters fellow, Oxford U. Writer Fgn. Affairs, N.Y. Rev. Books; bur. chief New Delhi, 1988—91, Tokyo, 1992—96; sr. writer Fortune; v.p. ctrs. and content Infoseek; editor, pres. eCompany Now, 1999—2001, Bus. 2.0 mag., pres., 2001—02; exec. editor Time Inc. Interactive, 2002—. Office: American Online Inc 22000 Aol Way Dulles VA 20166-9032

DESMOND-HELLMANN, SUSAN, medical products manufacturing executive; b. 1958; BS in Pre-Medicine, MD, U. Nev.; M in Epidemiology and Biostats., U. Calif. Sch. Pub. Health, Berkeley. Bd. cert. internal medicine and med. oncology. Trainee U. Calif., San Francisco; assoc. dir. clin. cancer rsch., project team leader Taxol Bristol-Myers Squibb Pharm. Rsch. Inst.; clin. scientist Genentech, Inc., South San Francisco, 1995-96, sr. dir. clin. sci., 1996, v.p. med. affairs, 1996, chief med. officer, 1996—, v.p. devel., 1997, sr. v.p. devel., 1997, exec. v.p. devel. and product ops., 1999, pres., product devel. Vis. faculty Uganda Cancer Inst.; asst. prof. hematology-oncology U. Calif. San Francisco, adj. assoc. prof. epidemiology and biostats; adv. com. regulatory reform, HHS, 2002; bd. dirs. Biotechnology Industry Orgn., 2001. Named one of Top 50 Most Powerful Women in Business, FORTUNE, 2001, 2003, 2004, 100 Most Powerful Women in World, Forbes Mag., 2005. Office: Genentech Inc One DNA Way South San Francisco CA 94080 Office Fax: 650-225-6000.*

DESNICK, ROBERT JOHN, human geneticist; b. Mpls., July 12, 1943; s. Theodore David and Celia Janice (Marcus) D.; Julie E. Herzig, Oct. 23, 1988; 1 child, Jonathan Phillips. BA, U. Minn., 1965, PhD, 1970, MD, 1971; DSc (hon.), Mt. Sinai Sch. Medicine/NYU, 2004. Diplomate Am. Bd. Med. Examiners, Am. Acad. Pediat., Am. Bd. Med. Genetics (bd. dirs. 1990-93, treas. 1991-93). Rsch. assoc. U. Minn., 1970-72, intern and resident dept. pediat., 1971-73, asst. prof. lab. medicine and pathology, 1973-75; asst. prof. pediat. U. Minn. Dight Inst. Human Genetics, 1973-75, assoc. prof. pediat., 1975—77; assoc. prof. genetics and cell biology U. Minn. Coll. Biol. Sci., 1975-77. Arthur J. and Nellie Z. Cohen prof. pediat. and genetics Mt. Sinai Sch. Medicine, N.Y.C., 1977—2000, chief divsn. med. and molecular genetics, 1977—, chair dept human genetics, 1990—99; med. adv. bd. Nat. Neurofibromatosis Found., 1978—81; dir. Mt. Sinai Ctr. Jewish Genetic Diseases, 1981—; program dir. Mt. Sinai Gen. Clin. Rsch. Ctr., 1993—2003; attending physician pediat. Mt. Sinai Hosp.; cons. physician pediat. Beth Israel Med. Ctr., N.Y.C., City Ctr. Hosp., Elmhurst, NY; med. adv. bd. Nat. Found. Jewish Genetic Diseases, 1981—2002; mem. N.Y. Gov.'s Adv. Com. on Genetics, 1982—92; med. adv. bd. Mucolipidosis IV Found., 1984—; sci. adv. bd. Dysautonomia Found., 1990—2005, Nat. Niemann-Pick Found., 1992—; med. adv. bd. Internat. Incontinenta Pigmenti Found., 1993—; mem. mental retardation study sect. NIH, 1995—98; sci. adv. bd. Ara Parshegian Med. Rsch. Found., 1995—2002, Bachman-Strauss Dystonia & Parkinson Found., 1997—; chmn. organizing com. Internat. Congresses Inherited Metabolic Diseases, 1990—; mem. NCRR adv. coun. NIH, 2000—04. Editor: Enzyme Therapy in Genetic Diseases, 1973, Molecular Genetic Modification of Eucaryotes, 1978, Enzyme Therapy in Genetic Diseases, 1980, Gaucher Disease: A Century of Delineation and Research, 1982, Animal Models of Inherited Metabolic Disorders, 1982; mem. editl. bd. Clinica Chemica Acta, 1984—96; editor: Recent Advances in Inborn Errors of Metabolism, 1987, Treatment of Genetic Diseases, 1991, Tay-Sachs Disease, 2001; mem. editl. bd. Enzyme, 1979—98, Am. Jour. Human Genetics, 1980—84, Pediatrics, 1991—96, Human Mutation, 1991—, Biochem. Medicine and Metabolic Biology, 1991—97, Jour. Clin. Investigation, 1992—97, Jour. Inherited Metabolic Disease, 1996—, Jour. Human Genetics, 1998—, Molecular Genetics and Metabolism, 1998—, Molecular Medicine, 2002—, Human Genome, 2003—; contbr. articles to profl. jours. Pres. fifth Internat. Congress of Inborn Errors of Metabolism, 1990. Recipient Ross award Soc. Pediat. Rsch., 1972, C.J. Watson award U. Minn. Med. Sch., 1973, Rsch. E. Mead Johnson award Am. Acad. Pediatrics, 1981, Outstanding Faculty award Mt. Sinai Sch.of Medicine, 1991, NIH Merit award, 1992, J. Lester Gabrilove award for med. rsch., 2003, Jacobi award Mt. Sinai Sch. Medicine Alumni Assn., 2003, E.H. Ahrens Jr. Disting. Rsch. award Assn. Patient-Oriented Rsch., 2004, Disting. Alumni award U. Minn. Med. Sch., 2004, Clin. Rsch. Excellence award Nat. Ctr. Clin. Rsch., NIH, 2005, Albion O. Bernstein award N.Y. State; USPHS fellow, 1968-70; grantee NIH, 1975-80. Fellow AAAS (sr.); mem. Nat. Acad. Scis. (mem. inst. medicine 2004), Am. Soc. Human Genetics, Genetics Soc. Am., Am. Acad. Pediat., Minn. Human Genetics League (dir. 1970-77), Soc. Complex Carbohydrates, Behavior Genetics Assn., Am. Fedn. Clin. Rsch., Am. Coll. Med. Genetics (founding fellow, chair hon. membership com. 1990-98, chair biochem. and molecular resource com. 1993-2002, chmn. accreditation com. 1998-2000), Am. Coll. Med. Genetics Found. (bd. dirs. 1998—), Am. Soc. Biochemistry and Molecular Biology, Assn. Profs. Human/Med. Genetics (pres-elect 1994, pres. 1996-98), Ea. Soc. Pediatric Rsch., Soc. Pediatric Rsch., Soc. Exptl. Biology and Medicine, Am. Soc. Exptl. Pathology, Ctrl. Soc. Clin. Rsch., Soc. Study Social Biology, Soc. Study Inborn Errors of Metabolism, N.Y. Acad. Sci., European Soc. Human Genetics, Harvey Soc. (sec. 1984-89), Am. Porphyria Assn. (med. adv. bd. 1984—), Soc. Inherited Metabolic Diseases (bd. dirs. 1983-92, pres. 1989-91), Am. Pediatric Soc., Am. Soc. Microbiology, Assn. Am. Med. Colls. (adminstrv. bd., coun. acad. socs. 2001—, chmn.-elect, 2004, chmn., 2005), Nat. Tay-Sachs and Allied Diseases Assn. (med. adv. bd. 1975—, chmn. 1990-92), Nat. MPS Soc. (med. adv. bd. 1987—), Am. Assn. Physicians, Am. Soc. Clin. Investigation, Assn. Patient-Oriented Rsch. (founding 1998—), Am. Soc. for Gene Therapy, Japanese Soc. Inherited Diseases (hon.), Società Italiana di Pediatrica (hon.), Peripatetic Club, Sigma Xi, Inst. Medicine, 2004. Office: Mt Sinai Sch Medicine Dept Human Genetics 5th Ave & 100th St New York NY 10029 Business E-Mail: rjdesnick@mssm.edu.

DESNOYERS, MEGAN FLOYD, archivist, educator; b. N.Y.C., Oct. 31, 1945; d. Lawrence Clifford and Frances Irene Floyd; m. David George Desnoyers, Sept. 2, 1967; 1 child, Adam O'Neil. AB, Vassar Coll., 1967; MLS, Rutgers U., 1968. Cert. archivist. Libr. John Jay H.S., Wappingers Falls, N.Y., 1968-69; archivist Franklin D. Roosevelt Libr., Hyde Park, N.Y., 1969, John F. Kennedy Libr., Boston, 1970—, curator Ernest Hemingway Collection, 1987—96, 2000—01; instr. in archives adminstrn. Nat. Archives Modern Archives Inst., Washington, 1982-2000. Lectr. archives adminstrn. U. Mass., Boston, 1978-80; lectr. on Hemingway, 1992—2000; mem. Archives Adv. Commn., Boston, 1977-2000; archival advisor Girl Scouts U.S., N.Y.C., 1991—. Contbr. chpt. to book, articles to profl. jours. Mem. adv. bd., chmn. com. Voluntary Action Ctr., Mass. Bay United Way, Boston, 1974-80; mem., chair bd. trustees Randall Libr., Stow, Mass., 1976-80; mem. Mass. Hist. Records Adv. Bd., 1979-2000. Nat. Def. fellow, 1967-68. Fellow Soc. Am. Archivists; mem. New Eng. Archivists (sec. 1976-78), Soc. Am. Archivists (workshop instr. 1978-2000), Acad. Cert. Archivists (task force on recert. 1991-92), Beta Phi Mu. Democrat. Roman Catholic. Office: John F Kennedy Libr Columbia Point Boston MA 02125

DESOER, BARBARA J., bank executive; BA in Math., Mount Holyoke Coll.; MBA, U. Calif., Berkeley. Various positions to mng. strategy devel. and implementation, consumer banking unit Bank Am. Corp., 1977—96, exec. v.p., Calif. retail banking group, 1996—98, pres., No. Calif. banking, 1998, mktg. exec., 1999—2001, pres. consumer products, 2001—04, chief technology, svc. and fulfillment exec., 2004—. Chmn. internat. diversity adv. coun. Bank Am. Corp.; mem. adv. coun. Haas Sch. Bus. U. Calif., Berkeley; mem. bus. adv. coun. Belk Coll. Bus. Adminstrn. U. NC, Charlotte. Bd. dir. NC Dance Theatre, Presbyn. Hosp. Found., United Way Ctrl. Carolinas. Office: Bank Am Corp 100 N Tryon St Charlotte NC 28255

DE SOFI, OLIVER JULIUS, data processing executive; b. Havana, Cuba, Dec. 26, 1929; came to U.S., 1956; s. Julius A. and Edith H. (Zsuffa) DeS.; m. Phyllis H. Dumich, Feb. 14, 1971; children: Richard D., Stephen R., Kerri L. BS in Math. and Physics, Ernst Lehman Coll., 1950; postgrad. in agronomy, U.Havana, 1952; BS in Aero. Engring., 1956. Dir. EDP tech. svcs. and planning Am. Airlines, N.Y.C., 1968-70; dir. Sabre II, Tulsa, 1970-72; v.p. data processing and comms. Nat. Bank N.Am., Huntington Sta., NY, 1972-76; sr. v.p. data processing and comms., 1976-78; sr. v.p. sys. and ops., 1978-79; sr. v.p. adminstrn., 1979—82; exec. v.p. adminstrn. group Nat. Westminster Bank, N.Y.C., 1982—84; exec. v.p. data processing methodologies and arch. Anacomp, Inc., Ft. Lee, NJ, 1982—84; v.p. copr. devel. Computer Horizons Corp., N.Y.C., 1984-86; pres., CEO Coast to Coast Computers, Inc., Sarasota, Fla., 1986—; CEO, 1993-94. Chief data processing cons. Arab Nat. Bank, Riyadh, Kingdom of Saudi Arabia, 1991-92; CEO,; bd. dirs. The Bentley Group, San Francisco, Innovative Mgmt. Systems, Inc., Sarasota, Doks Enterprises, Inc., Carson City, C.C. Lawn Care, Inc., Sarasota; lectr. program for women Adelphi Coll. Mem. AAAS, Am. Mgmt. Assn., NRA, Internat. Platform Assn., Data Processing Mgmt. Assn., Computer Exec. Round Table, Sales Execs. Club, Bank Adminstrn. Inst., Masons (Havana). E-mail: dsfi@aol.com.

DE SOTO, ERNEST FRANK, artist, writer; b. Tucson, Oct. 26, 1923; s. Robert Carlos and Artemisa Ortiz Soto; m. Rosalind Braun, Dec. 15, 1950 (div. June 1962); m. Josephine Mary Panyk, Aug. 6, 1962. Cert., Chouinard Art Sch., L.A., 1942-43, 46-48; BFA, U. Ill., 1961. Owner, dir. Ernest F. de Soto Workshop, San Francisco, 1978-93; master printer Edits. Press, San Francisco, 1972-76, Collectors Press, San Francisco, 1967-72. Pub.: (graphics) Limited Editions, 1978-93; book illustrator: Robin Crusoe, Folk Tales of Mexico, 1957-58. Bd. trustees Mex. Mus., San Francisco, 1987-93; art instr. Western Res. U., Cleve., 1952-53, U. Ill., Urbana, 1954-62. Sgt. USAF, 1943-46, PTO. Recipient Award of Honor, San Francisco Arts Commn., Bank of Am., 1982; rsch. tech. lithography grantee Ford Found., U. Ill., 1958, Master Printer Ford Found. grantee Tamarind Lithography Workshop, 1965-67. Avocations: art, painting, graphics. Home: 915 S La Huerta Green Valley AZ 85614-2120 Office Phone: 520-625-0128. E-mail: dsotowrkshopart@aol.com.

DE SOTO, HERNANDO, pediatric anesthesiologist; b. San Juan, P.R., Mar. 17, 1956; s. Moises and Rosario (Carreno) De S.; m. Hortensia Zeno, July 14, 1979; children: Lara, Pedro Urena. BS, U. P.R., 1977; MD, U. Pedro Humena, 1982. Diplomate Am. Bd. Anesthesia. Intern, resident Mt. Sinai Hosp., N.Y.C., 1985; fellow Children's Hosp., Washington, 1986; asst. prof. anesthesia Med. Coll. Ga., Augusta, 1986-88; chief anesthesia Riverside Hosp., Jacksonville, Fla., 1988-92; dir. pediat. anesthesia U. Fla., Jacksonville, 1992—. Fellow Am. Acad. Pediatrics; mem. Am. Soc. Anesthesiologists, Interam. Soc. Physicians, Soc. Pediat. Anesthesia, Soc. Ambulatory Anesthesia (pubs. com. 1990—), Fla. Soc. Anesthesiology. Avocations: computers, golf, music. Office: Univ Med Ctr 655 W 8th St Jacksonville FL 32209-6511

DESOTO, LEWIS DAMIEN, art educator; b. San Bernardino, Calif., Jan. 3, 1954; s. Lewis Dan and Albertina (Quiroz) DeS. BA, U. Calif., Riverside, 1978; MFA, Claremont Grad. Sch., 1981. Tchr. Otis Parsons, L.A., 1982-85; chmn. art dept. Cornish Coll. of Arts, Seattle, 1985-88; prof. art San Francisco State U., 1988—95; dir. grad. studies Calif. Coll. Arts and Crafts, Oakland, 1993-95; prof. art San Francisco State U., 1995—. Exhibitions include New Mus., N.Y.C., 1992, Centro Cultural De La Raza, San Diego, 1993, Moderna Museet, Stockholm, Sweden, 1993, Christopher Grimes Gallery, Santa Monica, Calif., 1994, Denver Art Mus., 1994, Columbus Mus. Art, 1994, Des Moines Art Ctr., 1995, Fundacao Serralves, Opporto, Portugal, 1995, MetronÒm, Barcelona, Spain, 1997, Public Art Commn., San Francisco Courthouse, 1998, San Francisco Internat. Airport, 2000, San Jose Animal Care Ctr. Public Commn., Calif., 2004, U. Tex., San Antonio, 2003, Public Art Commn., List Visual Art Ctr., MIT, Cambridge, 1998, Bill Maynes Gallery, N.Y.C., 1999, 2000, Mus. of Contemporary Religious Art, St. Louis, 2000, Mus. Contemporary Art, San Diego, 2001, Worcester Art (Mass.) Mus., 2001, Bill Maynes Gallery, N.Y.C., 2002, Samek Art Ctr., Bucknell U., Lewisburg, Pa., 2002, N.C. Mus. Art, Raleigh, 2003, Newhouse Ctr. for Contemporary Art, S.I., 2003, Harn Mus. Art, Gainesville, Fla., 2003, Vanderbilt Art Gallery, Vanderbilt U., Nashville, 2003, San Diego Mus. Contemporary Aft, LaJolla, 2004, Columbus Mus. of Art, 2004. Mem. photo coun. Seattle Art Mus., 1987-88, Eureka Fellowship, vis. arts, 1999. Recipient New Genres award Calif. Arts Coun., 1992, NEA fellow, 1996, recipient Visual Arts award Flintridge Found., Pasadena, Calif., 2004. Mem. L.A. Ctr. for Photographic Studies (bd. dirs. 1983-85), CameraWork (exec. bd. dirs. 1991-93), Ctr. for Arts (adv. bd. 1993-95), Friends of Photography (peer award bd. 1991-96). Office: San Francisco State U Art Dept 1600 Holloway Ave San Francisco CA 94132-1722 Personal E-mail: Sotolux@sbcglobal.net.

DE SOUZA, ISMENIA SALES, language educator; b. Alto-Longa, Brazil, Nov. 28, 1954; arrived in U.S., 1974; d. João Pereira and Neusa Sales de Sousa; m. Geraldo Soares De Souza, Apr. 30, 1973; children: Patricia, Lesley, Geraldo Jr. BA in Fgn. Lang., Auburn (Ala.) U., 1987; MA in Hispanic Studies, Auburn (Ala.) U, 1990; MEd, Auburn (Ala.) U., 1991; PhD student in Spanish, Ala. U., 2002—. Tchr. Portuguese Auburn (Ala.) U., 1988—90; instr. Faulkner U., Montgomery, Ala., 1991; tchr. Spanish and French Auburn City Schs., 1992—2002; tchg. asst. Spanish U. Ala., Tuscaloosa, Ala., 2002—. Tchr. Portuguese Columbus (Ga.) Coll., 1997; translator South Ala. Select Soccer Team, Guatemala, 1996; referee Nat. Outstanding Tchr. Com., Colo., 1996—98; clin. instr. Coll. Edn. Auburn U., 1996—97; presenter in field. Chmn. honor soc. Auburn (Ala.) Jr. HS, 1994—97; referee Ala. HS Athletic Assn., 1997; chmn. tchr. morality com. Auburn (Ala.) Jr. HS, 1995—96. Recipient Class Act award, TV 12, Montgomery, Ala., 1994; grantee, Auburn (Ala.) City Schs., 1996—2001. Mem.: Am. Assn. Tchrs. Spanish and Portuguese (named Nat. Tchr. of Yr. 1995—96), Sigma Delta Di, Omicron Delta Kappa, Phi Beta Delta, Alpha Epsilon Lambda (chmn. academic excellence and leadership com. 2003, pres. 2004—). Avocations: weightlifting, swimming, walking, reading. Office: Alabama Univ Dept Modern Lang Classics PO Box 870246 Tuscaloosa AL 35487-0154 Office Phone: 205-348-5055.

DESOUZA, KEVIN, think-tank executive, researcher, academic administrator; BSc, U. Ill. at Chgo., 2000; MBA, Ill. Inst. Tech., 2001. Pres. The Engaged Enterprise, Chgo., 2004—; dir. Inst. Engaged Bus. Rsch., Chgo., 2004—. Office Phone: 312-829-8447. Personal E-mail: desouza@engagedenterprise.com.

DESOUZA, KEVIN CLYDE, application developer; BSc with dist. in acctg., info. decision, U. Ill., 2000; MBA, Stuart Grad. Sch. of Bus., Ill. Inst. of Tech., 2001. Software engr. CCC Info. Services, Chicago, Ill., 1998—2001. Contbr. articles various profl. jours. and papers. Office: Engaged Enterprise Ste 1 1349 W 16th St Chicago IL 60608 E-mail: desouza@engagedenterprise.com.

DE SOUZA, MARCELA, language educator; arrived in U.S., 1995; BA in English and Edn., U. Nacional Mar del Plata, Buenos Aires, 1994; MA Edn. in Curriculum Devel., Chapman U., 2000; MA Edn. in Cultural Perspectives, U. Calif., Santa Barbara, 2004. Cert. tchr. Calif., bilingual cross-cultural lang. and acad. devel. ESL tchr. El Sausal Mid. Sch., Salinas, Calif., 1995—2002, Santa Barbara (Calif.) City Coll., 2004—; tchg. asst. U. Calif., Santa Barbara, 2003—05. Nominee Outstanding Tchg. Asst. award, U. Calif., Santa Barbara, 2005. Mem.: Calif. TESOL, Am. Ednl. Rsch. Assn.

DESPINS, LUC, lawyer; b. 1960; LLL, U. Ottawa, 1981, LLB, 1982; LLM, Harvard Law Sch., 1985. Bar: Quebec 1983, NY 1986, US Dist. Ct., So. Dist. NY 1987, US Ct. Appeals, Second Circuit 1993, US Dist. Ct., No. Dist. NY 1996, US Ct. Appeals, Third Circuit 2001. Assoc. Kirkland & Ellis; ptnr. & co-chmn. Fin. Restructuring Group Milbank, Tweed, Hadley & McCloy LLP, 1999—. Named one of Top 45 Lawyers in Country Under 45, Am. Lawyer Mag., 2003. Office: Milbank Tweed Hadley & McCloy LLP 1 Chase Manhattan Plaza New York NY 10005-1413 Office Phone: 212-530-5660. Office Fax: 212-530-5219. Business E-Mail: ldespins@milbank.com.

DESPOMMIER, DICKSON DONALD, microbiology educator, parasitologist; b. New Orleans, June 5, 1940; s. Roland Medd and Beverly (Wood) D.; children— Bruce, Bradley BS, Fairleigh Dickinson U., 1962; MS, Columbia U., 1964; PhD, U. Notre Dame, 1967. Postdoctoral fellow Rockefeller U., 1967-71; Asst. prof. pub. health Columbia U., N.Y.C., 1971-75, assoc. prof., 1975-77, prof. pub. health and microbiology, 1982—. Cons. NIH, 1980-84, Gen. Food Corp., 1976, Cordis Corp., 1973-74, Bionetics Rsch. Inc., 1986-89, Eco-Chem, Inc., 1993; Theobald Smith lectr. 1993; pres. Apple Trees Prodns., LLC, N.Y.C. Author: Parasitic Diseases, 4th edit., 2000, Parasite Life Cycles, 1988, West Nile Story, 2001. Bd. dirs., chmn. edn. com. Catskill Flyfishing Ctr. and Mus., 1994—, dir., 1994—. Named Tchr. of Yr. Columbia U., 1980, 81, 83, 84; recipient Career Devel. award Nat. Inst. A.I.D., 1971-75, Disting. Tchr. award Med. Coll. Ohio, 1980, Deans' Disting. Tchr. award Columbia U., 1989, Golden Apple Tchr. of Yr. award Am. Med. Students Assn., 2003. Mem. AAAS, Am. Soc. Parasitologists, Am. Soc. Tropical Medicine and Hygiene, Harvey Soc., N.Y. Soc. Tropical Medicine (pres. 1980), Internat. Commn. on Trichinellosis. Clubs: Trout Unltd. (bd. dirs. 1976-78), Salmagundi Club, Aglers Club. Office: Dept Environ Health Scis Columbia U 60 Haven Ave Rm 100 New York NY 10032 Office Phone: 212-781-6670. Business E-Mail: ddd1@columbia.edu.

D'ESPOSITO, JULIAN C., JR., lawyer; b. NYC, Aug. 6, 1944; BS, Loyola U., 1966; JD cum laude, Northwestern U., 1969. Bar: Ill. 1969, U.S. Dist. Ct. (no. dist.) 1969. With Ross, Hardies, O'Keefe, Babcock & Parsons, 1970—76, ptnr., 1976; counsel to Gov. Ill., 1977-81; ptnr. Isham, Lincoln & Beale, 1981—87, Mayer, Brown, Rowe & Maw, 1988—, ptnr. in charge Chgo. office, 2002—. Chmn. Winnetka Plan Commn., 1985-89; mem. Ill. Med. Ctr. Commn., 1987-94; dir. Ill. Capital Devel. Bd., 1994-95, Chgo. Ctrl. Area Com., 2004-; chmn. Ill. State Toll Hwy. Authority, 1995-99. Co-editor-in-chief Jour. Criminal Law, Criminology & Police Sci., Northwestern U., 1968-69. Mem. ABA, Nat. Assn. Bond Lawyers. Office: Mayer Brown Rowe & Maw LLP 71 S Wacker Dr Chicago IL 60606

DESPRES, LEO ARTHUR, sociologist, anthropologist, educator, academic administrator; b. Lebanon, N.H., Mar. 29, 1932; s. Leo Arthur and Madeline (Bedford) D.; m. Loretta A. LaBarre, Aug. 22, 1953; children— Christine, Michelle, Denise, Mary Louise, Renee. BA, U. Notre Dame, 1954, MA, 1956; PhD, Ohio State U., 1960. Research assoc. Columbia Psychiat. Inst. and Hosp., 1957-60; postdoctoral fellow Social Sci. Research Council, Guyana, 1960-61; asst. prof. Ohio Wesleyan U., 1961-63; faculty Case Western Res. U., Cleve., 1963-74, prof. anthropology, 1967-74, chmn. dept., 1968-74; prof. sociology, anthropology U. Notre Dame, Ind., 1974-97, chmn. dept., 1974-80, fellow Kellogg Inst. Internat. Studies, 1982—, prof. emeritus, 1997—. Cons. in field. Author: Cultural Pluralism and Nationalist Politics in British Guyana, 1968; editor: Ethnicity and Resource Competition in Plural Societies, 1975, Manaus: Social Life and Work in Brazil's Free Trade Zone, 1991. Fulbright scholar, U. Guyana, 1970—71, Brazil, 1986, rsch. grantee, NSF, 1984. Mem. Am. Anthrop. Assn., Am. Ethnol. Soc., Latin Am. Studies Assn., Cen. States Anthrop. Soc. (pres. 1976-77), AAUP. Office: U Notre Dame Dept Anthropology Notre Dame IN 46556 Home: PO Box 6752 South Bend IN 46660-6752 Business E-mail: ldespres@nd.edu.

DESPRES, LEON MATHIS, lawyer, former city official; b. Chgo., Feb. 2, 1908; s. Samuel and Henrietta (Rubovits) D.; m. Marian Alschuler, Sept. 10, 1931; children— Linda Baskin, Robert Leon. PhB, U. Chgo., 1927, JD, 1929; DLitt, Columbia Coll., 1990, U. Ill., 2000. Bar: Ill. 1929. Ptnr. Despres, Schwartz and Geoghegan, Chgo.; trial examiner NLRB, Chgo., 1935-37; instr. U. Chgo., 1936, U. Wis., summers 1946-49; alderman 5th Ward Chgo. City Council, 1955-75, parliamentarian, 1979-87. Author: Challenging the Daley Machine, 2005. Mem. Chgo. Plan Commn., 1979-89. Mem. Am., Ill., Chgo. bar. assns., Chgo. Council Lawyers, Order of Coif, Phi Beta Kappa. Home: 5830 S Stony Island Ave Apt 10A Chicago IL 60637-2024 Office: 77 W Washington St Chicago IL 60602-2801 E-mail: DSG777@aol.com.

DESPRIET, JOHN G., lawyer; b. Kortrijk, Belgium, Aug. 12, 1949; BS with honors, U. Fla., 1971, JD with honors, 1978; MBA, U. Utah, 1976. Bar: Ga. 1979, Fla. 1979. Mem. Smith, Gambrell & Russell, Atlanta. Sr. student editor U. Fla. Law Review, 1978. Capt. USAF, 1971-76. Mem. State Bar Ga., Fla. Bar. Office: Smith Gambrell & Russell 1230 Peachtree St NE Ste 3100 Atlanta GA 30309-3592

DESROSIERS, APRYLLE LYNN, director, consultant; b. Cheverly, Md., Apr. 4, 1955; d. Arthur Herrmann and Marjorie de Cuba; m. Michael Wakefield, Oct. 16, 1976 (div. Sept. 1993); children: Travis Wakefield, Tucker B. Wakefield; m. Reed Barry Desrosiers, Feb. 19, 1995. AA in Chem. Dependency, BS in Health, Keene State Coll., 1983, MEd in Curriculum and Instrn., 1990, postgrad. Cert. health edn. N.H., trainer emergency mgmt. preparedness Fed. Emergency Mgmt. Agy., childbirth edn. Internat. Childbirth Edn. Assn. Health and substance abuse educator Greenfield (Mass.) Sch. Dist., 1987-92; substance abuse prevention educator Keene (N.H.) Sch. Dist., 1992-96; safe schs. coord. Manchester (N.H.) Sch. Dist., 1996—. Tng. family and peer mediation Franklin County Mediation Svcs., Greenfield; tng. advanced peer mediation and violence intervention program N.Mex. Inst. Dispute Resolution; tng. orgnl. conflict mgmt. Woodbury (Vt.) Inst. Dispute Resolution; tng. marital mediation Alternatives, Keene. Musician: (albums) Bits and Pieces, 1997, Into the Winter's Night, 1999, A Little Renaissance and Baroque and Romantic, 2003. Mem.: ASCD, N.H. Mediators Assn. (v.p. 1999—2000, pres. 2000—01, Exemplary Work in Conflict Resolution award 1997), Educators Social Responsibility. Democrat. Avocations: exercising, swimming, running, reading, weaving. Home: 64 Cove Woods Rd Munsonville NH 03457 Office: Manchester Pub Sch Dist 530 S Porter St Manchester NH 03103-3198 E-mail: aprylled@hotmail.com.

DESROSIERS, MICHELE L., curator; b. Carthage, N.Y., Mar. 9, 1953; d. Russell and Geraldine Ethel Desrosiers; children: Eric Travis Rattan, Kristina Lynn Rattan Champ. AA, Jefferson C.C., Watertown, N.Y., 1991; BA, SUNY, Oswego, 1993; M of Human Rels., U. Okla., 1996. Archives assoc. Graceland Divsn., Memphis, 1998—2000; collections mgr. U. Miss., Oxford, 2000—01; curator Umatilla County Hist. Soc., Pendleton, Oreg., 2001—02; program dir. Ct. Appointed Spl. Advs. of Jefferson County, Watertown, NY, 2003—04; support and devel. staff Big Bros., Big Sisters of No. N.Y., Watertown, 2004—05; collections asst. Geneva Hist. Soc., NY, 2004—05. Presenter in field. Avocations: reading, writing fiction. Home: 4 High St Carthage NY 13619

DESSAUER, CARIN, journalist; b. Pottstown, Pa., Dec. 31, 1963; d. Ralph and Margot (Abrams) D.; m. Marc Richard Engel, May 29, 1988. BA cum laude, Bucknell U., 1985; postgrad., George Washington U., 1987. Reporter The Polit. Report, Washington, 1986-87; off-air reporter ABC News Polit. Unit, Washington, 1988; assoc. editor Congl. Quarterly's Politics in Am., Washington, 1989; contbg. editor Campaigns and Elections mag., Washington, 1989-91; head Washington polit. unit Cable News Network, 1990-91; assoc. polit. dir. CNN, Washington, 1991-95, dep. pol. dir., 1995-98; election dir. CNN website, Washington, 1998-99, exec. editor Washington and election dir., 1999—; prof. Sch. Media and Pub. Affairs George Washington U., Washington, 2001—02; CONS., 2002—. Lectr. in field; spkr. in field; co-chmn. Bus. and Profl. Women's Divsn. United Jewish Fedn., Washington, 1997—99, mem. exec. coun., 1999—2002, co-chmn. Bus. and Entrepreneur's Divsn., 2002—03, bd. dir., mem. cabinet Nat. Young Leadership, 2001—; bd. trustees adv. com. comms. and mktg. Bucknell U., 2001—; mem. adv. bd. The Media Ctr. Am. Press Inst., 2002—. Co-author: (monograph) Running to Win, 1988, Society Online: The Internet in Context, 2003. Co-chair UJA Women's Bus. and Profl. Divsn., D.C. chpt., bd. dirs., cabinet, 1997=99, exec. com., 1994-97; mem. exec. coun. USA Fedn. Washington, 1999—; active alumnus Make A Wish Found., New Endeavors by Women. Mem. Phi Beta Kappa. Avocations: design, exercise, art, theater, photography, travel.

DESSEM, R. LAWRENCE, dean, law educator; b. Berea, Ohio, May 16, 1951; s. Ralph Eugene and Jane Elizabeth (Brightbill) D.; m. Beth Ann Taylor, May 20, 1973; children: Matthew, Lindsay, Emily. BA, Macalester Coll., 1973; JD, Harvard U., 1976. Bar: Ohio 1976, D.C. 1979, Tenn. 1985, Mo., 2002. Law clk. to presiding judge U.S. Dist. Ct. (no. dist.) Ohio, Cleve., 1976-78; asst. gen. counsel NEA, Washington, 1978-80; trial atty. civil div. U.S. Dept. Justice, Washington, 1980-84, sr. trial counsel, 1984-85; assoc. prof. law coll. of law U. Tenn., Knoxville, 1985-92, prof. law coll. of law, 1992-95, assoc. dean, 1993-95; dean Mercer U., Macon, Ga., 1995—2002; dean & prof. law U. Mo.-Columbia, Sch. Law, 2002—. Mem. faculty Legal Edn. Inst., U.S. Dept. Justice, San Francisco, 1985, Nat. Inst. for Trial Adv., Chgo., 1987-90; reporter Adv. Group on Litigation Cost and Delay, Tenn., 1991-95; mem. Tenn. Supreme Ct. Commn. on Dispute Resolution, 1992-94. Author: Pretrial Litigation, 1991, 2d edit., 1996, 3d edit. 2001, Pretrial Litigation in a Nutshell, 3d edit. 2001; contbr. articles to profl. jours. Nat. Merit scholar 1969. Fellow Am. Bar Found., Lawyer's Found. of Ga.; mem. ABA (co-chair dean's workshop 1998-99), Tenn. Bar Found., Am. Law Inst., Assn. Am. Law Schs. (mem. review com., chair, 2005—), Phi Beta Kappa. Office: U Mo 230 Hulston Hall Columbia MO 65211-4300 Office Phone: 573-882-3246. E-mail: DessemRL@missouri.edu.

DESSLER, ALEXANDER JACK, astrophysicist, educator; b. San Francisco, Oct. 21, 1928; s. David Alexander and Julia (Shapiro) D.; m. Lorraine Hudek, Apr. 18, 1952; children: Pauline Karen, David Alexander, Valerie Jan, Andrew Emory. BS, Calif. Inst. Tech., 1952; PhD, Duke U., 1956. Sect. head Lockheed Missiles & Space Co., 1956-62; prof. Grad. Rsch. Ctr., Dallas, 1962-63, prof. space physics and astronomy, 1963-82, 86-93; chmn. dept. Rice U., Houston, 1963-69, 79-82, 87-92, campus bus. mgr., 1974-76; dir. space sci. lab. MSFC NASA, Huntsville, Ala., 1982-86; sr. rsch. scientist Lunar and Planetary Lab. U. Ariz., Tucson, 1993—. Sci. adviser Nat. Aeros. and Space Coun., 1969-70; pres. Univs. Space Rsch. Assn., 1975-81. Editor Jour. Geophys. Rsch., 1965-69, Revs. of Geophysics, 1969-74, The John Wiley Space Sci. Text Series, 1968-76, Geophys. Rsch. Letters, 1986-89, Atmospheric and Space Sci. Series, 1986—; adv. bd.: Planetary and Space Sci., 1963-92; assoc. editor Space Solar Power Rev., 1980-85. Served with USN, 1946-48. Recipient Outstanding Young Scientist award Tex. Wing Air Force Assn., 1964, medal for contbns. to internat. geophysics Soviet Geophys. Com., 1984, Stellar award for acad. devel., Rotary Nat., 1988. Fellow AAAS, Am. Geophys. Union (Macelwane award 1963, John Adam Fleming medal 1993, William Kaula award for publs. 2003); mem. Am. Astron. Soc., Internat. Assn. Geomagnetism and Aeronomy (v.p. 1979-83), Royal Swedish Acad. Scis. (fgn.), Cosmos Club (Washington). Home: 1434 E Seneca St Tucson AZ 85719-3645 Office: Univ Ariz Lunar Planetary Lab Sonett Bldg Tucson AZ 85721-0063 Business E-Mail: dessler@arizona.edu.

DESSOYE, FRANCIS JOSEPH, special education educator; b. Pittston, Pa., Jan. 4, 1952; s. Francis Joseph and Mary Elizabeth Dessoye; m. Angela C. Alba, June 28, 1975; 1 child, Amy Elizabeth. BS in Elem. Edn. with Endorsement in Spl. Edn., King's Coll., Wilkes Barre, PA, 1975; MS in Rehab. Counseling, U. Scranton, 1986. Instrnl. II cert. in elem. and spl. edn. Pa., cert. in cooperative edn. Pa. Spl. edn. tchr., phys. support class Luzerne Intermediate Unit 18, Kingston, Pa., 1976—2000, work study coord., 2000—. New membership chmn. Wyo. (Pa.) Area Fed. Credit Union, 1985—2005. Mem.: NEA, Assn. Career and Tech. Edn., Pa. Coop. Edn. Assn., Pa. Assn. Vocat. Spl. Needs Pers., Nat. Assn. Vocat. Spl. Needs Pers., Luzerne Intermediate Unit 18 Edn. Assn., Pa. State Edn. Assn. Democrat. Roman Catholic. Avocations: golf, fishing, travel. Home: 123 Front St Pittston PA 18640 Office: Luzerne Intermediate Unit 18 368 Tioga Ave Kingston PA 18704 Office Phone: 570-825-0639. Office Fax: 570-287-5721. Personal E-mail: fdessoye@liu18.org.

DESTEFANO, JENNIFER LYNN, veterinarian; b. Bridgeport, Conn., June 27, 1972; d. Richard and Paula DeStefano; m. Russell Dean Teeters, Feb. 16, 2002; children: Isaiah Teeters, Isabella Teeters. BSc, Messiah Coll., Grantham, Pa., 1994; DVM, U. Fla., Gainesville, 1998. Assoc. veterinarian Banfield, Clearwater, Fla., 1998—2002, Vet. Ctrs. Am.-Antech, Oldsmar, Fla., 2002—03; med. dir. VCA-Antech, St. Petersburg, 2003—. State veterinarian Tampa Bay Downs, Fla., 1999—2002. Mem.: Am. Vet. Med. Assn. Office: VCA-Antech St Petersburg Animal Hosp 3295 62d Ave N Saint Petersburg FL 33702

DESTEFANO, L. TIMOTHY, music educator, conductor; b. Canton, Ohio, July 28, 1939; s. James John and Lucille Rita (Catalano) DeStefano; m. Elizabeth Anne French, July 19, 1974; children: Jennifer Leigh, Kathleen Elizabeth, Timothy James. BS in Pub. Sch. Music, Kent State U., 1961, MEd in Adminstrn., 1969. Cert. K-12 music educator Ohio. H.s. band dir., instrumental music grades 5-12 W. Br. Local, Beloit, Ohio, 1961—73, N.W. Local, Canal Fulton, Ohio, 1973—74, Jackson Local, Massillon, Ohio, 1974—95; asst. prof. music, band dir. Mt. Union Coll., Alliance, Ohio, 1995—. Dept. head music curriculum K-12 Jackson Local, Massillon, 1974—95, others, 1961—73; participant Internat. Jazz Festival, Montrex, Switzerland, 1972—73. Author: (textbooks) Fundamentals of Brass, Music Methods, Basic Rhythms from Scratch; contbr. articles to profl. jours. Mem. levy com. W. Br., Jackson, 1961—95. Named Great Tchr., Mt. Union Coll., 2004; named to Hall Fame, We. Br. Local, 2004, Wall Fame, Jackson Local, 2005. Mem.: Am. School Band Dirs. Assn. (state chmn., natl. dues chmn.), Ohio Music Educators (adjudicator 1973—98), Music Educators Nat. Assn., Kappa Kappa Psi (historian), Pi Kappa Lambda, Phi Beta Mu. Achievements include the distinction of being 1 of 4 high school bands in the world to perform in all national bowl parades and the International Jazz Festival in Switzerland. Avocations: yard work, civil war, old cars. Office: Mt Union Coll 1972 Clark Ave Alliance OH 44601

DESTLER, I. M(AC), political scientist, foreign policy writer; b. Statesboro, Ga., Aug. 21, 1939; s. Chester McArthur and Katharine (Hardesty) D.; m. Harriett Kirkham Parsons, July 27, 1968; children: Mark Dodson, Katharine Elizabeth. BA magna cum laude, Harvard U., 1961; MPA, Princeton U., 1965, PhD, 1971. Peace Corps vol. U. Nigeria, Nsukka, 1961-63; asst. Senator Walter Mondale Washington, 1965-67; staff assoc. Pres.'s Task Force on Govt. Orgn., Washington, 1967; analyst, acting coord. for Asia Internat. Agrl. Devel. Svc., USDA, Washington, 1967-69; Internat. Affairs fellow Coun. Fgn. Rels., Washington, 1969-70; vis. lectr. Woodrow Wilson Sch., Princeton U., 1971-72; rsch. assoc. Brookings Inst., Washington, 1972-76, sr. fellow, 1976-77; sr. assoc. Carnegie Endowment for Internat. Peace, Washington, 1977-83; sr. fellow Inst. Internat. Econs., Washington, 1983-87; prof. Sch. Pub. Affairs U. Md., College Park, 1987—, acting dean, 1994-95, dir. Ctr. Internat. and Security Studies, 1991-99, dir. PhD program, 2000—; dir. Md. seminar in U.S. fgn. policymaking, 1987-95. Cons. U.S. Office Mgmt. and Budget, 1977, 79, U.S. Dept. State, 1976, 93, U.S. Agy. for Internat. Devel., Ctrl. Asia, 1999-2000; vis. prof. Internat. U. Japan (Urasa), spring, 1986; vis. fellow Inst. Internat. Econs., 1987—. Author: Presidents, Bureaucrats and Foreign Policy - The Politics of Organizational Reform, 1972, 74, (with others) Managing an Alliance - The Politics of U.S.-Japanese Relations, 1976, (with Fukui and Sato) The Textile Wrangle - Conflict in Japanese-American Relations, 1969-71, 1979, Making Foreign Economic Policy, 1980, (with Gelb and Lake) Our Own Worst Enemy: The Unmaking of American Foreign Policy, 1984, American Trade Politics, 1986 (Gladys M. Kammerer award Am. Polit. Sci. Assn. 1987), 4th edit., 2005, (with Odell) Anti-Protection: Changing Forces in U.S. Trade Politics, 1987, (with Henning) Dollar Politics: Exchange Rate Policy Making in the United States, 1989, The National Economic Council: A Work in Progress, 1996, Renewing Fast-Track Legislation, 1997, (with Kull) Misreading the Public: The Myth of a New Isolationism, 1999, (with Balint) The New Politics of American Trade, 1999, (with others) Protecting the American Homeland, 2002, 03; co-editor: Coping with U.S.-Japanese Economic Conflicts, 1982, Beyond the Beltway: Engaging the Public in U.S. Foreign Policy, 1994. Mem. Coun. Fgn. Rels., Am. Polit. Sci. Assn., Nat. Acad. Pub. Adminstrn. Democrat. Presbyterian. Home: 701 River Bend Rd Great Falls VA 22066-2712 Office: U Md Sch Pub Affairs College Park MD 20742-1811 Office Phone: 301-405-6357. E-mail: mdestler@umd.edu.

DESTLER, WILLIAM W., academic administrator; BS, Stevens Inst. Tech., 1968; PhD, Cornell U., 1972. Former chair dept. elec. engring. U. Md., College Park, former dean sch. engring., former v.p. rsch., former dean grad. sch., sr. v.p. acad. affairs and provost. Contbr. numerous articles to profl. jours. Recipient award for excellence in engring. edn. for Mid-Atlantic states, AT&T, 1989. Fellow: IEEE, Am. Phys. Soc. Office: U Md 1119 Main Adminstrn Bldg College Park MD 20742-5031 Office Phone: 301-405-1603. E-mail: wdestler@umd.edu.

DE SYON, GUILLAUME PAUL SAM, history educator; b. Paris, Mar. 2, 1966; came to U.S., 1994; s. Michel and Joelle Suzanne Juliette (Carpano) de S.; m. Maria Dee Mitchell, Aug. 27, 1994. BA, Tufts U., 1987; MA, George Washington U., 1989; PhD, Boston U., 1994. Contbg. editor Einstein Papers Project, Boston, 1992-94; asst. prof. history Albright Coll., Reading, Pa., 1995-2001, assoc. prof., 2001—. Dir. Johnson Ctr. for Interdisciplinary Studies, Reading, 1997-98, 99-2000; chmn. faculty Albright Coll., Reading, Pa., 2004—. Author: Zeppelin! Germany and the Airship, 2001; contbg. editor: Collected Papers of Albert Einstein Vol. 8: Correspondence 1914-1918, 1998, One Hundred Years of Motoring Progress, 2005. With Swiss Air Force, 1984. Mem. Nat. Coun. for History Edn., Royal Aeronautical Soc., Soc. for the History of Tech., Am. Hist. Assn. Office: Albright Coll 13th & Bern Sts Reading PA 19612-5234

DETELS, ROGER, epidemiologist, retired dean; b. Bklyn., Oct. 14, 1936; s. Martin P. and Mary J. (Crooker) D.; m. Mary M. Doud, Sept. 14, 1963; children: Martin, Edward. BA, Harvard U., 1958; MD, NYU, 1962; MS in Preventive Medicine, U. Wash., 1966. Diplomate Am. Bd. Preventive Medicine. Intern U. Calif. Gen. Hosp., San Francisco, 1962-63; resident U. Wash., Seattle, 1963-66; med. officer, epidemiologist Nat. Inst. Neurol. Diseases, Bethesda, Md., 1969-71; assoc. prof. epidemiology Sch. Pub. Health UCLA, 1971-73, prof. Sch. Pub. Health, 1973—, dean, 1980-85, head divsn. epidemiology Sch. Pub. Health, 1972-80, chair, dept. epidemiology, 2001—05. Guest lectr. various univs., profl. confs. and med. orgns., 1969—; sci. adv. com. Am. Found AIDS Rsch.; dir. UCLA/Fogarty AIDS Internat. Tng. and Rsch. Program, 1988—, Tng. Program in Epidemiology of HIV/AIDS, 1995—; cons. Ministries of Health, Thailand, Myanmar, Philippines, 1989, Global Program on AIDS, 1995, Singapore, 1996, China, 2002—, WHO, 1999, U.S. AID, 1998, 99, 2000, 01, Cambodia, 1998, 99, 2000, 02, 03, 04, UN Devel. Program, 2001, St. Thomas Med. Sch., London, 1993-94, Myanmar, 1997, UN Devel. Program, Myanmar, 2001; mem. Nat. Adv. Environ. Health Scis. Coun., 1990-94; com. to study transmission of HIV through blood products Inst. Medicine, 1994-95; external examiner Nat. U. Singapore, 1994, 2004. Editor: Oxford Textbook of Public Health, 1985, 2d edit. 1991, 3d edit., 1997, 4th edit., 2002; contbr. articles to profl. jours. Lt. comdr. M.C. USN, 1966-69. Grantee in field. Fellow AAAS, Am. Coll. Preventive Medicine, Am. Coll. Epidemiology (coun. 1987-89), Faculty Pub. Health Medicine Royal Coll. Physicians of U.K. (hon.); mem. Am. Epidemiol. Soc., Soc. Epidemiologic Rsch. (pres. 1977-78), Assn. Tchrs. Preventive Medicine (chmn. essay com. 1969-75), APHA, Am. Assn. Cancer Edn. (membership com. 1978-85), Internat. Epidemiol. Assn. (exec. com. 1984-99, treas. 1984-90, pres. 1990-93), Assn. Schs. Pub. Health (sec.-treas. 1980-85), Sigma Xi, Delta Omega. Office: UCLA Dept Epidemiology Ctr for Health Scis Box 951772 Los Angeles CA 90095-1772 Office Fax: 310-206-6039. Business E-Mail: detels@ucla.edu.

DETER, RUSSELL LEE, II, obstetrical ultrasonographer; b. Dallas, Jan. 14, 1936; s. Russell Lee and Virginia (Peden) D.; m. Susan Tipery, Dec. 14, 1981. BS, Baylor U., Waco, Tex., 1958; MS, MD, Baylor U., Houston, 1963. Postdoctoral fellow Rockefeller U., N.Y.C., 1964-66, U. Louvain, Belgium, 1966-67; asst. prof. anatomy Baylor Coll. Medicine, Houston, 1967-72, asst. prof. cell biology, 1973—, asst. prof. ob-gyn., 1975-80, dir. obstet. ultrasonography, 1977-95, assoc. prof. ob-gyn., 1981-84, prof., 1985—. Med. dir. outpatient ultrasound program Harris County Hosp. Dist., Houston, 1986—. Co-author: Quantitative Obstetrical Ultrasonography, 1986; editor-in-chief Jour. Clin. Ultrasound, 1982-96; contbr. articles to profl. jours., chpts. to books. Recipient rsch. grants Frankel Found., 1979-84, March of Dimes, 1979-83, 84-87, Joseph H. Holmes award Jour. Clin. Ultrasound, 1987. Mem. ACOG, Am. Inst. Ultrasound in Medicine (assoc.), Soc. Maternal-Fetal Medicine (assoc.), Internat. Soc. Ultrasound in Ob-Gyn. Home: 1721 Hawthorne St Houston TX 77098-1605 Office: Baylor Coll Medicine 1 Baylor Plz Houston TX 77030-3411 Office Phone: 713-524-2877. E-mail: russelld@bcm.tmc.edu.

DETERDING, PAUL E., pastor; b. Jacksonville, Ill., Feb. 19, 1953; s. George H and Velda F Deterding; m. Donna Marie Janosov, Feb. 4, 1989; children: Stephen Michael, Andrew Joseph, Jason Daniel. ThD, Concordia Sem., St. Louis, 1981. Pastor Our Savior Luth. Ch., Satellite Beach, Fla., 1981—94, Christ Luth. Ch., Jackson, Miss., 1994—2000, Bethlehem Luth. Ch., Carson City, Nev., 2000—. Bd. dirs. Sierra Luth. H.S., Minden, Nev., 2002—. Author: (Biblical commentary) Colossians, 2003, (Bible study guide) Daniel: Encouragement for Faith, 1996; contbr. articles to profl. jours. Lutheran. Avocations: family, reading, sports. Office: Bethlehem Luth Ch 1837 Mountain St Carson City NV 89703 Business E-Mail: bethlehempastor@blcs.org.

DETERMAN, DON PAUL, lawyer; b. Sacramento, Nov. 9, 1938; s. Charles Kenneth and Winnifred Ann D. BS, U. Calif., 1961, Sacramento State, 1963; JD, Calif. Western, 1967. Bar: Calif. 1968, U.S. Cir. Ct. (9th cir.) 1970, U.S. Tax. Ct. 1973; CPA. Acct. Touche, Ross & Co., San Diego, 1966-67; counsel Irvin Kahn Orgn., San Diego, 1967-72; treas. U.S. Elevator, San Diego, 1972; v.p., counsel Shelterl Island Properties, San Diego, 1973-74; v.p. Vidcom, San Diego, 1975-90; pvt. practice San Diego, 1990—. Dir. Sail Bay Shores, San Diego, 1975-80. Author: Grand Larceny by Power, 1970, What is Gambling?, 1973. Dir. Rep. Advocates, San Diego, 1970-80. With USAFR, 1961-67. Recipient Bank of Am. award, 1958. Mem. Tau Kappa Epsilon (pres. 1964-65). Roman Catholic. Avocations: stamp collecting/philately, tennis, golf, sports cards. Home: 3920 Riviera Dr Apt R San Diego CA 92109-5838

DETERMAN, JOHN DAVID, lawyer; b. Mitchell, S.D., Feb. 18, 1933; s. Alred John and Olive Gertrude (Lovinger) D.; m. Gloria Esther Rivas, Nov. 15, 1980; children by previous marriage: James Taylor, Mark Sterling. BEE cum laude, U. So. Calif., 1955; LLD magna cum laude, UCLA, 1961. Electronics engr. Hughes Aircraft Co., L.A., 1955-60; sr. ptnr. Tuttle & Taylor, Inc., L.A., 1961-86; gen. counsel Provena Foods Inc., Chino, Calif., 1986-92, CEO, 1992-98, chmn. bd., 1992—2004. Founder Carl D. Spaeth Scholarship Fund, Stanford U. Law Sch., 1972; mem. nat. panel arbitrators Am. Arbitration Assn., L.A., 1962—, mem. adv. coun., 1982—, mem. nat. panel of mediators, 1986—, mem. large complex case panel of arbitrators, 1993—. Mem. Am. Coll. Constrn. Arbitrators (charter 1982—), Order of Coif, Eta Kappa Nu, Tau Beta Pi. Home: 25 S El Molino St Alhambra CA 91801-4102 Office: Provena Foods Inc 5010 Eucalyptus Ave Chino CA 91710-9216
Tolerate even intolerance but never cruelty.

DETERRA, SANDRA LEE SHIVERS, secondary school educator; b. Hattiesburg, Miss., Dec. 23, 1946; d. George Evan Shivers, Jr. and Zulma (Dubuisson) Shivers; m. Raymond James DeTerra, June 3, 1972; children: Andrea L., David J., Michael A. BS cum laude and spl. honors in Math., Miss. U. for Women, 1968; MA, La. State U., 1969. Secondary tchrs. lic. math. Alaska. Math. tchr. Natchez-Adams County H.S., Natchez, Miss., 1969—70, Gulfport (Miss.) Pub. Schs., 1974; math. instr. Miss. Gulf Coast C.C., Gulfport, 1970—71, 1974—78; adj. math. tchr. Ctrl. Tex. C.C., Ft. Richardson, Ark., 1978—84, Chapman Coll., Elmendorf AFB, Alaska, 1978—84, Panama City (Fla.) C.C., 1984—85, U. Alaska, Anchorage, 1978—84, 1986—; math. tchr. 9-12 Bartlett H.S., Anchorage, 2001—. Mem. St. Andrew Cath. Ch., Eagle River. Mem.: NEA, Math. Assn. Am., Anchorage Edn. Assn., Alaska Fedn. Tchrs., Nat. Coun. Tchrs. Math. Avocations: bowling, camping, church activities. Home: 9550 Dinaaka Dr Eagle River AK 99577-8519 Office: Bartlett High Sch 25-500 N Muldoon Anchorage AK 99506 Business E-Mail: deterra_sandra@asdk12.org. E-mail: deterrasandra@aol.com.

DETERS, THOMAS C., publishing executive, educator; BA in Sociology, U. Mich., 1982; degree with hons. in Human Biology, Nat. Coll. Chiropractic, 1986, DSc with hons. in Chiropractic, 1984. Assoc. pub. Men's Pub. Group of Weider Pubs., Inc., 1997, Flex; group publisher, editor-in-chief Muscle and Fitness mag., 2002—03; exec. v.p. Am. Media Inc., 2003—; pub. dir. WeiderPubs. Enthusiast Group, Woodland Hills, Calif., 2003—. Cons. to many profl. athletes. Appeared numerous TV segments and videos; contbr. various articles; author: books; contbr. video cassettes. Dir. edn. Muscle and Fitness Tng. Camp, L.A. Mem.: Internat. Chiropractors Assn. (life Lifetime Achievement award, 1st ever lifetime membership award Coun. on Fitness and Sports Health Sci.). Office: Muscle and Fitness Mag 21100 Erwin St Woodland Hills CA 91367 also: Weider Publications Inc PO Box 864 Woodland Hills CA 91365-0864

DETERT, MIRIAM ANNE, chemical analyst; b. San Diego, Calif., Sept. 16, 1925; d. George Bernard and Margaret Theresa Zita (Lohre) D. BS, Dominican Coll., San Rafael, Calif., 1947. Chem. analyst Shell Devel. Co., Emeryville, Calif., 1947-72, Houston, 1972-86. Photo participant Wax Rsch.: Quest, 1981; exhibited etchings Sight and Insight Art Studio, Mill Valley, Calif., 2002; contbr. poetry to books including The International Library of Poetry - Best Poems of the 90's, Spirit of the Age, The Nightfall of Diamonds, The Long and Winding Road, Through Oceans of Time. Vol. Falkirk Cultural Ctr., San Rafael, 1987-91, M.D. Anderson Tumor Inst., Houston, 1978-86, Rep. Party, San Rafael, 1990, 94; mem. Jewish Comm. Ctr. Recipient Disting. Alumni award Dominican Coll., 1994. Mem. Marin Geneal. Soc. Republican. Roman Catholic. Avocations: etching, painting, genealogy, swimming. Personal E-mail: mdetert@ix.netcom.com.

DETHERO, J. HAMBRIGHT, banker; b. Chattanooga, Jan. 2, 1932; s. Jacob Hambright and Rosalie Frances (Gasser) D.; m. Charlotte Nixon Lee, Sept. 19, 1959; children: Dinah Lee, Charles Drew. BS in Bus. Adminstrn., U. Fla., 1953; BFT, Am. Grad. Sch. Internat. Mgmt., Phoenix, 1958. With Citibank, N.Y.C., P.R., Caracas, Venezuela, San Francisco, 1958-69; mgr. First Nat. City Bank (Internat.), San Francisco, until 1969; v.p. internat. div. Crocker Nat. Bank, San Francisco, 1969-75; sr. v.p. London, 1976-80, San Francisco, 1980-84, Bank America World Trade Corp., San Francisco, 1984-85; 1st v.p. Security Pacific Nat. Bank, Los Angeles, 1986-87; regional mgr. Calif. Export Fin. Office, Calif. State World Trade Commn., San Francisco, 1988-93; sr. v.p. Comml. Bank of San Francisco, 1994-98. Internat. bus. cons., instr., 1998—; adj. prof. Grad. Sch. Bus., St. Mary's Coll., Moraga, Calif., 1988-2000, John F. Kennedy U., Walnut Creek, Calif., 1997-2000. Author: Exporting Guide for California, 1993, 2d edit., 1999. Bd. dirs. Calif. Coun. Internat. Trade, 1972-77, 82-98, pres., 1974-76; trustee World Affairs Coun. No. Calif., 1971-77, 88-93; chmn. dist. Export Coun. No. Calif., 1983-93; dir. Internat. Diplomacy Coun., San Francisco, 1995-2002, treas., 1997-2000, pres., 2000-01; mem. San Francisco Host Com., 2000-02, chair, past pres. Com., 2005-. Recipient Export Citizen of the Year award No. Calif. Export Coun./San Francisco Bus. Times, 1996. Home and Office: 694 Old Jonas Hill Rd Lafayette CA 94549-5214 Personal E-mail: hamdethero@aol.com.

DETHLOFF, HENRY CLAY, historian, educator; b. New Orleans, Aug. 10, 1934; s. Carl Curt and Camelia (Jordan) Dethloff; m. Myrtle Anne Elliott, Aug. 27, 1961; children: Clay, Carl. BA, U. Tex., Austin, 1956; MA, Northwestern State U., Natchitoches, La., 1960; PhD, U. Mo., Columbia, 1964. From instr. to assoc. prof. history U. So. La., 1962—66, assoc. prof., 1966—69; from mem. faculty to prof. emeritus Tex. A&M U., College Station, 1969—99, prof. emeritus history, 1999—. Author: (book) Our Louisiana Legacy, 1968, The Centennial History of Texas A&M University, 1976-1976, 1975, Americans and Free Enterprise, 1979, A History of the American Rice Industry 1685-1985, 1988, Suddenly, Tomorrow Came: A History of Johnson Space Center, 1993, The U.S. and the Global Economy, 1945-1995, 1997, A Bookmark: The Texas A&M University Press, 1999; co-author: A History of American Business, 1983, Timeless Heritage, A History of the Forest Service in the Southwest, 1988, Pattillo Higgins and the Search for Texas Oil, 1989, A Special Kind of Doctor: A History of Veterinary Medicine in Texas, 1991, Louisiana: A Study of Diveristy, 1998, Voyager's Grand Tour: To the Outer Planets and Beyond, 2003; co-editor: American Business History: Case Studies, 1987, Aerial Navigation, 1783-1903, 2003. Served to lt. (j.g.) USNR, 1956—58. Mem.: La. Hist. Assn., Tex. Hist. Assn., So. Hist. Assn., Econ. History Assn., Agrl. History Assn., Sigma Chi, Phi Alpha Theta, Phi Kappa Phi. Republican. Methodist. Home: 8709 Bent Tree Dr College Station TX 77845-5561

DETHOMAS, JOSEPH MICHAEL, former ambassador; b. Easton, Pa., June 1951; BA, MA, Pa. State U.; MPA, Harvard U.; Disting. Grad., Nat. War coll. Former dir. Office of European Union and Regioanl Affairs and Bur. of Polit.-Mil. Affairs; former prin. dep. asst. sec. of state Bureau of Nonproliferation US Dept. State, US amb. to Estonia, 2001—04. Recipient Meritorious Honor award for earthquake rescue work in Mexico, U.S. Dept. of State, numerous honor awards and citations.

DE THOUARS, VICTOR IVAN CHARLES, performance artist, educator; b. Pare'/kediri, East Java, Indonesia, Sept. 25, 1941; s. Marquis Henry Alexandre and Susanna de Thouars; m. Jane Fischer, May 7, 1999; children: Valerie, Vincent, Marcus, Daniel. Grad. Mechanical Engineer, THS, Netherlands, 1960. Sr. mech. engr. Cooper Industries, Sumter, SC, 1998—2000; founder, chief instr. VDT Acad., Bellflower, Calif., 2000—. Dir. VDT Acad., Bellflower, Calif., 2000—; prodr. VDT Comm., 2000—; internat. dir. Internat. Silat Fedn., 2000—. Author: Personal Automation, 1995 (Automation award, 1995), The System of Serak, 2001, Serak the Tsunami, 2001, Sera the Last Butterfly, 2002, The Treshold of the Tsunami, 2002; composer: (Songs) Softwind, 1965; prodr.: (Video) The Edges of Sera, 2001, The Art of Serak, 2002, Kuntao Mang Po, 2002, Pentjak Silat Soempat, 2002. Republican. Avocations: surfing, scuba diving, skiing, hunting. Home: PO Box 1663 Bellflower CA 90707-1663 Office: VDT Acad 17165 Bellflower Blvd Bellflower CA 90706 Personal E-mail: Lavaseur@aol.com. Business E-Mail: vdtacademy@aol.com.

DETJEN, DAVID WHEELER, lawyer; b. St. Louis, Jan. 25, 1948; s. Don Wheeler and Shirley (Pence) Detjen; m. Barbara Louise Morgan, Jan. 6, 1973; children: Andrea Marlene, Erika Alexandra. AB magna cum laude, Washington U., 1970, JD with honors, 1973; postgrad., Eberhard-Karls-Universitaet, Tuebingen, Germany, 1969—70. Bar: Mo. 1973, U.S. Ct. Appeals (8th cir.) 1976, U.S. Supreme Ct. 1976, N.Y. 1981. Law clk. to chief judge U.S. Ct. Appeals (8th cir.), St. Louis, 1973-75; assoc. Lewis, Rice, Tucker, Allen & Chubb, St. Louis, 1975-80, Walter, Conston, Alexander & Green, P.C., NYC, 1980-83; ptnr. Walter, Conston, Alexander & Green, NYC, 1983-2000, Alston & Bird LLP, NYC, 2001—, co-chmn. internat. practice group, 2001—04. Lectr. law Washington U., St. Louis, 1975—80; bd. dirs. Felix Schoeller Tech. Papers, Inc. Author: (book) Distributorship Agreements in the US, 1983, 2d edit., 1989, The Germans in Mo. 1900-1918: Prohibition, Neutrality and Assimilation, 1985, Licensing Tech. and Trademarks in the US, 1988, 1997, Establishing a US Joint Venture with a Fgn. Ptnr., 1988, 2d edit., 1989, 3d edit., 1993, US Joint Ventures with Internat. Partners, 2000. Sec. German Forum, N.Y.C., 1988—, bd. dirs., 1995—; co-pres. King-Merritt cmty. Assn., Greenwich, Conn., 1997—; mem. Am. Coun. Germany, N.Y.C., Atlantik-Bruecke, Berlin, St. Louis County Rep. Cen. Com., 1976—83, Representative Town Meeting, Greenwich, 2000—, vice-chmn. labor contracts com., 2002—; mem. nat. coun. Washington U. Law Sch., St. Louis, 1989—; trustee Washington U., 2004—, Am. Inst. Contemporary German Studies, Johns Hopkins U., 1999—, corp. sec., 2000—, vice chmn., 2004—. Recipient Disting. Alumnus award, Washington U. Law Sch., 1998, Regional Disting. Leadership award, Washington U., 2003. Mem.: ABA, Order of Coif, German Am. Law Assn., Assn. Bar City of NY, NY State Bar Assn. (exec. editor Internat. Law Practicum 1988—, mem. exec. com. internat. law and practice sect. 1999—, editor-in-chief Internat. Law Practicum 2004—, vice chmn. internat. law and practice sect. 2004—), German-Am. C. of C. (bd. dirs. 2003—), William G. Eliot Soc. Washington U. (N.Y. chmn. 1993—, nat. membership chair 2004—), German Am. Round Table, Deutscher Verein Club NYC (bd. dirs. 1994—97, 1999—2005, v.p., sec. 2000—03), Delta Phi Delta. Presbyterian. Office: Alston & Bird LLP 90 Park Ave Fl 14 New York NY 10016-1301 Fax: 212 210-9444. E-mail: ddetjen@alston.com.

DETMER, DON EUGENE, health informatics, management and policy researcher; b. Winfield, Kans., Feb. 3, 1939; s. Lawrence Oscar and Esther Beulah (McCormick) Detmer; m. Mary Helen McFerson, Aug. 26, 1961; children: Mary Catherine, Emily Anne. Student, U. Kans., 1957—59, U. Durham, 1959—60; MD, U. Kans., Kansas City, 1965; MA, U. Cambridge, 2002. Intern, then resident in surgery Johns Hopkins U., Balt., 1965—67; clin. assoc. surg. br. Nat. Heart Inst. NIH, Bethesda, Md., 1967—69; resident in surgery Duke U., Durham, NC, 1969—72; Global Cmty. Health fellow Dept. HEW, Inst. Medicine/NAS, Washington, 1972—73; prof. preventive medicine and surgery U. Wis., Madison, 1973—84; v.p. health scis., prof. surgery and med. info. U. Utah, Salt Lake City, 1984—88; univ. prof. health policy, prof. surgery and health evaluation scis. U. Va., Charlottesville, 1988—93, v.p., provost for health scis., 1988—96, sr. v.p., 1996—98, Louise Nurancy prof. health scis. policy, 1996—99, prof. emeritus, prof. med. edn., 1999—; Dennis Gillings prof. health mgmt. Cambridge U., 1999—2003; dir. Cambridge U. Health, 1999—2003; sr. assoc. Judge Inst. Mgmt. Cambridge U., 2004—; pres., CEO Am. Med. Informatics Assn., Bethesda, Md., 2004—. Mem. commn. on systemic interoperability U.S. Dept. HHS, Washington, 2004—; bd. dirs. MedBiquitious; cons. Hong Kong Hosp. Authority, Markle Found., N.Y.C., Australasian Coll. Surgeons, U. Algeria, Robert Wood Johnson Found., Princeton, NJ; vice chmn. China Med. Bd. N.Y., Inc., 2002—04; chmn. bd. healthcare svcs. Inst. Medicine, Washington, 1994—2000; chmn. nat. com. vital health stats. HHS, Washington, 1996—99; chmn. Blue Ridge Acad. Health Group, 1997—, co-chmn., 2002—; regent Nat. Libr. Medicine, NIH, Bethesda, Md., 1987—91; trustee Nuffield Trust, 2000—; bd. dirs., developer adminstrv. medicine U. Wis., Madison; membership com. chmn. sect. 12 Inst. Medicine, Washington, 2002—04; chair Nat. Libr. Medicine NIH, Bethesda, 1989—91; assoc. Nat. Acads., 2002; cons. in field; vis. prof. Chime U. Coll. London, 2005—. Contbr. articles on nat. health info. sys., compartment syndromes, health svcs. rsch. and policy to profl. jours. Chmn. pub. svc. com. bd. dirs. United Way, Salt Lake City, 1986—88, Charlottesville, 1992—97; with USPHS, 1967—69; pres. Peace Luth. Ch., 1996—99. Recipient Global Cmty. Health fellowship, HEW, 1972—73; fellow, Clare Hall, Cambridge U., 2000—. Fellow: ACS (vice chmn. com. allied health pers. 1989—90, chmn. 1990—94, internat. health com. 1996—2002), AAAS, Acad. Health, Am. Coll. Sports Medicine; mem.: Royal Soc. Medicine, Soc. Med. Adminstrs. (treas. 1997—2000), Am. Hosp. Assn. (chmn. coun. hosp. med. staffs 1984—87), Am. Acad. Physician Assts. (hon.), Inst. of Medicine of NAS, Assn. Acad. Health Ctrs. (bd. dirs. 1996—98), Am. Med. Informatics Assn. (bd. dirs. 1996—98, chair internat. com. 2004), Cosmos Club Washington, Alpha Omega Alpha. Lutheran. Avocations: fly fishing, painting, horseback riding, crafts, reading. Home: 5245 Browns Gap Tpke Crozet VA 22932-1613 Office Phone: 301-657-1291. Business E-Mail: detmer@virginia.edu.

DETOLLA, LOUIS JAMES, research scientist, veterinarian; b. Phila., Nov. 18, 1947; s. Louis James and Linda Liberatore DeTolla; m. Setsu Nakai, June 28, 1975; 1 child, Leonardo Nakai. BA, Temple U., 1970; MS, Rutgers U., 1974, PhD, 1978; VMD, U. Pa., 1982. Instr. biology Rutgers U., New Brunswick, N.J., 1975-78, tchg. asst. in immunology, endocrinology and genetics, 1973-78, postdoctoral fellow, 1978; NSF fellow U. Pa., Phila., 1979-82; rsch. veterinarian Sloan-Kettering Inst., N.Y.C., 1982-83; veterinarian Fox Chase Cancer Ctr., Phila., 1983-85; rsch. veterinarian Merck, Sharp & Dohme Labs., Rahway, N.J., 1985-88; dir. comparative medicine U. Md. Sch. Medicine, 1988—; vet. med. officer Balt. VA Med. Ctr., 1988—. Rsch. fellow Nat. Aquarium, Balt., mem. bd. govs., chmn. animal policy com., 1993—. Contbr. articles to profl. jours. Recipient Nat. Rsch. Svcs. award NIH, 1983; Nat. Needs Manpower fellow NSF, 1980; NIH fellow in immunobiology, 1982; grantee NIH, 1990—, Dept. Def., 1995. Mem. AAAS, AVMA, Assn. Primate Veterinarians, Am. Soc. Lab. Animal Practitioners, Md. Vet. Med. Assn., Am. Coll. Lab Animal Medicine (bd. cert.), Phi Zeta. Office: U Maryland MSTF Bldg Rm G-100 10 S Pine St Baltimore MD 21201-1116 Business E-Mail: detolla@vetmed.umaryland.edu.

DE TONNANCOUR, PAUL ROGER GODEFROY, library administrator; b. Fall River, Mass., May 22, 1926; s. R. Godefroy and Emilie (St. Germain) de T.; m. Mary E. Fenno, Apr. 9, 1955; children— Paul Godefroy, Camille Marie. AB cum laude, Providence Coll., 1952; MS, Simmons Coll., 1953; postgrad., Western Res. U., U. So. Cal. Asst. librarian Enoch Pratt Library, Balt., 1953-54; chief librarian, tech. analyst Armco Steel Corp., Balt., 1954-56; dir. rsch. library Gen. Dynamics (Ft. Worth div.), 1956—, dir. tech. information programs, 1964-87, with Proposal Devel. Ctr., 1987—. Cons. MLA, U.S. Office Edn. on sci. info. pers.; John Cotton Dana lectr., 1966 Singer, Ft. Worth Opera Assn. Chorus; Author: The Exploitation of Technical Information, 1966; co-author: Science Information Personnel, 1963; Contbr. articles to profl. jours. Active United Fund and Community Council; mem. exec. com. Big Bros. Tarrant County.; Trustee Cosmopolitan Internat., 1961-63. Served with USNR, 1943-46. Named Boss of Year Am. Bus. Women's Assn., 1965 Mem. ALA, AAAS, Am., Nat. mgmt. assns., Ft. Worth Art Assn., Spl. Libraries Assn., Am. Soc. Information Sci., Delta Epsilon Sigma. Clubs: Mason, Fort Worth Boat. Episcopalian. Home: 6332 Genoa Rd Fort Worth TX 76116-2028 Office: PO Box 748 Fort Worth TX 76101-0748 *Above all, don't take yourself too seriously; Seek wisdom for itself and nurture a sense of humor. Together, they will serve you well.*

DE TORNYAY, RHEBA, nursing educator, retired dean; b. Petaluma, Calif., Apr. 17, 1926; d. Bernard and Ella Fradkin; m. Rudy de Tornyay, June 4, 1954. Student, U. Calif., Berkeley, 1944-46; diploma, Mt. Zion Hosp. Sch. Nursing, 1949; AB, San Francisco State U., 1951, MA, 1954; Ed.D., Stanford U., 1967; Sc.D. (hon.), Ill. Wesleyan U., 1974; LHD (hon.), U. Portland, 1974, Georgetown U., 1994. Mem. faculty San Francisco State U., 1957-67, prof. nursing, 1966-67, chmn. dept., 1959-67; assoc. prof. U. Calif. Sch. Nursing, San Francisco, 1968-71, prof., 1971; dean, prof. Sch. Nursing UCLA, 1971-75; dean emeritus, prof. U. Wash., Seattle, 1986—. Author: Strategies for Teaching nursing, 1971, 3rd edit., 1987, Japanese transl., 1974, Spanish edit., 1986; co-author: (with Heather Young) Choices: Making a Good Move to a Retirement Community, 2001. Trustee emeritus Robert Wood Johnson Found. Mem. ANA, Am. Acad. Nursing (charter fellow, pres. 1973-75), Inst. Medicine (governing coun. 1979-81). Home: 4540 8th Ave NE Apt 1001 Seattle WA 98105-4795 Business E-Mail: rheba@u.washington.edu.

DETORO, IRVING JOHN, management consultant; b. New Haven, Conn., June 24, 1934; s. Armand and Frances (Paceill) DeT.; m. Evelyn V. Fadden, Oct. 3, 1959; children: Gail Ann, Janice Ellen, Jeffrey Armand. BS in Econs., U. Pa., 1956; MBA, U. Rochester, 1965. Sales, br., product mktg., N.E. region ops, mgr. Xerox Corp., Rochester, N.Y., 1985-86; chmn. The Quality Network, Palm Harbor, Fla., 1987—97. Mem. White House Conf. on Productivity, Washington, 1982. Author: Doing It Right, 1990; co-author: Total Quality Management: Three Steps to Contiuous Improvement, 1991, Process Redesign, 1996; contbr. article to publ. Vice chair Pinellas Habitat for Humanity, 1998—2005; dir. East Lake Cmty Libr. Mem. Am. Soc. for Quality Control, Assn. for Quality and Participation. Avocation: sailing. Office: Quality Network 4075 Capitol Dr Palm Harbor FL 34685-4020 E-mail: irv.detoro@knology.net.

DETRE, THOMAS, psychiatrist, educator; b. Budapest, Hungary, May 17, 1924; came to U.S., 1953, naturalized, 1958; m. Katherine Maria Drechsler, Sept. 15, 1956; children: John Allan, Antony James. BA, Gymnasium of Piarist Fathers, Kecskemet, Hungary, 1942; postgrad., Horthy Miklos U. and Pazmany Peter U., Hungary, 1945-47; MD, Rome U., 1952. Diplomate: Am. Bd. Psychiatry and Neurology (assoc. examiner). Intern Morrisania City Hosp., N.Y.C., 1953-54; resident in psychiatry Mt. Sinai Hosp., N.Y.C., 1954-55, Yale U., 1955-57, chief resident, instr., 1957-58, instr., 1958-59, asst. prof., 1959-62; dir. psychiat. inpatient service Yale-New Haven Hosp., 1960-68, assoc. prof., 1962-70, asst. chief psychiatry div., 1965-68, psychiatrist in chief, 1968-73, prof., 1970-73; prof., chmn. dept. psychiatry U. Pitts., 1973-82, assoc. sr. vice chancellor, 1982-84, disting. svc. prof. health scis., 1982—, disting. prof. psychiatry and neurosci., 1993—, sr. v.p. health scis., 1984-92, sr. vice chancellor for health scis., 1992-98, pres. med. and health care div., 1986-90, pres. med. ctr., 1990-92; dir. Western Psychiat. Inst. and Clin. Western Psychiat. Inst. and Clin., 1973-94; exec. v.p. internat. and acad. programs, dir. internat. med. affairs UPMC Health Sys., Pitts., 1998—2002, med. dir. internat. programs, 2002—04. Mem. Nat. Adv. Mental Health Coun., NIH, 1994-97; pres. bd. regents Nat. Libr. Medicine, 2005. Author: (with H.G. Jarecki) Modern Psychiatric Treatment, 1971; contbr. chpts. to books. Fellow Am. Coll. Psychiatrists, Am. Coll. Neuropsychopharmacology (pres. 1994), Am. Psychiat. Assn. (life fellow); mem. Inst. Medicine, Collegium Internat. Neuropsychopharmacologicum, Pan Am. Med. Assn., Am. Soc. Clin. Pharmacology and Therapeutics, Phi Beta Kappa. Office: UPMC Health Sys 3811 Ohara St Pittsburgh PA 15213-2593 Office Phone: 412-246-6555. Business E-Mail: detretp@upmc.edu.

DETTBARN, WOLF-DIETRICH, neurochemist, pharmacologist, educator; b. Berlin, Jan. 30, 1928; came to U.S., 1958, naturalized, 1968; s. Erwin Bruno and MariaMagdalena (Conrady) D.; children: Donata-Andrea, Henning-Christian. MD, Dr. med., D. Göttingen, 1953. Intern Univ. Clinic, Göttingen, 1953-54; research assoc. biol. dept. Ciba Co., Basel, 1954-55; research assoc. Physiol. Inst., U. Saarland, Homburg, Saar, 1955-58; research assoc. neurology Columbia U., N.Y.C., 1958-61, asst. prof., 1961-67, assoc. prof., 1967-68; prof. pharmacology Vanderbilt U., Nashville, 1968-96, prof. pharmacology emeritus, 1996—, prof. neurology, 1985—. Mem. com. on toxicology of anticholinesterase chems. NRC. 1981-83; cons. U.S. Army Med. R & D Command, 1981-82. Contbr. articles to profl. jours. Mem. internal rev. bd. Vanderbilt U., 1991-93. Recipient Career Devel. award, 1965; grantee NIH, 1958—. Mem. AAAS, Am. Physiol. Soc., Am. Soc. Pharmcology and Exptl. Therapeutics, Am. Soc. Neurochemistry, Soc. for Neurosci., Corp. Marine Biology Lab. (Woods Hole, Mass.). Home: 4422 Wayland Dr Nashville TN 37215-4024 Office: Emeritus Faculty 209 Oxford House Vanderbilt U Med Ctr Nashville TN 37232-4245 Office Phone: 615-322-1474. Business E-Mail: wolf-d.dettbarn@vanderbilt.edu.

DETTER, CARLA RENEE, media specialist; b. Lincolnton, N.C., Apr. 29, 1958; d. Carl Lester and Betty Ruth Detter. BS in Edn., Gardner-Webb Coll., Boiling Springs, NC, 1982; MEd, U. N.C., Charlotte, 1985; MLS, Appalachian State U., 1999. Bd. cert. tchr. early childhood - young adult Nat. Bd. Profl. Tchg. Standards, 2002. Tchr. grade 6 North Brook Elem. Sch., Lincolnton, NC, 1982—83; tchr. grade 4 Love Meml. Sch., 1983—84; tchr. grade 6 North Brook Elem., 1984—85; tchr. grade 7 East Lincoln Mid. Sch., Iron Station, 1985—99; libr. media specialist Catawba Springs Elem., 1999—2005. Treas. Rhyne Heights United Meth. Women, 1998—; lay leader Rhyne Heights United Meth. Ch., Lincolnton, NC, 2001—03, nurture/evangelism chairperson, 2004—. Grantee, State Libr. N.C., 2002—03. Mem.: ALA, N.C. Sch. Libr. Media Assn. Home: 1272 Pleasant Grove Ch Rd Crouse NC 28033 Office: Catawba Springs Elem Sch 206 N Little Egypt Rd Denver NC 28037 Office Phone: 704-736-1895. E-mail: cdetter@lincoln.k12.nc.us.

DETTER, GERALD L., transportation executive; b. York, Pa. m. Iris Detter; 3 children. Student exec. mgmt. program, Columbia U. Dockman Consol. Freightways subs. CNF Transp. Svcs., York, 1964, line-haul dispatcher, various other positions, 1965, mgr. terminal Richfield, Ohio, 1971-76, divsn. mgr. Detroit, 1976-82, pres., CEO Con-Way Express, 1982, pres. CEO Con-Way Transp. Svcs., sr. v.p. Palo Alto, Calif. Active Mission of Hope Cancer Fund, Jackson, Mich., Boy Scouts of Am., Girl Scouts of Am., United Way. Office: CNF Transp Inc 3240 Hillview Ave Palo Alto CA 94304-1201

DETTERBECK, FRANK C., cardiothoracic surgeon; b. Detroit, Jan. 14, 1955; s. Frank Joseph and Inge (Wals) D.; m. Judit Farkas, Sept. 20, 1980; children: Sabine, Roland. BS, U. Mich., 1976; MD, Northwestern U., 1983. Diplomate Am. Bd. Surgery, Am. Bd. Thoracic Surgery. Intern Va. Mason Clinic, Seattle, 1983-84, resident in gen. surgery, 1984-88; resident in cardiothoracic surgery U. N.C., Chapel Hill, 1988-91, fellow in thoracic transplantation, clin. instr., 1991-92, asst. prof., 1992—. Author: (with others) Surgical Critical Care, 1994; contbr. articles to profl. jours. Fellow Am. Coll. Chest Physicians, Am. Coll. Surgeons; mem. Am. Thoracic Soc., Internat. Soc. Heart Lung Transplant, CALBG Thoracic Surgery Subcom., Gen. Thoracic Surg. Club. Office: Univ North Carolina 108 Burnett Womack Cb 7065 Chapel Hill NC 27599-0001

DETTERLINE, MILTON E., JR., minister; b. Bethlehem, Pa., Nov. 16, 1929; s. Milton Elmer Detterline, Sr. and Mary Elizabeth Detterline; m. Nancy Jane Day, June 26, 1954 (div. July 1976); children: James Lee, Jon Scott, Peter Kirk. BA, Moravian Coll., 1951; MDiv, Drew U., 1954. Ordained to ministry Evang. Congl. Ch., Pa. Conf., 1954. Pastor Pottsville Evang. Congl. Ch., Pa., 1954—57, St. John Evang. Congl. Ch., Allentown, Pa., 1957—61, St. John United Ch. of Christ, Tamaqua, Pa., 1961—69; pastoral fellow in ecumenics Yale U., New Haven, 1968; spl. asst. to pres., chaplain, alumni dir. Ursinus Coll., Collegeville, Pa., 1969—74; sr. pastor St. Peters United Ch. of Christ, Pa., 1972—. Dir. sch. methods Evang. Congl. denomina, bd. christian edn., various other offices. Contbr. articles to newspapers, reports and publs. Past pres. Allentown Area Coun. Chs.; chmn. Lehigh County Child Care Commn., Schuylkill County Child Care Commn., numerous other offices; moderator, co-founder Coventry-Warwick Ministerium; bd. Christian concern PSE Housing for Elderly, bd. Jefferson Apts.; pres., mem. bd. Orion Cmtys., Inc. Named Citizen of Yr., City of Tamaqua, 1968, Bldg. named in honor, St. Peter United Ch. of Christ, 2001; fellow, Westar Inst. Office: St Peter United Ch of Christ 1100 Mt Pleasant Rd Saint Peters PA 19470 Home: Box 156 Saint Peters PA 19470 Office Phone: 610-469-9690. E-mail: medetterline@aol.com.

DETTERMAN, ROBERT LINWOOD, financial planner; b. Norfolk, Va., May 1, 1931; s. George William and Jeanneille (Watson) D.; m. Virginia Armstrong; children: Janine, Patricia, William Arthur. BS in Engring., Va. Poly. Inst., 1953; PhD in Nuclear Engring., postgrad., Oak Ridge Sch. Reactor Tech., 1954; cert. in fin. planning, Coll. Fin. Planning, Denver, 1986. Registered investment advisor, Calif. Engring. test dir. Foster Wheeler Co., N.Y.C., 1954-59; sr. research engr. Atomics Internat. Co., Canoga Park, Calif., 1959-62; chief project engr. Rockwell Internat. Co., Canoga Park, Calif., 1962-68, dir. bus. devel., 1968-84, mgr. internat. program, 1984-87; pres. Bo-Gin Fin., Inc., Thousand Oaks, Calif., 1987—; owner Bo-Gin Arabians, Thousand Oaks, 1963—. Nuclear cons. Danish Govt., 1960, Lawrence Livermore Lab., Calif., 1959. Trustee, mem. exec. com. Morris Animal Found., Denver, 1984—, chmn., 1984-88, now trustee emeritus; mem. pres.' adv. com. Kellog Arabian Ranch, U. Calif. Poly., Pomona; treas., trustee Arabian Horse Trust, Denver, 1979-94, now trustee emeritus; chmn. Cal Bred Futurity. Named to Arabian Tent of Honor, Arabian Horse Trust, 1997. Mem. Nat. Assn. Personal Fin. Advisers, Fin. Planning Assn., Acad. Magical Arts, Am. Horse Shows Assn., Am. Horse Coun., Magic Castle Club, Internat. Arabian Horse Assn. Club, Tau Beta Phi, Eta Kappa Nu, Phi Kappa Phi. Republican. Avocations: collecting stamps, growing orchids. Office: 3609 E Thousand Oaks Blvd Ste 220 Westlake Village CA 91362-6941 Office Phone: 805-494-1844. Business E-Mail: boginfin@aol.com.

DETTINGER, GARTH BRYANT, surgeon, physician, retired military officer, public health service officer; b. Syracuse, NY, Dec. 23, 1921; s. Maurice and Maxine Bryant (giddings) D.; m. Gladys Ruth Hickingbotham, Aug. 5, 1939 (dec. Aug. 1996); children: Holly Maxine Dettinger Dixon-Keane, Ronald Mark, Michael James; m. Jeffa Taylor, July 26, 1997. AB, Harvard U., 1948; MD, Columbia U., 1952; MS in Surgery, Baylor U., 1956. Diplomate Am. Bd. Surgery. B-17 instr. pilot, B-29 aircraft comdr. U.S. Army Air Corps, 1941—45; Commd. officer U.S. Air Force, 1952, advanced through grades to maj. gen., 1977; intern Valley Forge Army Hosp., Phoenixville, Pa., 1952-53; resident in surgery Brooke Army Hosp., San Antonio, 1953-57; chief surgery MacDill Hosp., Tampa, Fla., 1957-59, Elmendorf Hosp., Alaska, 1959-62, Davis-Monthan Hosp., Tucson, 1962-64; hosp. comdr. Roswell, N.Mex., 1964-67; prime recovery helicopter surgeon Project Gemini, Cape Kennedy, Fla., 1964—67; chief profl. services Air Forces Europe, 1967-70; hosp. comdr. Vandenberg, Calif., 1970-72; surgeon Air Force Mil. Personnel Center, San Antonio, 1972-74; command surgeon Air Tng. Command, 1974-75; dir. plans and resources U.S. Air Force, Washington, 1975-77, dep. surgeon gen., 1977-80; asst. health dir. Fairfax County, Va., 1980—. Surg. cons. Surgeon Gen. U.S., CIA, 1978-99; clin. assoc. prof. Georgetown U. Med. Sch., 1983— Editor-in-chief: Surgeons Comments, 1967-70. Recipient Disting. Svc. medal, USAF, 1977. Fellow A.C.S. (bd. govs.); mem. Soc. Med. Cons. to Armed Services, Alpha Omega Alpha. Republican. Episcopalian. Home: #M-116 9120 Belvoir Woods Pkwy # M-116 Fort Belvoir VA 22060-2721 Office: Fairfax County Dept Health 10777 Main St Ste 203 Fairfax VA 22030-6900 *I've always tried to leave anyone, anything or anyplace a little better than before I had been there.*

DETTINGER, WARREN WALTER, lawyer; b. Toledo, Feb. 13, 1954; s. Walter Henry and Elizabeth Mae (Zoll) Dettinger; children: John Robert, Laura Marie. BS cum laude, U. Toledo, 1977, JD magna cum laude, 1980. Bar: Ohio 1980, U.S. Dist. Ct. (no. dist.) Ohio 1980, U.S. Ct. Appeals (6th cir.) 1980, U.S. Tax Ct. 1981. Law clk. to presiding judge U.S. Ct. Appeals (6th cir.), Grand Rapids, Mich., 1980-81; assoc. Fuller & Henry, Toledo, 1981-84; atty. Sheller-Globe Corp., Toledo, 1984-87; v.p., gen. counsel, sec. Diebold, Inc., Canton, Ohio, 1987—. Mem. ABA, Ohio Bar Assn., Stark County Bar Assn., Am. Corp. Counsel Assn., Mfrs. Alliance (law coun. II), Brookside Country Club, Phi Kappa Phi. Roman Catholic. Avocations: golf, travel, photography, tennis. Home: 5237 Birkdale St NW Canton OH 44708-1825 Office: Diebold Inc 5995 Mayfair Rd PO Box 3077 North Canton OH 44720-8077 Office Phone: 330-490-5037. Business E-Mail: dettinw@diebold.com.

DETTMANN, DAVID ALLEN, lawyer; b. Milw., Mar. 30, 1949; s. Karl F. and Beverly J. (Rusdal) D.; m. Jenee A. Nelson, June 26, 1971; children: Justin, Lisa, Jacob. BA in Acctg./Econs., Luther Coll., 1971; MBA, JD, Drake U., 1974. Bar: Iowa 1974, U.S. Dist. Ct. (so. dist.) Iowa 1974, U.S. Tax Ct. 1974, U.S. Ct. Appeals (8th cir.) 1989, Ill. 1993; CPA, Iowa; accredited estate planner, Am. Coll. Real Estate Lawyers, 1994, Am. Coll. Trust and Estate Counsel, 2000. Ptnr. Lane & Waterman LLP, Davenport, Iowa, 1974—. Bd. dirs. Cmty. Found. Great River Bend, chair, 2004; former mem. ch. coun. Redeemer Luth. Ch.; trustee, vice chair, chair Miss. Valley Regional Blood Ctr., Davenport, 1984—; bd. dirs. Am. Inst. Commerce, Davenport, 1986-98, Quad-City Estate Planning Coun., pres., 1990-91, 02-; mem. cmty. adv. bd. Augustana Coll. Ctr. Study of Ethics, 2003-; mem. adult edn. adv. com. Scott C.C., 1998-; mem. com. Luther Coll., 2002—; mem. cmty. adv. bd. Augustana Coll. Ctr. Study Ethics, 2003—. Recipient Disting. Svc. award, Luther Coll., 2001. Mem. ABA, AICPA, Iowa Bar Assn. (title stds. com. 1985-94, real estate and title law sect. coun. 1993-96, 2001-04, chair 1994-95, chmn. title guaranty subcom. 1990-94), Real Estate Modernization Com.(chmn. 2002-2003), Iowa Soc. CPAs, Scott County Bar Assn. (chmn. abstract/real estate com. 1985-95). Avocations: travel, photography, golf. Office: Lane & Waterman LLP 220 N Main St Ste 600 Davenport IA 52801-1987 Office Phone: 563-324-3246. Business E-Mail: ddettmann@l-wlaw.com.

DETTMER, ROBERT GERHART, retired beverage company executive; b. Parsons, Kans., Sept. 11, 1931; s. Ira Gerhart and Dema (Hinze) D.; m. Patricia Isabel York, Aug. 20, 1955; children: Stephanie, Constance, Robert Brantley. Student, U.S. Naval Acad., 1949-52; B in Bus. and Engring. Adminstrn., MIT, 1955; MBA, Harvard U., 1957. Engr. Lincoln Electric Co., Cleve., 1957-60; assoc. Booz, Allen & Hamilton, Cleve., 1960-64; propr. Robert G. Dettmer, Investment Mgmt., Cleve., 1964-66; v.p. ops. Tasa Corp., Pitts., 1966-68; pres. Scott Aviation div. A-T-O, Lancaster, N.Y., 1968-70, George J. Meyer Mfg. div. A-T-O, Milw., 1970-72, N.Am. Van Lines subs. PepsiCo, Inc., Fort Wayne, Ind., 1973-76; v.p. fin. mgmt. and planning PepsiCo, Inc., Purchase, N.Y., 1976-79; pres. Pepsi Cola Bottling Group subs., Purchase, N.Y., 1979-86; exec. v.p., CFO PepsiCo, Purchase, N.Y., 1986-96. Chmn. bd. Am. Movers Conf., 1974-76; trustee Miss Porter's Sch., 1978-84; trustee Manhattanville Coll., 1986-93, chmn. bd. trustees, 1988-92. Mem. Delta Tau Delta, Tau Beta Pi. Clubs: Harvard Bus. Sch. of Westchester-Fairfield County (chmn. bd. 1977-80), Harvard Bus. Sch. of Greater N.Y. (chmn. bd. 1982-83). Home: 80 Round Hill Rd Greenwich CT 06831-3743

DETTWYLER, WILLIAM KARL, medical technologist; b. Silverton, Oreg., Mar. 24, 1933; s. Karl Henry and Lydia Mae (Stadeli) D.; m. Mary Jane Kaufman, May 7, 1960; children: Nancy, Brian, Kelvin, Judith, Marlin, Arden, Roseann, Mark, Karla, Melissa. AAS, Oreg. Inst. Tech., 1959.

Registered med. technologist. Med. technologist Salem Meml. Hosp., Oreg., 1959—65; lab. dir. D.F. Taylor Med. Lab., Salem, 1965—75; sr. technologist Ctrl. Clin. Lab., Salem, 1975—79; lab. cons. Aetna Oreg. Med. Carrier, Portland, Oreg., 1981—83; procedure code analyst Wolfgang Assocs., Portland, 1986—88, Medicode, Salem, 1971—99; lab. and x-ray cons. State of Oreg., Salem, 1971—86; med. technologist West Salem Clinic, 1984—91; sr. coding analyst Health Sys. Concepts, Inc., Longwood, Fla., 1989—; pres. Codus Medicus, Inc., 1999—. Med. asst., instr. Cascade Vocat. Ctr., Salem, 1972-75; bd. dirs. Northwest Human Svcs., Salem, 1994—. Contbr. articles to profl. jours. Mem. adv. com. Sheriff's Adv. Commn., Salem, 1980-84, Marion County Traffic Safety, Salem, 1984-90; bd. dirs. NW Human Svcs., Salem. With U.S. Army Med., 1956-58. Recipient Disting. Achievement award Am. Med. Technologists, 1961, Charles E. Martin award Oreg. State Soc., 1988. Mem. Am. Med. Technologists, Oreg. State Soc. (pres. 1959-60), Am. Soc. Clin. Lab. Scientists, Am. Assn. Clin. Chemists, Med. Group Mgmt. Assn., Clin. Lab. Mgmt. Assn. Avocations: history, silviculture, genealogy, parasitology. Home and Office: 5555 Sunnyview Rd NE Salem OR 97305-3264 E-mail: wdettwcpt@aol.com.

DETWEILER, DAVID KENNETH, veterinary physiologist, educator; b. Phila., Oct. 23, 1919; s. David Rieser and Pearl Irene (Overholt) Detweiler; children: Ellen, Diane, Judith, Inge, Kenneth, David. VMD, U. Pa., 1942, MS, 1949; ScD (hon.), Ohio State U., 1966; MVD (hon.), U. Vienna, Austria, 1968; DMV (hon.), U. Turin, Italy, 1969. Asst. instr. physiology and pharmacology Sch. Vet. Medicine, U. Pa., Phila., 1942—43, instr., 1943—45, assoc. in physiology, pharmacology, 1945—47, asst. prof., 1947—51, assoc. prof., 1951—62, assoc. prof. Grad. Sch. Arts and Scis., chmn. dept. vet. med. scis. Grad. Sch. Medicine, 1956—68, dir. comparative cardiovasc. studies unit, 1960—90, prof., head lab. physiology and pharmacology, 1962—68, prof., head lab. physiology, 1968—90, prof. faculty arts and scis., 1968—90, chmn. grad. group comparative med. scis., 1971—87, prof. emeritus, 1990—. Mem. Inst. Medicine of NAS, 1974—; guest USSR Acad. Sci.; cons. cardiovasc. toxicology, 1950—. Contbr. articles to profl. jours. Recipient Disting. Veterinarian award, Pa. Vet. Med. Assn., 1989, Disting. Practitioner award, Nat. Acads. of Practice in Vet. Medicine, 1989, D.K. Detweiler prize in cardiology established in his honor, German Group of World Vet. Med. Assn., 1982, David K. Detweiler Conf. Rm. named in honor, Veterinary Sch. U. Pa., 1993, Centennial medal, Sch. Vet. Medicine, U. Pa., 1994, cert. appreciation, FDA, 1998; fellow Guggenheim Found. Fellow: AAAS; mem.: Vet. Med. Alumni Soc. (Merit award U. Pa. 1981), Am. Coll. Vet. Internal Medicine (diplomate, cardiology group), Acad. Vet. Cardiology (pres.), Am. Heart Assn., Coun. Basic Scis., Am. Vet. Med. Assn. (Gaines award and medal 1960, Honor Roll award 1990), N.Y. Acad. Scis., Am. Assn. Vet. Physiology and Pharmacology (pres.), Am. Physiol. Soc., Phi Zeta, Sigma Xi. Office Phone: 610-645-8964. Home Fax: 610-645-8719.

DETWEILER, GREG JEFFREY, music educator; b. Harrisburg, Pa., Dec. 31, 1951; s. Roderick Leon and Betty Mae Detweiler; m. Rebecca Ann Finley, Mar. 3, 1985 (div. Dec. 20, 1999); children: Jaron Matthew, Aaron Nathaniel. BS, Lebanon Valley Coll., Annville, Pa., 1973; MusM, U. Ill., 1978, DMA, 1985. Vocal music tchr. Susquehanna Twp. Mid. Sch., Harrisburg, Pa., 1973—74; vis. dir. choral-vocal studies Mercer U., Macon, Ga., 1980—81; dir. choral activities Idaho State U., Pocatello, 1982—86, Southeastern La. U., Hammond, 1986—88, Albertson Coll. Idaho, Caldwell, 1989—97, Morehead (Ky.) State U., 1998—. Condr., artistic dir. Boise (Idaho) Master Chorale, 1993—95; choral dir. 1st Bapt. Ch., Morehead, 1999—; prof., choral condr. Ky. Inst. for Internat. Studies, Salzburg, Austria, 2001, 03; founder, dir. cmty. choir Idaho State Chorale, Pocatello, 1985—86, Albertson Coll. Choral Union, Caldwell, 1989—97. Specialist 6 U.S. Army, 1974—77. Named Outstanding Young Man of Am., 1983, Ky. Coll.-Univ. Tchr. of Yr., Ky. Music Educators Assn., 2002; recipient Outstanding Svc. award, Gen. Commn. Chaplains and Armed Forces Pers., 1977. Mem.: Nat. Assn. Tchrs. of Singing, Music Educators Nat. Conf. (dist. festival mgr. 2003—, Ky. Tchr. of Yr. 2002), Am. Choral Dirs. Assn. (chmn. youth and student activities N.W. divsn. 1992—96, Ky. 2003—), Phi Kappa Phi. Southern Baptist. Achievements include research in investigation of resonance source of the singer's formant; psychoacoustic ramifications of singer's formant; laryngeal configuration in pulse register phonation: MRI and stroboscopic data; relationship of music and content area reading and writing. Avocations: mountain biking, hiking, reading. Home: 45 Windy Cove Morehead KY 40351 Office: Morehead State U Dept Music Morehead KY 40351 Office Phone: 606-783-2480. E-mail: g.detweiler@moreheadstate.edu.

DETWEILER, RICHARD ALLEN, college president; b. L.A., Nov. 14, 1946; s. James Irvin and Dorothy Elizabeth D.; m. Carol Sue D., Aug. 26, 1967; children: Jerusha, Natasha, Carrick. BA, Calif. Western U., 1968; MA, Princeton U., 1972, PhD, 1973. Structural draftsman Young's Iron Works, Burbank, Calif., 1962-64; peace corps volunteer U.S. Peace Corps, Truk, Caroline Islands; prof. psychology Drew U., Madison, N.J., 1973-92, vice pres., 1985-92; pres. Hartwick Coll., Oneonta, N.Y., 1992—, prof. psychology. Vis. fellow Princeton (N.J.) U., 1973-74; internat. edn. cons. to various non-profit and govt. orgns., 1977—; vis. scholar U. Calif., Berkeley, Calif., 1980; profl. assoc. East West Ctr., Honolulu, HI, 1978. Contbr. numerous articles and speeches in the fields of psychology, edn. and info. tech. Recipient Outstanding Contbn. and Leadership award, Carnegie Mellon U., 1991; disting. scholar, Coun. on Libr. and Info. Resources, life fellow, Oxford U. Mem. Coun. Ind. Colls., Ind. Col. Fund., Am. Coun. on Edn. Office: CIR Ste 500 1755 Massachusetts Ave NW Washington DC 20036-2124

DETWEILER, STANLEY BRUCE, music educator; b. Denver, May 28, 1951; s. Stanley Howe and Bernadine Marie Detweiler; m. Kelly Kathleen Lynch, Sept. 22, 1983; children: Chelsea Elise, Sonja Marie. MusB, Calif. State U., 1975, MA in Music, 1981. Single subject tchg. credential State of Calif., 1976. Army bandsmen U.S. Army, Fort Sill, Okla., 1976—2000, ret., 2000; sr. tech. writer, developer Armed Forces Sch. of Music, Little Creek, Va., 1986—94; prof. Ctrl. Tex. Coll., Panama City, Panama, 1995—97; instr. Pikes Peak C.C., Fort Sill, Okla., 2000—05; prof. Cameron U., Lawton, 2002—; band dir. Lawton Christian Sch., 2003—. Presenter Nat. Assn. Music Merchandisers, Anahiem, Calif., 1994—94. Lead alto saxophone player Cameron U./Lawton Ft. Sill Cmty. Jazz Band; 1st alto saxophone player Cameron U./Lawton Ft. Sill Cmty. Concert Band; vocalist Cameron U./Lawton Ft. Sill Cmty. Chorus (Messiah); sanctuary choir mem. New Post Chapel; choir mem. Calif. State U., Long Beach. Decorated Army Achievement medal US Army, Meritorious Svc. medal, First Oak Leaf Cluster, Meritorious Svc. medal, Humanitarian Svc. medal, Good Conduct award, Seventh award, Army Commendation medal, Third Oak Leaf Cluster, Army Achievement medal, Second Oak Leaf Cluster. Mem.: Okla. Music Educators Assn., Music Educators Nat. Councel, Harley Owners Group, Kappa Delta Pi, Phi Delta Gamma. Liberal. Methodist. Achievements include research in Researched, developed, and wrote a video script Rhythm Section Techniques, 42 Self Development Tests for Career Management Field 97, Army Bands. Avocations: fly fishing, fly rod building, trout fishing, hiking, motorcycling. Home: 124 SE Chruchill Way Lawton OK 73501-6413 Office: Lawton Christian Sch 1 NW Crusader Dr Lawton OK 73505-9598 Office Phone: 580-536-6885. Office Fax: 580-536-5242. Personal E-mail: sdetweiler@sbcglobal.net.

DETWILER, CHRISTINA LEFEVRE, elementary school educator; b. Richmond, Va., July 27, 1968; d. Michael Roy and Linda Harris LeFevre; m. Scott Douglas Detwiler, Aug. 1, 1998; children: Sarah Catherine, Grayson Scott. Student, Longwood Coll., 1986—88, J. Sargeant Reynolds, Richmond, 1988—90, Va. Commonwealth U., 1990—91, BS in Psychology, MT in Elem. Edn., 1994. Postgrad. profl. lic. in early edn. NK-4. Kindergarten tchr. Elmont Elem., Ashland, Va., 1995—97, 1st grade loop tchr., 1997—98, 1st grade tchr., 1998—99, Acquinton Elem., King William, Va., 1999—2001. Active March of Dimes, Aylett, Va., 1998—, VFW, 1998—, Save the Mattaponi Orgn., King William, 1999—2004, Sept. 11 Fund, 2001, Va. Food Bank, 2003—. Mem.: NEA, Psi Chi, Sigma Kappa.

DETWILER, CHRISTINE WENDLER, special education educator; b. Phila., Nov. 7, 1947; d. Frederick Lawrence Wendler, Jr. and Eileen Casey Wendler; m. Barry Russell Detwiler, Dec. 9, 1967 (div. 1993); children: B.R. Brendan Jr., Benjamin Jonathan(dec.). AAS in Early Childhood Edn. summa cum laude, Montgomery County C.C., 1985; BS in Spl. Edn. cum laude, Gwynedd-Mercy Coll., 1990; MA in Edn., U. Arts, Phila., 1994. Cert. tchr. for mentally or physically handicapped Pa. Instrnl. asst., spl. edn. North Pa. Sch. Dist., Lansdale, 1983—90, spl. edn. tchr., all levels, 1990—99, program tchr., ann. young authors' conf., 1998—, learning support tchr., co-tchg. inclusion tchr., 1999—; tchr. elem. Walton Farm Sch., 1996—. Writer, implemented various ednl. programs; presenter in field; lectr. in field; program tchr. Ann. Young Authors Conf., 2005. Contbr. articles to profl. jours. and newspapers. Tour guide narrator Independence Nat. Hist. Park, Phila., 1987—90; mem. North Penn Sch. Dist. Cmty. Forum Steering Com. Named to, Mont. County C.C. Hall of Fame, 2004; grantee, North Penn Sch. Dist. Ednl. Found., 2001—, North Pa. Cmty. Health Found., 2003—05; scholar, Charlotte W. Newcombe Found., 1988, 1989, Lansdale Bus. and Profl. Women's Club, 1989. Avocations: travel, photography, writing for children, reading, antiques. Office: PO Box 453 Montgomeryville PA 18936 Office Phone: 215-896-0710.

DETWILER, JEAN M., music educator; d. William C. and Lucy M. (Winkler) Mellott; m. Richard F. Detwiler, Nov. 15, 1958; children: Peggy, Daniel, Matthew, Paul, Carol. MusB (magna cum laude), U. Akron, 1986. Cert. tchr. Ohio. Youth dir. of music Jerusalem Ch., Seville, Ohio, 1972—87; music tchr. Cloverleaf Schs., Lodi, Ohio, 1987—2002; pvt. music tchr. Joyful Music, Seville, Ohio, 1982—. Dir. Westfield Symfunics, 1986—2002. Singer: Cloverleaf Singers, 1974—90, Medina County Chorus, 1974—90, Akron Symphony Chorus, 1980—90. Pres. Cloverleaf Edn. Assn., Lodi, Ohio, bldg. rep.; mem. steering com. Comprehensive Plan, Seville, Ohio, 2003. Grantee Jennings Grant, Martha Holden Jennings Found., 1989; Jennings Scholar, 1999—2000. Mem.: Town and Country Guild. Republican. Lutheran. Avocations: sewing, travel, walking, community service. Home: 144 Sherwood Ct Seville OH 44273

DEUKMEJIAN, GEORGE, lawyer, retired governor; b. Albany, N.Y., June 6, 1928; s. C. George and Alice (Gairdan) D.; m. Gloria M. Saatjian, 1957; children: Leslie Ann, George Krikor, Andrea Diane. BA, Siena Coll., 1949; JD, St. John's U., 1952. Bar: N.Y. 1952, Calif. 1956, U.S. Supreme Ct. 1970. Mem. Calif. Assembly, 1963-67, Calif. Senate, 1967-79, minority leader; atty. gen. State of Calif., 1979-82, gov., 1983-91; former dep. county counsel Los Angeles County.; former ptnr. Sidley & Austin, 1991-2000. Served with U.S. Army, 1953-55. Republican. Episcopalian. Office: 5366 E Broadway Long Beach CA 90803-3549

DEULL, CHARLES BRIAN, publishing executive, lawyer; b. 1959; BA, Tufts U.; JD, Boston (Mass.) U. Sr. v.p. legal and bus. affairs Scholastic Corp., N.Y., 1995—99, sr. v.p., 1999—, gen. counsel, 1999—, sec., 1999—. Office: Scholastic Corp 557 Broadway New York NY 10012*

DEUPREE, MARVIN MATTOX, financial consultant; b. Woodbine, Iowa, Oct. 8, 1917; s. Archie Orin and Pearl (Mattox) D.; m. Katherine Anita Beard, Aug. 18, 1951; children: Marvin Mattox, Meredith Ann. BA with high distinction, State U. Iowa, 1941; MBA with distinction, U. Pa., 1948. C.P.A., N.Y., Ill., Mich., La., Iowa, Va., N.C. Instr. acctg. U. Pa., 1947-48; with Arthur Andersen & Co. (C.P.A.s), 1948-75, partner, 1960-75, mem. policy com. on acctg. and auditing, 1962-72; bus. cons., 1975—; pres. Emporium Specialties Co., Inc., 1977—. Adj. asso. prof. NYU Grad. Sch. Bus. Adminstrn., 1973-76 Contbr. articles to profl. jours. Served as officer USNR, 1943-46. Mem. AICPA, N.Y. State, Ill. Socs. CPA's, Nat. Assn. Accts., Am. Acctg. Assn., Execs. Club (Chgo.), Wharton Grad. Bus. Sch. Club (Chgo.), Univ. Club (Chgo.), Phi Beta Kappa. Episcopalian. Home: 5 Academy Rd Ho Ho Kus NJ 07423-1301

DEUTCH, JOHN MARK, chemistry professor, former CIA Director; b. Brussels, July 27, 1938; came to U.S., 1940, naturalized, 1946; s. Michael Joseph and Rachel Felicia (Fisher) D.; m. Pat Lyons; children: Philip, Paul, Zachary. BA, Amherst Coll., 1961, D.Sc. and Humane Letters (hon.), 1978; B. Chem. Engring, M.I.T., 1961, PhD in Phys. Chemistry, 1965; D.Litt. (hon.), U. Lowell, 1986. System analyst Office Sec. Def., 1961-65; fellow Nat. Acad. Scis./NRC, Nat. Bur. Standards, 1966-67; asst. prof. Princeton U., 1967-70; mem. faculty MIT, 1970—, prof. chemistry, 1971—, chmn. chemistry dept., 1976—77, dean sci., 1982—85, provost, 1985—90, inst. prof., 1990—; dir. Office Energy Rsch., US Dept. Energy, Washington, 1977—79, acting asst. sec. for energy tech., 1979, under sec., 1979—80; under sec. for acquisition & tech. US Dept. Def., Washington, 1993-94, dep. sec., 1994—95; dir. CIA, Washington, 1995—96. Chmn. adv. panel on chemistry NSF, 1974; mem. Def. Sci. Bd., 1977—, Pres.'s Nuclear Safety Oversight Com., 1980-81; mem. Army Sci. Adv. Panel, 1975-78, Pres.'s Commn. on Strategic Forces, 1983, The White House Sci. Coun., 1985-89; Pres.'s Fgn. Intelligence Adv. Bd., 1990-94, Pres. Commn. on Aviation Safety & Security, 1996, Commn. on Reducing & Protecting Govt. Secrecy, 1996, Pres. Com. of Advisors on Sci. & Tech., 1997-2001; chair Commn. to Assess the Orgn. of the Fed. Govt. to Combat the Proliferation of Weapons of Mass Destruction, 1998-99; bd. dirs, Citigroup Inc., 1987-93, 1996-, Citibank, N.A., 1987-93, 1996-98 Author research articles. Sloan fellow, 1969-71; Guggenheim fellow, 1974; Disting. Intelligence medal, CIA 1996, Intelligence Community Disting. Intelligence medal, 1996, Greater Boston Fed. Exec. Bd. Speaker Thomas P. O'Neill award, 2002. Mem. Am. Phys. Soc., Am. Chem. Soc., Council Fgn. Relations, Am. Acad. Arts and Scis. Avocations: tennis, reading. Office: MIT Chemistry Dept 77 Massachusetts Ave Rm 6-208 Cambridge MA 02139-4307 E-mail: jmd@mit.edu.

DEUTSCH, BARRY JOSEPH, consulting and management development company executive; b. Gary, Ind., Aug. 10, 1941; s. Jack Elias and Helen Louise (La Rue) D. BS, U. So. Calif., 1969, MBA magna cum laude, 1970. Lectr. mgmt. U. So. Calif., L.A., 1967-70; pres., founder The Deutsch Group, Inc., L.A., 1970—; founder, CEO, chmn. bd., bd. dirs. Investment Planning Network, Inc., 1988—. Author: Leadership Techniques, 1969, Recruiting Techniques, 1970, The Art of Selling, 1973, Professional Real Estate Management, 1975, Strategic Planning, 1976, Employer/Employee: Making the Transition, 1979, Managing by Objectives, 1980, Conducting Effective Performance Appraisal, 1982, Advanced Supervisory Development, 1984, Managing a Successful Financial Planning Business, 1988, How to Franchise Your Business, 1991. Chmn. bd. govs. Am. Hist. Ctr., 1980—; mentor U. S.C. Career Advancement Program, 1999—. Mem. ASTD, Am. Mgmt. Assn., Am. Soc. Bus. and Mgmt. Cons., Internat. Mgmt. by Objectives Inst., Internat. Soc. for Performance Improvement, Organization Devel. Network, Planning Execs. Inst., Sponsors for Ednl. Advancement of Asians (bd. dirs.). Office: 1140 Highland Ave Ste 200 Manhattan Beach CA 90266-5335 Office Phone: 562-596-5544. E-mail: deutschbj@aol.com.

DEUTSCH, DONNY, advertising executive; s. David Deutsch; m. Stacy Josloff. Grad., U. Pa. Chmn., CEO Deutsch, Inc., NYC, 1984—; and mng. ptnr. Deutsch Open City prodn. company. Host The Big Idea with Donny Deutsch, CNBC, 2004—; mem. Clinton/Gore comm. team, 1992. Author: Often Wrong, Never in Doubt: Unleash the Business Rebel Within, 2005. Bd. dir. Michael J. Fox Parkinson's Found.; exec. com. U. Pa. Sch. Social Work. Democrat. Office: Deutsch Inc 111 8th Ave Fl 14 New York NY 10011-5295*

DEUTSCH, HARVEY ELLIOT, lawyer; b. Bklyn., Aug. 18, 1940; s. Harry Deutsch and Beulah (Deutsch) Koft; m. Paula Kantor, Nov. 26, 1964; children— Stacia Francine, Steven Harold, Karen Gail. B.A., So. Methodist U., 1962; LL.B., U. Tex., 1966. Bar: U.S. Dist. Ct. Colo. 1967, U.S. Ct. Appeals (10th cir.) 1967. Assoc., Holland & Hart, Denver, 1967-69; ptnr. Isaacson, Rosenbaum, Spiegleman & Friedman, Denver, 1970-82; v.p., gen. counsel Bill L. Walters Cos., Englewood, Colo., 1982-84; ptnr. Deutsch & Sheldon, Englewood, 1984—; lectr. in field. Contbr. chpts. to books. Bd. dirs. Anti-Defamation League of B'nai B'rith, Denver, 1976—; commr. Colo. Civil Rights Commn., 1972-80, chmn., 1976-78. Served with USNR, 1962-70. Mem. Tex. Bar Assn., Colo. Bar Assn. Home: 255 Cook St Denver CO 80206-5304

DEUTSCH, HERBERT ARNOLD, music educator; b. Baldwin, N.Y., Feb. 9, 1932; s. Barnet Baruch and Miriam (Meyersburg) D.; m. Margaret Ann Carbray, Oct. 10, 1955 (dec.); children: Lisbeth Ann, Edmund Barnet; m. Nancy DiNapoli Blau, Sept. 14, 1997. BS in Edn., Hofstra U., 1956; MusM, Manhattan Sch. Music, 1961; postgrad., NYU, 1973-75. Music faculty East Meadow (N.Y.) Pub. Schs., 1959-60; freelance musician N.Y.C. area, 1960-61; lectr. music Hofstra Univ., Hempstead, NY, 1961-63, instr., 1964-68, asst. prof., 1969-73, assoc. prof., 1974-79, prof., 1983—, dept. chair, 1995—2001, prof. emeritus, 2001—; dir. mktg. Moog Music div. Norlin Corp., Buffalo, 1980-81, dir. sales/mktg., 1981-83. Cons. Pulse Concepts, L.I., N.Y., 1971—, Jim Henson's Muppets, N.Y.C., 1983-86, Norlin Corp., Chgo., 1976-79; edn. cons. Music and Computer Educator, 1989-91. Author: Synthesis, 1975, 2d rev. edit., 1984, Electroacoustic Music: Its First Century, 1993; composer numerous mus. works; contbr. articles to profl. jours., 1972—, Am. Record Guide, 1987-93 Mem. Huntington (N.Y.) Spl. Edn. PTA, 1976-88; bd. dirs. Huntington Symphony, 1973-75, Suffolk County (N.Y.) Family Services, 1975-77; founding tech. com. mem. NY State Sch. Music Assn., 1992-, composition adj., 1999-. Served with U.S. Army, 1956-58. Recipient grad. assistantship, Manhattan Sch. Music, 1961, Estabrook Disting. Alumni award, Hofstra U., 1996, award for alumni achievment, 2001; grantee, Meet the Composer, 1976, 1986—88, 1990—98, 2000—03. Mem.: AAUP, ASCAP (awards 1992—), Music and Entertainment Industry Edn. Assn., Am. Fedn. Musicians, L.I. Composers Alliance (bd. dirs. 1972—91, v.p. 1991—95, pres. 1998—2000, archivist 2000—, founder, pres. 2003—).

DEUTSCH, JAMES BERNARD, lawyer; b. St. Louis, Aug. 24, 1948; s. William Joseph and Margaret (Klevorn) D.; m. Deborah Marie Hallenberg, June 26, 1976; children: Michael, Gabriel. BA, Southeast Mo. State U., 1974; JD, U. Mo., 1978. Bar: Mo. 1978, U.S. Dist. Ct. (we. dist.) Mo. 1978, U.S. Ct. Appeals (8th cir.), 1989, U.S. Supreme Ct., 1990. Assoc. Gt. Plains Legal Found., Kansas City, Mo., 1978-79; pvt. practice, Kansas City, 1979-81; gen. counsel Mo. Dept. Revenue, Jefferson City, Mo., 1981-83; commr. Mo. Adminstrv. Hearing Commn., Jefferson City, 1983-89; dep. atty.-gen State of Mo., Jefferson City, 1989-93; ptnr. Riezman & Blitz, P.C., Jefferson City, Mo., 1993-99; Ptnr. Blitz Bardgett & Deutsch LC, Jefferson City, 2000—. Served to lance cpl. USMC, 1968-70, Vietnam. Named one of Men of Yr. in Constrn. Industry, Engring. News, McGraw-Hill Pub., N.Y.C., 1985. Mem. ABA (jud. adminstrn. com.), ASCE (hon. fellow), Mo. Bar Assn. (council mem. taxation com. 1985—, adminstrn. law and jud. adminstrn. coms.), Mo. Inst. for Justice (bd. dirs. 1977—), VFW, Marine Corps League. Office: Blitz Bardgett & Deutsch LC 308 E High St Jefferson City MO 65101-3237 Office Phone: 573-634-2500. E-mail: jdeutsch@blitzbardgett.com.

DEUTSCH, JAMES I., curator; b. N.Y.C., June 9, 1948; s. Joseph and Ethel Weiner Deutsch. BA, Williams Coll., Williamstown, Mass., 1970; MA, U. Minn., 1976; MLA, Emory U., 1979; PhD, George Washington U., 1991. Newspaper reporter The Indpls. Star, 1970—71; monorail operator Walt Disney World, Lake Buena Vista, Fla., 1971—72; park ranger-archaeologist U.S. Nat. Park Svc., Camp Verde and Clarkdale, Ariz., 1972—73; cmty. info. specialist Fairbanks North Star Borough Libr., Fairbanks, Alaska, 1973—74; forest naturalist Chugach Nat. Forest, Portage, Alaska, 1974; newspaper reporter, photographer People's Press, Yazoo City, Miss., 1977; park ranger, historian U.S. Nat. Park Svc., Vicksburg, Miss., 1977; bookmobile driver W.A. Percy Meml. Libr., Greenville, Miss., 1977—78; head ext. svcs. Parmly Billings (Mont.) Libr., 1979—82; foodways coord. Smithsonian Folklife Festival, Washington, 1991—92; hist. cons. Nat. Coun. on the Aging, Washington, 1991—94; dir. Learning Resource Ctr. Marymount U., Arlington, Va., 1995—96; census enumerator U.S. Bur. Census, Washington, 2000; program coord. Smithsonian Instn., Washington, 2001—02; acad. specialist U.S. Dept. State, Washington, 2000—03; program curator Nat. WW II Reunion, Washington, 2003—04; program curator Folklife Festival Smithsonian Inst., Washington, 2004—. Adj. prof. George Washington U., Washington, 1985—; Fulbright prof. U. Hannover, Germany, 1992—93, U. Leipzig, Germany, 1993—94, U. Veliko Turnovo, Bulgaria, 1998—99, Norwegian Ministry Edn., Oslo, 2002—03; rschr., presenter Smithsonian Folklife Festival, Washington, 1995—96; vis. prof. U. Lodz, Poland, 1997—98. Fulbright scholar, Coun. for the Internat. Exch. of Scholars, 1992—94, 1998—99, 2002—03. Office Phone: 202-275-1844. Business E-Mail: deutschj@si.edu.

DEUTSCH, JOHN LUDWIG, chemistry educator, researcher; b. N.Y.C., May 5, 1938; s. James Erwin and May (Pomerantz) D.; m. Edna Wishart Robertson, July 31, 1961; children: Karin Anne, Erik Robertson. BS with honors, Tulane U., 1959; DPhil, Oxford (Eng.) U., 1963. Chartered chemist, U.K. Lab. instr. Tulane U., New Orleans, 1956-59; vis. asst. prof. chemistry Pomona (Calif.) Coll., 1964-66; assoc. prof. SUNY, Geneseo, 1966-77, prof., 1977—, acting chmn. dept., 1974-75, 95-96. Vis. researcher Inst. Physics, U. Stockholm, 1973, Phys. Chemistry Lab., Oxford, summers 1980-81, 83; vis. scientist Herzberg Inst. Astrophysics, Ottawa, Ont., Can., summers 1986-87; vis. prof. U. Rochester, N.Y., 1987-88, 95. Honor scholar Tulane U., 1955-59, Rhodes scholar Rhodes Trust, Oxford, 1959-62; postdoctoral fellow NSF, Oxford, 1963-64. Fellow Royal Soc. Chemistry, Am. Inst. Chemists; mem. AAAS, Am. Chem. Soc., N.Y. Acad. Sci., Phi Beta Kappa, Sigma Xi, Sigma Pi Sigma.

DEUTSCH, MARSHALL E(MANUEL), medical products company executive, inventor; b. NYC, Aug. 17, 1921; s. David and Madeline Lea (Roth) D.; m. Judith Greene, June 27, 1947; children: Pamina Margret, Ethan Amadeus, Freeman Sarastro. BS, CCNY, 1941; PhD, NYU, 1951. Tech. dir. NEN-Picker Radiopharms., Boston, 1966-68, Picker-Hoechst Inc., Bedford, Mass., 1968-70, Mead Diagnostics, Inc., Bedford, 1970-72, CIS Radiopharms., Bedford, 1972-74, Thyroid Diagnostics Inc., Bedford, 1972-85; chmn. Marshall Diagnostics Inc., Bedford, 1985-87; tech. adv. J&S Med. Assocs., Framingham, Mass., 1989—2004, cons., 2004—. Bd. dirs., corp. sec., v.p. Health Svcs. Internat., Washington, 1983-96; contractor Joint Publs. Rsch. Svc., Arlington, Va., 1984-92. Inventor self-contained technetium generator, 1971, various radiopharm. products, 1973, various clin. chem. test kits, devices, 1953-96; contbr. articles to mags. Cons. AID, Zaire, 1979, UN Capital Devel. Fund, Benin, 1977. 1st lt. A.C., U.S. Army, 1942-45, ETO. Fellow AAAS (life); mem. Am. Assn. Clin. Chemistry (emeritus, chmn. pub. rels. com. 1962), Am. Chem. Soc. (sr., emeritus), NY Acad. Scis., Sci. Rsch. Soc. Am. Unitarian Universalist. Avocations: folk dancing, growing exotic mushrooms. Home: 41 Concord Rd Sudbury MA 01776-2328 Office Phone: 978-443-5837. E-mail: med41@aol.com.

DEUTSCH, MARTIN BERNARD JOSEPH, editor, publishing executive; b. Karlsruhe, Fed. Republic of Germany, Apr. 7, 1931; came to U.S., 1939, naturalized, 1948; s. Benedikt and Margarethe (Zivi) D.; 1 son, Kenneth; m. Denise Elaine Brosius, Sept. 24, 1994; 1 adopted child, Ariel Jade YunXin. Student in history and journalism, CCNY, 1953; student in Eng. lit., Columbia U., summer 1955. CCNY coll. corr. N.Y. Times, 1951-53; mng. editor The Beachcomber, Long Beach Island, N.J., summers 1952, 53; reporter Southwest American, Ft. Smith, Ark., 1954-55; mng. editor Travel Courier and Travel Weekly, 1955-67; pres., editor, pub. travel mags. divsn. Ofcl. Airline Guides, N.Y.C., 1967-93; editor, pub. Reed Travel Mags., Secaucus, N.J., 1993-94; cons. Travel Industry Shows (Cruise Tour World), Pleasanton, Calif., 2002—; ptnr., database promotions, mktg. Morrell Wine Travel Experience, Harney Tea Tours, 2003—. CEO DB Prodns., Bedford, N.Y.; guest instr. U. Mass., 1975; cons., spkr. to travel and transp. industry. Monthly columnist: Up Front, Frequent Flyer mag., 1980-94; editor-at-large, monthly columnist Travel Agent mag., 1995-2001, pres. trade show divsn., 1995-99; pub. Selling North America, 1995-2000, CEO & columnist Travel Content on Demand, 2002—. Mem. Upper Manhattan Cmty. Planning Bd., 1965; mem. travel adv. bd. U.S. Dept. Commerce, U.S. Travel Svc., 1977-81; delegate White House Conf. on Travel and Tourism, 1995; officer Ctr. for Internat.

Health and Coop., N.Y.C. With U.S. Army, 1953-55. Recipient various awards for travel journalism. Home and Office: 15 W 72nd St New York NY 10023-3402 Office Phone: 212-787-5759. E-mail: mbjdeutsch@aol.com.

DEUTSCH, MAURICE MAYER, healthcare educator, consultant, medical librarian; s. Armand and Rosalie Deutsch; m. Diane Perkins, June 15, 1971. BSc magna cum laude, Bklyn. Coll., 1966; MLS, Pratt Inst., 1967; MSc in Zoology, U. Toronto, 1970; grad., B.C. Conservation and Outdoor Recreation, 1976. Sr. libr., tchr., cons. Simon Fraser U. Libr., Burnaby, 1971—97, acting dir. distance edn. info. svc., 1990—95; weight-loss cons., lectr. Creative Weight Loss Techniques., Tucson, 2000—. Portrait photographer MD Studios, Burnaby, B.C., Canada, 1978—82; sci. info. resources cons., 1986—93; weight-loss cons., tchr. Oasis Inst., Tucson, 2002—, Tucson Open U., 2003—05, Pima C.C., 2004; cons. Take Off Pounds Sensibly, Tuscon, 2004; host TV show Lose Weight Forever Access Tucson, 2004—. Author: Lose Weight Forever-Take It Off & Keep It Off! Success Strategies for PErmanent Weight Loss, 2005. Vol. Carnegie Cmty. Ctr. Kitchen, Vancouver, 1999—2000; weight-loss cons. El Pueblo Clinic Pima County Health Dept., Tucson, 2004—; weight-loss cons., tchr. St. Philip's Episcopal Ch., 2003—05. Mem.: Tucson Macintosh Users Group, Beta Phi Mu, Phi Beta Kappa. Avocations: weightlifting, walking, music, gardening. Home: 2660 W Dante Way Tucson AZ 85741-2516 Office: Creative Weight Loss Techniques 2660 W Dante Way Tucson AZ 85741-2516 Office Phone: 520-850-5975. Business E-Mail: maurice@excel.com.

DEUTSCH, NINA, musician, vocalist; b. San Antonio, Mar. 15; d. Irvin and Freda (Smukler) Deutsch. BS, Juilliard Sch. Music, 1964; MMA, Yale U., 1973. Concert pianist internat. and U.S. tours, 1965-82; entertainer, solo pianist Holland Am. Cruise Lines, 1987, 89-90; freelance pianist, lectr. music, 1990—; pianist Royal Caribbean Cruise Lines, 2004. Exec. v.p. Internat. Symphony, N.Y.C., 1978—82. *Nina Deutsch achieved the first musical exchange on stage in the history of the People's Republic of China in 1982. As executive vice president of International Symphony for World Peace in 1982, she represented her organization in a series of concerts on that theme. ISWP had collected musical scores on the theme of Peace, Friendship, and Humanity. Her tour was endorsed by former U.S. President George Bush, and his brother Prescott Bush. Nina is also the first woman to have recorded the massive solo piano repertoire of Charles Ives. She presents lectures on leaders in American music and lectures with musical illustrations.* Musician (pianist): (albums) Charles Ives, 1976; author: (plays) Portrait of Clara Schumann, 1987, Portrait of Liberace, 1995; contbr. articles to mags. and newspapers. Bd. dirs. Metzner Found. Overseas Relief; Ft. Lee coord. Channel 13, 1974. Recipient award for Am. music, Nat. Fedn. Music Clubs, 1975; grantee, Philips Petroleum Found., 1982; scholar, Oberlin Coll.; Tanglewood fellow, Wulsin Fellowship, 1966. Mem.: Yale Alumni Assn. Bergen County. Achievements include first American pianist to play all American music in communist China, 1982; first woman pianist to entertain for Holland America; first and only woman to record complete solo piano music of Charles Ives. Avocations: swimming, hiking, baking. Home: PO Box 405 Leonia NJ 07605-0405 Office Phone: 201-947-0087. E-mail: ianist100@aol.com.

DEUTSCH, PETER R., former congressman; b. Bronx, NY, Apr. 1, 1957; m. Lori Ann Coffino; children: Jonathan Michael, Danielle Brooke. BA in Psychology, Swarthmore Coll., 1979; JD, Yale U., 1982. Atty., 1983—; mem. Fla. Ho. Reps., 1983—93, U.S. Congress 20th Fla. dist., 1993—2005; mem. energy and commerce com. Dir., founder Medicare Info. Program, Broward County, Fla., 1981-82. Recipient Humanitarian award Deborah Hosp., 1984, Torch of Liberty award Anti-Defamation League, 1985, Appreciation award Paralyzed Vets Assn., 1987, Scroll of Hon. Jewish Fedn., 1988; named Legislator of Yr. Broward County Chiropractic Soc., 1984, 85, Man of Yr. Lauderhill Regular Dem. Club, 1990, Alzheimer's Assn., 1990; Swarthmore Nat. scholar, 1975-79; J. Roland Pennock fellow, 1979. Mem. W. Broward Dem. Club, Broward Young Dems., Lauderhill Dem. Club, Pembroke Pines Dem. Club, Davie Dem. Club, United Dem. Club, Plantation Club, Sunrise C. of C., Tamarac C. of C., Margate Knights of Pythias, B'nai B'rith (Israeli award, Sunrise 1983), Jewish Fedn., Gold Key, Phi Beta Kappa. Democrat.

DEUTSCH, ROBERT WILLIAM, physicist; b. Far Rockaway, N.Y., Mar. 21, 1924; s. Nathan and Lena (Berger) D.; m. Florence Kadish, Sept. 11, 1949; children: Jane Lisa, David Jeffrey. BS, MIT, 1948; PhD, U. Calif., 1953; LLD (hon.), U. Balt., 1999; LHD (hon.), Towson U., 1998; DSc (hon.), U. Md. Baltimore County, 2000. Registered profl. engr., Md., Mich. Physics cons. Martin-Marietta Corp., Balt., 1962-64; prof., chmn. dept. nuclear sci. and engring. Cath. U. Am., 1963-71; chmn. bd., CEO Gen. Physics Corp., Columbia, Md., 1966-87, RWD Tech. Inc., Balt., 1988—2004, chmn., 2005—. Contbr. articles to profl. jours.; author newspaper articles and pub. info. booklets on nuclear power. Bd. visitors U. Md. Baltimore County. Fellow Am. Nuclear Soc.; mem. NAE, AAAS, Am. Soc. Engring. Edn. Achievements include the founding of world class companies dedicated to improving human performance in high technology workplaces. Office: RWD Tech Inc 5521 Research Park Dr Baltimore MD 21228 E-mail: rdeutsch@rwd.com.

DEUTSCH, SID, biomedical engineer, educator; b. N.Y.C., Sept. 19, 1918; s. Elias and Gussie (Hazen) D.; m. Ruth Appleman, Nov. 15, 1941 (div. June 1969), remarried, 1984; children: Alice, Phyllis, Naomi; m. Jane Arieti, Aug., 1969 (dec. Mar., 1978); m. Annette Page, Apr., 1979 (div. Dec., 1984). BEE, Cooper Union, 1941; MEE, Bklyn. Poly. Inst., 1947, PhD, 1955. Designer Fairchild Camera & Instrument Co., N.Y.C., 1943-44; instr. Madison Inst., Newark, 1946-50; engr. Poly. R & D Co., Bklyn., 1950-54; mem. faculty Bklyn. Poly. Inst., 1954-72, prof. elec. engring., 1962-72; prof. bioengring. Rutgers U. Med. Sch., Piscataway, N.J., 1972-79; vis. prof. U. S.Fla., Tampa, 1983-98. Vis. prof. Tel Aviv U., Israel, 1977, prof. bioengring, 1979-84; cons. Lewyt Mfg. Corp., 1958-60; affiliate Rockefeller Inst., 1961-64. Author: Theory and Design of TV Receivers, 1951, Models of the Nervous System, 1967, Return of the Ether: When Theory and Reality Collide, 1999, Are You Conscious, and Can You Prove It? Short Science Essays, 2003; co-author: Biomedical Instruments: Theory and Design, 1976, 2d edit., 1992, Neuroelectric Systems, 1987, Understanding the Nervous System: An Engineering Perspective, 1993; assoc. editor: IEEE Transactions on Biomedical Engring., 1991-96; patentee pseudorandom dot scan for TV. Mem. adult edn. com. Roslyn (N.Y.) Pub. Schs., 1955-58. With USNR, 1944-46. Fellow IEEE, Soc. for Info. Display; mem. Sigma Xi, Tau Beta Pi, Eta Kappa Nu. Home: 3967 Oakhurst Blvd Sarasota FL 34233-1447

DEUTSCH, STACIA, rabbi, director, writer; b. Denver, July 8, 1968; d. Harvey E. and Paula L. (Kantor) D.; m. Richard M. Steinberg, Aug. 22, 1993; children: Jacob, Zachary. BA, Scripps Coll., 1990; MAHL, Hebrew Union Coll., Cin., 1993. Ordained rabbi, 1995. Asst. rabbi Beth Abraham Congregation, Dayton, Ohio, 1995-97; program dir. Hebrew Union Coll., Cin., 1997-99, dir. outreach edn., 1999—. Author: Kiss Me Quick, 1999, My Hero, 2000, (children's books)(Blast to the Past series with Rhody Cohon) Lincoln's Legacy, 2005. Mem. Ctrl. Conf. Am. Rabbis. Address: c/o Literary Group Internat Ste 1505 270 Lafayette St New York NY 10012*

DEUTSCH, STANLEY, retired anesthesiologist, educator; b. N.Y.C., Apr. 4, 1930; s. Elias and Estelle (Press) D.; m. Margaret R. Zuanic, July 11, 1971; children: Susan, Ellen, Nina, Eva. BA, NYU, 1950; MA, Boston U., 1951, PhD, 1955, MD, 1957. Diplomate Am. Bd. Anesthesiology. Rsch. and teaching fellow in physiology Boston U. Sch. Medicine, 1951-55; intern U. Pa. Grad. Hosp., 1957-58; resident in anesthesiology Hosp. U. Pa., 1958-61; asst. prof. anesthesiology U. Pa., 1963-65; asst. prof. Harvard U., 1965-69; prof. U. Chgo., 1969-71; prof., head. dept. anesthesiology U. Okla. Health Scis. Center, 1971-82; prof. anesthesiology U. Tex. Med. Sch., Houston, 1982-89, George Washington Sch. Medicine, Washington, 1989-98, prof. emeritus, 1998—. Cons. VA Med. Center, Oklahoma City. Contbr. articles to profl. publs. Capt., M.C. USAR, 1961-63. Mem. AMA, Am. Soc. Anesthesiologists, D.C. Med. Assn., Sigma Xi, Alpha Omega Alpha. Home: 1508 Colonial Ct Arlington VA 22209-1439 Office: George Washington U Hosp 901 23rd St NW Washington DC 20037-2327

DEUTSCH, THOMAS FREDERICK, physicist; b. Vienna, Apr. 24, 1932; came to U.S., 1939; s. George and Sabina (Edel) D.; m. Judy Foreman, May 5, 1990. B. Enging Physics, Cornell U., 1955; AM, Harvard U., 1956, PhD, 1961. Prin. rsch. scientist Raytheon Co., Lexington, Mass., 1960-74; staff mem. Mass. Inst. Tech., Lexington, 1974-84; physicist Mass. Gen. Hosp., Boston, 1984—; assoc. prof. Harvard Med. Sch., Boston, 1987—. Contbr. articles to profl. jours.; patentee in field. Recipient of R.W. Wood Prize, 1991, Optical Soc. Am. Fellow Am. Phys. Soc., Optical Soc. Am. (Wood prize 1991), Am. Soc. for Lasers in Medicine; mem. IEEE (sr.). Office: Bar 703 Wellman Labs Mass Gen Hosp Boston MA 02114-2605

DEUTSCHE, KIRSTEN HANSEN, pharmaceutical company executive; b. Snartemo, Norway, June 2, 1949; came to U.S., 1952; d. Fridjof and Gerda Hansen; m. Donald Edgar Deutsche, Mar. 28, 1982 (div. Mar. 2000). BA, Central Coll., Pella, Iowa, 1971; MBA, NYU, 1998. Tchr. math. and sci. St. John's Sch., Dunellen, N.J., 1971-74; chemist BOC Inc., Murray Hill, N.J., 1974-82; regulatory affairs mgr. Anaquest/BOC Inc., Murray Hill, 1982-87, CIBA Geigy, Summit, N.J., 1987-88; regulatory affairs asst. dir. Organon/AKZO, West Orange, N.J., 1988-93; regulator affairs dir. Gynopharma, Somerville, N.J., 1993-95; pres., cons. Kearstin Pharm. Contracting, Summit, 1995—. Patentee in field. Active vol. Helpline, CASA, Supervised Visitation. Mem. Nat. Assn. Investors, Scandinavian House Assoc., Regulatory Affairs Profl. Soc., Am. Contract Bridge League (life master). Avocations: reading, travel, gardening, investing, exercise.

DEUTSCHMAN, LOUISE TOLLIVER, curator; b. Taylorville, Ill., Sept. 6, 1921; m. Paul Eugene Deutschman, Dec. 20, 1941 (div. 1966); 1 child, Deborah Elliott. BA MacMurray Coll., 1937; postgrad., Northwestern U., Sorbonne, Paris, 1950—66. Assoc. dir. Waddell Gallery, NYC, 1966—74, Sidney Janis Gallery, NYC, 1975—78; dir. Alex Rosenberg Gallery, NYC, 1978—80; assoc. Sidney Janis Gallery, NYC, 1980—2000; curator PaceWildenstein, NYC, 2000—. Guest curator Nasher Sculpture Ctr., Dallas, 2004.

DEUTZ, NATALIE RUBINSTEIN, actress, consultant; b. Plymouth, Mass., Sept. 26; d. Louis and Lillian Rubinstein; m. Nov. 29, 1947 (dec.). Student, Simmons Coll., Modern Sch. Applied Art. Fashion buyer Wm. Filene's Sons Co., Boston, 1940-47; asst. to corp. pres. Columbia Textiles, Inc., NYC, 1956-58; dir. John Robert Powers Sch., NYC, 1968-72; v.p., nat. dir. fashion merchandising, dir. advt. workshop Barbizon Internat., Inc., NYC, 1972-83. Cons., 1983—. Films include Arthur on the Rocks, Crocodile Dundee, Moonstruck, Six Degrees of Separation; appeared on (TV) Sopranos; appeared in Super Elderly People for Japanese TV; commls. include Rogaine, Levis, Blockbuster. Mem.: AFTRA, SAG.

DEVAAN, JON S., information technology executive; BS in Math. & Computer Sci., Oreg. State U., 1985. From mgr. to sr. v.p. Microsoft, Redmond, Wash., sr. v.p. TV divsn., 1999—2002, sr. v.p., software engring. strategy, 2003—. Spkr. in field; panelist UN World TV Forum, 2000. Achievements include patents for simplifying user interface elements in PC applications. Office: One Microsoft Way Redmond WA 98052-6399

DEVAN, DEBORAH HUNT, lawyer; b. Allentown, Pa., Jan. 22, 1950; d. Valerio R. and Audrey (Miller) H.; m. Mark S. Devan, May 30, 1981; children: Emily, David, Eric. BA in Econs. magna cum laude, U. Md., 1972, JD cum laude, 1975. Bar: Md. 1975, D.C. 1976, U.S. Dist. Ct. Md. 1976, U.S. Dist. Ct. D.C. 1987, U.S. Ct. Appeals (4th cir.) 1988, U.S. Ct. Appeals (2d cir.) 1991, U.S. Supreme Ct. 1980, Md. Ct. Appeals 1975, D.C. Ct. Appeals 1976. Ptnr. Weinberg and Green, Balt., 1974-94; prin. Neuberger, Quinn, Gielen, Rubin & Gibber, P.A., Balt., 1994—. Bd. dirs. Lutheran Hosp. Md., Inc., 1981-86, Cystic Fibrosis Found., 1983 (Community Svc. Gold award), Lutheran Health Care Corp., 1988-91, U. Md. Law Sch. Fund, 1991, Balt. Devel. Corp., 1999—, U. Md. Sch. Law Alumni Assn., 2000—; trustee Merry-Go-Round Enterprises, Inc. Named one of Top 100 Md. Women, 2005. Fellow Am. Coll. Bankruptcy; mem. ABA (bus. bankruptcy com., subcommittee bankruptcy litigation, subcommittee claims and priorities), Am. Bankruptcy Inst., Turnaround Mgmt. Assn., Women's Bar Assn., Assn. Comml. Fin. Attys., Md. State Bar Assn., Inc. (subcommittee creditor's rights, bankruptcy and insolvency), Bankruptcy Bar Assn. Md. (corp. sec., bd. dirs., pres. 1996-97), Exec. and Profl. Women's Coun. Md. (1st v.p. 1984), Network 2000, Comml. Real Estate Women, Bar Assn. Balt. City (profl. ethics com. 1980, publicity com. 1981). Office: Neuberger Quinn Gielen Rubin & Gibber 1 South St Fl 27 Baltimore MD 21202-3282

DEVANE, MINDY KLEIN, financial planner; b. Detroit, May 4, 1954; d. Myer and Maxine (Gold) Klein; m. Kenneth Manuel DeVane, Nov. 20, 1993. BS in Journalism, U. Fla., 1976, MBA in Fin., 1981. CFP. Mktg. rep. IBM, Tampa, 1981-85; account exec. Thomson McKinnon, Tampa, 1985-88, Smith Barney, Miami, 1988-89; underwriter Cigna, North Miami, Fla., 1989-92; sr. account exec. Cohig & Assocs., Tampa, 1992-93; v.p. Josephthal Lyon & Ross, Tampa, 1993-96; v.p. investments Raymond James, Tampa, 1996-99; fin. planner Griffith Bowles Fin. Mgmt. First Union Securities, Tampa, 1999—2001; proprietor DeVane Fin. Advisors, Tampa, 2001—. Allocations com. mem. United Way, Pinellas County, Fla., 1998, Hillsborough County, Fla., 1999; founder Hyde Park Exec. Women Leader Club, 1999-2002; bd. dirs. Vivo Fla. Orch. Guild, Sword of Hope; mem. ACS Guild. Recipient Outstanding Fin. Advisor award Asset Mgmt. Svcs. RJF, 1996-97. Mem. Fin. Planners Assn. (pres.-elect), Bus. and Profl. Women (editor 1986-88). Avocations: bicycling, swimming, collectibles. Home: 6308 Jacqueline Arbor Dr Temple Terrace FL 33617-3164 Office: PO Box 16626 Tampa FL 33687 E-mail: mdevane@tampabay.rr.com.

DEVANEY, DENNIS MARTIN, lawyer, educator; b. Cheverly, Md., Feb. 25, 1946; s. Peter Paul and Alice Dorothy (Duffy) D.; m. Caryn Joanne; children: Jeanne Marie, Susan Theresa. BA in History, U. Md., 1968, MA in Govt. Politics, 1970; JD, Georgetown U., 1975. Bar: Md. 1976, D.C. 1976, Fla. 1977, Mich. 1999, U.S. Supreme Ct. 1980. Instr. European div. U. Md., Bremerhaven, Fed. Republic Germany, 1971-72; legis. asst. Md. Senate Jud. Commn., Annapolis, 1973-74; asst. gen. counsel U.S. Brewers Assn., Washington, 1975-77; counsel Food Mktg. Inst., Washington, 1977-79; ptnr. Randall, Bangert & Thelen, Washington, 1979-81; assoc. Tighe, Curhan & Piliero, Washington, 1981-82; mem. U.S. Merit System Protection Bd., Washington, 1982-88; gen. counsel Fed. Labor Relations Auth., Washington, 1988; mem. NLRB, 1988-94; commr. US Internat. Trade Commn., 2001; of counsel Winston & Strawn, 1995-97, Butzel Long, 1997—2001; ptnr. Williams, Mullen Clark and Dobbins, 2002—04; counsel Varnum, Riddering, Schmidt & Howlett, LLP, 2004—05; shareholder Strobl Cunningham @ Sharp, Bloomfield Hills, Mich., 2005—. Adj. prof. George Washington U., Washington, 1982—90, Boston U., 1992—94, 2002, Cornell U., 1995, Tulane U., 1995; assoc. prof. Wayne State U., 1995—2001, Thomas Cooley Law Sch., 2004. Served with USN, 1970-72, ETO. Mem. ABA, Md. Bar Assn., D.C. Bar Assn., Fla. Bar Assn., Mich. State Bar, Fed. Bar Assn., Phi Alpha Theta, Pi Sigma Alpha, Delta Theta Phi, Omicron Delta Kappa. Roman Catholic. Home: 5240 Buell Dr Commerce Township MI 48382 Office: Strobl Cunningham & Sharp 300 E Long Rd Ste 200 Bloomfield Hills MI 48304-2376 Office Phone: 248-205-2766. Business E-Mail: ddevaney@stroblpc.com.

DEVANEY, DONALD EVERETT, law enforcement official; b. Providence, Nov. 21, 1936; s. William Francis and Elizabeth Florence (Hill) D.; m. Tokiko Yoshida, May 19, 1960; 1 child, George Y. AA in Edn., El Paso C.C., 1973; BA, SUNY, Albany, 1979. Sgt. maj. U.S. Army, 1954-83; customs inspector U.S. Customs Svc., Honolulu, 1983-84; provost marshal Tripler Army Med. Ctr., Honolulu, 1984—; past regional chair Europe and Asia Internat. Assn. Healthcare Security and Safety, 1989—93, 1997—2001. Past dir. Kalihi-Palama Immigrant Svc. Ctr.; extraordinary min. of the eucharist Tripler Cath. Cmty., 1985—2002; sec. Friends Tipler Med. Ctr., Inc. Nat. co-chair NAUS, 2003—; bd. dirs. Coalition for a Drug Free Hawaii, 1996—2000; sec. USO-Hawaii, 1998—2001; bd. dirs. U.S. Army Hawaii Housing Found., 2003—; sec. bd. dirs. Newtown Cmty. Assn., 2004; vice chair U.S. Army Hawaii Retiree Coun., 1985—. Decorated Legoin of Merit; named to Hawaii Joint Police Hall of Fame, 1998, Nelson W. Aldrich H.S. Hall of Honor, 1998; recipient Disting. Svc. award, Hawaii Joint Police, 1977, 1986, George Washington Honor medal, Freedom's Found., 1973, Order Mil. Merit, 1996, Elwood J. McGuire award, Hawaii, 1997. Mem.: KC, DAV (life), Internat. Assn. Chiefs of Police, Hawaii Coun. Police and Pvt. Security, Nat. Assn. for Uniformed Svcs. (v.p. Hawaii chpt., nat. bd. dirs. 1996—2000, co-chmn. bd. nat. 2003—), CID Agt. Assn., Hawaii Joint Police Assn. (pres. 1985, 1998, 1999), Friend Med. Regt., Ret. Enlisted Assn. (life), Noncommd. Officer Assn. (life), Rotary (pres. Pearl Harbor chpt. 1991—92, dir. cmty. svc. Dist. 5000 1992—93). Roman Catholic. Avocation: coin and stamp collecting. Home: 98-911 Ainanui Loop Aiea HI 96701-2766 Office: Office Provost Marshal Tripler Army Med Ctr Honolulu HI 96859-5000 Office Phone: 808-433-4465. E-mail: donald.devaney@amedd.army.mil, ddevaney@hawaii.rr.com.

DEVANEY, EARL E., federal agency administrator; m. Judith Devaney; 2 children. BA in Govt., Franklin & Marshall Coll., 1970; grad. exec. devel. program, George Washington U., 1990. Joined Secret Svc., 1971, various positions including spl. agt. in charge Office Investigations Washington, spl. agt. in charge Fraud Divsn.; dir. Office Criminal Enforcement, Forensics and Tng. EPA, 1991—99; inspector gen. U.S. Dept. Interior, Washington, 1999—. Office: US Dept Interior Inspector Gen 1849 C St NW Washington DC 20240

DEVANEY, ROBERT L., mathematician, educator; BA, MA, Holy Cross Coll., 1969; PhD, U. Calif., Berkeley, Calif., 1973. Instr. Northwestern U., Tufts U., U. Md.; prof. Dept. Math. Boston (Mass.) U., 1980—. Dir. Dynamical Sys. and Tech. Project NSF, 1989—, dir. Regional Geometry Inst., 1990—93. Author (or editor): 10 books. Recipient Deborah and Franklin Tepper Haimo award, 1994, Disting. Tchg. award, N.E. Sect. Math. Assn. Am., 1994, Dir.'s award, NSF, 2002, Excellence award, ICTCM, 2002. Office: Dept Math Boston Univ MCS 164 111 Cummington St Boston MA 02215 E-mail: bob@bu.edu.

DEVANNY, CARYN BETH, elementary school educator; b. Warren, Ohio, Nov. 22, 1976; d. John Joseph and Lynnette Eileen Devanny. BS in Elem. Edn., Youngstown (Ohio) State U., 2000, MS in Edn., 2004. Cert. tchr. Ohio, 2000. Tchr. Hartford (Ohio) Elem. Sch. Joseph Badger Local Sch. Dist., 2002—. Tchr. saturday enrichment Trumbull County Ednl. Svc. Ctr., Warren, Ohio, 2000—, liaison lang. arts and sci., 2004—, writer curriculum standards guides, 2004—; tchr. summer sch. Joseph Badger Local Sch. Dist., 2000—. Nominee Bonnie Chambers award, Hartford (Ohio) Elem. Sch., 2004. Mem.: Internat. Reading Assn., ACSD, Mahoning Valley Profls. 20/30 (trustee 2004—05), Phi Kappa Phi, Beta Sigma Phi Internat. Sorority (v.p. 2003—05, named Girl of the Yr. 1998, 2002, Perfect Attendance award 1996—2002). Avocations: reading, swimming, travel. Home: 3073 B Ivy Hill Circle North Cortland OH 44410-9359 Office Phone: 330-772-2401. Personal E-mail: cbeth76@aol.com.

DEVANNY, LOUISE BELL, public relations executive; b. Bklyn., Oct. 6, 1959; d. Robert Lloyd and Helen Louise (Matthews) Bell; m. Scott William Devanny. BA, Washington and Jefferson Coll., 1980. Mem. White House Staff, Washington, 1981-89, corr. analyst, 1981-82, mem. photo office staff, 1982-85; staff asst. First Lady's office Washington, 1985-89; assoc. campaign dir. Ketchum Inc., Pitts., 1990-91, campaign dir., 1991-92; project dir. Nat. Cmty. Devel. Svcs., Inc., Atlanta, 1993-94; fundraising cons. L&S Enterprises, Inc., Annapolis, Md., 1994—. Asst. Portrait Project, Washington, 1982—85; show coord. photography exhbn. Corcoran Gallery Art, Washington, 1985. Asst. photo editor: People and Power, 1985. Trustee Linden Hall Sch. Girls, 1996—2002, treas. bd. dirs., 1999—2002; bd. dirs. Annapolis Symphony, 1996—2003, Chesapeake Youth Symphony Orch., Inc., 1996—99; sustainer Jr. League, Annapolis; trustee Hammond Hardwood House, 2000—; mem. admissions bd. Washington and Jefferson Coll., 1981—, mem. devel. coun., 1985—88, trustee, 1990—93. Recipient Secret Svc. award, 1984, Outstanding Alumnae award, Linden Hall, 1986. Mem.: DAR (regent Petty Stewart Tea Party chpt. 2002), World Affairs Coun., Art Barn Assn., Hammond Hardwood House (chair aux.), Washington and Jefferson Coll. Washington Area Alumni (bd. dirs. 1986—90, mem. exec. alumni com. 1988—90, Disting. Alumni award 1994). Republican. Presbyterian. Avocations: sailing, golf. Home and Office: L&S Enterprises Inc 363 Kingsberry Dr Annapolis MD 21409 Fax: 410-349-1485. Personal E-mail: weezer1@worldnet.att.net.

DEVANTIER, PAUL W., communications executive, broadcast executive; b. Wausau, Wis., Mar. 25, 1946; w. Walter Herman and Ella Marie (Mundt) D.; m. Ellen Stapel, Aug. 2, 1970; children: Richard, John, Andrew, Katie, Susan. BA, Concordia Coll., 1968; MDiv, Concordia Sem., 1972; M in Mass Comm., So. Ill. U., Edwardsville, 1993; LLD, Concordia U., 1998. Radio announcer Sta. WXCO, Wausau, 1965-68, Sta. KRCH, St. Louis, 1968-72; dir. devel. Sta. KFUO-AM-FM, St. Louis, 1972-74, gen. mgr., 1974-82; exec. dir. comms. Luth. Ch.-Mo. Synod, St. Louis, 1982-2000; chief comm. officer Bethesda Luth. Homes and Svcs., Watertown, Wis., 2000—02; nat. dir. Infant Adoption Awareness Tng. Program, Washington, 2002—. Spkr. By the Way (internat. syndicated radio program) 1974—. Author: By the Way, 1993, By the Way, Encore, 1999; exec. prodr.: (religious documentary film) Hymn A Celebration of Change, 1984 (Angel award), (TV spl.) Easter Alive 'Round the World, 1993 (Emmy award nomination), (TV spl.) Not Without Hope, 1994 (Angel award), Martin Luther Promo, 1998 (Telley award), Message of Hope, 1998 (Angel award DeRose Hinkhouse award), Just in Time For Christmas, 1999 (Angel award De Rose Hinkhouse award), Message of Love, 2000 (Angel award); (radio) Lutheran School Spots, 1999 (Angel award), Classical Radio Station of the Year in America, 1999 (Marconi award), (video) Free to Voice the Gospel, 2000 (Angel award), syndicated radio By The Way, 2001 (Angel award), television spl. So Much Like Us, 2002 (Angel award, Wis. Coun. on Devel. Disabilities award), television campaign, Thanks for Considering Adoption, 2004 (Angel award), Adoption Awareness, 2005 (Angel award); exec. dir. Luth. Witness mag., 1999 (Associated Ch. Press Best of Class award). Trustee, pres. Luth. Film Assocs., N.Y.C., 1982-2000; bd. dirs. Excellence in Media, Hollywood, 2001—. Recipient Outstanding Parent award, Adoption and Foster Care Coalition, 2002. Office: Nat Coun for Adoption 225 N Washington St Alexandria VA 22314-2520 Office Phone: 866-212-3678. Personal E-mail: pdevantier@msn.com.

DEVARD, JERRI, marketing professional; BA in Econs., Spelman Coll., 1979; MBA in Mktg., Atlanta U., 1983. Mktg. asst. The Pillsbury Co., Mpls., 1983—92, group mktg. mgr. cake mixes divsn., 1992—93; dir. suites mktg. Minn. Vikings, 1993—94; v.p. mktg. Harrah's Entertainment, New Orleans, 1994—96; v.p. mktg. Color Cosmetics Revlon, 1996; with Citigroup, chief mktg. officer e-Consumer line of bus.; sr. v.p. brand mgmt. and mktg. comm. Verizon Comms., N.Y.C., 2003—. Bd. dirs. Exec. Leadership Coun. Found. Mem.: Nat. Black MBA Assn., Spelman Coll. Alumnae Assn. Office: Verizon Communications Inc 1095 Ave of the Americas New York NY 10036-6797

DEVARIS, JEANNETTE MARY, psychologist; b. Burbank, Calif., Jan. 7, 1947; d. Nicholas Propper Klein and Elizabeth (Von Lichtenberg) Schaeffer; m. Robert Lee Blake, May 20, 1967 (div. 1979); 1 child: Brendon; m. Panayotis Eric DeVaris, Dec. 5, 1988. BA, Adelphi U., 1968; MA, Fairleigh Dickinson U., 1977; PhD, Seton Hall U., 1987. Lic. psychologist, N.J. Caseworker N.Y.C. Welfare Dept., 1968-72; alcohol and drug rehab. counselor U.S. Army, Ft. Monmouth, NJ, 1972-76; psychol. intern N.J. State Intern Program, Trenton, 1977-78; psychologist Greystone Psychiat. Hosp., Greystone Park, NJ, 1979; sr. psychologist R. Hall Cmty. Mental Health Ctr., Bridgewater, NJ, 1979-90; pvt. practice South Orange and Somerset, NJ, 1988—. Tng. supr. Grad. Sch. Applied and Profl. Psychology; adj. prof. Seton Hall U.; sponsor and participant in Cable TV program; mem. South Orange Critical Support Team Vol. Group of Psychologists. Contbr. articles to profl.

jours. Mem. APA, Nat. Register Health Svc. Providers, N.J. Psychol. Assn. (bd. dirs., interprofl. rels. com.), Soc. Psychologists in Pvt. Practice (bd. dirs., spkrs. bur. com.). Avocations: travel, reading. Office Phone: 973-762-3149. Personal E-mail: drdevaris@aol.com.

DEVARIS, PANAYOTIS ERIC, architect; b. Lefkas Island, Greece, Dec. 29, 1932; came to U.S., 1960; M.Arch, Ecole des Beaux Arts, Paris, 1960; grad. cert. in bus. adminstrn., L.I. U., 1981. Registered architect; cert. Nat. Council Archtl. Registration Bds.; cert. profl. planner. Sr. corp. architect AT&T, N.Y.C., 1972-90, PSE&G, N.J., 1990-93, cons., 1990-93; pres. DeVaris/Workspace Planning & Design, Inc., 1990-97. Prin. works include projects in N.Y.C.: World Trade Ctr., Park Lane Hotel, The Gershwin Theatre, The Sovereign Apts., The Uris Office Bldg.; in Conn.: Wesleyan U. Dormitories, 1960-72; for AT&T: Microelectronics Hdqs., Berkeley Heights, N.J., Network Software Ctr., Lisle, Ill., AT&T Corp. Ctr., Chgo., Materials Mgmt. Ctrs., Sacramento, Calif., Wichita, Kans., Ramapo, N.Y., AT&T Techs. Offices, Tokyo, 1972-90; author, internat. lectr. in field of work environments; juror furniture design competition Corp. Design mag., Annual Design Awards N.Y. State Assn. Architects; contbr. articles to trade mags. Mem. exec. com. Architects for Social Responsibility, 1988-90; village trustee Orange Village, NJ. Recipient tech. excellence award Western Electric Co., Inc., 1983. Fellow AIA (chmn. corp. architects com. N.Y. chpt. 1978, nat. chpt. 1986, N.J. chpt. 1992, mem. steering com. 1983-90, rep. to Internat. Union of Architects 1985-91). Home: 18 Harding Dr South Orange NJ 07079-1203

DE VARON, LORNA COOKE, choral conductor; b. Western Springs, Ill., Jan. 17, 1921; d. Vernon Walter and Hazel Mildred (Watts) Cooke; m. Jose de Varon, May 14, 1944; children: David, Joanna, Cristina, Alexander. BA, Wellesley Coll., 1942; MA, Radcliffe Coll., 1945; MusD honoris causa, New Eng. Conservatory, 1988. Asst. condr. Radcliffe Choral Soc., Radcliffe-Harvard Choir, 1942-44; condr. Bryn Mawr Coll. Choir, 1944-47; condr. chorus, chmn. choral dept. New Eng. Conservatory Music, Boston, 1947-88, condr. chorus for concerts with Boston Symphony Orch., 1952-86; concert performer New Eng. Conservatory Chorus, tours in U.S., Europe, Russia, Israel, China; condr. Israel Summer Festival, 1977-79; condr., tchr. choral conducting Tanglewood Festival Chorus, 1952-66; condr. New Eng. Conservatory Camerata, 1989—; prof. emerita New Eng. Conservatory; condr. Longy Chamber Chorus, 1989—2005. Guest condr. Cameron Singers, Israel, 1984, Beijing Radio Chorus and Orch., Beijing, 1987; chmn. Choral Inst. of Composers Conf., 1983-85; mem. choral adv. panel Nat. Endowment for Arts; condr. New Eng. Conservatory Chamber Singers, summers 1982-87, Monadnock Music Festival. Editor, arranger choral works, E.C. Schirmer and Galaxy Pubs., Boston. Mem. Cambridge Arts Council. Recipient medal for Disting. Achievement City of Boston, 1967, medal for Disting. Achievement Radcliffe Grad. Soc., 1972, medal for Disting. Achievement Wellesley Coll., 1978, medal of Israel, 1977, Ludi award New Eng. Conservatory, 1983, Harvard Glee Club medal, 1987. Mem. Am. Choral Condrs. Assn., Pi Kappa Lambda. Home: 94 Lake View Ave Cambridge MA 02138-3326 Personal E-mail: ldevaron@aol.com.

DE VARONA, DONNA, sports reporter, former Olympic swimmer; b. San Diego, Apr. 26, 1947; m. John Pinto; 2 children. BA in polit. sci., UCLA; four doctoral degrees (hon.). On-air analyst, commentator, host, writer ABC Sports, 1965—76, 1983—98, Olympic Coverage NBC, 1976—83; radio host Donna de Varona on Sports. Chair Women's World Cup Soccer Tournament Organizing Com., 1999; served on US Sec. Edn. Commn. on Opportunity in Athletics, 2002—03; founding mem., first pres. Women's Sport Found., 1979—84; served four terms Pres. Coun. Physical Fitness and Sports. Named Most Outstanding Female Athlete World, AP, 1964, United Press Internat. (UPI), 1964; named to US Olympic Hall Fame, Bay Area Hall Fame, San Jose Hall Fame, Woman's Hall Fame, 2003; recipient Internat. Swimming Hall Fame Gold Medallion, Olympia Award for contbn. to Olympic Movement, Olympic Order, Internat. Olympic Com., Susan B. Anthony Trailblazer award, Overcoming Obstacle award, Cmty. Edn. Found., 2002, Theodore Roosevelt (Teddy) award, Nat. Collegiate Athletic Assn. (NCAA), Emmy award for Special Olympics coverage, 1991. Achievements include youngest competitor at 1960 Olympics games; broke 18 world swimming records; won 2 Olympic Gold medals, 400-meter individual medley and 4 by 100 meter relay, 1964 Olympics; won 37 national championships; first female sports broadcaster on network TV, 1965; first woman to do TV commentary on Olympics, 1968; active in passing 1978 Amateur Sports Act by US Congress and 1972 landmark "Title IX" legis.

DEVAUL, DIANE D., financial planner; b. Ames, Iowa, July 12, 1943; d. Wayne Allen DeVaul and Ruth Louise Dana; m. Thomas Andrew Twomey, June 6, 1965 (div. Oct. 1978); children: Heather B. Twomey, Antonio DeVaul; m. Hagos Alemayehu, Apr. 30, 1982; 1 chlid, Victor Hagos DeVaul. BA, U. Iowa, 1965; MA, U. Md., 1972, PhD, 1998. Instr. Am. U., George Mason U., U. Md., 1976-77; policy analyst N.E.-Midwest Inst., Washington, 1978-86, dir. policy, 1986—; cons. to asst. sec. U.S. Dept. HUD, Washington, 1979. Dir. N.E. Regional Resource Ctr. for Innovation, U.S. Dept. Energy, Washington, 1997-2002, mem. grant rev. panel, 1998-2001; presenter in field. Author poetry book, 1979; contbr. articles to profl. jours. Recipient Commendation, Gov. of N.H., 1998. Mem. Am. Studies Assn. Office: NE-Midwest Inst 218 D St SE Washington DC 20003 E-mail: ddevaul@nemw.org.

DEVAULT, JOHN ANDREW, III, lawyer; b. Knoxville, Tenn., Oct. 17, 1942; s. John Andrew and Bobbie Candus (Pollack) DeV.; m. Laurie Sue Sheppard, Aug. 14, 1965; children— Carol Sue, Andrew Michael, Allan Livingston. B.S. in Broadcasting, U. Fla., 1964, J.D., 1967. Bar: Fla. 1967, U.S. Dist. Ct. (mid. dist.) Fla. 1967, U.S. Ct. Appeals (5th cir.) 1967, U.S. Supreme Ct. 1975, U.S. Claims Ct. 1980, U.S. Ct. Appeals (11th cir.) 1982. Law clk. to judge U.S. Dist. Ct., 1967-68; assoc. Bedell, Bedell, Dittmar & Smith, Jacksonville, Fla., 1968-70; ptnr. Bedell, Bedell, Dittmar, Smith & Zehmer, Jacksonville, 1970-83; mng. ptnr. Bedell, Dittmar, DeVault, Pillans and Cox, P.A., Jacksonville, 1983— . Exec. editor Law Rev.; mem. Univ. Fla. Moot Team, Fla. Blue Key; pres. Fla. Bar, 1995-96; mem. Ho. of Del., 1994-2000; Fellow Am. Coll. of Trial Lawyers, Imternat. Soc. Barristers; mem. ABA. Office: Bedell Bldg 101 E Adams St Jacksonville FL 32202-3303 Office Phone: 904-353-0211. Business E-Mail: jad@bedellfirm.com.

DEVAULT, JOHN LEE, oil industry executive, geophysicist; b. Kansas City, Mo., Aug. 4, 1937; s. Isaac Henderson and Evelyn Margaret (Rowell) DeVault; m. Janet Ann Miller, Sept. 11, 1968; children: Bryan Charles, Chris Lee. BSChE, Case Inst. Tech., 1959; BS, MacMurray Coll., 1961; MS, U. Houston, 1975. Lic. geophysicist Calif., Tex., Am. Assn. Petroleum Geologists, Soc. Ind. Profl. Earth Scientists. Geophysicist United Geophys., Europe, Africa, Middle East, Australia-Asia, Alaska, Houston, 1961—74; pres. Sercel Inc., Houston, 1974—88; chmn. bd. dirs. Jade Corp., Houston, 1988—. Contbr. articles to profl. jours. Trustee Culver Legion-Culver Academies; downstate v.p. Young Rep. Club, Springfield, 1960; bd. dirs. Jaycees, Springfield, Ill., 1960, Honors Coll., U. Houston, 1990—, McMurray Coll. Mem.: Am. Inst. Profl. Geologists (pres. Tex. sect., lic. geophysicist), Soc. Exploration Goephysics, Geophys. Soc. Houston (hon.; pres. 1987), Culver Club Greater Houston (pres.). Mem. Disciples Of Christ. Home: 703 Queensmill Ct Houston TX 77079-2411 Office: Jade Corp PO Box 218567 Houston TX 77218-8567

DEVEER, ROBERT KIPP, JR., investment banker; b. Englewood, NJ, Apr. 22, 1946; s. Robert Kipp and Patricia Ann (Mulcare) deV.; m. Sally J. Staub, Dec. 21, 1968 (dec. Jan. 1994); children: Robert Kipp III, James Britten; m. Mary Louise Leaf, Feb. 18, 1995. BA in Econs., Yale U., 1968; MBA, Stanford U., 1973. Assoc. The First Boston Corp., N.Y.C., 1973—78, v.p., 1978—85, mng. dir., 1985—, dir. east coast investment banking, 1988—92, head natural resources group, 1992—93; alternate dir. YPF, s.a., 1993—96; dir. TheraTech Inc., 1996—2000, Palatin Techs., Inc., 1998—. Pres.deVeer Capital LLC, 1996—. Lt. USN, 1968-71. Arjay Miller scholar Stanford Bus. Sch., 1973. Mem. SC Yacht Club, East Chop Beach Club (Martha's Vineyard). Avocations: skiing, golf. E-mail: deVeer46@aol.com.

DEVELLANO, JAMES CHARLES, professional hockey manager, baseball executive; b. Ont., Can., Jan. 18, 1943; came to U.S., 1979; s. James Joseph and Jean (Piter) D. Ont. scout St. Louis Blues NHL, Toronto, 1967-72; eastern Can. scout N.Y. Islanders, Toronto, 1972-74, dir. scouting, 1974-82; asst. gen. mgr. Islanders, L.I., N.Y., 1981-82; gen. mgr. Detroit Red Wings, 1982-90, sr. v.p., 1990—; v.p., gen. mgr. Indpls. Checkers, 1979-81; sr. v.p. Detroit Tigers, 2001—. Alternate gov. for Detroit Red Wings. Winner Stanley Cup with N.Y. Islanders, 1979-80, 80-81, 81-82, with Detroit Red Wings, 1996-97, 97-98, 2001-2002, Pres.'s Trophy with Detroit Red Wings, 1994-95, 95-96, 2001-2002, 2003-04. Mem. Nat. Hockey League (bd. govs.). Office: Detroit Red Wings Hockey Club Joe Louis Arena 600 Civic Center Dr Detroit MI 48226-4419

DEVENOT, DAVID CHARLES, human resources specialist, artist; b. Indpls., May 27, 1939; s. Charles Joseph and Pearl (Geodry) Devenot; m. Hillary Mock; children: Daniel, Mark. BBA, U. Hawaii, 1962. Dir. indsl. rels. USP Corp subs. Consol. Foods, Sara Lee, San Jose, Calif., 1964-70; mgr. human resources cons. and rsch. Hawaii Employers Coun., Honolulu, 1970. Adj. prof. U. Hawaii. Bd. dir. Hawn Humane Soc., Honolulu, 1975—, Am. Cancer Soc., 1989, pres. Pacific divsn.; active Hawaii Cmty. Svcs. Coun., 2004—. Mem.: Soc. Human Resource Mgmt., Santa Clara Valley Pers. Assn. (pres. 1968—69). Avocations: travel, photography, art, painting. Home: 2803 Puuhonua St Honolulu HI 96822-1765 Office: Hawaii Employers Coun 2682 Wai Wai Loop Honolulu HI 96819-1938 E-mail: ddevenot@hecouncil.org.

DEVENS, JOHN SEARLE, natural resources administrator; b. Shickshinny, Pa., Mar. 31, 1940; s. John Ezra and Laura (Bulkley) D.; m. Sharon I. Snyder (div. 1979); children: John, Jerilyn, James, Janis. BS, Belmont Coll., 1964; MEd, Emory U., 1966; PhD, Wichita State U., 1975. Dir. speech and hearing Columbia Coll., Columbia, SC, 1967—70; head dept. audiology Inst. Logopedics, Wichita, Kans., 1970—71; supr. audiology State of Alaska, Fairbanks, 1971—73; asst. prof. U. Houston, Victoria, Tex., 1975—77; pres. Prince William Sound C.C., Valdez, Alaska, 1977—92, Sterling Coll., Craftsbury Common, Vt., 1993—96; dir. Valdez Hearing and Speech Ctr.; exec. dir. Prince William Sound Regional Citizens' Adv. Coun., 1997—; prin., owner The Lake House a Country Inn, Valdez, 2000—. Owner, operator Valdez Hearing and Speech Ctr., 1977—92, Lake House Country Inn, 2000—. Prodr. films on hearing problems; contbr. articles to profl. jours. Mayor City of Valdez, 1985-89, mem. city coun., 1980-89; nat. chmn. adv. com. Horsemanship for Handicapped, 1964-67; mem. Alaska Gov.'s Coun. for Handicapped, 1980-82; pres. Valdez chpt. Alaska Visitors Assn., 1980; mem. small cities adv. coun. Nat. League Cities, 1983-87, mem. internat. econ. devel. task force; mem. Nat. Export Coun.; bd. dirs. Resource Devel. Coun.; Dem. nominee U.S. Ho. Reps., 1990, 92; hosted internat. conf. on oil spills for mayors; exec. dir. Prince William Sound Regional Citizens Adv. Coun., 1997—. Mem. Am. Speech-Lang. Hearing Assn. (cert. clin. competence in audiology and speech and lang. pathology), Am. C. of C. in Korea, Valdez C. of C., Alaska Mcpl. League (bd. dirs. 1984-89). Methodist. Avocation: charter boat operator. Home: PO Box 770 Valdez AK 99686-0770 Office: PO Box 3089 Valdez AK 99686-3089 Office Phone: 907-834-5060. E-mail: jhdvns@aol.com.

DEVENS, PAUL, lawyer; b. Gary, Ind., June 8, 1931; s. Zenove and Anna (Brilla) Dewenetz; m. Setsuko Sugihara, Aug. 14, 1955; children: Paula, Vladimir, Mignon. BA in Econs. cum laude, Ind. U., 1954; LLB, Columbia U., 1957. Bar: N.Y. 1958, U.S. Dist. Ct. Hawaii 1960, Hawaii 1961, U.S. Ct. Appeals (9th cir.) 1962, U.S. Ct. Internat. Trade 1963, U.S. Supreme Ct. 1970. Pvt. practice law, N.Y.C., 1958-60; ptnr. Lewis, Saunders & Key, Honolulu, 1960-69; corp. counsel City and County of Honolulu, 1969-72, mng. dir., 1973-75; ptnr. Devens, Nakano, Saito, Lee, Wong & Ching, Honolulu, 1975-94, of counsel, 1994—2002; ret., 2002. Judge Nuclear Claims Tribunal, Majuro, Republic of the Marshall Islands, 1988-90. Mem. Japan-Hawaii Econ. Coun., 1975-95, Honolulu Charter Reorgn. Com., 1979-80, Pacific and Asian Affairs Coun., 1983; trustee Japan-Am. Soc. Honolulu, 1981—, pres., 1987-89; chmn. bd. dirs. Nat. Assn. Japan-Am. Socs., 1989-91; mem. bd. govs. Japanese Cultural Ctr., Hawaii, 1989-94, mem. bd. dirs., v.p., 1994-96, chmn. bd. dirs., 1996-97. Decorated Imperial Order of the Sacred Treasure, Gold Rays with Neck ribbon Govt. of Japan, 1993. Mem.: Phi Beta Kappa. Democrat. Eastern Orthodox. Office: Devens Nakano Saito Lee Wong & Ching 220 S King St Ste 1600 Honolulu HI 96813-4597 Office Phone: 808-521-1456. Business E-Mail: pdevens@dnslwc.com.

DEVER, JOHN THOMAS, academic administrator, language educator; b. Lebanon, Ky., Nov. 10, 1945; s. Garland Ray and Mary Frances (O'Sullivan) D.; m. Peggy Elaine Bryant, June 16, 1976; children: Seth, Sarah. BA in History summa cum laude, Bellarmine Coll., 1968; MA in English, U. Ky., 1974; PhD in English, U. Va., 1991. Prof. English Thomas Nelson Community Coll., Hampton, Va., 1975—, head dept. English, 1986-88, chair div. communications & humanities, 1988; v.p., academic and student affairs Tidewater CC, Va.; exec. v.p. No. Va. CC, Annandale, Va., 2004—. Pres. Thomas Nelson Community Coll. Facutly Forum, Hampton, 1979-80. Mem. Regional Literacy Coordinating Com., Va. Peninsula, 1988—. DuPont Fellow U. Va., 1981-82. Mem. MLA, Southeastern MLA, Southeastern conf. on English in the Two-Yr. Coll., Va. Community Coll. Assn., English-Speaking Union (mem. Ky. br., fellow U. Birmingham, Stratford-Upon-Avon, Eng., 1973). Office: Northern Va Comm Coll 4001 Wakefield Chapel Rd Annandale VA 22003-3796

DEVER, MERRILL THOMAS, academic administrator, retired protective services official; b. Erie, Pa., Oct. 31, 1930; s. Merrill Franklin and Rose Elenore (Miller) D.; m. Barbara Ann Snyder, Sept. 21, 1957; children: Christopher, Lori Ann, Robin Alane, James Joseph, Beth Anne. BS, U. Va., 1973, Kans. State U., 1950. Cert. in firearms. Chief of police Millcreek Twp. Police Dept., Erie, 1980-86; dir. security Mercyhurst Coll., Erie, 1986—97; br. mgr. U.S. Security Assocs., Inc., Erie, Pa., 1998—. Tng. and edn. dir. Northwestern Chiefs of Police, 1978—. Contbr. articles to mags. and newspapers. Dir. FEMA (Millcreek Twp.), Erie County, Pa., 1975-82; pres. Family Crisis Intervention, Erie County, 1979-81; pres. citizens adv. bd. Pa. Bd. Parole, 1984-86; bd. dirs. Times Newsies, 1980—. Lt. U.S. Army, 1952-55. Recipient medal of valor, other medals and awards. Mem. Chiefs of Police (life), Fraternal Order of Police (life mem., pres. 1966- 69). Democrat. Roman Catholic. Avocations: history and civil war roundtables, firearms, hunting, gardening. Office: US Security Assocs Inc 11 W 33rd St Erie PA 16508 E-mail: mdever@greatguards.com.

DEVERA, GERTRUDE QUENANO, education educator; b. Malasiqui, Pangasinan, Philippines, Dec. 15, 1924; came to U.S., 1950; d. Paulino Castro and Filomena (del Rosario) Magsanoc; m. Perfecto Tamondong DeVera, June 23, 1946 (dec. Sept. 1976). BA, San Francisco State U., 1952; postgrad., U. Calif., Berkeley, 11952-54; MA in English Lit., San Francisco State U., 1956. Calif. tchrs. cert. and life diploma. Tchr. San Francisco Unified Sch. Dist., 1956-88, demonstration tchr., 1958-59; mem. aux. bd. trustees Don Adriano Geslani Montessori Sch., Malasiqui, Luzon, The Philippines, 1997—. Tchr. participant Project Read Behavioral Rsch. Labs., Palo Alto, Calif., 1967-68; cert. demonstrator Astra's Magic Math-Alphaphonics, 1987-88; rschr. in preventive medicine, San Francisco, 1975—. Editing chmn.: Guidelines for Use of the Eudcational Facilities Planning model, 1968 (NDEA award 1968). Summer Inst. grantee NDEA, U. Wash., Seattle, 1968; recipient Hon. Svc. awards Calif. Congress Parents and Tchrs. Inc., Sacramento, 1975, San Francisco 2nd Dist., 1980. Mem. AAUW (legis. interview com. 1970's), Internat. Platform Assn., World Affairs Coun. No. Calif., Libr. of Congress. Democrat. Roman Catholic. Avocations: reading, creative writing, public speaking, attending lectures, various cultural pursuits.

DEVERAUX, JUDE (JUDE GILLIAM WHITE), writer; b. Louisville, Sept. 20, 1947; d. Harold J. and Virgina (Berry) Gilliam; m. Richard G. Sides, 1967 (div. 1969); m. Claude B. White, 1970 (div. 1993). BS Fine Arts, Murray State U., 1970; Cert. in Teaching, Coll. Santa Fe, 1973. Cert. remedial reading tchr. Tchr. elem. sch., Santa Fe, 1970-76; writer, 1976—. Author novels including: The Enchanted Land, 1978, The Black Lyon, 1980, The Velvet Promise, 1981, Casa Grande, 1982, Highland Velvet, 1982, Velvet Song, 1983, Velvet Angel, 1983, Sweetbriar, 1983, Countefeit Lady, 1984, Lost Lady, 1985, River Lady, 1985, Twin of Ice, 1985, Twin of Fire, 1985, The Temptress, 1986, The Raider, 1987, The Princess, 1987, The Maiden, 1988, The Awakening, 1988, The Taming, 1989, A Knight in Shining Armor, 1990, Wishes, 1990, Mountain Laurel, 1990, The Conquest, 1991, The Duchess, 1991, Sweet Liar, 1992, Eternity, 1992, The Invitation, 1993, Remembrance, 1994, Legend, 1996, An Angel for Emily, 1998, The Blessing, 1999, High Tide, 2000, Temptation, 2000, Twin of Fire/Twin of Ice, 2001, The Summerhouse, 2001, A Knight in Shining Armor, 2002, The Mulberry Tree, 2002, Forever, 2002, Wild Orchids, 2003, Forever and Always, 2003, Holly, 2003, Eternity, 2004, The Princess, 2004, Wishes, 2004, River Lady, 2004, Always, 2004. Mem. Costume Soc. Am. Avocations: cooking, computers, travel, collecting books on costume history, reading english history. Office: Pocket Books Simon & Schuster Inc 1230 Avenue Of The Americas New York NY 10020-1586*

DEVEREUX, OWEN FRANCIS, retired metallurgy educator; b. Lexington, Mass., Aug. 23, 1937; s. George Francis and Mildred Anna (Gleeson) D.; m. Sally Williamson, June 15, 1957 (div. June 1969); children: Owen M., Amy L., Jonathan W., Nancy J.; m. Olivia Elaine Marin, June 13, 1969. BS, MIT, 1959, MS, 1960, PhD, 1962. Rsch. chemist Chevron Rsch. Co., La Habra, Calif., 1962-64, Corning (N.Y.) Glass Works, 1964-66, Chevron Oil Field Rsch. Co., La Habra, 1966-68; assoc. prof. metallurgy U. Conn., Storrs, 1968-76, prof., 1976-99, head dept., 1983-98; ret., 1999. Author: Topics in Metallurgical Thermodynamics, 1983; contbr. articles to profl. jours. Rsch. grantee NSF, 1970-76, U.S. Dept. Energy, 1976-86, NSF Industry/Univ. Corp. Rsch. Ctr. for Grinding Rsch. and Devel., 1990-98. Mem. AIME, AAUP, Electrochem. Soc. (div. editor 1987-90), Nat. Assn. Corrosion Engrs. Avocations: quarter horses, carriage driving, saddle making, classical guitar. Home: 99 Summit Rd Storrs Mansfield CT 06268-1421

DEVEREUX, TIMOTHY EDWARD, advertising executive; b. Chgo., Jan. 13, 1932; s. James Matthew and Nellie (Fitzmaurice) D.; m. Ann Sullivan, Apr. 2, 1956; children: Timothy Jr., Colette Marie, Jennifer Ann, Peter Gerard, Nora Marie, Matthew. BA in Communication Arts, U. Notre Dame, 1955. Copywriter Montgomery Ward & Co., Chgo., 1957-58; pub. relations dir. Victor Comptometer Corp., Chgo., 1958-60; sales promotion mgr. Bankers Life & Casualty Co., Chgo., 1960-61; dir. advt. and pub. relations Mid-America Foods, Inc., River Forest, Ill., 1961-62; mdse. mgr. Marshall John & Assos., Chgo. also Northbrook, 1962-65; acct. supr. Marshall John/Action Advt., Northbrook, Ill., 1965-70, exec. v.p., chief exec. officer, 1970-77, also dir.; pres. Devereux Direct, Ltd., 1977-79; v.p. direct response group Frankel & Co., Chgo., 1979-85; pres. Timothy E. Devereux & Assocs., Oak Park, Ill., 1985—. Served to 1st lt. USMCR, 1955—57. Home and Office: 1185 S Oak Park Ave Oak Park IL 60304-2048 Office Phone: 708-383-5544.

DEVERS, GAIL, track and field athlete; b. Seattle, Nov. 19, 1966; BA in Sociology, UCLA, 1988. Mem. U.S. Olympic Team, Barcelona, 1992, Atlanta, 1996, Sydney, 2000, Athens, 2004; Gold medalist, 100m Track and Field Barcelona Olympic Games, 1992; Gold medalist 100m, 100m Hurdles World Track and Field Championships, Stuttgart, Germany, 1993; Gold medalist, 100m Track and Field Atlanta Olympic Games, 1996, Gold medalist 4x100m relay, 1996, World Championships, 1997; founder, CEO Gail Force, Inc. Founder Gail Devers Found. Named Nat. champion 100m hurdles, 1991, 1992, 1993, 1993, 1995, 1996, Nat. indoor champion 60m, 1993, World indoor champion 60m, 1993, World champion 100m, 1993, 1995, World champion 100m hurdles, 1993, Athlete of Yr., Women's Sports Found., 1997; recipient Espy Award for Best Female Track and Field Athlete, 1994, 2003, 2004. Achievements include overcoming Graves disease to win multiple Olympic medals. Office: Elite Intl Sports Mkt PO Box 69047 Saint Louis MO 63169-0047

DEVETAK, IGOR, engineering educator; b. Beograd, Serbia-Monteneg (Yugoslavia), Dec. 5, 1975; s. Dusan and Sonja Devetak. PhD, Cornell U., 2002. Post-doctoral rschr. IBM T.J. Watson Rsch. Ctr., Yorktown Heights, NY, 2002—04; asst. prof. U. So. Calif., L.A., 2005—. Contbr. articles to profl. jours. Achievements include research in coding theorems for quantum information theory. Office: U So Calif EE Systems EEB532 Los Angeles CA 90089 Office Phone: 213-740-9264. E-mail: devetak@usc.edu.

DEVEY, RICHARD H., language educator; s. Samuel Richard Devey and Clara Catherine Kneip; m. Donna Jane Haggerty, June 19, 1982. BA, Thiel Coll., 1966; MA, U. Pitts., 1971, MAT, 1974. Cert. tchr. Spanish Pa., tchr. French Pa., tchr. English Pa. Tchr. Spanish, French and English Commodore Perry Sch., Hadley, Pa., 1978—93; lectr. Spanish Shenango campus Pa. State U., Sharon, 1993—. Deacon Emmanuel Christian Ch. Mem.: SPEBSQSA (Lawrence County chpt.). Office: Pa State U Shenango Campus 147 Shenango Ave Sharon PA 16146-1537

DE VIDO, ALFREDO EDUARDO, architect; b. N.Y.C., Mar. 19, 1932; s. Eduardo and Maria (Zanucco) DeV.; m. Catherine Nelligan, 1962; children: Roberto, Antonio J. BArch, Carnegie Mellon U., 1954; MFA, Princeton U., 1956. Registered arch., N.J., N.Y., Conn., Mass., Pa. Arch. Archs. Collaborative, Rome, 1960-61, Marcel Breuer, N.Y.C., 1961-62, Ernest Kump, N.Y.C., 1963-67, McFadyen & Knowles, N.Y.C., 1967-69, DeVido Archs., N.Y.C., 1969—. Author: Designing Your Clients' House, 1983, Innovative Management Techniques for Architectural Design and Construction, 1984, House Design: Art and Practice, 1996, Master Architect III: Alfredo De Vido, 1999, Ten Houses/Alfredo De Vido, 1999. Recipient Solar award HUD, 1979, Bard award City Club N.Y., 1983, 89, award Am. Solar Energy Soc., 1982, Design award Interfaith Forum on Religion, Art and Arch., 1989, Design award Conn. Soc. Archs., 1991, Queens C. of C. award, 1993, Interior Design award Restaurants and Instns., 1997. Fellow AIA (honor award 1968, N.Y. chpt. design awards 1971, 77, 81, 94); mem. N.Y. State Assn. Archs. (design awards 1980, 81, 82, 86, 92, 95), Am. Inst. Steel Constrn. (award 1977), Am. Wood Coun. (award 1993). Office: Alfredo De Vido Architects 412 E 85th St New York NY 10028-6302 Business E-Mail: adevido@devido-architects.com.

DEVILLE, DONALD CHARLES, accountant; b. New Roads, La., Sept. 18, 1953; s. Sterling Joseph and Barbara J. (Beaud) DeV.; m. Michelle L. Rinaudo, Apr. 14, 1984; children: Ariel Elizabeth, Stewart Charles, Olivia. BS in Acctg., La. State U., 1976. CPA, La. Auditor State of La., Baton Rouge, 1976—78; mgr. Hawthorn Waymouth & Carroll, Baton Rouge, 1978—89; pvt. practice Baton Rouge, 1989—. Pres. Baton Rouge Work Exch., 1988; publicity dir. Baton Rouge Opera, 1989-90, treas., 1991-95; liturg. min St. George Cath. Ch., Baton Rouge, 1987—; bd. dirs. Capital Area Safety Coun. La., treas., 1994-95; bd. dirs. Baton Rouge Boys Club; chmn. fin. com. St. George Sch.; mem. Sisters of St. Joseph Congl. Devel. Com. Recipient Freedom award La. Farm Bur. Mem. AICPA, La. Soc. CPA, SAR (sec. 1990-93, pres. 1994, treas. La. 1998—, La. Meritorious Svc. award, Silver Good Citizenship award). Republican. Roman Catholic. Avocations: outdoor cooking, boating. Home: 18002 Inverness Ave Baton Rouge LA 70810-5979

DEVILLION, KEVIN JOHN, information scientist, consultant; b. St. Paul, Dec. 30, 1963; s. Lee Samuel and Freda Marcel (Loving) DeV.; m. Rosie L. Radin, June 28, 1996; children: Damien, Brandon, Nicholaus, Stepen. A in Computer Sci., Augsburg Coll., Mpls., 1983; B in Computer Sci., MIT, 1985; M in Computer Sci., U. Minn., 1987, PhD in Computer Sci. and Physics, 1989. Jr. analyst Oracle Corp., Redwood Shores, Calif., 1989-91; sr. analyst FTP Software Inc., Andover, Mass., 1991-92, Livermore Software Lab. Internat., Houston, 1993; sr. systems adminstr. On Tech. Corp., Cambridge, Mass., 1993-95, DeVillions Industries, Brainerd, Minn., 1995—. Maj. U.S. Army, 1979—. Republican. Avocations: bowling, painting, animation, native american pow-wows. Home: 1111 Highway 73 Moose Lake MN 55767-9452

DEVIN, LEE (PHILIP LEE DEVIN), dramaturg, author; b. Glendale, Calif., Apr. 28, 1938; s. Philip Lee Sr. and Bernice Hermoine (Rogers) D.; m. Barbara Kathleen Norton, June 22, 1958 (div. 1986); children: Siobhan Kathleen, Sean Michael. AB, San Jose State Coll., 1958; MA, Ind. U., 1961, PhD, 1967. Lectr. Ind. U. extension, Indpls., 1960-62; instr., tech. dir. U. Va., Charlottesville, 1962-66; instr., assoc. dir. Exptl. Theatre Vassar Coll., Poughkeepsie, N.Y., 1966-67, asst. prof., assoc. dir., 1967-70; assoc. prof., dir. theatre Swarthmore (Pa.) Coll., 1970-79, prof., dir. theatre, 1979-98, prof., 1998—2003, sr. rsch. scholar, 2003—. Electrician, state mgr., prodn. stage mgr. Honey in the Rock, Beckley, W.Va., 1962-64; artist-in-residence Ball State U., Muncie, Ind., 1968, U. Calif. San Diego, La Jolla, 1973; assoc. artist People's Light and Theatre Co., Malvern, Pa., 1977—, dramaturg, 1985—. Author: (with Rob Austin) Artful Making: What Managers Need to Know About How Artists Work, 2003, (radio plays) Elegy for Irish Jack, 1973, When the Time Comes, 1978, Frankenstein, 1981 (WHA, Earplay Purchase awards); (with S. Hodkinson) (drama with music) Lament: for Guitar and Two Lovers, 1963; (active oratorio) Vox Populous, 1973; (opera) St. Carmen of the Main, 1987 actor various roles stage, film, TV; translator (with A. Adams) A Doll House, 1987, Oedipus, 1988. Recipient 1st prize WGBH Radio Drama, Boston, 1968, James S. Helms Playscript award, 1964, Calif. Olympiad of the Arts, 1965, Elliot Hayes award for dramaturgy, 2005; librettist's grantee NEA, Washington, 1974, 75, 77; grantee Mellon Found., 1973, 77; Lang fellow 1990. Mem. Actors' Equity Assn., Assn. for Theatre in Higher Edn., Literary Mgrs. and Dramaturgs of the Ams. Avocation: fly fishing. Home: 603 Hillborn Ave Swarthmore PA 19081-1123 Business E-Mail: ldevin1@swarthmore.edu.

DEVIN, ROBIN B., librarian, anthropologist; b. Milw., May 9, 1948; d. John H. and Betty J. (Armour) Block; m. Carl E. Devin, Mar. 8, 1980; children: C. Eric, Darton B. BA, U. Wis., 1970, MLS, 1971; MA, U. R.I., 1984; PhD, U. Conn., 1995. Libr. Temple U. Librs., Phila., 1976-80, U. R.I. Libr., Kingston, 1980—. Rschr. Haitian Health Found., Jeremie, Haiti, 1993, 97. Contbr. articles to profl. jours. Bd. dirs. Longworthy Libr., 1989—2002. Fellow Soc. for Applied Anthropology (Peter K. New award 2d place 1995); mem. AAUP (local newsletter editor 1995-2000), Am. Anthrop. Assn. (Beth Dillingham award 1990), Assn. of R.I. Health Scis. Librs. (instl. rep. 1994—, pres. 1999-2000), North Atlantic Health Scis. Librs., Med. Libr. Assn. (instnl. rep.), Beta Phi Mu, Phi Kappa Phi. Home: PO Box 145 Hope Valley RI 02832 Office: U RI Libr 15 Lippitt Rd Kingston RI 02881-2011 Business E-Mail: rdevin@uri.edu.

DEVINATZ, ALLEN, retired mathematician, educator; b. Chgo., July 22, 1922; s. Victor and Kate (Bass) D.; m. Pearl Moskowitz, Sep. 16, 1956; children: Victor Gary, Ethan Sander. BS, Ill. Inst. Tech., 1944; A.M., Harvard U., 1947, PhD, 1950. Instr. Ill. Inst. Tech., 1950-52; NSF Postdoctoral fellow, 1952-53; fellow Inst. Advanced Study, Princeton, 1953-54; asst. prof. U. Conn., 1954-55; mem. faculty Washington U., St. Louis, 1955-67, prof. math., 1961-67, acting chmn. dept., 1963-64; prof. math. Northwestern U., Evanston, Ill., 1967-92, prof. emeritus, 1992—, asst. chmn. dept., 1968-70, acting chmn. dept., 1991. Vis. mem. Weizmann Inst., Israel, 1980, Inst. Hautes Etudes Sci., Paris, 1982, Inst. for Applications of Calculus-Mauro Picone, Rome, 1988; vis. scholar U. Calif., Berkeley, 1985; Disting. lectr. Hebrew U., Jerusalem, 1993. Contbr. articles profl. jours. Sr. NSF Postdoctoral fellow, 1960-61 Mem. Am. Math. Soc. (translation com. for Russian 1985-88), Sigma Xi, Tau Beta Pi. Office: Northwestern U Dept Math Lunt Bldg Evanston IL 60208-0001

DEVINATZ, VICTOR GARY, industrial engineering educator; b. St. Louis, Oct. 19, 1957; s. Allen and Pearl (Moskowitz) D. BSE, Northwestern U., 1979, MA, 1980; MS, U. Mass., 1986; PhD, U. Minn., 1990. Lectr. U. Minn., Mpls., 1990-91; asst. prof. Ill. State U., Normal, 1991-94, assoc. prof., 1994-98, prof., 1998—. Contbr. articles to profl. jours. Grantee, Henry J. Kaiser Family Found., Walter P. Reuther Libr., Wayne State U., 1989; Caterpillar scholar, 1999, 2004, Merl E. Reed fellow in so. labor history, 2003. Mem.: Labor and Employment Rels. Assn., United Assn. Labor Edn. Home: 102 S Oak St Apt 3 Normal IL 61761-3053 Office: Ill State U Dept Mgmt & Quant Methods Normal IL 61790-5580 Office Phone: 309-438-3403. Business E-Mail: vgdevin@ilstu.edu.

DEVINE, BRIAN KIERNAN, pet food and supplies company executive; b. Washington, Mar. 1, 1942; s. William John and Rita Marie (Kiernan) D.; m. Silvija Viktorija Kutlets, June 13, 1964; children— Brian Jr., Brooke BA, Georgetown U., 1963; postgrad., Am. U., 1964-65, Yale U., 1965. Statis. adv. USPHS, Washington, 1963-70; with Toys "R" Us, 1970-88; gen. mgr. San Jose, Calif., 1970-75; regional gen. mgr. Chgo., 1975-77; v.p. Saddle Brook, N.J., 1977-82; sr. v.p. Rochelle Park, N.J., 1982-88; pres. of furniture mfr./retailer Krause's Sofa Factory, Fountain Valley, Calif., 1988-89; pres. Petco, San Diego, 1990—, CEO, 1990—2004, chmn., 1994—. Bd. dirs. Nat. Retail Fedn., Students in Free Enterprise, Wild Oats Markets, Inc.; mem. coll. bd. advisers, bd. regents Georgetown U. Contbr. articles to profl. publs. Mem. Internat. Mass Retail Assn. (bd. dirs.). Republican. Roman Catholic. Office: Petco 9125 Rehco Rd San Diego CA 92121-2270 Business E-Mail: briand@petco.com.*

DEVINE, DONALD C., manufacturing executive; BS, U.S. Mil. Acad. From v.p., gen. mgr. Bag Ops. to v.p., mgr. Packaging Ivex Packaging Corp., 1993—96, v.p., mgr. Packaging, 1996—97; pres., CEO Kimble Glass, 1998—2001, Jacuzzi Inc., 2002—03; pres. Jacuzzi Brands Inc., 2003—. With U.S. Army.

DEVINE, DONALD F. (DON), lawyer; b. Dubuque, Iowa, 1939; BA, Univ. Iowa, 1967; JD, Harvard Univ., 1970; MBA, NYU, 1979. Bar: DC 1972, NY 1973. Adminstrv. ptnr. Jones Day, NYC. Mem.: Assn. of the Bar of NYC, DC Bar Assn., Phi Beta Kappa. Office: Jones Day 222 E 41st St New York NY 10017-6702 Office Phone: 212-326-3635. Office Fax: 212-755-7306. Business E-Mail: dfdevine@jonesday.com.

DEVINE, DONALD J., management and political consultant; b. Bronxville, N.Y., Apr. 14, 1937; s. John and Frances M. D.; m. Ann Delia Smith, Aug. 29, 1959; children: William, J. Michael, Patricia, Joseph. BBA, St. John's U., Jamaica, N.Y., 1959; MA, CUNY, 1965; PhD, Syracuse (N.Y.) U., 1967. Assoc. prof. govt. and politics U. Md., 1967-81; dir. U.S. Office Personnel Mgmt., 1981-85; pres. Donald Devine Co., 1985—. Columnist Washington Times; adj. scholar Heritage Found.; Grewcock chair Bellevue U., 2001—. Author: The Attentive Public, 1970, The Political Culture of the United States, 1972, Does Freedom Work? Liberty and Justice in America, 1978, Reagan Electionomics, 1983, Reagan's Terrible Swift Sword, 1991, Restoring the Tenth Amendment, 1996, In Defense of the West, 2004; editor Western Vision and American Values, 2002. Parliamentarian, mem. exec. com. Md. Rep. Com., 1974-79; Md. chmn. Reagan for Pres., 1976, 80; sr. cons. Dole for Pres., 1988, 96; cons. Steve Forbes for pres., 1999-2000; mem. rules com. Rep. Nat. Com., 1973-75, platform com., del., 1976-88, 96; vice chmn. Am. Conservative Union; Rep. nominee Md. State Comptroller, 1976, 5th Congl. Dist., 1994. With USAR, 1960-66. Mem. Am. Polit. Sci. Assn., Am. Assn. Public Opinion Research, Mt. Pelerin Soc., Phila. Soc. Roman Catholic. Office: 4805 Idlewilde Rd Shady Side MD 20764-9768

DEVINE, DONN, lawyer, genealogist, municipal official; b. South Amboy, N.J., Mar. 30, 1929; s. Frank Edward and Emily Theresa (DeRevere) D. m. Elizabeth Cecilia Baldwin, Nov. 23, 1951; children: Edward (dec.), Mary Elizabeth, Martin Joseph. BS, U. Del., 1949; JD with honors, Widener U., 1975. Bar: Del. 1975, US Dist. Ct. Del. 1976, US Supreme Ct. 1997; cert. genealogist and cert. genealogy instr. Bd. for Cert. Genealogists; cert. Am. Inst. Cert. Planners. Devel. chemist Allied Chem. Corp., Claymont, Del., 1950-52; newspaper writer, editor corp. publs. Atlas Powder Co., Wilmington, Del., 1952-60; mgmt. cons., 1960-68; dir. renewal planning City of Wilmington, 1968-79, dep. dir. planning, 1979-80, dir. planning, 1981-85; cons. Wilmington City Coun., 1985-01; pvt. practice, 1985-00; archival cons. Cath. Diocese Wilmington, 1989—; of counsel City of Wilmington Law Dept., 2001—. Spl. counsel Del. Div. Alcoholism, Drug Abuse and Mental Health, 1990-93; trustee Bd. for Cert. Genealogists, 1992—; mediator Del. Superior Ct., 1998—. Author: Delaware National Guard, A Historical Sketch, 1968, DeRevere Family of Peekskill, NY, 1982; editor Del. Geneal. Soc. Jour., 1980-81, Cultural Resources Survey of Wilmington, Del., 1982-84; assoc. editor Del. Jour. Corp. Law, 1974-75; assoc editor Professional Genealogy: A Manual for Researchers, Writers, Editors, Lecturers and Librarians, 2001. Past bd. dir. Wilmington Small Bus. Devel. Corp., Wilmington Econ. Devel. Corp.; past officer Delmarva Ecumenical Agy.; emeritus bd. dirs., past officer Generations Home Care (formerly Geriatric Svcs. Del.); past officer Christina Cultural Arts Ctr., Cath. Interracial Coun., Del. chpt. ACLU, Maplewood Housing for Elderly, St. Mary's-St. Patrick's Parish Coun. With USAR, 1950-54; brig. gen. Del. Army N.G., 1954-84, ret. Decorated Meritorious Svc. medal. Mem. Am. Planning Assn. (Peter Larson Achievement award 2002), Am. Chem. Soc., Del. Bar Assn., Del. Soc. SAR (past pres.), Nat. Geneal. Soc. (bd. dir. 1994-2002), Assn. Cath. Diocesan Archivists (bd. dir. 1993-95), Del. Geneal. Soc. (past pres.), Ft. Delaware Soc. (recognition award), Old Bohemia Hist. Soc. (bd. dirs. 1992—), Univ. and Whist Club, Chemists Club NYC, Ancient Order Hibernians, Phi Kappa Phi, Delta Theta Phi. Democrat. Home: 2004 Kentmere Pkwy Wilmington DE 19806-2014 E-mail: donndevine@aol.com.

DEVINE, EDMOND FRANCIS, lawyer; b. Ann Arbor, Mich., Aug. 9, 1916; s. Frank B. and Elizabeth Catherine (Doherty) DeV.; m. Elizabeth Palmer Ward, Sept. 17, 1955; children: Elizabeth Palmer, Stephen Ward, Michael Edmond, Suzanne Lee. AB, U. Mich., 1937, JD, 1940; LLM, Cath. U. Am., 1941. Bar: Mich. 1940, U.S. Dist. Ct. (ea. dist.) Mich. 1940, U.S. Ct. Appeals (6th cir) 1974, U.S. Supreme Ct. 1975. Spl. agt. FBI, 1941-43; chief asst. prosecutor Washtenaw County (Mich.), Ann Arbor, 1947-53, prosecuting atty., 1953-58; ptnr. DeVine & DeVine, Ann Arbor, 1958-74, DeVine, DeVine, Kantor & Serr, Ann Arbor, 1974-84; sr. ptnr. Miller, Canfield, Paddock & Stone, Ann Arbor, 1984-92, of counsel, 1992—. Asst. prof., adj. prof. U. Mich. Law Sch., 1949-79. Co-author: Criminal Procedure, 1960. Lt. USNR, 1943—46, PTO. Decorated Bronze Star with combat v. Fellow Am. Bar Found. Am. Coll. Trial Lawyers, Mich. Bar Found.; mem. ABA, State Bar Mich. (bd. commrs., chmn. judiciary com. 1976-85, mem. rep. assembly, chmn. rules and calendar com.1971-76, co-chair U.S. Cts. com. 1986-87), Internat. Assn. Def. Counsel, U.S. Supreme Ct. Hist. Soc., Ann Arbor C. of C. (chmn. bd. 1971), Detroit Athletic Club, Barton Hills Country Club, Pres.'s Club. U. Mich., Varsity M Club, Order of Coif, Barristers, Phi Delta Phi, Phi Kappa Psi. Republican. Roman Catholic. Avocations: golf, running, reading. Home: 101 Underdown Rd Ann Arbor MI 48105-1078 Office: Miller Canfield Paddock & Stone 101 N Main St Fl 7 Ann Arbor MI 48104-5507 Office Phone: 734-663-2445. Business E-Mail: devinee@millercanfield.com.

DEVINE, HUGH JAMES, JR., marketing executive, consultant; b. Buffalo, N.Y., May 8, 1938; s. Hugh James Sr. and Ruth D. Devine; m. Bernice Riley Cushing, May 27, 1984; children: Hugh James III, Thomas C., Catherine D. Whitaker, Kent T., Diane C. Alleborn, Linda C. Hughes, Karen C. Krueger. AB in Econs., Bethany Coll., 1961; MBA, U. Bridgeport, 1971. Mgr. mktg. intelligence Winchester-Western Div. Olin Corp., New Haven, 1961-71; sr. v.p., dir. mktg. Rsch. Data Svcs., Inc., Princeton, NJ, 1971-75, exec. v.p., dir. mktg., 1975—93, dir., 1978-97, pres., 1993-96; COO Total Rsch. Corp., Princeton, N.J., 1996; mktg. cons.; pres. Hugh J. Devine & Assocs., 1997—. Speaker Am. Mgmt. Assn., N.Y.C., 1974-76, Assn. Nat. Advertisers, Washington, 1985, Fin. Independence Day, Princeton, 1986, U. N.C., Chapel Hill, 1989, 91, others. Author newsletter Strategic Goals Should Govern Mktg. Rsch. Budget, 1981; co-author newsletter The Value of Predictive Research, 1989; contbr. articles to mags. Sgt. USAR, 1961-67. Mem. Coun. Am. Survey Rsch. Orgn. (membership chmn. 1985, career planning chmn. 1986, survey quality com. 1990-91, 96), Am. Mktg. Assn., Inst. Mgmt. Consultants (v.p. membership 2000-02, chmn. leadership devel. 2004—), SPEBSQSA (mktg. task force 2002-03). Republican. Avocations: barbershop style singing, walking, reading. Home and Office: 49 Krebs Rd Plainsboro NJ 08536-1104 Office Phone: 609-799-8170. Personal E-mail: HJDevine@aol.com.

DEVINE, JAMES I., lawyer; b. Darby, Pa., July 31, 1958; s. Martin J. and Gabrielle M. Devine. BS, U. Notre Dame, 1980; JD, Widener U., 1983. Bar: Pa. 1983, U.S. Dist. Ct. (ea. dist.) Pa. 1983, U.S. Ct. Appeals (3d cir.) 1985. Jud. law clk. Hon. Joseph L. McGlynn Jr. U.S. Dist. Ct. (ea. dist.) Pa., Phila., 1983—84; atty. Dilworth Paxson, 1984—85; ptnr. O'Brien & Ryan, Plymouth Meeting, 1985—91; shareholder James I. Devine & Assocs., 1991—96; pvt. practice Phila., 1996—2000, Norristown, 2000—. Office: 509 Swede St Norristown PA 19401 Office Phone: 610-292-9300.

DE VINE, JOHN BERNARD, lawyer; b. Ann Arbor, Mich., Feb. 5, 1920; s. Frank Bernard and Elizabeth Catherine (Doherty) DeVine; m. Margaret Louise Burke, Apr. 23, 1949; children: Margaret DeVine Mumby, Ann DeVine Klein, Kathleen DeVine Brilliant, Susan DeVine Baglien, John Kennedy. AB, U. Mich., 1941; JD, Harvard U., 1948. Bar: Mich. 1948. Ptnr. DeVine, DeVine, Kantor and Serr, Ann Arbor, 1948—84, Miller, Canfield, Paddock and Stone, Ann Arbor, 1984—, head health law sect., 1984—90. Asst. pros. atty. County of Washtenaw, Mich., 1948—52; dir. NBD, Ann Arbor, 1963—90. Founder NCCJ, Ann Arbor; chmn. Cath. Social Svcs., Washtenaw County, 1960—64, Leadership Giving Assn., Washtenaw United Way, 1988—89, Nat. Inst. Burn Medicine; chmn. emeritus Marnee and John DeVine Found. Cath. Social Svcs.; chmn. Washtenaw County chpt. ARC, 1995; trustee Paul Oliver Meml. Hosp. Found. Lt. USN, 1942—46. Mem.: ABA, Mich. Soc. Hosp. Attys. (past pres.), Am. Acad. Hosp. Attys. (pres. 1981), Washtenaw County Bar Assn., Mich. Bar Assn., Crystal Downs, Barton Hills Country Club. Roman Catholic. Home: 1908 Boulder Dr Ann Arbor MI 48104-4164 Office: Miller Canfield Paddock & Stone 101 N Main St Fl 7 Ann Arbor MI 48104-5507 E-mail: devinej@millercanfield.com.

DEVINE, JOHN MARTIN, automotive company executive; b. Pitts., May 13, 1944; s. John Patrick and Camilla (Durkin) D.; m. Patricia McGee Devine; children: Sean, Bridget. BS in Econs., Duquesne U., 1967; MBA, U. Mich., 1972. Various fin. positions Ford Motor Co., 1968-80, contr. product devel. Europe, 1981-83; staff dir. fin. Asia, Asia, 1983-85; v.p. no. Pacific ops. Ford Motor Co., Asia, 1985-86, exec. dir. no. Pacific bus. devel., 1986-87; contr. truck ops. U.S., U.S., 1988; pres. First Nationwide Bank, 1988-91; contr. Ford Motor Co., 1994, CFO, 1994-99, Gen. Motors Corp., Detroit, 2000—. Office: Gen Motors Corp 300 Renaissance Ctr Detroit MI 48265*

DEVINE, MICHAEL BUXTON, lawyer; b. Des Moines, Oct. 25, 1953; s. Cleatie Hiram, Jr., and Katherine Ann (Buxton) D. Student, St. Peter's Coll., Oxford U., 1975; BA cum laude, St. Olaf Coll., 1976; MPA, JD, Drake U., 1980; diploma in Advanced Internat. Legal Studies, U. Pacific, Salzburg, Austria, 1986; LLM in Internat. Bus. Legal Studies, U. Exeter, 1988, postgrad., 1997. Bar: Iowa 1980, U.S. Dist. Ct. (no. and so. dists.) Iowa 1980, U.S. Ct. Appeals (8th cir.) 1980, Nebr. 1985, Supreme Ct. 1985, Minn. 1986, D.C. 1986., N.Y. 1987, Wis. 1987, Colo. 1988, N.Y. 1990, U.S. Ct. Appeals (fed. cir.) 1990, U.S. Ct. Internat. Trade 1990, Eng. and Wales, 1995, U.K. Ho. of Lords, 1995, Ct. Justice of European Com., 1995, No. Ireland, 2000. Assoc. Bump & Haesemeyer, P.C., Des Moines, 1980—85; jud. law clk. Jud. Dept. State of Iowa, 1987—88; assoc. Christianson, Hohnbaum & George, Des Moines, 1989, Pavelic & Levites, P.C., N.Y.C., 1989—92; with chambers Alan Tyrrell, Q.C., London, 1993—94; with legal dept. Philips Electronics U.K., Ltd., London, 1994; with Lafili, Van Crombrugghe & Ptnrs., Brussels, 1995; pvt. practice Des Moines/N.Y.C./London, 1997—; of counsel Pavelic & Levites, P.C., N.Y.C., 1997—. Internat. legal intern Herbert Oppenheimer, Nathan & Vandyk, London, 1986; lectr. law U. Kent, Canterbury, Eng., 2000-01; lectr. law, course leader Robert Gordon U., Aberdeen, Scotland, 2001—; asst. prof. bus. law U. Wis.-La Crosse, 2005— Contbr. articles to profl. jours. Nat. alt. U.S. Presdl. Mgmt. Intern Program, 1980. Scholar St. Olaf Coll., 1972-76 Mem. ABA (sect. internat. law), Fed. Bar Assn. (chmn. state of Iowa SBA export assistance program 1983-85, treas. Iowa chpt. 1984-85, exec. com. 1985-87), N.Y. State Bar Assn. (sec. internat. law),D-C.ar Assn., Colo. Bar Assn., Nebr. State Bar Assn., Iowa State Bar Assn., Minn. State Bar Assn., Wis. Bar Assn., Assn. of Bar of City of N.Y. (coun. internat. affairs 1990-92), Soc. Legal Scholars Gt. Britain and Ireland, Acad. Legal Studies in Bus., Phi Alpha Theta, Pi Alpha Alpha. Presbyterian. Home: 2611 40th St Des Moines IA 50310-3949 Office: 865 3rd Ave New York NY 10022-6202 E-mail: mikedevinelawyer@aol.com, devine.mich@uwlax.edu.

DEVINE, RICHARD A. (DICK DEVINE), lawyer; b. Chgo., Ill., July 5, 1943; m. Charlene DeVine; children: Matt, Karen, Tim, Pete. BA cum laude, Loyola U., 1966; JD cum laude, Northwestern U., 1968. Bar: Ohio 1968, Ill. 1969, U.S. Dist. Ct. (no. dist.) Ill. 1973, U.S. Ct. Appeals (7th cir.) 1983, U.S. Supreme Ct. 1983. Assoc. Squire, Sanders & Dempsey, Cleve., 1968-69; adminstrv. asst. to mayor of Chgo., 1969-72; assoc. Pope, Ballard, Shepard & Fowle, 1972-74; assoc., ptnr. Foran, Wiss & Schultz, 1974-80, ptnr., 1983-85; 1st asst. state's atty. Cook County State's Atty.'s Office, 1980-83; ptnr. Phelan, Pope, Cahill, DeVine & Quinlan, Ltd., 1985-95, Shefsky Froelich & DeVine Ltd., 1995-96; state's atty. Cook County, 1996—. Lectr. continuing legal edn. IIT Kent Coll. Law, John Marshall U.; co-chair courses on damages in bus. litigation Law Jour. Seminar; judge moot ct. programs Northwestern Law Sch., John Marshall Law Sch.; appointed mem. State Commn. on Accreditation of Criminal Justice; appointed mem. Spl. Commn. on Adminstrn. of Justice in Cook County, chmn. task force on misdemeanor and preliminary hearing cts., chmn. task force on jud. adminstrn.; appointed mem. profl. adv. com. Office of State's Atty. of Cook County, 1984-89; bd. dirs. Cook County Criminal Justice Project; mem. Chgo.-Cook County Criminal Justice Commn., 1971-78; hearing officer Chgo. Bd. Election Commrs., 1984. Mem. editl. bd. Northwestern U. Law Rev., 1966-68, mng. editor, 1967-68; contbr. to law jours. Bd. commrs. Chgo. Park Dist., 1989-93, pres. bd., 1990-93; bd. trustees Loyola Acad., 1982-88, St. Scholastica H.S.; bd. dirs. Chgo. Hist. Soc., 1990-93, Adler Planetarium; pro bono mem., pres. Chgo. Park Dist, 1989-93. Russell Sage fellow in law and social scis. Mem. ABA, Am. Coll. Trial Lawyers (elected), Ill. State Bar Assn., Chgo. Bar Assn. (com. jud. evaluation 1983-88, chmn. legis. assistance and evaluation com., young lawyers sect. 1973-74, vice-chmn. 1974-76, chmn. 1976-77, urban affairs com., mem. local govt. com. 1974-76, faculty young lawyers sect. trial advocacy program, lectr. on continuing legal edn.), Northwestern Law Sch. Alumni Assn. (bd. dirs. 1993—), Ill. State Attys. Assn. (bd. dirs.), Nat. Dist. Attys. Assn. (bd. dirs.). Office: Cook County State Atty 69 W Washington St Ste 3200 Chicago IL 60602 Office Phone: 312-603-5106. E-mail: stateattorny@cookcountygov.com.

DEVINENI, MOHAN, pharmacist; b. Hyderabad, India, Aug. 15, 1957; arrived in U.S., 2001; s. Ranga Rao and Venkata Rathnam Devineni; m. Nirmala Devineni, May 21, 1983; children: Ramya, Abhilash. B Pharmacy, Coll. Pharmacy, Manipal, India, 1980; DPM, Indian Inst. Sci., Bangalore, 1984; MS in Pharmacy, Birla Inst. Tech., Pilani, India, 1989. Registered pharmacist India. Sr. chemist Kanpha Labs., Bangalore, 1982—88; dir. Strides Pharms., Bangalore, 1988—91; v.p. Strides Arcolab Ltd., Bangalore, 1991—96, sr. v.p., 1996—2000; dir. Murty Pharms., Inc., Lexington, Ky., 2001—02; v.p. Capricorn Pharma, Inc., Frederick, Md., 2002—. Bd. dirs. Pharmacon (India) Pvt., Ltd., Bangalore, Dry Cool (India) Pvt., Ltd., Bangalore; cons. in field. Recipient Disting. Alumni award, Coll. Pharmacy, 2000. Mem.: Sci. Adv. Bd., Am. Assn. Pharm. Scientists, Indian Pharm. Assn. Achievements include design of several pharmaceuticals. Avocations: painting portraits and landscapes, cricket. Home: 6372 Lambert Ct Frederick MD 21703 Office: Capricorn Pharma Inc 6900 Unit A English Muffin Way Frederick MD 21703 Office Phone: 301-696-8520 ext. 2807.

DEVINEY, MARVIN LEE, JR., science administrator, director; b. Kingsville, Tex., Dec. 5, 1929; s. Marvin Lee and Esther Lee (Gambrell) D.; m. Marie Carole Massey, June 7, 1975; children: Marvin Lee III, John H., Ann-Marie K. Deviney Bowen. BS in Chemistry and Math., S.W. Tex. State U., San Marcos, 1949; MA in Phys. Chemistry, U. Tex., Austin, 1952, PhD in Phys. Chemistry, 1956. Cert. profl. chemist. Devel. chemist Celanese Chem. Co., Bishop, Tex., 1956-58; rsch. chemist Shell Chem. Co., Deer Park, Tex., 1958-66; sr. scientist, head group phys. and radio-chemistry Ashland Chem. Co., Houston, 1966-68, mgr. sect. phys. and analytical chemistry, 1968-71, mgr. sect. phys. chemistry div. rsch. and devel. Columbus, Ohio, 1971-78; rsch. assoc., supr. applied surface chemistry Ashland Ventures Rsch. and Devel., Columbus, 1978-84, supr. electron microscopy, advanced aerospace composites, govt. contracts, 1984-90; inst. scientist, mem. internal R & D com. SW Rsch. Inst., San Antonio, 1990-97; pres. MLD Polymers/Composites, Inc., 1997—; R&D dir. Nuresco Polymers, 1998—; cons. polymer divsn. Tex. State U., San Marcos, 1998—. Adj. prof. U. Tex., San Antonio, 1973-75, Ohio State U., 1990-91; mem. sci. adv. bd. Am. Petroleum Inst. Rsch. Project 60, 1968-74. Contbr. numerous articles to profl. jours.; patentee in field. Mem. ednl. adv. com. Columbus Tech. Inst., 1974-84, Cen. Ohio Tech. Coll., 1975-82, Hocking Tech. Coll., 1989-91. Lt. col., USAR, retired. Humble Oil Rsch. fellow, 1954. Fellow Am. Inst. Chemists (pres. Ohio Inst. 1978-82); mem. Tex. Acad. Sci., Am. Def. Preparedness Assn., Electron Microscopy Soc. Am., Materials Rsch. Soc., SAMPE Composites Soc., N.Am. Catalysis Soc., Am. Soc. Composites, Soc. Plastics Engrs., Soc. Automotive Engrs., Am. Chem. Soc. (chmn. chpt. exec. bd. 1969, bus. mgr. nat. div. Petroleum Chemistry, 1986-90, Best Paper award rubber div. 1967, 70, Honorable Mention awards 1968, 69, 73, symposia co-chmn., co-editor books on catalysis-surface chemistry 1985, carbon-graphite chemistry 1975), Engrs.' Coun. Houston (sr. councilor 1970-71), Sigma Xi, Phi Lambda Upsilon, Alpha Chi, Sigma Pi Sigma. Methodist. Home and Office: 106 Pecos Ct Georgetown TX 78628-4231 Office Phone: 512-864-1518. E-mail: deviney_marvin@hotmail.com.

DE VINK, LODEWIJK J. R., healthcare consultant, former consumer pharmaceutical products company executive; b. Amsterdam, Netherlands, Feb. 14, 1945; married; two sons. BBA, Washburn U, 1968; MBA, Am. U., Netherlands Sch. of Bus., 1969. Internat. mgmt. assoc. Schering-Plough/Schering Internat., 1969—70, mktg. planning assoc., 1970—71, product planning mgr.-instl. market, 1972—73, group planning mgr., Rx products, 1973—74, mktg. mgr., 1974—77, gen. mgr., 1977—78; dir. of mktg. for Europe, Middle East, Africa Schering-Plough Corp., 1978—81, vice pres., Schering Labs., 1981—84, sr. vice-pres., Schering Internat., 1984—86, pres., Schering Internat., 1986—88; v.p., pres. internat. ops. Warner-Lambert Co., Morris Plains, NJ, 1988-90, exec. v.p., pres. US ops., 1990-91, pres., COO, 1991-2000, chmn. bd. pres., CEO, 1999—2000. Bd. dirs. Meml. Hosp., Pharm. Rsch. & Mfrs. Assn. (chmn. 1995), Internat. Fedn. of Pharm. Mfrs. Assns. (chmn. 1998-1999); mem. supervisory bd. of Royal Ahold, Bd. of Alcon, Inc., European Adv. Coun., Rothschild & Cie.; chmn. of global health care ptnr. Credit Suisse First Boston, 2000-02; chmn. Internat. Health Care Ptnrs., 2002-03; founding mem., cons. Blackstone Healthcare Ptnrs., 2003-. Trustee Nat. Found. Infectious Diseases, 1992—; bd. dirs. Nat. Actors Theatre, NYC, 1993—, Friends of Hassenfeld, United Negro Coll. Fund, Nijenrode U.

DE VISSCHER, FRANCOIS MARIE, investment banker; b. Louvain, Belgium, Sept. 24, 1953; m. Maura Michaela Nicholson, Oct. 4, 1980; children: Patrick-Michel, Luke-Michel. BA in Applied Econs., U. Louvain, 1975; MBA, Rutgers U., 1977. CPA, N.Y. Staff asst. Coopers & Lybrand, Brussels, 1975-76, staff acct. N.Y.C., 1977-79, sr. acct., 1979-80, supr. audit, 1980; assoc. Smith Barney, Harris Upham & Co., Inc., N.Y.C., 1981-82, 2nd v.p., 1983-84, v.p., 1985-88, mng. dir., 1988-90; pres. de Visscher & Co., Greenwich, Conn., 1990-98; ptnr. de Visscher, Olson & Allen LLC, Greenwich, 1998—. Bd. dirs. Bekaert Corp. Pres. Family Firm Inst., Brookline, Mass.; chmn. European Family Office Conf., London. Mem. AICPA, Nat. Assn. Securities Dealers (registered rep.), N.Y. Soc. CPAs, Belgium Am. C. of C. (bd. dirs.), Bekaert N.V. Belgium (bd. dirs.), Larchmont (N.Y.) Yacht Club, Westchester Country Club (Rye, N.Y.), Pawling (N.Y.) Mt. Club. Avocations: sailing, shooting, fishing, golf. Office: de Visscher Olson & Allen 104 Field Point Rd Greenwich CT 06830-6481 E-mail: francois@devisscher.com.

DEVITO, DANNY MICHAEL, actor, film director; b. Asbury Park, NJ, Nov. 17, 1944; s. Daniel and Julia DeV.; m. Rhea Perlman, Jan. 8, 1982; children: Lucy Chet, Gracie, Daniel Jacob. Grad., Am. Acad. Dramatic Arts,

1966. Co-founder Jersey Films. Theater appearances include The Man With a Flower in His Mouth, Sheridan Sq. Playhouse, 1969, The Shrinking Bride, 1971, One Flew Over the Cuckoo's Nest, 1971, DuBarry Was a Lady, 1972, A Phantasmagoria Historia of D. Johann Fauster Magister, Ph.D, M.D., D.D., D.L., etc., 1973, The Many Wives of Windsor (N.Y. Shakespeare Festival), 1974, Where Do We Go From Here?, 1974; motion picture appearances include Lady Liberty, 1971, Hurry Up, or I'll Be 30, 1973, Scalawag, 1972, One Flew Over the Cuckoo's Nest, 1975, Car Wash, 1976, Hot Dogs for Gaugin, Goin' South, 1978, Swap Meet, 1979, Going Ape!, 1981, Terms of Endearment, 1983, Romancing the Stone, 1984, Johnny Dangerously, 1984, Jewel of the Nile, 1985, Wise Guys, 1986, My Little Pony (voice), 1986, Ruthless People, 1986, Tin Men, 1987, (dir. debut) Throw Momma from the Train, 1987, Twins, 1988, The War of the Roses (also dir.), 1989, Other People's Money, 1991, Batman Returns, 1992, Hoffa, (also producer, dir.) 1992, Jack the Bear, 1993, The Last Action Hero (voice), 1993, Renaissance Man, 1994, Junior, 1994, Get Shorty, (also prodr.), 1995, Matilda, (also dir.), 1996, Mars Attacks!, 1996, The Rainmaker, 1997, Hercules (voice), 1997; co-exec. prodr.: Reality Bites, 1994, Pulp Fiction, 1994; prodr.: Feeling Minnesota, 1996, Gattaca, 1997, Living Out Loud (also prodr.), 1998 The Virgin Suicides, 1999, The Big Kahuna, 1999, Man On the Moon, 1999 (also prodr.), Drowning Mona, 2000, Screwed, 2000, Erin Brokovich (prodr.), 2000, How High, 2001, Camp, 2003, Marx Brothers, 2003, What's the Worst That Could Happen, 2001, Heist, 2001, Death to Smoochy (also dir.), 2002, Anything Else, 2003, (voice) Big Fish, 2003, Duplex (also dir.), Family of the Year, 2004, (voice) Catching Kringle, 2004, Christmas in Love, 2004, Marilyn Hotchkiss' Ballroom Dancing Charm School, 2005, Be Cool, 2005 (also prodr.); appeared in role of Louie in TV series Taxi, 1978-83; guest voice: The Simpsons, 1989; directed and appeared in cable TV movie The Ratings Game, 1984; TV appearances include Starsky and Hutch, 1977, Police Woman, 1977, Amazing Stories, 1986, (voice) The Simpsons, 1991, 92, Pearl, 1997, Ed, 2002, Karen Sisco, 2003, Friends, 2004, (voice) Father of the Pride, 2004. Recipient Golden Globe award for TV series, Taxi, 1979; Emmy award 1981 Office: care Fred Specktor Creative Artists Agy Inc 9830 Wilshire Blvd Beverly Hills CA 90212-1804*

DEVITO, KAREN SMITH, French educator; b. Milw., July 25, 1953; d. Harry Earle and Helen Eilene (Knapp) S.; m. Lee Carl DeVito, Nov. 8, 1986. BA, U. Maine, 1975; MA, Boston U., 1977; PhD, U. Conn., 1992. Grad. asst. Boston U., 1975-76; teaching asst. U. Conn., Storrs, 1980-82; instr. French Milton Jr.-Sr. High Sch., Milton, Vt., 1978-80; instr. French, U.S. History Lake Region High Sch., Bridgton, Maine, 1985-89; instr. French St. Joseph's Coll., Windham, Maine, 1987-2000, mem. faculty senate, 1989-90; sales exec. Compass Techs., Cadillac, Mich., 2005—. Grantee, French Govt., 1982, Assn. D'Auvergne, 1982, U. Conn. 1982. Mem. MLA, NEA, Fgn. Lang. Assn. Maine, Northeastern Assn. Modern Langs., Medieval Acad., Maine Tchrs. Assn., Lake Region Tchrs. Assn. (pres. 1987-88, mem. negotiating team 1986—), Harrison Bus. and Profl. Assn. Republican. Congregationalist. Home: PO Box 536 Harrison ME 04040-0536 Office: Compass Tech Po Box 717 Cadillac MI 49601

DEVITO, MATHIAS JOSEPH, retired real estate executive; b. Trenton, NJ, Aug. 23, 1930; s. Charles P. and Margaret L. DeV.; m. Rosetta Kormuth, July 28, 1956; children: Ann DeVito Walker, Charles Michael. BA, U. Md., 1954, LL.B. with highest honors, 1956; L.H.D., Salisbury State Coll., 1984. Bar: Md. Asst. atty. gen. State of Md., 1963-64; ptnr. Piper & Marbury, Balt., 1965-70; sr. v.p., gen. counsel, then exec. v.p. Rouse Co., Columbia, Md., 1968-73, pres., CEO, bd. dirs., 1973-84, chmn. bd. dirs., pres., CEO, 1984-93, chmn. bd. dirs., CEO, 1993-95, chmn. bd. dirs., 1995-97, chmn. exec. com. bd., 1997-2001, chmn. emeritus, 1997—. Bd. dirs. Mars Supermarkets, Inc., Sitel Corp., Triton PSC; chmn. Greater Balt. Com., 1990—92. Editor Md. Law Rev., 1955-56. Chmn. bd. trustees Md. State Colls., 1970-73; trustee Johns Hopkins U., 1983-89, Md. Inst. Coll. Art, 1995—. Mem. Adirondack League, Elkridge Club, Order of Coif. Roman Catholic. Office: Ste 220 Village Sq II Baltimore MD 21210-1935 Office Phone: 410-433-7109. E-mail: mnrdevito@aol.com.

DEVITO, TERESA MARIE, artist; b. Bangoli del Tigino, Italy, June 11, 1920; came to U.S., 1924, naturalized, 1926; d. Bartolomeo and Santo Donatello Cimaglia; m. Americao DeVito; children: Richard (dec.), Sandra Ann DeVito King. BA inEdn., Fairmont State Coll., 1960; MA, W.Va. U., 1964; postgrad., Wagner Coll., 1968; D (hon.), Minsitry Fgn. Affairs of Malta. Tchr. East Fairmont (W.Va.) High Sch., 1960-68, Miller Jr. High Sch., Rivesville, W.Va., 1969-70; instr. art Fairview H.S., 1970-86, Barrockville H.S., Farmington H.S. One-woman shows include Lynn Katler Gallery, N.y.C., 1975; exhibited at group shows at Morgantown Art Assn. Exhbn., 1960; commd. work includes paintings on cloth at Immaculate Conception Ch., Fairmont, Fairmont Bowling Ctr., 1988, Disney World. Recipient Internat. Statue of Victory, Einstein Peace Medal, Rhodeodendron Festival award, Honoris Causea, Internat. Found., 1987. Mem. AAUW, NEA, Nat. Art Edn. Assn., Tole Painters Am., W.Va. Art Assn., W.Va. Artist and Craftsman Guild, Artists Equity, League Ind. Artists (past v.p.), Village Garden Club, Cath. Daus. Am. (State Ct. of W.Va. award, Nat. Merit award for "Face in a Cloud" entry in poster contest, 2000), Quota Internat. Orgn. Roman Catholic. Home: 417 Newton St Fairmont WV 26554-5218

DEVITT, WILLIAM LOUIS, retired lawyer; b. St. Paul, Minn., May 25, 1923; s. Louis James and Nora Gertrude Devitt; m. Mary McNulty Devitt, May 24, 1952; children: Christopher, Sean, Mary, Anne, Nicholas, Matthew, William, Sarah. BBA, U. Minn., 1960, LLB, 1955. Bar: Minn. Acct. Shell Oil co., Mpls., 1948—49; lawyer Thomas Spence - Lawyer, St. Paul, 1955—57, Allen & Counrtny Lawyers, St. Paul, 1958—61, Harvest States Coop., St. Paul, 1961—88, ret., 1988. Author: Shoretail, the Odyssey of an Infantry Lieutenant in World War II, 2001. Capt. U.S. Army, 1943—46, capt. U.S. Army, 1950—52. Decorated Bronze Star U.S. Army, Purple Heart. Roman Catholic. Avocation: reading. Home: 6812 Indian Hills Rd Minneapolis MN 55439

DEVIVO, ANGE, retired small business owner; b. Bay Shore, NY, Oct. 20, 1925; d. Romeo Zanetti and Karolina (Hodapp) King; m. John Michael DeVivo, Dec. 30, 1950; 1 child, Michael. Student, Washington Sch. for Secs., N.Y.C., 1945-46. Sec. Am. Airlines, N.Y.C., 1946-51; exec. sec. W.C. Holzhauer, N.Y.C., 1951-52; dist. sales mgr. Emmons Jewelers, Inc., Bound Brook, N.J., 1952-53; exec. sec. NJ Rep. State Com., 1960—64; dist. office supr. 19th Decenniel census U.S. Dept. Commerce, Charlotte, NC, 1970; adminstrv. sec. Mercy Hosp., Charlotte, NC, 1973—81; pres. Secs., Plus, Convs., Plus, Charlotte, 1983—91; prin. Ange DeVivo & Assocs., Inc., Charlotte, 1991—92; ret., 1992. Editor: The North Carolina Republican Woman, 2d edit., 1994, 3d edit., 1995; author Precinct Training Manual, 1971. First woman chair Mecklenburg County Rep. Party, 1976; adminstrv. sec. Nat. Broadcast Assn. for Cmty. Affairs, 1987-90; active in local politics, NJ, 1956-64, Conn., 1964-68, NC, 1968-96; active Human Svcs. Coun., Charlotte, 1984-88; conf. mgr., 8th Nat. Recycling Congress, 1989; active Emergency Med. Svc. Adv. Coun., Charlotte, 1981-92, chmn., 1988-90; active Charlotte Women's Polit. Caucus, 1972-96; chair Mecklenburg County Rep. Party, 1976-77; mem. Mecklenburg Evening Rep. Women's Club, Charlotte, 1996—, pres., 1973-74, 93-94; mem. Mecklenburg County Women's Commn., 1990-96, Women's Roundtable, 1994-95; citizens adv. com. Conv. and Visitors Bur., 1986-90; coord. Women's Equality Day celebration Mecklenburg County Women's Commn., 1990, coord., fin. chair, 1991-92, co-chmn., fin. chair, 1993-96, adv. bd. 1993-96, vice-chair bd., 1995; fundraiser March of Dimes and Leukemia, Ala., 1999, 2002; active Rep. Women Today Ala., 1997-2001, tel. com., 2001; pres. Cardinal Bus. and Profl. Women's Club, 1979-81. Recipient Order of Long Leaf Pine award Gov. of N.C., 1974, Entrepreneur of Yr. award Women Bus. Owners, 1987, Spl. Recognition award for devotion, dedication and untiring efforts Mecklenburg County Women's Commn., 1996; honoree N.C. Fedn. Rep. Women, 1987; nominee Cmty. Svc. award Mecklenburg County Women's Commn., 1994, Hall Fame, N.C. Rep. Party, 1995. Mem.: Rep. Women of the South (mem. telephone com. 2004—05). Roman Catholic. Avocations: politics, community service. Personal E-mail: jmdevivo531@cs.com.

DE VIVO, DARRYL CLAUDE, pediatrician, neurologist; b. Everett, Mass., Aug. 28, 1937; children: Cynthia, Jessica, Kristin. BA, Amherst Coll., 1959; MD, U. Va., 1964. Diplomate Am. Bd. Psychiatry and Neurology (dir. neurology 1991-99, pres. 1999). Intern Univ. Hosp., Boston, 1964—65; resident in pediat. and neurology Mass. Gen. Hosp., Boston, 1965—67; clin. assoc. NIH, 1967—69; fellow in pediatric neurology St. Louis Children's Hosp., 1969—70; mem. faculty Wash. U. Sch. Medicine, St. Louis, 1970—78, prof. pediat. and neurology, 1977—78; Sidney Carter prof. neurology and prof. pediatrics Coll. Physicians and Surgeons, Columbia U., N.Y.C., 1979—; dir. pediatric neurology Columbia-Presbyn. Med. Ctr., N.Y.C., 1979—2000, assoc. chmn. child neurology and devel. neurobiology, 1998—. Mem. coun. NANDS, 1997—2000. Assoc. editor Rudolph's Textbook of Pediatrics, 17th edit., 1982, 18th edit., 1987, 19th edit., 1990, 20th edit., 1996, 21st edit., 2000, Annals of Neurology, 1979—83, Advances in Pediatrics, 1989—; contbr. articles to profl. jours. With With USPHS, 1967—69. Grantee NIH. Mem.: Soc. Neurosci., Internat. Child Neurology Assn., Am. Soc. Neurochemistry, Soc. Pediatric Rsch., Am. Pediatric Soc., Child Neurology Soc. (pres. 1989—91), Am. Acad. Neurology (sec. 1993—97, trustee Rsch. and Edn. Found. 1997—), Am. Neurol. Assn., Alpha Omega Alpha. Office: Presbyn Hosp Neurology Inst 710 W 168th St New York NY 10032-2603

DEVIVO, SAL J., newspaper executive; b. Saratoga Springs, N.Y., Feb. 3, 1937; s. Salvatore and Sabine (Lobombardo) DeV.; m. Carolyn Ann Turney, Dec. 17, 1961; children: Sally, Karen, Michael, Darin. BA in Journalism, St. Bonaventure U., 1962. Reporter The Saratogian, Saratoga Springs, 1956-58, Schenectady Gazette, 1959, Niagara Falls Gazette, N.Y., 1962, Sunday editor Niagara Gazette, 1964, city editor, 1966-68, editor, pub., 1974-75; mng. editor The Saratogian, 1968-72, editor, pub., 1972-74; editor Camden Courier-Post, N.J., 1975, pub., 1976-79; exec. editor, assoc. pub. Binghamton Press and Sun-Bull., N.Y., 1979-80; pres., pub. Utica Observer-Dispatch and Daily Press, N.Y., 1980-85, Wilmington Morning News and Evening Jour., Del., 1985-94, The Daily Jour., Vineland, N.J., 1994-96. Pres. Saratoga County United Way, 1973; gen. campaign chmn. Niagara Falls United Givers Fund, 1975, Utica United Way, 1985; pres. adv. council St. Bonaventure U., 1978-79; bd. dirs. Cooper Med. Center, Camden, 1978-79; trustee Wilmington Coll., 1989-2005. Mem. N.Y. State Soc. Newspaper Editors (past pres.), Md., Del., D.C. press assns., N.J. Press Assn. (dir.), Am. Newspaper Pubs. Assn., Am. Soc. Newspaper Editors. Roman Catholic. Home: 10 Summerknoll Cir Newark DE 19711-2488

DEVLIN, BARBARA JO, school district administrator; b. Milw., 1947; m. John Edward Devlin, 1973; 2 children. BA, Gustavus Adolphus Coll., 1969; MA, U. Mass., 1971; PhD, U. Minn., 1978. Cert. tchr., sch. prin., supt., Minn.; cert. supt., Ill., Minn. Tchr. Worthington (Minn.) High Sch., 1971-75; rsch. assoc. Ednl. R & D, Mpls.-St. Paul, 1975-76, 76-77; coord. edn. svcs. Ednl. Coop. Svc., Mpls.-St. Paul, 1977-79; dir. personnel Minnetonka Pub. Schs., Excelsior, Minn., 1979-85, asst. supt., 1985-87; supt. Sch. Dist. 45, Villa Park, Ill., 1987-95, Ind. Sch. Dist. 280, Richfield, Minn., 1995—. Editor working papers Gov.'s Coun. on Fluctuating Enrollments, St. Paul, 1976. Contbr. articles to ednl. jours. Bd. dir. Richfield Found., 1995—. Named Ill. Supt. of Yr., 1994, Region 9 Adminstr. of Excellence, Minn. Assn. Sch. Adminstrs., 2004; recipient Disting. Alumni award, Gustavus Adolphus Coll., 1994; Ednl. Policy fellow, George Washington U., 1977—78, mem. fellow program, Bush Found. Pub. Schs., 1984—85. Mem. Minn. Assn. Sch. Adminstrs., Rotary Internat. (membership chair Villa Park unit 1989-91, vocat. dir. 1991-92, sec. 1992-93, pres. 1994-95), Optimists Internat. Methodist. Office: Richfield Pub Schs 7001 Harriet Ave Richfield MN 55423-3061 Office Phone: 612-798-6010. E-mail: Barbara.Devlin@richfield.k12.mn.us.

DEVLIN, CYNTHIA M., air transportation executive, consultant; b. Freeport, Tex., Dec. 13, 1949; d. Kellon Sherrell and Janiece (Chambers) Marshall; m. Philip Devlin. Archaeool. cert., U. London, 1988; BA in Anthropology, U. Houston, 1991; paralegal cert., Southwestern Paralegal Inst., 1994; postgrad., Austin STate U., 2004—. Flight attendant Trans-Tex. Airways/Tex. Internat., Houston, 1969—73; office mgr. Mark Stevens Co., Houston, 1973—76, 1981—86, Foster Testers and Oil Drilling, Odessa, Tex., 1977—80; sales sec. Sys. One/Ea. Airlines, Miami and Houston, 1987—88, Continental Ea. Sales, Houston, 1988—89; sales adminstr. Continental Airlines, Houston, 1989—91, spl. events coord., 1991—94; specialist tech. publs. Continental Express, Houston, 1995; pres. PJD Airworthiness Cons., Inc., Houston and Zavalla, Tex., 1998—. Mem. adv. bd. Tenneco Marathon, Houston, 1994—96; cons. in field. Author: Fahrenheit 6000, 2002, When the Sun Hides the Moon, 2003. Vol. Toys for Tots, Houston, Am. Cancer Soc., Spring, Tex.; mem. USO, Washington, Friends of Archaeology, U. St. Thomas, Houston, 1999—2003. Scholar, Assn. Women in Mgmt., 1989. Mem.: Tex. Archaeology Soc., East Tex. Hist. Assn., U. Houston Alumni Assn. (life), Golden Key, Phi Alpha Theta. Republican. Avocations: painting, gardening, sewing, cooking. Home: 421 Chambers Rd Zavalla TX 75980 Office: PJD Airworthiness Cons Inc PO Box 46 Zavalla TX 75980

DEVLIN, FRANCIS JAMES, lawyer; b. NYC, Apr. 12, 1943; dual citizen, Ireland, U.S., 2005; s. Francis James and Marie A. D.; m. Patricia Ann Scheid; children: Christopher James, Kimberley Ann. BA magna cum laude, Providence Coll., 1964; JD, Fordham U., 1967. Bar: N.Y. 1968, Tex. 1979, U.S. Ct. Appeals (5th and 11th cirs.) 1981, U.S. Supreme Ct. 1993. Assoc. Rogers and Wells, N.Y.C., 1967-72; counsel Standard Oil Co. N.J., N.Y.C., 1972, Exxon Corp., N.Y.C., 1973-78, Exxon Co., U.S.A., Houston, 1978-90, sr. counsel, 1990-99, coord. gen. comml. practice group, 1996-99; sr. counsel, coord. mktg. Exxon Mobil Corp., Fuels Mktg. Co., Fairfax, Va., 1999—2002; spl. counsel Duane Morris, LLP, Houston, 2003—04. Adj. prof. Fordham U., 1978. Articles editor Fordham Law Rev., 1966-67. Bd. dirs. Our Lady of Guadalupe Sch., Houston, 1994-2000, chmn., 1998-2000. Fellow: Am. Bar Found., Coll. State Bar Tex.; mem.: ABA (vice-chmn. 1997—2003, chmn. 2003—05, oil and natural gas downstream com., environment, energy and resources sect., vice-chmn. 2005—), Houston Bar Assn., Brit.-Am. Bus. Coun., Tex. Mid-Continent Oil and Gas Assn. (chmn. mktg. subcom.legal com. 1982—2000), Am. Petroleum Inst. (chmn. 1990—92, vice-chmn. 1992—94, chmn. 1997—98, vice-chmn. 1998—99, counsel, gen. com. on mktg. 2001—02, founding chmn. subcom. on mktg. law, gen. com. law, emeritus mem.), Tex. State Bar (unauthorized practice of law com. 1989—92, Bar Jour. com. 1995—98), Soc. Friendly Sons of St. Patrick in City N.Y. Republican. Roman Catholic. Home: 12625 Memorial Dr Houston TX 77024-4819 Office: 12625 Memorial Dr Ste 112 Houston TX 77024-4819 E-mail: francisdevlin@msn.com.

DEVLIN, JAMES RICHARD, lawyer; b. Camden, N.J., July 7, 1950; s. Gerald William and Mary (Hand) D.; children: Grace, Jennifer, Kristen. BS in Indsl. Engring., N.J. Inst. Tech., 1972; JD, Fordham U., 1976. Bar: N.J. 1976, N.Y. 1977, Kans. 2002, U.S. Ct. Appeals (D.C. cir.) 1982. Various mgmt. positions in Long Lines Sect. AT&T, NYC, 1972-76, counsel Long Lines Sect. Bedminster, N.J., 1976-82, counsel NYC, 1982-83, gen. atty. comm. sect. Basking Ridge, N.J., 1983-86; v.p., gen. counsel telephone United Telecomm., Inc., Westwood, Kans., 1987-88; exec. v.p. gen. counsel and external affairs Sprint Corp., Westwood, Kans., 1989—2003. Past pres., bd. dirs. Ctr. for Mgmt. Assistance, Kansas City, Mo., 1993-96 Mem. ABA (past chmn. comm. com. pub. utility law sect.), Am. Arbitration Assn., Fed. Comm. Bar Assn. Home: 12300 Catalina St Leawood KS 66209-2220

DEVLIN, JOHN GERARD, lawyer, writer; b. Phila., Apr. 26, 1955; s. John and Catherine (Flannery) D.; m. Maureen Borneman, June 17, 1978; children: Caitlin, Colin, Courtenay, Conor. BA, Temple U., 1977, JD, 1980, LLM, 1996. Bar: Pa. 1980, N.J. 1992. Assoc. Spencer, Sherr & Moses, Norristown, Pa., 1980-82, Deasey, Scanlan & Bender, Phila., 1982-84; mng. atty. Devlin Assocs., P.A., Phila., 1984—. Author: Tort Liability for Bad Faith Claims, 1995. Mem. Union League Club, Phi Beta Kappa. Office: 1515 Market St Ste 2010 Philadelphia PA 19102-1920

DEVLIN, KARIN L, education educator; b. Los Angeles, Calif., Jan. 18, 1966; d. Bernard L and Janice M Frankhouser; m. Ned P Devlin, May 18, 1996. BS in edn., Calif. U. of Pa., 1988, M in edn., 1990. Reading specialist Hempfield Area Sch. Dist., Irwin, Pa., 1990—91; reading specialist/instr. Mt. Pleasant Area Sch. Dist., Mt. Pleasant, Pa., 1991—93, Connellsville Area Sch. Dist., Connellsville, Pa., 1993—96; gen. edn./bus. instr. Berks Tech. Inst., Wyomissing, Pa., 2000—. Cons. Berks Country Chiropractic Assn., Wyomissing, Pa., 2000—; mem. adv. bd. Berks Tech. Inst., Wyomissing, Pa., 2001—; coord. of acad. study skills ctr.; coord. of placement entrance exam; prometric adminstr. Adv. Students in Free Enterprise, 2002—03, Student Coun. Berks Tech. Inst., 2003—. Mem.: Nat. Bus. Edn. Assn. Avocations: travel, interior decorating, gardening, research. Office: Berks Tech Inst 2205 Ridgewood Rd Reading PA 19610 Office Fax: 610-376-4684. Business E-Mail: kdevlin@berkstech.com.

DEVLIN, MICHAEL COLES, bass-baritone; b. Chgo., Nov. 27, 1942; s. John Stott and Jane (Coles) D. Mus.B., La. State U., 1965. Debut, N.Y.C. Opera, 1966, appeared with, Santa Fe Opera, Houston Opera and Symphony, San Francisco Symphony, symphonies in, Los Angeles, Phila., Boston, Chgo., New Orleans, Washington, N.Y. Philharm., opera cos. in, Boston, New Orleans, Washington, Ft. Worth, English debut, Glyndebourne Festival, 1974; appeared at, Covent Garden, 1975, 77, European debut, Holland Festival, 1977; appeared with, Frankfurt and Munich operas, 1977, Can. opera and symphony work in, Winnipeg, Toronto and Ottawa, debut, Met. Opera, 1978, San Francisco Opera, 1979, Hamburg and Paris operas, 1980, Miami and Monte Carlo operas, 1981, Dallas opera, 1983, Chgo. Opera, 1984, Los Angeles Opera, 1986.

DEVLIN, PATRICIA, lawyer; b. Vallejo, Calif., July 25, 1945; BA magna cum laude, U. Wash., 1968; JD, U. Calif., 1977. Bar: Calif. 1977, Hawaii 1978, U.S. Dist. Ct. Hawaii 1978. With Carlsmith Ball LLP, Honolulu. Mem. ABA, State Bar Calif., Hawaii Soc. Corp. Planners (pres. 1992-93), Phi Beta Kappa. Office: Carlsmith Ball LLP Pacific Tower # 2200 1001 Bishop St Honolulu HI 96813-3429 E-mail: pdevlin@carlsmith.com.

DEVLIN, PETER J., lawyer; BS, Clarkson Coll., 1980; JD magna cum laude, Suffolk U., 1985. Bar: Mass. 1985, US Patent and Trademark Office. Elec. engr., patent atty. Raytheon Co.; with Fish & Richardson PC, Boston, 1987—, pres., prin., 1993—. Contbg. author Inside the Minds: The Innovative Lawyer, 2003. Office: Fish & Richardson PC 225 Franklin St Boston MA 02110-2804 Office Phone: 617-521-7018. Office Fax: 617-542-8906. E-mail: devlin@fr.com.

DEVLIN, ROBERT MANNING, diversified financial services company executive; b. Bklyn., Feb. 28, 1941; s. John Manning and Norma (Hall) D.; m. Katharine Bareis, Sept. 13, 1961; children: Michael Hall II, Matthew Bareis. BA in Econs., Tulane U., 1964. Various positions Mut. of N.Y., 1964-77; v.p., asst. to pres. Calif. Western States Life Ins. Co., Sacramento, 1977-80, sr. v.p., 1980; exec. v.p., dir. Am. Gen. Life and Accident Ins. Co., Nashville, 1980-85; pres., CEO Am. Gen. Life Insurance Co., Houston, 1986—93; vice chmn., bd. dir. Am. Gen. Corp., Houston, 1993—95, pres., CEO, 1995—2001, chmn., bd. dirs., 1997—2001; chmn. Curragh Capital Ptnrs. LLC, 2001—. Bd. dirs. Cooper Industries Inc., LKQ, Corp. Blaylock Ptnrs., LLC, FFS Holdings Inc.; bd. trustees Boston Coll., Tulane Coll.; exec. com., bd. dirs. Internat. Insurance Soc. Inc.; exec. com., bd. dir. Am. Irish Historical Soc. Dir. Fin. Svcs. Roundtable; mem. Bus. Roundtable; bd. dirs. America's Promise-Alliance for Youth. Mem. Saratoga Reading Rooms, N.Y., Winged Foot Golf Club, N.Y., Met. Club, N.Y., Univ. Club, N.Y., Caves Valley Golf Club, Owings Mill, Md. Roman Catholic. Office: Curragh Capital Ptnrs LLC 730 5th Ave Ste 2102 New York NY 10019

DEVLIN, THOMAS MCKEOWN, biochemist, educator; b. Phila., June 29, 1929; s. Frank and Ella Mae (McKeown) Devlin; m. Marjorie Adele Paynter, Aug. 15, 1953; children: Steven James, Mark Thomas. BA, U. Pa., 1953; PhD, Johns Hopkins U., 1957. Rsch. assoc. Merck Inst., Rahway, NJ, 1957-61, sect. head, 1961-66, dir. enzymology, 1966-67; prof., chmn. dept. biochemistry Coll. Medicine Drexel U. (formerly Hahnemann U.), 1967-94, prof., 1994-95, prof. emeritus, 1995—. acting dean, Sch. Allied Health Professions, 1972-74, 80-81. Vis. scientist U. Brussels, 1964—65, Inst. Genetics, Naples, Italy, 1965; mem. rev. panels NSF, 1976—77; mem. com. sci. and arts Franklin Inst., 1977—90; mem. test com. Nat. Bd. Med. Examiners, 1983—85; chair Med. Biochemistry Edn. Bd., 1986—93. Editor: Textbook of Biochemistry (J. Wiley), 1982, 1986, 1992, 1997, 2002; contbr. articles to profl. jours. Mem. commn. evaluation, retention and selection of judges Phila. Bar Assn., 1976—79, vice chmn., 1979; mem. selection panel for magistrate judges, 1993, 1995; mem. vis. com. Lehigh U., 1982—90; mem. tech. adv. com. Ben Franklin Tech. Ctr., 1991—2000. Mem.: Biochemal Soc., Biophys. Soc., Soc. Exptl. Biology and Medicine, Am. Soc. Cell Biology, Am. Assn. Cancer Rsch., Am. Soc. Biochemistry and Molecular Biology, Greate Bay Golf Club, Ocean City (N.J.) Yacht Club, Sigma Xi, Phi Beta Kappa. Episcopalian. Home: 159 Greenville Ct Berwyn PA 19312-2071 Office: Drexel U Coll Medicine 159 Greenville Ct Berwyn PA 19312-2071 Business E-Mail: tdevlin@drexel.edu.

DEVLIN, WENDE DOROTHY, writer, artist; b. Buffalo, Apr. 27, 1918; d. Bernhardt Phillip Wende and Elizabeth May Buffington; m. Harry Devlin, Aug. 30, 1941; children: Harry, Wende, Jeffrey, Alexandra, Brian, Nicholas, David. BFA, Syracuse U., 1940. Author: (children's books) Old Black Witch, 1963, Old Witch and the Polkadot Ribbon, 1963, The Knobby Boys to the Rescue, 1965, Aunt Agatha, There is a Lion Under the Couch, 1968, How Fletcher was Hatched, 1970, (N.J. English Tchrs. award), A Kiss for a Warthog, 1970, Cranberry Thanksgiving, 1971, Old Witch Rescues Halloween, 1973 (Chgo. Book Fair award for excellence 1974), Cranberry Christmas, 1973, Cranberry Mystery, 1979, Hang on Hester, 1980, Cranberry Summer, 1991, Cranberry Valentine, 1986, Cranberry Autumn, 1994, The Trouble with Henriette, 1995; artist, painter comic strip Ragg Mopp, 1969-72; contbr. of many poems to Good Housekeeping mag.; one person show at Schering Plough, N.J.; represented in permanent collections at Midlantic Bank of N.J., Nat. Westminster Bank of N.J., also many private collections. Mem. Rutgers Adv. Coun. on Children's Lit., 1980—. Recipient Arents award Syracuse U., 1977; named to N.J. Literary Hall of Fame, 1989. Congregationalist. Office: Simon & Schuster 866 3rd Ave New York NY 10022-6221 Home and Office: 100 W Dudley Ave Westfield NJ 07090-4002

DEVOE, DAVID, SR., publishing executive; Group internal auditor News Corp., 1983; dep. fin. dir. News Corp. Ltd., NYC, 1985—90; CFO, fin. dir. News Corp., NYC, 1990—, exec. v.p. News Am. Inc., 1991—98, sr. exec. v.p., 1996—, sr. exec. v.p. News Am. Inc., 1998—. Dir. William Collins Holdings, Harper Collins, British Sky Broadcasting Group, NDS Group, The News Corp. Office: News Corp Ste 300 1211 Avenue Of The Americas New York NY 10036-8795*

DEVOGEL, STEPHEN BERT, research scientist; s. Nancy and Donald DeVogel. BS, U. South Fla., 1996—2000; MSc, U. of Colo., 2000—03. Profl. scientist INSTAAR, Boulder, Colo., 2003—. Grad. Student fellowship, Dept. of Geol. Sciences; Univ of CO, 2000—01, Grad. Student Rsch. grant, Geol. Soc. of Am., 2002. Mem.: Golden Key. Achievements include research in Paleomonsoon changes over last 10, 000 years in Yemen; ecosystem changes, extinctions, and human impact in Australia over the last 125, 000 years; the rate of small ice cap melting on northern Baffin Island over the last 50+ years. Avocations: travel, fly fishing, hiking, cycling, skiing. Office: Inst of Arctic and Alpine Research 1560 30th St; UCB 450 Boulder CO 80309-0450 Office Phone: 303-492-5075. E-mail: stephendevogel@hotmail.com.

DEVOGT, JOHN FREDERICK, management science and business ethics educator, consultant; b. Detroit, Oct. 20, 1930; s. Leo Henry and Dorothy Helen (Gibbs) D.; m. Ann Marie Berby, Aug. 29, 1959; children— Joanne Elise, Linda Christine BS, U. N.C., 1957, PhD, 1966. Instr. Washington and Lee U., Lexington, Va., 1962-66, asst. prof., 1966-67, assoc. prof., 1967-70, prof., 1970-2000, head dept., 1968-90, prof. emeritus, 2000—; acad. dir. Washington and Lee Family Bus. Inst., 1987—89. State judge Blue Chip Enterprise Initiative, 1991-96; acad. Jonah A.Y. Goldratt Inst., 1991—; chmn. adv. bd. Lexington office CorEast Savs. Bank, Richmond, 1976-90. Chmn. Lexington City Sch. Bd., 1973; pres. Va. Sch. Bds. Assn., Charlottesville, 1974; v.p. Henry St. Playhouse, Lexington, 1985, Friends Rockbridge Choral Soc., 2000—04; deacon, elder Lexington Presbyterian Ch.; bd. dirs. Lexington Indsl. Devel., 2004—. Served to staff sgt. USAF, 1951—55. Vis. fellow, Univ. Coll., Oxford, Eng., 1983. Mem. So. Mgmt. Assn. (pres. 1975-76), Lexington Golf and Country Club (bd. dirs. 2004—), Phi Beta Kappa, Phi Eta Sigma, Beta Gamma Sigma Presbyterian. Avocations: golf, amateur dramatics, singing. Home: 617 Stonewall St Lexington VA 24450-1947 Office: Washington and Lee Univ Lexington VA 24450 Personal E-mail: jdevogt@rockbridge.net. Business E-Mail: devogtj@wlu.edu.

DEVOLITES, JEANNEMARIE ARAGONA, state legislator; b. Swindon, England, Feb. 28, 1956; children: Nichole, Ashley, Cassandra, Alexandra; m. Tom Davis. BA in Math., U. Va., 1978. Mem. Va. State Legis., 1998—, mem. privileges & elections com., mem. transp., gen. laws and rehab. and social svcs. coms. Republican. Roman Catholic. Office: Gen Assembly Bldg PO Box 406 Richmond VA 23218-0406 Office Phone: 703-938-7972. E-mail: jdevolites@aol.com.

DEVONS, SAMUEL, physicist, educator; b. Bangor, N.Wales, U.K., Sept. 30, 1914; came to U.S., 1959; s. David Isaac and Edith (Edlestein) D.; m. Celia Ruth Toubkin, Sept. 7, 1938; children— Susan Danielle, Judith Rosalind, Amanda Jane, Cathryn Ann Julie. BA, Trinity Coll., Cambridge (Eng.) U., 1935, MA, PhD (Exhbn. 1851 scholar), 1939; M.Sc., Manchester (Eng.) U., 1959. Sr. sci. officer Air Ministry, Ministry Supply, U.K., 1939-45; fellow, dir. studies, lectr. physics Trinity Coll., 1946-49; prof. physics Imperial Coll., London, Eng., 1950-55; Langworthy prof. physics, dir. phys. labs. U. Manchester, 1955-60; prof. physics Columbia U., 1960-84, prof. emeritus, spl. rsch. scientist, 1985—, chmn. dept., 1963-67. Royal Soc.-Leverhulme vis. prof., Andhra, India, 1967-68; Racah vis. prof. physics Hebrew U., Jerusalem, 1973; Balfour vis. prof. history of sci. Weizmann Inst., Israel, 1974, bd. govs., 1971—; Royal Soc. Rutherford Meml. Lectr., Australia, 1989; mem. Tech. Assistance-UNESCO Team of UN to S. Am., 1957 Author: Excited States of Nuclei, 1949; Editor: Biology and the Physical Sciences, 1969, High Energy Physics and Nuclear Structure, 1970. Served with RAF, 1944-45. Recipient Rutherford medal and prize Inst. Physics, U.K., 1970 Fellow: Phi Beta Kappa, The Joseph Priestley Assn. (founder, convenor 1986—), N.Y. Acad. Scis., Am. Phys. Soc., Royal Soc. London. Home: 34 Lewis Rd Irvington NY 10533-2005 Office: Columbia U Nevis Lab PO Box 137 Irvington NY 10533-0137 E-mail: devons@nevis1.columbia.edu.

DEVORE, C. BRENT, college president, educator; b. Zanesville, Ohio, Sept. 3, 1940; s. Carl Emerson and Helen Elizabeth (Van Atta) DeVore; m. Linda Mospens, July 2, 1966; children: Krista, Matthew. BSJ., Ohio U., 1962; MA, Kent State U., 1971, PhD, 1978. Dir. devel. Am. Heart Assn., Cleve., 1965-68; exec. dir. Kent State U. Found., Ohio, 1968-72; v.p. Hiram Coll., Ohio, 1972-82; pres. Davis and Elkins Coll., Elkins, W.Va., 1982-84, Otterbein Coll., Westerville, Ohio, 1984—. Pres. Higher Edn. Coun., Columbus, 1985; trustee Nationwide Investing Found., 1990; bd. dirs. Coun. Ind. Colleges, 2004-. Producer and moderator film series on liberal arts edn. Pres. Hiram (Ohio) Village Council, 1981; chmn. E. Cen. Colls., 1990; pres. Nat. Assn. Schs. and Colls., United Meth. Ch., 1991. Mem. Am. Assn. Advancement of Humanities, AAUP, Ohio Council of Fund Raising Execs. (pres. 1976), Ohio Coll. Assn. (pres. 1987), W.Va. Assn. Coll. and Univ. Pres. (pres. 1984), Westerville C. of C. (pres.). Clubs: University (Columbus, Ohio); University (NYC). Lodges: Rotary. Office: Otterbein Coll Pres Office 27 S Grove St Westerville OH 43081-2004

DEVORE, DALE PAUL, research and development company executive; b. Phillipsburg, N.J., Mar. 31, 1943; s. David Henry DeVore and Anna Elizabeth DeVore-Iskra; m. Sandra Bernice Grebowiec, Dec. 27, 1965; children: Mychelle Leigh, Braden Patrick. BS, Rutgers U., 1966, MS, 1972, PhD, 1973. Prin. biochemist Battelle Meml. Inst., Columbus, Ohio, 1972-79; sr. rsch. specialist 3M, St. Paul, 1979-85; v.p. sci. affairs MedChem Products, Woburn, Mass., 1985-88; chief sci. officer Autogenesis Tech., Inc., Acton, Mass., 1988-96; chief sci. officer, co-founder, sr. v.p. R&D, dir. Collagenesis, Inc., Beverly, Mass., 1996—. Cons. Auto Immune, Lexington, Mass., 1993-94; dir. biomaterials Organogenesis, Inc., Canton, Mass., 1994-95; chief tech. officer Keratoform, Inc., Westerly, R.I., 1994-98, Xium, Westerly, 1998—, Keracon Corp., 2000—; tech. advisor Pericor Sci., Inc., 1999—. Patentee 51 inventions; contbr. over 60 articles to profl. jours.; presenter in field. Mem. AAAS, Assn. Rsch. Vision Ophthalmology, Soc. Biomaterials, Am. Coll. Rheumatology, Am. Urol. Soc., Kiwanis (treas. 1978), Lions Club (v.p. 1984). Home: 3 Warwick Dr Chelmsford MA 01824-3769 Office: Collagenesis Inc 500 Cummings Ctr Beverly MA 01915-6142

DEVORE, DAUN ALINE, lawyer; b. Ft. Worth; Student, U. Paris IV; BA magna cum laude, U. Calif., Irvine; JD, U. San Francisco; MPA, Harvard U.; postgrad., Oxford U. Bar: Calif., U.S. Ct. Appeals (fed. and 9th cirs.), U.S. Ct. Internat. Trade, U.S. Dist. Ct. (ctrl. dist.) Calif., U.S. Ct. Vets. Appeals. Law clk. U.S. Environ. Protection Agy. Region IX, Constitution Sub-Com., U.S. Senate Jud. Com.; honors clk. civil rights div. fed. enforcement U.S. Dept. Justice; summer atty. Office Pub. Defenders for the City and County, San Francisco; lectr. law coll. Seoul (Republic of Korea) Nat. U.; assoc. Cen. Internat. Law Firm, Seoul; U.S. prin. Othniel H.K. Ltd., Cambridge (Mass.), L.A., and Hong Kong; ptnr. Internat. Bus. Law Firm, Palm Springs, Calif. and Washington. Conf. and seminar presenter, Korea, Singapore, Hong Kong; Fulbright fellow judge, Seoul. Contbr. articles to legal publs. City commr. Hist. Site Preservation Bd., Palm Springs, Appeals Bd., Palm Springs; mem. legis. com. San Francisco Commn. on Status of Women. Named Ms. Mass., 1997, Beauty and Talent Queen, Ams. Miss US, 1999. Mem. ABA (chair internat. law com. gen. practice sect., com. internat. svcs., chmn. subcom. on Asia-Pacific sect. internat. law, internat. law com. gen. practice sect., chmn., mem. standing com. liaison to fgn. and internat. bars.), Internat. Inst. Strategic Studies, Calif. Bar Assn. (com. internat. law), Armed Forces Comm. and Electronic Assn., Harvard Club (bd. dirs. Korea), Toastmasters (numerous speech awards), Phi Delta Phi. Achievements include recognized constitutional law expert; worked on Russian and Nigerian constitutions, asked to work on Iraqi constitution. Avocations: operatic singer, songwriter, flutist. Office Phone: 760-773-2257. Personal E-mail: daundevore@yahoo.com.

DEVORE, KIMBERLY K., healthcare executive; b. Louisville, June 19, 1947; d. Wendell O. and Shirley F. DeV. Student, Xavier U., 1972-76; AA, Coll. Mt. St. Joseph, 1979; BA, Internat. U. Metaphysics, 1999. Patient registration supr. St. Francis Hosp., Cin., 1974-76; cons., bus. mgr. Family Health Care Found., Cin., 1976-77; exec. dir. Hospice of Cin., Inc., 1977-80; pres. Micro Med, 1979-86; v.p. Sycamore Profl. Assn., 1979-86; ptnr. Enchanted House, 1979-86, sec., 1979-80, treas., 1980-83; dist. sales rep. Control-O-Fax, 1986; br. sales mgr., 1987; nat. dealer devel. rep., 1987; nat. computer field sales trainer, 1987-90; pres. U.S. Exec. Leasing and U.S. Med. Leasing, Inc., 1991—2001, Accu Svcs., Inc., 1993—2003, U.S. Med. Mgmt., Inc., 1994-98. Pres. U.S. Med. Mgmt. of Ga., Inc., 1996—. Pres. Saddle Creek Homeowners Assn., Inc., 1992-95, parliamentarian, 1995-96; chairperson Citizen's Police Adv. Com. City of Roswell, 1997-99; chairperson found. grants Orch. Atlanta, 1998-99, pres., 1999-03, vice-chmn., pres. & CEO, chaplin Unity N. Atlanta, 2000-02, emeritus, 2003; bd. dirs., membership chairperson Smith Plantation City of Roswell, 1996-97; pres. Roswell Citizen's Police Acad., Inc., 1994-95; mem. City of Roswell Med. Devel. Dist. Coun., 1995—; mem. North Fulton Civic League, Inc., 1995-96, 2001-; bd. dirs. Nat. Hospice Orgn., 1979-82, chmn. long-term planning com., fin. com., ann. meeting com., 1979-82, sec., 1980-81, treas., 1981-82; bd. dirs. Hospice of Miami Valley, Inc., 1982-86, also chmn. pers. com., by-laws com.; bd. dirs. Orch. Atlanta, 1998—. Mem. Greater Clin. Soc. Fund Raisers, Better Housing League; mem. service and rehab. com. Hamilton County Unit, Am. Cancer Soc., 1977-78; chair road com. Saddle Creek Homeowners Assn., 1991-92. Mem. Ohio Hospice Assn. (co-founder, state chmn., pres., 1978-83), Nat. League for Nursing, Ohio Hosp. Assn., Nat. Fedn. Bus. and Profl. Women's Clubs, Ohio Fedn. Bus. and Profl. Women's Clubs, Cin. Bus. and Profl. Women's Clubs (pres. 1973-75).

DEVORE, PAUL CAMERON, lawyer; b. Great Falls, Mont., Apr. 25, 1932; s. Paul Theodore and Maxine (Cameron) DeV.; m. Roberta Humphrey, Feb. 3, 1962; children: Jennifer Ross, Andrew Cameron, Christopher Humphrey. BA, Yale U., 1954; MA, Cambridge U., 1956; JD, Harvard U., 1961. Bar: Wash. 1961. Assoc. Wright, Innis, Simon & Todd, Seattle, 1961-66; ptnr. Davis Wright Tremaine, Seattle, 1967—, chmn. exec. com., 1983-95. Mem. adv. bd. BNA Media Law Reporter, 1978—. Chmn. Seattle C.C., 1967-68, Bush Sch., Seattle, 1976-79, Virginia Mason Med. Found., 1984-85, Virginia Mason Rsch. Ctr., 1983-84, Seattle Found., 1985-87, Children's Hosp. Found., 1993-2005; trustee Lakeside Sch., 1995—2004; chmn. bd. visitors U. Wash. Sch. Comm., 1989-98; pres. A Contemporary Theatre, Seattle, 1972-74; sec. Seattle Art Mus., 1973-2000. Mem. ABA (chmn. forum on comm. law 1981-84), Wash. State Bar Assn. (chmn. sect. corp. bus. and banking law 1981-82, bench, bar, press com. 1984-90), Seattle-King County Bar Assn. (trustee 1975-76), Seattle Tennis Club, Phi Beta Kappa, Beta Theta Phi. Home: 5740 27th Ave NE Seattle WA 98105-5512 Office: Davis Wright Tremaine 2600 Century Sq 1501 4th Ave Ste 2600 Seattle WA 98101-1688 E-mail: camdevore@dwt.com.

DE VORE, PAUL WARREN, computer scientist, educator; b. Parkersburg, W.Va., July 18, 1926; s. Harry and Eleanor Sarah (Dunn) De Vore; m. Eleanor Jean Condron, Apr. 7, 1952; children: Harry Edwin, Michelle Ann, Phillip Charles. BS, Ohio U., 1950; MA, Kent State U., 1954; EdD, Pa. State U., 1961; postgrad., Ohio State U., 1983. Cert. homeland security angel flight pilot first responder 2005. Postdoctoral fellow U. Md., 1965-66; instr. pub. schs. Chagrin Falls, Ohio, 1950-53; asst. prof. engring. Grove City Coll., 1953-56; asst. prof. SUNY-Oswego, 1956-60, dir. div. indsl. arts and tech., 1960-67; prof. tech. edn. W. Va. U., Morgantown, 1967-75, prof., chmn. tech. edn., 1975-85, prof., coord. rsch. project offices, dept. technology, 1985-92; dir. Appalachian Tech. Edn. Consortium, 1990-95; dir. div. edn. and tng. Nat. Tech. Transfer Ctr., 1992-93. Tech. cons., pres. PWD Assocs., Morgantown, W.Va., 1974—; cons. NSF, U.S. Dept. Edn., AID, pub. schs., colls., univs.; mem. com. technol. literacy Nat. Acad. Engring., 1999—; pres. Aviation Resources Inc., 1999—; pres. Hart Field Coalition, 1998-2003; mem. Morgantown Airport Com., 2004—. Author: Technology: An Intellectual Discipline, 1964, Education in a Technological Society, 1971, Technology and the New Liberal Arts, 1976, Technology: An Introduction, 1980, Introduction to Transportation, 1983; cons. editor: Tech. Edn. Series, 1974-93. Mem. nat. commn. Tech. for All Ams., 1994—95; chmn. campaign United Fund, Oswego, 1962—63; mem. Monongalia County Devel. Authority, 2000—04. Served with USN, 1944—46. Named Outstanding Tchr., W.Va. U., 1970-71, 89, W.Va. U. Coll. Resources and Edn., 1988; recipient Outstanding Rsch. award Phi Delta Kappa, 1978; recognized as one of individuals who has contbd. most to tech. edn., 1985. Mem. Coun. on Tech. Tchr. Edn. (life), Soc. History of Tech., Internat. Tech. Edn. Assn. (Acad. of Fellows 1987), Epsilon Pi Tau (Disting. Svc. award 1976, Paul T. Hiser Exemplary Publ. award 1988, 99, Bill Hart Aviation award 2001). Office: W Va U Tech Edn Rsch Proj Offices Morgantown WV 26506-6680 Home: 6000 Riverside Dr Apt A 332 Dublin OH 43017-5113 *Seek quality in all you do and conduct your personal and civic affairs in a responsible and civil manner.*

DE VOS, GEORGE ALPHONSE, psychologist, anthropologist; b. Detroit, July 25, 1922; s. Medard Joseph and Marina Marie (Tack) De V.; m. Winifred Olsen, May 4, 1944 (div. 1974); m. Suzanne Lake, Nov. 18, 1974; children: Laurie, Susan, Eric, Michael. BA in Sociology, U. Chgo., 1946, MA in Anthropology, 1948, PhD in Psychology, 1951. Chief psychologist, dir. psychol. tng. Elgin (Ill.) State Hosp., 1951-53; asst. prof. psychology U. Mich., Ann Arbor, 1955-57; assoc. prof. social welfare U. Calif., Berkeley, 1957-63, prof. anthropology, 1963-91, prof. emeritus, 1991—. Vis. prof. U. Rome, 1975, U. Paris, 1979, Cath. U. Leuven, Belgium, 1986, U. Barcelona, 1992; exch. prof. U. Leningrad (now U. St. Petersburg), 1990; chmn. Ctr. for Japanese and Korean Studies U. Calif., 1965—91; cons. Family Planning Rsch., Korean Inst. Behavioral Scis., Seoul, Republic of Korea, 1970—71; rsch. assoc. Ecole des Hautes Etudes en Scis. Sociales, U. Paris, 1973—91; sr. cons. series prodn. The Japanese Film PBS, 1975; dir. NSF project The Korean Minority in Japan; cons. on Japanese culture Human Rels. Area File, New Haven, 1975—82; cons. Cultural Learning East-West Center, Hawaii, 1978—79. Author: 22 books, including Oasis and Casbah, 1960, Japan's Invisible Race, 1966, Socialization for Achievement, 1973, Ethnic Identity, 1975, 3d edit., 1995, Responses to Change, 1976, Koreans in Japan, 1981, Heritage of Endurance: Delinquency in Japan, 1984, Culture and Self, 1985, 1984, Religion and the Family in East Asia, 1986, Symbolic Analysis Cross Culturally: The Rorschach Test, 1989, Status Inequality, 1990, Social Cohesion and Alienation, 1992, Confucianism and The Family, 1998, Basic Dimensions in Conscious Thought, 2003, Cross Cultural Dimensions in Conscious Thought, 2004. Fulbright fellow, Nagoya, Japan, 1953-55, NIMH fellow French Min. Justice, 1963, NSF fellow UN Social Def. Rsch. Inst., Rome, 1972-73; Fulbright Sr. Rsch. Sch. Cath. U. Rio Grande do Sul, Brazil, 1992. Mem. APA (pres. Soc. for Psychol. Anthropology 1984-85), Assn. Asian Studies, Am. Anthropology Assn. Home: 2835 Morley Dr Oakland CA 94611-2547 E-mail: devos@sscl-berkeley.edu.

DE VOS, PETER JON, ambassador; b. San Diego, Dec. 24, 1938; BA, Princeton U., 1960; MA, Johns Hopkins U., 1962. Consular officer Am. Consulate, Recife, Brazil, 1962-64; fgn. service officer for Brazil Dept. State, Washington, 1964-66; polit. officer Am. Consulate, Naples, 1966-68; dep. prin. officer Am. Embassy, Luanda, 1968-70; polit. officer Am. Consulate, Sao Paulo, 1970-71, Am. Embassy, Brasilia, 1971-73; spl. asst. Bur. Inter-Am. Affairs Dept. State, Washington, 1973-75; polit. officer Am. Embassy, Athens, 1975-78, Nat. War. Coll., 1978-79; dep. dir. So. African Affairs Dept. State, Washington, 1979-80; U.S. ambassador to Republic of Guinea-Bissau and to Republic of Cape Verde, 1980-83, Mozambique, Maputo, 1983-87; dep. asst. sec. of state U.S. Dept. State, Washington, 1987-89, prin. dep. asst. sec. state Bur. Oceans and Internat. Environ. and Sci. Affairsv, 1989-90, amb. to Republic of Liberia, 1990-92, appointed U.S. spl. envoy to Somalia, 1992, amb. to Republic of Tanzania, 1992-94, amb. to Republic of Costa Rica, 1994-97. Disting. guest lectr. U. Chgo., 1997—; Rivers chair prof. East Carolina U., 2000—01; bd. dirs. Old Theater Corp. Bd. dirs. Pamlico Music Soc. Home: 410 Point Of View Dr Merritt NC 28556-9624

DEVOTO, MARK BERNARD, music educator; b. Cambridge, Mass., Jan. 11, 1940; s. Bernard Augustine and Helen Avis (MacVicar) DeV.; m. Deanna Mirsky (div.); children: Emily Julia, Marya Ellen. BA, Harvard Coll., 1961; MFA, Princeton U., 1963, PhD, 1967. Tchr. Reed Coll., Portland, Oreg., 1964-68, U. N.H., Durham, 1968-81; tchr. dept. music Tufts U., Medford, Mass., 1981-2000. Bd. mem. Internat. Alban Berg Soc., N.Y.C., 1975—; pres. Lili Boulanger Meml. Fund, Boston, 1985-96. Author: Debussy and Veil of Tonality, 2004; co-author: (with Walter Piston) Harmony, 5th edit., 1987; compiler: Mostly Short Pieces, 1992; translator, editor: Berg Guides, 1995 (ASCAP Deems Taylor 1995); mem. editl. bd. Perspectives of New Music, 1972—; composer many unpublished works. Mem. Am. Musicol. Soc., Soc. Music Theory, Soc. for Am. Music, New Eng. Conf. Music Theorists. Democrat. Jewish. Avocations: writing fiction, cooking. Home: 33 West St Medford MA 02155-4340 Office: Tufts U Music Dept 48 Professors Row Medford MA 02155-5807

DE VRIES, CAROL N., singer, music educator; b. Fresno, Calif., Dec. 20, 1938; d. John and Georgia C. (Lofgren) de V. BA, Calif. State U., 1960, MA, 1988. Tchr. Madera (Calif.) Sch. Dist., 1960-61; music educator Fresno (Calif.) City Schs., 1963-68; voice faculty Calif. State U., Stanislaus, 1972-74, Fresno Pacific Coll., 1978-80, Clovis (Calif.) Unified Sch. Dist., 1985—; profl. singer, dancer and actress N.Y.C./L.A./San Francisco, 1962—. Pvt. voice tchr., Fresno, 1969—; guest lectr. Calif. State U., Fresno, 1989-92. Mem. Am. Choral Dirs. Assn., Calif. Music Educators, Equity. Avocations: travel, cross country skiing, backpacking. Office: Cole Sch 615 W Stuart Ave Clovis CA 93612-0799

DEVRIES, DAVID JOHN, mathematician, educator; b. Grand Rapids, Mich., Sept. 22, 1942; s. John and Janet DeVries; m. Mary Elaine Vander Molen, Jan. 1, 1965. PhD, Penn State U., Univ. Pk., Pa, 1965—69; BA, Calvin Coll., Grand Rapids, Mich., 1962—65. Asst. prof. of math. Hobart & William Smith Colleges, Geneva, NY, 1969—71; assoc. prof. of math. Mars Hill Coll., Mars Hill, NC, 1971—83; prof. of math. Ga. Coll. & State U., Milledgeville, Ga., 1983—2003, emeritus prof. math., 2005—. Mem.: AAUP, Assn. of Rsch. in Undergraduate Math. Edn., Math. Assn. of Am. Office: Georgia College & State University Hancock Street Milledgeville GA 31061 Office Phone: 478-445-5213.

DEVRIES, JAMES E., historian, educator; b. East Chicago, Ind., Nov. 26, 1941; s. Tunis and Evelyn DeVries; m. Chang Cha Yi (div.); children: Adrienne Nelson, Christopher, Derk; m. Sharon Burns, Aug. 22, 1982; children: Corinne Alane, Cassandra Rae. BA in History, Hope Coll., Holland, Mich., 1964; MA in History, Ball State U., 1968, EdD in Social Sci., 1978. Prof. history Monroe County CC, Monroe, Mich., 1970—. Author: Race & Kinship in a Midwestern Town, 1984. Mem. Arthur Lesow Cmty. Ctr. Bd., Monroe, 1977—88, Monroe County Hist. commn., 1980—97, Monroe County Opportunity Program Bd., 1980—82, Monroe Pub. Sch. Bd., 1990—94. With U.S. Army, 1964—66, Korea. Mem.: Soc. Anthropology CC, Am. Anthrop. Assn., Orgn. Am. Historians. Avocations: reading, camping, hiking, canoeing. Home: 2975 W Country Ln Monroe MI 48162 Office: Monroe County CC 1555 S Rainsinville Rd Monroe MI 48161 Office Phone: 734-384-4237. Office Fax: 734-384-4160. Business E-Mail: jdevries@monroeccc.edu.

DEVRIES, JAMES HOWARD, lawyer; b. Chgo., Mar. 17, 1932; s. James and Ruth Frances (Heuman) DeV.; m. Eleanor Newport Smith, Mar. 3, 1956; children: Sara, James, Peter, Adam, Mary. BS in Bus. Mgmt., U. Colo., 1954; JD with distinction, U. Mich., 1961. Bar: Ill. 1961. Assoc. Hopkins & Sutter, Chgo., 1961-62; ptnr. McBride & Baker, Chgo., 1963-82; chmn., chief exec. officer LaserVideo, Inc., Chgo., 1982-88; vice chmn. Disc Mfg. Inc., Chgo., 1991-97; exec. v.p., sec. Quixote Corp., Chgo., 1969-97, ret., 1997, also bd. dirs., 1969—; pres. Legal Techs. Inc., Chgo., 1993-96, also bd. dirs. Pres. Library Internat. Relations, Chgo., 1980-83; dir. Internat. Trade Club, Chgo., 1974-76, Chg. Commons, 1999—. Served to lt. USN, 1954-58. Mem. Univ. Club (Chgo.), Am. Corp. Counsel Assn., Michigan Shores Club (Wilmette, Ill.), Chgo. Literary Club. Avocations: photography, flying. Home: 467 Willow Rd Winnetka IL 60093-4140 Office: Quixote Corp 35 E Wacker Dr Ste 1100 Chicago IL 60601-2108

DE VRIES, KENNETH LAWRENCE, mechanical engineer, educator; b. Ogden, Utah, Oct. 27, 1933; s. Sam and Fern (Slater) DeV.; m. Kay M. McGee, Mar. 1, 1959; children: Kenneth, Susan. AS in Civil Engring., Weber State Coll., 1953; BSME, U. Utah, 1959, PhD in Physics, Mech. Engring., 1962. Registered profl. engr., Utah. Rsch. engr. hydraulic group Convair Aircraft Corp., Fort Worth, 1957-58; prof. dept. mech. engring. U. Utah, Salt Lake City, 1969-75, 1976-91, disting. prof., 1991—, chmn. dept., 1970-81, pres. acad. senate, 2004—05; sr. assoc. dean U. Utah Coll. Engring., Salt Lake City, 1983-97, acting dean, 1997-98. Program dir. div. materials rsch. NSF, Washington, 1975-76, pres. academic senate, 2004-05; materials cons. Browning, Morgan, Utah, 1972—; cons. 3M Co., Mpls., 1985—; tech. adv. bd. Emerson Electric, St. Louis, 1978-2002; mem. Utah Coun. Sci. and Tech., 1973-77; trustee Gordon Rsch. Conf., 1989-97, chair, 1992-93 Co-author: Analysis and Testing of Adhesive Bonds, 1978; contbr. chpts. to books, articles to profl. jours. Fellow ASME, Am. Phys. Soc.; mem. Am. Chem. Soc. (polymer div.), Am. Soc. for Engring. Edn. (nat. officer), Adhesion Soc. Mem. Lds Ch. Office: U Utah Coll Engring 50 S Central Campus Dr Salt Lake City UT 84112-9249 Office Phone: 801-581-7101. Business E-Mail: kldevries@mech.utah.edu.

DE VRIES, MADELINE, public relations executive; Founder, pres. DeVries Pub. Rels., N.Y.C., 1978—; chmn., CEO DeVries Pub. Rels. (acquired by Interpublic Group), N.Y.C.; public relations dir. Bergdorf Goodman, N.Y.C. Bd. dirs. and trustee Brooklyn Botanic Garden. Named an honoree Matrix Award, New York Women in Communications, 2002. Mem.: Cosmetic Exec. Women (mem. exec. com., chair, mktg. com.). Office: DeVries Public Relations 30 E 60th St New York NY 10022-1008

DE VRIES, RIMMER, economist; b. Utrecht, Netherlands, Jan. 20, 1929; came to U.S., 1951, naturalized, 1957; s. Jacob and Mettje (Verburg) de V.; m. Ruth Berg, May 24, 1958; children— Rimmer D., Jacqueline R., Joyce C. BA, Netherlands Sch. Econs., 1951; MA, Ohio State U., 1952, PhD, 1955. Economist Fed. Res. Bank N.Y., 1956-61; economist, then v.p. Morgan Guaranty Trust Co., N.Y.C., 1961-78, sr. v.p., 1978-88, chief economist, 1988-94, mng. dir., 1990-94; cons. J.P. Morgan & Co. Inc., 1994-97. Bd. dirs. AGF Cos. Ltd.; mem. Pres. Reagan Commn. on Competitiveness, 1984-86. Mem. Coun. Fgn. Rels. Republican. Home: 804 Holbeck Dr Camano Island WA 98282-7366 E-mail: rdevries@wavecable.com.

DEVRIES, ROBERT ALLEN, foundation administrator; b. Chgo., May 12, 1936; s. Robert and Mildred (Burgess) DeV.; m. Eleanor Rose Siems, Aug. 16, 1958; children: Susan E., Robert S., Laura H., Steven P. BS in Physiology, U. Chgo., 1958, MBA in Hosp. Adminstrn., 1961. Adminstrv. resident, asst. Miami Valley Hosp., Dayton, Ohio, 1959-61, asst. dir., 1961-67; adminstr. McPherson Community Health Ctr., Howell, Mich., 1967-71; program dir. W.K. Kellogg Found., Battle Creek, Mich., 1971-88, program dir., dir. Kellogg Internat. Fellowship Programs, 1988-90, program dir., dir. Internat. Study Grants and Exchanges, 1990-97, mem. adminstrv. coun., 1995-97, program dir., mem. fellowship com., 1997-99; ret., 1999. Cons. on domestic and internat. programs W.K. Kellogg Found., 1999—; mem. com. vis. Sch. Nursing, U. Mich., 2000—; assisting min. St. Peter Luth. Ch.; chmn. quality com. bd. trustees Battle Creek Health Sys., 2001—, chmn., 2004—; bd. dirs. Lifecare Ambulance, chmn. bd., 2004—; bd. dirs. North Pointe Woods, Mich. Health Coun.; lectr. nursing orgn., adminstrn. Sch. Nursing Miami Valley Hosp., 1961-67, Grad. Sch. Pub. Health U. Mich., 1967—; adj. prof. Coll. Health and Human Svcs., Western Mich. U., 1986—; advisor Sch. Pub. Health Beijing Med. U., 1986—, Med. Coll. Health Staff, Shanghai, 1986—, 1st People's Hosp., Shanghai, 1986—; mem. nat. adv. com. on rural health U.S. Dept. Health and Human Svcs., Washington, 1988-92; mem. adv. panel acad. health scis. ctr. U.N.C., Chapel Hill, 1992-94; mem. policy coun. Nat. Inst. Rural Health Policy, 1987-90; mem. health planning and cert. of need workgroup Mich. Dept. Mgmt. & Budget, Mich. Dept. Pub. Health, 1986-87; vice chmn. adv. coun. Hosp. Rsch. & Ednl. Trust, Chgo., 1974-85; treas. coun. practice Am. Assn. Nurse Anesthetists, 1978-84; mem. Southwest Mich. Health Sys. Agy. Bd., 1980-83; guest lectr. King's Fund Coll., London, U. Leeds, Eng., French Nat. Sch. Pub. Health, Rennes, U. Toronto, Pan Am. Health Orgn., Washington and Brasilia, Brazil, Katholieke Universiteit Leuven, Belgium, Internat. Hosp. Fedn., London, Elton Mayo Sch. Mgmt., Adelaide, Australia, Ministry Pub. Health, Beijing, Indian Hosp. Assn., New Delhi. Editorial bds. Inquiry, Hosp. & Health Svcs.; contbr. articles to profl. jours., also book chpts. Counselor Baxter Am. Found. Prize in Health Svcs. Rsch., 1986—; assoc. trustee Florence Nightingale Mus. Trust, London. Recipient Disting. Svc. award Am. Soc. Allied Health Professions, 1989, Med. Group Mgmt. Assn., Denver, 1990, Ohio State U. Alumni Assn., 1998; Monsignor Griffin award for disting. writing Ohio Hosp. Assn., 1965, Civic Achievement award Jr. C. of C., Chgo., 1955, recognition award for contbns. to svcs. to handicapped Commn. on Accreditation of Rehab. Facilities, 1976, Cmty. Health Leadership award Hosp. Rsch. and Ednl. Trust, 1994, Spl. Recognition award Mich. Health and Hosp. Assn., 1999, Cert. of Honor, Peking U., China, 2003, Red Rose award for disting. cmty. svc. Gr. Battle Creek Rotary, 2004, U. Chgo. Pub. Svc. citation, 2005; named Outstanding Young Men in Am. Howell, Mich. Area C. of C. and Jaycees, 1970; Nat. Health Svcs. rsch. fellow U. Mich., 1970-71. Fellow Am. Coll. Healthcare Execs.(life), U.S. China Ednl. Inst., Can. Sch. Mgmt. (hon.); mem. APHA, Am. Hosp. Assn. (hon. life, vice chair R&D coun. 1974-85, adv. panel multi-hosp. systems 1977-85, Living the Vision award 1999), Internat. Hosp. Fedn., Nat. Rural Health Assn., Mich. Hosp. Assn. (assn. governance and strategic planning com. 1986-89, pub. policy and govt. com. 1981-83), U. Chgo. Hosp. Adminstrn. Alumni Assn. (pres. 1982-83), Leila Arboretum Soc. (pres. 2003-04). Lutheran. Avocations: music, writing, travel, gardening.

DEVRIES, ROBERT CHARLES, research scientist; b. Evansport, Ohio, Oct. 10, 1922; s. Charles and Rebecca (Goethe) DeV.; m. Ruth Elizabeth Wood, Oct. 30, 1943; children: David, Peter, Charles, Jonathan, Katherine. BA, DePauw U., 1948; PhD, Pa. State U., 1953. Topographer U.S. Geol. Survey, Washington, 1943-46; postdoctoral fellow Pa. State U., State College, 1953-54; staff scientist rsch. lab. GE, Schenectady, N.Y., 1954-61, staff scientist corp. R& D Ctr., 1965-88; assoc. prof. Rensselaer Poly. Inst., Troy, N.Y., 1961-65; cons. P-T-X, Burnt Hills, N.Y., 1988—. Adj. prof. Pa. State U., 1992-95; cultural exch. visitor, Japan, 1974; Coolidge fellow R&D Ctr. CE, 1981. Editor: The Reactivity of Solids, 1968, contbr. numerous articles to profl. jours.; patentee in field. With USAF, 1943. Rector scholar DePauw U., 1941; recipient Engring. Materials Achievement award Am. Soc. Metals, 1973. Fellow Am. Ceramic Soc., Am. Mineral Soc.; mem. AAAS, Am. Assn. Crystal Growth, Materials Rsch. Soc., Nat. Acad. Engring., Materials Rsch. Soc. (hon. Japan 1993), Mineral Soc. London, Sigma Xi. Avocations: gemmology, beekeeping, biking, reading, wood carving. Home and Office: P-T-X 17 Van Vorst Dr Burnt Hills NY 12027-9712 Office Phone: 518-399-5225. Personal E-mail: rcdvriesptx@worldnet.att.net.

DEVRIES, ROBERT K., writer, consultant; b. Sully, Iowa, July 6, 1932; s. Fred G. and Selena Irene (Willetts) DeV.; m. Carolyn Jo Schroeder, June 2, 1962 (div. 1978); children: Stephen Robert, Suzanne Mishael Dahill; m. Carolyn Gail Bergmans, May 26, 1979; children: Staci Ann McKellar, Keri Gail Bailey. AB, Wheaton Coll., 1954; ThM, Dallas Theol. Sem., 1958, ThD, 1969. Asst. registrar Dallas Theol. Sem., 1959-63; editor-in-chief Moody Press, Chgo., 1963-68; dir., v.p. pubs. Zondervan Pub. House, Grand Rapids, Mich., 1968-76, exec. v.p. book div., 1976-85; exec. v.p., publisher Zondervan Book Group, Zondervan Corp., Grand Rapids, Mich., 1985-86; pub., bd. dirs. Discovery House Pubs., Grand Rapids, 1987-2000, sr. publisher, bd. dirs., 2000—; cons., bd. dirs. Serendipity House, Littleton, Colo., 1990-99; bd. dirs. Serendipity House Found., Littleton, 1999—2003. Bd. dirs. Oswald Chambers Pub. Assn. Ltd., Eng. Bd. dirs. Ligonier Valley Study Ctr., Stahlstown, Pa., 1979-83, Bd. Publ., Evang. Covenant Ch. Am., Chgo., 1989-94, chmn., 1992-94; advisor Internat. Coun. Bibl. Inerrancy, Walnut Creek, Calif., 1978-87. Recipient Outstanding Young Men in Am. award Jaycees, 1965 Republican. Mem. Evangelical Covenant Ch. Avocation: model railroading. Home: 7554 Lime Hollow Dr SE Grand Rapids MI 49546-7439 Office: 3000 Kraft Ave SE Grand Rapids MI 49512-2024 Office Phone: 616-974-2714. Business E-Mail: rdevries@rbc.org.

DEVYLDER, EDGAR PAUL, JR., lawyer; b. Waterbury, Conn., Jan. 7, 1945; s. Edgar Paul Sr. and Lillian (Cordett) DeV.; m. Elaine Jordan, Jan. 8, 1972; children: Joseph Steven, Jordan Edgar. AB, Yale U., 1967; JD, U. Mich., 1974. Bar: Conn. 1974, U.S. Dist. Ct. Conn. 1975, U.S. Ct. Appeals (2nd cir.) 1975, Fla. 1978, U.S. Supreme Ct. 1979. Assoc. Cummings & Lockwood, Stamford, Conn., 1974-79; counsel Gen. Signal Corp., Stamford, 1979-85, sr. atty., 1985-87; v.p., gen. counsel, sec. BTR, Inc., Stamford, 1988-99; ptnr. Cummings & Lockwood, Stamford, 2000—01, Pepe & Hazard, Southport, Conn., 2001—02; v.p. adminstrn., gen. counsel, sec. Raytech Corp., Shelton, Conn., 2002—. Lt. USN, 1967-71. Mem.: Yale Club of Stamford (pres. 2000—), Assn. Yale Alumni (del. 2000—). Office Phone: 203-952-4300. E-mail: edevylder2@aol.com.

DEW, CHARLES BURGESS, historian, educator; b. St. Petersburg, Fla., Jan. 5, 1937; s. Jack Carlos and Amy (Meek) Dew; m. Robb Reavill Forman, Jan. 26, 1968. AB, Williams Coll., 1958; PhD, Johns Hopkins, 1964. Instr. Wayne State U., 1963-64, asst. prof., 1964-65, La. State U., 1965-68; assoc. prof. U. Mo., Columbia, 1968-72, prof., 1972-78; vis. assoc. prof. U. Va., 1970-71; vis. prof. history Williams Coll., Williamstown, Mass., 1977-78, prof. history, 1978-85, Class of 1956 prof. Am. Studies, 1985-96, chmn. dept. history, 1986-92, dir. Francis C. Oakley Ctr. for Humanities and Social Scis., 1994-97; prof. social scis. W. Van Alan Clark Third Century, 1996—2002, Charles R. Keller prof. history, 2002—03, Ephriam Williams prof. Am. history, 2003—. Author: Ironmaker to the Confederacy: Joseph R. Anderson and the Tredegar Iron Works, 1966, rev. edit., 1999, The Meanings of American History, 1972, Bond of Iron: Master and Slave at Buffalo Forge, 1994, Apostles of Disunion: Southern Secession Commissioners and the Causes of the Civil War, 2001; contbr. chapters to books. Recipient Fletcher Pratt award, N.Y. Civil War Round Table, 1966, 2001, award of merit, Am. Assn. State and Local History, 1967, hon. mention Peter Seaborg award for Civil War scholarship, George Tyler Moore Ctr. for Study the Civil War, Shepherd Coll., Shepherdstown, W.Va., 2002, Disting. Svc. award, Woodberry Forest Sch., 2004. Mem.: Orgn. Am. Historians (Elliott Rudwick award 1995), Am. Hist. Assn., Phi Beta Kappa, Delta Psi. Home: 218 Bulkley St Williamstown MA 01267-2023 Office: Williams Coll Stetson Hall History Dept Williamstown MA 01267 Office Phone: 413-597-2394. Personal E-mail: Charlesdew37@aol.com. Business E-Mail: charles.b.dew@williams.edu.

DEW, THOMAS EDWARD, lawyer; b. Detroit, Feb. 13, 1947; s. Albert Nelson and Irene Theresa (Morris) D.; m. Gail Ruth Tuesink, June 27, 1970. BA, U. Mich., 1969; JD, Detroit Coll. Law, 1974. Bar: Mich. 1974, U.S. Dist. Ct. (ea. dist.) Mich. 1974, U.S. Tax Ct. 1980. Agt. IRS, Detroit, 1969-74; trust officer Ann Arbor (Mich.) Trust Co., 1974-75, asst. v.p., 1975-78; ptnr. Conner, Harbour, Dew, Ann Arbor, 1978-83, Harris, Lax, Guenzel & Dew, Ann Arbor, 1983-87; private practice Thomas E. Dew Profl. Corp., Ann Arbor, 1987-88; prin. Dever and Dew Profl. Corp., Ann Arbor, 1988-99, Wise & Marsac, Detroit, 1999-2001, Berry Moorman, PC, Detroit, 2001—. Lectr. Am. Coll., Bryn Mawr, Pa., 1979-82, Am. Inst. Paralegal Studies, Detroit, 1982; adj. prof. Ave Maria Sch. Law, 2003—. Mem. Ann Arbor Housing Commn., 1979-81, pres. 1981; trustee Ann Arbor Area Cmty. Found. Named Law scholar, Sigma Nu Phi, 1974. Fellow Mich. State Bar Found.; mem. State Bar Mich., Washtenaw County Bar Assn., Washtenaw Estate Planning Coun. (pres. 1979-80), New Enterprise Forum. Republican. Presbyterian. Office: Berry Moorman PC 900 Victors Way Ste 300 Ann Arbor MI 48108 Office Phone: 734-668-4100. E-mail: tdew@berrymoorman.com.

DE WAAL, FRANS B.M., biologist, psychology professor; b. Netherlands, 1948; B in Biology, U. Nijmegen, Netherlands, 1970; D in Biology, U. Groeningen, Netherlands, 1973; PhD in Biology, U. Utrecht, Netherlands, 1977. Rsch. assoc. U. Utrecht, 1973—81; vis. asst. scientist Wis. Nat. Primate Rsch. Ctr., 1981—82, asst. scientist, 1982—85, assoc. scientist, 1985—91, affiliate scientist, 1991—; adj. prof. biol. scis. U. Wis., Milwaukee, 1988—91; assoc. prof. psychology Emory U., 1991—93, Charles Howard Candler prof. psychology, 1996—; rsch. prof. psychobiology Yerkes Nat. Primate Rsch. Ctr., 1991—, dir. Living Links Ctr., 1997—. Author: Chimpanzee Politics, 1982, Peacemaking Among Primates, 1989, Good Natured: The Origins of Right and Wrong in Humans and Other Animals, 1996, Bonobo: The Forgotten Ape, 1997, The Ape and the Sushi Master, 2001; consulting editor: Jour. of Comparative Psychology, mem. editl. bd.: Greater Good, PloS Biology, Evolutionary Psychology, Primates, Primatologie, Internat. Jour. of Primatology, Politics, and the Life Sciences. Recipient LA Times Book award, 1989, Presdl. Citation, APA, 2001; fellow, Carl Friedrich von Siemens Stiftung, 1995. Fellow: Japan Soc. for the Promotion of Sci.; mem.: Royal Dutch Acad. Scis. (corr.), Nat. Acad. Scis. (assoc.). Office: Living Links Ctr Yerkes Nat Primate Ctr 954 N Gatewood Rd Atlanta GA 30329

DEWAHL, DUNCAN COMRIE, stockbroker; b. North Tarrytown, N.Y., Oct. 31, 1958; s. David Allen and Lois (Dann) DeW.; m. Lael Elizabeth Wilcox, Sept. 23, 1989; children: Alexander Macmillian, John Comrie. BA, Franklin and Marshall Coll., 1980; MBA, Northeastern U., 1987. Mgmt. trainee The Bank of N.Y., N.Y.C., 1980-83; sys. analyst U.S. Trust Co., N.Y.C., 1983-85; treasury mgr. Analog Devices, Boston, 1987-90; br. mgr. Securities Rsch., Orlando, Fla., 1990-93, regional mgr., 1993—2004; wealth advisor Morgan Stanley, Inc., Winter Park, Fla., 2004—. Bd. mem. lakes adv. com. City of Maitland, Fla., 1997. Mem. Winter Park Raquet Club (bd. mem.). Republican. Presbyterian. Avocations: golf, wake boarding. Home: 541 Dommerich Dr Maitland FL 32751-4502 Office: Morgan Stanley 200 E New England Ave Winter Park FL 32789 Office Phone: 407-740-4937.

DEWALD, BRUCE WAYNE, lawyer; b. Tripp, S.D., Apr. 10, 1955; s. Maynard W. and Adaline (Mehlhaff) D.; m. Sherry L. Messina, Aug. 27, 1978; children: Paul S., Melinda L. BS in Econ., U. S.D., 1977; JD, U. Chgo., 1980. Bar: Colo. 1981, U.S. Dist. Ct. Colo. 1981, U.S. Claims Ct. 1984, U.S. Ct. Appeals (10th cir.) 1988. Atty. Grant, McHendrie, Haines & Crouse, Denver, 1980-82, Canges, Shaver, Volpe & Licht, Denver, 1982-83, Shaver & Licht, Denver, 1983-99, Bombardier Capital, 1999; pvt. practice Littleton, Colo., 2000—05; ptnr. Hudgins & Dewald, Greenwood Village, Colo., 2005—. Mem. Cherry Creek Luncheon Optimists (sec.-treas. 1989-93). Avocations: biking, hiking. Office: 5105 DTC Pkwy Greenwood Village CO 80111 Office Phone: 303-347-8906. E-mail: dewaldlaw@msn.com.

DEWALD, PAUL ADOLPH, psychiatrist, educator; b. N.Y.C., Mar. 12, 1920; s. Jacob Frederick and Elsie (Wurzburger) D.; m. Eleanor Whitman, Sept. 1, 1961; children: Jonathan S., Ellen F. BA, Swarthmore Coll., 1942; MD, U. Rochester, 1945; cert. psychoanalysis, SUNY, 1960. Intern, Strong Meml. Hosp., Rochester, N.Y., 1945-46, resident, 1948-52; instr. U. Rochester, 1952-57, asst. prof. psychiatry, 1957-61; pvt. practice psychoanalysis St. Louis, 1961-99; asst. clin. prof. psychiatry Washington U., St. Louis, 1961-65, 96—; asso. clin. prof. St. Louis U., 1965-69, clin. prof. psychiatry, 1969—. Dir. treatment svc. Psychoanalytic Found. St. Louis, 1961-72, med. dir., 1972-83 St. Louis Psychoanalytic Inst., 1973-83, supervising and tng. analyst, 1973—; mem. faculty Chgo. Inst. Psychoanlysis, 1961-75, supervising and tng. analyst, 1965-73; vis. prof. U. Cin., 1968-80; mem. Mo. State Mental Health Commn., 1978-83, chmn., 1981-83; asst. prof. clin. psychiatry Washington U., 1995—. Author: Psychotherapy: A Dynamic Approach, 1964, 2d edit., 1969, The Psychoanalytic Process, 1972, Learning Process in Psycho-analytic Supervision, 1987; co-editor: Ethics Case Book of the American Psychoanalytic Assn., 2001; contbr. articles to profl. jours. Served to capt. M.C., AUS, 1946-48. Fellow Am. Psychiat. Assn. (life); mem. Mo. Psychiat. Assn. (pres. 1970-71), Eastern Mo. Psychiat. Assn. (pres. 1969-70), Am. Psychoanalytic Assn. (life), St. Louis Psychoanalytic Soc. (pres. 1970-71, 86-88) Home: Apt 3H 8600 Delmar Blvd Saint Louis MO 63124-1961 Office: 8600 Delmar Blvd Saint Louis MO 63124 Office Phone: 314-994-9608. Personal E-mail: padewald@charter.net. *I was encouraged by my parents to see my career as a potential source of creative enjoyment, fulfillment and self-esteem. I was fortunate to choose a field that encouraged those attitudes, and a wife who supported me in them. I have other interests and sources of fulfillment, but when there is nothing better or more enjoyable to do, I work.*

DEWALD, WILLIAM GUENTHNER, economist; b. Sioux City, Iowa, Nov. 9, 1928; s. William Frederick and Leah (Guenthner) D.; m. Ann Peterson, Mar. 6, 1952 (div. 1981); children: Jane Dewald Smirniotopoulos, Ruth Dewald Baginski, Charlotte Dewald O'Brien, Robin Dewald Yarinsky; m. Aileen Lee, Mar. 9, 1984 (div. 2003). BS, Northwestern U., Evanston, Ill., 1950; PhD, U. Minn., 1963. Assoc. economist Fed. Res. Bank, Mpls., 1957-60; assoc. prof. St. Olaf Coll., Northfield, Minn., 1960-62; asst. prof. U. Chgo., 1962-64; prof. Ohio State U., Columbus, 1964-85; sr. economist, dep. dir. planning and econ. analysis staff U.S. Dept. of State, Washington, 1985-92; sr. v.p., dir. rsch. Fed. Res. Bank of St. Louis, 1992-98; ret. Vis. scholar Res. Bank Australia, Sydney, NSW, 1966-67, Fed. Res. Bank, Kansas City, 1978-79, Fed. Res. Bank, San Francisco, 1981; vis. expert European Ctrl. Bank, Frankfurt, 2002-2003; dir. fgn. econ. rsch. U.S. Labor Dept., Washington, 1973-74; cons. IMF, 1984-85, Fed. Res. Bank of St. Louis, 1999; adv. bd. Jour. Money, Credit and Banking, 1984—; exec. in residence No. Ariz. U., Flagstaff, 2001; advisor Ctrl. Bank Iraq, Baghdad, 2004, 2005. Editor Jour. Money, Credit and Banking, 1975-83; contbr. articles to profl. jours. With U.S. Army, 1951-53. Recipient faculty fellowship Ford Found., 1969-70, Jour. Money, Credit and Banking grant NSF, 1983-84. E-mail: dewald@columbus.rr.com.

DEWALL, RICHARD ALLISON, retired surgeon; b. Appleton, Minn., Dec. 16, 1926; s. Herman H. and Grace G. (Gardner) DeW.; m. Diane B. Prettyman, Oct. 24, 1952; children— Beth B., Amy, Melissa. BA, U. Minn., 1949, BS, 1950, B.M., 1952, MD, 1953, MS in Surgery, 1960; D.Sc. (hon.), Wright State U., 1986. Diplomate Am. Bd. Surgery, Am. Bd. Thoracic Surgery. Rsch. asst. dept. surgery U. Minn., 1954-56, instr. surgery, 1960-62, asst. prof., 1962—; rsch. fellow Am. Heart Assn., 1956-58, advanced rsch. fellow, 1958-60, established investigator, 1960-62; prof. surgery, chmn. dept. Chgo. Med. Sch., 1962-66; chief surgery Cox Heart Inst., Kettering, Ohio, 1966-82; mem. staff Kettering Hosp., 1982-87; ret., 1987. Chmn. bd. Med., Inc., 1976-86; coord. surgery residency tng. program Kettering Meml. Hosp., 1968-75; co-chmn. med. sch. planning com. Wright State U., Dayton, Ohio, 1968-73, clin. prof. surgery, 1975-87, clin. prof. emeritus, 1987—. Recipient award U.S. Jr. C. of C., 1957, Appreciation award Wright State U. Sch. Medicine, 1989. Fellow A.C.S., Am. Coll. Cardiology; mem. Soc. for Thoracic Surgery, AMA, AAAS (co-recipient Ida B. Gould Meml. award 1956), Soc. Univ. Surgeons, Am. Assn. Thoracic Surgery, Dayton Surg. Soc., Nu Sigma Nu, Sigma Chi., Rotary. Achievements include research on perfusion techniques as an aid to open heart surgery. Home: 421 Thornhill Rd Dayton OH 45419-2932

DEWALT, BILL, museum director; BA in Sociology and Anthropology, U. Conn., 1969, PhD in Anthropology, 1975. Dir. Carnegie Mus. Natural History, Pitts., 2001—. Cons. World Wildlife Fund, World Bank, Inter-Am. Devel. Bank, Internat. Fin. Corp., U.S. Agy. for Internat. Devel., Latin Am. Scholarship Program in Am. Univs. Contbr. articles to profl. jours. Office: Carnegie Mus Natural History 4400 Forbes Ave Pittsburgh PA 15213

DEWALT, DEBORAH N., lawyer; b. Bismarck, ND, Oct. 18, 1954; BA summa cum laude, U. ND, 1976; JD cum laude, U. Minn., 1983. Bar: ND 83, Minn. 83. Law clk. U.S. Dist. Ct. (we. dist.) ND, Bismarck, 1983—84; assoc. Horvei & Krueger, Roseville, Minn., 1984—85, Reidenberg & Ormond, Mpls., 1985—87; ptnr. Ormond & Dewalt, Mpls., 1987—96; pvt. practice Dewalt Law Office, Burnsville, Minn., 1996—. Author: Family Law Ripples Newsletter, 2002—. Fellow: Acad. Matrimonial Lawyers; mem.: Assn. Family and Conciliation Cts., Minn. Assn. Conflict Resolution, Nat. Assn. Conflict Resolution, Dakota County Bar Assn., Hennepin County Bar Assn., Minn. State Bar Assn., Collaborative Law Inst. (bd. dirs. 1999—2003). Office: Dewalt Law Office 2412 117th St Ste 100 Burnsville MN 55337 Office Phone: 952-895-5543.

DEWALT, MARK WILLIAM, education educator, researcher; s. Marvin E. and Gloria L. Dewalt; m. Carolyn Ann Kepple, Mar. 27, 1978; children: Philip Mark, Peter William. AB, Muhlenberg Coll., 1976; MEd, U. S.C. Columbia, 1982; PhD, U. Va. Charlottesville, 1986. Tchr. Clarendon Sch. Dist. #2, Manning, SC, 1980—84; grad. asst. U. Va., Charlottesville, 1984—86; asst. prof. edn. and dept. chair Susquehanna U., Selinsgrove, Pa., 1986—90; asst. prof. to assoc. prof. edn. Lenoir-Rhyne Coll., Hickory, NC, 1990—96; prof. edn. and dir. grad. studies Winthrop U., Rock Hill, SC, 1996—. Dir. Christian edn. Wesley Meth. Ch., Charlottesville, Va., 1987—88. Coach Hickory Recreation Dept. and Catawba Valley Blast, NC, 1990—96; vol. Gaston County Sch., Gastonia, 2003—05; mem. Gaston County Commn. on the Family, 2000—, chair, 2004—; Sunday sch. tchr. Meth. Ch., Manning, SC, 1980—84; lay spkr. United Meth. Ch., Hickory, NC, 1993—95. Recipient Cmty. Svc. award, Winthrop U., 2004; fellow, 2005—. Mem.: Am. Ednl. Rsch. Assn., Phi Delta Kappa. Independent. Avocations: running, gardening, woodworking, Amish education. Home: 3063 Colony Ridge Dr Gastonia NC 28056 Office: Winthrop U 106 Withers Rock Hill SC 29733 Office Phone: 803-323-2151. E-mail: dewaltm@winthrop.edu.

DEWAR, ROBERT EARL, artist; b. Chgo., May 18, 1943; s. William James and Dorothy Ann (Haupt) D.; m. Cynthia Ann Waldman, Apr. 24, 1982; 1 child, John Starr. BFA, Calif. State U., L.A., 1971. Computer analyst, programmer Jet Propulsion Lab., Pasadena, Calif., 1968-78, computer art specialist, 1981; computer graphics programmer CADAM, Inc., Burbank, Calif., 1983-90, computer graphics tech. support, 1990-91, IBM, Santa Monica, Calif., 1992-94; artist Tehachapi, Calif., 1994—. Author: A Technical Catalog of Computer Halftones, 1972; inventor in field. With U.S. Army, 1962-65. Home: 11600 Bonanza Dr Tehachapi CA 93561-9312

DE WECK, OLIVER, engineering educator, researcher; M in Aeronautics and Astronautics, Mass. Inst. Tech., 1999; Diplom Ingenieur degree, Swiss Fed. Inst. Tech., 1993; PhD in Aerospace Systems, Mass. Inst. Tech. Liaison engr. to engring. program mgr. Swiss F/A-18 program McDonnell Douglas (now Boeing), St. Louis, 1993—97; prof. aeronautics, astronautics and engring. systems Mass. Inst. Tech., Cambridge, Robert N. Noyce career devel. prof. Contbr. articles to profl. jours. Recipient Carroll L. Wilson award, 1998; Pellegrini-Medicus Fellowship. Mem.: IEEE, AIAA (mem. multidisciplinary design optimization specialist com. 2002—), Sigma Xi. Office: Mass Inst Tech 77 Massachusetts Ave Bldg 33-410 Cambridge MA 02139 Office Phone: 617-253-0255. Business E-Mail: deweck@mit.edu.

DEWEES, DONALD CHARLES, security firm executive; b. Phila., Sept. 7, 1931; s. John Coleman and Elva (Burke) DeW.; m. Martha V. Folk, July 31, 1954; children: Donald C., Suzanne C., Gretchen F. BS in Commerce and Finance, Bucknell U., 1953; MBA, U. Pa., 1954. Data processing rep. Nat. Cash Register Co., Wilmington, Del., 1954-62; account rep. Francis I. duPont Co., Investments, Wilmington, 1962-67, br. mgr. Balt., 1968, Butcher & Singer, Wilmington, 1969-71, v.p., 1971-76, 1st v.p., 1977, sr. v.p., 1978—, resident mgr., 1969-76, ltd. ptnr., 1976-87, exec. v.p., 1987, sr. exec. v.p., 1988—, mng. dir., 1988—, also bd. dirs. Mng. dir. Butcher & Singer, 1986-98, Wheat Securities, 1998-2004; dir. Mgmt. Scis. Inc., 1978-92, Bus. Trends Inc., 1977-91, Computer Terminals and Tapes Ltd., 1970-98, Wheat Securities, mng. dir. Wheat Securities Butcher & Singer, 1986-2004, Lloyds of London, 1985-2000, First Union Bank, 1998-2004; underwriting mem. Lloyds of London, 1985-02; cons. in field. Author sales tng. publs. Active Wilmington YMCA; bd. dirs. Del. Ctr. of Contemporary Arts, 1992-94, Ingleside Nursing Home, 1989-2004, Ch. Home Found., 1986-92, Episcopal Home Del., 1983-90, Kalmar Nyckle Found., 2000-05, Del Marva Boy Scouts Am., 1989-2003, chmn. endowment com., 1993-2003; vice chmn. Nat. Assn. Christians and Jews, 1991-98; mem. allocation com. United Way, 1994; bd. dirs. Am. Cancer Soc., 1994-2005, Leukemia Soc., 1994-2005; chmn. Edgar A. Thronson Charitable Found., 1995—. Served with AUS, 1952-53, 58-59, Korea. Mem. Fin. Analysts Soc., Am. Philatelic Soc., Phi Kappa Psi, Univ. Club (Wilmington), Collectors Club (N.Y.), Rodney Square Club, Masons, Shriners, Greenville Country Club, Bonita Bay Country Club. Home: 4200 Pyles Ford Rd Wilmington DE 19807-1734 also: 25 Kelly Ln Bethany Beach DE 19930-9549 Office: Wheat Securities 3801 Kennett Pike Greenville DE 19807-2321

DEWEES, JENNIFER T., lawyer; b. St. Paul, Minn., Mar. 13, 1968; d. Guy Bryan Dewees III and Elizabeth Weathersby Barron; m. Daniel James Bolongaro, Oct. 16, 1999; 1 child, Frederick Dewees Bolongaro. BA, Millsaps Coll., 1990; JD, U. Miss. Sch. Law, 1997. Bar: Ala. 2000, Miss. 1997. Lawyer Tucker, Selden, L. L. C., Tunica, Miss., 1997—98, Webb, Sanders, Deaton, Smith & Balducci, Tupelo, Miss., 1998—99, Nakamura, Quinn & Walls, Birmingham, Ala., 1999—2000, Gaines, Wolter & Kinney, 2000—02, Cin. Ins. Co., 2002—. Pres. of parent group First United Meth. Child Devel. Ctr., Birmingham, Ala., 2004; sunday sch. tchr. - 2yr old St. Mary's-on-the-Highlands Episcopal Ch., 2003; mem. Memls. Com., 2003; bd. mem. First United Meth. Child Devel. Ctr., 2004—; guild mem. St. Marys-on-the-Highlands Episcopal Ch., 1999—. Mem.: Ala. Bar Assn. (life), Miss. State Bar (life), ABA (life). Episcopalian. Avocations: tennis, heirloom sewing, painting, reading. Home: 137 East Glenwood Drive Homewood AL 35209 Office: Cincinnati Insurance Company 2001 Park Place North Ste 911 Birmingham AL 35203 Office Phone: 205-251-9958. Office Fax: 205-251-9848. Personal E-mail: dbolongaro@hotmail.com. E-mail: jennifer_dewees@staffdefense.com.

DEWEESE, ELDONNA ROSE, librarian, editor; b. Mo., Nov. 7, 1940; d. Osborne Kuhn and Helena Elizabeth DeWeese. MLS, Emporia State U., 1969; BS in Edn., Southwest Mo. State U., 1962; MA, Southwest Mo. State, 1984. Tchr. English, speech, libr. Pierce City (Mo.) H.S., 1962-68; ref. libr. Southwest Bapt. Coll., Bolivar, Mo., 1969-72, adminstrv. libr., 1972-82; grad. asst./ref. libr. Southwest Mo. State U., Springfield, 1982-85; computer software distbr. Micro Magic Systems, Bolivar, 1985-88; collection devel. libr. Southwest Bapt. U., Bolivar, 1991—2000, 2002—03, interim dean univ. libr., 2000—02. Editor/prodn. mgr. So. Bapt. Periodical Index, 1987—. Mem. ALA, Am. Soc. Indexers, Mo. State Poetry Soc., Mo. Libr. Assn., So. Bapt. Libr. Assn. Baptist. Avocations: reading, church choir, poetry writing. Office: Southwest Bapt Univ Libr 1600 University Ave Bolivar MO 65613-2578 Office Phone: 417-328-1614. Business E-Mail: edeweese@sbuniv.edu.

DEWEESE, JAMES ARVILLE, surgeon, educator; b. Apr. 5, 1925; s. Arville Ottis and Vergie (Jenkins) DeW.; m. Margaret Brown, June 20, 1950 (dec. 1960); children: James Arville Jr., Margaret Ann, Elizabeth Lynn, Joanne Spencer; m. Patricia Bidwell, May 5, 1962; children: Robert Bidwell, Jamie Susan. Student, Harvard U., 1942-43, Kent State U., 1943-44; MD, U. Rochester, 1949. Diplomate Am. Bd. Surgery (bd. dirs. 1986-91), Am. Bd. Thoracic and Cardiovascular Surgery (bd. dirs. 1987-91); cert. spl. qualifications gen. vascular surgery. Intern Strong Meml. Hosp., Rochester, N.Y., 1949-50, resident, 1950-52, 54-56; instr. surgery U. Rochester (N.Y.) Sch. Medicine and Dentistry, 1955-58, asst. prof. surgery, 1958-63, assoc. prof. surgery, 1963-69, prof. surgery, 1969-74, prof. cardiothoracic surgery, 1975—, chmn. div. cardiothoracic surgery, 1977-91, assoc. chmn. dept. surgery, 1986-90, chief sect. vascular surgery, 1987-91. Bd. dirs. Jour. Vascular Surgery, 1983—; editor: Vascular Surgery, 1985; contbr. over 200 articles to sci. jours. and over 60 chpts. to books. Mem. bd. trustees Clifton Springs (N.Y.) Hosp., 1980—. Mem. Am. Heart Assn. (bd. dirs. 1982-86, chmn. coun. cardiovascular surgery 1982-84), Ea. Vascular Soc. (pres. 1988), Internat. Soc. Cardiovascular Surgery (pres. N.Am. chpt. 1984-85, sec.-gen. 1987-95, pres. 1995-97), Pan Pacific Surg. Assn. (pres. 1989-91), Soc. Vascular Surgery (pres. 1977-78), Am. Venous Forum (pres. 1993-94), Sr. Cardiovascular Surg. Soc. (pres. 1996), Oak Hill Country Club (bd. govs. 1978-81). Home: 601 Crittenden Blvd Rochester NY 14642-0001 Office: U Rochester Dept Surgery M&D Cardiothoracic Div 601 Elmwood Ave Rochester NY 14642-0001 E-mail: deweesepnj@aol.com.

DEWERD, LARRY ALBERT, medical physicist, educator; b. Milw., July 18, 1941; s. Anthony Lawrence and Dorothy M. (Heling) DeW.; m. Vada Mary Anderson, Sept. 14, 1963; children: Scott, Mark, Eric. BS, U. Wis., Milw., 1963; MS, U. Wis., 1965, PhD, 1970. Rsch. assoc. U. Wash., Seattle, 1970-72, rsch. asst. prof., 1973-75; vis. asst. prof. U. Wis., Madison, 1975-76, clin. asst. prof., 1976-79, clin. assoc. prof., 1979-86, prof., 1990—. Mgr. product devel. Radiation Measurements, Middleton, Wis., 1986-90; dir. Radiation Calibration Lab., Madison, 1983-86, 90—; cons. Instrumentarium, Milw., 1990; v.p. Standard Imaging, Madison, 1990—; presenter in field; cons. IAEA. Contbg. author: Brachytherapy, Ionization Chambers and Dosimetry, Thermoluminescence and Mammography; also numerous articles. Science chmn. Am. Cancer Soc. State of Wis., 1986-90. Grantee Nat. Cancer Inst., 1979-86, 94-98. Fellow Am. Assn. Physicists in Medicine (pres. 1990-92), Health Physics Soc., Am. Phys. Soc., Coun. Ionizing Radiation Measurements and Standards (pres. 1995-98), Sigma Xi (bd. dirs. 1984-86). Avocations: golf, fishing, backpacking, hunting. Home: 13 Pilgrim Cir Madison WI 53711-4033 Office: U Wis 1530 Med Sci Ctr 1300 University Ave Madison WI 53706-1510

DEWERTH, GORDON HENRY, management consultant; b. Milw., Sept. 3, 1939; s. Henry Andrew and Elizabeth Barbara (Schlitt) DeWerth; m. Karen Lillian Overson, July 7, 1962 (div.); children: Julie, Christine, Amy. BBA, U. Wis., 1961; MBA, Bradley U., 1965. Asst. to treas. Jos. Schlitz Brewing Co., Milw., 1965—71; with ITT, N.Y.C., 1971—76; treas. Macmillan, Inc., N.Y.C., 1976—82; sr. v.p. fin. Cowles Media Co., Mpls., 1982—85; sr. v.p.

fin., treas. U. Hartford, Conn., 1985—89; v.p., gen. mgr. Gestra Inc., West Caldwell, NJ, 1989—90; v.p. David Werner Internat. Corp., N.Y.C., 1990—94; mng. ptnr. Round Table Ptnrs. Cons. Group, Framingham, Mass., 1994—. With U.S. Army, 1961-63. Mem. Assn. Corp. Growth, Mensa. Office: Round Table Ptnrs Cons Group 146 Maynard Rd Ste 503C Framingham MA 01701

DEWEY, ARTHUR EUGENE, federal agency administrator; b. Mainesburg, Pennsylvania, Feb. 18, 1933; s. Glenn Cecil and Florence (Tice) D.; m. Priscilla Ann (Parce), June 24, 1956; 1 child, Elisabeth Parce Ainsworth. BSE, U.S. Mil. Acad., 1956; MSE, Princeton U., 1961; post grad., Grad. Inst. Internat. Studies, Geneva, Switzerland, 1972-73. Officer U.S. Army, 1956; White House fellow Dept. State, Washington, 1968-69, dir. Pres. Commn. on White House Fellowships, 1971-72; advanced through grades to coll. U.S. Army, 1973, ret., 1981; dep. asst. sec. state, Bur. Refugee Program Dept. State, Washington, 1981-86; asst. sec. gen., dep. high commr. for refugees UN, Geneva, 1986-90; exec. dir. Congl. Hunger Ctr., 1993—97; asst. sec. for population, refugees, and migration Dept. State, Washington, 2002—. Decorated DFC, Legion of Merit with two oak leaf clusters, Air medal with nine oak leaf clusters, Army Commendation medal with three oak leaf clusters. Mem.: Cosmos Club, Army and Navy Club. Republican. Presbyterian. Home: 5219 Westbard Ave Bethesda MD 20816-1411 Office: US Dept State Bur Population Refugees and Migration 2201 C St NW Washington DC 20520 E-mail: deweyg56@hotmail.com.

DEWEY, CLARENCE FORBES, JR., engineering educator; b. Pueblo, Colo., Mar. 27, 1935; s. Clarence F. and Elsie (Hafermalz) D.; m. Carolyn Miller, Aug. 3, 1963; 1 child, Devan Forbes. BE, Yale U., 1956; MS, Stanford U., 1957; PhD, Calif. Inst. Tech., 1963. Aero. rsch. scientist NASA-AMES, Moffet Field, Calif., summer 1956; tech. staff aeronutronic divsn. Ford, Newport Beach, 1957-59; rsch. asst. Calif. Inst. Tech., Pasadena, Calif., 1959-63; asst. prof. mech. engring. U. Colo., Boulder, 1963-68; assoc. prof. MIT, Cambridge, 1968-76, prof., 1976-98, prof. mech. engring. and bioengring., 1998—, head fluid mechanics lab., 1975—83, head microfluids lab., 2001—03; assoc. in pathology Peter Brent Brigham Hosp., Boston, 1978-95. Vis. scientist Inst. Plasma Physics, Garching, Germany, 1966—67; vis. prof. Harvard U. Med. Sch., 1978—79, Hefei Poly. U., China, 1986, Imperial Coll. Ctr. Med. and Biol. Sys., London, 1992, London, 2001; biomed. engr. Mass. Gen. Hosp., Boston, 1975—76, cons. in medicine, 1976—80; founder Concurrent Computer Corp., 1981; co-dir. Internat. Consortium for Med. Imaging Tech., 1992—; path. cons. Brigham and Women's Hosp., 1982—96. Contbr. articles to profl. jours. Chmn. MIT United Way, 1996—97; trustee Fidelity Non-Profit Mgmt. Found., 2001—. Grantee NIH, Bethesda, Md., 1971—, Office Naval Rsch., San Diego 1970-75, 1987-89, Air Force Office Sci. Rsch., Washington, 1976-79, Dept. of Energy, 2003—. Fellow Am. Inst. Med. Biol. Engring. (founding), Am. Phys. Soc.; mem. Biomed. Engring. Soc. (sr.). Achievements include patents in field. Avocations: trout fishing, skiing. Office: 77 Massachusetts Ave Rm 3-254 Cambridge MA 02139-4301 Office Phone: 617-253-2235. Business E-Mail: cfdewey@mit.edu.

DEWEY, DONALD ODELL, dean, academic administrator; b. Portland, Oreg., July 9, 1930; s. Leslie Hamilton and Helen (Odell) D.; m. Charlotte Marion Neuber, Sept. 21, 1952; children: Leslie Helen, Catherine Dawn, Scott Hamilton. Student, Lewis and Clark Coll., 1948-49; BA, U. Oreg., 1952; MS, U. Utah, 1956; PhD, U. Chgo., 1960. Mng. editor Condon (Oreg.) Globe-Times, 1952-53; city editor Ashland (Oreg.) Daily Tidings, 1953-54; asst. editor, assoc. editor The Papers of James Madison, Chgo., 1957-62; instr. U. Chgo., 1960-62; from asst. prof. to prof. Calif. State U., L.A., 1962-96, dean Sch. Letters and Sci., 1970-84, dean Sch. Natural and Social Sci., 1984-96, dean emeritus, prof. emeritus, 1996—; v.p. acad. affairs Trinity Coll. Grad. Studies, Anaheim, Calif., 2000—. Author: The Continuing Dialogue, 2 vols., 1964, Union and Liberty: Documents in American Constitutionalism, 1969, Marshall versus Jefferson: The Political Background of Marbury v. Madison, 1970, Becoming Informed Citizens: Lessons on the Constitution for Junior High School Students, 1988, revised edit., 1995, Invitation to the Dance: An Introduction to Social Dance, 1991, Becoming Informed Citizens: The Bill of Rights and Limited Government, 1995, That's a Good One: Cal State L.A. at 50, 1997, The Federalist and Antifederalist Papers, 1998, Controversial Elections, 2001; contbr. chpts. to books. Recipient Outstanding Prof. award Calif. State U., 1976 Mem. Am. Hist. Assn. (exec. com. Pacific Coast br. 1971-74), Orgn. Am. Historians, Am. Soc. Legal History (adv. bd. Pacific Coast br. 1972-75), Gold Key, Calif. State U. Emeriti and Ret. Faculty Assn. (v.p. 2005—), Phi Alpha Theta, Pi Sigma Alpha, Phi Kappa Phi, Sigma Delta Chi. Office: Calif State U Dept History 5151 State University Dr Los Angeles CA 90032-4226 Office Phone: 323-343-2022. Business E-Mail: ddewey@calstatela.edu.

DEWEY, ELIZABETH R., lawyer; b. Phoenix, Ariz., Nov. 29, 1967; Student, Univ. Madrid, Spain, 1989; BA cum laude, Univ. Tulsa, 1990; JD summa cum laude, Am. Univ. of Washington, 1993. Bar: Md. 1993, DC 1995, US Dist. Ct. (DC, Md. dist.), Md. Ct. Appeals, US Ct. Appeals (Fed. cir.). Law clk. Hon. Noel Anketell Kramer DC Superior Ct.; pro bono ptnr. DLA Piper Rudnick Gray Cary, Washington, 1999—. Adj. prof. law Am. Univ. Wash. Coll. of Law. Founder, editorial bd. mem. Journal of Gender and the Law, Am. Univ. of Washington; contbr. articles to profl. jours. Hon. trustee AYUDA Inc. Named co-winner, Young Guns category, Washington Bus. Jour., 2004. Mem.: ABA, DC Women's Bar Assn., Mortar Board, Phi Beta Kappa. Office: DLA Piper Rudnick Gray Cary 1200 Nineteenth St NW Washington DC 20036-2412 Office Phone: 202-861-6218. Office Fax: 202-223-2085. Business E-Mail: elizabeth.dewey@dlapiper.com.

DEWEY, JOEL ALLEN, lawyer; b. Balt., Dec. 17, 1956; s. Allen Leonard and Mary Louise (Karcher) D.; m. Martha Dayle Nesbitt, Aug 25, 1979; children: Samuel Everett, Sarah Radcliffe. SBCE, MIT, 1977; JD, Harvard U., 1980. Bar: Calif. 1980, Md. 1981, D.C. 1981, U.S. Dist. Ct. Md. 1981, U.S. Ct. Appeals (4th cir.) 1981, N.Y. 1993, Va. 1994. Law clk. to presiding justice U.S. Dist. Ct. Md., Balt., 1980-81; assoc. Piper & Marbury, Balt., 1981-88, ptnr., 1989—. Mem. Chi Epsilon, Tau Beta Pi. Republican. Presbyterian. Avocation: running. Home: 1428B W Joppa Rd Towson MD 21204-3618 Office: DLA Piper Rudnick Gray Cary US LLP 6225 Smith Ave Baltimore MD 21209-3600 Office Phone: 410-580-4135. Business E-Mail: joel.dewey@dlapiper.com.

DEWEY, RALPH JAY, school system administrator; b. NYC, Feb. 8, 1944; s. Ralph Morris and Evelyn Elizabeth (Karle) D.; m. Vivian V. Barone Dewey, Dec. 20, 1970; children: Gabriella Maria, Meredith Elizabeth, Ralph Stephen. BS, Holy Cross Coll., Worcester, Mass., 1965; MAT, Brown U., Providence, 1968; EdS, Rutgers U., 1985. Teaching Cert., N.Y. Tchr. Moses Brown Sch., Providence, 1965-68; founding head of mid. sch. Portledge Sch., Locust Valley, N.Y., 1968-74; head of lower sch. Rutgers Preparatory Sch., Somerset, N.J., 1974-83; founding headmaster The Winston Sch., Summit, N.J., 1983-87; headmaster St. James Episc. Sch., Corpus Christi, 1987-95; headmaster, bd. dirs. Cape Fear Acad., Wilmington, NC, 1995—2001; founding dir. Schechter Regional HS, Bergen County, NJ, 2002—. Regional coord. Southwestern Assn. Episcopal Schs., Corpus Christi, Tex., 1989-93, stds. com. Southwestern Assn. Episcopal Schs., 1994-95, cons., Dallas, 1990-92; presenter in field Author, editor: Winston Newsletter, 1983-87, St. James Episcopal School Newsletter, 1987-95; author: Classical Vocabulary, 1990; contbr. articles to profl. jours. Treas. Coastal Bend Soc. Friends, 1988-95; sec., v.p. Harbor Playhouse, Corpus Christi, Tex., 1989-92; mem. Com. of 100, Wilmington, 1995; mem. exec. coun. Leadership Wilmington, 1996; bd. dirs. Ea. Plains Ind. Conf. Recipient U.S. Dept. Blue Ribbon Sch. Excellence award, Salute to Prins. award Nat. Assn. Elem. Sch. Prins. Mem. NC Assn. Ind. Schs. (bd. dirs. 1998-2002, membership chmn. 1998-2001), SAR, ASCD, Assn. Children with Learning Disabilities, Nat. Assn. for Edn. of Young Children, Nat. Coun. for Tchrs. English, Tex. ASCD, Assn. Leadership Educators, Internat. Leadership Assn., Loyal Order St. Andrew's Brewers, Network of Progressive Educators, Rotary, Leadership Wilmington, Wilmington Execs. Club, City Club de Rossette. Mem. Soc. Friends. Avocations: russian literature, furniture building. Office: Solomon Schechter Regional H S 800 Broad St Teaneck NJ 07666 Home: 296 Myrtle Ave New Milford NJ 07646-1910 Office Phone: 201-837-8357. Personal E-mail: jvdewey@optonline.net. Business E-Mail: jdewey@schechter.info.

DEWEY-BALZHISER, ANNE ELIZABETH MARIE, lawyer; b. Balt., Mar. 16, 1951; d. George Daniel and Elizabeth Patricia (Mohan) Dewey; m. Richard J. Balzhiser; children: Brendan M. Barnett, Andrew P. Barnett, Meghan E. Barnett. BA, Mich. State U., 1972; JD, U. Chgo., 1975; grad., Stonier Grad. Sch. Banking, East Brunswick, N.J., 1983. Bar: D.C. 1976. Legal clk. and atty. FTC, Washington, 1975—78; atty., sr. atty. Comptr. of Currency, Dallas and Washington, 1978—86; assoc. gen. counsel, gen. counsel, spl. counsel Farm Credit Adminstrn., McLean, Va., 1986—92; counsel, closed bank litig. and policy sect. FDIC, Washington, 1993—94; gen. counsel, spl. advisor Office of Fed. Housing Enterprise Oversight, HUD, Washington, 1994—2004; pres. Women Lead LLC, 2003—. Mem. D.C. study devel. coun. Mich. State U., 1999—. Mem.: FBA (bd. dirs. D.C. chpt. 1988—91, banking law com. exec. coun. 1995—2001), ABA (coun. 2002—, gen. and pub. sect. law divsn., bus. law sect., banking law com., liaison to com. on women in the profession, adminstrv. law and regulatory practice sect.), D.C. Bar Assn., Women in Housing and Fin. (bd. dirs. 1982—83, gen. counsel 1991—93, co-chair, profl. devel. com. 2002—), Exchequer Club. Roman Catholic. Office: Women Lead LLC PO Box 1414 Falls Church VA 22041 Office Phone: 703-933-2444. E-mail: womenlead@womenlead.net.

DEWHURST, CHARLES KURT, museum director, curator, language educator; b. Passaic, N.J., Dec. 21, 1948; s. Charles Allaire and Minn Jule (Hanzl) D.; m. Marsha MacDowell, Dec. 15, 1972; 1 dau., Marit Charlene. BA, Mich. State U., 1970, MA, 1973, PhD, 1983. Editorial asst. Carlton Press, N.Y.C., 1967; computer operator IBM, N.Y.C., 1968; project dir. Mich. State U. Mus., 1975, curator, 1976-83, dir., 1982—. Guest curator Mus. Am. Folk Art, N.Y.C., 1978—83, Artrain, Detroit, 1980—83; dir. Festival of Mich. Folklife, 1987—95, Ctr. for Great Lakes Culture, 2000—. Author: Reflections of Faith, 1983, Artists in Aprons, 1979, Rainbows in the Sky, 1978, Michigan Folk Art, 1976 (Am. Assn. State and Local History award 1977), Art at Work: Folk Pottery of Grand Ledge, Michigan, 1986, Michigan Quilts, 1987, Michigan Folklife Reader, 1988, To Honor and Comfort: Native Quilting Traditions, 1998, MSU Campus: Buildings, Places and Spaces, 2002. Coord. South African-U.S. Partnership Project, 1967—; mem. and chair adv. com. Smithsonian Ctr. for Folklife and Cultural Heritage; pres. bd. dirs. Fund for Folk Culture. Recipient Disting. Svc. and Humanities award, 1994. Fellow Mich. State U.; mem. Am. Folkore Soc.(Americo Padres proze, 2004), Mich. Folklore Soc., Midwest Soc. Lit., Popular Culture Assn., Mich. Hist. Soc., Mich. Mus. Assn., Am. Assn. Mus., Internat. Coun. Mus. Home: 1804 Cricket Ln East Lansing MI 48823-1225 Office: Mich State U Mus W Circle Dr East Lansing MI 48824 Office Phone: 517-355-2370. Business E-Mail: dewhurs1@msu.edu.

DEWHURST, DAVID, lieutenant governor; b. Tex., Aug. 18, 1945; BA, U. Ariz. With CIA, U.S. State Dept.; founder Falcon Seaboard, 1981; ptnr. Falcon Seabord Diversified Energy and Investments Co.; commr. Tex. Gen. Land Office; lt. gov. State of Tex., 2003—. Chmn. Gov.'s Task Force on Homeland Security, 2001—03; mem. Gov.'s Bus. Coun., Pres.'s Commn. on Capabilities of U.S. Intelligence Cmty.; chmn. State Product Devel. Bd. Active civic and charitable bds., Houston. Officer USAF. Republican. Presbyterian. Office: Capitol Sta PO Box 12068 Austin TX 78711*

DEWILDE, DAVID MICHAEL, management consultant, retired executive recruiter, lawyer, finance company executive; b. Bridgeton, N.J., Aug. 11, 1940; s. Louis and Dorothea (Donnelly) deW.; m. Katherine August, Dec. 30, 1984; children: Holland Stockdale, Christian DuCroix, Nicholas Alexander, Lucas Barrymore. AB, Dartmouth Coll., 1962; LLB, U. Va., 1967; MS in Mgmt., Stanford U., 1984. Bar: N.Y. 1968, D.C. 1972. Assoc. Curtis, Mallet-Prevost, Colt & Mosle, N.Y.C., 1967-69; assoc. gen. counsel HUD, Washington, 1969-72; investment banker Lehman Bros., Washington, 1972-74; dep. commr. FHA, Washington, 1974-76; pres. Govt. Nat. Mortgage Assn., Washington, 1976-77; mng. dir. Lepercq DeNeuflize & Co., N.Y.C., 1977-81; exec. v.p. policy and planning Fed. Nat. Mortgage Assn., Washington, 1981-82; pres. deWilde & Assocs., Washington, 1982-84; mng. dir., dir. fin. svcs. Boyden Internat., San Francisco, 1984-88; CEO Chartwell Ptnrs. Internat., San Francisco, 1989-97; mng. dir. LAI Worldwide, San Francisco, 1998-99; mng. ptnr. TMP Worldwide, San Francisco, 1999-2001; mgmt. cons., 2001—. Bd. dirs. Berkshire Realty Investment Trust, Fritzi of Calif., Silicon Valley Bankshares; bd. dirs. St. Luke's School, San Francisco, chair, 2001-03. Editor-in-chief Va. Jour. Internat. Law, 1966-67. Lt. USN, 1962-64. Mem. Pacific Union Club (San Francisco), Villa Taverna (San Francisco), Met. Club (Washington), Belvedere Tennis Club. Republican. Personal E-mail: ddewilde@pacbell.net.

DEWINE, R. MICHAEL, senator, lawyer; b. Springfield, Ohio, Jan. 5, 1947; s. Richard and Jean DeWine; m. Frances Struewing, June 3, 1967; children: Patrick, Jill, Rebecca, John, Brian, Alice, Mark, Anna. BS in Edn., Miami U., Oxford, Ohio, 1969; JD, Ohio No. U., 1972. Bar: Ohio 1972, U.S. Supreme Ct. 1977. Asst. pros. atty. Greene County, Xenia, Ohio, 1973-75, pros. atty., 1977-81; mem. Ohio Senate, 1981-82, 98th, 99th, 100th, 101st Congress from 7th Ohio dist., Washington, 1983-90; lt. gov. State of Ohio, Columbus, Ohio, 1991-94; U.S. senator from Ohio, 1995—. Mem. judiciary com., labor and human resources com., intelligence com., Health Edn. Com., Labor and Pensions Com. Republican. Roman Catholic. Office: US Senate 140 Russell Senate Bldg Washington DC 20510-0001*

DEWITT, BARBARA JANE, journalist; b. Glendale, Calif., Aug. 5, 1947; d. Clarence James and Irene Brezina; m. Don DeWitt, Apr. 21, 1974; children: Lisa, Scarlett. BA in Journalism, Calif. State U., Northridge, 1971. Features editor The Daily Ind. Newspaper, Ridgecrest, Calif., 1971-84; fashion editor The Daily Breeze, Torrance, Calif., 1984-89; freelance fashion reporter The Seattle Times, 1990; fashion editor, columnist The Los Angeles Daily News, L.A., 1990—. Instr. fashion writing UCLA, 1988, Am. InterContinental U., L.A., 1996—. Dir. Miss Indian Wells Valley Scholarship Pageant, 1980-84. Recipient 1st Pl. Best Youth Page, Calif. Newspaper Pubs. Assn., 1980, 1st Pl. Best Fashion, Wash. Press Assn., 1989, The Internat. Aldo award for fashion journalism, 1995, 96. Republican. Lutheran. Avocations: antiques, reading, swimming. Office: The Daily News 21221 Oxnard St Woodland Hills CA 91367-5081 Home: PO Box 2518 Agoura Hills CA 91376-2518

DEWITT, CAROL A., publishing executive, writer; b. Indpls., Ind., Nov. 4, 1942; d. Robert William Kollmeyer; m. Robert Knox DeWitt, Oct. 27, 1983; m. Roy L. Bruner, Dec. 6, 1958 (div. May 0, 1973); 1 child, Robin Renee Chaffee. Associates, Applied Sci., Univ. Louisville, Louisville, KY, 1982. Sales rep. Br. Motor Freight, Louisville, 1975—77, Spector Freight Sys., Louisville, 1977—81; sales mgr. Atlantic Container Line, Jeffersonville, 1981—83; owner Land-Sea-Air, Louisville, 1983—85; sales exec. Ctrl. Transport, Inc., Louisville, 1985—87, Am. Pres. Dist., Louisville, 1987—89; writer StarPoint Pub., Sebring, 2001—02. Dir. nat. bd. Transp. Clubs Internat., Louisville, 1978—81, Kentuckiana World Commerce Coun., Louisville, 1977—80; pres. Women's Traffic Club, Louisville, 1981. Author: (book) God 101, composer christian music. Dir. St. Elizabeth's Home, New Albany, Ind., 1988—91, Indianapolis, Ind., 1991; mem. Louisville Forum, Louisville, Ky., 1986. Recipient Transp. Queen, Women's Traffic Club, Louisville, KY, 1976. Mem.: Ch. Women United, Span, Country Club of Sebring. United Church Of Christ. Avocations: golf, painting, travel. Home: 2851 Briarwood Lane Sebring FL 33875 Office: Starpoint Publishing Co 2851 Briarwood Lane Sebring FL 33875

DEWITT, CHARLES BARBOUR, federal official; b. L.A., Mar. 13, 1950; s. Homer Charles and Gwenyth Deakin (Barbour) DeW.; m. Bonnie St. Clair; 1 child, Anna. BA with univ. distinction and dept. honors, Stanford U., 1972; postgrad., Cambridge U., 1972-73. Dep. sheriff City of San Jose, Calif., 1973-74, specialist regional crime bd., 1974-78, dir. justice div., 1978-84; fellow U.S. Dept. of Justice, 1984-89; advisor White House, Washington, 1989-90; dir. Nat. Inst. Justice, 1990-93; ptnr. Lafayette Group, Inc., Vienna, Va., 1993—. Faculty Nat. Acad. Corrections, Boulder, Colo., 1986-90, Nat. Inst. Corrections, Washington, 1986-90; cons. Police Found., 1993-94. Author: National Directory of Corrections, 1986, 1988, Building on Experience, 1987, Prison Expansion, 1988. Adv. coun. The Ditchley Found. With USMCR, 1968-71. Recipient Atty. Gen's Achievement award, 1993, Dist. Attys. award, 1993, Am. Jails award, 1993. Mem. Am. Correctional Assn., Internat. Assn. Chiefs Police, Nat. Sheriffs Assn., Nat. Dist. Attys. Assn. Republican. Episcopalian. Avocations: jogging, skiing, tennis. Home: 5058 Sedgwick St NW Washington DC 20016-1940 Office: Lafayette Group Inc 8150 Leesburg Pike Ste 900 Vienna VA 22182-7749 Office Phone: 703-760-8866. Business E-Mail: cbdewitt@lafayettegroup.com.

DEWITT, DALE, secondary school educator, state representative; b. Blackwell, Okla., Jan. 17, 1950; s. Ed and Ramona DeWitt; m. Carol Grell; children: Garrett, Camille Holt. BS In Agr. Edn., Okla. State U., 1972. Tchr. of agr. Braman (Okla.) Schs., 1974—; rep. Ho. of Reps., State of Okla., 2001—. Mem. agr. and rural devel., common edn., econ. devel. and wildlife coms. Okla. Ho. of Reps., 2001—; adv. com. Okla. State U. Extension. Past chmn., developer Pete Gailey Plan; minuteman Kay Electric Coop. Named Outstanding Tchr., Nat. Agr. Edn. Tchrs. Assn.; recipient State and Nat. Hon. Degrees, Future Farmers Am. Mem.: Okla. Agr. Edn. Tchrs. Assn. (bd. dirs., chmn.ethics com.), Okla. Cattleman's Assn., Kay Cattleman's Assn. (pres.). Republican. Office: Capitol Bldg 2300 N Lincoln Blvd Oklahoma City OK 73105 Home and Office: 14235 W Stateline Rd Braman OK 74632 E-mail: dewittda@lsb.state.ok.us.

DEWITT, DAVID B., political scientist, educator, political organization worker; b. London, Sept. 11, 1948; BA, U. Brit. Columbia, 1971; MA, Stanford U., 1973, PhD, 1977. Dir. York Ctr. Internat. Security Studies York U., 1988—, prof. polit. sci., 1993—. Office: York Ctr Internat and Security Studies 375 York Lanes York Univ 4700 Keele St Toronto ON Canada M3J 1P3

DEWITT, DIANA LEIGH, retired secondary school educator; b. Campbellsville, Ky., Nov. 21, 1941; d. Robert Tally and Opal Joy (May) DeW. BA, Georgetown (Ky.) Coll., 1964; MA, Western Ky. U., 1969; postgrad., U. Louisville, 1984. Cert. elem. and secondary guidance counseling, psychology, English; lic. realtor into escrow, Ky. Tchr. Shelbyville (Ky.) City Schs., 1964-66, Jefferson County Schs., Louisville, 1966-91, ret., 1991; realtor Paul Semonin Realty, 1992-94. Supr. title 9 Jefferson County Schs., 1974—83. Vol. Jewish Hosp., Louisville, 1972-73, Humana Hosp. Audubon, Louisville, 1981-83, Bapt. East Hosp., Louisville, 1988-94, Ky. Ctr. for Arts, Louisville, 1988-94, Taylor County Hosp. Vol. Aux., 1994-2000, sec., 1998, pres., 1999-2000 Mem. NEA, Jefferson County Ret. Tchrs. Assn., Taylor County Ret. Tchrs. Assn., Ky. Ret. Tchrs. Assn., Ky. Real Estate Commn., Red Hat Soc. Democrat. Baptist. Avocations: gardening, travel, theater, needlecrafts, music.

DEWITT, KATHARINE CRAMER, museum administrator; BA, Manhattenville Coll. of Sacred Heart. Docent Cin. Art Mus. Co-chair Presdl. Inaugural Com., 2001; mem. Nat. Coun. Arts., Nat. Endowment for Arts, 2002—. Trustee Cin. Children's Hosp. Med. Ctr., Beechwood Home, Stratford Hall Plantation, Va.; co-chmn. Cin. Antiques Festival, 1990, Garden Club of Am., 1995—97. Mem.: Cin. Fine Arts Fund (co-chmn. Individual Gifts 1985, 1993, mem. Allocation Com. 1991—94). Office: Cin Art Mus 953 Eden Park Dr Cincinnati OH 45202 Office Phone: 513-721-2787.*

DEWITT, TIMOTHY LEE, music educator, conductor, actor; b. Oakland, Md., May 3, 1958; s. Paul Edward and Virginia Emelee DeWitt. MusB, W.Va. U., 1980; MusM in Performance, Bowling Green State U., 1982; D of Musical Arts in Performance and Lit. (Trumpet), Eastman Sch. of Music, Rochester, NY, 2003. Second trumpet W.Va. Symphony Orch., Charleston, W.Va., 1985—2001; prof. of music Alderson-Broaddus Coll., Philippi, W.Va., 1983—. Musician: (compact disc recording) Passions of the Soul; Music of the Baroque for Trumpet and Organ; dir.(alderson-broaddus college brass choir): (compact disc recording) Reflections in Brass. Recipient, Alderson-Broaddus Coll., Employee of the Month. Mem.: Music Tchrs. Nat. Assn., Internat. Trumpet Guild. Democrat-Npl. Avocations: kayaking, skiing. Office: Alderson-Broaddus Coll Box 2126 A-B Philippi WV 26416 Office Phone: 304-457-6236.

DEWITT-MORETTE, CÉCILE, physicist; b. Paris, Dec. 21, 1922; came to U.S., 1948; d. André and Marie Louise (Ravaudet) Morette; m. Bryce S. DeWitt, Apr. 26, 1951; children: Nicolette, Jan, Chris, Abigail. BS, U. Caen, 1943; PhD, U. Paris, 1947. With Centre Nat. de la Recherche Sci., 1944-65, Maitre de Confs. prof., 1965-88. Mem. Inst. Advanced Studies, Dublin, 1946—47, Copenhagen, 1947—48, Princeton, 1948—50; lectr. U. Calif., Berkeley, 1952—55, U. N.C., Chapel Hill, 1956—71; prof. U. Tex., 1972—93, Jane and Roland Blumberg Centennial prof. physics, 1993—2000, prof. emeritus, 2000—; founder, dir. Ecole d'ete de Physique Theorique, Les Houches, France, 1951—72. Author: Particules Elementaires, 1951, (with Y. Choquet-Bruhat and M. Dillard-Bleick) Analysis, Manifolds and Physics, 1977, rev. edit., 1982, (with A. Maheshwari, B. Nelson) Path Integration in Non Relativistic Quantum Mechanics, 1979, (with Y. Choquet Bruhat) Analysis, Manifolds and Physics, Part II, 92 Applications, 1989, rev. edit., 2000, also articles. Decorated chevalier Ordre Nat. du Mérite, chevalier Ordre des Palmes Académiques; chevalier Ordre Nat. Legion d'Honneur; Rask-Oersted fellow, 1947-48, Prix des Sciences Physiques et Mathematiques (Comite du Rayonnement Français, 1992); recipient (with Bryce DeWitt) Marcel Grossman award, 2000. Fellow Am. Phys. Soc.; mem. Internat. Astron. Union, European Phys. Soc., Inst. Hautes Etudes Scientific (trustee), French Soc. Physics (membre d'honneur). Home: 2411 Vista Ln Austin TX 78703-2343 Office: U Tex Austin Dept Physics 1 University Station C1600 Austin TX 78712-0268 E-mail: cdewitt@physics.utexas.edu.

DE WOLF, DAVID ALTER, physicist, educator; b. Dordrecht, The Netherlands, July 23, 1934; came to U.S., 1962; m. Peggy Louise Lumpkin; 1 dau., Sarah Eleonora; children by previous marriage: Naomi, Jiska. BS in Physics, U. Amsterdam, The Netherlands, 1955, MS in Physics, 1959; PhDEE, U. Eindhoven, The Netherlands, 1968. Rsch. scientist Edgewood (Md.) Arsenal U.S. Army Chem. Ctr., 1962; mem. tech. staff RCA Labs.-David Sarnoff Rsch. Ctr., Princeton, N.J., 1962-82; prof. elec. engring. Va. Tech., Blacksburg, 1982—2003, prof. emeritus, 2003—. Commn. B and F U.S. Nat. Com. Internat. Union Radio Sci., sec. 1985-89. Author 2 books and contbr. numerous articles on wave propagation, electron optics to profl. jours. Fellow IEEE, Optical Soc. Am. (assoc. editor JOSA 1969-81); mem. Am. Assn. Physics Tchrs., Dutch Physics Soc., Electromagnetics Acad., Sigma Xi, Eta Kappa Nu. Avocations: music, piano, literature, tennis. Office: Va Tech Bradley Dept Elec and Computer Engring Blacksburg VA 24061-0111 Office Phone: 540-231-4874. Business E-Mail: dadewolf@vt.edu.

DEWOLFE, JOHN CHAUNCEY, JR., lawyer; b. Chgo., June 9, 1913; s. John Chauncey and Mabel (Spafford) DeW.; m. Dorothy Fulton, May 9, 1942; children: John Chauncey, III, George F. BS, U. Ill.; JD, U. Wis., 1939. Bar: Wis. 1939, Ill. 1940. Ptnr. firm DeWolfe, Poynton & Stevens and predecessor firms, 1946—. Contbr. articles to profl. jours. Trustee Village of Riverside, Ill., 1963-70; Chmn. West Suburban Mass Transit Dist., 1974-76. Served from lt. to maj. AUS, 1942-45, 51-52; lt. col. USAR ret. Mem. ABA, Ill. Bar Assn., Wis. Bar Assn., Chgo. Bar Assn. (chmn. corp. law com. 1973-74), Univ. Clug (Chgo.), Sigma Phi Epsilon. Republican. Episcopalian. Home: 1448 N Lake Shore Dr Chicago IL 60610-6655 Office: 135 S La Salle St Chicago IL 60603

DE WOLFF, LOUIS, management consultant; b. NYC, Dec. 21, 1929; s. Maurice and Minnie (Konrad) De W.; m. Grace Elise Sorrentino, Apr. 27, 1957 (dec. Dec. 2000); children: Douglas Louis, Cynthia Ann. AS, Bklyn. Coll., 1960; BS in Acctg., CCNY, 1962. Officer Lykes Bros. S.S. Co., New Orleans, 1950-57; export mgr. Cory Mann George Corp., N.Y.C., 1957-60;

dist. supt. F&M Schaefer Brewing Co., N.Y.C., 1960-64; product and material mgr. Del Labs., Inc., Farmingdale, N.Y., 1965-69; exec. cons., exec. v.p. Pennington (N.J.) Industries, 1969-73; dir. ops. Alexander Proudfoot Co., Chgo., 1973-86; mgr. ops. Metra Proudfoot Ltd., Brussels, 1986-87; CEO, chmn. DeWolff Boberg & Assocs., Charleston, SC, 1987—. Lt. (j.g.) USMS and USNR, 1950-57, PTO, Mem.: U.S. Navy League, U.S. Naval Inst., Charleston Concert Assn. (bd. dirs.). Republican. Lutheran. Avocations: carpentry, sailing, gardening. Home: 53 Waterway Island Dr Isle Of Palms SC 29451 Office: DeWolff Boberg & Assocs PO Box 21989 Charleston SC 29413-1989 Office Fax: 843-886-5323.

DEWOODY, BETH RUDIN, film producer; b. NYC; d. Lewis Rudin. Studied Anthropology & Film Studies, U. Calif. Santa Barbara; BA, New Sch. Social Rsch. Pres. May & Samuel Rudin Found. Inc.; exec. v.p. Rudin Mgmt. Co.; contbg. editor Hampton's Cottages & Garden's Mag. Dir.(asst. dir.): (TV series) Born Free; prodn. asst. Annie Hall, The Front, Hair, co-prodr. Enter Juliet. Bd. dir. Creative Time Inc., Whitney Mus. Am. Art, Bklyn. Mus. Am. Art, New Sch. U.; bd. adv. Eos Music Inc. Mailing: Whitney Mus Am Art 945 Madison Ave New York NY 10021*

DEWS, P(ETER) B(OOTH), pharmacology educator, physician; b. Ossett, Yorkshire, Eng., Sept. 11, 1922; s. G.A. and E. (Booth) D.; m. Grace Miller, Dec. 1949; children: Pamela, Kenneth, Alan, Michael. MBChB, U. Leeds, Eng., 1944; PhD, U. Minn., 1952; MA, Harvard U., 1959. House physician Grimsby Hosp., England, 1944-45; lectr. pharmacology U. Leeds, England, 1945-47; rsch. assoc. Wellcome Rsch. Labs., Tuckahoe, NY, 1948-49, Mayo Found., Rochester, Minn., 1950-52; from instr. to prof. Harvard Med. Sch., Boston, 1953-93, prof. emeritus, 1993—. Mem. Nat. Adv. Mental Health Coun., Washington, 1985-88, Nat. Adv. Space Coun., Washington, 1982-86; v.p. Internat. Life Scis. Inst., Washington, 1977-97. Mem. Inst. of Medicine. E-mail: peter_dews@hms.harvard.edu.

DEWSBURY, DONALD ALLEN, psychologist; b. Bklyn., Aug. 11, 1939; s. Edwin Leroy and Carol Wieler (Neil) D.; children: Bryan Bradley, Laura Alison. AB, Bucknell U., 1961; PhD, U. Mich., 1965. NSF postdoctoral fellow U. Calif., Berkeley, 1965-66; mem. faculty dept. psychology U. Fla., Gainesville, 1966—, prof., 1973—. Author: Comparative Animal Behavior, 1978, Comparative Psychology in the Twentieth Century, 1984, Monkey Farm: A history of Yerkes Laboratories of Primate Biology, 1930-1965, 2005; editor (with D. Rethlinghshafer): Comparative Psychology: A Modern Survey, 1973; editor: (with T. McGill, B. Sachs) Sex and Behavior: Status and Prospectus, 1978; editor: Mammalian Sexual Behavior, 1981, Foundations of Comparative Psychology, 1984, Leaders in the Study of Animal Behavior, 1985, Studying Animal Behavior, 1989, Contemporary Issues in Comparative Psychology, 1990, Unification Through Division: Histories of the Divisions of the American Psychological Association, vol. 1, 1996, vol. 2, 1997, vol. 3, 1998, vol. 4, 1999, vol. 5, 2000; editor: (with W. Pickren) Evolving Perspectives on the History of Psychology, 2002; editor: (with L.T. Benjamin, Jr. and M. Westheimer) Portraits of Pioneers in Psychology, 2005. Fellow APA (pres. divsn. 6 1992-93, pres. divsn. 26 1997-98), AAAS, Animal Behavior Soc. (pres. 1978-79); mem. Psychonomic Soc., History of Sci. Soc., Cheiron Soc., Phi Beta Kappa, Psi Chi. Home: 4004 NW 59th Ave Gainesville FL 32653-8358 Office: Univ Fla Dept Psychology Gainesville FL 32611-2250 Office Phone: 352-392-0601 ext. 279. Business E-Mail: dewsbury@ufl.edu.

DEWSNUP, RALPH L., lawyer; b. Salt Lake City, Mar. 13, 1948; s. Edwin Grant and Mary Jeannette (Fairbanks) D.; m. Mary C. Dewsnup, Mar. 26, 1971; children: Emily, Rebecca, Hillary, Nathan, Heidi. BA, U. Utah, 1972; JD, Brigham Young U., 1977. Bar: Utah, 1977; U.S. Dist. Ct. Utah, 1977, U.S. Ct. Appeals (10th cir.) 1978, U.S. Supreme Ct., 1985. Asst. trust officer Tracy Collins Bank and Trust, Salt Lake City, 1971-74; brig. gen. Utah Air Nat. Guard, Salt Lake City, 1967—; law clk. Hansen & Orton, Salt Lake City, 1975-77; assoc. Hansen & Thompson, Salt Lake City, 1977-80; ptnr. Hansen, Thompson & Dewsnup, Salt Lake City, 1980-83, Hansen & Dewsnup, Salt Lake City, 1983-90; shareholder, officer Wilcox, Dewsnup & King, Salt Lake City, 1990-97; pres. Dewsnup, King & Olsen, 1998—. Stake pres. LDS Ch., Salt Lake City, 1988-97, bishop, 1985-88; chmn. prelitigation task force Divsn. of Occpl. and Profl. Lics., Salt Lake City, 1995-96. Mem.: ATLA, Am. Inns of Ct. Found. (trustee 1987—88, sec. 1985—96, treas. 1996—98, mem. exec. com. 1988—98), Utah Trial Lawyers Assn. (pres. 1990—92), Temple Bar Found. (trustee 1996—98), Utah State Bar (gov. 1987—2001), Aldon J. Anderson Am. Inn of Ct. (pres. 1991—92). Republican. Avocations: music (piano, banjo and guitar), woodworking, basketball. Home: 1407 E Stratford Ave Salt Lake City UT 84106-3527 Office: Dewsnup King & Olsen 36 S State St Salt Lake City UT 84111-1401

DEWULF NICKELL, KAROL, editor; m. Don Nickell; children: Lauren, Alexander. BA in Journalism, Iowa St. U. Furnishings editor Better Homes and Gardens mag., 1979—87; editor-in-chief Traditional Home mag., 1987—2001; columnist Country Home mag., 1987—2001; editor-in-chief Better Homes and Gardens mag., 2001—. Editor Renovation Style mag., Decorator Showhouse mag. Avocations: gardening, reading, cooking. Office: 1716 Locust St Des Moines IA 50309-3023

DEXHEIMER, LARRY WILLIAM, advertising agency executive; b. Hackensack, N.J., Aug. 8, 1941; s. Harold Dexheimer and Gretchen Bartell; m. Carol Frances Martin, May 1, 1965 (div. 1983); children— Lynda Anne, Susan Carol BS in Mktg. and Advt., Fairleigh Dickinson U. Broadcast media buyer Doyle, Dane, Bernback, N.Y.C., 1964-67; media group head BBDO, N.Y.C., 1967-71; mktg. svcs. dir. Ally & Gargano, Inc., N.Y.C., 1972-89; ptnr., media dir. Messner, Vetere, Berger, McNamee & Schmetterer, N.Y.C., 1989-99, mng. dir., COO, 1999—. Mem. Internat. TV and Radio Soc. Avocations: tennis, reading, travel, art.

DEXTER, DONALD HARVEY, surgeon, educator; b. Maywood, Ill., Apr. 8, 1928; s. Harry Malcolm and Theodora Jane (Trelawny) D.; m. Esther Ruth Reeve, May 16, 1953; children: Donald Harvey, Scott Reeve, Bryce Malcolm, Margaret Helen. BS, Tulane U., 1948; MD, Northwestern U., 1950; LHD (hon.), Western Ill. U., 1993. Diplomate: Am. Bd. Surgery. Intern Cook County Hosp., Chgo., 1950-51; resident in surgery Ill. Central Hosp., Chgo., 1951-52, Cook County Hosp., 1955-58; practice medicine specializing in surgery Macomb, Ill., 1958—89; prof. dept. health scis. Western Ill. U., 1975—89; physician surveyor Joint Commn. on Accreditation Healthcare Orgns., 1989-93; chief of staff Beu Health Ctr., Western Ill. U., 1993-2001, physician, 2001—. Sr. mem. Macomb Clinic; team physician; coroner McDonough County, Ill., 1964-76; mem. gov. bd., chmn. devel. coun. McDonough Dist. Hosp., 1995—. Mem. Western Ill. U. Found. Served with USNR, 1953-54. Named Outstanding Citizen of Macomb Jaycees, 1972, Outstanding Citizen of Macomb Macomb Area C. of C., 1973; recipient award of recognition Devel. Center of Western Ill. U. and Macomb Area C. of C., 1977, Hon. Alumni award Western Ill. U., 2004; named to Hall of Fame Western Ill. U., 1991. Fellow ACS (pres. Ill. chpt. 1972, gov.-at-large Ill. chpt. 1983-88), state chmn. field liaison program commn. on cancer, 1983-89); mem. AMA, Ill. Med. Soc., (Outstanding Team Physician award 1985), Ill. Surg. Soc., M.W. Surg. Assn., Rotary (Paul Harris fellow 1987), Phi Beta Kappa. Republican. Episcopalian. Home: 1601 Tower Rd RR 1 Macomb IL 61455-9801

DEXTER, HELEN LOUISE, dermatologist, consultant; b. Cin., July 28, 1908; d. William Jordan and Katherine (Weston) Taylor; m. Morrie W. Dexter, Jan. 27, 1937; children: Katharine, Helen Dexter Dalzell, Elizabeth Taylor, William Taylor. AB, Bryn Mawr Coll., 1930; MD, Columbia U., 1937; postgrad., U. Cin., 1948-50. Intern Jersey City (N.J.) Med. Ctr., 1938-39; internist Cin. Babies Milk Fund Maternal Health Clinic, 1938-45; clinician U. Cin. Med. Sch., 1938-48; lectr. dept. dermatology, 1948-53; practice in medicine specializing in dermatology Clearwater, Fla., 1954—. Dermatology cons. VA, 1955—; investigation of carcinogenic effects of shale oil U.S. Bur. Mines, Rifle, Colo., 1950. Contbr. articles to profl. jours. Mem. Clearwater Power Squadron Aux.; commr. Town of Belleair, 1980. Recipient Ina Clay trophy Intercollegiate Ski Champion, 1928-30. Mem. AMA, Soc. Investigation Deramtology, Am. Acad. Dermatology, S.E. Dermatol. Assn. (v.p. 1963-65), Fla. Dermatol. Soc., Pan-Am. Dermatol. Soc., Am. Archaeol. Soc., Soc. Tropical Dermatology, Clearwater Yacht CarioueI Yacht. Presbyterian. Address: 409 Bayview Dr Belleair FL 33756-1409

DEXTER, ROBERT PAUL, lawyer; b. Halifax, N.S., Can., Dec. 11, 1951; s. Carl Edmund and Jean Rankin (Collins) D.; 1 child, Angela Elizabeth. BComm, Dalhousie U., 1973, LLB, 1976. With firm Stewart McKelvey Stirling Scales, Halifax, 1977—; chmn., CEO Maritime Travel, Halifax, Canada, 1978—; chmn. Empire Co. Ltd., Stellarton, Canada, 2004—. Vice chmn. N.S. Bus. Devel. Corp., 1992-94; bd. dirs. Empire Co. Ltd., Wajax Ltd., Sobeys Inc., High Liner Foods Inc., Corpora Tel, Aliant Inc.; pres. Halifax Bd. Trade, 1993-94. Chmn. Metro United Way Campaign, 1997. I.W. Killam scholar, 1973, Sir James Dunn scholar, 1976. Mem. N.S. Barristers Soc., Can. Bar Assn., Young Pres. Orgn. Avocations: sailing, skiing, tennis. Home: 1028 Ridgewood Dr Halifax NS Canada B3H 3Y4 Office: Maritime Travel 2000 Barrington St Ste 202 Halifax NS Canada B3J 2X2

DEXTER, THEODORE HENRY, chemist; b. Preston, Cuba, June 1, 1923; parents Am. citizens; s. Harry Malcolm and Theodora Jane (Trelawny) D.; m. Marilyn Ann Cantara, July 26, 1952; children: Carol Dexter, Martha Dexter Rogala, John Dexter. BS, Tulane U., 1944; MS, 1947; PhD, U. Ill., 1950. Tchg. asst. chemistry Tulane U., New Orleans, 1943-44, 46-47; chemist E.I. du Pont de Nemours, Inc.; Okla. Ordnance Works, 1944-45; gen. aniline chem. rsch. asst. U. Ill., Urbana, 1947-49; group leader chem. rsch. Mathieson Chem. Corp., Niagara Falls, N.Y., 1949-55, sect. chief rsch., 1955-60; rsch. supr. Hooker Chem. Corp., Grand Island, N.Y., 1960-75; program leader, 1975-76; sr. rsch. chemist Hooker Indsl. and Splty. Chems div. Occidental Chem. Corp., 1976—85. Cons. Dexter Cons. Svcs., 1986—; lect., rsch. adv. Joe Berg Found., 1960-61; mem. photoreactivity task force Mfg. Chemists Assn., 1966-68; lectr. in field. Contbr. articles to profl. jours.; U.S., fgn. patentee inorganic chemistry and processes. Violinist Niagara Falls Philharm. Orch., 1950-72, Niagara Cmty. Orch., 1988-92, Niagara Symphony, 1992—2001; group chmn. in-house steering com. United Givers Fund., 1970-73; mem. exec. com. Episc. Diocese We. N.Y., 1977-81, nursing home ministry, 1972—; lay reader, vestryman Episc. Ch., warden, 1967-68, 77-80, 92-94; vol. tax counselor AARP, 1998—. With USNR, 1945—46. Mem. Am. Chem. Soc. (chmn. Western N.Y. 1969-70, N.E. regional meeting divisional chn. 1971, founder Western N.Y. Inorganic Chemistry Group 1967, Schoellkopf Award jury chmn. 1970-72), Soap and Detergent Assn. (del. internat. conf. 1979, com. chmn.), Electrochem. Soc., Sigma Xi, Alpha Chi Sigma (Niagara Frontier pres. 1954), Phi Lambda Upsilon. Home and Office: 850 Hillside Dr Lewiston NY 14092-1828

DEY, CHARLOTTE JANE, retired community health nurse; b. Benson, Minn., Dec. 14, 1927; d. Elmer Ellsworth and Charlotte Iona (Eastman) Bowers; m. Thomas A. Dey, June 25, 1948 (dec. Mar. 1973); children: Thomas A. Jr., Scott E. (dec.). Grad., St. Luke's Hosp. Sch. Nursing, 1948; student, Kansas City (Kans.) Jr. Coll., 1968; BS in Nursing with distinction, U. Kans., 1970; MPA, U. Mo., Kansas City, 1975. RN, Mo.; ordained deacon, Episcopal Ch., 1993. Head nurse communicable disease ward St. Luke's Children's Hosp., Kansas City, Mo., 1948-49; head nurse newborn nursery Providence Hosp., Kansas City, Kans., 1949-51; pub. health nurse Johnson County Health Dept., Olathe, Kans., 1951-52, 66-68, pub. health nurse, supr., 1970-72; evening supr. Olathe Community Hosp., 1953-55; office nurse B. Albert Lieberman, Jr., MD, Kansas City, Mo., 1960-66; coord. clin. confs. ANA, Kansas City, 1973-76; chief Bur. Community Health Nursing Mo. Dept. Health, Jefferson City, 1976-93; ret., 1993. Sem. expert panel to review and update criteria to estimate future requirements for nursing pers. div. nursing Dept. Health and Human Svcs., 1984, mem. nat. adv. coun. nursing edn. and practice div. nursing, 1998-2002; chair Mid-Am. Community Health Nursing Leadership Group. Recipient award of merit Assn. State and Territorial Dirs. Nursing, 1992. Mem. ANA (cert. nursing adminstrn. advanced, chairperson exec. com. coun. community health nursing 1989-92), APHA, Nat. League Nursing, Nat. Perinatal Assn., Am. Acad. Health Adminstrn. (pres. Mo. chpt. 1980-82), Mo. State Nurses Assn. (coun. nursing svc. facilitors exec. com. 1983-92), Mo. Pub. Health Assn., Mo. League Nursing, Mo. Perinatal Assn., Kans. State Nurses' Assn. (vice chairperson community health conf. group), Kans. Pub. Health Assn. (legislative com.), Sigma Theta Tau. Mem. Episcopal Ch. Home: 8090 Granite Falls Ct Redmond OR 97756-7389

DEY, DEBABRATA, education educator; s. Gangadhar and Abharani Dey; m. Sumana Dey, Aug. 10, 1990; 1 child, Trisha Riya. PhD, U. of Rochester, 1989—94. Prof. U. of Wash., Seattle, 1997—; asst. prof. La. State U., Baton Rouge, 1993—97. Office Phone: 206-543-1855.

DEY, RADHESHYAM CHANDRA, cytologist; b. Calcutta, India, Jan. 30, 1950; arrived in US, 1978; s. Bhairab and Satyabala D.; m. Indrani Roy Chowdhury, July 5, 1981; children: Smita, Anita, Ishan. BSc, Bangabasi Coll., Calcutta, 1970; MSc, U. Calcutta, 1972, cert. in life sci., 1974; CT, Brooke Army Med. Ctr., San Antonio, 1983; cert. leaderhsip mgmt., ednl. devel., quality improvement and equal opportunity, Walter Reed Army Med. Ctr., 1989; postgrad., Laval U., Quebec City, Can., 1995, Albert Einstein Sch. Medicine, N.Y.C., 1997; student in quality assurance, Inspector's Inspection Lab., Coll. Am. Pathologists, 2005. Registered cytotechnologist, Am. Soc. Clin. Pathologists, Internat. Acad. Cytology, Calif., Md. Rsch. fellow U. Calcutta, 1975-77; with Anthropol. Survey of India Indian Mus. Calcutta, India, 1977—78; biol. sci. asst. Army Inst. Rsch., Washington, 1980—83; cytology specialist U.S. Army Hosp., Ft. Campbell, Ky., 1983-85, SHAPE Med. Ctr., Mons, Belgium, 1985—87; cytotechnologist Nat. Health Lab., Vienna, Va., 1988; supervisory cytologist Walter Reed Army Med. Ctr., Washington, 1988—. Vis. Indian Statis. Inst., Calcutta, 1999; presenter in field; mem. European Congress Cytology, Athens, Greece, 2004. Contbr. articles to profl. jours. Decorated U.S. Army Commendation medal, Achievement medal, Good Conduct medals; recipient Decree of Merit for outstanding contbn. to medicine and health care, 1995, Excellence in Tchg. award Nat. Capital Region Consortium Pathology Residency, 1997, Comdr.'s award US Army Walter Reed Med. Ctr., 1997. Mem.: AAAS, Md. Assn. Cytopathology, Washington Met. Assn. Cytology, Indian Anthropol. Soc., Ind. Sci. Congress, Md. Assn. Cytopathology, Belge de Cytologie Clinique (del. visit to People's Republic China 1987, internat. team cytologists exch. sci. knowledge with USSR 1990, del. visit to People's Republic China 1991, vis. Athens, Greece for European Congress of Cytology, 2005), Soc. of Armed Forces Med. Lab. Scientists, N.Y. Acad. Scis., Am. Soc. for Cytotech., Am. Soc. Clin. Pathologists, Am. Soc. Cytopathology, Am. Anthropol. Assn., Internat. Acad. Cytology, Am. Legion. Avocations: soccer, swimming, running, travel, theater. Home: 10110 Treble Ct Rockville MD 20850 Office: Walter Reed Army Med Ctr Dept Pathology Cytology Lab Washington DC 20307-0001 Office Phone: 202-782-1126. Personal E-mail: dey_rad@hotmail.com.

DE YOE, DAVID P., lawyer; b. Muskegon, Mich., July 18, 1948; s. Frank A. and Mildred E. (Jensen) DeY.; m. Ilene L. Nevel, May 26, 1979; children: Andrew, Mary, Emily, Peter. BA in Econs., U. Mich., 1970; JD, Stanford U., 1973. Bar: Ill. 1973, U.S. Dist. Ct. (no. dist.) Ill. 1973, Cal. 1975. Assoc. McDermott, Will & Emery, Chgo., 1973-79, ptnr., 1979—. Contbr. articles to profl. jours. Office: McDermott Will & Emery 227 W Monroe St Ste 4700 Chicago IL 60606-5096

DE YOUNG, DAVID SPENCER, astrophysicist, educator; b. Colorado Springs, Colo., Nov. 29, 1940; s. Henry C. and Zona L. (Church) DeY.; m. Mary Ellen Haney. BA, U. Colo., 1962; PhD, Cornell U., 1967. Rsch. physicist Los Alamos (N.Mex.) Nat. Labs., 1967-69; astronomer Nat. Radio Astronomy Obs., Charlottesville, Va., 1969-80, Kitt Peak Nat. Obs., Tucson, 1980—, assoc. dir., 1983-88, dir., 1988-94. Organizer numerous sci. confs.; mem. adv. bd. Aspen (Colo.) Ctr. Physics, 1977—, trustee, 1992—, pres., 2001—; mem. exec. com. steering com. San Diego Supercomputer Ctr., 1985-98, chmn., 1989-91; mem. steering com. Nat. Virtual Obs., 2000—, project scientist, 2001-, exec. com., 2001—; mem. Nat. Optical Astronomy Obs., Tucson, 1982—, assoc. dir., 1988-94; bd. dirs. WIYN Telescope Consortium, Tucson; mem. exec. com. Internat. Virtual Obs. Alliance, 2001—. Contbr. articles to profl. jours. NASA grantee. Fellow Am. Phys. Soc.; mem. Astron. Soc. Pacific, Am. Astron. Soc., Internat. Astron. Union, Internat. Union Radio Soc., Phi Beta Kappa. Office: Kitt Peak Nat Obs 950 N Cherry Ave Tucson AZ 85719-4933

DEYSHER, PAUL EVANS, retired management consultant; b. Reading, Pa., Oct. 16, 1923; s. Paul Stauffer and Ida Estelle (Evans) D.; m. Myrtle Constance Stover, June 17, 1950 (dec. Feb. 2003); children: David Paul, Mark Edward. BS, Albright Coll., 1945; M in Ednl. Adminstrn., Temple U., 1949. Math. and sci. tchr. Lebanon City (Pa.) Sch. Dist., 1950-56; asst. h.s. prin. Ocean City Sch. (N.J.) Dist., 1956-57; h.s. prin. Yeadon Sch. (Pa.), Dist., 1957-60; mgr. pers. adminstrn. Philco Corp., Phila., 1960-66; tng. specialist AMP, Inc., Harrisburg, Pa., 1966-80, supr. mgmt. tng., 1980-85, mgr. mgmt. tng. and devel., 1986, ret., 1986. Cons. and lectr. in field. Author: (poems) Anthologies of International Library of Poetry, 1999, 00; co-author: Transistor Fundamentals, 1962; contbr. chpts. to books and articles to profl. jours. Pres. Albright Coll., Lebanon County Alumni chpt., 1979—; trustee Albright Coll., Reading, Pa., 1985-89. Mem. NEA (life), Am. Soc. Pers. Adminstrn. (cert., sr. prof. in human resources), ASTD (past pres.), Internat. Soc. Poets (Disting. mem.), Phi Delta Kappa. Republican. Lutheran. Home: 39 S Mill St Lebanon PA 17042-3124

DE ZEGHER, CATHERINE, museum director, curator; b. 1955; Co-founder Kanaal Art Found., Kortrijk, Belgium, 1985, dir., 1987—2000; visiting curator Inst. of Contemporary Art, Boston, 1995—97; exec. dir. Drawing Center, NYC, 2000—. Lecturer U. of Leeds, Royal Coll. of Art, London, U. of London. Author: Inside the Visible: An Elliptical Traverse of Twentieth Century Art, in, of, and from the Feminine, 1996, The Precarious: Art and Poetry of Cecilia Vicuna and Quipoem, 1997, Mona Hatoum, 1997, Martha Rosler: Rights of Passage, 1997. Office: Drawing Ctr 35 Wooster St New York NY 10013

DEZII, CHRISTOPHER MICHAEL, medical/surgical nurse, medical researcher; b. Philadelphia, Pa., Nov. 14, 1958; s. Randolph and Margherita Dezii; m. Karen Ann Charlton, July 25, 1987; children: Allyson Michelle, Alexis Nicole. MBA, La Salle U., Phila., 1994. RN Phila., 1981. Dir. of patient care svcs./clin. coord. Hahnemann U. Hosp., Phila., 1990—94; sr. mgr. health econ. Bristol-Myers Squibb Co., Plainsboro, 1995—97, sr. mgr., outcomes rsch., 1997—2001, assoc. dir., sci. ops. virology, 2001—04, assoc. med. dir., 2004—. Contbr. articles to profl. jours. Recipient Pres.'s award, Bristol-Myers Squibb, 2001. Conservative. Avocation: music. Home: 36 Joanne Rd Holland PA 18966 Office: Bristol-Myers Squibb Co 777 Scudders Mill Road Plainsboro NJ 08536 Office Phone: 609-897-2718. Business E-Mail: christopherdezii@aol.com.

DEZURKO, EDWARD ROBERT, art educator; b. N.Y.C., Mar. 25, 1913; s. Edward and Hattie (Lehman) DeZ.; m. Madith Smith, July 30, 1938 (div. 1962); children: Robin Klein, Sandra Krchnak; m. Grace Crump, Sept. 5, 1964. BS in Edn., U. Ill., 1939, BS in Arch., 1940; MS in Arch., Columbia U., 1942; PhD, NYU, 1954. former registered arch. Tchr. Champaign (Ill.) H.S., 1941; tchr. arch. Kans. State Coll., Manhattan, 1942-47, Rice U., Houston, 1947-62; head dept. art Austin Coll., Sherman, Tex., 1962-66; prof. art, grad. coord. U. Ga., Athens, 1966-79, emeritus prof. art, 1979—. Draftsman, illustrator U.S. Naval Ordnance Lab., Washington, 1943-44. Author: Early Kansas Churches, 1949, Origins of Functionalist Theory, 1957, Vistas and Mazes, 1997, Through Cracks in the Wall, 2001; co-author: Man and the Cultural World, 1947; contbr. articles to profl. jours. Recipient Ga. Poet of Yr. award Nat. League Am. Pen Women, 1997, Internat. Order of Merit award. Mem. AIA, Ga. Poetry Soc., Author's Club Athens, Pi Delta Phi, Zeta Zeta. Avocations: poetry, gardening, travel. Office: Lamar Dodd Sch Art U Ga Athens GA 30602 Home: 350 Wilkinson Pky Apt 20 Toccoa GA 30577 Office Fax: 706-542-0226.

D'HAITI, FELICIA KATHLEEN (FELICIA KATHLEEN MESSINA), fine arts educator; BA, Georgetown U., 1991; MA, Rutgers U., 1995. Cert. Advanced Profl. Md. State Bd. of Edn., nat. bd. cert. tchr. art/early adolescence through young adulthood. Edn. program specialist Smithsonian Office of Edn., Washington, 1995—97; contractor Smithsonian Mag., Washington, 1997—98; fine arts tchr. Prince George's County Pub. Schools, Forestville, Md., 1999—. Recipient Armed Forces Comm. and Electronics Ednl. award, Dept. Def., 1987, Smithsonian Instn. award, 1996, Letter of Commendation, Andrew Jackson Mid. Sch., 2000, 2001; Georgetown U. grantee, 1987-1991, Md. State scholar, 1989, Ralph J. Bunche fellow, Rutgers U., 1992-1994, Trustees fellow, 1994-1995, U. Md. Student Support grantee, 1997-1999, Fulbright Meml. Fund Tchr. Program scholar, 2002. Mem.: ASCD, NEA, Am. Assn. Museums, Am. Ednl. Rsch. Assn., Prince George's County Educators Assn., Md. State Tchrs. Assn., Nat. Art Edn. Assn., Alpha Delta Kappa, Phi Delta Kappa. Independent. Roman Catholic. Avocations: travel, piano, museums, theater. Personal E-mail: fkmdhaiti@aol.com. E-mail: felicia.dhaiti@pgcps.org.

DHALIWAL, HERB (HARBANCE SINGH), legislator, former Canadian government official; b. Punjab, India, Dec. 12, 1952; BA Commerce, U. B.C., 1971. Mem. Ho. of Commons, Ottawa, 1993—, parliamentary sec to min. of fisheries & oceans, 1993—96, min. of nat. revenue, 1997-99, min. fisheries and oceans, 1999—2002, min. nat. resources, 2002—03, min. with polit. responsibility for B.C., 2002—03. Office: Ho of Commons Rm 121 E Block Ottawa ON Canada K1A 0A6

DHAR, PROMILA, researcher; b. Anantnag, Kashmir, India, Jan. 6, 1962; arrived in U.S., 1999; d. Triloki Nath and Shanta Raina; m. Soman Dhar, Oct. 5, 1990; children: Jyotsna, Archit. BSc in Biophysics with honors, Punjab U., Chandigarh, India, 1985, MSc in Biophysics with honors, 1987; PhD in Biomechanics, Indian Inst. Tech., New Delhi, 1996. Sr. rsch. asst. Indian Inst. Tech., New Delhi, 1988-93, sr. rsch. fellow, 1993-95; rsch. assoc. All India Inst. Med. Scis., New Delhi, 1996-98, rsch. scientist Coun. for Sci. and Indsl. Rsch., 1998—2000. Contbr. articles to profl. jours. and procs. Mem. AAAS, Indian Biophys. Soc. (life), Assn. Physiologists and Pharmacologists India. Avocations: photography, gardening, reading. Home: 2308 Sedgewick Ct Naperville IL 60564-4385 E-mail: promilaska@yahoo.com.

D'HARNONCOURT, ANNE, museum director, museum administrator; m. Joseph J. Rishel, June 19, 1971. BA, Radcliffe Coll., 1965; MA with distinction, Courtauld Inst. Art, U. London, 1967. Curatorial asst. Phila. Mus. Art, 1967-69; asst. curator 20th Century art Art Inst. Chgo., 1969-71; curator 20th Century art Phila. Mus. Art, 1971-82, George D. Widener dir., 1982—. Mem. mus. panel NEA, 1976-78, mem. indemnity panel, 1985-88, mem. mus. program overview panel, 1986-87; mem. Indo-U.S. Subcommn. Edn. and Culture, 1983-87; bd. advs. Ctr. Advanced Study in the Visual Arts Nat. Gallery Art, 1987-89. Organizer: (with McShine) exhbn. Marcel Duchamp, 1973-74, (with others) Philadelphia: Three Centuries of American Art, 1976, Eight Artists, 1978, (with Percy) Violet Oakley, 1979, Futurism and the International Avant-Garde, 1980, (with Sims) John Cage: Scores and Prints, 1982; author: (with Walter Hopps) Etant Donnes. Reflections on a New Work by Marcel Duchamp, 1969, The Cubist Cockatoo: Preliminary Exploration of Joseph Cornell's Hommages to Juan Gris, 1978, John Cage: Paying Attention, 1993, also prefaces for various books. Bd. dirs. Henry Luce Found., Inc., N.Y.C.; trustee Fairmount Park Art Assn. Phila., Georgia O'Keeffe Found.; bd. trustees Japan Soc. N.Y.C.; bd. regents Smithsonian Instn. Fellow AAAS; mem. Am. Philos. Soc., Pa. Coun. Arts, 1992-99, Assn. Art Mus. Dirs. Office: Phila Mus Art Benjamin Franklin Pkwy & 26th St PO Box 7646 Philadelphia PA 19130 Office Phone: 215-684-7701.

DHAWAN, ATAM PRAKASH, engineering educator, dean; b. Moradabad, India, Mar. 30, 1956; came to U.S., 1985; s. Chandar Bhan Dhawan and Shanti Devi Kapoor; m. Nilam Dhawan, Mar. 5, 1982; children: Anirudh, Akshay. B of Engring., U. Roorkee, India, 1977, M of Engring., 1979; PhD,

U. Man., Winnipeg, Can., 1985. Asst. prof. elec. engring. U. Houston, 1985-88; from asst. prof. elec. and computer engring. to assoc. prof. U. Cin., 1988-95, prof. elec. engring., computer engring. and computer sci., 1995-96, dir. Ctr. Intelligence Vision Sys., 1994-96; prof./chmn. elec. engring. U. Tex., Arlington, 1996-97; adj. prof. radiol. scis. U. Tex. S.W., Dallas, 1996-98; prof. bioengring. U. Toledo, 1998-2000, asst. dean grad. studies/coll. engring., 1998-99, assoc. dean rsch. and grad. studies/coll. engring., 1998-2000; prof., chmn. elec. and computer engring. N.J. Inst. Tech., Newark, 2000—. Adj. assoc. prof. radiology U. Cin., 1990-95; mem. sci. adv. com. Life Spec Inc., Houston, 1997-99; mem. nat. adv. com. Rsch. Resource for Pharmacokinetic Studies, U. Wash., Seattle, 1999-2001; mem. external adv. com. Ohio Aerospace Inst., Cleve., 2000-01; dir. N.J. Ctr. for Multimedia Rsch., 2000-02; dir. NSF-NJ Inst. Tech. Industry Univ. Coop. Rsch. Ctr. Next Generation Video, 2000-02, N.J. Ctr. for Wireless Networking and Internet Security, 2002--. Author: (textbook) Medical Image Analysis, 2003; editor Internat. Jour. Computing Info. and Tech., 1997—; assoc. editor Internat. Jour. Pattern Recognition, 1999—; contbr. articles to profl. jours Recipient NIH F.I.R.S.T. award Nat. Cancer Inst., 1988-93, Martin N. Epstein award Student Paper Competition at Symposium of Computer Applications in Med. Care, 1984; Can. Commonwealth fellow U. Man., 1982-85. Fellow IEEE (assoc. editor Transactions on Biomed. Engring. 1996-2001, 2004—, asst. editor Transactions on Rehab. Engring. 1994-2001, workshop chair 1996-97, Engring. in Medicine and Biology Early Career Achievement award 1995), IEEE Engring. in Medicine and Biology (chmn. emerging techs. com. 1998-2000, chair workshop on Intelligent Med. Image Analysis: Principles to Recent Advances, Cancun, Mex. 2003, San Francisco 2004, conf. chair 2005), World Congress on Med. Physics and Biomed. Engring. (chmn. New Frontier in Med. Physics and Biomed. Engring. Track 1999-2000), Eta Kappa Nu Avocations: swimming, music, reading. Office: Chair ECE Dept NJ Inst Tech University Heights Newark NJ 07102 Office Phone: 973-596-5442. Business E-Mail: dhawan@adm.njit.edu.

DHAWAN, VIKAS, plastic surgeon; s. Satpal and Sudershan Dhawan; m. Veronika Georgiyevna Naumchenko; 1 child, Kalinda. MD, Moscow Med. Stomatological Inst., 1994, PhD, 1997. Rsch. fellow in plastic surgery U. Louisville, 1997—99; clin. fellow in hand and microsurgery Christine M. Kleinert Inst., U. Louisville, 1999—2000; cons. plastic surgeon European Med. Ctr., Am. Med. Ctr., Moscow, 2000—01; clin. fellow in brachial plexus surgery Ogori Daiichi Gen. Hosp., U. Yamaguchi, Japan, 2001—02; clin. instr. Ctrl. Inst. Stomatology, Moscow, 2003—; vis. fellow Plastic Surgery Ctr., Buffalo, 2004—. Contbr. articles to profl. jours. Mem.: Japanese Soc. for Surgery of the Hand, Assn. Plastic Surgeons India, Am. Soc. for Surgery of the Hand (assoc.), Indian Soc. for Surgery of the Hand (life). Office: Plastic Surgery Ctr 405 E Mich Ave 4 Au Gres MI 48703 E-mail: dr_vikasdhawan@hotmail.com.

D'HEURLE, FRANÇOIS MAX, research scientist, engineering educator; b. Paris, Nov. 23, 1925; came to U.S., 1946; s. Albert Emile and Odette (Valentini) d'H.; m. Adma Jeha, May 6, 1950; children: Amal, David, Alain. BSc Arts et Metiers, U. Paris, 1946; MS, Mich. Tech. U., 1948; PhD, Ill. Inst. Tech., 1958; D honoris causa, Royal Inst. Tech., Stockholm, 1995. Rsch. asst. U. Chgo., 1948-55; scientist IBM, Yorktown Heights, N.Y., 1958—. Prof. Royal Inst. Tech., Stockholm, 1995. Contbr. numerous articles to profl. jours.; holder 10 patents. Recipient award Am. Inst. Physics, 1991, Theory to Practice Prize Minerals, Metals and Materials Soc., 1998. Fellow IEEE (Cledo-Brunetti award 1989); Am. Vacuum Soc. (Gaede-Langmuir award 1990); mem. Minerals, Metals and Materials Soc., Materials Rsch. Soc. Home: Spring Valley Rd Ossining NY 10562 Office: IBM Rsch PO Box 218 Yorktown Heights NY 10598-0218 Office Phone: 914-945-1701. Business E-Mail: dheurle@us.ibm.com.

DHIR, VIJAY K., mechanical engineering educator; b. Giddarbaha, Panjab, India, Apr. 14, 1943; arrived in US, 1969; s. Harnand Lal and Parsinni Devi (Sofat) D.; m. Komal Lata Khanna, Aug. 31, 1973; children: Vinita, Vashita. BScME, Punjab Engring. Coll., India, 1965; MTechME, Indian Inst. Tech., 1969; PhD in Mech. Engring., U. Ky., 1972. Asst. devel. engr. Jyoti Pumps, Ltd., Baroda, India, 1968-69; postgrad. engr. Engring. Rsch. Ctr. Tata Engring. & Locomotive Co., Poona, India, 1969; rsch. asst. U. Ky., Lexington, 1969-72, rsch. assoc., 1972-74; asst. prof. chem., nuclear & thermal engring. dept. UCLA, 1974-78, assoc. prof., 1978-82, prof. mech., aerospace & nuclear engring. dept., 1982—, vice chmn. mech., aerospace & nuclear engring. dept., 1988-91, chmn. dept., 1994-2000, assoc. dean Henry Samueli Sch. Engring. and Applied Sci., 2001—02, interim dean, 2002—03, dean, 2003—. Cons. Nuclear Regulatory Commn., Seabulk Corp., Ft. Lauderdale, Fla., Argonne (Ill.) Nat. Lab., Pickard, Lowe & Garrick, Inc., Irvine, Calif., Rockwell Internat., Canoga Park, Calif., GE Corp., San Jose, Calif., Battelle N.W. Lab., Richland, Wash., Phys. Rsch., Inc., Torrance, Calif., Nat. Bur. Stds., Gaithersburg, Md., Los Alamos (N.Mex.) Nat. Lab., Sci. Applications Inc., El Segundo, Calif., Brookhaven Nat. Lab., Upton, N.Y.; chmn. numerous conf. sessions. Contbr. over 130 articles to profl. jours., over 130 papers to procs./conf. & symposia records; assoc. editor Applied Mechs. Rev., 1985-88, Jour. Heat Transfer, Transactions ASME, 1993-96, editor, 2000—; assoc. editor ASME Symposium Vol., 1978; referee numerous jours. Recipient Max Jakob award, ASME/AIChE, 2004. Fellow: AIChE (Donald Q. Kern award 1999), ASME (sr. tech. editor Jour. Heat Transfer 2000—05, Heat Transfer Meml. Award Sci. Category 1992), Am. Nuclear Soc. Office: Sch of Engring & Applied Sc U Calif 46-147 K Engineering IV Los Angeles CA 90024 Business E-Mail: vdhir@seas.ucla.edu.

DHRYMES, PHOEBUS JAMES, economist, educator; b. Cyprus, Oct. 1, 1932; s. Demetrios and Kyriaki (Neophytou) Dhrymiotis; m. Beatrice Bell Fitch, Dec. 10, 1972; children: Phoebus James, Philip Andrew, Alexander Robert. BA with highest honors, U. Tex., 1957; PhD, MIT, 1961. Asst. prof. econs. Harvard U., 1962-64; assoc. prof. econs. U. Pa., 1964-67, prof., 1967-73; prof. econs. Columbia U., N.Y.C., 1973—. Vis. prof. fin. Wharton Sch. U. Pa., 1984 Author: Econometrics: Statistical Foundations and Applications, 1970, 74, Distributed Lags: Problems of Estimation and Formulation, 1971, 81, Russian edit., 1982, Introductory Econometrics, 1978, Mathematics for Econometrics, 1978, 3d edit., 2000, Topics in Advanced Econometrics: Probability Foundations, 1989, Tropics in Advanced Econometrics: vol. II Linear and Non Linear Simultaneous Equations, 1994, Theoretical and Applied Econometrics: The Selected Papers of Phoebus J. Dhrymes, 1995, Time Series, Unit Roots and Cointegration, 1998; mng. editor, editor Internat. Econ. Rev., 1965-72; co-editor Jour. Econometrics, 1972-77, exec. coun., 1993—. Served with U.S. Army, 1952-54. Fellow Econometric Soc., Am. Stats. Assn.; mem. Am. Econ. Assn. Office: Columbia U Dept Econs New York NY 10027 E-mail: b.pid1@columbia.edu.

DHUE, STEPHANIE, television producer, reporter; BA in Comm., George Mason U. Prodr. The Insiders with Jack Anderson, Fin. News Network; prodr. CNBC, Ft. Lee, N.J.; sr. prodr., reporter Nightly Bus. Report, Washington. Office: NBR 1325 G St NW Ste 1005 Washington DC 20005-3126 Office Phone: 202-682-9029.

DIAISO, ROBERT JOSEPH, civil engineer; b. Jersey City, N.J., Jan. 3, 1940; s. Dominick A. and Marie M. (Sarno) DiA.; m. Elaine Ricca, June 8, 1963; 1 child, Michael. BS, U.S. Naval Acad., 1962; MCE, NYU, 1964; M in Urban and Regional Planning, U. Pitts., 1971; PhD, 1971, 1972; AA (hon.), Anne Arundel C.C., 1998. Engr. Clarke, Hartman & Dunn, 1955-57, 69; project dir. Inst. Urban Policy Analysis, 1970-71; assoc. partner Dewberry, Nealon & Davis, Annapolis, Md., 1971-81; sr. assoc. Dewberry & Davis, Annapolis, 1981-82; prin. Dewsberry & Davis, 1983-84; pres. Property Improvement Collaborative, Inc., 1984-90, LandScope, 1985—2000; dir. LandTech Corp., 1985-88, mng. dir., 1988-94; CEO, FM Tech Corp., 1991-94; pres., CEO The Tech Group, 1993—. Organizer, dir. Bay Nat. Bank; Land Tech. Corp., 1986—; bd. dirs. Scotts Seaboard Corp.; pres. Peacock Mgmt. Systems. Pres., Crofton Civic Assn., 1973, trustee emeritus, 1998; chmn. bd. trustees by 3 govs. Anne Arundel C.C., 1974-98, trustee emeritus, 1998; mem. County Zoning Adv. Task Force, 1983-84; mem. county coun. adv. com. on adequate facilities, 1977-78; bd. dirs. Anne Arundel Trade Coun.; chmn. Public Works Rev. Bd.; mem. Sewer Allocation Task Force; chmn. County Exec. Transition Task Force, 1982; mem. County Exec. Transition Team, 1991, County Exec. USN David Taylor Naval Facility Reuse Com., 1996; mem. Gov's. com. on Affordable Housing, 1976-78; mem. adv. bd. Patuxent Water Reclamation Plant; mem. adv. com. Crofton on Municipal Incorp.; bldg. com. St. Elizabeth Ann Seton Ch. Served with USAF, 1962-69. Named Bus. Leader of Yr., Anne Arundel Trade Coun., 1982; HEW fellow, 1970-72. Mem. ASCE, Am. Planning Assn., Am. Inst. Certified Planners, Nat. Soc. Profl. Engrs., Assn. County Engrs. Roman Catholic. Office: 147 Old Solomons Island Rd Annapolis MD 21401-0903

DIAKOS, MARIA LOUISE, lawyer; b. Buffalo, Jan. 31, 1959; d. Louis K. and Deanna (Doerr) D.; m. Michael Manolitsas. BA in Polit. Sci., SUNY, Buffalo, 1979, JD, 1982. Bar: N.Y. 1983. Assoc. counsel divsn. corps. N.Y. Dept. of State, Albany, 1982-84; assoc. Sargent & Repka, P.C., Cheektowaga, N.Y., 1984-85; pvt. practice, Amherst, N.Y., 1985—. Hearing officer small claims assessment rev. 8th Jud. Dist. N.Y. Supreme Ct., Buffalo, 1986-97; sr. closing atty. Pub. Abstract Corp., Ticor Title Ins. Co., Niagara Sq. Abstract Co., Buffalo, 1995—. Founding mem. joint pub. policy com. Hellenic Am. Women, Washington; mem. parish coun. Hellenic Orthodox Ch. of Annunciation, Buffalo, 1985-88, 93-98, parish legal advisor, 1995-98, treas., 1995, interim treas., sec., 1996; founding mem., legal advisor Hellenic Charitable Found., Inc., Buffalo. Mem. Women's Philoptochos Com. (recording sec. 1984-85, corr. sec. 1995-97), Buffalo and Western N.Y. Women in Travel, Variety Club Women. Democrat. Eastern Orthodox. Avocations: travel, cruising, spectator sports, sewing, cooking. Home: 9 Omega Dr Rochester NY 14624-5415 Office: 1449 Eggert Rd Amherst NY 14226-3356

DIAL, DAVID EMORY, librarian; b. Cleve., Apr. 17, 1955; s. Robert Joel and Donna Louise (Hudson) D.; m. Sharon Ann Takacs, May 18, 1985; children: Andrew J., Amy Elizabeth, Melissa Marie. BA, Baldwin-Wallace Coll., 1977; M of Libr. and Info. Sci., Clarion State U., 1978. Cert. netware adminstr. Dir. New Madison Pub. Libr., Ohio, 1978-82, Grafton-Midview Pub. Libr., 1982-96; internet trainer Stow-Munroe Falls Pub. Libr., Stow, 1997—2000; tech. libr. Wayne Co. Pub. Libr., Wooster, 2000—03; libr. Ind. Wesleyan U., Independence, 2003—. Coord. automation and tech. divsn. Ohio Libr. Coun., 2000. Mem. ALA, Ohio Libr. Coun., Libr. and Info. Tech. Assn., Reference and User Svcs. Assn. Republican. Avocations: reading, computer programming, public relations. Home: 382 Chapel Cir Berea OH 44017-2343 Office: Indiana Wesleyan University Cleveland Education and Conferencing Ctr 4100 Rockside Road Independence OH 44131 Office Phone: 216-525-6160. E-mail: davedial@att.net.

DIAMA, BENJAMIN, retired secondary school educator, artist, composer; b. Hilo, Hawaii, Sept. 23, 1933; s. Agapito and Catalina (Buscas) D. BFA, Sch. Art Inst. Chgo., 1956. Cert. tchr., Hawaii. Tchr. art, basketball coach Waimea (Kauai, Hawaii) High Sch., 1963-67; tchr. music and art Campbell High Sch., Honolulu, 1967-68; tchr. math. and art Waipahu High Sch., Honolulu, 1968-69; tchr. art and music Palisades Elem. Sch., Honolulu, 1969-70; tchr. typing, history, art and music Honokaa (Hawaii) High Sch., 1970-73; tchr. music Kealakehe Sch., Kailua, 1973-74; ret., 1974. Author, writer, composer: Hawaii, 1983; author: Poems of Faith, 1983-88, School One vs. School Two On The Same School Campus, 1983, The Calendar-Clock Theory of the Universe with Faith-- Above and Beyond, 1984-90, Phonetic Sound-Musical Theory, 1990; contbg. author: Benjamin Diama-- The Calendar Clock Theory of the Universe, 1991, 92, (poetry) Celebration of Poets, 1998, Poets Elite, Internat. Soc. of Poets, 2000; prodr., composer (Cassette) Hawaii I Love You, 1986; inventor universal clock, double floater boat, Gardener's Water Box, Full Court Half Court 6 vs. 6, 3 Offense-3 Defense Basketball Game. Recipient Achievement award Waimea Dept. Edn., 1964-67, Purchase award State Found. Arts on Culture and the Arts, 1984, State Found. Arts and Culture Acquisition Painting Art award State of Hawaii Govt. Art Collection, Lifetime Achieve. award Internat. Biographical Ctr., 2005 Mem. NEA, Hawaii Tchrs. Assn., Hawaii Edn. Assn., AAAS, Nat. Geog. Soc., Smithsonian Assocs., ASCAP, N.Y. Acad. Scis., Nat. Libr. Poetry (assoc.), Internat. Soc. Poets, Am. Geophysical Union. Mem. Salvation Army. Achievements include design of slip on-pull a step lace walking aid foot or shoe slipper supporter. Avocations: singing, writing science, coaching basketball. Home: PO Box 2997 Kailua Kona HI 96745-2997 Office Phone: 808-329-9789.

DIAMAN, NICKOLAS ANTONY, writer, photographer; b. San Francisco, Nov. 1, 1936; s. Petros Nikolaos Diamantides and Evanthia Chrisopoulos. BA, U. So. Calif., L.A., 1958. Coord. Queer Blue Light, N.Y.C., 1971-72, San Francisco, 1973-77, The Antares Found., San Francisco, 1976-79; dir. Persona Prodns., San Francisco, 1976-99; exec. dir. Aegean Friends, San Francisco, 2000—. Author: Ed Dean is Queer, 1978, The Fourth Wall, 1980, Second Crossing, 1982, Reunion, 1983, Castro Street Memories, 1988, Private Nation, 1997; prodr. (videos) Ohio Gay Pride Week, 1972, Larry Goldman Works, 1976, Cut Sleeve, 1991. Home: 2950 Van Ness Ave #4 San Francisco CA 94109-1036 Home Fax: 707-922-1236. E-mail: nadiaman@aol.com.

DIAMANDIS, PETER H., foundation administrator; Undergraduate and graduate degree in Aerospace Engring., MIT; MD, Harvard Med. Sch. Founder Intenat. MicroSpace, Inc. (acquired by CTA Inc.); v.p., commercial space CTA Inc.; founder, pres., chmn. X PRIZE Found., Inc., (originally in Rockville, Md., but now in St. Louis), 1995—; pres., COO Angel Technologies Corp. Co-founder, trustee Internat. Space U., Strasbourg, France, 1987—; co-founder Space Adventures, Zero Gravity Corp. (ZERO-G). Founded Students for the Exploration and Development of Space (SEDS). Recipient Kresge award, MIT, Space Industrialization Fellowship award, 1986, Aviation Week and Space Technology Laurel, 1988, Pioneer award, Space Frontier Found., 1993, K.E. Tsiolkovsky award, 1995. X PRIZE Foundation developed the X PRIZE in May, 1996. This prize is a $10,000,000 prize to jumpstart the space tourism industry through competition among the most talented entrepreneurs and rocket experts in the world. In 2004, the X PRIZE was officially re-named the ANSARI X PRIZE. Office: X Prize Found Inc 722-A Spirit of St Louis Blvd Chesterfield MO 63005 Address: X Prize Found inc Sonnenschein Laura L Carley One Metropolitan Sq Ste 3000 Saint Louis MO 63102

DIAMANT, ANITA, writer; b. NYC, June 27, 1951; d. Maurice and Helene Diamant; m. James R. Ball, June 11, 1982; 1 child, Emilia. AB, Washington U., St. Louis, 1973; MA, SUNY, Binghamton, 1975. Sr. staff writer Boston Mag., 1986-88; columnist Boston Globe mag., 1988-95; freelance writer, 1988—; columnist Jewishfamily.com., Boston, 1998-99; commentator WBUR-FM, Boston, 1994-96; contbg. editor Parenting Mag., 1994-95. Author: The New Jewish Wedding, 1985, Living a Jewish Life, 1991, The New Jewish Baby Book, 1994, Bible Baby Names, 1996, Choosing a Jewish Life: A Handbook for People Converting to Judaism and Their Family and Friends, 1997, The Red Tent, 1997, Saying Kaddish: How to Mourn as a Jew, 1998, How to be a Jewish Parent, 2000, Good Harbor, 2001, Pitching My Tent, 2003, The Last Days of Dogtown, 2005; editor: Equal Times, 1977—78; contbr. to profl. publs. and mags. Founder, pres. Mayyim Hayyim Living Waters and Cmty. Mikveh and Edn. Ctr., 2000—. Recipient Book of Yr. award Boston Author's Club, 1998, Significant Jewish Book of Yr. award UAHC Reform Judaism Mag., 1999, Booksense Book of Yr. award, 2001. Jewish. E-mail: anitaweb@aol.com.

DIAMOND, ARTHUR MANSFIELD, JR., economics professor; b. South Bend, Ind., May 23, 1953; s. Arthur Mansfield and Dagny (Lenon) D.; m. Jeanette N. Medewitz, 1991; 1 child, Jennifer Nicole Medewitz Diamond. BA, Wabash Coll., 1974; MA in Philosophy, U. Chgo., 1975, MA in Econs., PhD in Philosophy, U. Chgo., 1978. Asst. prof. econs. Ohio State U., Columbus, 1981-86; assoc. prof. econs. U. Nebr., Omaha, 1986-91, Frederick W. Kayser prof., 1991-97, Noddle prof., 1997—2003, Lucas prof., 2003—. Sr. rsch. assoc., Ctr. for Human Resource Rsch., Columbus, 1981-83. Contbr. articles to profl. jours. Postdoctoral fellow U. Chgo., 1978-81; NSF grantee, 1983-84, 92-95. Mem. Am. Econ. Assn., Western Econ. Assn., So. Econ. Assn., History of Econs. Soc., Phi Beta Kappa. Libertarian. Office: U Nebr Coll Bus Adminstrn Omaha NE 68182-0048 Office Phone: 402-554-3657. Business E-Mail: adiamond@mail.unomaha.edu.

DIAMOND, BERNARD ROBIN, lawyer; b. Bronx, N.Y., July 3, 1944; m. Elizabeth Heimbuch, Oct. 20, 1976; children: Jessica, Carey, Erin. BA, Rutgers U., 1966; JD, Bklyn. Law Sch., 1972. Bar: N.Y. 1973, U.S. Dist. Ct. (so. and ea. dists.) N.Y. 1973, U.S. Ct. Appeals (2d cir.) 1974. Gen. counsel The Trump Orgn., N.Y.C., 1995—. Mem. Assn. of the Bar of the City of N.Y. Office: Trump Orgn 725 5th Ave Fl 26 New York NY 10022-2520

DIAMOND, BRIAN, lawyer; BA, SUNY, Stony Brook, 1978; JD, Bklyn. Law Sch., 1982. Bar: NY 1983. Ptnr., real estate practice Stroock & Stroock & Lavan LLP, NYC, mem., operating exec. com. Editor-in-chief Bklyn. Law Rev. Mem.: Comml. Mortgage Securities Assn., NY State Bar Assn. Office: Stroock & Stroock & Lavan LLP 180 Maiden Ln New York NY 10038-4982 Office Phone: 212-806-5569. Office Fax: 212-806-6006. Business E-Mail: bdiamond@stroock.com.

DIAMOND, CASEY See DAMJANOVICH, CHASLAV

DIAMOND, DAVID HOWARD, lawyer; b. N.Y.C., June 24, 1945; s. Philip and Betty (Resnikoff) D.; m. Barbara R. Jacobs, Sep. 6, 1969; children: John, Andrew, Jill. BA, SUNY, Binghamton, 1967; JD, Georgetown U., Washington, D.C., 1970. Bar: Va. 1970, D.C. 1971, N.J. 1972, N.Y. 1973, U.S. Supreme Ct. 1982, U.S. Dist. Ct. Asst. gen. counsel Nat. Treas. Employees Union, Washington, D.C., 1970-71; trial atty. Nat. Labor Relations Bd., Newark, N.J., 1971-73; assoc. Putney, Twombly, Hall & Hirson, N.Y.C., 1973-76; ptnr. Guggenheimer & Untermeyer, N.Y.C., 1976-86, Summit, Rovins & Felderman, N.Y.C., 1986-89, Patterson, Belknap, Webb & Tyler, N.Y.C., 1989-91, Proskauer, Rose LLP, N.Y.C., 1991—. Contbg. editor: Developing Labor Law, 1975-82, The Fair Labor Standards Act, BNA, 2000. Pres., dir. Birchwood Civic Assn., Jericho, N.Y., 1985-95; trustee Jericho Libr. Bd., 1994—, pres. 2004—. Mem. ABA (sect. labor and employment law, com. fed. labor standards), N.Y. State Bar Assn. (com. on individual and employee rights). Avocations: biking, tennis, whitewater rafting. Home: 18 Briar Ln Jericho NY 11753-2212 Office: Proskauer Rose LLP 1585 Broadway Fl 27 New York NY 10036-8299

DIAMOND, DIANA LOUISE, editor, graphic artist; b. Floral Park, NY, Feb. 4, 1937; d. Louis Bartholomew and Helen Stephanie (Strzelecki) Chmielewski; m. Horace Williams Diamond, Jr., June 29, 1958 (div. 1975); children: Bruce Williams, Scott Kenneth, Kent Christopher, Mark Patrick. BA in English, U. Mich., 1958. Reporter Lerner Newspapers, Highland Park, 1970-72, mng. editor, 1972-78, suburban coord., 1974-78; corr. (part-time) The N.Y. Times, 1975-78; prof. journalism fellow Stanford U., 1978-79, sr. writer, editor, spl. asst. to pres., 1983-88, exec. asst. to v.p. and dean Sch. of Medicine, 1988-89; writer, editl. bd. San Jose (Calif.) Mercury News, 1979—81; editor, sect., spl. projects editor Sunday Opinion, 1981; editor-in-chief Calif. Lawyer, 1981—83; spl. asst. to pres. Stanford U. Hosp., 1990-93, mgr. publs., 1993-94; pres. Diamond Comm. and Design, Palo Alto, Calif., 1994—2005. Columnist Palo Alto Daily News, 2001—, exec. editor Daily News Newspaper, 2005—. Bd. dirs. Midpeninsula Citizens for Fair Housing, pres., 1983-86; bd. dirs. New Forum, 1985-90, pres., 1987-89; bd. dirs. Pacific Art League, 1989-94, Palo Alto Centennial '94, 1990-94, Palo Alto chpt. ARC, 2000—; founder, chmn. bd. dirs. RotaCare Internat., 1992—. Recipient Nat. Blue Ribbon Newspaper award, 1976-78; 3rd pl. Ill. Editor of Yr. contest, 1974; 1st pl. for best feature story, Ill. Press Assn., 1976, Suburban Newspapers Am., 1977; 2d pl. for best column Nat. Newspaper Assn., 1977, Maggie award We. Pubs. Assn., Silver Six award Internat. Bus. Comm., 1996, Crystal award Communicators Group, 1998, 1st pl. best column Pa. Press Assn., 2002. Mem. Palo Alto Red Cross (bd. dirs.), Rotary (pres. Palo Alto chpt. 1999-2000). Home: 2512 Cowper St Palo Alto CA 94301-4218 Office: Daily News 324 High St Palo Alto CA 94301 E-mail: diana@dianadiamond.com.

DIAMOND, EUGENE CHRISTOPHER, lawyer, health facility administrator; b. Oceanside, Calif., Oct. 19, 1952; s. Eugene Francis and Rosemary (Wright) D.; m. Mary Theresa O'Donnell, Jan. 20, 1984; children: Eugene John, Kevin Seamus, Hannah Rosemary, Seamus Michael, Maeve Therese. BA, U. Notre Dame, 1974; MHA, St. Louis U., 1978, JD, 1979. Bar: Ill. 1979. Staff atty. AUL Legal Def. Fund, Chgo., 1979-80; adminstrv. asst. Holy Cross Hosp., Chgo., 1980-81, asst. adminstr., 1981-82, v.p., 1982-83, counsel to adminstr., 1980—, exec. v.p., 1983-91; exec. v.p., COO, St. Margaret Mercy Healthcare Ctrs., Hammond, Ind., 1991-93, pres., CEO, 1993—2004, regional COO, 2001—04, regional CEO, 2004—. Cons. Birthright of Chgo., 1979—, mem. benefit com., 1981—; bd. dirs. Hammond C. of C., 1993, North West Ind. Forum. Mem.: Chgo. Bar Assn. Roman Catholic. Office: St Margaret Mercy Healthcare Ctrs 5454 Hohman Ave Hammond IN 46320-1999 Office Phone: 219-933-2178. Business E-Mail: gene.diamond@ssfhs.org.

DIAMOND, GUSTAVE, federal judge; b. Burgettstown, Pa., Jan. 29, 1928; s. George and Margaret (Solinsky) D.; m. Emma L. Scarton, Dec. 28, 1974; 1 dau., Margaret Ann; 1 stepdau., Joanne Yoney. AB, Duke U., 1951; JD, Duquesne U., 1956. Bar: Pa. bar 1958, U.S. Ct. Appeals bar 1962. Law clk. to judge U.S. Dist. Ct., Pitts., 1955-61; 1st asst. U.S. atty. Western Dist. Pa., 1961-62, U.S. atty., 1963-69; partner firm Cooper, Schwartz, Diamond & Reich, Pitts., 1969-75; formerly individual practice law Washington, Pa.; former solicitor Washington County, Pa.; judge U.S. Dist. Ct. Western Dist. Pa.; chief judge U.S. Dist. Ct. (we. dist.) Pa., 1992-94, sr. judge, 1994—. Chmn. Jud. Conf. Com. on Defender Svcs. Mem. ABA, Fed. Bar Assn., Pa. Bar Assn., Allegheny County Bar Assn., Washington County Bar Assn. Office: US Dist Ct 821 US Courthouse 7th St Rm 2 Pittsburgh PA 15219

DIAMOND, HEIDI JANICE, marketing professional; b. Washington, Dec. 8, 1958; d. Lawrence David and Vicky (Katz) D. BS, U. Md., 1979; postgrad., Boston U., 1976-78; MBA, Am. U., 1989. Account exec. Abramson Assocs., Washington, 1980-82; account exec., media dir. KMD Media, Arlington, Va., 1982-83; mktg. mgr. Hardee's Food Systems, Annapolis, Md., 1983-84, sr. mktg. mgr., 1984-86; dir. field advt. planning and devel. Erols, Inc., Springfield, Va., 1986, dir. advt., planning and devel., 1986-88, dir. mktg., 1988—; sr. v.p. mktg., creative and bus. develop. The Food Network, 1998—2000, sr. v.p. strategic network planning/develop., 2001; exec. v.p. AMC Networks and Rainbow Media, 2001—02; exec. v.p., pres. TV Martha Stewart Living Omnimedia, NYC, 2002—05, cons., 2005—. Named Washington Woman of Yr. Washington Woman Mag., 1986, 87; recipient Viddies award, 1989. Mem. Women in Advt. and Mktg. (bd. dirs. 1983-86). Democrat. Jewish. Office: Martha Stewart Living Omnimedia Inc 11 W 42nd St New York NY 10036*

DIAMOND, JARED MASON, biologist, writer; b. Boston, Sept. 10, 1937; m. Marie Cohen; children: Max, Joshua. BA in biochemical sciences, Harvard U., 1958; PhD in physiology, Cambridge (Eng.) U., 1961. Jr. fellow, Soc. Fellows Harvard U., 1962—65; assoc. in biophysics Harvard Med. Sch., 1965—66; assoc. prof. physiology UCLA Med. Sch., 1966—68, prof., 1968—; now prof. geography UCLA. Rsch. assoc. ornithology Am. Mus. Natural History, 1973—, LA County Mus. Natural History, 1985—; contbg. editor Discover mag., 1984—; bd. dirs. World Wildlife Fund, 1993—. Author: The Avifauna of the Eastern Highlands of New Guinea, 1972, The Third Chimpanzee: The Evolution and Future of the Human Animal, 1992 (Rhone-Poulenc Science Book Prize, 1992), Why is Sex Fun? The Evolution of Human Sexuality, 1997, Guns, Germs, and Steel: The Fates of Human Societies, 1997 (Phi Beta Kappa Sci. Book Prize, 1997, Pulitzer Prize, 1998, Cosmos Prize, Japan, 1998, Rhone-Poulenc Science Book Prize, 1998), Collapse: How Societies Choose to Fail or Succeed, 2004; co-author: Birds of New Guinea, 1986, The Birds of Northern Melanesia: Speciation, Ecology, and Biogeography, 2001; co-editor (with M.L. Cody): Ecology and Evolution of Communities, 1975; co-editor: (with T.J. Case) Community Ecology, 1986.

Recipient Disting. Achievement Award, Am. Gastroent. Assn., 1975, Bowditch Prize, Am. Physiol. Soc., 1976, Burr Medal, Nat. Geog. Soc., 1979, Carr Medal, 1989, Coues Award, Am. Ornithologists' Union, 1998, Nat. Medal Science, 1999, Tyler Prize for Environ. Achievement, 2001; MacArthur Found. Fellowship, 1985. Fellow: Am. Acad. Arts and Scis.; mem.: NAS, Am. Philos. Soc. Office: UCLA Med Ctr Dept of Physiology 10833 Le Conte Ave Los Angeles CA 90095-3075*

DIAMOND, JESSICA, artist; b. Bronx, N.Y. BFA, Sch. Visual Arts, N.Y.C., 1979; MFA, Columbia U., N.Y.C., 1981. One-woman shows include Standard Graphic, Cologne, Germany, 1990, Jablonka Gallery, Cologne, 1991, Gallery Fahnemann, Berlin, 1991, Gallery Massimo DeCarlo, Milan, 1993, Ynglingagatan 1, Stockholm, 1994, Rix, Linköping, Sweden, 1996, Galerie Analix, Geneva, 1996, Deitch Projects, N.Y., 1996, le Consortium, Dijon, France, 1997, Vera Van Laer Gallery, Antwerp, Belgium, 1998, Ota Fine Arts, Tokyo, 1999, Mus. Het Domein, Sittard, The Netherlands, 1999, Birmingham (Ala.) Mus. of Art, 2000, Art Gallery-York U., Toronto, 2001, Montreal Mus. Fine Arts, 2002; exhibited in group shows at Mus. van Hedendaagse Kunst Ghent, Belgium, 1993, Venice (Italy) Biennale, 1993, Vorarlberger Kunstverein, Bregenz, Austria, 1993, Corner House, Manchester, Eng., 1994, Deichtorhallen Hamburg, Germany, 1994, Mus. Contemporary Art, Sydney, Australia, 1994, Serpentine Gallery, London, 1994, Watari-um Mus., Tokyo, 1995, Kunsthalle Bern, Switzerland, 1995, Galerie Fahnemann, Berlin, 1996, Whitney Mus. Am. Art, N.Y.C., 1997, Stedelijk Mus. voor Actuele Kunst, Ghent, Belgium, 1999, Paula Cooper Gallery, N.Y.C., 1999, Tate Gallery Liverpool, Eng., 1999, Kunstmuseum Bonn, Germany, 1999, Kunstlerhaus Wien, Vienna, 2000, Sonsbeek 9, Arnhem, The Netherlands, 2001, The Tang Tchg. Mus. and Art Gallery, Skidmore Coll., Saratago Springs, N.Y., 2001, Casino Luxembourg, 2002, Neues Mus., Germany, 2002, MIT List Visual Arts Ctr., Cambridge, Mass., 2003, Inst. of Contemporary Art, Phila., 2004. Recipient award Nat. Endowment for Arts, 1989; John Simon Guggenheim Meml. Found. fellow, 2000. Home: 549 83d St Brooklyn NY 11209-4503

DIAMOND, LARRY, political scientist; BA, Stanford Univ, 1974, MA, 1978, PhD, 1980. Prof Vanderbilt Univ, 1980—85; sr fellow Hoover Inst, Stanford, Calif., 1985—; prof Stanford Univ, 1985—. Coord, Democracy Prog Inst for Internat Studies, Stanford Univ; co-dir Forum for Democratic Studies, Nat Endowment for Democracy; Fulbright vis. lectr. Bayero Univ., Kano, Nigeria, 1982—83; vis. scholar Academia Sinica, Taiwan, 1997—98; cons US Agency for Internat Devel, 2001—02; sr advisor Coalition Provisional Authority, Iraq, 2004. Co-editor: Journal of Democracy, 1990—; author: Developing Democracy: Toward Consolidation, 1999, Promoting Democracy in the 1990s: Actors and Instruments, Issues and Imperatives, 1999, Class, Ethnicity and Democracy in Nigeria: The Failure of the First Republic, 1988, Squandered Victory: The American Occupation and Bungled Effort to Bring Democracy to Iraq, 2005; contbr. articles to profl jours. Office: Hoover Institution Room 1202 Hoover Tower Stanford CA 94305-6010 Business E-Mail: diamond@hoover.stanford.edu.*

DIAMOND, M. JEROME, lawyer, retired state attorney general; b. Chgo., Mar. 16, 1942; s. Leo and Sonya (Pevsner) D.; m. Carol English Robinson; 8 children. AB, George Washington U., 1963; MA, U. Tenn., 1965, JD, 1968. Bar: Vt. 1968, U.S. Supreme Ct. 1975. Law clk. U.S. Dist. Judge Ernest Gibson, 1968-69; assoc. Kristensen, Cummings & Price, Brattleboro, Vt., 1969-70; state's atty. Windham County, Vt., 1970-74; atty. gen. State of Vt., 1975-81; atty., sr. ptnr. Diamond & Robinson, P.C., Montpelier, Vt., 1981—. Trustee Brooks Meml. Library, 1970-73; bd. trustees Vt. Law Sch., 2004-; chmn. Putney Zoning Bd. Adjustment, 1971-74; mem. Vt. Criminal Justice Tng. Council, 1974-81, Vt. Commn. Adminstrn. of Justice, 1975-81; mem. Vt. Adv. Group, U.S. Civil Rights Commn.; gen. campaign chmn. United Way Washington County, 1986-87, 88-89; bd. dirs. Nat. Coun. on Aging, 1990-93, Vt. Bar Found., 1997—, Vt. State Employees Credit Union, 1997—; internat. commr. Anti-Defamation League, 1988-93. Mem. Vt. State's Attys. Assn. (past pres.), Vt. Bar Assn., Vt. Bar Found. (bd. dirs. 1997—), Washington County Bar Assn., Nat. Assn. Atty. Gens. (v.p. 1978-79, pres. 1980), Ea. Regional Conf. Attys. Gen. (chmn. 1975-76), B'nai B'rith (internat. commr. anti-defamation league 1988-93, internat. bd. govs. 1990-92), Jewish Inst. for Nat. Security Affairs (bd. dirs. 1993—), Am. Judicature Soc. (bd. dirs., Vt. rep. 1994-00), Vt. State Employees Credit Union, 1997 (bd. dirs., v.p. of bd. VSECU 2000—, pres. bd. dirs. 2004-), Shriners, Masons, Montpelier Rotary Club (bd. dirs. 1998—, v.p. 2001-02, pres.-elect 2002-03, pres. 2003-04). Democrat. Jewish. Office: Diamond & Robinson PC PO Box 1460 Montpelier VT 05601 Office Phone: 802-223-6166. Business E-Mail: mjd@diamond-robinson.com.

DIAMOND, MARIAN CLEEVES, anatomy educator; b. Glendale, Calif., Nov. 11, 1926; d. Montague and Rosa Marian (Wamphler) Cleeves; m. Richard M. Diamond, Dec. 20, 1950 (div.); m. Arnold B. Scheibel, Sept. 14, 1982; children: Catherine, Richard, Jeffrey, Ann. AB, U. Calif., Berkeley, 1948, MA, 1949, PhD, 1953. With Harvard U., Cambridge, 1952-54, Cornell U., Ithaca, N.Y., 1954-58, U. Calif., San Francisco, 1959—62, prof. anatomy Berkeley, 1962—. Asst. dean U. Calif., Berkeley, 1967-70, assoc. dean, 1970-73, dir. The Lawrence Hall of Sci., 1990-95, dir. emeritus, 1995—; vis. scholar Australian Nat. U., 1978, Fudan U., Shanghai, China, 1985, U. Nairobi, Kenya, 1988. Author (with J. Hopson): Magic Trees of the Mind, 1998; author: Enriching Heredity, 1989; co-author: The Human Brain Coloring, 1985; editor: Contraceptive Hormones Estrogen and Human Welfare, 1978; contbr. over 155 articles to profl. jours. V.p. County Women Dems., Ithaca, 1957; bd. dirs. Unitarian Ch., Berkeley, 1969. Recipient Calif. Gifted award, 1989, C.A.S.E. Calif. Prof. of Yr. award, Nat. Gold medalist, 1990, Woman of Yr. award Zonta Internat., 1991, U. medal La. Universidad Del Zulia, Maricaibo, Venezuela, 1992, Alumna of the Yr. award U. Calif., Berkeley, 1995; Calif. Acad. Scis. fellow, 1991, Calif. Soc. Biomedical Rsch. Dist. Svc. award, 1998, Alumnae Resources-Women of Achievement Vision and Excellence award, 1999, Benjamin Ide Wheeler award 1999, Achievement award Calif. Child Devel. Adminstrs. Assn., 2001; named Disting. Scholar America, Am. Assn. U. Women, 1997; named to Internat. Educators Hall of Fame, 1999. Fellow AAAS, AAUW (sr.; fellowship chair 1970-85, 1st Sr. Scholar award 1997); mem. Am. Assn. Anatomists, Soc. Neurosci., Philos. Soc. Washington, The Faculty Club (Berkeley, v.p. 1979-85, 90-95). Avocations: hiking, sports, painting. Home: 2583 Virginia St Berkeley CA 94709-1108 Office: U Calif Dept Integrative Biology 3060 Valley Life Sciences Bldg Berkeley CA 94720-3116 Office Phone: 510-642-4547. Business E-Mail: diamond@berkeley.edu.

DIAMOND, NEIL LESLIE, singer, composer; b. Bklyn., Jan. 24, 1941; m. Marcia Murphey, 1975; children: Jesse, Micah; children by previous marriage: Marjorie, Elyn. Student, NYU. Formerly with Bang Records, Uni, MCA Records, Los Angeles, now rec. artist, singer, composer, Columbia Records; songs include Solitary Man, Cherry, Cherry, Kentucky Woman, I'm a Believer, September Morn, Sweet Caroline, Holly Holy, A Little Bit Me, A Little Bit You, Longfellow Serenade, Song Sung Blue, America, I Am, I Said; albums include: The Feel of Neil Diamond, 1966, Just for You, 1967, Neil Diamond's Greatest Hits, 1968, Velvet Gloves and Spit, 1968, Touching You, Touching Me, 1969, Brother Love's Travelling Salvation Show, 1969, Gold, 1970, Tap Root Manuscript, 1970, Shilo, 1970, Stones, 1971, Do It!, 1971, Hot August Nights, 1972, Moods, 1972, Rainbow, 1973, Jonathan Livingston Seagull, 1973, Greatest Hits, 1974, Serenade, 1974, Gold 1, 1974, Gold 2, 1974, Diamonds, 1975, Focus On, 1975, Beautiful Noise, 1976, And the Singer Sings His Song, 1976, Live at the Greek, 1977, I'm Glad You're Here With Me Tonight, 1977, You Don't Bring Me Flowers, 1978, 20 Golden Greats, 1978, Neil Diamonds, 1979, September Morn, 1980, Jazz Singer, 1980, Best Of, 1981, Solitary, 1981, Love Songs, 1981, On the Way to the Sky, 1981, Live Diamond, 1982, Heart Light, 1982, Song Sung Blue, 1982, Primitive, 1984, Headed For the Future, 1986, Hot August Night II, 1987, The Best Years of Our Lives, 1989, Lovescape, 1991, Neil Diamond The Greatest Hits, 1966-92, 1992, The Christmas Album, 1992, Neil Diamond Glory Road 1968-72, 1992, Live in America, 1994, His 12 Greatest Hits, 1996, As Time Goes By-Movie Album, 1998, Best of Neil Diamond, 1999, Best of The Movie Album, 1999, Three Cord Opera, 2001, The Essential, 2001, Play Me, 2002, Gold, 2005; (videos) Neil Diamond: Greatest Hits Live, 1988, Neil Diamond: Under a Tennessee Moon, 1996 (with others) Tennessee Moon, 1996; composer film scores Jonathan Livingston Seagull (Grammy award 1973), Every Which Way but Loose, 1978, The Jazz Singer (also actor), 1980; guest artist network TV shows; (TV specials) Neil Diamond's Christmas Special, HBO, 1992, ABC, 1993. Recipient 19 platinum albums, 28 gold albums.*

DIAMOND, PAUL STEVEN, federal judge, lawyer, educator; b. Bklyn., Jan. 2, 1953; s. George and Anna (Jaeger) D.; m. Robin Nilon. BA magna cum laude, Columbia U., 1974; JD, U. Pa., 1977. Bar: Pa. 1977, U.S. Dist. Ct. (ea. dist.) Pa, 1979, U.S. Ct. Appeals (3d cir.) 1979, U.S. Supreme Ct. 1983. Asst. dist. atty. Phila. Dist. Atty. Office, 1977-83; law clk. Supreme Ct. Pa., Phila., 1980; assoc. Dilworth, Paxson, Kalish & Kauffman, Phila., 1983-85, ptnr., 1986-91, Obermayer, Rebmann, Maxwell & Hippel, Phila., 1992—2004; judge U.S. Dist. Ct. (ea. dist.) Pa, 2004—. Lectr. Temple U. Sch. Law, Phila., 1990—92; mem. civil procedural rules com. Supreme Ct. Pa., 1995—98, treas. Pa. lawyers fund for client security bd., 1999—, chmn. Pa. lawyers fund for client security bd., 2002—; mem. civil procedural rules com. fed. jud. nominating commn., 1993, 1995—2000; vice chmn., chmn. Amicus Curiae Briefs Com., 1995—99. Author: Federal Grand Jury Practice and Procedure, 1990, rev. 4d edit., 2001. Mem. ABA (criminal justice sect., Amicus Curiae briefs subcom. 1984-99, grand jury subcom. 1991-93), Am. Law Inst., Pa. Bar Assn., Phila. Bar Assn. Republican. Jewish. Office: US Courthouse 601 Market St Rm 2609 Philadelphia PA 19106-1797

DIAMOND, RICHARD, retired secondary education educator; b. NYC, June 23, 1936; s. Oscar and Frieda (Rosenfeld) D.; m. Donna Jean Berkshire Wilson, June 14, 1961 (div. June 1974); m. Betty Ruth Jane Foster, Nov. 17, 1975; children: Thomas, Laura, Rick, Jeff. BA, U. Calif., Berkeley, 1958. Cert. tchr., Calif. Tchr. Riverside (Calif.) Unified Schs., 1959-67, 73-99, coord. social studies, 1967-69, program dir. compensatory edn., 1969-72, attendance officer, 1972-73; project mgr. Biotech. Sch., 1999—2001. Creater curriculum programs Afro-Am. history and Chicano studies, 1968; developer law and youth H.S. course, 1978, track coach, 1975-88. Contbr. articles and photographs to profl. jours. Co-creator h.s. vol. program, h.s. svc. learning coord., 1995—; active Riverside County Hist. Commn., 1997-2003; Dem. Party worker, 1964-72; Rep. Party worker, 1992—; historic commn. liaison Riverside County Archives Commn., 1998-2002; bd. dirs. Calif. Citrus Hist. State Park, 2000-02, sec., 2000-03; pres. Vail Ranch Restoration Assn., Inc., Temecula, Calif., 2000-02; journalist Tillamook Headlight Herald, 2004-; budget com. Bay City, Oreg., 2005— Named Social Studies Tchr. of Yr., Inland Empire Social Studies Assn., 1980, Tchr. of Yr., Arlington H.S., Riverside, 1992; recipient hon. svc. award Dist. Coun. PTA, Riverside, 1993, Johnny Harris Youth Action award City of Riverside, 1998. Mem. NEA, Calif. Tchrs. Assn., Riverside County Tchrs. Assn. Presbyterian. Avocations: gardening, travel, reading, woodworking. Office Phone: 503-812-9585. E-mail: diamond@where-eagles-soar.com.

DIAMOND, RICHARD MARTIN, nuclear chemist; b. L.A., Jan. 7, 1924; divorced; 4 children. BS, UCLA, 1947; PhD in Nuclear Chemistry, U. Calif. Berkeley, 1951. Instr. chemistry Harvard U., 1951-54; asst. prof. Cornell U., 1954-58; mem. sr. staff Lawrence Berkeley Lab., U. Calif., 1958—, sr. scientist emeritus, 1995—. Mem. U.S. Physics del. to Russia, 1966, rev. com. physics divsn. Oak Ridge Lab., 1972-74, Dept. of Energy rev. com. Brookhaven (n, gamma) Facility and Isotope Separator, 1983, 8pi Gamma Spect. Com., Chalk River, Canada, 1983, adv. com. Ind. Cyclotron Facility, 1980-83, Tandem-Linac Facility Argonne Nat. Lab., 1983-86, Holifield Rsch. Facility, 1988-90, Holifield Radioactive Ion Beam Facility, 1994-97; chmn. Gordon Conf. on Nuclear Chemistry, 1965, Gordon Conf. on Ion Exch., 1969, rev. com. UNISOR, Oak Ridge Nat. Lab., 1974-75, subcom. high spin and nuclei far from stability Dept. Energy-NSF, 1983; vis. fellow Japan Soc. for Promotion of Sci., 1981; co-organizer Int. Conf. Nuclear Physics, 1980, workshop on nuclear str., 1986, workshop Nat. Gamma-Ray Facility, 1987. Guggenheim fellow, 1966-67, Fullbright fellow, 1977. Fellow AAAS, Am. Phys. Soc. (shared Tom W. Bonner award 1980); mem. Am. Chem. Soc. (award in nuclear chemistry 1993). Achievements include research in nuclear spectroscopy, coulomb excitation, high-spin nuclear structure. Home: 574 Santa Clara Ave Berkeley CA 94707-1647 Office: Lawrence Berkeley Nat Lab One Cyclotron Rd MS88R0192 Berkeley CA 94720-8101 Office Phone: 510-486-5720. Business E-Mail: rmdiamond@lbl.gov.

DIAMOND, ROBERT E., JR., investment company executive; b. Concord, Mass. married; 3 children. BA, Colby Coll., 1974; MBA, Univ. Conn., 1977. Lectr. Univ. Conn. Sch. Bus., 1976—77; with Morgan Stanley, 1979—92, dir. mgmt. info., asst. to CFO, NYC, mng. dir. head European/Asian fixed income trading, London; with Credit Suisse First Boston, 1992—96, chmn. pres. & CEO, CS First Boston Pacific, Tokyo, vice chmn., head global fixed income & fgn. exch. NYC; pres., CEO investment banking & investment mgmt. Barclays plc, London, 1996—, mem. bd. & exec. com., 1997—. Trustee Colby Coll., Am. Sch., London; mem. adv. bd. Judge Inst., Cambridge Univ.; co-chmn. capital campaign Royal Coll. Music, London. Office: Barclays plc 5 The North Collonade Canary Wharf London E14 4BB England*

DIAMOND, ROBERT MACH, higher education administrator; b. Schenectady, N.Y., Mar. 5, 1930; s. Henry Gordon and Ruth Ada (Mach) D.; m. Dolores Lou Jacobs, Apr. 14, 1957; children: Harli Fait, H. Gordon. AB, Union Coll., Schenectady, 1951; MA, NYU, 1953, PhD, 1962. Secondary sch. tchr. math., TV tchr., TV project dir. Schenectady Pub. Schs., 1956-59; assoc. prof. edn., instructional TV prodn. supr. San Jose State U., 1959-63; dir. instructional rsch., vis. prof. U. Miami, Coral Gables, Fla., 1963-66; dir. instructional resources ctr., prof. edn. SUNY, Fredonia, 1966-71; asst. vice chancellor instrnl. devel., dir., prof. edn. Syracuse (N.Y.) U. Ctr. for Instructional Devel., 1971-97, rsch. prof., dir. Inst. Change in Higher Edn., 1998-99; rsch. prof. Syracuse U., 1999—; pres. Nat. Acad. Academic Leadership, St. Petersburg, Fla., 1999—. Nat. adv. bd. Bur. of Handicapped, Office of Edn.; dir. Focus in Tchg. Project, Fund for Improvement of Postsecondary Edn., Washington; Fulbright sr. lectr., 1976; dir. Nat. Project on Instnl. Priorities and Faculty Rewards, Lilly Endowment and Pew Charitable Trusts, Indpls., Phila., 1989-95; cons. NIH, NSF, Office of Edn., various colls., univs. and assns.; lectr. in field. Author: A Guide to Instrnl. Television, 1964, Designing and Improving Courses and Curricula in Higher Edn., 1989, Serving on Promotion Tenure, and Faculty Review Coms., A Faculty Guide, 1994, 2002, Preparing for Tenure Promotion and Ann. Rev., 1995, 2004; co-author: Instrnl. Development for Individualized Learning in Higher Edn., 1975, Nat. Study of Tchg. Assts., 1987, A Nat. Study of Rsch. Univs. on the Perceived Balance Between Rsch. and Undergraduate Tchr., 1991, 93, 95; editor: Field Guide to Academic Leadership, 2002; co-editor: Recognizing Faculty Work: Reward Systems for the Year 2000, 1993, Changing Priorities at Rsch. Univs., 1997, Designing & Assessing Courses and Curriculum, 1998, Aligining Faculty Records With Inst. Mission, 1999, The Disciplines Speak, Vol. I, 1995, Vol. II, 2000; mem. editl bd. Jour. Higher Ednl. Rsch. and Devel., South African Jour. Edn.; contbr. chpts. to books and articles to profl. jours. Bd. dir. Temple Adath, 1990-94, Jewish Family Svcs., Syracuse, 1975-83. With U.S. Army, 1973-75. Recipient award for Outstanding Practice in Instructional Devel., Assn. Ednl. Comm. and Tech., 1989. Mem. Am. Assn. Higher Edn. (cited innovations in the improvement of higher edn. 1994). E-mail: r.m.diamond@verizon.net.

DIAMOND, ROBERT MICHAEL, lawyer; b. NYC, Dec. 23, 1948; s. Meyer and Libby (Leventhal) Diamond; m. Amy B. Pullman, July 5, 1987; children: Michael Israel, Philip Brenner, Julia Rose. Student, Vassar Coll., 1969—70; AB, Colgate U., 1970; JD, Columbia U., 1974. Bar: DC 1974, Va. 1976, Md. 1982. Assoc. Fried, Frank, Harris, Shriver & Kampelman, Washington, 1974-75; from assoc. to ptnr. Reed Smith, LLP, Falls Church, Va., 1975—. *Robert Diamond practices real property law, with special emphasis on the planning, development, and financing of condominiums, mixed-use projects and planned unit developments, he prepares community association documents for developers and builders, reviews documents for lenders, ensures compliance with secondary mortgage market requirements, negotiates and litigates warranty and construction defect claims, and represents community associations. He has been active in the development of legislation concerning condominiums and planned communities since 1975. He is one of four drafters of the Uniform Condominium Act, and he also drafted portions of the Virginia and D.C. Condominium Acts. He also has authored a number of articles in the field.* Contbr. articles to profl. jours. and industry publs. Trustee Cmty. Assns. Inst., Alexandria, Va., sec., 1993, treas., 1994, pres.-elect, 1995; liaison to joint editl. bd. Uniform Real Estate Acts, 1997—. Recipient Oustanding Leadership award, Cmty. Assns. Inst., 1989, Pres.'s award for outstanding leadership, 1989—90, others. Mem.: Coll. Cmty. Assn. Lawyers. Avocations: scuba diving, classic automobiles. Office: Reed Smith LLP 3110 Fairview Park Dr Ste 1400 Falls Church VA 22042-4536 Office Phone: 703-641-4273. Business E-Mail: rdiamond@reedsmith.com.

DIAMOND, SEYMOUR, physician; b. Chgo., Apr. 15, 1925; s. Nathan Avruum and Rose (Roth) D.; m. Elaine June Flamm, June 20, 1948; children: Judi, Merle, Amy. Student, Loyola U., 1943-45; MB, Chgo. Med. Sch., 1948, MD, 1949. Intern White Cross Hosp., Columbus, Ohio, 1949-50; gen. practice medicine Chgo., 1950—; founder, dir. Diamond Headache Clinic, Ltd., Chgo., 1970—; dir. inpatient headache unit St. Joseph Hosp., Chgo.; prof. neurology Chgo. Med. Sch. at Rosalind Franklin U. Medicine & Sci., 1970-82, 85—, adj. prof. cellular and molecular pharmacology North Chicago, 1985—, clin. prof. family medicine, 1999—; clin. prof. dept. family medicine U. Medicine and Dentistry N.J. Sch. Osteo. Medicine, Stratford, NJ, 1994-98; cons. mem. FDA Orphan Products Devel. Initial Rev. Group. Lectr. dept. cmty. and family medicine Loyola U. Stritch Sch. Medicine, 1972-78; lectr. Falconbridge lecture series Laurentian U., Sudbury, Ont., Can., 1987; disting. lectr. neurology U. Tenn., 1992; AMA cons. on drug evaluation, 1993; mem. sci. com. neurology Internat. Jour. Pain Therapy, 1993; mem. panel Nat. Ctr. on Addiction and Substance Abuse, Columbia U., N.Y.C., 2003. Author: A Pain Specialist's Approach to the Headache Patient, 1994; (with Bill and Cynthia Still) The Hormone Headache, 1995; Diagnosing and Managing Headaches, 1994, 4th edit., 2004; (with Donald J. Dalessio) The Practicing Physician's Approach to Headache, 5th edit., 1992, More Than Two Aspirin: Help for Your Headache Problem, 1976, (with Judi Diamond-Falk) Advice from the Diamond Headache Clinic, 1982, (with Mary Franklin Epstein) Coping with Your Headaches, 1982, 2d edit., 1987, (with Arnold P. Friedman MD) Headache in Contemporary Patient Management series, 1983; (with Amy Diamond Vye) Headache and Diet, 1990; (with Michael Maliszewski) Sexual Aspects of Headaches, 1992; (with Mary A. Franklin) Conquering Your Migraine, 2001; (with Amy Diamond) Headache and Your Child, 2001; (with Merle L. Diamond) Contemporary Diagnosis and Management of Headache and Migraine, 2d edit., 2000, (with Mary A. Franklin) Headache Through the Ages, 2005; contbg. author: Wolff's Headache and Other Head Pain, 6th edit., 1993, Handbook of Pain Management, 2d edit., 1994, Nonsteroidal Anti-Inflammatory Drugs, 2d edit., 1994, Current Review of Pain, 1994, New Advances in Headache Research, 1994, Conn's Current Therapy, 1998, Advanced Therapy of Headache, 1999, Diamond and Dalessio's Practicing Physician's Approach to Headache, 6th edit., 1999; editor: Migraine Headache Prevention and Management; editor-in-chief Headache Quar., 1990-2002; editor-in-chief Headache and Pain, 2003—; mem. internat. editl. bd. Pediat. Drugs, 2001—; editl. cons. BIOSIS, 1986-90; contbr. numerous articles on headache and related fields to profl. jours. Bd. govs. Chgo. Med. Sch. at Rosalind Franklin U. Medicine & Sci. Recipient Disting. Alumni award Chgo. Med. Sch., 1977; Nat. Migraine Found. lectureship award, 1982, award Headache Consortium of New Eng., 1997, Cert. Appreciation, Chgo. Med. Soc., 1998, Presdl. award Alumni Assn. Chgo. Med. Sch., 2002; 1st recipient Migraine Trust lectureship, 1988; Brit. Migraine Trust 7th Internat. Migraine Symposium, London; Nat. Headache Found. Seymour Diamond fellow, 1993; Disting. lectr. in neurology U. Tenn., 1992. Fellow Royal Soc. Medicine; mem. AMA (Physicians Recognition awards 1970-73, 74, 77, 79, 82, 87, del. sect. clin. pharmacology and therapeutics 1987-89, mem. health policy agenda for Am. people, mem. cost effectiveness conf., del. reference com. "C" on edn., reference com. C, 1988), Am. Coun. on Sci. and Health (bd. sci. and policy advisors), Am. Assn. Study of Headache (exec. dir. 1971-85, pres. 1972-74, #1 regent mem. 1984, svc. award 1971-85, Lifetime Achievement award 1999), Nat. Headache Found. (pres. 1971-77, exec. dir. 1977-95, exec. chmn. 1995—, 1st recipient cert. of added qualification in headache mgmt. Nat. Bd. Cert. in Headache Mgmt. 2001), Assn. Applied Psychophysiology and Biofeedback (Presidl. Recognition award 2005), World Fedn. Neurology (exec. officer 1980-95, research group on migraine and headache), Ill. Acad. Gen. Practice (chmn. mental health com. 1966-70), Ill. Med. Soc., Chgo. Med. Soc., Assn. for Applied Psychophisiology and Biofeedback, Internat. Assn. Study of Pain, Am. Soc. Clin. Pharmacology and Therapeutics (chmn. headache sect. 1982-89, mem. com. coordination sci. sects. 1983-89), Postgrad. Med. Assn. (pres. 1981). Office: 467 W Deming Pl Ste 500 Chicago IL 60614-1726 Office Phone: 773-388-6390. Personal E-mail: MACF48@aol.com. Business E-Mail: clinic@diamondheadache.org. *I derive great satisfaction from helping a person who is totally disabled from pain to again lead a normal, functional life.*

DIAMOND, SHARI SEIDMAN, law professor, psychology professor; b. Chgo., Mar. 17, 1947; d. Leon Harry and Rita (Wolff) S.; m. Stewart Howard Diamond, Nov. 1, 1970; 1 child, Nicole. BA in Psychology, Sociology, U. Mich., 1968; MA in Psychology, Northwestern U., 1970, PhD in Social Psychology, 1972; JD with honors, U. Chgo., 1985. Bar: Ill. 1985. Rsch. assoc. Sch. Law U. Chgo., 1972-73; asst. prof. psychology and criminal justice U. Ill., Chgo., 1973-79, assoc. prof., 1979-90, prof., 1990-2000; assoc. Sidley & Austin, Chgo., 1985-87; sr. rsch. fellow ABF, Chgo., 1987—; lectr. U. Chgo. Law Sch., 1994-96; prof. law and psychology Northwestern U., 1999—, Stanton Clinton sr. rsch. prof., 2000-01, Howard J. Trienens prof. law, 2002—. Cons. govtl. and pub. interests groups including Rsch. Adv. Panel for U.S. Sentencing Commn., 1987-91; acad. visitor dept. law London Sch. Econs., 1981; hon. fellow Ctr. for Urban Affairs Northwestern U., Evanston, Ill., 1973-73; hon. rsch. assoc. U. London, 1970; speaker, lectr. in field; mem. NAS panel on sentencing rsch., 1981-83, panel on forensic DNA evidence, 1994-96. Editor Law and Soc. Rev., 1988-91; past mem. editorial bd. Law and Soc. Rev., 1983-88, Law and Human Behavior, Crime and Justice Annual, Evaluation Rev.; reviewer NSF; contbr. articles to profl. jours. Chair Coll. Edn. Policy Com., 1979-80; dir. tng. grant NIMH Crime and Delinquency, 1979-80. Fellow Northwestern U., 1968-69, NIMH, 1969-71; grantee Spencer Found., 1972-74, disting. scholar, grantee, U. Ill., 1995-98, Law Enforcement Assistance Adminstrn., 1974-76, Ctr. for Crime and Delinquency NIMH, 1976-81, NSF, 1980-83, 90-92, 99—; B. Kenneth West U. scholar, 1995-98. Fellow APA (Award for Disting. Contbns. to Rsch. in Pub. Policy 1991), ABA, Am. Psychol. Soc.; mem. Am. Psychology-Law Soc. (pres. 1987-88), Law and Soc. Assn. (trustee 1979-82). Office: Northwestern U Law Sch 357 E Chicago Ave Chicago IL 60611 Business E-Mail: s-diamond@law.northwestern.edu.

DIAMOND, SIDNEY, chemist, educator; b. N.Y.C., Nov. 10, 1929; s. Julius and Ethel D.; m. Harriet Urish, May 2, 1953; children: Florence, Julia. BS, Syracuse U., 1950; M.F., Duke U., 1951; PhD, Purdue U., 1963. Research engr. U.S. Bur. Public Rds. (now Fed. Hwy. Adminstrn.), Washington, 1953-61, research chemist, 1961-65; assoc. prof. engring. materials Purdue U., 1965-69, prof., 1969—2002, prof. emeritus, 2002—; pres. Sidney Diamond and Assocs., Inc. Mem. Nat. Materials Adv. Bd. Com. on Status of Research in U.S. Cement and Concrete Industries; chmn. Internat. Symposium on Durability of Glass Fiber Reinforced Concrete, Chgo., 1985; mem. adv. com. NSF Ctr. for Advanced Cement-Based Materials, 1989—. Contbr. numerous articles on cement and concrete to profl. jours.; editor: Cement and Concrete Research. Served with U.S. Army, 1951-53. Fellow Am. Ceramic Soc. (past trustee, Copeland award), Am. Concrete Inst., Am. Concrete Inst. (anderson award 1993); mem. ASTM, Internat. Congress on Chemistry of Cement (pres. sect. 6 of 8th congress), Materials Rsch. Soc. Home: 819 Essex St West Lafayette IN 47906-1534 Office: Purdue U Sch Civil Engring West Lafayette IN 47907 E-mail: diamond@ecu.purdue.edu.

DIAMOND, STANLEY JAY, lawyer; b. LA, Nov. 27, 1927; s. Philip Alfred and Florence (Fadem) D.; m. Lois Jane Broida, June 22, 1969; children: Caryn Elaine, Diana Beth. BA, UCLA, 1949; JD, U. So. Calif., 1952. Bar: Calif. 1953. Practiced law, LA, 1953—; dep. Office of Calif. Atty. Gen., LA, 1953; ptnr. Diamond & Tilem, LA, 1957-60, Diamond, Tilem & Colden, LA, 1960-79, Diamond & Wilson, LA, 1979—. Lectr. music and entertainment law UCLA; mem. nat. panel arbitrators Am. Arbitration Assn. Bd. dirs. LA Suicide Prevention Ctr., 1971-76. Served with 349th Engr. Constrn. Bn. AUS, 1945-47. Mem. ABA, Calif. Bar Assn., Los Angeles County Bar Assn., Beverly Hills Bar Assn., Am. Judicature Soc., Calif. Copyright Conf., Nat. Acad. Rec. Arts and Scis., Zeta Beta Tau, Nu Beta Epsilon. Office: 12304 Santa Monica Blvd Fl 3D Los Angeles CA 90025-2551 Office Phone: 310-820-7808. E-mail: standimond@aol.com.

DIAMOND, STUART, lawyer, educator; b. Camden, N.J., June 20, 1948; s. Irving H. and Ruth (Safran) D. BA in English, Rutgers U., 1970; JD, Harvard U., 1990; MBA, U. Pa., 1992. Bar: N.J. 1990, N.Y. 1991. Mcpl., investigative, polit., energy, tech. and fin. reporter Home News, New Brunswick, NJ, 1969—73, Newsday, L.I., NY, 1973—84, The N.Y. Times, N.Y.C., 1984—88; assoc. Morgan Stanley, N.Y.C., 1989, Sullivan & Cromwell, N.Y.C., 1989; assoc. dir. Harvard negotiation project, exec. dir. Conflict Mgmt. Group Harvard U. Sch. Law, Cambridge, Mass., 1990—92; v.p. MerOil, 1990—92; CEO Global Strategy Group, L.I., L.A., Phila., NY, 1991—; prof. Wharton Sch. U. Pa., Phila., 1993—, adj. law prof., 1994—; pres., CEO First Manhattan Capital Group, 1996—; pres. The Andean Group, 1997—2002; chmn., CEO i-Luxury.com, 2000—01; chmn. Summus, Inc., 2001, Digital Theatre Group, 2002—03, First Phila. Capital Group, 2003—. Lectr., TV commentator, 1978—, cons. U.N., 1991-97. Author: It's In Your Power, 1978, No-Cost, Low-Cost Energy Tips, 1980; documentary films: The Energy War, 1980, The Future is Now, 1981. Recipient Amos Tuck award nat. econ. reporting, 1978, 80, 82, Polk award nat. reporting, 1980, Pulitzer Prize, 1987, Tchg. award Wharton, 1997, 98, 2001, 02, 05. Mem. ABA. E-mail: sd@gsg.b2.

DIAMOND, SUSAN ZEE, management consultant; b. Okla., Aug. 20, 1949; d. Louis Edward and Henrietta (Wood) Diamond; m. Allan T. Devitt, July 27, 1974. AB, U. Chgo., 1970; MBA, DePaul U., 1979. Dir. study guide prodn. Am. Sch. Co., Chgo., 1972—75; supr. publs. Allied Van Lines, Broadview, Ill., 1975—78, sr. account svcs. rep., 1978—79; pres. Diamond Assocs. Ltd., Bensenville, Ill., 1978—. Author: Records Management: A Practical Guide, 3d edit., 1995, Seventeen Steps to Slimness: A Sherlockian Guide to Dieting, 2002; editor: The Serpentine Muse, 1996—, Serpentine Muse-ings, 2004, 2005. Mem.: Assn. Record Mgrs. and Adminstrs., Inst. Mgmt. Accts., Baker St. Irregulars, Adventuresses of Sherlock Holmes.

DIAMONSTEIN-SPIELVOGEL, BARBARALEE, writer, television producer; b. N.Y.C. d. Rubin Robert and Sally H. Simmons; m. Alan A. Diamonstein, July 22, 1956; m. Carl Spielvogel, Oct. 27, 1981. BA, BC, MA, Doctorate, NYU, 1963; DHL (hon.), Md. Inst. Coll. Art, 1990, Longwood U., 1995, PHL (hon.). Staff asst. The White House, Washington, 1663—1966; 1st dir. dept. cultural affairs City of New York, 1966—67; dir. of forums McCall Corp., 1967—69; editor spl. supplements, columnist Harper's Bazaar, 1969—71; spl. project dir., guest editor Art News, 1971—93. Columnist Ladies Home Jour., 1979-84; contbr. to Saturday Rev., Vogue, Ms., Partisan Rev., N.Y. Times, Condé Nast, Traveller, House and Garden, others; mem. faculty Hunter Coll., City U. N.Y., 1974-76, New Sch., 1976-84, Duke U. (Inst. Policy Sci.), 1978; arts cons. Sunday Morning CBS-TV, 1978-82; curator Buildings Reborn, Collaborations, Visions and Images, Remaking America, The Landmarks of N.Y. I, II, and III (internat. travelling museum exhibitions.), 1978—, and numerous others. Author: Open Secrets: 94 Women in Touch With Our Time, 1972; editor: Our 200 Years: Tradition and Renewal, 1975; TV interviewer, prodr. About the Arts, WNYC-TV, 1975—79; author: The World of Art, 1902-77, 75 Years of Art News, 1977; Leo Castelli Gallery, 1978; author: Buildings Reborn: New Uses, Old Places, 1978, Inside New York's Art World, 1979; editor: MOMA at 50, 1980; TV interviewer, prodr. ABC-TV Arts, 1980—88, A and E Network, 1980—89; author: Collaboration: Artists and Architects, 1981, Visions and Images: Am. Photographers on Photography, 1981, Interior Design: The New Freedom, 1982, Handmade in Am., 1983; Leo Castelli Gallery, 1984; author: Fashion: The Inside Story, 1985, Am. Architecture Now, 1985, Remaking Am., 1986; Leo Castelli Gallery, 1988; author: The Landmarks of N.Y., 1988, 18 Wonders of the N.Y. World, 1992, The Landmarks of N.Y.: Vol. II, 1993, The Landmarks of N.Y., The Municipal Art Society, 2005; Leo Castelli Gallery, 1994; author: Inside the Art World: Conversations with Barbaralee Diamonstein, 1994, Skills, Values, Dreams, 1995, Singular Voices: Americans Who Make a Difference, 1997, The Landmarks of N. Y.: Vol. III, 1998, Barbaralee's Rules of the Rd.: 59 Simple Ways to Cope with a Complex World, 2001, The Landmarks of New York: An Illustrated Record of the City's Historic Buildings, 2005. Nat. juror Vietnam Vet. Meml. Edn. Ctr. Competition, 2004; juror High Line Competition, 2004; bd. advisors Film Anthology Archives, 1969—; mem. Caramoor Ctr. for Music and Arts, 1981—92; Commr. N.Y.C. Landmarks Preservation Commn., 1972—87, N.Y.C. Cultural Commn., 1975—86; vice-chmn. N.Y. Landmarks Conservancy, 1983—87; mem. Pres. coun. Rockefeller U., 1987—; bd. visitors Pub. Policy Inst. Duke U., Durham, NC, 1987—93; mem. U.S. Holocaust Meml. Mus., 1987—93; chmn. N.Y. Landmarks Preservation Found., 1987—95; chair art pub. spaces com. Holocaust Mus., 1987—96; mem. drawing com. Met. Mus. Art, 1990—; Commr. N.Y.C. Arts Commn., 1991—94; trustee Ctrl. Pk. Conservancy, 1993—95, N.Y. Hist. Soc., 1993—95; mem. drawing com. Whitney Mus. Am. Art, 1995—98; mem. U.S. Commn. Fine Arts, 1996—2005; bd. trustees Mus. of Women, the Leadership Ctr., N.Y.C., 1999—; co-chair NGO Assn. Culture Edn. and Comm., 2001—; vice chmn. U.S. Commn. Fine Arts, 2001—02; mem. N.Y. State Travel and Tourism Bd.; bd. dir. PEN Am. Ctr., 1983—96, Mcpl. Art Soc., 1973—83, Am. Coun. Arts, 1982—89, N.Y.C. Bicentennial Commn., 1973—77, Bklyn. Acad. Music, 1969—74, N.Y. Landmarks Conservancy, 1973—97, Fresh Air Fund, 1983—, Big Apple Circus, 1989—92, Corcoran Gallery Art, Washington, 1992—99, N.Y. State Hist. Archive's Partnership Trust, 1994—, Whitney Mus. Am. Art, 1995—98, White House Endowment Fund, 1995—98, Friends of the High Line, 2002—; chair Hist. Landmarks Preservation Ctr., 1995—, Nat. Competition for Low Cost Housing, N.Y.C., 2004. Recipient Founder's Day award Pratt Inst., 1994, Outstanding Citizen award Citizen Ctr., 1996, Visionary in Arts award, Mus. Contemporary Crafts, 1996, Heritage Trails award, 1998, Spirit of the City award Women's City Club, 1998, Manhattan award, 1999, New Millenium Humanitarian award HELP, 1999, Gen. Milan R. Stefanik award Slovak Am. Cultural Ctr., 2002, Aging in Am. Humanitarian award, 2003, Gold medal of the Ministry of Fgn. Affairs of Slovakia, 2004, Humanitarian award Jewish Women's Found. N.Y., 2005. Mem.: Nat. Am. Inst. Architects (hon.). Home: 720 Park Ave New York NY 10021-4954

DIANA, JOHN NICHOLAS, physiologist; b. Lake Placid, N.Y., Dec. 19, 1930; s. Alphonse Walton and Dolores (Mirto) D.; m. Anita Louise Harris, May 8, 1966; children: Gina Sue, Lisa Ann, John Nicholas. BA, Norwich U., 1952; PhD, U. Louisville, 1965. Asst. prof. physiology Mich. State U. Med. Sch., 1966-68; assoc. prof., then prof. U. Iowa Med. Sch., 1969-78; prof. physiology, chmn. dept. La. State U. Med. Ctr., Shreveport, 1978-85; dir. cardiovasc. rsch. ctr. U. Ky., 1985-87, assoc. dean rsch. and basic sci., 1987-88, prof. emeritus, 1997—. Dir. T&H Rsch. Inst., 1988—; cons. Nat. Inst. Neurol. Diseases and Stroke, 1973-75, Nat. Heart, Lung and Blood Inst., 1974—, mem. cardiovasc. and renal study sect., 1980-85, mem. clin. scis. study sect., 1986-91, chmn. 1989-91; rsch. com. Iowa Heart Assn., 1974-77, bd. dirs., 1977-79; mem. cardiovasc. study sect. Am. Heart Assn., 1981-84. Author papers, abstracts in field. Served with AUS, 1952-54; Served with USAR, 1961-62. NIH postdoctoral fellow, 1965-67 Mem. Am. Fedn. Clin. Research, Am. Physiol. Soc. (editorial bd. jour. 1974-78), Microcirculation Soc. (pres. 1977-78, editorial bd. jour. 1979-85), Am. Heart Assn. (fellow council circulation), N.Y. Acad. Scis., La. Heart Assn. (dir. 1979-81, research com. 1978-82), Sigma Xi. Democrat. Achievements include patent for coronary vasodilator. Home: 7332 Saint Georges Way Bradenton FL 34201-2353 *Progress related to the health and welfare of any nation can only be accomplished by programs directed at the development of human thought and human thought processes. The ultimate fate of man will rest upon the success of all societies to stimulate human vital curiosity, talents. energies. basic scholarship and research to address those factors which will preserve man's natural cultural heritage and his ability to lead a free and independent existence.*

DIANA, JOSEPH A., retired foundation executive; b. New Castle, Pa., June 26, 1924; s. Joseph Anthony and Emma (Eardly) D.; m. Kathryn June Matthews, June 26, 1946; children: Mark Steven, Chris Joseph, Todd Francis, Paul Jeffrey. Student, Notre Dame U., 1942; BA, U. Mich., 1950, postgrad., 1950-51. Mem. adminstrv. staff U. Mich., 1950-56, sec. to faculty Med. Sch., 1956-69, asst. controller, 1969-70; v.p. fin. and mgmt. SUNY, Stony Brook, 1970-75; vice chancellor adminstrv. affairs, assoc. v.p. bus. affairs U. Ill., Champaign-Urbana, 1975-79; v.p., treas. emeritus John D. and Catherine T. MacArthur Found., Chgo.; pres. Dianaid Ltd., 1985-91. Interim pub. Harper's mag.; sec., treas. Harper's Mag. Found., 1980-82. Republican. Roman Catholic. Home: 2310 Saint Francis Dr Ann Arbor MI 48104-4807

DI ANGELO, CHRISTOPHER J., lawyer; b. Poughkeepsie, N.Y., Mar. 24, 1957; BA, Williams Coll., 1979; JD, Columbia Univ., 1984. Bar: N.Y. Staff N.Y. State Housing Fin. Agency; assoc. Dewey Ballantine LLP, N.Y.C., 1984—92, ptnr. & chmn. structured fin. group, 1992—. Office: Dewey Ballantine LLP 1301 Ave of the Americas New York NY 10019-6092 Office Phone: 212-259-6718. Office Fax: 212-259-6333. Business E-Mail: cdiangelo@dbllp.com.

DIAO, YIXIN, electrical engineer, researcher; b. 1970; BS, Tsinghua U., 1994, MS, 1997; PhD, Ohio State U., 2000. Grad. rsch. assoc. Elec. Engring. dept. Ohio State U., Columbus, 1997—2000; rsch. staff mem. T.J. Watson Rsch. Ctr. IBM, Hawthorne, NY, 2001—. Author: Feedback Control of Computing Systems; contbr. articles various profl. jours and conf. papers (various best papers awards). Session co-chair Am. Control Conf., 2004. Recipient Siemens prize, Siemens, 1996. Mem.: IEEE. Achievements include invention of method and system for model-based management using abstract models; optimization with unknown objective function; system and methods for control discovery in computing systems; fast oscillation avoidance through bit-vector analysis; dynamic online optimization method for autonomic computing systems.

DIAO, YUANAN, mathematics professor; b. Anlong County, Guizhou Province, China, Mar. 19, 1958; s. Caolian Diao and Xianyun Gu; m. Yanqing Sun, Apr. 24, 1985; children: Liyang, Kevin. BS, Wuhan U. Sci. and Tech., China, 1981; MS, Beijing U. Sci. and Tech., 1984; PhD, Fla. State U., 1990. Assoc. prof. Kennesaw State U., Marietta, Ga., 1990—96; prof. UNC Charlotte, NC, 1996—. Contbr. articles to profl. jours. NFS Rsch. grant, Nat. Sci. Found., 2003—. Mem.: Am. Math. Soc. (assoc.). Avocations: bridge, tennis, chess, reading. Home: 3401 Thistle Bloom Ct Charlotte NC 28269 Office: Univ NC Charlotte 9201 University City Blvd Charlotte NC 28223 Office Phone: 704-687-2887. Personal E-mail: ydiao@uncc.edu.

DIAS, FIONA P., retail executive; m. Floyd Dias. Grad., Harvard U., 1987; MBA, Stanford U. Sr. fin. analyst Merrill Lynch Capital Markets, Inc.; sr. asst. brand mgr. Fixodent and Fasteeth denture adhesives Proctor and Gamble Co., 1996; v.p., corp. develop. Pennzoil Quaker State Co., 1996—99; v.p., mktg. and develop. Frito-Lay Co., 1999—2000; chief mktg. officer Stick Networks, Inc., 2000; sr. v.p., mktg. Circuit City, 2000—05; pres. Circuit City Direct, 2003—; sr. v.p., chief marketing officer Circuit City Stores, Inc., 2005—. Office: Circuit City 9950 Mayland Dr Richmond VA 23233-1464*

DIAS, LYNETTE, psychologist, researcher; d. Abilio and Vera Dias. BA, St. Xavier's Coll., Bombay, 1991; MA, SUNY, Stony Brook, 1994, PhD, 1998. Advanced cert. health care mgmt. N.Y., 1996. Instr. psychology SUNY, Stony Brook, 1992—96, myopia study coord., 1998—, instr. med. students, 2001—, instr. preventive medicine resident physicians, 2002—; pregnancy rsch. coord. Stony Brook Pregnancy Project, 1993—98; prenatal testing project dir. Stony Brook Primary Care Ctr., 1996—98. Data analysis cons.-student affairs SUNY, Stony Brook, 1997—97; HIV/AIDS trainer APA, 2002—; presenter in field. Reviewer: Health Psychology, Jour. Adolescence, Jour. Applied Social Psychology; contbr. articles to profl. jours. Tutor, tester Literacy Vols. Am., 2003; vol., event organizer Social Svc. League, Bombay, 1988—91. Recipient Rsch. award for the Integration of Rsch. and Edn., NSF, 1997; scholar Grad. Assistantship and Tuition Waiver, SUNY at Stony Brook, 1992—96; Psychosomatic Medicine traineeship, Germany, 1993. Mem.: APA, assn. for Rsch. in Vision and Ophthalmology, Am. Psychol. Soc. Personal E-mail: lynette_dias@yahoo.com.

DIAS GRIFFIN, ANNE, investment advisor; MBA, Harvard Bus. Sch.; grad. summa cum laude, Georgetown U. Analyst, Banking Dept. Goldman Sachs; investment analyst Fidelity Investment Ltd., London; analyst & portfolio mgr. Soro Fund Mgmt.; analyst Viking Global Investors; founder, v.p., mng. ptnr. Aragon Global Investors. Trustee Chgo. Symphony Orchestra, Whitney Mus. Am. Art. Mailing: c/o Whitney Mus Am Art 945 Madison Ave New York NY 10021*

DIASIO, ILSE WOLFARTSBERGER, volunteer; b. Linz, Austria, Nov. 12, 1946; came to U.S., 1967; d. D.I. Gottfried and Elfriede (Stuchlik) Wolfartsberger; m. Robert B. Diasio, July 4, 1970; children: Christoph, Thomas, Michael. Grad. in Phys. Therapy, U. Vienna, 1967. Phys. therapist Yale-New Haven Hosp., 1968—71, Vis. Nurse Assn., Rochester, NY, 1971—72; symposium coord. dept. pharmacology U. Ala., 1988. Vol. tchr. German, Pemberton Elem. Sch., Richmond, Va., 1980-84, Vestavia Hills Elem. and H.S., 1985-93; organizer student exch. program between Vestavia Hills H.S. and Seebacher Gymnasium, Graz, Austria, 1990, 91, 94. Bd. dirs. Pemberton (Va.) Elem. Sch. PTA, 1979-84, pres., 1982-84; bd. dirs. Va. Commonwealth U. Faculty Woman's Club, 1978-84, Greater Birmingham Ministries, chmn. direct svcs. work group, 1999-2002, Ala. chpt. Fulbright Assn., 1999—; pres. Childrens Svc. League, 1992-93, treas. 1991-92, asst. treas. 1990-91, 2d v.p., rec. sec., 1998-99; vol. Our Lady Queen of the Universe and Sacred Heart of Jesus Cath. Chs., 1988-90; St. Peter's rep. Ala. Arise, diocesan rep., rec. sec., 1988-94; mem. Peace and Justice Commn. of the Cath. Diocese of Birmingham, 1989-95, chair of commn., 1994-95; bd. dirs. Be an Apostle of Christ, vice chair, 2003—; chair human concerns com. St. Peter's Outreach Commn., 1988—; mem. Direct Svc. Network, 1989—; active Greater Birmingham Ministries, 1989—, treas. Greater Birmingham UNA-USA chpt., 1982-2004, pres., 2005—, CCD steering com. South Atlantic region rep., 2002—; mem. COMPEER Bd., Birmingham, Ala., 1990-99; mem. WOC, Call to Action, Bread for the World, CALC, Pax Christi, Amnesty Internat., Nat. Conf. of Cmty. and Justice, Smithsonian Inst., UNICEF, Coalition Against Hate Crimes, 1997—, Birmingham Com. on Fgn. Rels., 1998—; organizer Christmas gift drive for needy families Angel Tree project St. Peter's Cath. Ch., 1988—; bd. dirs., sec. World of Opportunity, 2002—; vol. tchr. for GED preparation Recipient resolution City of Birmingham, 1999. Mem. AAUW, Nat. Mus. of Women in the Arts, U.S. Holocost Mus., Vereinigung Ehemaliger Körnerschülerinnen, LWV (bd. dirs. Greater Birmingham 1999-2000). Roman Catholic. Avocations: reading, music, skiing, cooking, travel. Home: 1225 Branchwater Ln Birmingham AL 35216-2001 Personal E-mail: idiasio@aol.com.

DIATTA, JOSEPH, Nigerian diplomat; b. Fadama, Niger, May 15, 1948; s. Emmanuel and Saha (Sani) D.; m. Haoua Oumarou, Dec. 28, 1975; children— Sylvia, Amadou, Myriam, Linda. Licence en Droit, U. Abidjan, Ivory Coast, 1970; diplome, Institut International d'Admnistration Publique, Paris, 1971. Permanent sec. Ministry Fgn. Affairs, Niamey, Niger, 1975-79; amb. to Ethiopia, Niger Embassy, Addis-Abeba, 1979-82, amb. to U.S. Washington, 1982—88, 1997—; permanent rep. to UN, Permanent Mission of Niger, N.Y.C., 1985—88; amb. to China, 1988-90; sec. gen High Com. for the Restoration of Peace, 1994—96; spl. advisor to Pres. of Niger, 1996—97. Office: Embassy of Niger Chancery 2204 R St NW Washington DC 20008

DIAZ, ALPHONSO VINCENT, aerospace executive; BS in Physics, St. Joseph U.; MS in Physics, Old Dominion U.; MS in Mgmt., MIT. With NASA, 1964-88, dep. assoc. adminstr. for space sci., 1994-96; divsn. v.p. space and aeronautics svcs. GE Govt. Svcs. Divsn., Cherry Hill, N.J., 1988-89; dept. assoc. adminstr. Office of Space Sci. and Applications, 1989-93; dep. dir. Goddard Space Flight Ctr., Greenbelt, Md., 1996-98, dir., 1998—. Fellow AIAA (assoc.).

DIAZ, ANGELA, pediatrician, educator; b. Dominican Republic, Oct. 2, 1954; MD, Columbia Coll. Physicians and Surgeons, 1994. Diplomate Am. Bd. Pediatrics with subspecialty in adolescent medicine. Intern Mt. Sinai Med. Ctr., N.Y.C., 1981—82, resident in pediats., 1982—84, fellow, 1984—85, prof. dept. pediats., 1985—. Mem.: SAM, Am. Acad. Pediats. (Founders of Adolescent Health award 2001). Office: Mount Sinai Med Ctr 320 E 94th St New York NY 10128-5604

DIAZ, CAMERON, actress; b. Long Beach, Calif., Aug. 30, 1972; Grad. high sch., Long Beach, Calif. Appeared in (films) The Mask, 1994, Feeling Minnesota, 1996, She's the One, 1996, The Last Supper, 1996, Keys to Tulsa, 1996, Head Above Water, 1996, My Best Friend's Wedding, 1997 (Blockbuster Entertainment award), a Life Less Ordinary, 1997, (TV) Space Ghost Coast to Coast, 1994, Very Bad Things, 1998, Fear and Loathing in Las Vegas, 1998, There's Something About Mary (Golden Globe nomination Best Performance by an Actress in a Comedy or Musical Motion Picture), 1998 (N.Y. Film Critics Cir. award, MTV Movie award, Am. Comedy award), Invisible Circus, 1999, Being John Malkovich (Golden Globe nomination Best Supporting Actress in a Motion Picture), 1999, Any Given Sunday, 1999, Charlie's Angels: The Movie, 2000, Things You Can Tell Just by Looking at Her, 2000, Shrek (voice), 2001, Vanilla Sky, 2001, The Sweetest Thing, 2002, Gangs of New York, 2002, Charlie's Angels: Full Throttle, 2003, Shrek 2 (voice), 2004; (TV Series) Trippin, 2005. Named Female Star of Tomorrow, Nat. Theatre Owners Assn., 1996, Boston Soc. of Film Critics best supporting actress award, 2001, Chicago Film Critics Award for best supporting actress, 2002.*

DIAZ, DAVID, illustrator; married; 3 children. Degree, Ft. Lauderdale (Fla.) Art Inst. Illustrator of children's books including Neighborhood Odes (Gary Soto), 1992, Smoky Night (Eve Bunting), 1994 (Caldecott medal 1995), Anansi's Narrow Waist (Len Cabral), 1994, Wilma Unlimited: How Wilma Rudolph Became the World's Fastest Woman (Kathleen Krull), 1996, Passing Strange: True Tales of New England Hauntings and Horrors (Joseph Citro), 1996, Just One Flick of the Finger (Marybeth Lorbiecki), 1996, The Inner City Mother Goose (Eve Merriam), 1996, Going Home (Eve Bunting), 1996, December (Eve Bunting), 1997, The Disappearing Alphabet (Richard Wilbur), 1999, The Little Scarecrow Boy (Margaret Wise Brown); one-man shows include Thurber Ctr. Gallery. Recipient awards Parents' Choice, Am. Illustrations, Comm. Arts, Am. Inst. Graphic Arts, N.Y. Art Dirs. Club.

DIAZ, FERNANDO GUSTAVO, neurosurgeon; s. Fernando Diaz Calderon and Susana (Barriga) D.; children: Fernando Austin, David Frederick, Sean Christopher, Patrick Aaron. BS, Centro Universitario Mex., 1963; MD, Univ. de Mex., 1969; MA, U. Kans., Kansas City, 1973; PhD, U. Minn., 1979; MA in Bus., Cen. Mich. U., Mt. Pleasant, 1987; JD, Wayne State U., 1995. Diplomate Am. Bd. Neurological Surgery; lic. physician and surgeon Mex., Can., Ill., Mich., Fla.; mem. Michigan Bar, 1995. Intern Regina Gen. Hosp., Sask., Can., 1969-70, resident in anethesia, 1971; resident in gen. surgery U. Kans., Kansas City, 1971-73; resident in neurosurgery U. Minn. Hosps., Mpls., 1973-78; staff neurosurgeon Henry Ford Hosp., Detroit, 1978-87; chmn. Neurosci. Inst. Santa Fe, Gainesville, Fla., 1987-90; prof., chmn. dept. neurol. surgery Wayne State U., Detroit, 1990—; chief med. officer Detroit Med. Ctr., 2000—; cert. physician exec. ACPE, 2002. Neurosurg. nat. cons. to U.S. Surgeon Gen., USAF, 1991; coord. neurosurgery resident edn. Henry Ford Hosp., 1979—; clin. assoc. prof. surgery U. Mich., 1986—; mem. working group in neurosurgery WHO. Mem. editl. bd. Neurosurgery Jour.; contbr. articles to profl. jours. Lt. col. USAFR. Recipient awards Lily Pharms., Merck, Sharp & Dome Pharms., Organon Labs. Fellow Am. Chem. Soc., Interam. Coll. Physicians, Internat. Coll. Surgeons (vice regent U.S. sect. 1985); mem. AMA, Neurosurg. Soc. Am., Soc. Neurol. Surgeons, Mich. Med. Soc., Wayne County Med. Soc., Am. Assn. Neurol. Surgeons (cerebrovascular sect.), Congress of Neurol. Surgeons, Mich. Assn. Neurol. Surgeons (sec.-treas. 1984-86, v.p. 1986, pres. 1997-98), Detroit Neurosurg. Acad. (v.p. 1986-90), Soc. Critical Care Medicine, Mich. Heart Assn. (chmn. stroke com. 1984-86, cmty. site ad-hoc com. 1984, cmty. programs and edn. com. 1986), Mich. Assn. Neurosurgery (chmn. bd.), L.Am. Fedn. Neurosurgery (sec. gen., 1999-2002), Council State Neurological Soc.(vice chair) U. Minn. Alumni Assn. Roman Catholic. Office: Wayne State U Neurol Surg 4201 Saint Antoine St Detroit MI 48201-2153 Business E-Mail: fdiaz@unsg.com.

DIAZ, FRANCISCO GIL, minister of finance for Mexico; b. Mexico City, Mex., Sept. 2, 1943; m. Margarita White; 4 children. BA in Econs., ITAM; M, PhD, U. Chgo. Various pub. svc. positions Ctrl. Bank and Treasury; under-sec. of the Treasury, in charge of revenues Finance and Public Credit Secretariat, 1988—94; mem. bd. governors Ctrl. Bank Mex., 1994—98; CEO Avantel, 1998—2000; min. of fin. and pub. credit Govt. of Mexico, Col Centro, 2000—. Taught econs. various inst.; chmn. econs. dept. ITAM, prof. emeritus; prof. econs., mem. governing bd. Iberoamericana U., mem. governing bd.; exec. coun. Mex. Ctr., U. of Tex., Austin; bd. govs. Ctrl. Bank; bd. visitors Andreson Sch. Bus., UCLA. Author on pub. fin., exchange rate policy, monetary and fin. policy, macroeconomic management and deregulation of econ. activity. Avocations: bicycling, windsurfing, Alpine skiing. Office: Ministry Fin Public Credit Palacio Nacio 1er Patio Mariano Piso 3 Centro 06000 Mexico City Mexico

DIAZ, HERIBERTO, medical products executive; BSc in elec. engring., U. PR. With Prime Computer, 1981—90, Guidant Corp., 1990—; gen. mgr. and v.p. ops. Guidant del Caribe, Ltd., PR. Recipient Mfg. Exec. Yr., PR Mfg. Assn., 2003. Office: Guidant del Caribe Ltd Rd 698 Lot #12 Dorado PR 00646

DIAZ, JUAN C., communications executive, consultant; s. Bertha Diaz. M, Columbus State U., 1999. Cert. computer graphics ROP, Calif., 1994. Chmn., CEO iNTERTAINMENT.NETWORK inc., Las Vegas, Nev., 1999—. Cons. Am. Votes, DC, 2004. Personal E-mail: intertainment@intertainment.net.

DIAZ, MANUEL A., mayor; b. Havana, Cuba, Nov. 5, 1954; arrived in U.S., 1961; m. Robin Smith; children: Manny, Natlie, Bobby, Elisa. Grad. with high honors, Miami-Dade C.C., 1975, Fla. Internat. U., 1977; JD, U. Miami. Bar: Fla., U.S. Ct. Appeals (5th cir.), U.S. Dist. Ct. Appeals (11th cir.), U.S. Dist. Ct. (so. dist.) Fla., U.S. Supreme Ct. With Coopers & Lybrand; founder, mng. ptnr. Berkowitz & Diaz; former exec. v.p., gen. counsel Terremark Investment Svcs., Inc.; v.p., gen. counsel Monty's Restaurant Holdings; gen. counsel Fla. Worker's Compensation Ins. Guaranty Assn.; ptnr. Diaz & O'Naghten, L.L.P.; elected mayor City of Miami, 2001—05. Cons. U. Chgo. Law Sch., Nat. Assessment of Ednl. Progress. Founding bd. mem. State Bd. C.C.'s, Fla.; apptd. mem. Fla. Residential Property & Casualty JUA, chmn. investment com.; chmn. Dade County Com. for Fair Representation; bd. mem. numerous cmty. orgns.; founding mem. Little Havana Activities and Nutrition Ctr.; past mem. Little Havana Devel. Authority; founding mem. Coalition Hispanic Am. Women; past chmn. Spanish Am. League Against Discrimination; founding mem. Gtr. Miami United; co-chair Music Fest Miami; past bd. dirs. United Way Hispanic Leadership Devel. Program, Miami's for Me Com. of 100; Leadership Miami; City of Miami Bds. & Coms. Rev. Com.; City of Miami City Atty. Selection Com.; City of Miami Bond Underwriters Selection Com. Office: City Hall 3500 Pan American Dr Miami FL 33133

DIAZ, MARLENE CARMEN, retired language educator; d. Inez Longo. BA, Hunter Coll., 1968; MA, CCNY, 1972; MS in Ednl. Adminstrn. and Supervision, Pace U., 1982. Tchr. Spanish Intermediate Sch. 131, Bronx, NY,

1968—70, Adlai Stevenson H.S., Bronx, 1970—84; interim-acting asst. prin., fgn. lang. and ESL depts. Andrew Jackson H.S., Queens, NY, 1984—85; asst. prin., fgn. lang. and ESL dept. DeWitt Clinton H.S., Bronx, NY, 1985—2002; full time instr. of Spanish, modern fgn. langs. dept. Coll. of Mt. St. Vincent, Riverdale, NY, 2002—04; ret., 2004. Mentor in the asst. prin. leadership program Bronx H.S. Superintendency, 1994—2001, participant bilingual/ESL staff devel. acad. for raising stds., 1998—2000; supr. Title VII programs DeWitt Clinton H.S., 1990—99, mem. accreditation com., 1990—98; presenter in field. Named Supr. of Yr., Bronx H.S. Superintendency, 1990, Supr. of Yr., 1997; scholar, NY State Coun. for the Humanities, 1991. Mem.: Am. Assn. Tchrs. of Spanish and Portuguese (Theodore Huebener Svc. award 1992), Sigma Delta Pi, Phi Delta Kappa, Phi Beta Kappa.

DIAZ, NELSON, lawyer; b. NYC, May 23, 1947; s. Luis Diaz and Maria (Cancel) Rodriguez; children: Vilmarie, Nelson M.V., Delia Lee. AAS, St. John's U., 1967, BS, 1969; JD, Temple U., 1972; LLD (hon.), LaSalle Coll., 1982, St. John's U., 1987, Temple U., 1990, Albright Coll., 1995, Lincoln U., 1996. Bar: Pa. 1972, D.C. 1978, U.S. Supreme Ct. 1978, N.Y. 1998. Legal intern Camden (N.J.) Regional Legal Svcs., 1970-71; asst. defender Defender Assn. Phila., 1972-73; asoc. counsel Temple U. Legal Aid Office, Phila., 1973-75; assoc. Fell, Spalding, Goff & Ruben, Phila., 1976-77; exec. dir. Spanish Mchts. Assn., Phila., 1973-77; White House fellow v.p. of U.S., 1977-78; assoc. Wolf, Block, Schorr & Solis-Cohen, Phila., 1978-81; adminstrv. judge Phila. Ct. of Common Pleas, 1981-93; gen. counsel HUD, Washington, 1993-97; ptnr. Blank, Rome, Comisky & McCauley, Phila., 1997—2001; city solicitor City of Philadelphia, Pa., 2001—. Lectr. Sch. Law Temple U., Phila., 1983—; bd. dirs. Exelon; adv. bd. PNC. Columnist Phila. Sun and Evening Bull., 1973-75; contbr. articles on Japanese, Peruvian legal system to various publs. Founder Phila. Leadership Prayer Breakfast, 1984-93; bd. dirs., com. chmn. Revitalized Neighborhood, 1983-87; participant, hon. chair Soviet Jewry Coun., 1985; com. mem. Charter Rev. Phila., 1986; chmn. Nat. Assn. Hispanic Elderly, L.A., 1978-93; trustee Young Life, 1989-93, Temple U., 1997—, Phila. Mus. Art; bd. govs. Temple Hosp., Phila., 1975-93; founder, bd. dirs. Nat. P.R. Coalition, 1978-86; co-chmn., bd. dirs. Urban Affairs Partnership, Phila., 1984-90; bd. dirs. USHLI, Chgo., 1982-93, 97—, World Affairs Coun., 1997-2001, Phila. (Pa.) Indsl. Corp., Pa. Convention Ctr., Red Cross Phila., 2002-04, Phila. Conv. Ctr.; chair Greater Phila. Billy Graham Crusade, Nat. Bar Assn. Jud. Coun., 1993, Frederick Douglass Soc. Found., 1995, Salvation Army, 1995, Boricua Coll., 1995; Mayor's St. Police Discipline Task Force, Phila., Pa. Recipient Life Achievement award Nat. Puerto Rican Coalition, Washington, 1988, Judge of the Yr. award Pa. Trial Lawyers Assn., 1989, Man of the Yr., NAACP, North Phila., 1990, Found. Improvement Justice award, 1992, Cesar Chavez award, 1995, Spirit of Excellence award ABA, 2001, William Hall award Barristers, 2003, Lifetime Achievement award Minority Bar, 2003, Learned Hand award Am. Jewish Com., 2003, Outstanding Recognition award Phila. (Pa.) Multicultural Congress, 2004; named Grand Marshall, P.R. Milburne (Fla.) Parade; Japan Soc. fellow, Fulbright fellow, 1990. Mem. Pa. Bar Assn. (chair DOC Hispanic Caucus, exec. com., bylaws and rules com., Martin Luther King Barrister award 2003), Phila. Bar Assn., D.C. Bar Assn., Pa. Trial Lawyers Assn., State Conf. Trial Judges, Hist. Soc. (bd. dirs.). Democrat. Avocation: sports. Office: Blank Rome LLP One Logan Square Philadelphia PA 19103 Office Phone: 215-569-5734. E-mail: diaz@blankrome.com.

DIAZ, NILS JUAN, federal agency administrator; b. Moron, Cuba, Apr. 7, 1938; came to US, 1961; s. Rafael Octavio Diaz and Rosa Dalia (Rojas) Chao; m. Zenaida G. Gonzalez, Oct. 9, 1960; children: NIls, Ariadne, Allene. BSME, U. Villanova, Havana, 1960; MS in Nuclear Engring. Sci., U. Fla., 1964, PhD in Nuclear Engring. Sci., 1969. Rsch. assoc. nuclear engring. sci. U. Fla., Gainesville, 1965-69, asst. prof., reactor supr., 1969-74, assoc. prof., dir. nuclear facilities, 1974-79, prof., dir. nuclear facilities, 1979-84; assoc. dean for rsch. Sch. of Engring. Calif. State U., Long Beach, 1984-86; prof. nuclear engring. scis. U. Fla., Gainesville, 1986-96; dir. Innovative Nuclear Space Power and Propulsion Inst., Calif. and Fla., 1985-96; commr. U.S. Nuclear Regulatory Commn., Washington, 1996—, chmn., 2003—. Sr. cons. Exxon Nuclear, Fla. Power and Light-Fla. Power Corp., Bellevue, Wash. and Fla., 1974-79; pres., chief engr. Fla. Nuclear Assocs., Inc., Gainesville, 1976-96; prin. advisor Nuclear Safety Coun., Madrid, 1981-83; internat. energy cons., Argentina, Brazil, Mex., Santo Domingo, Spain; commr. U.S. Nuclear Regulatory Commn. Contbr. articles to profl. jours. Chmn. Minority Engr. Program Adv. Bd., Long Beach, 1984-86. Recipient Disting. Svc. Award Math. Engring. Sci. Achievements and Minority Engring. Program State of Calif., Long Beach, 1983, Hispanic Bus. Fed. Elite award, HispanicBusiness.com, 2002; named Hispanic Engr. of Yr. for Outstanding Tech. Contbns., Hispanic Engr. Nat. Achievement Com., Houston, 1990, Top 50 Hispanics in Business and Tech., Hispanic Engr. & Information Tech., 2003. Fellow AAAS, ASME, Am. Nuclear Soc.; mem. Am. Soc. for Engring. Edn., Cuban-Am. Engring. Soc. (Engr. of Yr. 1993), Hispanic Assn. Profl. Engrs. Republican. Roman Catholic. Achievements include patents for heterogeneous gas core reactors, gamma ray flaw detection system; invention of vapor core nuclear rocket propulsion system. Office: US Nuclear Regulatory Commn Offices Of The Commr Washington DC 20555-0001

DIAZ, OLIVER E., JR., state supreme court justice; b. Biloxi, Miss., Dec. 16, 1959; s. Oliver E. Sr. and Sylvia (Fountain) D. AA, Miss. Gulf Coast Jr. Coll., 1979; BA, U. S. Ala., 1982; JD, U. Miss., 1985. Bar: Miss., U.S. Dist. Ct. (no. and so. dists.) Miss., U.S. Ct. Appeals (5th cir.). Assoc. Holkins Logan Vaughn & Anderson, Gulfport, Miss., 1985-86, Gerald R. Emil PA, Gulfport, 1986-88; mem. Miss. House of Reps., 1988—94; ptnr. Diaz Davis & Emil, Gulfport, 1988—95; judge Miss. Ct. of Appeals, Jackson, 1995—2000; justice Miss. Supreme Court, Jackson, 2000—. Mem. Harrison County Rep. exec. com., 1987—; treas. Miss. State Young Reps., 1987-88; pres. Miss. Gulf Coast Young Reps., Harrison County, 1987-88. Mem. Assn. Trial Lawyers Am., Miss. Trial Lawyers Assn., Am. Legis. Exchange Com., Jaycees. Office: Mississippi Supreme Ct Gartin Justice Bldg PO Box 249 Jackson MS 39205

DIAZ, OSCAR, JR., voice educator, music institute director; b. Havana, Cuba, Apr. 7, 1961; s. Oscar and Esther Diaz; life ptnr. Javier Julian Ferrer. Bachelors Degree, University of Texas at Arlington, Arlington, Texas, 1978—88. Choir dir., cantor, music tchr. St. Maria Goretti Cath. Ch. and Sch., Arlington, Tex., 1983—87; voice instr. Performer's Music Inst., Miami, Fla., 1988—; voice instr. adj. faculty New World Sch. of Arts, Miami, 2000—03. Exec. dir. Performer's Music Inst., Miami, 1988—. Singer: (operas and mus.) Fla. Grand Opera, 1988—2001, Ft. Worth Opera, 1984—87, Dallas Symphony Chorus, 1984—87, (leading roles) U. Tex. Opera Theatre, Arlington Opera, Coral Gables Opera. Mem.: Nat. Guild Piano Tchrs., Nat. Assn. Tchrs. Singing (pres. South Fla. chpt. 2003—), Miami Music Tchrs. Assn. (2d v.p. 1995—97). Office Phone: 305-757-7725. Personal E-mail: pmimusic@bellsouth.net.

DIAZ, PAUL J., service industry executive; With Arthur Andersen LLC; atty. pvt. practice; CEO Allegis Health Svcs., Inc.; exec. v.p., COO Mariner Health Group, Inc., 1996—98; chmn., CEO Capella Sr. Living, LLC; mng. mem. Falcon Capital Partners, LLC; pres., CEO Kindred Healthcare, Louisville, 2002—. Mem.: Johns Hopkins Bloomberg Sch. Pub. Health. Office: Kindred Healthcare 680 S Fourth St Louisville KY 40202*

DIAZ, ROBYN WHIPPLE, lawyer; b. Queens, N.Y. d. David and Felicia Whipple; m. Geoffrey Carlos Diaz, July 27, 2001. BA magna cum laude, Brandeis U., 1998; JD cum laude, Georgetown U., 2003. Bar: N.Y. 2004, D.C. 2004. Rsch. specialist Health Care Adv. Bd., Washington, 1998—99, rsch. mgr., 1999—2000; project specialist Ctr. for Studying Health Sys. Change, Washington, 2000—02; assoc. Crowell & Moring LLP, Washington, 2003—. Contbr. articles to profl. jours. Mem.: Women's Bar Assn. D.C., Am. Health Lawyers Assn., ABA (health law sect.). Office: Crowell & Moring LLP 1001 Pennsylvania Ave NW Washington DC 20004 Office Phone: 202-624-2763. Business E-Mail: rdiaz@crowell.com.

DIAZ, SHARON, education administrator; b. Bakersfield, Calif., July 29, 1946; d. Karl C. and Mildred (Lunn) Clark; m. Luis F. Diaz, Oct. 19, 1968; children: Daniel, David. BS, San Jose State U., 1969; MS, U. Calif., San Francisco, 1973; PhD (hon.), St. Mary's Coll. Calif., 1999. Nurse Kaiser Found. Hosp., Redwood City, Calif., 1969-73; lectr. San Jose (Calif.) State Coll., 1969-70; instr. St. Francis Meml. Hosp. Sch. Nursing, San Francisco, 1970—71; pub. health nurse San Mateo County, 1971—72; instr. Samuel Merritt Hosp. Sch. Nursing, Oakland, Calif., 1973—76; asst. dir. Samuel Merritt Hosp. Sch. of Nursing, Oakland, 1976—78, dir., 1978—84; founding pres. Samuel Merritt Coll., Oakland, 1984—; interim pres. Calif. Coll. Podiatric Medicine, 2001. V.p. East Bay Area Health Edn. Ctr., Oakland, 1980-87; mem. adv. com. Calif. Acad. Partnership Program, 1990-92; mem. nat. adv. com. Nursing Outcomes Project; bd. dirs. Calif. Workforce Initiative, U. Calif. San Francisco Ctr. for the Health Professions, 2000--. Bd. dirs. Head Royce Sch., 1990-98, vice chair, 1993-95, chair, 1995-97; bd. dirs. Ladies Home Soc., 1992—, sec. 1994-95, treas., CFO 1995-97, 2nd v.p. 1997-99; bd. dirs. George Mark Children's House, 2001--; mem. adv. bd. Ethnic Health Inst., 1997—; mem. com. minorities higher edn. Am. Coun. Edn., 1998—. Named Woman of Yr., Oakland YWCA, 1996. Mem. Am. Assn. of Pres. Ind. Colls. and Univs., Sigma Theta Tau (Leadership award Nu Xi chpt. 2001, Philanthropy award 2005). Office: Samuel Merritt Coll 450 30th St Oakland CA 94609-3302 E-mail: sdiaz@samuelmerritt.edu.

DIAZ, TERESITA PEREZ, chemist; b. Placetas, Las Villas, Cuba, Sept. 2, 1956; arrived in U.S., 1974; d. Pedro Angel and Gladys (Teresita) Perez; m. Luis Diaz, Jr., Sept. 2, 1984; children: Tiffany Marie, Luis III. BS in Chemistry, Monclair U., 1979. Asst. scientist baby products Johnson & Johnson, Raritan, NJ, 1979—81; assoc. scientist, 1981—84, assoc. scientist toiletries Skillman, NJ, 1984—86, scientist R & D, 1986—96, sr. scientist rsch, devel. and engring., 1996—2001, staff scientist, 2001—02, group leader, 2002—. Piano tchr., Perth Amboy, NJ, 1975—; coach, trainer Johnson & Johnson Skillman U., 2001—04. Class mother Perth Amboy Cath. Schs., 1989—2003. Recipient Grandview award, Johnson & Johnson, 2000, 2002, 2004, Engring. Excellence award, 2002. Mem.: Nat. Guild Piano Tchrs., Soc. Cosmetic Chemists. Achievements include co-inventor skin toning formulation; co-inventor relaxing personal care composition; co-inventor delivery system for topical skin care agents. Avocations: art, theater, museums, music, films. Office: Johnson and Johnson 199 Grandview Rd Skillman NJ 08558

DIAZ-BALART, LINCOLN, congressman, lawyer; b. Havana, Cuba, Aug. 13, 1954; m. Cristina Fernandez; children: Lincoln Gabriel, Daniel. BA in Internat. Rels., New Coll. of U. So. Fla., 1976; diploma in Brit. Politics, Cambridge (Eng.) U.; JD, Case Western Res. U., 1979. Lawyer Legal Svcs. of Greater Miami, Fla.; asst. state atty. State of Fla.; mem. Fla. Ho. of Reps. from 110th Dist., 1986-89, Fla. State Senate from Dist. 34, 1989-92, U.S. Congress from 21st Fla. dist., 1993—, Select Com. on Homeland Security; mem. Rules com. Mem. rules com.; vice chmn. subcom. on rules of the house. Mem. exec. com. Congl. Human Rights Caucus; vice chmn. Nat. Rep. Congl. Com. Mem. ABA, Fla. Bar Assn., Dade County Bar Assn., Cuban-Am. Bar Assn., Rep. Nat. Lawyers Assn., Lions. Republican. Roman Catholic. Office: US Ho of Reps 2244 Rayburn Ho Office Bldg Washington DC 20515-0921

DIAZ-BALART, MARIO, congressman; b. Ft. Lauderdale, Fla., Sept. 25, 1961; Student, U. South Fla. Pres. Gordeon, Sloan and Diaz-Balart; adminstrv. asst. to Mayor Xavier Suarez City of Miami, 1985-88; mem. Fla. Ho. of Reps., Tallahassee, 1988-92, 2001—03, Fla. State Senate, Tallahassee, 1992—2000, U.S. Ho. of Reps from 25th Fla. dist., 2003—. Vice chmn. Rules and Calendar Com.; chmn. Banking and Ins. Com.; mem. Subcom. E Fin. and Tax Ways and Means Com., Natural Resources Com., Edn. Com. Commerce and Econ. Opportunities Com. Mem. consultive com. Children's First; mem. Dade Ptnrs. for Safe Neighborhoods, Spanish-Am. League Against Discriminations; mem. Hispanic adv. bd. Rep. Nat. Com.; advisor nat. human rights commn. Municipios en el Exilio; bd. dirs. Fla. Entertainment Commn.; former mem. Fla. bd. dirs. Spl. Olympics Recipient award Fla. Assn. C.C.'s, award of honor, Pub. Svcs. award MADD, 1994, Furtherance of Justice award Fla. Attys. Assn., 1994, Govt. Recognition awrd Am. Assn. Poison Control Ctrs., 1996, Disting. Leadership award Police Benevolent Assn., 1996, Leadership award Fla. Assn. State Troopers, 1996, Resolution of Appreciation Fla. Conf. of Dist. Cts. of Appeal Judges, 1996. Mem. Nat. Assn. Latino Elected Officials, Asociacion Integral Mambisa, Westchester Lions Club. Republican. Roman Catholic. Avocations: reading, biking, diving. Office: 313 Cannon Ho Office Bldg Washington DC 20515-0925

DIAZ-CRUZ, MARIO, III, lawyer; b. Havana, Cuba, 1946; BBA cum laude, Univ. Miami, 1967; JD, Harvard Univ., 1970. Bar: NY 1971. Ptnr., corp. dept., chair, Latin Am. dept. Dorsey & Whitney LLP, NYC, 1995—. Chmn., pres. Spain-US C of C, Girls' Vacation Fund. Mem.: ABA, Assn. of Bar City NY, NY State Bar Assn. Office: Dorsey & Whitney LLP 250 Park Ave New York NY 10177-1500 Office Phone: 212-415-9250. Office Fax: 212-953-7201. Business E-Mail: diaz.cruz.mario@dorsey.com.

DIAZ MEYER, CHERYL, photojournalist; b. Phillipines; arrived in US, 1981; BA in German, U. Minn., 1990; BA in journalism, Western Ky. U., 1994. Staff photographer Mpls. Star Tribune, 1994—2000; sr. staff photographer Dallas Morning News, 2000—. Named Minn. Photographer Yr., 1999; recipient Pulitzer Prize for breaking news photography, 2004. Office: Dallas Morning News 508 Young St PO Box 655237 Dallas TX 75265-5237

DIAZ-TORRES, MARIA R., research scientist; d. Alvaro Diaz Arocha and Concepcion Torres; 1 child, Laura Claverie. BSc in Biology, U. de La Laguna, Spain, 1978, MS in Microbiology, 1979; PhD, Nat. U. Ireland, Dublin, 1984. Post doctoral assoc. U. Ga., 1984—88; rsch. assoc. Tufts U. Med. Sch., Boston, 1988—92; sr. scientist Genencor Internat., Palo Alto, Calif., 1993—. Recipient Presdl. Green Chemistry Challenge Award, US EPA, 2003, DuPont Sustainable Growth Excellence award, 2005. Achievements include patents in field; discovery of new gene functions; development of new tecniques in Molecular Biology; genetic strain improvement. Avocations: poetry, painting, drawing. Office: Genencor Internat 925 Page Mill Rd Palo Alto CA 94304

DIAZ-ZUBIETA, AGUSTIN, nuclear engineer, engineering executive; b. Madrid, Mar. 24, 1936; came to U.S., 1953; s. Emilio Diaz Cabeza and Maria Teresa Zubieta Atucha; m. Beth Lee Fortune, Sept. 6, 1958; children: Walter Agustin, Michael Joel, Anthony John. B, U. Madrid, 1953; BSc in Physics, U. Tenn., 1958; MSc in Mech. Engring., Duke U., 1960; PhD in Nuclear Engring., U. Md., 1981. Nuclear engr. Combustion Engring., Tenn., 1954-58; instr. engring. Duke U., Durham, N.C., 1958-60; nuclear physicist Allis Chalmers Co., Washington, 1960-64, country mgr. South Africa, 1964-66; mgr. internat. power generation projects GE, N.Y.C., 1966-69, mgr. Europe and Middle East strategic planning, 1969-71, dir. internat. constrn. planning Westport, Conn., 1971-75, dir. constrn., 1975-83; CEO GE Affiliate, Westport, 1983-87; v.p. internat. sales, devel. Internat. Tech. Corp., L.A., 1987-94. Mng. dir. IT Italia S.P.A., IT Spain, S.A. Author: Measurement of Subcriticality of Nuclear Reactors by Stocastic Processes, 1981. Pres. Fairfield (Conn.) Assn. Condo Owners, 1983-87. Named Astronomer of Yr. Barnard Astronomical Soc., Chattanooga, 1957; fgn. exchange scholar U.S. Govt., 1953-58; grantee, NSF, 1958-60, U.S. Office of Ordinance Rsch. U.S. Army, 1958-60. Mem. Am. Nuclear Soc., Am. Soc. Mech. Engrs., Am. Soc. Profl. Engrs., Sigma Xi. Republican. Roman Catholic. Avocations: golf, tennis, swimming, sailing, music. Home: 47 Country Meadow Rd Rolling Hills Estates CA 90274

DIBACCO, T. JAY, financial services planner, retired military officer; b. Casper, Wyo., June 8, 1954; s. Albert Joseph and Evelyn DeBacco; m. Nadine Louise Allen, June 1, 1976. MusB, cert. in edn., U. Wyo., 1976; MBA, Almeda Coll. and U., 2003; diploma, US Army Command and Gen. Staff Coll., Ft. Leavenworth, Kans., 1994. Life Underwriter Tng. Coun. fellow Nat. Assn. Life Underwriters, cert. sr. advisor Soc. Cert. Sr. Advisors; registered rep. Nat. Assn. Securities Dealers. Music tchr. St. Agnes Acad., Alliance, Nebr., 1976-77; instrumental music Gering (Nebr.) Pub. Schs., 1977-79; sales assoc. Panhandle Co-op, Scottsbluff, 1980-81; advanced underwriter Security Mut. Life Nebr., Scottsbluff, 1981-99; sr. assoc. Hi-Plains Fin. Svcs. Inc., Scottsbluff, 1985-99; pres., CEO DiBacco & Assoc.-WealthMaker$ Ltd., Scottsbluff, 1999—. Adj. faculty Western Nebr. C.C., Scottsbluff, 1989—90; gen. agt. Ohio Nat. Fin. Svcs., 2000—; gen. practitioner Cir. of Wealth Sys., 2000—; rep. Ohio Nat. Equity Sales Co., 1999—. Contbr. articles to profl. jours.; writer local newspaper column. Adv. bd. Regional West Med. Ctr. Found., Scottsbluff, 1989—; MBA catalyst group U. Nebr. Panhandle Sta., Scottsbluff, 1990-92; dist. commr. Longs Peak Coun. Boy Scouts Am., 1980-83; active emergency comms. Amateur Radio Emergency Svc., Scottsbluff, 1990—; founding pres., bd. dirs. Panhandle Estate Planning Coun., Scottsbluff, 1982-92. Lt. col. U.S. Army N.G., 1985-2004 Decorated Meritorious Svc. medal, Army Commendation medal with oak leaf cluster; recipient Scouter Tng. award, Longs Peak coun. Boy Scouts Am., 1977, Vigil Honor award, 1977, Assn. Achievement award, Nebr. Assn. Life Underwriters, 1988. Mem.: Gen. Agts. and Mgrs. Assn., Soc. Fin. Svc. Profls., Nat. Assn. Ins. and Fin. Advisors (past local pres.), Fin. Planning Assn., Nebr. N.G. Officers Assn. (life), N.G. Officers Assn. of US (life; Nebr. del. 1990—92), Sugar Valley Singers (pres. 2002—04, Barbershopper of Yr. 1997), Scottsbluff Gering United C. of C. (diploma, founding chmn.), Barbershp Harmony Soc., Soc. Creative Anachronism (regional safety officer 1995—99, Regional Svc. award 1995), Valley Vintners (pres. 2002—), Scottsbluff County Club, Elks, Am. Legion. Avocations: music, history, archery, travel, wine making. Home: PO Box 158 Gering NE 69341-0158 Office: PO Box 840 Scottsbluff NE 69363-0840 Fax: 308-220-3938. Office Phone: 308-220-3255. E-mail: info@wealth-makers.com.

DIBAIYAN, FATEMEH MARIAM, artist; b. Saveh, Iran, Sept. 21, 1937; d. Soltan Ali Dibaiyan and Mariam Vakili; widowed; children: Nasser, Danesh, Sadaf, Donna Rahimi. Student, U. Utah, 1993. Exhibited in group shows at Moon Flower Gallery, Salt Lake City, 1994, Phillips Gallery, Salt Lake City, 1994-95, Kimball Gallery, Park City, Utah, 1996, Amir Kabir Gallery, Tehran, Iran, 1994-96, Art of Utah, Salt Lake City, 1996—, Bellevue Art Mus., Wash., 1998; represented in permanent collections at U. Utah, Children's Mus., Salt Lake City, Kimball Gallery, Univ. Hosp., Tehran, Salt Lake C.C. Home: 408 S 1300 E #5 Salt Lake City UT 84102 Office Phone: 801-582-1057. Personal E-mail: fatemeh_diba2003@yahoo.com. Business E-Mail: fatemeh_diba@ms.com.

DIBATTISTE, CAROL A., former federal agency administrator; b. Phila., Dec. 28, 1951; d. Peter Martin DiBattiste and Hilda Yolanda (Battilana) Mignogna. BA magna cum luade, LaSalle U., 1976; JD, Temple U., 1981; LLM, Columbia U., 1986. Bar: Pa. 1982, U.S. Ct. Mil. Appeals 1982, U.S. Supreme Ct. 1985, N.Y. 1989, D.C. 1989, Fla. 1990, U.S. Dist. Ct. (so. dist.) Fla. 1991, U.S. Ct. Appeals (11th cir.) 1991. Commd. 2d lt. USAF, 1976, advanced through grades to maj., 1987, cir. trial counsel Pacific Region, 1982—85; mem. faculty USAF JAG Sch., Maxwell AFB, Ala., 1986—89; chief recruiting atty. Office of Judge Advocate Gen. USAF, Washington, 1989—91; asst. U.S. atty. (So. Dist.) Fla. US Dept. Justice, Miami, 1991—92, dir. Office of Legal Edn., 1992—93; prin. dep. gen. coun. USN, 1993—94; dir. Exec. Office for U.S. Attys., Washington, 1994—98; dep. U.S. atty. (So. Dist.) Fla. US Dept. Justice, Miami, 1998—99; undersec. USAF, Arlington, Va., 1999—2001; ptnr. Holland & Knight, LLP, 2001—03; chief of staff Transp. Security Adminstrn., 2003—04, dep. adminstr., 2004—05; chief credentialing compliance & privacy officer ChoicePoint Inc., Washington, 2005—. Adj. faculty U. Miami Sch. Law Trial Skills, 1998—99; bd. dirs. Holland & Knight Cons. Editor: The Reporter, 1986—87; mem. editl. bd.: Air Force Law Rev., 1984; contbr. articles to profl. jours. Bd. visitors Temple U. Sch. Law, 1996-99; trustee USAF JAG Sch. Found., 1993-96, Air Force Falcon Found., 2004—. Mem. ABA (chmn. standing com. on mil. law 1989-91), Fed. Bar Assn. (Young Fed. Lawyer award 1985), Nat. Inst. for Trial Advocacy (faculty 1986-92), USAF Assn. Roman Catholic. Business E-Mail: carol.dibattiste@choicepoint.net.

DIBB, DAVID WALTER, research association administrator; b. Draper, Utah, July 4, 1943; s. Walter and Mary (Lisinsky) D.; m. Vivian Berrett, Dec. 15, 1966; children: Stephanie, Gregory, Steven, Rebecca. BS, Brigham Young U., 1970; PhD, U. Ill., 1974. Cert. profl. agronomist, cert. profl. soil scientist. Rsch. asst. U. Ill., Urbana, 1970-74, tchg. asst., 1971-74; vis. asst. prof. N.C. State U., Raleigh, 1974-75; rsch. dir. Potash & Phosphate Inst., Atlanta, 1982-89, regional dir. Columbia, Mo., 1975-82, coord. Latin Am. Atlanta, 1982-85, v.p. North Am. West Lafayette, Ind., 1985-86, sr. v.p., 1987-88, pres. Atlanta, 1989—. Pres. Agronomic Sci. Found., Madison, Wis., 1983-85; mem. fertilizer industry adv. com. Food and Agrl. Orgn. of UN, Rome, 1988-94; exec. industry rev. group TVA, Muscle Shoals, Ala., 1989-94; adj. prof. Purdue U., West Lafayette, 1985-88; hon. prof. Chinese Acad. Agrl. Scis., 1996. Contbr. author: Potassium in Agriculture, 1985; editor: Fertilizer Research, 1989-90; contbr. articles to profl. jours. Instnl. rep. Boy Scouts Am., West Lafayette, 1982-85, asst. scoutmaster, Norcross, Ga., 1989-90; youth coach for basketball, baseball, and soccer, Mo., Ind., Ga., 1980-89; active PTA, Mo., Ind., Ga., 1978-96. Fellow AAAS, Am. Soc. Agronomy (chmn. budget and fin. com. 1988), Soil Sci. Soc. Am.; mem. Coun. for Agrl. Sci. and Tech., Internat. Soil Sci. Soc., Gamma Sigma Delta, Alpha Zeta. Office: Potash and Phosphate Inst 655 Engineerring Dr Ste 110 Norcross GA 30092 E-mail: ddibb@ppi-far.org.

DIBBLE, DAVID VAN VLACK, visually impaired educator, lawyer; b. San Francisco, Feb. 5, 1928; s. Oliver and Isabelle (Bishop) D.; m. Frances Bauer, May 3, 1984; 1 child, T.C. Clark. AA, San Mateo Jr. Coll., 1948; student, Mexico City Coll., 1950; BA, U. Calif., Berkeley, 1952; JD, U. Calif., San Francisco, 1962; grad. in Edn., Calif. State U., Hayward, 1969; MA, San Francisco State U., 1981. Bar: Calif., 1962; cert. elem. tchr., spl. edn. visually impaired, Calif. Tchr. Marine Corps Inst., Washington, 1953-54; purser Am. Pres. Lines, San Francisco, 1955, passenger agt. Honolulu, 1956-58, San Francisco, 1958-60; trial lawyer Barfield, Barfield & Dryden, San Francisco, 1963-65; ptnr. Thorpe & Dibble, Hayward, Calif., 1966-69; part time tchr. various Calif. sch. dist., 1970-74; lawyer and vision tchr. pvt. practice, San Francisco, 1974-82; sec., dir. Original Sixteen to One Mine, Inc., Alleghany, Calif., 1978-81; vision tchr. Oakland Pub. Sch., Calif., 1982-89; cons. vision edn. pvt. practice, Oakland, 1989—. Author: The Pelton Wheel, 2003; contbr. articles on Art of Seeing to various pubs. Pub. defender Legal Aid Soc., San Francisco, 1965-66; bd. dir. Healing Ctr., San Francisco, 1974-78; vol., 1974-90; bd. dir., v.p. Calif. Heritage Coun., 1970—, Telegraph Hill Dwellers, 1979-88, pres., 1976, San Francisco; bd. dirs., v.p. Diamond Improvement Assn., Oakland, 1987-88; vestry and warden St. Paul's Episcopal Ch., Oakland, 1989-92; dir. Internat. Maritime Ctr., Oakland, 1995—; docent Oakland Mus., 1992, presdl. yacht. U.S.S. Potomac, Jack London Mus., Hugenot Soc. Calif., Thomas Jefferson chpt. SAR. Recipient Cert. Appreciation, Calif. Heritage Coun., San Francisco, 1990. Mem. Bar Assn. Calif., Oakland Tchrs. Assn., Calif. Assn. Orientation and Mobility Specialists, Calif. Alumni Assn., Nat. Audubon Soc., Bay Area Assn. Disabled Sailors, San Francisco Bay Wildlife Soc., E.C.V. YB#1, History Soc., Sierra Club, Calif. Mus. History (docent coun.), Calif. Hist. Soc., Alameda County Hist. Soc., Bates-Corbett Tchr. Assn., Phi Gamma Delta. Republican. Episcopalian. Home: 2806 Bellaire Pl Oakland CA 94601-2010 Personal E-mail: daviddibble@aol.com.

DIBBLE, ELIZABETH JEANE, lawyer, educator; b. Hammond, Ind., May 26, 1958; d. Harold Richard and Janet Deliah (Lane) Elsey; m. John Taylor Dibble, June 7, 1980; children: James Taylor, Katherine Elizabeth. BS in Learning Disabilities cum laude, MacMurray Coll., Jacksonville, Ill., 1979; JD, So. Ill. U., 1983. Bar: Ill. 1983. Tchr. learning disabilities Sedgwick (Kans.) Sch. System, 1979-80; atty. Powless & Brocking, Marion, Ill., 1984-85, Randy Patchett & Assoc., Marion, 1985-86; sole practice Marion, 1987-96. Dir. paralegal studies program Belleville (Ill.) Area Coll., 1996—; part-time lectr. So. Ill. U., Carbondale, 1985—. Fundraiser Rep. Party, Williamson County, Ill, 1986; bd. dirs. So. Ill. Epilepsy Found., Mt. Vernon, 1984-86; mem. Episcopal Ch. Women; religious edn. dir. St. James Episcopal Ch., Marion, 1983-86. Cartwright scholar for women MacMurray Coll.,

1976-79. Mem. Williamson County Bar Assn., Ill. State Bar Assn. Republican. Avocations: racquetball, volleyball, basketball, reading. Home: 6495 Schiermeier Rd Freeburg IL 62243-2035 Office: 400 N Market St Marion IL 62959-2316

DIBBLE, FRANCIS DANIEL, JR., lawyer; b. Holyoke, Mass., Mar. 1, 1947; s. Francis Daniel and Rita (Egan) D.; m. Mary Harris Dibble, June 26, 1971. AB, Amherst Coll., 1971; JD magna cum laude, Suffolk U., 1974. Bar: Mass. 1974, U.S. Dist. Ct. Mass. 1975, U.S. Dist. Ct. Conn. 1978, U.S. Dist. Ct. (ea. dist.) Mich. 1984, U.S. Ct. Appeals (1st cir.) 1987, U.S. Ct. Appeals (D.C. cir.) 1981, U.S. Supreme Ct. 1984. Law clk. to justice Supreme Jud. Ct. of Mass., Boston, 1974-75; from assoc. to mng. ptnr. Bulkley, Richardson and Gelinas, Springfield, Mass., 1975-94, chmn., exec. com., 1997—. Instr. Western New Eng. Law Sch., Springfield, 1979. Contbr. articles to profl. jours. Mem. civil justice adv. bd. U.S. Dist. Ct. Mass.; spl. counsel. Fellow Mass. Bar Found. (life); mem. ABA (antitrust law sect.), Mass. Bar Assn., Hampden County Bar, Boston Bar Assn., The Colony Club, Longmeadow Country Club, East Chop Assn., East Chop Yacht Club, East Chop Tennis Club. Office: Bulkley Richardson and Gelinas LLP 1500 Main St Ste 2700 Springfield MA 01115-0001 Office Phone: 413-781-2820. E-mail: fdibble@bulkley.com.

DIBELLA, RUSSELL THOMAS, federal investigator; b. Phila., Mar. 21, 1934; s. Carmen and Erina (Louden) DiB.; m. Mary Sarah McGivern, Feb. 9, 1957; children: Diane Hanna, Carole Yates, Kathleen Tower, Russell Carmen, Michael Bernard. BS in Bus., LaSalle U., 1962. Bank clk. 1st Pa. Bank, Phila., 1951—62; spl. agt. U.S. Treasury Dept., Phila., 1962—87; criminal investigator N.J. Atty. Gen., Trenton, 1987—89; state investigator N.J. Taxation, Trenton, 1989—97; investigator Def. Security, Tabernacle, NJ, 2002—04; spl. investigator FBI - Background Inestigations Contract Svcs., Tabernacle, 2000—. Ch. organist St. Mary of the Lakes Ch., Medford, NJ, 1980—85; accordionist Aqua String Band, Phila., 1949—50. With USN, 1952—56. Mem.: Fed. Criminal Investigators (regional v.p. 1984—86, pres. 1986—87), Assn. Former Spl. Agts. (nat. pres. 2001—02), Tabernacle Rep. Club (treas. 2001—02), VFW, Am. Legion. Republican. Roman Catholic. Avocations: piano, accordion, competitive pistol shooting. Home: 30 Powell Place Rd Tabernacle NJ 08088 Office: FBI-BICS 30 Powell Place Rd Tabernacle NJ 08088

DIBENEDETTO, GARY, composer, educator; m. Althea Jean Wetzel, May 19, 1984; children: Amy, Colin. BA, Alma White Coll., Zarepath, NJ, 1972; MA, NYU, NYC, 1993. Tchr. cert. State of NJ. Artist-in-residence Hunterdon Cent. HS, Flemington, NJ, 1976—78; instrumental music tchr. Bridgewater Schs., NJ, 1992—93. Adj. instrumental tchr. Hillsborough Schs., NJ, 1993—94; adj. music tchr. Warren CC, Warren City, NJ, 1996—97, Middlesex CC, NJ, 1996—98. Composer: (albums) Season of Adjustment, 1998, Drop in the Bucket, 2000, Twin Towers, 2005. DC3 USN. Recipient Midwest Composers Honorarium, 2000; Composition fellowship, NJ State Coun. on Arts, 2002. Mem.: Soc. Electro-Acoustic Music in US, Internat. Computer Music Assn., Electronic Music Found. Avocations: boating, fishing. Office: Diversity Music PO Box 1296 Belle Mead NJ 08502 Business E-Mail: music@garydibenedetto.com.

DIBENEDETTO, ROBERT LAWRENCE, retired obstetrician, retired gynecologist, insurance company executive; b. New Orleans, Apr. 14, 1928; s. Salvador and Eunice Madeline (Frisch) DiB.; m. Mary Nathalie Roeling, June 20, 1951; children: Madeline E., Robert R., Lawrence W. Student, Tulane U., 1945-47; BS, La. State U., 1948, MD, 1952. Diplomate Am. Bd. Ob-Gyn. Intern Mercy Hosp., New Orleans, 1952-53; resident in pathology La. State U. Med. Sch., 1955-56, clin. assoc. prof. ob-gyn., 1963; resident ob-gyn. Charity Hosp., New Orleans, 1956-59; practice medicine specializing in ob-gyn. Baton Rouge, 1959—94; pres., CEO La. Med. Mutual Ins. Co., New Orleans, 1994—99; ret., 2000. Founding chmn. Mid-La. Health Systems Agy., 1976-77; chmn. bd. dirs., med. dir. Woman's Hosp., Baton Rouge, 1999—; pres. Capitol Area Health Planning, 1975-76; mem. Perinatal Commn. La., Bd. Health, Edn. Authority La., State Health Coord. Council. Served with USPHS, 1953-55. Mem. AMA (past del.), ACOG (past chmn. La. sect.), South Ctrl. Ob-Gyn. Soc., La. Med. Soc. (co-chmn. polit. action com., past pres.), East Baton Rouge Parish Med. Soc. (past pres.), City Club (Baton Rouge), So. Yacht Club (New Orleans), Baton Rouge Country Club. Republican. Roman Catholic. Home: 6666 Pikes Ln Baton Rouge LA 70808-4272 E-mail: RLdiB@cox.net.

DIBERARDINO, MARIE ANTOINETTE, developmental biologist, educator; b. Phila., May 2, 1926; d. Henry and Adelina (Belfi) DiB. BS in Biology, Chestnut Hill Coll., 1948, JD (hon.), 1990; PhD in Zoology, U. Pa., 1962. Rsch. asst. Fox Chase Cancer Ctr. (formerly Inst. Cancer Rsch.), 1948-58, rsch. assoc., 1960-64, asst. mem., 1964-67; assoc. prof. anatomy Drexel U. Coll. Medicine, Phila., 1967-71, prof. anatomy, 1971-81, prof. physiology, 1981-92, prof. biochemistry, 1992-96, prof. emerita, 1996—. Adv. bd. Internat. Rev. of Cytology, 1976-2000, Differentiation, 1981-2004, Series: Developmental Biology, A Comprehensive Synthesis, 1982-94; assoc. editor Jour. Exptl. Zoology, 1984-86; Contbr. articles on devel., genetics and cell biology to sci. jours.; contbr. book revs. in field. Mem. NIH Fogarty Internat. Fellowship Study Group, 1984. NSF grantee, NIH grantee; recipient Jean Brachet Meml. award. Fellow AAAS; mem. Am. Soc. Cell Biology (emerita), Soc. for Devel. Biologists (emerita, treas., trustee 1975-78), Internat. Soc. Devel. Biologists, Internat. Soc. of Differentiation (emerita, exec. com. 1978-85, 87-90, bd. dirs. 1980-94). Home: The Quadrangle 7311 3300 Darby Rd Haverford PA 19041 E-mail: mdiberar@drexelmed.edu.

DIBERT, ROSALIE, elementary school educator; Graduate, Calif. U. of Pa., 1964. Tchr. Pitts. Pub. Schs., 1964—2002; coord. Pitts. Initiative, 2002—. Chmn. Exceptional Needs Com.; Gov. at Large for Tchrs. CEC Exec. Bd.; liaison Profl. Standards Com. Finalist Tchr. of Yr., Pa., 1986; named Clarissa Hug Internat. Spec. Educator of Yr., 1990; recipient Bernice Baumgartner Meml. award; Jordan Fundamentals grant, 2000. Mem.: Nat. Coun. for Exceptional Children Com., Pa. Tchrs. Forum, Pa. State Adv. Bd., Western Region Chpt. #104 (pres.), Pa. Fed. Coun. for Exceptional Children, Pa. Chpt. Tchr. of Yr. Chpt. (pres. 1992), Nat. Bd Profl. Tchg. Standards.

DIBIAGGIO, JOHN A., university president; b. San Antonio, Sept. 11, 1932; s. Ciro and Acidalia DiBiaggio; married; children: David John, Dana Elizabeth, Deirdre Joan; m. Nancy Cronemiller, May 27, 1989. AB, Eastern Mich. U., 1954, D (hon.) of Edn., 1985; DDS, U. Detroit, 1958, LHD (hon.), 1985; MA, U. Mich., 1967; DSc (hon.), Fairleigh Dickinson U., 1981; LLD (hon.), Sacred Heart U., Bridgeport, Conn., 1984; LLD (hon.), U. Md., 1985; DHL (hon.), U. New Eng., 1987; DHL (hon.), Tokyo U. Agr., 1991; LLD (hon.), U. Nigeria, Nsukka, 1992; LHD (hon.), Fitchburg State Coll., 1994; LHD (hon.), Amer. Coll. Greece, 1998; LLD (hon.), Tufts U., 2002. Pvt. practice, New Baltimore, Mich., 1958—65; asst. prof., asst. to dean, dept. chmn. sch. dentistry U. Detroit, 1965—67; asst. dean student affairs U. Ky., Lexington, 1967—70; prof., dean sch. dentistry Va. Commonwealth U., Richmond, 1970—76; v.p. for health affairs, exec. dir. health ctr. U. Conn., Farmington, 1976—79, pres. Storrs, 1979—85, Mich. State U., East Lansing, 1985—92, Tufts U., Medford, Mass., 1992—2001, now pres. emeritus, 2001—; bd. trustees U. Mass., 2003—. Bd. dirs. Kaman Corp.; mem. Knight Found. Commn. on Intercollegiate Athletics, 1990—2001, PEW Health Professions Commn., 1990—93; cons. in field. Author (with others): Applied Practice Management: A Strategy for Stress Control, 1979; contbr. articles to profl. jours. Bd. nominators Am. Inst. Pub. Svc., 1989—92; bd. dirs. Nat. Italian Am. Found., 1988—94; active Bus. Higher Edn. Forum, 1996—2002, WGBH Ednl. Found., 1992—2001, chmn. governance com., 1997—98; trustee U. Detroit, 1979—86, Am. Film Inst., 1988—, Forsyth Dental Ctr., 1993—, Am. Cancer Soc. Found., 1993—, pres., 1999; trustee Oral Health Am., 1995—97; chmn. adv. com. dental scholars R.W. Johnson Found.; pres. com. Argonne Nat. Lab. 6, 1986—92; coun. pres. Univs. Rsch. Assn., 1989—92; bd. dirs. Black Child and Family Inst., 1990, Coun. for Aid to Edn., 1994—96, Mass. Nat. and Cmty. Svc. Commn., 1994—97, Am. Coun. on Edn., 1995—2001, vice-chmn., 1998, chmn., 1999; exec. com. Mass. Campus Compact, 1995—2001, exec. dir. search com., 1996—2000, chmn. devel. com., 1996—, governance com., 1996—98, chmn., 1998; bd. assocs. Whitehead Inst. for Biomed. Rsch., 1995—2001. Decorated Order of Merit Italy; named Disting. Profl. of Yr., Mich. Assn. Profls., 1985, Disting. Alumni, Ea. Mich. U., 1986, Man of Yr., City of Detroit, 1985; recipient Leadership award, Sacred Heart U., Pierre Fauchard Gold Medal award, 1989. Fellow: Internat. Coll. Dentists, Am. Coll. Dentist; mem.: NCAA (found. bd. dirs. 1988—2001, found. divsn. III pres.'s coun. 1997—2001), APHA, ADA, Nat. Assn. State Univs. and Land Grant Colls. (chmn. 1986—87), Internat. Assn. Dental Rsch., Am. Assn. Dental Schs., Mass. Automobile Assn. (bd. dirs. 1992—2002), Am. Automobile Assn. (bd. dirs. 1994—2002), Am. Film Inst., Phi Beta Kappa, Golden Key, Alpha Lambda Delta, Alpha Sigma Chi, Alpha Omega Alpha (Achievement award 1993), Beta Gamma Sigma, Omicron Kappa Upsilon, Phi Kappa Phi. Avocations: golf, antique automobiles, skiing. Home: PO Box 5346 Snowmass Village CO 81615-5346 Business E-Mail: john.dibiaggio@tufts.edu.

DIBIAGIO, THOMAS MICHAEL, lawyer, former prosecutor; b. Balt., June 1960; BA, Dickinson Coll., 1982; JD, U. Richmond, 1985. Bar: Md. 1985, DC 1986. Assoc. Semmes, Brown and Semmes, Balt., 1986—91; asst. U.S. atty. U.S. Dept. Justice, Md., 1991—2000, U.S. atty., 2001—04; ptnr. Dyer, Ellis & Joseph, Washington, 2000—01; shareholder Beveridge & Diamond P.C., Balt., 2005—. Contbr. articles to profl. jours. Office: Beveridge & Diamond PC 201 N Charles St Baltimore MD 21201

DIBIASE, CATHERINE PRISCILLA, nurse; d. Alden Smith Hull and Margaret Antoinette Langley; m. Nicholas Francis DiBiase, Feb. 8, 1986. BS in nursing, 1983. RN, Fla. State Bd. Nursing, 1983, ACLS (Advanced Cardica Life Support), AHA (Am. Heart Assn.), Brevard County, FL, 1989, TNCC (Trauma Nursing Core Course), Health First, FL, 2003, Space Operations Med. Support Tng., Dept. of Def. Manned Spaceflight Office, 1996. Telemetry, staff nurse Boca Raton Cmty. Hosp., Boca Raton, Fla., 1985—87; icu relief charge nurse Parrish Med. Ctr., Titusville, Fla., 1987—89; telemetry, icu staff nurse Humana Hosp., Daytona Beach, Fla., 1989—90; critical care nurse Delray Cmty. Hosp., Delray Beach, Fla., 1989—90; nurse case mgr. Paragon Home Healthcare, Daytona Beach, Fla., 1991—91; critical care clinician and preceptor Bethesaeda Meml. Hosp., Boynton Beach, Fla., 1991—94; aerosapce nurse The Bionetics Corp., Kennedy Space Ctr., Fla., 1994—. Lead and rep. Contract Safety Com., Kennedy Space Center, Fla., 1998—2005. Author: (newsletter) Aerospace Medicine and Resident Organization, On Call column, (brief) Occupational Health Topic - The Aging Workforce. Mem. planning team Ann. Easter Meal for the Needy, Cocoa, Fla., 1996—2000; musician, choir Cath. Ch., Fla., 1976—2001. Recipient NASA Space Flight Awareness Honoree, NASA/Kennedy Space Ctr., 2002, Group Achievement, 2000, KSC Teamwork, 1997, 1998 (2), ARC Appreciation, ARC, 1997, 2000, Vol. Svc. award, Leukemia Soc., 1996, Pub. Svc. Group Achievement, NASA/Kennedy Space Ctr., 2000. Mem.: Aerospace Med. Assn. (corr.), Aerospace Nursing Soc. (corr.), Soc. of NASA Flight Surgeons (hon. Hon. Membership 2002). Avocations: reading, musician, bicycling. Office: The Bionetics Corp Mail Code: BIO-1 Kennedy Space Center FL 32899 Office Phone: 321-867-7462. Personal E-mail: cathydibiase@yahoo.com.

DIBIASIO, ADOLF R, entertainment company executive; BS in elec. engring., U. Rhode Island; MBA, Wharton Bus. Sch. Sr. dir. McKinsey & Co., 1969—2000; exec. v.p., strategy and investments Time Warner, Inc., 2001—. Past trustee Brunswick Sch., Greenwich, Conn., New Canaan Country Sch.; past chmn. Fairfield County March of Dimes; trustee A Better Chance; dir. Wharton Exec. Bd. of Pa. Office: Time Warner Inc 75 Rockefeller Plaza New York NY 10019

DI BISCEGLIE, LAUREEN GAIL, pianist, accompanist, educator; b. Johannesburg, Gauteng, South Africa, Oct. 27, 1955; came to U.S., 1985; d. Peter Cyril and Mavis Gladys (Campbell) Pinn; m. Adrian Michael Di Bisceglie, Dec. 9, 1978; children: Michael James, Anne-Marie Hope. MMus cum laude, U. Witwatersrand, Johannesburg, 1987. Cert. tchr. music. Music tchr. Kingsmead Coll., Johannesburg, 1977-82, head dept. music, 1980-82; pvt. piano tchr. Washington, 1985-95; tchr. music, head music program Barrie Day Sch., Washington, 1987-90; accompanist Wilson Sch., St. Louis, 1987—; pvt. piano tchr. St. Louis, 1995—. Contbr. articles to profl. jours. Vol. music dept. Washington Nat. Cathedral, 1986-87; advisor search com. Christ Episc. Ch., Rockville, Md., 1992-93, outreach com., 1991-92; bd. dirs. Woman's Club, SLU Sch. of Medicine, 1997, chmn. com., 1997—; mem. steering com. Parents Assn., 1997—; co-chair Wilson Sch.'s Thistle Auction, 1998-99, 99-2000; hon. mem. Liver Found's. Ann. Auction com.; mem. outreach com. Ch. of St. Michael and St. George Clayton, St. Louis. Anglo-Am. scholar, 1973-78; Royal Coll. of Ch. Music grantee, Croydon, Eng., 1985. Mem. Music Tchrs. Nat. Assn., St. Louis Area Music Tchrs. Assn. (chair dist. auditions 2002-03, bd. dirs., chair 2002-04, co-chair 2005), Piano Tchrs. Round Table (bd. dirs., v.p. programs, pres.), Suzuki Assn. Am., Fedn. Music Tchrs., Woman's Club (sec. 1998—). Episcopalian. Avocations: reading, travel, gardening, walking. Home: 5 Deer Creek Woods Saint Louis MO 63124-1411

DIBLASI, DIANNE CLARK, editor; b. Bklyn., May 3, 1960; d. Arthur J. and Constance C. (Clark) Mandick; m. Paul J. DiBlasi; 1 child, Bryan Gene. BA in Journalism, NYU, 1982. Asst. editor Random House/Fodor's Travel Guides, N.Y.C., 1983-85; writer, editor Constrn. Products Rev. Mag., Boston, 1986-88; prodn. editor Prentice Hall, Englewood Cliffs, N.J., 1988-91; owner, cons. D. DiBlasi Editl. Svcs., Allendale, NJ, 1991—. Copy editor: Take My Word For It, 1986; prodn. editor: Creativities! Elementary Curriculum Art Activities, 1991, Parenting Toward Solutions, 1997; editor, writer Constrn. Products Rev., 1986-88. Mem. Hillsdale Playground Assn., 1994-96, Hillsdale Centennial Com., 1996; mem. mem., chair com. Meadowbrook Faculty and Family Assn., Hillsdale, 1996—; host Fresh Air Fund, 1997—; docent Wildlife Conservation Soc., Bronx Zoo. Mem.: Editl. Freelancer Assn., Brookside Music Assn. (chmn.). Avocations: animal wildlife outreach programs, fundraising. Home and Office: 222 E Crescent Ave Allendale NJ 07401

DIBLASI, GANDOLFO VINCENT, lawyer; b. Bklyn., July 7, 1953; s. Rudolph Francis and Theresa (Restivo) DiB.; m. Roberta Wilson, Sept. 13, 1980; children: Richard, William. BA, Yale Coll., 1975, JD, 1978. Bar: N.Y., 1979, U.S. Ct. Appeals (2d cir.), 1982, U.S. Ct. Appeals (4th cir.), 1991, U.S. Ct. Appeals (9th cir.), 1981, U.S. Supreme Ct., 1990, U.S. Dist. Ct. (so. dist.) N.Y., 1979, U.S. Dist. Ct. (ea. dist.) N.Y., 1982, U.S. Dist. Ct. (no. dist.) Calif., 1989. Assoc. Sullivan & Cromwell, N.Y.C., 1978-85, ptnr., 1985—. Home: 200 E End Ave Apt 15I New York NY 10128-7887 Office: Sullivan & Cromwell 125 Broad St Fl 28 New York NY 10004-2489 Office Phone: 212-558-3836.

DIBLE, DAVID D., retail executive; m. Gloria Dible; children: Shawn, Bradley. BS in Phys. Edn., Ft. Hays State U., 1969. Dept. mgr. Wal-Mart Stores, Inc., Lebanon, Mo., asst. store mgr. Waynesville, Mo., 1972—73, Monett, Mo., 1972—73, Junction City, Kans., 1972—73, store mgr. Sikeston, Mo., 1973—81, Rolla, Mo., 1973—81, Waynesville, Mo., 1973—81, sporting goods buyer Bentonville, Ark., 1981—82, v.p. divisional merchandise mgr., 1982—85, gen. merchandise mgr. and sr. v.p., 1985—93, exec. v.p. merchandising and sales, 1993—95, exec. v.p. splty. groups Bentonville, 1995—. Active Children's Miracle Network, Spl. Olympics, United Way, Ark. Children's Hosp., N.W. Ark. Crisis Intervention Ctr., Youth Ctr. Recreational Activities. With U.S. Army. Recipient Spl. Recognition, ASDA Stores U.K. Mem.: Nat. Assn. Chain Drug Stores, Internat. Mass Retailers Assn. Office: Wal-Mart Stores Inc 702 SW Eighth St Bentonville AR 72716*

DIBNER, DAVID ROBERT, architect, writer; b. N.Y.C., May 29, 1926; s. Harry Jesse and Masha Leah (Goldberg) D.; m. Dorothy Joyce Siegel, June 22, 1947; children: Mark Douglas, Amy Lauren. B.Arch., U. Pa., 1949. Registered architect, N.Y., Md., Va., D.C. Ptnr. Fordyce & Hamby Assocs., N.Y.C., 1956-66, The Grad Ptnrship., Newark, 1966-77; pres. Grad-Hoffman, Inc., 1971-75; v.p. Walker-Grad, N.Y.C., 1972-77; exec. v.p. Grad Assocs. P.A., Newark, 1975-77; asst. commr. design and constrn. GSA, Washington, 1977-82; sr. v.p. Bernard Johnson Inc., Bethesda, Md., 1982-89; v.p. and prin. architect Sverdrup Corp., Arlington, Va., 1989-92. Adj. prof. Seton Hall U., South Orange, N.J., 1972-77; mem. Bldg. Rsch. Bd. of Nat. Acad. Sci., com. chmn., 1984-92. Author: Joint Ventures for Architects and Engineers, 1972, You and Your Architect, 1973, (with Amy Dibner-Dunlap) Building Additions Design, 1985; editor (with Andrew Lemer) The Role of Public Agencies in Fostering New Technology and Innovation in Building, 1992, Dreams and Schemes: Stories of People and Architecture, 2001; chmn. editorial bd. Architecture/N.J., 1968-71; contbr. articles to profl. jours. Mem. West Orange Bd. of Adjustment, N.J., 1970-77, Nat. Trust for Historic Preservation. Served with USN, 1944-46, PTO. Fellow AIA (Washington chpt.). E-mail: drdibs@cox.net.

DIBONA, CHARLES JOSEPH, retired trade association executive; b. Quincy, Mass., Feb. 26, 1932; s. Guido Ralph and Helen Elizabeth (Pangraze) DiB.; m. Evelyn Rauch, July 2, 1959; children: Caroline Anne, Charles J. BS, U.S. Naval Acad., 1956; MA (Rhodes scholar), Oxford U., Eng., 1962. Pres., chief exec. officer Center for Naval Analyses, 1967-73; spl. cons. to Pres. U.S., dep. dir.; White House Energy Policy Office, 1973-74; exec. v.p., chief oper. officer Am. Petroleum Inst., Washington, 1974-78, pres., chief exec. officer, 1979-98; ret., 1998. Hon. dir. Am. Petroleum Inst.; mem. Fed. City Coun. Lt. comdr. USN, 1956-67. Mem. Cosmos Club, Met. Club, Chevy Chase Country Club. Roman Catholic. Home: 9306 Georgetown Pike Great Falls VA 22066-2725 Personal E-mail: dibonac@erols.com.

DIBONAVENTURA, LORENZO, film company executive; b. 1957; m. Kimberly DiBonaventura; 2 children. Attended, Harvard U. Production exec. to production v.p. Warner Bros., Inc., Burbank, Calif., 1989—93, sr. v.p. production, 1993—95, exec. v.p. production, 1995—96, co-pres. Worldwide Theatrical Prodn., 1996—98, pres. worldwide production, 1998—2002, exec. v.p. worldwide motion pictures, 1998—2002; pres. DiBonaventura Pictures, Los Angeles, Calif., 2002—. Office: Warner Bros Inc 4000 Warner Blvd Burbank CA 91522-0002

DICAMILLO, GARY THOMAS, manufacturing executive; b. Niagara Falls, N.Y., Dec. 10, 1950; s. Joseph John and Olga Marie (Parenti) DiC.; m. Susan Christine Whitaker, Sept. 13, 1975; children: David, John, Benjamin. BSChemE, Rensselaer Poly. Inst., 1973; MBA, Harvard U., 1975. Brand mgr. Procter & Gamble, Cin., 1975-80; mgr. Mckinsey & Co., Chgo., 1980-83; v.p., gen. mgr. Culligan Internat. Co., Northbrook, Ill., 1983-86; pres. Worldwide Power Tools Group Black & Decker Corp., Towson, Md., 1986-95; chmn., CEO Polaroid Corp., Cambridge, Mass., 1995—2002; pres., CEO TAC Worldwide Cos., 2002—. Bd. dirs. Whirlpool Corp., Pella Corp., Sheridan Group, 3Com Corp. Mem. bd. govs. New Eng. Aquarium, 1996-2003; commr. Md. Pub. Broadcasting Commn., 1988-93; trustee St. Paul's Sch., 1988-95, Greater Balt. Com., Md. Sci. Ctr.; bd. dirs. Leadership Balt., 1991-93; trustee Mus. of Sci., Boston, Rensselaer Poly. Inst.; mem. bd. trustees The Conf. Bd., 1999-2002. Recipient Albert Demers medal, Livingston Houston prize, Rensselaer Poly. Inst., 1973; Buffalo Alumni scholar Buffalo area Rensselaer Poly. Inst. Alumni, 1969; Chirurg Advt. fellow Harvard U. Bus. Sch., 1974; recipient Rensselaer Poly. Inst. Dirs. award, 1989. Mem. Water Quality Assn. (bd. dirs. 1985-86), Md. Acad. Scis. (bd. dirs. 1991-96), Rensselaer Poly. Inst. Club (bd. dirs. 1987-91, pres.), Rensselaer Alumni Assn. (bd. dirs. 1989-93, Alumni Key award 1990), Hardware Mktg. Coun., DIY Rsch. Inst. (bd. dirs. 1989-90), Skokie Country Club, Elkridge Club, Md. Club, L'Hirondelle Club, Willowbend Club, Wianno Club, Brae Burn Country Club, Harvard Club, Ocean Reef Club Republican. Avocations: golf, squash, antique furniture, italian cooking. Home: 113 Cliff Rd Wellesley MA 02481-3017 Office: TAC Worldwide Cos 888 Washington St Dedham MA 02026

DICAMILLO, KATE, writer; b. Phila. Degree, U. Fla., Gainesville, Fla. Author: (children's books) Because of Winn-Dixie, 2000 (named Newbery Honor Book, 2001, Dorothy Canfield Fisher Children's Book award, 2002, NY Times Bestseller, Publishers Weekly Bestseller children's fiction list, 2005), The Tiger Rising, 2001 (Nat. Book award finalist, 2000), The Tale of Despereaux: Being the Story of a Mouse, a Princess, Some Soup, and a Spool of Thread, 2003 (Newbery medal, 2004, NY Times Bestseller, USA Today Bestseller, Book Sense Bestseller, Publishers Weekly Bestseller), Mercy Watson to the Rescue, 2005. Grantee McKnight Artist fellowship, 1998. Office: Candlewick Press Inc 2067 Massachusetts Ave Cambridge MA 02140*

DICANDILO, MICHAEL D, corporate financial executive, accountant; BSc in acctg., Wharton Sch., U. Pa. CPA. With Ernst & Young, 1982—90; regional v.p. of fin. AmeriSource, 1990—95, v.p., 1995—2001; v.p., corp. contr. AmerisourceBergen Corp., 2001—02; sr. v.p., CFO Amerisource Bergen Corp., 2002—.

DICAPRIO, LEONARDO, actor; b. Hollywood, Calif., Nov. 11, 1974; s. George and Irmelin DiC. Actor: (films) Critters III, 1991, This Boy's Life, 1993, What's Eating Gilbert Grape?, 1993 (Academy award nomination best supporting actor 1993), The Quick and the Dead, 1995, The Basketball Diaries, 1995, Total Eclipse, 1995, Romeo and Juliet, 1996, Marvin's Room, 1996, Titanic, 1997, The Man in the Iron Mask, 1998, Celebrity, 1998, The Beach, 2000, Dons Plum, 2001, Gangs of New York, 2002, Catch Me If You Can, 2002; actor, prodr., The Aviator, 2004 (Golden Globe award for best actor, 2005); exec. prodr. The Assassination of Richard Nixon, 2004; (TV series) Parenthood, 1990, Growing Pains, 1991-92. Founder The Leonardo DiCaprio Charitable Found., 1998—. Named Commdr. Order of Arts & Letters, Govt. France, 2005; named one of 50 Most Powerful People in Hollywood, Premiere mag., 2003—05; recipient Green Cross Millenium award for Entertainment Ind. Environ., Global Green USA, 2003, Platinum award, Santa Barbara Internat. Film Festival, 2005.*

DICARLO, MICHAEL ALEXANDER, library director; b. Lake Charle, La., Feb. 9, 1953; s. Secondo Lawrence DiCarlo, Eugenia Bernadette DiCarlo; m. Rebecca Lynn McKillips; 1 child, Carrifrances. BA in History, Tulane U., 1975; MLS, La. State U., 0197. Info. svcs. libr. bus./social scis., instrnl. Northeast La. U., Monreo, 1978—81; head libr. automation La. Tech. U., Ruston, 1983—87, head reference & libr. automation, 1987—91, asst. dir. pub. svcs., 1991—96, interim dir. librs., 1996—97, assoc. dir. libs., 1997—. Recipient Certificate of Recognition, Sigma Xi, La. Tech.chpt., 1992. Mem.: La. Libr. Assn. (Anthony H. Benoit Mid-Career award, New Mem. Round Table 1995), Beta Phi Mu, Phi Alpha Theta. Roman Catholic. Office: La Tech Univ- Prescott Libr Everett St at The Columns Ruston LA 71272 Office Phone: 318-257-2577. Office Fax: 318-257-2579. Business E-Mail: miked@latech.edu.

DICCIANNI, MITCHELL B., oncologist, research scientist; AS, Suffolk C.C., 1980; BS, Stony Brook U., 1983; PhD, U. Cin., 1989. Rsch. scientist U. Calif., San Diego, 1992—. Vis. scientist Tokyo U., 1990—92. Contbr. scientific papers. Fellow, Japan Soc. Promotion Sci., 1990. Mem.: U. Calif. San Diego Moores Cancer Ctr., Childrens Oncology Group, Am. Assn. Cancer Rsch. Achievements include research in Pediatric Cancer Research. Office: U Calif 200 W Arbor Dr San Diego CA 92103-8447 Office Phone: 619-543-6844. Office Fax: 619-543-5413. Personal E-mail: mdiscover@hotmail.com. E-mail: mdiccianni@ucsd.edu.

DICE, BRUCE BURTON, gas industry executive; b. Grand Rapids, Mich., Dec. 24, 1926; s. William and Wilma (Rose) D.; children: Karen, Kevin, Kirk. BS in Geology, U. Mich., 1950; MS in Geology, Mich. State U., 1956. With El Paso Natural Gas, 1956—62, Drilling and Exploration Co., 1962—63, Ocean Drilling and Exploration, New Orleans, 1963—75; pres. Transco Exploration Co., Houston, 1975—82, Dice Exploration Co., Inc., Houston, 1982—95, Wadi Petroleum, Inc., Houston, 1996—. Cons. in field. Mem.:

Shepherd Soc., Houston Geol. Soc., Am. Assn. Petroleum Geologists. Home: 1907 Grand Valley Dr Houston TX 77090-1052 Office: Wadi Petroleum Inc 14405 Walters Rd Houston TX 77014-1337 Business E-Mail: sgc@wadipetroleum.com.

DICELLO, FRANCIS P., lawyer; b. Waukegan, Ill., May 5, 1941; s. Anthony M. and Mary Dicello; m. Mary Janice Dicello; children: Anthony, Andrew, Carlotta. BA, U. Notre Dame, 1963; JD, Fordham U., 1966. Bar: Conn. 1966, D.C. 1967, Md 1984, Va 1982. Trial atty. U.S. Dept. Justice, Washington, 1970-76; dep. asst., gen. counsel U.S. Railway Assn., Washington, 1976-78; asst., chief trial & settlement rev. sects. tax divsn. U.S. Dept. Justice, Washington, 1978-79; U.S. trustee ea. dist. Va. and D.C., 1979—82; ptnr., owner Hazel & Thomas, P.C., Washington, 1982-94; ptnr. Reed Smith, LLP, Washington, 1994—. Fellow Am. Coll. Bankruptcy; mem. Am. Bankruptcy Inst. Office: Reed Smith LLP 1301 K St NW Ste 1100E Washington DC 20005-3373 Office Phone: 202-414-9200. E-mail: fdicello@reedsmith.com.

DICELLO, JOHN FRANCIS, JR., physicist, researcher; b. Bradford, Pa., Dec. 18, 1938; s. John Francis and Nicolina Camille (Costello) D.; m. Shirley Ann Rodgers, Aug. 25, 1962; children: John Francis III, Paul T. BS, St. Bonaventure U., 1962-63; MS, U. Pitts., 1962; PhD, Tex. A&M U., 1968. Instr. St. Bonaventure U., 1962-63; Univ. grad. fellow Tex. A&M U., College Station, 1963-65; AEC-Assoc. Western Univs. grad. fellow Los Alamos Nat. Lab., 1965-67, staff scientist, 1973-84; rsch. assoc., rsch. scientist Columbia U., N.Y.C., 1967-73; faculty U. N.Mex., Los Alamos, 1980-82; faculty fellowship Northwest Coll. and Univ. Assn. for Sci., Pacific N.W. Labs., 1989; prof. physics Clarkson U., Potsdam, N.Y., 1982-95; dir. med. physics and prof. oncology, joint appointment Johns Hopkins U., Balt., 1995—. Mem. peer rev. panel NASA specialized ctrs. of rsch. and tng., 1991—; mem. ad hoc com. NIH/Dept. Energy, 1991—; vis. prof. Johns Hopkins Oncology Ctr., 1992-93. Bd. dirs. N.Mex. divsn. Am. Cancer Soc., 1978-82; mem. sci. com. #88 and #93, Nat. Coun. on Radiation Protection and Measurements, 1992—; mem. task group on biol. effects of space radiation NRC NAS, 1996. Mem. AAUP, IEEE (nuc. and plasma scis. divsn.), Am. Assn. Physicists in Medicine, Radiation Rsch. Soc. (editl. bd., assoc. editor Radiation Rsch. jour. 1992-96), Am. Inst. Biol. Scis. (radiation health peer rev. panel to NASA 1990-94), Am. Phys. Soc. (com. on space rsch.), Sigma Xi (pres. Clarkson U. chpt. 1991-92), Sigma Pi Sigma. Roman Catholic. Achievements include research in field of physics, dosimetry, microdosimetry, radiation biology, cancer research, integrated circuits, accelerator and nuclear physics, heavy-particle radiation therapy. Office: Johns Hopkins U Sch Medicine Oncology Ctr Divsn Radiation Oncology 600 N Wolfe St Baltimore MD 21287-0005

DI CHIERA, DAVID, opera company director; b. McKeesport, Pa., Apr. 8, 1935; s. Cosimo and Maria (Pezzaniti) DiC.; m. Karen VanderKloot, July 20, 1965 (div. 1992); children: Lisa Maria, Cristina Maria. BA in Music summa cum laude, UCLA, 1956, MA in Composition (scholar), 1958, PhD in Musicology, 1962; certificate in composition and piano (Fulbright Research grantee), Naples Conservatory of Music, 1959; D (hon.), U. Mich., 1998. Instr. music U. Calif., Los Angeles, 1960-61; asst. prof. music, asst. dean Oakland U., Rochester, Mich., 1962-65, chmn. music dept., 1966-73; founding gen. dir. Mich. Opera Theatre, Detroit, 1971—; founding dir. Music Hall Center for the Performing Arts, Detroit, 1973—. Artistic dir. Dayton Opera Assn., 1981-92; founding gen. dir. Opera Pacific, Costa Mesa, Calif., 1985-97; trustee Nat. Opera Inst.; adj. prof. Oakland U., Wayne State U. Producer, dir.: Overture to Opera series for Detroit Grand Opera series, 1963-71; Composer various works for piano, violin, orch., voice; author articles on Italian opera for various encyclopedias; contbr. revs. and articles to music jours. Mem. Arts Com. New Detroit, Inc.; trustee, mem. exec. com. Music Center for Performing Arts; mem. Arts Task Force City of Detroit. Recipient Atwater Kent award U. Calif., Los Angeles, 1961; Certificate of Appreciation City of Detroit, 1970; citation Mich. Legislature, 1976; Michaelangelo award Boys' Town of Italy, 1980; award Arts Found. of Mich., 1981; President's Cabinet award U. Detroit, 1982; George Gershwin fellow, 1958; named A Michiganian of Yr., 1980; cavaliere della Repubblica Italiana. Mem. Am. Arts Alliance (exec. com.), Nat. Opera Assn., Internat. Assn. Lyric Theatre (v.p.), Am. Symphony League, Am. Musicol. Soc., OPERA Am. (pres. 1979-83), AAUP, Phi Beta Kappa, Phi Mu Alpha Sinfonia. Clubs: Detroit Athletic. Office: Mich Opera Theatre 1526 Broadway St Detroit MI 48226-2115 Office Phone: 313-237-3420. E-mail: ddd@motopera.org.*

DICHTER, BARRY JOEL, lawyer; b. Brookline, Mass., Feb. 19, 1950; s. Irving Melvin and Arlene Dichter; m. Judith Rand, Oct. 22, 1972; children: Rebecca Lynn, Jason Benjamin. AB magna cum laude, Harvard U., 1972, JD cum laude, 1975. Bar: Mass. 1975, N.Y. 1976, U.S. Dist. Ct. (so. and ea. dists.) N.Y. 1976, D.C. 1980, U.S. Dist. Ct. D.C. 1980, U.S. Ct. Appeals (D.C. cir.) 1985. Assoc. Webster & Sheffield, N.Y.C., 1975-82, Cadwalader, Wickersham & Taft, N.Y.C., 1983-84, ptnr., 1984—. Lectr. in field. Contbg. editor: Collier on Bankruptcy, 15th edit., rev. Vice chmn. Harvard Law Sch. Fund, Cambridge, Mass., 1984-88, class agt., 1988-99; bd. dirs. Children's Corner, Inc., 1990-95, treas., 1992-95; mem. exec. com., bankruptcy and reorgn. group of lawyers divsn. N.Y. United Jewish Appeal. Mem. ABA (mem. task force on Sect. 110 1991-92, mem. task force on emerging issues in the transp. industry 1992-96, mem. task force on Article 9 securitization issues), Assn. of Bar of City of N.Y. (mem. bankruptcy com. 1986-89, 91-94). Office: Cadwalader Wickersham & Taft LLP One World Financial Ctr New York NY 10281

DICHTER, MARC ALLEN, physician; b. N.Y.C., Dec. 1, 1943; m. Carole Dichter; children: Harold, Eric. BS, Queen Coll. CUNY, 1964; MD, PhD, NYU, 1969. Asst. prof., assoc. prof. neurology Harvard Med. Sch., Boston, 1975-86; prof. neurology U. Pa., Phila., 1986—. Lt. comdr. USPHS, 1970-72. Office: Hosp U Pa Dept Neurology 3400 Spruce St Philadelphia PA 19104-4206 Office Phone: 215-349-5166.

DICHTER, MARK S., lawyer; b. Phila., Jan. 22, 1943; s. Harry B. and Mollie (Silverstein) D.; m. Tobey Gordon, Aug. 17, 1969; children: Aliza, Melissa. BSEE, Drexel U., 1966; JD magna cum laude, Villanova U., 1969. Bar: Pa. 1969, U.S. Ct. Appeals (3d cir.) 1969, U.S. Supreme Ct. 1979. Assoc. Morgan, Lewis & Bockius, LLP, Phila., 1969-76, ptnr., 1976—, chmn. labor and employment law practice group. Co-author: Employee Dismissal Law: Forms and Procedures, 1986-91; editor-in-chief Ann. Supplement Employment Discrimination Law, 1984-89; co-editor: Employment-at-will, 1985, 86, State-by-State Survey, 1984-89; adv. bd. Disability Law Reporter. Bd. dirs. Urban League Phila.; bd. dirs., chmn. Wilma Theater; bd. consultors Villanova U. Sch. Law; bd. dirs. Pub. Interest Law Ctr. Phila. Mem. ABA (labor and employment law sect., chmn. 2000-01, mem. governing coun. 1991-2000, co-chmn. equal opportunity com. 1986-89, employment law com. litigation sect.), FBA (vice chmn. equal employment com. 1983-86), Nat. Employment Law Inst. (adv. bd. 1984—), Am. Employment Law Counsel (bd. dirs.), Am. Coll. Employment Lawyers, Def. Rsch. Inst. (chmn. employment law com. 1989-93). Office: Morgan Lewis & Bockius LLP 1701 Market St Philadelphia PA 19103-2903 Office Phone: 215-963-5291. Office Fax: 215-963-5001. Business E-Mail: mdichter@morganlewis.com.

DICICCO, TONY, soccer coach; b. Wethersfield, Conn., Aug. 5, 1948; m. Diane; children: Anthony, Andrew, Alex, Nicholas. Grad., Springfield Coll., 1970; M in Phys. Edn., Ctrl. Conn. State U.; advanced nat. diploma, Nat. Soccer Coaches Assn. Am. Lic. U.S. Soccer A. Profl. soccer player Conn. Wildcats, RI Oceaneers; asst. coach US Women's Nat. Soccer Team, 1991-94, head coach, 1994-99; asst. coach Under 20 Men's Nat. Team, 1993. Founder Soccer Plus, Inc., Specialty Stores, 1981—, Soccer Plus Goalkeeper Schs., 1981—; region I boys goalkeeper dir.; goalkeeper specialist Nat. Soccer Coaches Assn. Am.; conductor US Soccer and Nat. Soccer Coaches Assn. Am. nat. licensing camps.; former commr. Women's United Soccer Assn.; mem. Fedn. Internat. Football Assn. Panel of Instrs. and Lectrs. for Coaching, 2002-; commentator in the field. Started HS soccer progams Bellows Falls HS, Bellow Falls, Vt., South Catholic HS, Hartford, Conn. Achievements include guided the team to a third place finish at the 2nd Fedn. Internat. Football Assn. (FIFA) Women's World Championship in Sweden in 1995 and to first place in the U.S. Women's Cup in the years 1995-99; leading the US Nat. Team to the first ever gold medal in Olympic women's soccer in 1996, Pan Am Games in 1998 and World Cup Championship in 1999. Office: #202 11 Executive DR Farmington CT 06032-2854

DICINTIO, MICHELLE S., lawyer; BA in Polit. Sci. and Bus., U. Redlands, 1986—90; JD, U. Va. Sch. of Law, 1990—93. Bar: D.C., Va. 1993. Assoc., corp. & securities group Dechert Price & Rhoads, Washington, 1993—95, Dickstein Shapiro Morin & Oshinsky, Washington, 1995—2000; counsel, corp. & securities group Jenner & Block, Washington, 2000—01; dir., sr. counsel Gen. Dynamics Corp., Falls Church, Va., 2001—03, staff v.p., asst. gen. counsel, 2003—. Mentor Everybody Wins, Washington, 2001—05. Mem.: ABA, Compliance and Ethics Leadership Counsel, Am. Corp. Counsel Assn., Phi Beta Kappa. Office: Gen Dynamics Corp 2941 Fairview Pk Dr Ste 100 Falls Church VA 22042 Office Phone: 703-876-3000. Office Fax: 703-876-3554. E-mail: mdicintio@gd.com.

DICK, BERNARD MARTIN, human resources specialist, political organization worker; b. Chgo., July 3, 1924; Owner, operator Ill. Wholesale, Oak Park, 1946—72, Rudd Ford Inc., Cobden, Ill., 1972—83; sales mgr. J. M. Pumtial, Hollywood, Fla., 1983—89; with U.S. Peace Corps, Quito, Ecuador, 1993—96; job developer Easter Seals, Paducah, Ky., 1993—. Job developer Sr. Citizen Spl. Employment Program, Washington, 1993—. Vol. U.S. Peace Corps, Ecuador, 1992; mem. U.S. Peace Coalition, Ill., 1989; vol. Vets. United, Washington, 1992—2005, Dem. Com., Washington, 1948. Sgt. U.S. Army, 1942—45. Recipient diploma on svc., Garchi Province, 1993, Achievement award, State of Ill., 2001. Mem.: NAACP, VFW, DAV. Avocations: reading, gardening, travel, carpentry. Home: 610 Heern Rd Cobden IL 62920 Office: Eastern Seals 213 S 13th St Murphysboro IL 62966

DICK, BERTRAM GALE, JR., physics professor; b. Portland, Oreg., June 12, 1926; s. Bertram Gale and Helen (Meengs) D.; m. Ann Bradford Volkmann, June 23, 1956; children— Timothy Howe, Robin Louise, Stephen Gale. BA, Reed Coll., 1950, Wadham Coll., Oxford (Eng.) U., 1953, MA, 1958; PhD, Cornell U., 1958. Rsch. assoc. U. Ill., 1957-59; mem. faculty U. Utah, 1959-98, prof. physics, 1965-98, prof. emeritus, 1998—, Univ. prof., 1979-80, chmn. dept., 1964-67, dean grad. sch., 1987-93. Cons. Minn. Mining and Mfg. Co., 1960-67; vis. prof. Technische Hochschule, Munich, 1967-68; vis. scientist Max Planck Institut für Festkörperforschung, Stuttgart, Fed. Republic Germany, 1976-77; faculty Semester at Sea, fall 1983, 86. Mem. Alta Planning and Zoning Commn., 1972-76; pres. Chamber Music Salt Lake City, 1974-76; bd. trustees Citizen's Com. to Save Our Canyons, 1972—, Coalition for Utah's Future Project 2000, 1989-96. Served with USNR, 1944-46. Rhodes scholar, Oxford U., 1951—53. Fellow Am. Phys. Soc.; mem. Am. Alpine Club, Phi Beta Kappa, Sigma Xi. Achievements include research in solid state theory. Home: 1377 Butler Ave Salt Lake City UT 84102-1803 E-mail: gdick@xmission.com.

DICK, DEBBIE ANN, elementary school educator; b. Hillsboro, Kans., Feb. 9, 1962; d. Gordon Dale and Doris Delue Dalke; m. Douglas Bradley Dick, June 4, 1983; children: Daniel, Devin, David. BA, Tabor Coll., 1984. Tchr. Hillsboro Elem. Sch., 1984—. Mennonite Brethern. Home: 206 S Wilson Hillsboro KS 67063

DICK, HAROLD LATHAM, manufacturing executive; b. Wichita, Kans., Oct. 24, 1943; s. Harold G. and Evelyn (Spines) D.; m. Jeanne Marie Luczai, Aug. 25, 1973; children: Harold Campbell, Edward Latham. BA, Washburn U., 1966; MBA, Harvard U., 1968. Exec. asst. to treas. Skelly Oil Co., Tulsa, 1968-70; mgmt. cons. McKinsey & Co. Inc., Chgo., Dallas, Houston, 1970-77; dir. planning Frito-Lay Inc., Dallas, 1977-80; v.p. Norton Simon Inc., N.Y.C., 1980-83; founder Summit Ptnrs., Wichita, Kans., 1983-85; pres., chief exec. officer Doskocil Cos. Inc., Hutchinson, Kans., 1985-88; founder, pres. The Summit Group, Hutchinson, 1988—. Adv. bd. dirs. Garvey Industries, Wichita, 1987-94, Petroleum Inc., Wichita, 1993—. Trustee Kanza coun. Boy Scouts Am., 1989-97, exec. bd., 1995-97, v.p 1997—, exec. bd. dirs. Quivira coun., 1997—, v.p., 1997-98, coun. commr., 1998-2002, coun. pres., 2002-04, nat. coun. rep., 2004-; Stephen minister, 1987-94; mem. bd. regents Washburn U., 1995—2003, chmn. bd. regents, 2001-02, chmn. fin. com., 1998-2001, mem. presdl. search com., 1987-88; chmn. Washburn Regents Soc., 2003—; trustee Washburn Endowment Assn., 1990- . Mem. Washburn Alumni Assn. (bd. dirs. 1986-89, Disting. Svc. award), Washburn Regents Soc. (chmn. fin. com. 2004—), Former Regents Soc. (chmn. 2004—). Republican. Episcopalian. Office: The Summit Group PO Box 3216 Hutchinson KS 67504-3216 Personal E-mail: hldick@yahoo.com.

DICK, HENRY HENRY, minister; b. Russia, June 1, 1922; s. Henry Henry and Mary (Unger) D.; m. Erica Penner, May 25, 1946; children— Janet (Mrs. Arthur Enns), Judith (Mrs. Ron Brown), James, Henry. Th.B., Mennonite Brethren Bible Coll., 1950. Ordained to ministry Mennonite Brethren Ch., 1950; pastor in Orillia, Ont., Can., 1950-54, Lodi, Calif., 1954-57, Shafter, Calif., 1958-69; faculty Tabor Coll., 1954-55; gen. sec. Mennonite Brethren Conf. of U.S.A., 1969-72; pres. Mennonite Brethren Bibl. Sem., Fresno, Calif., 1972-76; vice moderator Gen Conf. Mennonite Brethren Ch., 1975-78, moderator, 1979-84; pastor Reedley Mennonite Brethren Ch., 1976-88; ret., 1989; dir. ch. and constituency relations Mennonite Brethren Biblical Sem., 1987-89; dist. min. emeritus Mennonites, 2002—. Moderator Pacific Dist. Conf., 1959-60, 61-63, 75-77; mem. exec. com. Mennonite Central Com. Internat., 1967-75, mem. bd. reference and counsel, 1966-69, 72-75, mem. bd. missions and services, 1969-72; exec. sec. Bd. Edn. Mennonite Brethren, 1969-72; chmn. Bd. Missions and Services, 1985-91; pastor emeritus Reedley Mennonite Brethren Ch., 1987. Columnist bi-weekly publ. Christian Leader, 1969-75. Bd. dirs. Bob Wilson Meml. Hosp., Ulysses, Kans., 1969-72; dist. minister Pacific Dist. Conf. Mennonite Brethren, 1989—. Recipient Humanitarian award Shafter C. of C., 1969, Citation bd. dirs. Bibl. Sem. Mem.: Kiwanis, Reedley Rotary. Mem. Mennonite Brethren Ch. Home: 783 W Carpenter Ave Reedley CA 93654-3903 Office: 1632 L St Reedley CA 93654-3340

DICK, JAMES CORDELL, concert pianist; b. Hutchinson, Kans., June 29, 1940; s. George Gerhard and Dorothy Lois (Ulsh) Dick., 1958-63; studied with, Dalies Frantz; MusB with spl. honors, U. Tex., 1963; studied with Sir Clifford Curzon, 1963-65; postgrad., Royal Acad. Music, London, 1963-65. Concert pianist Sol Hurok Presents, N.Y.C., 1968-70, Shaw Concerts, N.Y.C., 1970-75, Columbia Artists, N.Y.C., 1975-89, A.G. Declert and Assocs., Round Top, Tex., 1989—. Founder, artistic dir. Internat. Festival-Inst., Round Top, 1971—; judge internat. rec. competition Nat. Guild Piano Tchrs., 1970—71; nat. cons. music com. Inst. Internat. Edn., N.Y.C., 1971—72; mem. internat. jury Tschaikovsky Competition, Moscow, 1974, Van Cliburn Competition, Ft. Worth, 1975, Ft. Worth, 78; chmn. Fulbright Panel in Music, N.Y.C., 1978. Commd. (Am. piano concerto) Shiva's Drum, (nominated Pulitzer Prize in music), 1994. Recipient First Prize award Shreveport Symphony Competition, 1958-60, San Angelo Symphony Competition, 1958-60, Dallas Symphony, 1961-62, Nat. Guild Piano Tchrs., 1961-62, Tschaikovsky Internat. Competition, 1965-66, Leventritt Piano Competition, 1965-66, Busoni Internat. Piano Competition, 1965-66, Citation cert. Tex. Ho. Reps., 1975, award Japan Soc. Houston, 1975, Presdl. citation Nat. Fedn. Music Clubs, 1979, Round Top award Gov. William. P. Clements, Tex., 1980, Headliner of Yr. award Headliners Club, 1983, Tex. State Musician award, 2003; honoree Pres. Lyndon B. Johnson, 1965-66; nominee Pulitzer Prize in Music, 1974; commd. Amb. of Goodwill, State of Tex., 1978; named Hon. Texan, Gov. Dolph Briscoe, 1978, Chevalier des Arts et Lettres French Ministry Culture, 1994; Fulbright scholar, Tobias Matthay fellow, Royal Acad. Music, Hon assoc., 1969, recipient Merit cert., 1965, Beethoven prize, Recital medal, Chevalier des Arts et Lettres, French Ministry of Cult., 1994; named Tex. State Musician, 2003. Mem.: Tex. Lyceum Assn. (adv. dir. 1978—), Tex. Fedn. Music Clubs (hon. life), Philos. Soc. Tex. (treas. 1976—), English Speaking Union, Bohemians Club (N.Y.C.), Tuesday Mus. Club (hon.), Rotary Internat. (hon. life), Sigma Alpha Iota (hon. nat. patron 2001). Avocations: architecture, landscaping, literature, poetry, woodworking. Office Phone: 979-249-3129. Office Fax: 979-249-5078. Business E-Mail: jamesd@festivalhill.org.

DICK, JOHN R., information technology executive; m. Mary Valenta; 2 children. Grad., U. Va., 1979. Exec. GMAC, Detroit; exec. v.p. and chief info. officer Regions Fin. Corp., Birmingham, Ala., 2001—. Named one of top tech. innovators, Info. Week mag., 2004. Office: EVP & CIO Regions Fin Corp 417 N 20th St Birmingham AL 35202

DICK, RAYMOND DALE, psychologist, educator; b. Toledo, Ohio, July 16, 1930; s. Floyd Edward and Clara Belle (Spilker) D.; m. Beverly Ann Sparks, June 18, 1955; children: Gregory Dale, Jeffrey Clayton. BS, Northwestern U., 1952; MA, U. Mo., 1955, PhD, 1958. Asst. prof. psychology Ft. Hays (Kans.) State Coll., 1958-62; assoc. prof. Fort Hayes (Kans.) State Coll., 1962-64, prof., 1964-66, acad. chmn. psychology dept., 1959-66; prof. psychology U. Wis., Eau Claire, 1966-98, dean Sch. Grad Studies, 1966-81, prof. emeritus, 1998—. Assoc. Danforth Found., 1962-84, also chmn. Upper Midwest selection com., 1969-72; mem. com. liberal arts edn. North Central Assn. Colls. and Secondary Schs., 1963-66, coordinator liberal arts com., 1965-68, cons-examiner, 1971— Contbr. profl. jours. Mem. APA, AAAS. Home: 2823 Irene Dr Eau Claire WI 54701-6692 E-mail: rddick@uwec.edu.

DICK, RICHARD IRWIN, environmental engineer, educator; b. Sanborn, Iowa, July 18, 1935; s. Laurence Irwin and Lillian Marie (Riesser) D.; m. Delores Kay Den Beste, Aug. 31, 1958; children: Natalie Ann, Kevin Irwin, Laura Lynn, Craig David. BS, Iowa State U., 1957; MS, State U. Iowa, 1958; PhD, U. Ill., 1965. Sanitary engr. USPHS, Kansas City, Mo., 1958-60; sanitary engr. Clark, Daily and Dietz (Cons. Engrs.), Urbana, Ill., 1960-62; instr. to prof. civil engring. U. Ill., 1962-72; prof. civil engring. U. Del., Newark, 1972-77; Joseph P. Ripley prof. engring. Cornell U., Ithaca, NY, 1977—2002, Joseph P. Ripley prof. emeritus, 2002—; Thomas R. Camp lectr. Boston Soc. Civil Engrs., 1981. Disting. vis. scientist U.S. EPA Water Engring. Rsch. Lab., Cin., 1986-89; vis. engr. Water Pollution Rsch. Lab., Stevenage, Eng., 1970-71; hon. rsch. fellow Univ. Coll. London, 1990; vis. prof. U. B.C., Vancouver, 1991, McGill U., Montreal, 1991. Contbr. over 200 articles to profl. jours. Served with USPHS, 1958-60. Recipient Disting. Alumnus award, U. Ill., 1996, Daniel M. Lazar '29 Excellence in Tchg. award, 1996, James M. and Martha D. McCormick award for excellence in advising, 1999. Mem.: ASCE (Rudolph Hering medal 1986), Charted Instn. Water and Environ. Mgmt., Am. Water Works Assn., Water Environment Fedn. (Harrison Prescott Eddy medal 1968), Internat. Water Assn. (past mem. exec. com., bd. govs.), Assn. Environ. Engring. Profs. (past pres., Disting. lectr. 1980, Outstanding Pub. award 1986, 1987, Founder's award 1998), Phi Kappa Phi, Chi Epsilon (U. Ill. Chpt. Honor mem. 1980, Cornell U. Prof. of Yr. 1995, 2002), Tau Beta Pi, Sigma Xi. Home: 115 W Upland Rd Ithaca NY 14850-1415 Office: Cornell U 105 Hollister Hall Ithaca NY 14853-3501 Business E-Mail: rid@cornell.edu.

DICK, WILLIAM ALLEN, engineering educator; b. Belleville, Ill., June 7, 1956; s. William Allen and Ruth Anne (Racine) D.; children: Allen, Corinth, Barrett. B.Mech.Engring., U. Del., 1979; MBA, U. Ill., 1992. Composites engr. Ctr. Composite Materials, U. Del., 1979-82, dep. dir., 1982-86; asst. dir. engring. Coll. Engring., U. Ill., Urbana, 1986-90, dir. corp. programs, 1990-97, asst. dean, 1994-97, mng. dir., 1997—. Cons. Composites Tech. Assocs., Newark, 1979-86, Pi-d 2020, Champaign, 1999—; dir. Mfg. Extension Rsch. and Tech. Ctr., State of Ill., 1995—, dir. Ill. Ctr. for Indsl. Tech., 1987-92 Contbr. articles to profl. jours. Active Boy Scouts Am., Champaign, 1992—; audit dir. Empty Tomb Social Svcs., Champaign, 1989-93; deacon Windsor Rd. Christian Ch., Champaign, 1990-92. Exec. MBA scholar, 1990-92. Mem. AAAS, IEEE, AIAA, Am. Soc. Engring. Edn. (mem. coun., regional exec. com. 1996-97). Republican. Home: 706 Ashton Ln N Champaign IL 61820-7303 Office: Univ of Illinois 1304 W Springfield Ave Urbana IL 61801-2910 Office Phone: 217-244-7235. Business E-Mail: wdick@uiuc.edu.

DICKE, JAMES FREDERICK, II, manufacturing executive; b. San Angelo, Tex., Nov. 9, 1945; s. James Frederick and Eilleen (Webster) D.; m. Janet St. Clair, July 6, 1968; children: James F. III, Jennifer S. BS, Trinity U., 1968. Intern U.S. Ho. of Reps., Washington, 1966; sales coord. Crown Controls Corp., New Bremen, Ohio, 1968-69, v.p. internat., 1970-78; exec. v.p. Crown Equipment Corp., New Bremen, Ohio, 1979-80, pres., CEO, 1980—2002, chmn., CEO, 2003—. Chmn. Crown Australia Pty. Ltd., Sydney, 1980—, Crown Ltd., Galway, Ireland, 1980—; bd. dirs. Dayton (Ohio) Power and Light Co. Chmn. bd. trustees Dayton (Ohio) Art Inst., 1998—; trustee, v.p., sec. Culver (Ind.) Ednl. Found., 1981-2001; Midwest dir. Boys and Girls Clubs Am., Chgo., 1987-2001; co-chmn. Ohio Rep. Fin. Com., 1995—. Recipient Disting. Svc. award Culver Acads., 1989, Disting. Alumnus award Trinity U., 1991; honoree Nat. Acad. Design, 1999. Mem. Young Pres.' Orgn. (bd. dirs. 1985-94, internat. pres. 1992-93), Cum Laude Soc. Culver Acads., Key Largo Anglers CLub (chmn. bd. dirs. 1999-2001). Mem. United Ch. of Christ. Office: Crown Equipment Corp PO Box 97 New Bremen OH 45869-0097

DICKENS, ALYCIA THOMPSON, nurse practitioner; b. Norfolk, Va., July 31, 1968; d. Freeman Robert and Doris Kennedy Thompson; m. Byron Patrick Dickens, Mar. 20, 1991; children: Schuyler Kennedy, Logan Alexandria. BSN, Hampton U., 1995, MS, 1997. RN, Va.; cert. family nurse practitioner. Nurse Ea. State Hosp., Williamsburg, Va., 1995-96, Med. Coll. Va. at Va. Commonwealth U., Richmond, 1996—; nurse bon secours Med. ICU, Depaul Med. Ctr., 1997-99; nurse practitioner infectious disease divsn. Ea. Va. Med. Sch., 1999—. Recipient grant Ea. State Hosp., 1994, 95, William Freeman scholarship Hampton U., 1995. Mem. ANA, Assn. Reproductive Health Profls., Va. Nurses Assn., Va. Coun. for Nurse Practitioners, Sigma Theta Tau, Alpha Kappa Alpha. Democrat. Baptist.

DICKENS, BERNARD MORRIS, law educator; b. London, Nov. 4, 1937; emigrated to Can., 1974; s. David and Rose (Jacobs) D.; m. Rebecca J. Cook, Apr., 1987. LL.B., King's Coll., U. London, 1961, LL.M., 1965, PhD, 1971; LL.D., U. London, 1978. Barrister, Inner Temple, 1963; barrister and solicitor, Law Soc. Upper Can. (Ont. bar), 1977. Tutorial student King's Coll., U. London, England, 1962-63; lectr. Coll. Law, London, 1964-68, sr. lectr., 1968-72, prin. lectr., 1972-74; rsch. prof. law U. Toronto, Canada, 1974-80, prof. law, 1980—2003, prof. emeritus, 2003—; chair rsch. ethics bd. Health Can., 2001—. Cons. panel human rsch. WHO/Coun. Internat. Orgns. Med. Scis., Geneva, 1979-83, 91-93, prin. investigator epidemiol. rsch. and human organ transplantation, 1990-91; legal cons. reproduction law Commonwealth Secretariat, London, 1976—; project cons. Ont. Law Reform, Toronto, 1982-84; cons. mem. com. on ethics Can. Med. Assn., Ottawa, 1982-89; mem. rsch. ethics com. NRC Can., Ottawa, 1992-99, chair 1995-99; adj. faculty Ctr. for Population and Family Health, Faculty Medicine, Columbia U., 1987—; mem. WHO task force on organ transplantation, 1996-99. Author: Abortion and the Law, 1966, Medico-Legal Aspects of Family Law, 1979, (with R.J. Cook) Abortion Laws in Commonwealth Countries, 1979, Emerging Issues in Commonwealth Abortion Law, 1982, Medicine and the Law, 1993, (with D. Roy, J. Williams) Bioethics in Canada, 1993; (with R.J. Cook, M.F. Fathalla) Reproductive Health and Human Rights, 2003; dept. editor Health Policy and Ethics, Am. Jour. Pub. Health, 2005—; mem. internat. editl. bd. Am. Jour. Law and Medicine; mem. editl. adv. bd. Bibliography of Bioethics, Kennedy Inst., 1978—; legal articles editor Jour. Law Medicine and Ethics, 1986—. Connaught grantee U. Toronto, 1974, 78; Julius Silver fellow Columbia Law Sch., 1987. Fellow Royal Soc. Medicine (London), Royal Soc. Can.; mem. Am. Soc. Law, Medicine and Ethics (bd. dirs. 1986-92, sec. 1987-89, pres. 1990-91), World Assn. Med. Law (bd. dirs. 1994—, v.p. 1996—). Jewish. Home: 31 Walmer Rd #10 Toronto ON Canada M5R 2W7 Office: U Toronto Faculty of Law 84 Queen's Pk Toronto ON Canada M5S 2C5 E-mail: bernard.dickens@utoronto.ca.

DICKENS, CHARLES HENDERSON, retired social sciences educator; b. Thomasville, NC, Nov. 22, 1934; s. Argie Marshall and Edna (Sullivan) D.; m. Jane McClung, Aug. 27, 1965; children: Martha Jane, Anne Elizabeth. BS, Duke U., 1957, MEd, 1964, ED, 1966. Asst. prof. Wake Forest U., Winston-Salem, N.C., 1965-67; planning specialist NSF, Washington, 1967-69, assoc. program dir. undergrad. instrnl. program, 1969-73, study dir. sci. edn. studies group, 1973-83, sect. head scientific and tech. pers. studies sect., 1983-86, sect. head surveys and analysis sect., 1986-90; sr. policy analyst Fed. Coordinating Coun. for Sci., Engring., and Tech., Washington, 1990-92, exec. sec., 1992-93, ret., 1993. Adv. bd. Am. Men and Women of Sci., New Providence, NJ, 1991—, C.C. Cameron Applied Rsch. Ctr. U. NC, Charlotte, 1994-99, Buncombe County Coun. on Aging, 2000—; cons. Stanford Rsch. Internat., 2002—, Sr. Tar Heel Legis., 2005—. With U.S. Army, 1958-59. Recipient Angier B. Duke prize Duke U., 1953-57; Woodrow Wilson fellow Woodrow Wilson Fellowship Found., 1963, James B. Duke fellow Duke U., 1963-64. Fellow: AAAS; mem.: Nat. Assn. Ret. Fed. Employees (v.p. chpt. 156 1995—96, pres. 1996—97, v.p. N.C. area I 1997—2001). Republican. Presbyterian. Avocations: computing, reading. Home: 4 Arrow Pl Asheville NC 28805-9748 E-mail: chas34@juno.com.

DICKENS, JOYCE REBECCA, addictions therapist, educator; b. Roanoke Rapids, NC; d. Lydia Marie Dickens. M in Addiction Psychology with honors, Capella U., 2000, PhD in Psychology with honors, 2003. Cert. addiction profl. Adj. instr. Broward CC, Ft. Lauderdale, Fla., 1991—; primary therapist addictions Treatment Works, Ft. Lauderdale, 2002—. Mem.: AAUW, Phi Theta Kappa, Alpha Chi. Avocations: tennis, travel, public speaking. Office Phone: 561-662-3732. Personal E-mail: joyced@bellsouth.net. E-mail: joycedickens@faithfarm.org.

DICKENS, JUSTIN KIRK, nuclear physicist; b. Syracuse, N.Y., Nov. 2, 1931; s. Milton Clifford and Jennette Martin (Holmes) D.; m. Marcay Cosette Jordan, Dec. 21, 1957; children: Alan Russell, Leonard Raymond, Steven Kenneth, Michael Loren. AB in Physics, U. So. Calif., L.A., 1955, PhD in Physics, 1962; MS in Physics, U. Chgo., 1956. Engring. assoc. Collins Radio Co., Burbank, Calif., 1955; electronic technician Enrico Fermi Inst. for Nuclear Studies, Chgo., 1956-57; grad. teaching asst. U. So. Calif., L.A., 1957-61, rsch. assoc., 1961-62; rsch. staff mem. Oak Ridge (Tenn.) Nat. Lab., 1962-78, sr. rsch. staff mem., 1978-94, cons., 2000—; private cons., 1995; rsch. prof. physics U. Tenn., Knoxville, 1996-99, 2001; cons. Oak Ridge Nat. Lab., 2000—. Gen. chmn. Internat. Conf. on Nuclear Data for Sci. and Tech., Gatlinburg, Tenn., 1994. Author: The Descendants of Ephraim Dickens (Jr.) and Thomas Dickens, 1992, rev. edit., vol. I, 2005, vol. II, 2005, Memoirs...and Memories, 2002; co-author (tech. standard) Am. Nat. Standard on Decay Heat; contbr. 200 articles to profl. jours. Bd. dirs. Oak Ridge Community Playhouse, 1972, 85. With U.S. Army, 1950-52. Recipient Lifetime Achievement award Oak Ridge Comty. Playhouse, 1996, Lockheed Martin Energy Rsch. Tech. Achievement award, 1997. Mem. Am. Phys. Soc., Am. Nuclear Soc., Phi Beta Kappa, Sigma Xi. Office: Ctr of Excel Bldg 6010 Inst Heavy Ion Rsch MS 6354 Oak Ridge TN 37831-6354 Office Phone: 865-482-1920. E-mail: jkdickens@aol.com.

DICKENS, STEPHEN A, medical practice executive; s. Wesley A and Doris S Dickens; m. Cindy A Porterfield; children: Reagan E, Rylie A. BS, Tenn. Technol. U., 1985—89, MA, 1989—91. Diplomate Certified Healthcare Executive Am. Coll. of Healthcare Executives, 2004, Certified Medical Practice Executive Am. Coll. of Med. Practice Executives, 2005, Certified Home and Hospice Care Executive Nat. Assn. for Home Care, 2002. Coo/adminstr. Cumberland River Hosp./PHC Home Health Care, Celina, Tenn., 1993—2002; ceo Carthage Family Practice Specialists, PC, Carthage, Tenn., 2002—. Recipient John W. Hines award/Homecare Adminstr. of the Yr., Tenn. Assn. for Home Care, 2001, President's award, 2002. Mem.: Rotary Internat., Pi Kappa Alpha Frat. (chpt. pres., alumni pres., chpt. advisor 1895—2005, internat. alumni commr. 2003—05, Regional Chpt. Advisor of the Yr., Regional Alumnus of the Yr.). Office: Carthage Family Practice Specialists PC 130 Lebanon Highway Ste B Carthage TN 37030 Office Phone: 615-735-0700. Office Fax: 615-735-5451. E-mail: steve.dickens@carthagefamilypractice.com.

DICKENS, WILLIAM THEODORE, economic researcher; b. Chgo., Dec. 31, 1953; s. William James and Estelle Geraldine (Schmidt) D.; m. Maureen Ellen Finegan, June 18, 1982; 1 child, Christopher James. BA, Bard Coll., 1976; PhD, MIT, 1981. Econometric computing cons. MIT, Cambridge, Mass., 1978-80; from asst. to assoc. prof. econ. U. Calif., Berkeley, 1980-95, prof. econ., 1995. Vis. asst. prof. MIT, Cambridge, 1985-86; cons. World Bank, Washington, 1987-88, Calif. State Employees Assn., Oakland, Calif., 1988-89; sr. economist, pres. Coun. Econ. Advisors, 1993-94; vis. fellow The Brookings Instn., 1994-95, sr. fellow, 1995—; faculty rsch. fellow NBER, 1982-86, rsch. assoc., 1986-97. Editor, author: (with Laura Tyson) Dynamics of trade and Employment, 1988, (with Lloyd Uimon and Barry Eichengreen) Labor and an Integrated Europe, 1993, The U.S. Labor Market Effects of European Economic Integration, 1993, (with Kent Weaver) Looking Before We Leap: Social Science and Welfare Reform, 1995, (with Ronald Ferguson) Urban Problems and Community Development, 1999; contbr. articles to profl. jours. including The Brookings Papers on Econ. Activity, 1996, Psychol. Rev., 2001. Grad. fellow NSF, 1976; recipient numerous grants. Mem. Am. Econs. Assn. Democrat. Avocation: flying. Home: 9813 Ashburton Ln Bethesda MD 20817-1723 Office: The Brookings Instn 1775 Massachusetts Ave NW Washington DC 20036-2103 Business E-Mail: wdickens@brookings.edu.

DICKENSON, KATHARINE HORN, historic preservationist; b. Newburgh, N.Y., Oct. 31, 1945; d. John Harold and Eleanor (Hamway) Horn; m. David Blaine Dickenson, July 12, 1969; children: Blaine, John David, Daniel. BEd, U. Miami, Coral Gables, Fla., 1967; MEd, U. Miami, 1968. Pres., trustee Boca Raton (Fla.) Hist. Soc., 1974; pres. Boca Raton Jr. League, 1980; chmn. Fla. Historic Preservation Adv. Coun., Tallahassee, 1985, Palm Beach (Fla.) County Preservation Bd., 1986-88; dir. Bonnet House, Ft. Lauderdale, Fla., 1984—, Seaboard Rwy. Sta., West Palm Beach, 1988—, Preservation Action, Washington, 1986—. Trustee Nat. Trust Hist. Preservation, Washington, 1991—2000; chmn. bd. Boca Raton (Fla.) Hist. Soc.; mem. Fla. Arts Coun., 2001—. Recipient Disting. Svc. in Historic Preservation award, Fla. Trust, 1989, Judge Knott Hist. award. Roman Catholic. Avocations: gardening, tennis. Office: Dickenson & Co Inc 980 N Federal Hwy Ste 410 Boca Raton FL 33432-2704 Office Phone: 407-391-1900. Personal E-mail: lkatboca@aol.com.

DICKENSON, MOLLIE M., freelance writer; b. Sioux City, Iowa, Aug. 9, 1935; d. Earl Dale and Norma Elizabeth (Hunt) McCauley; m. James Richard Dickenson, 1963; children: Elizabeth Anne Lerch Oxley, John Hunt Lerch. BA, U. Iowa, 1962, postgrad., 1962-63. Adminstrv. asst. Planned Parenthood, Washington, 1963-69; pvt. practice speaker's agt. Kensington, Md., 1976-78; writer freelance, 1978—. Commentator on Pacifica and RadioAmerica. Author: (book) Thumbs Up the Life and Courageous Comeback of Whte House Press Secretary Jim Brady, 1987; contbr. articles to popular mags. Mem. Nat. Press Club.

DICKERMAN, ROB DALE, biomedical scientist; b. Ft. Worth, Feb. 29, 1968; s. Donald Wayne and Peggy Jean (Barrentine) D.; m. Paula Kay Mabra, May 30, 1992. BS in Chemistry, Tex. Wesleyan U., 1992; postgrad., U. North Tex. Health Sci. Ctr., 1992—. Medicinal chemist Alcon Labs., Ft. Worth, 1993-95. Cons. on steroid abuse Royal Australian Physicians, Sydney, 1996-97; apptd. mem. dean's subcom. U. North Tex. Health Sci. Ctr., Ft. Worth, 1996-97. Contbr. articles to profl. jours. including Cardiology, European Heart Jour. Fellow Glaxo-Wellcome, 1995, So. Med. Soc., 1996; grantee U. North Tex. Health Sci. Ctr., 1996, Am. Assn. Clin. Chemistry, 1996. Mem. Internat. Soc. for Neurochemistry, Soc. for Exptl. Biology and Medicine, Soc. for Neurosci., Assn. for Rsch. in Nervous and Mental Disease, Tex. Med. Assn. (apptd. com. mem. 1996-97), Ft. Worth Zool. Assn. (rsch. com. mem. 1992—), DO/PhD Assn. (pres. 1996-97), Sigma Sigma Phi. Republican. Achievements include development of neuronal cell culture technique for monitoring steroid-responsive neurotransmitters, and assessing age-related central nevous system disease. Home: 3500 Camp Bowie Blvd Fort Worth TX 76107-2644

DICKERSON, CLAIRE MOORE, lawyer, educator; b. Boston, Apr. 1, 1950; d. Roger Cleveland and Ines Idelette (Roullet) Moore; m. Thomas Pasquali Dickerson, May 22, 1976; children: Caroline Anne, Susannah Moore. AB, Wellesley Coll., 1971; JD, Columbia U., 1974; LLM in Taxation, NYU, 1981. Bar: N.Y. 1975, U.S. Dist. Ct. (ea. and so. dists.) N.Y. 1975, U.S. Ct. Appeals (2d cir.) 1975, U.S. Supreme Ct. 1980. Assoc. Coudert Brothers, N.Y., 1974-82, ptnr., 1983-86, Schnader, Harrison, Segal & Lewis, N.Y., 1987-88, of counsel, 1988—; assoc. prof. law St. John's U., Jamaica, N.Y., 1986-88, prof., 1989-2000; prof law Rutgers U., Newark, 2000—. Author: Partnership Law Adviser; contbr. articles to profl. jours. Scholar Arthur L. Dickson scholar. Mem.: ABA, Soc. for Advancement of Socio-Econs., Law and Soc. Assn., Assn. of Bar of City of N.Y., Shenorock Club. Democrat. E-mail: cmdckrsn@rci.rutgers.edu.

DICKERSON, CLAUDIA THOMPSON, psychologist; b. Greenville, SC, Aug. 11, 1953; d. Claude Vehorn and Bobbie (Swindell) Thompson. BA, Furman Univ., Greenville, SC, 1974; MA, Wake Forest Univ., Winston-Salem, NC, 1976; PhD, NC State Univ., Raleigh, NC, 1988. Sch. psychologist Gwinnett Co., Pub. Sch., Lawrenceville, Ga., 1982—, Wake County Pub. Sch. Sys., Raleigh, NC, 1980—82. Bd. dirs. Advent Spirituality Ctr. Mem.: Calif. Assn. of Sch. Psychologists, Southwestern Psychol. Assn., Am. Psychol. Soc., Nat. Assoc. of Sch. Psychol., Am. Psychol. Assoc. Baptist. Home: 2465 Sunset Dr Atlanta GA 30345 Office: Psychol Svc Gwinnett Co Sch PO Box 343 Lawrenceville GA 30046-0343

DICKERSON, DENNIS CLARK, SR., historian, educator; b. McKeesport, Pa., Aug. 12, 1949; s. Carl O'Neal and Oswanna (Wheeler) D.; m. Mary Anne Eubanks, Aug. 6, 1977; children: Nicole Denise, Valerie Anne, Christina Marie, Dennis Clark Jr. BA, Lincoln U., 1971; MA, Washington (Mo.) U., 1974, PhD, 1978; LHD (hon.), Morris Brown Coll., 1990; postgrad., Hartford Sem., Memphis Theol. Seminary. Instr. history Forest Park C.C., St. Louis, 1974, Memphis Theol. Seminary, Pa. State U. Ogontz, Abington, 1975-76; from asst. to assoc. prof. history Williams Coll., Williamstown, Mass., 1976-85, assoc. prof., 1987-88, prof., 1988-99, Stanfield prof. history, 1992-99; assoc. prof. history Rhodes Coll., Memphis, 1985—87; prof. history and grad. dept. religion Vanderbilt U., Nashville, 1999—. Mem. com. examiners GRE History test Ednl. Testing Svc., Princeton, 1990-96; corporator Williamstown Savs. Bank, 1992-99; vis. prof. Payne Theol. Sem., Wilberforce, Ohio, 1992, 96, 98, 2002, 04; vis. prof. Am. religious history Yale Div. Sch., 1995. Author: Out of the Crucible, 1986, Religion, Race and Region: Research Notes on A.M.E. Church History, 1995, Militant Mediator: Whitney M. Young, Jr., 1998, A Liberated Past: Explorations in A.M.E. Church History, 2003; historiographer, exec. dir. rsch. and scholarship, editor A.M.E. Ch. Rev; contbr. articles to profl. jours. Historiographer, African Meth. Episcopal Ch., 1988—, min. 1977—; trustee Mass. Coll. Liberal Arts, 1992-95. Rockefeller Found. fellow U. Va., 1987-88. Mem. Am. Bible Soc. (vice-chmn. bd. trustees), Am. Soc. Ch. History (pres. 2004), Elks, Alpha Phi Alpha. Office: Vanderbilt U Dept History Nashville TN 37235-0001 Office Phone: 615-343-4329. Business E-Mail: dennis.c.dickerson@vanderbilt.edu.

DICKERSON, JAMES ALAN, psychologist; b. Mpls., Minn., July 8, 1948; s. Joseph Holmes and Millicent Friyze Dickerson; m. Kristy Ann Elfe, Oct. 6, 1979; children: Joseph James, Matthew David. BA, U. Md., 1970; MA, U. Iowa, 1972; PhD, U. Md., 1975. Lic. Psychologist. Chief psychologist Human Svc. Ctr., 2005—; pvt. practice, 2004—05. Mem.: Am. Psychological Assn. Avocation: travel. Office: NE Human Svc Ctr 151 South 47th St State 40 Grand Forks ND 58203 Office Phone: 701-795-3095.

DICKERSON, JOHN ROBERT, retired automotive engineer; b. Detroit, Oct. 8, 1930; s. James Eldridge and Edith Barrie Dickerson; m. Jacqueline Bowman, June 14, 1952 (div. Sept. 1967); children: Robert Floyd, Diane Lynn; m. Barbara Marie Gannon, Feb. 7, 1969; 1 child, Edward Michael Gannon. Cert., Wayne State U., 1950, N.D. State U., 1951, Chrysler Inst. Engring., 1956, Cert., 1964. Sr. stylist designer Chrysler Corp., Highland Park, Mich., 1957—61, 1961—64, sr. stylist designer, engr., 1964—69, engr. product devel., 1978—84, mgr. vehicle build ops., 1984—88; owner, CFO J. Robert Dickerson & Assocs., Detroit, 1969—72; supr. fleet engring. Am. Motors Corp., Detroit, 1972—78. Stylist designer cons. Creative Industries, Detroit, 1970—71; cons. Wayne State U. Consortium, Detroit, 1971—72; design cons. J. Robert Dickerson & Assocs., Detroit, 1969—73; chmn. adv. com. Tech. Comms., 2001—02; engring. rep. to G.S.A. Automotive Vehicle Bid Consortium, Washington, 1974—78; signatory party to UN for Am. Motors Corp., 1974—78. Author: One Goal is Not Enough, 2001, How to Build a 50 Foot Yacht, 1972. Charter mem. Rep. Nat. Com., Washington, 2000—; mem. Rep. Presdl. Task Force, Washington, 2000—. With USAF, 1950—52. Recipient Design award, GSA, 1980. Mem.: Am. Soc. Body Engring., NRA, Sr. Mens Club of Grosse Pointe. Republican. Achievements include patents for automotive design; first to introduction and homologation of first Pacer vehicle into Europe; created concept engineering test and show vehicle development from tooling to complete running vehicles; prototype vehicle build coordinator in Italy for Chrysler Maserati Program; first to Named first Dodge Charger, 1962; development of show cars from preproduction vehicles for Nat. Press Shows. Avocations: flying, boating, golf, travel, gardening.

DICKERSON, LON RICHARD, library administrator; b. Ypsilanti, Mich., Dec. 16, 1941; s. Lon E. and Maxine A. (Merryfield) D.; m. Anne Elizabeth Bryan, Aug. 24, 1968; children: Robert Lon, Sarah Elizabeth, Peter Bryan. AB, Albion Coll., 1964; MLS, U. Pitts., 1968. Dir. U. Liberia Librs., Monrovia, 1968-72, Lake Agassiz Regional Libr., Moorhead, Minn., 1972-85, Timberland Regional Libr., Olympia, Wash., 1985-92, Omaha Pub. Libr., 1993-96, Chatham-Effingham-Liberty Regional Libr., Savannah, Ga., 1996—. Pres. Adv. Coun. to State Libr., Minn., 1977-78, Minn. Regional Pub. Libr. Systems Adminstrs., 1980, No. Lights Libr. Network Adv. Coun., Minn., 1981-82; v.p. Ga. Coun. Pub. Librs., 1998-00, pres., 2000—. Contbr. articles to profl. jours. Libr. vol. Peace Corps Sierra Leone Libr. Bd., Freetown, 1964-67; mem. planning commn. City of Lacey, Wash.,1985-93; vice-chair planning commn. City of Lacey, 1991-93, mem. various sch. dist. coms.; bd. dirs. Clay-Wilkin Opportunity Coun., Moorhead, Minn., 1982-85; mem. steering com. Omaha 2000, 1993-96, Omaha Free-Net, 1994-96, United Way of the Midlands Com., Omaha, 1996. Mem. ALA (internat. rels. com. 1974-75), Wash. Libr. Assn. (co-chmn. legis. planning com. 1987-92, Pres.'s award 1988), Ga. Libr. Assn., Pub. Libr. Assn. (nominating com. 1989-90), Rotary, Tau Kappa Epsilon. Democrat. Congregationalist. Office: CEL Regional Libr 2002 Bull St Savannah GA 31401-8564

DICKERSON, MARTIN LEE, vice principal; b. Wilson, N.C., Mar. 30, 1961; s. Joelene Armwood; m. Barbara Gail Lutterloh; 1 child, Lamont Lee. BS, Rutgers U., 1983; MA, Montclair State U., 1997; EdD, U. Pa., 2006. Cert. tchr. N.H., prin. N.H., supt. N.J. Tchr. Newark Bd. Edn., 1986—99; vice prin. Sampson G. Smith Sch., Somerset, NJ, 1999—2005. Trace and field coach Arts H.S., Newark, 1986—94. Vol. United Way, Newark, 2003—05; v.p. Fairview Apt. Tenant Assn., East Orange, NJ, 1994. Named Track and Field Coach of Yr., Newark Star Ledger, 1990, Cross Country Coach of Yr., Nat. Fedn. Interscholastic Athletics, Kansas City, 1991. Mem.: Am. Ednl. Rsch Assn., N.J. Prin. and Supervisors Assn. (com. mem. 1999—2005), Gideons (camp pres. 1997—2000). Independent. Avocations: reading, fishing, basketball. Office: Franklin Twp Pub Sch 1755 Amwell Rd Somerset NJ 08873

DICKERSON, ROLAND NELSON, pharmacy educator, health science association administrator; b. Plattsburgh, NY, June 26, 1956; s. Nelson Donald and Shirley Mae (LaPierre) D.; m. Erin Kristine Walker, July 19, 1980; children: Robert Nelson, Anne Louise, Gillian Rose. BS in Pharmacy, Temple U., 1979; Dr of Pharmacy, U. Tenn., Memphis, 1982. Diplomate Bd. Pharm. Specialties. Resident Thomas Jefferson U. Hosp., Phila., 1979-80; fellow U. N.C., Chapel Hill, 1982-83; clin. pharmacist in nutrition Hosp. U. Pa., Phila., 1983-88; asst. prof. pharmacy Phila. Coll. Pharm. Sci., 1988-92; prof. pharmacy U. Tenn., Memphis, 1992—. Mem. editl. bd. Nutrition, 1989—, Nutrition in Clin. Practice, 1996—, Jour. Parenteral and Enteral Nutrition, 2004—; contbg. editor Hosp. Pharmacy, 1987—; contbr. over 120 articles to profl. jours. Vol. Ronald McDonald House, Memphis, 1996-. Am. Soc. Hosp. Pharmacists Pharmacy Nutrition Support fellow, 1982; PHS grantee, 1992, others. Fellow Am. Coll. Nutrition, Am. Coll. Clin. Pharmacy. Achievements include to demonstrate net protein anabolism with hypocaloric high protein parenteral nutrition in obese stressed patients. Office: U Tenn 26 S Dunlap St Memphis TN 38103-4909

DICKESON, ROBERT CELMER, retired academic administrator, foundation executive, political scientist, educator; b. Independence, Mo., June 28, 1940; s. James Houston and Sophie Stephanie (Celmer) D.; m. Ludmila Ann Weir, June 22, 1963; children: Elizabeth Ann, Cynthia Marie. AB, U. Mo., 1962, MA, 1963, PhD, 1968; postgrad., U. No. Colo., 1971, 72; postgrad. inst. ednl. mgmt., Harvard U., 1973. Adminstrv. asst. U. Mo., Columbia, 1962-64, dir. student activities, 1964-68, asst. dean students, 1968-69; dean student affairs No. Ariz. U., Flagstaff, 1969-70, assoc. prof. polit. sci., 1970-76, prof., 1976-81, on leave, 1979-81, v.p. student affairs, 1970-79, v.p., univ. relations, 1973-79; dir. Ariz. Dept. Adminstrn., Phoenix, 1979-81; pres. U. No. Colo., Greeley, 1981-91, prof. polit. sci., 1981-87, 88-91; chief of staff to gov., exec. dir. Office of State Planning and Budgeting State of Colo., 1987; pres. Noel/Levitz Ctrs. Inc., Iowa City, 1991-97; divsn. pres. USA Group Found. for Edn., Indpls., 1995-97. Sr. v.p. Lumina Found. for Edn., 1997—; adj. prof. U. Colo., Denver, 1987, Ariz. State U., Tempe, 1979-81; nat. vice-chmn. Cert. Public Mgr. Policy Bd., 1980-81; planning and mgmt. cons.; mem. univ. adv. council Am. Council on Life Ins.; dir. United Bank of Greeley; mem. Pres.' Commn. NCAA, 1989-91; mem. Nat. Commn. on Minorities in Higher Edn., 1989-91; nat. cons. Office of Women in Higher Edn., Am. Coun. on Edn., 1989-97; vis. scholar U. Mich., 2003. Author: Prioritizing Academic Programs and Services, 1999; contbr. articles to profl. jours. Active Boy Scouts Am., v.p. Grand Canyon council, Flagstaff, 1974-76, pres., 1976-79, mem. nat. council, 1976-81, T. Roosevelt council, 1979-81, v.p. Long's Peak Council, 1981-87; mem. state com. Ariz. Democratic Com., 1970-72; chmn. Gov.'s Commn. on Merit System Reform, 1979-80, Gov.'s Regulatory Rev. Council, 1980-81, Gov.'s Commn. Higher Edn., 1983-86; mem. Gov.'s Commn. Excellence in Edn., 1983-86, Gov.'s Coun. on Creative Schs., 1989-91; commr. from Colo. to Edn. Commn. of the States, 1987-91; internat. trustee Sigma Alpha Epsilon Found., 1993-97. Recipient Dist. award of Merit., 1973, Silver Beaver award, 1975, Disting. Service award Sigma Alpha Epsilon, 1969, Merit Key award 1997, Disting. Alumnus award U. Mo.-Columbia, 1988, Outstanding Pres. award Am. Assn. Colls. of Tchrs. Edn, 1991, Bus. Excellence award U. No. Colo., 1996, Faculty-Alumni U. Mo. award, 1999, Disting. Svc. award Am. Coun. Edn., 2000; named to N. Crtrl. Athletic Conf. Hall of Fame, 1991. Mem. Am. Polit. Sci. Assn., Am. Soc. Public Adminstrn. (Ariz. exec. bd., Superior Svc. award 1981), Am. Acad. Polit. and Social Sci., Coll. Student Pers. Inst. (acad. coun. 1969-73), Assn. Pub. Coll. and Univ. Pres. (pres. 1985-87), Assn. Pub. Coll. and Univ. Pres. (pres. 1985-87), Nat. Assn. Student Pers. Adminstrs. (regional coun. 1974-79), Am. Assn. State Colls. and Univs. (chmn. coun. on doctoral granting instns., Meritorious Svc. award 1991), Columbia Club (Indpls.), Newcomen Soc., Phi Kappa Phi. United Methodist (pres. bd. trustees 1974). Lodges: Kiwanis (pres. 1975-76); Rotary. Office Phone: 317-951-5755. E-mail: rdickeson@luminafoundation.org.

DICKEY, BETTY C., state supreme court justice; b. 1940; m. Jay Dickey, 1960 (div. 1987); 1 adopted child, John 1 foster child, Cindy children: Laura, Ted, Rachel. BA in English, U. Ark., 1962, JD, 1985; attended, Nat. Coll. Dist. Attorneys Executive Program, 1994, FBI Nat. Law Inst., 1994. Former tchr. Pine Bluff High Sch., Ark., Watson Chapel Elementary Sch., Ark.; pvt. practice atty. Pine Bluff, Ark., 1985—86, Little Rock, 1990—91; asst. atty., 1986—90, 1993—94; city atty., 1988—94; atty. State Soil and Water Commn., Ark., 1991—93; prosecutor 11th Jud. Dist., 1995—99; commr. Ark. Pub. Svc., 1999—2003; chief legal counsel Ark. Gov.'s Office, 2003; chief justice Ark. Supreme Ct., 2004, assoc. justice, 2004—. Recipient Atty. Gen.'s Top Prosecutor award, 1997, Top 100 Women in Ark. award, 1998, 1999. Mem.: Jefferson County Bar Assn., Pulaski County Bar Assn., Texas Bar Assn., Ark. Bar Assn. Office: Adminstrv Office of the Cts 625 Marshall St 120 Justice Bldg Little Rock AR 72201*

DICKEY, DAVID HERSCHEL, lawyer, accountant; b. Savannah, Ga., Dec. 31, 1951; s. Grady Lee and Sara (Leon) D.; children: David Bradford, Carolyn Amanda. BBA in Acctg. and Fin., Armstrong State Coll., 1974; M in Accountancy, JD, U. Ga., 1977. CPA; bar: Ga. 1978, U.S. Dist. Ct. (no. dist.) Ga. 1980, U.S. Ct. Claims 1978, U.S. Tax Ct. 1978, U.S. Ct. Appeals (5th and 11th cirs.) 1978, U.S. Supreme Ct. 1981. Assoc., acct. Thompson and Benken, Attys., Savannah, 1977-79; pub. acct. Arthur Andersen & Co., Atlanta, 1979-81; assoc. Oliver Maner & Gray, LLP, Savannah, 1981—82, ptnr., 1982—. Pres. Savannah Estate Planning Coun., 1986-87, chmn. bd., 1987-88; bd. dirs. Chatham-Savannah Citizen's Advocacy; mem. legal adv. bd. Small Bus. Coun. Am., Inc., 1989—; pres. Seminar Group, Inc., 1989—, Hist. Investment Properties, Inc., 1991—. Pres. L'Alliance Francaise de Savannah, 2001—03; bd. dirs. Savannah Theatre Co., 1984, Savannah chpt. Am. Cancer Soc., 1986—91, Hist. Savannah Found., Inc., 1988—94, Candler Hosp. Found., 2003; chmn., trustee Armstrong State Coll. Alumni Endowment Fund, Inc., 1991; chmn. lawyers divsn. Chatham County United Way, 1992; dir., v.p. Armstrong Atlantic State U. Found., 2001—03; bd. trustees The Candler Found., 2001—03. Recipient Outstanding Svc. award Am. Cancer Soc., 1987, Outstanding Alumni Svc. award Armstrong State Coll., 1992; named to Leadership Savannah, Savannah C. of C., 1984-86. Fellow: Am. Coll. Trust and Estate Counsel; mem.: S.R. (pres. Ga. chpt. 2001—03), SAR (pres. Ga. 1999), AICPA, ABA (estate and gift tax com. taxation sect. 1990—), Mil. Order of the Stars and Bars (Lafayette McLaws chpt. comdr. 2005—), Am. Assn. Atty.-CPAs, Ga. Soc. CPAs, Savannah Bar Assn., Ga. Bar Assn., St. Andrew's Soc., Soc. Colonial Wars, Sons Confederate Vets (comdr. Francis S. Bartow camp no. 93 1997—98), Chatham Club, First City Club (bd. dirs. Savannah 1987—90). Avocations: history, genealogy, music, computers, historic rehab. Home: 4 Springfield Pl Savannah GA 31411 Office: Oliver Maner & Gray LLP 218 W State St Savannah GA 31401-3232 Office Phone: 912-236-3311. Business E-Mail: ddickey@omg-law.com.

DICKEY, ELIZABETH BROWN, journalism educator; b. Charleston, S.C., Aug. 18, 1945; d. Joseph Andrew and Nettie Catherine (Bouknight) Brown; m. Gary Clinton Dickey, Jan. 5, 1971; two children. BA, U. S.C., 1967, MA, 1978. Reporter, editor Charleston (S.C.) News, Evening Post and Courier, 1967-71, Columbia Record, 1971-73; from tchg. assoc. to assoc. prof. U. S.C., Columbia, 1973—; exec. dir. Southern Interscholastic Press, chmn. advt. and pub. rels. sequence, 2004—. Faculty advisor Bateman Pub. Rels. Acad. Team, 2002—. Mem. Assn. in Edn. for Journalism & Mass Comms., Scholastic Journalism Divsn., Journalism Edn. Assn., SC Soc. Assn. Execs., Pub. Rels. Soc. Am. Lutheran. Office: Coll Mass Comm and Info Studies Journalism U SC Columbia SC 29208-0001

DICKEY, ERIC JEROME, writer; b. Memphis, Tenn., 1961; BS, Univ. Memphis, 1983. Computer programmer; middle sch. tchr.; actor, standup comic. Author: (novels) Sister, Sister, 1996 (#1 Blackboard Bestseller), Friends and Lovers, 1997 (#1 Blackboard Bestseller), Milk in My Coffee, 1998 (#1 Blackboard Bestseller), Cheaters, 1999 (#1 Blackboard Bestseller), Liar's Game, 2000 (NY Times Bestseller), Between Lovers, 2001 (NY Times Bestseller), Thieves' Paradise, 2002 (NY Times Bestseller, nominee NAACP Image award, 2003), Black Silk, 2002, The Other Woman, 2003 (NY Times, Publishers Weekly Bestseller), Naughty or Nice, 2003 (NY Times Bestseller), Drive Me Crazy, 2004 (NY Times Bestseller), Genevieve, 2005 (Publishers Weekly Bestseller), (collections) Griots Beneath the Baobab: Tales from Los Angeles, 2002. Named Author of Yr., African Am. Lit. awards show, 2004. Office: c/o Author Mail Dutton/NAL 375 Hudson St New York NY 10014 E-mail: ejdickeyfanmail@aol.com.*

DICKEY, GEORGE EDWARD, economist, educator, water transportation executive; b. Sewickley, Pa, Jan. 27, 1940; s. George Otto and Frances Marie (Dougherty) D.; m. Susan Emma Veigel, July 14, 1966; children: Paul Edward, George Louis. BA, Johns Hopkins U., 1961; MA, Northwestern U., 1964, PhD, 1968. Operation rsch. analyst Office Sec. Def., Washington, 1967-69; asst. prof. U. Md., Balt., 1969-73; mem. staff Office Sec. of Army, Washington, 1973-75, econ. advisor, 1976-83; dep. for policy and evaluation Office of Asst. Sec. of Army for Civil Works, Washington, 1983-90, acting prin. dep., 1990-93; acting asst. sec., 1993-94; chief planning divsn. US Army Corps of Engr., Washington, 1994-98; affiliate prof. econ. Loyal Coll., Md., 1998—. Vis. prof. Indsl. Coll. Armed Forces, Washington, 1967-70; cons. in field of water resources; sr. adv. Dawson & Assocs., 1998—. Author: Money, Prices and Growth: The American Experience 1869-1896, 1977; contbr. articles to profl. publ. Capt. US Army, 1965-67. Recipient award for Meritorious Civil Svc., 1981, Presdl. Rank award for Meritorious Svc., 1988, Presdl. Rank award for Disting. Svc., 1993, award for Exceptional Civilian Svc., 1998, Silver Order of the Fluery medal, 1998; Harold E. Stonier fellow, 1964-65. Mem. SAR, Soc. of colonial Wars, Soc. of Sons of Revolution in State of Md., Cath. League for Religious and Civil Rights, Engring. Soc. Balt., Soc. Mil. Engrs., Md. Hist. Soc., Johns Hopkins Club, Omicron Delta Epsilon. Home: 3 Stratford Rd Baltimore MD 21218-1145 Office Phone: 410-467-9545, 202-289-2060. Business E-Mail: gedickey@jhu.edu.

DICKEY, GLENN ERNEST, JR., sportswriter; b. Virginia, Minn., Feb. 16, 1936; s. Glenn Ernest and Madlyn Marie (Emmert) D.; m. Nancy Jo McDaniel, Feb. 25, 1967; 1 son, Kevin Scott. BA, U. Calif., Berkeley, 1958. Sports editor Watsonville (Calif.) Register-Pajoronian, 1958-63; sports writer San Francisco Chronicle, 1963-71, sports columnist, 1971—. Author: The Jock Empire, 1974, The Great No-Hitters, 1976, Champs and Chumps, 1976, The History of National League Baseball, 1979, The History of American League Baseball, 1980, (with Dick Berg) Eavesdropping America, 1980, America Has a Better Team, 1982, The History of Professional Basketball, 1982, The History of the World Series, 1984, (with Jim Tunney) Impartial Judgment: The Dean of NFL Referees Calls Football As He Sees It, 1988, San Francisco Forty-Niners: The Super Year, 1989; (with Bill Walsh) Building a Champion, 1990; Just Win, Baby, Al Davis and His Raiders, 1991; Sports Hero Kevin Mitchell (juvenile), 1993, Sports Hero Jerry Rice (juvenile), 1993, San Francisco 49ers: 50 Years, 1995, San Francisco Giants: 40 Seasons, 1997, Glenn Dickey's 49ers, 2000, Champions: The History of the Oakland A's; contbr. stories to Best Sports Stories, 1962, 68, 71, 75, 76. Home: 120 Florence Ave Oakland CA 94618-2249 Office: Chronicle Pub Co 901 Mission St San Francisco CA 94103-2905

DICKEY, JENA KAY SOWARD, music educator; b. Beaumont, Tex., Aug. 5, 1950; d. J W and Mary Lou Chance Soward; children: Bradley Tyler, Jennifer Anne. MusB, U. of Tex., Austin, Texas, 1968—72; MusM, U. of Colo., 1977—81. Artist Teacher Certificate Choral Music Experience, 1994. Founder and artistic dir. Young Voices of Colo., Littleton, Colo., 1990—. Bd. of dir. Colo.Chpt. of Am. Choral Directors Assn., Colo., 2003—. Mem.: Chorus Am., Internat. Fedn. of Choral Musicians, Colo. Music Educators Assn., Music Educators Nat. Conf., Am. Choral Directors Assn. (life; bd. mem. (state level-colorado) 2003—05), Jr. League of Denver, Tex. Exes (life), Main St. Players, Pi Kappa Lambda, Alpha Lambda Delta, Alpha Delta Pi (life). Avocation: theater. Home: 2432 W Sunset Dr Littleton CO 80120 Office: Young Voices of Colo P O Box 1234 Littleton CO 80160 Office Phone: 303-797-7464.

DICKEY, JOHN HARWELL, lawyer; b. Huntsville, Ala., Feb. 22, 1944; s. Gilbert McClain and Marjorie Loucille (Harwell) D.; m. Nancy Margaret Eagar, Nov. 24, 1984; children: Marjorie Ruth, Gilbert Charles. BA, Samford U., 1966; JD, Cumberland Sch. of Law, 1969. Bar: Tenn. 1971, U.S. Dist. Ct. (ea. dist.) Tenn. 1972. Adminstrv. asst. Dist. Atty.'s Office, Huntsville, 1969-70; law clerk domestic and juvenile divsn. Cir. Ct., Huntsville, 1970-72; trial lawyer Legal Aid Soc., Chattanooga, 1972-75; pvt. practice Chattanooga, 1975-77, Fayetteville, Tenn., 1977-89; dist. pub. defender 17th jud. cir. State of Tenn., Fayetteville, 1989-98; pvt. practice, Fayetteville, Tenn., 1998—. Mem. continuing edn. com. Pub. Defenders Conf., Tenn., 1990-92, mem. long range planning com., 1991-93, mem. legis. com., 1990-93, mem. exec. com., Mid. Tenn. rep., 1993-94. Lectr. Fayetteville-Lincoln County Leadership Tng. Program, 1989—; mem. adv. bd. Community Correction South Ctrl. Tenn., Fayetteville, 1989—; mem. Bedford County Dem. Club, 1989—. Mem. Nat. Assn. Criminal Def. Lawyers, Tenn. Bar Assn., Tenn. Assn. Criminal Def. Lawyers (membership com. 1989—, juvenile law com. 1988—, Disting. Svc. award 1990, 91, 92), Marshall County Bar Assn., Fayetteville-Lincoln County Bar Assn. (treas. 1977, sec. 1978, v.p. 1979, pres. 1980), Fayetteville-Lincoln County C. of C., Elks, Masons (jr. steward 1991, sr. steward 1992, jr. deacon 1993, jr. warden 1994, sr. warden 1995, worshipful master 1996), York Rite Mason, Scottish Rite Mason (32d degree), Shriners (sgt.-at-arms 1993, v.p. 1994, dir. pub. rels. 1994, 96—, pres. 1995), Internat. Platform Assn., Order of Ea. Star (chaplain 1993-94), Tenn. 4-H Found., Gideons Internat. Democrat. Methodist. Avocations: hunting, fishing, canoeing, kayaking. Home: 122 Brookmeade Dr Fayetteville TN 37334-2046 Office: 105 Main Ave S Fayetteville TN 37334-3057

DICKEY, JOSEPH WILLIAM, utilities executive, engineer; b. Decatur, Ill., Sept. 20, 1944; s. Lawrence Wayne and Helen Marie (Van Horn) D. BS in Chem. Engring., MIT, 1966, MS in Civil Engring., 1967; postgrad., U. Va., 1978. Registered profl. engr., Tenn., Fla. Plant mgr. Fla. Power & Light Co., Miami, 1973-76, mgmt. positions in nuclear energy and power resources, 1976-85, v.p. nuclear energy and nuclear ops., 1985-88, v.p. power resources, 1988-91; sr. v.p. fossil and hydro power TVA, Chattanooga, 1991-94, chief operating officer Knoxville, 1994-98; pres., CEO FGS & Assocs. LLC, 1999—. Mem. subcom., chmn., officer EEI Prime Movers Com., Washington, 1980-85; mem. subcom., officer S.E. Electric Exch., Atlanta, 1988-91; speaker in field. Contbr. numerous articles to jours. and trade mags. Chmn. for Broward County MIT Ednl. Coun., 1978-91; bd. govs. Dept. Energy Robotics Program, 1987-88; mem. industry adv. coun. U. Fla. Coll. Engring., Gainesville, 1987-91; trustee, chmn. FPL Polit. Action Com., 1981-85, 83-84. Recipient Ishikawa medal Am. Soc. Quality Control, 1996. Fellow Fla. Engring. Soc.; mem. NSPE, ASCE (br. pres. 1974-75).

DICKEY, LUCY JANE, elementary school educator; b. LaPorte, Ind., Apr. 5, 1953; d. Walter Ellsworth and Jane Ann Wilson; m. Wayne Edward Dickey, Aug. 1, 1982; children: Mary Jane, Laura Elizabeth. BSc, Manchester Coll., 1975; MA, Ball State U., 1981. Dir./tchr. North Liberty Ch. of Christ Day Sch., Ind., 1975—77; elem. tchr. Middlebury Cmty. Schools, Ind., 1977—87, 1988—95, title one tchr., 1996—. Mem. parent adv. club 4-H, Middlebury, Ind., 1996—. Recipient Sch. Project award for the Effective Tchg.of Reading, Indiana U., 1985. Mem.: Middlebury Teachers Assn. (treas., exec. bd.). Avocations: reading, gardening, needlecrafts. Office: Middlebury Elem P O Box 26 412 So Main Middlebury IN 46540 Business E-Mail: dickeyl@mcsin-k12.org.

DICKEY, NANCY WILSON, chancellor, physician; b. Watertown, SD, Sept. 10, 1950; m. Franklin Champ; children: Danielle, Wilson, Elizabeth. BA, Stephen F. Austin State U.; MD, U. Tex., 1976. Diplomate Am. Bd. Family Practice. Resident family medicine Meml. Hosp. System, Houston, 1976-79; pres., vice chancellor health affairs TAMUS Health Sci. Ctr.; prof. family medicine TAMUS Coll. Med., College Station, Tex., 1996—. Hon. staff Polly Ryon Meml. Hosp., Richmond; active staff Coll. Sta. (Tex.) Med. Ctr., St. Josephs Hosp., Bryan, Tex. Reviewer Jour. of AMA; editl. adv. bd. Patient Care, Med. World News, Med. Ethics Advisor, Archives of Family Medicine. Coach youth soccer, 1986-88; sponsor United Meth. Youth Fellowship, 1991-95; bd. dirs. Hastings Ctr., Office of Early Childhood Devel., Am. Heart Assn.; mem. Christ United Meth. Ch., College Station. Recipient Disting. Alumni award U. Tex. Med. Sch., Citation of Merit Tex. Soc. of Pathologists, 1995. Mem. AMA (pres. elect 1997, pres. 1998, chair bd. trustees 1995-97, vice chair 1994-95, bd. trustees 1989-97, sec. treas. 1993-94, exec. com. 1991, other coms.), Tex. Acad. of Family Physicians, Tex. Med. Assn., Alpha Omega Alpha. Office: 301 Tarrow St #7th Flr College Station TX 77840-7896

DICKEY, ROBERT MARVIN (RICK DICKEY), property manager; b. Charleston, S.C., Dec. 3, 1950; s. John Lincoln II and Ruth (Marvin) D.; m. Teresa Ann Curry, Dec. 19, 1969 (div. 1979); 1 child, Gena Lynette; m. Martha Suzanne Coup, July 21, 1999; 1 child, Dylan Thomas. A of Computer Sci., USMC Degree Program, Washington, 1975. Cert. apt. property supr. Nat. Apt. Assn., Wash., occupancy specialist Nat. Ctr.for Housing Mgmt., Wash. Enlisted USMC, 1968, advanced through grades to staff sgt., 1968-78; shop mgr., bookkeeper Amalgamated Plant Co., Las Vegas, Nev., 1978-79; supr. constrn. Joseph Yousem Co., Las Vegas, 1979-80; apt. mgr. Robert A. McNeil Corp., Las Vegas, 1980, comml. bldg. mgr., leasing agt., 1980-82; asst. v.p., regional property mgr. Westminster Co., Las Vegas, 1982-87, Weyerhaeuser Mortgage Co., Las Vegas, 1988-89; pres., ptnr. Equinox Devel., Inc., Las Vegas, 1989-91; dir. residental properties R.W. Robideaux & Co., Spokane, Wash., 1992-97; mgr. residential divsn. G&B Real Estate Svcs., Spokane, 1997—. Contbr. articles to profl. jours. Mem. Nat. Assn. Realtors, Wash. Assn. Realtors, Spokane Assn. Realtors, Inst. Real Estate Mgmt. (accredited residential mgr., legis. chmn. 1987-88, Accredited Residential Mgr. award 1985, 86, 90), Nev. Apt. Assn. (v.p. 1985, pres. 1988—, bd. dirs.), So. Nev. Homebuilders Assn., Las Vegas Bd. Realtors (mgmt. legis. com. 1988).

DICKEY, ROBERT PRESTON, writer, educator, poet; b. Flat River, Mo., Sept. 24, 1936; s. Delno Miren D. and Naomi Valentine (Jackson) D.; children: Georgia Rae, Shannon Ezra, Rain Dancer. BA, U. Mo., 1968, MA, 1969; PhD, Walden U., 1975. Instr. U. Mo., 1967-69; asst. prof. English and creative writing U. So. Colo., 1969-73; assoc. mem. faculty Pima Coll., Tucson, 1975-78. Author: (with Donald Justice, Thomas McAfee, Donald Drummond) poetry Four Poets, 1967, Running Lucky, 1969, Acting Immortal, 1970; Concise Dictionary of Lead River, Mo., 1972, The Basic Stuff of Poetry, 1972, Life Cycle of Seven Songs, 1972, McCabe Wants Chimes, 1973, Admitting Complicity, 1973; opera librettos Minnequa, 1976, The Witch of Tucson, 1976; Jimmie Cotton!, 1979, Way Out West, 1979, The Poetica Erotica of R.P. Dickey, 1989, The Little Book on Racism and Politics, 1990, The Way of Eternal Recurrence, 1994, Ode on Liberty, 1996, The Lee Poems, 1998, Self-Liberation, 1998, Exercise Anytime, 1998, Collected Poems, 1999, (with Lee Foster) Taos and Other Works of Art, 2002; contbr. poetry to popular mags., Poetry, Saturday Rev., Commonwealth, Prairie Schooner; founder, editor: The Poetry Bag quar., 1966-71; poetry editor: So. Colo. Std., 1973-74. With USAF, 1955-57. Recipient Mahan award for poetry U. Mo., 1965-66 Home: PO Box 87 Ranchos De Taos NM 87557-0087

DICKFELD, TIMM-MICHAEL, electrophysiologist, cardiologist, educator; s. Lutz Heiner and Renate Dickfeld. MD, J.W. v.G-University, Frankfurt, Germany, 1995, PhD, 1997. Asst. prof. medicine U. Md., Balt., 2005—; dir. electrophysiology VA Balt., 2005—. Adj. asst. prof. Johns Hopkins U., Balt. Recipient Silverman Award for Creative Rsch., Johns Hopkins U., 2001. Mem.: AMA, Soc. Cardiovasc. Magnetic Resonance (Best Abstract award 2003), Am. Heart Assn. (Melvin Judkins Young Investigator award 2002). Achievements include research in the feasibility of image integration for real-time guidance of radiofrequency ablations; visualization of ablation lesions using magnetic resonance imaging; real-time CT guidance for percutaneous placement of left ventricular leads; validation of image integration for clinical ablation procedures; patents pending for visualization of radiofrequency ablation lesions. Office: Univ Maryland 22 S Greene St Baltimore MD 21201 Office Phone: 410-328-6056.

DICKIE, GEORGE THOMAS, philosopher, educator; b. Palmetto, Fla., Aug. 12, 1926; s. George Harrison and Emily Neal (Brown) Dickie; m. Ruth Joyce Petty, Aug. 5, 1950 (dec. Apr. 1975); children: Garrick George, Blake Allen; m. Suzanne Ruth Cunningham, June 25, 1977. BA, Fla. State U., 1949; PhD, UCLA, 1959. From instr. to assoc. prof. Wash. State U., Pullman, 1956—64; assoc. prof. U. Houston, 1964—65; assoc. prof. to prof. U. Ill. Chgo., 1965—95, prof. emeritus, 1995—. Pres. Ill. Philosophy Assn., 1990—91. Author: The Art Circle, 1984, The Century of Taste, 1996, Art and Value, 2001, Evaluating Art, 1988, Art and the Aesthetic, 1974, Introduction to Aesthetics, 1971. Pfc USMC, 1944—46. Fellow, NEH, 1971—72, 1989—90, Guggenheim Found., 1978—79. Mem.: Am. Philos. Assn., Am. Soc. Aesthetics (pres. 1993—94). Democrat. Home: 3110 43rd St W Bradenton FL 34209 Personal E-mail: GeoTDickie26@aol.com.

DICKIE, ROBERT BENJAMIN, lawyer, educator; b. Glendale, Calif., Sept. 10, 1941; s. John A. and Dorothy C. Dickie; m. Susan J. Williams, Jan. 28, 1967 (div. 1987); children: Amy, John, Thomas. BA, Yale U., 1963; JD, U. Calif., Berkeley, 1967. Bar: Calif. 1967, N.Y. 1970, Mass. 1971. Assoc. Shearman & Sterling, N.Y.C., 1969-71, Sullivan & Worcester, Boston, 1971-77; asst. prof. mgmt. policy Boston U., 1977-83, tenured assoc. prof., 1983-94; prin The Dickie Group, 1994—. Cons. World Bank, Washington, Fortune 100 Cos., leading law firms in U.S., Europe and Asia. Author: Financial Statement Analysis and Business Valuation for the Practical Lawyer, ABA, 1999; contbr. numerous articles to Nat. Law Jour., Strategic Mgmt. Jour., Columbia Jour. World Bus., others. Mem.: ABA, Calif. Bar Assn., Boston Bar Assn., Longwood Cricket Club, Yale Club Boston. Office: The Dickie Group Reservoir Pl 1601 Trapelo Rd Waltham MA 02451 Office Phone: 781-290-2222.

DICKINSON, CAROL RITTGERS, arts administrator, writer, executive director; b. Des Moines, Apr. 16, 1933; d. Robert Johnson and Cecil Marjorie (Snyder) Rittgers; m. Donald Ira Dickinson, June 6, 1959; 1 child, Lauren Lucy. *Paternal relatives were descendants of John Augustus Rittgers, who immigrated from Prussia to Virginia in 1799. They settled homestead in 1840 along Des Moines river in Iowa. Developed extensive farm, beautiful park and family cemetery still in use. Mother, Marjorie Snyder Rittgers, and her two siblings, Thelma and J.B., graduated from Drake University in art and music. Credits mother for supporting two girls through college by teaching art in Des Moines schools. Also taught multiple arts and crafts to myself and sister Mary Ann Roberts via hands-on approach. Formative teachers included W.L. Reese, philosophy, Prithwish Neogy and Jean Charlot, art, and Andrew Sarris, film.* BA in English with honors, Drake U., 1954; MA in Art History, U. Hawaii, 1964. Lydia Roberts fellow Columbia U., N.Y.C., 1954-56; instr. Iowa State U., U. Hawaii, Colo Women's Coll., U. Petroleum and Minerals, Dhahran, Saudi Arabia, Colo. Sc. Mines, Golden, 1956-76; dir. pub. programs Denver Art Mus., 1980-83; dir. publicity and edn. Mus. Western Art, Denver, 1985-86; freelance writer, 1979—. Lectr., panelist numerous mus., univs. and profl. groups, Colo., 1980—. Co-editor, contbg. author: Colorado and the American Renaissance, 1980, Walking in Beauty, 1990, The Art of Dean Mitchell, 1999; founding editor Denver Urban Design Forum Newsletter, 1984, 85; contbr. more than 400 articles to nat. and regional newspapers and mags.; art critic Denver Rocky Mountain News, 1990-92. Exec. dir. Foothills Art Ctr., Golden, 1992-2003. Recipient Denver Mayor's Award for Excellence in Arts, 2000, 1st Cultural award, Jefferson Symphony, 2000, medal, Colorado Sch. Mines, 2000, Living Landmarks award, Golden Landmarks Assn., 2005, 1st pl. awards, revs./features, Colo. Press Women; Honoree in naming of The Carol and Don Dickinson Sculpture Garden, Foothills Art Ctr., Golden, Colo., 2004. Mem. Golden Fortnightly Club, Asian Art Assn. Democrat. Episcopalian. Avocations: Asian philosophies and history, Chinese brush painting, films. Home: 1908 Pinal Rd Golden CO 80401-1744 Office Phone: 303-278-1357.

DICKINSON, CHRISTINE Z., nuclear medicine and nuclear cardiologist, medical educator; b. American Fork, Utah, Oct. 23, 1952; d. James Hershel and Helen Evatz Zunich; 1 child, William Claiborne. BS, U. Utah, 1974, MD, 1978; cardiology fellow, U. Calif. Davis, 1990. Diplomate Am. Bd. Internal Medicine, Am. Bd. Nuclear Medicine. Resident in internal medicine Vanderbilt U. Sch. Medicine, Nashville, 1981, fellow in nuc. medicine and nuc. cardiology, 1981—85; fellow in cardiology U. Calif., Davis, 1990; asst. prof. radiology, divsn. nuc. medicine U. Calif. Davis Med. Ctr., Sacramento, 1985—87; dir. nuc. medicine San Jose Imaging Ctr., Calif., 1990—92; asst. clin. prof. radiology U. Calif. Davis, Sacramento, 1991; staff physician nuc. medicine Covina Intercmty. Hosp., 1992; dir. nuc. cardiology, dept. nuc. medicine William Beaumont Hosp., Royal Oak, Mich., 1992—. Clin. asst. prof. dept. radiology Mich. State U., Lansing, 2000—; mem. admissions com., cardiology fellowship program William Beaumont Hosp., Royal Oak, Mich., 2000—, lectr. nuc. medicine residency tng. and oncology fellowship tng., 1999—, coord. nuc. cardiology faculty/divsn. cardiology, 1992—; sci. program com. moderator Soc. Nuc. Medicine, 2001. Contbr. articles to profl. jours. Mem. Joint Rev. Com. on Ednl. Programs in Nuc. Medicine Tech., Mont., 2003—; mem. women's legacy luncheon Am. Heart Assn., Detroit, 2002—03, bd. dirs., 2003—. Grantee, Am. Heart Assn., 1989—90; Presdl. scholar, U. Utah, 1974—78. Mem.: Am. Coll. Nuc. Physicians, Am. Soc. Nuc. Cardiology, Soc. Nuc. Medicine, Mortar Board, Phi Kappa Phi. Office: William Beaumont Hosp 3601 West 13 Mile Rd Royal Oak MI 48073 Office Phone: 248-898-4123. Business E-Mail: cdickinson@beaumont.edu.

DICKINSON, DONALD CHARLES, library science professor; b. Schenectady, N.Y., June 9, 1927; s. Charles William and Stella Barney (Sheldon) D.; m. Colleen Eleanor Schindler, Aug. 7, 1954; children: Ann, Jean, Ellen, Mary, Kathleen, Sheila. AB, SUNY, Albany, 1949; MLS, U. Ill., 1951; PhD, U. Mich., 1964. Ref. librarian Cen. Mo. State Coll., Warrensburg, 1951-53, Eastern Mich. U., Ypsilanti, 1953-56; asst. acquisitions U. Kans., Lawrence, 1956-58; head librarian Bemidji (Minn.) State Coll., 1958-66; dir. reader service U. Mo., Columbia, 1966-69; dir. grad. library sch. U. Ariz., Tucson, 1969-78, prof. grad. library sch., 1979-96, prof. emeritus, 1996—. Author: Bio-bibliography Langston Hughes, 1967, 2d edit., 1972, Hellmut Lehmann-Haupt, 1975, Dictionary of American Book Collectors, 1986, George Watson Cole, 1990, Henry E. Huntington's Library of Libraries, 1995, Dictionary of American Antiquarian Bookdealers, 1998, John Carter, Taste and Technique of a Bookman, 2004. Am. Philos. Assn. grantee, 1969; Andrew W. Mellon fellow Henry E. Huntington Libr., 1989; Helm fellow Ind. U., 1999; C.P. Snow travel fellow U. Tex., 2000; Huntington/Brit. Acad. fellow, 2000. Mem. ALA (coun. 1972-73, travel grantee 1960), Bibliographic Soc. Am., Ariz. Libr. Assn. (pres. 1978-79), Grolier Club (N.Y.C.), Zamorano Club (L.A.). Democrat. Business E-Mail: dickinsd@u.arizona.edu.

DICKINSON, ELEANOR CREEKMORE, artist, educator; b. Knoxville, Tenn., Feb. 7, 1931; d. Robert Elmond and Evelyn Louise (Van Gilder) C.; m. Ben Wade Oakes Dickinson, June 12, 1952; children: Mark Wade, Katherine Van Gilder, Peter Somers. BA, U. Tenn., 1952; postgrad., San Francisco Art Inst., 1961—63, Academié de la Grande Chaumière, Paris, 1971; MFA, Calif. Coll. Arts, Crafts, 1982, Golden Gate U., 1984. Cert. Recognition El Consejo Mundial de Artistas Plasticos, 1993. Escrow officer Security Nat. Bank, Santa Monica, Calif., 1953-54; mem. faculty Calif. Coll. of the Arts, Oakland, 1971—2001, assoc. prof. art, 1974—84, prof., 1984-2001, prof. emerita, 2001—, dir. galleries, 1975-85. Artist-in-residence U. Tenn., 1969, Ark. State U., 1993, Fine Arts Mus. of San Francisco, 2000; faculty U. Calif. Ext., 1967-70; lectr. in field. Co-author, illustrator: Revival, 1974, That Old Time Religion, 1975; also mus. catalogs; illustrator: The Complete Fruit Cookbook, 1972, Human Sexuality: A Search for Understanding, 1984, Days Journey, 1985; author, illustrator: Elkmont, the Heart of the Great Smoky Mountain National Park, 2005; commissions: University of San Francisco, 1990-2001, U. Tenn. Downtown Gallery, 2005; solo shows include Corcoran Gallery Art, Washington, 1970, 74, San Francisco Mus. Modern Art, 1965, 68, Fine Arts Mus. San Francisco, 1969, 75, Poindexter Gallery, NY, 1972, 74, Smithsonian Inst., 1975-81, U. Tenn., 1976, 2005, Galeria de Arte y Libros, Monterrey, Mex., 1978, Oakland Mus., 1979, Interart Ctr., NY, 1980, Tenn. State Mus., 1981-82, Hatley Martin Gallery, San Francisco, 1986, 89, Michael Himovitz Gallery, Sacramento, Calif., 1988-89, 91, 93, 97-98, Gallery 10, Washington, 1989, Diverse Works, Houston, 1990, Ewing Gallery, U. Tenn., 1991, G.T.U. Gallery, U. Calif., Berkeley, 1991, Mus. Contemporary Religious Art, St. Louis, 1995, Thacher Gallery, U. San Francisco, 2000; represented in permanent collections Nat. Collection Fine Arts, Corcoran Gallery Art, Libr. of Congress, Smithsonian Instn., San Francisco Mus. Modern Art, Butler Inst. Am. Art, Oakland Mus., Santa Barbara Mus., Nat. Mus. Women in Arts, Washington; prodr. (TV) The Art of the Matter-Professional Practices in Fine Arts, 1986—. Bd. dirs. Calif. Confedn. of the Arts, 1983—; bd. dirs., v.p. Calif. Lawyers for the Arts, 1986—; mem. coun. bd. San Francisco Art Inst., 1966-91, trustee, 1964-67; sec., bd. dirs. YWCA, 1955-62; treas., bd. Westminster Ctr., 1955-59; bd. dirs. Children's Theater Assn., 1958-60, 93-94, Internat. Child Art Ctr., 1958-68. Recipient Disting. Alumni award San Francisco Art Inst., 1983, Master Drawing award Nat. Soc. Arts and Letters, 1983, Pres.'s award Nat. Women's Caucus for Art, 1995, Allgemeines Kunstlerfexidon, 2001, Lifetime Achivement award Nat. Women's Caucus for Art, 2003; grantee Zellerbach Family Fund, 1975, NEH, 1978, 80, 82-85, Thomas F. Stanley Found., 1985, Bay Area Video Coalition, 1988-92, PAS Graphics, 1988, San Francisco Cmty. TV Corp., 1990, Skaggs Found., 1991. Mem.: NOW, Nat. Women's Caucus for Art (nat. Affirmative Action officer 1978—80, nat. bd. dirs. 2000—, Pres.'s award, Lifetime Achievement award 1995), Arts Advocates, Artists Equity Assn. (nat. v.p., dir. 1978—92), San Francisco Art Assn. (sec., dir. 1964—67), Calif. Lawyers for Arts (v.p. 1986—2004, bd. dirs. 1986—), Calif. Confederation of Arts (bd. dirs. 1983—89), Coll. Art Assn. (chair com. on Women in the Arts 2004—), Coalition Women's Art Orgns. (dir. 1978—80, v.p. 2000—01), AAUP. Democrat. Episcopalian. Office: Calif Coll of the Arts 1111 8th St San Francisco CA 94107-2247 Office Phone: 415-922-3733. Personal E-mail: eleanordickinson@mac.com.

DICKINSON, JANE W., social services administrator; b. Sept. 27, 1919; d. Charles Herman and Rachel (Whaler) Wagner; m. E. F. Sherwood Dickinson, Oct. 23, 1943; children: Diane Jane Gray Clem, Carolyn Dickinson Vane. BA, Duke U., 1941; MEd, Goucher Coll., 1965. Exec. sec. Petroleum Industry Com., Balt., 1941-43, Sherwood Feed Mills Inc., Balt., 1943-79. Mem. exec. com. Children's Aid Md., 1960-61; mem. bd. women's aux. Balt. Symphony Orch., 1958-60; dist. chmn. Balt. Cancer Drive, 1957; co-chmn. Balt. United Appeal, 1968; bd. mgrs. Pickersgill Retirement Home. Mem. Three Arts Club (Balt., sec. 1958-60, bd. govs. 1960-64, 67-70, pres. 1970-72), Women's Club of Roland Park (bd. govs. 1960-64, 86-88, 92-94), Cliff Dwellers Garden Club, Alpha Delta Phi Home: Apt 609 1055 W Joppa Rd Baltimore MD 21204-3748

DICKINSON, JESS H., state supreme court justice; b. Charleston, Miss., 1947; m. Janet Holiman; 4 children. BS, Miss. State U., 1978; JD, U. Miss. Sch. of Law, 1982. Bar: Miss. 1982. Atty. priv. practice, Jackson, Miss., 1982—83, Gulfport, Miss., 1984—2003; judge Forrest and Perry County Circuit Ct.; justice Miss. Supreme Ct., 2004—. Mem.: Miss. Bar Assn. (Ethics Com., Professionalism Com.). Office: Miss Supreme Ct PO Box 249 Jackson MS 39205

DICKINSON, JOSHUA CLIFTON, JR., museum director, educator; b. Tampa, Fla., Apr. 28, 1916; s. Joshua Clifton and Mary (Martin) D.; m. Lucy Jackson, Apr. 13, 1936 (wid. June 10, 1997); children: Joshua Clifton III, Martin Freeman, Susan Ellissa; m. Sarah Donnovin Hadley, Nov. 1, 1997. Student, U. Va., 1936-39, Cornell U., 1938; BS, U. Fla., 1940, MS, 1946, PhD, 1950. Faculty U. Fla., 1946—, asst. prof. biology, 1950-55, assoc. prof. biology, 1955, prof. zoology, 1973-79; curator Fla. State Mus. (name changed to Fla. Mus. of Natural History-U. Fla.), 1952-79, chmn. natural scis., 1953-60, acting dir., 1959-61, dir., 1961-79, dir. emeritus, 1979—. Vis. investigator Woods Hole Oceanographic Inst., 1952; expdns. to, Honduras, 1946, Bahamas, 1958-62, 66-67, Jamaica, 1946, Baffin Island, 1955, Sombrero Island, 1964, Navassa Island, 1967, Turks and Caicos Islands, 1974. Contbr. articles to profl. jours. Chmn. Fla. Bd. Archives and History, 1967-69; mem. mus. adv. panel Nat. Endowment for Arts, 1970-72, co-chmn., 1972-74; panelist fellowship program NSF, 1966-68; mem. Nat. Council on Arts, 1976-82, also chmn. com. planning and policy; bd. dirs. Fla. Arts Celebration, 1984-92, vice chmn., 1985-86. Comdr. USCGR, 1942-46, ret. Grantee Nat. Park Service, 1954, NSF, 1955-57; Rsch. fellow Harvard U., 1951-52; recipient Disting. Alumnus award U. Fla., 1977, Presdl. Medallion U. Fla.,

1979; Dickinson Hall named in his honor U. Fla. Mem. Am. Ornithologists Union, Am. Soc. Naturalists, Am. Assn. Museums (chmn. sci. mus. sect. 1961, mem. council 1964-70, sec. 1970), Am. Soc. Zoologists, Wilson Ornithol. Soc., Am. Assn. Sci. Mus. Dirs. (v.p. 1967-69), Assn. Systematic Collections (pres. 1972-75, bd. dir. 1974-76, chmn. membership com. 1976-79), Bahamas Nat. Trust, Assn. S.E. Biologists (sec. 1955-58), Fla. Acad. Scis. (chmn. biology sect. 1952, editor quar. jour. 1955-63), Conf. Dirs. Systematics Collections (pres. 1976-78), Fla. Audubon Soc. (bd. dir. 1958-64, 79-84), S.E. Museums Conf. (v.p. 1971-72, pres. 1972, James L. Shortt award 1987), Internat. Council Museums (exec. com. 1974-77), Am. Assn. Museums (vis. accreditation team 1973-75), Rotary (pres. Gainesville 1967-68), Sigma Xi, Phi Sigma, Alpha Tau Omega. Democrat. Presbyterian. Home: 9517 SW 40th Ln Gainesville FL 32608-4647

DICKINSON, MARGERY ELSIE, missionary, clinical psychologist; b. Petoskey, Mich., Oct. 29, 1940; d. David Eugene and Beryle Mae (Herrington) L.; m. Hugh Dickinson, July 30, 2005. BS with honors, Taylor U., Upland, Ind., 1962; MA with high honors, Wheaton (Ill.) Coll., 1983; student, U. Paris Sorbonne, 1970. Lic. psychologist, Pa., limited lic. psychologist, Mich. Tchr. Waterford (Mich.) Sch. Sys., 1962-64; ednl. missionary, county dir. BCM Internat., Union County, NJ, 1965-69; ednl. missionary BCM Internat. and AIM Internat., Albertville and Paris, France, 1969-70, ednl. missionary, technician Watsa, Democratic Republic of Congo, 1970-81; counselor, therapist BCM Internat./AIM Internat. Amani Counseling Ctr., Nairobi, Kenya, 1983-84; organizer, dir. counseling dept., counselor, cons. BCM Internat., Upper Darby, Pa., 1985-97, psychol. testing and assessment of mission candidates, 1986—95, organizer, dir. mem. care ministries, 1998—2000, mem. care ministries, cons., 2000—. Organizer/facilitator Missions and Mental Health-East, Mt. Bethel, Pa., 1995-97; lectr. in field; spkr. in field. Editor: Commit Thy Way, 1994; author: (Bible study series) Living in Community, 1980, translator (illustrator) Bible lessons from English to Lingala for use in Congo; contbr. articles to profl. jours. Facilitator Bible Club work, Democratic Republic of Congo, 1985—; fundraiser, facilitator printing and distbn. Christian lit., 2001—; leader grief support group First Congl. Ch., Rockford, Mich., 2003; Bible study leader Rockford (Mich.) Bapt. Ch., 2004; cons. Congo Internat. Mission, Grand Rapids, Mich., 2004—. Billy Graham Evangelistic Assn. scholar, 1981-83. Mem.: APA (assoc.), Midwest Mem. Care Network (charter), Christian Therapists Bible Study, Assn. N.Am. Missions, Am. Assn. of Christian Counselors (charter, spkr. regional conf. 1999). Baptist. Avocations: writing songs and poetry, clarinet, walking, aerobic weight-lifting, swimming. Office: 309 Colonial Dr Box 249 Akron PA 17501-0249 also: BCMI Western Mich 710 Baldwin St Jenison MI 49428-9706 Office Phone: 616-799-4047. Business E-Mail: worship@rockfordbaptist.com, membercare@bcmintl.org.

DICKINSON, MICHAEL, physiologist; ScB, Brown U., 1984; PhD, U. Wash., 1989. Postdoctoral trainee Roche Inst. Molecular Biology, 1990—91; mem. faculty dept. organismal biology and anatomy U. Chgo., 1991—96; prof. integrative biology U. Calif., Berkeley, 1996—. Vis. scholar Max Planck Inst. Biol. Cybernetics, 1991, 93. Recipient Larry Sandler award, Genetic Soc. Am., 1990, George Bartholomew award for physiology, Soc. Integrative and Comparative Biology, 1995; fellow, NSF, 1985, Packard Found., 1992; John D. and Catherine T. MacArthur fellow, 2001. Office: Calif Inst Tech M/C 138 78 1200 E California Blvd Pasadena CA 91125 Office Phone: 626-395-3906. Business E-Mail: flyman@caltech.edu.

DICKINSON, RICHARD DONALD NYE, clergyman, theology studies educator; b. Monson, Mass., Aug. 1, 1929; s. Richard Donald Nye and Phoebe Abigail (Naylor) D.; m. Nancy Leland Stone, Nov. 26, 1955; children: Elizabeth Stone, Richard Donald Nye III, Edward David McCrea. BA, Am. Internat. Coll., 1950, MA, 1951; STB, Boston U., 1954, PhD, 1959; cert., Institut Oecumenique, Geneva, 1955. Ordained to ministry United Ch. of Christ; chaplain, instr. Wheaton Coll., Norton, Mass., 1957-62; assoc. dir. Quaker Confs. in So. Asia, 1962-64; sr. research officer Inst. for Social Studies, The Hague, Netherlands, 1964-67; sec. for specialized assistance World Council Chs., 1967-68; now cons.; prof. Christian social ethics Christian Theol. Sem., Indpls., 1968-74, v.p., dean, 1974-86, acting pres., 1986-87, pres., 1987-97. Chmn. devel. commn. World Coun. Chs.; mem. edn. commn. Nat. Coun. Chs., 1972-74; mem. ch. world service com.; incorporating mem. Center for Exploration Values and Meaning.; bd. dirs. internat. affairs div. Am. Friends Service Com., div. overseas ministries of Christian Ch. Author: The Christian College and National Development, 1967, Line and Plummet, 1968, The Christian College in Developing India, 1969, To Set at Liberty the Oppressed, 1975, Poor, Yet Making Many Rich, 1983, Economic Globalization: Challenge for Christians. Bd. dirs. Ind. Opera Theatre, Internat. Ctr. Indpls., The Gemmer Found., Ind. Com. Econ. Edn., Martin Luther King Multiservice Ctr., Ind.-Ky. Conf. United Ch. of Christ, bd. dirs., chair fin. com.; mem. Greater Indpls. Progress Com.; moderator First Congl. Ch.; chmn. Ch. World Svc. Bd. Ind.-Ky. Mem. Am. Soc. for Christian Ethics, Soc. for Sci. Study Religion, Econs. Club of Indpls. (bd. dir.), Rotary. Mem. United Ch. Of Christ. Home: 5173 N Kenwood Ave Indianapolis IN 46208-2619 E-mail: rdndjnsd@aol.com, rdndjnsd@earthlink.net.

DICKINSON, RICHARD HENRY, accountant; b. June 16, 1944; s. Everett I. and Gertrude T. (Frear) D.; m. Georgette M. Turner, Jan. 27, 1968 (dec. June 1998); children: Eric, Christine, Brent; m. Barbara J. Jones, Oct. 16, 2004 BS, U. Wis.; BBA, Siena Coll., 1973; MBA, Dartmouth Coll., 1995. Assoc. acct. Alexander Varga, CPA, Catskill, N.Y., 1973; contr. Hocker Power Brake Co., Inc., Evansville, Ind., 1974; dep. contr. Watervliet (N.Y.) Arsenal, Dept. Def., 1975-76; auditor Melvin I. Weiskopf, CPA, Saratoga Springs, N.Y., 1977; owner, prin. Richard H. Dickinson, CPA, Ballston Spa and Saratoga Springs, N.Y., 1978-83; owner Dickinson & Co., CPAs, Saratoga Spring, 1984—. Lectr. Siena Coll., Loudonville, N.Y., 1983-89, Skidmore Coll., 1990-96. With U.S. Army, 1967-70. Decorated Silver Star, Bronze Star. Mem. ABA (assoc.), Am. Inst. CPAs, N.Y. State Soc. CPAs, Inst. Mgmt. Accts., Masons, Rotary (pres. Ballston Spa chpt. 1979), Delta Epsilon Sigma, Alpha Kappa Alpha. Republican. Lutheran. Home: 60 Locust Grove Rd Saratoga Springs NY 12866 Office: 439 Maple Ave Saratoga Springs NY 12866-5503 also: 2 Washington Sq Greenwich NY 12834-1319 Office Phone: 518-587-1136. E-mail: rdcpa44@hotmail.com.

DICKINSON, RICHARD RAYMOND, retired oil company executive; b. Orange, Calif., Jan. 28, 1931; s. Raymond Russel and Florence Marie (Jacobson) D.; m. Barbara Jean Morrison, June 16, 1957; children: Roderick, Christine. BS, Calif. Inst. Tech., 1952; MS, U. So. Calif., 1960. Chem. engr. L.A. Refinery Texaco, 1952-68, gen. mgr. supply and distbn. London, 1968-76, plant mgr. Eagle Point plant Westville, N.J., 1976-79, gen. mgr. alternate energy group White Plains, N.Y., 1979, v.p. strategic planning, 1979-82; sr. v.p. U.S. refining, mktg., supply and transp. Texaco U.S.A., Houston, 1982-87; v.p. tech. Texaco, Inc., White Plains, N.Y., 1988-94. Served with USNR, 1955-58. Home: 944 Hills Creek Dr Mc Kinney TX 75070-5232

DICKINSON, ROBERT EARL, atmospheric scientist, educator, retired science administrator; b. Millersburg, Ohio, Mar. 26, 1940; s. Leonard Earl and Carmen L. (Ostby) D. AB in Chemistry and Physics, Harvard U., 1961; MS in Meteorology, MIT, 1962, PhD in Meteorology, 1966. Rsch. assoc. MIT, Cambridge, 1966-68; scientist Nat. Ctr. Atmospheric Rsch., Boulder, Colo., 1968-73, sr. scientist, 1973-90, head climate sect., 1975-81, dep. dir. A.A.P. divsn., 1981-86, acting dir., 1986-87; prof. atmospheric physics U. Ariz., 1990-93, regents prof., 1993-99; prof. earth and atmospheric scis. Ga. Inst. Tech., Atlanta, 1999—; chair Ga. Power/Ga. Rsch. Alliance. Mem. climate rsch. com. NRC, Washington, 1985-90, chmn., 1987-90, com. earth sci., 1985-88, global change com., 1985-92; mem. WCRP sci. steering group GEWEX, 1988-92; UNU steering com. Climatic, Biotic and Human Interactions in Humid Tropics, 1984-88, steering com. Internat. Satellite Land Surface Climatology project, 1984-89. Editor: The Geophysiology of Amazonia, 1986; contbr. articles to profl. jours. Recipient G. Unger Vetlesen prize, 1996. Fellow AAAS, Am. Meteorol. Soc. (chmn. com. biometeorol. and aerobiol. 1987-89, Meisinger award 1973, Editors award 1976, Jule Charney award 1989, Walter Orr Roberts lectr. in interdisciplinary sci. 1995, Carl-Gustaf Rossby award 1997), Am. Geophys. Union (atmospheric sci. sect. 1986-88, pres.-elect 1988-90, pres. 1990-92, pres.-elect 2000-02, pres. 2002-04, Revelle medal 1996); mem. NAS, NAE, European Geoscis. Union (hon.). Democrat. Home: 1074 Peachtree Walk B311 Atlanta GA 30309 Office: Ga Inst Tech EAS 311 Ferst Dr Atlanta GA 30332-0340

DICKINSON, ROGER ALLYN, business administration educator; b. Bklyn., Sept. 8, 1929; s. Robert Albert and Esther (Odland) D.; m. Ruth Nordis, June 1, 1957; children: Robert Allyn, Roger Perry, Todd Charles, Bruce Gregory. AB, Williams Coll., 1951; MBA, UCLA, 1955; PhD, Columbia U., 1967. Lectr., asst. prof. bus. adminstrn. U. Calif., Berkeley, 1964-69; assoc. prof. Rutgers Grad. Sch. Bus., Newark, N.J., 1969-70, prof., 1970-75; prof. Coll. Bus. Adminstrn. U. Tex., Arlington, 1975-79, prof. mktg., 1979—; dean Coll. Bus., U. Tex., 1975-79. Author: Retail Management: A Channels Approach, 1974, (with others) A Basic Approach to Executive Decision Making, 1978, Retail Management, 1981; book note editor Jour. Retailing, 1970-92, Jour. Macromktg., 1992—; mem. editl. bd. Jour. Consumer Mktg., Jour. Macromktg., Jour. Mktg. Channels; contbr. chpts. to books and articles to profl. jours. Mem. Am. Collegiate Retailing Assn. (pres. 1980-82) Office: U Tex Coll Bus Arlington TX 76019-0001 Home: 17600 SE Covington Cir 88 The Villages FL 32162 Office Phone: 817-272-2284. E-mail: rogerd@uta.edu.

DICKINSON, WADE, oil industry executive, educator; b. Sharon, Pa., Oct. 29, 1926; s. Ben Wade Orr and Gladys Grace (Oakes) D.; m. Eleanor Creekmore, June 12, 1952; children: Mark, Katherine, Peter. Student, Carnegie Inst. Tech., 1944-45; BS, U.S. Mil. Acad., 1949; postgrad., Oak Ridge Sch. Reactor Tech., 1950-51. Commd. 2d lt. USAF, 1949, advanced through grades to capt., 1954, resigned, 1954; cons. physicist Rand Corp., Santa Monica, Calif., 1952-54; engring. cons. Bechtel Group, Inc., San Francisco, 1954-87; tech. advisor U.S. Congress, Washington, 1957-58; pres. Agrophysics, Inc., San Francisco, 1968—, Petrolphysics Inc., San Francisco, 1975—; ptnr. Radialphysics Ltd., San Francisco, 1980—, Robotphysics Ltd., San Francisco, 1983—; mng. mem. The Spark Group, 2000—, Petro Jet Co, LLC, Solid Gas Techs. Lectr. engring. and bus. U. Calif., Berkeley, 1984—; cardiology cons. Mt. Zion Med. Ctr., U. Calif., San Francisco, 1970-95; chmn. bd. Calif. Med. Clin. Psychotherapy. Contbr. articles to profl. jours; patentee in field. Trustee World Affair Coun., 1958-62; mem. San Francisco Com. Fgn. Rels., Young Republicans, Calif. Mem. Am. Phys. Soc., Am. Soc. Petroleum Engrs. Clubs: Bohemian (San Francisco), Chit Chat (San Francisco). Lodges: Masons, Guardsmen. Episcopalian. Home: 2125 Broderick St San Francisco CA 94115-1627 Office: Petrolphysics Inc 1388 Sutter St Ste 603 San Francisco CA 94109-5452 Office Phone: 415-626-6020. Personal E-mail: petrojet@ix.netcom.com.

DICKINSON, WILLIAM BOYD, JR., media consultant; b. Kansas City, Mo., Feb. 21, 1931; s. William Boyd and Aileen (Robinson) D.; m. Betty Ann Landree, Feb. 1, 1953; children: William Boyd IV, David Alan. AB, U. Kans., 1953; student, George Washington U. Law Sch., 1957-58. With U.P.I., 1955-59, mem. staff overnight desk Washington, 1957-59; staff writer Editorial Research Reports, Washington, 1959-66, editor, 1966-73; editor, v.p. Congl. Quar., Inc., 1972-73; gen. mgr., editorial dir. Washington Post Writers Group, 1973-91; cons., 1991-96, Biocentric Inst., 1991—. Resident profl. Journalism Sch. U. Kans., 1993-99; manship chair Journalism Sch. La. State U., 1999-2003, disting. prof., 2003—; Winston Churchill Traveling fellow, summer 1968. Supervisory editor: Congl. Quar.'s Complete Guide to Congress. Served with AUS, 1953-55. Press fellowship Knight Internat., 1998. Mem. William Allen White Found. (trustee), Alpha Tau Omega, Omicron Delta Kappa. (Washington). Home and Office: 1617 Alvamar Dr Lawrence KS 66047-1715 also: LSU 221B Journalism Bldg Baton Rouge LA 70803-0001 Office Phone: 785-832-1899. E-mail: wdicki2@lsu.edu.

DICKINSON, WILLIAM TREVOR, hydrologist, educator; b. Toronto, Ont., Can., Aug. 30, 1939; s. Clarence Heber and Katie Isobel (Kneen) D.; m. Sharon Lucille Tutt, Aug. 24, 1963; children: Michael Trevor, Cathryn Ruth. BSA., U. Toronto, 1961, BASci., 1962, MSA., 1964; PhD, Colo. State U., 1967. Research assoc. Colo. State U., 1964-67; asst. prof. engring. U. Guelph, Ont., 1967-70, assoc. prof., 1970-78, prof., 1978-94, prof. emeritus, 1995—, coordinator instructional devel., 1979-82, Sc. Tchg. and Learning Higher Edn. and 3M teaching fellow, coord. univ. teaching program, 1991—93; pvt. cons. water resources engring. Contbr. articles to profl. jours. Recipient Conservation Pioneer award, Conservation Ont., 2000. Mem. Assn. Profl. Engrs. Ont., Can. Assn. Univ. Tchrs., Soc. Tchg. Learning High Edn. Mem. United Ch. of Can. Home: 68 Pine Ridge Dr Guelph ON Canada N1L 1J1 Office: Univ Guelph Guelph ON Canada N1G 2W1 E-mail: wdickins@ucguelph.ca.

DICKISON, ALEXANDER KANE, physical science educator; b. Jamaica, NY, Oct. 16, 1943; s. William and Eileen S. (Kane) D.; m. Lois Jean Tansley, Mar. 21, 1967; children: Stephen William, Jonathan Harry. BS, Western Ill. U., 1965; MS, Mont. State U., 1968, EdD, 1972. Instr. U. Wis., Green Bay, 1969-72, Mont. State U., Bozeman, 1972-73, Seminole C.C., Sanford, Fla., 1973—, dept. chmn. phys. scis., 1986—. Adj. prof. U. Ctrl. Fla., Orlando, 1972-83; del. U.S.-Japan-China Confs. on Physics Tchg., 1989, 91, 93; mem. Fla. Statewide Com. on Common Course Numbering, 1981—; reader, table leader Advance Placement Test Readings, 1988-2001; mem. com. on career planning Am. Inst. Physics, 1991-95. Chair Seminole County Hist. Commn., Sanford, 1982—; mem. Citizen com., Expressway Authority, Seminole County, 1989-93; county liason St. John's Water Mgmt. Dist., Seminole County, 1981-91; energy com. East Fla. Regional Planning Com., Seminole county, 1976-82. Mem. NSTA, Am. Physics Soc., Am. Assn. Physics Tchrs. (exec. bd. 1991-95, treas. 1996-2002, Outstanding Physics Tchr. of Yr. award Fla. sect. 1990, Disting. Svc. award 2003), Fla. Assn. Physics Tchrs. (chmn. 1975-76), Fla. Acad. Scis. (exec. sec. 1986-91, Disting. Svc. award 1993), Fla. Assn. Sci. Tchrs., Sigma Pi Sigma. Avocations: history, outdoors, travel, reading, golf. Home: 4851 Hester Ave Sanford FL 32773-9402 Office: Seminole Community Coll 100 Weldon Blvd Sanford FL 32773-6132 Business E-Mail: dickisoa@scc-fl.edu.

DICKMAN, CRAIG STEVEN, retail, distribution-consulting company executive; b. Oshkosh, Wis., July 23, 1960; s. Llewellyn Herman and Betty Jane (Klemp) D.; m. Karen Jean Thomson, June 4, 1983; children: Megan, Brenden. BS, U. Wis., Green Bay, 1982; MBA, U. Wis., Oshkosh, 1987. Ops. supr. Schneider Nat., Inc., Green Bay, 1983-86, regional mgr., 1986-87; mgr. ops. Catenation, Inc. a SHADE Co., Green Bay, 1987-88; mgr. logistics svcs. SHADE Info. Systems, Inc., Green Bay, 1988-92, dir. strategic planning, 1992-94; pres. The MD2 Group, Inc., Green Bay, 1994-97; v.p. Space Explorers, Inc., 1997-98; dir. human resources Schneider Nat. Inc., 1998-2000, v.p. info. tech., 2000—. Bd. dirs. Space Edn. Initiatives, Inc., Schneider Technol. Svcs. LLC. Mem. Green Bay Housing Authority, 1990-94, Brown County (Wis.) Solid Waste Bd., 1992-94, Green Bay City Coun., 1990-92, Brown County Criminal Justice Bd., 1992-94, Brown County Bd. Suprs., 1990-92; 1st vice chmn. Rep. Com. Green Bay, 1994—. Mem. Coun. Logistics Mgmt., World Future Soc. Home: 2914 Westline Rd Green Bay WI 54313-8264 Office: 3101 Packerland Dr Green Bay WI 54313-6187 E-mail: dickmanc@earthlink.net.

DICKMAN, FRANCOIS MOUSSIEGT, former foreign service officer, educator; b. Iowa City, Dec. 23, 1924; s. Adolphe Jacques and Henriette Louise (Moussiegt) D.; m. Margaret Hoy, June 3, 1947; children: Christine, Paul. BA, U. Wyo., 1947; MA, Fletcher Sch. Law & Diplomacy, 1948; student, U.S. Army War Coll., Carlisle, Pa., 1968—69. Rsch. asst. Brookings Instn., Washington, 1950; with U.S. Fgn. Svc., 1951-84, consular/comml. officer Barranquilla, Colombia, 1952-54, Arabic lang. trainee Beirut, 1955-57, econ., comml., consular officer Khartoum, Sudan, 1957-60; Egyptian-Syrian affairs desk officer Dept. State, 1961-65, econ. officer Tunis, Tunisia, 1965-68; econ. counselor Jidda, Saudi Arabia, 1969-72; dir. Arabian Peninsula affairs Dept. State, 1972-76, amb. to United Arab Emirates, 1976-79, amb. to Kuwait, 1979-83; diplomat in residence Marquette U., 1984; adj. prof. polit. sci. U. Wyo., Laramie, 1985—2004. Lectr. in field. Served with AUS, 1943-46, 50-51. Recipient Dept. State Meritorious Honor award, 1965, Disting. Alumni award U. Wyo., 1980; named Exemplary Alumnus U. Wyo., 1993. Mem. VFW, U.S. Army War Coll. Alumni Assn., U. Wyo. Alumni Assn., Phi Beta Kappa, Phi Kappa Phi. Office: U Wyo Polit Sci Dept Laramie WY 82071-3197 Personal E-mail: fmdmhd@aol.com.

DICKMAN, JAMES BRUCE, photojournalist; b. St. Louis, Mar. 25, 1949; s. Joseph Edward and Isabel Catherine (Brown) D.; m. Mary Kay Thomas, Sept. 23, 1968 (div.); children: Kristi Michele, Gavin Thomas; m. 2d Rebecca Lauren Skelton, Sept. 16, 1983; children: Matthew Benjamin, Margaret Catherine Anne. Student, U. Tex., 1967-69. Photographer McKinney Job Corps., Tex., 1969-70, Dallas Times Herald, 1970-86. Founder First Light photography workshops, France, 2003, Scotland, 04. Worked on photo projects Day in the Life of Can., Day in the Life of Am., Day in the Life of Spain, Day in the Life of the Soviet Union, Day in the Life of China; (book and CD-ROM) Passage to Vietnam, 1994, Day in the Life of Africa, 2002; contbg. editor Am. Way Mag. Recipient Pulitzer prize for photography Columbia U., 1983; recipient World Press Photo of Yr. award World Press Photo Orgn., Holland, Amsterdam, 1983, 89, awards Dallas Press Club, AP and UPI, Tex. Headliners, Damascus Syria, Internat. Orgn. of Photography, 1st place, Sigma Delta Chi Disting. Service award, Bronze Medallion, others Mem. Am. Soc. Mag. Photographers. Office Phone: 303-730-2894. E-mail: jaybec@comcast.net. *I've always felt that I've had a guardian angel pointing me in the correct directions. But it's always been up to me to do something with the opportunities once they're presented.*

DICKMAN, JAMES EARL, financial services executive; m. LaTricia P. Schendel, May 10, 1997. BS in Fin., Va. Tech., 1985. CFP. Agt., registered rep. Life of Va., Charlottesville, 1985-86; fin. cons. Merrill Lynch, Pierce Fenner and Smith, Roanoke, Va., 1986-90; v.p. Horton Fin. Svcs. Inc., Charlottesville, 1990—. Office Horton Fin. Svc. Inc., Charlottesville. Republican. Presbyterian. Avocations: photography, tennis.

DICKMAN, MARTIN J., federal agency administrator; b. Chgo. BS, U. Ill., 1966; JD, DePaul U., 1969. Asst. corp. counsel City of Chgo., 1970—72; counsel to minority leader Ill. Ho. Reps., 1972—73; mem. Bd. Trade, Chgo., 1972—91; asst. Peter Fitzpatrick and Assocs., 1973—89; hearings ref. Ill. Dept. Revenue, 1976—80; prosecutor Cook County Ill. State's Atty.'s Fin. and Govtl. Crimes Task Force, 1991—94; inspector gen. Railroad Retirement Bd., 1994—. Office: US Railroad Retirementt Bd 4th Fl 844 N Rush St Chicago IL 60611-2092 Office Phone: 312-751-4690. Business E-Mail: mdickman@oig.rrb.gov.

DICKMAN, ROBERT S., aerospace institute administrator, retired military officer; b. Brooklyn, N.Y. BS in Physics, Union Coll., 1966; MS in Space Physics, Air Force Inst. Tech., 1968; MA in Mgmt., Salve Regina Coll.; grad. (dist.), Naval War Coll., 1983. 2nd. lt. USAF, 1966, advanced through grades to major gen., 1966-2000; prog. mgr. USAF Office Sci Rsch., Arlington, Va., 1968-72; prog. element monitor USAF Hdqs., Washington, D.C., 1972-73; terminal sys. mgr. USAF, Los Angeles AFB, Calif., 1973-75; operational mgr. USAF Hdqs., Washington, 1976-79; space Def. Opers. Ctr. Hdrs. Aerospace Def. Command, Cheyenne Mtn. AFB, Colo., 1979-82; dir. space sys., dep. chief staff ops. Hdqs. Air Force Space Command, Peterson AFB, Colo., 1983-84; chief comdr. group Hdqs. N. American Aerospace Def. Command, Space Command, Peterson AFB, Colo., 1984-85; vice comdr. 2d space wing Schriever AFB, Colo., 1985—86; asst. to dir. ops., then dir. missile warning Space Command, Colo., 1986-87; chief Space Sys. Divsn., Washington, 1987-89; dep. dir. space progams Office of Asst. Sec. USAF for Acquisition, Washington, 1987-92; dir. plans Hdqs. USAF Space Command, Peterson AFB, Colo., 1992-93; comdr. 45th Space Wing, Patrick AFB, Fla., 1993-95; dir. Eastern Range, Cape Canaveral Air Sta., Fla., 1993-95; dir. space programs Office Asst. Sec. USAF for Acquisition, Washington, 1995; space architect US Dept. Def., Washington, 1995-98; dir. Office Plans and Analysis and Sys. of Sys. Architect Nat. Reconnaissance Office, Washington, 1998-2000, dir. corp. ops., chief info. officer, 2000; aerospace cons., 2001—01; dep. for military space, Office of Under-Sec., USAF, Washington, 2002—05; exec. dir. Am. Inst. Aeronautics & Astronautics Inc., Reston, Va., 2005—. Decorated Def. D.S.M., Air Force D.S.M., Def. Superior Svc. Medal, Legion of Merit; recipient Astronautics award Nat. Space Club, master space badge. Office: Am Inst Aeronautics & Astronautics Inc 1801 Alexander Bell Dr Reston VA 20191*

DICKS, NORMAN DE VALOIS, congressman; b. Bremerton, Wash., Dec. 16, 1940; s. Horace D. and Eileen Cora D.; m. Suzanne Callison, Aug. 25, 1967; children: David, Ryan. BA, U. Wash., 1963, JD, 1968; LLD (hon.), Gonzaga U., 1987. Bars: Wash. 1968, D.C., 1978. Salesman, Boise Cascade Corp., Seattle, 1963; labor negotiator Kaiser Gypsum Co., Seattle, 1964; legis. asst. to Senator Warren Magnuson of Wash., 1968-73, adminstrv. asst., 1973-76; mem. U.S. Congress from 6th Wash. Dist., Washington, 1977—; mem. appropriations com., homeland sec. com. Mem. U. Wash. Alumni Assn., Sigma Nu. Democrat. Lutheran. Office: US Ho Reps 2467 Rayburn Ho Office Bldg Washington DC 20515-0001*

DICKSHEET, SHARADKUMAR, plastic surgeon; b. Pandharpur, Mumbai, India, Dec. 13, 1930; s. Sitaram Ganpat and Malati Sitaram Dixit; children: Shari, Sharad, Supriya. BMus, Bhatkmande U., 1943; BS, Osmania U., Hyperabad, India, 1951; MBBS, Naqpur U., India, 1956. Pvt. practice, Fairbanks, Ala., 1969—78; fellow cosmetic surgery Guadalahara Inst. of Plastic Surgery, Mexico, 1979—80, Manhattan EET Hosp., N.Y.C., 1980—81, Trudi Vogt Inst., Zurich, Switzerland, 1981—82; resident plastic surgery Downstate Med. Ctr., Bklyn., 1982—84; pvt. practice Bklyn., 1984—94. Residency tchg. Downstate Med. Ctr., Bklyn., 1984—94; classical music vocalist, India, 1948—58; founder Plasti Surgery India Project, 1968. Contbr. articles to profl. jours. Mem.: Bhavatiya Jaih Soc., Giants Club, Lions Club, Rotary Club. Hindu. Home: 17 C 135 Ocean Pkwy Brooklyn NY 11218

DICKSON, ALAN T., mill and holding company executive; b. 1931; married BS, N.C. State Coll., 1953; MBA, Harvard U., 1955. With Ruddick Corp., Charlotte, N.C., 1968—, now pres., dir., Chmn.; pres. Am. and Efird Mills, Inc. (subs.), Mount Holly, N.C., 1957-69, chmn., 1969—, also dir. Dir. NCNB Corp., Chatham Mfg. Co., N.C. Textile Found., Sonoco Products Co., Harris-Teeter Super Markets Trustee John Motley Morehead Found.; trustee, dir. Central Piedmont Community Coll. Served with U.S. Army, 1955-57 Office: American & Efird Inc 22 American St Mount Holly NC 28120-2150

DICKSON, BRENT E., state supreme court justice; b. July 18, 1941; m. Jan Aikman, June 8, 1963; children: Andrew, Kyle, Reed. BA, Purdue U., 1964; JD, Ind. U., Indpls., 1968; LittD, Purdue U., 1996. Bar: Ind. 1968, U.S. Ct. Appeals (7th cir.) 1972, U.S. Supreme Ct. 1975; cert. civil trial adv., NBTA. Pvt. practice, Lafayette, Ind., 1968-85; sr. ptnr. Dickson, Reiling, Teder & Withered, 1977-85; assoc. justice Ind. Supreme Ct., Indpls., 1986—. Adj. prof. Sch. of Law Ind. U., 1992-. Past pres. Tippecanoe County Hist. Assn.; mem. dean's adv. coun. Sch. Liberal Arts Purdue U., 1990-94; mem. adv. bd. Heartland Film Festival, 1995-2000. Mem. Am. Inns Ct. (founding pres. Sagamore chpt.), Am. Law Inst. Office: Ind Supreme Ct 313 Ind Statehouse Indianapolis IN 46204-2213*

DICKSON, JAMES FRANCIS, III, surgeon; b. Boston, May 4, 1924; s. James Francis Jr. and Mary Elizabeth (Rich) Dickson; m. Vivian Joan Franco, Dec. 23, 1977. AB, Dartmouth Coll., 1944; MD, Harvard Med. Sch., 1947. Diplomate Am. Bd. Surgery. Intern and resident Boston City Hosp., 1947—51; practice in thoracic and cardiovascular surgery Boston, 1951—61; NIH spl. fellow MIT, Cambridge, 1961—65; dir. engring. in biology and medicine program NIH, Bethesda, Md., 1965—75; asst. surgeon gen. HHS, Washington, 1976—89. Sr. advisor to dean Harvard Med. Sch., 1992—2001, vis. com., 1992—2001; bd. overseers Dartmouth Med. Sch., 1990—2003, C. Everett Koop Inst., 1992—. Fellow: IEEE, ACS; mem.: Inst. Medicine of NAS.

DICKSON, JIM, writer, theater producer; b. Chgo., Mar. 25, 1949; s. Vincent Brackley and Carol Lois (Schaffner) D.; m. Helen Denise McEachrane, Feb. 11, 1984 (div. 1988). BA, Harvard U., 1970. Artistic adminstr. Santa Fe Opera, 1978-80; mng. dir. Chamber Opera Theatre, 1982; gen. mgr. Opera Festival of N.J., 1982-85; mng. dir. N.J. State Opera, 1985-89; exec. dir. Newark Arts Coun., 1989-95. Propr. The Dickson Office, 1991—. Author: Monmouth, 1968, Fear of Success, 1971, Summer in the Midwest, 1975, Chiliasm, 1972, The Princess of the Suburbs, 1973, Banjo, 1981, A Couple Interviews With A Couple Czars, 1991; (musical) Pippin, 1969, Appetite and Embarrassment, 1998. Recipient Phyllis Anderson award, 1969 Office: PO Box 1337 Newark NJ 07101-1337

DICKSON, JOHN T., information technology executive; b. Sheffield, Eng. Degree (hon.) in Elec. Engring., U. Sheffield, 1966, postgrad. in Bus. studies. With ICL, plc., bd. dir.; with Texas Instruments (UK and France); pres. microelectronics group Lucent Tech., COO, v.p. integrated circuits divsn., v.p., CEO; CEO Headland Tech., Inc., bd. dir.; CEO SHOgraphics, Inc., Sunnyvale, Calif., bd. dir.; joined Agere Systems, Inc., Allentown, Pa., 1993, pres., CEO. Bd. dir. Tandon Computer Corp., Inc., LSI Logic Europe, Inc., Internat. Network Svcs. Ltd., EO, Inc., Mettler-Toledo Internat., Inc., 2000—; bd. dir. (current) Semiconductor Industry Assn. Recipient Mensforth medal, Inst. Elec. Engrs., 1990. Office: Agere Systems Inc 1110 American Pkwy NE Allentown PA 18109-9138*

DICKSON, KATHLEEN M., language educator; d. Warren Charles and Barbara Nobrega Moore; m. Dennis Robert Dickson, June 4, 1977; children: Kevin, Aaron, Steven. BA in Edn., St. Mary U., Leavenworth, Kans., 1977; MS in Edn., Kans. State U., Manhattan, 1999. Home econs. tchr. Immaculata HS, Leavenworth, 1978—83, Leavenworth Pub. Schs., 1985—87; ELL tchr. Turner Pub. Schs., Kansas City, 1994; Spanish tchr. grades 10-12 Olathe North HS, Kans., 1994—. Mem. YWCA, Leavenworth, 1983—89. Mem.: Am. Coun. Tchg. Fgn. Langs. Democrat. Avocations: sewing, cooking, speaking and reading in Spanish. Business E-Mail: kdicksonon@olatheschools.com.

DICKSON, LESLEY R., psychiatrist, educator; d. Richard Warren and Ruthe Miriam (Wrighton) McKesson; 1 child, Michelle Dickson Sulkowski. BA, UCLA, 1968; MD, U. Ky., 1982. Diplomate Am. Bd. Psychiatry. Asst. to assoc. prof. U. Ky., Lexington, 1986—93; clin. assoc. prof. N.Y. U., N.Y.C., 1993—2002, U. Nev. Sch. Medicine, Las Vegas, 2002—. Staff psychiatrist Southern Nev. Veteran's Affairs Med. Ctr., Las Vegas, 2002—. Recipient Creativity award, Am. Coll. Psychiatrists, 1993. Fellow: Acad. Psychosomatic Medicine; mem.: So. Nev. Psych. Assn. (sec. 2003—). Avocation: writing. E-mail: lesley.dickson2@med.va.gov.

DICKSON, MARKHAM ALLEN, wholesale company executive; b. Shreveport, La., June 10, 1922; s. Claudius Markham and Marjorie (Fields) D.; m. Margaret Shaffer, Sept. 4, 1943 (div. Mar. 1981); m. June Baldwin, Apr. 19, 1981; children: Louise Dickson Cravens, Claudius Markham, Markham Allen, Paul Meade. BS, MIT, 1947; MS, Calif. Inst. Tech., 1952; DD, Cranmer Theol. House Sem., 1996, Nashotah Ho. Sem., 2004. Registered profl. engr., La.; ordained priest Episcopal Ch., 1973. Prodn. engr. Brewster Co., Shreveport, 1948-51; pres. Shreveport Druggists, 1951-52, Morris & Dickson Co. Ltd., Shreveport, 1952-95, chmn., 1995—. Capt. USAAF, 1941-46. Recipient Conservationist of Yr. award DAR. Mem. Nat. Wholesale Druggists Assn. (tech. award 1991), La. Wholesale Drug Distbrs. (pres. 1981-90), Shreveport Club, Masons (32d degree), Shriners, Kappa Alpha, La Confrerie des Chevaliers du Tastevin. Office: Morris & Dickson Co Ltd 410 Kay Ln Shreveport LA 71115-3611

DICKSON, NANCY STARR, retired elementary school educator; b. Frankfort, Ind., Apr. 3, 1936; d. Harley Ledger and Geneve (Daugherty) Fickle; m. Sam W. Dickson, Aug. 23, 1959; 1 child, Hal S. BS, Ball State U., 1958, MA, 1964, cert. reading specialist, 1972. Cert. elem. tchr., Ind. Tchr. Edgelea Elem. Sch., Lafayette, Ind., 1958-59, McKinley Elem. Sch., Muncie, Ind., 1959-65; tchr. spl. reading Garfield Elem. Sch., Muncie, Ind., 1967-78, reading specialist, 1996-98, Garfield Elem., Muncie, Ind., 1978-96; reading supr., tutor trainer 4 elem. schs., Muncie, Ind., 1978—96; ret., 1998. Author (tchr.'s edition textbook): Our Language Today- Grade 3, 1966, Our Language Today- Grade 4, 1966. Mem. NEA (life), Internat. Reading Assn. (literacy award 1986), Ind. Reading Assn. (pres. 1996-97, coord. 6 couns. 1975—, outstanding svc. award 1986, 89), Muncie Area Reading Coun. (membership dir. 1974-96, past pres.), Ind. Tchrs. Assn., Muncie Tchrs. Assn., Ball State U. Women, Pi Lambda Theta (pres. 1988-90), Delta Kappa Gamma (pres. 1990-92), Alpha Sigma Alpha (pres. alumnae 1986-87, advisor 1986-95). Democrat. Methodist. Avocations: reading, sewing, swimming. Home: 3315 W Petty Rd Muncie IN 47304-3271

DICKSON, PAUL WESLEY, JR., physicist; b. Sharon, Pa., Sept. 14, 1931; s. Paul Wesley and Elizabeth Ella (Trevethan) D.; m. Eleanor Ann Dunning, Nov. 17, 1952; children: Gretchen Ann, Heather Elizabeth, Paul Wesley. BS in Metall. Engring., MS, U. Ariz., 1954; PhD in Physics, N.C. State U., 1962. With Westinghouse Electric Corp., Large, Pa., 1963-84, mgr. weapon systems, 1965-68, mgr. advanced projects, 1969-72, mgr. reactor analysis and core design Madison, Pa., 1972-79, tech. dir. Oak Ridge, 1979-84; with EG & G Idaho, Idaho Falls, 1984-89, mgr. new tech. devel., 1984-87, mgr. reactor projects and programs, 1987-88; dir. Ctr. for Nuclear Engring. and Tech., 1988-89; tech. dir. reactor restart div. Westinghouse Savannah River Co., 1989-92; chief engr. nuclear materials processing div. Westinghouse, 1992-95; pvt. cons., 1995—. Mem. adv. com. on advanced propulsion systems NASA, Washington, 1970-72; mem. adv. com. reactor physics AEC/Dept. Energy, 1974-79; mem. rev. com. applied physics Argonne (Ill.) Nat. Lab., 1978-83, chmn., 1980; mem. rev. com. engring. physics Oak Ridge Nat. Lab., 1982-86, chmn., 1986; mem. fellow selection com. Dept. Energy, 1981-82; mem. rev. com. EBR II Argonne Nat. Lab., 1984, sci. and tech. adv. com., 1985-91. Contbr. numerous sci. articles to profl. publs. Capt. USAF, 1955-63. Fellow Am. Nuclear Soc.; mem. Am. Phys. Soc., N.Y. Acad. Scis., AIME, AAAS, Scabbord and Blade, Sigma Xi, Phi Kappa Phi, Tau Beta Pi, Phi Lambda Upsilon, Sigma Pi Sigma. Republican. Home: 4005 Woodvalley Dr Aiken SC 29803-8421 E-mail: pwdickson@scescape.net.

DICKSON, THOMAS WALTER, textile company executive; b. Charlotte, N.C., Aug. 17, 1955; s. Rush Stuart and Joanne (Shoemaker) D.; m. Billie Cecelia Seddinger, Sept. 22, 1984; children: William Thomas, Michael Alan. BA in Econs., U. Va., 1977, MBA, 1980. Project mgr. spinning div. Am. & Efird, Inc., Mount Holly, N.C., 1980-81, project mgr. internat. Manchester, Eng., 1981-82, plant mgr. spinning div. Gastonia, N.C., 1982-84, mgr. Far East ops. Hong Kong, 1984-87, v.p. internat. ops. Mount Holly, 1987—; CEO Ruddick Corp. Bd. dirs. Am. & Efird (Hong Kong) Ltd., Am. & Efird Mills Singapore, Am. & Efird (Great Britain) Ltd. Bd. dirs. Dickson Found., Charlotte, 1983—. Mem. Charlotte Country Club, Linville Golf Club. Republican. Baptist. Office: Ruddick Corp Ste 1800 301 S Tryon St Charlotte NC 28202 Office Phone: 704-372-5404. Office Fax: 704-372-6409.

DICKSON, TIM, music educator; b. Covington, Ky., Apr. 1, 1952; s. Ray and Dorthea Dickson; m. Valerie McBeath, Nov. 29, 1986; 1 child, Melody. MusB in Edn., Morehead (Ky.) State U., 1974; MusM in Edn., Ea. Ky. U., 1980. Cert. tchr. Fla. Dept. of Edn. Band dir., chorus dir. Deming HS, Mount Olivet, Ky., 1977—79; grad. asst. Ea. Ky. U., Richmond, Ky., 1979—80; band dir., chorus dir. Ft. Campbell (Ky.) HS, 1980—88; band dir. Jefferson HS, Tampa, Fla., 1988—89, Chamberlain HS, Tampa, Fla., 1989—98, B. T. Wash. Magnet Mid. Sch., Tampa, Fla., 1998—2003, William Mid. Magnet Sch. for Internat. Studies, Tampa, 2003—05; mgr. Shell Point Marina, Ruskin, 2005—. Sec., treas. Region IX Band Dirs. Assn., Ashland, Ky., 1977—78, pres., 1978—79. Mem.: Fla. Sch. Music Assn. (assoc.), Fla. Music Educators Assn. (assoc.), Music Educator's Nat. Conf. (assoc.), Fla. Bandmasters Assn. (assoc.). Home: 827 Birdie Way Apollo Beach FL 33572 Office: Shell Point Marine LLC 3440 W Shell Point Rd Ruskin FL 33570 Business E-Mail: newshellpoint@aol.com.

DICKSON, WILLIAM ROBERT, academic administrator; b. Framingham, Mass., Apr. 9, 1935; s. Leo Elwood adn Edith Isabel (McCormick)D.; m. Patricia Ann Lingley, June 30, 1956; children: William Christopher, Jeffrey Lee, Julie Ann. BS, MIT, 1956. Registered profl. engr. Staff engr. Linclon Lab. MIT, Lexington, Mass., 1956-58; assoc. scientist AVCO Corp., Wilmington, Mass., 1958-60; asst. to dir. Phy Plant MIT, Cambridge, Mass., 1960-71, dir. plant, 1971-80, v.p. ops., 1980-82, sr. v.p., 1982—. Chmn. bd. examiners City of Cambridge; CEO, chmn., bd. dirs. Harvard Coop. Soc., Cambridge. Served to capt. USAR, 1956-65. Recipient Medal for Excellence, Am. Soc. Mil. Engrs., 1956, Meritorious Svc. award Assn. Phys. Plant Adminstrs., 1980. Mem. Am. Inst. Plant Engrs. (cert. plant engr.), Masons, Algonquin Club. Congregationalists. Office: MIT 77 Massachusetts Ave Rm 10-200 Cambridge MA 02139-4307

DICKSTEIN, HARVEY LEONARD, pharmaceutical executive, researcher; b. Springfield, Mass., Jan. 19, 1936; s. David and Ruth (Stein) D.; m. Judith Marie Barton, Mar. 26, 1966; children: Jason Adam, Debra Ann. BA in Biology, Am. Internat. Coll., 1957; MD, Tufts U., 1961. Diplomate Nat. Bd. Med. Examiners. Intern then resident Bronx Mcpl. Hosp. Ctr., 1961-63; surg. resident Springfield (Mass.) Hosp., 1963-64; surg. resident, then chief resident Boston U. Med. Ctr., 1964-66; med. monitor Baxter Labs., Morton Grove, Ill., 1968-69; assoc. dir. hosp. products div. Abbott Labs., North Chgo., Ill., 1969-72, assoc. dir. exptl. therapy, 1972-73; dir. clin. rsch. Johnson & Johnson, New Brunswick, N.J., 1973-83; group leader surg. anesthetic and dental products FDA, Rockville, Md., 1983-85; dir. regulatory med. affairs E.R. Squibb, New Brunswick, 1985-87; v.p. regulatory affairs Parke-Davis Div. of Warner-Lambert, Morris Plains, N.J., 1987-89, v.p. med. rsch., 1989-91, v.p. med. affairs, 1992-93, v.p. med. and regulatory affairs, consumer products R&D, 1993-96; v.p., med. dir. Metaworks, Inc., Boston, 1996-97; v.p. clin. rsch. Transcend Therapeutics, Inc., Cambridge, Mass., 1997-98. Pharm. cons., Cohasset, Mass., 1999—. Lt. comdr. USPHS, 1966-68. New England Arthritis and Rheumatism Found. summer scholar, 1959. Avocations: weightlifting, skiing, jogging. Home: 393 Beechwood St Cohasset MA 02025-1521 Office Phone: 781-383-7058. Personal E-mail: Harveydickstein@comcast.net.

DICKSTEIN, JACK, chemist; b. Phila., Dec. 14, 1925; s. Harry and Anna A. (Anselevitz) D.; m. Pauline M. Gotheif, Dec. 24, 1950; children: Jeffrey L., John F., Andrea E. BS in Biochemistry, Pa. State U., 1946; MA in Organic Chemistry, Temple U., 1951; PhD in Polymer Chemistry, Rutgers U., 1958. Rsch. assoc. E.R. Squibb & Sons, New Brunswick, NJ, 1951—56; mgr. lab. Borden Chem. Co., Phila., 1958—61, devel. mgr. thermoplastics divsn. Leominster, Mass., 1961—67, dir. R&D Phila., 1967—74; group mgr. R&D Haven Chem. Co., Phila., 1974—77; v.p., dir. R&D Seal Inc., Naugatuck, Conn., 1977—79; pres. Kibow Biotech Inc., Phila., 1997—, Monomer-Polymer & Dajac Labs., Inc., Feasterville, Pa., 1979—. Tech. cons. Avery Internat., Pasadena, Calif., 1978-81, Painesville, Ohio, 1981-83, Avmor Inc., Montreal, Can., 1982-84, Wesley Jessen, Chgo., Ill., 1980-90. Patentee in field; contbr. articles to profl. jours. Mem. AAAS, Am. Chem. Soc., Am. Inst. Chemists, N.Y. Acad. Scis., Franklin Inst., Sigma Xi, Phi Lambda Upsilon, Phi Eta Sigma. Jewish. Avocations: sports statistics, photography. Home: 318 Keats Rd Huntingdon Valley PA 19006-3029 Office: Monomer-Polymer & Dajac Labs 1675 Bustleton Pike Feasterville Trevose PA 19053 Office Phone: 215-364-1155. Personal E-mail: featherpoo@comcast.net.

DICKSTEIN, JOAN BORTECK, arbitrator, consultant; b. Phila., June 20, 1919; d. Joseph and Mary (Leibovitz) Borteck; m. Benjamin Dickstein, Dec. 24, 1939; children: Howard, Kenneth, Mary. BA, Antioch Coll., 1974; MA in Sociology, U. Pa., 1978. Phila. coord. Gt. Books Found., Chgo., 1960-64; moderator, panelist Panel of Am. Women, Phila., 1964-73; trainer sensitivity courses Phila. Fellowship commn., 1966-69; rsch. assoc., cons. U. Pa. Human Resources Ctr., Phila., 1969-73; arbitrator comty. disputes Am. Arbitration Assn., Phila., 1969-82, Mcpl. Ct. of Phila., 1974-80, Commn. on Human Rels., Phila., 1979-82; facilitator interfaith dialogue Elkins Park (Pa.) Interfaith Dialogue, 1987—. Guest lectr. conflict mgmt. La Salle Coll., Phila., 1971-74; mem. adv. com. Episcopal Comty. Svcs., Phila., 1972-73; cons. staff devel. Covenant House Health Svc., Phila., 1979-80. V.p. Phila. chpt. Am. Jewish Com., Phila., 1970-73; study tour mem. Scandinavia, World Future Soc., Washington, 1974; study tour mem. Mid. East, United Presbyn. Ch., Roman Cath. Conf., Am. Jewish Com., N.Y.C., 1976; bd. dirs. Or Hadash Congregation, Ft. Washington, Pa., 1990-93; peer counselor Women's Ctr., Jenkintown, Pa., 1987—. Recipient Human Rights award City of Phila. Commn. on Human Rels., 1982. Democrat. Jewish. Avocations: great books discussion programs, interfaith dialogue, aerobics, crossword puzzles, volunteering at women's ctr. Home: 1250 Greenwood Ave Apt 307 Jenkintown PA 19046-2901

DICKSTEIN, MICHAEL ETHAN, lawyer, mediator, arbitrator; b. Montreal, Can., Sept. 8, 1959; s. Joseph and Barbara Dickstein AB, Harvard U., 1981, JD, 1985. Bar: Calif. 1985. Assoc. Heller, Ehrman, White & McAuliffe, San Francisco, 1985-91, ptnr., 1992; mediator, arbitrator, atty., cons. in pvt. practice dispute resolution, 1993—. Judge pro tem/mediator San Francisco and Alameda Superior and Mcpl. Cts., 1992—; adj. prof., U. San Francisco, 2003—; mediation and negotiation instr. Stitt, Feld, et al, 1996—; lectr. in appellate advocacy Boalt Law Sch., U. Calif., Berkeley, 1990. Mem.: Assn. Conflict Resolution (nat. co-chmn. workplace sect. 2001—04, adv. bd. 2004—).

DICKSTEIN, MORRIS, language educator, writer; b. N.Y.C., Feb. 23, 1940; s. Abraham and Anne (Reitman) D.; m. Lore Willner, Jan. 3, 1965; children: Jeremy Elliot, Rachel Ariela. AB, Columbia U., 1961; MA, Yale U., 1963; postgrad., Cambridge (Eng.) U., 1963-64; PhD, Yale U., 1967. Instr. English Columbia U., N.Y.C., 1966-67, asst. prof. English, 1967-71; assoc. prof. English Queens Coll., CUNY, 1971-75, prof. English, 1976—, CUNY Grad. Ctr., 1974—; dir. Humanities Ctr., 1993—; disting. prof. English CUNY Grad. Ctr., 1994—. Vis. prof. U. Paris VIII, 1980-81; humanities cons. Basic Books, Inc., N.Y.C., 1972-80; adv. bd. Revue Francaise d'Etudes Americaines, Paris, 1986—; bd. dirs. N.Y. Coun. Humanities. Author: Keats and His Poetry, 1971, Gates of Eden, 1977, Double Agent, 1992, Leopards in the Temple: The Transformation of American Fiction, 1945-1970, 2002, A Mirror in the Roadway: Literature and the Real World, 2005; co-editor: Great Film Directors, 1978; contbg. editor Partisan Rev., Boston, 1972—. Fellow, J.S. Guggenheim Found., 1973-74, ACLS, 1977, Rockefeller Found., 1981-82, NEH, 1986-87, Nat. Humanities Ctr., 1989-90. Mem. MLA, Nat. Soc. Film Critics, Am. Studies Assn., Nat. Book Critics Circle (bd. dirs. 1983-89). Office: CUNY Grad Sch Humanities Ctr 33 W 42nd St New York NY 10036-8003 Office Phone: 212-817-7210. Business E-Mail: mdickstein@gc.cuny.edu.*

DICLAUDIO, JANET ALBERTA, health information administrator; b. Monroeville, Pa., June 17, 1940; d. Frank and Pearl Alberta (Wolfgang) DiC. Cert. in Med. Rsch. Libr. Sci., Luth Med. Ctr., 1962; BA, Thiel Coll., 1975; MS, SUNY, Buffalo, 1978. Registered record adminstr. Dir. med. records Bashline Hosp., Grove City, Pa., 1962, St. Clair Meml. Hosp., Pitts., 1963-73; asst. prof. Ill. State U., Normal, 1976-81; corp. dir. med. records Buffalo Gen. Hosp., 1981-85; dir. med. records Candler Hosp., Savannah, Ga., 1985-94, med. records analyst, 1994-98; pres. prn Assocs., Savannah, Ga., 1998—. Med. record cons. White Cliff Nursing Home, Greenville, Pa., 1973—75; mgmt. cons. Gifford W. Lorenz MD, Savannah, 1992—94; Medicare compliance officer and coder Health Claims, Inc., Savannah, 1999—2001; mgmt. cons. John D. Northup, Jr., MD, Savannah, 2001—02; auditor, cons. Healthpac Computer Sys., Inc., 2001—. Contbr. articles to periodicals. Bd. dirs. Mid-Ill. Areawide Health Planning Corp., Normal, 1979-81. Mem. Am. Health Info. Mgmt. Assn., Ga. Health Info. Mgmt. Assn., S.E. Ga. Health Info. Mgmt. Assn. Avocations: painting, story telling, dance, reading. Office: Ste 705 PMB 153 7400 Abercorn St Savannah GA 31406 Office Phone: 912-352-8383. E-mail: JDCprn@aol.com.

DICLERICO, JOSEPH ANTHONY, JR., federal judge; b. Lynn, Mass., Jan. 30, 1941; s. Joseph Anthony and Ruth Adel (Cummings) DiC.; m. Laurie Breed Thomson, July 27, 1975; 1 child, Devon Thomson. BA, Williams Coll., Williamstown, Mass., 1963; LLB, Yale U., 1966. Bar: N.H. 1967, U.S. Dist. Ct. N.H. 1967, U.S. Ct. Appeals (1st cir.) 1973, U.S. Supreme Ct. 1975. Law clk. to presiding justice U.S. Dist. Ct. N.H., Concord, 1966-67, N.H. Supreme Ct., Concord, 1967-68; assoc. Cleveland Waters & Bass, Concord, 1968-70; asst. atty. gen. State of N.H., Concord, 1970-77; assoc. justice N.H. Superior Ct., Concord, 1977-91, chief justice, 1991-92; chief judge U.S. Dist. Ct. N.H., Concord, 1992-97. Chmn. Superior Ct. sentence rev. disvn., 1987-92. Fellow Am. Bar Found. (life), N.H. Bar Found. (jud.); mem. N.H. Bar Assn (nat. conf. state trial judges 1986-92, nat. conf. fed. trial judges, 1992-96, mem. com. on codes of conduct jud. conf. of U.S. 1994-2002, dist. judge rep. from 1st cir. to Jud. Conf. of U.S. 1997-2000, 1st cir. jud. coun. mem. 1992-94, 98-2004), Phi Beta Kappa. Republican. Roman Catholic. Avocation: gardening. Office: 55 Pleasant St Concord NH 03301-3954

DICONTI, MICHAEL ANDREW, trade organization executive; b. Glendale, Calif., Aug. 19, 1958; s. Andrew Raphael Jr. and Diane Rose (Carlotti) DiConti; m. Veronica Donahue, Aug. 6, 1988; 1 child, Nolan James. AB in Psychology magna cum laude, Occidental Coll., 1980; MBA in Acctg./Fin., UCLA, 1983; MA in Polit. Sci., Johns Hopkins U., 1987, PhD in Polit. Sci., 1990. Tax advisor Arthur Young, L.A., 1983-85; instr. C.C. of Balt., 1985-90, Johns Hopkins U., Balt., 1987-90; exec. asst. to pres. The Bus. Roundtable, Washington, 1990-93, dir. ops. & pub. policy, 1993—2004; dir. strategic partnerships Am. Coun. for Tech., Fairfax, Va., 2005—. Author: Entrepreneurship in Training, 1992. Mem. Fairfax County Info. Tech. Policy Adv. Com., 2004—. Fellow Inst. for Study of World Politics, Washington, 1987-88. Mem. Phi Beta Kappa, Psi Chi (pres. Occidental Coll. chpt. 1979-80). Home: 3110 Pine Oaks Way Oak Hill VA 20171 Office: Am Coun for Tech 11350 Random Hills Rd Ste 120 Fairfax VA 22030 Office Phone: 703-218-1955. Business E-Mail: mdiconti@actgov.org. E-mail: mdiconti@cox.net.

DICORCIA, PHILIP-LORCA, artist, photographer; b. Hartford, Conn., 1953; Diploma, Sch. Mus. Fine Arts, Boston, 1975, postgrad. cert., 1976; MFA, Yale U., 1979. One-man shows include Zeus Arts, Milan, 1985, Photographer's Gallery, London, 1991, 1996, Galeria Palmira Suso, Lisbon, Portugal, 1993, Mus. Modern Art, N.Y.C., 1993, Ctr. Cultural Rocher, Lyon, France, 1993, Nikon Salon, Tokyo, 1994, Art and Pub., Geneva, 1995, Galerie Klemens Gasser, Cologne, Germany, 1995, 1996, 1998, Pace Wildenstein Macgill, N.Y.C., 1996, 1998, Theoretical Events, Naples, Italy, 1996, Pace Wildenstein, L.A., 1998, Mus. Nat. Ctr. Arts Reina Sofia, Madrid, 1998, Galerie Rodolphe Janssen, Brussels, 1998, Galerie Almine Rech, Paris, 1998, exhibited in group shows at Enjay Gallery Photography, Boston, 1977, Balt. Mus. Art, 1987, 1991, Mus. Modern Art, N.Y.C., 1987, 1991, Artists Space, N.Y.C., 1990, Art Gallery York U., Toronto, Ont., Can., 1991, Met. Mus. Art, N.Y.C., 1991, L.A. County Mus. Art, 1991, 1992, Galeria Tanjia Grunert, Cologna, 1992, Luhring Augustine Gallery, N.Y.C., 1993, San Francisco Mus. Modern Art, 1993, Robert Klein Gallery, Boston, 1994, Foto Manifestabe, Eindhoven, The Netherlands, 1994, Ansel Adams Ctr., San Francisco, 1995, Portland (Maine) Art Mus., 1995, 1997, Art and Pub., Geneva, 1995, Inst. Contemporary Art, Boston, 1995, Galerie Agnes B, Paris, 1996, Whitney Mus. Am. Art, 1997, Reykjavik (Iceland) Mcpl. Art Mus., 1997, Gemente Mus., Helmond, Germany, 1997, Mus. Contemporary Art, Chgo., 1997, Howard Greenberg Gallery, N.Y.C., 1998, Galerie Fotohof, Salzburg, Austria, Galerie Sfeir-Semler, Hamburg, 2000, Monika Sprüth Philomene Magers, Munich, 2001, Neue Galerie Graz am-Landesmuseum Joanneum, Graz, 2003, Whitechapel Art Gallery, London, 2003, Mus. Modern Art, Queens, N.Y., 2004, Represented in permanent collections Boston Mus. Fin Arts, Chgo. Mus. Contemporary Photography, Dreyfus Corp., N.Y.C., L.A. County Mus. Art, Met. Mus. Art, Mus. Fine Art, Houston; actor: (Operas) Nikon Salon, 1994. Fellow Artist fellow, Nat. Endowment for the Arts, 1980, 1986, 1989; John Simon Guggenheim Meml. Found. fellow, 1987.

DICUFFA, PATRICIA BAYLEY, retired literature and language professor; b. Petersburg, Tex., Apr. 18, 1939; d. Spencer Alanson and Gaynelle Smith Bayley; m. Wilson W. DiCuffa, June 2, 1962; children: Julie Carol DiCuffa Wilson, Anthony Wilson. BA, West Tex. A&M U., 1961, MEd, 1974. Cert. secondary tchr. Tex. Edn. Agy., 1961. Elem. educator Dimmitt Ind. Sch. Dist., 1961—62; secondary English educator Lubbock Ind. Sch. Dist., 1962—63, Dimmitt Ind. Sch. Dist., 1963—65, Bovina Ind. Sch. Dist., Tex., 1965—76, Fredericksburg Ind. Sch. Dist., 1976—95; writing cons. U. Writing Ctr., Tex. A&M U., College Station, 2002—. Leader Gillespie County 4H Club, Fredericksburg, 1976—82. Mem.: DAR (treas. 2003—04), Delta Kappa Gamma (rec. sec. 1967—96). Home: 2905 River Oaks Cir Bryan TX 77802-4752 Office: U Writing Ctr Texas A&M U College Station TX Office Phone: 979-458-1455. Personal E-mail: wwdicuffa@cox.net.

DICUS, BRIAN GEORGE, lawyer; b. Kansas City, Mo., Oct. 29, 1961; s. Clarence Howard and Edith Helen (George) D.; m. Vali Ann Venner, Dec. 14, 1985; children: Brian George, Cady Alyssa. BA, So. Meth. U., 1984, JD, 1987. Bar: Tex. 1987, U.S. Dist. Ct. (no. dist.) Tex. 1988; bd. cert. estate planning and probate law Tex. Bd. Legal Specialization. Assoc. Thorp & Sorenson, Dallas, 1987-89, Joseph E. Ashmore Jr., P.C., Dallas, 1989-92; pvt. practice Dallas, 1992—. Chmn. local alumni student recruiting program So. Meth. U., Dallas, 1989-90. Fellow Tex. Bar Found.; mem. Tex. Bar Assn., Dallas Bar Assn., Phi Alpha Delta, Pi Sigma Alpha. Home: 2336 Serenity Ln Heath TX 75032-1922 Office: 5910 N Central Expy Ste 920 Dallas TX 75206-5159

DICUS, STEPHEN HOWARD, lawyer; b. Kansas City, Mo., Mar. 3, 1948; s. Clarence Howard and Edith Helen (George) D.; m. Jolene Purcell; children: Brett S., Adam J. AB, U. Mo., 1970; JD, U. Mo., Kansas City, 1973. Bar: Mo. 1973, U.S. Dist. Ct. (we. dist.) Mo. 1973. Ptnr. Dietrich, Davis, Dicus, Rowlands, Schmitt & Gorman, Kansas City, 1979—89; shareholder Dicus Davis Sands & Collins, P.C., Kansas City, 1991—2004, Farchmin Dicus PC, 2005—. Mem. Kansas City Met. Bar Assn., The Missouri Bar, Estate Planning Soc. Kansas City, Rotary Club, Mission Hills Country Club. Meth. Avocations: tennis, golf. Home: 14011 Pawnee Leawood KS 66224-1069 Office: Farchmin Dicus PC 2 Emanual Cleaver II Blvd Ste 425 Kansas City MO 64112 Office Phone: 816-931-1984. Business E-Mail: sdicus@farchmindicus.com.

DIDDY, See COMBS, SEAN

DIDENKO, YURI, chemist; b. Korsakov, Russia, Jan. 24, 1953; s. Trophim M. and Nadezhda M. (Guseva) D.; m. Nataliya Y. Ovsannikova, June 10, 1999 MS, Moscow State U., 1975, PhD, 1985. Rschr. Pacific Oceanol. Inst., Vladivostok, Russia, 1975-87, sr. scientist, 1987-93; head of lab. Pacific Oceanol. Inst, Vladivostok, Russia, 1993-95. Sr. rsch. scientist. U. Ill., Urbana, 1995—; vis. scientist Nat. Rsch. Coun., Ottawa, Can., 1990; com. mem. trade union Pacific Oceanol. Inst., 1983-85. Reviewer Jour. of Phys. Chemistry, 1995; contbr. articles to profl. jours. Com. mem. chemistry dept. students trade union Moscow State U., 1973-74. Recipient Golden Medal for High Edn. Russian Ministry of Edn., 1970; travel grant Internat. Sci. Foun., 1994, 95. Mem. Acoustical Soc. of Am., European Soc. of Sonochemistry, Am. Inst. of Ultrasound Medicine. Avocations: sport, photography, folk music. Office: U Ill at Urbana-Champaign CLSL Box 276 600 S Mathews Ave Urbana IL 61801-3602

DIDION, JOAN, writer; b. Sacramento, Calif., Dec. 5, 1934; d. Frank Reese and Eduene (Jerrett) D.; m. John Gregory Dunne, Jan. 30, 1964; 1 child, Quintana Roo. BA, U. Calif., Berkeley, 1956. Assoc. feature editor Vogue mag., 1956-63; former columnist Saturday Evening Post, Life, Esquire; now contbr. The N.Y. Rev. of Books, The New Yorker. Novels include Run River, 1963, Play It As It Lays, 1970, A Book of Common Prayer, 1977, Democracy, 1984, The Last Thing He Wanted, 1996; books of essays: Slouching Towards Bethlehem, 1968, The White Album, 1979, After Henry, 1992; nonfiction Salvador, 1983, Miami, 1987, Political Fictions, 2001, Fixed Ideas, 2003,

Where I Was From, 2003, (non-fiction) The Year of Magical Thinking, 2005; co-author: (with John Gregory Dunne) Screenplays for films The Panic in Needle Park, 1971, Play It As It Lays, 1972, A Star Is Born, 1976, True Confessions, 1981, Hills Like White Elephants, 1991, Broken Trust, 1995, Up Close and Personal, 1996. Recipient 1st prize Vogue's Prix de Paris, 1956, Morton Dauwen Zabel prize AAAL, 1978, The Edward MacDowell medal, 1996, Columbia Journalism award, 1999. Mem. Am. Acad. Arts and Letters (Gold medal in Belle Lettres and Criticism, 2005), Am. Acad. Arts and Scis., Coun. Fgn. Rels. Office: care Janklow & Nesbit 445 Park Ave New York NY 10022-2606

DI DOMENICA, ROBERT ANTHONY, musician, composer; b. N.Y.C., Mar. 4, 1927; s. Angelo and Philomena (Mosca) DiD.; m. Leona Knopf, Feb. 6, 1951 (dec. 1998); children— David, Peter Josef, Claude Robert; m. Ellen Bender, Apr., 1999. BS, N.Y. U., 1951. Mem. theory-composition faculty New Eng. Conservatory, 1969-92, assoc. dean performing orgns., 1973-76, dean, 1976-78. Flutist, N.Y.C. Ctr. Opera, N.Y. Philharm., Symphony of Air, soloist, Composers Forum, 20th Century Innovations, rec. artist, RCA, Columbia, Colpix, MGM, Atlantic, Deutsche Grammophon records; recs. include Leona DiDomenica In Live First Performance of the Solo Piano Music of Robert DiDomenica, GM/200/CD; compositions include Symphony, 1961, Concerto for Violin and Chamber Orch., 1962, Quintet for Clarinet and String Quartet, 1965, Sonata for Violin and Piano, 1966; opera The Balcony, 1972, Black Poems (baritone, piano and tape), 1976, The Holy Colophon for Orch., Chorus, Soprano and Tenor, 1980, Piano Concerto No. 2, 1982, Dream Journeys for Orch., 1984, The Scarlet Letter (opera), 1986, Opera The Balcony given its world premier by The Opera Co. of Boston, 1990, performed at Moscow's Bolshoi Theater, 1991, (operatic trilogy) Francesco Cenci, 1996, Beatrice Cenci, 1993, The Cenci, 1995. Served with USNR, 1944-46. Guggenheim fellow, 1972-73; grantee Rockefeller Found., 1965; commd. by Goethe Inst., Boston, 1975 Mem. Broadcast Music Inc. Home: 159 Valley Rd Needham MA 02492-4724 Office Phone: 781-455-9175. Personal E-mail: marblefaun@aol.com.

DIDOMENICO, MAURO, JR., communications executive; b. Bronx, N.Y., Jan. 12, 1937; s. Mauro and Elizabeth DiD.; m. Angela M. Carracino, Aug. 29, 1964; children— Catherine Lee, David M. BS, Stanford U., 1958, MS, 1959, PhD, 1963. Mem. tech. staff Bell Labs., Murray Hill, N.J., 1962-66, supr., 1966-70, head optical device dept., 1970-80, dept. head integrated circuit customer service dept., 1980-82; divsn. mgr. strategic planning AT&T, Basking Ridge, N.J., 1982-84; divsn. mgr. applied rsch. BellCore, Morristown, NJ, 1984-85; exec. dir. tech. liaison office Bell Comms. Rsch., Morristown, N.J., 1985-92, ret., 1992; pres. CommTech Internat., Bernardsville, N.J., 1993-95; pres., founder FreeLinQ Comm., N.Y.C., 1995—99; founder, exec. v.p. eVideo Incorporated, 2000—; prin. UltraPro Internat., 2000—03. Contbr. numerous articles to profl. lit. Fellow IEEE, Am. Phys. Soc.; mem. N.Y. Acad. Scis., Sigma Xi, Tau Beta Pi. Roman Catholic. Personal E-mail: maury.dido@verizon.net.

DIDRIKSEN, CALEB H., III, lawyer; b. Cleve., Nov. 3, 1955; s. Caleb H. Jr. and Eleanore Ann (Hoepli) D.; m. Sondra L. Brown, Apr. 21, 1993; children: Severin, Spencer, Luke. BS in Engring., U. Ill., 1977; JD, Tulane U., 1982. Bar: La. 1982, Tex. 1995, U.S. Dist. Ct. (ea., mid. and we. dists.) La. 1982, U.S. Ct. Appeals (5th cir.) 1982, U.S. Supreme Ct. 1987. Assoc. McGlinchey, Stafford, New Orleans, 1982-84, Monroe & Lemann, New Orleans, 1984-88; pvt. practice New Orleans, 1988-89; sr. ptnr. Didriksen & Carbo, New Orleans, 1989—98, Didriksen Law Firm, 1998—. Mem. Boy Scouts-Eagle; scout leader; soccer coach; mem SPR com. Munholland United Meth. Ch; bd. mem. Raintree Svcs. Inc. Mem. ABA, La. Bar Assn. (asst. grader), New Orleans Bar Assn., Tau Beta Pi, Gamma Epsilon. Republican. Office: 3114 Canal St New Orleans LA 70119 Office Phone: 504-822-3114.

DIDZEREKIS, PAUL PATRICK, lawyer; b. Chgo., Mar. 17, 1939; s. Louis Joseph and Estelle (Traczyk) D.; m. Judith V. Wright, June 30, 1962 (div. 1968); children: Ann Frances, Paul Patrick; m. Heather Joy Izod, Aug. 1969 (div. 1993); children: Alexandria, Alexis; m. Kathleen A. Breier, Mar. 31, 1994. BBA, Loyola U., Chgo., 1963; JD, Loyola U., 1964. Bar: Ill. 1964, U.S. Supreme Ct. 1971. Atty. govt. affairs law and tax depts. Sears, Roebuck & Co., 1960-65; mem. Ashcraft & Ashcraft, Chgo., 1965-72; sole practice Chgo., 1972-74; pres., ptnr. Didzerekis & Douglas Ltd., Chgo., 1972-74; sole practice Chgo., Wheaton, Ill., 1978—. Mem. paraprofl. adv. bd. Lewis U. Coll. Law, Glen Ellyn, Ill., 1975, adj. prof. legal ethics in action program, 1976-77; chmn. bd., pres. Real Estate Profls. Am. Inc., 1989—; bd. dirs., gen. counsel The Eleanor Assn., 1970-88, pres., 1983-84; comnr. DuPage County Bd., 1998-2002. Pres. United Way, Wheaton, 1987-88; chmn. Milton Twp. Rep. Cen. Com., 1996-98; park dist. commr. Wheaton, 1991-98, pres., 1995-97; pub. adminstr. DuPage County, Ill., 01998—; commr. DuPage County Forest Preserve, 1998-2002. Recipient David C. Hilliard award Chgo. Bar Assn., 1973-74. Fellow Am. Acad. Matrimonial Lawyers; mem. DuPage County Bar Assn., Kiwanis (dir. 1989-93, 2d v.p.). Home: 411 Hevern Dr Wheaton IL 60187-7395 Office: 610 W Roosevelt Rd Ste 2B Wheaton IL 60187-2303 Office Phone: 630-653-7710. E-mail: paul@pauldidzerekis.com.

DIEBOLD, FRANCIS X., economist, educator; b. Nov. 12, 1959; m. Susan S. Diebold; 3 children. BS in Fin. and Econs., U. Pa., 1981, PhD in Econs., 1986. Rsch. economist, mem. bd. govs. FRS, 1986—89; asst. prof. econs., J.M. Cohen term chair U. Pa., 1989—92, assoc. prof., 1992—96, prof., 1996—99, prof. stats. Wharton Sch., 1996—, dir. Inst. Econ. Rsch., Lawrence R. Klein prof. econs., 1999—; faculty rsch. fellow Nat. Bur. Econ. Rsch., 1993—99, rsch. assoc., 1999—2001; prof. fin. Wharton Sch. U. Pa., 2001—, W.P. Carey prof. econs., 2000—. Charter mem. Oliver Wyman Inst., 1996—; vis. prof. fin., econ., stats. Stern Sch. Bus., NYU, 1998-2000; vis. prof. Cambridge U., 1998, Princeton U., 1997, Johns Hopkins U., 1995, U. Chgo., 1993, London Sch. Econs., 1992, U. Minn., 1990; Benedum lectr. W.Va. U., 1992; mem. organizing com. Computational Fin., 1999—; mem. econs. panel NSF, 1998-2000, chmn. forecasting seminar, 1995—. Author: (with G. Rudebusch) Business Cycles: Durations, Dynamics and Forecasting, 1999, Elements of Forecasting, 1998, Empirical Modeling of Exchange Rate Dynamics, 1988; assoc. editor Rev. Econs. and Stats., 1993—, Jour. Bus. and Econ. Stats., 1993—, Jour. Forecasting, 1994—, Stata Tech. Bull., 1994—, Econometrica, 1994-97, Jour. Applied Econometrics, 1991-97, Jour. Empirical Fin., 1992-95, Econometric Revs., 1989-92; mem. adv. bd. Econ. Policy Rev., Fed. Res. Bank N.Y., 1997—, Macroecon. Dynamics, 1996—; co-editor Internat. Econ. Rev., 1993-99, Jour. Forecasting, 1990-94; contbr. articles to econ. and bus. jours.; spkr. at many profl. meetings and confs. Mem. bd. sr. scholars Nat. Ctr. for Ednl. Quality of Workforce, 1993-95. Fellow Wharton Fin. Instns. Ctr., 1997—; Alfred P. Sloan Found. rsch. fellow, 1992-94; grantee NSF, 1989-92, 92-94, 95-98, 98—, Pew Found., 1995-96, NSF and Cornell Super Computer Ctr., 1992-92, Alexander von Humboldt award, Fed. Rep. Germany, 2004, Gugenheim fellow, 2003-2004, Fellow, Am. State. Assn., 2004. Fellow Econometric Soc. (program com. N.Am. winter mtg. 1999, program com. time-series econometrics 1993); mem. Am. Statis. Assn. (mem. editl. selection com. Jour. B sec., Econ. Stats., 1994, 2000, Zellner award selection com. 1995, sec./treas. bus. and econ. stats. sect. 1994, program chair 1991), Am. Econ. Assn., Am. Fin. Assn. Office: U Pa Dept Econs 3718 Locust Walk Philadelphia PA 19104-6297 E-mail: FDiebold@sas.upenn.edu.

DIECK, DANIEL WILLIAM, search company executive; b. Clintonville, Wis., July 19, 1951; s. Harold Gustav and Jean Lucille (Rohan) D.; children: Ryan Patrick, Benjamin James, Angela Marie, Timothy Daniel; m. Lesa F. Guderyon, May 16, 2003; stepchildren: Joshua J. Dillahunty, Jacy N. Dillahunty. BA cum laude in Mktg. Communications and Drama, U. Wis., Stevens Point, 1973. Cert. pers. cons. Dist. sales rep. Mass. Mutual, Springfield, 1973-76, Paul Bunyan Co., Mpls., 1976-82; nat. sales mgr. Browning, Morgan, Utah, 1982-83; v.p. sales and mktg. HCA, Green Bay, Wis., 1983-85; pres. The Dieck Group, Mauston, Wis., 1985—. Mem. TAPPI, Paper Industry Mgmt. Assn., Wis. Pers. Cons., Internat. Assn. Profl. Recruiters. Independent. Avocations: hunting, fishing, golf, tennis, travel. Office: 114 West Monroe St Mauston WI 53948

DIECKHOFF, JASON ELLIS, agricultural studies educator; b. Lexington, Mo., Aug. 25, 1980; s. Ellis Alfred and Teresa Marie Dieckhoff. BS in Agrl. Econ., U. Mo., Columbia, 2002, BS in Agrl. Edn., 2003. Cert. tchr. State of Mo., 2003. Grad. tchg. asst. U. Mo., Columbia, 2001—02; tech. asst. U. Mo. Ext. Svc., 2000—03; agr. instr. Harrisonville Cass R-IX Schools, Harrisonville, 2003—. Pres. elect Cass County Jr. Livestock Producers, Harrisonville, Mo., 2003—. Grantee, Friends NRA, 2004. Mem.: KC, NEA (assoc.), Nat. Assn. Agrl. Educators, Mo. Vocat. Agr. Tchrs. Assn. (assoc.), Am. Career and Tech. Educators (assoc.), Alpha Gamma Sigma (life; treas. 1999—). Roman Catholic. Home: 306 E Pearl Harrisonville MO 64701 Office: Harrisonville Cass R-IX Schs 1600 E Elm Harrisonville MO 64701 Office Phone: 816-380-3253. Personal E-mail: dieckhoffj@harrisonville.k12.mo.us.

DIEDERICH, J(OHN) WILLIAM, internet publisher; b. Ladysmith, Wis., Aug. 30, 1929; s. Joseph Charles and Alice Florence (Yost) D.; m. Mary Theresa Klein, Nov. 25, 1950; children: Mary Theresa Diederich Evans, Robert Douglas, Charles Stuart, Michael Mark, Patricia Anne Diederich Irelan, Donna Maureen (dec.), Denise Brendan, Carol Lynn Diederich Weaver, Barbara Gail, Brian Donald, Tracy Maureen, Theodora Bernadette Diederich Davidson, Tamara Alice Diederich Williams, Lorraine Angela. PhB, Marquette U., Milw., 1951; MBA with high distinction, Harvard U., 1955. With Landmark Comm., Inc., Norfolk, Va., 1955-90, v.p., treas., 1965-73, exec. v.p. fin., 1973-78, exec. v.p. community newspapers, 1978-82, exec. v.p., CFO, 1982-90, fin. cons., 1990—; internet pub. Wide World Web Internat., Incline Village, 1996—. Chmn. bd. dirs. Landmark Cmty. Newspapers, Inc., 1977-88; pres. Exec. Productivity Sys., Inc., 1982-88, LCI Credit Corp., 1991-93, Landmark TV Inc., 1991—, LTM Investments, Inc., 1991—; v.p., treas., KLAS, Inc., 1994-95; v.p. Internet Express, Inc., 1994-2000; pres., bd. dirs. Wide World Web Internat., 1995—, TWC Holdings, Inc., 1996—; instr. Boston U., 1954, Old Dominion U., 1955-59; mgr. No. Neck Newspaper Group LLC, 2002—; pres. City News Inc., 2004—. Lt. col. USMC, 1951-53, USMCR, 1953-71. Baker scholar Harvard U., 1955. Mem. SAR, Nat. Assn. Accts., Am. Numismatic Assn., Nat. Geneal. Soc., Wis. Geneal. Soc., Pa. Geneal. Soc., Sigma Delta Chi. Roman Catholic. Home and Office: PO Box 7677 925 Jupiter Dr Incline Village NV 89451

DIEDERICH, MICHAEL DAVID, JR., lawyer; b. Bronxville, N.Y., June 14, 1954; s. Michael and Dorothy Elizabeth Diederich; m. Brigitte M. Gulliver, Sept. 24, 1988; children: M. Patrick, Victoria, Sean. BS, U. Vt., 1976; JD, Northwestern U., Portland, Oreg., 1980; LLM, Pace U., White Plains, N.Y., 1992. Bar: N.Y. 1981, Mass. 1981, U.S. Dist. Ct. (so. dist.) N.Y. 1982, U.S. Ct. Appeals (2d cir.) 1989, U.S. Supreme Ct. 1991. Pvt. practice, Stony Point, N.Y., 1981-84, 93—; assoc. Witte, Lestz & Hogan, P.C., Bronxville, N.Y., 1988-89; asst. county atty. Westchester and Rockland County Atty.'s Office, White Plains, New City, N.Y., 1989-93. Contbr. articles to profl. jours. Mem. Stony Point Planning Bd., 1994-95; mem., chmn. Rockland County Environ. Mgmt. Coun., New City, 1982-84. LTC. JAGC USAR, 1984—. Mem. ABA, Assn. Trial Lawyers Am., N.Y. State Bar Assn., Rockland County Bar Assn., Natl. Employment Lawyers Assn. Avocation: alpine ski racing. Office: 361 Rte 210 Stony Point NY 10980-3500

DIEDERICHS, JANET WOOD, public relations executive; b. Libertyville, Ill. BA, Wellesley Coll, 1950. Sales agt. Pan Am. Airways, Chgo., 1951-52; regional mgr. pub. relations Braniff Internat., Chgo., 1953-69; pres. Janet Diederichs & Assocs., Inc.; pub. rels. cons. Chgo., 1970—. Com. mem. Nat. Trust for Historic Preservation, 1975—79, Marshall Scholars (Brit. Govt.), 1975—79; trustee Sherwood Conservatory Music, 2000—04, Northwestern Meml. Hosp., 1985—2005, mem. exec. com., 1995—2000, life trustee; founder Com. of 200; founders coun. Field Mus., 1999—; mem. exec. com. Vatican Art Coun., Chgo., 1981—83; pres. Jr. League Chgo., 1968—69; trustee Fourth Presbyn. Ch., mem. bd. dirs., 1990—93; bd. dirs., mem. exec. com. Chgo. Conv. and Visitors Bur., 1978—87; bd. dirs. Internat. House, U. Chgo., 1978—84; bd. dirs. Latino Inst., 1986—89, Albert Pick Jr. Found. Mem. Chgo. Assn. Commerce and Industry (bd. dirs. 1982-89, exec. com. 1985-88), Internat. Women's Forum, Woman's Athletic Club of Chgo., Comml. Club of Chgo., The Casino Club (Chgo.), Wellesley Coll. Bus. Leadership Coun. Office: Janet Diederichs & Associates 208 S La Salle St Ste 1240 Chicago IL 60604-1111 Office Phone: 312-346-7886.

DIEDERICHSEN, MARK A., artist, art director; b. San Diego, May 4, 1957; s. Raymond and Barbra Diederichsen. Cert. in Gen. Studies, Truckee Meadows C.C., Reno, Nev., 1987. Designer Pk. Pl. Entertainment, Las Vegas, Nev., 1997—2000; art dir. Sta. Casinos, 2000—, Bell Tower Editions, Santa Fe, 2002—; painter Am. Eagle Fine Art, Scottsdale, Ariz., 2005—. Freelance graphic designer Las Vegas Art Mus., Las Vegas, Nev., 1996—. One-man shows include Recent Works, Santa Fe, 2003, New Land, 2004, Fifteen Santa Fe Artists. Recipient Best of Show, Reno Ad Club, 1982. Mem.: Calif. Art Club (assoc.). Home: #291 4616 W Sahara Ave Las Vegas NV 89102

DIEDRICH, RICHARD JOSEPH, architect; b. South Bend, Ind., May 8, 1936; s. Arthur Joseph and Lucille D.; m. Francyne L. Diedrich (div. 1980); children: Dawn Marie, Lisa Lee, Andrea Lynn; m. Linda P. Diedrich. BArch, U. Ill., 1961, MArch, 1962. Archtl. designer Richardson Severns Scheeler & Assocs., Champaign, Ill., 1961-62; design critic U. Ill. Sch. Architecture, Champaign, 1961-62; archtl. designer Swensson & Kott, Nashville, 1963-64; architect, v.p. Miller Waltz Diedrich, Architects, Milw., 1965-77; pres. MWD Archs., Atlanta, 1978-80, Diedrich Archs., Atlanta, 1980-97; pres., exec. v.p. Diedrich/NBA, Atlanta, 1997—2002; pres. Diedrich LLC, Atlanta, 2002—. Instr. profl. devel. course Harvard Grad. Sch. Design, 1990-2004 Author: Building Type Basics for Recreational Facilities, 2005; co-author: Golf Course Development and Real Estate; archtl. works include: Avondale Sta., Med. Ctr. Sta., Atlanta Rapid Transit, S. Miami Sta. of Miami Rapid Transit, Vt. Sunset Sta., L.A. Rapid Transit, Student Ctr., U. Ga., Bloomingdale's Stores, Boca Raton, Palm Beach Gardens, Mall of Am., Neiman Marcus Stores, Scottsdale, Ariz., Troy, Mich., Honolulu, Short Hills, N.J., King of Prussia, Pa., Paramus, N.J., Tampa, Fla., Coral Gables, Fla., Plano, Tex., Orlando, Fla., Grand Cypress Clubhouse, Orlando, English Turn Clubhouse, New Orelans, Golf Club Ga., Atlanta, Country Club North, Dayton, Old Overton Club House, Birmingham, Cherokee Country Club, Atlanta, Naples Nat. Golf Club, Sun City Hilton Head amenity facilities, Aerial Tram, Stone Mountain Park, Atlanta, Village Clubhouse, Kapaulua, Maui, Hawaii. Mem. Whitefish Bay Bd. Appeals, 1968-71; v.p. North Decatur Youth assn., 1975-76; bd. dirs. Lake Burton Civic Assn., 2002-05 Margaret T. Biddle scholar, 1960. Mem. AIA (past pres. Milw. chpt., six design awards, two S.E. regional awards, four Ga. AIA awards), Wis. Architect (past pres.). Home and Office: 8 Brookhaven Dr Atlanta GA 30319

DIEDRICHS, CAROL PITTS, librarian; b. New Orleans, Mar. 8, 1958; d. Leland Bascom and Mae Nell (Harper) Pitts; m. Frank M. Diedrichs. BA, Baylor U., 1980; M of Libr. and Info. Sci., U. Tex., 1981. Serials cataloger U. Houston Librs., 1981-82, head acquisition dept., 1982-87, Ohio State U. Librs., Columbus, 1987-97; asst. dir. for tech. svcs. and collections Ohio State U., Columbus, 1997—2003; dea librs. U. Ky., Lexington, 2003—. Mem. editorial bd. Libr. Collections, Acquisitions and Tech. Svcs., 1989-90, editor-in-chief, 1990-2003; contbr. articles to profl. jours. Chair acquisitions serial control com. OhioLink, asst. dir. for policy devel., 1991-92, chair database mgmt. and stds. com.; mem. OCLC Mems. Council, 2001-03, SOLINET Bd. Dirs., 2005—. Mem. ALA (chairperson discussion group, com. mem., sec. mem.-at-large, chmn. sect., pres., Esther J. Piercy award 1991, Leadership in Acquisitions award 1999), N.Am. Serials Interest Group (mem.-at-large), INNOVATIVE Users' Group (com. mem.), Assoc. Libr. Collections and Tech. Svcs. (pres.). Office: 1-85 WM T Young Libr U Ky Lexington KY 40506-0456 Office Phone: 859-257-0500 ext. 2087. Business E-Mail: diedrichs@uky.edu.

DIEFENBACH, DALE ALAN, retired law librarian; b. Cleve., Aug. 14, 1933; s. Walter Ewald and Alice Naomi (Austin) D.; m. Olga Maspaitella, Jan. 20, 1973; 1 stepson, Andrew Ivan Ward. BA, Baldwin-Wallace Coll., 1955; MLS, U. Hawaii, 1970. Fgn. svc. officer U.S. Dept. State, 1961-68; reference libr. Cornell U. Law Libr., Ithaca, N.Y., 1970-87; sr. reference libr. Harvard U. Law Libr., Cambridge, Mass., 1987-97, ret., 1997; reference libr., adj. assoc. prof. law libr. Barry U. Sch. Law Euliano Law Libr., 1998—2003. Lt. (j.g.) USNR, 1956-60, Philippines. Recipient Ficken Meml. award Baldwin-Wallace Coll., Berea, Ohio, 1988. Mem. ALA, Am. Assn. Law Librs. Democrat. Home: 500 Windmeadows St Altamonte Springs FL 32701-3572 E-mail: deepbrook@earthlink.net.

DIEFENDERFER, DAN, filmmaker; s. Raymond Gernard Diefenderfer, Jr. and Jean Francis Magerstadt. Student, U. Miami, 1972. Prodr.(director, co-writer): (5 hour PBS documentary series) Uniquely Kansas City; editor (post- production supervisior): (motion picture) Ninth Street (Ind. Film Channel award, 1999); prodr.: (U.S. EPA film) Dioxin Destruction, (director, co-writer) (motion picture) Timesweep. Recipient Press Club award, Kans. City Star newspaper, 2000, EMMY award for Best Direction- Documentary, NATAS, 2001, 2d pl. documentary category, Kan Film Fest- Kansas City, Mo., 2001, PBS Series of Yr., Nat. Ednl. Telecom. Assn., 2001, Preservation award, Kans. City Hist. Found., 2001, Gold award, The Aurora Awards, 2002, 2-Platinum Best of Show, 2002, 2 Gold finalist awards, The Telly Awards, 2002, Gold finalist, 2003. Mem.: KC Screenwriters. Achievements include first to Produced, Directed and Co-Wrote Uniquely Kansas City, the first locally originated PBS series shot and nationally broadcast in High Defintion video; Produced & directed the motion picture Timesweep, documented by The New York Times: first use of new film stock specifically designed for conversion of 16mm film to 35mm theatrical exhibition prints. Office Phone: 816-294-8735.

DIEFFENBACH, OTTO WEAVER, III, real estate company executive; b. Key West, Fla., Aug. 4, 1953; s. Otto, Jr. and Alice Jean Thompson D.; m. Susan S., Jan. 16, 1982 (div. May 1997); children: Otto Weaver IV, Claire T., Bryan V.; m. Elisabeth I., June 12, 1997 (div. Sept. 2002). BSEM, USAF Acad., 1975; MBA, Golden Gate U., 1977; MS in Aeronautics, USAF Test Pilot Sch., 1978. With USAF, 1975-81, advanced through ranks to capt., 1979; flight test engr. Air Force Flight Test Ctr., Edwards AFB, Calif., 1975-78; sys. test engr. USAF Armament Divsn., Eglin AFB, Fla., 1979-81; sr. staff engr. Martin Marietta, Denver, 1981-83; regional ops. mgr. air traffic control divsn. Lockheed Martin, LA, 1984-93; mgr. bus. devel. Advanced Devel. Ops., San Diego, 1993-96; dir. bus. devel. L3 Comm., Anaheim, Calif., 1997-99; dir. mktg. Racal Comm., Bonn, Germany, 1999—2000; v.p. mktg. Spirent Comm., Calabasas, Calif., 2000—01; dir. Lockheed Martin, Lawndale, Calif., 2002—03; ptnr. Dieffenbach Real Estate, Rancho Santa Fe, Calif., 2003—. CEO Ariel Ltd., San diego, 1988-90. Developer autonomous precision approach and landing sys. (Best of Whats New award Popular Sci. 1997). Vol. Children's Hosp. and Health Ctr. Recipient Nat. Conservation award Dept. of Energy, 1980, Industry Leadership award Dubai-Partnership 21, 1995, Outstanding Tech. Paper award Air Traffic Control Assn., 1995, Aviation & Space award Popular Sci., 1996. Mem.: Rotary Internat. Avocations: sailing, car restoration, water-skiing. Home: PO Box 990 Rancho Santa Fe CA 92067 Office: Dieffenbach Real Estate 6013 La Granada Rancho Santa Fe CA 92067 Office Phone: 858-756-2345. Personal E-mail: otto3@sbcglobal.net.

DIEHL, CAROL LOU, retired library director, library consultant; b. Milw., Aug. 10, 1929; d. Gilbert Fred and Erna Lou (Braeger) Doepke; m. Russell Phillip Diehl, Aug. 8, 1953; children: Holly Lou Diehl Nelson, Jeffrey Phillip. BS, U. Wis., Madison, 1951; MA, U. Wis., Oshkosh, 1971. Tchr. English, libr. Port Washington (Wis.) High Sch., 1951-54, Minoqua (Wis.) High Sch., 1954-55; libr. Ozaukee High Sch., Fredonia, Wis., 1964-65, Vernon County Tchrs. Coll., Viroqua, Wis., 1965-67; libr. media coord. Manawa (Wis.) Sch. Dist., 1973-77; dir. libr. media svcs. Sch. Dist. of New London, Wis., 1977-95; ret., 1995; lectr. U. Wis., Oshkosh, 1993, 95—. V.p. Coun. on Libr. and Network Devel., Madison, 1979; pres. Lake Forest Bd. Dirs., Eagle River, Wis., 1987-89; libr. cons. Thern Design Ctrs. Inc., 1994. Author: (with others) School Library Media Annual, 1985-87; news corr. Appleton (Wis.) Post Crescent, 1971-81; contbr. articles to profl. jours. Past mem. Fox Valley Symphony League; mem. exec. com. Waupaca and Winnebago County Grand Ole Party, chair, 1994-97, vice chmn., 1991-94; del.-at-large White House Conf. Libr. and Info. Svcs., 1991; trustee Sturm Meml. Libr., 1996-2002, treas., 1998—; mem. bd. edn. Sch. Dist. of Manawa, 1997-2004; mem. Manawa City Appeals Bd., 1999-2002; mem. U.S. Nat. Commn. on Librs. and Info. Sci., 2003—. Named Wis. Sch. Libr. Media Specialist of Yr., Assn. Ednl. Comm. and Tech., 1992. Mem. ALA (councilor-at-large 1998-2003, legis. com. 1986-91, ALA White House Conf. Libr. and Info. Svcs., 1995—, chair, 1992-95, legis. assembly chair 1989-90, membership com. 1995-99, ALTA legis. com. 1998-99, chair, 1999—, Outstanding Libr. Advocate of 20th Century 2000), AASL (legis. chmn. 1987-95, planning and implementation task force White House Conf. 1990-92, Disting. Sch. Adminstrs. chair 2001-02), Wis. Libr. Assn. (fed. rels. coord. 1990-91), Assn. Wis. Sch. Adminstr., Wis. Edn. Media Assn. (legis. com. 1986-93, Excellence award 1992), Futurae Club of Manawa, Manawa Federated Women's Club, Appleton Women's Shrine Club, Phi Delta Kappa. Republican. Lutheran. Office Phone: 920-277-1021. E-mail: cdieh1@new.rr.com, cdieho7@comcast.net.

DIEHL, DEAN R., engineering company executive; b. Abbottstown, Pa., Oct. 28, 1934; s. Samuel J. and Bessie E. Diehl; m. Eileen Anna Diehl, Feb. 1, 1959; children: Michael P., Cathy D. Budd, Brian J. BS in Engring., Pa. State U., 1956. Sales engr. Jeffrey Mfg. Co., Columbus, Ohio, 1956-68; dist. mgr. Fairfield Engring. Co., Marion, Ohio, 1968-79; ENCO divsn. mgr. Derkin & Wise Inc., Toledo, 1979-86; pres. Diehl Innovative Conveyor Engring. Inc., Toledo, 1986—. With U.S. Army, 1957-64. Mem. Mensa Ltd. Office: Diehl Inc 6848 Woodmeadow Dr Toledo OH 43617

DIEHL, DEBORAH HILDA, lawyer; b. Troy, N.Y., Feb. 13, 1951; d. Warren S. and Norma K. (Apple) D.; 1 child, Alexandra Ellen. Student, U. de Rouen, France, 1971-72; BA, St. Lawrence U., 1973; JD, Syracuse U., 1976; postdoctoral, George Washington U., 1978-79. Bar: N.Y. 1977, D.C. 1981, Ohio 1982, Md. 1987. Atty. USDA, Washington, 1976-81; assoc. Thompson, Hine & Flory, Columbus, Ohio, 1981-87, Semmes, Bowen & Semmes, Balt., 1987-90, ptnr., 1990-95, Whiteford, Taylor & Preston, Balt., 1995—. Pres. Mt. Royal Improvement Assn., 1995—97; chair Midtown Cmty. Benefits Dist. Mgmt. Authority, 1998—2000, dir., 1995—2001, Midtown Devel. Corp., 2000—; participant Leadership Md., 1997; mem. U. Md. Balt. County Tech. Ctr. Adv. Bd., 2001—. Mem.: ABA, Bar Assn. City Balt., Md. State Bar Assn. (bus. law sect. coun. 1998—, chair 2002—03). Avocations: bicycling, travel, economic development. Office Phone: 410-347-8766.

DIEHL, DOLORES, performing company executive; b. Salina, Kans., Dec. 28, 1927; d. William Augustus and Martha (Frank) Diehl. Student pub. schs., Kans. Bus. rep. Southwestern Bell Telephone Co., St. Louis and Kansas City, Mo., 1948-49, Mountain States Telephone Co., Denver, 1949-50; edn. coord. pub. rels. Pacific Telephone/AT&T, L.A. and San Diego, 1950-83; cons. Bus. Magnet High Sch., L.A. Unified Sch. Dist., 1977-79; pres. First Calif. Acad. Decathlon, 1979; owner Community Connection, L.A., 1983—; mgr., dir. DelMar Media Arts, Burbank, Calif., 1985-89; mgr. Susan Blu workshops Blupka Prodns., L.A., 1989—; ptnr., dir. animation and commls. voiceover workshops Elaine Craig Voicecasting, Hollywood, Calif., 1989—; freelance performer, voiceover L.A., 1990—; mgr. Sounds Great Film Looping Workshops, L.A., 1992-93; owner Voiceover Connection, L.A., 1994-95; pres. Voiceover Connection, Inc., L.A., 1995—. V.p. pub. rels. San Diego Inst. Creativity, 1965—67. Pub. rels. dir. Greater San Diego Sci. Fair, 1963—68; mem. exec. com. San Diego's 200th Anniversary Celebration, 1967; mem. Better Bus. Bur. Named one of Seven Top Voiceover Trainer, Animation Mag., 1999; recipient Dedication to Edn. award, Industry Edn. Coun., Calif., 1964. Mem.: Industry Edn. Coun. Calif., L.A. and San Diego (past pres.), Magnet Sch. Consortium Cities (chairperson), L.A. Area C. of C. (bd. dirs.

women's coun.), Bus. and Profl. Women's Club, Delta Kappa Gamma (hon.). Republican. Methodist. Home and Office: 691 Irolo St Apt 212 Los Angeles CA 90005-4110 Office Phone: 213-384-9251. E-mail: doloresdiehl@speakeasy.net.

DIEHL, JAMES HARVEY, church administrator; m. Dorothy Diehl; 4 children. BA, Olivet Nazarene U., 1959; DD, N.W. Nazarene U., 1990. Adminstr. MidAm. Nazarene U., 1973-76; dist. supt. Ch. of Nazarene, Nebr. and Colo., 1979-89; pastor Atlanta First Ch., 1976-79, Nazarene chs. in Iowa, Denver First Ch. of Nazarene, 1989-93; gen. supt. Ch. of the Nazarene, Kansas City, Mo., 1993—. Contbr. articles to Herald of Holiness, Preacher's Mag., Bread, World Mission, others; condr. daily radio program, weekly TV broadcast. Bd. trustees MidAm. Nazarene U., Nazarene Theol. Sem., Nazarene Bible Coll., N.W. Nazarene U.; chmn. bd. N.W. Nazarene U. Mem. Ch. Of Nazarene. Office: Ch of the Nazarene 6401 Paseo Blvd Kansas City MO 64131-1213 Office Phone: 816-333-7000.

DIEHL, LOUIS F., hematologist; b. Trenton, N.J., Apr. 8, 1948; s. Louis and Anna D.; m. Anna Mae, Dec. 3, 1973; children: Megan, Erin. BS, Georgetown U., 1970, MD, 1975. Oncologist Johns Hopkins Oncology Ctr., Balt., 1975—2004, Duke U. Med. Ctr., 2004—.

DIEHL, NANCY J., lawyer; b. 1953; d. Robert and Anne Diehl. B, Western Mich. Univ.; JD, Wayne State Univ., 1978. Trial prosecutor Recorder's Ct., Detroit, 1981—84; spl. assignment trial prosecutor Cir. Ct., 1984—87; dir. Child Abuse Unit, 1987—94; dep. chief Child and Family Abuse Bur., 1994—2000; chief Projects and Training Divsn., 2000—04, Felony Trial Divsn., 2004—. Mem. Gov. Task Force on Children's Justice (exec. com.), State Bar Rep. Assembly, 1992—96, 1996—2005. Author, illustrator with Lynda Baker (booklet) It is Good to Tell the Truth, 1988, Kids and Secrets, 1992, author, photographer with Lynda Baker Kids Go to Court, 1988; author (with Lynda Baker): (booklet) Sometimes It Is Sad to Be at Home, What Is a Kid to Do About Domestic Violence, 1997. Recipient Leonard Gilman award, 1999. Mem.: Detroit Met. Bar Assn. (Champion of Justice award 2004), State Bar of Mich. (pres. 2004). Office: Wayne County Prosecutor's Office 1441 St Antoine Detroit MI 48226-2302 Office Phone: 313-224-5742. Business E-Mail: ndiehl@co.wayne.mi.us.

DIEHL, RICHARD KURTH, retail executive, consultant; b. Chgo., July 6, 1935; s. George Henry and Agnes Martha (Kurth) D.; m. Barbara Louise Clark, June 9, 1957; children— Clark Kurth, Scott Richard, Stacy Louise. BA, Beloit Coll., 1957; postgrad., Harvard U., 1957-58; MBA, U. Chgo., 1959. With brand mgmt. staff Procter & Gamble, Cin., 1959-62; v.p., account supr. Needham, Harper & Steers, Chgo., 1963-68; Dir. mktg. Kimberly-Clark Corp., Neenah, Wis., 1968-70; pres., chief exec. officer Purnell, Inc., Santa Monica, Calif., 1970-72; v.p., chief operating officer Theta Cable TV, Santa Monica, 1972-74; exec. v.p., chief savs. officer Western Fed. Savs. and Loan Assn., Los Angeles, 1974-80; exec. v.p., a founding officer Centurion Savs. and Loan Assn., Century City, Calif., 1980-82; founder Diehl & Assocs., Los Angeles, 1983—; pres., CEO Stockwell and Binney/Royale, La Habra, Calif., 1992—. Mem. Citizens Adv. Council Los Angeles Schs., 1970-72. Woodrow Wilson fellow, 1957-58; Harvard Austin fellow, 1957-58; Sears Roebuck Found. fellow, 1958-59 Mem. Phi Beta Kappa, Sigma Alpha Epsilon. Clubs: Riviera Tennis, Santa Monica Tennis Patrons. Lodges: Rotary. Home: 17117 Ave Herradura Pacific Palisades CA 90272-2002

DIEHL, STEPHEN ANTHONY, human resources consultant; b. N.Y.C., Mar. 15, 1942; s. Anthony Stephen and Paula (Kula) D.; m. Barbara Lynn Marschman, Aug. 3, 1968. BS, L.I. U., 1963; postgrad. in bus., NYU, 1967-73. V.p. mktg. dir. Green Point Savs. Bank, Bklyn., 1969—77; sr. v.p., human resources dir. Green Point Bank, N.Y.C., 1977—95. Dir. Human Resources N.Y. Road Runners Club (N.Y. City Marathon), 1996-2001; officer, dir. Soc. for Human Resources Mgmt., N.Y. chpt., 1995-2001. Mem. Savs. Banks Mktg. Forum N.Y. State (chmn. 1973-74), N.Y.C. Mktg. Forum (chmn. 1975-76), Human Resources Officers Forum (chmn. 1980-81), Savs. Banks Officers Forum (pres. 1986-87). Avocations: photography, video, stereo. E-mail: sadiehl@aol.com.

DIEHM, JAMES WARREN, lawyer, educator; b. Lancaster, Pa., Nov. 6, 1944; s. Warren G. and Verna M. (Hertzler) D.; m. Cathleen M. Hohmeier; children: Elizabeth Ann, Rebecca Jane. BA, Pa. State U., 1966; JD, Georgetown U., 1969. Bar: D.C. 1969, V.I. 1975, Pa. 1988. Asst. U.S. atty., Washington, 1970-74; asst. atty. gen. Atty. Gen.'s Office U.S. V.I., St. Croix, 1974-76; from assoc. to ptnr. Isherwood, Hunter & Diehm, St. Croix, 1976-83; U.S. atty. U.S. V.I., 1983-87; prof. law Widener U., 1987—. Bar examiner U.S. V.I. Bar, 1979-87. Mem. ABA. Republican. Lutheran. Office: Widener U Sch Law 3800 Vartan Way PO Box 69382 Harrisburg PA 17106-9382 Office Phone: 717-541-3939.

DIEHR, BEVERLY HUNT, lawyer; b. Tampa, Fla., Aug. 19, 1954; d. Carl William Jr. and Helen Fern (Rouse) Hunt; children: Erin Elizabeth, Sara Katherine, Dana Marie. BA with high honors, U. So. Fla., 1975; JD with high honors, U. Fla., 1978. Bar: Fla. 1978, U.S. Dist. Ct. (mid. dist.) Fla. 1979. Staff atty. Three Rivers Legal Svcs. Inc., Gainesville, Fla., 1979-82; assoc. Sessums and McCall, Tampa, 1982-83; asst. dist. legal counsel dist. 6 Fla. Dept. Health and Rehab. Svcs., Tampa, 1983-84; pvt. practice law Tampa, 1984—. Mem. Fla. Bar Assn., Hillsborough County Bar Assn., Fla. Assn. Women Lawyers, Hillsborough Assn. Women Lawyers, Order of Coif. Home: 4301 W Cleveland St Tampa FL 33609-3867 Office: State Fla Dept Children and Families 9393 North Florida Ave Ste 902 Tampa FL 33612

DIEKEMA, ANTHONY J., college president, consultant; b. Borculo, Mich., Dec. 3, 1933; m. Jeane Waanders, Dec. 20, 1957; children: Douglas, David, Daniel, Paul, Mark, Maria, Tanya. BA, Calvin Coll., Grand Rapids, Mich., 1956; MA in Sociology and Anthropology, Mich. State U., 1958, PhD in Sociology, 1965. Field interviewer Bur. Bus. Research Mich. State U., East Lansing, 1955-56, asst. dir. housing, 1957-59, instr., lectr. sociology and anthropology, 1959-64, admissions counselor, 1959-61, asst. dir. admissions and scholarships, 1961-62, asst. registrar, 1962-64; asst. dean admissions and records, research assoc. in med. edn. and asst. prof. sociology U. Ill. Med. Center, Chgo., 1964-66, dir. admissions and records, asst. prof. sociology and edn., 1966-70, asso. chancellor, asso. prof. med. edn., 1970-76; pres. Calvin Coll., 1976-96, pres. emeritus. Mem. bd. trustees, chmn., Russian-Am. Christian U.; adv. bd. NBD Grand Rapids, 1983-95; chmn. bd. Russian-Am. Christian U., Moscow, 2005-. Trustee Blodgett Meml. Med. Center, Grand Rapids, 1979-91; bd. dirs. Met. YMCA, 1979-93, Project Rehab, 1978-84; treas. Back-to-God Hour Radio Com., 1970-76; chmn. Synodical Com. on Race Relations, 1973-75; pres. Strategic Christian Ministry Found., 1969-73; mem. bd. curators Trinity Christian Coll., 1969-73, chmn., 1972-73, mem. presdl. search com., 1972-73, NCAA coun. 1983-87, Pres'. commn. 1987-91. Mem. Am. Assn. Pres.'s Ind. Coll. and Univs. (bd. dirs. 1978-84, 88-91), Nat. Assn. Ind. Colls. and Univs. (bd. dirs. 1991-94), Assn. Ind. Colls. and Univs. Mich. (exec. com. 1979-84), Am. Assn. Higher Edn., Am. Sociol. Assn., Soc. Health and Human Values, Soc. Values in Higher Edn., Nat. League Nursing (accreditation com. 1974-79), Alpha Kappa Delta, Rotary. Office: Calvin Coll Grand Rapids MI 49546 Office Phone: 616-402-6898. Personal E-mail: ajdiek@aol.com.

DIEKEMPER, RITA GARBS, landscape company executive; d. Donald Richard and Carol Ann Garbs; m. Gregory Robert Diekemper, Feb. 14, 1987; children: Madelyn Garbs, Thomas Garbs, Grace Rickert. BS in Acctg., U. Mo., 1983. CPA Mo. Auditor Touche Ross & Co., St. Louis, 1983—89, Aslage Kiefer and Co., St. Louis, 1990—95; pres., owner Gardens of Grace LLC, St. Louis, 1995—. Chmn. For Our Future...For Our Kids, St. Louis, 1987—2000; chmn. citizen's adv. com. Mehlville Sch. Dist., St. Louis, 1988—89, bd. dirs., 2001—, pres. bd. dirs., 2005—; chmn. Homes for Holidays Ho. Tour, St. Louis, 2001, 2004; treas. Renew Oakville, St. Louis, St. Mark's Episcopal Ch., St. Louis, 1986—2000, vestry mem., 1986—89, endowment pres., 2000—. Recipient Disting. Svc. award, Mehlville Sch. Dist., 2000. Avocations: gardening, half-marathon runner, triathelete, travel. Home and Office: 2571 Cripple Creek Dr Saint Louis MO 63129 Office Phone: 314-846-3850.

DIEKMAN, MARK A., animal science educator; b. Vincennes, Ind., Sept. 16, 1948; s. Earl William and Dorothy Marie Diekman; m. Patti L. O'Callaghan, Dec. 17, 1977; children: Casey, Brian. BS, Purdue U., 1970, MS, 1972; PhD, Colo. State U., Ft. Collins, 1978. Rsch. assoc. Iowa state U., Ames, 1978-79; asst. prof. animal sci. Purdue U., West Lafayette, Ind., 1979-84, assoc. prof. animal sci., 1984-89, prof. animal sci., 1989—. Contbr. articles to profl. jours.; mem. editl. bd., Jour. Animal Sci., 1998—. Coach, West Lafayette Youth Baseball, 1988-98, Athletic Amateur Basketball, 1992-96. Recipient Outstanding Faculty Alumni award, Vincennes U., 2000; named Outstanding Counselor in Sch. Agr., 2001. Mem. AAAS, Am. Soc. Animal Scis., Biology of Reprodn. Assn. (reviewer 1994--), Alpha Zeta. Avocations: golf, softball, basketball, house repairs. Home: 927 N Salisbury St West Lafayette IN 47906 Office: Purdue U Dept Animal Scis West Lafayette IN 47907 Office Phone: 765-494-4829. E-mail: mdiekman@purdue.edu.

DIEKMANN, GILMORE FREDERICK, JR., lawyer; b. Evansville, Ind., Jan. 14, 1946; s. Gilmore Frederick Sr. and Mabel Pauline (Daniel) K.; children: Anne Westlake, Andrew Gilmore, Matthew Frederick. BSBA, Northwestern U., 1968, JD, 1971. Bar: Calif. 1972, U.S. Dist. Ct. Calif. (no., ea., cen. and so. dists.) Calif. 1972, U.S. Ct. Appeals (9th cir.) 1972, U.S. Supreme Ct. 1978. Assoc. Bronson, Bronson & McKinnon, San Francisco, 1971-78, ptnr. labor and employment law, 1979-99, chmn., mng. ptnr., 1991-93, chmn. labor, employment dept., 1993-99; ptnr. Seyfarth Shaw, San Francisco, 1999—, chmn. no. Calif. labor dept., 1999—2005. Author and speaker in field. Mem. ABA, Def. Rsch. Inst., Am. Employment Law Coun., Order of Coif. Republican. Lutheran. Home: 901 Powell St # 6 San Francisco CA 94108 Office: Seyfarth Shaw 560 Mission St Fl 31 San Francisco CA 94105-2907 Office Phone: 415-544-1070. Business E-Mail: gdiekmann@seyfarth.com.

DIEM, RICHARD A., social studies educator, educational consultant; b. Kansas City, Mo., Dec. 13, 1945; s. William M. and Rose (Chawkin) D.; m. Roberta Ann Lewin, July 12, 1970; children: Joshua, Sarah. BS, Bradley U., 1967; MS, So. Ill. U., 1969; MA, Colo. State U., 1971; PhD, Northwestern U., 1975. Cert. tchr. Tex., Mo., Colo., Ill. Tchr. Maine North High Sch., Des Plaines, Ill., 1971-75; clin. prof. No. Ill. U., DeKalb, 1974-75; prof. U. Tex., San Antonio, 1975—, vice provost, dean honors coll. Contbr. articles to profl. jours.

DIEMAND, KIM EUGENE, human resources executive; b. Camden, N.J., Nov. 5, 1953; s. Eugene August and Ruth (Maute) D.; m. Jan Elizabeth Ratcliffe, Oct. 7, 1975; children: Megan, Michael, Andrew. AA, Coll. DuPage, 1977; BS, No. Ill. U., 1978. Office mgr. Diemand Printing Co., Chgo., 1978-79; indsl. engr., estimator Henry Pratt Co., Aurora, Ill., 1979-80; personnel mgr. Marmon/Keystone Corp., Lemont, Ill., 1980-81; plant personnel mgr. Gen. Mills Inc. Package Foods Div., Lodi, Calif., 1981-83; employee rels. mgr. The Gorton Group div. Gen Mills, Gloucester, Mass., 1983-90; dir. human resources McKesson Drug Co., Romeoville, Ill., 1990-94, distbn. ctr. mgr. St. Peters, Mo., 1994-96, v.p., gen. mgr. nat. customer support ctr. Westlake, Tex., 1996-97; v.p. human resources Tri-Gas Indsl. Gases, Irving, Tex., 1997-99; v.p., gen. mgr. D&K Healthcare Resources, Inc., Mpls., 1999—. Chief spokesman, mem. personnel bd. Town of Essex (Mass.), 1985-86. Sgt. USMC, 1971-75; dir. youth ministry Crown of Life Luth. Ch., Colleyville, Tex., 1997-98. Mem. Am. Soc. Human Resource Mgrs., Rolling Green Country Club Office: D&K Healthcare Resources Inc 800 N 3rd St Minneapolis MN 55401-1104

DIEMER, EMMA LOU, composer, educator; b. Kansas City, Mo., Nov. 24, 1927; d. George Willis and Myrtle (Casebolt) D. MusB, Yale U., 1949, MusM, 1950; PhD, Eastman Sch. Music, 1960; LHD (hon.), Ctrl. Mo. State U., 1999. Composer-in-residence Arlington (Va.) Schs., 1959-61; composer, cons. pub. schs., Arlington and Balt., 1964-65; prof. theory and composition U. Md., College Park, 1965-70, U. Calif., Santa Barbara, 1971-91. Organist Ch. of the Reformation, Washington, 1962—71, Ch. of Christ, Santa Barbara, 1973—84, 1st Presbyn. Ch., Santa Barbara, 1984—2001. Composer of over 100 choral and instrumental compositions including Music for Woodwind Quartet, 1976, Four Poems of Alice Meynell for Soprano and Chamber Ensemble, 1977, Symphony No. 2, 1980, Suite for Orchestra, 1981, Suite of Homages, 1985, Church Rock, 1986, Variations for Piano, 4 Hands, 1987, String Quartet No. 1, 1987, Serenade for String Orch., 1988, Concerto for Marimba, 1990, Concerto for Piano, 1991, Sextet, 1992, Four Biblical Settings for Organ, 1992, Fantasy for Piano, 1993, Kyrie for Mixed Chorus, Organ, and Piano - 4 Hands, 1993, Santa Barbara Overture, 1995, Gloria for Mixed Chorus, 2 Pianos and Percussion, 1996, Psalm 122 for Bass Trombone and Organ, Psalm 121 for Organ, Brass and Percussion, Psalms for Flute and Organ, Psalms for Trumpet and Organ, Psalms for Percussion and Organ, 1998, Latin Mass, 2000, Homage to Tschaikovsky, 2000, Piano Trio, 2000, Quartet for Piano and Brass, 2001, Songs for the Earth, 2002, Toccata for Six, 2004, Requiem for woodwind quintet and string quintet, 2004, Chumash Indian Dance Celebration, 2004, Homage to Poulenc, Mozart, and MacDowell, 2004, Oxford Town Hall for organ, 2005; composer-in-residence Santa Barbara Symphony, 1990-92. Fulbright scholar, 1952-53; grantee Ford Found. Young Composers, 1959-61, Kindler Found. Commn., 1963, Nat. Endowment Arts, 1980-81; Kennedy Ctr. Friedheim award, 1992. Mem. ASCAP (ann. awards 1962—), Am. Guild Organists (Composer of Yr. 1995), Internat. Alliance for Women in Music, Am. Music Ctr., Mu Phi Epsilon (award of merit 1995). Democrat. Presbyterian. Avocations: reading, electronic and computer music. E-mail: eldiemer@cox.net. *A composer who succeeds in some measure must have talent, encouragement, strong self-motivation, an almost obsessive need for self-expression through music, a belief in the importance of one's own contribution, the ability to appraise one's own work, the desire, at least part of the time, to communicate.*

DIENELT, JOHN F., lawyer; b. Alexandria, Va., Nov. 24, 1943; BA, U. Va., 1965; MA, Fletcher Sch. Law and Diplomacy, Tufts Univ., 1966; LLB, Yale U., 1969. Law clk. to Hon. G.A. Gessell U.S. Dist. Ct. D.C., 1969-70; asst. to Solicitor Gen. U.S. Dept. Justice, 1970-71; counsel Environ. Def. Fund, Washington; mem. Reed Smith Shaw & McClay, Washington; ptnr., chmn. Franchise Litigation practice group DLA Piper Rudnick Gray Cary, Washington, 1996—. Instr. Nat. Inst. Trial Advocacy, Georgetown Univ.; mem. steering com. Nat. Franchise Mediation Program. Mng. editor Yale Law Jour., 1968-69; contbr. articles to profl. jours. Mem. ABA (chmn. Forum on Franchising 2000-2001), DC Bar, Order of Coif, Phi Beta Kappa. Office: DLA Piper Rudnick Gray Cary 1200 19th St NW Washington DC 20036-2412 Office Phone: 202-861-3880. Office Fax: 202-223-2085. Business E-Mail: john.dienelt@dlapiper.com.

DIENER, BETTY JANE, business educator; b. Washington, Sept. 15, 1940; d. Edward George and Minnie (Feild) Diener; m. Robert D. Bell, 1987 (dec. 1993). AB, Wellesley Coll., 1962; MBA, Harvard U., 1964, DBA, 1974. Account exec. Young & Rubicam, Inc., N.Y.C., 1964-70; product mgr. Am. Cyanamid Co., Wayne, NJ, 1970-72; asst. dean Sch. Bus. Case Western Res. U., Cleve., 1974-79; dean Sch. Bus. Adminstrn. Old Dominion U., Norfolk, Va., 1986-87; provost, vice-chancellor acad. affairs U. Mass., Boston, 1987-88, prof. mktg., 1987—2002, spl. asst. to chancellor econ. devel., 1993-94; prof., mgmt. Barry U., Miami Shores, Fla., 2002—. Pres. Environ. Bus. Coun. New Eng., Inc., 1995—97. Contbr. articles to profl. publs. Mem. Citizens Coun. Chesapeake Bay, 1986—87; adviser Jr. League, 1963—64, Plans for Progress, 1968—70, Leadership Met. Richmond, 1980—82; mem. Mass. Gov.'s Adv. Com. Sci. and Tech., 1988—90, Mayor's Task Force Empowerment Zones, 1994; mem. cmty. working group Mass. Mil. Reservation, 1997—2000; pres. Provincetown (Mass.) Repertory Theater, 2002, bd. dirs., 2001—03; commr. Norfolk Indsl. Devel. Authority, 1979—82; bd. dirs. Norfolk Conv. and Visitors Bur., 1979—82, Norfolk C. of C., 1979—82, Greater Norfolk Corp., 1986—87, Va. Orch. Group, 1982—87, Va. Stage Co., 1986—87, Karamu Ho., 1975—79, Woodruff Hosp., 1975—79, Women's City Club Cleve., 1976—79, Coun. Sustainable Fla., 2003—, Bainbridge Grad. Inst., 2003—05; mem. adv. com. state and local govt. programs John F. Kennedy Sch. Govt., Harvard U., 1986—88. Named Outstanding Working Woman, Glamour Mag., 1979; named one of 10 Outstanding Career Women of Decade, 1984; recipient Honor award, Soil Conservation Soc., 1984; Fulbright scholar, 2001. Democrat. Home: 9304 NE 9th Pl Miami Shores FL 33138 Office: Barry Univ Andreas Sch of Business Miami Shores FL 33138 E-mail: bejade@aol.com.

DIENER, ERWIN, immunologist; b. Lucerne, Switzerland, Jan. 6, 1932; arrived in Can., 1970; s. Reinhold and Alice (Treichler) D.; m. Eva Schaufelberger, 1957. PhD, U. Zurich, 1963. Rsch. fellow Inst. for Radiobiology, Zurich, 1960-64; Roche fellow Walter and Eliza Hall Inst., Melbourne, Australia, 1964-67, rsch. fellow, 1967-70; prof. U. Alta., Edmonton, Can., 1970-73, prof., head dept. immunology, 1973-88, prof. emeritus, 1989—. Fellow Royal Soc. Can.

DIENER, ROYCE, retired health products executive; b. Mar. 27, 1918; s. Louis and Lillian (Goodman) Diener; m. Jennifer S. Flinton; children: Robert, Joan, Michael, Dianne. BA, Harvard U.; LLD (hon.), Pepperdine U. Comml. lending officer, ivnestment banker, various locations, 1972; pres. Am. Med. Internat., Inc., Beverly Hills, Calif., 1972—75, pres., CEO, 1975—78, chmn., CEO, 1978—85, chmn. bd., chmn. exec. com., 1986—89. Bd. dirs. Calif. Econ. Devel. Corp., Acuson, Inc., Advanced Tech. Venture Funds, Am. Health Properties, AMI Health Svcs., plc., Constorium 2000. Author: Financing a Growing Business, 1966, 4th edit., 1995. Mem. bd. visitors Grad. Sch. Mgmt., UCLA Med. Ctr.; mem. vis. com. Med. Sch. and Sch. Dental Medicine, Harvard U.; bd. dirs. L.A. Philharm. Assn.; bd. dirs. L.A. chpt. ARC; bd. dirs. Heritage Sq. Mus., Santa Monica, Calif.; trustee Contemporary Mus., Honolulu; chmn. bd. UCLA Med. Ctr. Capt. USAF, 1942—46, PTO. Decorated D.F.C. with oak leaf cluster. Mem.: Calif. Bus. Round Table (bd. dirs.), Calif. C. of C. (bd. dirs.), L.A. C. of C. (bd. dirs.), Outrigger Canoe Club (Honolulu), Marks Club (London), Riviera Country Club (L.A.), Calif. Yacht Club, Regency Club, Harvard Club.

DIENER, THEODOR OTTO, plant pathologist, researcher; b. Zurich, Switzerland, Feb. 28, 1921; arrived in 1949, 1949, naturalized, 1955; s. Theodor Emanuel and Hedwig Rosa (Baumann) D.; m. Sybil Mary Fox, May 11, 1968; children from previous marriage: Theodor W., Robert A., Michael S. Diploma, Swiss Fed. Inst. Tech., 1946; DSc, Nat. Swiss Fed. Inst. Tech., 1948. Asst. Swiss Fed. Inst. Tech., Zurich, 1946—48; plant pathologist Swiss Fed. Exptl. Sta., Waedenswil, 1949—50; asst. prof. plant pathology RI State U., Kingston, 1950; asst. plant pathologist Wash. State U., Prosser, 1950—55, assoc. plant pathologist, 1955—59; rsch. plant pathologist agr. rsch. svc. USDA, Beltsville, Md., 1959—88, collaborator agr. rsch. svc., 1988—97; prof. botany, sr. staff sci. Ctr. Agr. Biotech., dept. Botany U. Md., College Park, 1988—98, acting dir. Ctr. Agr. Biotech., 1991—92, Disting. Univ. prof., 1994—98; Disting. prof. U. Md. Biotech. Inst., 1998, Disting. Univ. prof. emeritus, 1999—. Univ. lectr., rsch. instr.; Regent's lectr. U. Calif., Riverside, 1970; A.W. Dimock lectr. Cornell U., 1975, Andrew D. White prof.-at-large, 1979—81; James Law disting. lectr. NY State Coll. Vet. Medicine, 1981; disting. lectr. Boyce Thomson Inst. for Plant Rsch., 1987, Hong Kong U. Sci. and Tech., 1992; Ernest Everett Just Meml. lectr. Howard U., Washington, 1990; guest lectr. Israel Soc. for Microbiology, Rehovot, 1994, Royal Swedish Acad. of Scis., Stockholm, 1997, Swedish Agrl. U., Uppsala, 1997, Royal Netherlands Acad. Arts and Scis., Amsterdam, 1998, Alexander von Humboldt Assn., Washington, 1999. Author: Viroids and Viroid Diseases, 1979; editor: The Viroids, 1987; assoc. editor: Virology, 1967—71, mem. editl. com.: Ann. Rev. Phytopathology, 1970—74, Annales de Virologie, 1980—88; contbr. articles to profl. jours. Named to USDA Sci. Hall of Fame, 1989; recipient Campbell award, Am. Inst. Biol. Scis., 1968, Superior Svc. award, USDA, 1969, Disting. Svc. award, 1975, Alexander von Humboldt award, 1975, Wolf prize in Agr., 1987, U.S. Nat. medal of Sci., 1987, Gov.'s citation, State of Md., 1988, E.C. Stakman award, U. Minn., 1988. Fellow: Am. Acad. Arts and Scis., NY Acad. Scis., Am. Phytopath. Soc.; mem.: AAAS, NAS, German Acad. Natural Scientists, Leopoldina. Achievements include discovery of novel class of pathogens (viroids), 1971. Home: 11711 Battersea Dr PO Box 272 Beltsville MD 20704-0272 Office: U Md Biosystems Rsch Ctr College Park MD 20742-0001 E-mail: diener@umbi.umd.edu.

DIENES, LOUIS ROBERT, lawyer; b. New Brunswick, N.J., Apr. 17, 1966; s. Louis S. and Rosemary T. D. AB, U. Calif., Berkeley, 1990; JD, Stanford U., 1994. Bar: Calif. 1994. Ptnr. Alschuler Grossman Stein & Kuhan, LLP, L.A. Mem. adv. bd. L.A. Bus. Tech. Ctr., L.A., 2002—. Mem.: Pasadena Angels. Office: 1620 26th St North Tower 4th Fl Santa Monica CA 90404 Office Phone: 310-255-9097. Business E-Mail: LDienes@agsk.com.

DIENST, DANIEL W., metal products executive; BA, Wash. Univ.; JD, Brooklyn Law Sch. With Jeffries and Co., Inc., 1995—98, CIBC World Markets Corp., 1999—2000; chmn. bd. Metals USA, 2003—. Office: Metals USA 10891 Forbes Ave Garden Grove CA 92843*

DIENSTAG, JULES LEONARD, dean, gastroenterologist, medical researcher; b. NYC, Dec. 10, 1946; m. Judy Iris Gordon, Feb. 3, 1974; children: Josh, Jonathan. AB magna cum laude, Columbia Coll., 1968; MD, Columbia U., 1972. Diplomate Am. Bd Internal Medicine. Intern in medicine U. Chgo., 1972-73, resident in medicine, 1973-74; postdoctoral fellow, rsch. assoc. NIH, Bethesda, Md., 1974-76; clin. and rsch. fellow Mass. Gen. Hosp., Boston, 1976-78, clin. asst. medicine, 1978-79, asst. in medicine, 1979-82, asst. physician, 1983-87, assoc. physician, 1988-93, physician, 1993—; asst. prof. of medicine Harvard Med. Sch., Boston, 1978-82, assoc. prof., 1982—2002, faculty assoc. dean for admissions, 1998—2003, Carl W. Walter prof. medicine, 2002—, assoc. dean Academic and Clin. Programs, 2003—05, dean Med. Edn., 2005—. Vis. scientist Lab. of Epidemiology, The Lindsley F. Kimball Rsch. Inst. of the N.Y. Blood Ctr., 1980-82; expert panelist on viral hepatitis Lister Hill Nat. Ctr. for Biomed. Comm., Nat. Libr. Medicine, 1980-82, advisor, 1982-86; numerous tchg. appointments; lectr. in field. Mem. editl. bd. Jour. Clin. Microbiology, 1977-86, Hepatology, 1980-86, Infectious Disease Series, Marcel Dekker Med. divsn., 1981-85, Gastroenterology, 1981-86, Jour. Viral Hepatitis, 1993—; editor: Gastroenterology Series, Marcel Dekker, 1983-86, Mass. Gen. Hosp. Liver-Biliary-Pancreas Ctr. Newsletter, 1990—; assoc. editor: Gastroenterology, 1986-91, 96—, Viral Hepatitis Knowledge-Base, New Eng. Jour. Medicine, 1986-89. With USPHS res., 1976-83, surgeon, 1983—. Recipient Clin. Investigator award USPHS, 1978-79. Fellow ACP; mem. AAAS, Internat. Assn. Study of the Liver, European Assn. Study of the Liver (corr.), Am. Soc. Microbiology, Am. Fedn. Clin. Rsch. Am. Assn. Immunologists, Am. Assn. Study Liver Diseases (abstract selection com. hepatitis, immunology 1979-85, 89—, tng. and edn. com. 1980-83, mem. nominations com. 1989-90, mem. publs. com. 1993-96), Am. Gastroent. Assn. (abstract selection com., liver-biliary-bile 1983-84, 89—), Mass. Med. Soc., Phi Beta Kappa. Office: Harvard Med Sch Off Dean for Med Edn / Gordon Hall 25 Shattuck St Boston MA 02115 also: Mass Gen Hosp 55 Fruit St Ste 148 Boston MA 02114-2696 Office Phone: 617-432-6250. Office Fax: 617-432-6253. E-mail: jules_dienstag@hms.harvard.edu.*

DIERBERG, JAMES F., bank executive; b. 1937; s. William and Genevieve Dierberg; m. Mary Dierberg; 2 children. BS, BA, Univ. Mo.; JD, Univ. Wash. Pres. First Bank, Inc., St. Louis, 1966—99, former CEO, chmn.; owner Hermanhoff Winery, Hermann, Mo., 1978—. Dierberg Vineyards, Santa Barbara, Calif., 1996—. Served U.S. Air Nat. Guard, France. Office: First Bank Inc 11901 Olive Blvd Saint Louis MO 63141*

DIERCKS, WALTER ELMER, lawyer; b. Irvington, NJ, July 6, 1945; s. Elmer Jules and Evelyn Sophie (Lauster) D.; m. Mary-Jane Atwater, Apr. 16, 1977; children: Emily Jane, Gillian Ruth. B.Chem. Engring., Rensselaer Poly. Inst., 1967; JD, U. Va., 1972. Bar: Va. 1972, DC 1973, US Supreme Ct. 1984. Engr. Bethlehem Steel Corp., Balt., 1968-69; Devel. engr. Diamond Shamrock Corp., Balt., 1969-70; pub. Charlottesville (Va.) Consumer, 1970-72; atty. FTC, Washington, 1972-76; dep. asst. dir. compliance Bur. Consumer Protection, 1976-77; gen. counsel, sec. Washington Star Co., 1977-81; ptnr. Rubin, Winston, Diercks, Harris & Cooke, LLP, Washington, 1981—. Chmn. Alexandria (Va.) Landlord-Tenant Relations Bd., 1976; mem. Alexandria Charter Rev. Commn., 1980-81, Alexandria Democratic Com., 1979-81, 83-85. Recipient award excellence FTC, 1977 Mem. ABA Unitarian Universalist. Home: 304 Lamond Pl Alexandria VA 22314-4907 Office: 6th Fl 1155 Connecticut Ave NW Washington DC 20036-4306 Office Phone: 202-861-0870. Business E-Mail: wdiercks@rwdhc.com.

DIERDORF, DANIEL LEE (DAN DIERDORF), sports commentator, football analyst, former professional football player; b. Canton, Ohio, June 29, 1949; m. Debbie D.; children: Dana, Kelly(dec.), Katherine; children: Dan, Kristen. Student, U. Mich. Football player St. Louis Cardinals, 1971—83; with Sta. KMOX, St. Louis, 1974—; sports dir. Sta. KMOV-TV, St. Louis, 1987—; football analyst CBS NFL broadcasts, 1985—87, ABC Monday Night Football broadcasts, 1987—99; NFL football analyst CBS Sports, 1999—. Named to NFL Pro-Bowl Team, 1974—78, 1980, Pro Football Hall of Fame, 1996. Office: CBS Sports 51 W 52nd St New York NY 10019-6119*

DIERICKX, CONSTANCE RICKER, psychologist, management consultant; b. Evanston, Ill, June 26, 1952; d. Benjamin Franklin Ricker and Betty June Caldwell; m. Michael James Dierickx; children: Amy Gambill, April Gambill. PhD, Ga. State U., Atlanta, GA, 1998. Psychologist self employed, Marietta, Ga., 1990—98; cons. RHR Internat.Co., Atlanta, 1998—. Spkr. in field; presenter in field. Vol. Save the Park, Marietta, 2001; member, vol., adv. Ga. Coun. for Hearing Impaired., Atlanta, 1995—98; vol. Citizens to Rescind the Resolution, Marietta; Chair, Selection Com/ Habitat for Humanity, Asheville, NC, 1989—90. Grantee, Undergraduate Research Council - University of North Carolina - Asheville, NC, 1989. Mem.: APA, Soc.for Consulting. Psychology, Bd. Dirs. Network (bd. mem.), National Assn. Corp. Dirs. Unitarian Universalist. Avocations: cooking, reading, walking, boxing fan. Office: RHR Internat Co 1355 Peachtree St Ste 1400 Atlanta GA 30064 Business E-Mail: cdierickx@rhrinternational.com.

DIERKS, RICHARD ERNEST, veterinarian, academic administrator; b. Flandreau, SD, Mar. 11, 1934; s. Martin and Lillian Ester (Benedict) D.; m. Eveline Carol Amundson, July 20, 1956; children— Jeffrey Scott, Steven Eric, Joel Richard. Student, S.D. State U., 1952-55; BS, U. Minn., 1957, DVM, 1959, MPH, PhD, U. Minn., 1964; MBA, U. Ill., 1985. Diplomate Am. Coll. Vet. Microbiologists, Am. Coll. Vet. Preventive Medicine. Supervisory microbiologist Communicable Disease Ctr., Atlanta, 1964-68; prof. coll. veterinary medicine Iowa State U., Ames, 1968-74; head dept. veterinary sci. Mont. State U., Bozeman, 1974-76; dean Coll. Veterinary Medicine U. Ill., Urbana, 1976-89, prof., dean emeritus, 1989—; dean Coll. Veterinary Medicine U. Fla., Gainesville, 1989-97, prof., dean emeritus, 1997—. Mem. tng. grant rev. com. Nat. Inst. Allergy and Infectious Diseases, 1973-74 Contbr. articles on virology, immunology and epidemiology to profl. jours. Served with USPHS, 1964-67. Career Devel. awardee Nat. Inst. Allergy and Infectious Diseases, 1969-74, Nat. Acad. Practitioners, 1995. Mem. Am. Vet. Medicine Assn., Am. Soc. Virology, Am. Soc. Microbiologists, Am. Assn. Immunologists, Am. Assn. Vet. Lab. Diagnosis, Colo. Vet. Medicine Assn., Soc. Exptl. Biology and Medicine, Gamma Sigma Delta, Phi Kappa Phi, Phi Zeta. Clubs: Rotary. Republican. Lutheran. Office: 13651 N 115th St Longmont CO 80504-8017 Office Phone: 303-774-1897. Personal E-mail: dierksrichardcar@msn.com.

DIERNA, JOSEPH BIAGIO, construction company executive, land development consultant; b. Bklyn., June 19, 1959; s. Joseph Michael and Anna (DeVito) D.; m. Camille DiPerna, Oct. 6, 1979; children: Andrea Lynn, Tina Marie, Nicole Suzanne. Student, Orange County Coll., 1979. Supr. Steverand, Inc., Builders, Monroe, N.Y., 1978-84; project mgr. Sherman Builders, Monroe, 1984-86, Solart Builders, Monroe, 1984-86; treas./gen. mgr. Pine Tree Lake Corp., Developers, Monroe, 1986-89; project mgr. Fieldcrest Corp., home builders, Chester, N.Y., 1989—; owner, pres. Orange & Rockland Bldg. Corp., 1994—, Orange & Rockland Realty, 1994—, also bd. dirs.; v.p., owner Maple Tree Assn., Washingtonville, NY. Sec. Weathervane Condo I, Washingtonville, N.Y., 1981-84; cons. D.E. P. Resources, Monroe, 1985—, U.S. One Corp., N.Y.C., 1986—, N.Y. Archdiocese Bldg. Commn., 1991. Mem. Interact, Monroe, 1977; jr. varsity hockey coach Washingtonville HS, 1998—2002. Mem.: Bear Mountain Hockey Coub (Highland Falls, NY, coach), Builders Assn. Hudson Valley, NY State Builders Assn., Nat. Assn. Builders. Republican. Roman Catholic. Avocations: gardening, tennis, hockey. Office: 371 Orchard Dr Monroe NY 10950

DIERNISSE, HANS VILHELM (VILLY DIERNISSE), writer, mechanical engineer; b. Gudbjerg, Denmark, Feb. 11, 1928; arrived in U.S., 1948; s. Aage Madsen Diernisse and Anna Jensine (Kirstine) Rasmussen; m. Anita Rosella Lumm, Aug. 13, 1983; children: Lloyd, Lisa stepchildren: Robert, Sharon, Kevin; m. Lisa Mina Erma Karspeck (div.). BME, Polytechnic Inst., Bklyn., 1961. Ship Master Saetterskipperskolen/ Denmark, 1946. Seaman Mcht. Marine, 1942—48; laborer, 1949—54; engr., 1955—64; sr. chief engr.; plant mgr., 1964—75; gen. mgr; CEO Ronthor & Corona Plastics, NJ, 1976—78; self-employed writer Westwood, NJ, 1979—. Dir. Star Products, Hackensack, NJ, 1960—63, Laal Cos., 1978—94; cons. to plastic industry, 1964—90. Author: Johnny Music, 2002, Letters, 2002; inventor (ergonomic computer keyboard), 1989. Coun. mem. Boy Scouts USA, Westwood, NJ, 1971—80; vol. Girl Scouts of Am., Westwood, 1975—76; vol. civic orgns. With U.S. Army, 1951—52. Avocations: outdoor activities, travel, concerts, genealogy, photography. Home: 9 Kaufman Dr Westwood NJ 07675 Office Fax: 201-664-6222.

DIESCH, STANLEY LA VERNE, veterinarian, educator; b. Blooming Prairie, Minn., May 16, 1925; s. John Herman and Emma Lillian (Erickson) D.; m. Darlene Ardis Witty; July 22, 1956; children: Lauren, Stephanie. BS, U. Minn., 1951, DVM, 1956, MPH, 1963. Diplomate Am. Coll. Vet. Preventive Medicine and Epidemiology. Asst. prof. Coll. Vet. Med., U. Iowa, Iowa City, 1963-66; asst. prof. U. Minn. Coll. Vet. Medicine, St. Paul, 1966-69, assoc. prof., 1969-73, prof., 1973-95, prof. emeritus, 1995—, dir. internat. programs, 1985-98; prof. Sch. Pub. Health, U. Minn., Mpls., 1973-95. Advisor Pan Am. Health Orgn., Washington, 1971— Contbr. more than 100 articles to profl. jours., 4 chapters to books. Mem. East Buchanan County Sch. Bd., Winthrop, Iowa, 1960; Rep. del., Minn., 1970-85; co-chair nat. Outdoor Speedskating, St. Paul, 1973; dir. CENSHARE, Mpls., 1981-82; chmn. Veterinarians for Re-election of Durenberger, Minn., 1982, 88; bd. dirs. Minn.-Uruguay Ptnrs. Ams., 1981—, pres., 1990-94, chmn. bd., 1995-99; hon. consul of Uruguay in Minn., 1991-96. Recipient Am. Express award Nat. Assn. Ptnrs. Ams., 1984, Internat. Castricone U. Linkage award Nat. Assn. Ptnrs. Ams., 1998, Dummond Peck Hill Lifetime Achievement award Ptnrs. Ams., 2002; WHO travel fellow, 1974; grantee EPA, 1968-71, USDA, 1978. Mem. AVMA (Pub. Svc. award 1987, Internat. Vet. Congress award 1998), APHA (coun. 1971-84), U.S. Animal Health Assn. (com. chair, Appreciation award 1986), Internat. Soc. Animal Hygiene (exec. bd. 1988-2000, pres. 1991-94, Honor award 2000), Minn. Vet. Medicine Assn. (com. chair 1970-75, Disting. Svc. award 1996). Lutheran. Avocations: fishing, hunting, boating. Home and Office: 743 Heinel Dr Saint Paul MN 55113-2152 Office Phone: 651-484-8635. Business E-Mail: diesc001@umn.edu.

DIESEL, VIN (MARK VINCENT), actor; b. NYC, July 18, 1967; Student, Hunter Coll. Actor, dir., prodr., writer: (films) Multi-facial, 1994; Strays, 1997; actor, exec. prodr. XXX, 2002; A Man Apart, 2003; actor, prodr. The Chronicles of Riddick, 2004; actor: Saving Private Ryan, 1998, (voice) The Iron Giant, 1999, Boiler Room, 2000, Pitch Black, 2000, The Fast and the Furious, 2001, Knockaround Guys, 2001, Be Cool, 2005; (TV films) Into Pitch Black, 2000. Office: c/o Endeavor Talent Agency 9701 Wilshire Blvd Beverly Hills CA 90212*

DIESTE, TONY, marketing professional; b. Mex. m. Stephanie Dieste; children: Alejandro, Ashley. Founder Hawaiian Products, Inc., 1981—84; mgr. several key accts. and new bus. DDB Needham Worldwide Dallas Group; with BBDO; mng. ptnr., dir. devel. and execution of all client Hispanic mktg. activity O&A; pres., founder Dieste Harmel & Partners, Dallas, 2002—. Active mem. Hispanic cmty., several Hispanic coms., employee assns., and 2 bds. Named Ad Star of Yr., Am. Adv. Fed., 1993, one of 100 most influential Hispanics in USA, 2000, Hispanic Agy. Exec. of Yr., Assn. Hispanic Adv. Agys., 2001; named to Adv. Hall of Achievement, 1996; recipient Multicultural Agy. of the Yr., AdAge, 2003. Mem.: Assn. Hispanic Adv. Agys. Office: Dieste Harmel & Partners 3102 Oaklawn Ste 109 Dallas TX 75219

DIETEL, WILLIAM MOORE, former foundation executive; b. Islip, N.Y., Aug. 14, 1927; s. Frederick William and Zillah Yolanda (Vannuccini) D.; m. Linda Remington, June 16, 1951; children: Elizabeth Lynn, Cynthia Lyon, Lisa Remington, John Frederick, Victoria Moore. AB, Princeton U., 1950; MA, Yale U., 1952, PhD, 1959; postgrad., London U. Inst. Hist. Research, 1953-54. Instr. history U. Mass., Amherst, 1954-59; asst. dean of coll., asst. prof. humanities Amherst Coll., 1959-61; prin. Emma Willard Sch., Troy, N.Y., 1961-70; pres. Rockefeller Bros. Fund, N.Y.C., 1975-87. Pres. Pierson-Lovelace Found., L.A.; chmn. FB Heron Found., N.Y.C., Brain Mapping Med. Rsch. Orgn., L.A.; chmn. Guidestar Internat., Williamsburg, Va.; adv. counsel Inst. for Philanthropy, London; internat. adv. com. Johns Hopkins UN; co-chair pres.'s adv. coun. Am. Farmland Trust. Mem. Nat. Campaign Leadership Coun., Coun. for America's First Freedom, Univ. Club (N.Y.C.), Cosmos Club (Washington). Office: PO Box 309 Flint Hill VA 22627-0309

DIETER, GEORGE ELWOOD, JR., academic administrator; b. Phila., Dec. 5, 1928; m. Nancy Joan Russell, June 21, 1952; children: Carol Joan, Barbara June. BS in Metall. Engring, Drexel Inst. Tech., 1950; Sc.D., Carnegie Inst. Tech., 1953. Research engr. E.I. duPont Engring Research Lab., Wilmington, Del., 1955-59, research supr., 1959-62; prof., head dept. metall. engring. Drexel Inst. Tech., 1962-69; dean Coll. Engring. Drexel U., 1969-73; dir. Processing Research Inst., Carnegie-Mellon U., 1973-77; dean Coll. Engring. U. Md., College Park, 1977-94, dir. continuous quality improvement, 1994-2000, Glenn L. Martin prof. engring., 2000—. Cons. in field. Author: Mechanical Metallurgy, 1961, 3d edit., 1986, Engineering Design, 1983, 3d edit., 1999. Mem. 1953-55, AUS. Recipient Pres. medal, U. Md., 2004. Fellow AAAS, Am. Soc. Metals (A.E. White award 1986, Sauver award 1992), Am. Soc. Engring. Edn. (pres. 1993, Lamme award 1996), Minerals, Metals and Materials Soc. (educator award 1994); mem. NAE, AIME, Soc. Mfg. Engrs. (educator award 1987), Fedn. Materials Socs. (pres. 1990-92), Sigma Xi, Tau Beta Pi. Home: 1 Locksley Ct Silver Spring MD 20904-6321 Office: U Md Dept Mech Engring College Park MD 20742-0001 Office Phone: 301-405-5248. Business E-Mail: gdieter@eng.umd.edu.

DIETER, MELVIN EASTERDAY, retired minister, educator; b. Cherryville, Pa., Oct. 12, 1924; s. Harold David Dieter and Laura Esther Easterday; m. Hallie Arline Kirtz, Dec. 27, 1945; 1 child, Judith Patrice. Grad. Cantonese, Naval Oriental Lang. Sch., U. Colo., 1946; AB in Modern Languages summa cum laude, Muhlenberg Coll., 1947; BTh in Bible and Theology summa cum laude, Ea. Pilgrim Coll., 1950; MA in Am. History, Lehigh U., 1951; MST in Church History andTheology, Temple U., 1953; LLD (hon.), Houghton Coll., 1964; PhD in Religion, Temple U., 1973. Ordained to ministry Wesleyan Ch., 1952. From instr. to pres. Ea. Pilgrim Coll., Allentown, Pa., 1946-65; acad. dean Houghton (N.Y.) Coll., 1968; pastor Chichester Wesleyan Ch., Boothwyn, Pa., 1965—67; gen. sec. edn. The Wesleyan Ch., Marion, Ind., 1968-75; prof. ch. history and hist. theology, provost, v.p. Asbury Theol. Sem., Wilmore, Ky., 1975-90. Dir. Pew Foundations' Wesleyan Holiness Study Project Asbury Theol. Sem., 1987-90; pres. Wesleyan Theol. Soc., 1977; chair Houghton Coll. Bd. Trustees, 1992-99. Author: The Holiness Revival of the Nineteenth Century, 1980; co-editor: The Church, 1984; (with Hallie Dieter): God is Enough, 1986; editor: The Christian's Secret of a Holy Life, 1994, The 19th Century Holiness Movement, 1998; contbr.: Mandate for Mission, 1970, Aspects of Pentecostal-Charismatic Origins, 1975, Five Views on Sanctification, 1987, John Wesley:Contemporary Perspectives, 1988, Reformers and Revivalists, 1992, Theological Education in the Evangelical Tradition, 1996, Christianity in Appalachia, 1999; contbr. articles to profl. jours Pres. William J. Harley Found., Allentown, 1961-85, Lehigh Valley Pub. Rels. Club, 1965; treas. Allentown Sch. Bd. Authority, 1963-65, Rotary, Waynesboro, Va.; chaplain Kiwanis Club, Allentown, Pa Lt. N.G. USNR, 1942—51. Recipient Outstanding Alumnus award, United Wesleyan Coll., 1976. Mem.: Wesleyan Theol. Soc. (Disting. Lifetime Svc. award 1996—), Conf. on Faith and History, Am. Soc. Ch. History. Independent. Wesleyan. Avocations: genealogy, gardening. Home: 400 Chinquapin Dr Lyndhurst VA 22952-2911 Office Phone: 540-949-6506.

DIETER, RAYMOND ANDREW, JR., physician, thoracic and vascular surgeon; b. Chebanse, Ill., June 19, 1934; s. Raymond Augustus Sr. and Emma Rose Mayme (Witt) D.; m. Bette René Myers, Sept. 29, 1961; children: Raymond III, David, Lisa, Lynn, Deanna, Robert. Student, U. Ill., 1952-56, Olivet Nazarene Coll., 1954; MA in Physiology, U. Ill., Chgo., 1966; BS in Chemistry, U. Ill., Champaign, 1994; MD, Loyola U., 1960. Diplomate Am. Bd. Thoracic Surgery, Am. Bd. Surgery. Intern Cook County Hosp., Chgo., 1960-61; resident in gen. surgery VA Hosp., Hines, Ill., 1963-67, sr. resident in cardiopulmonary surgery, 1967-69; practice specializing in thoracic, cardiovascular surg. Glen Ellyn (Ill.) Clinic, 1969—, pres., 1982-85, also bd. dirs.; mem. staff Hines (Ill.) VA Hosp., 1963-74, Cen. DuPage Hosp., Winfield, Ill., 1969—, pres. staff, 1987-89; mem. staff Loyola U. Med. Ctr., Maywood, Ill., 1969-80, Meml. Hosp. DuPage County, Elmhurst, Ill., 1969—, Delnor Hosp., St. Charles, Ill., 1970-79, Community Hosp., Geneva, Ill., 1970—, Alexian Bros. Med. Ctr., Elk Grove Village, Ill., 1975-79, 93—, Good Samaritan Hosp., Downers Grove, Ill., 1976—, pres. staff, 1979; mem. staff Glendale Heights (Ill.) and Glen Oaks Cmty. Hosp., 1980—, St. Mary's Hosp., Streator, Ill., 1997—. Clin. instr. Stritch Sch. Medicine Loyola U., 1966-71, clin. asst. prof., 1971-80; trustee Ctr. Bank, Glen Ellyn, 1978-90, Lake Shore Bank, Glen Ellyn Found.; internat. lectr. on med. topics; chmn. Glen Ellyn Clinic Facilities, 1987-98, Physicians Benefit trust, 1988-92; pres., chmn. bd. No. Ill. Surg. Ctr., 1989—; pres. DuPage Doctors, Inc., Ctr. for Surgery; bd. dirs., co-founder Cmty. Bank of Wheaton Glen Ellyn, 1993—, Cmty. Bank Wheaton-Glen Ellyn, 1998; co-founder, pres. Northeast DuPage Surgicenter, 1997—; chmn. bd. dirs., CEO, pres. Masterile, Inc., 1997-99; mem., chmn. negotiating com. Glen Ellyn Clinic, 1999. Author: (with B.R. Dieter and A.C. Mickelson) Mickelson and Peterson Family Sketch, 1970, (with M.C. Sorensen and E.R. Dieter) A Sorensen and Jensen Family Tree, 1975, (with B.R. Dieter, C. Myers, U. Myers, and D. Dieter) A Myers and Remley Family Tree, 1978, (with others) A Witt and (von) Ruehle Family Sketch, 1976, A Hofeling, Janssen, Lehnert, and Meier Family Sketch, 1979, A Dieter Family Tree: Sketches of German Families, 1981, Thoracoscopy for Surgeons, 1994; editor: Thoracoscopy for Surgeons-Diagnostic and Therapeutic, 1995; contbr. numerous articles to profl. jours. and chpts. in med. book. Mgr. Glen Ellyn baseball team, 1970, 71, 78-82; asst. leader 4-H Club, 1975-83; mem. Glenbard South High Sch. Boosters, World Fedn. Drs. Who Respect Human Life, 1980—; pres., bd. dirs. DuPage Med. Found.; mem. Econ. Devel. Coun. Glen Ellyn, sec., 2000, v.p., 2001-02, pres., 2003; bd. dirs. Farm Safety Just 4 Kids, 2004—. Served with USPHS, 1961-63, with Res., 1982—. Named Hon. Citizen, Quito Ecuador, La Paz, Bolivia; recipient Key to City of Manila, Philippines. Fellow ACS, Internat. Coll. Angiology (editl. bd. 1995—), Internat. Coll. Surgeons (exec. com. 1991—, treas. 1993-94, pres. elect 1995-96, pres. 1997-98, U.S. sect., corp. sec. 1997-2000, pres.-elect 2001-02, pres. 2003-2004, chmn. internat. surg. teams. program 2005—, World body); mem. AMA (Physician's Recognition awards, mem. ho. dels.), Internat. Mus. Surg. Sci. (chmn. bd. dirs. 1991—), Internat. Soc. Circumpolar Health, Internat. Soc. Outdoor Health, Global Acad. for Tropical Surgery (co-founder 2004), Am. Coll. Angiology, Am. Coll. Chest Physicians, Assn. Acad. Surgeons, Am. Soc. Circumpolar Health (charter), Assn. Mil. Surgeons, Assn. Res. Officers, Am. Heart Assn. (coun. 1974—), Soc. Med. Hist. Chgo., Soc. Critical Care Medicine, Soc. Thoracic Surgeons (membership com.), Ill. State Med. Soc. (trustee 1983-92, chmn. Ill. hosp. med. staff sect. 1985-87, pres., med. adminstrs. ctr. for surgery 1994—), Ill. Thoracic Surg. Soc. (sec. 1981-83, pres. 1984-85), DuPage County Med. Soc. (pres. 1977, mem. numerous coms.), Chgo. Med. Soc., Charles B. Puestow Surg. Soc. (sec., treas. 1966-67, v.p. 1968), Good Samaritan Soc., Ala. Geographic Soc., Kankakee Valley Geneal. Soc., Ill. Geneal. Soc., U. Ill. Alumni Assn.(bd. dirs.), Am. Rabbit Breeders Assn., Silver Marten Club, Century Club (Elmhurst), Chebanse Lions (charter), Resurrection Bay (Alaska) Lions. Republican. Roman Catholic. Avocations: alaska, large game animals, outdoor health, farming, fishing. Office: Glen Ellyn Clinic 454 Pennsylvania Ave Glen Ellyn IL 60137-4496 Office Fax: 630-545-7853. Personal E-mail: brdrad@aol.com.

DIETERT, RODNEY REYNOLDS, immunology and toxicology educator; b. Ft. Lee, Va., Dec. 6, 1951; s. Ralph O. and Beverly (Reynolds) D.; children: Grant C., Matthew W; m. Janice M. Dietert. BS, Duke U., 1974; PhD, U. Tex., 1977. Asst. prof. immunogenetics Cornell U., Ithaca, N.Y., 1977-83, assoc. prof., 1983-89, prof., 1989—, prof. immunotoxicology, 1997—; adj. prof. N.C. State U., 1992—; head grad. program in immunology Cornell U., Ithaca, N.Y., 1989-92, dir. Inst. for Comparative and Environ. Toxicology, 1992-97, prof. immunotoxicology, 1997—, dir. program on breast cancer and environ. risk factors, 2000—; sr. fellow Ctr. for the Environment, 1993-96. Cons. pesticide program EPA, Washington, 1984-86, Embrex, Inc., Research Triangle Park, N.C., 1991-95; panelist Nat. Inst. Environ. Health Scis. (AIDS Therapeutics), Research Triangle Park, 1988, mem. oxidative damage panel, 1997; USDA grant panel mgr., Washington, 1993-94; mem. Am. Inst. Biol. Scis.-Gulf War Illnesses panel Dept. Def., 1995, 97; invited testimony U.S. Congress Clean Water Act, 1995; spkr. at profl. confs. Jour. editor CRC Press, Inc., Boca Raton, Fla., 1986-90, editor book series, 1990—; editor jour. Elsevier Sci. Publs., Ltd., Oxford, U.K., 1990-95; contbr. to profl. publs. Bd. dirs. Wesley Found., Ithaca, 1979-84; chmn. Minority Edn. Com., Ithaca, 1980; chmn. Environ. Com. on Native Americans, Ithaca, 1994-95. Mem. Am. Assn. Immunologists, Soc. Toxicology. Office: Cornell U Dept Microbiology/Immunol Coll Vet Med C5-135 UMC Ithaca NY 14853-5601 Office Phone: 607-253-4015. Business E-Mail: rrd1@cornell.edu.

DIETHELM, ARNOLD GILLESPIE, surgeon; b. Balt., Jan. 13, 1932; s. Oskar Arnold and Grace (Gillespie) D.; m. Nancy Lee Lane, June 21, 1951; children: Nancy Elizabeth, Linda Lane, Eugene Arnold (dec.), Ellen Jeanette, Richard Gillespie. AB, Wash. State U., 1953; MD, Cornell U., 1958; DSc (hon.), U. Ala., 1993. Intern, then resident in surgery N.Y. Hosp., 1958-65; asst. in surgery, research fellow Peter Bent Brigham Hosp., Boston, 1965-66; research fellow surgery Harvard U. Med. Sch., 1966-67; instr. Cornell U. Med. Sch., 1964-65; mem. faculty U. Ala. Med. Center, Birmingham, 1967—, prof. surgery, 1973—, vice chmn. dept., 1973-82, chmn. dept. surgery, 1982-2000; prof. emertius dept. surgery Univ. Ala. Sch. Medicine. Mem. residency rev. com. for surgery Accreditation Coun. for Grad. Med. Edn., 1994—, chmn., 1997-99. Contbr. articles med. jours. Mem. AAAS, ACS., AMA, Am. Soc. Nephrology, Am. Soc. Transplant Surgeons (pres. 1991-92), Am. Surg. Assn., Am. Bd. Surgery (dir. 1987-93), Assn. Acad. Surgery, Transplantation Soc., So. Surg. Assn. (pres. 1989). Home: 3248 Sterling Rd Birmingham AL 35213-3508 Office: U Ala Hosp Dept Surgery 619 19th St S Birmingham AL 35233-0001

DIETLER, CORTLANDT S., oil company executive; b. Tulsa, Okla. Grad., U. Tulsa; degree (hon.), Hillsdale Coll. Founder, CEO Associated Natural Gas Corp.; chmn., CEO TransMontaigne Oil Co.; CEO TransMontaigne, Inc., Denver, 1995—99, chmn., 1995—, also chmn., compensation com. and mominating and corp. governance com. Dir. Hallador Petroleum Co., Cimarex Energy Co.; mem. Nat. Petroleum Council; dir. Am. Petroleum Inst.; former dir. Independent Petroleum Assn. of Am.; former pres. Rocky Mountain Oil & Gas Assn. Trustee Denver Art Museum, Denver Museum of Nature and Sci., Buffalo Bill Memorial Assn. Served in U.S. Army. Office: TransMontaigne Inc 1670 Broadway Ste 3100 Denver CO 80217-5660*

DIETMEYER, DONALD LEO, retired electrical engineering educator; b. Wausau, Wis., Nov. 20, 1932; s. Henry Joseph and Erna M. (Zastrow) D.; m. Carol White, Jan. 26, 1957; children: Karl Peter, Elizabeth Mary, Anne Katherine, Diana Lee. BSEE, U. Wis., Madison, 1954, MS, 1955, PhD, 1959. Mem. faculty U. Wis., Madison, 1958-63, 64-98, prof. elec. and computer engring., 1967-98, prof. emeritus, 1998—, assoc. dean Coll. Engring., 1983-95. Sr. engr. IBM Corp., Poughkeepsie, N.Y., 1964 Author: Logic Design of Digital Systems, 1978, 3rd rev. edit., 1988, Conlan Report, 1983. With AUS, 1957. Recipient Western Electric Fund award, 1972 Fellow IEEE; mem. Computer Soc., Assn. Computing Machinery, Sigma Xi. Home: 2211 Waunona Way Madison WI 53713-1619 Office: 1415 Engineering Dr Madison WI 53706-1607 Personal E-mail: dld@engr.wisc.edu.

DIETRICH, BRUCE LEINBACH, museum administrator, astronomer, educator; b. Reading, Pa., Oct. 10, 1937; s. Harold Richard and Emily Jeannette (Leinbach) D.; m. Renee Carol Long, Nov. 25, 1959; children: Dodson Bruce, Katie Ellen. BS, Kutztown U., 1960; MS, SUNY, Oswego, 1969. Tchr. Reading Pub. Schs., 1960-67; curator space sci. Reading Mus., 1967-69, dir. planetarium, 1969-92, dir., 1976-92, dir. emeritus, 1992—; instr. astronomy Reading Area C.C., 1972-75, asst. prof., 1975-82, prof., 1982—. Contbr. articles to profl. jours. Trustee Berks County Hist. Soc., 1994—, pres., 1996-98; sec. Interactive Video Sci. Consortium; sec. Reading Musical Found., 1980-88, trustee, 1989-98, hon. trustee, 1998—. Named Kellogg Mus. Profl., 1987; NSF grantee, 1965-67. Fellow: Internat. Planetarium Soc.; mem.: SAR, AAAS, Pa. Soc., Am. Assn. Mus., Mid-Atlantic Planetarium Soc., Can. Assn. Planetariums, Torch Club (Reading, pres. 1987). Home and Office: 1546 Dauphin Ave Reading PA 19610-2118

DIETRICH, DANIEL KEITH, music educator; b. Pekil, Ill., Mar. 24, 1955; s. Donald Earl and Ruth Eileen Dietrich; m. Christine Vandre, July 24, 1993; children: Abigail, Alex. B in Music Edn., Ill. State U., 1977, M in Music Edn., 1985. Cert. profl. tchr. Ill. Dir. bands Bement (Ill.) Sch., 1977—80, Ill. Valley Ctrl. H.S., Chillicothe, 1980—. Recipient Friends of Youth award, Optimists Club, Chillicothe, 2003. Mem.: Ill. Music Educators Assn., Music Educators Nat. Conf., Internat. Assn. Jazz Educators, Ill. Music Educators (equipment mgr. 1990—), Ill. H.S. Assn. (asst. to dir. 1977—2004), Phi Beta Ma. Avocation: woodworking. Home: 1516 Beech St Peoria IL 61615 Office: Ill Valley Ctrl High Sch 1300 W Sycamore St Chillicothe IL 61523

DIETRICH, DEAN FORBES, academic administrator; b. Davenport, Iowa, Jan. 10, 1966; s. Dean Willis and Carolyn (Brandhorst) Dietrich. AB summa cum laude, Dartmouth Coll., 1988; MA, U. Va., 1990, PhD, 1997. Viewer info., edn. svcs. asst. C-SPAN, Washington, 1988, 89; grad. instr. U. Va., Charlottesville, 1990-97, computer, video cons. Law Sch., 1995-97; vis. asst. prof. English Hanover (Ind.) Coll., 1998-99; sr. rsch. advancement SUNY, Stony Brook, 2000—03; prospect rsch. mgr. U. Nev., Reno, 2003—. Gov.'s fellow U. Va., 1990-91, 92-93. Mem. MLA, Assn. Profl. Rschrs. Advancement, Coun. Advancement and Support Edn., Greater N.Y. Assn. Profl. Rschrs. Advancement (sec. 2002-03), Phi Beta Kappa. Office: U Nev Devel & Alumni Rels Mail Stop 007 Reno NV 89557

DIETRICH, JOSEPH EDWARD, III, lawyer; b. Buffalo; s. Joseph Edward and Kathleen Nora Dietrich; m. Colleen Patricia Dietrich, Dec. 21, 1997; children: Grace Marie, Liesl Monica, Joseph Edward III. BBA, Temple Univ., Phila., 1991; JD, State Univ. N.Y., Buffalo, 1995. Bar: N.Y., 1996, U.S. Dist. Ct. (we. dist.) N.Y., 1997. Asst. dist. atty. Erie County Dist. Atty., Buffalo, 1996—98; first asst. dist. atty. Cattaraugus County Dist. Atty., Little Valley, NY, 1998—99; ptnr. Cellino and Barnes, P.C., Buffalo, 1999—. Legal counsel Dietrich Funeral Homes, Inc., Amherst, NY, 1996—. Mem.: ATLA, Bar Assn. Erie County. Avocations: skiing, water-skiing, windsurfing, telemark skiing. Home: 120 Wood Acres Dr East Amherst NY 14051 Office: Cellino and Barnes PC 17 Court St 7th Flr Buffalo NY 14202 Office Phone: 716-854-2020.

DIETRICH, JOSEPH JACOB, retired chemist, research executive; b. Bismark, N.D., Oct. 31, 1932; s. Jacob Peter and Elizabeth (Janzer) D.; m. Florence Kolodziejczak, June 27, 1959; children: Ann Marie, Michael, John, James. BA in Chemistry, St. John's U., Collegeville, Minn., 1953; PhD in Organic Chemistry, Iowa State U., 1957. Rsch. chemist PPG, Inc., Barberton, Ohio, 1957-59, Spencer Chem. Co., Kansas City, Kans., 1960-64; with Diamond-Shamrock Corp., Cleve., 1964-82, dir. rsch., 1973-78, dir. tech. devel., 1978-82; dir. tech. Eltech Systems Corp., Painesville, Ohio, 1982-85, dir. tech. and comml. devel./ Europe, Chardon, Ohio, 1986-90; pres. Eltech Internat. Corp., 1990-94, Elgard Corp., 1994; ret., 1994. Contbr. articles to profl. jours; patentee in field. Mem. Am. Chem. Soc., Soc. Plastic Engrs., Serra Club. Republican. Roman Catholic. Home: 6958 Pennywhistle Cir Painesville OH 44077-2141

DIETRICH, MELINDA, art director, curator; b. Bklyn., July 2, 1943; d. Charles Porter and Ethel Dietrich; children: Charles, Daniel, Vinton. Cert., Parsons Sch. Design, 1964; BFA, U. Hartford, 1968; MBA, Boston Coll., 1986. Art and graphics asst. J.B.W. Graphics, N.Y.C., 1968—69; art dir. Chiquita Brands Inc., Boston, 1970-75; designer James Perry Contractor, Lexington, Mass., 1977-83; cons. Small Bus. Devel. Ctr., Boston, 1986-87; co-founder, designer John Vinton Arch., Lexington, 1988-91; exec. dir. Arts Lexington, 1992-94, Munroe Ctr. Arts, Lexington, 1994—; founder Munroe Gallery, 2001; curator Spiritual Mosaic exhbn., 2002, Journey of the Spirit, R. True Exhibit, 2003. Request for Proposal cons. Lexington Friends Arts, 1994; prof. devel. Mass. Cultural Coun., Lexington, 1993. Exhibited in numerous exhbns., 1960—, including Journey of the Spirit, 2003. Pub. rels. advisor Lexington Pub. Schs., 1988-91, elected Lexington Town Mtg. mem., 1988-2000; steward Lexington Conservation Com., 1996-99. Recipient numerous awards and grants. Mem. Lexington C. of C., Art Ctrs. Consortium, Appalachian Mountain Club. Avocations: writing, poetry, bookmaking, gardening, painting. Office: Munroe Ctr Arts 1403 Mass Ave Lexington MA 02420-3804 E-mail: mcelticd@hotmail.com, munroe@ziplink.net.

DIETRICH, RICHARD VINCENT, geologist, educator; b. LaFargeville, N.Y., Feb. 7, 1924; s. Roy Eugene and Mida Amy (Vincent) D.; m. Frances Elizabeth Smith, Dec. 28, 1946; children: Richard Smith, Kurt Robert, Krista Gayle Brown. AB, Colgate U., 1947; MS, Yale U., 1950, PhD, 1951. Geologist Iowa Geol. Survey, 1947, N.Y. State Sci. Service, summers 1949-50; asst. prof. geology Va. Poly. Inst., Blacksburg, 1951, assoc. prof., 1952-56, prof., 1956-69, mineral technologist Va. Engrng. Exp. Sta., 1951-58; Fulbright rsch. prof. Oslo U., Norway, 1959-60; asso. dean arts and scis. Va. Poly. Inst., 1966-69, dean, 1969; prof. geology Central Mich. U., Mt. Pleasant, 1969-86, prof. emeritus, 1986—, dean arts and scis., 1969-75. Dir. Econ. Geol. Pub. Co., 1966-72. Author or co-author over 20 sci. books and textbooks in field (transl. into German, Malaysian, Russian, and Japanese); also poems, haiku, essays, cartoons; editor Mineral Industries Jour., 1953-61; mng. editor Bull. Econ. Geology, 1966-73; exec. editor Rocks and Minerals, 1980-88, petrology adv. editor, 1988—; mem. editl. bd. Mineral Record, 1969-74; contbr. over 300 articles to profl. jours.; composer, performer music. Organizer N. Am. for Mineral. Abstracts, 1976-80. Served with U.S. Air Corps, 1943-46. Recipient Acad. Citation Mich. Acad. Sci., Arts and Letters, 1978, Children's Sci. Book award N.Y. Acad. Scis., 1981; Fulbright rsch. prof. U. Oslo, 1958-59; Pres.'s scholar, 1941-42, Austin Colgate scholar Colgate U., 1943, Newton Lloyd Andrews scholar, 1943, Colgate U. scholar, 1946; Edward S. Binney fellow, 1948-49, James Dwight Dana fellow Yale U., 1950-51. Fellow Am. Mineral. Soc. (assoc. life), Soc. Econ. Geol. (sr.); mem. Norsk Geologisk Forening (life), Geol. Soc. Finland (life), Am. Geol. Inst. (gov. 1972-74), Assn. Earth Sci. Editors (pres. 1972-73), Phi Beta Kappa, Sigma Xi, Phi Kappa Phi, Sigma Gamma Epsilon. Presbyterian. Home: 1323 Center Dr Mount Pleasant MI 48858-4103 Business E-Mail: dietr1rv@cmich.edu. *My parents were supportive although they had hoped for a different direction. Education, the work ethic, and retention of individualism and imagination were promoted.*

DIETRICH, ROBERT ANTHONY, pathologist, consultant, medical association administrator; b. Buffalo, May 24, 1933; s. Charles Thomas and Mary Evelyn (Shoecraft) D.; m. Alison Elinor D'Arcy, June 13, 1959; children—Anne Marie, Alison D'Arcy, Karen Elizabeth, Kathleen Murray, Patricia Evelyn, Ellen Kiley BS, Canisius Coll., Buffalo, 1955; MD, Georgetown U., Washington, 1959; MS in Surg. Pathology, U. Minn., Mpls., 1964; JD, George Washington U., Washington, 1974. Diplomate Am. Bd. Pathology, Am. Bd. Nuclear Medicine. Intern D.C. Gen. Hosp., Washington, 1959-60; resident Mayo Clinic, Rochester, Minn., 1960-64; chief pathology svc. U.S. Army Hosp., Fort Gordon, Augusta, Ga., 1964-66; pathologist O.B. Hunter Meml. Lab., Washington, 1966-78; chmn. dept. pathology, chief div. nuclear medicine Montgomery Gen. Hosp., Olney, Md., 1972-78; vice chmn. dept. pathology, chief divsn. nuclear medicine Sibley Meml. Hosp., Washington, 1978-89; sec. Am. Soc. Clin. Pathologists, Chgo., 1981-88, exec. v.p./chief staff, 1982-92; cons., 1992—. Served to capt. U.S. Army, 1964-66. Noble Found. grantee Mayo Clinic, 1964 Fellow Am. Coll. Legal Medicine, Coll. Am. Path., Am. Soc. Clin. Path.; mem. Med. Soc. D.C. (sec. 1984-86, pres. 1988). Home and Office: 5506 Parkston Rd Bethesda MD 20816-3326

DIETRICH, WILLIAM ALAN, reporter, writer; b. Tacoma, Sept. 29, 1951; s. William Richard and Janice Lenore (Pooler) D.; m. Holly Susan Roberts, Dec. 19, 1970; children: Lisa, Heidi. BA, Western Wash. U., 1973. Reporter Bellingham (Wash.) Herald, 1973-76, Gannett News Svc., Washington, 1976-78, Vancouver (Wash.) Columbian, 1978-82, Seattle Times, 1982-97; freelance writer, 1998—. Author: The Final Forest, 1992, Northwest Passage, 1995, Ice Reich, 1998, Getting Back, 2000, Dark Winter, 2001, Natural Grace, 2003, Hadrian's Wall, 2004, The Scourge of God, 2005. Recipient Paul Tobenkin award Columbia U., 1986, Pulitzer prize for nat. reporting, 1990; Nieman fellow Harvard U., 1987-88.

DIETRICH, WILLIAM GALE, lawyer, real estate developer, consultant; b. Kansas City, Mo., Mar. 6, 1925; s. Roy Kaiser and Gale (Gossett) D.; m. Marjorie Nell Reich, July 14, 1945; children: Meredith G. Dietrich Steinhaus, Ann. E. Dietrich Cooling, Walter R. AB with high honors, Yale U., 1948, LLB, 1951. Bar: Mo. 1951. Ptnr. Dietrich, Davis, Dicus, Rowlands, Schmitt & Gorman (and predecessors), 1953-73; project dir., gen. counsel Blue Ridge Shopping Ctr., Inc., Kansas City, 1955-73, pres., gen. mgr., 1964-73, Blue Ridge Tower, Inc., Kansas City, 1967-73; sec.-treas. A. Reich & Sons, Inc., Kansas City, 1973-88, chmn., 1988—; pvt. practice law Kansas City, 1973—; sec., treas. A. Reich & Sons Gardens, Inc., 1973-89; pres. J&D Devel., Inc., 1987—; gen. ptnr. J & D Enterprises, 1986—; gen. mgr. The Farm Shopping and Office Ctr., 1994-98; pres. BBJ Treats, L.L.C., 1994-98; mem. WGD Properties, LLC, 1999—. Sec., bd. dirs. Rsch. Med. Ctr., Kansas City, 1977, vice-chmn., 1980-83, chmn., 1983-87; bd. dirs. The Rsch. Found., 1980-91, vice-chmn., 1989-91; bd. dirs. Rsch. Health Svcs., 1980-81, vice chmn., 1983-87, chmn. 1987-89; bd. dirs. Mahana Condominium Assn., Maui, Hawaii, 1977-96, Blue Ridge Bank and Trust Co., Kansas City, 1982-94; vestry mem. Grace & Holy Trinity Cathedral, Kansas City, 1972-95, former treas. 1st lt. AUS, 1943-46, PTO. Recipient Army Commendation Ribbon, 1946. Mem. ABA, Mo. Bar Assn., Kansas City Bar Assn., Blue Ridge Mall Mchts. Assn. (dir. 1958-73), Internat. Coun. Shopping Ctrs. (past dir. for Mo., Kans, Iowa, cert. shopping ctr. mgr.), Lawyers Assn. Kansas City, Mission Hills Country Club, Yale Club, Kansas City (Mo.) Club, Rotary (bd. dirs., sec. found. Kansas City 1978—), Phi Beta Kappa (pres. Kansas City chpt. 1989-91), Phi Delta Phi. Home: 1000 Huntington Rd Kansas City MO 64113-1346 Office: 6155 Oak St Profl Bldg Ste A Kansas City MO 64113-2266 Office Phone: 816-822-2600. E-mail: wgdlo@sbcglobal.net.

DIETZ, ARTHUR TOWNSEND, investment counseling company executive; b. Mt. Vernon, N.Y., Oct. 30, 1923; s. William Arthur and Adele Townsend (Dods) D.; m. Mary Archer, June 29, 1947 (dec. 1980); children; Adele Archer Dietz, Laura Townsend Burke, Amelia Edmunds Williams; m. Mary Laura Peavy, Sept. 16, 1982 (dec. 1992); m. Margie Nell Lee Baghose, Oct. 4, 1992. AB, Wesleyan U., Middletown, Conn., 1946; MA, Princeton U., 1948, PhD, 1953. Instr. Princeton U., 1948-49; asst. prof. Wesleyan U., 1949-54; Mills Bee Lane prof. fin. and banking, dir. MBA program Emory U., Atlanta, 1954—88; dir. Alpha Fund, Atlanta, 1972-85, Enterprise Funds, Atlanta, 1985—, Enterprise Accumulation Trust, 1995—, Car Trax Security Systems, 2000—. Pres. ATD Adv. Corp., 1996-2003, Strategic Portfolio Mgmt., 1988-95; trustee Emory U. Resolution in Honor, 1983, Amherst Coll., 1953-54; vis. prof. Internat. Inst. Mgmt. Devel., 1965-66; Robert Morris prof., Va., 1984-85. Author books; mem. editl. bd. Jour. of Mktg., 1950, Jour. of Pub. Law, 1950; contbr. articles to profl. jours. Pres. Fernbank PTA, DeKalb County, Ga., 1959-60; mem. DeKalb County Inflation com., 1974, DeKalb County Devel. Authority, 1980-84; Retirement Facility for Elderly Authority, DeKalb County, 1982-84. Sgt. AUS, 1942-45, ETO. Named one of Outstanding Educators of Am., 1972; recipient Emory Williams Disting. Tchg. award Emory U., 1983, Disting. Achievement award Emory Bus. Alumni Assn., 1985; Woodrow Wilson fellow, 1946. Fellow Fin. Analysts Soc.; mem. Phi Beta Kappa (pres. Gamma chpt. 1964-65). Methodist. Avocations: tennis, bridge. Personal E-mail: arthurdietz_17@msn.com.

DIETZ, JANIS CAMILLE, business educator; b. Washington, May 26, 1950; d. Albert and Joan Mildred (MacMullen) Weinstein; m. John William Dietz, Apr. 10, 1981. BA, U. R.I., 1971; MBA, Calif. Poly. U., Pomona, 1984; PhD, Claremont Gard. Sch., 1997. Customer svc. trainer People's Bank, Providence, 1974-76; salesman, food broker Bradshaw Co., L.A., 1976-78; salesman Johnson & Johnson, L.A., 1978-79, GE Co., L.A., 1979-82; regional sales mgr. Leviton Co., L.A., 1982-85; nat. sales mgr. Jensen Gen. divsn. Nortek Co., L.A., 1985-86; retail sales mgr. Norris divsn. Masco, L.A., 1986-88; nat. sales mgr. Thermador Waste King divsn. Masco, L.A., 1988-91; nat. accounts mgr. Universal Flooring divsn. Masco, 1991-92; western regl. mgr. Peerless Faucet divsn. Masco, 1992-95; performance devel. cons. Delta Faucet divsn. Masco, 1995—. Assoc. prof. bus. adminstrn. U. LaVerne, 1995-2002, prof., 2002—; sales trainer, Upland, Calif., 1985—; instr. Calif. Poly. U., 1988-91; lectr. Whittier Coll., 1994. Dir. pub. rels. Jr. Achievement, Providence, 1975-76; trustee Soc. Calif. chpt. Nat. Multiple Sclerosis Soc. Recipient Sector Svc. award GE Co., Fairfield, Conn., 1980, Outstanding Achievement award, 1980. Mem. NAFE, Sales Profls. L.A. (v.p. 1984-86), Toastmasters (adminstrv. v.p. 1985). Unitarian Universalist. Office Phone: 909-593-3511 ext. 4213. E-mail: dietzj@ulv.edu.

DIETZ, JOHN RAPHAEL, engineering executive, consultant; b. Carbondale, Pa., Jan. 31, 1912; s. John A. and Bridget (Barrett) D.; m. Elizabeth Harding Bezilla, Mar. 15, 1983; children by previous marriage: Robert J., Elizabeth Dietz Brown. BS in Civil Engrng., Drexel U., Phila., 1934. Registered profl. engr., Pa. Contract estimator J.A. Dietz Co., 1934-35; designer Pa. Dept. Hwys., 1935-38; designer, resident engr. Pa. Turnpike Commn., 1938-40; san. engr. for J.E. Greiner Co., Camp Meade, Md., 1940; designer Caribbean Architect-Engrs., 1941-42; chief designer for Gannett Eastman & Fleming, Inc., Andrews Air Field, Washington, 1942-43; civilian with U.S. Engr. Corps on study Potomac River Basin flood control, 1943-44; with Gannett Fleming Corddry and Carpenter, Inc., cons. engrs., 1942—, dir. hwy. div., then pres. Harrisburg, Pa., 1950-76, chmn. bd., 1970-83, chmn. emeritus, 1983—. Dir. CCNB Bank (N.A.) Trustee Drexel U. Bd.; dirs. Holy Spirit Hosp., Camp Hill, Pa., 1965—, pres., 1983; bd. dirs. Villa Teresa Nursing Home, Harrisburg, Pa., 1973—, pres., 1973-75. Recipient A.J. Drexel Paul award Drexel U., 1973; named Knight of St. Gregory, Pope John Paul II, 1983; selected in 100 Most Outstanding Men Drexel U. Alumni, 1992. Life fellow ASCE (past pres. Central Pa. chpt.); mem. Am. Council Cons. Engrs., Nat. Soc. Profl. Engrs., Am. Road and Transp. Builders Assn. (past dir.), Pa. Hwy. Info. Assn. (past pres.), Pa. Soc. Profl. Engrs. (Profl. Engrs. Disting. Service award Harrisburg chpt. 1965) Roman Catholic. Home: PO Box 485 Camp Hill PA 17001-0485 Office: PO Box 67100 Harrisburg PA 17106-7100

DIETZ, WILLIAM HARRY, pediatrician; b. Phila., Oct. 6, 1944; s. William H. and Margaret (Shoemaker) Dietz; m. Nancy Fenn, May 6, 1966. BA, Wesleyan U., 1966; MD, U. Pa., 1970; PhD, MIT, 1981. Diplomate Am. Bd. Pediatrics. Intern Children's Hosp. Phila., 1970-71; resident Upstate Med. Ctr., Syracuse, NY, 1974-76; rsch. assoc. NIH, 1971-74, MIT, Cambridge, 1976-81; assoc. prof. Tufts U. Sch. Medicine, Boston, 1986-96, prof., 1996-98; dir. clin. nutrition New England Med. Ctr., Boston, 1983-97. Adj. prof. Tufts U. Sch. Medicine, Boston, 1998—. Fellow: Am. Acad. Pediat. (chmn. task force on children and TV, Elk Grove Village, Ill. 1984—87); mem.: Nat. Acad. Scis., Inst. Medicine, Am. Dietetic Assn. (hon.), N.Am. Assn. Study Obesity (pres. 1993—94), Am. Soc. Clin. Nutrition (v.p. 1998—99, pres. 1999—2000, counselor). Office: CDC Divsn Nutrition/Phys Act 4770 Buford Hwy NE # MS-K24 Atlanta GA 30341-3717 Office Phone: 770-488-6042. Business E-Mail: wcd4@cdc.gov.

DIETZ, WILLIAM RONALD, corporate management consultant; b. Seattle, Nov. 25, 1942; s. William Phillip and Helen Mae (Wilson) D.; 1 child, David Phillip. BA, U. Wash., 1964; MBA, Stanford U., 1968. Fin. cons. 1st Nat. City Bank, NYC, 1968-70; v.p., mgr. Citicorp Subs. Mgmt. Office, Citicorp, NYC, 1971-74; chmn. Citicorp Factors, Inc., NYC, 1974-75; v.p., mgr. N.Y., N.J. and Conn. comml. banking Citibank N.A., NYC, 1976-78, sr. v.p., gen. mgr. Eastern region corp. banking, 1978-81, sr. v.p., head Caribbean Basin div., 1982-84; pres. Charter Assocs. Ltd., 1985-89; chmn. and chief exec. officer CorEast Savs. Bank, Richmond, Va., 1989-91; pres., CEO Am. Savs. Bank, White Plains, NY, 1991-92, Mo. Bridge Bank, Kansas City, 1992-93, Anthem Fin., Inc., Indpls., 1993-96; ptnr. Concord Ptnrs., 1997—2003; mng. ptnr. Customer Contact solutions, LLC, 1999—; pres. W.M. Putnam Co., 2001—. Bd. dirs. Capital One Fin. Corp., Stratis Corp., Baker Hill, W.M. Putnam Co.; mem. policy com. Bank Mgmt. Inst., SUNY-Buffalo. Contbg. author: Customer-Focused Marketing of Financial Services. Trustee Children's Mus. of Indpls.; bd. advisors Ind. U./Purdue U., Indpls.; bd. trustees Indpls.-Marion County Pub. Libr. Found. Lt. USNR, 1964-66. Mem. Woodstock Country Club, Delta Tau Delta. Office: WM Putnam Co 1625 Commerce Pky Bloomington IL 61704 Personal E-mail: contactsolutions@earthlink.net. Business E-Mail: rdietz@wmputnam.com.

DIETZE, GOTTFRIED, political science professor; b. Kemberg, Germany, Nov. 11, 1922; came to U.S., 1949; s. Paul and Susanne (Pechstein) D. Dr.Jur., U. Heidelberg, Germany, 1949; PhD, Princeton U., 1952; SJD, U. Va., 1961. Instr. polit. sci. Dickinson Coll., 1952-54; mem. faculty Johns Hopkins U., Balt., 1954—, prof. polit. sci., 1962—. Vis. prof. U. Heidelberg, 1956, 58-60, Brookings Instn., 1960-61, 67. Author: Ueber Formulierung der Menschenrechte, 1956, The Federalist, 1960, In Defense of Property, 1963, Magna Carta and Property, 1965, America's Political Dilemma, 1968, Youth, University and Democracy, 1970, Bedeutungswandel der Menschenrechte, 1971, Academic Truths and Frauds, 1972, Two Concepts of the Rule of Law, 1973, Deutschland-Wo Bist Du?, 1980, Kant und der Rechtsstaat, 1981, Kandidaten, 1982, El Gobierno Constitucional, 1983, Liberalism Proper and Proper Liberalism, 1984, Reiner Liberalismus, 1985, Konservativer Liberalismus in Amerika, 1987, Liberaler Kommentar zur Amerikanischen Verfassung, 1988, Amerikanische Demokratie, 1988, Politik-Wissenschaft, 1989, Der Hitler-Komplex, 1990, Liberale Demokratie, 1992, American Democracy, 1993, Problematik der Menschenrechte, 1995, Briefe aus Amerika, 1995, Begriff des Rechts, 1997, Deutschland, 1999, 1999, Deutschland: besser und schöner, 2001, Amerikas Schuldgefuehl, 2005; editor: Essays on the American Constitution, 1964. Mem.: Acad. Human Rights, Phi Beta Kappa. Lutheran. Office: Johns Hopkins U Dept Polit Sci Baltimore MD 21218

DIETZE, JOACHIM, librarian; b. Dresden, Germany, Oct. 16, 1931; s. Richard and Meta (Reh) D. Diploma, U. Leipzig, Fed. Republic Germany, 1954, PhD, 1964, Dr. phil.habil., 1971. Cert. Slavistic diplomate, sci. libr. Jr. libr. Univ. Libr., Leipzig, 1954-55, German State Libr., Berlin, 1955-56; libr. Regional Libr. of Thuringia, Weimar, Fed. Republic Germany, 1956-59, Univ. Libr., Leipzig, 1959-65; chief libr. Univ. and State Libr. of Sachsen-Anhalt, Halle, 1965-96. Author: August Schleicher als Slawist, 1966, Die Sprache der 1. Novgoroder Chronik, 1975, Naukowa informacja i dokumentacja, 1977, Frequenzwörterbuch zur Synodalhandschrift der 1. Novgoroder Chronik, 1977, Frequenzwörterbuch zur jüngeren Redaktion der 1. Novgoroder Chronik, 1984, Frequenzwörterbuch zur 4. Novgoroder Chronik, 1984, Einführung in die Informationslinguistik, 1989, Texterschließung, 1994, Frequenzwörterbuch der russischen Schriftsprache des 18 Jh., 1997, B. Travens Wortschatz, 1998, Der Wortschatz Karl Mays, 1999; editor, translator: Die 1. Novgoroder Chronik (Synodalhandschrift), 1971. Avocation: sailing. E-mail: prof.dietze@12move.de.

DI FALCO, GERARD A., artist; b. Camden, N.J., Sept. 26, 1952; s. Horace Giovanni Robilotta-Di Falco and Marie Ann Mazur-Di Falco. BA in Visual Art, Rutgers U., 1974; MS in Arts Adminstrn., Drexel U., Phila., 1985. Teaching Certificate in Art Dept. of Edn., N.J., 1977. Visual artist DiFALCO Studios, Phila., 1978—; visual artist: juried into group Nexus Gallery/Found. for Today's Art, Phila., 1984—98; mus. curator The Port of History Mus., Phila., 1988—90; visual artist: juried into group Creative Artists Network, Phila., 1994—96; resident artist art futures project Phila. Mus. of Art, 2002—03. Ind. curator, 1973—; curator, chair, group and exch. show com. Nexus Gallery/Found. for Today's Art, Phila., 1984—90. One-man shows include The Midas Touch, The Spanish Paintings, Phila., The Madrid Paintings, Phila., The Spanish Paintings, Societal Genres, Art Golf Installation, Paintings and Installations by Di Falco, Paintings: A Thirteen Year Retrospective, U. of Pa., The Strega Dance, Davinci Art Alliance, Phila., Installation Called Relics, 2000—, exhibited in group shows at DiFalco, Reese-Horvitz & Wheeling, Phila., CAN Artists In Soho, Majority Rules, Scotland, Creative Artists Network Gallery, exhibited in group shows, Borowsky Gallery, Phila., exhibited in group shows, Across USA and Madrid, exhibited in group shows, State Mus. Harrisburg, Pa., 2004, Del. Ctr. Contemporary Art, Wilmington, 2004, Phila. City Hall, 2004, BoxHeart Gallery, Pitts., 2005 (Best of Show award), show of furniture, 10 Couturier, LA. Donating artist for ann. auction MANNA Met. AIDS Neighborhood Nutrition Alliance, Phila., 1994—2003; mem. Del. Valley Pagan Network, Phila., 2002—03, Clements Episc. Ch., Phila., 2004—; bd. mem. World AIDS Day/Day With(out) Art Com., Phila., 1995—2003. Grantee Individual Artist's Grant, Pa. Coun. on the Arts, 1992, Fellowship Grant, The Pollock-Krasner Found., Inc., N.Y.C., 2002; scholar Grad. Assistantship in Arts Adminstrn., Drexel U., 1984—85. Mem.: DaVinci Art Alliance. Independent. Avocations: researching folklore, herbology, paranormal investigation, reading art history/literature, lecturing/workshop presentation. Home: 2201 Cherry St #902 Philadelphia PA 19103 Office Phone: 215-640-0765. Personal E-mail: phillysbestartist@yahoo.com. E-mail: gerarddifalco@msn.com.

DIFALCO, JOHN PATRICK, lawyer, arbitrator; b. Steubenville, Ohio, Nov. 24, 1943; s. Pat John and Antoinette (Ricci) DiF.; m. Carolyn L. Otten, June 11, 1977; children: Elizabeth Ann, Jennifer Ann, Kevin John. BA, Ohio State U.; MA, U. No. Colo.; JD, Ohio State U. Bar: Ohio 1968, Colo. 1972, U.S. Dist. Colo. 1972, U.S. Ct. Appeals Colo. 1972, U.S. Supreme Ct. 1972, U.S. Ct. Appeals (fed. cir.) 1986, D.C. 1989. Atty., hearing officer, dir. U.S. Postal Svc., Washington, 1970-77; labor rels. specialist City and County of Denver, 1977-80; city atty. City of Greeley, Colo., 1980-87; pvt. practice Greeley, 1987—; prin. John P. DiFalco & Assocs., P.C., Ft. Collins, Colo., 1987—. Instr. Regis U., Denver, U. Phoenix, Denver, Aims Community Coll., Greeley, Arapahoe Community Coll., Littleton, Colo., Pikes Peak Community Coll., Colo. Springs, Tri-State Coll., Angola, Ind.; arbitrator, 1980—; speaker in field. Contbr. Postmaster Advocate mag., also articles to profl. jours. Named an Outstanding City Atty. Colo., 1986. Mem. ABA (com. on pub. employee bargaining), Colo. Bar Assn. (labor law sect., Spl. Achievement award 1987), Fed. Bar Assn. (coms. on pub. sector labor rels., arbitration and office mgmt.), Colo. Trial Lawyers Assn., Indsl. Rels. Rsch. Assn., Nat. Pub. Employer Labor Rels. Assn., Nat. Acad. Arbitrators, Am. Arbitration Assn., Nat. Inst. Mcpl. Law Officers (com. on law office mgmt.), Larimer County Bar Assn., Colo. Mcpl. League (chmn. attys. sect., mcpl. govt. issues and open meeting coms.), Met. Denver City Attys. Assn. (pres.), Ohio State U. Pres.'s Club, Rotary. Republican. Roman Catholic. Avocations: reading, sports, model railroading, historical studies. Office: 5821 Langley Ave Ste 101 Loveland CO 80538-8828 Office Phone: 970-667-3424. Business E-Mail: difalco@difalcolaw.com.

DIFEO, SAMUEL X., automotive executive; Exec. v.p. DiFeo Group United Auto Group, Inc., Detroit, 1992-98, pres., COO DiFeo Group, 1998—. Mailing: United Auto Group Inc 2555 S Telegraph Rd Bloomfield Hills MI 48302-0954

DIFFIE, WHITFIELD (WHIT), computer and communications engineer; b. June 5, 1944; m. Mary L. Fischer. BS in Math., MIT, 1965; postgrad. in elec. engrng., Stanford U., 1975-78; D in Tech. Scis. honoris causa, Swiss Fed. Inst. Tech., Zurich, 1992. Rsch. asst. The Mitre Corp., Bedford, Mass., 1965-69; rsch. programmer artificial intellingence lab. Stanford U., Palo Alto, Calif., 1969-73, rsch. asst., 1975-78, rsch. programmer, 1975; self-supported researcher in cryptography, 1973-74; mgr. secure syss. rsch. No. Telecom, Mountain View, Calif., 1978-91; disting. engr., adv. computer and comm. security Sun Microsystems, Palo Alto, Calif., 1991—, v.p., Sun fellow and chief security officer. Organizer conf. Crypto '81, '83; mem. program com. Crypto 89; mem. program com. Status and Prospects of Rsch. in Cryptography '93, First ACM Conf. on Comms. and Computer Security, 1993; mem. adv. bd. Electronic Privacy Info. Ctr.; presenter in field. Author (with Susan Landau) Privacy on the Line (Donald McGannon award for Social and Ethical Relevance in Comm. Policy Rsch. and the IEEE-USA award for Disting. Literary Contbn. Furthering Public Understanding of the Profession); Contbr. numerous articles to scientific jours.; featured in Sci.Am., Sci., Time, Omni, Newsweek, NY Times mag., others. G.C. Steward fellow Gonville and Caius Coll., 1996; recipient award for Disting. Contbn. to Consumer Protection Calif. State Psychol. Assn., 1978, Nat. Computer Sys. Security award Nat. Inst. Stds. and Tech. and Nat. Security Agy., 1996, Louis E. Levy medal Franklin Inst., 1997, First Paris Kanellakis award ACM, 1997, Fellow Marconi Found, 2000, Chairman's award for Innovation and Fellow Internat. Assn. for Cryptologic Rsch. 2004. Mem. IEEE (Info. Theory Soc. Paper award 1979, Donald G. Fink award 1981, conf. organizer 1983). Achievements include discovery of the concept of public key cryptography, 1975; devel. of Mathlab symbolic manipulation sys., of Lisp 1.6 sys.; rsch. on interactive debugging and extensible compiling, proof of correctness of programs, proof checking and extensible compilers, on cryptography and its applications; patents (with Martin E. Hellman and Ralph Merkle) for cryptographic apparatus and method, 1980, (with Ashar Aziz) on security of mobile comm., 1993. Office: Sun Microsystems MAK 15-214 901 San Antonio Rd Palo Alto CA 94303-4900

DIFORIO, ROBERT GEORGE, literary agent; b. Mamaroneck, NY, Mar. 19, 1940; s. Richard John and Mildred (Kuntz) Diforio; m. Birgit Rasmussen; children: Stephen Christopher, Danielle Alexandra. BA, Williams Coll., 1964; AMP, Harvard U., 1978. From book sales rep. to v.p. book Kable News Co., 1964—72; with New Am. Libr./E.P. Dutton, NYC, 1972—80, exec. v.p., 1980—81, chmn., CEO, 1983—89; sr. v.p. book sales and mktg. Arcata Graphics Co., 1990-91; founder, prin. D4EO Lit. Agy., 1991—. Served USCGR. Mem.: Conn. Golf Club. Home: 7 Indian Valley Rd Weston CT 06883-1018 Office Phone: 203-544-7180. E-mail: d4eo@optonline.net.

DIFRANCESCO, DONALD T., lawyer; b. Scotch Plains, N.J., Nov. 20, 1944; grad. Pa. State U., 1966; J.D., Seton Hall U., 1969; m. Diane Dragovic, June 17, 1967; children: Marie, Tracy, Marci. Bar: N.J. 1969. Practices in Warren, N.J.; ptnr. Bivona, Cohen, Kunzman, Coley, Yospin, Bernstein & DiFrancesco; mem. N.J. Assembly, 1976-79; mem. N.J. State Senate, 1979-2001, pres. State Senate, 1992-2001; acting gov., 2001; lawyer DiFrancesco, Bateman, Coley, Yospin, Kunzman, Davis & Lehrer, P.C., 2001-. Trustee N.J. Symphony; bd. dirs. Resolve Counseling Ctr., Children's Specialized Hosp., N.J.; mem. exec. com. Nat. Conf. State Legislators. Office: DiFrancesco, Bateman, Coley, Yospin, Kunzman, Davis & Lehrer 15 Mountain Blvd Warren NJ 07059-6327

DIFRANCO, ANI, music executive, musician; b. Buffalo, N.Y., Sept. 23, 1970; Founder Righteous Babe, 1990—. Albums include: Ani DiFranco, 1989, Not So Soft, 1991, Imperfectly, 1992, Puddle Drive, 1993, Out of Range, 1994, Like I Said, 1994, Not A Pretty Girl, 1995, More Joy Less

Shame, 1996, Dilate, 1996, Living in Clip, 1997, Little Plastic Castle, 1998, Up, 1999, Little Plastic Remixes, 1999, Fellow Workers, 1999, To the Teeth, 1999, Swing Set, 2000, Revelling/Reckoning, 2001, So Much Shouting, So Much Laughter, 2002, Evolve, 2003, Educated Guess, 2003. Office: c/o Righteous Babe Records PO Box 95 Buffalo NY 14205-0095

DIFRONZO, FRANCIS G., painter; b. 1969; BFA, Calif. State U., Fullerton, 1994; MFA, Pa. Acad. Fine Arts, Phila., 1998. Solo exhibitions, Phila. Cathedral, 2000, Common Disaster, Artists' House Gallery, Phila., 1999, Segue, 2000, Rosenfeld Gallery, Phila., 2002, 2004. Recipient Art in Am. Scholarship Award, Liquitrex, 1993; So. Calif. Art Alliance Fellowship, 1991, Stobbart Found. Fellowship in the Arts, 1998, Pew Fellowship in the Arts, 2004.*

DIFRUSCIA, ANTHONY R., lawyer, real estate developer; b. Lawrence, Mass., June 5, 1940; s. Carmine and Sebastina (Tine) DiF.; m. Kathleen Sullivan; children: Marc Anthony, Kara Ann, Tamra Lee, Daniel Anthony. B, Emerson Coll.; JD, New Eng. Sch. Law, 1966. Bar: Mass. 1967. Sr. ptnr., Lawrence, 1967—. Pres. A.D. Devel., Inc., Lawrence; pres., treas. A.D. Mgmt., Lawrence. Mem. Mass. Ho. of Reps., 1967-72; commerce com. N.H. Ho. of Reps., 1998—. Roman Catholic. Office: 302 Broadway Methuen MA 01844-1208 Office Phone: 978-687-1777. E-mail: adirfuscia@aol.com.

DIGANCI, TODD T., stock exchange executive; B in acctg. and computer info. sys., Drake U., 1982, M in fin., 1984. Various sr. fin. positions Marriott Corp.; corp. controller NASD, Wash., DC, 1995—99, sr. v.p., controller, 1999—, exec. v.p., CFO. Mem. bd. dirs. Securities Dealers Insurance Co., Ltd. (SDIC). Office: NASD 1735 K St NW Washington DC 20006 Office Phone: 202-728-8000. Office Fax: 202-293-6260.

DIGANGI, FRANK EDWARD, academic administrator; b. West Rutland, Vt., Sept. 29, 1917; s. Leonard and Mary Grace (Zafonti) DiG.; m. Genevieve Frances Colignon, June 27, 1946; children: Ellen (Mrs. Philo David Hall), Janet (Mrs. W. Dale Greenwood). BS in Pharmacy, Rutgers U., 1940; MS, Western Res. U., 1942; PhD, U. Minn., 1948. Asst. prof. U. Minn. Coll. Pharmacy, 1948-52, asso. prof., 1952-57, prof. medicinal chemistry, 1957—, also asso. dean adminstrv. affairs. Author: Quantitative Pharmaceutical Analysis, 7th edit, 1977, The History of the Minnesota Pharmacists Association, 1883-1983, 2004; Contbr. articles to pharm. jours. Served with USNR, 1943-46, PTO. Recipient Alumni Assn. Disting. Pharmacist award, 1977, Faculty Recognition award Coll. of Pharmacy Alumni Soc., 1981, Lawrence and Delores M. Weaver medal, 1997. Mem. Am. Pharm. Assn., Minn. Pharm. Assn. (pres. 1971, chmn. bd. 1972-73, Pharmacist of Yr. award 1972, Harold R. Popp Meml. award 1979, hon. mem. 1994), Mpls. Soc. Profl. Pharmacists (hon.), AAUP, Am. Chem. Soc., Am. Assn. Colls. Pharmacy, Univ. Campus Club (Mpls.), Univ. Faculty Golf Club (Mpls., Gownin-Town Club (Mpls.), Sigma Xi, Phi Beta Phi, Phi Lambda Upsilon, Rho Chi. Home: 1666 Coffman St Apt 234 Saint Paul MN 55108-1343 Office: Univ Minn Coll of Pharmacy Minneapolis MN 55455

DIGAVALLI, SIVARAO V., pharmacologist, research scientist; s. Ratnam V. and Vijayalakshmi Digavalli; m. Neeta Mehrotra, Apr. 2, 1967. BS, Univ. Coll. of Pharm. Scis., Kakatiya U., Warangal, India, 1988; PhD, LSU Med. Sch., New Orleans, 1997; Postdoctoral Fellowship, Harvard Med. Sch., Boston, 2000. Sr. rsch. investigator Bristol Myers Squibb Co., Wallingford, Conn., 2000—. Cons. Thomas Jefferson Med. Sch., Phila., 2003—03. Contbr. articles to sci. jours. Mem.: Am. Gastroenterology Assn., NY Acad. of Sci. Avocations: hiking, canoeing. Office: Bristol Myers Squibb Co 5 Rsch Pky Wallingford CT 06492 Office Phone: 203-677-7439. Office Fax: 203-677-7569. Business E-Mail: siva.digavalli@bms.com. E-mail: sivarao_digavalli@yahoo.com.

DIGENOVA, JOSEPH E., lawyer; b. Wilmington, Del., Feb. 22, 1945; s. Egidio Joseph and Elizabeth (Castelline) diG.; m. Victoria Toensing, June 27, 1981; children: Todd, Brady, Amy. BA, U. Cinn., 1967; JD, Georgetown U., 1970. Bar: D.C. 1970, U.S. Dist. Ct. D.C. 1970, U.S. Ct. Appeals (D.C. cir.) 1972. Law clk. to assoc. judge D.C. Ct. Appeals, 1970-71; dir., gen. counsel U. Cin. Project, 1971-72; asst. U.S. atty. Office of U.S. Atty., Washington, 1972-75, prin. asst. U.S. atty., 1982-83; U.S. atty. D.C., 1983-88; counsel on intelligence matters Office of U.S. Atty. Gen., Washington, 1976; counsel for select com. on intelligence U.S. Senate, Washington, 1975-76, counsel for subcommittee on D.C., com. govt. affairs, 1976, counsel for com. on judiciary, 1978, chief counsel, staff advisor for com. on rules and adminstrn., 1981; adminstrv. asst., legis. counsel U.S. Senator Charles Mathias, Washington, 1979; U.S. Atty. for D.C., 1983-88; ptnr. Bishop, Cook, Purcell & Reynolds, 1988-90, Manatt Phelps & Phillips, 1991-95; founding ptnr. diGenova & Toensing, 1996—. Ind. counsel Clinton passport file search matter, 1992-95; apptd. grievance com. U.S. Dist. Ct. D.C., 1994. Contbr. articles to profl. jours. Mem.: ABA (com. grand jury 1983—87, criminal justice sect. 1982—, white collar crime com. 1988—), Gridiron Club. Republican. Roman Catholic. Avocations: golf, music, singing. Office: diGenova & Toensing 901 15th St NW Ste 430 Washington DC 20005-2327 Office Phone: 202-289-7701.

DIGGINS, PETER SHEEHAN, arts administrator; b. Rochester, N.Y., June 23, 1938; s. Bartholomew A. and Mona (Sheehan) D. BA in English, Georgetown U., 1959. guest artist cons. San Francisco Opera, 1997. Staff reporter Washington Post, 1960-65; asst. artistic adminstr. Met. Opera, NYC, 1965-72; dir. dance programs NY State Coun. on the Arts, 1972-75; gen. adminstr. The Joffrey Ballet, NYC, 1975-79; pres. Peter S. Diggins Assocs., 1979—; Am. entertainment coord. Winter Olympics, Nagano, Japan, 1998; artistic adminstr. Ballet Pacifica, 2004—. Cons. in arts mgmt. dance and opera cos.; cons. for guest dancers San Francisco Opera, 1996; casting cons. Broadway and tour prodns. of Carousel, Titanic, Victor/Victoria, Cats, Red Shoes, Christmas Carol, 1993-98. Contbr. articles to Opera Mag. Recipient grant for European work-study tour Met. Opera, 1968 Home: 133 W 71st St New York NY 10023-3834 Office Phone: 212-874-4534. Personal E-mail: Festspiel@aol.com.

DIGGS, DARNELL E., physicist, researcher; b. Ala. BS in Physics, MS in Physics, PhD in Physics, Alabama A&M U. Rsch. physicist U.S. Air Force Rsch. Lab., 2002—. Named Most Promising Scientist in Govt., Black Engr., 2004; named one of 50 Most Important Blacks in Rsch. Sci., Sci. Spectrum mag., 2004. Office: AFRL/PA Bldg 15 Room 225 WPAFB Wright Patterson Afb OH 45433-7131

DIGGS, DAVID B., music educator; b. Lubbock, Tex., Mar. 20, 1947; s. Bill H and Adele Krueger Diggs; m. Grace Louise Meade, Jan. 2, 1982; children: Christina Susan, Gordon Meade. MusB, Okla. City U., 1965—69; MusM, SUNY at Stony Brook, 1972—74. Tchg. asst. SUNY at Stony Brook, NY, 1972—74; woodwind specialist (oboist) NYC Musical Organizations, 1974—; dir. of winds Lehigh U., Bethlehem, Pa., 1998—. Cons. Moravian Music Found., Winston-Salem, NC, 2002—; rschr. Band of HM Coldstream Guards, London, 2003—. Prodr.(condr.): (cd) Lehigh Glory, Rhapsody; author: (book) The Dalton Recorder Book; composer: (musical suite) Echoes of Glory; transcriber (overture) Henry the Fifth Overture; editor (transcriber): (music) The Eley Project; composer: (musical suite) Trooping the Colour Suite, Highland Pipes Medley; prodr. (condr.): (cd) American Overture; prodr.(condr.): (cd) Incantation, Tempered Steel, Pipes & Band:Music of Ireland & Scotland. Grantee Rsch. grant, Henry Lawrence Gipson Inst., 2004—05; Faculty Rsch. grant, Lehigh U., 2001—03, Rec. grant, Mary Gordon Roberts Fund, 1999—. Mem.: Am. Fedn. of Musicians, Coll. Band Directors Nat. Assn. Achievements include research in band music of the civil war era; music of the 18th century foot guards bands. Avocation: computers. Office: Lehigh Univ 420 East Packer Ave Bethlehem PA 18015 Office Phone: 610-758-3831. Office Fax: 610-758-6470. Personal E-mail: dbd2@lehigh.edu.

DIGGS, WALTER WHITLEY, health science facility administrator; b. Memphis, Tenn., June 8, 1932; s. Lemuel Whitley and Beatrice (Moshier) D.; m. Ann C. Thobae, Nov. 29, 1958; children: Jennie, Thomas, Andrew. BS, Washington and Lee U., 1954; MHA, U. Minn., 1956. Adminstrv. resident Stormont-Vail Hosp., Topeka, 1955-56; asst. dir. The Johns Hopkins Hosp., Balt., 1959-66; adminstr. Med. Coll. Ga. Hosp., Augusta, 1966-70; asst. prof. Med. Coll. Ga., Augusta, 1970-71, U. Tenn. and U. Memphis, 1971-97; field rep. Joint Commn. Hosps., Chgo., 1981-88, 93—; supt. Memphis Mental Health Inst., 1987-93. Cons. Tenn. Dept. Mental Health, 1993-95. Pres. Delta Found., Miss., 1987—, Ballet South, Memphis Ballet, Augusta Civic Ballet. Lt. USNR, 1956-59. Recipient Peter Cooper award, Unitarian Ch., Memphis, 1975, Forrest Fletcher, Washington and Lee, Lexington, Va., 1954. Fellow Am. Coll. Healthcare Execs. (life). Avocation: seniors track and field. Home: 5282 Shady Grove Rd Memphis TN 38120-2404 E-mail: cordovawwd@aol.com.

DI GIACINTO, SHARON, artist, educator; d. Vendal and Virginia Di G.; m. Richard K. Hillis. BFA, Ohio U., 1981; MFA, Tex. Woman's U., 1983. Teaching asst. art Stephen F. Austin State U., Nacogdoches, Tex., 1981, Tex. Woman's U., Denton, 1982-83; art instr. Phoenix Coll., 1983-84, Glendale (Ariz.) C.C., 1985-88; ind. artist Peoria, Ariz. Solo exhbns. include Glendale C.C. Art Gallery, 1984, Phoenix Coll. Art Gallery, Scottsdale (Ariz.) C.C., 1989, Sun Cities Art Mus., 1989, Phoenix Visual Arts Gallery, 1990, Madison House, Sun City West, 1990, Fine Art Gallery, Phoenix Coll., 2000, Heffernon Rm., West Valley Art Mus., Surprise, Ariz., 2001; group exhbns. include 2-person exhbn. Chandler (Ariz.) Ctr. for Arts, 1991, Peoria (Ariz.) City Hall, 1995, Narthex Art Exhibit, Phoenix, 1996, Udinotti Gallery, Scotsdale, 1986, Casa Grande (Ariz.) Art Mus., 1997; illustrations included in City of Peoria (Ariz.) Annual Fin. Report, 1994, The Best of Colored Pencil 2, 1994, The Best of Oil Painting, 1996, The Best of Sketching and Drawing, 1998, others; represented in collections Hill Country Arts Found., Ingram, Tex., Peru (Nebr.) State Coll., Paradise Valley (Ariz.) C.C., Glendale (Ariz.) Pub. Libr., City of Mesa, Ariz., Glendale C.C., and pvt. collections. Co-chair Peoria Arts Commn., 1988-91. Mem. Coll. Art Assn. Am., Phoenix Art Mus., San Diego Zoo. Democrat. Roman Catholic. Avocation: animals.

DI GIACOMO, FRAN, artist; b. Miami, Ariz., Oct. 24, 1944; d. B.J. and LaVenia Marilyn (Beavers) Fain; m. Len DiGiacomo, May 9, 1970; children: Marc, Eric. Student, Scottsdale Artist's Sch., 1985—2000; studied, with David Leffel, with Joe Anna Arnette, with Greg Kreutz, with Howard Terpning. Artist, 1970—; represented by Gallerie Amsterdam, Carmel, Calif., Southwest Gallery, Dallas, Heritage Gallery, Scottsdale, Ariz., Downey Gallery, Santa Fe. Commissions include portraits of Supreme Court Chief Justice Warren E. Burger, Dist. Atty., 1994, Henry Wade, 1995, Haggar Apparel, Dallas Cowboys' Emmitt Smith, 1993; author: I'd Rather Do Chemo Than Clean Out the Garage, 2003; subject of numerous articles. Recepient 2nd place, 1993, Hon. Mention, 1994, 1st place, 1996, Plano Art Assn.,1st place, 1994, Assoc. Creative Artists, Grumbacher Gold, 1997, 2nd place, 1994, Trinity Arts Guild, 1st place, 1998, 3rd place, 1999, Richardson Civic Art, 3rd place, 1995, Tex. and Neighbors 5 state. Mem. Oil Painters Am. (assoc., signature), Am. Soc. (assoc.), Classical Realism, Portrait Soc. Am., Assoc. Creative Artists (signature). Avocation: tennis.

DI GIACOMO, MICHAEL, historian, educator; b. Ururi, Campobasso, Italy, Jan. 10, 1954; s. Antonio and Elvira Maria Di Giacomo; m. Janet Ruth Ursel, May 3, 1980; children: Daniel Frederick, Cristina Maria, Paul Antonio, David Richard, Joel Michael. Diploma, Collège Biblique Québec, Quebec City, Can., 1980; MA, Laval U., Quebec City, 1994, PhD, 1999. Ordained to ministry Pentecostal Assemblies of Can., 1985, Assemblies of God, 2003. Asst. pastor Carrefour Chrétien de la Capitale, Quebec City, 1979—82; scholar in residence Ctr. for Rsch. on French Can. Culture, Ottawa, Canada, 1999—2000; assoc. prof. history Valley Forge Christian Coll., Phoenixville, Pa.; sr. pastor Assemblée Chrétienne des Bois-Francs, Victoriaville, Canada, 1982—93; adj. prof. Institut biblique du Québec, Montreal, Canada, 1990—; lectr. U. Ottawa, 1999—2000. Author: Les Assemblées de la Pentecôte du Canada: Leur origine, leur évolution, leur théologie distinctive. Scholar, Canadian-Italian Businessmen and PA, 1995, 1996, 1997; Fonds pour la Formation de Chercheurs et l'Aide à la Recherche fellow, Govt. of Que., 1997. Mem.: Soc. Pentecostal Studies, Am. Soc. Ch. History. Office: Valley Forge Christian Coll 1401 Charlestown Rd Phoenixville PA 19460 E-mail: m_digiacomo@vfcc.edu.

DIGILIO, JOHN THOMAS, JR., healthcare executive, consultant; b. Kew Gardens, N.Y., Oct. 18, 1944; s. John Thomas and Gloria Marie (Valenzio) D.; m. Dianne E. (Pilgrim), July 12, 1969; children: Susan Elizabeth, Sandra Marie, John Thomas III. Diploma, U.S. Army War Coll., 1966; BA, LaSalle Univ., 1967; MBA, Wagner Coll., 1969. Lic. nursing home adminstr., N.Y. Adminstr. VA Med. Ctr., Northport, N.Y., 1971-72; ambulatory care adminstr. Southside Hosp., Bay Shore, N.Y., 1972-75; rschr., faculty of med. Coll. Physicians and Surgeons, Columbia Univ., N.Y.C., 1975-76; hosp. adminstrn. N.Y. Dept. of Health, 1976-81; adminstr. Brunswick Nursing Home, Amityville, N.Y., 1981-88, Luth. Ctr. for Aging, Smithtown, N.Y., 1988-92, Sunharbor Manor, Roslyn, N.Y., 1992-95; cons. Helme Assoc., Providence, 1995-99; adminstr. Patchogue Nursing Ctr., N.Y., 1999; exec. dir. John Foley SNF, Yapnank, N.Y., 1999—. Contbg. author: Organizing Health Care for Children, 1977. Chmn. bd. L.I. Arthritis Found., 1992. Brig. gen. U.S. Army-N.G., 1969-99. Decorated Legion of Merit, Bronze Star, Order of Mil. Med. Merit; recepient Joel T. Boone award, Assn. Mil. Surgeons U.S., 1997. Fellow Am. Coll. Health Care Adminstrs.; mem. Am. Legion Post 365 (trustee 1998—), La Sociètè des Quarante Hommes Et Huit Chavaux (cnat. omdr. 1976—), Mil. and Hospitalier Order of St. Lazarus of Jerusalem (comdr. 2001—), Sovereign Mil. Order of the Temple of Jerusalem (knight comdr. 1998—). Home: 1430 Manor Ln Bay Shore NY 11706 Office: John J Foley SNF 14 Glover Dr Yaphank NY 11980 E-mail: johntd@aol.com.

DIGIOVANNA, AUGUSTINE GASPAR, biologist, educator; BS, St. John's U., 1965; MS, U. Md., 1970, PhD, 1972. Prof. biology Salisbury (Md.) U., 1972—. Vis. prof. U. Md., College Pk., 1980—88; tchg. assoc. Maine Geriat./Gerontology Edn. Ctr., Biddeford, 2001—. Author: Human Aging: Biological Perspectives, 2001. Mem.: Human Anatomy and Physiology Soc., Gerontol. Soc. Am., Phi Kappa Phi. Office: Salisbury Univ 1101 Camden Ave Salisbury MD 21801 Business E-Mail: agdigiovanna@salisbury.edu.

DI GIOVANNI, ANTHONY, retired coal mining company executive; b. Phila., May 10, 1919; s. Charles and Josephine (Giacobbe) Di Giovanni; m. Rose Persichetti, July 28, 1946 (dec. Mar. 2003); children: Joanne, Diane, Rosemary, Charles. BS in Bus. Adminstrn, St. Joseph's U., 1940. CPA Pa. Acct. Service Supply Corp., Phila., 1940-42; account supr. Ernst & Ernst, 1942-51, mgr. Phila., 1952—65; former v.p., dir. United Eastern Coal Sales Corp.; exec. v.p. finance and adminstrn. Barnes & Tucker Co., Valley Forge, Pa., 1965-72, pres., 1972-84; group pres. resources div. Alco Standard Corp. (now Ikon Office Solutions, Inc.), 1973-85, v.p., 1976-85; pres. Alco Standard Canadian Coal Corp., 1976-85; v.p. Tri County bentures, Inc., Ebensburg, Pa., 1985—. Dir. Upshur Coals Corp. Bd. dirs. St. Joseph U., 1983—85. Mem.: AICPA, Pa. Inst. CPA (past bd. dirs., chmn. com.), Nat. Coal Assn. (bd. dirs. 1973—85, fin. com. 1978—83), Sons of Italy (treas., policy com. Commonwealth Lodge #1949 1989—91), Phoenixville Country Club. Roman Catholic.

DIGIUSTINI, ANTONETTA ANNA, educational association administrator, educator; b. Boston, July 10, 1961; d. Luigi and Elisa Carolina (Castrucci) DiGiustini. AB, Harvard U., 1997. Tchr., arts adminstr. Charles River Creative Arts Program, Dover, Mass., 1977—92; program asst. Nazzaro Cmty. Ctr., Boston, 1989—90; asst. dir. pub. programs and edn. Bostonian Soc., Boston, 1991—93; stewardship coord. Radcliffe Inst. for Advanced Study, Cambridge, Mass., 1995—2003; co-founder, dir., tchr. The Advent Sch.'s LearningBoston, 1999—; tchr., mem. faculty The Saturday Course, Milton Acad., Milton, Mass., 2000—. Contbr. poetry to anthologies, 1976—. Account mgr., loaned exec. United Way of Mass. Bay, Boston, 2004—05. Recipient Am. Registry of Outstanding Profl., 2002—. Mem.: Assn. Fund-raising Profls., Orgn. Am. Historians, Am. Hist. Assn. Avocations: poetry, photography, running, reading. Home: 107 Beacon St Apt 7 Boston MA 02116 Personal E-mail: antonetta_digiustini@yahoo.com.

DIGMAN, LESTER ALOYSIUS, management educator; b. Kieler, Wis., Nov. 22, 1938; s. Arthur Louis and Hilda Dorothy (Jansen) D.; m. Ellen Rhomberg Pfohl, Jan. 15, 1966; children: Stephanie, Sarah, Mark. BSME, U. Iowa, 1961, MSIE, 1962, PhD, 1970. Registered profl. engr., Mass. Mgmt. cons. U.S. Ameta, Rock Island, Ill., 1962-67; mgmt. instr. U. Iowa, Iowa City, 1967-69; head applied math. dept. U.S. Ameta, Rock Island, Ill., 1969-74, head managerial tng. dept., 1974-77; assoc. prof. mgt. U. Nebr., Lincoln, 1977-84, dir. grad. studies in mgmt., 1982—, prof. mgmt., 1984-87, Leonard E Whittaker Am. Charter disting. prof. mgmt., 1987-93, Met. Fed. Bank disting. prof. mgmt., 1993-95, First Bank disting. prof. mgmt., 1995-98, U.S. Bank disting. prof. mgmt., 1998—2002, Harold J. Laipply coll. prof., 2002—; dir. Ctr. for Tech. Mgmt. and Decision Scis., 1992-94; interim dir. Gallup Rsch. Ctr., 1994-95; mem. adv. bd. Ctr. for Albanian Studies, 1992—. Cons. various orgns., 1963-72; sec. treas. Mgmt. Svcs. Assocs. Ltd., Davenport, Iowa, 1972-77; owner L.A. Digman and Assocs., Lincoln, 1977—; gen. ptnr. Letna Properties, Madison, Wis., 1978—. Author: Strategic Management: Concepts, Decisions, Cases, 1986, 2d edit., 1990, Strategic Management: Concepts, Processes, Decisions, 1995, 2d edit., 1999, Strategic Management: Cases, 1995, 2d edit., 1997, 3d edit., 1999, Network Analysis for Management Decisions, 1982, Strategic Management: Cases for the Global Information Age, 2002, Strategic Management: Competing in the Global Information Age, 2002; contbr. articles to profl. jours.;: 2d edit., 2004. Recipient Dist. award SBA, 1980, Certs. of Appreciation Dept. of Def., 1972. Fellow Decision Scis. Inst. (charter, program chmn. 1986, pres. 1987-88, coord. doctoral consortium 1989, strategy/policy track chmn. 1991, v.p. 1992-94, strategic mgmt. track chmn. internat. meeting 1993, chair long-range planning com. 1995-96, adv. com. for internat. meeting 1997, chair fellows com., 1999-2000), Pan Pacific Bus. Assn. (bd. adv. 1999—); mem. IEEE, Strategic Mgmt. Soc. (founding), Acad. of Mgmt., Strategic Leadership Forum, Inst. for Ops. Rsch. and Mgmt. Scis. (founding), MBA Roundtable (charter, steering com.), Nebr. Club, Firethorn Country Club, Confrerie de la Chaine Rotisseurs. Roman Catholic. Avocations: gardening, photography, wine tasting. Home: 7520 Lincolnshire Rd Lincoln NE 68506-1635 Office: U Nebr 277 CBA Lincoln NE 68588 Business E-Mail: ldigman1@unl.edu.

DIGNAC, GENY (EUGENIA M. BERMUDEZ), sculptor; b. Buenos Aires, June 8, 1932; came to U.S., 1954; d. Jose Victor Marenco and Margarita Eugenia D.; m. Jose Y. Bermudez, Apr. 7, 1958; children— Alexander, Melanie. Ed., U. Buenos Aires, 1952-54. Lectr. in field. Exhibited in one-woman shows at Galeria 22, Caracas, Venezuela, 1967, Michael Berger Gallery, Pitts., 1969, Cinema 2, Caracas, 1971, Pyramid Gallery, Washington, 1971; exhibited in numerous group shows including Corcoran Gallery of Art, Washington, 1958, 59, Inst. Contemporary Arts, Washington, 1967, Bklyn. Mus., 1968, Mus. Modern Art, Buenos Aires, 1971, Mus. Fine Arts, Boston, 1971, Palais des Beaux Arts, Brussels, 1974, Inst. Contemporary Arts, London, 1974; represented in permanent collections including Fundacio Joan Miro, Barcelona, Spain, Palazzo Dei Diamanti, Ferrara, Italy, Museo La Tertulia, Cali, Colombia, Galeria del Banco Central, Guayaquil, Ecuador, The Latinoamerican Art Found., San Juan, P.R., and others in Argentina, Chile, Germany, Italy, Ireland, Spain, U.S. and Venezuela; works include 27 Fire Gestures-, 1970-2000; radio and TV interviews, U.S. and abroad; works with lights, fire and temperatures; subject of profl. articles, films. Recipient prize for light sculpture IX Festival of Art, 1969 Home: 4109 E Via Estrella Phoenix AZ 85028-4515 Office: Osuna Art 7200 Wisconsin Ave Bethesda MD 20814 Office Phone: 602-996-3239. E-mail: gdignac@aol.com.

DIGNAM, WILLIAM JOSEPH, obstetrician, gynecologist, educator; b. Manchester, N.H., Aug. 11, 1920; s. Walter Joseph and Margaret Veronica (Lowe) D.; m. Winifred Kennedy, June 7, 1947; children— Mary Brett, Kevan Jean, Erin Margaret, Meighan Ann AB, Dartmouth Coll., 1941; MD, Harvard U., 1943. Intern Boston City Hosp., 1944; resident in ob-gyn U. Kans. Med. Ctr., Kansas City, 1947-50; from asst. prof. to prof. ob-gyn UCLA, 1951—. Affiliated with UCLA Med. Ctr., Cedars-Sinai Med. Ctr., Harbor-UCLA Med. Ctr. Roman Catholic. Home: 820 Alma Real Dr Pacific Palisades CA 90272-3704 Office: UCLA Sch Medicine Dept Ob-Gyn 10833 Le Conte Ave Los Angeles CA 90095-3075 Business E-Mail: wdignam@mednet.ucla.edu.

DIGNAN, THOMAS GREGORY, JR., lawyer; b. Worcester, Mass., May 23, 1940; s. Thomas Gregory and Hester Clare (Sharkey) D.; m. Mary Anne Connor, Sept. 16, 1978; children: Kellyanne E., Maryclare E. BA, Yale U., 1961; JD, U. Mich., 1964. Bar: Mass. 1964, U.S. Supreme Ct. 1968. Assoc. Ropes & Gray, Boston, 1964—74, ptnr., 1974—2000, of counsel, 2001—. Spl. asst. atty. gen. State of Mass., 1974-76; trustee NSTAR. Asst. editor: Mich. Law Rev., 1963-64; contbr. articles to profl. jours. Bd. dirs. Family Counseling and Guidance Ctrs., Inc., 1967-76, 78-94, v.p., 1983-87, pres., 1987-89; trustee Cath. Charitable Bur. of Boston, Inc., 1994-97, Dana Hall Sch., 1994-2005; bd. dirs. Gov.'s Mgmt. Task Force, 1979-81, Mass. Moderator's Assn., 1994-2000; mem. fin. com. Town of Sudbury, 1982-85, moderator, 1985-2003; bd. advisors Environ. Law Ctr., Vt. Law Sch., 1981—; mem. vis. com. U. Mich. Law Sch.; corporator Emerson Hosp., 1989-2004. Mem. Nashawtuc Country Club, Shadow Wood Country Club, Order of the Coif, Phi Delta Phi. Republican. Roman Catholic. Home: 9053 Windswept Dr Bonita Springs FL 34135 Personal E-mail: Tdignanjr@aol.com.

DIGORGIO, KENNETH, lawyer; MBA, UCLA; JD, UCLA Anderson Grad. Sch. Mgmt. Regulatory counsel The First Am. Corp., Santa Ana, Calif., 1999—2003; exec. v.p., gen counsel First Advantage Corp. (subsidiary of First Am. Corp), 2003—04; gen. counsel The First Am. Corp., Santa Ana, Calif., 2004—. Office: First American Corp 1 First American Way Santa Ana CA 92707-5913

DIGREGORIO, VINCENT R., plastic surgeon; s. Nicholas J. and Anne M. DiGregorio; m. Jennifer E. Ruys, Apr. 26, 2003; 1 child, Nicole C. BA, Hobart Coll., Geneva, N.Y., 1964; MD, Albany Med. Coll., 1968. Plastic surgeon Long Island Plastic Surgery Group, Garden City, NY, 1978—; chief plastic surgery Winthrop U. Hosp., Mineola, NY, 1978—, pres. med. staff, 1984—88. Pres. Day Op Ctr. of L.I., Mineola, NY, 1988—. Oils and watercolors. Maj. Us Army, 1970—71, m. Home: 110 Sixth St Garden City NY 11530 Office: Long Island Plastic Surgery Group 999 Franklin Ave Garden City NY 11530 Office Phone: 516-742-3404. Personal E-mail: vincentdig@cs.com. E-mail: vincentdig @cs.com.

DIKA, SANDRA LOREE, educational association administrator; b. Spirit River, Alta., Can., Dec. 6, 1970; d. Jeffrey Michael and Linda Lee Dika; m. Miguel Angel Pando, May 26, 1999; 1 child, Diego Alejandro Pando Dika. EdB, U. Alta., Edmonton, Can., 1993, MS, 1996; PhD, Va. Tech U., 2003. Vis. asst. prof. Va. Tech, Blacksburg, 2002—; asst. rsch. prof. U. of P.R., Mayaguez, PR, 2003—04; rsch. and evaluation specialist Edn. Alliance at Brown U., Providence, 2004—. Contbr. articles to profl. jours. Fellow, Social Scis. and Humanities Rsch. Coun. of Can., 2000—02; McComas-Chambless scholar, Va. Tech, Dept. of Ednl. Leadership and Policy Studies, 2002, Doris Badir Grad. fellow in Human Ecology, U. of Alta., Dept. of Human Ecology, 1995. Fellow: Kappa Delta Pi; mem.: Ea. Ednl. Rsch. Assn., Am. Sociol. Assn., Am. Ednl. Rsch. Assn., Phi Delta Kappa. Home: 910 Parque Forestal Mayaguez PR 00682 Office: Edn Alliance at Brown U 222 Richmond St Providence RI 02903-4226 Office Phone: 401-274-9548 402. Home Fax: 787-265-4001; Office Fax: 401-421-7650. Personal E-mail: sandra_dika@brown.edu.

DIKE, RAD (EDWARD CONRAD DIKE), artist; b. Maywood, Nebr., June 9, 1945; s. Raymond Hadyn and Mary Dorothy (Popp) D.; m. Laurel Ellen Rathbun, 1970 (div. 1971); m. Ann Doherty Langenbach, Feb. 14, 1985. Think tank dir. Henry Dreyfuss Assn., N.Y.C., 1970-72; vis. prof. Pratt Inst. Sch. of Architecture, N.Y.C., 1970-72, adj. prof., 1972-77; organizer Nat

Indsl. Design Conf., Pa., 1971; mentor prof. PhD leadership program NYU, 1974-77; guest lectr. CCNY, Cooper Union, N.Y. Sch. Interior Design, 1975-77; vis. prof. Parsons Sch. Design, 1976-77; spkr. Harvard Grad. Sch. Design, 1983. Exhibited in shows at Pratt Inst., N.Y.C., 1968, 69, U.S. Embassy, Stockholm, 1970, Smithsonian Air & Space Mus., Washington, 1971, Gotham Book Mart Gallery, N.Y.C, 1973, Field Taos, N.Mex., 1976, Nat. Peace Garden Travelling Show, 1989-92, Boston Athenaeum, 1992, 94, 96, Nat. Arts Club (Pres. award), 1995, Flickinger Arts Ctr., 1995, HGTV Arts Video, 1995, Virtuosity Art Internat. 3D CD ROM Mus., 1996; author: Architectural Common Sense, 1983; represented in permanent collections; inventor Mr. McCogitator robot, 1959, balcony-autogyro/boat/car balcony, 1969, naturally refined architecture, gesso/metal dusts paint tech.; prin. archtl. works include N.Y.C. Dept. Gen. Svc. Gardens, 1981, Hell's Kitchen Seedling Greenhouse, 1983, Whole Tree Cottage, 1988, Trussed Arched Tree Branches (Vt. Gov.'s Spl. Merit award), 1989, Arch Keystone Tree, 1990, Suspension Tree Facade, 1991, Chez Ploix, France, 1994—, others. Cons., organizer First Earth Day, N.Y.C, 1970; laborer Green Guerillas, 1976-82; regional planning commr. So. Windsor (Vt.) County, 1989-90; bd. dirs. Hist. Windsor, 1991-93, trustee, 1994-95; founder Conservation Commn., West Windsor, 1990; commr. Vt. Road & Bridges Agy., 1990, Vt. Assn. Planners & Developers Agys., 1990; bd. advisors Preservation Inst. Bldg. Crafts, 1994—; bd. dirs. Am Inst. Wine & Food New England, 1993-95. Batchelder grantee, 1964-70, Ford Motor grantee, 1967-70, Travel grantee U.S. Dept. Commerce, Pratt Inst., 1969; recipient Armco Steel prize, 1969, Merit award NEA, 1984, Outstanding Electronics award USAF, 1959, Poetry award Quill & Scroll USA, 1960. Mem. Nat. Arts Club, Vt. Land Trust (life). Achievements include scientific research and demonstration on Squared Circle of da Vinci's Man, Disproof of Le Corbusier's Modular Man, Human Golden Trinity, Skyscraper as Garden-Engine, Heat chimney Skyscraper Cooling, Laws of Branches, Natural Refinement. Home: Dike Outlook Reading VT 05062 Office Phone: 802-484-3339.

DIKEMAN, MAY, writer; b. Baldwin, N.Y., Sept. 8, 1923; d. James Bradley and Elsie Isabel (Helmrich) Dikeman; m. Norman Edward Hoss, Sept. 12, 1946; children: Antonie Kyrie, Kurt, Talara Kristin. BA, Vassar Coll., 1945. Instr. writers workshops New Sch. Social Rsch., N.Y.C., 1968-69. Author: (novel) The Pike, 1954, The Angelica, 1971, The Devil We Know, 1973; contbr. to Best in Am. Stories, 1963, 64; contbr. short stories to lit. publs. Atlantic "First" Ingram Merrill grantee Atlantic Monthly. Home: 70 Irving Pl New York NY 10003-2205 Office Phone: 212-475-4533.

DIKER, CHARLES M., investment advisor; b. NYC; m. Valerie Diker. B, Harvard U., 1956, MBA, 1958. Mng. ptnr. Diker Mgmt. LLC. Dir. Loews Corp.; mem. fund reunion gift steering com. Harvard U., com. on U. resources, visiting com. to art mus.; dir. Cantel Medical Corp., 1985—, chmn. bd., 1986—. Named one of Top 200 Collectors, ARTnews Mag., 2004. Mem.: Antique Tribal Art Dealers Assn. Inc., George Gustav Heye Ctr. (co-chmn. bd., mem. nat. bd.), Nat. Mus. Am. Indian. Avocation: Collector of Native Am. Art; Modern & Contemporary Art. Office: 767 Fifth Ave 26th Floor New York NY 10153 Office Phone: 212-904-0321. Office Fax: 212-308-6891. Business E-Mail: charles.diker@wpginvest.com.*

DIKMAN, MICHAEL, lawyer; b. Jamaica, N.Y., Oct. 23, 1936; s. Leo and Dorothy (Meyerson) D.; m. Harriet Schnitzer, Aug. 16, 1987; children by previous marriage: David, Donna. AB, Dartmouth Coll., 1958; LLB, Cornell U., 1961. Bar: N.Y. 1961, U.S. Dist. Ct. (ea. and so. dists.) N.Y. 1964, U.S. Supreme Ct. 1965. Ptnr., Jamaica, 1962—, Dikman & Dikman, Jamaica, 1969—, Lake Success, N.Y., 1998—. Contbr. articles to profl. jours. Mem. Jamaica Lawyers Club (past pres. 1965-66), Brandeis Assn. (past pres. 1974-75), Fed. Lawyers Club (past pres. 1972-73), Queens County Bar Assn. (past pres. 1978-79), N.Y. State Bar Assn. (bd. dirs. family law sect.), Am. Acad. Matrimonial Lawyers (bd. dirs., v.p.), Lions (past pres. 1967). Democrat. Jewish. Avocations: magic, handball, tennis, squash, bridge. Home: 98 Shrub Hollow Rd Roslyn NY 11576 Office: Dikman & Dikman 5 Dakota Dr Ste 208 New Hyde Park NY 11042-1109 also: Dikman & Dikman 161-10 Jamaica Ave Jamaica NY 11432

DILCHER, DAVID LEONARD, paleobotany educator, researcher; b. Cedar Falls, Iowa, July 10, 1936; m. Katherine Swanson, 1961; children: Peter, Ann. BS in Natural History, U. Minn., 1958, MS in Botany, Geology and Zoology, 1960; postgrad., U. Ill., 1960-62; PhD in Biology, Geology, Yale U., 1964; participant OTS course field dendrology, Costa Rica, 1968. Teaching asst. U. Minn., Mpls., 1958-60, U. Ill., Urbana, 1960-62, Yale U., New Haven, Conn., 1962-63, Cullman-Univ. fellow, 1963-64, instr. biology, 1965-66; NSF postdoctoral fellow Senckenberg Mus., Frankfurt am Main, Fed. Republic of Germany, 1964-65; asst. prof. botany Ind. U., Bloomington, 1966-70, assoc. prof., 1970-76; Guggenheim fellow Imperial Coll., Univ. London, 1972-73; assoc. prof. geology Ind. U., Bloomington, 1975-77, prof. paleobotany, 1977-90, adj. prof. biology, adj. prof. geology, 1990—; grad. rsch. prof. Fla. Mus. Natural History, U. Fla., Gainesville, 1990—. Panel mem. for systematic biology program, NSF, 1977-79, panel mem. for selecting NATO postdoctoral fellow, 1982, mem. adv. com. Earth Sys. History, 1997-2000, bd. mem. on earth scis. and resources NRC, 2001-04; vis. lectr. to People's Republic of China Nat. Acad. Sci. com. on scholarly communications with China, 1986; corr. mem. Senckenberg Mus., Frankfurt, Fed. Republic Germany, 1989; hon. prof. Nanjing Inst. Geology and Paleontology, Acad. Sinica, China, 1998—, Jilin U., Changchau, China, 2001—; adj. prof. biology U. Tenn., Martin, 2000—; hon. prof., vice chmn. sci. com. rsch. ctr. paleontoloty and stratigraphy Jilin U., Changchun, China, 2001—; bd. dirs. Smithsonian Inst., 1998-; prof. Rsch. Found. Univ. Fla., 2004—. Author: (with D. Redmon, M. Tansey and D. Whitehead) Plant Biology Laboratory Manual, 1973, 2d edit., 1975; editor: (with Tom Taylor and Theodore Delevoryas) Plant Reproduction in the Fossil Record, symposium vol., 1979; (with T. Taylor) Biostratigraphy of Fossil Plants: Successional and Paleoecological Analysis, 1980; (with William L. Crepet) Origin and Evolution of Flowering Plants, Symposium Volume, 1984; (with Michael S. Zavada) Phylogeny of the Hamamedidae, symposium vol., 1986; (with Patrick S. Herendeen) Advances in Legume Systematics Part 4, The Fossil Record, 1992; contbr. over 200 articles to profl. jours. Mem. utilities bd. City of Bloomington, 1974-76; ruling elder First Presbyn. Ch. Bloomington, 1975-77; bd. dirs. United Campus Ministries, 1971-72, Smithsonian Mus. Natural History, 1998—; mem. coun. Monroe County United Ministries, 1975-77. Dist. Vis. Rsch. scholar U. Adelaide, Australia, 1981, 88; Vis. Rsch. scholar Birbal Sahni Palaeonbot. Inst., Lucknow, India, 1992; grantee Sigma Xi, 1961-62, 66, Ind. U., 1967-68, Orgn. Tropical Studies, 1971, Travel grantee Ind. U., 1968, 71, 77, 80, Rsch. grantee NSF, 1966-89, 96—, Amax Coal Found., 1980-81, NATO Coop, 1991-93; Eaton-Hooker fellow, 1963, Cullman-Univ. fellow, 1963-64, Guggenheim fellow, Giessen, Fed. Republic of Germany, 1972-73, Ind. U., 1972-73, Brit. Mus. Natural History, London, 1988-89; recipient Tracey M. Sonneborn award for disting. rsch. and excellenc in tchg. Ind. U., 1978-88, Bot. Soc. Am. Merit award, 1991, Birbal Sahni Found. award, 1998, U. Fla. Rsch. Found. Professorship award, 2004—. Fellow Ind. Acad. Sci.; mem. NAS, AAAS, Bot. Soc. Am. (chmn. paleobot. sect. 1974, sec.-treas. 1975-77, rep. to jour. editl. bd. 1978-79, jour. editl. bd. 1981-82, conservation com. 1978-81, chmn. conservation com. 1981, 82, program dir. 1982-84, exec. bd. 1982-91, sec. 1984-88, pres.-elect 1988-89, pres. 1989-90), Paleontol. Soc., Paleontol. Assn., Internat. Orgn. Paleobotany (N.Am. rep. 1975-81, v.p. 1987-93), Assn. Tropical Biology, Am. Inst. Biol. Scis., Am. Assn. Stratigraphic Palynologists, Internat. Assn. Angiosperm Paleobotany (pres. 1977-80), Geol. Soc. Am. (com. on collection and collecting 1978-85), Ky. Acad. Scis., Senckenberg Natur Mus. und Forschungsgeshellshaft Frankfurt am Main (corr. mem. 1990), Sigma Xi (pres.-elect Ind. cpt. 1985-86, pres. 1986-87). Office: U Fla Dept Natural Sci Fla Mus Natural History PO Box 117800 Gainesville FL 32611-7800 Office Phone: 352-392-1721 ext. 460. Business E-Mail: dilcher@flmnh.ufl.edu.

DI LELLA, ALEXANDER ANTHONY, biblical studies educator; b. Paterson, N.J., Aug. 14, 1929; s. Alessandro and Adelaide (Grimaldi) Di L. BA, St. Bonaventure U., 1952; S.T.L., Cath. U. Am., 1959, PhD, 1962; S.S.L., Pontifical Bibl. Inst., Rome, 1964. Entered Franciscan Order, Roman Catholic Ch., 1949; ordained priest, 1955. Lectr. O.T. and bibl. Greek Holy Name Coll., Washington, 1964-67; asst. prof. Semitic lang. Cath. U. Am., 1966-68, assoc. prof., 1968-76, assoc. prof. Bibl. studies, 1976-77, prof., 1977-92, Andrews-Kelly-Ryan disting. prof. bib. studies, 1992—2004, prof. emeritus, 2004—; vis. prof. Biblical studies Facoltà teologica di Sicilia, Italy, 2005. Adj. prof. O.T., Washington Theol. Union, 1969-72; vis. prof. O.T., Theol. Faculty of Sicily, 2005; mem. Rev. Standard Version Bible Com., 1982—; chmn. bd. of control New Am. Bible, 1988—; vis. prof. Old Testament Facolta Teologica de Sicilia, 2005 Assoc. editor, translator New American Bible, 1965-87; editor New Revised Standard Version Bible Cath. Edit., 1993; author: The Hebrew Text of Sirach: A Text-Critical and Historical Study, 1966, The Book of Daniel, 1978, Proverbs in the Old Testament in Syriac According to the Peshitta Version, 1979, The Wisdom of Ben Sira, 1987, Il Libro di Daniele (1-6), 1995, (7-14), 1996, Daniel: A Book for Troubling Times, 1997, El libro de Daniel (1-6), 2000, (7-14), 2001; contbr. articles and revs. to scholarly and popular publs. Mem. instnl. rev. bd. Dubroff Eye Ctr., Silver Spring, Md., 1982-94; cancer care continuum group Washington Hosp. Ctr., 1995-96. Am. Sch. Oriental rsch. fellow, 1962-63; Guggenheim fellow, 1972-73. Mem. Soc. Bibl. Lit. (pres. Chesapeake Bay region 1972-73), Cath. Bibl. Assn. (pres. 1975-76, del. Coun. on Study of Religion 1971-72) Home: Curley Hall Cath U Am Washington DC 20064-0001 Office: Cath U Am Rm 420 Caldwell Hall Washington DC 20064 E-mail: dilella@cua.edu. *Most of my adult life I have been a student of Biblical languages and literatures, interpretation and theology. Teaching, research and publications enable me to convey to others the value of the Bible as a primary document of Judaism and Christianity and as a significant factor in Western culture and civilization.*

DILEO, CHERYL, music therapist; d. Noble Joseph and Frieda Grace Dileo; 1 child, Jeffrey Noble. MusB in Music Therapy, Loyola U., New Orleans, 1971, MusM in Music Therapy, 1975; PhD, La. State U., Baton Rouge, 1981. Cert. bd. music Therapist Certification Bd. for Music Therapy, 1984. Prof. of music therapy, dir arts and quality of life rsch. ctr. Temple U., Phila., 1984—; McAndless disting. prof. and chair in the humanities Ea. Mich. U., Ypsilanti, Mich., 2002; dir. Arts and Quality Life Rsch. Ctr., Temple U., 2004—. Music therapy cons. Pvt. Practice, Cherry Hill, NJ, 1990—; editor in chief Jeffrey Books, Cherry Hill, NJ, 1993—; music therapy dir. Temple U. Hosp., Phila., 2000—; grant reviewer NIH, Bethesda, Md., 2000—, Nat. Cancer Inst., Bethesda, Md., 2001, Nat. Ctr. for Alternative and Complementary Medicine, Bethesda, Md., 2001; music therapist Compassionate Care Hospice, Cherry Hill, NJ, 2003—. Author (editor): (professional text) Methods of Teaching and Training the Music Therapist, 1988, Music Therapy at the End of Life, 2005; author: (professional text) Ethical Thinking in Music Therapy, 2000, (professional text and cd-rom) Medical Music Therapy: Present Status and Future Trends, 2005; editor: (professional text) Applications of Music in Medicine, 1990, Music therapy: International Perspectives, 1993, Music Vibration and Health, 1997, Music Therapy and Medicine, 1999. Cantor St. Pius X Ch., Cherry Hill, NJ, 1990—2003; bd. mem. Arts Adv. Coun., Cherry Hill, NJ, 1989—90, Phila. Assn. for Retarded Citizens: Ctr. for Creative Arts, Phila, 1989—95, Christ the King Sch., Haddonfield, NJ, 1990—97. Recipient Award for Music Therapy, Werlein, 1971, Award for Music, Lincoln Ctr., 1967, McAndless Disting. Prof. and Chair in the Humanities, Ea. Mich. U., 2002, Award of Merit, Am. Music Therapy Assn., 1985, Hon. Membership, Catalan Assn. for Music Therapy, 2000, Voluntas Assn. for the Handicapped, 1995, Polish Assn. for Music Therapy, 1997, Appreciation for Svc., Nat. Assn. for Music Therapy, 1998, Included in Men and Women of Distinction, Internat. Biog. Ctr., 1992, Best Paper, Internat. Communication Assn., 1991, Disting. Resch. Publ. award, Am. Music Therapy Assn., 2003; grantee Collaborative Rsch. Grant, Temple U., 2001, Music Therapy and Heart Failure, Music Merchants Assn., 2000, Travel/Rsch. Grant, Ctr. for Asian Studies, Temple U., 1993-4, NJ. Coun. for the Arts Block Grant, NJ. Coun. for the Arts, 1984-5, Music in Spl. Edn. Grant, La. Bur. of Elem. and Secondary Edn., 1982-3, Boyer Coll. Dean's Grant, Temple U., 2003, Prin. Investigator: Formula Fund Grant, State Pa. Fellow: Nat. Assn. for Music Therapy (pres. 1988—90, Plaque of Appreciation 1990), World Fedn. of Music Therapy (pres. 1993—96); mem.: Medart, USA (vice-president 1990—93), Internat. Soc. for Music in Medicine (internat. sci. com. 1993—2003). Roman Catholic. Office: Temple Univ Presser Hall 13th & Norris Philadelphia PA 19122 Personal E-mail: cdileo@temple.edu.

DILER, RASIM SOMER, psychiatrist, researcher; s. Kemal and Leman Cercel Diler; m. Hacer Aytas, Sept. 3, 1995; 1 child, Simge Su. MD, Istanbul U., Turkey, 1993. Cert. specialist in child and adolescent psychiatry Child and Adolescent Psychiatry Bd., 1999, Crisis Mgmt. in Psychiatry U. of Pitts., 2000, eye movement desensitization and reprocessing Internat. Soc. EMDR, 2001, Autism Diagnostic Interview Turkish Soc. of Child and Adolescent Psychiatry, 2003, Treatment of Pervasive Developmental Disorders Turkish Soc. of Child and Adolescent Psychiatry, 2003. Asst. prof. psychiatry Cukurova U. Faculty of Medicine, Child and Adolescent Psychiatry, Adana, Turkey, 1999—2003, assoc. prof. psychiatry, 2003—. Dir. outpatient svcs. Cukurova U. Faculty of Medicine, Child and Adolescent Psychiatry, Adana, Turkey, 1999—, co-dir. and supr. of rsch. studies, 1999—, co-dir. residency tng., 1999, web dir. of ofcl. child psychiatry univ. homepage, 1998—; bd. mem., Ctr. Hearing and Communication Disabilities Cukurova U. Faculty of Medicine, Adana, Turkey, 2003—; site coord. tech. and rsch. cooperation Xi'an U. (China) and Cukurova U., 2003—; bd. mem. and cons. Gov. Oguz Kaan Koksal Residential Treatment Ctr.(the first juvenile residential treatment ctr. of Adana city), Turkey, Adana, Turkey, 2002—; bd. mem. Bridging Ea. and Western Psychiatry Orgn., Pisa, Italy, 2002—. Co-dir. Commn. Planning Core Edn. For Grad. Students, Adana, Turkey, 2002—03; cons., bd. mem., and policy maker State Coun. for Preventing Youth from Harmful Environment and Activities, Adana, Turkey, 2001—03; coord. Commn. Planning Core Edn. For Grad. Students, Adana, Turkey, 2002—03. Named Hon. Prof. and Prof. Emeritus, Xi'an (China) Jiaoton U., 2003—; recipient Young Minds in CNS (Ctrl. Nervous Sys.) Award in Depressionand Anxiety category, AstraZeneca, 2001; fellow XII. World Congress of Psychiatry, World Psychiat. Assn., 2002; Disting. Rsch. grantee, Sci. and Tech. Rsch. Coun. of Turkey (TUBITAK), 2003—. Mem.: AAAS, Pa. Med. Soc. (licentiate), Bridging Ea. and Western Psychiatry (corr.; site coord. 2001), Turkish Psychiatry Soc. (life), Turkish Soc. of Child and Adolescent Psychiatry (life). Achievements include research in Pharmacotherapy and changes in regional cerebral blood flow in children with obsessive compulsive disorder; Emotional and behavioral problems in migrant children; Efficacy of Risperidone in Children with Autism; Efficacy of paroxetine in children with obsessive compulsive disorder; discovery of presence of selective serotonin reuptake inhibitor discontinuation syndrome in children; selective serotonin reuptake inhibitors induced mania in children with obsessive compulsive disorder; an atypical antipsyhotic agent which may be used adjunctively for obsessions, can induce obsessive compulsive symptoms in children; research in efficacy of moclobemide in young adolescents with major depressive disorder. Avocations: music, dance, travel, international cuisine, movies. Office: Cukurova U Faculty Medicine Balcali 01130 Adana Turkey also: 3811 O'Hara St Pittsburgh PA 15213 Office Phone: +90.322.3386060/3246. Personal E-mail: dilerrs@yahoo.com.

DILG, JOSEPH CARL, lawyer; b. Dallas, Apr. 1, 1951; s. Millard John and Helen Mary (Gill) D.; m. Alexandra Gregg, Aug. 5, 1972; children: Helen Lane, Mary Saunders. BA in economics, So. Meth. U., 1973; JD with high honors, U. Tex., 1976. Bar: Tex. 1976. Assoc. Vinson & Elkins, Houston, 1976—83, ptnr., 1983—2002, mng. ptnr., 2002—. Editor U. Tex. Law Rev., 1976. Trustee U. Tex. Law Sch. Found.; dir. Bus. Com. for the Arts Inc., Greater Houston Partnership, Ctrl. Houston Inc. Named Outstanding Editor, U. Tex. Law Rev., 1976; named one of The Top 100 Tex. Super Lawyers, Tex. Monthly, 2003—04. Mem. ABA, Tex. Bar Assn., Houston Bar Assn., Order of Coif. Office: Vinson & Elkins LLP 3401 First City Tower 1001 Fannin St Ste 2300 Houston TX 77002-6760 Business E-Mail: jdilg@velaw.com.

DILIBERTI, LARA MARIE, music educator; d. Mark Michael Medvedev and Ludmilla Sokolov; m. Charles Ernest DiLiberti, July 24, 1983 (div.). BS, William Paterson State U., 1980; MA, Columbia U., 1985. Cert. gen. edn. grades K-8. Band dir. Ben Franklin Jr. H.S., Teaneck, NJ, choir dir.; musical dir. Teaneck H.S.; gen. music tchr. Radburn Sch., Fairlawn, NJ; tchr. summer music theatre Fairlawn H.S.; summer vocal dir. Summit (N.J.) H.S., vocal musical dir.; choral dir. Matawan (N.J.) Regional H.S. Mem.: Music Educators Nat. Conf., Am. Choral Dirs. Assn., Adoptees Liberty Movement Assn., Reunited Twins Assn., Kappa Delta Pi. Avocations: writing, running, target shooting. Office Phone: 732-290-2800.

DILIBERTO, RICHARD ANTHONY, JR., lawyer; b. Hazleton, Pa., July 19, 1961; s. Richard A. Sr. and Marija (Vukcevich) D.; m. Faith Ann Petrovich, Sept. 4, 1982. BS in Edn. cum laude, Bloomsburg U. of Pa., 1982; JD cum laude, Widener U., Wilmington, Del., 1986. Bar: Del. 1986, Pa. 1987, N.J. 1987, U.S. Dist. Ct. Del. 1987. Law clk. Superior Ct. Del., Wilmington, 1986-87; ptnr. Young, Conaway, Stargatt & Taylor, Wilmington, 1987—. Adj. prof. paralegal program Widener U., 1987-90; rep. Del State House of Reps., 1992-2002. Contbr. articles to profl. jours. Coach basketball YMCA, softball, 1994—. Recipient Advocacy award ATLA, Outstanding Alumni Svc. award Widener U. Law Sch., 1999. Mem. ABA, Del. Bar Assn. (Disting. Legis. award 1999), Del. Trial Lawyers Assn. (pres. 2005—) Roman Catholic. Home: 311 Winterthur Ln Newark DE 19711-4136 Office: Young Conaway Stargatt & Taylor LLP PO Box 391 Wilmington DE 19899-0391 Fax: (302) 576-3290. E-mail: rdiliberto@ycst.com.

DILIBERTO, SAM MICHAEL, business educator; b. Cleve., Nov. 26, 1957; s. Menno DiLiberto and Marilyn (Lamont) Skinner. BS in Journalism, Ohio U., 1980, MEd in Higher Edn., 1988. Cert. tchr., Ohio. Bus. mgr. Haffa's, Athens, Ohio, 1979-81, cons., 1981-86; admissions counselor Hocking Coll., Nelsonville, Ohio, 1981-84, vets. cons., 1984-86, graphic designer, asst. to evening dir., 1985-86, prof. bus., 1986—. Recipient Excellence in Instrn. award Hocking Coll., 1991, Student Choice award, 1993. Avocations: golf, collecting music, photography, home repair. Home: 204 Mound St The Plains OH 45780-1077 Office: Hocking Coll JL 353 Hocking Pky Nelsonville OH 45764 Office Phone: 740-753-3591. Business E-Mail: diliberto_s@hocking.edu.

DILL, BONNIE THORNTON, sociology educator; BA in English, U. Rochester, 1965; MA in Human Relations/Edn., PhD in Sociology, NYU, 1979. Trainer and course asst. Ctr. for Human Rels. NYU, 1969-71; adj. lectr. Black and Hispanic Studies Program Bernard M. Baruch Coll., 1972-73; tchg. asst. Sociology Dept. NYU, 1974-75, adj. instr. Sociology Dept., 1976-77; counselor/lectr. Dept. Compensatory Programs Bernard M. Baruch Coll., CUNY, 1970-77; dir. and founder Ctr. for Rsch. on Women Memphis State U., 1982-88, prof. sociology Dept. Sociology and Social Work, 1978-91; prof. dept. women's studies, affiliate prof. sociology U. Md., 1991—, dir. Consortium on Race, Gender & Ethnicity. Mem. adv. bd. on rsch., scholarship and edn. Ms. Mag., 1985-91; mem. editl. bd. Signs: Jour. of Women and Culture in Soc., 1979-89, mem. selection adv. com. U. Chgo. Press; cons. numerous orgns.; presenter and lectr. in field. Co-editor: Women of Color in U.S. Society, 1994, Across the Boundaries of Race and Class: An Exploration of Work and Family Among Black Female Domestic Servants, 1994; contbr. numerous articles to jours. in field. Recipient numerous grants and fellowships including The Ford Found., 1988-89, 1989-91, 1992-94, 1999-2003, Jessie Bernard Disting. Contributions to Teaching, Am. Soc. Assn., Robin Williams Jr. Lectr. Women & Achievement. Mem. Am. Sociol. Assn. (com. on status of women in sociology, com. on noms. 1984-85, task force on minority fellow program 1986-87, Jessie Bernard award com. 1986-89, chair com. on coms. 1995, numerous others), Assn. Black Sociologists (bd. dirs. 1977-79), Nat. Coun. Rsch. on Women (bd. dirs. 1983-86), Nat. Women's Studies Assn., Soc. for the Study of Social Problems (editl. and publs. com. 1986-89, Lee-Founder's award com. 1985, 87, C. Wright Mills award com. 1980-81). Office: U of Md Womens Studies Program 2101 Woods Hall College Park MD 20742-0001 Business E-Mail: bd36@umail.umd.edu.

DILL, ELLIS HAROLD, university dean; b. Pittsburg County, Okla., Dec. 31, 1932; s. Harold and Mayme Doris (Ellis) D.; m. Cleone June Granrud, Sept. 12, 1953; children: Michael Harold, Susan Marie. AA, Grant Tech. Jr. Coll., 1951; BS in Civil Engring, U. Calif. at Berkeley, 1954, MS in Civil Engring, 1955, PhD, 1957. Asst. prof. to prof. aeros. and astronautics U. Wash., 1956-77, chmn. dept. aeros. and astronautics, 1976-77; dean engring. Rutgers U., New Brunswick, N.J., 1977-98, univ. prof., 1998—. Mem. Soc. Natural Philosophy. Achievements include research, numerous publications on mechanics of solids. Home: 436 Brentwood Dr Piscataway NJ 08854-3608 Office: Rutgers U Coll Engring 98 Brett Rd Piscataway NJ 08854-8058

DILL, KENNETH AUSTIN, pharmaceutical chemistry educator; b. Oklahoma City, Dec. 11, 1947; s. Austin Glenn and Margaret (Blocker) D. SB, SM, MIT, 1971; PhD, U. Calif., San Diego, 1978. Fellow Damon Runyon-Walter Winchell Stanford (Calif.) U., 1978-81; asst. prof. chemistry U. Fla., Gainesville, 1981-82; asst. prof. pharm. chemistry and pharmacy U. Calif., San Francisco, 1982-85, assoc. prof., 1985-89, prof., 1989—, co-dir. program in quantitative biology, assoc. dean rsch. Sch. Pharmacy, 2001—. Adj. prof. pharmaceutics U. Utah, 1989—. Contbr. numerous sci. articles to profl. publs.; patentee in field. Recipient Hans Neurath award Protein Soc., 1998; PEW Found. scholar. Fellow AAAS, Am. Phys. Soc. (physics policy coun. 2002—), Biophys. Soc. (nat lectr. 1996, pres. 1998); mem. Am. Chem. Soc., Protein Soc. Office: Univ Calif Pharm Chemistry Dept San Francisco CA 94143-0001

DILL, LADDIE JOHN, artist; b. Long Beach, Calif., Sept. 14, 1943; s. James Melvin and Virginia (Crane) D.; children: Ariel, Jackson Caldwell. BFA, Chouinard Art Inst., 1968. Chmn. of visual arts The Studio Sch., Santa Monica, Calif. Lectr. painting and drawing UCLA, 1975-88. Exhibitions include San Francisco Mus. Modern Art, 1977—78, Albright Knox Mus., Buffalo, 1978—79, Charles Cowles Gallery, N.Y.C., 1983—85, Sonnabend Gallery, The First Show, L.A., Represented in permanent collections Mus. Modern Art, N.Y.C., Laguna Mus. Art, Los Angeles County Mus., Mus. Contemporary Art, L.A., Santa Barbara Mus., San Francisco Mus. Modern Art, Seattle Mus., Newport Harbor Art Mus., Oakland Mus., Smithsonian Instn., IBM, Nat. Mus., Seoul, Republic of Korea, San Diego Mus. Art, La. Mus., Denmark, Am. Embassy, Helsinki, Finland, Corcoran Gallery Art, Washington, Chgo. Art Inst., Greenville County (S.C.) Mus., Palm Springs Desert Mus., Phoenix Art Mus., William Rockhill Nelsen Mus., Kansas City, Phillips Collection. Nat. Endowment Arts grantee, 1975, 82; Guggenheim Found. fellow, 1979-80; Calif. Arts Council Commn. grantee, 1983-84 Personal E-mail: laddiejohndill@comcast.net.

DILL, WILLIAM RANKIN, college president; b. Sewickley, Pa., Aug. 18, 1930; s. Frederick Hayes and Caroline (Rankin) D.; m. Jean McLeod, June 13, 1953; children: Jens McLeod, Holly Ruth, Harrison Rankin, Cynthia Wightman. AB, Bates Coll., 1951, LLD (hon.), 1987; MS, Carnegie Inst. Tech., 1953, PhD, 1956; postgrad., U. Oslo, 1953-54; LHD (hon.), Babson Coll., 1991. Faculty mem. Carnegie-Mellon U., Pitts., 1955—65; program dir. edn. R & D IBM, White Plains, NY, 1965-70; dean Grad. Sch. Bus. Adminstrn., NYU, NYC, 1970-80, U.S.-Chinese Nat. Ctr. for Mgmt. Devel., Dalian, China, 1980-81; pres. Babson Coll., Wellesley, Mass., 1981-89; dir. Office of Global Enterprise U. So. Maine, Portland, 1989-91, cons., 1991-94; pres. Anna Maria Coll., 1995-96, Boston Arch. Ctr., 1996-97; bd. dirs. Maine Coll. Art, Portland, 1999—, interim pres., 2005—. Bd. dirs. Salomon Bros. Mut. Funds; chmn. overseers Boston Architectural Ctr. Author: The New Managers, 1962, The Carnegie Tech. Management Game, 1964, The Organizational World, 1973, Running the American Corporation, 1978, Planning in the US and USSR, 1978. Fulbright scholar, 1953-54; recipient Disting. Achievement award Carnegie-Mellon U., 1989. Fellow AAAS; mem. Phi Beta Kappa, Sigma Xi, Delta Sigma Rho, Beta Gamma Sigma. Unitarian Universalist. Home: 25 Birch Ln Cumberland Foreside ME 04110-1225 Office: Maine Coll Art 97 Spring St Portland ME 04101 E-mail: wdill1@maine.rr.com.

DILLABER, PHILIP ARTHUR, financial analyst, consultant; b. Springfield, Mass., Aug. 24, 1922; s. Ralph E. and Grace (Holman) D.; m. Jacqueline M. Bertin, July 16, 1946; children: Anne Erline (Mrs. Donald Youngblood), Katherine Marie, John Philip, Patricia Elizabeth (dec.). BA with honors, Am. Internat. Coll., 1949; MBA, Ind. U., 1950; postgrad., U. Mich., Ind. U., 1950-54; PhD, Pacific Western U., 1985. Cert. govt. fin. mgr. Clk. rsch. and devel. div. Springfield Armory, 1946-47; rsch. asst. dept. econs. Ind. U., 1951, lectr. econs., 1955-57; orgn. and methods examiner USAF, Gulfport, Miss., 1952-53; mgmt. analyst 5th U.S. Army, Chgo., 1954-61; program progress and resources mgmt. analyst Continental Army Command, Ft. Monroe, Va., 1962-66; adminstrv. officer U.S. Army NIKE-X System Office, Alexandria, Va., 1967; program analyst Office Asst. Chief Staff Force Devel. Dept. Army, Washington, 1967-71, budget analyst Office Dep. Chief Staff Logistics, 1971-74; budget analyst Office Dep. Chief Staff Rsch., Devel. and Acquisition, Washington, 1974-80; sr. analyst Info. Spectrum, Inc., Arlington, Va., 1980-87; mem. Nat. Def. Exec. Reserve, Washington, 1985-97; cons. Profl. Group, Inc., 1992-99; del. Citizen Amb. Program Pub. Budgeting and Fin. Mgmt., People's Republic of China, 1995; mem. Nat. Exec. Svc. Corp., N.Y.C., 1997. Guest lectr. econs. Purdue U., 1959-61. Decorated Commendation medal Regional Coun., Normandy, France, 1994, Wall of Liberty Meml. Mus., Caen, France, 1994; mem. Exceptional WWII Fin. Unit displayed U.S. Army Fin. Corps Mus., Ft. Jackson, S.C. Mem. Am. Econ. Assn., Nat. Contract Mgmt. Assn., Nat. Def. Indsl. Assn., Am. Assn. Budget Program Analysis, Project Mgmt. Inst., Assn. Govt. Accts. (cert. govt. fin. mgr.), Am. Soc. Pub. Adminstrn., Sons. of Am. Revolution, Assn. Def. and Emergency Resources, Beta Gamma Sigma. Home: 3003 Arkendale St Woodbridge VA 22193-1223 E-mail: 103264.2265@compuserve.com.

DILLAHUNTY, GEORGE ROBERT, minister; b. Bklyn., Sept. 22, 1943; s. George Robert and Ruth Jean (Creighton) Bull; m. Mary Anna Cutler (div. Apr. 1996); children: Cheryl Ann, Pamela Jean, Kevin Michael; m. Alice Pearl Bender, Apr. 27, 1996; children: Earle Allen, Jeffrey Harold. AS, Mohegan C.C., 1977. Magistrate State Supreme Ct., Va.; ordained deacon AME Ch., 2002. Chief petty officer USN, 1961-85; bailiff Norfolk (Va.) Sheriff's Dept., 1985; magistrate Supreme Ct. of Va., Norfolk, 1985-94; rental mgr. Ford Rent-A-Car, Morehead City, NC, 1994—99; preacher Ame Zion Ch., 1999—2001; travelling min., 2001—; asst. pastor Morris Chapel Ame Zion Ch., Pollocksville, NC, 2001—02, Piney Grove AME Zion Ch., 2002—. Decorated Vietnam Combat Action Ribbon, Navy Achievement medal USN, 1982, Commendation medal, 85. Mem.: Assn. Naval Aviation, Masons. Democrat. Avocations: writing, bowling. Office: 1430 Temples Point Rd Trenton NC 28532 Home: PO Box 405 Havelock NC 28532-0405

DILLARD, DEAN INNES, English language educator, academic administrator; b. Melvern, Kans., Aug. 13, 1947; s. Alva Everett and Dorothy Marie (Whitney) D. BS in Edn., Emporia (Kans.) State U., 1969, MA, 1975, postgrad., 1977, Ft. Hays State U., Hays, Kans., 1980. Tchr. English, Unified Sch. Dist. 379, Clay Center, Kans., 1969-70; tchr. English and social studies Unified Sch. Dist. 208, WaKeeney, Kans., 1972-84; instr. English, Neosho County C.C., Chanute, Kans., 1984—, chair divsn. liberal arts, 1996-99, interim v.p. acad. and student affairs, 1997-98, 99-00. Fine arts task force Neosho County C.C., Chanute, 1990-91. With U.S. Army, 1970-71. Mem.: MLA, VFW (life), Nat. Acad. Advising Assn., Neosho County C.C. Educators Assn., Kans. Assn. Tchrs. English (exec. bd. 1981—84), Midwest Modern Lang. Assn., The Assn. Lit. Scholars and Critics (life), Nat. Coun. Tchrs. English, Kans. Assn. Scholars, Nat. Assn. Scholars, Assembly on Lit. for Adolescents (life), Kans. Acad. Advising Network, Am. Legion, C.C. Humanities Assn., Chanute Lions Club (zone chmn. 1988—90), Kappa Delta Pi. Republican. Home: 732 S Washington Ave Chanute KS 66720-2713 Office: Neosho County C C 800 W 14th St Chanute KS 66720-2639 Office Phone: 620-431-2820 235.

DILLARD, FAYE GRAHAM, education educator; b. Thaxton, Miss., Jan. 27, 1933; s. Bud and Sudiebet Graham; m. Roy Dillard, June 24, 1955. AA in edn., Holmes Jr. Coll., 1952; BA in edn., U. of Miss., 1954, MA in edn., 1959. Tchr. Randoph HS and Ranolph Mid. Sch., Randolph, Miss., 1952—57; tchr. 6th grade Pontotoc City Schs., Pontotoc, Miss., 1957—95; tchr./tutor Functional Literacy Exam Skills, Pototoc, 1996—2004. Mem. adv. bd. Pontotoc County Leadership, 1994—; mem. Foster Care Rev. Bd., 1995—99; mem. of edn. com. Miss. Commn. Vol., Jackson, Miss., 1996—99. Gov. appointee Miss. Chpt. Adv. Bd., 1992—94; mem. chmn. Leadership Team Miss., Jackson, 1992—2000; mem. Pontotoc County C. of C., 1996; chmn. Rep. Party, 1989—2004, vice chmn., 2004—. Recipient Miss. Hall of Master Teachers, U. for Women, 2000, No. Miss. Educator of the Yr., Phi Delta Kappa, 1992. Mem.: U. Miss. Alumni Assn., Holmes Jr. Coll. Alumni Assn. Republican. Bapt. Home: 4760 Thaxton Rd Thaxton MS 38871 Office Phone: 662-489-2290.

DILLARD, GEORGE STEWART, III, minister; b. Jacksonville, Fla., Dec. 17, 1958; s. George Stewart II and Carolyn Faye (Brown) D.; m. Reneé Cheryl Barnes, Mar. 26, 1988; children: Tiffany Reneé, Alexis Nichole. BS, Atlanta Christian Coll., 1983; postgrad., Emmanuel Sch. Religion, 1983-85; M in Ministry magna cum laude, Evang. Theol. Sem., 1996, postgrad., 1998—. Ordained to ministry Christian Ch., 1980. Min. Countyline Christian Ch., Brooks, Ga., 1980-82, New Hope Christian Ch., Rogersville, Tenn., 1983-85; sr. min. 1st Christian Ch., Rincon, Ga., 1985-93; min. preaching, Evangelism Peachtree City (Ga.) Christian Ch., 1993—, sr. min., 1999—. Pres. Min. Asst., Christian Ch., Savannah, Ga., 1986-88; v.p., treas., bd. dirs. Bd. Coastal Empire Christian Camp, Sylvania, Ga., 1986-93; com. mem. Ga. Christian Youth Conv., Atlanta, 1987, Ga. Christian Missionary Rally, Atlanta, 1989-93; chaplain Effingham County (Ga.) Sheriffs Dept., 1986-93, Effingham County High Sch. Football, 1986-93; chaplain McIntosh High Football, 1997—. Author column Mins. Thoughts, 1985-93, This Week (Peachtree City), 1995—. Chmn. com. George Bush for Pres., 1988; chmn. Victims/Witness Asistance Program, Effingham County, 1989-93; mem. Tidelands Coun. Prevention of Drug Abuse, Effingham County, 1989-93; pres. Effingham County Athletic Booster Club, 1990-93; exec. bd. dirs. Fayette Ballet, 1998—. Recipient Outstanding Young Mins. award N.Am. Christian Conv., Louisville, Ky., 1990; named one of Outstanding Young Men in Am., 1996, Hon. Chaplain Ho. of Reps., 105th Congress, 1997. Mem. Rotary (bd. dirs. 1989-91, co-chmn. tel. dir.), Peachtree Christian Conv. (founder, chmn. 1992). Home: 335 Little Creek Dr Sharpsburg GA 30277-1739 Office: Peachtree City Christian Ch Wisdom Rd Peachtree City GA 30269 *Have this attitude in yourselves which was in Christ Jesus. (Phil. 2:5). The world needs a Church which understands and lives this truth, that there is no price to great to pay in order to be obedient to the Father.*

DILLARD, JOHN JAMES, librarian; b. Lubbock, Tex., Nov. 30, 1950; s. Tillman Robert and Mary Lenora Dillard; m. Sara Frances Hammett, May 20, 1989. MS, U. of North Tex., Denton, Texas, 1986—88; MA, U. of Tex. at Arlington, Arlington, Texas, 1978—81. Profl. libr. U. of Tex., Arlington, Tex., 1988—. Recipient Star award, UTA Friends of Librs., 1997, Recognition Outstanding Libr. Resource Svcs., UTA Sch. Social Work, 1998. Mem.: Tex. Libr. Assn. Home: 6551 Locke Ave Fort Worth TX 76116-4303 Office: U Texas at Arlington 211 South Cooper St Room A-111 Arlington TX 76019-0497 Personal E-mail: dillard@uta.edu.

DILLARD, JOHN MARTIN, lawyer, pilot; b. Long Beach, Calif., Dec. 25, 1945; s. John Warren and Clara Leora (Livermore) D.; m. Patricia Anne Yeager, Aug. 10, 1968; children: Jason Robert, Jennifer Lee. Student, U. Calif., Berkeley, 1963-67; BA, UCLA, 1968; JD, Pepperdine U., 1976. Bar: Calif. 1976. Instr. pilot, Norton AFB, Calif., 1973-77; assoc. Magana, Cathcart & McCarthy, L.A., 1977-80, Lord, Bissell & Book, L.A., 1980-85; of counsel Finley, Kumble, Wagner, 1985-86, Schell & Delamer, 1986—94, Law Offices of John M. Dillard, 1985—, mediator, arbitrator, 1994—; v.p., gen. counsel, dir. Resort Aviation Svcs., Inc., Calif., 1988—93; mng. ptnr. Natkin & Weisbach, Calif., 1988—89; arbitrator Orange County Superior Ct. Atty. settlement officer U.S. Dist. Ct. Ctrl. Dist. Calif.; trained mediator Straus Inst. Active Am. Cancer Soc.; bd. dirs. Placentia-Yorba Linda Ednl. Found., Inc. Capt. USAF, 1968-73, Vietnam. Mem. ATLA (aviation litigation com.), Am. Bar Assn. (aviation com.), Orange County Bar Assn., Fed. Bar Assn., L.A. County Bar Assn. (aviation com.), Century City Bar Assn., Internat. Platform Assn., Res. Officers Assn., Orange County Com. of 100, Sigma Nu. Home: 19621 Verona Ln Yorba Linda CA 92886-2858 Office: 313 N Birch St Santa Ana CA 92701-5263 Office Phone: 714-953-9936. Personal E-mail: leegal1@aol.com.

DILLARD, MICHAEL E., lawyer; b. Shreveport, La. BA summa cum laude, So. Meth. Univ., Dallas, 1979, JD cum laude, 1982. Bar: Tex. 1982. Co-chair firmwide mergers and acquisitions practice group and head of corp. practice Houston Akin Gump Strauss Hauer & Feld LLP, Houston, 1989—, ptnr. Mng. editor Jour. of Air Law and Commerce, 1981—82. Mem.: Dallas Bar Assn., State Bar of Tex. (former sec., venture capital com. of Bus. Law Sect.), Phi Beta Kappa, Order of Coif. Office: Akin Gump Strauss Hauer & Feld LLP 44th Fl 1111 Louisiana St Houston TX 77002-5200 Office Phone: 713-220-5821. Office Fax: 713-236-0822. Business E-Mail: mdillard@akingump.com.

DILLARD, MIKE, retail executive; s. William Dillard. Exec. v.p. Dillard's Dept. Store, Little Rock. Office: Dillard Department Stores Inc 1600 Cantrell Rd Little Rock AR 72201-1110

DILLARD, RODNEY JEFFERSON, real estate executive; b. Short Hills, N.J., Jan. 1, 1939; s. Albert Jefferson and Anne E. (Willingham) D.; m. Anne Palfrey Lanston, June 10, 1961 (div.); children: Courtney Lanston, Carter Jefferson. BA, Rollins Coll., 1961. Account exec. A.M. Kidder Co., N.Y.C., 1961-62; v.p. Previews, Inc, Palm Beach, Fla., 1963-76; pres., chmn. bd. Illustrated Properties, Inc., Palm Beach, Fla., 1976-79; sr. v.p., bd. dirs. Sotheby's Internat. Realty Corp., Palm Beach, Fla., 1979-91; pres. John's Island Real Estate Co., Vero Beach, Fla., 1991-95, vice chmn., 1995-97; pres. The Dillard Investment Corp., Palm Beach, Fla., 1996, Illustrated Properties Internat. Inc., 1998—. Mem. Bath and Tennis Club (Palm Beach), Spouting Rock Club (Newport, R.I.), The Travellers Club (Paris). Office: Illustrated Properties Real Estate Inc 249 Royal Palm Way Palm Beach FL 33480 Office Phone: 561-366-1121. E-mail: rodneyipi@aol.com, rdillard@ipintl.com.

DILLARD, STEPHEN C., lawyer; b. Tyler, Tex., Nov. 1, 1946; BA, Baylor U., 1968, JD, 1971. Bar: Tex. 1971. Ptnr. Fulbright & Jaworski LLP, Houston, 1978—, chair, firmwide litig. dept., 2004—, mem. exec. com. Named a Tex. Super Lawyer, Tex. Monthly Mag., 2003, 2004. Fellow: Am. Bd. Trial Advs., Internat. Assn. Def. Counsel, Am. Coll. Trial Lawyers (life), Tex. Bar Found. (life); mem.: ABA, Houston Bar Assn., Tex. Assn. Def. Counsel, State Bar Tex., Phi Alpha Delta (v.p. 1984—87). Office: Fulbright & Jaworski LLP 1301 McKinney St Ste 5100 Houston TX 77010-3031 Office Phone: 713-651-5151, 713-651-5507. Office Fax: 713-651-5246. E-mail: sdillard@fulbright.com.

DILLARD, W. THOMAS, lawyer; b. Dothan, Ala., Nov. 28, 1941; s. William T. and Gladys (Harris) D.; m. Susan Jean Jakuboski, Oct. 26, 1974. BA, U. Tenn., 1963, JD, 1964. Bar: Tenn. 1965; cert. criminal trial specialist Nat. Bd. Trial Advocacy. Asst. U.S. atty. Dept. Justice, Knoxville, Tenn., 1967-76, chief asst. U.S. atty., 1978-83, U.S. atty., 1981, Tallahassee, 1983-86; ptnr. Ritchie, Fels, and Dillard, P.C., Knoxville, 1987—; U.S. magistrate, 1976-78. Adj. prof. East Tenn. State U., Knoxville, 1979-80, U. Tenn. Coll. Law, 1993—; instr. Knoxville Police Acad., 1979-82, Nat. Inst. Trial Advocacy, Chapel Hill, N.C. and Boulder, Colo., 1985-2001, U. Tenn. Trial Advocacy Program, 1992-2001 mem. Tenn. Bar Profl. Stds. com.; pres. Fed. Def. Svcs., 2001. Deacon Presbyn. Ch., Knoxville, 1972-76, elder, 1978-82, 88-91, 95-98, 2000-03; mem. Mayor's Commn. on Police; mem. Leadership Knoxville, 1998; bd. dirs. Helen Ross McNabb Ctr. Fellow Am. Coll. Trial Lawyers, Tenn. Bar Found.; mem. ABA, Am. Judicature Soc., Knoxville Young Lawyers (pres. 1972-73), Nat. Assn. Criminal Def. Lawyers, Tenn. Assn. Criminal Def. Lawyers (bd. dirs.), Nat. Assn. Former U.S. Attys. (bd. dirs.), Knoxville Bar Found. (bd. govs.). Avocations: reading, hiking, travel. Home: 8667 Ellijay Way Strawberry Plains TN 37871 Office: Ritchie Fels & Dillard 606 W Main St Knoxville TN 37902-2617 Office Phone: 865-637-0661. E-mail: dillard@rfdlaw.com.

DILLARD, WILLIAM, II, department store chain executive; b. 1945; married. Grad., U. Ark.; MBA, Harvard U. With Dillard Dept. Stores, Little Rock, 1967—, dir., 1968—, exec. v.p., 1973-77, pres. and COO, 1977—98, CEO, 1998—, chmn., 2002—. Nat. adv. bd. JPMorganChase & Co., Dallas Region adv. bd.; dir. Acxiom Corp. Office: Dillard Dept Stores Inc 1600 Cantrell Rd Little Rock AR 72201-1110*

DILLBERGER-BEY, ROSE ALEXANDRA, artist; b. St. Louis, May 26, 1918; d. Louis Jerome and Katherine Elizabeth (Von Pozojevic) Mirjanich; m. Howard Bassford Bowen, May 24, 1946 (div. Jan. 1957); m. Hugo Dillberger, Jan. 30, 1958 (dec. 1983); 1 child, Alexandra Maria; m. Everett Edward Bey, Jan. 1, 1995 (dec. May 2001). BFA, Washington U., St. Louis, 1941; postgrad., Pierce Coll., 1972—76, U. Calif., Northridge, 1986—87. Comml. artist Advertisers Artists, St. Louis, 1941—42; artist Wolf Printing Co., St. Louis, 1943—44, Gardner Advt. Co., St. Louis, 1944—46; mgr. advt. Kessler Fur Co., St. Louis, 1944; instr. fine arts Washington U., 1946—56; freelance artist, 1956—. One woman show at West Valley Art Mus., Sun City, Ariz., 1993; exhibited in group show at Sun City Art Mus., 1989; represented in collection at West Valley Art Mus., Sun City; numerous commd. portraits in pvt. collections abroad and in U.S. Art dir. Am. Women's Group, Teheran, Iran, 1976-79; treas. Advertising Artists, St. Louis, 1953-56. Mem. Ariz. Artists Guild, Vanguards (pres., treas.), Nat. Assn. Women in Arts, Am. Acad. Women Artists. Eastern Orthodox Catholic. Home: 10826 W Thunderbird Blvd Sun City AZ 85351-2646

DILLE, JOHN ROBERT, retired physician; b. Waynesburg, Pa., Sept. 2, 1931; s. Charles Emanuel and Ruth Emma (South) D.; m. Joan Marie Sirtosky, Dec. 17, 1955 (wid. Mar. 1996); children: Paul Andrew, John Alan. BS, Waynesburg Coll., 1952; MD, U. Pitts., 1956; M in Indsl. Health, Harvard U., 1960. Diplomate Am. Bd. Preventive Medicine; cert. correctional health profl. Intern Akron City Hosp., 1956-57; resident in aerospace medicine USAF Sch. Aerospace Medicine, San Antonio, 1960-62; program adv. officer FAA Civil Aeromed. Rsch. Inst., Oklahoma City, 1961-64; western region flight surgeon FAA, L.A., 1965; chief FAA Civil Aeromed. Inst., U.S. Dept. Transp., Oklahoma City, 1966-87, ret., 1987; med. dir. Okla. Dept. Corrections, Oklahoma City, 1990-93. Assoc. prof. U. Okla., 1961-98, dir. tng. residency in aerospace medicine, 1967-72; state surgeon Okla. Army N.G., 1990-91; surveyor Nat. Commn. on Correctional Health Care, 2000-04. Assoc. editor: Ag Pilot Internat. mag., 1980-98, Conservation Aeronautics mag., 1989-92, Above All mag., 1992; mem. editorial bd. Aviation, Space and Environ. Medicine, 1987-94; contbr. chpts. to textbooks and articles to profl. jours. With USAF, 1957-59; col. M.C., U.S. Army N.G., 1976-91. Recipient Meritorious award William A. Jump Found., 1968; named Army N.G. Flight Surgeon of Yr. 1987, Master Flight Surgeon, 1987. Fellow: Am. Coll. Preventive Medicine (regent 1974—77), Aerospace Med. Assn. (mem. exec. coun. 1978—81, chmn. history and archives com. 1982—90, chmn. sci. program com. 1985, 1st v.p. 1990—91, pres. 1992—93, mem. exec. coun. 1993—98, chmn. nominating com. 1997—98, Theodore C. Lyster award 1978, Harry G. Moseley award 1987, Armstrong lectr. 1997); mem.: Civil Aviation Med. Assn., Am. Soc. Aerospace Medicine Specialists, Acad. Correctional Health Profls., Soc. Correctional Physicians, Res. Officers Assn. (state surgeon Okla. dept. 2002—), Am. Air Mail Soc. (bd. dirs. 1990—92), Mil. and Hospitaller Order St. Lazarus of Jerusalem, Soc. U.S. Army Flight Surgeons (bd. govs. 1990—92, Order Aeromed. Merit), Internat. Acad. Aviation and Space Medicine, Nu Sigma Nu, Sigma Xi. Presbyterian. Home: 335 Merkle Dr Norman OK 73069-6429 E-mail: jrobtdille@aol.com.

DILLE, ROLAND PAUL, college president; b. Dassel, Minn., Sept. 16, 1924; s. Oliver Valentine and Eleanor (Johnson) D.; m. Beth Hopeman, Sept. 4, 1948; children— Deborah, Martha, Sarah, Benjamin. BA summa cum laude, U. Minn., 1949, PhD, 1962, LHD (hon.), 1995. Instr. English U. Minn., 1953-56; asst. prof. St. Olaf Coll., Northfield, Minn., 1956-61; asst. prof. English Calif. Lutheran Coll., Thousand Oaks, Calif., 1961-63; mem. faculty Moorhead (Minn.) State U., 1964-94, pres., 1968-94; ret., 1994. Author: Four Romantic Poets, 1969; contbr. numerous articles and revs. to profl. jours. Treas. Am. Assn. State Colls. and Univs., 1977-78, bd. dirs., 1978-80, chmn., 1980-81; mem. Nat. Coun. for Humanities, 1980-86; vice-chair Commn. on Higher Edn., North Cen. Assn., 1989-91, chair, 1991-93. With inf. AUS, 1944-46. Disting. Svc. to Humanities award given by Minn. Humanities Commn. named in his honor; named one of 100 most effective Am. coll. pres., 1987. Mem. Phi Beta Kappa. Home: 516 9th St S Moorhead MN 56560-3519 Office: Minn State U Moorhead 11th St S Moorhead MN 56560-9980 Office Phone: 218-477-2612. Business E-Mail: dille@mnstate.edu.

DILLENBECK, MARIANNE FRANCES, elementary school educator; d. Walter M and Marian Elizabeth Reitz; m. Kevin John Dillenbeck, Apr. 15, 1978; children: Daniel, Elizabeth. AAS, Herkimer County C.C., 1975; BS, Plattsburgh State U., 1977; M, Cortland State U., 1983. Tchr. Oppenheim-Ephratah Ctrl. Sch., St. Johnsville, NY, 1977—. Bldg. rep. Oppenheim-Ephratah, 1978—; v.p. Teachers Assn., 1978—. Mem.: Salisbury Grange, Herkimer County Pomona Grange (sec. 2000—). Republican. Cath. Avocations: cross country skiing, travel, camping, reading. Office: Oppenheim Ephratah Ctrl Sch 6486 Hwy 29 Saint Johnsville NY 13452 Personal E-mail: kmstmich@localnet.com.

DILLENBERG, JACK, dean; b. N.Y.C., Nov. 22, 1945; m. Marianna Dillenberg. BA in Psychology, Tulane U., 1967; DDS, NYU, 1971; MPH, Harvard Sch. Pub. Health, 1978. Dental officer USN, 1971—73; dentist Southbury (Conn.) Tng. Sch., 1973-75; mgr. dental clinic, Jamaica, 1975-77; vis. lectr. Cape Cod C.C., 1978-84; tutor dept. population scis. Harvard Sch. Pub. Health, 1978-81; cons. Mass. Dept. Mental Health, 1978-84; pvt. practice Beacon St. Dental Assocs., Brookline, Mass., 1980-84; instr. Harvard Sch. Dental Medicine, 1980-84; cons. Pan Am. Health Orgn., 1993-97; acting dir. Ariz. Dept. Health Services, 1993—94, dir., 1994—97; area health officer west area L.A. County Dept. Health Services, Santa Monica, Calif., 1997-99; assoc. dir. pub. health programs Calif. Dept. Health Services; dean Ariz. Sch. Dentistry and Oral Health A.T. Still U. of Health Sciences, 2001—; pres. Dillenberg & Friends Health Services Consulting. Cons. Dillenberg & Friends, Inc., 1979-84; pres. Dentanomics, Inc., 1984-86; pub. health cons. World Bank, 1978-99. Recipient Presdl. Citation ADA, 1992, Nat. Fluoridation award CDC, 1991, Alunmi award of Merit, Harvard Sch. Pub. Health, 1997; named Marketer of the Yr., Am. Mktg. Assn., 1997, CEO of Yr., Am. Pub. Adminstrn. Assn., 1997. Mem. ADA, Assn. State and Territorial Dental Dirs., Ariz. Pub. Health Assn. Office: AT Still U Health Scis Ariz Sch Dentistry & Oral Health 5850 East Still Cir Mesa AZ 85206 E-mail: jdillenberg@dhs.co.la.ca.us.

DILLENBURG, CAROLYN EVA LAUER, retired secondary education educator; b. Adair County, Iowa, May 13, 1934; d. Harvey Francis and Lorna Orilda (Gilbert) Lauer; m. Dale Everett Dillenburg, May 29, 1954; children: Candace Dee Brotherton, Shari Sue Eivins, Jeffrey Dale Dillenburg. AA, Creston Jr. Coll., 1954; BS, Iowa State Coll., 1956; MSEd., Drake U., 1968. Cert. secondary tchr. Engr.'s aide GM, Indpls., 1955; math. and sci. tchr. Afton (Iowa) Independent Sch., 1957-58, Runnells (Iowa) Independent Sch., 1958-59; math. and English tchr. Winterset (Iowa) Community Sch., 1959-61; math. and sci. tchr. O-M Community Sch., Orient, Iowa, 1961-63; math. and English tchr. Creston (Iowa) Community Sch., 1964-65; math. tchr. Lenox (Iowa) Community Sch., 1968-94; ret., 1994. Adj. math. tchr. Southwestern C.C., Creston, 1977-81; curriculum coord. Green Valley AEA 14 Schs., 1994—. Treas. Iowa Town & Country YWCA, southwest Iowa, 1981-2001; pres. Creston YWCA Coun., 1981—2001; bd. trustees Greater Cmty. Hosp., 1997—. Mem. NEA (life), S.W. Uniserv (bd. dirs. 1988-92, mem. contract advancement cadre 1992-94, mem. ret. tchrs. cadre 1994—2000), Iowa State Edn. Assn. (life, ret., mem. standing com. for ret. tchrs. 1994—2000), Creston Area Ret. Sch. Personnel Assn., P.E.O., Elzivirs Women's Reading Group, Delta Kappa Gamma, Pi Mu Epsilon, Psi Chi. Mem. United Ch. of Christ. Avocations: antique collecting, travel. Home: 1392 150th St Creston IA 50801-8406

DILLER, BARRY, broadcast executive; b. San Francisco, Feb. 2, 1942; s. Michael and Reva (Addison) D. V.p. feature films and movies of week ABC, 1971-73, ABC (prime time TV ABC Entertainment), 1973-74; chmn. bd. Paramount Pictures Corp., 1974-84; pres. Gulf & Western Entertainment and Comm. Group, Simon and Schuster, Inc., Madison Sq. Garden Corp., SEGA Enterprises, Inc., 1983-84; chmn., CEO Twentieth Century Fox Film Corp., TCF Holdings, L.A., 1984-85, Fox, Inc., 1984-92, QVC Network, Inc., 1992-94; CEO, bd. chair, chmn. Silver King Comm., Inc., 1995-98; chmn. bd. dirs., CEO Home Shopping Network, Inc., 1996-98; dir., chmn., CEO IAC / InterActiveCorp (formerly USA Networks, Inc., USA Interactive), N.Y.C., 1995—; co-CEO Vivendi Universal, 2002—03. Bd. dirs. Washington Post Co., Coca-Cola Co., News Corp Ltd., FCC Adv. Com. on Advanced TV Svcs., Mus. TV and Radio, Calif. Inst. Arts, Acad. Arts and Scis. Found., Ticketmaster Online-Citysearch, Inc., Seagram Co. Ltd., Channel 13/WNET, Washington Post.; bd. councilors Sch. Cinema-TV U. So. Calif.; exec. bd. med. scis. UCLA; bd. trustees NYU.; dean's coun. Tisch Sch. Art; mem. adv. bd. Ctr. Health Comm. Harvard U. Sch. Pub. Health. Mem. Pres. Export Coun.; bd. dirs. N.Y. Pub. Libr., Conservation Internat., Mus. TV and Radio. Office: US InterActive Corp 152 W 57th St Fl 42 New York NY 10019-3310*

DILLER, EDWARD DIETRICH, lawyer; b. Pandora, Ohio, Aug. 7, 1947; s. Hiram D. and Selma G. (Warkentin) D.; m. Karen Esmonde, June 1, 1968; children: Jason, Anna. BA, Bluffton Coll., 1969; postgrad., U. Oreg., 1969-70; JD cum laude, Harvard U., 1976. Assoc. Taft, Stettinius & Hollister, Cin., 1976-84, ptnr., 1984—, chmn. dept. bus. & fin., 1998—. Chmn. Gen. Conf. Coun. on Higher Edn., 1990-93, 96-2001, vice chmn., 1993-94; lectr. numerous seminars; mem. women's initiative adv. bd. Deloitte & Touche, Cin., 2000—. Tchr. Mennonite Ctrl. Com., Frankfield, Jamaica, 1970-73; chmn. edn. integration com. Mennonite Ch. USA, 1997-2001; trustee Mental Health Svcs. East, 1977-85, Bluffton Coll., 1979-2002, mem. exec. com., 1987-2002, chmn. bd., 1991-2002; mem. Family Svc. of Greater Cin. Area, 1989-96, chmn., 1992-95; trustee Habitat for Humanity (Southwestern Ohio and No. Ky. affiliate), 1995-2000; trustee Working in Neighborhoods, 1991-94, Dan Beard Coun. Boy Scouts of Am., 1996-, chmn. 2003-, Leadership Cin. Alumni Assn., 2001-02; mem. Leadership Cin. Class XVI; trustee Found. Family Svc., 1997-, chmn. 2002-. Mem. Ohio State Bar Assn., Cin. Bar Assn., Ohio Harvard Law Sch. Assn. Office: 1800 Firstar Tower 425 Walnut St Cincinnati OH 45202-3923 E-mail: diller@taftlaw.com.

DILLER, ELIZABETH E., architect, educator, artist; b. Poland, 1954; B in Arch., Cooper Union Sch. of Arch., 1979. Ptnr. Diller & Scofidio (now Diller Scofidio & Renfro), NYC, 1979—; assoc. prof. arch. design Princeton U., NJ, 1990—, prof. arch. Works include Inst. of Contemporary Art, Boston, Seagrams, NY, Mus. of Art & Tech., NY, Blur Bldg. (Progressive Architecture Design award), media pavillion for Swiss EXPO 2002, designed viewing platform for Ground Zero, NYC, Brasserie Restaurant, NY (James Beard Found. award for Best New Restaurant Design), Slither, Gifu, Japan, Loophole, Mus. Contemporary Art, Chgo., 1992, Apparatus Drawing, Mus. of Modern Art, NY, 1993, Case#00-17164, New Mus., 1993, Dysfunction, Ctr. d'Art Contemporian de Castres, France, 1993, Desiring Eye, I' dentity and Difference, Triennale, Milan, 1994, Pelts, Thaddeus Ropac Gallery, Paris, France, 1997, Non-Place, San Francisco Mus. Modern Art, 1997, Slow House, At the End of the Century: One Hundred Years of Architecture, Mus. Contemporary Art, LA, 1998, The American Lawn: Surface of Everyday Life, Canadian Centre for Architecture, Montreal, 1998, Public Faces/Private Places, Pusan Internat. Arts Festival, Korea, 1998, His/Her Bathroom, Thomas Healy Gallery, NY, 1998, Dress Code, Landesmuseum, Linz, Austria, 1998, (permanent collections) Travelogues, Internat. Arrivals Terminal 4, JFK Airport, NY, (installation) The Desiring Eye: Reviewing the Slow House, Gallery MA, Tokyo, 1992, Master/Slave, Fondation Cartier, Paris, InterClone Hotel, Ataturk Airport for Istanbul Biennial, 1997, (dance collaborations with the Lyon Ballet Opera of France and Charlerol/Danses of Belgium (touring exhbn.) EJM1:Man Walking at Ordinary Speed and EJM2: Inertia, 1998, (web project) Refresh, Dia Art Found., (video installation) Pageant, Johannesburg Biennial & Rotterdam Film Festival, 1997, (permanent installation) X,Y, Kobe, Japan, 1997, (multi-media work for stage in collaboration with Builders Assn.) Jet Lag, 1998 (Obie award for Creative Achievement), (pub. art commn., permanent video marques) Jump Cuts, United Artists Cineplex, San Jose, Calif., (collaborative dance work with Charlerol/Danses) Moving Target, (collaborative theater work with Dumb Type and Hotel Pro Forma) Business Class, Copenhagen Cultural Capital, (interactive video installation) Indigestion, Barbican Art Gallery, London, Walter Phillips Gallery, Banff, Canada, Biennial Nagoya, Japan, 1997, (electronic project) Subtopia, ICC Gallery, Tokyo, 1997, and several others, installations commissioned by Mus. of Modern Art, Whitney Mus., New Mus. of Contemporary Art, Walker Art Ctr., Minn., Cartier Found., Palais des Beaux-Arts Brussels, and Gallery Ma Tokyo, works are in the permanent collections of Mus. of Modern Art, Mus. Modern Art San Francisco, Fond Nat. d'Art Contemporain, several FRACs in France, Musee de la Mode in Paris, and many private collections, co-pub. with Ricardo Scofidio Back to the Front: Tourisms of War, FRAC Basse-Normandie, 1994, Flesh: Architectural Probes, Princeton Architectural Press, 1995, Blur: The Making of Nothing, Abrams, 2002. Recipient Chrysler award for Innovation in Design, 1988—89, MacArthur Found. award, 1999, Brunner prize in Arch., AAAL, 2003, MacDermott award for Creative Achievement, MIT; Graham Found. Fellowship, 1998—99, Chgo. Inst. for Architecture and Urbanism Fellowship. Office: Princeton U Sch Architecture 5116 Architecture Princeton NJ 08544-0001 Address: Diller Scofidio & Renfro 36 Cooper Sq New York NY 10003 Office Phone: 212-260-7971.*

DILLER, PHYLLIS (PHYLLIS ADA DRIVER DILLER), actress, writer; b. Lima, Ohio, July 17, 1917; d. Perry Marcus and Frances Ada (Romshe) Driver; m. Sherwood Anderson Diller, Nov. 4, 1939 (div. Sept. 1965); children: Peter III, Sally, Suzanne Diller Mills, Stephanie Diller Waldron, Perry; m. Warde Donovan, Oct. 7, 1965 (div. July 1975). Student, Sherwood Music Conservatory, Chgo., 1935-37, Bluffton (Ohio) Coll., 1938-39; D.H.L., Nat. Christian U., 1973; PhD (hon.), Bluffton Coll., 1993. (Best TV Comedienne award TV Radio Mirror 1965); Author: Phyllis Diller Tells All About Fang, 1963, Phyllis Diller's Housekeeping Hints, 1966, Phyllis Diller's Marriage Manual, The Complete Mother, The Joys of Aging and How to Avoid Them, 1981, (with Richard Buskin) Like A Lampshade in a Whorehouse: My Life in Comedy, 2005; Accompanied Bob Hope entertainment group to, South Vietnam, Christmas, 1966, symphony appearances soloing on piano.; Theatrical prodns. include Dark at the Top of the Stairs, 1961, Wonderful Town, 1962, Happy Birthday, 1963, Hello, Dolly!, 1970, Everybody Loves Opal, 1972, What Are We Going to Do With Jenny, 1977, Nunsense, 1989, The Wizard of Oz, 1990-92; numerous appearances TV and radio, concerts, supper clubs and hotels, 1955-; producer, writer: Phyllis Diller Shows, 1963, 64; rec. artist, Verve Records, Columbia Records, pres., BAM Prodns., Ltd., from 1965, PhilDil Prodns., Ltd., 1966-; motion pictures include Eight on the Lam, 1967, The Private Navy of Sergeant O'Farrell, Hungry Reunion, 1981, Pink Motel, 1983, The Nutcracker Prince, 1990, The Boneyard, 1991, The Perfect Man, 1993, The Silence of the Hams, 1994, A Bug's Life (voice), 1998, The Debtors, 1999, Everything's Jake, 2000, The Last Place on Earth, 2002, Hip! Edgy! Quirky!, 2002, West From North Goes South, 2002, Motocross Kids, 2004, West From North Goes South, 2004, Forget About It, 2005; star: TV series The Pruitts of Southampton, 1966-67, Beautiful Phyllis Diller Show, 1968-69 (Recipient honors including Star of Year award Nat. Assn. Theatre Owners), The Bold and the Beautiful (recurring role), 1995-, Titus, 2002; video appearance: How to Have a Moneymaking Garage Sale, 1987. Recipient Minuteman award U.S. Treasury Dept., Disting. Service citation Ladies Aux. VFW, Woman of Year award Variety Club Women Balt.; Golden Apple Hollywood Women's Press Club, 1967, Woman of Year award St. Louis chpt. Nat. Bus. and Profl. Women's Club, 1971; named hon. mayor Brentwood, Calif., 1971; Hon. life mem. San Francisco Press and Union League Club; named Walk of Fame Star on Hollywood Blvd., 1975, Hon. Chair for Outstanding Svc. to Calif. State U. at Los Angeles, Friends of Music Scholarship Auction, 1982; recipient Doctor of Comedy award Kent State U., 1980, AMC Cancer Rsch. Ctr. Humanitarian award, 1981, Child-Help USA Woman of Yr. award, 1989; City of Los Angeles Proclamation of Phyllis Diller Week Mayor Tom Bradley, 1979; named to Ohio's Hall of Fame, 1981; Commonwealth scholar, 1964. Office: c/o The Sychin Co Ste 208 12747 Riverside Dr Valley Village CA 91607-3303*

DILLEY, WHITNEY CROTHERS, language educator; d. Robert and Judith Crothers; m. Larry Allan Dilley, Sept. 21, 1996; 1 child, Emma Judith. BA in English, Oberlin Coll., 1987; MA, U. Wash., 1992, PhD in Comparative Lit., 1998. Tchg. asst. dept. Asian langs. and lit. U. Wash., Seattle, 1994—98; asst. prof. dept. English Shih Hsin U., Taipei, Taiwan, 1998—. Editor: Feminism/Femininity in Chinese Literature, 2002; contbr. articles to profl. jours.; guest editor: Tamkang Rev., 1999—2000. Fellow Taiwan U. fellow, U. Wash., 1992—99; scholar K.C. Hsiao scholar, 1995—96; Taiwan Nat. Rsch. fellowship, 2004—05. Mem.: MLA, Comparative Lit. Assn. Republic of China, English Am. Lit. Assn. Republic of China. Office: Shih Hsin U English Dept 1 Lane 17 Mu-cha Rd Sect 1 Taipei 116 Taiwan Business E-Mail: wdilley@cc.shu.edu.tw.

DILLIN, JOHN WOODWARD, JR., retired editor, reporter; b. Miami, Fla., July 6, 1936; s. John Woodward and Alberta (Thompson) D.; m. Gay Andrews, Oct. 1, 1966 (div. 1988); 1 child, Katherine. BSJ. with honors, U. Fla., 1958, postgrad. in U.S. history, 1961-63. Reporter St. Augustine Record, Fla., 1958, Tampa Tribune, Fla., 1960-61; with Christian Sci. Monitor, 1964—, reporter Boston, 1964-66, corr. Saigon, Vietnam, 1966-67, city editor Boston, 1967-71, corr. Atlanta and Washington, 1971-79, mng. editor for news Boston, 1979-83, nat. polit. corr. Washington, 1983-94, mng. editor Boston, 1994-99, assoc. editor, Washington bur. chief Washington, 1999—, ret., 2001. Mem. advd. bd. UF Florida/Today, 2004—. Served with AUS, 1958-59 Recipient Sigma Delta Chi award for Washington Corr., 1993; named Alumnus of Distinction, Coll. Journalism and Comms., U. Fla., 2002. Christian Scientist. Home: 5525 15th St N Arlington VA 22205-2712 Office: 910 16th St NW Washington DC 20006-2903 E-mail: dillinj@csmonitor.com.

DILLINGHAM, JOHN ALLEN, marketing professional; b. Kansas City, Mo., Jan. 9, 1939; s. Jay B. and Frances (Thompson) D.; m. Nancy Jane Abbott, Sept. 4, 1965; children: Allen Edwards, William Kemp. AS, Wentworth Mil. Acad., 1958; AB in Polit. Sci., U. Mo., 1961, MS in Pub. Adminstrn., 1962. Br. mgr. Rudy-Patrick divsn. W.R. Grace Co., Mt. Vernon, Ill., 1964-68; pres. Sho-Hawk Industries, Kansas City, Mo., 1968-72; v.p. comml. loans Traders Nat. Bank, Kansas City, 1972-79; sr. v.p. sales and mktg. Garney Constrn. Co., Kansas City, 1979-95; pres., bd. dirs. Jo Dill, Inc., 1985—, Dillingham Enterprises, 1997—. Bd. dirs. Waddell and Read Advisor Funds 1997-00, Inc., Kansas City; chmn. Clay County Indsl. Devel. Authority, 1980-2003, Clay County EDC, 1972-74; adv. bd. for extension U. Mo., 1972-80; cons. CMSU Grad. Sch., Warrensberg, Mo., 1996-97; dir., cons. McDougal Constrn., Kansas City, 1996-97; adv. dir. Northland Bd. United Mo. Bank, 1998—, Synergy Svcs. Trustee Wentworth Mil. Acad., Lexington, 1978-80, 93-00; state chmn. Mo. 4H Found., Columbia, 1985-90; mem. ctrl. governing bd. Children's Mercy Hosp., Kansas City, 1987-92; bd. dirs. Kansas City Conv. and Vis. Bur., 1976-80, Northland Cmty. Fund, Kansas City, 1988-97, Kansas City Sports Commn., 1990-93; treas. Harry S. Truman Scholarship Nat. Alumni Assn., 1979-90; mem., v.p. Kansas City Bd. Police Commrs., 1990-95; chmn. Kansas City Mcpl. Asst. Corp., 1984—, Alex Doniphan Meml. Hwy. Naming, 1998, Naming I635 Harry Darby Meml. Pkwy; hon. co-chair St. Plus X H.S. Capital campaign, 1997-98; coordinating bd. task force on affordability of higher edn. State of Mo., 1999; mem. Nat. 4H Resource Devel. Com., 1990-92, mem., pres. Kansas City Mayor's Fast Forward Commn., 1996—; mem. exec. com. Metro C. C. Found., Kansas City, 1996—; exec. bd. Heart of Am. coun. Boy Scouts Am., 1993-01; 1st bd. dirs. alumni assn. U.S. Command and Gen. Staff Coll., Ft. Leavenworth, Kans., 1993—; dir. DARE of Greater Kansas City, 1995-98, CMSU Found. Warrensburg, 1995-97, Am. Royal, Kansas City, Mo., 1997-03; co-chmn. K.C. Storm runoff campaign, 1998. With U.S. Army, 1964. Recipient Faculty Alumni award U. Mo., Columbia, 1981, Silver Beaver award Boy Scouts Am. Heart Am. coun., 1992, Harry S. Truman Scholarship Appreciation plaque, 1993, Cmty. Svc. award Park Coll., 1993, Pub. Svc. award Ctrl. Mo. State Univ., 1994; named one of 100 Most Influential Kans. Citizens, Ingrams Mag., 1993, Spirit award Kansas City, 1999. Mem. SAR, VFW, Am. Legion, Sons of the Confederate Officers, Decendents of Magna Charta, Plantenegent Soc., Northland C. of C. (Quality of Life award 1990), KC Kings, Gold Coaters (pres. 1979-89), Mt. Vernon Ill. C. of C. (pres. 1968), Native Sons Kansas City (bd. dirs., pres., 1991-92, 98—), Sigma Alpha Epsilon (KC Alumni Assn. pres. 1976, Honor Man 1988, trustee Nat. Found. 1987-93, Nat. Disting. Svc. award 1993). Democrat. Mem. Christian Ch. (Disciples Of Christ). Avocations: fishing, landscaping, family geneaology. Home: 4040 NW Claymont Dr Kansas City MO 64116-1751 Office: 924 Livestock Exch Bldg Kansas City MO 64102 Office Fax: 816-842-6803.

DILLINGHAM, KATHERINE HALL, musician, educator; d. M. Frank and Eve Harlan Dillingham. MusB summa cum laude, Rutgers U., 1990, MusM, 1992; diploma, Moscow (Russia) Conservatory, 1998. Co-editor (owner): Sonatas For Cellow and Keyboard, 2005—; musician: (albums) The Moscow Chamber Orchestra, 2001, 2003, 50th Anniversary Party, 2003, Salzburg Festival, 2004, Carnegie Recital Hall, 2005, U. N.C., 2005, Lincoln Ctr. Festival, 2005—, (invited) U.S. Supreme Ct., 2005—. Grantee, Conn. Alliance Music, 2003—05; scholar, Rutgers U., 1985—92. Mem.: Chamber Music Am., Musical Am., Am. Fedn. Musicians. Avocations: cooking, outdoors.

DILLINGHAM, WILLIAM BYRON, literature educator, author; b. Atlanta, Mar. 7, 1930; s. Cornelius Howard and Emerald (Storey) D.; m. Marion Elizabeth Joiner, July 3, 1952; children: Rebecca Lynn, Judith Ann, Paul Christopher. BA, Emory U., 1955, MA, 1956; PhD, U. Pa., 1961. Instr. Emory U., Atlanta, 1956-62, asst. prof., 1962-66, assoc. prof., 1966-68, prof., 1968-84, chair. dept. English, 1979-82, 85-86, 90-91, Charles Howard Candler prof. Am. lit., 1984-96; prof. emeritus, 1996—. Author: Frank Norris: Instinct and Art, 1969, An Artist in the Rigging, 1972, Melville's Short Fiction, 1977, Melville's Later Novels, 1986, Melville and His Circle: The Last Years, 1996, Rudyard Kipling: Hell and Heroism, 2005; co-author: Humor of the Old Southwest, 1964, 3d edit., 1994, Practical English Handbook, 10th edit., 1996; mem. editl. bd. Nineteenth-Century Lit., 1990-97, South Atlantic Rev., 1986-89, Frank Norris Studies, 1986-94. Served with U.S. Army, 1950—52. Recipient Fulbright award, U.S. Govt., 1964—65, award of distinction, Emory U., 2000, Disting. Emeritus award, 2004; fellow, Guggenheim Found., 1982—83; Sr. fellow, NEH, 1978—79, Heilbrun Disting. Emeritus fellow, 2002—03. Mem. MLA (mem. adv. coun. Am. lit. sect. 1988-90), Nat. Assn. Scholars, Soc. Lit. Scholars and Critics, Frank Norris Soc., Melville Soc. (pres. 1987), Kipling Soc., Phi Beta Kappa, Omicron Delta Kappa. Home: 1416 Vista Leaf Dr Decatur GA 30033-2012 also: 3258 Esperanza Ave Daytona Beach FL 32118-6231 Business E-Mail: wdillin@emory.edu.

DILLMAN, DONALD ANDREW, sociologist, educator, survey methodologist; b. Chariton, Iowa, Oct. 24, 1941; BS, Iowa State U., 1964, MS, 1966, PhD, 1969. Rsch. assoc. Iowa State U., Ames, 1967-69; asst. prof. Wash. State U., Pullman, 1969-73, assoc. prof., dept. chair, 1973-81, prof., 1978—2003, dir. social and econ. scis. rsch. ctr., 1986-96, dep. dir. R&D Social Econ. Sci. Rsch. Ctr., 1996—, Thomas S. Foley disting. prof. govt. and pub. policy, 2000—, Regents prof., 2003—. Guest prof. German Ctr. for Survey Methods Rsch., Mannheim, Fed. Republic of Germany, 1985, 87, 2000; sr. survey methodologist Office of Dir. US Bur. Census, 1991-95; sr. scientist Gallup Orgn., 1995—; cons. and lectr. in field. Author: Mail and Telephone Surveys, 1978, Mail and Internet Surveys, 2000; co-author 5 books; contbr. articles to profl. jour. Recipient Alumni Disting. Achievement citation Iowa State U., 2001, Lester F. Ward for Disting. Contbns. to Applied Sociology, Soc. for Applied Sociology, 2002; Kellogg fellow, 1981-83; grantee in field. Fellow AAAS, Am. Statis. Assn. (Roger Herriot award 2000); mem. Am. Sociol. Assn., Rural Sociol. Soc. Am. (pres. 1983-84, Outstanding Svc. award 1983, Excellence in Rsch. award 1998), Am. Assn. Pub. Opinion Rsch. (sec.-treas. 1995-97, councillor-at-large 1999, pres. 2001, AAPOR Award for Exceptionally Distinguished Achievement, 2003) Home: 705 SW Mies St Pullman WA 99163-2056 Office: Wash State U Wilson Hall 133 Pullman WA 99164-4014 E-mail: dillman@wsu.edu.

DILLMAN, LINDA, retail executive; Student, U. Indpls. With Hewlett-Packard, Wholesale Club (acquired by Wal-Mart Stores, Inc.), Indpls.; application devel. mgr. Wal-Mart Stores, Inc., 1991—97, dir. applications devel., 1997—98, v.p. applications devel., 1998—99, v.p. internat. sys., 1999—2002, sr. v.p., CIO info. sys. divsn., 2002—03, exec. v.p., CIO, 2003—. Bd. dirs. Northwest Ark. Community Coll. Mem.: Uniform Code Council (bd. mem.). Office: Wal-Mart Stores Inc 702 SW Eighth St Bentonville AR 72716

DILLON, COREY, professional football player; b. Oct. 24, 1975; married; 1 child, Cameron. Student, U. Wash. Football player Cin. Bengals, 1997—2003, New England Patriots, 2004—. Named to NFL Pro-Bowl, 1999—2001, 2004. Achievements include mem. Super Bowl XXXIX Champion New England Patriots, 2004. Office: c/o New England Patriots 1 Patriot Place Foxboro MA 02035*

DILLON, DAVID ANTHONY, editor, educator; b. Fitchburg, Mass., Aug. 24, 1947; s. John Joseph and Lauretta Irene (Morris) D.; m. Sally Ann Hall, June 5, 1971; children: Christopher, Catherine. BA, Boston Coll., 1963; MA, Harvard U., 1965, PhD, 1970. Asst. prof. So. Meth. U., Dallas, 1970-77; mag. editor D Mag., Dallas, 1978-81; archtl. editor Dallas Morning News, 1983—. Author: Experience and Expression, 1976, Dallas Architecture, 1986, Extending the Legacy: Planning America's Capital in the 21st Century, 1997, The Architecture of O'Neil Ford, 1999; contbg. editor Texas Architect, Landscape Architecture, 1990—, Archtl. Record, 1996—. Loeb fellow Harvard U., 1986-87; NEA Critic's grantee, 1980; recipient AP award for criticism, 1988, 90, 91, 2002. Democrat. Roman Catholic. Home: PO Box 3323 Amherst MA 01004-3323 Office: The Dallas Morning News 508 Young St Dallas TX 75202-4828 Office Phone: 214-977-8471. Business E-Mail: ddillon@dallasnews.com.

DILLON, DAVID BRIAN, retail grocery executive; b. Hutchinson, Kans., Mar. 30, 1951; s. Paul Wilson and Ruth (Muirhead) D.; m. Dee A. Ehling, July 29, 1973; children: Jefferson, Heather, Kathryn. BS, U. Kans., 1973; JD, So. Meth. U., 1976. V.p. Fry's Food Stores of Ariz. Inc. div. Dillon Cos. Inc., Phoenix, 1978-79, exec. v.p., 1979-83; v.p. Dillon Cos. Inc. (subs. of Kroger Co.), Hutchinson, 1983-86, pres., 1986-95; exec. v.p. Kroger Co., Cin., 1990-95; chmn. bd. Dillon Cos., Inc. (subs. Kroger Co.), Cin., 1993—95; pres., COO The Kroger Co., Cin., 1995—99, pres., 1999—2000, pres., COO, 2000—03, CEO, 2003—, chmn., 2004—. Bd. dirs. Convergys. Chmn. Leadership Hutchinson, 1986-87, Leadership Kans., 1988; bd. dirs. Bethesda Hosp., Cin., 1996—; trustee U. Kans. Endowment Assn., 1993—, U. Cin. Found., 1997—, Dan Beard coun. Boy Scouts Am., 1996—; bd. advisors U. Kans. Bus. Sch., 1990—. Recipient Brotherhood-Sisterhood award Kans. region NCCJ, 1992. Mem. U. Kans. Alumni Assn., Urban League of Greater Cin. (trustee 1998—), Order of Coif, Sigma Chi (Balfour award 1973). Republican. Presbyterian. Office: The Kroger Co 1014 Vine St Cincinnati OH 45202-1100

DILLON, DONALD F., data processing executive; Co-founder, pres. Info. Tech., Inc., 1976—95; vice chmn. Fiserv, Inc., Brookfield, Wis., 1995—2000, chmn. bd., 2000—. Chmn. bd. Info. Tech., Inc. Office: Fiserv Inc 255 Fiserv Dr Brookfield WI 53045

DILLON, DONALD WARD, management consultant; b. Wichita, Kans., Jan. 31, 1936; s. Maurice B. and Helen M. (Ward) D.; m. Jacquelyn A. Hicks, Dec. 28, 1958; m. Brenda Marie Rager, July 9, 1983. B.Music Edn., Wichita State U., 1959, M.Music Edn., 1961; D.Music. Edn., U. Okla., 1970. Tchr. music Derby (Kans.) public schs., 1959-66; mem. faculty Southeastern La. U., Hammond, 1968-69; exec. dir. Okla. Arts and Humanities Council, 1969-73; asst. dir. fed.-state partnership Nat. Endowment Arts, Washington, 1973-79, dir. grants office, 1979; exec. dir. Music Educators Nat. Conf., Reston, Va., 1979-83; pres. Don Dillon Assocs. Inc., Dallas, 1983—. Exec. mgmt. cons., bd.dirs. Fund Advancement Music Edn., 1979—. Exec. editor: Music Educators Jour, 1979—, Design for Arts Edn, 1980—; Contbr. articles profl. jours. Bd. dirs. Nat. Com. Arts for Handicapped, 1980— . Mem. Am. Soc. Assn. Execs., Inst. Assn. Mgmt. Cos., Meeting Planners Internat. Methodist. Home: 6204 Trailwood Dr Plano TX 75024-6023 Office: 13140 Coit Rd Ste 320 LB120 Dallas TX 75240-5737 Office Phone: 972-233-9107. E-mail: don@dondillon.com.

DILLON, DORIS (DORIS DILLON KENOFER), artist, art historian, educator; b. Kansas City, Mo., Dec. 1, 1929; d. Joseph Patrick and Geraldine Elizabeth (Galligan) D.; m. Calvin Louis Kenofer, Aug. 25, 1950; children: Wendy Annette Kenofer Barnes, Bruce Patrick Kenofer. BA in Art, U. Denver, 1950, MA in Art History, 1965. Stewardess United Air Lines, 1950-51; founder, chmn. fine arts dept. Regis Coll., Denver, 1970-74; cons. Sarkisian's Oriental Imports, Denver, 1975-93; mus. curator Van Vechten-Lineberry Taos Art, Taos, N.Mex., 1995. Coord. Inter-Relationship Between the Fine Arts and Science Seminars, 1970-74, Colo. Coun. on Arts & Humanities, Denver, 1980, adv. panel, 1981; permanent consular rep. United Cultural Conv., 2004; dep dir. gen. Internat. Biog. Ctr., Eng., 1997-2004; rsch. bd. advisors Am. Biog. Inst., 1997; lectr. Outer Space and Inner Man, Mensa Chpts., Asheville, N.C., 2003; lectr. in field. One-woman shows include Heard Mus., Dallas, 1984, El Pueblo Art Gallery/Mus., Pueblo, Colo., 1970, Nelson Rockefeller Collection, N.Y.C., 1984, Amparo Gallery, Denver, 1985, Veerhoff Gallery, Washington, 1986, Colo. Gallery the Arts Mus., Littleton, 1987, Highland Gallery, Atlanta, 1988, The Earth Sci. Mus., Asheville, N.C., 2003, Turchin Ctr. for Visual Arts, Appalachian State U., Boone, N.C., 2005, two-person shows, E Margo Gallery, N.Y.C., 2003, exhibited in group shows at U. Denver, 1970, Denver Art Mus., 1970, Denver Mus. Natural History, 1976, U. Colo., 1986, Denver C. of C., 1987, Cadme Gallery, Phila., 1987, Internat. Platform Assn., Washington, 1998—2001 (Best of Show painting), Internat. Exhbn. Gallery, Lisbon, 2000, Turchin Ctr. for Visual Arts, Boone, N.C., 2005, exhibitions include St. Johns Coll., Cambridge, Eng., 2001, Vancouver, Can., 2002, 30th Internat. Congress on Sci., Culture and Arts in the 21st Century, Dublin, Ireland, 2003 (Congress Medallion for distinctive participation), World Forum at Oxford U., Eng., 2005. Named Woman of Yr., ABI, 1998; recipient 1st place drawing award, 4 States Conf. Ctr., Colo., 1960, Salute to Women award, AAUW, 1997, Key award, Excellence Arts, Rsch., Tchg., 1997, Best of Show award, Internat. Platform Assn., Washington, 2001, 2002, Internat. Visual Artist of the Yr., 2004, Congress medallion, Dublin Congress. Mem.: Denver Art Mus., Asian Art assn. (bd. dirs. 1982—84, treas. 1985), Fine Arts Guild (v.p. 1982), Soc. for Arts, Religion and Contemporary Culture, Nat. Mus. for Women in the Arts (assoc.), Mensa (scholarship juror 1993—94). Avocations: piano, travel, bridge, swimming, hiking. Home and Office: 135 Delphia Dr Brevard NC 28712 Office Phone: 828-883-3623.

DILLON, JAMES JOSEPH, lawyer; b. Rockville Ctr., NY, June 18, 1948; s. James Martin and Rosemary (Peter) D.; m. Martha Stone Wiske, Mar. 19, 1977; 1 child, Eleanor. BA, Fordham U., 1970; JD, Harvard U., 1975; MA, Oxford U., 1982. Bar: Mass. 1975, U.S. Dist. Ct. Mass. 1976, N.Y. 2000, D.C. 2004, U.S. Ct. Appeals (1st cir.) 1978, U.S. Ct. Appeals (5th cir.) 1986, U.S. Ct. Appeals (6th cir.) 1996, U.S. Ct. Appeals (11th cir.) 1995, U.S. Supreme Ct. 1990. Assoc. Goodwin Procter LLP, Boston, 1975-83, ptnr., 1983—2002, Foley Hang LLP, 2002—. Dir. Beth Israel Deaconess Med. Ctr. Obstetrics and Gynecology Found., Inc.; trustee Huntington Theatre Co. Mem. ABA, Boston Bar Assn. Democrat. Office: Foley Hoag LLP 155 Seaport Blvd Boston MA 02210 Office Phone: 617-832-1109. Business E-Mail: jdillon@foleyhong.com.

DILLON, JEAN KATHERINE, executive secretary, small business owner; b. Birmingham, Ala., May 18, 1925; d. Andrew Crawford and Nell (Cook) Dillon; m. Roy Lerone Morris, June 12, 1946 (div. May 1969); children: Norma Jean, Elizabeth Annell. BA in Bus. and Edn., Huntingdon Coll., 1950. Cert. tchr. secondary edn., Ala. Sec./bookkeeper H.T. Fitzpatrick CPA, Atty., Montgomery, Ala., 1948-50; sec., budget technician Dir. Budget, HQ Air Univ., Maxwell AFB, Ala., 1950-58; exec. sec., adminstrv. asst. Comptroller, HQ Air Univ., Maxwell AFB, Ala., 1958-86; adminstrv. asst. Family Violence Program, State Coalition, Montgomery, 1986; owner/operator The William Cook House, Nauvoo, Ala., 1989—. Pres. Nauvoo Hist. Soc., Inc., 1989—98, bd. dirs., 1998—2001; mem., patron Birmingham Hist. Soc., 1991—; mem. Nat. Hist. Preservation Forum, 1995—; mem.-at-large, bd. dirs. Jasper Scottish Heritage Soc., 1999—2001; sec., bd. dirs. Ofcl. State of Ala. Highland Games, Montgomery, 1992—2001; treas. Capital City Rep. Women, 1995—96, v.p., 1997—98, chmn. budget and fin. com., 1997—2003, mem. budget and fin. com., 2003—, Montgomery County Ala. Rep. Exec. Com., 2003—, active, 1998—; bd. dirs. St. Andrew's Soc., Montgomery, 1995—, Walker County Arts Coun., 1996—, Montgomery Landmarks Found., Nat. Trust for Hist. Preservation, Nat. Parks Svc. Mem. Huntingdon Coll. Alumni Assn. (life), Walker County C. of C. (sec.-treas., vice chair tourism task force 1990-98). Methodist. Avocations: travel, geneology, historical research, writing, heritage. Home and Office: 929 Parkwood Dr Montgomery AL 36109-1228

DILLON, JIMI, protective services official; b. Totota, Monrovia, Bong Co., Liberia, Dec. 12, 1948; s. Jimmy Trybest and Vonne Shebikollie Dillon; m. Pamela Denise Dillon, Oct. 12, 1985; children: Oleg, Jimmy Jr., Jerry, Paul Andrew; m. Bessie M. King, July 12, 1976 (div. Aug. 10, 1982); 1 child, Yeaetha Monete. Assoc. in Law Enforcement, Owens Tech. Coll., Oregon, Ohio, 1977. Police officer State Mental Health Bd., Toledo, Ohio, 1982—82; indsl. engr. Portside Assoc. Market Pl., Toledo, Ohio, 1984—86; corrections officer Harris County Juvenile Probation, Houston, Tex., 1994—. Counceling Harris County Juvenile Probation, Houston, 1994—. Author: (book) Calamity Of The Heathens. Scholar Ednl. Sholarship, Bapt. Gen. Conv., 2001. Democrat-Npl. Christian Baptist. Avocations: soccer, jogging, swimming. Office: Gateway International Christian Churdh 4270 SKirkwood Houston TX 77072 Home: 3105 Ashton Park Dr Pearland TX 77584-1272 Personal E-mail: pdhcd@aol.com.

DILLON, JOHN ROBERT, III, communications executive; b. Valdosta, Ga., Oct. 7, 1941; s. John Robert and Mary (Murphey) D.; m. Joyce F. Dillon, Sept. 2, 1967 (div. 1978); 1 child, John Robert IV; m. Ann Hudgins, Apr. 17, 1982; children: Philip JOnes, Ansley Jones, Jennifer Jones. BEE, Ga. Inst. Tech., 1963; MBA, Harvard U., 1968. Gen. mgr. cable divsn. Sci. Atlanta, Inc., 1970-74, treas., 1978-81; exec. v.p. Fuqua Nat., Inc., Atlanta, 1974-78, pres., 1981-82; v.p. fin. Cox Comm., Inc., Atlanta, 1982-85; v.p. CFO Cox Enterprises, Inc., Atlanta, 1985-90, sr. v.p., 1990-96; mng. dir. Cravey Green & Wahler. Bd. dirs. Cox Comm., Inc, Teleport Comm. Group. Mem. Nat Adv. Bd. Ga. Tech; bd. trustees Ga. Ctr. for Advanced Telecom. Tech. 1st It. U.S. Army, 1964-66. Mem. Cherokee Town and Country Club, Wade Hampton Golf Club (Cashiers, N.C.), Island Golf and Beach Club, Rotary. Presbyterian. Home: 100 Beachside Dr Apt 302 Vero Beach FL 32963-9566 Office: Cravey Green & Wahlen 12 Piedmont Ctr NE Atlanta GA 30305-1749

DILLON, MATT, actor; b. New Rochelle, N.Y., Feb. 18, 1964; s. Paul and Mary Ellen Dillon. Appeared in films including Over the Edge, 1979, Little Darlings, 1980, My Bodyguard, 1980, Liar's Moon, 1982, Tex, 1982, The Outsiders, 1983, Rumblefish, 1983, The Flamingo Kid, 1984, Target, 1985, Rebel, 1986, Native Son, 1986, Big Town, 1987, Kansas, 1988, Bloodhounds of Broadway, 1989, Drugstore Cowboy, 1989 (Independent Spirit award best actor 1989), A Kiss Before Dying, 1991, Singles, 1992, The Saint of Fort Washington, 1993, Mr. Wonderful, 1993, Golden Gate, 1994, To Die For, 1995, Frankie Starlight, 1995, Grace of My Heart, 1996, Beautiful Girls, 1996, Albino Alligator, 1996, In and Out, 1997, Wild Things, 1998, There's Something About Mary, 1998, One Night at McCool's, 2001, Deuces Wild, 2002, Employee of the Month, 2004, Crash, 2004, Loverboy, 2005, Factotum,

2005, Herbie: Fully Loaded, 2005; actor, writer, dir. City of Ghosts, 2002; dir. episode of TV Series Oz, 1997; TV appearances include The Great American Fourth of July, Women and Men 2: In Love There Are No Rules; actor stage play Boys of Winter, 1985. Office: Endeavor 9701 Wilshire Blvd 10th Fl Beverly Hills CA 90212*

DILLON, MERTON LYNN, historian, educator; b. nr. Addison, Mich., Apr. 4, 1924; s. Henry J. and Cecil Edith (Sanford) D. BA, Mich. State Normal Coll., 1945; MA, U. Mich., 1948, PhD, 1951. Asst. prof. history N.Mex. Mil. Inst., Roswell, 1951-56; asst. prof. Tex. Tech. Coll., Lubbock, 1956-59, asso. prof., 1959-63, prof., 1963-65; asso. prof. Northern Ill. U., DeKalb, 1965-67; prof. Ohio State U., Columbus, 1967-91, prof. emeritus, 1991—. Author: Elijah P. Lovejoy, Abolitionist Editor, 1961, Benjamin Lundy and the Struggle for Negro Freedom, 1966, The Abolitionists, the Growth of a Dissenting Minority, 1974; Ulrich Bonnell Phillips, Historian of the Old South, 1985, Slavery Attacked: Southern Slaves and Their Allies, 1619-1865, 1990; contbr. articles to profl. jours. NEH fellow, 1973-74 Mem.Orgn. Am. Historians, So. Hist. Assn. (bd. editors 1959-63). Home: 10460 Addison Rd Jerome MI 49249-9723 Personal E-mail: mertondillon@yahoo.com.

DILLON, MICHAEL A., lawyer; BA in comm. and sociology, U. Calif., San Diego; JD, Santa Clara U., 1984. Various positions Sun Microsystems Inc., Santa Clara, Calif., 1993—99, v.p. products law group, 2002—04, sr. v.p., gen. counsel, sec., 2004—; v.p., gen. counsel ONI Systems Corp., San Jose, Calif., 1999—2002, sec., 2000—02. Office: Sun Microsystems Inc 4150 Network Cir Santa Clara CA 95054

DILLON, MICHAEL EARL, engineering executive, mechanical engineer, educator; children: Bryan Douglas, Nicole Marie, Brendon McMichael. BA in Math., Calif. State U., Long Beach, 1978, postgrad. Registered profl. engr., Ala., Alaska, Ariz., Ark., Calif., Colo., Conn., Del., Fla., Ga., Hawaii, Idaho, Ill., Ind., Iowa, Kans., Ky., La., Md., Mass., Mich., Minn., Miss., Mo., Mont., Nebr., Nev., NJ, N.Mex., NY, NC, Ohio, Okla., Oreg., Pa., SC, Tenn., Tex., Utah, Va., Wash., W.Va., Wis., Wyo., chartered engr., U.K. Journeyman plumber Roy E. Dillon & Sons, Long Beach, 1967-69, ptnr., 1969-73; field supr. Dennis Mech., San Marino, 1973-74; chief mech. official City of Long Beach, 1974-79; mgr. engr. Southland Industries, Long Beach, 1979-83; v.p. Syska & Hennessy, L.A. and N.Y., 1983-87; prin. Robert M. Young & Assoc., Pasadena, Calif., 1987-89; pres. Dillon Cons. Engrs., Long Beach, 1989—. Mech. cons. in field; instr. in field; lectr. in field UCLA, U. Calif. San Diego, U. Calif., Irvine, U. So. Calif., U.S. Mil. Acad., West Point. Author: numerous poems; contbr. articles to profl. jours., chapters to books. Former chair Mechanical, Plumbing. Elec. and Energy CodeAdv. Commn. of Calif. Bldg. Stds. Commn.; former vice chmn. bd. examiners Appeals and Condemnations, Long Beach; mem. adv. bd. City of LA; mem. bus. adv. bd. City of Long Beach. Recipient Environ. Ozone Protection award, U.S. EPA, 1993, John Fies award, Internat. Conf. Bldg. Ofcls., 1995. Fellow Chartered Inst. Bldg. Svc. Engrs. Gt. Britain and Ireland, Inst. Refrigeration, Heating, Air Conditioning Engrs. of New Zealand, Inst. Advancement Engring.; mem. ASCE, ASME, IEEE, ISA, Internat. Soc. Fire Safety Sci., Nat. Inst. for Engring. Ethics, Nat. Fire Protection Assn., Internat. Assn. Bldg. Ofcls., Internat. Fire Code Inst., Internat. Code Coun., Soc. Fire Protection Engrs., Tau Beta Pi, Pi Tau Sigma, Chi Epsilon, others. Avocation: poetry. Office: Dillon Cons Engrs Inc 671 Quincy Ave Long Beach CA 90814-1818 Office Phone: 562-434-4640. Business E-Mail: medillon@dillon-consulting.com. *Rather I live and love in coventry than lust and rust in the public reign of insouciant sycophancy.*

DILLON, MILLICENT GERSON, writer; b. May 24, 1925; AB, Hunter Coll., 1944; MA, San Francisco State U., 1966. Author: Baby Perpetua and Other Stories, 1971, The One in the Back Is Medea, 1973, A Little Original Sin: The Life and Work of Jane Bowles, 1981, After Egypt, Isadora Duncan and Mary Cassatt, 1990, The Dance of the Mothers, 1991, You Are Not I: A Portrait of Paul Bowles, 1998, Harry Gold, 2000, A Version of Love, 2003. Home: 2571 Yarmouth Ln Tallahassee FL 32309 E-mail: millicentd@mindspring.com.

DILLON, PHILLIP MICHAEL, real estate developer, construction executive; b. Ypsilanti, Mich., July 15, 1944; s. Robert Timothy and Maxine Helen (Elliott) Dillon; m. Phyllis Louise Brooks, Jan. 21, 1978; children: Richard, Debora, Michael, Robert, Karen. Student, Mich. State U., 1962—66. Lic. realtor Fla. . Store mgr. Morse Shoe, Inc., Detroit, 1964—68, asst. dir. store planning Boston, 1968—72; asst. dir. store planning and constrn. Stride Rite Corp., Boston, 1972—74; sr. v.p. Capitol Cos., Inc., Arlington Heights, Ill., 1974-81; chmn. bd., chief exec. officer Std. Cos., Inc., Palatine, Ill., 1982-83; co-owner, sr. v.p. Eagle Constrn. Corp., 1983-88; chief exec. officer Dillon Enterprises, Ltd., Lemont, Ill., 1988—2000, also bd. dirs.; mem. Nationwide Constrn. Svcs. LLC, Ft. Walton Beach, Fla., 1999—2001; developer, ptnr. Valrico Assocs., 2001—; developer N. Taylor Rd. Assocs., 2001—; real estate agt. Keller Williams Realty, Clearwater, Fla., 2002—; developer Keysville Rd. Assocs. LLC, 2003—. Bd. dirs., sr. ptnr. Internat. Developers Partnership. Mem.: Inst. Store Planners. Roman Catholic. E-mail: pdillon1@tampabay.rr.com.

DILLON, RICHARD HUGH, librarian, author; b. Sausalito, Calif., Jan. 16, 1924; s. William T. and Alice M. (Burke) D.; m. Barbara A. Sutherland, June 9, 1950; children: Brian, David, Ross. AA with hon. mention, U. Calif.-Berkeley, 1943, AB with honors in History, 1948, MA, 1949, BS in LS, 1950. Head Sutro Library, San Francisco, 1953-79; tchr. summer sessions UCLA, 1964, U. San Francisco, 1959—, prof. history, Fromm Inst., 1980—; tchr. summer sessions U. Hawaii, 1962. Author: Embarcadero, 1959 (2d place nonfiction Phelan awards 1959), The Gila Trail, 1960, Shanghaiing Days, 1961, California Trail Herd, 1961, The Hatchet Men, 1962, Meriwether Lewis, 1965 (Gold medal Commonwealth Club Calif. 1966), J. Ross Browne, 1965, The Legend of Grizzly Adams, 1966, Fool's Gold, 1967 (Silver medal Commonwealth Club Calif. 1967), Humbugs and Heroes, 1970, Burnt-Out Fires, 1973 (Spur award Western Writers Am., 1973), Exploring the Mother Lode Country, 1974, Siskiyou Trail, 1975, We Have Met the Enemy, 1978, High Steel, 1979, Great Expectations, 1980, Delta Country, 1982, San Francisco: Adventurers and Visionaries, 1983, North American Indian Wars, 1983, Iron Men, 1984, North Beach, 1985, Impressions of Bohemia, 1986, Texas Argonauts, 1988, Artful Deeds, 2002, Napa Valley Heyday, 2004 Served with inf. AUS, World War II, ETO. Decorated Purple Heart; recipient awards of merit Calif. Hist. Soc., awards of merit Am. Assn. State and Local History for all-around research and pub.; Laura Bride Powers award for disting. service to city of San Francisco, 1970, Oscar Lewis award Book Club Calif., 1997, award of merit San Francisco Hist. Soc., 1997. Fellow Calif. Hist. Soc., Gleeson Libr. Assocs., U. San Francisco; mem. Western History Assn., Book Club Calif. (pres. 1977-79), Soc. Calif. Pioneers (hon.), Phi Beta Kappa Home: 98 Alta Vista Ave Mill Valley CA 94941-1316

DILLON, ROBERT SHERWOOD, retired diplomat; b. Chgo., Jan. 7, 1929; s. Dale Crowell and Viola May (Sherwood)D.; m. Caroline Sue Burch, June 16, 1951; children: Dale, Robert Jr., John, Elizabeth, Thomas. BA, Duke U., 1951; postgrad., Princeton U., 1958-59. Ops. officer CIA, 1951-56; fgn. svc. officer (including U.S. Amb. Lebanon, 1981-83) Dept. State, Washington, 1956-84; asst. sec. gen. UN, Vienna, Austria, 1984-88; pres. Am.-Mideast Ednl. & Tng. Svcs., Washington, 1988-95. UN spl. envoy for Rwanda and Burundi, 1994; advisor Dept. of State, 1995-96. Cpl. U.S. Army, 1947-48. Recipient Presdl. Honor award, White House, 1983.

DILLON, TERRI L., consulting firm executive; b. Winston-Salem, N.C., Sept. 12, 1962; d. Dallas Eugene and Opal Wall Shields; m. Victor Ray Dillon, Apr. 18, 1992; children: Mary Abigail, Leslie Gray, Summer Rae, Dalton Levi. Student, High Point U., 1984-88, Vanderbilt U., 1998, U. N.C., Greensboro, 1999. Proof operator, teller, customer svc. and consumer loan rep. Northwestern Bank (First Union Nat. Bank), Winston-Salem, N.C., 1979-86; adminstrv. asst., grant writer, sr. project mgr. Whitney jones, Inc., Winston-Salem, 1986-97, v.p. fin. and adminstrn., 1997-2001; v.p. adminstrn. Management Recruiters of Greensboro, 2001—. Mem. steering com., chair spkrs. bur. Leave A Legacy of the Triad, Winston-Salem, 1998-99; com. mem. Colfax (N.C.) Inc. Com., 1999; grad. Winston Class of Leadership, Winston-Salem, 2001. Mem. Nat. Ctr. for Non-Profit Bds., Nat. Soc. Fund Raising Execs. (cert., chair 1999 fund-raising day conf. 1999, charter N.C.-Triad chpt., treas. and 1st v.p. 1996-99, pres. 1999-2001), New Garden Moose Lodge, Jr. Achievement N.W. N.C., Inc. (bd. dirs. 1999-2000), Rotary Club of Winston-Salem (sec. 2001). Republican. Methodist. Office: Management Recruiters Greensboro 324 W Wendover Ave Ste 230 Greensboro NC 27408

DILLON, TONI ANN, emotional support educator; b. Point Pleasant, N.J., Jan. 7, 1962; d. Thomas Joseph and Anita Marie Dillon. BA in Edn., Mercyhurst Coll., 1983; M, 1991. Cert. elem. educator Pa., tchr. mentally and/or physically handicapped Pa. Emotional support tchr. Sch. Dist. of the City of Erie, Pa., 1983—. Contbr. articles to profl. jours.; author: (1 page in storybook) GoFish! The Offishial Tale, 2001. Walktahon participant Crop-Walk, Erie, 1990—92, Am. Cancer Society, Erie, 2001—03, Presque Isle State Pk., Erie, 2002—03, March of Dimes, Erie, 1997—; leader Penn Lakes Girl Scout Coun., Erie, 1979—. Nominee Disney's Am. Tchr. award, 2000; named Tchr. of Yr., Burton Elem. Sch., 1989, Lincoln Elem. Sch., 1992; recipient St. Elizabeth Ann Seton award, Penn Lakes Girl Scouts, 1990, Outstanding Leader award, 1991, Class Rm. award, Erie Met. Transit Authority, 1997—98, Arts in Edn. award, Lincoln Elem. Parent Tchr. Assn., 1998—99, Bread Box award, Second Harvest Food Bank, 2000. Avocations: photography, gardening, collecting N.Y. Yankee baseball cards, arts and crafts. Personal E-mail: teacherinpink@aol.com. E-mail: tdillon@eriesd.iu5.og.

DILLON, WILLIAM HENRY, retired secondary school educator; b. Pearisburg, Va., Nov. 4, 1941; s. Ernest Henry and Mary (Robertson) D.; m. Doris Jean Elliott, Jan. 3, 1964; 1 child, Mary Elliott. BA, Emory and Henry Coll., 1973; MS, Radford U., 1979. Cert. tchr., Va. English educator Castlewood (Va.) H.S., 1973—81, Riverheads H.S., Staunton, Va., 1981—2001. Adj. English instr. Blue Ridge C.C., Weyers Cave, Va., 1984-92. With USAR, 1966-72. Fellow Masons; mem. Schola Cantorum (pres. 1996-2000). Avocations: reading, herb and flower gardening. Home: 1501 Tuckahoe Rd Waynesboro VA 22980-3520

DILLON, WILTON STERLING, anthropologist, foundation administrator; b. Yale, Okla., July 13, 1923; s. Earl Henry and Edith Holland (Canfield) D.; m. Virginia Leigh Harris, Jan. 20, 1956; 1 child, James Harris. BA, U. Calif.-Berkeley, 1951; postgrad., Inst. Ethnology, U. Paris, U. Leyden, 1951-52; PhD, Columbia U., 1961. News reporter Holdenville (Okla.) Daily News, 1936-41; info. specialist, civilian mem. Civil Info. and Edn. Sect. SCAP, Tokyo, 1946-49; vis. lectr. sociology and anthropology Hobart and William Smith colls., Geneva, N.Y., 1953-54; staff anthropologist Japan Soc. N.Y.; also lectr. Japanese studies Fordham U., 1954; dir. Clearinghouse for Research in Human Orgn., Soc. Applied Anthropology, N.Y.C., 1954-56; exec. sec., dir. research Phelps-Stokes Fund N.Y.; including dir. research project on higher edn. and African nationhood U. Ghana, 1957-63; vis. lectr. Columbia U., New Sch. Social Research, 1957-63; staff dir. Nat. Acad. Scis., 1963-69; dir. symposia and seminars Smithsonian Instn., Washington, 1969-85, dir. interdisciplinary studies, 1986-90, sr. scholar, 1990—; sr. scholar emeritus. Dir. internat. commemoration of 250th anniversary of birth of Thomas Jefferson, 1992—; adj. prof. U. Ala., 1971—; chmn. Oxford U.-Smithsonian Seminars, 1985. Author: Gifts and Nations, 1968; editor: (with John F. Eisenberg) Man and Beast: Comparative Social Behavior, 1971, The Cultural Drama, 1974, (with Neil G. Kotler) The Statue of Liberty Revisited: Making a Universal Symbol, 1993; contbr. articles to profl. jours.; editl. bd. Ala. Heritage. Del. numerous internat. confs. including UNESCO, Pugwash; mem. adv. coun. on Africa Dept. State, 1964-68; hon. commr. Internat. Year of Child, 1979-80; pres. bd. dirs. Inst. Intercultural Studies, N.Y.C.; trustee emeritus Phelps-Stokes Fund, 1985—; sec.-treas., bd. dirs. Inst. Psychiatry and Fgn. Affairs; bd. visitors Wake Forest U., 1978-81; adv. com. Hubert Humphrey Inst. for Pub. Affairs, 1988-94; bd. dirs. Delta Rsch. and Ednl. Found., 1987-95; trustee Friends of Raoul Wallenberg Found., 1995-97, Lives and Legacies Inc., 1995—; advisor Nation's Capital Bicentennial Celebration 1999-2000, Margaret Mead Centenary 2001, Historic Mt. Vernon 1999, Benjamin Franklin Creativity Found., 2002. With USAAF, 1943-46. Decorated Chevalier de l'ordre des arts et lettres; Woodrow Wilson Internat. Center for Scholars guest scholar, 1970. Fellow AAAS, Am. Anthrop. Assn., Royal Soc. Arts; mem. Lit. Soc. Washington (pres. 1990), Anthrop. Soc. Washington, Cosmos Club (Washington). Episcopalian (lay reader N.Y. diocese 1958-60). Home: 1446 Woodacre Dr Mc Lean VA 22101-2536 Office: Smithsonian Instn Nat Mus Natural History Rm 445 MRC 124 PO Box 37012 Washington DC 20013-7012 Office Phone: 202-633-1081. Business E-Mail: dillon.wilton@nmnh.si.edu.

DILLOW, JOHN DAVID, lawyer; b. Bremerton, Wash., Aug. 17, 1946; s. Garold Maurice and Margaret (Roediger) D.; m. Alison Wenke, Sept. 19, 1977; children: Gwen, Jake, Claire BS magna cum laude, U. Wash., 1968; JD, Duke U., 1971. Bar: Calif. 1972, Wash. 1975, U.S. Dist. Ct. (Ctrl. Dist.) Wash. 1972, U.S. Dist. Ct. (We. Dist.) Calif. 1975, U.S. Ct. Appeals (9th Cir.) 1972, U.S. Supreme Ct. 1975, N.Y. 1981. Assoc. O'Melveny and Meyers, L.A., 1971-75, Perkins Coie, LLP, Seattle, 1975-77, ptnr., Product Liability Area, 1977—. Editor Duke Law Jour. Bd. dirs. ARC King County, Seattle, 1987—; mem. coun. fund raising Duke U., Durham, N.C., 1975—. Mem. ABA (aviation & space law com.), Wash. State Bar Assn., King County Bar Assn., Barristers Club, Seattle Tennis Club, Order of Coif, Tau Beta Pi. Avocations: tennis, skiing. Office: Perkins Coie LLP 1201 3rd Ave Fl 40 Seattle WA 98101-3029 Office Phone: 206-359-8476. Office Fax: 206-359-9000. Business E-Mail: jdillow@perkinscoie.com.*

DILLS, JAMES ARLOF, retired publishing company executive; b. Guelph, Ont., Can., Aug. 11, 1930; s. George Arlof and Isma Marie (MacPherson) D.; m. Shirley Jean Elliott, Aug. 16, 1952; children— Steven George, James Mark, Paul David, Catherine Jane, Carolyn Shirley. Grad. in journalism, Ryerson Poly. Inst., 1951. Pub. The Can. Champion, Milton, Ont., 1966-78, The Georgetown (Ont.) Ind., 1973-78; sec.-treas. Dills Printing and Pub. Co. Ltd., Acton, Ont., 1954—; exec. dir. Can. Community Newspapers Assn., Toronto, Ont., 1979-87; mem. adv. com. journalism program Sheridan Coll., 1965-78; pres. Ont. Weekly Newspapers Assn., 1975-76; pub. County Chronicles Press, 1992—2003; ret., 2003. Dir. Milton Evergreen Cemetery Co., 1997. Author: Moments in History, 1993; editor: Time Capsules from Milton's Past 1890-1894, 2002. Pres. Milton Hist. Soc., 1977-80; dir. emeritus MacKenzie Printery and Newspaper Mus, 2004. Named Citizen of Yr., Milton, 1978; recipient Lifetime Achievement Cmty. award, Milton C. of C., 1999, Lifetime Achievement cert., Ont. Heritage Found., 2005. E-mail: jdills@idirect.com.

DILORENZO, FRANCIS X., bishop; b. Phila., Apr. 15, 1942; s. Samuel and Anna (Porrino) DiLorenzo. Ed., St. Charles Borromeo Sem.; STD, Pontifical U. of St. Thomas Aquinas, 1975. Ordained priest, 1968; served Archdiocese Phila., 1968—71; chaplain & instr. theology St. Pius X H.S., Pottstown, Pa., 1975—77; chaplain & assoc. prof. moral theology Immaculata Coll., Pa., 1977—83; vice rector St. Charles Borromeo Sem., Wynnewood, Pa., 1983—85, rector, 1985—88; Titular Bishop of Tigia, 1988—93; Aux. Bishop of Scranton, 1988—93; apostolic adminstr. Diocese of Honolulu, Hawaii, 1993-94; Bishop of Honolulu, 1994—2004; Bishop of Richmond, 2004—. Mem.: US Conf. Cath. Bishops (mem. adminstrv. com., chmn. com. on sci. & human values). Roman Catholic. Office: Diocese of Richmond 811 Cathedral Pl Richmond VA 23220-4801*

DI LORENZO, JOHN FLORIO, JR., retired lawyer; b. Paterson, N.J., May 18, 1940; s. John F. and Ida (Cona) Di L.; m. Ernestine R. De Rose, Nov. 15, 1969; children: Christina P., Roberta J. BA, Seton Hall U., 1962; LLB, MBA, Columbia U., 1966. Bar: N.J. 1967, N.Y. 1968, Ohio 1981. Assoc. Stryker, Tams & Dill, Esqs., Newark, 1966-68; atty. Am. Electric Power Svc. Corp., N.Y.C., 1968-79, asst. gen. counsel, asst. v.p., exec. asst. to pres., 1979-81, assoc. gen. counsel, v.p., sec. Columbus, Ohio, 1981-2001; ret., 2001. Sec. various Am. Electric Power Sys. cos., 1987-2001, asst. sec. 1979. Trustee Ballet Met. Columbus, 1981-87. Mem. ABA (chmn. subcom. on pub. utility holding co. act of fed. regulation of securities com. 1985-94), Knights of Malta, Knights of the Holy Sepulchre of Jerusalem, Scioto Country Club. Roman Catholic. Avocations: skiing, travel. Home: 2756 Elginfield Rd Columbus OH 43220-4248 Office Phone: 614-459-0047. E-mail: jfdilorenzo@att.net.

DILORENZO, SHARON HIESTAND, professional management services specialist, architect, real estate broker; b. Jennings, La., Oct. 11, 1946; d. Garland and Annabelle (Carter) H.; m. Frank Clifford DiLorenzo, Feb. 5, 1965; children: Anthony Garland, Michael Russell. B in Urban Planning, Design, Mgmt., U. Hartford, 1969; MFA in Design and Arch., Sch. Art Inst. Chgo., 1978; PhD in Indsl. Psychology, U. Conn., 1981; CFP, Roosevelt U., 1990. Real estate investment planning profl. Prof. interior architecture Sch. of Art Inst. Chgo., 1975—78; prof. archtl. history Barat Coll., Lake Forest, Ill., 1979-80; constrn. mgr. Taubman Devel., Bloomfield Hills, Mich., 1980-84; facilities devel. mgr. Pritzger Sch. Medicine U. Chgo. Hosps. Ill. Capital Constrn. Mgmt., 1984-92; v.p. real estate devel. Enviro Technics Ltd., Barrington, 1965—80. City planning hist. downtown rehab. specialist Yale Grad. Sch. Arch., New Haven, 1968—70, Art-Tech Images Bus. Svcs., 1992—2001. Exhibitions include Hartford Atheneum, 1968 (Prudential Ins. award). Recipient Supermarket of Yr., Enviro-Technics Ltd., Cert. Grocers Midwest, 1970, Frank Lloyd Wright Home and Studio Found. award, 1977; making connections scholar, Brown U., 1987. Mem. AAUW, AARP, LWV, Barrington C. of C., Nat. Trust for Hist. Preservation, Architecture Soc. of Art Inst. Chgo., Graham Found. for Advanced Studies in Fine Arts. Roman Catholic. Avocations: model making, kite flying, swimming, boating, family camping. Studio: Ste 311 3170 W Monroe St Waukegan IL 60085-3066 Office: PO Box 8172 Waukegan IL 60079-8172 E-mail: shdilorenzo@comcast.net.

DILTZ, JERRY DWAINE, computer science educator, consultant; b. Bluefield, W.Va., Oct. 21, 1948; s. Eugene Gearheart and Mary Francis House; life ptnr. Thomas Michael Quealy, Mar. 27, 1985. Facilitator Convergys CMG TSS, Ft. Pierce, Fla., 1998—. Del. Volusia County Dem. Exec. Com., Daytona Beach, 1991-93. Mem. N.Y. Bd. of Scientists. Home: 389 N W Grandadeer St Port Saint Lucie FL 34983-8706

DILWORTH, ROBERT LEXOW, career military officer, educator; b. Chgo., Aug. 19, 1936; s. Robert Oliver and Linda Agnes (Lexow) D.; m. Doris Elthea Smith, Sept. 1, 1981; children by previous marriage: Alexa, Robert. BS in Advt., U. Fla., 1959; MS in Mil. Sci., U.S. Army Command and Gen. Staff Coll., 1971; MA in Pub. Adminstrn., U. Okla., 1975; MEd, EdD, Columbia U., 1993. Commd. 2nd lt. U.S. Army, 1959, advanced through grades to brig. gen., 1986, chief adminstrn. div. office chief of staff Washington, 1968-70, chief mgmt. analysis br. office chief of staff, 1971-75, chief of staff 2nd infantry div. Republic of Korea, 1975-76, chief mgmt. div. adj. gen. ctr. Washington, 1976-77, chief compt. div. Nat. Guard Bur., 1978-81, dep. comdr. 1st pers. command Schwetzingen, Fed. Republic of Germany, 1981-84, dir. resource mgmt. U.S. Mil. Acad. West Point, N.Y., 1984-86, adjutant gen. army Alexandria, Va., 1986-88, dep. chief of staff base ops. support tng./doctrine command Ft. Monroe, Va., 1988-91; assoc. prof. emeritus adult edn., human resource devel. Va. Commonwealth U., Richmond, 1993—. Guest lectr. Hungarian Mil. Acad., 1989. Contbr. articles to profl. jours. Mem. ASPA (exec. com. mgmt. sci. and policy analysis sect. 1992-96), ASTD (chair nat. rsch. to practice com. 2000-2002), Acad. Human Resource Devel., Assn. U.S. Army, Mil. Officer Assn., Internat. Soc. Quality Govt. (nat. dir. 1992-93). Mem. Lds Ch. Avocation: writing for publication. Home: PO Box 29 Gum Spring VA 23065-0029 Personal E-mail: lexter@earthlink.net.

DIMAGGIO, FRANK LOUIS, civil engineering educator; b. N.Y.C., Sept. 2, 1929; s. Serafino and Maria (Barbuto) DiM.; m. Irene C. Koehn, Dec. 15, 1963 (dec. June 1998); children: Samuel, Peter. BS, Columbia U., 1950, MS, 1951, PhD, 1954. Registered profl. engr., N.Y. Prof. civil engring. Columbia U., 1956—, chmn. dept., 1975-78, Carleton prof., 1978—. Cons. in field, 1956— Served with AUS, 1954-56. NSF sr. postdoctoral fellow, 1962-63; guest scholar Kyoto U., Japan, 1986. Fellow ASCE (chmn. exec. com. engring. mech. div. 1982-83, chmn. adv. bd. engring. mechanics div. 1985-86); mem. Sigma Xi. Home: 138 Van Orden Ave Leonia NJ 07605-1521 Office: Columbia Univ Dept Civil Engring and Engring Mechanics New York NY 10027 Office Phone: 212-854-3751. E-mail: dimaggio@civil.columbia.edu.

DIMAIO, FRANK R., orthopedic surgeon; b. Whitestone, N.Y., Oct. 6, 1962; s. Frank Paul and Jennie DiMaio; m. Claire J. DiMaio, Oct. 9, 1993; children: Breanna, Nicholas, Christian. BS in Biology, U. Scranton, 1984; MD in Rsch., SUNY Health Sci. Ctr. Downstate, 1988. Surg. resident SUNY Health Sci. Ctr. Downstate, Bklyn., 1988—89, orthopedic resident, 1989—93; fellow adult joint reconstrn. U. Calif., San Diego, 1993—94; chief adult joint reconstrn. Wintrhop U. Hosp., Mineola, NY, 1999—2001, vice-chmn. dept. orthopedic surgery, 2001—03, chmn. dept. orthopedic surgery, 2003—; assoc. clin. prof. dept. orthop. surgery SUNY, Stony Brook, NY, 2003—. Asst. clin. prof. dept. orthopedic surgery SUNY, Stony Brook, 1999—. Contbr. articles to profl. jours. Orthopedic surgeon Nassau County Police Dept., Mineola, 1998—. Grantee NIH Summer Rsch. grantee, Bklyn. VA Hosp., 1988, 1989. Fellow: Am. Bd. Orthopedic Surgery, Am. Assn. Hip and Knee Surgeons, Am. Acad. Orthopedic Surgery. Republican. Roman Catholic. Avocation: golf. Office: Winthrop U Hosp 259 1st St Mineola NY 11501

DIMANCESCU, MIHAI D., neurosurgeon, researcher, educator; b. Maidenhead, Berkshire, Eng., Mar. 27, 1940; arrived in US, 1956, naturalized, 1963; s. Dimitri D. and Alexandra Irina (Radulescu) D.; m. Joan E. Brenner, Mar. 17, 1966; children: Stefan, Marc-Mihai. BA, Yale U., 1962; MD, U. Toulouse, France, 1968. Diplomate Am. Bd. Neurol. Surgery. Rotating intern Purpan Hosp., Toulouse, 1968-69; jr. resident in gen. surgery Hartford Hosp., Conn., 1969-70; jr. resident neurosurgery Albert Einstein-Montefiore Hosp., Bronx, NY, 1970-72; rsch. fellow in spasticity and movement disorders U. Miami VA Hosp., Miami, Fla., 1972-74; sr. resident in neurosurgery U. Miami, 1972-76, asst. instr. in neurol. surgery, 1975-76; pvt. practice Freeport, NY, 1976—2003, Garden City, 1976—2003; v.p. med. affairs OmniCorder Tech., Inc., Bohemia, NY, 2004—. Dir. Internat. Coma Recovery Inst., Garden City, 1977—2003; faculty, dir. brain studies Internat. Sch. Evan Thomas Inst., Phila., 1980—2003; staff, dir. dept. neurosurgery Franklin Hosp. Med. Ctr., Valley Stream, NY; staff neurosurgery South Nassau Cmtys. Hosp., Oceanside, NY, Mercy Med. Ctr., Rockville Ctr., NY, St. Francis Hosp., Rockville Ctr., NY, Winthrop U. Hosp., Mineola, NY, North Shore U. Hosp., Manhasset, NY, continuing med. edn. lectr., 1977—2003; cons. neurosurgery Inst. Achievement Human Potential, Phila., 1977—; surg. core faculty Health Sci. Ctr., Sch. Medicine, SUNY Stony Brook, 1980—2003; med. coun. LI Health Network; v.p. med. affairs Advanced BioPhotonics, Inc., Bohemia, NY, 2004—; bd. dirs. South Nassau Cmty. Hosp. Contbr. articles profl. jours. Bd. dirs. Inst. Achievement Human Potential, 1990—, Princess Margarita Romania Found., chmn., 1998—. Recipient Golden medal, World Orgn. Human Potential, 1978; grantee, Verterans Adminstration, 1972—74. Fellow: Royal Soc. Arts, ACS; mem.: Nassau Physicians' Rev. Orgn., Nassau County Med. Soc., World Med. Assn., NY State Head Injury Providers' Council (rotating chmn. 1986—87), Med. Soc. State NY (neurosurg. de. interspclty. com. 1983—88), NY State Neurosurg. Soc. (bd. dirs. 1983—88, pres. elect 1986—87, pres. 1988), Coma Recovery Assn. (chmn. bd. dirs. Garden City chpt. 1983), Congress Neurol. Surgeons (Sci. Exhibit award 1974), Am. Assn. Neurol. Surgeons, AMA. Office Phone: 631-244-8244. Personal E-mail: mdimancescu@aol.com.

DIMANDJA, JEAN-MARIE D., chemistry professor, consultant; b. Oxford, Ohio; s. Antoine R. and Denise K. Dimandja; m. Shuenae Ann Smith; 1 child, Cady Alexandra. PhD, So. Ill. U., Carbondale, Ill. Vis. rschr. CDC, Atlanta, 1997—2002; prof. Spelman Coll., Atlanta, 2002—. Cons. LECO Corp., St

Joseph, Mich., 2002—03. Grantee MBRS/SCORE, NIH, 2004-2008, IIS, NSF, 2004-2007. Mem.: NOBCChE. Office: Spelman Coll 350 Spelman Ln SW Box 279 Atlanta GA 30314 Office Phone: 404-270-5743. Business E-Mail: jdimandja@spelman.edu.

DIMANT, JACOB, internist; b. Rehovot, Israel, Apr. 27, 1947; came to U.S., 1972, naturalized, 1977; s. Simcha and Ita D.; m. Rose Bea Jearolmen, Sept. 11, 1974. MD, Hebrew U., Jerusalem, 1972. Diplomate Am. Bd. Internal Medicine and Rheumatology and Geriatric Medicine, Am. Bd. Quality Assurance and Utilization Rev. Physicians. Intern Maimonides Med. Ctr., Bklyn., 1972-73, resident in medicine, 1973-75, chief resident in medicine Bklyn., 1975-76; fellow in rheumatology SUNY Downstate Med. Ctr., Bklyn., 1976-78; practice medicine specializing in internal medicine and rheumatology Bklyn., 1975—; dir. rheumatology Maimonides Med. Ctr., Bklyn., 1978-89, assoc. dir. med. edn., 1978-80; med. dir. Clove Lakes Nursing Home, S.I., N.Y., 1985-97; dir. divsn. of geriatrics Luth. Med. Ctr., Bklyn., 1998—. Med. dir. Prospect Park Nursing Home, Bklyn., 1977—87, Crown Nursing Home, Bklyn., 1983—2001, Hillside Manor Nursing Ctr., Queens, NY, 1993—98, Augustana Luth. Ctr. for Extended Care, Bklyn., 1996—; pres. Crown Nursing Home Assocs., Inc., Bklyn., 1989—; asst. prof. medicine SUNY, Bklyn., 1978—; pres. Crest Hall Care Ctr. and Oak Hollow Nursing Ctr., Middle Island, NY, 1999—. Contbr. articles to profl. jours. Named hon. police surgeon N.Y.C. Police Dept., 1982; fellow Arthritis Found. of N.Y., 1977-78. Fellow: ACP; mem.: N.Y. Med. Dirs. Assn. (bd. dirs. 1990—, pres. 1994—96), Am. Med. Dirs. Assn. (bd. dirs. 1995—97, treas. 1997—99, v.p. 2000—01, pres.-elect 2001—02, pres. 2002—03), Am. Geriatric Soc. Office: Crown Nursing and Rehab Ctr 3457 Nostrand Ave Brooklyn NY 11229-5194

DI MARCO, BARBARANNE YANUS, principal; b. Jersey City, Nov. 16, 1946; d. Stanley Joseph and Anne Barbara (Dalack) Yanus; m. Charles Benjamin DiMarco, Mar. 15, 1986; 1 child, Charles Garrett. BA in Music Edn., Trenton State Coll., 1968; MA in Spl. Edn., Kean Coll., 1971, elem. edn. cert., 1974, adminstrv. cert., 1976. Cert. elem., music, adminstrn., spl. edn., N.J. Vocal music educator Roselle (N.J.) Bd. Edn., 1968-69, tchr. trainable mentally retarded, 1969-76, tchr. multiple handicapped, 1976—95, tchr. neurologically impaired, 1995—2003; prin. Grace Wilday Jr. H.S., Roselle, 2003—. Color guard instr. Roselle Bd. Edn., 1973—88, elem. tutor, 1976—92, adminstrv. asst. to supt., 1980—85; program dir., sec. Expanded Dimensions in Gifted Edn., Westfield, NJ, 1978—85. Vestryperson St. Luke's Ch., Roselle, 1989-91. Recipient Govs. Tchr. Recognition award, Gov. Florio, N.J., Trenton, 1992-93. Mem. NEA, N.J. Edn. Assn., Roselle Edn. Assn., N.J. Assn. for Retarded Children, Eastern Star (25-yr award 1991), Delta Omicron. Republican. Episcopalian. Avocations: skiing, flying, painting, travel, swimming. Home: 13 Gentore Ct Edison NJ 08820-1029 Office: Grace Wilday Jr HS 400 Brooklawn Ave Roselle NJ 07203 Office Phone: 908-298-2066. Personal E-mail: btdtbarb@aol.com.

DIMARCO, CHRISTIAN, professional golfer; b. Huntington, NY, Aug. 23, 1968; m. Amy DiMarco; children: Cristian Alexander, Amanda Elizabeth. Student, U. Fla. Mem. Pres. Cup, 2003, Ryder Cup, 2004. Named winner, NIKE Ozarks Open, 1997, SEI Pa. Classic, 2000, Buick Challenge, 2001, Phoenix Open, 2002, CVS Charity Classic, 2002; recipient All-America, NCAA, 1990. Office: c/o PGA Tour 112 PGA Tour Blvd Ponte Vedra Beach FL 32082

DIMARCO, DAVID, mathematician, educator; s. Jeanette Mary and Joseph Paul DiMarco. BS, Stevens Inst. of Tech., Hoboken, N.J., 1975—79; MS, Stevens Inst Tech., Hoboken, N.J., 1981, PhD, 1988; MS, Iona Coll., New Rochelle, N.Y., 1995—95. Instr. math. Various Colleges, 1983—; adj. asst. professor-math NYC Tech. Coll., Brooklyn, NY, 1994—2002; adj. instr. math Fairleigh Dickinson U., Teaneck, NJ, 1997—2002; asst. prof. math Neumann Coll., Aston, Pa., 2002—. Contbr. articles to profl. jours. Mem.: Am. Math. Soc. Avocations: cross training, jogging. Office: Neumann Coll Div of Arts and Sci One Neumann Dr Aston PA 19014

DIMARIO, FRANCIS JOSEPH, neurologist, medical educator, researcher; s. Francis Joseph and Elizabeth Catherine DiMario; m. Sandra Lynn Sergeant, Sept. 1, 1984; children: Trevor Douglas, Tyler Francis. BA, U. Mass., Amherst, Mass., 1976; MD, Tufts Sch. of Medicine, Boston, Mass., 1981. Asst. prof. pediat. and neurology U. Conn., Sch. of Medicine, Farmington, Conn., 1988—94, assoc. prof. pediat. and neurology, 1994—2000, prof. pediat. and neurology, 2000—. Chief, divsn. of pediatric neurology Conn. Children's Med. Ctr., Hartford, Conn., 1994—; assoc. chair, dept. of pediat. for academic affairs U. Conn., Sch. of Medicine at Conn. Children's Med. Ctr., Hartford, Conn., 2002—; chair, instl. rev. bd. Conn. Children's Med. Ctr., Hartford, Conn., 2002—, rsch. integrity officer, 2003—. Contbr. articles pub. to profl. jour. Past pres. Mid. Sch. PTO, Simsbury, Conn.; past chief, indian guides YMCA of Farmington Valley, Simsbury, Conn.; coach Little League and Babe Ruth Baseball, Simsbury, Conn. Fellow: Am. Bd. of Psychiatry & Neurology, Am. Acad. of Pediat.; mem.: Am. Neurol. Assn., Am. Acad. of Neurology, Child Neurology Soc. Office: Conn Children's Med Ctr 282 Washington St Hartford CT 06106 Office Phone: 860-545-9489. Office Fax: 860-545-9484. Business E-Mail: fdimari@ccmckids.org.

DIMARZIO, NICHOLAS ANTHONY, bishop; b. Newark, June 16, 1944; s. Nicholas Anthony and Grace (Grande) DiMarzio. BA, Seton Hall U., 1966; STB, Catholic U., 1970; MSW, Fordham U., 1980; PhD, Rutgers U., 1985. Ordained to ministry Roman Cath. Ch., 1970, ordained to bishop Roman Cath. Ch., 1996. Divsn. dir. spl. svcs. Cath. Cmty. Svcs., Newark, 1976-85, assoc. exec. dir., 1991-92, exec. dir., 1992-97, Migration & Refugee Svcs. U.S. Cath. Conf., Washington, 1985-91; bishop Camden, NJ, 1999—2003; pontifical coun. pastoral care of migrants and itinerant people, 1999—; bishop Brooklyn Diocese, 2003—. Vicar human svcs. Archdiocese of Newark, 1991—99; mem. global commn. internat. migration, 2004—; cons. in field. Co-author: (book) Profiling Unapprehended Undocumented Aliens in the New York Metropolitan Area: An Exploration into Their Social and Labor Market Incorporation, 1986; contbr. articles to profl. jours., mags., and newspapers. V.p. Internat. Cath. Migration Commn., 1989—92; chmn. bd. dirs. Nat. Immigration, Refugee and Citizenship Forum, Washington, 1986—89; bd. dirs. Ctr. Migration Studies, Washington, 1988—93, Am. Com. Italian Migration, 1989—91, Cath. Relief Svcs. Decorated Knight of the Italian Republic N.Y., Prelate of Honor Pope John Paul II, Vatican; recipient Spl. award, N.Y. Assn. New Ams. Mem.: NASW. Office: Brooklyn Diocese 75 Greene Ave PO Box C Brooklyn NY 11202

DIMAS, MARILYN J., health products executive; b. Portland, Oreg., Jan. 24, 1944; d. John Davidson Dow and Gladys Victoria (Lewis) Thompson;m. John F. Bass, m. George Dimas (div. 1981); children: Ron Farr, Kimberly Farr. BS, U. Oreg., 1967, MSN, 1970; MPA, NYU, 1978. Dir. Psychiat. Crisis Unit Med. Sch. U. Oreg., Portland, 1970-73; dep. dir. Nat. Coun. on Alcoholism, N.Y.C., 1973-74; asst. dir. Am. Lung Assn., N.Y.C., 1974-76; exec. dir. Richmond Fellowship of N.Y., N.Y.C., 1978-84; pres. Marilyn Dimas & Assocs., N.Y.C., 1978-88; exec. dir. Boley Manor, St. Petersburg, Fla., 1984-86; assoc. exec. dir. Woodhall Hosp., Bklyn., 1986-90; pres. Healthcare Quality Improvement Resources, Inc., N.Y.C., 1988—. Dir. Western Inst. Drug Problems Summer Sch., Portland, 1970-72; cons. Am. Lung Assn., N.Y.C., 1974, Nat. Health Coun., N.Y.C., 1975-76. Author: Standards for State Alcoholism Associations, 1971, Standards for Voluntary Health Organizations, 1976. Recipient Gold plaque Nat. Inst. on Alcoholism and Alcohol Abuse/NIAAA, 1974; named one of Outstanding Young Women of Am., 1980. Mem. Am. Hosp. Assn., Nat. Assn. Quality Assurance Profls., N.Y. State Quality Assurance Profls. Avocations: swimming, horseback riding, jogging, cooking. Office: Healthcare Quality Improvement Resources 1401 51st Ave NE Saint Petersburg FL 33703

DIMASCIO, JOHN PHILIP, lawyer; b. Bklyn., Feb. 4, 1944; s. Eugenio and Stella (Scheuermann) DiM.; m. Angela Piccininni, Apr. 2, 1967 (div. 1980); children: John Philip, Jr., Christine Pagano, Thomas; m. Linda Nick, Oct. 19, 1997. BA, C.W. Post Coll., 1975; MA, L.I. U., 1976; postgrad., NYU, 1976-79; JD, St. John's U., 1983. Bar: N.Y. 1984, U.S. Dist. Ct. (ea. and so. dists.) N.Y. 1984, U.S. Ct. Appeals (2d cir.) 1984, U.S. Supreme Ct. 1997, U.S. Ct. Appeals for Armed Forces 1997, U.S. Ct. of Fed. Claims, 1997, U.S. Ct. Appeals (fed. cir.) 1997. Sr. ct. officer N.Y. State Supreme Ct., Mineola, 1970-82; assoc. Joel R. Brandes, PC, Garden City, N.Y., 1984; pvt. practice N.Y., 1984-87; ptnr. Di Mascio, Meisner & Koopersmith, Carle Place, 1987-93; pvt. practice Garden City, 1993—2004; ptnr. John P. DiMascio & Assocs., Garden City, 2004—. Lectr. Nassau Acad. Law; barrister, NY family law chpt. Am. Inns of Ct. With USN, 1962—69. Recipient acad. awards. Mem.: Nassau County Bar Assn. (family ct. com. 1984—, past chmn. matrimonial com., past editor Recent Decisions, contbg. author), N.Y. State Bar Assn. (family law com. 1982—). Avocations: photography, boating, target shooting. Office: John P DiMascio & Assoc LLP 300 Garden City Plz Garden City NY 11530-3302 Office Phone: 516-747-4343. Business E-Mail: jpdlawoff@msn.com.

DIMASHKIEH, HAYTHAM, pathologist; s. Hicham and Hind Dimashkieh; m. Dania Zantout, June 1, 1979; 1 child, Hisham. BS, Am. U. of Beirut, 1994, MD, 1998. Lic. anatomic and clin. pathology U. of Cin., surg. pathology Mayo Clinic. Clin. intern Am. U. of Beirut, 1998—99; resident in anatomic and clin. pathology U. of Cin., 1999—2003; fellow in surg. pathology Mayo Clinic, Rochester, Minn., 2003—04; fellow in cytopathology M.D. Anderson Cancer Ctr., Houston, 2004—. Mem.: ASC, ASCP (Sheard Sanford award 2003), USCAP (Stowell Orbison award 2002), Coll. Am. Pathologist. Achievements include research in NK cells; Eye Melanoma; Thinprep technique for bile duct brushins; ER on breast cancer aspirates; GLut-1 in infantile liver vascular lesions; Lymph node involovement in renal cell carcinoma; CDX2 in neuroendocrine tumors; Indirect evaluation of NK cells using CD2-CD3 in flow cytometry; role of bone marrow natural killers cells in acute leukemia following chemotherapy. Home: Apt 3087 1 Hermann Museu Circle Dr Houston TX 77004 Office: MD Anderson Cancer Ctr Unit 53 1515 Holcombe Blvd Houston TX 77030 Office Phone: 713 404 0562 (pager).

DI MASSA, ERNANI VINCENZO, JR., communications executive, television producer, writer; b. Phila., Sept. 12, 1947; s. Ernani Vincenzo and Rita C. (Iacovoni) Di M.; divorced; 1 child, Michael Colin. BS, La Salle Coll., 1970; MS, Temple U., 1972. Producer, writer Mike Douglas Show, Phila. and L.A., 1969-81, Regis Philbin Show, NBC-TV, 1981, Fantasy NBC-TV, L.A., 1981-83; exec. producer, writer Thicke of the Night, L.A., 1983-84, Tony Orlando Show, 1985-86; supervising producer Hollywood Squares, L.A., 1987-89; sr. v.p. programming and devel. King World Prodns., L.A., 1989-97; pres. DiMassa Prodns., 1998—. Supervising prodr. Candid Camera; exec. in charge prodn. Rolonda; exec. prodr. Terry Bradshaw-Fox TV; exec. in charge of programming and distbn. for The Oprah Winfrey Show, Wheel of Fortune, Jeopardy!, Inside Edition, Am. Jour., Instant Recall, The Arts and Entertainment Rev. Recipient Emmy award NATAS, 1982. Mem. Producers Guild Am., Writers Guild Am. Roman Catholic. Avocations: car collecting and restoring, photography. Office: Di Mass Prodns 374 Newport Glen Ct Ste 1000 Newport Beach CA 92660 E-mail: ernani-d@usa.net.

DI MASSA, RUDOLPH J., JR., lawyer; b. Phila., July 14, 1956; BA, Lehigh U., 1978; JD, U. Pa., 1981. Bar: Pa. 1981, US Ct. Appeals 3rd Cir., US Dist. Ct. Ea. Dist. Pa. Assoc. Duane Morris LLP, Phila., 1981—88, ptnr., 1989—, chair firm reorganization & fin. restructuring practice group, 2001—. Staff writer The Legal Intelligencer, 2000—. Pro-bono atty. Support Ctr. for Child Advocates, Phila.; vol. atty. St. Thomas More Soc., Archdiocese Phila.; bd. dirs. Filitalia. Mem.: ABA (bus. law sect.), Justinian Soc., Comml. Law League Am., Ea. Dist. Pa. Bankruptcy Conf., Phila. Bar Assn. (bus. law sect.), Pa. Bar Assn., Am. Bankruptcy Inst. (co-chair mid-atlantic conf.). Office: Duane Morris LLP One Liberty Pl Philadelphia PA 19103-7396 Office Phone: 215-979-1506. Office Fax: 215-979-1020. Business E-Mail: dimassa@duanemorris.com.

DIMBERG, LENNART AXEL, medical researcher, physician; b. Vanersborg, Sweden, Aug. 28, 1947; arrived in U.S., 1998; s. Sven Inguar and Eva Ingrid Dimberg; m. Kerstin Aline Dimberg, Nov. 17, 1952; children: Asa, Ida, Emelie. Diploma in Occpl. Health, Arbet Arskydds Styrelsen, Stockholm, 1978; diploma in Gen. Medicine, Norra Alusborgs Stuuhms, Trollhattan, Sweden, 1978; D in Orthop. Surgery, Goteborg U., Sweden, 1991. Intern then resident Trollhattans Sjulhns, Trollhattan, Sweden, 1975—78; mgr. health promotion Volvo Flygmotor, 1978—98; corp. medical dir. Volvo AB, Goteborg, 1989—94; occpl. health specialist World Bank, Washington, 1998—. Chmn. Assn. Volvo Physicians, Goteborg, Sweden, 1993—98; Swedish coord. Volvo-Renault Heart Study, 1993—2004; assoc. prof. Sahlgrenska Acad., 2004; co-task mgr. first symposium on travel and stress World Bank, Washington, 2004. Contbr. chapters to books, articles to profl. jours. Coord. table tennis team Volvo AG, Goteborg, Sweden, 1980—90; vol. instr. Tennis Club, Vanersborg, 1988—89; bd. mem PTA, Vanersborg, 1997—98. Mem.: Swedish Med. Assn. (sec. 1982—85), Am. Coll. Occpl. and Environ. Medicine. Avocations: tennis, ping pong/table tennis, guitar, piano. Office: World Bank Occpl Health Svcs 1818 H St NW Washington DC 20433-0001

DIMEDIO, MICHAEL JOSEPH, secondary school educator; b. Phila., Aug. 27, 1951; s. Robert Michael and Dorothy Emma (Goodman) DiM.; m. Marcia Louise Heminway, Sept. 26, 1970; children: Nicole Louise, Liza Darlene, Adam Michael. BA in Environ. Scis., Richard Stockton Coll., 1981. Cert. tchr., N.J. Varsity golf coach Wildwood (N.J.) H.S., 1982-86, class advisor, 1986, student coun. adviser, 1986-95, sci. dept. chmn., 1992—, biology tchr., 1981—. Editor: Hawk Watch: A Guide for High School Students, 1983. Commr. Lower Twp. (N.J.) Environ. Commn., 1986—. Staff sgt. USAF, 1970-74. Recipient Region 2 Environ. Quality award EPA, 1989. Mem. NSTA. Episcopalian. Avocations: backpacking, camping, surfing, golf, hunting. Home: 100 Briarwood Dr Cape May NJ 08204-3813 Office: Wildwood HS 4300 Pacific Ave Wildwood NJ 08260-4625

DIMEGLIO, DAVID J., lawyer; b. San Pedro, Calif. BA, U. Calif., Los Angeles, 1984; JD, Stanford U., 1987. Bar: Calif. 1987, Calif. Ninth Circuit Ct. of Appeals. Ptnr., civil litigation Jones Day, Los Angeles, Calif. Mem.: ABA, Calif. State Bar Assn. Office: Jones Day 555 W Fifth St Ste 4600 Los Angeles CA 90013 Office Phone: 213-243-2551. Office Fax: 213-243-2539. Business E-Mail: djdimeglio@jonesday.com.

DI MEO, DOMINICK, artist, sculptor, painter; b. Niagara Falls, NY, Feb. 1, 1927; s. Antonio and Michelina (Sandonato) Di M.; m. Judith S. Cousins, Dec. 26, 1963. B.F.A., Sch. Art Inst., Chgo., 1952; M.F.A., State U. Iowa, 1953. Vis. artist Sch. of Art Inst. Chgo., 1977; instr. Chgo. Acad. Fine Arts, 1967-69 One man shows include Lake Forest (Ill.) Coll., 1955, Bemidji (Minn.) Coll., 1963, Fairweather-Hardin Gallery, Chgo., 1964, 68, 71, Barat Coll., Lake Forest, 1966, Chgo. Public Libr., 1966, Kendall Coll., Evanston, Ill., 1967, Westbroadway Gallery, NYC, 1973, 75-76, Project Studios One, Long Island City, NY, 1982, group exhbns. include, Albright-Knox Art Gallery, Buffalo, 1953-54, Art Inst. Chgo, 1959-61, 63, 65-68, 71, 76, 79, 89-90, Whitney Mus. Am. Art, NY, 1967-68, Mus. Contemporary Art, Chgo., 1969, Joan Miro Internat. Drawing Prize Competition, Barcelona, Spain, 1977-80, Centro Cultural/Arte Contemporaneo, Mexico City, 1986-1987, Art Inst. Chgo., 1989-90; represented in permanent collections Art Inst. Chgo., Whitney Mus. Am. Art, NYC, U. Mass., Amherst, Nat. Collection Fine Arts, Smithsonian Instn., Elmhurst (Ill.) Coll. Fellow Guggenheim Found., 1972, sculpture fellow Nat. Endowment for Arts, 1983. Mem. Momentum (founding mem.), Participating Artists Chgo.), Artists Collaborative. Address: 429 Broome St New York NY 10013-2686 Office Phone: 212-966-6037.

DIMICCO, DANIEL R., manufacturing executive; BS in Engring., Metallurgy and Materials Sci., Brown U., 1972; MS in Metallurgy and Materials Sci., U. Pa., 1975. Rsch. metallurgist, project leader Republic Steel, Cleve., 1975—82; plant metallurgist, mgr. quality control Nucor Steel, Plymouth, Utah, 1982—88, mgr. melting and casting Utah divsn., 1988—91; gen. mgr. Nucor-Yamato, Blytheville, Ark., 1991—92, v.p., 1992—99, exec. v.p., 1999—2000; pres., CEO Nucor Corp., 2000—, vice chmn., 2001—. Office: Nucor Corp 2100 Rexford Rd Charlotte NC 28211*

DIMICELI, VINCENT EDWARD, mathematician, educator; b. Port Arthur, Tex., Aug. 18, 1962; s. Vito Emanuel and Betty Lee Dimiceli; m. Linda Marie Kleihege, Aug. 11, 1990; 1 child, Emma Grace Marie; 1 child, Peter Vincent Emanuel. BS, Lamar U., Beaumont, Tex., 1986; MS, Tex. A&M U., 1989, PhD, 1999. Math. tchr. asst. Tex. A&M U., College Station, 1987—89, math. lectr., 1989—96; math. tchr. Bryan (Tex.) H.S., 1996—97; asst. prof. of math. Oral Roberts U., Tulsa, 1997—. Faculty advisor for Okla.-Delta chpt. of Kappa Mu Epsilon Oral Roberts U., Tulsa, 1997—, treas. of arts and scis. faculty senate, 2000—02, advisor for Coll. Reps., 2002—, v.p., pres.-elect of arts and scis. faculty senate, 2002—03, pres. of arts scis. faculty senate, 2003—04. Author: (abstracts for Okla. Academy Sci. Meeting) Biostatistics Applied to Tulsa Forensic Palynology, 2004. Treas. for campaign for Michael Bates for city coun. Rep. Party, Tulsa, 2001—02, del. to county conv., 2000, del. to state conv., 2000, chmn. precinct 124, 2004—; exec. com. Tulsa County Reps., 2003—; bd. dirs. Mt. Horeb Ch., Bryan, 1995—97; dir. Brazos Valley Mar. for Jesus, Bryan and College Station, 1996—97; worship leader for Sunday sch. class Victory Christian Ctr., Tulsa, 1999—2003, actor in Christmas and Easter dramas, 2001—02; voice-over for character in outdoor theater Impact Prodns., Tulsa, 2002; bd. dir. COTEAM, Inc. Named Outstanding Math. and Computer Sci.Tchr., Oral Roberts U., 2003; recipient undergrad. rsch. fellowship, U.S. Govt., 1987, Outstanding Comp. Sci./Math. Prof., ORU, 2003—04, Professionalism in the Classroom award, 2003. Mem.: Nat. Coun. of Tchrs. of Math., Math. Assn. of Am., Phi Kappa Phi, Kappa Mu Epsilon (corr. sec. Okla.-Delta chpt. 1997—), Alpha Phi Omega (life). Conservative. Charismatic Christian. Achievements include first to First teacher at Texas A&M University to develop a college algebra course utilizing calculator graphing technology to teach concepts in algebra; In the group of teachers to first implement computer laboratories for calculus at Texas A&M University; First to develop and implement computer laboratories for calculus at Oral Roberts University. Avocations: photography, reading, singing, acting. Office: Oral Roberts U 7777 S Lewis Ave Tulsa OK 74171 Office Phone: 918-495-6700. E-mail: dimiceli@oru.edu.

DIMICHELE, DONNA, medical educator, researcher; MD, McGill U., 1978. Cert. Am. Bd. Pediat., 1985, Am. Bd. Pediatric Hematology/Oncology, 1987. Instr. pediat. U. Colo. Med. Sch., Denver, 1982—83, Tufts U. Sch. Medicine, Boston, 1988—90; asst. prof. pediat. Northwestern U. Med. Sch., Chgo., 1990—95, Weill Med. Coll. Cornell U., N.Y.C., 1995—2000, assoc. prof. clin. pediat., 2001—04, assoc. prof. pediat., 2004—. Attending pediatrician Children's Meml. Hosp., Chgo., 1990—95, N.Y. Presbyn. Hosp., N.Y.C., 1995—2001; assoc. attending pediatrician Hosp. Spl. Surgery, 1999—; assoc. prof. pediat. and pub. health Weill Coll. Cornell U., N.Y.C., 2005—. Co-author: Thrombosis and Hemorrhage, Anticoagulants: Physiologic, Pathologic and Pharmacologic, Pediatric Clinics of North America, Thrombosis and Hemorrhage, Hematology/Oncology Clinics of North America, Disorders of Hemostasis and Thrombosis, Inhibitors in Patients with Haemophilia, Thrombosis and Hemorrhage, Hematology: Basic Principles and Practice, Textbook of Hemophilia, Best Practice and Research Clinical Hematology, Current Pediatric Therapy. Recipient David W. Smith Pediat. Trainee Rsch. award, Western Soc. Pediatric Rsch., 1987; grantee Altered Coagulation Pediatric Stem Cell Patients, Am. Cancer Soc., 1998—2000. Mem.: Nat. Hemophilia Found. (med. and sci. adv. coun. 2002—), Internat. Soc. Thrombosis and Haemostasis (subcom. chair 2000), World Fedn. of Hemophilia (med. specialist adv. 2000). Office: NY Presbyn Hosp 525 East 68th St Payson 695 New York NY 10021

DI MINO, ANDRÉ ANTHONY, manufacturing executive, consultant; b. Bklyn., Aug. 24, 1955; s. Alfonso and Nancy (Zarbo) DiM.; m. Jenny DiCapua, May 30, 1981. BS in Indsl. Engring., Fairleigh Dickinson U., 1978, MBA in Fin., 1981. Engr. ADMTronics Inc., Emerson, NJ, 1977—79, dir. tech., 1979—82, sec./treas. Northvale, NJ, 1982—86, exec. v.p. and dir., 1986—2001; pres. ADMTronics, Northvale, NJ, 2002—; founder, dir. Enviro-Pack Devel. Corp., Northvale, 1991—2002. Ptnr., cons. Tech. Mgmt. Cons., Woodcliff Lake, NJ, 1978-94; v.p., dir. Pegasus Labs., Inc., Northvale, NJ, 1989—, Sonotron Med. Sys., Inc., Northvale, 1988—, VET-Sonotron Sys., Inc., Northvale, 1988-2002; pres. AANorthvale Med. Assocs., Inc., 1998-2004, chmn. bd. dirs., 2004—; pres. Ivivi Tech., Inc., 2004-. Inventor in field. Mem. coun. Borough of Woodcliff Lake, 1984-97, pres., 1987-93, 97, cable adv. com., 1999-; corr. sec. Office N.E. Rep. Orgn., 1989-93, treas., 1992-93, vice chmn., 1993; co-chmn. privatization subcom. Bergen County Cost Containment Rev. Team, 1991; open space com. Bergen County, 1997, 98; fundraising dir. Our Lady Mother of the Ch., Woodcliff Lake, 1990-99; founding mem., 1st v.p. Woodcliff chpt. Unico Nat. Svcs. Orgn., 1990-92, pres., 1992-94, 97-00; dep. dist. gov., 1993-94, dist. gov., 1994-96, nat. treas., 2002—05, 3d v.p. 2005-; founder, pres. Cmty. Access TV studio WCL-TV, 1990—; pres. Woodcliff Lake Rep. Club, 1994-96; devel. chmn. NW Bergen chpt. Am. Heart Assn. (vice chmn. 1995-96), 1994; founder, chmn. Woodcliff Lake Sr. Assn., 1989-99; trustee Pascack Hist. Soc., 1995-99; vice chmn. Pascack Valley Region Cmty. Devel. com., 1997; computer sci. adv. bd. Fairleigh Dickinson U., Madison, NJ, 2000-; chmn. Marconi Sci. Award Com., 2000—. Named Vol. of Yr. Bergen County, N.J., 1991, 93, Citizen of Yr. Pascack Valley C. of C., 1993. Mem. Woodcliff Lake Vol. Fire Assn. (hon.). Republican. Roman Catholic. Avocations: classic cars, antiques, video and photography. Office: ADMTronics Inc 224S Pegasus Ave Northvale NJ 07647-1904 E-mail: andre@adtronics.com.

DIMINO, JOSEPH C., lawyer; b. Rochester, NY, 1952; BA summa cum laude, U. Rochester, 1973; JD, U. Va., 1976. Aty. Norfolk So. Corp., Va., corp. gen. counsel, 2000—02, sr. gen. counsel, 2002—05, v.p., corp. counsel, 2005—. ABA Office: Norfolk Southern Corp 3 Commerical Pl Norfolk VA 23510-2191 Office Phone: 757-629-2816.

DIMITRI, ELIA CHARLES, retired medical educator; b. Jenkins, Ky., Aug. 29, 1936; s. Charles Z. and Sofia (Kosova) D.; m. Candace Love, Feb. 14, 1963; children: George E., Sara C., C. Robert. BA, East Tenn. State Coll., 1958; MD, U. Tenn., 1960; MPH, U. N.C., 1978. Diplomate Am. Bd. Pediatrics. Intern Nashville Gen. Hosp., Nashville, 1961; U.S. Army Tripler Gen. Hosp. U.S. Army, Honolulu, 1961-62; pediatric resident Vanderbilt U. Hosp., Nashville, 1964-66; fellow in child psychiatry Children's Hosp. Med. Ctr., Boston, 1966-67; asst. prof. Pediatrics U. Va. Sch. Medicine, Charlottesville, 1967-70; pediatrician Reynolds Meml. Hosp., Winston-Salem, N.C., 1970-72; pediatric cons. N.C. Div. Health Svcs., Winston-Salem, 1972-81; assoc. prof. Family Practice and Community Medicine U. Tex. Southwestern Med. Sch., Dallas, Wichita Falls, Tex., 1981—2003; ret., 2003. Dir. pediat. edn. Family Practice Residency Program, Wichita Falls, 1981-2003; assoc. med. dir. Wichita Falls City/County Health Dept., 1987-2003; assoc. program dir. Wichita Falls Family Practice Residency, 1992-2003; clin. prof. pediatrics Vanderbilt U. Dept. Pediatrics, 2005-; vol physician Siloam Family Health Ctr Capt. U.S. Army, 1961-64. Fellow Am. Acad. Pediat.; mem. AMA, APHA, Tex. Pediat. Soc. (chmn. membership com. 1987-94), Tex. Med. Assn., Nashville Acad. Medicine, Tenn. Pediat. Soc., Ambulatory Pediat. Assn. Home: 6820 Hwy 70 South 307 Nashville TN 37221 Personal E-mail: edimitri@comcast.net.

DIMITRIADIS, ANDRE C., health care executive; b. Istanbul, Turkey, Sept. 29, 1940; s. Constantine N. and Terry D. BS, Robert Coll., Istanbul, 1964; MS, Princeton U., 1965; MBA, NYU, 1967, PhD, 1970. Analyst Mobil Oil Internat., N.Y.C., 1965-67; mgr. TWA, N.Y.C., 1967-73; dir. Pan Am. Airways, N.Y.C., 1973-76, asst. treas., 1976-79; v.p., chief fin. officer Air Calif., Newport Beach, 1979-82; exec. v.p. fin. and adminstrn., chief fin. officer Western Airlines, Los Angeles, 1982-85, dir.; sr. v.p. (fin) Am. Med. Internat., from 1985, chief fin. officer, 1985-89, exec. v.p., 1988-89; dir., exec. v.p. fin., chief fin. officer Beverly Enterprises Inc., Ft. Smith, Ark., 1989-92;

chmn., CEO LTC Properties, Inc., 1992—. Bd. dirs. Assisted Living Concepts, Inc. Democrat. Greek Orthodox. Home: 4470 Vista Del Preseas Malibu CA 90265-2540 Office: LTC Properties Inc 300 E Esplanade Dr Ste 1860 Oxnard CA 93030-1286

DIMITRIOU, DOLORES ENNIS, computer consultant; b. Phila., Apr. 7, 1932; d. Charles Adair and Rubye Stanton (Greene) Ennis; m. John Alexander Dimitriou, Sept. 25, 1954 (div. Aug. 1983); 1 child, Sandra Irene Dimitriou Falor. BS in Math., U. Miami, 1954; MA in Linguistics, U. Tex., 1994. Jet engine supr. GE, Evendale, Ohio, 1954-58; rsch. aide Marine Lab. U. Miami, Coral Gables, 1959-65; supr. tests Weathering Rsch. Svc., Princeton, Fla., 1959-87; income tax preparer H&R Block, Homestead, Fla., 1981-83; small bus. cons., pres., co-founder Facts & Figures Svcs., Homestead, 1983-87; computer cons., trainer Wycliffe Bible Translators, Orlando, Fla., 1987-97. Sec., treas., co-founder Weathering Rsch. Svcs., Princeton, Fla., 1959—95; treas. GILLBT, Ghana, 1994—96. Tax aide Am. Assn. Ret. Persons, 1998—, instr., 2002—; long-term care ombudsman state coun., 2000—01, 2003—05; dist. chmn., 2000—01, 2003—04; bd. dirs. Ch. Women United, 1999—2003; ch. rels. Wycliffe Bible Translators, 1998—2003. Named Outstanding Woman in Religion YWCA, U. Miami, 1953-54. Mem.: Cutler Ridge Woman's Club, Mortar Board, Phi Mu Epsilon. Democrat. Avocations: computers, travel, reading, crafts. Home and Office: 10381 SW 209 Ln Miami FL 33189-3612 Personal E-mail: dolores-dimitriou@att.net.

DIMITRY, JOHN RANDOLPH, academic administrator; b. Detroit, Feb. 15, 1929; s. Dracos Alexander and Elizabeth Stanton (Bisland) D.; m. Audrey Oktavec, Aug. 20, 1952; children: Mark, Jane, Kate. Student, Spring Hill Coll., 1948-49; BA, Wayne State U., 1952, MS, 1954, Ed.D., 1966. Tchr., Highland Park (Mich.) Jr. Coll., 1954-61; asst. to pres. Macomb County C.C., Warren, Mich., 1963-65; dean center campus Macomb County Community Coll., 1966-67, pres., 1967-75, Northern Essex Community Coll., Haverhill, Mass., 1975—; mem. Gov.'s Commn. on Higher Edn., 1973-75. Pres. Mich. C.C. Assn., 1972-73; mem. Mass. Gov.'s State Job Tng. Coordinating Coun., 1983-91; mem. Mass. Commn. for Occupational Edn., 1982-88; chmn. NE Consortium of Colls. and Univs. in Mass., 1985-86, Mass. C.C. Pres. Assn., 1986-87, New England Regional Student Exch. Program ADv. Coun., 1992—. Bd. dirs. Lawrence Boys Club, Lawrence Yough Commn. Lt. U.S. Army, 1947-48, 52-53. Kellogg Found. fellow Community Coll. Adminstrn., 1961-63; recipient Leadership award Prudential Ins. Co. Am., 1992. Mem. Greater Haverhill C. of C. (pres. 1985-86). Home: Old Wharf Rd West Newbury MA 01985 Office: No Essex Community Coll Office of the Pres Elliott Way Haverhill MA 01830-2399

DIMITRY, THEODORE GEORGE, retired lawyer; b. New Orleans, Jan. 15, 1937; s. Theodore Joseph and Ouida Marion (Seiler) D.; m. S. Elizabeth Warren; children: Mary Elizabeth Hyry, Theodore Warren. BS, Tulane U., 1958, JD, 1960. Bar: La. 1960, Tex. 1964. Assoc. firm Phelps, Dunbar, Marks, Claverie & Sims, New Orleans, 1965-69, ptnr., 1969-75; ptnr. firm Vinson & Elkins, Houston, 1975-98; ret., 1998; pvt. arbitrator and mediator, 1999—. Rsch. fellow Southwestern Legal Found., Dallas, 1973-98; spkr. on maritime law, offshore contracting, ins. and resource devel. at profl. seminars, 1975— Contbr. articles to profl. jours. Mem. permanent adv. bd. Tulane U. Admiralty Law Inst., 1985—2000. Served with USN, 1960—64. Mem.: Maritime Law Assn. U.S. Fax: 713-877-1963. Personal E-mail: crossjack@sbcglobal.net.

DIMLING, JOHN ARTHUR, marketing executive; b. Pitts., Apr. 9, 1938; s. John Arthur and Elizabeth (Powell) D.; m. Marilyn Jean O'Connor; children: Courtney O'Connor, Meredith O'Connor. AB, Dartmouth Coll., 1960; MS, Carnegie Mellon U., 1962; JD, George Washington U., 1977. Bar: Md. 1977, D.C. 1978. Group mgr. Spindletop Rsch. Corp., Lexington, Ky., 1965-69; v.p. rsch. analysis Nat. Assn. Broadcasters, Washington, 1969-79; v.p. rsch., planning and analysis Arbitron Co., 1979; dir. planning & policy Corp. Pub. Broadcasting, Washington, 1979-82; exec. dir., CEO Electronic Media Rating Coun., N.Y.C., 1982-85; sr. v.p. A.C. Nielsen Co., N.Y.C., 1985-88, exec. v.p., 1988-93, pres., 1993—2001, chmn., 2001—. Chmn. Coltram, NYC, 1969-79; asst. treas. Broadcasting Rating Coun., NYC, 1971-79; cons. Western Broadcasting Corp., Missoula, Mont., 1981; sec., treas. Electronic Media Rating Coun., NYC, 1970-72; bd. dirs. Advt. Rsch. Found., 1989-95, sec., 1992, chmn., 1993-94; exec. com. Market Rsch. Coun., 1995-96; chmn. bd. dirs. NetRatings, Inc. Author: (with others) The Role of Analysis in Regulatory Decision Making-- The Case of Cable Television, 1973; contbr. articles to profl. jours. Bd. dirs. Ctr. for Comm., 1994—, St. Christopher's Sch., 2002—; trustee Masters Sch., 2000—. 1st lt. U.S. Army, 1963-65. Mem. ABA, Radio-TV Rsch. Coun., Ardsley Country Club (bd. govs. 1987-94, 2003-), Dartmouth Club (NY). Avocation: tennis. Home: 198 Judson Ave Dobbs Ferry NY 10522-3028 Office: Nielsen Media Rsch 770 Broadway New York NY 10003

DIMMA, WILLIAM ANDREW, real estate executive; b. Montreal, Que., Can., Aug. 13, 1928; s. William Roy and Lillian Norine (Miller) D.; m. Katherine Louise Vacy Ash, May 13, 1961; children: Suzanne Elizabeth Irene, Katherine Lillian Louise. BA in Sci., U. Toronto, Can., 1948; postgrad., Harvard U., 1956, DBA, 1973; MBA, York U., Toronto, 1969; LLD (hon.), York U., 1998; D of Commerce (hon.), St. Mary's U., 1991. Registered profl. engr., Ont. With Union Carbide Can Ltd., 1948-70, exec. v.p., bd. dirs., 1967-70; prof., dean faculty adminstrv. studies York U., 1974-76; pres., bd. dirs. Torstar Corp., Toronto Star Newspapers Ltd., Toronto, 1976-78; pres. A.E. LePage Ltd., Toronto, 1979-84; pres., CEO Royal LePage Ltd., Toronto, 1984-86, dep. chmn., 1986-93. Bd. dirs. Brascan Corp., Home Trust Co., Magellan Aerospace Corp.; chmn. bd. dirs. Home Capital Group, Malibu Engring. and Software Ltd., Royal Le Page Comml.; dir. York U. Devel. Corp.;dir. adv. group Inst. Chartered Accts., Best Bus. Book of Yr., jury. Author: Canada Development Corporation: Diffident Experiment on a Large Scale, 1973, Excellence in the Boardroom, 2002. Hon. dir. Niagara Inst., chmn. 1983-86; hon. gov. York U., chmn., 1992-97; hon. trustee Hosp. for Sick Children; gov. Jr. Achievement of Met. Toronto, chmn., 1992-93; gov. Can. Journalism Found. Decorated Order of Can., Order of Ont.; knight comdr. Order of St. Lazarus of Jerusalem; Elmslie Meml. scholar, 1944; Stevens gold medal Harvard Bus. Sch., 1971; Can. Coun. fellow, 1970-73; recipient York U. award Outstanding Corp. Leadership, 2001, Schulich Sch. Bus. Outstanding Leadership award, 1992, Queen's Golden Jubilee medal, 2002. Fellow Inst. Corp. Dirs. (bd. dirs.); mem. Toronto Club, Toronto Golf Club, York Club, Harvard Club Toronto, Bellair Country Club, Beta Theta Pi. Avocations: swimming, bicycling, writing. Home: Apt 302 407 Walmer Rd Toronto ON Canada M5R 3N2 E-mail: wdimma@brascancorp.com.

DIMMICK, CAROLYN REABER, federal judge; b. Seattle, Oct. 24, 1929; d. Maurice C. and Margaret T. (Taylor) Reaber; m. Cyrus Allen Dimmick, Sept. 10, 1955; children: Taylor, Dana. BA, U. Wash., 1951, JD, 1953; LLD, Gonzaga U., 1982, CUNY, 1987. Bar: Wash. 1953. Asst. atty. gen. State of Wash., Seattle, 1953-55; pros. atty. King County, Wash., 1955-59, 60-62; sole practice Seattle, 1959-60, 62-65; judge N.E. Dist. Ct. Wash., 1965-75, King County Superior Ct., 1976-80; justice Wash. Supreme Ct., 1981-85; judge U.S. Dist. Ct. (we. dist.) Wash., Seattle, 1985-94, chief judge, 1994-97, sr. judge, 1997—. Chmn. Jud. Resources Com., 1991—94, active, 1987—94. Recipient Matrix Table award, 1981, World Plan Execs. Coun. award, 1981, Vanguard Honor award King County of Wash. Women Lawyers, 1996, Disting. Alumni award U. Wash. Law Sch., 1997, Outstanding Jurist award King County Bar Assn., 2003; named Wash. Women of Yr. Seattle U. Women's Law Caucus, 2004. Mem. ABA, Am. Judges Assn. (gov.), Nat. Assn. Women Judges, World Assn. Judges, Wash. Bar Assn., Am. Judicature Soc., Order of Coif (Wash. chpt.). Office: US Dist Ct 16134 US Courthouse 700 Stewart St Seattle WA 98101 Office Phone: 206-370-8850. E-mail: carolyn_dimmick@wawd.uscourts.gov.

DIMMOCK, JOHN OLIVER, physicist, educator; b. Mineola, N.Y., Nov. 24, 1936; s. Clarence Oliver and Eleanor Stevens (Waste) D.; m. Barbara Welch Clark, June 21, 1958 (div. Nov. 1973); children: Leanne, Cynthia, John; m. Cynthia Kalliope Vouros, May 12, 1974 (div. 2000); children: Jonathan, Justin, James; m. Linda R. Leslie, June 30, 2001. BS in Physics, Yale U., 1958, PhD in Physics, 1962. Mem. staff rsch. div. Raytheon, Waltham, Mass., 1962-63, MIT Lincoln Lab., Lexington, 1963-66, leader applied physics group, 1966-71, leader applied optics group, 1971-74; dir. electronics and solid state scis. Office Naval Rsch., Arlington, Va., 1974-81, dep. dir., dir. tech. programs, 1981-84; tech. dir. Air Force Office Sci. Rsch., Washington, 1984-89; staff v.p. for rsch. McDonnell Douglas Corp., St. Louis, 1989-92; tech. dir. strategic technologies McDonnell Douglas Corp., St. Louis, 1992-93; dir. Ctr. Applied Optics, 1993—2003; prof. physics U. Ala., Huntsville, 2003—. Author: Properties of the Thirty-Two Point Groups, 1963; contbr. over 60 articles to sci. jours.; patentee in field. Recipient Superior Civilian Svc. award USN, 1984. Fellow AIAA (assoc.), Am. Phys. Soc.; mem. IEEE (sr.), AAAS, Sigma Xi. Office: U Ala Huntsville Ctr Applied Optics Huntsville AL 35899-0001 Business E-Mail: dimmockj@uah.edu.

DIMODICA, KATHLEEN ANNE, science educator; b. Mass. d. John and Jeanne Murphy; m. Paul DiModica. BS in Microbiology, U. R.I., 1983; MED in Secondary Adminstrn., Providence Coll., 1991. Cert. prin. curriculum coord. K-12, chemistry, biology, gen. sci. State of R.I. Sci. tchr. Norton (Mass.) H.S., 1986—2000, Dedham (Mass.) H.S., 2000—01, Cumberland (R.I.) H.S., 2001—. Mem. Sch. Improvement Team, Cumberland; mem. steering com. New Eng. Assn. Sch. Accreditation, Cumberland. Mem.: Network Educators in Sci. and Tech. at MIT, ASCD, Nat. Sci. Tchrs. Assn. Avocations: playing and attending sporting events, science, attending musicals. Office: Cumberland H S 2600 Mendon Rd Cumberland RI 02864

DIMON, JAMES L. (JAMIE DIMON), bank executive; b. N.Y.C., Mar. 13, 1956; s. Theodore and Themis Dimon; m. Judith Kent, May 21, 1983; children: Julia, Laura, Kara. BA, Tufts U., 1978; MBA, Harvard U., 1982. V.p., asst. to pres. Am. Express Co., N.Y.C., 1982-85; sr. v.p., CFO Comml. Credit Co., Balt., 1986-88; exec. v.p., CFO Primerica Corp., N.Y.C., 1989—90, pres., 1990—93; pres., COO Travelers Inc.; pres., COO, CFO The Travelers Inc, 1993—98; chmn, co-CEO Salomon Smith Barney Holdings Inc., 1998—2000; pres. Citigroup Inc, 1998—2000; chmn., CEO Bank One Corp., Chicago, 2000—04; pres., COO JPMorgan Chase & Co., N.Y.C., 2004—. Bd. dirs. Yum! Brands, Inc. Bd. dirs. Nat. Ctr. Addiction and Substance Abuse; mem. Coun. Fgn. Rels.; bd. dirs. U. Chgo., Econ. Club Chgo.; civic com. Comml. Club Chgo.; bd. dirs. Mt. Sinai Med. Ctr. and Health Systems. Office: JPMorgan Chase & Co 270 Park Ave New York NY 10017

DIMOND, EDMUNDS GREY, medical educator; b. St. Louis, Dec. 8, 1918; s. Edmunds Grey and Gertrude Ruth (Schmidt) D.; m. Mary Dwight Clark, Nov. 28, 1968 (dec. June 1983); children: Sherri Grey Byrer, Lea Grey Dimond, Lark Grey Dimond-Cates. Student, Purdue U., 1938—39; BS, Ind. U., 1942, MD, 1944. Mem. faculty Med. Ctr., U. Kans., Kansas City, 1950-60, prof., chmn. dept. medicine, 1953-60, dir. cardiovasc. lab., 1950-60; mem., dir. Inst. for Cardiopulmonary Diseases, Scripps Clinic and Rsch. Found., 1960-67; rsch. assoc. physiology Scripps Inst. Oceanography, La Jolla, Calif., 1960-68; prof. in residence Sch. Medicine, U. Calif., San Diego, 1967-68; scholar in residence Nat. Libr. Medicine, 1967; spl. asst. to asst. sec. HEW, Washington, 1968; Disting. univ. prof. medicine U. Mo., Kansas City, 1968-98, provost for health scis., 1968-79. Fulbright prof., The Netherlands, 1956; vis. prof., Israel, 1978; scholar in residence Rockefeller Found. Study Ctr., Bellagio, Italy, 1978; chmn. overseas edn. team Dept. State, 1962, 64-66, 73; guest lectr. Chinese Med. Assn., 1971-73, 76-80, 82-92; pres. Edgar Snow Fund, Inc., Diastole-Hospital Hill, Inc. Author: Electrocardiography, 1952, rev. edits., 1955, 60, 64, Digitalis, 1957, Exercise Electrocardiograms, 1961, More Than Herbs and Acupuncture, 1975, Inside China Today, 1981, Take Wing, 1991, Dr. Horse of China, 1992, Reverend Whitehead, Mississippi Pioneer, 1987, Letters from Forest Place, 1993, Essays By An Unfinished Physician, 1995, Milepost Eighty, 2000; editor: Diastole on Hospital Hill Audiotape, 1980-86; editor-in-chief Accel, 1968-77; contbr. articles to profl. jours. Bd. dirs. Truman Med. Ctr., Kansas City, Mo., Eye Found., Kansas City, Sci. Edn. Partnership, Kansas City. With M.C., AUS, 1945-47. Paul Dudley White Traveling scholar, 1956-57. Master Am. Coll. Cardiology (pres. 1962, Disting. Svc. award 1969). Home and Office: 2501 Holmes St Kansas City MO 64108-2742 E-mail: gdimond@planetkc.com.

DIMOND, ROBERT B., food products executive; BS in acctg., U. Utah. Cert. CPA. Group v.p., admin. contr. Smith's Food & Drug Ctrs., Inc.; group v.p., CFO, western region The Kroger Co.; sr. v.p., CFO Nash Finch Co., Mpls., 2000—02, exec. v.p., CFO, 2002—. Office: Nash Finch Co 7600 France Ave S Minneapolis MN 55440-0355

DIMOND, THOMAS, investment company executive, consultant; b. Scarsdale, N.Y., Jan. 24, 1916; s. George A. and Jessie (Kennedy) D. BA magna cum laude, Princeton U., 1939; MBA, Harvard U., 1941. Mem. faculty Wharton Sch. Fin., U. Pa., 1948; economist, account mgr. Lionel D. Edie & Co., 1948-50; economist, mgr. comml. rsch. Youngstown Sheet & Tube Co., Ohio, 1951-56; sr. account mgr., security analyst deVegh & Co., N.Y.C., 1956-60; pres. Humes-Schmidlapp Assocs., N.Y.C., 1960—. Bd. dirs. Mercer Mgmt. Corp., co-mgr. Mercer Fund, 1963-67; bd. dirs. Scudder Spl. Fund, 1967-72, Scudder Duv-Vest, 1968-71; gen. ptnr. HS Spl. Fund. Contbr. articles to profl. publs. Trustee, Humes Found., 1963—. Capt. USAAF, 1941-46. Mem. N.Y. Soc. Security Analysts, Racquet & Tennis Club, Down Town Assn. (N.Y.C.). Episcopalian. Home: 200 E 66th St Apt C1703 New York NY 10021-9187 Office: Humes-Schmidlapp Assoc 375 Park Ave Ste 3505 New York NY 10152-0002

DIMOPOULOS, LINDA J., food service executive; b. 1951; With Darden Restaurants, Inc., 1982, sr. v.p. fin. ops. Red Lobster, 1993—98, sr. v.p., corp. controller, bus info. sys., 1998—99, sr. v.p., chief info. officer, 1999—2002, chief fin. officer, 2002—. Office: Darden Restaurants Inc 4800 Lake Ellenor Dr Orlando FL 32809

DIMOPOULOS, VASSILIOS GEORGIOS, physician, researcher; s. Georgios Vassilios and Chrysoula Dimopoulos; m. Polyxeni Mouhtouri, Jan. 6, 2001; 1 child, George. MD, Med. Sch. Patras, 1989—95. Gen. practitioner Kalamata Hosp., Androusa, Greece, 1996—97, gen. surgery resident Greece, 1999—2000; neurosurgical resident U. Hosp. Patras, Greece, 2001; neurosurgical fellow Med. Ctr. Ctrl. Ga., Macon, 2001—. Contbr. articles to profl. jours. Dr. Hellenic Air Force, 1997—98, Athens, Kalamata. Mem.: AMA, Hellenic Med. Assn., Patras Med. Assosiation, Gen. Med. Coun., So. Med. Assn. Achievements include research in the use of transintracranial ultrasound in neurosurgery; the proposal of third nerve palsy scale; the proposal of recurrent laryngeal nerve intraoperative irritation scale. Avocations: travel, weightlifting, movies, track and field. Office: Ga Neurosurgical Inst 840 Pine St Ste 880 Macon GA 31201 Office Phone: 478-743-7092. Office Fax: 478-743-0523.

DIMSDALE, JOEL EDWARD, psychiatry educator; b. Sioux City, Iowa, Apr. 16, 1947; s. Lewis J. and Phyllis (Green) D.; m. Nancy Kleinman, Sept. 17, 1978; 1 child, Jonathan Jared. BA in Biology, Carleton Coll., 1968; MA in Sociology, Stanford U., 1970, MD, 1973. Diplomate Am. Bd. Psychiatry. Resident in psychiatry Mass. Gen. Hosp., Boston, 1973-76; instr. psychiatry Harvard U. Sch. Medicine, Boston, 1976-80, asst. prof., 1980-84, assoc. prof., 1984-85; assoc. prof., now prof. psychiatry U. Calif., San Diego, 1985—2002, chair acad. senate, 2002—03. Cons. to Pres.'s Commn. on Mental Health, Washington, 1977-78, NIH, Washington, 1980—. Editor: Survivors, Victims and Perpetrators, 1980, Quality of Life in Behavior Medicine Rsch., 1995; editor-in-chief Psychosomatic Medicine, 1992-02; mem. editl. bd. Internat. Jour. Behavioral Medicine, 1993—, Applied Biobehavioral Rsch., 1994—, Am. Jour. Human Biology, 1994-2003, Psychosomatics, 1996—; contbr. articles to profl. jours. Fellow Am. Psychopathol. Assn., Acad. Behavioral Med. Rsch. (coun. 1988-91, 2004—, pres. 1991-92), Soc. of Behavioral Medicine (pres. 2000), Disting. fellow Am. Psychiat. Assn.; mem. Am. Psychosomatic Soc. (coun. 1982-85, pres. 1999), Sigma Xi. Home: 4435 Ampudia St San Diego CA 92103 Office: U Calif San Diego 9500 Gilman Dr La Jolla CA 92093-0804 Office Phone: 619-543-5592. Business E-Mail: jdimsdale@ucsd.edu.

DI MUCCIO, MARY-JO, retired librarian; b. Hanford, Calif., June 16, 1930; d. Vincent and Theresa (Yovino) DiMuccio. BA, Immaculate Heart Coll., 1953, MA, 1960; PhD, U.S. Internat. U., 1970. Tchr. parochial schs., Los Angeles, 1949-54, San Francisco, 1954-58; tchr. Govt. of Can., Victoria, 1958—60; asst. libr. Immaculate Heart Coll. Libr., Los Angeles, 1960-62, head libr., 1962—72; adminstrv. libr. City of Sunnyvale, Calif., 1972-88; ret., 1988. Instr. Foothill C.C., Los Altos, 1977—95. Mem. exec. bd., past pres. Sunnyvale Cmty. Svcs.; chair for Chefs Who Care, Cmty. Svcs. Agy., 1999— Mem. ICF (past pres.), Cath. Libr. Assn. (past pres.), Sunnyvale Bus. and Profl. Women, Peninsula Dist. Bus. and Profl. Women (past pres.). Home: 736 Muir Dr Mountain View CA 94041-2509 E-mail: JO736@aol.com. *My goal has been to become a universal person, and that is my responsibility as a professional person-to see that the society we are building for tomorrow is appropriate to the needs of the people we serve.*

DIMUCCIO, ROBERT A., insurance company executive; b. Providence; Grad., Providence Coll. CPA; cert. CPCU. With KPMG Peat Marwick, Providence, 1978—92; v.p., sr. v.p., treas., to CFO Amica Mutual Ins. Co., Lincoln, RI, 1992—2004, exec. v.p., 2004—05, pres., CEO, 2005—. Bd. dir. Inst. Bus. & Home Safety, 2005—, RI Pub. Expenditure Coun. Phi Class Leadership RI, 2001. Office: Amica Mutual Ins Co 100 Amica Way Lincoln RI 02865 Office Phone: 800-652-6422.*

DIMURO, BERNARD JOSEPH, lawyer; b. Boston, Mar. 3, 1954; s. Bernard P. and Katherine (Deuce) D. BA, Northwestern U., 1976; JD, George Washington U., 1979. Bar: Va. 1979, U.S. Dist. Ct. (ea. dist.) Va. 1979, U.S. Ct. Appeals (4th cir.) 1979, Ill. 1980, D.C. 1985, U.S. Ct. Appeals (9th cir.) 1986, U.S. Ct. Appeals (8th cir.) 1987. Ptnr. Hirschkop, DiMuro & Mook, Alexandria, Va., 1979—89; found. ptnr. Dimuro, Ginsberg & Mook PC, Alexandria, Va., 1990—. Founder, pres. The Civil Workplace, 1996—. Mem. ABA, Va. State Bar Assn. (mem. com. to implement pro bono report, chmn. 8th dist. grievance com., disciplinary bd. 1988-95, chair 1993-95, exec. com. 1995-97, 2000-, chair task force on public access to the disciplinary system, mem. task force on corp. counsel 2001-, Va. model rules com. 1995-99, lawyers serving as fiduciaries com. 1993-94, vice chair publications/public info. com. 1996-2001, faculty for the professsionalism course 1995-98, pres. 2002-03), Ill. State Bar Assn., D.C. Bar, Va. Trial Lawyers Assn. (bd. govs. 1997-2000), Assn. Trial Lawyers Am.; fellow Va. Law Found. 1995, ABA 1998 Roman Catholic. Office: DiMuro Ginsberg & Mook PC 908 King St Ste 200 Alexandria VA 22314-3018

DINAKAR, CHITRA, immunologist, allergist; MD, Jawaharlal Inst. of Postgrad. Med. Edn. and Rsch., Pondicherry, India, 1991; diploma in Child Health, Pondicherry U., India, 1992. Diplomate Pondicherry State Med. Bd., India, 1993, Am. Bd. of Pediat., 1996, Am. Bd. of Allergy, Asthma and Immunology, 1999. Asst. prof. pediat. U. Mo., Kansas City, 1999—; faculty, sect. of allergy, asthma and immunology Children's Mercy Hosp., Kansas City, Mo., 1999—. Mem. instl. rev. bd. (pediat.) U. Mo., Kansas City. Mem. editl. bd.: Allergy and Asthma Procs., reviewer: jour. Annals of Allergy, Asthma, Immunology, Jour. of Allergy and Clinical Immunology. Recipient Instl. Rsch. Day Award for rsch. on exhaled nitric oxide, Children's Mercy Hosp., 2002; Rsch. on exhaled nitric oxide in children grant, Katharine B. Richardson Found., 2001, 2002. Fellow: Am. Coll. Allergy, Asthma, Immunology, Am. Acad. of Pediat. (pediatric rsch. com.), Am. Acad. of Allergy, Asthma, Immunology (sec. health care delivery edn. and quality, chair new allergists immunologists group, vice chair women in AAAAI com., vice chair internat. health care delivery com., vis. prof. panel, Clemens Von Pirquet award for best abstract 1998, Outstanding Pediatric Allergy and Immunology Abstract award 2005, Fellows-in-tng. Rsch. grant 1997); mem.: Indian Acad. of Allergy (ann. conf. planning com. 2004—05, internat. adv. bd. 2004—05), Mo. State Med. Assn. (alt. del. to internat. med. grads. sect.), Ednl. Commn. for Fgn. Med. Grads. Office: Children's Mercy Hosp 2401 Gillham Rd Kansas City MO 64108 Office Phone: 816-234-3097. Office Fax: 816-346-1301. Business E-Mail: cdinakar@cmh.edu.

DINAN, ROBERT MICHAEL, lawyer; b. Quebec City, Que., Can., Aug. 12, 1956; s. John H.T. and Lorraine (Matte) D.; m. Alicia Soldevila, June 11, 1983; children: Karina, Philippe, John. LLB, U. Laval, Que., 1978. Bar: Que., 1980. Assoc. Pothier Begin et al, Quebec City, 1980-87, ptnr., 1987-94, Lepage Dinan, Quebec City, 1994—2002; chmn. bd. TeleFilm Can., Montreal, 1993-98; ptnr. O'Brien, Avocats, Quebec City, 2003—. Mem. exec. com., v.p., pres. Jeffery Hales Hosp., Quebec City, 1992-95, bd. dirs., 1992—, chmn. bd. dirs., 1996—; bd. dirs. Duke of Edinburgh's award, bd. dirs. Voice of English Que., 1992-98, mem. exec. com., 1995-98, v.p., 1997-98; v.p. St. Brigid's Home, 1985-89, pres., 2002-; v.p. Danse Partout, 1989-91; v.p. Morrin Coll. Found., 1997-2000, fin. com. 1997-2000, bldg. com. 1997-2000; mem. Centre Aide Que., 1985—, Assemblée Regie Régional Santé et Svcs. Sociaux, 1992-97, appt. Queen's Coun., 1992; bd. dirs. Can. TV and Cable Prodn. Fund, 1996-98. Recipient Bursery award Minister of Justice, Can., 1978. Mem. Can. Bar Assn., Que. Bar Assn. (external rels. com. 1993-96, libr. com. 1986-88), Que. C. of C. Avocations: gardening, painting, skiing, bicycling. Home: 2391 Marie-Victorin Sillery PQ Canada G1T 1K2 Office Phone: 418-648-1511. Personal E-mail: rdinan@obrienavocats.qc.ca.

DINCECCO, JENNIE ELIZABETH WILLIAMS SWANSON, healthcare administrator, mentor, healthcare educator, volunteer; b. Atlanta, Aug. 5, 1932; d. Chester Arthur and Cleo Annie Williams; m. Richard Edward Swanson, Apr. 24, 1954 (dec. 1994); children: Laurel Dee Swanson, Jeffrey Richard Swanson, Scott Edward Swanson; m. Thomas M. Dincecco, Aug. 26, 2000. BS, Northwestern U., 1954; MS, No. Ill. U., 1972, EdD, 1976. Pub. sch. tchr., 1954-69; psycho-ednl. diagnostician, 1969-72; faculty Loyola U., Chgo., 1976-82, asst. prof. ob-gyn and pediat., 1979-82; dir. pre-start project depts. ob-gyn and pediat. Stritch Sch. Medicine, 1978-82; dir. spl. svcs. Cmty. Unit Sch. Dist. 220, 1982-92. Hospice bereavement vol., 1997—; coun. mem., mentor Cong. Unitarian Ch.; antique dealer; mem. Gov. Ill. Com. Preventive Svcs., 1979-80; chair B-3 subcom. First Chance Consortium, 1978-80; chair INTER-ACT, 1979-80; cons. in field. Author: Dying With Open Eyes: Alzheimer's Disease, 2005; co-author: Partners in Child Development, 1978 Vol. Latino Coalition, Alzheimer's Assn. Grantee HEW, 1973-76, 78-82. Mem.: Ret. Tchrs. McHenry County, Nat. Assn. Edn. Young Child, Nat. Acad. Neuropsychology, Nat. Perinatal Assn., Assn. Maternal and Child Health, Coun. Exceptional Children, Golden Cir., Woodstock Opera House Commn. (chairperson 2001—), Northwestern U. Alumni Assn., Nu Alumni Club, Delta Kappa Gamma (scholar 1974), Delta Delta Delta (life; golden cir.). Unitarian Universalist.

DINCULEANU, NICOLAE, mathematician, educator; b. Padea, Romania, Feb. 26, 1925; came to U.S., 1976. s. Nicolae and Frusina (Lusca) Dobrescu; m. Elena Constantinescu, Feb. 9, 1959. Engr., Poly. Inst., Bucharest, 1950; licencie math., U. Bucharest, 1951; PhD in Math, U. Bucarest, 1957; Doctor honoris causa, U. Craiova, 1995, U. Bucharest, 2001. Prof. math. U. Bucharest, 1950-77; vis. prof. Queen's U., Kingston, Ont., Can., 1966-67, U. Rennes, France, U. Erlangen, Germany, 1970; Disting. vis. prof. U. Pitts., 1970-71; vis. research prof. U. Fla., Gainesville, 1972-77, prof. math., 1977—2003. Author: Vector Measures, 1967, Integration on Locally Compact Spaces, 1974, Textbook of Mathematical Analysis, 2 vols, 1962, Vector Integration and Stochastic Integration in Banach Spaces, 2000; also articles. Mem.: Romanian Acad. (hon.). Mem. Romanian Orthodox Ch. Club: Torch. Office: U Fla Math Dept Little Hall # 450A Gainesville FL 32611-2082 Business E-Mail: nd@math.ufl.edu.

DINE, JIM, artist; b. Cin., June 16, 1935; m. Nancy Minto, 1957; 3 children. Student, U. Cin., Boston Mus. Sch.; B.F.A., Ohio U., 1958. Instr. Yale U., 1965. Artist-in-residence Oberlin (Ohio) Coll., 1965, Cornell U., Ithaca, N.Y., 1966-67; instr. Royal Coll. Art, London, 1967-68 Painter, sculptor, author, illustrator: Welcome Home Lovebirds, 1969; co-author: Work from the Same House, 1969; co-author, illustrator: The Adventures of Mr. and Mrs. Jim & Ron, 1970; illustrator: The Poet Assassinated, 1968; prod. happenings, including Car Crash, 1960; one-man shows, 1959—, including: N.Y.C., Milan, Brussels, Paris, Chgo., Washington; exhibited in groups shows: Venice, London, Dallas, Buenos Aires, Phila., Pasadena, Tokyo, The Hague, Brussels, Vienna, Buffalo, Munich, W.Ger., Stockholm, Atlanta, Los Angeles, others, The Hague, Chgo., London, N.Y.C.; represented in permanent collections: Brandeis U., Mus. Modern Art, Guggenheim Mus., Albright Mus., N.Y. U., Tate Gallery, London, Stedelijk Mus., Amsterdam, Whitney Mus., N.Y.C., others. Recipient Norman Harris Silver medal Art Inst. Chgo., 1964; named, Nat. Academician, Nat. Academy of Design, 2002 Mem. Am. Acad. and Inst. Arts and Scis. Address: 59 Barrow St New York NY 10014-3701*

DINEEN, JOHN K., lawyer; b. Gardiner, Maine, Jan. 21, 1928; s. James J. and Eleanor (Kelley) D.; m. Carolyn Foley Reardon (dec. 1982); children: Jane, Martha, Louisa, Jessica, John; m. Susan Lowell Wales, Aug. 15, 1986; children: Theodore, Ralph, Andrew. BA, U. Maine, 1951; JD, Boston U., 1954; DHL (hon.), Cambridge Coll., 2001. Bar: Maine 1954, Mass. 1954. Ptnr. Weston, Patrick & Stevens, Boston, 1954-67, Gaston & Snow, Boston, 1970-91, Peabody & Arnold, Boston, 1967—70, ptnr., 1991—2000, counsel, 2000—02; sr. counsel Nutter McClennen & Fish, 2002—. Spl. asst. atty. gen. Commonwealth of Mass., Boston, 1965-67; dir. Dingle Am. Properties Ltd., Dingle, County Kerry, Ireland, 1973—; pres., trustee Boston Local Devel. Corp., 1982—. Trustee emeritus Waring Sch., Beverley, Mass., 1981—, Cambridge (Mass.) Coll.; life trustee U.S.S. Constn. Mus., 1993—; trustee, chmn. Nahant (Mass.) Pub. Libr., 1996—; former trustee Boston U. Med. Ctr., Winsor Sch. Emmanuel Coll., Boston, Hebron Acad., Maine, Boston Aid to the Blind, 1994-2000. With U.S. Army, 1946-48. Mem. Boston Bar Assn., Mass. Bar Assn., Boston Law Sch. Alumni Assn. (exec. com. 1989-91), Marshall Street Hist. Soc., Tavern Club, Union Club, Cary Street Club, Apollo Club, Norway Weary Club. Republican. Roman Catholic. Home: 40 Pleasant St Nahant MA 01908-1632 Office: Nutter McClennen & Fish LLP World Trade Ctr West 155 Seaport Blvd Boston MA 02110-2604 Office Phone: 617-439-2804. E-mail: jdineen@nutter.com.

DINEEN, JOSEPH LAWRENCE, legal association administrator, consultant; b. Jersey City, Sept. 25, 1942; s. Cornelius P. and Dolores (Fitzsimmons) D.; m. Andrea J. Manzone, Nov. 20, 1965; children: Jacqueline, Kimberley A. BA in Polit. Sci., Fordham U., 1964; MBA in Human Resources, St. John's U., Springfield, La., 1984, PhD in Indsl. Psychology, 1988. Tchr. Xavier H.S., N.Y.C., 1964-67; adminstrv. mgr. Royal Globe Ins., N.Y.C., 1967-72; pers. mgr. U. Ga., Athens, 1972-74; v.p., dir. Fowler Products Co., Athens, 1974-85; sr. v.p. Scovill, Inc., Clarksville, Ga., 1985-88; dir. human resources Charter Med. Corp., Macon, Ga., 1988-93, G&O Mfg. Co., Jackson, Miss., 1993-96; chief compliance officer Union (S.C.) Hosp. Dist., 1996-2000, Spartanburg (S.C.) Regional Healthcare Sys., 2000—05; ret., 2005. Dir., chmn. bd. N.E. Ga. Employee Assistance Program, Athens, 1974-85, Employer Assistance Group-Dept. of Labor, Athens, 1988-93; mem., cert. tchr. Dept. Labor, 1986—; budget dir. United Way of N.E. Ga., Athens, 1985-88; cons. Gov.'s Com., Jackson, 1995-96. Author: Management in 21st Century, 1995, Management in the Twenty First Century - A Primer. Dir. United Way, Athens and Jackson, 1974-93, Employee Assistance Program, Athens, 1974-85; mem. Pres. Carter's Roundtable of Businessmen, Dept. of Commerce, 1978. Mem. Soc. Human Resource Mgmt. Avocations: teaching seminars, racquetball, tennis, reading. Home: 440 Savanna Plains Dr Spartanburg SC 29307-3160

DINEL, RICHARD HENRY, lawyer; b. L.A., Sept. 16, 1942; s. Edward Price and Edith Elizabeth (Rheinstein) D.; m. Joyce Ann Korsmeyer, Dec. 26, 1970; children: Edward, Alison. BA, Pomona Coll., 1964; JD, Stanford U., 1967. Bar: Calif. Owner Richard H. Dinel, Profl. Law Corp., L.A., 1971-79; ptnr. Richards, Watson & Gershon, L.A., 1979-92, of counsel, 1992-93; pres. R.H. Dinel Investment Counsel, Inc., L.A., 1992—. Chmn. bd. Pomona Coll. Assocs., 1987-89; ex-officio trustee Pomona Coll., 1987-89; arbitrator Chgo. Bd. Options Exch., 1978—, Pacific Stock Exch., 1979—; bd. govs. Western Los Angeles County coun. Boys Scouts Am., 1993—. Mem. Securities Ind. Assn. (speaker compliance and legal div. 1978-92), Pomona Coll. Alumni Assn. (chmn. alumni fund and continuing edn. com. 1972-73), Nat. Assn. Securities Dealers (mem. nat. bd. arbitrators 1978-90). Office: 11661 San Vicente Blvd Ste 400 Los Angeles CA 90049-5112

DINER, BRYAN C., lawyer; b. Livingston, NJ, Dec. 22, 1962; BSChemE, NJ Inst. Tech., 1984; JD, Seton Hall U., 1987. Bar: DC 1988, NJ, US Dist. Ct. (Dist. NJ), US Patent & Trademark Office. Resident & mng. ptnr. Brussels Office Finnegan, Henderson, Farabow, Garrett & Dunner LLP, 1998—2003, ptnr. Washington, mem. exec. com. Spkr. in field. Mem.: NJ State Bar Assn., DC Bar Assn., Am. Inst. Chem. Engrs., Am. Chem. Soc., Am. Intellectual Property Law Assn., ABA. Fluent in French. Office: Finnegan Henderson Farabow Garrett & Dunner LLP 901 New York Ave NW Washington DC 20001-3315 Office Phone: 202-408-4000. Office Fax: 202-408-4400. Business E-Mail: bryan.diner@finnegan.com.

DINERMAN, MIRIAM, social work educator; b. NYC, Apr. 13, 1925; d. Abraham J. and Frances (Shostac) Goldforb; m. Harold Dinerman, June 12, 1951 (dec. June 1976); children: David, Ellen, Ruth. BA with honors, Swarthmore Coll., 1945; MSW, Columbia U., 1949, D of Social Work, 1972. Youth dir. Jewish Assn. for Neighborhood Ctrs., N.Y.C., 1949-50, program dir., 1951-54; various social work part time positions, 1955-60; asst. prof. Rutgers U. Grad. Sch. Social Work, New Brunswick, NJ, 1961-72, assoc. prof., 1972-76, prof., 1976-99, asst. dean for acad. planning, 1973-75, assoc. dean, 1975-81, acting dean, 1978, chmn. health care sequence, mem. New Brunswick faculty coun., 1989-93, chair, 1991-92; dir. PhD program Rutgers U. Sch. Social Work, 1992-97, emerita, 1999—. Mem. grants rev. panel Office Human Devel. Svcs., HHS, 1986—90; cons. on health and social svcs. N.J. Legis. Task Force on 21st Century; mem. task force on std. of need N.J. Divsn. Econ. Assistance, 1989—91; manuscript rev. editor Longman's Press, Methuen Press; dir. Ctr. for Internat. and Comparative Social Work, 1977—99; adj. prof. Yeshiva U. Sch. Social Work, 1999—. Editor: Social Work Futures, 1983; mem. editl. bd. Affilia: Jour. Women and Social Work, 1985-94, 95—, book rev. editor., 1995-00, editor-in-chief, 2000—; contbr. articles to profl. jours., chpts. to books. Bd. dirs. Def. for Children Internat., 1980—88. Grantee NIMH, 1966-67, Rutgers U. Rsch. Coun. and Samuel Silberman Fund, 1979-80. Mem.: NJ AAUP (N.J. task force on health care policy), NASW (chpt. pres. 1984—86, nat. com. on nominations and leadership identification 1988—97, editl. com. 1991—95, NYC steering com. polit. action for candidate election 1996—2001, bd. dirs. N.Y.C. chpt. 1999—2001, sec. bd. dirs. 2003—, bd. dirs. N.Y.C. chpt. 2003—), Group for Advancement of Doctoral Edn. (sec. steering com. 1990—96), Coun. on Social Work Edn. (program planning com. 1984—89, ednl. policy and planning commn. 1989—94), Internat. Assn. Schs. Social Work (agt. 1988—95, bd. dirs.), Acad. Cert. Social Workers. Home: 353 W 29th St New York NY 10001-4784 Office Phone: 212-960-5289. Business E-Mail: dinerma@ymail.yu.edu.

DINES, DAVID MICHAEL, surgeon, educator; b. N.Y.C., Feb. 4, 1948; s. Aaron and Yuche Yvette Harriet Dines; m. Judith Lori Dines, Jan. 29, 1973; children: Joshua Scott, Alison Kate. BA in Biology, Lehigh U., 1970; MD, N.J. Coll. Medicine, 1974. Diplomate Am. Bd. Surgery. Resident in orthop. surgery N.Y. Hosp. Cornell, N.Y.C., 1974—76, Hosp. Spl. Surgery, N.Y.C., 1976—79, fellow, 1980, Am. Acad. Orthop. Surgery, Chgo., 1981; adj. Cornell U. Med. Coll., N.Y.C., 1983—; clin. prof. orthop. surgery Albert Einstein Coll. Medicine, N.Y.C., 1998—, chmn. dept. orthop. surgery, 1996—. Team physician N.Y. Mets, 1991—97, USTA, 1999—; med. advisor Assn. Tennis Profls., Punte Verde, Fla., 1994—; team physician U.S. Davis Cup Tennis Team, 2000—04. Contbr. articles to profl. jours. Fund raiser Hosp. Spl. Surgery, N.Y.C., 1979—, Rep. Nat. Com., Washington, 1994—. Named one of Best Drs. in N.Y., N.Y. Mag., 1997—, 2002, Best Drs. in Am., 1999—2002; recipient John Chanley Meml. award, U. Liverpool, Eng., 1996. Fellow: Am. Acad. Orthop. Surgeons; mem.: Assn. Tennis Profls. (med. dir. 2005—), Assn. Team Profl. Med. Soc. (assoc. dir. 1991), Am. Orthop. Assn. (mem. membership com. 1998—), Acad. Orthop. Soc. Am., Am. Shoulder and Elbow Soc. (mem. exec. com. 1999—, pres. 2005, pres.-elect, Neer award 2004). Avocations: tennis, golf, politics. Office: Albert Einstein Coll Med 935 Northern Blvd Ste 303 Great Neck NY 11021 Office Phone: 516-482-1037. E-mail: ddinesmd98@aol.com.

DING, HONGMING, mathematician, educator; b. Shanghai, Apr. 27, 1941; s. Kunyan Ding and Fengying Gu; m. Xiufang Yu, Oct. 14, 1972; 1 child, Jian. BA, Fudan U., Shanghai, China, 1964; MS, Shanghai Jiaotong U., China, 1982; PhD, U. Ga., Athens, 1989. Asst. prof., math. Shanghai Jiaotong U., 1982—84, U. Vt., Burlington, 1989—92, St. Louis U., 1992—96, assoc. prof., math., 1996—. Co-author: (books) Special Functions, 2000, The Mathematical Legacy of Harish-Chandra, 2000. Grantee, NSF, 1992—95, 1995—99, 1999—2003. Mem.: Am. Math. Soc. (organizer, spl. session 1995). Office: St Louis Univ 221 N Grand Blvd Saint Louis MO 63103

DING, JIANCHI, embryologist, researcher; b. Jiangyin, Jiangsu, Peoples Republic of China, Oct. 24, 1957; came to U.S., 1996; s. Xufu and Xiujin (Gao) D.; m. Mingxian Shen, Nov. 15, 1983; children: Helen Guangning, Jennifer Guangting. BSc, Jiangsu Agrl. Coll., Yangzhou, 1982, MSc, 1985; PhD, U. Alta., Edmonton, Can., 1993. Cert. high complexity lab. dir. Am. Bd. Bioanalysis . Instr. Jiangsu Agrl. Coll., Yangzhou, 1985-87; Natural Sci. and Engring. Rsch. Coun. postdoctoral fellow U. Guelph, Guelph, Ont., Can., 1993-95, rsch. assoc., 1993-96; sr. rschr. Inst. for the Study and Treatment of Endometriosis, Oak Brook, Ill., 1996—; lab. dir. Oak Brook Fertility Ctr., 1996—. Contbr. articles to profl. jours. including Biology of Reprodn., Molecular Reprodn. Devel., and Human Reprodn.; assoc. editor: New Technics to Animal and Poultry Production, 2003. Recipient scholarship Jiangsu Edn. Com., China, 1987-88. Mem. Am. Assn. Bioanalysts, Am. Soc. for Reproductive Medicine, Am. Soc. Andrology, Soc. for Study Reprodn., Coll. Reproductive Biology. Home: 117 Hawkins Cir Wheaton IL 60187-8564 Office: Oak Brook Fertility Ctr 2425 W 22nd St Ste 102 Oak Brook IL 60523-4643 Office Phone: 630-954-0054.

DING, JINWEN, biomedical researcher; MD, Tongji Med. U., Wuhan, China, 1983; PhD, Lund U., Sweden, 1993. Rsch. scientist U. of Toronto, Canada, 1993—99; asst. prof. Loyola U. Med. Ctr., Maywood, Ill., 1999—2004, U. Chgo., 2004—. Recipient Rsch. award, Am. Cancer Soc., 2004; grantee, Can. Assn. Gastroenterology, 1997, Ill. Transplant Soc., 2002; Sheila Sherlock Basic Rsch. grant, The U. of Toronto, 1997. Mem.: World Assn. of HPB Surgery, Am. Gastroent. Assn. Achievements include research in Immunological and molecular mechanisms of liver injury. Office Phone: 773-702-5520.

DINGELL, JOHN DAVID, congressman; b. Colorado Springs, Colo., July 8, 1926; s. John D. and Grace (Bigler) D.m. Deborah Insley; 4 children. BS in Chemistry, Georgetown U., 1949, JD, 1952. Bar: DC 1952, Mich. 1953. Pk. ranger U.S. Dept. Interior, 1948-52; asst. pros. atty. Wayne County, Mich., 1953-55; mem. U.S. Ho. of Reps. from 15th Mich. dist., 1955-65, 2003—, U.S. Ho. of Reps. from 16th Mich. dist., 1965—2002. Mem. migratory bird conservation commn.; ranking mem. energy and commerce com. 2nd lt. inf. AUS, 1945-46. Democrat. Office: US Ho of Reps 2328 Rayburn Bldg Washington DC 20515-2216 also: 19855 W Outer Dr Ste 103-E Dearborn MI 48124*

DINGER, ANN MONROE, association executive, interior designer; d. Hoke Jefferson and Florence Parsons Monroe; m. Donald Brackett Dinger, Aug. 13, 1960; 1 child, Lynn Ann Dinger Edmonds. BA in Edn. and Art, Mary Washington Coll. U. Va., Fredericksburg, 1958. Cert. tchr. Va. Art tchr. Alexandria (Va.) Pub. Schs., 1958—61; pvt. interior design cons. Alexandria, Charlottesville, Great Falls, Va., 1958—. Docent Robert E. Lee Boyhood Home, Alexandria, 1967—68; chair D.C. Embassy Tour Alexandria Jr. Women's Club, 1967—68; floral chmn. Pres. James Monroe Home, Charlottesville, Va., 1982—86; hospitality chmn. Newcomers Great Falls, 1987—88; dir., pres., adv. bd. mem. Clan Munro Assn., 1992—, mem. Scottish coun., 1992—. Fellowship com. chmn. Immanuel Presbyn. Ch., McLean, Va., 1994—98. Mem.: Clan Munro Assn., Great Falls Hist. Soc., Great Falls Citizens' Assn. Republican. Presbyterian. Avocations: antiques, gardening, travel. Home: 9100 Potomac Woods Ln Great Falls VA 22066

DINGES, RICHARD ALLEN, entrepreneur; b. Englewood, N.J., June 17, 1945; m. Kathie A. Headley; children: Kelly, Courtney, Daniel. Grad., Jersey City State Coll., 1967; MEd, U. Hawaii, 1972; postgrad., William Peterson Coll., 1974-79. Cert. sch. adminstr.; cert. sch. spl. services dir., N.J., Ariz., Hawaii. Pres. Def. Industry Assocs., Sierra Vista, Ariz., 1979—, Fed. Career Cons., Sierra Vista, Ariz., 1985; dir. Nat. Scholarship Locators, Sierra Vista, 1985—. Spl. needs counselor Pinelands Regional Sch. Dist. Editor: Guide to U.S. Defense Contractors, 1985, 87, 10 Step Guide to College Selection, Salary Negotiations for Military, How to Survive the Job Interview. Vice prin. Little Egg Harbor Primary Sch.; founder Families in Touch, 1992. Mem. Cochise County Merit Commn. (vice-chmn.), Platform Soc. Speakers' Assn. Office: 37 Olena St Hilo HI 96720-1867 E-mail: Richard_Dinges@hotmail.com.

DINGLE, CAROL A., state agency administrator, writer; b. Winchester, Mass., May 12, 1943; d. Leon B. and Lillian Dingle; m. Melvin Green (dec. Mar. 1989). BA, Merrimack Coll., North Andover, Mass., 1965. English tchr. Springbrook H.S., Silver Spring, Md., 1965—67; program dir. USO, Okinawa, Japan, 1967—69, dir. vols. Frankfurt, Germany, 1970—72, dir. fleet canteens Athens, Greece, 1973—74; bus. owner D&D Advertising, Arlington, Mass., 1975—92; grant adminstr. Commonwealth of Mass., Boston, 1992—; owner Memorable Quotations.com, Intelligentsia Network.com. Editor: (books) Memorable Quotations: Philosophers of Western Civilization, 2000, Memorable Quotations: English Writers of the Past, 2000, Memorable Quotations: French Writers of the Past, 2000, Memorable Quotations: Irish Writers of the Past, 2001, Memorable Quotations: Massachusetts Writers of the Past, 2001, Memorable Quotations: Jewish Writers of the Past, 2003; author: (screenplays) Megan McShane, 2003, Escape from Quiet Desperation, 2003, Tina Toscano, 2004, The Carriage House, 2004; co-author Mel's Boarding House, 2004. Personal E-mail: caroladingle@aol.com.

DINGLE, PHILIP, oil industry executive; BSCE, U. Calgary, Can., 1970. With drilling and prodn. Imperial Oil Ltd., 1970; engring. mgr. Esso Prodn. Malaysia, Inc., 1981, offshore divsn. mgr., 1984; v.p. corp. planning Imperial Oil Ltd., v.p. exploration and prodn.; mng. dir. Esso Exploration and Prodn. UK, 1993; chmn. and CEO Esso Malaysia, 1995; pres. ExxonMobil Saudi Arabia, 2001—03, ExxonMobil Gas and Power Mktg., 2003—; v.p. Exxon-Mobil Corp., 2003—. Office: ExxonMobil Gas & Power Mktg 5959 Las Colinas Blvd Irving TX 75039-2298*

DINGMAN, LINDA SUSAN, special education educator; b. LA, Mar. 23, 1942; d. Harold Hadley Story and Esther Pidgeon (Van Vleet) Schou; m. Roger Vincent Dingman, Aug. 21, 1965; children: Charles, Margaret, Zachary, Andrew. BA summa cum laude, UCLA, 1964; MA, Brandeis U., 1965. Cert. sec. tchr., Mass.; cert. sec. English tchr., severely handicapped credential, Calif., Colo. Prin. St. Clare's Family Care Ctr., Redondo Beach, Calif., 1983-86; edn. specialist Urban League Child Care Ctr., Colorado Springs, Colo., 1988-89; primary tchr. Infant-Toddler Devel. Ctr., Calif. State U., Dominguez Hills, 1986-88, head tchr., 1989—96; infant devel. specialist Harbor Regional Ctr., Harbor City, Calif., 1996—. Faculty mem. Grad. Sch. Edn., Calif. State U., Dominguez Hills; cons. on spl. edn. Marineland, Palos Verdes, Calif., 1987; mem. coord. coun. L.A. County Implementation Pub. Law 99-457, 1988. Cub Scout leader Boy Scouts Am., Lexington, Mass. and L.A., 1970-85; vol. L.A. Unified Sch. Dist., 1971-82; leader Girl Scouts U.S.A., L.A., 1975-82. Woodrow Wilson fellow, 1964. Mem. Assn. for Edn. Young Children, Coun. for Exceptional Children, Phi Beta Kappa, Kappa Delta Pi. Democrat. Roman Catholic. Avocations: reading, needlecrafts, stained glass. Home: 1532 238th St Harbor City CA 90710-1305

DINGMAN, MICHAEL DAVID, manufacturing executive, investor; b. New Haven, Sept. 29, 1931; s. James Everett and Amelia (Williamson) D.; children from 1st marriage: Michael David, Linda Channing (Mrs. Michael S. Cady), James Clifford; m. 2d, Elizabeth G. Tharp; children: James Tharp, David Ross, Patrick Michael. student, DSc Bus. Mgmt. (hon.), U. Md. Various mgmt. positions Sigma Instruments, Inc., Braintree, Mass., 1954-64; gen. and ltd. ptnr. Burnham & Co., N.Y.C., 1964-70; pres., CEO, bd. dirs. Wheelabrator-Frye Inc., Hampton, N.H., 1970-83, chmn. bd., 1977-83; pres., bd. dirs. The Signal Cos., Inc., La Jolla, Calif., 1983-85, AlliedSignal, Morristown, N.J., 1985-86; chmn. bd., CEO The Henley Group, Inc. and affiliates, Hampton, N.H., 1986-92; chmn. bd. Fisher Sci. Internat. Inc., Hampton, 1991-98; chmn. bd., CEO Abex Inc., Hampton, 1992-95; pres., CEO Shipston Group Ltd., Nassau, Bahamas, 1994—. Bd. dirs. Ford Motor Co., Fisher Sci. Internat. Inc. Trustee The John A. Hartford Found. Mem. IEEE (adv. bd.). Clubs: Links, Yacht (N.Y.C.); Union (Boston); Cruising of Am. (Conn.); Bohemian (San Francisco); Lyford Cay (Nassau); La Jolla Country, San Diego Yacht. Office: Shipston Group Ltd Lyford Cay PO Box N7776 Nassau The Bahamas

DINH, THIN VAN, electronics specialist; b. Saigon, Vietnam, Apr. 7, 1939; came to U.S., 1975; s. Hoi Dinh and Ut Thi Tran; m. Mo Tran Dinh, Dec. 10, 1962; children: Truong An, Uyen, Huan, Tram. LLB, U. Saigon, 1974; PhD in Counseling (hon.), Progressive Universal Life Ch., 1994. Tchr. Dept. Edn., Danang, Vietnam, 1959-63, Lythaito Sch., Saigon, 1972-75; garage worker Car Body Clinic, portland, Oreg., 1975-78; electronic technician Tektronix, Beaverton, Oreg., 1978-95; specialist, tester Maxim Integrated Cir., Beaverton, 1995—. Author Tung Canh Dieu Bay, also articles in Vietnamese. Spkr. to chs., schs. and Vietnamese cmty. Officer Vietnamese Army, 1963-72. Avocations: music, economics research. Office: Maxim Integrated Products 14320 SW Jenkins Rd Beaverton OR 97005-1155

DINH, VIET D., law educator; b. Saigon, Vietnam, Feb. 22, 1968; came to U.S., 1978; s. Phong Hong Dinh and Thunga Thi Nguyen. AB, Harvard U., 1990, JD, 1993. Legal methods instr. Harvard Law Sch., Cambridge, Mass., 1991-93; law clk. to Hon. Laurence Silberman U.S. Ct. Appeals, Washington, 1993-94; law clk. to Justice Sandra Day O' Connor U.S. Supreme Ct., Washington, 1994-95; assoc. spl. counsel Whitewater Com. U.S. Senate, Washington, 1995-96; prof. law Georgetown U., Washington, 1996—; asst. atty. gen. legal policy U.S. Dept. Justice, Washington, 2001—03. Pres. Viet D. Dinh, LLC, Alexandria, Va., 1996—; mem. bd. dirs. News Corp. Ltd. Contbr. articles, essay to profl. publs. Dep. issues dir. legal policy Wilson for Pres., 1996; mem. Dole/Kemp Econ. Policy Adv. Com., 1996. Republican. Roman Catholic. Avocations: tennis, golf, chess. Office: Georgetown U Law Ctr 600 New Jersey Ave NW Washington DC 20001-2075 E-mail: dinhv@law.georgetown.edu.*

DINICOLA, ROBERT, consumer products company executive; With Macy's Dept. Store, N.Y.C., 1973-89, Federated Stores, N.Y.C., 1989-91; chmn. bd., CEO Bon, Seattle, 1991-94; chmn., CEO Zale Corp., Irving, Tex., 1994—2000, chmn., 2001—05, CEO, 2001—02; ret., 2004; exec. chmn. GNC Corp., Pitts., 2004—, interim CEO, 2005. Office: GNC Corp 300 Sixth Ave Pittsburgh PA 15222

DINITTO, ANDREW JOSEPH, political scientist, educator; b. Gaeta, Italy, Mar. 19, 1943; s. Paul F. and Clara S. DiNitto; m. Maria Remencsik, Aug. 28, 1966; children: Paul, Marcus. BA in Polit. Sci., Binghamton U., N.Y., 1965, MA in Comparative and Internat. Politics, 1967; PhD in Am. Govt. and Politics, U. Albany, 1978. Pub. adminstrn. intern State Govt. of N.Y., Albany, 1967—68; pres. X & O Reality Corp., Johnstown, NY, 1974—2002; prof. SUNY, Johnstown, 1968—, assoc. prof. Empire State Coll. Saratoga, 1985—. Contbr. articles to profl. jours. Co-chair Govt. Consolidation, Fulton County, NY, 1992—93; chair Bd. of Ethics, Gloversville, NY, 1993—97; bd. mem. Mountain Valley Hospice, Fulton County, NY, 2000—03. Recipient Coach of Yr., Nat. Soccer Coaches Assn., 1963. Mem.: Am. Polit. Sci. Assn., Loyal Order of Moose. Avocations: soccer, music. Home: 122 Little Rd Johnstown NY 12095 Office Phone: 518-762-4651. Business E-Mail: andrew.dinitto@esc.edu.

DINKEL, JOHN GEORGE, automotive executive, consultant; b. Bklyn., Aug. 1, 1944; s. Charles Ernest and Loretta Gertrude D.; m. Leslie Hawkins, Oct. 25, 1969; children: Meredith Anne, Kevin Carter. BS in Mech. Engring, U. Mich., 1967, MS in Mech. Engring, 1969. Staff engr. Chrysler Corp., Highland Park, Mich., 1967-69; engring. editor Car Life Mag., Newport Beach, Calif., 1969-70, Road & Track Mag., Newport Beach, 1972-79, editor, 1979-88, editor in chief, 1988-91, editor at large, 1991-92; dir. product communications Hill-Holliday, 1991-92; pres. John Dinkel & Assocs., 1991—; editor-at-large Sports Car Internat., 1992—; v.p. editl. ops. Calcar, 1995-97; group mgr. member info. and comm. svcs. Automobile Club So. Calif., Costa Mesa, 1998-2000; pub. Westways, 1998-2000; v.p. pub. Driving Media, Inc./Driving.com, 2000—02; asst. pub. relations dir. Pirelli Tire and Saleen, Inc., 2002—05; exec. v.p. product planning, devel. and testing Visionary Vehicles, 2005—. Commencement spkr. U. Mich., Dearborn, 1987; hon. judge Meadow Brook Hall Concourse D'Elegance, 1985-86, Hillsborough Concourse D'Elegance, 1989, Palo Alto Concours D'Elegance, 1990; spkr. Direct Mktg. Club So. Calif., 1992; SCCA competition driving instr., 2000—. Author: Road & Track Auto Dictionary, 1977, Road & Track Illustrated Auto Dictionary, 2000; co-author: RX-7: Mazda's Legendary Sports Car, 1991, Mazda MX-5 Miata, 1998, The Mazda RX-8: World's First 4-Door, 4-Seat Sports Car, 2003; editor-at-large Westways, 2003—; contbg. editor No. New Eng. Journey, 2000—, European Car, 2003—; co-host daily radio show Auto Report, 1986-88; host weekly radio show Drive Time, 1996—; contbr. articles to profl. jours.; patentee method and sys. for adjusting settings of vehicle functions, 2000 Nat. chmn. U. Mich. Ann. Fund, 1988—; commr. Irvine (Calif.) Baseball Assn.; sec. Irvine Pony Baseball-Softball, 1995—; organizer clothing drive victims of Armenia earthquake, 1988; soccer coach AYSO, 1984-90, Irvine Soccer Club, 1991—; baseball coach Northwood Little League, 1994—; basketball coach Irvine Boys and Girls Club, 1993—; vol. mem. corp. alliance com. Orange County chpt. Nat. Multiple Sclerosis Soc., 2002. Honored by Colden Ctr. for the Performing Arts, Queens Coll., N.Y.C., 1990. Mem. SAE (panelist conf. on impacts of intelligent vehicle hwy. systems 1990, organizer, chmn. sessions on fuel economy and small cars 1978-79, chmn. pub. affairs Future Transp. Conf. 1997), Am. Racing Press Assn., Internat. Motor Press Assn., Sports Car Club Am., Internat. Motor Sports Assn., Motor Press Guild (pres. 1991), Pi Tau Sigma. Achievements include being the Four-time winner of SCCA Nelson Ledges 24-hour endurance auto race. E-mail: jdinkel3@cox.net.

DINKINS, CAROL EGGERT, lawyer; b. Corpus Christi, Tex., Nov. 9, 1945; d. Edgar H. Jr. and Evelyn S. (Scheel) Eggert; m. Bob Brown; children: Anne, Amy. BS, U. Tex., 1968; JD, U. Houston, 1971. Bar: Tex. 1971. Prin. assoc. Tex. Law Inst. Coastal and Marine Resources, Coll. Law U. Houston, Tex., 1971-73; assoc., ptnr. Vinson & Elkins LLP, Houston, 1973-81, 83-84, 85—, mem. mgmt. com., 1991-96, chair Adminstrv. and Environ. Law practice; asst. atty. gen. environ. and natural resources Dept. Justice, 1981-83, U.S. dep. atty. gen., 1984-85. Chmn. Pres.'s Task Force on Legal Equity for Women, 1981-83; mem. Hawaiian Native Study Commn., 1981-83; dir. Nat. Consumer Coop. Banks Bd., 1981 Contbr. articles to profl. jours. Chmn. Gov.'s Conservation Task Force, 2000, Tex. Gov.'s Flood Control Action Group 1980-81; commr. Tex. Parks and Wildlife Dept., 1997-2001; bd. govs. The Nature Conservancy, 1996—, chmn. 2003-04; dir. Oryx Energy Co., 1990-95, U. Houston Law Ctr. Found., 1985-89, 96-98, Environ. and Energy Study Inst., 1986-98, Houston Mus. Natural Sci., 1986-98, 2000—; bd. govs. Tex. Nature Conservancy, 1985—, chmn., 1996-99. Mem. ABA (ho. of dels., past chmn. state and local govt. sect., past chair sect. nat. resources, energy, and environ. law, standing com. on fed. judiciary 1997-98, chair 2002-03, bd. editors ABA Jour., chair 2003—), Fed. Bar Assn. (bd. dirs. Houston chpt.

1986), State Bar Tex., Houston Bar Assn., Tex. Water Conservation Assn., Houston Law Rev. Assn. (bd. dirs. 1978). Republican. Lutheran. Office: Vinson & Elkins 2300 First City Tower 1001 Fannin St Houston TX 77002-6706 Business E-Mail: cdinkins@velaw.com.

DINNEEN, GERALD PAUL, electrical engineer, retired federal official; b. Elmhurst, N.Y., Oct. 23, 1924; s. Walter James and Anna Constance (Costello) D.; m. Mary Purington, June 28, 1947; children: Patricia Dinneen Mooney, Barbara Dinneen Sehr, Michael. BS, Queens Coll., 1947; MS, U. Wis., 1948, PHD, 1952. Teaching asst. U. Wis., 1947-51; sr. devel. engr. Goodyear Aircraft, 1951-53; with MIT, Lexington, 1953-77, prof. elec. engring., dir. Lincoln Lab.; asst. sec. of def., 1977-81; corp. v.p. sci. and tech. Honeywell Inc., Mpls., 1981-89; fgn. sec. NAE, Washington, 1988-95; chair policy and global affairs divsn. Nat. Rsch. Coun., Washington, 1997—2004. Cons. Def. Dept. NASA, USN, USAF. Served with AC, AUS, 1943-46. Recipient Disting. Pub. Service award Dept. Def., 1981. Mem. NAE, Engring. Acad. Japan, Swiss Acad. of Engring. Scis., Royal Acad. of Engring. (U.K.), Am. Math. Soc., Math. Assn. Am., Cosmos Club (Washington), Sigma Xi, Phi Beta Kappa. Home: 1010 Waltham St Apt D434 Lexington MA 02421 Personal E-mail: gdinneen@comcast.net.

DINNERSTEIN, HARVEY, artist; b. NYC, Apr. 3, 1928; s. Louis and Sarah (Kobilansky) D.; m. Lois Behrke, May 25, 1951; children: Rachel, Michael. Student of, Moses Soyer, 1944-46; student, Art Students League, 1946-47, Tyler Art Sch., Temple U., 1950; D (hon.), Lyme Acad. Fine Arts, 1998. Instr. drawing and painting Sch. Visual Arts, N.Y.C., 1963—80, N.A.D., 1974-92, Art Students League, 1980—. One-man shows include Davis Galleries, N.Y.C., 1955, 60-61, 63, Kenmore Galleries, Phila., 1964, 66, 69-70, F.A.R. Galleries, N.Y.C., 1972, 79, Sindin Galleries, 1983, Deutsch Galleries, 1989, Capricorn Galleries, 1990, Butler Inst. Am. Art, Youngstown, Ohio, 1994, Gerold Wunderlich Galleries, 1997, Frey Norris Gallery, San Francisco, 2003, 05; exhibited in group shows at Whitney Mus. Am. Art, N.Y.C., 1955, New Britain (Conn.) Mus. Am. Art, 1964, Am. Acad. and Inst. Arts and Letters, N.Y.C., 1974, Pa. State U. Mus. Art, 1974, others; works represented in collections Met. Mus. Art, Lehman Coll., Whitney Mus. Am. Art, Martin Luther King Labor Ctr., N.Y.C., New Britain Mus. Art, Fleming Mus. at U. Vt., Burlington: author: A Portfolio of Drawings, 1968, Harvey Dinnerstein-Artist at Work, 1978. Served with U.S. Army, 1951-53. Recipient Temple Gold medal Pa. Acad. Fine Art, 1950; Allied Artist Gold medal, 1977; President's award Audubon Artists, 1978; Arthur Ross award Classical Am., 1983; others; Tiffany Found. grantee, 1948, 61 Mem. N.A.D. (Samuel F.B. Morse medal 2003). Home: 933 President St Brooklyn NY 11215-1603

DINNERSTEIN, LEONARD, historian, educator; b. N.Y.C., May 5, 1934; s. Abraham and Lillian (Kubrik) D.; m. Myra Anne Rosenberg, Aug. 20, 1961; children: Andrew, Julie. B of Social Scis., CCNY, 1955; MA, Columbia U., 1960, PhD, 1966. Instr. N.Y. Inst. Tech., N.Y.C., 1960-65; asst. prof. Fairleigh Dickinson U., Teaneck, NJ, 1967-70; prof. Am. history U. Ariz., Tucson, 1970—, dir. Judaic studies, 1993-2000. Adj. prof. Columbia U., summers 1969, 72, 74, 81, 87, 89, NYU, summers 1969-70, 82, 86. Author: The Leo Frank Case, 1968 (Anisfield-Wolf award 1969), America and the Survivors of the Holocaust, 1982, Uneasy at Home, 1987; (with David M. Reimers) Ethnic Americans: A History of Immigration and Assimilation, 1987, 4th edit., 1999; (with R.L. Nichols, D.M. Reimers) Natives and Strangers, 1996, 4th edit., 2003, Antisemitism in America, 1994 (Nat. Jewish Book prize 1994); contbr. articles to profl. jours.; editor: (with Fred Jaher) The Aliens, 1970; (with Kenneth T. Jackson) American Vistas, 1971, 7th edit., 1995; (with Mary Dale Palsson) Jews in the South, 1973; (with Jean Christie) Decisions and Revisions: Interpretations of 20th Century American History, 1975, America Since World War II, 1976. Mem. Orgn. Am. Historians, Am. Hist. Assn., Am. Jewish Hist. Assn. Democrat. Jewish. Home: 1981 E Miraval Cuarto Tucson AZ 85718-3032 Office: U Ariz Dept History Tucson AZ 85721-0027 Office Phone: 520-615-8585. Business E-Mail: dinnerst@u.arizona.edu.

DINNERSTEIN, SIMON ABRAHAM, artist, educator; b. Bklyn., Feb. 16, 1943; s. Louis and Sarah (Kobalansky) Dinnerstein; m. Renée Sudler, Aug. 28, 1965; 1 child, Simone. BA, CCNY, 1965; postgrad., Bklyn. Mus. Art Sch., 1964-67, Hochschule für Bildende Kunst, Kassel, Fed. Republic Germany, 1970-71. Instr. in fine arts New Sch. Social Rsch., Parsons Sch. of Design, N.Y.C., 1975—. Adj. lectr. N.Y.C. Tech. Coll., Bklyn., 1979—88; vis. prof. Pratt Inst., Bklyn., 1986—87; vis. artist Calhoun Sch., NY, 1988—89; lectr. Am. Acad. Rome, 1977—78, USIS, Barcelona and Madrid, Spain, 1979, Pa. State U., 1984, Pt. Washington Pub. Libr., 1990, St. Paul's Sch., Concord, N.H., 1991, Nassau County C.C., 1994, NAD, 2000, Walton Arts Ctr., Fayetteville, Ark., 1999, U. Richmond, Va., 2000. One-man shows include Staempfli Gallery, N.Y.C., 1975, 1979, 1988, Inst. Internat. Edn., 1976—77, 1979, Am. Acad. Rome, 1977, Pratt Inst., 1987, New Sch. Social Rsch., 1981, 1993, Martin Luther King, Jr., Labor Ctr., N.Y.C., 1985, St. Paul's Sch., Concord, 1991, N.J. Ctr. for Visual Art, Summit, 1994, ACA Galleries, N.Y., Bread and Roses Gallery, N.Y. and St. Peter's Church, N.Y., 1999, Walton Arts Ctr., Fayetteville, Texarkana Regional Arts Ctr., Tex./Ark., Marsh Art Gallery, U. Richmond, 2000, Arnot Art Mus., 2003; subject of monographs: The Art of Simon Dinnerstein, 1991, Simon Dinnerstein: Paintings and Drawings, 2000; included in anthology Drawing from Life, 1992, Drawing from Life (Clint Brown), 1997, Centennial Directory of Fellows, Am. Acad. Rome, 1995, Hooked on Drawing: Illustrated Lessons and Exercises for Grades 4 and up, 1996, Community of Creativity, A Century of MacDowell Colony Artists, 1996, Drawing Dimensions, 1999, Ont. Rev., 1998, St. Ann's Rev., 2000, Rattapallax Jour., 2000, Bklyn. Jews, 2001, Great Am. Writers, 2001, City Secrets, Rome, 2000, City Secrets, Florence, Venice and the Towns of Italy, 2001, City Secrets, New York, 2002, Hanging Loose, 2003; represented, ACA Galleries, N.Y.C. Recipient Rome prize Am. Acad. in Rome, 1976-78, Ingram Merrill Found. award for painting, 1978-79, Cannon prize NAD, 1988, Ralph Fabri prize NAD, 1997, Bertelsen award NAD, 1998; Childe Hassam purchase award Am. Acad. Arts and Letters, 1976-78; fellow Fulbright Found., Germany, 1970-71, Louis Comfort Tiffany Found., 1976, MacDowell Colony, 1969, 79, N.Y. Found. for Arts, 1987; E.D. Found. grantee, 1977-78, 78-79; composer Gabriela Lena Frank composed a quintet based on his art; to premiere, Trinity Ctr. for Performing Arts, Phila., 2005. Mem.: NAD, Soc. Fellows Am. Acad. Rome. Democrat. Jewish. Avocations: reading, film, walking, travel, dreaming. Home: 415 1st St Brooklyn NY 11215-2507 Office Phone: 718-788-4387. E-mail: pturtle58@aol.com.

DINNIMAN, ANDREW ERIC, internation studies and history professor, director, commissioner; b. New Haven, Oct. 10, 1944; s. Harold and Edith (Stephson) D.; m. Margo Portnoy, June 8, 1969; 1 dau., Alexis. BA, U. Conn., 1966; MA, U. Md., 1969; EdD, Pa. State U., 1978. Student pers. worker U. Md., 1969-71, U. Denver, 1971-72; prof. West Chester (Pa.) State U., 1972—, dir. Ctr. for Internat. Programs, 1986-2001; commissioner Chester County, 1992—. Author: Book of Human Relations Readings, 1980, Education for International Competence in Pennsylvania, 1988; contbr. articles to profl. jours. Chmn. Chester County Dem. Com., 1979-85; mem. Pa. Dem. State Com., 1982-89, mem. exec. com., 1984-89; chmn. Eastern Pa. Dem. County Chmn. Assn., 1982-85; mem. Dem. Nat. Com., 1984-89; del. Dem. Nat. Conv., 1984, 88, 92, 96; pres. Pa. Coun. on Internat. Edn., 1989-91; v.p. Downingtown Area (Pa.) Sch. Bd., 1975-79; mem. Ctrl. Chester County Vocat.-Tech. Sch. Bd., 1978-79; mem. Chester County Conservation Dist., 1992—; mem. Pa. State Transp. Adv. Com., 1992-95, mem. Chester County Econ. Devel. Bd., 1992-96; mem. Nat. Assn. Counties Com. on Globalization, 1997-98, Chester County Internat. Trade Coun., 1999—. Recipient Bicentennial award Pa. Sch. Bds. Assn., 1976, Outstanding Acad. Svc. award Commonwealth Pa., 1977, Human Rights award W. Chester State U. chpt. NAACP, 1980, Cmty. Svc. award Coatesville NAACP, 1997, Mil. Order of Purple Heart Nat. citation for outstanding svc., 1998, Excellence in Local Govt. award Commonwealth of Pa., 1998, Grange award for pub. svc., 1999, Regional Leadership award Exton Regional C. of C., 1999, Leadership award Chester County Water Resources Authority, 2003, Cmty. Builder award, Melton Arts and Edn. Ctr, 2004, Cert. Appreciation, Borough West Chester, 2004, People That Make A Difference award, Hutchinson UAME Ch., 2004; Proclamation for Dedicated Svc., City of Coatsville, 2004, Appreciation Inspirational Moments award, 2004, Building Better Cmtys. award, Housing Partnership Chester County, 2004. Mem. Chester County Hist. Soc., Pa. Soc. Jewish. Home: 471 Spruce Dr Exton PA 19341-2025 Office: Courthouse 2 N High St West Chester PA 19380-3025 Office Phone: 610-344-6199. E-mail: adinniman@chesco.org.

DINOSO, VICENTE PESCADOR, JR., physician, educator; b. San Marcelino, Philippines, Oct. 17, 1936; came to U.S., 1961, naturalized, 1973; s. Vicente Dinoso and Eugenia Corpus (Pescador) D.; m. Alice M. Dinoso, June 19, 1965; children— Vincent, David. BS, U. Philippines, 1955, MD, 1960. Intern Mt. Sinai Hosp., Hartford, Conn., 1961-62; resident St. Mary's Hosp., Waterbury, Conn., 1962-64, Lahey Clinic Found., Boston, 1964-65; research fellow Temple U. Sch. Medicine, Phila., 1965-66, 68-69, instr. medicine, 1969-72, asst. prof., 1972-74; assoc. prof. medicine Hahnemann U. Sch. Medicine, Phila., 1974-78, prof. medicine, assoc. prof. physiology, 1978—. Practice medicine specializing in gastroenterology, 1969— Co-editor: Gastrointestinal Emergencies, 1976; contbr. articles to med. jours. Mem. Am. Gastroenterol. Assn., Am. Physiol. Soc., Am. Fedn. for Clin. Research, AAAS, Sigma Xi. Republican. Home: 1421 Granary Rd Blue Bell PA 19422-2124 Office: Hahnemann U Hosp Broad and Vine St Philadelphia PA 19102-5087

DINSE, JOHN MERRELL, lawyer; b. Rochester, N.Y., June 26, 1925; s. Frank John and Lois Vanlora (Merrell) D.; m. Ann Thompson (Goodenough), Dec. 27, 1948; children— Jeffrey P., Pamela D. Johnston AB, U. Rochester, 1947; LL.B., Cornell U., 1950. Bar: N.Y. 1950, Vt. 1951, U.S. Dist. Ct. Vt. 1952, U.S. Ct. Appeals (2d cir.) 1957. Assoc. firm Austin & Edmunds, Burlington, Vt., 1950-57; ptnr. Dinse, Erdmann, & Clapp (and predecessor firms), Burlington, 1957-90; of counsel Dinse, Knapp, & McAndrew (and predecessor firms), Burlington, 1990—. Mem. Med. Ctr.Hosp. Assocs.; dir. Vt. Mcpl. Bond Bank, 1980—83; past trustee Burlington (Vt.) YWCA; past bd. govs. Med. Ctr. Hosp. Vt.; past bd. dirs. Vt. Diabetes Assn., Arthritis Found.; bd. dirs. Vt. Symphony Orch., v.p., 1995—, chmn. bd., 2001—; mem. Vt. Waterways Commn., 1962—63; chmn. Jud. Nominating Bd., 1967—77; campaign chmn. Gov. Deane C. Davis, 1968, 1970; mem. Waterways Commn. on Champlain Basin. With USAR, 1943—46. Decorated Bronze Star U.S. Army. Fellow Am. Coll. Trial Lawyers, Am. Bar Found., Am. Coll. Trust and Estate Counsel; mem. ABA, New Eng. Bar Assn. (bd. dirs. 1977-80), Chittenden County Bar Assn., Vt. Bar Assn. (bd. mgrs. 1974—, pres. 1978-79), Am. Bd. Trial Advs. (bd. dirs. 1990-92), Am. Judicature Soc. (dir. 1975-79), Am. Acad. Hosp. Attys., No. New Eng. Def. Counsel Assn. (pres. 1971-72), Assn. Def. Attys., Internat. Assn. Def. Counsel, Def. Research Inst. (dir. 1975-81, pres. 1980, chmn. bd. 1981), Am. Law Inst., Nat. Assn. Coll. and Univ. Attys. Clubs: Lake Champlain Yacht (commodore 1961-62); Malletts Bay Boat (master 1957-58). Home: Harbor Rd Shelburne VT 05482 Office: Dinse Knapp & McAndrew PO Box 988 209 Battery St Burlington VT 05402 Office Phone: 802-864-5751.

DINSMOOR, JAMES ARTHUR, psychology educator; b. Woburn, Mass., Oct. 4, 1921; s. Daniel Stark and Jean Erskine (Masson) D.; m. Anne Darrow Berninger, July 17, 1943 (div. Mar. 1953); 1 son, Daniel Stark; m. Marise Kay Sawyer, Jan. 1, 1956; children: Mara Jean, Robert Scott. BA, Dartmouth Coll., 1943; MA, Columbia U., 1945, PhD, 1949. Instr. Newark Colls., Rutgers U., 1945-46; lectr. Columbia U., N.Y.C., 1946-51; asst. prof. Ind. U., Bloomington, 1951-58, assoc. prof., 1958-63, prof. psychology, 1963-86, prof. emeritus psychology, 1987—. Author: Operant Conditioning: An Experimental Analysis of Behavior, 1970. Mem. nat. bd. Nat. Com. for a Sane Nuclear Policy, Washington, 1966-68. Fellow APA (divsn. v.p. 1977-80, divsn. pres. 1992-93); mem. Soc. Exptl. Analysis of Behavior (pres. 1979-81), Midwestern Psychol. Assn. (coun. 1973-82, pres. 1980-81), Assn. for Behavior Analysis (orgnl. com. 1974-76). Home: 1511 E Maxwell Ln Bloomington IN 47401-5144 Office: Ind U Dept Psychology 1101 E 10th St Bloomington IN 47405-7007 E-mail: dinsmoor@indiana.edu.

DINSMORE, PHILIP WADE, architect; b. Gilroy, Calif., Nov. 4, 1942; s. Wilbur Allen and Elizabeth Eleanor (Hill) D.; m. Mary Kathryn Mead; children: Robert Allen, Kerry Philip. BArch, U. Ariz., 1965. Registered arch., Ariz., Calif., Nev., S.C., N.C., Wyo. Nat. Coun. Archtl. Registration Bds. Designer William L. Pereira & Assocs., L.A., 1965-67; assoc. CNWC Archs., Tucson, 1967-69; prin., ptnr. Arch. One Ltd., Tucson, 1970-90; pres. Durrant Archts. Ariz., Phoenix, Tucson, 1995—. Bd. dirs. Durrant Group, 1992—. Mem., chmn. Archtl. Approval Bd., City of Tucson, 1974-75, 77; bd. dirs. Tucson Met. YMCA, 1993—, U. Ariz. Coll. Arch., environ. design coun.; trustee AIA Benefit Ins. Trust, 1997—, Durrant Found., 1998—; founding mem. Environ. Design Coun., Tucson, 1998—; mem. Ariz. State Bd. Tech. Registration, 2000—. Recipient Tucker award Bldg. Stone Inst., 1986, U. Ariz. Alumni assn. Centennial Recognition award, 1997. Fellow AIA (nat. bd. dirs. 1981-84, nat. sec. 1984-88, regional fellows rep. 1990-96, Ariz. Archs. medal 1985, Western Mountain Region Citation award 1973, 76, 78, Award of Honor 19983, Silver medal 1992); mem. Am. Archtl. Found. (bd. regents 1988-92), Constrn. Specifications Inst., Ariz. Soc. Archs. (citation 1977-80, 89). Office: Durrant Ariz 2980 N Campbell S-130 Tucson AZ 85719-2897

DINSMORE, ROBERTA JOAN MAIER, library director; b. Phila., Sept. 30, 1934; d. Bert Faust and Emma Baker (Keen) Maier; m. Ray W. Dinsmore, Sr., Oct. 20, 1956; children: Ray Wilson Jr., Jeffrey Maier, Debra Joan, Matthew Bert. BA, Pa. State U., 1956; MLS, Clarion U. Pa., 1990. Proofreader Aluminum Co. Am., Pitts., 1957-60; office mgr. Dinsmore, Lithographer, Punxsutawney, Pa., 1969—; dir. Punxsutawney Meml. Libr., 1978—. Freelance writer Greenburg (Pa.) Tribune Rev., 1980—81; adult edn. tchr. Jeff Tech., Reynoldsville, Pa., 1981—82; freelance writer Punxsutawney Spirit, 2003—. Mem. Jefferson County Constrn. Com., Jefferson County Heritage Com.; mem. sch. dist. strategic planning com.; chair Police Civil Svc. Commn., Punxsutawney; exec. bd. Theatre Arts; ch. libr. Punxsutawney Presbyn. Ch., 1985—; elder Presbyn. Ch.; mem. com. on ministry Kiskiminetas Presbytery; head hostess Welcome Wagon Internat., Memphis, 1976—80; mem. libr. sci. accreditation team Clarion U., Pa.; mem. exec. bd. Punxsutawney Theatre Arts Guild; hospice vol.; tchr. adult discussion class; mem. coun., vice chair Cmty. Action Svc. Corp.; vice chair numerous orgns. Mem.: AAUW (pres., Woman of the Yr. 1987), ALA, Goschenhoppen Historians, Punxsutawney Area Hist. and Geneol. Soc. (charter), Clarion Dist. Libr. Assn. (pres. 1984—86), Pa. Libr. Assn. (past chair pub. libr. divsn.), Punxsutawney Hosp. Aux., Friends of Libr., Pa. Citizens for Better Libs., Irving Club (past pres., v.p.), Garden Club (past pres. Punxsutawney chpt.), PEO. Republican. Avocations: reading, making and selling crafts in small, self-owned business, genealogy. Home: 808 E Mahoning St Punxsutawney PA 15767-2320 Office: Punxsutawney Meml Libr 301 E Mahoning St Punxsutawney PA 15767-2142 Office Phone: 814-938-5020. E-mail: punxlib@adelphia.net.

DINWIDDIE, MOLLIE MICHELLE, school librarian; d. Walter Curtis and Priestly Carlton Dinwiddie; m. Ronald Duane Niemeyer, June 27, 1975 (div. May 23, 1991); children: Elise Claire Barry, Erin Michelle Niemeyer. BA, Bethel Coll., 1967—70; MLS, Peabody Coll. (Vanderbilt U.), 1971—72; Edn. Specialist, Ctrl. Mo. State U., 1986—89. Catalog libr. Mitchell Meml. Libr. Miss. State U., 1972—73; spl. collections libr., 1973—75; asst. law libr. Miss. Coll. Sch. of Law, 1975—79; catalog libr. Kirkpatrick Libr. Ctrl. Mo. State U., 1985—89, dir. of tech. services, 1990—2003; dean of libr. services (interim) Ctrl. Mo. State U., 2003—. Mem.: Mo. Libr. Assn. (pres. 1999—2000), ALA, Beta Phi Mu (chpt. pres. 1997—98), Phi Kapph Phi (chpt. pres. 1997—99). Independent. Ch. Of Christ. Avocations: reading, travel. Home: 1006 Walnut Lane Warrensburg MO 64093 Office: James C Kirkpatrick Libr CMSU 601 S Missouri St Warrensburg MO 64093 Office Phone: 660-543-4140. Personal E-mail: mollie@iland.net.

DIODOSIO, CHARLES JOSEPH, lawyer; b. Pueblo, Colo., Apr. 27, 1951; s. Warren Joseph and Lucille Julia Diodosio. BSChemE, U. Colo., 1973; JD, Northwestern U., 1976. Assoc. McDermott, Will & Emery, Chgo., 1976-80; internat. counsel Beatrice Co., Chgo., 1980-84, v.p. Asia devel., 1984-88; chmn. TMGC Ltd., Chgo., 1988—, Meadow Gold Investment Holding Co., Beijing, 1993—; chmn. L&D International Corp., Beijing, 1993—. Chmn. L&D Internat. Corp., Beijing, China, 1993—. Mem. ABA, Ill. Bar. Home: 1387 Calle de Maria Palm Springs CA 92264-8503 Fax: 760-327-1200. E-mail: meadgo@aol.com.

DIOGUARDI, RICHARD JAMES, psychologist, researcher; b. White Plains, N.Y., July 12, 1974; s. Richard Joseph and Louise Mary DioGuardi; m. Lea Athena Theodore, June 6, 2004. BA in Psychology, Cornell U., 1996; MA in Child Clin. Psychology, St. John's U., 2000, PhD in Child Clin. Psychology, 2003. Cert. sch. psychologist N.Y. Intern Inst. Living, Hartford (Conn.) Hosp., 2001—02; SAMSHA psychologist N.Shore U. Hosp., Manhasset, NY, 2003—04; project dir. Weinman/Schoee, Inc., N.Y.C., 2005. Adj. asst. prof. St. John's U., Jamaica, NY, 2003—05; presenter in field. Contbr. articles to profl. jours. Recipient Grace Lauw Meml. award, N.Y. State Psychol. Assn., 2000, Cert. Acad. Excellence, St. John's U., 1999, 2003. Mem.: Am. Psychol. Assn. (conv. proposal reveiwer 2000, chair-elect 1998—99, chair 1999—2000, Travel award 2001). Avocations: drums, disc jockey.

DION, CELINE, musician; b. Charlemagne, Quebec, Can., Mar. 30, 1970; m. Rene Angelil, 1994; 1 child. Singer: (albums) Unison, 1990 (album of the year, 1990), Celine Dion, 1992, Colour of My Love, 1993 (multi-platinum, 1994), Premieres Anees, 1994, Dion Chante Plamondon, 1994, Des Mots Qui Sonnent, 1995, Power of Love, 1995, French Album, 1995, Live A Paris, 1996, Falling Into You, 1997 (Grammy award album of the yr. & best pop album, 1997), C'est Pour Vivre, 1997, The Collection, 1982—88, 1997, Let's Talk About Love, 1997 (Billboard Music award best album, 1998), S'il suffisait d'aimer, 1998, These are Special Times, 1998 (Grammy & Juno awds., 1999), All The Way, 1999, The French Album, 2001, Classique: A Love Collection, 2001, A New Day Has Come, 2002, One Heart, 2003, 1 Fille & 4 Types, 2003, Miracle, 2004, (Soundtracks) Real Love, 1979, Beauty & the Beast, 1991 (Grammy award, 1992, best selling single, 1992, Acad. award, 1992), Sleepless in Seattle, 1993, Through the Fire, 1994, Titanic (single My Heart Will Go On), 1999 (Grammy award record of yr., 1999, Grammy award best female pop vocal, 1999, Billboard Music award best soundtrack single, 1998), (shows) The Colosseum, Caesars Palace, Las Vegas, 2003—. Recipient Favorite Female Pop/Rock Artist award, Music awards, 1999, Favorite Adult Contemporary Artist award, Am. Music awards, 1999, Album of Yr. for Titanic, Billboard Music awards, 1999, Album Artist, Billboard Music award, 1999, Adult Contemporary Artist Billboard Music award, 1999.

DION, STÉPHANE, legislator; b. Quebec, Can., Sept. 28, 1955; married; 1 daughter. BA in Polit. Sci., U. Laval, 1977, MA in Polit. Sci., 1979; D in Sociology, Inst. Polit. Paris. Prof. polit. sci. U. Moncton, Can., 1984, U. Montréal, Can., 1984-96; mem. Ho. Commons, Canada, 1996—; pres. Privy Coun., Canada, 1996—2003; min. Intergovernmental Affairs, Canada, 1996—2003, Environment, Canada, 2004—. Vis. prof. Lab. Econ. Pub., Paris; sr. rsch. fellow Brookings Inst., Washington; rsch. fellow Can. Ctr. Mgmt. Devel. Co-dir. Can. Jour. Polit. Sci.; contbr. articles to profl. jours. Office: 750 Marcel Laurin Blvd Ste 440 Saint Laurent PQ Canada H4M 2M4 E-mail: dions@parl.gc.ca.

DIONISOPOULOS, GEORGE ALLAN, lawyer; b. Santa Monica, Calif., July 31, 1954; s. P. Allan and Christine (Nassios) D.; m. Sandra Doreen Jordan, June 11, 1977; children: Sarah, Elaina. BA summa cum laude, U. Ill., 1976; JD cum laude, Harvard U., 1980. Bar: Wis. 1980, U.S. Dist. Ct. (ea. and we. dists.) Wis. 1980. Ptnr. Foley & Lardner LLP, Milw., 1980—, co-chmn. estates & trusts practice group. Mem. ABA (real property and probate sect., taxation sect.), Wis. Bar Assn. (speaker 1984—), Milw. Young Lawyers Assn., Phi Beta Kappa. Greek Orthodox. Office: Foley & Lardner LLP 777 E Wisconsin Ave Ste 3800 Milwaukee WI 53202-5367 Office Phone: 414-297-5750. Office Fax: 414-297-4900. Business E-Mail: gdionisopoulos@foleylaw.com.

DIONNE, E.J., JR., columnist; b. Boston, Apr. 23, 1952; m. Mary Boyle; children: James, Julia, Margot. BA summa cum laude, Harvard Univ, 1973; DPhil, Oxford Univ, 1982. Correspondent New York Times, 1977—89, Washington Post, 1990—92, columnist, 1993—; sr fellow Brookings Inst, Washington, 1996—. Prof Georgetown Univ; co-founder & co-chmn Pew Forum on Religion & Public Life, 2000—. Contbr. articles to polit jours, columns in newspapers, commentary on TV & radio programs; author: Why Americans Hate Politics, 1991 (Los Angeles Times Book prize, National Book Award nominee), They Only Look Dead: Why Progressives Will Dominate the Next Political Era, 1996, Community Works: The Revival of Civil Society in America, 1998, What's God Got to Do With the American Experiment, 2000, Bush v Gore: The Court Cases and the Commentary, 2000, Sacred Places, Civic Purposes: Should Government Help Faith-Based Charity?, 2001, United We Serve: National Service and the Future of Citizenship, 2003. Rhodes scholar. Mem.: Phi Beta Kappa. Office: The Brookings Institution 1775 Massachusetts Ave NW Washington DC 20036 Business E-Mail: edionne@brookings.edu.*

DIONNE, GERALD FRANCIS, research physicist, educator, consultant; b. Montreal, Can., Feb. 5, 1935; arrived in U.S., 1964, naturalized, 1980; s. Louis Philip and Clare Isabel (Flood) D.; m. Claudette Leblanc, June 29, 1963; 1 child, Stephen. BS summa cum laude, Loyola Coll., U. Montreal, 1956; B of Engring. magna cum laude, McGill U., Montreal, 1958, PhD in Physics, 1964; MS, Carnegie-Mellon U., 1959. Jr. engr. IBM Corp., Poughkeepsie, NY, 1959-60; sr. engr. Sylvania Electric Products, Woburn, Mass., 1960-61; rsch. asst., lectr. McGill U., 1964; sr. rsch. assoc. Pratt & Whitney Aircraft, North Haven, Conn., 1964-66; mem. rsch. staff Lincoln Lab., MIT, Lexington, Mass., 1966—96, expert svcs. pers., 1996—; rsch. affiliate dept. materials sci. and engring. MIT, Cambridge, 2005—. Grad student rsch. advisor, sci. and tech. advisor to industry and govt.; rsch. affiliate dept. mats. sci, and engring. MIT, Cambridge, Mass., 2005-. Contbr. articles to sci. jours. NRC of Can. fellow. Fellow IEEE, Am. Phys. Soc.; mem. Materials Rsch. Soc., Corp. Profl. Engrs. Que., Sigma Xi. Achievements include numerous research advances in magnetism and magnetic materials; research in magnetoelastic and magneto-optic phenomena; magnetic spin transport; magnetoresistance; superconductivity theory and devices; microwave and submillimeter-wave physics and instrumentation; physics of electron emission; patents for microwave, superconducting, and magnetic devices. Home: 182 High St Winchester MA 01890-3366 Office: 244 Wood St Lexington MA 02421-6426

DIONYSIOU, DIONYSIOS DEMETRIOU, adult education educator, researcher; s. Demetris Dionysiou and Kyriaki Christoforou; m. Polymnia Ioannou Antoniou; children: Marianna children: Stella. BS in Chem. Engring., Nat. Tech. U., Athens, Greece, 1991; MS in Chem. Engring., Nat.Tech. U., Athens, Greece, 1991, Tufts U., 1992—95; PhD in Environ. Engring., U. of Cin., 1995—2001. Rsch. engr. W. R. Grace, Cambridge, Mass., 1994—95; asst. prof., environ. engring. U. of Cin., 2000—. Author: (ph.d. dissertation) Engineered Process for the Photocatalytic Oxidation of Hazardous and Toxic Organic Contaminants in Water (Am. Water Works Association's First Pl. 2002 Academic Achievement Award for Best Dissertation, 2002); contbr. numerous articles to profl. jours. Mem., internat. organizing com. Internat. Conferences on TiO2 Photocatalysis, 2001—02; mem., adv. com. Cin. Water Works, 2000; mem., young professionals com. Ohio Am. Water Works Assn. (OAWWA), Ohio Water Environment Assn. (OWEA), 2001. Recipient Recognition as a Mem. of Good Standing by ACS Pres., Am. Chem. Soc., 2001, Grad. Student Rsch. Paper Award for Excellence in Rsch. and Presentation in Environ. Sci., Divsn. of Environ. Chemistry, Am. Chem. Soc., 2001, Grad. Student Award for Excellence in Grad. Studies in Environ. Sci., 2001, First Pl. Student Rsch. Paper Award and Presentation, Ohio Water Environment Assn. (OWEA), 2001, Dr. Pasquale V. and Flora Jean Scarpino and Family Award for The Best PhD Dissertation, Environ. Engring. Divsn., U. of Cin., 2001; grantee Gerondelis Found. Fellowship, Gerondelis Found. Inc., 1992-1994, Rsch. on Ionic Liquids, NSF, 2000-2002, Rsch. on MTBE,

EPA, 2001, Rsch. on Mercury Pollution in Aquatic Systems, 2000-2001, Rsch. on Pollution Treatment in Estuarine Systems, The Coop. Inst. for Coastal and Estuarine Environ. Tech. (CICEET), 2002; scholar Tuition/Rsch., U. of Cin., 1995-2000, Tufts U., 1992-1994, Hellenic Nat. Scholarship Found. (I.K.Y.) Fellowship, Hellenic Nat. Scholarship Found. (I.K.Y.), Greece, 1986-1991, Hellenic Nat. Scholarship Found. (I.K.Y.) Award for Excellent Performance, 1998-1991. Mem.: Water Environment Fedn., Tri-State Catalysis Soc., North Am. Catalyst Soc., Internat. Ultraviolet Assn., Fed. Water Quality Assn., Assn. of Environ. Engring. and Sci. Professors, Am. Water Works Assn., ASEE, AIChE, ACS (recognition as member of good standing by ACS pres. 2001), Sigma Xi. Achievements include development of Novel Photocatalytic Reactors; research in Transition Metal Chemical Oxidation; Membrane Biofouling; Novel Properties of Ionic Liquids in Environmental Engineering; development of Efficient Photocatalytic Reactors; New Green Processes for Treating Water; research in Advanced Oxidation Technologies; Novel Methods for Treating Drinking Water; development of Advanced Water Treatment Systems; discovery of Novel Photochemical Reactions in Ionic Liquids; research in Mercury Pollution in Aquatic Systems. Avocations: swimming, fishing, dance. Home: 1122 Scarborough Way Cincinnati OH 45215 Office: Univ of Cincinnati Civil and Environ Engring Dept 765 Baldwin Hall MS 0071 Cincinnati OH 45221-0071 E-mail: dionysios.d.dionysiou@uc.edu.

DIPADOVA, LAURIE NEWMAN, social services administrator, educator; b. Portsmouth, Va., July 31, 1945; d. Everett Hale Newman Jr. and Evelyn Naomi Moore; m. Theodore Anthony DiPadova Mar. 25, 1972 (div.); children: Audra Mae, Joseph Russell; m. Hugh Grant Stocks, July 8, 1995. BA in Sociology, Mary Washington Coll., U. Va., 1967; MS in Sociology, U. Utah, 1970; PhD in Pub. Adminstrn. & Policy, SUNY, Albany, 1995. Instr. sociology Ricks Coll., Rexburg, Idaho, 1969-71, Old Dominion U., Norfolk, Va., 1971-76; trainer human svcs. grad. sch. social work SUNY, Albany, 1980-81; tng. assoc. N.Y. State Dept. Social Svcs., Albany, 1981-83; assoc. faculty SUNY, Saratoga Springs, N.Y., 1991-96; vis asst. prof. polit. sci. U. Utah, Salt Lake City, 1995-97, adj. assoc. prof. polit. sci., 1997—, dep. dir. Ctr. Pub. Policy and Adminstrn., 1997-99, faculty outreach fellow, exec. dir. office of profl. edn., 1999—; policy fellow Ctr. Pub. Policy and Adminstrn., 1999—. Editor-in-chief Employability Devel. pubs. series; contbr. articles to profl. jours. Bd. dirs. Pk. Pl. Cmty. Mental Health Ctr., Norfolk, 1974-75, Citizen's Assn. Justice Va., 1975; elected ofcl. Holladay-Cottonwood Cmty. Coun., Salt Lake County, 1998. Mem. Am. Soc. Pub. Adminstrn., Utah Nonprofits Assn., Acad. Mgmt., Assn. Rsch. Nonprofit & Voluntary Assns., Pi Alpha Alpha. Mem. Lds Ch. Avocations: Am. Civil War, Genealogy, running, travel. Office: U Utah Rsch Park 423 Wakara Way Ste 203 Salt Lake City UT 84108-1242

DIPADOVA, REGINA MARIA, counselor; b. Flushing, N.Y., Oct. 24, 1959; d. Anthony and Carmela DiPadova. AA, Pikes Peak C.C., 1982; BA, U. So. Colo., 1984; MA in Sociology, U. Colorado Springs, 2004. Cert. addiction counselor, Colo., therapeutic recreation specialist. Counselor Emily Griffith Ctr., Colorado Springs, 1984-87, Comty. Learning Ctr., Colorado Springs, 1987-90; program dir., founder Inside/Out, Colorado Springs, 1990-99; adolescent counselor El Paso Health Dept., Colorado Springs, 1990—; recreation dir. Comcor Inc., Colorado Springs, 1999—. Founder, dir. Learning Through Challenges, Colorado Springs, 1990—; HIV outreach dir. Inside/Out, Colorado Springs, 1998—; presenter in field; trainer, educator on gay issues, 1990—. Editor, writer New Phazes Mag., 1988-96; contbr. poetry to anthologies. Bd. dirs. Pikes Peak Gay Cmty., 1999-2000, Urban Peak, 2000-2001. Recipient Equality Pride award Equality Colo., 1998, Paul Hunter award Human Rights Campaign, 1999. Democrat. Buddhist. Avocations: rock climbing, triathlons, racquetball, hiking, reading. Office: 301 S Union Blvd Colorado Springs CO 80910-3123 E-mail: reginadipadova@elphealth.org.

DI PALMA, JOSEPH ALPHONSE, investment company executive, lawyer; b. NYC, Jan. 17, 1931; s. Gaetano and Michela May (Ambrosio) Di P.; m. Joycelyn Ann Engle, Apr. 18, 1970; children: Joycelyn Joan, Julianne Michelle. BA, Columbia U., 1952; JD, Fordham U., 1958; LLM in Taxation, NYU, 1959. Bar: N.Y. 1959. Tax atty. CBS, N.Y.C., 1960-64; v.p. tax dept. TWA, N.Y.C., 1964-74; pvt. practice law N.Y.C., 1974-87; investor, exec. dir. Di Palma Family Holdings, Las Vegas and N.Y.C., 1987—. Cons. in field; head study group Comprehensive Gaming Study, N.Y.C. and Washington, 1990—; think tank exec. dir. Di Palma Position Papers; founder Di Palma Forum, U. Nev., Las Vegas; established The Di Palma Ctr. for Study of Jewelry and Precious Metals at Cooper-Hewitt, Nat. Design Mus., Smithsonian Instn., N.Y.C. Contbr. articles to profl. jours. Bd. dirs. Friends of the Henry St. Settlement, N.Y.C., 1961-63, Outdoor Cleanliness Assn., N.Y.C., 1961-65; chmn. Air Transport Assn. Taxation Com., 1974. With U.S. Army, 1953-54. Recipient Disting. Svc. and Valuable Counsel commendation award, Air Transport Assn., 1974, spl. commendation, NYC mayor Rudolph Giuliani, 1997, U. Nev., Las Vegas, 1999, Tiffany Smithsonian Benefactors Circle award, 2001, WNET/Thirteen Pub. Spirit award, 2002. Mem. Internat. Platform Assn., N.Y. State Bar Assn., N.Y. Athletic Club. Roman Catholic. Home: 3111 Bel Air Dr Apt 21B Las Vegas NV 89109-1506 Office: 930 5th Ave # 4 J&H New York NY 10021-2651 Office Phone: 212-861-1945.

DIPALMA, JOSEPH RUPERT, pharmacology educator; b. N.Y.C., Mar. 21, 1916; s. Frank and Anna (Attanasio) DiP.; m. Mary Solowey, June 26, 1948; children: Maria, Dorothea, Joan, Yvonne, Mary-Jo. BS, Columbia U., 1936; MD, SUNY, Bklyn., 1941; DSc (hon.), Hahnemann U., 1980. Intern, resident in internal medicine Kings County Hosp., Bklyn., 1942-44; asst. prof. medicine and pharmacology State U. N.Y. Downstate Med. Sch., 1946; prof. pharmacology, chmn. dept. Hahnemann Med. Coll. and Hosp., Phila., 1951-67, dean, 1967-82, v.p., 1971-82, sr. v.p., 1972-82, prof. pharmacology and medicine, 1982-86, emeritus prof. pharmacology and medicine, 1986—, emeritus dean, 1986—. Mem. bd. Regional Med. Program Southeastern Pa., 1967-75, Health Systems Agy., 1977-82, Hahnemann Hosp., 2000-, St. Davids Instnl. Rev., 1975-. Editor: Pharmacology in Medicine, 1971, Basic Pharmacology in Medicine, 1976, 4th edit., 1994; contbr. med. jours. Bd. dirs. Hahnemann U. Hosp., 2000—. Recipient Alumni medallion SUNY, Downstate Med. Sch., 1966, Corp. medal Hahnemann U., 1990 Mem. Coll. Physicians Phila. (council 1969-78), AMA, Pa., Phila. County Med. socs., Am. Physiol. Soc., Am. Soc. Pharmacology and Exptl. Therapeutics, Am. Soc. Clin. Investigation, Am. Soc. Clin. Pharmacology, Alpha Omega Alpha. Home: 100 Pembroke Ave Wayne PA 19087-4819 Office: 235 N 15th St Philadelphia PA 19102-1101 Personal E-mail: josephdipalma@yahoo.com. *The creation of new ideas and approaches is always the ultimate goal.*

DIPALMA, RAYMOND ANTHONY, writer, literature educator; b. New Kensington, Pa., Sept. 27, 1943; s. Raymond Alphonso and Nancy Monica DiPalma; m. Elizabeth Anita Brandfass, May 27, 1976. BA, Duquesne U., 1966; MFA, U. Iowa, 1968. Adj. faculty mem. Sch. Visual Arts, N.Y.C., 1995—. Author: Provocations, 1994, Motion of the Cypher, 1995, Letters, 1998; contbr. poetry Harvard Rev., Chgo. Rev., Paris Rev., Partisan Rev., Action Poetique, Iowa Rev., Verse, others. Fellow, Nat. Endowment for Arts, 1980, NY State Coun. on Arts, 1990, Fund for Poetry, 1998. Home: 301 W 108th St Apt 6B New York NY 10025-2723

DI PAOLO, JOSEPH AMEDEO, geneticist; b. Bridgeport, Conn., June 13, 1924; s. John Anthony and Nancy (Montagano) Di P.; m. Arleta Mae Schreib, June 14, 1952; children: Nancy, John. BA, Wesleyan U., 1948; MS, Western Res. U., 1949; PhD, Northwestern U., 1951; MD (hon.), U. Cagliari, Italy, 1991. Instr. genetics bacteriology dept. biology Loyola U., Chgo., 1951-53; instr. clin. and exptl. pathology Northwestern U. Med. Sch., Chgo., 1953-55; sr. cancer research scientist Roswell Park Meml. Inst., Buffalo, 1955-63; research pharmacologist, cell biologist biology br., div. chem. and phys. carcinogenesis program Nat. Cancer Inst., Bethesda, Md., 1963-76, chief lab. biology, divsn. basic scis., 1976—99; emeritus, 1999. Assoc. prof., lectr. anatomy George Washington U., Washington, 1973-96; chmn. U.S.-Germany Cancer Program Area for Environ. Carcinogenesis, 1979-85, U.S.-USSR Mammalian Sometic Cell Genetics Relation to Neoplasia Program, 1973-76; cons. U.S.-Poland Cancer Program, 1979-91; mem. Coun. of the European Rsch. Orgn. on Genital Infection and Neoplasis, 1994; co-chmn. Cervical Cancer Prevention and Therapy Symposium UICC, New Delhi, 1994; co-organizer 16th Internat. Papillomavirus Conf., Siena, Italy, 1997; mem. Sci. Com. European Environ. Hygiene, 1996; sci. advisor divsn. biol. scis. NCI Frontiers in Sci., 1999—. Editor, co-author: Chemical Carcinogenesis, 1974; assoc. editor: Jour. of Nat. Cancer Inst., 1968-71, Cancer Rsch., 1970-78, Teratogenesis, Carcinogenesis, Mutagenesis, 1982-92; editl. acad. Internat. Jour. Oncology, 1992—; guest editor Cancer Investigation, 2000-01; sci. adv. mem. CCR Frontiers in Sci., 2000--. With USN, 1943-46 Fellow N.Y. Acad. Sci., AAAS; mem. Am. Assn. Cancer Rsch. (bd. dirs. 1983-86), Coun. of European Rsch., Orgn. Genital Infection and Neoplasia, Am. Soc. Human Genetics, Am. Soc. for Investigation of Pathology, Genetics Soc. Am., Teratology Soc., Hamster Soc., Tissue Culture Assn., Am. Assn. Pathology, European Assn. for Cancer Rsch., Sigma Xi. Achievements include research on ribozyme and antisense patents for cervical cancer; patent for identification of transforming fragment of HSV-2 and its detection in clinical specimens. Home: 6605 Melody Ln Bethesda MD 20817-3154 Office: Nat Cancer Inst 37-2014 Convent Dr Bethesda MD 20892-4256 Office Phone: 301-496-6441. Business E-Mail: jd8la@nih.gov.

DIPAOLO, MARCELLA KAY, elementary school educator; b. Wood River, Ill., June 2, 1950; d. William Harvey and Grace Pauline Marie (Highlander) Dorsey; m. Robert Dale DiPaolo, Nov. 29, 1969; children: Tony, Gina, John, Nick. BS, So. Ill. U., Edwardsville, 1980, MS, 1987, Cert. of Math., 1988. Tchr. 3rd, 6th, 7th and 8th grades St. Kevin Sch., East Alton, Ill., 1980—. Tchr. math. Lewis & Clark Community Coll., Godfrey, Ill., 1989—; coach baseball St. Kevin Sch., 1989—. Roman Catholic. Avocations: reading, swimming, writing. Office: St Kevin Sch 4 Saint Kevins Dr East Alton IL 62024-1872

DIPARDO, ANNE, English language educator; BA in English magna cum laude, Calif. State U., Northridge, 1976; MA in English, UCLA, 1977; EdD in Lang. and Literacy, U. Calif., Berkeley, 1991. Assoc. prof. English and edn. U. Iowa, Iowa City, 1991—2002, prof., 2002—. Author: A Kind of Passport, 1993, Teaching in Common, 1998; co-editor Research in the Teaching of English, 2003—; contbr. articles to profl. jours. Recipient Outstanding Scholarship award Nat. Writing Ctrs. Assn., 1993; NAE/Spencer postdoctoral fellow, 1995—. Fellow Nat. Conf. Rsch. in Literacy; mem. MLA, Am. Ednl. Rsch. Assn., Nat. Coun. Tchrs. English (Promising Rschr. award 1992, Meade award 2000). Office: U Iowa N246 Linquist Ctr Iowa City IA 52242 Business E-Mail: anne-dipardo@uiowa.edu.

DIPASQUALE, LAURENE, physician; b. Bklyn., Dec. 17, 1957; d. Anthony and Josephine (Gangi) DiP. BS, Bklyn. Coll., 1979; MD, U. Cen. del Este, Dominican Republic, 1982. Flexible intern St. Michael's Med. Ctr., Newark, 1984-85; resident in internal medicine Mountainside Hosp., Montclair, N.J., 1985-88; fellow in pulmonary and critical care Bronx Lebanon Hosp., 1988-90. Mem. ACP, Am. Thoracic Soc., Am. Coll. Chest Physicians, AMA. Office: Bronx Lebanon Hosp 400 Old Hook Rd Ste 1-4 Westwood NJ 07675-3020

DIPASQUALE, LINDA JO, reading specialist, educator; d. Joe and Helen Gorecki; m. August DiPasquale, Aug. 23, 1975; children: Angela, Dennis. BE, Calif. State Coll., California, Pa., 1974; ME, U. Pitts., 1976. Cert. reading specialist. Tchr., reading specialist Shaler Area Sch. Dist., Glenshaw, Pa., 1974—. Mem. Three Rivers Reading Coun. Business E-Mail: dipasqualel@sasd.k12.pa.us.

DIPENTIMA, RENATO ANTHONY, corporate executive; b. Jan. 17, 1941; s. Victor and Mary (Cadolino) DiP.; m. Patricia Ellen Gillespie, July 24, 1965; children: Margaret Ellen, Katherine Alice. BA, NYU, 1963; MA, George Washington U., 1979; PhD, U. Md., 1984. With Social Security Adminstrn., N.Y.C., 1963—95, exec. officer Nat. Commn. Social Security Reform Balt., 1979—82, dep. assoc. commr. for sys. requirements, 1982-84, dep. assoc. commr. for sys. integration, 1984-88, assoc. commr. for sys. design and devel., 1988-90, dep. commr. for sys., 1990-95; v.p., chief info. officer Sys. Rsch. and Applications Corp., Arlington, Va., 1995-97; pres. SRA Fed. Sys., 1997-98, SRA Govt. Sector, 1999—2000, SRA Cons. and Sys. Integration, 2001—03, pres., COO, 2003—05, pres., CEO, 2005—. Bd. dirs. MCDATA Corp., NVTC, ITAA. Mem. Coun. on Excellence, vice-chmn. industry adv. coun., 2002-04. Recipient Under Sec.'s Spl. citation HEW, 1972, Sec.'s citation, 1974, Commr.'s citation Social Security Adminstrn., 1974, Dir.'s citation, 1979, Dep. Commr.'s citation, 1984, Commr.'s citation, 1991, Sec.'s Exec. Mgmt. citation Health and Human Svcs., 1987, Presdl. Meritorious Rank award, 1989, Presdl. Disting. Rank award, 1990. Mem. Nat. Acad. of Soc. Ins. Home: 4 Weems Creek Dr Annapolis MD 21401- Business E-Mail: renny_dipentima@sra.com.

DIPERNA, FRANK PAUL, photographer, educator; b. Pitts., Feb. 4, 1947; s. Frank Paul and Virginia Carmella (DeRenna) DiP. BS in Mech. Engring., Va.Polytech. Inst., 1970; student, Visual Studies Workshop, 1971-72; MA in Photography, Goddard Coll., 1977. Assoc. prof. art and photography Corcoran Coll. Art and Design, Washington, 1974-94, prof., 1994—, chmn. photography dept., 1978—81, 1984—87, 1999—2002. Instr. photography No. Va. C.C., Alexandria, 1973-78, George Washington U., Washington, summer 1974; lectrs. and workshops Smithsonian Inst., 1976, Maine Photog. Inst. Rockport, 1977, Am. U., Washington, 1977, 78, 79, Internat. Ctr. Photography, N.Y.C., 1979, U. Del., 1981, James Madison U., Harrisonburg, Va., 1982, Rice U., Houston, No. Va. C.C., Sterling, 1991; resident Vt. Studio Ctr., Johnson, Vt., 1993, 2002; vis. prof. U. Ga, Study Abroad Program, Cortona, Italy, 2005. Solo exhbns. include Kathleen Ewing Gallery, Washington, 1982, 84, 89, 95, 98, 2000, Diane Brown Gallery, Washington, 1977, 78, 80, Bird in Hand Gallery, Alexandria, 1973, Corcoran Gallery Art, 1974, 77, Recontres Internationales de la Photographie, Arles, France, 1981, Rice Univ., Houston, 1986; group exhbns. include Athenaeum Mus., Alexandria, 1972, Photo Impressions Gallery, Washington, 1974, Va. Mus. Fine Arts, Richmond, 1973, 75, 80, The Franklin Inst., Phila., 1978, Susan Spiritus Gallery, Newport Beach, Calif., 1979, Mus. Fine Arts, Houston, 1979, Decordova Mus., Lincoln, Mass., 1979, Mpls. Inst. Arts, 1979, L.A. Inst. Contemporary Art, 1979, Denver Art Mus., 1979, Art Inst. Chgo., 1979, Phila. Coll. Art, 1980, Brown U., Providence, R.I., 1980, Arlington (Va.) Arts Ctr., 1981, Everson Mus. Art, Syracuse, N.Y., 1985, Comfort Gallery Haverford (Pa.) Coll., 1986, Washington Ctr. Photography, 1992, Nat. Mus. Am. Art, 1992, Smithsonian Inst., 1992, Carnegie Mus. Art, 1992, New Orleans Mus. Art, 1992, Corcoran Gallery of Art, 1994, 96, 98, Virginia's Photographers, Longwood Ctr. for the Visual Arts, Farmville, Va., 1997, Kathleen Ewing Gallery, Washington, 1999, Art Mus. Western Va., Roanoke, 2002, Smithsonian AM. Art Mus., 2003, 1708 Gallery, Richmond, Va., 2003, Room Full of Mirrors, U. Md., 2004, Images of Itay, Kathleen Ewing Gallery, 2004, many others; represented in permanent collections Chrysler Mus., Norfolk, Va., Recontres Internationale de la Photographie, Arles, France, Bibliotheque Nationale, Paris, Libr. Cong., Washington, Polaroid (Euopa) Amsterdam, The Netherlands, Corcoran Gallery of Art, Va. Mus. Fine Arts, Smithsonian Inst., Balt. Mus. Art, Nat. Mus. Am. Art, Washington, Met. Mus. Art, N.Y., Ctr. for Creative Photography, U. Ariz. Artist-in-Residence Lightwork, Syracuse, N.Y., 1982, Camargo Found., Cassis, France, 1980, Vt. Studio Ctr., Johnson, 1992; Graduate fellow Va. Mus. Fine Arts, 1975. Avocations: tennis, fishing, playing guitar, birdwatching, furniture making. Office: Corcoran Coll Art & Design 500 17th St NW Washington DC 20006-4804

DIPIAZZA, SAMUEL, JR., finance company executive; Degree acctg./econs., U. Ala.; MS Tax Acctg., U. Houston. Joined Coopers & Lybrand, 1973, ptnr., 1979, mem. firm coun., 1986, midwest regional mng. ptnr., 1992, regional mng. ptnr., client svc. vice chmn. N.Y. metro region, 1994, leader Ams. tax and legal svs., 1998—2000, mem. internat. tax bd., global tax and legal svc. exec., Pwc consulting global bd.; chmn, sr. ptnr. U.S. firm PricewaterhouseCoopers, 2000—02, mem. global leadership team, CEO, 2002—. Trustee Fin. Acctg. Found. Mem. exec. coun. Inner City Sholarship Fund; mem. exec. com. Nat. Corp. Theatre Fund; pres. Big Bros./Sisters, NYC., 2001; mem. internat. adv. bd. Jr. Achievement; mem. bd. dirs. NYC Ballet. Named Acct. of Yr., Beta Alpha Psi Soc.; recipient Ellis Island medal of honor, INROADS Leadership award. Mem.: Mergers and Acquistions Group (Frankfurt). Office: PricewaterhouseCoopers 1301 Avenue of the Americas New York NY 10036

DIPIERO, ANDREW EDWARD, JR., lawyer; b. Phila., Nov. 26, 1952; s. Andrew E. and Edna M. (Gulla) DiPiero; m. Janet Doris Eggert, Oct. 26, 1975; children: Andrew, Michael, Kristin. BA, LaSalle U., 1974; JD, Del Law Sch., 1981. Bar: Pa. 1981, N.J. 1981, U.S. Dist. Ct. (ea. dist.) Pa. 1981, U.S. Dist. Ct. N.J. 1981, U.S. Ct. Appeals (3d cir.) 1987. Asst. city solicitor City of Phila., 1981-82; assoc. Rutter, Turner, Stein & Solomon, Phila., 1982-86; ptnr. Rutter, Turner, Solomon & DiPiero, Phila., 1986—97, Master, Weinstein, Schnoil & Dodig, 1997—. Bd. dirs. Quaint Oak Savs. Bank. Mem.: ABA, Phila. Bar Assn., Pa. Bar Assn., Justinian Club (Phila.), Vince Lombardi, Sons of Italy. Democrat. Roman Catholic. Home: 3879 Whitman Rd Huntingdon Valley PA 19006-2350

DIPIETRO, MARK JOSEPH, lawyer; b. Memphis, Aug. 25, 1947; s. Joseph Mark and Anne E. (Dorsey) DiP.; m. Kathleen Ann (Rafferty), June 22, 1968; children: Mark, Lora, Matthew. BA in Chemistry, So. Ill. U., 1969; JD, John Marshall Law Sch., 1976. Bar: Ill. 1976, Minn. 1983. Chemist Univ. Conn. Med. Sch., Hartford, 1969-70, VA Hosp., Indpls., 1970-71, U.S. Steel Corp., Gary, Ind., 1971-76; atty. Standard Oil of Ind. (now BP-Amoco), Chgo., 1976-81; from assoc. to ptnr. Merchant and Gould PA, Mpls., 1981-91; sr. v.p., sec. Merchant & Gould PA, St. Paul, 1992—. Mem. Met. Airport Sound Abatement Com., Mpls., 1984. Mem. ABA, AAAS, Internat. Bar Assn., Am. Intellectual Property Assn., Minn. Intellectual Property Assn., Ramsey County Bar Assn. Roman Catholic. Avocations: reading, bicycling, aerobics, piano. Home: 815 Fairview Ave S Saint Paul MN 55116-2161 Office: Merchant & Gould 3100 Norwest Ctr 80 S 8th St Ste 3200 Minneapolis MN 55402-2215 Fax: 612 371-5323.

DIPIETRO, RALPH ANTHONY, management consultant, educator, marketing consultant; b. NYC, Oct. 27, 1942; s. Joseph and Marie (Borelli) DiP. BBA, CUNY, 1964, MBA, 1966; PhD, NYU, 1972. Chmn., prof. mktg. and internat. bus. dept. Sch. Bus. Montclair State U., Upper Montclair, N.J., 1972—. Adj. prof. mgmt. NYU, 1976-97, mgmt. tng. dir. Inst. Retail Mgmt., 1976-86; cons. Mfrs. Hanover Trust, N.Y.C., 1979-85, Sharp Electronics, N.Y.C., 1980-94, Battus Corp., N.Y.C., 1982-85, AT&T Bell Labs., 1989-91; program dir. Bally of Switzerland, N.Y.C., 1981-93, Fortunoff's, N.Y.C., 1984-86. Author: Managerial Effectiveness: A Review and an Empirical Testing of a Model, 1973; contbr. articles to profl. jours. Mem. Am. Mktg. Assn., Acad. Mktg. Scis., Internat. Assn. Applied Psychology, Omicron Delta Epsilon. Avocations: tennis, swimming, opera. Home: 12 Manor Dr Warren NJ 07059 Office Phone: 973-655-7218. Business E-Mail: dipietror@mail.montclair.edu. E-mail: ralphd01@optonline.net.

DIPKO, THOMAS EARL, retired minister, retired religious organization administrator; b. St. Michael, Pa., June 26, 1936; s. John and Sarah Jane (Gittins) D.; m. Sandra Jane Faust, Nov. 19, 1960; children: Lisa Renee, Sarah Marie. BA, Otterbein Coll., 1958; MDiv, United Theol. Sem., 1961; PhD in Ecumenical Theology, Boston U., 1969; LLD (hon.), Heidelberg Coll., 1987; DD (hon.), United Theol. Sem. of the Twin Cities, 1992; LHD (hon.), The Defiance Coll., 1992; DD (hon.), Elmhurst Coll., 1993, Ursinus Coll., 1994. ordained min. Youth min. First United Methodist Ch., Dayton, Ohio, 1958-61; ecumenical intern social action office Ch. Rhineland-Westphalia, Germany, 1962; asst. pastor First Ch. Congregational, Swampscott, Mass., 1963-64; pastor First United Methodist Ch., East Conemaugh, Pa., 1964-66; asst. pastor South Ch. Congregational, Andover, Mass., 1966-68; sr. pastor Christ Ch. United in Lowell, Mass., 1969-77, Grace Congregational Ch., Framingham, Mass., 1977-84; conf. min. and exec. Ohio conf. United Ch. of Christ, Columbus, 1984-92; exec. v.p. United Ch. Bd. for Homeland Ministries, Cleve., 1992-2000. Mem. bd. trustees The Defiance Coll., 1985—; mem. exec. com. Consultation on Church Union, 1989—2002; del. Seventh Assembly World Coun. Churches, Canberra, Australia, 1991; mem. bd. dirs. Ryder Meml. Hosp., Humacao, Puerto Rico, 1993-96. Author: (first draft, book) United Church of Christ Book of Worship, 1986; contbr. chpts. to books, articles to profl. jours. Chmn. Lowell Drug Action Com., 1971-74; mem. bd. dirs. Internat. Inst., 1971-77. Samaritans (suicide intervention), 1983-84; del. gen. coun. World Alliance Reformed Chs., Debrecen, Hungary, 1997; bd. trustees LeMoyne-Owen Coll. Fellow Coll. Preachers, 1983. Mem. N.Am. Acad. Ecumenists (mem. exec. com. 1981-83), Christians Associated for Rels. in Eastern Europe, Consultation on Common Texts. Avocations: swimming, perennial gardening, canoeing.

DIPLAS, PANAYIOTIS, civil engineering educator; b. Athens, Jan. 28, 1954; came to U.S., 1980; s. Anthony and Vasiliki (Sassalou) D.; m. Ageliki Brackoulia, Jan. 26, 1980; children: Anthony, Katherina, Bill. BSCE, Nat. Tech. U. Athens, 1979; MSCE, U. Minn., 1983, PhD in Civil Engring., 1986. Grad. rsch. asst. St. Anthony Falls Hydraulic Lab./Univ. Minn., Mpls., 1980-85; postdoctoral fellow dept. civil engring. U. Canterbury, Christchurch, New Zealand, 1985-86; postdoctoral assoc. Iowa Inst. Hydraulic Rsch./U. Iowa, Iowa City, 1986-88; asst. prof. dept. civil engring. Va. Poly. Inst. and State U., Blacksburg, 1988-93, assoc. prof., 1993—. Reviewer NSF, 1989—; cons. No. State Power Co., Mpls., 1986, Comminco, Ltd., Can., 1987; lectr. worldwide. Reviewer jours. in field; contbr. articles to profl. jours. Recipient Rsch. Initiation award NSF, 1989, Nat. Young Investiagor award NSF, 1992, U.S. Geol. Survey award, 1992; grantee NASA, 1990, Army Rsch. Office, 1990. Mem. ASCE (assoc. editor Jour. Hydraulic Engring.), Internat. Assn. Hydraulic Rsch., Am. Geophys. Union, U.S.-Japan Sci. Rsch. Exch. Program on River Mechanics. Office: Virgina Tech Inst Dept Civil Engring Blacksburg VA 24061

DIPRIMA, ANNE, middle school educator; b. Bklyn. d. Anthony and Grace D BS, Adelphi U., 1970; MS, Hofstra U., 1973; postgrad., C.W. Post Coll. of L.I. U. Cert. sch. dist. adminstr., sch. adminstr.-supr. Varsity softball and volleyball coach Bethpage (N.Y.) High Sch., 1970—; tchr. John F. Kennedy Mid. Sch., Bethpage, 1970—, athletic coord., 1990—. Named Coach of Yr. finalist Nat. H.S. Athletic Coaches Assn., 1994, 2001, 2005. Mem. Nassau County Volleyball Coaches Assn., Nassau County Softball Coaches Assn., Nassau Bd. Women's Ofcls. Office Phone: 516-644-4271. E-mail: adiprima@bethpage.ws.

DIPRIMA, RICHARD JOSEPH, neuropsychologist; s. Michael T. and Kathleen M. DiPrima; m. Erin Kathleen Cashin, Aug. 14, 1999. BA, Marquette U., 1995; MA, Argosy U., 1999, D Psychology, 2002. Lic. psychologist NY. Job coach supportive rehab. and tng. Lifetime Asst., Rochester, NY, 1997; psychologist Alexian Bros. No. Mental Health Ctr., Palatine, Ill., 1998—99; psychotherapy/day ctr. practice in neuropsychology Neuropsychol. and Rehab. Cons., Chgo., 1999—2000; cons., diagnostician U.S. Family Counseling Ctr., Chgo., 1999—2001; predoctoral intern U. Rochester Med. Ctr., 2001—02, postdoctoral resident in neuropsychology, 2002—04, faculty mem., sr. instr., 2004—. Program aide in support rehab. and tng. Crestomathy Ctr., Mpls., 1996; program counselor Dungarvin, St. Paul, 1996. Acad. scholar, Marquette U., 1991, Dean's Acad. scholar, Argosy U., 1999, APA Conf. Student Rep. scholar, 1999. Mem.: APA, Psi Chi. Avocations: soccer, tennis, golf, writing.

DIR, DAVE, professional soccer coach; b. June 23, 1959; Student, Western Ill. U. Profl. soccer player Chgo. Sting, 1980-84; soccer coach Trinity Prep Luth. Sch., Orlando, Fla., 1984-90; coach Regis U., Denver, 1990-92; head coach Colo. Foxes, 1992-93; dir. player devel. Major League Soccer, 1993-95; head coach Dallas Burn, 1995—. Goalkeeper coach U.S. Youth Soccer Assn. Region IV Olympic Devel. Program. Named Coach of the Yr., Colo. Athletic Conf., 1991. Office: c/o Dallas Burn 14800 Quorum Drive #300 Dallas TX 75254

DIRADO, LINDA MARIE, mathematician, educator; b. Danville, Pa., Apr. 8, 1952; d. Harry Matthais and Winifred Orpha Williams; m. Anthony DiRado, Apr. 1, 1979; children: Amber Wynn, Shannon Lynn. BS in Edn., Bloomsburg (Pa.) U., 1973; MS in Edn., Johns Hopkins U., 1979. Cert. tchr. Pa. Dept. Edn., 1982. Tchr. math. Joppatowne Jr.-Sr. H.S., Joppa, Md., 1974—77, Magnolia (Md.) Mid. Sch., 1977—79, Sullivan County Jr.-Sr. H.S., Laporte, Pa., 1979—84, 1999—, Benton (Pa.) Jr.-Sr. H.S., 1993—99. Avocations: crocheting, gardening. Office: Sullivan County Jr Sr High Sch Beech and South Sts PO Box 98 Laporte PA 18626-0098

DIRECTOR, STEPHEN WILLIAM, electrical and computer engineering educator, academic administrator; b. Bklyn., June 28, 1943; s. Murray and Lillian (Brody) D.; m. Lorraine Schwartz, June 20, 1965; children: Joshua (dec.), Kimberly, Cynthia, Deborah. BS, SUNY, Stony Brook, 1965; MS, U. Calif., Berkeley, 1967, PhD, 1968. Prof. elec. engring. U. Fla., Gainesville, 1968-77; vis. scientist IBM Rsch. Labs., Yorktown Heights, N.Y., 1974-75; prof. elec. and computer engring. Carnegie-Mellon U., Pitts., 1977-96, U.A. and Helen Whitaker Univ. prof. electrical and computer engring., 1980-96, prof. computer sci., 1981-96, head dept. elec. and computer engring., 1982-91, univ. prof., 1992-93, dean Carnegie Inst. Tech., 1991-96; Robert J. Vlasic dean of engring. U. Mich., Ann Arbor, 1996—2005, prof. elec. engring. and computer science, 1996—2005; provost, sr. v.p. Drexel U., Phila., 2005—. Advisor info. and comm. tech. Techno Venture Mgmt., 1999—2002; sr. rsch. fellow IC2 Inst., 1996—; sr. cons. editor McGraw-Hill Book Co., N.Y.C., 1976—; dir. Rsch. Ctr. Computer-Aided Design, Pitts., 1982—89; mem. tech. adv. bd. Nextwave, Inc., 1990—95, CAD Framework Initiative, 1991—93, Aspect Devel. Corp., 1991—92, JW2 Inc., 1991—94, LSI Logic, 1994, Autogate Logic, 1994—96, EDF Ventures, 1999—, MobileWebSurf Inc., 2002—; bd. dirs. Job Gravity, 1999—; hon. prof. Shanghai Jiao Tong U., 2003; mem. adv. coun. Lutron Electronics Inc., 1999—; cons. in field. Author: Introduction to System Theory, 1972, Circuit Theory, 1975, VLSI Design for Manufacturing: Yield Enhancement, 1989, Principles of VLSI System Planning: A Framework for Conceptual Design, 1991; editor: Computer-Aided Design, 1974; co-editor: Advances in Computer-Aided Design for VLSI: vol. 8, Statistical Approach to VLSI, 1994. Chair bd. dirs. Am. Soc. Engring. Edn., Engring. Deans Coun., 1999-2001. Named Distinguished Alumnus, SUNY, Stony Brook, 1984; Recipient Aristotle award Semicondr. Rsch. Corp., 1996, Outstanding Alumnus award in Elec. Engring. U. Calif., Berkeley, 1996, Berkeley Disting. Engring. Alumnus award U. Calif., 1999; fellow Am. Soc. Engring. Edn., 2004. Fellow IEEE (W.R.G. Baker prize 1979, Edn. Soc. Outstanding Achievement award 1995, Edn. medal 1998, Millennium medal 2000), Am. Soc. Engring Edn. (Frederick Emmons Terman award 1976, Benjamin Garver Lamme award 2004); mem. NAE (chair com. on engring. edn.), IEEE Cirs. and Sys. Soc. (pres. 1981, assoc. editor jour. 1973-75, best paper award 1970, 85, 89, 92, Centennial medal 1984, soc. award 1992, Golden Jubilee medal 1999). Office: Drexel Univ Office of Provost 3141 Chestnut St Philadelphia PA 19104 E-mail: director@drexel.edu.

DIRENZO, GORDON JAMES, sociologist, psychologist, educator; b. North Attleboro, Mass., July 19, 1934; s. Santo and Giulia (Petti) DiR.; m. Mary Kathleen Ryan, July 6, 1968; children: Maria Giulia, Chiara Veronica, Marco Santo. BA, U. Notre Dame, 1956, MA, 1957, PhD, 1963; postgrad., Harvard U., 1959, Columbia U., 1963-65, U. Colo., 1964. Lic. psychologist, Del.; cert. social psychologist. Instr. Coll. of St. Rose, Albany, NY, 1957-59; Instr. U. Portland, Oreg., 1961-62; asst. prof. Fairfield (Conn.) U., 1962-66; assoc. prof. Ind. U., South Bend, 1966-70; prof. sociology U. Del., Newark, 1970—; mem. faculty Siena Coll., Albany (N.Y.) Med. Ctr., 1958-59, U. Notre Dame, 1960-61, Coll. White Plains, 1963-65, Bklyn. Coll., 1965, Western Conn. State U., 1964, SUNY, Stony Brook, 1980, Cortland, 1966; affiliate mem. med. and dental staff Med. Ctr. Del., Wilmington, 1976-80, St. Francis Hosp., Wilmington, 1980—, Northeastern Hosp., Phila., 1982-85, Rockford Ctr., Wilmington, 1995—. Pres. Behavior Cons., Newark, Del., 1975—; dir. Sociol. Cons. Group, North Attleboro, Mass., 1963-75; Fulbright-Hays prof. U. Rome, 1968-69, U. Bologna, Italy, 1980-81; mem., exec. sec., bd. examiners psychologists State of Del., 1991-99, 2003—. Author: Concepts, Theory and Explanation in the Behavioral Sciences, 1966, Personality, Power and Politics, 1967, Personalità Potere Politico, 1967, Personality and Politics, 1974, We, the People: American Character and Social Change, 1977, Sociological Perspectives, 1987, Human Social Behavior, 1990, Personality and Society, 2001, The Social Individual, 2002, Individuo e Società, 2003, Conoscenza e Spiegazione, 2004, La Persona Sociale, 2004; contbr. articles to profl. jours. Recipient Disting. Svc. award Am. Assn. Family Practice, 1980, 82, 84, Excellence in Teaching award U. Del., 1991; fellow U. Notre Dame, 1959-60, Italian Ministry Edn., 1960, NSF, 1964; grantee Ford Found., 1960, NEH, 1975, Del. Inst. Med. Edn. and Rsch., 1975, Hon. Command, Dover AFB, 2005. Fellow Am. Sociol. Assn. (diplomate); mem. APA, AAUP, AAAS, Assn. Behavioral Scis. in Med. Edn., Soc. Personality and Social Psychology, Soc. for Advancement Social Psychology (bd. dirs. 1988-94), Am.-Italian Hist. Assn. (nat. exec. council 1977-80), Fulbright Alumni Assn., Internat. Sociol. Assn., Clin. Sociology Assn., Internat. Soc. Polit. Psychology (charter), Soc. Psychologists in Medicine, Internat. Polit. Sci. Assn., Soc. for Study Social Problems, Soc. Psychol. Study Social Issues, Eastern Sociol. Soc., Am. Sociol. Assn., Nat. Assn. Scholars, Alpha Kappa Delta. Home: 28 Deer Run Little Baltimore Farms Newark DE 19711 Office: U Del Dept Sociology Newark DE 19716 Office Phone: 302-239-4975. Business E-Mail: gdirenzo@udel.edu.

DIRKS, KENNETH RAY, medical educator, army officer; b. Newton, Kans., Feb. 11, 1925; s. Jacob Kenneth and Ruth Viola (Penner) D.; m. Betty Jean Worsham, June 9, 1946; children: Susan Jan, Jeffrey Mark, Deborah Anne, Timothy David, Melissa Jane. MD, Washington U., St. Louis, 1947. Diplomate: Am. Bd. Pathology. Rotating intern St. Louis City Hosp., 1948, asst. resident in gen. surgery, 1948-49; resident in pathology VA Hosp., Jefferson Barracks, Mo., 1951-53, resident in pathology, asst. chief lab. service Indpls., 1953-54; resident in pathology Letterman Army Hosp., San Francisco, 1956-57; fellow in tropical medicine and parasitology La. State U., Central Am., 1958; asst. in pathology Washington U. Sch. Medicine, 1952-53; asst. chief lab. service VA Hosp., Jefferson Barracks, 1953; instr. pathology U. Ind. Med. Center, Indpls., 1953-54; commd. capt. M.C. U.S. Army, 1954, advanced through grades to maj. gen., 1976; dir. research Med. Research and Devel. Command, Washington, 1968-69, dep. comdr., 1969-71, comdr., 1973-76; asst. surgeon gen., research and devel. U.S. Army, 1973-76; dep. comdr., comdr. Med. Research Inst. Infectious Diseases, Ft. Detrick, Frederick, Md., 1972-73; comdr. Fitzsimons Army Med. Center, Denver, 1976-77; supt. Acad. Health Scis., Ft. Sam Houston, Tex., 1977-80; assoc. prof. to prof. pathology and lab. medicine Coll. Med. Tex. A&M U., College Station, 1980-95; interim head dept. Coll. Medicine, Tex. A&M U., College Station, 1990-91; prof. emeritus pathology, 1995—; asst. dean coll. Coll. Medicine, Tex. A&M U., College Station, 1985-88; dir. dept. student health svcs. and A.P. Beutel Health Ctr. Tex. A&M U., College Station, 1989-95; dir. student health svcs. emeritus, 1995—. Contbr. articles to med. jours. Decorated D.S.M., Legion of Merit with oak leaf cluster, Meritorious Service medal, Army Commendation medal with oak leaf cluster. Fellow Coll. Am. Pathologists, Internat. Acad. Pathology, Am. Soc. for Clin. Pthology (emeritus). Republican. Baptist. Address: 2513 Oak Cir Bryan TX 77802-2009 *1) Know your job and work hard. 2) Respect all persons. 3) Be candid and honest always. 4)Persevere in the face of adversity. 5) Love God, country, and other people. 6) Help others.*

DIRKS, LEE EDWARD, newspaper executive; b. Indpls., Aug. 4, 1935; s. Raymond Louis and Virginia Belle (Wagner) Dirks; m. Barbara Dee Nutt, June 16, 1956 (div. Jan. 1985); children: Stephen Merle, Deborah Virginia, David Louis; m. Judith Ann Putman, Dec. 28, 2001. BA, DePauw U., 1956; MA, Fletcher Sch. Law and Diplomacy, 1957. Reporter Boston Globe, 1957, Nat. Observer, Washington, 1962-65, news editor, 1966-68; securities analyst specializing in newspaper stocks Dirks Bros., Ltd., Washington, 1969-71, Delafield, Childs, Inc., Washington, 1971-75, C.S. McKee & Co., Washington, 1975-76; asst. to pres. Detroit Free Press, 1976-77, v.p., gen. mgr., 1977-80; chmn. Dirks, Van Essen & Murray, Santa Fe, N.Mex., 1980—. Author: Religion in Action, 1965; pub. Newspaper Newsletter, 1970-76. Bd. dirs. Nat. Ghost Ranch Found., Santa Fe, 1973-97, Santa Fe Opera, 1998-2004; pres. Georgia O'Keeffe Mus., Santa Fe, 2000-04. Named Religion Writer of Yr. Religious Newswriters Assn., 1964 Fellow Religious Pub. Relations Council; mem. Phi Beta Kappa, Lambda Chi Alpha, Nat. Press Club (Washington), Oakland Hills Country Club (Detroit), Las Campanas(Santa Fe). Presbyterian. Home: 11 E Arrowhead Cir Santa Fe NM 87506-8248 Office: 119 E Marcy St Ste 100 Santa Fe NM 87501-2046 E-mail: lee@dirksvanessen.com.

DIRLAM, DAVID KIRK, education educator; b. Corning, NY, Jan. 13, 1942; s. Arthur Clinton and Edith Lor (Kirk) D.; m. Annette Isaacs, Dec. 31, 1981; children: David, Djuna, Lydia, Gareth. BA, Northwestern U., 1964; MA, McMaster U., 1967, PhD, 1970. Asst. prof. St. Norbert Coll., DePere, Wis., 1969—74; dir. edn. rsch. and demo ctr. Plattsburgh State U., NY, 1974—82; owner Dirlam Data Systems, San Marcos, Calif., 1982—88; vis. scholar U. of Calif., San Diego, 1997—98; owner David K. Dirlam Cons., Carlsbad, Calif., 1998—2002, The Folk Traditions Store, Savannah, Ga., 2002—; with Memetics Cons., 2003—. Cons. The Second R, Bd. of Coop. Edn. Services, Malone, NY, 1979—80, Memetics Consulting, Savannah, Ga., 2003—04. Contbr. articles; author: Standardized Developmental Ratings, 1978, (book) Memes in your Life, 2002; contbr. (book) Toward a Theory of Psychological Development, 1980, (series of books) The Second "R":K-12 Writing Curriculum, 1980—81. Pres. Mt. Rogers Appalachian Trail Club, Abingdon, Va., 1990—; mem. bd. managers Appalachian Trl. Conf., Harpers Ferry, W.Va., 1993—. Recipient James McKeen Cattell Fund Fellow, 1997—98; grant, Appalachian Coll. Assn., 1998, 1999, 2000. Mem. Am. Psychol. Soc. Jewish. Achievements include finding that the age of appearance of general drawing and discourse skills can be modeled Lotka-Voterra competing species equations, with means several yrs. apart; yet individual children use skills from widely diverse parts of the sequence from one week to the next. Avocations: flute, harp, singing, hiking, torah chanting. Home: 17 Oak Park Pl Savannah GA 31405 Office: The Folk Traditions Store 12 Price St Savannah GA 31401 Office Phone: 912-341-8898.

DIRNT, MIKE (MICHAEL RYAN PRITCHARD), musician, singer; b. Berkeley, Calif., May 4, 1972; m. Anastasia Dirnt, 1999 (div.); 1 child, Estelle Desiree. Played with the bands Screeching Weasel, Crummy Musicians, Squirtgun; currently bassist with side band The Frustrators; co-founder, musician, back-up vocals Sweet Children (name changed to Green Day in 1989), 1988—. Musician (bassist): How to Make Enemies and Irritate People (with Screeching Weasel); musician, back-up vocals (first EP) 1,000 Hours, (albums) 1,039/Smoothed Out Slappy Hour, 1991, Kerplunk, 1992, Dookie, 1994 (Grammy award for Best Alternative Music Performance, 1994), Insomniac, 1995, Nimrod, 1997, Warning, 2000, American Idiot, 2004 (Viewers Choice award, MTV Video Music Awards, 2005), voice (films) Live Freaky Die Freaky, 2003; composer: (films) Angus, 1995, Godzilla, 1998, Varsity Blues, 1999, Austin Powers: The Spy Who Shagged Me, 1999; guest appearances Saturday Night Live, 1994, 2005, Mad TV, 2001, (voice) King of the Hill, 1997, and several others. Recipient Video of Yr., Best Group Video, Best Rock Video, Best Editing in a Video, Best Direction in a Video for Boulevard of Broken Dreams, MTV Video Music Awards, 2005.*

DIROSA, STEVEN JOSEPH, primary and secondary school educator; b. Phila. s. Joseph and Patricia (Bealer) D. BS, Temple U., 1989; MS in Ednl. Technologies, Rosemont Coll., 1996. Cert. elem., secondary tchr., Pa. Tchr., dept. head Chester-Upland (Pa.) Sch. Dist., 1989-2000; spl. assignmnet middle sch. tchr. Penn-Delco Sch. Dist., 2000—. Tech. dir. STEP Summer Student Prog., Chester, Pa., 1990-95; intramural sports asst. dir. Chester-Upland Sch. Dist., 1993-96. Author: Travel Tales (Billy the Shoe), 1989 (best children's short story award Pa. Tchr. Pages 1990). Recipient Pres.' award Pres.' Acad. Excellence Com., Rosemont, Pa., 1992, outstanding svc. award S.E. Pa. STEP Prog., Chester, Pa., 1994. Fellow Smithsonian Instn.; mem. World Wildlife Fund, Nat. Coun. Tchrs. Math., Sierra Club, Audubon Soc. Home: 232 Talbot Dr Broomall PA 19008-3729 Office: EDCO 232 Talbot Dr Broomall PA 19008

DIRSCHL, DOUGLAS RAY, surgeon, educator; b. Klamath Falls, Oreg., May 16, 1962; s. Raymond Bernard and Sandra Helen Dirschl; m. Virginia Lee Pereira, July 27, 1985; children: Katherine Cord, Douglas Kirk, Margaret Alexandra. BS, Stanford U., 1984; MD, Oreg. Health Scis. U., 1988; cert., Kenan Flagler Grad. Sch. Bus., 1998, MIT, 2000, Northwestern U., 2005. Diplomate U.S. Med. Licensing Exam., Am. Bd. Orthopedic Surgery. Resident in orthop. surgery U. N.C. Sch. Medicine, Chapel Hill, 1988—93, asst. prof. orthops., 1993—99, assoc. prof., 1999—2001, prof., chmn. dept. orthop., 2003—; dir. dept. orthop. Wake Area Health Edn. Ctr., Raleigh, NC, 1996—2001, exec. dir., 1998—2001; prof., chmn. dept. orthops. Oreg. Health & Sci. U., Portland, 2001—03. Chief orthops. VA Med. Ctr., Portland, 2001—03; cons. surgeon EBI Med. Sys., Parsippany, NJ, 1996—. Author: Orthopaedics: PreTest, Self-Assessment, and Review, On Call Orthopaedics: Principles and Protocols; mem. editl. bd. Jour. Orthop. Trauma, Jour. Am. Acad. Orthop. Surgeons, cons. reviewer Jour. Bone and Joint Surgery; contbr. articles to profl. jours., chapters to books. Mem., bd. dirs. Thomas Dameron Found. Orthop. Edn., Raleigh, 1996—2001; mem. exec. com. OHSU Med. Group, Portland, 2001—03; mem. fin. com., mem. exec. com., manged care com. UNC Physicians and Assocs., Chapel Hill, 2003—05; specialist site visitor Accreditation Coun. Grad. Med. Edn., Chgo., 2002—05. Named Edwin J. Bovill Jr. MD Meml. lectr., Orthopaedic Trauma Assn., 1998; recipient Lange Book award for Academic Excellence, Oreg. Health & Scis. U., 1986, Tchg. award for Resident Instrn., U. N.C. Dept. Orthops., 1990, Musculoskeletal cup for Outstanding Faculty Instrn., 2004, Frank C. Wilson Faculty Tchg. award, 1998, Musculoskeletal Cup for Outstanding Faculty Instrn. to med. students, 1994, Jr. Faculty Devel. award, U. N.C., 1994; Nathan Womack scholar, U. N.C. Dept. Surgery, 1993, Tchg. scholar, U. N.C. Sch. Medicine, 1997—99. Fellow: Am. Acad. Orthop. Surgeons (mem. edn. com., mem. program com. 1995—2005); mem.: Interurban Orthop. Soc. (mem. edn. com., mem. program com. 2001—05), Am. Orthop. Assn. (mem. various coms., program chair 2001—05, Travelling fellow 2001), Orthop. Trauma Assn. (mem. various coms., bd. dirs. 1996—2005), Nathan Womack Surg. Soc., Alpha Omega Alpha, Tau Beta Pi. Avocations: baseball, reading, tennis, bicycling. Office: U NC Dept Orthop CB #7055 3147 Bioinformatics Bldg Chapel Hill NC 27599-7055 Office Phone: 919-966-9072. Office Fax: 919-966-6730.

DIRSMITH, RONALD, architect; m. Suzanne Roe Dirsmith. BS, Architectural Engineering, MA, Architecture Design, U. of Il. Cert. Il., Fl., NCARB. With Perkins & Will; principal Ed Dart & Assoc.; founder, principal architect Dirsmith Group, 1971—. Named Nat. Academician, Nat. Academy of Design, 1999; fellow Rome Prize in Architecture. Office: c/o The Dirsmith Group 318 Maple Avenue Highland Park IL 60035*

DIRVIN, GERALD VINCENT, retired consumer products company executive; b. Phila., Mar. 28, 1937; s. Vincent A. and Mary (Fitch) D.; m. Polly Burnett, June 27, 1959; children: John, David, Barbara. BA, Hamilton Coll., Clinton, N.Y., 1959. With Procter & Gamble Co., 1959-94, sales mgt., then v.p. coffee divsn., 1975-80, group v.p. Cin., 1980-89, exec. v.p., 1990-94, dir., 1981-94. Bd. dirs. Cintas Corp. Bd. trustees Hamilton Coll. Mem. Comml. Club, Plantation Golf Club, Commonwealth Club, Camargo Club, Pine Valley Golf Club, Double Eagle Golf Club, Confrerie des Chevaliers du Tastevin, Pablo Creek Golf Club, Kingsley Golf Club. Republican. Roman Catholic. E-mail: gdirvin@aol.com.

DISAIA, PHILIP JOHN, obstetrician, gynecologist, radiology educator; b. Providence, Aug. 14, 1937; s. George and Antoinette (Vastano) DiS.; children: John P., Steven D.; m. Patricia June; children: Dominic J., Vincent J. BS cum laude, Brown U., 1959; MD cum laude, Tufts U., 1963; MD (hon.), U. Genoa, Italy, 1999. Diplomate Am. Bd. Ob-Gyn. (examiner 1975—, bd. dirs. 1994, v.p. bd. dirs. 1997—), Am. Bd. Gynecologic Oncology (bd. dirs. 1987—). Intern Yale U. Sch. Medicine, New Haven Hosp., 1963-64, resident in ob-gyn., 1964-67, instr. ob-gyn., 1966-67; fellow in gynecologic oncology U. Tex. M.D. Anderson Hosp. and Tumor Inst., Houston, 1969-70, NIH sr. fellow, 1969-70, instr. ob-gyn., 1969-71; asst. prof. ob-gyn. and radiology U. So. Calif. Sch. Medicine, L.A., 1971-74, assoc. prof., 1974-77; prof., chmn. dept. ob-gyn. U. Calif. Irvine Med. Ctr., Calif. Coll. Medicine, 1977-88, prof., 1977—, prof. radiology, radiation therapy div., 1978—, assoc. vice chancellor for health scis. Irvine Coll. Medicine, 1987-89, Dorothy Marsh chair of reproductive biology, 1989—; dep. dir. cancer ctr. U. Calif, Irvine Med. Ctr., Calif. Coll. Medicine, 1989—; pres. med. staff U. Calif. Irvine Med. Ctr., Calif. Coll. Medicine, 1993-97; pres. UCI Clin. Practice Group, 1994—. Dir. div. gynecol. oncology Am. Bd. Obstetrics & Gynecology, 1995—, bd. dirs., 1994—, chair-elect 2002; bd. dirs. U. Calif. Irvine Med. Ctr., 1995, chair health sys. steering com., 1995, chair health sys. capital planning group, 1995, health sys. bd. dirs., 1995; clin. enterprise adv. coun. to pres. U. Calif., 1995; academic planning task force U. Calif. Irvine, 1994, continuing med. edn. com., 1991-94; cancer liaison commn. on cancer Am. Coll. Surgeons, 1981-94; bd. dirs., dir. at large Am. Cancer Soc., 1985—; clin. prof. dept. ob-gyn. U. Nev. Sch. Medicine, Reno, 1985—; chmn. site visit team for surgery br. Nat. Cancer Inst. NIH, 1983, subcom. surg. oncology rsch. devel., 1982-83, mem. sci. counselors div. cancer treatment, 1979-83; mem. gov.'s adv. coun. on cancer State of Calif., 1980-85; vis. prof., lectr., speaker various sci. meetings, confs., courses. Recipient Disting. Alumnus award M.D. Anderson Hosp. and Tumor Inst. U. Tex., 1980, Silver Apple award U. Calif. Med. Students, 1983, Lauds and Laurels Profl. Achievement award U. Calif. Alumni Assn., 1983, Hubert Haussel's award Long Beach Meml. Hosp., 1983, Dist. Faculty Lectureship award for Teaching, U. Calif. Irvine Acad. Senate, 1993-94, also various rsch. awards. Fellow Am. Coll. Obstetricians and Gynecologists (com. on human rsch. for cancer 1979—, chmn. 1984—, chmn. subcom. on gynecologic oncology 1984-85, prolog editorial and adv. com. 1986—, v.p. 1997-99, various others), ACS (bd. govs. 1998—), Commn. on Cancer Liaison, Western Assn. Gynecologic Oncologists (founder 1971, pres. 1978-79), Am. Gynecol. and Obstet. Soc. (exec. coun. 1986—), Am. Gynecologic Soc., Pacific Coast Ob/Gyn Soc., South Atlantic Assn. Obstetricians and Gynecologists (hon.); mem. AMA, Am. Cancer Soc. (bd. dirs L.A. County unit 1975-77, Orange County 1979, unit pres. 1993—; bd. dirs. Calif. div. 1985—, chmn. med. scientific com. 1993-94), Nat. Am. Cancer Soc. (dir.-at-large, bd. dirs. 1985—, chmn. program com. for nat. conf. 1986, vice-chmn. detection and treatment adv. group gynecol. cancer 1993-94, active in others), Am. Coll. Radiology (commn. on cancer 1984-85), Am. Soc. Clin. Oncologists, Soc. Gynecologic Oncologists (exec. coun. 1975-80, pres. 1982-83), Internat. Gynecologic Oncology Cancer Soc., Italian Soc. Ob-Gyn. (Camillo Golgi prof. U. Brescia 1991), Calif. Med. Assn., NCI, Ctrl. IRB, Academic Senate, (chair 2000-), Gynecologic Oncology Group, (chair 2002-), ABOG, (pres.2002-), Alpha Omega Alpha. Office: U Calif Irvine Med Ctr 101 The City Dr S Bldg 56 Rm 265 Orange CA 92868-3201 E-mail: pjdisaia@uci.edu.

DISALVATORE, WILLIAM P., lawyer; b. 1966; BA cum laude, Hofstra U., 1987; JD cum laude, Pace U., 1991. Bar: Ct. 1991, New York 1992. Ptnr. Wilmer, Cutler, Pickering, Hale, and Dorr, LLP, New York. Named one of Top 40 Under 40, Nat. Law Journal, 2002. Mem.: Am. Intellectual Property Law Assoc., Federal Circuit Bar Assoc., N.Y. City Bar Assoc., Am. Bar. Assoc. Office: Wilmer Cutler Pickering Hale and Dorr LLP 399 Park Ave New York NY 10022

DISANDRO, LINDA ANITA, counselor; b. Phila., Aug. 23, 1950; d. Anthony and Frances Helen (Lopinski) D. BA, Holy Family Coll., 1972. Exec. sec. dept. radiology Episcopal Hosp., Phila., 1972-77; sr. sec. dept. radiology Hosp. U. Pa., Phila., 1977-89; faculty Cheltenham Township Adult Evening Sch., Wyncote, Pa., 1982-84; admissions counselor Holy Family Coll., Phila., 1989-96, assoc. dir. admissions, 1996-98; dir. coll. counseling St. Basil Acad., Fox Chase Manor, Pa., 1998—. Mem. AAUW, Nat. Assn. Coll. Admission Counselling (co-chair Phila. Nat. Coll. Fair 1995-97), Pa. Assn. Secondary Sch. and Coll. Admissions Counselors, Pa. Assn. Cath. Colls. Admission Officers (adv. bd. 1991-98), Phila. Area Cath. Colls. (adv. bd./transp. coord., 1991-98), Polish Am. Congress, Assoc. Polish Home Phila. Democrat. Roman Catholic. Avocations: arts and crafts, travel, theater. Home: 4542 Edgemont St Philadelphia PA 19137-2002 Office: Saint Basil Acad 711 Fox Chase Rd Jenkintown PA 19046-4197

DISBROW, SIDNEY ARDEN, JR., chiropractor; b. Ann Arbor, Mich., Sept. 22, 1946; s. Sidney Arden Sr. and Leona Irene (Reinhart) D.; m. Marilyn Ann Musson, Dec. 28, 1968 (div.); 1 child, Mary Elizabeth; m. Kathleen Riemesma, Oct. 3, 1998. BA, Hope Coll., 1968; MA, U. Mich., 1971; DC, Nat. Coll. of Chiropractic, 1975. Diplomate Am. Bd. Chiropractic Examiners. Tchr. Plymouth (Mich.) Community Schs., 1968-72; psychotherapist Milan (Mich.) Fed. Correctional Instn., 1970-72; pvt. practice Plymouth, 1975—99, Grand Haven, 1998—. Lectr. continuing edn. program U. Mich. Med. Sch., Ann Arbor, 1980; adv. comt. Muskegon Community Coll. Massage Therapy Prog. Pres. Plymouth Rotary Found., 1990; chair fundraising com. United Way, Plymouth, 1990—, pres., 1996, campaign chmn. Tri-Cities United Way. Recipient Night of 100 Stars, 2002, Dabridge Community Service award, 2003. Mem. Am. Chiropractic Assn., Internat. Coll. Applied Kinesiology, Mich. Chiropractic Assn., Coun. on Diagnostic Imaging, Alumni Assn. Nat. Coll. Chiropractors, U. Mich. Alumni Assn., Masons, Rotary (pres. 1997), Rotary Club Grand Haven (dist. conf. chmn. Rotary Dist. 9290, 2003-), Delta Tau Alpha. Presbyterian. Avocations: running, painting, skiing, sailing, trumpet. Office: 518 S Beacon Blvd Grand Haven MI 49417-1954 also: 518 S Beacon Blvd Grand Haven MI 49417-1954

DISCALA, JAMIE LYNN, actress; b. Jericho, NY, May 15, 1981; m. A.J. DiScala. Student, NYU. Actor: (films) A Brooklyn State of Mind, 1997, Campfire Stories, 2001, Death of a Dynasty, 2003; (TV films) Call Me: The Rise and Fall of Heidi Fleiss, 2004; (TV series) The Sopranos, 1999—; (Broadway plays) Beauty and the Beast, 2002—03; author: (autobiography) Wise Girl, 2002. Achievements include started acting at NY regional theaters; starred in over two dozen theatrical prodns. including Annie, The Wizard of Oz, The Sound of Music, The Wiz, and Gypsy. Office: 1100 Ave of the Americas New York NY 10036

DISCIULLO, ALAN MICHAEL, lawyer; b. Long Branch, N.J., Mar. 18, 1950; s. Peter Michael and Marion (Kaney) DiS.; m. Mary Jo Coppola, Oct. 13, 1979; children: Megan Eileen, Corinne Leigh. AB cum laude, Georgetown U., 1972, JD, 1977; MBA, NYU, 1986; M in Corp. Real Estate with honors, NACORE Inst., 1997. Bar: N.J. 1977; U.S. Dist. Ct. N.J. 1977, D.C. 1980, N.Y. 1980. Law clk. to presiding justice U.S. Tax Ct., Washington, 1975-76; assoc. Shanley & Fisher, Newark, 1977-78; asst. v.p. Paine Webber Jackson, N.Y.C., 1978-83; v.p., 1st v.p. Morgan Stanley, N.Y.C., 1983—2005; of counsel Sills, Cummis, Epstein & Gross, P.C., Newark, 2005—. V.p., dir. Wall St. Realty, N.Y.C., 1981—83; bd. dirs., gen. counsel, sec. Dean Witter polit. action com., N.Y.C., 1986—91; prof. masters real estate program NYU, 1991—; v.p. North Brunswick (N.J.) Tenants Assn., 1979—81; mem. task force Pres.'s Pvt. Sector Survey on Cost Control, Grace Commn., Washington, 1982—83; mem. land use adv. com. 12th Congl. Dist. N.J., 1999—; spkr., panelist comml. real estate & planning issues; lectr. Practicing Law Inst., 1996—, Strategic Rsch. Inst., 1996—98, NACORE Inst. for Corp. Real Estate, Corenet Global, 2002—; mem. Corenet Learning Adv. Bd., 2002—; vice chmn. Negotiating Comml. Leases Panel, 2000—. Co-author: (treatise) Negotiating and Drafting Office Leases, 1995; co-editor: Met. Corp. Counsel Real Estate Corner column, corp. counsel adv. com., 1997—99; bd. editors: Jour. of Corp. Real Estate Mgmt., 1998—, exec. mem.:, 2003—, mem. edtl. bd.: Comml. Leasing Law and Strategy, 1999—, Comml. Tenant's Lease Insider, 2003—; contbr. articles to profl. jours., book chpt. Treas., dir., coach West Windsor Plainsboro Soccer Assn., 1990—97; mgr. West Windsor Little League, 1993—2000; coach West Windsor Wildcats Traveling ASA Team, 1998—2001; dir. Princeton Soccer Assn., 2001—02; lectr. Sobelsohn Sch.; advisor site plan rev. com. West Windsor Twp., 1987—88, mem. growth mgmt. planning com., 1988—90, mem. growth mgmt. adv. com., 1991—93, zoning bd., 1997—98; chmn. West Windsor Planning Bd., 1993—97; co-chair Mayor's N.Y.C. Bus. Task Force, 2003—; mem. West Windsor Plainsboro sch. redistricting com., 1995; trustee West Windsor Plainsboro

Sch. Dist. Edn. Found., Inc., 1996—2002, v.p., 1999—2001; mem. Mayor's (NYC) Bldg. Industry Adv. Com., 2003—; dir. N.J. Planning Ofcls., 1997—. Recipient O'Connor award for disting. legal writing, 1987, 89, 91, Individual Achievement in Planning award N.J. Planning Ofcls., 1996, Outstanding Svc. award NYU, 1998, Outstanding Tchr. award NYU, 2002, Covenet Top Faculty award, 2001, 04. Fellow: Am. Coll. Real Estate Lawyers, Am. Bar Assn. Found.; mem.: ABA (chmn. young lawyers divsn. 1985—86, vice chair office lease sect. 1994—98, chmn. task force bldg. safety 1995—, chair 1998—, v.p. securities law divsn., corp. banking and bus. law sect., comml. leasing subcom., exec. com. mem., chmn.coms. on tenant equity participation, subrogation, idemnification, office lease sect.), Georgetown U. Wall Street Alliance (mem. adv. bd. 2003—), Practising Law Inst. (real estate adv. bd. mem. 1996—), N.Y. County Lawyers Assn. (exec. com. corp. law sect. 1994—95, co-chair 1996—98), Internat. Assn. Attys. in Corp. Real Estate, NACORE Internat. (dir. N.Y. chpt. 1996, pres. N.Y.C. chpt. 1997—98, internat. bd. dirs. 1997—2002, dir. NACORE Inst. 1999—2002, pres.-elect 2001—02, pres. 2002), Young Lawyers of N.Y.C. (treas. 1982—83, chmn. 1983—85), Mensa, Gavel Club, Princeton (N.J.) Athletic Rugby Club, Carnegie Lake Rowing Club (chair nominating com.), Pi Sigma Alpha. Democrat. Roman Catholic. Avocations: athletics, photography, reading. Home: 19 Taunton Ct Princeton Junction NJ 08550-2164 Office Phone: 973-643-6199. Business E-Mail: adisciullo@sillscummis.com. E-mail: Adisciu9@comcast.net.

DISESSA, ANDREA A., education educator; b. June 3, 1947; m. Melinda M. diSessa; children: Kurt, Nicholas. AB in Physics, Princeton U., 1969; PhD in Physics, MIT, 1975. Mem. A.I. lab. logo group MIT, Cambridge, Mass., 1972—82, spl. lectr. edn., 1975—77, from asst. prof. to assoc. prof. edn., 1977—82, prin. scientist lab. for computer sci., 1982—84, sr. scientist lab. for computer sci., leader ednl. computing group, 1984—85; assoc. prof. edn. U. Calif., Berkeley, 1985—88, prof. edn., 1988—, chmn. SESAME grad. program, 1988—89, assoc. dean for acad. affairs Grad. Sch. Edn., 1989—91, chair cognition and devel. edn., 1998—2000. Vis. rschr. World Ctr. for Computers and Human Resources, Paris, 1982; spkr. divsn. edn. and math., sci. and tech. edn. U. Calif., Berkeley, 1992—93; vis. prof. media lab. MIT, Cambridge, 1993—94; convenor Ctr. for Study of Critical Transitions, 1997—2002; fellow Ctr. for Advanced Study in Behavioral Scis., 1997—98; cons. in field; founding mem. adv. bd. SIG in Edn. in Sci. and Tech., 1989—; mem. adv. bd. Handheld Assessment Project, 1999—. Contbg. editor: Jour. Math. Behavior, 1982—; editor: Instructional Science, 1984—89; mem. editl. bd.: Jour. Learning Scis., 1990—, Interactive Learning Environments, 1990, Jour. Sci. Edn. and Tech., 1993—. Recipient grants in field. Mem.: NAE, Math. Assn. Am., Jean Piaget Soc., Internat. Soc. of Learning Scis., Cognitive Sci. Soc., Am. Ednl. Rsch. Assn., Nat. Consortium on Uses of Computers in Math. Scis. Edn. (steering com. 1984—86), Phi Beta Kappa. Achievements include research in computers in education; learning/genetic epistemology; instruction in physics and mathematics; programming languages for non-professionals. Office: 4533 Tolman Hall #1670 Grad Sch Edn U Calif Berkeley CA 94720-1670*

DISHER, DAVID ALAN, lawyer, consultant; b. Chgo., Apr. 15, 1944; s. Hugh George and Beatrice Rose (Selmanovitz) D.; children: Karl Theodore, Carol Ann, Kathy; m. Clara Hoffman, Sept. 17, 1991. BSEE, MIT, 1965, MSEE, 1966; JD, U. Houston, 1983. Bar: Tex. 1984, U.S. Ct. Appeals (5th cir.) 1984, U.S. Tax Ct. 1984, U.S. Dist. Ct. (so. dist.) 1986, U.S. Supreme Ct. 1987. Mathematician Shell Devel., Houston, 1966—68; sr. engr. Tex. Instruments, Stafford, 1968; dir. rsch. GEOCOM, New Orleans, 1969—70; cons., inventor Disher Consulting Svc., Houston, 1970—73; pres., chmn. bd. Seismic Programming Internat., 1973—84; pvt. practice law LaMarque, Tex., 1994—99; pvt. practice Houston, 1999—. Ind. geophys. rsch. cons. Contbr. articles to Geophysics. Mem. crime control com. Houston C. of C., 1974—76. Mem. ACLU, Coll. State Bar Tex., Tex. Criminal Def. Lawyers Assn., Galveston County Bar Assn., Harris County Bar Assn., Harris County Criminal Lawyers Assn., Houston Geophys. Soc., Houston Bar Assn. Office: 3318 Mercer St Houston TX 77027-6020 Fax: 713-961-9402. Office Phone: 713-355-1191. E-mail: disherdave@aol.com.

DISHEROON, FRED RUSSELL, lawyer; b. Hot Springs, Ark., Nov. 21, 1931; s. Andrew Russell and Ruth Fayrene (Bearden) D.;children: Terri Suzanne, John Frederick; m. Diane L. Donley, Apr. 8, 1989; 1 child, Travis William. AB, Hendrix Coll., 1953; JD, So. Meth. U., 1956; LLM in Environ. Law, George Washington U., 1976. Bar: Tex. 1956, Va. 1974, U.S. Ct. Appeals (1st, 4th, 5th, 6th, 8th, 9th, 10th, 11th, D.C. and fed. cirs.), U.S. Supreme Ct. 1964. Atty. Superior Ins. Co., Dallas, 1960-64; claims atty. Sentry Ins. Co., Dallas, 1964-67; litigation counsel Stigall, Maxfield & Collier, Dallas, 1967-69; sole practice Dallas, 1969-70; asst. gen. counsel for litigation C.E. U.S. Army, Washington, 1970-75; spl. litigation counsel Dept. Justice, Washington, 1975—. Instr. environ. law U. Ala.-Huntsville, 1979-82; lectr. law George Washington U., 1981-86; vis. rsch. specialist U. Calif., Davis, 1990. Co-author: Sustainable Environmental Law, 1993, Water Law, Trends, Policies and Practice, 1995; editor Southwestern Law Jour., 1955-56. Col. JAGC, USAR. Recipient Sr. Exec. Svc. Meritorious award Dept. Justice, 1984, Outstanding Civilian Svc. medal Dept. Army, Disting. Svc. award Atty. Gen., 2004, and numerous outstanding performance awards U.S. Army, Dept. Justice Mem. Sr. Execs. Assn. Home: 3508 Riverwood Rd Alexandria VA 22309-2720 Office: Dept Justice Environ & Natural Resources Divsn 601 D St NW Washington DC 20004 E-mail: fred.disheroon@usdoj.gov.

DISHMAN, ROSE MARIE RICE, academic administrator, researcher; BS in Physics with honors, U. Mo., 1966; MS in Physics, U. Calif., Riverside, 1968, PhD, 1971; MBA, San Diego State U., 1979. Physics instr., elem. particle rsch. assoc. U. Tenn., Knoxville, Oak Ridge, 1968-71; computer programmer, analyst Signal Processing Divsn. Sys. Ctrl., Inc., Palo Alto, Calif., 1971-72; instr. physics San Diego State U., 1974-75; instr. algebra, calculus, physics San Diego C.C., Navy Tng. Ctr., Marine Corps Recruit Depot, 1975-78; instr. Grossmont Coll., San Diego, 1976-77; prof., dept. head Sch. Engring. and Applied Sci. U.S. Internat. U., San Diego, 1977-92, dean Sch. Engring. and Applied Sci., 1989-92, acting provost, v.p. acad. affairs, 1991-92; dean acad. affairs DeVry Inst. Tech., Pomona, Calif., 1992-94, pres. Pomona, Long Beach, Calif., 1994—. Supr. world-wide acad. progs. including campuses in Mex., Eng., Kenya, U.S. Internat. U., primary supr. deans Schs. of Edn., Bus., Visual and Performing Arts, Human Behavior, Hotel and Restaurant Mgmt., Libr., Learning Resource Ctr., developer civil engring., engring. mgmt., electronics tech., elec. engring. progs. resulting in Engring. Accreditation Commn. of the Accreditation Bd. for Engring. and Tech. accreditation for civil engring. prog. for San Diego, London campuses, mem. curriculum coun. for all univ. progs., advisor U.S. Internat. U. Engring. Club; elected mem. Calif. Engring. Liaison Com., pres. pvt. univ. segment. Named outstanting engring. educator Am. Soc. Engring. Edn., 1989; rsch. grantee Fulbright-Hayes, 1972-73, grantee Am. Soc. Engring. Edn., NASA, 1979, Am. Soc. Engring. Edn., Dept. Energy, 1981, 82, 1984-85, Fed. Emergency Mgmt. Agy., 1983, 86. Office: DeVry Inst Tech Univ Ctr 901 Corp Ctr Dr Pomona CA 91768-2642 Fax: 909-623-5666.

DISHONG, LINDA S., estate planner; b. Bluffton, Ind., July 2, 1948; d. George William Dishong and Mary Kathryn Randol; children: Loni Marie, Marlou Reneé. Student various schs. for estate and fin. planning, Ind. Cert. estate planning specialist, sr. adv., real estate rep., NASD Series 7 & 63 broker. Pres. estate planning Genesis Projects, Indpls., 1982—89; adminstrn. and customer svc. rep. MR, Inc., Indpls., 1990—99; real estate profl. Coldwell Banker, Indpls., 1998—2000; broker Charles Schwab, Indpls., 2000—01; estate planning, regulation dir. United Fin. Sys. Corp., Indpls., 2001—. Motivational svc. profl., bus. cons. Genesis Projects, Indpls., 1982—89. Mem.: Westfield-Washinton Kiwanis Club, N.W. Kiwanis Club (sec. 1989—95, v.p. 1995—96, pres. 1996—97, Disting. Sec. 1989—95, Disting. Pres. 1996—97). Republican. Avocations: family, hiking, bicycling, travel, whitewater rafting.

DISHONG, MORRIS WILLIAM, forensic specialist, nurse; b. Canton, Ohio, Aug. 13, 1953; s. Morris W. and Vera M. Dishong; 1 child, Jeffery. Cert. death investigator, St. Louis U., 1997. Firefighter Plain Twp. Fire Dept., North Canton, Ohio, 1975-85; staff nurse emergency rm. Massillon (Ohio) Cmty. Hosp., 1986—; forensic investigator Stark County Coroner, Massillon, 1997—. Mem. Am. Assn. Critical Care Nurses. Republican. Avocations: travel, land exploration. Office: Stark County Coroner 400 Austrin Ave NW Massillon OH 44646 Office Fax: 330-837-3380. E-mail: headtotoe@raex.com.

DISHY, BOB, actor; b. Bklyn. s. Nathan and Amy (Barazani) D.; m. Judy Graubart; 1 child, Samuel Nathan. Ed. in drama, Syracuse U. Appeared in Broadway plays Damn Yankees, 1955, From A to Z, Flora The Red Menace, The Unknown Soldier and His Wife, Something Different, The Goodbye People, A Way of Life, The Creation of the World and Other Business, An American Millionaire, Sly Fox, Murder at the Howard Johnsons, Grown Ups, Cafe Crown, The Tenth Man, The Price, Morning's at Seven, Sly Fox (revival); off-Broadway plays Chic, There Is A Play Tonight, Can-Can, By Jupiter, The Shawl; actor, dir. N.Y. Second City Co.; also appeared in various regional theaters, Stratford Shakespeare Festival, Mark Taper Forum, Am. Repertory Theatre, The Public Theatre, Berkshire Theatre Festival, Williamson Theatre Festival, Westport Country Playhouse; appeared in films including The Tiger Makes Out, Lovers and Others Strangers, The Big Bus, Last Married Couple in America, First Family, Author, Author, Brighton Beach Memoirs, Critical Condition, Stay Tuned, Used People, My Boyfriend's Back, Don Juan DeMarco and the Centerfold, Jungle 2 Jungle, The Fish in the Bathtub, Judy Berlin, Labor Pains, Along Came Polly; numerous network and PBS shows including Frasier, Columbo, Law and Order, Jonny Zero, All in the Family, Mary Tyler Moore, Barney Miller, The Good Doctor, The Cafeteria; mem. TV series co. That Was The Week That Was; actor, dir. TV series Story Theatre. Served with U.S. Army 1957-59. Winner All-Army Entertainment Contest; Tony award nomination; recipient Drama Desk award, Chancellor's medal for disting. achievement Syracuse U., Outer Critics Cir. award. Mem. Acad. Motion Picture Arts and Scis.

DI SIMONE, ROBERT NICHOLAS, radiologist, educator; b. Canton, Ohio, Nov. 15, 1937; s. Nicholas Joseph and Margaret Elizabeth (Karas) DiS.; m. Patricia Anne Zwigard, June 22, 1963; children: Christopher, Angela, Elizabeth. BSc summa cum laude, Ohio State U., 1959, MSc, MD cum laude, Ohio State U., 1963. Diplomate Am. Bd. Radiology, Am. Bd. Nuclear Medicine. Intern, fellow Johns Hopkins U. Hosp., Balt., 1963-64, asst. resident, fellow in internal medicine, 1964-65, asst. resident, fellow in radiology, 1967-70, instr., radiologist, 1970-71; dir. nuclear medicine Aultman Hosp., Canton, 1971-95, pres., med. staff, 1986-87, vice-chmn. dept. radiology, 1988-96, sec.-treas. med. staff, 1977-79; chmn. nuclear medicine sect. Northeastern Ohio Univs. Coll. Medicine, Rootstown, 1979-97; chmn. dept. radiology Northeastern Ohio Univs. Coll. of Medicine (NEOUCOM), Rootstown, 1992-93; diagnostic radiologist Aultman Health Found., Canton, Ohio, 1971-2000; radiology cons. North Canton, Ohio, 2000—. Author: Imaging of the Endocrine System in Organ System Radiology, 1984; contbr. articles to profl. jours. Fellow Am. Coll. Radiology; mem. AMA, Soc. Nuclear Medicine, Ohio State Med. Soc. (del. 1983-95), Radiol. Soc. N.Am., Stark County Med. Soc. (trustee 1979-95, chmn. bd. censors 1980-82, pres. 1993), Unique Club Stark County, Phi Beta Kappa, Sigma Xi, Alpha Omega Alpha, Phi Lambda Upsilon. Avocations: playing bluegrass guitar music, collecting antique old trains, travel, hiking. Home and Office: 2465 Oakway St N North Canton OH 44720-5886

DISIPIO, ROCCO THOMAS, writer; b. Phila., Dec. 17, 1949; s. Rocco Benjamin and Rita Elizabeth DiSipio. BS in Police Adminstrn., Mich. State U., 1971. Chief tour guide Mich. State U., 1970-71; probation, parole officer Pa. Ct. Common Pleas, 1971-79; gen. mgr. Poniard Books, Inc., Broomall, Pa., 1980-82; ops. mgr. Myles Med. Equip., Ardmore, Pa., 1982-85; editor-in-chief Merit Industries, Bensalem, Pa., 1985-87; freelance writer, 1987—. Prodr. Fgn. Films Enterprises, L.A., 1995—. Author: (world's 1st internet novel) Arcadia Ego, 1996 (USA Today award), (novel) Darkness. Paradise. 1997. Avocation: target shooting. Office: PO Box 405 New Kingstown PA 17072-0405 Office Phone: 717-691-8150.

DISKANT, GREGORY L., lawyer; b. Phila., June 7, 1948; s. Robert and Eda (Grunberg) D.; m. Sandra S. Baron, Feb. 29, 1980; children: Edward, Benjamin. AB, Princeton U., 1970; JD, Columbia U., 1974. Bar: N.Y. 1975. Law clk. to Hon. J. Skelly Wright, U.S. Ct. Appeals for D.C. Cir., Washington, 1974-75; law clk. to Hon. Thurgood Marshall, U.S. Supreme Ct., Washington, 1975-76; asst. U.S. atty. for so. dist. N.Y., Dept. Justice, N.Y.C., 1976-80, chief appellate atty., 1980; assoc. Patterson, Belknap, Webb & Tyler, N.Y.C., 1981—82, ptnr., 1982—, co-chmn., 1997—2002, chmn., 2003—. Editor-in-chief Columbia Law Rev., 1973-74. Kent scholar, 1972, Stone scholar, 1973, 74. Fellow Am. Coll. Trial Lawyers; mem. ABA, N.Y. State Bar Assn., Assn. Bar of City of N.Y. Office: Patterson Belknap Webb & Tyler Rm 2400 1133 Avenue of the Americas Fl 22 New York NY 10036-6731 Office Phone: 212-336-2710. Business E-Mail: gldiskant@pbwt.com.

DISMUKES, ROBERT KEY, medical researcher; b. Dahlonega, Ga., June 21, 1943; s. Camillus Jackson and Marion (Mullen) D.; children: Antony, William, Renee. BS, North Ga. Coll., Dahlonega, 1964; MA, Vanderbilt U., 1966; PhD, Pa. State U., 1971. Staff fellow NIH, Bethesda, Md., 1973-75; staff scientist neurosciences rsch. program MIT, Brookline, Mass., 1977-79; dir. study com. vision Nat. Acad. Scis., 1979-83; dir. life scis. Air Force Office Sci. Rsch., Bolling AFB, 1983-89; chief rsch. divsn. aerospace human factors NASA, Moffett Field, Calif., 1989-91, chief scientist aerospace human factors, 1991—. Vis. faculty mem. Free Univ., Amsterdam, 1975-76; with interagy. com. low vision Nat. Inst. Handicapped Rsch. Washingotn, 1981-84; with forum on rsch. mgmt. Fedn. Behavioral, Psychol. and Cognitive Scis., 1983-89. Editor: (with Robert Sekuler, Donald Kline) Aging and Human Visual Function, 1982, (with Guy Smith) Facilitaiton and Debriefing in Aviation Training and Operations, 2000; contbr. articles to profl. jours. Vol. pilot, Lighthawk, San Francisco, 1994—. With U.S. Army, 1966-68. Fellow Nat. Endowment for Humanities, NSF, Inst. Society, Ethics and Life Scis., 1976-77. Home: 1357 Harrison St Santa Clara CA 95050 Office: NASA Ames Rsch Ctr Mailstop 262-4 Moffett Field CA 94035 E-mail: kdismukes@mail.arc.nasa.gov.

DISNEY, ANTHEA, publishing executive; b. Dunstable, Eng., Oct. 13, 1946; naturalized, U.S., 1973; d. Alfred Leslie and Elsie (Wale) Disney; m. Peter Robert Howe, Jan. 28, 1984. Ed., Queen's Coll., Eng. Fgn. corr. London Daily Mail, N.Y.C., 1973-75, features editor London, 1975-77, bur. chief N.Y.C., 1977-79; columnist London Daily Express, N.Y.C., 1979-84; dep. mng. editor N.Y. Daily News, N.Y.C., 1984-87; editor Sunday Daily News, 1984-87, US Mag., 1987-88; editor-in-chief Self mag., 1988-89; mag. developer Murdoch Mags., 1989-90; exec. producer Fox TV's A Current Affair, 1990-91; editor-in-chief TV Guide mag., N.Y.C., 1991-95; editorial dir. Murdoch Mags., 1993-95; editor-in-chief I-Guide, Newscorp's Internet Svc., 1995-96; pres., CEO Harper Collins Publishers, 1996-97; chmn., CEO News Am. Pub. Group, N.Y.C., 1997—99, TV Guide, Inc., 1999; exec. v.p. content The News Corp Ltd., N.Y.C., 1999—; exec. chmn. Gemstar-TV Guide International Inc., LA, 2004—. Bd. dirs. Household Internat. Inc., 2001—. Office: The News Corp Ltd Ste 300 1211 Avenue Of The Americas New York NY 10036-8795

DISNEY, RALPH L(YNDE), retired industrial engineering educator; b. Balt., Feb. 27, 1928; BE, Johns Hopkins U., 1952, MSE, 1955, DEng., 1964. Engr. Industrial Diecraft Inc., 1953-55, rsch. analyst Ops. Rsch. Office, 1955-56; asst. prof. Lamar State Coll., Beaumont, 1956-59; assoc. prof. U. Buffalo, 1959-63; vis. assoc. prof. U. Mich., Ann Arbor, 1963-64, assoc. prof., 1964-68, prof. indsl. engring., 1968-77; Charles O. Gordon prof. indsl. engring. Va. Polytech Inst. & State U., Blacksburg, 1977-87; prof. indsl. engring. dept. Tex. A&M U., College Station, 1988-96; ret., 1996. OAS vis. prof. Inst. Aeron. Tech., Brazil, 1970-71; disting. vis. prof. Grad. Sch. Ohio State U., Columbus, 1974-75; vis. prof. dept. math. and stats. U. São Paulo, Brazil. Author 2 books; editor sects. in books; contbr. more than 70 articles to profl. jours. Erskine fellow Canterbury U., Christchurch, New Zealand, 1995. Fellow Am. Inst. Indsl. Engrs. (A.G. Holzman award 1986, David Baker award 1972, Frank and Lillian Gilbreth Indsl. Engring. award 1993); mem. ORSA (mem. coun. 1978-82), INFORMS (founder sect. on applied probabilities, sect. pres. 1979), NAE. Home (Summer): 1395 Locust Ave Blacksburg VA 24060 E-mail: rdisneyva@adelphia.net.

DISNEY, ROY EDWARD, broadcasting company executive; b. Los Angeles, Jan. 10, 1930; s. Roy Oliver and Edna (Francis) D.; m. Patricia Ann Dailey, Sept. 17, 1955; children: Roy Patrick, Susan Margaret, Abigail Edna, Timothy John. BA, Pomona Coll., 1951. Apprentice film editor Mark VII Prodns., Hollywood, 1942; guest relations exec. NBC, Hollywood, Calif., 1952; asst. film editor, cameraman prodn. asst., writer, producer Walt Disney Prodns., Burbank, Calif., 1954-77, dir., 1967—77; pres. Roy E. Disney Prodns. Inc., Burbank, 1978—; chmn. bd. dir. Shamrock Broadcasting Co., Hollywood, 1979—; chmn. bd. dir., founder Shamrock Holdings Inc., Burbank, 1980—; chmn. Walt Disney Animation, 1984—2003; vice chmn. Walt Disney Co., Burbank, 1984—2003, dir. emeritus, cons., 2005—. Trustee Calif. Inst. of the Arts, Valencia, 1967—. Author: novelized adaptation of Perri; producer (film) Pacific High, Mysteries of the Deep exec. producer Cheetah, 1989, The Little Mermaid, 1989, Beauty and the Beast, 1991, The Lion King, 1994, Pocahontas, 1995, Fantasia 2000;(TV show) Walt Disney's Wonderful World of Color, others; writer, dir., producer numerous TV prodns. Bd. dirs. Big Bros. of Greater Los Angeles, U.S. com. UNICEF, Ronald McDonald House charities, chmn. emeritus, Peregrine Fund; mem. adv. bd. dirs. St. Joseph Med. Ctr., Burbank; mem. U.S. Naval Acad. Sailing Squadron, Annapolis, Md.; fellow U. Ky. Recipient Acad. award nomination for Mysteries of the Deep, Mort Walker award for Outstanding Contbn. to the Cartoon Industry, Boca Raton Internat. Mus. of Cartoon Art, 1997, Internat. Creative Achievement. award, Cinema Expo, 1997, Elizabeth Ann Seton award, Nat. Catholic Edn. Assn. 1999, Henry Bergh Humane award, ASPCA, 1999, Inaugural Environ. Leadership award, Audubon Soc. 2000, Lifetime Achievement in Animation, Santa Clarita Internat. Film Festival, 2002 Mem. Dirs. Guild Am. West, Writers Guild Am. Clubs: 100, Confrerie des Chevaliers du Tastevin, St. Francis Yacht, Calif. Yacht, San Diego Yacht, Transpacific Yacht, Los Angeles Yacht. Republican.*

DISPALTRO, FRANKLIN L., plastic surgeon; MD with honors, N.Y. Med. Coll., 1965. Diplomate Am. Bd. Plastic Surgery. Intern New Rochelle Hosp., NY; resident in gen. surgery Met. Hosp. Ctr. N.Y.; resident in plastic surgery St. Barnabas Med. Ctr., Livingston; chief resident plastic surgery Bellevue Hosp. Ctr., NY; fellow in plastic surgery NYU Med. Ctr., 1973; pvt. practice plastic surgery West Orange, NJ. Attending and clin. instr. gen. surgery N.Y. Med. Coll., 1980—90, NYU, 1980—90; cons. in plastic and reconstructive surgery N.J. Rehab. Hosp., East Orange, 1972—2000; full attending St. Barnabas Med. Ctr., Livingston, 1979—, assoc. and clin. chief, chair dept. plastic and reconstructive surgery, 1980—87, chmn. dept. plastic and reconstructive surgery, 1987—93, bd. trustees, 1992—; chmn., founder, CEO Metrowest, 1984—92. Bd. govs. Nat. owment for Plastic Surgery, 1999—; bd. trustees N.Y. Med. Coll., 1982—92. Fellow: ACS; mem.: rgery, Internat. Soc. Clin. Plastic Surgery, N.Y. Regional Soc. Plastic and Reconstructive Surgeons (pres. 1983—84), Northeastern Soc. Plastic Surgery, Am. Bd. Plastic Surgery, Internat. Plastic Reconstructive Aesthetic Surgery, Internat. Soc. Aesthetic Plastic Surgery, Aesthetic Surgery Edn. and Rsch. Found. (bd. dirs. 2000—01), Lipoplasty Soc. N.Am., Plastic Surgery Ednl. Found., Am. Soc. Aesthetic Plastic Surgery (pres.-elect 2001—02, v.p. 2000—01, bd. dirs. 1990—, treas. 1999—2000, parliamentarian 1997—98), Am. Soc. Plastic Surgeons. Office: 101 Old Short Hills Rd Ste 510 West Orange NJ 07052

DISPENZIERE, RICHARD JOHN, music educator; b. Denville, NJ, May 8, 1966; s. Salvatore and Lorraine Dispenziere; m. Karen Sue Jensen, Dec. 15, 1990; children: Katelyn Noel, Ashley Kayla. MusB, William Paterson Coll., 1988. Band dir. West Essex Pub. Schools, North Caldwell, 1988—91, Frankford Twp. Sch., Branchville, NJ, 1991—. Religious educator St. Marie's Ch., 2001—. Recipient Governor's Tchr. Recognition award, Frankford Twp. Bd. Edn., 2000. Republican. Roman Cath. Avocations: golf, travel.

DI SPIGNO, GUY JOSEPH, industrial psychologist, international management consultant; b. Bklyn., Mar. 6, 1948; s. Joseph Vincent and Jeanne Nina (Renna) DiS.; m. Gisela Riba, May 23, 1979; children: Michael Paul, Abie Francis. *Wife, Gisele Riba DiSpigno, a native of Havana, Cuba, is director of contracts and negoations for IBM. She has over twenty-five years of line and staff experience in direct sales and management, strategic planning, business practices, and contracts for IBM. In addition to Spanish, Gisele also speaks Catalan and Italian. Gisele holds a M.A. from Northwestern University and a B.A. from Mundelein College of Loyola University. She is president of the Spanish Coalition for Jobs, Inc., and served on the board of directors of the Girl Scouts of Chicago and Hispanic Alliance for Career Enhancement. Son, Abie DiSpigno received his B.S. in 1995 from the University of Illinois in Engineering. Abie currently works in the Information Technology field for Aglient in Chicago. Son, Michael DiSpigno recieved a B.A. in marketing communications from Kendall College, Evanston, Illinios. He currently works as marketing representative for Ice Mountain in Chicago.* BS, Carroll Coll., 1969; MA, No. Ill. U., 1972; MEd, Loyola U., 1974; PhD, Northwestern U., 1977. Instr. No. Ill. U., DeKalb, 1969-70; chmn. humanities dept. Quincy (Ill.) Boys' H.S., 1970-71; dir. religious edn. St. Mary's Ch., DeKalb, 1971-72; dir. edn. Immaculate Conception Parish, Highland Park, Ill., 1972-77; dir. human resources Am. Valuation Cons., Des Plaines, Ill., 1977-79; psychologist Hay Assocs., Chgo., 1979-80; v.p. mktg. Exec. Assets Corp., Chgo., 1980-82; dir. mgmt. devel. and pers. svcs. Borg-Warner Corp., Chgo., 1982-84; ptnr., cons. psychologist Medina & Thompson, Chgo., 1984-91; pres. Exec. Synergies, Inc., Northbrook, Ill., 1991—. Coun. regents Loyola U., Chgo., 2004—; adv. bd. Northwestern U. Sch. Continuing Studies, 2005—. *Guy is a broad based, results oriented consultant and industrial psychologist with a pragmatic approach to achieving maximum organizational effectiveness. Over the last 20 years, he has developed an extensive background in organizational planning and development, executive assessment, succession planning, performance systems, and management education. As president of Executive Synergies, Inc., Guy assists major North American and international companies to integrate strategic vision with executive development and succession planning. Develop customized computer based education programs, and executive development tracking systems.* Contbr. articles to profl. jours. Mem. Highland Park Human Rels. Commn., 1975-77, Home Owners and Businessmen's Assn., Highland Park, 1976-77; mem. legis. com. Vernon Hills (Ill.) Sch. Bd., alumni coun. Carroll Coll., 1981-83; soccer coach Am. Youth Soccer Orgn., Glenview, Ill.; chmn.'s cabinet Ill. Dem. Party, 1988-92; benefactor Jesuit Partnership, Chgo. province, 1995—. Clifford B. Scott scholar, 1967; fellow No. Ill. U., 1970-72; named to Order Ky. Cols. Mem. APA, Cmty. Religious Edn. Dirs. (nat. vice chmn. 1971-73), Ill. Psychol. Assn., Nat. Registry Health Svc. Providers in Psychology, Am. Pers. and Guidance Assn., Soc. Indsl. and Orgnl. Psychology, Carroll Coll. Alumni Counsel, Phi Alpha Theta, Sigma Phi Epsilon. Office: 555 Skokie Blvd Ste 260 Northbrook IL 60062-2889 Office Phone: 847-272-3420. Business E-Mail: guyd@executivesynergies.com.

DISSEN, JAMES HARDIMAN, lawyer; b. Pitts., Jan. 26, 1942; s. William Paul and Kathryn Grace (Reilly) D.; m. Shirley Ann Stark, Dec. 17, 1976; children: Elizabeth Ann, William Stark, Anna Kathryn. BS, Wheeling (W.Va.) Jesuit U., 1963; MBA, Xavier U., Cin., 1966; JD, Duquesne U., Pitts., 1972. Bar: Pa. 1972, U.S. Dist. Ct. (we. dist.) Pa. 1972, W.Va. 1973, U.S. Dist. Ct. (so. dist.) W.Va. 1973, U.S. Supreme Ct. 1976. Spl. agent Counter Intelligence U.S. Army Intelligence Corps, 1963-66; personnel mgr. Columbia Gas of Pa., Inc., Uniontown, 1969-73; dir. labor rels. Columbia Gas Transmission Corp., Charleston, W.Va., 1973-84, dir. personnel and labor rels., 1984-87, dir. employee rels., 1987-96; v.p. Columbia Natural Resources, Charleston, W.Va., 1996-2001; v.p., ptnr. Triana Energy, Charleston, W.Va., 2001—03; sr. v.p. Columbia Natural Resources, LLC, Charleston, 2003—. Adj. prof. W.Va. Grad. Coll., 1996-97, Wheeling Jesuit U., 1997, U. Charleston, 1998; chmn., exec. com., bd. dirs. Star U.S.A. Fed. Credit Union. V.p., bd. trustees

Highland Hosp., 1991—; chmn. bd. dirs. Inroads/W.Va., 1995-2001, Christmas in April, 2000-01; pres. Cath. Bus. Network, 2002—. Mem. ABA, W.Va. State Bar, Soc. Human Resource Mgmt., W.Va. C. of C. (chmn. human resource com., bd. dirs.), St. Thomas Moore Soc., Berry Hills Country Club. Republican. Roman Catholic. Avocation: golf. Home: 1501 Brentwood Rd Charleston WV 25314-2307 Office: Columbia Natural Resources LLC 900 Pennsylvania Ave PO Box 6070 Charleston WV 25362 Office Phone: 304-353-5112. E-mail: jdissen@trianaenergy.com.

DISTASIO, RICHARD P., manufacturing executive; married; 4 children. BS in Acctg., U. Ill., Chgo. Former contr., sr. v.p. ops. GRI Corp.; former CFO, exec. v.p. Maurice Sporting Goods; former CFO Reyes Holdings, LLC, former pres. U.S. ops. Martin-Brower Co. subs., former pres., CEO; pres., CEO USF Corp., Chgo., 2003—; also bd. dirs. Mem. bus. adv. bd. U. Ill. Chgo.; active Cath. Charities. Office: USF Corp 8550 W Bryn Mawr Ave Ste 700 Chicago IL 60631

DISTEFANO, GREGORY JOHN, marketing professional; b. Providence, Mar. 25, 1966; s. Joseph Robert and Barbara Ann (D'Ambra) DiStefano. BA cum laude, Brown U., 1998; MBA, Columbia U., 1990. Mgr. Citibank, N.A., N.Y.C., 1990—92; pres. In Public PR, N.Y.C., 1992—95; sr. v.p. DeVries Pub. Rels., N.Y.C., 1995—98; sr. ptnr. J. Walter Thompson, N.Y.C., 1998—2001; pub. rels. dir. David Yurman, N.Y.C., 2001—02; exec. dir. Newport (RI) Internat. Film Festival, 2002—03. Cons. RI Econ. Policy Coun., Providence, 2003—04, Lookig Glass Theater, Providence, 2004. Vol. cons. RI Coun. for Humanities, Providence, 2004. Recipient Silver Anvil award, Pub. Rels. Soc. Am., 2000. Mem.: Dunes Club. Avocations: tennis, cooking, travel, writing, reading. Home: 276 East Shore Rd Jamestown RI 02835

DISTEFANO, PHILIP, academic administrator; BA in Humanities Edn., Ohio State U., 1968, PhD in Humanities Edn., 1974; MA in English Edn., W.Va. U., 1971. Joined U. Colo., Boulder, 1974, dean, 1986—96, vice chancellor, 1998—2000, exec. vice chancellor, provost, 2000—05, interim chancellor, 2005—. Office: VC Acad Affairs Univ Colo Boulder 40 UCB Boulder CO 80309-0400

DISTEFANO, TONY E., communications executive; BS in Elec. Power Engring., MS in Elec. Power Engring., Rensselaer Poly. Inst.; MBA, Stanford U. V.p. corp. devel Pacific Telesis Corp.; pres. PacTel Cable U.K. Ltd.; head unregulated subs. PG&E Enterprises, 1994, sr. v.p. corp. devel.; sr. v.p. PG&E Corp.; CFO PG&E Energy Svcs., 1997—; CEO Arrival Comm., San Francisco. Bd. dirs. Pacific Exch., World Affairs Coun. of No. Calif.

DISTELHORST, GARIS FRED, trade association administrator; b. Columbus, Ohio, Jan. 21, 1942; s. Harold Theodore and Ruth (Haywood) D.; m. Helen Cecilla Gillen, Oct. 28, 1972; children: Garen, Kristen, Alison. BSc, Ohio State U., 1965. V.p. Smith, Bucklin & Assocs., Washington, 1969-80; chief staff exec., CEO, pres. Nat. Assn. Coll. Stores, Oberlin, Ohio, 1980-98; pres. Assn. Initiatives, Inc., Westlake, Ohio, 1998—2002; pres., CEO Conv. Industry Coun., 1999—2001, Marble Inst. Am., 2002—. Mem. book and libr. adv. com. USIA, 1990-93; bd. dirs. FirstMerit Bank, N.A., Holcombs, Inc. Pres. Oberlin Cmty. Improvement Corp., 1985-88; bd. dirs. Leadership Lorain County, 1988-89, Access Program, 1994-97, Conv. and Visitors Bur. Greater Cleve., 1994-2003, Lorain County C.C. Found., Lorain County United Way, 1991-97, v.p., 1993-94, pres., 1994-96, campaign chmn., 1993; bd. dirs. Project Love, 2003—, Avon Lake Cmty. Improvement Corp., 2003—. Decorated USN Achievement medal, 1969 Mem. Inst. Assn. Mgmt. Soc. (treas. 1979-80, award of merit), Am. Soc. Assn. Execs. (bd. dirs. 1981-84, vice chmn. 1985, chmn.-elect 1994, chmn. 1995-96, bd. dirs. found. 1990-94, vice chmn. found. 1991-92, chmn. found. 1992-93, Key award 1984, chmn. Assn. Advance Am. 1993-94), Oberlin Area C. of C. (pres. 1987-90, bd. dirs. 1987-90), Greater Cleve. Soc. Assn. Execs. (bd. dirs. 2003—). Republican. Roman Catholic. Office: Marble Inst Am 28901 Clemens Rd Ste 100 Cleveland OH 44145 Office Phone: 440-250-9222. Business E-Mail: gdistelhorst@marble-institute.com. *Leadership isn't about having followers, but rather about providing an inspiring vision of a better future for your associates & colleagues.*

DI SUVERO, MARK, sculptor; b. Shanghai, Sept. 18, 1933; s. Vittorio and Matilde (Millo) Di Suvero. BA, U. Calif., Berkeley, 1957. Co-founder Park Place Gallery, N.Y.C., 1963. Founder Socrates Sculpture Pk., N.Y.C., 1986; one-person shows include Green Gallery, N.Y., 1960, Park Place Gallery, N.Y., 1966, Van Abbemuseum, Eindhoven, Netherlands, 1972, City of Chalon-sur-Saone, France, 1974, Jardin des Tuileries, Paris, 1975, Whitney Mus., N.Y.C., 1975, Oil and Steel Gallery, N.Y.C., 1983, Storm King Art Ctr., 1985, 95, 96, Wurttembergischer Kunstverein, Stuttgart, 1988, City of Valence, France, 1990, Musee d'Art Moderne et d'Art Contemporain de Nice, France, 1991, City of Chalon/Saône, France, 1992, IVAM Centre Julio Gonzalez, Valencia, Spain, 1994, XLVI Venice Biennial, 1995, City of Paris, 1997, Hiroshima Mus. Contemporary Art, 1998, Gagosian Gallery, N.Y.C., 2001, others; represented in permanent collections, Art Inst. Chgo., Whitney Mus., N.Y.C., Museum of Modern Art, N.Y.C., Nat. Gallery Art, Washington, Hirshhorn Mus. and Sculpture Garden, Washington, Mus. of Contemporary Art, L.A., others. Recipient Art Inst. Chgo. award, 1963, Creative Arts award, Brandeis U., 1969, Skowhegan Sch. award, 1974, Heinz Award in the Arts and Humanities, 2005; grantee Longview Found., Walter K. Gutman Found. Business E-Mail: disuvero@spacetimecc.com.*

DITELBERG, DENNIS LEONARD, lawyer; b. Chelsea, Mass., June 2, 1932; s. Richard and Dorothy (Berkovitz) D.; m. Frances Dion, Sept. 3, 1961 (dec. Aug. 1995); children: Joshua Lee, Jeremy Stuart, Julia Dion; m. Bonnie Sashin, Mar. 25, 2000. BFA, Mass. Coll. Art, 1954; JD, Boston Coll., 1961. Bar: Mass. 1961, U.S. Dist. Ct. Mass. 1962, U.S. Supreme Ct. 1969, U.S. Ct. Appeals (1st cir.) 1976, U.S. Tax Ct. 1976, U.S. Ct. Internat. Trade 1981. Assoc. Poitrast, Carney and Moore, Boston, 1961-66; ptnr. Callas, Felopulos and Ditelberg LLP, Boston, 1967—; asst. atty. gen., chief contracts div. Mass. Atty. Gen., Boston, 1972-75. Mem. bd. editors Boston Coll. Comml. and Indsl. Law Rev. and Ann. Survey of Mass. Law Rev., 1960-61. Chmn. Newton (Mass.) Conservation Commn., 1970-91; pres. Norumbega coun. Boy Scouts Am., 1984-86, N.E. area one v.p. Boy Scouts Am., 1993—. Capt. inf. U.S. Army, 1954-57. Fellow: Mass. Bar Found. (life); mem.: Boston Bar Assn. Avocations: art, camping, youth activities.

DITKA, MICHAEL KELLER, former professional football coach; b. Carnegie, Pa., Oct. 18, 1939; s. Mike and Charlotte (Keller) D.; m. Margery Ditka, Jan. 21, 1961 (div. 1973); children: Michael, Mark, Megan, Matthew; m. Diana S. Ditka, July 8, 1977. Student, U. Pitts. Profl. football player Chgo. Bears, 1961-66, Phila. Eagles, 1967-68, Dallas Cowboys, 1969-72, asst. coach, 1973-81; head coach Chgo. Bears, 1982-93; coach Chgo. Bears Superbowl Championship Team, 1985; owner Ditka's Restaurant, Chgo., 1986—; head coach New Orleans Saints, 1997-99. Actor: (films) Up, Michigan!, 2001, Kicking & Screaming, 2005; (TV films) Maximum Surge Movie, 2003; host (TV series) Mike Ditka Show, 1982, guest appearances L.A. Law, 1990, Cheers, 1993, Coach, 1996, 3rd Rock from the Sun, 1996, 1997, Becker, 2001, According to Jim, 2002, ESPN Sports Century, 2001—05. Named Rookie of Yr., NFL, 1961; named to Pro Bowl, 1962-66; inducted into Hall of Fame, 1988; named coach of the year, NFL, 1988. Roman Catholic.*

DITKOFF, EDWARD CHARLES, reproductive endocrinologist; b. N.Y.C., Jan. 12, 1960; s. Jerome Lionel and Adele Helen (Liebermann) D.; m. Patricia Marie Hansen, May 1, 1988; children: Rebecca, Erica. BS in Biology, Emory U., 1981; MD, Chgo. Med. Sch., 1985. Intern. ObGyn. Brookdale Med. Ctr., Bklyn., 1985-86; resident ObGyn. Albany Med. Ctr., N.Y.C., 1986-87; resident Washington Med. Ctr., 1987-90; fellow reproductive endocrinology U. So. Calif., L.A., 1990-92; asst. prof., med. dir. divsn. asst. reproduction Columbia U., N.Y.C., 1992-98; physician Advanced Fertility Svcs., N.Y.C., 1998—. Asst. instr. George Washington Med. Sch., 1987-90. Contbr. articles to profl. jours. Fellow Am. Coll. ObGyn.; mem. Am. Soc. Reproductive Medicine, Soc. Laproscopic Surgeons, Endocrine Soc. Office: 1625 Third Ave New York NY 10128 also: 30 Davis Ave White Plains NY 10605 E-mail: reproed@aol.com.

DITMAS, BRUCE, musician, composer, music producer; b. Atlantic City, Dec. 12, 1946; s. Abraham and Maude Ditmas; m. Patricia Burgess, June 20, 1987. Student in summer jazz program, Ind. U., 1962—63, Mich. State U., 1963. Drummer, composer: record Yellow, What If, Aeray Dust, Spontaneous Combustion, drummer: Fountainbleu Hotel Show Band, 1963—65, Ira Sullivan Quartet, 1964—65, Judy Garland, 1965—67, Barbara Streisand's TV spl. The Belle of 14th Street, 1967, Central Park Concert, 1967, Latin Quarter Show Band, 1967—68, Merv Griffin Show Studio Band, 1967—69, various jingles many clients, 1967—2005, Copacabana Show Band, 1968—69, NY Neophonic Orch., 1969—70, Zoot Sims Band of the Century, 1970—71, Pit Orch., 1970—71, Johnny Coles Band, 1971, Jazz Rock Band, 1971—72, Gil Evans Orch., 1971—85, various famous jazz musicians, 1971—2005, Steve Kuhn Quartet, 1972—73, Stan Getz Quartet, 1973, Paul Bley Quartet, 1973—75, Enrico Rava Band, European Tours, 1975—86, composer, drummer, performer: Live Concert Drums and Electronics; composer: House of Candles Theatre Group, 1987—89, Toon Theatre, 1989—90, (theme song) Atlantic 10 Basketball Conf., 1993—94, (jazz music package) Bravo TV Network, 1995; composer, prodr.: Insync Prodn., 1995—2005, Charles Morrow Assocs., 1999—2000, nickelodeon.com, CD original score The Day The Rabbi Disappeared, record Bootleg Milkshake, Industry of Cool, vol. 2, Still Cool, prodr., orchestrator: Operas Reflections of the Watermoon, orchestrator: Operas The Dream of the Four Directions, 1992, musician, featured soloist: films Oggetti Smaretti/Bernardo Bertolucci, creative dir., prodr., composer: Pomposello Prodns., 1996—98; prodr.: various singers and bands, 2001—05. Avocation: sports car racing. Home: 2 Pleasant Grove Rd Schooleys Mountain NJ 07870 Office: Insync Prodns Box 51 Schooleys Mountain NJ 07870 Personal E-mail: bd1212@aol.com.

DI TRAPANI, MARCIA A., health facility administrator, community health nurse, educator; b. Madison, Wis., Mar. 7, 1938; d. Alfred H. and Margaret E. Dvorak; m. Anthony R. Di Trapani, Nov. 12, 1960; children: Anthony R. Di Trapani, Jr., Laura M. Clairmont, Nancy A. Erickson. BSN, U. of Wis., 1960; MA, George Mason U., 1994. RN Va., 1974, Wash., DC, 2000. Staff nurse U. Hosps., Madison, Wis., 1960, D.C. Dept. Pub. Health, Washington, 1961—62, Columbia Hosp. for Women, Washington, 1966—68; case mgr. Internat. Rehab. Assn., Inc., Towson, Md., 1976—77; pub. health nurse Arlington (Va.) County Health Dept., 1978—83, Fairfax (Va.) County Health Dept., 1983—90, nursing supr., 1990—95; cmty. health cons. No. Va. C.C., Annandale, Va., 1995—97; exec. v.p., sec., treas. T&MCorp, Reston, Va., 1997—. Profl. practice adv. bd. mem. Va. State Bd. of Nursing, Richmond, Va., 1992—95; nurses leadership planning group mem. Child Devel. Resources, Norge, Va., 1998—2001; instr. George Mason U., Fairfax, 1998—2004. Contbr. articles to profl. jours. Sec. Marjorie F. Hughes Fund for Children, Arlington, Va., 1996—; family assistance coord. Herndon/Reston (Va.) FISH, Inc., 2003; mem. Giving Cir. of Hope, 2004—. Mem.: DAR, ANA (del. to nat. conv. 2001—03), Coalition Va. Nurses, Va. Nurses Assn. (various positions 1994—2003, pres. dist. 8 2001—03, named one of 99 Outstanding Nurses in Va. 1999, Dist 8 Outstanding Nurse award in Nursing Edn. 2000), Va. Pub. Health Assn., Sigma Theta Tau (corr. sec., eta alpha 2002—). Avocations: travel, genealogy, knitting, geocaching. Home: 11500 Drop Forge Lane Reston VA 20191

D'ITRI, FRANK MICHAEL, environmental research chemist; b. Flint, Mich., Apr. 25, 1933; s. Dominic and Angelina D'Itri; m. Patricia Ann Ward, Sept. 10, 1955; children: Michael Payne, Angela Kathryn, Patricia Ann, Julie Lynn. BS in Zoology, Mich. State U., 1955, MS in Analytical Chemistry, 1966, PhD, 1968. Lab. technician Dow Industry Service Labs., Midland, Mich., 1960-62; research asst. dept. chemistry Mich. State U., East Lansing, 1963-68, asst. prof. dept. fisheries and wildlife, 1968-72, assoc. prof. dept. fisheries and wildlife, 1973-76, prof. dept. fisheries and wildlife, 1977—; assoc. dir. Inst. Water Rsch., 1987—; asst. dir. Mich. Agrl. Exptl. Sta., 1996—2000; ind. studies and programs, 2004—. Cons. U.S. Dept. Energy, Washington, 1983-85, EEC, UN, Geneva, 1982—; vis. prof. U. Bahia, Brazil, 1978, Tokyo U. Agr., 1980, 84-85, 87, 94, 2000, 01; mem. adv. bd. Lewis Pubs., Inc., Springer-Verlag. Author: The Environmental Mercury Problem, 1972, (with P.A. D'Itri) Mercury Contamination: A Human Tragedy, 1977, (with A.W. Andren, R.A. Doherty, J.M. Wood), Assessment of Mercury in the Environment, 1978, Acid Precipitation, 1982, Artificial Reefs, 1985; editor (with J. Aguirre M., M. Athie L.), Municipal Wastewater in Agriculture, 1981, Land Treatment of Municipal Wastewater: Vegetation Selection and Management, 1982, Acid Precipitation: Effects on Ecological Systems, 1982, (with M.A. Kamrin) PCBs: Human and Environmental Hazards, 1983, Artificial Reefs: Marine and Freshwater Applications, 1985, A System Approach to Conservation Tillage, 1985, (with H.H. Prince) Coastal Wetlands, 1985; (with L.G. Wolfson) Rural Groundwater Contamination, 1987, Chemical Deicers And The Environment, 1992, (with H.W. Belcher) Subirrigation and Controlled Drainage, 1995, Zebra Mussels and Aquatic Nuisance Species, 1997, (with Y. Itakura) Integrated Environmental Management, 1999; contbr. numerous articles to profl. jours. Mem. critical materials adv. subcom. Mich. Water Resources Commns. Mich. Dept. Natural Resources, 1971-79, mem. solid waste com., 1971-79; mem. subcom. Mich. State U. Waste Control Authority Chem. Waste, 1971—; mem. tech. adv. com. Great Lakes Protection fund tech. adv. com., 1990-93; mem. Great Lakes Commn., 1992—; mem. subirrigation steering com. Mich. Soil Conservation Svc., 1986—; mem. fluctuating lake levels com. Internat. Joint Commn., 1992-93; mem. internat. rsch. group mercury pollution in Amazon, Brazil, 1992—. NIH summer fellow, 1964-67, Socony-Mobil fellow Mich. State U., 1967-68, Japan Soc. Promotion Sci. fellow, 1980; Rockefeller Found. Bellagio Resident scholar, 1972, 75. Mem. Am. Chem. Soc., Am. Soc. Limnology and Oceanography, Assn. Analytical Chemists, Water Pollution Research Soc., Midwest Univs. Analytical Chemists Conf., Mich. Acad. Sci., Arts and Letters, Sigma Xi, Setac. Office: Mich State U 4A Internat Ctr East Lansing MI 48824-1035 Office Phone: 517-355-2350. Business E-Mail: ditri@msu.edu.

DITROLIO, JOSEPH, controller; BS in Acctg., St. Joseph's U. CPA. With Peat Marwick, Phila., PricewaterhouseCoopers, Comcast, Phila., 1992—, former asst. corp. contr., v.p., corp. contr., 2000—. Mem.: AICPA, Pa. Inst. CPAs. Office: Comcast 1500 Market ST Philadelphia PA 19102

DITTENHAFER, BRIAN DOUGLAS, banker, economist; b. York, Pa., Aug. 15, 1942; s. Nathaniel Webster and Evelyn Romaine (Myers) D.; m. Miriam Marcy, Aug. 22, 1964; 1 child. BA, Ursinus Coll., 1964; MA, Temple U., 1966, postgrad., 1967—71. Pers. asst. Philco Corp., Phila., 1965-66; teaching asst. Temple U., Phila., 1966-67, rsch. assoc., 1968-69; bus. economist Fed. Res. Bank of Atlanta, 1971-76; v.p., chief economist Fed. Home Loan Bank of N.Y., N.Y.C., 1976-79, sr. v.p., CFO, 1979-80, exec. v.p., 1980-85, pres., 1985-92, Collective Fed. Savs. Bank, 1992-94, Collective Bancorp, 1992-94; chmn. MBD Mgmt. Co., 1994—. Vice chmn. Fin. Instns. Thrift Plan, 1991-92, chmn., 1992; trustee Fin. Instns. Retirement Fund, 1985-92, vice chmn., 1991, chmn., 1992; bd. dirs. Investors Savs. Bank, 1997—. Bd. dirs. Social Compact, 1990-99, sec., 1995-99; mem. FNMA Found. Adv. Group, 1994; deacon Ctrl. Presbyn. Ch., 1981-84; bd. dirs. N.Y. Coun. Econ. Edn., 1983-89; chmn. Resolution Funding Corp., 1989-92. Temple U. fellow, G.E. Found. fellow Temple U. Mem. Nat. Assn. Bus. Economists, Forecaster's Club N.Y. (sec.-treas. 1982-84), Suntree Country Club (dir., treas. 2000-03), Omicron Delta Epsilon.

DITTER, J. WILLIAM, JR., federal judge; b. Phila., Oct. 19, 1921; BA, Ursinus Coll., 1943, LL.D., 1970; LL.B., U. Pa., 1948. Bar: Pa. 1949. Clk. Ct. Common Pleas, Montgomery County, Pa., 1948-51; asst. dist. atty. Montgomery County, 1951, 53-55; 1st asst. dist. atty., 1956-60; mem. firm Ditter and Jenkins and predecessor firm, Ambler, Pa., 1953-63; judge Ct. Common Pleas, Montgomery County, 1964-70, U.S. Dist. Ct. Ea. Dist. Pa., Phila., 1970-86, sr. judge, 1986—; lectr. Villanova U. Past pres. bd. trustees Calvary Methodist Ch.; charter pres. Ambler Jaycees, 1954-55; bd. dirs. Riverview Osteo. Hosp., Norristown, Pa., 1964-71; bd. consulters Villanova U. Sch. Law, 1977—. Served to capt. USNR, 1943-68. Recipient Disting. Alumnus award Ambler High Sch., 1986; named Alumnus of Yr., Ursinus Coll., 1980. Mem. Am., Fed., Pa., Montgomery County bar assns., Hist. Soc. U.S. Dist. Ct. Eastern Dist. Pa. (incorporator, bd. dirs.) Office: US Dist Ct 3040 601 Market St Philadelphia PA 19106-1713

DITTMAN, ROBERT ALLAN, retired music educator; b. Springfield, Ohio, Aug. 25, 1933; s. Charles Thomas Dittman and Helen Louise Watkins; m. Mina Marie Gilliland, Dec. 20, 1959; children: James Michael, Lee Patrick, Daniel Dale, Gary Allan. MusB, Sherwood Music Sch., 1955; MEd, Miami U., Oxford, Ohio, 1956. Cert. tchr. Ohio State Bd. Edn., Fla. State Bd. Edn. Band dir. Kennard Jr. H.S., Cleve., 1956—57; vocal dir. Manatee H.S., Bradenton, Fla., 1957—61, West Carrollton H.S., Ohio, 1961—70, Palmetto H.S., Fla., 1970—87, Lincoln Mid. Sch., Palmetto, 1987—95; ret., 1995. Composer: Fla. Vocal Assn. Sight Reading Music, 1977—2005, Christmas Cantata, 1991, 1992. Lutheran. Avocation: antiques. Home: 1141 Beale Court Dr Blairsville GA 30512 Office Phone: 706-745-6209. E-mail: rmdittman@alltel.net.

DITTMAR, DAWN MARIE, lawyer; b. Aberdeen, Md., Dec. 13, 1955; d. Robert William Grady and Diane Elizabeth (Canepi) Katz; m. Walter BA in Polit. Sci., SUNY, 1982; JD, U. Bridgeport, 1985. Rsch. asst. Tuv Rheinland, Mt. Kisco, N.Y., 1982; clk. Danbury (Conn.) Superior Ct, 1985-86; pvt. practice Ridgefield, Conn., 1986-98, Brookfield, Conn., 1998—. Mem. Conn. Bar Assn. Republican. Roman Catholic. Avocations: ballet, yoga, reading, theater. Office: 60 Old New Milford Rd Brookfield CT 06804-2430 Home: 168 W Palmer Ave West Long Branch NJ 07764-1231

DITTMER, FRANCES R., curator; m. Thomas Henry Dittmer (div.). Former curator Refco Collection; pvt. cons.; curator of modern & contemporary art Art Inst. Chgo. Bd. dir. Drawing Ctr. Inc., Whitney Mus. Am. Art, NYC; bd. trustees Menil Collection, Dia Art Found., Art Inst. Chgo., 1988—. Named one of Top 200 collectors, ARTnews Mag., 2004. Avocation: Collector of Contemporary Art. Mailing: Art Inst Chicago 111 S Michiagn Ave Chicago IL 60603-6110*

DITTMER, JOHN AVERY, history professor; b. Seymour, Ind., Oct. 30, 1939; s. J. Avery and Melba Roberta (Ahlbrand) D.; m. Ellen Ann Tobey, June 3, 1961; children: Julia Susan, John David. BS in Edn., Ind. U., 1961, MA in History, 1964, PhD in History, 1971. Asst. prof. Tougaloo (Miss.) Coll., 1967-68, acad. dean, 1968-70, assoc. prof., 1971-79; assoc. prof. history DePauw U., Greencastle, Ind., 1985-92, prof., 1993—2004, prof. emeritus, 2004—. Vis. assoc. prof. Brown U., Providence, 1979-80, 81-82, 83-84, MIT, Cambridge, 1982-84; cons. NEH, Washington, 1980-83, PBS Series, Eyes on the Prize, Boston, 1986. Author: Black Georgia in the Progressive Era, 1900-1920, 1977, Local People: The Struggle for Civil Rights in Mississippi, 1994 (Lillian Smith book award, 1994, Bancroft prize Columbia U. 1995); contbr. articles to profl. jours. Younger Humanist fellow NEH, 1973-74, fellowship-in-residence NEH, Vanderbilt U., 1976-77, Rockefeller Found., 1980-81, Am. Coun. Learned Socs., 1983-84, Ctr. for Study of Civil Rights, U. Va., 1988-89, NEH, 2000-01, Nat. Humanities Ctr., 2001-01. Mem. Orgn. of Am. Historians (Frederick Jackson Turner award finalist 1972), So. Hist. Assn., Am. Hist. Assn. Avocations: tennis, golf, jazz music. Home: 230 Westwood Rd Fillmore IN 46128-9621 Office: DePauw U Dept History Greencastle IN 46135 Office Phone: 765-658-4590. Business E-Mail: rip@depauw.edu.

DITTON, ROBERT BROWNING, education educator; b. New York, NY, Jan. 22, 1943; s. Robert Edward and Flora Marie Ditton; m. Wheeler Penelope Jane; children: Allison, Megan. BS, State U. of NY Coll. at Cortland, 1964; MS, U. Ill., 1966, PhD, 1969. Asst. prof. U. Wis. at Green Bay, 1969—73; assoc. prof. Tex. A&M U., 1974—80, prof., 1980—. Mem. Ocean Studies Bd. Nat. Rsch. Coun., Washington, 2003—05; mem. bd. dirs. Gulf and Caribbean, Miami, Fla., 1997—. Mem.: Am. Fisheries Soc., Acad. Leisure Sci. Home: 1807 Lamar Dr College Station TX 77840

DITTRICH, STEVEN MICHAEL, lawyer; b. Winona, Minn., Apr. 23, 1969; s. Daniel Willard Dittrich and Kathy Mary Chafos; m. Andrea Turner; 1 stepchild, Jasmine Chantel Bush. BA, Gustavus Adolphus Coll., 1991; JD, U. Ark., 1999. Bar: Minn. 1999. Assoc. atty. Lawrence Downing & Assocs., Rochester, Minn., 1999—. Home: 4107 4 Pl NW Rochester MN 55901 Office: Lawrence Downing and Assocs 330 Wells Fargo Ctr 21 1st Ave SW Rochester MN 55902 Office Phone: 507-288-8432.

DITTRICK, WILLIAM G., lawyer; b. 1947; BA in Bus. Adminstrn., Univ. Neb., 1969, JD, 1974. Law clerk Hon. Warren K. Urbom, Chief US Dist. Judge, 1974—76; mem. Baird, Holm, McEachen, Pedersen, Hamann & Strasheim LLP, 1976—. Exec. ed.: editorial bd. Neb. Law Review, 1973—74. Past pres., bd. dirs. Big Brothers/Big Sisters, Midlands. Fellow: Am. Coll. of Trial Lawyers; mem.: ABA, Robert M. Spire Inns of Ct., Neb. State Bar Assn. (pres.-elect 2005). Office: Baird Holm McEachen Pedersen Hamann & Strasheim LLP 1500 Woodmen Tower Omaha NE 68102

DI TURI, CHRISTOPHER, dentist, educator; b. N.Y.C., Dec. 21, 1961; s. Dominic and C. Paula (DiRaffaele) Di T. BS in Biochemistry, SUNY, Stony Brook, 1983; DDS, NYU, 1987; MS in Combined Prosthodontics, N.J. Dental Sch., 1990. Resident Richmond Meml. Hosp., S.I., 1987-88; prof. prosthodontics and biomaterial sci., rschr. U. Medicine Dentistry of N.J., Newark, 1990—; pvt. practice Fair Haven, N.J., 1994—; dir. implant residency Monmouth Med. Ctr. Bd. dirs. Columbus Hosp., 2000-. Editor: Introduction to the Dental Industry, 1992; contbr. articles to profl. jours. Recipient scholarship Richmond County Dental Soc., NYU, 1983-84. Mem. ADA, Am. Coll. Prosthodontics (bd. dirs., pres. N.J. sect. 1997-), Acad. Osseointegration, Northeast Gnathological Soc., N.J. Acad. Medicine, Boys Town Italy (N.Y.C.), Columbus Citizens Found., Theatre Devel. Found., Nat. Italian Am. Found., Coalition Italo-Am. Orgns., Italian Welfare League Republican. Roman Catholic. Home: 133 Hooper Ave Staten Island NY 10306-3752 Office: 600 River Rd Fair Haven NJ 07704-3221

DITZ, TOBY LEE, history educator; b. N.Y.C., May 1, 1951; d. Leo M. and Florence B. (Winkler) D.; m. Mark Edward Martin; 1 child, Rebecca. BA, Northwestern U., 1972; MA, Columbia U., 1975, PhD, 1982. Asst. prof. history Johns Hopkins U., Balt., 1982-87, assoc. prof., 1987—. Author: Property and Kinship: Inheritance in Early Connecticut, 1750-1820, 1986. Mem. Am. Hist. Assn., Berkshire Conf. Women Historians. Office: Johns Hopkins U Dept History Baltimore MD 21218

DIVAC, VLADE, professional basketball player; b. Serbia-Montenegro, Feb. 3, 1968; m. Ann Divac; 1 adopted child. Profl. basketball player in Yugoslavia, Sloga, Partizan; profl. basketball player L.A. Lakers, 1989—96, 2004—, Charlotte Hornets, 1996—98, Sacramento Kings, 1998—2004. Founder Divac Found. Named to, NBA All-Rookie First Team, 1990, NBA All-Star game, 2001. Achievements include won Olympic Silver medal with Team Yugoslavia, 1988, 1996; appeared in movies Space Jam, Eddie, Juwanna Mann and TV series Driving me Crazy. Office: c/o Los Angeles Lakers 555 N Nash St El Segundo CA 90245

DIVENERE, ANTHONY JOSEPH, lawyer; b. Bari, Italy, June 20, 1941; s. Joseph and Donna (Montini) DiV.; m. Sylvia Kathleen Scarnati, June 19, 1965; children: Anthony, Diana, John. AB, John Carroll U., 1964; JD, Ohio State U., 1967. BAr: Ohio 1967. Atty. in charge Cleve. Legal Aid Soc., 1967-70; prin., v.p. Burke Haber & Berick Co., L.P.A., Cleve., 1971; shareholder McDonald, Hopkins, Burke & Haber. Recipient Claude E. Clark award Cleve. Legal Aid. Soc., 1968, Cmty. Svc. aard North Olmsted Jaycees, 1972. Mem. ABA, Ohio Bar Assn., Cleve. Bar Assn. (Appreciation award 1979-80), Cleve. Assn. Trial Attys. (pres. 1979-80), Def. Rsch. Inst., Vermilion Yacht Club. Avocations: sailing, marathon running, squash, opera.

Home: 310 Rye Gate St Cleveland OH 44140-1272 Office: McDonald Hopkins Co 600 Superior Ave Ste 2100 Cleveland OH 44114 Business E-Mail: adivenere@mcdonaldhopkins.com.

DIVER, COLIN S., academic administrator, educator; b. 1943; BA, Amherst Coll., 1965; LLB, Harvard U., 1968; MA, U. Pa., 1989; LLD, Amherst Coll., 1990. Bar: Mass. 1968. Spl. counsel Office of the Mayor, Boston, 1968-71; asst. sec. consumer affairs Exec. Office Consumer Affairs, Boston, 1971-72; undersec. adminstrn. Exec. Office Adminstrn. and Fin., Boston, 1972-74; assoc. prof. Boston U., 1975-81, prof., 1981-89, from assoc. dean to dean, 1985-89; dean, Bernard G. Segal prof. U. Pa., Phila., 1989—99, Charles A. Heinbold, Jr., prof., 1999—2002; pres. Reed Coll., Portland, Oreg., 2002—. Cons. Adminstrv. Conf. of U.S., 1980-88. Chmn. Mass. State Ethics Com., 1983-89; mem. adv. com. on enforcement policy NRC, 1984-85. Office: Reed Coll 3203 SE Woodstock Blvd Portland OR 97202 E-mail: presidentsoffice@reed.edu.*

DI VESTA, FRANCIS JOHN, psychologist, educator; b. Bridgeport, Conn., Mar. 8, 1920; s. Patrick and Marion (Lepore) Di V.; children: Carol Lynn, Laurence Aldrich. BS, U. Conn., 1942; MS, Cornell U., 1945, PhD, 1948. Asst. prof. edn. Bucknell U., 1948-49; assoc. program dir. Human Resources Research Ctr. (USAF), 1949-54; assoc. prof. to prof. Syracuse U., 1954-64; prof. edn. and psychology Pa. State U., University Park, 1964—; cons. to govt. and industry; lectr. Author: (with G.G. Thompson) Educational Psychology, 1970, Language, Learning and Cognitive Processes, 1974; editorial: (with G.G. Thompson and J. Horrocks) Social Development and Personality, 1971; bd. cons. editors: Jour. Ednl. Psychology, 1966—; assoc. editor Ednl. and Communication Tech. Jour., 1975—, Research and Devel. in Edn., 1978-85, Interam. Jour. Psychology, 1982—; contbr. articles to profl. and tech. jours. Fellow Am. Psychol. Assn. (exec. com. 1975-78), AAAS; mem. Am. Ednl. Research Assn., Soc. Research in Child Devel., Psychonomic Soc., Sigma Xi Office: Pa State U 314 Cedar Bldg University Park PA 16802-3110

DIVINE, ROBERT ALEXANDER, history professor; b. Bklyn., May 10, 1929; s. Walter E. and Emily (Mable) D.; m. Barbara C. Renick, Aug. 6, 1955 (dec.); children: J. Douglas, Elisabeth T., Richard L., Kirk M.; m. Darlene S. Harris, June 1, 1996 (dec.). BA, Yale U., 1951, MA, 1952, PhD, 1954. Instr. U. Tex., Austin, 1954-57, asst. prof., 1957-61, assoc. prof., 1961-63, prof. history, 1963-96, chmn. dept. history, 1963-68, Piper prof., 1972, George W. Littlefield prof. Am. history, 1981-96, prof. emeritus, 1996—. Fellow Center for Advanced Study in Behavioral Scis. Stanford, Calif., 1962-63; Albert Shaw lectr. in diplomatic history, Johns Hopkins, 1968 Author: American Immigration Policy, 1924-52, 1957, The Illusion of Neutrality, 1962, The Reluctant Belligerent, 1965, Second Chance, 1967, Roosevelt and World War II, 1969, Foreign Policy and U.S. Presidential Elections, 1940-60, 2 vols., 1974, Since 1945: Politics and Diplomacy in Recent American History, 1975, Blowing on the Wind, 1978, Eisenhower and the Cold War, 1981, The Sputnik Challenge, 1993, Perpetual War for Perpetual Peace, 2000; co-author: America Past and Present, 1984, 7th edit., 2005. Mem. Orgn. Am. Historians, Soc. for Historians of Am. Fgn. Rels. Methodist. Home: 10617 Sans Souci Pl Austin TX 78759-6185 E-mail: rdivine@austin.rr.com.

DIVINEY, CRAIG DAVID, lawyer; b. Keokuk, Iowa, July 19, 1953; s. William Thomas and Ella (Michel) D.; m. Astrid Maria Kost, Oct. 6, 1975; children: Adam Thomas, Elliot Michel, Lisa Anne. BA, Augustana Coll., Rock Island, Ill., 1975; JD, U. Iowa, 1979. Bar: Minn. 1979, U.S. Dist. Ct. Minn. 1980, U.S. Ct. Appeals (8th cir.) 1984, U.S. Ct. Appeals (7th cir.) 1987, U.S. Ct. Appeals (fed. cir.) 1990. Assoc. Dorsey & Whitney, Mpls., 1979-84, ptnr., trial, intellectual property litig., 1985—, and chmn., life sci. and health care group. Adj. prof. William Mitchell Coll. Law, 1983-85; faculty Minn. Advocacy Inst., 1989—. Mem. fed. practice com. Dist. Minn., 1990-91; mem. adv. com. U.S. Dist. Ct., 1991—. Mem. ABA, Order of Coif. Office: Dorsey & Whitney 50 S 6th St Minneapolis MN 55402-1498 Office Phone: 601-340-2873. Office Fax: 612-340-2868. Business E-Mail: diviney.craig@dorsey.com.

DIVITA, JAMES J., retired social studies educator, writer, researcher; b. Chgo., Jan. 20, 1938; s. Charles V. and Theresa Rohde Divita; m. Mary Frances Beckmeyer, Aug. 22, 1964; children: Lawrence, Mary Theresa, Michael, Anne. BA, DePaul U., Chgo., 1959, AM, 1960; PhD, U. Chgo., 1972. Instr. history Marian Coll., Indpls., 1961—64, asst. prof. history, 1964—70, assoc. prof. history, 1970—76, prof. history, 1976—2003, prof. emeritus history, 2003—, chmn. dept. history and polit. sci., 1974—75, 1983—2002. Pres. Ind. Religious History Assn., Indpls., 1987—97; chmn. Am. Cath. Hist. Assn. Regional Meeting, Indpls., 1998. Author: Slaves to No One, 1981, The Italians of Indianapolis, 1984, Indianapolis Cathedral, 1986, Ethnic Settlement Patterns in Indianapolis, 1989, Rejoice and Remember, 1992, Workers' Church, 1994 (IRHA Excellence award, 1995), History of St. Christopher, Speedway, 1998, Splendor of the South Side, 2000 (IRHA Excellence award, 2001), Return to Splendor, 2003; contbr. chapters to books, articles pub. to profl. jour., encyclopedia. V.p. Italian Heritage Soc. of Ind., Indpls., 1998—2004, pres., 2004—; participant ICIP Faculty Tour. Recipient Marian Coll. Franciscan Values award, 2003, Marian Coll. Tchg. Excellence award, 1998; grantee NEH faculty study grants, 1977, 1981, 1984. Mem.: Ind. Hist. Soc. (libr. com. chmn. 1983—94), Am. Hist. Assn. (life), Indpls. Literary Club (asst. sec. 1989—92). Roman Catholic. Home: 3208 Acacia Dr Indianapolis IN 46214 Office: Marian Coll Dept History 3200 Cold Springs Rd Indianapolis IN 46222-1997

DIVITA-FROMMERT, ANGELA MARIE, music educator; b. Lewiston, NY, June 28, 1978; d. Michael Louis and Jessie Wrobel DiVita; m. Derek Frommert. B of Music Edn., SUNY, Potsdam, 2000; M of Music Edn., U. Ill., Urbana-Champaign, 2003; MSc in Ednl. Adminstrn. and Supervision, Niagara U., 2005. Cert. music tchr. K-12 Ga., music tchr. K-12 permanent N.Y., elem. tchr. pre-K-6 provisional N.Y. Freelance clarinet, woodwind tchr., 2000—; music tchr. Niagara Falls (NY) City Schs., 2000—02, 2004—, band dir., 2002—04, Cobb County Sch. Dist., Marietta, Ga., 2002—04. Instrumental adjudicator NY State Sch. Music. Wish coord. Make-A-Wish Found., Marietta, 2002—04; French horn player Cobb Wind Symphony, Marietta, 2002—04. Mem.: N.Y. State Sch. Music Assn. (woodwind judge 2005—), NY State Band Dirs. Assn., NY Sch. Music Assn. (cert. adjudicator), Music Educators Nat. Conf., Ga. Music Educator's Assn. (chair all-state auditions 2002), Kappa Delta Pi, Sigma Alpha Iota. Republican. Roman Catholic. Avocations: reading, remodeling homes. Home: 3927 Washington St Niagara Falls NY 14305

DI VITTORIO, SALVATORE, composer, conductor; b. Palermo, Italy, Oct. 22, 1967; s. Giuseppe and Caterina (Chiello) Di Vittorio. MusB, Manhattan Sch. Music, 1997; MA, Columbia U., 2000; postgrad. certificate, Rome Workshop for Young Condrs., 2003; apprenticeship, Piero Bellugi, 2003. Dir. music dept. Loyola Sch., N.Y.C., 2002—. Composer/asst. condr. Accademia Musicale Siciliana, Florence Symphonietta Chamber Ensemble of Rome, 1998; apprenticeship with P. Bellugi, 2003; guest condr./music dir. Danbury Symphony Orch., 2004—05; judge IBLA Inst. Culture, N.Y., 2003. Composer: Sinfonia No.2 Lost Innocence, 1997—2000, Sinfonia No.1 Isolation, 1994—2000; composer: (and librettist) (opera) Romeo E Giulietta, 2003; performer (premier): N.Y. Symphony, 1997, 2003, Rome Symphony, 2003, Florence Symphony, 2002, 2003, San Jose Symphony, 2003, Perugia Symphony, 2002, Venice Symphony, 2001, Palermo Symphony, 1998, 1999, 2000, Orvieto Symphony, 1997. Finalist ASCAP awards, N.Y., 2002, 2004; grantee, Italian Inst. of Culture of N.Y., 2002. Mem.: SIAE, ASCAP (assoc. Std. awards 1999—2002), Coll. Music Soc., Am. Symphony Orch. League (assoc.), Condrs. Guild (assoc.). Roman Catholic. Office: Loyola Sch 980 Park Ave New York NY 11105 Home: 305 E 63d St Apt 4K New York NY 10021-7790 Personal E-mail: sdvittorio@yahoo.com.

DIVO, EDUARDO ALEJANDRO, engineering educator, research scientist; b. Valencia, Venezuela, Apr. 19, 1971; s. Eduardo Abraham Divo and Milagro Materan. Degree in mechanics, degree in computer engring., UNITEC, Valencia, 1990, diploma in mech. engring., 1992; MSME, U. Ctrl. Fla., 1996, PhD in Mech. Engring., 1998. Statistical Control Analyst, ITESM, Monterrey, Mex., 1993. Prof. UNITEC, Valencia, Venezuela, 1992—94; rsch. scientist U. Ctrl. Fla., Orlando, 1996—, prof., 2001—. V.p. rsch. Computational Engring. Techs., Oviedo, Fla., 1996—. Contbr. articles to profl. jours. Named valedictorian, UNITEC, 1992; Order Antonio Jose de Sucre scholar, Govt. of Venezuela, 1993. Mem.: Soc. Hispanic Profl. Engrs. (assoc.; faculty advisor U. Ctrl. Fla. chpt. 2003). Achievements include research in generalized boundary integral formulation for anisotropic-heterogeneous diffusion. Avocations: piano, soccer, golf. Office: U Ctrl Fla PO Box 162450 Orlando FL 32816-2450 Office Phone: 407-823-4753. Office Fax: 407-823-4746. Personal E-mail: edivo@mail.ucf.edu.

DIVON, MICHAEL Y., obstetrican and gynecologist; b. Cheb, Czechoslovaki, Oct. 6, 1947; s. David and Friei D.; m. Ruth Divon Barkai, Jan. 3, 1956 (div.). BS summa cum laude, Northrop Inst. Tech., 1973; MD cum laude, Technion Israel Inst., 1978. Dir. ob-gyn Albert Einstein Coll. Medicine, Bronx, N.Y., 1989-97, Lenox Hill Hosp., N.Y.C., 1997—. Maj. USAF, 1966-83. Office: 130 E 77th St Fl 2 Black Hall New York NY 10021

DIWEKAR, URMILA, engineering educator, consultant, researcher; b. Paratwada, India, Dec. 16, 1961; came to U.S., 1988; d. Murlidhar Hari and Leela Murlidhar (Bhawalkar) D.; m. Sanjay Vasudev Joag, Jan. 26, 1995. BS, Indian Inst. Tech., Mumbai, 1982, MS, 1984, PhD, 1988. Rsch. engr. computer aided design ctr. Indian Inst. Tech., Bombay, 1985-88; postdoctoral fellow Carnegie Mellon U., Pitts., 1988-91; devel. engr. Simulation Scis. Inc., Fullerton, Calif., 1990-91; rsch. asst. prof. Carnegie Mellon U., Pitts., 1991-94, rsch. assoc. prof., 1994-98, rsch. prof., 1998—. Vis. sci.-UNDP fellow Washington U., St. Louis, 1986, U. Wis., Madison, 1986; cons. Hindustan Organic Chems., India, 1984-85, Herdillia Chems., India, 1984-85, Gujarat State Fertilizer Corp., India, 1986-88, Batch Process Techs. Inc., West Lafayette, Ind., 1993—, Oak Ridge (Tenn.) Nat. Lab., 1993—, Pacific N.W. Lab., Richland, Wash., 1994—, Simulation Scis. Inc., Aurora, Colo., 1994—, Amoco Chems., Naperville, Ill., 1994—, Midwest Rsch. Inst., Kans., 1996—, Mich. Recovery Systems, 1997—; presenter nat. and internat. confs. in field; participant indsl. workshops in field. Author: Batch Distillation: Simulation, Optimal Design and Control, 1995, Ency. Environ. Analysis and Remediation, 1997; contbr. articles to profl. jours.; reviewer Indsl. and Engring. Chemistry Rsch., 1992—, Computers and Chem. Engring., 1992—, Chem. Engring. Comm., 1992—, Chem. Engring. Sci., 1993—, The Chem. Engr., 1994—, Chem. Engring. Rsch. and Design, 1996—, Carnegie Mellone U. Patents, 1992, European Symposium on Computer Aided Process Engring., 1996—. Fellow UN Devel. Program, 1986; Acad. Excellence scholar Govt. India, 1978-82; rsch. grantee Dept. of Energy, 1992-97, Ben Franklin Rsch. Ctr., 1993-94, Amoco Corp., 1995-97, Calif. Air Resources Bd., 1996-97, Faculty Rsch. Fund, 1996, NSF, 1997, EPA, 1997. Mem. AIChE (reviewer AIChE Jour. 1991—). Achievements include development of BATCH-DIST, a comprehensive package for simulation, design, optimization and optimal control of multicomponent batch distillation columns; MultiBatch DS professional multibatch distillation systems for multiple column configurations, multiple operating modes, multiple fractions and multiple products with multiple levels of models. Home: 921 Harvest Ridge Dr Wexford PA 15090-6820 Office: Carnegie Mellon U EPP Dept BH 131C Pittsburgh PA 15213

DIX, DIANA LYNN, elementary school educator, consultant; d. Janice and Darryl Baker; m. Joseph LeRoy Dix, July 14, 1984; children: Jessica, Darren. BS, No. State Coll., SD, 1984; M in Ednl. Leadership, City U., 2005. Continuing Tchg. Cert. Wash., 1988. Vision specialist Clover Pk. Sch. Dist., Lakewood, Wash., 1984—85, lang. arts, fine arts tchr., 1985—89, spl. edn. tchr., 1989—99, instrnl. facilitator, 1999—2004, elem. advisor, 2005—; tchr., leader start-up sch. 5-12 Learning Cmty., 2004—05, prin. intern, 2005—. Literacy and tech. cons. Literacy 4 All, Roy, Wash., 2000—. Sunday sch. dir. Pioneer Valley Bapt. Ch., Graham, Wash., 1999—2002. Mem.: ASCD. Office: Literacy 4 All 29317 30th Avenue East Roy WA 98580 Office Phone: 253-847-3224. Personal E-mail: literacy4all@excite.com.

DIX, RICHARD D., medical educator, virologist, researcher; s. Delmas D. and Juanita B. Dix. BS, Youngstown State U., Ohio, 1973; PhD, Baylor Coll. of Medicine, Houston, 1978; post doc., U. Calif., San Francisco, 1978—82, San Francisco Gen. Hosp., 1982—85. Asst. prof. to prof. U. of Miami Sch. of Medicine Bascom Palmer Eye Inst., Miami, Fla., 1985—99; prof. U. of Ark. for Med. Scis. Jones Eye Inst., Little Rock, 1999—2003. Dir., Walker Eye Rsch. Ctr. U. Ark. Med. Scis., Jones Eye Inst., Little Rock, 1999—2003. Grantee Individual Rsch., NIH, 1985—. Office: Jones Eye Inst UAMS 4301 West Markham St #523 Little Rock AR 72205 E-mail: drrichardd@uams.edu.

DIX, ROLLIN C(UMMING), mechanical engineering educator, consultant; b. NYC, Feb. 8, 1936; s. Omer Houston and Ona Mae (Cumming) D.; m. Elaine B. VanNest, June 18, 1960; children: Gregory, Elisabeth, Karen. BSME, Purdue U., 1957, MSME, 1958, PhD, 1963. Registered profl. engr., Ill. Asst. prof. mech. engring. Ill. Inst. Tech., Chgo., 1964-69, assoc. prof., 1969-80, prof., 1980—2004, assoc. dean for computing, 1980-96; pres. Patpending Mktg., Inc., 1996—. 1st lt. U.S. Army, 1960—61. Fellow: ASME. Achievements include patents in field. Home: 10154 S Seeley Ave Chicago IL 60643-2037 Office: Ill Inst Tech 10 W 32d St Chicago IL 60616-3729 Business E-Mail: dix@iit.edu.

DIX, SAMUEL MORMAN, industrial engineer, economist, appraiser; b. Grand Rapids, Mich., Nov. 20, 1916; s. Horace Philip and Helen (Morman) D., m. Dorothy Swanson, Jan. 1951 (dec. 1981); children: Stephen, Peter, Pamela. BA, Dartmouth, 1939, MCS, 1940; postgrad., Univ. Calif., 1941-42. Plant industrial engr. Am. Box Board Co., Buffalo, N.Y., 1940-41; staff engr. Albert Ramond & Assocs., 1946-48; asst. to chief industrial engr. Gen. Foods Corp., N.Y., Can., 1948-52; ceo S.M. Dix & Assocs., Grand Rapids, 1952-86; farmer, mfg. and mktg. cons., Belmont, Mich., 1988—. Author: Energy: A Critical Decision for the United State Economy, 1977, The Cost of Future Freedom, 1982. Energy adv. to Pres. Ford, 1974-76, Congress Subcom. Energy and Power, 1976-78. With USNR, 1941-46. Mem. N.Y. Acad. Scis., Nat. Assn. Accts. (officer 1954-56), Am. Mktg. Assn., Am. Soc. Appraisers, Indsl. Mgmt. Soc. (founder West Mich. chpt.), World Future Soc. (contbr.). Avocations: tennis, golf, camping, music, farming.

DIXIT, BALWANT NARAYAN, pharmacology and toxicology educator; b. Kerawade, India, Jan. 7, 1933; came to U.S., 1962; s. Narayan V. and Janakibai N. (Gokhale) D.; m. Vidya B. Ghanekar, Dec. 26, 1969; children: Sunil, Sanjay. BS in Chemistry and Biology, Fergusson Coll., Poona, India, 1954; BS in Chemistry with honors, U. Poona, 1955; MS in Biochemistry with honors, U.Poona, 1956; MS in Pharmacology with honors, U. Baroda, India, 1962; PhD, U. Pitts., 1965, MBA, 2001. Sr. research fellow Baroda U., 1960-61; asst. prof. pharmacology U. Pitts., 1965-68; assoc. prof., 1968-74; prof., 1974—; asst. chmn., 1969-74; acting dean, 1976-78; chmn., 1974-87; assoc. dean, 1974-84; dir. Ctr. for the Performing Arts of India, 1992—. Recipient Disting. Alumnus award U. Pitts. Sch. Pharmacy, 1982; fellow Internat. Union Physiological Scis., 1962 Mem. Am. Soc. Pharmacology and Explt. Therapeutics, Soc. Neurosci., Internat. Soc. Xenobiotic Metabolism Home: 608 Ravencrest Rd Pittsburgh PA 15215-1120 Office: U Pitts 559 Salk Hall Pittsburgh PA 15261-1905 Fax: (412) 648-8475. E-mail: bdixit@pitt.edu.

DIXIT, SANJAY, cardiologist, researcher; b. Jabalpur, Madhya Pradesh, India, Feb. 27, 1966; s. Shakun and Suman Shankar Dixit; m. Pragati Shukla, Apr. 22, 1996; children: Sanjana, Pranav. MBBS, Moti Lal Nehru Med. Coll., Allahabad, U.P., India, 1983—88, MD, 1989—92. Cardiovascular Disease Am. Bd. of Internal Medicine, diplomate Am. Bd. Internal Medicine. Instr. U. of Pa. Sch. of Medicine, Phila., 2002—03, asst. prof., 2003—. Dir., electrophysiology laboratories Veterans Affairs Med. Ctr., Phila., 2002—04. Author: (cardiovascular rsch. presentation) Mechanisms Underlying Sustained Pulmonary Vein Firing. Tech. com. mem. Nat. Pacemaker Rev. Com. for all V.A.M.C Hospitals. Recipient Career Devel. Award in Arrhythmias, Am. Coll. of Cardiology, 2004, David Haack Meml. award, Astra Zeneca, 2002, Post Grad. Med. award, Pfizer, 1999, D.B. Chandra Gold medal, 1989, Kamla Nehru Gold medal, 1989, Jadubir Singh Gold medal, 1989; Scientist Devel. grant, Am. Heart Assn., 1999. Mem.: Heart Rhythm Soc., Assn. of Am. Physicians of Indian Origin, Am. Coll. of Cardiology, Alpha Omega Alpha Soc. Achievements include research in mechanisms underlying initiation and maintenance of atrial fibrillation; developing criteria for identifying sites of origin of outflow tract tachycardias; identifying patterns of activation for localizing triggers of atrial fibrillation; implications of lesion distribution during pulmonic vein isolation and its impact on flow velocities in patients with atrial fibrillation. Avocations: long distance running, tennis, nature and wild life, public speaking. Office Phone: 215-615-4337. Office Fax: 215-615-4350. Personal E-mail: sanjay.dixit@uphs.upenn.edu.

DIXON, ANDREW DERART, retired academic administrator; b. Belfast, No. Ireland, Oct. 27, 1925; arrived in came to U.S., 1963, naturalized; s. Andrew and Martha (Stewart) Dixon; m. Mary Elizabeth Hernderson, Oct. 14, 1948; children: Penelope Jane, Melinda Sara, Alison Mary. Licentiate in Dental Surgery, Queens U., Belfast, 1948, B in Dental Surgery, 1949, M.Dental Surgery, 1953, BS (Nuffield Found. dental fellow), 1954, D.Sc., 1965; PhD, U. Manchester, 1958. Asst. lectr. anatomy U. Manchester, 1954—56, lectr., 1956—62, sr. lectr., 1962—63; 1vis. assoc. prof. anatomy U. Iowa, 1959—61; prof. dental sci. U. N.C., Chapel Hill, 1963—65, prof. dental sci., anatomy, 1965—69, prof. oral biology and anatomy, 1969—73, asst. dean, coordinator research Sch. Dentistry, 1966—69, dir. Dental Research Ctr., 1967—73, assoc. dean research, 1969—73; prof., dean UCLA, 1973—80, assoc. dean for faculty affairs, 1985—92, assoc. dean adminstrn., 1989—92; prof. emeritus, 1993—. Chmn. dental tng. com. Nat. Inst. Dental Rsch., 1972—73; mem. No. Ireland Partnership. Author sci. texts; contbr. articles to profl. jours.; Studies on early devel. and growth of the jaws, sex chromatin in oral smears as a diagnostic tool, nerve supply to oral mucous membrane, facial tissues and temporomandibular joint, craniofacial skeletal growth, trigeminal pathway. Grantee Fulbright Sr. Fellow award, 1959—61, Commonwealth Fund Travel fellow, 1961. Fellow: AAAS, Internat. Coll. Dentists, Am. Coll. Dentists; mem.: Pierre Fauchard Acad., Internat. Soc. Craniofacial Biology, N.Y. Acad. Sci., Am. Soc. Cell Biology, AAAS, Internat. Assn. Dental Rsch., Am. Assn. Anatomists, Anat. Soc. Gt. Britain and Ireland (sr.), Western Conf. Dental Examiners and Dental Deans, Pacific Coast Soc. Orthodontists (hon.), Inst. of Medicine, ADA, Psi Omega, Omicron Kappa Upsilon, Sigma Xi. Home: 2213 Quail Point Terr Medford OR 97504 Personal E-mail: addixRVM@charter.net.

DIXON, ARMENDIA PIERCE, school program administrator; b. Laurel, Miss., July 15, 1937; d. L.E. and Denothras (Pickens) Pierce; m. Harrison D. Dixon Jr., Aug. 28, 1971; 1 child, Harrison D. III BS in Edn., Jackson (Miss.) State U., 1960; postgrad., No. Ill. State U., 1965-66; MEd, Edinboro (Pa.) U., 1978; PhD, PhD, Kent State U., 1994. Cert. English and secondary edn., Miss. Tchr. English, libr. Laurel City Schs., 1962-67; tchr. English, dir. summer pre-sch. Erie (Pa.) Pub. Schs., 1967-72; tchr. English, drama, journalism, forensic coach Crawford Cen. Schs., Meadville, Pa., 1972-85, asst. prin., facilitator sch. improvement coun., 1985-89, coord. successful student partnership, 1988—; prin. Meadville Area Sr. High, 1993; prof. Edinboro U., Pa., 2002—. Chair acad. support svcs. Edinboro U. Pa., 2005—; exec. dir. Meadville Latch-Key Program, 1985—; coord. Urban Tchrs. Project, Kent State U., adj. asst. prof., 1989—, dir. Prospective Tchrs. Program for Phi Delta Kappa; charter mem. Results chpt., Kent State U., 1990; dir. HS edn. sch. dist. City of Erie, 1993-2001; instr. English Edinboro U. Pa Fundraiser Cystic Fibrosis Found., Pitts., 1976. 79, 81, Sickle Cell Anemia, Erie, 1978-83; pres. Martin Luther King Jr. Scholarship Fund, Inc., 1979-89; bd. dirs. ARC, Erie, 1996—, Villa Marie Coll., Erie, 1995—, Internat. Inst., 1994—; mem. adv. bd. Am. Enterprise, Erie, 1993—; mem. alumni bd. dirs. Edinboro U. Alumni, 1997—. Named to Oak Park Hall of Fame, Laurel, Miss., 2004. Mem.: NAACP (pres. Meadville chpt. 1984—), Nat. Assn. Secondary Sch. Prins., Pa. Assn. Secondary Sch. Prins., Navy Mothers, Rainbow lll, Burres, Order Eastern Star (worthy matron), Phi Delta Kappa, Alpha Kappa Alpha. Methodist. Avocations: collecting dolls, writing, gardening. Office: Crawford Ctrl Schs 847 N Main St Meadville PA 16335-2655 Home: 716 Jefferson Street Meadville PA 16335 Office Phone: 814-732-2288. Business E-Mail: adixon@edinboro.edu. E-mail: armendia1@alltel.net.

DIXON, ARTHUR RAY, retired secondary school educator, minister; b. Brownsville, Tenn., Feb. 14, 1935; s. James Arthur and Alla Jeanette (Waddell) D.; m. Kathryn Carie Smith, June 14, 1980. BS, Union U., 1962; MA, Memphis State U., 1972; postgrad., Cumberland U., 1985, Bethel Coll., 1986-87. Tchr. Hardeman County Schs., Bolivar, Tenn., 1962-63; min. Fulton (Tenn.) Bapt. Ch., 1959-69; tchr. Haywood County Schs., Brownsville, 1963-95; min. Antioch Bapt. Ch., Brownsville, 1969-80; assoc. prof. Union U., 1985—2005; ret. Adj. faculty mem. Union U., Jackson, Tenn., 1985—, St. Francis Coll., Joliet, Ill., 1987—, Cumberland U., Gallatin, Tenn., 1988-89. Author: Nutbush to Orange, 1992. Pres. Haywood County Hist. Com., Brownsville, 1974—; mem. Sister Cities Commn., Brownsville, 1988—; mem. Sel. Svc. Bd., Tenn. Served with USN, 1954-58, Korea, Guam. Recipient Burnley award Chas. A. Burnley, Inc., 1958, Man of Yr. award Brownsville Jaycees, 1979. Mem. Tenn. Edn. Assn. (del.), Haywood County Edn. Assn. (past v.p., pres.), Brownsville Exch. Club (sec.-treas. 1980-86), Brownsville Country Club, VFW (comdr. 2002—), English Speaking Union. Republican. Avocations: photography, travel, sports, geneological research, computers. Home: 915 Lee Ave Brownsville TN 38012-2819

DIXON, BARBARA BRUINEKOOL, academic administrator; b. Sparta, Wis., June 14, 1943; MusB magna cum laude in Applied Piano, Mich. State U., 1966, MusM, 1969; MusD, U. Colo., 1991. Instr. vocal music K-12 Capac (Mich.) Cmty. Schs., 1970-71; tchr. dept. music Ctrl. Mich. U., Mt. Pleasant, 1971-89, assoc. dean coll. arts and scis., 1989-95, interim dean coll. arts and scis., 1995-97; provost, v.p. acad. affairs SUNY, Geneseo, 1997—2003; pres. Truman St. U., Kirksville, Mo., 2003—. Rep. acad. senate exec. bd., acad. senate liaison com., univ. acad. planning coun. Ctrl. Mich. U., 1986-89; dir. tchr. edn. search com., 1990, 95; chair faculty load equity study com., 1988-89, undergrad. curriculum com., 1992-93, formal hearing com. for grievance under senate rules, 1988-89; mem. profl. edn. coun., 1990-95, honors coun., 1989-94, task force on distance learning, 1992-93, piano search com., 1989, 90, 92, 95, music awards policy com., 1980-81, numerous others. One-woman performances include Kirtland C.C., Roscommon, Mich., 1986, Lansing (Mich.) C.C. Artist Series, 1987, Wurlitzer Hdqs., Holly Springs, Miss., 1989, Benefit for Cmty. Arts Coun., Pigeon, Mich., 1991, Beethoven Festival, Lansing, 1993, and others; accompanying performances include Backstage Recital Series, Jasper, Ind., 1984, Bridgeport (Mich.) Voice Symposium, 1986, Manistee (Mich.) Opera House, 1986, Saginaw (Mich.) Choral Soc., 1987, Alma (Mich.) Coll. Faculty, 1995, Black Forest Music Festival (Broadway rev.), Harbor Springs, Mich., 1995, and others. Active Art Reach Mid-Mich. (gallery com. 1995-96, chamber music com. 1995-97, fund drive com. 1996-97, bd. dirs. 1995-97, treas. 1996-97), Lions Club (chair spl. events com., bd. dirs. 1995-97), United Way (liaison to campus campaign); vol. Mich. Spl. Olympics. Mem. Mich. Music Tchrs. Assn. (bd. of certification 1976-79, 84-90, 95-97, chair 1996-97, pres. local chpt. 1991-92; chmn. collegiate activities 1979-81; mem. spkrs. bur. 1974-97, adjudicators bur. 1975-97, exec. bd. 1979-81, 96; rep. Mich. Youth Arts Festival bd. 1976-81, Mich. Alliance for Arts in Edn. 1988-89), Dalcroze Soc. Am., Delta Omicron, AAUW, Am. Assn. Higher Edn., Phi Beta Delta, Pi Kappa Lambda, Phi Kappa Phi Mortar Bd. Office: Truman St U 100 E Normal St MC200 Kirksville MO 63501 E-mail: dixon@truman.edu.

DIXON, BEN HAROLD, musician, educator; b. Gaffney, SC, Dec. 25, 1934; s. O.C. Marcus Dixon and Evelyn Pinder Pryor; m. Minnie Cordelia Davis (dec. 1960); children: Dawnelle, Beneé, Velori; m. Ollie Olivia Priester, Oct. 27, 1972; children: Richard, Qadir, Kameelah. Diploma, Armstrong Tech. High, 1953. Drummer Real Jazz Sextet, Bklyn., 1997—. Musician Jacksonville (Fla.) Jazz Festival, 2005, St. Albans (NY) Jazz Festi, 2005.

Musician: (albums) numerous recordings since 1961 with Blue Note Records including most recently, Lost Sessions, 1999, Blues For Lou, 1999, Man With A Horn, 1999, Have Guitar Will Travel, 1999, Party Jazz, 1999, 32 Gems From 32 Jazz, 1999; musician, arranger, composer (albums) Say Yes To Your Best, 2000. Basketball coach Say Yes to Success Found., Bklyn., 1990—93, Crown Heights Youth Collective and Peace Acad., Bklyn., 1992—95, EKB Scouting Svc., East Orange, NJ, 1991—97. Recipient 6 Gold Records, Gold Album, Devotion to Jazz award, Greater Jamaican Devel. Corp., 2001, You Make A Difference award, Masjid Abdul Muhsi Khalifah, 2004, coaching award, Say Yes to Success Found., 1990, Crown Heights Youth Collective and Peace Acad., 1994; Basketball scholar, Ctrl. State U., Wilberforce, Ohio, 1955. Mem.: Internat. Assn. Approved Basketball Ofcls. (cert. pub. sch. athletic league ofcl.), African Am. Jazz Caucus, Internat. Assn. Jazz Educators. Democrat. Islamic.

DIXON, BILLY GENE, academic administrator, educator; b. Benton, Ill., Oct. 25, 1935; s. John and Stella (Prowell) D.; m. Judith R. McCommons, June 7, 1957; children: Valerie J., Clark A. BS, So. Ill. U., 1957, PhD, 1967; MS, Ill. Wesleyan U., 1961. Tchr. math., chmn. dept. Cahokia (Ill.) High Sch., 1960-61; tchr. Univ. Sch., So. Ill. U., Carbondale, 1961-67, chmn. dept. math., 1963-67; dir. rsch. and evaluation ESEA Title II Project Uplift, Mt. Vernon, Ill., 1967-69; coordinator profl. edn. experiences Coll. Edn. So. Ill. U., Carbondale, 1968-75, mem. faculty, coord. grad. program in secondary edn., 1975-78, departmental exec. officer curriculum and instrn., 1978—2001, asst. to dept. exec. officer for spl. projects, 2001—04, asst. to dean profl. devel. Coll. Edn. and Human Svcs., 2004—. Bd. dirs. Holmes Partnership. Pres. Benton Cmty. Pk. Dist., 1974—95; bd. dirs. United Meth. Children's Home, 2004—. Named Citizen of Yr., Benton C. of C., 1982; recipient Liberty Bell award, 1995. Mem. Ill. Assn. Tchr. Educators (pres. 1973, exec. coun. 1976-79, Disting. mem. 1984), Assn. Tchr. Educators (chmn. nat. rev. panel Disting. Program in Tchr. Edn. 1976-86, exec. bd. 1983-86, pres. 1988-89, Pres.'s award 1983, 84, 95, 99, 2004, 05, Disting. mem. 1992), Pi Mu Epsilon, Phi Kappa Phi, Phi Delta Kappa, Kappa Delta Pi. Democrat. Methodist. Home: 9793 Stuyvesant St Benton IL 62812-5916 Office: So Ill U Coll Edn Human Svcs Carbondale IL 62901-4624

DIXON, BONNIE LYNN, lawyer; b. Pitts., Aug. 21, 1955; d. Kenneth Harold and Margaret Louise Dixon. BA, U. Mich., 1978, JD, 1981. Bar: N.Y. 1982. Fgn. assoc. Nagashima & Ohno, Tokyo, 1981-84; assoc. Mudge, Rose, Guthrie, Alexander & Ferdon, N.Y.C., 1984-89, Breed, Abbott & Morgan, N.Y.C., 1989-91, Schulte, Roth & Zabel LLP, N.Y.C., 1991-94, ptnr., 1995—2001, Morgan, Lewis and Bockius LLP, Tokyo, 2002—03, Dorsey & Whitney LLP, Tokyo, 2004, Atsumi & Ptnrs., Tokyo, 2005—. Adj. prof. U. Mich. Law Sch., 1989-91; founder, pres. Roppongi Bar Assn., Tokyo, 1982-84; founder Japan Women's Profl. Network, 1996. Founder, sec. Internat. Friends Kabuki, Tokyo, 1982-84. Mem. ABA, N.Y. State Bar Assn., Phi Beta Kappa, Zeta Tau Alpha. Avocation: translating japanese kabuki and bunraku drama. Office: Atsumi & Ptnrs Fukoku Seimei Bldg 2-chome, Chiyoda=ku 8F 2-2 Uchisaiwai-cho Tokyo 100-0011 Japan Office Phone: 813-5501-2111. E-mail: b.dixon@apap.gr.jp.

DIXON, DANIEL ROBERTS, JR., retired lawyer; b. Rocky Mount, N.C., Feb. 22, 1911; s. Daniel Roberts and Ida Louise (Mason) D.; children: Daniel Roberts III, Carolyn Roy Dixon Dyess. AB, Coll. William and Mary, 1937; JD, Duke U., 1941; LLM in Taxation, NYU, 1951. CPA, N.C.; bar: N.C. Atty. Hamel, Park & Saunders, Washington, 1951-52; asst. prof. N.C. State U., Raleigh, 1954-76; pvt. practice Raleigh, 1953—. Author: Graphic Guide Fundamental Accounting; inventor building block; contbr. articles to profl. jours. Mem. Internat. Visitors Coun., Raleigh, N.C. Capt. U.S. Air Corps., 1942-46. Mem. Navy League of U.S. (judge advocate 1990-96), N.C. Triangle Coun., N.C. Bar Assn., Wake County Bar Assn., Phi Beta Kappa (pres. Wake County), Omicron Delta Epsilon. Avocations: carpentry, organist. Home: 1022 Shelley Rd Raleigh NC 27609-4332 Office: 4610 Holly Tree Rd Apt 322 Wilmington NC 28409-8555

DIXON, DAVID ADAMS, chemistry professor, researcher; b. Houston, Dec. 3, 1949; s. John Wilburn Dixon and Nancy Eddy Wilder; m. Christine Diane Powless-Dixon, June 2, 1983; children: Michell Dawes, Nicole Dawes, Jessica Dawes. BS in Chemistry, Calif. Inst. Tech., 1971; PhD in Phys. Chemistry, Harvard U., 1976. Asst. prof. chemistry dept. U. Minn., Mpls., 1977—83; mem. rsch. staff ctrl. rsch. and devel. dept. E.I. du Pont de Nemours and Co., Inc., Wilmington, Del., 1983—95, rsch. leader, 1990—95; assoc. dir. theory, modeling & simulation Environ. Molecular Sci. Lab., Pacific Northwest Nat. Lab., 1995—2002; prof. chemistry U. Ala., Tuscaloosa, 2004—, Robert Ramsay chair dept. chemistry, 2004—. Vis. assoc. chemistry Calif. Inst. Tech., Pasadena, 1977; adj. faculty chemistry dept. U. Pa., Phila., 1986; adj. prof. chemistry dept. U. Del., Newark, 1989—99, U. Utah, Salt Lake City, 1997—2003. Contbr. articles to profl. jours. Recipient ACS award for Creative Work in Fluorine Chemistry, 2003; fellow, Harvard U., 1974, 1975—77, DuPont Ctrl. Sci. and Engring. Labs., Exptl. Sta., Wilmington, 1992—95; scholar, Autonomous Met. U., Mexico City, 1997; Alfred P. Sloann Rsch. fellow, 1977—81, Battelle fellow, Pacific Northwest Nat. Lab., 2002—03, Camille and Henry Dreyfus Tchr. scholar, 1978—83. Fellow: AAAS, Am. Phys. Soc.; mem.: Mat. Assn. Am., Soc. Indsl. & Applied Math., Assn. Computing Machinery, Am. Chem. Soc. (Leo Hendrik Backeland award 1989). Avocations: art collecting, swimming, reading, surfing. Office: U Ala Chemistry Dept Shelby Hall Box 870336 Tuscaloosa AL 35487-0336

DIXON, DONNA SUE, secondary school educator; b. Beaumont, Tex., Nov. 26, 1945; d. Jackson Daries and Wanda Melvo (Brown) Beasley; m. Raymond Douglas Dixon, Aug. 27, 1966. B.A. in History, Lamar U., Beaumont, 1966, M.A. in History, 1970; M.L.S., North Tex. State U., 1979. Cert. learning resources specialist, Tex. Instr. Spanish, Bridge City (Tex.) Ind. Sch. Dist., 1968-70, Streator (Ill.) Twp. High Sch., 1970-71, Blackhorse Pike Schs., Blackwood, N.J., 1971-73; instr. social studies Trinity Heights Acad., Shreveport, La., 1973-77; learning resources specialist Irving (Tex.) Ind. Sch. Dist., 1978-81, Carrollton (Tex.)-Farmers Branch Ind. Sch. Dist., 1981; instr. social studies and sci. Ft. Bend Ind. Sch. Dist., Missouri City-Tex., 1981-82; learning resources specialist John Foster Dulles High Sch., Stafford, Tex., 1982-88; instr. Spanish Hodges Bend Mid. Sch., Houston, 1992-94, Stafford Mcpl. Sch. Dist., 1994—. Alpha Delta Kappa scholar, 1963-66; Woodrow Wilson fellowship nominee, 1966; NDEA fellow, 1966-67; recipient Audio-Visual Prodn. award Tex. Assn. Sch. Librarians, 1979; fgn. lang. grantee, 1993. Mem. ALA, Tex. Library Assn., North Tex. State U. Sch. Library Sci. Alumni Soc., Phi Kappa Phi, Beta Phi Mu, Alpha Lambda Sigma. Methodist. Author: (with Sherry DeBorde) Library Skills Handbook, Grades 6-8, 1981. Office: Stafford Mid Sch 1625 Staffordshire Stafford TX 77477 E-mail: ddixon@stafford.msd.esc4.net.

DIXON, FRANK JAMES, pathologist, educator; b. St. Paul, Mar. 9, 1920; s. Frank James and Rose Augusta (Kuhfeld) D.; m. Marion Edwards, Mar. 14, 1946; children: Janet Wynne, Frank, Michael. BS, U. Minn., 1941, MB, 1943, MD, 1944; DS (hon.), Med. Coll. Ohio, 1983; DSc (hon.), Washington U., 1992. Diplomate: Am. Bd. Pathology. Intern U.S. Naval Hosp., Great Lakes, Ill., 1943-44; research asst. dept. pathology Harvard, 1946-48; instr. dept. pathology Washington U., 1948-50, asst. prof., 1950-51; prof., chmn. dept. pathology U. Pitts. Med. Sch., 1951-60; chmn. dept. exptl. pathology Scripps Clinic and Research Found., La Jolla, Calif., 1961-74, chmn. biomed. research depts., 1970-74, dir. research inst., 1974-86, dir. emeritus, 1987—. Rsch. assoc. dept. biology U. Calif., San Diego, 1961-64, prof. in residence dept. biology, 1965-68, adj. prof. dept. pathology, 1968-96; sci. advisor NIH, Nat. Found., Helen Hay Whitney Found., St. Jude's Med. Ctr., Christ Hosp. Inst., Cin.; mem. expert adv. panel on immunology WHO; sci. adv. bd. Nat. Kidney Found.; Pahlavi lectr. Ministry of Sci. and Higher Tech., Iran, 1976; mem. adv. com. Lupus Rsch. Inst., Nat. Multiple Sclerosis Soc., Harold C. Simmons Arthritis Rsch. Ctr., Irvington House Inst. Editor: Advances in Immunology; mem. editorial bd. Excerpta Medica, Jour. Exptl. Medicine, Am. Jour. Pathology, Cellular Immunology, Kidney Hosp. Practice, Perspectives in Biology and Medicine, Jour. Exptl. Clin. Cancer Rsch., Springer Seminars in Immunopathology, Immunological Revs.; contbr. articles to profl. jours. Served with M.C. USNR, 1943-46. Recipient Theobald Smith award, 1952, Parke-Davis award in exptl. pathology, 1957, Disting. Achievement award Modern Medicine, 1961, Martin E. Rehfuss award in internal medicine, 1966, Von Pirquet medal Ann. Forum on Allergy, 1967, Bunim medal Am. Rheumatism Assn., 1968, Internat. award Gairdner Found., 1969, Mayo Soley award Western Soc. Clin. Research, 1969, Albert Lasker Basic Med. Research award, 1975, Dickson prize U. Pitts., 1975, Homer Smith award N.Y. Heart Assn., 1976, Rous-Whipple award Am. Assn. Pathologists, 1979, So. Calif. Permanente Med. Group Immunology award, 1979, Regents award U. Minn., 1985, H.P. Smith award Am. Soc. Clin. Pathologists, 1985, Gold-Headed Cane award, 1987, Distinguished Service award Lupus Found. Am., 1987, 88; Flame of Hope award Terri Gotthelf Rsch. Inst., 1987, Paul Klemperer award N.Y. Acad. Medicine, 1989, Jean Hamburger award Internat. Soc. Nephrology, 1990. Fellow Am. Coll. Allergists, Am. Acad. Allergy, Royal Coll. Pathologists (hon.); mem. NAS, N.Y. Acad. Scis. Western Assn. Physicians, Western Soc. Clin. Research, Soc. Exptl. Biology and Medicine, Transplantation Soc., AAAS, Am. Soc. Clin. Investigation, Am. Acad. Allergists, Interurban Path. Soc., Harvey Soc. (lectr. 1962), Am. Soc. Exptl. Pathology (pres. 1966), Am. Assn. Immunologists (pres. 1972), Am. Assn. for Cancer Research, Assn. Am. Physicians, Am. Acad. Arts and Scis., Am. Heart Assn., Coun. on the Kidney in Cardiovascular Disease, Fedn. Am. Scientists, Internat. Acad. Pathology, U.S. Acad. Pathologists, Can. Acad. Pathologists, Scandinavian Soc. for Immunology (hon.), Japanese Nephrology Soc. (hon.), Sigma Xi, Nu Sigma Nu, Alpha Omega Alpha. Office: Scripps Rsch Inst 10550 N Torrey Pines Rd La Jolla CA 92037-1000

DIXON, FREDERICK DAIL, architect; b. Raleigh, N.C., Dec. 18, 1942; s. Frederick Dail (dec.) and Mary Isabel (Richbourg)(dec.) D.; m. Artemis Markatos, July 7, 1968; children: Frederick Markatos. BArch, Clemson (S.C.) U., 1966; MFA in Sculpture, U. N.C., 1970. Intern Leslie Boney, Architects, Wilmington, NC, 1966—68; arch. John D. Latimer & Assocs., Durham, NC, 1968—72, Cogswell/Hausler Assocs., Chapel Hill, NC, 1972—74; founding ptnr. Designworks, Carrboro, NC, 1974—82; dir. Dixon Weinstein Architects, PA, Chapel Hill, 1982—. Instr. Boston Archtl. Ctr., 1970-71; vis. prof. arch. N.C. State U. Coll. Design, Raleigh, 1983-2004. Recipient 1st Place award (with sculptor Patrick Dougherty) Pines Portico Competition, Penland Sch. Crafts, 2005; HUD grantee. Fellow AIA, South Atlantic Region AIA (award for Excellence in Arch. 1991, 92, Merit award 1998), N.C. AIA (Merit award 1991, 92, 95, 98, Honor award 2002, Outstanding Firm award 2003). Democrat. Office: Dixon Weinstein Architects PA #25 The Courtyard 431 W Franklin St Chapel Hill NC 27516-2319 Office Phone: 919-968-8333. Business E-Mail: dail@dixonweinstein.com.

DIXON, GLENN, art critic; Former arts editor Washington City Paper; art critic Washington Post.com, 2004—. Contbr. to Artnet.com Mag. Recipient 3rd Place for Art Criticism, Assn. of Alternative Newsweeklies, 1997, Honorable Mention for Art Criticism, 2003. Office: Washington Post 1150 15th St NW Washington DC 20071*

DIXON, GORDON HENRY, biochemist, educator; b. Durban, South Africa, Mar. 25, 1930; naturalized, Can., 1951; s. Walter James and Ruth (Nightingale) Dixon; m. Sylvia W. Gillen, Nov. 20, 1954; children: Frances Anne, Walter Timothy, Christopher James, Robin Jonathan. MA with honors, U. Cambridge, Eng., 1951; PhD, U. Toronto, 1956. Rsch. assoc. U. Wash., 1954-58, U. Oxford, Eng., 1958-59; asst. prof. biochemistry U. Toronto, 1959-61, assoc. prof., 1961-63; prof. U. B.C., 1963-72; prof., chmn. dept. biochemistry U. Sussex, Eng., 1972-74; prof. med. biochemistry U. Calgary, Alta., Can., 1974-94; emeritus, 1994—; chmn. U. Calgary, Alta., Can., 1983-88. Contbr. over 250 articles to prof. jours. Flying officer Royal Can. AFR 5001 Air Intelligence, 1952—54. Decorated officer Order of Can.; recipient Steacie prize, Steacie Found., 1966, Killam Meml. prize, Can. Coun., 1991, Queens Golden Jubilee medal, 2002. Fellow: Royal Soc. Can. (Flavelle medal 1980), Royal Soc. London; mem.: Internat. Union Biochemistry (mem. exec. coun. 1988—94), Pan-Am. Assn. Biochem. Socs. (v.p. 1984—87, pres. 1987—90), Can. Biochem. Soc. (pres. 1982—83, Ayerst award 1966). Avocations: hiking, gardening. E-mail: gordon.dixon@shaw.ca.

DIXON, HARRY D., JR., (DONNIE DIXON), former prosecutor; b. Waycross, Ga., Nov. 6, 1953; s. Harry D. Sr. and Ruth (Starling) D.; m. Elizabeth Tonning, Apr. 19, 1980; 2 children. AB in History, Valdosta State Coll., 1974; JD, U. Ga., 1977. Bar: Ga. 1977, U.S. Dist. Ct. Ga. 1978, U.S. Ct. Appeals 1979. Law clk. to Hon. Marvin Hartley, Jr. Superior Ct. for Mid. Jud. Cir., 1977-78; asst. dist. atty. Waycross Jud. Cir, 1977-79, dist. atty., 1983-94; atty. Bennett, Pedrick and Bennett, 1979-83; U.S. atty. for so. dist. Ga. U.S. Dept. Justice, Savannah, 1994—2001; atty. Oliver Maner & Gray LLP, Savannah, Ga., 2002—04, Donnie Dixon Atty. at Law, 2004—. His profl. assoc. include the Nat. Assoc. of Former US Atty., the Nat. Assoc. of Criminal Defense Lawyers, the fGa. Assoc. of Criminal Defense Lawyers, the Savannah Bar Assoc. and the Savannah Assoc. of Criminal Defense Lawyers. Office: Donnie Dixon Atty at Law 304 E Bray St Savannah GA 31412 Office Phone: 912-644-6700.

DIXON, JACK EDWARD, biological chemistry professor, consultant; b. June 16, 1943; BA, UCLA, 1966; PhD, U. Calif., Santa Barbara, 1971. NSF Found. postdoctoral rsch. fellow U. Calif., San Diego, 1971—73; from asst. prof. to assoc. prof. biochemistry Purdue U., West Lafayette, Ind., 1973—82, prof. biochemistry, 1982—86, Harvey W. Wiley disting. prof. biochemistry, 1986—91; Minor J. Coon prof. biol. chemistry, chmn. dept. U. Mich., Ann Arbor, 1991—2003, co-dir. Life Scis. Inst., 2001—02, dir. Life Scis. Inst., 2002—03; prof. pharmacology, cellular medicine, chemistry and biochemistry U. Calif., San Diego, 2003—, dean sci. affairs Sch. Medicine, 2003—. P.T. Varandani Meml. lectr. Wright State U., Dayton, Ohio, 1987; chmn. rsch. rev. com. Ind. affiliate Am. Heart Assn., 1983; Nathan O. Kaplan lectr. U. Calif., San Diego, 1991; Vestling lectr. U. Iowa, 1991; Edmund Fischer lectr. U. Wash., Seattle, 1993; Árets Novo Nordisk lectr. U. Copenhagen, 1994; adj. prof. Salk Inst., 2003—; presenter in field. Recipient Rsch. award, Ind. affiliate Am. Diabetes Assn., 1985—86, Merit award, NIH, 1987, 1996, 2004, Lions award for cancer rsch., 1990, William Rose award, ASBMB, Merck award in Biochemistry and Molecular Biology. Fellow: Am. Acad. Arts and Sci., Mich. Soc. Fellows U. Mich. (sr.); mem.: Am. Acad. Arts and Scis., Inst. of Medicine, Nat. Acad. Sci., Am. Soc. Cell Biology, Am. Soc. Biochemistry and Molecular Biology (program chmn. 1994—, pres. 1996—97), Sigma Xi. Office: U Calif San Diego 9500 Gilman Dr 0602 La Jolla CA 92093-0602

DIXON, JOANNE ELAINE, music educator; b. Lancaster, Pa., July 3, 1944; d. William Russell and Anna Mary (Allen) D. B Music Edn., Westminster Choir Coll., Princeton, N.J., 1966; MEd, Trenton State Coll., 1982. Cert. music tchr., N.J. Music tchr. Warren (N.J.) Twp. Sch. Dist., 1966-67; vocal music tchr. Branchburg Twp. Sch. Dist., Somerville, N.J., 1967—, handbell dir., 1985—97. Music edn. handbell cons. Somerset County Dept. Edn., 1988-90; handbell dir., cons. Music Educator's Nat. Conf., Washington, 1990; N.J. rep. Com. for Handbells in Music Edn., Dayton, Ohio, 1990—. Handbell ringer First United Meth. Ch., Somerville, 1985—, mem. visions com., 1992-94, substitute handbell dir., 1992-2001; condr. N.J. Schs. Handbell Festival, 1995, 96. Recipient Excellence in Tchg. award State of N.J. Dept. Edn., 1988. Mem. Am. Guild English Handbell Ringers (area II N.J. rep. 1993-96, N.J. state rep. 1993-96, handbell workshop dir. 1993—), Branchburg Fedn. Tchrs. Democrat. Avocations: ringing handbells, painting, reading, stitchery. Office: Old York Sch 580 Old York Rd Somerville NJ 08876-3785 Home: 977 Robin Rd Hillsborough NJ 08844-4440

DIXON, JOHN JAMES, music educator; b. Rockford, Ill., Oct. 26, 1953; s. John Henry Dixon and Sarah Rosemary Intravaia; m. Debra Ann Flanders-Dixon, Aug. 8, 1981. MusB, Northern Ill. U., DeKalb, 1975, MusM, 1979. Cert. tchr. elem. and secondary Ill. State Tchr. Cert. Bd., tchr. music Ill. State Tchr. Cert. Bd. Tchr. instrumental music, band, jazz band and orch. Rockford (Ill.) Sch. Dist. #205, 1975—. V.p. bd. dir. Rockford Wind Ensemble, 2002—; mem. Sphear Saxaphone Quartet, 2000—. Nominee Golden Apple award, Golden Apple Found. Rockford, 2002; recipient Alumnus of Month, Rock Valley Coll., 1981. Mem.: Nat. Music Educators Conf., Ill. Music Educators Assn. Avocations: pottery, print collecting. Home: 5420 Pebble Creek Trl Loves Park IL 61111-4329 E-mail: dixon.john@ingishtbb.com.

DIXON, JOHN MORRIS, magazine editor; b. Long Branch, N.J., June 22, 1933; s. Abram C. and Emily (Minton) D.; m. Carol Ruth Nipomnich, Dec. 27, 1959; children: Peter, Susannah. B.Arch., MIT, 1955. From asst. editor to sr. editor Progressive Architecture, 1960-65, editor, 1971-96; assoc. editor Archtl. Rsch. Quar., 1999—2002. Sr. editor Archtl. Forum, 1965-71 Author: Architectural Design Preview, U.S.A, 1962, (with N. White and E. Willensky) A.I.A. Guide to New York City, 1967, Urban Spaces, 1999, Urban Spaces No. 2, 2001, Urban Spaces No. 3, 2004, The World Bank, 2002. Served to 1st lt. AUS, 1955-57. Fellow A.I.A. (chmn. exhibits com. N.Y. chpt. 1964-65, co-chmn. visitors com. N.Y. chpt. 1965-66, chmn. pub. relations com. N.Y. chpt. 1970-71, mem. design com. 1978—, chmn. 1983), Gen. Svcs. Adminstrn. (peer rev. panelist 2001—). Home: 382 Sound Beach Ave Old Greenwich CT 06870-2223 E-mail: jmdixon@optonline.net.

DIXON, JOHN MORRIS, JR., retired judge, lawyer; b. Gulf Shores, Ala., Apr. 3, 1940; s. John Morris Sr. and Margaret (Herndon) D.; children: John M. III, Kathryn D. BS, U. Ky., 1962, JD, 1965. Bar: Ky. 1965, Ark. 1968. Assoc. Bridges, Young, Matthews & Davis, Pine Bluff, Ark., 1968-70; ptnr. Turner & Dixon, Hopkinsville, 1970-75, Turner, Dixon, Kemp & Fletcher, Hopkinsville, 1975-77, Turner, Dixon & Kemp, Hopkinsville, 1977-89; prin. John M. Dixon Jr., Atty., Hopkinsville, 1989; ptnr. Dixon & Kemp, Hopkinsville, 1989-91; U.S. magistrate judge Bowling Green, Ky., 1971—98; of counsel Fletcher and Redd, Hopkinsville, 1999—, Resolute Systems, Inc., 1998—; pres. John M. Dixon Jr., P.S.C., 2004—. Capt. U.S. Army, 1965-68. Mem. ABA, Ky. Bar Assn. Personal E-mail: jdixonjr@earthlink.net.

DIXON, JOHN SPENCER, international executive; b. London, Apr. 23, 1957; s. Richard Kennedy and Elizabeth Ann (Flaxman) D.; m. Karen Beth Swanson, Aug. 18, 1984; children: Katherine Elizabeth, John Spencer Jr. BA with honors, Oxford U., 1979, MA, 1985; MBA, Harvard U., 1982. Supply exec. Hi-Tec Sports Ltd., Essex, England, 1982-86; pres. Hi-Tec Internat. Ltd., Taichung, Taiwan, 1983-84; founder, ptnr. Transatlantic Mktg. Co., Essex, England, 1985-2000; exec. v.p. Decipher, Inc., Norfolk, Va., 1988-90; pres. Waller Whittemore & Co., Virginia Beach, Va., 1992—, PH Internat., Virginia Beach, Va., 1997—2001; organist, composer-in-residence Providence Presbyn. Ch., Virginia Beach, Va., 1998—; exec. dir. Acad. of Music, Norfolk, Va., 2003—. Mem.: Am. Guild Organists. Presbyterian. Avocations: music, sports. Home: 4829 Berrywood Rd Virginia Beach VA 23464-5874 Office: 5497 Providence Rd Virginia Beach VA 23464

DIXON, LARRY DEAN, state legislator; b. Aug. 31, 1942; s. Chesley Lafayette and Charlene (Walker) D.; m. Gaynell Kimbrough, Dec. 23, 1967; children: Katherine Dixon Hert, Elizabeth Walker. AAS, Columbia Basin Jr. Coll., 1966; BS in Police Sci., Wash. State U., 1968, MA in History, 1970. Cons. Ala. State Dept. Edn., 1970-72; dir. dept. edn. Med. Assn. State of Ala., Montgomery, 1972-76; dir. Montgomery Family Practice Residency Program, 1976-78, Jackson Hosp. Found., Montgomery, 1978-81; exec. dir. Ala. Bd. Med. Examiners, Montgomery, 1981—. Mem. Montgomery City Coun., 1975-78, Ala. Ho. of Reps., 1978-82, Ala. Senate, 1982—; past mem. steering com. Nat. Clearinghouse on Licensure, Enforcement and Regulation; past bd. dirs. Fedn. State Med. Bds.; presdl. appointee Intergovt. Agy. Coun. on Edn., 1986-90, 90-94, 2002–; mem. legis. adv. bd. So. Regional Edn. Bd., 1986-90; mem. Med. Scholarship Bd., State of Ala., 1988-98; past trustee Tuskegee U.; commr. So. Assn. Colls. and Schs., 1998-2001. With U.S. Army, 1961-64. Mem. Nat. Conf. State Legislatures, Adminstrs. in Medicine Soc. (pres. 1984-85), Edn. Commn. of the States, Ala. Ex POWs (hon.), Blue Gray Assn., Lions. Republican. Methodist. Home and Office: 820 E Fairview Ave Montgomery AL 36106-1818 also: PO Box 946 Montgomery AL 36101-0946

DIXON, MICHAEL WAYNE, designer, writer, researcher; b. Honolulu, May 3, 1942; s. Gordon Alvin and Terry (Mendes) Dixon; m. Janis Marie Travis, Jan. 4, 1963 (div. Jan. 1977); children: Kimberlee Ann, Gregory Page, Morgan Ashley; m. Harlene Miller, Dec. 15, 1997. Tech. illustrator Rockwell Internat., Anaheim, Calif., 1962-66, Western Gear Corp., Lynwood, Calif., 1966-69; ind. biochem. rschr., 1968—; owner Unisex Clothing Store, Norwalk, Calif., 1969-71; mgr. Am. Health Industries, Downey, Calif., 1971-72; police officer Vernon Police Dept., LA Police Dept., 1972-81; designer, pres. Dornaus and Dixon Enterprises, Inc., Huntington Beach, Calif., 1979-88; freelance writer Huntington Beach, 1986—; founder, pres., CEO Gusty Winds Corp., 1991—, Maxcelint Labs. Inc., 2000—, Maxcelint Health Inc., 2000—, Maxcelint Internat., 2000—; founder, dir. The Health Ctr., 2001—. Founder, dir. The Rsch. Lab, 1991—, The Health Ctr., 2001—. Author: Bren Ten Owner's Manual, 1982, BodyShaping, 1985, BodyQuest, 1993, BodyLanguage, 1993, Courtroom Rapport, 1993, Naked Truth, 1995, There is a Magic Bullet After All, 1996, Cardiovasc. Disease, Potent. Magnesium and the True Fountain of Youth, 1999, pMg and Heart Wellness, 2000, Potentiated Magnesium--The Super Mineral for Super Good Health, 2001, Nature's Magic Bullet, 2001, The Finest Handgun Ever Made, 2002. Founder, dir. Street Smart Pepper Spray Hdqs. of Calif. With USN, 1959—62. Mem.: Rsch. Coun. Scripps Clinic and Rsch. Found., Am. Film Inst., NY Acad. Sci., Linus Pauling Inst. Sci. and Medicine, LA County Mus. Art, Smithsonian Instn. Achievements include invention of firearm safety devices; 10mm auto cartridge; Just'n Case police holster; MAWB cutter police bullet; BodyHugger holsters and ammunition holders; piper nigrum and acetic acid lachrymator; nutritional supplement formula that prevents atherosclerosis; potentiated magnesium; patents for first double ligand compounded coordination complex; potentiated calcium; holds 48 U.S. and internat. patents. Office Phone: 949-855-3776.

DIXON, MICHEL L., educational administrator; b. Norman, Okla., Oct. 2, 1945; s. Gerald R. and Erma M. (Fischer) D.; m. Mary Dee Brown, July 12, 1970 (div. 1995); children: Terri, Kelly, Kristi, Johanna. BA, Athens Coll., 1968, BE, 1972; MEd, U. Ala., 1976. Ins. adjustor Gen. Adjustment Bur., Birmingham, Ala., 1968-71; tchr. Adamsburg Sch., DeKalb County, Ala., 1971-72, Decatur (Ala.) City Schs., 1972-80; pubs. rep. Economy Pub. Co., Oklahoma City, 1980-82, Jostens Printing & Pub. Div., Mpls., 1982-84; course dir. AS100 Air Force ROTC, Maxwell AFB, Ala., 1984-85; pub. Civil Air Patrol News Aux. USAF, Maxwell AFB, 1985-86; tng. specialist, course mgr. Corps Engrs. Tng. div. U.S. Army, Huntsville, Ala., 1986-89; adminstr. Lawrence County High Sch., Moulton, Ala., 1989-90, Dept. Defense Dependent Sch., Nuernburg, Fed. Repub. Germany, 1990-91; dir. edn. programs in all western states U.S. Army 6th Recruiting BDE, Ft. Baker, Calif., 1991-94; prin. Round Valley H.S., Covelo, Calif., 1994-95; asst. prin. Calexico (Calif.) H.S., 1996-97, Capistrano Adult Sch., 1997-98; dir. cmty. edu. Mt. Brook (Ala.) Schs., Ala., 1998-1999; instrnl. sys. specialist in tech. specialized tng. program Pension Benefit Guaraty Corp., 1999—. With Pension Benefit Guaranty Corp., Washington, 1999—. Author: textbook AS 100, 1984; editor The Air Force Today, 1985; author, editor 3 slide briefings Aircraft and Weapons of AF, Vietnam, Korea, 1984-85; pub. Civil Air Patrol News, 1985-86. Test proctor Am. Mensa Soc. Presbyterian. Avocations: photography, electronics, country dancing, woodworking, bicycling. Office: Pension Benefit Guaranty Corp 1200 K St NW Fl 4 Washington DC 20005-4026 Home: 9340 Cherry Hill Rd Apt 1 College Park MD 20740-1263 E-mail: dixon.mike@pbgc.gov.

DIXON, MILDRED KELLEY, podiatrist; b. Phila., Sept. 7, 1916; d. Spencer Paul and Annie B. (West) Kelley; widowed; children: James, Denise. DPM, Ohio Coll. Podiatric Med., 1944; MD (hon.), U. St. Kitt. Founder, dir. podiatric residency program VAH, Tuskegee, Ala., 1956—85; pvt. practice Tuskegee Inst., Ala., 1948—. Cons. podiatry VA Montgomery, Montgomery, Ala., 1977—84, VA, Tuscaloosa, 1982—84; presenter in field. Contbr. articles to profl. med. jours. Pres. AARP; vol. RSVP, Tuskegee, Ala.; chaplain Ch. Women United; pres. Missionary Circle. Mem.: AAUW, NAACP, APHA, Nat. Acads. Practice, AWP, Assn. Podiatrists in Fed. Svcs. (past. pres.), Nat. Podiatry Med. Assn. (past pres.). Avocations: travel, reading. Home: 1103 Thompson St PO Box 753 Tuskegee Institute AL 36087

DIXON, PAUL EDWARD, lawyer, metal products executive, manufacturing executive; b. Bklyn., Aug. 27, 1944; s. Paul Stewart and Bernice (Mathisen) D.; m. Kathleen Constance Kayser, Sept. 23, 1967; children: Jennifer Pyne, Paul Kayser, Meredith Stewart. BA, Villanova U., 1966; JD, St. Johns U., 1972. Bar: N.Y. 1972, U.S. Supreme Ct. 1976. Assoc. mem. firm Rogers & Wells, N.Y.C., 1972-77; sec., asst. gen. counsel Volvo of Am. Corp., Rockleigh, N.J., 1977-79, v.p., gen. counsel, 1979-81; v.p., gen. counsel, sec. Reichhold Chems. Inc., 1981-88; sr. v.p., gen. counsel, sec. The Warnaco Group Inc., 1988-91; v.p., gen. counsel, sec. Handy & Harman, Rye, N.Y., 1992-97, sr. v.p., gen. counsel, sec., 1997—. Chmn. Teeches Ltd., Bermuda. Mem. ABA, Assn. Bar City N.Y., N.Y. State Bar Assn., U.S. Supreme Ct. Hist. Soc., Am. Corp. Counsel Assn., Bedford Golf and Tennis Club. Office: Handy & Harman 555 Theodore Fremd Ave Rye NY 10580-1451

DIXON, PAUL WILLIAM, psychologist, educator; b. N.Y.C., Aug. 1, 1936; s. Edward Everet and Esther (McCracken) D.; children: Michael H., Theodore K., Eleanor T., Aaron T. BA in English, Blackburn Coll., 1960; MA in Gen. Exptl. Psychology, U. Hawaii, 1963, PhD in Gen. Exptl. Psychology, 1966. Cert. tchr., Ill. Prof. psychology Coll. Arts and Scis. U. Hawaii, Hilo, 1965—, chmn. dept. liberal studies Coll. Arts and Scis., 1972-82, chmn. dept. psychology Coll. Arts and Scis., 1972-75. Vis. assoc. prof. psychology internat. divsn. Sophia U., Tokyo, 1971-72; vis. prof. dept. microbiology and immunology, UCLA, 1978-79; all-campus faculty pers. com. U. Hilo, 1967-68, pers. com. social scis. and edn. divsn., 1968-69, faculty senate, 1970-71, libr. com., 1970-71, acad. freedom, privilege and tenure com., 1973-74, dissertation com. dept. polit. sci., 1974-78, Rsch. Coun., 1977-78, chmn. all-coll. faculty pers. com., 1970, libr. com., 1973-74, liberal studies com., 1973-82. Contbr. numerous articles to psychol. and ednl. jours. Presenter, demonstrator Frequency Transfer Hearing Aid to Action Group for the Hearing Impaired, Honolulu, 1980, also to State Hearing and Visual Handicapped Svc., Hilo, Hawaii, 1980; chmn. commn. on anthropology of math. Internat. Union Anthrop. and Ethnol. Scis. Nominee Nobel prize in physics, 1986, 95, 98; NDEA fellow, 1963-66; aid grantee U. Hwaii Rsch. Coun., 1965-70, U. Hawaii Hilo Fund, 1970. Fellow Am. Anthrop. Assn., Soc. for Applied Anthropology; mem. AAAS, APA (travel grantee 1972), Internat. Congress of Anthrop. and Ethnographic Scis. Achievements include pioneering immunotherapy of cancer with levamisole, cancer vaccine, and pyrogen; life extension with immortalized autograft; generation of supernovae via high-energy physics experimentation; solution to Last Theorm of Fermat and Continuum Hypothesis of Gregor Cantor; research in linguistry. Home: PO Box 244 Volcano HI 96785-0244 Office: U Hawaii Coll Arts and Scis 200 W Kawili St Hilo HI 96720-4075 Business E-Mail: dixon@hawaii.edu.

DIXON, PHILLIP RAY, SR., lawyer; b. Wake Forest, NC, Mar. 26, 1949; s. Milton R. Dixon and Lottie Belle (Tippett) Larson; m. Candace (Mamie) Cicerone, Nov. 26, 1977; children: Phillip Ray Jr., Joseph David, Jonathan Scott. BSBA, East Carolina U., 1971; JD, U. NC, 1974. Bar: NC 1974, U.S. Dist. Ct. (ea. dist.) NC 1976, U.S. Ct. Appeals (4th cir.) 1981, U.S. Supreme Ct. 1981. Law clk. to assoc. justice NC Ct. Appeals, Raleigh, 1974-75; assoc. Gaylord & Singleton, Greenville, NC, 1975-78; ptnr. Dixon, Duffus & Doub, Greenville, 1978-90; N/A Dixon Doub Conner and Foster P.L.L.C, Greenville, 1990—. Instr. police sci. paralegal program Pitt C.C. and Pitt Tech. Inst., 1975-79, advisor 1982—; 981; bd. dirs., counsel PBC Ctr. Bank and Trust Co., Greenville, bd. dirs. RBC Centura Bank. Editor-in-chief NC Law Record, 1972-73, assoc. editor 1973-74. Atty. Greenville City Schs. and Greenville City Bd. Edn., 1978-86, Pitt County Schs. and Bd. of Edn., 1978—; local and state hearing officer NC Dept. Pub. Instrn.; atty. Greenville Utilities Commn., 1981—; mem. Pitt County Area Mental Health Mental Retardation and Substance Abuse Bd., 1983-87, chmn. bd. dirs. 1984-86; chancel choir mem. 1st Christian Ch. of Greenville, 1975-77, Sunday sch. supt., 1977, deacon, 1978-82, elder, 1983-87, guest minister, 1984, vice chmn. bd. dirs. 1981, chmn. 1982; bd. dirs., trustee Pitt-Greenville Arts Coun., Inc., 1979-81; exec. bd. Pitt County United Way, Inc., 1981, sec., campaign chmn., pres. 1982, 1986; mem. Downtown Greenville Assn., 1980—, Greenville Mus. Art, 1980—, treas. 1986-87, v.p., 1987-88, trustee, 1986—; pres. 1988—; bd. dirs. Greenville Jaycees 1975-77; past pres. East Carolina U. Ednl. Founds., Inc., 1987; del. county, dist. and state Dem. Convs., 1984, del. NC State Dem. Conv., Pitt. County campaign chmn. lt. gov.'s race, 1983-84; bd. govs. U. N.C., 2005—. Named one of Outstanding Young Men of Am., 1974-83. Mem. ABA, NC Bar Assn. (sustaining mem., family law sect., criminal law sect., real estate sect., probate sect., practical tng. com., instr. and seminar spkr. on topic appeals, practical skills course 1975-81, bd. govs.), Pitts County Bar Assn. (sec. law libr. com. 1976-77, chmn. 1976-82), NC Acad. Trial Lawyers, NC Coll. Advocacy, NC Coun. Sch. Bd. of Attys. (bd. dirs. 1982—, chmn. 1984-85, v.p. 1983-84, chmn. ins. com. 1983-84, Disting. Svc. award 2003), Nat. Coun. Sch. Bd. Attys., Greenville C. of C. (chmn.), Greenville-Pitt County Home Builders Assn. (chmn.), East Carolina Univ. Alumni Assn. (Outstanding Alumnus award 1984), Phi Sigma Pi., Greenville Sports Club (chartered, sec., treas. 1975-77, pres. 1979-80), Rotary (chartered, bd. dirs. Greenville chpt. 1981-83, dist. sec. 1982, v.p. 1983, pres. 1986-87, Paul Harris fellow 1982), East Carolina U. (sec. 1995-97, vice chair, 1997-99, chair, bd. trustees, 1999-01), Pitts. CC (vice chair, 1989-91, bd. trustees, 1991-99), NC Ctr. Pub. Policy Rsch (chair, 2002-03), Greenville City Bond Advocay Com (co-chair, 2004). Democrat. Office: Dixon Doub Conner and Foster LLC PO Box Drawer 8668 110 Arlington Blvd Greenville NC 27835 Office Phone: 252-355-8100. E-mail: phildixon@coastalnet.com.

DIXON, RICHARD WAYNE, retired communications company executive; b. Hubbard, Oreg., Sept. 25, 1936; s. Harlow C. and Mabel (Nilsson) D.; m. Rosina O. Berry, July 4, 1970; children: Erica, Douglas, Andrew. BA summa cum laude, Harvard U., 1958, MA, 1960, PhD, 1964. Tech. staff mem. AT&T Bell Labs., Murray Hill, N.J., 1965, supr. lightwave lasers group, 1968-79, head optoelectronics devices dept., 1979-83, dir. lightwave devices lab., 1983-90, dir. platforms and new products labs., 1991-93; now expert witness and tech. cons., Bernardsville, N.J. Contbr. articles to various publs. Nat. scholar Harvard U., 1955-58; NSF fellow, 1959-63. Fellow IEEE (editor Electronic Device Letters 1980-90, Medal of Engrng. Excellence 1993); mem. AAAS, Am. Phys. Soc. Home: 43 Old Wood Rd Bernardsville NJ 07924-1416 Personal E-mail: rdixon@worldnet.att.net.

DIXON, ROBERT F., telecommunications executive; b. Newport, R.I., July 5, 1948; s. Robert and Helen (Dowd) D. BFA, R.I. Sch. Design, 1970, BArch, 1971. Intern architect State of Conn., Hartford, 1971-72, engrng. asst., 1972-73, mgmt. analyst I, 1973-75, mgmt. analyst II, 1975-78, mgmt. analyst assoc., 1978-80; prin. analyst telecommunications Office of the Comptroller, Hartford, 1980-83, dir. telecommunications div., 1983-89; dir. telecommunications Office of Info. and Tech., Hartford, 1989-96; dir. planning and architecture dept. info. tech. State of Conn., 1997—2000, dir. ops., dept. info. tech., 2001—03; prin. Advantech Group LLC, Glastonbury, Conn., 2003—. Trustee R.I. Sch. Design, Providence, 1989—; pres. Rope Ferry Commons, a part of the Jordan Village Historic Dist., Waterford, 1987—. Mem. R.I. Sch. Design Alumni Assn. (pres. 1989-91), Coun. of State Govts. (strategic planning com. 1991—), Nat. Assn. State Telecommunications Dirs. (pres. 1991-93), Conn. Telecommunications Assn. (pres. 1985-86). Avocation: whitewater paddle-rafting. Office: 2620 New London Tpke Glastonbury CT 06033 Office Phone: 860-430-1509. E-mail: rdixon@advantechgrp.com.

DIXON, ROSINA BERRY, physician, pharmaceutical development consultant; b. Columbus, Ohio, Dec. 3, 1942; d. Loren C. and Florence H. (Bateson) Berry; m. Richard W. Dixon, July 4, 1970; children: Erica H., Douglas R., Andrew D. BA in Chemistry, Radcliffe Coll., 1964; MD, Columbia U., 1968. Diplomate Am. Bd. Internal Medicine. Intern, resident, and chief med. resident Roosevelt Hosp., N.Y.C., 1968-72; from sr. assoc. to exec. dir. Ciba-Geigy, Summit, N.J., 1972-81; med. dir. Schering Labs., Kenilworth, N.J., 1981-84; v.p. Med. Market Spltys., Boonton, N.J., 1985-86; cons. pharm. devel. Bernardsville, N.J., 1986—. Bd. dirs. Cambrex Corp., East Rutherford, N.J., Enzon Pharms., Inc., Piscataway, N.J., Church & Dwight Co., Inc., Princeton, N.J.; instr. medicine Coll. Phys. and Surg., Columbia U., 1972-99; preceptor in family practice Overlook Hosp., Summit, 1979—; governing bd. Daytop, N.J., 1991—; trustee Bonnie Brae, N.J., 1992-; bd. advisors Fairleigh Dickinson Silberman Coll., 2003—. Mem. Am. Coll. Clin. Pharmacology, Am. Soc. Clin. Pharmacology and Therapeutics, Nat. Assn. Corp. Dirs. Home and Office: 43 Old Wood Rd Bernardsville NJ 07924-1416

DIXON, SAMUEL B., retired comedian, film director, film producer; s. Paul Dixon and Thomas G Elzie; m. Rita F Lusk, June 1, 1991; children: Smauel Jr., Karla, Cedrick, Derrick children: Renetta F Lesure, Sherita L Peterson, Charles R Peterson. BAAS, Stephen F. Austin State U., 1980. Cert. electronic technician Lee Coll. Tex., 1978. Author (actor, dir., prodr.): (movie script) Hanging With the Big Boys; composer: (poetry) Wake Up America (Nat. Mag. Publ., 2002), (country western music selection) Lost Respect For Love (Nat. Mag. Publ., 2002), (rythym and blues musical selection) Gotta Go On (Nat. Mag. Publ., 2002). Newsletter pub. Lion's Club Internat., Plano, Tex., 1994—96; mem. Leadership Memphis, 1990—2003. With U.S. Army, 1967—71. Named to Internat. Hole-In-One Hall-of-Fame. Mem.: U.S. Golf Assn. Home: 109 N Main Apt #1701 Memphis TN 38103 Office: Center Stage Prodns 109 N Main Ste 1701 Memphis TN 38103 Office Phone: 901-527-2482.

DIXON, SHIRLEY LEE, emergency physician; b. NYC, Dec. 10, 1947; d. Henry Ester and Ethel Mae (Samuels) D. BS in Biology, CCNY, 1969; MD, Howard U., 1976; MPH, Columbia U., 1983. Intern Harlem Hosp. Ctr., NYC, 1976-77, resident in internal medicine, 1979-81, attending physician dept. ambulatory care, 1981-83; attending physician La Guardia Med. Group PC, 1983-85; emergency rm. attending Interfaith Med. Ctr., 1985-87; med. dir. Triboro Divsn. US Postal Svc., Flushing, NY, 1986-93, med. officer, 1993-96; attending emergency room VA Hosp., Bronx, 1993-96. Mem. cmty. adv. bd. Harlem Hosp., 1981—83; attending physician night screening clinic Lincoln Hosp., 1989—91. Active People to People Citizen Amb. Program, Spokane, Wash., 1991; mem. People to People Internat. Commd. officer USPHS, 1977-79. Scholar Health Professions scholar; USHPS scholar, Nat. Med. fellow. Fellow: Fgn. Policy Rsch. Assn., Am. Acad. Experts in Traumatic Stress (cert. illness trauma 2001, cert. disability trauma 2001, cert. stress mgmt. 2001, diplomate, fellow 2004), Am. Bd. Forensic Examiners (life; diplomate); mem.: APHA, Assn. Clinicians for Underserved (charter), Am. Profl. Practice Assn. (life), Am. Bd. Disability Analysts (life; diplomate, sr. analyst), NY Acad. Sci. Home: 752 West End Ave New York NY 10025-6230 Personal E-mail: vze34pbn@msn.com.

DIXON, STEWART STRAWN, lawyer, consultant; b. Chgo., Nov. 5, 1930; s. Wesley M. and Katherine (Strawn) D.; m. Romayne Wilson, June 24, 1961 (dec. July 1993); children: Stewart S. Jr., John W., Romayne W. Thompson; m. Ann Wilson Grozier, Sept. 15, 1997. BA, Yale U., 1952; JD, U. Mich., 1955. Bar: Ill. 1957, U.S. Dist. Ct. 1957, U.S. Ct. Appeals 1974, U.S. Supreme Ct. 1974. Ptnr. Kirkland & Ellis, Chgo., 1957-67, Wildman, Harrold, Allen & Dixon, Chgo., 1967—. Dir. Lord, Abbett & Co. Managed Mut. Funds, N.Y.C., 1976-2002, ret. Dec. 31, 2002; dir. Otho Sprague Inst., Chgo. Trustee, past chmn. Chgo. Hist. Soc., 1982-87. 1st lt. U.S. Army, 1955-60. Mem. Am. Bar Assn., Am. Law Inst., Ill. Bar Assn., Chgo. Bar Assn. Clubs: Chgo., Commonwealth, Commercial, Met., Univ., Old Elm, Onwentsia, Rolling Rock. Republican. Episcopalian. Office: Wildman Harrold Allen & Dixon 225 W Wacker Dr Chicago IL 60606-1224

DIXON, TAMECKA, professional basketball player; b. Dec. 14, 1975; Grad., Kans. State U., 1997. Basketball player Los Angeles Sparks Women's NBA, Inglewood, Calif., 1997—. Mem. Olympic Festival Team South, 1995. Avocations: dance, shopping.

DIXON, TIMOTHY KAINE, music educator; b. Rocky Mount, N.C., Mar. 2, 1959; s. John Smith Jr. and Ida M. Dixon. BSc, Norfolk State U., 1981, MA, 1997. Band dir. Indian River Jr. H.S., Chesapeake, Va., 1983—84; elem. music tchr. Thurgood Marshall Elem. Sch., Chesapeake, Va., 1984—. Treas. Voices of Norfolk, 1991; chair sub-com. Elem. Music Chorus, Chesapeake, 2002; sec. Men's Chorus, 1st Bapt. Ch., Norfolk, 2003. Recipient Apple for the Tchr., Iota Phi Lambda Sorority, 2003, Tchr. of the Yr., Chesapeake Pub. Schools, 2002—03, Outstanding Young Man of Am., Outstanding Young Men, 1989. Mem.: Gospel Music Workshop of Am., Nat. Va. Chesapeake Edn. Assn., Music Educators Nat. Conf. Avocations: photography, cake decorating. Home: 910 Joyce St Norfolk VA 23523 Office: Thurgood Marshall Elem Sch 2706 Border Rd Chesapeake VA 23324 Office Phone: 757-494-7515.

DIXON, WHEELER WINSTON, film and video studies educator, writer; b. New Brunswick, NJ, Mar. 12, 1950; s. Percival Vincent and Hilda-Barr (Wheeler) D.; m. Gwendolyn Audrey Foster, Dec. 23, 1985. AB, Livingston Coll., 1972; MA, MPhil, Rutgers U., 1980, PhD, 1982. Instr. English Rutgers U., New Brunswick, 1974-84; lectr. film studies The New Sch. for Social Rsch., 1983, 97, 98; asst. prof. English and art U. Nebr., Lincoln, 1984-88, assoc. prof. English, 1988—92, chmn. film studies program, 1988—2003, prof. English, 1992—2002; series editor Cultural Studies in Cinema Video Series SUNY Press, 1995—2004, endowed chair, Ryan prof. of film studies, 2000—. Guest programmer, lectr. Nat. Film Theatre of Brit. Film Inst. and Mus. of Moving Image, London, 1991; guest programmer Nat. Film Theatre of Brit. Film Inst., London, 1992; mem. ad hoc curriculum rev. com. dept. English, U. Nebr., Lincoln, 1992, mem. faculty devel. fellowship com., 1992-95, chmn. Robinson Prize com., spring 1994, chmn. faculty devel. fellowship com., 1994, mem. various MA thesis and PhD coms.; panelist NEH, 1993—; presenter papers in field; lectr. Lincoln Ctr., Mus. Modern Art, N.Y.C., New Sch. Univ., N.Y.C., 1997; guest lectr. on digital theory, U. Amsterdam, 1999. Author: The "B" Directors: A Bibliographical Directory, 1985, The Cinematic Vision of F. Scott Fitzgerald, 1986, The Films of Freddie Francis, 1991, The Charm of Evil: The Films of Terence Fisher, 1991, The Films of Reginald Le Borg: Interviews, Essays and Filmography, 1992, The Early Film Criticism of François Truffaut, 1993, Re-Viewing British Cinema 1900-1992: Essays and Interviews, 1994, It Looks at You: The Returned Gaze of Cinema, 1995, The Films of Jean-Luc Godard, 1997, The Exploding Eye: A Re-visionary History of 1960s Experimental Cinema, 1997, The Transparency of Spectacle, 1998, Disaster and Memory, 1999, The Second Century of Cinema, 2000, Film Genre 2000, 2000, Collected Interviews: Voices from 20th Century Cinema, 2001, Experimental Cinema: The Film Reader, 2002, Straight: Constructions of Heterosexuality in the Cinema, 2003, Visions of the Apocalypse: Spectacles of Destruction in the American Cinema, 2003, Film and Television after 9/11, 2004, Lost in the Fifties, 2005; editor-in-chief Quarterly Review of Film and Video, 1999—; guest editor Film Criticism, Fall-Winter 1991-92, mem. editl. bd., 1991—, article reviewer, 1991—; article reviewer Jour. of History of Sexuality, 1991-93, Cinema Jour., 1993—; mem. adv. bd. Jour. Popular Brit. Cinema; manuscript reviewer SUNY Press, 1993—; contbr. articles and revs. to profl. jours. and essays to various publs., including Film Criticism, Films in Rev., Cineaste, Interview, others; writer, dir., prodr. Coming Attractions: A History of the Motion Picture Trailer, 1986-88, (feature film) What Can I Do?, 1993 (Layman Fund award 1993-94); co-prodr., co-dir., co-writer: Women Who Made The Movies, 1988-90; dir./prodr.: (feature film) Squatters, 1994; exhibited in group shows at U. Nebr.-Lincoln, 1985-86, 87-88, 89-90, Syracuse U., 1986, W.Va. U., 1986, Lincolnshire Coll. Art, Lincoln, Eng., 1988-89; performances include That's Different: Tales of Nebraska, 1987; exhibitions of films include Whitney Mus. Am. Art, 1972, Mus. Modern Art, 1994, Mus. Moving Image, London, 1994, Millennium Film Workshop, 1997, Mus. Modern Art, 2003; complete films archived exclusively at Mus. of Modern Art, 2003, Career Retrospective, 2003; author (notes) Home Vision DVDs, 2004—. Recipient Outstanding Rsch. and Creative Achievement award, 2003; grantee Royal Film Archive of Belgium, 1974, N.J. State Arts Coun., 1972, Rsch. Coun., U. Nebr., 1984-85, Ind. Filmmaker, S.W. Alt. Media Project, 1985, Interdisciplinary Arts Fellowship Program, Rockefeller Found. and NEA, 1987, Rsch. Coun., 1987, 89, S.W. Alt. Media Project Ind. Prodn. Fund, 1993, John C. and Nettie V. David Meml. Trust, 2003; George Holmes Faculty fellow, 1989. Mem.: Soc. for Cinema Studies (exec. coun. 2004—). Office: U Nebraska Dept English 202 Andrews Hall Lincoln NE 68588-0333 Office Phone: 402-472-6064. Business E-Mail: wdixon@unlserve.unl.edu.

DIXON, WILLIAM ROBERT, musician, educator; b. Nantucket, Mass., Oct. 5, 1925; s. William Robert and Louise Ann (Wade) D.; children: William, Claudia Gayle, William. Diploma, Hartnette Conservatory Music, 1951. Clk., internat. civil servant UN Secretariat, N.Y.C., 1956-62; free lance musician, composer N.Y.C., 1962-67; mem. faculty Columbia U. Tchrs. Coll., 1967-70; composer-in-residence George Washington U., Washington, 1967; dir. Conservatory of Univ. of the Streets, N.Y.C., 1967-68; guest artist in residence Ohio State U., 1967; mem. faculty dept. dance Bennington (Vt.) Coll., 1968-95, chmn. dept. black music, 1973-86. Vis. prof. U. Wis., Madison, 1971-95; lectr. painting and music Mus. Modern Art, Verona, Italy, 1982, Palast, Nuremberg, Fed. Republic Germany, 1990; lectr. workshop on contemporary music Pori, Finland, 1991, Jerusalem, Tel Aviv, Israel, 1990; lectr. in Black Art Music Maison du Livre et du Son, Villeurbanne, France, 1994; tchr. Master Classes in Improvisation Ecole Nationale de Musique, Villeurbanne, France, 1994, Master Class Composition and Performance NYU, 1996; in residence Wesleyan U., 2005. Recs. include Archie Shepp-Bill Dixon Quartet, 1962, Bill Dixon 7-Tette, 1963, Intents and Purposes: The Bill Dixon Orchestra, 1967, For Franz, 1976, New Music, Second Wave, 1979, Bill Dixon in Italy, 2 vols., 1980, considerations 1 and 2 Bill Dixon, 1980, 82, November: 1981, 1982, Bill Dixon in the Labyrinth, 1983, Collection, 1985, Thoughts, 1986, Son of Sisyphus, 1990, Bill Dixon: Vade Mecum, 1994, Vade Mecum II, 1996, (6-CD set) Bill Dixon: Solo Trumpet, 1998, PAPYRUS vol. 1 and 2, compositions for trumpet, percussion & piano, 1999, Berlin Abbozzi, 2000; retrospective of music compositions 1963-91 by Radio Sta. WKCR, Columbia U., 1991-92; trumpet soloist Celebration Orchestra, Berlin, Germany, 1994; concert performance of original compositions Espace Tonkin, Villeurbanne, France, 1994, Teatro Colosseo, Rome, Italy, 1996, Nickelsdorf, Austria, 1997; composed orch. piece Cologne (Germany) Radio Sta., 1998; performer new compositions Festival of New Music for Trumpet, 2004, Donaueschingen, Guiramers and Royal Festival Hall, London, 2004; paintings exhibited, Ferrari Gallery, Verona, Italy, 1982, Multimedia Contemporary Art Gallery, Brescia, Italy, 1982, Uferpalast, Nuremberg, Germany, 1990, Cite de la Musique, Paris, 2002; exhibited lithographs Villeurbanne, France, 1994, Chittenden Bank, Bennington, Vt., 1994-95, Skoto Gallery, N.Y.C., 1996; retrospective of paintings 1968-91, So. Vt. Coll., 1991; author: L'Opera, (bio-discography by Ben Young) Dixonia, 1998; prodr. lithographs Union Regionale pour le Devel. de la Lithographie d'Art, Lyon, France, 1994; orchestral work Index, 2000; artist album cover, 2002. Mem. adv. com. New Eng. Found. of the Arts. Served with U.S. Army, 1944-46. Recipient Disting. Visitor in the Arts Middlebury Coll., 1986. Fellow Vt. Acad. Arts and Scis.; mem. Am. Fedn. Musicians, Duke Ellington Jazz Soc. (hon.) Office Phone: 802-442-4490. Personal E-mail: billdixon@adelphia.net. *Were it possible to live for three thousand years, one could lay around the house and do nothing for the first five hundred years, go to school for the next five hundred and then have two thousand years left to find a way to do work, etc., of substance. Since that is NOT the case (and even if one crosses with the green and not in between and manages to live to be one hundred--in cosmic or universal time akin to attempting to spit in the Atlantic Ocean from a height of 50,000 feet and expecting a ripple to follow) there is another reality extant. And from the time THAT reality dawned on me, I have endeavoured (albeit not always with success) to do everything one hundred percent. Those things I felt I COULDN'T (for whatever reason) expend that kind of energy upon, I have left alone.*

DIXON, W(ILLIAM) ROBERT, retired psychologist; b. Hudson, Pa., Sept. 16, 1917; s. William Robert and Mary (George) D.; m. Carol Everson Lewis, Dec. 20, 1940; children: William R., Barbara Ann. AB, Syracuse U., 1938, MA, 1939; PhD (Horace H. Rackham fellow 1947-48, Burke Aaron Hinsdale scholar 1948), U. Mich., 1948. Tchr., prin. W. Canada Valley Central Schs., Middleville, N.Y., 1940-42; asst. prof. U. Ill., 1948-49, U. Mich., 1949-52, asso. prof., 1952-56, prof. ednl. psychology, 1956-86, ret., 1986. Vis. prof. edn. U. Bombay, India, 1964-65 Contbr. articles to profl. jours. Dir. Mich. Interdisciplinary Research Tng. Program, 1967-72. Served with USAAF, 1942-45. Decorated Air Medal with 10 oak leaf clusters, D.F.C. Fellow Am. Psychol. Assn., AAAS; mem. Am. Ednl. Research Assn. Achievements include being nationally ranked tennis player Men's Singles, 1945, Vets. Singles, 1962. Home: 2793 W Fairway Loop Dunnellon FL 34434-4829

DIXSON, DIANE ELIZABETH, acquisitions librarian, tax preparation business owner; b. Washington, Sept. 26, 1943; d. Charles Hanan and Doris (Cover) D. BA in English and German, George Mason U., 1978; grad., Fin. Mgmt. Sch., 2002. Bibliographic technician Libr. Congress, Washington, 1966-68, preliminary cataloger, 1968-72, sr. acquisitions libr., 1973—, sr. acquisitions specialist, 1997—, bd. dirs., 1998—. Chair supervisory com. Libr. Congress Fed. Credit Union, 1982—90, bd. dirs., 1991—94, 2001—, chmn. credit. com., 1994—. Recipient Edward A. Filene award Credit Union Nat. Assn., 1992, Vol. Assistance Program award, 1994, numerous credit union svc. awards, 1982-2002. Roman Catholic. Avocations: travel, classical music, beach, tennis, financial planning. Office: Libr Congress 1st & Independence Ave SE Washington DC 20540-4183 Business E-Mail: mschef@erols.com.

DIXSON, J. B., communications executive; b. Norwich, N.Y., Oct. 19, 1941; d. William Joseph and Ann Wanda (Teale) Barrett. BS, Syracuse U., 1963; postgrad. in bus. adminstrn., Wayne State U., 1979-81; MBA, Ctrl. Mich. U., 1984. Pub. rels. editl. asst. Am. Mus. Natural History, N.Y.C., 1963-64; writer, prodr. Norman, Navan, Moore & Baird Advt., Grand Rapids, Mich., 1964-67; prin. J.B. Dixson Comm. Cons., Detroit, 1967-74; dir. Pub. Info. Svcs. divsn. Mich. Employment Security Commn., Detroit, 1974-82; news rels. mgr. Burroughs Corp., 1982-83, dir. creative svcs., 1983-85, dir. pub. rels., 1985-86; prin. Dixson Comm., Detroit, 1986-93, Durocher Dixson Werba, LLC, Detroit, 1994—. Lectr., spkr. in field at colls, univs., cmty. orgns. Author: Guidelines for Non-Sexist Verbal and Written Communication, 1976, Sexual Harassment on The Job, 1979, The TV Interview: Good News or Bad?, 1981. Mem. Detroit Mayor's Transition Com. of 100, 1972; mem. bd. mgmt. Detroit YWCA, 1974; chmn. Detroit Women's Equality Day Com., 1975; bd. dirs., founding mem. Feminist Fed. Credit Union, Detroit, 1976; centennial chair Indian Village Assn., 1993-95; founding mem. Mich. Women's Campaign Fund, 1980; active Mich. Task Force on Sexual Harassment in Workplace, Mich. Women's Com. of 100, Mich. Women's Polit. Caucus, Mich. Women's Found. Named Outstanding Sr. Woman in Radio and TV, Syracuse U., 1963; recipient Five Watch award Am. Women in Radio and TV, Mich., 1969, 75, Outstanding Women in Comm. Women's Advt. Club, 1998, cert. of recognition Detroit City Coun., 1976, Feminist of Yr. award NOW, 1977, City of Detroit Human Rights Commn., 1988, Design in Mich. award Mich. Coun. of Arts/Gov. William G. Milliken, 1977, Achievement award U.S. Dept. Labor, 1979, Spirit of Detroit award Detroit City Coun., 1980, PR Casebook, 1983, PR News Case Study, 1986, Pinnacle award Mich. Hosp. Pub. Rels. Assn., 1987, award Nat. Sch. Pub. Rels. Assn., 1992, 21st Century award Corp. Detroit Mag., 1995, Creativity in Advt. award Detroit Newspapers Assn., 2000; subject of Mich. Senate Resolution 412, 1979. Fellow Pub. Rels. Soc. Am. (accredited, pres. chpt. 1983-84, Dist. award and citation 1984, 86, 87, 93, exec. com. corp. sect. 1996-2001, Disting. Svc. award 1999), Internat. Assn. Bus. Communicators (Silver Quill award chpt. 1987, 88, 91, 93, dist. 1987, Renaissance award 1988, 91, Mercury award 1987), Nat. Assn. Govt. Communicators (Blue Pencil award 1977, Gold Screen award 1980), Automotive Press Assn., Women's Advt. Club (Top 75 Women in Comm. 1999), Econ. Club Detroit, Maple Grove Gun Club, Detroit Athletic Club. Office: 21920 River Ridge Trl Farmington MI 48335-4680 E-mail: dixson@ddwpr.com.

DIZDAROGLU, MIRAL, chemist; b. Dortyol, Turkey, Apr. 7, 1945; s. Muhterem and Muzeyyen Dizdaroglu; m. Emel Seckin Koksal, May 21, 1979; children: Ata Murat Dizdar, Sila Emel Dizdar. MS in Chem. Engring., U. Ankara, Turkey, 1967; PhD, U. Karlsruhe, Germany, 1971. Lic. Chem. Engr., U. Ankara, Turkey, 1967. Adj. prof. U. Md., Balt., 1980—86; sr.

scientist Nat. Inst. of Standards and Tech., Gaithersburg, Md., 1986—; scientist Max-Planck-Institut, Mulheim a.d. Ruhr, Germany, 1971—78, US Army Natick Lab., Natick, Mass., 1978—80. Group leader Nat. Inst. of Standards and Tech., Gaithersburg, Md., 2000—. Lt. U.S. Army, 1976, Turkey. Recipient Hillebrand Prize, Wash. DC Sect. of the Am. Chem. Soc., 1989, Sci. Award, Govt. of The Republic of Turkey, 1993, Silver Medal Award, Dept. of Commerce, US Govt., 1993, Turkish-American of The Yr., Assembly of The Turkish-American Assn. in USA, 1993, Hon. Doctorate, Med. U., Bydgoszsz, Poland, 2000, Award for Excellence in Sci., Assembly of the Turkish-Am. Assn. in USA, 2001. Mem.: Soc. for Free Radical Rsch. (editor 1991—2005). Achievements include research in 186 Pub. in Scientific Jour; 125 Invited Talks at Scientific Meetings and Inst; 8700 Citations to his Pub. in the Scientific Lit. Office: Nat Inst of Standards and Tech 100 Bureau D r Bldg 227 MS 8311 Gaithersburg MD 20899 Office Phone: 301-975-2581. Office Fax: 301-975-8505. Business E-Mail: miral@nist.gov.

DIZON, DON STEVEN, oncologist, educator; b. Tamuning, Guam, Feb. 12, 1970; s. Modesto Millari and Millionita Dongon Dizon; life ptnr. Henry Wilson Stoll; 1 child, Isabelle Dizon-Stoll. BA, U. Rochester, N.Y., 1991, MD, 1995. Cert. internal medicine Am. Bd. Internal Medicine, 1998, medical oncology Am. Bd. Internal Medicine, 2002; sex educator Planned Parenthood, 2005. Resident internal medicine Yale-New Haven Hosp., 1995—98; clinician and educator Yale Primary Care Program, Waterbury, 1998—99; fellow med. oncology Meml. Sloan-Kettering Cancer Ctr., N.Y.C., 1999—2001, clin. asst. attending, 2001—03; fellow medicine Weill Med. Coll. Cornell U., 1999—2001, instr. medicine, 2001—03; dir. med. oncology Program in Women's Oncology, Women and Infants' Hosp., Providence, 2003—; asst. prof. Brown U. Med. Sch., 2003—. Mem. devel. therapeutics com. Gynecologic Oncology Group, Buffalo, 2005—; dir. ctr. for sexuality, intimacy, and fertility Program in Women's Oncology, Providence, 2005—. Author: 100 Questions and Answers About Ovarian Cancer, 2003. Mem.: ACP, Am. Assn. Cancer Rsch., Am. Soc. Clin. Oncology (Career Devel. award 2002). Office: Program Womens Oncology Women and Infants' Hosp Brown Med Sch 101 Dudley St Providence RI 02382 Office Phone: 401-453-7520. Office Fax: 401-453-7529. E-mail: ddizon@wihri.org.

DJANG, ARTHUR H.K., pathologist, health facility administrator; b. Beijing, Feb. 12, 1925; arrived in U.S., 1948; s. Wei-Fang DJang and Sujen Liu; m. Mary Helen Winston; divorced; children: Philipp, Douglas, Lincoln, David; m. Tina Marie Barone, 1980-98; 1 child, Anna Claire. MD, Harbin (China) Med. U., 1944; MPH, U. Minn., 1951; PhD in Infectious Diseases, UCLA, 1955. Cert. specialist in Clin. Pathology, Anatomic Pathology, Nuclear Medicine Clin. Faculty UCLA Sch. Medicine, 1955. Chief state epidemiologist, dir. chronic & communicable diseases State Dept. Pub. Health, Santa Fe, 1956-58; pres., dir. Biomedical Sci. Labs., Albuquerque, 1962-74; chmn. dept. pathology & nuclear med. Jamestown (N.Y.) Gen. Hosp., 1975-85; clin. prof. of molecular biology SUNY, Fredonia (N.Y.), 1977-86; pres. Internat. Health Inc., Jamestown, 1987—90; pres., CEO Santé Internat. Inc., Jamestown (N.Y.) and Tianjin, China, 1994—; pres. Environ. Scis. Internat., Jamestown and Tianjin, China, 1993—. Cons. prof. in pathology N. Mex. State U., University Park, 1962-74; cons. physician NASA White Sands Facility, N. Mex., 1966-74; med. dir., cons. physician Medina Meml. Hosp., 1991—93; disting. vis. prof. Grad. Sch. Health Scis. Dalian (China) U., 1988—, bd. dirs.; hon. chmn. Sci. and Tech. Commn., Zhuhai. Author monographs in field; cons. editor Jour. Gerontology, 1988—. Bd. dirs. Am. Heart Assn., Albuquerque, 1965-75, Am. Cancer Soc., 1965-74, Chautauqua Bd. Health, Mayville, N.Y., 1976-84; coun. mem. SUNY, Fredonia, 1978-86. Named hon. chmn. Scis. Tech. Commn., hon. pres. Yantai Internat. Red Cross Hosp., hon. pres. Dalian Inst. Gerontology, 1988, hon. prof. Harbin Med. U., 1981; recipient First Nation Gold Medal award outstanding contbn. health scis., 2004. Fellow Am. Coll. Pathologists, Am. Coll. Nuclear Med. (chmn. Internat. com. 1984-85), Am. Coll. Preventive Med. (mem. by-laws com. 1983-85); mem. AAAS, Am. Coll. Physician Execs., N.Y. Acad. Scis., Sigma Xi. Achievements include discovery of main ingredients used in Lysol, 1955; holder of 5 patents related to Anti-Aging and Cancer Prevention and Treatment (3 U.S., 1 Canadian, and 1 European) and 1 U.S. pending patent; inventor of Oncolyn (anti-cancer plant extract); Longevity Crystal (for life extension); Nasbesilin (for particle and inhalation injury and respiratory diseases); Mellinol (for blood sugar and weight balance); Evergreen (for protection of UV damage and antimutation); Memory Gold+ (for prevention and treatment of pre-dementia and Alzheimer); Cardio-CP (for cardiovascular health); Bariatol (weight management); Rejuvenin (skin anti-aging and UV damage); Viranox (HIV and other viral infections); Pomecran (anti-cancer); Mégrani (anti-aging). Avocations: coins, stamps, paintings. Office: Santé Internat Inc 111 W Second St Ste 4000 Jamestown NY 14701 Office Phone: 716-664-7255. E-mail: santedjang@netscape.net.

DJANG, DAVID S.W., physician; b. Seattle, Jan. 24, 1970; s. Mary Helen Surovik; m. Eleanor Yu-Chen Lo, Mar. 3, 2001. BA, U. Tex., 1992; MD, U. Tex. S.W. Med. Sch., Dallas, 1998. Cert. ABNM. Intern U. Wash. Med. Ctr., Seattle, 1998—99, resident, 1999—2003; staff physician Swedish Hosp., Seattle, 2003—. Vol. U.S. Peace Corp., Malawi, Africa, 1992—94. Recipient Rsch. in Tng., RSNA, 2002, WRSNM, 2002. Mem.: SNM (Soc. of Nuc. Medicine), AMA.

DJAWAD, SAID TAYEB See JAWAD, SAID

DJEDDAH, RICHARD NISSIM, investment banker; s. Joseph N. and Nelly (Serper) D.; m. Rachel Ruth Baron; 1 child, Esteevered. BS in Physics, CCNY, 1971; MBA, CUNY, 1986, PhD in Fin., 1990. Notary pub., N.Y. Prin., pres. Richard N. Djeddah & Assocs., N.Y.C., 1976—. Author: The Impact of Advertising on Security Prices, 1990. Mem. N.Y. Acad. Scis., Alliance Francaise, Baron Rothchild Golf and Country Club (Caesaria). Republican. Avocations: skiing, golf, chess, collecting ancient coins and art. Home: 346 Heathcote Rd Scarsdale NY 10583-7132 Office: RN Djeddah & Assocs 4 Park Ave New York NY 10016-5339

DJERASSI, CARL, writer, retired chemistry professor; b. Vienna, Oct. 29, 1923; s. Samuel and Alice (Friedmann) Djerassi; m. Virginia Jeremiah (div. 1950); m. Norma Lundholm (div. 1976); children: Dale, Pamela(dec.); m. Diane W. Middlebrook, 1985. AB summa cum laude, Kenyon Coll., 1942, DSc (hon.), 1959; PhD, U. Wis., 1945, DSc (hon.), 1995, Nat. U. Mex., 1953, Fed. U., Rio de Janeiro, 1969, Worcester Poly. Inst., 1972, Wayne State U., 1974, Columbia U., 1975, Uppsala U., 1977, Coe Coll., 1978, U. Geneva, 1978, U. Ghent, 1985, U. Man., 1985, Adelphi U., 1993, U. S.C., 1995, Swiss Fed. Inst. Tech., 1995, U. Md.- Balt. County, 1997, Bulgarian Acad. Scis., 1998, U. Aberdeen, 2000, Polytechnic U., 2001, Cambridge U., 2005. Rsch. chemist Ciba Pharm. Products, Inc., Summit, NJ, 1942—43, 1945—49; assoc. dir. rsch. Syntex, Mexico City, 1949—52, rsch. v.p., 1957—60; v.p. Syntex Labs., Palo Alto, Calif., 1960—62, Syntex Rsch., 1962—68, pres., 1968—72, Zoecon Corp., 1968—83, chmn. bd. dirs., 1968—86; prof. chemistry Wayne State U., 1952—59, Stanford (Calif.) U., 1959—2002. Founder Djerassi Resident Artists Program, Woodside, Calif. Author: The Futurist and Other Stories, 1988; author: (novels) Cantor's Dilemma, 1989, The Bourbaki Gambit, 1994, Marx Deceased, 1996, Menachem's Seed, 1997, NO, 1998; author: (poetry) The Clock Runs Backward, 1991; author: (plays) An Immaculate Misconception, 1998, BBC World Svc. Play of Week, 2000, Calculus, 2003, ICSI--a pedagogic wordplay for 2 voices, 2002, Ego, 2003, Three on a Couch, 2004, Phallacy, 2005, Fertility Rites, 2005, Taboos, 2005; author: (with Roald Hoffmann) Oxygen, 2001, BBC World Svc.Play of Week, 2001; author: (with Pierre Laszlo) NO--a pedagogic wordplay for 3 voices, 2003; author: (autobiography) The Pill, Pygmy Chimps and Degas' Horse, 1992; author: (memoir) This Man's Pill, 2001; author: (with D. Pinner) Newton's Darkness: Two Dramatic Views, 2004; author: 9 other books; mem. editl. bd. Jour. Organic Chemistry, 1955—59, Tetrahedron, 1958—92, Steroids, 1963—2001, Procs. NAS, 1964—70, Jour. Am. Chem. Soc., 1966—75, Organic Mass Spectrometry, 1968—91, contbr. numerous articles to profl. jours., poems, memoirs and short stories to lit. publs. Decorated Austrian Cross of Honor 1st class, Great Cross of Merit Germany; named to Nat. Inventors Hall of Fame; recipient Intrasci. Rsch. Found. award, 1969, Freedman Patent award, Am. Inst. chemists, 1970, Chem. Pioneer award, 1973, Nat. medal of Sci. for first synthesis of oral contraceptive, 1973, Wolf prize in Chemistry, 1978, John and Samuel Bard award in Sci. and Medicine, 1983, Roussel prize, Paris, 1988, Discovers award, Pharm. Mfg. Assn., 1988, Nat. medal Tech. for new approaches to insect control, 1991, Nev. medal, 1992, Thomson medal, Internat. Soc. Mass Spectroscopy, 1994, Prince Mahidol award, Thailand, 1995, Sovereign Fund award, 1996, Othmer Gold medal, Chem. Heritage Found., 2000, Author's prize, German Chem. Soc., 2001, Erasmus medal, Acad. Europeae, 2003, Gold medal, Am. Inst. Chemists, 2004, Sevono prize for lit., Rome, 2005. Mem.: NAS (Indsl. Application of Sci. award 1990), Acad. Europeae, Bulgarian Acad. Scis. (fgn. mem.), Mex. Acad. Scis., Brazilian Acad. Scis., Royal Swedish Acad. Engring. (fgn. mem.), Royal Swedish Acad. Scis. (fgn. mem.), German Acad. Leopoldina, Am. Acad. Arts and Scis., Royal Soc. Chemistry (hon. fellow, Centenary lectr. 1964), Am. Chem. Soc. (award pure chemistry 1958, Baekeland medal 1959, Fritzsche award 1960, award for creative invention 1973, award in chemistry of contemporary tech. problems 1983, Esselen award 1989, Priestley medal 1992, Gibbs medal 1997), NAS Inst. Medicine, Am. Acad. Pharm. Scis. (hon.), Sigma Xi (Proctor prize for sci. achievement 1998), Phi Beta Kappa, Phi Lambda Upsilon (hon.). Office: Stanford U Dept Chemistry Stanford CA 94305-5080 E-mail: djerassi@stanford.edu.

DJERASSI, ISAAC, medical researcher; b. Sofia, Bulgaria, July 27, 1925; came to U.S., 1954, naturalized, 1962; s. Rahamim and Adela (Tadjer) D.; m. Nira Eskenazy, Jan. 31, 1954; children— Ram Isaac, Ady Lynn. Student, Sofia U. Med. Sch., 1944-49; MD, Hebrew U., Jerusalem, 1952; DH (hon.), Villanova U., 1977. Intern Hadassah Hosp., Tel Aviv, 1951-52, resident, 1953-54; rsch. assoc. Med. Sch. Harvard U., Boston, 1955-60; asst. prof. pediats. U. Pa., Phila., 1960-69; dir. rsch. oncology-hematology Mercy Cath. Med. Ctr., Phila., 1969-98. Prof. oncology Med. Sch. U. Tel Aviv, Israel, 1986, dir. Djerassi-Elias Oncology Inst., 1987. Contbr. articles to profl. jours. Mem. med. advisory bd. Nat. Hemophilia Found., Phila., 1964-75; mem. med. advisory bd. Leukemia Soc., 1970-75. Recipient Albert Lasker Found. award, 1972, E. Cohn-De Laval award, 1990. Mem. Am. Soc. Cancer Rsch., Am. Soc. Clin. Oncology, Am. Assn. Blood Banks. Inventor filtration leukopheresis system and machine for white blood cell transfusions, 1970; discoverer high methotrexate-citrovorum rescue chemotherapy of cancer, 1964-77; developer platelet and white cells transfusions and supportive care, 1955-71; developed curative treatments for acute childhood leukemia, non-Hodgkin lymphoma, 1964-68, osteogenic sarcoma, 1971, effective brain gliomas, 1983-99. Home: 1820 Rittenhouse Sq Philadelphia PA 19103 Office: Mercy Cath Med Ctr PO Box 19709 Philadelphia PA 19143-0709

DJEREJIAN, EDWARD PETER, academic administrator, retired diplomat; b. N.Y.C., Mar. 6, 1939; s. Peter Minas and Mary (Yazudjian) D.; m. Francoise Andrée Haelters, July 31, 1971; children: Gregory, Francesca. BS in Fgn. Svc., Georgetown U., 1960, doctorate (hon.), 1992; LLD (hon.), Middlebury Coll., 2004. Staff asst. to sec. of state U.S. Dept. of State, 1963-64; Political officer Am. Embassy, Beirut, Lebanon, 1965-69; political/labor officer Am. Consulate Gen., Casablanca, Morocco, 1969-72; spl. asst. Under Sec. of State, Washington, 1973-75; prin. officer Am. Consulate Gen., Bordeaux, France, 1975-77; political counselor Am. Embassy, Moscow, USSR, 1979-81, dep. chief of mission Amman, Jordan, 1981-84; dep. spokesman & dep. asst. sec. Dept. of State, Washington, 1984-85; spl. asst. to the pres., dep. press sec. The White House, 1985-86; prin. dep. asst. sec. for Near East/South Asia, 1987-88; Am. ambassador Am. Embassy, Damascus, Syria, 1988-91; asst. sec. Near Eastern and South Asian Affairs bur. Dept. State, Washington, 1991-93; amb. to Israel Tel Aviv, 1993-94; dir. James A. Baker III Inst. for Pub. Policy Rice U., Houston, 1994—. Bd. dirs. Occidental Petroleum Corp., Global Industries, Ltd., Baker Hughes. 1st Lt. U.S. Army, 1961-62 (Korea). Recipient Presdl. award, Presdl. Meritorious Svc. award, 1988, Superior Honor award Dept. State, 1984, Disting. Honor award, 1993, Presdl. Disting. Svc. award, 1994, Ellis Island medal of honor, Moral Statesman award ADL, 1994. Mem. Coun. on Fgn. Rels. Armenian Apostolic. Avocations: writing, skiing. Office: Baker Inst Pub Policy Rice Univ 6100 Main St Houston TX 77005-1827 Office Phone: 713-348-4981. Business E-Mail: epd@rice.edu.

DJEREJIAN, ROBERT ASBED, architect; b. N.Y.C., July 6, 1931; s. Peter Minas Djerejian and Mary Yazudjian; children: Linda, Madeline, Pier; m. Marian Patrice Lair, Sept. 14, 1997. B in Architecture, Pratt Inst., 1955. Registered arch., N.Y., planner, N.J. Plans and project officer U.S. Army Corp. Engrs., 1955-57; dir. design Haines Lundberg Waehler, N.Y.C., 1965-75, ptnr., 1976, mng. ptnr., 1977—82; sr. mng. ptnr. HLW Internat., N.Y.C., 1983—95, sr. cons., 1996—. Bd. adv. Pa. State U., 1982—; trustee Pratt Inst., 1992—, bd. dirs. Delaware Coll. Arts & Design. Bd. dir. Fonar Corp., Chmn. bd. of zoning and appeals, Yonkers, N.Y., 1972. Recipient Excellence in Design Nat. Honor award Nat. Endowment of the Arts, 1989; named Architect of Yr. N.J. Contractors Assn., 1986 Mem. AIA (emeritus, chmn. com. natural environment 1974, N.Y. State AIA chpt. excellence in design award 1992), Am. Arbitration Assn., Union League Club. Avocations: mountain climbing, skiing, vintage auto racing. Home: 303 E 57th St Apt 16L New York NY 10022 Office: HLW International 115 5th Ave New York NY 10003-1004 E-mail: rdjerejian@hlw.com.

DJOKIC, WALTER HENRY, lawyer; b. Schwaforden, Germany, Sept. 12, 1947; came to U.S., 1951, naturalized, 1959; s. Radovan and Martha (Schulenburg) D.; married; 1 child, Joshua David. B.A., U. Ill., 1969; J.D., DePaul U., 1972. Bar: Ill. 1972, Ariz. 1980, Fla. 1994. Assoc. Wachowski & Wachowski, Chgo., 1972-73; atty. Pretzel & Stouffer, Chartered, Chgo., 1973-79, ptnr., 1979-85; ptnr. Wood, Lucksinger & Epstein, Chgo., 1985-86, Finley Kumble Wagner, Heine, Underberg, Manley, Myerson & Casey, Chgo., 1986-88; of counsel McCullough, Campbell & Lane, 1988-93, Conrad, Scherer & James, 1994-95, Miller, Kagan, Rodriguez & Silver, 1995-2000; atty. McIntosh, Sawran Peltz & Cargaya, 2000-02, ptnr., 2002—. Mem. Chgo. Bar Assn., Ill. State Bar Assn., State Bar of Ariz., State Bar of Fla. Office: 625 N Flagler Dr Ste 502 West Palm Beach FL 33401 Home: 2077 Carambola Rd West Palm Beach FL 33406-5314 Office Phone: 561-655-7520. Business E-Mail: wdjokic@mspcesq.com.

DJORDJEVIC, DIMITRIJE, historian, educator; b. Belgrad, Yugoslavia, Feb. 27, 1922; came to U.S., 1970, naturalized, 1977; s. Vladimir and Jelena (Rasic) D.; m. Nan Fletcher, June 1981; 1 child, Jelena Grad., U. Beograd, 1954, PhD, 1962. Sr. staff mem. Inst. History, Serbian Acad. Scis. and Arts, 1958-69, Inst. Balkan Studies, 1969-70; prof. U. Calif., Santa Barbara, 1970-91, prof. emeritus, 1991—, chmn. Russian area studies, 1976-82. Mem. Nat. Com. to Promote History of Habsburg Monarchy, 1973-79 Author: Austro-Serbian Customs War 1906-1911, in Serbian, 1962, Revolutions nationales des peuples balkaniques, 1804-1914, 1965, Scars and Memory, 1997; co-author: The Balkan Revolutionary Tradition, 1981, also papers, essays, revs.; editor: The Creation of Yugoslavia, 1914-1918, 1980; editorial bd. profl. jours. Mem. Am. Hist. Assn., Am. Assn. Advancement Slavic Studies, Conf. Slavic and East European History (pres. 1984), Serbian Acad. Scis., N. Am. Assn. Serbiam Studies (pres. 1986-88). Serbian Orthodox. Personal E-mail: vmarkovic@msn.com.

DJORDJEVIC, MICHAEL M., lawyer; b. Rochester, Pa., Sept. 20, 1952; s. Vlastimir and Vera D.; m. Mary C. Prodromov, Aug. 24, 1974; children: Charles, Thomas, Gregory. BA, Allegheny Coll., 1974; JD, Case We. Res. U., 1977. Bar: Ohio 1977. Assoc. Smith & Smith, Avon Lake, Ohio, 1977-86, Jacobson, Maynard, Tuschman & Kalur, Cleve., 1986-87, prin., 1987-94, Michael M. Djordjevic Attys. at Law, Akron, Ohio, 1994—. Alden scholar Allegheny Coll., 1972-73. Mem. Am. Trial Lawyers Assn., Ohio Acad. Trial Lawyers, Pi Gamma Mu. Avocation: motorcycle sports riding. Office: 17 S Main St # 201 Akron OH 44308-1803

DJORDJEVICH, MIROSLAV-MICHAEL, bank executive; b. Belgrade, Yugoslavia, 1936; arrived in U.S., 1956; s. Dragoslav and Ruzica Georgevich; m. Marie Louise Hohman, 1963; children: Marie, Alexander, Michelle. BS, U. Calif., Berkeley, 1960; MBA, San Francisco State U., 1963; cert. advanced fin., U. Stanford. Fin. analyst Fireman's Fund Ins. Co., San Francisco, 1962-68, asst. v.p. investments, 1972-76, v.p. investments, 1976-78, v.p., treas., 1978-84; pres., CEO U.S. Fidelity and Guaranty Fin. Co., San Francisco, 1985-86; chmn., pres., CEO Capital Guaranty Ins. Co., San Francisco, 1986-94; pres., CEO Monad Fin., San Rafael, Calif., 1994-97, Bank S.E. Europe Internat., San Juan, PR, 1997—2004; chmn. devel. Bank of South-East Europe, Bosnia-Herzegovina. Author: About Happy Living, 1985. State pres. Calif. Young Reps., 1965-66; commr. Statue of Liberty Ellis Island Centennial Commn., 1986; pres. Serbian Unity Congress, 1990-93, Coun. for Dem. Changes, 1998-01, Studenica Found., 1995-; dir. World Affairs Coun. of Am., 2002-04. With U.S. Army, 1961-63. Recipient Excellence award Am. Security Coun., 1967, Americanism medal Nat. Soc. DAR, 1969. Mem.: First Serbian Benevolent Soc. (treas. 1978—82). Avocations: reading, tennis, politics. Office: Monad Fin 535 4th St Ste 203 San Rafael CA 94901-3314 Business E-Mail: monadf@ix.netcom.com.

DJURDJANOVIC, DRAGAN, mechanical engineer, educator; b. Nis, Yugoslavia, Nov. 8, 1973; s. Miroslav and Olivera Djurdjanovic; m. Swee Paw Shum, Mar. 14, 2003; 1 child, Danica. BSME, U. Nis, Serbia, 1997; BS in Applied Math., U. Nis, Serbia, 1997; MS, Nanyang Technol. U., 1999; MSEE, PhD in Mech. Engring., U. Mich., 2002. From rsch. fellow to adj. asst. prof. Dept. Mech. Engring. U. Mich., Ann Arbor, Mich., 2002—04, adj. asst. prof. Dept. Mech. Engring., 2004—. Lead rschr. Intelligent Maintenance Sys. NSF I/UCRC, Ann Arbor, 2002—. Contbr. articles to profl. jours. (Outstanding Paper award, 2003). Recipient Jan. 11th award, City of Nis, 1998; Next Generation High Yield Fab grant, Semiconductor Rsch. Corp., 2004, Learning Model Based Diagnostics grant, ETAS Inc., 2004. Mem.: ASME, Soc. Mfg. Engrs. Achievements include invention of learning model based diagnostics. Office: Univ of Michigan Dept of Mech Eng 235 Hayward Street Ann Arbor MI 48109-2125 Office Phone: 734-763-9975. Personal E-mail: ddjurdja@umich.edu.

DLAB, VLASTIMIL, mathematics professor, researcher; b. Bzi, Czech Republic, Aug. 5, 1932; arrived in Can., 1968; s. Vlastimil Dlab and Anna (Stuchlikova) Dlabova; m. Zdenka Dvorakova, Apr. 27, 1959 (div.); children: Dagmar, Daniel Jan; m. Helena Briestenska, Dec. 18, 1985; children: Philip Adam, David Michael. R.N.Dr., Charles U., 1956, C.Sc., 1959, Habilitation, 1962, DSc, 1966; PhD, U. Khartoum, 1962. Rsch. fellow Czechoslovak Acad. Sci., Prague, 1956—57; lectr., sr. lectr. Charles U., Prague, 1957—59, reader, 1964—65, dir. Grad. Inst., 1992—94; lectr., sr. lectr. U. Khartoum, Sudan, 1959—64; rsch. fellow, sr. rsch. fellow Inst. Advanced Studies, Australian Nat. U., Canberra, 1965—66; prof. math. Carleton U., Ottawa, Canada, 1968—98, chmn. dept., 1971—74, 1994—97, disting. rsch. prof., 1998—, prof. emeritus; professorem hospitem Charles U., 1995—. Vis. prof. U. Paris VI, Brandeis U., U. Bonn, Monash U., U. Tsukuba, U. Sao Paulo, U. Stuttgart, U. Poitiers, Nat. U. Mex., U. Essen, U. Bielefeld, Hungarian Acad. Sci., Budapest, U. Warsaw, U. Normal Beijing, U. Vienna, UCLA, U. Va., Czechoslovak Acad. Sci., U. Trondheim, U. Paderborn, U. St. Petersburg, U. Reims, U. Sao Paulo, Osaka U., Yamaneashi U., Shinshu U., Eotvos U., Budapest, Charles U., Prague, U. Murcia, Spain, Erdos Rsch. Ctr., Budapest, Australian Nat. Univ., Canberra, Gadjah Mada U., Jogjakarta; presenter in field. Author: Representations of Valued Graphs, 1980, An Introduction to Diagrammatical Methods, 1981, Quasi-hereditary Algebras, 1994; editor: procs. internat. confs., 1974, 1979, 1984, 1987, 1990, 1992, 1993, 1994, 1996, 2004, Algebra and Representation Theory, 1998—, procs. internat. confs., 2002, Algebra and Discrete Mathematics, 2002—, Southeast Asian Bulletin of Mathematics; contbr. numerous articles to profl. jours. Recipient Diploma of Honour Union Czechoslovak Mathematicians, 1962; Can. Coun. fellow, 1974; Japan Soc. Promotion of Sci. sr. rsch. fellow, 1981; sci. exch. grantee Nat. Sci. and Engring. Rsch. Coun. Can., 1978, 81, 83, 85, 88, 91. Fellow Royal Soc. Can. (convenor 1977-78, 80-81, coun. 1980-81, editor-in-chief Comptes rendus mathematiques-Math. Reports 1997—); mem. Am. Math. Soc., Math. Assn. Am., Can. Math. Soc. (coun., chmn. rsch. com. 1973-77, editor Can. Jour. Math. 1988-93), European Math. Soc., London Math. Soc., Czech Math. Union. Roman Catholic. Avocations: sports, music. Home: 277 Sherwood Dr Ottawa ON Canada K1Y 3W3 Office: Carleton U Sch Math & Stat Math Dept Ottawa ON Canada K1S 5B6 Office Phone: 613-520-2600 ext 2616. E-mail: vdlab@math.carleton.ca.

D'LEON, OMAR, artist; b. Managua, Nicaragua, Mar. 5, 1933; arrived in U.S., 1986, naturalized; s. David and Guillermina Lacayo. D in Fine Arts, U. Managua, Nicaragua, 1957. Artist: one man exhibitions include: Museo de Tauroentum, France, 1982, Carnegie Mus., Calif., 1983, Ethinos Gallery, Calif., 1986, Gallery Qualli, Mexico City, 1987, Gallery Costa de Oro, Calif., 1988, Gallery Fernandez, Calif., 1989, Palm Street Gallery, Calif., 1990, Museo Galeria Omar d'León, Managua, Nicaragua, 1990, The Americas Collection, Miami Fla. Bond Gallery, San Francisco, 1993; numerous group exhibitions include: Bienial in Spain, Madrid, 1950, Bienial in France, N.Y. World's Fair, 1950, Bienial de Sao Paulo, Brazil, 1969, Galeria Tagüe, Managua, 1975, Fisherman's Wharf, San Francisco,1980, Moss Gallery, San Francisco, 1980, Segund Bienal, Mexico City, 1980, Presidential Collection, White House, Washington, 1983, Art Inst., Chgo., 1987, Christie's, Manson and Woods, Internat., N.Y.C., 1989, 90, The Armand Hammer Mus., L.A., 1991, William Doyle Galleries, N.Y., 1991, Gallery Los Pipitos, Managua, 1993, Galleries Contil, Josefina, Managua, Christie's, William Doyle, N.Y.C., 1992; permanent collections include: Mus. Modern Art of Latin Am., Washington, 1980, Gallery of Carole R. Korn Asid, Miami, 1982, Carnegie Art Mus., N.Y.C.; represented in permanent collection Mus. of Latin Am. Art, Calif., Sotheby's Auction, N.Y.C., Mus. Jose Luis Cueva, Mexico City, Hist. and Art Mus., Ventura City, Calif., Gallery Salinas, Beverley Hills, Calif., Mus. MOLAA Song Beach, Calif., 2000; authhor: Lapiel del Sigmo, 2001; his poetry is included in Treasured Poems of America, Cenizas Literature, Poesia Nicaragüense and other anthologies; art included in (book) Latin American Art in XX Century. Recipient Gold medal Managua, Nicaragua, early 1950's, Silver medal Juegos de Guatemala, Honorable mention, Bogota, Colombia, 3d prize Camarillo Art Ctr., 1984, 1st, 2d and best overall, 1983; special diploma from Consul Gen. Nicaragua, 1994. Achievements include invention of poineer of modern art in Nicaragua considerate agnostic and master top noch as painter, as poet and fighter for Freedom and Peace of the World. Avocations: writing, archaeology, classical music, philosophy, botanics. Home: PO Box 3125 Camarillo CA 93011-3125

DLOTT, SUSAN JUDY, judge, lawyer; b. Dayton, Ohio, Sept. 11, 1949; d. Herman and Mildred (Zemboch) D.; m. Austin E. Knowlton, July 11, 1986 (div. 1988); m. Stanley M. Chesley, Dec. 7, 1991. BA, U. Pa., 1971; JD, Boston U., 1973. Bar: Ohio 1973, U.S. Dist. Ct. (so. dist.) Ohio 1975, U.S. Ct. Appeals (6th cir.) 1976, U.S. Supreme Ct. 1980, U.S. Dist. Ct. (ea. dist.) Ky. 1984, U.S. dist. Ct. (no. dist.) Ohio 1989, Ky. 1990. Law clk. Ohio Ct. of Appeals, Cleve., 1973-74; asst. U.S. atty. U.S. Dist. Ct. (so. dist.) Ohio, Dayton, 1975-79; ptnr. Graydon, Head & Ritchey, Cin., 1979-95; dist. judge U.S. Dist. Ct. for So. Dist. Ohio, Cin., 1995—. Legal reporter Multimedia Program Prodn., Inc., 1982-84. Mem. Ohio Bldg. Authority, 1988-93, vice chmn., 1990-93, Jewish Fedn. Cin., trustee and mem. com. 1979-93, Jewish Cmty. Rels. Coun. Cin., 1980-90, Hamilton County Park Dist. Vol. in Parks, 1985-86 Recipient U.S. Postal Serv. Commendation, 1977, Service award Dayton Bar Assn., 1975-76. Mem. ABA, FBA (asst. treas. 1981-82, treas. 1982-83, sec. 1983-84, v.p. 1984-86), Ohio Bar Assn., Ky. Bar Assn., Cin. Bar Assn., Leadership Cin. Alumni Assn., Queen City Dog Tng. Club, 6th Cir. Jud. Conf. (life), NAACP (life), Hadassah (life), Potter Stewart Inn of Ct. (pres. 1997—), Cavalier King Charles Spaniel Club Jewish. Office: 100 E 5th St Cincinnati OH 45202-3927 Office Phone: 513-564-7630.

D'LOWER, DEL, manufacturing executive; b. Sept. 21, 1912; s. Max and Estere (Gerlatky) D.; m. Helen Fuchs, June 5, 1937 (dec. Mar. 1980); 1 child, Esther Ann. Student, U. Tulsa, 1942-44, New Sch., N.Y.C., 1960-63. Cosmetologist Seligman & Latz, N.Y.C., 1936-41, Del's, Tulsa, 1941-46; owner Delby beauty salon, N.Y.C., 1946-76; greeting card mfr., 1972; diversified bus. exec., pres., CEO Delby Sys., N.Y.C., 1975—; personal care products mfr., 1976. Author: Ginny the Pretty White Doe, 1973; composer:

High Cheek bones, 1960, Only the Ashes Remain, The Wedding Waltz, Good Bye Diane, 1990, m' Dina Dinosaurian Coquette, 1993; patentee in field. Fellow ASCAP, 1992. Jewish. Avocations: creative writing, composing, poems, plays.

DLUGACH, ELENA, psychiatrist; MD, Sechenov Moscow Med. Acad., 1993. Diplomate in psychiatry Am. Bd. Psychiatry and Neurology, 2001, in child and adolescent psychiartry Am. Bd. Psychiatry and Neurology, 2003. Gen. psychiatry resident Robert Wood Johnson Med. Sch. U. Medicine and Dentistry N.J., Piscataway, NJ, 1996—99, child and adolescent psychiatry resident Robert Wood Johnson Med. Sch., 1999—2001; child and adolescent psychiatrist Cmty. Care, Bangor, 2001—. Mem.: APA. Office: Cmty Care PO Box 936 Bangor ME 04402-0936 Office Phone: 207-945-4240. Personal E-mail: edlugach@hotmail.com.

DLUGOFF, MARC ALAN, lawyer; b. NYC, Oct. 6, 1955; s. Arnold M. and Ruth B. (Schnall) D. AB, Colgate U., 1976; JD, Hofstra U., 1980; LLM in Taxation, NYU, 1981. Bar: N.Y. 1981, D.C. 1985, Calif. 1988. Law clk. to presiding justice U.S. Tax Ct., Washington, 1981-83; assoc. Mudge, Rose, Guthrie, Alexander & Ferdon, NYC, 1983-85, Milbank, Tweed, Hadley & McCloy, NYC, 1985-89, ptnr., 1989—92; counsel Roberts & Holland, NYC, 1993-94; pres., CEO, Atlantic Adv. Corp., NYC, 1995—. Fundraiser lawyers divsn. United Jewish Appeal, N.Y.C. chpt., 1986-90. Charles Dana scholar Colgate U., 1976. Mem. ABA, N.Y. State Bar Assn., Assn. Bar City N.Y., State Bar Calif., Phi Beta Kappa. Jewish. Home and Office: 130 Water St Ste 5-G New York NY 10005-1625 E-mail: marcnyc130@hotmail.com.

DLUHY, DEBORAH HAIGH, dean; b. Summit, NJ, Mar. 4, 1940; d. Richard Hartman Haigh and Elin Frederika Anderson Neumann; m. Robert George Dluhy, June 11, 1962; 1 child, Leonore Alexandra. BA, Wheaton Coll., 1962; postgrad., Boston U., 1962—63, U. Heidelberg, Germany, 1963—65; PhD, Harvard U., 1976. Instr. fine arts Wheaton Coll., Norton, Mass., 1975—76, Radcliffe Coll., Cambridge, Mass., 1977, Boston Coll., Newton, Mass., 1976—78; devel. officer Mus. Fine Arts, Boston, 1978—84, asst. dir. devel., 1984—86; assoc. dean adminstrn. Sch. Mus. Fine Arts, Boston, 1986—87, dean acad. programs and adminstrn., 1987—93, dean, 1993—; dep. dir. Mus. Fine Arts, Boston, 1999—. Trustee Cultural Edn. Collaborative Boston, 1987—90, Wheaton Coll., Norton, Mass., 1988—, mem. exec. com., vice chair fin. and facilities, 2001—02, chair faculty/staff com., mem. governance bd., 2004—, vice chair presdl. search com., 2003—04, chair bd. trustees, 2005—; pres. Wheaton Coll. Alumni Assn., Norton, Mass., 1994—2000; visitor Walnut Hill Sch., Natick, Mass., 1996—; pres. Pro Arts Consortium, 1999—2000; bd. dirs. Boston Arts Acad., 1999—. Woodrow Wilson fellow, 1963. Mem.: Assn. Ind. Coll. Art and Design (program com. 1995—2001, bd. dirs., exec. com., chair), Copley Soc. Boston (hon. trustee 1997—), Nat. Assn. Schs. Art and Design (rsch. com. 1990—96, evaluator 1996—, bd. dirs. 1996—, sec. bd. dirs. 2001—, exec. com. 2001—). Office: Sch Mus of Fine Arts 230 Fenway Boston MA 02115-5534 Office Phone: 617-369-3611. Personal E-mail: ddluhy@earthlink.net. E-mail: ddluhy@mfa.org.

D'LUHY, JOHN JAMES, investment banker; b. Passaic, N.J., Sept. 18, 1933; s. John George and Leonara (Fila) D'L.; m. Gale Rainsford, Dec. 7, 1968; children: Amanda, Pamela. AB, Trinity Coll., 1955; MBA, The Wharton Sch., U. Pa., 1959. Lic. amateur radio operator K2EXI, comml. pilot (instrument-rated). Jr. exec. trainee Merrill Lynch, N.Y.C., 1956—58, with over-the-counter rsch. dept., 1959—60; assoc. syndicate dept., investment mgmt., investment banking Lazard Freres & Co., N.Y.C., 1960—68; sr. v.p., ptnr., dir. money mgmt. and venture capital divsn. R.W. Pressprich & Co., N.Y.C., 1968—72; dir. money mgmt. and pvt. placements Wood Walker & Co., N.Y.C., 1972—73; pres. U.S. Oil Co., 1973—83, founder, pres., 1983—84; pvt. investor Dominick & Dominick, N.Y.C., 1983—86; fin. advisor Robert Thomas Securities divsn. Raymond James Assocs., N.Y.C., 1990—2002; pvt. investor Spring Lake, NJ, 2002—. Trustee Collier Svcs. Found., Marlboro, N.J., 1986-92; bus. coun. Monmouth Univ., West Long Branch, N.J., 1994-98. Hon. usher St. Patrick's Cath., N.Y.C., 1969—, chief hon. usher, 1975-76; founding mem. U.S. Naval War Coll. Found., 1969—, Newport, R.I., trustee, 2001—, fin. com. 2002—, chmn. audit com., 2004-05, treas., 2004—; co-chmn. Spring Lake Centennial Com., 1990-92; pres. Spring Lake Chorus, 1990-92; mem. Bond Club N.Y., 1963-91, Thurs. Evening Club, 1981-87, Chorus of Atlantic, 2000—, barbershop chorus; 1st pilot, aux. air arm, U.S. Coast Guard Aux., flotilla air officer, 2001-2003, vice comdr., 2003-04. Served with USN, 1955. Mem. Investment Assn. N.Y. (bd. dirs. 1967, chmn. capital and money mktgs. com.), Assn. Investment Mgmt. and Rsch., N.Y. Soc. Security Analysts (sr. analyst, high net worth investors com. 2000-02, career devel. com. 2000-02), Am. Radio Relay League, Aircraft Owners and Pilots Assn., Univ. Club N.Y.C. (coun. 1977-83, exec. com., treas. 1979-83), Spring Lake Bath and Tennis Club, Jersey Aero Club (chmn. rules com. 1992), Blue Hill (N.Y.C.) Troupe, Penn Club N.Y., Clayton (N.Y.) Yacht Club. Roman Catholic. Home: 115 Ludlow Ave Spring Lake NJ 07762-1547 Home (Summer): Club Island Clayton NY 13624 E-mail: johngale@worldnet.att.net.

DLUHY, ROBERT GEORGE, physician; b. Montclair, N.J., Jan. 23, 1937; s. John George and Leona (Fila) D.; m. Deborah Haigh; 1 child, Leonore Alexandra. AB magna cum laude, Princeton U., 1958; MD, Harvard Med. Sch., 1962. Intern/resident Peter Bent Brigham Hosp., Boston, 1962, 65-67, endocrine fellow, 1967-69; instr. med. Harvard Med. Sch., Boston, 1969-74, asst. prof. med., 1974-80, assoc. prof. med., 1980-98, prof. med., 1998—. Assoc. editor New Eng. Jour. Medicine. Capt. med. corp. U.S. Army, 1964-66, Germany. Fellow: Endocrine Soc., Hypertension Coun. AHA; mem.: Phi Beta Kappa. Office: Endocrine Hypertension Divs 221 Longwood Ave # Rfb2 Boston MA 02115-5804 Office Phone: 617-732-5011. Business E-Mail: rdluhy@partners.org.

DMITROVSKY, ETHAN, oncologist, medical educator, researcher; b. Phila., 1954; BS, Harvard Coll., 1976; MD, Cornell U. Med. Coll., 1980. Intern NY Hosp. - Meml. Sloan-Kettering Cancer Ctr., NYC, 1980—81, resident in internal medicine, 1981—83; med. staff fellow Nat. Cancer Inst., NIH, Bethesda, Md., 1983—86, fellow in biotechnology, Molecular Genetics Section-Navy Med. Oncology Br., 1986—87; clin. asst. physician Meml. Sloan-Kettering Cancer Ctr., 1987—89, asst. prof., 1989—92, named head lab. molecular medicine, 1992, named assoc. mem. Sloan Kettering Inst. molecular pharmacology and therapeutics program, 1994; named assoc. prof. medicine Cornell U., 1992; Andrew G. Wallace Prof., chmn. dept. pharmacology and toxicology Dartmouth Med. Sch., 1998—, acting dean, 2002—03. Spkr. in field. Contbr. articles to profl. jours., more than 100 pubs.; mem. editl. bds. (major oncology jours.) Jour. Nat. Cancer Inst., Cancer Rsch., Clin. Cancer Rsch., Jour. Clin. Oncology, Molecular Cancer Therapeutics; assoc. editor: Encyclopedia of Cancer. Mem.: Am. Soc. Clin. Investigation, Am. Soc. Clin. Oncology (young investigator award), Am. Assn. Cancer Rsch., Am. Cancer Soc. Achievements include research on mechanisms of human tumor cell growth and differentiation helping to advance cancer therapy and prevention; helped clone the abnormal retinoid receptor found in acute promyelocytic leukemia and led the team that developed the molecular test used to diagnose this disease. Office: Dartmouth Med Sch 1 Rope Ferry Rd Hanover NH 03755-1404

DMYTRYSHYN, BASIL, historian, educator; b. Poland, Jan. 14, 1925; arrived in U.S., 1947, naturalized, 1951; s. Frank and Euphrosinia (Senchak) Dmytryshyn; m. Virginia Roehl, July 16, 1949; children: Sonia, Tania. BA, U. Ark., 1950; MA, U. Ark, 1951; PhD, U. Calif., Berkeley, 1955; diploma (hon.), U. Kiev-Mohyla Acad., 1993. Asst. prof. history Portland (Oreg.) State U., 1956-59, assoc. prof., 1959-64, prof., 1964-89, prof. emeritus, 1989—, assoc. dir. Internat. Trade and Commerce Inst., 1984-89. Vis. prof. U. Ill., 1964-65, Harvard U., 1971, U. Hawaii, 1976, Hokkaido U., Sapporo, Japan, 1978-79; adviser U. Kiev-Mohyla Acad., 1993. Author books including: Moscow and the Ukraine, 1918-1953, 1956, Medieval Russia, 900-1700, 4th edit., 2000, Imperial Russia, 1700-1917, 4th edit., 1999, Modernization of Russia Under Peter I and Catherine II, 1974, Colonial Russian America 1817-1832, 1976, A History of Russia, 1977, U.S.S.R.: A Concise History, 4th edit., 1984, The End of Russian America, 1979, Civil and Savage Encounters, 1983, Russian Statecraft, 1985, Russian Conquest of Siberia 1558-1700, 1985, Russian Penetration of the North Pacific Archipelago, 1700-1799, 1987, The Soviet Union and the Middle East, 1917-1985, 1987, Russia's Colonies in North America, 1799-1867, 1988, The Soviet Union and the Arab World of the Fertile Crescent, 1918-1985, 1994, Imperial Russia, 1700-1917, 1999, Medieval Russia, 850-1700, 2000; contbr. articles to profl. jours. U.S., Can., Yugoslavia, Italy, South Korea, Fed. Republic Germany, France, Eng., Japan, Russia, Ukraine. State bd. dirs. PTA, Oreg., 1963-64; mem. World Affairs Coun., 1965-92. Named Hon. Rsch. Prof. Emeritus, Kyungnam U., 1989—; Fulbright-Hays fellow W. Germany, 1967-68; fellow Kennan Inst. Advanced Russian Studies, Washington, 1978; recipient John Mosser award Oreg. State Bd. Higher Edn., 1966, 67; Branford P. Millar award for faculty excellence Portland State U., 1985, Outstanding Retired Faculty award, 1994; Hillard scholar in the humanities U. Nev., Reno, 1992. Mem. Am. Assn. Advancement Slavic Studies (dir. 1972-75), Am. Hist. Assn., Western Slavic Assn. (pres. 1990-92), Can. Assn. Slavists, Oreg. Hist. Soc. (hon. mem. coun.), Nat. Geog. Soc., Conf. Slavic and East European History (nat. sec. 1972-75), Am. Assn. for Ukrainian Studies (pres. 1991-93), Ctr. Study of Russian Am. (hon.), Assn. Study Nationalities (bd. mem.-at-large USSR and Ea. Europe 1993—), Czechoslovak Soc. Arts and Scis., Soc. Jewish-Ukraine Contacts Assn., Salem City Club. Home: 5291 Woodscape Dr SE Salem OR 97306

DO, TAM HUU, health educator, academic counselor; b. Nhatrang, Vietnam, Aug. 31, 1954; s. Mau Do and Hai Thi Nguyen; m. Thuy Thi Nguyen, June 1, 1986; children: Namgiao, Tonhu, Nhan, Hoa. BA, CSU Fullerton, 1980; M in pub. health, Loma Unda U., 1982; M in edn., UC Los Angeles, 1989; M, CSU, Dominguez Hills, 1996; D in edn., UCLA, 2004. Health educator Calif. Dept. of Health Svcs., 1982—84; project dir. Bachviet Assn., Sacramento, 1985—86; program specialist City of Irvine, 1994—95; acad. counselor for internat. students Irvine Valley Coll., 1996—. Co-dir. Giaodiem Humanitarian Project, 1995—; project Vietnam, 2000—03. Green Party. Buddhist. Avocation: Aikido. Home: 4161 Loma St Irvine CA 92604 Personal E-mail: tamdo831@hotmail.com.

DO, THI D., lawyer; arrived in U.S., 1980; s. Thang D. and Xuan Thi Minh Au; m. Dominque T. Tran, May 23, 1998; 1 child: Nicholas Duy. BS, Va. Commonwealth U., 1992, MS, 1994; JD, St. Louis U. Sch. of Law, 1998. Bar: Wash. 2002, U.S. Ct. Appeals (9th cir.) 2002. Asst. prof. Va. Commonwealth U., Richmond, 1994—95; immigration specialist Intel Corp., Folsom, Calif., 2000—01; attorney pvt. practice Law Offices of Thi Do, Sacramento, 2002—. Recipient Pro Bono Publico Svc. commendation, Wash. State Bar Assn., Olympia, 2003. Mem.: Am. Health Lawyers Assn., Am. Immigration Lawyers Assn. Buddhist. Office: Law Offices of Thi Do 2831 Fruitridge Rd Ste k Sacramento CA 95820 Office Fax: 916-456-7527. E-mail: thi_d_do@yahoo.com.

DO, TWEE T., orthopedist; BS in Microbiology, U. Iowa, 1989, MD, 1993. Diplomate Am. Bd. Orthop. Surgeons. Resident in orthop. surgery U. Colo., Denver, 1993—98; fellow in pediat. orthopedics Hosp. for Spl. Surgery, NYC, 1998—99; asst. prof. orthop. surgery Children's Hosp. Med. Ctr., Cin., 1999—; clin. affiliate U. Cin. Orthopedics, 1999—. Mem. adv. bd. Girls on the Run, Cin., 2002—03; dir. neuromuscular orthop. Children's Hosp., Cin., 2002—. Contbr. articles to profl. jours., chapters to books. Mentor Cin. Youth Collaborative, 2003—. Fellow Travelling fellow, Japanese Orthop. Assn., 2004; grantee Allergon Rsch. grantee, Allergon Corp., 2003, Rsch. grantee, U. Cin. Orthop. Rsch. and Edn. Fund, 2003. Fellow: Am. Acad. Orthop. Surgeons, Am. Acad. Pediats.; mem.: Pediat. Orthop. Soc. N.Am. Avocations: camping, gardening, baking, running, mountain biking. Office: Cincinnati Children's Hosp 3333 Barnet Ave Cincinnati OH 45229 Office Phone: 513-636-4785. E-mail: twee.do@cchmc.org.

DOAK, WESLEY ALLEN, school librarian, educator; b. Oberlin, Ohio, Jan. 19, 1939; s. Homer Alson and Mary Jane (Flynn) Doak; m. Mary Carolyn Schipper, Sept. 19, 1970; m. Patricia Jean Macfarlane, June 0, 1965 (div.); 1 child, Patrick Brian. BA, Yankton (S.D.) Coll., 1960; MLS, U. Mass., 1963; degree, U. Calif., Davis, Calif., 1976. Cert. fund raiser Assn. Fundraising Execs., 1993, registered profl. librarian Mass. Bd. Libr. Examiners, 1963. Libr. Cary Meml. Libr., Lexington, Mass., 1960—63; sr. libr. Bruggemeyer Meml. Libr., Monterey Park, Calif., 1964—68; prin. libr. L.A. (Calif.) Pub. Libr., 1968—73; chief libr. devel. Calif. State Libr., Sacramento, 1973—83; state libr. Oreg. State Libr., Salem, Ohio, 1983—91; prof. Calif. State U., Sacramento, 1996—. Instr. Grad. Sch. Libr. and Info. Sci. U. Calif., L.A., 1971—73; chmn., CIO Mouse Magic!, Sacramento, 1991—; exec. dir. Oreg. Ctr. for Book, Salem, Ohio, 1987—91, Oreg. Econ. Info. Network, Salem, Ohio, 1988—91; instr. U. San Francisco, 1996—, Sacramento (Calif.) City Coll., 1996—. Editor (pub.): Film Review Index (Media & Methods award, 1970); composer: (films) Fifth Freedom (Cine Golden Eagle award, 1964); prodr.: (films) Wheels of Eden, (host): (TV series) Live Wire; designer: website. Spkr. Townwatch 80, Sacramento, 1980—80; citizen amb. People to People; developer Francis Ho., Sacramento, 2003—05, Family Services Agy., Sacramento, 2000—02. With U.S. Army, 1956—62. Named Oreg. Educator of the Yr., Oreg. Edn. Assn., 1990; recipient Boyle-Hutchinson award, Calif. Libr. Assn., 1977, McCarthy award, Nat. Coun. State Govts., 1990, Good Govt. award, Gov.'s Office, Oreg., 1991; fellow, Harvard U., MIT, 1990. Fellow: Am. Leadership Forum (past bd. dirs.); mem.: ALA (life; various positions), Assn. Fundraising Profls. (licentiate; info. tech.), Alliance Cmty. Media (assoc.; mem. regional bd.). Independent. Presbyn. Avocations: music, travel, reading. Office: Mouse Magic PO Box 19260 Sacramento CA 95819 Office Phone: 916-669-8376. Personal E-mail: wesdoak@surewest.net. E-mail: wesdoak@mousemagic.com.

DOAN, KIRK HUGH, lawyer; b. Independence, Iowa, Jan. 30, 1953; s. Arthur Nelson and Kathlyn (Kingsley) D.; m. Laura Leah Brown, M.D., Sept. 25, 1982. BS, Iowa State U., 1975; JD, U. Iowa, 1978. Bar: Mo. 1978, U.S. Dist. Ct. (we. dist.) Mo. 1978, U.S. Dist. Ct. Kans. 1998, U.S. Dist. Ct. Appeals (8th cir.) 1989, U.S. Supreme Ct. 1990. Assoc. Stinson Morrison Hecker, LLP, Kansas City, Mo., 1978-83, ptnr., 1983—. Contbr. articles to profl. jours. Advisor Heart of Am. coun. Boy Scouts Am., 1982—; counsel Met. Med. Soc. Greater Kansas City; capt. U.S. CAP. Mem. Mo. Bar Assn., Kansas City Met. Bar Assn., Lawyers Assn. Kansas City (pres. young lawyers sect. 1984-85, treas. sr. sect. 1991-94, bd. dirs. 2004-), Greater Kans. City Soc. Health Care Attorneys (pres. 2004)Order of Coif, Lakewood Oaks Country Club. Republican. Methodist. Home: 4300 NW Lake Dr Lees Summit MO 64064-1425 Office: Stinson Morrison Hecker LLP 1201 Walnut Ste 2600 Kansas City MO 64106-2150 Business E-Mail: kdoan@stinsonmoheck.com.

DOAN, MARY FRANCES, advertising executive; b. Vallejo, Calif., Apr. 16, 1954; d. Larry E. and Dudley (Harbison) D.; m. Timothy Warren Hesselgren, Mar. 19, 1988; children: Edward Latimer, Clinton Robert. BA in Linguistics, U. Calif., Berkeley, 1976; M in Internat. Mgmt., Am. Grad. Sch. Internat. Mgmt., 1980. Trading asst. The Capital Group, L.A., 1980-81; fin. analyst Litton Industries, Beverly Hills, 1981-82; account exec. Grey Advt., San Francisco, L.A., 1982-84, J. Walter Thompson, San Francisco, 1984-85, Lowe Marshalk, 1985-86; account supr. Young & Rubicam, 1986-89; acct. mgr. Saatchi & Saatchi, 1989—95, CEO, pres., 1995—96, worldwide dir. client svc. applications, 1997—98; cons., 1999; v.p. mktg. Roundl, San Francisco, 1999-2000; cons., 2001—02; v.p. mktg. and advt. Good Guys, 2002—04, cons., 2005—. Office Phone: 415-504-6977. Personal E-mail: mfdoan@hotmail.com.

DOAN, MICHAEL FREDERICK, editor; b. Oakland, Calif., Feb. 5, 1942; s. Philip Melville and Agnes Blair (Gee) Doan; m. Mary Pickett Craddock, May 11, 1985; 1 child, Sara. BA in Journalism, U. Calif., Berkeley, 1963. Corr. AP, Las Vegas, 1968-69, econs. corr. Washington, 1970-79; assoc. editor U.S. News and World Report, Washington, 1979-87; editor Satellite Orbit mag., Vienna, Va., 1987-92; sr. assoc. editor Kiplinger Washington Editors, 1992-99; editor Kiplinger Calif. Letter, 2000—. Treas. United Meth. Ch., Washington. With USAR, 1964—70. Mem.: Washington Press Club (chmn. membership, sec. 1980—87). Methodist. Avocations: skiing, biking, jazz piano. Home: 3316 21st Ave N Arlington VA 22207-3821 Office: Kiplinger Washington Editors 1729 H St NW Washington DC 20006-3925 E-mail: mdoan@kiplinger.com.

DOAN, SHANE, professional hockey player; b. Halkirk, Alta., Can., Oct. 10, 1976; s. Bernie; m. Andrea Doan; children: Gracie, Joshua. Profl. hockey player Winnipeg Jets (now Phoenix Coyotes), 1995—96, Phoenix Coyotes, 1996—. Player Team Can., World Championships, 2003, Team Can., World Cup of Hockey, 2002. Charity work United Blood Svcs. Named to, Western Conf. All-Star Team, 2004. Achievements include won Gold medal with Team Canada, World Championships, 2003; mem. World Cup Champion Team Can., 2004. Avocations: golf, horseback riding. Office: c/o Phoenix Coyotes Hockey Club Alltel Ice Den 9375 E Bell Rd Scottsdale AZ 85260

DOAN, TAI DANH, social worker, director; b. Thuy Loi, Vietnam, July 14, 1936; arrived in U.S., 1975; s. Cuc Danh Doan and Bong Thi Chu; m. Thu Minh Thi Nguyen, 1962; children: Trinh Thuy, Trang Thuy, Hoai Thu, Minh Danh. Grad., Vietnamese Naval Acad., 1957; MS in Mgmt., US Naval Acad., 1974. Skipper Navy ships Vietnamese Navy Fleet, 1962—68; chief bur. naval ops. Vietnamese Navy Hdqrs., Saigon, 1968—72, chief bur. naval personnel, 1974—75; project dir. title XX Vol. Agys. Employment Svc. Consortium, San Diego, 1979—81; social work supr. Health & Human Svcs. Agy., San Diego, 1981—. Adj. faculty Mesa Coll., San Deigo, 1997—. Commr. Equal Opportunity Commn., San Diego, 1987—91; employment equal opportunity com. Dept. Social Svcs., San Diego, cultural awareness com.; chair San Diego Refugee Coalition; vice chair adv. bd. Pan Asian Parents Edn. Project; adv. bd. Indochinese bilingual edn. program San Diego City Schs.; adv. bd. ESSA; adv. bd. family planning project Linda Vista Health Ctr.; adv. bd. Indochinese Continuing Edn. Project San Diego C.C., San Diego; adv. bd. tchr. corps. Coll. Edn., San Diego State U.; adv. bd. nat. project Indochinese document evaluation Calif. State U., Long Beach; adv. bd. Indochinese needs assessment survey project Social Sci. Rsch. Lab., San Diego State U.; bd. dirs. Bayside Settlement Ho. Home: 14335 Bourgeois Way San Diego CA 92129 Office: HHSAA 4370 54th St San Diego CA 92115

DOANE, CHERI LYNN, education educator; b. Newton, Iowa, Aug. 21, 1954; d. Les and La Vola Trout; m. Marty Doane, Feb. 11, 1978; children: Emily Hotchkin, Andrew. AA, Des Moines Area C.C., Newton, Iowa, 1997; BA, Ctrl. Coll., Pella, 1998; MSc, Iowa State U., 2003. Dir. cmty.-based learning Ctrl. Coll., Pella, 1999—. Cons. various colls. and corps. Trustee Skiff Med. Ctr., Newton, Iowa, 1994—2001, Newton Cmty. Ednl. Found., 1990—2001, Progress Industries, Newton, 1992—98; chmn. state conv. Iowa PTA, Des Moines, 1998—98; bd. dirs. Positively Pella, 2003—05, Pella C. of C., 2002—04. Recipient Outstanding Alumni award, Des Moines Are C.C. Alumni Assn., 2004. Mem.: Iowa Campus Compact (steering com. mem. 2002—05). Democrat. Quaker. Office: Central Coll 812 University Pella IA 50219 Office Phone: 641-628-5332.

DOANE, EILEEN MALONEY, learning disabilities teacher consultant; b. Welcome, Md., Dec. 5, 1933; d. John Laurence and Lillian Marion (Posey) Maloney; m. Allan Hammond Doane, June 12, 1954; children: Kathleen, Sharon, Elizabeth. BA in Speech Arts, George Washington U., 1955; MA in Edn., Seton Hall U., 1983; postgrad. studies Learning Disabilities, Kean Coll., 1987; PhD, Berne U., 2002. Cert. tchr. of handicapped, speech correction, prin., supr., learning cons., N.J. Mem. child study team Elizabeth (N.J.) Bd. Edn. Spl. Svcs., 1990-95; learning disability tchr. cons., instrnl. supr. Matheny Sch. and Hosp., Peapack, N.J., 1995—; owner, dir. Randolph Denville Ednl. Ctr., Denville. Mem. Outreach Com. St. Peter's Episcopal Ch., Mountain Lakes, N.J., adult edn. com. Mountain Lakes. Recipient cert. appreciation Vol. Action Ctr., Morristown, N.J, Mental Health Players, Morris County Mental Health Assn., Madison, N.J., 1987, Benefactor award Rotary Found., Evanston, Ill., 1995; named Paul Harris fellow Rotary Found., 1984. Mem. AAUW, N.J. Assn. Learning Cons., Coun. Exceptional Children, Kappa Delta Pi. Democrat. Avocations: bridge, reading, travel. Home: 38 Cobb Rd Mountain Lakes NJ 07046-1143 Office: Randolph Denville Ednl Ctr 3125 Rt 105 Denville NJ 07834 Office Phone: 973-328-8088.

DOANE, TIM, travel company executive; BBA in Mktg. and Mgmt., U. Cin., 1979; MBA in Mktg. and Fin., Miami (Ohio) U. With Travel Centers of Am., Westlake, Ohio, 1995—, sr. v.p., mktg., pres., COO, 2003—05, pres., CEO, 2005—. Office: Travel Centers of Am 24601 Center Ridge Rd Westlake OH 44145

DOBB, LINDA SUE, academic administrator, librarian; b. Reading, Pa., Aug. 6, 1952; d. Rhea Beverly Blachman; m. Arthur Michael Small, Aug. 14, 1985; 1 child, Lorelei Small. AB, U. Calif., Berkeley, 1973; MLS, Simmons Coll., 1974; JD, Hastings Coll., 1983. Cataloging libr., instr. libr. sci. City Coll. San Francisco, 1974-83; processing libr. Libr. Congress, Washington, 1984-85; chief bibliographic control sect. Govt. Printing Office, Washington, 1985-87; asst. univ. libr. San Francisco State U., 1990-95; dean librs. Bowling Green (Ohio) State U., 1995-99, exec. v.p., 2000—. Fellow Coro Found-City Focus Program, San Francisco, 1993-94; adv. bd. Kent (Ohio) State Sch. Libr. and Info. Sci., 1997—; reviewer NSF and Inst. for Mus. and Libr. Svcs., Washington, 1998-2000. Bd. dirs. Calif. Libr. Authority for Sys. and Svcs., San Jose, Calif., 1990-95, OhioNet, Columbus, 1996-2000, Horizon Youth Theatre, Bowling Green, 1999-2001. Mem. ALA, AFTRA, Libr. Adminstrn. and Mgmt. Assn. (v.p./pres.-elect 2001—), Kiwanis. Avocation: acting. Office: Bowling Green State U McFAll Ctr 220 Bowling Green OH 43403 Home: PO Box 743 Bowling Green OH 43402-0743 Fax: 419-372-7723. E-mail: ldobb@bgnet.bgsu.edu, bgsulib@wcnet.org.

DOBBEN, AMY MARKAY, music educator; d. Gerald W. and Margaret L. McGuffey; m. James M. Dobben, Sept. 27, 1997. BA in Applied Music, Lee U., 1997. Min. music West A St. Ch. God, Kannapolis, NC, 2000—01, Dixie Valley Ch. God, Louisville, 2001—04; instr. piano Forte Piano Studio, LLC, 2004—. Vol. emer. fin. assistance Shively Area Ministries, Louisville, 2001—05. Recipient Music Departmental award, Lee U. Sch. Music, 1997. Mem.: Nat. Guild Piano Tchrs., Music Tchrs. Nat. Assn., Pi Kappa Lambda. Personal E-mail: amy@fortepianostudio.com.

DOBBIN, EDMUND J., university administrator; b. Bklyn., 1935; BA in Philosophy, Villanova U., 1958; MA, Augustinian Coll., 1962; SDT, U. Louvain, Belgium, 1971. ordained priest Roman Cath. Ch., 1962. Tchr. math. and religion, prefect of students Malvern Prep. Sch., 1962-67; tchr. systematic theology Washington Theol. Union, 1971-87, asst. prof., assoc. prof.; assoc. prof. Villanova U., Pa., 1987—, pres., 1988—. Trustee Villanova U., 1979-87, Merrimack Coll., North Andover, Mass., 1971-89, chmn. bd., 1986-89; mem. provincial coun. Augustinian Province of St. Thomas of Villanova, 1982-89. Mem. Am. Acad. Religion, Cath. Theol. Soc. Am. Office: Villanova U Office of the President 800 E Lancaster Ave Villanova PA 19085-1603

DOBBINS, DAVID FOSTER, lawyer; b. Cleve., Aug. 22, 1928; s. Verne Foster and Ida Wells (Smith) D.; m. Iris McKee, Sept. 27, 1953 (div. 1983); children: David Jr., Carol, James. BA, Yale U., 1950; LLB, Columbia U., 1956. Bar: N.Y. 1957, U.S. Ct. Appeals (2nd cir.) 1957, U.S. Dist. Ct. (so. and ea. dists.) N.Y. 1958, Ohio 1961, U.S. Ct. Appeals (9th cir.) 1978, U.S. Ct. Appeals (1st cir.) 1980, U.S. Ct. Appeals (5th cir.) 1980, U.S. Ct. Appeals (3rd cir.) 1981, U.S. Ct. Appeals (8th cir.) 1982, U.S. Supreme Ct. 1983, U.S. Ct. Appeals (10th cir.) 1985. Assoc. Dwight, Royall, Harris, Koegel & Caskey, N.Y.C., 1956-57; law clk. to Hon. Leonard P. Moore U.S. Ct. Appeals (2nd cir.), N.Y.C., 1957-58; assoc. Dwight, Royall, Harris, Koegel & Caskey, N.Y.C., 1958-60, Lane, Krotinger & Santoka, Cleve., 1961-62; assoc. to ptnr. Royall, Koegel, Rogers & Wells, Cleve., 1962-77; ptnr. Patterson, Belknap, Webb & Tyler LLP, Cleve., 1977—2000, of counsel, 2001—. Bd. dirs. All-O-Matic Inds., Jackson Heights, N.Y., 1988. Mem. bd. govs. Young Republican Club, N.Y.C., 1962-68. Lt. (j.g.), USN, 1950-53. Mem. ABA,

Assn. of Bar of City of N.Y., Ken Court Club, Phi Delta Phi. Republican. Episcopalian. Avocations: jogging, climbing, skiing. Office: Patterson Belknap Webb & Tyler LLP 1133 Ave Americas New York NY 10036

DOBBINS, FREDA JANE, librarian; b. Hutchinson, Kans., June 1, 1940; d. Mahlon F. and Verna (Detter) Stauffer; m. James R. Dobbins, Aug. 3, 1968; children: Jared S., Janelle K. BA, Southwestern Coll., 1962; MA, U. Denver, 1963. Head adult svcs. Hutchinson Pub. Libr., 1964-67; sys. cons. S. Ctrl. Kans. Libr. Sys., Hutchinson, 1967-68; reference libr. Main Post Libr., Fort Knox, Ky., 1968-69; from dir. ext. to legis. reference libr. Kans. State Libr., Topeka, 1970-78; dir. Pottawatomie Wabaunsee Regional Libr., St. Marys, Kans., 1985—. Mem. ALA, Kans. Libr. Assn. Methodist. Avocation: reading. Office: Pottawatomie Wabaunsee Regional Libr 306 N 5th St Saint Marys KS 66536-1404 Home: 1473 St Hwy 9 Goff KS 66428

DOBBINS ALBERSON, SHARON KAY, lawyer, educator; b. Akron, Ohio, Dec. 10, 1955; d. Richard Dean and Zelda Dolores (Shumate) D.; m. Ramsey Bancroft Alberson, Mar. 3, 1990; children: Heather, Renée. MusB summa cum laude, Kent State U., 1982; JD, U. Akron, 1985; M of Theol. Studies, Harvard U., 1987; diploma in Law, Oxford U., 1989. Bar: Ohio 1985. Vis. asst. prof. philosophy and humanities Wesleyan U., Middletown, Conn., 1991, 92; adj. prof. philosophy U. New Haven, West Haven, Conn., 1990, So. Conn. State U., New Haven, Conn., 1990—; atty. Akron, 1985—. Bus. ethics cons. Haluch & Assocs., Trumbull, Conn., 1990—; assoc. min. Southport Congl. Ch., 2002—. Author (booklet) How to Protect the Children and Keep the Church out of Court, 1988, (musical) The Law of Love, 1993, The Trial of Job, 1995, Lost and Found, 1996, Found and Forgiven, 1998, A Star for Freedom, 1999, Forever Love, 2000; contbr. articles to profl. jours. Treas. Greater Bridgeport Luth. Ministry Coalition, Bridgeport, Conn., 1992; v.p. Interfaith Vol. Caregivers of Greater Bridgeport; exec. sec. Greater Bridgeport Coun. of Ch. Mem. Ohio Bar Assn., Soc. of Law and Medicine. Avocations: singing, playing piano, composing. Home and Office: 452 Fisher Ct Shelton CT 06484-2836

DOBBS, DAN BYRON, lawyer, educator; b. Ft. Smith, Ark., Nov. 8, 1932; s. George Byron and Gladys Pauline (Stone) D.; m. Betty Jo Teeter, May 31, 1953 (div. 1978); children: Katherine, George, Rebecca, Jean. BA, LL.B., U. Ark., 1956; LL.M., U. Ill., 1961, J.S.D., 1966. Bar: Ark. 1956. Partner firm Dobbs, Pryor & Dobbs, Ft. Smith, 1956-60; asst. prof. law U. N.C., Chapel Hill, 1961-63, assoc. prof., 1963-66, prof., 1967, Aubrey L. Brooks prof. law, 1975-77; Rosenstiel prof. law U. Ariz., 1978—, Regents prof., 1992—. Vis. asst. prof. U. Tex., summer 1961; vis. prof. U. Minn., 1966-67, Cornell Law Sch., 1968-69, U. Va. Law Sch., 1974, U. Ariz. Law Sch., 1977-78 Author: Handbook on the Law of Remedies, Damages, Equity, Restitution, 1973, Problems in Remedies, 1974, The Law of Remedies, 3 vols., 2d edit., 1993, The Law of Torts, 2000; co-author: Prosser and Keeton on Torts, 5th edit., 1984, Torts and Compensation, 1985, 4th edit., 2001, (with Paul Hayden), 1997; contbr. articles to legal jours. Office: U Ariz Law Coll Tucson AZ 85721-0001

DOBBS, GREGORY ALLAN, journalist; b. San Francisco, Oct. 9, 1946; s. Harold Stanley and Annette Rae (Lehrer) D.; m. Carol Lynn Walker, Nov. 25, 1973; children: Jason Walker, Alexander Adair. BA, U. Calif., Berkeley, 1968; MSJ, Northwestern U., 1969. Assignment editor, reporter Sta. KGO-TV, San Francisco, 1966-68; news dir. San Francisco Tourist Info. Program Service, 1968; editor ABC Radio, Chgo., 1969-71; prodr. ABC News, Chgo., 1971-73, corr., 1973-77, London, 1977-82, Paris, 1982-86, Denver, 1986-92; host The Greg Dobbs Show/Sta. KOA Radio, 1992—98; corr. Nat. Geographic TV, 2001—03; host The Greg Dobbs Morning Show KNRC Radio, Denver, 2002—04; host Colo. State of Mind Rocky Mt. PBS, 2003—; corr. HDNet TV, 2004—. Adj. prof. Northwestern U. Sch. Journalism, 1975, 76; prof. U. Colo. Sch. Journalism, 1996—; corr. Nat. Geog. TV, HD Net TV. Columnist The Denver Post, 1996—2001, Rocky Mountain News, 2001—, nationally syndicated columnist Scripps Howard, 2001—. Recipient Sigma Delta Chi Disting. Svc. award for TV reporting Soc. Profl. Journalists, 1980, Emmy award for the best news reporting on a network 1980, outstanding documentary, 1989, award of excellence Colo. Broadcasters Assn., 1993, 94, award for best talk show Colo. Soc. Profl. Journalists, 1994, Emmy Best Interview/Discussion program, 2003; Lippmann fellow Ford Found., 1975; named Best Talk Show Host in Denver, Westword Mag., 2002 Office: 1153 Bergen Pkwy Ste M150 Evergreen CO 80439-9501 Office Phone: 303-670-1977. E-mail: dobbs@newslike.com.

DOBBS, HERBERT HOTALING, automotive executive, consultant, research scientist, retired military officer; b. Mpls., July 5, 1931; s. Willis Clark and Mary Evalyn (Hotaling) D.; m. Joyce Belle Roberts, Mar. 20, 1954; children: Herbert H., Jr., Douglas Edwin, Graeme Clark. BSME, U. Minn., 1954; MSME, U. Mich., 1961, PhD in Mech. Engring., 1972; grad., U.S. Army Command and Gen., 1972, U.S. Army War Coll., 1977. Registered profl. engr., Mich. Commd. 2d. lt. U.S. Army, 1954, advanced through grades to col., 1977, assigned to Italy, 1955-57, assigned to Vietnam, 1966—67, assigned to Taiwan, 1975—76, ret., 1983; tech. dir. U.S. Army Tank-Automotive Command, 1983-85; chmn. Torvec, Inc., Pittsford, NY, 1998—2002. Design engr. Aerojet Gen. Corp., Sacramento, 1957; mem indsl. adv. bd. mech. engring. dept. Wayne State U., 1986—, Oakland U., 1986—; cons. Dobbs Assocs., Rochester Hills, Mich., 1986—; cons. Office Naval Rsch. USN, 1997; mem. or cons. U.S. Army Sci. Bd., 1994—; various govt. adv. bds., 1986—; mem. adv. bd. Nat. Jr. Sci. and Humanities Symposium, 1995—. Contbr. articles to profl. jours.; patentee for turbulent flow research work and military research and development work. State chmn. MSPE Mathcounts, 1986—. Mem. AIAA, ASME, AAAS, NSPE, Mich. Soc. Profl. Engrs., Soc. Automotive Engrs., Soc. Mfg. Engrs., Assn. Unmanned Vehicle Systems Internat., Res. Officers Assn., Assn. U.S. Army, Detroit chpt., exec. bd. 1985-99, chmn. jr. sci. and humanities seminar 1988-99, Armor Assn., Nat. Def. Indsl. Assn. Avocations: reading, mathematics, woodworking, opera. Home: 448 Maryknoll Rd Rochester Hills MI 48309 Office: Torvec Inc Powder Mills Office Pk 1169 Pittsford-Victor Rd Ste 125 Pittsford NY 14534-9501 Office Phone: 248-375-2558. E-mail: dr.hh.dobbs@earthlink.net.

DOBBS, JOHN BARNES, artist, educator; b. Nutley, NJ, Aug. 2, 1931; s. John Montgomery and Catherine (Barnes) D.; m. Anne Baudement, 1959; children: Nicolas, Michel. Student, R.I. Sch. Design, 1949, Bklyn. Mus. Art Sch., 1950-52, Skowhegan Sch., 1952. Prof. studio art John Jay Coll. CUNY, N.Y.C., 1974-96. Thirty one-man shows in U.S. and France; group exhbns. include Am. Acad. Arts and Letters (Childe Hassam purchase prize 1972, Art award 1994), Whitney Mus., Nat. Acad. Design (Ranger Fund purchase prize 1966, 90, Benjamin Altman prize 1980, Edwin Palmer prize 1991, Obrig prize 2003), Mus. Modern Art, Butler Inst. Am. Art, Salon des Independents. Cpl. U.S. Army, 1952-54, ETO. Louis Comfort Tiffany grantee, 1967 Mem. NAD (academician), Century Club. Home: 463 West St Apt B339 New York NY 10014-2032

DOBBS, LOU, television executive, managing editor; b. Childress, Tex., Sept. 24, 1945; m. Debi Segura; children: Chance, Jason, Hilary, Heather. Degree in econs., Harvard U., 1967. Copy reader LA Times; chief econs. corr., anchor Moneyline CNN, NYC, 1980-81, anchor Primenews, 1981, v.p., mng. editor bus. news, 1984-97, pres. news, exec. v.p., 1997-98, anchor Moneyline Tokyo, 1989; host TV spl. Nobel Minds Stockholm, 1993; anchor Moneyline Chgo., 1992-1999; sr. v.p., 1992-97; exec. v.p., 1997-98; founder, CEO., chmn. space.com, 1999—2001; pres. CNNfn, 1995—99; exec. v.p. CNNfn.com, 1995—99; anchor, mng. editor CNN's Lou Dobbs Tonight, 2001—; anchor syndicated fin. news radio report Lou Dobbs Fin. Report, 2001—. Mem. Loeb Award judges com.; bd. mem. Soc. Profl. Journalists Found., Horatio Alger Assn., Nat. Space Found., Space.com. Columnist Money mag., NY Daily News, US News and World Report. Recipient George Foster Peabody award for coverage of 1987 stock market crash, Luminary award Bus. Journalism Rev., 1990, CableAce award, Front Page award, NY Film Festival award, Janus award, Daniel Webster award, Emmy awards, Award for Disting. Am., Horatio Alger Assn., 1999, Media award, Nat. Space Club, 2000; named Father Yr., Nat. Father's Day Com., 1993. Mem. NATAS, Investigative Reporters and Editors Assn., Am. Econ. Assn., Nat. Acad. TV Arts and Scis., Overseas Press Club, Planetary Soc., Sigma Delta Chi.*

DOBBS, MICHAEL E., management educator, researcher; b. Houston, Aug. 25, 1966; s. Curtis E. and Sue (Castleberry) D. BA, U. North Tex., Denton, 1988; MBA, Baylor U., 1991; PhD, U. Tex., Dallas, 1999. Computer technician Garland (Tex.) Ind. Sch. Dist., 1985-86; mgmt. trainee Color Tile, Inc., Dallas, 1989-90; grad. asst. Baylor U., Waco, Tex., 1990-91; sale assoc. Slaughter Distbg., Inc., Dallas, 1991-94; grad. asst. U. Tex., Dallas, 1994-99; asst. prof. mgmt. Ark. State U., Jonesboro, 1999—. Mem. Acad. of Mgmt., S.W. Acad. Mgmt., Am. Sociol. Assn., Acad. Internat. Bus. Avocation: canine frisbee. Office: Ark State U PO Box 59 State University AR 72467-0059

DOBBS, STANLEY, military officer, information quality engineer; s. Nancy Mae Miles; m. Cecily A. Williams, Mar. 13, 1993 (div. Aug. 1, 2001); children: Nia, Naomi, Niles Stanley, Fentrice A. A in sci. Nuclear Engring. Tech. (hon.), Naval Nuclear Power Sch., Orlando, Fla., 1986; BSEE, U. of Memphis, 1991; MBA, Fla. Inst. of Tech., Melbourne, 1999; MS in Ops. Rsch. Engring., Naval Postgrad. Sch., Monterey, Calif., 2001. Cert. nuclear quality assurance, Chief Naval Edn. and Tng., data quality engring., MIT, info. tech. program mgmt., George Wash. U. Instr. Naval Nuclear Power Program, Ballston Spa, NY, 1984—86; officer candidate Broadened Opportunity for Officer Selection and Tng., San Diego, 1986—87; profl. naval instr. Naval Air Sta. Millington, Tenn., 1987—91; logistics quality assurance officer USS Holland (AS 32), Agana, 1992—94; chief logistics officer USS Sunfish (SSN 649), Norfolk, Va., 1994—97; fed. contracts negotiator/ officer Naval Sea Sys. Command, Washington, 1997—99; ops. rsch. engr. Naval Postgrad. Sch., Monterey, Calif., 1999—2001; dep. dir. ops. rsch. Naval Inventory Control Point, Phila., 2001—02; dir. Data Integrity Mgmt. Ctr., Phila., 2002—. Dir. Data Integrity Mgmt. Ctr., Pa., 2001—; program mgr. Info. Quality Support Engring., Phila., 2001—03. Author (presenter): (quality engring. support sys.) Information Quality: When Profit is NOT the Bottom-line; author: (edn. cons.) Re-engineering the Forecasting Enrollment Management System for the MPUSD (Superior Svc. award, 2001). Distinguished chpt. mem. Alpha Phi Alpha, Memphis, Tenn., 1989—91. Lt. comdr. US Navy, 1983, Naval Inventory Control Point. Recipient Superior Svc. Bronze award, Fed. Exec. Bd., 2001, Superior Svc. Silver award, 2001, EEO/Diversity award, Phila. Area Human Resource, 2003. Master: Student Govt. Assn. (assoc.; v.p. student govt. 1989—90, Man of the Yr. 1989); mem.: Toastmasters Internat. (assoc.; club founder 2001—02), Alpha Phi Alpha (life; dean of pledges 1989—90, Brother of the Yr. 1990). Achievements include first to Information Centric Quality Management Methodology; Information Quality Support Management Circles of Excellence. Avocations: golf, youth development, computers, motivational speaking. Home: Ste N20 9601 Ashton Rd Philadelphia PA 19114 Office: Naval Inventory Control Point 700 Robbins Ave Philadelphia PA 19111 Personal E-mail: stan_dobbs@yahoo.com.

DOBELIS, INGE NACHMAN, editor, writer; b. Würzburg, Germany, Nov. 16, 1933; came to U.S., 1938, naturalized, 1951; d. Rudolf Hugo and Resi (Hamburger) Nachman; m. Miervaldis C. Dobelis, May 4, 1969; 1 child, Arthur N. BA in English, U. Ga., 1956. Editl. positions Buttenheim Publs. and Crowell-Collier, 1956-64; copy editor Gen. Book divsn. Readers Digest, N.Y.C., 1965-72, assoc. editor, 1973-79, sr. editor, 1979-85, 1979-85, sr. staff editor, 1985-97. Freelance writer, editor, 1998—; bd. dirs. Barnstable Assoc. editor: Reader's Digest Family Encyclopedia of American History, 1975, Reader's Digest Family Health Guide and Medical Encyclopedia, 1976, Reader's Digest Illustrated Guide to Gardening, 1978; editor: Readers Digest Family Legal Guide, 1981, Quick and Thrifty Cooking, 1984, Magic and Medicine of Plants, 1986, Great Recipes for Good Health, 1988, America: Land of Beauty and Splendor, 1992, Legal Problem Solver, 1994, Know Your Rights, 1995. Mem. exec. bd., officer Murray Hill Dem. Club, 1968-74; mem. exec. bd. Cmty. Bd. No. 6, N.Y.C., 1973-78, sec., 1976, chmn. health and hosps. com., 1974-78; trustee, officer Brotherhood Synagogue, 1983—, pres., 1993-95, hon. pres., 2001; mem. N.Y. Dem. County Com., 1967-74. Mem. Nat. Arts Club (N.Y.C.), Phi Beta Kappa. Home: 201 E 17th St New York NY 10003-3607 E-mail: inged@ix.netcom.com.

DOBELL, BYRON MAXWELL, magazine consultant; b. Bronx, N.Y., May 30, 1927; s. Jacob and Marie (Schaeffer) D.; m. Edith Spielberg, 1952 (div. 1957); m. Ande Rubin, 1958 (dec. 1967); 1 dau., Elizabeth; m. Elizabeth Rodgers Dempster, 1969 (dec. 1992); m. Alexandra Mayes Birnbaum, 1999. AB, Columbia U., 1947. Picture editor U.S. Camera, 1952-55; assoc. editor Popular Photography, 1956-57; feature editor Pageant, 1957-58, This Week, 1958-60; sr. editor Time-Life Books, 1960-62, assoc. dir. editl. planning, 1971-72; mng. editor Esquire mag., N.Y.C., 1962-67, 79-82, editor-in-chief, 1977, Book World (weekly lit. supplement Chgo. Tribune and Washington Post), 1967-69; editor-in-chief book divsn. McCall Pub. Co., 1969-71; editl. dir. New York mag., 1972-77; sr. editor Life mag., N.Y.C., 1978-79; editor-in-chief Am. Heritage mag., 1982-90, Am. Heritage of Invention & Tech. mag., 1984-90; mag. cons. N.Y.C., 1990—. Bd. dirs. Am. Soc. Mag. Editors, 1987-91. Editor: Life Guide to Paris, A Sense of History. Bd. advisors Libr. of Am., 2003—. Served with U.S. Army, 1946—47. Named to Am. Soc. of Mag. Editor's Hall of Fame, 1998. Mem. Century Assn. Home and Office: 145 E 76th St New York NY 10021-2843 Office Phone: 212-861-0256.

DOBELLE, EVAN SAMUEL, academic administrator; b. Washington, Apr. 22, 1945; s. Martin and Lillian (Mendelsohn) Dobelle; m. Edith Huntington Kit, June 7, 1970; 1 child, Harry Huntington. BA, U. Mass., 1983, MEd, 1970, EdD, 1987; MPA, Harvard U., 1984. Exec. asst. U.S. Senator Edward Brooke, Boston, 1971—73; mayor City of Pittsfield, 1973—76; commr. environ. mgmt. State of Mass., Boston, 1976—77; chief protocol U.S., Washington, 1977—78; treas. Dem. Nat. Com., 1978—79, dep. chair, 1980—81; chairman Carter-Mondale Presdl. Com., 1979—80; v.p. Bear Stearns and Co., N.Y.C., 1984—87; pres. Middlesex Cmty. Coll., Mass., 1987—90; chancellor City Coll. San Francisco, 1991—95; pres. Trinity College, Hartford, Conn., 1995—2001, U. Hawaii, Honolulu, 2001—04, New England Bd. Higher Edn., Boston, 2005—. Jewish. Avocations: reading, travel, history. Office Phone: 617-357-9620. Business E-Mail: edobelle@nebhe.org.

DOBERENZ, ALEXANDER R., nutrition educator, chemist; b. Newark, Aug. 17, 1936; s. Alexander J. and Marie (Zink) D.; m. Angela Rajoppi, June 7, 1958; children: Annamarie Wexler, Judith Lynn, Hoke Jr. BS in Chemistry, Tusculum Coll., 1958; MS, U. Ariz., 1960, PhD in Biochemistry and Nutrition, 1963. Rsch. assoc. dept. physics U. Ariz., Tucson, 1963-69; vis. assoc. prof. nutrition U. Hawaii, 1969; assoc. prof. nutritional scis. U. Wis., Green Bay, 1969-71, prof., 1971-76, assoc. dean Coll. and Sch. Profl. Studies, 1969-76, prof. growth and devel., 1975-76; prof. food sci. and human nutrition U. Del., Newark, 1976-97, dean Coll. Human Resources, 1976-93, coord. home econs. rsch., 1978-93, spl. asst. to the pres., 1993, interim v.p. for student life, 1994-95, prof. nutritional scis., Coll. of Health and Nursing Scis., 1997-99, prof. emerita, 1999—. Cons. food industry, 1976-93; mem. nat. steering com. new initiatives for home econs. U.S. Dept. Agr., 1979-81, USDA Planning com. Workshops on Improving Health Maintenance, 1984-87. Contbr. numerous articles on food chemistry and nutrition to profl. publs. Head underwater recovery unit Pima County Sheriff's Dept., 1966-68; warrant officer CAP, 1965-69; mem. Brown County Comprehensive Health Planning Coun., 1973-76; bd. dirs. Pima County Sheriff's Search and Rescue, 1968. Recipient Rsch. Career Devel. award NIH, 1966-69; named Outstanding Educator Am., 1971, 72. Fellow Am. Inst. Chemists; mem. Am. Chem. Soc., Am. Home Econs. Soc., Am. Inst. Nutrition (Mead Johnson award nominating com. 1973-76), Nutrition Soc. Today, Soc. for Nutrition Edn., Nutrition Soc. London Soc. Exptl. Biology and Medicine, Am. Soc. Clin. Nutrition, AAAS, Assn. Adminstrs. of Home Econs., Del. Gerontol. Soc. (exec. com. 1978), Nat. Coun. Adminstrs. Home Econs. (exec. bd. 1982-83), APHA, Del.-Panama Ptnrs. of Ams., Assn. for Devel. Computer Based Instruction, Del. Acad. Sci., Univ. and Whist Club, Sigma Xi, Phi Lambda Upsilon., Phi Kappa Phi. Roman Catholic. Business E-Mail: ard@udel.edu.

DOBEY, JAMES KENNETH, banker; b. Vallejo, Calif., June 20, 1919; s. Austin E. and Margaret (Hansen) D.; m. Jean Smith, Apr. 18, 1942; children: James A., Peter M. AB, U. Calif., Berkeley, 1940; postgrad., Rutgers U., 1956. With Shell Oil Co., Comml. Credit Corp., 1940-42, Wells Fargo Bank, San Francisco, 1946-72, exec. v.p., 1965-72, vice chmn. bd., 1973, chmn. bd., 1977-80, ret. Capt. airborne inf. AUS, 1942-46. Mem. Delta Chi. Mailing: Carmel Valley Manor 8545 Carmel Valley Rd Carmel CA 93923-9556

DOBIS, CHARLES, JR., systems administrator; s. Charles Edward Dobis and Betty Louise Mozisek. AA in Liberal Studies, Fullerton Coll., 1993. Aircraft maintenance adminstrn. USMC, Hawaii, 1980—84, Tustin, Calif., 1984—86, aircraft controller El Toro, 1986—89, aircraft maintenance adminstr., 1989—90; maintenance supr. Gold Key Landscape, 1990—94; adminstrn. clerk Nat. Park Svc., Stanton, ND, 1994—96; house mgr. Harmony Ho., Home for Disabled Men Ages 25-60, Fullerton, Calif., 2003—04. Sgt. USMC, 1977—90. Recipient Achievement medal, Sec. Navy, 1984, Commendation medal, 1986. Mem.: Smithsonian Inst. (assoc.), Calif. Rep. Party, Nature Conservancy, Am. Legion. Republican. Presbyterian. Achievements include five western pacific deployments including two in support of the Iran hostage crisis in Afghanistan between 1980-81. Avocations: trout fishing, hiking, reading, gardening.

DOBLER, DONALD WILLIAM, retired dean, management consulting executive; b. Rocky Ford, Colo., Apr. 18, 1927; s. William L. and Anna (Nelson) D.; m. Elaine Carlson, Dec. 27, 1951; children: Kathleen, David, Daniel. BS in Engring., Colo State U., 1946-50; MBA, Stanford U., 1958, PhD, 1960. Application and sales engr. Westinghouse Elec. Corp., Pitts. and Phila., 1950-53; mgr. purchasing and materials FMC Corp., Green River, Wyo., 1953-57; guest lectr. Stanford Sch. Bus., 1960; asst. prof. mgmt. State U. Utah, Logan, 1960-63, assoc. prof., 1964-66, head dept. bus. adminstrn., 1964-66; vis. prof. mgmt. Dartmouth Coll., 1963-64; dean Coll. Bus., Colo. State U., Ft. Collins, 1966-86; ind. mgmt. cons. Ft. Collins, 1986-91; corp. v.p. for cert. and program devel. Inst. Supply Mgmt., Tempe, Ariz., 1990-94. Past bd. dirs. U. Nat. Bank, Home Fed. Savs. Bank; pres. Parklane Arms, Inc., 1967-77; part-time mgmt. cons., 1960-86; cons. European Logistics Mgmt. Program, 1970, 72, 77, European Fedn. Purchasing, 1970; faculty Mgmt. Center Netherlands, 1972; dean's adv. coun. logistics mgmt. program Ariz. State U., 1991-94; mem. adv. bd. Mgmt. Inst. U. Wis., 1992-97. Sr. author: Purchasing and Supply Management, 1965, 6th edit., 1996; co-author: The Purchasing Handbook, 1993; mem. editl. bd. European Jour. Purchasing and Supply Mgmt., 1993—; contbr. articles on mgmt. to profl. jours., chpts. to books. Mem. Colo. Gov.'s Adv. Com., 1968-77, Ft. Collins Mayor's Budget Com., 1968-71; dist. chmn. Boy Scouts Am., 1974-77; mem. adv. council Colo. Region, SBA, 1973-79, No. Region, Colo. Div. Employment, 1975-77; bd. dirs., div. chmn. Ft. Collins United Way, 1973-80, pres., 1977; bd. dirs. Ft. Collins Jr. Achievement, 1973-87; bd. dirs. Colo. Assn. Commerce and Industry Ednl. Found., 1988-91. Served with USNR, 1945-46. Mem. Acad. Mgmt., Nat. Assn. Purchasing Mgmt. (Shipman Medalist 1987, chmn. nat. acad. plan com. 1976-81, mem. profl. cert. bd. 1981-86, chmn. 1985-86, assoc. editor Internat. Jour. Purchasing and Materials Mgmt. 1975-80, editor 1980-97), Denver Purchasing Mgmt. Assn. (dir. 1975-83, v.p. 1977, pres. 1979), Am. Prodn. and Inventory Control Soc., Green River Jr. C. of C. (pres. 1955), Am. Assn. Collegiate Schs. Bus. (nat. com. continuing accreditation 1972-78, nat. standards commn. 1978-81, dir. 1980-83, chmn. fin. and audit com. 1983), Sigma Tau, Phi Kappa Phi (editorial cons. Nat. Forum, 1988-94), Rotary, Beta Gamma Sigma (nat. gov. 1975-78) Methodist.

DOBNER, NANCY S., microbiologist, immunologist; b. Oak Park, Ill., Aug. 1, 1949; d. Elinor S. and Roland Radford Reed; m. Duane E. Dobner, Aug. 18, 1979; children: Amanda Marie, Derek Andrew. BA, So. Ill. U., 1976. Cert. med. technologist Mercy Hosp., 1978. Mgr. microbiology/immunology Consol. Med. Lab., Lake Bluff, Ill., 1996—2000, Lake Forest (Ill.) Hosp., 2000—. Sch. bd. mem. Wauconda (Ill.) Dist. 118, 1992—. Mem.: Am. Soc. Clin. Pathologists, Ill. Soc. Microbiologists, Am. Soc. Microbiologists (assoc.). Home: 29651 N Garland Rd Wauconda IL 60084 Office: Lake Forest Hosp 660 N Westmoreland Rd Lake Forest IL 60045 Office Phone: 847-535-6216. Personal E-mail: nsdobner@msn.com. E-mail: ndobner@lakeforesthospital.com.

DOBRANSKI, BERNARD, law educator; b. Sept. 3, 1939; s. Walter John and Helen Dolores (Rudnick) Dobranski; m. Caroll Sue Wood, Aug. 31, 1963; children: Stephanie, Andrea, Christopher. BBA in Fin., U. Notre Dame, 1961; JD, U. Va., 1964. Bar: Va. 64, U.S. Supreme Ct. 68, U.S. Ct. Appeals (DC cir.) 71. Legal advisor to bd. Nat. Labor Rels. Bd., 1964—67; profl. staff mem. Pres.'s Adv. Commn. on Civil Disorders, 1967—68; adminstrv. asst. U.S. Ho. of Reps., 1968—71; gen. counsel Washington Met. Area Transit Commn., 1971—72; mem. faculty Creighton U. Sch. of Law, Omaha, 1972—77, U. Notre Dame, 1977—83; prof., dean U. Detroit Sch. of Law, 1983—95, Cath. U. Am. Sch. of Law, 1995—99; prof., pres., dean Ave Maria Sch. of Law, Ann Arbor, Mich., 1999—. Labor arbitrator Fed. Mediation and Conciliation Svc. Contbr. articles to profl. jours. Mem.: ABA, Am. Arbitration Assn., Detroit Athletic Club, Hurlingham Club, Frank Murphy Honor Soc. Roman Catholic. Office: Ave Maria Sch of Law 3475 Plymouth Rd Ann Arbor MI 48105 Office Phone: 734-827-8043. Business E-Mail: bdobranski@avemarialaw.edu.

DOBRIANSKY, LEV EUGENE, economist, educator, diplomat; b. NYC, Nov. 9, 1918; s. John and Eugenia (Greshchuk) Dobriansky; m. Julia Kusy, June 29, 1946; children: Larisa Eugenia, Paula Jon. BS (Charles Hayden Meml. scholar), NYU, 1941, MA, 1943, Hirshland polit. sci. fellow, 1943—44, PhD, 1951; LLD, Free Ukrainian U. at U. Munich, 1952. Mem. faculty NYU, 1942—48; from asst. prof. econs. to prof. Georgetown U., Washington, 1948—86; prof. emeritus, 1986—; chmn. dept. Georgetown U., 1953—54; exec. mem. Inst. Ethnic Studies, 1957—65; dir. Inst. Comparative Econ. and Polit. Sys., 1970—86; grad. faculty Nat. War Coll., 1957—58; U.S. ambassador to Bahamas, 1982—86; pres. Global Economic Action Inst., 1987—92; chmn. Victims of Communism Meml. Found., Inc., 1994—2003. Lectr. on Soviet Union, Communism, U.S. Fgn. Policy; chmn. Nat. Captive Nations Com., Inc., 1959—; pres. Ukrainian Congress Com. Am., 1949-82, Am. Coun. for World Freedom, 1976-79; mem. Economists Nat. Com. on Monetary Policy; strategy staff Am. Security Coun., 1962-70; econs. editor Washington Report; mem. Pres.'s Commn. on Population, 1974-75; cons. Corpus Instrumentation, Kreber Found., Dept. State, 1971-75, USIA, 1971-74; mem. Am. Com. to Aid Katanga Freedom Fighters, Emergency Com. Chinese Refugees; Internat. mem. Pacific Rim Cmty. Inst., 1992-96; hon. pres. Ukrainian Congress com. Am., 1992—. Author: A Philosophico-Economic Critique of Thorstein Veblen, 1943, The Social Philosophical System of Thorstein Veblen, 1950, Free Trade Ideal, 1954, Communist Takeover of Non-Russian Nations in USSR, 1954, Veblenism: A New Critique, 1957, Captive Nations Week Resolution, 1959, Shevchenko Statue Resolution, 1960, Vulnerabilities of USSR, 1963, The Vulnerable Russians, 1967, U.S.A. and the Soviet Myth, 1971; co-author: The Great Pretense, 1956, The Crimes of Khrushchev, 1959, Decisions for a Better America, 1960, Nations, Peoples, and Countries in the USSR, 1964; pub.: Revista Americana, 1977; editor: Europe's Freedom Fighter: Taras Shevchenko, 1960, Tenth Anniversary of the Captive Nations Week Resolution, 1969, The Bicentennial Salute to the Captive Nations, 1977, Twentieth Observance and Anniversary of Captive Nations Week, 1980; assoc. editor: (1946-62) Ukrainian Quar., chmn. editorial bd., 1962-94; contbr.: Peace and Freedom Through Cold War Victory, 1964, Nationalism in the USSR and Eastern Europe, 1977, Ukraine in a Changing World, 1978; contbr. articles to profl. jours. Planning mem. Freedom Studies Center, Boston; asst. sec. Republican Nat. Conv., 1952; adviser Rep. Nat. Com., 1956; mem. Com. on Program and Progress of Rep. Party, 1959; asst. to chmn. Rep. Nat. Conv., 1964; vice chmn. nationalities div. Rep. Nat. Com., 1964; sr. adviser United Citizens for Nixon-Agnew, 1968; exec. mem. ethnic div. Com. to Reelect the Pres., 1972; advisor to Gov. Reagan, 1980; issues dir. Republican Nat. Com., 1980; chmn. Ukrainian Catholic Studies Found., 1970-73; bd. govs. Charles Edison Youth Fund, 1976-87; mem. expert adv. bd. NBC, Washington, 1977-80. chmn. Victims of Communism Meml. Found. Inc. Lt. col. (res.) 352d Mil. Govt. Civil Affairs 1958; col. U.S. Army Res., 1966. Recipient Freedoms Found.

award, 1961, 73; Shevchenko Freedom award Shevchenko Meml. Com., 1964; Shevchenko Sci. Soc. medal, 1965; Hungarian Freedom Fighters' Freedom award, 1965; Latvian Pro Merito medal, 1968; Freedom Acad. award Korea, 1969; Wisdom award of honor Calif., 1970; named Outstanding Am. Educator, 1973; decorated M.S.M., 1973; Georgetown U. Centennial medal of honor, 1982; Ellis Island medal of honor, 1986; Thomas C. Corcoran award, 1987; Lifetime Achievement award, 2005; Truman, Reagan Freedom award, 2005. Mem. Free World Forum (exec. com.), Citizens for Democracy, Acad. Polit. Sci., Nat. Acad. Econs. and Polit. Sci., AAUP, Am. Acad. Polit. and Social Sci., Am., Cath. econ. assns., Am. Finance Assn., Nat. Soc. Study Edn., Shevchenko Sci. Soc., U.S. Global Strategy Council, Social List of Washington, Council Am. Ambassadors, NYU Alumni Assn., Georgetown U. Alumni Assn. (hon.), Reagan Alumni Assn., Internat. Cultural Soc. Korea (hon.), Am. Legion, Res. Officers Assn., Nat. War Coll. Alumni Assn., University Club of Washington (hon.), Capitol Hill Club, Internat. Club, Gold Key Soc., Beta Gamma Sigma, Delta Sigma Pi.

DOBRIANSKY, PAULA JON, federal agency administrator; b. Sept. 14, 1955; d. Lev Eugene and Julia Kusy Dobriansky. BS summa cum laude, Georgetown U., 1977; MA, Harvard U., 1980, PhD, 1991; LHD (hon.), Fairleigh Dickinson U., 2002; LLD (hon.), Flagler Coll., 2003; LHD (hon.), Westminster Coll., 2005, Roger Williams U., 2005. Adminstrv. aide Dept. Army, Washington, 1973-76; staff asst. Am. Embassy, Rome, 1976; rsch. asst. joint econ. com. U.S. Congress, Washington, 1977-78; NATO analyst Bur. Intelligence and Rsch. Dept. State, Washington, 1979; staff mem. NSC, White House, Washington, 1980-83, dep. dir. European and Soviet affairs, 1983-84, dir. European and Soviet affairs, 1984-87; dep. asst. sec. of state Human Rights and Humanitarian Affairs, 1987-90; dep. head U.S. Del. to Conf. on Security and Cooperation in Europe, Copenhagen, 1990; assoc. dir. for policy and programs U.S. Info. Agy., 1990-93; co-chair internat. TV coun. Corp. Pub. Broadcasting, 1993-94; sr. internat. affairs and trade advisor Hunton and Williams, Washington, 1994-97; sr. v.p., dir. Washington Office Coun. on Fgn. Rels., 1997—2001; under sec. state for global affairs U.S. State Dept., Washington, 2001—. Commr. U.S. Adv. Commn. on Pub. Diplomacy, 1997-2001; adj. fellow Hudson Inst., 1993-2001. Host: Freedom's Challenge, Nat. Empowerment Television, 1994-96; co-host: Worldwise, 1997. Bd. dirs. Congl. Human Rights Found., 1994-95, Freedom House, 1999-2001, Western NIS Enterprise Fund, 1994-2001, Am. Com. for Aid to Poland, 1994-95, ABA Ctrl./East European Law Initiative, 1994-99; mem. bd. visitors George Mason U., 1994-98; mem. adv. bd. Horton Internat. Inc., 1998-99. Decorated Grand Cross of Comdr. Order of Lithuanian Grand Duke Gediminas, Star of Romania; named Ethnic Woman of Yr., 1990; named one of 10 Most Outstanding Young Women in Am., 1982, 10 Outstanding Working Women of 1990; recipient Georgetown U. Alumni Achievement award, 1986, State Dept. Superior Honor award, 1990, Poland's Highest medal of Merit, 1998, Democracy Svc. medal, Nat. Endowment Democracy, 2002, Dialogue on Diversity Internat. award, 2001; fellow, Rotary Found., 1979, Ford Found., 1980; scholar Fulbright-Hays scholar, 1978. Mem. Internat. Inst. Strategic Studies, Coun. Fgn. Rels., Am. Polit. Sci. Assn., Fulbright Assn., Nat. Endowment for Democracy (bd. dirs. 1993-2001, vice-chmn. 1995-2001), Am. Coun. on Young Polit. Leaders (trustee 1993-2001), U.S. Environ. Tng. Inst. (bd. adv. 1992-93), Harvard Club (bd. dirs. 1982-85), Univ. Club, Phi Beta Kappa, Phi Alpha Theta, Pi Sigma Alpha. Office: US State Dept Washington DC 20520

DOBRINSKY, SUSAN ELIZABETH, human resources director; b. Warren, N.J., Sept. 25, 1943; d. Samuel Henry Jr. and Janet Adeline (Ryder) Christie; m. Stanley Dobrinsky, Feb. 12, 1972; children: David Stanley, Mark Alan. BA, Lycoming Coll., 1965. Cert. for Sr. Execs., John F. Kennedy Sch. of Govt. of Harvard U., 1994, PHR Cert. by SHRM, Profl. in Human Resources, 1997—. Pers. asst. County of Somerset, Somerville, N.J., 1970-74, pers. mgr., 1974-82, pers. dir., 1982-90, dir. adminstrn., 1991-95, dir. human resources, 1995—. Gov. apptd. Pub. Employees Occupl. Safety and Health Adv. Bd., Dept. of Labor, Trenton, N.J., 1984—; bd. trustees N.J. Pub. Employer Labor Rels. Assn., Somerville, N.J., 1993—, treas., 1995—; mem. Soc. Human Resource Mgmt. Cen. Jersey, Somerset, 1978—; pres. Comty. Indsl. Rels. Orgn., Somerset, 1990-92; apptd. senate pres., mem. Pension Adv. Commn., Trenton, 1992-2001. Mem., dep. mayor Green Brook Twp. Commn., 1987-88, mayor, 1989-92; v.p. Somerset County Governing Offcls., 1990, pres., 1991; elected mem. Somerset County Mcpl. Com., 1999-01, 2002-2004, 2005, vice chmn., 2005—; sec. Rep. Club, Green Brook, 1977; mem. staff parish com. Meth. Ch., 2002-2004, bd. trustees, 2005—. Recipient N.J. Alumni award 4-H Youth Devel. Program, 1992, United Way Star award, 2005. Mem. Nat. Pub. Employer's Labor Rels. Assn., N.J. Pub. Employer Labor Rels. Assn. (bd. trustees, treas. 1993—, treas. 1995—), Soc. Human Resource Mgmt., Ctrl. N.J. Soc. Human Resource Mgmt., Internat. Personnel Mgmt. Assn., N.J. Pension and Health Commn., Cmty. Indsl. Rels. Orgn. (treas. 1988-90, pres. 1990-92), Pub. Pers. Orgn. (pres. 1990-2000), DAR (Elizabeth Snyder chpt. regent 1998-99, 2001-2004, registrar 2004-). Republican. Methodist. Avocations: skiing, genealogy, reading, crafts. Home: 11 Glenn Ave Green Brook NJ 08812-2431 Office: County of Somerset 20 Grove St Somerville NJ 08876-2306

DOBRONSKI, MARK WILLIAM, judge, justice of the peace; b. Detroit, Oct. 8, 1957; s. Clarence Robert and Jean (Shotey) D.; m. Susan Kay Roach, Sept. 12, 1980; children: Clarence Robert III, Juli E. AS, Henry Ford C.C., 1980. Cert. engr. Nat. Assn. Radio and Telecomm. Engrs. V.p. Mobilfone, Inc., Dearborn, Mich., 1977-79; asst. v.p. RAM Broadcasting Corp., N.Y.C., 1979-86; adminstr. State of Ariz., Phoenix, 1986-88, 89-97; divsn. comdr. City of Peoria (Ariz.) Police Dept., 1991; assoc. presiding justice of the peace Maricopa County, Ariz. Cons., expert witness Teletech, Inc., Dearborn, 1980-98. Mem., bd. dirs. Congl. Ch. of the Valley, United Ch. of Christ, Scottsdale, Ariz., 1994-98; mem. Maricopa County Sheriff's Exec. Posse, Phoenix, 1996-98. Mem. ABA, Am. Judicature Soc., Ariz. Justice of the Peace Assn., Maricopa County Bar Assn., Scottsdale Bar Assn., Am. Pvt. Radio Assn. (dir. 1989-98). Republican. Office: Scottsdale Justice Court 8230 E Butherus Dr Scottsdale AZ 85260-2520

DOBRYNINA, GALINA, mathematics professor, researcher; b. Moscow, Jan. 2, 1953; d. Ninel Dobrynina; m. Yefim Abram Kogan, May 8, 1974; children: Alex, David. EdD, Boston U., 2001. Math. instr. Regis Coll., Weston, Mass., 1996—99; asst. prof. Wheelock Coll., Boston, 1998—. Grad. rsch. asst. Boston U., Chelsea Pub. Schs., 1994—97; vis. cons. The Consortium for Math. and its Applications, Lexington, Mass., 1996. Contbr. chapters to books; presenter numerous confs. and proceedings. Grantee, Wheelock Coll., 2002—04. Mem.: Assn. Math. Tchr. Educators, Assn. Tchrs. Math. in Mass., Nat. Coun. Suprs. Math., Internat. Group for Psychology of Math. Edn., Matematical Assn. Am., Am. Ednl. Rsch. Assn., Nat. Coun. Tchrs. Math., Pi Lambda Theta (hon.). Achievements include research in algebraic thinking of elementary school students and preservice teachers. Office: Wheelock Coll Boston MA Personal E-mail: gdobrynina@wheelock.edu.

DOBRZANSKI, SLAWOMIR, musician; arrived in U.S., 1992; s. Joseph and Ewa Dobrzanski; 1 child, Angelina Sophie Dominici. MusM, Chopin Acad. Music, Warsaw, 1991; D in Musical Arts, U. Conn., 2001. Asst. prof. piano Concordia Coll., Moorhead, Minn., 2002—; guest artist, tchr. of piano Univ. R.I., 2004—05; asst. prof. piano Kans. State Univ., 2005—. Vis. artist Nat. Conservatory Music, Lima, Peru, 2000; guest artist, tchr. of piano U. RI, Kingston, RI, 2004. Mem.: RI Music Tchrs. Assn. (pres-elect 2004—), Polish Inst. Arts and Scis. Am., Music Tchrs. Nat. Assn., Coll. Music Soc., Chopin Soc. Conn. (pres. 1998—2001). Avocations: travel, languages, enviroment. E-mail: slawomir@usu.edu.

DOBRZHINETSKAYA, LARISSA, geoscience educator; d. Felix Dobrzhinetsky and Jozefine Dobrzhinetskaya. MSc, PhD, St. Petersburg U., 1978; DSc in Geology and Mineralogy, Supreme Commn. Edn., 1990; DSc, Supreme Com. Edn., 1993. Sci. dept. head Inst. Lithosphere, Russian Acad. Scis., Moscow, 1980—92; sr. scientist Geol. Survey Norway, Trondheim, 1992—93; rsch. geophysicist Inst. Geophysics and Planetary Physics, Riverside, 1993—2002; prof. geology and mineralogy U. Calif., Riverside, 2002—, workshop organizer, 2004. Vis. rschr. Los Alamos Nat. Lab., N.Mex., 1999; ultradeep continental crust subduction task group chair Internat. Lithosphere Program; conf. spkr. in field. Recipient Disting. Rschr. award, U. Calif., 2002, award, Soros Found., NSF, Collaborative Rsch. award, Women Internat. Sci.; fellow, Norwegian Royal Found. for Promotion in Scis. Rsch., 1993, Basic Rsch. Program grant, Los Alamos Nat. Lab., 1999. Fellow: Japanese Soc. Promotion of Sci. (fellow 2004); mem.: Mineral. Soc. Am., Geol. Soc. Am., Am. Geophys. Union (meeting convener, mem. edn. and outreach com.). D-Liberal. Achievements include discovery of Discovery of microdiamonds in Norway; research in rocks from earth's mantle. Avocations: swimming, travel, tennis, reading, writing. Office: Univ Calif Dept Earth Sciences Riverside CA 92521

DOBRZYNSKI, JUDITH HELEN, journalist, commentator; b. Rochester, N.Y., Mar. 8, 1949; d. Francis Anthony and Theresa (Contino) Dobrzynski. BS cum laude, Syracuse U., 1971. Corr. McGraw-Hill, San Francisco and N.Y.C., 1971—75, Bus. Week, Washington, 1976—79, London, 1979—83, corp. strategies editor, assoc. editor N.Y.C., 1983—88, sr. writer, 1988—91, sr. editor, 1991—94; bus. reporter N.Y. Times, N.Y.C., 1995—97, culture reporter, 1997—2000, dep. bus. editor and editor Sunday Money and Bus. sect., 2000—03; mng. editor CNBC, Englewood Cliffs, NJ, 2003—05, exec. editor, 2005—. Adj. instr. Columbia U. Sch. Journalism, 2002—; mem. New Founds. Corp. Governance Group Harvard U., Boston, 1992—95; adv. panel Corp. Investment Project U.S. Coun. on Competitiveness, Washington, 1990—92. Contbr. articles to profl. jours. and book revs. Trustee CEC Internat. Ptnrs., N.Y.C., 1993—96; bd. dirs. City Lights Youth Theatre, N.Y.C., 1994—96. Recipient Nat. Headliner award 1st Pl. in Bus. and Consumer TV Journalism, 2004, 2005; Knight Found. fellow, Salzburg Seminar, 2002. Mem.: Syracuse U. Newhouse Sch. Alumni Assn. (bd. dirs. 1991—94, pres. 1992—93), Century Assn. Office: CNBC 900 Sylvan Ave Englewood Cliffs NJ 07632 Office Phone: 201-735-3001. E-mail: jhdobrzynski@nyc.rr.com.

DOBS, ADRIAN SANDRA, endocrinologist, educator; b. June 27, 1952; m. Martin Auster; children: Nina Auster, Becky Auster, Harry Auster, Paul Auster. BS in Nutrition Scis., Cornell U., 1973; MD, Albany Med. Coll., 1978; MHS in Cardiovascular Epidemiology, Johns Hopkins U., 1990. Diplomate Nat. Bd. Med. Examiners, Am. Bd. Internal Medicine, Am. Bd. Endocrinology and Metabolism. Resident in internal medicine Montefiore Hosp. Med. Ctr./Albert Einstein Coll. Medicine, Bronx, N.Y., 1978-81, chief resident, 1981-82; instr. medicine, physicians asst. program CCNY, N.Y.C., 1981-82; endocrinology fellow Johns Hopkins U., Balt., 1982-84, instr. divsn. endocrinology and metabolism, 1984-87, asst. prof. medicine, 1987-93, assoc. prof. medicine, 1993—, vice chair dept. medicine, clin. rsch., 1996—. Mem. study sect., adv. com. Nat. Inst. Aging, 1992, NIH, 1993, 94; lectr. in field. Reviewer Am. Jour. Clin. Nutrition, Am. Jour. Medicine, Diabetes Care, Jour. AMA, Jour. Clin. Endocrinology and Metabolism, New Eng. Jour. Medicine; contbr. articles, abstracts to profl. jours., chpts. to books. Recipient Rsch. award Women Physicians Stetler Found., 1986-87; scholar Leopold Schepp Found., 1975, Vanderbilt U., 1976, Carnegie-Mellon Found., 1984-85, Robert Glassner Found. Diabetes Rsch., 1985-86; grantee Merck, Inc., 1991-93, TheraTech, Inc., 1991-94, NIH, 1992-93, 92—, Diabetes Rsch. and Edn. Found., 1992-93, Johns Hopkins Out-patient Clin. Rsch. Ctr., 1992-93. Mem. ACP, Am. Coll. Nutrition, Am. Diabetes Assn. (award Md. chpt. 1986-87), Am. Fedn. Clin. Rsch. (Johns Hopkins rep. 1990—, sch. coun. 1990—), Am. Heart Assn. (epidemiology coun. 1985, grantee 1990-94), Endocrine Soc. Home: 3510 Anton Farms Rd Baltimore MD 21208-1703 Office: Johns Hopkins Hosp 906B Blalock Bldg 600 N Wolfe St Baltimore MD 21287-0005

DOBSON, BRIDGET MCCOLL HURSLEY, television executive, writer; b. Milw., Sept. 1, 1938; d. Franklin McColl and Doris (Berger) Hursley; m. Jerome John Dobson, June 16, 1961; children: Mary McColl, Andrew Carmichael. BA, Stanford U., 1960, MA, 1964; CBA, Harvard U., 1961. Assoc. writer General Hospital ABC-TV, 1965-73, head writer General Hospital, 1973-75; producer Friendly Road Sta. KIXE-TV, Redding, Calif., 1972; head writer Guiding Light CBS-TV, 1975-80, head writer As the World Turns, 1980-83; creator, co-owner Santa Barbara NBC-TV, 1983—, head writer Santa Barbara, 1983-86, 91, exec. producer Santa Barbara, 1986-87, 91, creative prodn. exec. Santa Barbara, 1990-91; pres. Dobson Global Entertainment, L.A., 1994—. Bd. dirs. Emory U. Carlos Mus.; bd. advisors Atlanta Internat. Sch., 1997-2000. Author, co-lyricist: Slings and Eros, 1993; prodr. Confessions of a Nightingale, 1994; exhibited in gallery show acrylic paintings Swan Coach House, Atlanta, 1997, exhibited oil paintings Raymond Lawrence Gallery, Atlanta, 1999, Fay Gold Gallery, Atlanta, 1999, Tippy Stern Fine Art, Charleston, S.C., 2002; one-woman shows include Mus. S.W., Midland, Tex., 2001, Midwest Mus. Am. Art, Elkhart, Ind., 2001, Charles Allis Art Mus., Milw., 2001, Albrecht-Kemper Mus. Art, St. Joseph, Mo., 2001, Walter Wickiser Gallery, N.Y.C., 2001, Danville (Va.) Mus. Fine Art, 2002, Burroughs-Chapin Art Mus., Myrtle Beach, S.C., 2002, Tippy Stern Fine Art, 2002, Anderson (Ind.) Fine Art Ctr., 2002, Ella Sharp Mus., Jackson, Miss., 2002. Bd. dirs. Carlos Mus., 1998-2001. Walter Wickiser Gallery, N.Y.C., 2003. Recipient Emmy award, 1988. Mem. Nat. Acad. TV Arts and Scis. (com. on substance abuse 1986-88), Writers Guild Am. (award for Guiding Light 1977, for Santa Barbara 1991), Am. Film Inst. (mem. TV com. 1986-88). Office: PO Box 52813 Atlanta GA 30355-0813

DOBSON, CARL WILHELM, education educator; b. Nuremburg, Germany, Jan. 6, 1958; arrived in U.S., 1959; s. Charles William and Stella Flora (Smith) Dobson. BS in Polit. Sci., Charleston So. U., 1981; postgrad., U. N.C., MA in History, 1986; AAS in Paralegal Studies, Cecils Coll., 1989; postgrad., U. N.C., 2001—, Erskine Sem., 2005—. Instr. Cecils Jr. Coll., Asheville, NC, 1990—98, Shaw U., 2003. Author of poems. Republican. Presbyterian. Home: 16 Graystone Rd Asheville NC 28804-1320

DOBSON, DONALD ALFRED, retired electrical engineer; b. Evanston, Ill., Feb. 19, 1928; s. Alfred Topping and Agnes Lucille (Park) D. BSEE, Northwestern U., 1950, PhD, 1955; MSEE, MIT, 1951. Research assoc. Northwestern U., Evanston, 1951-54; engr. Indsl. Research Products, Franklin Park, Ill., 1952; sr. engr. Sperry Gyroscope Co., Great Neck, N.Y., 1954-59; sr. tech. specialist N.Am. Aviation, Columbus, Ohio, 1959-63; research staff mem. Inst. for Def. Analyses, Arlington, Va., 1963-90, adj. staff mem., 1990-98, ret., 1998. Instr. physics Adelphi Coll., Garden City, N.Y., 1956 Mem. IEEE, Sigma Xi, Tau Beta Pi, Eta Kappa Mu, Pi Mu Epsilon Home: 6800 Fleetwood Rd Apt 420 Mc Lean VA 22101-3607

DOBSON, DOROTHY LYNN WATTS, elementary school educator; b. Santa Monica, Calif., Nov. 29, 1954; d. Seymour Locke and Margaret (Cheeseman) Watts; m. J. Cody Dobson, June 5, 1982; children: Jeremiah, Hannah. BS, Utah State U., 1975; MEd, U. Utah, 1982. Cert. tchr. intellectually handicapped and behaviorally handicapped, elem., Utah. Tchr. San Juan Sch. Dit., Blanding, Utah, 1974-76; behavioral specialist Salt Lake Sch. Dist., Salt Lake City, 1976-77; tchr. Granite Sch. Dist., Salt Lake City, 1977-82; instr. Utah State U., Logan, 1987—; tchr. Edith Bowen Lab. Sch., Logan, 1982—. Team coord. First Amendment Schs., Bowen Lab. Sch., Logan, 2002—. Author: Utilizing Newspapers in Social Studies, Math. and Science and Language Arts, 1983; also articles. Mem. Nat. Coun. for Social Studies (bd. dirs. 1996-99, Nat. Elem. Tchr. of Yr. 1992, State Farm Good Neighbor award 1993), Utah Coun. for Social Studies (State Elem. Tchr. of Yr. 1991), Nat. Assn. Lab. Schs. Episcopalian. Office: Edith Bowen Sch Utah State U Logan UT 84322-0001

DOBSON, EDWARD TAUSCHER, mathematician; b. Athens, Ga., Aug. 20, 1965; s. Gerard Ramsden and Kay Ann Tauscher Dobson; m. Susan Deborah Cook, July 16, 1994; children: Beatrice Rose Cook children: Magdalen Ruth Cook. BS, U. North Tex., 1988, MA, 1989; PhD, La. State U., Baton Rouge, 1995. Vis. scholar U. Cambridge, England, 1991—94; instr. La. State U., Baton Rouge, 1995—97; vis. asst. prof. Okla. State U., Stillwater, 1997—98; assoc. prof. Miss. State U., Mississippi State, 1998—. Contbr. articles to profl. jours. Home: 2009 Buckner St Starkville MS 39759 Office: Dept Math and Stats Miss State U Mississippi State MS 39762 E-mail: dobson@math.msstate.edu.

DOBSON, JOHN MCCULLOUGH, historian, educator; b. Las Cruces, N.Mex., July 20, 1940; s. Donald Duane and Carolyn Margaret (Van Anda) D.; m. Cynthia Davis, Aug. 29, 1963; children: David, Daniel. BS, MIT, 1962; MS, U. Wis., 1964, PhD, 1966. Asst. prof. history Calif. State U., Chico, 1966-67; fgn. service officer U.S. Dept. State, Washington, 1967-68; asst. prof. history Iowa State U., Ames, 1968-72, assoc. prof., 1972-78, prof., 1978—, asst. dean, 1987-91, asst. vice provost, 1991-92, interim vice provost, 1991-92; assoc. vice provost, 1992—. Vis. assoc. prof. history U. Md., 1972, 76; Fulbright lectr. Univ. Coll., Dublin, 1979-80 Author: Politics in the Gilded Age: A New Perspective on Reform, 1972, Two Centuries of Tariffs: The Background and Origins of the U.S. International Trade Commission, 1977, America's Ascent, 1978, A History of American Enterprise, 1987, Reticent Expansionism, 1988. Grantee U.S. Internat. Trade Commn., 1976 Mem. Am. Hist. Assn., Orgn. Am. Historians, Soc. Historians of Am. Fgn. Relations, AAUP Home: 1524 Fairway Dr Stillwater OK 74074-1320 Office: Iowa State U Dept History 211 Beardshear Hl Ames IA 50011-0001

DOBSON, NEIL CUNNINGHAM, marine archaeologist; b. Dunfermline, Fife, Scotland, July 18, 1956; s. Norman Walker and Elsie Young Dobson; life ptnr. Iona Shonagh Potter; children: Skye Potter, Luthais Potter. M.Litt., St Andrews U., Scotland, 1996. Cert. in ONC nautical sci., leith Nautical Coll., Scotland, 1973, in offshore survival tech., Robert Gordons U., Aberdeen, Scotland, 1995, ROV pilot, technician, IMCA UK, 1999, HSE SCUBA surface supply comml. diver, HSE UK, 1999, Oceaneering ROV pilot, Oceaneering USA, 2002; NVQ Skills trainer, assessor Perth Coll. Scotland, 1998. Deck officer Ben Line Steamers Ltd., Edinburgh, Scotland, 1973—77; pub. ho. mgr. Free Ho., Strathkinness, Scotland, 1977—79; stability officer, barge engr. Various Offshore Oil Companies, 1979—90; offshore marine survival instr. RGIT Ltd, Dundee, 1990—95; marine archaeologist St Andrews (Scotland) U., St Andrews, 1995—2001; dir. field archaeology Odyssey Marine Exploration, Tampa, Fla., 2001—; freelance cons. marine archaeologist Rovarch, St Andrews, 2002—. Nat. boathandling and chartwork coord. Sub Aqua Assn., Liverpool, England, 1996—; dir. Connect Archaeology Ltd, St Andrews; chmn. Cosmos Cmty. Centre, St Andrews, 1999—. Contbr. articles to marine exploration training manuals. Chmn. Cosmos Cmty. Centre, St Andrews, 1999—2005. Acting sub. lt Royal Navy Res., 1987—88, Scotland. Grantee, Andrew Carnagie Trust, 1995. Mem.: Sub Aqua Assn. (nat. coord, diving officer 1990—2005), Junior C. of C (bd. dirs.), Royal Yachting Assn. (powerboat instr. 1989—2005), St Andrews Golf Club. Home and Office: 38 Winram Pl Fife Saint Andrews KY16 8XH Scotland Office Phone: 01334 477171. Personal E-mail: rovarch@hotmail.com.

DOBSON, RICHARD LAWRENCE, dermatologist, educator; b. Boston, Apr. 12, 1928; s. Joseph William and Celia Beatrice (Siegler) D.; children: Richard Lawrence, Pamela Blair, Lisa Marie; m. Rhoda H. Freda, Feb. 14, 2004. MD, U. Chgo., 1953; BS, U. N.H., 1981. Diplomate Am. Bd. Dermatology (v.p. 1987-88, pres. 1988-89). Intern Cin. Gen. Hosp., 1953-54; resident Hitchcock Clinic, Hanover, N.H., 1954-57; asst. prof. dermatology U. N.C., Chapel Hill, 1957-61; prof. U. Oreg., Portland, 1961-72, SUNY-Buffalo, 1972-79, Med. U. S.C., Charleston, 1980-98, acting dean, 1985-86, chmn. dept. anatomy and cell biology, 1991-92, prof. emeritus, 1998—. Vis. prof. U. Nijmegen, The Netherlands, 1969-70; hon. prof. Shanghai 2d Med. U.; hon. cons. Royal Prince Alfred Hosp., Sydney, Australia. Editor: Year Book of Dermatology, 1979-82, Clinical Dermatology, 1972-82, Contemporary Review, 1973-87; asst. editor: Jour. Am. Acad. Dermatology, 1979-87, editor, 1988-98; mng. editor Arch. Dermatol. Research, 1982-87 . Served with USN, 1946-47. Fellow ACP, Am. Acad. Dermatology (pres. 1983-84); mem. Am. Dermatologic Assn. (treas. 1977-82), Soc. Investigative Dermatology (pres. 1975-76), Oreg. Dermatol. Soc. (pres. 1971-72); hon. mem. Brit. Assn. Dermatology, Spanish Assn. Dermatology, French Dermatology Soc., Polish Dermatology Soc., Finnish Dermatology Soc., Dutch Dermatology Soc., German Dermatology Soc., N.Am. Dermatology Soc., Ga. Dermatology Soc., Iowa Dermatology Soc., Snee Farm Club. Republican. Roman Catholic. Office: Med U SC 171 Ashley Ave Charleston SC 29425-0001 Office Phone: 803-792-5858. Personal E-mail: rowda@aol.com.

DOBSON, RICK, energy executive; BS in bus. admin., U. Wis.; MBA in fin., U. Nebr. Cert. CPA. Audit mgr. Arthur Andersen, 1981—89; v.p., contr. Aquila Merchant Svcs., 1989—95; v.p., risk mgmt. acctg. Aquila, Kans. City, Mo., 1997, interim CFO, 2002—03, CFO, 2003—. Office: Aquila 20 W 9th St Kansas City MO 64105-1711

DOBSON, ROBERT ALBERTUS, III, lawyer, volunteer; b. Greenville, SC, Nov. 27, 1938; s. Robert A. Jr. and Dorothy (Leonard) D.; m. Linda Josephine Bryant, Nov. 18, 1956; children: Robert, William, Michael, Daniel, Jonathan, Laura (dec.); m. Catherine Elizabeth Cornmesser, Sept. 17, 1983; children: Andrew, Thomas, Juana. BS in Acctg. summa cum laude, U. S.C., 1960, JD magna cum laude, 1962; DPS, Limestone Coll., 2002. Asst. dean of students U. S.C., 1960-62; pvt. practice pub. acctg. Greenville, 1962-64; ptnr. Dobson & Dobson, Greenville, 1964-93. Chmn., bd. trustees Limestone Coll., 1987-89, founder Christian edn. and leadership program; trustee The King's Coll., 2003—. Contbr. articles to profl. jours. Sr. warden St. Francis Episcopal Ch., Greenville; chmn. bd. Dobson Tape Ministry, Homeless Children Internat., Inc.; bd. dirs. A Child's Haven, Inc.; chmn. Walker Found. for the SC Sch. for the Multihandicapped, Deaf and Blind, Spartanburg, SC; adv. bd. Salvation Army, Greenville; chmn. bd. Sch. Ministries, Inc.; active History's Handful Campus Crusade for Christ; founder Dobson Vol. Svc. Program, U. SC. Mem. ABA, S.C. Bar Assn., AICPAs, Am. Assn. Attys. and CPAs, S.C. Assn. Pub. Accts., Block C Assn. The Group, U. S.C. Alumni Assn. (cir. v.p.), Kappa Sigma (chmn. legal com. 1989-93, dist. grand master 1971-2002, Nat. Dist. Grand Master of the Yr. 1986, John G. Tower Disting. Alumni award 2000, Stephen Alonzo Jackson award 1998), Phi Beta Kappa. Lodges: Sertoma Internat. (dist. treas.), Sertoma Sunrisers (pres. Greenville club). Episcopalian. Home: 1207 Pelham Rd Greenville SC 29615-3643 Office Phone: 864-284-6042.

DOBSON, WENDY KATHLEEN, economics professor; BSN, U. B.C., 1963; MPA, Harvard U., 1971, SM, 1972; PhD in Econs., Princeton U., 1979. Pres. C.D. Howe Inst., Toronto, 1981—87; assoc. dep. min. Dept. Fin. Govt. Can., Ottawa, 1987—89; prof., dir. Inst. Internat. Bus. Rotman Sch. Mgmt. U. Toronto, 1993—. Bd. dirs. Toronto-Dominion Bank, TransCan. Pipelines, Can. Pub. Accountability Bd.; steering com. Pacific Trade Devel. Network; adv. com. Inst. Internat. Econs., Washington; mem. Trilateral Commn. Author: Japan in East Asia: Trade and Investment Strategies, 1993, Multinationals and East Asian Integration, 1997 (Ohira prize, 1998), Financial Services Liberalization in the WTO, 1998, Shaping the Future of North American Economic Space: A Framework for Action, 2002, Taking a Giant's Measure: Canada, NAFTA and an Emergent China, 2004, (chpts.) Bretton Woods: Looking to the Future, 1994, A Part of the Peace, 1994, Trade Technology and Economics: Essays in Honour of Richard G. Lipsey, 1997, Fifty Years After Bretton Woods: The Future of the IMF and the World Bank, 1995, The Growing Importance of the Asia Pacific Region in the World Economy: Implications for Canada, 1997, Trade Technology and Economics, 1997, Whither APEC?, 1997, Prisoners of the Past: Canada's Policy Framework for the Financial Services Sector, 1999; co-editor: Shaping Comparative Advantage, 1987, East Asian Capitalism: Diversity and Dynamism, 1996, Managing U.S. Japanese Trade Disputes, 1996, The People Link, 1997, Fiscal Framework and Financial Systems in East Asia, 1998, East Asia in Transition, 1999; contbr. articles to profl. jours. Office: Rotman Sch Mgmt U Toronto 105 St George St Toronto ON M5S 3E6 Canada Business E-Mail: dobson@rotman.utoronto.ca.

DOBY, JOHN THOMAS, social psychologist; b. Gray, Ky., May 29, 1920; s. Daniel W. and Minnie (Farris) D.; m. Rose Catherine Hopper Doby, Dec. 21, 1942; children: Mary Catherine, Nancy H. AB cum laude, Union Coll.,

Barbourville, Ky., 1946; MS, U. Wis., 1950; PhD, 1956. From assoc. prof. to prof. sociology and anthropology Wofford Coll., Spartanburg, SC, 1950-57; assoc. prof. sociology and anthropology Emory U., Atlanta, 1958-63, prof., 1963-85, chmn. dept. sociology and anthropology, 1960-69, chmn. dept. sociology, 1980-85, prof. emeritus sociology, 1985; cons. engring. Ga. Inst. Tech., Atlanta, 1960-62; cons. Ednl. Testing Svc., Princeton, N.J., 1969; mem. faculty Grad. Sch. Consumer Banking, U. Va., summer 1972-75. Vis. scientist/lectr. NSF, 1965-66; chair tech. sci. adv. com. on mental retardation Ga. Dept. Health, 1965-66; dir. NSF Summer Inst. for Coll. Tchrs. of Sociology, Emory U., 1965-66; mem. sci. faculty panel Am. Coun. Learned Socs., Nat. Sci. Postdoctoral Panel, 1976-77. Author: Introduction to Social Research, 1954, Introduction to Social Psychology, 1966, Introduction to Social Research, 1967; editor, author: Sociology: A Study of Man in Adaptation, 1973; contbr. articles to profl. jours., chpt. to book. Maj. USAF, 1941-46. Grantee NIMH, 1960, NSF, 1964, 65, 71, OEO, 1966-67, NICHD, 1979-80. Mem.: So. Sociol. Assn. (pres. 1969—70), Am. Sociol. Assn. Methodist. Home: 473 Ky-1629 Corbin KY 40701-9469 Office Phone: 606-523-0850.

DOBYNS, BETH MCCURDY, clergy member; b. Hot Springs, Ark., July 7, 1952; d. Melvin Jr. and Wilma Lou (Prichard) McC.; m. Bruce Warren Dobyns, Aug. 18, 1979; Leslie Ann, Nicole Kristine. BS in Med. Tech., Tex. Christian U., Ft. Worth, 1974, MDiv, 1979; DMin, St. Paul Sch. Theology, Kansas City, Mo., 1995. Ordained minister, Christian Ch., 1979. Med. technologist Palo Pinto Gen. Hosp., Mineral Wells, Tex., 1974-76, Johnson County Hosp., Cleburne, Tex., 1976-77, Med. Plaza Hosp., Ft. Worth, 1977-79; assoc. minister 1st Christian Ch., Cedar Rapids, Iowa, 1979-81; co-minister Forest Ave and Univ. Christian Chs., Buffalo, N.Y., 1981-83, 1st christian Ch., Perry, Iowa, 1983-93; assoc. regional minister interim Christian Ch. in the Upper Midwest, Des Moines, 1993—2000; dir., sr. svcs. Luth. Social Svcs. Ill., West Peoria, 2000—. Trustee Dallas County Hosp., Perry, Iowa, 1985-91; assoc. regional min. Christian Ch., Ill., 2003— Mem. Assn. Christian Ch. Educators. Democrat. Avocations: quilting, photography, antiques.

DOBYNS, BROWN MCILVAINE, retired surgeon, retired educator; b. Jacksonville, Ill., May 14, 1913; s. Henry D. and Leah (McIlvaine) D.; married; children— Mary Meredith, Courtney Sara, Brown McIlvaine. BA with hons., Ill. Coll., 1935; MD, Johns Hopkins, 1939; MS, U. Minn., 1944, PhD, 1946. Diplomate: Am. Bd. Surgery. Intern surgery Johns Hopkins Hosp., 1939-40; fellow surgery Mayo Found., 1940-43; resident surgery Kahler Hosp., Mayo Clinic, 1943-45, 1st asst. surgery, 1945-46, asst. surg. staff, 1946; research fellow surgery, med. sch. Harvard, 1946-48, asst. prof. surgery, 1948-51; grad. asst. surgery Mass. Gen. Hosp., 1946-48, asst. surgery, 1946-51; assoc. prof. surgery Case Western Res. U. Med. Sch., 1951-58, prof. surgery, 1958—88, prof. emeritus, 1984—88; ret., 1988. Asst. chief surg. service Cleve. Met. Gen. Hosp., 1951-88, assoc. chief surg. service, 1967-88; asst. surgeon Univ. Hosp., Cleve., 1951-88; Fulbright lectr., Australia, 1966. Mem. fellowship subcom. Com. on Growth NRC, 1950-54; mem. fellowship com. NSF, 1954-61, chmn., 1955-61; adv. screening com. med. scis. Fulbright, 1955-58; adv. com. research on etiology cancer Am. Cancer Soc., 1956-59, chmn. adv. com. on instnl. grants, 1963-65; mem. Dernham Scholarship com. Calif. Cancer Soc., 1964-74; cons. Markle Found. Selection Com., 1961-62. Recipient Van Meter prize, 1946, award of merit, 1954, Disting. Service award, 1978; all Am. Thyroid Assn.; citation for disting. public service Ill. Coll.; elected to Cleve. Med. Hall of Fame, 1997. Fellow ACS; mem. AAAS, Soc. Univ. Surgeons, Am. Soc. Clin. Investigation, Am. Surg. Assn., Ctrl. Surg. Assn., Am. Thyroid Assn. (pres. 1956-57), Cleve. Surg. Soc. (pres. 1966-67), Halstead Soc., Socíeté Internationale de Chirurgie, Endocrine Soc., Sigma Xi, Phi Beta Kappa. Home: 9930 Kirtland Rd Chardon OH 44024-9746 *Try to have a new experience every day.*

DOBYNS, HENRY F(ARMER), anthropology consultant, educator; b. Tucson, July 3, 1925; s. Henry F. and Susie K. (Comstock) D.; children: Henry, William, Maritha, Mark, York. BA, U. Ariz., 1949, MA, 1956; PhD, Cornell U., 1960. Lectr. Cornell U., Ithaca, N.Y., 1964-66; prof., chmn. anthropology dept. U. Ky., Lexington, 1966-70; prof. Prescott (Ariz.) Coll., 1970-73; vis. prof. U. Wis.-Parkside, Kenosha, 1974-75, adj. prof., 1983-84; vis. prof. U. Fla., Gainesville, 1977-79; rschr. Newberry Libr., Chgo., 1979-81; cons. Gila River Indian Community, Sacaton, Ariz., 1983—. Adj. prof. U. Okla., Norman, 1989—. Author: Spanish Colonial Tucson, 1976, From Fire to Flood, 1981, Their Number Becomme Thinned, 1983, The Pima-Maricopa, 1989; also numerous others. With U.S. Army, 1943. Co-recipient Anisfeld-Wolff award Saturday Rev., 1968, award Ariz. Hist. Soc., 1977. Fellow AAAS, Am. Anthrop. Assn., Soc. for Applied Anthropology (Bronislaw Malinowski award 1951), Ariz.-Nev. Acad. Sci.; mem. Ariz. Archaeol. and Hist. Soc. (life, Stoner award 1990), Western Hist. Assn. (life).

DOCARMO, JERRY SOARES, academic administrator; b. Sao Paulo, Brazil, Aug. 15, 1967; s. Benedito Do Carmo, Marina Soares Docarmo; m. Ana Oliveira Docarmo; children: Andrew children: Kevin. BA in Mgmt., Hamilton U., 2000, M in Mgmt., 2002. Dir. internat. fair preparation The Chinese Porcelain Co., N.Y.C., 1995—96; travel dir. Ark Travel Corp, Parsipanny, NJ, 1996—98; v.p. Am. English Ctr., Newark, 1997—99; pres., CEO Harvest Inst., Newark, 1999—. Cons. Welb Franshising, Sao Jose dos Campos, Sao Paulo, Brazil, 1999—. Contbr. Age of Galantry in Deutch Art in the 16th century, 1997. Recipient Outstanding Svc. to Cmty. award, Civil Svc. Leader Newspaper, 1999, 2000, 2001, 2002. Avocations: travel, reading. Office: Harvest Inst 128 Wilson Ave Newark NJ 07105 Business E-Mail: harvest@harvestinstitute.net.

DOCKENDORFF, ROBERT LAWRENCE, computer graphics designer; b. Bronx, N.Y., May 19, 1930; s. Lawrence Christian and Madeline (Krollmann) D.; m. Geraldine Neyens, Oct. 10, 1954 (div. Aug. 1978); m. Kathleen Rose McGlynn, July 27, 1980. Student, Pratt Inst., Bklyn., 1949-51, Cornell U., 1955-56. Tech. illustrator GE Advanced Electronics Ctr., Ithaca, N.Y., 1956-65; indsl.-graphics designer Electronics Lab. GE, Syracuse, N.Y., 1965-69; human factors designer GE Genigraphics, Syracuse, 1969-77, cons. trainer, 1975-79; pres., cons. DK: Assocs., Syracuse, 1979, Basking Ridge, N.J., 1979-80, Sparta, N.J., 1980-85; pres., chief exec. officer Computer Arts, Inc., Sparta, 1985-1992. Cons. Aetna Ins. Co., Hartford, Conn., 1979-85; cons., trainer Digital Equipment Corp., Bedford, Mass., 1979-85, Exxon Rsch., Houston, 1979-85, Nat. Security Agy., Ft. Meade, Md., 1979-84. Author, designer: (trade periodical) Police Vehicle Concept, 1969; author: (tng. course) Genigraphics System, 1971-74, (trade periodical) History-Genigraphics Devel., 1987. Chmn. publicity com. United Fund, Ithaca, 1963-65. Staff sgt. USAF, 1951-55, Korea.Chmn. local road commn., 1993-1996. Local v.p. mktg. and comm. Am. Cancer Soc., 1993-1995. Dir./Advisor Morongo Basin Shack Attack program, 1996—. Advisor Homestead Valley Pk. & Recreation, 1997—; dir. Basin Wide Found., 2001—; oversight com. Copper Mountain Coll., 2005—; mgr. Calif. Welcome Ctr., Yucca Valley, Calif., 2004—. Recipient Computer Graphics Pioneer award Computer Graphics Pioneers, Chatsworth, Calif., 1988. Mem.: Homestead Valley Cmty. Coun. (pres. 1997—2002). Republican. Avocations: camping, marksmanship, motorcycling, woodworking. Home: 159 Geronimo Trl Yucca Valley CA 92284-1491

DOCKERY, J. LEE, retired medical school administrator; b. Amity, Ark., 1932; MD, U. Ark., 1957. Rotating intern Jackson Meml. Hosp., Miami, Fla., 1957—58; resident in ob-gyn. U. Miami, 1958—61; active attending staff Jackson Meml. Hosp., Miami, Fla., 1963—75; active staff Doctor's Hosp. Miami, 1963—75; active staff, chmn. dept. ob-gyn. Bapt. Hosp. Miami, 1972—73; staff Shands Hosp., Gainesville, Fla., 1975—91; prof. ob-gyn. U. Fla., Gainesville, 1980—92, assoc. dean, 1980—86, exec. assoc. dean, 1986—88, interim dean, assoc. v.p. clin. affairs, 1988—91; exec. v.p. Am. Bd. Med. Specialties, 1991—97. Clin. adj. prof. dept. ob-gyn. Northwestern U. Med. Sch., 1992—; clin. prof. dept. ob-gyn. U. Fla. Coll. Medicine, 1992—2000; trustee McKnight Brain Rsch. Found., 1999—; prof. emeritus U. Fla. Coll. Medicine, 2000—; mem. Accreditation Coun. for Grad. Med. Edn., 1984—89, Liaison Com. for Med. Edn., 1989—91, Fla. Bd. Medicine, 1988—92; mem. exam. bd. Fed. State Med. Bds., 1991—94; mem. U.S. Med. Licensing Exam. Composite Com., 1996—2002, Nat. Com. on Fgn. Med. Edn. and Accreditation, 2001—. Mem.: AMA (mem. coun. med. edn. 1983—92, chmn. 1987—88), Fla. Med. Assn. (pres. 1983—84), So. Med. Assn. (pres. 1987—88), Alpha Omega Alpha.

DOCKERY-SCHILLIG, LINDA, writer; b. Louisville, Sept. 23, 1952; d. Willie Dockery and Minnie Cotton; m. Roger Lee Schillig. Freelance consulting tchr., Louisville, 1975—2002; spkr. in field; past columnist Banner Gazette. Author: Distant Drums, 1997 (Can.n Fiction award, 1997), Three Little Words, 2002 (Adcott Publishing award Fiction, 2002), Anna Claus: The Woman Behind the Legend, 2003, Cowgirl Up, 2004, Trail of No Return, 2004, An Angel for Christmas, 2003, North Pole Kitchen, 2003, Trusty Steads of Film & TV, 2004, Once Upon A Time, Renegades, Rebels and Rogues of The Old West, 2005, My Book of Thoughts-Poetry From The Heart, 2005, (screenplays) My Special Angel, 1977, Wilderness Love, 1976 (Lippincott award for most promising new screenplay, 1976), Children of Darkness, 1977, Inherit the Devil, 1978 (Sun Burst award Best Screenplay, 1978), Welcome to Hell, 1978, Rain Softly Till Then, 1984, (TV series) A Time for Love, 1981, (film) Inherit the Devil, 1985, (documentary film) For Our Land, 1991, singer country music; contbr. articles to profl. jours.; editor: Pen Works. Named to, Nat. Cowgirl Hall of Fame, Women Who Write the West Hall of Fame, 2002; recipient Faith and Love award Best Christian Short Story, 1980, Golden pen, 1991, Marshal award Poetry, 1992. Mem.: Ind. Film Makers Guild (founding bd. dirs., v.p.), American Film Inst., Ind. Film Inst., Nat. Hist. Soc., Women Writing the West, Women's Writers Guild. Home and Office: 11117 E Old 56 Scottsburg IN 47170 Personal E-mail: dockery2004@aol.com.

DOCKING, THOMAS ROBERT, lawyer, former state lieutenant governor; b. Lawrence, Kans., Aug. 10, 1954; s. Robert Blackwell and Meredith (Gear) D.; m. Jill Sadowsky, June 18, 1977; children: Brian Thomas, Margery Meredith BS, U. Kans., 1976, MBA, JD, 1980. Bar: Kans. 1980. Assoc. Regan & McGannon, Wichita, Kans., 1980-82, ptnr., 1983-90, Ayesh, Docking, Herd & Theis, Wichita, 1990, Morris, Laing, Evans, Brock & Kennedy, Wichita, 1990—; lt. gov. State of Kans., Topeka, 1983-87. Dem. nominee for Gov. of Kans., 1986; chmn. adv. bd. Docking Inst. Pub. Affairs, Ft. Hays State U. Mem. steering com. Campaign Kans.; chmn. campaign com. Coll. Liberal Arts and Sci., 1988-91; bd. dirs. Kans. Easter Seals-Goodwill Industries, 1987-93, chmn. 1989 Telethon, vice-chair, 1991-93; bd. dirs. Wichita Conv. and Visitors Bur., 1988-2002; chmn., bd. dirs. St. Francis Found., 1988-94; trustee Emporia State U. Sch. Bus.; chmn. Wichita Water Conservation Task Force, 1991—; mem. Wichita/Brookes Water Task Force, 1997; chmn. allocation com. United Way of the Plains, 2003; mem. bd. govs. U. Kans. Sch. Law, 1998—2000; bd. dirs. Wichita Downtown Devel. Corp., 2001—, Fin. Fitness Found., 1999—, United Way of the Plains, 2004—. Recipient Bob Brock award, Kansas Dem. Party, 2003. Mem. ABA, Kans. Bar Assn., Pi Sigma Alpha, Beta Gamma Sigma, Beta Theta Pi. Presbyterian. Home: 125 S Crestway St Wichita KS 67218-1309 Office: Morris Laing Evans Brock & Kennedy 300 N Mead St #200 Wichita KS 67202-2744 Office Phone: 316-262-2671.

DOCKSTADER, DEBORAH RUTH, minister; b. Elmira, N.Y., Oct. 12, 1948; d. E. Stanley and Ruth Emery Dockstader. BA, Mercyhurst Coll., 1974; MDiv, Princeton Theol. Sem., 1977. Ordained to ministry Presbyn. Ch., 1977. Pastor Lake Champlain Islands Parish, North Hero, Vt., 1977—79, East Greene Presbyn. Ch., Erie, Pa., 1979—84; dir. edn. St. Stephen's Ch., Fairview, 1984—85; assoc. exec. dir. Inter-Ch. Ministries Northwestern Pa, Erie, 1985—93; interim pastor Ross Meml. Presbyn. Ch., Binghamton, NY, 1993—96; pastor Southside Presbyn. Ch., Niles, Ohio, 1997—, First Presbyn. Ch., Girard, 1997—. Perm. jud. commn. Eastminster Presbytery, Youngstown, Ohio, 1999—, mem. com. ministry, 2000—04, mem. comms. com., 2005—; commr. synod assembly Covenant Synod, 1997—2001. Bd. dirs. WQLN Pub. TV & Radio, Erie, 1987—90; mem. Erie Tanzania Project Bd., 1987—90, Allegany Nature Pilgrimage Bd., 1988—93; trustee Erie Rotary Club Scholarship Found., 1990—93; sec. bd. dirs. Niles Cmty. Svcs., 1997—; treas. Friends McKinley Libr., 2000—01; mem. Presbyn. Media Mission Bd., 1983—87, Ecumenical Theol. Ctr. Bd., 1987—90; trustee Susquehanna Valley Presbytery, 1994—96; bd. dirs. Manhoning Valley Assn. Chs., 2000—02; mem. Presbytery Self Study Com., 2001—02. Avocations: reading, birdwatching. Office Phone: 330-505-1192. Personal E-mail: drdockstader@sbcglobal.net.

DOCKSTADER, EMMETT STANLEY, civil engineer, construction executive; b. Elmira, NY, Nov. 7, 1923; s. Roy S. and Gertrude (Everts) D.; m. Ruth Norma Emery, May 11, 1946 (dec.); children: Deborah Ruth, David Stanley; m. Muriel Thomas Fearnot, Oct. 31, 1999. BCE cum laude, Syracuse U., 1947. Registered profl. engr. R.I., Pa., W.Va., Ga., N.C. Engr. Am. Bridge Co., Elmira, 1948-50; field engr. Sessinghaus & Ostergaard, Inc., Erie, Pa., 1950-53; project mgr., 1953-58; v.p., 1958-69; sr. v.p., sec., 1972-79; pres., 1984-86; gen. mgr. constrn. divsn. H.H. Roberston Co., Ambridge, 1969-71; constrn. exec. Gilbane Bldg. Co., Providence, R.I., 1979-84; pres. Dockstader Constrn. Assocs., 1986—. Dir. Erie Constrn. Coun.; mem. Erie Port Commn., 1967—69; chmn. N.W. Pa. Rail Authority; mem. Erie City Wter Authority. Dir. Erie Civic Music Assn.; trustee Ch. of the Covenant. Inductee Hall of Achievement, Thomas A. Edison H.S. Alumni Assn., 2000. Mem. Nat. Soc. Profl. Engrs. (life), Am. Arbitration Assn. (arbitrator), Soc. Profls. in Dispute Resolution, Nat. Railway Hist. Soc. (bd. dirs. Lakeshore chpt.), Erie Mannerchor (life), SAR, The Pa. Soc., Masons (32nd degree), Rotary (Paul Harris fellow), Erie Yacht Club, Y Mens Club (past pres.), Tau Beta Pi. Office: 125 Lincoln Ave Erie PA 16505-2441

DOCKSTEADER, KAREN KEMP, marketing professional; b. Salisbury, Md., Feb. 11, 1953; d. Robert George and Laverne (Briggs) Kemp; m. Gerald Hugh Docksteader, Apr. 3, 1997; children from previous marriage: Daniel Richard Arrington IV, James William Arrington. BS, Iowa State U., 1975; MEd, Salisbury U., 1979. Dir. horticultural project Chesapeake Rehab. Ctr., Easton, Md., 1975-76; mgr. greenhouses Bountiful Ridge Nurseries, Inc., Princess Anne, Md., 1976-77; instr. horticulture Dorchester Bd. Edn., Cambridge, Md., 1978-80, Fredrick (Md.) Bd. Edn., 1980-87; instr. agronomy Frederick C.C., 1985; treas. Kemp's Ltd., Inc., Martinsburg, W.Va., 1985-87, pres. Frederick, 1987—2001; mgr. U.S. retail sales Kord Products, Ltd., Brampton, 1995-98; sales and mktg. dir. Angelica Nurseries, Inc., Kennedyville, Md., 2001—03; published photographer, author Garden Writers Assn., 2003—. Keynote spkr. Vocat. Counseling Orgn., Md., 1980—88; cons. retail and comml. mktg. groups, 1977—91; dir. Russian-Georgian Rose Project, Tblissi, Georgia, 1993. Editor: (newsletter) The Spreader, 1990; featured narrator: (documentaries) Our Land, Our Future, 1980; exhibitor Assn. Nurserymen, Balt. and King of Prussia, Pa., 1986—2003. Coach 4-H, FFA, NJHA, and other youth orgns., 1977—98; state chair Soil Conservation Poster Competition, Md., 1990—91; judge horticulture county fairs, state and nat. 4-H and FFA activities, 1977—91; co-founder Windows of Opportunity Found., 2000—. Named Conservation Tchr. of the Yr., State Soil and Water Conservation Svc., 1984. Mem.: DAR, Somerset Pa. Hist. Soc., Hackers Creek Hist. Soc., Md. Hist. Soc., New Market Grange, Md. Greenhouse Growers Assn. Avocations: geneaology and historical research, writing, needlepoint, gardening. Office: Kemp's Ltd Inc 26875 Mallard Rd Chestertown MD 21620 Business E-Mail: kkemp@angelicanurseries.com.

DOCKTERMAN, MICHAEL, lawyer; b. Davenport, Iowa, Dec. 14, 1954; s. Jerome and Elaine (Epstein) D.; m. Laura Di Giantonio, Sept. 25, 1983; 1 child, Eliana. BA, Yale U., 1975; JD, Duke U., 1978. Bar: Ill. 1978, US Dist. Ct. (no. dist.) Ill. 1978, US Ct. Appeals (7th cir.) 1978, US Dist. Ct. (ea. dist.) Mich. 1986, US Dist. Ct. (ctrl. dist.) Ill. 1988, US Ct. Appeals (4th, 6th and fed. cir.) 1990, US Dist. Ct. (so. dist.) Ill. 1991, US Supreme Ct. 1992, US Ct. Appeals (2d cir.) 1993, US Dist Ct. (we. dist.) Mich. 1995, US Dist. Ct. (ea. dist.) Mo. 1996, US Ct. Appeals (9th cir.) 2004; registered fgn. lawyer U.K., 2004—. Ptnr. Wildman, Harrold, Allen and Dixon, ILP, Chgo., 1978—. Co-author: IICLE Class Actions, 1986, 92, 2000; contbg. author: ABA Criminal Antitrust Litigation Manual; contbr. articles to profl. jours. Active Chgo. Vol. Legal Svc., 1983—, The Chgo. Com., Chgo. Coun. on Fgn. Rels., Am. Refugee Com.; adult bd. dir. Greater Midwest region B'nai B'rith Youth Orgn., 1985—; bd. dir. KAM Isaiah Israel Congregation, 1993-96, 2002-03; bd. dir. Duke Law Alumni Assn., 1994-2003, pres., 2000-02; bd. of visitors, 2003-; trustee Max and Gretel Janowski Fund, Chgo., 1992-99. Recipient Award for Advocacy Internat. Acad. Trial Lawyers, Charles A. Dukes award for vol. svc., Leadership Devel. award B'nai B'rith Youth Orgn., Fellow Pvt. Adjudication Found., Am. Bar Found.; mem. ABA (chair corp. governance subcom. Corp. Counsel com. Bus. Law Sect. 1997-2003), Chgo. Bar Assn., Lawyers Club Chgo., B'nai B'rith Justice Lodge. Office: Wildman Harrold Allen Dixon 225 W Wacker Dr Chicago IL 60606-1229 E-mail: dockterm@wildmanharrold.com.

DOCTER, CHARLES ALFRED, lawyer, retired state legislator; b. Hamburg, Germany, Aug. 5, 1931; s. Alfred Joseph and Annie Beatrice D.; m. Marcia Kaplan, Nov. 27, 1958; children: Henry David Will, Michael Warren, Adina Jo. BA magna cum laude, Kenyon Coll., 1953; JD, U. Chgo., 1956. Bar: D.C. 1959, Md. 1962, U.S. Supreme Ct. 1959. Former aide to late Sen. Paul H. Douglas, U.S. Senate, Washington; practice law, specializing in bankruptcy and reorgn., Washington, 1959—; sr. ptnr. Docter, Docter, Lynn, P.C., Washington, 1967—. Presdl. appointee to bd. Pa. Ave. Devel. Corp., 1995-96; pres. Montgomery County (Md.) Com. for Fair Representation, 1962-65. Pres. Western Suburban Democratic Club, 1965-66; mem. Md. Ho. of Dels., 1967-78; serving variously as chmn. Montgomery and Prince George's counties Bi-County Dels.; bd. dirs. Met. Washington Coun. Govts., 1970, Downtown D.C. Bus. Improvement Dist., 1997—; chmn. Downtown Housing Now Com., 1997—; D.C. adv. neighborhood commr. for Dist. 6C 09, 2003—. Lt. USNR, 1956-59. Fellow Am. Coll. Bankruptcy, Walter Chandler Am. Inn of Ct. (master emeritus). Achievements include sponsoring Md. tenants' rights laws, Md. Pub. campaign financing law, Md. revolving credit law and other consumer measures. Home: 1101 Market Sq W 801 Pennsylvania Ave NW Washington DC 20004-2615 Office: Docter Docter & Lynn PC 666 11th St NW Ste 1010 Washington DC 20001-4525 Office Phone: 202-628-6860. Business E-Mail: ddl@bankruptcy-docter.com.

DOCTOR, ALLAN, physician, researcher; b. Norfolk, Virginia, Sept. 21, 1962; s. Donald Harvie and Susanna (Schorr) Doctor; m. Dahven Eliotte White, Feb. 15, 1997; children: Reid Haefen, Chase Morgan. BA, U. of Va., 1980—84, MD, 1985—89. Diplomate Nat. Bd. of Med. Examiners, 1990, Am. Bd. of Emergency Medicine, 1994, Sub bd., Pediatric Emergency Medicine, 1994, Am. Bd. of Pediat., 1997, Sub bd., Pediatric Critical Care, 2000. Resident in emergency medicine U. Pitts., 1989—92; fellow in pediatric emergency medicine Harvard U., Boston Children's Hosp., Boston, 1992—94, resident in pediat., 1994—95, fellow in pediatric critical care anesthesia, 1995—99; asst. prof. of pediat. and anesthesia U. of Va. Sch. of Medicine, Charlottesville, Va., 1999—. Dir., tng. program in pediatric critical care U. of Va. Sch. of Medicine, Charlottesville, Va., 2000—. Author: (med. rsch.) Pediat., Jour. of Applied Physiology, Critical Care Medicine, Jour. of Thoracic and Cardiovasc. Surgery. Youth mentor Thomas Jefferson Meml. Unitarian Ch., Charlottesville, Va., 2003. Recipient Ronald Stewart Award for Excellence in Tchg., U. of Pitts., 1992, Scholar's Award for Rsch. in Pediat., U. of Va., 2004; grantee Grant in Aid, U. of Va. Dept. of Pediat., 2001, Fund for Excellence in Sci. and Tech., U. of Va., 2001, Child Health Rsch. Scholar, NIH, 2001—03, Mentored Physician Scientist Award, 2004, R and D Fund, U. of Va., 2004. Fellow: Am. Acad. of Pediat.; mem.: Am. Thoracic Soc., Soc. for Critical Care Medicine. Unitarian Universalist. Achievements include development of perflubron assisted high frequency oscillatory ventialtion; research in pulmonary blood flow derangement in disease; nitric oxide signaling in the pulmonary circulation. Avocations: swimming, sailing, cultural studies. Office: U of Va HSC Box 800386 Charlottesville VA 22908 Business E-Mail: ad4j@virginia.edu.

DOCTOR, KENNETH JAY, publishing executive; b. L.A., Jan. 5, 1950; s. Joseph and Ruth (Kazdoy) D.; m. Katherine Conant Francis, June 14, 1971; children: Jenika, Joseph, Katy. BA in Sociology, U. Calif., Santa Cruz, 1971; MS in Journalism, U. Oreg., 1979. Editor, pub. Willamette Valley Observer, Eugene, Oreg., 1975-82; mng. editor Oreg. Mag., Portland, 1982-84; mng. editor, features Boulder (Colo.) Daily Camera, 1984-86; assoc. editor, features St. Paul Pioneer Press, 1986-90, mng. editor, features, 1990-94, mng. editor, 1994-97; v.p. editl. Knight Ridder New Media, San Jose, Calif., 1997-99; v.p. strategy Knight-Ridder.com., 1999-2001; v.p. content svcs. Knight-Ridder Digital, 2001—. Chair Knight-Ridder Task Force on Family Readers, Miami, Fla., 1991, Knight-Ridder mgmt. devel. program, Harvard U., 1993. Pres. Alumni Assn. U. Calif., Santa Cruz. Recipient Achievement award Oreg. Civil Liberties Union, Eugene, 1982. Mem. Soc. Newspaper Design, Am. Soc. Newspaper Editors. Avocations: baseball, travel. Office: Knight Ridder Digital 35 S Market St San Jose CA 95113 E-mail: kdoctor@smail.com.

DOCTOROFF, DANIEL L., municipal official; m. Alisa Doctoroff; children: Jacob, Ariel, Jenna. BA, Harvard Coll.; JD, Law Sch. U. Chgo. Investment banker Lehman Bros.; mng. ptnr. Oak Hill Capital Ptnrs.; dep. mayor for econ. devel. and rebuilding City of NY, 2002—. Founder, pres. NYC2012, 2000; bd. mem. NYC and Co., NYC Partnership. Bd. mem. YMCA Greater NY. Office: NYC2012 1 Liberty Plz 34th Fl New York NY 10006 also: City Hall New York NY 10007 Office Phone: 212-953-2012, 212-788-3000. Office Fax: 212-788-2460.

DOCTOROW, EDGAR LAWRENCE, writer, English educator; b. NYC, Jan. 6, 1931; s. David Richard and Rose (Levine) D.; m. Helen Esther Setzer, Aug. 20, 1954; children: Jenny, Caroline, Richard. AB in Philosophy with honors, Kenyon Coll., 1952; student, Columbia U., 1952-53; LHD (hon.), Kenyon Coll., 1976; LittD (hon.), Hobart and William Smith Coll., 1979; LHD (hon.), Brandeis U., 1989. Script reader Columbia Pictures, Inc., NYC; sr. editor New Am. Libr., NYC, 1959-64; editor-in-chief Dial Press, NYC, 1964-69, v.p., pub., 1968-69; mem. faculty Sarah Lawrence Coll., Bronxville, NY, 1971-78; creative writing fellow Sch. Drama Yale U., New Haven, 1974-75; Glucksman Prof. English and Am. Letters NYU, 1982—. Writer-in-residence U. Calif, Irvine, 1969-70; vis. prof. U. Utah, 1975; vis. sr. fellow Coun. on Humanities Princeton U., 1980. Author: (novels) Welcome to Hard Times, 1960, Big as Life, 1966, The Book of Daniel, 1971 (Nat. Book award nominee 1972), Ragtime, 1975 (Nat. Book Critics Circle award 1976, Arts and Letters award 1976), Loon Lake, 1980 (Nat. Book award nomiee 1980), Lives of the Poets: Six Stories and a Novella, 1984, World's Fair, 1985 (Nat. Book award 1986), Billy Bathgate, 1989 (Nat. Book award nominee 1989, Nat. Book Critics Circle award 1990, PEN/Faulkner award 1990, William Dean Howells medal Am. Acad. and Inst. Arts and Letters 1990), The Waterworks, 1994, City of God, 2000, The March, 2005; (play) Drinks Before Dinner, 1979; (screenplay) Daniel, 1983; (essays) Jack London, Hemingway, and the Constitution: Selected Essays 1977-92, 1993. With AUS, 1953-55. Recipient Arts and Letters award Am. Acad. and Nat. Inst. Art, 1976; Guggenheim fellow, 1973, Creative Artists Program Svc. fellow, 1973-74; Edith Wharton citation of merit for fiction and N.Y. State Author, 1989-91, Nat. Humanities medal, 1998, Commonwealth award, 2000. Mem. Authors Guild, Am. Acad. Arts and Letters, Am. Acad. Arts and Scis., Am. PEN, Writers Guild Am. East, Century Assn. Office: NYU English Dept Rm 221 Faculty Arts and Scis 19 University Pl New York NY 10003-6607*

DODD, CHRISTOPHER J., senator; b. Willimantic, Conn., May 27, 1944; s. Thomas J. and Grace (Murphy) D. BA in English Lit., Providence Coll., 1966; JD, U. Louisville, 1972. Bar: Conn. 1973. Vol. Peace Corps, Dominican Republic, 1966-68; atty. Suisman, Shapiro, Wool & Brennan, New London, Conn., 1973-74; mem. 94th-96th Congresses from 2d Conn. Dist., 1975-80; sen. from Conn. U.S. Senate, Washington, 1980—, mem. fgn. rels., banking, housing & urban affairs coms., rules com., 1981—, mem. subcom. edn., arts & humanities, founder & co-chmn. Senate Children's Caucus, 1983—, ranking mem. Western Hemisphere subcom., mem. subcom. children & families, labor com., randing mem. subcom. securities, banking com. Chmn. Dem. Nat. Com.; mem. Whitewater com. Served with AUS, 1969-75.

Recipient Hubert H. Humphrey Pub. Svc. award, Outstanding U.S. Senator award, Nathan Davis award AMA, Head Start Senator of Decade award. Democrat. Roman Catholic. Office: US Senate 448 Russell Senate Bldg Washington DC 20510-0001

DODD, GERALD DEWEY, JR., radiologist, educator; b. Oaklyn, N.J., Nov. 18, 1922; s. Gerald Dewey and Anne Aloysius (Keveney) D.; m. Helen Carolyn Glenzing, Apr. 5, 1946; children: Patricia, Michael, Barbara, Gerald Dewey III, Anne, Susan, Thomas. AB, Lafayette Coll., 1945; MD, Jefferson Med. Coll., 1947; DSc (hon.), Lafayette Coll., 1991. Diplomate Am. Bd. Radiology. Intern Fitzgerald Mercy Hosp., Darby, Pa., 1947; resident Jefferson Med. Coll., Phila., 1948—50; asst. radiologist, instr. radiology Jefferson Med. Coll. and Hosp., Phila., 1952—55, asst. radiologist, clin. prof. radiology, 1961—66; asst. radiology, roentgenologist Thomas Jefferson U., Phila., 1952—54, assoc. radiology, 1954—55; assoc. prof. radiology, assoc. radiologist U. Tex. M.D. Anderson Cancer Ctr., Houston, 1955—61, prof., 1966—89, chmn. dept. diagnostic radiology, 1966—89, prof., head divsn. diagnostic imaging, 1984—92, Robert D. Moreton Chair Diagnostic Radiology, 1988—93, chair emeritus, 1996—; prof. radiology U. Tex. Med. Sch., Houston, 1971—, chmn. dept. radiology, 1971—74, prof. radiology Sch. Allied Health Scis., 1971—94. Cons. radiologist St. Luke's Hosp., Tex. Children's Hosp., Houston, 1966—, Singleton Prof. Radiology, 1995-99; vis. mem. grad. faculty Tex. A&M U., College Station, 1969-93; adj. prof. radiology Baylor Coll. Medicine, 1983—. Cons. to editor Radiology, 1977—86, cons. editor The Cancer Bull., 1979—89, assoc. editor Cancer, 1991—2000; editor: Breast Diseases, 1993—2004; referee CRC Critical Revs. in Radiol. Scis., 1969—95; contbr. articles to profl. jours. Dir.-at-large Am. Cancer Soc., 1977-90, pres., 1990-91, past officer dir.; mem. coun. Nat. Coun. Radiation Protection and Measurement, 1979-91, bd. dirs., 1981-91. Fellow Am. Coll. Radiology (bd. chancellors 1976-81, 82-85, chmn. bd. chancellors 1982-84, pres. 1984-85, Gold medal 1989); mem. Radiol. Soc. N.Am. (Gold medal 1986), Am. Roentgen Ray Soc. (Gold medal 1992), Soc. Gastrointestinal Radiologists (Cannon medal 1995), Assn. Univ. Radiologists, Tex. Med. Assn., Tex. Radiol. Soc. (Gold medal 1988), Soc. Breast Imaging (Gold medal 1995), Harris County Med. Soc., Houston Radiol. Soc., Phila. Roentgen Ray Soc. (hon.), Alpha Omega Alpha, Phi Delta Theta, Phi Chi. Republican. Roman Catholic. Office: M D Anderson Hosp 1515 Holcombe Blvd Houston TX 77030-4009

DODD, JACK GORDON, JR., physicist, researcher; b. Spokane, Wash., June 19, 1926; s. Jack Gordon and Mary Ida (Stuart) D.; m. Mary Ann Howell, June 11, 1951; children— Jeffrey John, Laura Jean. Student, State Coll. Wash., 1946-48; BS in Physics, Ill. Inst. Tech., 1951; MS in Physics, U. Ark., 1957, PhD in Physics, 1965. With Argonne (Ill.) Nat. Lab., 1951-53; tchr. Fourche Valley High Sch., 1953-55, 56-57; asst. prof. Drury Coll., 1957-60; assoc. prof. Ark. Poly. Coll., 1960-65, U. Tenn., Knoxville, 1965-69; Charles A. Dana prof. physics and astronomy Colgate U., Hamilton, N.Y., 1969-87, ret., 1988; v.p. Spectrum Sq., Ithaca, N.Y., 1987—; bd. trustees McCrone Rsch. Inst., Chgo., 1999—. Cons. on phys. optics, microscopy, detonation theory, spectral and image data processing Served with USN, 1944-46. Mem. Am. Assn. Physics Tchrs., Am. Phys. Soc., Am. Astron. Soc., Optical Soc. Am., Sigma Xi. Office: 213 Sears Pond Rd Sherburne NY 13460-5018 Business E-Mail: jackdodd@clarityconnect.com.

DODD, JAMES B., internet executive; BA in Econs., Stanford U.; MBA, Harvard U. CPA. With Sprint; pres., CEO Nat. Info. Consortium Inc., Overland Park, Kans. Office: National Information Center 10540 S Ridgeview Rd Olathe KS 66061-6440

DODD, JAN EVE, lawyer; b. Kansas City, Mo., May 24, 1964; d. Raymond Thomas and Eva Faith (McCorkle) D. BA in Polit. Sci. & Journalism, U. Mo., Columbia, 1985; JD, U. Mo., Kansas City, 1988. Bar: Mo. 1988, Ill. 1989, U.S. Dist. Ct. (so. dist.) Ill. 1989, U.S. Dist. Ct. (ea. dist.) Mo. 1989, U.S. Ct. Appeals (7th cir.) 1991, U.S. Ct. Appeals (8th cir.) 1994. Rsch. asst. Prof. Jack M. Balkin, Kansas City, Mo., 1986-87; jud. law clk. Judge Edward D. Robertson Jr. Mo. Supreme Ct., Jefferson City, Mo., 1988-89; sr. assoc. def. litigation Sandberg, Phoenix & Von Gontard, St. Louis, 1989—; former special state atty gen. State of Mo.; now ptnr., litigation dept. Kaye Scholer, Los Angeles, Calif. Recipient diploma Nat. Inst. for Trial Adv., Mid-Am. Regional, 1994. Mem. Def. Rsch. Inst., Bar Assn. Met. St. Louis, Tower Grove Neighborhood Assn. Office: Kaye Scholer 1999 Ave of Stars Ste 1700 Los Angeles CA 90067 Office Phone: 310-788-1000. Office Fax: 310-788-1200. Business E-Mail: jdodd@kayescholer.com.

DODD, JEFF C., lawyer; b. St. Louis, 1955; BA magna cum laude, U. Houston, 1976, JD summa cum laude, 1979. Bar: Tex. 1979. Ptnr., Corp./Securities Practice Andrews Kurth LLP, Houston, mem. mgmt. com. Adj. prof. law U. Houston, 1994, 95, 99, 2000, 01, S. Tex. Coll. Law, 1989, 90. Editor: Houston Law Rev., 1978—79. Adv. bd. Honors. Coll. U. Houston. Mem.: ABA (Bus. Law Sect., Taxation Sect., Sci. & Tech. Sect., Forum on Franchising), State Bar Tex. (Bus. Law Sect., electronic com. subcom.), Houston Bar Assn. (Bus. Law Sect., electronic commerce subcom.), Phi Kappa Phi. Office: Andrews Kurth LLP 600 Travis St Ste 4200 Houston TX 77002-3090 also: Andrews Kurth LLP 111 Congress Ste 1700 Austin TX 78701 Office Phone: 713-220-4736, 512-320-9252. Office Fax: 713-220-4285. Business E-Mail: jeffdodd@andrewskurth.com.

DODD, JERRY LEE, lawyer; b. Bakersfield, Calif., Nov. 16, 1953; s. James Luther and Juanita Louise (Holmes) D.; m. Phena Fite, Jan. 9, 1972; children: Jody, Kimberly, Kristy, Julie, Timothy, Andrew, Matthew, Lindsey, Allison, Daniel. BS magna cum laude, U. Ark., 1975; MBA, Monmouth Coll., 1978; JD, Rutgers U., 1979. CPA; bar: N.J. 1979, Pa. 1983, Minn. 1988. Commd. 2d. lt. USAF, 1975, advanced through grades to capt., auditor A.F. Audit Agy. Wrightstown, N.J., 1975-78, base counsel Alexandria, La., 1979-81, def. counsel, 1981-82, contract trial atty. A.F. Contract Law Ctr. Dayton, Ohio, 1982-86, ret., 1986; govt. contracts counsel U.S. Army 7th Signal Command, Ft. Richie, Md., 1986-87; group counsel Honeywell, Mpls., 1987-90; divsn. counsel Harsco-BMY Wheeled Vehicles Divsn., Marysville, Ohio, 1990—. Mem.: ABA (com. mem.), Ark. Soc. CPAs, Assn. Corp. Counsels Am. (bd. dirs.). Home: 700 Kirkpatrick Rd Malvern AR 72104 Office: Harsco BMY Wheeled Vehicles 700 Kirkpatrick Rd Malvern AR 72104 Office Phone: 501-332-7173. Personal E-mail: jerryleedodd@yahoo.com.

DODD, JOHN ROBERT, non-profit organization administrator; b. Dallas, Oct. 15, 1951; s. Carlos Lestor and Betty (Ayers) D.; m. Mary Teresa Parsons, Nov. 12, 1983; children: Katherine Howard, Mary Alexandra. BA, Coll. William and Mary, 1975; MA, U. N.C., 1980. Tchr. Cinnaminson (N.J.) H.S., 1975-78; grad. asst. U. N.C., Chapel Hill, 1978-80; PAC coord. Nat. Congl. Club, Raleigh, N.C., 1981-82; v.p. Coalition for Freedom, Raleigh, 1982-85; pres. J & T Dodd Assocs., Fairfax, Va., 1985-94, Jesse Helms Ctr, Wingate, N.C., 1994—. Cons. to various mems. of Congress. Bd. dirs. Fellowship of Christian Athletes, Washington, 1991-94, Turning Point Women's Shelter; del. Rep. Nat. Conv., 2000, 04; pres. Lacrosse Camps, Inc., 1993— Named Deep South Conf. Coach of Yr., 2001, coach North-South Coll. All-Star Game, 2001. Fellow: Am. Leadership Forum (sr.). Republican. Office: Jesse Helms Ctr PO Box 247 Wingate NC 28174-0247 Office Phone: 704-233-1776.

DODD, LISA LEHR, writer, literature educator; b. Palo Alto, Calif., Jan. 29, 1958; d. Wendell John and Joyce Browne Lehr. BA in EPO Biology, U. Colo., 1980. Basic Literacy and English as a Second Language Literacy Coun., 2003. Quality control technician Syva Co., Palo Alto, Calif., 1981—84; tchr. writing Sierra Emeritus Coll., Grass Valley; instrnl. aide Grass Valley Sch. Dist.; freelance writer. Pro bono grant writing AnimalSave, Grass Valley, Calif. Esl tutor Literacy Coun., Grass Valley, Calif.; vol. instr. Saddle Pals Therapeutic Horseback Riding, Grass Valley, Calif.; cat cuddler Nev. County Animal Shelter, Grass Valley, Calif.; pub. sch. art docent Pleasant Ridge Sch. Dist., Grass Valley, Calif.; mem. and former deaconess Calvary Bible Ch., Grass Valley, Calif., 1991—. Recipient Art Docent Five-Year Pin, Nev. County Supt. of Schools, 2002. Mem.: Turning Memories Into Memoirs (TM). Conservative. Protestant. Avocations: animals, art, reading, walking, outdoors. Office: Grass Valley CA Office Phone: 530-274-1727. E-mail: reachlisa@myway.com, lisa@ljlcopywriting.com.

DODD, LOIS, artist, art educator; b. Montclair, NJ, Apr. 22, 1927; d. Lawrence Dodd and Margaret Vanderhoff; m. William Dickey King (div.); 1 child, Eli Benjamin. Student, Cooper Union, 1945-48. Tchr. art Bklyn. Coll., 1971-92. One-woman shows include Tanager Gallery, N.Y.C., 1954—62, Green Mountain Gallery, 1969—76, Fischbach Gallery, 1978—2002, Washington (Conn.) Art Assn., 1977, Cape Split Pl., Maine, 1977—83, N.J. State Mus., Trenton, 1981, Lyman Allyn Mus., Conn., 1980, La. State U., Baton Rouge, 1984, Anne Weber Gallery, Maine, 1987, Caldbeck Gallery, 1990, 1995, 1998, 2001—03, Dartmouth (N.H.) Coll., 1990, 2004, Rider (N.J.) U., 1993, Montclair Art Mus., 1996, Farnsworth Art Mus., Rockland, Maine, 1996, Trenton City Mus., Alexandre Gallery, 2002—, 2004, Bowdoin Coll. Mus., Maine, 2004, Represented in permanent collections Colby Coll. Mus., Cooper Hewitt Mus., Farnsworth Mus., Kalamazoo Art Ctr., Montclair Art Mus., NAD, AT&T, Chase Manhattan Bank, Commerce Bancshares Inc., Met. Life Ins. Co., Readers Digest, R.V. Reynolds Security, Pacific Nat. Bank, First Nat. City Bank, Hood Mus., Dartmouth, Rider U., NJ. Bd. govs. Skowhegan Sch. of Painting and Sculptures, 1980—. Recipient Disting. Alumni citation Cooper Union, 1987; Ingram Merrill Found. grantee, 1971. Mem. NAD, AAAL (award 1986). Office: c/o Alexandre Gallery Fuller Bldg 41 E 57th St New York NY 10022 Office Phone: 212-254-7159.*

DODD, ROGER J., lawyer; b. Sewickley, Pa., Sept. 15, 1951; s. Carl Roger and Dorothy Maude (Barley) Dodd; m. Marcia J. Dodd; children: Matthew A., Andrew J., Kristin. BA in Econs., Bucknell U., 1973; JD, U. Pitts., 1976, Ga., 1976, Fla., 1977. Ptnr. Blackburn, Bright, Edwards Dodd & Joseph, Valdosta, Ga., 1976-87; prin. Roger J. Dodd Lawyers, P.C., Valdosta, 1987—; spl. asst. atty. gen. State of Ga., 1979-85; mem. faculty Ga. Inst. Trial Advocacy, 1986—92, chmn. of bd., 1988—91; mem. faculty Nat. Coll. Criminal Def., 1986—. Mem. faculty Nat. Coll. Criminal Def., 1986—, Advance Cross Exam., Advance Trial Inst.; adj. prof. Valdosta State Coll.; guest lectr. sch. law Mercer U. Ga. State U.; mem. family law sect. exec. com., 1985-88, criminal law sect., mem. family law sect., exec. com. 1985-88; mem. ABA family law sect., criminal law sect. exec. coms., 1992—; internat. lectr. in field. Co-author: Cross Examination: Science and Techniques, 1993; guest commentator on Court TV; peer rev. lawyer Trial Mag., 1991—; contbr. articles to profl. jours., newspapers; videos: Killer Cross-Examination (6 hrs. of audio & video tapes) The Art and Science of Cross Examination, 2 parts, 1990, How to Dominate a Courtroom on Cross Examination, 4 parts, 1994. Bd. dirs. Lowndes Country Assn. Retarded Citizens, Valdosta, 1977, Valwood Sch., Valdosta, 1984-86, Nat. Bd. Trial Advocacy, 1989, civil trial specialist, criminal trial specialist, 1990; peer rev. lawyer Trial Mag., 1991; mem. Boy Scouts Am., sustaining mem. Alapaha Coun. Mem.: Am. Acad. Matrimonial Lawyers, Internat. Acad. Matrimonial Lawyers. Libertarian. Presbyterian. Home: 5634 Danieli Dr N Lake Park GA 31636 Office: PO Box 1066 613 N Patterson St Valdosta GA 31601-4609 Office Phone: 229-242-4470. Office Fax: 229-245-7731. E-mail: doddlaw@doddlaw.com.

DODD, WAYNE D., poet, editor; b. Clarita, Okla., Sept. 23, 1930; s. Homer Dewey and Maggie Mathilda Dodd; m. Betty Coshow, June 7, 1958 (div. Nov. 1980); children: Elizabeth Caroline, Hudson Callahan; m. Joyce Barlow, June 27, 1981. BA with distinction, U. Okla., 1955, MA, 1957, PhD, 1963. Asst. prof. U. Colo., Boulder, 1960-68; asst. editor Abstracts of English Studies, Boulder, 1961-68; prof. English Ohio U., Athens, 1968-94, disting. prof., 1994—; editor Ohio Rev., Athens, 1971—2001. Mem. adv. bd. Coordinating Coun. Lit. Mags., N.Y.C., 1975-77. Author: We Will Wear White Roses, 1974, Made in America, 1975, A Time of Hunting, 1975, The Names You Gave It, 1980, The General Mule Poems, 1981, Sometimes Music Rises, 1986, Echoes of the Unspoken, 1990, Toward the End of the Century, 1993, Of Desire & Disorder, 1994, The Blue Salvages, 1998, IS, 2003. Mem. adv. bd. Ohio Arts Coun., Columbus, 1970-79. With USN, 1948-52. Recipient Krout award Ohioana Found., 1991, Ohio Gov.'s award Ohio Arts Coun., 2001; Poetry fellow Nat. Endowment Arts, 1982, Artist's fellow Ohio Arts Coun., Isabella Gardner Poetry award, 2003, Residency fellow Rockefeller Found., 1995. Mem. Phi Beta Kappa. Democrat. Home: 11292 Peach Ridge Rd Athens OH 45701 Business E-Mail: doddw@ohio.edu.

DODDS, CHRISTOPHER V., finance company executive; m. M. J. Dodds; children: William, Andrew. Degree magna cum laude, Clemson U.; MBA in Fin., U. Pitts. With Treasury Dept. Gulf Oil, Exxon; from various fin. positions to exec. v.p., CFO The Charles Schwab Corp., San Francisco, 1986—98, exec. v.p., 1998—, CFO, 1999—. Mem. exec. com. The Charles Schwab Corp. Office: The Charles Schwab Corp 101 Montgomery St San Francisco CA 94104

DODDS, ROBERT JAMES, III, lawyer; b. San Antonio, Sept. 19, 1943; s. Robert James Jr. and Kathryn (Bechman) D.; m. Deborah N. Detchon, June 25, 1966 (div. Mar. 1989); children: Zachary Bechman, Seth Detchon; m. D.J. Knowles, Dec. 27, 1990. BA, Yale U., 1965; LLB, U. Pa., 1969. Assoc. Reed Smith Shaw & McClay, Pitts., 1969-77, ptnr., 1978-91; ptrn. Davenport & Dodds, LLP, Santa Fe, 1992—; of counsel Strassburger, McKenna, Gutnick & Potter, Pitts., 1991—. Bd. dirs. ATP Inc., Davison Sand & Gravel Co., Pitts.; pres. Homewood Cemetery, Pitts., 1980-91, bd. dirs. Trustee Mus. Art, Carnegie Inst, 1974-84, Westmoreland Mus. Art, Greensburg, Pa., YMCA of Pitts., Carnegie-Mellon U.; dir., pres. Pitts. Plan for Art, 1981-85; dir., chmn. West Pa. Hosp. Found., Carnegie Mellon Art Gallery; bd. dirs. Western Pa. Hosp., Western Pa. Healthcare Systems Inc., Pitts. Athletic Assn., Inst. Am. Indian Arts Found., Santa Fe; mus. panel Pa. Coun. on the Arts. Mem.: Yale Club (NYC), Duquesne Club (Pitts.). Democrat. Episcopalian. Home: 3101 Old Pecos Trl Unit 687 Santa Fe NM 87505-9547 Office: Davenport & Dodds LLP 721 Don Diego Ave Santa Fe NM 87505 Office Phone: 505-982-0080. E-mail: dod@newmexico.com.

DODDS-METTS, REBECCA, antique jewelry wholesale company executive; b. Salem, Mo., Dec. 9, 1950; d. Paul Durham and Rosemary (Frazier) D. BA, S.W. Mo. State U., 1973. Dir. pub. rels. Dodds Truck Line, Springfield, Mo., 1973-79; owner, mgr. Silver Flute, Ft. Lauderdale, Fla., 1983—. Bd. dirs. Dodds Investment Co., West Plains, Mo.; mem. adv. bd. Schroeder's Antiques Price Guide, Paducah, Ky., 1983—. Com. co-chmn., vol. Kids in Crisis, Ft. Lauderdale, 1989—90; serving in music ministry Faith Farm Tabernacle, Ft. Lauderdale, 1999—. Avocation: playing flute.

DODGE, ADRIANA, real estate investor, educator; arrived in US, 1986; d. Luis and Carmenza de Villarraga; m. Nathan Dodge (div. Mar. 2001). Hotel mgmt., Inuniversitas, 1985; B in bus. adminstrn., Met. State U., 1992. Lic. real estate broker Fla. Pres. Katzen LLC, Clearwater, 2000—, Home Realty LLC, Clearwater, 2000—. Owner, tchr. No Cash No Credit Pub. LLC, Fla., 2004—; cons. in field. Author: No Cash No Credit Home Buying System, 2005; contbr. articles to newspapers. Avocations: equestrian, aerobics, reading, writing. Office: No Cash No Credit Pub LLC Ste 140 611 S Fort Harrison Clearwater FL 33756

DODGE, ARTHUR BYRON, JR., b. Lancaster, Pa., June 13, 1923; s. Arthur Byron and Marion Frances (Cochran) D.; m. Margaretha Gerbert, Dec. 28, 1954; children: Arthur B., Andrew Nikolaus. Student, Williams Coll., 1942; BS in Econs., Franklin and Marshall Coll., 1947. With Dodge Cork Co., 1947-89, product mgr., 1947-50, factory mgr., 1952-57, mgr. fgn. divsn., 1958-61, v.p., sec., 1961-81, pres., 1981-90. Bd. dirs. Dodge-Regupol, Inc., 1989—, chmn., 1990—; bd. dirs., sec. Gerbert, Ltd., Lancaster, 1979—, Intertrade, Inc., Lancaster, 1979-91. Trustee Episcopal Ch. Sch. Found., 1958-85, Lancaster Theol. Sem., 1998—; pres. Friends of SOS Children's Villages, 1979-85, bd. dirs., 1979-93; bd. dirs., treas. SOS Children's Villages USA, 1993-98; bd. dirs. 88th Inf. Divsn. Assn., 1988—, pres., 1996-97; bd. dirs. Meml. Trust, 1992—. Capt. AUS, 1942-45, 50-52. Decorated Bronze Star with cluster, Purple Heart with cluster, Meritorious Svc. award; battlefield commn. Italy, 1944. Mem. ASTM, Cork Inst. Am. (treas. 1980—), Newcomen Soc., Pa. Soc., Pa. Commn. Employment of Handicapped, Delta Upsilon, Hamilton Club, Lancaster Country Club. Republican. Office: 715 Fountain Ave Lancaster PA 17601-4547 E-mail: gwd@regupol.com.

DODGE, CALVERT RENAUL, education and training executive, author, educator; b. Chgo., Apr. 15, 1921; s. Lawrence Frank and Anna Rose (Manke) D.; m. Mary Irene Dodge, Apr. 2, 1951; children: Lawrence Wesley, Laura Irene, Valarie Le, James Calvert. BS in Agrl. Sci., U. Wyo., 1947, MA in Sociology, 1957; cert., Air U., Montgomery Ala., 1968; PhD in Speech Comm., U. Denver, 1971; BA in Video and Film Prodn., U. Md., 1998. Cert. supr. edn., Calif.; masters lic. 25 ton ships USCG; cert. USAF Parachute Jump Sch., 1969. Dir. youth, ednl. activities Standard Oil Ind. AMOCO, Chgo., 1948—51, dir. employee, pub. rels., 1951—55; pres. Western Concrete Products Inc., Laramie, Wyo., 1955—64; dir. state tng. ctr. State of Colo. Youth Svcs., Denver, 1964—71; dir. rsch. Ky. Manpower Devel. Commn., Louisville, 1971—76; instr. U. Ky., 1974—75; assoc. prof. U. D.C., Washington, 1979—82; instr. in Japan, Korea, Turkey, Germany, Spain and U.K. U. Md., 1976—82; exec. v.p. Human Equations, Inc., Balt., 1982—87; pres. Dodge-Marck Assocs., Balt., 1991—. Pres. Seminars at Sea, Balt., 1983-97; dir. pub. affairs Md. Motorcycle Safety Program, Balt., 1990-92, asst. chief tng. and employee devel., dir. videography Md. Transp. Authority, 1992-96. Author: Power Machinery Maintenance, 1955, A World Without Prisons, 1979, Executive Communication Development, 1986, Profit Recovery Management, 1986, Strategic Sales Development System, 1986; editor: A Nation Without Prisons, 1975, New Mind Power, Increasing Your Brain Powers for Lifetime Change with Malcolm E. Bernstein, 1999; producer videos. Sponsors com. Nat. 4H, Nat. FFA, Nat. Jr. Achievement. Grantee U.S. Dept. Justice, 1966, 69; recipient Outstanding Cmty. Svc. award, Am. Assn. Cmty. Resource Devel., 1990, Cmty. Svc. award USAFR, 1968. Mem. ASTD (v.p. 1969-71), Md. Assn. Adult Edn., Inter-Am. Assn., Dodge Family Assn., Annapolis Naval Sailing Assn., Am. Soc. Group Psychotherapy and Psychodrama, Internat. TV Assn., Masons, Alpha Zeta, Omicron Delta Kappa, Tau Kappa Epsilon. Buddhist. Avocations: teaching sailing, painting, video and film production. Home: 8 S Broadway Baltimore MD 21231-1713 Office: Dodge-Marck Assocs Baltimore MD 21231 Office Phone: 410-276-8775. Personal E-mail: granitewyo@aol.com.

DODGE, CLAYTON WILLARD, mathematics professor; b. Stoneham, Mass., Nov. 15, 1931; s. Lyman Riford and Ruth E.R. (Higgins) D.; m. Donna Rhoda, Feb. 4, 1956 (div. 1978); 1 child, Kathy; m. Dorothy Robertson, July 18, 1981; children: Faith, Patricia. BA in Math., U. Maine, 1956, MA in Math., 1960; postgrad., Brown U., 1960-61. Tchr. Brecksville (Ohio) High Sch., 1956; prof. math. U. Maine, Orono, 1956—97. Author: The Circular Functions, 1966, Sets, Logic and Numbers, 1969, Numbers and Mathematics, 1969, 2d edit., 1975, Euclidean Geometry and transformations, 1972; author software; problems editor Am. Math. Monthly, 1968-75, Pi Mu Epsilon Jour., 1981—2000. NSF fellow, 1960-61. Mem. Math. Assn. Am. (instnl. rep. 1988—), Nat. Coun. Tchrs. Math., Am. Math. Assn. 2-Yr. Colls., Assn. Tchrs. Math. in Maine, Assn. Tchrs. Math. in New Eng. Avocations: computers, electronics. Home: 350 Main St Orono ME 04473-3434

DODGE, CLEVELAND EARL, JR., retired manufacturing executive, director; b. N.Y.C., Mar. 7, 1922; s. Cleveland Earl and Pauline (Morgan) D.; m. Phyllis Boushall, Dec. 19, 1942 (dec. Jan. 2004); children: Alice Berkeley, Sally Mole, Cleveland Earl III. BS in Mech. Engring., Princeton U., 1943; D in Humanics, Springfield Coll., 1996. With DeLaval Steam Turbine Co., 1942, GE, 1946-51; v.p., dir. Warren Wire Co., Pownal, Vt., 1951-55; pres., dir. Dodge Industries, Inc., Hoosick Falls, NY, 1955-67; v.p., dir. Engineered Yarns, Inc., 1962-68; pres., dir. Circuit Materials Corp., 1962-68; pres., treas., dir. Internat. Dodge, Inc., 1968—2005; pres., dir. Dodge Machine Co., 1968—2005; pres., bd. dirs. Alta Energy Corp., 1980-89, Amex Plastics Inc., 1972-74, Am. Hydride Corp., 1991—2005; ret., 2005. Bd. dirs. Display Sys., Inc., Imetrix Corp., Internat. Dodge, Inc., Cleeland Corp., Am. Hydride Corp., Dodge Machine Co., Inc., Wild Goose Island Corp., Imetrix, Inc.; bd. dirs. emeritus Phelps Dodge Corp., Atlantic Mut. Ins., Key Bank. Patentee in field. Chmn., bd. dirs. Cleveland H. Dodge Found.; vice chmn. emeritus YMCA Retirement Fund; bd. dirs. emeritus Springfield Coll., Bennington Mus., Antique Boat Mus., Brisbee Coun. on Arts and Humanities, Silver City Mus., YMCA Retirement Fund. Lt. USNR, 1943-45. Mem. Princeton Engring. Assn., Princeton Rowing Assn., Laurentian Lodge (Shawbridge, Que., Can.), Taconic Golf Club (Williamstown, Mass.), Kiwanis. Congregationalist. Avocations: skiing, golf, travel. Office: Internat Dodge Inc PO Box 178 Hoosick Falls NY 12090-0178 Office Phone: 518-686-7841.

DODGE, EDWARD JOHN, retired insurance company executive; b. Malone, NY, Mar. 28, 1935; s. Harry Gilman and Marjorie Dietz (Wright) Dodge; m. Ann Louise Cupps. Grad. hs, 1953. Map clk. N.Y. Underwriters, San Francisco, 1956-57; underwriter Reliance Ins., San Francisco, 1957-58; agt. Am. Hardware Mut., San Francisco, 1958; investigator Retail Credit Co., 1963-68; claims adjuster Allstate Ins., Arlington Heights, Ill., 1968-70, Epiic Ins., Phoenix, 1974; claims examiner GEICO, Chgo., 1970-73; multi-line adjuster Ariz. Adjustment, Phoenix, 1973-74; investigator Equifax, Chgo., 1974-78; sales br. mgr. Hooper Holmes, Chgo., Springfield, Ill., 1978-80; multi-line agt. Met. Ins., Springfield, 1980-81; subrogation examiner Horace Mann Ins., Springfield, 1982-97; ret., 1997. Author: Relief is Greatly Wanted, The Battle of Fort William Henry, 1998; contbr. articles to hist. publs. Commr. Boy Scouts Am., Arlington Heights, Ill., 1971—78, vice chmn. scouting, 1977—79, vice chmn. exploring, 1988—90, commr. Springfield, 1981—92, Phoenix, 1983—84. Recipient Dist. Commrs. award, Boy Scouts Am., 1978, Scouter of the Month award, 1978, Bronze Big Horn award, 1989. Mem.: Masons, Princess of Wale's Royal Regtl. Assn. (licentiate), Queen's Regtl. Assn. (life). Republican. Methodist. Avocations: historical research, historical writing. Home: 1223 N Rutledge St Springfield IL 62702-2524

DODGE, GEOFFREY A., magazine publisher; b. Newburyport, Mass., Aug. 14, 1960; s. Edward and Sandra (Whitley) D. BA, Babson Coll., Wellesley, Mass., 1983. Ad sales rep. IDG, Boston, 1985-86; pub. Boston Computer News, 1986; sales rep. Fortune, N.Y.C., 1987-89, Washington mgr., 1989-92, N.Y. advt. dir., 1992-94, eastern advt. dir., 1994-95; pub. Money mag., N.Y.C., 1995—2000; CEO mediospacebank.com, 2000—02; assoc. pub., v.p. U.S. advt. BusinessWeek mag. The McGraw Hill Cos., N.Y.C., 2002, pub. (North Am.), sr. v.p. BusinessWeek mag. Mem. exec. com. Jr. Achievement, N.Y.C., 1988—. Mem. N.Y. Athletic Club, Rockefeller Center Club, Sleepy Hollow Country Club (Scarborough, N.Y.). Office: Business Week The McGraw Hill Cos Bldg 1221 Avenue of the Americas New York NY 10020 Office Phone: 212-412-4611. Office Fax: 212-512-2277. E-mail: geoff_dodge@businessweek.com.*

DODGE, JAMES WILLIAM, lawyer, educator; b. Springfield, Ill., Sept. 14, 1967; s. James U. and Nancy C. (Donaldson) D.; m. Cynthia Joy Selby, July 19, 1991; children: James A., Adrienne R.M. BS, U. Ill., 1989; JD, So. Ill. U., 1992. Bar: Ill. 1992, U.S. Dist. Ct. (ctrl. dist.) 1992, U.S. Ct. Appeals (7th cir.) 1993, U.S. Tax Ct. 1993. Pvt. practice, Springfield, 1992-93; asst. atty. gen. Ill. Atty. Gen.'s Office, Springfield, 1993-97; first asst. state's atty. Christian County State's Atty.'s Office, Taylorville, Ill., 1997-99; legal counsel judiciary com. Ill. Senate Dem. Leader's Office, Springfield, Ill., 1999—; instr. MacMurry Coll., Jacksonville, 1998-99. Instr. Robert Morris Coll., Springfield, 1993—. Author: A Brief Survey of Limited Liability Partnership Law in Illinois, 1996; contbr. articles to profl. jours. Ky. Col., Commonwealth of Ky., 1994. Fellow Ill. Bar Found.; mem. ABA, Ill. State Bar Assn. (mem.law-related edn. to pub. com. 1994-97, Christian County Bar Assn. (v.p. 1998—), Ask a Lawyer Day vol. 1994—, h.s. mock trial evaluator 1994—), Sangamon County Bar Assn. (dir. Young Lawyer's divsn. 1993-98), Acad. Legal Studies in Bus., Sangamo Club, Masons, Phi Alpha Delta. Episcopalian. Office: Ill Senate Dem Leader's Office State Capitol Rm 309 Springfield IL 62706-0001

DODGE, PAUL CECIL, academic administrator; b. Granville, N.Y., Mar. 25, 1943; s. Cecil John Paul and Elsie Elizabeth Dodge Rogers; m. Margaret Mary Kostyun, June 6, 1964 (div. Sept. 1985); 1 child, Cynthia Ruth; m. Cynthia Dee Bennett, Apr. 26, 1986; children: Michelle Lynn, Jason Paul, Benjamin Charles. BA in Math., U. Vt., 1967. Mgr. data processing Thermal Wire & Electronics, South Hero, Vt., 1967-70, DDSV divsn. Vt. Cos., Burlington, 1970-73, Revere Copper & Brass, Clinton, Ill., 1973-78, Angelica Corp., St. Louis, 1978-81; pres. chief ops. officer Dodge Mgmt., St. Louis, 1981-82; mgr. systems and programming Terra Internat., 1982-87; pres., COO Mo. Tech, 1987—. Mem. Mo. Assn. Pvt. Career Schs. (pres. 1993-94), Nat. Rehab. Assn., Mo. Rehab. Assn. Republican. Presbyterian. Avocations: amatuer radio, chess. Office: Mo Tech Sch 1167 Corporate Lake Dr Saint Louis MO 63132-1716

DODGE, PHILIP ROGERS, neurologist, educator; b. Beverly, Mass., Mar. 16, 1923; s. Israel R. and Anna (McCarthy) D.; children: Susan, Judith. Student, U. N.H., 1941-43, Yale, 1943; MD, U. Rochester, 1948. Diplomate: Am. Bd. Psychiatry and Neurology. Intern Strong Meml. Hosp., 1948-49; asst. resident neurology Boston City Hosp., 1949-50, resident, 1950, sr. resident, 1951-52; practice medicine, specializing in child neurology Boston, 1956-67, St. Louis, 1967—; teaching fellow neurology Harvard Med. Sch., 1950, 51-53, instr. neurology, 1956-58, assoc. in neurology, 1958-61, asst. prof., 1962-67; asst. neurologist Mass. Gen. Hosp., 1956-59, dir. pediatric neurology program, 1958-67, assoc. neurologist, 1959-63, neurologist, 1963-67, assoc. pediatrician, 1961-62, pediatrician, 1962-67; investigator Joseph P. Kennedy, Jr. Meml. Labs. for Study Mental Retardation, 1962-67; pediatric neurologist Boston Lying-In Hosp., 1961-67; cons. in neurology Walter E. Fernald State Sch. for Retarded Children, 1963-67; med. dir. St. Louis Children's Hosp., 1967-84, pediatrician-in-chief, 1967-86; assoc. neurologist Barnes Hosp., 1967—; chmn. Mallinckrodt Dept. Pediatrics, Washington U. Sch. Medicine, 1967-86, prof. pediatrics and neurology, 1967-93; prof. emeritus pediatrics and neurology Washington U. Sch. Medicine, 1993—; lectr. in pediatrics, 1993-99. Vis. scientist Clin. Research Center, U. P.R., 1965-66, hon. vis. prof. physiology, 1967; cons. collaborative project on cerebral palsy Nat. Inst. Neurol. Diseases and Blindness, 1958; bd. dirs., chmn. research adv. com. Mass. Soc. for Prevention Cruelty to Children, 1961-67; mem. sci. research adv. bd. Nat. Assn. for Retarded Children, 1963-67; bd. dirs. Central Midwestern Regional Lab., Inc., 1968-70; mem. gen. clin. research centers adv. com. USPHS, 1971-74; mem. Mo. Gov.'s Council on Developmental Disabilities, 1971-74; chmn. Mo. Mental Health Commn., 1974-78; mem. nat. adv. child health and human devel. council NIH, 1974-77; chmn. panel on neurol. disorders, developmental, long-range program strategies NINCDS, 1977-79; panel chmn., consensus devel. conf. on diagnosis and treatment of Reye's Syndrome, 1981; vis. prof. pediatrics and adolescent medicine, Royal Postgrad. Med. Sch., U. London, 1986—; hon. vis. fellow dept. pathology U. Western Australia, Nedlands, Australia, 1986-87; vis. prof. neurology Columbia U. Coll. Physicians and Surgeons, N.Y.C., 1987-88; spl. asst. to dir. for mental retardation Nat. Inst. Child Health and Human Devel., NIH, Washington, 1987-88. Author: (with others) Nutrition and the Developing Nervous System, 1975; Editorial bd.: (with others) Jour. Developmental Medicine and Child Neurology, 1965—, Jour. Pediatrics, 1970-80, Pediatric Research, 1970-78, Current Problems in Pediatrics, 1969-84, Neurology, 1973-76; Contbr. (with others) articles to profl. jours. Served from 1st lt. to maj. M.C. U.S. Army, 1950-56. Mem. Am. Pediatric Soc. (coun. 1972-78, chmn. coun. 1978-79), Am. Acad. Neurology (past com. chmn.), Am. Neurol. Assn., Child Neurology Soc., Assn. for Rsch. in Nervous and Mental Disease, Soc. Pediatric Rsch., Soc. Biol. Psychiatry, St. Louis Soc. Neurol. Scis., Assn. Med. Sch. Pediatric Dept. Chmn. (pres. 1975-77), Alpha Omega Alpha. Home: 410 N Newstead Ave Saint Louis MO 63108-2654 Office: 1 Childrens Pl Saint Louis MO 63110-1002

DODGE, R(ALPH) EDWARD, JR., physician; b. Salamanca, NY, Jan. 14, 1936; s. Ralph Edward and Eunice Elvira (Davis) D.; m. Nancy Lou De Lay, Aug. 14, 1957 (dec. 1999); children: Randall, Jeffrey, Amy; m. Carol Marie Fitzgerald, Dec. 17, 1999. BA, Taylor U., 1958; MD, Ind. U., 1962; MPH, Johns Hopkins U., 1967. Diplomate Am. Bd. Preventive Medicine, Am. Bd. Family Practice. Rotating intern L.A. County Gen. Hosp., 1962-63; resident gen. preventive medicine sch. hygiene & pub. health Johns Hopkins U., 1966-69; asst. prof. pub. health Haile Sellassie U., Gondar, Ethiopia, 1967-69; staff physician Frontier Nursing Svc., Hyden, Ky., 1970-71; med. dir. Citrus-Levy County Health Dept., Inverness, Fla., 1971-74; physician emergency dept. Waterman Meml. Hosp., Eustis, Fla., 1974-75; pvt. practice Inverness, 1975-96; med. dir. Citrus Primary Care Network, 1994-96. Clin. asst. prof. U. Fla., 1994-98. Author: Tim's Story-A Spiritual Perspective of Health, 2005; contbr. articles to med. jours.; editor Fla. Family Physician, 1991-95, 97-99; newspaper columnist: Health Simplicity, 1988-90, Life and Health, 1990-2000, A Passion for Health, 2005. Bd. dirs. Marion-Citrus Mental Health Ctrs., Ocala, Fla., 1972—74, North Ctrl. Fla. Health Planning Commn., Gainesville, 1979—80, Fla. divsn. Am. Cancer Soc., 1988—90, Citrus Meml. Health Found., Inverness, 1988—94, Citrus County Edn. Found., 1998—2002, Citrus County Assn. for Retarded Citizens, 1998—, v.p., 1999—; trustee Old Courthouse Heritage Mus., 1999—2000; active Citrus County Hist. Soc.; trustee Unity Ch. of Citrus County, 2000—03, pres., 2001—03. Lt comdr. USPHS, 1964—66. Recipient Disting. Svc. award Fla. Assn. Emergency Med. Technicians, 1976, Community Svc. award Seventh Day Adventist Ch., Inverness, 1978, Citizen of Yr. award Citrus County Chronicle, 1987, Svc. Above Self award Rotary Club Inverness, 1998. Mem. AMA, Am. Coll. Preventive Medicine, Am. Acad. Family Physicians, Fla. Acad. Family Physicians (bd. dirs. 1994-96), Fla. Med. Assn., Citrus County Med. Soc. (pres. 1977, sec.-treas. 1981-86). Democrat. Avocations: tennis, chess, gardening.

DODGE, WILLIAM DOUGLAS, risk management consultant; b. Savannah, Ga., Sept. 26, 1937; s. Kenneth Douglas and Bettie Wilbur (Sadler) D.; m. Susan Penny, Dec. 27, 1958 (div. 1976); children: Gregory D., Phillip C., Warren D., Andrew L.; m. Marian Elizabeth Monroe, Apr. 2, 1983. BS, Ga. Inst. Tech., 1959; MBA, Ga. State U., 1966. CPCU, ARM. Underwriter Liberty Mutual Ins. Co., Atlanta, 1960-66; ins. adminstr. Lockheed Corp., Marietta, Ga., 1966-78; risk mgr. Schlumberger Ltd., Atlanta, 1978-79; v.p. ins. Fuqua Industries, Inc., Atlanta, 1979-90, v.p. ins. and benefits, 1991-92; pres. Fuqua Ins. Co. Ltd., Hamilton, Bermuda, 1978-92, Fuqua Risk Retention Group, Atlanta, 1989-92; ind. risk mgmt. cons. Atlanta, 1992-95. Adv. bd. Risk Mgmt. Inc., N.Y.C., 1978-92; chmn. bd., mem. investment com. J&H WF Syndicate B., N.Y. Ins. Exch., N.Y.C., 1984-88. Co-author: The Hold Harmless Agreement, 1968. Mem. Exec. Com. Reorgn. and Mgmt. Improvement State of Ga., 1971, Agts. Licensing Exam. Revision Bd. State Ga., 1970; bd. dirs. Ga. State U. Ednl. Found., 1980-88; lt. comdr. USPS/Tybee Light Power Squadron, 1999, comdr., 2000—. Republican. Methodist. Avocations: gardening, boating. Office: Mickey Dodge & Assocs Inc 12 Pipers Pond Ln Savannah GA 31404-1122 Personal E-mail: savdodges@aol.com.

DODGEN, ANDREW CLAY, lawyer; b. LaGrange, Ga., Apr. 8, 1961; s. Walter Eugene Dodgen and Mary Lucy (Thomason) Lott; m. Lisa Jean Morris, July 7, 1979; children: Andrew Lee, Alexander Morris, Benjamin Michael. BA in History and Religion, LaGrange (Ga.) Coll., 1983; JD, Mercer U., 1986. Bar: Ga. 1986, U.S. Dist. Ct. (mid. dist.) Ga. 1986. Ptnr. Moore & Dodgen, Columbus, Ga., 1986—. Mem. ABA, State Bar Ga., Ga. Trial Lawyers Assn., Columbus Lawyers Club. Baptist. Office: Moore & Dodgen 846 Second Ave PO Box 1297 Columbus GA 31902-1297

DODGEN, DANIEL W., health policy advisor, psychologist; s. David W Dodgen and Marye Dodgen Settles. BA in Psychology, BA in Spanish, U. of So. Calif., L.A., 1986; MA in Clin. Psychology, U. of Houston, 1990, PhD in Clin. Psychology, 1995. Lic. clin. psychologist D.C., 2000. Clin. psychologist Didi Hirsch CMHC, L.A., 1992—96; congl. fellow U.S. Ho. of Reps., Washington, 1996—97; sr. fed. affairs officer APA, Washington, 1997—2003; emergency mgmt. coord. U.S. Dept. of Health & Human Services/SAMHSA, Washington, 2003—. Chair Pentagon Mental Health Response Coalition, Washington, 2001—03, Nat. Child and Adolescent Mental Health Coalition, Washington, 1997—2003; mental health steering com. Met. Wash. Coun. of Govts., Washington, 2003—05. Recipient Early Career Contbn. award, APA, 2005, Scholar in Rehab. Policy, Mary Switzer Found., 2000; fellow Congl. Sci. fellow, APA. Mem.: APA, Smithsonian Instn., US Holocaust Meml. Mus., Phi Beta Kapa (life). Office: US Dept of Health & Human Services 1 Choke Cherry Rockville MD 20857 Office Phone: 240-276-2237.

DODGEN, JOHN N., manufacturing executive; b. Sapulpa, Okla., June 22, 1926; s. Claude W. and Pearl M. (Glass) D.; m. Wanda Lou Edwards; children: James, Mary Lou, John C.T., Lori. BA, Ottawa U., 1956; PMD, Harvard U., 1961. V.p. distbn. farm equipment Dodgen & Co., Fort Dodge, Iowa, 1947-56; v.p. mfg. and distbn. farm equipment Dodgen Associated Mfrs., Sioux City, Iowa, 1956-58; pres. mfg. and distbn. farm equipment Silbaugh Mfg., Humboldt, Iowa, 1958-61; pres. mfg. farm and indsl. equipment Dodgen Industries, Inc., Humboldt, 1961—; pres., owner Rib Case, Ft. Dodge. Pres., founder John N. Dodgen Found., 1960—; pres. Dodgen Leasing Corp., Humboldt, 1964—, Born Free, Inc., Humboldt, 1969—, Fiberglass Fabricators, Inc., Humboldt, 1984—, Dodgen Mobile Technologies, Humboldt, 1990—, Custom Cabinets, Humboldt, Born Free Fla., 1998—, Born Free Nev., 1999—; bd. trustees Ottawa (Kans.) U., 1964-99; bd. dirs. Iowa Assn. Bus. and Industry. Licensed Bapt. lay min., 1954—; trustee Ctrl. Bapt. Sem., 1963-73; chmn. campaign Humboldt Area Family Aquatic Ctr; pres. Humboldt County Taxpayers Assn., 2002. Named one of One Thousand Gt. Ams., 2003. Mem. Rotary. Avocations: hunting pheasants, geese and ducks, golf, fishing, public speaking. Office: Dodgen Industries Inc Hwy 169 N Humboldt IA 50548 Office Phone: 515-332-3755.

DODGEN, LARRY J., career military officer; b. New Orleans, June 12, 1949; BS, La. State U., 1972; MBA in Pub. Adminstrn., U. Mo.; MS in Nat. Security and Strategy, US Navel War Coll. Commd. U.S. Army; comdr. 8th Battalion, 43d Air Defense Artillery, 1989—91, 69th Air Defense Artillery Brigade, Germany, 1993; comdr.-in-chief U.S. Army Europe; brigadier gen., 1996; dep. asst. sec. defense for policy and missions; dir. Joint Theater Air Missile Def. Orgn., Washington, 1998—2001; commdg. gen. U.S. Army Aviation and Missile Command, 2001—03, U.S. Army Space and Missile Defense Command / U.S. Army Forces Strategic Command, Arlington, Va., 2003—. Decorated Defense Disting. Svc. Medal with Oak Leaf Cluster, Legion of Merit (two Oak Leaf Clusters), Meritorious Svc. Medal (four Oak Leaf Clusters), Army Commendation Medal, Army Achievement Medal. Office: Commdg Gen USASMDC/ARSTRAT PO Box 15280 Arlington VA 22215-0280 Office Phone: 703-607-1874. Office Fax: 703-607-1879.*

DODGE ROBBINS, DOROTHY ELLIN, language educator; b. Aug. 16, 1958; MA, U. S.D., 1991; PhD, U. Nebr., 2000. Lectr. Tex. A&M, College Station, 1987—88; asst. prof. English Dakota Wesleyan U., Mitchell, SD, 1995—99; instr. speech comm. La. Tech. U., Ruston, 1999—2000, asst. prof. English, 2000—. Co-editor: Christmas Stories from Louisiana, 2003, Christmas on the Great Plains, 2004, Christmas Stories from Georgia, 2005. Office: PO Box 3162 Ruston LA 71272-0001 Office Phone: 318-257-2418. Business E-Mail: drobbins@garts.latech.edu.

DODOHARA, JEAN NOTON, music educator; b. Monroe, Wis., Feb. 21, 1934; d. Albert Henry and Eunice Elizabeth (Edgerton) Noton; m. Laurence G. Landers, June 7, 1955 (div.); children: Theodore Scott Landers, Thomas Warren Landers, Philip John Landers; m. Edward R. Harris, Nov. 27, 1981 (dec.); stepchildren: Adrianne, Erica; m. Takashi Dodohara, Aug. 7, 1988; 1 stepchild, Eve D. BA, Monmouth (Ill.) Coll., 1955; MS, U. Ill., 1975, adminstrv. cert., 1980, EdD, 1985. Tchr. music schs. in Ill. and Fla., 1955—76; tchr. ch. music for children, 1957—72; tchr. music Dist. 54, Schaumburg, Ill., 1976—93; teaching asst. U. Ill., 1979. Named Outstanding Young Woman of Yr., Jaycee Wives, St. Charles, Mo., 1968, charter mem., Nat. Mus. Women in Arts. Mem.: AAUW, NEA (life), Elgin Area Ret. Tchrs. Assn., Music Educators Nat. Conf. (life), Ill. Educators Assn. (life), U. Ill. Alumni Assn. (life), Mortar Bd., Mensa, Delta Kappa Pi. Mem. United Ch. Of Christ. Home: Friendship Village 350 W Schaumburg Rd D 300 Schaumburg IL 60159

DODSON, BRUCE J., funeral director; b. Alma, Mich., Oct. 9, 1937; s. Floyd S. and Bertha M. (Van Vynck) D.; m. Carolyn K. McCracken, Jan. 24, 1970; children: Eric, Joshua. AA, Northwood Inst., Midland, Mich., 1961; cert. Mortuary Scis., Wis. Inst. Mortuary Scis., Milw., 1962. Automobile dealer, Edmore, Mich., 1955-58; mgr. Stebbins Funeral Home, Stanton, Mich., 1962-69; owner Dodson Funeral Home, St. Ignace, Mich., 1969—. Pres. Dist. Funeral Dirs. 9, 1974-78. Mem. Stanton City Coun., 1963-68, St. Ignace City Coun., 1981-83; mem. Gov.'s Task Force for Mackinac Bridge Fin., 1986-87; mayor City of St. Ignace, 1983—; chmn. Mackinac Straits Hosp. Bd., 1989-91, vice chmn., 1991-92; co-founder St. Ignace Antique Auto Show, 1976—; mem. Mackinac County Bldg. Authority, 1993-98; chair, 1995-96. Named St. Ignace Citizen of the Yr. C. of C., 1992. Mem. Nat. Funeral Dirs. Assn., Mich. Funeral Dirs. Assn. (bd. govs. 1978-81), Mich. Assn. Mayors, Automobile Club Am. (life, nat. judge), Classic Car Club Am., Motor City Packard Club (charter), Family Motor Coach Assn. (life), Great Lakes Cruising Club. Methodist. Avocations: antique automobiles, model trains, great lakes boating. Home and Office: 240 Mccann St Saint Ignace MI 49781-1651

DODSON, DARYL THEODORE, ballet administrator, consultant; b. Warrensburg, Mo., Oct. 9, 1934; s. Theodore and Ada Marie (Ayres) D. BS, Ctrl. Mo. State U., 1956. Mem. Gov. S.C.'s Coun. of the Arts, 1974; mem. adv. panel Vt. Coun. on Arts, 1978; mgr. Am. tour 1st cultural exch., People's Republic of China and U.S., 1978, Nat. Ballet Cuba, 1979, Royal Ballet Eng., 1981; pres. Pine Cone Enterprises, Ltd., 1977-81; propr. Pine Cone Inn, Haverhill, N.H., 1978-81; mgr. Opera House, John F. Kennedy Ctr., Washington, 1981; mgr. U.S. and Can. tour Sweeney Todd, 1982; mgr. U.S. tours Amadeus, 1982-83, The Wiz, 1983-84, Les Miserables, 1988-92, Phantom of the Opera, 1992-2003; mgr. N.Y. engagement The Golden Land, 1985; mgr. Porgy and Bess, 1986-87, La Cage Aux Folles, 1987, N.Y. and U.S. tour Paris Opera Ballet, 1988; gen. mgr. John Curry Skating Co., 1984. Asst. dir. The Mikado, N.Y.C. Opera, 1959; regisseur Chgo. Opera Ballet, 1960, asst. stage mgr. Am. Ballet Theatre, N.Y.C., 1960, stage mgr., 1961, prodn. stage mgr., 1961, prodn. mgr., 1963, gen. mgr., 1968-77. Served with U.S. Army, 1957-59. Recipient Nat. Touring Broadway Achievement award, 2003. Mem. Theta Chi, Theta Alpha Phi. Episcopalian. Office: PO Box 89 East Saint Johnsbury VT 05838-0089

DODSON, HERSHA RHEE, psychiatric and mental health nurse; b. Pecos, Tex., Feb. 18, 1939; d. Herschel W. and Marjorie E. (Jarrell) Woods; m. Louis Dean Dodson, July 2, 1962 (dec. Nov. 1973); children: Raina Elise, Farley Duane. Diploma, Shannon Sch. Nursing, San Angelo, Tex., 1963; B in Applied Arts and Sci., Midwestern State U., Wichita Falls, Tex., 1986; M in Counseling, St. John's U., Springfield, La., 1996. RN, Tex.; cert. psychiat. and mental health nurse. Shift nurse supr. Wichita Falls State Hosp.; adolescent nurse coord. Red River Psychiat. Hosp.-HCA, Wichita Falls; staff nurse adolescent unit Sun Valley Regional Hosp.-HCA, El Paso, Tex.; coord., psychiat. nurse Tex. Dept. Mental Health and Mental Retardation, Van Horn, 1990—; part-time nurse El Paso (Tex.) State Ctr., 1994-98, El Paso Psychiat. Ctr., 1998. Home: PO Box 234 Van Horn TX 79855-0234

DODSON, JOHN THOMAS, orchestra conductor; b. Dayton, Ohio, Jan. 17, 1957; s. James Henry and Anita Faye Dodson; m. Amy Elizabeth Simpson, June 14, 1990. MusM in Orchestral Conducting, Johns Hopkins U., 1981. Music dir. Philharmonia Orch. of Tucson, 1984—89, Coronado Music Festival, Tucson, 1985—87, Orch. N.Y., N.Y.C., 1990—93; faculty Tenn. Technol. U., Cookeville, 1993—2001; music dir. Bryan Symphony Orch., Cookeville, Tenn., 1993—2001; faculty Adrian Coll., Mich., 2001—; music dir. Adrian Symphony Orch., Mich., 2001—. Guest condr. Budapest Philharm., Hungary, 1987; adminstrv. dir. The Yard: A Colony for Performing Artists, N.Y.C., 1990—93; guest condr. Rochester Philharm., NY, 1994; cover condr. St. Louis Symphony Orch., 1995—97; condr. Sewannee Summer Music Ctr., Tenn., 1995—98, Tenn. Gov.'s Sch. for Arts, Murphreesboro, 1996—; guest condr. Rochester Philharm. Pops, NY, 1997; condr. Colo. Symphony Orch. Summer Orch. Tng. Program, Denver, 1997; guest condr. Albany Symphony Orch., Ga., 1998, Orquesta Sinfonica UANL, Monterrey, Mexico, 1998—99, Nat. Philharm. Orch. of Russia, Tomsk, 1999, Irkutsk Philharm., Russia, 1999; faculty condr. Okla. Arts Summer Inst., Norman, 1999; guest condr. Omsk Philharm., Russia, 1999—2004, Nat. Symphony Orch. of Bashkortostan, Ufa, Russia, 2000—04, Bialystok Symphony Orch., Poland, 2002. Recipient Outstanding Young Alumni award, Tenn. Technol. U., 1985, Golden Book award, Budapest Philharm., 1987, Sally Parker Edn. award, Am. Symphony Orch. League, 1995, 1998; Music Club of Am. scholarship, Peabody Conservatory of Music, 1981 - 1983, Conducting fellowship, Aspen Music Sch., 1983. Home: 1117 College Ave Adrian MI 49221 Office: Adrian Symphony Orch Rush Hall 110 S Madison St Adrian MI 49221 Office Phone: 517-264-3121. Office Fax: 517-264-3833. Personal E-mail: jdodson@adrian.edu. E-mail: john@aso.org.

DODSON, SAMUEL ROBINETTE, III, investment banker; b. Nashville, Feb. 24, 1943; s. Samuel Robinette and Helen Elizabeth (Maiden) D.; m. Marsha Robertson Moody, Aug. 2, 1969; children— Bradley John, Andrew Caldwell. Student, Yale U., 1961-63; BS, Vanderbilt U., 1966; MBA, U. Chgo., 1968; MS, London Sch. Econs., 1968. Various fin. and planning positions Exxon Corp. and Affiliates, Houston, 1968-81; v.p. First Boston Corp., 1981-84, mng. dir., 1984-93, Merrill Lynch, Houston, 1993—. Served to 1st lt. U.S. Army, 1963-64 E-mail: sam_dodson@ml.com.

DODSON, W(ILLIAM) EDWIN, child neurology educator; b. Durham, N.C., Dec. 23, 1941; s. Howard William and Mildred (Sorrell) D.; m. Doreen Carol Davis, June 4, 1964 (div. May 1976); children: Anna Elizabeth, William Edwin Jr., Jason David; m. Sandra Schorr (div. Mar. 1993); children: Steven Gage, Matthew Sorrell; m. Karen Leigh Pursel. AB, Duke U., 1963, MD, 1967. Intern Children's Hosp., Boston, 1967-68, resident in pediat., 1970-71; resident, fellow in child neurology Barnes Hosp. and St. Louis Children's Hosp., 1971-75; asst. prof. child neurology Washington U., St. Louis, 1975-80, resident in pediat., 1970-71, assoc. prof., 1980-86, prof. child neurology, 1986—; assoc. dean admissions and fin. aid Washington U. Sch. Medicine, St. Louis, 1990—. Assoc. vice-chancellor for continuing edn., admissions and fin. aid Washington U. Sch. Medicine, St. Louis, 1997—; bd. dirs. Family Resource Ctr., St. Louis, Physicians Corp., Washington U. Alliance Corp., First Tier Health Corp., Grace Hill Health Ctr., Nat. Com. to Prevent Child Abuse, Mo.; pres. bd. dirs. St. Louis Child Abuse Network, v.p. Family Support Network. Mem. editl. bd. Annals of Neurology and Clinical Neuropharmacology; contbr. articles to profl. jours. Bd. dirs. City St. Louis Bd. Children's Welfare, 1984-86, (life) Family Support Network, 2005—; mem. profl. adv. bd. Epilepsy Found. Am., 1987-94, chmn.-elect, 1991-93, pres.-elect, 1993-95, pres. 1995-97, chmn. bd., 1997-98; co-chmn. Blue Ribbon Commn. on Future Svcs. to Children & Families, Mo., 1987-88; chmn. Children's Trust Fund Mo., 1989-91, bd. dirs., 1985-91; bd. dirs. Epilepsy Found. St. Louis, 2000—; sec. bd. dirs. Epilepsy Found. St. Louis, 2005; mem. Mayor's Commn. on Children, Youth and Families, 2005 Recipient Spl. Recognition award State of Md., 1971, Career Acad. Devel. award NIH, 1975, Disting. Social Svcs. award Mo. Dept. Social Svcs., 1988, Child Adv. award St. Louis Child Abuse Network, 1990, Child Adv. award Family Resource Ctr., 1991, 29th Ann. honoree, 1999; Spl. Recognition award Epilepsy Fedn. St. Louis, 1992, Guardian Angel award St. Louis Family Support Network, 1999, Samuel Clemmens award Epilepsy Found., St. Louis, 1999, J. Kiffin Penney award Am. Epilepsy Soc., 2003-. Fellow Am. Acad. Neurology, Am. Acad. Pediat.; mem. Child Neurology Soc. (bd. dirs. 1985-87), Am. Neurol. Assn., Soc. Pediat. Rsch., Cen. Soc. Neurol. Rsch. (sec., treas. 1985, pres. 1989), Alpha Omega Alpha. Avocations: fly fishing, water sports, photography. Office: St Louis Childrens Hosp One Childrens Pl Saint Louis MO 63110-1014 E-mail: ed.dodson@wustl.edu.

DODSWORTH, ROY W., pharmaceutical company executive; b. Norwood, Mass., Sept. 6, 1948; s. James W. and Beulah G. Dodsworth; m. Genevieve Dodsworth, June 26, 1971; children: Dawn Terri, Roger H. Whitford Jr. BA, Drew U., 1970. Asst. dir. Ayerst Labs. Inc., N.Y.C., 1983-86; dir., N.Am. head regulatory affairs Organon, Inc., West Orange, NJ, 1986-94; sr. assoc. dir. Sandoz, East Hanover, NJ, 1995-97, dir. N.Am. head, Regulatory CMC, 1995-97; from dir., regional area head-asthma, hormone replacement therapy, bone to v.p. global therapeutic area head neurosci. Novartis Pharm. Co., East Hanover, NJ, 1997—2004, v.p. global therapeutic area head neurosci., 2004—. Contbr. numerous tech. publs. Active Budd Lake Rescue Squad, 1992-93; adv. com. Mt. Olive Township Multiple Family Dwelling, Budd Lane, 1980-83. Fellow Am. Inst. Chemists; mem. Regulatory Affairs Profl. Soc., Am. Chem. Soc., Drug Info. Assn., Parenteral Drug Assn. Republican. Methodist. Avocations: raquetball, basketball, football, softball, fishing. Home: 10 Crossing Dr Flanders NJ 07836-4709 Office: Novartis Pharm Co 1 Heatlh Plz East Hanover NJ 07936 Office Phone: 862-778-3250.

DOE, WILLO, critic, writer; arrived in U.S., 1982; d. Wantack Kong and Hanae Yang. BA, Yonsei U., 1979; student, Heidelberg (Germany) U., 1980—81. Corr. N.Y. Art Monthly, Seoul, Republic of Korea, 1995—99, Art & Arch., Seoul, Republic of Korea, 1996—99; contbg. editor The N.Y. Art World, 1999—2000, The Fiber Arts Mag., Asheville, NC, 2001—03; corr. N.Y. The Nat. Mus. Contemporary Art Korea, N.Y., 2003—. Guest curator The Korean Cultural Svc., N.Y., 1995—98; cons. Roseline Koener Gallery, Westhampton, NY, 1999—2004. Recipient The Nat. Art Criticism award, Cho Sun Daily, 1995. Avocations: art, swimming, running. Home: 355 West 85th St New York NY 10024

DOEBBLER, CURTIS F.J., lawyer; b. Buffalo, N.Y., 1961; BA, BFA, So. Meth. U., 1983; JD, NYU Law Sch., 1988; LLM, U. Nijmegen, 1993; PhD in Internat. Law, London Sch. Econs. & Polit. Sci., 1998; diploma, Hague Acad. Internat. Law, 2000. Bar: Washington, DC, U.S. Ct. Appeals, 4th Cir., U.S. Ct. Fed. Claims. Internat. human rights lawyer, 1988—; legal asst. Van Driel & Verraats, Netherlands, 1993; legal cons. UNICEF, Sudan, 1997; of counsel Law Office of Ghazi Suleiman, Khartoum, Sudan, 1997—2002; advisor Adv. Coun. Human Rights Min. Justice, Govt. Sudan, 1997—99. Cons. on humanitarian projects Former Yugoslavia, 1992—97; instr. London Sch. Econs. and Polit. Sci., 1995—97; vis. prof. U. Tuzla, Bosnia-Herzegovina, 1996, Khartoum U., Sudan, 1997—98, U. Pristina, Kosovo, 2002—03, Tashkent State Inst. Law, Uzbekistan, 2004—05, An-Najah Nat. U., Nablus, Palestine; disting. lectr. Dept. Polit. Sci. Am. U., Cairo, 2000—02. Recipient Human Rights Award, Acad. Internat. Human Rights and Humanitarian Law, 2001; rsch. fellow, Hague Acad. Internat. Law, 1988, law dept. tchg. fellowship, London Sch. Econs., 1995—97. Office Phone: 206-984-4734. E-mail: human_rights_lawyer@writeme.com, cdoebbler@gmail.com.

DOEBLER, BETTIE ANNE, language educator, researcher, poet; b. Atlantic City; d. Willoughby Foster and Ann (Ratledge) Young; m. John W. Doebler, Sept. 1, 1954 (dec. Aug. 26, 1994); 1 child, Mark B. BA, Duke U., 1953, MA, 1955; PhD, U. Wis., 1961. From instr. to assoc. prof. Dickinson Coll., Carlisle, Pa., 1961-70; assoc. prof. Ariz. State U., Tempe, 1971, prof., 1975, prof. emeritus, 1994—, dir. interdisciplinary humanities program, 1989-94. Vis. prof. English Grand Canyon U., Ariz. Author: The Quickening Seed: Death in the Sermons of John Donne, 1974, Rooted Sorrow: Dying in Early Modern Eng., 1994; co-author: Book of the Mermaid: Poems by Doebler, Slotten, Thiem, 2001, Nine Waves: Poems by Doebler, Slotten, Thiem, 2003; co-editor: Funeral Sermons Publ. for Women (1600-1630), 6 vol., 1993—2004; author: A Sermon from Constantinople, 1619, 7th vol., 2005; contbr. East of Auden, South: An Anthology of the Southern Counties, Eng., 2002, poetry in Passages North, The Awakenings Rev., articles to profl. jour. Angier B. Duke Grad. fellow Duke U., 1954; recipient Faculty Rsch. award Ariz. State U., 1984. Episcopalian. E-mail: bettieadoebler@aol.com.

DOEBLER, PAUL DICKERSON, publishing management executive; b. Milw., July 3, 1930; s. Paul Henry and Grace Elizabeth (Whittaker) D.; m. Aileen Mary Hunt, May 15, 1958 (dec. 1966); m. Terry Gerda Moss, Dec. 15, 1967 BS in Journalism, Northwestern U., 1953; BS in Printing Mgmt.,

Carnegie-Mellon U., 1956. Editor-in-chief Book Prodn. Industry mag. Penton Pub. Co., N.Y.C., 1965-71; pub. mgmt. cons. N.Y.C., 1972-80; mgr. bus. devel. R.R. Bowker subs. Xerox, N.Y.C., 1980-82, editor-in-chief profl. books, 1983-84; pub. cons. Xerox Systems Group, El Segundo, Calif., 1984-85, mgr. documentation cons. services, 1985-86, mgr. documentation systems mktg., 1986-89; pres. Paul Doebler Enterprises, Camarillo, Calif., 1990—. Instr. Assn. Am. Pubs., 1985, CCNY, 1980-85; guest lectr. The Writing Program MIT, 1988-90; instr. learning Tree U., 1997—. Contbr. articles to mags. Mem. Carnegie Printers Alumni Assn. (pres. 1972) Home: 6343 Gitana Ave Camarillo CA 93012-8135

DOEDE, JOHN HENRY, investment company executive; b. Chgo., Sept. 29, 1937; s. Clinton Milford and Dorothy Ruth (Hagemeyer) D.; m. Jean Anne Dabbs, May 6, 1983; children: Danna, Tina, Timothy. AB in Chemistry, Harvard U., 1959; MS in Phys. Chemistry, U. Chgo., 1962, PhD in Phys. Chemistry, Physics, 1963. Physicist Argonne (Ill.) Nat. Lab., 1963-65; mgr. EMR computer div. (electro magnetic rsch). Schlumberger Corp., Mpls., 1965-67; pres. Data Internat. Inc., Mpls., 1967-70; v.p. Heizer Corp., Chgo., 1970-72; v.p., dir. 1st Chgo. Investment Corp., 1972-83; pres. Polaris Capital Group, San Diego, 1983—88; chmn. JDJD, Inc., Palm Beach, Fla., 1992-97, Blue Eagle Golf Ctrs., Inc., Wayne, Pa., 1996-98, AIG Silk Road Fund, NYC, 1997—, Am. European Industries, Inc., 1999—2004, Answer System, Inc., 1999—2004; mng. mem. Bilter Inc. LLC, 2004—. Republican. Home: 7525 E Gainey Ranch Rd Unit 197 Scottsdale AZ 85258-1610 E-mail: john@johndoede.com.

DOELL, MARGARET J., art educator; d. Peter Doell and Elizabeth Reimer; life ptnr. Jennifer D. Stoughton. BFA, U. Man., Winnipeg, Can., 1989; MFA, Concordia U., Montreal, Can., 1993. Lectr. Concordia U., Montreal, Canada, 1992—93, Mt. Allison U., Sackville, Canada, 1993—94; instr. U. Coll. of Cariboo, Kamloops, Canada, 1995—95; prof. art Adams State Coll., Alamosa, Colo., 1996—. Artist in residence West Baffin Eskimo Co-op, Cape Dorset, Nunavut, Canada, 1990—00; faculty senate rep. Adams State Coll., Alamosa, Colo., 2001—05; juror Creede Nat. Small Print Show, Colo., 2003—03. Exhibition, Self Portrait with Small Feet, Delta National Small Print Show (Lindquist Purchase Prize, 2003), MAP, Learning to Watch Television, On the Horizon. V.p. Cattails Golf Course, Alamosa, Colo., 2004—05. J.W. McConnell fellowship, Concordia U., 1990-1992. Mem.: Coll. Art Assn. Mennonite. Avocations: golf, skiing, travel, gardening. Office Phone: 719-587-7822.

DOENECKE, CAROL ANNE, artist; b. Chgo., July 9, 1942; d. George John and Irene Victoria (Ostrowski) Soukup; m. Justus Drew Doenecke, Mar. 21, 1970. Student, U. Chgo., 1960-63; BFA, Sch. of the Art Inst., Chgo., 1964. Group exhbns. include Polk Pub. Mus. All Fla. Biennial, Lakeland, 1985, Longboat Key Art Ctr. Show, Fla. State Sen. Office Bldg., Talahassee, 1985, Vantage Gallery, Ithaca, NY, 1986, Lake Worth (Fla.) Art League, 1987, Pastel Soc. Can., Toronto, 1987, Hull, 1992, Ottawa, Ont., 1994, Ctr. for the Arts, Vero Beach, Fla., 1987, 90, Pastel Soc. of S.W., Dallas, 1988, 90, Hilltop Gallery, Nogales, Ariz., 1989, La. Art and Artist's Guild, Baton Rouge, 1989, Northwest Pastel Soc., Issaquah, Wash., 1989, 90, Southeastern Pastel Soc., Moultrie, Ga., 1990, 92, Pastel Soc. Oreg., Roseburg, 1990, 92, Pastel Soc. North Fla., Pensacola (Fla.) Mus. Art, 1992, Pastel Soc. New Mexico, Albuquerque, 1992, 93, West Bank Art Guild, New Orleans, 1992, Fla. Soc. Fine Arts, Fla. Mus. Hispanic and Latin Am. Art, Miami, 1993, Conn. Pastel Soc., Paul Mellon Arts Ctr., Choate Rosemary Hall, Wallingford, Conn., 1993, 94, Women's Caucus for Art, Sarasota, Fla., 1993, 2000, Tallahassee, Fla., 1996, Miami, Fla., 1996, Venice, Fla., 1997, The Arts Ctr., St. Petersburg, Fla., 1994, Daytona Beach Art League, Fla., 1989, Fla. Mus. Hispanic and L.Am. Art, Miami, 1994, 96, NJ Ctr. Visual Arts, 1995, Art Janet Reid Hodges Gallery, Art League of Manatee County, Bradenton, Fla., 1995, 98, Boca Raton Mus. Art, 1995, Visual Arts Ctr. Northwest Fla., Panama City, 1995, Nat. Congress Art and Design, Salt Lake City, 1995, Swann Gallery, Detroit, 1996, Women's Caucus for Art Nat. 25th Ann. Show, Artemisia Gallery, Chgo., 1996-97, Pastel Painters Cape Cod, Chatham, Mass., 1996, Fla. Art Ctr., Havana, Fla., 1996, 97, Ridge Art Assn., Winter Haven, Fla., 1997, Soho Gallery, Pensacola, Fla., 1999, Women's Resource Ctr., 1999, Galerie Montcalm, Hull, Que., 1992, 99, Tex. Artists' Mus. Port Arthur, 1997, Palm Springs Desert Mus., 2004, many others; one-woman shows include Women's Resource Ctr., Sarasota, Fla., 1987, Arts Ctr. At Maas Bros., St. Petersburg, Fla., 1990, Fine Arts Gallery, New Coll., U. South Fla., Sarasota, 1991, Fine Arts Gallery at The Edn. Ctr., Longboat Key, Fla., 1999, Harmony Gallery, Beatrice Friedman Symphony Ctr., Sarasota, Fla., 2004; two-person shows include Polk C.C., Winter Haven, Fla., 1991 Recipient numerous others awards, 1981—, 1st Pl. award, 2d Internat. Art Competition, Palm Beach Art Galleries, 1983, 3d Internat. Competition, Palm Beach Art Galleries, New Orleans, 1984, Nepenthe Mundi Soc./ Emerald City Classic, Wichita, Kans., 1984, merit award, Art Ctr. Sarasota/ Fla., 1985, 46th Ann. Nat. Jury Competition, Lake Worth Art League, 1987, award of merit, Pastel Soc. West Coast, Carmichael, 1991, Third Pl., Northern Trust Bank of Fla. Exhibit, 1982, award of merit, No. Calif. Arts, Inc., Sacramento Fine Arts Ctr./Carmichael, Calif., 2002, hon. merit award, Art Ctr. Sarasota, 2002, Northern Trust Bank of Fla. Exhibit, 2000, Award of Merit, Fla. Pastel Assn., 1984, 1st Pl. award, 1988, Honorable Mention, Art League of Manatee County, 2003, General Pencil Co., Inc. award, Palm Springs Desert Mus., 2004. Mem. Pastel Soc. Can. (hon.), Art League Manatee County (bd. govs. 1994-97). Episcopalian. Home: 3943 Riverview Blvd W Bradenton FL 34209-2000 E-mail: doenecke@ncf.edu.

DOENGES, BYRON FREDERICK, former government official, finance educator; b. Ft. Wayne, Ind., June 18, 1922; s. Arthur Philip and Elsie (Mesing) D.; m. Elaine Aiken, June 15, 1947. Diploma, Internat. Bus. Coll., 1941; student, DePauw U., 1943—44; AB, Franklin (Ind.) Coll., 1946; MBA, Ind. U., 1948, PhD, 1962; LittD (hon.), Franklin Coll. of Ind., 1985. Instr., headmaster boarding dept. Punahou Sr. Acad., Honolulu, 1948-50; dir. scholarships and loans Ind. U., Bloomington, 1951-56, asst. dean Coll. Arts and Scis., 1955-65; prof. econs., dean Coll. Liberal Arts Willamette U., 1965-71; econ. cons. Gov. Oreg., 1971-72; dep. asst. dir. ACDA, Washington, 1972-73, chief econs. and spl. studies divsn., 1973-76; sr. econs. advisor U.S. Arms Control and Disarmament Agy., 1976-93; ind. writer and internat. econ. cons., 1993—. Program devel. head Title II NDEA, U.S. Office Edn., Washington, 1958-59; assoc. dir. Salzburg (Austria) Seminar Am. Studies, 1962-64; mem. Higher Commn. N.W. Assn. Secondary and Higher Schs., 1968-71; mem. exec. bd. N.W. Assn. Pvt. Colls. and Univs., 1969-70; chmn. planning com. Navy V-12 Nat. Colloquium, 1989; conduct spl. rsch. on internat. capital movements, econs. higher edn., econs. arms control, Soviet and successor states to former Soviet Union economies, econ. impact of def. spending. Editor: Accountability, 1973, World Military Expenditures and Arms Transfers, 1981-84, Arms Control Ann. Report, 1981-91, Arms Control Impact Statement for the Congress, 1991; contbr. articles to profl. jours. Lt. comdr. USNR, 1943-46, PTO. Recipient alumni citation Franklin Coll., 1977. Mem. Am. Econ. Assn., Cosmos Club (Washington), Lambda Chi Alpha (mem. nat. fellowship bd. 1965-2000, Meritorious Svc. award 1984), Pi Gamma Mu, Omicron Delta Kappa. Home: 1002 Fearrington Post Pittsboro NC 27312-5503 Office: 4 E Madison Pittsboro NC 27312 E-mail: byron-doenges@mindspring.com.

DOENGES, RUDOLPH CONRAD, finance educator; b. Tonkawa, Okla., Dec. 7, 1930; s. Rudolph Soland and Helen Elizabeth (Lower) D.; m. Ellen Ione Gummere, Oct. 5, 1963; children: Rudolph Conrad, John Soland, William Gummere. AB magna cum laude (scholar 1948-54), Harvard U., 1952, MBA, 1954; D.BA (Ford Found. fellow 1963-64), U. Colo., Boulder, 1965. Mktg. analyst Ford Motor Co., Dearborn, Mich., 1954; gen. mgr. Doenges-Long Motors and Western Auto Rentals, Colorado Springs, 1958-61; mem. faculty U. Tex., Austin, 1964-2000, prof. fin., 1974-2000, Arthur Andersen & Co. prof. fin., 1983-2000, assoc. dean Grad. Sch. Bus., 1972-76, chmn. dept. fin., 1976-80, assoc. dean Coll. Bus. Adminstrn., 1987-97. Author: (with E. W. Walker) Case Problems in Financial Management, 1968, Consumer Credit in Texas, 1970; editor: Readings in Money and Banking, 1968, (with H. A. Wolf) Corporate Planning Models, 1971; contbr. articles in field to profl. jours. Gen. Bd. Pensions United Meth. Ch., 1988-96; trustee Iliff Sch. Theology, 1992-96. Served with USN, 1955-58. Mem. Austin C. of C., Fin. Mgmt. Assn. (dir. 1980-82), Southwestern Fin. Assn. (pres. 1973-74), Southwestern Fedn. Adminstrv. Disciplines (pres. 1975-76), Austin Soc. Fin. Analysts, El Paso Club (Colorado Springs), Austin Club, Garden of the Gods Club. Republican. Methodist. Home: 3500 Hillbrook Cir Austin TX 78731-4036 Office: U Tex Dept Finance Austin TX 78712

DOERFFEL, MARK ALBERT, music educator; s. George Alfred and Constance Joan Doerffel. BA in Music Edn., La. State U., Baton Rouge, 1993—97; MA in Music Edn., Appalachain State U., Boone, N.C., 2000—01. Band dir. Laney H.S., Wilmington, NC, 2001—. Ednl. dir. Wilmington Symphony Orch., NC, 2002—05. Avocations: scuba diving, running, music, bicycling. Office Phone: 910-350-2089 248.

DOERFLER, RONALD JOHN, communications company executive; b. Jersey City, July 15, 1941; s. Louis S. and Ann E. (Dubiak) D.; m. Beatrice Mary Corbett, Jan. 4, 1942; children: Stephanie, Nicholas. B in Acctg., Fairleigh Dickinson U., 1967, MBA magna cum laude, 1972. CPA N.Y., 1967. Fin. analyst ITT, N.Y.C., 1966—69; asst. contr. Capital Cities Comm., N.Y.C., 1969—76, treas., 1977—80, sr. v.p., CFO, 1980—85, Capital Cities/ABC, N.Y.C., 1986—98, HEARST, N.Y.C., 1998—, also bd. dirs. Trustee Fairleigh Dickinson U.; bd. dirs. Arts and Bus. Coun. Named one of Ams. Best CFO's, Instnl. Investor mag., 1986. Mem. AICPA, Internat. Radio and TV Soc., Inst. Newspaper Fin. Execs., Broadcast Cable Fin. Mgmt. Assn. (pres. 1979-80, former chmn. bd.). Office: Hearst 1345 Sixth Ave New York NY 10105

DOERING, PAUL LOUIS, pharmacist, educator; b. Miami, Feb. 25, 1949; s. Juanita Brown and Ernest Doering; m. Cheryl Rainey, Aug. 22, 1970; children: Christopher, Tracy, Jennifer. BS in Pharmacy, U. Fla., 1972, MS in Pharmacy, 1975. Asst. prof. pharmacy practice U. Fla., Gainesville, 1976—81, assoc. prof. pharmacy practice, 1981—88, prof. pharmacy practice, 1988—95, disting. svc. prof. pharmacy practice, 1995—2002. Co-dir. Drug Info. and Pharmacy Resource Ctr., Gainesville, 1988—2002. Contbr. articles to profl. jours. Lectr.- drug abuse prevention Various, Various, Fla., 1976—2002. Mem.: Fla. Pharmacy Assn., Am. Coll. Clin. Pharmacists, Am. Assn. Colls. Pharmacy, Am. Soc. Health Sys. Pharmacists, Am. Pharm. Assn. Democrat. Methodist. Office: U Fla Coll Pharmacy Box 100486 Gainesville FL 32610 Home Fax: (352)-338-9860. Business E-Mail: doering@shands.ufl.edu.

DOERMANN, HUMPHREY, writer, consultant; b. Toledo, Nov. 13, 1930; s. Henry John and Alice (Robbins Humphrey) D.; m. Elisabeth Adams Wakefield, Jan. 7, 1956; children: Elisabeth M., Eleanor H., Julia L. AB, Harvard U., 1952, MBA, 1958, PhD, 1967; LLD (hon.), Xavier U., La., 1990, U. Minn., 1997; LHD (hon.), Coll. St. Scholastica, 1993, U. St. Thomas, 1996, Ctrl. Coll., 1998. Asst. to com. on admissions and scholarships Harvard, 1955-56; reporter Mpls. Star, 1958-60; asst. to bus. mgr. Mpls. Star & Tribune Co., 1960-61; dir. admissions Harvard, 1961-66; asst. to dean Harvard (Faculty of Arts and Scis.), 1966-69, asst. dean for financial affairs, 1970-71; lectr. on edn. Harvard (Grad. Sch. Edn.), 1967-71; exec. dir. Bush Found., St. Paul, 1971-78, pres., 1978-97; vis. prof. Macalester Coll., 1997-2000, rsch. assoc., 2000—. Cons. Coun. Higher Edn. Va., 1969, W.Va. Bd. Regents, 1970; bd. overseers Harvard Coll., Harvard U., 1973-79; trustee St. Paul Acad. and Summit Sch., 1997—; bd. dirs. Coun. on Founds., Washington, 1985-92, chmn. bd. 1990-92; trustee Found. Ctr., N.Y.C., 1975-83, chmn. bd. 1982-83; chmn. Minn. Coun. on Founds., 1981-85, Coll. Bd., N.Y.C., 1994-99; chmn. Minn. Legis. Task Force on Student Aid, 1993; chair regents candidate adv. coun. U. Minn., 1997-99; chmn. Minn. Humanities Commn., 2004—. Author: Crosscurrents in College Admissions, rev. edit, 1970, Toward Equal Access, 1978; co-author (with Henry N. Drewry) Stand and Prosper, 2001. Mem. Belmont (Mass.) Town Meeting, 1969-70. Served to lt. (j.g.) USN, 1952-55. Home: 736 Goodrich Ave Saint Paul MN 55105-3524 Office: Macalester Coll 1600 Grand Ave Saint Paul MN 55105-1801 E-mail: doermann@macalester.edu.

DOERPER, JOHN ERWIN, journal editor, publishing executive; b. Würzburg, Germany, Sept. 17, 1943; came to U.S., 1963, naturalized resident, 1973; s. Werner and Theresia (Wolf) D.; m. Victoria McCulloch, Dec. 2, 1970. BA, Calif. State U., Fullerton, 1968; postgrad., U. Calif., Davis, 1972. Writer/author, Seattle, 1984—; food columnist Washington, Seattle, 1985-88, Seattle Times, 1985-88; food editor Wash.-The Evergreen State Mag., Seattle, 1989-94, Pacific Northwest mag., 1989-94, Seattle Home and Garden, 1989-91; pub., editor, founder Pacific Epicure, Quarterly Jour. Gastronomy, Bellingham, Wash., 1988—. Dir. Annual N.W. Invitational Chef's Symposium. Author: Eating Well: A Guide to Foods of the Pacific Northwest, 1984, The Eating Well Cookbook, 1984, Shellfish Cookery: Absolutely Delicious Recipes from the West Coast, 1985, Pacific Northwest Wine Country, 2001, author: Washington: A Compass Guide, 2002, Fodor's Pacific Northwest, 2002, Fodor's Seattle, 2000, California Wine Country, 2004, Oregon Wine Country, 2004, Washington Wine Country, 2004; author, illustrator: The Blue Carp, 1994, Wine Country: California's Napa and Sonoma Valleys, 1996, Pacific Northwest, 1997, Coastal California, 1998 (Lowell Thomas Travel Journalism Competition Gold medal 1999); contbr. articles to profl. jours., intro. and chpts. to books. Recipient Silver medal, White award for city and regional mags. William Allen White Sch. Journalism, U. Kans., Lowell Thomas award Gold medal for best guide book, 1999. Mem. Oxford Symposium Food and Cookery (speaker 26th Ann. Pacific N.W. Writer's Conf. 1982, 92). Avocations: food, wine, travel, painting, printmaking. E-mail: jdoerper@mac.com.

DOERR, JOHN, venture capitalist; b. St. Louis, Mo. BS, MS in electrical engineering, Rice U.; MBA, Harvard U. Joined Intel Corp., 1974; ptnr. Kleiner Perkins Caulfield & Byers, Menlo Park, Calif., 1980—; founder, CEO Silicon Compilers, 1981. Mem. bd. dirs. Intuit, Amazon.com, Drugstore.com, Homestore.com, PalmOne, Sun Microsystems, Google, Good Technology, Segway, Elance, EndForce. Office: Kleiner Perkins 2750 Sand Hill Rd Menlo Park CA 94025-7020

DOERRIE, BOBETTE, secondary school educator; b. Albuquerque, June 22, 1944; d. Neill and Dorothy Madelyn (Jones) Patterson; m. Edward Lewis Horton, Aug. 21, 1966 (div. 1990); children: Leah, James, Carol, Neill; m. Jerome Lee Doerrie, July 28, 1991; children: Jennifer, Elena. BA, McMurry Coll., 1966; MEd, DePaul U., 1977. Cert. sec. broadfield sci. Tchr. physics and phys. sci, environ. edn., TAKS Remed. G/T coord. Perryton (Tex.) H.S.; tchr. Summit Sch., Dundee, Ill., 1974-77, Lamesa Middle Sch., 1980-85, Lamesa H.S., 1968-69, 85-91, Perryton High Sch., 1991—. Co-dir. Dawson County Sci. Fair, 1981-91; coach Odyssey of the Mind, 1988-91; mem. McMurry U. Ednl. Adv. Bd., 1991-97, engrng. team faculty advisor, 1993-2004, sci. olympiad coach, 1998-2000, sci. bowl advisor, 2001-05; mem. Mus. Bd. Dawson County, 1983-90; mem. Libr. Bd. Ochiltree County, v.p., 1993-95; bd. dirs. Perrytown Crisis Ctr., 2005—. Bd. dirs. Crisis Ctr., 2005. Recipient Excellence in Teaching award Tex. State Assn. for Physics Tchrs., 1992, Nat. Tchg. award RadioShack, 2001; NSF/Tex. Edn. Assn. Christa McAuliffe grantee, 1993, Outstanding Sci. Educator, Tex. Acad. Sci., 2002, Nat. Tchg. award Health Physics Soc., 2002; named Tchr. of Yr., Region XVI Gifted and Talented Tchrs., 1994, Perryton H.S., 2004. Mem.: Sci. Tchrs. of Tex. (treas. 1998—2001), South Plains Sci. Soc. (pres. 1988, Sharon Christa McAuliffe Tchr. of Yr. 1987), Delta Kamma Gamma (past pres.). Avocations: amateur radio, painting, astronomy, reading, writing. Home: 13925 CR B Booker TX 79005-9713 Office: Perryton High Sch 1200 S Jefferson St Perryton TX 79070-3700 Office Phone: 806-439-3633. Business E-Mail: bdoerrie@perrytonsd.com.

DOERRIES, REINHARD RENÉ, historian, educator; b. Berlin, Sept. 25, 1934; came to U.S., 1954; s. Hermann and Annemarie (Kochendoerffer) D.; m. Elaine Sulli, Jan. 20, 1963; 1 child, Chantal-Aimée. BA, Concordia Coll., 1958; MFA, Ohio U., 1960; MA, Yale U., 1962; MBA, Inst. Europèen d'Adminstrn. des Affaires, Fontainebleau, France, 1965; PhD, Bochum U., 1971; habilitation, U. Hamburg, 1982. With internat. divsn. 1st Nat. Bank of Boston, 1962-64; internat. mgmt. cons. Booz Allen & Hamilton Internat., Zurich, Switzerland, 1965-68; asst. prof. modern history Hamburg U., Germany, 1970-73, 75-83, prof., 1983-86, U. Kassel, Germany, 1986-88, U. Erlangen-Nuremberg, Germany, 1988—. Guest prof. U. Southampton, Eng., 1986; internat. fellow Am. Council Learned Socs., N.Y.C., 1973-75; lectr. in field. Author: Washington-Berlin 1908/1917, 1975, Iren und Deutsche in der Neuen Welt, 1985, Imperial Challenge, 1989, Prelude to the Easter Rising, 2000, Hitler's Last Chief of Foreign Intelligence, 2003; editor: Memoirs of Erika von Watzdorf-Bachoff, 1997, Diplomaten und Agenten, 2001; co-editor: Amerikastudien, 1990—2003, American Studies Book Series, 1990—; adv. editor: Perspectives in Intelligence History, 1991—95; contbr. articles to profl. jours. Bd. dirs. Internat. Sch., Hamburg, 1979-80; bd. dirs. Am. House Nuremberg, 1995—, vice chmn., 1996—. Danforth Found. fellow Yale U., 1962. Mem. German Soc. for Am. Studies (dir. 1976-84, pres. 1987-90, dir. 1990—), Am. Hist. Assn., German Soc. for Can. Studies, Immigration History Soc., Intelligence History Study Group (dir. 1993-2000), Soc. for Historians of Am. Fgn. Rels., German Hist. Assn., Group 65 Club (founder), Yale Club. Avocation: painting. Office: U Erlangen-Nuremberg Findelgasse 9 90402 Nuremberg Germany

DOERSAM, CHARLES HENRY, JR., engineer, educator, entrepreneur; b. N.Y.C., Nov. 1, 1921; s. Charles Henry, Sr. and Mary Emily (Davenport) D.; m. Cynthia Ann Wick, Dec. 7, 1954 (div. dec. 1980); children: Charles Henry III, Donna Davenport, Dean Robert. BS in Engr., Columbia U., 1942, MSME, 1944; post grad., MIT, U. Mich., N.Y.U. Registered profl. engr., N.Y. Indsl. engr. Pratt & Whitney, East Hartford, Conn., 1941-42; mem. tech. staff Bell Telephone Labs, N.Y.C., 1942-44; with Combined Rsch. Group, Naval Rsch. Lab., 1944—46; sr. project engr Spl. Devices Ctr., Sands Point, NY, 1946-53; project mgr. Sperry Gyroscope Co., Lake Success, N.Y., 1953-60; new product planning mgr. Potter Instrument Co., Plainview, N.Y., 1960-62; dir. mktg. chief engr. Instruments for Industry, Hicksville, N.Y., 1962-64; prof. Polytech. Instit. of Bklyn., 1964-69; pres. Com Comp Inc, Hauppauge, N.Y., 1969-71; chmn., CEO Fiber Optic Sensors, Inc., Old Lyme, Conn., 1983—. Pres. DOERCO Cons., CUB Computer Co., NUTEK Corp., Princeton Automated Labs., Pedagogy Rsch. Inst.; nat. chmn. IRE Profl. Group on Space Electronics, 1950. Pantentee in field; contbr. articles to profl. jours. Bd. Advisors Waldorf Sch., Garden City, N.Y., 1964-68, Portledge Sch., Locust Valley, N.Y., 1977. Lt. (j.g.) USNR, 1944-46. Mem. North Shore Yacht Club (commn. 1968-69), Point O'Woods Club. Republican. Congregationalist. Avocations: tennis, sailing, woodworking, gardening, construction. Home and Office: 67 Shore Rd PO Box 927 Old Lyme CT 06371-0927 Office Phone: 860-434-0666. Personal E-mail: fosi5@aol.com.

DOESCHER, WILLIAM FREDERICK, communications executive; b. Utica, N.Y., Dec. 9, 1937; s. Frederick William and Katherine Ann (Kipp) D.; m. Linda Blair, Nov. 25, 1977; children: Michelle Blair, Douglas C., Marc H. Blair, Cinda L. BA in Econs., Colgate U., 1959; MS in Journalism, Syracuse (N.Y.) U., 1961; postgrad. in advanced mgmt., Columbia U., 1973. Pub. rels. assoc., editor Chase Manhattan News Chase Manhattan Bank, N.Y.C., 1961-65; mgr. press rels. Inmont Corp., 1965-66; asst. corp. rels. mgr. U.S. Plywood Corp., 1966-67; pub. affairs mgr. ea. region Champion Internat. Corp., 1967-69, mgr. advt. svcs., then dir. corp. advt., 1969-71; v.p. pub. rels. and advt. Drexel Heritage Furnishings, Inc., 1971-78; v.p. comms. Dun & Bradstreet, Inc., 1978-83, v.p. pub. rels. and advt., 1983-96, sr. v.p. global comm., 1992—; sr. v.p., chief comm. officer Dun & Bradstreet Corp., 1996—; also pub. D&B Reports mag., N.Y.C., 1978-94. Author numerous articles in mags., periodicals. Bd. dirs. Direct Mktg. Assn., Jackie Robinson Found., BBBonline, PRSA Found.; mem., adv. com. S.I. Newhouse Sch. Pub. Comm. and its Distant Learning Program at Syracuse U.; bd. govs. Scarsdale (N.Y.) Golf Club; bd. dirs. N.Y.C. divsn. N.Y. Easter Seal Soc.; past pres. Nat. Combined Health Appeal; past pres. Scarsdale, N.Y. Civic Club; past bd. dirs. Colgate Alumni Corp., Nat. Easter Seal Soc., N.Y. Easter Seal Soc., N.Y.C. divsn. Am. Cancer Soc. With USAR, 1959-65. Mem. Pub. Rels. Seminar, Arthur Page Soc., Pub. Rels. Soc. Am., Wisemen. Office: 1 Diamond Hill Rd New Providence NJ 07974-1200

DOETSCH, VIRGINIA LAMB, former advertising executive, writer; b. NYC, Oct. 12, 1920; d. Andrew Thomas and Cameola Weeden (Burns) Lamb; m. Gunter H. Doetsch, Oct. 12, 1953 (div. Feb. 1972); 1 child, Hugo. BS, Northwestern U., 1941; postgrad., Columbia U., 1943—44, postgrad., 1946—47. Writer, dir. pub. rels. J. Walter Thompson, Frankfurt, Germany, 1953-56; creative group head, v.p. to ptnr. Tatham-Laird & Kudner (now Euro RSCG Tatham Ptnrs.), Chgo., 1959—76; v.p. Needham Harper & Steers (now DDB Chgo.), Chgo., 1976-83; free-lance advt. writer and prodr. Chgo., 1983—; writer, rschr. OmniTech Cons. Group now Diamond Tech. Ptnrs., Chgo., 1992-99. Mem. Chgo. Symphony Orch. Women's Assn., 1992—; fundraiser, subscription sales Goodman Theatre, Chgo., 2003—; bd. dirs. Better Bus. Bur., Chgo., 1973—76, Jr. Achievement, Chgo., 1973, Chgo. Symphony Orch. Women's Assn., 2002—. With ARC, 1944—46, China, Burma, India. Decorated Bronze Star; named Woman of Yr., Am. Advt. Fedn., 1973. Mem. Women's Advt. Club Chgo. (Woman of Yr. award 1973), Chgo. Advt. Club (bd. dirs. 1973-76). Home: 400 E Randolph St Apt 828 Chicago IL 60601-7309

DOFT, BERNARD HARVEY, ophthalmologist; b. N.Y.C., Aug. 13, 1946; children: Michelle, Amy, Jennifer. Student, Cornell U., 1964—67; MD, NYU, 1971. Diplomate Am. Bd. Internal Medicine, Am. Bd. Ophthalmology. Intern, asst. resident in internal medicine Barnes Hosp., Washington U. Sch. of Medicine, St. Louis, 1971—73; rsch. assoc. NIH, Nat. Heart & Lung Inst. and Bur. of Biologics, Bethesda, Md., 1973—75; resident in ophthalmology Bascom Palmer Eye Inst., U. Miami Sch. Medicine, 1975—78, fellowship in diseases and surgery of retina and vitreous, 1978—79; asst. prof. ophthalmology U. Pitts. Sch. Medicine, 1979—84, clin. assoc. prof. ophthalmology, 1984—99, clin. assoc. prof. epidemiology, 1989—99, clin. prof. ophthalmology, 1999—; pvt. practice Retina Vitreous Cons, Pitts., 1984—. Cons. vision rsch. rev. com. NIH Nat. Eye Inst., 1985, protocol rev. com, 2003; apptd. ophthalmic steering com., diabetic control and complications trial NIH, 1983; quality assurance com. Bascom Palmer Eye Inst., Ann Bates Leach Eye Hosp., U. Miami Sch. Medicine, 1977—78; co-dir., retina svc. Eye and Ear Hosp., U. Pitts., 1979—84, operating rm. com., 1982—87, chmn. com. on lasers, 1982—85; clinic coord. com. Eye and Ear Hosp., Pitts., 1982—85, ad hoc. com. for adminstrn./staff rels., 1983—85, chmn. oversight com. outpatient testing and laser ctr., 1983—85, med. staff nursing oversight com., 1983—98; study chair the endophthalmitis vitrectomy study Nat. Eye Inst., Bethesda, 1989—99; SurgiCenter task force U. Pitts. Med. Ctr., 1995, ophthalmology search com. dept. of ophthalmology chmn., 95; network cons. Diabetic Retinopathy Clin. Rsch. Network, 2003; rsch. adv. com. for steroids in ctrl. vein occlusion study NIH, 2003—. Vitreoretinal Surgery and Technology, 1989—99; contbr. articles to profl. jours. Parent coun. Emory U., Atlanta, 1998—2002. With USPHS, 1973—75. Grantee in field. Fellow: ACS, Am. Acad. Ophthalmology; mem.: AMA, Pa. Acad. Ophthalmology (coun. mem. 1990—91), Retina Soc., Vitreous Soc., Macula Soc., Allegheny County Med. Soc., Pa. Med. Soc., Pitts. Ophthalmology Soc. (exec. com. 1980—91, program co-chmn. 1982—83, program chmn. 1983—87, v.p., pres.-elect 1987—88, pres. 1989—91, chmn. nominating com. 1991—93), Bascom Palmer Eye Inst. Alumni Assn., Alpha Omega Alpha. Avocation: tennis. Home: 123 South Dr Pittsburgh PA 15238-2313 Office: Retina-Vitreous Cons Ste 500 3501 Forbes Ave Pittsburgh PA 15213-3317 Office Phone: 412-683-5300. E-mail: doft@pitt.edu, bdoft@aol.com.

DOGANÇAY, BURHAN C., artist, photographer, sculptor; b. Istanbul, Turkey, Sept. 11, 1929; s. Adil and Hediye Dogançay; m. Angela Hausmann, Dec. 11, 1978. Student, Acad. de la Grande Chaumière, 1955; PhD in Econs., U. Paris, 1956. Dir. dept. tourism Govt. of Turkey, Ankara, 1959-62, dir. Turk Info. N.Y.C., 1962-64; artist N.Y.C., 1964—. Author: Dogancay, 1986, Dessine-Moi L'Amour, 1992, Bride of Dreams, 1999, Dogancay: A Retrospective, 2001, Dogancay: Works on Paper, 2003, Walls of the World, 2003, Blue Walls of New York, 2003; exhibitions include Ctr. Georges Pompidou, Paris, 1982, Mus. St.-Georges, Liége, Belgium, 1982, Mus. Art Contemporain, Montreal, 1983, Seibu Mus. Art, Tokyo, 1989, State Russian Mus., Leningrad, 1992, Artists' Union, Moscow, 1992, JFK Internat. Airport, 1998—, Ofcl. Opening of Dogançay Mus., Istanbul, 2004, Aubusson tapestry, —. Recipient Cert. of Appreciation, City of N.Y., 1964, medal of appreciaiton Ministry of Culture Russia, 1992, Nat. Medal of Arts for Lifetime Achievement and Cultural Contbn., Pres. of Turkey, 1995; fellow Tamarind Lithography Workshop, 1969; design selected for UNICEF cards, 1974, 96 E-mail: Dogancay@aol.com. *Mostly unshattered self-confidence, hard work and the willingness to meet new challenges are the basis of my success and happiness.*

DOGGETT, JOHN MARTIN, JR., (MARTY DOGGETT), headmaster; m. Patti Doggett. BA in Am. Civilization, Williams Coll., 1973; MA in History, NYU, 1981. History and economics teacher, housemaster and coach then assoc. headmaster and dean of students Lawrenceville Sch., Lawrenceville, NJ, 1974—98; headmaster Gov. Dummer Acad., Byfield, Mass., 1999—. Mem. bd. dirs. City Prep, Inc. Office: Gov Dummer Acad 1 Elm St Byfield MA 01922*

DOGGETT, JOHN NELSON, JR., clergyman; b. Phila., Apr. 3, 1918; s. John Nelson and Frances Brown Doggett; m. Juanita Toley, Aug. 2, 1973; children from previous marriage: Lorraine, John, William, Kenneth, Riddick. BA, Lincoln U., Pa., 1942; MDiv, Union Theol. Sem., NYC, 1945; MEd, St. Louis U., 1969, PhD, 1971. Ordained to ministry United Meth. Ch. 1943. Civilian chaplain South Gate Cmty. Ch., San Francisco, 1945—47; organizing pastor Downs Meml. Meth. Ch., Oakland, Calif., 1947—49; chaplain Calif. Nat. Guard, 1947—49; pastor Scott Meml. Meth. Ch., Pasadena, Calif., 1950—53, Hamilton Meml. Meth. Ch., L.A., 1953—64, Union Meml. United Meth. Ch., St. Louis, 1964—76; dist. supt. United Meth. Ch., St. Louis, 1976—82; sr. pastor Grace United Meth. Ch., St. Louis, 1982—85; ret. pastor Cabanne United Meth. Ch., 1986—89; mem. staff Pastoral Counseling Inst., St. Louis, 1968—89; pres. Midwest Cons., 1989—. Instr. founds. edn. Harris Tchrs. Coll., St. Louis, 1971—75; assoc. prof. practical theology Met. Coll., St. Louis, 1976—77; bd. dirs. Mentor St. Louis, 1996; commr. Nat. Coun. Chs. of Christ, 1981—84. *Juanita Doggett served 50 years in teaching and administration positions. She was principal of Sherman School in the Shaw neighborhood for 24 years and received the Lifetime Achievement Award. The city of St. Louis constructed Juanita Park, near Sherman, in honor of her service to children, parents, and the community. A tree was planted in Tower Grove Park for her effort to improve race relations and quality of life for all. She is a Life Member recipient of the NAACP Humanitarian Award. She received the YMCA Zealot 2004 Award, Dr. Martin Luther King Humanity 2005 Award, Urban League Lifetime, Friends of Tower Grove Park, and Alpha Kappa Sorority, Inc.* Pres. St. Louis NAACP, 1971—81; bd. dirs. St. Louis United Way, 1974—81; mem. Commn. on Alternatives to Prison, 1981, Citizens Com. Mo. Dept. Corrections; mem. Mo. Minority Health Task Force, 1986—88; trustee Mo. Hist. Soc., 1986—, John N. Doggett St. Louis Internist program, 1996; mem. adv. com. St. Louis U. Sch. Social Work, 1982—88; St. Louis U. Pres. Coun.; project friend St. Louis Drug Free Schs., 1992—95; bd. dirs. Mentor St. Louis, 1997—; advisor John and Juanita Doggett Scholarships, St. Paul Sch. Theology, Kansas City, Mo., Lincoln U.; mem. Interfaith Clergy Coun., 1980—85, World Meth. Coun.; pres. bd. dirs. Retirement Village Ctr. St. Louis Ctrl. Med. Ctr., 1973—86; pres. bd. dirs. Ctrl. Med. Ctr. Hosps., 1973—86. Named Minister of Yr., St. Louis Argus Newspaper, 1971, hon. citizen, Huntsville, Ala., 1993, J.N. Doggett Day in his honor, Mayor of St. Louis, 1996; recipient Outstanding Alumni award, St. Louis. U., 1981, Human Rights award, E.P. Lovejoy Soc., 1982, Drum Major award, Nat. Conf. Cmty. Justice, 1994, award of merit, Urban Met. League, St. Louis, 1994, Outstanding Alumni award, Lincoln U., 1996, Founder's Day award, 1996, Black Alumni Outstanding Svc. award, St. Louis U., 1999, Griot Gala Tribunal honors, Black World History Mus., 2004, Humanitarian plaque, NAACP, 2004. Mem.: Interreligious and Internat. Fedn. for Peace (Amb. for Peace 2001), UN Assn. (clergy pub. edn. com.), Am. Assn. Pastoral Counselors, Masons, Shriners, Phi Delta Kappa, Alpha Phi Alpha (nat. chaplain emeritus, D. Bowles/R. Anderson Svc. award, inducted into regional hall of fame 1987, Renaissance IV Excellence Svc. plaque Epsilon Lambda chpt. 1994). Home: 4466 W Pine Blvd Apt 2C Saint Louis MO 63108-2327 E-mail: jndoggett@sbcglobal.net.

DOGGETT, LLOYD ALTON, II, congressman, retired judge; b. Austin, Tex., Oct. 6, 1946; s. Lloyd A. and Alyce (Freydenfeldt) D.; m. Elizabeth Belk, 1969; children: Lisa, Catherine. BBA in Bus., U. Tex., 1967, JD with honors, 1970. Bar: Tex. 1971, U.S. Ct. Appeals (5th cir.) 1972, U.S. Dist. Ct. (we. dist.) Tex. 1972. Mem. Tex. State Senate, Dist. 14, 1973-85; ptnr. Doggett and Jacks, Austin, 1975-88; justice Tex. Supreme Ct., Austin, 1989-94; mem. U.S. Congresses from 25th Tex. dist., Washington, 1995—; mem. Ways and Means com. Adj. prof. U. Tex. Sch. of Law, 1989-94; chair Supreme Ct. Task Force on Jud. Ethics, 1992-94; co-founder Info. Tech. Working Group; mem. Congl. Task Force on Tobacco and Health. Named one of Five Outstanding Young Texans Tex. Jaycees, 1977, Outstanding Young Lawyer of Austin, 1978, one of Best Legislators, Tex. Monthly, 1979, 81, Outstanding State Senator, Common Cause, 1980, Disting. Alumnus, Bus. Adminstrn. Honors program U. Tex., 1989, Outstanding Jurist in Tex., Mex. Am. Bar Assn., 1993; recipient James Madison award Freedom of Info. Found. Tex., 1990, First Amendment award Nat. Soc. Profl. Journalists, 1990, Arthur B. DeWitty award for outstanding achievement in human rights Austin NAACP, others. Mem. Consumers Union U.S. (bd. dirs. 1976-79, 80-81, 86-89), Tex. Consumer Assn. (pres. 1973). Democrat. Methodist. Office: US House Reps 201 Cannon Ho Office Bldg Washington DC 20515-4310*

DOGGRELL, HENRY PATTON, lawyer; b. Memphis, July 3, 1948; s. Frank Ernest Doggrell Jr. and Martha (Patton) Brown; m. Beverly Gay Rhoda, Jan. 22, 1983; children: Henry Patton Jr., Dana Scott, Adrian Edward. BS in Commerce, U. Va., 1970; JD, Vanderbilt U., 1976. Bar: U.S. Dist. Ct. (mid. dist.) Tenn. 1977, U.S. Ct. Appeals (6th cir.) 1977, U.S. Dist. Ct. (we. dist.) Tenn. 1978, U.S. Ct. Appeals (fed. cir.) 1985. Law clk. to Judge Harry W. Wellford, U.S. Dist. Ct., 1975; assoc. Boult, Cummings, Conners & Berry, Nashville, 1976-78; ptnr. Burch, Porter & Johnson, Memphis, 1978-88, Baker, Donelson, Bearman & Caldwell, Memphis, 1988—96; gen. counsel Buckeye Techs., Inc., 1996—97, sr. v.p. corp. devel., 1998—2001; v.p. gen coun. GTx, Inc., Memphis, 2001—, sec., 2001—. Chmn. ad hoc com. Citizens on Govtl. Consolidation, Memphis, 1978; chmn. Brooks Mus. Art, 2000-02; bd. dirs. Calvary St. Ministry, 1996—. lt. (j.g.) USN, 1970-71. Mem. ABA, Tenn. Bar Assn. (chmn. real estate sect., sec. com. on real estate 1988-90). Republican. Unitarian. Avocations: backpacking, fishing, hiking, skiing, reading, golf. Home: 1657 Peabody Ave Memphis TN 38104-3829 Office: GTx Inc 3 N Dunlap 3rd FL Memphis TN 38163 Office Phone: 901-523-9700. E-mail: hdoggrell@gtxinc.com.

DOGOLOFF, LEE ISRAEL, clinical social worker, psychotherapist, consultant; b. Balt., Oct. 19, 1939; s. Mark and Minnie Lottie (Gresser) D.; m. Jane Roberta Greenberg, June 17, 1962 (div. 1973); children: Jody, Ilene; m. Mary Louise Gumpper, Feb. 3, 1974; 1 child, Kathryn Ann. BA in Sociology, U. Md., 1961; MSW, Howard U., 1964. Lic. social worker, Md., Del.; bd. cert. diplomate in Clin. Social Work, 1990—. Dep. adminstr. Narcotics Treatment Adminstrn., Washington, 1970-72; dir., govt. asst. Spl. Action Office on Drug Abuse Prevention, Washington, 1972-73; dir. div. community assistance Nat. Inst. Drug Abuse, Rockville, Md., 1974-75; dep. fed. drug mgmt. program Office Mgmt. and Budget, Washington, 1975-76; assoc. dir. White House Domestic Policy, Washington, 1977-80; exec. dir. Am. Coun. Drug Edn., Rockville, 1981-92; pres. Employee Health Programs, Inc., Bethesda, Md., 1992-93; psychotherapist, pvt. practice, 1980—. Ind. counselor drug abuse treatment; field instr. Sch. Social Work, U. Md., 1986-92; moderator edn. sect. White House Conf. for Drug Free Am., 1987-88; Presdl. appointee Pres.'s Drug Adv. Coun., 1989-94. Contbr. numerous articles to profl. publs. Mem.: NASW, Drug Watch Internat. (bd. dirs.).

DOHANIAN, DIRAN KAVORK, art historian, educator; b. Somerville, Mass., Mar. 26, 1931; s. Hagop Mardiros and Esther (Babigian) D. BFA, Mass. Sch. Art, 1952; MA in Tchg., Harvard U., 1953, MA, 1955, PhD, 1964. Instr. art Ea. Nazarene Coll., Wollaston, Mass., 1952—55; reader in fine arts Harvard U., Cambridge, Mass., 1954—57, tchg. fellow fine arts, 1955—57; vis. asst. prof. history art U. Ala., 1957—58; vis. asst. prof. history Oriental art U. Hawaii, 1959—60; asst. prof. fine arts, dir. course in Oriental humanities U. Rochester, NY, 1960—65, assoc. prof. fine arts, 1965—71, prof., 1971—87, prof. art history, 1988—2001, acting chmn. dept. fine arts, 1977—78, chmn. dept. fine arts, 1980—83, mem. faculty coun. Coll. Arts and Sci., 1991—94, sec. faculty coun., 1992—94, prof. art history emeritus, 2002—. Cons., curator Oriental art The Meml. Art Gallery, Rochester, 1976—88, bd. mgrs., 1977—78, 1980—83; Cooke-Daniels Meml. lectr. Cooke-Daniels Found. and Denver Art Mus., 1965; Louise Weiser lectr. Mt. Holyoke Coll., 1983; ind. scholar, cons. to art collections, 2003—. Author: The Mahayana Buddhist Sculpture of Ceylon, 1977; contbr. articles to profl. jours. C.R.B. fellow Belgian Art Seminar, Brussels and Antwerp, 1956, Fulbright fellow India, 1958-59, sr. rsch. fellow Am. Inst. Ceylonese Studies, Colombo, 1968, Am. Coun. Learned Socs. fellow India, 1973; fine arts rsch. scholar, 2002—. Fellow Am. Philos. Soc.; mem. Am. Inst. Indian Studies (trustee 1964-65), Am. Com. for History South Asian Art (dir. 1969-71). Home: 269 Payson Rd Belmont MA 02478-3406 Office Phone: 781-933-0157. E-mail: dkdn@netzero.com.

DOHENY, MICHAEL K., music educator; b. Camden, NJ, Sept. 13, 1970; s. Edward L. and Ellen B. Doheny; m. Jessica Schwartz, Sept. 15, 2001; 1 child, Patrick M. MusB, Rowan U., Glassboro, NJ, 1994. Music tchr. Edgewood Regional H.S., Atco, NJ, 1994—2001, Edgewood Regional Jr. H.S., 1994—96, Overbrook Regional H.S., Pine Hill, NJ, 1996—98, Winslow Twp. H.S., Atco, NJ, 2001—. Dir.: (festival honors chorus) Salem County Chorus, 2000, South Jersey Senior High Chorus, 2004; actor(singer): (musical theatre prodn.) Smokey Joe's Cafe (Outstanding Performance by a Featured Actor In a Musical, 2004). Mem.: South Jersey Choral Dirs. Assn., NJ. Music Educators' Assn., Am. Choral Dirs. Assn., Music Educators' Nat. Conf. Office: Winslow Twp High Sch 10 Coopers Folly Rd Atco NJ 08004 Office Phone: 856-767-1850 8644. Office Fax: 856-767-5670. E-mail: dohenymi@winslow-schools.com.

DOHERTY, BARBARA WHITEHURST, chemical purchasing manager; b. Charlotte, Jan. 18, 1935; d. Frank Joseph and Geneva Kathryn (Pease) Whitehurst; m. Martin William Doherty, Sr., June 23, 1956 (div. June, 1975); children: Martin William, Jr., Frank Whitehurst. BA in Religion magna cum laude, Duke U., 1956. Cert. notary pub., 1982-97. Rsch. asst., dept. sociology Duke U., Durham, N.C., 1953-56; sec. Pelham (N.Y.) Visiting Nurse & Family Svc., 1958-59; adminstrv. asst. Mecklenburg Times, Charlotte, N.C., 1972-73; bookkeeper Carolina Waterbed Co., Charlotte, N.C., 1972-74; mgr., purchasing and inventory control Reagents, Inc., Charlotte, N.C., 1974-97. Author: poems appear in: Southern Poetry Review, 1992, 1993, 1995, Charlotte Observer, 1993, Sparrowgrass Poetry Forum, 1997. Treas. Charlotte (N.C.) Fair Housing, 1968-70; mem. Charlotte-Mecklenburg Schs. Emergency Sch. Assistance Adv. Com., 1972; Co-chair Paul Leonard for City Council Campaign, Charlotte, 1970; friend of the ct. Swann vs. Bd. Edn., Charlotte, 1972; vol. Marylyn Huff for Sch. Bd., Charlotte, 1970, 74; founder ACLU, Charlotte, 1980 (sec., 1980-82, treas., 1982-84); vol. Harvey Gantt for Mayor campaign, Charlotte, 1983, 85; co-founder, treas. Parents and Friends of Lesbians and Gays, Charlotte, 1988-90; bd. mem. Metrolina Cmty. Svc. Project, Charlotte, 1990-93 (treas., 1992-93). Mem. Phi Beta Kappa, Sigma Delta Pi. Democrat. Avocations: politics, african travel. Home: 1419 Ferncliff Rd Charlotte NC 28211-2220

DOHERTY, BRIAN GERARD, alderman; b. Chgo., Oct. 25, 1957; s. Daniel Joseph and Kathleen (McDonagh) D.; m. Rose Mary Gillespie, 1986; children: Kathleen Marie, Kevin Michael. BA, U. N.E. Ill., 1984; MA in Urban Studies, Loyola U., Chgo., 2005. Alderman 41st Ward, Chgo., 1991—. Boxing champ Chgo. Pk. Dist., 1972, 73, Chgo. Golden Gloves champion Tribune Charities, 1973. Mem. Alpha Chi Honor Soc. Roman Catholic. Home: 7805 W Catalpa Ave Chicago IL 60656-1640 Office: 6650 N Northwest Hwy Chicago IL 60631-1307

DOHERTY, CHARLES VINCENT, investment advisor; b. Pitts., Dec. 17, 1933; s. Charles V. and Emma (Lager) D.; m. Marilyn Bongiorno, Oct. 17, 1964; children: Charles, Michelle, Kristen. BS, U. Notre Dame, 1955; MBA, U. Chgo., 1967. CPA, Ill. Tax specialist Haskins & Sells, CPA, Chgo., 1960-67; ptnr. Lamson Bros. & Co., Chgo., 1968-73; pres. Doherty Zable & Co., Chgo., 1974-85, Chgo. Stock Exch., Inc., 1986-92; mng. dir. Madison Adv. Group, Chgo., 1993—. Bd. dirs. Lakeside Bank, Howe Barnes Securities, Inc., Banc of Am. Fin. Products, Brauvin Capital Corp., Knight Capital Group, Inc; trustee Wayne Hummer Investment Trust, AHA Investment Funds. Office Phone: 312-280-9231. Personal E-mail: cdoherty@ameritech.net, milfordtrek@msn.com.

DOHERTY, JOHN JOSEPH, librarian, educator; s. John James and Kathleen Doherty; m. Lisa Anne Clark, June 20, 1992; children: Nicole Anne, Meghan Kathleen, Sarah Viola. BA in English with honors, U. Ulster, Coleraine, Northern Ireland, 1989; MA in English, U. Wales, Bangor, 1991; MA in Libr. Sci., U. Ariz., 1995. Asst. prof., reference libr. Mont. State U., Bozeman, 1996—98; undergraduate services libr. No. Ariz. U., Flagstaff, 1998—2003, libr. arts and letters, 2003—. Contbr. articles to profl. publs., chapters to books. Mem.: ALA, Prog. Librarians Guild, Am. Ednl. Rsch. Assn., Internat. Arthurian Soc., Ariz. Libr. Assn. (exec. bd. 2000—04, Intellectual Freedom award 2004). Office: No Ariz U Cline Library Flagstaff AZ 86011-6022 Office Phone: 928-523-8569. E-mail: john.doherty@nau.edu.

DOHERTY, KATHERINE MANN, librarian, writer; b. N.Y.C., July 11, 1951; d. Jack Howard Mann and Glenn (Ellis) Andrews; m. Craig A. Doherty, June 16, 1973; 1 child, Meghan Corinne. BA, U. N.Mex., 1973; MSLS, Simmons Coll., 1976. Cataloger Mass. Hist. Soc., Boston, 1976-79; libr. media specialist Zuni (N.Mex.) Pub. Sch.s, 1982-86; libr. dist. Zuni Pub. Schs., 1985-86; unified media specialist Nantucket (Mass.) Elem. Sch., 1986-87; dir. learning resources Fortier Libr., N.H. Cmty. Tech. Coll., Berlin, 1987—. Author: (children's books) Apaches and Navajos, 1989, Iroquois, 1989, (young adult books) Benazir Bhutto, 1990, The Zunis, 1993, Arnold Schwarzenegger, 1993, The Huron, 1994, The Narragansett, 1994, The Chickasaw, 1994, The Ute, 1994, The Chuilla, 1994, The Sioux, 1994, The Golden Gate Bridge, 1995, Hoover Dam, 1995, Mount Rushmore, 1995, Washington Monument, 1995, Gateway Arch, 1995, The Wampanoag, 1995, The Penobscot, 1995, The Astrodome, 1996, The Erie Canal, 1996, the Empire State Building, 1997, The Alaska Pipeline, 1997, Richard I and the Crusades, 2002, New Hampshire, 2005, Massachusetts, 2005, Rhode Island, 2005, others; pub. Field Trial Mag. Office: NH Com Tech Coll Libr 2020 Riverside Dr Berlin NH 03570-3717 Office Phone: 603-752-1113. E-mail: kdoherty@nhctc.edu.

DOHERTY, LARRY JOE, lawyer; b. Hillsboro, Tex., July 29, 1946; s. Johnnie Adrian Doherty and Thelma Francis King; m. Joanne Marie Johnson; children: Megan Elaine, Austin Duffy. BS, U. Houston, 1968, JD, 1970. Cert.: Tex. Bd. Legal Spec. (bd. cert. P.I. trial law) 1978. Lawyer Brown, Kronzer, Abraham, Watkins & Steel, Houston, 1969—74; ptnr. White, Wallace, Doherty & Powell, Houston, 1974—75, Denson, Vela, Doherty & Collins, Houston, 1975—76, Doherty, Vela, Poser, Sears & Collins, Houston, 1976—80, Doherty, Long, Wagner, Houston, 1980—. Chmn. grievancecom. State Bar, Houston, 1980—86; spkr. in field; mem. staff Trial Lawyers Coll., Wyo., 2000—. Lawyer: (TV series) Tex. Justice, 2000—04; contbr. poems to jours. Mem. exec. com. Tex. Dem. Party, 1980—82. Recipient Tex. Justice Day award, City of Houston, 2003, Disting. Svc. award, U. Houston Alumni Org., 2003. Mem.: Tex. Quail Coun., Wash. County Wildlife Soc. (pres. 2004). Avocations: wildlife, hunting, fishing, writing. Office: Doherty Long Wagner LLP 13810 Champion Forest Blvd 225 Houston TX 77069

DOHERTY, PETER CHARLES, immunologist; b. Brisbane, Australia, Oct. 15, 1940; s. Eric C. and Linda Doherty; m. Penelope Stephens, 1965; children: James, Michael. B.V.Sc, U. Queensland, Australia, 1963, MVSc, 1966; PhD, U. Edinburgh, Scotland, 1970; hon. doctorates from, 16 univs. Vet. officer Animal Rsch. Inst., Brisbane, Australia, 1963—67; sci. officer Moredun Rsch. Inst., Edinburgh, 1967—71; postdoctoral fellow John Curtin Sch. Med. Rsch., Canberra, Australia, 1972—75, prof., head dept. exptl. pathology, 1982—88; from assoc. prof. to prof. The Wistar Inst., Phila., 1975—82; mem., chmn. dept. immunology St. Jude Children's Rsch. Hosp., Memphis, 1988—2001; laureate prof. dept. microbiology and immunology U. Melbourne, Australia, 2002—. Bd. dirs. Internat. Lab. Animal Diseases, Nairobi, 1986—92; mem. exptl. virology study sect. NIH, 1982—83, 1990—. Contbr. chapters to books, articles to profl. jours. Co-recipient Nobel Prize for medicine, 1996; recipient Paul Ehrlich prize, Fed. Republic Germany, 1983, Gairdner Internat. award for med. sci., Can., 1986, Lasker award for Basic Med. Rsch., 1995. Fellow: Australian Acad. Sci., Royal Soc. London. Avocations: walking, reading. Office Phone: 61-3-8344-7968. Office Fax: 61-3-8344-7990. E-mail: peter.doherty@stjude.org, pcd@unimelb.edu.au.*

DOHERTY, ROBERT CUNNINGHAM, retired advertising executive; b. N.Y.C., Sept. 30, 1930; s. Francis Joseph and Helen (Utley) D.; m. Brucie Rial (div. 1961); children: Michael Bruce, Robert Kelly; m. Kerstin Brigetta Karlsson; children: Andrew Seger, Thomas Nils. BA, Princeton U., 1952. Account exec. Needham Harper Steers, N.Y.C., 1958-62, v.p., account supr., 1962-65; exec. v.p. John Rockwell and Assocs., N.Y.C., 1965-73, ptnr., chmn. bd., 1973-75; v.p. mgmt. group Wells, Rich & Greene, N.Y.C., 1975-79; sr. v.p. McKinney & Silver, Raleigh, N.C., 1979-83, exec. v.p., 1983-87, pres., 1987-90, chief exec. officer, 1991-97, chmn., 1993-98; ret., 1998. Trustee, mem. exec. com. N.C. Symphony, 1991—, chmn. bd. 2001-03; trustee, mem. exec. com. NC Mus. History, 1997—; trustee NC Mus. History Found., 2004-. Served to 1st lt. USMC, 1952-54, Korea. Mem. Figure Eight Yacht Club (Wilmington, NC), Ivy Club (Princeton, NJ), Cardinal Club (Raleigh, NC). Episcopalian. Office: 5 W Hargett St Raleigh NC 27601 Office Phone: 919-831-4761.

DOHERTY, SHANNEN, actress; b. Memphis, Apr. 12, 1971; d. Tom and Rosa D.; m. Ashley Hamilton, Sept. 24, 1993 (div. 1994); m. Rick Salomon, Jan. 25, 2003 (annulled 2003). Actor TV series Little House: A New Beginning, 1982-83, Our House, 1986-88, Beverly Hills, 90210, 1990-94, Charmed, 1998-2001, Scare Tactics, 2003, North Shore, 2004, Love, Inc., 2005; TV movies The Other Lover, 1985, Robert Kennedy and His Times, 1985, Obsessed, 1992, Rebel Highway: Jailbreakers, Showtime, 1994, A Burning Passion: The Margaret Mitchell Story, 1994, Gone in the Night, 1996, Sleeping with the Devil, 1997, The Ticket, 1997, Satan's School for Girls, 2000, Another Day, 2001, Hell on Heels: The Battle of Mary Kay, 2002, Nightlight, 2003; TV guest appearances include Father Murphy, 1981, Magnum, P.I., 1983, Airwolf, 1984, Highway to Heaven, 1985, 21 Jump Street, 1989, Life Goes On, 1989; films: Night Shift, 1982, (voice) The Secret of Nimh, 1982, Girls Just Want to Have Fun, 1985, Heathers, 1989, Blindfold: Acts of Obsession, 1993, Almost Dead, 1994, Mallrats, 1995, Nowhere, 1997, Striking Poses, 1999, The Rendering, 2002. Baptist.*

DOHERTY, STEVE, lawyer, state legislator; b. Great Falls, Mont., May 5, 1952; s. Arthur Frederick and Myra M. Doherty. BA, U. Pa., 1975; JD, Lewis & Clark Law Sch., 1984. Assoc. Spears, Lubersky, Campbell, Bledsoe, Anderson & Young, Portland, 1984-86; from assoc. to ptnr. Graybill, Ostrem, Warner & Crotty, Great Falls, Mont., 1986-92; assoc. Smith & Guenther, Great Falls, Mont., 1992-97; mem. Mont. Senate, Dist. 24, Great Falls, 1991—2003; majority whip, chmn. jud. com. Mont. Senate, Great Falls, Mont., 1993-94, mem. taxation and nat. resources com., 1991-94, mem. environ. quality coun. com., 1991-94, mem. edn. com., 1995, mem. fish and game and ethics com., 1997, minority leader, 1999-2001, mem. rules com., 1999—; ptnr. Smith & Doherty, Great Falls, 1998—2002, Smith, Doherty & Belcourt, P.C., Great Falls, 2003—. Chmn. Mont. Fish, Wildlife, and Parles Commn., 2005—. Mem. legis. del. to Taiwan, 2000, Mont. del. to Mnsfield Ctr. Conf. on Environment, Kumamoto, Japan, 2000; chmn. Mont. Fish, Wildlife and Parks Commn., 2003—; bd. dirs. Rural Employment Opportunities, Helena, 1990—92. Recipient Conservation Eagle award, N.W. Energy Coalition, 1999, Pub. Svc. award, Mont. Trial Lawyers Assn., 2001; Flemming fellow, Ctr. for Policy Alts., 1998, Eleanor Roosevelt Global fellow, Chile, 2001. Mem. Great Falls Pub. Radio Assn. (bd. dirs. 1986-91). Democrat. Avocations: hunting, fishing, hiking, skiing, western history. Office: Smith Doherty & Belcourt PC 410 Central Ave Ste 522 Great Falls MT 59401-3128 Fax: 406-452-9787. Office Phone: 406-452-9791.

DOHERTY, THOMAS, publisher; b. Hartford, Conn., Apr. 23, 1935; Thomas and Elizabeth (Story) D.; m. Barbara Slocum, Feb. 14, 1958 (dec.); children: Thomas, Kathleen, Linda; m. Tatiana Pachina, July 19, 1991; 1 stepchild, Elena. Student, Trinity Coll., 1953-57. From salesman to divsn. sales mgr. Pocket Books, 1958—68; nat. sales mgr. Simon & Schuster, 1968—70; pub. Tempo Books, 1971-75; pub., gen. mgr. Ace and Tempo divsns. Grossett & Dunlap Inc., 1976-80; founder, pres. Tom Doherty Assocs., Inc., N.Y.C., 1980-87; pres., pub. Tor & Forge Imprints of Tom Doherty Assocs. LLC, A Holtzbrinck Co., N.Y.C., 1987—, Tor and Forge Books. Winner Skylark award, Locus award for best pub. sci. and fantasy, annually, 1987—. Mem. World Sci. Fiction Assn. (charter), Nat. Space Inst. Roman Catholic. Home: 280 Park Ave S Apt 15A New York NY 10010-6131 Address: 23 Terry's Trl East Hampton NY 11937 Office: Tor Books 175 Fifth Ave New York NY 10010-7703 Office Phone: 646-307-5503. Personal E-mail: tom.doherty@tor.com.

DOHERTY, WILLIAM THOMAS, JR., historian, retired educator; b. Cape Girardeau, Mo., Mar. 30, 1923; s. William Thomas and Kittie (Baird) D.; m. Dorothy Ashley Huff Zienowicz, Aug. 13, 1947; children: Victor Sargent, Dorothy Ashley, Catherine Baird, Julia Holbrook, William Thomas III. AB, BS, S.E. Mo. State U., 1943; MA, Am. U., 1950; PhD, U. Mo., 1951. Instr. history Westminster Coll., Fulton, Mo., 1947-48, Christian Coll., 1949-50, U. Mo., 1948-49, 50-51; asst. prof. history U. Miss., 1951-53, assoc. prof. history, 1956-58, prof., chmn. dept. history, 1958-61; asst. prof., then assoc. prof. history U. Ark., 1953-56; prof. history, dir. Ford Found. 3 yr. Master's program Kan. State U., Manhattan, 1961-63; prof. history, chmn. dept. W.Va. U., Morgantown, 1963-79, univ. historian, 1979-88, prof. emeritus, 1988—. Author: Louis Houck: Missouri Historian and Entrepreneur, 1960, Berkeley, U.S.A.: A Bicentennial History of a Virginia and West Virginia County 1772-1972, 1972, West Virginia History, 1974, West Virginia University: Symbol of Unity in a Sectionalized State, 1982, West Virginia Studies, 1984, West Virginia: Our Land, Our People, 1990; editor: Minerals, Vol. IV in Conservation History of the United States, 1971; editor in chief West Virginia History Jour., 1979-88; contbr. numerous articles to profl. jours. Served with AUS, 1943-46. Decorated Bronze star medal, 1946. Mem. Am. Hist. Assn., So. Hist. Assn., Orgn. Am. Historians, AAUP, Kappa Delta Pi, Sigma Tau Delta, Phi Alpha Theta. Democrat. Home: 15115 Interlachen Dr Apt 214 Silver Spring MD 20906-5638

DOHMAN, GLORIA ANN, librarian; b. Vermillion, S.D., June 19, 1949; d. Marlyn Doyle and Dorothy Marie (Peterson) Edman; student Ball State U., 1973; B.A., Sioux Falls Coll., 1971; M.S., Tri-Coll. U., 1984; m. Terry L. Dohman, Aug. 16, 1970; children— Robb Quincy, Kristin LeeAnn. Librarian/audio visual coordinator U.S. Dependent Schs., Hahn AFB, W.Ger., 1973-74; library coordinator/dir. Wahpeton (N.D.) Public Schs. and Leach Public Library, Wahpeton, 1974-76; periodicals/media librarian N.D. State Sch. Sci., Wahpeton, 1976—; del. White House Conf. Libraries and Info. Services, 1979; del. N.D. Gov.'s Conf. on Libraries and Info. Services, 1978. Trustee, Leach Public Library, 1977-83, chmn. bd., 1978-80. Mem. ALA, N.D. Library Assn. (sec. acad. sect. 1981-83), LWV (chpt. dir. 1977-79), Mountain Plains Library Assn., AAUW. Lutheran. Home: 1502 14th Ave N Wahpeton ND 58075-5013

DOHMEN, FREDERICK HOEGER, retired pharmaceutical executive; b. Milw., May 12, 1917; s. Fred William and Viola (Gutsch) D.; m. Gladys Elizabeth Dite, Dec. 23, 1939 (dec. 1963); children: William Francis, Robert Charles; m. Mary Alexander Holgate, June 27, 1964. *Great-grandfather, Frederick Dohmen, a German immigrant, founded The F. Dohmen Co. in 1858, 147 years ago. It has been both owned and managed by five successive* *generations of Dohmens, which makes it unique in America. Begun in Milwaukee, it now has four wholesale distribution centers stretching from Alabama to Minnesota, plus three pharmacy-related subsidiaries. Son, Robert, together with his cousin, constitute the fifth generation and the present top management.* BA in Commerce, U. Wis., 1939. With F. Dohmen Co., Milw., 1939—82, pres., 1952—82, dir., 1947—2004, chmn. bd., 1952-82; ret., 2004. Travel lectr. various orgns., 1980—. Bd. dirs. St. Luke's Hosp. Ednl. Found., Milw., 1965-83, pres., 1969-72, chmn. bd., 1972-73; bd. dirs. U. Wis. Milw. Found., 1976-79, bd. visitors, 1978-88, emeritus mem., 1988—; assoc. chmn. Nat. Bible Week, Laymen's Nat. Bible Com., N.Y.C;., 1968-82, mem. coun. of advisors, 1983—; elder Presbyn. Ch.; bd. dirs. Riveredge Nature Ctr., Newburg, Wis., 1993-94. Mem. Nat. Wholesale Druggists Assn. (chmn. mfr. rels. com. 1962, resolutions com. 1963, bd. control 1963-66), Nat. Assn. Wholesalers (trustee 1966-75), Druggists Svc. Coun. (dir. 1967-71), Wis. Pharm. Assn., Miss. Valley Drug Club, Univ. Club Town Club (Milw.), Beta Gamma Sigma, Phi Eta Sigma, Delta Kappa Epsilon. Home: 3903 W Mequon Rd Mequon WI 53092-2727

DOHMEN, JOHN F., pharmaceutical executive; From mem. staff to pres., CEO F. Dohmen, Germantown, Wis., 1980—95, pres., 1995—, CEO, 1995—. Finalist, Ernst & Young Entrepreneur of Yr., 2003. Mem.: Healthcare Distbn. Mgmt. Assn. (chmn. 2001), Nat. Wholesale Druggist's Assn. (chmn. 2000). Office: F Dohmen W 194 N 11381 McCormick Dr Germantown WI 53022

DOHMEN, MARY HOLGATE, retired primary school educator; b. Gary, Ind., July 28, 1918; d. Clarence Gibson and Margaret Alexander (Kinnear) Holgate; m. Frederick Hoeger Dohmen, June 27, 1964; children: William Francis, Robert Charles. BS, Milw. State Tchrs. Coll., 1940; M of Philosophy, U. Wis., 1945. Cert. tchr., Wis. Tchr. primary grades Baraboo (Wis.) Pub. Schs., 1940-43, Whitefish Bay (Wis.) Pub. Schs., 1943-64. Contbr. articles, story, poems to various pubs. Bd. dirs. Homestead H.S. chpt. Am. Field Svc., Mequon, Wis., 1970-80; mem. Milw. Aux. VNA, 1975—, 2d v.p., 1983-85, Milw. Pub. Mus. Enrichment Club, 1975—, Boys and Girls Club of Greater Milw., 1986—; vol. Reading is Fun program, 1987—, Milw. Symphony Orch. League, 1960—, Ptnrs. in Conservation, World Wildlife Fund, Washington, 1991—, Milw. Art Mus. Garden Club, 1979—, com. chmn., 1981-86; mem. Chancellor's Soc. U. Wis.-Milw., 1991—; travel lectr. various orgns., 1980—. Mem. AAUW, Milw. Coll. Endowment Assn. (v.p. 1987-90, pres. 1991-93), Bascom Hill Soc. (U. Wis.), Woman's Club Wis., Alpha Phi (pres. Milw. alumnae 1962-64), Pi Lambda Theta (pres. Milw. alumnae 1962-64), Delta Kappa Gamma. Republican. Presbyterian. Avocations: writing, travel, nature. Home: 3903 W Mequon Rd Mequon WI 53092-2727

DOHNANYI, CHRISTOPH VON, musician, conductor; b. Berlin, Sept. 8, 1929; s. Hans and Christine (Bonhoeffer) Von Dohnányi. Student, U. Munich, Hochschule fuer Musik, Munich, Fla. State U., Berkshire Music Ctr.; doctorate (hon.), Oberlin Coll., Cleve. Inst. Music, Kent State U., Case Western Res. U., Eastman Sch. Music, 1998. Coach, condr., asst. to Sir George Solti Frankfurt (Germany) Opera, 1952-57, gen. music dir., artistic dir., 1968-77; gen. music dir. Lubeck, Germany, 1957-63, Kassel, Germany, 1963-66; chief conductor West German Radio Symphony Orch., Cologne, 1964-70; artistic dir., chief condr., intendant Hamburg (Germany) State Opera, 1977-84; music dir. designate Cleve. Orch., 1982-84, music dir., 1984—2002; prin . guest conductor Philharmonia Orch., London, 1995—97, prin. condr., 1997—. Guest conductor Salzburg Festival, Chatelet Paris, Zurich Opera House, Israel Philharm., Orchestre de Paris, Vienna Philharm., Berlin Philharm. Recordings with Vienna Philharmonia include opera Wozzeck, Lulu, Fidelio, Flying Dutchman, Salome, 5 Mendelssohn symphonies, works by Stravinsky, Tschaikovsky, Glass, Schnittke, recordings with Cleve. orch. include symphonies of Beethoven, Brahms, Schumann, Bruckner, Dvorak, Mahler, Mozart, Schubert, orchestral works by Bartok, Lutoslawski, R. Strauss, Webern, Ives, Ruggles, Birtwistle, opera Rheingold, Walkure. Recipient Scopus award, Am. Friends of Hebrew U. in Jerusalem, 1996, Scroll of Remembrance for Von Dohnányi and Bonhoeffer Families in German resistance U.S. Holocaust Mus., Washington, 1995, Condr. of Yr. award Musical Am., 1992, Comdr.'s Cross Republic of Austria, 1992, Comdr. de L'Ordre des Arts et des Lettres, France, Cross Order of Merit, Cross Order of Merit, Germany, Bartok prize, Hungary, 1982, Goethe medal City of Frankfurt, 1979, Richard Straus prize Munich, 1951, Torch of Liberty award Anti Defamation League, 2001. Address: Colbert Artists Mgmt 111 W 57th St Ste 1416 New York NY 10019-2211 Office: Philharmonia Orch 125 High Holborn 1 FL London WCIV6QA England

DOHNER, JOHN MICHAEL, lawyer; b. Akron, Ohio, June 9, 1955; BS, U. Akron, 1980, JD, 1986. Atty. Umbaugh, Sharp & Dohner, Hudson, Ohio, 1986-90, Buckingham, Doolittle & Burroughs, Akron, 1990—. Asst. prosecuting atty. Portgage County, Ohio, Ravenna, 1987; bd. mem. Arc of Summit and Portage Counties, Akron, 1987—, pres., 1992—; bd. mem. Citizen Adv. Bd. N.E. Ohio Devel. Ctrs., 1980-83. Named Vol. of Yr., State of Ohio, Dept. Mental Retardation and Devel. Disabilities, Columbus, 1980. Mem. ABA (family law sect.), Ohio State Bar Assn. (family law sect.), Akron Bar Assn. (vice chair family law sect. 1992, chair family law sect. 1993). Office: Buckingham Doolittle & Burroughs PO Box 1500 Akron OH 44309-1500

DOHRENWEND, BRUCE PHILIP, epidemiologist, social sciences educator; b. N.Y.C., July 26, 1927; s. Gustav John and Gertrude Elise (Funke) D.; m. Barbara Anne Snell, Sept. 21, 1951 (dec. June 1982); m. Catherine J. Douglass, June 1, 1985 BA, Columbia U., 1950, MA, 1952; PhD, Cornell U., 1955. Cert. psychologist, N.Y. Research assoc. Cornell U., Ithaca, N.Y., 1954-58; research assoc. Columbia U., N.Y.C., 1958-63, asst. prof., 1963-67, assoc. prof., 1967-70, prof., 1970—; chief of rsch. dept. social psychiatry N.Y. State Psychiat. Inst., N.Y.C., 1979—. Mem. task panel on problems, scope and boundaries Presl. Commn. on Mental Health, Washington, 1977-78; head task group on behavioral effects Presl. Commn. on Accident at Three Mile Island, Washington, 1979; mem. tech. evaluation bd. Vietnam Era Veterans study, VA, Washington, 1983-89. Author: (with others) Social Status and Psychological Disorder, 1969, Mental Illness in the United States, 1980, (with others) Socioeconomic Status and Psychiatric Disorders, 1992; editor: (with others) Stressful Life Events, 1974, Stressful Life Events and Their Contexts, 1981 Served with USNR, 1945-46 Recipient Research Scientist award NIMH, 1971, 76, 81, 86, 91, Emily Mumford award Columbia U., 1992; NIMH grantee, 1964-82, 77—. Fellow AAAS (co-recipient prize for behavioral rsch. 1990), APA (co-recipient disting. contbns. div. community psychology award 1980), Am. Psychopathol. Assn. (Hamilton award 1994); mem. Am. Pub. Health Assn. (co-recipient Rema Lapouse Mental Health Epidemiology award 1981), Am. Sociol. Assn. (Leo G. Reeder award for disting. contbn. med. sociology sect. 1999), Soc. for Study of Social Problems (Disting. Contbrs. award divsn. psychiat. sociology 1994). Home: 1056 5th Ave New York NY 10028-0112 Office: NY State Psychiat Inst 1051 Riverside Dr Unit 8 New York NY 10032-1013

DOHRMANN, RUSSELL WILLIAM, manufacturing executive; b. Clinton, Iowa, June 29, 1942; s. Russell Wilbert and Anita Doris (Miller) D.; m. Rita Marie Meade, Dec. 26, 1964 (dec. Feb. 1978); m. M. Jean Stapleton, Aug. 18, 1979. BS, Upper Iowa U., 1965; MBA, Drake U., 1971. Acct. Chamberlain Mfg. Corp., Clinton, 1965-66, plant controller Derry, Pa., 1967-68; fin. analyst Frye Copysystems Inc., Des Moines, 1968-71, v.p., controller, 1971-77, pres., 1980-97, also bd. dirs.; internat. controller Wheelabrator-Frye, N.Y.C., 1977-78; pres. FryeTech, Inc., Des Moines, 1997-98; group controller Wheelabrator-Frye, Des Moines, 1978-80; cons., 1998—. Mem. Nat. Assn. Accts., Des. Moines C. of C. Republican. Methodist. Personal E-mail: windyridge@mchsi.com.

DOHRN, BERNARDINE, law educator, advocate; BA, U. Chgo., 1963, MA, JD, 1967. Atty. Sidley & Austin, New York, 1984—88; litig. legal assoc. Office of Pub. Guardian, Cook County Juvenile Div., 1988—90; legal rschr. Children's Rights Project, Roger Baldwin Found., ACLU, 1990—91, Legal Assistance Found., Homeless Advocacy Project, 1991; dir. Juvenile Ct. Project Northwestern U. Sch. Law, 1991—92, dir. Children and Family Justice Ctr., 1992—, clin. assoc. prof. Bluhm Legal Clinic, 2000—. Adj. faculty U. Ill./Chgo., Dept. Criminal Justice, 2000—02; vis. law faculty Vrieje U., Amsterdam, 2002—; assoc. prof. Coll. of U. Chgo., 2003, 04; steering com. Ill. Family Violence Coordinating Com., 1994—, Ill. State Ct. Improvement Project, 1996—; adv. bd. Kellogg Sch. Mgmt. Non-Profit Prog., 1997—; mem. Expert Work Group Adoption 2002 Project, U.S. Dept. Health and Human Svcs. Contbr. articles to law jours.; author: Zero Tolerance: Resisting the Drive for Punishment in Our Schools, 2001, A Century of Juvenile Justice, 2002. Mem.: ABA (founding co-chair Task Force on Children 1992—96, adv. com. Immigration Pro Bono Devel. and Bar Activation Prog. 2001—), Human Rights Watch (bd. mem. Children's Rights Project 1995—), Chgo. Reporter (co-chair 1997—, bd. dirs. 1999—). Office: Northwestern U Sch Law 357 E Chicago Ave Chicago IL 60611-3069 E-mail: b-dohrn@law.northwestern.edu.

DOIG, JAMESON WALLACE, political science professor; b. Oakland, Calif., June 12, 1933; s. James Rufus and Mary (Jameson) D.; m. Joan Nishimoto, Oct. 8, 1955; children: Rachel, Stephen, Sean. AB, Dartmouth Coll., 1954; M.P.A., Princeton U., 1958, MA, 1959, PhD, 1961. Research asst. N.J. Republican Com., 1957; staff mem. Brookings Instn., 1959-61; from asst. prof. to prof. politics and pub. affairs Princeton U., 1961—2004, prof. emeritus, 2004—, sr. rsch. scholar, 2004—; assoc. dean Woodrow Wilson Sch., Princeton U., 1972-73, dir. univ. research program in criminal justice, 1973-93. Dir. grad.studies dept. polit. sci. Princeton U., 1988—90, chair undergrad. studies, 1991—94, chair dept. polit. sci., 1997—2000; dir. Mamdouha S. Bobst Ctr. for Peace and Justice, 2000—04, chair Can. studies, 2002—04, chair athletics com., 2002—03; cons. Fels Fund, 1966—68, Daniel and Florence Guggenheim Found., 1970—, Nat. Prison Overcrowding Project, 1983, Lavenburg Found., 1983—90; vis. prof. John Jay Coll. Criminal Justice, 1967—68, 1970—72; mem. adv. com. Gov. N.J., 1965—71, Vera Inst. Justice, 1986—92; mem. NRC/Trans. Rsch. Bd., 1990—92; mem. adv. coun. N.J. Dept. Corrections, 1974—82, vice-chmn., 1980—82, cons. on parole to gov. of N.J., 1975—78; dir. Guggenheim Summer Intern. Program, 1997—. Author: Metropolitan Transportation Politics and the New York Region, 1966, (with D.E. Mann) The Assistant Secretaries, 1965, (with D.T. Stanley and D.E. Mann) Men Who Govern, 1967, (with M. Danielson) New York: The Politics of Urban Regional Development, 1982, Empire on the Hudson, 2001; co-author, editor: Criminal Corrections: Ideals and Realities, 1983, Leadership and Innovation, 1987, 90, Combating Corruption/Encouraging Ethics, 1990; contbr. Governing the States and Localities, 1969, Agenda for a City, 1970, Metropolitan Politics, 1971, Urban Politics and Policy-Making, 1973, Crime and Criminal Justice, 1975, Public Administration of Law Enforcement Policies, 1979, Politics of Urban Development, 1987, Public Authorities and Public Policy, 1991, Landscape of Modernity, 1992, Studies in American Political Development, 1993, Technology and Culture, 1994, Building the Public City, 1995, Seaport, 2001, Innovation, 2002, Art of Structural Design, 2003, Textual Studies in Canada, 2004. Served to lt. (j.g.) USNR, 1954-56. Recipient Herbert Kaufman award, 1989, A.P. Usher prize, 1995, A. Wildavsky award, 1997, Abel Wolman award, 2001, Humanities Honor award, 2002. Mem. Am. Correctional Assn., Am. Polit. Sci. Assn., Am. Soc. Pub. Adminstrn., Law and Soc. Assn., Soc. History of Technology, Policy Studies Orgn., Pub. Works Hist. Soc. (bd. dirs. 2003—), Can. Studies Assn., Phi Beta Kappa. Office: Princeton U Bobst Hall Princeton NJ 08544-0001 Office Phone: 609-258-4808. Business E-Mail: jimdoig@princeton.edu.

DOIRON, MATTHEW ROBERT, band director, music teacher; b. Sanford, Maine, Feb. 25, 1968; s. Wilfred Lionel and Susan Marie (McIntyre) D.; children: Kelsey Lauren, Jensen Kylie; m. Jennifer L. Thompson, June 26, 2004 MusB in Music Edn., Keene State Coll., 1990. Cert. tchr. gen. edn. and choral music, Maine, N.H., Vt. Dir. music Sch. Adminstrv. Dist. # 6, Claremont, N.H., 1990-92; dir. instrumental music Sanford H.S., 1992—. Band mgr. Maine Dist. Concert Band, York County, 1994-2002; music dir. Strafford Wind Symphony, 1995—. Mem. Maine Band Dirs. Assn., Nat. Band Assn. (state chair), Music Educators Nat. Conf. E-mail: mdoiron@gwi.net, mdoioron@sanford.org.

DOKE, MARSHALL J., JR., lawyer; b. Wichita Falls, Tex., June 9, 1934; s. Marshall J. and Mary Jane (Johnson) D.; m. Betty Marie Orsini, June 2, 1956; children: Gregory J., Michael J., Laetitia Marie. BA magna cum laude, Hardin-Simmons U., 1956; LLB magna cum laude, So. Meth. U., 1959. Bar: Tex. 1959. Founding ptnr. Rain Harrell Emery Young & Doke, Dallas, 1965-87; assoc. Thompson, Knight, Wright & Simmons, Dallas, 1959, 62-65; founding ptnr. Doke & Riley, Dallas, 1987-92; ptnr. McKenna & Cuneo, 1993-96, Gardere Wynne Sewell L.L.P., Dallas, 1996—. Gen. counsel Tex. Rep. Party, 1976-77; mem. adv. coun. U.S. Ct. Fed. Claims, 1982—; mem. fed. acquisitions adv. panel U.S. OMB, 2005—. Author: Ann. Procurement Rev., Govt. Contractor Briefing Papers, Contract Changes, Fed. Contract Mgmt., 1982—, also articles; editor-in-chief: Southwestern Law Jour., 1958-59. Pres. Hope Cottage-Children's Bur., Inc., 1969-70, Hope Cottage Found., 1997-2002, pres., 1998-2002; bd. visitors Law Sch., So. Meth. U., 1966-69, McDonald Obs., U. Tex., 1990—; dir. Tex. Hist. Found., 1993—, v.p., 1996-98, pres. 2000-2004, chmn., 2004—; law com., bd. trustees So. Meth. U., 1977-78; bd. dirs., pres. World Trade Assn., Dallas-Ft. Worth, 1979-80; chmn. bd. dirs. Internat. Trade Assn. Dallas/Ft. Worth, 1993-94; bd. dirs., sec. Mayor's Internat. Com., City of Dallas, 1984-87, mem. Judicial Nominating Commn., Dallas, 1997—, vice chair, 1998-2000, chair, 2000—. 1st lt. JAGC, U.S. Army, 1959-62. Fellow Am. Bar Found., Tex. Bar Found.; mem. ABA (chmn. sect. pub. contract law 1969-70, ho. of dels. 1970-72, 74-2003, bd. govs. 1980-82, nominating com. 1988-91, 2000-2003, chmn. conf. sect. dels. 1991-2003, standing com. on audit 2003—), Tex. Bar Assn., U.S. Ct. of Fed. Claims Bar Assn. (bd. govs. 1987-2001, pres. 1996), Bd. of Contract Appeals Bar Assn. (pres. 1988-90, bd. govs. 1988—), Am. Bar Retirement Assn. (bd. dirs., trustee 1980-84, pres 1982-84), Nat. Conf. Lawyers and CPAs (co-chmn. 1983-85), Nat. Contract Mgmt. Assn. (nat. bd. advisors 1983—), Dallas C. of C. (chmn. internat. com. 1979-83). Home: 11 Glenmeadow Ct Dallas TX 75225 Office: Gardere Wynne Sewell LLP Thanksgiving Tower 1601 Elm St Ste 3000 Dallas TX 75201-7254 Office Fax: 214-999-3733. Business E-Mail: mdoke@gardere.com.

DOKIC, SINISA, library and information scientist; b. Vinkovci, Croatia, Jan. 22, 1964; s. Selimir Dokic and Sofija Vukov; m. Shira Loewenberg, June 28, 1997; children: Gavrilo Loewenberg, Emanuilo, Rafailo. BA, Faculty of Philosophy, U. Belgrade, Belgrade, 1997; MS in libr. and info sci., Pratt Inst., 2000; MA in philosophy, New Sch. U., 2002; post grad, U. Belgrade. Freelance translator, interpreter, editor, Zagreb, Croatia, 1988—94; info. and lang. asst. United Nations, Topusko, Croatia, 1995—96, asst. editor, dtp operator Vukovar, Croatia, 1996—97; database adminstr. Paul, Weiss, Rifkind, Wharton & Garrison, N.Y.C., NY, 1998; libr. info. asst. NY Pub. Libr., N.Y.C., NY, 1998—2001; head of history and polit. sci., supervising libr. Mid-Manhattan Libr., NY Pub. Libr., N.Y.C., NY, 2002—04, head of gen. reference svc., supervising libr., 2004—. Project leader, editor Open Soc. Inst., Zagreb, Croatia. Contbr. periodical (philosophy);, musician various guitar performances; editor: (book (philosophy, asian studies) Sudesika. Recipient Pratt Merit award, Pratt Inst., 1999-2000; fellow, Royal Asiatic Soc., 1994; grantee, Open Soc. Inst., 1994-1998; scholar, New Sch. U., Grad. Faculty of Polit. and Social Sci., 2000-2002, NY Pub. Libr., 1999-2002, Pratt Libr. Sch. Grad. Assn., 1999-2000, H. W. Wilson, 1999-2000. Fellow: Royal Asiatic Soc.; mem.: Am. Oriental Soc., Serbian Philos. Assn., Am. Philos. Assn., ALA. Office: Mid Manhattan Libr 455 Fifth Ave New York NY 10015 Office Phone: 212-340-0824.

DOKURNO, ANTHONY DAVID, lawyer; b. Gardner, Mass., Mar. 14, 1957; s. Anthony Chester and Damey Anteena (Aleson) D. BA, Holy Cross Coll., 1979; JD, Vt. Law Sch., 1982; postgrad., Johns Hopkins U., 1993-94. Bar: Mass. 1982, U.S. Ct. Appeals for the Armed Forces 1986, U.S. Supreme Ct. 1987. Pvt. practice, Fitchburg, Mass., 1982-86; appellate counsel Navy-Marine Corps Appellate Rev. Activity, Navy JAG, Washington, 1986-88; atty. admiralty law divsn. Navy JAG, Washington, 1988-90, atty. ops. and mgmt., 1991-93. Assoc. counsel, bd. vets. appeals Dept. Vets. Affairs, 1994-96; analyst Dept. of Def., 1996—. Comdr. USNR, 1998—. Mem.: Nat. Cryptologic History Found., Maritime Law Assn., Mensa, Naval Res. Assn., Amnesty Internat., Am. Legion, Phi Beta Kappa.

DO KYUNG, KIM, materials scientist, researcher; b. Seoul, Korea (South), Mar. 22, 1970; s. Kim Tae Yoon and Choi Jung Sook. Bsc, Myong Ji U., KyungKiDo, South Korea, 1989—92, Msc., 1993—95; Tech. Licentiate, Royal Inst. of Tech. (KTH), Stockholm, 1999—2001, PhD, 2001—02. Sr. rschr. Dept. of Materials Sci. and Engring., Royal Inst. of Tech., Stockholm, 2002—03; vis. scientist Dept. of Ceramics and Materials Engring., Rutgers U., NJ, 2003—; postdoctoral fellow Dept. of Elec. Engring. and Computer Sci., MIT, Cambridge, Mass., 2004—. Pres. Eurokorean Network, Seoul, Korea (South), 1999—. Author: (journal) Applied Physics Letters, Langmuir, Chemistry of Materials, Macromolecular Rapid Communications, Journal of Nanoparticle Research, Scripta Materials, J. Magn. Magn. Mater. Pvt. U.S. Army, 1995—97, South Korea. Recipient Best poster presentation award, MRS 2001 spring meeting, San Francisco, USA, 2001, Nano2000, Sendai, Japan, 2000; scholar A Tchg. Assistantship, Myong Ji U., 1993, 5 Fellowship Awards, 1989-1992. Achievements include patents for Gold coated superparamagnetic iron oxide nanoparticle for biomedical applications. Home: 109 -801 World 3rd APT Janggi Dong Kyung Gi Do Kimpso-Si 415-744 Republic of Korea Office: MIT Dept of Electrical Engring and Comp Sci 155 Massachusetts Ave N10-202 Cambridge MA 02139 Home Fax: +82-31-981-6182. Personal E-mail: scoop_kim@hanmail.net. Business E-Mail: dokyung@mit.edu.

DOLAN, ANDREW KEVIN, lawyer; b. Chgo., Dec. 7, 1945; s. Andrew O. and Elsie Dolan; children: Andrew, Francesca, Melinda. BA, U. Ill., Chgo., 1967; JD, Columbia U., 1970, MPH, 1976, DPH, 1980. Bar: Wash. 1980. Asst. prof. law Rutgers-Camden Law Sch., N.J., 1970-72; assoc. prof. law U. So. Calif., L.A., 1972-75; assoc. prof. pub. health U. Wash., Seattle, 1977-81; ptnr. Bogle & Gates, Seattle, 1988-93; pvt. practice law, 1993—. Commr. Civil Svc. Commn., Lake Forest Park, Wash., 1981; mcpl. judge City of Lake Forest Park, 1982-98. Russell Sage fellow, 1975. Mem. Order of Coif, Washington Athletic Club. Avocation: book collecting. Office: 5500 Columbia Ctr 701 5th Ave Seattle WA 98104-7096 Office Phone: 206-623-9803.

DOLAN, CHARLES FRANCIS (CHARLES "CHUCK" DOLAN), media and entertainment company executive; b. Cleveland, Ohio, Oct. 16, 1926; m. Helen Ann Burgess; children: Patrick, Tom, James, MariAnne, Kathleen, Deborah. Student, John Carroll U. Founder Sterling Manhattan Cable, 1961, Teleguide, Inc., HBO, 1971, Cablevision, Sterling Manhattan Cable, 1973; mng. gen. ptnr. Cablevision and predecessor firms, 1973—85; chmn. Cablevision Systems Corp., Woodbury, NY, 1985—. Mng. dir. Met. Opera, N.Y.C.; majority owner Madison Square Garden Properties, 1995—, also bd. dirs. Bd. dirs., bd. govs. St. Francis Hosp., L.I., NY; bd. dirs. Cold Spring Harbor Lab.; trustee Fairfield U., Conn. Served USAF. Avocation: sailing. Office: Cablevision Systems Corp 1111 Stewart Ave Bethpage NY 11714-3581 Office Phone: 516-803-2300. Office Fax: 516-803-2273.*

DOLAN, DENNIS JOSEPH, pilot, lawyer; b. St. Louis, Mar. 19, 1946; s. Robert Glennon and Lucille Anne (Stanley) D.; m. Aura Maritza Vargas, June 8, 1974; children: Dennis J. Jr., Rebecca and Robert (twins). BSc, Spring Hill Coll., Mobile, Ala., 1967; JD cum laude, St. Louis U., 1985. Bar: Mo. 1985, U.S. Dist. Ct. (ea. dist.) Mo. 1987. Commd. 2nd lt. USMC, 1967, advanced through grades to capt., 1970, resigned, 1976; served to maj. USMCR; flew in numerous combat missions, 2 combat tours Vietnam; airline pilot Western Air Lines, LA, 1976-87, Delta Air Lines, Inc., Atlanta, 1987—; pvt. practice law Clayton, Mo., 1985-88. Mem. ABA, ATLA, Air Line Pilots Assn. (bd. dirs. 1992-94, exec. v.p. 1994-96, chmn. Delta Master exec. coun. 1996-98, 1st v.p. 1999—), Internat. Fedn. Airline Pilot Assns. (prin. v.p. profl. affairs 2000-03, pres., 2003—). Roman Catholic. Avocations: skiing, woodworking. Home: PO Box 906 Roswell GA 30077-0906

DOLAN, EDWARD CHARLES, lawyer; b. N.Y.C., Sept. 25, 1953; s. Eamonn Ignatius and Mary Theresa (Golden) D.; m. Margaret Mary Vaughan, Nov. 29, 1980; children: Caroline, William. BA, Columbia U., 1975; JD, Georgetown U., 1978. Bar: Md. 1978, D.C. 1979, U.S. Dist. Ct. Md. 1980, U.S. Dist. Ct. D.C. 1980, U.S. Supreme Ct. 1983, U.S. Ct. of Appeals (4th cir.), U.S. Dist. Ct. Colo. 1997. Intern Office of U.S. Atty., ea. dist., N.Y., 1977; law clk. Dept. Justice Drug Enforcement Adminstrn., Washington, 1978; assoc. Beckett Cromwell & Myers, Bethesda, Md., 1978-84, Hogan and Hartson L.L.P., Washington, D.C., 1984-87, counsel, 1987-89, ptnr., 1989—. Chandler Bankruptcy Inn of Ct., Washington, 1990—; mem. standing com. local rules Bankruptcy Ct., Md., 1984—, chair, 1996-97. Author: (with others) The Law of Distressed Real Estate, 1988, Practice Manual for the Maryland Lawyer, 1989, 3d edit., 2001; contbg. author: Environmental Aspects of Real Estate Transactions, 1995. Pres. De Chantal Parish Home and Sch. Assn., Bethesda, 1990-92; active De Chantal Parish Sch. Bd., Bethesda, 1992-96, pres., 1994-96; mem. parents' coun. St. Anselm's Abbey Sch., Washington, 1995—2002, co-pres. 2001-02; active Columbia Coll. Secondary Schs. Com., N.Y.C., 1978-92; class co-chmn. Columbia Coll. Club, Washington, 1990-92. Mem. ABA, Fed. Bar Assn. (dir. Md. chpt., 2002—), Am.Bankruptcy Inst., Md. State Bar Assn., Montgomery County Bar Assn. (chmn. bankruptcy com. 1990-91), Prince George's County Bar Assn. (spl. com. on professionalism 1988-90), Bankruptcy Bar Assn. (Md. pres. 1989-90, dir. 1988—), D.C. Bar Assn. (chmn. bus. bankruptcy com. 1995—)99. Office: Hogan and Hartson LLP Columbia Square 555 13th St NW Ste 800E Washington DC 20004-1109

DOLAN, EDWARD FRANCIS, writer; b. Oakland, Calif., Feb. 10, 1924; s. Edward Francis Sr. and Zelda Olympia (Vieira) D.; m. Rose Esther Puddefoot, Nov. 17, 1945 (dec.); children: Timothy L. (dec.), Wendy Anne Irving. Student, U. So. Calif., L.A., 1942-43, U. San Francisco, 1958-59. Free-lance writer KRON-TV, Bay Area Pub. Schs. TV Coun., Pub. Svc. telecasts for Archdiocese, San Francisco, 1949-53; instr. dept. speech and drama Monticello Coll., Alton, Ill., 1953-56; writer, 1957—. Author: Pasteur and the Invisible Giants, 1958, White Battleground: The Conquest of the Arctic, 1961, Disaster 1906: The San Francisco Earthquake and Fire, 1967, Legal Action: A Layman's Guide, 1972; A Lion in the Sun: The Rise and Fall of the British Empire, 1973, Amnesty: The American Puzzle, 1976, Gun Control: A Decision for Americans, 1978, Child Abuse, 1980, revised edit., 1992, Adolf Hitler: A Portrait in Tyranny, 1981, History of the Movies, 1983, The Simon & Schuster Sports Question and Answer Book, 1984, Hollywood Goes to War, 1985, Drugs in Sports, 1986, revised edit., 1992, The Old Farmer's Almanac Book of Weather Lore, 1988, MIA: Missing in Action, 1989, America after Vietnam: Legacies of a Hated War, 1989, (with M.M. Scariano) Nuclear Waste: The 10,000-Year Challenge, 1990, Our Poisoned Sky, 1991, America in World War II: 1941, 1991, America in World War II: 1942, 1992, America in World War II: 1943, 1992, Animal Folklore: From Black Cats to White Horses, 1992, The American Wilderness and Its Future, 1992, America in World War II, 1944, 1993, Folk Medicine: Cures and Curiosities, 1993, America in World War II: 1945, 1994, Your Privacy: Protecting It in a Nosy World, 1994, Teenagers and Compulsive Gambling, 1994, (with M.M. Scariano) Illiteracy in America, 1995, The American Revolution: How We Fought the War of Independence, 1995, America in World War I, 1996, (with M.M. Scariano) Shaping U.S. Foreign Policy, 1996, In Sports, Money Talks, 1996, Our Poisoned Waters, 1997, The Civil War: A House Divided, 1997, America in the Korean War, 1998, Beyond the Frontier: the Story of the Trails West, 1999, The Spanish-American War, 2001, The Irish Potato Famine, 2003, The American Indian Wars, 2003, 113 non-fiction titles. With U.S. Army, 1943-45, ETO. Mem. Calif. Writers Club (pres. Redwood br. 1976-77, 83-84). Avocation: golf.

DOLAN, JAMES L, communications executive; m. Kristin Dolan; 5 children. Past advt. sales v.p. Cablevision Sys. Corp., past advt. corp. dir. Rainbow Advt. Sales Corp., past CEO Rainbow Programming Holdings, Inc. (now Rainbow Media Holdings LLC), CEO, pres. Woodbury, NY, 1995—, also bd. dirs.; creator Rainbow Advt. Sales Corp. Chmn. Madison Sq. Garden; creator, mgr. Sta. WKNR-AM, Cleve. Trustee WNET; bd. dirs. Lustgarten

Found. for Pancreatic Rsch., Allan Houston Found. Avocations: music, sailing. Office: Cablevision Sys Corp 1111 Stewart Ave Bethpage NY 11714-5310 Office Phone: 516-803-2300. Office Fax: 516-803-2273.*

DOLAN, JOHN E., retired utilities executive, consultant; b. N.Y.C., May 9, 1923; s. John A. and Marie C. (Comiskey) D.; m. Anne Dolan, Feb. 16, 1952; children— John E., Bryan, Vincent, Robert, Raymond, Philip, Lawrence, Paul. Student, Rensselaer Poly. Inst., 1946-47; BSM.E., Columbia U., 1950. With Am. Electric Power Service Corp., Columbus, Ohio, 1950-88, chief mech. engr., 1966, chief engr., 1967, sr. exec. v.p. engring., 1975-79, vice chmn. engring. and constrn., 1979-88; ret.; bd. dir., v.p. subs. cos. and Am. Electric Power Service Corp.; cons., 1988—. Bd. dirs. Dravo Corp. Served to 1st lt. USAAF, 1942-46. Decorated Air medal (4). Fellow ASME (James N. Landis medal 1990); mem. NAE, Tau Beta Pi. Roman Catholic. Home: 14448 Mark Dr Largo FL 33774-5102

DOLAN, JOHN RALPH, retired electronics executive; b. Peabody, Mass., Apr. 20, 1926; s. John L. and Ethel M. D.; m. Lois M. Burkhart, Jan. 24, 1948 (dec.); children: Mary Ellen, Geraldine, Dorothy, John, Peter; m. Barbara C. Gleason, Dec. 22, 1995; stepchildren: Janet Rogers, Barry, David, Julie Doyle. Student, Boston Coll., 1943, Bryant and Stratton Coll., 1945-46, Bentley Coll., 1948-50. Passenger accountant Cunard Steamship Co., 1947-50; office mgr. Dolan Tanning Co., 1950-56; gen. mgr. Flash Sportswear, 1957-59; budget mgr. CBS Electronics Co., 1959-62; controller/treas. Am. Polymer & Chem. Co., 1962-63; dir. financial planning E.G. & G., Inc., Bedford, Mass., 1963-71, controller, 1971-86; sr. v.p., chief fin. officer EG&G Inc., Wellesley, Mass., 1986-91. Mem. Town Meeting, Danvers, Mass., 1964-70, Sch. Bldg. Com., Danvers, 1966-69. Served with USNR, 1943-45. Mem. Financial Execs. Inst. Home: 56 Summer St Danvers MA 01923-1549

DOLAN, LOUISE ANN, physicist; b. Wilmington, Del., Apr. 5, 1950; BA, Wellesley Coll., 1971; PhD in Physics, MIT, 1976. Jr. fellow in physics Harvard U., 1976-79; asst. prof. physics Rockefeller U., N.Y.C., 1979-82, assoc. prof., 1983-90, lab. head, 1990; prof. physics U. N.C., Chapel Hill, 1990—. Program dir. for theoretical physics NSF, 1995. Recipient Wellesley Alumna Achievement award, 2004; John Simon Guggenheim fellow, 1988. Fellow Am. Phys. Soc. (Maria Goeppert-Mayer award 1987). Office: U NC Dept Physics Chapel Hill NC 27599-0001

DOLAN, MARY ANNE, journalist, columnist; b. Washington, May 1, 1947; d. William David and Christine (Shea) D. BA, Marymount Coll., Tarrytown, N.Y., 1968; HHD (hon.), Marymount Coll., %, 1984; student, Queen Mary, Royal Holloway colls., U. London, London Sch. Econs., Kings Coll., Cambridge U., 1966-68. Reporter, editor Washington Star, 1969-77; asst. mng. editor, 1976-77; mng. editor L.A. Herald Examiner, 1978-81, editor, 1981—, now commentator. Mem. Pulitzer Prize Journalism Jury, 1981—82; bd. selectors for Neiman Fellows Harvard U. Recipient Golden Flame award, Calif. Press Women, 1980, Woman Achiever award, Calif. Fed. Bus. and Profl. Women's Clubs, 1981. Mem.: Am. Soc. Newspaper Editors, NOW. Office: MAD Inc 1033 Gayley Ave Ste 205 Los Angeles CA 90024-3417

DOLAN, MICHAEL, entertainment company executive, former advertising agency executive; married; 2 children. Grad., Fordham U.; MBA, Columbia U.; PhD, Cornell U. With J.P. Morgan; ptnr. strategy practice Booz Allen & Hamilton, 1985-87; corp. exec. v.p. Continental Can Co. subs. Peter Kiewet Sons, Inc., 1987-91; sr. v.p. worldwide ops. PepsiCo Foods Internat., from 1991; pres., CEO Snack Ventures Europe (joint venture PepsiCo and Gen. Mills); vice chmn., CFO Young & Rubicam Inc., 1996—2000; pres., COO Young & Rubicam Inc, 2000—01; CEO Young & Rubicam Inc., N.Y.C., 2000—03; exec. v.p., CFO Viacom Inc., 2005—. Office: Viacom Inc 1515 Broadway New York NY 10036

DOLAN, MICHAEL F., lawyer; b. Dougherty, Iowa, 1949; BS magna cum laude, Loras Coll., 1971; MS, So. Ill. Univ., 1973; MBA, JD with high distinction, Univ. of Iowa, 1981. Bar: Ill. 1982; cert. Industl. Hygienist (ret.), safety profl., 1977-2001. Compliance safety and health officer Iowa State OSHA program; ptnr., chair, environ., health & safety practice Jones Day, Chgo. Co-author: (books) Legal Guide for Handling Toxic Substances in the Workplace, 1992; author: numerous articles in profl. publications; mem. (editorial adv. bd.) Environmental Management News. Mem.: ABA, Am. Conf. of Govtl. Indsl. Hygienists, Am. Soc. of Safety Engineers, Am. Indsl. Hygiene Assn., Environ. Law Inst., Ill. State Bar Assn. Office: Jones Day 77 W Wacker Chicago IL 60601-1692 Office Fax: 312-782-8585.

DOLAN, MICHAEL JOHN, psychologist; b. Ashland, Pa., June 16, 1958; s. William J. and Elizabeth A. (Bolich) D.; m. Debra Lee Sharpless, May 16, 1987; children: Jamie Elizabeth, Michael John. BA in Psychology, Penn State U., 1980; MA in Counseling Psychology, Kutztown U., 1988. Diplomate addiction counseling Pa. Chem. Abuse Cert. Bd.; cert. of proficency in substance use disorders Bd. Govs. APA Profl. Psychology. Counselor On Drugs Inc., State Coll., Pa., 1979-81; drug and alcohol counselor Good Samaritan Hosp., Pottsville, Pa., 1981-82; counselor, program dir. Endeavor Inc., Bethlehem, Pa., 1982-88; clin. supr. Lehigh Valley Behavioral Health Ctr., Allentown, Pa., 1988-91; psychologist Community Psychol. Svcs. Consultants Inc., Allentown, 1989—. Mem. APA. Avocations: reading, my kids. Home: 3155 Shakespeare Rd Bethlehem PA 18017-2731 Office: Community Psychol Svcs 2341 Walbert Ave Allentown PA 18104-1351

DOLAN, MICHAEL WILLIAM, lawyer; b. Kansas City, Mo., Dec. 13, 1942; s. William Michael and Vivian (Bush) D.; m. Laurel C. Cummings, June 13, 1964 (div. 1984); children: Matthew, Abigail. BA, U. Kans., 1964; JD with honors, George Washington U., 1969; LLM, Georgetown U., 1981. Bar: Va. 1969, D.C. 1970, U.S. Ct. Claims 1981, U.S. Tax Ct. 1981, U.S. Supreme Ct. 1973. Atty. Dept. Justice, Washington, 1971-73, dep. legis. counsel, 1973-79, dep. asst. atty. gen., 1979-85; with Fed Exec. Devel. Program, 1978-79; assoc. Winthrop, Stimson, Putnam & Roberts, Washington, 1985-94; chief Article III Judges divsn. Adminstrv. Office of U.S. Ct., Washington, 1994—2002; atty. Michael W. Dolan, PLLC, 2003—. Contbr. numerous articles to profl. jours. 1st lt. U.S. Army, 1964-66. Recipient John Marshall award Dept. Justice, 1978 Democrat. Office: 2021 L St NW 2d Fl Washington DC 20036 Office Phone: 202-293-2776. E-mail: mwdolan@att.net.

DOLAN, PETER BROWN, lawyer; b. Bklyn., Mar. 25, 1939; s. Daniel Arthur and Eileen Margaret (Brown) D.; m. Jacqueline Elizabeth Gruning, Sept. 9, 1961; children: Kerry Anne, Peter Brown Jr. BS, U.S. Naval Acad., 1960; JD, U. So. Calif., 1967. Bar: Calif. 1967, U.S. Ct. Appeals (9th cir.) 1967, U.S. Dist. Ct. (no. and ctrl. dists.) Calif. 1967, U.S. Dist. Ct. (ea. dist.) Calif. 1972, U.S. Dist. Ct. (so. dist.) Calif. 1973, U.S. Claims Ct. 1982, U.S. Supreme Ct. 1986. Dep. L.A. County counsel, 1967-69; assoc. Macdonald, Halsted & Laybourne, L.A., 1969-71, ptnr., 1972-77, Overton, Lyman & Prince, L.A., 1977-87, Morrison & Foerster, L.A., 1987-93, Morgan, Lewis & Bockius LLP, L.A., 1993-99; prin. The Dolan Law Firm, L.A., 1999—. Active Pasadena (Calif.) Tournament Roses Assn., 1973-05; pres. West Pasadena Residents Assn., 1979-81. Served to lt. USN, 1960-64, comdr. USNR, 1964-86. Mem.: ABA, L.A. County Bar Assn., Assn. Bus. Trial Lawyers, State Bar Calif., Chancery (LA), Bel-Air Bay Club, Phi Delta Phi. Roman Catholic. Fax: 213-680-9889. Office Phone: 213-689-0333. E-mail: dolanlaw@sbcglobal.net, peterbrowndolan@netscape.net.

DOLAN, PETER ROBERT, pharmaceutical executive; b. Salem, Mass., Jan. 6, 1956; s. John Ralph and Lois D. (Burkhart); m. Katherine Helen Lange, Sept. 12, 1981; children: Christopher Lange, Timothy Lange. B, Tufts U., 1978; MBA, Amos Tuck Sch. Bus. Dartmouth Coll., 1980. Asst. product mgr. Gen. Foods Corp., White Plains, N.Y., 1980-81, assoc. product mgr., 1982-83, product mgr., 1983-84, sr. product mgr., 1985, group product mgr., 1986-87, category mgr., 1987-88; v.p. mktg. Bristol-Myers Co., N.Y.C., 1988-90, sr. v.p. mktg. & sales, 1990-91, sr. v.p. mktg., sales & ops., 1991-92, exec. v.p., 1992, pres., 1993-94, Mead Johnson Nutritional Group, Evansville, Ind., 1995-96; group pres. nutritionals and med. devices Bristol-Myers Squibb Co., 1997—98, pres. Europe, Worldwide medicines, 1998, sr. v.p. strategy and orgnl. effectiveness, 1998—2000, pres., 2000—, chmn., 2001—05, CEO, 2001—. Bd. dirs. Old Nat. Bank, Am. Express Comp., Pharm. Rsch. and Mfrs. of Am.; bd. overseers Tufts Medical Sch. Bd.; mem. Bus. Coun., Bus. Roundtable. Co-author: Insider's Guide to the Top Ten Business Schools, 1982. Bd. dirs. NY Botanical Garden, Nat. Center on Addiction and Substance Abuse at Columbia U., C-Change; bd. trustee Tufts U. Mem.: Young Pres. Orgn., Non-Prescription Drug Mfrs. Assn. (bd. dirs. 1993). Avocations: triathlons, tennis, scuba diving. Office: Brystol Meyers Squibb 345 Park Ave New York NY 10154

DOLAN, RAYMOND BERNARD, insurance executive; b. Chgo., Feb. 13, 1923; s. Christopher P. and Florence M. (Taylor) D.; m. Theresa, May 25, 1946; children— Paul, Ronald, Donald, Sharon. Student, No. Mich. U., 1942; D.Arts and Scis. (hon.), Mt. Marty Coll., Yankton, S.D., 1980. With Equitable Life Assurance Soc. U.S., 1946—, v.p., chief line ops. N.Y.C., 1971-74, sr. v.p. corp. communications, 1974-79, exec. v.p., chief agy. officer, 1979—; chmn. bd. Equitable of Del., 1985—. Inst. Life Ins. prof. in residence, econs. dept. St. Olaf Coll., 1975; dir. Equitable Variable Life Ins. Co., Equitable Capitol Mgmt. Corp., Equitable Life Leasing Corp., Equico Securities Corp., Donaldson, Lufkin & Jennette Inc., U.S. Marshalls Found. Vice chmn. Holy Spirit Ch. Parish Council, Stamford, Conn., 1968-71; chmn. Stamford dist. Boy Scouts Am., 1970-73; past trustee, vice chmn. bd. dirs. Teledaga Coll., Ala.; chmn. bd. dirs. Nat. Council Better Bus. Burs. Served to lt. col. USAF, 1942-45, 51-52, 61-62. Decorated D.F.C., Air medal with 4 oak leaf clusters. Mem. Nat. Assn. Life Underwriters, C.L.U.'s N.Y., Nat. Guard Assn. (life), Consumer Council, Am. Council Life Ins., Res. Officers Assn., Conf. Bd., Pub. Affairs Research Council. Clubs: K.C. (4th deg.). Republican. Roman Catholic. Home: 5 Kings Grant 377 Main St New Canaan CT 06840-5941 Office: Equitable Life Assurance Soc US 787 7th Ave Fl 38 New York NY 10019-6018

DOLAN, REGINA A., security firm executive; BS, St. John's U. With Ernst & Young, 1975—86, ptnr., 1986—92; sr. v.p. fin. and controls Paine Webber Group Inc., 1992—94, CFO, 1994—97, CFO, chief adminstrv. officer, 1997—2001; chief adminstrv. officer pvt. clients and asset mgmt. divsn. UBS Warburg, 2001—02; global head strategic planning and bus. devel. UBS Investment Bank, 2002—. Bd. dirs. Bus. Coun. Southwestern Conn. Office: Paine Webber Group Inc Ste 302 1285 Avenue Of The Americas Fl Sconc New York NY 10019-6096

DOLAN, ROBERT J., dean; b. Peabody, Mass. m. Kathleen Splaine-Dolan; children: Hilary, Nicholas. BA in math. magna cum laude, Boston Coll., 1969; MS in bus. adminstrn., Grad. Sch. Mgmt., U. Rochester, 1976; PhD in bus. adminstrn., Grad. Sch. Adminstrn., U. Rochester, 1977. Asst. prof. mgmt. scis. and mktg. U. Chgo., 1976—80; assoc. prof. bus. adminstrn. Harvard U. Grad. Sch. Bus. Adminstrn., 1980—85, prof. bus. adminstrn., 1985—90, mktg. area chmn., 1986—94, mktg. tchr. Advanced Mgmt. Program, 1990—95, Edward W. Carter prof. bus. adminstrn., 1990—2001, faculty chmn. MBA program, 1996—97; pres. William David Inst. U. Mich. Ann Arbor Bus. Sch., 2001—, Gilbert and Ruth Whitaker prof. bus. adminstrn., 2001—, dean, 2001—. Mem. Mktg. Sci. Inst. Adv. Coun., 1986—89, Harvard Bus. Sch. Press Publ. Review Bd., 1989—92; vis. prof. IESE, Barcelona, 2001. Editor (field studies section): Marketing Science, 1989—94; mem. editl. review bd.:, 1982—88, Jour. Mktg., 1978—84, 1990—98, Jour. Pub. Policy and Mktg., 2001—; author: (books) Managing the New Product Development Process, 1993, Marketing Management: Text and Cases, 2001; co-author (with John Quelch and Benson Shapiro): Marketing Management Readings: From Theory to Practice, 1985, Marketing Management: Strategy, Planning and Implementation, 1985, Marketing Management: Principles, Analysis, and Application, 1985; co-author: (with John Quelch and Thomas Kosnik) Marketing Management, 1993; co-author: (with Hermann Simon) Power Pricing: How Managing Price Transforms the Bottom Line, 1996; editor: Strategic Marketing Management, 1992; contbr. articles to numerous jour. Office: U Mich Bus Sch 701 Tappan St Ann Arbor MI 48109-1234 Office Phone: 734-764-1361. Business E-Mail: rjdolan@umich.edu.

DOLAN, TERESA A., dean, educator, researcher; MPH, UCLA; BA Zoology, Rutgers U., 1979; DDS, U. Tex., 1983; cert. gen. practice, L.I. Jewish Med. Ctr., 1985; cert. geriatric dentistry, Vets. Adminstrn., 1989; cert. dental pub. health, U. Fla., 1991; grad., Pub. Health Leadership Inst. Fla., 1998; grad. cert., U. Fla., 2001. Diplomate Am. Bd. Dental Pub. Health, 1994. Resident in gen. dentistry dept. dentistry L.I. Jewish Med. Ctr., 1983—84, chief resident in gen. dentistry dept. dentistry, 1984—85; fellow geriatric dentistry Vets. Adminstrn. Med. Ctr., Sepulveda, Calif., 1987—89; asst. prof. U. Fla. Coll. Dentistry, 1989—93, assoc. prof. with tenure, 1993—98, acting assoc. dean acad. affairs, 1996—97, assoc. dean acad. affairs, 1997—2001, prof. with tenure, 1998—, assoc. dean edn., 2001—03, interim dean, 2002—03, dean, 2003—. Rschr., tchr., spkr. in field, lectr. various seminars; vis. asst. prof. U. Calif., 1985—87, adj. asst. prof., 1987—89; faculty discipline com. Fla. Dept. Edn., Statewide Course Numbering Sys., 1998—; reviewer grants in field; participant NIH Summer Inst. Rsh. on Minority Aging, 1991. Contbr. articles to profl. jours.; exec. prodr.: (ednl. satellite videoconf.) Dental Care for the Developmentally Disabled Patient, 1991, Challenges in Geriatrics: Moving on- Rehabilitation After Stroke, 1991, How Much is Enough? Dental Tretament Decisions for Older Adults, 1992; author (dir.): Five Steps to Improving the Oral Health of Your Older Patients: A Guide for Non-dental Health Professionals, 1994. Adv., treating dentist cmty. nursing homes, 1989—96; dentist to low income elderly participants U. Fla. Geriatric Dental Demonstration Project, Jacksonville, 1990—92; dir. dental svcs. to older and medically compromised patients U. Fla. Geriatric Dental Group, 1990—95. Named honorable mention AARP Healthy Order Adults, 2000 Recognition Programs Exemplary Contbns. to Healthy Aging, 1992; recipient numerous grants and awards; fellow Vets. Adminstrn. Geriatric Dentistry; scholar Rsch., Robert Wood Johnson Found. Dental Health Svcs., 1985—87, L.I. U., 1984—85. Mem.: APHA, Am. Coll. Dentists, Phi Beta Kappa, Am. Soc. Geriatric Dentistry (ad hoc reviewer Spl. Care in Dentistry 1992—93, judge Saul Kamen Sci. Report award competition 1993—, chmn. ann. sci. session 1996), Fla. Coun. Aging, Fla. Pub. Health Assn., Am. Assn. Pub. Health Dentistry (abstract reviewer 1987, co-chmn. local arrangements ann. meeting 1992, ad hoc reviewer Jour. Pub. Health Dentistry 1994, session co-chmn. ann. meeting 1996, judge grad. student merit award projects 1997, mem. at large exec. coun. 1997—2000, mem. awards and nominations com. 2000, Pres.'s award 1999), Am. Dental Assn. (com. G Coun. Dental Edn. and Licensure 1999—, Geriatric Dental Care award 1991), Internat. Assn. Dental Rsch. (v.p. abstract reviewer geriat. oral rsch. sect. 1992—93, dir. behavioral sci. and health svcs. rsch. sect. 1992—95, pres.-elect program chmn. geriat. oral rsch. sect. 1993—94, pres. symposium organizer geriat. oral rsch. sect. 1994—95), Am. Assn. Women Dentists (chmn. com. student and component chpts. 1986—88, trustee dist. XIII Calif. 1986—89, contbg. editor Chronicle 1986—91), Acorn Clinic (v.p., acting pres. 1996—97, pres. 1997—99, past pres. 1999—2000), Fla. Coun. Aging (bd. trustees 1993—95), U. Health Sci. Ctr., Edn. Task Force, U. Curriculum Com., Geriatric Rsch., Edn. and Clin. Ctr., ACORN Clinic, Internat. Assn. Dental Rsch. (session co-chmn., abstract reviewer geriat. oral rsch. sect. 1991—92, immediate past-pres., chmn. nominations com. geriat. oral rsch. sect. 1995—96, mem. awards com. geriat. oral rsch. sect. 1996—97, constn. and bylaws com. 1996—), Am. Bd. Dental Pub. Health (dir.-elect 2000—01), Am. Dental Edn. Assn. (chair-elect spl. interest group in geriatric dentistry 1991—92, editl. rev. bd. Jour. Dental Edn. 1991—94, chmn. spl. intertest group in geriatric dentistry 1992—93, immediate past chmn. sect. on gerontology and geriat. edn. 1993—94, abstract reviewer ann. session 1998—2000, ann. session planning com. 2002—), Beta Beta Beta, Omicron Kappa Upsilon (Xi Omicron chpt. 1998), Phi Beta Kappa. Office: U Fla Coll Dentistry 1600 SW Archer Rd D Box 100405 JHMH Gainesville FL 32610-0405

DOLAN, THOMAS CHRISTOPHER, professional society administrator; b. Chgo., Dec. 31, 1947; s. Thomas Christopher and Bernice Mary (Doyle) D.; m. Georgia Ann Siebke, Feb. 14, 1983; children: William, Barbara, Lauren. BBA, Loyola U., Chgo., 1969; PhD, U. Iowa, 1977. Instr. U. Iowa, Iowa City, 1971-72; vis. fellow U. Wash., Seattle, 1973-74; asst. prof. U. Mo., Columbia, 1974-79; assoc. prof., dir. St. Louis U., 1979-86; v.p. Am. Coll. Healthcare Execs., Chgo., 1986-87, exec. v.p., 1987-91, pres., 1991—. Mem. Accrediting Commn. on Edn. for Health Svcs. Adminstrn., Washington, 1985-86; chmn. Assn. Univ. Programs in Health Adminstrn., Washington, 1983-84; cons. HEW, Kansas City, Mo., 1974-79, State of Mo., Jefferson City, 1974-79. Author: Systems for Health Care Administration: A Model for the Education of Health Manpower, 1975; contbr. articles to profl. jours. Pres. Mental Health Assn. Boone County, Columbia, Mo., 1977—78, Mental Health Assn. Mo., Jefferson City, 1980—82; chair Inst. for Diversity in Health Mgmt., 2002, Assn. Forum, 1999—2000, Am. Soc. Assn. Execs. Found., Washington, 2000—01; bd. dirs. Alexian Bros. Hosp., St. Louis, 1980—86. Fellow: Am. Soc. Assn. Execs. (cert. assn. exec., bd. dirs.), Am. Coll. Healthcare Execs. Roman Catholic. Avocations: golf, motorcycling, photography. Office: Am Coll Healthcare Execs 1 N Franklin St Ste 1700 Chicago IL 60606-4425

DOLAN, THOMAS JOSEPH, judge; b. Bronx, NY, Oct. 24, 1943; s. Joseph William and Helen Winnifred (Hannigan) D.; m. Barbara Louise Nuesell, Apr. 6, 1968; children: Claire Jean, Claudia Barbara. BS, Fordham U., 1965; JD, St. John's U., 1968. Bar: N.Y. 1968, U.S. Ct. Mil. Appeals 1969, U.S. Dist. Ct. (so. and ea. dists.) N.Y. 1975, U.S. Supreme Ct. 1980. Asst. dist. atty. Office of Dist. Atty., Dutchess County, Poughkeepsie, N.Y., 1973-92; county ct. judge Dutchess County, 1993—; acting judge N.Y. State Supreme Ct., 2001—. Served to capt. JAGC, U.S. Army, 1968-73. Decorated Bronze Star (2), Army Commendation medal (2). Mem. N.Y. State Bar Assn., Dutchess County Bar Assn. Clubs: So. Dutchess Exchange (Fishkill, N.Y.). Republican. Home: Neville Rd Wappingers Falls NY 12590 Office: County Court 10 Market St Ste 7 Poughkeepsie NY 12601-3233 Office Phone: 845-486-2210. Personal E-mail: btdolan@aol.com. Business E-Mail: tdolan@courts.state.ny.us.

DOLAN, TIMOTHY MICHAEL, archbishop; b. Feb. 6, 1950; s. Robert and Shirley Radcliffe Dolan. BA in Philosophy, Cardinal Glennon Coll.; attended, Pontifical N. Am. Coll., Rome; License in Sacred Theology, Pontifical U. of St. Thomas; PhD in Am. Church History, Catholic U. of Am. Ordained to priesthood, 1976; assoc. pastor Immaculata Parish, Richmond Heights, Mo., 1976—79; served in parish ministry, liaison for Archbishop John L. May St. Louis, 1983—87; secretary Apostolic Nunciature, Washington, 1987—92; vice rector, dir. of spiritual formation & prof. of church history Kenrick-Glennon Seminary, St. Louis, 1992—94; rector Pontifical N. Am. Coll., Rome, 1994—2001; auxiliary bishop St. Louis, 2001—02; archbishop of Milwaukee, 2002—. Former adjunct prof. of theology St. Louis U.; visiting prof. of church history Pontifical Gregorian U., Rome; faculty mem. dept. of ecumenical theology Pontifical U. of St. Thomas Aquinas, Rome. Office: Archdiocese of Milwaukee 3501 S Lake Dr PO Box 070912 Milwaukee WI 53207*

DOLAN, WILLIAM D., III, lawyer; b. Washington, Nov. 20, 1943; AB, Marquette U., 1967; JD, Cath. U. Am., 1972. Bar: Va. 1972, D.C. 1974. Ptnr., commercial litigation Venable LLP (formerly Venable, Baetjer and Howard), McLean, Va. Adj. prof. med. malpractice law Georgetown U., 1982-, former pres., Va. Com. on Women & Minorities in Legal System. Fellow Am. Bar Found., Am. Coll. Trial Lawyers, Internat. Acad. Trial Lawyers, Va. Law Found.; mem. ABA (former deleg.), Am. Law Inst., Va. State Bar (pres. 1984-85, chair criminal law section), D.C. Bar, Assn. Trial Lawyers Am., Va. Trial Lawyers Assn. Office: Venable LLP 8010 Towers Crescent Dr Ste 300 Vienna VA 22182 Office Phone: 703-760-1680. Office Fax: 703-821-8949. Business E-Mail: wddolan@venable.com.

DOLAN, WILLIAM J., media company executive; b. Portland, Oreg., Feb. 8, 1959; s. John Lee and Dolores Maureen Dolan; m. Camilla Anne Derby, Aug. 1, 1981; children: Heather, Brittain, Courtney, William, Keenan. Student, Mt. Hood Coll., 1977-79, Portland State U., 1979—80. CFP. Dir. KATU-TV, Portland, 1979-92; pres., creative dir. Spirit Media, Portland. Prodr. (TV documentary) Foundations of Freedom, 1999 (The Vision award 2000), (TV spl.) Luis Palau Festival, 1999 (Emmy nomination 2000). Speech scholar Mt. Hood Coll., 1977. Mem.: Media Comm. Assn. Internat. (bd. dirs.), Oreg. Media Prodn. Assn., Nat. Religious Broadcasters. Office: Spirit Media #700F 10117 SE Sunnyside Rd Portland OR 97015 Office Fax: 503-698-8408. E-mail: bill@spiritmedia.com.

DOLAS, EVELYN ANN, poet, musician; b. Chicago, Ill., Oct. 2, 1960; d. George Evangelos and Clara Dolas. English Composition, City Colleges Chgo., Chicago, IL; Cert. Graduation, Automation Acad., 1982. Author: (book of poetry) America at the Millennium: The Best Poems and Poets of the 20th Century, Poetry's Elite: The Best Poems of 2000, Echoes of Yesteryear, Rainstorms and Rainbows, Nature's Echoes, By the Light of the Moon, Mythology of the Heart, A Secret Language. Recipient Achievement award, Chgo. Pk. Dist. Dept. Recreation, 1973, Cert. Achievement, Chgo. Pub. Schools, Cert., Curie Concert Chorus 1973-1977, Cert. Excellence, Curie Chamber Chorus, 1977, seven Editor's Choice awards, 2000—02, Internat. Poet of Merit award, 2002. Mem.: Internat. Soc. Poets. Home: PO Box 4763 Hailey ID 83333

DOLBERG, DAVID SPENCER, lawyer; b. L.A., Nov. 28, 1945; s. Samuel and Kitty (Snyder) D.; m. Katherine Blumberg, Feb. 22, 1974 (div. 1979); 1 child, Max; m. Sarah Carnochan, May 23, 1992 (div. 1995); m. Elana Mann, June 15, 1997; children: Kayla, Sophia. BA in Biology with honors, U. Calif., Berkeley, 1974; PhD in Molecular Biology, U. Calif., San Diego, 1980; JD, U. Calif., Berkeley, 1989. Bar: Calif. 1989, U.S. Dist. Ct. (no. dist.) Calif. 1989, U.S. Patent and Trademark Office, 1990. Staff biologist, postdoctoral fellow Lawrence Berkeley Lab. U. Calif., 1980-85; assoc. Irell & Manella, Menlo Park, Calif., 1989-91; v.p. EROX Corp., Menlo Park, Calif., 1991-92; v.p. sci. and patents Pherin Corp., Menlo Park, Calif., 1992-94; pvt. practice Berkeley, 1994-98, N.Y.C., 1996-97, Richmond, Calif., 1998—2004; dir. intellectual property Sanaria Inc., Rockville, Md., 2004—, Protein Potential LLC, Rockville, Md., 2004—. Speaker in field. Contbr. articles to Jour. Gen. Virology, Jour. Virology, Nature, Science, Psychoneuroendocrinology. Address: 37 Terrace Ave Richmond CA 94801-3937 Office Phone: 510-685-6405. E-mail: dsdol@pacbell.net.

DOLBY, RAY MILTON, engineering company executive, electrical engineer; b. Portland, Oreg., Jan. 18, 1933; s. Earl Milton and Esther Eufemia (Strand) Dolby; m. Dagmar Baumert, Aug. 19, 1966; 1 child, Thomas Eric; 1 child, David Earl. Student, San Jose State Coll., 1951-52, 55, Washington U., St. Louis, 1953—54; BSEE, Stanford U., 1957; PhD in Physics (Marshall scholar 1957-60, Draper's studentship 1959-61, NSF fellow 1960-61), Cambridge (Eng.) U., 1961, ScD (hon.), 1997; Doctor of the U. (hon.), U. York. Lic. Comml. pilot instrument rating FAA. Electronic technician/jr. engr. Ampex Corp., Redwood City, Calif., 1949—53, engr., 1955—57, sr. engr., 1957; PhD research student in physics Cavendish Lab., Cambridge U., 1957—61, research in long wavelength x-rays, 1957—63; fellow Pembroke Coll., 1961—63; cons. U.K. Atomic Energy Authority, 1962—63; UNESCO adviser Central Sci. Instruments Orgn., Chandigarh, Punjab, India, 1963—65; owner, chmn., CEO Dolby Labs., Inc., San Francisco and Wootton Bassett, U.K., 1965—. Mem. Marshall Scholarship selection com., 1979—85; Trustee Univ. High Sch., San Francisco, 1978—84; bd. dirs. San Francisco Opera; bd. govs. San Francisco Symphony. Served with U.S. Army, 1953—54. Decorated officer Most Excellent Order of Brit. Empire; named Man of Yr., Internat. Tape Assn., 1987, Nat. Inventors Hall of Fame, U.S. Patent and Trademark Office, 2004; recipient Beech-Thompson award, Stanford U., 1956, Emmy award, 1957, 1989, Trendsetter award, Billboard, 1971, Emile Berliner Maker of the microphone award, Emile Berliner Assn., 1972, Lyre award, Inst. High Fidelity, 1972, Top 200 Execs. Bi-Centennial award, 1976, Sci. and Engring. award, Acad. Motion Picture Arts and Scis., 1979, Pioneer award, Internat. Teleprodn. Soc., 1988, Edward Rhein Ring award, Edward Rhein Found., 1988, Oscar award, 1989, Life Achievement award, Cinema Audio Soc., 1989, Grammy award, NARAS, 1995, Nat. medal Tech., U.S.

Dept. Commerce, 1997, medal of Achievement, Am. Electronics Assn., 1997, Festival medal Cannes, Cannes Internat. Film Festival, 2004; fellow Pembroke Coll., Cambridge U., 1983. Fellow: Inst. Broadcast Sound, Soc. Motion Picture and TV Engrs. (Samuel L. Warner award 1979, Alexander M. Poniatoff Gold medal 1982, Progress award 1983), Brit. kenematograph, Sound and TV Soc. (Outstanding Tech. and Sci. award 1995), Audio Engring. Soc. (bd. govs. 1972-74 1979—84, Silver medal 1971, Gold medal 1992); mem.: NATAS (Charles F. Jenkins Lifetime award 2003), Consumer Electronics Assn. (Consumer Electronics Hall of Fame 2000), Internat. Broadcasting Conv. (John Tucker award 2000), IEEE (Ibuka award 1997), Pacific Union Club, St. Francis Yacht Club, Tau Beta Pi. Achievements include research in Achievements include inventing dolby stero, rsch., publs. in video tape recording, x-ray microanalysis, noise reduction and quality improvements in audio and video systems; holder 50 U.S. patents. Office: Dolby Labs 100 Potrero Ave San Francisco CA 94103-4886*

DOLCE, CARL JOHN, education administration educator; b. New Orleans, June 3, 1928; s. John and Nina (Puglia) D.; m. Nancy Lockwood, July 27, 1955; children: Carla, John. BA, Tulane U., 1947; MEd, Loyola U., New Orleans, 1955; EdD, Harvard U., 1963. Elem. sch. tchr. New Orleans Pub. Schs., 1948-54, secondary sch. tchr., 1954-55, jr. high sch. prin., 1955-63, supt. schs., 1965-69; rsch. assoc., lectr. Harvard Grad. Sch. Edn., Cambridge, Mass., 1963-65; dean Coll. Edn. and Psychology, N.C. State U., Raleigh, 1969-88, dean emeritus, prof. edn. adminstrn., 1989—. Chair adv. com. aesthetic edn. Cen. Midwest Regulatory Lab., St. Louis, 1968-71; chair exptl. schs. selection com. Office Edn., Washington, 1971-72; pres. Coun. Basic Edn., Washington, 1972-79; vice chmn. nat. assn. Elem. and Secondary Edn. Act Title IV state adv. councs., 1978-79 Editorial bd. Ednl. Forum, 1988; author book chpts., monograph, articles. Chmn. Wake County (N.C.) Sch. Study Com., Raleigh, 1978-79; chmn. tech. advisors Durham City/County Merger Task Force, 1988. Sgt. U.S. Army, 1950-52. Grantee U.S Office Edn. grantee, 1981—82, 1986—87;, 1971—78. Mem. Raleigh Chamber Music Guild (pres. 1978-1980, Phi Kappa Phi (pres. N.C. State U. chpt. 1982-83). Avocations: gardening, reading, mysteries, puzzles. Home: 801 Macon Pl Raleigh NC 27609-5552

DOLCH, GARY D., pharmaceutical executive; BS in Chemistry, Ursinus Coll.; MS in Chemistry, Fairleigh Dickinson U.; PhD in Med. Chemistry, Purdue U. Quality mgr. Ayerst Labs., Am. Home Products, 1979—85, asst. v.p., 1986—88; various mgmt. positions quality control Genetech, Inc., Boehringer-Ingelheim Pharms., 1988—92; v.p. quality affairs and tech. ops. Knoll Pharms., BASF, 1992—2001; sr. v.p. quality and regulatory affairs ARC, 2001—02; exec. v.p. quality and regulatory affairs Cardinal Health, Inc., 2002—. Mem. dean's coun. Sch. Pharmacy Purdue U., 2004—; dir. PDA Found., 1987—94. Office: Cardinal Health Inc 7000 Cardinal Pl Dublin OH 43017 Office Phone: 614-757-5697.

DOLD, ROBERT BRUCE, journalist; b. Newark, Mar. 9, 1955; s. Robert Bruce and Margaret (Noll) Dold; m. Eileen Claire Norris, July 10, 1982; children: Megan, Kristen. BS in Journalism, Northwestern U., 1977, MS in Journalism, 1978. Reporter Suburban Tribune, Hinsdale, Ill., 1978—83, Chgo. Tribune, 1983—90, mem. editl. bd., 1990—95, dep. editl. page editor, columnist, 1995—2000, editl. page editor, 2000—. Pulitzer Prize juror, 1997—98; columnist Chgo. Enterprise, 1991—95; critic Downbeat Mag., 1980—84; commentator Chgo. Week in Rev., 1987—. Bd. dirs. Jazz Inst. Chgo., 1980—83. Recipient Peter Lisagor award, Sigma Delta Chi, 1988, Pulitzer Prize for editl. writing, 1994, Scripps Howard Found. Nat. award for commentary, 1999. Mem.: Am. Soc. Newspaper Editors, Econ. Club of Chgo. Roman Catholic. Avocations: golf, basketball, jazz. Home: 501 N Park Rd La Grange Park IL 60526-5516 Office: Chgo Tribune 435 N Michigan Ave Chicago IL 60611-4066 Office Phone: 312-222-4438. E-mail: bdold@tribune.com.

DOLE, ARTHUR ALEXANDER, former psychology professor, department chairman; b. San Francisco, Oct. 25, 1917; s. Arthur Alexander and Ella Elizabeth (Duncan) D.; m. Marjorie Elizabeth Welsh, Mar. 19, 1949; children: Peter, Steven, Barbara. BA, Antioch Coll., 1946; MA, Ohio State U., 1949, PhD, 1951; MA (hon.), U. Pa., 1973. Diplomate Am. Bd. Examiners Profl. Psychology. Asst. psychology, edn. Antioch Coll., 1946-48; counselor Ohio State U., 1948-51; dir. Bur. Testing and Guidance, U. Hawaii, 1951-60, asst. prof., prof. psychology, 1951-67; prof. psychology edn. U. Pa., 1967-88, chmn. divsn., 1967-88, prof. emeritus, 1988—. Mem. internat. adv. bd. Univ MSG, Romero, El Salvador. Author articles in field.; cons. editor profl. jours. Bd. dirs. PEACE, Internat. Celtic Studies Assn. Fellow APA, AAUP, ACA, Am. Ednl. Rsch. Assn., Internat. Coun. Psychologists, Internat. Assn. Applied Psychology, Nat. Rehab. Assn. E-mail: aadole@adelphia.net.

DOLE, BOB (ROBERT JOSEPH DOLE), lawyer, retired senator; b. Russell, Kans., July 22, 1923; s. Doran R. and Bina Dole; m. Phyllis Holden, 1948 (div. 1972); 1 child, Robin; m. Elizabeth Hanford, Dec. 6, 1975. Student, U. Kans., 1941—43, U. Ariz., 1948—49; AB, LLB, Washburn Mcpl. U., Topeka, 1952; LLD (hon.), Washburn U., Topeka, 1969. Bar: Kans. 1952. Mem. Kans. Ho. of Reps., 1951—53; sole practice Russell, Kans., 1953—61; atty. Russell County, 1953—61; mem. 87th Congress from 6th Dist. Kans., 1961—63, 88th-90th Congresses from 1st Dist. Kans., 1963—69; U.S. senator from Kans., 1969—96; Senate majority leader, 1985—87, 1995—96; Senate minority leader, 1987—95; chmn. Rep. Nat. Com., 1971—73; of counsel Verner, Liipfert, Bernhard, McPherson & Hand, 1999—, Alston & Bird, 2003—. Advisor US Del. to the UN Food & Agrl. Orgn., 1965, 68, 74, 75, 77, 79, President's Del. to Study the Food Crisis in India, 1966, US Del. to Study the Arab Refugee Problem, 1967, GATT Ministerial Trade Conf., 1982; mem. US Nat. Commn. for the UN Ednl., Scientific, & Cultural Orgn., 1970, 73, Commn. on Security & Cooperation in Europe, 1977, Nat. Commn. on Social Security Reform, 1983, Martin Luther King Jr. Fed. Holiday Commn., 1984; chmn. Internat. Commn. on Missing Persons in the Former Yugoslavia, 1997—2001; Rep. vice-presdl. candidate, 1976; Rep. presdl. candidate, 96. Author: Great Political Wit: Laughing (Almost) All the Way to the White House, 1998, Great Presidential Wits (...I Wish I Was in the Book): A Collection of Humorous Anecdotes and Quotations, 2001, One Soldier's Story: A Memoir, 2005 (NY Times Bestseller list, 2005); co-author (with George McGovern, Donald Messer): Ending Hunger Now: A Challenge to Persons of Faith, 2005; co-author: (with Elizabeth Dole Richard Norton Smith and Kerry Tymchuk) (autobiography) Unlimited Partners: Our American Story, 1996. Chmn. Nat. WWII Meml., 1997—2004, Dole Found. Served with U.S. Army, WW II. Decorated Purple Heart (2), Bronze Star with oak cluster; recipient Horatio Alger award, Horatio Alger Assn. Disting. Ams., 1988, Presdl. Medal of Freedom, 1997. Mem.: DAV, VFW, 4-H Fair Assn., Am. Legion, Kiwanis, Elks, Shriners, Masons, Kappa Sigma. Methodist. Office: Office of Sen Dole c/o Alston & Bird 601 Pennsylvania Ave NW Washington DC 20004 Business E-Mail: bdole@alston.com.*

DOLE, ELIZABETH HANFORD, senator, former secretary of labor; b. Salisbury, NC, July 29, 1936; d. John Van and Mary Ella (Cathey) Hanford; m. Robert Joseph Dole (former U.S. Senator from Kans.), Dec. 6, 1975. BA with honors in Polit. Sci., Duke U., 1958; postgrad., Oxford (Eng.) U., summer 1959; MA in Edn. and Govt., Harvard U., 1960, JD, 1965. Bar: DC 1966. Staff asst. to asst. sec. for edn. HEW, Washington, 1966-67; practiced law Washington, 1967-68; assoc. dir. legis. affairs, then exec. dir. Pres.'s Com. for Consumer Interests, Washington, 1968-71; dep. asst. to Pres. The White House, Washington, 1971-73; commr. FTC, Washington, 1973-79; chmn. Voters for Reagan-Bush, 1980; dir. Human Services Group, Office of Exec. Br. Mgmt., Office of Pres.-Elect, 1980; asst. to Pres. for pub. liaison, 1981-83; sec. U.S. Dept. Transp., 1983-87; with Robert Dole Presdl. Campaign, 1987-88; participant 1988 Presdl. and Congl. campaigns; sec. U.S. Dept. Labor, 1989-90; pres. ARC, 1991-99; U.S. senator from N.C., 2003—; mem. armed services, agr., banking and aging coms., 2003—. Mem. nominating com. Am. Stock Exch., 1972, N.C. Consumer Coun., 1972. Author (with Bob Dole Richard Norton Smith and Kerry Tymchuk): (autobiography) Unlimited Partners, 1996. Trustee Duke U., 1974-88; mem. coun. Harvard Law Sch. Assocs., mem. vis. com. Harvard Sch. Pub. Health, 1992-95; mem. bd. overseers Harvard U., 1989-95. Recipient Arthur S. Flemming award U.S. Govt., 1972, Humanitarian award Nat. Commn. Against Drunk Driving, 1988, Disting. Alumni award Duke U., 1988, N.C. award, 1991, Lifetime Achievement award (Breaking The Glass Ceiling) Women Execs. in State Govt., 1993, North Carolinian of the Yr. award N.C. Press Assn., 1993, Radcliffe medal, 1993, Leadership award LWV, 1994, Maxwell Finland award Nat. Found. Infectious Diseases, 1994, Disting. Svc. award Nat. Safety Coun., 1989, Raoul Wallenberg award for Humanitarian Svc., 1995, Christian Woman of Yr. award, 1996; named one of Am.'s 200 Young Leaders, Time mag., 1974, one of World's 10 Most Admired Women, Gallup Poll, 1988, one of 10 most fascinating people 1996 Barbara Walter's Spl., most inspiring polit. figure 1996 MSNBC, 3rd most admired woman in Am. Good Housekeeping, 1996, 98, one of most powerful women, Forbes mag., 2005; selected for Safety and Health Hall of Fame Internat., 1993; inducted into Nat. Women's Hall of Fame, 1995. Mem. Phi Beta Kappa, Pi Lambda Theta, Pi Sigma Alpha. Republican. Office: US Senate 555 Dirksen Office Bldg Washington DC 20510 also: 310 New Bern Ave Ste 122 Raleigh NC 27601 Office Phone: 703-525-9100, 202-224-6342.*

DOLE, JANICE GAIL ARNOLD, literacy educator; b. Boston, Jan. 31, 1947; d. Walter Francis and Jenny Clare (Sapuppo) Arnold; m. Patrick John Brennan, Dec. 30, 1992; 1 child, Melissa Erin. BA, U. Mass., Boston, 1969; MA, U. Colo., 1974, PhD, 1977. Cert. elem. tchr., Mass., Calif. Elem. tchr. Medford (Mass.) Sch. Sys., 1969-70, Ridgecrest (Calif.) Sch. Dist., 1970-73; rsch./tchg. asst. U. Colo., Boulder, 1974-77; asst. prof. U. Denver, 1978-84; asst. vis. prof. Ctr. for Study of Reading U. Ill., 1984-86; asst. prof. Mich. State U., East Lansing, 1986-88, U. Utah, Salt Lake City, 1988—. Adv. bd. Reading Rsch. Quarterly, Contemporary Edn. Psychology, Jour. Lit. Rsch.; mem. devel. panel Nat. Assessment Ednl. Progress, Princeton, N.J., 1992—; co-dir. Utah Reading Excellence Act, 1999-2001; mem. Rand Panel Reading, 2000—, cons. to numerous sch. dists. Author: Elementary Language Arts, 1984; contbr. articles to profl. publs. Mem. Am. Edn. Rsch. Assn., Nat. Reading Conf., Internat. Reading Assn., Soc. for Sci. Study of Reading. Avocations: skiing, hiking, reading, running. Office: U Utah 1705 E Central Campus #120 Salt Lake City UT 84112-1169 E-mail: dole@ed.utah.edu.

DOLEAC, CHARLES BARTHOLOMEW, lawyer; b. New Orleans, Sept. 20, 1947; s. Cyril Bartholomew and Emma Elizabeth (St. Clair) D.; m. Denise Kilfoyle, Feb. 2, 1972; children: Keith Gabriel, Jessa Lee. BS cum laude, U. N.H., 1968; JD, NYU, 1971. Bar: Mass. 1972, N.H. 1972, Maine 1973. Law clk. to Justice Grimes N.H. Supreme Ct., Concord, 1972-73; assoc. Boynton, Waldron, Dill & Aeschliman, Portsmouth, N.H., 1973-76; ptnr. Boynton, Waldron, Doleac, Woodman & Scott, Portsmouth, 1977—. Apptd. mediator N.H. Superior Ct., 1992—; del. to tour Chinese legal system Chinese Ministry Justice, 1982; del. to People's Republic of China/U.S. joint session on trade investments and econ. law Chinese Ministry Justice/U.S. Dept. Justice, Beijing, 1987; propr. Portsmouth Athenaeum; moderator seminars on ethics for Leaders & Comparative Cultures and Values/East & West and Exec. Seminar Aspen Inst., 1990-95; moderator exec. sem. Aspen Inst., 1997-2000; mem. faculty Southwestern Legal Found. Internat. & Comparative Law Ctr., 1997—; ofcl. guest Fgn. Ministry Japan, Tokyo, 1998; developed Asian Seminar, Aspen Inst., 2000; spkr. ethics Ann. Nat. Conf. Appellate Ct. Clks., 1999-2000. Contbr. articles to profl. jours. Mem. citizens adv. coun. Portsmouth Cmty. Devel. Program, 1976-77; incorporator N.H. Charitable Found.; pres., bd. dirs. Seacoast United Way; chmn. Portsmouth Bd. Bldg. Appeals, 1976-77; chmn. stewardship com. Soc. Preservation New Eng. Antiquities, 1980-84, also trustee; pres. bd. trustees Strawbery Banke Mus., 1985-88; founder Daniel Webster Inn of Ct., 1993, Charles C. Doe Inn of Ct., 1994, Portsmouth Peace Treaty Forums I-IV, 1994-2000; chmn. Portsmouth Peace Treaty 100th Ann. Com., 1993-; founder, pres. Japan-Am. Soc. N.H., 1988; develop Asian seminar, Aspen Inst., 2000. Named Citizen of Yr., Portsmouth, N.H., 1991; recipient John E. Thayer III award, Japan Soc. Boston, 2001. Fellow N.H. Bar Found; mem. ATLA, Mass. Bar Assn., Maine Bar Assn., N.H. Bar Assn., N.H. Trial Lawyers Assn., Maine Trial Lawyers Assn. Avocation: masters swimming. Home: Little Harbor Rd Portsmouth NH 03801 Office: Boynton Waldron Doleac Woodman & Scott PA 82 Court St Portsmouth NH 03801-4414 Office Phone: 603-436-4010. Business E-Mail: cdoleac@nhlawfirm.com.

DOLEN, WILLIAM KENNEDY, allergist, immunologist, pediatrician, educator; b. Memphis, Oct. 16, 1952; s. William Smith and Dorothy DeWitt (Kennedy) D.; m. Carolyn Canon, Dec. 21, 1974; children: John William, Susan Elizabeth. BS in Biology with distinction and honors, Rhodes Coll., 1974; MD, U. Tenn., 1977. Cert. Nat. Bd. Med. Examiners, Am. Bd. Pediatrics, Am. Bd. Allergy and Immunology. Commd. 2d lt. U.S. Army, 1974, advanced through grades to maj., 1982; intern in pediatrics U. Tenn. Hosp., Knoxville, 1977-78; med. officer SHAPE Med. Ctr., Belgium, 1978-79; comdr. U.S. Army NATO Health Clinic, Belgium, 1979-80; resident in pediatrics Letterman Army Med. Ctr., San Francisco, 1980-82; pediatrician Bassett Army Community Hosp., Ft. Wainwright, Alaska, 1982-84; fellow allergy and clin. immunology Fitzsimons Army Med. Ctr., Aurora, Colo., 1984-86; allergist, immunologist Ochsner Clinic, New Orleans, 1988-89, Allergy Respiratory Inst. Colo., Denver, 1989-92; chief pediatric allergy sect. allergy-immunology svc. Fitzsimons Army Med. Ctr., Aurora, Colo., 1986-88; clin. assoc. prof. medicine Ctr. for Health Scis. U. Colo., Denver, 1990-92; assoc. prof. pediatrics and medicine Med. Coll. Ga., Augusta, 1992-98, prof., 1998—. Presenter in field. Author: (with others) Rhinolaryngoscopy, 2d edit., 1989; mem. editl. bd. Annals of Allergy, 1993-99; contbr. articles to profl. jours., chpts. to books. Assoc. dir. Augusta Choral Soc. Fellow Am. Coll. Allergy, Asthma and Immunology (bd. regents 1993-96, exec. com. 1995-96, chair comm. coun. 1993-96, disting. fellow, pres.-elect 2004-2005), Am. Acad. Allergy and Immunology (com. computers and tech. 1994-97, workshop com. 1993-96), Am. Acad. Pediats.; mem. AMA, Allergy, Asthma and Immunology Soc. of Ga. (pres. 2001-2003), Southeastern Allergy, Asthma and Clin. Immunology Soc. (pres. 2002-03), European Acad. Allergology and Clin. Immunology, Am. Guild of Organists. Episcopalian. Office: Sect Allergy Immunology Med Coll GA Augusta GA 30912

DOLENZ, MICKEY (GEORGE MICHAEL DOLENZ, MICKEY BRADDOCK), entertainer, actor, television producer; b. LA, Mar. 8, 1945; s. George and Janelle (Johnson) Dolenz; m. Samantha Just, 1967-1975 (div.) 1 daughter, m. Trina Dow, 1977-91 (div.) 3 daughters, m. Donna Quinter, 2002-. Student, Valley Coll., Los Angeles Tech. Inst. Ind. actor, musician, 1958-66; mem. The Monkees, 1966-70, 85—, star TV series, 1966-68; cartoon voice-over artist, actor, musician, 1970-77; TV dir., producer, 1977-85; solo artist, 1990—92; actor theater productions; morning host CBS-FM 101.1, NYC, 2005. Rec. artist: (The Monkees: Dolenz, Mike Nesmith, Davey Jones, Peter Tork) The Monkees, 1966, More of the Monkees, 1967, Headquarters, Pisces, Aquarius, Capircorn & Jones Ltd., 1967, The Birds, the Bees & the Monkees, 1968, (film soundtrack) Head, 1968, Instant Replay, 1969, The Monkees Present, 1969, Changes, 1969, The Monkees Greatest Hits, 1969, The Monkees Golden Hits, (The Monkees: Dolenz, Jones, Tork) Then and Now, 1986, Missing Links, 1987, vol. 2, 1990, Listen To The Bard, 1991, JustUs, 1996; hit singles include Last Train to Clarksville, Daydream Believer, Valerie, Peter Percival and his Pet Pig Porky, I'm a Believer, Steppin' Stone, Pleasant Valley Sunday; other TV series appearances include My Three Sons, Adam 12, Pacific Blues, 1995; (cartoon series) Scooby Doo, Devlin, The Funky Phantom, 1971, The Tick, 1995; (TV movies) 33 1/3 Revolutions per Monkee, 1969, Hey, Hey, It's the Monkees, 1997, The Love Bug, 1997; (films) Head, 1968, Keep off my Grass!, 1971, Night of the Strangler, 1972, Keep Off! Keep Off!, 1975, Linda Lovelace for President, 1976, Deadfall, 1993, The Brady Bunch Movie, 1995, Mom, Can I keep Her?, 1998; stage appearances include Tom Sawyer, Sacramento, 1976, The Point by Harry Nilsson, London; author: I'm a Believer: My Life of Monkees, Music and Madness, 1993.*

DOLE-RECIO, LECIA, artist; b. San Francisco, 1971; BFA, RI Sch. Design; MFA, Art Ctr. Coll. Design. Exhibited in group shows at Whitney Biennial, Whitney Mus. Am. Art, 2004, one-woman shows include, Richard Telles Fine Art, LA, Adamski Gallery Contemporary Art, Aachen, Germany, Represented in permanent collections, Mus. Contemporary Art, LA, Walker Art Ctr., Mpls., LA County Mus. Art. Mailing: c/o Whitney Museum American Art 945 Madison Ave New York NY 10021*

DOLEV, JACQUELINE, physician, researcher; b. Feb. 25, 1975; d. Sharon and Mark Dolev. BA, U. Calif, Berkeley; MD, Yale U. Sch. Medicine. Lic. Calif. Internal medicine resident Stanford U. Hosp., Calif.; dermatology resident and fellow UCSF, San Francisco. Dir. Looking with Care; med. observational skills curriculum, Stanford Med. Sch., The Cantor Center for Visual Arts, Calif.; healthcare fellow U.S Senate, Washington; co-founder Med. observational skills curriculum, Yale Ctr. for Brit. Art, New Haven; eDerm co-dir. UCSF online curriculum. Contbr. articles various profl. jours. and chpts. to books; author: (resolution) AMA Policy Compendium; author: (illustrator) (children's book) Around the World. Mem.: AMA, San Francisco Med. Soc. (editor), Calif. Med. Assn., Psi Chi Nat. Honor Soc. in Psychology.

DOLEY, HAROLD EMANUEL, JR., securities company executive; b. New Orleans, Mar. 8, 1947; s. Helena C. Doley; children: Harold E. III, Aaron M. BS, Xavier U., New Orleans, 1968; DHL (hon.), Bishop Coll., Dallas, 1983; DL (hon.), Clark Atlanta U., 1984; postgrad. bus. sch. mgmt. program, Harvard U., 1987-90; DHL (hon.), Shaw U. Div. Sch., 1992. Account exec. Bache & Co., N.Y.C. and New Orleans, 1968-73; mem. N.Y. Stock Exchange, 1973—; v.p. Howard, Weil, Labouisse & Fredericks, New Orleans, 1973-76; pres. Doley Securities Inc., New Orleans, 1976-82, 85-86, chmn., 1986—; dir. minerals mgmt. service Dept. Interior, Washington, 1982-83; U.S. rep. to African Devel. Bank and Fund, 1983-85. Instr. So. U., 1970-77; mem. La. Mineral Bd., Baton Rouge, chmn. royalty acctg. com., 1980-81. Treas. Greater New Orleans Ednl. TV, 1975-81; trustee Clark Atlanta U., 1985—, Shaw U., 1992—, African Am. Inst., 1992. Named Outstanding Stockbroker of Yr. Shareholders Mgmt. Co., 1972; winner Stock Pickers' Choice contest Wall Street Jour., 1989. Mem. N.Y. Options Exchange, Lloyds of London, Population Resource Ctr. (bd. dirs.), U.S.-Africa C. of C., Sigma Phi Phi. Republican. Office: Doley Securities 616 Baronne St New Orleans LA 70113

DOLEZAL, DALE FRANCIS, truck manufacturing company executive; b. Ronan, Mont., Apr. 9, 1936; s. Henry Lewis and Regina Marie (Nedjelski) D.; m. Patricia Louise Johnson, Aug. 27, 1960 (div. Dec. 1980); children: Craig, Kelly, Kathleen, Kari. BS in Indsl. Engring., Mont. State U., 1961; student Exec. Program for Mgmt. Devel., Bus. Sch., Harvard U., 1974. Registered profl. engr., Oreg. Indsl. and methods engr. Westinghouse Electric Corp., Sunnyvale, Calif., 1962—63; chief indsl. engr. Clarke Equipment Corp., Spokane, Wash., 1963—65; mgr. materials Freightliner Corp., Portland, Oreg., 1965—67; dir. purchasing and inventory mgmt. Internat. Harvester Co., Chgo., 1977—80, dir. materials and ops. planning, 1980—81; gen. mgr. parts and retail Indsl. Trucks div. Eaton Corp., Phila., 1981—84; pres. Modern Group, Phila., 1984—86; group v.p., gen. mgr. Holland Atlantic Hitch. Co. of Denmark, Whitehouse Sta., NJ, 1986—2001; COO Holland U.S.A., 2001—03; pres., CEO Road Guard Systems, LLC, 2003—. Pres. Positive Prints, Inc.; dir. Real Am. Corp.; mem. bd. bus. and indsl. advisers U. Wis., Madison; bd. dirs. Ops. Tng. Inst., Ea. Leadership Mgmt., Inc. Contbr. articles to trade jours. Mem. parents adv. bd. Naperville (Ill.) Central High Sch., 1977—; mem. adv. bd. Sch. Dist. 203, Naperville, 1978—; mem. New Hope (Pa.) Solebury Sch. Bd., 1982-87; mem. bd. dirs "Am. Moisture Monitoring Sys. LLC, Westland Seed, Inc., Mission Mountain Country Club. Served with USMC, 1954-57. Mem. Am. Inst. Indsl. Engrs., Am. Prodn. and Inventory Control. Soc. (pres. 1968-74), Am. Soc. Indsl. Engrs., Rotary (Paul Harris fellow 1992, bd. dirs. 1988—, pres. 1989-90), K.C. (pres.), Harvard Club. Republican. Avocations: golf, hunting, fishing. E-mail: jmartin512@aol.com, nedjelskidfd@ronan.net, ddolezal@roadguardsystems.com.

DOLGEN, JONATHAN L., former motion picture company executive; b. N.Y.C., Apr. 27, 1945; m. Susan Dolgen; children: Tamar, Lauren. Grad., Cornell U., 1966; JD, N.Y.U. Law Sch., 1969. Lawyer Fried, Frank, Harris, Shriver & Jacobson, N.Y.C, 1969-76; asst. gen. counsel, deputy gen. counsel Columbia Pictures Industries, 1976-85, sr. v.p. Worldwide Bus. Affairs, 1979, exec. v.p., 1980, pres. Pay Cable & Home Entertainment Group, 1983—85; sr. exec. v.p. Fox Inc., 1985—88, pres. Beverly Hills, 1988—90, chmn. Twentieth Century TV, 1988—90; pres. Columbia Pictures, 1990-94; pres. motion picture group Sony Pictures Entertainment, 1991—94; chmn., CEO Viacom Entertainment Group, N.Y.C., 1994—2004. Bd. fellows Claremont U. Ctr. and Grad. Sch.; founder Friends of the Cornell U. Theater Arts Ctr.; mem. Alumni Coun. N.Y.U. Law Sch.; founding mem. Edn. First; adv. Calif. State Summer Sch. for the Arts.; bd. dirs. Sony Pictures, Charter Comm. Named Pioneer of Yr., Will Rogers Motion Picture Pioneers Found., 2002.

DOLGON, COREY, sociology educator, political activist; b. Bklyn., Dec. 13, 1961; s. Fred Stewart and Arlene (Fromberg) D. BA in English/Sociology, Boston U., 1984; MA in Am. Studies, Baylor U., 1986; PhD in Am. Culture, U. Mich., 1993. Organizer Pub. Interest Rsch. Group, Ann Arbor, Mich., 1986-87; instr. U. Mich., Ann Arbor, 1987; asst. prof., Am. Studies Southampton Coll, Long Island Univ.; vis. asst. prof., social studies Worcester State Coll., Mass., assoc. prof., sociology. Coord. Wade McCree Scholar Incentive program, Ann Arbor, 1990-92. Author: The End of the Hamptons: Scenes from the Class Struggle in America's Paradise, 2005; editor: Humanity and Society, jour. of Assn. for Humanist Sociology. Organizer Students Against U.S. Intervention in the Mid. East, Ann Arbor, 1990, Homeless Action Com., Ann Arbor, 1990-92; chair Mich. Student Assemby, Students Rights Commn., Ann Arbor, 1989-90; steering com. Grad. Employees Orgn. MFT Local 3550. Mem. Homeless Action Com., Grad. Employees Orgn. Avocations: music, sports. Office: Sociology Dept Worcester State Coll 486 Chandler St Worcester MA 01602-2597 Office Phone: 508-929-8534. Business E-Mail: cdolgon@worcester.edu.*

DOLGOPYAT, MAX, microbiologist; b. Kiev, Ukraine, Sept. 26, 1978; s. Leonid and Yelena Dolgopyat; m. Dawn R. Scott, July 17, 2004. BS in Biology, Rutgers U., 2000; AS in Chemistry, Middlesex County Coll., 1998. Quality control analyst ImClone Systems, Somerville, NJ, 2003—04; quality control sr. analyst ImClone Sys., Somerville, NJ, 2004—. Musician: (concerts) Rock Guitarist. Mem.: Am. Soc. Microbiology, Perenteral Drug Assn. Avocations: music, reading, new age philosophy. Office: ImClone Sys 33 Chubb Way Somerville NJ 08876 Office Phone: 908-541-2922. E-mail: max.dolgopyat@imclone.com.

DOLHANCYK, DIANA See PAMIN, DIANA DOLHANCYK

DOLIBER, DARREL LEE, retired engineering consultant, hotel executive; b. Mpls., June 19, 1940; s. Russell Clifford Doliber and Helen Carol (Homa) Price; m. Ethel Lorraine Dzivi, June 17, 1962; children: Wendy Lorraine, Heather Leigh; m. Helga Renate Miggo, Oct. 31, 1986. AA, Palomar Coll., 1973. Prodn. engr. Hughes Aircraft Co., Carlsbad, Calif., 1969-74; sr. engr. I.T.T., Roanoke, Va., 1974-77; dir. mfg. Gainsboro Elec. Mfg. Co., Inc., Roanoke, Va., 1977-78; mfg. engr. Litton Industries, Tempe, Ariz., 1978-82; sr. engr. Datagraphix, Inc., San Diego, 1982-84; lab. mgr. S.A.I.C., San Diego, 1984-98; cons. in photon counting detectors, UHV sys. Cleanroom Design, Med. Devices, Alpine, Calif., 1996—2002; propr. Victoria Rock Bed and Breakfast, 1995—. Contbr. articles in field; patentee in field. Mem. Soc. Photo-Optical and Instrumentation Engrs. Roman Catholic. Avocations: art, soaring. Home and Office: 2952 N Victoria Dr Alpine CA 91901-3673

DOLICH, ANDREW BRUCE, sports marketing executive; b. Bklyn., Feb. 18, 1947; s. Mac and Yetta (Weiselter) D.; m. Ellen Andrea Fass, June 11, 1972; children: Lindsey, Caryn, Cory. BA, Am. U., 1969; MEd, Ohio U., 1971. Adminstrv. asst. to gen. mgr. Phila. 76ers, NBA, Pa., 1971-74; v.p. Md. Arrows Lacrosse, Landover, Md., 1974-76; mktg. dir. Washington Capitals, NHL, Landover, Md., 1976-78; exec. v.p., gen. mgr. Washington Diplomats Soccer, 1978-80; v.p. bus. ops. Oakland A's Baseball, Calif., 1980-92, exec. v.p., 1993-95; pres., COO Golden State Warriors NBA, Oakland, Calif., 1995-98; pres. Dolich & Assoc. Sports Mktg., Alameda, Calif., 1996—; exec.

v.p. Tickets.com, 1998—; pres. Memphis Grizzlies, 2000—. Nat. fundraising chmn. sports adminstrs. program Ohio U., Athens, dir., 1978-82; lectr. sports mktg. U. Calif. Ext. Bd. dirs. Bay Area Sports Hall of Fame, 1982—, Grizzlies Found, Sports Exec. Leadership Coun., 2000-04, MIFA, Memphis Art Coun. Recipient Alumni of Yr. award Ohio U. Sports Adminstrs. Program, Athens, 1982; recipient Clio award Am. Advt. Fedn., 1982 Mem.: Memphis C. of C., Memphis Sports Commn. Office Phone: 901-205-1234. Business E-Mail: adolich@grizzlies.com.

D'OLIMPIO, JAMES THOMAS, oncologist; b. Quincy, Mass., June 3, 1950; s. Orlando James D'Olimpio and Marie Johanna Ricciuti; m. Louise Mary Simon, May 30, 1980 (div. Apr. 1994); children: Matthew, Christopher; m. Mary Suzanne Clifford, Dec. 30, 1995; 1 child, John. BA, Boston U., 1972; MD, U. Guadalajara, 1978. Diplomate Am. Bd. Internal Medicine and Med. Oncology, and Hospice/Palliative Medicine. Intern, resident Mt. Sinai Hosp., N.Y.C., 1979—82; resident Oncology, fellow Montefiore Med. Ctr., Bronx, NY, 1982—84; rsch. fellow Albert Einstein Coll. Medicine, Bronx, 1984—85; dir. Hospice Care Network North Shore L.I. Jewish Health Sys., Westbury, NY, 1992—97, dir. Supportive Oncology and Palliative Medicine Program Manhasset, NY, 1997—. Asst. prof. medicine NYU Sch. Medicine. Contbr. articles to profl. jours. Grantee, United Hosp. Fund, 2000—02. Mem.: Cancer and Leukemia Group B, Multinat. Assn. Supportive Care in Cancer, Am. Acad. Hospice and Palliative Medicine (cert. 1997), Am. Pain Soc., Am. Soc. Clin. Oncology. Avocations: jazz, painting, golf. Office: North Shore Univ Hosp 300 Community Dr Manhasset NY 11030

DOLIN, LONNY H., lawyer; b. Youngstown, Ohio, Jan. 24, 1954; d. Lawrence Joseph and Sonya (Sacks) Heselov; m. Gordon S. Black, Aug. 20, 1988; children: Nathaniel, Brooke, Aaron, Benjamin, Lindsay. AB, Georgetown U., 1976; JD, Cath. U., 1979. Bar: Vt. 1980, N.Y. State Bar 1984, U.S. Dist. Ct. (we. dist.) N.Y. 1984. Assoc. Downs, Rachlin & Martin, Burlington, Vt., 1979-81; pvt. practice Burlington, 1981-84; assoc., then ptnr. Harris, Beach, Wilcox, Rubin & Levey, Rochester, N.Y., 1984-90; ptnr. Harris, Beach & Wilcox, Rochester, N.Y., 1990-93; former of counsel to U.S. Congressman Fred J. Eckert, N.Y.; ptnr. Lonny H. Dolin and Assocs., Rochester, 1993—. Bd. dirs. Monroe County Legal Services Corp.; faculty mem. Nat. Adv. Inst.; co-chair 2d and 3d Ann. Nat. Inst. on Sexual Harassment; spkr. in field. Asst. editor ABA's Sect. of Labor and Employment Law Newsletter; contbr. chpts. and articles to profl. jours. Mem. Pittsford Town and County Com., N.Y., 1983—, Town of Pittsford Bd. of Zoning Appeals, N.Y., 1984—, vice chair 1990; chmn. Monroe County Comparable Worth Task Force, Rochester, 1985—, Fred J. Eckert Women's Adv. Council, Rochester, 1985—; del. The Jud. Dist. N.Y., Rochester, 1985—, chair 1990; bd. dirs. Nat. Council Jewish Women. Recipient Corpus Juris Secundum award West Pub. co., 1979. Fellow Coll. Labor and Employment Lawyers; mem. ABA (plaintiff's chair labor and amployment law sect., co-chair nat. CLE/Inst. and Meetings Com., nat. co-chair employee's rights and responsibilities ethics subcom., nat. vice chair tort and ins. practice sect., spkr. ann. meetings), Nat. Employment Law Assn. (co-chair disabilities rights com.), Vt. Bar Assn., N.Y. Bar Assn., Monroe County Bar Assn. (mem. practice and perf. com.), Greater Rochester Women's Bar Assn. (treas. 1986), Assn. Trial Lawyers Am., N.Y. State Trial Lawyers Assn., Genesee Valley Trial Lawyers Assn. (treas. 1990). Republican. Avocations: golf, skiing, tennis. Home: 9 Hidden Springs Dr Pittsford NY 14534-2897 Office: Dolin Thomas & Solomon LLP 693 E Ave Rochester NY 14607 Fax: 716-272-0574. E-mail: ldolin@dts.esg.com.

DOLIN, MITCHELL F., lawyer; b. Augusta, Ga., Feb. 6, 1956; s. Martin and Harriet Dolin; m. Monica P. Dolin; 2 children. BA, Tufts U., 1978; JD, NYU, 1981. Bar: DC 1982, registered: US Supreme Ct. 1986. Clk. to chief judge U.S. Ct. Appeals (5th cir.), 1981-82; assoc. Covington & Burling, Washington, 1982-89, ptnr., 1989—, chmn. Arbitration & Alternative Dispute Resolution Practice Group, chmn. client devel. com. Mem.: ABA, Human Rights First (past bd. dir.), Am. Judicature Soc. (past bd. dir.), Am. Law Inst. Office: Covington & Burling 1201 Pennsylvania Ave NW Washington DC 20004-2401

DOLIN, RAPHAEL, medical educator; b. Kaunas, Lithuania, Aug. 31, 1941; came to the U.S., 1950; s. Simon and Sara (Zolkov) D.; m. Kelly Millar, June 17, 1989; children: Eric, Nathaniel, Brooke, Allison. BS, Harvard U., 1963, MD, 1967. Intern Boston City Hosp., 1967—68, resident, 1968—69; rsch. assoc. Nat. Inst. Allergy and Infectious Diseases, NIH, Bethesda, Md., 1969-72, fellow in infectious disease, 1972-73, head med. virology sect., 1972-78; prof. medicine U. Vt., Burlington, 1978-82; prof. medicine, head infectious disease unit U. Rochester, N.Y., 1982-91, prof. microbiology and immunology, 1982-98, Charles A. Dewey prof., chair dept. medicine, 1991-98; physician in chief Strong Meml. Hosp., Rochester, NY, 1991—97; dean for clin. programs Harvard Med. Sch., 1997—2003, dean for academic and clin. programs, 2003—, Maxwell Finland prof. medicine. Editor: Principles and Practice of Infectious Disease, 1995, AIDS Therapy, 1999. Fellow Infectious Disease Soc. Am.; mem. Am. Soc. for Clin. Investigation, Assn. Am. Physicians. Office: Harvard Med Sch 25 Shattuck St Rm 101 Boston MA 02115-6027

DOLINER, NATHANIEL LEE, lawyer; b. Daytona Beach, Fla., June 28, 1949; s. Joseph and Asia (Shaffer) D.; m. Debra Lynn Simon, June 5, 1983. BA, George Washington U., 1970; JD, Vanderbilt U., 1973; LLM in Taxation, U. Fla., 1977. Bar: Fla. 1973. Assoc. Smalbein, Eubank, Johnson, Rosier & Bussey, PA, Daytona Beach, Fla., 1973-76; vis. asst. prof. law U. Fla. Law Sch., Gainesville, 1977-78; assoc. Carlton, Fields, Ward, Emmanuel, Smith & Cutler, PA, Tampa, Fla., 1978-82; shareholder Carlton Fields, PA, Tampa, 1982—, chair bus. transactions practice group, 1984—. Spkr. in field. Adv. bd. Mergers and Acquisitions Law Report, pub. Bur. Nat. Affairs. Dist. commr. Gulf Ridge coun. Boy Scouts Am., 1983—84; bd. dirs. Kol Ami Synagogue, Tampa, 2003—04, Big Bros./Big Sisters Greater Tampa, Inc., 1980—82, Child Abuse Coun., Inc., 1986—95, asst. treas., 1987—88, treas., 1988—89, pres.-elect, 1989—90, pres., 1990—91; bd. dirs. Tampa Jewish Fedn. Bd., 1988—91, Mus. Sci. and Industry, Tampa, 1994—2002, 2004—, exec. com., 1994—2002, sec., 1995—97, first vice-chmn., 1997—99, chair, 1999—2001; mem. alumni bd. Vanderbilt Law Sch., 1999—2000; bd. dirs. Hillel Sch., Tampa, 1998—, first v.p., 1999—2000, pres., 2001—03. Fellow: Am. Coll. Tax Counsel, Am. Bar Found. (bus. law sect., mem. coun.); mem.: ABA (chmn. task force preliminary and ancillary agreements 1992—95, acquisition rev. task force 1992—95, co-chmn. various presdl. showcase programs 1994—, chmn. programs subcom. 1995—98, vice-chmn. 1997—98, chmn. 1998—2002, mem. coun. 2002—, chair coun. com. on com. support and structure, panelist confs., negotiated acqusitions com., bus. law sect.), Tampa C. of C. (chmn. Ambassadors Target Task Force of Com. of 100 1984—85, 1987—88, vice-chmn. govt. fin. and taxation coun. 1987—88, chmn. 1988—89, chair geographic task force 1989—90, bd. govs. 1991—93, exec. com. 1992, chmn. govtl. affairs com. 1992), Fla. Bar Assn. (exec. coun. tax sect. 1980—82, tax cert. com. 1987—88, vice-chmn. 1988—89, chmn. 1989—90), Am. Law Inst., Anti-Defamation League (regional bd. dirs. 1986—90, exec. com. 1987—90), Tampa Club (sec. 1987—89, bd. dirs. 1987—92, pres. 1990—91). Home: 13341 Golf Crest Cir Tampa FL 33624-4648 Office: Carlton Fields Ward Emmanuel Smith & Cutler PA 4221 W Boy Scout Blvd Tampa FL 33607-5736 Office Phone: 813-229-4208. Business E-Mail: ndoliner@carltonfields.com.

DOLINICH-MATUSKA, CHRISTINE, artist; b. Elizabeth, N.J., Feb. 24, 1950; d. Anton J. and Irene Marie (Kutay) Dolinich; m. John A. Matuska, Jr., Aug. 14, 1993. Student, Oxford U., England, 1970-71; BA in Studio Art, Rutgers U., 1973; postgrad., Westminster Choir Coll., 1984, 86. Dir. Union County Conservatory, Rahway, N.J., 1987—, Linden (N.J.) Art and Music Studio, 1983-87; critiquer Union County Teen Arts Festival, Union Coll., Cranford, N.J., 1986-94; curator visual arts Merck and Co., Inc., Rahway, 1989; profl. rev. panelist Union County Arts Grants Com., 1990-94. Exhibited in group shows at Los Angeles Women's Ctr., Houston U., Utah U., 1977, Newark Mus., 1982, City Without Walls Gallery, Newark, 1982, 83, 84, 85, 86, Morris Mus., Morristown, N.J., 1987, Merck & Co., Rahway, 1989-93, Douglass Coll.; one-woman shows include Caldwell (N.J.) Coll., 1976, 82, 89, Middlesex Coll. Art Gallery, Edison, N.J., 1985, Douglass Coll. Women Artists Series, 1986-87, Rutgers U., New Brunswick, N.J., 1987, Brookdale Coll, 1988; artists books Rutgers U., U. of Delaware, Newark Library, New Brunswick, 1982-83. Fellow N.J. State Coun. on the Arts, 1984-85; recipient Frist prize Art with Mus. Subjects Cover Contest, Best Mixed Media Work, 1992. Mem. AAUW (radio host Sta. WFMU Women in Music and Art Series 1984-85, lectr., slide and tape presentation Women in Art and Music 1985), Women's Caucus for Art, Music Tchr. Nat. Assn. (1st prize Am. Music Tchr. 1981, 83), Piano Tchrs. Soc. Am. (Genia Robinor Pedagogy award 1989-94, cert. in piano pedagogy). Home: 1348 Pierce St Rahway NJ 07065-3932

DOLINKO, ROBERT A., lawyer; b. New York, NY, Oct. 9, 1953; married; 2 children. BS in Indsl. & Labor Relations, Cornell U., 1974; JD, NYU, 1977. Bar: Calif. 1977. Assoc. Littler Mendelson, San Francisco, 1977—80; labor atty. Merck & Co. Inc., Whitehouse Station, NJ, 1980—82; assoc. Epstein, Becker & Green, San Francisco, 1982—86, ptnr., 1986—94; ptnr., labor & employment dept. Thelen Reid & Priest LLP, San Francisco. Lectr. Cornell U. Sch. Indsl. & Labor Relations, Ithaca, NY, 1980—82. Bd. trustees Seven Hills Sch., Walnut Creek, Calif., 1992—. Mem.: ABA (Labor Sect.), State Bar Calif. (Labor Sect.). Office: Thelen Reid & Priest LLP 101 Second St Ste 1800 San Francisco CA 94105-3606 Office Phone: 415-369-7180. Office Fax: 415-371-1211. Business E-Mail: radolinko@thelenreid.com.

DOLL, LYNNE MARIE, public relations agency executive; b. Glendale, Calif., Aug. 27, 1961; d. George William and Carol Ann (Kennedy) D.; m. David Jay Lans, Oct. 11, 1986. BA in Journalism, Calif. State U., Northridge, 1983. Freelance writer Austin Pub. Rels. Systems, Glendale, 1978-82; asst. account exec. Berkhemer & Kline, L.A., 1982-83; pres. Rogers & Assocs., L.A., 1983—. Exec. dir. Suzuki Automotive Found. for Life, Brea, Calif., 1986-91; mem. strategic planning com. Gateway to Indian Am. Corp. for Am. Indian Devel., San Francisco, 1988-90. Pub. rels. cons., Rape Treatment Ctr., L.A., 1986—. Mem. Ad Club L.A. (bd. dirs., pres. 1994-95), Pub. Rels. Soc. Am. (L.A. chpt. Outstanding Profl. 1999), So. Calif. Assn. Philanthropy, Coun. on Founds., Internat. Motor Press Assn., Nat. Conf. for Cmty. and Justice (L.A. region bd. dirs. 1996—, nat. bd. dirs. 2002—). Democrat. Office: Rogers & Assocs 1875 Century Park E Ste 300 Los Angeles CA 90067-2504

DOLLAR, DAVID RICHARD, economist; b. St. Louis, Nov. 21, 1954; s. John Gabriel and Muriel Irene Dollar; m. Lesley Paige Whitley, Sept. 13, 1987; children: Isabel Lord, Evan Whitley. BA, Dartmouth Coll., Hanover, NH, 1972—75; PhD, NY Univ., N.Y.C., 1978—84. Asst. prof. Univ. Calif. at Los Angeles, 1984—89; country economist for Vietnam World Bank, Washington, 1989—95, rsch. mgr., 1995—2003, dir. of devel. policy, 2003—04, country dist. for China and Mongolia, 2004—. Author: (econ. rsch. books and articles) Globalization, Growth, and Poverty; Assessing Aid; jour. articles in Am. Econ. Rev., Quar. Jour of Econ., Rev. of Economics and Stats., Econ. Jour., Jour of Devel. Economics. Mem.: Am. Econ. Assn. Office: World Bank 1818 H St NW Washington DC 20433 Business E-Mail: ddollar@worldbank.org.

DOLLARHIDE, MARY C., lawyer; b. Long Beach, Calif., Jan. 28, 1957; BA with distinction, Occidental Coll., 1979; OTH, Circle Sq. Theatre Sch., N.Y.C., 1981; JD, U. Southern Calif., 1988. Bar: Calif. 1988, D.C. 1991, Conn. 1996. Ptnr. Paul, Hastings, Janofsky & Walker LLP, San Diego, chmn. recruiting. Author: Workers & the Web: Employment Pitfalls Related Email & Internet, 1999, What Bus. Must Know About Americans With Disabilities Act, 1991. Mem.: ABA-Planning Com. EEO Com. Mid-Winter Meeting (mgmt. co-chmn. 2003—04), ABA-Nat. Planning Com. EEO Basics Program (mgmt. chm. 2001—02). Office: Paul Hastings Janofsky & Walker LLP 3579 Valley Center Dr San Diego CA 92130 Office Phone: 858-720-8660. Office Fax: 858-647-3660. Business E-Mail: marydollarhide@paulhastings.com.

DOLLENS, RONALD W., pharmaceutical executive; b. Ind., Dec. 17, 1946; s. William Franklin and Louise Anna (Davis) D.; m. Susan Stanley, Aug. 30, 1969; children: Stephanie, Grant. BS, Purdue U., 1970; MBA, Ind. U., 1972. From sales rep. to dir. bus. devel. Eli Lilly & Co., Indpls., 1972-85; sr. v.p. Advanced Cardiovasc. Sys., Santa Clara, 1985—88, pres., CEO Santa Clara, 1988—94; pres. med. devices divsn. Eli Lilly & Co., 1991-94; pres., CEO Guidant Corp., Indpls., 1994—. Mem., Adv. Com. on Regulatory Health US Dept. Health & Human Svcs., 2002—; memb. bd. Ind. Health Industry Forum, Kinetic Concepts Inc., Beckman Coulter Corp. Bd. dir. Butler U., Indpls., Eiteljorg Mus., Indpls., St. Vincent Hosp. Found. Mem.: AdvaMed, Alliance for Aging Rsch., Healthcare Leadership Coun. (chmn. 2003—05). Office: Guidant 111 Monument Cir 29th Fl Indianapolis IN 46204*

DOLLIVER, ROBERT HENRY, psychology professor; b. Fort Dodge, Iowa, Oct. 15, 1934; BA, Cornell Coll., 1958; MA, Ohio State U., 1963, PhD, 1966. Social worker Bd. Child Welfare, Elyria, Ohio, 1958-59; social worker Cleve. Boys Sch., 1959-61; asst., then assoc. prof. psychology U. Mo., Columbia, 1966-77, prof., 1977-99, prof. emeritus, 1999—. Office: U Mo Dept Psychology Columbia MO 65211-0001 E-mail: SnoopyRHD@aol.com.

DOLMAN, EDWARD JAMES, auction house executive; b. Feb. 24, 1960; m. Clare Dolman; 2 children. Student, Dulwich Coll., London, Southampton U. Various positions including porter, specialist, dir. and dept. head Christie's Fine Art Auctioneers, South Kensington, 1984—89; mng. dir. Christie's Amsterdam, Netherlands, 1995—97, Christie's Europe, 1997—99, Christie's Ams., NY, 1999—; CEO Christie's Internat., 2000—. Office: Christies Fine Art Auctioneers 20 Rockefeller Plaza New York NY 10020

DOLMAN, JOHN PHILLIPS, JR., (TIM DOLMAN), communications company executive; b. Phila., May 22, 1944; s. John Phillips and Dodie Lewis (Porter) D.; m. Rebecca Critchlow, Oct. 29, 1977; children— John P. III, Timothy Chadwick (dec.). AB in History, Wagner Coll., 1966; MBA. in Internat. Bus, U. Pa., 1971. Asst. account exec. Benton & Bowles Inc., N.Y.C., 1971-72, account exec., 1972-73, account dir Amsterdam and London, 1973-75, v.p., account supr., 1975-78; pub. Motor Boating & Sailing mag., 1978-80; gen. mgr. mag. devel. Hearst Mags., N.Y.C., 1980-82; v.p., asst. pub. Pub. div. Playboy Enterprises, Inc., Chgo., 1983-84, sr. v.p., 1984-88; pres. Dolman & Co., New Canaan, Conn., 1988-92; sr. v.p. mktg. Championship Auto Racing Teams, Inc. dba IndyCar, 1992-94; v.p. mktg. and bus. devel. OCC Sports Inc. subs. ESPN, Inc. subs. ABC, Inc. subs. Walt Disney Co., 1994-99; v.p. dir., bus. ops. ESPN, ABC Sports Mktg. and Sales, 1999—2005; v.p. strategy and bus. devel. ESPN New Media, 2005—. Contbr.: Marine Bus. mag, 1977-78. 1st lt. U.S. Army, 1966-69, Vietnam; lic. capt. USCG, 1988. Decorated Bronze Star. Mem. VFW, N.Y. Yacht Club. Republican. Episcopalian. Office Phone: 212-448-4814. E-mail: TDolman@aol.com.

DOLMATCH, THEODORE BIELEY, management consultant; b. N.Y.C., Apr. 22, 1924; s. Aaron and Diana (Bieley) D.; m. Blanche Ormont, Dec. 28, 1948; children: Karen Ann, Stephen Joseph. BA, NYU, 1947, MA, 1948; student, Columbia U., N.Y.C., 1948-50. Tchr. Queens Coll., 1948-50; asst. supr. Sch. Gen. Studies, Bklyn. Coll., 1950-55; publs. bus. mgr. Am. Mgmt. Assn., 1955-62; pres. Pitman Pub. Corp., N.Y.C., 1962-71, Intext Publishers Group, N.Y.C., also Intext Ednl. Devel. Group, N.Y.C., 1971-75, Info. Please Pub., Inc., N.Y.C., 1976-80, Dolmatch Publs., Inc., N.Y.C., 1979-85; cons. to govt. agys. and corps., 1981—; chmn. ISD/Shaw, Inc., Washington, 1986-2000. Author (sometimes under pseudonym Stephen Josephs) books and articles. Home: 15 Pond View Ln Ossining NY 10562 E-mail: t.dolmatch@verizon.net.

DOLMATOV, VALERIY KONSTANTINOVICH, physicist, researcher; MSc in Physics, Tashkent State U., 1977, PhD in Theoretical and Math. Physics, 1985. Engr. S.V. Starodubtsev Phys.-Tech. Inst., Tashkent, 1977, sr. engr., 1977-78, jr. scientist, 1978-86, scientist, 1986-88, sr. scientist, 1989-91, Inst. Materials Sci., Tashkent, 1991-97; leading scientist S.V. Starodubtsev Phys.-Tech. Inst., Tashkent, 1997—2002; asst. prof. U. North Ala., Florence, Ala., 2002—. Assoc. prof. Inst. Ry. Transport Engrs., Tashkent, 1988-89; contracted referee Internat. Assn., Brussels, 1998—; external referee PhD theses Supreme Attestation Com. on PhD Theses, Cabinet Mins. of Uzbekistan, Tashkent, 1995—. Contbr. articles to profl. jours. Alexander von Humboldt rsch. fellow, 1991-93, vis. scientist fellow Royal Soc. London, 1996; NSF Internat. Supplementary grantee, 1997-98, Collaborative Linkage grantee NATO, 1999, Expert Visit grantee NATO, 2000. Mem. Am. Phys. Soc., European Phys. Soc. Avocations: soccer, ping pong/table tennis, hiking, swimming. Office: U North Alabama Dept Physics and Earth Science PO Box 5101 Florence AL 35632 Business E-Mail: vkdolmatov@una.edu.

DOLNICK, BRUCE JEFFREY, research scientist, consultant; s. Daniel Harold and Evelyn Harriette Dolnick; m. Ree Young Lee, Apr. 10, 1993; 1 child, Jessica Elaine. BS, SUNY, Stony Brook, 1973; PhD, SUNY, Buffalo, 1977. Assoc. prof. Roswell Pk. Cancer Inst., Buffalo, 1988—92, prof., 1992—. Expert witness in field. Recipient Faculty Rsch. award, Am. Cancer Soc., 1987—92. Fellow: AAAS. Achievements include patents pending for a high throughput assay to identify thymidylate synthase modulators; rts signaling pathway for regulation of cellgrowth. Office: Roswell Park Cancer Inst Elm and Carlton Sts Buffalo NY 14263 Office Phone: 716-845-5828. E-mail: bruce.dolnick@roswellpark.org.

DOLORES, FIDISHUN, librarian, educator; b. East Stroudsburg, Pa., Dec. 7, 1955; d. John M. Fidishun, Dolores A. Fidishun; m. Albert J. Labonis. BS, Kutztown U., 1976; MS Libr. Sci., Drexel U., 1982; MEd, Widener U., 1993, EdD, 1996. Libr. Bensalem Sch. Dist., 1976—77; libr., media specialist Palisades Sch. Dist., Kintnersville, 1977—85; head audiovisual svcs. Montgomery County-Norristown Pub. Libr., Norristown, 1985—87, Widener U., Chester, 1987—95; head libr. Pa. State Great Valley Sch. Grad. Profl. Studies, Malvern, 1995—. Cons. Sch. Dist. of Borough of Morrisville, Computer Tng., 1997—98. Recipient Library Sci. award, Kutztown U., Pa., 1976. Mem.: ALA, Libr. Info. and Tech. Assn., Libr. Adminstrn. and Mgmt. Assn., Assn. Ednl. Comm. and Tech., Assn. Coll. and Rsch. Librs. (women's studies sect. chair 2002), Phi Kappa Phi. Roman Catholic. Office: Pa State U Great Valley Libr 30 E Swedesford Rd Malvern PA 19355 Office Phone: 610-648-3227. Office Fax: 610-725-5223.

DOLPH, WILBERT EMERY, lawyer; b. Palatka, Fla., Dec. 29, 1923; s. Wilbert Emery and Ophelia (Reynolds) D.; m. Roberta Hundley; children: Wilbert Emery III, Kenneth Alan, Scott Marshall, Cheryl Karlsson. Student, U. Ariz., 1941-42, LL.B., 1949. Bar: Ariz. 1949. Asst. city atty., Tucson, 1949-50; asst. atty. gen. Ariz., 1950-51; pvt. practice Tucson, 1951—93; counsel. jud. com. Ariz. Senate, 1952; shareholder Bilby & Shoenhair, P.C., 1953-89; ptnr. Snell & Wilmer, Tucson, 1989-93, of counsel, 1992-93; ret., 1993. Pres. Pima County Young Dems., 1952-53; v.p. Ariz. Young Dems., 1952-53; trustee Tucson Med. Ctr., pres., 1973-75; mem. U. Ariz. Found., U. Ariz. Pres.'s Club; past chmn. bd. dirs. Friends of Libr., U. Ariz., 1995-97; past bd. visitors U. Ariz. Law Coll.; past bd. dirs. Ariz. Sonora Desert Mus., Ariz. Heart Assn., So. Ariz. Heart Assn., Tucson Festival Soc., Ariz. Children's Home Assn., Tucson YMCA, Ariz. Coun. Econ. Edn.; past vestryman, parish warden St. Phlips in the Hills Episcopal Ch., 1974-76. With USNR, 1942-44, to capt. USMCR, 1944-46. Decorated Air medal. Mem. ABA, Ariz. Bar Assn., Pima County Bar Assn. (exec. com., pres. 1974-75), Coronado Hosp. Found., Rotary Club, Coronado Roundtable, Coronado Yacht Club, Phi Delta Phi, Sigma Chi. Personal E-mail: wedolph@san.rr.com.

DOLUISIO, JAMES THOMAS, pharmacy educator; b. Bethlehem, Pa., Sept. 28, 1935; s. Dominic and Sue (Powell) D.; m. Phyllis M. Sabolski, June 20, 1959; children— Thomas, James, Rebecca. BS in Pharmacy, Temple U., 1957, MS, 1959; PhD, Purdue U., 1962; DSc, Phila. Coll. Pharmacy and Sci., 1983; DSc (hon.), Purdue U., 1995, Wilkes U., 2000. From asst. prof. to assoc. prof. pharmacy Phila. Coll. Pharmacy and Sci., 1961-67, also assoc. dir. dept., 1965-67; prof., chmn. dept. pharmacy U. Ky., Lexington, 1967-73; prof., dean U. Tex., Austin, 1973-98. Bd. dirs. Eckerd Corp., 1986-96, COR Therapeutics, 1994-02; cons. Smith Kline & French Labs., Phila., 1962-67, McNeil Labs., Ft. Washington, Pa., 1967-72, Hoechst Labs., Somerville, N.J., 1973-93, Nat. Inst. Drug Abuse, 1976-78, HEW, U.S. Surgeon Gen., 1975-83; cons. Merck-Medco, Franklin Lakes, N.J., 2000-2001. Contbr. to profl. and sci. jours. Active Pharmacists Against Drug Abuse Found, 1984; chmn. U.S. Pharmacopeial Conv., Inc., 1990-95; v.p. Fedn. Internat. Pharmaceutique, 1994-98. NSF fellow, 1959-61; Am. Found. Pharm. Edn. fellow, 1957-59 Mem. Am. Pharm. Assn. (Remington Honor medal 1995), Am. Assn. Colls. Pharmacy, Am. Soc. Hosp. Pharmacy, Am. Assn. Pharm. Scientists, Fed. Internat. Pharmacists (Lifetime Achievement award 2000), Rho Chi. Office: U Texas College of Pharmacy Austin TX 78712 Office Phone: 512-471-3718. Business E-Mail: doluisio.jt@mail.utexas.edu.

DOMAN, ELVIRA, retired science administrator; b. NYC; d. Andrew and Lillian (McClary) Hand; m. John H. Holder (div.); children: Paula Holder Simpkins, Rodney M. BA in Chemistry, CUNY, 1955; MA in Biochemistry, Columbia U., 1959; MS in Molecular Biology, NYU, 1960; PhD in Physiology and Biochemistry, Rutgers U., 1965. Jr. tech. U. Hosp. N.Y.U. Bellevue Med. Ctr., 1955; rsch. asst. Coll. Physicians and Surgeons, N.Y.C., 1959-60, Sloan-Kettering Inst. Cancer Rsch., N.Y.C., 1959-60, postdoctoral assoc., postdoctoral fellow, 1965; rsch. assoc. Rockefeller U., N.Y.C., 1965-68; lectr. Douglass Coll. Rutgers U., New Brunswick, N.J., 1970-73; asst. prof. Seton Hall U., South Orange, N.J., 1973-77; assoc. program dir. NSF, Washington, 1978-92, program dir., 1992-99; ret., 1999. Vis. scientist Rutgers U., 1989; reader Gates Millenium Scholars, Fairfax, Va., 2002—; sci. fair judge pub., pvt. schs., colls. Bd. dirs. Math. Sci., Computer Learning Ctr. of Shiloh Bapt. Ch., Washington, 1989—. Recipient Achievement award NSF, 1986, 92, Outstanding Mentor award U. Md. Balt. County, 2000; grantee Seton Hall U., 1975. Fellow Am. Inst. Chemists; mem. AAAS, Am. Chem. Soc., Assn. Women Sci., Minority Women Sci., Orgn. Black Sci. (pres. 1990-93).

DOMAR, ALICE DIANE, psychologist, educator; b. Balt., May 1, 1958; d. Evsey David and Carola Rosenthal Domar; m. David Allen Ostrow, Aug. 26, 1990; children: Sarah Domar Ostrow, Katherine Domar Ostrow. BA, Colby Coll., Waterville, Maine, 1980; MA, Yeshiva U., N.Y., 1984, PhD, 1986. lic. psychologist, Mass. Staff psychologist Deaconess Hosp., Boston, 1988-96; sr. scientist Mind/Body Med. Inst., Boston, 1994—2002, dir. ctr. women's health, 1994—2002; dir. Mind/Body Ctr. Women's Health, Boston IVF, 2002—. Asst. prof. Harvard Med. Sch., Boston, 1994—. Author: (book) Healing Mind, Healthy Woman, 1996, Self-Nurture, 2000, Conquering Infertility, 2002; co-author: Six Steps to Increased Fertility, 2000; adv. bd.: Parent's Mag., columnist: Health Mag. Bd. experts Lluminari. Recipient Young Investigators award, Mass. Dept. Pub. Health, 1993; grant Nat. Inst. Mental Health, 1990, 94. Mem. Mental Health Profl. Group (chair), 1997-98. Avocations: travel, cooking, reading. Office: 40 Second Ave Ste 300 Waltham MA 02451 Business E-Mail: alice.domar@bostonivf.com.

DOMBECK, HAROLD ARTHUR, insurance company executive; b. Bronx, NY, Mar. 23, 1941; s. Max J. and Rose R. (Schefren) D.; m. Cynthia E. Kofoed, May 14, 1983; children: Mark J., Glenn D., David S. BCE, NYU, 1962, MCE, 1963. Profl. engr., N.Y., N.J., Conn., Ga. Instr. San Antonio Coll., 1964-65, SUNY, Farmingdale, 1965-68; project mgr. H2M Group, Melville, NY, 1965-74, dir. environ. engring., 1971-81, dir. mktg., 1982-85, exec. v.p., 1986-88, pres., 1989-91, pres., CEO, chmn., 1991-94; CEO Dombeck Assocs. Inc., Duluth, Ga., 1995—. Chmn., CEO Archs. and Engrs. Ins. Co., Naperville, Ill., 1987—; v.p., CFO, Dod/Pritchard Comms. Inc., Norcross, Ga., 1998-2001; dir., Perceptive Solutions, Inc., Norcross, 2001-03; chmn. bd. dirs. Am. Cons. Engrs. Pension Trust, St. Louis, 1991-94; chmn. ACEC Bus. Inst. Trust, St. Louis, 1994-96. Pres. High Woods Civic Assn., St. James, N.Y., 1971-73, River Plantation Homeowners Assn., 1999-2001. 1st lt. USAF, 1963-65. Fellow ASCE, Am. Cons. Engrs. Coun. (pres. L.I. 1982-84); mem. Am. Acad. Environ. Engrs. (diplomate), NSPE (dir. 1982-85), N.Y. State Water Pollution Control Assn. (dir. 1980-83), N.Y. State Soc. Profl. Engrs.

(pres. 1983-84, pres. Suffolk County chpt. 1978-80, Engr. of Yr. 1989, 90, Outstanding Svc. awards 1988, 89). Avocations: reading, golf, history. Office: AEIC 2056 Westings Ave Naperville IL 60563 Personal E-mail: hadombeck@yahoo.com.

DOMBROSKI, RICHELLE BRAGG, secondary school educator; b. Bloomington, Ill., Nov. 19, 1960; d. Raymond Jack Bragg and Joanne (Phillips) Saravia; m. Ronald E. Dombroski, July 2, 1994. BA in History, U. N.C., 1984. Cert. secondary educator N.C. Interim tchr. John T. Hoggard H.S., Wilmington, N.C., 1984-85; tchr. Williston Jr. H.S., Wilmington, N.C., 1985-88; tchr., dept. chmn. E.A. Laney H.S., Wilmington, N.C., 1986. Chmn. Laney Sch. Improvement Team, Wilmington, 1989-97; mem. County Curriculum Com., Wilmington, 1992-93, Laney Sch. Adv. Bd., 1992-93. Vol. Rape Crisis Ctr., Wilmington, 1985-90; mem. Rape Crisis Adv. Bd., Wilmington, 1985-90; tchr. Sunday sch. St. Mary's Cath. Ch., Wilmington, 1992—. Recipient Cram Map award, 1989, Raleigh (N.C.) Gov.'s award, 1991, State Farm Good Neighbor Teaching award, 1995. Mem. Nat. Coun. Social Studies, Nat. Coun. Geographic Edn. (awards com. 1990-94), N.C. Coun. Social Studies (bd. dirs. 1992-95), N.C. Geog. Alliance (steering com. 1987-92, cons. 1987—). Democrat. Avocations: reading, scrapbooks, travel.

DOMBROWSKI, ANNE WESSELING, retired microbiologist, researcher; b. Cin., Jan. 26, 1948; m. Allan Wayne Dombrowski, Apr. 17, 1982; children: Amy, Alicia. BA summa cum laude, Xavier U., 1970; MS, U. Cin., 1972, PhD, 1974. Fellow Scripps Clinic and Rsch. Found., La Jolla, Calif., 1974-76; sr. rsch. microbiologist Merck & Co., Inc., Rahway, N.J., 1976-87, rsch. fellow, 1987-96, sr. rsch. fellow, 1996—2003, ret., 2003. Contbr. articles to profl. jours. Mem.: Am. Soc. Microbiology, Soc. Indsl. Microbiology (sec. 1982—85, dir. 1998—2001). Achievements include patents in field. Avocations: reading, gardening. Home: 51 Landsdowne Rd East Brunswick NJ 08816-4156 Personal E-mail: annewd@aol.com.

DOMBROWSKI, BOB, artist, writer; b. Buffalo, Feb. 16, 1944; s. Edward A. and Mary Ann Dombrowski. BS, SUNY, Buffalo, 1965; postgrad., Cornish Inst., Seattle, 1975-76. Artist, N.Y.C., 1976—; owner, mgr. GB Art Co., N.Y.C., 1994—. Cons. Cementex Corp., N.Y.C., 1989—. Creator, prodr. Ode to Birth of Shiva, 1987, Elegy for the Republic, 1991, Hwy. 17, 1993, On Thinking Thoughts, 1997; author: Theme Show, 2002, A Delicate Membrane, 2002; contbr. chpts. to books; author numerous poems; exhibited in group shows at Albright-Knox Art Mus., Buffalo, 1980, Ashford Hollow (NY) Found., 1980, Storefront for Art and Architecture, N.Y.C., 1985, Franklin Furnace, NYC, 1986, Nelson-Atkins Mus., Kansas City, 1989, Shedhalle (Rote Fabrik), Zurich, 1989, Barking Legs Dance Theater, Chattanooga, 1995 (Daimler-Chrysler Spirit of the Word award 1999), Mus. of New Art, Detroit; represented in permanent collections including Bruce Kaplan Collection, Chattanooga, Tenn., NYC Cmty. Bd. #3, Nico Smith Gallery, NYC, Mus. Modern Art Libr., NYC, Bettina Riedel Ltd., Phila., Pernod Corp., NYC, La Perla Garden, NYC, Francis Pratt Usui, Nicholson, Pa., Dorah Rosen Birmingham, Ala., Cleve. Art Inst., Linda Woodall, Chattanooga Bd. dirs. La Perla Cmty. Garden, N.Y.C.; treas. Keep Dade Beautiful Com.; mem. design com. Better Hometown Cmty., Trenton, Ga; coord. Picture Dade County project Mem. N.Y. Artists Equity (bd. dirs. 1989-90), The Unbearables Poet Group. Avocations: photography, walking. Home and Office: 19740 Hwy #11N Wildwood GA 30757 Office Phone: 706-657-8858. E-mail: d.p.productions@earthlink.net, dombrowski@webbittown.net.

DOMBROWSKI, MITCHELL PAUL, obstetrician, researcher; b. Detroit, Apr. 24, 1953; s. Mitchell Stanley and Dorothy Julia (Silarski) D.; m. Jocelyn McKinley, Mar. 7, 1981; children: Michael, Jacqueline, David, Elizabeth. BS, U. Mich., 1975; MD, Wayne State U., 1979. Diplomate Am. Bd. OB-Gyn, Am. Bd. Perinatology. Resident in obstetrics and gynecology, Detroit, 1979-84; fellow in perinatology, 1984-86; from asst. to assoc. prof. Wayne State U. Sch. Medicine, Detroit, 1986-98, prof., 1998, chmn., chief, 1996-98; chief St. John Hosp., 2002. Prin. investigator maternal fetal medicine network units Nat. Inst. Child Health and Human Devel., 1996. Contbr. articles to med. publs.; patentee fetal blood sampling device, reagent test strip, digital medication device, self-capping needle assemblies, amnicentesis needle. Recipient Research award Nat Insts Hlth. Recipient Nat. Inst. Alcohol Abuse and Alcoholism award, AMA; grantee Nat. Heart, Lung and Blood Inst./NICHD, 1994; fellow Am. Coll. Obstetrics and Gynecologists, Soc. Perinatal Obstetricians; Diabetes Rsch. Office: St John Hosp & Med Ctr 22151 Moross Rd Detroit MI 48236-2114 Office Phone: 313-343-7798. Personal E-mail: wsuserver@hotmail.com.

DOMBROWSKI, ROBERT THEODORE, materials scientist, information scientist; b. New Brunswick, N.J., Jan. 8, 1956; s. Theodore Frank and Grace (Keri) D.; m. Karen Marie Thornton. BS in Biol. Scis., Rutgers U., 1979, MS in Materials Sci., 1988. Jr. rsch. scientist Carter Wallace, Cranbury, N.J., 1979-84; scientist, rsch. scientist Colgate Palmolive, Piscataway, N.J., 1984-91; rsch. assoc., microscopy lab. mgr. Novon Products divsn. Warner Lambert, Morris Plains, N.J., 1991-93; pres., prin. scientist Microview Consultancy, Inc., Mendham, N.J., 1993—; adminstr. Rutgers Internet Inst., Piscataway, NJ, 1999; dir. ops. N.J. Ctr. for Biomaterials, Piscataway, 2000; chief web officer The Pharma Network, Woodcliff Lake, NJ, 2001; vis. scientist, adj. prof. Med. Device Concept Lab., NJ Inst. Tech., Newark, 2004—. Mem. characterization sub-team Biodegradable Packaging and Materials Consortium, Natick, Mass., 1991-93; instr., creator tng. course Microscopy for the New Millennium, 1999. Pub., webmaster Bobby D's Mysterious Sci., 1998. Recipient Colgate Palmolive Chmns. You Can Make a Difference award, Baxter Edu Net & Critical Mass award, 1999, Wisdom award, The Blue Ribbon award, Golden Web Awards, 2000-01; nominee Pirelli INTERNETional award 2001. Mem. Microscopy Soc. Am., Am. Chem. Soc., N.Y. Microscopical Soc., Biogradable Polymer Soc., HTML Writers Guild, Internat. Assn. Web Masters and Designers. Achievements include development of state-of-the-art materials characterization methods using optical analytical microscopy, chemical microscopy, video microscopy, image analysis, SEM, TEM, AFM, EDS and CLSM to determine the microstructure of starch based biodegradable polymers; first to use automated image analysis to determine the degree of starch destructurization in biodegradable materials; development of unique iodine based staining method to observe the ultrastructural elements of destructured starch used in combination with TEM; determination of the precise phase morphology of starch/synthetic biodegradable polymer blends using micro-milling, epi-DIC and FESEM. Office: Microview Consultancy Inc PO Box 148 Mendham NJ 07945-0148 Office Phone: 732-979-7833. Personal E-mail: gammux@yahoo.com. Business E-mail: principal@microviewconsult.com.

DOMBY, ARTHUR H., lawyer; b. Lafayette, Ind., 1951; BA, Hamilton Coll., 1973; MS, Univ. Ga., 1976; JD, Union Univ., 1973. Bar: Ga. 1979, NY 1980. Assoc. Troutman Sanders LLP, Atlanta, 1979—86, ptnr., environ. and natural resources, 1987—, and group practice leader, nuclear regulation. Adj. prof., natural resources law Emory Univ., Atlanta, 1987, 89. Mem.: ABA, Nuclear Energy Inst. Lawyers' Com. (chmn. 2000—01), State Bar Ga. (past chmn., environ. law sect.). Office: Troutman Sanders LLP One Logan Sq Ste 5200 600 Peachtree St NE Atlanta GA 30308-2216 Office Phone: 404-885-3130. Office Fax: 404-962-6546. Business E-mail: arthur.domby@troutmansanders.com.

DOMENECH, EDGAR A., government agency administrator; b. 1946; BS in Pub. Adminstrn., John Jay Coll. Criminal Justice. Spl. agent Bur. Alcohol, Tobacco, and Firearms, Ft. Lauderdale, Fla., 1985, supr. firearms enforcement group, supr. High Intensity Drug Trafficking/Organized Drug Enforcement Task Force, various positions Washington, 1995—2004, spl. agent in charge spl. programs br., asst. to spl. agent in charge office of inspection, asst. spl. agent in charge NY field divsn., 1998, dep. asst. dir. field ops., 2002—03, acting dep. dir., 2003—04, dep. dir., 2004—. Apptd. sr. exec. svc. Fed. Govt., 2001; founder, former pres. Hispanic Agents Assn. Office: Bur Alcohol Tobacco Firearms and Explosives Office Pub and Govtl Affairs 650 Massachusetts Ave NW Rm 8290 Washington DC 20226

DOMENICI, PETE V. (VICHI DOMENICI), senator; b. Albuquerque, May 7, 1932; s. Cherubino and Alda (Vichi) D.; m. Nancy Burk, Jan. 15, 1958; children: Lisa, Peter, Nella, Clare, David, Nanette, Helen, Paula. Student, U. Albuquerque, 1950-52; BS, U. N.Mex., 1954, LLD (hon.); LLB, Denver U., 1958; LLD (hon.), Georgetown U. Sch. Medicine; HHD (hon.), N.Mex. State U. Bar: N.Mex. 1958. Tchr. math. pub. schs., Albuquerque, 1954-55; ptnr. firm Domenici & Bonham, Albuquerque, 1958-72; chmn., ex-officio mayor Albuquerque, 1967; city commr., 1966-68; U.S. senator from N.Mex., 1973—. Mem. appropriations com., energy and natural resources com., chmn. subcom. on energy rsch. and devel.; mem. com. on environ. and pub. works, mem. govtl. affairs com.; chmn. budget com., com. on Indian affairs; mem. Presl. Adv. Com. on Federalism; senate Rep. policy com. Mem. Gov.'s Policy Bd. for Law Enforcement, 1967-68; chmn. Model Cities Joint Adv. Com., 1967-68. Recipient Nat. League of Cities award Outstanding Performance in Congress; Disting. Svc. award Tax Found., 1986, Legislator of Yr. award Nat. Mental Health Assn., 1987, public sector leadership award, 1996. Mem. Nat. League Cities, Middle Rio Grande Council Govts. Republican. Office: US Senate 328 Hart Senate Office Bldg Washington DC 20510-0001*

DOMEÑO, EUGENE TIMOTHY, elementary education educator, principal; b. L.A., Oct. 22, 1938; s. Digno and Aurora Mary (Roldan) D. AA, Santa Monica (Calif.) City Coll., 1958; BA, Calif. State U., 1960, MA, 1966. Cert. elem. tchr., gen. sch svcs, special secondary tchr. Elem. tchr. L.A. Unified Sch. Dist., 1960-70; asst. prin. Pomona (Calif.) Unified Sch. Dist., 1970-71, prin., 1971—. Cons. testing and evaluation Pomona Unified Sch. Dist., 1990—. With USNR, 1958-65. Recipient PTA Hon. Svc. award Granada Elem. PTA, Granada Hills, Calif., 1960, Armstrong Sch. PTA, Diamond Bar, Calif., 1990, Calif. Disting. Sch. Calif. Dept. Edn., 1989, Nat. Blue Ribbon Sch. U.S. Dept. Edn., Washington, 1990, Prin. and Leadership award, 1990. Mem. ASCD, Nat. Assn, Elem. Sch. Prins. (Prin. of Leadership award with Nat. Safety Com., 1991), Nat. Assn. Year Round Sch., Assn. Calif. Sch. Administrs., Diamond Bar C. of C. (edn. com.). Avocations: golf, dance, church, playing the flute. Office: Neil Armstrong Elem Sch 22750 Beaverhead Dr Diamond Bar CA 91765-1566 E-mail: auroratlc@aol.com.

DOMER, FLOYD RAY, pharmacologist, educator; b. Cedar Rapids, Iowa, July 12, 1931; s. William Ray and Caroline Anne (Zimmer) D.; m. Judith Elaine Kofroth, 1965. BS, State U. Iowa, 1954, MS, 1956; PhD, Tulane U., 1959. Life Ins. Med. Research Fund postdoctoral fellow Nat. Inst. Med. Research, London, 1959-60; with USAF Research and Devel. Command Istituto Superior di Sanita, Rome, 1960-61; asst. prof. pharmacology U. Cin., 1961-62, Tulane U., New Orleans, 1963-64, assoc. prof., 1965-74, prof., 1974-97; adj. prof. biology Appalachian State U., Boone, N.C., 1998—. Author: Animal Experiments in Pharmacological Analysis, 1971, Practical Anesthetic Pharmacology, 2d edit. 1986. Recipient award for teaching Owl Club, 1982, 83, 91, 94, 96. Mem. Am. Soc. Pharmacology and Exptl. Therapeutics, Soc. Neurosci., Soc. Exptl. Biology and Medicine. Clubs: Trojan. Home: # 2 194 Hill Beck Rd Boone NC 28607-7955 Personal E-mail: domerje@charter.net.

DOMINGO, CORA MARIA CORAZON ENCARNACION, minister; b. Urdaneta City, Philippines, Mar. 25, 1917; arrived in US, 1961, naturalized, 1967; d. Martin Cantaoe and Casimira Agbanlog Echalas; m. Nicanor Barrientos Domingo, Oct. 29, 1950; m. Teofilo Alonzo Manzano, July 8, 1935 (div. Sept. 26, 1950); children: Don Leonardo Manzano, Teddy Teofilo Manzano. BMin. and Practical Theology, Word of Faith Leadership & Bible Inst., Dallas, 1985. Ordained minister Ministry Salvation Ch., 1986. Tchr. Public Sch., Urdaneta City, Philippines, 1939—46; assoc. pastor The Assembly of the First Born, Kahului, Hawaii, 1993—; pres./founder Christ Tabernacle of Praise, Cabuloan, Philippines, 1999—; missionary pastor Cabuloan Village Chapel, Cabuloan, Philippines, 1971—99; child evangelist Child Evangelism Fellowship, Honolulu, 1980—92; pastor Maui Evang. Ch., Kahului, Hawaii, 1970—74; landlord and bus. woman Kahului, Hawaii, 1962—. Dir. of Filipino lang. radio program KNUI/KMVI, Kahului, Hawaii. Mem. Friendship Bible com., coord. Maui Christian Women's Club; pres., host Great Commn. Fellowship, 1980—95; mem. Maui Retarded Children's Assn., Big Bros./Big Sisters of Hawaii, Humane Soc.; treas., bd. dirs. Maui Adult Day Care Ctr., 1974—94; pres. Filipino Mins. Fellowship Maui, 1976—98; mem. Maui Christian Mins. Assn.; leader Girls Scout Am. Troop 78, 1953—63; bd. dirs. Status of Women, Com. on Aging, Wailuku, Hawaii. Named one of Maui's Filipino Heroes, 1998; recipient Outstanding Citizen of Filipino Ancestry, Maui Filipino Cmty. Assn., 1965, Milady of the Valley Isle award, 1968, Worthy Matron of Order, Maui Chpt. 5 Order of the Ea. Star of Maui Hawaii, 1975, 1980, 1993, Conservative Patriotic award, Young Am. Found., 2003. Mem.: Maui Filipino Ladies Cir., Bus. & Profl. Women's Club (vp & chmn. 1965—69). Republican. Avocations: reading, sewing, gardening, travel. Home and Office: 739 Iluna Pl Kahului HI 96732

DOMINGO, PLACIDO, tenor; b. Madrid, Jan. 21, 1941; s. Placido and Pepita (Embil) Domingo; m. Marta Ornelas; children: Jose, Placido, Alvaro Maurizio. Student, Conservatory in Mexico City; hon. degree, Royal Coll. Music, 1982, Complutense de Madrid, 1989; doctorate (hon.), Oxford U. Gen. dir. Washington Nat. Opera, 1994—, L.A. Opera, 2000—. Singer: (Operas) made operatic debut in La Traviata, 1961, debut Met. Opera, 1968, (star tenor with opera cos. including) La Scala, Covent Garden, Hamburg State Opera, Vienna State Opera, N.Y.C. Opera, San Francisco Opera, Nat. Hebrew Opera in Tel-Aviv, (leading roles 120 opera including) Don Rodrigo, Ofello, Walkure, Tosca, Andrea Chenier, Don Carlo, Carmen, La Boheme, Errani, Parsifal, Idomeneo, (films) Traviata, 1983, Carmen, 1984, Otello, 1986, (made more than 100 recs. including 93 full-length opera) BMG (formerly RCA), DGG, Sony, Decca/London, Philips, Time Warner, EMI (Angel), made more than 50 videos, (performed in concert) PBS TV spl. (with José Carreras & Luciano Pavorotti) The Three Tenors, 1994; condr. numerous performances at major opera houses including: Met. Opera, London's Covent Garden, Vienna State Opera, music dir.: Seville World's Fair, active: Operalia internat. vocal competition. Performed concerts to benefit victims of 1985 Mexican earthquake. Named Kennedy Ctr. honoree, 2000; recipient 9 Grammy awards, 2 Latin Grammy awards, Legion of Honor, France, 2002, Medal of Freedom, U.S., 2002, Gran Cruz de la Orden del Merito Civil, 2002, Knight Comdr. of the Brit. Empire, 2002. Address: care Vincent & Farrell Assocs 165 E 83d St Apt 5E New York NY 10028 Mailing: The Washington Opera 2600 Virginia Ave NW Ste 104 Washington DC 20037: Los Angeles Opera 135 North Grand Ave Los Angeles CA 90012*

DOMINGUE, EMERY, retired consulting engineering company executive; b. Scott, La., Jan. 9, 1926; s. Lucien and Mathilde (Hebert) D.; m. Beatrice Broussard, Dec. 30, 1950; children: Dave, Cal James, Kevin Drew. BS, U. Southwestern La., 1949; MS, U. Ill., 1955. Engr. La. Dept. Hwys., 1949-50, East Tex. Constrn. Co., 1950-51; tchr. civil engring. U. Southwestern La., 1951-61; prin. Domingue, Szabo & Assocs., Inc., Lafayette, La., 1957-96, ret., 1996. Mem. Lafayette Parish Planning Commn.; pres. La. Intracoastal Seaway Assn. With U.S. Army, 1944-46, ETO. Fellow ASCE (pres., cert. of appreciation Baton Rouge br.), Am. Cons. Engrs. Coun.; mem. Am. Soc. Profl. Engrs., Profl. Engrs. Pvt. Practice, Am. Concrete Inst., Am. Congress Surveying and Mapping, Am. Pub. Works Assn., Am. Ry. Engring. Assn., Cons. Engrs. Coun. La. (A.E. Wilder award), C. of C. (exec. com., dir.), Kiwanis (pres.), Ragin Cajun Club. Republican. Roman Catholic. Home: 203 Beverly Dr Lafayette LA 70503-3107 Office: 400 E Kaliste Saloom Rd Lafayette LA 70508-8508

DOMINGUE, GERALD JAMES, medical scientist, microbiologist, immunologist, educator, urologist, researcher, bacteriologist; b. Lafayette, La., Mar. 2, 1937; s. Edgar Paul and Sarah Ann (Prejean) D.; m. Marie H. Dugas, Aug. 30, 1958 (div. 1980); children: Andrea, Yvonne, Michelle, Gerald Jr., Marcel; m. Kathryn H. Colbert, June 20, 1981 (div. 1985). BS in Bacteriology, U. La., Lafayette, 1959; PhD in Med. Microbiol. and Immunology, Tulane U., 1964. Post-doctoral research fellow Children's Hosp., asst. research instr. pediatrics SUNY, Buffalo, 1965-66; dir. microbiol. Snodgras Lab. of Pathology and Bacteriology, St. Louis, 1966-67; instr. microbiology St. Louis U., 1966-67; asst. prof. microbiology, immunology and urology Tulane U., New Orleans, 1967-70, assoc. prof. microbiology, immunology and urology, 1970-74, prof. microbiology, immunology and urology, 1974-97, prof. emeritus, 1997—. Lectr. microbiology sch. dentistry Washington U., St. Louis, 1966-67; vis. prof., lectr. Peruvian Urol. Assn., Lima, 1973, First Internat. Congress Bacteriology, Jerusalem, 1973, Internat. Convocation Immunology, Buffalo, 1974, World Health Orgn. Conf. on Sperm Immunology, Aarhus, Denmark, 1974, European Soc. Exptl. Urol. Research, Wurzburg, Fed. Republic Germany, 1976, Internat. Seminar L-Forms, Montpellier, France, 1976, U. Melbourne, Royal Melbourne Hosp., Australia, 1978, XII Internat. Congress Microbiology, Munich, 1978, Internat. Symposium Vaccines and Vaccinations, Institut Pasteur, Paris, 1985; speaker U. Montpellier Sch. Medicine, 1985, 4th Internat. Congress on Pyelonephritis, Goteborg, Sweden, 1986, Orion Diagnostica, Helsinki, Finland, 1986, Nat. Inst. Hygiene, Warsaw, Poland, 1986, Symposium on Molecular Biology and Infectious Diseases, Institut Pasteur, 1987; mem. com. for infection control So. Bapt. Hosp., 1971-75, Charity Hosp. La., 1977—, Tulane U. Hosp., 1977—; mem. infectious disease com. St. Louis City Hosp., 1966-67; mem., reviewer, visitor project sites NIH Grant Review Study Sects., 1967-97, NSF, Kaiser Rsch. Found., Kidney Found. of Can.; cons. bacteriology So. Bapt. Hosp., New Orleans, 1968-84, Tulane U. Hosp., 1978-83, Med. Tech. Corp., Somerset, N.J., 1983—; research cons. VA Hosp., New Orleans, 1970-78; cons., mem. tech. adv. bd. Analytab Products, Inc., N.Y.C., 1972-77; expert witness to subcom. on dept. investigation oversight and research for Animal Cancer Research Act, U.S. Ho. of Reps., 1980. Author, editor: Cell Wall-Deficient Bacteria, 1962; editorial bd. cons. numerous jours.; contbr. over 160 articles to profl. jours. and chpts. to books. Pres. France-Louisiane de la Nouvelle Orleans, 1985—, pres. fondateur, 1988; apptd. mem. Gov.'s Council for Devel. of French Lang. in La., 1985, 88; mem. Met. Area Com., New Orleans, 1987, Bur. Govtl. Research, New Orleans, 1987; mem. Mayor's Com. New Orleans-Paris Cultural Exchange, 1988; chmn. scholar's com. La. Com. on French Revolution, 1988; mem. Alliance for Good Govt., 1980-84; mem. Greater New Orleans French Bd., 1987—; rep. Coun. for Devel. French and France Louisiane for celebration of French Bicentennial, Paris, 1989. Served with La. N.G., USAR, 1955-63. Guaranty scholar U. Southwestern La., 1958; grantee NIH, 1970-97, Schlieder Found., Armour Pharm. House, VA, Cadwallader Family Found., Med. Tech. Corp., Orion Diagnostica; decorated chevalier Order of Palmes Academiques (France); recipient French Medal, 1996. Fellow Am. Acad. Microbiology, Infectious Disease Soc. Am.; mem. Am. Soc. Microbiology (divisional lectr. 1978, found. lectr. 1979-80, symposium lectr. 1994), Soc. Basic Urologic Rsch. (state of art lectr. 1994), Soc. for Exptl. Biology and Medicine, AAAS, AAUP, Fedn. Am. Scientists, Southwestern Assn. Clin. Microbiology (editor newsletter 1983-85, pres. 1985-86), N.Y. Acad. Scis., Am. Assn. Lab. Animal Sci., Soc. Basic Urological Rsch. (nominating com. 1988), Am. Urol. Assn. (affiliate mem.), French-Am. Bus. Assn., Am. Acad. Poets (assoc.), Am. Acad. Poets, Sigma Xi. Independent. Roman Catholic. Avocations: painting, writing. Home: PO Box 51999 New Orleans LA 70151-1999 Office: Tulane U Sch Medicine 1430 Tulane Ave New Orleans LA 70112-2699

DOMINGUEZ, CARI M., government agency administrator; BA, MA, Am. U.; fellow advanced study Program in Pub. Mgmt., MIT; D in Humanitarian Svc. (hon.), Loma Linda U., 2003. Dir. exec. programs Bank Am. Corp.; partner Heidrick & Struggles; dir. Spencer Stuart, San Francisco; principal Dominguez & Associates, 1999; chair U.S. Equal Employment Opportunity Comm., 2001—. Named one of 80 Elite Hispanic Women, Hispanic Bus. mag., 100 Most Influential Hispanics in the Country; recipient Eagle Award, Bank America CEO, Chmns. 2002 award for excellence, Nat. Image, Inc. Mem.: Human Resources Planning Soc. (bd. mem.), Leadership Found. Internat. Women's Forum (bd. mem.). Office: Equal Employment Opportunity Comm 1801 L Street NW Washington DC 20507

DOMINGUEZ, DANIEL R., judge; b. San Juan, PR, 1945; BA, Boston U., 1967; LLB cum laude, U. P.R., 1970. Bar: P.R. Atty. Hector M. Laffitte Law Offices, 1970—72; ptnr. Laffitte, Dominguez & Totti, 1973—84, Dominguez & Totti, 1983—94; judge U.S. Dist. Ct. P.R., San Juan, 1994—. Gov. Adv. Com. on Labor Policy, 1984; mem. bd. Fed. Bar Examiners U.S. Dist. Ct. P.R., 1989—94; mem. Civil Justice Reform Act Adv. Group, 1991—94; mem. merit selection com. Appointment of U.S. Magistrate Judge, 1993; mem. com. for jud. reform Gov. P.R., 1993—94. With USAR, 1967. Mem.: Hyatt Dorado Beach Country Club, Berwind Country Club. Office: US Dist Ct PR US Courthouse CH-129 150 Ave Carlos Chardon San Juan PR 00918-1703

DOMINGUEZ, EDDIE, artist; b. Tucumcari, N.Mex., Oct. 17, 1957; BFA, Cleve. Inst. Art, 1981; MFA, Alfred U., 1983. Grad. asst., ceramics and visual design courses Alfred (N.Y.) U., 1981-83; artist-in-residence, lectr. Ohio State U., Columbus, 1984; artist-in-edn. N.Mex. Arts Divsn., Santa Fe, 1985-86; artist-in-residence Cleve. Inst. Art, 1986; artist-in-residence, lectr. U. Mont., Missoula, 1988; asst. prof. art U. Nebr., Lincoln, 1998—. Lectr., presenter workshops, mem. panels Ill. Arts Coun., Chgo., 1994, NEA, Washington, 1994, Ariz. Commn. on the Arts, 1994, Concordia U., Montreal, Que., Can., 1994, Mass. Coll. Art, Boston, 1994, Bennington (Vt.) Coll., 1994, 95, 96, Peters Valley, Layton, N.J., 1994, Firehouse Art Ctr., Norman, Okla., 1994, Haystack Mountain Sch. Arts & Crafts, Deer Isle, Maine, 1994, Ghost Ranch, Abiquiu, N.Mex., 1995, We. States Arts Fedn., Santa Fe, 1995, Colo. Coun. on the Arts, Boulder, 1995, Durango (Colo.) Art Ctr., 1995, Tamarind Inst., Albuquerque, 1995, 96, Kansas City (Mo.) Ar Inst., 1995, Hallmark Cards, Kansas City, 1996, Wichita (Kans.) Ctr. Arts, 1996, La. State U., Baton Rouge, 1996, Idaho State Arts Coun. Grants, Boise, 1996, Mattie Rhodes Counseling and Art Ctr., Kansas City, 1996, Southwest Ctr. Crafts, San Antonio, 1997, Very Spl. Arts, Albuquerque, 197, Topeka (Kans.) and Shawnee County Pub. Libr., 1997, U. Alaska, Anchorage, 2000, Craft Guild of Tex., Dallas, RISD, 2001, S.W. Ctr. for Crafts, San Antonio, 2002, numerous others; mem. fellowship panelist Colo. Coun. on the Arts, Denver, Penland Sch. of Crafts, N.C., 2001. Solo exhbns. include Pro Art Gallery, St. Louis, 1990, Mobilia Gallery, Cambridge, Mass., 1990, Munson Gallery, Santa Fe, 1990, 92, 94, 95, 97, 99, 2001, Mariposa Gallery, Albuquerque, 1990, Joanne Rapp Gallery, Scottsdale, Ariz., 1991, 93, 95, Felicita Found., Escondido, Calif., 1991, Tucumcari (N.Mex.) Area Vocat. Sch., 1992, Manchester Art Ctr., Pitts., 1993, Wetsman Collection, Detroit, 1993, Clovis (N.Mex.) C.C., 1993, Firehouse Art Ctr., 1994, Kavesh Gallery, Sun Valley, Idaho, 1995, Jan Weiner Gallery, Kansas City, 1995, 96, 2000, Jan Weiner Gallery, 2000, Gallerymateria, Scotsdale, Ariz., 2001, Munson Gallery, Santa Fe, 2001, Univ. Tulsa, Okla., 2001, Roswell (N.Mex.) Mus. and Art Ctr., 2002, numerous others; group exhbns. include Fred Jones Mus. Art, U. Okla., Norman, 1995, Roswell (N.Mex.) Mus. & Art Ctr., 1995, Nancy Margolis Gallery, N.Y.C., 1995, Sharadin Art Gallery, Kutztown (Pa.) U., 1995, Richard Kavesh Gallery, 1995, Jan Weiner Gallery, 1995, Ariz. State U. Art Mus., Tempe, 1995, Islip (N.Y.) Mus., 1995, Bruce Kapson Gallery, Santa Monica, Calif., 1996, Site Sante Fe Gallery, 1996, Johnston County C.C., Overland Parks, Kans., 1996, Jane Haslem Gallery, Washington, 1996, Karen Ruhlen Gallery, Santa Fe, 1996, Margo Jacobson Gallery, Portland, Oreg., 1996, Very Spl. Arts Gallery, Albuquerque, 1997, Joanne Rapp Gallery, 1997, Munson Gallery, 1999, numerous others; pub. art project include, among others, murals at Great Brook Valley Health Ctr., Worcester, Mass., 1994, Mass. Gen. Hosp., 1996, (mural) Island Nursing Home, Deer Isle, 2000, (mural) Big Red, Lincoln, Nebr., 2000, Washington Park, Albuquerque, 2002; represented in many permanent collections, including Sheldon Meml. Art Mus, Lincloln, Nebr., Mus. Nebr. Art, Kearney, Nebr., Cooper-Hewitt, N.Y.C., Mus. Fine Arts, Santa Fe, Cleve. Inst. Art, Fed. Reserve Bank, Dallas, Roswell Mus. and Art Ctr., Albuquerque Mus. Fine Arts, City of Tucson (Ariz.), Phoenix Airport, Renwick Gallery Nat. Mus. Am. Art Smithsonian Inst., Washington, Detroit Inst. Art, Hallmark Cards Corp., Kansas City, State Capitol Art Collection, Santa Fe, pvt. collections. Recipient numerous grants, including NEA fellowships, 1986, 88, Kohler Arts-in-Industry grant, Sheboygan, Wis., 1988, 2000, Percent for Art Project grant, Phoenix Arts Coun., 1990, 1992, artist-in-residence grantee Roswell (N.Mex.) Mus. and Art Found., 1986, 2001.

DOMINGUEZ, JORGE IGNACIO, political scientist, educator; b. Havana, Cuba, June 2, 1945; arrived in US, 1960; s. Jorge Jose and Lilia Rosa (de la Carrera) D.; m. Mary Alice Kmietek, Dec. 16, 1967; children: Lara Lisa, Leslie Karen. AB, Yale U., 1967; AM, Harvard U., 1968, PhD, 1972. From asst. prof. to prof. govt. Harvard U., Cambridge, Mass., 1972—93, Frank G. Thomson prof. govt., 1993—96, chmn. Latin Am. and Iberian studies, 1979—83, 1990—93, acting dir. ctr. for internat. affairs, 1995, Clarence Dillon prof. internat. affairs, 1996—, dir. Weatherhead Ctr. for Internat. Affairs, 1996—, Harvard Coll. prof., 1998—2003; chmn. Harvard Acad. for Internat. and Area Studies, 2004—. Active Coun. on Fgn. Rels., Club de Madrid, Inter-Am. Dialogue, 1982—, sr. fellow, 1993-94, assoc. fellow, 1995—. Author: Cuba: Order and Revolution, 1978, Insurrection or Loyalty, 1980, To Make the World Safe for Revolution: Cuba's Foreign Policy, 1989, Democratic Politics in Latin America and the Caribbean, 1998; editor: Democracy in the Caribbean, 1993, Technopols: Freeing Politics and Markets in Latin America in the 1990s, 1997, Democratic Transitions in Central America, 1997, The Future of Inter-American Relations, 2000, Mexico, Central and South America: New Perceptions, 5 vols., 2001, Constructing Democratic Governance in Latin America, 2003, The Cuban Economy at the Start of the Twenty-First Century, 2004, Mexico's Pivotal Democratic Election: Candidates, Voters, and the Presidential Campaign of 2000, 2004, Between Compliance and Conflict: East Asia, Latin America, and the "New" Pax Americana, 2005; co-author: Democratizing Mexico: Public Opinion and Electoral Choices, 1996, The United States and Mexico: Between Partnership and Conflict, 2001; mem. editl. bd. Am. Polit. Sci. Rev., 1979—81, Foreign Affairs en español, Polit. Sci. Quar., 1984—, Cuban Studies, 1991—, Latin Am. Rsch. Rev., 2003—, series editor Crisis in Central America: A Four-Part Special Report, Frontline, PBS (Peabody award), 1985—, chief editl. adv. 3-part spl. report Mexico, 1988. Chmn. bd. trustees Latin Am. Scholarship Program of Am. Univs., Cambridge, Mass., 1981-82. Recipient Joseph Levenson Meml. Tchg. award, Harvard U., 1991; jr. fellow, 1969—72, Fulbright-Hays fellow, 1983, 1988. Mem. Latin Am. Studies Assn. (pres. 1982-83), New Eng. Coun. Latin Am. Studies (pres. 1980), Inst. Cuban Studies (pres. 1990-94). Office: Harvard U Ctr Weatherhead Internat Affairs 1737 Cambridge St Cambridge MA 02138

DOMINGUEZ, KATHRYN MARY, economist, educator; b. Santa Monica, Calif., Nov. 26, 1960; d. Frederick A. and Margaret M. (McGauren) D. AB, Vassar Coll., 1982; MA, Yale U., 1984, M in Philosophy, 1985, PhD, 1987. Researcher Congl. Budget Ofice, Washington, summer 1984; rsch. scholar bd. of govs. FRS, Washington, 1985—86; asst. prof. pub. policy Kennedy Sch. Govt. Harvard U., Cambridge, Mass., 1987—91, assoc. prof. pub. policy, 1991—97; assoc. prof. pub. policy and econs. U. Mich., Ann Arbor, 1997—2004, prof., 2004—. Rsch. cons IMF, Washington, 1989; vis. asst. prof., asst. dir. internat. fin. sect. dept. econs. Princeton U., 1990-91; Nat. Bur. Econs. Rsch. Olin fellow, 1991-92. Author: (monograph) Oil and Money, 1989; Exchange Rate Efficiency and the Behavior of International Asset Markets, 1992; (with Jeff Frankel) Does Foreign Exchange Intervention Work?, 1993. Mem. Nat. Bur. Econ. Rsch. (rsch. assoc. 2000—), Am. Econ. Assn., Am. Fin. Assn., Phi Beta Kappa. Democrat. Office: U Mich Sch Pub Policy Lorch Hall 611 Tappan Ave Ann Arbor MI 48109-1220 Office Phone: 734-764-3490.

DOMINGUEZ, MICHAEL L., civilian military employee; BS, U.S. Mil. Acad., West Point, N.Y., 1975; MBA, Stanford U., 1983; program for sr. ofcls. in nat. security, Harvard U., 1989. Commd. 2d lt. U.S. Army, 1975; program analyst for program analysis and evaluation Office of Sec. Def., Washington, 1983—88; exec. asst. for program analysis and evaluation Asst. Sec. Def., Washington, 1988—91; dir. for planning and analytical support for program analysis and evaluation Office of Asst. Sec. Def., Washington, 1991—94; assoc. dir. for programming Office of Chief of Naval Ops., Washington, 1994—97; gen. mgr. Tech 2000 Inc., Herndon, Va., 1997—99; rsch. project dir. Ctr. for Naval Analyses, Alexandria, Va., 1999—2001; asst. dir. for space, info. warfare, and command and control Office of Chief Naval Ops., Washington, 2001; asst. sec. Manpower and Res. Affairs USAF, US Dept. Def., Washington, 2001—, acting sec., 2005. Decorated Army Commendation medal, Def. Meritorious Civilian Svc. medal, Def. medal for Civilian Svc., Medal for Superior Civilian Svc. Dept. Navy, Presdl. Meritorious Exec. Rank award. Office: US Dept Def Manpower and Res Affairs 1660 Air Force Pentagon Washington DC 20330-1660

DOMINI, AMY LEE, portfolio manager; b. N.Y.C., Jan. 25, 1950; d. Enzo Vice and Margaret Cabot (Colt) D.; m. Peter D. Kinder, Sept. 28, 1980 (div.); 1 child, Peter D. CFA. Stockbroker Tucker Anthony & RL Day, Cambridge, Mass., 1975-80, Moseley Securities, Cambridge, 1980-85; portfolio mgr. Franklin R & D Corp., Boston, 1985-87; pvt. trustee Loring, Wolcott & Coolidge, Boston, 1987—. Pres. Domini Social Equity Fund, N.Y.C., 1996—; chair of bd. Linder, Lydenberg, Domini & Co., Cambridge, 1991—; ptnr. Domini Social Investments LLC, Boston, 1997—. Co-author: (books) Ethical Investing, 1984, Challenges of Wealth, Social Investment Almanac, 1992, Investing for Good. Bd. dirs. Social Investment Forum, Washington, 1994—, ch. pension fund Episcopal Ch., N.Y.C., 1994—; governing bd. Interfaith Ctr. on Corp. Responsibility, N.Y.C., 1985-95; mem. social responsibility investments com. Episcopal Ch., N.Y.C., 1985-91. Recipient Accioniste award Accion Internat., 1992, Money's 100 Best Mut. Funds award Money Mag., 1998, SRI Svc. award 1st Affirmative Fin. Network, 1996; named one of World's 100 Most Influential People, Time Mag. 2005. Mem. Nat. Comty. Capital Assn. (assoc., bd. dirs. 1987-91), Boston Security Analysts Soc., Social Investment Forum, Somerset Club, Cambridge Boat Club. Democrat. Episcopalian. Avocations: day-sailing, gardening. Office: Loring Wolcott & Coolidge 230 Congress St Fl 12 Boston MA 02110-2437

DOMINIAK, GERALDINE FLORENCE, retired accounting educator; b. Detroit, Sept. 28, 1934; d. Benjamin Vincent and Geraldine Esther (Davey) D. BS, U. Detroit, 1954, MBA, 1956; PhD, Mich. State U., 1966. CPA Mich. Audit supr. Coopers & Lybrand, 1958-63; asst. prof. U. Detroit, 1965-68; assoc. prof. Mich. State U., 1968-69; prof. acctg. Tex. Christian U., Ft. Worth, 1969-97, chmn. dept. acctg., 1974-83, prof. emeritus, 1997; Arthur Young prof. acctg. Fla. A&M U., 1977. Author: (with J. Edwards and T. Hedges) Interim Financial Reporting, 1972; (with J. Louderback) Managerial Accounting, 1975, 9th edit., 2000. Ford Found. fellow, 1964-65. Mem. AICPA, Am. Acctg. Assn., Inst. Mgmt. Accts., Tex. Soc. CPAs, AAUP, ACLU, Beta Alpha Psi, Beta Gamma Sigma. Roman Catholic. Home: 4401 Cardiff Ave Fort Worth TX 76133-3513 *To teach is to learn.*

DOMINICK, CHARLES ALVA, college official; b. Canton, Ohio, Mar. 31, 1943; s. Joseph and Dorthy (Hawkins) D.; m. Nancy Unkefer, July 26, 1969; 1 child, Timothy Joseph. BA, Coll. of Wooster, 1965; MA, Ohio State U., 1968; PhD, U. Mich., 1987; postgrad., Harvard U., 1988. Admissions counselor Davis and Elkins (W.Va.) Coll., 1965-67, Mt. Union Coll., Alliance, Ohio, 1967-68; admissions asst. U. Mich., Ann Arbor, 1977-78, rsch. assoc. Project Choice, 1978-79; asst. dean admissions Wittenberg U., Springfield, Ohio, 1972-77, assoc. dir. for univ. advancement, 1979-80, asst. to pres., 1980-85, v.p. for instnl. rels., 1985—. Contbg. author: Managing Change in Higher Education, 1990, Student Recruitment, 1991. Mem. Com. Housing Resources Bd., Springfield, 1986—92; bd. dirs. Clark County Labor-Mgmt. Rels. Com., Springfield, Ohio, 1987—90, Jr. Achievement, 1990—95, Aid for Coll. Opportunities; trustee Oakwood Village, Springfield, 1988—96, Clark County Hist. Soc., 1986—94, 2001—, pres., 1989—92; bd. dirs. Cmty. Hosp. Found., 1996—, Cmty. Hosp., 2000—. Mem.: Springfield Country Club, Springfield Polo Club (pres. 1999—2001), Springfield Univ. Club (v.p. 1991—92, pres. 2002—03), Rotary. Home: 829 Linmuth Ct S Springfield OH 45503-1903 Office: Wittenberg U PO Box 720 U Ward St at N Wittenberg Springfield OH 45501

DOMINICK, PAUL ALLEN, lawyer; b. Orangeburg, SC, Feb. 13, 1954; s. Allen Etheredge and Ruby Estelle (Pardue) D.; m. Sharon Norment, May 15, 1982. BA, U. S.C., 1976; JD, Washington & Lee U., 1979. Bar: S.C. 1979, U.S. Dist. Ct. S.C. 1980, U.S. Ct. Appeals (4th cir.) 1982. Assoc. Nexsen, Pruet, Jacobs & Pollard, Columbia, S.C., 1979-85, ptnr., 1985—91, Nexsen Pruet, Charleston, SC, 1991—. Bd. dirs., Columbia Forum; bd. dirs., participant Leadership Columbia-Columbia C. of C., 1986. Mem. ABA (chair bus. torts com. tort and ins. practice sect. 1995-96), SC Bar Assn., Charleston County Bar Assn., Columbia Forum, Com. of 100, Columbia 100 (pres. 1983-84), Sertoma (pres. 1987-88), Phi Beta Kappa. Presbyterian. Home: 670 Hobcaw Bluff Dr Mount Pleasant SC 29464 Office: Nexsen Pruet PO Box 486 Charleston SC 29402-0486

DOMINICK, PETER HOYT, JR., architect; b. N.Y.C., June 9, 1941; s. Peter Hoyt and Nancy Parks D.; m. Philae M. Carver, Dec. 9, 1978; children: Philae M., James W. BA, Yale U., 1963; MArch, U. Pa., 1967. Registered architect, Colo. Project designer John R. Wild, Pty., Ltd., Papau, New Guinea, 1968-69, Spence Robinson, Hong Kong, 1969-71, W.C. Muchow & Ptnrs., Denver, 1971-74; pres. Wazee Design/Devel., Denver, 1973-75; prin. Dominick Architects, Denver, 1975-88; sr. prin. Urban Design Group, Inc. (now 4240 Arch., Inc.), Denver, 1988—. Pres., chmn. bd. Urban Design Group, Inc., 2001—, Trustee Downtown Denver, Inc., Civic Ventures, 1984-94, Met. Denver Arts Alliance, 1983-84; active Mayor's Commn. on the Arts, 1983; juror Gov.'s awards, Denver, 1982; nat. com., exec. com. Whitney Mus. Am. Art.; bd. trustees Denver Art Mus., 2002. Fellow AIA (nat. com. on design, bd. dirs.); mem. Colo. Soc. Architects, Cactus Club, Arapahoe Tennis Club. Republican. Episcopalian. Office: Urban Design Group Inc 4240 Architecture Inc 1621 18th St Ste 200 Denver CO 80202-1267 Office Phone: 303-292-3388. E-mail: pdominick@urbandesigngroup.com, pdominick@4240arch.com.

DOMINO, CONSTANCE MAE, genetics researcher; b. Winnebego, Minn., Mar. 12, 1950; d. Virgil Dean Domino and Loretta Antonette Zahorski; 1 child, Kirk. AA, North Hennepin Cmty. Coll., 1976, Mpls. Cmty. Coll., 1981; BS, U. Minn., 2002. RN Minn., 1981. Surgical nurse U. Minn. Hosp., Mpls., 1981—82; med-surg nurse Fairview Hosp., Mpls., 1982—85; float pool nurse Staff Builders, Mpls., 1985—90; triage nurse Group Health, Mpls., 1990—92; rschr. Ind., Mpls., 1982—; sales assoc. Target Corp., Mpls., 1997—. Sperzem scholarship, U. Minn. Nursing Sch., 1994. Mem.: NY Acad. of Scis., AAAS. Democrat. Roman Catholic. Achievements include discovery of use of bone marrow transplants for genetic diseases, 1985. Home: 727 15th Ave SE Minneapolis MN 55414

DOMINO, FATS (ANTOINE DOMINO), pianist, singer, songwriter; b. New Orleans, Feb. 26, 1928; Pianist since youth; performer: with groups in clubs, for dances, in theaters, composer (blues); recording artist (albums) Here Comes Fats Domino, 1963, Fats on Fire, 1965, Fats '65, Getaway With Fats Domino, Fats Domino, 1966, Stompin' Fats Domino, 1967, Trouble in Mind, Fats is Back, 1968, Live in Montreux, 1973, Sleeping on the Job, 1978, The Best of Fats, 1990, All Time Greatest Hits, Fats Domino, 1991, Best of Fats Domino Live, Antoine "Fats" Domino, 1992, The Fat Man, 1995, Live in Concert, Early Imperial singles 1950-52, 1996, Fabulous Mr. D./Swings, 1998, Here Stands/this is, vol. 3 Imperial Singles, 1998, Live at Gilleys, 1999, Collector's Edition, 2000, toured Britain, 1967, appeared (films) Shake, Rattle & Rock, Disc Jockey Jamboree, The Big Beat, The Girl Can't Help It, Any Which Way You Can, appeared on TV spl (TV films) Fats Domino & Friends, 1987. Named to Rock and Roll Hall of Fame, 1986; recipient Nat. Medal Arts, 1998, Grammy Lifetime Achievement award, 1987. Office: care Atlantic Records 1290 Ave of the Ams New York NY 10104-0101 also: SMS Records 14134 NE Airport Way Portland OR 97230-3443*

DOMJAN, JOSEPH, artist; b. Budapest, Hungary, Mar. 15, 1907; s. Paul and Maria (Lika) D.; m. Evelyn A. Domjan, Mar. 13, 1944; children— Alma Domjan Melbourne, Michael P., Daniel G. BA, Hungarian Royal Acad. Fine Arts, 1940, MA, 1942. Founder Domjan Mus., Sarospatek, Hungary, 1977. Exhibited in over 550 one-man shows including Ernst Mus., Budapest, 1955, Mus. Art and History, Geneva, 1975, Cin. Art Mus., 1958, 74, N.J. State Mus., Trenton, 1966, 73, Dallas Pub. Libr., 1964, 77, Mueso della Bellas Artes, Mexico City, 1966, Cuyuga Mus., Auburn, N.Y., 1975; represented in numerous permanent collections including Met. Mus., Victoria and Albert Mus., Tate Gallery, London, Mus. Modern Art, Paris, Albertina Graphische Sammlung, Vienna, Nat. Gallery Fine Arts, Libr. of Congress, Washington, Nat. Mus., Stockholm, Mus. Modern Art, Tokyo; author, illustrator 24 books; author: The Proud Peacock, 1966, The Little Cock, 1966, The Artist and the Legend, 1975, Bellringer, 1975, Wing Beat, 1976, Edge of Paradise, 1979. Rockefeller Found. grantee, 1958; Recipient numerous prizes Soc. Illustrators, numerous prizes Am. Inst. Graphic Arts, numerous prizes Print Club of Albany, numerous prizes Am. Color Print Soc. Mem. Nat. Acad. Design, Soc. Am. Graphic Artists, Soc. Illustrators, Print Council Am., Silvermine Guild, Internat. Platform Assn. Address: West Lake Rd Tuxedo Park NY 10987

DOMJAN, LASZLO KAROLY, editor; b. Kormend, Hungary, Apr. 19, 1947; arrived in U.S., 1956; s. Frank and Violet Domjan; m. Louise Replogle, June 6, 1969; children: Andrew P., Eric S. BJ, U. Mo., 1969. Copy editor St. Louis Globe-Democrat, 1969; reporter, bureau chief UPI, St. Louis, 1969-81; reporter, night city editor St. Louis Post-Dispatch, 1981-87, exec. city editor, 1987-96, projects editor, 1996-97, asst. mng. editor, 1997-99, sr. editor, 1999—. Author, editor: Dioxin: Quandary for the 80s, 1983; author: (reporter series) Hungary: Thirty Years After, 1986; editor: (series) Prosecutorial Corruption (1993 Pulitzer prize finalist). Active Leadership, St. Louis. Recipient Herb Trask award Sigma Delta Chi, St. Louis, 1968. Mem. Press Club of Met. St. Louis, Investigative Reporters and Editors. Roman Catholic. Avocations: reading, freelance writing, music. Office: St Louis Post-Dispatch 900 N Tucker Blvd Saint Louis MO 63101-1099 Personal E-mail: ldomjan@hotmail.com. Business E-Mail: ldomjan@post-dispatch.com. *Always do right. Always do your best. Always make time for romance.*

DOMMEN, ARTHUR JOHN, agricultural economist, historian; b. Mexico City, Mex., June 24, 1934; came to U.S., 1940, naturalized, 1958; s. John Henry and Sarah (Hall) D.; m. Phan Thi Hong Loan. B.Sc., Cornell U., 1955; PhD, U. Md., 1975. Mem. staff UPI, 1957-63, bur. chief, 1959-61, Hong Kong, 1961-63; mem. staff Los Angeles Times, 1965-71; bur. chief Japan, 1965—66, Los Angeles Times, New Delhi, 1966-68, Saigon, Vietnam, 1968-71; agrl. economist Intech, Inc., Silver Spring, Md., 1975-77; mem. AID mission to Tunisia, 1977-79; with USDA, Washington, 1980-96; affiliate prof. Indochina Inst., George Mason U., Fairfax, Va., 1996-98; ind. rschr., 1998—. Author: Conflict in Laos, The Politics of Neutralization, 1964, Laos: Keystone of Indochina, 1985, The Indochinese Experience of the French and the Americans, 2001. Served with AUS, 1955-57. Press fellow N.Y. Council Fgn. Relations, 1963-64 Home and Office: 7716 Radnor Rd Bethesda MD 20817-6282 Office Phone: 301-229-5883.

DOMMERMUTH, WILLIAM PETER, marketing consultant, educator; b. Chgo. s. Peter R. and Gertrude Dommermuth; m. H. Joan Hasty, June 6, 1959; children: Karin, Margaret, Jean. BA, U. Iowa; PhD, Northwestern U., 1964. Advt. copywriter Sears, Roebuck & Co., Chgo., sales promotion mgr.; asst., then asso. prof. mktg. U. Tex., Austin, 1961—67; assoc. prof. U. Iowa, Iowa City, 1967—68; prof. So. Ill. U., Carbondale, 1968—86, U. Mo., St. Louis, 1986—; CEO Optiphonics, Inc. Cons. in field. Author (with Kernan and Sommers): Promotion: An Introductory Analysis, 1970, (with Andersen) Distribution Systems, 1972, (with Marcus and others) Modern Marketing, 1975, Modern Marketing Management, 1980, Promotion: Analysis, Creativity and Strategy, 1984, 2d edit., 1989; contbr. articles to profl. jours. Mem. Am. Mktg. Assn., Phi Beta Kappa, Beta Gamma Sigma, Theta Xi, Delta Sigma Pi. Home: 11 Paris Ct Lake Saint Louis MO 63367-1506 Personal E-mail; willdo@mail.com. Business E-Mail: optomizer@consultant.com.

DOMNITZ, AVIN MARK, not-for-profit association executive; Owner bookstore, Milw.; exec. dir., CEO Am. Booksellers Assn., Tarrytown, NY. Exec. com. The Quills. Office: Am Booksellers Assn 828 S Broadway Tarrytown NY 10591 Office Phone: 914-591-2665 ext 1205, 800-673-0037. Office Fax: 914-591-2720. Business E-Mail: avin@bookweb.org.*

DOMOWITZ, IAN, finance company executive; b. N.Y.C., Nov. 29, 1951; s. Jacob and Marilyn (Raffer) D.; m. Marguerite Morton, Sept. 25, 1984. BA, U. Conn., 1977; PhD, U. Calif., San Diego, 1982. Asst. prof., assoc. prof., prof. econs. Northwestern U., Evanston, Ill., 1982-98, mem. rsch. faculty Inst. for Policy Rsch., 1987-98; Mary Jean and Frank P. Smeal chaired prof. fin. Pa. State U., University Park, 1998—2002; mng. dir. analytical products and rsch., global head rsch. ITG, Inc., 2001—. Rsch. dir. K2 Capital Mgmt., 1992-94; cons. IMF, 1992, World Bank, 1993-96, 98-99, to various internat. fin. markets with respect to automated exch. structures, 1991-97; cons. U.S. Commodity Futures Trading Commn., 1991, 95-96; mem. sci. adv. bd. ITG, Inc., 1997-, mem. sci. adv. bd. ITG Europe, 2003—; bd. mgrs. Inference Group LLC, 2002-04. Contbr. more than 80 articles to profl. jours., chpts. to books. Sgt. U.S. Army, 1972-75, Germany. NSF grantee, 1984, 85, 87, 90. Mem. Am. Fin. Assn., Fin. Mgmt. Assn., Nat. Assn. Securities Dealers (econ. adv. bd. 1998-2000, chair 1998-2000, bond market transparency com. 1998-99). Home: 684 Broadway # 4E New York NY 10012 Office Phone: 212-444-6279. Business E-Mail: idomowitz@itginc.com.

DOMZALSKI, JOHN F., city health department administrator; BS, Bloomsburg State Coll.; MPH, U. Pitts.; JD, Temple U. Dep. health commr. for pub. health svcs. Phila. Dept. Pub. Health, dir., correction health, chief, field opers., dist. health dir., exec. dep. health commr., chief of staff, 1998—2002, commr., 2002—; adj. assoc. prof., sch. of biomed. engrng. sci. and health sys. Drexel U., Phila. Mem. City of Phila. Emergency Mgmt. Planning Group, 1996—; mem., steering com. U.S. Pub. Health Svc. Bicentennial Celebration; participant The Pres.'s Summit for Am.'s Future. Fellow: Coll. Physicians of Phila.; mem.: ABA, Prisoner's Family Welfare Assn. (past pres.), Phila. Bar Assn., Am. Pub. Health Assn. Office: Dept Pub Health 1101 Market St Philadelphia PA 19107

DOMZALSKI, RONALD LAURENCE, audio-visual specialist, educator; b. Wilkes-Barre, Pa., Feb. 12, 1971; s. Ronald Laurence and Jacqueline Ann (Leiby) Domzalski. AAS in broadcasting, Luzerne CC, 1991, AAS in photography, 1994, AAS in journalism, 2003; BA, MA in digital media, Marywood U., 2005. Student asst. Luzerne CC, Nanticoke, Pa., 1990—91; film devel., printer Camera Pro, Forty Fort, Pa., 1994; radio personality WARD, WKQV AM-FM, Pittston, Pa., 1992—95; actor Entertainment Partners, Burbank, Calif., 1997—2000; film svcs. Fotokem Film and Video, Burbank, 1999; master control operator WOLF/WSWB-TV, Plains, Pa., 2001—03; tchr. West Side Vo-Tech, Pringle, Pa., 2002—. Dir.: (promotional video) St. Pius X Seminary, 1991; performer: (radio recording) Ron Domzalski, 2001; contbr. articles various profl. jours. Rail tech., vol. Marywood Performing Arts Ctr., Scranton, 2004; audio engr., vol. TV Marywood, Scranton, Pa., 2003; air talent, vol. WVMW-FM, Scranton, 2003; vol. Students Against Drunk Driving, 1988—89; Walk-a-thon March of Dimes, 1995. Mem.: Screen Actors Guild, People for the Ethical Treatment of Animals, Amnesty Internat. Democrat. Roman Catholic. Avocations: photography, music, volleyball, computers, electronics. Office: DZL Productions 26 E Grand St Nanticoke PA 18634-3202

DOMZELLA, JANET, retired library director; b. Marquette, Mich., Mar. 22, 1935; d. Jack Carl and Alice Margaret (Blom) Messenger; m. Theodore S. Wodzinski (div. 1974); children: Christopher, Joseph, Daniel; m. Perry Landon Domzella, July 15, 1977; stepchildren: Perry, Pamela. BS, No. Mich. U., 1973; MLS, U. Buffalo, 1979. Sch. libr. media specialist Niagara Falls (N.Y.) Bd. Edn., 1974-75, Iroquois Ctrl. Sch., Elma, N.Y., 1975-77; dir. Lewiston (N.Y.) Pub. Libr., 1977-2000, libr. emeritus, 2001—; ret., 2000. Mgr. LaSalle br. Niagara Falls Pub. Libr., NY, 2002. Co-author: Lewiston: Self Guided Tour, 1986. Vol. firefighter Upper Mountain Vol. Fire Co., Lewiston, 1980—90, treas., 1984—90; mem. Town of Lewiston Bur. Fire Prevention, 1988—90; mem. adv. bd. Documentary Heritage Program, 1991—93; mem. pub. libr. program Coll. of Charleston (S.C.) Conf., 1998, 2000, 2001. Democrat. Roman Catholic. Avocations: rosemaling, watercolor.

DONABEDIAN, AVEDIS, physician, educator; b. Beirut, Jan. 7, 1919; arrived in U.S., 1955, naturalized, 1960; s. Samuel and Maritza (Der Hagopian) Donabedian; m. Dorothy Salibian, Sept. 15, 1945; children: Haig, Bairj, Armen. BA, Am. U., Beirut, 1940, MD, 1944; MPH, Harvard U., 1955. Physician, acting supt. English Mission Hosp., Jerusalem, 1945—47; instr. physiology, clin. asst. dermatology and venereology Am. U. Med. Sch., 1948—51, univ. physician, dir. univ. health service, 1949—54; med. assoc. United Community Services Met. Boston, 1955—57; asst. prof., then assoc. prof. preventive medicine N.Y. Med. Coll., 1957—61; mem. faculty U. Mich. Sch. Pub. Health, Ann Arbor, 1961—, prof. med. care orgn., 1964—79, Nathan Sinai disting. prof. public health, 1979—89, emeritus. Author: A Guide to Medical Care Administration: Medical Care Appraisal--Quality and Utilization, 1969, Aspects of Medical Care Administration, 1973, Benefits in Medical Care Programs, 1976, The Definition of Quality and Approaches to Its Assessment, 1980, Medical Care Chartbook, 1986, The Criteria and Standards of Quality, 1982, Methods and Findings of Quality Assessment and Monitoring, 1985; co-author: Striving for Quality in Health Care: An Inquiry into Policy and Practice, 1991. Recipient Dean Conley award, Am. Coll. Hosp. Adminstrs., 1969, Norman A. Welch award, Nat. Assn. Blue Shield Plans, 1976, Elizur Wright award, Am. Risk and Ins. Assn., 1978, Nat. Merit award, Delta Omega, 1978, Richard B. Tobias award, Am. Coll. Utilization Rev. Physicians, 1984, Outstanding Contbns. in Health Svcs. Rsch. award, Assn. Health Svcs. Rsch., 1985, Baxter Am. Found. Health Svcs. Rsch. prize, 1986, Gold medal award, Med. Alumni Assn., Am. U. Beirut, 1986, The Ernest A. Codman award, Joint Commn. on Accreditation of Healthcare Orgns., 1997. Fellow: APHA (Sedgewick Meml. medal 1999), Am. Coll. Med. Quality, Am. Coll. Healthcare Execs. (hon.), Am. Coll. Utilization Rev. Physicians (hon.), Royal Coll. Gen. Practitioners (hon.); mem.: Inst. Medicine NAS, Internat. Soc. Quality Assurance in Health Care (hon.), Nat. Acad. Medicine of Mex. (hon.), Avedis Donabedian Found. (Barcelona, hon. pres. 1990—, Buenos Aires, hon. pres. 1994—). Office: HMP-SPH II 109 Observatory St Ann Arbor MI 48109-2029*

DONADIO, DONALD A., lawyer; b. Hampton, Va., Jan. 3, 1943; BA cum laude, Wake Forest U., NC, 1965; JD cum laude, Wake Forest U. Law Sch., 1967. Bar: NC 1972, US Eastern and Middle District Courts, NC. Mem. mgmt. com. Womble Carlyle Sandridge & Rice, PLLC, NC, mem. recruiting com., mng. mem. Raleigh, NC. Counsel NC Partnership for Econ. Development; lectr. in field. Assoc. editor Wake Forest Law Review, 1966—67; contbr. articles to profl. jours. Bd. dir. Greater Raleigh CofC. Capt., Judge Advocate General's Corp (JAGC) U.S. Army, 1967—72. Mem.: Wake Country Econ. Development Bd., NC Econ. Developers Assn., Am. Coll. of Real Estate Lawyers, Nat. Ass. of Bond Lawyers, ABA (mem. bus. sect.), NC Bar Assn. (mem. bus. sect.), Wake County Bar Assn., Phi Delta Phi. Office: Womble Carlyle Sandridge & Rice PLLC 150 Fayetteville St Mall Ste 2100 Raleigh NC 27601 Mailing: Womble Carlyle Sandridge & Rice PLLC PO Box 831 Raleigh NC 27602 Office Phone: 919-755-2102. Office Fax: 919-755-6049. Business E-Mail: ddonadio@wcsr.com.

DONADIO, ROBERT EUGENE, lawyer; b. Indianapolis, May 24, 1932; s. Anthony Prosper and Violet Camelina (Panden) D.; m. Frances LaVerne Strutner, Feb. 1, 1934; children: Robert E., Anne Frances, Jean, Diane, Janet, William, Gregory. BS, Mt. St. Mary Coll., Emmitsburg, Ind., 1958; JD, U. Baltimore, 1964. Asst. state's atty. Baltimore Co., Towson, Md., 1979-82; house counsel Govt. Employees Insurance Co., Towson, 1964-65; pvt. practice atty. Towson, 1965-99. Pfc., U.S. Army, 1953-55. Mem. Am. Arbitration Assn. (panel judge). Republican. Roman Catholic. Avocation: piano. Home: 2426 Eastridge Rd Timonium MD 21093-2510 E-mail: bob.donadio@aol.com.

DONAGHY, HENRY JAMES, literature educator, academic administrator; b. N.Y.C., Apr. 11, 1930; s. Joseph Peter and Catherine (McQuaid) D.; m. Joyce Aasen, Dec. 7, 1968 (div. Oct. 1986); children: Nora, Martin. BA in Philosophy and Classics magna cum laude, Stonehill Coll., 1954; theology student, Holy Cross Coll., 1954-58; MA in English, Fordham U., 1960; PhD in English, NYU, 1966. Priest Roman Catholic Ch., N.Y.C., Bridgeport,

Conn., 1958-1966; asst. prof. Ga. State U., Atlanta, 1966-69; assoc. prof. SUNY-Oswego, 1969-71, dir. grad. studies English, 1970-71; assoc. prof. Calif. State U., Fresno, 1971-73, supr. student tchrs., 1972-73; assoc. prof. to prof. English, chmn. dept. Idaho State U., Pocatello, 1973-83, assoc. dean Coll. Liberal Arts, 1982-83, dir. Dr. Arts teaching internship, 1973-75, dir. grad. studies English, 1975-76, vice chmn. Univ. Grad. Council, 1977-79, chmn. Dept. English and Philosophy, 1977-82; prof., head English Dept. Kans. State U., Manhattan, 1983-88, Miss. State U., Miss. State, 1988—97; ret., 1997. Dir. NEH grant offering interdisciplinary courses in sci. and humanities, Idaho, 1980-81; sr. Fulbright lect. U. Damascus, Syria, 1979-80; vis. prof. Meisei U., Tokyo, 1995-96. Author: James Clarence Mangan, 1974, Graham Greene: An Introduction to His Works, 1982; editor: Opposing Visions: Byron's and Southey's Vision of Judgement, 1976, Conversations with Graham Greene, 1992, Vessels of Clay: The Seductive Life of the Priesthood (a memoir), 2003; contbr. articles and revs. to profl. jours. and publs. Recipient Founders Day award NYU, 1966, Grand prize for fiction Memphis Mag., 1996. Mem.: MLA, Miss. Philological Assn. (pres. 1989—91). Democrat. Avocations: jazz, dodger baseball, notre dame football, reading, and writing. Mailing: 7612 Hudson Ln Las Vegas NV 89128 Personal E-mail: hdonaghy@cox.net.

DONAGHY, JAMES K., construction executive, contractor; Chmn. Structure Tone, NYC. Bd. dirs. Exenet Technologies. Office: Structure Tone Inc 770 Broadway Fl 9 New York NY 10005-9511 Office Fax: (212) 685-9267.

DONAHO, JOHN ALBERT, management consultant; b. Chgo., Sept. 9, 1917; s. John and Pauline (Langdon) D.; m. Patricia A. Maguire, Sept. 23, 1961. BA, Ctrl. YMCA Coll., 1941; cert. pub. adminstrn., MA, U. Chgo. Asst. to contr. Commonwealth Edison Co., Chgo., 1935-42; asst. dir. work simplification and measurement U.S. Bur. Budget, Exec. Office of Pres., Washington, 1943-47; v.p. devel. Roosevelt U., Chgo., 1947-48; budget dir., city mgr. City of Richmond, Va., 1948-52; pres. John A. Donaho & Assocs. Inc., Reisterstown, Md., 1953—. Cons. to Mayor of Balt. and Gov. of Md., 1952-54, 74-87, 88-89; chmn. Md. Local Govt. Ins. Trust, 1987-88; ins. commr. State of Md., 1989-93; lectr., mem. faculty Am. U., Washington, Washington U., Goucher Coll., Balt., Johns Hopkins U., Balt., U. Balt., Fgn. Svc. Inst., Va. Commonwealth U., Roosevelt U., Chgo.; chmn. Va. State Commn. on Uniform Fin. Reporting; cons. UN and Econ Commn., Asia, Far East, 1959-60. Contbr. articles to profl. jours. Pres., dir. Univ. Club, Balt.; dir. United Reisterstown Residents; pres. Lakeview Club, Inc., Reistertown, Civitan Club Balt., Civitan Club Richmond; mem., sec. Balt. City Com. on Workers' Compensation, Balt. City Com. on Ins. and Risk Mgmt.; mem. Md. Gov.'s Task Force on Liability Ins., Md. Gov.'s Blue Ribbon Task Force on Self-Ins., Gov.'s Blue Ribbon Commn. on Ins., Gov.'s Prescription Drug Commn.; chmn. Ad Hoc Com. on Liability Ins. for Md.; mem. Balt. County Restructuring Commn.; trustee Balt. Internat. Culinary Coll., Balt. Street Car Mus.; mem. Baltimore County Redistricting Commn. Fellow Soc. for Advancement Mgmt. (pres. Balt. regional chpt., v.p. Richmond chpt., chmn. round table on work simplification DC chpt.), ASPA (sr. mem., pres. Md. chpt., dir. Olympia chpt.); mem. Nat. Assn. Ins. Commrs. Office: 2525 Pot Spring Rd S352 Timonium MD 21093 Office Phone: 410-252-4059. E-mail: donassoc@bellatlantic.net.

DONAHOO, WILLIAM TROY, medical educator; s. Darrell Donahoo and Rose Dafoe; m. Julie Johnson, July 31, 1994; 1 child, Carissa Nicolle. MD, U. Colo., 1991. Diplomate Am. Bd. Internal Medicine, 1995. Asst. prof. UCHSC, Denver, 1999—2004, U. Vt., Burlington, Vt., 2004—. Dir. weight mgmt. clinic UCHSC, 1999—2002. Office: University of Vermont Given C331 89 Beaumont Ave Burlington VT 05405 Office Phone: 802-656-2530.

DONAHUE, ANN M., television producer; Student, Ohio State U. Legal asst., Century City, Calif.; writer China Beach, Picket Fences, Murder One; prodr. 21 Jump St., Street Justice; writer CSI NBC, LA, 2000—. Author: (plays) Home Fires, (films) Those Beaumont Girls, Three Girls in the Air Force, Three Girls Pose for Playboy. Home: 1412 Warnall Ave Los Angeles CA 90024

DONAHUE, CHARLES, JR., law educator; b. NYC, Oct. 4, 1941; s. Charles James and Rosemary (Spang) Donahue; m. Sheila Finn, Aug. 22, 1964; 1 child, Sarah. AB in Classics & English, Harvard Coll., 1962; LLB, Yale U., 1965. Bar: NY 1966, Mich. 1969, US Supreme Ct. 1971. Atty.-adv. Office Gen. Counsel of Air Force, Washington, 1965-67; asst. gen. counsel Pres.'s Commn. on Postal Orgn., Washington, 1967-68; asst. prof. law U. Mich., 1968-70, assoc. prof., 1970-73, prof., 1973-79; prof. law Harvard Law Sch., Cambridge, Mass., 1980—, Paul A. Freund prof. law, 1995—. Acad. vis. law dept. London Sch. Economics and Polit. Sci., 1972-73; vis. prof. law Vrije Universiteit Brussel, 1975, Columbia U., 1976, U. Calif. Boalt Hall, 1976, Harvard U., 1978-79, Boston Coll., 1987; articles editor Yale Law Jour., 1963-65; bd. editors Am. Jour. Legal History, 1977-82. Editor: The Records of the Medieval Ecclesiastical Courts Part I: The Continent, 1989, The Records of the Medieval Ecclesiastical Courts Part II: England, 1994, Samuel Edmund Thorne: 1907-1994, 1995; co-editor: Lex Mercatoria and Legal Pluralism: A Late Thirteenth-Century Treatise and Its Afterlife, 1998; author (commentary): Year Books of Richard II: 6 Richard II, 1382-83, 1996; co-author: A Course in Basic Property, 1975, 1993, Cases and Materials on Property: An Introduction to the Concept and the Institution, 1974, 1993. Served with USAF, 1965-68. Mem. Am. Law Inst., Am. Soc. Legal History (dir. 1977-79, v.p. 1981-85), Selden Soc. (v.p. 1985-87, Am. treas. 1987—, councillor 1987—), Société d'histoire du droit, Société pour l'histoire des droits de l'antiquité, Medieval Acad. Am. Roman Catholic. Office: Harvard Law Sch 1563 Massachusetts Ave Cambridge MA 02138 Office Phone: 617-495-2944. Office Fax: 617-496-4913.*

DONAHUE, CHARLES BERTRAND, II, lawyer; b. Hampton, Iowa; s. Charles B. and Alta M. (Sykes) D.; m. Brenda K. Kumpf (div. Dec. 1980); children: Kaylie Elizabeth, Megan E. (dec.); m. Kathleen L. Komnenovich, June 27, 1987. AB, Harvard U., 1959; JD cum laude, Cleve. State U., 1967. Bar: Ohio 1967, Fla. 1970. Commd. 2d lt. USAF, 1959, advanced through grades to capt., 1962, res., 1969, contracting officer McGuire AFB, NJ, 1959—62; subcontract adminstr. Westinghouse, Pitts., 1962—63; contract adminstr. TRW, Inc., Cleve., 1963—67; atty., ptnr. Calfee Halter & Griswold, Cleve., 1967—79; founder, ptnr. Donahue & Scanlon, Cleve., 1979—99; legal counselor in field. Trustee Cleve. Artists Found., 1999; civil svc. commn. City Westlake, Ohio, 1995-96. Mem.: Chautauqua Lake Power Boat Club. Avocations: cooking, reading, travel, boating. Home and Office: 827 Brick Mill Run Westlake OH 44145-1602 Office Phone: 440-331-3232. E-mail: cbdonahue@prodigy.net.

DONAHUE, CHARLOTTE MARY, lawyer; b. Columbus, Ohio, Sept. 29, 1954; d. Patrick Henry and Helen Donahue. AB, Holy Cross Coll., 1976; JD, U. Toledo, 1983. Bar: Pa. 1984, D.C. 1985, U.S. Dist. Ct. (ea. dist.) Pa. 1985, U.S. Ct. Appeals 3d cir.) 1985, U.S. Supreme Ct. 1990, Mass. 1992. Jud. clk. to presiding justice Commonwealth Ct. Pa., Phila., 1983-84; spl. asst. U.S. atty. U.S. Dist. Ct. (ea. dist.) Pa., Phila., 1987-90; atty. HUD, Phila., 1984-93, Boston, 1993—. Mem. Fed. Bar Assn., Pa. Bar Assn., Mass. Bar Assn., D.C. Bar Assn., Order of Barristers, Internat. Platform Assn., Supreme Ct. Hist. Soc. Home: 40 Meredith Cir Milton MA 02186-3916 Office: HUD Thomas P O'Neill Jr Fed Bldg 10 Causeway St Boston MA 02222-1092

DONAHUE, JOHN DAVID, federal agency administrator, educator; b. Alexandria, Indiana, June 17, 1956; s. Thomas Edward and Judith Ann (Wheatley) D.; m. Margaret Ann (Pax), Aug. 23, 1986; children: Kathleen, Benedict. BA, Ind. U., 1979; M in Pub. Policy, Harvard U., 1982, PhD, 1987. Asst. prof. to assoc. prof. Harvard U., Cambridge, Mass., 1987—93; asst. sec. U.S. Dept. Labor, Washington, 1993—94, counselor to sec., 1994—95; assoc. prof. pub. policy Harvard U., Cambridge, Mass., 1995—99, Raymond Vernon lectr. in pub. policy, 1999—; dir. Weil Program on Collaborative Governance, 2003—. Econ. cons., Cambridge, Mass., 1985-2002; adv. com. on shareholder responsibiity, Harvard U., 1998—. Editor: Cost Benefit Analysis and Project Design, 1980; co-author: (book) New Deals: The Chrysler Revival, 1985; author: The Privatization Decision, 1989, Disunited States, 1997, Hazardous Crosscurrents, 1998; editor: Making Washington Work: Tales of Innovation in the Fed. Govt., 1999; co-editor: Governance in a Globalizing World, 2000, Governance Amid Bigger, Better Markets, 2001, Market Based Govt. Supply Side, Demand Side, Upside, and Downside, 2002; book rev. editor Jour. Policy Analysis and Mgmt., 2002—; co-editor: For the People, 2003. Advisor Clinton presdl. transition, Washington, 1993. Doctoral fellow NSF, 1980, fellow Dively Found., 1984. Office: Harvard Univ 79 JFK St Cambridge MA 02138-5801

DONAHUE, JOHN EDWARD, physician; b. Revere, Mass., Apr. 27, 1966; s. Edward Francis and Camille (Santoro) D. BS summa cum laude, Tufts U., Medford, 1984—88, MD, 1988—92. Diplomate Am. Bd. Psychiatry and Neurology, Am. Bd. Pathology, Nat. Bd. Med. Examiners. Intern St. Elizabeth's Med. Ctr., Boston, 1992-93; resident New Eng. Med. Ctr., Boston, 1993-96; fellow R.I. Hosp., Providence, 1996-99; dir. neuropathology NJ Neuroscience Inst., Edison, 1999—2003; asst. prof. neuroscience Sch. Grad. Med. Edn. Seton Hall U., Orange, 1999—2003; asst program dir. neurology residency program NJ Neuroscience Inst., 2001—03; attending neuropathologist RI Hosp., 2003—. Asst. prof. pathology Brown U. Sch. Medicine, 2003—. Contbr. articles to profl. jours. Recipient David L. Kasdon prize Tufts U. Sch. Medicine, 1992, Second Place award Gustaf Retzius Neuroanatomy Competition, 1997, 98, champion 1999. Mem.: AAAS, Neuroplex Inc., Soc. Neurosci., Coll. Am. Pathologists, Am. Assn. Neuropathologists, Am. Acad. Neurology, Mass. Med. Soc., Phi Beta Kappa. Roman Catholic. Achievements include research in breakthroughs in Alzheimer's disease rsch. Avocations: swimming, computers. Office: RI Hosp Dept Pathology 593 Eddy St Providence RI 02903 Office Phone: 401-444-5057. Business E-Mail: JDonahue3@Lifespan.org.

DONAHUE, JOHN FRANCIS, investment company executive; b. Pitts., 1924; Grad., U.S. Mil. Acad., 1946. Chmn. Federated Investors, Inc., Pitts. Office: Federated Investors Federated Investors Tower 1001 Liberty Ave Pittsburgh PA 15222-3779

DONAHUE, JOHN JOSEPH, park and recreation director; b. Bklyn., Nov. 20, 1952; s. John and Anna Donahue; m. Sarah Grassi, July 2, 1977; 1 child, John Vincent. Degree in natural resource mgmt., Calif. State U., Sonoma, 1986. Instr. Bklyn. Bot. Garden, 1977-78; supr. N.Y.C. Parks Dept., 1978-79; gardener Cape Cod Nat. Seashore, 1980-83, John Muir Nat. Hist. Site, 1983-86; specialist nat. resource mgmt. Morristown (N.J.) Nat. Hist. Park, 1986-89; specialist environ. protection Nat. Park Svc., Washington, 1989-94; supt. Thomas Stone Nat. Hist. Site, Charles County, Md., 1994—, George Washington Birthplace Nat. Monument, Washington's Birthplace, Va., 1994—. Adv. bd. mem. Olmsted Ctr. Landscape Preservation, Valley Forge Archeol. Ctr.; bd. dirs., treas. George Wright Soc.; chief visitor protection and resource mgmt. Cape Cod Nat. Seashore, 1993. Spkr. in field; contbr. articles to profl. jours. Fax: 804-224-2142.

DONAHUE, JOSEPH GERALD, lawyer; b. Waterville, Maine, Oct. 16, 1951; s. Gerald L. and Gertrude (Poulin) D.; m. Rita P. Bouchard, Aug. 31, 1974; children: Kathryn, Joseph, James. AB, Bowdoin Coll., Brunswick, Maine, 1974; JD, Boston U., 1977. Bar: Mass. 1977, Maine 1978, U.S. Dist. Ct. Maine 1978, U.S. Ct. Appeals (1st cir.) 1984, U.S. Supreme Ct. 1985, U.S. Ct. Appeals (D.C. cir.) 1986. Law clk. Maine Supreme Jud. Ct., Portland, 1978-79; atty. examiner Maine Pub. Utilities Commn., Augusta, 1979-82, gen. counsel, 1982-89; assoc. Preti, Flaherty, Beliveau, Pachios & Haley, Augusta, Maine, 1989-93, ptnr., 1994—. Mem. Fed. Comm. Bar Assn. Home: 74 Lincoln Ave Gardiner ME 04345-2518 Office: Preti Flaherty Beliveau Pachios & Haley PO Box 1058 Augusta ME 04330-6494 Office Phone: 207-623-5300. E-mail: jdonahue@preti.com.

DONAHUE, SHIRLEY OHNSTAD, elementary school educator; b. Darlington, Wis., Aug. 29, 1937; d. Joseph and Edna L. (Peterson) Ohnstad; m. John V. Donahue, Aug. 20, 1960; children: Roger K., Jeffrey J. BS, U. Wis., Platteville, 1959; MS, No. Ill. U., 1978. Cert. tchr., Ill. Tchr. Freeport (Ill.) Sch. Sys., 1959-62, Belvidere (Ill.) Sch. Sys., 1962-64, Pecatonica (Ill.) Sch. Sys., 1964-66, Orangeville (Ill.) Sch. Sys., 1966-67, Rock Falls (Ill.) Sch. Sys., 1967-93; ret. Rock Falls (Ill.) Sch. System, 1993. Co-author gifted student curriculum materials. Mem. Liturgical com. St. Mary's Ch., Sterling, Ill., 1980-84, aux. min., 1980-94; mem. Friends of Sterling Pub. Libr., v.p. 1990-93, 96, pres. 1995; bd. dirs. YWCA, sec. bd. dirs., 1994-95, pres. bd. dirs. 1997-99; mem. Cmty. Gen. Hosp. Med. Ctr. Aux., 1993—, co-chair sr. health ins. program, 1994-2000, pres. 1995-99, v.p. ways and means, 1999-2004, v.p. gift shop, 2004—; pres. YWCA, 1997-99; bd. dirs. ARC, Lincolnland chpt., 1996-99. Recipient Western Ill. Master Tchr. award, 1991. Mem. NEA, Rock Falls Elem. Edn. Assn. (chmn. polit. action com. for edn. 1985-87), Ill. Edn. Assn. Roman Catholic. Avocation: bicycling. Home: 1720 Avenue E Sterling IL 61081-1124

DONAHUE, THOMAS REILLY, trade union official; b. N.Y.C., Sept. 4, 1928; s. Thomas Reilly and Mary E. (Purcell) D.; children: Nancy Angela, Thomas Reilly III. BA, Manhattan Coll., 1949; JD, Fordham U., 1956; LLD (hon.), U. Notre Dame, 1980, Loyola U., Chgo., 1984, SUNY, 1988, Manhattan Coll., 1988, U. Mass., 1990, Nat. Labor Coll., 2001. Dir. edn., bus. agt. local 32B Bldg. Svc. Employees Internat. Union, AFL-CIO, 1949-52, dir. contract dept., 1952-57; European labor program coord. Free Europe Com., Paris, 1957-60; asst. to pres. Bldg. Svc. Employees Internat. Union, AFL-CIO, 1960-67; asst. sect. for labor-mgmt. rels. U.S. Dept. Labor, 1967-69; exec. sec. Svc. Employees Internat. Union, 1969-71, v.p., 1971-73; exec. asst. to pres. AFL-CIO, 1973-79, sec.-treas., 1979-95, pres., 1995. Chmn. adv. com. to Sec. of State and Pres. on Labor Diplomacy, 1999-2005; co-chmn. Found. for Prevention and Early Resolution of Conflict, 1996-97; vice-chmn. Nat. Endowment for Democracy, 1999—; chmn. bd. dirs. Am. Heary Lift Shipping Co., 2001— Former mem., bd. dirs. U.S. Cath. Conf. Com. on Social Devel., Coun. on Fgn. Rels., Carnegie Corp., Nat. Urban League, Brookings Instn., Muscular Dystrophy Assn., African Am. Inst., Work in Am. Inst., Nat. Planning Assn., Inst. Multi-Track Diplomacy. With USNR, 1945-46. Sr. fellow Work in Am. Inst., 1997—. Democrat. Home: 613 G St SW Washington DC 20024-2439 Office: AFL-CIO 1717 K St NW Ste 707 Washington DC 20036-5331

DONAHUE, TIMOTHY M., telecommunications industry executive; BA in English Lit., John Carroll U. Pres., paging div. McCaw Cellular Comm., 1986—89; pres., U.S. ctrl. region McCaw Cellular Comm. (now AT&T Wireless), 1989—91; N.E. regional pres., gen. mgr. AT&T Wireless, 1991-96; pres., COO Nextel Comms. Inc., Reston, Va., 1996—99, pres., CEO, 1999—2005; exec. chmn. Sprint Nextel Corp., 2005—. Dir. NII Holdings, Nextel Partners, Eastman Kodak Co. Mem.: Cellular Telecommunications & Internet Assoc. (past chmn.). Office: Nextel Comm Inc 2001 Edmund Halley Dr Reston VA 20191-3421*

DONAHUE, WILLIAM JOSEPH, writer; b. Vinita, Okla., Mar. 29, 1949; s. Woodrow Leonidas and Doretha Ellen-Jane (Grimes) Donahue; m. Vickie Lynn Hegi, Sept. 15, 1985; 1 child, Robert Kenneth. Degree in bus., Capitol City Coll., Little Rock, 1971; BA in Fine Arts, U. Ark., 1979. Cert. med. supply tech. Office clk. Piffer-Dillards Dept. Stores, Little Rock, 1969—70; publ. dir. Landmark Publ., North Little Rock, Ark., 1978—81; med. supply tech. VA, Little Rock, 1981—99; ret., 1999. Author: (screenplays) Nightvasion, 2001, Rogue Star, 2004, (short stories) Sand, 1984, Doppleganger, 1986 (1st pl. Twilight Zone Mag., 1986), Lights in the Sky, 1999. Active United Way, Little Rock, 1986. With USN, 1971—75, Vietnam. Mem.: VFW. Democrat. Baptist. Avocations: photography, painting, art, filmmaking. Home: 1616 S Rice St Little Rock AR 72202 Personal E-mail: kronospsi@netscape.com.

DONAIS, GERALD ALAN, manufacturing executive; b. Portland, Oreg., Oct. 17, 1959; s. Don Martin Donais and Joyce Vincent, Lynda LoAnn Donais (Stepmother); m. Cheryl Lynn Stevens, Apr. 18, 1982; 1 child, Jamie Marie Allen. Respiratory therapy tech, Apollo Coll., 1992—94. Emergency Medical Tech 2-D Oreg., 1986. Ceo Tri-County Ambulance, Inc., Portland, Oreg., 1994—98, D&S Appliance Svc., Inc, Salem, Oreg., 2002—. Author: Not Just a Touch: Living a Childhood of Sexual Abuse and Growing up Intersexed, 2003. With US Army N.G., 1976, Portland, Oreg. Roman Catholic. Avocations: writing, singing, walking, travel, meteorology. Home: 452 45th Ct NE Salem OR 97301 Office: D&S Appliance Service Inc 452 45th Ct NE Salem OR 97301 Office Phone: 503-362-5630. E-mail: g.donais@comcast.net.

DONALD, AIDA DIPACE, retired publishing executive; d. Victor E. and Bessie DiPace; m. David Herbert Donald; 1 child, Bruce Randall. AB cum laude, Barnard Coll.; MA, Columbia U.; PhD, U. Rochester. Instr. history dept. Columbia U., N.Y.C.; cons. and series editor Hill and Wang Pubs., N.Y.C.; editor Mass. Hist. Soc., Boston, 1960-64, Johns Hopkins U. Press, Balt., 1972-73; social sci. editor Harvard U. Press, Cambridge, Mass., 1973-79, exec. editor, 1979-89, editor in chief, 1989—2000, asst. dir., 1990—2000; ret., 2000. Editor: John F. Kennedy and the New Frontier, 1966, (with David Herbert Donald) Charles Frances Adams Diary, 2 vols., 1965. Columbia U. Dibblee fellow, 1952-53, U. Rochester fellow, 1953-55, 56-57, Oxford U. Fulbright fellow, 1959-60. Fellow AAUW; mem. Am. Hist. Assn., Orgn. Am. Historians. Avocations: writing, tennis, first editions, antique silver, coins.

DONALD, ALEXANDER GRANT, psychiatrist, educator; b. Darlington, S.C., Jan. 24, 1928; s. Raymond George and Chesnut Evans (McIntosh) Donald; m. Emma Louise Coggeshall, Oct. 25, 1958; children: Sandy, Mary Chesnut, Marion Lide. BS, Davidson Coll., 1948; MD, Med. U. S.C., 1952. Diplomate Am. Bd. Psychiatry and Neurology. Intern Jefferson Med. Coll., 1952-53; resident in psychiatry Walter Reed Hosp., 1956-59; dir. Mental Health Clinic, Florence, SC, 1962-66; dept. commr. S.C. Dept. Mental Health, 1966-67; dir. William S Hall Psychiat. Inst., Columbia, 1967-90; prof., chmn. dept. neuropsychiatry and behavioral scis. Sch. Medicine, U. S.C., Columbia, 1975-90, Disting. prof. neuropsychiatry, assoc. dean ednl. planning, 1990-91, Disting. prof. emeritus, 1991—. Bd. dirs. Health Resource Found.; trustee Richland Meml. Hosp., 1993—2002, vice-chmn., 1997, chmn., 1999; bd. dirs. S.C. Inst. Med. Edn. and Rsch., pres., 1992—96; trustee Palmetto Health Alliance, 1999—2004, vice-chmn., 2003; steward United Way of the Midlands, 2003—. Fellow: Am. Psychiat. Assn., Am. Coll. Psychiatrists (pres. S.C. chpt. 1967); mem.: AMA, So. Psychiat. Assn. (v.p.), Columbia Med. Soc. (v.p. 1981, del. 1981, pres. 1989—90), Evening Music Club, Alpha Omega Alpha. Presbyterian. Office: U SC Sch Medicine 3555 Harden St Ext Ste 104 Columbia SC 29203-6894 Personal E-mail: grantd@aol.com. *Accepting responsibility for ones' actions - using one's mind to understand one's self is the highest function of mankind.*

DONALD, ARNOLD W., food products executive; m. Hazel Donald; children: Radiah, Alicia, Zachary. BA, Carleton Coll.; BSME, Washington U., St. Louis; MBA, U. of Chgo. Grad. Sch. Bus. From indsl. chem. sales to positions of increasing responsibility Monsanto Co., St. Louis, 1977—98, sr. v.p., 1998-99; CEO Merisant Co., 2000—03, chmn., 2000—. Apptd. President's Export Coun. internat. trade; bd. dirs. Crown Cork & Seal Co., Oil-Dri Corp. Am., Belden Inc., Carnival Corp., Laclede Group, Scotts Co., St. Louis Sports Commn. Bd. dirs. United Way of Greater St. Louis, Carleton Coll., Dillard U., Wash. U., St. Louis Art Museum, Mo. Botanical Garden, St. Louis Sci. Ctr., Opera Theatre of St. Louis, Boy Scouts of Am., Greater St. Louis Area Coun. Named one of 50 Most Powerful Black Executives in Am., Fortune mag., 2002; recipient Exec. of the Year, Black Enterprise mag., 1997, Disting. Alumni award, Wash. U., 1998, Eagle award, Nat. Eagle Leadership Inst., 1999, Black Engineers President's award, 2000. Office: One N Brentwood Saint Louis MO 63105

DONALD, BERNICE B., judge; b. Miss., Sept. 17, 1951; d. Perry and Willie Bell (Hall) Bowie; m. W. L. Donald, Oct. 9, 1973. BA in Sociology, Memphis State Univ., 1974, JD, 1979; student, Nat. Judicial Coll., 1983, 84. Bar: Tenn. 1979, U.S. Fed. Ct. 1979, U.S. Supreme Ct. 1989. Clk. South Central Bell Telephone Co., 1971-75, mgr., 1975-80; staff atty. Memphis Area Legal Svcs., 1980, Shelby County Public Defenders Office, 1980-82; judge Gen. Sessions Criminal Ct. of Shelby County, Tenn., 1982-88; bankruptcy judge U.S. Bankruptcy Ct. (we. dist.) Tenn., Memphis, 1988-96; U.S. dist. judge U.S. Dist. Ct. (we. dist.) Tenn., 1996—. Mem. adv. com. on bankruptcy rules Jud. Conf., 1996—; faculty mem. Fed. Judicial Ctr., 1991—, Nat. Judicial Coll., 1992—; adj. prof. Shelby State C.C., 1980-84, Cecil C. Humphreys Sch. of Law, 1985-88; lectr., presenter in field. Featured in Essence mag., Ebony mag., Jet mag., Memphis mag., Dollars and Sense mag., Black Enterprise mag. Bd. dirs. Midtown Mental Health, 1990-92, 94-96, Memphis in May, 1994-97, Leadership Memphis, Inc., 1993-96, U. Memphis Alumni Bd., 1994—, Memphis Race Rels. and Diversity Inst., 1994—, Fed. Jud. Ctr.; former bd. dirs. numerous religious and civic orgns. including Calvary St. Ministry, Memphis Literacy Coun., YWCA. Recipient Cmty. Svcs. award Nat. Conf. on Christians and Jews, 1986, Martin Luther King Cmty. Svc. award, Young Careerist award State of Tenn. Raleigh Bureau of Profl. Women, plaques and certs.; named Citizen of Yr. Excelsior Chpt. of Eastern Star, Woman of Yr. Pentecostal Ch. of God in Christ. Mem. ABA (mem. standing com. on Gavel awards 1989-95, mem. adv. com. Ctrl. and Ea. European Law Initiative 1999—, mem. ho. dels. 1993-95, 99—, bd. govs. 1999—, liason labor and employment law sect. 1999—, Law Libr. Congress 1999—, Appellate Judges Conf. 1999-2000, Africa Legal Tech. Assistance Project 2000—, mem. legal opportunity scholarship com. 2000—, Mus.'s bd. dirs. 2000—, numerous jud. adminstrn. divsn. coms.), Nat. Assn. of Women Judges (treas. 1986-87, sec. 1987-88, v.p. 1988-89, pres. elect 1989-90, pres. 1990-91), Am. Judges Assn., Nat. Ctr. for State Cts., Am. Bar Assn., Nat. Bar Assn., Tenn. Bar Assn. (bd. dirs. 1997-98), Memphis County Bar Assn., Shelby County Bar Assn., Am. Trial Lawyers Assn., Assn. of Women Attys. (pres. 1991, bd. dirs.), Nat. Conf. of Bankruptcy Judges (bd. dirs. 1993-96), Nat. Conf. of Women's Bar Assn. (bd. mem.), Nat. Conf. of Spl. Ct. Judges (sec.), Leadership Memphis (pres. 1987, bd. dirs.), Internat. Women's Forum, Memphis Bar Assn. (bd. dirs. 1993), Zeta Phi Beta (Alpha Eta Zeta chpt.). Avocations: reading, crossword puzzles, music, bicycling, walking. Office: Federal Building 167 N Main St Ste 1111 Memphis TN 38103-1831

DONALD, BRUCE R., computer science educator; b. June 25, 1958; BA summa cum laude, Yale U., 1980; MS in EE and Computer Sci, MIT, 1984, PhD in Computer Sci., 1987. Research analyst in computer graphics and spatial analysis Lab. for Computer Graphics and Spatial Analysis, Harvard U., Cambridge, Mass., 1978-84; research staff Artificial Intelligence Lab. MIT, 1984; asst. prof. dept. computer sci., dir. robotics lab. Cornell U., Ithaca, N.Y., 1987—. Cons. in field; lectr. in field. Contbr. articles to profl. jours. Grantee MIT, 1985-88, Cornell U., 1988—; named Presdl. Young Investigator, Nat. Sci. Found., 1989. Mem. ACM, Am. Math. Soc., Math. Assn. Am., IEEE, Sigma Xi. Office: Cornell U Dept Computer Sci Ithaca NY 14853-7501

DONALD, DAVID HERBERT, writer, history professor; b. Goodman, Miss., Oct. 1, 1920; s. Ira Unger and Sue Ella (Belford) D.; m. Aida DiPace, 1955; 1 son, Bruce Randall. Student, Holmes Jr. Coll., 1937-39; AB, Millsaps Coll., 1941, LHD, 1976; AM, U. Ill., 1942, PhD, 1946, LHD (hon.), 1992; MA (hon.), U. Oxford, 1959, Harvard U., 1973; LittD (hon.), Coll. Charleston, 1985; D in History, Lincoln U., 1996; LHD, U. Calgary, 2000; LLD, Ill. Coll., 2002; LittD, Middlebury Coll., 2003. Teaching fellow U. N.C., 1942; research asst. history U. Ill., 1943-45, research assoc., 1946-47; fellow Social Sci. Research Council, 1945-46; instr. history Columbia U., 1947-49; assoc. prof. history Smith Coll., 1949-51; asst. prof. history Columbia U. Grad. Faculty, 1951-52, assoc. prof., 1952-57, prof. history, 1957-59, Princeton U., 1959-62; prof. Am. history Johns Hopkins U., Balt., 1962-73, Harry C. Black prof., 1963-73, dir. Inst. So. History, 1966-72; Charles Warren prof. Am. history and prof. Am. civilization Harvard U., 1973-91, prof. emeritus, 1991—, chmn. grad. program in Am. civilization, 1979-85. Vis. assoc. prof. Amherst Coll., 1950; Fulbright lectr. Am. history U. Coll. North Wales,

1953-54; mem. Inst. Advanced Study, 1957-58; Harmsworth prof. Am. history Oxford U., 1959-60; John P. Young lectr. Memphis State U., 1963; Walter Lynwood Fleming lectr. La. State U., 1965; Benjamin Rush lectr. Am. Psychiat. Assn., 1972; Commonwealth lectr. Univ. Coll., London, 1975; Samuel Paley lectr. Hebrew Univ. of Jerusalem, 1991; mem. U.S. del. to UNESCO, 2003. Author: Lincoln's Herndon, 1948, Divided We Fought, A Pictorial History of the War, 1861-65, 1952, Inside Lincoln's Cabinet: The Civil War Diaries of Salmon P. Chase, 1954, Lincoln Reconsidered: Essays on the Civil War Era, 1956, rev. 3d edit., 2001, A Rebel's Recollections, (G.C. Eggleston), 1959, Charles Sumner and the Coming of the Civil War, 1960 (Pulitzer prize in biography), Why the North Won the Civil War, 1960, rev. edit., 1996, (with J.G. Randall) The Civil War and Reconstruction, 2d edit., 1961, rev., enlarged edit., 1969, (with Jean H. Baker and Michael F. Holt) rev. edit., 2001, The Divided Union, 1961, The Politics of Reconstruction, 1863-67, 1965, The Nation in Crisis, 1861-1877, 1969, Charles Sumner and the Rights of Man, 1970, (with Sidney Andrews) The South Since the War, 1970, Gone for a Soldier, 1975, (with others) The Great Republic, 1977, rev. edit., 1981, 3rd edit., 1985, 4th edit., 1992, Liberty and Union, 1978, Look Homeward: A Life of Thomas Wolfe, 1987 (Pulitzer prize 1988), Lincoln, 1995 rev. edit., 1996, Charles Sumner, 1997, Lincoln at Home: Two Glimpses of Abraham Lincoln's Domestic Life, 1999, We Are Lincoln Men: Abraham Lincoln and His Friends, 2003; editor: War Diary and Letters of Stephen Minot Weld, 1979; gen. editor: Documentary History of American Life, The Making of America Series, 6 vols.; co-editor: (with wife) Diary of Charles Francis Adams, 2 vols., 1964, (with Harold Holzer) Lincoln: Original News Coverage from the New York Times, 2004; contbr. articles to periodicals. Recipient Abraham Lincoln Lit. award Union League Club N.Y.C., 1977, C. Hugh Holman prize MLA, 1988, Joseph R. Levenson award Harvard U. 1993, Benjamin L.C. Wailes award Miss. Hist. Soc., 1994, Barondess-Lincoln prize, 1996, Award of Achievement, Lincoln Group N.Y.C., 1995, 2003 Christopher award, 1996, Lincoln prize Gettysburg Coll., 1996, Jefferson Davis award Mus. of Confederacy, 1996, Nevins/Freeman award Chgo. Civil War Round Table, 1999, Life-time Achievement award Abraham Lincoln Presdl. Mus., Springfield, 2005; Guggenheim fellow, 1964-65, 85-86, fellow Am. Coun. Learned Socs., 1969-70, Ctr. for Advanced Study Behavioral Scis., 1969-70, George A. and Eliza G. Howard fellow, 1957-58, sr. fellow NEH, 1971-72. Fellow Am. Acad. Arts and Scis.; mem. Orgn. Am. Historians, Am. Hist. Assn., So. Hist. Assn. (v.p. 1968, pres. 1969), Soc. Am. Historians, Mass. Hist. Soc., Am. Antiquarian Soc., Phi Beta Kappa, Phi Kappa Phi, Pi Kappa Delta, Pi Kappa Alpha, Omicron Delta Kappa. Clubs: Harvard (N.Y.C.); Cosmos, Signet, Fox. Episcopalian. Home: 41 Lincoln Rd PO Box 6158 Lincoln MA 01773-6158 Business E-Mail: donald@fas.harvard.edu.

DONALD, JACK C., gas industry executive; b. Edmonton, Alta., Can., Nov. 29, 1934; s. Archibald Scott and Margaret Catherine (Cameron) D.; m. Joan M. Schultz, Oct. 29, 1955. Student, Southern Alta. Inst. Tech., 1959. Owner, operator Parkdale Auto Svc., Edmonton, 1959—62; sales mgr. Sanford Oil Ltd., Edmonton, 1962—64, Pacific Petroleums, Edmonton, 1964—71; pres., gen. mgr. Parkland Oil Products, Red Deer, 1971—76; v.p. mktg. Turbo Resources, Calgary, 1977—2002; pres., CEO Parkland Industries Ltd., Red Deer, 1977—, founder, chmn. emeritus, 1993—. Chmn., bd. dirs. Can. Western Bank, Edmonton, Can. Western Trust; v.p., bd. dirs. Deermart Equipment Sales Ltd., Red. Deer, Brandt Industries Ltd., Regina, 2003—, Sifton Energy Inc., Calgary; bd. dirs. Ensign Svcs., Inc., Can. Direct Ins.; past coun. Inst. Chartered Accts. Alta. Alderman City of Red Deer, 1971-77. Mem.: Rotary. Office: Parkland Properties Ltd 5102 58th St #110 Red Deer AB Canada T4N 2L8 Business E-Mail: jackdonald@telus.net.

DONALD, JAMES, food service executive; Trainee Publix Super Mkts., Inc., 1971-76; mgmt. exec. Fla., Ala. and Tex. divsns. Albertson's, 1976-91; key exec. Wal-Mart, 1991-94; sr. v.p., mgr. 130 store ea. divsns. Safeway, Inc., 1994-96; CEO, pres., chmn. Pathmark Stores, Inc., Carteret, NJ, 1996—2002, also chmn. bd. dirs.; pres, North Am. div. Starbucks Corp., Seattle, 2002—05, pres., CEO & dir., 2005—. Office: Starbucks Corp 2401 Utah Ave S Seattle WA 98134

DONALD, JAMES EDWARD, retired career officer, government agency executive; b. Jackson, Miss., Apr. 20, 1949; m. August S. Green; children: Jeff, Cheryl. BA in Polit. Sci. and History, U. Miss., 1970; MPA, U. Mo., 1983; grad., Command Gen. Staff Coll., Nat. War Coll. Commd. 2nd lt. US Army Inf., 1970, advanced through grades to maj. gen., bn. adj./comdr. C Co. 1st Bn., 87th Inf. Regiment Baumholder, Germany, inf. advisor Readiness Group Stewart NY, inspector gen., inspection team chief 101st Airborne Divsn. Ft. Campbell, Ky., bn. exec. officer 2d Bn., 502d Inf. Regiment, bn. comdr. 1st Bn., 502d Inf. Regiment, chief forces team War Plans divsn., Office Dep. Chief Staff, comdr. 1st Brigade, 101st Airborne divsn., chief mil. support divsn., dep. dir. ops./JE U.S. Pacific Command Camp Smith, Hawaii, asst. divsn. comdr. ops. 25th Inf. Divsn. Schofield Barracks, Hawaii; dep. commdg. gen. US Army Pacific, Ft. Shafter, 1998—2000; dep. chief of staff over personnel and installations (ret.) US Army Forces Command, Fort McPherson, Ga., 2000—03; corrections commr. Ga. Dept. of Corrections, Ga. State Gov., Atlanta, 2003—. Decorated Def. Superior Svc. medal, Legion of Merit with oak leaf cluster, Bronze Star, Meritorious Svc. medal with four oak leaf clusters, Army Commendation medal with oak leaf cluster, Nat. Def. Svc. medal with svc. star, Armed Forces Expeditionary medal, Kuwait Liberation medal, S.W. Asia Svc. ribbon. Office: Off of Commissioner GA Dept of Corrections 2 Martin Luther King Jr Dr Atlanta GA 30334

DONALD, JAMES ROBERT, federal agency administrator, writer, economist; b. Omega, Ga., Dec. 31, 1933; s. Clinton Ernest and Lorena (Branan) D.; m. Nancy Ripple, Sept. 16, 1961; children: James Gordon, Mary Carol. Cert., Abraham Baldwin Agrl. Coll., 1952; BS, U. Ga., 1954; MS, N.C. State U., 1956; cert. in govt. tng., Mich. State U., 1975. Economist Econ. Rsch. Svc., USDA, Washington, 1957-76, outlook officer World Agrl. Outlook Bd., 1977-81; retired, 1994; chairperson USDA, Washington, 1982-94. Freelance writer on fishing affairs, 1972—. With U.S. Army, 1957-63. Recipient Superior Svc. award USDA, 1968, Presdl. rank award, 1989. Mem. Am. Agrl. Econs. Assn. (Best Info. Bull. award 1976), Bass Angler's Soc. Am. Home: 584 Laurelwood Dr Mineral VA 23117-4734 E-mail: nrd33@ns.gemlink.com.

DONALD, NORMAN HENDERSON, III, lawyer; b. Denver, Nov. 1, 1937; s. Norman Henderson Jr. and Angelene (Pell) D.; m. Alice Allen, Oct. 31, 1970 (div. Aug. 1980); children: Norman H. IV (dec.), Helen P.; m. Kathryn Akers, Sept. 26, 1981 (div. Jan. 1998). AB, Princeton U., 1959; LLB, Harvard U., 1962. Bar: N.Y. 1962. Assoc. Davis, Polk & Wardwell, N.Y.C., 1962-67, Skadden, Arps, Slate, Meagher & Flom, N.Y.C., 1967-68, ptnr., 1968-94. Chmn. bd. dirs. Norwil Holdings, Inc., N.Y.C., Atlanta and Sarasota. Mem. Assn. of Bar of City of N.Y., Practising Law Inst. (editor Reit Restructuring 1977—), St. Paul's Sch. Alumni Assn. (v.p., bd. dirs. 1984-86), Union Club (N.Y.C.), Rotary, Gold Creek Club (Dawsonville, Ga.). Republican. Episcopalian. Home: Mistral Farms 1544 Bailey Waters Rd Dawsonville GA 30534-1807 Office: care Brock & Silverstein 800 3d Ave New York NY 10022 Fax: 706-265-2810. E-mail: mistral@syclone.net.

DONALDSON, COLEMAN DUPONT, aeronautical engineer, consultant, aerospace engineer; b. Phila., Sept. 22, 1922; s. John W. and Renee (duPont) Donaldson; m. Barbara Goldsmith, Jan. 17, 1945; children: B. Beirne, Coleman duPont, Evan F., Alexander M., William M. BS in Aero. Engring., Rensselaer Poly. Inst., 1943; MA, Princeton U., 1954, PhD, 1957. Staff, NACA, Langley Field, Va., 1943-44, head aerophysics sect., 1946-52; gen. aerodynamics USAC, Wright Field, Ohio, 1945-46; aerodynamic evaluation Bell Aircraft, Niagara Falls, N.Y., 1946; sr. cons., pres. Aero Research Assos. of Princeton, N.J., 1954-79, chmn. bd., 1979-86; group gen. mgr. Aero Research Assocs. Princeton Inc., 1986-87; v.p. Titan Systems, Inc., 1986-87; ret., 1987. Cons. missile guidance and control Gen. Precision Equipment Corp., 1957—68; cons. magnetohydro-dynamics Thompson Ramo Wooldridge, Inc., 1958—61; cons. aerodynamic heating, gen. aerodynamics Martin Marietta Corp., 1955—72, adv. devel. and tech. ops., 1989—96; gen. editor Princeton series on high speed aerodynamics and jet propulsion, 1955—64; cons. boundary layer stability, aerodynamic heating, missile and ordnance sys. dept. GE, 1956—72; cons. Grumman Aerospace Corp., 1959—72; Robert H. Goddard vis. lectr. with rank of prof. Princeton (N.J.) U., 1970—71, chmn. adv. coun. dept. aerospace and mech. scis., 1973—78; mem. rsch. tech. adv. coun. panel rsch. NASA, 1969—76, hypersonic tech. com., 1986—90; mem. indsl. profl. adv. com. Pa. State U.; mem. Pres.' Air Quality Adv. Bd., 1973—74; chmn. lab. adv. bd. for air warfare Naval Rsch. Adv. Com., 1986—89, DARPA Tech. Adv. Panel on Hydrodynamics and Acoustics, 1991—94; cons. Ctr. Naval Analysis, 1990—98; mem. adv. panel NASA Ctr. Turbulence Rsch., 1993—95. Contbr. articles to profl. jours. Recipient Meritorious Pub. Svc. award, Chief Naval Rsch., 1990. Fellow: AIAA (gen. chmn. 13th aerospace scis. meeting 1975, Dryden Rsch. lectr. award 1971); mem.: NAE, Am. Phys. Soc., Delta Phi, Sigma Xi. Home: Apt 1066 955 Harpersville Rd Newport News VA 23601-1093 Office Phone: 757-926-4293.

DONALDSON, EDWARD MOSSOP, research scientist, marine biologist, consultant; b. Whitehaven, Cumbria, Eng., June 1939; arrived in Can., 1961; s. Edward and Margaret (Mossop) D.; m. Judith Selwood, Aug. 8, 1964; 1 child, Heather. BSc with honors, Sheffield (Eng.) U., 1961, DSc, 1975; PhD, U. B.C., Vancouver, Can., 1964. Rsch. scientist Dept. Fisheries and Oceans, West Vancouver, 1965-97, sect. head fish culture rsch., 1981-89, sect. head biotech., genetics and nutrition, 1989-97, head Ctr. of Disciplinary Excellence for Biotech. and Genetics in Aquaculture, 1987-97, scientist emeritus, 1997—; cons. in aquaculture and the environment, 1997—; dir. Ed Donaldson & Assocs. Ltd. Aquaculture and Fisheries Cons., 2001—. Hon. rsch. assoc. U. B.C., 1979-88, adj. prof., 1988—; cons. finfish aquaculture FAO, UN Devel. Program, Can. Internat. Devel. Agy., Internat. Devel. Rsch. Ctrs., U.S. AID, Office of Tech. Assessment of the U.S. Congress, Can. Exec. Svc. Overseas, Sci. Com. on Problems of Environment, WHO, U.S. Seagrant, Portugese Ministry Sci. and Tech., 2002; mem. Nat. Scis. and Engring. Rsch. Coun. Can., mem. strategic grant selection com. for food agr. and aquaculture, 1988-93; mem., active in strategic planning for applied rsch. and knowledge com. biotech. B.C. Sci. Coun. Mem. editl. bd. Gen. and Comparative Endocrinology, 1971-78, Can. Jour. Fisheries and Aquatic Sci., 1985-88, Aquaculture, 1983—, sect. editor, 1999—; mem. editl. bd. Can. Jour. Zoology, 1986-91, Revista Italiana de Acquacoltura, 1991-96; contbr. over 400 articles to sci. jours. and conf. procs.; contbr. to books on endocrinology, biotech. and aquaculture; patentee in field. Bd. dirs. Vancouver Aquarium Marine Sci. Ctr., 1992—. Recipient award for best publs. in Transactions of Am. Fisheries Soc., 1977, Ministerial Merit award Min. of Fisheries and Oceans, 1989, B.C. Sci. Coun. Gold medal, 1992, Commendation award Dep. Minister, 1997; B.C. Sugar Co. scholar, 1961; NIH fellow, 1964-65; recipient Thomas W. Eadie medal Royal Soc. Can., 1995. Fellow Acad. Sci. of Royal Soc. Can. (mem. Rowmanoswky medal com. 1994, Thomas W. Eadie medal com. 1995-96, life sci. fellowship selection com., 2001-04); mem. Can. Soc. Zoologists (councilor 1980-83), Aquaculture Assn. Can. (Rsch. Excellence award 2004). Office: Dept Fisheries & Oceans 4160 Marine Dr Vancouver BC Canada V7V 1N6 Office Phone: 604-666-7928. Business E-Mail: donaldsone@pac.dfo-mpo.gc.ca.

DONALDSON, JAMES NEILL, banker; b. Washington County, Pa., Mar. 25, 1940; s. James Reed and Mary Alice (Neill) D. BA in Polit. Sci., Westminster Coll., 1962; MEd, U. Pitts., 1965, postgrad. in law, 1962-64. cert. trust and fin. advisor, corp. trust specialist; accredited estate planner. Trust adminstr. Bankers Trust Co., N.Y.C., 1967-70, asst. trust officer, 1970-73, trust officer White Plains, N.Y., 1973-76, officer-in-charge Trust Adminstrv. Unit, 1976, v.p., 1976-78, head trust office, 1978-82, with Trust Adminstrn. Unit, 1982-83; head new bus. devel., trust and estates group Chem. Bank, N.Y.C., 1983-88, head trust and estates adminstrn. mgmt., 1989-90; sect. head mgr. trust and estates adminstrn. Chase Manhattan Bank, N.Y.C., 1990-2001, personal trust sales Global Trust and Fiduciary Unit, 1996-2000; wealth transfer and succession planning J.P. Morgan Chase & Co., N.Y.C., 2001; sr. v.p. regional mgr. wealth mgmt. Hudson United Bank, 2002—. Chase rep. to Corp. Fiduciaries Assn. of N.Y.C.; editl. mini-adv. bd. Trusts & Estates Mag., 1997-2002; lectr. Bank Mktg. Assn. Conf., 1995, 99; mem. Estate Planning Coun. Westchester County (N.Y.), 1975—, bd. dirs., 1980-85, treas. 1986-87, v.p., 1988-89, pres. 1989; mem. Estate Planning Coun. Rockland County (N.Y.), 1973—, pres., 1984-85; mem. Estate Planning Coun. N.Y.C., 1983—, bd. dirs., 1988-91, 97-2000, sec., 2001-02, treas., 2002-03, v.p., 2003-04, pres., 2004—, estate adminstrn. Trust Div., N.Y. State Bankers Assn., 1975, 90, 93, 96, mem. estate planning com., 1980-83, mem. mktg. com., 1984—, chmn. 1989-94. Contbr. articles to profl. publs. Mem. Planned Giving Com., U. Pitts.; mem. planned giving com. N.Y. chpt. Arthritis Found. Mem. Am. Bankers Assn. (adv. com. for trust, asset mgmt. and mktg. conf. 2001—03), Phi Kappa Tau. Office: Hudson United Bank Wealth Management 90 Post Road East Westport CT 06880 Office Phone: 203-291-6705 ext 308.

DONALDSON, JAMES OSWELL, III, neurologist, educator; b. Butler, Pa., July 19, 1942; s. James Oswell Jr. and Estelle Mathilda (Unverzagt) D.; m. Mary Hoopingarner, Aug. 23, 1969 (div. Dec. 1983); 1 child, Andrew Robert; m. Susan McKernin, Nov. 3, 1984; stepchildren: Brendan McDonald, Ian McDonald. BS, Haverford Coll., 1964; MD, U. Pa., 1968. Diplomate Am. Bd. Psychiatry and Neurology, Am. Bd. Internal Medicine. Intern in medicine Hosp. of U. Pa., Phila., 1968-69, resident, 1969-70, resident in neurology, 1974-76; hon. house physician Nat. Hosp. for Nervous Diseases, London, 1973-74, sr. vis. fellow, 1991; asst. prof. neurology U. Conn. Sch. Medicine, Farmington, 1977-82, assoc. prof., 1982-88, prof., 1988—. Author: Neurology of Pregnancy, 1978, 2nd edit., 1989. Maj. M.C., U.S. Army, 1970-73. Fellow ACP, Am. Acad. Neurology; mem. Am. Neurol. Assn. Office: U Conn Health Ctr 263 Farmington Ave Farmington CT 06030-1840 Office Phone: 860-679-3186.

DONALDSON, JOHN CECIL, JR., consumer products company executive; b. Bklyn., Dec. 8, 1933; s. John Cecil and Josephine (Greason) D.; m. Marilyn J. Smith, Aug. 29, 1959; children: Susan, John III. AB, Brown U., 1956; MBA, U. Pa., 1959; postgrad., Bentley Sch. Acctg., 1957, LaSalle Law Sch., 1959. Various positions Gen. Motors Corp., Flint, Mich., 1960-71, zone mgr. Buffalo, 1971-76, Newark, 1976-77, mgr. forward product planning, 1977-78; from dir. sales and mktg. to v.p. Corbin Ltd., 1979-85; exec. v.p. and gen. mgr. TMG Corp., N.Y.C., 1986—. Pres. Gen. Motors Exec. Club, Newark, N.J., 1977-78. Mem. Am. Mktg. Assn. Republican. Avocations: ice skating, tennis, golf. Home: 36 Nottingham Way Millington NJ 07946-1917 Office: TMG Corp 1290 Avenue Of The Americas New York NY 10104-0101 Address: 101 Baxters Neck Rd Marstons Mills MA 02648

DONALDSON, MARCIA JEAN, lay worker; b. Wilmington, Del., June 20, 1925; C. Aubrey Smith and Marcia Allen (Hall) Whitman; m. Robert Donald Donaldson, Jan. 8, 1944; children: Robert Gary, Pamela Lynn, David Keith. Student pub. schs., Wilmington. Sunday Sch. tchr., Del., N.J., 1943-70; tchr. Child Evangelism Fellowship, Wilmington, 1943-55, tchr., bd. dirs. N.J., 1955-64, dir. Ocean County, N.J., 1964-73; pres., exec. dir. Christian Children's Assocs., Toms River, NJ, 1964—. Writer radio and TV syndicated programs worldwide for children; author: (booklet) A 30 Year Adventure; producer, hostess radio and TV program Adventure Pals. Mem. Nat. Religious Broadcasters Assn., Gideons Aux. Office: Christian Children's Assn Inc PO Box 446 Toms River NJ 08754-0446 Office Phone: 732-240-3003. Personal E-mail: adventurepals@juno.com. *Of all the important achievements one can accomplish in this life I believe the most rewarding is to be able to introduce another person to the one true and living God, who alone can give us real joy and hope and peace.*

DONALDSON, MICHELE V., marketing professional; B in Comm. and Bus., Ariz. State U.; M in Journalsim and Telecomm., U. Ariz. Dir. mktg. and programming Peple's Choice TV Corp., Shelton, Conn., 1992—96; v.p. mktg. DirectTV/Direct Connect LLP, Boston, 1997—98, TVN Entertainment Corp., LA, 1998—2000; dir. mktg. and sales interactive TV Sony Pictures Digital Entertainment, Culver City, Calif., 2000—02; exec. dir. distbn. GSN Sony Pictures Entertainment Corp., LA, 2000—. Home: 1214 S Citrus Ave Los Angeles CA 90019

DONALDSON, MYRTLE NORMA, music educator, musician; b. Priddy, Tex., Feb. 9, 1923; d. Emil Otto and Brunhilda Eleanore (Riewe) Schneider; m. Fletcher William Donaldson, Feb. 12, 1943; children: Patricia Annette, Rebecca Joyce. BA, U. Ariz., 1970; MA, Middle Tenn. State U., 1982. Cert. profl. piano tchr. Tenn. Music Tchrs. Assn., profl. piano tchr.'s cert. Nat. Music Tchrs.' Assn. Organist Luth. chs., Aleman and Austin, Tex., 1937-42, 43-50, Kinston, N.C., 1943, Los Alamos, N.Mex., 1951-53; Ft. Worth, 1954-56; organist Tullahoma, Tenn., 1969-81; piano tchr., 1972-2001. Composer: sonata, 1981, theme and variations, 1980. Mem. Cmty. Concert Bd., Tullahoma, 1973-99; mem. Cmty. Concert Membership Ch., 1974-78, pres., 1978-80, 89-93. Mem. Music Tchrs. Nat. Assn. (coms. 1983-99, cert. 1991), Mid. Tenn. Music Tchrs. Assn. (sec. Murfreesboro chpt. 1975-77, chair membership state 1977-78, pres. Mid. Tenn. chpt. 1979-81, 87-89), Delta Phi Alpha. Republican. Lutheran. Avocations: knitting, sewing, creative memories album, national background of grandparents.

DONALDSON, PATRICIA ANNE DARCY, secondary educator; b. Hartford, Conn., Mar. 17, 1949; d. Edward Alison and Priscilla Hinckley (Matthews) Darcy; m. Kent Regan Donaldson, May 28, 1983. BA in English, Elizabethtown (Pa.) Coll., 1971; MEd in English, Shippensburg (Pa.) U., 1975. Cert. tchr., Pa. Tchr. Howell High Sch., Freehold (N.J.) Regional High Sch. Dist., 1971-72; tchr. Cornwall-Lebanon (Pa.) Sch. Dist., 1973; tchr. English, Derry Twp. Sch. Dist., Hershey, Pa., 1973—2004, subject coord., 1985-92, lead tchr., 1992-93. Bd. dirs. Capital Area Writing Project, Harrisburg, Pa., 1992—; part-time instr. Pa. State U., Harrisburg, 1993-1998. Trustee Leukemia & Lymphoma Soc., Harrisburg. Democrat. Episcopalian. Avocations: landscaping, travel, walking, reading. Home: 91 Bowling Rd Harrisburg PA 17112-4235

DONALDSON, ROBERT CHARLES, history educator; b. San Francisco, Jan. 28, 1924; s. Donald and Cora Priscilla (Donaldson) Wood; m. Persis Chapple, Jan. 4, 1975. Student, U. Ariz., 1942; BA, U. So. Calif., 1950, MA, 1951; PhD, U. Mich., 1954; Fulbright scholar, U. Brussels, 1953-54. Asst. prof. Eastern Ky. State Coll., 1954-57; asst. prof. history Calif. State U., Sacramento, 1957-62, assoc. prof., 1962-67, prof., 1967—86, chmn. dept., 1969-75, chmn. acad. senate, 1968-69, coll. ombudsman, 1969-70, presiding officer faculty, 1972-75, faculty emeritus, 1986—. Senator Acad. Senate of Calif. State Univs. and Colls., 1970-76; real estate broker, 1990-2005. Pres. Gold Country Chamber Orch., 2000-2001. Served with AUS, 1943-46. Recipient Meritorious Performance award for outstanding svc. to univ. community, 1988. Mem. Am. Hist. Assn., Faculty Emeritus Assn. (pres. 1995-97), Town and Gown (dir. 1989-2005), Am. Contract Bridge League (gold life master), Phi Kappa Phi (pres. campus chpt. 1963-64, 74-76, 92-94, 2003-05), Phi Alpha Theta, Blue Key, Phi Beta Delta, Phi Kappa Phi Democrat. Home: 1516 Little Ct Carmichael CA 95608-5915

DONALDSON, ROBERT FROST, minister; b. Charlevoix, Mich., May 29, 1945; s. Howard Earl and Lois Marie (Frost) D.; m. Suzanne Alzina Trowbridge, Dec. 22, 1973 (div. Nov. 1986); children: Samantha, Roberta; m. Karen Mae Hoisington, Feb. 14, 1987; children: Cathy, David, Laura. DDiv, Universal Life Ch., 1994, PhD in Religion, 1995; BS in Pastoral Counseling, Am. Internat. U., 1996. Ordained minister Am. Fellowship, 1988, Ministers for Christ Assembly of Churches, 1994. Owner East Jordan Zephyr Svc., 1965-67; mechanic, assembler East Jordan (Mich.) Iron Works, Inc., 1967—; owner Donaldson Machine Shop, Ellsworth, Mich., 1975-90; pastor, counselor Discovery Ministries, East Jordan, 1988—. Sec. South Arm Twp. Planning and Zoning Bd., East Jordan, 1986-89; candidate for sch. bd. Ellsworth Schs., 1984; mem. arts couns. East Jordan, Petoskey, Traverse City and Cadillac, Mich. Mem. UUCOP (founder, sec. 1993-97). Avocations: protection of children, wellness in the workplace. Home: 701 Division St East Jordan MI 49727-9747

DONALDSON, ROBERT HERSCHEL, university administrator, educator; b. Houston, June 14, 1943; s. Herschel Arthur and Vera Edith (True) D.; m. Judy Carol Johnston, June 27, 1964 (div. Apr. 30, 1984); children: Jennifer Gwynne, John Andrew; m. Sally S. Abravanel, Mar. 31, 1985; children: Mark Elliot, Ryan Scott. AB, Harvard U., 1964, A.M., 1966, PhD, 1969. Prof. polit. sci. Vanderbilt U., 1968-81, assoc. dean Coll. Arts and Sci., 1975-81; provost, v.p. acad. affairs, prof. polit. sci. Herbert H. Lehman Coll. CUNY, 1981-84; pres. Fairleigh Dickinson U., Rutherford, N.J., 1984-90, U. Tulsa, 1990-96, trustees prof. polit. sci., 1996—. Vis. research prof. U.S. Army War Coll., 1978-79; pres. Am. coms. fgn. rels., 2002-. Author: Stasis and Change in Revolutionary Elites, 1971, Soviet Policy toward India, 1974, The Soviet-Indian Alliance: Quest for Influence, 1979, The Soviet Union in the Third World: Successes and Failures, 1981, Soviet Foreign Policy since World War II, 1981, 85, 88, 92, The Foreign Policy of Russia: Changing Systems, Enduring Interests, 1998, 2002, 05. Council Fgn. Relations fellow, 1973-74 Mem. Coun. on Fgn. Rels., Phi Beta Kappa. Republican. Methodist. Home: 6449 S Richmond Ave Tulsa OK 74136-1669 Office: Univ Tulsa 600 S College Ave Tulsa OK 74104-3126 Office Phone: 918-631-2409. Business E-Mail: robert-donaldson@utulsa.edu.

DONALDSON, SAMUEL ANDREW, journalist; b. El Paso, Tex., Mar. 11, 1934; s. Samuel Andrew and Chloe (Hampson) Donaldson; m. Billie Kay Butler, Nov. 30, 1963 (div. 1981); children: Samuel, Jennifer, Thomas, Robert; m. Janice Claire Smith, Apr. 16, 1983. BA, Tex. Western Coll. (now UTEP), 1955; postgrad., U. So. Calif., 1955—56. Radio/TV news reporter/anchorman WTOP, Washington, 1961—67; Capitol Hill corr. ABC News, Washington, 1967—77, White House corr., 1977—89; panelist This Week With David Brinkley, 1981—96; co-anchor This Week With Sam Donaldson and Cokie Roberts, 1996—2002, Prime Time Live, ABC, 1989—98; chief White House corrs. ABC News, 1998—99; co-anchor 20/20 ABC, 1998—99; anchor SamDonaldson@abcnews.com, 1999—2002, The Sam Donaldson Show, ABC Radio Network, 2001—04; co-anchor ABC News Now, 2004—. Bd. mem. Acad. Achievement, 2003—. Author: (book) Hold On, Mr. President, 1987 (internat. best seller). Chmn. adv. bd. Moffitt Cancer Ctr.; mem. Ariz. Meml. Bd. Capt. U.S. Army, 1956—59. Named a UTEP Distinguished Alumnus, 1976; named Best TV White House Corr. in Bus., The Washington Journalism Rev., 1985, Best TV Corr. in Bus., 1986; recipient, 1987, 1988, 1989, 4 Emmy awards, 3 George Foster Peabody awards, others, Broadcaster of Yr. award, Nat. Press Found., 1998; UTEP's Ctr. for Comm. Studies named in his honor, 2002. Mem.: AFTRA (past pres. Washington-Balt. chpt.), Nat. Acad. of Achievement. Office: ABC 1717 Desales St NW Washington DC 20036

DONALDSON, SARAH SUSAN, radiologist; b. Portland, Oreg., Apr. 20, 1939; BS, RN, U. Oreg., 1961; MD, Harvard U., 1968. Intern U. Wash., 1968—69; resident in radiol. therapy Stanford (Calif.) Med. Ctr., 1969—72; fellow in pediatric oncology Inst. Gustave-Roussy, 1972—73; prof. radiol. oncology Stanford U. Sch. Medicine., 1973—. Mem.: NIH. Office: Stanford U Med Ctr Dept Radio/Oncology 875 Blake Wilbur Dr Stanford CA 94305-5847

DONALDSON, STEPHEN REEDER, author; b. Cleve., May 13, 1947; s. James R. and Mary Ruth (Reeder) D. BA, Coll. of Wooster, 1968; MA, Kent State U., 1971; LittD (hon.), Coll. of Wooster, 1993. Asst. dispatcher Akron City Hosp., 1968-70; tchg. fellow Kent State U., 1971; acquisitions editor Tapp-Gentz Assos., West Chester, Pa., 1973-74; instr. Ghost Ranch Writers Workshops, N.Mex., 1973-77. Author: Lord Foul's Bane, 1977, The Illearth War, 1977, The Power That Preserves, 1977, The Wounded Land, 1980, The One Tree, 1982, White Gold Wielder, 1983, Daughter of Regals, 1984, The Mirror of Her Dreams, 1986, A Man Rides Through, 1987, The Real Story, 1991, Forbidden Knowledge, 1991, A Dark and Hungry God Arises, 1992, Chaos and Order, 1994, This Day All Gods Die, 1996, Reave The Just, 1999, The Man Who Fought Alone, 2001, The Runes of the Earth, 2004, (as Reed Stephens) The Man Who Killed His Brother, 1980, The Man Who Risked His Partner, 1984, The Man Who Tried to Get Away, 1990; editor: Strange Dreams, 1993. Recipient John W. Campbell award best new writer World Sci. Fiction Conv., 1979, Best Novel award Brit. Fantasy Soc., 1979, Balrog award for best novel, 1981, 83, for best collection, 1985, Saturn award for best fantasy novel, 1983, Book ofYr. award Sci. Fiction Book Club, 1987, 88, World Fantasy award, Best Collection,2000. Mem. Am. Contract Bridge League, Internat. Assn. for the Fantastic in the Arts, N.M. Shotokan, Life - Dance Kajukenbo. Office: care Howard Morhaim Rm 604 11 John St Ste 407 New York NY 10038 Office Phone: 212-529-4433.

DONALDSON, THOMAS, finance educator; b. Wichita, Kans., July 23, 1945; s. Paul J. and Louisene (Sadler) D.; m. Sally Leisure, May, 1970 (div. 1973); m. Jean Shephard, Sept. 3, 1977 (dec. June 2002); children: Paul, Keith, Paige. Student, U.S. Naval Acad., 1963-65; BS, U. Kans., 1967, PhD, 1976. Asst. prof. Loyola U., Chgo., 1976-81, assoc. prof., 1981-84, Henry J. Wirtenberger prof. ethics, 1984-88; C. Stewart Sheppard vis. prof. bus. adminstrn. U. Va., Charlottesville, 1988-89; John Carroll prof. bus. ethics Georgetown U., Washington, 1989-92, John F. Connelly prof. bus. ethics, 1992-96; Mark O. Winkelman endowed prof. Wharton Sch., U. Pa., Phila., 1996—. Testified in U.S. Congress (Senate Judiciary Com.) on Sarbanes-Oxley legis., 2002; participant World Econ. Forum, Davos, Switzerland, 2003. Editor: Issues in Moral Philosophy, 1986, Case Studies in Business Ethics, 1987,Ethical Issues in Business, 1979, 83, 87, 92; author: The Ethics of International Business, 1989, Corporations and Morality, 1982, (with Thomas W. Dunfee) Ties That Bind: A Social Contracts Approach to Business Ethics, 1999; assoc. editor Acad. of Mgmt. Rev., 2002—, mem. editl. bd., 1996-2002; contbr. articles to profl. jours.; mem. editl. bd. Bus. Ethics Quar., 1990—. Mem. Haverford Friends Meeting, 1998—. With USN, 1963-68. Fellow Bus. Enterprise Trust; mem. Ctr. for Advanced Study Ethics (coun. scholars 1990—), Phila. Country Club. Avocations: music, skiing. Home: 518 Lynmere Rd Bryn Mawr PA 19010-2818 Office: U Pa Wharton Sch Philadelphia PA 19104 E-mail: donaldst@comcast.net.

DONALDSON, WILLIAM HENRY, former federal agency administrator, corporate financial executive, insurance company executive; b. Buffalo, June 2, 1931; s. Eames and Guida (Marx) D.; m. Sept. 17, 1960; children: Adam, Kimberly, Matthew. BA, Yale U., 1953, MA (hon.), 1970; MBA with distinction, Harvard U., 1958; LLD (hon.), Webster U., 1992; DPhil (hon.), St. Lawrence U., 1995; DHL (hon.), Alfred U., 1995. Chmn., chief exec. Donaldson, Lufkin & Jenrette, Inc., N.Y.C., 1959-73; under sec. U.S. Dept. State, Washington, 1973—75; spl. cons. to v.p. of U.S. The White House, Washington, 1975; dean, Beinecke prof. mgmt. Yale Grad. Mgmt. Sch., New Haven, 1975-80; chmn., CEO Donaldson Enterprises, Inc., N.Y.C., 1980-90; chmn., chief exec. N.Y. Stock Exch., N.Y.C., 1990-95; founder, sr. advisor Donaldson, Lufkin and Jenrette, Inc., 1996-2000; chair., pres., CEO Aetna Inc., Hartford, 2000—02; chair., CEO Donaldson Enterprises, 2001—; chmn. SEC, 2003—05. Bd. dirs. Aetna Life & Casualty, Honeywell Inc., Bright Horizons Family Solutions, Inc. Trustee, chmn. fin. com. Ford Found., N.Y.C., 1968-80; trustee Yale U., New Haven, 1970-75; ptnr. N.Y.C. Partnership; bd. dirs. Bus. Coun. of State of N.Y., 1990-96, Lincoln Ctr. for Performing Arts, N.Y.C.; trustee N.Y. Police Found., Marine Corps Univ. Found., Aspen Inst.; gov. Fgn. Policy Assn.; chmn. Carnegie Endowment for Internat. Peace, 1999-2003. 1st lt. USMC, 1953-55. Recipient Pres.'s Disting. Svc. award SUNY, 1976; named Businessman of Yr., AP, 1969. Mem. Inst. CFAs, Yale Mgmt. Sch. (chmn. bd. advisors 1995-2003), Coun. on Fgn. Rels. E-mail: bdonaldson@denterprise.com.

DONALDSON, WILMA CRANKSHAW, elementary school educator; b. Havre de Grace, Md., Aug. 28, 1942; d. John Hamilton and Wilma Chaffee (Thurlow) Crankshaw; m. James Neill Donaldson, Aug. 5, 1967. BA in Edn. cum laude, Westminster Coll., 1964; MA in Edn., Fairfield U., 1976. Educator Hurlbutt Elem. Sch., Weston, Conn., 1964-78, 92—, Weston Mid. Sch., 1979-91; tchr. Greek Mythology Elem. Sch., 1999—. Team leader Hurlbutt Elem. Sch., 1967—68, 1976—78, sci. rep., 1992—99, developer of curriculum; judge Odyssey of the Mind, Conn., 1995—2001; presenter of photography and Greek myth courses elem. sch., 2002—; tchr. pvt. student art courses; tchr. Music/Lit./Theater Workshop, 1997—; presenter in field; sci. cons. Greenwich Pub. Schs., 2002—. Author: (filmstrip script) Sci. Series, 1972, Metric Math Series, 1973. Chairperson fine arts New England Sch. Accreditation Com., Weston, 1990-91; trainer Project CHEM, Exxon Corp., 1991—; state planning com., program/site chmn. Conn. Elem. Sci. Day Conf., 1994—; organizer, advisor Student Elem. Sch. Environ. Orgn., 1992-2003, sci. cons. for Pub. Schs. Greenwich, Conn., 2002-; co-organizer, co-founder Elem. Family Sci. Night, Weston, 2000; dir./tchr. Camp Invention, Weston, 2002-, mem. Silvermine Arts Enrichment Com. Recipient Faculty Mem. Presdl. Recognition Sch. award U.S. Dept. Edn., 1987-88, Celebration of Excellence award State of Conn., 1989, 92, 95, 98. Mem. NEA, Nat. Sci. Tchrs. Assn. (workshop presenter Moscow 1991, NASA-NEWEST awardee 1997), ASCD, Conn. Edn. Assn., Conn. Alliance Arts Edn. (Weston Tchr. of Yr. 1994-95, Conn. Alliance for Art Edn. Disting. Tchr. of Yr. 1995), Conn. Elem. Sci. Internat. (com. chmn. 1991-98), Delta Zeta. Avocations: art, theater, photography, travel.

DONATHAN, DAVID ALLEN, dean, retired military officer; s. William Richard and Tokuko Donathan (Stepmother); m. April Dauphine Surber, Mar. 31, 1972; 1 child, Colleen Katherine Duval. BA in Bus. Adminstrn., Columbia Coll., 1979; MS, Chapman U., 1992; diploma, U.S. Army Command and Gen. Staff Coll., 1992. Cert. rank I instr. Ky. Dept. Edn., 2005. Commd. lt. U.S. Army, 1971, advanced through grades to maj., ret., 1992; instr., chmn. Army Jr. ROTC Rockcastle County H.S., Mt. Vernon, Ky., 1995—98; one-stop coord. Somerset (Ky.) C.C., 1999—2000; instr., coord. Dept. Bus. Sullivan U., Lexington, Ky., 2003, assoc. dean academic affairs, 2003—05; chair of bus. St. Catherine Coll., 2005—. Pres., chief oper. office Diversified Activities, Inc., Somerset, 1992—95. Author: Subaqua Diving Supervisors Handbook, (handbook) Human Resource Management/Development, 1984. Decorated Joint Svc. Commendation medal Dept.f Def., Def. Meritorious Svc. medal; Go the Distance scholarship, Chela Found., 2004. Mem.: MENSA (locsec 1989—90), Nat. Assn. Underwater Instrs. (instr. 1988), Mil. Officers Assn. (life). Home: 10595 North Highway 27 Eubank KY 42567 Office: 227 East Main St Lebanon KY 40033 Office Phone: 859-276-7681. Home Fax: 859-276-1153; Office Fax: 859-276-1153. E-mail: ddonathan@hotmail.com.

DONATI, ROBERT MARIO, physician, educational administrator; b. Richmond Heights, Mo., Feb. 28, 1934; s. Leo S. and Rose Marie (Gualdoni) D. BS in Biology, St. Louis U., 1955, MD, 1959. Diplomate Am. Bd. Nuclear Medicine. Intern St. Louis City Hosp., 1959-60; asst. resident John Cochran Hosp., St. Louis, 1960-62; fellow in nuclear medicine St. Louis U., 1962-63; pvt. practice specializing in nuclear medicine St. Louis, 1963-93; mem. staff St. Louis VA Med. Ctr., 1963-83, chief nuclear medicine svc., 1968-79, chief of staff, 1979-83; mem. staff St. Louis U. Hosps., 1963-93, interim chief exec. officer, 1987-88; mem. staff St. Mary's Health Ctr., 1984-93; mem. faculty Sch. Medicine St. Louis U., 1963—, asst. prof. internal medicine, 1965-68, assoc. prof., 1968-74, prof., 1974-93, prof. emeritus internal medicine, 1993—, prof. radiology, 1979-93, prof. emeritus radiology, 1993—, dir. div. nuclear medicine Sch. Medicine, 1968-87, sr. assoc. dean Sch. Medicine, 1983-93; exec. assoc. v.p. Med. Ctr., 1985-93, acting v.p., 1986; adj. prof. medicine Washington U. Sch. Medicine, 1979-83. Rschr. in clin. investigative nuclear medicine and humoral control of cellular proliferation; fin. com. del. Am. Bd. Med. Spltys., 1984-90. Editor: (with W.T. Newton) Radioassay in Clinical Medicine, 1973, (with J. Edwards) Current Medical Practice, 1992, rev., 2001; contbr. articles to profl. jours. Mem. Presdl. Adv. Commn. on VA, 1972, Inst. Medicine com. to estimate VA physician needs, 1988-90; bd. dirs. Alliance for Cmty. Health, Inc., 1986-96, Healthline Mgmt. Svcs., Inc., 1986-94, chmn., 1988-93, Healthline Corp. Health Metro St. Louis, 1992-94, Ctrl. Med. Ctr., Inc., 1988-89, Healthlink, Inc., 1987-93, Abbott Ambulance Co., Inc., 1989-94, chmn., 1992-94; cabinet mem. Cath. Cmty. Svcs., St. Louis, 2000-04; mem. HEW Task Force on Health Effects Ionizing Radiation, 1978-79; desegregation monitoring and adv. com. U.S. Dist. Ct., 1980. Decorated Army Commendation medal; recipient VA Disting. Service award, 1983, alumni Merit award St. Louis U., 1996. Mem. AMA (residency rev. com. for nuclear medicine 1978-80, coun. on med. schs. 1984-94), AAUP, Am. Bd. Nuclear Medicine (life, bd. dirs. 1980—, vice chmn. 1984-85, chmn. 1985-86), St. Louis Med. Soc., Am. Fedn. for Clin. Rsch. (councilor 1967-70), Ctrl. Soc. Clin. Rsch., NY Acad. Scis., Soc. Nuclear Medicine (acad. coun. 1970—, trustee 1977-81, 90-92, assoc. chmn. sci. program 1978, publs. com. 1979-83, chmn. 1982-83, bus. advisors com. 1989-93, chmn. 1990-92), Am. Coll. Nuclear Physicians, Internat. Socs. Hematology, Soc. Med. Cons. to Armed Forces, Cosmos Club, Mo. Athletic Club, Phi Beta Kappa, Sigma Xi, Alpha Omega Alpha. Roman Catholic. Home: 5335 Botanical Ave Saint Louis MO 63110-3123 Office: St Louis U Sch Medicine 1402 S Grand Blvd Saint Louis MO 63104-1004 Office Phone: 314-772-5335. Personal E-mail: rmdonati5335@webtv.net.

DONAWAY, CARL D., messenger service executive; BA, Calif. State U., Northridge; MBA, U. Minn. Ops. supr. Airborne, L.A., 1977—78, sales rep., 1978—79, ops. mgr., 1979—80, L.A. sta. mgr., 1980, dist. ops. mgr. Midwest, dist. sales mgr. Midwest region, 1985, mktg. devel. dir. Seattle, 1987—88, customer support dir., 1988—90, v.p. customer support, 1990—92, v.p. bus. analysis, 1992, pres. ABX Air, 1992—99, sr. exec. v.p. field and air svcs., 1999—2002, pres., CEO, 2002—, chmn. bd., 2002—; exec. chmn. DHL Holdings (USA), Plantation, Fla., 2003—. Office: DHL Holdings USA Ste 600 1200 South Pine Island Road Fort Lauderdale FL 33324

DONDANVILLE, JOHN WALLACE, lawyer; b. Moline, Ill., Nov. 29, 1937; s. Laurence A. and Eva C. Dondanville; m. Maureen C. Ryan, Apr. 16, 1966; children: Edward John, Julie Ann. AB in History, Holy Cross Coll., 1959; JD, Northwestern U., 1962. Bar: Ill. 1962. Ptnr. Baker & McKenzie, Chgo., 1965-97; ret., 1997. Author: Product Liability Trends & Implications, 1970. Mem.: Ill. Bar Assn. Avocation: hiking.

DONDANVILLE, PATRICIA, lawyer; b. Anchorage, Alaska, Mar. 21, 1956; d. Leo John and Ann Louise (Mosey) D.; m. James F. Berman; children: Emily Grace, Edward James. BA in Am. Studies, U. Notre Dame, 1978; JD, U. Va., 1981. Bar: Ill. 1981. Assoc. Schiff Hardin & Waite, Chgo., 1981-87, ptnr., 1988—. Bd. dirs. Nat. Ctr. for Laity, Chgo., 1986-98 Mem. ABA, Chgo. Bar Assn., Notre Dame Club Chgo. (bd. govs., scholarship found. 1988—), The Economic Club Chgo. Office: Schiff Hardin LLP 6600 Sears Tower Chicago IL 60606 Office Phone: 312-258-5709. Business E-Mail: pdondanville@schiffhardin.com.

DONDYSH, VICTORIA, pianist; b. Moscow, July 8, 1963; arrived in U.S., 1976; d. Leon Michael Dondysh and Zhanna N. Stepanitskaya-Dondysh; m. Gary Katz, June 28, 1991; children: Samuel Katz, Elizabeth Katz. Prep. divsn., Julliard Sch. of Music, NYC, 1976—78, Mannes Coll. of Music, 1979—81; MusB, Manhattan Sch. of Music, NYC, 1986, MusM, 1988. Musician: (concerts) Ctrl. Hall Arts, 1975, 2000, Hubbard Hall, 1986, Paul Hall, 1976—78, Soesterberg Music Festival, 2001, Free Libr. of Westhampton, 2001, Clayton - Liberatore Gallery, 2002, Fairleigh Dickenson U., 2002, Roger Meml. Libr., 2003, (albums) Victoria Dondysh Piano Recital, (CDs) Complete Bach Partitas, 2004; appearances: on radio and TV; author: Children's Art Composer edit., 1992. Recipient Young Artists Competition, Hoppauge, NY, 1978; grantee scholarship, Julliard Sch. of Music, 1976—79, Mannes Sch. of Music, 1979—81. Mem.: MTNA, Piano Tchr. Congress. Home: 141 Oakdene Ave Leonia NJ 07605 Personal E-mail: katzga@yahoo.com.

DONEGAN, CHARLES EDWARD, lawyer, educator; b. Chgo., Apr. 10, 1933; s. Arthur C. and Odessa (Arnold) D.; m. Patty Lou Harris, June 15, 1963; 1 son, Carter Edward. BSC., Roosevelt U., 1954; MS, Loyola U., 1959; JD, Howard U., 1967; LL.M., Columbia, 1970. Bar: NY 1968, DC 1968, Ill. 1979. Pub. sch. tchr., Chgo., 1956-59; with Office Internal Revenue, Chgo., 1959-62; labor economist U.S. Dept. Labor, Washington, 1962-65; legal intern U.S. Commn. Civil Rights, Washington, summer 1966; asst. counsel NAACP Legal Def. Fund, N.Y.C., 1967-69; lectr. law Baruch Coll., N.Y.C., 1969-70; asst. prof. law State U. N.Y. at Buffalo, 1970-73; assoc. prof. law Howard U., 1973-77; vis. assoc. prof. Ohio State U., Columbus, 1977-78; asst. regional counsel U.S. EPA, 1978-80; prof. law So. U., Baton Rouge, 1980—; sole practice law Chgo. and Washington, 1984—. Arbitrator steel industry, 1972, U.S. Postal Svc., New Orleans, D.C. Superior Ct., 1987—, Fed. Mediation and Conciliation Svc., 1985—, N.Y. Stock Exch.; vis. prof. law La. State U., 1981, N.C. Cen. U., Durham, 1988—, So. U., Baton Rouge, spring 1992; real estate broker; mem. bd. consumer claims Dist. D.C., 1988—; mem. Mayor's Transition Task Force, Washington, 1995; moot ct. judge Georgetown U. Law Sch., Washington, 1987—, Howard U. Law Sch., Washington, 1987—, Balsa, 1987—; spkr. in field. Author: Discrimination in Public Employment, 1975; editor Nat. Bar Assn. Arbitration Section newsletter. 1997-; contbr. articles to profl. jours. Active Ams. for Dem. Action; adv. com. DC Bd. Edn. Named one of Top 42 Lawyers in Washington Area, Washington Afro-Am. Newspaper, 1993-96; Ford Found. scholar, 1965-67. Columbia U., 1972-73, NEH Postdoctoral fellow in Afro-Am. studies Yale U., 1972-73. Mem. ABA (vice-chmn. edn. and curriculum com. local govt. law sect. 1972-80, pub. edn. com. sect. local govt. 1974-84, chmn. liaison com. AALS, 1984, chair arbitration sect., editor arbitration sect. newsletter 1997-), Nat. Bar Assn. (labor and employment law sect., steering com.), D.C. Bar Assn., Washington Bar Assn. (chmn. legal edn. com.), Chgo. Bar Assn., Fed. Bar Assn., Cook County Bar Assn., Am. Arbitration Assn. (arbitrator), D.C. Fee Arbitration Bd. (bd. govs. 1990—), Nat. Conf. Black Lawyers (bd. organizers), Nat. Futures Assn. (arbitrator), Nat. Assn. Securities Dealers (arbitrator), Assn. Henri Capitant, Roosevelt U. Alumni Assn. (rep. at George Washington U. 175th anniversary charter day convocation 1996), Loyola U. Alumni Assn. (v.p. Washington), Howard U. Alumni Assn. (rep. at Hunter Coll. Centennial 1970), Columbia U. Alumni Assn. (v.p. law Washington), Alpha Phi Alpha (life), Phi Alpha Kappa, Phi Alpha Delta. Home: 4315 Argyle Ter NW Washington DC 20011-4243 Office: 601 Pennsylvania Ave NW Ste 900 Washington DC 20004-3615 also: 10 S Riversie Plz Ste 1800 Chicago IL 60606 Office Phone: 202-434-8210. *I have always tried to do my best and never give in to obstacles. I have also been blessed with wonderful parents, relatives, friends, teachers and mentors who had confidence in me.*

DONEGAN, MARK, metal products executive; Pres., airfoil divsn. Precision Castparts Corp., pres., structural divsn., pres., Wyman-Gordon, 1999, pres., COO Portland, Oreg., 1999—2002, pres., CEO, dir., 2002—. Office: Precision Castparts Corp 4650 SW Macadam Ave Ste 440 Portland OR 97239-4262*

DONEGAN, WILLIAM LAURENCE, retired medical educator; b. Jacksonville, Fla., Nov. 3, 1932; s. William Elton and Mildred Louise (Bullock) D.; m. Judith Fae Higgins, Dec. 21, 1963; children: William David, Elizabeth Kathleen. BA, Yale U., 1955, MD, 1959. Diplomate Am. Bd. Surgery. Resident surgery Barnes Hosp., St. Louis, 1959-64; staff surgeon Ellis Fischel State Cancer Hosp., Columbia, Mo., 1964-74; prof. surgery Med. Coll. Wis., Milw., 1974—2003; ret., 2004. Clin. prof. surgery Med. Coll. Wis., Milw., 2003—. Editor: Cancer of the Breast, 1967-2002; editorial bd. Cancer, Jour. Surg. Oncology, 1988-2003. Pres. Wis. div. Am. Cancer Soc., 1990-91. Recipient Disting. Svc. award, Med. Coll. Wis., 1999, St. George medal, Am. Cancer Soc., 2001. Personal E-mail: wilado@aol.com.

DONEHEY, MARILYN MOSS, foundation administrator; b. Malad City, Idaho, Sept. 5, 1946; d. Ray Wesley and LaRue Camp Jones; m. Robert David Donehey, Apr. 15, 1966 (div. June 1989); children: Troy Robert, David Ray, Calli-Anne, Suzanne, Erin. AA, Elgin Cmty. Coll., 1987; BA, Judson Coll., 1992. Sec., receptionist Fox Valley Ctr. for Ind. Livng, Elgin, Ill., 1987-88, devel. dir., 1990-91; cmty. outreach specialist Tri-County Ind. Living Ctr., Akron, Ohio, 1993-94; program dir. Soc. of the Blind, Akron, 1997—2002. Subs. tchr. dispatcher, Ill. Sch. Dist. 300, Carpentersville, 1972-81. Precinct com. person Rep. Cen. Com., Kane County, Ill., 1977-90; pres. Consumer Advocacy coun., Akron, 2000-2002.; participant blindness adjustment program La. Ctr. Blind. Mem. Nat. Fedn. of the Blind (vice chair 1997-2001, sec. 2001-2002, scholar 1987). Republican. Mem. Lds Ch. Avocations: music, writing. Office: Soc of the Blind 325 E Market Akron OH 44304 E-mail: mmoss325@aol.com, Lynssom@aol.com.

DONEHUE, JOHN DOUGLAS, interdenominational ministries executive; b. Cramerton, NC, July 5, 1928; s. John Sidney and Annie (Shepherd) D.; m. Mary Phelps, Jan. 9, 1952 (dec. 1964); children: Teresa Jean, Marilyn Phelps; m. Sylvia Louise McKenzie, Feb. 11, 1966 (dec. Nov. 1971); children: Hayden Shepherd, John Douglas; m. Virginia Kirkland, June 28, 1975; children: Anne Mikell, Robertson Carr. Student, Am. Press Inst., Columbia U., 1965, 71-73; LHD (hon.), Charleston So. U., 1985. Sports editor Orangeburg (S.C.) Times and Dem., 1948-50; polit reporter Montgomery (Ala.) Advertiser, 1954-55; sports editor Charleston (S.C.) News and Courier, 1956, copy editor, 1958, state editor, 1959-62, city editor, 1962-68, mng. editor, 1968-71, promotion dir., 1971-75, v.p. for corp. pub. rels., 1975-96; v.p. corp. comm., adminstr. The Post and Courier Found., 1996—; bd. dirs. Star Gospel Mission, Charleston, 1962-80, chmn. bd. dirs., 1980-96, exec. dir., 1996—. Faculty advisor Student Newspaper, Charleston So. U.; lectr.; spl. adviser comdt. 7th USCG dist. for establishment of dist.-wide pub. info. program, 1960-61; journalism lectr. Charleston So. U.; sec. 1st bd. founders, 1969. Author: Charleston on the Air, A History of Radio Broadcasting in Charleston, 2000; compiler: News and Courier Style Books, 1969; guest commentator Nat. Pub. Radio. Chmn. adv. bd. Salvation Army; chmn. regional adv. coun. S.C. Dept. Youth Svc.; chmn. planning bd. United Way; pres. Palmetto Safety Coun.; chmn. bd. Charleston County Libr. Found.; lay reader, vestryman, sr. warden Episc. Ch.; bd. dirs. Charleston Mus., S.C. Tricentennial Parade Com., 1972, S.C. Humanities Coun. Served with S.C., N.G., 1948—50 USAF, 1950—54 USMCR, 1955—56 USAR, 1956—59 USCGR, 1959—66, served with USNR, 1966—75. Recipient Freedoms Found. award, 1969, S.C. Family of Yr. award, Am. Advt. Fedn., Silver Medal award, 1987, VA citation for meritorious svc., 1971, La Societe Francaise de Bienfaisance Humanitati medal of Honor, 2001. Mem. John Ancrum Soc. of Soc. Prevention Cruelty to Animals, Carolina Art Assn., Internat. Newspaper Promotion Assn., S.C. Press Assn. (pres. 1985), Air Force Assn. (dir. Charleston coun.), Naval Civilian Mgrs. Assn., Navy league (v.p. Charleston coun.), Charleston Trident C. of C. (pres. 1983), Toastmasters Internat. (charter mem. Okinawa club), Okinawa Soc., Downtown Athletic Club, Pacific Stars and Stripes Alumni Assn. (bd. dirs.), Rotary Charleston (pres. 1974-75). Achievements include only person serve in all 5 branches of armed forces per Def. Dept. records. Home: 66 Bull St Charleston SC 29401-1303 Office: Star Gospel Mission PO Box 20235 474 Meeting St Charleston SC 29403-4831 Office Phone: 743-722-0980. Personal E-mail: ddonehue@charleston.net.

DONELAN, MARK ANTHONY, physicist; b. Grenada, West Indies, Mar. 27, 1942; came to Can., 1960, naturalized, 1969; s. William Gregory and Ivy (Payne) D.; B.Engring., McGill U., 1964; Ph.D., U. B.C., 1970; m. June Lynch, June 10, 1967; children: Laura, Maxwell. Project engr. Procter & Gamble Can., Hamilton, Ont., 1964-66; Killam postdoctoral fellow Cambridge (Eng.) U., 1970-71; rsch. scientist Environ. Can., Burlington, Ont., 1971-96; prof. Rosenstiel Sch. Marine and Atmospheric Sci. U. Miami, 1996—; asso. prof. civil engring. McMaster U., Hamilton, Ont., 1979-85, prof. civil engring., 1985-93; adj. prof. Waterloo (Ont.) U., 1979—, Laval U., Que., 1990-94, U. Miami, Fla., 1992-96; emeritus scientist Environ. Can., Burlington, Ont., 1997—. Humboldt research fellow Max-Planck-Institut für Meteorologie, Germany, 1984. Fellow Am. Meteorol. Soc. (Sverdrup Gold medal 1994), Royal Soc. Can.; mem. AAAS, Can. Meteorol. and Oceanographic Soc., Am. Geophys. Union, The Oceanography Soc. Office: U Miami Rosenstiel Sch Marine/Sci 4600 Rickenbacker Cswy Miami FL 33149-1031

DONELSON, JOHN EVERETT, biochemistry professor, molecular biologist; b. Ogden, Iowa, May 23, 1943; s. Mervin E. and Christine (James) D.; m. Linda Meyers, Sept. 16, 1966; children: Christina, Loren, Lyn, Emory. BS, Iowa State U., 1965; PhD, Cornell U., 1971. Postdoctoral fellow MRC Lab. Molecular biology, Cambridge, Eng., 1971-74, Stanford (Calif.) U., 1974; from asst. prof., assoc. prof. to prof. biochemistry U. Iowa, Iowa City, 1975-89, Disting. prof. biochemistry, 1989—, chmn. dept. biochemistry, 1998—; investigator Howard Hughes Med. Ctr. Howard Hughes Med. Inst., Iowa City, 1989-97. Contbr. numerous articles to profl. jours., sci. mags. Vol. Am. Peace Corps, Dormaa, Ghana, 1965-67. Recipient Molecular Parasitology award Burroughs-Wellcome Found., N.C., 1983, Medal of Sci. Achievement award Iowa Gov., 1990. Office: U Iowa Dept Biochemistry Iowa City IA 52242

DONELY, GEORGE ANTHONY THOMAS, III, economist, consultant; b. New Orleans, Aug. 14, 1934; s. George A.T. and Valerie Clare (Burmaster) D.; m. Lisa Suzanne Young, June 30, 1963; 1 child, Valerie Jennie Young. AB in Econs. cum laude, Williams Coll., 1956; MA in Econs., Columbia U., 1958; PhD, U. Mashad, Iran, 1967. Economist Lionel D. Edie & Co., NYC, 1959-60; instr. La. State U., New Orleans, 1960-61; joined Fgn. Svc., Dept. State, 1961-69; economist IMF, Washington, 1969-91; mng. dir. sr. vol. program St. Mary's County, Md., 2000—. Cons. Miss Lisa's Sugarless Foods, Inc., Washington, 1985-92. Contbr. articles to profl. jours. Mem. steering com. Friends of Music at Smithsonian, Washington, 1972—; vol. Md. Hist. Trust, Annapolis, 1982—85; mem. restoration adv. bd. Patuxent River NAS; bd. dirs., treas. Chamber Orch. So. Med., 1998—2000; bd. dirs. St. Mary's County Arts Coun., 2002—. Ford Found. fellow Columbia U., 1958. Mem. Am. Econ. Assn., Econ. History Assn., Round Table, St. Mary's River Yacht Club, Met. Club, Williams Club, Rotary (Paul Harris fellow). Home: St Richard's Manor 22880 Old Manor Ln Lexington Park MD 20653-2146 also: Résidence Panorama Rte Du Village CH 1884 Villars sur Ollon Switzerland Business E-Mail: srmanor@mac.com.

DONENFELD, KENNETH JAY, management consultant; b. Nov. 2, 1946; s. Israel James and Anne (Puretz) D.; m. Sharon Etta Kamer, June 23, 1968; children: Elissa Meredith, Jonathan Lloyd. BA, CUNY, 1967; MA, Syracuse U., 1968; postgrad., N.Y. Inst. Fin., 1971. Mgmt. cons. Georgeson & Co., N.Y.C., 1969-79; exec. v.p., dir. investor rels. divsn. Robert Marston and Assocs., N.Y.C., 1979-89; pres. Robert Marston Investor Rels., Inc., N.Y.C., 1988; exec. v.p. D.F. King and Co., Inc., N.Y.C., 1989-91; pres. The Donenfeld Group, Inc., N.Y.C., 1991—, DGI Investor Rels., Inc., N.Y.C., 1996—. N.Y. State Regents scholar, 1963-67. Merm. Nat. Investor Rels. Inst. (adv. bd. IR mag.), N.Y. Assn. for Internat. Investment, Swedish C. of C., N.Y. Soc. Security Analysts, The Bd. Rm. Club, Media Club. Republican. Home: 15 Maplewood Dr Northport NY 11768-3431 Personal E-mail: donfgroup@aol.com.

DONEY, BRENT CLIFFORD, industrial hygienist, public health service officer; b. Havre, Mont., June 5, 1954; s. Clifford Doney and Isla Cottrell; m. Bobbi Jean Doney, June 10, 1983; children: Skye Brent, Megan Noelle, Mindee Nichole. AS in Water Quality Tech., No. Mont. Coll., 1981; MS in Microbiology, Mont. State U., 1983; MS in Indsl. Hygiene, Mont. Tech, 1985. Cert. indsl. hygienist Am. Bd. Indsl. Hygiene, registered sanitarian W.Va. Bd. Registration Sanitarians. Indsl. hygienist N.D. State Dept. of Health, Bismarck, 1984—86, U.S. Dept. of Labor/OSHA, Billings, Mont., 1986—2000, CDC/NIOSH, Morgantown, W.Va., 2000—. Lt. col, pub. health officer W.Va. Air N.G. USAF, 2003—, Charleston, WV. Mem.: Am. Conf. Govtl. Indsl. Hygienists. Office: CDC/NOISH 1095 Willowdale Rd Morgantown WV 26505 Office Phone: 304-285-6357.

DONFRIED, KARL PAUL, theology studies educator, minister; b. NYC, Apr. 6, 1940; s. Paul and Else (Schmuck) D.; m. Katharine E. Krayer, Sept. 10, 1960; children: Paul Andrew, Karen Erika, Mark Christopher. AB, Columbia U., 1960; BD, Harvard U., 1963; STM, Union Theol. Sem., 1965; ThD, U. Heidelberg, Germany, 1968. Ordained to ministry Lutheran Ch. in Am., 1963; named ecumenical canon Christ Ch. Cathedral, Springfield, Mass., 1977. Assoc. pastor ch., N.Y.C., 1963-64; acting Luth. chaplain (Columbia U.), 1963-64; mem. faculty Smith Coll., Northampton, Mass., 1968—, prof. New Testament and early Christianity, 1968—2000, chmn. dept. religion, 1980-83, 97-00, dir. ancient studies, 1994-95, Elizabeth A. Woodson prof. religion and bibl. lit., 2000—. Mem. New Testament panel Nat. Luth.-Roman Cath. dialogue 1971-73, 75-78, vis. prof. Assumption Coll., Worcester, Mass., 1975, Amherst Coll., 1976, 78, 85, 2002, St. Hyacinth Coll. and Sem., Granby, Mass., 1976, Brown U., 1979, Mt. Holyoke

Coll., 1983, U. Hamburg, 1985, Yale U. Div. Sch., New Haven, 1993, U. Geneva, 2001; Fulbright vis. prof. Hebrew U., Jerusalem, 1997; vis. chaplain Ho. of Reps., 1999; ofcl. rep. Evang. Luth. Ch. in Am. to Signing of Joint Declaration on Justification between Luth. World Fedn. and the Vatican, Augsburg, Germany, 1999; Fulbright vis. prof. Freie U. Berlin, 2004, Humboldt U. Berlin, 2004; pres. Colloquium Oecumenicum Paulinum, Benedictine Abbey St. Paul, 2004—. Author: (with R.E. Brown, J. Reumann) Peter in the New Testament, 1973, The Setting of Second Clement in Early Christianity, 1974, (with others) Mary in the New Testament, 1978, The Dynamic Word, 1981; editor: The Romans Debate, 1977, The Romans Debate: New and Expanded Edition, 1991, (with I.H. Marshall) The Shorter Pauline Epistles, 1993, (with Peter Richardson) Judaism and Christianity in First-Century Rome, 1998, (with Johannes Beutler) The Thessalonians Debate: Methodological Discord or Methodological Synthesis?, 2000, Paul, Thessalonica and Early Christianity, 2002; mem. editl. bd. Jour. Bibl. Lit., 1975-81. Mem. Am. Acad. Religion (dir. 1972-73, pres. New Eng. region 1971-72), Studiorum Novi Testamenti Societas (chmn. Paul seminar 1975-78, exec. com. 1979-83, chmn. New Testament Texts in Their Cultural Environment seminar 1990-94, chmn. Thessalonian Correspondence seminar 1995-2000), Soc. Bibl. Lit. (pres. New Eng. region 1975-76), Cath. Bibl. Assn. (participant internat. congresses scholars in Aberdeen, Basel, Bern, Bielefeld, Bonn, Cambridge, Canterbury, Copenhagen, Edinburgh, Einhoven, Göttingen, Heidelberg, Frankfurt, Jerusalem, Louvain, Milan, Montreal, Newcastle, Oxford, Prague, Rome, Sigtuna, Strasbourg, Toronto, Tubingen). Office: Smith Coll Dept Religion Northampton MA 01063-0001 Business E-Mail: kdonfrie@smith.edu. *As the son of immigrant parents, I learned early the value of hard and honest work, the necessity for integrity in all human relations and the blessings of generosity to those less fortunate. These values, together with my commitment to Christianity, have shaped, and continue to shape, my life.*

DONG, HANMIN, forest products executive; b. Hebei, China, Nov. 11, 1960; s. Hongsen Dong and Dabiao Zhang; m. Jun Wen, Dec. 18, 1989; children: Michael, James. Bachelor's degree, Cen. China Agrl. U., Wuhan, 1981; M. Forestry, U. B.C., Vancouver, Can., 1986; PhD, Tex. A&M U., 1990. Project leader Internat. Paper, Bainbridge, 1990-95, China resource mgr. Shanghai, 1995-97; chief rep. Internat. Paper (Asia) Ltd., Shanghai, 1997-2000; gen. mgr. Shanghai Internat. Paper Trading Co., Ltd., Shanghai, 1999-2000; mgr. bus. analysis and planning Masonite Corp., Chgo., 2001; mgr. internat. sales CraftMaster Mfg., Inc., Chgo., 2002—, dir. internat. sales, 2002—04; mgr. Internat. Forestry, Internat. Paper, 2004—. Mem. Soc. of Am. Foresters. Avocation: badminton. Home: 838 N Kenilworth Oak Park IL 60302 Office Phone: 901-419-6000. E-mail: hanmin.dong@ipaper.com.

DONG, JUN, mechanical engineer, researcher; b. Danjiangkou City, Hubei Province, China, Oct. 2, 1972; s. Tongxue Dong and Xiurong Zhang. BSc in Vehicle Engring., Beijing (China) Inst. Tech., 1993; MS in Automotive Engring., Wuhan (China) Inst. Tech., 1996; PhD in Mech. Engring., U. Iowa, 2004. Registered profl. engr., Ministry of Machinary Industry, China, 1999. Rsch. engr. China Automotive Tech. and Rsch. Ctr., Tianjin, China, 1996—2000; computer aided engring. Engring. Tech. Associated, Inc, Troy, Mich., 1997—98; rsch. asst. Ctr. Computer Aided Design U. Iowa, Iowa City, 2000—04; R&D engr. computer aided engring. divsn. LMS Internat., Coralville, Iowa, 2004—. Mem.: ASME (Best Paper award 2003), Soc. Automotive Engrs. Achievements include development of unique method to conduct the design sensitivity analysis and optimization of high frequency structure-borne noise. Home: 1047 22d Ave Coralville IA 52241 Office: CAE Division LMS International 2651 Crosspark Road Coralville IA 52241 Office Phone: 319-626-6700 205. Office Fax: 319-626-3488. Personal E-mail: jundong@ccad.uiowa.edu. E-mail: jun-dong2000@yahoo.com.

DONG, KUI, music educator, composer; d. Naixing Dong and Jiaxin Sun; m. Duo Huang, June 1990. BA, Ctrl. Conservatory of Music, Beijing, China, 1983—87; MA, Ctrl. Conservatory of Music, 1988—89; MusD, Stanford U., 1991—97. Prof. of music Dartmouth Coll., Hanover, NH, 1997—. Composer: The Blue Melody (1st prize Alea III Internat. Composition Competition for Chamber Music, 1994), (3-act ballet) Imperial Concubine Young (Commd. by Ctrl. Ballet Group of China, 1988), Flying Apples (Hon. mention, Prix Ars Electronica Internat. competitions for Computer Music and Art, Linz, Austria, 1996), Pangu's Song (League of Composers/Internat. Soc. of Contemporary Music Internat. composition competition, 2001), Three Voices (Internat. Music Competitions of the Val Tidone, Italy, 1999), Shui Tiao Ge To (Dale Warland Singers New Chorus Music Competition, 2000), Four Image Songs (The Nat. Ann. Collegiate Art Song Competition, first prize, Beijing, China, 1990), Three Piano Pieces (3d prize 1st Nat. Piano Works Competition, 84), Zhan Jing Tang (The Third Nat. Dance & Music Competition, First Music award, Beijing, China, 1989). Recipient Commissioning Award, Koussevitsky Music Found. & Libr. of Congress, 2001, Commissioning award, Mary Cary Flagler Trust Fund, 1999, Commissioning Program Award, Meet The Composer/USA, 1997, ASCAP Award for Young Composers, the Am. Soc. of Composers, Authors and Publishers., 1995; fellow Fellowship for Composers, Santa Clara Art Coun., 1995, Composer Resident Program, Djaressi Found., Bellagio Artist Residency Program, Rockefeller Found., 2000, Gerald Oshita Stipend Fellowship, Djaressi Found., 1995; grantee Rsch. Grant, Asia-Pacific Ednl. Rsch. Grant, Md., ME, 1993, Dickey Ctr. for Internat. Understanding, Dartmouth Coll., Dickey Fundation, 1998, Short-term Travel grant, Internat. Rsch. & Exch. Bd., 2000. Office: Music Dept Dartmouth Coll 6187 Hopkins Ctr Hanover NH 03755 E-mail: kui.dong@dartmouth.edu.

DONG, MABEL H, music educator; d. Siu-tong Hau and Yim-ching Chan; m. Tony K Dong, Aug. 10, 1988; 1 child, Vanessa W. MusB, Hong Kong Bapt. U., 1977—81; MusM, SW Tex. State U., 1984—85; DMA in Progress, U. of Colo., 1986—88. Single Subject Tchg. Credential, Music Calif. Teacher's Credential Commn., 1997, Ill. Tchg. Cert., Music Chgo. Bd. of Edn., 1995. Music tchr. Tak Ngai Cath. Sch., Hong Kong, China, 1977—78, Alliance Elem. Sch., Hong Kong, China, 1981—83; job tng. coord. Chinese Mut. Aid Assn., Chgo., 1990—91; music dir. St. Barbara H.S., Chgo., 1991—94; piano/voice instr. Moraine Valley C.C., Palos Hill, Ill., 1992—95; music tchr. Florence Nightingale Sch., Chgo., 1995—96; chinese bilingual tchr. Glenview Elem. Sch., Oakland, Calif., 1996—97; music tchr. Jefferson Sch. Dist., Daly City, Calif., 1997—99, Berkeley Unified Sch. Dist., Berkeley, Calif., 1999—. Com. mem. Berkeley Districtwide Music Curriculum Com., Berkeley, Calif., 2000—; music teacher's workshop presenter Jefferson Sch. Dist., Daly City, Calif., 1997—99. Recipient Second Pl. in Singing (Grad. Divsn.), Nat. Assn. of Teachers Singing, 1985. Mem.: Trinity Coll., London (licentiate LTCL 1983), Associated Bd. of Royal Schools of Music (licentiate LRSM 1981), Internat. Fedn. for Choral Music (assoc.), Chinese Music Tchr. Assn. of No. Calif. (assoc.), Am. Choral Dir. Assn. (assoc.), Music Educator Nat. Conf. (assoc.). Office: Berkeley Unified School District 1500 Derby St Rm 509 Berkeley CA 94704 Personal E-mail: mabelhdong@sbcglobal.net.

DONG, MICHAEL HON, toxicologist; b. Hong Kong, China, Dec. 17, 1948; s. Henry and L-G Dong; m. Ivy Tze-Wah To, Apr. 15, 1977; children: Jennifer Ivy, Stephanie Michelle. BSc, U. Calif., Davis, Calif., 1972; MPH, UCLA, 1973; BSc, Calif. State U., 1976; PhD in Pub. Adminstrn., U. So. Calif., 1981, U. Pitts., 1984. Diplomate Am. Bd. Toxicology, NC, 1999, cert. nutrition specialist Am. Coll. Nutrition, Fla., 1994. Commd. officer U.S. Army Med. Svc. Corps, San Francisco, 1977—80, Fort Gordon, Ga., 1980—81; rsch. asst. U. Pitts., 1981—84; occupl. toxicologist epidemiologist U.S. Occupl. Health and Safety Adminstrn., DC, 1985; lt. comdr. U.S. FDA, Rockville, Md., 1986—89; staff toxicologist Calif. Dept. Pesticide Regulation, Sacramento, 1989—. Lectr. in field. Editor: Jour.Environ. Geochemistry and Health, 2005—. Mem.: Am. Soc. Toxicology. Office: California Dept of Pesticide Regulation 1001 I Street Sacramento CA 95814 Office Phone: 916-445-4263. Business E-Mail: mdong@cdpr.ca.gov.

DONG, NELSON G., lawyer; b. 1949; AB, Stanford Univ., 1971; JD, Yale Univ., 1974. Bar: Calif. 1974, Minn. 1992. Ptnr., corp. dept, chair, Asian dept. Dorsey & Whitney LLP, Mpls. Legal counsel IEEE. Bd. trustees Stanford Univ., 1978—82; bd. dir. Com. 100, NYC, 1998—, gen. counsel, secy., 1999—2003; bd. dir. White House Fellows Assn., 2004—06. Grantee White House Fellow, 1978—79. Mem.: Asian Am. Bar Assn. (secy. 1984, bd. mem. 1985). Office: Dorsey & Whitney LLP Ste 3400 US Bank Ctr 1420 Fifth Ave Seattle WA 98101-4010 Office Phone: 206-903-8871. Office Fax: 206-903-8820. Business E-Mail: dong.nelson@dorsey.com.

DONG, QUAN, ecologist, educator; b. Beijing, July 18, 1954; came to U.S., 1986; s. Chung Cai and Duan Fang (Jiang) D. MS, Duke U., 1992; PhD, Vanderbilt U., 1994. Rsch. asst. Inst. Zoology, Chinese Acad. Scis., Beijing, 1974—77, rsch. fellow, 1982—85; vis. scholar Can. Wildlife Svc., Edmonton, Canada, 1985—86; rsch. asst., teaching asst. Sch. of the Environment, Duke U., Durham, NC, 1986—89; hon. fellow U. Wis., Madison, 1991; fellow Electric Power Rsch. Inst., 1991—93; teaching asst. Vanderbilt U., Nashville, 1993—95; rsch. assoc. U. Miami, Fla., 1995—96, sr. scientific assoc., 1996; environtl. scientist South Fla. Water Mgmt. Dist., 1997—98; rsch. scientist Fla. Internat. U., 1998—2001; ecologist U.S. Nat. Park Svc., Homestead, Fla., 2002—. Sci. advisor U.S.-China Found., 1999—. Writer TV sci. documentary Ctrl. TV Sta. of China, 1983 (Milky Way award 1984); editor Chinese Jour. Applied Ecology, 1996—; author one book; editor Acta Ecologia Sinica; contbr. chpts. to books, articles to profl. jours. Gen. sec., chief editor newsletter Sino-Eco Club, 1994, pres., 1995. Recipient Tng. award World Univ. Svc. of Can., 1985-86. Mem. AAAS, Ecol. Soc. Am., Ecol. Soc. China (coun. mem. 1995), Sigma Xi. Avocations: travel, photography, reading, music, sports. Office: NPS SF Ecosystem Office 950 N Korme Ave 3d Fl Homestead FL 33030

DONG, YU REN, English language educator, researcher; PhD, U. Ga., 1995. Assoc. prof. Queens Coll., CUNY, Flushing, NY, 1995—. Mem.: Am. Ednl. Rsch. Assn., Tchrs. of English to Spkrs. of Other Langs., Nat. Coun. Tchrs. of English. Office: Queens Coll 65-30 Kissena Blvd Flushing NY 11367 Office Phone: 718-997-5171. Personal E-mail: yurendong@earthlink.net.

DONIGER, PAUL EDWARD, literature and language educator, theater educator, actor; b. NYC, Jan. 5, 1947; s. Arthur and Florence Lavsky Doniger; m. Nancy Newill, Dec. 23, 1979; children: Colin Newill, Nicholas Newill, Alexandra Newill. MusB in Music Theory, Manhattan Sch. of Music, 1968; MA in English, Western Conn. State U., 2000. Cert. English Teacher - Grades 7-12 State of Conn. Bd. of Edn., 1994. Actor/mgr./founding mem./instr. CSC Repertory Theatre, New York, NY, 1968—75; v.p. Flormel Adhesive Products, West Haven, Conn., 1982—94; dept. chair Ancestors Cmty. Charter H.S., Waterbury, Conn., 1997—99; English tchr., dir. of drama The Gilbert Sch., Winsted, Conn., 1999—; English tchr. ELI - U. of Bridgeport, Conn., 1996—97; adj. English tchr. Western Conn. State U., Danbury, 2001—. Composer: (guitar solo) Piccola Musica Mattina, (choral composition) Spirit Voices, 3 for string quartet, (composition for voice and small ensemble) sono una creatura, (Small ensemble composition) Daughter of the reconcillers; actor: stage, film and TV; contbr. articles to profl. jours., chapters to books. Sec. ATEG, 2000—05; founding mem. CSC Repertory Theatre, NYC, 1968—75, Monroe Arts Coun., Conn., 1980—82. Recipient Outstanding Achievement award, CSC Repertory Theatre, 1969. Mem.: MLA (assoc.), ASCD (assoc.), NCTE (assoc.), Phi Delta Kappa. Democrat. Avocations: classical guitar, gardening, cooking. Office Phone: 860-379-8521.

DONILON, THOMAS E., federal official; b. Providence, May 14, 1955; m. Catherine Russell, Dec. 14, 1991. BA summa cum laude, Cath. U., 1977; JD, U. Va., 1985. Bar: D.C. With office congrl. liaison White House, 1977-79; nat. del. selection coord., nat. conv. dir. Carter-Mondale Presdl. Campaign, 1979-80; lectr. politics Cath. U. Am., 1981; nat. campaign coord. Mondale for Pres. Campaign, 1983-84; assoc. O'Melveny & Myers, Washington, 1985-92, ptnr., 1992-93; asst. sec. pub. affairs bur. pub. affairs Dept. of State, Washington, 1993—96; chief of staff to sec. of state Washington, 1994-99; gen. counsel Fannie Mae, Washington, 1999—. Cons. CBS News, 1988; presdl. debate coord. Clinton-Gore Presdl. Campaign, 1992; mem. Clinton-Gore Presdl. Transition Team, 1992-93. Mem. editorial bd. U. Va. Law Rev., 1982-83. Mem. ABA, Coun. on Fgn. Rels., Phi Beta Kappa. Office: Fannie Mae 3900 Wisconsin Ave NW Washington DC 20016-2892

DONKERVOET, RICHARD CORNELIUS, architect; b. Detroit, Oct. 8, 1930; s. Cornelius and Anna Eva Hendrika (Boer) D.; m. Carolyn Eugenia Moore, May 4, 1957; children: Carolyn Daralice Donkervoet Boles, Sharon Elisabeth Donkervoet Credit, John Cornelius. BArch, U. Mich., 1952; MArch, MIT, 1953. Fulbright fellow Tech. U., Delft, Holland, 1954-55; arch. Cochran, Stephenson & Wing, Balt., 1957-63; ptnr. Cochran, Stephenson & Donkervoet, Inc., Balt., 1963-68, exec. v.p., 1968-83, pres., 1983-96, chmn., 1996—. Trustee Roland Park Country Sch., Balt., 1968-75, Balt. Mus. Art, 1970—; pres. bd. trustees Westminster House, Balt., 1975—; pres. bd. dirs. Citizens League Balt., 1980-82. With U.S. Army, 1956-58. Fellow AIA (pres. Balt. chpt., treas. 1966, bd. dirs. 1973, Disting. Svc. awards 1977, 99); mem. Hamilton St. Club (mem. steering com. 1983-88). Avocations: reading, travel, tennis. Home: 13801 York Rd Unit M-12 Cockeysville Hunt Valley MD 21030- Office: C S & D Inc 323 W Camden St Ste 700 Baltimore MD 21201-8601 Office Phone: 410-539-2080. E-mail: csd@csdarch.com.

DONLEAVY, JAMES PATRICK, writer, artist; b. Bklyn., Apr. 23, 1926; m. Valerie Heron (div.); children: Philip, Karen; m. Mary Wilson Price (div.); children: Rebecca, Rory. Student, Trinity Coll., Dublin, Ireland. Author: novel, later adapted as play The Ginger Man, 1955; drama Fairy Tales of New York, 1960; A Singular Man novel, later adapted as play, 1963, Meet My Maker the Mad Molecule, short stories, sketches, 1964, The Saddest Summer of Samuel S, novella, later adapted as play, 1966, The Beastly Beatitudes of Balthazar B, novel, later adapted as play, 1968, The Onion Eaters, 1971, The Plays of J.P. Donleavy, 1972; novel A Fairy Tale of New York, 1973; The Unexpurgated Code, A Complete Manual of Survival and Manners, 1975, The Destinies of Darcy Dancer, Gentleman, 1977; novel Schultz, 1979, Leila, 1983, Are You Listening Rabbi Löw, 1987; De Alfonce Tennis, The Superlative Game of Eccentric Champions: Its History, Accoutrements, Rules, Conduct and Regimen, 1984, J.P. Donleavy's Ireland: In All Her Sins and in Some of Her Graces, 1986 (Gold award Worldfest Houston 1993, Cine Golden Eagle award), A Singular Country, 1989, That Darcy, That Dancer, That Gentleman, 1990, The History of The Ginger Man, 1994, Wrong Information is Being Given Out at Pinceton, 1998, (novella) The Lady Who Liked Clean Rest Rooms, 1996, An Author and His Image, 1997; contbr. to numerous mags. and jours. including Times of London, N.Y. Times, Washington Post, Atlantic Monthly, The Daily Telegraph, The New Yorker, Rolling Stone, others; art exhbns. include: Painter's Gallery, St. Stephen's Green, Dublin, 1950, 51, Bronxville, N.Y., 1959, Langton Galleries, London, 1975, Godolphin Gallery, Dublin, 1986, Caldwell Galleries, Belfast, 1987, Anna Mei Chadwick Gallery, London, 1989, 91, 94, Alba Fine Art Gallery, London, 1991, Front Lounge Gallery, 1995, Walton Gallery, London, 2002. Served with USNR, WWII. Recipient Creative Arts award Brandeis U., 1961-62; AAAL grantee, 1975. Home: Levington Park Mullingar County Westmeath Ireland

DONLEVY, JOHN DEARDEN, lawyer; b. Chgo., May 29, 1933; s. Frank and Alice Genevieve (O'Connor) D.; m. Kristin Bach Minnick, Apr. 20, 1963 (div. Sept. 1985); 1 son, John Dearden. Student, Stanford U., 1950-52; BS, Northwestern U., 1954; JD, U. Chgo., 1957; postgrad., Northwestern U., 1958. Bar: Ill. 1957, U.S. Dist. Ct. (no. dist.) 1957, U.S. Ct. Appeals (7th cir.) 1969, U.S. Supreme Ct. 1972. Asst. state's atty. Cook County Criminal Divsn., Chgo., 1958-61; city prosecutor City of Evanston, Ill., 1961; assoc. Mayer, Brown & Platt, Chgo., 1962-73, ptnr., 1973-90; pvt. practice law Chgo., 1990—. Participant Hinton Moot Ct. Competition U. Chgo., 1955-56, judge, 1972. Active Rep. Orgn., 1958—60; bd. dirs. English-Speaking Union, Chgo., 1964—65. Recipient Disting. Legal award Am. Legion, Chgo., 1960; named spl. prosecutor-labor racketeering Cook County State's Atty., Chgo., 1959-61; profiled in Lindberg "Summerdale--35 Year Anniversary", 1995. Mem. ABA, Ill. Bar Assn., Chgo. Bar Assn. (criminal law com., chair def. of prisoners com., criminal law and in-court criminal def. panels), Chgo. Athletic Assn. Office: Ste 2040 30 N La Salle St Chicago IL 60602-2506 Office Phone: 312-201-0227. Business E-Mail: jdonlevy@core.com. *I always try to examine problems carefully to obtain a good understanding of them, as with understanding, nothing in life need be feared.*

DONLEY, BILLY MARTIN, lawyer; b. Spartanburg, S.C., Oct. 15, 1964; s. Vernon Clinton Donley and Molly Laverne Huffman; m. Denise Michelle Miller, Nov. 12, 1994; children: Kristen, Katie, Jake. AA, San Jacinto Coll., 1987; BS, U. Houston Clearlake, 1989; JD, South Tex. Coll. Law, 1991. Bar: Tex., U.S. Dist. (no. dist. Tex.), U.S. Dist. Ct. (so. dist. Tex.). Assoc. counsel Texaco Inc., Houston, 1991—94; assoc. McFall, Sherwood & Sheehy, Houston, 1994—96; ptnr. Baker & Hostetler, Houston, 1996—. Team capt. MS Soc., Houston, 2004. Named Rising Star Tex., Tex. Monthly, 2004, Rising Star Houston, Houston Mag., 2004. Mem.: Rep. Nat. Lawyers Assn. Republican. Baptist. Avocations: hunting, fishing, bicycling. Office: Baker & Hostetler LLP 1000 Louisiana Ste 2000 Houston TX 77002 Office Phone: 713-646-1382. Office Fax: 713-751-1717. E-mail: bdonley@bakerlaw.com.

DONLEY, DEEDRA ANN, medical educator; b. Jacksonville, N.C., Aug. 1966; d. E. Alexander and Martha A. (Turner) Donley. BS in Adminstrn. of Criminal Justice, BA in Psychology, U. N.C., Chapel Hill, 1988; MS in Orgn. Mgmt., Pfeiffer U., 2001; MEd in Adult Edn., Pa. State U.; PhD in Bus. and Tech. Health Care Mgmt. Concentration, North Ctrl. U., Ariz. Cert. in tng. and devel./adult edn. N.C. State U., notary pub. N.C. AHEC coord. U. N.C. Sch. Medicine, Chapel Hill, 1994—95, registrar, 1995—96, program coord., 1997—98, ops. mgr., 1999—2000, assoc. dir., 2001—. Mem. employee forum U. N.C., Chapel Hill, 1996—2000; pres. Legion Rd. Homeowners Assn., Chapel Hill, 2001—. N.C. scholar, State of N.C., 1984. Mem.: N.C. Substance Abuse Profls., Alliance for Continuing Med. Edn., Am. Coll. Healthcare Execs. Avocations: entertaining, refinishing furniture, reading, writing, dachshunds. E-mail: deedradon@intrex.net.

DONLEY, DENNIS LEE, school librarian; b. Port Hueneme, Calif., July 19, 1950; s. Mickey Holt and Joan Elizabeth (Smith) D.; m. Ruth Ann Shank, June 10, 1972; children: Eric Holt, Evan Scott. AA, Ventura Coll., 1970; BA with honors, U. Calif., Santa Barbara, 1973; MLS, San Jose State U., 1976. Cert. secondary tchr., Calif. Tchr. libr. media San Diego Unified Sch. Dist., 1975—. Lectr. Calif. State U., L.A., 1987-89; libr. cons. San Diego C.C. Dist., 1990; chmn. sch. adv. com. Point Loma H.S., San Diego, 1986-87; coop. book rev. bd. San Diego County, 1984-86; creator adult sch. curriculum, 1984-86; contbr. Deadbase X, Deadbase 94, The Deadhead's Taping Compendium, Vols. 1-3, The Deadhead's Taping Addendum. Mem. ALA, Calif. Libr. Media Educators Assn. Avocations: reading, music, exercise. Office: Hoover HS 4474 El Cajon Blvd San Diego CA 92115-4312 Office Phone: 619-283-6281 2183. Personal E-mail: dennisd@well.com. Business E-Mail: ddonley@sandi.net.

DONLEY, JAMES WALTON, management consultant; b. Cleve., June 27, 1934; s. Howard Russell and Mary Louise (Mullikin) D.; m. Frances Elizabeth Jordan, July 5, 1963 (div. Oct. 1983); children: Dana, Elizabeth; m. Mary Todd Mann Goodspeed, May 25, 1985; children: Bennett, Mary Todd, Emily, Jonathan Goodspeed. BA, Denison U., 1958; MBA, U. Pa., 1960. Asst. to pub. Time Mag., N.Y.C., 1960-67; sr. v.p. Thomas J. Deegan Co., N.Y.C., 1967-71; asst. commr. N.Y.C. Dept. Commerce, 1971-72; asst. sec. U.S. Dept. Treasury, Wash., 1972-74; chmn. Donley Comm., N.Y.C., 1974—; country dir. Bulgaria Internat. Exec. Svc. Corps, Sofia, 1995—2003; v.p. Donley Farm Co., Boston Mills, Ohio, 1998—. Bd. dirs. Technoserve, Inc. Mem. bd. visitors Western Res. Acad., Hudson, Ohio; mem. bd. advisors Internat. Exec. Svc. Corps, Stamford, Conn.; bd. dirs. Greenwich C. of C., 1999—. With U.S. Army, 1954-56, Germany. Mem. Round Hill Club, Belle Haven Club. Republican. Congregationalist. Home: 28 Wooddale Rd Greenwich CT 06830-3824 E-mail: james_w_donley@hotmail.com.

DONLEY, RUSSELL LEE, III, former state legislator; b. Salt Lake City, Feb. 3, 1939; s. Lee and Leona (Sherwood) Donley; m. Karen Kocherhans, June 4, 1960; children: Tammera Sue, Tonya Kay, Christina Lynn. BSCE with honors, U. Wyo., 1961; MS in Engring., U. Fla., 1962. From mem. to spkr. of house Wyo. Ho. of Reps., 1969-84; chmn. bd. Nat. Ctr. Constl. Studies, Wyo. region, 1983-87; CEO Constitution Schs. Inc., Casper, 1987—; owner Russell L. Donley & Assocs., 1988—. Chmn. appropriations com. Wyo. Ho. of Reps., 1975—78, chmn. legis. mgmt. coun., 1983—84. Pres. bd. dirs. YMCA, Casper, 1976—77; chmn. western region Coun. State Govts., 1982—83; Rep. candidate for Gov. Wyo., 1986; precinct committeeman Rep. Ctrl. Com., 1987—96; chmn. Wyo. Young Reps., 1968; fin. chmn. Natrona County Rep. Ctrl. Com., 1970; state chmn. Initiative 3 dr. Invest in Wyo. not Wall St., 1994. Named Wyo. Outstanding Young Engr., Sigma Tau, 1974, Disting. Wyo. Engr., Tau Beta Pi, 1976; recipient award for engring. excellence, Am. Cons. Engrs. Coun., Legislator of the Yr. award, Nat. Rep. Legislators Assn., 1981. Republican. Mem. Lds Ch. Home: 1102 Carriage House Way Williamsburg VA 23188-2746 Office: 240 S Wolcott St Ste 234 Casper WY 82601-2552 Office Phone: 307-235-1789. Business E-Mail: russ-rlda@cox.net.

DONLON, CLAUDETTE, performing company executive; Gen. mgr. Am. Ballet Theatre, finance dir.; exec. v.p. Kennedy Center for the Performing Arts. Office: Kennedy Center for the Performing Arts 2700 F St NW Washington DC 20566

DONLON, JAMES D, III, controller, corporate financial executive; b. Seattle, Wash., Oct. 1, 1946; BSc in bus. adminstrn., Calif. State U., 1968; MBA, U. So. Calif., 1969. Mgr., investment analysis Chrysler Corp., 1979; dir., internat. planning and new venture develop. Chrysler Motor Internat. Ops., 1989—90; v.p., fin. controls Chrysler Fin., 1990—92; corp. contr. Chrysler Corp., 1992—94, v.p., contr., 1994—98; sr. v.p., corp. controlling and acctg. Daimler Chrysler, Stuggart, Germany, 1998—2000, sr. v.p., contr., 2000—03.

DONLON, WILLIAM JAMES, retired lawyer; b. Colorado Springs, Colo., Apr. 22, 1924; s. John Andrew and Kathleen M. D; m. Josephine A. Janssen, July 19, 1946; children: William James, Gregory A., Michele, Dru Ann Gazelle. Student, Colo. Coll., 1941-43; BS, U. Denver, 1949, JD, 1950. Bar: Colo. 1950, Ohio 1964, Ill. 1969, U.S. Dist. Ct. Colo. 1956, U.S. Dist. Ct. (no. dist.) Ill. 1974, U.S. Ct. Appeals (10th cir.) 1957, U.S. Ct. Appeals (5th cir.) 1970, U.S. Ct. Appeals (7th cir.) 1974, U.S. Ct. Appeals D.C. 1979, U.S. Supreme Ct. 1965. Dep. clk. Dist. Ct., Denver, 1949-50; pvt. practice Denver, 1953-63; gen. counsel Brotherhood Ry. Airline & S.S. Clks., Freight Handlers, Express & Sta. Empl., Rosemont, Ill., 1963-84, Rockville, Md., 1963-86; ret., 1985. Instr. labor U. Ill., 1972-78. With USAAF, 1942-45. Decorated Air medal with 2 oak leaf clusters; named Ky. Col. Mem. ABA (coun. sect. labor and employment law 1977-86, co-chmn. railroad and airline com., 1974-76, co-chmn. equl employment com., 1976-77), Ill. Bar Assn., D.C. Bar Assn., Am. Legion, VFW, KC (Grand Knight coun. 10329 1991-93), 34th Bomb Group Assn., Phi Alpha Delta, Phi Delta Theta. Democrat. Roman Catholic. Office: PO Box 2212 Pineland FL 33945-2212

DONNALLY, PATRICIA BRODERICK, writer; b. Cheverly, Md., Mar. 11, 1955; d. James Duane and Olga Frances (Duenas) Broderick; m. Robert Andrew Donnally, Dec. 30, 1977; 1 child, Danielle Christine. BS, U. Md., 1977. Fashion editor The Washington Times, 1983-85, The San Francisco Chronicle, 1985-2000; sr. fashion and beauty editor eLuxury.com, 2000; mng. editor PaperCity mag., 2002—04; co-editor Washington Spaces mag., 2004—, editor-in-chief, 2005—. Recipient Atrium award U. Ga., 1984, 87-89, 90, 94-98, 99, Lulu award U. Ga., 1985, 87, award Am. Cancer Soc., 1991, Aldo award, U. Ga., 1994, George A. Hough III award, U. Ga., 1999. Avocation: travel. Office Phone: 703-992-1196. Business E-Mail: tdonnally@washingtonspaces.com.

DONNALLY, ROBERT ANDREW, lawyer; b. Washington, July 10, 1953; s. Reaumur Stearnes and Katherine Ann (Sutliff) D.; m. Patricia Kane Broderick, Dec. 30, 1977; 1 child, Danielle Christine. BA in Psychology, U.

Md., 1976; JD, U. Balt., 1980; cert. in bus., Stanford U., 1996. Bar: Md. 1980, Calif. 1986. Pvt. practice, Oxen Hill, Md., 1980-81; rsch. contract staff officer Dept. Def., Ft. Meade, Md., 1981-85; with legal and contractual ops. ARGOSystems, Inc., Sunnyvale, Calif., 1985-90; asst. dir. Inst. Def. Analyses, San Diego, 1990-91; dep. chief counsel ARGOSystems, Inc., 1991-93, chief counsel, corp. sec., 1993-98; chief counsel comms. and infomanagement divsn. Boeing Co., 1997-98; gen. counsel, mng. ptnr. BT Comml. Real Estate, Palo Alto, Calif., 1998-99; assoc. gen. counsel Inhale Therapeutic Sys. Inc., San Carlos, Calif., 1999—2003. Editor-in-chief The Forum, 1979-80. Active The Pillars Soc./United Way, 1991-98. Waxter Legal scholar U. Baltimore, 1978. Mem. Am. Corp. Counsel, Nat. Contract Mgmt. Assn., Md. Bar Assn., Calif. Bar Assn., Assn. of Silicon Valley Brokers, Tae Kwon Do Assn. (Black Belt), Black Belt, Kukkiwon World Tac Kwon Do Assn. Avocations: martial arts, marathons and triathlons, hiking, travel, reading. Home: 14720 Georgia Ave Rockville MD 20852 E-mail: robertdonnally@hotmail.com.

DONNELL, BEN ADDISON, lawyer; b. Wichita Falls, Tex., Nov. 18, 1936; s. Ralph Shirley and Anita (Crocker) D.; m. Elinor Drake, Aug. 16, 1958; children: Allison Donnell Mantor, Amy Donnell Greenwood. BBA, U. Tex., 1958, JD, 1961. Bar: Tex. 1961, U.S. Dist. Ct. (so., we., ea. dist.) Tex., 1961, U.S. Ct. Appeals (5th cir.), 1961, U.S. Supreme Ct., 1961. Legis. asst. U.S. Senate, Washington, 1959-60; clk. Supreme Ct. of Tex., Austin, 1961-62; assoc., ptnr. Keys, Russell, Watson, Seaman, Corpus Christi, Tex., 1962-68; ptnr. Meredith, Donnell, Abernathy, Corpus Christi, Tex., 1973—2003, Donnell, Abernathy, Kieschnick LLP, 2003—. Chmn. Zoning and Planning Commn. of Corpus Christi, 1978-84; mem. vestry Ch. of Good Shepherd; mem. exec. com. Chancellor's Coun., U. Tex. Sys.; mem. bd. visitors M.D. Anderson Cancer Ctr. Fellow Tex. Bar Found.; mem. Corpus Christi C. of C. (dir.), Rotary, Corpus Christi Yacht Club (dir.), Corpus Christi Country Club (dir.), disting. alumnus, Phi Kappa Psi, 2005. Episcopalian. Avocations: golf, hunting, tennis. Home: 205 Jackson Pl Corpus Christi TX 78411-1215 Office: Donnell Abernathy and Kieschnick LLP 555 N Carancahua Ste 400 Corpus Christi TX 78478 Office Phone: 361-866-8102. E-mail: bdonnell@dakpc.com.

DONNELL, HAROLD EUGENE, JR., retired professional society administrator; b. Balt., Mar. 12, 1935; s. Harold Eugene and Ruth Elizabeth (Meeth) D.; m. Rosemary Gatch, Apr. 25, 1959; children— David Crawford, Laurette Butler. BA, Amherst Coll., 1957. Field asst., agt. Equitable Life Assurance Soc., Balt., 1958-61; salesman Eastern Products Corp., Balt., 1961-64, asst. nat. sales mgr., 1964-66; exec. dir. Md. State Dental Assn., Towson, 1966-74, Acad. Gen. Dentistry, Chgo., 1974—2003. Trustee Am. Fund for Dental Health, 1976-84 . Served with U.S. Army, 1957-58. Recipient Disting. Service award N.C. Acad. Gen. Dentistry, 1980; ann. Walter E. Levine Meritorious Service award Alpha Omega, 1970, 93. Fellow Acad. Gen. Denistry (hon.); mem. ADA, Am. Soc. Assn. Execs. (cert. assn. exec.), Assn. Forum, Acad. Gen. Dentistry (Albert Borish award 2003). Republican. Lutheran. *Any degree of success I have achieved in this life is a result of dedicatedly applying the talents I have been given or acquired with single minded drive to accomplish specific goals.*

DONNELL, WILLIAM RAY, small business owner, communications executive; b. Lewiston, Maine, Oct. 3, 1931; s. William Thomas and Gladys Mae (Spinney) Donnell; m. Mayra Cintia Colon, June 16, 1962 (div. Jan. 1996); children: William Thomas, Jose Ismael, Ariadne Elizabeth. BA, U. Maine, 1959. Comml. capt. lic. Comml. fisherman, Maine, 1948-52, 55-60; tchr. Bath (Maine) Jr. HS, 1962, substitute tchr., 1963; tchr. Deer Isle (Maine) HS, 1965, 71, tchr. adult edn., 1976; tchr. St. Jude Integrated HS, St. Fintons, Canada, 1972, Stonington (Maine) Elem. Sch., 1973; v.p., bd. dirs. Fisheries Comm., Inc., 1977—; owner, operator Donnell's Clapboard Mill, Sedgwick, Maine, 1983—. Recreational dir. City of Bath, 1963; capt. prin. comml. passenger schooner, 1965—71; remedial instr. Harpwell Islands Sch., Maine, 1965; farmer, Deer Isle, 1968—71, Deer Isle, 1972—78, Highlands, Nfld., 1971—72, Sedgwick, 1978—; lectr. in field; guest spkr. TV Can.-U.S. offshore boundary issue. Contbg. editor: Comml. Fisheries News, 1981—83; editor: Maine Comml. Fisheries, 1979—80, Fisheries Fed. Register Rev., 1981—82; author: numerous poems. Active Gov.'s Lobster Adv. Coun., Maine, 1980—85, Downeast Resource Conservation & Devel. Coun., 1994—, Sedgwick Budget Com., 1995—; co-chmn. Hancock County 4-H Citizenship Com., 1987—88; exec. com. Hancock County Extension, 1988—; moderator Sedgwick Town Meeting, 1993—94, 2002—; v.p. Brooklin Sedgwick Hist. Soc., 2000—02, 2004—; candidate state legis. from Bath area Sagadahoc County, Maine, 1969; charter mem., bd. dirs. Maine Fishermen's Forum, Inc., 1985; lectr. discussion team Thelme's, Laguna Beach, Calif., 1985. Sgt. U.S. Army, 1952—54, Korea. Decorated Bronze Star, Korean Svc. medal with 2 bronze stars, Combat Infantryman's Badge; recipient Poetry award, Nfld. and Labrador Arts and Letters Contest, 1972. Mem.: Sigma Chi (pres.). Avocations: antique vehicles, vessels and machinery. Home and Office: Donnells Clapboard Mill Box 1560 County Rd Sedgwick ME 04676 Office Phone: 207-359-2036.

DONNELLAN, ANDREA, geophysicist; BS in Geology, Ohio State U., 1986; MS in Geophysics, PhD in Geophysics, Calif. Inst. Tech., 1991; MS in Computer Sci., U. So. Calif., 2003. NRC postdoctoral assoc. NASA Goddard Space Flight Ctr., Greenbelt, Md., 1991—93; mem. tech. staff Jet Propulsion Lab., Pasadena, Calif., 1993—99, supr. data understanding systems group, 1999—2000, dep. mgr. exploration systems autonomy sect., 2000—02, dep. mgr. sci. divsn., 2002—. Editor: (jour.) Computational Earthquake Sci. Parts I and II. Recipient Presdl. Early Career award, White Ho., 1996, Outstanding Achievement award, Women in Aerospace, 2003, medal of honor, Women at Work, 2004; postdoctoral fellow, NRC, 1991—93. Mem.: Am. Geophys. Union. Office: Jet Propulsion Lab 4800 Oak Grove Dr Pasadena CA 91109

DONNELLAN, ANDREW B., JR., lawyer; b. Rockville Centre, N.Y., Jan. 24, 1952; AB cum laude, Georgetown U., 1973; MBA, Rensselaer Polytechnic Inst., 1977; JD cum laude, Albany Law Sch., 1977. Assoc. Dewey, Ballantine, Bushby, Palmer & Wood, N.Y.C., 1977-86; with Reliance Group Holdings, Inc., N.Y.C., 1986—, v.p., chief litigation counsel, 1995—, dep. gen. counsel, 2000—. Bd. dirs. Larchmont Shore Club Corp. Office: Reliance Group Holdings Inc 5 Hanover Sq New York NY 10004

DONNELLEY, JAMES RUSSELL, printing company executive; b. Chgo., June 18, 1935; s. Elliott and Ann (Steinwedell) D.; m. Nina Louis Herrmann, Apr. 11, 1980; children: Niel J., Nicole C. BA, Dartmouth Coll., 1957; MBA, U. Chgo., 1962. With R.R. Donnelley & Sons Co., Chgo., 1962-2000, v.p., 1974-75, group pres. fin. svcs. group, 1985-87, group pres. corp. devel., 1987-90, vice chmn. bd., 1990-2000, also bd. dirs. Bd. dirs. Sierra Pacific Resources, PMP Inc., Melbourne, Australia. Office: Stet & Query LTD Partnership Ste 1009 360 N Michigan Ave Chicago IL 60601-3803 E-mail: james.donnelley@stetandquery.com.

DONNELLEY, STRACHAN, philosopher; b. Chgo., Mar. 22, 1942; s. Gaylord and Dorothy Ranney Donnelley; m. Vivian Hilst, Aug. 24, 1968; children: Inanna, Naomi, Aidan, Ceara, Tegan. BA, Yale U., 1964; MA, New Sch. for Social Rsch., 1972, PhD, 1977. Mem. faculty Valparaiso (Ind.) U., 1967—69, Seminar Coll., New Sch., N.Y.C., 1978-85; dir. edn. Hastings Ctr., Garrison, NY, 1986-96, assoc. environ. ethics, 1989-96, pres., 1996-99, dir. humans and nature program, 1999—2002; pres. Ctr. for Humans and Nature, N.Y.C., 2003—. Mem. animal care and use com. Cornell Med. Sch., 1990-96; advisor Ctr. for Biodiversity, Am. Mus. Natural History, N.Y.C., 1995—, Inst. Biospheric Studies, Yale U., 1995—. Editor spl. supplements Hastings Ctr. Report, 1990-98; contbr. articles to profl. jours. Trustee Nat. Humanities Ctr., Raleigh, N.C., 1993-2003, Union Inst., Cin., 1980-92, U. Chgo., 1993—, New Sch., N.Y.C., 1994—, Hotchkiss Sch., Lakeville, Conn., 1988-98, The Land Inst., Salna, Kans., 2005—; chmn. Gaylord and Dorothy Donnelley Found., Chgo., 1992-2003, vice chmn., 2003—. Recipient Pres.' award, Union Inst., 1999, Disting. Alumni award, New Sch. Univ., 2001. Mem. Am. Philos. Assn., World Conservation Union. Democrat. Avocations: music, skiing, fly fishing, collecting. Office Phone: 212-362-7170. Business E-Mail: strachandonnelley@humansandnature.org.

DONNELLY, BARBARA SCHETTLER, retired medical technologist; b. Sweetwater, Tenn., Dec. 2, 1933; d. Clarence G. and Irene Elizabeth (Brown) Schettler; children: Linda Ann, Richard Michael. AA, Tenn. Wesleyan Coll., 1952; BS, U. Tenn., 1954; cert. med. tech., Erlanger Hosp. Sch. Med. Tech., 1954; postgrad., So. Meth. U., 1980-81. Med. technologist Erlanger Hosp., Chattanooga, 1953-57, St. Luke's Episcopal Hosp., Tex. Med. Ctr., Houston, 1957-58, 62; engring. R&D SCI Systems, Inc., Huntsville, Ala., 1974-76; cons. hematology systems Abbott Labs., Dallas, 1976-77; hematology specialist Dallas, Irving, Tex., 1977-81; tech. specialist microbiology systems Irving, Tex., 1981-83; coord. tech. svc. clin. chemistry systems, 1983-84; coord. customer tng. clin. chemistry systems, 1984-87; supr. clin. chemistry tech. svcs., 1987-88; supr. clin. chemistry customer support ctr., 1988-93; supr. clin. chemistry and x-systems customer support ctr., 1993-97; ret., 1997. Contbr. articles on cytology to profl. jours. Mem. Am. Soc. Clin. Pathologists (cert. med. technologist), Am. Soc. Microbiology, Nat. Assn. Female Execs., U. Tenn. Alumni Assn., Chi Omega. Republican. Methodist. Home: 204 Greenbriar Ln Colleyville TX 76034-8616

DONNELLY, CHARLES ROBERT, retired college president; b. Allen, Mich., Apr. 3, 1921; s. Peter Joseph and Florence Veronica (Stitt) D.; m. Marilynn Elaine Jones, Sept. 15, 1945; children— Maureen, Michael, Mark, Bridget, Patrick, Kathleen. BA, Hillsdale (Mich.) Coll., 1941; MA, U. Mich., 1947, PhD, 1961. Tchr. English Rockwood (Mich.) High Sch., 1941-42; tchr. English, baseball coach Flint (Mich.) Community Jr. Coll., 1947-60, dean, then pres., 1960-70; pres. Community Colls. of U. Nev. System, 1970-77, Alpena (Mich.) Community Coll., 1977-88, pres. emeritus, 1988—; interim pres. Mott C.C., Flint, Mich., 1992. Mem. Western States Regional Manpower Adv. Com., 1970-74; pres. Mich. Assn. Jr. Colls., 1964-65 Served with AUS, 1942-46. Recipient Alumni Achievement award Hillsdale Coll., 1968; Athletic award Nat. Assn. Jr. Colls., 1970 Mem. Am. Vocat. Assn., Mich. Community Coll. Assn. Clubs: Kiwanis, K.C. Democrat. Roman Catholic. Home: 4420 E Shomi St Phoenix AZ 85044-4005

DONNELLY, DENNIS WILLIAM, psychiatrist; b. Phila., Aug. 13, 1942; s. William J. and Elizabeth (Giambrone) D.; m. Marie Alik Radna, Dec. 18, 1982; children: Robert, Susan, Alexander, Christina. BA, Duke U., 1964; MD, Hahnemann U., 1968. Cert. psychiatrist. Intern Bryn Mawr Hosp., 1968—69; resident Hahnemann U., 1968—72; pvt. practice psychiatrist Paoli, Pa., 1975—. Dir. psychiat. svcs. Paoli (Pa.) Meml. Hosp., 1990—; chmn. dept. psychiatry Mainline Health Hosps., 1996—. Mem. Am. Psychiat. Assn., Am. Psychoanalytic Assn., Internat. Psychoanalytic Assn. Home: 425 Homestead Rd Wayne PA 19087-2433 Office: Paoli Medical Bldg Ste 224 Paoli PA 19301-1763 Office Phone: 610-687-3098.

DONNELLY, EDWARD J., JR., pharmaceutical executive; b. Phila. m. Caren Donnelly; 4 children. Chemist DuPont Marshall R & D Lab., Phila.; rsch. chemist DuPont Troy Lab., Troy, Mich.; tech. supr. DuPont, Fort Madison, Iowa; rsch. supr. automotive and refinish DuPont Troy Lab., Troy, Mich., 1976—78; personnel and employee rels. div. DuPont, Wilmington, Del., 1979—80; personnel and facilities mgr. DuPont Marshall R & D Lab., Phila., 1980—82; group mgr. DuPont Automotive Finishes, Mt. Clemens, Mich., 1986—88, gen. mktg. and sales mgr., 1988—98, dir. planning Wilmington, Del., 1998—99, v.p., gen. mgr. Global Refinish and Indsl. Coatings and DuPont Performance Coatings Am., 1999—2001; group v.p. DuPont Performance Coatings, 2001—02, DuPont Coatings & Color Technologies, 2002—. Office: DuPont Corp Info Ctr Barley Mill Plz PIO Wilmington DE 19880-0010

DONNELLY, EDWIN F., radiologist; s. Kenneth G. and Carole A. Donnelly; m. Jennifer M Klug, May 18, 1996; children: Lauren N, Jacob A, Elizabeth A. BS, U. Cin., 1992, MD, 1996; PhD., Vanderbilt U., 2003. Lic. Tenn., 1997, Radaiology Am. Bd. Radiology, 2000. Asst. prof. of radiology Vanderbilt U. Med. Ctr., Nashville, 2001—. Chief resident radiology Vanderbilt U. Med. Ctr., Nashville, 1999—2000. Recipient Roentgen Ray scholar, Am. Roentgen Ray Soc., 2001, Rsch. Trainee Prize, Radiol. Soc. North Am., 1999, New Investigator award, Am. Inst. Ultrasound Medicine, 2002. Mem.: Am. Coll. of Radiology, Assn. U. Radiologist, Am. Roentgen Ray Soc., Radiol. Soc. North Am., Soc. Thoracic Radiology, Golden Key Nat. Honor Soc. (cin. local chpt. pres. 1991—92), Phi Beta Kappa. Achievements include research in Phase-contrast radiography; Tumor blood flow assessment. Office: Dept Radiology Vanderbilt UMC 1161 21st Ave Nashville TN 37232-2675 Office Phone: 615-322-3190.

DONNELLY, GERARD KEVIN, marketing and retail executive; b. N.Y.C., July 2, 1933; s. Joseph R. and Margaret M. (Siefert) D.; m. Maria McAlllister, Aug. 29, 1964; children: Gerard K., Peter F., Deirdre A., Patrick J., James V. BBA in Acctg., Pace U., 1957; cert. in Indsl. Rels., Colgate U., 1966. Asst. contr. Allied Stores Corp., N.Y.C., 1957-65; gen. auditor Lone Star Industries, N.Y.C., 1965-67; contr., asst. sec. Computer Applications Inc., N.Y.C., 1967-70; pres. Rhodes S.W., Phoenix, 1970-75; sr. v.p. Hart Schaffner & Marx, Chgo., 1975-81; CEO, chmn. bd. dirs. Hughes & Hatcher Inc., Phila., 1981-83; sr. v.p., dir. Macys-N.E. Inc., N.Y.C., 1983-90; pres., CEO H.C. Prange Co., Green Bay, Wis., 1990-94; mng. cons. Houlihan, Lokey, Howard & Zukin, N.Y.C., 1994—99; mng. dir. GeKayDee Assocs., 1994—. Bd. dirs. Frederick Atkins, Inc., N.Y.C., Younkers Inc., Des Moines, Mottahedeh & Co., N.Y.C., H.C. Prange Co., Green Bay, Saks, Inc., Birmingham, Ala. Mem. County Com., Queens County, N.Y., 1955-64; commr. pks. and recreation, Manalapan Twp., N.J., 1967-68; bd. dirs. Ctrl. Bus. Dist. Assn., Detroit, 1981-83, U. Wis. Green Bay Founders Assn., 1991-94. With USN, 1951-53. Mem.: Menswear Retailers Am., Internat. Coun. Shopping Ctrs., Am. Mgmt. Assn., Nat. Retail Fedn., Due Process Golf Club, Celtic Soc. Football (referee), N.Y. Athletic Club, U.S. Power Squadron, Cherry Valley Country Club, KC (4th degree). Roman Catholic. Home: 160 Spring Hill Rd Skillman NJ 08558-1418 Office: 2490 Pennington Rd Ste 201 Pennington NJ 08534 Office Phone: 609-737-2077.

DONNELLY, GLORIA FERRARO, university dean; b. Phila. Grad., Villanova U., U. Pa.; PhD in Human Devel., Bryn Mawr Coll., 1985. With Eastern Pa. Psychiat. Hosp., Inst. Pa. Hosp.; mem. faculty U. Pa. Sch. Nursing, Trenton (N.J.) State Coll., Villanova U.; founding dean of nursing La Salle U.; dean Sch. Nursing MCP Hahnemann U., Phila., 1996—98, Col. Nursing and Health Professions Drexel U., Phila., 1998—. Editor Holistic Nursing Practice Jour.; author 4 books. Recipient Am. Jour. Nursing Book of Yr. awards. Fellow Am. Acad. Nursing; mem. Nat. League for Nursing (bd. govs. 1995-97, chmn. coun. baccalaureate and higher degree programs, mem. exec. com.). Office: Drexel U Coll Nursing and Health Professions 245 N 15th St # 501 Philadelphia PA 19102-1192 Business E-Mail: gloria.donnelly@drexel.edu.

DONNELLY, JAMES CORCORAN, JR., lawyer; b. Newton, Mass., June 10, 1946; s. James C. and Margery J. (MacNeil) D.; m. Carol R. Burns, June 28, 1968; children: James C. IV, Sarah Y. BA, Dartmouth Coll., 1968; JD, Boston Coll., 1973. Bar: Mass. 1973, U.S. Dist. Ct. Mass. 1974, U.S. Ct. Appeals (7th cir.) 1979, U.S. Ct. Appeals (1st cir.) 1983, U.S. Tax Ct. 1988, U.S. Dist. Ct. (no. dist.) Ohio 1991, U.S. Ct. Appeals (2d cir) 1994, U.S. Ct. Appeals (3d cir.) 1999. From assoc. to ptnr. Hale & Dorr, Boston, 1973-84; sr. ptnr. Mirick, O'Connell, DeMallie & Lougee, Worcester, Mass., 1985—, chmn. litig. dept., 1993-97. Editor-in-chief 1972 Ann. Survey of Mass. Law. Corporator Greater Worcester Cmty. Found., 1986—, monitoring and evaluation com., 1997—; trustee Higgins Armory Mus., Worcester, 1985—, pres. 1994-97; corporator Worcester Art Mus., 1986—, pres., mem. coun., 1987-88; councilor Am. Antiquarian Soc., 1996—, treas., 1997—; bd. overseers Supreme Jud. Ct. Hist. Soc., 2004—; club officers exec. com. Dartmouth Coll., 1997-2005, pres., 1999-2002, alumni coun., 2000-2005, coll. rels. group, 2002-2005, com. on alumni orgn., 2000-2005, chmn. 2002-2003; bd. overseers Supreme Judicial Ct. Hist. Soc. Lt. U.S. Army, 1968-70. Decorated Army Commendation medal for meritorious svc., 1970. Fellow Mass. Bar Found. (life); mem. ABA, Mass. Bar Assn. (appellate bench bar com. 1994-1995, bus. law sect. coun. 2003—), Worcester County Bar Assn. (co-chmn. fed. ct. com. 1995-98), Dartmouth Lawyers Assn., Worcester Club (bd. dirs. 1995-98), Worcester Fire Soc. (clk. 2004-05), Dartmouth Club Ctrl. Mass. (exec. com. 1996—, pres. 1997-2002), Worcester Fir Soc. (clk. 2004), Shakespeare Club of Worcester. Avocations: sailing, bicycling, hiking, history. Home: 285 Salisbury St Worcester MA 01609-1661 Office: Mirick O'Connell 100 Front St Worcester MA 01608-1425

DONNELLY, JOHN F., automotive part company executive; m. Barbara Donnelly; children: JOhn, Aisling, Saraid. BA, U. Mich.; M Sci. Mgmt., MIT. With Donnelly Corp., Holland, Mich., 1967—, mfg. mgr., current bus. group mgr. automotive vision sys., bus. group mgr. modular windows, v.p. modular window sys., sr. v.p. modular window sys. group, 1992—. Bd. dirs. Lakeshore Boys and Girls Club, Holland Hist. Trust. Office: Donnelly Corp 49 W 3d St Holland MI 49423

DONNELLY, KEVIN WILLIAM, lawyer; b. Rockville Centre, N.Y., Sept. 25, 1954; s. William Lorne and Marie Grace (Busch) D.; m. Judith Marcia Brier, July 19, 1986; children: Lisa, Jennifer. BS, Boston Coll., 1976, JD, 1979; MBA, Dartmouth Coll., 1982. Bar: N.Y. 1980, Mass. 1980, U.S. Supreme Ct. 1999. Tax atty. Exxon Corp., N.Y.C., 1979-80; assoc. Hemenway & Barnes, Boston, 1982-83; v.p., gen. counsel The Yankee Cos. Inc., Boston, 1983-88; v.p., gen. counsel, sec. Nortek, Inc., Providence, 1989—. Mem. ABA, Mass. Bar Assn. Home: 11 Foxhunt Trl Walpole MA 02081-2270 Office: Nortek Inc 50 Kennedy Plz Ste 1700 Providence RI 02903-2393 E-mail: donnelly@nortek-inc.com.*

DONNELLY, PATRICK L., broadcast executive, lawyer; b. 1962; AB, Lafayette Coll., 1984; JD, Cornell Law Sch. Atty. Simpson Thacher & Bartlett LLP, NYC; assist. gen. counsel ITT Corp. (aquired by Starwood Hotels & Resorts Worldwide, Inc.), 1995—97, v.p. & deputy gen. counsel, 1997—98; exec. v.p. & gen. counsel Sirius Satellite Radio, NYC, 1998—, acting CFO, 1999—2001. Former editor Cornell Law Review. Recipient Wall Street Journal prize, Am. Jurisprudence award in Debtor & Creditor Law. Office: SIRIUS Satellite Radio 1221 Ave of the Americas New York NY 10020 Office Phone: 212-584-5100.

DONNELLY, PETER F., art association administrator; s. Peter Francis Donnelly and Marjorie Isobel Gale/Donnelly. BFA, Boston U., 1960. Asst. to prodr. Barter Theatre, Abingdon, Va., 1960—61; gen. mgr. Seattle Repertory Theatre, 1964—69, producing dir., 1969—85; exec. mng. dir. Dallas Theatre Ctr., 1986—89; pres., CEO ArtsFund (formerly Corp. Coun. Arts), Seattle, 1989—. Vice chair Americans for Arts, Washington, 1990—; chair Theatre Comm. Group, N.Y.C., 1966—2002; bd. dirs. Nat. Coalition United Arts Funds, Washington, 1990—, past pres. Contbr. articles to profl. jours. Com. mem. Governor's Task Force Arts, Olympia, Wash. With U.S. Army, 1961—62. Recipient President's award Individual Achievement Theatre, Wash. Assn. Theatre Artists, 1980, Sch. Fine Arts Outstanding Alumni award, Boston U., 1988, Michael Newton award Excellence Outstanding Leadership, Nat. Coalition United Arts Fund, 1995, Howard S. Wright award Outstanding Support Arts, Seattle Arts Commn., 1996; fellow, The Ford Found., 1963. Mem.: The Rainier Club (bd. dirs. 1999—2002). Achievements include development of Creation of statewide capital building fund for arts related buildings. Over $40 milllion of state money given to arts organizations during the last decade. Office: ArtsFund 10 Harrison St #200 Seattle WA 98109 Personal E-mail: peterd@artsfund.org.

DONNELLY, ROSEMARIE, lawyer; b. Dallas, 1956; BA cum laude, Tex. A&M U., 1978; JD, U. Houston, 1988. Bar: Tex. 1988, admitted to practice: US Ct. Appeals (5th Cir.), US Dist. Ct. (No. Dist.) Tex., US Dist. Ct. (So. Dist.) Tex., US Dist. Ct. (Ea. Dist.) Tex., US Dist. Ct. (We. Dist.) Tex. With Andrews Kurth LLP, Houston, 1988—, ptnr., litig. dept. Contbr. articles to profl. jour. Mem.: State Bar Tex., Houston Bar Assn., Order of Barons. Office: Andrews Kurth LLP 600 Travis St Ste 4200 Houston TX 77002-3090 Office Phone: 713-220-4004. Office Fax: 713-238-7253. Business E-Mail: rdonnelly@andrewskurth.com.

DONNELLY, RUSSELL JAMES, physicist, researcher; b. Hamilton, Ont., Can., Apr. 16, 1930; naturalized 2000; s. Clifford Ernest and Bessie (Harrison) D.; m. Marian Card, Jan. 21, 1956 (dec. 1999); 1 son, James. BSc, McMaster U., 1951, MSc, 1952, LLD, 1999; MS, Yale U., 1953, PhD, 1956. Faculty U. Chgo., 1956-66, prof. physics, 1965-66, U. Oreg., Eugene, 1966—, chmn. dept., 1966-72, 82-83; vis. prof. Niels Bohr Inst., Copenhagen, Denmark, 1972; co-founder Pine Mountain Obs., 1967. Cons. GM Co. Rsch. Labs., 1958—68, NSF, 1968—76, mem. adv. panel for physics, 1970—73, chmn,, 1971—72, mem. adv. coms. on materials rsch., 1979—84; mem. task force on fundamental physics and chemistry in space, space sci. bd. NRC; cons. Jet Propulsion Lab., Calif. Inst. Tech., Pasadena, 1973—82; chmn. Sci. Adv. Com. Low Temp. Facilities in Space, 1990—91; mem. fluid dynamics discipline working group NASA, 1992—95; gen. chmn. 20th Internat. Conf. on Low Temp. Physics, 1993; Chia-Shun lectr. U. Mich., 1995; Fritz London meml. lectr. Duke U., 1996, 2002; Howard Vollum award Reed Coll., 1997. Author: (with Parks, Glaberson) Experimental Superfluidity, 1967, (with Francis) Cryogenic Science and Technology: Contributions of Leo Dana, 1985, Quantized Vortices in Helium II, 1991; editor: (with Herman, Prigogine) Non-Equilibrium Thermodynamics Variational Techniques and Stability, 1966, High Reynolds Number Flows Using Liquid and Gaseous Helium, 1991, Procs. 20th Internat. Conf. Low Temperature Physics, Physica B, 1994; editor: (with Sreenivasan) Flow at Ultra-High Reynolds and Rayleigh Numbers, (with Barenghi and Vinen) Quantized Vortex Dynamic and Superfluid Turbulence; mem. editl. bd. Physics of Fluids, 1966-68, Phys. Rev. E, 1978-84, assoc. editor, 1987-93; mem. editl. bd. Jour. Phys. and Chem. Ref. Data, 1989-92, Handbook of Chemistry and Physics, 1989-98, Royal Soc. London; contbr. articles to profl. jours. Bd. dirs. U. Oreg. Found., 1970-72, 88-91, investment com., 1990-91; bd. dirs. Oreg. Mus. Park Commn., 1975-87, chmn., 1975-82; bd. dirs. Oreg. Bach Festival, 1975-87, Oreg. Mozart Players, 1990-93. Recipient Disting. Alumnus award, McMaster U., 1992, Lars Onsager medal, Norwegian U. Sci. and Tech., 1996, Fritz London prize, Internat. Union Pure and Applied Physics, 2002; Alfred P. Sloan fellow, 1959—63, sr. vis. fellow, Sci. Rsch. Coun., Eng., 1978. Fellow: AAAS, Inst. of Physics (London), Am. Phys. Soc. (exec. com. divsn. fluid dynamics 1966—72, 1980—84, 1988—91, sec.-treas. 1967—70, 1988—91, chmn. 1971—72, 1983—83, Otto Laporte award 1974), Am. Acad. Arts and Scis.; mem.: Soc. Archtl. Historians, Nat. Trust for Scotland, Cosmos Club. Episcopalian. Achievements include research on physics of fluids, especially hydrodynamic stability, turbulence and superfluidity. Home: 2175 Olive St Eugene OR 97405-2837 Office: Univ Oreg Dept Physics Eugene OR 97403-1274 Business E-Mail: russ@vortex.uoregon.edu.

DONNELLY, SHARLOTTE K. B. NEELY, anthropology educator, writer; b. Savannah, Ga., Aug. 13, 1948; d. Joseph Bowden and Kathleen Bell Neely; m. Thomas Christian C. Donnelly, June 21, 1980; 1 child, Bridgette. BA, Ga. State U., 1970; MA, U. NC, 1971, PhD, 1976. Prof. of anthropology No. Ky. U., Highland Heights, 1974—, anthropology coord., 1992—2000, 2004—05. Author: (book) Snowbird Cherokees, 1991; co-author: This Land Was Theirs, 1996, 1999; contbr. articles to profl. jours., chpts. to books. Pres. League for Animal Welfare, Cincinnati, Ohio, 1984—85. Recipient Strongest Influence Award, No. Ky. U. Alumni Assn., 1996. Fellow: Am. Anthrop. Assn.; mem.: Anthropologists and Sociologists of Ky. (pres. 1979—80). Democrat-Npl. Roman Catholic. Avocations: writing, travel. Office: No Ky U Nunn Dr Highland Heights KY 41099 Office Phone: 859-572-5259. Personal E-mail: donnelly@one.net. E-mail: neelys@nku.edu.

DONNELLY, SHAUN EDWARD, government agency administrator; b. Culver, Ind. m. Susan Buesing; children: Alex, Eric. BA in Econs., Lawrence U., Appleton, Wis., 1968; MA in Econs., Northwestern U., 1971. With U.S.

Fgn. Svc., 1972—, econ./comml. officer, fin. economist Office of Devel. Fin. Washington; dep. asst. sec. for energy and econ. sanctions State Dept. Bur. of Econ. and Bus. Affairs, Washington, 1994—95, dep. asst. sec. for trade policy, 1996—97; amb. to Sri Lanka and Republic of Maldives U.S. Dept. State, Colombo, 1997—2000, prin. dep. asst. sec. for econ. and bus. affairs Washington, 2001—. Office: Economic and Business Bureau Room 6828 US Department of State Washington DC 20520 Office Phone: 202-647-5991. E-mail: donnellyse@state.gov.

DONNELLY, THOMAS CHRISTIAN, lawyer, athletic director; b. Cin., July 8, 1956; s. Thomas Meiners and Mary Margaret Stauber Donnelly; m. Sharlotte Neely, June 21, 1980; 1 child, Bridgette. BA, No. Ky. U., 1978; MA, U. Ky., 1981; JD, U. Cin., 1985. Bar: Ohio, Ky.; registered athletic adminstr. Nat. Interscholastic Athletic Adminstrs. Assn. Atty. Dinsmore and Shohl, Cin., 1985—90, Benesch, Friedlander, Copland and Aronoff, Cin., 1990—93; pvt. practice Cin., 1993—; athletic dir. Clark Montessori HS, Cin., 2001—. Charter trustee law alumni U. Cin., 1987. Editor: U. Cin. Law Rev., 1984—85; author: Growler, 2002. Pres. Cmty. Coun., Clifton Heights, 1985—87, University Heights, Fairview, Ohio, Svcs. United for Mothers and Adolescents, Cin., 1994—97, 2000—03; chmn. found. scholarship oversight com. No. Ky. U., 2000—02, mem. alumni lecture com., 2000—, mem. presdl. and alumni dir., screening com., 1997, 2002. Recipient Spl. Recognition award, No. Ky. U. Alumni Assn., 1992. Mem.: No. Ky. U. Pres.'s Soc. (co-chmn. 2002—), No. Ky. U. Anthropology Alumni Club (pres. 1999—), Lambda Alpha (life). Avocations: basketball, hiking, travel. Office: Clark Montessori HS 3030 Erie Ave Cincinnati OH 45208 Office Phone: 513-363-7138. E-mail: donnelly@one.net.

DONNELLY, THOMAS JOSEPH, lawyer, director; b. Pitts., Mar. 4, 1925; s. Thomas E. and Ruth L. (Beitzer) D.; m. Marilyn A. Pfohl, Apr. 16, 1955; children: Thomas C., Elizabeth A., Daria, Heather, Michael, Marilyn, Peter. Student, MIT, 1943-44; BS in Engring., U. Mich., 1946, JD, 1950. Bar: Pa. 1951. Student engr. Westinghouse Electric Corp., 1946-47; since practiced in Pitts. Trustee Carlow U., Pitts.; bd. dirs. Weston Jesuit Sch. Theology, Cambridge, Mass., Pitts. Symphony Soc. With USNR, 1943-46. Mem. ABA, Barristers Soc., Pa. Bar Assn., Allegheny County Bar Assn., Tau Beta Pi. Clubs: Knight of Malta, Toastmasters U. Mich. Lawyers (Ann Arbor); Univ., Duquesne, Chatham (Mass.) Yacht. Roman Catholic. Home: 1085 Shady Ave Pittsburgh PA 15232-2912 Office: 650 Smithfield St Ste 1810 Pittsburgh PA 15222-3907

DONNELLY, THOMAS M., lawyer; BA summa cum laude, Tufts U., 1985; JD, Harvard U., 1988. Bar: Calif., Am. Bar Assoc. Atty., shareholder Heller Ehrman LLP, San Francisco, 1988—; co-chair, Consumer and Environ. Litigation Heller, Ehrman, White, & McAuliffe LLP, San Francisco. Office: Heller Ehrman 333 Bush St San Francisco CA 94104 Office Phone: 415-772-6611. Office Fax: 415-772-6268. Business E-Mail: tdonnelly@hewm.com.

DONNEM, ROLAND WILLIAM, retired lawyer, real estate developer, health facility administrator; b. Seattle, Nov. 8, 1929; s. William Roland and Mary Louise (Hughes) D.; m. Sarah Brandon Lund, Feb. 18, 1961; children: Elizabeth Donnem Sigety, Sarah Madison. BA, Yale U., 1952; JD magna cum laude, Harvard U., 1957. Bar: NY 1958, U.S. Dist. Ct. (ea. and so. dists.) NY 1959, U.S. Ct. Appeals (2d cir.) 1959, U.S. Ct. Claims 1960, U.S. Tax Ct. 1960, U.S. Supreme Ct. 1963, U.S. Ct. Appeals (3d cir.) 1969, DC 1970, U.S. Ct. Appeals (DC cir.) 1970, Ohio 1976, U.S. Dist. Ct. (no. dist.) Ohio 1980, U.S. Ct. Appeals (7th cir.) 1980, U.S. Ct. Appeals (6th cir.) 1984. With Davis Polk & Wardwell, NYC, 1957-63, 64-69; law sec. appellate divsn. NY Supreme Ct., NYC, 1963-64; dir. policy planning antitrust divsn. Justice Dept., Washington, 1969-71; v.p., sec., gen. counsel Std. Brands Inc., NYC, 1971-76; from v.p. law to sr. v.p. law and casualty prevention Chessie Sys., Cleve., 1976-86; ptnr. Meta Ptnrs., real estate devel., 1984—2002, mng. ptnr., 1989—2002, registered security rep., 1985-90; gen. counsel Acorn Properties, Inc., Cleve., 1985—2002, pres., 1989—2002; gen. counsel Meta Devel. Corp., Cleve., 1985—2002, pres., 1989—2002; gen. counsel Meta Properties, Inc., Cleve., 1988—2002, pres., 1989—2002. Founding mem., bd. dirs. Assn. Sheraton Franchisees N.Am., 1997—2002. Mem. editl. bd. Harvard Law Rev., 1955-57. Bd. dirs., fin. v.p. Presbyn. Home for Aged Women, NYC, 1972-76; bd. dirs., treas. James Lenox Ho., Inc., 1972-76; trustee Food and Drug Law Inst., 1974-76; trustee, sec. Brick Presbyn. Ch., NYC, 1974-76; sec. class of 1952, Yale U., 1992-97; bd. dirs. Yale Alumni Fund, 1990-95; chmn. Cleve. Area Yale Campaign, 1991-97. Lt. (j.g.) USNR, 1952-54. Fellow Timothy Dwight Coll., Yale U., 1987—. Mem. Am. Law Inst. (life), Am. Arbitration Assn. (nat. panel arbitrators), Def. Orientation Conf. Assn. (bd. dirs. 1996-99), Yale U. Alumni Assn. Cleve. (treas. 1982-84, del. 1984-87, trustee 1984-93, adv. coun. 1993-2002), Yale U. Alumni Assn. (bd. govs. 1987-90), Union Club (NYC and Cleve.), Washington Chevy Chase Club, Cleve. Racquet Club, Kirtland Country Club (Cleve.), Met. Club (Washington), Carolina Yacht Club, The Country Club of Charleston, Mory's Assn. (New Haven), Phi Beta Kappa. Republican. Presbyterian. Home: Ft Sumter Ho 1 King St Apt 307 Charleston SC 29401

DONNEM, SARAH LUND, financial analyst, non-profit and political organization consultant; b. St. Louis, Apr. 10, 1936; d. Joel Y. and Erle Hall (Harsh) Lund; m. Roland W. Donnem, Feb. 18, 1961; children: Elizabeth Prince Donnem Sigety, Sarah Madison. BA, Vassar Coll., 1958. Tech. aide, computer programmer Bell Labs, Whippany, N.J., 1959-60; chmn. placement vol. opportunities N.Y. Jr. League, 1972-73, asst. treas., 1974-75, chmn. urban problems relating to mental health, 1967-69, mem. project rsch. com., 1967-70, chmn., 1973-74, mem. bd. mgrs., 1973-74. Chmn. cmty. rsch. Washington Jr. League, 1970-71, mem. bd. mgrs., 1970-71; mem. Stratford Hall (N.Y.) Com., 1970—; bd. dirs. East Side Settlement House, Bronx, N.Y., 1972-2004, hon., 2005—, v.p., 1975-76, chmn. Nat. Horse Show Benefit, 1976, winter antiques show com., 1994—, co-chmn. adv. com., 1991-94, chmn. VIP Day, 1999—, mem. nominating com., 1990-2000, mem. investment com., 1993-2003, mem. fin. com., 2004—; bd. dirs. Stanley M. Isaacs Neighborhood Ctr., N.Y.C., 1973-76, v.p., 1975-76; bd. dirs. Presbyn. Home for Aged Women, N.Y.C., 1974-76, v.p., 1976; mem. exec. bd. N.Y. Aux. of Blue Ridge Sch., 1971-75, sec. 1965-67, pres., 1973-75; budget and benevolence com. Brick Presbyn. Ch., N.Y.C., 1973-76, mem. social svc. com., 1973-74, chmn. fgn. students com., 1963-64; bd. dirs. Search and Care, N.Y.C., 1973--76, Project LEARN, cleve., 1990-96, 2000—; chmn. Literacy Fund, 1991-95, mem., 1995—; mem. Friends of Project LEARN, 1986—, mem. Fedn. Cmty. Planning, Cleve., coun. on Older Persons, 1978-82, mem. future Planning task Force, 1980-81, commn. on social concerns, 1982-84; trustee Golden Age Ctrs. Greatr cleve., 1979-92, investment com., 1993, 1st v.p., 1980-81, pres. 1981-85, chmn. Western Res. Antiques show, 1979, 80; chmn. cleve. antiques Show Silver Anniv., 2000; mem. women's adv. coun. Westrn Res. Hist. Soc., 1977—, coord. sec., 1978; mem. women's com. Cleve. Orch., 1979-85, Vassar Coll. cleve. sec. 1980-82, v.p., 1983, pres. 1984-86; mem. AAVC Club Liaison com., 1986-89, chmn. regional program com., 1987-89; bd. dirs. Cleve. Ballet, 1980-2001, exec. com. 1981, fin. com. 1982-88, 95-98, nominating com., 1988-90, 95-2000, co-chmn. 1997-99; co-chmn. Yale Ball, 1983; bd. advisors Ret. Sr. Vol. Program, 1982, trustee, 1983-90, chmn. long range planning comm., 1986, sec. 1987-89; mem. Family Friends Adv. Coun., 1987-89; trustee Fairmount Presbyn. Ch., 1985-88; mem. long range planning com. United Way, Cleve., 1985-87; coord. Friends of Voinovich, 1987-89; womens adv. com. Voinovich for Gov., 1990, Voinovich for Senate, 1997-98, chmn. Voinovich Task Force on Aging, 1990-91, Ohio Adv. Coun. on Aging, 1991-2002, legis. com., 1994-2000; chmn. legis. com. Cuyahoga County Rep. Party, 1994-2000, mem. policy com., mem. fin. com., 1999—, Plain Dealer adv. counsel for elderly coverage, 1991-93; chmn. Johns Hopkins Parents Fund, 1986-88, Project LEARN 15th Anniversary celebration (with Barbara Bush, hon. chmn.), 1989-90; coord. Decorative Arts Trust Cleve. Symposium, 1996; mem. Leadership Cleve. Class 1992; del. White House Conf. on Aging, 1995. Named Vol. of Yr. N.Y. Jr. League, 1975; recipient Sustainer Svc. award Jr. League Cleve., 1990. Mem. Nat. Inst. Social Scis. (membership com. 1972-92, trustee 1984-96), Nat. Soc. Colonial Dames, Colony Club (N.Y.C.), Chevy Chase Club (Washington), Intown club, Vassar Club, Kirtland Club (Cleve.), Historic Charleston Found. (hon. chmn. internat. Charleston ann. antique show 2004, 05) Home (Winter): 2945 Fontenay Rd Shaker Heights OH 44120 Home (Summer): 1 King St Apt 307 Charleston SC 29401

DONNESON, SEENA SAND, artist; b. N.Y.C. d. Max and Ann (Silber) Sand; children: Erika, Lisa. Attended, Pratt Inst., Art Students League. Guest artist Tamarind Lithography Workshop; vis. artist Clayworks, N.Y.C. One-woman shows include Lauren Rogers Mus. Art, Laurel, Miss., Greenville (N.C.) Mus. Art, Galerie #836, Sante Fe, N.Mex., Lehigh U., Princeton U., Portland (Maine) Mus. Art, Piertrantonio Gallery, N.Y.C., U. Calif., L.I. U., George Washington U., Danville (Va.) Mus. Fine Arts and History, others; exhibited in group shows at SUNY, N.Y.C., Quietude Sculpture Garden, N.J., A.F.A. Pier/92, N.Y.C., Sculpture in Color, N.Y.C., Ft. Lauderdale (Fla.) Mus., Norfolk Mus. Arts and Scis., Bklyn. Mus., San Francisco Mus. Art, DeCordova Mus., Alternate Spac, Belgrade Lakes, Maine Mod Art Foundry, N.Y.C., fgn. traveling exhbns., USIS, Mcpl. Art Mus., Tokyo, also on tour throughout Japan, Musseo de Belles Artes, Buenos Aires, Argentina, Scotland, Eng.; represented in permanent collections Va. Mus. Fine Art, Bklyn. Mus., Doris Freidman Sculpture garden, Albright U., Reading, Pa., Norfolk Mus., USIA Art in Embassies, L.A. County Mus. Art, Mus. Modern Art, N.Y.C., Smithsonian Mus., Ft. Lauderdale Mus. Fine Art, Snug Harbor Cultural Ctr., N.Y.C., N.Y. Pub. Libr., Cornell Med. Sch., N.Y.C., others; also pvt. collections; revs. Newsday, The N.Y. Times, The N.Y. Post, Art News, Conran Octopus Ltd., others. Recipient numerous art awards; fellow Edward MacDowell Found., guest artist Tamarind Lithography Workshop, Creative Artists Pub. Svc. grant N.Y. State Coun. on Arts, 1983-84; grantee Mcpl. Art Soc., N.Y. Art in Park, 1974, Queens Coun. on Arts, 1992. Mem. Artists Equity, Nat. Assn. Women Artists (bd. dirs.), L.I.C. Artists (bd. dirs.). Studio: 20 Sutton Pl S New York NY 10022 Office Phone: 212-753-5328. Fax: 212-753-4967. E-mail: elaici@aol.com.

DONOFF, R. BRUCE, dean, oral surgeon, dental educator; BSc cum laude, Bklyn. Coll., 1963; DMD, Harvard U., 1967, MD, 1973. Clin. fellow in oral surgery Harvard U. Sch. Dental Medicine, Boston, 1969-71, asst. prof. oral surgery, 1974-78, assoc. prof. oral and maxillofacial surgery, 1978-83, acting chmn. dept. oral and maxillofacial surgery, 1982-83, chmn., 1983-93, prof., 1983—, dean and Walter C. Guralnick disting. prof. oral and maxillofacial surgery, 1991—. Contbr. articles to profl. jours. Recipient William J. Gies Found. award, 1993, 2d place award Am. Soc. Oral Surgeons, 1969. Fellow AAAS; mem. Omicron Kappa Upsilon.

DONOFRIO, NICHOLAS M., computer engineer; BS, Rensselaer Polytech., 1967; MS, Syracuse Univ., 1971; PhD in engring. (hon.), Polytechnic U., 1999; DSc (hon.), Warwick U., 2000. Designer Internat. Bus. Mach., 1967-83; dir. Semiconductor Devel. Lab., Burlington, Vt., 1983-85, sec., exec. mgt., 1985-86; gen. mgr. site ops. Semiconductor Devel. & Mfg., 1986-87; dir. hardware devel. Corp. Headquarters, 1987-88; v.p., corp. v.p., pres. Personal Computer Prod. Devel., 1988-91; sr. v.p., group exec. Server Group Internat. Bus. Mach., 1995-97, sr. v.p. tech., mfg., 1997—. Chmn. Nat. Action Coun. for Minorities in Engring., 1997—2002. Mensforth Internat. Gold Medal, 2002; Named Tech. Exec. of the Year, Ariz. Coll. of Engring.& Eller Coll. of Bus.& Pub. Adminstrn., 2003, Rodney D. Chipp Meml. award, Soc. of Women Engineers, 2003. Fellow IEEE; mem. Nat. Acad. Engr., Sigam Xi, N.Y. Acad. Sci. Office: IBM Mail Drop 131 New Orchard Rd Armonk NY 10504

DONOFRIO, PETER DANIEL, neurology educator; b. Syracuse, NY, June 5, 1950; s. Carmin Peter and Donna Marie (Powers) D.; m. Kathleen Ann Fitzgerald, May 29, 1976; children: Molly, Emily, Julie. BS, U. Notre Dame, 1972; MD, Ohio State U., 1975. Diplomate Am. Bd. Internal Medicine, Am. Bd. Neurology, Am. Bd. Emergency Medicine. Resident internal medicine Good Samaritan Hosp., Cin., 1978; resident neurology U. Mich. Med. Ctr., Ann Arbor, 1981, instr., 1982-84, V.A. Hosp., Ann Arbor, 1982-84, asst. prof., 1984-85, U. Mich. Med. Ctr., Ann Arbor, 1984-85; asst. prof. neurology Wake Forest U. Sch. Medicine, Winston-Salem, N.C., 1986-89, assoc. prof., 1989-97, prof., 1997—, vice chmn. dept., 1993—. Cons. in neurology, Winston-Salem, 1984—. Contbr. articles to profl. jours. Dept. rep. United Way, Winston-Salem, N.C., 1989— Scholar U. Notre Dame U., 1968. Fellow Am. Acad. Neurology; mem. Am. Assn. Electrodiagnostic Medicine, Am. Neurological Assn. Roman Catholic. Avocations: woodworking, piano, hi-fidelity, landscaping. Home: 3509 Donegal Dr Clemmons NC 27012-8678 Office: Wake Forest Univ Medical Center Blvd Winston Salem NC 27157-0001 Business E-Mail: donofrio@wfubmc.edu.

DONOGHUE, DENIS, language professional, educator; b. Tullow, County Carlow, Ireland, Dec. 1, 1928; came to U.S., 1979; s. Denis and Johanna (O'Neill) D.; m. Frances Rutledge, Dec. 1, 1951; children— David, Helen, Hugh, Celia, Mark, Barbara, Stella, Emma. BA, Univ. Coll., Dublin, 1949, MA, 1952, PhD, 1957; MA, Cambridge (Eng.) U., 1964. Adminstrv. officer Dublin Dept. Fin., 1951-54; fellow King's Coll., univ. lectr. English Cambridge U., England, 1964-65; prof. modern English and Am. lit. Univ. Coll., England, 1965-79; Henry James prof., English, Am. Letters NYU, 1979—. Author: The Third Voice, 1959, Connoisseurs of Chaos, 1964, Jonathan Swift, 1965, Emily Dickinson, 1966, The Ordinary Universe, 1968, Thieves of Fire, 1973, The Sovereign Ghost, 1976, Ferocious Alphabets, 1981, The Arts without Mystery, 1983, The Practice of Reading, 1998, Words Alone: The Poet T.S. Eliot, 2000, Adam's Curse, 2001, Speaking of Beauty, 2003, The American Classics: A Personal Essay, 2005; editor: An Honoured Guest, 1965, Yeats, Memoirs, 1967. Mem. Internat. Assn. U. Profs. English (exec. com.), Roman Catholic. Office: Dept of English NYU 19 University Pl New York NY 10003-4556 Office Phone: 212-998-8800. Business E-Mail: dd1@nyu.edu.*

DONOGHUE, JOHN CHARLES, application developer, consultant; b. Oswego, NY, Sept. 19, 1950; s. James Charles and Marian Louise (Farrell) Donoghue; m. Ann Marie Perry, Dec. 20, 1969; children: John Charles II, Kelly Anne. BS in Electronic Tech., Chapman Coll., 1981; postgrad., U. Calif., Irvine, 1981-82, Western State U. Coll., 1988-89, Azusa Pacific U., 1991-93; MA, U. Redlands, 1987. Enlisted USAF, 1969, advanced through grades to staff sgt., 1977, resigned, 1979; mgr. Lockheed Aircraft, Ontario, Calif., 1979-85; project engr. Northrop Corp., Pico Rivera, Calif., 1985-99; sr. prin. software engr. Raytheon Missile Syss., Tucson, 1999—; Raytheon cert. Six Sigma expert, 2001—. Cons., Fontana, Calif., 1981—2001; mem. software coun. Northrop Corp., Hawthorne, Calif., 1987—97; mem. software improvement network U. Calif., Irvine, 1988—2000; mem. capability maturity model coor. group Software Engring. Inst., Pitts., 1993—; mem. L.A. software improvement network U. So. Calif, 1994—2000; mem. Tucson Software Process Improvement Network, 2000—. Active PTA, 1975—85; mem. Block Parent Assn., 1981—87, Parent to Parent Support Group, 1982—87; vol. cons. S.W. Antropol. Assn., Calif. State U., L.A., 1996—97, Resource Conservation Dist., Rancho Cucamonga, Calif., 1996—, S.W. Mus., L.A., 1997—2000. Decorated USAF Commendation medal; named to Outstanding Young Men of Am., 1983. Mem.: IEEE Computer Soc., IEEE, Nat. Space Soc., N.Y. Acad. Scis., Software Inspection and Rev. Orgn. Avocations: motorcycling, snorkeling, photography. Office: Raytheon Missile Systems Bldg 807/L6 PO Box 11337 Tucson AZ 85734-1337 Office Phone: 520-794-3239. Personal E-mail: jcd28@cox.net.

DONOGHUE, JOHN FRANCIS, archbishop; b. Washington, Aug. 9, 1928; s. Daniel and Rose (Ryan) Donoghue. Student, St. Charles Coll., Catonsville, Md., St. Mary's Sem., Balt., Cath. U. Ordained priest St. Matthew Cathedral, Washington, 1955; asst. pastor St. Bernard's Ch., Riverdale, Md., 1955—61, Holy Face parish, Great Mills, Md., 1961—64; chancellor and vicar gen. Archdiocesan Chancery, Washington, 1965—84; given papal rank of Chaplain to his Holiness with the title Monsignor, 1970; given rank of Prelate of Honor, 1971; elevated to bishop, 1984; bishop Diocese of Charlotte, 1984—93; archbishop Diocese of Atlanta, 1993—2004, archbishop emeritus, 2004—. Roman Cath.*

DONOGHUE, JOHN PHILLIP, neuroscience educator, neurotechnology company executive; b. Cambridge, Mass., Mar. 22, 1949; s. John P. and Nanette L. (Maxwell) D.; m. Karen L. Kerman, Oct. 9, 1982; children: Jacob, Noah. AB, Boston U., 1971; MS in Anatomy, U. Vt., 1976; PhD in Neurosci., Brown U., 1979. Asst. prof. Brown U. Ctr. Neural Sci., Providence, 1984-88, assoc. prof., 1988-91; chmn., dept. neuroscience Brown U., Providence, 1991—, Henry Merritt Wriston prof., exec. dir., Brain Science Program, 1998—; founder, chief scientific officer, dir. Cyberkinetics Neurotechnology Systems, Inc., Foxborough, Mass., 2001—. Mem. advisory panel NIH Neurology and Mental Health Inst.; mem., space med. panel NASA. Assoc. editor Jour. Neurosci., 1995—, Metabolic Brain Disease, 1989-93; contbr. articles to profl. jours. Basil O'Connor fellow March of Dimes Found., 1985; nominee Rave award in Medicine, WIRED, 2005. Mem. AAAS, Am. Physiological Soc., Soc. Neurosci., Internat. Brain Rsch. Orgn, Fedn. Am. Socs. for Exptl. Biology. Office: Brown U Dept Neurosci PO Box 1953 Providence RI 02912-1953 also: Brown U Dept Neurosci PO Box 1953 Providence RI 02912-1953 also: Cyberkinetics Neurotechnology Systems Inc 100 Foxborough Blvd Ste 240 Foxboro MA 02035 Office Phone: 508-549-9981. Office Fax: 508-549-9985.

DONOGHUE, MILDRED RANSDORF, education educator; b. Cleve. d. James and Caroline (Sychra) Ransdorf; m. Charles K. Donoghue (dec.); children: Kathleen, James. EdD, UCLA, 1962; JD, Western State U., 1979. Asst. prof. edn. and reading Calif. State U., Fullerton, 1962-66, assoc. prof., 1966-71, prof., 1971—. Founder, dir. Donoghue Children's Lit. Ctr., Calif. State U., Fullerton, Calif., 2001—. Author: Foreign Languages and the Schools, 1967, Foreign Languages and the Elementary School Child, 1968, The Child and the English Language Arts, 1971, 75, 79, 85, 90, Using Literature Activities to Teach Content Areas to Emergent Readers, 2001; co-author: Second Languages in Primary Education, 1979; contbr. articles to profl. jours. and Ednl. Resources Info. Ctr. U.S. Dept. Edn. Mem. AAUP, AAUW, Nat. Network for Early Lang. Learning, Nat. Coun. Tchrs. English, Nat. Coun. Tchrs. Math., Nat. Coun. Social Studies, Nat. Sci. Tchrs. Assn., Am. Ednl. Rsch. Assn., Nat. Soc. for Study of Edn., Internat. Reading Assn., Nat. Assn. Edn. Young Children, Assn. for Childhood Edn. Internat., Phi Beta Kappa, Phi Kappa Phi, Pi Lambda Theta, Alpha Upsilon Alpha. Address: Calif State U 800 State Coll Blvd Fullerton CA 92834

DONOHEW, ROBERT LEWIS, SR., communications educator; b. Owingsville, Ky., May 9, 1929; s. Butler Ford and Ethel (Couchman) D.; m. Ethel Cox, Sept. 6, 1950 (div. Oct. 1974); children: Robert L. Jr., Susan Kerry Donohew Schneider, John Patrick; m. Phyllis A.M. Aileen, Oct. 19, 1998. AA, Cumberland Coll., 1949; AB, U. Ky., 1951, MA, 1961; PhD, U. Iowa, 1965. Editor Pikeville (Ky.) Daily News, 1951-52; city editor Owensboro (Ky.) Messenger & Inquirer, 1954-57; pub. info. officer U. Ky., Lexington, 1957-61, from instr. to prof. comm., 1962-70, prof. comm., 1970—, dir. Sch. Comm., assoc. dean Coll. Arts and Scis., 1971-73. John F. Murray vis. prof. U. Iowa, Iowa City, 1979-80; pres. Bloomsbury Consulting and Rsch., Lexington, 1988—, Media Rsch. Assocs., Inc., Lexington, 1991-95. Editor: Communication, Social Cognition and Affect, 1988, Persuasive Communication and Drug Abuse Prevention, 1990, others; contbr. more than 100 articles to profl. jours. With USAF, 1952-54. Rsch. grantee Nat. Inst. Drug Abuse, 1985-2001, Ctr. for Substance Abuse Prevention, 1991-95, Nat. Inst. on Alcohol Abuse and Alcoholism, 1995-2001; recipient Health Commn. Scholar of Yr., Nat. Commn. Assn., 2001, others; scholar Old Gold. Mem. Nat. Comm. Assn., Internat. Comm. Assn. Democrat. Avocations: writing, travel, vineyards. Office: Dept Comm Univ Ky Lexington KY 40506-0001 Business E-Mail: Donohew@uky.edu.

DONOHO, TIM MARK, not-for-profit executive; b. St. Louis, Sept. 25, 1955; s. James O. and Jean (Dace) D.; m. Deborah Ann Peeples, Feb. 26, 1981; children: Drew Morgan, Jourdan Alexis. BABA, Columbia Coll., 1979. Editor U.S. Army, Okinawa, Japan, 1973-77; sales mgr. Unival Investments, Okinawa, 1975-77; nat. dir. mktg. Pyramid Life Ins. Co., Springfield, Mo., 1978-82; chmn., owner Ins. Mktg. Group, Springfield, 1982-90; pres., owner Am. Dental Program, Inc., Ft. Lauderdale, Fla., 1984-97, Donoho Gruppe Cos., Ft. Lauderdale, 1985—; owner Advantage Dental Health Plans, Ft. Lauderdale, Fla., 1984-97; pub., editor, owner Prime Years News Mag., Ft. Lauderdale, 1985-92; chmn., owner Bus. Healthcare Coalition Inc., 1995-98; chmn. Express Bakery, 1998—. Bd. dirs. So. Fla. chpt. Nat. Multiple Sclerosis Soc., 1996-97; founder, chmn. bd. dirs. Pastors Closet, 2000—, chmn., founder, Film the Bible, Inc., 1996—; bd. govs. Graves Archael. Mus., 1998-2000, chmn. founder Pasters Golf Tour, 2004—, chmn. founder World's Largest Choir Project, 2004-. With U.S. Army, 1973—77. Mem.: Nat. Assn. Dental Plans (chmn. bd. dirs. 1996—97). Republican. Baptist. Avocations: tennis, golf, loudspeaker design. Home: 1075 Hillsboro Mile Hillsboro Beach FL 33062 Office: Film The Bible 8100 N Univ Dr Fort Lauderdale FL 33321

DONOHOE, CATHRYN MURRAY, journalist; b. Bronx, N.Y. d. Harry and Helen (Crowley) Murray; m. Thomas W. Donohoe, Dec. 1, 1962. BA cum laude in Am. Lit., Middlebury Coll., 1958; student in Russian lit., Columbia U., 1958—60; student in journalism, American U., 1983—84; cert. in Russian Lang. and Culture, Gornyi Inst., St. Petersburg, Russia, 1993. Rsch. and policy coord. Radio Liberty, N.Y.C., 1963—74; freelance journalist, 1977—84; reporter Potomac Almanac, Potomac, Md., 1985, Washington Times, Washington, 1985—94, deputy editor, features, 1994—. Recipient Nat. Mag. award for pub. svc., 1985. Office: Washington Times 3600 New York Ave NE Washington DC 20002-1996

DONOHOE, CHARLES RICHARD, lawyer; b. Iowa City, Apr. 29, 1941; s. Charles Joseph and Sarah Henrietta D.; m. Nancy Christy, Sept. 27, 2003; children: Kelly, Patrick, Mark, Charles Jr., Thomas. BSEE, Ohio State U., 1964, MSEE, 1965; JD, George Washington U., 1970. Bar: Md. 1970, D.C. 1973. Engr. GM, Milford, Mich., 1965-68; patent engr. Burroughs Corp., Washington, 1968-70; assoc. atty. Pennie & Edmonds, N.Y.C., 1970-73; ptnr. Cushman, Darby & Cushman, Washington, 1973-89; gen. patent consul, exec. v.p. Samsung Electronics Co. Ltd., Washington and Seoul, 1989—2003; patent expert witness advisor, 2004—. Lectr. Patent Resources Group, Washington, 1977-88, Kyoto U. Comparative Law Conv., Tokyo, 1984. Co-author: Advanced Patent Prosecution, 1977; patentee in field. Mem. adv. bd. G.W. Law Sch. Recipient Caldwell scholarship Ohio State U., 1964. Mem. ABA, Am. Intellectual Property Assn., Md. Bar Assn., Customs and Internat. Trade Bar Assn., Seoul Club, Am. C. of C., Manor Country Club. Roman Catholic. Avocations: golf, tennis. Home: 15309 Basswood Ct Rockville MD 20853-1801 Office: Samsung Electronics 2445 M St NW Washington DC 20037-1435 Office Phone: 202-907-5700. E-mail: charlesdonohoe@aol.com.

DONOHOE, JAMES DAY, lawyer; b. Rochester, N.Y., Aug. 10, 1943; s. James Vincent and Constance Traganza (Day) D.; m. Laurel Andrews, Aug. 8, 1987; children by previous marriage: J. Douglas, Jeffrey, Cynthia. BS, Cornell U., 1965; JD, Cath. U. Am., 1969; MBA, Case Western Res. U., 1979. Bar: N.Y. 1970, Ohio 1974, Pa. 1988., S.C. 2002. Assoc. Pennie & Edmonds, N.Y.C., 1967-73; house counsel Republic Steel Corp., Cleve., 1973-84, LTV Corp., Dallas, 1984-89, Republic Engineered Steels Inc., Massillon, Ohio, 1989-98; atty. Squire, Sanders & Dempsey, Cleve., 1998-99, Legal Affairs Adminstrn. LLC, Massillon, 1999—2003, Law Offices Edward E. Bullard, Hilton Head, SC, 2003—. Mem.: ABA, S.C. Bar Assn. Home: 1587 Breining St Pittsburgh PA 15226-1940 Office: 8 Lafayette Pl Hilton Head Island SC 29925 Office Phone: 843-689-2525.

DONOHOE, JEROME FRANCIS, lawyer; b. Yankton, S.D., Mar. 17, 1939; s. Francis A. and Ruth D. Donohoe; m. Elaine Bush, Jan. 27, 1968; 1 child, Nicole Elaine. BA, St. John's U., 1961; JD cum laude, U. Minn., 1964. Bar: Ill. 1964, S.D. 1964. Atty. Atchison, Topeka & Santa Fe Ry. Co., Chgo., 1967-73, gen. atty., 1973-78; gen. counsel corp. affairs Santa Fe Industries Inc., Chgo., 1978-84; v.p. law Santa Fe Industries, Inc., Chgo., 1984-90, Santa Fe Pacific Corp., Chgo., 1984-94; ptnr. Mayer, Brown, Rowe & Maw, Chgo., 1990-99, sr. counsel, 1999—. Bd. dirs. Evanston Cmty. Found., 2000—. Capt.

JAGC U.S. Army, 1964—67. Fellow: Ill. Bar Found.; mem.: ABA (pub. utility, comm. and transp. law sect.), Northwestern U. Assocs., Mich. Shores Club (Wilmette, Ill.), Chgo. Athletic Assn., Chgo. Club. E-mail: jdonohoe@mac.com.

DONOHUE, BRADLEY C., psychology professor; b. N.Y.C., Aug. 17, 1965; s. Brian and Jolene Donohue; m. Denise Rosati; children: Shannon, Devin. BA, U. Kans., Lawrence, 1989; PhD, Nova Southeastern U., Ft. Lauderdale, Fla., 1995. Co-investigator, program dir. Nat. Inst. on Drug Abuse, Bethesda, Md., 1991—93, Nat. Inst. Mental Health, Bethesda, Md., 1993—95; adj. prof. Nova Southeastern U., Ft. Lauderdale, Fla., 1995—98; asst. prof. U. Nev., Las Vegas, 1998—2004, assoc. prof., 2004—. Prin. investigator Clark County Bus. Devel. Divsn., Las Vegas, 2001—04; cons. Family Devel. Found., Las Vegas, 2004—; McNair Scholarship mentor U. Nev., Las Vegas, 2004. Contbr. articles to profl. jours.; editor: Jour. Child & Adolescent Substance Abuse, 1999—. Recipient Applied Rsch. Initiative award, State of Nev., 2001. Mem.: We. Psychol. Assn. Avocations: basketball, boxing, skiing, travel. Office: Univ Nevada - Las Vegas 4505 Maryland Pkwy Las Vegas NV 89154

DONOHUE, CLAIRE P., retired school librarian; b. Glen Cove, NY, Mar. 6, 1941; d. Hubert Aloysius Donohue and Catherine Teresa Scarlett; m. John T. Sexton, Aug. 30, 1975 (div. Apr. 1, 1983). BA, St. John's U., Jamaica, NY, 1965, MA, 1967; MLS, L.I. U., 1974. Cert. secondary English tchr. NY, 1967, sch. libr. media specialist NY, 1974, sch. dist. adminstr. NY, 1995. English tchr. St. Peter Alcantara Sch., Port Washington, NY, 1966—68; libr. media dir. St. Agnes Acad. HS, College Point, NY, 1969—77; libr. media specialist Bethpage Union Free Sch. Dist., Bethpage, NY, 1977—91, libr. media chair, 1991—2003; ret., 2003—; part time ref. libr. St. Joseph's Coll., Patchogue, NY. Adj. instr. NYC Tech. Coll., Bklyn., 1975—79, Palmer Sch. L.I. U., Greenvale, NY, 1991—95; acting interim dir. Nassau BOCES Sch. Libr. Sys., Massapequa, NY, 2003; part-time ref. libr. St. Joseph's Coll., Patchogue, 2004—. Mem.: ALA, Nassau Sch. Libr. Sys. Adv. Coun. (chair 1992—94), L.I. Sch. Media Assn. (bd. mem. 1991—93), NY Libr. Assn. Home: 15 Tojan Dr East Islip NY 11730 Personal E-mail: clairedonohue@optonline.net.

DONOHUE, CRAIG S., stock exchange executive; married; 3 children. BA, Drake U.; LLM in Fin. Svcs. Regulation, Ill. Inst. Tech., Chgo.; JD, John Marshall Law Sch.; M in Mgmt., Northwestern U. Bar: Ill. Assoc. McBride, Baker & Coles, Chgo.; corp. atty. Chgo. Mercantile Exch., Inc., 1989—95, v.p., assoc. gen. counsel, 1995—97, v.p. market regulation, 1997—98, sr. v.p., gen. counsel, 1998—2000, mng. dir., bus. devel. and corp./legal affairs, 2000—01, mng. dir., chief adminstrv. officer, 2001—02; exec. v.p., chief adminstrv. officer, Office of the CEO Chgo. Mercantile Exch. Holdings Inc. and Chgo. Mercantile Exch. Inc., 2002—03, CEO, 2004—. Bd. dir. Nat. Council on Economic Ed. Office: CME 30 S Wacker Dr Chicago IL 60606*

DONOHUE, DAVID PATRICK, engineering executive, retired military officer; b. N.Y.C., May 7, 1931; s. Patrick Joseph and Beatrice Anna (Bligh) D.; m. Dolores Theresa Bowen, Nov. 24, 1956; children: Christine, David, Steven, Joanne, Denise. AB, Holy Cross Coll., 1953; MSEE, U.S. Naval Postgrad. Sch., 1961; postgrad., Harvard Bus. Sch., 1969, Kennedy Sch. Nat. Security, 1986. Design advisor Vietnam Naval Shipyard, Saigon, Vietnam, 1965-66; plan/estimating supt. Puget Sound Naval Shipyard, Bremerton, Wash., 1966-69; ship projects officer, supr. shipbuilding USN, Seattle, 1969-71; ship systems engr. Staff Naval Air Forces Pacific, San Diego, 1971-75; exec. dir. surface platforms Naval Sea Systems Command, Washington, 1975-77; prodn., planning officer Pearl Harbor (Hawaii) Naval Shipyard, 1977-80; shipyard commdr. Norfolk Naval Shipyard, Portsmouth, Va., 1980-83; rear adm., dir. maintenance U.S. Atlantic Fleet USN, Norfolk, Va., 1983-89; engring. mgr. The Jonathan Corp., Norfolk, 1989-91, program mgr., 1991-93, v.p., gen. mgr. shipyard Norfolk, 1993-95; corp. tech. dir. Integrated Sys. Analysts, Inc., Chesapeake, Va., 1995—2002; chmn. bd. dirs. Cen. Mgmt. Sys., 2000—01; corp. tech. dir. Thermal Spray & Machine, Inc., Norfolk, 2002—. Exec. adv. coun. Old Dominion U. Coll. Bus. and Pub. Adminstrn., 1996-99; bd. dirs. Unitech Corp., Hampton. Va., Lockring Corp. Pres. Portsmouth Area United Way, 1981-82, com. mem. South Hampton Roads chpt., Norfolk, 1983-88; chmn. Portsmouth Armed Svcs. YMCA, 1981-82. Mem. Am. Soc. for Quality Control (vice-chmn. Tidewater, Va. sect. 1995-97, chmn. 1997-98, sec. 1998-2000), Am. Soc. Naval Engrs. (councillor Tidewater sect. 1981-84, 2005—, chmn. Tiewater sect. 2004-2005, ret. nat. councillor 1990-93, 2002—), Soc. Naval Architects and Marine engrs. (Hampton Rds. sect. chmn. 1985-86, chmn. ship prodn. com. nat. shipbuilding rsch. program 1990-95, Va. gov.'s commn. on base retention 1995), Norfolk Naval Shipyard Portsmouth Assn. (pres. 1998-2000), Town Point Club (bd. govs. 1994-2002). Republican. Roman Catholic. Home: 216 Brackenridge Ave Norfolk VA 23505-4322 Office: Thermal Spray and Machine Inc 2400 Hampton Blvd Norfolk VA 23517-1004 Office Phone: 757-623-6484. E-mail: donohued6@cox.net, dave.donohue@tsmnorfolk.com.

DONOHUE, EDITH M., human resources specialist, educator; b. Nov. 10, 1938; d. Edward Anthony and Beatrice (Jones) McParland; m. Salvatore R. Donohue, Aug. 23, 1960; children: Kathleen, Deborah. BA, Coll. Notre Dame, Balt., 1960; MS, Johns Hopkins U., 1981; postgrad., CASE (cert. adv. study edn.), 1985; PhD in Human Resources, CASE, 1990. Cert. counselor, national, sr. profl. human resources. Dir. pub. rels. Coll. Notre Dame, Balt., 1970—71, dir. continuing edn., 1981—86; program coord. bus. and industry Catonsville C.C., Balt. County, Md., 1986—88; mgr. tng. and devel. Sheppard Pratt Hosp., Balt., 1988—90; assoc. prof., Sch. Edn. Barry U., 1993—98; cons. in human resources Stuart, Fla., 1985—. Adj. faculty Loyola Coll. Grad. Studies Program, Fla. Inst. Tech., Indian River C. of C. Co-author: Communicate Like a Manager, 1989, Life After Layoff, 2003; contbg. author career devel. workshop manual, 1985; contbr. articles to profl. jours. Pres. Cathedral Sch. Parents Assn., 1972-74; asst. treas., treas. Md. Gen. Hosp. Aux., 1975-78; dir. sect. Exec. Women's Network, Balt., 1983-85; adv. bd. Mayor's Commn. on Aging, 1981-86; bd. dirs. Md. Assn. Higher Edn., 1985-88; vol. trainer United Way Martin County, co-chair campaign, 1994—, strategic planning com., 1998—, bd. dirs., 2004—; steering com. Chautaugua South. Recipient Mayor's Citation, City of Balt. Council, 1985, Woman of Distinction, Martin County, 1999 Mem. AAUW (dir., v.p. 1980-83), Am. Assn. Tng. and Devel. (bd. dirs.), Am. Counseling Assn., Soc. Human Resources Mgmt., Martin County Personnel Mgt. Assn. (edn. chmn. 1991-94), Martin County Libr. Assn. Inc. (pres. 2001-2003), Martin County C. of C. (edn. com. 1991-94), Friends of Lyric (bd. dirs. chmn., strategic planning, pres.), United Way of Martin County Found. (bd. dirs. 2003—), Martin Meml. Health System (patient safety comr. 2003-), Chi Sigma Iota (pres.), Phi Delta Kappa. Republican. Roman Cath. Avocations: tennis, performing arts, reading, wellness. Home: Apt 3103 144 NE Edgewater Dr Stuart FL 34996-4477 E-mail: edonohue@gate.net.

DONOHUE, GEORGE L., mechanical engineer, educator; b. Wichita, Kans., July 8, 1944; s. George Edward and Dorothy Mae (Cunningham) Custer; m. Andreana Grillis, June 7, 1969; children: Carmen, Kathleen, Georgiana, Caroline. Student, Ga. Inst. Tech., Atlanta, 1962-64; BSME, U. Houston, 1967; MS, Okla. State U., 1968, PhD, 1972. Coop student NASA, Clear Lake, Tex., 1963-67; postdoctoral fellow Naval Undersea Ctr., Pasadena, Calif., 1972-73; br. head Naval Ocean Sys. Ctr., San Diego, 1973-76, divsn. head, 1977-79; prog. mgr. Def. Adv. Rsch. Project Agy., Arlington, Va., 1976-77, office dir., 1988-89; v.p. Dynamics Tech. Inc., Torrance, Calif., 1979-84; prog. mgr. Rand Corp., Santa Monica, Calif., 1984-88, v.p., 1989-94; assoc. adminstr. rsch. and acquisition FAA, Washington, 1994-98; prof. George Mason U., Fairfax, Va., 2000—. Vis. prof. air transp. tech. and policy Sch. IT & Engring. George Mason U., Fairfax, 1998—2000, prof. sys. engring., 2000—. Author: Air Transportation Systems Engineering, 2001; contbr. articles to profl. jours. Treas. YMCA Girls Gymnastics Team, San Pedro, Calif., 1983; adult advisor Girl Scouts U.S., Torrance, 1987—88. Recipient Merit Civil Svc. medal, Dept. of Def., 1977; NDEA fellow, 1967, NRC fellow, 1972. Fellow: AIAA (mem. policy com. 1990—94); mem.: Air Traffic Control Assn., Exptl. Aircraft Assn., Aircraft Owners & Pilots Assn., Elks, Sigma Xi, Pi Tau Sigma, Omicron Delta Kappa, Tau Beta Pi. Roman Catholic. Avocations: flying, skiing, sailing, backpacking. Office Phone: 703-993-2093.

DONOHUE, JAMES J., lawyer; b. N.Y.C., Dec. 3, 1947; s. Joseph P. and Constance (Anderson) D.; m. Carol A. Mager, July 29, 1973; children: Jay Mager, Megan Constance. AB, Dartmouth Coll., 1969; JD, U. Pa., 1972. Atty. Fed. Defender Phila., 1972-76; ptnr. White and Williams, Phila., 1976—. Mem.: ABA (chair trial evidence com., litigation sect. 1995—99, judiciary task force 2000—03, fed. practice task force 2004—), Phila Bar Found. (trustee 1992—97), WYCK (bd. dirs. 1996—, treas. 1998—), Rotary Club Phila. (bd. dirs. 1993-95), (bd. dirs. 1993—95), Phila. Cricket Club, Phila. Racquet Club. Avocations: skiing, golf. Office: White and Williams 1800 One Liberty Pl 1650 Market St Philadelphia PA 19103-7395 Office Phone: 215-864-7037. Business E-Mail: donohuej@whiteandwilliams.com.

DONOHUE, JOHN JOSEPH, law educator; b. Alexandria, Va., Jan. 30, 1953; s. Mildred (Sileo) Donohue; m. Marijke Rijsberman, Dec. 27, 1986 (div.); 1 child, Lauren Elizabeth; m. Maureen O'Kicki, Oct. 25, 1995; children: Aidan John, Patrick John. BA, Hamilton Coll., 1974; JD, Harvard U., 1977; PhD, Yale U., 1986. Bar: Conn. 1977, D.C. 1978. Assoc. Covington & Burling, Washington, 1978-81; fellow Civil Liability Program, Law Sch. Yale U., New Haven, 1985-86; rsch. fellow Am. Bar Found., Chgo., 1986-95; Class of 1967 James B. Haddad prof. law Northwestern U., Chgo., 1994-95; prof. Stanford (Calif.) Law Sch., 1995—2004, William H. Neukom prof. law, 2002—04; Leighton Homer Surbeck prof. law Yale Law Sch., New Haven, 2004—. Vis. prof. Harvard Law Sch., 2003. Contbr. articles to profl. jours. Mem. ABA, Am. Econ. Assn., Phi Beta Kappa. Office: Yale Law Sch PO Box 208215 New Haven CT 06520-8215 Office Phone: 203-432-1994. Business E-Mail: j.donohue@yale.edu.

DONOHUE, JOHN PATRICK, lawyer; b. N.Y.C., Sept. 16, 1944; s. Joseph Francis and Catherine Elizabeth (Feeney) D.; m. Patricia Ann Holly, June 11, 1977; children: Eileen Mary, Anne Catherine. BA, Providence Coll., 1966; JD, Catholic U. Am., 1969. Bar: N.Y. 1973, U.S. Ct. Appeals (2d cir.) 1973, U.S. Ct. Appeals (fed. cir.) 1974, N.J. 1975, U.S. Dist. Ct. N.J. 1975, U.S. Dist. Ct. (so., ea. dists.) N.Y. 1975, U.S. Supreme Ct. 1978, D.C. 1981, Pa. 1986. Spl. agt. FBI, Washington, 1969-71; assoc. Donohue & Donohue, N.Y.C., 1971-74, ptnr., 1974—; of counsel Kittredge Donley Elson Fullem & Embick. Adj. prof. law internat. bus. transactions Seton Hall U. Sch. Law, Newark, 1986-94, 2002—. Author book sect. Customs Fraud Section on Business Crimes, 1982; co-author: The Prevention and Prosecution of Computer and High Technology Crime. Bd. dirs. Maritime Exch. Delaware River and Bay, 1989—; mem. bd. regents Cath. U. Am., 1990-2000, chmn., 1997-2000; trustee Rosemont (Pa.) Sch., 1995—, chmn., 1996-2001; mem. bd. visitors Cath. U. Sch. Law, 1998—; mem. Congress of Fellows, Ctr. for Internat. Legal Studies, Salzburg, Austria. Named Man of Yr., Phila. Customs, Brokers and Forwarders Assn., 1984. Mem. Customs and Internat. Trade Bar Assn., Pa. State Bar Assn., Republican. Roman Catholic. Office: Kittredge Donley Elson Fullem & Embick 400 Market St Ste 200 Philadelphia PA 19106 Office Phone: 215-829-9900. Business E-Mail: Jdonohue@kdefe.com.

DONOHUE, KATHLEEN GRACE, history professor; b. Munich, July 12, 1958; d. Gerard Anthony and Edith May Donohue; m. Bronwyn Laird Blair Aidan. BA, Fla. State U., 1980, MA, 1982, U. Va., 1989, PhD, 1994. Prof. history Ctrl. Mich. U., Mt. Pleasant, Mich., 2004—. Author: Freedom from Want: Am, 2003. Grantee, NEH, 2004. Mem.: Am. Polit. Sci. Assn., Am. Hist. Assn. Office: Central Michigan Univ Dept History Mount Pleasant MI 48859

DONOHUE, MARC DAVID, chemical engineering professor; b. Watertown, N.Y., Sept. 10, 1951; s. Paul Francis and Beverly Gertrude D.; m. Mary Ann Chamberlain, July 20, 1974; children: Paul, Megan, Ian. BS, Clarkson Coll. Tech., 1973; PhD, U. Calif., Berkeley, 1977. Asst. prof. chem. engring. Clarkson Coll. Tech., Potsdam, N.Y., 1977-79; asst. prof. Johns Hopkins U., Balt., 1979-83, assoc. prof., 1983-87, prof., 1987—, chmn. dept., 1984-95, assoc. dean, 1999—. Treas. Coun. Chem. Rsch., 1993—. Recipient Adminstr.'s Pollution Prevention award for Region III, U.S. EPA, 1992, Md. sect. Outstanding Engring. Achievement award, NSPE, 1989. Mem. Am. Inst. Chem. Engrs., Am. Chem. Soc. (Md. chemist 1999), Am. Soc. Engring. Edn. (Outstanding Young Engr. award 1984), Tau Beta Pi. Office Phone: 410-516-5262. Business E-Mail: mdd@jhu.edu.

DONOHUE, MARY, lieutenant governor; b. Rensselaer County, N.Y. children: Sara, Justin. B.Edn., Coll. New Rochelle, 1968; MS in Edn., Russell Sage Coll., Troy, N.Y., 1973; JD, Union U., 1983. Bar: NY 1983. Tchr. elem., jr. h.s. Rensselaer and Albany County (N.Y.) sch. dists., Albany, 1969-78; law clk., intern U.S. Atty.'s Office, Albany, 1980-83; assoc. O'Connell & Aronowitz, Albany, 1983-88; pvt. practice Troy, 1988-92; asst. county atty. Rensselaer County, 1990-92, dist. atty., 1992-96; justice N.Y. Supreme Ct., 3rd Jud. Dist., 1996-98; lt. gov. State of N.Y., Albany, 1998—. Chair Govs. Task Force on Sch. Violence, 1999—, Task Force on Quality Cmtys., 2000—, Govs. Task Force on Small Bus. Chair Capital Dist. Women's Adv. Coun., 1996; mem. Gov.-elect Pataki's Transition Team for Criminal Justice, 1994-96. Republican. Office: Office of Lt Governor State Capitol Rm 246 Albany NY 12224

DONOHUE, PATRICIA CAROL, academic administrator; b. St. Louis, Jan. 11, 1946; d. Carroll and Juanita Donohue; m. James H. Stevens Jr., Aug. 27, 1966 (div. Mar. 1984); children: James H. Stevens III, Carol Janet Stevens. AB, Duke U., 1966; MA, U. Mo., 1974, PhD, 1982. Tchr. math. in secondary schs., Balt., St. Louis and Shawnee Mission, Kans., 1966-71; lectr. U. Mo., Kansas City, 1975-76, rsch. asst. affirmative action, 1976-79, coord. affirmative action, 1979-82, instl. rsch. assoc., 1982-84, acting dir. affirmative action and acad. pers., 1984; dir. instl. rsch. Lakeland C.C., 1984-86; asst. dean acad. affairs, math., engring. and tech. Harrisburg Area C.C., 1986-89, dean sch. bus., engring., and tech., 1989-93, dean Lebanon campus, v.p. cmty. devel. and external affairs, 1993; vice chancellor edn. St. Louis C.C., 1993—2002, acting pres. Florissant Valley campus, 1998-99; pres. Luzerne County C.C., 2002—. Active Pa. Coun. on Vocat. Edn., 1989—93; v.p. St. Louis Sch. to Work, Inc., 1994—96, pres., 1996—2002; chairperson Pa. Occupl. Deans, 1988—93; bd. dirs., chmn. edn. com. Humane Soc. Mo., 1997—2002; cons. evaluator North Ctrl. Assn., 2000—; bd. dirs. Diamond City Partnership, 2003—05, Greater Wilkes-Barre (Pa.) Chamber Bus. and Industry, 2004—, The Luzerne Found., 2004—, Northeastern Pa. Tech. Inst., 2004—, pres., 2004—; bd. dirs. F.M. Kirby Ctr. Bd. dirs., v.p. Am. Cancer Soc. Jackson County, 1975—84; mem. adv. coun. Ben Franklin Partnership, 1988—93; sec. Ctrl. Pa. Tech. Coun., 1992—93; mem. steering com. New Baldwin Corridor Coalition, 1991—93, chair edn. task force, 1992—93; mem. Leadership St. Louis, 1996—97, Exec. Leadership Wilkes-Barre, 2003; mem. strategic planning com. Penns Woods Girl Scout Coun., 2003—04, bd. dirs., 2004—; mem. Exec. Leadership Scranton, 2004; bd. dirs. PTA, 1975—77, Cmty. Lebanon Assocs., Ctrl. Pa. Tech. Coun., 1989—93, Mantec, 1988—93, Delta Gamma Ctr. for Children with Visual Impairments, 2001—03, Osterhout Libr., 2003—, Hemlock coun. Girl Scouts U.S.A., 2004—. Recipient Outstanding Service and Achievement award U. Mo. Kansas City, 1976, Outstanding Svc. award Ctrl. Pa. Tech. Coun., 1993; Jack C. Coffey grantee, 1978; named Outstanding Woman AAUW, 1989, one of Outstanding Leaders Nat. Inst. Leadership Devel., 1986, Exec. Leadership Inst., 1990, Cmty. Woman of Yr. Wilkes-Barre, Am. Bus. Women Assn., 2005. Mem.: Assn. Inst. Rsch., Women's Network, Nat. Assn. Student Pers. Adminstrs., Women's Equity Project, Soc. Mfg. Engrs. (chmn. 1989—90), Am. Assn. Women in Cmty. and Jr. Colls. (Pa. state coord. 1988, bd. dirs. Region 3 1989—91, 2005—), Nat. Coun. for Occupl. Edn. (chairperson diversity task force 1991, chairperson job tng. 2000 task force 1992, v.p. programs 1992—93, bd. dirs. 1992—2000, v.p. membership 1993—94, pres. 1995—96, past pres. 1996—97), Am. Assn. Cmty. Colls. (coun. affiliated chairpersons 1994—2000, commn. on cmty. and workforce devel. 1995—97, chairperson coun. 1996—2000, commn. on cmty. and workforce devel. 1998—2001, acad. pres. 2003, bd. dirs. 1988—91, 2005—), Am. Vocat. Assn., Math. Assn. Am., Nat. Coun. Tchrs. of Math., ASCD, Delta Gamma (v.p., del. nat. conv. 1988, pres. 1989-91, bd. dirs. Delta Gamma Ctr. for Children with Visual Impairment 2001-) (del. nat. conv. 1988, pres. 1989—91, v.p., Cream Rose Outstanding Svc. award 1970), Pi Lambda Theta, Phi Kappa Phi, Phi Delta Kappa (pres. 1975, Read fellow 1989). Home: 40 Elmcrest Dr Dallas PA 18612 Office: Luzerne County C C 1333 S Prospect St Nanticoke PA 18634 Office Phone: 570-740-0388. Business E-Mail: pdonohue@luzerne.edu.

DONOHUE, THERESE BRADY, artistic director, choreographer, set designer; b. Washington, Jan. 13, 1937; d. John Bernard and Mary Catherine (Rupert) B.; m. Joseph W. Donohue Jr., June 13, 1959 (div. 1987); children: Sharon Marie, Maura Cathleen (dec.), Sheila Patricia. BA, Coll. of Notre Dame Md., 1958. Cert. tchr. ballet Royal Acad. Dance London. Advt. artist Kronstadt Advt. Agy., Washington, 1958; instr. art The Maret Sch., Washington, 1958-60, Princeton (N.J.) U., 1967-71; artist dir. Amherst (Mass.) Ballet Theatre Co., 1977—2000; founder, dir. Amherst Ballet Centre, 1971—2000. Sch. adminstr. Amherst Ballet, 1999-2004; co-dir., founder Pioneer Valley Ballet, Northampton, Mass., 1972-77; dancer, tchr. Princeton Ballet, 1962-71; animal masks Charleston (SC) Ballet, 1985—90; choreographer Roanoke (Va.) Ballet Theatre, 1983; chair N.E. Region Craft Choreography Conf., Amherst, 1979; artist/chorcographer Nat. Gallery Art, 1986, 88, Guggenheim, 1986, Nat. Mus. Am. Art, 1989, Hirshhorn Mus. and Sculpture Garden, 1993. Choreographer (ballets for children) Peter & the Wolf, 1973, One Thousand Cranes, 1974, Punch & Judy, 1975, Amherst Poets, 1977, Uncle Wiggily & the Duck Pond, 1979, (Springfield Symphony) History of Dance, 1983, (Project Opera) Hansel & Gretel, 1983, Sea Study (included in Aberdeen Internat. Youth Festival in Scotland), 1994, Peter Pan Amherst Cmty. Theater, 1995, Aida Commonwealth Opera, 1996, Flower Fairy Ballet, 1997, Ribbon Festival Ballet, 1997; rechoregraphed Matisse's Circus, Dancing with Dubuffet; toured Maui Hawaii Elem. Schs. (Amherst Ballet Theatre Co.), 1996; spl. projects dir. Amherst Ballet, 2003-05; prodr., costumer Eric Carle's The Very Lonely Firefly, 2003, Russian Nat. Dances, 2003, Eric Carle's The Honeybee and the Robber, 2004, The Eric Carle Museum of Picture Book Art; costumer Amherst Ballet's Shim Chung, 2005. Mem. Amherst Arts Coun., 1983-89. Recipient Town of Amherst Arts and Supplemental Edn. award, 1997, Mass. Senate Citation, 2002, C.C. Dakin Medallion award in edn., 2002. Mem. Amherst Club. Avocation: travel. Home and Office: 17 Juniper Ln Amherst MA 01002-1227 E-mail: tbd@crocker.com.

DONOHUE, THOMAS JOSEPH, federal agency administrator, transportation association executive; b. N.Y.C., Aug. 12, 1938; s. Thomas Joseph Sr. and Ruth (Ahern) D.; m. Elizabeth Schulz, June 29, 1963; children: Thomas, Keith, John. BA, St. John's U., 1963, PhD (hon.), 1985; MBA, Adelphi U., 1965; PhD (hon.), Marymount U., 1991. V.p. Fairfield (Conn.) U., 1967-69; dep. asst. postmaster gen. U.S. Postal Svc., Washington, 1969-71, asst. regional postmaster gen. San Francisco, 1971-73, dist. mgr. N.Y.C., 1973-75; asst. regional postmaster gen. U.S. Postal Service, N.Y.C., 1975-76; group v.p. U.S.A. C. of C., Washington, 1976-84; pres., CEO U.S. C. of C., Wash., DC, 1997—, Am. Trucking Assns., Alexandria, Va., 1985—. Bd. dirs. Sunrise Assisted Living, Fairfax, Va., Internat. Planning and Analysis Ctr., Arlington, Va., Newmyer Assn., Marymount U., Hwy. Users Fedn., Washington, Hudson Inst., Indpls.; mem. Nat. Commn. on Intermodal Transp., Transp. Rsch. Bd.; mem. adv. com. transp. Northwestern U. Bd. dirs. Marymount U. Office: US Chamber of Commerce 1615 H St NW Washington DC 20062-0001

DONOHUGH, DONALD LEE, physician; b. LA, Apr. 12, 1924; s. William Noble and Florence Virginia (Shelton) D.; m. Virginia Eskew McGregor, Sept. 12, 1950 (div. 1971); children: Ruth, Laurel, Marilee, Carol, Greg; m. Beatrice Ivany Redick, Dec. 3, 1976; stepchildren: Leslie Ann, Andrea Jean. BS, U.S. Naval Acad., 1946; MD, U. Calif., San Francisco, 1956; MPH and Tropical Medicine, Tulane U., 1961. Diplomate Am. Bd. Internal Medicine. Intern U. Hosp., San Diego, 1956—57; resident Monterey County Hosp., 1957—58; dir. med. svc. U.S. Dept. Interior, Am. Samoa, 1958—60; instr. Tulane U. Med. Sch., New Orleans, 1960—63; resident Tulane Svc. VA and Charity Hosp., New Orleans, 1961—63; cons. Internat. Ctr. for Rsch and Tng., Costa Rica, 1961—63; asst. prof. medicine and preventive medicine La. State U. Sch. Medicine, 1962—63, assoc. prof., 1963—65; vis. prof. U. Costa Rica, 1963—65; faculty advisor, head of AID program U. Costa Rica Med. Sch., 1965—67; dir. med. svcs. Med. Ctr. U. Calif. (formerly Orange County Hosp.), Irvine, 1967—69; assoc. clin. prof. U. Calif., Irvine, 1967—79, clin. prof., 1980—85; pvt. practice Tustin, Calif., 1970—80; with Joint Commn. on Accreditation of Hosp., 1981; cons. Kauai, Hawaii, 1981—. Author: The Middle Years, 1981, Practice Management, 1986, Kauai, 1988, 4th edit., 1992, Our Ancestors, 1995, The Story of Koloa, 2001, (second edition, 2002); co-translator; Rashomon (Ryonosuke Akutagawa), 1950; also numerous articles. Lt. USN, 1946-52, capt. USNR, 1966-84. Fellow ACP (life); mem. Delta Omega. Republican. Episcopalian. Home: 4890 Lawai Beach Rd Koloa HI 96756-9675 E-mail: dldondhugh1@verizon.net.

DONOVAN, ANDREW JOSEPH, financial consultant; b. N.Y.C., Nov. 22, 1952; s. Andrew Joseph and Marion (Cooley) D.; m. Margaret Mary Dowd, June 17, 1984; children: Andrew, John, Daniel. BA, Fordham U., 1974, MA, 1976, PhD, 1983; grad., Coll. Fin. Planning, 1996, Naval War Coll., 2000. Adj. instr. Fordham U., Bronx, N.Y., 1976-78; ops. mgr. Merrill Lynch, Pierce, Fenner & Smith, N.Y.C., 1978-79, stockbroker Mt. Kisco, N.Y., 1984-88, Kidder Peabody, White Plains, N.Y., 1988-89; dir. devel. N.Y. Med. Coll., Valhalla, 1989-93, U.S. Merchant Marine Acad. Found., Inc., Kings Point, N.Y., 1993-96; fin. cons. Chase Investment Svcs. Corp., 1996-2001, Donovan Fin., 2001—. Chmn. N.Y. State 4-H Found., Inc., 1990-92. Author: The Political Clock, 1983. Councilman Town of Yorktown, N.Y., 1990-93; legislator Westchester County, N.Y., 1994-97. Lt. cmdr. USNR, 1979—. Fellow H.B. Earhart Found., 1976. Republican. Roman Catholic. Avocation: collecting books. Home: 168 Country Club Rd Hopewell Junction NY 12533 Office Phone: 914-526-7288.

DONOVAN, ANNE, professional basketball coach; b. Ridgewood, N.J., Nov. 1, 1961; Asst. coach Old Dominion U.; head coach women's basketball E. Carolina U., Greenville, 1995-98; head coach Phila. Rage, 1998-99, Indiana Fever, Indianapolis, 1999—. Recipient Naismith Player of Yr. award, 1983, Olympic Team Gold medal, 1984, 88, World Championship Team Gold medal, 1986. Mem. USA Basketball Com. (exec. bd. dirs. 1996—). Achievements include Three time All-Am. selection; led nation in rebounding, 1982; all-time leading scorer, blocker and rebounder Old Dominion Univ.; Olympian, 1980, 84, 88; World Championship team, 1983, 86.

DONOVAN, BEVERLY SUE, psychologist; b. Toledo, Feb. 16, 1947; d. Henry John Merce and Helen Clara Ufer; m. Duane Lee Donovan, June 14, 1969; children: Gregory Michael, Matthew Ryan. PhD, Kent State U., 1993. Staff psychologist Brecksville divsn. Louis Stoke DVA Med. Ctr., Cleve., 1991—. Contbr. articles to profl. jours. Recipient Angel Almedina award, 12th Ann. Conf., 1994, Hearts and Hands, VA Med. Ctr., 2001. Mem.: Ohio Psychol. Assn., Internat. Soc. Traumatic Stress Studies. Avocations: exercise, reading, travel. Home: 76 Ghasset Dr Hudson OH 44236 Office: VA Med Ctr 10000 Brecksville Rd Brecksville OH 44141

DONOVAN, BILLY, university basketball coach; b. May 30, 1965; m. Christine D'Auria; children: William, Hasbrouck, Bryan. BA, Providence Coll., 1987. Profl. basketball player N.Y. Knicks, NBA, 1987-88; grad. asst. coach U. Ky., Lexington, 1989-90, asst. coach, 1990-93, assoc. coach, 1993-94; head coach Marshall U., 1994-96, U. Fla., Gainesville, 1996—. Named Nat. Rookie Coach of Yr., Basketball Times, 1994, W.Va. Coll. Coach of Yr., 1994, So. Conf. Coach of Yr., 1994. Office: U Fla Basketball Office PO Box 14485 Gainesville FL 32604-2485

DONOVAN, BRIAN, freelance/self-employed journalist; b. Syracuse, N.Y., Mar. 11, 1941; children: Gregg, Becky. BA, Syracuse U., 1963. With Dem. and Chronicle, Rochester, NY, 1964—67; investigative reporter Newsday,

Melville, NY, 1967—2001. Recipient Pulitzer Prize for investigative reporting, 1995, George Polk award for Nat. Reporting, 1980, John Hancock award for Fin. Reporting, 1985, others. E-mail: briandonovan26@hotmail.com.

DONOVAN, BRUCE ELLIOT, literature educator, dean; b. Lawrence, Mass., Mar. 8, 1937; s. Harry Albert and Ruth Hannah (Kent) D.; m. Doris Louise Stearn, Sept. 7, 1959; children: Gregory Stearn, Erika Ruth. AB, Brown U., 1959; postgrad., U. Bristol, Eng., 1959-60; MA, Yale U., 1961, PhD, 1965; postgrad., Rutgers Center for Alcohol Studies, 1976. Instr. Yale U., 1962-65; from instr. to prof. classics Brown U., Providence, 1965—2003, assoc. dean for chem. dependency, 1977—2003, dean freshmen and sophomores, 1981-87, assoc. dean coll., 1977—2003. Instr. summer sch. alcohol studies Rutgers U.; cons. on collegiate alcoholism and other drug abuse. Author: Euripides Papyri from Oxyrhynchus, 1969; author articles and revs. on ancient Greek lit. and alcohol and other drug issues. Bd. dirs. Vols. in Action, 1975-90, R.I. Coun. on Alcoholism and Other Drug Dependence, 1973-94, New Eng. Inst. Alcohol Studies, 1978-91; founding mem. New Eng. Coll. Alcohol Network, Academics Recovering Together; steering com. Network Colls. and Univs. Committed to the Elimination of Substance Abuse, 1988-93. Fulbright fellow, 1959-60; Woodrow Wilson fellow, 1960-61; fellow Center for Hellenic Studies, Washington, 1971-72 Mem. Am. Philol. Assn., Assn. Recovery Sch. Home: 261 President Ave Providence RI 02906-5537 E-mail: bruce_donovan@brown.edu.

DONOVAN, DAVID P., lawyer; b. June 26, 1958; BS with honors, Iowa State Univ., 1980; JD magna cum laude, Georgetown Univ., 1984. Bar: DC 1984, Va. 2002, US Supreme Ct. Law clk. Judge Thomas A. Flannery, US Dist. Ct. (DC dist.), 1984—85; ptnr., comml. litigation, product liability practices, co-chmn. recruiting com. Wilmer Cutler Pickering Hale & Dorr, McLean, Va. Editor (in chief): Georgetown Univ. Law Jour.; contbr. articles to profl. jours. Recipient Pro Bono award, NAACP Legal Def. & Edn. Fund, 1992. Mem.: ABA, Def. Rsch. Inst., DC Bar Assn., Phi Beta Kappa. Office: Wilmer Cutler Pickering Hale & Dorr Suite 1000 1600 Tysons Blvd Mc Lean VA 22102 Office Fax: 703-251-9760, 703-251-9797. Business E-Mail: david.donovan@wilmerhale.com.

DONOVAN, DAVID WILLIAM, physics professor, researcher; b. Framingham, Mass., Oct. 16, 1960; s. William Patrick and Doris Lorrain Donovan. BS in Physics and Math., Hampden-Sydney Coll., 1982; PhD in Physics, Pa. State U., 1991. Vis. asst. prof. physics Norwich U., Northfield, Vt., 1991—92; vis. rsch. assoc. Materials Rsch. Lab., Pa. State U., State College, 1992; asst. prof. physics No. Mich. U., Marquette, 1992—97, assoc. prof. physics, 1997—2003, prof. physics, 2003—. Grantee, NSF, 1997-2002. Mem.: Am. Assn. of Physics Tchrs., Am. Phys. Soc., Pi Mu Epsilon, Chi Beta Phi, Sigma Xi, Omicron Delta Kappa, Phi Beta Kappa, Alpha Chi Sigma. Roman Catholic. Avocations: reading, trivia games, star gazing, movies, sports. Home: 713 Northland Dr Marquette MI 49855 Office: No Mich Univ Dept Physics 1401 Presque Isle Ave Marquette MI 49855 Office Phone: 906-227-2453. Business E-Mail: ddonovan@nmu.edu.

DONOVAN, DENNIS DALE, priest; b. Nyack, NY, Feb. 26, 1954; s. Thomas A. and Helen I. (Rudolph) D. BA in Philosophy, Don Bosco Coll., 1977; MA in Theology, MDiv in Theology, Pontifical Coll. Josephinum, 1983. Joined Soc. St. Francis de Sales, Roman Cath. Ch., 1973, ordained priest, 1983; cert. tchr. N.Y., N.J. Asst. adminstr. Salesian Sch., Goshen, N.Y., 1983-85; adminstr. Salesian Ctr., Columbus, Ohio, 1985-94, vicar, 1998—2004; dir. devel. Salesians of Don Bosco Province of St. Philip the Apostle, New Rochelle, N.Y., 1994-98; assoc. pastor St. Anthony Ch., Nanuet, N.Y., 1994-98; vicar Salesian Provincial House, New Rochelle, N.Y., 1994-98, Salesian Ctr., Columbus, Ohio, 1998—2004; assoc. pastor St. Joseph Cathedral, Columbus, Ohio, 1998—2004, St. Catherine Ch., Bexley, Ohio, 2002—04. Assoc., youth min. St. Andrew Parish, Upper Arlington, Ohio, 1985-94; mem. Nat. Cath. Devel. Conf., 1995—; chmn. Ea. province Salesian Centennial Com., 1995-98; mem. youth commn. adv. bd. City Columbus, Ohio, 2001-04, youth adv. commn. Cath. Diocese of Columbus, Ohio, 2003-04. Chaplain Ohio Senate, Columbus, 1987-94, 2002-04, Don Bosco Ladies Guild, Larchmont, NY, 1994-98; trustee Salesian Boys and Girls Club Columbus, 1993-04, Boys & Girls Club, Tampa Bay, 2004-; active Juvenile Delinquency Task Force, Franklin County, 1988-90, Westchester chpt. Crohn's and Colitis Found. Am., 1980-2000, Ctrl. Ohio chpt., 2000-04; exec. dir. Salesian Boys and Girls Club, Columbus, Ohio, 1998-2004; mem. Profl. Adv. Coun. United Way Franklin County, Columbus, 1998-2004, Ohio Alliance of Boys & Girls Clubs, 1998-2004; growth and measurement best practices task force Boys & Girls Clubs Am., Atlanta, 2002—; bd. trustees Discovery Dist. Devel. Corp., Columbus, 1998-2004; race rels. vision coun. United Way Franklin County, 1999-2003, Columbus Met. Area Ch. Coun., 1999-2004; mem. Columbus Truancy Task Force, 2000-02; blue ribbon panel Jefferson Awards, Columbus, 2003-04, treas. Mary Help of Christians Sch., Tampa, 2004—, dir. Mary Help of Christians Boys & Girls Club, Tampa, 2004—; assoc. pastor Good Shepherd RC Ch., Tampa, 2005-. Recipient Senate Resolution award Ohio Senate, 1988. Mem. Acad. Boys & Girls Club Profls., Nat. Soc. Fundraising Execs., Am. Guild Organists (bd. dirs., chaplain 1986-2004), KC (chaplain 1987-2004), Assn. Boys and Girls Clubs Profls. (disting. exec. level); mem. cmty. adv. bd. Jr. League of Columbus, 2001-04). Business E-Mail: frdennis@maryhelptampa.org.

DONOVAN, DENNIS M., manufacturing executive; b. Mass. BA, MBA, Univ. Mass.; JD, Western New Eng. Coll. of Law Sch. Various positions including v.p. human resources Gen. Electric Co., 1972—98; sr. v.p. human resources Raytheon Co., 1998—2001; exec. v.p. human resources Home Depot, 2001—. Industrial rels. com. U.S. Coun. for Internat. Bus.; bd. advisors Employment Policy Found., Ctr. for Adv. Human Resources Studies, Human Resource Inst.; bd. dirs. Job's for Am. Grad., Inc. Recipient HR Exec. of the Yr., Human Resources Exec. Mag. Fellow: Nat. Acad. of Human Resources (bd. dirs.); mem.: Personnel Roundtable, Human Resources Policy Inst., Human Resources Roundtable Group, Cowdrick Group. Office: The Home Depot Inc 2455 Paces ferry Rd N W Atlanta GA 30339-4024*

DONOVAN, DIANNE FRANCYS, journalist; b. Houston, Sept. 30, 1948; d. James Henry and Doris Elaine (Simerly) D.; m. Anthony Charles Burba; children: Donovan Anthony, James Donovan. Student, Trinity Coll., Dublin, Ireland, 1969; BA, Spring Hill Coll., 1970; MA, U. Mo., 1975, U. Chgo., 1982. Fgn./nat. copy desk supr. Chgo. Tribune, 1979-80, asst. editor for news/features, 1980-83, lit. editor, 1985-93, mem. editl. bd., 1993-99, sr. editor for recruitment, 2000—02; v.p., editl. page editor The Balt. Sun, 2002—. Vis. prof. U. Oreg. Sch. Journalism, Eugene, 1983-85; adj. faculty Northwestern U. Sch. Journalism, 1980-81, 89-90; bd. dirs. Chgo. Tribune Found. Bd. dirs. Nelson Algren/Heartland lit. awards, Chgo., 1986-93; judge Nat. Headliners' Club Awards, Atlantic City, N.J., 1983. Recipient award for editl. writing Am. Soc. Newspaper Editors, 1999, Media award Chgo. Bar Assn., 1999. Episcopalian. Office: 501 N Calvert St Baltimore MD 21278

DONOVAN, GEORGE JOSEPH, transportation executive, consultant; b. Jersey City, Apr. 15, 1935; s. Matthew T. and Jean (Wilson) D.; m. Susan M. Tamborini; children— Marybeth, George Joseph Jr., Amy BS in Chemistry, St. Peter's Coll., Jersey City; postgrad. in organic chemistry, Seaton Hall U.; postgrad. in fin. and mktg., NYU; postgrad. in internat. relations, U. Pa. Research chemist Reaction Motors, Inc., Denville, N.J., 1956-58; research and devel. tech. rep. Thiokol Corp., Washington, 1961-63, asst. mgr. midwest regional office, 1963-65, mgr., dir. aerospace mktg., 1965-74, asst. to pres., 1974-75, corp. dir. mktg., 1975-77, v.p., 1977-82; dep. asst. sec. for systems Office of Asst. Sec. Air Force for Research Devel. and Logistics, Washington, 1983-85, prin. dep. asst. sec., 1985-86; pres. Prime Resources, 1986-87; v.p. Washington ops. Tex. Instruments Inc., 1988-91; v.p. govtl. rels. Smiths Industries, 1991—2003, Prime Resources, 2003—. Cons. to industry and govt., Def. Sci. Bd.; mem. Naval Rsch. Adv. Com.; bd. dirs. USO Capital, Smith Aerospace. Patentee liquid and solid propellant ingredients and formulations (13); contbr. articles to profl. jours. Recipient Exceptional Civilian Svc. award USAF. Mem. AIAA, Navy League, Air Force Assn. (bd. dirs.), Navy League (exec. com.), Assn. US Army, Navy League (bd. dirs.), Nat. Def. Indsl. Assn. (bd. dirs., chmn. pub. policy com.), Congl. Country Club. Avocations: hunting, fishing, golf, boating, reading. Home: 4632 Charleston Ter NW Washington DC 20007-1900 Business E-Mail: g.gjdonovan@verizon.net.

DONOVAN, GERALD ALTON, retired academic administrator, retired dean; b. Hartford, Conn., Feb. 10, 1925; s. Gerald Joseph and Alice Gertrude (Gleason) D.; m. Barbara Ann Hue, Feb. 1, 1948; children: Deborah E. (Mrs. Alan Abare), Clayton H., Bruce G. BA, U. Conn., 1950, MS, 1952; PhD, Iowa State U., 1955. Poultry nutritionist Charles Pfizer & Co., Inc., Terre Haute, Ind., 1955-60; prof., chmn. poultry sci. dept. U. Vt., 1960-66; asso. dir. U. Vt. (Vt. Agrl. Expt. Sta.); asso. dean Coll. Agr. and Home Econs., U. Vt., 1966-73; dean Coll. Resource Devel., U. R.I., Kingston, 1973-89, dir. Internat. Ctr. Marine Resource Devel., 1975-89, ret., 1989—; exec. dir. Northeastern Region Aquaculture Ctr., Southeastern Mass. U., 1988-90, ret., 1990. Mem. U.S. AID/BIFAD Joint Research Council, 1979-83. Contbr. articles to profl. jours. Bd. dirs. Vt. C.C., 1970-73, Operation Clean Govt., 1997—; tech. specialist AARP-Tax Aide Program, 1993-2001; chairperson Narragansett Rep. Com., 1991-93; vol. tax cons. to the elderly. With USN, 1943-46. Mem. Am. Inst. Nutrition, Agrl. Research Inst., Assn. Agrl. Expt. Sta. Dirs., Sigma Xi, Alpha Zeta, Alpha Gamma Rho. Home: 65 Wyndcliff Dr Saunderstown RI 02874-2408

DONOVAN, HELEN W., newspaper editor; Graduated from, Mount Holyoke Coll., 1969. Exec. editor Boston Globe, 1993—. Adv. bd., Nat. Arts Journalism Program. Office: Boston Globe Newspapers PO Box 2378 Boston MA 02107-2378*

DONOVAN, JAMES ALBERT, writer, consultant, volunteer; b. Utica, N.Y., Jan. 20, 1949; s. James Hubert and Esther (Moretti) D.; m. Janet Ann Liesch, Apr. 19, 1974; children: Kelly, Katie. BA, Wadhams Hall Sem. Coll., 1972. Dir. campaign United Way, Utica, N.Y., 1972-74; dir. devel. United Negro Coll. Fund, N.Y.C., 1975-77, Tusculum Coll., Greenville, Tenn., 1977-78; asst. dir. devel. East Tenn. State U., Johnson City, 1978-80; dir. devel., exec. dir. U. Central Fla. Found., Orlando, 1980-84; assoc. v.p. devel. Clemson U., S.C., 1985—. Author: Take the Fear out of Asking for Major Gifts, 50 Ways to Motivate Your Board. Trustee Wadhams Hall Sem. Coll.; bd. dirs. Human Rights Inst., St. Thomas U., Miami. Recipient Gov.'s award Am. Legion Boys State, 1967. Mem. Nat. Soc. Fund Raising Execs. (founder Central Fla. chpt. 1982). Republican. Roman Catholic. Avocations: photography, golf, jogging. Home: 415 Flatwood Dr Winter Springs FL 32708-6149 Office: Donovan Mgmt Inc PO Box 195068 Winter Springs FL 32719-5068

DONOVAN, JAMES M., librarian, anthropologist; b. Chattanooga, Ten., June 6, 1959; s. Dennis Howard Donovan and Yvonne Marie Fino. BA, U. Tenn., Chattanooga, 1981; M of Libr. Info. Scis., La. State U., 1989; PhD U., Tulane U., 1994; JD, Loyola University, New Orleans, LA, 2000—03; MA, La. State U., 2000. Libr. asst. Chattanooga-Hamilton County Bicentennial Libr., Chattanooga, 1978—84; libr. Tulane Law Libr., New Orleans, 1985—96; libr. Law Library U. Ga., 2003—. Contbr. articles to profl. jours.; author: Anthropology and Law, 2003. Chair Mayor's Adv. Com. for Lesbian, Gay, Bisexual and Transgender Issues, New Orleans, 1998—99; bd. dirs. AIDSLaw of La., New Orleans, 2001—03. Mem.: Am. Assn. Law Librs., Am. Anthropol. Assn., Pi Kappa Alpha. None. Home: 2360 W Broad St Apt R1 Athens GA 30606 Office: U Ga Law Libr Athens GA 30602 Office Phone: 706-542-5077. Personal E-mail: JamesMDonovan@aol.com.

DONOVAN, JAMES MICHAEL, history educator; b. Huntington, N.Y., Aug. 11, 1948; s. Michael James and Beverly Ann (Martin) D. BA, Yankton (S.D.) Coll., 1971; MA, N.Mex. State U., 1977; PhD, Syracuse U., 1982. Asst. prof. history Pa. State U., Mont Alto, 1983-92, assoc. prof. history, 1992—2002. Contbr. articles to profl. jours. Tutor, Hanover Area (Pa.) Literacy Coun., 1992-02. Mem. Am. Hist. Assn., Soc. for French Hist. Studies, Western Soc. for French History, Nat. Assn. of Scholars, Phi Alpha Theta, Am. Soc. for Legal History. Office: Pa State Univ Dept Of History Mont Alto PA 17237 E-mail: jmd9@psu.edu.

DONOVAN, JAMES ROBERT, business equipment company executive; b. Wichita, Kans., Apr. 11, 1932; s. Karl Genevay and Louise (Silcott) D.; m. Ottille Schreiber, July 2, 1955; children: Amy Louise, Robert Silcott; m. Margaret Jones Esty, Ot. 31, 1981. AB, Harvard U., 1954, MBA, 1956. Mgr. sales adminstrn., market rschr. Hickok, Inc., Rochester, N.Y., 1956-59, reginal sales mgr., 1959-62, asst. nat. sales mgr., 1963-65; group program mgr. Xerox Corp., Stamford, Conn., 1965-68, mktg. mgr. spl. products, 1968-70, mgr. copier products, 1970-72, dir. corp. pricing and competitive activity, 1972-78, dir. corp. mktg. strategy and planning, 1978-83; sr. v.p. corp. mktg. McDonnell Douglas Automation Co., St. Louis, 1983-84; v.p. mktg. and planning info. sys. group McDonnell Douglas Corp., St. Louis, 1984-87; pres. Bus. Adv. Svcs., Inc., Naples, Fla., 1987—. Vice pres. Family Svc., Rochester, 1971-72; dir. Family and Children's Svcs., Stamford, 1972-79; mem. mktg. adv. bd. Columbis U. Bus. Sch., 1978-86; v.p. United Way New Canaan, 1982-83; bd. dirs. Family Svc. Am., 1986-91. Mem. Harvard U. Alumni Assn. (bd. dirs. 1978-83), Harvard U. Bus. Sch. Alumni Assn. (bd. dirs. 1982-85), Pelican Bay Property Owners Assn. (bd. dirs. 1994—), Harvard Club (pres. Rochester 1971-72, pres. Fairfield County 1976-78, pres. St. Louis 1986-87, pres. Naples 1991-93), Harvard Bus. Sch. Club (pres. Rochester 1972, chmn. Westchester/Fairfield 1973-74), Woodway Country Club (Darien, Conn.), Club at Palican Bay, Hole-in-Wall Country Club.

DONOVAN, JOHN ARTHUR, lawyer; b. N.Y.C., Apr. 11, 1942; children: Lara, Alex. AB, Harvard U., 1965; JD, Fordham Law Sch., 1967. Bar: N.Y. 1967, U.S. Tax. Ct. 1968, U.S. Ct. Appeals (2nd cir), 1968, U.S. Dist. Ct. (so., no. dists.) N.Y. 1969, U.S. Supreme Ct. 1971, U.S. Ct. Appeals (10th cir.) 1972, U.S. Ct. Appeals (9th cir.) 1976, Calif. 1982, U.S. Dist. Ct. (so., no. dists.) Calif. 1982, U.S. Ct. Appeals (5th cir.) 1983, Alaska 1993. Assoc. Hughes, Hubbard & Reed, N.Y.C., 1967-74, ptnr. N.Y.C., L.A., 1974-85, Skadden, Arps, Slate, Meagher & Flom, L.A., 1985—. Mem. adj. faculty law sch. U. So. Calif., L.A., 1986-87. Office: Skadden Arps Slate Meagher & Flom 300 S Grand Ave Ste 3400 Los Angeles CA 90071-3109

DONOVAN, NOWELL, academic administrator; BS, King Edwards VII Sch.; PhD, U. Newcastle-upon-Tyne. Faculty U. Newcastle-upon-Tyne, Okla. State U.; joined faculty Tex. Christian U., Ft. Worth, 1986, provost, vice chancellor, 2004—. Contbr. articles to profl. jours. Recipient I. Leverson award, Am. Assn. Petroleum Geologists. Office: Provost and Vice Chancellor Acad Affairs TCU Box 297040 Fort Worth TX 76129

DONOVAN, RICHARD EDWARD, lawyer; b. Cleve., Dec. 3, 1952; s. Richard A. and Eileen (Karthaus) D.; m. Ellen Brode, June 16, 1979; children: Colin, Ryan Michael, Patrick. BS, U. Notre Dame, 1974; JD, Rutgers U., 1977. Bar: N.Y. 1978, U.S. Dist. Ct. (ea. dist.) N.Y. 1978, N.J. 1985, U.S. Dist. Ct. N.J. 1985, U.S. Ct. Appeals (2d cir.) 1987, U.S. Supreme Ct. 1990. Assoc. Breed, Abbott & Morgan, N.Y.C., 1977-80, Kelley, Drye & Warren LLP, N.Y.C., 1980-86, ptnr., 1987—. Mem. ABA, Assn. Bar City N.Y. (com. prof. and jud. ethics 1996-99), N.J. Bar Assn., Rutgers Alumni Coun., N.Y. State Bar Assn. (sec. comml. and fed. litigation sect. 1988-90), Fed. Bar Coun., Assn. Fed. Bar N.J. Home: 61 Oak Ridge Ave Summit NJ 07901-4306 Office: Kelley Drye & Warren LLP 101 Park Ave New York NY 10178 Office Phone: 212-808-7800. E-mail: rdonovan@kelleydrye.com.

DONOVAN, ROBERT ALAN, language educator; b. Chgo., Sept. 27, 1921; s. John Elmer and Dorothy (Dickey) D.; m. Hope Elaine Taussig, Sept. 15, 1942; children: Faith, Peter Alan, Brian Roger. PhB, U. Chgo., 1948, MA, 1950; PhD, Washington U., St. Louis, 1953. Instr. English Cornell U., Ithaca, N.Y., 1953-56, asst. prof., 1956-62; prof. English SUNY, Albany, 1962-91, prof. emeritus, 1991—, chmn. dept. English, 1981-84. Author: The Shaping Vision: Imagination in the English Novel from Defoe to Dickens, 1966; contbr. articles to profl. jours. Sgt. U.S. Army, 1942-46, ETO. Mem.: MLA, Phi Beta Kappa. Office: SUNY Dept English Albany NY 12222-0001 Home: 214 Glen Eddy Dr Niskayuna NY 12309

DONOVAN, TIMOTHY JAMES, school system administrator; b. Bay Shore, N.Y. s. Thomas James and Elizabeth Donovan; m. Mary Margaret Stadler. BS in Speech Comm., No. Ariz. U., 1993; EdM in Curriculum and Instrn., Loyola Coll. of Md., 2001. Cert. secondary social studies tchr. Md. Tchr. Rosa Parks-St. Ambrose, Balt., 1993—94, St. Frances Acad., Balt., 1994—2003; dir. Lasallian programs, assoc. edn. dir. Bros. of the Christian Schs.-Balt. Dist., 2003—. Lasallian animator St. Frances Acad., Balt., 1995—2003. Editor: (newspaper) Together and By Association, 2003—, (website) FSC Baltimore.org, 2003—. Vol. Campuchin Franciscan Vol. Corps, Balt., 2003—04; mem. Regional Edn. Bd., Landover, Md., 2003—; bd. dirs. Dist. Mission Coun., Adamstown, Md., 2004—. Mem.: Lasallian Leadership Inst. Office: Balt Dist Edn Office 3225 Wilkens Ave Baltimore MD 21229 Office Phone: 410-644-4784. Business E-Mail: donovan@fsc.baltimore.org.

DONOVAN, TIMOTHY R., automotive executive, lawyer; b. 1955; BS, Ohio State U.; JD cum laude, Capital U., Columbus, OH, 1981. Bar: 1981. Assoc. Jenner & Block, ptnr., 1989—99, chmn. corp. securities group; sr. v.p. Tenneco Automotive Inc., Lake Forest, Ill., 1999—2001, gen. counsel, 1999—, exec. v.p., 2001—, mng. dir. internat. group, 2001—. Dir. John B. Sanfilippo Sons Inc. Mem.: Chgo. Bar Assn. (securities law com.), ABA. Office: Tenneco Automotive Inc 500 N Field Dr Lake Forest IL 60045*

DONOVAN, WILLARD PATRICK, retired elementary school educator; b. Grand Rapids, Mich., Sept. 1, 1930; s. Willard Andrew and Thelma Alfreda (Davis) D.; m. Dorothy Jane Nester, Nov. 27, 1954 (dec. May 1981); children: Cindy Jane, Kimberly Sue. BS, Ea. Mich. U., 1965, MA, 1969. Cert. grades K-8, Mich. Enlisted U.S. Army, 1947, advanced through grades to master sgt., 1953; platoon sgt. U.S. Army of Occupation, Korea, 1947-48, 1948-50, U.S. Army Korean War Svc., 1950-51; ret. U.S. Army, 1964; pharm. sales Nat. Drug Co., Detroit, 1964-66; tchr. Cromie Elem. Sch. Warren (Mich.) Consol. Schs., 1966—, ret., 1995. Reading textbook and curriculum devel. com. Warren (Mich.) Consol. Schs., 1969-73, sci. com., 1970-95; curriculum and textbook com. Macomb County Christian Schs., Warren, 1982-95. Decorated Combat Infantry badge U.S. Army, Korea, 1947-50, Purple heart with three clusters, Korea-Japan Svc. medal, 1951, Presdl. citation, 1951, Korean medal with three campaign clusters, 1951, Nat. Def. Svc. medal, 1951, Bronze star, Silver star; Chosin few Army and Marines Assn. 31st Inf. Assn. Mem. NRA, Am. Quarterhouse Assn., Assn. U.S. Army, Detroit Area Coun. Tchrs. Math., Met. Detroit Sci. Tchrs. Assn., The Chosin Few (U.S. Army), Nat. Edn. Assn., Mich. Edn. Assn., Warren (Mich.) Edn. Assn., U.S. Army Assn. Avocations: theater, arts, horsemanship, travel, pistol shooting. Home: PO Box 563 8440 Mission Hills Arizona City AZ 85223

DONOVAN, WILLIAM ALAN, retired librarian; b. Rochester, N.Y., Jan. 29, 1937; s. Joseph Leo and Wilhelmina (Fawcett) D. BA, St. John Fisher Coll., 1958; MA, U. South Fla., 1981. Libr. Chgo. Pub. Libr., 1961—93. Cartoon gagwriter; contbr. articles and book revs. to profl. jours. With U.S. Army, 1958-61. Mem. ALA, Phi Kappa Phi, Beta Phi Mu. Roman Catholic. Home: 2233 Ednor St Port Charlotte FL 33952-4314 E-mail: proficient@myway.com.

DONOVAN-JOHNSON, D. J., artist, educator; b. Thayer, Kans., June 14, 1940; d. Lawrence R. and Pauline Rosilind (Shearer) Hague; m. John Thomas Donovan, June 4, 1960 (dec. 1969); 1 child, Erik; m. Gregory B. Johnson, Dec. 29, 1972; children: Ruthie, Julie. BS, Western Mich. U., 1962; MA, Wash. State U., 1965. Instr. pub. schs., Mont., Mich. and Wash. Juror for art shows; workshop instr. One-woman shows include Salmagundi Club, State of the Art, N.Y.C., Water Media U.S., Open Facet, Taos, N.Mex., Gallery of Interior, Washington, House Gallery, Oklahoma City, U. Denver, Colorado Springs Art Ctr., Art Expo/Calif., L.A., published in Award Winning Paintings, 1996, Floral Inspirations, 1998, one-woman shows include Mitchell Mus., Trinidad, Colo. Bd. dirs., founding pres. Flatirons Ctr. for Arts, Boulder, 1986-89;ch. sch. tchr. Calvary Bible Ch., Boulder, 1998—. Recipient Best of Boulder, Artist Choice award Daily Camera, 1992, Wash. State W.S. award, 1994, Kans. State W.S. award, 1994, Red River W.S. Silver medal award, 1994. Mem. Nat. Painters in Casein and Acrylic, Nat. League Am. Pen Women, Studio Six Artists Coop. (founding mem.). Avocations: platform tennis, reading, travel. Home: 225 Bristlecone Way Boulder CO 80304-0467 Office Phone: 303-449-1692.

DONSON, ANDREW C., history professor; b. Tarrytown, N.Y., Apr. 8, 1968; s. Theodore Bertram and Gail Ann (Grollman) Donson; m. Erin Holman, June 11, 2005. BA, Cornell U., Ithaca, N.Y., 1991; MA, U. Mich., Ann Arbor, 1995, PhD, 2000. Vis. asst. prof. U. Nev., Reno, 2000—01, Marquette U., History Dept., Milw., 2001—04, U. Mass., German Dept., Amherst, 2004—. Office: Univ Mass 161 Presidents Dr Amherst MA 01003

DONZIS, PAUL BENNETT, lawyer, finance educator, ophthalmologist, educator; b. LA, Calif., July 7, 1956; s. Harold Kritt and Julia Bernice Donzis; m. Robin Carla Donzis, Aug. 29, 1999; children: Elizabeth, Lauren. BA, Princeton U., Princeton, NJ, 1978; MD, Washington U., Saint Louis, Mo., 1982; MBA, William Howard Taft U., Santa Ana, Calif., 1999; JD with honors, Law Office Judges Chamber Study Program, LA, 2000. Bar: Calif. 2000, US Dist. Ct. (ctrl. dist. Calif.) 2000, US Ct. Appeals (9th Cir.) 2000. Ophthalmologist Eye Inst. Marina Del Rey, Calif., 1988—; atty. Vialla & Donzis, LA, 2000—. Assoc. clin. prof. medicine UCLA, Calif., 1986—; prof. bus. William Howard Taft U., Santa Ana, Calif., 2002—. Contbr. over 40 sci. articles, papers, book chpts. in field. Heed fellowship, Heed Opthalmic Found., 1987. Mem.: ABA, Am. Trial Lawyers Assn., Am. Acad. Ophthalmology. Avocations: photography, tennis, golf. Office: Paul Donzis MD ESQ 4644 Lincoln Blvd Ste 102 Marina Del Rey CA 90292 Office Phone: 310-822-0022. Business E-Mail: pdonzis@donziseye.com.

DOODY, AGNES G., communications educator, management and communication consultant; b. New Haven; d. Daniel M. and Carrie Mae (Goodrich) D.; m. Arthur D. Jeffrey, Dec. 22, 1962 (dec. Sept. 1985); children: Andrew N., Jill; m. Ellis H. Maris, Jr., June 28, 1991. BA, Emerson Coll., 1952; MA, Pa. State U., 1954, PhD, 1961; cert. program on negotiation, Harvard U. Prof. communications U. R.I., Kingston, 1958—; pres. Arthur Assocs. Bd. dirs., co-chairperson PierBank, Narragansett, R.I., 1994. Mem. Soc. Profls. in Dispute Resolution, Internat. Comm. Assn., Nat. Comm. Assn., Ea. Comm. Assn. (pres. 1967-68), Rotary (newsletter editor Wakefield 1989-90). Avocations: photography, travel, gardening. Home: One Post Rd Wakefield RI 02879

DOODY, JOHN, lawyer; b. Bklyn., 1964; BS, Bklyn. Coll. CUNY, 1989; JD, Fordham U., 1992. Bar: NY 1993, Conn. 1993, US Dist. Ct. So., Ea., & No. Districts NY, US Ct. Appeals 2nd Cir. Ptnr. Wilson, Elser, Moskowitz, Edelman & Dicker LLP, NYC. Office: Wilson Elser Moskowitz Edelman & Dicker LLP 23rd Fl 150 E 42nd St New York NY 10017-5639 Office Phone: 212-490-3000 ext. 2107. Office Fax: 212-490-3038. Business E-Mail: doodyj@wemed.com.

DOODY, LOUIS CLARENCE, JR., retired accountant; b. New Orleans, Feb. 5, 1940; s. Louis Clarence and Elsie Clair (Connors) D.; m. Barbara Virginia Pettett, Oct. 9, 1982; children by previous marriage: Dana Lori, Mary Lyn, Kathleen Louise. BCS, Tulane U., 1963. CPA, La., Tex., Miss. Acct. Louis C. Doody, C.P.A., 1963-68; ptnr. Doody and Doody, C.P.A.'s, Metairie, La., 1969—. Mem. AICPA, La. Soc. CPA's. Home: 36 Cypress Rd Covington LA 70433-4306 Address: PO Box 1000 Covington LA 70434

DOODY, MARGARET ANNE, English language educator; b. St. John, N.B., Can., Sept. 21, 1939; came to U.S., 1976; d. Hubert and Anne Ruth (Cornwall) D. BA, Dalhousie U., Can., 1960; BA with 1st class hons., Lady

Margaret Hall-Oxford U., Eng., 1962, MA, 1965, D.Phil., 1968; LLD (hon.), Dalhousie U., 1985. Instr. English U. Victoria (B.C., Can.), 1962-64, asst. prof. English, 1968-69; lectr. Univ. Coll. Swansea, Wales, 1969-76; assoc. prof. English U. Calif.-Berkeley, 1976-80; prof. English dept. Princeton U., N.J., 1980-89; Andrew W. Mellon prof. humanities, prof. English Vanderbilt U., Nashville, 1989-99, dir. comparative lit. program, 1992-99; John and Barbara Glyn Family prof. lit. U. Notre Dame, 2000—, dir. PhD in Lit. program, 2001—. Author: A Natural Passion: A Study of the Novels of Samuel Richardson, 1974, The Daring Muse: Augustan Poetry Reconsidered, 1985, Frances Burney: The Life in the Works, 1988, The True Story of the Novel, 1996, (novels) Aristotle Detective, 1978, The Alchemists, 1980, Aristotle e la giustizia poetica, 2000, Aristotle and Poetic Justice, 2002, Poison in Athens, 2004, Mysteries of Eleusis, 2005; author: (with F. Stuber) (play) Clarissa, 1984; editor (with Peter Sabor): Samuel Richardson Tercentenary Essays, 1989; co-editor (with Douglas Murray): Catharine and Other Writings by Jane Austen, 1993; co-editor: (with Wendy Barry and Mary Doody Jones) Anne of Green Gables, 1997. Guggenheim postdoctoral fellow, 1979; recipient Rose Mary Crawshay award Brit. Acad., 1986. Episcopalian. Office: U Notre Dame PhD in Literature Program Notre Dame IN 46556 Office Phone: 574-631-0465. Business E-Mail: mdoody@nd.edu.

DOODY, WILLIAM E., secondary school educator; b. Latrobe, Pa., Jan. 3, 1977; s. William D. and Romayne S. Doody. BA in History and Spanish, St. Vincent Coll., 1998; MA in Tchg., U. Pitts., 2000. H.S. tchr. Indiana (Pa.) Area Sch. Dist., 2000—. Instr. Westmoreland County C.C., Indiana, 2005—. Coun. mem. Pa. Hist. Assn., Harrisburg, 2004—05. Mem.: Am. Hist. Assn. Avocation: travel. Office Phone: 724-463-8562.

DOOGE, JAMES CLEMENT IGNATIUS, civil engineer, hydrologist; b. Birkenhead, Eng., July 30, 1922; s. Denis Patrick and Veronica Catherine (Carroll) D.; m. Roni O'Doherty, Nov. 25, 1946 (dec. Nov. 1991); children: Colm, Diarmuid, Cliona, Dara, Meliosa (dec. Feb. 2000). CBS, Dun Laoghaire; BE, BSc., Univ. Coll., Dublin, 1942, ME, 1952; MS, U. Iowa, 1956; DrAgrSci (hon.), U. Wageningen, 1978, DrTech (hon.), 1980; DSc (hon.), U. Birmingham, Eng., 1985, U. Dublin, 1988; D Engring. (hon.), Heriot-Watt U., 2000; Dr. (hon.), Cracow Tech. U., 2000; DSc (hon.), Nat. U., Ireland, 2001, Madrid, 2001. Jr. civil engr. Irish Office Pub. Works, 1943-46; design engr. E.S.B., 1946-58; prof. civil engring. Univ. Coll., Cork, Ireland, 1958-70, Dublin, 1970-81, 82-84; minister for fgn. affairs Ireland, 1981-82; leader Irish Senate, 1983-87; mem. Coun. of State, 1973-77. Recipient Horton award Am. Geophys. Union, 1959, Bowie medal, 1986, Ven Te Chow award ASCE, 1993, John Dalton medal European Geophys. Soc., 1998, Internat. Meteorology prize WMO, 1999. Mem. Instn. Civil Engrs. Ireland (pres. 1968-69, Kettle Premium and Plaque awards 1948, Mullins medal 1951, 62), Royal Irish Acad. (pres. 1987-90), Polish Acad. Sci. (fgn.), Russian Acad. Scis. (fgn.), Spanish Acad. Sci. (fgn.), Internat. Assn. Hydrological Scis. (pres. 1975-79), Internat. Coun. Sci. Unions (pres. 1993-96), Royal Acad. Engring. (fgn., Prince Philip Gold medal 2005). Roman Catholic. Home: 2 Belgrave Rd Monkstown County Dublin Ireland Office: U Coll Earlsfort Terr Dublin 2 Ireland

DOOLAN, WENDY, professional golfer; b. Sydney, Australia, Dec. 16, 1968; Winner LPGA Champions Classic, 2001, Welch's/Fry's Championships, 2003, Evian Masters, 2004. Competed Futures Tour, Women Profl. Golfers' European Tour, 1992—95, Asian Ladies Tour, 1993—95; rep. Australia seven times internat.; runner-up British Amateur Championships, 1991. Avocations: swimming, tennis. Office: c/o LPGA 100 International Golf Dr Daytona Beach FL 32124-1092

DOOLE, ROBERT JAMES, music educator; b. Columbia, Mo., Oct. 29, 1966; BA in Music Edn., Washburn U., Topeka, Kans.; MA in Music Edn., Kans. State U., Manhattan. Music educator Alma-Wabannsee HS, Alma, Kans., 1991—94, Royal Valley HS, Maretta, Kans., 1994—2002, Shawnee Heights, Tecumseh, Kans., 2002—. Choral dir. Westside Christian Ch., 1994—2002, Country Side Meth., 2002—04. Mem.: Am. Choral Dirs. Assn. Democrat. Baptist. Avocation: basketball. Home: 2921 SE Granger St Topeka KS 66605 E-mail: dooler1@cox.net.

DOOLEY, ALTON CLINE, JR., curator; b. Roanoke, Va., Mar. 4, 1969; s. Marjorie Ellen and Alton Cline Dooley, Pamela Dawn Dooley (Stepmother); m. Brett Samantha Kessler, June 12, 1994; 1 child, Timothy Connor. BA, Carleton Coll., Northfield, Minn., 1991; PhD, La. State U., 1998. Asst. curator of paleontology Va. Mus. of Natural History, Martinsville, 1999—. Achievements include description of new fossil whale species. Office: Va Mus of Natural History 1001 Douglas Ave Martinsville VA 24112 Office Phone: 276-666-8600. Business E-Mail: butchd@vmnh.net.

DOOLEY, ANN ELIZABETH, freelance writers cooperative executive, editor; b. Mpls., Feb. 19, 1952; d. Merlyn James and Susan Marie (Hinze) Dooley; m. John M. Dodge, May 8, 1983; children: Christopher Dooley Dodge, Kathryn Dooley Dodge. BA in Journalism, U. Wis., 1974. Free-lance journalist, 1974-75; photo editor C.W. Communications, Newton, Mass., 1975-77, writer, photographer, 1977-79; editor Computerworld O A, Framingham, Mass., 1979-83; editorial dir. Computerworld Focus, Framingham, 1983-92; pres. freelance writers coop. Dooley & Assocs., West Newbury, Mass., 1992—. Speaker, chmn. mem. editorial adv. bd. various computer confs. Mem. Pub. Relations Soc. Am., Women in Communications (sec. 1982-84). Democrat. Home and Office: 1 Old Parish Way West Newbury MA 01985-1222

DOOLEY, CALVIN MILLARD, former congressman; b. Visalia, Calif., Jan. 11, 1954; m. Linda Phillips; children: Brooke, Emily. BS, U. Calif., Davis, 1977; MA, Stanford U., 1987. Mem. U.S. Congresses from 17th Calif. dist., 1991-93, U.S. Congresses from 20th Calif. dist., 1993—2005; mem. agriculture com.; mem. natural resources com.; pres., CEO Nat. Food Processors Assn., Washington, 2005—. Democrat. Methodist. Office: Nat Food Processors Assn 1350 I St NW Ste 300 Washington DC 20005

DOOLEY, CRAIG IRWIN, entrepreneur; b. Dallas, July 10, 1951; s. Clyde Edward and Dorothy Louise Dooley; m. Linda Susan Bowman, Aug. 9, 1975; children: Ryan, Erin, Megan, Shannon. BBA, Sam Houston State U., Huntsville, Tex., 1977. Sales and mktg. staff IBM, 1977; project mgr. Gen. Homes, 1980; pres. Dooley Homes, 1985; stockbroker Merrill Lynch, 1986; area pres. Royce Homes, Inc., Houston, 1987-89; pres., CEO, Polybutylene Specialists, Inc., Spring, Tex., 1989-98; COO, Safe Home, Inc., Conroe, Tex., 1998—2002; pres., CEO Capital Recovery Group, 2002—. Scoutmaster, founder troop 136 Boy Scouts Am., Spring, 1988-98; life mem. Houston Livestock Show and Rodeo, 1991—; bd. dirs. Brisket Cases, Houston, 1992—; com. chmn. Houston Golf Assn., The Woodlands, Tex., 1996—. Named One of Top 25 Entrepreneurs of Yr., Ernst & Young, Houston, 1997; recipient Inc. 500 1997 award Inc. mag., 1997, Houston 100 award Houston Bus. Jour., 1997, Remodeler 100 award Remodeler mag., Houston, 1999. Mem. Sigma Phi Epsilon. Republican. Roman Catholic. Avocations: golf, tennis, travel, participating in his children's activities. Home: 5502 Linden Ct Spring TX 77379-8864 Office: Capital Recovery Group 14614 Falling Creek Ste 202 Houston TX 77068 Fax: 281-444-2497. E-mail: cidooley@hotmail.com.

DOOLEY, DONALD JOHN, retired publishing executive; b. Des Moines, Aug. 16, 1921; s. Martin and Anne Marguerite (Barger) D.; m. Beverly Frederick, Dec. 21, 1955 (div. 1977); children: Nancy Elizabeth, Katherine Anne(dec.), Mary Bridget, Robert Frederick; m. Patricia Connell, Dec. 28, 1996. BA, U. Iowa, 1947; postgrad., Drake U., 1949-50. Gen. Promotion and pub. relations mgr. Meredith Corp., Des Moines, 1953-59, dir. pub. relations, 1960-65; art and editorial dir. Better Homes & Gardens Books & Spl. Interest Publs., Des Moines, 1965-77; dir. editorial planning and devel. Better Homes and Gardens Books (Meredith Corp.), Des Moines, 1977-84; cons., 1985. Chmn. bd. adv. com. Sch. Vol. Program, Des Moines; steering com. Intercultural Affairs program to Desegregate Dist. Schs., 1975-77; treas. Iowa U. Parents Assn., 1977-79; bd. dirs. Iowa Cystic Fibrosis Found., 1979-87, v.p., 1981-85; trustee Citizens Scholarship Found. Am., 1976-85, Iowa Freedom of Info. Council, 1977-87; adv. bd. Adult and Community Edn., Des Moines Pub. Sch., 1982—99; cons. White House Conf. on Families, 1981. Officer USAAF, 1942-46. Decorated 2 battle stars; recipient Dorothy Dawe award Home Furnishings Industry, 1973. Mem. Pub. Rels. Soc. Am. (accredited, pres. chpt. 1969, dir. chpt. 1965-76), ACLU, Beyond War (co-dir. Iowa office 1987-88), Friendship Force, Ams. for Dem. Action, Sigma Nu (comdr. chpt. 1946-47), Found. for Global Community, 1991—. Clubs: Echo Valley Country. Democrat. Home and Office: 3711 Oak Creek Pl West Des Moines IA 50265-7968

DOOLEY, DOUGLAS JOHN, bank executive; b. Lakeview, Oreg., June 9, 1955; s. Delmer John and Thalia (Doty) D.; m. Stephanie Snyder McClain, May 20, 1978 (dec. Sept. 1996); children: Carolyn J., Justin S.; m. Cynthia Stix, Aug. 20, 2000; JC, Brittany Bennett. BS, Am. U., 1977; MBA, Columbia U., 1979. Investment rsch. Morgan Guaranty Trust Co., N.Y.C., 1979-84, v.p., 1983-94, portfolio mgr., 1984-90, dir. internat. rsch., 1986-90, emerging internat. markets mgr., head emerging internat. equity mgmt., 1990-2000, lead adv. global trusts JP Morgan Pvt. Bank, N.Y.C., 2000—, dir. external due diligence, 2002-05, portfolio mgr. internat. clients pvt. bank; mng. dir. J.P. Morgan Investment Mgmt., N.Y.C., 1994—. Mem. N.Y. Soc. Security Analysts. Office: JP Morgan Private Bank 345 Park Ave New York NY 10154 Office Phone: 212-464-1318. E-mail: doug@douglasdooley.com.

DOOLEY, JAMES C., newspaper editor, director of photography; m. Susan Levy; children: David, Marc, Steven, Thomas. From reporter to state editor The Ariz. Republic, 1966-78; photo assignment editor, dep. dir. photography L.A. Times, 1978-86; dir. photography Newsday, N.Y.C., 1986—. Office: Newsday Inc 235 Pinelawn Rd Melville NY 11747-4250 Office Phone: 631-843-2829. E-mail: james.dooley@newsday.com.

DOOLEY, JAMES H., product company executive; BS in Agrl. Engring., Calif. Poly., San Luis Obispo, 1971; M in Engring., U. Calif., Davis, 1972; PhD in Forest Resources/Forest Engring., U. Wash., 2000. Registered profl. engr., Hawaii, Wash. Dir. control and devel. Puna Papaya Inc., Keaau, Hawaii, 1973-77; mgr. nursery, seed orchard and greenhouse sys. unit-silvicultural engring. dept. Weyerhaeuser Co., Tacoma, 1977-82, biomech. engring unit, diversified r & d, 1982-85, dir. rsch. and engring., nursery products div., 1986-89, product engring. mgr., sensor and simulation products div., 1989-90, program mgr., corp. r & d div., 1991-94, interim mgr. strategic biol. scis. program, 1994-95; pres., CEO Silverbrook Ltd., Federal Way, Wash., 1995—. Exptl. sta. com. on orgn. and policy Nat. Assn. State U. and Land Grant Colls., 1986, plant biol. engring., strategic planning com., 1989-94; task force on univ., industry and govt. coop. ASAE, 1989; emerging technologies devel. com. ASAE, 1994-95; emerging technologies adv. com. chair ASAE, 1995-96; adv. com. past chmn. biol. engring ASAE, 1992-93; engring and tech. accreditation com. ASAE, 1984—; comprehensive review team U.S. Dept. Agr., Coop. State Rsch. Svc., Auburn U., 1989, Pa. State U., 1991, U. Ga., 1993; adv. com. forest biology project Inst. Paper Sci. Tech., 1994; adv. group biol. engring. program indsl. adv. group Wash. State U., 1994—, agrl. engring. dept. Calif.Poly, 1992—; engring. accreditation commn. ABET, 1990-95, sec., 2005; presenter in field Contbr. articles to profl. jours., local newspapers. Recipient Am. Soc. Agrl. Engrs. fellow award, 1996. Fellow Am. Soc. Agrl. Engrs. (Pres. Citation, 1994, Dirs. award, 1994, Dir. Citation, 1996, Fellow award 1996); mem. Inst. Biol. Engring. (pres. 2000), Licensing Execs. Soc. Achievements include patents for a Seed Planter a double-row vacuum precision sower for foresty and other densely planted seeds, Seed Supply Sytem for Multiple Row Sower a method of ensuring all rows of a sower run out of seed at the same time, engineered wood structure for watershed restoration, wood-strand erosion control material. Address: 1911 SW Campus Dr # 545 Federal Way WA 98023-6473 Office Phone: 253-838-4759. E-mail: jdooley@seanet.com.

DOOLEY, JOHN AUGUSTINE, III, state supreme court justice; b. Nashua, N.H., Apr. 10, 1944; s. John A. and Edna Elizabeth (Elwell) D.; m. Sandra C. Sapp, Dec. 19, 1970 BS, Union Coll., 1965; LLB, Boston Coll., 1968. Bar: Vt. 1968. Law clk. to presiding judge U.S. Dist. Ct. Vt., 1968-69; asst. dir. Vt. Legal Aid, 1969-72, dir., 1972-78; legal counsel to gov. of Vt., 1985; sec. of adminstrn. State of Vt., 1985-87; assoc. justice Vt. Supreme Ct., 1987—. Part-time U.S. magistrate for Vt., from 1971. Co-author: Cases and Materials on Urban Poverty Law, 1974. Mem. Vt. Bar Assn. Office: Vt Supreme Ct 109 State St Montpelier VT 05609-0001

DOOLEY, MICHAEL P., law educator; b. Iowa City, 1939; BA, U. Iowa, 1960, JD, 1963. Bar: Iowa 1963, N.Y. 1964, Ill. 1971, Va. 1979. Assoc. Dewey, Ballantine, Bushby, Palmer & Wood, 1963-68; assoc. prof. U. Ill., 1968-71, prof., 1971-72; vis. prof. U. Va., 1971-72, prof., 1972-80, Doherty prof., 1980-90, William S. Potter prof. and dir. grad. studies, 1990—. Mem. Saltzburg Seminar in Am. Studies, 1986; mem. legal adv. com. N.Y. Stock Exch. Author: Fundamentals of Corporation Law, 1995, A Practical Guide for Corporate Directors, 1996, Model Business Corporation Act Annotated, 1997. Named Ruby R. Vale Disting. Academic, Widener U. Sch. Law, 1996. Mem.: Am. Assn. Law Sch. (chmn. bus. sect., formerly), ALI, ABA (com. corp. laws 1983—91, corp. practice com. 1995—, com. corp. laws 1996—, reporter Model Bus. Corp. Act 1996—). Office: U Va Sch Law 580 Massie Rd Charlottesville VA 22903-1738 Office Phone: 434-924-3864. E-mail: mpd@virginia.edu.*

DOOLEY, PATRICK JOHN, graphic designer, design educator; b. Cleve., May 29, 1950; s. John William and Edna Ann (Mellick) D.; m. Mary Leah Spicer, Apr. 3, 1982; children: Claire Adele, Grace Ellen, James Joseph. BFA, U. Iowa, 1975, MA, 1977, MFA, 1978. Designer J. Paul Getty Mus., LA, 1980-89; design mgr. J. Paul Getty Mus., J. Paul Getty Trust, LA, 1987-89; designer, owner Patrick Dooley Design, Santa Monica, Calif., 1989-93, Lawrence, Kans., 1993—; mem. faculty Otis Parsons Sch. Art and Design, LA, 1988-93; prof. dept. design Sch. Fine Art U. Kans., Lawrence, 1993—, Gretchen Van Bloom Budig tchg. prof., 1997. Freelance graphic designer, LA, 1978-80, designer, cons. Walt Disney Co., Burbank, Calif., 1989-93, Lannan Lit. Found., LA, 1991—, The Lapis Press, Venice, Calif., 1989-93, Nelson-Atkins Mus., Kansas City, Mo., 1995-96; spkr. Assn. Am. U. Presses ann. conf., 1994, Art Dirs. Club Tulsa, 1996; judge 42nd Art Dirs. Club LA Show, 1988. Designer: (poster) Illuminated Manuscripts, 1984 (NY Type Dirs. Club award of excellence 1985), (books) Whisper of the Muse, 1986 (NY Art Dirs. Club award of merit 1987), Pierre Dubreuil, 1988 (Am. Inst. Graphic Arts Book Show cert. of excellence 1989), The Surrealists Look at Art, 1990 (NY Art Dirs. Club award of merit 1991), Explorations, 1992 (Am. Inst. Graphic Arts 50 Books of 1992), Pacific Wall, 1992 (Am. Inst. Graphic Arts Cover Show 1994), Walter Evans: The Getty Museum Collection, 1996 (Assn. Am. Univ. Presses cert. of excellence 1996). Recipient over 70 awards from Comm. Arts Mag., Print Mag., Am. Assn. Museums, Art Mus. Assn. Am., Am. Fedn. Arts, Univ. and Coll. Designer's Assn., others; Fulbright sr. scholar Fachhochschule, Trier, Germany, 2003. Mem.: Am. Inst. Graphic Arts. Office: U Kans Dept Design 300 Art And Design Bldg Lawrence KS 66045-0001 Business E-Mail: pdooley@ku.edu.

DOOLEY, WENDY BROOKE, vocalist, music educator, administrative assistant; b. Paragould, Ark., Apr. 7, 1976; d. Garry Don and Nina Doris Dooley. MusB, U. Ctrl. Ark., 1999. Lic. tchr. Ark. Dept. Edn., 2000. Clk., employee trainer Crockett Oil Co., Rector, Ark., 1991—97; choral libr. U. Ctrl. Ark., Conway, 1997—99; music tchr. Cabot (Ark.) Jr. High North & South, 1999—2000, Eastside Elem. Sch., Cabot, 2000—01; tchr. Clarkton (Mo.) C-4 Pub. Schs., 2001—; adminstrv. asst. Ark. Govs. Mansion, 2004—. Curriculum devel. com. Cabot Pub. Schs., 2000—01, Clarkton (Mo.) C-4 Pub. Schs., 2001—, cons., 2001—; caterer Simply the Best Catering, Little Rock. Entertainer C. of C., Rector, Ark., 1992—95; mem. Moark Gen. Bapt. Assoc., Campbell, Mo., 1989—2002. Mem.: Ark. Choral Dirs. Assn., Mo. Band Dirs. Assn., Clarkton Tchrs. Assn. (profl. devel. com. mem. 2002—03), Mo. State Tchrs. Assn., Music Educator's Nat. Conf. (sec. collegete chpt. 1998—99). Mem. Assembly Of God. Achievements include first to began a volunteer program to teach children music through the area libraries summer reading programs; started a traveling Vacation Bible School music program. During the summer I travel to different churches and handle all of the music for their VBS. This is a volunteer program without pay; entertain and lead group activities at area retirement centers; entertain at festivals, fair, and other special events. Avocations: travel, singing, reading, gardening. Home: 19 Deerwood Dr Conway AR 72034 Office: Ark Govs Manson 1800 Center St Little Rock AR 72206 E-mail: the_singing_dooley@sbcglobal.net.

DOOLEY, WILLIAM CHESNUT, oncologist, researcher, surgeon; b. Waynesboro, Miss., Sept. 6, 1956; s. B. J. and Ann Chesnut Dooley; m. Kathryn Hage Hage; children: Alexander, Rees. BS with hon., Sanford U.; MD, Vanderbilt U., 1982. Diplomate Am. Bd. Surgery, 1989. Intern Johns Hopkins Hosp., 1982—85; resident Oxford U., 1985—88; dir. the Johns Hopkins breast ctr. The Johns Hopkins Hosp., Balt., 1982—2000; chmn. of surgical oncology & breast inst. U. of Okla., Okla. City, 2001—. Office: U Okla Breast Inst 825 NE 10th St Ste 5200 Oklahoma City OK 73104 Fax: 405-271-4443. Office Phone: 405-271-7867. Business E-Mail: william-dooley@ouhsc.edu.

DOOLITTLE, JESSE WILLIAM, JR., lawyer; b. Wheaton, Ill., May 19, 1929; s. Jesse William and Selma Caroline (Schacht) D.; m. Annette Danforth Bush, May 5, 1962; children: Danforth Bush, Alice Walters. AB, DePauw U., 1951; LLB magna cum laude, Harvard, 1954. Bar: D.C. 1954. Law clk. to U.S. Supreme Ct. Justice Felix Frankfurter, 1957-58; assoc. firm Covington & Burling, Washington, 1958-61; asst. to solicitor gen. of U.S. Dept. Justice, Washington, 1961-63, 1st asst. civil div., 1963-66; gen. counsel Dept. Air Force, Washington, 1966-68, asst. sec. for manpower and res. affairs, 1968-69; partner firm Prather Seeger Doolittle & Farmer, Washington, 1969-94. Editl. cons. Lexis-Nexis, 1995-98; comml.arbitrator, 1992-. Mem.: Harvard Law Rev, 1952-54. Pres. bd. trustees Nat. Child Rsch. Ctr., Washington, 1972-74; mem. bd. overseers com. to visit ROTC programs Harvard, 1967-69; com. to visit Law Sch., 1969-75; mem. governing bd. Nat. Cathedral Sch. for Girls, Washington, 1979-85, vice-chmn., 1981-82, chmn., 1982-85; mem. chpt. Washington Nat. Cathedral, 1982-85; mem. policy bd. Legal Counsel for the Elderly, Washington, 1992-97; bd. dirs. Westchester Corp., Washington, 2000-2003. 1st lt. AUS, 1954-57. Recipient Career Service award Nat. Civil Service League, 1968, Exceptional Civilian Service award Dept. Air Force, 1969 Mem. Am. Law Inst., Harvard Law Sch. Assn. (coun. 1964-68), Harvard Law Rev. Assn. (bd. overseers 1967-72, 92-98), Phi Beta Kappa, Delta Chi. Democrat. Episcopalian (sr. warden 1973-75, past vestryman). Clubs: Metropolitan, Chevy Chase. Home: 4000 Cathedral Ave NW Apt 444B Washington DC 20016-5282

DOOLITTLE, JOHN TAYLOR, congressman; b. Glendale, Calif., Oct. 30, 1950; s. Merrill T. and Dorothy Doolittle; m. Julia Harlow Doolittle, Feb. 17, 1979; children: John Taylor, Jr., Courtney A. BA with hons. in History, U. Calif., Santa Cruz, 1972; JD, U. Pacific, 1978. Mem. Calif. State Senate, 1980—90, U.S. Congress from 4th Calif. dist., 1991—; mem. appropriations and house adminstrn. coms., joint com. on printing. Mem. agr. com. U.S. Congress, mem. resource com., chmn. water and power resources subcom. Republican. Mem. Lds Ch. Office: Ho of Reps 2410 Rayburn Ho Office Bldg Washington DC 20515-0504

DOOLITTLE, WARREN T., retired federal official; b. Webster City, Iowa, July 24, 1921; s. Edward and Rhoda Leone (McGuire) D.; m. Jane Anne Beddow, Dec. 29, 1942; children: Linda Jane, Randolph James, Steven Eric. BS in Forestry, Iowa State U., 1946; MS in Forestry, Duke U., 1950; PhD in Forestery, Yale U., 1955. Enlisted USAF, 1943, advanced through grades to lt. col., 1969, navigator, 1943-45, 1951-52; rsch. scientist USDA Forest Svc., Asheville, N.C., 1946-57, Washington, 1957-59, from asst. dir. to dir. Upper Darby, Pa., 1959-74, assoc. dep. chief Washington, 1974-80, ret., 1980. Contbr. articles to profl. jours. Moderator Congrl. Ch., Asheville, N.C., 1956-57. Lt. col. USAF, 1943-69. Decorated DFC. Fellow Soc. Am. Foresters (pres. 1986, John Beale Meml. award 1983); mem. Am. Forests (pres., B.E. Fernow award 1993), Internat. Soc. Tropical Foresters (pres. 1984-01), Res. Officers Assn. Republican. Avocations: golf, skiing. Home: 5328 Trevino Drive Haymarket VA 20169

DOONE, MICHELE MARIE, chiropractor; b. Oak Park, Ill., Oct. 3, 1942; d. Robert Emmett and Tana Josephine (Alioto) D. Cert., Valley Coll. of Med. and Dental Careers, 1962; student, L.A. Valley Coll., 1960-63, Dallas County Community Coll., 1983-84; D in Chiropractic summa cum laude, Parker Coll. of Chiropractic, 1986. Lic. chiropractic, Calif., Tex.; cert. Nat. Bd. Chiropractic Examiners, impairment rater; diplomate Am. Acad. Pain Mgmt., Am. Bd. Disability Analysts. Med. asst. William Orlando M.D., Edwin Crost, M.D., 1962-65; nursing supr., chief radiologic technologist Vanowen Med. Group, North Hollywood, Calif., 1965-76; radiologic technologist/purchasing agt. Lanier-Brown Clinic, Dallas, 1976-83; faculty mem./ chief radiologic technologist Parker Coll. of Chiropractic, Irving, Tex., 1983-85; exam and X-Ray doctor Margolies Chiropractic Ctr., Richardson, Tex., 1986; clinic staff doctor, assoc. prof. Parker Coll. of Chiropractic, Irving, Tex., 1986-87; doctor/ mgr. contractor Accident Ctrs. of Am., Garland, Tex., 1987; clinic dir. Back Pain Chiropractic, Carrollton, Tex., 1988-91; assoc. in group practice Mullican Chiropractic Ctr., Addison, Tex., 1991-97; co-owner, COO, pres. Health North Chiropractic Rehab Ctr PC, Addison, Tex., 1997—2002; assoc. med. dir. Intracorp., Carrolton, 2002—. Adviser health-related matters Inner Devel. Inst., Dallas, 1977—; seminar com. Back Pain Chiropractic, Inc., Metairie, La., 1989-91, clinic dir., 1988-91. Mem.: Parker Chiropractic Rsch. Found., Metroplex Neurospinal Diagnostic Med. and Surg. Group (med. adv. com. 1989—95), Tex. Chiropractic Assn. (chmn. radiology com. 1990—94), Parker Coll. Alumni Assn. (bd. dirs. 1988—90, 1993—94, 1995—2000, 2001—03, Dr. of Yr. 1990), Pi Tau Delta. Home: 11083 Lockshire Dr Frisco TX 75035-3765 Office Phone: 214-763-0412. E-mail: drdoone@comcast.net.

DOONER, JOHN JOSEPH, JR., advertising executive; b. Mt. Vernon, NY, Aug. 3, 1948; s. John Joseph and Elizabeth Ann (Forrest) D.; m. Cynthia Ann Stewart, Aug. 16, 1975; children: Miriam, Jaclyn. BA, St. Thomas Villanova U., Miami, Fla.; postgrad., Iona Coll. Advt. media supr. Grey Advt., NYC, 1970-73; assoc. media dir. The Marschalk Co., NYC, 1973-74, account mgr., 1974-84; exec. v.p. McCann-Erickson, NYC, 1984—88, gen. mgr. N.Y. office, 1984-88, pres. N.Am. region, 1988-94; pres., COO McCann-Erickson Worldwide, NYC, 1992-94; chmn., CEO McCann-Erickson WorldGroup, NYC, 1995—2000, 2003—. Bd. dirs. The Interpublic Group. Bd. trustees Sound Shore Med. Ctr., 1993—, Coll. New Rochelle; bd. dirs. Nat. Multiple Sclerosis Soc., 1998—. Mem. Pelham Country Club, Lago Mar Club (Ft. Lauderdale, Fla.). Avocations: tennis, boating. Office: McCann-Erickson Worldwide 622 3rd Ave New York NY 10017-2798*

DOORLEY, JOHN, public relations executive, educator; b. Uniontown, Pa., May 25, 1942; s. John T. Doorley, Sr. and Mary Grasinger; m. Carole Tierney Doorley, Aug. 27, 1972; children: Nanci, Jonathan. BS in Biology, St. Vincent Coll., 1964; MA in Journalism, NYU, 1980; cert. in Exec. Mgmt. Program, Harvard U., 1999. Social worker Pa. Dept. Pub. Assistance, Uniontown, 1964—66; with sales and mktg. Sterling Drug Inc., N.Y.C., 1966—81; dir. corp. comm. Hoffmann-LaRoche, Nutley, NJ, 1981—87; exec. dir. corp. comm. Merck & Co., Inc., Whitehouse Station, NJ, 1987—2000; freelance developer comprehensive reputation mgmt., 2003—. Instr. Rutgers U., New Brunswick, NJ, 2001—; chmn. N.J. Health Products Com., Union, 1988; dir. ann. summer inst. pub. rels. NYU, N.Y.C., 2001—04. Bd. dirs. Emmanuel Cancer Found., Summit, NJ, 1983—93, Little League Baseball, Mountainside, NJ, 1994—98. Mem.: AAUP, Nat. Comm. Assn. Roman Catholic. Avocations: running, golf. Office: Rutgers U 4 Huntington St New Brunswick NJ 08901-1071 Office Phone: 908-232-6340.

DOORLEY, THOMAS LAWRENCE, III, management consulting firm executive; b. Sewickley, Pa., Aug. 15, 1944; s. Thomas Lawrence and Emma Lou (Sage) D.; m. Gail Lynn Schwartz, Feb. 3, 1968; children: Christopher Sage, Scott Frederick. BSChemE, Pa. State U., BA in Arts and Sci., 1967;

MBA in Mktg., Columbia U., 1969. Cons. Westvaco, N.Y.C., 1968-69; sr. cons. A D Little, Cambridge, Mass., 1969-74, bus. unit mgr., 1974-76; founder, exec. v.p. Braxton Assocs., Boston, 1977-84; sr. ptnr. Deloitte Consulting, 1984-99, Deloitte Consulting Braxton Assocs., Boston, 1996—. Author: Teaming up for the 90's, 1991, Value-Creating Growth, 1999; contbr. articles to profl. jours. Chmn., bd. dirs. The Soccer Network, Boston, 1987—; mem. leadership club United Way Mass., Boston, 1986-90; coach Wellesley (Mass.) United Soccer Club, 1977-90; deacon Wellesley Congregational Ch., 1970's, sr. high youth advisor, 1970's. Woodrow Wilson fellow Columbia U., 1969. Mem. Columbia Bus. Sch. Club, Wellesley Country Club, Alliance Analyst and World Econ. Found. (advisory bd.). Avocations: running, exercise, reading, children. Home: 34 Arnold Rd Wellesley MA 02481-2841 Office: Deloitte Consulting Braxton Assocs 200 Clarendon St Ste 2000 Boston MA 02116-5021

DOORY, ANN MARIE, legislator; b. Yonkers, N.Y., Aug. 19, 1954; d. Gerard R. and Patricia M. Lowe; m. Robert Leonard Doory Jr., Sept. 29, 1979; children: Brian Robert, Elizabeth Lowe. BA in Polit. Sci., Towson State U., 1976; JD, U. Balt., 1979. Bar: Md. Counsel to majority leader Md. State Senate, 1980—81; vol., arbitrator Better Bus. Bur., 1984-86; dep. spkr. pro tem Md. Ho. of Dels., 1999—2003, parliamentarian, 1993—94; mem. Ho. Econ. Matters Com. Md. Gen. Assembly, 1987—94, vice-chair Ho. Judiciary Com., 1995—2003, vice-chair Ho. Econ. Matters Com., 2003—. Mem. Dem. State Ctrl. Com. 43d Legis. Dist., Baltimore City, 1982-86. Mem. Women's Bar Assn., Md. Bar Assn. Democrat. Roman Catholic. also: Md Ho of Dels State Capitol Annapolis MD 21401 Office Phone: 410-841-3476. Office Fax: 410-841-3558. Business E-Mail: annmarie_doory@house.state.md.us.

DOPF, GLENN WILLIAM, lawyer; b. NYC, June 6, 1953; s. William Bernard and Doris Virginia (Roxby) D. BS cum laude, Fordham Coll., 1975; JD, Fordham U., 1979; LLM, NYU, 1983. Bar: N.J. 1979, U.S. Dist. Ct. N.J. 1979, N.Y. 1980, U.S. Dist. Ct. (so. and ea. dists.) N.Y. 1980, U.S. Ct. Appeals (2d cir.) 1980, U.S. Ct. Internat. Trade 1981, U.S. Supreme Ct. 1983. Assoc. Martin, Clearwater & Bell, N.Y.C., 1980-81; ptnr. Kopff, Nardelli & Dopf LLP, N.Y.C., 1982—. Mem. ABA, Assn. Bar City N.Y. Office: Kopff Nardelli & Dopf LLP 440 9th Ave Fl 15 New York NY 10001-1688

DOR, GEORGE W. K, music educator; b. Alavanyo Wudidi, Ghana, July 11, 1954; s. Seth Kwasi and Lucia Afua Dor; m. Rose Ama Nimo; children: Dzidefo Kokutse, Nyuiemedi Yawa, Mozart Nuku, Lilian Seyram, Senyoagbe Koku. MusB, U. of Ghana, Legon, Accra, Ghana, 1982—86; MPhil, U. of Ghana, 1989—92; PhD, U. of Pitts., 1996—2001. Certfied Teacher Ghana Edn. Svc., 1977. Music master Kadjebi Secondary Sch., Kadjebi, Ghana, 1977—80, St Aquinas Secondary Sch., Accra, Ghana, 1980—82; tchg. asst. U. of Ghana, Music Dept., Legon, Accra, Ghana, 1986—88; lectr. U. of Edn., Winneba, Ghana, 1992—96; tchg. fellow and part time faculty U. of Pitts., Music Dept., 1996—2001; chair in ethnomusicology and asst. prof. of music U. of Miss. (Sally McDonnell-Barksdale Honors Coll., and Dept. of Music), Oxford, 2001—. Resident dir./condr. Ghana Nat. Symphony Orch., Accra, Ghana, 1996; music dir. Cmty. of Reconciliation Ch., Pitts., 1999—2001; nat. choir dir. Evang. Presbyn. Ch., Ghana, 1995—96; founder and dir. Goethe Inst. Choir, Accra, Ghana, 1993—96; choir dir./organist North La E. P. Ch., Accra, Ghana, 1980—96; first row cellist Ghana Nat. Symphony Orch., Accra, 1988—96; 2nd v.p. Ghana Assn. of Choral Conductors, Accra, Ghana, 1984—86; founder and dir. Ole Miss African Drum and Dance Ensembel, U. of Miss., Oxford, Miss., 2003—. Editor (conributor): (festschrift) Dynamics of Creativity and Knowledge in African Music Traditions: A Festschrift in Honor of Akin Euba; contbr. article, encyclopedia; author: (ph.d. dissertation) Tonal resources and Compositional Processes in Ewe Traditional Vocal Music. Mem. of hymbook rev. com. Evang. Presbyn. Ch., Ghana, 1992—2003; adjucator of singing competitions Ministry of Edn. and Culture, Ghana. Summer Rsch. grant, U. of Pitts., 1998, Grad. scholarship, U. of Ghana, 1989—91, Andrew Mellon GraduateTeaching fellowship, U. of Pitts., 1996—98, 2000, Summer Rsch. grant, U. of Miss., 2002, 2003. Mem.: Soc. for Ethnomusicology (life; intercultural music arts 2002). Christian. Achievements include introduce the field of ethnomusicology at the University of Mississippi, formed the first african and drum ensemble in a college in the state of Mississippi. Avocations: reading, travel, music. Home: 1015 Benbow Cir #5 Oxford MS 38655 Office: Univ of Miss Music Dept Scruggs Hall University MS 38677 Office Phone: 662-915-7269. Office Fax: 662-915-1230. Personal E-mail: gwkdor@olemiss.edu. E-mail: gwkdor1@olemiss.edu.

DORADO, MARIANNE GAERTNER, lawyer; d. Wolfgang Wilhelm and Marianne L. Gaertner; m. Richard Manuel Dorado, Oct. 1, 1982; children: Marianne Christine, Kathleen Gina. BA, Yale U., 1978; JD, U. Mich., 1981. Bar: N.Y. 1982, U.S. Supreme Ct. 1993. Ptnr. The Dorado Law Group, LLC, N.Y.C., 1998—. Contbr. articles to profl. jours. Extern office legal advisor U.S. Dept. State, Washington, 1980. Republican. Roman Catholic. Office: The Dorado Law Group LLC 74 Trinity Pl Ste 1204 New York NY 10006 E-mail: mdorado@doradolaw.com.

DORAI, THAMBI, oncologist, researcher; b. Tirupattur, India, Feb. 28, 1950; arrived in U.S., 1983; s. Devarajan and Radha; m. Bhuvaneswari Dorai, Sept. 5, 1982; children: Arvind, Vinod. BS, Sacred Heart Coll. (Madras Univ.), 1970; MS, Christian Med. Coll. (Madras Univ.), Vellore, India, 1973; PhD, Madras Univ., 1980. Sr. scientist Indian Inst. Chem. Biology, Calcutta, Ind., 1980—83; rsch. fellow USC, Sch. Medicine, L.A., 1980—84; rsch. assoc. Rockefeller Univ., N.Y.C., 1984—88; vis. fellow Mt. Sinai Sch. Medicine, N.Y.C., 1988—91, rsch. asst. prof., 1991—94; sr. rsch. assoc. Columbia Univ. Coll. of Physicians and Surgeons, N.Y.C., 1994—2000; rsch. assoc. prof. N.Y. Med. Coll., N.Y.C., 2000—. Contbr. over 40 articles to profl. jours. Recipient Edwin Beer award, N.Y. Acad. Medicine, 1997; grantee Rsch. in Urology, Elsa U. Pardee Found., 1999; Irwin White Fellowship, Columbia Univ., N.Y., 1995. Mem.: Am. Assn. for Advancement of Sci., Am. Assn. for Cancer Rsch. Achievements include characterization of novel prevention and treatment strategies for bone metastasis in prostate cancer; research on the molecular mechanisms of kidney cancer. Avocation: travel. Home: 92 E Allison Ave Nanuet NY 10954 Office: Comprenhensive Cancer Ctr Our Lady of Mercy Med Ctr 600 E 233rd St Bronx NY 10466 Office Phone: 718-920-1137.

DORAN, CHARLES FRANCIS, political scientist, consultant; b. Mankato, Minn., Jan. 31, 1943; s. George Francis and Harriet Jennetta (Wallace) Doran; m. Barbara Giusti, Dec. 30, 1967; children: Charles Francis, Brent Richard, Kirk Bennett, Connemara. *Wife Barbara, BA 1966 Rice U., PhD 1972 Johns Hopkins U., is a consultant in research design and an author in history, philosophy, and science. Son Charles, AB/AM 1992, PhD 1999 Harvard U., is a professor of mathematics at University of Washington, Seattle. Son Brent, AB/AM 1997 Harvard U., PhD 2003 Princeton U., also a mathematician, is a Glasstone Research Fellow in science at U. Oxford, England. Son Kirk, AB/SM 2002 Harvard U., is pursuing a PhD in economics at Princeton U. Daughter Connemara, Harvard class of 2009, is interested in mathematical sciences, music, and the humanities.* AB in History and Sci., Harvard U., 1964; MA in Internat. Rels., Johns Hopkins U., 1966, PhD in Polit. Sci., 1969. Asst. prof. Tex. A&M U., 1968—70; from asst. prof. to prof. Rice U., Houston, 1970—79; prof. dir. Canadian studies, internat. rels., global theory and history Johns Hopkins U., Washington, 1979—90, Andrew W. Mellon prof. internat. rels., 1991—. Founder, dir. internat. programs Jones Grad. Sch. Adminstrn., 1977—79; sr. assoc. Ctr. for Strategic and Internat. Studies, Washington, 1995—; Claude T. Bissell chair U. Toronto, 1985—86; working group, standing com. on the Western Hemisphere, congrl. and dept. briefings NSF, 1981—83; lectr. in field. Author: Politics of Assimilation: Hegemony and Its Aftermath, 1971, Myth, Oil and Politics, 1976, Forgotten Partnership, 1984, Systems in Crisis, 1991, Why Canadian Unity Matters, 2001, Power Cycle Theory and Global Politics, 2003; contbr. articles to profl. jours. Elected Can.-Am. Com., 1982; trade dipute resolution mechanisms Jt. C. of C., 1985—86; N.Am. com. Atlantic Coun. US, 1982. Recipient Gov. Gen. Internat. award, Can., 1999, medal, Internat. Soc. Scholars, Mex., 2001; Rsch. grantee, Woodrow Wilson Found., 1968, NSF, 1981—83, MacArthur and Ford Found., 1988—91, Donner Found., 1990—95, ACLS/DAAD, 1993—95. Mem.: Internat. Polit. Sci. Assn., Internat. Commn. of the History Internat. Rels., Internat. Studies Assn. (editl. bd.), Am. Polit. Sci. Assn., German Studies Assn., Mid. East Studies Assn., Assn. for Canadian Studies in the US (v.p. 1985—87, pres. 1987—89), Coun. Fgn. Rels., Harvard Club, Cosmos Club. Achievements include research in power cycle theory of historical change and fgn. policy behavior, principles of relative power dynamics. Avocations: sailing, skiing. Home: 8544 Brickyard Rd Potomac MD 20854-4833 Office: Johns Hopkins SAIS 1740 Massachusetts Ave NW Washington DC 20036 Office Phone: 202-663-5715. Office Fax: 202-663-5717. Business E-Mail: cfdoran@jhu.edu.

DORAN, JAMES EDWARD, adult education educator, consultant; b. Ephrata, Wash., May 27, 1949; s. Samuel M. and Mary I. Doran; m. Meredith Fry, Mar. 13, 1973; children: Jarod, Brittney. BA in Bus. Adminstrn., Wash. State U., 1971, BA in Agrl. Econs., 1975; MBA, City U. Washington, 1992; cert. in Project Mgmt., George Washington U., 2000; MEd in Adult Edn., We. Wash. U., 2005. Mgr. Johnson Orchards, Quincy, Wash., 1975—77; loan officer Seattle (Wash.) First Nat. Bank, 1977—85; pres. Doran Investments, Inc., Edmonds, Wash., 1985—88; lead process improvement Boeing, Seattle, 1988—2003; instr. math., coord. program Edmonds (Wash.) C.C., 2004—05; test examiner USN, Everett, Wash., 2005—. Student adv. com. We. Wash. U., Bellingham, Wash., 2003—05; presenter in field; designer curriculum, instr. Skag Valley Coll., Mt. Vernon, Wash., 2004; judge sr. project Arlington H.S.; mem. delegation, China. Vol. tour guide Dept. Interior AMTRAK, Wash., 2004—05. Recipient Customer Svc. awards, Boeing Computer Svcs., 1988—2003. Mem.: Am. Soc. of Tng. and Devel., Assn. of Career and Tech. Edn., Internat. Soc. of Productivity Improvement, Am. Assn. Adult and Continuing Educators. Independent. Avocations: antique mustang restoration, motorcycle restoration, motorcycling. Home: 1617 200th Pl SW Lynnwood WA 98036 Personal E-mail: jimdoran1@juno.com.

DORAN, JAMES MARTIN, retired food products company executive; b. Toronto, Ohio, Apr. 21, 1933; s. Hugh John and Mary Agnes (Murray) D.; m. Peggotty Hanks Namm, Dec. 9, 1967 (dec. Dec. 1978); children— Beth Doran Putnam, Wendy Harrison Doran. BS in Bus. Adminstrn., John Carroll Univ., 1955. C.P.A., Pa., Ohio. Sr. acct. Deloitte, Haskins & Sells, Pitts., 1956-60; sr. corp. acct. Revere Copper & Brass, Rome, N.Y., 1960-64; contr. A.C. Gilbert Co., New Haven, 1964-67, Heublein Spirits & Wine, Farmington, Conn, 1967-83; sr. v.p. fin. Heublein, Inc., Farmington, 1983-89, ret. V.p., trustee Namm Found., N.Y.C., 1970—; mem. Leadership Greater Hartford, 1977—; trustee, Julie Edn. Ctr., 1996—; pres., trustee The Dornam Found. Mem. AICPA. Roman Catholic. Avocations: investing, platform tennis, tennis, golf. Home: 83 Rumford St West Hartford CT 06107-3754

DORAN, KATHLEEN BREWER, dean, consultant; b. Glen Ridge, N.J., Mar. 5, 1955; d. Ambrose Benedict and Marjorie Westgate Doran. AB, Dartmouth Coll., 1976; MBA, U. of Va., 1978; PhD, McGill U., Montreal, Que., Can., 2000. Sr. sales rep. Internat. Paper Co., Chgo., 1978—80, sr. fin. analyst Dallas, 1980—81, strategic planning specialist, 1981—82; sr. assoc. Harbidge House, Denver, 1982; owner Eagle Valley Aviation, Vail, Colo., 1982—86, Condor Aviation, Oceano, Calif., 1986—90; lectr. Calif. Poly. State U., San Luis Obispo, 1986—90, McGill U., Montreal, 1991—95; asst. prof. Babson Coll., Wellesley, Mass., 1995—2000; dean Sch. Bus. and Info. Sci. Lasell Coll., Newton, Mass., 2000—. Instr. Tsinghua U., Beijing, 2001—02; prin. Narod Enterprises Consulting, Vail, 1982—86. Contbr. articles to profl. jours. Named Outstanding Scholar in Chinese Mktg., Soc. for Mktg. Advances, Chinese Golden Tripod Com., 2002; recipient Sr. fellowship, Dartmouth Coll., 1975—76, Rsch. fellowship, U. of Nairobi, Inst. of African Studies, 1975—76, Rsch. scholarship, McGill U., 1990—91, Rsch. fellowship, McGill and Renmin Univs., 1994—95, Babson Coll., 1997—99, Sr. Specialist grant, Fulbright Fgn. Scholarship Bd., 2003. Mem.: Assn. for Consumer Rsch., Acad. of Internat. Bus. Liberal. Episcopalian. Avocations: travel, skiing, cooking. Home: 241 Captain Eames Cir Ashland MA 01721 Office: Lasell Coll 1844 Commonwealth Ave Auburndale MA 02466 Office Phone: 617-243-2105. E-mail: bdoran@lasell.edu.

DORAN, MARK RICHARD, real estate financial executive; b. Chgo., June 17, 1954; s. Paul George and Mae (Olson) D.; m. Wendy Carole Beckham, Dec. 17, 1977; children: Blake, Barrett, Hayley. BBA in Acctg., Baylor U., 1975, MBA, 1976. From asst. acct. to supr. Peat, Marwick, Mitchell & Co., Dallas, 1977-81; sr. v.p. fin. Lincoln Property Co., Dallas, 1982-89; exec. v.p., CFO Prentiss Properties Trust, Dallas, 1990-98, Transwestern Comml. Svcs., 1999—2002, COO, 2002—. Deacon Park Cities Bapt. Ch., Dallas, 1988—. Mem. The Urban Land Inst., Baylor U. Alumni Assn. Avocations: basketball, golf, skiing. Office: Transwestern Comml Svcs 5001 Spring Valley Ste 600W Dallas TX 75244

DORAN, ROBERT STUART, mathematician, educator; b. Winthrop, Iowa, Dec. 21, 1937; s. Carl Arthur D. and Imogene (Ownby) Doran Nodurft; m. Shirley Ann Lange, June 27, 1959; children: Bruce Robert, Brad Christopher. BA with hons., U. Iowa, 1962, MA, 1964; MS, U. Washington, 1967, PhD, 1968. Instr. U. Wash., 1968; asst. prof. U. No. Iowa, Cedar Falls, 1968-69; asst. to prof. math. Tex. Christian U., Ft. Worth, 1969—, chmn. dept. math., 1990—, John William and Helen Stubbs Potter prof. math., 1995—. Vis. prof. U. Tex., Austin, 1979; cons. in field. Author: Approximate Identities and Factorization in Banach Modules, 1979, Characterizations of C*-Algebras: The Gelfand-Naimark Theorems, 1986, Representations of Locally Compact Groups and Banach *-Algebraic Bundles, 1988; editor: Cambridge U. Press, 1987, Selfadjoint and Nonselfadjoint Operator Algebras and Operator Theory, 1991, C*-Algebras: A Fifty Year Celebration, 1994, Automorphic Forms, Automorphic Representations and Arithmetic, 1999, The Mathematical Legacy of Harish-Chandra, 2000, Operator Algebras, Quantization, and Non-commutative Geometry, 2004; contbr. articles to profl. jours. Chmn. bd. deacons Birchman Bapt. Ch., Ft. Worth, 1987; vol. Van Cliburn Internat. Piano Competition, 1984—, Am. Cancer Soc., 1987—. Recipient Burlington No. award for Disting. Tchg., 1988, Top Ten Prof. award Ho. of Reps., 1986, 87, 91, Mortar Bd. Preferred Prof. award, 1983, 87, 91, 93, 95, Gold medal for Prof. of Yr. Coun. for Advancement and Support of Edn., 1989, Honors Prof. of Yr. award, 1993, Coll. Sci. and Engring. Chancellor's award for disting. rsch., 2003; vis. scholar MIT, 1981, Oxford U., 1988; Minnie Stevens Piper prof., 1989, Chancellor's Dist. Rsch. award Coll. Sci. Engring., 2003. Mem. Inst. Advanced Study (chmn. we. U.S. 1984—), Assn. Mems. Inst. for Advanced Study (pres. bd. trustees 1990-99), Am. Math. Soc., Math. Assn. Am. (vis. lectr. 1990—, Beckenbach Book award prize com. 1990-94), Phi Beta Kappa, Sigma Xi, Pi Mu Epsilon. Republican. Avocations: chess, running, swimming. Home: 4204 Ridglea Country Club Dr Fort Worth TX 76126-2224 Office: Tex Christian U Dept Math Fort Worth TX 76129-0001 Office Phone: 817-257-7335. Business E-Mail: r.doran@tcu.edu.

DORAN, THOMAS GEORGE, bishop; b. Rockford, Ill., Feb. 20, 1936; Licentiate in Sacred Theology, Pontifical Gregorian U., Rome, 1962, PhD in Canon Law, 1978. Ordained priest Roman Cath. Ch. 1961, bishop 1994. Asst. pastor St. Joseph Parish, Elgin, Ill., St. Peter Parish, South Beloit; various admin. duties Diocese of Rockford, Ill., rector diocesan cathedral; prelate auditor Roman Rota, 1986—94; bishop Rockford, 1994—. Mem. Supreme Tribunal of the Apostolic Signatura, 2000. Mem.: Congregation for the Clergy. Roman Catholic. Office: Diocese of Rockford PO Box 7044 Rockford IL 61125-7044 Office Phone: 815-399-4300. Business E-Mail: officeofthebishop@rockforddiocese.org.

DORAN, TIMOTHY PATRICK, academic administrator; b. NYC, July 1, 1949; s. Joseph Anthony and Claire (Griffin) D.; m. Kathleen Matava, Aug. 1, 1981; children: Claire Marie, Bridget Anne. BA in Econs., Le Moyne Coll., 1971; MA in Tchg., U. Alaska, 1984, Edn. Specialist, 1990. Cert. type A secondary, econs., type B K-12 prin., supt. Svc. rep. Emigrant Savs. Bank, NYC, 1971-72; exec., dir. Project Equality Northwest, Seattle, 1972-73, Jesuit Vol. Corps., Portland, Oreg., 1973-75, adminstv. advisor Kaltag City (Alaska) coun., 1975-77; program developer Diocese Fairbanks, Alaska, 1978-81, adminstr., supt. St. Mary's Cath. H.S., 1981-83; prin. intern U. Alaska, Fairbanks, 1984, vis. instr., 1990-94; tchr. Anthony A. Andrews Sch., St. Michael, Alaska, 1984-86; prin., tchr. James C. Isabell Sch., Teller, Alaska, 1986-88; prin. Unalakleet (Alaska) Schs., 1988-90, Denali Elem. Sch., Fairbanks, 1992—. Acad. coord. U. Alaska, Fairbanks, summers, 1984—86; instr. Elderhostel, 1991—; docent U. Alaska Mus., 1991—; sch. edn. adv. bd. U. Alaska, 1998—, adj. instr., Anchorage, 2001—. Active nat. com. Campaign for Human Devel., 1980-83; mem. manpower planning coun. Tanana Chiefs Conf., 1976-77, parish coun. Sacred Heart Cathedral, 1979-81; Sunday Sch. tchr. St. Mark's Univ. Parish, 1990-97, adv. coun., 1998-2001; mem. com. chair Fairbanks Arts and Culture in Edn., 1995—; bd. dirs., v.p., pres. Literacy Coun. Alaska, 1997-2002. Recipient Merit awards Alaska Dept. Edn., 1986-90; named Alaska Disting. Prin., 1998, Fairbanks Elem. Prin. of Yr., 2003. Mem. ASCD, Nat. Assn. Elem. Sch. Prins., Alaska Assn. Elem. Sch. Prins. (v.p., pres.-elect, pres. 2000-02, state rep. 2004—), Fairbanks Prins. Assn. (v.p. 1998-99, pres. 1999-2000), Alaska Math. Consortium (bd. dirs. 1992-99), Alaska Coun. Sch. Adminstrs. (bd. dirs. 1998-2002, 04). Home: 512 Windsor Dr Fairbanks AK 99709-3439 Office: Denali Elem Sch 1042 Lathrop St Fairbanks AK 99701-4124 Office Phone: 907-452-2456. Business E-Mail: tdoran@northstar.k12.ak.us.

DORATO, PETER, electrical and computer engineering educator; b. NYC, Dec. 17, 1932; s. Fioretto and Rosina (Lachello) D.; m. Marie Madeleine Turlan, June 2, 1956; children: Christopher, Alexander, Sylvia, Veronica. BEE, CCNY, 1955; MSEE, Columbia U., 1956; DEE, Poly. Inst. N.Y., 1961. Registered profl. engr., Colo. Lectr. elec. engring. dept. CCNY, 1956-57; instr. elec. engring. Poly. Inst. N.Y., Bklyn., 1957-61, prof., 1961-72; prof. elec. engring., dir. Resource System Analysis U. Colo., Colorado Springs, 1972-76; Gardner-Zemke prof. elec. and computer engring. U. N.Mex., Albuquerque, 1984—2004, chmn. dept., 1976-84, prof. emeritus, 2005—. Hon. chaired prof. Nanjing Aero. Inst., 1989; vis. prof. Politecnico di Torino, Italy, 1991-921 dir. Ctr. for Intelligent Systems Engring. U. N.Mex., 2001. Author: Analytic Feedback Systems Design, 2000; co-author Linear Quadratic Control, 1995, Robust Control for Unstructured Perturbations, 1992, Robust Control-System Design, 1996, Italian Culture—A View from America, 2001; editor: Robust Control, Recent Results in Robust Control and Advances in Adaptive Control, reprint vols., 1987, 90, 91, IEEE Press Reprint Vol. Series, 1989-90; assoc. editor Automatica Jour., 1969-83, 89-92, editor rapid publs., 1994-98; assoc. editor IEEE Trans on Edn., 1989-91; contbr. articles on control systems theory to profl. jours. Recipient John R. Ragazzini edn. award Am. Automatic Control Coun., 1998 Fellow IEEE (3rd Millenium medal); mem. IEEE Control Systems Soc. (Disting. Mem. award)., World Automation Congress (Life Achievement award 2002). Democrat. Home: 1514 Roma Ave NE Albuquerque NM 87106-4513 Office: U NMex Dept Elec Computer Eng Albuquerque NM 87131-1356 Business E-Mail: peter@ece.unm.edu.

DORCHAK, GLENDA, electronics company executive; Various positions IBM Canada, 1974—92; dir. sales and svc. AMBRA, 1993; various exec. positions in sales, mktg. and planning IBM US, 1993; pres. Value Am., Inc., Charlottesville, Va., 1998—99, chmn., CEO, 2000; v.p., COO Communications Group Intel Corp., v.p., Desktop Platforms Group, gen. mgr., Consumer Electronics Group. Named one of top 25 execs. of new millennium Computer Reseller News, 1999. Office: Intel Corp 2200 Mission College Blvd Santa Clara CA 95052-8119

DORDELMAN, WILLIAM FORSYTH, food company executive; b. Glen Ridge, N.J., Oct. 18, 1940; s. Wilbert E. and Dorothy F. (Forsyth) D.; m. Barbara Ann Gaddis, Sept. 16, 1959; children: Dorothy Ann, William Edward, Patricia Lynne, Lauren Forsyth. BA in Econs, U. Va., 1962; MBA, Harvard U., 1964. With Gen. Foods Corp., White Plains, N.Y., 1965—, advt. and merchandising mgr. Birdseye divsn., 1972-73, gen. mgr. main meal strategic bus. unit, 1973-77, v.p. corp., pres. food products divsn., 1977-80, corp. group v.p., 1980-86; pres. Fairfield Capital, Rowayton, Conn., 1986-92; co-CEO B. Manischewitz Co., 1992-93; chmn., CEO Colo. Prime Foods, 1993-98; prin. Kohlberg & Co., Mcht. Bankers, 1998—. Bd. dirs. Bailey & Alling Lumber Co., Oscar Mayer, Entemanns, B. Manischewitz Co., Color Spot Nursery, United Signature Foods, Colo. Prime Food, S.W. Supermarket, Urgrocer.com.; chmn. Am. Homecare Supply, Orion Food Supply. Innotek Inc.; bd. dirs. Internat. Cancer Screening Lab. Bd. dirs. Mid-Fairfield Youth Hockey Assn., 1973-77, St. Vincent's Hosp. Mem. Am. Mgmt. Assn., Am. Mktg. Assn., Young Pres. Orgn. (bd. dirs. N.Y. chpt. 1982), Weeburn Country Club, Ocean Reef Club, Westchester/Fairfield County Club, Harvard Bus. Sch. Club (dir. 1978—), Zeta Psi. Episcopalian. Home: 9 Woodley Rd Darien CT 06820-2622

DORE, ANITA WILKES, English language educator; b. N.Y.C., Dec. 16, 1914; d. Abraham P. and Rose (Hirsch) Wilkes; m. Robert M. Dore, June 26, 1938; children: Marjorie Dore Allen, Elizabeth. BA, Vassar Coll., 1935; MA with honors, Columbia U., 1937. Cert. English tchr., N.Y. Tchr. H.S. English, Bd. Edn., N.Y.C., 1937-41, 56-59, TV broadcaster, producer, 1961-65, coordinator English jr. high sch. div., 1959-61, chair English dept., 1965-67, asst. dir. English, 1967-73, dir. English, N.Y.C. schs., 1973-83, cons., 1983—; cons. Young Playwrights Dramatists Guild, N.Y.C., 1983-87. Author: Premier Book of Major Poets, 1970, Emerging Woman, 1974; co-author: Distrust of Authority, 1981; also articles. Pres., bd. dirs. Sch. Settlement House, Bklyn., 1951-53; mem. edn. com. NOW, N.Y.C., 1972-75; chair Child Study Children's Book Com. Bank St. Coll., 1983-98; sec., bd. dirs. Westport-Westport Arts Ctr., Conn., 1983-93; trustee Westport Libr., Conn.; 1985-92; chair adv. com. young poets and playwrights festivals of Conn. Westport Arts Ctr., 1983—. Recipient Elizabeth Dana prize in English, Vassar Coll., 1934; named Honoree Salute to Women YWCA, 1991. Fellow N.Y. State English Council (v.p. 1970-75); mem. Nat. Council Tchrs. English Lit. Commn., N.Y.C. Assn. Tchrs. English (v.p. 1962-70), Alumnae Assn. Vassar (class 1935 pres. 1996—). Democrat. Avocations: theatre, traveling, politics. Home: 59 Fox Den Rd Mount Kisco NY 10549-3834

DORE, KATHLEEN A., broadcast executive; m. Keith Jepsen. BA in Film and Broadcasting, U. Iowa, 1972, MBA, 1984. Affiliate mktg. mgr. Rainbow Media Holdings, 1982—84, sales dir. Am. Movie Classics, 1984—86, regional dir. Am. Movie Classics, 1986, pres. Bravo Networks, 1996—2002, pres. Ind. Film Channel Cos., 2002—03, pres. Entertainment Svcs., 2003—. Named honoree, Girl Scouts Inc., 2002; named one of Fast 40, Fast Co., 100 Most Powerful Women in Hollywood, Hollywood Reporter, 2003; recipient Lee Salk Goodworks award, Theatreworks/USA, Disting. Alumni Achievement award, U. Iowa, 1998. Mem.: N.Y. Women in Film, Mktg. Soc. for Cable and Telecomm. Industry, Women in Cable and Telecomm. Found. (chair 2001—02, Woman of Yr. 2003). Office: Rainbow Media Holdings 200 Jericho Quadrangle Jericho NY 11753

DOREMUS, OGDEN, lawyer; b. Atlanta, Apr. 23, 1921; s. C. Estes and Mary (McAdory) D.; m. Carolyn Wooten Greene, Aug. 30, 1947 (dec. Aug. 1989); children: Celia Jane, Frank O., Dale Marie Doremus. BA, Emory U., 1946, JD, 1949. Bar: Ga. 1947; cert. U.S. postal mediator, 1999. Asst. solicitor gen., Atlanta, 1947-49; ptnr. firm Smith Field Doremus & Ringel, Atlanta, 1949-60, Falligant, Doremus and Karsman, Savannah, Ga., 1960-72, Doremus, Jones & Smith, P.C., Metter, Ga., 1972-94; of counsel Karsman, Brooks & Callaway, 1994—2000; judge State Ct. Candler County, Ga., 1985—2005; sr. judge State Cts., 2005—. Prof. Woodrow Wilson Sch. Law, Atlanta, 1948-50; judge State Ct. Candler County, Ga., 1985—, chair uniform rules com. Coun. State Cts., 1990-2004; pres. Ga. Coun. State Ct. Judges, 1990-91, chair legis. com., 1997-99; mem. Jud. Coun. State of Ga., 1989-91, Unified Trial Ct. Commn., 1997; mem. ct. futures com. State Bar Ga., 1996—; bd. dirs. Ctr. for Law in the Pub. Interest, 1996—, Lifetie Achievement, 2004; judge Mcpl. Ct., Metter, Ga., 1997-2001; mem. commn. on judiciary Supreme Ct. Ga., 1999—. Mem. editl. adv. bd. Environ. Law, Reporter, 1969-80. Scoutmaster Boy Scouts Am., Atlanta, 1951-60, commn., 1961-70; chmn. Ga. Day and Savannah Arts Festival, 1968-72; mem. Atlanta City Coun., 1950-53; mem. Savannah Govtl. Reorgn. Commn., 1960-61, Ga. Ct. Futures Commn., 1991-93, 97—; adv. com. Nat. Coastal Zone Mgmt. Coun., 1978-86; trustee Ga. Conservancy; bd. dirs. Legal Environ. Assistance Found., 1983-86, Ga. Hazardous Waste Authority, 1989—, Chatham Environ.

Forum, 1990-93; mem. strategic planning com. Coun. State Cts. Ga., 1996—; bd. dirs. Coastal Environ. Orgn. Ga., 1998—, Cancochee Riverkeeper. Served with USAAC, 1942-46, ETO. Named Young Man of Yr. Atlanta, 1951; recipient Thomas H. Gignilliat award Cultural Progress of Savannah, 1969, Tradition of Excellence award Ga. State Bar, 1988, 1st Ann. Coun. of State Cts. award named Ogden Doremus in his honor, 1993, River Pioneer award Chattahoochee Riverkeeper, 2003, Lifetime award Ga. Ctr. Law in Pub. Interest. Mem.: ABA (chmn. environ law com., gen. practice 1976—77), Atlanta Soc., Ga. Inst. Trial Advocacy (chmn. 1984—89), Savannah Bar Assn., State Bar Ga. (chmn. ins. law sect. 1963—67, 1977—83, mediator for U.S. Postal Svc. 1999—, cert. mediator Ga. commn. on dispute resolution), Izaak Walton League (founder Ga. chpt. 1950), Willow Lake Country Club, Chatham Tennis Club, Chatham Club, Sierra Club (exec. com. Chattahoochee chpt. 1965—75, chair legal com. Ga. chpt. 1997—2001, vice chair exec. com. Ga. chpt. 2004—, Lifetime Achievement Ga. environ. coun. Citizenship award 1997, Common Cause Citizenship award 1998, Lifetime Achievement Ga. environ. coun. Citizenship award 1999, Conservation Leadership award Ga. chpt. 1999, Lifetime Leadership award 2004). Home: RR 2 Box 188A Metter GA 30439-9570 Office: Doremus and Assocs PO Box 702 Metter GA 30439-0702 Office Phone: 912-685-6282. Personal E-mail: odoremus@excite.com. *It has been my experience that a love for this earth and all that it has is the most precious of our possessions. My hope is that love and kindness become universal.*

DORER, FRED HAROLD, retired chemistry educator; b. Auburn, Calif., May 3, 1936; s. Fred H. and Mary E. (Fisher) D.; m. Marilyn Pearl Young, Sept. 6, 1958; children: Garrett Michael, Russell Kenneth. BS, Calif. State U.-Long Beach, 1961; PhD, U. Wash., 1965; postgrad., U. Freiburg, (Germany), 1965-66. Rsch. chemist Shell Devel. Co., Emeryville, Calif., 1966-67; prof. chemistry Calif. State U., Fullerton, 1967-75; assoc. program dir. chem. dynamics NSF, Washington, 1974-75; chmn., prof. chemistry San Francisco State U., 1975-81; dean natural sci. Sonoma State U., Rohnert Park, Calif., 1981-82, provost, v.p., 1982-84; acad. v.p. Calif. State U., Bakersfield, 1984-99, provost v.p., 1996-99, ret., 1999, emeritus provost, v.p. acad. affairs, 2000—. Contbr. articles to profl. jours. Served with USMC, 1954-57. Grantee Research Corp., 1968; grantee NSF, 1969-75, Petroleum Research Fund, 1978, 80; fellow NSF, 1965 Mem. AAAS, Am. Chem. Soc. Home: 5704 Muirfield Dr Bakersfield CA 93306-9518

DOREY, WILLIAM G., construction company executive; BS in Constrn. Mgmt., Ariz. State U. Br. mgr. Granite Constrn., Inc., Santa Barbara, Calif., 1973-83, asst. divsn. mgr., br. divsn. mgr., sr. v.p., mgr. br. divsn., 1983—87; exec. v.p., COO Granite Constrn. Inc., 1998—2003, pres., COO, 2003—04, pres., CEO, 2004—. also: PO Box 50085 Watsonville CA 95077-5085 Office: Granite Constrn Inc PO Box 50085 Watsonville CA 95077-5085*

DORF, MICHAEL C., law educator; AB, Harvard U., 1986; attended, Victoria U., Wellington, New Zealand, 1986—87; JD magna cum laude, Harvard U., 1990. Bar: NY. Law clk. to Hon. Stephen Reinhardt US Ct. Appeals (9th Cir.), LA, 1990—91; law clk. to Justice Anthony M. Kennedy US Supreme Ct., 1991—92; asst. prof. Rutgers U. Sch. Law, Camden, 1992—94, assoc. prof., 1994—95, Columbia U. Sch. Law, NYC, 1995—97, prof. law, 1997—2004, vice-dean, 1998—2002, Michael I. Sovern prof. law, 2004—. Reporter NJ Supreme Ct. Ad Hoc Com. on Jury Selection, 1992—93. Co-author: On Reading the Constitution, 1991; editor: Constitutional Law Stories, 2004; columnist FindLaw.com; contbr. articles to law jours. Office: Columbia Law Sch 435 W 116th St New York NY 10027 Office Phone: 212-854-2672. Office Fax: 212-854-7946. E-mail: michael.dorf@law.columbia.edu.

DORFAN, JONATHAN MANNIE, physicist, researcher; b. Cape Town, South Africa, Oct. 10, 1947; came to U.S., 1969; s. Charles Archie and Esther (Levine) D.; m. Renee Bing, Dec. 15, 1969; children: Nicole Michelle, Rachel Lauren. BS, U. Cape Town, 1969; PhD, U. Calif., Irvine, 1976. Rsch. assoc. Stanford (Calif.) Linear Accelerator Ctr., 1976-78, staff physicist, 1978-83, assoc. prof., 1984-88, prof. physics, 1989—, assoc. dir., 1994-99, dir., 1999—. Mem. high energy physics adv. panel U.S. Dept. Energy, 1991—94; mem. exec. bd. BaBar, 1994—99; mem. adv. coun. Princeton Plasma Physics Lab., 2000—; mem. sci. adv. bd. Max Planck Inst., 2000—; mem. Internat. Com. Future Accelerators, 2000—. Fellow: Am. Phys. Soc., Am. Acad. Arts & Scis. Office: Stanford Linear Accelerator Ctr PO Box 20450 Stanford CA 94309

DORFMAN, ALLEN BERNARD, international management consultant; b. N.Y.C., Mar. 30, 1930; s. Harry and Jean (Schreiber) D.; m. Elaine Turbé, Jan. 9, 1955; children: Nancy Ann, Jeffrey David. BBA summa cum laude, 1952; postgrad. mgmt. studies, Harvard Bus. Sch. From mem. exec. tng. squad to sr. mgmt. R.H. Macy's, N.Y.C., 1954-67; asst. gen. mdse. mgr., v.p., mem. mgmt. com. N.Y. div. Allied Stores Corp., N.Y.C., 1967-69; v.p., gen. mdse. mgr. hard and soft goods, mem. exec. com. Town & Country Full Line Discount Stores div. Lane Bryant Corp., N.Y.C., 1969-71; pres., dir. Nat. Bellas Hess Inc., Kansas City, Mo., 1971-73; corp. sr. v.p. and pres., CEO retail div. Jewelcor, Inc., N.Y.C., 1973-77; corp. sr. v.p., dir. corp. ops., mem. exec. com. Vornado, Inc., Garfield, N.J., 1977-78; chmn. bd. dirs., CEO Allen B. Dorfman, Mgmt. Consulting Co., 1978—. Prof. Grad. Sch., L.I. Univ., NY. Bd. dirs., exec. v.p. Am. Cancer Soc., L.I.; bd. dirs. Kings Point (L.I.) Civic Assn. With AUS, 1952-54. Recipient award Advt. Club N.Y., Torch of Liberty award Nat. Anti-Defamation League. Mem. Mass. Retailing Inst., Nat. Retail Mchts. Assn., Nat. Assn. Catalog Showroom Merchandisers, Inc., Adelphi Coll. Found., Boy Scouts Am., Boys Club, Philhamonics Assn., Police Athletic League, Polo Club (Boca Raton, adv. bd. govs.-exec. com., chmn. coun. pres., chmn. emeritus coun. of pres.), Wildwood Country Club (Kings Point, NY, pres., bd. dirs.), Beta Gamma Sigma, Eta Mu Pi, Sigma Alpha. Achievements include patents pending for zippered ice and roller skates. Office: Allen B Dorfman Mgmt Consulting Co, Polo Club-Penthouse Villa 17588 Ashbourne Ln Ste C Boca Raton FL 33496-4434 Office Phone: 561-241-4642. Business E-Mail: AllenDorfman@webtv.net.

DORFMAN, CYNTHIA HEARN, government agency administrator; BA in English with honors, Skidmore Coll., 1970; M in English, Middlebury Coll. Sr. exec. fellow Kennedy Sch. Govt., Harvard U.; dir. OCRI Found.; mgr. Dept. Pubs. and Outreach Programs and Projects U.S. Dept. Edn., Washington, dir. media and info. svcs. Office Ednl. Rsch. and Improvement, comm. & develop. dir., Office Innovation and Improvement. Office: US Dept Edn IES Capital Place 555 New Jersey Ave NW Washington DC 20208*

DORFMAN, HOWARD DAVID, pathologist, educator; b. N.Y., July 20, 1928; s. Louis and Helen (Weingarten) D.; m. Esther Novick, June 21, 1952; children: Richard H., Peter W., Leslie Jane. BA, NYU, 1947; MD, SUNY, Bklyn., 1951. Resident in pathology Mt. Sinai Hosp., N.Y., 1952-54, Columbia Presby. Medical Ctr., N.Y., 1954-58; dir. pathology Sharon (Conn.) Hosp., 1958-60; assoc. pathologist Sinai Hosp. Balt., Baltimore, Md., 1960-64; dir. pathology Hosp. Joint Diseases, N.Y., 1964-74; pathologist-in-chief Sinai Hosp. Balt., 1974-85; prof. orthopedic pathology Johns Hopkins Sch. of Medicine, Balt., 1985; prof. pathology, radiology and orthopaedic surgery Albert Einstein Coll. Medicine, Bronx, N.Y., 1985—. Walter Putschar lectr. Mass. Gen. Hosp. Harvard Med. Sch., 1983; vis. prof. Wayne State U. Sch. Medicine, 1984, Baylor Coll. Medicine, Houston, 1984, Cleve. Clinic, 1984, SUNY, Stonybrook, 1994, Johns Hopkins U. Sch. Medicine, 1995, U. Mich. Sch. Medicine, 1997, Cornell U. Sch. Medicine, Meml.-Sloan Kettering Cancer Ctr., 1998, U. Pitts. Sch. Medicine, 1998, Brigham and Women's Hosp., Harvard Med. Sch., 1998, Yale U. Sch. of Medicine, 2003. Author: Bone Tumors, 1998; co-author: Tumors of Bone and Cartilage, 1971. Recipient Henry Jaffe award Hosp. Joint Diseases, 1984. Mem. N.Y. Pathological Soc. (pres. 1989-91), Internat. Skeletal Soc. (pres. 1986-88). Home: 201 E 79th St Apt 10G New York NY 10021-0836 Office Phone: 718-920-5622. Business E-Mail: hdorfman@montefiore.org.

DORFMAN, JOHN CHARLES, lawyer; b. Wilkinsburg, Pa., Feb. 3, 1925; s. Leo O. Dorfman; m. Ruth B. Davison; children: Beverly Dorfman Lenci, Laura Carolyn, Bradley. BEE, Yale U., 1945; JD, Cornell U., 1949. Bar: N.Y. 1949, U.S. Patent & Trademark Office 1949, Conn. 1950, Pa. 1956, U.S. Dist. Ct. (ea. dist.) Pa. 1957, U.S. Ct. Appeals (3d cir.) 1957, U.S. Supreme Ct. 1959, U.S. Ct. Appeals (fed. cir.) 1982. Patent counsel Machlett Labs. Inc., Springdale, Conn., 1950-54; assoc. Pennie & Edmonds, N.Y.C., 1949-55, Howson & Howson, Phila., 1955-59, ptnr., 1960-73; ptnr., chmn. Dann, Dorfman, Herrell & Skillman, Phila., 1974—. Elder Wayne Prebyn. Ch. Served to lt. (j.g.) USNR, 1943—46. Mem.: ABA (chmn. sect. patent, trademarkand copyright law 1984—85, hon. mem. coun.), Nat. Inventors Hall of Fame Found. (pres. 1977—78, bd. dirs. 1979—99, mem. joint bd. NIHF and Inveture Pl. 1997—2000, hon. mem. coun. 1999—), Phila. Patent Law Assn. (pres. 1974—76), Am. Intellectual Property Law Assn. (bd. dirs. 1973—76), Nat. Coun. Patent Law Assns. (chmn. 1978—79), Yale Club (Phila.) (pres. 1982—84), Union League Club (Phila.), St. David's Golf Club (Wayne), Phi Alpha Delta, Delta Tau Delta (bd. dirs. Cornell U. ho. corp. 1969—), Tau Beta Pi. Republican. Avocations: skiing, golf, travel. Home: 215 Midland Ave Wayne PA 19087-4108 Office: Dann Dorfman Herrell & Skillman 1601 Market St Ste 2400 Philadelphia PA 19103-2307 Office Phone: 215-563-4100. Business E-Mail: jdorfman@ddhs.com.

DORFMAN, WILLIAM M., dentist; children: Anna, Charlotte, Georgia. Grad., UCLA, 1980; DDS, U. of the Pacific, San Francisco, 1983. Dental resident, Lausanne, Switzerland, 1983—85; pvt. practice aesthetic and gen. dentistry L.A., 1985—; founder Discus Dental, Inc., L.A., 1989—; pvt. practice Century City Aesthetic Dentistry, L.A. Dental cons. ABC's Extreme Makeover, NBC's The Today Show, NBC's Entertainment Tonight, NBC's EXTRA, NBC's The Rosie O'Donnell Show, E! Entertainment TV; founder, program coord. P.A.C.-live, U. Pacific Dental Sch., San Francisco; lectr. in field. Author (and lectr.): The Smile Guide; past editor Jour. Am. Acad. Cosmetic Dentistry; contbr. articles to profl. jours.; guest appearances Channel 4 News, LA, Channel 7 News. Judge Miss S.C. beauty pageant; raised and donated with Crown Coun. of Dentists to St Jude's Children Rsch. Hosp., Children's Dental Ctr., & Garth Brooks' Teammates for Kids Found. Named Best Aesthetic Dentist in L.A., L.A. Mag.; recipient Lifetime Achievement awards (2). Fellow: Am. Acad. Cosmetic Dentistry; mem.: ADA. Recognized as one of the country's leading dentists and is responsible for creating smiles for famous Hollywood stars; developed products such as: Nite White, Day White, Zoom!, Breath Rx. Office: Discus Dental Inc Century City Aesthetic Dentistry 2080 Century Park E Ste 1601 Los Angeles CA 90067 Office Phone: 310-277-5678. Office Fax: 310-277-3294.*

DORGAN, BYRON LESLIE, senator; b. Dickinson, ND, May 14, 1942; s. Emmett P. and Dorothy (Bach) D.; m. Kimberly Olson Dorgan; children: Scott, Shelly (dec.), Brendon, Haley. B.S., U. N.D., 1965; MBA, U. Denver, 1966. Exec. devel. trainee Martin Marietta Corp., Denver, 1966-67; dep. tax commr., then tax commnr. State of N.D., 1967-80; mem. 97th-102nd congresses from N.D., Washington, 1981-92, U.S. Senate from N.D., Washington, 1992—; asst. Dem. floor leader U.S. Senate, Washington, 1996—. Mem. commerce, sci. and transp. com., select com. on Indian affairs, appropriations com., energy and natural resource com., chmn. Dem. policy com., 1992-, instr. econs. Bismarck (N.D.) Jr. Coll., 1969-71. Contbr. articles to profl. jours. Recipient Nat. Leadership award Office Gov. N.D., 1972 Mem. Nat. Assn. Tax Adminstrs. (exec. com. 1972-75) Democrat. Office: US Senate 322 Hart Senate Off Bldg Washington DC 20510-0001 E-mail: senator@dorgan.senate.gov.*

DORGAN, JAMES RICHARD, lawyer, educator; b. Jacksonville, Fla., Aug. 6, 1968; s. John Alston Jr. and Virginia (Zirkel) D. BA in English, Spring Hill Coll., Mobile, Ala., 1991; JD, Miss. Coll., 1995. Bar: Ala. 1996, Fla. 2004, U.S. Dist. Ct. (so. and mid. dists.) 1996. Pvt. practice, Fairhope, Ala., 1996—. Adj. prof. Spring Hill Coll., 1997—. Mem. Baldwin County Bar Assn., Fla. State Bar Assn. Office: 314 Magnolia Ave Ste B Fairhope AL 36532-2434 Office Phone: 251-928-0192. Personal E-mail: jrdorgan@aol.com.

DORIA, ANTHONY NOTARNICOLA, college dean, educator; b. Savona, Italy, June 2, 1927; s. Vito Sante and Jolanda (Giampaolo) Notarnicola. MBA, Wharton Sch., U. Pa., 1953; LL.M. (equivalent), U. Paris, 1960; D.Jr., U. Rome, 1962. Prof. history, bus. and internat. law Community Coll. at Suffolk County, Selden, N.Y., 1960-65, L.I. U., Southampton, N.Y., 1964-65; founder, pres. Royalton Coll. Sch. Internat. Affairs, S. Royalton, Vt., 1965-72; founder, dean Vt. Law Sch., 1972-74; dean Royalton Coll. Sch. Internat. Affairs (Royalton Coll. Law Study Center), 1974-92; prof. internat. law U. China, Beijing, 1992—; dir. grad. sch. program Internat. Bus. and Law - Hong Kong Ctr. Dir. grad. sch. program internat. bus. and law Hong Kong Ctr.; cons. internat. law and orgns.; panelist Am. Arbitration Assn.; mem. Vt. Gov.'s Commn. on Student Affairs, 1972-75 Author: Italy and the Free World, 1945, The Conquest of the Congo, 1947, Influences in the Making of Foreign Policy in the United States of America, Great Britain and France, 1953, Introduction to the Study of International Law, 1990. Candidate for U.S. Senate, 1986. Served with underground resistance movement World War II. Recipient Merit cert. UN; citation Boy Scouts Am., 1965 Mem. Am. Judicature Soc., Internat. Bar Assn., Internat. Law Assn., Am. Soc. Internat. Law, AAUP, Acad. Polit. Sci., Noble Assn. Chevaliers Pontificaux (life), Elysee (Paris), Penn and Pencil, Rotary (pres. 1990-91). Home: The Royalton Inn South Royalton VT 05068 Office: Royalton Coll Law Study Ctr South Royalton VT 05068

DORIA, CATALDO, transplant surgeon; b. Apr. 1, 1965; Degree in medicine and surgery, U. Perugia, Italy, 1990. Diplomate European Bd. Gen. Surgery. Fellow in transplantation surgery U. Pitts., 1997, 1997; asst. prof. surgery Presbyn. U. Hosp., Pitts., 1997—, Children's Hosp., Pitts., 1998—, VA Hosp., Pitts., Italy, 1998; clin. dir. transplant divsn. U. Pitts. Med. Ctr., Palermo, Italy, 1999—. Developer, implementer transplantation facility in So. Europe, U. Pitts. Med. Ctr., Palermo, Italy, 1998-99. Contbr. articles to profl jours. Grantee U. Perugia; 1991-92, 94, 95, Pfizer, Inc., 1997-98, U. Pitts., 1998.

DORIA, MARILYN L., lawyer; b. Boston, Jan. 15, 1944; AB, Brandeis U., 1965; MPA, Syracuse U., 1967; JD, Temple U., 1974. Bar: Pa. 1974, US Dist. Ct. (ea. dist.) Pa. 1974, Tex. 1986, US Dist. Ct. (so. dist.) Tex. 1986, US Ct. Appeals (5th cir.) 1986, US Ct. Appeals (DC cir.) 1986, DC 1993. Dep. asst. to asst. gen. counsel for enforcement FERC, 1980—83, dep. gen. counsel, 1983—85; former ptnr. oil and gas litig. Reynolds Allen & Cook, Houston; now ptnr. Akin, Gump, Strauss, Hauer & Feld, L.L.P., Washington, 1983—, and sect. mgr. energy, land use and environ. practice group. Mem.: Pa. Bar Assn., Tex. Bar Assn., DC Bar Assn., Fed. Energy Bar Assn. Office: Akin Gump Strauss Hauer & Feld Ste 400 1333 New Hampshire Ave NW Washington DC 20036-1564 Office Phone: 202-887-4000. Business E-Mail: mdoria@akingump.com.

DORIGHI, NANCY S., computer engineer; BS in Math., U. San Francisco, 1974; MSEE, Stanford U., 1976. Mgr. air traffic control tower simulator Future Flight Ctrl., Ames Rsch. Ctr. NASA, Moffett Field, Calif., 1976—. Fellow: AIAA (assoc.); mem.: ASME (assoc. editor ASME jour.). Avocations: hiking, skiing, gardening.

DORIN, DENNIS DANIEL, political science professor, researcher; b. Bklyn., May 11, 1942; s. Michael M. and Marie E. D.; m. Jo Ann Cannon, June 15, 1968; children: Daniel Brooks, Catherine Ann. BA in Polit. Sci. summa cum laude, Ariz. State U., 1964; MA in Govt., U. Va., 1965, PhD in Govt., 1974. Asst. prof. Am. U., Washington, 1967-72; from instr. to prof. polit. sci. U. N.C., Charlotte, 1972—2000, prof. emeritus, 2000—. Cons., expert witness in capital punishment litig. Contbr. articles to profl. jours., numerous newspapers. Mem. Supreme Ct. Hist. Soc. Guest scholar Brookings Instn., Washington, 1966-67; NDEA fellow, U.S. Govt., 1964-67. Mem. Am. Polit. Sci. Assn., John Marshall Found., Golden Key, Phi Beta Kappa, Phi Kappa Phi, Pi Sigma Alpha. Home: 6601 Wheeler Dr Charlotte NC 28211-4758

DORIO, MARTIN MATTHEW, JR., real estate company executive, investor; b. Bklyn., Nov. 12, 1945; s. Martin M. and Josephine V. (Marsala) D.; m. Gayle M. Morris, June 16, 1968; children: Paul, Jay. BS, SUNY, Stony Brook, 1967; PhD, U. Mass., 1975. Rsch. chemist Diamond Shamrock Corp., Painesville, Ohio, 1975-76, group leader, 1977-79; venture mgr. Gen. Electric Lighting Bus., Cleve., 1979-81, quality and mfg. tech. mgr., 1981-87; dir. quality and productivity FMC Corp., Chgo., 1987-90; v.p. worldwide product mgmt. and market strategy Case Corp., Racine, Wis., 1990-91; v.p. corp. planning and devel. J.I. Case Corp., Racine, Wis., 1992-95; pres., CEO, dir. CLARK Material Handling Co., Lexington, Ky., 1995-99, chmn., CEO, dir., 1999—2001; prin. ARGENT Internat., LLC, 2001—. Mem. adv. com. Dept. Energy, Washington, 1977-79, Am. Productivity and Quality Ctr., Houston, 1988-90; mem. adv. com. on quality Ency. Brit., 1988-90; mem. bd. examiners Malcolm Baldrige Nat. Quality Award, 1988-90; mem. adv. bd. Bioblend Lubricants Internat., Inc., 2001-03, Forintell Inc., 2002—; counselor Sr. Corps of Ret. Execs., 2002-03. Author: Multiple Electron Resonance Spectroscopy, 1979; contbr. articles to profl. jours.; patentee in field. Adv. bd. dirs. Mus. Culture and Diversity, 1997-99, chmn. elect; bd. dirs. Lexington Arts & Cultural Coun., 1996-99; co-chair advanced divsn. Lexington: Strides Ahead, 1998-99, counselor SCORE chpt. 573, 2002-2003; chmn. endowment com. Temple Shalom, 2003-05. Capt. USAF, 1968-71. Recipient Nat. Svc. award Nat. Inst. Sci. and Tech., 1988-90. Mem. Am. Soc. Quality Control (exec. com. 1984-85), Am. Mgmt. Assn. Avocations: tennis, raquetball, photography, reading, writing. Home and Office: 1472 Palma Blanca Ct Naples FL 34119-3368 Office Phone: 239-272-2279. E-mail: Marty@MartyDorio.com.

DORION, ROBERT CHARLES, entrepreneur, investor; b. N.Y.C., Dec. 28, 1926; s. William J. and Adelaide (Bacardi) D.; m. Ana Maria Ferber, Nov. 26, 1954; children: Robert Patrick, Marianne Michelle, Nicholas Christian, Kristel Alexia. Student, Columbia U., 1943-44; B of Naval Scis., Dartmouth Coll., 1946. Buyer Balfour, Guthrie and Co. Ltd., 1948-49; capt. M/V Assault Shark Industries div. Borden & Co., 1950-51; pres. Dorion, Rubio and Cia, 1952-57; mgr., ins., mining and chem. dept. Grace & Co., 1954-59; sales mgr. Gen. Tires, Guatemala, 1960-61; chmn. El Salto, S.A., 1962-78; pres. Tecnicos En Seguros, S.A., 1974—, Marcas Mundiales, S.A., 1978-99. Dir. emeritus Bacardi Ltd., Bermuda; pres. Marcas Mundiales S.A.; dir. Industrias Rio Dulce S.A.; pres. Fancap Found. of Inst. Nutricion de Centroamerica y Panama. Contbr. articles to profl. jours. Friend Am. Mus. of Nat. History, N.Y.C.; field assoc. Fla. Mus., Gainesville, Mote Marine Lab., Sarasota, Fla., Interamer. Scout Found., 1978-2004. Fellow Internat. Oceanographic Found. (life); mem. Rotary (Paul Harris fellow), World Scout Orgn. (Baden-Powell fellow), Internat. Scout Found. (dir. 1980-2004), U.S. Navy Meml. Found. (dir.), U.S. Naval Inst. (life), Audubon Soc. (life), Internat. Wildlife Soc., Order of The Bronze Wolf. Avocations: pre-columbian archaeology, cryptozoolical studies, shark research, deep sea fishing. Office: Sect 2870 PO Box 02-5339 Miami FL 33102-5339 also: Kristel SA Apt 195A Guatemala City Guatemala E-mail: kristel@terra.com.

DORIS, ALAN S(ANFORD), lawyer; b. Cleve., June 18, 1947; s. Sam E. and Rebecca D.; m. Nancy Rose Spitzer, Jan. 10, 1976; children: Matthew, Lisa. AB and BS in Bus. cum laude, Miami U., Oxford U., 1969; JD cum laude, Harvard U., 1972. Bar: Ohio 1972, U.S. Dist. Ct. (no. dist.) Ohio 1972, U.S. Tax Ct. 1972, U.S. Ct. Appeals (6th cir.) 1972. Assoc. Stotter, Familo, Cavitch, Elden & Durkin, Cleve., 1972-77; ptnr. Elden & Ford, Cleve., 1978-79, Benesch, Friedlander, Coplan & Aronoff, Cleve., 1980-2000, Squire, Sanders & Dempsey, 2000—. Editor: Ohio Transaction Guide. Treas. Hawthorne Valley Country Club, Cleve., 1984-85; chmn. Cleve. Tax Inst., 1994. Mem. ABA (chmn. capital recovery com. taxation sect. 1994-96). Avocation: golf. Office: Squire Sanders & Dempsey LLP 4900 Key Tower Cleveland OH 44114

DORIS, PETER A., biomedical scientist; b. Durham, Eng., July 1, 1956; came to U.S., 1976; m. Kinga Elzbieta Nurowska. BA, U. Calif., Riverside, 1979, PhD, 1981. Rsch. fellow M.R.C. Dunn clin. nutrition unit U. Cambridge, Eng., 1982-83; rsch. fellow U. Reading, Eng., 1982-83; asst. prof. Tex. Tech. U. Sch. Medicine, Lubbock, 1983-89, assoc. prof., 1989—. Recipient grant NIH, Am. Heart Assn. Mem. Am. Physiol. Soc. Office: Tex Tech Univ Sch of Medicine 3601 4th St Lubbock TX 79430-0001

DÖRKEN, UWE R., finance company executive; b. Schwelm, NRW, Germany, July 29, 1959; MBA, St. Gall U., Switzerland. With McKinsey & Co., Amsterdam, Netherlands, 1986—90, Zurich, Switzerland, Dusseldorf, Germany, Madrid, N.Y.C., Tokyo; mng. dir. internat. divsn. Deutsche Post, 1991; mem. bd. mgmt. DPWN, 1999; CEO, chmn. DHL Worldwide Express, Ft. Lauderdale, Fla., 2001—. Mem. exec. bd. Deutsche Post World Net. Named one of Elite for the Future, Wirtschaftswoche, 1995, Global Leader of Tomorrow, World Econs. Forum, 1997. Office: DHL Worldwide Express Ste 600 1200 South Pine Island Rd Fort Lauderdale FL 33324

DORKEY, CHARLES E., III, lawyer; b. Phila., June 23, 1948; s. Charles Edward and Peggy O'Neal D.; children: Charles Edward IV, John Hilliard, Marjorie Lyddon. AB cum laude, Dartmouth Coll., 1970; JD, Univ. Pa., 1973. Bar: Pa. 1974, N.Y. 1975, D.C. 1977. Law clk. to hon. Samuel J. Roberts Supreme Ct. of Pa., 1973-74; assoc. Sullivan & Cromwell, N.Y.C., 1975-81; ptnr. Reboul, MacMurray, Hewitt, Maynard & Kristol, N.Y.C., 1981-84, Richards & O'Neil, N.Y.C., 1984-91, Haythe & Curley, N.Y.C., 1992-99, Torys LLP, N.Y.C., 1999—. Approved mediator U.S. Dist. Ct. (so. dist.), N.Y. Panel Disting. Neutrals for Ctr. for Pub. Resources; mediator Supreme Ct., N.Y. County, Banking Dept., Jud. Hearing Office, State of N.Y.; chair Hudson River Park Trust. Trustee Citizens Budget Commn., 1993—98, N.Y. Hist. Soc., 1998—; mem. mayor's adv. com., housing ct. adv. coun. 1st Dept. Jud. Screening Com., 1995—99; mem. State Ct. of Claims Jud. Screening Com., 1995—99; mem. Departmental Disciplinary Com. 1st Jud. Dept.; trustee N.Y. Interest Lawyers Acct. Fund, 2000—03; overseer U. Pa. Law Sch., 1993—99; nat. chmn. Law Annual Giving, 1991—93; trustee Hist. Hudson Valley; bd. dirs. Empire State Devel. Corp., N.Y.C. Water Fin. Authority, N.Y. State Job Devel. Authority, Harlem Cmty. Devel. Corp., 42d St. Devel. Project, N.Y. State Mortgage Loan Enforcement and Adminstrn. Corp., N.Y. Parks and Conservation Assn., Liberty Devel. Corp.; mem. alumni coun. Dartmouth Coll., 1990—93, pres. class 1970, 1991—95. Mem. ABA, N.Y. State Bar Assn. (exec. com. comml. and fed. litigation sect. 1986—, fed. judiciary com. 1989—, internat. law and practice sect., com. internat. dispute resolution 1987—) Assn. of Bar of City of N.Y. (products liability com. 1983-86. fed. legis. com. 1990-93, state cts. of superior jurisdiction 1993-96, coun. jud. adminstrn. 1996-99, fed. judiciary 2000-03), N.Y. Athletic Club. Republican. Congregationalist. Home: 205 E 69th St Apt 6C New York NY 10021-5431 Office: Torys LLP 237 Park Ave Fl 20 New York NY 10017-3161 Office Phone: 212-880-6300. Business E-Mail: cdorkey@torys.com.

DORKIN, FREDERIC EUGENE, lawyer; b. Bridgeport, Conn., Feb. 1, 1932; s. William and Selma (Kraus) D.; m. Harriette A. Garfinkel, June 14, 1959; children: Rosalyn Gail, David Ira, Deborah Ruth. AB, Dartmouth Coll., 1953; LLB, Duke U., 1956; LLM, George Washington U., 1968. Bar: Conn. 1956, D.C. 1968, Wash. 1979. Atty. SEC, Washington, 1956-57; pvt. practice Bridgeport, 1960-61; asst. sec. CT Corp. Sys., N.Y.C., Washington, 1961-68; assoc. counsel, asst. sec. Susquehanna Corp., Alexandria, Va., 1968-69; sec., counsel Microdot Inc., Greenwich, Conn., 1969-72; gen. counsel Boeing Computer Svcs., Inc., Morristown, N.J., 1972-78; corp. counsel Boeing Co., Seattle, 1978-82, sr. corp. counsel, 1982-83, asst. gen. counsel, 1984-85; divsn. chief counsel Boeing Electronics Co., 1985-90; sr. counsel Boeing Def. & Space Group, Seattle, 1991-93, ret., 1993; legal cons., arbitrator-mediator Seattle, 1993—. With JAGC, U.S. Army, 1957-60. Mem. Phi Delta Phi, Tau Epsilon Phi. Home: 501 Kirkland Ave Apt 207 Kirkland WA 98033-6248

DORLAND, BYRL BROWN, retired volunteer; b. Apr. 25, 1915; d. David Alma and Ethel Myrle (Petersen) Brown; m. Jack Albert Dorland, June 11, 1944; children: Lynn Dorland Ballinger, Lee Allison. Cert. AA, Snow Jr. Coll., Ephraim, Utah, 1936; tchg. cert., Brigham Young U., 1937; BA, Utah State Coll., Logan, 1940; BS, Family Inst. Vassar Coll., Poughkeepsie, N.Y., 1978; grad., John Robert Powers, Sch. Profl. Women, N.Y.C., 1980. Sch. tchr., Utah, 1937-39, 40-42. Restored Washington Irving's graveplot in Sleepy Hollow (N.Y.) Cemetery (named Nat. Hist. Landmark 1972); nat. dir. Washington Irving Graveplot Restoration Program, 1968—, designer landmark plaque for grave; mem. Nat. Coun. State Garden Clubs,1959—; pres. Potpourri Garden Club, Westchester, N.Y., 1966—; nat. chmn. for graveplot programs Washington Irving Bicentennial, 1983-84; dir. Dorland Family Graveyard Restoration, N.J. Hist. Landmark, 1983—. Named Miss Congeniality, World's Fair Golden Gate Internat. Exposition, Treasure Island, Calif., 1939—40; recipient May Duff Walters trophy, Nat. Coun. State Garden Clubs, 1974, Nat. Trophy, Nat. Historic Landmark Com., 1974, citation, Keep Am. Beautiful, 1974, Disting. Alumni award for Cmty. Svc. Snow Coll., 1989. Mem. Nat. Trust for Historic Preservation (assoc., Pres.'s award 1977), Nat. Historic Soc. Am., Gen. Soc. Mayflower Desc., Am. Mus. Natural History (hon.), Internat. Washington Irving Soc. (founder, pres. 1981-), Nat. Assn. for Gravestone Studies (hon.), Herb Soc. Am., DAR, Internat. Platform Assn., Old Dutch Churchyard Restoration Assn., Am. Mus. Natural History (hon.), Nature Conservancy (hon.), Girls and Boys Town (hon.). Address: PO Box 12158 Scottsdale AZ 85267-2158

DORLAND, JOHN HOWARD, international management consultant; b. Washington, July 23, 1940; s. Gilbert Meding and Lillian (Okkerse) D.; m. Harriet Etter, June 12, 1965; children: John Henry, Howard Etter. BS, USMA, 1963; MS, U. So. Miss., 1968; MBA, U. Tenn., 1978. Commd. 2d lt. U.S. Army, 1963, advanced through grades to col., 1984, ret., 1985. Exec. v.p. Commerce Union Bank, Nashville, Tenn., 1973-81, FCB/FCBI, Pompano Beach, Fla., 1981-82; pres. Fla. Coast Bank, Pompano Beach, 1982-84; pres., CEO Hollywood (Fla.) Bank, 1984-90; CEO Suburban Bankshares, Inc., 1993-94; prin. Gemini Cons., 1994-95; pres. Dorland & Assocs., 1990—; dir. FCCS, Margate, Fla., FCB, Pompano Beach. Author: Duty Honor, Company-West Point Fundamentals for Business Success, 1992. Commr. Mid. Tenn. coun. Boy Scouts Am., 1979, Leadership Nashville, 1979; bd. dirs. YMCA, Ft. Lauderdale, 1983-89, Honda Golf Classics, Broward Econ. Devel., Com. of 100, United Way of Broward County. Decorated Bronze Star with 5 oak leaf clusters, Air medal with 5 oak leaf clusters, Purple Heart. Mem. Am. Bankers Assn., Fla. Bankers Assn. (bd. dirs.), Fla. League Fin. Instns., BEDC Broward County, Hollywood C. of C. Episcopalian. Republican. Home and Office: Dorland & Assocs 103 Heatherset Close Franklin TN 37069-7068 E-mail: dorlassoc@aol.com.

DORLEAC, CATHERINE See DENEUVE, CATHERINE

DORMAN, ALBERT A., engineering executive, consultant, architect; b. Phila., Apr. 30, 1926; s. William and Edith (Kleiman) D.; m. Joan Bettie Heiten, July 29, 1950; children: Laura Jane, Kenneth Joseph, Richard Coleman. BS, Newark Coll. Engring., 1945; MS, U. So. Calif., 1962; ScD (hon.), N.J. Inst. Tech., 1999. Registered profl. engr., Calif., N.Y., Ill., Oreg., Ariz., Pa., Nev., registered architect, Calif., Oreg. Owner firm Albert A. Dorman, Hanford, Calif., 1954-66; v.p. Daniel, Mann, Johnson & Mendenhall, Los Angeles, 1967-73, pres., chief oper. officer, 1974-77, pres., chief exec. officer, 1977-84, chmn., chief exec. officer, 1984-91, chmn. Los Angeles, 1991-99; chmn., chief exec. officer AECOM Tech. Corp., L.A., 1984-91, chmn., 1991-92; founding chmn. AECOM Tech Corp., L.A., 1992—; chmn. Holmes & Narver, Inc., Orange, Calif., 1991-97, Frederic R. Harris, Inc., N.Y.C., 1988-91, Consoer, Townsend and Assocs., Inc., Chgo., 1988-91. Pres., chmn. bd. dirs. Hanford Savs. & Loan Assn., 1963-72; chair com. on bus strategies for pub. capital investment NRC, 2002-04. Contbr. articles to profl. jours. Pres. Cmty. Concerts Assn., 1962-64; past mem. bd. councilors Sch. Urban and Regional Planning, U. So. Calif., Viterbi Sch. Engring., U. So. Calif., 2004—; trustee Harvey Mudd Coll., 1998-2005, J. David Gladstone Found., 1988—, Nat. Found. Advancement in Arts, 1988-99; bd. overseers N.J. Inst. Tech., 1989—; vice chmn. Los Angeles County Earthquake Fact-Finding Commn., 1980. With U.S. Army, 1945-47. Recipient Civil Engring. Alumnus award U. So. Calif., 1976, Edward F. Weston medal N.J. Inst. Tech., 1986, Golden Beaver Engring. award, 1991, Eponym, Albert Dorman Honors Coll., N.J. Inst. Tech., 1993, Disting. Award of Merit, ACEC, 1996, Medal, U. Calif., San Francisco, 1996. Fellow AIA, ASCE (hon. mem., Harland Bartholomew award 1976, Opal Outstanding Lifetime Achievement award 2000), Am. Cons. Engrs. Coun. (life); mem. NAE (elected mem.), Parcel-Sverdrup Civil Engring. Mgmt. award 1987, pres. L.A. sect. 1984-85), Real Estate Constrn. Industries (Humanitarian award 1986), Am. Pub. Works Assn. (life), Cons. Engrs. Assn. Calif. (bd. dirs. 1982-88, pres. 1985-86), Am. Water Works Assn. (life), Water Pollution Control Fedn. (life), Calif. C. of C. (bd. dirs. 1986-94), L.A. Area C. of C. (bd. dirs. 1983-88, exec. com. 1985-87), Calif. Club, Met. Club, Kiwanis (pres. 1962), Tau Beta Pi, Chi Epsilon. Office: AECOM Tech Corp Ste 3700 555 S Flower St Los Angeles CA 90071-2300

DORMAN, ANGELIA HARDY, writer; b. Moncks Corner, S.C., July 6, 1963; d. Dallas Mewborn Hardy and Jule Ann (Wyndham) Spencer; m. David Parris Dorman, July 4, 1983. BA in History, U. S.C., 1983, MA in Tchg., 1990; postgrad., U. Idaho, 1996—. Radio announcer Sta. WBER, Moncks Corner, 1980-81; radio announcer, writer WSCQ, Columbia, S.C., 1983; interlibr. loan libr. Thomas Cooper Libr., U. S.C., Columbia, 1989; asst. curator for edn. McKisick Mus., U. S.C., Columbia, 1989; tchr. Eau Claire H.S., Columbia, 1990, Alcorn Middle Sch., Columbia, 1990-92, Irving Jr. H.S., Pocatello, Idaho, 1992-96; adj. instr. Idaho State U., Pocatello, 1994-96; lead tchr. Moscow (Idaho) Alternative Sch. Ctr., 1996—2000, Warden (Wash.) HS, 2000—. Adj. prof. Big Bend (Wash.) C.C., 2000—; cons. in field. Author: 75th Anniversary History of Columbia YWCA, 1989, Martha Gellhorn and the Human Legacy of War, 1943-1945; contbr. articles to profl. jours. Mem. Martin Luther King Jr. Com., Pocatello, 1992—; com. mem. Women's Hist. Month com., Pocatello, 1992—; organizer Young women's Career Group, Pocatello, 1994—. Mem. U. S.C. Alumni Assn., Phi Alpha Theta.

DORMAN, ARTHUR, optometrist, state legislator; b. N.Y.C., Oct. 21, 1926; s. Harry and Stella (Shapiro) D.; m. Betty Jean Twery, June 5, 1949; children: Pamela R., Janet L., Barbara S., Matthew M. AA, George Washington U., 1949; DO, Pa. Coll. Optometry, 1953. Diplomate Am. Acad. Optometry. Pres. Vision Inst. Am., St. Louis, 1973-76, Vision Care SVcs., Chevy Chase, Md., 1978-82; practice optometry Silver Spring, Md., 1953—93; mem. Md. Ho. of Dels., 1965-75, Md. Senate, 1975—2003. Treas. So. Regional Edn. Bd., Atlanta, 1983-85; pres. Beth Torah Congregation, Hyattsville, Md., 1967; trustee Boys and Girls Clubs, Prince Georges County, 1958-65. Served with U.S. Army, 1945-47, Korea. Mem. Am. Optometric Assn. (Optometrist of Yr. 1967), Md. Optometric Assn. (Optometrist of Yr. 1967), Ctrl. Md. Optometric Assn., Kiwanis. Democrat.*

DORMAN, DAVID W., telecommunications industry executive; b. Atlanta, Jan. 1954; m. Susan Dorman, 1971; 3 children. BS in Indsl. Mgmt., Ga. Inst. Tech., 1975. Pres. Sprint Bus. Services, 1990—94; pres., chmn. bd. dirs., CEO Pacific Bell, 1994—97; exec. v.p. SBC Comm., 1997; chmn., pres., CEO PointCast Inc., 1997—98; CEO Concert Comm. Co., 1998—2000; pres. AT&T Corp., 2000—02, chmn., CEO, 2002—. Bd. dirs. AT&T, 2002—, Sci. Applications Internat. Corp., YUM! Brands, Inc., 2005—. Bd. dirs. Episcopal H.S., Alexandria, Va.; Ga. Tech. Found. Office: AT&T Corp One AT&T Way Bedminster NJ 07921

DORMAN, JEFFREY LAWRENCE, lawyer; b. Akron, Ohio, Feb. 6, 1949; s. Milton and Belle (Handler) D.; m. Bernadette Marie Pawlik, Sept. 2, 1988. BA, U. Mich., 1971; JD, Case Western Res. U., Cleve., 1974; MS, U. Wis., 1976. Bar: Ohio 1975, Ill. 1979, U.S. Dist. Ct. (no. dist.) Ill. 1980. Staff atty. U.S. Dept. Justice, Washington, 1976-79; assoc. Sonnenschein Nath & Rosenthal, Chgo., 1979-82, ptnr., 1982-2000, Freeborn & Peters, 2000—. Mem. ABA, Ohio Bar Assn., Chgo. Bar Assn. Avocation: mountain climbing. Home: 2639 N Southport Ave Chicago IL 60614-1227 Office: Freeborn & Peters 8000 Sears Tower 311 S Wacker Dr Ste 3000 Chicago IL 60606-6677

DORMAN, JO-ANNE, elementary school educator; b. Greenville, Miss. d. Joe Edward and Constance Bonita (Parks) D. BS, Delta State U., 1963. Cert. tchr., Fla. Tchr. Oakcrest Elem. Sch., Pensacola, Fla., 1963-93, 2005—. Traffic sch. instr., 1997—; substitute tchr. Sch. Dist. Escambia County, Pensacola, 1993-200; 5mem. tech. team Oakrest Sch. Hospitality Com., 2005— Sunday sch. tchr. Methodist Ch., Pensacola, Fla., 1963, 65, 68; voter precinct clk. Escambia County, 1997—; vol. Sr. Friends, 2000—. Named Local Sch. Tchr. of Yr., 1988. Mem.: U. West Fla. Leisure Learners Soc., Pensacola Dog Fanciers Assn., Papillon Club Am., Five Flags Dog Tng. Club. Democrat. Methodist. Avocations: travel, reading, photography, theater, dogs. Home: 188 Talladega Trl Pensacola FL 32506-3202 E-mail: jadpaps@yahoo.com.

DORMAN, JOHN FREDERICK, genealogist; b. Louisville, July 25, 1928; s. John Frederick and Sue Carpenter (Miller) D. BA, U. Louisville, 1950; MA, Emory U., 1955. Asst. archivist Coll. William and Mary, 1953-55; genealogist, 1955—; editor The Virginia Genealogist, 1957—; lectr. Nat. Inst. Geneal. Research, 1963-74, 77-93, Inst. Geneal. and Hist. Research Samford U., 1977-88. Trustee Bd. for Cert. of Genealogists, 1964-84, pres., 1979-82, exec. dir., 1983-96. Fellow Am. Soc. Genealogists (treas. 1959-66, pres. 1982-85), Va. Geneal. Soc.; mem. Soc. Cincinnati, Soc. Colonial Wars (dep. registrar gen. 1969-81, D.C. gov. 1980-82), SR (gen. registrar 1976-85, pres. D.C. chpt. 1982-84), SAR (D.C. pres. 1967-68), Nat. Geneal. Soc. (v.p. 1958-59, 68-70, libr. 1959-60), Children Am. Revolution (sr. nat. registrar 1960-62, sr. nat. treas. 1962-64, 66-68, sr. nat. 2d v.p. 1968-70), Descs. Colonial Govs. (gov. gen. 1973-76), Descs. Lords Md. Manors (pres. 1985-89), Sovereign Mil. Order Temple Jerusalem. Clubs: Cosmos (Washington). Republican. Episcopalian. Home: 175 Hulls Chapel Rd Fredericksburg VA 22406-5218

DORMAN, JOHN MERRILL, medical educator; b. Phila., Feb. 7, 1942; s. Daniel Bliss and Dorothy Merrill Dorman; m. Charlene Diane Tropeano, Aug. 15, 1964; children: Todd Trowbridge, Bianca Dorman Humphries, Lydia Fiore. BA, Williams Coll., 1963; MD, Harvard U., 1967. Clin. prof. medicine Stanford (Calif.) U. Sch. Medicine, 2003—. Comdr. USPHS, 1969—71. Fellow: Am. Coll. Health Assn. (Boynton award 1993). Republican. Office Phone: 650-725-1368.

DORMAN, LINNEAUS CUTHBERT, retired chemist; b. Orangeburg, SC, June 28, 1935; s. John Albert and Georgia D.; m. Phae Louise Hubble, June 21, 1958; children: Evelyn Suzanne, John Albert III. BS, Bradley U., 1956; PhD, Ind. U., 1961; DSc(hon.), Saginaw Valley State U., 1988. Chemist No. Regional Lab., U.S. Dept. Agr., Peoria, Ill., summers 1956-59; research chemist Dow Chem. Co., Midland, Mich., 1960-68, research specialist, 1968-76, research assoc., 1976-83, assoc. scientist, 1983-93, sr. assoc. scientist, 1993-94; ret., 1994. Lawrence lectr. Bradley U., 1990, mem. adv. bd., 1994, 2005; active Centurion Soc., 1993, Burgess award selection com., 1996-2000, chemistry dept. adv. bd.; cmty. adv. panel Dow Corning Midland Plant, 1995-2005. Contbr. articles to profl. jours.; patentee in field. Active NAACP, Midland Commn. on Cmty. Rels., 1963-73, vice-chmn., 1967; active Black Exec. Exch. Program, Urban League, 1971, 75; trustee Midland Found., 1980-90, v.p., 1987-90; dir.-at-large Midland Ctr. for the Arts, 1984, 85; bd. fellows Saginaw Valley State Coll., 1975-87, emeritus mem., 1987, v.p., 1981-83, pres., 1983-85, ann. fund drive, 1985-95, presdl. search com., 1989; chmn. Cen. Rsch. and Devel. Scientists Orgn., 1992; exec. coun. Ind. U. Alumni Assn., 2002—; bd. trustees Hidden Harvest, 2004. Paul Harris fellow Rotary, 1989; co-recipient Bond award Am. Oil Chemists Soc., 1960; recipient Cen. Rsch. Inventor of Yr. award Dow Chem. Co., 1982, Saginaw Valley State Univ. Disting. Svc. Medallion (with wife Phae), 2002. Mem. AAAS, Nat. Orgn. Black Chemists and Chem. Engrs. (Percy L. Julian award 1999), Am. Chem. Soc. (sect. treas. 1966, sec. 1967, dir. 1968-70, councilor 1971-76, 80-81, 84-92), Midland Rotary (sec. 1980-81, v.p. 1981-82, pres. 1982-83), Saginaw Valley Torch Club, Midland County Hist. Soc. (bd. mgrs. 2002), Little Forks Conservancy, Sigma Xi (chpt. treas. 1969, sec. 1970, pres. 1975), Phi Lambda Upsilon, Pi Kappa Delta, Omega Psi Phi. Mem. United Ch. of Christ. Home: PO Box 1732 Midland MI 48641-1732

DORMAN, RICHARD FREDERICK, JR., association executive, consultant; b. Peoria, Ill., June 3, 1944; s. Richard Frederick and Pauline Elizabeth (Dryfus) D.; children: Richard F., Kevin M.; m. Anne Marie Carlton, May 28, 1976. Student, Franklin U., Columbus, Ohio, 1963—65, student, 1968—69, New Sch. Social Reform, N.Y.C., 1979—80, U. Md., 1982. Field rep. Ohio Civil Svc. Employees Assn., Columbus, 1972-75; regional dir. St. Jude Children's Rsch. Hosp., N.Y.C., 1975-80; exec. dir. Assembly Govtl. Employees, Washington, 1980-85; with Quality Mgmt. Inst., Washington, 1985-86; exec. dir. Am. Congress on Surveying and Mapping, Falls Church, Va., 1986-90, Ohio Coun. for Home Care, 1991-93; exec. v.p., COO Assn. for Profls. in Infection Control and Epidemiology Inc., Washington, 1993-95; v.p. Assn. Mgmt. Group, Arlington, Va., 1995-96. Ptnr. McIntoch & Dorman, Washington, 1982-86; pres. Catalyst Group, Alexandria, 1996—. Founder, pres. Columbus Ind. Jr. High Football League, Ohio, 1970. Recipient Recognition for Contbn. to Women's Sports award Ohio Ho. of Reps., 1975, 76. Mem. Am. Soc. Assn. Execs. (cert. assn. exec., fellow 1988), Greater Washington Soc. Assn. Execs., Alexandria C. of C. (bd. dirs., vice chair). Republican. Presbyterian. E-mail: rfdorman@aol.com.

DORMANN, HENRY O., magazine publisher; b. N.Y.C., Mar. 5, 1932; s. Henry Maroni and Ivara (Soberg) D.; m. Alice Andreasen, Apr. 7, 1958; children: Kaari, Kristi. Chmn. bd. Nat. Enquirer, 1971-72, chmn. exec. com., 1987-89; chmn. Internat. Bd. Indsl. Advisors, 1964—; pres., editor-in-chief S.I.P.A. News Service, N.Y.C., 1966—; pres. U.S. Tech. Devel. Co., 1969-70; pres., editor-in-chief Holiday Mag., 1976-77; chmn. editor-in-chief Leaders Mag., 1977—. Adv. council Joint Legis. Com. on Met. and Regional Areas Study N.Y. State, 1969-72; chmn. N.Y. State Assembly Council on Econ. Devel., 1972-80. Author: A Millionaire's Guide to Europe or How to Save Money Like the Rich People Do, 1967, A Millionaire's Guide to Exotic Places or How to Save Money Like the Rich People Do, 1973, A Millionaire's Guide to Fun Places or How to Save Money Like the Rich People Do, 1978, The Speaker's Book of Quotations, 1987, 2000. Founder Libr. Presdl. Papers, Inst. for Study of Presidency; bd. dirs. Inst. Edn. Affairs, Washington; trustee IATA Internat. Airline Tng. Fund, 1988-2003, Am. U., Washington, 1981-92; founder, pres. Found. for Family Values, 1990-93. With USCG. Office: 59 E 54th St New York NY 10022-4211

DORMANS, JOHN PAUL, surgeon, educator; b. Ft. Wayne, Ind., Jan. 13, 1957; s. Paul M. and Viginia Ann Dormans; m. Nanette J. Dormans; children: Nicholas, Andrea, Laura, Kath. BA magna cum laude, Ind. U., 1979, MD, 1983. Diplomate Am. Bd. Orthopedic Surgery. Resident in orthop. surgery Mich. State U., Grand Rapids, 1988; pediat. orthop. fellow Hosp. Sick Children, Toronto, Canada, 1988; orthop. surgeon Children's Hosp. Phila., 1989—96, chief orthop. surgery, 1996—, pres. med. staff, 1999—2001, also trustee; from asst. prof. to assoc. prof. orthop. surgery U. Pa., 1991—2000, prof. orthop. surgery Sch. Medicine Phila., 2000—. Pres. Surg. Assoc. Rsch. and Edn. Found., 1997-98; dir. pediatric orthop. fellowship Children's Hosp. Phila. Editor: Caring for the Child with Cerebral Palsy, 1998; section editor: The Cervical Spine, 2004; assoc. editor Jour. Bone and Joint Surgery, 2000—; contbr. articles to profl. jours. Travelling fellow Am. Orthop. Assn. and Am. Acad. Orthop. Surgeons, 1996. Fellow ACS, Am. Acad. Orthop. Surgeons, Sooliosis Rsch. Soc.; mem. Am. Orthop. Assn., Pediatric Orthop. Soc. N.Am., Musculoskeletal Tumor Soc., Phi Beta Kappa. Lutheran. Avocations: fly fishing, painting, reading, history of medicine. Office: Childrens Hosp Phila Wood Bldg, 2d Fl 34th and Civic Center Blvd Philadelphia PA 19104-4399 Office Phone: 215-590-1527. Business E-Mail: dormans@email.chop.edu.

DORMINEY, HENRY CLAYTON, JR., allergist; b. Tifton, Ga., May 15, 1949; s. Henry Clayton and Virgina (Petty) D. BS, Davidson Coll., 1971; MD, U. Iowa, 1975. Diplomate Am. Bd. Internal Medicine, Am. Bd. Allergy and Immunology; lic. physician, Ga. Med. intern U. Iowa Hosps. and Clinics, Iowa City, 1975-76, med. resident, 1976-78, allergy and immunology fellow, 1978-80; practice medicine specializing allergy and clin. immunology Allergy & Dermatology Assocs. of Tiftone, Ga., 1981—99, Allergy, Asthma and Sinus Clinic of Tifton, 1999—. Mem. staff Tift Regional Med. Ctr.; bd. dirs. Brumby's Crossing, Dorminey Enterprises; chmn. and founder Tifton Mus. Arts and Heritage, 1991; mem. Allergy, Asthma & Sinus Clinic of Tifton. Assoc. editor, contbg. author Vital Signs, 1969-71. Bd. dirs. Tift County Found. Ednl. Excellence, 1996—, chmn. investment com., 1998-, v.p., 2004-2005, pres. elect., 2006-2006; bd. dirs. Tifton Heritage Found., pres., 1992; bd. dirs. Tifton Mus. Arts and Heritage, 1991—. Recipient Physician's Recognition award AMA, 1979, 85, Lee Willingham III trophy Davidson Coll., 1987, Tifton Main Street Program award, 1989, Best Adaptive Re-Use Project, Tifton Historic District, The Coca Cola Bldg., 1993; grantee Am. Coll. Allergy, 1980. Mem. Am. Acad. Allergy (travel grantee 1980), Tift County Med. Soc. (sec., treas. 1983-84, v.p., 1984-85, pres. 1985-86), Med. Assn. Ga., Am. Numismatic Soc., Forward Tifton, Tifton C. of C. Lodges: Rotary (Spl. Merit award, founder Tifton Directory, bd. dirs. 1988-93, pres.-elect 1989-90, pres. 1990-91, Paul Harris fellow 1993). Democrat. Home: 21 Duck Dr Tifton GA 31794-3953 Office: 820 Love Ave Tifton GA 31794-4071 Office Phone: 229-382-3720. E-mail: dorminey@friendlycity.net.

DORN, CHARLES MEEKER, art educator; b. Mpls., Jan. 17, 1927; s. Melville Wilkinson and Margaret (Meeker) D.; m. Virginia Josephine Coble, July 11, 1947; children: Mary Jan, Charles Meeker. BA, MA, George Peabody Coll. Tchrs., 1950; Ed.D., U. Tex., 1959. Asst. prof. art Union U., Jackson, Tenn., 1950-54; instr. art and edn. Memphis State U., 1954-57; lectr. edn. U. Tex., 1957-59; head art dept. Nat. Coll. Edn., Evanston, Ill., 1959-61; assoc. prof. art No. Ill. State U., 1961-62; exec. sec. Nat. Art Edn. Assn., Washington, 1962-70; prof., chmn. dept. art Calif. State U., Northridge, 1970-72; prof. creative arts Purdue U., Lafayette, Ind., 1972-86, head dept., 1972-76; prof., dir. Ctr. for Arts Adminstrn. Fla. State U., Tallahassee, 1986—, chmn. dept. art edn., 1986-90. Served with AUS, 1945-46. Recipient 25th Anniversary award for disting. service Nat. Gallery Art, 1966. Mem.: Internat. Soc. Edn. Through Art, Nat Art Edn. Assn. (pres. 1975—77, Disting. Svc. award 1979, Disting. fellow 1982, Southeastern Higher Edn. Art Educator award 1990, Higher Edn. award 1990, 1999, Nat. Art Educator of the Yr. 2003), Fla. Art Edn. Assn., Kappa Phi Kappa, Phi Delta Kappa. Home: 377 Castleton Cir Tallahassee FL 32312 Office: Fla State U Dept Art Edn Tallahassee FL 32306 Office Phone: 850-644-2158. E-mail: dornetal@aol.com, cdorn@mailer.fsu.edu.

DORN, DIANE M., science educator; b. Chilton, Wis., Jan. 11, 1966; d. Dennis and Marian Dorn; m. William Dowell, Feb. 13, 1993. AS in electronics, McHenry C.C., 1990; BS in natural environ. sys., No. Ill., 1994; MEd, Nat. Louis U., 1999. Sci. tchr. Woodstock HS, Woodstock, Ill., 1994—2001, Marian Ctrl. HS, Woodstock, Ill., 2001—. Bd. mem. Ringwood Planning Bd., Ringwood, Ill., 2000—. Recipient monetary award, Earth Watch, 2000. Mem.: NSTA, AAAS, Ill. Sci. Tchrs. Assn. Avocations: soccer, snowboarding, bicycling, backpacking, travel. Office: Marian Cath Ctrl HS 1001 McHenry Ave Woodstock IL 60098 E-mail: ddorn@marian.com.

DORN, GEORGETTE MAGASSY, library official; b. Budapest, Hungary, Aug. 13, 1934; arrived in U.S., 1955; d. Gabriel Luis and Georgette Gyorko Magassy; m. Paul Austin Dorn Jr., June 9, 1961; children: Georgette, Elizabeth, Susan, Paul Gabriel. Degree in pub. translation, U. Buenos Aires, 1955; BS, Creighton U., 1959; MA, Boston Coll., 1961; PhD, Georgetown U., 1981. Tchg. asst. Boston Coll., 1960—61; specialist in Hispanic culture Libr. of Congress, Washington, 1964—69, head Hispanic reading rm., 1969—94, chief Hispanic divsn., 1994—. Lectr. Ctr. Am. Studies, Georgetown U., Washington, 1982—; mem. adv. com. L.Am. project Ctr. Rsch. Librs., Chgo., 1994—; asst. editor Am. Quar. Rev., Washington, 1979—; chmn. history com. Pan Am. Inst. Geography and History, Washington, 2002—; cons. Andrew Mellon Found., 2001, 05; rec. L.Am., Caribbean and Latino authors Archive of Hispanic Literature on Tape. Translator (by Jose Francisco Ruiz): Report on the Indian Tribes of Texas, 1972; assoc. editor: Encyclopedia of Latin American History and Culture, 1996 (Waldo Leland award, 97); editor: Works by Miguel de Cervantes, 1994; contbr. articles to profl. publs. Organizer L.Am. Book Fair, Washington, 1984—85; curator archive Hispanic literature on tape Libr. of Congress, Washington, 1969—; chmn. disting. award com. Conf. on L.Am. History, 1998; chmn. U.S. History Commn., Pan Am. Inst. Geography and History, 2002—05; mem. exec. com. Conf. L.Am. History, 1991—96; mem. steering com. Consortium, L.Am. Studies Programs, 1992—96; mem. adv. com. D.C. Latino Cmty. Festival Exhibit, Washington, 1989; mem. adv. bd. Mex.-Am. Lit. Archives, UCLA, 1989—91; archivist Holy Trinity Ch., Washington, 1988—94. Travel grantee, Fulbright Commn., 1988. Mem.: Am. Cath. Hist. Assn., L.Am. Studies Assn. (mem. exec. coun. 1985—87, chmn. Bryce Wood Prize Com. 1990—91, regional liaison 1975—77), Am. Hist. Assn. (Premio de Rey prize 2004, Franklin Jameson prize 1995), Intern Am. Coun. Washington (pres. 1985—86), Phi Alpha Theta, Alpha Sigma Nu. Roman Catholic. Avocations: swimming, yoga, painting, films. Home: 4702 Essex Ave Chevy Chase MD 20815 Office: Libr Congress Hispanic Divsn 101 Independence Ave SE Washington DC 20540-4850 Office Phone: 202-707-2003. Office Fax: 202-707-2005. Business E-Mail: gdor@loc.gov.

DORN, JAMES ANDREW, editor; b. Buffalo, Aug. 26, 1945; s. Andrew William and Mary Carol (Gannon) D.; m. Carol Evans Cronmiller, Sept. 5, 1970; children: Andrea Yvonne, Heather Katherine. BS in Econs., Canisius Coll., 1967; MA in Econs., U. Va., 1969, PhD, 1976. Prof. Towson (Md.) U., 1973—; editor Cato Jour. Cato Inst., Washington, 1982—, v.p. for acad. affairs, 1989—; rsch. fellow Inst. Humane Studies George Mason U., Fairfax, Va., 1986-95. Editor: The Future of Money in the Info. Age, 1997, China in the New Millennium, 1998; co-editor (with Henry G. Manne): Econ. Liberties and the Judiciary, 1987; co-editor: (with Anna J. Schwartz) The Search for Stable Money, 1987; co-editor: (with William A. Niskanen) Dollars, Deficits and Trade, 1989; co-editor: (with Wang Xi) Econ. Reform in China, 1990; co-editor: (with Roberto Salinas-León) Money and Markets in the Americas, 1996; co-editor: (with Steve Hanke and Alan Walters) The Revolution in Devel. Economics, 1998; co-editor: (with T.G. Carpenter) China's Future, 2000; co-editor: (with D. Artana) Internat. Fin. Crises (in Spanish), 2004; contbr. articles to profl. jours. Mem. White House Commn. on Presdl. Scholars, Washington, 1984-90. Recipient Regent's Faculty Award for Excellence in Rsch./Scholarship Univ. Sys. Md., 1998; Hayek Fund grantee Inst. for Humane Studies, 1986-87, Earhart grantee 1969-70, 81; Thomas Jefferson Ctr. fellow U. Va., 1969-70. Mem. Am. Econ. Assn., Mont Pelerin Soc., West Side Rowing Club (Buffalo). Avocations: alpine hiking, photography, geology, jogging. Office: Cato Inst 1000 Massachusetts Ave NW Washington DC 20001-5400 Business E-Mail: jdorn@cato.org.

DORN, JENNIFER LYNN, federal agency administrator; b. Grand Island, Nebr., Dec. 7, 1950; d. Harold Clarence and Ethel Agnes D.; 2 children BA, Oreg. State U., 1973; MPA, U. Conn., 1977. Legis. asst. Senator M. Hatfield, Washington, 1977-81; com. staff Senate Appropriations, Washington, 1981-83; spl. asst. to Sec. Elizabeth Dole US Dept. Labor, Washington, 1983-84; dir. Comml. Space Transp., Washington, 1984-85; assoc. dep. sec. U.S. Dept. Transp., Washington, 1985-87; asst. sec. policy U.S. Dept. Labor, Washington, 1989-91; sr. v.p. pub. support ARC, Washington, 1991-98; pres. Nat. Health Mus., 1998—2001; adminstr. Fed. Transit Adminstrn. US Dept. Transp., Washington, 2001—. Mem. Washington Women's Forum, Cosmos Club. Republican. Lutheran. Office: US Dept Transp Fed Transit Adminstrn 400 7th St SW Washington DC 20590 E-mail: nrodj@aol.com.

DORN, LOUIS OTTO, retired minister; b. Detroit, July 1, 1928; s. Theodore Herman and Thekla Maria (Frederking) Dorn; m. Erna Ruth Koessel, June 14, 1953; children: Margaret Ligaya Dorn White, Peter Bayani, Martin Louis,

Judith Anne. BA, Concordia Theol. Sem., St. Louis, 1951, BD, 1962; MA in Linguistics, Ateneo de Manila U., Quezon City, The Philippines, 1974; PhD, Luth. Sch. Theology, Chgo., 1980. Ordained to ministry Luth. Ch.-Mo. Synod, 1953. Missionary Luth. Ch. in The Philippines, Manila, 1953-74; candidate Ohio dist. Luth. Ch. -Mo. Synod, 1975-80; candidate N.J. dist. Luth. Ch.-Mo. Synod, 1980-99; transls. rsch. assoc. Am. Bible Soc., N.Y.C., 1979-90; transl. cons. United Bible Socs., N.Y.C., 1990-99; ret., 1999. Chmn. Luth. Philippine Mission, Manila, 1962—63, Manila, 1971—72; sec. Luth. Ch. in the Philippines, Manila, 1962—63, commn. ecumenical affairs, 1964—74, dir. transls. dept., 1966—74; bd. dirs. Interchurch Lang. Sch., Quezon City, 1964—74, chmn. bd. dirs., 1967—74; hon. transls. advisor Philippine Bible Soc., Manila, 1968—74. Contbr. articles and revs. to religious publs. Grantee, Ctr. Dist. Luth. Ch.-Mo. Synod, 1944—53, Luth. Sch. Theology, Chgo., 1974—78. Mem.: Soc. Bibl. Lit. Home: 1414 N Gregson St Durham NC 27701-1110 *People often don't know how to live under God's grace because they can't forgive themselves and know only God's law. To accept God's grace, to be willing to be forgiven, results in an amazing life of freedom that honors the Savior.*

DORN, MARIAN MARGARET, educator, sports management administrator; b. North Chicago, Ill., Sept. 25, 1931; d. John and Marian (Petkovsek) Jelovsek; m. Eugene G. Dorn, Aug. 2, 1952 (div. 1975); 1 child, Bradford Jay. BS, U. Ill., 1953; MS, U. So. Calif., 1961. Tchr., North Chicago Cmty. H.S., 1954-56; tchr., advisor activities, high sch., Pico-Rivera, Calif., 1956-62; tchr., coach Calif. H.S., Whittier, 1962-65; prof. phys. edn., chmn. dept., coach, asst. chmn. div. women's athletic dir. Cypress (Calif.) Coll., 1966—; men's, women's golf coach; mgr. Billie Jean King Tennis Ctr., Long Beach, Calif., 1982-86; founder King-Dorn Golf Schs., Long Beach, 1984; pres. So. Calif. Athletic Conf., 1981; curriculum cons. Calif. Dept. Edn., 1989-92; spkr. Citizen Amb. Program China Conf. women, 1995; coach golf team state champions Women's Cypress Coll., 1997. Mem. del. to China Citizens Ambassador Program, 1995. Recipient cert. of merit Cypress Elem. Sch. Dist., 1976; Outstanding Svc. award Cypress Coll., 1986; named Women's Coach of Yr. Orgn. Empire Conf., 1995, Master Profl., 1996, Coll. Women's Golf Coach of Yr., Calif. Coaches Assn., 1998, L.P.G.A. Western Sect. Coach of Yr., 1998; nominated Coach of Yr., L.P.G.A. Western Sect., 1991-96. Mem. Calif. (v.p. So. dist.), San Gabriel Valley (pres.) Assns. Health, Phys. Edn. and Recreation, So. Calif. C.C. Athletic Coun. (sec., dir. pub. rels.), NEA, Calif. Tchrs. Assn., AAHPERD, Ladies Profl. Golf Assn. Conglist. Author: Bowling Manual, 1974. Office: 9200 Valley View St Cypress CA 90630-5805

DORN, MARK S., music educator, producer; b. Milwaukee, Wis, Aug. 5, 1957; s. Thomas John and Barbara Irene Dorn; children: Nathan, Emily, Nicole, Christopher. MusB in Edn., Ind. U., 1979, MusM in Trumpet Performance, 1981; MA in Biblical Counseling, Colo. Christian U., 1994. Assoc. prof. Colo. Christian U., Lakewood, 1995—. Free lance trumpet artist, Denver, 1993—. Prodr.: Kids From Wisconsin, 1996—. Mem.: Internat. Trumpet Guild, Internat. Assoc. of Jazz Ed., Music Ed. Nat. Conf. Avocations: racquetball, travel, reading, bicycling, hiking. Home: 11726 W Radcliff Ave Morrison CO 80465 Office Phone: 303-963-3133. E-mail: mdorn@ccv.edu.

DORN, MARY ANN, retired auditor; b. Overland, Mo., May 1, 1933; d. Bernard J. and Marie (Kunkler) Engler; children: Glennon (dec.), Pat Michael, Michelle; m. Donald Patrick Dorn, June 3, 2002. Student, Fontbonne Coll., 1951-52; AA, Sacramento City Coll., 1975; BS in Bus., Calif. State U., 1981. CPA, Calif.; cert. fraud examiner; cert. govt. fin. mgr. From asst. to acct. Mo. Rsch. Labs., Inc., St. Louis, 1953-55, adminstrv. asst., 1955-60; sec. western region fin. office Gen. Electric Co., St. Louis, 1960-62; credit analyst Crocker Nat. Bank, Sacramento, 1962-72; student tchr. Sacramento County Dept. Edn., 1979-81; acctg. technician East Yolo Community Services Dist., 1983; mgmt. specialist USAF Logistics Command, 1984; auditor Office Insp. Gen. U.S. Dept. Transp., 1984-92; auditor-in-charge Adminstrn. for Children and Families U.S. Dept. Health and Human Svcs., 1992—. Mem. Sacramento Community Commn. for Women, 1978-81, bd. dirs., 1980—; planning bd. Golden Empire Health Systems Agy. Mem. AARP (tax counselor), AAUW (fin. officer 1983—), AICPA, Nat. Assn. Accts. (dir., newsletter editor), Fontbonne Coll. Alumni Assn., Calif. State Alumni Assn., Assn. Govt. Accts. (chpt. officer), Calif. Soc. CPAs, German Geneological Soc. (bd. dirs. 1990—, publicity dir. 1994—), Sun City Lincoln Hills Assn., Beta Gamma Sigma, Beta Alpha Psi. Roman Catholic. Home: 815 Magnolia Ln Lincoln CA 95648-8429

DORN, NORMAN PHILIP, management consulting firm executive; b. Ithaca, NY, Jan. 29, 1945; s. Saul James and Pearl Dorn; m. Evelyn Mary Samonas, July 3, 1966; children: Paul, Ian, Nathan, Mark. BS, Carnegie-Mellon U., 1966; MS, U. Pitts., 1969. Engr. Westinghouse Electric, Pitts., 1969-78; sr. engr. GPU Svc. Corp., Forked River, NJ, 1978-79; mng. dir. Accountable Systems Co. Internat. Inc., Toms River, NJ, 1979—. Mem. Md./Del./D.C. Staff of Navy-Marine Corps Mil. Affiliate Radio Sys., Telephone Pioneers, Masons, Toastmasters. Achievements include inventions, quality improvements, requirements process engring., process controls devel., instruction, system stability analysis procedures, telecommunications tech., systems (applications) architecture and mfg. mgmt. Office Phone: 888-607-6267.

DORN, RYAN, sound recording engineer, small business owner, communications executive; b. Phila., Jan. 9, 1966; s. Joel Dorn and Florence Reese; m. Beth Adele Harnick Dorn; children: Ashley, Heather, Vaughn. Rec. engr., 1988—2005; pres. VVI/Visionary Video, Malibu, 1997—; acct. exec. West coast New World Sales, Hackensack, 2004—. Pres., co-founder VVI/Witkin Music Group; CEO Angels Wings for Autism, NPO. Democrat. Home: 31516 Anacapa View Dr Malibu CA 90265 Office Phone: 310-403-8647. E-mail: angelstar@earthlink.net.

DORN, SUE BRICKER, retired hospital administrator; b. Seattle, Apr. 1, 1934; d. Barney and Frances B. (Schnitzer) Bricker; m. Philip Henry Dorn, Dec. 31, 1955 (dec.); children: Charles, Martha Dorn. BA, Stanford U., Palo Alto, 1955; MA, Bank St. Coll., 1973. Cert. tchr., N.Y. Dir. promotion exec. compensation svc. Am. Mgmt. Assn., N.Y.C., 1956-58; tchr. spl. edn. N.Y.C. Bd. of Edn., 1969-77; assoc. dir. Yale U., New Haven, 1977—79; v.p. Bank St. Coll. of Edn., N.Y.C., 1979-81, Aspen Inst. for Humanistic Studies, N.Y.C., 1981-82; assoc. v.p. Yale U., New Haven, 1982-87; dep. dir. devel. and pub. affairs Mus. of Modern Art, N.Y.C., 1987-94; v.p., vice provost for devel. The N.Y. Hosp.-Cornell Med. Ctr., 1994—98. Mem. maj. gifts com. Stanford U.; cons. in field; bd. dirs. First Citicorp Life Ins. Co. Pres. LWV, Warren, Mich., 1962-65, Stanford Alumni Club of N.Y., N.J. and Conn., N.Y.C., 1968-70, 25 East 86th St. Corp., N.Y.C., 1989-93, 95—; mem. dirs. adv. bd. Yale Comprehensive Cancer Ctr., Yale U., 1990-94. Named Citizen of the Yr., Warren C. of C., 1962; recipient Citation, City of Warren, 1963, Gold Spike award and Cert. of Outstanding Achievement, Stanford U., 1976. Mem. Stanford Assocs., Univ. Club. Home: 25 E 86th St New York NY 10028-0553 E-mail: sdorn@nyc.rr.com.

DORNAGON, MANDY M., lawyer; b. Manila, Philippines, Feb. 28, 1958; s. Crispin and Rosina Dornagon; m. Valerie Mendoza; children: Robby, Lance. BSBA, U. of the East, Manila, 1979, LLB, 1984; postgrad., Bklyn. Law Sch., 1988—89, Touro Law Sch., 1992—93, NYU, 2004. Bar: Supreme Ct. of the Philippines 1985, Supreme Ct. N.Y. 1994, U.S. Tax Ct. 1994, U.S. Dist. Ct. (so. dist.) NY 1998. Legal asst. Banco Filipino Savs. & Mortgage Bank, Philippines, 1979—85; assoc. atty. N.C. Monteiro & Assocs., 1985—86; legal counsel Eagle Group of Cos., Philippines, 1986—87; sole practice Queens, NY, 1994—. Contbr. articles to profl. jours. Grantee, Nat. Scholarship Ctr., Manila, 1975—79. Mem.: ABA, Integrated Bar of the Philippines, Am. Immigration Lawyers Assn., UE Knights Fraternal Assn. Office: PO Box 260342 Bellerose NY 11426-0342 Office Phone: 718-468-8720. Business E-Mail: usimmigrationlawyer@attydornagon.com, mdornagon@attydornagon.com.

DORNAN, DONALD C., JR., lawyer; b. Columbus, Miss., Oct. 26, 1952; s. Donald C. and Virginia (Shelley) D.; children: Gloria Diana, Donald Patrick. BA, Miss. State U., 1974; JD, U. Miss., 1976. Bar: Miss. 1977, U.S. Dist. Ct. (no. and so. dists.) Miss. 1977, U.S. Ct. Appeals (5th and 11th cirs.) 1981, cert. civil trial advocate Nat. Bd. of Trial Advocacy. Atty. Page, Mannino & Peresich, Biloxi, Miss., 1976-80; ptnr. Dornan Law Office, Biloxi, 1980-87; sole practice Biloxi, 1987—; asst. city prosecutor City of Biloxi, 1977-80, city judge pro tem, 1982—; bd. dirs. Gulf Law Inst., 1981—. Mem. ABA, Fed. Bar Assn., Miss. Bar Assn. (pres. elect 2001, pres. 2002-03), Harrison County Bar Assn., Harrison County Young Lawyers (treas. 1980-81, v.p. 1981-82, pres. 1982-83), Miss. Trial Lawyers Assn., Assn. Trial Lawyers Am., Southeastern Admiralty Law Inst., Phi Delta Phi. Methodist. Office: PO Box 154 771 Water St Biloxi MS 39530-4219

DORNAN, JOHN NEILL, public policy center professional; b. Canonsburg, Pa., July 20, 1944; s. Carl Edward and Kathryn (Neill) D.; m. Jacquelin Riggs (div. 1971); children: Jodie Lynn, John Neill; m. Carol Michaels (div. 1976); m. Anne Marie Deegan (div. 1993). BA, Indiana U. of Pa., 1966; postgrad., U. Pitts., 1966-68. English tchr. Moon Twp., Coraopolis, Pa., 1966-69; field rep. NEA, Harrisburg, Pa., 1969-70, media rep. San Francisco, 1970-71; asst. exec. dir. Ill. Edn. Assn., Springfield, Ill., 1970-74; asst. to pres. AFSCME, Washington, 1974-75; assoc. exec. dir. Coalition of Am. Pub. Employees, Washington, 1975-76, N.Y. Edn. Assn., Albany, 1976-82; exec. sec. N.C. Assn. Educators, Raleigh, 1982-86; pres. Pub. Sch. Forum, Raleigh, 1986—. Cons. in field; adj. faculty Cornell U., Albany, 1981-82, Appalachian U., Boone, N.C., 1987-88, N.C. Prin's. Exec. Program, 1986-90. Contbr. numerous articles to profl. jours. Nat. bd. dir. Parents for Pub. Schs., The Columbia Group, Ctr. Tchr. Quality; bd. dir. N.C. Ctr. Internat. Understanding, N.C. in World, N.C. Math, Sci. and Tech. Ctr. Mem.: Raleigh C. of C. Democrat. Presbyterian. Avocations: reading, collecting antique posters. Home: 1409 Granada Dr Raleigh NC 27612-5109 Office: Koger Ctr Cumberland Bldg Ste 100 3739 National Dr Raleigh NC 27612-4844

DORNAN, READE WHITING, literature educator, writer; b. Denver, Dec. 7, 1940; d. William Foster and Lila Louise Day; m. David Benton Dornan, Mar. 7, 1964; children: Wythe Whiting, Ellen Kathlean. BA, U. Colo., 1963; MA, Mich. State U., 1980, PhD, 1988. Cert. tchr. Colo., 1963. Tchr. Hinckley H.S., Aurora, Colo., 1963—65; H.S. tchr., dept. head Fleur du Lac Sch., Homewood, Calif., 1965—66, The Garden Sch., Kuala Lumpur, Malaysia, 1972—74; prof. U. Mich., Flint, 1985—95, Purdue U., West Lafayette, Ind., 1995—96, Mich. State U., East Lansing, 1996—98, 2004, Ctrl. Mich. U., Mt. Pleasant, 1998—. Author: Arnold Wesker Revisited, 1995; co-author (with Lois Rosen and Marilyn Wilson): Multiple Voices, Multiple Texts: Reading in the Content Areas, 1997; co-author: (with Lois M. Rosen and Marilyn Wilson) Within and Beyond the Writing Process in the Secondary English Classroom, 2002; editor: Preserving the Game: Gambling, Mining, Hunting and Conservation in the Vanishing West, 1989, Arnold Wesker: A Casebook, 1998. Deutscher Akademischer Austauschdienst grantee, Heidelberg, Germany, 2001, Sr. Fulbright scholar, U. Heidelberg, Germany, 2005. Mem.: Ctr. for the Expansion of Lang. and Tchg., Soc. for Values in Higher Edn., Nat. Coun. Tchrs. English, Phi Kappa Phi. Mem. Soc. Of Friends. Avocation: weaving.

DORNBUSCH, ARTHUR A., II, lawyer; b. Peru, Ill., Nov. 8, 1943; s. Arthur A. Sr. and Genevieve C. (Knudtson) D.; children: Kimberly, Brendan, Courtney, Eric; m. Jacqueline Bahrs Montanus, Feb. 10, 1996. BA, Yale U., 1966; LLB, U. Pa., 1969. Bar: N.Y. 1970, U.S. Ct. Appeals. (2d cir.) 1971, U.S. Dist. Ct. (so. and ea. dists.) N.Y. 1971. Assoc. Dewey, Ballantine, Bushby, Palmer & Wood, N.Y.C., 1969-72; asst. gen. counsel Boise Cascade Corp., N.Y.C., 1972-75, Teleprompter Corp., N.Y.C., 1975-76, Engelhard Industries divsn. Engelhard Minerals and Chem. Corp., Edison, NJ, 1976-80; v.p., gen. counsel minerals and chems. divsn. Engelhard Corp., Edison, 1980—84, v.p., gen. counsel, sec. Iselin, NJ, 1984—. Mem. Pelham (N.Y.) Union Free Sch. Bd., 1979-82. Mem. ABA, N.Y. State Bar Assn., Assn. Bar City N.Y., Am. Corp. Counsel Assn., Am. Intellectual Property Law Assn., Am. Soc. Corp. Secs., Mfrs. Alliance for Productivity and Innovation. Office: Engelhard Corp PO Box 770 101 Wood Ave S Iselin NJ 08830-0770 Office Phone: 732-205-5527. Business E-Mail: arthur.dornbusch@engelhard.com.

DORNBUSH, K. TERRY, former ambassador, consulting company executive, educator; b. Atlanta, Oct. 31, 1933; m. Marilyn Pierce; 3 children. BA magna cum laude, Vanderbilt U.; postgrad., Emory U., N.Y. Inst. Fin. Former CEO, Hipolex Corp.; former pres. DOAG USA Inc.; former vice chmn. Am. Western Corp.; former ptnr. Courts & Co. & Investment Bankers; amb. to The Netherlands, Am. Embassy, The Hague, 1994-98; CEO Nalim Holdings BV, 1998—2003; mem. supervisory bd. RODAMCO Europe. Former prof. Nijenrode U., The Netherlands; chmn. Stichting Translational Rsch.; bd. dirs. Upaid.

DORNBUSH, VICKY JEAN, medical billing systems executive; b. Willowick, Ohio, Aug. 12, 1951; d. Charles W. and Josephine H. (Palumbo) Rader; m. Eric D. Erickson, Oct. 22, 1972 (div. June 1974); 1 child, Dana; m. Thomas Dornbush, Dec. 29, 1979 (div. 1987). Student, Kent State U., 1969-72, San Jose State U., 1982-84. Accounts receivable clk. MV Nursery, Richmond, Calif., 1975-76; accounts receivable and computer supr. Ga. Pacific, Richmond, 1976-78, acct. Tracy, Calif., 1978-79, Crown-Zellerbach, Anaheim, Calif., 1979-80, Interstate Pharmacy Corp., San Jose, Calif., 1981-83, contr., 1983-85; gen. ptnr. Med. Billing Systems, San Jose, 1984-89; regional billing mgr., co-ordinator St. Joseph's Med. Resources, Stockton, Calif., 1997—. Seminar trainer Systems Plus, Mountain View, Calif., 1987-89, MD Solutions, 1989-97; instr. med. program Sawyer Coll. Mem. San Jose Civic Light Opera, 1987—, San Jose Repertory Co., 1987-89; pres., bd. dirs. San Jose Stage Co., 1990—. Mem. AGPAM, Exec. Sales Women, Nat. Soc. Pub. Accts., Women in Bus., Univ. Women. Dem. Methodist. Office: St Josephs Med Resources 49 W Yokuts Ave Stockton CA 95207-5728

DORNE, DAVID J., lawyer; b. Chgo., Dec. 9, 1946; BS magna cum laude, U. Ill., 1969; MSc, London Sch. Econs., 1970; JD cum laude, Boston U., 1973. Bar: N.Y. 1973, U.S. Ct. Appeals (2d cir.) 1973, U.S. Tax Ct. 1973, U.S. Dist. Ct. (so. dist.) N.Y. 1975, Calif. 1978. Mem. Seltzer Caplan McMahon Vitek P.C., San Diego. Mem. City of San Diego Charter Rev. Commn., 1989—. Mem. ABA (taxation sect., corp., banking and bus. law sect.), State Bar Calif. (taxation sect., real property law sect., chmn. personal income tax subcom. 1982-84), San Diego County Bar Assn., Assn. of Bar of City of N.Y. (taxation sect.), Beta Gamma Sigma. Office: Seltzer Caplan McMahon Vitek PC 2100 Symphony Tower 750 B St San Diego CA 92101-8114 Office Phone: 619-685-3003.

DORNETTE, W(ILLIAM) STUART, lawyer, educator; b. Washington, Mar. 2, 1951; s. William Henry Lueders and Frances Roberta (Hester) D.; m. Martha Louise Mehl, Nov. 19, 1983; children: Marjorie Frances, Anna Christine, David Paul. AB, Williams Coll., 1972; JD, U. Va., 1975. Bar: Va. 1975, Ohio 1975, U.S. Dist. Ct. (so. dist.) Ohio 1975, D.C. 1976, U.S. Ct. Appeals (6th cir.) 1977, U.S. Supreme Ct. 1980. Assoc. Taft, Stettinius & Hollister, Cin., 1975-83, ptnr., 1983—. Instr. law U. Cin., 1980-87, adj. prof., 1988-91. Co-author: Federal Judiciary Almanac, 1984-87. Mem. Ohio Bd. Bar Examiners, 1991-93, Hamilton County Rep. Exec. Com., 1982—; bd. dirs. Zool. Soc. Cin., 1983-94, Cin. Parks Found., 1995-2004; bd. visitors U. Cin. Law Sch., 2002— Mem. FBA, Ohio State Bar Assn., Cin. Bar Assn., Am. Phys. Soc., Nat. Assn. Coll. and Univ. Attys. Methodist. Home: 329 Bishopsbridge Dr Cincinnati OH 45255-3948 Office: 1800 US Bank Tower 425 Walnut St Cincinnati OH 45202-3923 Office Phone: 513-357-9353. E-mail: dornette@taftlaw.com.

DORNFELD, DAVID ALAN, engineering educator; b. Horicon, Wis., Aug. 3, 1949; s. Harlan Edgar and Cleopatra D.; Barbara Ruth Dornfeld, Sept. 18, 1976. BS in Mech. Engring. with honors, U. Wis., 1972, MS in Mech. Engring., 1973, PhD in Mech. Engring., 1976. Asst. prof. dept. sys. design U. Wis., Milw., 1976-77; asst. prof. mfg. engring. U. Calif., Berkeley, 1977-83, assoc. prof. mfg. engring., 1983-89, vice-chmn. instrn. dept. mech. engring., 1987-88, dir. Engring. Sys. Rsch. Ctr., 1989-98, prof. mfg. engring., 1989—, Will C. Hall Family prof. engring., 1999—, assoc. dean interdisciplinary studies Coll. Engring., 2001—; assoc. dir. rsch. Ecole Nationale Superieure des Mines de Paris, Berkeley, 1983-84. Invited prof. Ecole Nationale Superieure D'Arts et Metiers, Paris, 1992-93; cons., expert witness for intellectual property issues, sensor systems, mfg. automation. Contbr. articles to profl. jours., chpts. in books; presenter numerous seminars, confs.; patentee in field. Recipient Dist. Svc. citation U. Wis. Coll. Engring, Madison, 2000. Fellow ASME (past editor, mem. editl. bd. Mfg. Rev. Jour., pres advisory com., Blackall Machine Tool and Gage Award 1990), Soc. Mfg. Engrs. (fellow editl. bd. Jour. Mfg. Systems, Outstanding Young Engr. award 1982, Frederick W. Taylor Rsch. medal 2004); mem. Am. Soc. Precision Engring., Acoustic Emission Working Group, N.Am. Mfg. Rsch. Inst. (past pres., scientific com.), Japan Soc. Precision Engring., Coll. Internat. pour l'Etude Scientifique des Techniques de Production Mechanique (CIRP). Avocations: hiking, travel, reading. Office: U Calif Dept Mech Engring Berkeley CA 94720-1740 Office Phone: 510-642-0906. E-mail: dornfeld@berkeley.edu.

DORNFELD, SHARON WICKS, lawyer; b. Detroit, Jan. 22, 1952; d. John Hoddard and Mary Catherine (Hogan) Wicks; m. William Harlan Dornfeld, Dec. 30, 1977; 2 children. BA, U. Mich., 1974, JD, 1981. Bar: Conn. 1982; U.S. Dist. Ct. Conn. 1983, U.S. Supreme Ct. 1996. Pvt. practice, Danbury, Conn., 1988—. Bd. dirs. A Better Chance in Ridgefield, Conn., 1986; parking violations hearing officer Town of Ridgefield, 1988—; mem. Office of Child Advocate Adv. Com., 1996-2000. Mem. ABA, Nat. Assn. Counsel Children, Conn. Bar Assn., Danbury Bar Assn. (pres. 1995). Democrat. Christian Scientist. Office: 70 North St Danbury CT 06810 Office Phone: 203-748-3363.

DORNFEST, BURTON SAUL, anatomy educator; b. N.Y.C., Oct. 31, 1930; s. Irving and Yetta (Rosengarten) D.; m. Eveline Drucker, June 13, 1954; children; Michael Barry. BA, NYU, 1952, MS, 1954, PhD, 1960. Rsch. asst. dept. biostats. Sloan-Kettering Inst. and Meml. Hosp., N.Y.C., 1952-53; rsch. asst. dept. biology NYU, 1953-54, 56-58, instr. gen. sci., 1958-63; instr. anatomy N.Y. Med. Coll., 1963-64, SUNY Health Sci. Ctr., Bklyn., 1964-67, asst. prof., 1967-73, assoc. prof., 1973-91; cons. study sect. Nat. Heart and Lung Inst., 1975; adj. prof. Med. Sch. CUNY, 1974-97; adj. prof. hematology sch. health scis. Hunter Coll., 1978-82, 90-91; adj. prof. anatomy Inst. Continuing Biomed. Edn., 1979-86, N.Y. Med. Coll., 1982-85, 91-96, Touro Coll. Ctr. Biomed. Edn., 1983-88, Einstein Coll. Medicine, 1991-99. Contbr. articles to profl. jours. Served with U.S. Army, 1954-56. NIH fellow, 1958-60, 61-63; Leukemia Soc., 1960-61; Nat. Inst. Arthritis and Metabolic Diseases grantee, 1964-71; Nat. Cancer Inst. grantee, 1973-75; Mildred Werner League for Cancer Research grantee, 1976-77; co-prin. investigator NIH Heart, Blood and Lung Inst., 1982-85. Mem. AAAS, N.Y. Acad. Scis., Am. Soc. Hematology, Am. Assn. Clin. Anatomists, Sigma Xi. Jewish. Home and Office: 96 Everett Rd Demarest NJ 07627-1225 Personal E-mail: burve35@aol.com.

DORNING, JOHN JOSEPH, nuclear engineering, physics, and applied mathematics educator; b. Bronx, N.Y., Apr. 17, 1938; s. John Joseph and Sarrah Cathrine (McCormack) D.; m. Helen Marie Driscoll, July 27, 1963; children: Michael, James, Denise. BS in Marine Engring., U.S. Mcht. Marine Acad., 1959; MS (AEC fellow), Columbia U., 1963, PhD (AEC fellow), 1967. Marine engr. U.S. Mcht. Marine, 1960-62; asst. physicist Brookhaven Nat. Lab., Upton, N.Y., 1967-69, assoc. physicist, group leader, 1969-70; assoc. prof. nuclear engring. U. Ill., Urbana, 1970-75, prof., 1975-84; Whitney Stone prof. nuclear engring., engring. physics and applied math. U. Va., Charlottesville, 1984—. NRC vis. prof. math. physics U. Bologna, Italy, 1975-76, 81, 85, 87; internat. prof. nuclear engring. Italian Ministry of Edn., 1983, 84, 86; physicist plasma theory group, div. magnetic fusion energy Lawrence Livermore (Calif.) Nat. Lab., 1977-78; cons. to U.S. nat. labs. and indsl. research labs., 1970— Contbr. articles to various publs. Served as ensign USN, 1959-60. Recipient Ernest O. Lawrence award U.S. Dept. Energy, 1990. Fellow AAAS, Am. Phys. Soc., Am. Nuclear Soc. (Mark Mills award 1967, Arthur Holly Compton award 1998, Eugene P. Wigner award 1999, Glenn T. Seaborg medal 2002); mem. Am. Soc. for Engring. Edn., (Glenn Murphy award 1988), Soc. Indsl. and Applied Math., N.Y. Acad. Scis., Sigma Xi.

DOROFTEI, MUGUR GIDEON, music educator, conductor, composer, musician; b. Bucharest, Romania, Oct. 11, 1943; arrived in US, 1980; s. Aristide and Venera Alexandrina Doroftei; m. Cornelia Mesinschi, Mar. 6, 1969; children: Andrei, Gabriel, Rebecca. MusM, Conservtorul Ciprian Porumbescu, Romania, 1970; PhD, Acadmia de Muzica, Romania, 1994. Violinist Opera and Opereta, Constaniza, Romania, 1960—61, Philharm. Orch., Ploiesti, Romania, 1961—62, Ciocirlia, Opera, Radio Orch. Opereta, Bucharest, Romania, 1962—70; prof. de Vioara Liceul de Muzica, Botosani-Suceava, Romania, 1970—80; strings, orch. Southwestern U., Keene, Tex., 1981—2004, Dallas Independent Sch. District, 2001—04. Author: Music Theory Made Clear, Music Theory Made Clear Workbood, Music Theory For The Young Musician, Music Theory For The Young Musician Workbook, Ear Trining Intervals & Chords, Solfeggio Sight Singing, Violin Method for Beginners Book On, with companion CD, Violin Method for Beginners Book Two with companion CD. Named Personalities of the South, Am. Biog. Inst., 1983. Achievements include development of metrical rhytmical transposition; the classification of measures, abbreviations and ornaments, classification of tempo marks, scales with fewer than seven sounds, ch. modes (analysis of the scales diatonic, mixed, chromatic); formation of major and minor scales, relationship between tonalities, chromatic system, classification of intervals. Home: P O Box 711 Keene TX 76059 Office Phone: 817-645-3921 ext. 6237.

DOROSCHAK, JOHN Z., dentist, consultant; b. Zalochiw, Ukraine, Feb. 11, 1928; arrived in US, 1950, naturalized, 1954; s. William and Anna (Stroczan) Doroschak; m. Nadia Zahorodny, June 30, 1962; children: Andrew, Michael, Natalie, Maria. Student, U. Minn., 1955—57, BS, 1959, DDS, 1961. Pvt. practice dentistry, Mpls., 1961—. Cons. St. Joseph's Home for Aged, Mpls., 1974—77, Holy Family Residence, St. Paul, 1977—84. Mem. steering com. St. Anthony West Neighborhood, Mpls., 1971—72, bd. dirs., 1988—89; chmn. Mpls. dentists Little Sisters of Poor Devel. Program, 1975; Webelos leader troop 50 Boy Scouts Am., 1975—76; pres. N.E. Regional Sch. Assn. Parents and Tchrs., 1978—79; bd. dirs. East Side Neighborhood Svc., 1972; treas. Ukrainian youth orgn. Plast Inc., Mpls., 1979—83; mem. Sr. Citizen Ctrs. Health Adv. Com., Mpls., 1979—83; mem. ch. com. Ukranian Cath. Ch., 1965—, chmn. new ch. campaign, 1966—80. With AUS, 1953—55. Fellow: Am. Soc. Geriatric Dentistry; mem.: Dental Health Edn. (com. mem. 1989—90), Ukrainian Med. Assn. (sec.-treas. Minn. chpt. 1971—75), Am. Soc. Dentistry for Children, Minn. Soc. Preventive Dentistry (dir. 1977—83, treas. 1979—83), Minn. Dental Assn. (com. dental care access 1980—83, ascending alt. del. ho. of dels. 1989, del. 1990, 1991, 1992), Am. Dental Assn., Mpls. Dist. Dental Soc. (nursing home com. 1974—, chmn. 1979—82, emergency care com. 1983—84, chmn. 1984—87, chmn. aquatenial health fair 1985, constn. and by-laws com. 1987—88, exec. coun. 1990—93), KC (4th degree), Ukrainian Profl. Club, U. Minn. Alumni Club (charter mem.), Psi Omega. Ukranian Cath. Home: 7254 Stage Coach Trail Lino Lakes MN 55014-1988 Office: Broadway and Univ Professional Bldg 230 Broadway St NE Minneapolis MN 55413-1902

DOROTHY, WAYNE FISER, music educator, band director; b. Oak Ridge, Tenn., May 13, 1956; s. Wesley Cole and Gayle Fiser Dorothy. BS Music Edn., U. Tenn., Knoxville, 1979, MS Music Edn., 1987; ArtsD in Conducting, Ball State U., 1996. H.s. band dir. East and Mid. Tenn., 1979—87; asst. band dir. Ball State U., Muncie, Ind., 1987—90; dir. of bands ND State U., Fargo, 1990—99; instrumental music edn. Morehead (Ky.) State U., 1999—2000, Kans. State U., Manhattan, 2000—02; dir. of bands Hardin-Simmons U., Abilene, Tex., 2002—. Bd. dirs. ND Music Educators Assn., 1995—97; chair collegiate activities com. Nat. Band Assn., 1996—2004; bd. dirs. East Tenn. Sch. Band and Orch. Assn., Tenn., 1982—84; univ. rep. Tex. Music Educators Assn., 2004—. Contbg. author (resource guide) Teaching Music Through Performance in Beginning Band, Teaching Music Through Performance in

Band, Vol. III, Teaching Music Through Performance in Band, Vol. IV; author: (research) An Assessment of Arts Education in Kansas: A State-Wide Survey; contbr. chapters to books. Emergency comm. specialist Abilene Emergency Mgmt., 2002—05. Recipient Citation of Excellence, Nat. Band Assn., 1999, Band Dir. of the Yr., Nat. Band Dirs. Assn., 1999, Arts Award, Abilene Cultural Affairs, 2003; grantee, Nat. Endowment for Arts, 2000. Mem.: Tex. Bandmasters Assn., Nat. Band Assn. (bd. dirs. 2004—), Coll. Band Dirs. Nat. Assn. (state chair 1999), Phi Beta Mu, Pi Kappa Lambda, Phi Mu Alpha Sinfonia. Presbyterian. Avocations: amateur radio, cooking, fishing, clarinet, saxophone. Home: 933 Westwood Dr Abilene TX 79603 Office: Hardin-Simmons University Box 16230 Abilene TX 79698 Office Phone: 325-670-1419. Office Fax: 325-670-5873. E-mail: wdorothy@hsutx.edu.

DORPAT, THEODORE LORENZ, psychoanalyst; b. Miles City, Mont., Mar. 25, 1925; s. Theodore Ertman and Eda (Christiansen) D.; married; 1 child, Joanne Katherine. BS, Whitworth Coll., 1948; MD, U. Wash., 1952; grad., Seattle Psychoanalytic Inst., 1964. Resident in psychiatry Seattle VA Hosp., 1953-55, Cin. Gen. Hosp., 1955-56; instr. in psychiatry U. Wash., 1956-58, asst. prof. psychiatry, 1958-59, assoc. prof., 1969-75, prof., 1976—; practice medicine specializing in psychiatry Seattle, 1958-64; practice psychoanalysis, 1964; instr. Seattle Psychoanalytic Inst., 1966-71, tng. psychoanalyst, 1971—, dir., 1984. Chmn. Wash. Gov.'s Task Force for Commitment Law Reform; trustee Seattle Cmty. Psychiat. Clinic; pres., trustee Seattle Psychoanalytic Inst. Contbr. numerous articles, books, revs. to profl. jours. Served to ensign USNR, 1943-46. Fellow Am. Psychiat. Assn.; mem. Am. Psychoanalytic Assn., AMA, Seattle Psychoanalytic Soc. (sec.-treas. 1965-67, pres. 1972-73), AAAS, Alpha Omega Alpha, Sigma Xi. Home: 7700 E Green Lake Dr N Seattle WA 98103-4971 Office: Blakely Bldg 2271 NE 51st St Seattle WA 98105-5713 Office Phone: 206-522-8553.

DORR, AIMEE, dean, education educator; b. Los Angeles, Sept. 20, 1942; d. Thomas Osborn and Mary Alice (Perkey) D.; m. Larry John Leifer, Dec. 19, 1962 (div.); 1 child, Simeon Kel Leifer; m. Donald Warren Bremme, Aug. 6, 1977 (div.); 1 child, John Thomas Dorr-Bremme; m. Donald Ross Simpson, Feb. 19, 1989. BS, Stanford U., 1964, MA, 1966, PhD in Psychology, 1970. Acting asst. prof. communication Stanford U., 1967-70, research assoc. in psychiatry and communication, 1970-71, research assoc. in psychiatry, acting asst. prof. communication, childcare policy analyst in Pres.'s Office, 1971-72; asst. prof. edn. Harvard U., Cambridge, Mass., 1972-76, assoc. prof., 1976-78; assoc. prof. communications Annenberg Sch. Communication U. So. Calif., Los Angeles, 1978-81, prof., 1981; prof. edn. UCLA, 1981—, dean Sch. Edn. & Info. Systems, 2005—. Cons. Children's TV Workshop, NBC, KCET, Children's Advt. Rev. Unit, others. Author: Television and Children: A Special Medium for a Special Audience, 1986; editor: (with Edward L. Palmer) Children and the Faces of Television-Teaching, Violence, Selling, 1980, 2d edit., 1981; contbr. articles to profl. jours. Fellow Am. Psychol. Assn., Am. Ednl. Research Assn., Soc. Research in Child Devel., Internat. Communication Assn., Amnesty Internat., Friends Com. on Nat. Legis. Democrat. Office: UCLA 2320 Moore Hall Los Angeles CA 90033 E-mail: dorr@gseis.ucla.edu.*

DORR, ANN PIERCE, science educator; b. Tulsa, Aug. 11, 1918; d. Oscar Charles Pierce and Grace Esther Myers; m. John Van Nostrand Dorr II, Feb. 5, 1946; children: John Van Nostrand Dorr III, Charles Pierce Dorr, Katherine Grace Dorr. BA, U. Kansas City, 1939; MEd, Am. U., 1968. Geol. asst. Ark. Geol. Survey, Little Rock, 1942-43; asst. rsch. analyst Petroleum Adminstrv. for War, Washington, 1943-44; geol. asst. Great Lakes Carbon Corp., Wichita, Kans., 1943-46; earth sci. tchr. Fairfax County Pub. Schs., Va., 1964-75; co-instr. course for earth sci. tchrs. U. Va. Sch. of Continuing Edn., Fairfax County, 1974-76; cons. crustal evolution Nat. Assn. Geology Tchrs., Washington, 1977; author course guide and faculty materials Internat. Univ. Consortium, Md., 1982-83. Mem. coms. in field, including Nat. Sci. Resources Ctr.-Smithsonian Instn.-Nat. Acad. Sci. adv. com. for Middle Sch. Project "Catastrophic Events", 1997-2000. Author: Minerals: Foundations of Society, 3d edit., 2002, numerous other publs. in field. Mem. natural resources com. LWV, Montgomery County, Md., 1974—, chair 1974-78; cons. editor: Science Activities, 1982-85; bd. dirs. Mineral Info. Inst., 1984-98, v.p. Southeastern Region, MII, 1984-89; mem. energy and environ. task force Woman's Nat. Dem. Club, 1986—, chair 1992-96, co-chair 1987-92, 92-97, others. Recipient numerous awards in field, including Outstanding Earth Sci. Tchr. of Va., Nat. Assn. Geology Tchrs., 1974, Outstanding Earth Sci. Tchr. in S.E. U.S., Nat. Assn. Geology Tchrs. Mem. Women in Mining, Assn. Women Geoscientists, Am. Inst. Mining, Metallurgy, Petroleum Engrs., Population Ref. Bur. Democrat. Avocations: writing, backcountry travel, music. Home: 9707 Old Georgetown Rd Apt 2514 Bethesda MD 20814-1761

DORR, DEBRA SUE, architecture educator; b. Sycamore, Ill., Mar. 22, 1955; d. Franklin Delano and Mary Jo Stojan; m. Vincent Joseph Dorr, Dec. 4, 1976; children: Anne Sue, Katy Marie. AAS in Archtl. Drafting, Phoenix Coll., 1992; BS in Indsl. Tech., Ariz. State U., 1995, MEd in Ednl. Media and Computers, 2000; postgrad., U. San Francisco, 2003—. Archtl. drafting/CAD faculty/program dir. Maricopa County C.C. Dist./Phoenix Coll., 1996—, chmn. dept., 2002—04. Mem. at-large Phoenix Coll. Alumni Assn., Phoenix, 2003. Mem.: MCCCD Drafting Instrnl. Coun., Ariz. Tech. Articulation Task Force (mcccd lead mem. 1998). Roman Catholic. Avocations: family, reading, sports, travel. Office: Phoenix Coll Indsl Tech 1202 W Thomas Rd Phoenix AZ 85013

DORR, LORNA BITGOOD, librarian; b. New London, Conn., May 2, 1941; d. Royal Earl and Frances Allen (Minson) Bitgood; m. Darwin Dorr, Apr. 25, 1964 (div. Mar. 1984); children: Benjamin Paul, Christopher Joseph. BA, Alfred U., 1963; postgrad., Washington U., St. Louis, 1973—74, Mars Hill Coll., 1980—82; MLS, U. S.C., 1985; MS, We. Carolina U., 1993. Tchr. elem. music Newburgh Pub. Sch., NY, 1963—65; libr. asst. R.M. Strozler Libr. Fla. State U., 1965—67, acting head circulation divsn. R.M. Strozler Libr., 1968—69; book orderer Ind. Study dept. U. Minn., 1967—68; supr. circulation Meml. Libr. Mars Hill Coll., 1979—82; chief reference asst. Ramsey Libr. U. N.C., Asheville, 1982—85; reference libr. We. Carolina U., 1986—. Instr. swimming Asheville YWCA, 1978; mem. Brevard Chamber Orch., NC, 1979—84, Asheville Symphony, 1981—83. Mem.: ALA, We. N.C. Libr. Assn., N.C. Libr. Assn., Pi Gamma Mu, Beta Phi Mu. Episcopalian. Home: 32 Pebble Creek Dr Asheville NC 28803-3256 Office Phone: 828-227-3416.

DORR, STEPHANIE TILDEN, psychotherapist; b. Orlando, Fla., Sept. 21, 1950; d. Luther Willis Tilden II and Lillian Murfee (Grace) Owen; m. Darwin Dorr, May 21, 1986. AA, El Camino Coll., 1975; BA, U. N.C., 1985; MA, Western Carolina U., 1991. Lic. clin. psychotherapist State Kans. Behavioral Scis. Regulatory Bd., 2000. Cons. psychologist Sylva (N.C.) Psychol. Assocs., 1991-92; staff psychologist Park Ridge Hosp., Naples, N.C., 1992, Blue Ridge Ctr., Asheville, N.C., 1991-93; pvt. practice psychology Asheville, 1991-93; project mgr. Sedgwick County Dept. Mental Health, Wichita, Kans., 1993-95; pvt. practice psychotherapy and psychol. assessment Counseling and Mediation Ctr., Wichita, Kans., 1995-98; therapist United Meth. Youthville Clinic, Wichita, 1998—2001; clin. therapist Wichita (Kans.) Pub. Schs. Greiffenstein Spl. Edn. Ctr., 2001—. Adj. faculty Kans. Newman Coll., Wichita, 1995—, Butler County (Kans.) Cmty. Coll., 1996-97; Assertive Cmty. Treatment (ACT) team clinician United Meth. Youthville, Wichita, 1997-98; presenter in field. Contbr. articles to profl. publs. Recipient Excellence in Tchg. award Butler County C.C., 1997, Outstanding Faculty Mem. award Butler County C.C., 1998. Mem. Soc. for Personality Assessment, Psychoanalytic Study Group (sec. 1989-93, award 1993), Western N.C. Psychol. Assn. (mem.-at-large 1985-93, pres.-elect 1993), Psi Chi, Pi Gamma Mu. Democrat. Episcopalian. Avocations: sewing, rock collecting, gardening. Office: Wichita Pub Schs Greiffenstein Spl Edn Ctr 1221 E Galena Wichita KS 67216 Office Phone: 316-973-6400. Personal E-mail: sdorr@usd259.net, stdorr@cox.net.

DORR, THOMAS C., federal agency administrator; BS, Morganside U. Mem. Iowa State Bd. Regents, 1991—97; pres., CEO Pine Grove Farm Co.; sr. advisor to sec. USDA, Washington, under sec. agr. & rural devel., 2005—, bd. dirs. Commodity Credit Corp. Mem.: Nat. Corn Growers. Assn. (officer), Iowa Corn Growers Assn. (officer). Office: USDA Jamie L Whitten Fed Bldg 14th and Independent Ave SW Rm 205W Washington DC 20250 Office Phone: 202-720-4581. Office Fax: 202-720-2080.*

DORRANCE, BENNETT, real estate company executive; married; 2 children. Grad., U. Ariz. Mng. dir. DMB Assoc., Scottsdale, Ariz. Bd. dirs. Campbell Soup Co., Camden, NJ, Larson Co., Tucson, Am. Grad. Sch. Internat. Mgmt. Governance com. Big Bros. Big Sisters; established scholarship Ariz. State U., Ariz.; sponsor Dorrance Merit Scholarship, Ariz.; bd. dirs. Ariz. Cmty. Found., Desert Botanical Garden. Office: DMB Assoc 7600 E Doubletree Ranch Rd Scottsdale AZ 85258

DORRELL, JOHN S., lawyer, insurance company executive; b. 1946; BS, Miami U. Ohio, 1969; JD, U. Toledo, 1974. Bar: Ohio 1975. Bailiff Lucas County Common Pleas Ct.; ptnr. Neipp, Dorrell, & Wingart, Toledo, Marshall & Melhorn, Toledo; v.p. Medchoice/HMO, legal counsel Med. Mutual Ohio, Cleve., 1986—89, v.p. alt. delivery systems, 1989—97, gen. counsel, v.p. legal affairs, 1997—. Mem.: ABA, Cleve. Bar Assn., Ohio State Bar Assn. Office: Med Mutual Ohio 2060 E Ninth St Cleveland OH 44115 Office Phone: 216-687-7476. Office Fax: 216-687-6164. E-mail: john.dorrell@mmoh.com.

DORRILL, WILLIAM FRANKLIN, political scientist, educator; b. Dallas, July 25, 1931; s. William Cumbie and Ruth (Esther Webb) D.; m. Martha Jeanne Brawley, Mar. 3, 1951; children: Jennifer Ruth, William Sidney, Rebecca Jeanne, Lisa Kathryn. BA, Baylor U., 1952; MA, U. Va., 1954; postgrad., Australian Nat. U., Canberra, 1954; PhD, Harvard U., 1972. Fgn. affairs analyst U.S. Govt., Washington, 1961-63; polit. scientist RAND Corp., Santa Monica, Calif., 1963-67; project chmn., sr. staff mem. Rsch. Analysis Corp., McLean, Va., 1967-68; dir. Asian Studies Ctr., assoc. prof. polit. sci. U. Pitts., 1969-77, chmn. dept. East Asian langs. and lits., 1972-77; dean Coll. Arts and Sci., prof. polit. sci. Ohio U., Athens, 1977-84; provost, prof. polit. sci. U. Louisville, 1984-88; pres. Longwood U., Farmville, Va., 1988-96, pres. emeritus, 1996—, prof. polit. sci. and history, 1988-96, bd. visitors, disting. prof., 1996—. Mem. faculty coll. mgmt. program Carnegie-Mellon U. and Nat. Ctr. for Higher Edn. Mgmt. Systems, summer, 1980; mem. com. on internat. edn. Am. Coun. on Edn., 1990, U.S. AID Univ. Ctr. Program Adv. Group, 1991; lectr. in field; higher edn. cons. U.S. Dept of State, China, 2000—01, Libya, 2004. Contbr. articles on East Asian politics and internat. relations to profl. jours., chpts. on Chinese politics and history to scholarly books. Mem. Athens County Bd. Mental Retardation and Devel. Disabilities, Ohio, 1982-84; chmn. bd. dirs. Kentuckiana Metroversity, 1986-88. Recipient Disting. Achievement medal Baylor U., 1980; Fulbright scholar, 1954; Soc. for Values in Higher Edn. Kent fellow, 1957-58; Ford Found. fgn. area fellow Taiwan, Hong Kong, 1959-61; Longwood U. Dorrill Dining Hall named in his honor, 2004. Fellow: Soc. for Values in Higher Edn.; mem.: Coun. on Postsecondary Edn. Environ. Task Force, Coun. for Internat. Exch. of Scholars (bd. dirs. 1992—96), Gov.'s Bus. Edn. Commn., Nat. Assn. State Univs. and Land Grant Colls. (acad. coun., exec. com. 1987—88), Southside Va. Bus. and Edn. Com. (exec. coun. 1992—2000), So. Assn. Colls. and Schs. (commn. on colls. 1986—88, chair vis. coms. 1990—, commn. on colls. 1991—96), Am. Assn. State Colls. and Univs. (com. on accreditation and instl. assessment 1989—96, chmn. 1990—96, gov.'s commn. econ. devel. in Southside Region Commonwealth Va. 1990—96, nominating com. 1993—94), Nat. Com. on U.S.-China Rels., Asia Soc. (adv. com. performing arts 1977—85), Assn. Asian Studies, Am. Conf. Acad. Deans (bd. dirs. 1980—84, vice chmn. 1981—82, chmn. 1982—83), Va. C. of C. (Va. emissary 1993—96), Rotary Internat. (gov.-elect dist. 7600 2002—03, gov. 2003—04). Democrat. Presbyterian. Achievements include Longwood U. building, Dorrill Dining Hall, named in honor of, 2004. Home: 1007 Fayette St Farmville VA 23901-2029 Office: Longwood U Dept History and Polit Sci Farmville VA 23909-0001 E-mail: wdorrill@ntelos.net.

DORRIS, GEORGE EDWARD, historian, educator, editor, author; b. Eugene, Oreg., Aug. 3, 1930; s. Benjamin Fultz and Klysta (Cornet) D. BA, U. Oreg., 1952; MA, Northwestern U., 1953, PhD, 1962. Instr. Duke U., Durham, NC, 1957—60, Rutgers U., New Brunswick, NJ, 1960—62; instr. Queen's Coll. CUNY, 1964—67, from asst. prof. to assoc. prof. York Coll., 1967—98. Presenter in field. Author: Paolo Rolli and the Italian Circle in London 1715-1744, 1967; editor: The Royal Swedish Ballet 1773-1998, 1999; co-editor, co-founder Dance Chronicle, 1977—; music editor Ballet Rev., 1967-77; record reviewer, Ballet Rev., 1993-; assoc. editor Internat. Ency. of Dance, 1981-98; sr. rschr. the Popular Balanchine Project of the Balanchine Found., 1999-2002. Sec. bd. dirs. Dance Perspectives Found., 1975—81. Mem. Dance Critics Assn. (bd. dirs. 1980-83, 96-99), Soc. Dance History Scholars (bd. dirs. 1979-82, 90-93, editl. bd. 2001-2004), World Dance Alliance Ams. (bd. dirs.) Home: 40 E 10th St New York NY 10003-6221

DORSEN, DAVID M(ILTON), lawyer; b. N.Y.C., Oct. 10, 1935; s. Arthur and Tanya (Stone) D.; m. Margaret L. Stern, Mar. 5, 1969 (div. Feb. 1976); m. Kenna D. Peusner, Jan. 24, 1997. AB, Harvard U., 1956, JD, 1959. Bar: N.Y. 1960, D.C. 1960, U.S. Supreme Ct. 1977. Assoc. Kaye, Scholer, Fierman, Hays & Handler, N.Y.C., 1960-64; asst. U.S. atty. U.S. Dist. Ct. (so. dist.) N.Y., 1964-69; dep. commr. and 1st dep. commr. N.Y.C. Dept. Investigation, 1969-73; asst. chief counsel Senate Watergate Com., Washington, 1973-74; ptnr. Sachs, Greenebaum & Tayler, Washington, 1974-91; of counsel Hughes Hubbard & Reed, Washington, 1991-94; pvt. practice Washington, 1994-98; of counsel Wallace King Marraro & Branson PLLC, Washington, 1998—; ptnr. The Nonsequitur Stable, LLC, 1994—. Vis. lectr. pub. policy studies Terry Sanford Inst. Pub. Policy, Duke U., Durham, N.C., 1995-2003; adj. prof. Georgetown U. Law Ctr., Washington, 2000-03, George Washington U. Law Sch., Washington, 2004-. Contbg. editor, wine and food editor The Washingtonian Mag., 1982—; assoc. prodr. Tolstoy, 1996; columnist The Hill, Washington, 1998-2000. Mem. D.C. Bar Assn. (chmn. arbitration bd. 1982-84), Internat. Club of Washington (chief counsel 1981-89). Home: 3501 Davis St NW Washington DC 20007-1426 Office Phone: 202-204-3706.

DORSEN, NORMAN, lawyer, educator; b. N.Y.C., Sept. 4, 1930; s. Arthur and Tanya (Stone) D.; m. Harriette Koffler, Nov. 25, 1965; children: Jennifer, Caroline Gail, Anne. BA, Columbia U., 1950; LLB magna cum laude, Harvard U., 1953; postgrad., London Sch. Econs., 1955-56; LLD (hon.), Ripon Coll., 1981, John Jay Coll. Criminal Justice, 1992. Bar: DC 1953, NY 1954. Law clk. to chief judge Calvert Magruder U.S. Ct. Appeals, Boston, 1956-57; law clk. to Justice John Marshall Harlan U.S. Supreme Ct., Washington, 1957-58; assoc. Dewey, Ballantine, Bushby, Palmer & Wood, N.Y.C., 1958-60; prof. law NYU Sch. Law, N.Y.C., 1961-81, Stokes prof., 1981—, dir. Hays civil liberties program, 1961—, dir. global law sch. program, 1994-96, chmn., 1996—2002; counselor to pres. NYU, 2002—. Vis. prof. law London Sch. Econs., 1968, U. Calif., Berkeley, 1974-75, Harvard U., 1980, 83, 84; cons. U.S. Commn. on Violence, 1968-69, Random House, 1969-73, B.B.C., 1969-73, U.S. Commn. on Social Security, 1979-80, Native Am. Rights Fund, 1978-89; exec. dir. spl. com. on courtroom conduct Assn. Bar N.Y.C., 1970-73; chmn. Com. for Pub. Justice, 1972-74; vice chmn. HEW sec.'s rev. panel on new drug regulation, 1975-76, chmn., 1976-77; mem. N.Y.C. Commn. on Status of Women, 1978-80; chmn. Sec. of Treasury's Citizen Rev. Panel on Good O' Boy Round-up, 1995-96. Author (with others): Political and Civil Rights in U.S., 3rd edit., 1967, Political and Civil Rights in U.S., 4th edit., Vol. I, 1976, Political and Civil Rights in U.S., 4th edit., Vol. II, 1979, Frontiers of Civil Liberties, 1968, Discrimination and Civil Rights, 1969, Comparative Constitution, 2003; author: (with L. Friedman) Disorder in the Court, 1973; author: (with S. Gillers) Regulation of Lawyers, 1985, Regulation of Lawyers, 2d edit., 1989; author: (with others) Constitutionalism Cases and Materials, 2003; editor: The Rights of Americans, 1971; editor: (with S. Gillers) None of Your Business, 1974; editor: Our Endangered Rights, 1984, The Evolving Constitution, 1987; editor: (with others) Human Rights in Northern Ireland, 1991, The Unpredictable Constitution, 2001, with P. Gifford: Democracy and the Rule of Law, 2001; editor: (with others) Comparitive Constitutionalism, 2003; editl. dir. Internat. Jour. Constl. Law, 2002—. 1st lt. JAGC U.S. Army, 1953—55. Recipient medal French Minister of Justice, 1983, Eleanor Roosevelt Human Rights award 2000; Fulbright Disting. Prof., Argentina, 1987, 88. Fellow Am. Acad. Arts and Scis.; mem. ABA (chmn. com. free speech and press 1968-70), ACLU (gen. counsel 1969-76, pres. 1976-91), Am. Law Inst., Coun. on Fgn. Rels., Lawyers Com. Human Rights (chmn. bd. dirs. 1995-2000), Lawyer Com. Civil Rights, Internat. Assn. Constnl. Law (exec. com. 1999-2003), U.S. Assn. Constnl. Law (pres. 1996-2003), Soc. Am. Law Tchrs. (pres. 1972-74, Tchg. award 1997), Thomas Jefferson Ctr. for Free Expression (trustee). Home: 146 Central Park W New York NY 10023-2005 Office: NYU Sch Law 40 Washington Sq S New York NY 10012-1005 Business E-Mail: norman.dorsen@nyu.edu.

DORSETT, JAMES K., III, lawyer; b. Raleigh, N.C., Nov. 10, 1951; BA, Davidson Coll., 1974; JD, Wake Forest U., 1977. Bar: N.C. 1977. Atty. Smith, Anderson, Blount, Dorsett, Mitchell & Jernigan, LLP, Raleigh, NC. Fellow: Am. Bar Found., Internat. Soc. Barristers (bd. govs., chair N.C. fellowship); mem.: ABA (del. ho. dels.), Wake County Bar Assn. (bd. dirs. 1982—84, 1988—90, vol. lawyers program 1990—93), Am. Bd. Trial Advs., N.C. Assn. Def. Attys., Am. Counsel Assn. (pres. 2005—06), N.C. State Bar (councilor 1992—, pres. 2002—03, chmn. grievance com.), N.C. Bar Assn., Phi Delta Phi. Office: Smith Anderson Blount Dorsett et al 2500 Wachovia Capitol Ctr PO Box 2611 Raleigh NC 27602-2611 Office Phone: 919-821-6649. Business E-Mail: jdorsett@smithlaw.com.

DORSEY, DOLORES FLORENCE, retired corporate treasurer, finance company executive; b. Buffalo, May 26, 1928; d. William G. and Florence R. D. BS, Coll. St. Elizabeth, 1950. With Aerojet-Gen. Corp., 1953—, asst. to treas. El Monte, Calif., 1972-74, asst. treas., 1974-79, treas., 1979—2001, ret., 2001. Mem. Cash Mgmt. Group San Diego (past pres.), Nat. Assn. Corp. Treas., Fin. Execs. Inst. (v.p.). Republican. Roman Catholic.

DORSEY, JAMES FRANCIS, JR., naval officer; b. Balt., May 28, 1934; s. James Francis Sr. and Elizabeth Rosalee (MacNamara) D.; m. Jeanne Lynch Hobbs, Aug. 16, 1958; children: James Francis III, Timothy Walker. Grad. in naval aviation, USN, Pensacola, Fla., 1956; degree in Polit. Sci., Naval Postgrad. Sch., Monterey, Calif., 1967. Commd. ensign USN, 1956, advanced through grades to VADM, 1991, comdg. officer 3 fighter squadrons, 1971-76, exec. officer USS Midway, 1976-78, comdg. officer USS Caloosehatchee, 1978-80, comdg. officer USS America, 1981-82, dir. joint program office, undersec. def. policy, dep. dir. def. mobilization systems planning activity, 1982-84, comdr. carrier group FOUR, and NATO comdr. carrier striking force Atlantic, 1984-85, dir. ops. U.S. European Command, 1985-87, dep. asst. chief naval ops. for plans, policy and ops., dep. ops. dep. for joint chief staff matters, 1987-89, comdr. 3d Fleet, 1989-91, ret., 1991; CEO Flag Ltd., Alexandria, Va., 1991—. Mem. Assn. Naval Aviation, U.S. Naval Inst., Chesapeake Bay Soc., Harbor Pt. Hoa (v.p.), Golden Eagle--The Early Pioneer Naval Aviators Assn. Office: PO Box 1119 Solomons MD 20688-1119

DORSEY, JEREMIAH EDMUND, pharmaceutical company executive; b. Worcester, Mass., Oct. 15, 1944; s. Jeremiah Edmund and Mary Theresa D.; m. Nadia S. Vidach, Dec. 6, 1970; children: Todd Edmud, Jaime Erin, Megan Elizabeth, Kelly Ann. AB, Assumption Coll., 1966; MBA, Farleigh Dickinson U., 1978. With Johnson & Johnson, New Brunswick, NJ, 1969-88, nat. indsl. engrng. mgr., 1975-76, supt. ops. and maintenance, 1976-88, dir. ops., mem. mgmt. bd., 1976-88; v.p. mktg., ops., gen. mgr. sales Johnson & Johnson Dental Products Co., New Brunswick, 1976-88; exec. v.p. The Kaelin Group, Bridgeton, NJ, 1988; pres. Towle Housewares Co., Newburyport, Mass., 1988-90; pres., CEO Foster Med. Supply, Inc., Dedham, Mass., 1990-92; group pres. Carvel Hall Corp., Crisfield, Md., 1990—; pres., COO West Pharm. Svcs. Inc., Lionville, Pa., 1992—. Corp. officer J.E. Dorsey Co., Carvel Hall Corp., Crisfield, Md.; bd. dirs. West Co. de Mex., Daikyo Seiko, Tokyo, Schubert Seals, Horsens, Denmark, DanBioSyst, Nottingham, Eng., Geschaftsfuherer West Co., Europe, Cardiotech Internat., Wilmington, Mass; mem. bd. dirs. Associated Internat. Corp., Wilmington, Mass. Editor: Spl. Forces Assn. News. Active N.J. Commn. for Discharge Upgrade, Appalachian Trail Conf.; mem. alumni bd. dirs. Assumption Coll., adv. com. U. PR Sch. of Pharmacy; mem. mil. acad. selection com. U.S. Senate; vice chmn. NJ Vietnam Vets Leadership Program; mem. Mercer County (NJ) Pvt. Industry Coun., NJ SR-92 Coalition. With U.S. Army, 1966-69, Vietnam. Decorated Silver Star, Bronze Star with 2 oak leaf clusters, Purple Heart with 4 oak leaf clusters, Army Commendation medal, Air medal with oak leaf cluster, Medal of Honor, Gallantry Cross, Vietnam; recipient Corp. Affirmative Action award 1981. Mem. DAV, KC, Sierra Club, Spl. Forces Assn., Smithsonian Assocs., Soc. First Divsn., Tiger Karate Soc. (Black Belt), Johnson & Johnson Mgmt. Club, Delta Epsilon Sigma. Roman Catholic. Office: 101 Gordon Dr Exton PA 19341-1320 Home: PO Box 910 Quechee VT 05059-0910

DORSEY, JOHN KEVIN, dean; b. NYC, 1943; Bachelor's degree, Fairfield U., Conn., 1964; PhD in physiologic chemistry, U. Wis., Madison, 1968; MD, So. Ill. U. Sch. Medicine, 1978; postgrad., The Johns Hopkins U., 1970—73. Diplomate internal medicine and rheumatology Am. Bd. Internal Medicine. Intern U. Iowa Hosps., Iowa City, 1978—79, resident in internal medicine, 1979—81; fellow in rheumatology U. Iowa, Iowa City, 1981—83; joined faculty as asst. prof. chemistry and biochemistry So. Ill. U., Carbondale, Ill., 1973, rejoined faculty as asst. prof. and coord. clin. affairs, 1983; med. dir. So. Ill. Arthritis Found.; attending rheumatologist Carbondale (Ill.) Clinic; consulting rheumatologist V.A. Hosp., Marion, Ill.; prof. internal medicine So. Ill. U. Sch. Medicine, Carbondale, Ill., assoc. provost so. region, 1998—2001, interim dean and provost Springfield, 2001—02, dean and provost, 2002—. Mem. Nuc. Magnetic Resonance Mgmt. Com. So. Ill. U., mem. Molecular Biology, Microbiology and Biochemistry com.; bd. trustees So. Ill. Healthcare. Co-host (edn. television program) Medically Speaking, reviewer Developmental Biology, Ill. Med. Jour., Tchg. and Learning in Medicine, Academic Medicine; contbr. articles to profl. jours. Named a Disting. Alumnus, So. Ill. U. Sch. Medicine, 1993; recipient John Templeton Spirituality in Medicine Curricular Award, 2000. Fellow: Am. Coll. Rheumatology, Am. Coll. Physicians; mem.: Alpha Omega Alpha, Sigma Xi. Office: So Ill Univ Sch Medicine 801 N Rutledge St Springfield IL 62794-9620

DORSEY, JOHN RUSSELL, journalist; b. Balt., Dec. 17, 1938; s. Charles Howard and Emma (Deputy) D. AB, Harvard U., 1961. Mem. staff Balt. Sun, 1962-81, 83-99, Sunday Sun book rev. editor, 1967-69, Sunday Sun restaurant critic, 1971-81, 84-86, Sun art critic, 1983-84, 86-99. Author: (with James D. Dilts) A Guide to Baltimore Architecture, 1973, Mount Vernon Place, 1983, (with James DuSel) Look Again in Baltimore, 2005; editor: On Mencken, 1980. Mem. Md. Club, 14 West Hamilton Street Club, Harvard-Radcliffe Club. Home: 600 Edgevale Rd Baltimore MD 21210-1904

DORSEY, JOHN WESLEY, JR., retired academic administrator, economist; b. Hagerstown, Md., June 13, 1936; s. John Wesley and Abbie Virginia (Wy) D.; m. Jeanne Ascosi; 1 child, Rachel Lynette. BS, U. Md., 1958; cert., London Sch. Econs., 1959; MA, Harvard U., 1962, PhD, 1964. Teaching fellow Harvard U., 1961, 62-63; asst. prof. econs. U. Md., 1963-66, asso. prof., dir. Bur. Bus. and Econ. Rsch., 1966-70, vice chancellor for adminstrv. affairs College Park, 1970-77, acting chancellor, 1974-75, prof. econs., 1976-2001, prof. emeritus, 2001—; chancellor U. Md. Baltimore County, 1977-86; asst. to pres. U. Md. System, 1986-89. Cons. to govt. Md. Employees Credit Union Bd., 1975—. Rotary Found. scholar, 1958-59; Brookings research fellow, 1961-63 Mem. Phi Beta Kappa, Phi Kappa Phi, Omicron Delta Kappa. Home: 8234 Bubbling Spg Laurel MD 20723-1079 Personal E-mail: jwd8234@comcast.net.

DORSEY, PETER COLLINS, federal judge; b. New London, Conn., Mar. 24, 1931; s. Thomas F., Jr. and Helen Mary (Collins) D.; m. Cornelia McEwen, June 26, 1954; children: Karen G., Peter C., Jennifer S., Christopher M. BA, Yale U., 1953; JD, Harvard U., 1959. Ptnr. Flanagan, Dorsey & Flanagan, New Haven, 1963-74; U.S. atty. Dept. Justice, New Haven, 1974-77; ptnr. Flanagan, Dorsey & Mulvey, New Haven, 1977-83; judge U.S. Dist. Ct. Conn., New Haven, 1983-99, chief judge, 1994-98, now sr. judge. Mem. Jud. Conf. of U.S. Cts., 1995-98; adj. prof. Quinnipiac Coll. Sch. Law, 1999—. Councilman Town of Hamden, Conn., 1961-69; town atty., 1973-74; commr. Bd. of Police, Hamden, 1977-81. Served to lt. comdr., USNR, 1953-56 Fellow Am. Coll. Trial Lawyers; mem. ABA (mem. house of dels. 1974-78), Conn. Bar Assn. (bd. govs. 1968-70, 74-78, pres. 1978), Am. Coll. Trial Lawyers, Conn. Def. Lawyers Assn. (pres. 1974), Am. Inns of Ct. Hartford (pres. 1991-93). Roman Catholic. Office: US Dist Ct 141 Church St New Haven CT 06510-2030 Office Phone: 203-773-2427.

DORSHOW-GORDON, ELLEN, epidemiologist; b. St. Paul, May 16, 1946; d. Bennie and Goldie (Salita) Dorshow; m. Charles Gordon, May 15, 1977; 1 child, Gayle. BS in Med. Tech., U. Minn., 1968, MPH, 1983; postgrad., Western Mich. U., 2002. Infection control coord. Samaritan Health Ctr., Detroit, 1980-83; cons Infection Control Resource Ctr., 1983-84; grad. rsch. asst. Rehab. Inst. Detroit, 1984-85; health and safety/mental health/nutrition coord. Renaissance Head Start, Detroit, 1984-86; infection control market specialist Calgon Vestal Labs., 1986-90; infection control coord. Sinai Hosp., Detroit, 1990-94; dir. quality svcs./infection control Great Lakes Rehab. Hosp., Southfield, Mich., 1994-95; epidemiologist Oakland County Health Divsn. Dept. Human Svcs., Pontiac, Mich., 1995-2000, Kalamazoo County Human Svcs. Dept., 2000—03, Jackson County Health Dept., Independence, Mo., 2003—. Mem. Nat. Sanitation Found. Task Group, 1997-99; mem. S.E. Mich. Epidemiology Com., 1995-2000, Coun. of State and Territorial Epidemiologists; mem. 5th Dist. Med. Response Coalition, 2002-03; presenter in field. Contbr. articles to profl. jours. Vol. B'nai Brith Women Twin Cities Coun., 1973-80, Hadassah, Am. Arab and Jewish Friends, 2002-03. U. Minn. Alumnae Freshman scholar, 1964; recipient Calgon Exec. Dir.'s award, 1986, Calgon Vestal Lab. Pacesetter award, 1987. Fellow Mich. Pub. Health Leadership Inst., Wall of Tolerance; mem. NOW, ACLU, AARP, NAFE, Minn. Soc. Med. Tech. (bd. dirs. 1972-75), Minn. Alumnae Assn., Assn. Practitioners Infection Control and Epidemiology (edn. com. chair greater Detroit 1983-85, legis. liason greater Kansas City 2004—), Women and AIDS com., Am. Pub. Health Assn., Mo. Pub. Health Assn., So. Poverty Law Ctr, Greater Kansas City TB Coalition, MARE Pub. Health Com., Metro. Official Health Agys. of Kansas City Area. Avocations: reading, net surfing, volunteering. Office: 313 S Liberty Independence MO 64050 Business E-Mail: ellen.dorshow-gordon@tmcmed.org.

DORSI, CRAIG R, education educator; b. Mineola, NY; s. Richard Salvatore and Diane Audrey Dorsi. BA, Molloy Coll., 2000; MA in hist. and edn., Columbia U., 2004. Tchr. NYS United Tchrs., Nassau County, NY, 2000—; mem. edn. team, rschr. Human Dignity and Human Studies, 2004—. Mediator Internat. Ctr. for Coop. and Conflict Resolution, NYC, 2004—. Democrat. Home: 115 Clayton Ave Massapequa NY 11758 Personal E-mail: craig798@aol.com.

DORSKY, NATHANIEL, filmmaker; b. NYC, 1943; Student, Antioch Coll., 1961, NYU, 1962. Instr. U. Calif., Berkeley, Stanford U. Filmmaker Bend in the River, 1955, Ingreen, 1964, A Fall Trip Home, 1965, Summerwind, 1965, Hours for Jerome, 1966—82, Gaugerion in Tahiti, 1968 (Emmy award), Triste, 1974—96, Revenge of the Cheerleaders, 1976, Pneuma, 1976—83, Alaya, 1976—87, Ariel, 1983, 17 Reasons Why, 1985—87, What Happened to Kerouac?, 1985 (Emmy award), Vacations, 1992—98, Night Waltz: The Music of Paul Bowles, 1999 (Emmy award), The Visitation, 2002, Monumental: David Brower's Fight for Wild America, 2004; editl. cons.: Hope Along the Wind: The Story of Harry Hay, 2002; actor: (films) Rembrandt Laughing, 1988. Grantee, NEA, Calif. Arts Coun.; Guggenheim fellow, 1997.

DORTON, TRUDA LOU, medical/surgical nurse, geriatrics nurse; b. Elkhorn Creek, Ky., Aug. 26, 1949; d. Clair Otis Parsons and Joyce Kidd; m. Eugene Anderson, Nov. 26, 1966 (dec. Apr. 1971); children: Gena Lynn, Richard Eugene; m. Leon Dorton, Dec. 15, 1972; children: Leondra Michelle, Jerald Thomas, Jonathan Layne. AS, student, Pikeville Coll., 1993. RN, Ky.; cert. ACLS, PALS. Instr. computer usage Lookout (Ky.) Elem. Sch., 1983; water/sewage technician McCoy & McCoy Environ. Cons., Pikeville, Ky., 1984; owner Signs of the Times, Elkhorn City, Ky., 1979-89; sec.'s asst. humanities and social scis. divsns. Pikeville Coll., 1989-92; nurse aide Mud Creek Clinic, Grethel, Ky., 1992-93; charge nurse Jenkins (Ky.) Cmty. Hosp., 1993-94; case mix coord. Parkview Manor Nursing Home, 1994-95, minimum data set and nursing care plan coord., 1995; acute care nurse Harrison Meml. Hosp., Cynthiana, Ky., 1996—2002; dir. nursing Robertson County Health Care Facility, Mt. Olivet, Ky.; long-term care charge nurse Trilogy Health Ctr. at Harrison Meml. Hosp., Cynthiana; med. inpatient svcs. Floyd Meml. Hosp., New Albany, Ind. Vol. nurse aide Mud Creek Clinic, Grethel, 1989-92. Founder free blood pressure clinic H.E.L.P.S. Community Action Program, Hellier, Ky., 1983; co-founder H.E.L.P.S. Community Action Group, Hellier, 1983; mem. Ellis Island Centennial Commn., N.Y., 1986. Appalachian Honors scholar Pikeville Coll., 1989-92. Mem. Nat. Geog. Soc., Ky. Nursing Assn., Order Ky. Cols. (Honorable Ky. Col. 1989), Smithsonian Inst., Nat. Trust Hist. Preservation, World Wildlife Fund, Pikeville Coll. Alumni Assn. Democrat. Mem. Worldwide Ch. of God. Avocations: creating indian jewelry and wall hangings, classical music, reading. Home: RR 1 Box 80 Hwy 539 Mount Olivet KY 41064-9510

DORTON-CHENEY, LORA GAIL, music educator; b. Trumann, Ark., May 14, 1963; d. Harold Elmo and Nancy Annette (Smith) Dorton; m. James Kenneth Cheney, Dec. 31, 1996. B of Music Edn., Ark. State U., 1985; MusM, U. Ill., 1988. Cert. tchr. Indpls. Cath. Edn. Tchr. Newman (Ill.) Cath. Unified Sch. Dist., 1988—90, Shiloh HS, Hume, Ill., 1988—90, Cross County HS, Cherry Valley, Ark., 1990—92, Ark. State U., Jonesboro, 1990—92, Marked Tree (Ark.) HS, 1992—94; piano tchr. Indpls., 1994—; tchr. St. Luke Cath. Sch., Indpls., 1994—. Mem. adv. bd. Paige's Music, Indpls., 2000—01; mem. profl. devel. com. St. Luke Cath. Sch., 2000—, mem. facilities com., 2000—. Bd. dirs. Lawrence Harrison Pk. Neighborhood Assn., 2001—03. Mem.: Music Educator's Nat. Conf., Ind. Music Educator's Assn., Ind. Bandmaster's Assn. Avocations: music, gardening, ethnic foods, travel, reading. Office: St Luke Cath Sch 7650 N Illinois Indianapolis IN 46260 Home: 11849 Serenity Ln Indianapolis IN 46229-3967 Office Phone: 317-255-3912. Personal E-mail: jambhi@comcast.net. Business E-Mail: ldortoncheney@stluke.org.

DORWART, BONNIE BRICE, historian, retired rheumatologist; b. Petersburg, Va., Jan. 27, 1942; d. Gratien Bertrand and Myrtle Elizabeth (Houser) Brice; m. William Villee Dorwart, Jr., June 22, 1963; children: William Bertrand, Brice Burdan, Michael Walter. AB, Bryn Mawr Coll., 1964; MD, Temple U., 1968. Diplomate Am. Bd. Med. Examiners, Am. Bd. Internal Medicine, Am. Bd. Rheumatology. Intern then resident in internal medicine Lankenau Hosp., Jefferson Med. Coll., Phila., 1968-72; instr. medicine Hosp. U. Pa., Phila., 1972-74; fellow rheumatology U. Pa. Sch. Medicine, Phila., 1974; instr. medicine Jefferson Med. Coll., Phila., 1974-76, asst. prof., 1976-81, assoc. prof., 1981-95, clin. prof., 1995—2003; assoc. investigator divsn. rsch. Lankenau Hosp., Wynnewood, Pa., 1978—88, chief arthritis clinic, 1982—86, chief connective tissue disorders, 1982—97; Civil War med. historian, writer, 2001—. Assoc. dir. Greater Delaware Valley Arthritis Control Program, 1975; mem. Gov.'s adv. bd. on Systemic Lupus Erythematosus, Phila., 1981-88. Author: Carson's Materia Medica of 1851: An Annotation, 2003; contbr. articles to med. jours., chpts. to books. Med. career advisor, active cells workshop Merion (Pa.) Elem. Sch., 1984-90; fund raiser Arthritis Found., Am. Cancer Soc., Phila., 1974-97; mem. resources com. Bryn Mawr Coll., 1985-90. Named Physician of Yr., 32 Carat Club, Phila., 1986; Janet M. Glasgow scholar Temple U. Sch. Medicine, 1968. Fellow ACP, Coll. Physicians Phila.; mem. AMA, Am. Coll. Rheumatology, Phila. Rheumatism Soc. (pres. 1981-82), Pa. Med. Soc., Philadelphia County Med. Soc. Lutheran. Avocations: cooking, gardening. Home and Office: 124 Maple Ave Bala Cynwyd PA 19004-3031

DORWART, DONALD BRUCE, lawyer; b. Zanesville, Ohio, Dec. 12, 1949; s. Walter G. and Katherine (Kachmar) D.; children: Claire Lauren, Hillary Beth. BA, Vanderbilt U., 1971; JD, Washington U., St. Louis, 1974. Bar: Mo. 1974, U.S. Dist. Ct. (ea. dist.) Mo. 1974. Assoc. Thompson Coburn LLP, St. Louis, 1974-79, ptnr., 1980—; dir. New Energy Corp. Ind., 1992-95. Contbr. articles to profl. jours. Mem.: ABA, FOCUS St. Louis (mem. selection com. 1990—91, mem. fin. com. 1990—2002, mem. cmty. policy com. 2000—02, bd. dirs. 2000—, treas. 2001—02, pres. 2002—04), Bar Assn. Met. St. Louis (chair securities regulation com. 1979), Maritime Law Assn. U.S. (mem. maritime fin. com. 1980—, proctor), Noonday Club. Office: Thompson Coburn LLP One US Bank Plz Ste 3300 Saint Louis MO 63101-1643 Office Phone: 314-552-6000. Business E-Mail: ddorwart@thompsoncoburn.com.

DOSAMANTES-BEAUDRY, IRMA, psychology professor; b. Mexico City; m. Walter A. Beaudry. BS, CUNY, 1959, MA, 1962; PhD, Mich. State U., 1967; postgrad., UCLA, 1972-73; grad. psychoanalyst, L.A. Inst./Soc. Psych. Studies, 1993. Assoc. dir., counselor SUNY, Stonybrook, 1968-71; assoc. prof. U. No. Colo., 1973-74, Calif. State U., L.A., 1974-77; prof. UCLA, 1977—. Dir. dance/movement therapy program UCLA, 1977—. Author: (book) Body-Image: A Cross-Cultural Perspective, 1993; editor-in-chief: (profl. jour.) The Arts in Psychotherapy Jour., 1998—, mem. editl. bd., 1986-87; mem. editl. bd. Am. Dance Therapy Jour., 1988-97. U. Calif. Pacific Rim Rsch. grantee, 1991-92. Mem. APA, Am. Dance Therapy Assn. (bd. dirs. 1974-84, pres. 1980-82, Chace Found. award 1997), Am. Assn. for Study of Mental Imagery (bd. dirs. 1982-86, pres. 1983-84), Internat. Psychoanalytic Assn., L.A. Inst. and Soc. for Psychoanalytic Studies. Avocations: tennis, gardening. Office: UCLA World Arts & Cultures Dept PO Box 951608 Los Angeles CA 90095-1608

DOSANJH, AMRITA, medical educator; BA magna cum laude, Brown U.; MD, UCSD. Lic. MD Calif., 1990, cert. pediatrics Am. Bd. Pediat., 1991. Asst. prof. Stanford U., Pal Alto, Calif., 1995—2000; assoc. prof. U. Tenn., St. Jude Coll. of Medicine, Memphis, 2001; adj. faculty Scripps Rsch. Inst., La Jolla, Calif., 2000—. Dir. pulmonary tchg. and rsch. CIT Coll. of Medicine, Memphis. Contbr. articles various profl. jours. Recipient Physician Investigation award, Am. Med. Assn., 1993. Mem.: Am. Thoracic Soc.

DOSIK, MICHAEL, breast cancer physician, hospital administrator, consultant; b. N.Y.C., Feb. 27, 0941; s. Albert and Helen Dosik; m. Lyn Boland Dosik, Feb. 12, 1984; 1 child, Diana; m. Antonia Atlas Dosik (div.); 1 child, Lia. AB, Cornell U., 1962, MD, 1966. Bd. cert. diplomate Am. Bd. Internal Medicine, cert. hematology, med. oncology. Pres. North Shore Hematology/Oncology Assn., Setauket, NY, 1974—2000; chief divsn. hematology and med. oncology St. Charles Hosp. and Mather Meml. Hosp., Pt. Jefferson, NY, 1980—2000; dir. Fortunato Breast Ctr. Mather Meml. Hosp., Pt. Jefferson, 1997—; pvt. practice cons. breast cancer Pt. Jefferson, 2000—; attending physician SUNY Med. Ctr., Stony Brook, NY, 2003. Chmn. Meml. Adj. Staff Oncology Bd., Sloan Kettering, N.Y.C., 1982—85. Contbr. articles to med. jours. Capt. USAF, 1968—70. Recipient Theodore Roosevelt award, Nassau-Suffolk Hosp. Coun., 1998. Fellow: ACP; mem.: L.I. Cancer Coun. (bd. dirs. 1977—79), Am. Cancer Soc. (bd. dirs. L.I. divsn. 1974—78), N.Y. Met. Breast Cancer Group, Am. Soc. Clin. Oncology. Achievements include patents for ELF3 gene composition and methods. Avocations: skiing, tennis, fishing. Office: SUNY Stony Brook Nicolls Rd Stony Brook NY 11794

DOSS, GREGORY S., music educator, musician; b. Atlanta, Nov. 24, 1957; s. Harold Edward and Martha E. Doss; m. Patricia A. Anderson, Aug. 6, 1982; children: Meghan Diane, Ellen Andera. BME, Shorter Coll. Music educator, choral dir. Towers H.S., Decatur, Ga., 1982—95; pianist White Oak Bapt. Ch., Lilburne, Ga., 1983—85, min. music, 1985—96; music educator, choral dir. Stone Mountain H.S., Ga., 1995—97, Meadows Mid. Sch., Granbury, Tex., 1997—98, Cleburne Mid. Sch., Tex., 1998—2000; assoc. music min. 1st Bapt. Ch., Cleburne, 1998—2003, organist, 2004—05; music educator, chorale dir. Acton Mid. Sch., Granbury, Tex., 2000—; organist Mayfield Bapt. Ch., Arlington, Tex., 2005—. Show choir festival chmn. Dekalb County Pub. Schs., Clarkston, Ga., 1993—94, h.s. choral festival coord., 1994—96; mid. sch. coord. Region VII Tex. Music Educators, Tex., 2001—03. Singer: (performance) Region VII Tex. Middle Edn. Assn. Reference CD for Middle School Region Choir, Holiday CD, O Holy Night. Named Tchr. of Yr., Acton Mid. Sch. Faculty, 2004. Mem.: Music Educators Nat. Conf., Tex. Choral Directors Assn., Am. Choral Directors Assn., Tex. Music Educators, Parent Tchr. Assn. (hon. hon. life mem. 1992), Phi Mu Alpha Symphonia. Conservative. Baptist. Office: Acton Mid Sch 1300 James Rd Granbury TX 76049 Office Phone: 817-408-4817. Office Fax: 817-408-4849. Personal E-mail: ssodpack@sbcglobal.net. E-mail: gregory_doss@granbury.k12.tx.us.

DOSS, JOANN TRAUERNICHT, elementary school educator; b. Litchfield, Ill., July 14, 1945; d. Edwin Walter and Helen Bernhardina (Mindrup) Trauernicht; m. Gary Eugene Doss; children: Angela Michelle, Kevin Michael. BS in Elem. Edn., Ill. State U., 1967; MEd in Elem. Edn., U. Ill., 1971. Tchr. Springfield Pub. Sch., 1967—71; spl. reading tchr. Farmer City Dist. 17, 1971—75; reading, lang. arts tchr. Rock Falls Dist. 13 Jr. HS, 1975—81; spl. reading tchr. Morrisonville Dist. 1 Jr. HS, 1981—83; tchr. Hillsboro Sch. Dist. 3, 1990—. Mem.: AFT, NEA, Litchfield Cmty. Food Pantry. Avocations: reading, sewing, crafts, piano, internet. Home: 69 Chatauqua Ln Hillsboro IL 62049-3436 Office: Beckemeyer Elem Sch 1035 Seymour Ave Hillsboro IL 62049 Office Phone: 217-532-6994. E-mail: gkak4@wamusa.com.

DOSS, SYLVIA M., psychologist, educator; b. Houston, Dec. 11, 1953; d. George Weston and Nancy George Doss. BA in Psychology and Rehab. Counseling, U. N.Tex., 1977; MEd in Rehab. Counseling, U. Mo., 1979; MA in Neuropsychology, Fielding Grad. Inst., 1994, PhD inClin. Psychology, 1996. Lic. psychologist, cert. rehab. counselor. Rehab. counselor Neurol. Disabilites Support Svcs., Tucson, 1987—95; pvt. practice Phoenix, 1996—. Dir., tng. cons. Cath. Cmty. Svc. So. Ariz., Tucson and Yuma, 1981—86; surveyor Commn. Accreditation Rehab. Facilities, 1983—89; master faculty U. Phoenix, 1992—; cons. Rehab. Svcs. Admin. Dept. Econ. Security, Tucson and Yuma, Ariz., 1998; adj. faculty Glendale C.C., Phoenix, 2001—; spkr. in field. Mem. Commn. for Handicapped, Tucson, 1981—82; mentor Fresh Start, 2003—. Recipient Disability Rights award, 1998. Mem.: APA, Am. Psychol. Soc., Psi Chi. Democrat. Methodist. Avocations: exercise, movies. Office: 515 E Carefree Hwy 110 Phoenix AZ 85085

DOSSIN, ALEXANDRE SAGGIN, pianist, educator; b. Porto Alegre, Rio Grande do Sul, Brazil, Sept. 13, 1970; s. Moacir Alexandre Dossin, Marli Elvira Saggin Dossin; m. Maria Loguinova, May 5, 1995; children: Victor children: Sophia. MFA, Moscow State Tchaikovsky Conservatory, 1996; D of Musical Arts, U. Tex., 2001. Cert. adv. postgrad. cert. in piano performance 1997. Assistantship Moscow State Tchaikovsky Conservatory, Russia, 1996—97; tchg. asst. U. Tex., Austin, 1999—2001, coord. piano project, 2000—01; asst. prof. piano U. La., Lafayette, 2001—02, U. Wis., 2002—. Soloist Brazilian Symphony Orch., Rio de Janeiro, 1992, Sao Paulo Symphony Orch., Sao Paulo, Brazil, 1991—92, Porto Alegre Symphony Orch., Rio Grande do Sul, Brazil, 1984—2005, Moscow State Tchaikovsky Conservatory Symphony Orch., 1996, Novossibirsk Philharmonic Orch., Siberia, Russia, 1994, Mozarteum Symphony Orch., Salzburg, Austria, 1995, Russian Min. of Defense Symphonic Orch., Moscow, 1994, Acadiana Symphony Orch., Lafayette, La., 2002, Montevideo Symphonic Orch., Montevideo, Uruguay, 1985, Yasi Philharmonic Orch., Athens, 1996, Buenos Aires Philharm. Orch., 2003. Musician: (CD recordings with) Musicians Showcase Recording, 2002, Blue Griffin Recording, 2005, Naxos, 2005. Named Ambassador of Rio Grande, State Gov. of Rio Grande do Sul, Brazil, 1997; recipient Silver Medal and 2nd Hon. Mention, Maria Callas Grand Prix, Athens, Greece, 1996, 3rd Prize and Spl. Prize from the Mozarteum Found., W.A.Mozart Internat. Piano Competition, Salzburg, Austria, 1995, 4th Prize, Mazara-del-Vallo Internat. Piano Competition, Mazara-del-Vallo, Italy, 1993, 1st Prize and two spl. prizes, First Edino Krieger National Piano Competition, Brusque, Brazil, 1988, 2d Prize, Santa Maria Internat. Piano Competition, Santa Maria, Brazil, 1988, Hours Concurs, Villa-Lobos Nat. Piano Competition, Bage, Brazil, 1987, 1st prize and spl. prize, Martha Argerich Internat. Piano Competition, Buenos Aires, Argentina, 2003; fellow Pre-Emptive Grad. fellowship, U. Tex., 1998—99. Mem.: Am. Liszt Soc., Music Tchrs. Nat. Assn., Coll. Music Soc. Roman Catholic. Avocations: reading, movies, travel. Office Phone: 715-836-5842. E-mail: dossin@dossin.net.

DOSSIN, ERNEST JOSEPH, III, credit manager; b. Detroit, May 24, 1941; s. Ernest Joseph and Jean (Dickson) D.; m. Mary Jane Mortimore, July 24, 1965; children: Ernest Joseph IV, Tobias Alfred. BA in Bus., Valparaiso U., 1963; MBA in Fin., Fairleigh Dickinson U., 1978; postgrad., Walden U., 1995-98. Asst. store mgr. W.T. Grant, Norfolk, Va., 1967-68; dir. acctg. Am. Express, Trenton, N.J., 1968-69; asst. to chmn. Americana Hotels, N.Y.C., 1969, dir. casinos, 1970-72, corp. dir. credit, 1972-79; v.p. Myers Group, Rouses Point, N.Y., 1979-92; exec. v.p. Global Collections Inc., Plattsburgh, N.Y., 1985-93; pres. Dossin's Consulting Assocs., Plattsburg, N.Y., 1993—. Guest lectr. Plattsburgh State U., 1995; leader seminars in improving credit practices, 1985-91; adj. faculty SUNY, Plattsburgh, 1993—, C.C. of Vt., 1993—. Author: Strictly Business, 1991. Corp. bd. mem. Champlaine Valley Physicians Hosp., 1998—; treas. New Eng. Synod Evang. Luth. Ch. Am., 1997—; congl. pres. Redeemer Luth. Ch., Plattsburh, 1985-8 9, congl. v.p., 1990-93; bd. dirs. Oratorio Soc., pres. 1996-98; bd. dirs. Plat tsburgh, 1986-90; treas. Luth. Coll., Teaneck, N.J., 1975-79; mem. exec. com. Boy Scouts Am., Clinton County, 1994—. Mem. Nat. Assn. Credit Mgrs. (cited 1984, 85), Internat. Credit Assn. (exec.), Soc. Cert. Consumer Credit Execs. (cert. exec.), Plattsburgh C. of C., Soc. for Preservation Barbershop Quartet Singing (v.p. 1990-93), Mgmt. Club Plattsburgh (bd. dirs. 1987-91). Republican. Lutheran. Avocations: boating, barbershop quartet singing, football. Office: Dossin's Consulting Assocs Plattsburgh NY 12901 E-mail: ernieD3@aol.com.

DOSS-QUINBY, EGLAL, language professional, educator; b. Alexandria, Egypt, July 19, 1953; arrived in U.S., 1965; d. Raouf and Suzanne (Sabbagh) Doss; m. David Quinby, Sept. 5, 1975; 1 child, Laura. BA, SUNY, Stony Brook, 1973; MA, NYU, 1976, PhD, 1982. Instr. French NYU, 1978-80; asst. prof. The Univ. of Tex., Austin, 1982-88; assoc. prof. Smith Coll., Northampton, Mass., 1990—2000, prof., 2000—. Speaker convs. in field. Author: Les Refrains chez les Trouvères, 1984, The Lyrics of the Trouvères: A Research Guide 1970-1990, 1994; co-editor: Songs of the Women Trouvères, 2001, The Old French Ballette, 2005; contbr. articles to profl. jours Grantee, U. Tex., 1984, Smith Coll., 1990—93, 1995—99, 2002—05; Penfield fellow, N.Y. U., 1977—78, Jean Picker fellow, Smith Coll., 1991—92, Presidl. fellow, 1998. Mem. Modern Lang. Assn. (speaker conv. 1988), Am. Assn. Tchrs. of French (speaker conv. 1982), Medieval Acad. of Am., Internat. Courtly Lit. Soc. Office: Smith Coll Dept French Northampton MA 01063-0001 E-mail: edoss@smith.edu.

DOSS-REED, HELEN GRIGSBY, writer; b. Sanderstead, Surrey, England, Aug. 9, 1915; (parents Am. citizens); d. Owen E. and Maude E. Grigsby; m. Carl M. Doss; adopted children: Don, Dorothy, Elaine, Ted, Lora, Susan, Tim, Rita, Diane, Alex, Richard(dec.), Greg(dec.); m. Roger W. Reed, 1986; stepchildren: John Reed, Jim Reed. Student, Santa Ana Coll., 1932—33, Eureka Coll., 1933—34; BA, U. Redlands, 1954; postgrad., UCLA, 1968. Author: The Family Nobody Wanted, 1954, 2001, A Brother the Size of Me, 1957, If You Adopt a Child, 1957, All the Children of the World, 1958, The Really Real Family, 1959, Friends Around the World, 1959, Jonah, 1964, King David, 1967, Where Can I Find God?, 1968, Young Readers Book of Bible Stories, 1970, All the Better to Bite With, 1976, Your Skin Holds You In, 1978, The U.S. Air Force, From Balloons to Space Ships, 1981. Mem.: AAUW. Methodist. Avocations: camping, reading. Home: 581 Scirocco Dr Yuba City CA 95991

DOST, MARK W., lawyer; b. Attleboro, Mass., May 22, 1955; s. Raymond and A. Louise (Fraser) D.; m. Karen M. Sullivan, Aug. 1976; children: Christopher, Stephen, Gregory, Isaac. AB summa cum laude, U. Mass., 1978; JD cum laude, Boston Coll., 1981. Bar: Conn. 1981, U.S. Tax Ct. 1985, U.S. Dist. Ct. Conn. 1986. Atty. Gager & Henry, Waterbury, Conn., 1981-95; ptnr. Tinley, Nastri, Renehan & Dost, Waterbury, 1995—. Author: (with John V. Galiette) Planning for Retirement Benefit Distributions, 1995, 2d revised edit., 1999. Fellow Am. Coll. Trust and Estate Counsel; mem. ABA, Conn. Bar Assn. (exec. com., elder law sect. 1991—, exec. com., estates and probate sect. 1991—, chair elder law sect. 1994-96, chair publs. com. 1997-2000), Nat. Acad. Elder Law Attys. Office: Tinley Nastri Renehan Dost 60 N Main St Waterbury CT 06702-1403 Office Phone: 203-596-9030. Business E-Mail: mdost@tnrdlaw.com.

DOSTART, PAUL JOSEPH, lawyer, investor, director, entrepreneur; b. Iowa, Nov. 12, 1951; s. Leonard A. and Lois M. Dostart; m. Joyce A. Dostart; children: Zachariah Paul, Samuel Paul. BS, Iowa State U., 1973; JD, U. Houston, 1977; LLM in Taxation, NYU, 1978. Bar: Tex, 1977, Calif. 1978; CPA, Ill. Mng. ptr. Dostart, Clapp & Coveney LLP. Adj. prof. U. San Diego, 1986—90; bd. dirs. Q3DM Inc. Editor Houston Law Rev. Founder U. Houston Tax Law Soc.; bd. dirs. Neuroscis. Rsch. Found. Lasker scholar, NYU, Nat. Merit scholar. Fellow Am. Bar Found. (life), Am. Coll. Tax Counsel; mem. ABA (chmn. various subcoms. sect. taxation 1982—, exempt orgns. com. 1977—), Calif. Bar Assn. (tax and bus. sects.), San Diego County Bar Assn. (chmn. tax sect. 1989), San Diego Tax Practitioners Group, Am. Electronics Assn. (San Diego coun. exec. com. 1993-95), World Trade Assn. (bd. dirs.). Presbyterian. Office: Dostart Clapp & Coveney LLP Ste 970 4370 La Jolla Village Dr San Diego CA 92122-1249 Office Phone: 858-623-4210. Business E-Mail: pdostart@sdlaw.com.

DOSTART, THOMAS J., lawyer; b. 1955; BS, Iowa State U., 1977; JD, U. Iowa, 1980. CPA; bar: 1981. Law clk. Iowa Supreme Ct.; atty. Arter & Hadden, Jones, Day, Reavis & Pogue, Diamond Shamrock, Inc., Amoco Corp., Chgo.; gen. counsel Lachman Tech. Corp., Interactive Systems Corp., Naperville, Ill., 1992—95; v.p., gen. counsel, sec. Nat. Auto Credit, Inc. (formerly Agency Rent-A-Car), 1995—97; gen. counsel, asst. sec. Alliance Coal, LLC, Lexington, Ky., 1997—2003; v.p., gen. counsel, sec. Massey Energy Co., Purchase, NY, 2003—. Former mng. editor: Iowa Law Review. Office: Massey Energy Co 2000 Purchase St Purchase NY 10577 Office Phone: 804-788-1800. Office Fax: 804-788-1870.

DOSTER, ROBERT FRANKLIN, music educator; b. Rothsville, Pa., July 13, 1935; s. Franklin Martin and Margrite Long Doster; m. Barbara Geltz; children: Brian Robert, Robyn Lynne. BA, Lebanon Valley Coll., 1958; MEd, U. Md., 1968. Tchr. Frederick County, Md. BOE, Frederick, Md., 1958—67; dir. of band, dept. chair Fairfax County BOE, Annandale, Va., 1967—77; dir. of band Towson State U., Towson, Md., 1978—85; pvt. cons. Md. Dept of Edn., Balt., 1986—99; percussion cons. Polk County C. C., Winter Haven, Fla., 2001—. Staff conductor, adj. Internat. Music Festival, Parchment, Mich., 1980—. Contbr. articles various profl. jours. V.p. Jaycees, Frederick, Md., 1965, Lions Club Internat., Annandale, Va., 1974; pres. Md. Band Dirs. Assn., 1965—67; Va. state chmn. Am. Sch. Band Dirs. Assn., 1968—75; Md. chmn. Coll. Band Dirs. Nat. Assn., 1980—84. Recipient Alumni award, Lebanon Valley Coll., 1975. Mem.: World Assn. Symphonic Bands, Coll. Band Dirs. Nat. Assn. Republican. Luth. Avocations: hist. rsch., freelance percussionists. Home: 1414 Wild Dunes Ct Winter Haven FL 33881

DOSTER, ROSE ELEANOR WILHELM, artist; b. Balt., May 11, 1938; d. Lewis Milford and Leeanora A. (Naylore) Wilhelm; m. Jesse Alfred Doster, Feb. 22, 1958; children: Jeffrey Allen, Roxane Elana. Cert. illustration and design, Art Instrn. Sch. Mpls., 1956; cert. design and painting, Md. Inst. Coll.

Art., 1960, postgrad., 1960-62. Tchr. drawing, painting and ceramics, 1968—; craft supt. Carroll County 4H Fair, 1982, 83, 84, 85. Exhibited in one-woman shows: Hampstead Library Gallery, 1969, 70, Aurora Fed. Gallery, Balt., 1969, Goodman Gallery, Ellicott City, Md., 1971, Central Savs. Gallery, Towson, Md., 1971, Parkville (Md.) Library Gallery, 1972, Equitable Trust Bank Reisterstown Gallery, Balt., 1973, Hanover Art Guild, 1981, Md. Ctr. Pub. Broadcasting, 1982, Kent Island Fedn. of Art Gallery, 1990, Heron Point Gallery, 2003, others; exhibited in group shows: St. John's Coll., Johns Hopkins, Goodman Gallery, Slayton House, Columbia, Md., Paynter Gallery, Rehoboth, Del., Hilltop House, Harpers Ferry, W.Va., 1974-86, Balt. Mus. Art Downtown Gallery, 1976, Towsontowne Arts Festival, 1977-79, 82, 84, McDonough Sch.'s Cleve. Gallery, 1978, Unicorn Gallery, 1979, Canon Bldg. U.S. Ho. of Reps., Washington, 1981-82, Md. State NLAPW, Art Exhibit, Balt., 1983, Annapolis, 1985, Md. chpt. Nat. League Am. Penwomen, 1983, Easton Art Acad., 1987-97, 2000-04, International Craft Show, Cordova, 1988, Dorchester County Art Showcase, 1989-97, Salisbury-Wicomico Arts Festival, 1993, St. Michaels Maritime Mus. Show, 1992-93, 94, 95, Chesapeake Coll. Art Show, 1987, 88, 89, 90, 91, 92, 93, 94, 95, Dorchester Educators Art Show, 1990, 91, 92, 94, 95, 96, 97, Working Artists Forum Juried show, 1995, 96, 97, 98, 99, Waterfowl Festival Art Show, 2003, 04, 05, Chestertown Wildlife Art Show, 2003, 04, Nat. League Am. Penwomen, 2004. Leader Shiloh Clovers 4-H Club, 1983-84; trustee Balt. Mus. Art; pres. Carroll County Arts Coun., 1975-76, 94; v.p. Caroline County Arts Coun., 1993, pres., 1994; judge Montgomery Cunty Fair, 1984, 86, 87, Howard County Fair, 1985, Balt. County 4-H Fair, Frederick County Fair, 1988, Caroline County Fair, 1989, 90, Easton Art Acad. Children's Exhibit, 1994, Federation Women's Club of Denton Children's Competition, 1992-93, 94, Md. State fair, 1993, 94, 95, Dorchester Educators Show, 2004; mem. bd. Carroll County Farmers Market—crafts; elected mem. Working Artists Forum, 1987-88, 89, 90, 91, 92, 93-, sec., 1992-93, treas., 1993— Recipient numerous awards including George Peabody award, 1960, Judges Choice award Dorchester Educators Art Show, 1990, Best of Painters award Artisan's Fair Queen Anne Rotary Club, 1992, Nat. Potpourri Contest winner Floral and Nature Crafts Mags., 1995, 96, medal from Gov. and First Lady of Md., 1998, 2nd prize Wash. Coll. Juried Art Show, 2000, 1st prize pastel, Washington Coll. Chestertown, Md., 2003, 2nd prize pastel, 2004, Cochran award Rehoboth Art League, 2003. Mem. Nat. League Am. Pen Women (bd. art chmn. 1970-72, 1st v.p. 1972-74, pres. Carroll br. 1974-76, br. historian 1976-96, branch achievement chmn. 1988-90, 92-94, br. newsletter editor 1992-93, 94, state historian 1982-84, 88-90, 93, chmn. tri-state miniature art show 1993, chmn. 50th anniversary Show 1995, Md. state pres., 2002-04, chmn. nat. slide/traveling art show, 2004—, treas. Carroll br. 2004—), Working Artist Forum (treas. 1994, 95, 96, 97, 98, 99, 2000, 2001, 2002, 2003, 2004, 2005, chmn. miniature painting show 1997), Nat. Oil/Acrylic Painters Soc., Portrait Soc. Am., Oil Painters Am., Kent Island Fedn. of Art, Chestertown Art League, Rehoboth Art League, Md. Inst. Art Alumni Assns., Balt. Watercolor Soc. (assoc.), Carroll County Hist. Soc. (bd. dirs. 1986—), Caroline County Hist. Soc., Betsy Patterson Doll Club, Lady Baltimore Doll Club, Miss Carroll's Doll Study Club (founder, pres.), Ea. Shore Miniature Enthusiasts Club (founder, pres.), Ea. Shore Doll Study Club (histroian 1993, libr. 1995, 96). Home: 9472 Quail Run Rd Denton MD 21629-1731 E-mail: rwdorlist@dmv.com.

DOSWALD, HERMAN KENNETH, language educator, retired academic administrator; b. Oakland, Calif., Mar. 24, 1932; s. Herman and Caroline Josephine (Mello) D.; m. Ruth Eugenie Hannes, Dec. 21, 1956; children: Caroline Susan, Stephanie Ann. AA, U. Calif., Berkeley, 1952, BA, 1955; MA, U. Wash., 1959, PhD, 1965. Instr., dept. German and Russian Oberlin (Ohio) Coll., 1959-60; instr., dept. German U. Wash., Seattle, 1960-61; instr., dept. fgn. langs. Seattle U., 1961-62; asst. prof. German U. Kans., Lawrence, 1964-67; asst., then assoc. prof., dept. fgn. langs. Fresno (Calif.) State U., 1967-72; prof., chmn. dept. German and Russian Kent (Ohio) State U., 1972-79; head dept. fgn. langs. Va. Poly. Inst. and State U., Blacksburg, 1979-84, assoc. dean adminstrn., Coll. Arts & Scis., 1984-86, interim dean Coll. Arts & Scis., 1986-87, dean, 1987-93, prof. German, 1993-96, prof. German, dean Coll. Arts & Scis. emeritus, 1996—. Contbr. articles to profl. jours. Served to 1st lt. U.S. Army, 1962-64. Adenauer scholar, Munich, Fed. Republic Germany, 1953-54; Fulbright fellow, Vienna, Austria, 1958-59. Mem. Phi Beta Kappa, Phi Kappa Phi, Omicron Delta Kappa. Home: 4592 Preston Forest Dr Blacksburg VA 24060-8660 Personal E-mail: doswald@vt.edu.

DOSWELL, CHARLES ARTHUR, III, meteorologist; b. Elmhurst, Ill., Nov. 5, 1945; s. Charles Arthur Jr. and Marie A. (Anderson) D.; m. Vickie A. Teel, Apr. 5, 1975; children: Charles Arthur IV, Heather L. BS, U. Wis., 1967; MS, U. Okla., 1969, PhD, 1976. Rsch. meteorologist Nat. Severe Storms Forecast Ctr. U.S. Dept. Commerce/NOAA/Nat. Weather Svc., Kansas City, Mo., 1976-82; rsch. meteorologist Weather Rsch. Program NOAA/Environ. Rsch. Lab., Boulder, Colo., 1982-86, meterologist Nat. Severe Storms Lab. Norman, Okla., 1986—. Adj. assoc. prof. Sch. Meteorology, Coll. Geoscis., U. Okla., Norman, 1989-96, prof., 1996—. Asst. scoutmaster troop 777 Boy Scouts Am., Norman, 1987—; mem. bicycle com. City of Norman, 1992—. With U.S. Army, 1969-72. Recipient Silver medal, U.S. Dept. Commerce, 1989, Outstanding Paper award, Environ. Rsch. Lab., 1996, Antonin Strnad Gold medal, Czech Hydrometeorol. Inst., 2002, Sergey Soloviev medal, European Geophys. Soc., 2005. Fellow Royal Meteorol. Soc.; mem. Am. Meteorol. Soc. (editor's award 1994), Nat. Weather Assn. (Rsch. Achievement award 1995), Sigma Xi. Achievements include research on the tornado and tornadic storms; development of objective analysis methods and forecast verification techniques. Office: CIMMS Rm 1110 56C 100 E Boyd St Norman OK 73019 Office Phone: 405-325-6093. E-mail: cdoswell@gcn.ou.edu.

DOTO, IRENE LOUISE, statistician; b. Wilmington, Del., May 7, 1922; d. Antonio and Teresa (Tabasso) D. BA, U. Pa., 1943; MA, Temple U., 1948, Columbia U., 1954; M of Quantitative Sys., Ariz. State U., 1986. Engring. asst. RCA-Victor, 1943-44; rsch. asst. U. Pa., 1944; actuarial clk. Penn Mut. Life Ins. Co., 1944-46; instr. math. Temple U., 1946-53; commd. lt. health svcs. officer USPHS, 1954, advanced through grades to capt., 1963; statistician Communicable Disease Ctr., Atlanta, 1954-55, Kansas City, Kans., 1955-67; chief statis. and publ. svcs., ecol. investigations program Ctr. for Disease Control, Kansas City, 1967-73, chief statis. svcs., divsn. hepatitis and viral enteritis Phoenix, 1973-83; statis. cons., 1984—. Mem. adj. faculty Phoenix Ctr., Ottawa U., 1982-98. Mem. APHA, Am. Statis. Assn., Ariz. Pub. Health Assn., Ariz. Coun. Engring. and Sci. Assn. (officer 1982-90, pres. 1988-89), Primate Found. Ariz. (mem. animal care and use com. 1986—), Bus. and Profl. Women's Club Phoenix, Mil. Officers Assn. Am. (state sec.-treas. 1995-96), Ariz. SPCA (bd. dirs. 2000-01), Sigma Xi, Pi Mu Epsilon. Office: PO Box 22197 Phoenix AZ 85028-0197

DOTO, PAUL JEROME, retired accountant; b. Newark, N.J., July 22, 1917; s. Anthony and Edith Margaret (Mascellaro) Doto. BS, NYU, 1947. CPA N.J., N.Y., registered mcpl. acct., N.J., pub. sch. acct., N.J. Acct. John Hewitt Foundry Co., East Newark, 1941—43, S.D. Leidesdorf & Co., N.Y.C., 1947—56; CPA Peat Marwick Mitchell & Co., N.Y.C., 1956—64; asst. controller Lincoln Ctr. for Performing Arts Inc., N.Y.C., 1964—69; controller Seton Hall U., So. Orange, NJ, 1969—74, Belart Products, Applied Coatings, Maddock, Inc., NJ, 1974—80, Internat. Trading Sales, Inc., Pan Atlantic Paper Co., N.Y.C., 1973—80. Cons. Controller's Office, City N.Y., 1966; bd. dirs. Parkway, Ltd., 1973—78. Mem. Nat. Police Hall of Fame. Served AUS, 1943—46. Mem. N.Y. State Soc. CPA's (chmn. govtl. acctg. com. 1963-64, chmn. internat. control quest on aid of municipalities, N.Y. State), AICPA, Cath. Accts. Guild (bd. govs. 1961-64), N.J. Soc. CPA's, Fin. Exec. Inst. Am. Acctg. Assn., N.Y. Assn. Profs., Smithsonian Assocs. (charter mem.), Nat. Wildlife Fedn., Am. Legion, Am. Mus. Nat. Hist. (assoc.). Address: 97 Norwich E West Palm Beach FL 33417-7910

DOTRICE, ROY LOUIS, actor; b. Guernsey Channel Isles, U.K., May 26, 1929; came to U.S., 1967; s. Louis and Neva (Wilton) D.; m. Kay Newman, May 8, 1947; children: Michele, Karen, Yvette. Student, Elizabeth Coll., Guernsey Channel Isles. Actor in leading roles Royal Shakespeare Co., Eng., 9 yrs.; actor 12 West End, London and Broadway prodns. including A Life (Tony award nomination), Moon for the Misbegotten (Tony, Critics Circle, Drama Desk, Jefferson awards), others; actor: (TV series) Beauty and the Beast, Going to Extremes, Picket Fences, Mr. and Mrs. Smith, Sliders, Madigan Men. With RAF, 1940-45, ETO. Recipient award Guiness Book of World Records for World's Longest Running One-Person Show "Brief Lives", Best Actor award "B.A.F.T.A.", 1969, Emmy award "Caretaker", 1966. Mem. Garrick Club (London). Avocations: fishing, riding. Office: Award Assocs 9720 Wilshire Blvd Beverly Hills CA 90212-2021 Office Phone: 310-550-1254. E-mail: RoyDotrice@aol.com.

DOTSON, ALBERT, not-for-profit fundraiser; b. Detroit; BS econ., Dartmouth Coll.; JD, Vanderbilt Univ. Bar: Fla. With 100 Black Men of America, Inc., 1994—, vice-pres., chmn., 2004—; ptnr. Bizlin Sumberg Baena Price & Axelrod LLP. Vice-chmn. Miami Dade Coll. Foundation; vice-pres Orange Bowl Com. Named one of Cmty. Leader Award, Wilke D. Ferguson, Jr. Bar Assn., 1999, corporate elite in practice of law in So. Fla., Fla. Bus. Jour., 1999, So. Fla. Top Lawyers, Miami Metro, 2001; recipient Cmty. Excellence in Real Estate award, March of Dimes, 2002. Office: 100 Black Men of America 141 Auburn Ave Atlanta GA 30303*

DOTSON, DONALD L., lawyer; b. Rutherford County, N.C., Oct. 8, 1938; s. Herman A. and Lottie E. (Hardin) D. AB, U. N.C., 1960; JD, Wake Forest U., 1968. Bar: N.C., Pa., D.C., U.S. Supreme Ct. Atty. NLRB, 1968-73, chmn., 1983-87; labor counsel Westinghouse Electric Corp., 1973-75; labor atty. Western Electric Co., 1975-76; chief labor counsel Wheeling-Pitts. Steel Corp., 1976-81; asst. sec. labor, 1981-83, 2001—; pvt. practice law, Washington, 1987-91; sr. v.p. Beverly Enterprises, 1991—2001; pvt. practice, 2001—. Served with USN, 1960-65. Republican. Episcopalian. Office: PO Box 25526 Washington DC 20027 Office Phone: 800-227-7140.

DOTSON, GEORGE STEPHEN, oil industry executive; b. Okemah, Okla., Dec. 25, 1940; s. Hilmer C. and Alma Lucille (McGee) D.; m. Phyllis A. Nickerson, Aug. 17, 1963; children: Sarah, Grant. BS, M.I.T., 1963; MBA, Harvard U., 1970. Asst. to pres. Helmerich & Payne, Inc., Tulsa, 1970-73; v.p. Helmerich & Payne (Peru) Drilling Co., 1974-75, Helmerich & Payne Internat. Drilling Co., 1976-77, pres., chief operating officer, 1977—; v.p. drilling Helmerich & Payne, Inc., 1977—, also bd. dirs. Bd. dirs. Atwood Oceanics, Inc; chmn. Internat. Assn. Drilling Contractors, 1995. Served to capt. U.S. Army, 1964-68. Decorated Bronze Star. Office: Helmerich Payne Internat Drilling Co 1579 E 21st St Tulsa OK 74114-1398

DOTSON, ROBERT CHARLES (BOB DOTSON), news correspondent; b. St. Louis, Oct. 3, 1946; s. William Henry and Dorothy Mae (Bailey) D.; m. Linda Gay Puckett, July 1, 1972; 1 child, Amy Michelle. BS in Journalism and Polit. Sci., Kans. U., 1968; MS in TV, Syracuse U., 1969. News dir. Sta. KANU-FM, Lawrence, Kans., 1966-68; reporter, photographer, documentary producer KMBC-TV, Kansas City, Mo., 1968; dir. spl. projects WKY-TV, Oklahoma City, 1969-75; corr. WKYC-TV, Cleve., 1975-77; network corr. NBC News, Dallas, 1977-79; corr. Prime Time Saturday Atlanta, 1979-80; corr. Today Show, 1980-85; nat. corr. NBC Nightly News, Atlanta, 1985-2000, Dateline NBC, 1985—; spl. nat. corr. NBC News Today Show, N.Y.C., 2000—. Vis. prof. journalism U. Okla., 1969-73; faculty affiliate Colo. State U., Ft. Collins; writer, host Bob Dotson's Am., travel channel and NBC Superchannel, 1996-98. Author: ...in Pursuit of the American Dream, 1985 (George Washington Honor medal Freedom Found. 1985), Make it Memorable, 2000; documentaries include Through the Looking Glass Darkly, 1974 (Emmy award, RFK award), The Urban Reservation, 1975 (RFK award DuPont-Columbia Journalism award), Still Got Life to Go, 1972, (Emmy nomination), Smoke and Steel, 1973 (Emmy nomination), The Sunshine Child, 1983 (Emmy nomination), People Who Make a Difference, 1987 (Emmy nomination), Bob Dotson's NBC Nightly News Stories, 1987 (Gabriel award 1987), Bob Dotson, 1987 (Media Acess award 1987), Assignment Am., 1989 (Nat. Headliners award 1990, Emmy nomination, 1989, Ohio State award 1989), El Capitan's Courageous Climbers, 1990 (Cine Golden Eale, Italian Film Festival grand prize, Union of Mountain Climbers grand prize, Wilbur award U.S. Film Festival 1990, 91, Cine Grand Prize Best Am. Non-Fiction Film, 1991, Bombay, India Internat. Film Festival Grand Prize, 1991, Japan, Spain Internat. Sprots Film Fest. Grand Prize, 1991, Juan Antonio Samaranch Spl. Citation, 1991), The River's Edge, Dateline NBC, 1994 (Emmy award), Susan Smith Coverage, 1994 (Clarion award), Bob Dotson's America Closeup, 1994 (Clarion award), The River's Edge, 1994 (Emmy award), Bob Dotson's Am., 1996. Recipient numerous awards including Elec. Media Grand Prize Nat. Assn. Yr. Round Edn., 1993, Gabriel Grand Prize Bob Dotson's Am. Diary, 1992, TV of Merit award DAR, 1985, Gabriel award Nat. Cath. Assn. Broadcasters, 1984, Clarion award Women in Communications, 1983, Epilepsy Found. Am. award, 1977, Silver medal Internat. Film and TV Festival of N.Y., 1976, Nat. Headliner award, NBC Today Show, 2001, Edward R. Murrow award for best network news writing Radio and TV News Dirs. Assn., 1999, for best reporting, 2001, 03, Diversity award, Columbia U., 2001, Emmy award for best story in regularly scheduled broadcast, 2003. Mem. Nat. Acad. TV Arts and Scis., Nat. Press Photographers Assn. (The Sprague Meml. award 1989), Writers Guild Am., Internat. Platform Assn., Radio and TV News Dirs., Explorers Club (N.Y.C.), Sigma Delta Chi. Avocation: writing. Office: NBC News-Today Show Ste 1028W 30 Rockefeller Plz New York NY 10112-0002 E-mail: dotson@nbc.com.

DOTT, ROBERT HENRY, JR., geologist, educator; b. Tulsa, June 2, 1929; s. Robert Henry and Esther Edgerton (Reed) Dott; m. Nancy Maud Robertson, Feb. 1, 1951; children: James, Karen, Eric, Cynthia, Brian. Student, U. Okla., 1946-48; BS, U. Mich., 1950, MS, 1951; PhD, Columbia U., 1956. Exploration geologist Humble Oil & Refining Co., Ariz., Oreg., Wash., 1954-56, 1958; mem. faculty U. Wis.-Madison, 1958-94, prof. geology, 1966-84, Stanley A. Tyler Disting. prof., 1984—, chmn. dept. geology and geophysics, 1974-77, emeritus prof., 1994—. Vis. prof. U. Calif., Berkeley, 1969; Cabot disting. vis. prof. U. Houston, 1986—87; NSF sci. faculty fellow Stanford U. and U.S. Geol. Survey, 1978, U. Colo., 1979; acad. visitor Imperial Coll., London, 1985—86, Oxford U., 1985—86, Adelaide U., Australia, 1992; cons. Roan Selection Trust, Ltd., Zambia, 1967, Atlantic-Richfield Co., 1983—85, Hubbard Map Co., 1984—86; lectr. Bur. Petroleum and Marine Geology, China, 1986; Erskine fellow, vis. prof. Canterbury U., New Zealand, 1987; Woodford-Ellis lectr. Pomona Coll., 1994. Co-author: Evolution of the Earth, 7th edit., 2003, Roadside Geology of Wisconsin, 2004; contbr. articles to profl. jours. 1st lt. USAF, 1956—57. Recipient Outstanding Tchr. award, Wis. Student Assn., 1969, Ben. H. Parker award, Am. Inst. Profl. Geologists, 1992; AEC fellow, Columbia U., 1951—55. Fellow: Edinburgh Geol. Soc. (hon. corr. 1997), Geol. Soc. Am. (chmn. history of geology divsn. 1990, councilor 1992—94, History of Geology award 1995, L.L. Sloss award 2001); mem.: AAAS, History of Earth Sci. Soc. (pres. 1990), Internat. Assn. Sedimentologists, Soc. Econ. Paleontologists and Mineralogists (sec.-treas. 1968—70, v.p. 1972—73, pres. 1981—82, hon., William H. Twenhofel medal 1993), Am. Assn. Petroleum Geologists (Pres.'s award 1956, Disting. Svc. award 1984, Disting. lectr. 1985), Sigma Xi (Disting. lectr. 1988—89). Unitarian Universalist. Office: U Wis Dept Geology and Geophysics 1215 W Dayton St Madison WI 53706-1600 E-mail: rdott@geology.wise.edu. *To understand the earth's past, which no human could witness, has been for me the most exciting challenge imaginable. It is like a great Sherlock Holmes mystery story.*

DOTTEN, MICHAEL CHESTER, lawyer; b. Marathon, Ont., Can., Feb. 23, 1952; came to U.S., 1957; s. William James and Ona Adelaide (Sheppard) D.; m. Kathleen Curtis, Aug. 17, 1974 (div. July 1991); children: Matthew Curtis, Tyler Ryan; m. Cheryl Calvin, Apr. 16, 1994. BS in Polit. Sci., U. Oreg., 1974, JD, 1977. Bar: Idaho 1977, Oreg. 1978, U.S. Dist. Ct. Idaho 1977, U.S. Dist. Ct. Oreg. 1978, U.S. Ct. Appeals (9th cir.), U.S. Ct. Appeals (D.C. cir.) 1987, U.S. Ct. Claims 1986, U.S. Supreme Ct. 1996. Staff asst. to Senator Bob Packwood, U.S. Senate, Washington, 1973-74; asst. atty. gen. State of Idaho, Boise, Idaho, 1977-78; chief rate counsel Bonneville Power Adminstrn., Portland, Oreg., 1978-83; spl. counsel Heller, Ehrman, White & McAuliffe, Portland, 1983-84, ptnr., 1985-98, 99—; gen. counsel PG&E Gas Transmission, N.W. Corp., Portland, 1998-99; co-chair Energy Nat. Practice Group, 2003—. Utility com. mem. Ctr. for Pub. Resources, N.Y.C., 1992—; Nat. Panel Arbitrators, Am. Arbitration Assn., 2005-. Coun. Emanual Hosp. Assocs., Portland, 1988-92; bd. dirs. William Temple House, 1995-99, chmn. devel. com., 1996-98, v.p., 1997-98, pres., 1998-99; active Portland Inter-neighborhood Trans. Rev. Commn., 1986-88; vestryman Christ Episcopal Ch., Lake Oswego, Oreg., 1999-2003, sr. warden, 2001-03. Hunter Leadership scholar U. Oreg., 1973, Oreg. scholar, 1970. Mem. ABA (chmn. electric power com. sect. natural resources 1985-88, coun. liaison energy com. 1990-93, coordinating group on energy law 1992-96), Fed. Bar Assn. (pres. Oreg. chpt. 1989-90, Chpt. Activity award 1990, Pres. award 1988-89), Oreg. State Bar (chmn. dispute resolution com. 1986-87), U. Oreg. Law Sch. Alumni Assn. (pres. 1989-92), Am. Arbitration Assn., Arlington Club, Multnomah Athletic Club. Democrat. Episcopalian. Avocations: skiing, golf, hiking, travel, racquetball. Office: Heller Ehrman White & McAuliffe 200 SW Market St Ste 1750 Portland OR 97201-5722 Office Phone: 503-227-7400. E-mail: mdotten@hewm.com.

DOTTO, PETER ATTILIUS, retired marine corps officer, defense consultant; b. Milan, June 30, 1949; s. Gianni Abraham and Renata Carla (Zagni) D.; m. July 15, 1978 (div. May 1994); children: John, Nicole, Regina, Anthony, Donna, Joseph; m. Marilyn Anne Capotosto, Sept. 12, 1999. BS in Biology, U. Dayton, 1971; MS in Govt., Campbell U., 1984; MA in Nat. Security-Strategic Studies, Naval War Coll., Newport, R.I., 1991. Commd. 2d lt. USMC, 1971, advanced through grades to col., 1992; dir. future ops. Unified Task Force, Somalia, 1992-93; comdr. Hdqs. Bn., 1st Marine Divsn., Camp Pendleton, Calif., 1993-94; vice dir. strategy, plans and policy U.S. So. Command, Panama, 1994-95; asst. chief staff for spl. ops. tng., exercises-simulations I Marine Expeditionary Force, Camp Pendleton, 1996-98, chief staff, 1998; ret., 1998; sr. exec. officer Avatar Sentry, Ltd., Hollywood, Fla., 1998; program dir. M2 Techs., Inc., West Hyannisport, Mass., 1999—. Adj. prof. Marine Corps U., San Diego, 1999—; cons. Naval Sea Sys. Command, Corona, Calif., 1999, Sierra Cybernetics, Yorba Linda, Calif., 1999. Contbr. articles to profl. jours. Decorated Def. Superior Svc. medal; recipient merit award U.S. Dept. State, 1993. Mem. DVA (life), Mil. Officers Assn., 1st Marine Divsn. Assn. (legal officer 1999-2000), Am. Legion, Marine Corps Assn. Republican. Roman Catholic. Avocations: hiking, travel. Office: M2 Techs Inc 1444 Eagle Glen Escondido CA 92029 Fax: 760-781-5539. Office Phone: 760-443-2366. E-mail: dottop@cox.net.

DOTY, DAVID SINGLETON, federal judge; b. Anoka, Minn., June 30, 1929; BA, JD, U. Minn., 1961; LLD (hon.), William Mitchell Coll. Law. Bar: Minn. 1961, U.S. Ct. Appeals (8th and 9th cirs.) 1976, U.S. Supreme Ct. 1982. V.p., dir. Popham, Haik, Schnobrich, Kaufman & Doty, Mpls., 1962-87, pres., 1977-79; instr. William Mitchell Coll. Law, St. Paul, 1963—64; judge U.S. Dist. Ct. for Minn., Mpls., 1987—. Mem. Adv. Com. on Civil Rules, 1992-98, Adv. Com. on Evidence Rules, 1994-98; trustee Mpls. Libr. Bd., 1969-79, Mpls. Found., 1976-83. Fellow ABA Found.; mem. ABA, Minn. Bar Assn. (gov. 1976-87, sec. 1980-83, pres. 1984-85), Hennepin County Bar Assn. (pres. 1975-76), Am. Judicature Soc., Am. Law Inst. Home: 23 Greenway Gables Minneapolis MN 55403-2145 Office: US Dist Ct 14 W US Courthouse 300 S 4th St Minneapolis MN 55415-1320 Office Phone: 612-664-5060. Business E-Mail: dsdoty@mnd.uscourts.gov.

DOTY, DONALD D., retired bank executive; b. Independence, Kans., June 30, 1928; s. Laton L. and Dorothy (Russell) D.; m. Cheri F. Montgomery, June 14, 1952; children: John Scott, Susan Dorothy, Mark Montgomery. BS, Okla. State U., 1950; postgrad., U. Wis. Grad. Sch. Banking, 1963. Rancher, nr. Bartlesville, Okla., 1950-94; asst. cashier First Nat. Bank, Bartlesville, 1956-58, asst. v.p., 1958-60, v.p., 1964-69, exec. v.p., 1969-74; pres. WestStar Bank, n.a. (formerly First Nat. Bank), Bartlesville, 1974-93; also bd. dirs.; retired, 1993. Pres. First Bancshares, Inc., Bartlesville, 1974-93, bd. dirs.; chmn. S.W. Cattlemen's Credit Corp., 1979-90; pres. Bartlesville Credit Bur., 1972—; pres. Bartlesville-Area Indsl. Devel. Co., 1970—; chmn. First Okla. Life Ins. Co., Oklahoma City, 1990-95; chmn. Coll. Bus. Assocs., Okla. State U., 1991-92. Chmn., trustees Jane Phillips Episcopal Meml. Med. Ctr., 1970—; trustee Washington County Indsl. Devel. Trust Authority, 1973-80; chmn. Frank Phillips Found., Bartlesville, 1975—2003; trustee St. John Hosp., Tulsa, 1995-2004; bd. dirs. St. John Health Sys., 2004. Capt. USAF, 1953-55. Named to Okla. State U., Coll. of Bus. Hall of Fame, 1994; recipient Disting. S c. award Bartlesville, 1957, Disting. Alumni award Okla. State U., 2000. Mem. Am. Bankers Assn., Okla. Bankers Assn. (pres. 1984-85), Bartlesville C. of C. (v.p., bd. dirs. 1965-81, pres. 1981-82), Jaycees (Outstanding Young Man Bartlesville 1957, Okla. 1958), Masons, Shriners, Rotary, Sigma Alpha Epsilon. Republican. Episcopalian. Avocations: skiing, hunting, golf. Home: 2407 Kyle Ct Bartlesville OK 74006-6340 Office Phone: 918-337-3461. E-mail: dotyd@sbcglobal.net.

DOTY, DUANE HAROLD, business educator; b. Wichita, Kans., July 5, 1960; s. David H. and Martha (Parker) D.; m. Susan Michal Smith, Dec. 30, 1991; children: Lindsey, Michala, Zachary, David. BA with honors, S.W. Tex. State U., San Marcos, Tex., 1982; MBA, U. Tex., Austin, 1987, PhD, 1990. Asst. prof. U. Ark., Fayetteville, 1990—95; chair dept. strategy and human resources Syracuse U. Sch. Mgmt., 1995; dean Coll. Bus. U. So. Miss., Hattiesburg, 2003—. Contbr. articles. Mem.: Acad. Mgmt. (mem. editl. bd. Acad. Mgmt. Jour., Best Article award 1993, Scholarly Achievement award human resouces divsn. 1997). Avocations: family, hunting, fishing, horses. Office: Univ So Miss Coll Bus PO Box 5021 Hattiesburg MS 39406 Office Phone: 601-266-4659. Business E-Mail: harold.doty@usm.edu.

DOTY, GRESDNA ANN, theatre historian, educator; b. Oelwein, Iowa, Feb. 22, 1931; d. James William and Gresdna (Wood) D.; m. James G. Traynham, Nov. 28, 1980. AA, Monticello Coll., Alton, Ill., 1951; BA, U. No. Iowa, 1953; MA, U. Fla., 1957; PhD, Ind. U., 1967. Instr. S.W. Tex. State U., San Marcos, 1957—61, asst. prof., 1964—65, La. State U., Baton Rouge, 1967-73, assoc. prof., 1973-79, dir. theatre, 1973-77, 81-91, prof., 1979-84, alumni prof., 1984—, alumni prof. emeritus, 1996—, chair dept. theatre, 1991-93, dean, 2004—. Author: Anne Brunton Merry in the American Theatre, 1971; co-editor: (with Billy J. Harbin) Inside the Royal Court Theatre, 1956-81: Artists Talk, 1990; contbr. articles to profl. jours. Bd. dirs. Arts Coun. Greater Baton Rouge, 1987-92, pres., 1990-91; mem. exec. com. Swine Palace Prodns. Rsch. grantee Nat. Endowment Humanities, 1981, Exxon Edn. Found., 1981. Fellow S.W. Theatre Assn.; mem. Am. Theatre Assn. (bd. dirs. 1977-80), Am. Coll. Theatre Festival (nat. chmn. 1976-79), Am. Soc. Theatre Rsch. (mem. exec. com. 1988-91, v.p. 1994-97), Nat. Theatre Conf. (sec. 1999-02), Coll. of Fellows of Am. Theatre (dean-elect 2003-04, dean 2004—). Home: 122 Highland Trace Baton Rouge LA 70810-5061

DOTY, JAMES EDWARD, minister, psychologist; b. Lakewood, Ohio, May 8, 1922; s. Ordello Luce and Margaret (McCurdy) D.; m. Mary Merciel Smith, Sept. 8, 1943; children: Mark Allen, David Wesley, Martha Suzanne. AB, Mt. Union Coll., Alliance, Ohio, 1944, DD (hon.), 1965; MDiv cum laude, Boston U., 1947, PhD, 1959; postgrad., Harvard U., Oxford U.; DD (hon.), DePauw U., 1966. Ordained to ministry Meth. Ch., 1945. Pastor in, Salem, Mass., 1947-51, Lynn, Mass., 1951-57; founder, dir. Greater Lynn Pastoral Care and Counselling Ctr., 1954-57; dir. pastoral care and counselling Ind. Area Meth. Ch., 1957-66; pres. Baker U., 1966-73; pvt. practice pastoral psychology Corpus Christi, Tex., 1973—2000; exec. dir. Corpus Christi Pastoral Counselling Ctr., 1973-84; interim sr. pastor First United Methodist Ch., Corpus Christi, 1988-89; interim pastor 1st Presbyn. Ch., Portland, Tex., 1991-98; pastor New Franklin (Ohio) United Meth. Ch., 2000—01; interim pastor Sebring (Ohio) Presbyn. Ch., 2001—03, Ch. of Silver Lake, Ohio, 2003—. Mem. staff Boston Ctr. Adult Edn., 1949—53; spl. lectr. Union Theol. Sem., Buenos Aires, 1962, Meth. Theol. Sem., Sao Paulo, Brazil, 1962, Epworth Theol. Sem., Salisbury, Rhodesia, 1963, Meth. Theol. Sem., Mulungwishi, Congo, 1964, Trinity Theol. Coll., Singapore, 1967, Union Theol. Sem., Manila, 1967, Cbanga Meth. Theol. Sem., Monrovia, Liberia, 1975, Meth. Theol. Sem., Suva, Fiji, 1986; mem. First Student

Christian Movement Conf. in postwar Germany Heidelberg U., 1947; del. World Family Life Consultation, Birmingham, England, 1966; chmn. World Family Life, 1981—86; mem. World Meth. Coun., London, 1966, Denver, 71, Dublin, 76, Honolulu, 81, del., Nairobi, Kenya, 86, Singapore, 1991—2001; chmn. exec. com., chmn. bd. visitors Sch. Theology Boston U. Author: The Pastor as Agape Counselor, 1964, Postmark Lambarene: A Visit with Albert Schweitzer, 1965; editor: Authentic Man Encounters God's World, 1967, Students Search for Meaning, 1971, (with Merciel S. Doty) For Heaven's Sake, 1993, Albert Schweitzer: Reverence for Life, 1993, With Schweitzer in Africa, 1994; producer, moderator weekly program Focus, Sta. KEDT-TV, 1984-95. V.p. Pike Twp. Sch. Bd., Marion County, Ind., 1960-66. Recipient Alumni of Yr. award, Mt. Union Coll., 1963, Alumni award of merit, Boston U., 1969. Mem. APA, S.W. Conf. United Meth. Ch., Tex. Bd. Profl. Counselors, Am. Bd. Sexology (diplomate), Am. Assn. Pastoral Counselors (diplomate, bd. dirs.), Am. Assn. Marriage and Family Therapy, Rotary, Sigma Alpha Epsilon, Zeta Chi. Home: 800 S 15th St Sebring OH 44672-2050 Office Phone: 330-928-2991.

DOTY, JAMES EDWARD, respiratory therapist; b. San Diego, Calif. s. James Bradford and Barbara Lee (Ceiplis) Doty; m. Sherrie Kay Lindner (div.); m. Ervie Me-Ann Amarille, Dec. 19, 1997; children: John Mark Paul Amarille Doty, James Ernesto Amarille Doty. AS in Respiratory Care, Gateway Coll., Phoenix, Ariz., 1993. Cert. respiratory care Gateway Coll., Ariz., 1993, respiratory tech. Gateway Coll., Ariz., 1992, nursing tech. Billings Vo-Tech, Mont., 1981, respiratory therapist Nat. Bd. for Respiratory Care, 1993. Tnr. tireman Trainer Tire, El Cajon, Calif., 1977—78; frontend tune-up mechanic Firestone Tire & Rubber, Prescott, Ariz., 1978—79; nursing patient technician St. Vincents Hosp., Billings, Mont., 1981—86; asst. foreman heavy equipment Concrete & Excavator, Inc., Billings, Mont., 1987—88; staff traveling therapist Immediate Respiratory Staffers, Phoenix, 1991—95; customer svc. rep. Carido-Sysytems Inc., Tempe, 1992—95; mgr. respiratory dept. Med. Ctr. Blount, Oneonta, Ala., 1995—2003. Smoking cessation trainer AHA, Birmingham, Ala., 2002—03; prod. usage trainer Cardio-Systems (in-hosp.), Tempe, 1992—95. Exhibited in group shows at Graphic Arts, Hill AFB, Utah, 1975 (honoriable mention). Counselor, house parent Montana Foster Parent, Billings, Mont., 1983—87; house parent devel. disabled Prescott Group Home, Prescott, Ariz., 1977—78; counselor summer programs YMCA, La Mesa, Calif., 1977; mem. Northeastern Ala. Cherokee Tribe. With USAF, 1974—77. Mem.: Nat. Coll. Level Tutors Assn., Lambda Beta Soc. (life). Republican. Zen. Achievements include patents for houseware redesign, 1985. Avocations: computers, art, gardening, woodworking, inventing.

DOTY, LEILANI, geriatric neuropsychologist, administrator; b. Everett, Mass., July 28, 1942; BA, U. Fla., 1976, PhD in Counselor Edn., 1986. RN, MGH, Mass.; nat. cert. counselor Am. Assn. Counseling and Devel.; cert. gerontology Ctr. for Gerontol. Studies, U. Fla. Adminstr. Alzheimer's Disease Initiative U. Fla. Memory Disorder Clinic, Gainesville, 1987—, mem. faculty dept. neurology Coll. Medicine, 1988—. Cons. Ctr. for Rsch. on Telehealth & Healthcare Comms. U. Fla., 2000—. Author: Basic Communication Skills and Assertiveness Training for Older Persons, 1982, Advanced Communication Skills and Selective Assertiveness Training for Older Persons, 1982, Life Satisfaction Determinants in Older Persons, 1986, Communication and Assertion for Older Persons, 1987, (with others) Helping People with Progressive Memory Disorders: A Guidebook for You and Your Family, 2d edit., 1998 (Nat. Health Info. Bronze award 1997); guest editor: (with N. S. Hardt) spl. issues Jour. Fla. Med. Assn., 1996, 97; contbr. chpts. to books; contbr. articles to profl. jours. Women's liason officer, U. Fla., 1995-2002; co-founder, 1st chair Cmty. Ptnrs., 1997; chair Nat. Women's Health Rsch. Conf., 1996-98; co-founder, bd. dirs. U. Fla. Inst. Women's Health. Recipient Pres. award Mental Health Assn. Alachua County, Fla., 1982, U. Fla. Women of Achievement award, 1998; postdoctoral fellow Geriat. Soc. Am., 1989, PhD Cmty. Svc. award, 2001. Office: Dept Neurology Box 100236 U Fla Brain Inst Gainesville FL 32610-0236 Office Phone: 352-273-5550. Office Fax: 352-273-5575. Business E-Mail: dotyl@neurology.ufl.edu.

DOTY, MARK A., author; b. Maryville, Tenn., Aug. 10, 1953; s. Lawrence Woodworth and Ruth S. Doty; life ptnr.: Paul Lisicky. BA, Drake U., Des Moines, 1978; MFA, Goddard Coll., Plainfield, Vt., 1980. Faculty Sarah Lawrence Coll., Bronxville, N.Y., 1990-94; vis. prof. Brandeis U., Waltham, Mass., 1994, U. Iowa, Iowa City, 1995-96; prof. U. Utah, Salt Lake City, 1996-98; prof. creative writing program U. Houston, 1998—. Author: Sweet Machine, 1998, Firebird, 1999, Still Life with Oysters and Lemon, 2001, Source, 2001. Recipient Nat. Book Critics Cir. award, 1994, Lila Wallace/Reader's Digest Writers award, 2000—; Nat. Ednowment for the Arts fellow, 1994, Guggenheim fellow, 1995. Home: 19 Pearl St Provincetown MA 02657 Office: Univ of Houston Dept of English Houston TX 77204

DOTY, PAUL MEAD, biochemist, educator, arms control specialist; b. Charleston, W.Va., June 1, 1920; s. Paul Mead and Maud (Stewart) D.; m. Margaretta Elenor Grevatt, Oct. 31, 1942 (div. Aug. 1953); 1 child, Gordon Sutherland; m. Helga Boedtker, Feb. 27, 1954; children: Marcia, Rebecca, Katherine. BS, Pa. State Coll., 1941; MA, Columbia U., 1943, PhD, 1944; DSc, U. Chgo., 1966. From instr. to asst. prof. chemistry Poly. Inst. Bklyn., 1943-46; Rockefeller fellow Cambridge (Eng.) U., 1946-47; asst. prof. chemistry U. Notre Dame, South Bend, Ind., 1947-48, Harvard U., Cambridge, Mass., 1948-50, prof. chemistry, 1950-68, Mallinckrodt prof. biochemistry, 1968-88, prof. pub. policy Kennedy Sch., 1988-90, prof. biochemistry emeritus, 1988—, prof. pub. policy emeritus, 1990—. Founder, dir. Ctr. for Sci. and Internat. Affairs, Harvard U., 1973-85, dir. emeritus, 1985—; mem. Pres.'s Sci. Adv. Commn., White House, Washington, 1961-64; mem. gen. adv. com. on arms control to Pres., White House, 1976-80; bd. dirs., vice chmn. Mitre Corp., Bedford, Mass., 1975-92; bd. dirs. Internat. Sci. Found., Washington, 1993-97. Editor: Defending Deterrence: Managing the ABM Treaty, 1989; founder, editor quar. jour. Internat. Security, 1975-85; author more than 350 articles. Bd. dirs. Aspen Inst. Berlin, 1981-2005, Harriman Inst., Columbia U., 1986-98; mem. Aspen Inst. for Humanitsic Studies, Wye, Md., 1969-85; mem. Pugwash Confs., 1957-97. Recipient Pure Chemistry award Am. Chem. Soc., 1956. Mem. Am. Acad. Arts and Sci. (commn. on internat. security), Nat. Acad. Sci. (com. on internat. security and arms control), Am. Philos. Soc. Home: 4 Kirkland Pl Cambridge MA 02138-2034 Office: Kennedy Sch Govt Harvard U 79 Jfk St Cambridge MA 02138-5801 E-mail: pauldoty@fas.harvard.edu.

DOTY, PETER S., artist, writer; b. Ravenna, Ohio, June 11, 1963; s. Charles Stewart and Jean Richards Doty. AA, City Coll. San Francisco, 1991. Exhibitions include San Francisco Mus. Mod. Art Artist's Gallery, Wingspread Gallery, Northeast Harbor, Maine, 1995—2005, Camera Club NY, 1996, Synchronicity Space, N.Y.C., 1997; author: (novels) Bikinie Jones and the Pinched Family Jewels; actor: (films) The Doors; (plays) Clue, 2004. Founding mem. San Francisco Cmty. Land Trust Task Force; founder Haight-Ashbury Land Trust. Mem.: Haight-Ashbury Preservation Soc., San Francisco Cacophony Soc. Democrat. Home: PO Box 170213 San Francisco CA 94117

DOTY, ROBERT WALTER, lawyer; b. Aliquippa, Pa., Sept. 19, 1942; s. David Lucien and Iona (Fox) D.; m. Joyce Marie Shaffalo, Sept. 10, 1961; children: Genie, Merrie Beth. BA cum laude, Wheaton Coll., 1963; JD, Vanderbilt U., 1966. Bar: Pa. 1966, U.S. Supreme Ct. 1982. Assoc. Eckert Seamans Cherin & Mellot, Pitts., 1966-74; solicitor Crescent Township, Allegheny County, Pa., 1969—; ptnr. Eckert Seamans Cherin & Mellot, Pitts., 1975-91; dir. Cohen & Grigsby, P.C., Pitts., 1991—2003, of counsel, 2004—. Arbitrator Am. Arbitration Assn., nat. panel, 1978—, spkr. in field; lectr. Westinghouse Internat. Sch. Environ. Mgmt., Ft. Collins, Colo., 1980-82. Mem. nat. com. on wills and trusts centennial campaign Vanderbilt U., 1977-81. Recipient Archie B. Martin Meml. scholarship medal Vanderbilt U., 1964, Robert F. Jackson Meml. scholarship prize, 1965, Founder's medal, 1966; 3 Am. Jurisprudence awards in contracts, civil procedure and criminal law The Lawyers Co-operative Pub. Co., Rochester, N.Y., 1964, 65; Mark Woodworth Walton scholar Vanderbilt U., 1965. Mem. Pa. Bar Assn., Allegheny County Bar Assn. (governing coun. civil litigation sect.), Wheaton Club (past pres.), Fox Chapel Racquet Club, Breckenridge Golf and Tennis Club, Estero Country Club, Racquet Club Memphis, Order of Coif, Phi Kappa Delta, Phi Alpha Delta. Avocations: swimming, tennis. Office: 11 Stanwix St 15th Floor Pittsburgh PA 15222 Office Phone: 412-297-4866. Business E-Mail: rdoty@cohenlaw.com. E-mail: lawyerbodd@aol.com.

DOTY, ROBERT WILLIAM, neuroscientist, physiologist, educator; b. New Rochelle, N.Y., Jan. 10, 1920; s. Earle Birdsell and Ethel Laurette (Mack) D.; m. Elizabeth Natalie Jusewich, Aug. 30, 1941; children— Robert William, Mary E., Cheryl A., Richard M. BS, U. Chgo., 1948, MS, 1949, PhD, 1950. Postdoctoral fellow U. Ill., Chgo., 1950-51; asst. prof. U. Utah, Salt Lake City, 1951-56; from asst. to assoc. prof. U. Mich., Ann Arbor, 1956-61; prof. U. Rochester, N.Y., 1961—. Vis. prof. U. Mex., 1975, U. Osaka, Japan, 1981; sci. adviser NIMH, Bethesda, Md., 1975-79, Yerkes Inst., Atlanta, 1975-78 Author: (with E.N. Doty) Man and Woman, War and Peace, 1941-1951, A Dual Auto Biography, 2004; assoc. editor: Acta Neurobiologiae, Warsaw, 1971—; contbr. articles to profl. jours. Served to capt. U.S. Army, 1942-46 Recipient Javits award, Nat. Inst. Neurol. and Communicative Disorders and Stroke., NIH, 1986. Fellow AAAS; mem. Am. Psychol. Soc. (pres. div. 6, 1984), Internat. Brain Research Orgn., Current Anthropology (assoc.), Soc. for Neurosci. (pres. 1975-76, councilor 1970-74) Avocations: photography, history, langs. Office: Box 603 U Rochester Med Ctr Neurobiology And Anatomy Ctr Rochester NY 14642-0001 Office Phone: 585-275-1922. Business E-Mail: robert_doty@urmc.rochester.edu.

DOTY, SHAYNE TAYLOR, organist; b. Memphis, Aug. 19, 1961; s. Robert and Janice Doty. BA, Duke U., 1983; diploma, Conservatoire Nat. Superieur Musique Lyon, 1986; MM, So. Meth. U., 1991. Rsch. assoc. Capital Campaign for Arts and Scis., Duke U., 1983-84; organist, choirmaster St. Paul's Episcopal Ch., Washington, 1991-98; organist Am. Cath., Paris, 1995-96; asst. dir. corp. and found. rels. U. Md., College Park, 1997-98; sr. major gift officer Met. Opera Assn., N.Y.C., 1998—2004; dir. devel. Washington Nat. Opera, 2004—. Organ recitalist including St. Denis, Paris, St. Paul's, Toronto, Nat. Cathedral, Washington. Mary Duke Biddle scholarship Duke U., 1979-83; Frank Huntington Beebe fellow, 1984-86. Mem. Am. Guild of Organists, Thomas S. Kenan Inst. for Arts (trustee). Episcopalian. Office: Washington Nat Opera Ste 104 2600 Virginia Ave NW Washington DC 20037

DOTY, VICTORIA SKOWER, elementary school educator; b. Stafford, Conn., Sept. 25, 1946; d. Frank Albert Jr. and Emily Marie (Jedziniak) Skower; m. Edwin Wilfred Doty, Oct. 14, 1978; 1 child, Peter Edwin. BA, Am. Internat. Coll., Springfield, Mass., 1969; MA, Elms Coll., 1991. Cert. elem. tchr., Mass., Conn. Coord. inventory control Hallmark Cards Inc., Enfield, Conn., 1969-89; substitute tchr. Enfield and Longmeadow, Mass., 1991—98; tchr., chair mid. sch. reading and lang. arts St. Gabriels Sch., Windsor, Conn., 1998—. Sec. Thompsonville Little League, 1991-94, fin. sec., 1988-89, 93-94; elected to parish coun. St. Adalbert Ch., 1994-98; coord. local and county dist. Modern Woodmen of Am. Oration Contest, 2000—. Mem. St. Adalbert Home and Sch. Assn. (historian 1991-93, fin. sec. 1988-89, 93-94, treas. 1987-88). Republican. Roman Catholic. Avocations: folk art, crafts, crocheting, reading. Home: 45 Alden Ave Enfield CT 06082-2866

DOUB, WILLIAM OFFUTT, lawyer; b. Cumberland, Md., Sept. 3, 1931; s. Albert A. and Fannabelle (Offutt) D.; m. Mary Graham Boggs, Sept. 12, 1959; children: Joseph Peyton, Albert A., II. AB, Washington and Jefferson Coll., 1953; LLB, U. Md., 1956. Bar: Md. 1956, D.C. 1974. With law dept. B. & O. R.R., 1955-57; assoc. Bartlett Poe & Claggett, Balt., 1957-61; ptnr. Niles Barton & Wilmer, Balt., 1961-71; commr. AEC, 1971-74; ptnr. LeBoeuf, Lamb, Leiby & MacRae, Washington, 1974-77, Doub, Muntzing and Glasgow, Washington, 1977-91, Newman & Holtzinger, P.C., Washington, 1991-94, Morgan Lewis & Bockius, Washington, 1995-2000. Chmn. Minimum Wage Commn., Balt., 1964-66; peoples' counsel Md. Pub. Service Commn., 1967-68, chmn., 1968-71; vice chmn. Washington Met. Area Transit Commn., 1968-71; mem. President's Air Quality Adv. Bd., 1970-71; mem. exec. adv. com. FPC, 1969-71, Nat. Gas Survey, 1975-78; pres. Great Lakes Conf. Pub. Utility Commrs., 1971; mem. nat. adv. bd. Am. Nat. Standards Inst., 1975-80; mem. Md. Adv. Com. Retardation, 1969-71 Mem. Adminstrv. Conf., U.S., 1973-75; chmn. U.S. Energy Assn., Inc., World Energy Conf., 1978-80, U.S. del., 1974, 77, 80, 83, 86, 89, 92, 95, 98; vice chmn. World Energy Conf., 1986-88, hon. vice chmn., 1988—; mem. adv. groups Nat. Acad. Pub. Adminstrn., NSF; presdl. appointee as rep. to So. States Energy Bd., 1983-90; bd. govs. Mid. East Inst. of U.S., 1982-86, 88-94, 95-2000; mem. exec. com. Thomas Alva Edison Found., 1983-90, 85-90; presdl. appointee 33d Ann. Conf. of Internat. Atomic Energy Agy., 1989. Recipient Nat. Energy award U.S. Energy Assn., 1998. Mem. Met. Club. Home (Winter): 512 Neapolitan Ln Naples FL 34103 Home (Summer): Box 449 Keedyville MD 21756 Personal E-mail: fudoub@aol.com.

DOUBEK, JOHN C., lawyer, educator; b. St. Louis, Apr. 30, 1951; s. John C. and Mary E. Doubek; m. John N. Doubek, Mar. 11, 1954; children: Andrew, Jake, Anna. BA in Polit. Sci., Carroll Coll., 1973; JD, U. Mont., 1976. Bar: Mont. 1976, U.S. Ct. Appeals (9th cir.) 1976. Trial atty. Mont. Consumer Counsel, Helena, 1976—78; ptnr. Small Hutch Doubke & Pyter, Helena, 1978—. Sec. Mont. Irrigators, 1981—93; assoc. prof. Carroll Coll., Helena, 1984—. Mem.: ATLA, Mont. Trial Attys. Achievements include over 12 cases with verdicts or settlements in excess of $1 million. Home: 640 S Harris Helena MT 59601 Office: Small Hatch Doubek & Pyter 307 N Jackson Helena MT 59601 E-mail: jdoubek@uswest.net.

DOUBLEDAY, CHARLES WILLIAM, dermatologist, educator; b. Houston, Oct. 1, 1954; s. Leonard Charles and Margaret (Walker) D.; m. Verlinde Van den Berge Hill, June 22, 1985; children: George Marchant, Julia Van den Berge, Walker Hill. BA with honors, U. Tex., Austin, 1976; MD, U. Tex., Houston, 1981. Diplomate Am. Bd. Dermatology, 1987. Rotating intern John Peter Smith Hosp., Ft. Worth, 1981-82; resident in dermatology U. Tex. Med. Sch., 1982-83, 85-87, fellow in dermatology, 1985, clin. asst. prof. dermatology, 1988—; pvt. practice, Houston, 1987—. Bd. dirs. The Park People. Contbr. articles to profl. jours. Recipient high sci. quality award Soc. for Investigative Dermatology, 1986; Rsch. fellow Dermatology Found., 1985. Fellow Am. Acad. Dermatology; mem. Tex. Med. Assn., Harris County Med. Soc., Tex. Dermatol. Soc., Houston Dermatol. Soc. (pres. 2005), U. Tex. Houston Health Sci. Ctr. (devel. coun., 1994-96), Houston Country Club. Republican. Episcopalian. Avocations: tennis, golf. Office: 515 Post Oak Blvd Ste 535 Houston TX 77027-9494

DOUCETTE, DAVID ROBERT, information technology executive; b. Pitts., Feb. 2, 1946; s. Adrian Robert and Mary Alyce (Newland) D. BSEE cum laude, Poly. Inst. Bklyn., 1968, MSEE, 1970, PhD, 1974. Asst. prof. elec. engring. Poly. Inst. NY (now Poly. U.), 1973-74, assoc. prof. computer sci., 1975-82, prof., 1982—, dir., 1994—2002, assoc. dean, 1997—2002; sr. staff specialist advanced planning Gruman Data Sys. Corp., Bethpage, NY, 1979-80, program mgr., 1979-80, mgr. graphics sys., 1980-84, from asst. dir. to dir. interactive sys. support, 1984-86, dir. interactive sys., 1986-94; pres., CEO D3Software Corp., 1994—. Active Nassau County Hist. Soc., Garden City Hist. Soc. Recipient Achievement award Engrs. Joint Coun. L.I., 1999. Mem. IEEE (past sect. chmn., Centennial medal, Third Millennium medal), Assn. Computing Machinery (past chpt. chmn.), Nat. Space Soc., Planetary Soc., Nat. Eagle Scout Assn. (chpt. bd.), Sigma Xi, Tau Beta Pi, Eta Kappa Nu, L.I. Early Fliers Club. Office: Poly U Dept Computer/Info Sci 6 Metrotech Ctr Brooklyn NY 11201

DOUCETTE, MARY-ALYCE, computer company executive; b. Pitts., Feb. 12, 1924; d. Andrew George and Alice Jane (Sloan) Newland; m. Adrian Robert Doucette, Feb. 6, 1945 (dec. June 1983); children: David Robert, Regis Robert. BS cum laude, U. Pitts., 1945. Mgr. Newland Bros., Millvale, Pa., 1946-53; gen. mgr. Newland-Ludlo, Pitts., 1953-72; mgmt. cons. D3 Software, Garden City, N.Y., 1972-80, sec., corp. officer, 1980—. Fin. sec. Cerebral Palsy Assn., Garden City, Helen Keller Svcs. for Blind, Garden City; mem. Winthrop-U. Hosp. Aux., Mercy League, Friends of Adelphi Univ. Libr., Friends of Hist. St. George Ch. of Hempstead, N.Y., Adv. Coun. for Continuing Edn., Garden City Sch. Dist., 1988—. Mem. AAUW, L.I. Panhellenic, Univ. Club, Nassau County Hist. Soc. (life), Garden City Hist. Soc., Community Club Garden City-Hempstead, Woman's Club Garden City, Alpha Delta Pi, Pi Lambda Theta. Home: 146 Washington Ave Garden City NY 11530-3013 Office: D3 Software PO Box 8051 Garden City NY 11530-8051

DOUD, DENNIS ADAIR, retired secondary school educator; b. Waukegan, Ill., Oct. 10, 1943; s. Webster Hawley and Adrienne D.; m. Mary Ann Loesch, July 11, 1970; children: Christopher, Tristan, Tiffany. BS, Loyola U., Chgo., 1965; MA, Loyola U., 1972. Cert. secondary tchr., Ill. Grad. asst. Loyola U., 1966-67; tchr., coach North Chicago (Ill.) H.S., 1967-72; tchr. modern European history, humanities, European hist. AP Evanston (Ill.) H.S., 1972—2002; parttime instr. Coll. of Lake County; ret., 2002. Jr. varsity sophmore basketball coach Evanston H.S., 1972-81. Basketball coach Waukegan Park Dist., 1985-96; coach Waukegan Baseball Assn., 1990—, Waukegan Soccer Assn.; soccer coach Gurnee (Ill.) Park Dist., 1989-93. Recipient Outstanding Tchr. award U. Chgo., 1986, 87, 89, spl. tchr. recognition Carleton Coll., 1987, influentia. tchr. recognition Wesleyan U., 1991; named One of Top 5 Tchrs., Evanston High Sch., 1989. Mem. IEA-NEA, Newberry Libr. Consortium for History Tchrs. Avocations: model building and railroading, stamp collecting/philately, reading, refereeing basketball, umpiring, classical cars. Home: 2012 Kingston Rd Waukegan IL 60087-2115

DOUD, WALLACE C., retired information technology executive; b. Bellingham, Wash., Feb. 25, 1925; s. Forrest Roy and Florence (Pollock) D.; m. Marjorie K. Fenton, Oct. 25, 1949 (dec. 1962); children: Forrest J., Mary, Margaret, Barbara, Melissa; m. Janice F. Freudenberg, June 15, 1963 (dec. 1978); children: Michael, Karen; m. Jean A. Kennedy, Oct. 13, 1979. BBA, U. Wis., 1948; DHL (hon.), Mercy Coll., 1983. Salesman IBM Corp., Milw., St. Paul, Detroit, dir. patent relations Armonk, N.Y., 1960-71, v.p. services staff, 1971-77, v.p. comml. and industry rels., 1977-85. Chmn. Bd. Parks and Recreation White Plains, N.Y., 1983-84; chmn., pres. United Way, White Plains, 1975-80. Recipient Youth Services award B'nai B'rith, 1972, Medallion Westchester Community Coll., 1980. Mem.: Rockland Golf Club, Megunticook Golf Club. Republican. Presbyterian.

DOUDNA, JENNIFER A., molecular biologist, educator; BA, Pomona Coll., 1985; PhD, Harvard U., 1989. Post-doctoral fellow Harvard Med. Sch., 1989-91, U. Colo., 1991-94; Henry Ford II prof. molecular biophysics and biochemistry Yale U., New Haven, 1994—2002, assoc. investigator Howard Hughes Med. Inst., 1997—; R. B. Woodward Visiting Prof. Harvard U., 2000—01; faculty scientist, physical biosciences div. Lawrence Berkeley Nat. Lab., 2003; faculty, biophysics grad. group U. of Calif., Berkeley, 2003—, prof. biochemistry and molecular biology, dept. chemistry, 2003—, prof. biochemistry and molecular biology, dept. molecular and cell biology, 2003—. Contbr. articles to profl. jours. Mem. bd. trustees Pomona Coll., 2001. Recipient award for initiatives in rsch., NAS, 1999, Alan T. Waterman award, NSF, 2000. Fellow: Am. Academy of Arts and Sciences; mem.: NAS. Achievements include structure and function of ribozymes and RNA-protein complexes. Office: UC Berkeley 305 Hildebrand Hall MS #3206 Berkeley CA 94720-3206

DOUGAL, ARWIN ADELBERT, electrical engineer, educator; b. Dunlap, Iowa, Nov. 22, 1926; s. Adelbert Isaac and Goldya (White) D.; m. Margaret Jane McLennan, Sept. 3, 1951; children: Catherine Ann, Roger Adelbert, Leonard Harley, Laura Beth. BS, Iowa State U., 1952; MS, U. Ill., 1955, PhD, 1957. Registered profl. engr., Tex. Radio engr. Collins Radio Co., Cedar Rapids, Iowa, 1952; research asst., research asso., asst. prof., asso. prof. U. Ill., Urbana, 1952-61; prof., mem. grad. faculty, dir. labs. for electronics and related sci. research U. Tex., Austin, 1961-67, prof., 1969—91; dir. Electronics Research Center, 1971-77, sec. grad. assembly, 1972-74; dir. Austron, Inc., 1977-82; prof. emeritus U. Tex., 1992—. Asst. dir. def. rsch. and engring. for rsch. Office Sec. Def., Washington, 1967-69; cons. Tex. Instruments, Inc., Dallas, Gen. Dynamics Corp., Ft. Worth, U. Calif. Los Alamos Sci. Lab., Battelle Meml. Inst. Contbr. articles to profl. jours Faculty sponsor U. Tex. Conservative Democrats Club, 1966-67; sr. mem. CAP, 1984—; elder local Presbyn. Ch.; commr., Mission Presbyn. With USAAF, 1946—49, with USAF, 1946—49, Airways & Air Commn. Svc. Recipient Teaching Excellence awards U. Tex. Students Assn., 1962, 63, Spl. award for outstanding service as program chmn. S.W. IEEE Conf. and Exhbn., 1967; Outstanding Grad. Adviser award Grad. Engring. Council, U. Tex., 1971; Disting. Advisor award Grad. Engring. Council, U. Tex., 1977, 84; Teaching Achievement award Grad. Engring. Council, U. Tex., 1977; Profl. Achievement citation in engring. Iowa State U. Alumni Assn., 1975 Fellow Am. Phys. Soc., IEEE (dir. 1980-81, Centennial medal 1984, Student Br. citation 1988, Outstanding Br. Counselor award, 1991, chmn. ctrl. Tex. sect. 1993-94)); mem. Am. Soc. Engring. Edn., Aircraft Owners and Pilots Assn., Exptl. Aircraft Assn., Sigma Xi, Phi Kappa Phi, Tau Beta Pi, Eta Kappa Nu, Pi Mu Epsilon, Phi Eta Sigma, Rockport Yacht Club Avocation: aviation. Home: 6115 Rickey Dr Austin TX 78757-4437 E-mail: aadougal@att.net.

DOUGALL-SIDES, LESLIE K., lawyer; b. Washington, Sept. 5, 1953; d. George Malcolm Richardson and Kathleen (Cahill) Dougall; m. Kenneth Jacob Sides, Feb. 19, 1994. BA, New Coll., Sarasota, Fla., 1975; JD cum laude, Florida State U., Tallahassee, 1978. Bar: Fla. 1981, DC 1981, Oreg. 1986, cert.: in city, county and local govt. law 1996, cert. profl. human resources 2001, bar: U.S. Dis. Ct. (middle and southern dist.) Fla., U.S. ct. appeals (11th cir.), U.S. Supreme Ct. Staff atty. Ctrl. Fla. Legal Svcs., Cocoa, 1982—85, dir. atty. Handicapped Law Ctr., 1985—87; asst. city atty., acting city atty. City of Key West (Fla.), 1987—95; asst. city atty. City of Clearwater (Fla.), 1995—; bd. dirs. IRRA, 2000—02; sec. West Ctrl. Fla. Chpt., Indsl. Rels. Rsch. Assn., 2003. Mem.: Indsl. Rels. Rsch. Assn. (sec. West Ctrl. Fla. chpt. 2003, bd. dirs. 2000—02), Soc. Human Resources, Clearwater Bar Assn., ABA. Avocation: sailing. Office: City of Clearwater City Atty's Office PO Box 4748 Clearwater FL 33758 Office Phone: 727-562-4010. Business E-Mail: leslie.dougall-sides@myclearwater.com.

DOUGAN, BRADY W., diversified financial services company executive; b. Urbana, Illinois, 1959; married; 2 children. AB in Econ., U. Chgo., 1981, MBA in Fin., 1982. With derivatives group to mng. dir. long term fin. Bankers Trust, Tokyo; joined Credit Suisse First Boston, 1990, co-head, fin. products' marketing effort in the Americas, co-head, global debt capital markets group, head equities divsn., 1996—2001, global head securities div., 2001—02, co-pres. institutional securities NYC, 2002—04, London, 2004, mem. exec. bd. and oper. com., 2003—; exec. bd. Credit Suisse Group, 2003—; CEO Credit Suisse First Boston, NYC, 2004—. Office: Credit Suisse First Boston 11 Madison Ave New York NY 10010 Office Phone: 212-325-2000. Office Fax: 212-325-6665.

DOUGHERTY, BEVERLY ANNE, mathematics educator; b. St. Louis, Oct. 28, 1950; d. John Morris and Louise Mary (Witeka) Martin; m. James Patrick Dougherty, Aug. 4, 1973; children: Erica, Bridget, Elizabeth. BA in Math./Philosophy magna cum laude, U. Mo., 1972; MA in Teaching, Webster U., 1974. Cert. math. tchr. Chmn. math. dept. Hazelwood Cen. High Sch., Florissant, Mo., 1975-79; math. tchr. Hazelwood Sch. Dist., Florissant, 1972-83; math. tutor St. Louis, 1984-88; math. tchr. Oakville Sr. High Sch., Oakville, Mo., 1988—. Adj. math. instr. St. Louis U., 1980-85, Harris-Stowe State Coll., St. Louis, 1984-86. Co-campaign mgr. Citizens to Re-elect Pat Dougherty, St. Louis, 1980—; bd. dirs. Friends of Tower Grove Park, St. Louis, Grand-Oak Hill Community Corp.; com. chair Old Fashioned St. Louis 4th of July Civic Celebration, 1991; participant Community Leadership Program for Tchrs., 1992-93. Recipient Vol. award St. Louis Pub. Schs., 1986-88, Lashley award for volunteerism Friends of St. Louis Pub. Libr., 1990, Citicorp Success Fund Innovator award, 1991, 92; Missouriana Study

Tour scholar Mo. State Coll., Warrensburg, 1990, 93, Ea. Mo. Econ. Study Tour scholar U. Mo.-St. Louis, 1992; Mehlville-Oakville Found. grantee, 1992, 93. Mem. NEA, Nat. Coun. Tchrs. Math., Math. Educators Greater St. Louis, Mo. Coun. Tchrs. Math. Democrat. Roman Catholic. Avocation: gardening. Office: Oakville Sr High Sch 5557 Milburn Rd Saint Louis MO 63129-3599

DOUGHERTY, CHARLES HAMILTON, pediatrician; b. St. Louis, June 1, 1947; s. Charles Joseph and Suzanne Louise (Hamilton) D.; m. Mary Laverty Peckham, July 7, 1972; children: Bridget, Matthew, Erin, Kelly. BA in Biology, Coll. of the Holy Cross, 1969; MD, U. Rochester Sch. of Medicine, N.Y., 1973. Pediatric resident St. Louis Children's Hosp., 1973-76, pres. med. staff, 2005—; pvt. practice pediatrics Primary Pediatric Care Group, St. Louis, 1976-86, Esse Health, St. Louis, 1986—. Fellow Am. Acad. Pediatrics. Roman Catholic. Avocations: marathon running, adventure vacations, computers, water sports, powered parachute pilot. Office: Esse Health 13303 Tesson Ferry Rd Saint Louis MO 63128-4062 Personal E-mail: cdoughe103@aol.com. Business E-Mail: cdougher@essehealth.com.

DOUGHERTY, CHARLES JOHN, university administrator, philosophy and medical ethics educator; b. N.Y.C., June 28, 1949; s. Charles Aloysius and Mary Elizabeth (Quinn) D.; m. Sandra Lee Drabik; children: Constance Marie, Justin Charles. BA, St. Bonaventure U., 1971; MA, U. Notre Dame, 1973, PhD in Philosophy, 1975. Prof. philosophy Creighton U., Omaha, 1975-88, dir., Ctr. for Health Policy and Ethics, 1988-95, v.p. acad. affairs, 1995-2001; pres. Duquesne U., Pitts., 2001—. Author: Ideal, Fact, and Medicine, 1985, (with R.P. Heaney) Research for Health Professionals, 1988, American Health Care: Realities, Rights and Reforms, 1988, (with Jerry Cederblom) Ethics at Work, 1990, (with A. Haddad and B. Edwards) Ethical Dilemmas in Perioperative Nursing, 1990, Back to Reform, 1996; contbr. articles to profl. jours.; mem. bd. editors Health Progress, 1989—. Chmn. Nebr. Com. for the Humanities, Lincoln, 1987-88; bd. dirs. Fedn. of State Humanities Couns., 1986-89; mem. disciplinary rev. bd. Nebr. Supreme Ct., 1988—, Nebr. Accountability and Disclosure Commn., 1991—; bd. dirs. Sisters of Charity Health Sys. of Cin., 1994-96; bd. trustees Cath. Health Assn., 1995—. Mem. Am. Philos. Assn., Am. Catholic Philos. Assn. (exec. council mem. 1987-90), Alpha Sigma Nu. Democrat. Roman Catholic. Office: Duquesne Univ 600 Forbes Ave Pittsburgh PA 15282

DOUGHERTY, DARIN DEAN, psychiatrist; b. Pensacola, Fla., Mar. 19, 1966; s. Darwin Dean Dougherty and Coletta Lue Rentschler; m. Christina Sjostrom Whiting, Oct. 5, 1996; 1 child, Emma. BS, BA, U. Ill., 1989; MD, U. Ill., Chgo., 1993; MS, Harvard U., 1999. Diplomate Am. Bd. Psychiatry and Neurology. Psychiatrist Mass. Gen. Hosp., Boston, 1994—, dir. trichotillomania clinic and rsch. unit, 1997—. Dir. med. edn. Obsessive-Compulsive Disorders Inst. McLean Hosp., Belmont, Mass., 1997—. Editor: Contemporary Strategies in Psychiatric Neuroimaging Research, 2000. Mem. Am. Psychiatric Assn., Soc. Biol. Psychiatry, Am. Neuropsychiatric Assn. Home: 26 Seaver St Wellesley MA 02481-6743 Office: Mass Gen Hosp Fruit St Boston MA 02114 Fax: 617-726-7541.

DOUGHERTY, DENNIS A., chemistry educator; b. Harrisburg, Pa., Dec. 4, 1952; s. John E. and Colleen (Canning) D.; m. Ellen M. Donnelly, June 3, 1973; children: Meghan, Kayla. BS, MS, Bucknell U., 1974; PhD, Princeton U., 1978. Postdoctoral fellow Yale U., New Haven, 1978-79; from asst. prof. to prof. Calif. Inst. Tech., Pasadena, 1979—2002, George Grant Hoag prof., 2002—. Contbr. articles to sci. jours. Recipient ICI Pharms. award for excellence in chemistry, 1991, Arthur C. Cope Scholar award, 1992; Alfred P. Sloan Found. fellow, 1983; Camille and Henry Dreyfus Tchr. scholar, 1984. Fellow AAAS, Am. Acad. Arts and Scis.; mem. Am. Chem. Soc., Biophys. Soc., Phi Beta Kappa. Home: 1817 Bushnell Ave South Pasadena CA 91030-4905 Office: Calif Inst Tech Div Chemistry & Chem Engring # 164-30 Pasadena CA 91125-0001

DOUGHERTY, ELMER LLOYD, JR., retired chemical engineering professor, consultant; b. Dorrance, Kans., Feb. 7, 1930; s. Elmer Lloyd and Nettie Linda (Anspaugh) Dougherty; m. Joan Victoria Benton, Nov. 25, 1952 (div. June 1963); children: Sharon, Victoria, Timothy, Michael(dec.); m. Ann Marie Da Silva (dec.). Student, Ft. Hays State Coll., 1946-48; BS in Chem. Engring., U. Kans., 1950; MS in Chem. Engring., U. Ill., 1952, PhD in Chem. Engring., 1955. Chem. engr. Esso Standard Oil Co., Baton Rouge, 1951-52; chem. engr. Dow Chem. Co., Freeport, Tex., 1955-58; research engr. Standard Oil of Calif., San Francisco, 1958-65; mgr. mgmt. sci. Union Carbide Corp., N.Y.C., 1965-68; cons. chem. engring. Stamford, Conn. and Denver, 1968-71; founder and owner Maraco, Inc., Monarch Beach, Calif., 1980—; prof. chem. engring. U. So. Calif., L.A., 1971-95, prof. emeritus, 1995—. Cons. OPEC, Vienna Austria, 1978-82, SANTOS, Ltd., Adelaide, Australia, 1980—, Kuwait Oil Co., 1995—. Contbr. numerous articles to profl. jours. Mem. Soc. Petroleum Engrs. (Disting. mem., chmn. Los Angeles Basin sect. 1984-85, Ferguson medal 1964, J.J. Arps award 1989), Am. Inst. Chem. Engrs., Internat. Assn. Energy Economists, Inst. Mgmt. Sci. Clubs: El Niguel Country (bd. dirs. 1976-78) (Laguna Niguel, Calif.). Republican. Avocation: golf. Home and Office: Maraco Inc 33531 Marlinspike Dr Monarch Beach CA 92629-4426 Office Phone: 949-388-6193. E-mail: eld@maraco-soft.com.

DOUGHERTY, F(RANCIS) KELLY, data processing executive; b. Lubbock, Tex., May 15, 1953; s. Francis Kelly and Mary Ann (Odell) D.; m. Bonnie Lee Burch, June 14, 1975; children: Anne Katherine, Margaret Erin, Mary Bridget, Kerry Meaghan, Frances Cara. BA in Math. and Physics summa cum laude, U. Dallas, 1975; MS in Computer Sci., U. Tex., Dallas, 1998; cert. assoc. customer svc., Life Office Mgmt. Inst., 1992. CLU; cert. computing profl.; chartered fin. cons.; Microsoft cert. programmer. Actuarial trainee Ranger Nat. Life Ins., Houston, 1976-77; mgr. time sharing svcs. Phila. Life Ins. Co., Houston, 1977-81; sys. engr. Electronic Data Sys., Dallas, 1981-85; IT analyst AEGON Direct Mktg. Svcs., Inc., Plano, Tex., 1985—. Pres. St. Elizabeth Seton Parish Bd. Edn., 1989-92. U. Dallas scholar, 1971-75; Rice U. fellow, 1975-76. Fellow Life Mgmt. Inst. (master); mem. IEEE, Assn. for Computing Machinery, K.C. Republican. Roman Catholic. Home: 2713 S Cypress Cir Plano TX 75075-3154 Office: AEGON Direct Mktg Svcs Inc 2700 W Plano Pky Plano TX 75075-8200 Office Phone: 972-881-6572. Business E-Mail: fdougher@comcast.net.

DOUGHERTY, JAMES, retired orthopedist; b. Lawrence, Mass., July 31, 1926; s. James A. and Maude D. (Dillard) D.; m. Marilyn Hays (dec.); m. Rita Buchman; children: James (dec.), Charles, Janice, Jonathan, Christopher. BS, Trinity Coll., Hartford, Conn., 1950; MD, Albany Med. Coll., N.Y., 1951. Diplomate, examiner and monitor Am. Bd. Orthopaedic Surgery, 1965-82; diplomate Am. Bd. Forensic Examiners, Am. Bd. Forensic Medicine. Intern U. Chgo. Clinics, 1951-52, resident, 1951-56, instr., 1955-56; founding chmn. divsn. orthop. surgery SUNY, Syracuse, 1958-60; prof. clin. surgery Albany Med. Coll., 1960-96, attending surgeon, 1961-94, chief of staff, 1987-89, prof. emeritus, 1996—. Trustee Albany Med. Ctr., 1993-95; cons. Subacute Care Alternative Project, Washington. Author: Ponies in The Window, 1998, (hymns) Life's Narrow Pathways, A Babe Was Born; mem. editl. bd.: Techniques in Orthops.; proponent and architect Fla. state program for pro-bono volunteerism of ret. physicians for medically disadvantaged, 2001; contbr. articles to profl. jours. and Ency. Brittanica. Mem. bd. edn. Ravena-Coeymans-Selkirk Ctrl. Schs., Ravena, NY, 1960—75; med. dir. N.Y. Sr. Games, 1986—89, Catskill Children's Orthop. Clinic, 1960—95; trustee Schaeffer Meml. Libr., 1990—92, Albany Med. Ctr., 1993—95; vol. coord. We Care Program, Lee County, Fla.; bd. dirs. Inst. for Study of Aging, 1990—95. Served with U.S. Army, 1944—46. Recipient Alumni medal Albany Med. Coll., 1951. Fellow: Am. Acad. Orthopaedic Surgeons; mem.: Sr. and Ret. Physicians' Assn. of Lee County Fla. (founder, pres. 1997—98), Albany Med. Coll. Alumni Assn. (trustee 1990—99, pres. 1994—96, Meritorious Svc. award 1996), Northeastern Regional Assn. Sports Medicine (chmn. 1984—89), Asean Orthop. Soc. (hon.), We. Orthop. Soc. (hon. honored guest, Scottsdale, Ariz. 2000), U. Chgo. Surg. Soc., Crawford Campbell Soc. (founder, pres. 1978—88), Sigma Nu, Sigma Psi, Alpha Omega Alpha. Presbyterian. Home: 3510 Pine Fern Ln Bonita Springs FL 34134-1918 Office Phone: 239-498-1209. *As an orthopaedic surgeon I have sometimes been tempted to exaggerate my role and massage my ego. But then I am reminded that I merely treated. The surgeon operates... God heals ... and the patient makes it work.*

DOUGHERTY, JAMES PATRICK, English language educator; b. Wichita, Kans., Mar. 20, 1937; s. James P. and Cora M. Dougherty; m. Jacqueline M. Centunzi, Aug. 18, 1962. BA, St. Louis U., 1959; PhD, U. Pa., 1962. Asst. prof. English U. Calgary, Alta., Can., 1962-66; from assoc. prof. to prof. English U. Notre Dame, Ind., 1966—. Author: The Fivesquare City, 1980, Walt Whitman and the Citizen's Eye, 1993; editor: Religion and Literature, 1984—. Bd. dirs. Renew, Inc., South Bend, Ind., 1984—. Roman Catholic. Office: U Notre Dame Dept English 356 O Shaugnessy Hall Notre Dame IN 46556-5639

DOUGHERTY, JOHN C., lawyer; b. Louisville, Ky., Nov. 30, 1963; BA, Catholic Univ., 1988, JD, 1991. Bar: Md. 1991, DC 1994. Ptnr., co-chmn. Patent Litigation practice group DLA Piper Rudnick Gray Cary, Balt. Editor (mng.): Jour. of Contemporary Health Law & Policy. Mem. bd. vis. Columbus Sch. Law, Catholic Univ. Named one of Top 15 Intellectual Property Lawyers in Md., Balt. Bus. Jour., 2001. Office: DLA Piper Rudnick Gray Cary 6225 Smith Ave Baltimore MD 21209-3600 Office Phone: 410-580-4140. Office Fax: 410-580-3001. Business E-Mail: john.dougherty@dlapiper.com.

DOUGHERTY, JOHN CHRYSOSTOM, III, retired lawyer; b. Beeville, Tex., May 3, 1915; s. John Chrysostom and Mary V. (Henderson) D.; m. Mary Ireland Graves, Apr. 18, 1942 (dec. July 1977); children: Mary Ireland, John Chrysostom IV; m. Bea Ann Smith, June 1978 (div. 1981); m. Sarah B. Randle, 1981 (dec. June 1997). BA, U. Tex., 1937; LLB, Harvard U., 1940; diploma, Inter-Am. Acad. Internat. and Comparative Law, Havana, Cuba, 1948. Bar: Tex. 1940. Atty. Hewit & Dougherty, Beeville, 1940-41; ptnr. Graves & Dougherty, Austin, Tex., 1946-50, Graves, Dougherty & Greenhill, Austin, 1950-57, Graves, Dougherty & Gee, Austin, 1957-60, Graves, Dougherty, Gee & Hearon, Austin, 1961-66, Graves, Dougherty, Gee, Hearon, Moody & Garwood, Austin, 1966-73, Graves, Dougherty, Hearon, Moody & Garwood, Austin, 1973-79, Graves, Dougherty, Hearon & Moody, Austin, 1979-93, sr. counsel, 1993—97; ret., 1997. Spl. asst. atty. gen., 1949-50; Hon. French Consul, Austin, 1971-86; lectr. on tax, estate planning, probate code, cmty. property problems; mem. Tex. Submerged Lands Adv. Com., 1963-72, Tex. Bus. and Commerce Code Adv. Com., 1964-66, Gov.'s Com. on Marine Resources, 1970-71, Gov.'s Planning Com. on Colorado River Basin Water Quality Mgmt. Study, 1972-73, Tex. Legis. Property Tax Com., 1973-75; adv. com. Mex. Ctr. Inst. of Latin-Am. Studies U. Tex., 1997—. Co-editor: Texas Appellate Practice, 1964, 2d edit., 1977; contbr. Bowe, Estate Planning and Taxation, 1957, 65; Texas Lawyers Practice Guide, 1967, 71, How to Live and Die with Texas Probate, 1968, 7th edit., 1995, Texas Estate Administration, 1975, 78; mem. bd. editors: Appellate Procedure in Tex., 1964, 2d edit., 1982; contbr. articles to profl. jours. Bd. dirs. Tex. Beta Students Aid Fund, 1949-84, Grenville Clark Fund at Dartmouth Coll., 1976-90, Umlauf Sculpture Garden, Inc., 1990-91, New Life Inst., 1993-2001; past bd. dirs. Advanced Religious Study Found., Holy Cross Hosp., Sea Arama, Inc., Nat. Pollution Control Found., Austin Nat. Bank; trustee St. Stephen's Episcopal Sch., Austin, 1969-83, Tex. Equal Access to Justice Found., 1986-90, U. Tex. Law Sch. Found., 1974-2002; mem. adv. com. Legal Assts. Tng. Inst., U. Tex., 1990-98; mem. vis. com. Harvard Law Sch., 1983-87. Capt. C.I.C., AUS, 1941-44, JAGC, 1944-46, maj. USAR. Decorated Medaille Française, France, Medaille d'honneur en Argent des Affairs Etrangeres, France, chevalier l'Ordre Nat. du Merite; recipient Wm. Reece Smith Spl. Svcs. to Pro Bono award Nat. Assn. of Pro Bono Coords., 2000. Fellow Am. Bar Found., Tex. Bar Found., Am. Coll. Trust and Estate Counsel, Am. Coll. Tax Counsel; mem. ABA (ho. of dels. 1982-88, standing com. on lawyers pub. responsibility 1983-85, spl. com. on delivery legal svcs. 1987-91, com. legal problems of the elderly 1997-2000, Sr. Lawyers divsn. Pro Bono Lawyer of 1999), Am. Arbitration Assn. (nat. panel arbitrators 1958-90), Travis County Bar Assn. (bd. dirs. 1974-76, pres. 1976-77), Internat. Acad. Estate and Trust Law (exec. coun. 1988-90), State Bar Tex. (chmn. sect. taxation 1965-66, pres. 1979-80, com. legal svcs. to the poor 1986-94), Am. Judicature Soc. (bd. dirs. 1985-87), Am. Law Inst. (adv. com. project law governing lawyers 1990-97), Tex. Supreme Ct. Hist. Soc. (trustee 1997—, chmn. 1999-2002), Philos. Soc. Tex. (pres. 1989, bd. dirs. 1989—), Harvard Law Sch. Assn. (com. on pub. svc. law 1990-95, chmn. 1990-95, coun. 1991-95, exec. com. 1992-95), Tex. Appleseed, Inc. (bd. dirs. 1996—), The Austin Project (bd. dirs. 1999—), Rotary. Presbyterian. Home: 1801 Lavaca St Apt 5J Austin TX 78701 Office: Frost Bank Tower Ste 2200 401 Congress Ave Austin TX 78701 also: PO Box 98 Austin TX 78767-0098 Office Phone: 512-480-5624. Business E-Mail: cdougherty@gdhm.com.

DOUGHERTY, JUDE PATRICK, philosopher, educator, dean; b. Chgo., July 21, 1930; s. Edward Timothy and Cecilia Anastasia (Loew) D.; m. Patricia Ann Regan, Dec. 28, 1957; children: Thomas, Michael, John, Paul. BA, Cath. U. Am., 1954, MA, 1955, PhD, 1960; LHD (hon.), Thomas More Coll., 1995, Cath. U. Lublin, Poland, 2000. Instr. Marquette U., 1957-58; instr. Bellarmine Coll., 1958-60, asst. prof., 1960-63, assoc. prof., 1963-66, Cath. U. Am., 1966-76, prof., 1976—; dean Cath. U. Am. (Sch. Philosophy), 1967-99. Vis. assoc. prof. Georgetown U., summer, 1965; vis. prof. Katholieke Universiteit te Leuven, Belgium, 1974-75 Author: Recent American Naturalism, 1960, Western Creed; Western Identity, 2000, The Logic of Religion, 2002, Jacques Maritain: An Intellectual Profile, 2003, Religion-Gesellschaft-Demokratie, 2003; co-author: Approaches to Morality, 1966; editor: (books) Theological Directions of the Ecumenical Movement, 1964, The Impact of Vatican II, 1966, The Good Life and Its Pursuit, 1985; editor Rev. of Metaphysics, 1971; gen. editor: Studies in Philosophy and the History of Philosophy, 1978; chpt. to book. Mem. bd. advisors Franklin J. Matchette Found., 1971—; trustee Bellarmine Coll., 1972-75, U. Bridgeport, 1995-99; mem. Pontifical Acad., St. Thomas, Rome, 1981—; mem. Academia Scientiarum et Artium Europae, Salzburg, 1991—. Decorated Knight of St. Gregory the Great, Pope John Paul II, 1999. Mem. Am. Philos. Assn. (program chmn. ea. divsn. 1988, exec. com. ea. divsn. 1989-93), Am. Cath. Philos. Assn. (pres. 1974-75, Aquinas medal 1994), Washington Philosophy Club (pres. 1968-69), Soc. for Philosophy Religion (pres. 1978-79), Metaphys. Soc. Am. (pres. 1983-84), Fellowship Cath. Scholars (exec. sec. 1994-97, treas. 1994-97, Cardinal Wright award 1994), Am. Maritain Assn. (scholarly achievement award 2000). Home: 9036 Rouen Ln Potomac MD 20854-3130 Office: Cath U Am Sch Philosophy 620 Michigan Ave NE Washington DC 20064-0001 Office Phone: 202-319-5589. Business E-Mail: dougherj@cua.edu. E-mail: judeandpat@aol.com.

DOUGHERTY, NEIL JOSEPH, physical education educator, safety consultant; b. Elizabeth, N.J., Apr. 7, 1943; s. Neil Joseph and Doris Burnett (Lindsay) D.; m. Margaret Ruth Quaranta, July 17, 1965; 1 child, Margaret Elizabeth. BS, Rutgers U., 1964, EdM, 1965; EdD, Temple U., 1970. Tchr. phys. edn. St. Joseph's Sch., Bound Brook, N.J., 1964-65; teaching assoc. Temple U., Phila., 1967-70; prof. Rutgers U., New Brunswick, N.J., 1970—. Mem. adv. bd. Youth Sports Rsch. Coun., New Brunswick, 1987—; nat. faculty mem. U.S. Sports Acad., 1988—. Co-author: Understanding and Assessing Human Movement, 1980, Management Principles in Sport and Leisure Scis., 1985, Contemporary Approaches to the Teaching of Physical Edn., 1979, 87, Sport, Physical Activity and the Law, 1993, 2002; editor: Physical Edn. and Sport for Secondary Sch. Students, 1983, 93, 2002, Principles of Safety in Physical Edn. and Sport, 1987, 93, 2002, Outdoor Recreation Safety, 1998, (jour.) The Reporter, 1977-81, (monograph series) Briefings, 1974-75; mem. editl. bd. Leisure Times Focus, 1984-88, Jour. of Tchg. in Phys. Edn., 1981-85, Safety Notebook, 1998—; contbr. to profl. jours. 1st lt. U.S. Army, 1965-67. Recipient Merit award Ea. Assn. for Health, Phys. Edn., Recreation and Dance, 1980, Honor award, 1982, Honor award Soc. for Study of Legal Aspects of Sport and Phys. Activity, 1998. Fellow N.Am. Soc. Health Edn., Phys. Edn, Recreation, Sport and Dance (charter); mem. Am. Assn. Active Lifestyles and Fitness (pres. 2001-03, Honor award 2005), Nat. Assn. Phys. Edn. Higher Edn. (pres. 1984-86), Sch. and Cmty. Safety Soc. Am. (pres. 1996-98, Profl. Svc. award 1991, 97, Scholar award 1994, hon. award 2004), N.J. Assn. of Dirs. of Health, Phys. Edn. and Recreation (pres. 1976-78), N.J. Assn. for Health, Phys. Edn., Recreation and Dance (pres. 1979-80, Honor fellow award 1983, Disting. Leadership award 1982), Coll. and Univ. Phys. Edn. Coun. (chmn. 1985-88). Avocations: fishing, water sports, golf. Home: 1655 East Dr Point Pleasant NJ 08742-5117 Office: Rutgers U Dept Exercise Sci/Sport Stu New Brunswick NJ 08903 Office Phone: 732-932-8673. Business E-Mail: njd@rci.rutgers.edu.

DOUGHERTY, PERCY H., geographer, educator, politician, planner; b. Kennett Square, Pa., Feb. 20, 1943; s. Percy H. Sr. and Anna (Cloud) D.; m. Anne Barbara Zinn, July 9, 1966; children: Thomas P., Robert J. BS in Geography, Biology, West Chester U., 1967, MEd in Phys. Geography, 1968; PhD in Phys. Geography, Geology, Boston U., 1980. Tchr. geography and earth sci. Plymouth Meeting (Pa.) Jr. H.S., 1967-68; asst. prof. West Chester (Pa.) U., 1968-70, Trenton (N.J.) State Coll., 1972-77, CUNY, 1977-78, U. Cin., 1978-83; vis. prof. Ohio U., Athens, 1983-84; vis. asst. prof. U. Ky., Lexington, 1984-85; assoc. prof. Kutztown (Pa.) U., 1985-90, prof. geography, 1990—. Editor of 2 books on karst; editor GEO2, 1980-88, Bulletin of the Nat. Speliological Soc., 1984-85; contbr. articles to profl. jours. Chmn. Lower Macungie Twp. Planning Commn., 1991-92; Allentown (Pa.) Art Mus., Allentown Symphony, Wildlands Conservancy; past chmn. comprehensive planning com., bd. dirs. Lehigh Valley Planning Commn. Lehigh and Northampton Counties, Pa., 1990, chmn. bd. dirs. 1995-97; Rep. committeeman Lower Macungie Twp. Dist. 2, 1990-96; elected mem. Lehigh County Commn., 1994—, chmn., 2000-03; bd. dirs. County Commn. Assn. Pa., 1998-2000, 02—, chair energy, environ. and land use com., 1998-2000; bd. mem. Nat. Assn. of Counties Energy/Environ./Land Use Com, 2002—; program chair Assn. Am. Geol. Annual Meeting, 2004. NSF fellow, 1971, 80, 92, NASA fellow, 1981, NOAA fellow, 1982. Fellow Nat. Speleol. Soc. (life), Miami Valley Grotto (hon. life), Ctrl. Jersey Grotto (hon. life); mem. Assn. Am. Geographers (life, mem. com. c.c.'s 2000-01, nat. councillor 2000-03, past pres., sec., treas., editor, bd. dirs., pres. wine specialty group 2004—), Delaware Valley Geog. Assn. (past pres., bd. dirs.), Nat. Coun. Geog. Edn. (life), Am. Water Resources Assn., Am. Soc. Photogrammetry and Remote Sensing, Conf. Latin Am. Geography, Pa. Geog. Soc. (past v.p., bd. dirs.), Am. Wine Soc. (cert. wine judge), Pa. Mapping Com. of the Pa. Geol. Survey. Achievements include research on remote sensing, air photo, geomorphology, karst, climatic geomorphology, groundwater diffusion, water resources, geographic education, planning. Office: Kutztown Univ Dept Geography 115 Grim Hall Kutztown PA 19530-9621 also: Lehigh County Courthouse PO Box 1548 Allentown PA 18105-1548 Office Phone: 610-683-4367. Personal E-mail: percydougherty@lehighcounty.org. Business E-Mail: dougherty@kutztown.edu.

DOUGHERTY, PETER JOSEPH, publisher; b. Phila., Feb. 25, 1949; s. Joseph Aloysius and Vera (Grohowski) D.; m. Elizabeth Rogers Hock, May 13, 1983; 1 child, Colman Rogers. AB, LaSalle Coll., 1971. Sales rep. Harcourt Brace Jovanovich, Balt., 1972-79, editor N.Y.C., 1979-82, McGraw-Hill, N.Y.C., 1982-83, W.H. Freeman, N.Y.C., 1983-84; sr. editor St. Martin's Press, N.Y.C., 1984-85; editorial dir. Basil Blackwell Inc., N.Y.C., 1985; sr. econ. editor to group publ. social sci. Princeton Press, Princeton, NJ, 1992—2005, dir., 2005—. Author: Who's Afraid of Adam Smith, 2002; contbr. articles to profl. journals. Mem.: Am. Assn. Univ. Presses, Am. Econ. Assn. Democrat. Roman Catholic. Office: Princeton Press 41 William St Princeton NJ 08540-5237 Office Phone: 609-258-6778. Office Fax: 609-258-6305. Business E-Mail: peter_dougherty@pupress.princeton.edu.*

DOUGHERTY, RAYMOND SYDNEY, radiologist, director; b. West Chester, Pa., Sept. 22, 1958; s. John F. and Dorothy Y. Dougherty; m. Lisa Jean Turicik, Oct. 22, 1983; children: Jonathon Andrew, Kevin Raymond, Jason Scott. BS in Biology, cum laude, Ursinus Coll., 1980; MD, Pa. State U., Hershey, 1984. Diplomate Am. Bd. Radiology, Am. Bd. Family Practice, Nat. Bd. Med. Examiners. Resident family practice USAF Regional Hosp., Carswell, AFB, Tex., 1984—87, chief resident family practice, 1986—87; physician family practice USAF Acad., Colo., 1987—90; clin. instr., dept. family medicine U. Colo. Health Scis. Ctr., Sch. Medicine, Denver, 1989—90; resident diagnostic radiology David Grant Med. Ctr., Travis AFB, Calif., 1990—94; fellow abdominal imaging U. Calif., Davis Med. Ctr., Sacramento, 1994—95; diagnostic radiologist David Grant Med. Ctr., Travis AFB, 1995—; asst. clin. prof. radiology U. Calif., Davis Med. Ctr., Sacramento, 1995—; program dir., diagnostic radiology residency David Grant Med. Ctr., Travis AFB, 1998—, chmn. diagnostic imaging flight comdr., 2001—. Med. dir., ultrasound technologist tng. program David Grant Med. Ctr., Travis AFB, 1995—2001, chmn., instl. rev. bd., 1998—2000, chmn., ultrasound working group, 1999—; med. malpractice expert reviewer Office of Surgeon Gen., Bolling AFB, DC, 2002—. Contbr. articles to profl. jours., chapters to books. Mid. sch. athletic dir. Notre Dame Sch., Vacaville, Calif., 1998—2003. Col. USAF, 1984—2003, Travis AFB, Calif. Decorated Meritorious Svc. Medal USAF, Commendation Medal; recipient Musculoskeletal Award for Acad. Excellence, David Grant Med. Ctr., 1994, Ob-Gyn Book Award, USAF Regional Hosp. Carswell, 1987, Lemmon Award for excellence in Family Practice, Pa. State U. Coll. Medicine, 1984; scholar Health Professions Scholarship, USAF, 1980—84, Hammond Meml. Scholarship Award for Acad. Performance, Pa. State U. Coll. Medicine, 1983. Mem.: Am. Roentgen Ray Soc., Radiol. Soc. N.Am., Am. Inst. Ultrasound in Medicine, Assn. Program Dirs. in Radiology, Am. Coll. Radiology. Office: David Grant Med Ctr 60 MDTS/SGQX 101 Bodin Circle Travis AFB CA 94535

DOUGHERTY, RICHARD HAMLEN, management and health care consultant; b. Boston, Dec. 15, 1952; s. John Bruce and Jean (MacDill) D.; m. Charlotte Louise Perry, Sept. 6, 1975; children: Cyra Perry, Alexa Starr. BA with honors, Colgate U., 1974; M in Social Services Admin., U. Chgo., 1977; PhD, Boston U., 1990. Counselor Phila. Child Guidance Clinic, 1974-75; clin. coord. Communities for People, Inc., Boston, 1977-79; evaluation specialist Mass. Dept. Pub. Welfare, Boston, 1979-80, rate liaison, 1980; program mgr. Mass. Dept. Social Services, Boston, 1980-82; CFO Nat. Mentor, Inc., Boston, 1982-85; sr. mgmt. cons. Seidman & Seidman, Boston, 1985-87; pres. DMA Health Strategies, Dougherty Mgmt. Assocs. Inc., Lexington, Mass., 1987—. Cons. health systems change; bd. dirs. Mass. Council Human Service Orgns., Boston, 1982-85. Ct. receiver Coastal Cmty. Counseling Ctr., Braintree, Mass., 1987-91; asst. treas. Cmty. Music Ctr. Boston, 1985-91, treas., 1991-95, pres., 1995-99, bd. dirs., 1995-2003; bd. dirs. Hole in the Sock Prodns., 1988-90; allocations com. United Way Massachusetts Bay, 1989-91, chmn. allocations coord. com., 1992-94; mem. Lexington Human Svcs. Com., 1989-91, Childrens Outcomes Roundtable, CMHS 2001—, Children in Managed Care Advisory Com., Ctr. for Healthcare Strategies, 2000—, Deacon and Sr. Deacon, Hancock United Ch. of Christ, congl. 1997-2000, treas. 2002—; treas. VanGo Prodns., Inc., 2001—; co-chmn. Lexington Health Benefits Adv. Com., 2005. Mem. Acad. Health, Am. Coll. Mental Health Adminstrn. (bd. dirs. 2002-05, treas. 2003-05), Boston Athenaeum Avocations: skiing, hiking, family activities, guitar. Office: DMA Health Strategies 9 Meriam St Ste 4 Lexington MA 02420-5312 Office Phone: 781-863-8003. E-mail: dickd@dmahealth.com.

DOUGHERTY, RICHARD MARTIN, library and information science professor; b. East Chicago, Ind., Jan. 17, 1935; s. Floyd C. and Harriet E. (Martin) D.; m. Ann Prescott, Mar. 24, 1974; children— Kathryn E., Emily E.; children by previous marriage— Jill Ann, Jacquelyn A., Douglas M. BS, Purdue U., 1959, LHD honoris causa, 1991; M.L.S., Rutgers U., 1961, PhD, 1963; LHD honoris causa, U. Stellenbosch, South Africa, 1995. Head acquisitions dept. Univ. Library, U. N.C., Chapel Hill, 1963-66; assoc. dir. libraries U. Colo., Boulder, 1966-70; prof. library sci. Syracuse U., N.Y., 1970-72; univ. librarian U. Calif-Berkeley, 1972-78; dir. univ. library U. Mich., Ann Arbor, 1978-88, acting dean. Sch. Library Sci., 1984-85, prof. sch. info., 1978-98, prof. emeritus, 1999—; pres. Dougherty & Assocs., 1994—. Cons., change mgmt. librs., Coll. DuPage; founder, pres. Mountainside Pub. Corp., 1974—; co-host live teleconferences. Author: Scientific Management of Library Organizations, 2d edit., 1982; co-author: Preferred Futures for Libraries II, 1993; editor Coll. and Research Libraries jour., 1969-74, Jour. Acad. Librarianship, 1975-94, Library Issues, 1981—. Trustee Ann Arbor

Dist. Libr., 1995—2002, pres. bd. trustees, 1998—2000. Recipient Esther Piercy award, 1968, Disting. Alumnus award Rutgers U., 1980, Acad. Librarian Yr., Assn. Coll. and Research Libraries, 1983, ALA Hugh C. Atkinson Meml. award, 1988, Blackwell Scholarship award, 1992, Joseph Lippincott medal, 1997; fellow Council on Library Resources. Mem. ALA (coun. 1969-76, 89-92, exec. bd. 1972-76, 89-92, endowment trustee 1986-89, pres. 1990-91), Assn. Rsch. Librs. (bd. dirs. 1977-80), Rsch. Librs. Group, Inc. (exec. com. 1984-88, chmn. bd. govs. 1986-87), Soc. Scholarly Pub. (bd. dirs. 1990-92, exec. com. 1991-92), Internat. Fedn. Libr. Assns. (round table of editors of library jours. 1985-87, standing com. univ. libr. sect. 1981-87). Home: 6 Northwick Ct Ann Arbor MI 48105-1408 Office: Dougherty & Assoc PO Box 8330 Ann Arbor MI 48107-8330 E-mail: rmdoughe@umich.edu.

DOUGHERTY, ROBERT ANTHONY, retired manufacturing company executive; b. St. Louis, May 3, 1928; s. Joseph A. and Venita E. (Gretline) D.; m. Rosemary Schmertmann, Jan. 29, 1955; children: Kevin, Patrick, Michael, Mary Ann, Timothy. BS in Mech. Engring, U. Notre Dame, 1952. Registered profl. engr., Calif. cert. mfg. engr. Sales engr. Robert R. Stephens Machinery Co., St. Louis, 1952-60, dist. mgr., 1961-72; pres. Dougherty & Assos., Prairie Village, Kans., 1972-99, ret., chmn. bd. dirs. Bd. dirs. Tech-Industry Cons., Lenexa, Kans.; exec. com. Kans. Industry/Univ./Govt. Engring. Edn. Consortium. Mem. adv. com. Pittsburg, Kans. Sch. Sci. and Tech., 1987—; coord. cons. Kans. U. Ctrs. Excellence for Kans. Tech. Enterprise Corp., 1991—. Served with U.S. Army, 1946-48. Recipient Productivity award Coll. and Univ. Mfg. Edn. Council, 1979, Soc. Mfg. Engrs. Joseph A. Siegel Meml. honor award, 1992; Outstanding Engring. Achievements award San Fernando Valley Engrs. Council, 1980. Fellow Instn. Prodn. Engrs. Gt. Britain (life); mem. ASME (state legis. fellow), Am. Soc. for Metals, Soc. Mfg. Engrs. (pres. 1980-81, dir. 1971-82, Region 5 award of merit 1969), Serra Club of Kansas City Kans. (pres. 2003—), Round Hill Bath and Tennis Club (pres. 1971), Hillcrest Country Club (v.p. 1982, pres. 1983—). Roman Catholic.

DOUGHERTY, THOMAS JAMES, lawyer; b. Boston, Apr. 26, 1948; s. Thomas Lawlor and Mary (Morse) D.; m. Jessie d'Entremont Bourneuf, Sept. 25, 1971; children— Thomas McKean, Jennie d'Entremont. BA, magna cum laude, Holy Cross Coll., 1970; BPhil in Econs., Oxford U., Eng., 1973; JD, cum laude, Harvard U., 1976. Bar: Mass. 1977, NY 1977, US Dist. Ct. Mass. 1977, US Dist. Ct. (ea. and so. dists.) NY 1977, US Ct. Appeals (1st cir.) 1977, US Ct. Appeals (6th cir.) 1981. Former law clk. to Hon. Stephen G. Breyer, US Ct. Appeals (1st cir.), 1980-81, now an assoc. justice, US Supreme Ct.; assoc. Cravath, Swaine & Moore, NYC, 1976-79; assoc. Skadden, Arps, Slate, Meagher & Flom, Boston, 1979-84, ptnr.,computer copyrights, litigation dept. 1984— . Author: Education at Holy Cross, 1970; Controlling the New Inflation, 1981. Marshall scholar Marshall Aid Commemoration Commn., London, 1970; Woodrow Wilson Found. fellow, 1970; Danforth Found. fellow, 1971. Mem. Acad. Polit. Sci., Soc. for Values in Higher Edn. Democrat. Roman Catholic. Office: Skadden Arps Slate Meagher et al 1 Beacon St Boston MA 02108 Office Phone: 617-573-4820. Office Fax: 888-329-6045. Business E-Mail: dougherty@skadden.com.

DOUGHERTY BUCHHOLZ, KAREN, communications executive; m. Carl Buchholz; 2 children. BS, Dickinson Collo.; MS, U. Pa. Mem. staff U.S. Sen. John Heinz, Gubernatorial candidate Barbara Hafer, 1990; supr. devel. Pyramid Club, Phila., 1991—93; sales exec. Comcast-Spectacor, 1993—97; pres. Phila. Host com. Rep. Nat. Convention, 1997—2000; v.p. corp. comms. Comcast Corp., Phila., 2000—03, v.p. adminstrn., 2003—. Bd. dirs. Phila. Convention and Vis. Bur.; trustee Crohn's and Colitis Found. Am.; bd. dirs. Millennium Phila.; bd. advisors Dickinson Coll.; bd. govs. Pyramid Club. Named PENJERDEL Coun. Citizen of Yr.; recipient Headliner award, Greater Phila. Hotal Assn., Take the Lead award, Girl Scouts U.S.A. Mem.: Nat. Assn. Women Bus. Owners (hon.). Office: Comcast 1500 Market St Philadelphia PA 19102

DOUGHTEN, MARY KATHERINE (MOLLY DOUGHTEN), retired secondary school educator; b. Belvidere, Ill., Apr. 26, 1923; d. Edwin Albert and Theora Teresa (Tefft) Loop; m. Philip Tedford Doughten, Oct. 15, 1947; children: Deborah Doughten Hellriegel, Susan Doughten Myers, Ann Doughten Fickenscher, Philip Tedford Jr., David, Sarah Doughten Wiggins. BA, DePauw U., 1945; MS, Western Res. U., 1947. Social worker Children's Svcs., Cleve., 1947, San Antonio, 1948-49; tchr. English Indian Valley High Schs., Gradenhutten, Ohio, 1962-66; tchr. English and sociology New Philadelphia (Ohio) High Sch., 1966-86; ret., 1986. Mem. Tuscarawas County Juvenile Judges Citizen's Rev. Bd., 1980—2003, United Way, 1960—67, ARC, PTA, 1955—58, coun. pres., 1960—62, mental health chmn. state bd., 1963—65, libr. chmn., 1966—68; mem. Hospice, 1987—; founding com. Kent State U. Tuscarawas campus, 1961—62; leader Girl Scouts, 1959—68; vol. Ohio Reads, 2000—; vol. reach for recovery Am. Cancer Soc., 2002—; mem. Tuscarawas Arts Coun.; vol. Tuscarawas County Job and Family Svcs., 2003—; mem. Tuscarawas Philharm. League, Dem. Women, 1986—; bd. dir. Tuscarawas Valley Guidance Ctr., 1950—62, Cmty Mental Health Care, Inc., 1974—82, 1984—92, pres., 1979—81; bd. dir. Alcohol, Drug and Mental Health Svcs. bd., Tuscarawas-Carroll County, 1992—2001, v.p., 1996—98; bd. mem. State CC, 1965—68; founder, bd. dir. Ohio Cmty. Mental Health Svcs., Columbus, Ohio, 1970—80; bd. dir. Mobile Meals, 1992—; bd. dirs. Kent-Tuscounty U. Found., 1996—, pres., 1998—2000. Named WJER Woman of the Yr., 2002; recipient Mental Health award, Cmty. and Profl. Svcs., 1978; Martha Holden Jennings scholar, 1975—76. Mem. AAUW (sec. 1962, v.p. 1996-98), New Philadelphia Edn. Assn., Friends of Libr., Chestnut Soc. (bd. dirs. 1987-89, 2001—), Tuscarawas County Med. Aux. (pres. 1959-60, 86-87, state bd. 1960-64), Union Hosp. Aux. (bd. dirs. 1986-98, editor 1986-98), DAR, Tuscarawas County Ret. Tchrs. Assn. (bd. dirs. 1999—), Coll. Club (scholarship chair 1989-91, 99-2001), Union Country Club, Atwood Yacht Club, Lady Elks, Mortar Bd., Phi Beta Kappa, Alpha Chi Omega, Theta Sigma Phi. Democrat. Presbyterian. Avocations: travel, golf, sailing, reading, photography. Home: 204 Gooding Ave NW New Philadelphia OH 44663-1727 Personal E-mail: philmoll@tusco.net.

DOUGHTY, A. GLENN, minister; b. Somers Point, N.J., Aug. 30, 1942; s. Alfred and Irene Dorothy (Colhouer) D.; m. Carole True, June 17, 1967; children: Matthew Glenn, Lynn Carole. BS in Bible Studies, Phila. Coll. of Bible, 1965; MDiv, Faith Theol. Sem., 1968. Ordained to ministry Fellowship Fundamental Bible Chs., 1970. Pastor Community Bible Ch., Barrington, N.J., 1968-70, The Bible Ch. of Westville, N.J., 1970—. Chmn. Bible Protestant Ch. Ext., 1970-73; sec. Fellowship of Fundamental Bible Chs., 1976-95, 2001—04, mem. ministerial qualifications com., 1980-95, Fundamental Bible Inst., 2001. Chmn. Cmty. Dispute Resolution Com., Westville, 1986—. Named Outstanding Vol. of Yr., Gloucester Co., 2003. Mem. Am. Coun. Christian Chs. (mem. exec. com. 1990—), Fellowship of Fundamental Bible Chs. (trustee 1985-95, pres. trustees 1985-91, chmn. trustees 1993-95, sec. Fundamental Bible Missions 1996-98, pres. 1998—2002). Home and Office: 142 Hess Ave Woodbury NJ 08096 E-mail: gcdoughty@quadnet.net.

DOUGHTY, GEORGE FRANKLIN, airport administrator; b. Wheeling, W.Va., Mar. 11, 1946; s. Ernest Heyward and Elizabeth Gertrude (Dei) D.; m. Jennifer L. Tyma; children: Susan Elizabeth, Jennifer Anne, Patrick George, Shannon Marie. BS in Aerospace Engring., W.Va. U., 1968. Asst. mgr. Cedar Rapids Mcpl. Airport, Iowa, 1975-78; dep. dir. Balt.-Washington Internat. Airport State of Md., 1978-80; dir. port control City of Cleve., Ohio, 1980-84; dir. aviation Stapleton Internat. Airport City and County of Denver, 1981-92; exec. dir. Lehigh-Northampton Airport Authority, Allentown, Pa., 1992—. Recipient Laurels award Aviation Week and Space Tech., 1988. Mem. Am. Assn. Airport Execs. (dir. 1980), Airports Coun. Internat. N.Am. (chmn. govtl. affairs com. 1985-86, bd. dirs. 1986-89, 1st vice chmn. 1992, chmn. 1993). Home: 2131 Stonewall Dr Macungie PA 18062-9064 Office: Lehigh Valley Intl Airport 3311 Airport Rd Ste 4 Allentown PA 18109-3040 Office Phone: 610-266-6001. E-mail: george@lnaa.com.

DOUGHTY, MARK ANTHONY, lawyer; b. Pasadena, Calif., Aug. 18, 1951; s. Lawrence Richard and Bertha Lou D.; children: Matthew James, Luke Anthony. BA in Bus. Law, Calif. State U., Chico, 1976; JD, U. Pacific, Sacramento, Calif., 1979. Bar: Calif. 1979, U.S. Dist. Ct. (ea. dist.) Calif. 1979; lic. real estate broker, cert. comml. investment mem, real estate developer. Law clk. Calif. Ct. Appeals (5th cir.), Fresno, Calif., 1979-80; assoc. Ashby and Guth, Yuba City, Calif., 1980-82; ptnr. Ashby, Guth and Doughty, Yuba City, 1982-86, Ashby & Doughty, Yuba City, 1986-92; prin. Law Offices of Mark A. Doughty, Yuba City, 1992—. Pres. Russian Radio Bible Inst. Mem. Consumer Attys. of Calif. (bd. govs. 19th dist.), Fellowship of Christian Businessmen, Yuba Sutter Bar Assn. (pres. 2001), Consumer Attys. Gold Country (pres. 1999—). Republican. Avocations: fathering, golf, private pilot, hunting, boating. Office: Law Offices of Mark A Doughty PO Box 3420 1528 Poole Blvd Ste A Yuba City CA 95992-3420 Home: 1528 Poole Blvd Ste A Yuba City CA 95993 Fax: 530-674-1180. E-mail: mark@golaw.com.

DOUGHTY-JENKINS, BONNIE-MARIE, middle school educator; b. New Britain, Conn., Mar. 12, 1967; d. Dennis John and Patricia Anne Doughty; m. John C. Jenkins, July 4, 2001. BS in Spl. Edn. and Elem. Edn., St. Joseph Coll., 1989, MA in Spl. Edn., 1995; EdD in Ednl. Leadership, Ctrl. Conn. State U., 2005. Tchr. 5th - 8th grades spl. edn. Plymouth Bd. Edn., Terryville, Conn., 1990—99, tchr. 8th grade sci., 1999—. Mem. sch. bd. St. Matthew Sch., Forestville, Conn., 2001—; adminstrv. intern Harry S. Fisher Mid. Sch., Terryville, 2003—04. Mem., scholar com. Harry S. Fisher Mid. Sch. PTA, Terryville, 1990—; mem. Nutmet Artists, Plymouth, 2004—; mem. exec. bd. dirs. Conn. Jr. Women, Inc., 1992—99; mem., chmn. Intersvc. Club Coun., Bristol, 1990—99. Named Jr. Woman of Yr., 1992; named to Subaru Tchr. Hall Fame, 2003; recipient Heart Saver award, Am. Heart Assn., 2003, 2005, Spirit of Am. award, Conn. PTA, 2005; grantee, Shopa Found., 2000, Thomaston Savs. Bank, Conn., 2001, Main St. Cmty. Found., Bristol, 2002. Mem.: ASCD, Plymouth Sch. to Career Action Com., Am. Edn. Rsch. Orgn. Roman Catholic. Avocations: travel, crafts, cooking. Office: Harry S Fisher Mid Sch 79 N Main St Terryville CT 06786

DOUGLAS, ASHANTI S. See ASHANTI

DOUGLAS, BARRY K., plastic surgeon; b. NYC, June 15, 1954; s. Leonard S. and Elaine K. Douglas; m. K. K. Koenigsberg, Mar. 28, 1983; children: Lauren, Robert. MD, Wake Forest U., 1980. Diplomate Am. Bd. Plastic Surgery. Attending physician plastic surgery L.I. Plastic Surg. Group, Garden City, NY, 1991—. Covers for art jours. and programs. Avocation: concert pianist. Office: LI Plastic Surg Group 999 Franklin Ave Garden City NY 11530 Office Phone: 516-742-3404. E-mail: bdouglas@lipsg.com.

DOUGLAS, BRUCE LEE, oral and maxillofacial surgeon, occupational and geriatric health educator, consultant; b. N.Y.C., July 14, 1925; s. William and Carrie (Basescu) D.; m. Janet Ramsden; children: Clifford, Steven, Jennifer, Sarah, Sandra. AB, Princeton U., 1947; D.D.S., NYU, 1948; postgrad. in oral surgery, Columbia U., 1949-51, MA in Edn, 1955, diploma in higher edn, 1957; M.P.H., U. Calif. at Berkeley, 1962. Diplomate Am. Bd. Oral and Maxillofacial Surgery. Prof. oral medicine and community dentistry Coll. Dentistry U. Ill., 1962-72, prof. preventive medicine Coll. Medicine, 1962-72; prof. health adminstrn. Sch. Pub. Health, 1972-98; prof. dental and oral surgery Rush Med. Coll., 1970-76; clin. prof. environ. and occupl. medicine Sch. Pub. Health, U. Ill. at Chgo., 1998—, health policy rsch., 2001—. Chief dentistry and oral surgery Rush-Presbyn.-St. Luke's Med. Ctr., Chgo., 1968-75; chief divsn. dental health, Ill. Dept. Pub. Health, 1976-78; chief sect. dentistry and oral surgery Lincoln Park Hosp. Chgo. (formerly Grant Hosp.), 1980-90, attending oral and maxillofacial surgeon, 1967—; Fulbright prof. oral surgery and anesthesiology Okayama (Japan) U. and Tokyo Med.-Dental U., 1959-61; WHO cons. to U. Antioquia, Colombia, Nat. U. and U. Zulia, Venezuela, 1964-69, Mahidol U., Bangkok, Thailand, 1973, Nat. Health Svc., Gt. Britain, 1977. Mem. Ill. Ho. of Reps., 11th Dist., 1971-72, 12th Dist., 1973-74; chmn. Ill. Coalition Against Tobacco, 1991-93; chief med. advisor, Sedgwick Claims Mgmt. Svcs., 1998-2002; sr. scholar in residence Wash. Bus. Group on Health, 2002-04. With USN, 1951—53, Japan, Korea, with USNR, 1943—53, lt. dental corps. USN, 1951—53. Fellow Chgo. Inst. Medicine (bd. dirs. 1970-80), Am. Dental Soc. Anesthesiology (past pres.); mem. Am. Assn. Hosp. Dentists (past pres., editor), Am. Assn. Oral and Maxillofacial Surgeons (assoc. editor Jour. Oral Surgery), Fulbright Assn. (pres. Chgo. chpt. 1990-92). Address: 2401 Duffy Ln Riverwoods IL 60015 Personal E-mail: brucedouglas@comcast.net. *A health professional career can be the portal through which an educated person can pass to a fuller and richer life. My health professional, education, and public health degrees have made it possible for me to broaden my involvement in the affairs of my community, my nation, my world, the world of business, and to serve individuals in need as well.*

DOUGLAS, CHARLES W., lawyer; b. Chgo., Apr. 1, 1948; BA, Northwestern U., 1970; JD, Harvard U., 1974. Bar: Ill. 1974, U.S. Dist. Ct. (no. dist.) Ill. 1974, U.S. Dist. Ct. (ea. dist.) Wis. 1997, U.S. Ct. Appeals (6th cir.) 1978, U.S. Ct. Appeals (9th cir.) 1981, U.S. Ct. Appeals (2nd cir.) 1983, U.S. Ct. Appeals (7th cir.) 1984, U.S. Ct. Appeals (11th cir.) 1999. Ptnr. Sidley Austin Brown & Wood LLP, Chgo., 1980—, exec. com., 1989—, mgmt. com. (chmn., 1999-), 1993—, and mng. ptnr. Chgo. office. Mem.: Phi Beta Kappa. Office: Sidley Austin Brown & Wood LLP Bank 1 Plz 10 S Dearborn St Chicago IL 60603 Office Phone: 312-853-7706. Office Fax: 312-853-7036. Business E-Mail: cdouglas@sidley.com.

DOUGLAS, CHRISTOPHER THOMAS, music educator, musician; b. Amsterdam, NY, Feb. 8, 1958; s. Donald David and Mary Gale Douglas; m. Susan Elaine Dye, Aug. 12, 1985; children: Sarah Elizabeth, David Stanley. BA, U. SC, Columbia, 1984. Cert. music tchr. Ga., 2000. Band dir. Princeton (NC) HS, 1986—88, Jordan-Matthews HS, Siler City, NC, 1988—96, SW Edgecombe H.S., Pinetops, NC, 1996—2000, Brunswick (Ga) H.S., 2000—. Chief judge All Am. Judges Assn, Hickory, NC, 1995—99. Ch. elder First Presbyn. Ch., Brunswick, Ga., 2003—05. Mem.: Ga. Music Educators Assn. Home: 248 South Teakwood Ct Brunswick GA 31525-8419 Office: Brunswick High School Band 3920 Habersham Street Brunswick GA 31520 Office Phone: 912-267-4200. Office Fax: 912-261-4433. E-mail: chdouglas@glynn.k12.ga.us.

DOUGLAS, DIANE MIRIAM, museum director; b. Harrisburg, Pa., Mar. 25, 1957; d. David C. and Anna (Barron) D.; m. Steve I. Perlmutter, Jan. 23, 1983; 1 child, David Simon. BA, Brown U., 1979; MA, U. Del., 1982. Oral history editor Former Members of Congress, Washington, 1979-80; assoc. curator exhibitions John Michael Kohler Arts Ctr., Sheboygan, Wis., 1982-83; dir. arts ctr. Lill Street Gallery, Chgo., 1984-88; exec. dir. David Adler Cultural Ctr., Libertyville, Ill., 1988-91; dir. Bellevue (Wash.) Art Mus., 1992—. Program chair, exec. bd. nat. Coun. for Edn. in Ceramic Arts, Bandon, Oreg., 1990-93; nat. adv. bd. Friends of Fiber Art, 1992; artists adv. com. Pilchuck Glass Sch., 1993—; mem. bd. dirs. Archie Bray Found., Helena, Mont., 1995—. Office: PO Box 1705 Bellevue WA 98009-1705

DOUGLAS, FRANK FAIR, architect, graphic designer; b. Mansfield, La., Oct. 27, 1945; s. Edward Osler and Minnie Merle (Flanders) D.; m. Judith Catherine Wainwright, Sept. 6, 1969; 1 child, Samuel Wainwright. Student, NYU; BArch, La. State U., 1968. Registered architect. Designer Eggers & Higgins, N.Y.C., 1968-69, Neuhaus & Taylor, Houston, 1969-70, dir. graphics, 1970-72, assoc., 1972-75, sr. assoc., 1975-77; v.p. 3D/Internat., Houston, 1977-81, sr. v.p., 1981-86, exec. v.p., 1986-87; chmn., pres. Douglas/Gallagher, Houston, Washington, Nashville, 1987—. Exhibit design and environ. prgaphic projects include Miss. Pavilion/Expoo '84, Singapore Pavilion/Expo '86, Conoco Retail Facilities Studies, 1987, Hotel Cheyenne and Santa Fe Disneyland Park, 1992, Environ. Graphics Stds. Entergy, Inc., 1994, Rangers Ballpark, 1994, N.Y. Yankees Spring Home Facility, 1996, Philippine Centennial Internat. Environ. Graphic, Anaheim Stadium for Disney Sports, Urban Graphics Syss. for cities of Mobile, Ala., San Antonio, San Juan, P.R., Salt Lake City, Galveston, Tex.; image cons. GM at Renaissance Ctr., Detroit, Mus. of Jewish Heritage, N.Y., 1997; Janet Annenberg Hooker Hall of Fame, Smithsonian, Independance Hall Visitors Ctr., Phila., Triple A Stadium for Oklahoma City Redhawks, Memphis Redbirds. Bd. dirs. Tex. Film Commn., Austin, 1982—; multi-media panelist Cultural Arts Coun. Houston, 1982-84; co-chair visual com. Houston Econ. Summit Host Com., 1990. Recipient awards for exhbns., 1985, 86, 88. Fellow AIA (bd. dirs. 1997—, exec. com. Houston chpt. 1989-90, pres. 1992, honor award 1985), Tex. Soc. Architects (v.p. 1994-96); mem. Soc. Environ. Graphic Designers (bd. dirs. 1971-72, Design award 1974), Rice Design Alliance (pres., bd. dirs. 1981-88, 91—), Soc. Mktg. Profl. Svcs. (bd. dirs. Houston chpt. 1982-92, Design award 1980O, Ind. Design Soc. Am., Houston City Club, Houston Club. Republican. Presbyterian. Home: 3822 Olympia Dr Houston TX 77019-3032 Office: Douglas Gallagher 3040 Post Oak Blvd Ste 510 Houston TX 77056-6521

DOUGLAS, GEORGE HALSEY, language educator, writer; b. East Orange, NJ, Jan. 9, 1934; s. Halsey M. and Harriet Elizabeth (Goldbach) D.; m. Rosalind Braun, June 19, 1961; 1 son, Philip. AB with honors in Philosophy, Lafayette Coll., 1956; MA, Columbia U., 1966; PhD, U. Ill., 1968. Tech. editor Bell Tel. Labs., Whippany, NJ, 1958—59; editor Agrl. Exptl. Sta. U. Ill., Urbana, 1961—66; instr. dept. English Agrl. Expt. Sta., U. Ill., Urbana, 1966—68, asst. prof. English, 1968—77, assoc. prof. English, 1977—88, prof. English, 1989—. Author: H.L. Mencken Critic of American Life, 1978, The Teaching of Business Communication, 1978, Rail City: Chicago and Its Railroads, 1981, Edmund Wilson's America, 1983, Women of the Twenties, 1986, The Early Days of Radio Broadcasting, 1987, The Smart Magazines, 1991, All Aboard: The Railroad in American Life, 1992, Education Without Impact: How Our Universities Fail the Young, 1992, Skyscraper: A Social History of the Tall Building in America, 1996, Postwar America, 1998, The Golden Age of the Newspaper, 1999; editor numerous books; contbr. articles to profl. jours., reference books, television documentaries. Mem. MLA, Am. Studies Assn., Am. Bus. Comm. Assn. (editor jour. bus. comm. 1968-80). Home: 809 Mendota Dr Champaign IL 61820-7566

DOUGLAS, JAMES (BUSTER), boxer; b. Columbus, Ohio; s. Billy and Lula Douglas; m. Bertha M. Douglas; children: Lamar, Cardaé, Arthur. Profl. boxer 1981—; defeated Mike Tyson, Feb. 1990 to become undisputed heavyweight champion. E-mail: mommiedog@chan-cor.com.

DOUGLAS, JAMES M., law educator, dean; BA in Math., Tex. So. U., 1966, JD, 1970; MS Law, Stanford U., 1971. Bar: Tex. 1970. Programmer analyst Singer Gen. Precision Co., Houston, 1966-70, 71-72; asst. prof. law Tex. So. U., Houston, 1972—74; asst. prof. Cleve.-Marshall Coll. Law, Cleve. State U., 1974—75, asst. prof., asst. dean student affairs, 1974-75; assoc. prof. law, assoc. dean Coll. Law Syracuse U., NY, 1975-80; prof. law Northea. U. Sch. Law, Boston, 1980-81; dean, prof. law Tex. So. U., Houston, 1981-95, interim provost, sr. v.p. acad. affairs, 1995, interim pres., 1995, pres., 1995—99, disting. prof. law, 1999—; interim dean Fla. A&M U. Coll. Law, 2005—. Contbr. articles to profl. jours. Mem. steering com. Houston Campaign Homeless, 1988—89; Bd. dirs. Sickle Cell Found. Tex., 1988—94, pres., 1990—91; bd. dirs. Boy Scouts Am., 1993—, Greater Houston Partnership, 1996—99. Mem.: Houston C. of C., Nat. Bar Assn., Houston Bar Assn. (chair law practice mgmt. sect. 1995—), Tex. Supreme Ct. Hist. Soc. (trustee 1990—), State Bar Tex., ABA. Home: 5318 Calhoun Rd Houston TX 77021-1714 Office: Tex So U 3100 Cleburne St Houston TX 77004-4501 Office Phone: 713-313-7352. Business E-Mail: jdouglas@tsulaw.edu.

DOUGLAS, JAMES MCCRYSTAL, lawyer; b. Wantagh, N.Y., 1956; Student, Bucknell U.; BA, SUNY, Binghamton, 1978; JD cum laude, Fordham U., 1981. Bar: N.Y. 1982. Ptnr. Skadden, Arps, Slate, Meagher & Flom LLP, NYC, head banking & instl. investing group. Mem. Fordham Law Rev., 1980-81. Office: Skadden Arps Slate Meagher & Flom LLP 4 Times Sq New York NY 10036-6595 Office Phone: 212-735-2868. Business E-Mail: jdouglas@skadden.com.

DOUGLAS, JANICE GREEN, physician, educator; b. Nashville, July 11, 1943; d. Louis D. and Electa Green. BA magna cum laude, Fish U., 1964; MD, Meharry Med. Coll., 1968. Intern Meharry Med. Coll., 1968-71; NIH tng. fellow in endocrinology, instr. internal medicine Vanderbilt U., Nashville, 1971-73; sr. staff fellow sect. on hormonal regulation NIH, 1973-76; asst. prof. medicine Case Western Res. U. Sch. Medicine, Cleve., 1976-81, assoc. prof. medicine, 1981-84, prof. medicine, 1984—; dir. hypertension renal ambulatory care svc. Univ. Hosps. Cleve., 1976-80; dir. divsn. endocrinology and hypertension dept. medicine Univ. Hosps. Cleve. and Case Western Res. U., 1988-93, vice chair acad. affairs dept. medicine, 1991-99, dir. divsn. hypertension dept. medicine, 1993—. Mem. numerous grant rev. coms.; lectr., presenter in field; atteding physician in medicine and endicrinology U. Hosps., 1987; vis. prof. SUNY, Kings County Hosp. and Health Sci. Ctr., Bklyn., 1987, Med. U. S.C., 1989, Harlem Hosp., N.Y.C., 1993, N.Y. Med. Coll., Valhalla, 1994. Mem. editl. rev. bd. Jour. Clin. Investigation, 1990—, Am. Jour. Physiology, Renal Fluid and Electrolytes, 1989-91; editl. bd. Hypertension, 1994—, Am. Soc. Clin. Investigation, 1990—, Ethnicity and Disease, 1990—, Circulation, 1993—; guest editor Jour. Clin. Investigation, U. Calif., San Diego, 1992—; assoc. editor Jour. Lab. and Clin. Medicine, 1986-90; reviewer numerous manuscripts and abstracts.; contbr. numerous articles, abstracts to profl. publs., chpts. to books. Fellow High Blood Pressure Coun., Am. Heart Assn., 1993—. Mem. Assn. Am. Physicians, Cleve. Med. Assn., Am. Soc. Hypertension, Kidney Found. Ohio, Women in Endocrinology, Inter-Am. Soc. Hypertension, Women in Nephrology, Assn. for Acad. Minority Physicians, Am. Physiology Soc., Endocrine Soc., Ctrl. Soc. for Clin. Rsch., Internat. Soc. Hypertension in Blacks, Inst. Medicine of NAS, Internat. Soc. Nephrology, Am. Soc. Nephrology, Am. Soc. Clin. Investigation, Am. Fedn. Clin. Rsch., Am. Heart Assn., Phi Beta Kappa, Alpha Omega Alpha (pres. Meharry chpt. 1968), Beta Kappa Chi. Office: Case Western U Sch Medicine 10900 Euclid Ave # 165 Cleveland OH 44106-1712

DOUGLAS, JEANNE MASSON, academic administrator, education educator; b. Albany, Vt., Oct. 9, 1938; d. Leonard Arnold and Helena Mary (LaRocque) Mason; m. Harlan L. Douglas, Dec. 2, 1960 (dec. Sept. 1978); children: Mason, Kimberly Jo (dec.). BS in Edn., Johnson State Coll., Johnson, Vt., 1960; MS Cert. Instrnl. Tech., U. So. Calif., 1968; MEd, U. Mass., 1978, EdD in Tchr. Edn., 1982. Dir. instrnl. devel. ctr. Burlington County Coll., Pemberton, N.J., 1969-72; dir. ednl. resources ctr. Reading (Pa.) C.C., 1972-75; dir. staff devel. ctr. Berks Heim Geriatrics Instn., Reading, 1975-76; measurement design specialist SIGNALS (sch. collaborative), Norton, Mass., 1978-79; dir. gifted edn. program Springfield (Vt.) Sch. Dist., 1981-83; dir. curriculum and instrn. Poultney (Vt.) Sch. Dist., 1983-85; coord. curriculum and instrn. and gifted/talented Orleans-Essex Supervisory, Union, Vt., 1987-90; coord. spl. edn. program for gifted School Adminstrn. Dist. #34, Belfast, Maine, 1990-92; coord. paraprofessional tng. program Kennebec Valley Cmty. Coll., Fairfield, Maine, 1993—. Cons. cmty. colls. in N.Y., Conn., Md., Pa., Ont., Can., 1971-84; evaluator Pub. Sch. Approval vis. team, South Burlington, Vt., 1990; adv. bd. PEDS project, Maine Child Devel. Svcs., 1993—; adv. bd. Rural Spl. Edn. project, U. Maine, 1993—. Author: Learning Environments/Rural Schs., 1982; contbr. articles to profl. jours. Spkr., learning disabled gifted advocate pub. info. meetings, Maine, Vt. sch. dists., 1988-92; mem., ext. program advocate U. New Eng., Belfast Acad. Forum, 1990-92; spkr., spl. edn. advocate pub. info. meetings, ctrl. Maine sch. dists., 1993—. Recipient gifted edn. programming grant U.S. Dept. Edn., 1982-83, spl. edn. technician program Maine Dept. Edn., 1994-95. Mem. ASCD, Maine Assn. Dirs. of Svcs. for Children with Exceptionalities, Vt. Network for the Gifted, Maine Educators of the Gifted and Talented, Poetry Soc. Vt. (editor Mountain Troubadour 1993—). Avocations: writing (nonfiction, poetry), collecting antiquarian books, reading, informal debate (history, polit. sci.). Home: PO Box 2901 Waterville ME 04903-2901 Office: Kennebec Valley Cmty Coll 92 Western Ave Fairfield ME 04937-1337 E-mail: jdouglas@kvcc.me.edu.

DOUGLAS, JIM (JAMES HOLLEY DOUGLAS), governor; b. Springfield, Mass., June 21, 1951; s. Robert James and Cora Elizabeth (Holley) D.; m. Dorothy Foster, May 24, 1975; children: Matthew James, Andrew Foster. AB, Middlebury Coll., 1972. Gen. mgr. Credit Bur. of Middlebury, Vt., 1972-76; exec. dir. United Way of Addison County, 1976-79; exec. asst. to Gov. of Vt., 1979-80; sec. of state State of Vt., Montpelier, 1981-93, treas., 1994—2002, gov., 2003—. Mem. Vt. Ho. of Reps., 1973-79, majority leader, 1975-77, 77-79 Mem. Nat. Assn. Secs. State (pres.). Lodges: Masons. Republican. Congregationalist. Office: Office of the Gov Pavilion, 109 State St Montpelier VT 05609*

DOUGLAS, J(OCELYN) FIELDING, toxicologist, consultant; b. Delta, Utah, Jan. 25, 1927; s. Benjamin and Amelia (Fielding) D.; m. Rose Mary Terrazzino, Sept. 16, 1951; children: David Benjamin, Pamela Susan, Jason Terrell. BS with high honors, U. Ill., 1948; MA, Columbia U., 1950, PhD, 1953. Project leader Johnson & Johnson, New Brunswick, N.J., 1952-58; dir. biochemistry Carter-Wallace, Cranbury, N.J., 1958-74; dep. dir. carcinogenesis testing program Nat. Cancer Inst., Bethesda, Md., 1976-80; chief ops. Nat. Toxicology Program, Bethesda, 1980-84; pres. Sci. Svcs., Inc., Front Royal, Va., 1984—. Expert cons. NIH, Bethesda, 1976-81; cons. in field; pres. High Knob Owners Assn. Inc., 1999—; bd. dirs. High Knob Utilities Inc., Front Royal, Va. Author, editor: Carcinogenesis and Mutagenesis Testing, 1984; contbr. numerous articles to profl. jours. Pvt. U.S. Army, 1944-46. Recipient Richard Neff award Richard Neff Soc., 1966, Dir. award Nat. Cancer Inst., 1979; USPHS fellow, 1950-52. Fellow AAAS; mem. Soc. Toxicology, Am. Soc. Pharmacology and Exptl. Therapeutics, Am. Chem. Soc. (chmn. biochem. sect. 1954). Avocations: gardening, reading, meditation. Home and Office: Sci Svcs Inc PO Box 533 Front Royal VA 22630-0533

DOUGLAS, JOHN LEWIS, lawyer; b. Atlanta, Sept. 23, 1950; s. Charles Lewis Jr. and Bettye Lee (Phelps) D.; m. Rebecca Ann Peterson, Aug. 16, 1974; children: Amber Lynne, Dianna Michelle, John Lewis Jr., Scott Foster, Charles Tillman, Alexander Peterson, Michael Lawrence, Jolanta Kuuzik, Tomas Kuuzik. BA in Econs., Davidson (N.C.) Coll., 1972; JD, U. Ga., 1977. Bar: Ga. 1977. Assoc. Alston and Bird, Atlanta, 1977-83, ptnr., fin. inst. regulation, mergers, acquistions Atlanta and Washington, 1990—; gen. counsel FDIC, Washington, 1987-89. Mem. steering com. Fin. Svcs. Vol. Corp. Contbr. articles to profl. jours. Republican. Mem. Lds Ch. Office: Alston & Bird LLP 1 Atlantic Ctr Atlanta GA 30309-3400 Office Phone: 404-881-7880. Business E-Mail: jdouglas@alston.com.

DOUGLAS, JOHN WOOLMAN, lawyer; b. Phila., Aug. 15, 1921; s. Paul H. and Dorothy S. (Wolff) D.; m. Mary Evans St. John, July 14, 1945; children: Katherine D. Torrey, Peter R. AB, Princeton U., 1943; LLB, Yale U., 1948; DPhil, Oxford U., 1950. Bar: N.Y. 1948, D.C. 1953. Law clk. to justice Harold H. Burton U.S. Supreme Ct., 1951—52; asst. atty. gen. U.S. Dept. Justice, 1963—66; from atty. to ptnr. Covington & Burling, Washington, 1950—. Chmn. Carnegie Endowment for Internat. Peace, 1978-86. Served to lt. (j.g.) USNR, 1943-46, MTO, PTO. Trustee Deerfield Acad., 1972-77; co-chair Citizens for McGovern com., 1972; chmn. Robert F. Kennedy Meml. Found., 1980-83. Rhodes scholar, 1948-50. Fellow Am. Coll. Trial Lawyers; mem. ABA, D.C. Bar Assn. (pres. 1974-75), Nat. Lawyers Com. for Civil Rights Under Law (co. chmn. 1969-71), Nat. Legal Aid and Defender Assn. (pres. 1970-71), Yale Law Sch. Assn. (pres. 1975-77). Democrat. Presbyterian. Home: 5700 Kirkside Dr Chevy Chase MD 20815-7116 Office: Covington & Burling 1201 Pennsylvania Ave NW PO Box 7566 Washington DC 20044-7566 Office Phone: 202-662-5622.

DOUGLAS, JON DAVID See OETJEN, DAVID

DOUGLAS, KARIN NADJA, engineer; b. Berlin, Sept. 2, 1931; came to U.S., 1963; d. Fritz and Irma (Rutke) Kruse; m. Karl Vonmoos, May 21, 1955 (div. Dec. 1961); m. Robert P. Douglas, Dec. 13, 1969. AS in Legal Adminstrn. magna cum laude, Sacred Heart U., Fairfield, Conn., 1984. Apprentice in tech. drafting and design Hasler AG., Bern, Switzerland, 1961-63; elec. designer UOP Air Correction Divsn., Norwalk, Conn., 1968-83; engring. cons. various engring. corps., Fairfield County, Conn., 1983-87; agy. compliance coord. ITT Flygt Corp., Trumbull, Conn., 1987—2005. Mem. univ. coll. coun. Sacred Heart U., 2000—. Sec. Friends of Boothe Park, Inc., mus. and rose garden, Stratford, Conn., 1985—; bd. dirs. Nat. Lympedema Network, Oakland, Calif., 1997—2002; creator Evelyn Conley scholarship for Sacred Heart U., 1988; also patient adv./activist, 1996—97; creator Dr. M. Palliser Endowment for Phys. Therapy for Sacred Heart U., 2001. Named Woman of Substance, Conn. Post, 1997; recipient D-Day award, Nat. Lymphedema Network, 1996, Disting. Alumni award, Sacred Heart U., 2002, Harold S. Geneen Cmty. Svc. award, ITT Industries, 2002. Achievements include invention of pink wristband for hospitals; lymphedema alert bracelet; design of lymphedema Awareness pin with turquoise ribbon. Avocations: sailing, fishing, cooking.

DOUGLAS, KENNETH JAY, food products executive; b. Harbor Beach, Mich., Sept. 4, 1922; s. Harry Douglas and Xenia (Williamson) D.; m. Elizabeth Ann Schweizer, Aug. 17, 1946; children: Connie Ann, Andrew Jay. Student, U. Ill., 1940-41, 46-47; JD, Chgo. Kent Coll. Law, 1950; grad., Advanced Mgmt. Program, Harvard, 1962. Bar: Ill. 1950, Ind. 1952. Spl. agt. FBI, 1950-54; dir. indsl. relations Dean Foods Co., Franklin Park, Ill., 1954-64, v.p. fin. and adminstrn., 1964-70, chmn. bd., chief exec. officer, 1970-87, chmn. bd., 1987-89, vice-chmn., 1989-92. Bd. dirs. Andrew Corp. Mem. Chgo. Com. With USNR, 1944-46. Mem. Chgo. Club, Econ. Club, Execs. Club, Comml. Club (Chgo.), Oak Park Country Club, River Forest Tennis Club, Old Baldy Country Club (Wyo.). Republican. Office: 1440 W North Ave Ste 207 Melrose Park IL 60160-1425 E-mail: kenmilk@aol.com.

DOUGLAS, KIMBERLY, university librarian; MS in libr. sci., Long Island U., Greenvale, NY, 1978. Position at Bigelow Lab. of Ocean Sci., Boothbay Harbor, Maine; dir. Hancock Libr. Biology & Oceanography U. So. Calif., LA, 1982—85, head Sci. & Engring. Libr., 1985—88; libr. staff Calif. Inst. Tech., Pasadena, 1988—, acting libr. dir., 2003—04, univ. libr., 2004—. Libr. adv. coun. IEEE; mem. vis. com. Goddard Space Flight Ctr. Libr. Mem.: Nat. Info. Std. Orgn., Libr. Info. and Tech. Assn. Office: Building 1-43 Calif Inst Tech 1200 E California Blvd Pasadena CA 91125 Office Phone: 626-395-6414. Office Fax: 626-431-2681. E-mail: kdouglas@caltech.edu.

DOUGLAS, KIRK (ISSUR DANIELOVITCH), actor, motion picture producer; b. Amsterdam, NY, Dec. 9, 1916; s. Harry and Bryna (Sanglel) Danielovitch; m. Diana Dill (div. Feb. 1950); children: Michael, Joel; m. Anne Buydens, May 29, 1954; children: Peter, Eric (dec. 2004) Anthony. AB, St. Lawrence U., 1938, D.F.A. (hon.), 1958; student, Am. Acad. Dramatic Arts, 1939-41. Appeared on Broadway in Spring Again, Three Sisters, Kiss and Tell, Wind is Ninety, Alice in Arms, Man Bites Dog; producer, star Broadway play One Flew over the Cuckoo's Nest; appeared in films: The Strange Love of Martha Ivers, 1946, Morning Becomes Electra, 1947, I Walk Alone, 1947, Out of the Past, 1947, Walls of Jericho, 1948, My Dear Secretary, 1948, A Letter to Three Wives, 1948, Champion, 1949, Young Man with a Horn, 1950, The Glass Menagerie, Ace in the Hole, Along the Great Divide, Detective Story, 1951, The Big Sky, 1951, The Big Trees, The Bad and the Beautiful, 1952, Equilibrium, 1952, The Story of Three Loves, The Juggler, 1953, Act of Love, Ulysses, 20,000 Leagues Under the Sea, 1954, Man Without a Star, The Racers, 1954, Lust for Life, 1956, Top Secret Affair, Gunfight at O.K. Corral, Paths of Glory, 1957, Last Train for Gunhill, 1958, Strangers When We Meet, 1958, The Devil's Disciple, 1959, Town Without Pity, Spartacus, 1960, The Last Sunset, 1961, Two Weeks in Another Town, 1962, The List of Adrian Messenger, For Love or Money, The Hook, 1963, In Harm's Way, Heroes of Telemark, 1965, Cast a Giant Shadow, Is Paris Burning?, 1966, War Wagon, The Way West, 1967, A Lovely Way to Die, 1968, The Arrangement, 1969, There Was a Crooked Man, 1970, The Light at the Edge of the World, Catch Me A Spy, 1971, A Man To Respect, 1972, Master Touch, 1972, Scalawag, 1973, Jekyl & Hyde, 1973, Posse, 1975, Once is Not Enough, 1975, Holocaust 2000, 1977, The Fury, 1978, The Villain, Saturn 3, Home Movies, 1979, The Man from Snowy River, 1982, Eddie Macon's Run, 1983, Tough Guys, 1986, Oscar, 1991, Greedy, 1994, Welcome to Veraz, 1990, A Song for David, 1996, (documentary) Once Upon A Time in Hollywood, 2004, Illusion, 2004; producer, dir. films Scalawag, 1973, Posse, 1975; pres. Bryna Co.; producer, actor films: The Final Countdown, Indian Fighter, 1955, Vikings, 1964, Spartacus, 1960, The Last Sunset, 1961, Lonely are the Brave, 1962, Summertree, 1963, Seven Days in May, 1964, The Brotherhood, 1968, A Gunfight, 1971, Oscar, 1991, The Secret, 1991, Take Me Home Again, 1994, Diamonds, 1999, It Runs in the Family, 2003; co-producer film One Flew Over the Cuckoo's Nest, 1975, The Final Countdown, 1979; TV miniseries appearance: Queenie, 1987; TV film appearance: Mousy (also dir.), 1973, The Money Changers, Victory at Entebbe, 1976, Remembrance of Love, 1982, Draw!, 1984, Amos, 1985, Inherit the Wind, 1988, Touched by An Angel, 2000; author: (autobiography) The Ragman's Son, 1988, Climbing the Mountain, 1997, My Stroke of Luck, 2002; (novels) Dance with the Devil, 1990, The Gift, 1992, Last Tango in Brooklyn, 1994, The Broken Mirror, 1997, (juvenile) Young Heroes of the Bible, 1999. Nominated for Acad. Award, 1949, 52, 56; nominated for Emmy, 1985, 98, 2000; recipient N.Y. Film Critics award, 1956, Hollywood Fgn. Press award, 1956, Heart and Torch award Am. Heart Assn., 1956, Splendid Am. award of merit George Washington Carver Meml. Found., 1957, cited in Congl. Record for service as goodwill ambassador, 1964, Cecil B. DeMille award for contbns. in entertainment field, 1967, Presdl. Medal of Freedom, 1981, elected to Cowboy Hall of Fame, 1984, Lifetime Achievement award Am. Film Inst., 1991; decorated Legion of Honor (France), 1985, Chevalier de la Legion d'Honneur, 1985, Officer de la Legion d'Honneur, 1990; Kennedy Center Honor, 1994; Honorary Oscar, Lifetime Achievement, 1996, Meltzer award for breaking blacklist Writers Guild Am., 1999, Lifetime Achievement SAG, 1999, Golden Boot award, 1999, Spencer Tracy award Outstanding Achievement in Drama, 1999, Lifetime Achievement Jerusalem Film Festival, 2000, Golden Bear award Berlin Film Festival, 2001, Nat. medal of Arts, 2002. Mem. UN Assn. (dir. Los Angeles chpt.) Achievements include making State Dept.-USIA tours around world; Kirk Douglas High School named in his honor, 2000, Kirk Douglas Theatre named in his honor, 2004, Kirk Douglas Way named in his honor, 2004. E-mail: mnewberger@warrencowan.com.

DOUGLAS, KYAN, television personality; b. 1970; Cert. in cosmetology, Aveda Inst., N.Y.C.; cert. in massage therapy, Blue Cliff Sch. Therapeutic Massage, New Orleans. Colorist Arrojo Studio, N.Y.C.; colorist TV project TLC's What Not to Wear, While You Were Out; colorist mag. project Child Mag.; grooming specialist TV series Queer Eye for the Straight Guy, 2003—. Co-author: Queer Eye for the Straight Guy: The Fab 5's Guide to Looking Better, Cooking Better, Dressing Better, Behaving Better, and Living Better, 2004. Office: Endeavor Talent Agy 270 Lafayette St Ste 605 New York NY 10012

DOUGLAS, LEE (CHARLES DOUGLAS), basketball team executive; b. Atlanta, Ga., Aug. 23, 1952; m. Nancy: children: Brent, Kelly. BA in Indsl. Mgmt., Ga. Inst. Tech., 1974; MBA, Ga. State U., 1978. From sales rep. to exec. v.p. Atlanta Hawks, 1978-89, exec. v.p., 1989—. Cons. Atlanta Braves, 1992—; mem. Mktg. Advisory Bd. NBA Properties. Bd. dirs. Atlanta Hawks Found. Office: One CNN Ctr Ste 405 S Tower Atlanta GA 30303

DOUGLAS, LESLIE, investment banker; b. Enon Valley, Pa., Mar. 14, 1914; s. Robert R. and Margaret M. (Mc Anlis) D.; m. Jean Wallace, Oct. 12, 1946; children— David, Ann and Joan (twins). BS, Geneva Coll., Beaver Falls, Pa., 1935; MBA, Harvard U., 1937. Investment mgr. Royal Liverpool Group, N.Y.C., 1937-41; investment banker Folger Nolan Fleming Douglas, Inc., Washington, 1946—, v.p., 1955—; bd. govs. Assn. Stock Exchange Firms, 1969-72, Securities Industry Assn., 1972-75. Trustee Holton Arms Sch., Washington, Landon Sch., Vis. Nurses Assn., Washington. Served to lt. comdr. USN, 1941-46. Mem.: Chevy Chase; Met. (Washington), Met. Club. Republican. Presbyterian. Home: 4733 Woodway Ln NW Washington DC 20016-3240 Office: 725 15th St NW Washington DC 20005-2109

DOUGLAS, LESLIE A., municipal official; b. Marting Ferry, Ohio, Feb. 18, 1931; s. Jesse Harrison and Helen Elizabeth Douglas; m. Betty Lou Briggs, Aug. 12, 1959; children: Charles, Richard, Kathryn Reed, James. BA, West Liberty (W.Va.) State Coll., 1958; MEd, Kent State U., 1964. Tchr., basketball coach Stanton local schs., Irondale, Ohio, 1958—60; guidance dir. Barnesville (Ohio) Exempted Village Schs., 1960—63; adminstr., guidance dir. Martins Ferry Schs., 1963—70, Martins Ferry City Schs., 1974—92; dir. job counseling & tng. Martins Ferry Model City Program, 1970—74; pres. coun. City of Martins Ferry, 1984—92, 1996—. Author: Martins Ferry Lodge Community Service, 1970 (Freedoms Found., 1971), Martins Ferry High School, 1970. Mem. Belmont County Dem. Ctrl. Com., St. Clairsville, Ohio, 1986—. Airman 1st class USAF, 1951—55, Korea. Mem.: Elks (state chmn. Hoop Shoot Program Ohio 1971—72, dist. dep. grand exalted ruler 1973—74, Elk of the Yr. 1970—71), Eagles (S.E. zone chmn. Ohio 1994—). Episcoplian. Avocations: exercise, running, walking, reading, coin collecting/numismatics. Home: 227 N 5th St Martins Ferry OH 43935-1530 Office: Martins Ferry City 5th St Martins Ferry OH 43935

DOUGLAS, MARJORIE MYERS, writer; b. Oxford, Ohio, Nov. 3, 1911; d. Walter Raleigh and Olinia May (Mattison) Myers; m. Donald Moats Douglas, June 19, 1937; children: Anne Marjorie Brothers, William Walter, Bruce David. BA, U. Minn., Mpls., 1933. Med. social worker Columbia Presbyn. Med. Ctr., N.Y.C., 1934-36; founder med. social work dept. Gillette Hosp. for Crippled Children, 1936-38; social worker Mpls. Pub. Schs., 1960-77. Author: Eggs in the Coffee, Sheep in the Corn, 1994 (Minn. book award), Barefoot on Crane Island, 1998. Named Alumni of Notable Achievement U. Minn., 1999. Home: 4344 Oakdale Ave S Edina MN 55424-1057

DOUGLAS, MARY TEW, anthropology and humanities educator; b. San Remo, Italy, Mar. 25, 1921; came to U.S., 1977; m. James Douglas, 1951; children: Janet, James, Philip. BA, U. Oxford, Eng., 1943, MA, 1947, BSc, 1948, PhD, 1951; hon. doctorate, U. Uppsala, U. Notre Dame, Jewish Theol. Sem., U. East Anglia, U. of Essex, U. Warwick, U. Pa., U. Surrey, Sigilo Doro U. Palermo; doctorate (hon.), U. Brunel, U. London. Rsch. fellow Internat. African Inst. for Fieldwork, Belgian Congo, 1949-50, 53, 87; lectr. anthropology Univ. Coll., London, 1951-62, prof. social anthropology, 1971—77; dir. rsch. on culture Russell Sage Found., N.Y.C., 1977-81; Avalon Found. prof. in humanities Northwestern U., Evanston, Ill., 1981-85; vis. prof. depts. religion and anthropology Princeton U., 1985-88. Author: Lele of the Kasai, 1963, Purity and Danger, 1966, Natural Symbols, 1970, Implicit Meanings, 1975, The World of Goods, 1979, Risk and Culture, 1982; In the Active Voice, 1982; editor: Essays in the Sociology of Perception, 1982, How Institutions Think, 1986, Risk Acceptability, 1987, Risk and Blame, 1992, In the Wilderness, 1993, Thought Styles, 1996, Missing Persons, 1998, Leviticus as Literature, 1999, Jacob's Tears, 2004. Hon. fellow U. Coll. London, 1994; decorated Comdr. British Empire, 1992. Fellow Royal Swedish Acad.; mem. AAAS, Am. Acad. Arts and Scis., Academia Europaea, Brit. Acad., Royal Swedish Acad. Humanities. Address: 22 Hillway Highgate London N66QA England E-mail: m.douglas@ucl.ac.uk.

DOUGLAS, MICHAEL KIRK, actor, film producer, director; b. New Brunswick, N.J., Sept. 25, 1944; s. Kirk and Diana Douglas; m. Diandra Morrell Luker, Mar. 20, 1977 (div. 2000); 1 child, Cameron Morrell; m. Catherine Zeta-Jones, Nov. 18, 2000; children: Dylan Michael, Carys Zeta. BA, U. Calif., Santa Barbara, 1967. Actor: films including (film debut) Cast a Giant Shadow, 1966, Hail Hero, 1969, Adam at 6 A.M., 1970, Summertree, 1971, Napoleon and Samantha, 1972, Coma, 1978, Running, 1979, The China Syndrome, 1979, It's My Turn, 1981, Star Chamber, 1983, A Chorus Line, 1985, Fatal Attraction, 1987, Wall Street, 1987 (Golden Globe award for best actor, Acad. award for best actor), Black Rain, 1989, The War of the Roses, 1989, Shining Through, 1992, Basic Instinct, 1992, Falling Down, 1993, Disclosure, 1994, The American President, 1995, The Ghost and the Darkness, 1996, A Song for David, 1996, The Game, 1997, A Perfect Murder, 1998, Wonder Boys, 1999, Still Life, 1999, Traffic, 1999, Don't Say a Word, 2001, The In-Laws, 2003; (TV series): Streets of San Francisco, 1972-76, Liberty's Kids: Est. 1776 (narrator), 2002; (TV appearances)This Is Your Life, 1958, the F.B.I., 1971, Medical Center, 1971, Will & Grace, 2002; producer, actor: (films) The China Syndrome, 1979, Romancing the Stone, 1984, Jewel of the Nile, 1985, One Night at McCool's 2001, It Runs in the Family, 2003; producer: (films) One Flew Over the Cuckoo's Nest, 1975 (Acad. award for best picture), Flatliners, 1990, Made in America, 1993, The Rainmaker, 1997, Godspeed, Lawrence Mann, 2004; exec. producer: (film) Starman, 1984, Eyes of an Angel, 1991, Radio Flyer, 1992, The Ghost and the Darkness, 1996, Face/Off, 1997; (TV series) Starman, 1986; co-prodr., Stone Cold, 1991, Double Impact, 1991; founder record label Third Stone/Atlantic. Cecil B. Demille award, 2004 Office: c/o Endeavor Talent Agy 9701 Wilshire Blvd 10th Fl Beverly Hills CA 90212

DOUGLAS, MICHAEL L., state supreme court justice; b. LA, Mar. 13, 1948; s. Elmer Walter and Lottie Lee (Nelson) D.; m. Frankie Haws, 1968 (div. Dec. 1970); 1 child, Christine; m. A. Martha Douglas, Jan. 13, 1971. BA in Polit. Sci., Calif. State U., Long Beach, 1971; JD, U. Calif., San Francisco, 1974. Bar: Pa. 1981, U.S. Dist. Ct. (ea. dist.) Pa. 1981, U.s. Ct. Appeals (2d cir.) 1983, Nev. 1983, U.S. Dist. Ct. Nev. 1983. Pvt. practice, Phila., 1981-82; directing atty. Nev. Legal Svcs., Las Vegas, 1982-84; dep. dist. atty. Clark County Dist. Atty., Las Vegas, 1984-96; dist. ct. judge State of Nev. 8th Dist. Ct., Las Vegas, 1996—2004, chief dist. ct. judge, 2003—04; justice Nev. Supreme Ct., 2004—. Instr. in law L.A. C.C. Dist., 1975-77; spkr. in field. Bd. dirs. Temporary Assistance for Domestic Crisis, 1983-85; mem. task force For Kids Sake/KLAS-TV, 1987-88; vol. Bridge Counseling, 1990-92; coach Ctrl. Valley Little League, 1991-95; bd. dirs. Nev. Law Found., 1991-93; mem. program com. H.P. Fitzgerald Sch., 1994-96. Recipient Svc. to Youth award YMCA L.A., 1971, Proclamation for Svc. to Youth award City of L.a., 1980, 81, Cmty. Svc. award Calif. State Assembly, 1981, Martin Luther King Com., L.a., 1980, Proclamation for Cmty. Svc. award Clark County, 1989, Mark of Excellence award Nat. Fedn. Black Pub. Adminstrs., 1996. Mem. ABA, NAACP (fundraising com. 1990-96, freedom fund budget com. 1990-93), State Bar Nev.(atty. grievance rev. com. 1986-95, mem. disciplinary bd. 1988-95), Clark County Bar Assn., Nat. Bar Assn. (sec. Las Vegas chpt. 1985-87, pres. 1987-88, scholarship chmn. 1989-95, scholarship budget com. 1987-94, Las Vegas Svc. award 1987, 91, Pres. Appreciation award 1988, 89, 90), Pa. Bar Assn., Phila. Bar Assn., Nat. Dist. Atty.'s Assn., Nev. Gaming Attys., Hastings Coll. of Law Alumni Assn., Calif. State U.-Long Beach Alumni Assn., Sigma Pi Phi, Alpha Phi Alpha. Presbyterian. Avocations: outdoor sports, camping, coaching youth sports. Office: Nev Supreme Ct 316 Bridger Ave Las Vegas NV 89101 Office Phone: 702-486-3225, 775-684-1755. Office Fax: 702-486-3231. Business E-Mail: mdouglas@nvcourts.state.nv.us.

DOUGLAS, ROBERT GORDON, JR., physician; b. N.Y.C., Apr. 17, 1934; s. Robert Gordon and Alice (Lewis) D.; m. Ann Castle Moses, Dec. 22, 1956; children: Robert Gordon, 3d, Timothy Stuart, Catherine Lewis. AB, Princeton U., 1955; MD, Cornell U., 1959. Diplomate Am. Bd. Internal Medicine. Successively intern, asst. resident in internal medicine, resident N.Y. Hosp., 1959-61, 62-63; asst. resident Johns Hopkins Hosp., 1961-62; USPHS clin. assoc., clin. investigator Nat. Inst. Allergy and Infectious Disease, 1963-66; asst. prof. microbiology and medicine Baylor Coll. Medicine, Houston, 1966-70; mem. faculty Sch. Medicine and Dentistry U. Rochester, N.Y., 1970-82, prof. medicine and microbiology Sch. Medicine and Dentistry, 1974-82, head infectious disease unit Sch. Medicine and Dentistry, 1970-82, sr. assoc. dean edn. Sch. Medicine and Dentistry, 1979-82; prof., chmn. dept. medicine Med. Coll. Cornell U., 1982-90; physician in chief N.Y. Hosp., 1982-90; sr. v.p. medi. and sci. affairs Merck Sharp & Dohme Internat., 1990-91; pres. Merck Vaccines, 1991-99; dir. strategic planning Vaccine Rsch. Ctr. NIAID, 1999—2004. Bd. dirs. Elusys Inc., Advancis Pharm. Corp., Iomai Inc., VaxInnate Inc., Internat. AIDS Vaccine Initiative, 1997-2003; chmn. bd. dirs. Vical Inc.; cons. in field; adj. prof. medicine Cornell U. Med. Coll., 1990—; hon. attending physician N.Y. Hosp., 1990—; chmn. Aeras Global TB Vaccine Found., 2001—. Editor: Principles and Practices of Infectious Diseases, 1979, 2d edit., 1985, 3d edit., 1990; contbr. articles to profl. jours. Recipient Hawkins award Assn. Am. Pubs., 1980. Fellow ACP, Infectious Diseases Soc. Am. (pres. 1991-92, Feldman award); mem. Inst. Medicine, Am. Soc. Clin. Investigation, Assn. Am. Physicians, Am. Clin. Climatol. Assn. (pres. 1999-2000), Nat. Found. for Infectious Disease (Maxwell Finland award 2000). Home and Office: 84 Old Black Point Rd Niantic CT 06357

DOUGLAS, STEVEN DANIEL, immunologist, educator, director; b. Jamaica, N.Y., Feb. 28, 1939; s. Albert H. and Felice (Berner) D.; m. Mary Ann Forciea, Feb. 29, 1980; children: Hope Felice, Anne Genevieve. BA, Cornell U., Ithaca, N.Y., 1959; MD, Cornell U. Med. Sch., N.Y.C., 1963; MA (hon.), U. Pa., 1982. Intern Mt. Sinai Hosp., N.Y.C., 1963-64; resident Mt. Sinai Sch. Medicine, N.Y.C., 1966-67; staff assoc. NIH, Bethesda, Md., 1964-66; rsch. fellow U. Calif., San Francisco, 1967-69; from asst. prof. to assoc. prof. medicine Mt. Sinai Sch. Medicine, N.Y.C., 1969-74; from assoc. prof. to prof. medicine and microbiology U. Minn., Mpls., 1974-80; prof. pediatrics and microbiology U. Pa., Phila., 1980—; dir. allergy-immunology-pulmonology Children's Hosp., Phila., 1980-89, dir. immunology lab., 1980—, dir. divsn. allergy-immunology-bone marrow transplantation, 1981-87, chief sect. immunology, 1989—; dir. clin. immunology lab., 1980—; dir. stem cell lab. Children's Hosp., Phila., 1994-99, dir. immunogenetics lab., 1996—; assoc. chmn. acad. affairs dept. pediatrics Sch. Medicine U. Pa., 1994—; chair AIDS immunology and pathogenesis study sect. Ctr. Sci. Rev. NIH, 2005—. Editor-in-chief: Clin. and Diagnostic Lab. Immunology, 1993—; editor: Jour. Clin. Microbiology, 1983—93, Jour. Leukocyte Biology, 1980—89; adv. bd.: Diagnostic Immunology, 1984—; editl. bd. Jour. Immunology, 1984—, Clin. Immunology Immunopathology, 1975—, Jour. Clin. Lab. Analysis, 1988—93; contbr.: over 410 articles in cellular and clin. immunology, particularly mononuclear phagocytes and immune deficiencies to profl. publs. With USPSH, 1964-66. Recipient Career Devel. award NIH, 1969-74, Abbott Labs. award, 1997, Erwin neter award, 2000. Fellow: AAAS; mem.: Reticuloendothelial Soc. (sec. 1980—82, program chmn. 1981, councilor 1984—87, pres. 1988—89), Am. Soc. Hematology, Am. Soc. Clin. Investigation, Am. Pediatric Soc., Soc. Pediatric Rsch., Am. Acad. Microbiology, Am. Soc. Cell Biology, Am. Assn. Immunologists, Soc. Leukocyte Biology (hon. life), Interurban Clin. Club (pres. 1994—95). Jewish. Home: 2122 Delancey St Philadelphia PA 19103-6512

DOUGLAS, THOMAS JOHN, healthcare educator; b. St. Louis, Dec. 21, 1946; s. Ernest Vetal and Helen Catherine Douglas; m. Linda Mary Schmid, Apr. 28, 1990; 1 child, Cassandra Elizabeth; m. Mary Eleanor Horvath, Oct. 13, 1967 (div.); children: Timothy James, Matthew John. BS in Math., St. Louis U., 1964—68; MBA, So. Ill. U., 1978; PhD in Bus. Adminstrn., U. Tenn., 1997. Dir. mktg. rsch. SBC Comm., St. Louis, 1967—93; asst. prof. U. Evansville, Ind., 1997—2000, Clemson U., Clemson, SC, 2000—05, So. Ill. U., Edwardsville, 2005—. Contbr. to profl. jours. Mem. Sertoma Internat., Clemson, SC, 2004. Lt. USN, 1970—73, Holyloch, Scotland. Recipient All Conf. Best Paper award, So. Mgmt. Assn., 2002. Mem.: Strategic Mgmt. Soc., Acad. Mgmt. Avocations: cooking, sailing. Home: 3457 Wilderness Dr Edwardsville IL 62025 Office: So Ill U 2134 Founders Hall Edwardsville IL 62026 Office Phone: 618-650-2731. Personal E-mail: td27@clemson.edu. E-mail: tomdouglas@yahoo.com.

DOUGLAS, VICTORIA JEAN, marketing professional, communications executive, educator; b. Wilmington, Del., Sept. 1, 1972; d. Richard Otto and Genevieve Douglas. Student, U. Caen, France, 1993, Oxford (Eng.) U., 1995, NYU Paris, 1996; BA in English/French, U. Del., 1996, MA in French Lit., 1999. Dir. comm. Mayor's Office, Wilmington, 1993—2001; mktg. and comm. chief cons. Met. Wilmington Urban League, 2001—; CEO Barracuda Comm., Wilmington, 2000—. Founder, chair Fgn. Lang. and Lit. Assn. Grad. Students, Newark, 1996—97; mem. mktg. com. Dept. Youth and Families, Wilmington, 1999—2000; supporting mem. Del. Ctr. for Contemporary Arts, Wilmington, 2001—; bd. mem. Kuumba Acad., Wilmington, 2001—; curriculum devel. staff, instr. English U. Caen Sch. Law, France, 1997—98;

account supr. Saatchi and Saatchi, Rowland, NY, 2001. Organizer Nat. Night Out, Wilmington, 1993—95, Mayor's Breast Cancer Awareness Campaign, Wilmington, 2001; mem. ball com. Am. Diabetes Assn., 2002, mem. leadership coun., 2002—; v.p. sales Wilmington Drama League. Recipient Tomorrow's Leaders Today award, Pub. Allies, 1994, proclamation, City of Wilmington, 2000, Apex Award for Excellence in Mktg. and Pub. Rels. Brochures, 2002, APEX award Design & Layout, 2003, Comm. award, 2003. Mem.: AAUW, Pub. Rels. Soc. Am., Met. Wilmington Urban League, Pi Delta Phi, Golden Key Nat. Honor Soc., Phi Sigma Tau, Sigma Tau Delta.

DOUGLAS, WILLIAM ERNEST, retired commissioner; b. Charleston, SC, Nov. 26, 1930; s. William Ernest and Helen A. (Fortune) D.; m. Nancy Anne (Gibson), July 18, 1980. BA cum laude (hon.), The Citadel, 1956; postgrad., U. SC, 1956—59. With IRS, 1959—80, divsn. chief Newark dist., 1970—72, asst. dir. Jackson (Miss.) dist., 1972-73, asst. dir. Atlanta dist., 1973-74, asst. commr. S.E. region, 1974-78, dir. Regional Svc. Ctr. S.E. region, 1978-80; commr. fin. mgmt. svc. U.S. Treasury Dept., Washington, 1980-91. Served in U.S. Army, 1948-52, Korean War, 1950-51. Recipient Exec. Excellence award Fed. Interagency Com. on Info. Resources Mgmt., 1985; Exec. Achievement award Sr. Exec. Svc., 1985; Am. Univ. Roger W. Jones Fed. Exec. Leadership award, 1986; Sec. of Treasury's Disting. Svc. award, 1991; Presdl. Exec. Disting. award, 1991. Home: 205 Settlers Rd Saint Simons Island GA 31522

DOUGLASS, BRUCE E., physician; b. Berwyn, Ill., Sept. 26, 1917; s. Frank Lionel and Helen Mary (Eccles) D.; m. Charlotte Maurer Natwick, Oct. 14, 1942; children: Jean N., Bruce G., John F. BA, U. Wis., 1938, MD, 1942; MS in Medicine, U. Minn., 1949. Intern Med. Coll. of Va., Richmond, 1942-43; resident in internal medicine Mayo Clinic, Rochester, Minn., 1947-50, mem. staff, 1949—, chmn. divsn. preventive medicine, 1962—; dir. Mayo Clinic (Mayo sect. of Patient and Health Edn.), 1976—. Dir. Occupational Health Inst., Chgo., 1968— Author: Anatomy of the Portal Vein and Its Tributaries, 1949, The Problem of Benign Bronchial Obstruction, 1954, Predicting Disease: Is It Possible? 1971, Health Problems of Hospital Employees, 1971, Examining Healthy Persons: How and How Often? 1980. Chmn. Rochester Music Bd., 1960-70; v.p. Minn. Zool. Soc., 1974-77. Served to capt. M.C. AUS, 1944-47. Fellow Am. Acad. Occupational Medicine (Keogh award 1981), Am. Occupational Med. Assn. (pres. 1977-78, Meritorious Service award 1979); mem. AMA (Physician's Recognition award 1974-77, chmn. sect. council on preventive medicine 1978-80, del. for occupational med. to ho. of dels. 1978-85), Minn. Med. Assn. (chmn. com. on public health edn. 1979), Ramazzini Soc., Assn. Tchrs. Preventive Medicine, Am. Coll. Preventive Medicine, Minn. Zool. Soc., Sigma Xi, Phi Kappa Phi, Sigma Phi, Nu Sigma Nu. Office: Mayo Clinic Rochester MN 55905-0001 Home: Charter House 211 2d St NW #1306 Rochester MN 55901 Office Phone: 507-284-2691.

DOUGLASS, GLORY L., music educator; b. Morristown, N.J., Nov. 12, 1953; d. Rodney Merrinet and Janet Ruth (Buker) Lanphear; children: Gregory Paul, Gwendolyn Jan. BS in Music Edn., U. Vt., 1975. Cert. tchr. Vt. Music educator Lamoille Union H.S., Hyde Park, Vt., 1975—81, North County Union H.S., Newport, Vt., 1983—99, Essex H.S., Essex, Vt., 1999—. Mem.: Am. Choral Dirs. Assn. (Vt. chpt. pres. 1999—2001), Vt. Music Educators Assn. (pres. 2001—, Vt. Music Educator of Yr. 1998), Music Educators Nat. Conf. Democrat. Protestant. Avocations: attending concerts, helping son's singing career, reading, walking, time at summer cottage. Office: Essex High School 2 Educational Drive Essex Junction VT 05452

DOUGLASS, JANE DEMPSEY, retired theology educator; b. Wilmington, Del., Mar. 22, 1933; d. Hazell Brownlie and Ethel Katherine (Smith) Dempsey; m. Gordon Klene Douglass, Aug. 23, 1964; children: Alan Bruce, Anne Lorine, John Gordon. AB, Syracuse U., 1954; postgrad., U. Geneva, Switzerland, 1954-55; AM, Radcliffe Coll., 1961; PhD, Harvard U., 1963; ThD (hon.), U. Geneva, 1994; LHD (hon.), Franklin and Marshall Coll., 1992; DD (hon.), U. St. Andrews, Scotland, 1992; STD (hon.), MacMurray Coll., 2000. Assoc. dir. Presbyn. Student Ctr., Columbia, Mo., 1955-58; teaching fellow Harvard Divinity Sch., Cambridge, Mass., 1959-62; from instr. to prof. Sch. of Theology at Claremont and Claremont Grad. Sch., Claremont, Ca., 1963-85; Hazel Thompson McCord prof. hist. theology Princeton (N.J.) Theol. Sem., 1985-98, emerita, 1998—. Pres. Am. Soc. Ch. History, 1983; v.p. World Alliance of Reformed Chs., 1989-90, pres. 1990-97, hon. mem. exec. com., 1997-2004. Author: Justification in Late Medieval Preaching: A Study of John Geiler of Keisersberg, 1966, 2d edit., 1989, Women, Freedom and Calvin, 1985; editor: (with Jack L. Stotts) To Confess the Faith Today, 1990, (with James F. Kay) Women, Gender and Christian Community, 1997, (with Páraic Réamonn) Partnership in God's Mission in the Middle East, 1998; contbr. articles to profl. jours. Presbyterian.

DOUGLASS, JOHN JAY, lawyer, educator; b. Lincoln, Nebr., Mar. 9, 1922; s. Edward Lyman and Edna Marie (Ball) D.; m. Margaret Casteel Pickering, Aug. 31, 1946; children: Carrie Bess, Timothy Pickering, Margaret Marie. AB with distinction, U. Nebr., 1943; JD with distinction, U. Mich., 1952; MA, George Washington U., 1963; LLM, U. Va., 1973; postgrad., Army War Coll., 1963. Bar: Nebr. 1952, Mich. 1952, Tex. 1975. Inf. officer U.S. Army, 1943-52, advanced through grades to col., 1966, judge adv., 1952-74, 1968-69, mil. judge Ft. Riley, Kans., 1969-70; comdt. U.S. Army JAG Sch., Charlottesville, Va., 1970-74; ret. U.S. Army, 1974; dean Nat. Coll. Dist. Attys., Houston, 1974-94; prof., dir. trial advocacy U. Houston, 1974—. Advisor on criminal law to Albania, 1991; advisor on elections to Ukraine, 1993; advisor Russian procuracy, 1994, Ukraine procuracy, 1995; named dist. mem. JAGC, 1994. Author: Ethical Concerns in Prosecution, 1988, 93; contbr. articles to profl. jours. Judge Harris County Absentee Voting, Houston, 1980-92. Decorated D.S.C., Legion of Merit, Bronze Star; recipient U. Nebr. Alumni Achievement award, 2003. Fellow Am. Bar Found. (life); mem. ABA (ho. of dels. 1980-96, chmn. standing com. on law and electoral process 1987-90, Nelson award 2001), Tex. Bar Assn. (penal code and criminal process com. 1988-90), Houston City Club, Army and Navy Club, Order of Coif, Alpha Tau Omega. Avocation: tennis. Home: 25 T 14 E Greenway Plz Houston TX 77046-1406 Office: Univ Houston Law Ctr 100 Law Center Houston TX 77204-6060 Office Phone: 713-743-1831. Personal E-mail: douglass.713@sbcglobal.net. Business E-Mail: jdouglass@uh.edu.

DOUGLASS, KRISTI ANN, special education educator; b. Chester, Pa. d. James and Patricia Lang; m. Jeff D. Douglass. BA, Allegheny Coll., Pa., 1997; MEd, Pa. State U., 2004. Spl. Edn. N-12 Cert. Pa., 2002. Spl. edn. tchr. Coatesville Area Sr. H.S., Pa., 2003—. Mem. Student Assistance Program, Coatesville, 2004—. Mem.: Pi Lambda Theta, Kappa Alpha Theta. Office Phone: 610-383-3730. Personal E-mail: douglassk@coatesville.k12.pa.us.

DOUGLASS, MELVIN ISADORE, middle school administrator, educator, clergyman; b. N.Y.C., July 21, 1948; s. Isadore Douglass and Esther L. Tripp. AS in Early Childhood Edn., Vincennes U., 1970; BS in Early Childhood and Elem. Edn., Tuskegee Inst., 1973; MS in Urban Elem. Edn., Morgan State U., 1975; MA in Orgn. Adminstrn. Supervision, NYU, 1977; MEd in Curriculum and Teaching, Columbia U., 1978, DEd, 1981; cert. in Urban Sch. Leadership, Harvard U., 2003. Cert. social studies tchr., N.Y.; cert. sch. dist. adminstr. and supr., N.Y.; cert. elem. tchr., N.Y.; ordained to ministry Bapt. Ch., 1987. Tchr., dean students Bronx Pub. Sch., NY, 1973-75; sch. age program dir. Amistad Child Day Care Ctr., Jamaica, 1976-77; head coach track and field CUNY, NYC, 1981—83; adminstrv. dir. Beck Meml. Day Care Ctr., Bronx, 1983—84; primary sch. dept. chair City of N.Y. Dept. Juvenile Justice, 1984-85, ombudsman, 1985-88; chmn. depts. English, reading and social studies Stimson Jr. High Sch., Huntington Station, N.Y., 1988—. Adj. instr. sociology and African Am. studies Coll. of New Rochelle, N.Y., 1992-2004, adj. asst. prof. Bklyn. Coll. Grad. Sch. of Edn., N.Y., 2000—, adj. prof. Metropolitan Coll of N.Y., 1999—; coord. various edn. confs., 1986—; CEO Minority Educators' Network, N.Y., 1999—, mem. community adv. bd. City of N.Y. Dept. of Correction, Queens House of Detention for Men, 1991-95; ednl. liaison N.Y. State Senator Alton R. Waldon, Jr., 1991-2000. Author: Black Winners: A History of Spingarn Medalists, 1915-1983, 1984, Carter G. Woodson: A Biography, 1987; contbr. articles to profl. jours. Assisting minister Calvary Bapt. Ch., 1987-91; co-chair edn. com. N.Y.C. Black Leadership Coun., 1987-88, N.Y. State Conf. NAACP, 1986-89; chmn. anti-drug com. Met. Coun. NAACP Brs., 1986-89; cons. Jamaica East/West Adolescent Pregnancy Consortium, 1986-89; mem. area policy bd. #12 subunit 2, 1987—97; mem. Queens adv. bd. N.Y. Urban League, 1988-93, adv. bd. Gerald W. Deas Professorship SUNY Downstate Med. Ctr., 2002— pres. bd. dirs. N.Y.C. Transit br. NAACP, 1984-89; bd. dirs. Queens Coun. on Arts, 1983-86, Black Exptl. Theatre, 1982—, United Black Men Queens County Inc., 1986-90, Dance Explosion, 1987-89, nat. adv. bd. The Principal's Ctr., Harvard Grad. Sch. of Edn., 2004-; mem. cmty. adv. bd. Pub. Sch. 40, Queens, 1992-95; mem. peer rev. com. Jour. Nat. Med. Assn., 2003—; co-chair youth com. Ptnrs. of the Ams., 2004—; bd. dirs. L.I. Head Start, 2004—; bd. dirs. USO of Metro. N.Y., 2005—; social policy advisor on children and families NY State Assemblyman William Scarborough; bd. dirs. USO Met. N.Y.C., 2005—. Recipient citation for cmty. svc. N.Y. State Gov. Mario Cuomo, 1986, citation award N.Y.C. Mayor Edward Koch, 1986, citation of honor Queens Borough Pres. Claire Shulman, 1986, Svc. award N.Y.C. Transit br. NAACP, 1986, Jefferson award Am. Inst. for Pub. Svc. and WNYW-Fox TV, 1987, Civil Rights award N.Y.C. Transit br. NAACP, 1988, citation N.Y.C. Coun., 1988, Alumni Faculty citation Vincennes U., 1991, resolution Senator A.R. Waldon, Jr., 1991, Svc. award Ea. Shore chpt. Links, 2001, Svc. award Suffolk County Human Rights Commn., 2004, citation Congressman Steve Israel, 2003, Proclamation, Legislator Allan Binder, 2003, Cert. Excellence Jour. Nat. Med. Assn., 2003, cert. of spl. recognition Oxford Round Table, U. Oxford, 2005; Henry M. Minton fellow, 2003; named Nu Omicron chpt. Omega Man of Yr., 1987. Mem. Nat. Black Child Devel. Inst., NEA, St. Albans C. of C., Am. Fedn. Sch. Adminstrs., Coun. Adminstrs. and Suprs., South Huntington Chairmen's Assn., L.I. Tuskegee Alumni Assn. (v.p. bd. dirs. 1987-89), Jamaica Track Club (pres., founder 1973—), Masons, Shriners, Kappa Delta Pi, Omega Psi Phi (basileus Nu Omicron chpt. 1986-89, bd. dirs. Nu Omicron chpt. Early Childhood Learning Ctr. 1984—), Phi Delta Kappa, Sigma Pi Phi, One Hundred Black Men. Address: 395 Stuyvesant Ave Brooklyn NY 11233

DOUGLASS, RAMONA ELIZABETH, medical sales professional; b. N.Y.C., Aug. 15, 1949; d. Howard William and Lena Verona (Belle) D. Student, Colo. Sch. Mines, 1966-68; BS in Physical Sci., Colo. State U., 1970. Adminstrv. asst. S.E. Queens Community Corp., Queens, N.Y., 1970-71; research editor Encyclopedia Britannica, Chgo., 1971-73; sales rep. Scott Foresman Co., Glenview, Ill., 1973-75, Am. Sci. Products, McGaw Park, Ill., 1975-78; mgr. New Eng. territory Hollister, Inc., Libertyville, Ill., 1978-81; mgr. midwest region Precision Dynamics Corp., San Fernando, Calif., 1981-95, mgr. Western region, bar code specialist, 1995—, mng. editor sales and mktg. newsletter, 1998—. Ptnr. Douglass/Sherod-Winter Assocs., Chgo., 1986-88, DMB Group, Internat., 1990-91; mem. Nat. Network Women in Sales, 1986-93, v.p. corp. rels., 1989-90; co-founder Healthy Concepts, Inc., 1993, mktg. v.p., cons., 1998—; apptd. to Fed. 2000 Census Adv. Com., 1995—, mem. Fed. Working Group on Racial and Ethnic Tabulations, 1997—; lectr., spkr. in field; appearances on radio and TV programs, including Oprah Winfrey Show, Jerry Springer Show, Mark Walberg Show, CBS Sunday Morning, Aaron Freeman Show, others. Contbr. poetry Great Am. Poetry Anthology, 1987; subject in The Rainbow Effect: Interracial Families, 1987, Heroes of Conscience: A Biographical Dictionary, 1996; contbg. author: The Multiracial Experience: Racial Borders as the New Frontier, 1995. Founding mem. The Nat. Alliance Against Racist & Polit. Repression, Chgo., 1972; bd. dirs., chair publicity The Biracial Family Network, Chgo., 1987-90, v.p., 1990-92, pres., 1992-93; v.p. pub. rels. Assn. Multi-Ethnic Ams., 1988-90, v.p. midwest region, 1991-94, pres., 1994—. Recipient Pioneer award for outstanding contbn. to multiracial issues U. Calif., Berkeley, 1997, Building Bridges award Racial Harmony award Multiracial Ams. of so. Calif., 1996. Mem. NAFE. Democrat. Avocations: creative writing, music, gourmet cooking, sailing. Office: Precision Dynamics Corp 13880 Del Sur St San Fernando CA 91340-3490

DOUGLASS, ROBERT JOSEPH, JR., computer scientist; b. Moline, Ill., June 8, 1951; s. Robert Joseph and Hattie Jane (Holmes) Douglass; m. Barbara Walker Mahan, June 3, 1973 (div. Aug. 1981); m. Cyndi Louise Wagner, Dec. 1, 1990. BEE magna cum laude, Princeton U., 1973; MS in Computer Scis., U. Wis., 1974, PhD in Computer Scis., 1978. Postdoctoral rschr. dept. physics and astronomy U. London, 1978; asst. prof. computer sci. U. Va., Charlottesville, 1978-81; assoc. group leader for rsch. Los Alamos (N.Mex.) Nat. Lab., 1981-85; machine intelligence unit head Martin Marietta, Denver, 1985, program mgr. Autonomous Land Vehicle, 1987-89, program mgr., 1989, program mgr. Automatic Radar Air-to-Ground Target Acquisition, 1990-93; co-founder, CEO DiamondBack Vision, Washington and Denver, 1998—; asst. dir. info. sys. Def. Adv. Rsch. Projects Agy., U.S. Dept. Def., Arlington, Va., 1995—98; co-founder, chief tech. officer SET Assocs., Inc., 2002—. Mem. panel Computer Architecture Pres.'s Sci. Adv. Nat. Acad. Sci., Washington, 1984. Editor: Characteristic of Parallel Algorithms, 1987; assoc. editor: Jour. Parallel and Distributed Processing, 1984—89; contbr. articles to profl. jours. Mem.: AAAS, IEEE, Assn. Computing Machinery. Achievements include patents for virtual reality interface to human-body, Salt Lake City, 93-95. Avocations: paleontology, alpine skiing, boxing, soccer. Office: 11600 Sunrise Valley Dr Ste 290 Herndon VA 20191-1410

DOUGLASS, ROBERT ROYAL, bank executive, lawyer; b. Binghamton, N.Y., Oct. 16, 1931; s. Robert R. and Frances (Behan) D.; m. Linda Ann Luria, June 2, 1962; children: Robert Royal, Alexandra Brooke, Andrew. BA with distinction, Dartmouth Coll., 1953; LL.B., Cornell U., 1959. Bar: N.Y. Asso. Hinman, Howard & Kattell, 1959-64; 1st asst. counsel to Gov. N.Y. State, Albany, 1964-65, counsel to gov., 1965-70, sec. to gov., 1970—72; partner Milbank, Tweed, Hadley & McCloy, 1972-76; exec. v.p., gen. counsel Chase Manhattan Bank, N.Y.C., 1976-83, exec. v.p., 1983-85, vice chmn., 1985-93; of counsel Milbank Tweed Hadley & McCloy, N.Y.C., 1994—. Dir. Rockefeller Ctr., Inc., 1976-82, Urstadt Biddle Properties, 1990—, Gryphon Holdings, 1993-95, Home Ins. Co., 1993-96; chmn. Cedel Internat., 1994—2002, Alliance for Downtown N.Y., 1995—, Clearstream Internat., 2000—04; chmn. Nelson Rockefeller's Campaign for Rep. Presdl. Nomination, 1968; commr. Port Authority of N.Y. State and N.J., 1972-76; trustee N.Y.C. Pub. Libr., 1972-86; bd. dirs., chmn. exec. com. Downtown-Lower Manhattan Assn., N.Y.C., 1973-91, chmn., 1991—; mem. vis. com. John F. Kennedy Sch. Govt., Harvard U., 1974-79; mem. N.Y. Landmarks Conservancy, 1977-80. Trustee Dartmouth Coll., 1983-93, Mus. of Modern Art, 1989-94. Served with M.C., U.S. Army, 1954-56. Recipient Wallace award Am.-Scottish Found., 1974 Mem. ABA, N.Y. State Bar Assn., Coun. Fgn. Rels. Clubs: Century Assn, Downtown Assn., Round Hill, Seal Harbor, Blind Brook. Roman Catholic. Office: Milbank Tweed Hadley & Mc Cloy 1 Chase Manhattan Plz Fl 47 New York NY 10005-1413

DOUGLASS, SUSAN LYNN, educational consultant, educator; b. East Cleveland, Ohio, Sept. 24, 1950; d. Howard Alfred Douglass and Mary Margaret Edler; m. Usama Al-Muhammady Amer, Feb. 1, 1983; children: Anas Usama Amer, Ayman Usama Amer, Maryam Usama Amer, Sarah Usama Amer. BA in History, U. Rochester, N.Y., 1968—72; MA in Arab Studies, Georgetown U., Washington D.C., 1990—93. Lic. tchr. in History & Social Sci. Commonwealth of Va., 1986. Social studies dept. chair Islamic Saudi Acad., Alexandria, Va., 1985—90; affiliated scholar Coun. on Islamic Edn., Fountain Valley, Calif., 1994—; rsch. team mem. World History for Us All Curriculum Project, San Diego, 2001—; academic coord. Edn. for Life, Annandale, Va., 2002—. Adv. bd. mem. First Liberty Inst., Fairfax, Va., 1990—93; ednl. cons. Amer/Douglass Ednl. Consulting, Falls Church, Va., 1993—; adv. bd. mem. Coun. on American-Islamic Rels., Washington, 1995—98; social studies curriculum adv. com. mem. Fairfax County Pub. Schools, Va., 1998—2002; governor's standards of learning revision task force mem. Va. Dept. Edn., Richmond, 2000—01; editl. bd. mem. Islamic Soc. N.Am.a-Islamic Horizons Mag., Plainfield, Ind. Contbr. reference volume; author: (book) Muslims in Our Community and Around the World, Where in the World Do Muslims Live?, Traders and Explorers in Wooden Ships, Islam and Muslim Civilization, (children's book) Ramadan, (book) Strategies and Structures for Teaching World History, I Am a Muslim: A Modern Storybook, Eid Mubarak! Islamic Celebration Around the World, Cities Then and Now. Academic reviewer Coun. on Islamic Edn., Fountain Valley, Calif., 1994—2004. Recipient Cmty. Svc. Award, Coun. on American-Islamic Rels., 2000. Mem.: First Liberty Inst. (adv. bd. mem. 1989—93), Edn. for Life (bd. dirs. 2002—05), Nat. Coun. for Social Studies, Am. Hist. Assn., World History Assn. (exec. coun. mem. 2002—05). Islam. Avocations: sewing, gardening, woodworking. Office Phone: 703-442-0638. E-mail: sldamer@aol.com.

DOUMANIAN, HERATCH OHANNES, radiologist; b. Beirut, Feb. 11, 1934; s. Ohannes Toros Doumanian and Hripsime Kupelian; m. Sonya L. Dermenjian, Mar. 17, 1967; children: Greta, John, Leo. MD, Am. U. Beirut, Lebanon, 1957. Diplomate Am. Bd. Radiology. Resident in radiology U. Chgo. Hosp., Chgo., 1962-65; fellow in cardiovascular radiology U. Minn. Hosp., Mpls., 1965-66; dir. radiology St. Mary Med. Ctr., Hobart, Ind., 1967-92. Capt. M.C., U.S. Army, 1960-62, Germany. Mem. AMA, Radiol. Soc. N.Am., Am. Coll. Radiology, Innsbrook Country Club. Armenian Orthodox. Home: 6451 Arthur St Merrillville IN 46410-3122 Fax: 219 980-0945.

DOUSE, STEVEN CARL, lawyer; b. Hastings, Mich., Sept. 9, 1948; s. Adolph, Jr. and Rose Marie (Laeder) D.; m. Karen Elizabeth Murray, Aug. 14, 1971; children: Katherine Emily, Christopher Murray. BA, Mich. State U., 1970; JD, U. Mich., 1973. Bar: Mich. 1973, Tenn. 1988, U.S. Dist. Ct. (ea. dist.) Mich. 1974, U.S. Dist. Ct. (mid. dist.) Tenn. 1988, U.S. Ct. Appeals (6th and 7th cirs.) 1995, U.S. Ct. Appeals (11th cir.) 1999, U.S. Supreme Ct. 1980. Law clk. to hon. judge John Feikens U.S. Dist. Ct. (ea. dist.) Mich., Detroit, 1973-74; trial atty., asst. sect. chief Antitrust Div. U.S. Dept. Justice, Washington, 1974-87; ptnr. King & Ballow, Nashville, 1987;, 1988—. Staff atty. Nat. Commn. for the Rev. of Antitrust Laws and Procedures, Washington, 1978-79; adj. prof. Vanderbilt Law Sch., 1996—. Note editor Mich. Jour. of Law Reform, 1972-73. Recipient Lewis Honigman Meml. award U. Mich. Law Sch., 1973. Mem. ABA, Tenn. Bar Assn., Soc. Barristers, Nashville Bar Assn., Fed. Bar Assn. (former pres. Nashville chpt.). Presbyterian. Avocation: running. Home: 5116 Woodland Hills Dr Brentwood TN 37027-5826 Office: King & Ballow 1100 Union St Plz 315 Union St Nashville TN 37201-1401 E-mail: sdouse@king-ballow.com.

DOUT, ANNE JACQUELINE, manufacturing and sales company executive; b. Detroit, Mar. 13, 1955; d. George Edwin and Virginia Irene Boesinger; m. James Edward Dout, July 16, 1977; 1 child, Brian Ross. Student, Macomb C.C., 1972-74; BBA, Western Mich. U., 1976; MBA, Duquesne U., 1982. Cert. cash mgr. Internal auditor Koppers Co. Inc., Pitts., 1976-78, cash analyst, 1978-79, supr. cash ops., 1979-80, mgr. cash ops., 1980-81, mgr. cash ops., asst. treas., 1981-87, dir. treasury svcs., asst. treas., 1987-88; corp. staff v.p., asst. treas. IMCERA Group Inc., Northbrook, Ill., 1988-91; v.p., treas. IMCERA Group, Inc., Northbrook, Ill., 1991-94; exec. v.p., CFO Champion Enterprises, Inc., Auburn Hills, Mich., 1994-98; pres. JJB Enterprises, Inc., Rochester Hills, Mich., 1998—2001; sr. v.p., CFO Pella (Iowa) Corp., 2002—. Bd. dirs. Cavco Industries Inc. Mem. allocations com. United Way, Pitts., 1979-83; bd. dirs. N.E. Lake County Coun. Boy Scouts Am., v.p. adminstrn., 1989-92; bd. dirs. Barat Coll., Lake Forest; Ill., 1992-94, U. Mich. Cancer Found.; bd. visitors Sch. Bus., Oakland U., 1994-2004; devel. com. Mich. Womens Fund, 1996-2000. Mem. Treas. Mgmt. Assn. (exec. com. 1988-90, govt. rels. com. 1984-86, bd. dirs. 1986-89, strategic plan com. 1987-90), Gov. Coun. Edu, Fin. Exec. Inst., Mid Am. Com., Econ. Club, Exec. Club, Womens Econ. Club. Protestant. Office: Pella Corp 102 Main St Pella IA 50219

DOUTY, LUCY EVELYN, sales and marketing executive; b. Boston, Sept. 22, 1951; d. Michael H. and Irma O. (Fusco) Gionfriddo; m. George E. Douty Jr., May 20, 1972. AS in Bus. Adminstrn., Northeastern U., 1988; postgrad., Simmons Coll., 1991-93. Mktg. mgr. Dynamics Rsch. Corp., Wilmington, Mass., 1974-85; natl. sales mgr. U.S. Law News, San Juan, Calif., 1986; client svcs. mgr. Price Waterhouse, Waltham, Mass., 1987-91; dir. mktg. Macdonald, Levin, Jenkin & Co., 1991-93. Total quality mgmt. seminar developer, presenter. Author: CNC Operating Manual, 1984, Sales Training Manual, 1986. Mem. vol. staff Nat. Multiple Sclerosis Soc. Mem. Boat U.S. Club. Roman Catholic. Avocations: sailing, skiing, reading, travel, golf.

DOUTY, ROBERT WATSON, minister, educator; b. Phila., June 20, 1943; m. MarshaLee Wood, Apr. 22, 1972. BA in Psychology, Calif. State U., Long Beach, 1969; MS in Edn., U. Bridgeport, 1974; MDiv, Alliance Theol. Sem., Nyack, N.Y., 1993. Ordained to ministry Am. Bapt. Chs., 1990; teaching cert., N.Y. Tchr. Garrison (N.Y.) Sch., 1980—2003; chmn. bd. deacons 1st Bapt. Ch., Ossining, N.Y., 1980-82, dir. Christian edn., 1985-91, assoc. pastor, 1990-96; dir. Christian edn. St. Philip's Episc. Ch., Garrison, N.Y., 1996-98; pastor Cold Spring (N.Y.) Bapt. Ch., 1998—. Deacon 1st Bapt. Ch., 1973-82, chmn. missions, 1990-95; chaplain Phelps Hosp., Tarrytown, N.Y., 1988—. Author: Star City: A Classroom Management System, 1989; author: (with others) In the Footsteps of Birdy Edwards, 1980; contbr. articles to mags. Victory 94 team leader to elect Gov. George Pataki, 1994. With U.S. Navy, 1962-65. Mem. Baker St. Irregulars (The Priory Sch.). Home: 138 Lindsey Ave Buchanan NY 10511-1610

DOVAN, CAROL See VAN SCHENKHOF, CAROL

DOVE, DONALD AUGUSTINE, city planner, educator; b. Waco, Tex., Aug. 7, 1930; s. Sebert Constantine and Amy Delmena (Stern) Dove; m. Cecelia Mae White, Feb. 9, 1957; children: Angela, Donald, Monica Gilstrap, Celine, Cathlyn, Dianna, Jennifer. BA, Calif. State U. L.A., 1951; MA in Pub. Adminstrn., U. So. Calif., 1966. Planning & devel. cons. D. Dove Assocs., L.A., 1959—60; supr. demographic rsch. Calif. Dept. Pub. Works, L.A., 1960—66; dir. transp. employment project State of Calif., L.A., 1966—71, chief L.A. Region transp. study, 1975—84; chief environ. planning Calif. Dept. Transp., L.A., 1972—75; dir. U. So. Calif., L.A., 1984—87; panelist, advisor Pres. Conf. Aging, Washington, 1970—; environ. coord. Calif. Dept. Pub. Works, Sacramento, 1971—75; panelist, advisor Internat. Conf. Energy Use Mgmt., 1981; ret., 1993. Guest lectr. univs. We. U.S., 1969—. Author: Preserving Urban Environment, 1976, Small Area Population Forecasts, 1966. Chmn. Lynwood City Planning Commn., Calif., 1982—2004; pres. Area Pastoral Coun., L.A., 1982—83; mem., del. Archdiocesan Pastoral Coun., L.A., 1979—86, Compton Cmty. Devel. Bd., Calif., 1967—71; pres. Neighborhood Esteem/Enrichment Techniques Inst., 1992—93. With U.S. Army, 1952—54. Mem.: Assn. Environ. Profls. (co-founder 1973), Am. Inst. Cert. Planners, Calif. Assn. Mgmt. (pres. 1987—88), Am. Inst. Planners (transp. chmn. 1972—73), Am. Planning Assn., Optimists Club (sec. 1978—79). Democrat. Roman Catholic. Home and Office: 11356 Ernestine Ave Lynwood CA 90262-3711 Business E-Mail: dondve@aol.com.

DOVE, G. MACK, transportation executive, director; s. John H. D.; m. Nancy; 1 child, Reid. Degree in Transportation, U. Tenn., 1958; completed the advanced studies program, Harvard U. Joined family bus. AAA Motor Lines, Inc., Ala., 1959—70; pres. Cooper Transfer Comp. (merged with AAA Motor Lines, Inc. in 1973, to become AAA Cooper), Brewton, Ala., 1970—89; pres., CEO AAA Cooper Transportation, Dothan, Ala., 1989—2002, chmn., CEO, 2002—. Bd. dir. Bus. Coun., Ala., Econ. Develop. Partnership, Ala. Civilian Aide to the Sec. of the Army (CASA), Ala., 2004—; mem. U. Tenn. Develop Coun., Chief Execs. Orgn., World President's Orgn., Ala. Heritage Trust Fund; bd. dir. Ala. Sports Hall of Fame; chmn. Governor's Commn. on Existing Industry; former mem. U. Tenn. Dean's Advisory Coun., Coll. Bus. Named to Ala. Bus. Hall of Fame, Culverhouse Coll. Commerce and Bus. Adminstrn., U. Ala., 2002; recipient Disting. Alumni award, U. Tenn., 1982; Paul Harris Fellow, Rotary Found. of Rotary Internat. Mem.: Am. Trucking Assn. (past chmn., mem. exec. com., bd. dir., chmn. litig. ctr., mem. policy and fin. com.), 1985—. Office: AAA Cooper Transportation 1751 Kinsey Rd P O Box 6827 Dothan AL 36303 Office Phone: 334-793-2284. Office Fax: 334-671-1507.

DOVE, RITA FRANCES, poet, language educator; b. Akron, Ohio, Aug. 28, 1952; d. Ray A. and Elvira E. (Hord) Dove; m. Fred Viebahn, Mar. 23, 1979; 1 child, Aviva Chantal Tamu Dove-Viebahn. BA summa cum laude, Miami U., Oxford, Ohio, 1973; postgrad., Universität Tübingen, Fed. Republic Germany, 1974-75; MFA, U. Iowa, 1977; LLD (hon.), Miami U., Oxford, Ohio, 1988, Knox Coll., 1989, Tuskegee U., 1994, U. Miami, Fla., 1994, Washington U., St. Louis, 1994, Case Western Res. U., 1994, U. Akron, 1994, Ariz. State U., 1995, Boston Coll., 1995, Dartmouth Coll., 1995, Spelman Coll., 1996, U. Pa., 1996, U. N.C., 1997, U. Notre Dame, 1997, Northeastern U., 1997, Columbia U., 1998, Washington & Lee U., 1999, SUNY, Brockport, 1999; LLD, Pratt Inst., 2001, Howard U., 2001; LLD (hon.), Skidmore Coll., 2004. Asst. prof. English Ariz. State U., Tempe, 1981-84, assoc. prof., 1984-87, prof., 1987-89, U. Va., Charlottesville, 1989-93, Commonwealth prof. English, 1993—; U.S. poet laureate, cons. in poetry Libr. of Congress, Washington, 1993-95, spl. cons. in poetry, 1999-2000; columnist Washington Post, 2000—02; poet laureate Va., 2004—. Writer-in-residence Tuskegee (Ala.) Inst., 1982; lit. panelist Nat. Endowment for Arts, Washington, 1984-86, chmn. poetry grants panel, 1985; judge Walt Whitman award Acad. Am. Poets, 1990, Pulitzer prize in poetry, 1991, Ruth Lilly prize 1991, Nat. Book award in poetry 1991, 98, Anisfield-Wolf Book awards, 1992—, Shelley Meml. award, 1997, Amy Lowell fellowship, 1997; poetry panel chmn. Pulitzer prize, 1997; final judge Brittingham and Pollack prizes, 1997; juror Christopher Columbus Fellowship Found., 1998-2002, Duke Ellington awards, 1999; bd. dirs. Poetry Daily, 2002. Author: (poetry) Ten Poems, 1977, The Only Dark Spot in the Sky, 1980, The Yellow House on the Corner, 1980, Mandolin, 1982, Museum, 1983, Thomas and Beulah, 1986 (Pulitzer Prize in poetry 1987), The Other Side of the House, 1988, Grace Notes, 1989 (Ohioana award 1990), Selected Poems, 1993 (Ohioana award 1994), Lady Freedom Among Us, 1994, Mother Love, 1995, Evening Primrose, 1998, On the Bus with Rosa Parks, 1999 (Ohioana award 2000), American Smooth, 2004; (verse drama) The Darker Face of the Earth, 1994 (W. Alton Jones Found. grant 1994, Kennedy Ctr. Fund for New Am. Plays award 1995, Geraldine Dodge Found. grant, 1997), completely rev. 2d edit., 1996, expanded 3d edit., 2000 (first performance Oreg. Shakespeare Festival 1996); (novel) Through the Ivory Gate, 1992 (Va. Coll. Stores Book award 1993); (short stories) Fifth Sunday, 1985 (Callaloo award 1986); (essays) The Poet's World, 1995, (song cycle) Seven for Luck (music by John Williams), 1st performance Boston Symphony Orch., Tanglewood, 1998; mem. editl. bd. Nat. Forum, 1984-89, Iris, 1989—; mem. adv. bd. Ploughshares, 1992—, N.C. Writers Network, 1992-99, Civilization, 1994-97; assoc. editor Callaloo, 1986-98; adv. and contbg. editor Gettysburg Rev., 1987—, TriQuarterly, 1988—, Ga. Review, 1994—, Bellingham Rev., 1996—, Internat. Quarterly, 1997—, Callaloo, 1998—, Mid-Am. Rev., 1998—; editor Best Am. Poetry, 2000. Commr. The Schomburg Ctr. for Rsch. in Black Culture, N.Y. Pub. Libr., 1987—; mem. Renaissance Forum Folger Shakespeare Libr., 1993-95, Coun. of Scholars Libr. of Congress, 1994—; mem. nat. launch com. AmeriCorps, 1994; mem. awards coun. Am. Acad. Achievement, 1994-2001; mem. adv. bd. Thomas Jefferson Ctr. Freedom of Expression, 1994—, U.S. Civil War Ctr., 1995-99, Va. Ctr. Creative Arts, 1995—, Student Achievement and Advocacy Svcs., 2002—; The Poets Corner elector Cathedral Ch. St. John the Divine, N.Y.C., 1991-2002; bd. govs. Humanities Rsch. Inst. U. Calif., 1996-99; bd. dirs. Poetry Daily, 2004—. Presdl. scholar, 1970, Nat. Achievement scholar, 1970-73; Fulbright/Hays fellow, 1974-75, rsch. fellow U. Iowa, 1975, teaching/writing fellow U. Iowa, 1976-77, Guggenheim Found. fellow, 1983-84, Mellon sr. fellow Nat. Humanities Ctr., 1988-89, fellow Ctr. for Advanced Studies, U. Va., 1989-92, fellow Shannon Ctr. for Advanced Studies, U. Va., 1995—; grantee NEA, 1977, 89; recipient Lavan Younger Poet award Acad. Am. Poets, 1986, GE Found. award, 1987, Bellagio (Italy) residency Rockefeller Found., 1988, Ohio Gov.'s award 1988, Literary Lion citation N.Y. Pub. Libr., 1991, Women of Yr. award Glamour Mag., 1993, NAACP Great Am. Artist award, 1993, Golden Plate award Am. Acad. Achievement, 1994, Disting. Achievement medal Miami U. Alumni Assn., 1994, Renaissance Forum award for leadership in the literary arts Folger Shakespeare Libr., 1994, Carl Sandburg award Internat. Platform Assn., 1994, Heinz award in arts and humanities, 1996, Charles Frankel prize/Nat. Humanities medal Pres. of U.S. and NEH, 1996; inducted Ohio Women's Hall of Fame, 1991, Nat. Assn. of Women in Edn. Disting. Woman award, 1997, Sara Lee Frontrunner award, 1997, Barnes & Noble Writers for Writers award, 1997, Levinson prize Poetry mag., 1998, John Frederick Nims Translation prize, 1999, Libr. Lion award N.Y. Pub. Libr., 2000, Duke Ellington Lifetime Achievement award, 2001, Emily Couric Women's Leadership award, 2003; named Phi Beta Kappa poet Harvard U., 1993, Poet Laureate of Commonwealth of Va., 2004-2006. Mem. PEN, ASCAP, Am. Philos. Soc., Poetry Soc. Am., Associated Writing Programs (bd. dirs. 1985-88, pres. 1986-87), Am. Acad. Achievement (mem. golden plate awards coun. 1994—2001), Phi Beta Kappa (senator 1994-2001), Phi Kappa Phi. Office: U Va Dept English 219 Bryan Hall PO Box 400121 Charlottesville VA 22904-4121 Business E-Mail: rfd4b@virginia.edu.

DOVER, SIR KENNETH JAMES, retired Greek scholar; b. Croydon, Eng., Mar. 11, 1920; s. Percy Henry and Dorothy Valerie (Healey) D.; student Balliol Coll., Oxford (Eng.) U., 1938-40, 45-47, MA, 1946, DLitt, 1974, student Merton Coll., 1948, hon. fellow; LLD, Birmingham U., St. Andrews U.; DLitt, U. Bristol, U. Liverpool, U. London, St. Andrews U., U. Durham; DHL, Oglethorpe U.; m. Audrey Ruth Latimer, Mar. 17, 1947; children: Alan Hugh, Catherine Ruth. Fellow, tutor Balliol Coll., Oxford (Eng.) U., 1948-55, hon. fellow, pres. Corpus Christi Coll., 1976-86, hon. fellow; prof. of Greek, St. Andrews U., 1955-76; chancellor St. Andrews U., 1981—; prof.-at-large Cornell U., 1983-89; vis. lectr. Harvard U., 1960; Sather vis. prof. U. Calif., 1967; prof. Stanford U., winter quarter, 1987-92. Served with artillery Brit. Army, 1940-45; mentioned in dispatches. Created Knight, 1977. Fellow Brit. Acad. (pres., 1978-81, Kenyon medal 1993); mem. Hellenic Soc. (pres., 1971-74), Classical Assn. (pres., 1975), Am. Acad. Arts and Scis., Netherlands Acad. Arts and Scis. Author: Greek Word Order, 1960; Lysias and the Corpus Lysiacum, 1968; Aristophanic Comedy, 1972; Greek Popular Morality in the Time of Plato and Aristotle, 1974; Greek Homosexuality, 1978; The Greeks, 1980; Greek and the Greeks (Collected Papers I), 1987; The Greeks and Their Legacy (Collected Papers II), 1988, Marginal Comment (memoirs), 1994, The Evolution of Greek Prose Style, 1997; contbr. to other books and articles; editor: Aristophanes' Clouds, 1968; Theocritus, 1971; Plato, Symposium, 1980, Perceptions of the Ancient Greeks, 1992, Aristophanes' Frogs, 1993. Home: 49 Hepburn Gardens Saint Andrews KY16 9LS Scotland

DOVIAK, INGRID ELLINGER, elementary school educator; b. New Britain, Conn., Feb. 10, 1971; d. John Leonard and Marjorie Chain Ellinger; m. Stephen Michael Doviak, June 8, 1996. BS, MA, So. Conn. State U., 1993. Tchr. head dept. enrichment grades k-8 Wntergreen Interdist. Magnet Sch., Hamden, Conn., 1998—. Adj. instr. deptl edn. Sacred Heart U., Fairfield, Conn., 2000—; adj. instr. So. Conn. State U., New Haven, 1998—; presenter Atomic Math Conf., 2001, 02, Conn. Assn. Math. Precocious Youth, 2000, 01, 02, Conn. Assn. Schs.

DOVRING, KARIN ELSA INGEBORG, writer, poet, playwright, media specialist; b. Stenstorp, Sweden, Dec. 5, 1919; arrived in US, 1953, naturalized, 1968; m. Folke Dovring, May 30, 1943. Grad., Coll. Commerce, Gothenburg, Sweden, 1936; MA, Lund (Sweden) U., 1943, PhD, 1951; Phil. Licentiate, Gothenburg U., 1947. Journalist several Swedish daily newspapers and weekly mags., 1940-60; tchr. Swedish colls.; rsch. assoc. of Harold Lasswell Yale U., New Haven, 1953-78; fgn. corr. Swedish newspapers, Italy, Switzerland, France and Germany, 1956-60; freelance writer, journalist, 1960—; rsch. prof. comms. and media studies U. Ill., Urbana, 2002. Vis. prof. Internat. U., The Vatican, Rome, 1958-60, Gottingen (W.Ger.) U., 1962; lectr. U.S. Army, Peace Corps, Yale U., U. Wis., McGill U., U. Iowa; rsch. assoc. U. Ill., Urbana, 1968-69, guest lectr., 2001-04; invited contbr. Social Sci. Rsch. Coun., 1988; speaker Conf. Law and Policy, Yale U. Law Sch., 1992-93, 99—; hon. mem. Profl. Women's Adv. Bd. Am. Biograph. Inst., Raleigh, NC, 2003; adv. coun. Internat. Biographical Ctr., Cambridge, Eng.; interviewee radio and TV programs; writer Ill. Alliance to Prevent Nuclear War, radio, theater; prof. comm. and media studies U. Ill. Coll. Comm., 2002—; moderator series U.S.A. Faces the World-Markets in Communications, 2004—; songwriter Hollywood and Nashville; plays for TV movies. Author: Songs of Zion, 1951, Land Reform as a Propaganda Theme, 3d edit., 1965, Road of Propaganda, 1959, Optional Society, 1972, Frontiers of Communication, 1975, English as Lingua Franca: Double Talk in Global Persuasion, 1997, (short stories) No Parking This Side of Heaven, 1982, Harold D. Lasswell: His Communication with a Future, 1987, 2d edit., 1988; (novel) Heart in Escrow, 1990; (poems) Faces in a Mirror, 1995, Changing Scenery, 2003, In the Service of Persuasion: English as Lingua Franca Across the Globe, 2001, Propaganda Is the Poetry of Politics, 2002, Propagandists: The Artists, 2004; contbr. chpts. to books, articles to mags.; author numerous poems. Named Poet of Yr., Internat. Libr. Poetry, 2000, 2001, 2002, 2003; named to, Internat. Poetry Hall of Fame, 1996; recipient Swedish Nat. award for short stories, Bonniers Pub. Ho., Stockholm, 1951. Mem. Soc. Jean Jacques Rousseau of Geneva (hon. life), Acad. Am. Poets. Democrat. Address: 613 W Vermont Ave Urbana IL 61801-4824

DOW, BRIAN CHRISTOPHER, geologist, educator; b. Westlake Village, Calif., Jan. 31, 1978; s. Richard Burnell and Carol Jean Dow; m. Jackie Margaret Birdsell, Aug. 27, 2005. BS in Geol. Sci., U. Calif., Santa Barbara, 2001. Geologist Douglas P. Imperato, Consulting Geologist, Santa Barbara, Calif., 2001—03, PW Environ., Santa Paula, 2003—04, Tetra Tech, Inc., Santa Barbara, 2004—. Educator geology Cmty. Environ. Coun., South Coast Watershed Resource Ctr., Santa Barbara, 2003—. Mem.: Assn. Engring. Geologists, Am. Assn. Petroleum Geologists. Office: Tetra Tech Inc 4213 State St Ste 100 Santa Barbara CA 93110 Office Phone: 805-681-3100. E-mail: brian.dow@tetratech.com.

DOW, DAVID SONTAG, retired ophthalmologist; b. Ann Arbor, Mich., Feb. 15, 1934; s. William Gould and Edna Lois (Sontag) D.; m. Gail Anita Bade, Feb. 11, 1961 (dec. Feb. 2000); children: Steven Michael, Bonnie Jean, William Herbert, James Patrick; m. Figes Flaherty, March, 17, 2001. BS with distinction, U. Mich., 1956, MD, 1958, MS in Ophthalmology, 1964. Diplomate Am. Bd. Ophthalmology. Intern Denver Gen. Comm. Hosp., 1958-59; psychiatrist USAF Med. Svc., Wichita Falls, Tex., 1959-61; resident in ophthalmology U. Mich. Med. Ctr., Ann Arbor, 1961-64; pvt. practice ophthalmology Scruggs, Dow, and Kannwischer ptnr., Waco, Tex., 1964-88, Cen. Tex. Eye Clinic, Waco, 1988-97; ret., 1997. Contbg. editor Waco Tribune Herald, 1983—; author pamphlets in field. City coun. mem., mayor Waco City Con., 1977—81; mem. Woodway City Coun., 1997—2001; bd. dir. Waco Symphony Assn., 1970—89, 1994—2001, pres., 1982—83; bd. dir. Tex. Med. Polit. Action Com., Austin, 1973—82; founding bd. dirs., chmn. Greater Waco Arts Coun., 1986—, chmn., 1992, 1994—2000. Capt. USAF, 1959—61. Mem. Am. Acad. Ophthalmology, Tex. Med. Assn., Ridgewood Country Club, Rotary. Episcopalian. Avocations: politics, musical theater, yard/garden construction, singing. Home: 400 Ivy Ann Ct Waco TX 76712-3629

DOW, ELIAS CHARLES, endocrinologist; b. Boston, Nov. 11, 1927; s. Charles A. Dow and Mary Shebaby; m. Jody Deroma Dow, June 15, 1957; children: Edward, Charles, Andrea. BA, Harvard Coll., 1948; MD, Tufts Med., 1953. Faculty Harvard Coll., Cambridge, Mass., Nat. Lancers, Framingham, Mass.; exec. coun. Tufts Med., Boston, 1979—. Trustee Boston (Mass.) Latin Sch.; bd. mem. NE Bapt. Hosp. Contbr. articles to various profl. jours. With U.S. Army, 1946—47, Pacific. Avocations: skiing, sailing, gardening, horseback riding. Office: 1101 Beacon St Brookline MA 02446

DOW, GARNETT MCCORMICK, geologist, consultant; b. Biddeford, Maine, Aug. 5, 1934; s. Derry Walter Fogg and Charlotte Adelade (Cousens) D.; m. Sigrid Irene Dow, May 26, 1972; children: Michael Eric, Tod McCormick, Erin Renee. BA, U. Maine, 1959; MS, U. Ill., 1962, PhD, 1965. Geophysicist, geologist Amoco, Oklahoma City, 1964-67; sr. rsch. scientist Amoco Rsch. Ctr., Tulsa, 1967-73; geol. supr. Amoco Internat., Chgo., 1973-76; regional chief geologist Amoco Europe, London, 1976-80; exploration mgr. Amoco Indonesia, Jakarta, 1980-83; sr. geol. assoc. Amoco, Houston, 1983-92; exploration cons. Noble Energy, Inc., Houston, 1995—2004, geol. advisor, 2004—. Cons. in field. Sustaining mem. Repu. Nat. Com., 1990's. With U.S. Army, 1954-56. Mem. Am. Assn. Petroleum Geologists, Am. Geophys. Union, Assn. Internat. Petroleum Negotiators, Houston Geol. Soc., Planetary Soc. Avocations: sailing, photography, amateur astronomy. Office Phone: 281-876-6500.

DOW, JOSEPH SHEFFIELD, lawyer; b. Boston, Mar. 18, 1925; s. John Abraham Dow and Yamna Maloof; children: Rachel Mary Dow-Tehrani, Sarah Yameen. AB cum laude, Bates Coll., Lewiston, ME, 1948; LLB, JD, Harvard, Cambridge, Mass., 1951. Bar: Mass. 1951, U.S. Dist. Ct. 1954. Pvt. practice, Boston & Brookline, Mass., 1951—. Contbr. articles to profl. jours. O1erseer of pub. welfare, Boston, 1960-70; 1st Lt. U.S. Army., Korea. Mem. VFW, DAV, Nicholas G. Beram Vets. Orgn., Brookline Town Meeting, Brookline Arts Coun.,Harvard Club, Boston Host Lions Club. Harvard Club, Boston Host Lions Club. Home and Office: 92 Newton St Brookline MA 02445-7407

DOW, LOIS WEYMAN, physician; b. Cin., Mar. 11, 1942; d. Albert Dames and Elsie Marion (Krug) Weyman; m. Alan Wayne Dow, July 23, 1966 (div. Aug. 1979); children: Elizabeth Suzanne, Alan Wayne. BA summa cum laude, Cornell U., 1964; MD cum laude, Harvard U., 1968. Diplomate Am. Bd. Internal Medicine, Am. Bd. Hematology, Am. Bd. Oncology, Am. Bd. Pathology in Hematopathology. Intern Bronx Mcpl. Hosp. Ctr., N.Y.C., 1968-69; resident in internal medicine Presbyn. Hosp., N.Y.C., 1969-70; fellow in hematology Columbia U. Coll. Physicians and Surgeons, 1970—72; instr., research assoc. U. Tenn., Memphis, 1972-73, asst. prof., 1973-74; research assoc. in hematology and oncology St. Jude Children's Research Hosp., Memphis, 1974-77, asst. mem., 1977-80, assoc. mem., 1980-88; assoc. prof. pediatrics U. Tenn., Memphis, 1983-88; mem. staff St. Jude Children's Research Hosp., Bapt. Mem. Hosp., 1972-88, Med. Ctr. Del., Newark, 1988-98; pvt. practice Newark, 1988-98; dir. hematology lab. Med. Ctr., Wilmington, Del., 1993-98; mem. staff Alfred I Dupont Inst., 1988—, St. Francis Hosp., 1996-98. Assoc. prof., Jefferson Med. Coll., Phila., 1988—; cons., Nat. Cancer Inst. Contbr. articles to profl. jours. Fellow ACP; mem. Am. Soc. Clin. Oncology, Am. Fedn. Clin. Rsch., Am. Soc. Hematology, Am. Assn. for Cancer Rsch., Am. Soc. Clin. Pathologists, Cornell Club, Harvard Club. Office: 3917 Heather Dr Wilmington DE 19807-2117

DOW, MARTHA ANNE, academic administrator, biology professor; b. Little Rock, Jan. 3, 1939; d. Clarence Edgar and Gretchen Devron (Gable) Eudy; m. Gary Eugene Dow, Aug. 28, 1960; children: Julie, Kevin, Jerilyn. BS in Biology, No. Mont. Coll., 1961; MS in Microbiology, Mont. State U., 1969; PhD in Microbiology, U. Hawaii, 1989. Registered microbiologist. Prof., chair biology No. Mont. Coll., Havre, 1986-90, v.p. acad. affairs, 1990-92; provost Oreg. Inst. Tech., Klamath Falls, Oreg., 1992—98, pres., 1998—. Dir. Mont. Environ. Tng. Ctr., EPA, No. Mont. Coll., 1989; pres. Nat. Environ. Tng. Assn., Phoenix, Oreg., 1990-92. Recipient Disting. Svc. award, Klamath County C. of C., 2000, Candice Richard award, Klamath County Econ. Develop. Corp., 2000. Mem. Am. Assn. for Advancement of Sci., Am. Assn. State Coll. & Univ., Am. Soc. for Engring. Edn., Am. Soc. Microbiology, Am. Water Works Assn., Water Environment Fedn. Methodist. Office: Oreg Inst Tech 3201 Campus Dr Klamath Falls OR 97601-8801*

DOW, PETER ANTHONY, advertising agency executive; b. Detroit, Oct. 7, 1933; s. Douglas and Mary Louise (Murray) D.; m. Jane Ann Ottaway, Mar. 21, 1959; children— Jennifer Dow Murphy, Peter Kinnersley, Thomas Anthony BA, U. Mich., 1955. Account exec. Campbell-Ewald Co., Detroit, 1958-66, exec. v.p., 1979-82, pres., 1982-93, vice chmn., 1993-95, ret., 1995; account supr. Young & Rubicam, Detroit, 1966-68; advt. dir. Chrysler Corp., Detroit, 1968-77, dir. mktg., 1977-79. Bd. dirs. Techno Brands, Inc., Masco Corp. Trustee emeritus Lawrenceville Sch., N.J. Served to lt. (j.g.) USNR, 1955-58. Mem. Mich. Advt. Industry Alliance (past pres.), Grosse Pointe Club, Detroit Athletic Club, Adcraft Club (past pres.), Country Club Detroit, Old Club. Republican. Presbyterian.

DOW, RONALD F., librarian; b. Deadwood, S.D., Jan. 26, 1949; s. Fay Ellsworth and Aldeen Faye (Decker) D.; m. Susan White, Apr. 24, 1982; children: Wesley E., Eleanor W. BA, Augustana Col., 1971; MLS, Syracuse U., 1972; PhD, Penn. State U., 1997. Asst. reference librarian Hamilton Col., Clinton, N.Y., 1972-76; asst. bus. and engring. librarian Dartmouth Col., Hanover, N.H., 1976-80; dir. grad. bus. adminstrn. libr. N.Y.U., 1980-83; first v.p. & dir. libraries Shearson Lehman Am. Express, N.Y.C., 1983-90; assoc. dean of libraries Penn. State U., U. Park, 1990-96; dean River Campus Libararies U. Rochester (N.Y.), 1996—. Mem. editl. bd. U. Rochester Press; contbr. articles to profl. jours. Mem. ALA, Am. Assn. Higher Edn. Office: U Rochester Rush Rhees Library Rochester NY 14627

DOW, SIMON, artistic director, choreographer; b. Australia; Diploma, Australian Ballet Sch. Joined Australian Ballet, Stuttgart (Germany) Ballet; joined, prin. dancer Wash. Ballet, 1979; prin. dancer Australian Ballet, 1982-85, San Francisco Ballet, 1985-88, Boston Ballet, 1988-90; freelance guest artist and master tchr., 1990; assoc. artistic dir. Wash. Ballet, 1992-93, 96-97; art dir. Milw. Ballet Co., 1999—2002; artistic dir. West Australian Ballet, Perth, Australia, 2003—. Master tchr. Australian Ballet, Australian Ballet Sch., Sydney Dance Co., NSW Coll. Dance, Am. Ballet Theatre, Boston Ballet, Met. Opera Ballet, Feld Ballet, Milw. Ballet, Internat. Tanz Wochen, Vienna, Austria, Frankfurt Ballet, Germany, Les Grands Ballet Cans.; tchr. Wash. Sch. Ballet, David Howard Sch. Dance, NY; jury mem. 4th Internat. Ballet Competition, Helsinki; bd. dirs. Ausdance WA; apptd. to dance bd. Australia Coun., 2004—; choreographer Milw. BAllet, West Australia Ballet, Theaterhaus, Stuttgart, Joyce Soho, N.Y.C., Steps Beyond, N.Y.C., St. Mark's Ch., N.Y.C., NY Festival Ballet, Florentine Opera, Milw., Jackson Internat. Ballet Competition. Guest appearances include Mann Performing Arts Ctr., Phila., Spoleto Festival, Wolf Trap Farm park, Jacob's Pillow Dance Festival, Pendleton Music Festival, Detroit Symphony; choreographer (ballets) Wash. Ballet, N.Y. Festival Ballet, Boston Ballet, Theater Artaud, San Francisco, Cin. Dance Pl., Theaterhaus, Stuttgart, Germany, St. Mark's Ch., N.Y.C., The Joyce Soho. Recipient Cecchetti Jr. medal, Best Ptnr. award, Internat. Ballet Competition, 1981. Office: West Australian Ballet PO Box 7228 Cloisters Sq Perth 6850 Australia Office Phone: 08-9481-0407.

DOW, STEVEN BENJAMIN, social studies educator; b. Washington, 1951; s. Thomas W and Priscilla M. Dow; m. Linda Lee Dow; children: T. Adam, Eric. BA, Bowling Green State U., 1973; JD, Ohio State U., 1978; MA, U. Mich., 1989, PhD, 1999. Bar: Ohio 1979. Counsel DeSelm, DeSelm, and Baker, Cambridge, Ohio, 1979; lectr. sch. bus. Mich. State U., East Lansing, 1979—80, asst. prof. sch. bus., 1980—85, assoc. prof. sch. bus., 1985—98, assoc. prof. sch. criminal justice, 1998—. Vis. assoc. prof. bus. sch. U. Mich., Ann Arbor, 1996—97, vis. prof. polit. sci. dept., 2000—04. Editor: (jour.) Am. Bus. Law, 1989—90; contbr. articles to profl. journals. Mem.: Am. Sociol. Assn., Midwest Polit. Sci. Assn., Tri State Acad. Legal Studies in Bus., Acad. Legal Studies in Bus., Am. Soc. Criminology, Acad. Criminal Justice Sci., Am. Polit. Sci. Assn., Law and Soc. Assn., Phi Kappa Phi. Avocations: music, bicycling, cooking. Office: Mich State Univ Sch Criminal Justice 534 Baker Hall East Lansing MI 48824

DOW, WILLIAM H., healthcare educator; PhD, Yale U., New Haven, Conn., 1991—95. Assoc. prof., health econs. U. Calif., Berkeley, 2004—.

DOWBEN, ROBERT MORRIS, physiologist, researcher; b. Phila., Apr. 18, 1927; m. Carla Lurie, June 20, 1950; children: Peter Arnold, Jonathan Stuart, Susan Laurie. AB, Haverford Coll., 1946; MS, U. Chgo., 1947, MD, 1949. Intern U. Chgo. Clinics, 1949-50; rsch. fellow U. Oslo, 1950-51; fellow Johns Hopkins Hosp., 1951-52; resident in medicine U. Pa. Hosp., 1952-53; instr. medicine U. Pa. and dir. radioisotope unit VA Hosp., Phila., 1953-55; asst. prof. medicine Northwestern U. Med. Sch., 1957-62; asso. prof. biology MIT, 1962-68; lectr. medicine Harvard U. Med. Sch., 1962-68; prof. med. sci. Brown U., 1968-72; prof. biochemistry U. Bergen, Norway, 1972; prof. physiology and neurology, dir. grad. program in biophysics U. Tex. Health Sci. Ctr., Dallas, 1972-88, prof. neurology, 1988-93; dir. Med. Cell Biology Lab. Baylor Rsch. Inst., Dallas, 1987-93; prof. physiology Brown U., Providence, 1993—. Cons. neurologist Children's Hosp., Dallas, Scottish Rite Hosp., Dallas, Presbyn. Hosp., Dallas, Baylor Hosp, Dallas, 1972-93; mem. corp. Haverford (Pa.) Coll., 1979-2001, Marine Biol. Lab., Woods Hole, Mass., 1964-79; trustee Mt. Desert Island Biol. Lab., 1994-98; adv. com. to the pres., Haverford Coll., 1997-2001; bd. dirs. Greenhill Sch., Dallas, 1974-77. Author: Biological Membranes, 1969, General Physiology, 1971, Cell Biology, 1972, also numerous articles; editor: Cell and Muscle Motility. Served to capt. M.C. USAF, 1955-57. Lalor fellow; recipient Disting. Svc. award Assn. Neuromusclar Diseases, 1964, Disting. Svc. award Alumni Assn. U. Chgo., 1980. Mem. Am. Physiol. Soc., Am. Soc. Biol. Chemists, Am. Chem. Soc., Soc. Exptl. Biology and Medicine, Biophys. Soc., Soc. Clin. Investigation, Ctrl. Soc. Clin. Rsch., Mass. Med. Soc., So. Med. Soc., Dallas County Med. Soc., Tex. Med. Assn., Biochem. Soc. London, Faraday Soc. (London), Phi Beta Kappa, Sigma Xi. Mem. Soc. Of Friends. Office: Brown U Physiology Dept PO Box G-B3 Providence RI 02912-9107

DOWD, CAROLYN LAY, social worker; b. Hagerstown, Md., May 1, 1940; d. James S. Jr. and Emily Graham (Miller) Lay; m. William J. Dowd, Sept. 1, 1962 (dec.); children: William J. Jr., James P. AB, Meredith Coll., 1962; MSW, Catholic U., 1987. Cert. social worker, clin. social worker. Social work cons. Bethesda (Md.) Fellowship House, 1987-89; social worker Family Svcs. Agy., Gaithersburg, Md., 1987-98, dir. svcs. for srs., 1991-98, clin. dir., 1996-98; pvt. practice Gaithersburg, 1991-98; clin. care mgr. Falls Church, Va., 1998—. Presenter in field. Past mem. bd. dirs. Alzheimer's Assn. of Greater Wash. Mem. NASW (register of clin. social work, diplomate), Acad. Cert. Social Workers. Home: 21913 Foxlair Rd Gaithersburg MD 20882-1306 Address: 12369 C Sunrise Valley Dr Reston VA 20191 E-mail: cnldowd@verizon.net.

DOWD, DAVID JOSEPH, banker, construction executive; b. Long Island City, N.Y., June 6, 1924; s. David Joseph and Elsie (Schaeffler) B.; children— Laury, David, Patrick, Carol. BS in Bus. Adminstrn, NYU, 1949. Asst. v.p. Irving Trust Co., N.Y.C., 1952-64; v.p. Franklin Nat. Bank, N.Y.C., 1964-66; sr. v.p. Security Nat. Bank, Huntington, N.Y., 1966-72; pres. Nassau Trust Co., Glen Cove, N.Y., 1972-75, Bankers Service Co., 1975—; pub. Long Island Financial Newsletter, 1976-82; pres. Victorian Homes, Inc., 1980-97. Pres. Suffolk County council Boy Scouts Am., 1969-70; chmn. Suffolk Community Devel. Corp., 1973-74; Trustee Stony Brook Found., State U. N.Y., 1972. Served with USMCR, 1942-45, 51-52. Mem. N.Y. State Bankers Assn. (chmn. group VII 1972-75), L.I. Bankers Assn. (dir. 1969-74), Suffolk County Bankers Assn. (pres. 1971-72), Empire State C. of C. (dir. 1969-75) Address: PO Box 1057 Shelter Island NY 11964

DOWD, EDWARD L., JR., lawyer, former prosecutor; s. Edward L. Dowd; m. Jill Goessling; 3 children. JD with distinction, St. Mary's Univ. With Dowd, Dowd & Dowd; from asst. U.S. atty. to chief narcotics sect., regional dir. south cen. region Pres.'s Organized Crime Drug Enforcement Task Force U.S. Atty.'s Office, 1979-84; pvt. practice, 1984-93; U.S. atty. ea. dist. of Mo. U.S. Dept. Justice, St. Louis, 1993-99; dep. spl. counsel to John C. Danforth Spl. Counsel Waco Investigation, 1999; ptnr. Bryan Cave, LLP, St. Louis, 1999—. Office: Bryan Cave LLP One Metropolitan Square 211 N Broadway Ste 3600 Saint Louis MO 63102-2733 E-mail: eldowd@bryancave.com.

DOWD, JOHN MAGUIRE, lawyer; b. Brockton, Mass., Nov. 2, 1941; s. Paul L. and Mary (Maquire) Dowd; m. Carole L. Folts, June 12, 1965; children: Thomas P., Anne M., Sarah E., Michael T., Daniel M. AB cum laude, St. Bernard Coll., Cullman, Ala., 1963; JD, Emory U., 1965. Bar: DC 1967, admitted to practice: US Ct. Appeals (DC Cir.) 1967, US Ct. Appeals (4th Cir.) 1967, US Ct. Appeals (5th Cir.) 1967, US Ct. Appeals (10th Cir.) 1967, US Ct. Appeals (11th Cir.) 1967, US Dist. Ct. (DC) 1967, US Ct. Internat. Trade 1967, US Supreme Ct. 1970, US Dist. Ct. (So. Dist.) Ga. 1987. Trial atty. Tax div. US Dept. Justice, Washington, 1969-72; chief strike force 18 Criminal div. US Dept. Justice, Washington, 1972-78; ptnr. Whitman &

Ransom, Washington, 1978-84, Heron, Burchette, Ruckert & Rothwell, Washington, 1984-90; ptnr., head criminal litig. group, mem. mgmt. com. Akin, Gump, Strauss, Hauer & Feld, L.L.P., Washington, 1990—. Arbitrator Internat. C. of C., Internat. Ct. Arbitration, 1994—; spl. counsel Commr. of Baseball, 1989—92; lectr. Nat. Inst. for Trial Adv. Georgetown U., 1979—81, lectr. continuing legal edn., 1987—88. Trustee Flint Hill Sch., Oakton, Va. Capt. USMC, 1965—69. Named one of 75 Best Lawyers, Washingtonian mag., 2002. Master: Edward Bennett Williams Inn of Ct.; fellow: Fellows of Young Lawyers of the Am. Bar; mem.: DC Bar Assn., ABA. Avocations: golf, swimming, walking, reading, teaching. Office: Akin Gump Strauss Hauer & Feld LLP Ste 400 1333 New Hampshire Ave NW Washington DC 20036-1564*

DOWD, MAUREEN, columnist; b. Washington, D.C., Jan. 14, 1952; BA English Lit., Catholic U., Washington D.C., 1973. From editl. asst. to feature writer The Washington Star, 1974-81; from corr. to writer Time mag., 1981-83; metro reporter N.Y. Times, 1983-86, D.C. reporter, 1986-95, opinion-editl. columnist, 1995—. Author: Bushworld: Enter at Your Own Risk, 2004 (Publishers Weekly Bestseller). Finalist Pulitzer Prize for nat. reporting, 1992; named one of Glamour's Women of the Yr., 1996; recipient Breakthrough Award, "Women, Men and Media", Columbia U., 1991, Matrix Award, NY Women in Comm., 1994, Pulitzer Prize for commentary, 1999, Damon Runyon Award, Denver Press Club, 2000. Office: NY Times 1627 I St NW Washington DC 20006-4007*

DOWD, MICHAEL PATRICK, lawyer; b. Los Alamitos, Mar. 25, 1970; s. Owen Joseph and Geraldine Ann Dowd; m. Dorena Joann Dominguez, Feb. 14, 1999. BA, Calif. State U., Long Beach, 1992; JD, U. of Houston Law Ctr., 1995. Prosecutor Ft. Bend Cty Dist. Atty, Richmond, Tex., 1994—95; atty. Law Offices of John Guerin, Huntington Beach, 1995—96; dep. dist. atty. San Bernardino Cty Dist. Atty., Rancho Cucamonga, 1996—. Com. mem. U. of La Verne Adv. Com., 2000—; legal advisor, cons. Gt. Western Gun Shows, Pomona, 1998—2001; com. mem. U. of La Verne Curriculum Devel. Com., 2000—. Campaign advisor Rep. Lawyers Assn., Orange, 1999—2000; founder San Bernardino Cty Dep. Dist. Atty. Assn., 2002; co-founder San Bernardino Cty Pub. Attorneys Assn., 2000. Mem.: ABA, Fed. Bar Assn., Orange Cty Rep. Lawyers Assn., Federalist Soc., Kiwanis Club. Republican. Roman Catholic. Avocations: baseball, reading, polit.activities. Office: San Bernardino Cty Dist Atty 8303 Haven Ave 4th Fl Rancho Cucamonga CA 91730-3848

DOWD, MORGAN DANIEL, retired political science professor, retired dean; b. Boston, Feb. 21, 1933; s. Joseph Francis and Marion Caroline (Calcari) D.; m. Dianne May Robichaud, Aug. 29, 1959; children: Megan Eileen, Sean Morgan, Colin Martin, Blaine Christopher, Roarke Terence. BA cum laude, St. Michael's Coll., 1955; JD, Catholic U. Am., 1958; MA, U. Mass., 1962, PhD, 1964. Instr. U. Maine, 1959-60, U. Mass., 1960-61; asst. prof. polit. sci. SUNY-Fredonia, 1963-67, assoc. prof., 1967-76, prof., 1976—, dean grad. studies and research, 1969-78, dean faculty for natural and social scis., 1978-84, joint prof. bus. and polit. sci., 1984—98, dist. svc. prof., 1995—98, ret., 1998; sr. assoc. Mendez Eng. and Assocs., Bethesda, Md., 1998—. Cons. Mid. States Assn. Colls. and Univs., 1977—; project dir. USIA grant, Albania, 1992-94, 95-96. Contbr. articles to law jours., 1956-78; co-editor: World Dictionary of Environmental Research Centers, 2d edit., 1974. Bd. dirs. com. Health Systems Agy. Western N.Y., 1986-87, mem. exec. com.; regional member N.Y. state commn. Bicentennial of Constn., 1987; convocation speaker West Chester U. Pa., 1991. Recipient Pres.'s Medallion award, West Chester U. Pa., 1991, Extraordinary Svc. to Commn. on Higher Edn. U. Rochester, 1994. Mem. Columbia U. Seminar on History of Legal and Polit. Theory, Torch Club, Delta Epsilon Sigma, Pi Sigma Alpha, Delta Theta Phi, Phi Eta Sigma Democrat. Roman Catholic. E-mail: dowd@fredonia.edu.

DOWD, PETER JEROME, public relations executive; b. Bklyn., Oct. 5, 1942; s. Jerome Ambrose and Mary Agnes (Young) D.; m. Brenda Badura, Nov. 25, 1972; 1 child, Kelly Ann. AB, Fordham U., 1964. Reporter UPI, N.Y.C., 1964-66; account exec. Hill and Knowlton, N.Y.C., 1966-71, v.p., 1971-74; sr. v.p., mgr. Hill and Knowlton (Los Angeles office), 1974-78, mng. dir. Western region, 1978-80, exec. v.p., 1980; ptnr. Haley, Kiss & Dowd, Inc., Los Angeles, 1980-83; group v.p. Am. Med. Internat., 1983-88; v.p. pub. rels. Texaco Inc., White Plains, N.Y., 1989-96; sr. v.p. corp. affairs Fidelity Investments, Boston, 1996-99; pub. affairs cons., 1999—. Instr. U. So. Calif., Calif. State U., Fullerton. Bd. dirs. Cath. Big Bros., Nature Conservancy (Lower Hudson chpt.). Mem. Pub. Rels. Soc. Am., Alan Page Soc., Town Hall West (v.p., dir.), Westchester County Assn. (bd. dirs.), Nature Conservancy (bd. dirs. Lower Hudson chpt.), U.S. Mil. Acad. Pub. Affairs (adv. com.). Republican. Roman Catholic. Office: Fidelity Investments 82 Devonshire St Boston MA 02109-3605

DOWD, SHEILA M., psychologist; b. Ill. d. Michael and Rita Dowd. PhD, U. Ill., Chgo., 2000. Lic. psychologist Ill., 2002. Psychologist Rush Med. Ctr., Chgo., 2004—. Mem.: APA. Achievements include research in food craving pattern scale. E-mail: sdowd@uic.edu.

DOWD, STEVEN MILTON, lawyer; b. Tyler, Tex., Feb. 1, 1951; s. Loyd Robertus and Roy Frances (Dickard) D.; m. Pamela Gayle Blacklock, Apr. 6, 1974; children: Anna Lisa, Lydia Caroline. BA, Austin Coll., 1973; JD, Baylor U., 1975; LLM, So. Meth. U., 1977. Bar: Tex. 1975, U.S. Dist. Ct. (so. dist.) Tex. 1983, U.S. Dist. Ct. (ea. dist.) Tex. 1985. Tax atty. Exxon Corp., Houston, 1977-79; assoc. Covington & Reese, Houston, 1982-84; pvt. practice Tyler, Tex., 1984-86; asst. gen. counsel Temple-Eastex, Inc., Diboll, Tex., 1986-92; co-owner Panola County Abstract and Title Co., 1992-99; pvt. practice, 1992—. Dist. judge 123rd Jud. Dist. Ct., Panola and Shelby Counties, 1995-97; pres. Lydianna Petroleum Co., Austin, Tex., 2000—. Bd. dirs. Noonday Holiness Camp, Hallsville, Tex. Baptist. Home and Office: 1 Oakmoore Round Rock TX 78664-9611

DOWD, THOMAS F., lawyer; b. Boston, 1943; AB, Harvard U., 1965; JD, Case Western Reserve U., 1974. Bar: Ohio 1974, DC 1989. Ptnr. Baker & Hostetler, Washington; named ptnr. Bryan, Cave, McPheeters & Roberts, Washington, 1989; v.p., gen. counsel, sec. Graybar Electric Co. Inc., St. Louis. Adv. coun. Nat. Assn. Minority and Women-Owned Law Firms, 2004—. Editor articles Case Western Reserve Law Review, 1973-74. Mem. Order of Coif. Office: Graybar Electric Co Inc 34 N Meramec Ave Saint Louis MO 63105

DOWDELL, DONNA RENEA, nurse; b. Indpls., Sept. 28, 1968; d. Ollie and Birdie Mae (McClendon) Strong; m. David Lee Dowdell, Jan. 28, 1991. BSN, Ind. U., Indpls., 1990; MS in Holistic Nutrition, Clayton Coll. Natural Health, 1999. RN, Ind.; TB and BLS, Ind.; cert. hypnotherapy, Atwood Inst., 1996. Student nurse technician VA Hosp., Indpls., 1988-89; student nurse extern Meth. Hosp., Indpls., 1989-90; staff nurse Riley Hosp., Indpls., 1991; staff home care nurse Pediatric Nursing Specialists, Indpls., 1991-94, Kimberly Quality Care, Indpls., 1992-94; clin. nurse supr. Olsten Kimberly Quality Care, Indpls., 1994, pediatric clin. mgr., 1994-95, case mgr. Las Vegas, 1995; staff RN Sunrise Hosp., Las Vegas, 1995-96; quality coord. Five Star Home Health, Las Vegas, 1997—. Pub. health nurse Health Hosp. Corp. Marion County, Indpls., 1992-94; nursing supr. home health Winona Hosp.-Pulse Health Svcs., Indpls., 1994; cons. holistic nutrition; hypnotherapist, N.V. Vol. Nat. Nurses Day, Indpls., 1992-94. Ind. U. Purdue U. scholar, 1990. Mem. Am. Assn. Nutritional Cons., Sigma Theta Tau Internat. Avocations: singing gospel music, arts and crafts, reading, watching movie videos, travel.

DOWDELL, RODGER B., JR., electronics executive; BSEE cum laude, Brown Univ., 1971; MSEE, Univ. Rhode Island. With Texas Instruments, Brown & Sharpe, Naval Underwater Sys. Ctr.; founder, pres. Independent Energy Inc.; cons. Am. Power Conversion (APC), W. Kingston, RI, 1985, pres., CEO, 1985—, and chmn. Bd. dir. Ctr. for Quality Mgmt., Cambridge, Mass. Named Entrepreneur of Yr., New England region, Ernst & Young, 1990, Merrill Lynch, 1990; recipient Thomas H. Lee Meritorious Svc. award, Ctr. for Quality Mgmt., 2001. Office: APC 132 Fairgrounds Rd West Kingston RI 02892 Office Phone: 401-789-5735. Office Fax: 401-789-3710.*

DOWDEN, THOMAS CLARK, telecommunication executive; b. Ridgetop, Tenn., May 6, 1935; s. James Robert and Anna Mary (Hunter) D.; m. Wendy Ellen Vereen, Jan. 27, 1962; children: Anna V. Dowden Tschetter, Constance H. Cobbs, John T. BA in Journalism, U. Ga., 1962, MA in Polit. Sci., 1963. Account exec. Corinthian Broadcasting, Houston, 1963-65; v.p., sec. Cox Cable Comm., Atlanta, 1965-76; owner, CEO Dowden Comm., Atlanta, 1977—. Mem. bd. dirs. Ga. Dept. Industry, Trade and Tourism, 1994-97; bd. dirs., chmn. George Foster Peabody Radio-TV-Cable awards, 1991-93. Organizer Cable TV's Role in 1976 Presdl. Election, Atlanta, 1975-76; trustee U. Ga., 1998-2004. Mem. Wade Hampton Golf Club (Cashiers, N.C.), Royal St. George's Golf Club (Sandwich, Kent, Eng.), Royal County Down Golf Club (Newcastle, No. Ireland), U.S. Sr. Golf Assn. Republican. Episcopalian. Avocations: golf, photography, travel. Office: Dowden Communications 650 Blackberry Ln Clarkesville GA 30523-4461 Home (Winter): 79655 Mandarina La Quinta CA 92253

DOWDLE, PATRICK DENNIS, lawyer; b. Denver, Dec. 8, 1948; s. William Robert and Helen (Schraeder) D.; m. Eleanor Pryor, Mar. 8, 1975; children: Jeffery William, Andrew Peter. BA, Cornell Coll., Mt. Vernon, Iowa, 1971; JD, Boston U., 1975. Bar: Colo. 1975, U.S. Dist. Ct. Colo. 1975, U.S. Ct. Appeals (10th cir.) 1976, U.S. Supreme Ct. 1978. Acad. dir. in Japan Sch. Internat. Tng., Putney, Vt., 1974; assoc. Decker & Miller, Denver, 1975-77; ptnr. Miller, Makkai & Dowdle, Denver, 1977—. Designated counsel criminal appeals Colo. Atty. Gens. Office, Denver, 1980-81; guardian ad litem Adams County Dist. Ct., Brighton, Colo., 1980-83; affiliated counsel ACLU, Denver, 1980—. Mem. Colo. Bar Assn., Denver Bar Assn. (various coms.), Porsche Club of Am. Avocations: scuba diving, photography, wine making, travel, skiing. Home: 3254 Tabor Ct Wheat Ridge CO 80033-5367 Office: Miller Makkai & Dowdle 2325 W 72nd Ave Denver CO 80221-3101 Office Phone: 303-427-7584. Business E-Mail: pdowdle@mmdlaw.us.

DOWDY, JOANNE KILGOUR, education educator; b. Port of Spain, Trinidad, Nov. 22, 1959; d. Lennox Stanislaus and Kathleen Louise (Armstrong) Kilgour; m. William Harold Dowdy, July 20, 1990 (div. Oct. 1999). BFA, Juilliard Sch., 1987; MA in Tchg., Columbia U., 1989; PhD, U. N.C., 1997. Cert. tchr., N.Y., N.C. Lectr. Shaw U., Wilmington, N.C., 1993; acad. cons. U. N.C., Chapel Hill, 1993-94; instr. N.C. State U., Raleigh, 1994-95; literacy cons. Literacy South, Durham, N.C., 1995-96; lectr. Durham Tech. C.C., 1996-97; asst. dir., asst. prof. Ga. State U., Atlanta, 1997—. Cons. Ga. State U., 1997; bd. dirs. N.C. Equity, Raleigh; mem. adv. bd. Tchrs. for Acad. Support Skills, Cin., 1997. Dir. (video prodn.) Noises in the Attic, 1997, Carmen Montana: A Story of Literacy in Motion, (stage and video prodn.) Brown Blues: Six Women Talk About their Experience of Integration. Recipient Derek Walcott scholarship Nobel Laureate Derek Walcott, 1982/83, Robin Williams award Juilliard Sch., 1994/95, Minority Presence award U. N.C., 1994. Mem. AAUW, NOW, Internat. Reading Assn. Avocations: sewing, correspondence, picture framing. Home: 447611 State Route 43 Kent OH 44240

DOWDY, ROBERT ALAN, lawyer, director; b. June 12, 1941; s. Andrew Hunter and Helen Marie (Brandes) Dowdy; m. Lynne Bryant, June 18, 1966; children: Roger Alan, Douglas John. BA, U. Calif., Berkeley, JD, 1966. Bar: D.C. 1967, Calif. 1968, Wash. 1974. Atty. Am. Airlines, NYC, 1969—72, Weyerhaeuser Co., Tacoma, 1972—74, sr. legal counsel, 1974—86, asst. gen. counsel, 1986—91, dep. gen. counsel, 1991—97, v.p., gen. counsel, 1997—2004, sr. v.p., gen. counsel, 2004—. Dir. Green Arrow Motor Co., Tacoma; mem. Wash. Bd. Bar Examiners, 1982—; arbitrator King County Superior Ct., 1986—; vis. com. U. Wash. Sch. Law, Seattle, 1986—. Contbr. articles to profl. jours. Bd. dir. N.W. Chamber Orch., Seattle, 1975—76; trustee St. James Sch., Kent, Wash., 1982—84; elder St. Elizabeth Episcopal Ch., Burien, Wash., 1976—78. Capt. U.S. Army, 1966—69. Decorated Army Commendation medal. Mem.: Am. Forest Products and Paper Assn. (gen. counsel com. 1997—), Assn. Gen. Counsel, Wash. Bar Assn. (exec. com. corp. sect. 1977—79, mem. legal edn. sect. 1982—84). Republican. Office: Weyerhaeuser Co CH5J PO Box 9777 Federal Way WA 98063-9777

DOWE, EMILY MAE, writer; b. Delway, N.C., Apr. 23, 1950; d. John Henry and Mae Haley Murphy; m. Irving Dowe Jr., June 6, 1975; childre: Darlene Renee, Deloris Renita. AA, Kittrell Coll., 1970; BA, Pembroke State U., 1972. Farm laborer, Sampson County, N.C., 1956-68; clerical asst. Kittrell (N.C.) Coll., 1968-69; acctg. N.J. Ins. Underwriting Assocs., Newark, 1970-71, E.I. duPont Co., Leland, N.C., 1973-87; freelance writer, 1988—. Author: (short story) Wellspring, 1994; author of poems. Recipient 2d pl. prize N.C. Writers Network Competition, 1994. Democrat. Methodist. Avocations: writing, reading, sewing.

DOWELL, EARL HUGH, dean, aerospace and mechanical engineering educator; b. Macomb, Ill., Nov. 16, 1937; s. Earl S. and Edna Bernice (Dean) D.; m. Lynn Cowell; children: Marla Lorraine, Janice Lynelle, Michael Hugh. BS, U. Ill., 1959; S.M., Mass. Inst. Tech., 1961, Sc.D., 1964. Rsch. engr. Boeing Co., 1962-63; rsch. asst. MIT, 1963-64, rsch. engr., 1964, asst. prof., 1964-65; asst. prof. aerospace and mech. engring. Princeton U., 1964-68, assoc. prof., 1968-72, prof., 1972-83, assoc. chmn., 1975-77, acting chmn., 1979; prof. Sch. Engring. Duke U., Durham, NC, 1983—, dean, 1983-99. Cons. to industry and govt Author: Aeroelasticity of Plates and Shells, 1974, A Modern Course in Aeroelasticity, 1978, 4th edit., 2004, Nonlinear Studies in Aeroelasticity, 1988, Dynamics of Very High Dimensional Systems, 2003; editl. bd.: AIAA Jour., 2000-, Jour. Sound and Vibration, 1988—, Jour. Fluids and Structures, 1987—, Jour. Nonlinear Dynamics, 1990—; contbr. articles to profl. jours. Chmn. N.J. Noise Control Council, 1972-76. Named outstanding young alumnus U. Ill. Sch. Aero. and Astronautical Engring., 1973, disting. alumnus, 1975; recipient Alumni Honor award Coll. Engring. U. Ill. Fellow: ASME, AIAA (hon.; v.p. publs. 1981—83, Structures, Structural Dynamics and Material award 1980, Theodore Von Karman lectr. 2002), Am. Acad. Mechs. (pres. 1991, Disting. Svc. award 1994); mem.: Nat. Acad. Engring., Acoustical Soc. Am., Am. Helicopter Soc. Office: Duke U Sch Engring Durham NC 27708 Home: 847 Inglerook Rd Durham NC 27707 Office Phone: 919-660-5321.

DOWELL, JAMES DALE, lawyer; b. Goose Creek, Tex., July 17, 1932; s. James Dale and Margaret (King) D.; m. Patricia Jo Skaggs, Feb. 2, 1957; children: Terry Dowell Owens, James Dale III. BA, Tex. A&M U, 1954; LLB, U. Tex., 1957. Bar: Tex. 1956, U.S. Dist. Ct. (ea. dist.) Tex. 1958, U.S Ct. Appeals (5th cir.) 1964, U.S. Supreme Ct. 1969. Assoc. King, Sharfstein & Rienstra, Beaumont, Tex., 1957-63, ptnr., 1963-68, Rienstra, Rienstra & Dowell, Beaumont, 1968-85, Rienstra, Dowell & Flatten, Beaumont, 1985—. Mem. Tex. Dem. Exec. Com., 1966-68, del. Nat. Conv., 1976—. Mem. ABA, State Bar Tex., Tex. Bar Found., Jefferson County Bar Assn. (pres. 1978-79, Blackstone award 2000), Def. Rsch. Inst., Tex. Assn. Def. Counsel, Beaumont Country Club, Beaumont Club (bd. dirs. 1975-77), Rotary (Paul Harris fellow 2000), Phi Gamma Delta. Methodist. Avocation: reading. Home: 6275 Wilchester Ln Beaumont TX 77706-4328 Office: 595 Orleans St Beaumont TX 77701-3214 Office Phone: 409-833-6317. Personal E-mail: riendf@aol.com.

DOWELL, MICHAEL BRENDAN, chemist; b. N.Y.C., Nov. 18, 1942; s. William Henry and Anne Susan (Cannon) D.; m. Gail Elizabeth Renton, Mar. 16, 1968; children: Rebecca S. Hall, Margaret A. Scott. BS, Fordham U., 1963; PhD, Pa. State U., 1967. Physicist U.S. Army Frankford Arsenal, Phila., 1967-69; rsch. scientist Parma (Ohio) Tech. Ctr., Union Carbide Corp., 1969-74, devel. mgr. carbon fiber applications, 1974-76, group leader metals and ceramics rsch., 1976-80, sr. group leader process rsch., 1980-82, mgr. market devel., 1982-92, Praxair Advanced Ceramics Inc. (formerly Union Carbide Corp), Ohio, 1992-93, Advanced Ceramics Corp., Cleve., 1993—, v.p. tech., 1999—2002; v.p. 5iTech, LLC, Cleve., 2003—. Mem. materials tech. adv. com. U.S. Dept. Commerce, 1994—2001; lectr. ops. mgmt. Case Western Res. U., 2001—03. Contbr. articles to profl. jours. Capt. ordnance AUS, 1967—69. Mem. Am. Chem. Soc., Am. Phys. Soc., U.S. Advanced Ceramics Assn. (bd. dirs. 1988-96), Am. Soc. Metals Internat. (govt. and pub. affairs com. 1989—), Soc. Prof. Fellows Case Western Res. U., Phi Lambda Upsilon. Roman Catholic. Home: 368 N Main St Hudson OH 44236-2246 Office: 5iTech LLC 1768 E 25th St Cleveland OH 44114 Office Phone: 216-391-7764. Personal E-mail: mbdowell@worldnet.att.net.

DOWER GOLD, CATHERINE ANNE, music history educator; b. South Hadley, Mass., May 19, 1924; d. Lawrence Frederick Dower and Marie (Barbieri) Barber; m. Arthur Gold, Mar. 24, 1994 (dec. Oct. 1998). AB, Hamline U., 1945; MA, Smith Coll., 1948; B in Liturgical Music, U. Mont., Gregorian Inst. Am., 1949; PhD, The Cath. U. Am., 1968. New England rep. Gregorian Inst. Am., Toledo, 1948-49; tchr. music, organist St. Rose Sch., Meriden, Conn., 1949-53; supr. music Holyoke (Mass.) Pub. Schs., 1953-55; instr. music U. Mass., Amherst, 1955-56; prof. music Westfield (Mass.) State Coll., 1956-90, prof. emerita, 1991—; columnist and freelance writer Holyoke Transcript Telegram, 1991-93. Organist St. Theresa's Ch., South Hadley, 1937-41, St. Michael's Ch., N.Y., 1945-46; concert series presenter Westfield State Coll., 1987-91, rschr. tchr.; vis. scholar U. So. Calif., 1969; vis. assoc. prof. music Herbert Lehman Coll. CUNY, 1970-71. Author: Puerto Rican Music Following the Spanish American War, 1898-1910, 1983; (monograph) Yella Pessl, 1986, Alfred Einstein on Music, 1991, Yella Pessl: First Lady of the Harpsichord, 1992, Fifty Years of Marching Together, 2001, Las actividades musicales en Puerto Rico: después de la guerra hispanoamericana 1898-1910, 2005; editor: (newsletter) Westfield State Coll., 2000—; presenter Irish Concert Springfield Symphony Orch., 1981 (plaque 1982); contbr. numerous pub. poems to anthologies. Pres. Coun. for Human Understanding Holyoke, 1981—83, Friends of Holyoke Pub. Libr., 1990—91; bd. dirs., chmn. nominating com. Holyoke Pub. Libr., 1987—89; bd. dirs. Holyoke Pub. Libr. Corp., 1991—94, Springfield Symphony Orch., 1992—94, Fla. Philharm. Orch., 2000—03, trustee, 2002—03; presiding officer inauguration Dr. Irving Buchman pres. of Westfield State Coll.; mem. ethics com. Holyoke Hosp., 1988—94; sec. Haiti Mission, 1982—94; bd. overseers Mullen U., 1993; hon. mem. bd. Coun. Human Understanding, 1994—; hon. mem. WSC Found., 1994—; co-chair United Jewish Appeal/Jewish Fed. Boca Lago Women's Divsn., South Palm Beach County, 1996—97; mem. St. Patrick's Com., Holyoke, Mass., 1991—; 1st v.p. fin. and adminstrn. Temple Beth El Women in Reformed Judaism, Boca Raton, 1997—99. Named Lady Comdr., Equestrian Order of the Holy Sepulchre of Jerusalem, 1987, with star, 1990, Career Woman of Yr., Quota Internat. Holyoke, 1988, Westfield State Coll. concert series named Catherine A. Dower Performing Arts Series in her honor, 1991; recipient citation, Academia InterAmericana de P.R., 1978, plaque, Mass. Tchrs. Assn., Boston, 1984, medal, Equestrian Order Holy Sepulchre of Jerusalem, Papal Knighthood Soc., Boston, 1984, Performance award, Gov. Dukakis, Mass., 1988, award, P.R. Jour. Al. Margens, 1992, Human Rels. award, Coun. for Human Understanding, Holyoke, 1994, 1st prize, Raddock Eminent Scholar Chair Essay Contest, Fla. Atlantic U., 1996, Internat. Poet of Merit Silver Bowl award, Internat. Libr. Poetry, 2002, 2003, 2004, 2005, 1st prize, Essay Contest on World Peace by Brotherly Love Press, Mass., 2002, Outstanding Achievement in Poetry award, Internat. Soc. Poets, 2003. Mem. Nat. Soc. Arts and Letters (chmn. violin competition 2005), Am. Musicol. Soc., Coll. Mus. Soc., Friends of Music of Lynn U. (life) (bd. dirs., editor music newsletter), Ch. Music Assn. Am. (journalist), Acad. Arts and Scis. P.R. (medal 1977), Internat. Platform Assn., Friends of the Holyoke Pub. Libr. (pres. 1990-91), Irish Am. Cultural Inst. (chmn. bd. 1981-89), Holyoke Quota (v.p. 1976-79, pres. 1979-81, 90-92, chmn. speech and hearing com. 1987-94), B'nai B'rith of Boca Lago (sec. bd. dirs. 1994-1999, newsletter editor 1999-2000), Lifelong Learning Soc. Fla. Atlantic U. (life, sec. 1994-97, bd. dirs. 1994-98, 2003—), Westfield State Coll. Found., Women's Symphony League (life), Philharm. Assn. Boca (pres. 2002-03), Univ. Club Fla. Atlantic U. (parliamentarian 2003-05, chmn. of bylaws 2005-), Nat. Soc. Art Letters (1st v.p.), Phi Beta Kappa. Democrat. Home: 8559 Casa Del Lago Boca Raton FL 33433-2107 Personal E-mail: cathig@juno.com.

DOWIE, IAN JAMES, management consultant; b. London, Mar. 3, 1938; came to U.S., 1980; s. James George and Ethel (Watker) Dowie; m. Barbara Eva Page, Jan. 9, 1960 (div. 1991); children: Paul James, David Ian; m. Nancy M. Pollard, 1993 (div. 2004). BSEE, A.City & Guilds Inst., U. London, 1958. Registered profl. engr., Ont., Can. Seismic engr. Seismograph Svcs. Ltd., Eng., 1958-61; design engr. GE, Toronto, Ont., 1961-62; v.p., div. dir. IBM Can., Toronto, 1962-80; v.p. field ops. Exxon Office Systems, Stamford, Conn., 1980-82; pres. Aregon Internat. Inc., Stamford, 1983-84, Benchmark East, Westport, Conn., 1985-96, Park City, Utah, 1993-97, Benchmark Pub. Inc., Park City, Utah; developer Goshawk Ranch, Park City, Utah, 1997—2005, The Overlook, Park City, Utah, 2000—02, Turnberry Condos, Midway, Utah. Pres. Benchmark-Goshawk, Inc., Park City, Utah; v.p. bus. develop. Interloci Inc., 2002—03. Pub. Once A Londoner, 1989, What's Love Got To Do With It?, 1993, From Womb to Tomb, 1994, Remuda Dust, 1994. Chmn. Credit Valley Assn. for Handicapped Children, Toronto, 1972-79. Mem. Shore and Country Club (Norwalk, Conn.), Jeremy Ranch Golf Club (Park City, Utah). Avocations: tennis, travel, skiing, golf. Office Phone: 801-647-9202. E-mail: ijd@benchmarkventures.com.

DOWIS, JAMES RICHARD, writer; b. Hamlet, N.C., Oct. 28, 1930; s. William Shafer Dowis Sr. and Patricia Letha Bunn; m. Ouida Woods, May 7, 1955; children: Dixie McGinty, James R. Jr. BA in Journalism, U. Ala., 1953. Editor, pub. various newspapers, Ala. and Ga., 1955-63; pub. rels. dir. Callaway Mills. Co., LaGrange, Ga., 1963-67; publs. mgr. Coca-Cola Co., Atlanta, 1967-69; sr. v.p. Manning, Selvage & Lee, Inc., Atlanta, 1969-91; pres., exec. dir. Soc. for Preservation of English Lang. and Lit., 1991—. Author: How to Make Your Writing Reader-Friendly, 1989, The Lost Art of Great Speech, 1999, Poor Farm Road, 2000; co-author: The Write Way, 1995, Sleeping Dogs Don't Lay, 1999. 1st. lt. U.S. Army, 1953-55. Methodist. Avocations: golf, chess, creating acrostic puzzles. Home and Office: 110 Bald Cypress Ct Waleska GA 30183-4200

DOWIS, LENORE, lawyer; b. N.Y., Nov. 7, 1934; d. Thomas and Julianna (Csitkovits) Esteves; children: Daniel, Lenore, Denise, Jonathan. AAS, Suffolk County Community Coll., 1981; BA, SUNY, Stony Brook, 1983; JD, Touro Coll., 1987. Bar: N.Y. 1988, N.J. 1988, U.S. Dist. Ct. N.J. 1988, U.S. Dist. Ct. (so. and ea. dists.) N.Y. 1992, U.S. Ct. Mil. Appeals 1993, U.S. Ct. Claims 1993, U.S. Ct. Appeals (fed. cir.) 1993, U.S. Supreme Ct. 1993. Tel. operator N.Y. Tel. Co., L.I., 1951-58; real estate sales agt. Gen. Devel. Corp., Hauppauge, N.Y, 1974-75; student law clk. to assoc. judge appellate div. U.S. Supreme Ct. N.Y., Bklyn., 1986; staff atty. Nassau/Suffolk Law Svcs., Bay Shore, N.Y., 1988; pvt. practice, Smithtown, N.Y., 1988—. Mem. ABA, Suffolk County Bar Assn., N.Y. State Bar Assn., Phi Theta Kappa, Alpha Beta Gamma. Republican. Home and Office: 33 Beverly Rd Smithtown NY 11787-5324

DOWLEY, JOEL EDWARD, transportation executive; b. Jackson, Mich., Apr. 27, 1952; s. William J. and Beth E. (Morell) D.; m. Janelle Smith, Nov. 12, 1983; children: Kara Marie, Alayna Kristine. BA, Spring Arbor Coll., 1974; JD, U. Notre Dame, 1977. Bar: Mich. 1977. Atty. Fraser, Trebilcock, Davis and Foster, P.C., Lansing, Mich., 1977-83; exec. v.p. and gen. counsel Dowley Mfg. Inc., Spring Arbor, Mich., 1983—87, chmn. and CEO, 1987—2003; pres. Integrity Moving Svcs., Inc., West Palm Beach, Fla., 2004—. Pub. mem. Mich. Bd. Psychology, 1978-82, vice chmn., 1980, chmn., 1981-82; pub. mem. ethics com. Am. Assn. Marriage and Family Therapy, 1980; mem. Ingham County Rep. Exec. Com., Mich., 1978-84, 3d Dist. Rep. Exec. Com., 1983-85; Rep. candidate for Ingham County commr., 1978, 82; trustee Highfield's, Inc., 1983-89, youth opportunity camp, Onondaga, Mich., 1983-89, sec., 1984-85, pres., 1986-87; trustee BoarsHead Theater, Lansing, 1982-92, treas., 1985-87, vice-chmn., 1987-89, Okemos Edn. Found., 1988-90, treas., 1989-90, Handicapped Children and Adults Found., trustee, 1994-2000, v.p., 1995-96, pres., 1996-97, treas., 1998-99; mem. elected ofcls. compensation commn. Meridian Twp., Mich., 1989—, elected chmn., 1993—. Mem. Mich. Bar Assn., Spring Arbor Coll. Alumni

Assn. (trustee 1979-82, pres. 1981-82, Young Leader award 1983), Hand Tools Inst. (bd. dirs. 1986-89, 90-2001, sec., treas. 1993-95, v.p. 1995-97, pres. 1997-99). Home: 1864 Cimarron Dr Okemos MI 48864-3810 Personal E-mail: dowleyj@aol.com.

DOWLEY, JOSEPH KYRAN, lawyer, congressman; b. L.A., Apr. 23, 1946; s. Michael F. and Charlotte (Moore) D.; m. Carol Walsh, Jan. 22, 1972; children: Kristin, Michael, Patricia. BA, Georgetown U., Washington, 1968, JD, 1976. Bar: Va. 1976, D.C. 1980. Adminstrv. asst. to Honorable Dan Rostenkowski U.S. Ho. of Reps., Washington, 1977-81, asst. chief counsel Com. on Ways and Means, 1981-84, chief counsel Com. on Ways and Means, 1985-87; ptnr. Dewey Ballantine, 1987—. 1st lt. U.S. Army, 1969-71. Mem. Bar Assn. Va., Bar Assn. D.C., Georgetown Univ. Alumni Club (pres. 1984-85). Roman Catholic. Office: Dewey Ballantine 1775 Pennsylvania Ave NW Washington DC 20006-4672

DOWLING, DEAN EDWARD, information scientist, educator; b. Daytona Beach, Fla., Feb. 17, 1942; s. Edward Moore and Josephine Frances Dowling; m. Brenda Graham Cameron, Aug. 15, 1976; children: Brian Edward, Julie Cameron children: Jo Anne Cameron Russo, Keith Robert; m. Karen Jorgensen Jorgensen, Feb. 29, 1964 (div. Nov. 0, 1975). BS, U.S. Mil. Acad., 1963; MA, Columbia U., 1970, PhD, 1972. Commd. lt. U.S. Army, 1963, advanced through grades to lt. col., 1979, ret., 1983; v.p. MUSE Technologies, Inc., Albuquerque, 1998—2001; pres. MUSE Fed. Systems Group, Inc., Arlington, Va., 1999—2001; prof. U. Phoenix (Ariz.) Online, 2003—. Adj. prof. Park U., Parkville, Mo., 1990—; cons. in field. Contbr. chapters to books. Decorated Cross of Gallantry Republic of Vietnam, Silver Star U.S. Army, Bronze Star, Purple Heart, Def. Superior Svc. medal, Meritorious Svc. medal, Army Commendation medal. Mem.: No. Va. Assn. Realtors. Republican. Avocations: golf, music. Home: 5904 Mt Eagle Dr 1210 Alexandria VA 22303 Office Phone: 703-329-0924. Personal E-mail: dean63@msn.com. E-mail: dean63@email.uophx.edu.

DOWLING, DORIS ANDERSON, business owner, educator, consultant; b. Clover Valley, Minn., Sept. 24, 1917; d. Gustaf Axel and Amanda Sophia (Karlsson) Anderson; m. John Joseph Dowling, Jan. 8, 1943 (dec. Feb. 1953); 1 child, Mary Kathryn. Home econs. degree, U. Minn., Virginia, 1937. Fashion coord., lectr. Fair Store/Montgomery Ward, Chgo., 1939-65, Marshall Field's, Chgo., 1967-82; founder, owner Doris Anderson Sewing Schs., 1948—. Cons. colls., textile industry, retail stores, 1948—; lectr. retail stores, 1954-94. Author: Simplified Systems of Sewing and Styling, 1948. Career counselor, trainer, Chgo., 1948-82. Recipient Future Farmers Am. award Duluth C. of C. Coun. Agr., 1934. Mem. Nat. Needlework Assn., Fashion Group Internat. Inc., Assn. Crafts & Creative Industries, Chgo. Apparel Ctr., Merchandise Mart. Avocations: designing, gardening, writing, research. Home and Office: Doris Anderson Sewing Schs 222 E Pearson St Apt 1108 Chicago IL 60611-7356

DOWLING, EDWARD THOMAS, economics professor; b. N.Y.C., Oct. 22, 1938; s. Edward Thomas and Mary Helen (Finegan) D. BA, Berchmans Coll., Philippines, 1962, MA in Philosophy, 1963; M.Div., Woodstock Coll., Md., 1969; PhD, Cornell U., Ithaca, N.Y., 1973. Asst. prof. econs. Fordham U., Bronx, 1973-79, assoc. prof., 1979-85, prof., 1985—, dean, 1982-86, chmn. dept., 1979-82, 88-94. Author: Development Economics, 1977, Mathematics for Economists, 1980, Calculus for Business, Economics, and the Social Sciences, 1990, Introduction to Mathematical Economics, 1992, 3d edit., 2000, Mathematical Methods for Business and Economics, 1993, Intermediate Statistics for Business and the Social Sciences, 2000. Mem. Am. Econ. Assn. Office: Fordham U Loyola Hall New York NY 10458-5198

DOWLING, JOHN CLARKSON, language educator; b. Strawn, Tex., Nov. 14, 1920; s. Albert Clarkson and Georgia Ann (Turrill) Dowling; m. Constance Guinevere Ford, Dec. 26, 1949; 1 child, Robert Clarkson. BA, U. Colo., 1941; MA, U. Wis., 1942, PhD, 1950. Instr. Spanish U. Wis., Madison, 1951-53; prof., head fgn. langs. Tex. Tech. U., Lubbock, 1953-63; prof., chmn. Spanish & Portuguese Ind. U., Bloomington, 1963-72; prof., head romance langs. U. Ga., Athens, 1973-79, dean grad. sch., 1979-89, prof. alumni found., 1980-91, prof. emeritus alumni found., 1992—. Vis. prof. romance langs. U. Tex., Austin, 1957; vis. prof. Spanish U. Iowa, Iowa City, 1993; interim dean arts & humanities Fla. Atlantic U., Boca Raton, 1995. Author: (book) Saavedra Fajardo, 1957, Saavedra Fajardo, 2d edit., 1977, Moratin, 1971, Jose Melchor Gomis, 1974; contbr. articles to profl. jours. Mem. exec. com. grad. deans African-Am. Inst., N.Y.C., 1985—92. Lt. (j.g.) USNR, 1942—46, lt. comdr. USNR, 1946—66. A. C. Markham Travel fellow, U. Wis., 1950—51, J. S. Guggenheim fellow, 1959—60, Rsch. grantee, Am. Philos. Soc., 1971, 1974. Mem.: Critica Hispanica Diechiocho, Am. Assn. Tchrs. Spanish & Portuguese, Hispanic Soc. Am. (corr.). Episcopalian. Home: 7101 Patriots Colony Drive Williamsburg VA 23188-0131

DOWLING, JOHN ELLIOTT, biology professor; b. Pawtucket, R.I., Aug. 31, 1935; s. Joseph Leo and Ruth W. (Tappan) D.; children by previous marriage: Christopher, Nicholas.; m. Judith Falco, Oct. 18, 1975; 1 dau., Alexandra. AB, Harvard U., 1957, PhD, 1961; MD (hon.), U. Lund (Sweden), 1982. Asst. prof. biology Harvard U., Cambridge, Mass., 1961—64, prof., 1971—87, Maria Moors Cabot prof. natural sci., 1987—2001, Llura and Gordon Gund prof. neurosci., 2001—; assoc. prof. Johns Hopkins Sch. Medicine, Balt., 1964—71. Pres. Marine Biol. Lab., 1998—. Author: The Retina: An Approachable Part of the Brain, 1987, Neurons and Networks: An Introduction to Neuroscience, 1992, 2d edit., 2001, Creating Mind: How the Brain Works, 1998, The Great Brain Debate: Is it Nature or Nurture, 2004; contbr. numerous articles on vision to profl. jours. Recipient ann. award N.E. Ophthal. Soc., 1979, award of merit Retina Rsch. Found., 1981, Prentice medal Am. Acad. Optometry, 1991, Von Sallman prize, 1992, The Helen Keller prize for vision rsch., 2000, Gund award Found. Fighting Blindness, 2001. Fellow Am. Acad. Arts and Scis., AAAS; mem. Am. Philos. Soc., Assn. Rsch. in Vision and Ophthalmology (Friedenwald medal 1970), NAS, Neurosci. Soc., Soc. Gen. Physiologists. Home: 135 Charles St Boston MA 02114-3264 Office: Harvard U Biology Labs Cambridge MA 02138 Office Phone: 617-495-2245. Business E-Mail: dowling@mcb.harvard.edu.

DOWLING, JOSEPH ALBERT, historian, educator; b. Dalmuir, Scotland, Nov. 10, 1926; came to U.S., 1940, naturalized, 1945; s. Joseph Albert and Maud Drury (Mitchell) D.; m. Sylvia Minkin, June 16, 1956; children—David, Kathryn, Juliet, Marc. AB, Lincoln Meml. U., 1948; MA, NYU, 1951, PhD, 1958. Instr. English and history Shorter Coll., Rome, Ga., 1951-52; instr. cultural heritage Bates Coll., Lewiston, Maine, 1955-58; asst. prof. history Lehigh U., Bethlehem, Pa., 1958-61, assoc. prof., 1961-67, prof., 1967-74, Disting. prof., 1974-93, chmn. dept., 1984-90. Mem. Citizens Adv. Com. to Upper Milford Zoning Commn., 1970-72, Pa. Humanities Council, 1983-87. Served with U.S. Army, 1945-46. Recipient Lindback award for disting. teaching Lehigh U., 1966, Student award for outstanding teaching, 1967, Stabler award for disting. teaching, 1981; Lehigh Yearbook dedication, 1973; Mellon faculty devel. grantee, 1977; Fulbright lectr. Katholieke U., Leuven, Belgium, 1987. Fellow Royal Soc. for Encouragement of Arts, Mfrs. and Commerce; mem. Orgn. Am. Historians. Democrat. Home: 6591 Corning Rd Zionsville PA 18092 Office: Lehigh U Dept History Maginnes 9 W Packer Ave Bethlehem PA 18015-3082

DOWLING, NADINE VALERY, college administrator, educator; b. Weymouth, Mass., Feb. 14, 1947; d. Clayton Ellsworth and Alise (Rostan) D. BS with high honors, Northeastern U., 1978, MBA, 1983, postgrad., 1986-87; EdM, Harvard U., 1992, EdD in Higher Edn. Adminstrn., 1997. Asst. dir. personnel Northeastern U., Boston, 1972-84, mem. faculty coll. bus., 1980-92; assoc. v.p. human resources/affirmative action Emerson Coll., Boston, 1984-93; chief adminstrv. officer Roxbury C.C., Roxbury Crossing, 1994—. Cons. Whale Communications, N.Y.C., 1978-80, Images, Hull, Mass., 1982-88; exec. v.p., cons. Mgmt. Concepts, Hull, Mass., 1989-91. Founder New Eng. Retirement Planners Council, 1974; co-chair Gov's. Adv. Coun. for Affirmative Action, Boston, 1990—; mem. pers. bd. Town of Hull, 1989-90. Mem. NAFE (dir. network 1985-86), Pers. Mgrs. Coun. (chair employment com. 1989—), Internat. Assn. Pers. Women (editor newsletter 1982-83, pub. rels. com. 1983-84, chair employment com. 1989—), Am. Soc. Pers. Adminstrs., Mass. Assn. Affirmative Actions Profls., Coll. and Univ. Pers. Assn., Small Coll. Pers. Mgrs. Assn. (founder), Fringe Benefits Adminstrs. Coun. (founder), Greater Boston C. of C. (speaker Bus. Expo 1985). Democrat. Methodist. Office: Roxbury C C 1234 Columbus Ave Rm 313 Roxbury Crossing MA 02120-3423 Home: 4993 Gunners Run NE Roswell GA 30075-1682 E-mail: ndowli@rcc.mass.edu.com.

DOWLING, THOMAS ALLAN, mathematics professor; b. Little Rock, Feb. 19, 1941; s. Charles and Esther (Jensen) D.; m. Nancy Lenthe D.; children: Debra Lynn, David Thomas. BS, Creighton U., 1962; PhD, U. N.C., 1967. Research assoc. U. N.C.-Chapel Hill, 1967-69, asst. prof., 1969-72; assoc. prof. math. Ohio State U., Columbus, 1972-82, prof., 1982—. Ops. researcher U.S. Govt., Patrick AFB, Fla., 1963-64; faculty fellow NASA at UCLA, Pasadena, summer, 1968; conf. organizer U. N.C., 1967, 70, Ohio State U., 1978, 82, 88, 92, 94, 98, 00, 02, 03. Editor: Combinatorial Mathematics and its Applications, 1967, 70; contbr. article to profl. jours.; discoverer Dowling lattices. NSF grantee, 1972-79 Mem. AAUP, Am. Math. Soc., Math. Assn. Am., Inst. Combinatorics and Applications. Democrat. Home: 2565 Sandover Rd Columbus OH 43220-2848 Office: Ohio State U Dept Math 231 W 18th Ave Columbus OH 43210-1101 Office Phone: 614-292-5013. E-mail: tdowling@math.ohio_state.edu, tdowlinh@columbus.rr.com.

DOWNEN, MADELINE ELIZABETH, hospital librarian; b. Pontiac, Mich., Aug. 17, 1930; d. Albert Oran and Hazel Marie (Fisk) Morgan; m. Evan Ray Downen, Dec. 3, 1949 (div. 1968); children: Charles Albert, Linda Carol Yedinak, Gregory Lyn. BS in Edn., Calumet Coll., 1978. Cert. hosp. libr. Am. Hosp. Assn., 1964. Asst. hosp. libr. St. Catherine Hosp., East Chicago, Ind., 1947-50, hosp. libr., 1962—95; ret., 1995. Med. libr. cons. Our Lady of Mercy Hosp., Dyer, Ind., 1969-70; bylaws com. Midwest Regional Med. Lib. Coun., 1971; adv. com. Midwest Regional Libr., 1974; state libr. cons. com. Ind. Univ. Sch. of Medicine, 1973; chmn. nominating com. Coun. of Health Sci. Librs. Midwest Health Sci. Libr. Network, 1974; bd. dirs. N.W. Ind. Area Libr. Svc. Authority Dist. 1, 1975-76, exec. bd. mem. 1976. Mem. First Christian Ch., Hammond. Ind. state rep. to Greater Midwest Regional Med. Libr. Network Coun., 1989-90. Democrat. Mem. Christian Ch. Avocations: swimming, creative arts, water aerobics, music, dance. Home: 2018 Davidson Pl Whiting IN 46394-2027 Office: St Catherine Hosp 4321 Fir St East Chicago IN 46312-3097

DOWNEN, ROBERT LYNN, international affairs analyst and political consultant, editor, writer; b. Wichita, Kans., Apr. 18, 1951; s. Lyndall and Ruth Downen; m. Holly Hutchens, Sept. 1, 1980; children: Heather, Lindsey. BA cum laude, Washington U., St. Louis, 1973; MA, George Washington U., Washington, 1975. Legis. asst. to Bob Dole, U.S. Senate, Washington, 1973-79; dir. Pacific stds. Ctr. for Strategic and Internat. Studies/Georgetown U., Washington, 1979-84; dir., spl. projects U.S. State Dept./Asia, Washington, 1984-89; v.p. Neill and Co., Washington, 1989-94, The Jefferson Group, Washington, 1994-98; pres. Downen Consulting, 1998—2004; v.p. APCO Worldwide, Washington, 2004—. Author: The Taiwan Pawn, 1979, To Bridge the China Strait, 1984; editor: Multi-System Nations and International Law, 1982, The Emerging Pacific Community, 1984. Mem. adv. group Dole for Pres., Washington, 1996, Reagan for Pres., Washington, 1980; bd. dirs. United Bapt. Ch. Named Kans. DeMolay of Yr., Order of DeMolay, 1969, DeMolay Legion of Honor award, 1983; recipient Wolcott Scholar award Internat. High Twelve Clubs, Mo., 1974, Hon. Mem. award Sojourners Lodge AF & AM, Panama Canal Zone, 1978. Mem. Masons, Phi Beta Kappa, Sigma Nu. Republican. Baptist. Avocations: photography, genealogy, study of american history and government, travel.

DOWNER, MICHAEL JOSEF, lawyer; b. Los Angeles, Feb. 25, 1955; s. Lowell Howard and Cora Marie (Masek) D. BA with honors, UCLA, 1977; JD, Southwestern U., 1981. Bar: Calif. 1982. Sr. v.p. fund bus. mgmt. group, coord. legal and compliance Capital Rsch. and Mgmt. Co., L.A., 1992—. Bd. dirs. Am. Fund Ins. Series, Capital Bank and Trust Co.; chmn. Investment Co. Inst. SEC Rules Com. and '40 Acts Group. Bd. dirs. Southwestern U. Sch. Law. Mem. ABA, Calif. Bar Assn., Los Angeles County Bar Assn., Beta Theta Pi (bd. dirs. Gamma Nu). Office: Capital Rsch and Mgmt Co 333 S Hope St 55th Fl Los Angeles CA 90071

DOWNER, ROBERT NELSON, lawyer; b. Newton, Iowa, July 15, 1939; s. Lowell William and Mabel Mary (Hannon) Downer; m. Jane Alice Glafka, May 29, 1971; children: Elise Michele, Andrew Nelson. BA, U. Iowa, 1961, JD, 1963. Bar: Iowa 1963, U.S. Dist. Ct. (so. dist.) Iowa 1963, U.S. Dist. Ct. (no. dist.) Iowa 1964, U.S. Supreme Ct. 1995, U.S. Ct. Appeals (8th cir.) 2001. Assoc. Meardon Law Office, Iowa City, 1963-68; mem. Meardon, Sueppel & Downer PLC and predecessor firms, Iowa City, 1969—. Dir., sec. KZIA, Inc., Cedar Rapids, Iowa, 1975—, Iowa City Tennis & Fitness Ctr., 1987—93; trustee The Oaknoll Found., Iowa City, 1990—98, Herbert Hoover Presdl. Libr. Assn., West Branch, Iowa, 2000—; dir. Christian Retirement Svcs., Inc., Iowa City, 1967—82, Iowa State Bar Found., 1996—2002, Iowa Law Sch. Found., 2000—; bd. regents State of Iowa, 2003—, pres. pro tem, 2004—. Mem. Iowa Supreme Ct. Task Force on Domestic Abuse, 1993—94; bd. dirs. Iowa City Area Devel. Group, 1993—2001, chmn., 1996—97, co-chair, 2000—01; bd. dirs., sec. Cmty. Found. Johnson County, Iowa, 2000—03; del. Rep. Nat. conv., New Orleans, 1988; mem. Iowa Supreme Ct. comm. Continuing Legal Edn., 1975—83; chair adminstrv. bd. First United Meth. Ch., Iowa City, 1985—87; pres. Greater Iowa City Area C. of C., 1979; bd. trustees Iowa City Pub. Libr., 1971—75, chair, 1973—74. Named to Iowa Legal Aid Hall Fame, 2005; recipient Excellence in Svc. award, Legal Svcs. Corp. Iowa, 1996. Fellow: Iowa State Bar Found., Am. Bar Found., Am. Coll. Trust and Estate Counsel (state chair 2000—05); mem.: ABA, Johnson County Bar Assn. (pres. 1976), Iowa State Bar Assn. (chair probate sect. 1990—93, v.p. 1993—94, pres.-elect 1994—95, pres. 1995—96, Merit award 2001), Rotary (pres. 1989—90). Republican. Methodist. Home: 2029 Rochester Ct Iowa City IA 52245-3246 Office: Meardon Sueppel & Downer PLC 122 S Linn St Iowa City IA 52240-1830 Office Phone: 319-338-9222. Business E-Mail: bobd@meardonlaw.com.

DOWNER, WILLIAM JOHN, JR., retired health facility administrator; b. Springfield, Ill., Sept. 29, 1932; s. William John and Geraldine (Foster) D.; m. Wanda M. Parson, Oct. 3, 1953; children: William E., Lawrence R. BA, Mich. State U., 1954; MHA, U. Mich., 1961. Various mgmt. positions Blodgett Meml. Med. Ctr., Grand Rapids, Mich., 1961-74, pres., CEO, 1974-84; pres., chief exec. officer Columbus Hosp., Great Falls, Mont., 1985-95, sr. cons., 1995-96. Contbr. articles to profl. jours. City commr. City of Gt. Falls, 1996—99; hosp. divsn. chmn. United Way Kent County, Grand Rapids, 1969; mem. cmty. adv. bd. N.W. Mont. for Horizon Air, 1990—97; bd. dirs. No. Rockies Easter Seals/Goodwill, 1995—2000; bd. dirs. Big Sky chpt. ARC, 1986—92, 1996—97; commr. 211th Gen. Assembly Presbyn. Ch. USA, 1999—2000; elder Westminster Presbyn. Ch., Grand Rapids, 1968—85, 1st Presbyn. Ch., Gt. Falls, 1985—2000, Oceanside, Calif., 2001—; mem. com. on ministry Glacier Presbytery, 1996—2000, moderator, 1997. Lt. col. AUS, ret. Fellow Am. Coll. Healthcare Execs. (life, regent for Mich. 1978-84, regent for Mont. 1986-89, Regent's award 1996); mem. Am. Hosp. Assn. (life, mem. governing coun. sect. for met. hosps. 1991-94), Mont. Hosp. Assn. (bd. dirs. 1987-90, chmn. 1989), Mich. Hosp. Assn. (bd. dirs. 1973-82, chmn. 1980-81, Homminga award 1982), Great Falls C. of C. (mem. exec. com. 1988, chmn. 1991-92, mil. affairs exec. com. 1995-99, vice chmn. 1998, chmn. 1999), Rotary, Phi Kappa Phi, Beta Gamma Sigma. Avocations: civil war history, golf, travel. Home: 4001 Arcadia Way Oceanside CA 92056-5139 E-mail: bwdowner@cox.net.

DOWNES, LAURENCE M., gas industry executive; b. Hackensack, N.J., Sept. 27, 1957; s. Laurence F. and Helene L. (Hart) D.; m. Mary Caroline Oliva, Oct. 3, 1981; 1 child, Thomas A. BBA, Iona Coll., 1979, MBA, 1981. Asst. v.p. Midlantic Nat. Bank, Edison, N.J., 1979-84; treas. NJ Resources Corp., Wall, NJ, 1985—90, sr. v.p., CFO, 1990—95, pres., CEO, NJ Nat. Gas, 1995—, pres., CEO, dir., 1995—, chmn., 1996—. Chmn., dir. Am. Gas Assn.; chmn. Natural Gas Council; trustee Am. Gas Found. Trustee Iona Coll.; chmn. Safe Child Consortium; dir., chmn. audit com. NJ Schools Construction Corp.; chmn. fin. council Diocese of Trenton. Republican. Roman Catholic. Office: NJ Resources Corp 1415 Wyckoff Rd Belmar NJ 07719*

DOWNES, PATRICIA ANN, minister; b. Sussex, N.J., Dec. 10, 1945; d. Leonard McGill and Violet McCarty; m. Randall Priest Jr., June 21, 1964 (div. May 20, 1988); children: Linda, Randall, Sarah-Elisabeth; m. Donald Downes, Oct. 17, 1992. AA, Brevard C.C., 1986; BSW, U. Ctrl. Fla., 1988; MDiv, Emory U., 1991; postgrad., So. Fla. Ctr. Theol. Studies, 2004—. Lic. practical nurse, Fla., 1965; ordained clergy, cert. in Christian edn. United Meth. Ch. Nurse Holmes Regional Hosp., Melbourne, Fla., 1965—67, therapeutic foster parent, 1967—88; pastor United Meth. Ch., Holly Hill, 1991—94, Miami, 1992—2001, Palm Bay, 2001—. Foster parent trainer Holmes Regional Hosp., Melbourne, 1980—88. Author: Foster Parent Manual, 1983. AIDS counselor, Melbourne, 1985—87; guardian ad litem GAL Program, Brevard County, 1981—86; bd. dirs. YMCA, Melbourne, 1975—79, Miami Urban Ministries, Miami, 1998—2000, Palm Bay Hosp., 2002—; grantwriter Foster Care Cmty. Edn., 1985. Named Child Advocate Yr., Children's Home Soc., 1983; recipient Cmty. Svc. award, Brevard C.C., 1986. Mem.: Dist. Bd. Ordained Ministry. Democrat. United Methodist. Avocations: writing, sewing, reading. Office: Palm Bay United Meth Ch 2100 Port Malabar Blvd Palm Bay FL 32905

DOWNES, RACKSTRAW, artist; b. Pembury, Kent, Eng., Nov. 8, 1939; came to U.S., 1961; s Henry Alfred and Rosa Kathleen (Rackstraw) D. BA, Cambridge U., 1961; MFA, Yale U., 1964. Asst. prof. U. Pa., Phila., 1967-78; mem.faculty Skowhegan Sch., Maine, 1975; mem. faculty N.Y. Studio Sch., N.Y.C., 1980-82. Editor Fairfield Porter: Art in Its Own Terms, 1979; bd. govs. Skowhegan Sch. Painting and Sculpture, 1981-95. One-man shows Kornblee Gallery, N.Y.C., 1972-82, Hirschl & Adler Modern, N.Y.C., 1982-94, Marlborough Galleries, N.Y.C., London, Madrid, 1996-99, Chinati Found., Marfa, Tex., 1999, Robert Miller Gallery, N.Y.C., 2000-04, Betty Cuningham Gallery, N.Y.C., 2004-; exhibited in group shows San Antonio Mus., 1981, Pa. Acad., Phila., 1981, Carnegie Internat., Pitts., 1983, Whitney Biennial, N.Y.C., 1981, Mus. Modern Art, N.Y.C., 2000, Snug Harbor Cultural Ctr., S.I., 2001; represented permanent collections, Mus. Modern Art, N.Y.C., Houston Mus. Fine Arts, Whitney Mus. Am. Art, N.Y.C., Hirschhorn Mus., Washington, Pa. Acad. Fine Art, Met. Mus. Art, N.Y.C., Phila. Mus. Art, Carnegie Inst., Pitts., Corcoran Gallery Art, Smithsonian Mus., Washington, Art Inst. Chgo., Nelson-Atkins Mus. Art, Kansas City, Ludwig Mus., Cologne; author: In Relation to the Whole, 2000; author Under the Gowanus and Razor-Wire Jour., 2000. Ingram Merrill fellow, 1974; grantee Nat. Endowment for Arts, 1980; recipient Creative Artist's Pub. Svc. award State of N.Y., 1978, Nat. Acad. Arts and Scis. award, 1989; Guggenheim fellow, 1998. Mem. Am. Acad. Arts and Letters. Office Phone: 212-334-8410.

DOWNES, WILLIAM F., federal judge; b. 1946; BA, U. North Tex., 1968; JD, U. Houston, 1974. Ptnr. Clark and Downes, Green River, Wyo., 1976-78; mem. Brown & Drew, Casper, Wyo., 1978-94; dist. judge US Dist. Ct. Wyo., Casper, Wyo., 1994—, chief judge. Capt. USMC, 1968—71. Mem.: Natrona County Bar Assn., Wyo. State Bar, Wyo. Athletic Club, Casper Petroleum Club. Office: US Dist Ct 111 S Wolcott St Rm 210 Casper WY 82601-2534*

DOWNEY, ARTHUR HAROLD, JR., lawyer, mediator; b. N.Y.C., Nov. 21, 1938; s. Arthur Harold Sr. and Charlotte (Bailey) D.; m. Gwen Vanden Berg, May 28, 1960; children: Anne Leigh, Neal Arthur, Drew Thomas. BA, Cen. Coll., Pella, Iowa, 1960; LLB, Cornell U., 1963. Bar: Colo. 1963, Wyo. 1991, U.S. Dist. Ct. Colo. 1963, U.S. Dist. Ct. Wyo. 1993, U.S. Ct. Appeals (10th cir.) 1963; diplomate Am. Bd. Forensic Examiners. From assoc. to ptnr. Weller, Friedrich, Ward & Andrew, Denver, 1963-82; ptnr., chief exec. officer Downey Law Firm P.C., Denver, 1982—. Trustee panel Colo. Hosp. Assn., 1988-93; del. Nat. Congress Hosp. Trustees, Am. Hosp. Assn., 1988-93. Contbr. articles to profl. jours. Past pres. Columbine Village Homeowners Assn., Trails End Homeowners Assn., Upper Village Homeowners Assn., Powderhorn Condo. Homeowners Assn., Breckenridge, Colo.; chmn. Promontory Point Homeowners Com., 2004—; vice moderator Presbytery of Denver, 1972; chmn. bd. trustees Bethesda Psychealth Sys., Inc., 1990—93. Fellow Internat. Soc. Barristers (emeritus); mem. ABA, Colo. Bar Assn., Larimer County Bar Assn., Wyo. Bar Assn., Def. Rsch. Inst. (disting. svc. award), Nat. Inst. Trial Advocacy (teaching faculty, team leader 1973—), Colo. Def. Lawyers Assn. (pres. 1977-78), Am. Coll. Legal Medicine (assoc. in law), Nat. Bd. Trial Advocacy (cert.), Am. Arbitration Assn. Republican. Mem. Christian Reformed Ch. In Am. Avocations: photography, woodworking, skiing. Office: Downey Law Firm PC 7688 Promontory Dr Windsor CO 80528-9305 Office Phone: 970-267-0925. E-mail: downeypc@comcast.net.

DOWNEY, ARTHUR THOMAS, III, lawyer; b. N.Y.C., Aug. 17, 1937; s. Arthur T. and Beatrice (Fortune) Downey; m. Mary S. Downey; children: Thomas, Allison, Paul stepchildren: Christopher, Sarah, Matthew. BA, St. Vincent, 1959; LLB, Villanova U., 1962; LLM, Georgetown U., 1963. Bar: D.C. 1964. Atty. U.S. Dept. State, Washington and Berlin, 1964-69; prof. staff The Nat. Security Coun., The White House, Washington, 1969-72; assoc. Morgan. Lewis & Bockius, Washington, 1972-75; dep. asst. sec. U.S. Dept. Commerce, Washington, 1975-77; ptnr. Sutherland, Ashill & Brennan, Washington, 1977-90; shareholder Johnson & Gibbs, 1990—92; v.p. Baker Hughes Inc., Washington, 1992—. Adj. prof. Georgetown U. Law Sch., Washington, 1978—90. Co-author: Freedom From Federal Establishment, 1964. Trustee Am. Univ. Sharjah, 2002—, Fgn. Bondholders Protective Coun., 2002—. Mem.: ABA (vice chmn. sec. internat. law 1984), UN Assn. of USA (bd. govs. 1985—90). Office: Baker Hughes Incorp 3900 Essex Ln Ste 1200 Houston TX 77027-5170

DOWNEY, BRUCE L., medical company executive, lawyer; Assoc. Bishop, Cook, Purcell and Reynolds; ptnr. Winston & Strawn; pres., COO, bd. dirs. Barr Labs., Inc., Blauvelt, N.Y., 1993—, chmn. bd. dirs., CEO, 1994—. Office: Barr Labs Inc Two Quaker Rd PO Box 2900 Pomona NY 10970-0519 Office Phone: 201-930-3300. E-mail: bdowney@barrlabs.com.

DOWNEY, GARY NEIL, marine corps officer; b. Rochester, N.Y., Nov. 3, 1957; s. Arnold Blaine and Barbara Ann (Quiggle) D. Assoc., Va. Coastal Cmty., Woodbridge, Va., 1978. Commd. USMC, advanced through grades to cwo-5, 1998—, security guard Casablanca, Morocco, 1980-86, pers. officer Camp Lejeune, N.C., 1986-89, Hqrs. USMC, Washington, 1989-94; course developer Marine Corps Inst., Washington, 1994-97; pers. officer Basic Sch., Quantico, Va., 1997-99; adjutant Marforlant, Norfolk, Va., 1999—. Author: (corr. courses) Supply Chiefs Guidebooks, 1994, Basic Pay Entitlements, 1995, Sassy Computer Classes, 1996. Scoutmaster Boy Scouts Am., 1978-94. Decorated Purple Heart, Meritorious Svc. medal. Mem. Internat. Soc. Performance Instrs. Democrat. Roman Catholic. Avocation: computers. Home: 1900 Dulles Ct Virginia Beach VA 23464-8709 Office: Adjutant 1348 Ingrahm St Norfolk VA 23551-0001 E-mail: GDowney@aol.com.

DOWNEY, JAMES CECIL, retired music and humanities educator; b. Grand Bay, Ala. s. James Fred and Thelma Hamilton Downey; m. Phyllis Barber, Jan. 25, 1952; children: James Vance, Joy Lyndell, Jennifer Anne, Robert Joel. BA, William Carey Coll., 1963; MMus, U. So. Miss., 1965; PhD, Tulane U., 1968. Prof. music William Carey Coll., Hattiesburg, Miss., 1966-96, prof. humanities, 1989-96, dean Gulfport (Miss.) campus, 1982-85, coord. continuing edn., 1985-86. State officer Am. Musicological Soc., 1966-96. Author: Mingo County Tales, 2003; contbr. articles to profl. jours. Founder, dir. Gulf Coast Cmty. Chorus, Biloxi, Miss., 1982. With U.S. Army, 1954-56. Recipient Jaap Kunst award Soc. for Ethnomusicology, 1964. Democrat. Baptist. Avocation: gentleman farmer. Home: 530 Knight Rd Sumrall MS 39482-3826

DOWNEY, JOHN ALEXANDER, physician, educator; b. Sept. 16, 1930; BSc in Medicine, U. Man., MD with honors, 1954; PhD, Oxford U., 1962. Diplomate Am. Bd. Phys. Medicine and Rehab. Intern Vancouver Gen. Hosp., Canada, 1953—54; resident phys. medicine and rehab. Columbia Presbyn. Med. Ctr., N.Y.C., 1954—56, resident, 1957—58; asst. resident internal medicine Peter Bent Brigham Hosp., Boston, 1956—57; asst. to med. dir., cons. phys. medicine Blythedale Children's Hosp., Valhalla, NY, 1957—59; rsch. assoc. Columbia U., 1958—59; vis. fellow Presbyn. Hosp., N.Y.C., 1958—59; sr. resident internal medicine Peter Bent Brigham Hosp., 1959—60; vis. worker Med. Rsch. Coun. Group for Body Temperature Control, Oxford, England, 1960—62; assc. prof. rehab. medicine Columbia U. Coll. Physicians ans Surgeons, 1962—64, assoc. prof., 1964—67, prof., 1967—74, Simon Baruch prof., 1974—, chair dept. rehab. medicine, 1974—90, asst. prof. medicine, 1963—64. Asst. attending Presbyn. Hosp., N.Y.C., 1962—64, assoc. attending, 1964—68, attending, 1968—, dir. rehab. medicine svc., 1974—90; vis. prof. dept. human physiology and pharmacology U. Adelaide, Australia, 1969. Author: Stroke: Two to Recover, 1969; co-editor: Physiological Basis of Rehabilitation Medicine, 1971, Physiological Basis of Rehabilitation Medicine, 2d edit., 1994, The Child with Disabling Illness: Principles of Rehabilitation, 1974, The Child with Disabling Illness: Principles of Rehabilitation, 2d edit., 1982, Bereavement of Physical Disability: Recommitment to Life, Health and Function, 1982; mem. editl. bd.: Benneman's Practice of Pediatrics, 1974; contbr. articles to profl. jours.; (films) Rehabilitation: A Patient's Perspective, 1973; I Had a Stroke, 1978; Physiatry: A Physician's Perspective, 1981. Fellow: Royal Coll. Physicians (Can.; mem.: AAAS, APA, AMA, NAS, N.Y. Acad. Medicine, N.Y. Acad. Scis., N.Y. Rheumatism Assn., Am. Rheumatism Assn. Office: Columbia U Dept Rehab Medicine 630 W 168th St New York NY 10032-3795

DOWNEY, KEVIN, advertising executive, publishing executive; BA in Comm. magna cum laude, Mercyhurst Coll., Erie, Pa.; M Pub. Affairs and Journalism with honors, Am. U., Washington; participant Internet Elect. Commerce Program, Gannon U.; participant Media Mgmt. and Entrepreneurship Program, Poynter Inst. Cert. Morgan yacht salesman. Pub. Warren County Guide, Warren, Pa., 1988—98; gen. mgr. Corry Jour., 1987—98; pub. Mineral Daily-News Tribune, Keyser, W.Va., 1998—2000; group advt. and bus. devel. mgr. Greater Niagra Newspapers, Niagra Falls, NY, 2000—01; classified advt. contracts supr. The Buffalo News, Buffalo, 2001—02; CEO Bright Hospitality, Inc., Titusville, Pa., 2002—03; consulting gen. mgr. Horizon Publs., Ridgeway, Pa., 2003; advt. dir. the Virgin Islands Daily News, Inc., St. Thomas, 2003—. Address: 230 E Pleasant St Corry PA 16407: 4029 Estate Thomas St Thomas VI 00802

DOWNEY, MARCESE ELLEN WALSH, librarian; b. Chgo., May 10, 1919; d. Cecil W. and Ellen T. (Benson) Walsh; m. Melvin C. Downey, Sept. 22, 1945 (dec. 1966); children: Maria Lisa, Rosemary T. Forsberg, Andrew M., Anna K. Davis. BS, Rosary Coll., 1942; MLS, Villanova U., 1969. Soc. editor Pictioral Rev., Oak Park, Ill., 1938-39; libr. Augustine Hist. Inst., Villanova (Pa.) U., 1972—92. Ensign USN WAVES, 1943-46. Avocations: gardening, painting, genealogy.

DOWNEY, MICHAEL PATRICK, lawyer; b. St. Louis; m. Elizabeth R. Downey. BA, Georgetown U., 1992; JD, Washington U., St. Louis, 1998. Bar: Mo. 1998, U.S. Ct. Appeals (8th cir.) 1998, Ill. 1999, U.S. Dist. Ct. (ea. dist.) Mo. 1999, U.S. Dist. Ct. (so. dist.) Ill. 1999, U.S. Dist. Ct. (cen. dist.) Ill. 2003, U.S. Dist. Ct. (we. dist.) Mo. 2004, U.S. Ct. Appeals (7th cir.) 2004. Law clk. to Chief Judge Pasco M. Bowman U.S. Ct. Appeals (8th cir.), Kansas City, Mo., 1998—99; sr. atty. Fox Galvin LLC, St. Louis, 2001—. Adj. prof. Washington U. Sch. of Law, 2000—. Exec. articles editor: Washington U. Law Quar., 1997—98. Mem.: ABA (leadership mentee law practice mgmt. sect. 2004—05), Ill. State Bar Assn. (standing com. on profl. conduct 2003—), Mo. Bar Assn. (spl. com. on lawyer advt. 2004—, spl. com. on ethics 2005, 2005), Bar Assn. Metro St. Louis (chmn. ethics com. 2003—). Office: Fox Galvin LLC 1 Memorial Dr Saint Louis MO 63102 Office Phone: 314-588-7000. Business E-Mail: mdowney@foxgalvin.com.

DOWNEY, RICHARD LAWRENCE, lawyer; b. Washington, Apr. 3, 1948; s. William G. and Laufey A. D.; m. Pamela L. Drewry, July 10, 1971; children: Anna Christine, Laura Michele, Richard Lawrence, Patricia Kathleen. BA, Randolph-Macon Coll., 1970; JD, Hamline U., 1977. Bar: Va. 1978, U.S. Dist. Ct. (ea. dist.) Va. 1978, U.S. Ct. Appeals (4th cir.) 1978, U.S. Supreme Ct. 1983, U.S. Tax Ct. 1990, U.S. Claims Ct. 1990; diplomate Nat. Bd. Trial Advocacy; bd. cert. civil trial advocacy. Assoc. Downey & Lennhoff, Springfield, Va., 1978-80; pvt. practice Fairfax, Va., 1980-82; sr. ptnr. Duvall, Blackburn, Hale & Downey, Fairfax, Va., 1982-92; prin. Richard L. Downey & Assocs., 1992—. Lt. col. USAR. Named Outstanding Young Man of Am. U.S. Jaycees, 1982. Mem. ABA, ATLA, Va. State Bar Assn., Va. Trial Lawyers Assn., Fairfax Bar Assn. (gen. dist. cts. com. 1984-86, cir. ct. com. 1988-89), Nat. Lawyers Assn., Christian Legal Soc., Fairfax County C. of C. (internat. trade com., planning and land use com., legis. com. 1984), Phi Alpha Delta, Rotary. Republican. Address: 4126 Leonard Dr Fairfax VA 22030-5118 Office Phone: 703-273-8800. E-mail: rldesq@aol.com.

DOWNEY, RICHARD RALPH, lawyer, consultant, accountant, management consultant; b. Boston, Mass., Apr. 22, 1934; s. Paul Joseph and Evelyn Mae (Butler) Downey; children: Richard Ralph (dec.), Janice M., Erin C., Timothy M. BS, Northeastern U., 1958; MBA, Harvard U., 1962; JD, Suffolk U., 1979; LLM, Boston U., 1981. Bar: Mass. 1979, Fed. 1980. Mem. audit staff Price Waterhouse & Co., Boston, 1962—64; assoc. Assocs. for Internat. Rsch., Inc., Cambridge, 1964—68, v.p., dir., 1968—. Treas. 1580 House Condominium Trust, 1979—80. Mem. ABA, Am. Inst. CPA's, Mass. Soc. CPA's, Mass. Bar Assn., Assn. Trial Lawyers Am., Boston Bar Assn., Phi Delta Phi, Algonquin Club, Harvard Club (Boston, N.Y.C.). Home: 25 Washington Ave Cambridge MA 02140-2834 Office: 1100 Massachusetts Ave Cambridge MA 02138-5241

DOWNEY, ROBERT, JR., actor, singer, musician; b. NYC, Apr. 4, 1965; s. Robert Downey and Elsie Ford; m. Deborah Falconer, May 29, 1992 (div. April 26, 2004); 1 child, Indio; m. Susan Levin, Aug. 27, 2005. Appeared in plays American Passion, 1983, Alms for the Middle Class, 1983, Fraternity, 1984; TV series Saturday Night Live, 1985-86; TV miniseries Mussolini: The Untold Story, 1985; films include Pound, 1970, Greaser's Palace, 1972, Up the Academy, 1980, Baby It's You, 1983, Firstborn, 1984, Deadwait, 1985, To Live and Die in L.A., 1985, Tuff Turf, 1985, Weird Science, 1985, America, 1986, Back to School, 1986, Less Than Zero, 1987, The Pick-Up Artist, 1987, Johnny Be Good, 1988, Rented Lips, 1988, 1969, 1988, True Believer, 1989, Chances Are, 1989, That's Adequate, 1990, Air America, 1990, Too Much Sun, 1991, Soapdish, 1991, Chaplin, 1992 (Acad. award nomination best actor), Heart and Souls, 1993, Short Cuts, 1993, The Last Party, 1993, Natural Born Killers, 1994, Only You, 1994, Restoration, 1994, Hail Caesar, 1994, Richard III, 1995, Home for the Holidays, 1995, Danger Zone, 1996, One Night Stand, 1997, Hugo Pool, 1997, Two Girls and a Guy, 1997, The Gingerbread Man, 1998, U.S. Marshals, 1998, In Dreams, 1999, Friends & Lovers, 1999, Bowfinger, 1999, Black and White, 1999, Wonder Boys, 2000, Auto Motives, 2000, Lethargy, 2002, The Singing Detective, 2003, Whatever We Do, 2003, Gothika, 2003, Eros, 2004, Game 6, 2005, Kiss, Kiss, Bang, Bang, 2005, Good Night and Good Luck, 2005; (TV films) Mr. Willowby's Christmas Tree, 1995; (TV series) Ally McBeal, 2000-2001; singer, musician Man Like Me, 2004, The Futurist, 2004; featured singer (movie and TV soundtracks) Chaplin, 1992, Heart and Sould, 1993, Ally McBeal-A Very Ally Christmas, 2000, Ally McBeal-For Once In My Life, 2001, The Singing Detective, 2003; featured in (music video) I Want Love by Elton John, 2001*

DOWNIE, LEONARD, JR., editor, writer; b. Cleve., May 1, 1942; s. Leonard and Pearl Martha (Evenheimer) D.; m. Barbara Lindsey, July 15, 1960 (div. 1971); children: David Leonard, Scott Leonard; m. Geraldine Rebach, Aug. 15, 1971 (div. 1997); children: Joshua Mark, Sarah Elizabeth; m. Janice Galin, Sept. 12, 1997. BA, Ohio State U., 1964, MA, 1965, LLD (hon.), 1993. Reporter, editor Washington Post, 1964-74, met. editor, 1974-79, London corr., 1979-82, nat. editor, 1982-84, mng. editor, 1984-91; dir. L.A. Times-Washington Post News Svc., 1991—; exec. editor Washington Post, 1991—; dir. Internat. Herald Tribune, 1985—2002. Author: Justice Denied, 1971, Mortgage on America, 1974, The New Muckrackers, 1976; author: (with Robert G. Kaiser) The News About the News, 2002. Trustee Georgetown Day Sch., 1988-93. Recipient Gavel award ABA, 1967; Alicia Patterson Found. fellow, 1971-72, Goldsmith award for the News About the News, Joan Shorenstein Ctr., Harvard U. John F. Kennedy Sch. of Govt., 2003. Fellow Soc. Profl. Journalists; mem. Am. Soc. Newspaper Editors. Office: Washington Post Co 1150 15th St NW Washington DC 20071-0002

DOWNIE, RICHARD DUNCAN, government agency administrator, retired military officer; BS, U.S. Mil. Acad., 1976; M In Internat. Rels., U. So. Calif., 1983, D in Internat. Rels., 1995. Fgn. area officer, Latin Am., Colombia, Panama, Mexico and Germany; exch. officer to Colombian Army; comdt. Western Hemisphere Inst. for Security Coop., 2001—04; dir. Ctr. Hemispheric Def. Studies USCG, Washington, 2004—. Author: Learning From Conflict: The U.S. Military in Vietnam, El Salvador and the Drug War, 1998; contbr. articles. Decorated Def. Superior Svc. Legion of Merit; named to Order Peruvian Cross; recipient Orden de Merito Academico, Colombia, Bosnia/Former Yugoslavia NATO medal; fellow, MIT. Office: Ctr Hemisphere Defense Studies USCG HQ Bldg Ste 118 2100 2d St SW Washington DC 20593-0001 Office Phone: 202-685-4670.

DOWNING, DARLENE L., non-for-profit organization executive; b. Cobleskill, N.Y., Jan. 30, 1946; d. Chester W. and Margie G. (Ronk) D.; 1 child, Zachary Boyd Sherry. BA, SUNY, Albany, 1981, postgrad., 1981-82. Program dir., dir. mktg. Rensselaerville (N.Y.) Inst., 1984-88; policy analyst N.Y. Assembly, Albany, N.Y., 1988-90; prin. policy analyst N.Y. Senate, Albany, 1991-97; exec. dir., editor newsletter and mag. Catskill Ctr. for Conservation Devel., inc., Arkville, N.Y., 1997—. Fundraiser Cedar Grove, Thomas Cole's hist. residence, Catskill, 1997-99. Office: Catskill Ctr for Conservation and Devel Rte 28 Arkville NY 12406 Home: PO Box 395 Pebble Beach CA 93953-0395

DOWNING, DAVID CHARLES, retired minister; b. South Gate, Calif., June 24, 1938; s. Kenneth Oliver and Edna Yesobel (Casaday) D.; m. Tommye Catherine Tew, July 11, 1959 (dec. Dec. 11, 1985); children: Sheri Lynn, Teresa Kay, Carla Jeane, Michael David. BA, N.W. Christian Coll., 1961; B in Divinity, Tex. Christian U., 1966, M in Theology, 1973; DMin, San Francisco Theol. Sem., 1987. Ordained to ministry Christian Ch., 1961. Min. Marcola (Oreg.) Ch. of Christ, 1958-59; assoc. min. First Christian Ch., Lebanon, Oreg., 1960-63, min. Ranger, Tex., 1963-65, Knox City, Tex., 1966-68, Fredonia, Kans., 1968-74, Ctrl. Christian Ch., Huntington, Ind., 1974-77; regional min., pres. Christian Ch. Greater Kansas City, Mo., 1978-94; sr. minister Univ. Christian Ch., Disciples of Christ, San Diego, 1994—2001; ret., 2001. Trustee Phillips Grad. Sem., Enid, Okla., 1988-94; bd. dirs. Ch. Fin. Coun., Indpls., Midwest Career Devel. Svc., Chgo.; v.p. bd. dirs. Midwest Christian Counseling Ctr., Kansas City. Author: A Contrast and Comparison of Pastoral Counseling in Rural and Urban Christian Churches, 1972, A Design for Enabling Urban Congregations to Cope with Their Fear of Displacement When Faced with Communities in Transition, 1987. Pres. Kansas City Interfaith Peace Alliance, 1980-82; interim regional min. Pacific S.W. Region Disciples Ch., 2002. Democrat. Mem. Christian Ch. Avocations: swimming, camping, fishing, water-skiing, collecting chalices. Home: 4325 Caminito De La Escena San Diego CA 92108-4201 E-mail: davidd624@cox.net.

DOWNING, KATHRYN M., former newspaper publishing executive, lawyer; b. Portland, Oreg., Mar. 24, 1953; BA in Econs., Lewis and Clark Coll., 1973; JD, Stanford U., 1979. Various positions Mead Data Ctrl., 1981—90, sr. dir. legal info. pub., 1988; pres., COO Electronic Pub. divsn. Thomson Profl. Pub., 1990—93; pres., CEO Lawyers Coop. Pub. divsn. Thomson Legal Pub., 1993—95, Mathew Bender, 1995—97; pres., CEO Mosby Matthew Bender unit, sr. v.p. Times Mirror, N.Y.C., 1997—99, vice pres., 1996—97, sr. v.p., 1997—98, exec. v.p., 1998—99; pres., CEO L.A. Times, 1998—99, pres., CEO, publisher, 1999—2000; CEO My Potential Inc., Santa Monica, Calif., 2000—01. Bd. dirs. Women's Found. Calif. Mem. Times Mirror Found., Jim Murray Meml. Found.; mem. bd. visitors Sch. Law Stanford U.; trustee Friends of Law Libr. of Congress; bd. visitors UCLA Anderson Sch. Bus.; pres. L.A. Times Fund; bd. trustees Lewis & Clark Coll. Fellow: Broad Urban Supt. Acad.; mem.: Newspaper Assn. Am., Am. Inns of Ct. (past pub. trustee), Am. Assn. Pubs. (bd. dirs.), L.A. C. of C.*

DOWNING, MARGARET MARY, newspaper editor; b. Altoona, Pa., June 3, 1952; d. Irvine William and Iva Ann (Regan) D.; m. Gary Beaver; children: Ian Downing-Beaver, Timothy Downing-Beaver, Abby Downing-Beaver. BA magna cum laude, Tex. Christian U., 1974. Reporting intern Corpus Christi Caller Times, 1973; reporter, bur. chief Beaumont (Tex.) Enterprise & Jour., 1974-76, Dallas Times Herald, 1976-80; reporter, asst. city editor, asst. bus., met. editor, mng. editor Houston Post, 1980—93; mng. editor Jackson (Miss.) Clarion-Ledger, 1993-97; editor-in-chief The Houston Press, 1998—. Jurist Pulitzer Prize Awards, 1992, 93; bd. dirs. News Media Credit Union, 1993, Santa's Helpers, 1992-93; mem. admissions com. Assn. Alternative Newspapers, 2000—. Respite foster parent vol. Harris County Children's Protective Svcs., 1993; chmn. landscape com. Windsor Hills Homeowners Assn.; active Madison Sta. Elem. PTA, 1993—98; coach South Madison County Soccer Orgn., 1997—98, First Colony Soccer Club, 2002—05; mem. runners club YMCA, 1994, mem. activities adv. bd., 1994, youth soccer and t-ball coach; coach Quail Valley Soccer Assn., 1999—2005; vol. Houston Taping for the Blind, 2000—02; coach First Colony Soccer Club, 2005—; vestry Grace Episcopal Ch., 2002—05, mem. children's edn. bd., 2003; bd. dirs. Alvin-Manvel Helping Hands Fund, 2001, Leadership Jackson, 1996—98. Recipient Rick Nelson soccer coaching award, 2001. Mem.: Nat. Soc. Newspaper Columnists, Investigative Reporters and Editors, Inc., Nat. Edn. Writers Assn., Nat. Youth Sports Assn. (cert. coach), Press Club Houston (bd. dirs. 1982—85, pres. 1984, bd. dirs. 2000—04), AP Mng. Editors Assn. (2d v.p. La./Miss. chpt. 1995—96, 1st v.p. 1996—97, pres. 1997—98), Quota Club (bd. dirs. 1996—97). Episcopalian. Home: 3215 Breckenridge Ct Missouri City TX 77459-4907 Office: The Houston Press 1621 Milam St Ste 100 Houston TX 77002-8017 Office Phone: 713-280-2470. Personal E-mail: downingmargaret@yahoo.com. Business E-Mail: margaret.downing@houstonpress.com.

DOWNS, ANTHONY, economist, consultant, real estate consultant; b. Evanston, Ill., Nov. 21, 1930; s. James Chesterfield and Florence Glassbrook (Finn) D.; m. Katherine Watson, Apr. 7, 1956 (dec.May 27, 1998); children: Katherine, Christine, Tony, Paul, Carol; m. Darian Olsen, Nov. 6, 1999. BA, Carleton Coll., 1952, LLD (hon.), 2002; MA, PhD, Stanford U., 1956. With Real Estate Rsch. Corp., Chgo., 1959-77, chmn. bd. dirs., 1973-77; asst. prof. econs. and polit. sci. U. Chgo., 1959-62; econ. cons. Rand Corp., Santa Monica, Calif., 1963-65; sr. fellow Brookings Instn., Washington, 1977—; visiting fellow Pub. Policy Inst. of Calif., 2004. Bd. dirs. NAACP Legal and Edul. Def. Fund., Inc., Gen. Growth Properties; mem. Nat. Commn. on Urban Problems, 1967—68, Adv. Commn. on Regulatory Barriers to Affordable Housing, 1990—91; adv. bd. Inst. for Rsch. on Poverty, 1970—78. Author: An Econ. Theory of Democracy, 1957, Inside Bureaucracy, 1967, Urban Problems and Prospects, 1970, 2d edit., 1976, Opening Up the Suburbs, 1973, Fed. Housing Subsidies, 1973, Racism in Am., 1970, Neighborhoods and Urban Devel., 1981, Rental Housing in the 1980s, 1983, The Revolution in Real Estate Fin., 1985, Stuck in Traffic, 1992, New Visions for Met. Am., 1994, A Re-Evaluation of Residential Rent Control, 1996, Polit. Theory and Pub. Choice, 1998, Urban Affairs and Urban Policy, 1998, Still Stuck in Traffic, 2004; co-author: Urban Decline and the Future of the Am. Cities, 1982, Costs of Sprawl, 2000, 2003, Sprawl Costs, 2005; co-editor: Do Housing Allowances Work, 1981, Energy Costs, Urban Devel. and Housing, 1984; editor: Growth Mgmt. and Affordable Houring: Do they Conflict. Served with USNR, 1956-59. Mem. Am. Econ. Assn., Am. Soc. Real Estate Counselors, Am. Acad. Arts and Scis., Urban Land Inst., Nat. Acad. Pub. Adminstrn., Anglo Am. Real Property Inst., Phi Beta Kappa, Lambda Alpha. Democrat. Roman Catholic. Home: 8483 Portland Pl Mc Lean VA 22102-1730 Office: 1775 Massachusetts Ave NW Washington DC 20036-2103 Office Phone: 202-797-6132. E-mail: anthonydowns@csi.com.

DOWNS, FLOELLA MCINTYRE, retired ferry pilot, instructor, flight examiner; b. Selmer, Tenn., Sept. 19, 1921; d. Edward N. and Ella Pearle (Byrd) McIntyre; m. James Harold Downs, May 27, 1946; children: Linda Downs Ulmer, William Edward, James Patrick. BA, LaVerne U., 1969. Flight instr., comml. pilot FAA, Memphis, 1945-46, pilot flight examiner, 1946; owner, mgr. Basic Tutoring Svc., Ventura, Calif., 1982-86. Civil air patrol pilot, 1956-57 Pres. Naval Officer's Wives, Patuxent River, Md., 1957; active charitable orgns., Md., Italy, Ventura, Calif., 1946—; vol. Children's Home Soc., Ventura and Carpenteria, Calif., 1962-70. Ferry pilot WASP, USAF, 1943-44, WWII, 1st lt. USAFR, 1952-56. Mem. AAUW (area rep. community issues VTA l980-82), Women's Air Force Svc. Pilots, Toastmistress (pres. Ventura l982-83). Democrat. Avocations: piano, painting, reading, gardening, theater. Home: 751 Montgomery Pl Ventura CA 93004-2169

DOWNS, HARTLEY H., III, chemist; b. Ridgewood, N.J., Oct. 21, 1949; s. Hartley Harrison and Jennie Mae (Smith) D.; m. Cindy Marie Millen, June 19, 1976; children: Kathryn Marie, Jennifer Anne, Susanna Jayne. BS, Grove City Coll., 1971; MS, Indiana U. of Pa., 1973; PhD, W. Va. U., 1978; postgrad., U. Colo., 1976-77. Postdoctoral rsch. assoc. chemistry dept. U. So. Calif., L.A., 1977-78; staff chemist corp. rsch. labs. Exxon Rsch. and Engring. Co., Linden, N.J., 1978-81, Houston, 1981-83, Annandale, N.J., 1983-86; rsch. scientist, surface chemistry and corrosion sci. group supr. Baker Performance Chems., Houston, 1986-91, rsch. mgr., 1991-92, tech. dir., 1992-97; tech. dir. fluids conditioning tech. Baker Petrolite, Houston, 1997—2004, dir. tech. worldwide oilfield ops., 2004—. Contbr. articles to profl. jours., chpt. to book; patentee in field. Recipient Award for Grad. Rsch., Sigma Xi, 1973, Union Carbide award W.Va. U., 1975, Stan Gillman award U. Colo., 1977, Tech. Merit award Baker-Hughes, 1989, 91, 93. Mem. Am. Chem. Soc., Soc. Petroleum Engrs., Offshore Operators Com. (task force on environ. sci.), NACE Internat. (chmn. task force on oil industry biocides 1996—, symposium chmn. mineral scale deposit control in oilfield ops. 1994, 98, chmn. corrosion/94 and corrosion/98 symposia, vice-chmn. microbiol. control in oil industry ops. corrosion/2000 symposium), Phi Lambda Upsilon. Office: Baker Petrolite 12645 W Airport Blvd Sugar Land TX 77478

DOWNS, JOHN B., anesthesiologist; b. Urbana, Ill., Dec. 5, 1943; s. Henry Burton and Evelyne (Valentine) D.; m. Dolores Porter, June 8, 1969; children: Kimberly Ann, Daniel Evan. BS, U. Ill., 1965; MD, U. Fla., 1969. Diplomate Am. Bd. Anesthesiology, Am. Bd. Critical Care Medicine. Intern U. Calif. Davis-Sacramento Med. Ctr., 1969-70; resident in anesthesiology U. Fla. Med. Ctr., Gainesville, 1970-73, fellow in critical care medicine, 1971-73; prof., chmn. dept. anesthesiology U. South Fla. Med. Ctr., Tampa, 1988—. Mem. staff Tampa Gen. Hosp. Contbr. over 200 articles to profl. jours.; inventor in field. Fellow Am. Bd. Anesthesiology, Am. Coll. Anesthesiologists, Am. Coll. Chest Physicians. Office: U South Fla Coll Medicine 12901 Bruce B Downs Blvd Tampa FL 33612-4742

DOWNS, JON FRANKLIN, drama educator, director, writer; b. Bartow, Fla., Sept. 15, 1938; s. Clarence Curtis and Frankie (Morgan) D. Student, Ga. State Coll., 1956-58; BFA, U. Ga., 1960, MFA, 1969. Drama dir. Ga. Perimeter Coll. (formerly DeKalb Coll.), Clarkston, 1969-99. Dir., author The Beastly Purple Forest (marionettes) U. Ga., 1968, Dracula: A Horrible Musical, DeKalb Coll., 1971; dir. A Streetcar Named Desire, DeKalb, 1974, Brigadoon, DeKalb, 1981, West Side Story, 1983, Amadeus, 1984, Noises Off, 1986, The Three Musketeers, 1988, A Midsummer Night's Dream, 1990, A Little Night Music, 1991, Hamlet, 1993, over 200 others; actor Wedding in Japan, N.Y.C., 1960, Dark at the Top of the Stairs, N.Y.C. and on tour, 1961, A Life in the Theatre, DeKalb Coll., 1981, numerous others; designer Sweeney Todd, DeKalb Coll., 1970, Romulus, 1971, Grass Harp, 1972, A Funny Thing Happened on the Way to the Forum, 1998, many others; writer, dir. plays Tokalitta, Gold!, The Vigil; on tour of Ga. summers 1973-76; author: The Illusionist, 1979, Rapunzel, 1997; film reviewer Southernflair mag., 1994-2005, arts editor, 2000-2005. Grantee arts sect. Ga Dept. Planning and Budget, 1973, 74, State Bicentennial Commn., 1975, Nat. Bicentennial Commn., 1975. Mem. Southeastern Theater Conf. (state rep. 1971-73), Ga. Theater Conf. (exec. bd. 1970-73, 79-82).

DOWNS, MARY ALANE, lawyer; BA summa cum laude, Mount St. Mary's Coll., 1979; JD, U. Md., 1982. Bar: Md. 1982, U.S. Ct. Appeals, Forth Cir. 1985. Ptnr. Morgan Shelsby Carlo Downs & Everton, P.A., 1985—. Mem. Nat. Moot Ct. Team; faculty mem. Md. Inst. Continuing Profl. Edn. of Lawyers (MICPEL). Mem.: ABA, Md. Assn. Defense Trial Counsel, Defense Rsch. Inst., Baltimore City Bar Assn., Md. State Bar Assn. Office: Morgan Shelsby Carlo Downs & Everton 4 North Park Dr Ste 404 Hunt Valley MD 21030 Office Phone: 410-584-2800. E-mail: MADowns@morganshelsby.com.

DOWNS, ROBERT K., lawyer; BA, Grinnell Coll.; JD, Stetson Univ. Law Sch. Ptnr. Downs Law Offices PC. Elected Ill. Ho. of Reps. 79th Gen. Assembly; chmn. emeritus Wednesday Journal Inc. Recipient Alumni Achievement award, Grinnell Coll., 1998, Ethel Parker award, Independent Voters of Ill., Best Legislator award. Mem.: Assn. of Family and Conciliation Cts., Justinian Soc. of Lawyers, North Suburban Bar Assn., DuPage County Bar Assn., West Suburban Bar Assn., Chgo. Bar Assn., Ill. Trial Lawyers Assn., Am. Bar Assn. (Pro Bono svc. award 1995), admitted to practice U.S. Supreme Ct., Fla. State Bar Assn., Ill. State Bar Assn. (bd. of gov. 1996—2002, pres.-elect 2004, pres. 2005—). Achievements include competing in and finishing NYC Marathon, 1992. Office: Downs Law Offices PC Ste 1870 150 N Wacker Chicago IL 60606

DOWNS, THOMAS K., lawyer; b. New Albany, Ind., Jan. 10, 1949; BA, Ind. U., 1977, JD magna cum laude, 1980. Bar: Ind. 1980. Ptnr., mcpl. fin. chmn. Ice Miller, Indpls. Mem. editl. bd. Mcpl. Fin. Jour., 1999—; editor Fundamentals of Mcpl. Bond Law: General Law and Professional Responsibility sects., 1994—; exec. editor Ind. Law Jour., 1979-80; contbr. articles to profl. jours. Pres. Ind. Assn. Cities and Towns Found., 1994—; mem. Lt. Gov.'s Jobs Coun. Fellow Am. Coll. Bond Counsel (founding mem., govt. rels. com., co-chmn. bond buyer midwest pub. fin. conf. 1998); mem. Nat. Assn. Bond Lawyers (steering com. 1985-86, 90, 92, 2000, 01, 02, chmn. bond banks workshop 1985-86, tax increment workshop 1989, panelist various workshops, faculty fundamentals mcpl. bond law, opinions and profl. responsibility 1989-90, chair Ann. Washington Conf. 1996, chmn. prof. responsibility com. 2001-03), Ind. Continuing Legal Edn. Forum (chmn. mcpl. law seminars 1984-92, practical impact tax reform act of 1986, panelist mcpl. utility fin. 1988, pub. law 10 1991), Ind. Mcpl. Lawyers Assn., Inc (bd. dirs. 1983—), Order of Coif, Assn. Ind. Counties (adv. com., gen. counsel), Ind. Assn. Cities and Towns (exec. com., special counsel), Ind. Comn. for the Purchase of Products and Svcs. of Persons with Disabilities (bd. dirs.). Office: Ice Miller Box 82001 1 American Sq Indianapolis IN 46282-0020 Business E-Mail: Thomas.Downs@icemiller.com.

DOWS, DAVID ALAN, chemistry professor; b. San Francisco, July 25, 1928; s. Samuel Randall and Rita M. (Bowers) D.; m. Wena Hunt Waldner, July 29, 1950; children— Janet Louise, Carol Marie, Joyce Ellen. BS, U. Calif. at Berkeley, 1952, PhD, 1954. Instr. chemistry Cornell U., 1954-56; instr. U. So. Calif., Los Angeles, 1956-57, asst. prof., 1957-59, assoc. prof., 1959-63, prof. chemistry, 1963—, chmn. dept., 1966-72; NATO prof., 1970. Contbr. articles profl. jours. NSF fellow, 1962-63 Mem. Am. Chem. Soc., Am. Phys. Soc., Phi Beta Kappa. Office: U So Calif Dept Chemistry University Park Los Angeles CA 90089-0482 Office Phone: 213-740-4121. Business E-Mail: dows@usc.edu.

DOWTY, ALAN KENT, political scientist, educator; b. Greenville, Ohio, Jan. 15, 1940; s. Paul Willard and Ethel Lovella (Harbaugh) D.; m. Nancy Ellen Gordon, Sept. 8, 1961 (div. 1972); children: Merav Aurli, Tamar Eliea,

Gidon Yair; m. Gail Gaynell Schupack, Jan. 1, 1973; children: Rachel Miriam, Rafael Jonathan; 1 stepchild, David Freeman. BA, Shimer Coll., 1959; MA, U. Chgo., 1960, PhD, 1963. Lectr. Hebrew U., Jerusalem, 1965-72, sr. lectr., 1972-75; assoc. prof. U. Notre Dame, Ind., 1975-78, prof. polit. sci., 1978—2004; Kahanoff chair Israeli studies U. Calgary, 2003—. Exec. dir. Leonard Davis Inst., Jerusalem, 1972-74; editl. bd. Middle East Rev., N.Y.C., 1977-90; project dir. Twentieth Century Fund, N.Y.C., 1983-85; reporter experts meeting Internat. Inst. Human Rights, Strasbourg, France, 1989. Author: The Limits of American Isolation, 1971, Middle East Crisis, 1984 (Quincy Wright award 1985), The Arab-Israel Conflict (with others), 1984, Closed Borders, 1987, The Jewish State, 1998, Israel/Palestine, 2005; book reviewer Jerusalem Post, 1964-75; contbr. articles to profl. jours. Exec. com. Am. Profs. for Peace in Mid. East, 1976-90; witness U.S. Senate Fgn. Rels. Com., Washington, 1976; nat. adv. com. Union of Couns. for Soviet Jews, Washington, 1980-91. Woodrow Wilson fellow, 1959-60; Rothschild fellow Hebrew U., 1963-64; resident fellow Adlai Stevenson Inst., Chgo., 1971-72; Skirball fellow Oxford Ctr. for Hebrew and Jewish Studies, 2000; recipient Charles W. Ramsdell award So. Hist. Assn., 1966; grantee Twentieth Century Fund, N.Y.C., 1983. Mem. Am. Polit. Sci. Assn., Internat. Polit. Sci. Assn., Internat. Studies Assn. (exec. com. 1977-79, Quincy Wright award 1985), Assn. Israel Studies (pres. 2005—). Jewish. Avocations: travel, jewish studies. Office: 615 S Greenlawn Ave South Bend IN 46615

DOXEY-TATE, SARAH ROLSTON, retired elementary school educator; b. Holly Springs, Miss., Mar. 13, 1933; d. Hindman and Mary Amis (Bitzer) Doxey; m. Lloyd O'Neil Tate, Dec. 25, 1960 (div. July 16, 1986); children: Katherine Bitzer Tate, William Hindman Tate, Marisa O. Tate Stone, Frances Tate Johnson. MS, Belhaven Coll., 1951; BA in Art Edn., U. Miss., 1954, postgrad., 1981—83, Miss. So. U., 1986—89. Tchr. 2d and 4th grades Canton Pub. Schs., Miss., 1954—59; tchr. 3d grade Holly Springs Schs., 1959—60; art supr. 5 schs. Clarksdale Pub. Elem. Schs., Miss., 1961—62; art supr. 5 elem. schs. Tupelo Pub. Schs. ETV Art, Miss., 1962—69; tchr. kindergarten and pvt. sch. Playhouse, Tupelo, 1970—73; tchr. h.s. art and journalism Tupelo Pub. Schs., 1974—75, tchr. jr. high gifted edn., 1977—80; tchr., libr./media ctr. Lee County Schs., Tupelo, 1985—96. Pianist receptions, rehearsal dinners Tupelo Country Club, 1985—. Grand marshal Tupelo Christmas Parade, 2002; pres. bd. Friends of Lee County Libr., 2001—04; elder 1st Presbyn. Ch.; past pres., moderator Presbyn. Women, Tupelo; bd. dirs., past pres. Faith Haven, Inc. Home for Children, 1976—; head counselor Camp DeSoto Camp for Girls, Mentone, Ala., 1972—95; founder Ch. After Sch. Assn., Lee County, 1982—, civic chmn. Fortnightly Musicale, 1963—, pres., 1965; pianist Salvation Army Ch. Svcs., Tupelo. Named one of Mississippians Who Have Made a Difference, Miss. Mag., 1985, Outstanding Women of Am., 1967; recipient Freedom Found. Valley Forge Tchr.'s medal, 1969, Outstanding Citizen award, Tupelo Jr. Aux., Inc., 1999. Mem.: DAR (regent 1970), N.E. Miss. Ret. Tchrs. Assn. (dist. pres. 1997—99), Tupelo-Lee County Miss. Assn. Educators. Presbyterian. Avocation: playing piano. Home: 2611 Lakeshire Dr Tupelo MS 38804

DOYLE, A. PATRICK, lawyer; b. Pitts., Sept. 6, 1948; BA, SUNY, Oswego, 1971; JD, Syracuse U., 1975. Bar: N.Y. 1976, D.C. 1985. Counsel multinational banking divsn. Office of Comptr. of Currency, 1979-81; dep. gen. counsel, acting gen. counsel Fed. Home Loan Bank Bd., 1982-83; mem. Arnold & Porter, Washington, 1983—93, ptnr., Fin. Svc. Practice Group, 1993—. Adj. prof. Morin ctr. banking law studies, sch. law Boston U., 1985-1993; mem bd. adv., Banking Law Inst, Univ N.C., 1998-. Mng. editor Syracuse Jour. Internat. Law and Commerce, 1974-75; contbr. articles to profl. jours. Mem. Fed. Bar Assn. (mem. exec. com., savs. instns. law com. 1984—). Office: Arnold & Porter Thurman Arnold Bldg 555 12th St NW Washington DC 20004-1206 Office Phone: 202-942-5949. Office Fax: 202-942-5999. Business E-Mail: a.patrick.doyle@aporter.com.

DOYLE, ANTHONY PETER, lawyer; b. Washington, July 13, 1953; s. Francis X. and Anna (Klekotka) D.; m. Maria H. Duda, Aug. 13, 1977; children: Jeffrey Anthony, Joseph Edward, Natalie Maria, Andrew Michael. AA, Berkshire Community Coll., Pittsfield, Mass., 1972-75; BS magna cum laude, Worcester State Coll., 1977; JD, Western New Eng. Coll., 1980. Bar: Mass. 1980; U.S. Dist. Ct. Mass. 1981; U.S. Ct. Appeals (1st cir.) 1981, U.S. Supreme Ct. 1999. Pvt. practice, Pittsfield, 1980-84; ptnr. Doyle & Cormier, Pittsfield, 1985-88, Barry, Doyle & Cormier, Pittsfield, 1989, Barry & Doyle, Pittsfield, 1989—. Pres. Hospice of Cen. Berkshire, Pittsfield, 1988-90; v.p. HospiceCare of the Berkshires, Pittsfield, 1990-92, pres. 1992-2002, bd. dirs., 2005—; bd. dirs. Dalton (Mass.) Youth Ctr., 1986-89, Community Recreation Assn., Dalton, 1989-95; exec. com. Appalachian Trails Dist. Boy Scouts Am., Dalton, 1989-96; mem. Zoning Bd. Appeals, Dalton, 1995—, chmn., 1997—, Dalton Coun. Aging, 1997—; bd. dirs. Berkshire Fund, 2002—. Recipient commendation Western Mass. Pro Bono Referral Svc., 1983-87. Mem. Mass. Bar Assn., Berkshire Bar Assn. (exec. com. 1989-91, v.p. 1997-99, pres. 1999-2001, Cmty. Svc. award 2004). Roman Catholic. Avocations: skiing, tennis, running. Home: 108 Barton Hill Rd Dalton MA 01226-2005 Office: Barry & Doyle 8 Bank Row Ste 2 Pittsfield MA 01201-6224 Office Phone: 413-499-1701. E-mail: doyleam@aol.com.

DOYLE, D. JOHN, anesthesiologist; arrived in US, 2002; m. Jo-Anne Taylor Williams, July 3, 1978; 1 child, Jonathan Taylor. BS in Physics, St. Francis Xavier U., Can., 1972; MD, U. Toronto, 1982; PhD, U. Toronto, Can., 1986. Bd. cert. Am. Bd. Anesthesiology, 1989. Intern, resident U. Toronto, Canada, 1982—86; staff anesthesiologist Cleve. Clinic Found., 2002—. Fellow: Royal Coll. Physicians Can. Avocations: travel, scuba diving. Office: Cleveland Clinic Foundation 9500 Euclid Ave Cleveland OH 44195 Office Phone: 216-444-1927. Office Fax: 216-444-9247. Business E-Mail: doylej@ccf.org.

DOYLE, DAVID C., lawyer; b. Nashville, Apr. 11, 1951; BA magna cum laude, U. Calif., San Diego, 1973; JD, UCLA, 1976. Bar: Calif. 1976. Law clk. to Hon. Gordon Thompson Jr. U.S. Dist. Ct. (so. dist.) Calif., 1976-78; asst. U.S. atty. So. Dist. of Calif., 1978-80; mem. Baker & McKenzie, San Diego; ptnr. Morrison & Foerster LLP, San Diego, co-leader patent practice group. Mem. editorial bd. UCLA Law Rev., 1974-76. Mem. State Bar Calif., San Diego County Bar Assn., Order of Coif. Office: Morrison & Foerster LLP 12636 High Bluff Dr Ste 300 San Diego CA 92130-2071 Office Phone: 858-720-1539. Office Fax: 858-720-5125. Business E-Mail: ddoyle@mofo.com.

DOYLE, DELORES MARIE, retired principal; b. Madison, SD, July 24, 1939; d. Martin N. and Pearl M. (Anderson) Berkelo; m. Patrick J. Doyle; children: Kathleen, Shawn, Tamara, Timothy. AS, Dakota State Coll., Madison, 1959; BS, Mid. Tenn. State U., 1966, MEd, 1968, EdS, 1975; PhD, Peabody/Vanderbilt U., 1980. Cert. career ladder III tchr. Tchr. 4th grade Meriden-Cleghorn Schs., Meriden, Iowa, 1960-62; tchr. 1st grade Hanover (Ill.) Sch., 1963-66; tchr. 2d grade Hobgood Sch., Murfreesboro, Tenn., 1969-70; tchr. 1st grade Reeves-Rogers Sch., Murfreesboro, 1972-80, tchr. 2d grade, 1981-97, prin., 1997-2000; ret., 2000. Cooperating tchr. Mid. Tenn. State U. Student Tchrs., Murfreesboro, 1972—97, mem. task force edn., 1992—93; summer sch. dir. Murfreesboro City Schs., 1986—98; lead project tutor Reeves-Rogers Sch., Murfreesboro, 1987—90. Active Edn. 2000 Com., Murfreesboro C. of C., 1993; trustee Mid Tenn State U. Found., 1995—2001; bd. dirs. Grace Luth. Ch., Murfreesboro, 1991—93, 2001—03, mem. choir, 1975—. Named Career Ladder III Tchr., Dept. Edn., Nashville, 1984; named to Tenn. Tchrs. Hall of Fame, 2001; recipient Tenn. Tchr. of the Yr. award, Dept. Edn., Nashville, 1992, Murfreesboro City Tchr. of the Yr. award, Murfreesboro City Schs., 1991, Mid-Cumberland Dist. Tchr. of the Yr. award, Dist. Dept. Edn., 1991, Trailblazer award, 1995; Creative Tchg. grantee, State Dept. Edn., 1992, 1993. Mem.: Murfreesboro Edn. Assn. (pres. 1981—82), Tenn. Edn. Assn. (Disting. Classroom Tchr. award 1992, Disting. Adminstr. award 2000), Tenn. State Tchr. of Yr. Orgn. (v.p. 2000—), Nat. State Tchr. of Yr. Orgn., Delta Kappa Gamma. Democrat. Avocations: bridge, travel, reading, bicycling. Home: 1710 Sutton Pl Murfreesboro TN 37129-6513 Personal E-mail: pandddoyle@comcast.net.

DOYLE, DENNIS T., lawyer; b. White Plains, N.Y., Apr. 9, 1943; BA, Boston Coll., 1965; JD, Fordham U., 1968. Bar: N.Y. State 1968, U.S. Dist. Ct. (so. and ea. dists.) N.Y. 1978, U.S. Supreme Ct. 1978. Ptnr. O'Connor, McGuiness, Conte, Doyle & Oleson, White Plains, 1969—. Author: You Haven't Got a Prayer. Mem. ABA, Am. Trial Lawyers Assn., N.Y. State Trial Lawyers Assn., Fedn. Ins. and Corp. Counsel, Appalachian Mountain Club, Adirondeck Mountain Club, Adirondeck Coun. Avocations: bicycling, religious education, hiking, golf. Office: O'Connor McGuiness Conte Doyle & Oleson One Barker Ave Ste 675 White Plains NY 10601-1517 Fax: 914 948-0645. E-mail: ddoyle@omcdoc.com.

DOYLE, DONALD VINCENT, retired state senator, lawyer; b. Sioux City, Iowa, Jan. 13, 1925; s. William E. and Nelsine E. (Sparby) D.; m. Jant E. Holtz, Aug. 9, 1963; 1 child, Dawn Renee. BS, Morningside Coll., Sioux City, 1951; JD, U. S.D., 1953. Bar: S.D. 1953, Iowa 1953. Pvt. practice, Sioux City, 1953—; mem. Iowa Ho. of Reps., 1956-80, Iowa Senate, 1981-93, chmn. judiciary com., 1982-90. Mem. law and justice com. Nat. Conf. State Legis., 1987-89, chmn., 1988-89; chmn. Iowa Boundary Commn., 1991, 92; mem. Commn. Accreditation Law Enforcement Agys., Inc., 1988-95. With USAF, 1943—46. Recipient award Woodbury County Peace Officers, 1974, Restoration Club Sioux City, 1964, Outstanding Elected Ofcl. award Iowa Corrections Assn., 1979. Mem. Iowa Bar Assn., S.D. Bar Assn. (50-Yr. plaque 2003), Woodbury County Bar Assn., CBI Vets. Assn. (past nat. judge adv., Iowa comdr. 1965), Am. Legion, VFW (comdr. post 1997-2001), DAV, 40 and 8 (chef de gare 1999-2001). Office: PO Box 941 Sioux City IA 51102-0941

DOYLE, EUGENIE FLERI, pediatrician, cardiologist, educator; b. Bklyn., Oct. 19, 1921; d. Paul Charles and Antoinette (Giovannetti) Fleri; m. Joseph Anthony Doyle, Aug. 19, 1944; children: Christopher, Stephen, Eugenie, Jane Marie, Richard. BS, Marymount Coll., Tarrytown, N.Y., 1943, DSc (hon.), 1993; MD, Johns Hopkins U., 1946; DSc (hon.), Coll. New Rochelle, 1975. Intern in pediatrics Johns Hopkins Hosp., Balt., 1946-47; pediatric resident Bellevue Hosp., N.Y.C., 1947-49; fellow pediatric cardiology NYU Med. Ctr., 1949-53, dir. pediatric cardiology, 1958-93; asst. prof. pediatrics NYU Sch. Medicine, 1953-58, assoc. prof., 1959-70, prof., 1970-92, prof. emerita, 1993—, clin. prof. pediatrics, 1994—. Mem. cardiac adv. com. N.Y. State Health Dept., 1983-92; dir. Vis. Nurse Svc., N.Y.C., 1984—. Editor: Pediatric Cardiology, 1985; contbr. articles to profl. jours. Trustee Marymount Coll., 1983-91, vice chair bd., 1988-91. Mem. Am. Acad. Pediatrics, Am. Pediatric Soc., Am. Coll. Cardiology, Am. Heart Assn., N.Y. Heart Assn. (bd. dirs. 1977-84, pres. 1979-81), Cosmopolitan Club. Roman Catholic. Avocations: gardening, travel, ballet. Home: 32 Washington Sq W New York NY 10011-9156 Office: NYU Med Ctr 550 1st Ave New York NY 10016-6402

DOYLE, FIONA MARY, metallurgical engineer, educator; b. Newcastle upon Tyne, Eng., Sept. 27, 1956; came to the U.S., 1983; d. Vincent Thomas and Teresa Mary (Lockey) D.; m. Stephen Craig Blair, Aug. 5, 1990; children: Katherine Nicole Blair, Ian James Blair. BA in Metallurgy and Materials Sci., U. Cambridge, 1978, MA in Natural Sci., 1982; MSc in Extractive Metallurgy, Imperial Coll., 1979, PhD in Metallurgy, 1983. Chartered engr., Great Britain. Grad. trainee metals and minerals div. Davy McKee, Stockton-on-Tees, United Kingdom, 1983; asst. prof. materials sci. and mineral engring. U. Calif., Berkeley, 1983-88, assoc. prof., 1988-94, prof., 1994—, acting assoc. dean coll. engring., 1990, dir. Inst. Environmental Sci. and Engring., 2001—02, chair dept. materials sci. and engring., 2002—. Cons. Placer Dome, U.S., San Francisco, 1989-90. Co-editor: Innovations in Materials Processing Using Aqueous Colloids and Surface Chemistry, 1989, Biotechnology in Minerals and Metal Processing, 1989, Mineral Processing and Extractive Metallury Rev., 1990—; editor: Mining and Mineral Processing Wastes, 1990; contbr. articles to profl. jours. Tech. cons. Sierra Club Legal Def. Fund, San Francisco, 1991. Grantee NSF, 1984, U.S. Dept. Interior, 1987, 91, U.S. Dept. Energy, 1990. Mem. Minerals, Metals and Materials Soc., Am. Inst. Mining, Metall. and Petroleum Engrs. (chair aqueous processing com. 1988-90), Instn. Mining and Metallurgy, Electrochem. Soc., Materials Rsch. Soc. Office: U Calif Berkeley Dept Materials Sci 325 Hearst Mining Bldg Berkeley CA 94720-1760 Office Phone: 510-642-2846.

DOYLE, FLORENCE ELIZABETH, retired secondary school educator; b. Mayville, N.D., Oct. 30, 1920; d. Ole Matias and Petra (Ulland) Kjelsberg; m. Joseph Patrick Doyle, Aug. 12, 1952. BA, Concordia Coll., 1942; MA, St. Thomas U., 1967. Tchr. pub. sch., Odessa, Minn., 1942—43, Pine Island, Minn., 1943—44, 1944—47, Montevideo, Minn., 1947—52, Royalton, Minn., 1952—53, Mahnomen, Minn., 1953—59, Richfield, Minn., 1959—79. Docent gov.'s residence, St. Paul, 1985—. Mem.: AAUW, Minn. Hist. Soc. (pres. Women's Orgn. 1990—92). Republican. Roman Catholic. Home: 1377 Maynard Dr W # 161 Saint Paul MN 55116-2951

DOYLE, FRANCES MARY, psychiatric social worker; d. Francis Joseph and Margaret Mary (O'Donnell) Barry; m. Eugene Francis Doyle, Aug. 8, 1997. BS, Adelphi U., 1989, MSW, 1990. LCSW Substance Abuse Svc. NY State Edn. Dept. Alcohol rehab. counselor I Nassau Co. Dept. Drug and Alcohol, Hempstead, NY, 1982—85; alcohol rehab. counselor II Nassau Co. Dept. Drug and Alcohol, Outpatient Unit, 1985—87, alcohol rehab. counselor III, 1987—92; psychiat. social worker I Nassau Co. Dept. Drug and Alcohol, Nassau County Jail, 1992—2001, psychiat. social worker II, 2001—02, dir. Stop DWI program, 2002—05; pvt. practice Uniondale, NY, 2001—. Co-author: (training manual) Treating Mandated Clients, 2003. Vol. Mineola (NY) Mustang Run, Fundraiser, 2000—02; bereavement counselor Sacred Heart Ch., No. Merrick, NY, 1999—. Named Social Worker of Yr., Elizabeth A. Doherty Scholarship Fund, 2002. Mem.: Eye Movement Desensitization and Reprocessing Internat. Assn., NY Fed. of Alcoholism Counselors, Nat. Assn. Social Workers. Avocations: crocheting, dog grooming, running marathon races. Home: 1342 Menard St Uniondale NY 11553 Office: Nassau County Dept Drug and Alcohol Nassau County Jail 100 Carman Ave East Meadow NY 11554 Office Phone: 516-576-7572. Personal E-mail: barrydoyle@msn.com.

DOYLE, FREDERICK JOSEPH, retired government research scientist; b. Oak Park, Ill., Apr. 3, 1920; s. John Frederick and Mary Elizabeth (Meyers) D.; m. Mary Blaskovich, June 18, 1955; children: Frederick J., Margaret, Mary Ellen, George. BCE, Syracuse U., 1951; postgrad., Internat. Tng. Ctr. Aerial Sur, Delft, The Netherlands, 1952; D Eng (hon.), Tech. U., Hannover, Germany, 1976; DSc (hon.), Ohio STate U., 1986, U. Bordeaux, France, 1987; D in Tech., Royal Tech. U., Sweden, 1987. Assoc. prof. geodetic sci. Ohio State U., 1952-60, chmn. dept., 1959-60; chief scientist Raytheon Autometric Co., Alexandria, Va., 1960-69; sci. advisor nat. mapping divsn. U.S. Geol. Survey, Reston, Va., 1969-89, dir. earth resources observation sys. program, 1978-80; ret., 1989. Geodesy cartography adv. com. nat. Acad. Scis., 1967-69; chmn. Apollo orbital Sci. photo team NASA, 1969-73, planetary cartography com., 1974-95; exec. com. divsn. earth sci. NRC, 1973-76. With C.E., AUS, 1943-48, PTO. Recipient Meritorious Svc. award Dept. Interior, 1977, Disting. Svc. medal, 1981, Silver medal City of Paris, 1978; Fulbright fellow Internat. Tng. Ctr. Aerial Survey, 1952, Internat. Tng. Ctr. fellow, 1986. Fellow AAAS; mem. NAE, Internat. Soc. Photogrammetry Remote Sensing (hon., pres. 1980-84, Brock award 1984), Am. Congress Surveying Mapping, Am. Geophys. Union, Am. Soc. Photogrammetry (hon., pres. 1969-70, contbg. author, editor publs., Fairchild Photogrammetric award 1968, Alan Gordon award 1985, Chancellors medal U.Calif. Santa Barbara 2000); mem. Nat. Acad. English. Home: 1591 Forest Villa Ln Mc Lean VA 22101-4132 E-mail: freddoyle@aol.com.

DOYLE, GERARD FRANCIS, lawyer; b. Needham, Mass., Oct. 25, 1942; s. John Patrick and Catherine Mary (Lawler) D.; m. Paula Marie Dervay, may 14, 1983; children: Laura Dervay, Meredith Lawler, Philip John. BS in Indsl. Adminstrn., Yale U., 1966; JD, Georgetown U., 1972. Bar: D.C. 1973, U.S. Dist. Ct. D.C. 1973, U.S. Ct. Fed. Claims 1976, U.S. Ct. Appeals (fed. cir.) 1982, U.S. Supreme Ct. 1982, Va. 2000. Group head for operating submarine reactors and reactor tech Div. Naval Reactors AEC, Washington, 1970-72; atty. Morgan, Lewis & Bockius, Washington, 1972-76; legal counsel Am. Nuclear Energy Coun., Washington, 1975-76; ptnr. Cotten, Day & Doyle, Washington, 1976-87, Doyle & Savit, Doyle, Simmons & Bachman, Doyle & Bachman LLP, Washington, 1987-99, Arlington, Va., 1999—. Legal counsel Assn. Fed. Data Peripheral Suppliers, Washington, 1979; dir. M Internat., Inc.; author and lectr. in field; columnist Federal Computer Week, 1989. Served in USN, 1966-71. Recipient outstanding young man of yr. award, 1976. Mem. ABA (coun. publ. contract law sect. 1989-92), D.C. Bar Assn., Fed. Bar Assn., Am. Arbitration Assn. (panel arbitrators), Nat. Contract Mgmt. Assn., Met. Club (Washington), Yale Club (Washington), Washington Golf & Country Club. Republican. Roman Catholic. Home: 901 Whann Ave Mc Lean VA 22101-1570 Office: Doyle & Bachman LLP 4350 N Fairfax Dr Arlington VA 22203-1637 Office Phone: 703-465-5440. Business E-Mail: gdoyle@doylebachman.com.

DOYLE, GILLIAN, actress; b. Maidenhead, Berkshire, Eng. came to U.S., 1977; d. John Joseph and Joan (Walker) D. BA in Theatre magna cum laude, Am. U., Washington. Appeared in (off Broadway) Ernest in Love, NYC, 1980; (plays) No Exit, Washington, 1985, Fefu and Her Friends, 1985, The Winters Tale, 1987, A Christmas Carol, 1987, Erpingham Camp, 1989, Turn of the Screw, 1989, Season's Greetings, 1986, Terra Nova, 1987, Mountain, 1990, Old Favorites, 1991, What the Butler Saw, 1993, Fawlty Towers, 1994, Last of the Red Hot Lovers, 1995, The Musical Comedy Murders of 1940, 1996, Move Over Mrs. Markham, 1997, Declarations: Love Letters of the Great Romantics, 1998, Present Laughter, 1999, Two, 1999, U.S.A., 2000, Blithe Spirit, 2002, A Midsummer Night's Dream, 2002, What The Butler Saw, 2003, Homebody/Kabul, 2003, Under Milkwood, 2004, My Boy Jack, 2004; (musical) The Cradle Will Rock, 2001; (films) Chances Are, 1989, Born Yesterday, 1993, North, 1993, Decade of Love, 1994, Wild Bill, 1994, The Tie That Binds, 1995, Independence Day, 1996, Play Me Again Sam, 1999, Love, 2000, Being Doctor Jack, 2005; (TV) Ancient Prophecies III, 1995, Friends, 1995, The Martin Short Show, 1995, Days of Our Lives, 1996, Love's Deadly Triangle: The Texas Cadet Murder, 1996, General Hospital, 1997, Port Charles, 1999, The Man Show, 1999, Titus, 2001; (music video) Johnny Sportcoat and the Casuals, 1987; (comml.) United Way, 1988. Mem. SAG, AFTRA, Actors Equity Assn., Phi Kappa Phi. Democrat. Roman Catholic. Avocations: equestrienne, golf, swimming, music, (cert.). Personal E-mail: gilliandoyle@hotmail.com.

DOYLE, JAMES EDWARD, governor; b. Washington, Nov. 23, 1945; s. James E. and Ruth (Bachhuber) Doyle; m. Jessica Laird, Dec. 21, 1966; children: Augustus, Gabriel. Student, Stanford U., 1963—66; AB in History, U. Wis., 1967; JD cum laude, Harvard U., 1972. Bar: Ariz. 1973, Wis. 1975, U.S. Dist. Ct. N.Mex. 1973, U.S. Dist. Ct. Ariz. 1973, U.S. Dist. Ct. Utah 1973, U.S. Dist. Ct. (we. dist.) Wis. 1975, U.S. Dist. Ct. (ea. dist.) Wis. 1976, U.S. Ct. Appeals (10th cir.) 1974, U.S. Ct. Appeals (7th cir.) 1985, U.S. Supreme Ct. 1989. Vol. Peace Corps, Tunisia, 1967—69; atty. DNA Legal Svcs., Chinle, Ariz., 1972—75; ptnr. Jacobs & Doyle, Madison, Wis., 1975—77; dist. atty. Dane County, Madison, 1977—83; ptnr. Doyle & Ritz, Madison, 1983—90; of counsel Lawton & Cates, Madison, 1990—91; atty. gen. State of Wis., Madison, 1991—2002, gov., 2003—. Mem.: ABA, 7th Cir. Bar Assn. (chmn. criminal law sect. 1988—89), Wis. Bar Assn. (bd. dirs. criminal law sect. 1988). Democrat. Roman Catholic. Office: Office of the Governor 115 E State Capitol Madison WI 53702

DOYLE, JAMES THOMAS, electronics engineer; b. Bklyn., Apr. 11, 1950; s. Leo James Doyle and Mary Ruth Welton; m. Baxanne Lowrance Hunt, June 9, 1995; children: Sheila Mary, Kory Lowrance, Michael James, Kelly Kegan Lowrance, John Patrick, MaryClaire Elizabeth. BSEE, U. Nebr., 1972; MBA, Nova Southeastern, Ft. Lauderdale, Fla., 1991. Registered profl. engr., Fla., 1978. Elec. engr. Honeywell, Freeport, Ill., 1973—76; staff rsch. engr. Motorola, Ft Lauderdale, Fla., 1976—85; mgr. cmos design BurrBrown/Tex. Instruments, Tucson, 1985—87; mem. tech. staff Motorola, Chandler, Ariz., 1987—89; acting pres. and chief engr. MCE Semiconductor, West Palm Beach, Fla., 1988—90; chief technologist, prin. engr. Intel Corp., Chandler, Ariz., 1990—2001; chief technologist pps and smts Nat. Semiconductor, Longmont, Colo., 2001—. Contbr. articles to profl. jours. Vol. Dairy Ctr. of Arts, Boulder, Colo., 2003—05. Engring. Honor scholarship, U. Miami, 1968. Master: IEEE; mem.: Profl. Engr. FES (Mem. #PE024719). Achievements include over 35 patents. Home: 300 Magnolia Dr Nederland CO 80466 Office: Nat Semiconductor 1820 Lefthand Cir Longmont CO 80466 Office Phone: 303-845-4064. Home Fax: 303-443-2418; Office Fax: 303-845-4005. Personal E-mail: jbkkdoyle1@aol.com. Business E-Mail: jim.doyle@nsc.com.

DOYLE, JOHN LAWRENCE, artist; b. Chgo., Mar. 14, 1939; s. John W. and Cecelia M. (Tarkowski) D.; children: Lynn, Sean, Morgan. BA, Sch. of Art Inst. Chgo., 1962; MA, No. Ill. U., 1967. Tchr. art Forest View High Sch., Arlington Heights, Ill., 1962-72. Bd. dirs. Toe River Arts Coun., Yancey Libr., Amy Regional Libr. Sys., Yancey History Assn., Yancey Evening Sch. Program, Steering Com., Yancey Mus./Visitor Ctr. Project. One-man shows of prints and/or paintings include: Denver Natural History Mus., Natural Am. Indian Mus., Spokane, Wash., Allen Galleries, Milw., U. N.D., U. S.D., Black Gallery, Taos, N.Mex., Vanderbilt U., Nashville, Tenn., Johns Hopkins U., Balt., Jockey Club Gallery, Miami, Fla., New West Whitney Gallery Western Art, Cody, Wyo., Harvard Med. Library, Lesch Gallery, Mpls., Clev. Clinic, Mayo Clinic, MGM Grand, Las Vegas, Yale U. Hosp., Now and Then Gallery, N.Y.C., Fine Print Unltd., Miami, Grand Gallery, Nev., Galerie Une, Puerto Vallarta, Mex., Welnetz Studio, Wis., Gallery G, Wichita, all 1981; group shows, latest being: U. Miami, Fla., Tex. Tech U., Amarillo and Lubbock, U. Iowa Hosp. and Clinic, Loma Linda U., Calif., Art Resources, Denver, Hayden Hayes Gallery, Colorado Springs, Colo., Southwestern Gallery, Dallas, Nat. Library of Medicine, Bethesda, Md., Cornell Med. Coll., N.Y.C., Columbia U., N.Y.C., U. Kans., Harvard Law Library, Denver Nat. Hist. Mus., William Mitchell Law Sch., Mpls., United Bank of Austin, Tex., others, 1982-85, Inter Art, Nice, France, Loyola U. Sch. Law, New Orleans, Fine Arts Ltd., Miami, U. Dubuque, Iowa, Art Expo Los Angeles, Art Expo N.Y., Degan Bella Gallery, San Antonio, U. Ariz., Tempe, Midwest Mus. Am. Art, Ind., 1986, U. Ill., Chgo., 1987, R. Volid Gallery, Chgo., 1987, Royce Gallery, Denver, 1987, Denver Mus. Nat. History, 1987, No. Ill. U., DeKalb, 1987, Art Expo, N.Y.C., 1987, U. Ill. Chgo., 1988, R. Volip Gallery, Chgo., 1988, Ramses II Denver Mus., N.H., 1988, Royce Gallery, Denver, 1988, Hayden-Hayes Gallery, Colorado Springs, 1988, World Trade Ctr., Mpls.-St. Paul, 1988, Bergren Gallery, Rockford, Ill., 1988, Red Carpet Gallery, Minn., 1988, Yancey County Hist. Mus., N.C., 1988, Minn. World Trade Ctr., St. Paul, 1989, U. Ill., Champaign, 1989, U. Wis., Madison, 1989, Jean Stephen Gallery, Mpls., 1989, New West Cont. Art, Buffalo Bill Hist. Ctr., Cody, Wyo., 1990, White Thunder World Gallery, Milw., 1990, D. Ehrlein Gallery, Milw., 1990, Bank One, Milw., 1990, White Hart Gallery, Steamboat Springs, Colo., 1991, Suzanne Brown Gallery, Scottsdale, Ariz., 1991, Midwest Mus. Am. Art, Elkhart, Ind., 1991, Scripps Meml. Hosp. Schaetzel Ctr., La Jolla, Calif., 1991, Suzanne Brown Gallery, Scottsdale, Ariz., 1992, Walker Art Ctr., Asheville, N.C., 1992; represented in permanent collections: Library of Congress, Washington, Art Inst. Chgo., Indpls., Mus. Art, Carnegie Inst., Pitts., Norton Gallery of Art, West Palm Beach, Fla., Birmingham (Ala.).Mus. Art, Canton (Ohio) Art Inst., Columbus Mus. Fine Art, Columbus, Ohio, Fort Lauderdale (Fla.) Mus. Art, Miss. Art Mus., Whitney Gallery Western Art, Jackson, Nat. Gallery of Art, Washington, U. Mich., Ann Arbor, Savannah (Ga.) Coll. Art and Design, Scripps Meml. Hosp., La Jolla. Bd. dirs. Family Violence Coalition Yancey County Vol. Coop, Toe River Arts Coun., Yancey Libr., Amy Regional Libr., Healthy Yancy; pres. Yancey History Assn.; sec., treas. Mus. Visitor Ctr. Project; chair subcom. Land Use Planning Commn.; mem. 21st century cmtys. action com. Yancey County Cultural Resource Commn., now pres.; chmn. Yancey Arts. Recipient Hon. Mention Internat. Printmakers, 1971; George Brown Travelling fellow, 1962 Address: PO Box 715 Burnsville NC 28714-0715

DOYLE, JOHN ROBERT, lawyer; b. Chgo., May 12, 1950; s. Frank Edward and Dorothy (Bolton) D.; m. Kathleen Julius, June 14, 1974; children: Melissa, Maureen. BA magna cum laude, St. Louis U., 1971; JD summa cum laude, DePaul U., 1976. Bar: Ill. 1976, U.S. Dist. Ct. 1976, U.S. Dist. Ct. (no. dist.) Ill. 1982, Ill. Trial Bar 1982, U.S. Ct. Appeals (7th cir.)

1982. Ptnr. McDermott, Will & Emery, Chgo., 1976—. Mem. ABA, Chgo. Bar Assn. (jud. investigative hearing panel 1986-88), Phi Beta Kappa. Office: McDermott Will & Emery 227 W Monroe St Ste 3100 Chicago IL 60606-5096

DOYLE, JOSEPH ANTHONY, retired lawyer; b. N.Y.C., June 13, 1920; s. Joseph A. and Jane (Donahue) D.; m. Eugenie A. Fleri, Aug. 19, 1944; children: Christopher, Stephen, Eugenie, Jane, Richard. BS, Georgetown U., 1941; LLB, Columbia U., 1947. Bar: N.Y. 1948. Assoc. Shearman & Sterling, N.Y.C., 1947-57, ptnr., 1957-79, 81-97; asst. sec. for manpower, res. affairs and logistics USN, Washington, 1979-81. Bd. dirs. The Fuji Bank and Trust Co. Bd. dirs. USO of Met. N.Y., 1982-90. Lt. USNR, 1941-45. Decorated Navy Cross, D.F.C. with 3 gold stars, Air medal with 7 gold stars; recipient Disting. Pub. Service award Sec. of Navy, 1980. Mem. Met. Club (Washington). Democrat. Roman Catholic. Home: 32 Washington Sq W New York NY 10011-9156

DOYLE, JUSTIN P., lawyer; b. Rochester, N.Y., Oct. 26, 1948; s. Justin Joseph and Jane Martha (Kreag) Doyle; children: Mary, Joe. BA, Dartmouth Coll., 1970; JD, Cornell U., 1974. Bar: N.Y. 1974. From assoc. to ptnr. Nixon, Hargrave, Devans & Doyle, Rochester, 1974-99; ptnr. Nixon Peabody LLP (formerly Nixon, Hargrave, Devans & Doyle), Rochester, 1999—. Mem.: Monroe County Bar Assn., N.Y. Bar Assn. Home: 252 Overbrook Rd Rochester NY 14618-3648 Office: Nixon Peabody LLP Clinton Sq PO Box 31051 Rochester NY 14603-1051

DOYLE, KRISTENE ANNE, psychologist, educator; b. N.Y.C., Oct. 5, 1972; d. Roger Christopher and Barbara Ann Doyle. BA, McGill U., 1994; MA with Distinction, Hofstra U., 1995, PhD, 1999. Lic. psychologist N.Y. Edn. Dept., 2000. Dir. clin. services Assn. Benefit Children, N.Y.C., 1999—2000; coordl. tng. and devel. Albert Ellis Inst., 2000—, dir. child and family svcs. clinic, 2000—, staff psychologist, 2000—, dir. clin. svcs., 2002—, assoc. exec. dir., 2003—. Adj. asst. prof. St. John's U., Jamaica, NY, 2000—. Co-author: Achieving Unconditional Self-Acceptance: Rational Emotive Behavior Therapy with a Depressed Woman; author: The Application of Rational Emotive Behavior Therapy In Women's Groups Therapy, My Idiosyncratic Practice of Rational Emotive Behavior Therapy, The Contribution of Social Psychology to Rational Emotive Behavior Therapy; mem. editl. bd.: Jour. Rational-Emotive and Cognitive-Behavior Therapy, 2002—. Fellow: Albert Ellis Inst.; mem.: APA, Assn. Advancement Behavior Therapy (chair inst. ann. psychol. conv. 2002—). Office: Albert Ellis Inst 45 East 65th St New York NY 10021 Office Phone: 212-535-0822. Personal E-mail: krisdoyle@msn.com.

DOYLE, L. F. BOKER, retired trust company executive; b. N.Y.C., Apr. 23, 1931; Luke Cantwell and Rita (Boker) D.; m. Susanna Stone, Jan. 31, 1959; children: Katharine, Nancy, Victoria, Jessica. BA, Yale U., 1953; postgrad., NYU, 1956-63. 1st v.p., dir., mgr. capital mgmt. dept. Smith Barney & Co., N.Y.C., 1956-74; exec. v.p. Fiduciary Trust Co. Internat., N.Y.C., 1974-83, pres., 1983-94, chmn. exec. com., 1994-96, also dir., 1978-96, cons., 1996. Dir. U.S. LIfe Ins. Co., 1996-97. Trustee Margaret Sanger Rsch. Bur., N.Y.C., 1962-68, N.Y.C. Sch. Vol. Program, 1979-90, New Sch. for Social Rsch., N.Y.C., 1983-91, Taconic Found., N.Y.C., 1989—, Hudson River Found., 1997—; trustee Am. Mus. Natural History, N.Y.C., 1968-2002, hon. trustee, 2003—; bd. dirs. Cultural Instns. Retirement Sys., N.Y.C., 1971-96, chmn. bd., 1980-96; trustee Nature Cons., N.Y. State, 1990-2003, chmn., 1993-96; trustee Frick Collection, N.Y.C., 1990, treas., 1992—; trustee Ea. N.Y. chpt. Nature Conservatory, 1998—, chmn., 2003-04. 1st lt. USMC, 1953-55. Mem. Century Assn., Anglers Club N.Y. (pres. 1976-77). Avocations: fishing, birding, natural history, conservation, antiques.

DOYLE, LAURIE ELLEN, art educator; b. Vernon, Tex., Sept. 25, 1959; d. Jerry Clinton and Lea Ellen Lawlis; m. David Glen Doyle, Dec. 20, 1982; children: Benjamin David, Adam Clinton. BA in Music, Lubbock Christian Coll., 1982; MA in Vocal Performance, Tex. Tech. U., 1985; PhD, Tex. Tech U., Lubbock, TX, 2000. Cert. tchr. State of Tex., 1982. Asst. prof. of fine arts Lubbock Christian U., Tex., 1982—2004, assoc. prof. of fine arts, 2004—. Ministry leader for adult drama Broadway Ch. of Christ, Lubbock, Tex., 1996—. Dir.: (play) The Ettiquette of Mourning, (musical) Quiliters (Achievement in Musical Direction, ACTF, 2000). Ministry leader Broadway Ch. of Christ, Lubbock, Tex., 1996—2005. Recipient Excellence in Musical Direction, Am. Coll. Theatre Festival, 1985, 1987, 2000. Mem.: Lubbock Music Tchrs. Assn., Assn. for Theatre in Higher Edn., Tex. Ednl. Theatre Assn., Christians in Theatre Arts, Tex. Music Educators Assn., Nat. Assn. of Teachers of Singing, Phi Kappa Phi. Office: Lubbock Christian University 5601 W 19th Lubbock TX 79407 Office Phone: 806-720-7428. Business E-Mail: laurie.doyle@lcu.edu.

DOYLE, MATHIAS FRANCIS, academic administrator, political scientist, educator; b. Malone, NY, Nov. 18, 1933; s. Francis J. and Madeline L. (Donnelly) D. BA, Siena Coll., 1955; MA, Cath. U. Am., 1965; PhD, U. Notre Dame, 1968; diploma, Pres.' Assn. of Am. Mgmt. Assn.; Inst. Edn. Mgmt., Harvard U. Lectr. St. Francis Coll., Rye Beach, N.H., 1963-65; assoc. prof. polit. sci. Siena Coll., Loudonville, N.Y., 1968-75; pres. St. Bonaventure (N.Y.) U., 1975-90, also trustee., prof. polit. sci., 1992—; Adminstr.'s fellow AID, Washington, 1990-92; dir. human svcs. St. Anthony Shrine, Boston. Trustee Commn. on Ind. Colls. and Univs. Contbr. articles periodicals. Trustee Siena Coll. Arthur Schmidt fellow, 1966-68 Mem. Am., Northeastern polit. sci. assns., Pi Gamma Mu, Delta Epsilon Sigma. Roman Catholic. Home: St Anthony Shrine 100 Arch St Boston MA 02110 Office: Dir of Human Resources Saint Anthony Shrine 100 Arch St Boston MA 02110 Office Phone: 617-542-6440. Business E-Mail: mdoyle@stanthonyshrine.org. *A lifetime spent in education and ministry has taught me how true it is that it is better to give then to receive.*

DOYLE, MICHAEL A., lawyer; b. Atlanta, Nov. 4, 1937; children: John, David, Peter.; m. Bernice H. Winter, Nov. 12, 1977. BA, Yale U., 1959, LLB, 1962. Bar: Ga. 1961, D.C. 1967, U.S. Dist. Ct. D.C. 1967, U.S. Dist. Ct. (no. dist.) Ga. 1962, U.S. Ct. Appeals (5th cir.) 1962, U.S. Ct. Appeals (11th cir.) 1982, U.S. Ct. Appeals (D.C. cir.) 1968, U.S. Supreme Ct. 1972, U.S. Ct. Appeals (4th cir.) 1985. Assoc. Alston, Miller & Gaines, Atlanta, 1962-67; ptnr. Alston & Bird and predecessor, Atlanta, 1967—; of counsel Alston & Bird LLP, Atlanta. Bd. dirs. Atlanta Legal Aid Soc., 1969-84, pres., 1975-76; bd. dirs. Ga. Legal Services Program; mem. Leadership Atlanta, 1974. Served to lt. USNR, 1964-69. Mem. ABA, State Bar Ga., Atlanta Lawyers Club, Assn. Yale Alumni, Yale Law Sch. Assn. (nat. v.p. 1982-85, mem. exec. com. 1978-85, chmn. planning com. 1988-90, pres. 1991-92, chmn. exec. com. 1992-94). Piedmont Driving Club, Commerce Club, Yale Club Ga. (pres. 1982-84), Yale Club N.Y. Office: Alston & Bird 4200 One Atlantic Ctr 1201 W Peachtree St NW Atlanta GA 30309-3424 Office Phone: 404-881-7340.

DOYLE, MICHAEL F., congressman; b. Swissvale, Pa., Aug. 5, 1953; s. Michael Sr. and Rosemarie (Fusco) D.; m. Susan Erlandson; children: Mike Jr., David, Kevin, Alexandra. BS, Pa. State U., 1975. Exec. dir. Turtle Creek (Pa.) Valley Citizens Union, 1977-79; chief of staff State Sen. Frank Pecora, Harrisburg, Pa., 1979-94; co-founder Eastgate Ins. Agy., Pitts., 1983-94; mem. U.S. Ho. of Reps. from 14th Pa. dist., Washington, 1995—; mem. energy and commerce com., founder Congl. Autism Caucus U.S. Ho. of Reps., Washington. Coun. mem. Swissvale (Pa.) Borough Coun., 1977-81. Active Lions Club, Leadership Pitts., Italian Sons & Daughters of Am. Mem.: Nat. Dem. Club. Democrat. Roman Catholic. Avocations: golf, italian cooking, piano. Office: US House Reps 401 Cannon HOB Washington DC 20515-3814 Address: 225 Ross St 5th flr Pittsburgh PA 15219 E-mail: doyle@mail.house.gov.*

DOYLE, MICHAEL PATRICK, microbiologist, educator, director; b. Madison, Wis., Oct. 3, 1949; s. Donald Vincent and Evelyn (Bauer) Doyle; m. Annette Marie Ripple, Dec. 27, 1971; children: Michael Patrick, Patrick Matthew, Kristen Anne. BS in Bacteriology, U. Wis., 1973, MS in Food Microbiology, 1975, PhD in Food Microbiology, 1977. Sr. project leader Ralston Purina Co., St. Louis, 1977-80; asst. prof. U. Wis., Madison, 1980-84, assoc. prof., 1984-88, prof., 1988-91; prof., dir. U. Ga., Griffin, 1991—, dept. head Athens, 1993-99. Mem. sci. bd. U.S. FDA, 2000—03; regents prof. Bd. Regents Ga. U. Sys., 1997—; nat. adv. com. on microbiol. criteria for foods USA, Washington, 1988—90, Washington, 1994—2000; trustee Internat. Life Scis. Inst.-N.Am., Washington, 1992—, sci. advisor, 1987—96; mem. Internat. Commn. on Microbiol. Specifications for Foods, 1989—2000; Wis. Disting. prof. bd. regents U. Wis., Madison, 1988—91; James M. Craig Meml. lectr. Oreg. State U., Corvallis, 1990; sci. lectr. Am. Soc. Microbiology Found., 1991—93, 1999—2001; Peter J. Shields lectr. U. Calif., Davis, 1993; G. Malcolm Trout vis. scholar Mich. State U., Lansing, 1994; sci. adv. coun. Refrigeration Rsch. and Edn. Found., 1997—2002; York Disting. lectr. Auburn U., 1999. Editor: Food Microbiology: Fundamentals and Frontiers, 1997, Food Microbiology: Fundamentals and Frontiers, 2d edit., 2001, Foodborne Bacterial Pathogens, 1989; contbr. articles to profl. jours. Named one of Top 100 Most Cited Rschrs. Agrl. Scis., Inst. Sci. Info., 2002; named to Inst. Med., 2003; recipient award for Profl. Excellence, Am. Agrl. Econs. Assn., 1992, Silver Plow Honor award, USDA, 1998, Ptnrs. in Pub. Health award, Ctrs. Disease Control and Prevention, 2001. Fellow: World Innovation Found., Am. Acad. Microbiology, Inst. of Food Technologists (Fred W. Tanner lectr. 1986, sci. lectr. 1987—90, exec. com. 2000—03, Samuel Cate Prescott award for rsch. 1987, Nicholas Appert award for preeminence in and contbns. to field of food tech. 1996), Internat. Assn. Food Protection (pres. 1992—93, Norbert F. Sherman article excellence award 1993, NFPA food safety award for outstanding contbn. to food safety rsch. and edn. 1999); mem.: NAS (assoc.), Inst. Medicine NAS (food and nutrition bd. 1991—97, com. to ensure safe food from prodn. to consumption 1998, chmn. rev. com. USDA E. coli 0157:H7 in ground beef risk assessment 2001—02, chmn. food forum 2003—, com. nat. needs rsch. in vet. scis. 2004—05, food and nutrition bd. 2005—), Am. Soc. for Microbiology (chmn. food microbiology divsn. 1987—89, pub. and sci. affairs bd. 2003—, P.R. Edwards award for outstanding career achievements 1994), Gamma Sigma Delta, Phi Kappa Phi. Roman Catholic. Achievements include patents for for monocional antibody to enterohemorrhagic E. coli; for competitive exclusion bacteria to reduce carriage of enterohemorrhagic E. coli by cattle and Listeria in floor drains; development of methods to control and detect foodborne pathogens. Office: U Ga Ctr Food Safety 1109 Experiment St Griffin GA 30223-1797 Office Phone: 770-228-7284. Business E-Mail: mdoyle@uga.edu.

DOYLE, MICHAEL W., international official, educator; b. Honolulu, 1948; Student, USAF Academy; AB, Harvard U, 1970; PhD, Harvard U., 1977. Lectr. internat. studies U. Warwick, England, 1975—76; asst. prof. pub. and internat. affairs Woodrow Wilson Sch. Princeton U., 1977—84, from assoc. prof. to Edwards S. Sanford prof. politics and internat. affairs, 1987—2003, dir. Ctr. Internat. Studies, 1997—2001; from asst. to assoc. prof. polit. sci. John Hopkins U., 1984—97; v.p. Internat. Peace Acad., NY, 1993—94; asst. sec.-gen. spl. adviser to sec. gen. Kofi Annan UN, 2001—03; Harold Brown prof. U.S. fgn. and security policy, prof. internat. and pub. affairs and law Columbia U., NYC. Mem. adv. coms. UN High Commr. for Refugees, Lessons Learned Unit, UN Dept. Peacekeeping Ops.; mem. Inst. for Advanced Study, Princeton, 1982-83; chmn. com. editors World Politics, 1997-2001; fellow Ctr. for Advanced Study in the Behavioral Scis., Stanford, 2000-01. Author: Empires, UN Peacekeeping in Cambodia: UNTAC's Civil Mandate, Ways of War and Peace; co-author: Alternatives to Monetary Disorder, (with Jean-Marc Coicaud and Anne-Marie Gardner) The Globalization of Human Rights, 2003; co-editor: Escalation and Intervention, Keeping the Peace, Peacemaking and Peacekeeping for the New Century, New Thinking in Internat. Relations Theorys. With Mass. National Air Guard. U Harvard awards include Detur Prize, John Harvard Scholar, Atherton Prize Fellowship; Ford Foundation Rsch. Fellowship, SSRC/MacArthur Found. Fellowship, Membership of the Inst. of Advanced Studies, Ctr. for Advanced Study in the Behavioral Scis. Fellow: Am. Acad. Arts and Scis. Office: Columbia Sch of Law 13th Fl IAB 420 West 118th St New York NY 10027 Office Phone: 212-854-3061. Office Fax: 212-854-7946. Business E-Mail: md2221@columbia.edu.

DOYLE, NANCY CAROLYN, writer; b. Taunton, Mass., Mar. 19, 1931; d. Herbert A. and Mildred (Sylvander) D. BA, Boston U., 1954; MA, Wellesley Coll., 1956. Rsch. and tng. asst. Wellesley (Mass.) Coll., 1954-56; press dir. United Fund Greater Boston, 1957-60; writer Mental Health Materials, N.Y.C., 1960-62, Nat. League Nursing, N.Y.C., 1962-65, Am. Lung Assn., N.Y.C., 1967-86; assoc. Am. Lung Assn. Greater Norfolk, Walpole, Mass., 1986-95. Author: The Dying Person and the Family, 1975, Smoking: A Habit to be Broken, 1979, Involuntary Smoking, 1987. Pres. Friends of Taunton (Mass.) Pub. Libr., 1993-95; bd. dirs. Star Players, Taunton, 1987-92. Mem. AAUW, Phi Beta Kappa, Sigma Xi. Avocations: tennis, travel, reading. Home: 20 Fairview Ave Taunton MA 02780-4413

DOYLE, NANCY HAZLETT, artist; b. Wilmington, Del., July 8, 1947; d. Theodore Jay and Catherine L. (Lynch) Hazlett; m. Michael Doyle, Nov. 20, 1982 (div. 1985). BS in Art Edn., Moore Coll. of Art, 1969; MFA in Painting, Pa. State U., 1975. Tchr. Chester County Juvenile Detention Home, Embreeville, Pa., 1972—73; instr. Pa. State U., State College, 1975—77; artist Chester County Art Assn., West Chester, Pa., 1977—78. One person shows include Pattee Meml. Libr., Pa. State U., University Park, 1974, Cygnet Framing Studio, West Chester, 1986, Va. Lippincott Gallery, Phoenixville, Pa., 1992, Agapè Gallery, Malvern, Pa., 1994; exhibited in group shows Coll. Arts and Arch., Zoller Gallery, Pa. State U., University Park, 1974-75, Erie (Pa.) Art Ctr., 1975, Corcoran Gallery, Washington, 1975, Juniata Coll., Huntingdon, Pa., 1976, Daisy Jamison Soroptomist Ann. Invitational Show, West Chester, 1979-82, Yellow Springs Ann. Art Show, Chester Springs, Pa., 1986-98, Chester County Art Assn. Invitational, 1986-88, Artworks Gallery, Kennett Square, Pa., 1992-95, Main Line Art Ctr., Haverford, Pa., 1994-96, Jun Gallery, Phila., 1994, Leslie Eadeh Art Gallery, Devon, Pa., 1995, Hardcastle Gallery, Wilmington, Del., 1996, Ctr. for Creative Arts, Hockessin, Del., 1997-2000, Del. Ctr. Contemporary Arts, Wilmington, 2001-03. Recipient grad. assistantships Pa. State U., 1973-75. Mem.: Del. Ctr. for Contemporary Arts, New Castle County Irish Soc. Democrat. Avocations: photography, crafts, reading, webmaster. Home: 5 Ruth Rd Apt G-5 Wilmington DE 19805 Personal E-mail: ndoylebus@cs.com.

DOYLE, PATRICK JOHN, otolaryngologist, department chairman; b. Moose Jaw, Sask., Can., Nov. 17, 1926; s. William E. and Bertha L. (Fisher) D.; m. Irene Strilchuk, May 21, 1949; children: Sharon, Patrick, Robert, Barbara, Joseph, Kathleen. BSc, U. Alta., 1947, MD, 1949. Diplomate Am. Bd. Otolaryngology (bd. dirs., v.p. 1986-88, pres. 1988-90). Intern U. B.C. Hosp., 1949-50; resident in medicine and pediatrics, 1950-51; resident in otolaryngology U. Oreg. Hosp., 1958-61; asst. prof., then asso. prof. U. Oreg. Med. Sch., 1965-70; mem. faculty U. B.C. Med. Sch., 1963—, prof. otolaryngology, 1972-91, prof. otolaryngology emeritus, 1992—, head dept., 1972-91, program dir. residency tng. program, 1972-91. Head div. otolaryngology St. Paul's Hosp., mem. numerous nat. med. coms. Author numerous articles in field; mem. editorial bds. profl. jours. Fellow Royal Coll. Surgeons Can., Am. Laryngol., Rhinol. and Otol. Soc. (v.p. western sect. 1988, pres. 1994), Am. Laryngol. Soc., Am. Acad. Otolaryngology-Head and Neck Surgery (v.p. 1984, bd. dirs. 1985-87), Am. Otol. Soc.; mem. Can. Soc. Otolaryngology-Head and Neck Surgery (pres. 1987), Pacific Coast Oto-Ophthal. Soc. (pres. 1977), Soc. Univ. Otolaryngologists, U. Oreg. Otolaryngology Alumni Assn. (pres. 1968-70), Am. Otological Soc., Centurion Club, Tinnitus Rsch. Found. Roman Catholic. Office: # 301-5704 Balsam St Vancouver BC Canada V6M 4B9

DOYLE, PAUL FRANCIS, lawyer; b. N.Y.C., Sept. 3, 1946; s. Paul Francis and Rita Lilian (Mulcahy) D.; m. Margaret Mary Sullivan, Aug. 23, 1969; children: Karen, Lynn. BA in English, Holy Cross Coll., 1968; JD cum laude, NYU, 1973. Bar: Mass. 1973, N.Y. 1975, U.S. Dist. Ct. (so. and ea. dists.) N.Y. 1975, U.S. Ct. Appeals (2d and 3d cirs.) 1975, U.S. Supreme Ct. 1991, U.S. Dist. Ct. Mass. 1992, U.S. Dist. Ct. (no. dist.) N.Y. 1995. Law clk. Superior Ct. Commonwealth of Mass., Boston, 1973-74; assoc. Kelley, Drye & Warren, N.Y.C., 1974-82, ptnr., 1983—. Instr. Nat. Inst. Trial Advocacy, 1994; mem. departmental disciplinary com. Supreme Ct. of N.Y., 1st Jud. Dept., 2003—; lectr. N.Y. State Bar Assn., 2001, 03. Assoc. editor Ann. Survey Am. Law, 1972-73. Mem. Planning Bd., Croton-on-Hudson, N.Y., 1989-92, mem. Comprehensive Plan Com., 1999—; mem. pres.'s coun. Holy Cross Coll. With U.S. Army, 1968-70, Vietnam. Mem. Am. Inns of Ct., Order of Coif. Roman Catholic. Office: Kelley Drye & Warren LLP 101 Park Ave New York NY 10178-0062

DOYLE, TOM, sculptor; b. Jerry City, Ohio, May 23, 1928; s. John Thomas and Kathleen (Solether) D.; m. Natalie N. Burdette (div. 1957); m. Eva Hesse (dec. 1970); m. Jane Miller. Student, Miami U., Oxford, Ohio, 1948-50; BFA, Ohio State U., 1952, MFA, 1953. Sculptor, N.Y.C., to date. Artist-in-residence La Napoule Art Found., France, 1989. One-man shows include Dwan Gallery, N.Y.C., 1966, 67, 55 Mercer Gallery, N.Y.C., 1972, 74, 76, Picker Art Gallery, Colgate U., Hamilton, N.Y., 1976, Sculpture Now, Inc., N.Y.C., 1978, The Sculpture Ctr., N.Y.C., 1988, Bill Bace Gallery, N.Y.C., 1991, 93-94, Long House Found., East Hampton, N.Y., 1995, Mattatuck Mus., Waterbury, Conn., 1996, Kouros Gallery, N.Y.C., 1999, Nicolaysen Art Mus., Casper, Wyo., 2001, New Arts Gallery, Litchfield, Conn., 2003, 05; exhibited in group shows at Whitney Mus., N.Y.C., 1967, Los Angeles County Mus., 1967, Taft Mus., Cin., 1974, Indpls. Mus. Art, 1974. Recipient commendation GSA, Fairbanks, Alaska, 1980, Jimmy Ernst Lifetime Art Achievement award AAAL, 1994, Ohioana Career award for Lifetime Achievement, 1996; Guggenheim fellow, 1982, Nat. Endowment for the Arts fellow, 1990-91; rsch. grantee CUNY, 1989-90. Mem. Am. Abstract Artists, Nat. Acad. Design. E-mail: tjmdoyle@charter.net.

DOYLE, WILLIAM ROBERT, finance educator; b. San Jose, Calif., July 6, 1974; s. William and Alice Doyle; m. Heather Leigh Jack, Aug. 15, 1999; children: Amelia Helen, Cora Anne. BA in Liberal Arts, BA in Philosophy, Villanova U., 1996; MA in Polit. Sci., PhD in Higher Edn., Stanford U., 2004. Rsch. asst. Calif. Higher Edn. Policy Ctr., San Jose, 1996—97; rsch. assoc. Nat. Ctr. Pub. Policy and Higher Edn., 1997—99, sr. policy analyst, 1999—2004; asst. prof. higher edn. Vanderbilt U., Nashville, 2004—. Cons. Nat. Ctr. Pub. Policy and Higher Edn., 2004—. Editor: (songs) Public and Private Financing of Higher Education. Mem.: Am. Ednl. Rsch. Assn., Association Study Higher Edn., Phi Beta Kappa. Avocations: rock climbing, mountain biking, trail running. Office: Vanderbilt U Peabody #514 230 Appleton Pl Nashville TN 37203-5721 Office Phone: 615-322-2904.

DOYLE, WILLIAM STOWELL, venture capitalist; b. Lowell, Mich., Aug. 14, 1944; s. William Stowell and Eunice Jane D.; m. Permele Elliott Frischkorn, Jan. 7, 1978; children: William Elliott, Permele Crawford. AB, Duke U., 1966. Copywriter Wallace-Blakeslee, Grand Rapids, Mich., 1966-68; dir. mktg. Wolverine Worldwide, Rockford, Mich., 1971-73; v.p., dir. mktg. Chase Manhattan Bank, N.Y.C., also London, Hong Kong, 1973-76, 79-82; pres. Doyle Graf Mabley, 1982-89, Ecomarine Inc., N.Y.C., 1989-92, Strategen, N.Y.C., 1992-95; pres., CEO Taishan Holdings Inc., 1995—2000; chmn. Taishan Pharms Ltd., Beijing, 1997—; vice chmn. Enzymatic Therapy, Inc., Green Bay, Wis., 2000—02; chmn. Phynova LLC, N.Y.C., 2001—, Phynova Ltd., Oxford, England, 2001—. Contbr. articles to profl. jours. Dep. commr. State of N.Y. Dept. Commerce, Albany, 1976-79; bd. dirs. Nat. Meals-on-Wheels Found., Washington; assoc. bd. dirs. Julliard Sch., N.Y.C. With USAF, 1968-69; 1st lt. U.S. Army, 1969-71. Mem. Internat. Inst. Strategic Studies (London), Racquet and Tennis Club (N.Y.C.), Union Club (N.Y.C.). Anglican. Office: Oxford Sci Park Magdalen Ctr Oxford OX4 4GA England Office Phone: 44 1865 784 880.

DOYLE, WILLIAM THOMAS, physicist, retired educator; b. New Britain, Conn., Dec. 5, 1925; s. Thomas William and Kathleen (McConn) D.; m. Barbara May Grant, June 16, 1951; children— Peter, Jeffrey. Sc.B. in Physics, Brown U., 1951; MA, Yale, 1952, PhD, 1955. Mem. faculty Dartmouth, 1955-97, prof. physics, 1964-97, chmn. dept., 1967-71. Served with USNR, 1943-46. NSF predoctoral fellow, 1953-54, 54-55; postdoctoral fellow, 1958-59 Mem.: AAPT, Sigma Xi. Home: 6 Tyler Rd Hanover NH 03755-2232

DOZIER, DAVID CHARLES, JR., advertising executive, public relations executive; b. Santa Fe, Dec. 4, 1938; s. David Charles Sr. and Zelma (Martin) D.; m. Dianne Flusche, June 1, 1960; children: Deborah, Mary Rebecca, Michael, Constance. BA, U. Dallas, 1960. Editor sports Tex. Cath., Dallas, 1960-70, gen. sales mgr., 1964-70; dir. classified advt. Dallas Times Herald, 1970-74; pres., chmn. DBG&H Unltd. Inc., Dallas, 1974-88; chmn. Dozier Co., Dallas, 1989—. Innovator, ptnr. Navi Pesanda Indian Blanket Creations, 1992. Author: A Compendium of Endurance, 1989. Mem. Am. Indian, Santa Clara Pueblo Tribe, N.Mex.; cert. athletic trainer Downtown YMCA, 1990-2003. Recipient Disting. Svc. award Pres. U.S. and HUD, 1984. Republican. Roman Catholic. Avocation: more than 132 completed marathons. Home: 7102 Wabash Cir Dallas TX 75214-3532 Office: 2547 Farrington St Dallas TX 75207-6607 Office Phone: 214-744-2800. Business E-Mail: david@thedoziercompany.com.

DOZIER, ELEANOR CAMERON, computer company executive, writer; b. N.Y.C., May 20, 1939; d. Robert Paul and Marion Gill MacNeil; m. Norman Garlan Dozier, June 23, 1989; children: Karen Gonzales, Robert Bennett, Heidi Bennett, Julia, Ian, Jordan. Rep. to British Isles Max Factor, Inc., Hollywood, Calif., 1966—71; co-owner; also songwriter and poet MacNeil Dozier Pub. Co., Ft. Lauderdale, Fla., 1988—2002; v.p. Computer Dimensions Network Corp., N.Y.C., 1998—. Mktg. dir. Prometheus Devel., San Jose, Calif., 1986—87. Author: (book) O For The Love Of God!, 2003. Recipient commn., Stephen Ministry, Order St. Luke. Episcopalian. Avocations: bicycling, golf, tennis, travel. Business E-Mail: call4ecd1@hotmail.com.

DOZIER, JAMES LEE, former army officer; b. Arcadia, Fla., Apr. 10, 1931; s. Joseph B. and Leota (Caruthers) D.; m. Judith I. Stimpson, June 30, 1956; children— Cheryl Lyn, Scott Lee BS, U.S. Mil. Acad., 1956; MS in Aerospace Engring., U. Ariz., 1964. Commd. 2d lt. U.S. Army, 1956, advanced through grades to maj. gen., 1984, comdr. 1st Squadron, 1st Cav., 1st Armored Div., 1971-73, staff officer Office of Dep. Chief of Staff for Research, Devel. and Acquisition Washington, 1974-76, also mil. asst. to asst. sec. of army, 1974-76, comdr. 2d Brigade, 2d Armored div. Fort Hood, Tex., 1976-78, chief of staff 2d Armored div., 1978-79, chief of staff III Corps and Ft. Hood, 1979-80, dep. chief of staff logistics and adminstrn. Allied Land Forces So. Europe Verona, Italy, 1980-82, asst. comdt. Armor Sch. Ft. Knox, Ky., 1982-83, dep. comdg. gen. III Corps and Fort Hood Fort Hood, Tex., 1983-85, ret., 1985; pres. Golden Grove Mgmt. Corp., Arcadia, Fla., 1985-87, Suncoast Media Group, Venice, Fla., 1987; gen. mgr. David C. Brown Enterprises, 1988-93; owner JCS Group, Ft. Myers, 1993—. Lectr., condr. seminars on kidnapping experience. Contbg. author: Winter of Fire, 1990; contbr. articles to mil. jours. Decorated Silver Star, Legion of Merit, Bronze Star with V device and 2 oak leaf clusters, Air medals, Purple Heart Avocations: fishing, boating, woodworking.

DOZIER, MONTY CHARLES, environmental scientist, educator; Student, Frank Phillips Coll., 1981; BS, Tex. A&M U., 1984; MEd, Tex. Tech U., 1986; PhD, Tex. A&M U., 1999. County ext. agt. Tex. Coop. Ext., Tex., 1984—95, ext. assoc. -water quality College Station, Tex., 1995—98, asst. prof., 1999—, ext. specialist, 1999—, ext. specialist emeritus Temple, Tex., 1997—99. Contbr. articles to profl. jours. Judge Franklin (Tex.) Elections, 2004—05; tchr. sunday sch. Shiloh Bapt. Ch., Franklin, 2004—05. Recipient Conservation medal, Tex. DAR, 2005. Fellow: Soil and Water Conservation Soc.; mem.: So. Weed Sci. Soc., Tex. Plant Protection Assn. (pres. 2003—04). Republican. Avocations: golf, camping, living history. Office: Texas Cooperative Extension 2474 Tamu College Station TX 77843-2474 Office Phone: 979-845-2761. Office Fax: 979-845-0604. Business E-Mail: m-dozier@tamu.edu.

DOZIER, WILLIAM EVERETT, JR., publishing executive, editor-in-chief; b. Delhi, La., June 12, 1922; s. William Everett and Harriet E. (Miles) D.; m. Eleanor Ruth Roye, Sept. 1, 1944; children: Martha Carolyn Dozier Hunnicutt (dec. July 1995), Sarah Rebecca, Dozeitdi Beratdino. BA in Journalism, La. Tech. U., 1943. Assoc. editor Delhi Dispatch, 1936-39; reporter, state editor New Orleans Times-Picayune, 1946-50; editor Courier-Times-Telegraph, Tyler, Tex., 1952-65; pres., editor, pub. Kerrville (Tex.) Daily Times, 1965-88; gen. ptnr. Frio-Nueces Publs. Ltd., 1976—94; pres. Hills o'Texas Publs., Inc., 1982—94. V.P. Kerrville Music Found. and Performing Arts Soc., 1978-84, also bd. dirs.; bd.d irs. Adm. Nimitz Ctr. Found., Fredericksburg, Tex., 1976—; founding dir. past pres. Riverside Nature Ctr.; assn. dir. Playhouse 2000, 2000-; chmn. United Fund campaign, Kerrville, 1967; mem. adv. bd. Salvation Army, 1967—; v.p. Tex. State Arts & Crafts Fair Assn., 1980-90, also bd. dirs., 1972-92; lay leader First United Meth. Ch., Kerrville, 1984-86, past chmn. bd. trustees, chmn. adminstrv. bd.; trustee Schreiner Coll., 1987-96, 97—, v.p., bd. trustees Sid Peterson Meml. Hosp., 1989-2002. Served with USN, 1943-46, 50-52, ret. comdr., 1973. Mem. Am. Soc. Newspaper Editors, Am. Newspaper Pubs. Assn., Nat. Newspaper Assn., Tex. AP Mng. Editors Assn. (pres. 1964-65), Tex. Press Assn. (pres. 1979-80), Tex. Daily Newspaper Assn. (dir. 1984-87), Tex. Press Found. (pres. 1982-92), So. Newspaper Pubs. Assn. (chmn. smaller newspaper com. 1983-84, dir. 1984-87), Kerr County C. of C. (pres. 1973-74), W. Tex. C. of C. (regional v.p. 1981-84, pres. 1985-86), Tex. C. of C. (founding dir. 1987-90), Masons (Tyler), Kiwanis (lt. gov. divsn. 5 Tex.-Okla. dist. 1974, pres. Kerrville 1973, Disting. Club Pres. 1973, Disting. Lt. Gov. 1974), Sigma Delta Chi. Home: 2428 Rock Creek Dr Kerrville TX 78028-6504 Office: 815 Jefferson St Ste A Kerrville TX 78028-4581

D. PRESTON, STEELE, adult education educator; b. Fort Smith, Ark., Oct. 23, 1975; s. Larray A. and Sharon F. Steele. MA in adult edn., U. South Fla., 2003. Program specialist Region IV Resource Ctr. - USF, Tampa, Fla., 2003—04, ednl. and tng. program dir., 2004—. Monetary grant, Fla. Dept. of Edn., 2. Mem.: ACE of Fla. (assoc.; n/a), ASCD (assoc.; n/a), Commn. on Adult Basic Edn. (assoc.; n/a), Am. Assn. for Adult and Continuing Edn. (assoc.; n/a). D-Liberal. Avocations: camping, fishing, beach and sun. Office: U S Fla 4202 E Fowler Ave HMS 421 Tampa FL 33620 Office Phone: 813-974-2904. Office Fax: 813-974-2780. Personal E-mail: prestons01@yahoo.com. E-mail: dsteele@coedu.usf.edu.

DRABBLE, MARGARET, writer; b. Sheffield, England, June 5, 1939; d. John Frederick and Kathleen Marie (Bloor) D.; m. Clive Swift, June 27, 1960 (div. 1975); children: Adam, Rebecca, Joseph; m. Michael Holroyd, 1982. BA with honors, Newnham Coll., Cambridge, 1960; DLitt (hon.), U. Sheffield, 1976, U. Manchester, 1987, U. Keele, 1988, U. Bradford, 1988, U. East Anglia, 1994, U. York, 1995. Author: (novels) A Summer Bird-Cage, 1963, The Garrick Year, 1964, The Millstone, 1965 (John Llewelyn Rhys Meml. award 1966), Jerusalem the Golden, 1967 (James Tait Black Meml. book prize 1968), The Waterfall, 1969, The Needle's Eye, 1972 (Yorkshire Post Book of Yr. award 1972), The Realms of Gold, 1975, The Ice Age, 1977, The Middle Ground, 1980 (ALA notable book citation 1981), The Radiant Way, 1987, A Natural Curiosity, 1989, Gates of Ivory, 1991, The Witch of Exmoor, 1996, Angus Wilson: A Biography, 1995, The Peppered Moth, 2001, The Seven Sisters, 2002, The Red Queen, 2004; (short stories) Hassan's Tower, 1966, The Reunion, 1968, The Gifts of War, 1970; (non-fiction) Arnold Bennett, A Biography, 1974, For Queen and Country: Britain in the Victorian Age, 1978, A Writer's Britain, 1979; (play) Bird of Paradise, 1969; (screenplays) Laura, 1964, Isadora, 1968, Thank You All Very Much, 1969; (criticism) Wordsworth, 1966; editor: Jane Austen, Lady Susan, The Watsons, and Sanditon, 1975, The Genius of Thomas Hardy, 1976, Oxford Companion to English Literature, 1985, 6th edit., 2000, The Concise Oxford Companion to English Literature, 1987, Angus Wilson a Biography, 1995. Mem.: Am. Acad. Arts and Letters (hon.; fgn. mem., E.M. Forster award 1973). Office: care Peters Fraser & Dunlop Drury House 34-43 Russell St London WC2B 5HA England

DRABKIN, CATHERINE LENORE, painter, educator; b. New Haven, Dec. 4, 1959; d. Irving Leo and Lenore Hannah (Hirshfield) D. Student, Amherst Coll., 1978; BFA, Md. Inst. Coll. Art, Balt., 1982; MFA, Queens Coll./SUNY, 1985. Adj. lectr. Queens Coll./SUNY, 1987; vis. asst. prof. Dartmouth Coll., Hanover, N.H., 1990, 92, 93; instr. Penland (N.C.) Sch. Crafts, 1994; vis. asst. prof. U. nebr., Omaha, 1994; adj. prof. So. Conn. State U., New Haven, 1995-96; instr., coord. fine art, coord. founds. Del. Coll. Art and Design, Wilmington, 1997—. Lectr. Spokane Falls C.C., Spokane, 1997, Buffalo State Coll., 1995; vis. artist St. Mary's Coll. Md., St. Mary's City, 1995. Exhibited paintings in solo shows at Marlboro (Vt.) Coll., 1994, Albright Knox Art Gallery, Buffalo, 1995, Kraushaar Galleries, N.Y.C., 1995, 98, 2000, 02, Lorinda Knight Gallery, Spokane, 1997. MacDowell Colony fellow, 1991, Vt. Studio Ctr. fellow, 1993, Va. Ctr. for Creative Art fellow, 1996. Office: care Kraushaar Galleries 724 5th Ave New York NY 10019-4106

DRABKIN, MURRAY, lawyer; b. N.Y.C., Aug. 3, 1928; s. Max Drabkin and Minnie Masin; m. Mary Elizabeth Hooper, Nov. 27, 1971. AB, Hamilton Coll., 1950; LLB, Harvard U., 1953. Bar: D.C. 1953, U.S. Ct. Appeals (D.C. cir.) 1954, N.Y. 1966, U.S. Supreme Ct. 1972. Counsel com. on judiciary U.S. Ho. of Reps., Washington, 1957-66; spl. asst. to mayor City of N.Y., 1966-68; pvt. practice N.Y.C. and Washington, 1968-82; ptnr. Cadwalader, Wickersham & Taft, Washington, 1983-92; ret., 1992; of counsel Hopkins & Sutter, Washington, 1992-2000. Dir. Conn. State Revenue Task Force, 1969-71; mem. adv. com. FRS, Washington, 1970-71, D.C. Tax Revision Com., 1976-77. Contbr. articles to profl. jours. Served with USN, 1953-57, to lt. comdr. USNR. Fellow Phi Beta Kappa (bd. dirs. 1996—, pres. 2001—); mem. Nat. Bankruptcy Conf. (chmn. com. on R.R. reorgn. 1984-2000, chmn. com on bankruptcy crimes, 1994-98), D.C. Bar Assn., Nat. Conf. Bankruptcy Judges (hon.), Harvard Club of Washington (pres. 2000-02, bd. dirs. 1996-2004), Harvard Club of N.Y.C., Chesapeake Bay Bermuda 40 Assn., Cosmos Club, Nat. Press Club, Delta Sigma Rho.

DRACH, JOHN CHARLES, research scientist, educator; b. Cin., Sept. 25, 1939; s. Charles Louis and Edrie B. Drach; m. E. Jean Flamm, June 20, 1964; children: Laura J., Diane E. BS in Pharmacy, U. Cin., 1961, MS in Pharm. Chemistry, 1963, PhD in Biochemistry, 1966. From assoc. rsch. scientist to rsch. scientist Parke, Davis and Co., Ann Arbor, Mich., 1966-70; asst. prof. U. Mich. Dental Sch., Ann Arbor, 1970-74; assoc. prof. U. Mich., Ann Arbor, 1974-80; assoc. prof. medicinal chemistry U. Mich. Coll. Pharmacy, Ann Arbor, 1978-80; prof. U. Mich., Ann Arbor, 1980—; chmn. dept. oral biology U. Mich. Dental Sch., Ann Arbor, 1985-87, chmn. dept. biologic and materials scis., 1987-95; vis. prof. divsn. virology Burroughs Wellcome Co., Research Triangle Park, N.C., 1994. Cons. Adria Labs., Am. Inst. Chem., Am. Pharm. Assn., AMA, Chartwell, Kimberly-Clark, 1976-83. Author: Clinical Pharmacology, 1986; mem. editorial bd. Elsevier Sci. Pubs., 1984—, Antiviral Chemistry & Chemotherapy, 1996—; contbr. articles to profl. jours.; patentee antiviral drugs. NSF summer fellow, 1963; NIH grad. fellow, 1964-66; NIH grantee, 1970—. Fellow: AAAS; mem.: Internat. Soc. Antiviral Rsch. (archivist 1992—, chair awards com. 1998—2002, pres. elect 2000—02, pres. 2002—04, immediate past pres., chmn. conf. com. 2004—), Am. Soc. Microbiology (mem. editl. bd. 1982—91), Am. Chem. Soc., Am. Assn. Oral Biology, Dental Edn. Assn. (pres. oral biology sect. 1990—91), Am. Assn. Dental Rsch., Sigma Xi, Omicron Kappa Upsilon, Rho Chi. Home: 1372 Barrister Rd Ann Arbor MI 48105-2875 Office: U Mich 1011 N University Ave Ann Arbor MI 48109-1078 Office Phone: 734-763-5579. E-mail: jcdrach@umich.edu.

DRACHMAN, DANIEL BRUCE, neurologist, educator; s. Julian Moses and Emily (Deitchman) D.; m. Jephta Piatigorsky, Aug. 28, 1960; children: Jonathan Gregor, Evan Bernard, Eric Edouard. AB summa cum laude (N.Y. State scholar), Columbia Coll., 1952; MD (N.Y. State Med. scholar), NYU, 1956. Cert. Neurology and Psychiatry 1962. Intern in internal medicine Beth Israel Hosp., Boston, 1956-57; asst. resident in neurology Harvard neurol. unit Boston City Hosp., 1957-58, resident in neurology, 1958-59; resident in neuropathology Harvard neurol. unit. and Mallory Inst. Pathology, 1959-60; teaching fellow in neurology Harvard U., 1957-60; clin. assoc. Nat. Inst. Neurol. Diseases and Blindness, NIH, Bethesda, Md., 1960-62, research asso. lab. neuroanat. scis., 1962-63; clin. instr. Georgetown U., 1961-63; asst. prof. neurology Tufts U., 1963-69; assoc. prof. Johns Hopkins U., 1969-73, prof., 1974—, prof. neurosci., 1980—, W.W. Smith Charitable Found. prof. neuroimmunology, 2003—. Attending neurologist Johns Hopkins Hosp.; adv. bd. Multiple Sclerosis Soc., 1981-85; pres. med. adv. bd. Myasthenia Gravis Found.; adv. bd. Familial Dysautonomia Found.; bd. sci. councillors Nat. Inst. Neurol. and Communicative Disorders and Stroke, NIH, 1985-90; med. adv. com. Muscular Dystrophy Assn., 1994-99. Clarinetist.; author over 200 publs. on myasthenia gravis, muscular atrophy, muscular dystrophy, clubfoot, devel. disorders, neurology, amyotrophic lateral sclerosis, chamber music; mem. editl. bd. Muscle and Nerve jour., Exptl. Neurology, Autoimmunity Served with USPHS, 1960-63. Recipient Founders' Day award NYU, 1956, Jacob Javits award, 1986, Berson Disting. Alumnus award NYU Sch. Medicine, 1999; NIH grantee, 1963—, Muscular Dystrophy Assn. grantee, 1969—. Fellow Am. Acad. Neurology, N.Y. Acad. Scis.; mem. AAAS, Internat. Soc. Devel. Biology, Balt. Neurol. Soc., Phi Beta Kappa, Alpha Omega Alpha. Achievements include defining pathogenesis of clubfoot (most common human congenital malformation) and arthrogryposis (rare form of similar disorder); first described the only currently useful treatment for Duchenne Muscular Dystrophy; basic work on botulinum toxin demonstrated its use to paralyze individual muscles, and led to the widespread clinical use of Botox; first defined pathogenic abnormalities in myasthenia gravis. Avocations: clarinet, fly fishing, bicycling. Office: Johns Hopkins U Sch Medicine Dept Neurology 600 N Wolfe St Baltimore MD 21287-7519 Office Phone: 410-955-5406. E-mail: dandrac@aol.com.

DRACHMAN, DAVID ALEXANDER, neurologist; b. NYC, July 18, 1932; s. Julian Moses and Emily Drachman; m. Eleanor Betsy Derby, Nov. 26, 1959; children: Laura Jeanne, Jessica Gail, Douglas Emmet. AB with highest honors, Columbia U., 1952; MD, NYU, 1956. Diplomate: Am. Bd. Psychiatry and Neurology. Intern Duke U. Med. Center, 1956-57; resident in neurology Mass. Gen. Hosp., Boston, 1957-60; clin. assoc. NIH, 1960-63; clin. instr. neurology Georgetown U. Med. Sch., 1961-63; mem. faculty Northwestern U. Med. Sch., 1963-77, dir. neurology clinics, 1963-77, prof. neurology, 1971-77, assoc. chmn. dept., 1972-75; attending physician Passavant Meml. Hosp., Chgo., 1964-72, Northwestern Meml. Hosp., 1972-77; prof. neurology, chmn. dept. neurology U. Mass.-Meml. Med. Ctr., 1977—2002, prof. neurology, chmn. emeritus dept. neurology, 2002—. Attending physician U. Mass. Med. Center, Worcester Med. Ctr., Worcester; mem. med. adv. bd. Chgo. Multiple Sclerosis Soc., 1971-77, Mass. Multiple Sclerosis Soc., 1979-87; mem. FDA adv. panel on control and peripheral nerve system drugs, 1996—2000; mem. working group on presdl. disability, 1994-96. Mem. editl. bd. Neurobiology of Aging, 1979-93, Neurology, Archives of Neurology, 1979-91, Jour. Geriat. Psychiatry and Neurology, Jour. Rehab. and Health; contbr. articles to profl. jours. Fellow Am. Acad. Neurology; mem. AAAS, Am. Neurol. Assn. (hon. mem., pres. 1994-95), Alzheimer's Disease Assn. (chmn. sci. adv. bd. 1986-90, trustee), Am. Neuro-otology Soc., Assn. Univ. Profs. Neurology, Assn. Rsch. Nervous and Mental Diseases, Mass. Assn. Neurology, N.Y. Acad. Scis., Boston Soc. Psychiatry and Neurology (pres. 1980-81), Phi Beta Kappa, Sigma Xi, Alpha Omega Alpha (counselor). Home: 111 Barretts Mill Rd Concord MA 01742-5519 Office: U Mass Med Sch Dept Neurology 55 Lake Ave N Worcester MA 01655-0002 Office Phone: 508-856-3081. Business E-Mail: david.drachman@umassmed.edu.

DRACHNIK, CATHERINE MELDYN, recreational therapist, artist, counselor; b. Kansas City, Mo., June 7, 1924; d. Gerald Willis and Edith (Gray) Weston; m. Joseph Brennan Drachnik, Oct. 6, 1946; children: Denise Elaine, Kenneth John. BS, U. Md., 1945; MA, Calif. State U., Sacramento, 1975. Lic. family and child counselor; registered art therapist. Art therapist Vincent Hall Retirement Home, McLean, Va., Fairfax Mental Health Day Treatment Ctr., McLean, Arlington (Va.) Mental Health Day Treatment Ctr., 1971-72, Hope for Retarded, San Jose, Calif., Sequoia Hosp., Redwood City, Calif., 1972-73; supervising tchr. adult edn. Sacramento Soc. Blind, 1975-77; ptnr. Sacramento Divsn. Mediation Svcs., 1981-82; instr. Calif. State U., Sacramento, 1975-82, 92-93, 1999, Coll. Notre Dame, Belmont, Calif., 1975-96; art therapist, mental health counselor Psych West Counseling Ctr. (formerly Eskaton Am. River Mental Health Clinic), Carmichael, Calif., 1975-93; instr. Sacramento City Coll., 1997—. Instr. U. Utah, Salt Lake City, 1988—89; lectr. in field. Author: Interpreting Metaphors in Children's Drawings, 1995; one-woman shows include Vacaville (Calif.) Art Gallery, 1995, Dublier Gallery, Sacramento, 1997, Thistle Dew Gallery, 1998, Jeffery Bldg. Gallery, 2001, Oldham Gallery, 2001, Juno Gallery, Auburn, Calif., 2004, Taylors Nouveau Art Gallery, 2005, exhibited in group shows at Art of Calif. Mag., 1993, Haggin Art Mus., Stockton, Calif., 1994, 1995, 1996, 1997, 1998, 1999, 2000, 2002, 2003, Calif. State Fair, Sacramento, 1995, 1997, 1998, 2000, 2001, 2005, Watercolor West, Brea, Calif., 1998, Rocky Mountain Nat. Watercolor, Golden, Colo., 1999, West Valley Art Mus., Phoenix, 1999, Elliot Fouts Art Gallery, Sacramento, 1999—2004, Am. Watercolor Soc., N.Y., 2000, Triton Mus. Art Biennial, Santa Clara, Calif., 2000, 2002, Calif. Watercolor Assn., San Francisco, 1999, 2001, 2005. Active charitable orgns. Mem.: Calif. Watercolor Assn. (signature status), Am. Assn. Marriage and Family Therapists, Nat. Art Edn. Assn., No. Calif. Arts, Inc. (master painter), No. Calif. Art Therapy Assn. (hon.; life), Am. Art Therapy Assn. (hon.; life, pres. 1987—89), Omicron Nu, Alpha Psi Omega, Kappa Kappa Gamma Alumnae Assn. (pres. Sacramento Valley chpt. 1991—92). Republican. Avocations: swimming, golf, theater. Home and Office: 4124 American River Dr Sacramento CA 95864-6025 Office Phone: 916-489-5138. Personal E-mail: cdrach@highstream.net.

DRACHTMAN, RICHARD ALLAN, pediatrician, educator; MD, U. Chgo, 1984. Diplomate Am. Bd. Pediat. Intern Northshore U. Hosp., Manhasset, NY, 1984—85, resident in pediat., 1987—88; fellow in pediat. hematology/oncology Mt. Sinai Med. Ctr., N.Y.C., 1988—91; physician divsn. pediat. hematology & oncology Cancer Inst. N.J., New Brunswick, NJ, 1998—. Office: Cancer Inst NJ 195 Little Albany St New Brunswick NJ 08903 Office Phone: 732-235-8862. Office Fax: 732-235-8234.

DRACOS, THEODORE MICHAEL, journalist, television producer; b. Boston, June 30, 1945; s. Harry M. and Helen C. (Dore) D.; m. Mary Jill Moore, Oct. 28, 1969 (div. June 1979); 1 child, Erin. BA in History, U. Wis., 1969. Host WMFM Radio, Madison, Wis., 1970—72; founder, CEO, dir. Small Planet Rsch. Assocs., Seattle, 1973-76; contbg. writer Seattle Weekly Mag., 1977-80; investigative reporter Harte-Hanks TV, San Antonio, 1980-82, editl. commentator, 1992-93; dir. investigative reporting Gannett Broadcast Group, Mpls., 1983; investigative reporter, prodr. McGraw-Hill TV, San Diego, 1984—89; S.W. bur. chief Orion Nat. Telepictures, San Antonio, 1990; journalism instr. Incarnate Word Coll., San Antonio, 1991; documentary prodr., writer San Antonio, 1994—. Author: Ungodly: the Passions, Torments and Murder of Atheist Madalyn Murray O'Hair, 2003; writer, prodr. (documentary) One Moment of Madness, 1981 (Best Nat. Reporting award Nat. Headliners 1982, Charles Green Best Feature award Tex. Headliners 1982), Poisoning Paradise, 1987, Johnny Massingale, 1986, Stainley Stress, 1985. Exec. com. Puget Sound Sierra Club, Seattle, 1974-76; citizen activity coord. U.S. EPA Region 10, Seattle, 1974-75; med. dir. Jimmy Carter Presdl. Campaign, Washington, 1976; vol. Child Advocates of San Antonio, 1993. Recipient Golden medallion for best legal reporting Calif. State Bar, 1986. Mem.: Aus. Guild.

DRACUP, KATHLEEN ANNE, nursing educator; b. Santa Monica, Calif., Sept. 28, 1942; d. Paul Joseph and Lucy Elizabeth (Milligan) Molloy; children: Jeffrey, Jonathan, Joy, Jan, Brian. BS in Nursing, St. Xavier's Coll., Chgo., 1967; M of Nursing, U. Calif., L.A., 1974; D of Nursing Sci., U. Calif., San Francisco, 1982. Clin. nurse Little Co. of Mary Hosp., Chgo., 1967-70, UCLA Med. Ctr., 1970-74; asst. clin. prof. U. Calif., L.A., 1974-78, rsch. fellow dept. medicine, 1979-81, asst. prof. to prof., 1982-99; clin. nurse U. Calif. San Francisco Med. Ctr., 1979; pvt. practice psychotherapist, 1980—; dean, sch. nursing U. Calif., San Francisco, 2000—. Editor Heart and Lung Jour., 1981-91, Am. Jour. Critical Care, 1991—; editor Critical Care Nursing Series; contbr. chpts. to books, articles to profl. jours. Recipient Eugene Brunwald Acad. Mentorship award Am. Heart Assn., 2003; Disting. Practitioner Nat. Acad., Washington, 1987; Fulbright Sr. scholar, 1995. Fellow Coun. Cardiovascular Nursing, Am. Heart Assn., Am. Assn. Cardiopulmonary Rehab.; mem. Inst. of Medicine, Am. Nurses' Assn., Am. Assn. Critical Care Nurses (life), Sigma Theta Tau. Office: UCSF Sch Nursing 2 Koret Way Rm N319 San Francisco CA 94143-0604 Office Phone: 415-476-1805. Business E-Mail: kathydracup@nursing.ucsf.edu.

DRAEGER, SUSANNE YARBROUGH, interior designer; b. Macon, Ga., July 16, 1950; d. Ceasar Augustus and Dorothy Anne (Patrick) Yarbrough; m. Charles Fred Newberry July 29, 1972 (div.); children: Catherine Neil, Charles Fred; m. Eric R. Stanley May, 1988 (div.); m. Lawrence William Draeger March 15, 1996. BSHE in Interior Design, U. Ga., 1972. Cert. ASID, IGD Am. Soc. Interior Designers, Inst. Bus. Designers. Interior designer Et Cetera, Inc., Athens, Ga., 1972-74; with Athens Federal Savings and Loan, Ga., 1974-77; co-owner, sr. designer Athens Interiors, Inc., Athens, Ga., 1974-77; independent interior designer Arlington, Va., 1978-82; interior designer Horizon Trading Co., Inc., Washington, 1983-84; pres., interior designer Nova Internat., Inc., Washington, 1984-94, Nova Europe, Inc., Washington, Paris, France, 1994-96; researcher Interior Design, 1996—. Selected NEA collection Nat. Endowment for the Arts, Am. Consulate Osaka, Japan, 1986. Significant projects with NOVA Europe include: Chevron Oil & Gas, Tengischevroil, Salans, Hertzfeld & Heilbronn, U.S. Agy. for Internat. Devel. in Budapest, Rabat, and Sofia, 1994-96; with NOVA Internat., Inc. U.S. consulate Bldg. Osaka, Japan, Am. consulate staff housing, Hong Kong, SATO for U.S. Mil. in Fed. Repub. West Germany, Mobil Oil, Aldwych House, London, UK, U.S. Dept. State staff housing worldwide, Turner Internat. Industries, N.Y., Peace Vector II Project, Beni Suef, Egypt, US Army Corps of Engrs., Transatlantic Divsn., Am. Internat. Contractors, Ins., Arlington, Va., Peace Vector IV Project, Sakara Egypt, 1984-94; others include Univ. Ga. Law Sch. Offices, Am. Embassies Cairo, Ankara, Islamabad, U.S. Consulate Building Osaka, Japan, Am. Consulate staff housing Hong Kong, Mobil Oil Aldwych House, London, Am. Embassies in Paris, Madrid, Islamabad, Minsk, Sofia and Athens. Vol. Alexandria Hosp., 1985-88. Episcopalian. Avocations: aerobic exercises, swimming, travel, painting. Home: 2409 Military Rd Arlington VA 22207-3907

DRAELOS, ZOE DIANA, dermatologist, consultant; b. Milw., Oct. 13, 1958; d. Dimitri Basil and Lorene June (Legan) Kececioglu; m. Michael Draelos, June 14, 1980; children: Mark, Matthew. BSME, U. Ariz., 1979, MD, 1983. Diplomate Am. Bd. Dermatology. Physician in solo dermatology practice, High Point, NC, 1988—. Cons., owner Dermatology Cons. Svcs., High Point, 1990—. Author: Cosmetics in Dermatology, 1995, Atlas of Cosmetic Dermatology, 2000. Rhodes scholar, Oxford, Eng., 1979. Office: Zoe Diana Draelos MD PA 2444 N Main St High Point NC 27262-7833 Office Phone: 336-841-2040.

DRAGAN, ALEXANDRA, mechanical engineer, consultant, environmental engineer, researcher, engineering educator; d. Ioan and Arety Elena Dragan; 1 child, Miruna Roxanna. BME, MME, U. Bucharest Polytechnica, Romania, 1964; M in Environ. Engring., U. So. Calif., 1993; DEng, U. Constrn., Bucharest, 1998. Registered profl. engr., Calif., N.Y. From engr. to sr. engr. Designing Inst. for Wood Industry, Bucharest, 1967—73; cons. engr. FOREXIM/Technoforest, Bucharest, 1973—76; engr. Jack Stone Engrs., N.Y.C., 1978—81; from sr. engr. to group leader Haines Lundberg Waehler, N.Y.C., 1981—84; from sr. engr. to assoc. Syska and Hennessy, L.A., 1984—86; pvt. practice L.A., Calif., 1984—; chief engr. Donald Dickerson Assoc., L.A., 1986—88; dir. engring. Nat. Air Sys., L.A., 1988; from sr. engr. to supervising mech. engr. III County of L.A. Dept. Pub. Works, Alhambra, Calif., 1988—. Pres. Dragan Engring., L.A., 1984—98; prof. mech. engring. U. Politehnica of Bucharest, 2000—01, prof. emeritus, 2001—. Author: Thermal Processes and Power Generation in Wood Industry, 1973. Recipient Value Engring. award, County of L.A., 1986, Environ. Sci. and Engring. fellow, AAAS and US EPA, 1992. Mem.: ASHRAE (Cert. of Appreciation 1993—94, Symposium Paper award 2001), Internat. Soc. Indoor Air Quality and Climate, Am. Romanian Acad. for Arts and Scis. (exec. com. 2001). Republican. Avocation: singing. Home: 350 N Palm Dr Apt 402 Beverly Hills CA 90210 Personal E-mail: draganalexandra@yahoo.com.

DRAGHICI, SORIN, computer science educator; b. Bucharest, Romania, Feb. 7, 1965; MS, Politecnica U., Bucharest, 1989; PhD, U. St. Andrews, Eng., 1995. Software developer Neosoft SRL, Rome, 2000—01; prof. Wayne State U., Detroit, 2001—. Recipient Overseas Rsch. award, Brit. Coun. Mem.: IEEE, AAAS, Inst. Neural Networks Soc., Assn. Computing Machinery. Office: Wayne State U Dept Computers 5143 Cass Ave Detroit MI 48202

DRAGNEV, PETER D., mathematician, educator; b. Varna, Bulgaria, Apr. 21, 1963; s. Dragni S. Dragnev and Liljana P. Dragneva; m. Blaga P. Kaltzova, Nov. 2, 1985; children: Peter P Dragnev Jr., Lilly P. BS, Sofia U., Bulgaria, 1987, MS, 1989; PhD, U. South Fla., 1997. Asst. prof. Ind.-Purdue U., Fort Wayne, 1998—2002, assoc. prof., 2002—. Contbr. articles to profl. jours. Recipient Pippert Sci. Rsch. award, Ind. Purdue Found., 2003; grantee, Purdue U., 2001, 2003. Mem.: Math. Assn. Am., Am. Math. Soc., Sigma Xi (chpt. pres. 2003, Rschr. of Yr. 2002). Eastern Orthodox. Office: Ind-Purdue U 2101 E Coliseum Blvd Fort Wayne IN 46805 Office Phone: 260-481-6382. Business E-Mail: dragnevp@ipfw.edu.

DRAGO, JOSEPH ROSARIO, urologist, educator; b. Jersey City, N.J., Oct. 28, 1947; m. Diane Lavacca; children: Andrea, Daniella, Denise. BS, U. Ill., 1968, MD, 1972. Diplomate Nat. Bd. Med. Examiners, Am. Bd. Urology; cert. Yag Laser, laparoscopic surgery. Intern Pa. State U. Milton S. Hershey Med. Ctr., 1972-73, resident in urology, 1973-77, instr. urology, 1976-77; asst. prof. urology, dir. urology oncology U. Calif., Davis, 1977-79, Milton S. Hershey (Pa.) Med. Ctr., 1979-80, assoc. prof. to prof. of surgery, dir. urologic oncology, 1980-85; assoc. staff Children's Hosp., Columbus, Ohio, 1985—; interim chief of staff elect, prof., dir. urologic oncology Ohio State U. Arthur G. James Cancer Hosp., Columbus, Ohio, 1990-92; with Easton (Pa.) Warren Urology, Easton, Pa., 1992-95; pvt. practice Washington, N.J., 1995—. Mem. editl. bd. In Vivo Jour.; advisor Internat. Urologic Svcs., Inc., 1987; cons. in field; vis. prof. more than 30 univs. and hosps. Author 12 book chpts.; reviewer various profl. jours., 1979—; contbr. articles to profl. jours. Recipient various rsch. grants, 1978-81. Fellow Internat. Coll. Surgeons in Urology; mem. AMA, Am. Coll. Surgeons, Am. Fertility Soc., Am. Inst. Ultrasound in Medicine, Am. Soc. Andrology, Am. Urologic Assn., Assn. Academic Surgery, Assn. Surgical Edn., Hershey Surgical Soc. (sec.-treas. 1983-85), Pa. Med. Soc., Phila. Urologic Soc., others. Home: 4559 Pinehurst Greens Ct Estero FL 33928 Office: 224 Roseberry St Phillipsburg NJ 08865-1632 Office Phone: 239-826-2151. Personal E-mail: igotagfe@aol.com.

DRAGON, WILLIAM, JR., footwear and apparel company executive; b. Lynn, Mass., Dec. 1, 1942; s. William and Anne (Stavru) D.; m. Suzanne Gail Behlmer, Feb. 24, 1968; children: Todd Christopher, Heather Anne, Paige Katherine (dec.). BS in Engring. Mgmt., Norwich U., Northfield, Vt., 1964; MS in Mgmt. Scis., Rensselaer Poly. Inst., Troy, N.Y., 1965. With mfg., sales and mktg. staff Gen. Electric Co., Mass. and Ky., 1967-73; dir. product planning and design Samsonite div. Beatrice Corp., Denver, 1973-75, dir. mktg. Samsonite div., 1975-78, v.p. mktg. and sales Buxton div. Springfield, Mass., 1978-81; gen. mgr. Johnston & Murphy Div. Genesco Inc., Nashville, 1981-85, exec. v.p., pres. U.S. Footwear Group, 1985-88, also dir.; v.p. Reebok Internat. Ltd., 1989-92; pres. Avia Group Internat. Inc., Portland, Oreg., 1989-92, Promotion Products Inc., Portland, 1992-94; dir. Deja, Inc., Portland, 1993-94; exec. v.p. DEJA Inc., Portland, 1994-95; pres. Pacific Trail divsn. London Fog Industries, 1995-99; pres., CEO London Fog Industries, 1999—2004, dir., 1999—2004; chmn., CEO Pacific Trail, 1999—2004; dir. Lucy, Inc., 2002. Dean's adv. coun. Oreg. State U., 1994-98. Bd. dirs. Nashville Youth Hockey League, 1983-85, Two/Ten Charity Found., 1988-92; vice chmn. Nashville United Way, 1985; mem. men's adv. bd. Cumberland

Valley coun. Girl Scouts U.S., 1985-86; mem. adminstrv. bd. Brentwood United Meth. Ch., 1986. 1st lt. U.S. Army, 1965-67, Vietnam. Decorated Bronze Star medal. Recipient Superior Achievement Recognition award Genesco Inc., 1984 Presbyterian. Personal E-mail: billdsuzanned@msn.com.

DRAGONETTE, RITA HOEY, public relations executive; b. Chgo., Nov. 4, 1950; d. Louis D. and Edith M. (Finnemann) Hoey; m. Joseph John Dragonette, Sept. 4, 1982 (dec.). BA in English and History, No. Ill. U., 1972. Asst. dir. Nat. Assn. Housing and Human Devel., Chgo., 1975; pub. rels. account exec. Weber Cohn & Riley, Chgo., 1975-76; publicity coord. U.S. Gypsum Co., Chgo., 1976-77; with Daniel J. Edelman, Inc., Chgo., 1977-84, sr. v.p., 1981-84; exec. v.p. Dragonette, Inc., Chgo., 1984-91, pres., 1991-99, GCI Dragonette, Chgo., 1999—2002, Dragonette Cons., 2002—. Home: Ste 422 680 North Lake Shore Dr Chicago IL 60611 E-mail: rmdragonette@ameritech.net.

DRAGOUMIS, PAUL, electric utility company executive; b. N.Y.C., Sept. 19, 1934; s. Andrew and Theologie (Pavlou) D.; m. Maria William, Sept. 15, 1957; children— Ann Marie Murtlow, Andrew Paul. BSEE, Poly. Inst. Bklyn., 1956; MS in Nuclear Engring., Internat. Sch. Nuclear Sci. and Engring., Argonne, Ill., 1959; MA in Philosophy, Georgetown U., 1986. Asst. v.p. Am. Electric Power Co., N.Y.C., 1956-70; gen. mgr. corp. exec. staff Allis Chalmers Corp., W. Allis, Wis., 1970-71; v.p. nuclear projects and fossil fuel supply group Potomac Electric Power Co., Washington, 1971-75, v.p. policy, 1976-78, sr. v.p., mem. exec. policy com., 1978-89, exec. v.p., 1989-95; dir. nuclear affairs USFEA, Washington, 1975-76; exec. dir. Pres. Ford's Energy Resources Coun., 1975-76. Mem. mgmt. com. PJM Interconnection, 1980-95; pres. PDA, Inc., 1995-2002. Chmn. emeritus Concert Soc. at Md.; trustee, mem. exec. com. The Washington Opera, 1980—, pres., 1990-94; trustee, mem. exec. com. Greater Washington Rsch. Ctr., 1978-97. Named U.S. Outstanding Young Elec. Engr. Eta Kappa Nu, 1964, Outstanding Young Man of Am. Jaycees, 1966; recipient award for meritorious service USFEA, 1976. Mem. Univ. Club (Washington). Republican. Greek Orthodox. Avocation: sailing. E-mail: dragoum@attglobal.net.

DRAGT, ALEXANDER JAMES, physicist, educator; b. Lafayette, Ind., Apr. 7, 1936; s. Gerrit and Beulah (Westra) D.; m. Lavonne Ann Wolters, Nov. 28, 1957; children: Alison Ann, Alexander James, William David. AB, Calvin Coll., 1958; PhD in Physics (NSF fellow), U. Calif., Berkeley, 1964. Sr. scientist Lockheed Missiles & Space Corp., Palo Alto, Calif., 1961-62; staff scientist Aerospace Corp., Los Angeles, 1963; mem. Inst. Advanced Study, Princeton, N.J., 1963-65; asst. prof. physics U. Md., 1965-68, assoc. prof., 1968-74, prof., 1974—, chmn. dept. physics and astronomy, 1975-78. Mem. vis. staff Los Alamos Sci. Lab., 1978-79, cons., 1979— vis. prof. Tex. A&M U., 1984; mem. vis. staff Tex Accelerator Ctr., 1984; guest scientist Lawrence Berkeley Lab., 1985, 2002, cons., 1985—, Stanford Linear Accelerator Center, 1995. Fellow Am. Phys. Soc.; Mem. Am. Geophys. Union, AAAS, Am. Math. Soc. Mem. Christian Reformed Ch. Achievements include research in theoretical physics and applied math. Office: U Md Dept Physics College Park MD 20742-0001 Business E-Mail: dragt@physics.umd.edu.

DRAGUNS, JURIS G., psychologist; b. Riga, Latvia, Apr. 8, 1932; arrived in US, 1950; s. Juris Karlis Draguns and Sophie Makarovs; m. Marie Gubaroff, Aug. 12, 1956; children: Julie, George. BA magna cum laude, Utica Coll. of Syracuse U., 1954; PhD in clin. psychology, U. Rochester, 1962; PhD (hon.), U. Latvia, Latvia, 2003. Lic. psychology Pa., 1977. Clin. psychologist Rochester State Hosp., Rochester, NY, 1958—62; prin. psychologist Worcester State Hosp., Worcester, Mass., 1963—67; assoc. prof. to prof. to emeritus Pa. State U., U. Pk., Pa., 1967—; vis. prof. Johannes Gutenberg U., Mainz, Germany, 1973—76, Flinders U., Bedford Pk., Australia, 1986; vis. scholar Nat. Taiwan U., Taipei, China, 1986; vis. prof. U. Latvia, Riga, Latvia, 1997. Sr. tchg. fellow East-West Ctr., Honolulu, 1987; master lectr. social sci. U. of the Am. in Puebla, Cholula, Mexico, 2000. Editor: Journal of Cross-Cultural Psychology, 1987—90; co-editor (with P. Pedersen): Counseling Across Cultures, 2002; co-editor: (with U. Gielen) Handbook of Culture, Therapy, and Healing, 2004; co-editor: (with U. Hentschel) Defense Mechanisms: Theoretical Research and Clinical Perspectives, 2004. Recipient Dist. Contribution to Internat. Advancement of Psychology, Am. Psychological Assn., 2001. Fellow: Soc. for Cross-Cultural Rsch., Am. Psychological Assn.; mem.: World Psychiatric Soc., Transcultural Studies Section. Greek Orthodox. Avocations: reading, travel, photography, stamp collecting/philately. Office: Pa State U 410 Moore Bldg University Park PA 16802 Office Phone: 814-863-1735. Office Fax: 814-863-7002. E-mail: jgd1@psu.edu.

DRAIN, ALBERT STERLING, business management consultant; b. Decatur, Tex., July 5, 1925; s. Albert S. and Bessie (Burk) D.; m. Mauvaline Joyce Beam, Apr. 18, 1946; children: Ronald Dale, Deborah Kay Drain Crawford. Student, Bellville (Ill.) Jr. Coll., Tex. Christian U., Iowa U., Milsaps Coll., Pittsburg (Kans.) Coll. With Armour & Co., 1945-79, regional mgr. Pitts., 1966-67, mgr. pork div. Chgo., 1967-68, fresh meats div. mgr., 1968-69, corporate v.p., 1968-75, exec. v.p., 1971-73, group v.p. food marketing div., 1973-75; pres. Armour Foods, 1975-79; also dir.; exec. v.p. for Iowa Beef Processors Inc., Dakota City, Nebr., 1979-80; group v.p. Greyhound Corp., Phoenix, 1977—; pres. Sterling Mktg. Inc. (ind. bus. cons. to meat industry), Phoenix, 1980-91; pvt. practice mgmt. cons. meat packing Phoenix, 1991-94; pvt. practice Al Drain Mgmt. Cons., Phoenix, 1994—. Served with USNR, 1943-45. Mem. Am. Soc. Agrl. Cons., Masons, Shriners. Baptist. Home and Office: 24 E San Miguel Ave Phoenix AZ 85012-1337 Fax: 602-266-4797. E-mail: AlDrainl@aol.com.

DRAIN, CECIL B., dean, nursing educator, retired military officer; b. Ft. Worth, Aug. 25, 1943; s. Harry Eugene and F. Colene (McDonald) D.; m. Cynthia M. Pfaff, Aug. 21, 1965; children: Timothy, Stephen, Kathryn. Diploma, St. Joseph Hosp. Sch. Nursing, Ft. Worth, 1967; BSN, U. Ariz., 1976, MS in Med.-Surg. Nursing, NS in Adult Pulmonary Nursing, U. Ariz., 1980; PhD in Ednl. Curriculum and Instrn. in Higher Edn., Tex. A&M U., 1986. RN, Va., Tex.; cert. RN anesthetist. Staff nurse recovery room, head nurse psychiatry St. Joseph Hosp., 1967; commd. 2d lt. U.S. Army, 1968, advanced through grades to col.; chief nurse anesthetist 121st Evacuation Hosp., Seoul, Republic of Korea, 1972—73; staff nurse anesthetist, chief respiratory therapy U.S. Gen. Leonard Wood Army Community Hosp., Ft. Leonard Wood, Mo., 1973-74; staff nurse anesthetist Tucson Med. Ctr., 1974—76, Brooke Army Med. Ctr., Ft. Sam Houston, Tex., 1976—78, spl. project officer, 1986-89; asst. program dir. U.S. Army-SUNY-Buffalo anesthesiology for ANC officers course U.S. Army Acad. Health Sciences, Ft. Sam Houston, 1980-83; program dir. program in anesthesia nursing U.S. Army-Tex. U.S. Army/Tex. Wesleyan U./Acad. of Health Scis., Ft. Sam Houston, 1989-92; dir. program in anesthesia nursing U. Tex. Health Sci. Ctr. Houston/AMEDD Ctr. and Sch., Ft. Sam Houston, 1992-93; prof. clin. nursing U. Tex. Health Sci. Ctr., Houston, 1992-93; prof. Va. Commonwealth U., Med. Coll. Va. Campus, Richmond, 1993—; chmn. dept. nurse anesthesia Med. Coll. Va., Richmond, 1993-96, interim dean Sch. Allied Health Professions, 1996-97, dean Sch. Allied Health Professions, 1997—. Teaching asst. U. Ariz., 1979-80; clin. instr. family medicine U. Okla., 1983; adj. prof. Tex. Wesleyan U., 1989-92; guest lectr. Tex. A&M U., 1986-93; numerous presentations in field; mem. long-term civilian profls. Schooling Selection Bd., Alexandria, Va., 1988; reviewer Clin. Rev. Series in Critical Care Nursing, 1988—. Author: Perianesthesia Nursing: A Critical Care Approach, 4th edit., 2003; mem. editl. bd.: Heart and Lung: Jour. Critical Care, 1977—92, Nurse Anesthesia, 1987—94, Am. Jour. Critical Care, 1992—, Jour. Am. Assn. Nurse Anesthetists, 1980—93, 1992—2000, Jour. Perianesthesia Nursing, 2002—; contbr. articles abstracts and book revs. to profl. jours., chpts. to books. Baseball commr., Ft. Sam Houston, 1980-81; bd. dirs. March of Dimes, San Antonio, 1981-83; umpire USTA, Bryan, Tex., 1985—; trustee Yankton Coll., 2003--. Decorated Legion of Merit, Meritorious Svc. medal with oak leaf cluster; named Alumni of Yr., Yankton Coll., 2003, Tex. A&M U., 2004 Fellow Am. Acad. Nursing; mem. ANA, AACN (cert. of achievement 1980), Am. Assn. Nurse Anesthetists (jour. faculty 1982-83, bd. dirs. Ednl. and Rsch. Found. 1983-91, cert. of profl. excellence 1976), Am. Soc. Post Anesthesia Nurses (rsch. com. 1986-87), Tex. Assn. Post Anesthesia Nurses (life), 38th Parallel Nurses Soc. (pres. 1971), So. Assn. Allied Health Deans of Acad. Med. Ctrs. (treas. 2002-04), Assn. Schs. Allied Health Profls. (treas. 2002-04), Ret. Officers Assn. (life), Ret. Army Nurse Corps Assn. (assoc.), Order of Mil. Med. Merit, Downtown Kiwanis, Sigma Theta Tau, Phi Delta Kappa, Sigma Epsilon Chi. Republican. Methodist. Home: 5511 W Bay Rd Midlothian VA 23112-2509 Office: Va Commonwealth U Med Coll Va Campus Sch Allied Health Profs Richmond VA 23298 Office Phone: 804-828-7247. Personal E-mail: cbdrain@vcu.edu.

DRAIN, DANNY, museum director; b. Bklyn., Nov. 10, 1964; s. Jacob Drain and Mary Simpson; m. Laura A. Sutton, Feb. 27, 2001; 1 child, Yolanda Darcel Layne. Diploma, County Schs., Inc., 1985, Royal Bus. Sch., Queens, N.Y., 1987, Ross U., St. John, Antigua, 1988. Ordained min. Ch. of Phila. Revival Ctr., Inc., 1993. Law clk. Morris D. Weintraub Law Firm, N.Y.C., 1988—95; news clk. WB Channel 11, N.Y.C., 1995—99; exec. dir. Slave Relic Mus., Walterboro, SC, 2000—. Black memorabilia chmn. York Coll., Jamaica, NY, 2001; pres. Preserving the Past, Jamaica, 1995—2000. Contbg. author: Captive Passage, 2001, Jubilee: The Emergence of African American Culture, 2002; contbr. articles to newspapers. Vol. African Burial Ground, N.Y.C., 2001—; asst. pastor Ch. of Phila. Revival Ctr., Jamaica, 1984—89, pastor, 1989—95. Mem.: Black Memorabilia Collectors Assn. (v.p. 1996—98). Achievements include ownership of 2,000 artifacts and rare documents and books regarding pre-Civil War African Americans. Home and Office: Slave Relic Mus 208 Carn St Walterboro SC 29488 Fax: 843-549-9130. Office Phone: 843-549-9130. E-mail: info@slaverelics.org.

DRAKE, ALBERT ESTERN, retired statistics educator, farming administrator; b. Stamping Ground, Ky., June 12, 1927; s. John L and Dullia Zena (Humphrey) D.; m. Katherine Ashby, June 22, 1952; children: Alan Sanford, Paul Steven, Jane, Philip David. Student, Georgetown Coll., 1946-47; BS, U. Ky., 1950, MS, 1951; PhD, U. Ill., 1958; postgrad., N.C. State U., 1959, 63, U. Fla., 1960. Rsch. asst. U. Ill., 1953-55, rsch. assoc., 1955-59; assoc. prof., assoc. biometrician Auburn U., 1959-62, prof., biometrician, 1962-63; dir. computer ctr. W.Va. U., 1963-65, acting coord. stats., 1965-66; prof. stats. U. Ala., 1966-92, coord. quantitative methods, 1966-72, acting head stats and mgmt. sci., 1981, interim assoc. dean undergrad. programs Coll. of Commerce and Bus. Adminstrn., 1988-90, assoc. dean undergrad. programs Coll. of Commerce and Bus. Adminstrn., 1990-92; prof. emeritus, 1992—; part-time mgr. farming enterprise and rock quarry Georgetown, Ky., 1992—. Cons. in field. Contbr. articles to profl. jours., papers to profl. meetings. Bd. dirs. Little League, Auburn, 1961-63; active local council Boy Scouts Am., 1962-63, 66-67. Served with USMC, 1945-46. NSF grantee, 1959, 60, 63; Venture Fund grantee, 1975, 76, 81; inducted to Coll. Commerce & Bus. Adminstrn. U. Ala. Faculty Hall of Fame, 1998. Mem. Biometrics Soc., Am. Statis. Assn. (pres. Ala. chpt. 1972), Decision Scis. Inst. (sec. 1973-74, coun. 1969-72, 75-77, mem. editl. bd. 1969-72), Am. Agrl. Econs. Assn., Pi Kappa Alpha (Disting. Alumni award Omega chpt. 2001). Republican. Home: 5533 E Desert Hills Dr Scottsdale AZ 85254 Office Phone: 502-863-0476.

DRAKE, ALMOND JERKINS, III, medical educator, department chairman; b. Rocky Mount, nc, May 21, 1957; m. Lori Rosenlof Rosenlog, Dec. 27, 1981; children: Jacquelyn Elizabeth, Almond, Andrea Lauren, Amanda Rosenlof, Joanna Christine, Lori Abigail. MD, Duke U. Sch. of Medicine, 1983. Chief, endocrinology Nat. Naval Med. Ctr., Bethesda, Md., 1996—2003, ECU Brody Sch. of Medicine, Greenville, NC, 2003—. Capt. USN, 1975—2003. Recipient Master Tchr. award, Am. Coll. of Physicians, 2000, Am. Soc. of Internal Medicine, 2000. Fellow: ACP, Am. Coll. of Endocrinology; mem.: Am. Soc. Internal Medicine. Office: ECU Brody Sch Medicine 3E129 Brody Med Scis Bldg Greenville NC 27834 Office Phone: 252-744-2567.

DRAKE, ANN M., consumer products company executive; d. James and Mary Lou McIlrath; m. John Drake, II; stepchildren: Joanna, Tracy. B in English, U. Iowa, 1969; MBA, Northwestern U., 1984. Founder, prin. Camwilde Interiors; exec. v.p. DSC Logistics, DesPlaines, Ill., 1990—92, CEO, 1992—. Bus. adv. com. Northwestern U. Transp. Ctr. Mem.: Chgo. Network, Com. of 200. Office: DSC Logistics 1750 S Wolf Rd Des Plaines IL 60018

DRAKE, CHARLES WHITNEY, physicist; b. South Portland, Maine, Mar. 8, 1926; s. Charles Whitney and Katharine Gabrielle (O'Neill) D.; m. Ellen Tan, June 15, 1952; children— Judith Ellen, Robert Charles, Linda Ann. BS, U. Maine, 1950; MA, Conn. Wesleyan U., 1952; PhD, Yale U., 1958. Scientist Westinghouse Atomic Power Div., 1952-53; instr. Yale U., New Haven, 1957-60, asst. prof., 1960-66, rsch. assoc., 1966-69; assoc. prof. Oreg. State U., 1966-74; prof., 1974-93; prof. emeritus, 1993—; chmn. dept. physics, 1976-84. Vis. prof. Oxford U. Clarendon Lab. and St. Peter's Coll., 1972-73, U. Tuebingen (W.Ger.), 1982 Contbr. articles to profl. jours. Served with USN, 1944-46. Recipient various fellowships and grants. Fellow Am. Phys. Soc.; mem. Am. Assn. Physics Tchrs., Sigma Xi, Tau Beta Pi, Sigma Pi Sigma. Office: Oreg State U Dept Physics Corvallis OR 97331

DRAKE, DAVID FULSTER, physical medicine and rehabilitation physician; b. Reno, Nev., Dec. 21, 1966; s. Don Ray and Joan Loraine Drake; m. Kelli Lynn Petersen, Jan. 11, 1992. BS, U. Nev., Reno, 1991, MD, 1997. Intern Va. Commonwealth U., Richmond, 1997—98, resident in phys. medicine and rehab., 1998—2000, chief resident, 2000—01, asst. prof. phys. medicine and rehab., 2001—, dir. musculoskeletal and sports medicine, 2001—, team physician athletics teams, 1998—. Dir. Massey Cancer Pain Ctr., Med. Coll. Va., Richmond, 2001—. Contbr. articles to profl. jours. Mem. World Affairs Coun. of Richmond, 1999—2001; mem. Commonwealth of Va. Med. Malpractice Rev. Bd., Richmond, 2000—. Mem. USCG Aux. Recipient Rsch. Enrichment award, NIDRR, 2001—; scholar, Rotary Club, 1993—94. Mem.: AMA, Va. Soc. Phys. Medicine and Rehab., Internat. Soc. Phys. and Rehab. Medicine, Physiatry Assn. Spine Sport Occupl. Rehab., Am. Coll. Sports Medicine, Am. Acad. Phys. Medicine and Rehab. (pres. 2000—01, presenter 2000, mem. health policy and legis. com. 1999—2000, Grand Rounds award 2000). Avocations: running, weightlifting, poetry, outdoor activities. Home: HHC 2nd Brigade CMR 464 Box 2800 APO AE 09226

DRAKE, DAVID LEE, electronics engineer; b. Campton, Ky., Mar. 15, 1960; s. Dudley and Sarah Ellen (Combs) D.; m. Bitha Mae Turner, June 10, 1983 (div.); children: Thomas Shelton, Rachel Leann. AAS, Morehead State U., 1981, BS, 1983. Electronics lab. technician Morehead (Ky.) State U., 1979-81; quality control technician Computer Peripherals, Campton, 1981; robotics rsch. engr. Morehead State U., 1981-83; personal computer test technician Campton Electronics, 1984-86; chief engr. Automation Svcs., Lexington, Ky., 1986—98; CEO D-TEK Computers, 1998—. Contbr. articles to profl. jours. Mem. IEEE, Sigma Tau Epsilon (parliamentarian 1982-83). Democrat. Home: PO Box 533 Campton KY 41301-0533 Office: D-Tek Computers 2670 Ky 191 Campton KY 41301

DRAKE, DIANA ASHLEY, retired financial planner; b. Poughkeepsie, N.Y., Apr. 28, 1937; d. Albert Jackson and Jane Ashley (Ketchum) D.; m. José Akel Abizaid, Dec. 2, 1956 (div. Nov. 1979); children: Cynthia A. Rush, Allison J. Abizaid, Linda A. Wiener, Carol Lynn Abizaid, Amanda Jo Abizaid, Richard Alan Abizaid; m. Sherrill Cleland, Sept. 3, 1988; stepchildren: Ann Cleland Feldmeier, Douglas S. Cleland, Sarah Cleland Allen, Scott C. Cleland. Student, Cornell U., 1955-56, Am. U. of Beirut, Lebanon, 1956-57; BS in Psychology cum laude, Vassar Coll., 1980; CFP, Inst. Fin. Planners, Denver, 1986. CFP. Divorce mediator Fin. Planning Corp. of Va., McLean, 1983-86; investment advisor Cert. Fin. Svc., McLean, 1986; ptnr. Koelz Drake Advisors, Falls Church, Va., 1987-89; pres. Drake Fin. Svcs., Falls Church, 1986-98; bronze distbr. Nikken health and wellness products, prin. Magnetic Living, 1998—2003; ret., 2003. Sec., mem. Bd. Equalization, Falls Church, 1992-94. Contbr. articles to various mags. Elder Falls Church Presbyn. Ch., 1993-96, chair Christian Edn. Com., 1996, planned giving com. 1997-99, revision com. 1997; co-chmn. 100 yrs. aquatics YMCA, New Orleans, 1986. Recipient Disting. Svc. award for 25 Yrs. svcs. Nat. YMCA, 1986. Mem.: DAR, AAUW, Inst. CFPs, No. Va. Inst. Cert. Fin. Planners (sec. 1994—97, bd. dirs. facilities), Sarasota Camera Club, Cornell Club (Sarasota), Zonta (dir. Arlington club 1992—99, cmty. svc. coord.), Cornell Club of Washington (mem. investment and audit com. 1990—99), Meadows Chorus (Sarasota), Vassar Club (Sarasota, Fla.), Highland Oaks Cir. Assn. (bd. dirs., pres. 2003), Delta Gamma. Republican. Avocations: swimming, bridge, writing, photography, travel. Home and Office: 4489 Highland Oaks Cir Sarasota FL 34235 E-mail: dadcleland@aol.com.

DRAKE, DONALD CHARLES, journalist, playwright; b. N.Y.C., Jan. 12, 1935; s. Albert E. and Gloria (Walters) D.; 1 child, Valerie; m. Molly Hindman; 1 step-child, Jennifer. Student, NYU, 1953-56. Copy boy New York Herald Tribune, 1954-55; reporter Patent Trader, Mt. Kisco, N.Y., 1956-57, New Haven Register, 1957-58, Newsday, Garden City, N.Y., 1958-65; med. writer Phila. Inquirer, 1966-93; narrative editor, 1993-2001. Author: Medical School, 1978, (plays) Words, Saintly Mother, Clear and Present Danger, Final Edition, The Last Appointment, Love Knot, The Passage, Aria, Thank You For The Flowers, Tom, Dick and Harriet. Recipient Russell L. Cecil Writing award Arthritis Found., 1968, John S. Packard award Pa. Tb. and Health Soc., 1968, Howard W. Blakeslee awards Am. Heart Assn., 1969, 76, 81, Walter J. Donaldson awards Pa. Med. Soc., 1970, 71, Keystone Press awards, 1974-81, 83, 84, 87, 88, 90, 93, 2002, Claude Bernard award Nat. Soc. for Med. Research, 1978, AP Mng. Editors award Pa., 1978, 81, 84, 93, Robert F. Kennedy Journalism award, 1982, Morse award Am. Psychiat. Assn., 1982, Gen. Motors Cancer Rsch. Found. prize, 1990, others. Mem. Nat. Assn. Sci. Writers, Dramatists Guild, Dramatists Ctr. *Journalism would serve a greater good if it sought the truth instead of just the facts, but that's a lot harder to do.*

DRAKE, ELISABETH MERTZ, chemical engineer, consultant; b. N.Y.C., Dec. 20, 1936; d. John and Ruth (Johnson) Mertz; m. Alvin William Drake, July 31, 1957 (div. 1984); 1 child, Alan Lee. SB in Chem. Engring., MIT, 1958, ScD in Chem. Engring., 1966. Registered profl. engr., Mass. Staff engr. Arthur D. Little Inc., Cambridge, Mass., 1958-64, sr. staff, 1966-76, mgr. risk analysis, 1977-82, v.p. tech. risk mgmt., 1980-82, 86-89, cons., 1990-94; assoc. dir. new tech. MIT Energy Lab., 1990-2000, dir., 1994-95, cons., 2000—; lectr. U. Calif., Berkeley, 1971; vis. prof. MIT, Cambridge, 1973-74; chmn. chem. engring. dept. Northeastern U., Boston, 1982-86. Corp. mgr. MIT, 1981-86; mem. tech. pipeline safety stds. com. U.S. Dept. Transp., 1980-85; mem. mng. bd. AIChE, 1988-90; vice chair com. on rev. and evaluation on army chem. stockpile disposal program NRC, 1993-98, mem., 2002-2004, vice chair com. on chem. demil., 2004—. Contbr. articles to profl. jours.; inventor fractionation method and apparatus, 1972. Fellow AIChE (bd. dirs. 1987-90); mem. AAAS, NAE, Am. Chem. Soc., Sigma Xi. Home: 30F Inman St Cambridge MA 02139-2411 E-mail: edrake@alum.mit.edu.

DRAKE, EVELYN DOWNIE, secondary school educator; b. Longmont, Colo., Aug. 23, 1940; d. Milford West and Colette Dorothy (Mraz) Downie; m. Sherman Hoffman Drake, May 18, 1963 (div. 1971); children: Marcella Colette Drake-Bettis, Sherman Downie Drake; m. Robert Dale Mager, July 14, 1975 (div. 1981). BS, U. Wyo., 1962; MA, U. No. Colo., 1980; postgrad., U. Edinburgh, Scotland, 1982, Cambridge U., Eng., 1986. Cert. tchr./vocat. tchr., Colo. Sec./receptionist Barnard Realty, Casper, Wyo., 1959-61, Pure Oil Co. (now UNOCAL), Casper, 1961; coord., tchr. St. Mark's Pre-Sch., Casper, 1965; reporter, feature writer Casper Star-Tribune, Casper, 1970-71; instr., tchr. Casper Coll., 1964-69; tchr. home econs. Kelly Walsh High Sch., 1971-72; tchg. asst. U. No. Colo., Greeley, 1979-80; tchr. of English, journalism, art, home econs. Jefferson County R-1 Schs., Golden, Colo., 1972—97. Cons., tchr. Casper North Side Ctr., 1969-71. Artist: weaving exhibit, Pub. Libr., Casper, 1968, others. Ctrl. com. Jefferson County Democrats, Lakewood, Colo., 1989—; candidate bd. dirs. Green Mt. Townhouse Corp. #1 Lakewood, 1987; tchr. Lakewood Sister Cities Exch. Program to Miranda, New South Wales, Sutherlandshire, Australia, 1995. Nominated Colo. Tchr. of Yr., Evergreen (Colo.) Jr. High, 1989. Mem. Colo. Lang. Arts Soc., Nat. Coun. Tchrs. of English (planning com. nat. conf. 1989-90), NEA (faculty rep.), Colo. Educators Assn. (faculty rep.), JCEA Edn. Assn. (faculty rep.), Denver Press Club, Phi Delta Kappa (sec. 1995-96), Delta Kappa Gamma, others. Avocations: art, writing, literature.

DRAKE, GEORGE ALBERT, academic administrator, historian; b. Springfield, Mo., Feb. 25, 1934; s. George Bryant and Alberta (Stimson) D.; m. Susan Martha Ratcliff, June 25, 1960; children: Christopher George, Cynthia May, Melanie Susan. AB, Grinnell Coll., 1956; Fulbright scholar, U. Paris, 1956-57; AB (Rhodes scholar), Oxford U., 1959, MA, 1963; BD, U. Chgo., 1962, MA, 1963, PhD (Rockefeller fellow), 1965; LLD (hon.), Colo. Coll., 1980, Ripon Coll., 1982; LHD (hon.), Ill. Coll., 1985, Ursinus Coll., 1988, Doane Coll., 1995, Morningside Coll., 1998. Instr. history Grinnell Coll., Iowa, 1960-61, pres., 1979-91, prof., 1979—, trustee, prof., 1991—2004; prof. emeritus, 2004—. Asst. prof., assoc. prof., prof. history Colo. Coll., Colorado Springs, 1964-79, acting dean of Coll., 1967-68, dean, 1969-73 Trustee Grinnell Coll., 1970-79, Penrose Hosp., 1976-79, 80-84, Grinnell Gen. Hosp., 1980-86, Doane Coll., 1995—; bd. dirs. Iowa Peace Inst., 1994—2004, chair, 1996-99, Fine Found., 1998-2004; vol. U.S. Peace Corps, Lesotho, 1991-93; commr. North Ctrl. Assn. Colls. and Schs., 1998-2001; bd. dirs. FINE Found., 1998—, chair 2003—. NEH fellow, 1974. Mem. Am. Hist. Assn., Am. Ch. History Soc., Nat. Coll. Athletic Assn. (pres. commn. 1984-89), Nat. Merit Scholarship Corp. Office Phone: 641-264-3720. Business E-Mail: Drake@Grinnell.edu.

DRAKE, GRACE L., retired state senator, cultural organization administrator; b. New London, Conn., May 25, 1926; d. Daniel Harvey and Marion Gertrude (Wiech) Driscoll; m. William Lee Drake, June 9, 1946 (dec.); 1 child, Sandra Drake Sparber. With Am. Photographic Corp., N.Y.C., 1944-72; senator State of Ohio, Columbus, 1984—2001; dir. Ohio Ctr. Advancement Women in Pub. Svc., 2001—. Chairwoman Cuyahoga County Rep. Exec. Commn.; alumnus Leadership Cleve.; mem. March of Dimes Metro and State Bd., HealthSpace Cleve. Bd., Masonic Learning Ctrs. Bd., Positive Edn. Program Bd., Coun. on Older Persons Bd., Northeast Ohio Nursing Initiative Bd. Named Legislator of the Yr., Nat. Rep. Legis.'s Assn., 1988; named to Ohio Women's Hall of Fame, 1995; recipient Meritorious Svc. award, Ohio State U., 2001, Ctr. for Health Affairs, 2001, Pub. Affairs award, March of Dimes, 2001. Roman Catholic. Avocations: bridge, golf. Home: 5954 Briardale Ln Solon OH 44139-2302 Office: Cleve State Univ 2121 Euclid Ave UR 140 Cleveland OH 44115 Office Phone: 216-687-4893. Business E-Mail: gdrake@urban.csuohio.edu.

DRAKE, HUDSON BILLINGS, aerospace transportation executive, electronics executive; b. LA, Mar. 3, 1935; s. Hudson C. and Blossom (Billings) Drake; m. Joan M. Johnson, Feb. 9, 1957 (dec. 1997); children: Howard Billings, Paul Marvin; m. Mary H. Vaugler, Nov. 1, 2000. BA in Econs., UCLA, 1957; MBA, Pepperdine U., 1976; exec. program mgmt., Anderson Sch.-UCLA, 1991. Mgr. Autonetics div. Rockwell Inc., Anaheim, Calif., 1958-68; exec. dir. Pres.'s Commn. White House Fellows, Washington, 1969-70; dep. under sec. U.S. Dept. Commerce, Washington, 1970-72; v.p., gen. mgr. Teledyne Ryan Electronics, San Diego, 1972-80, pres., 1980-84; pres., group exec. Teledyne Ryan Aero., San Diego, 1984-88; v.p., group exec. Teledyne Inc., L.A., 1987-88, sr. v.p., group exec., 1988-89, sr. v.p., pres. aerospace and electronics segment, 1989-96; pres. aerospace and electronics segment Allegheny Teledyne Inc., LA, 1996—97; ltd. ptnr. Carlisle Enterprises, La Jolla, Calif., 1997—. Mem. Def. Procurement Adv. Com. Trade, Washington, 1988—93; bd. dirs. Compass Aerospace Corp. Contbr. articles to profl. jours. Bd. dirs. Johnson Cancer Ctr. Found., UCLA, 1998—2005; vestry St. James by Sea, La Jolla, Calif., 1998—2002; trustee Children's Hosp., San Diego, 1981—86, chmn. rsch. corp., 1983—86; pres.'s coun. San Diego State U., 1984—90; bd. overseers U. Calif., San Diego, 1985—88. With USNR, 1953—61. Named Silver Knight of Mgmt., Nat. Mgmt. Assn., 1975, Gold Knight of Mgmt., 1986; recipient Exec. of the Yr. award, 1995, San Diego Bd. Suprs. resolution, 1988; White House fellow,

1968. Mem.: AIAA, IEEE, San Diego C. of C. (bd. dirs.), Navy League (life), Inst. Navigation, La Jolla Country Club. Republican. Episcopalian. Avocations: golf, fly fishing. Home: 1707 Soledad Ave La Jolla CA 92037 Personal E-mail: hdrake1@san.rr.com.

DRAKE, JOHN WARREN, aviation consultant; b. Chgo., July 5, 1930; s. Robert Warren and Winifred Elizabeth (Bramhall) D.; m. Miriam Anna Engleman, Dec. 19, 1960 (div. Dec. 1985); 1 child, Robert Warren; m. Mary Pat O'Kelly, Sept. 24, 2000. BS, Rensselaer Poly. Inst., 1952; MBA, Harvard U., 1954, D.BA, 1972. Research asso. Aero. Research Found., Cambridge, Mass., 1956-57; prin. United Research, Inc., Cambridge, 1957-61; v.p. Systems Analysis and Research Corp., Cambridge, 1961-69; prof. emeritus, air transp. area Sch. Aeros. and Astronautics, Sch. Engring., Purdue U., 1972-92, mem. president's council. Cons. in field; mem. Transp. Research Bd. NRC. Author: The Administration of Transportation Modeling Projects, 1973. Served with U.S. Army, 1954-56. Mem. Air Transp. Rsch. Internat. Forum (coun.), AIAA, Soc. Automotive Engrs. Clubs: University (Washington). Home and Office: 341 Riverview Dr Ann Arbor MI 48104-1847

DRAKE, KENNETH DAVID, geologist; b. Linton, Ind., Apr. 18, 1959; s. Kenneth Eugene and Marilyn Kay Drake; m. Kathleen Rose Smith, May 31, 1980. BS in Geology, Ind. U., 1984; MS in Urban Environ. Geology, U. Mo., 1999. Registered geologist Mo., profl. geologist Tenn. Geologist U.S. Army Corps Engrs., Kansas City, Mo., 1986—93; geologist, project mgr. U.S. EPA, Kansas City, Kans., 1993—. Contbr. articles to profl. jours. Pres. Lansing (Kans.) Lions Club, 1995. Recipient Bronze medal, U.S. EPA, 1999, Silver medal, 2001. Mem.: KC, Nat. Ground Water Assn., Assn. Engring. Geologists, Assn. Mo. Geologists, Geol. Soc. Am. Office: US EPA 901 N 5th St Kansas City KS 66101 Office Phone: 913-551-7626. Office Fax: 913-551-7063. E-mail: drake.dave@epa.gov.

DRAKE, MICHAEL V., academic administrator, ophthalmologist, educator; b. NYC; AB, BS, MD, U. Calif., San Francisco. Resident U. Calif., San Francisco, chief eye clinic Irvine, 1979—91, asst. prof. opthalmology, 1979—87, assoc. prof., 1991—93, prof., 1993—98, Stephen P. Shearing prof., 1998—, dir. vision care and clin. rsch. unit, 1991—93, asst. dean student affairs, 1991—93, vice chmn. dept. ophthalmology, 1998—2000, assoc. dean admissions and student programs, v.p. health affairs, 2000—05, chancellor, 2005—; sr. assoc. dean for admissions & extramural acad. prgrams U. Calif. Sch. Medicine, San Francisco, 1998—2000. Author: (with D.O. Harrington) The Visual Fields: Text and Atlas of Clinical Perimetry, 1990. Recipient Herbert W. Nickens award, Assn. Am. Medical Colleges, 2004. Office: The Chancellor's Office U Calif Irvine CA 92697-1900 Office Phone: 949-824-5111. Office Fax: 949-824-2087. E-mail: chancellor@uci.edu.*

DRAKE, MIRIAM ANNA, retired librarian, educator, writer, consultant; b. Boston, Dec. 20, 1936; d. Max Frederick and Beatrice Celia (Mitnick) Engleman; m. John Warren Drake, Dec. 19, 1960 (div. Dec. 1985); 1 child, Robert Warren. BS, Simmons Coll., Boston, 1958, MLS, 1971; postgrad., Harvard U., 1959-60; LHD (hon.), Ind. U., 1994; DLS (hon.), Simmons Coll., 1997. Assoc. United Rsch., Cambridge, Mass., 1958-61; with mktg. svcs. Kenyon & Eckhardt, Boston, 1963-65; cons. Boston, 1965-72; head rsch. unit libraries Purdue U., West Lafayette, Ind., 1972-76, asst. dir. libraries, prof. library sci., 1976-84; dean, dir. libraries, prof. Ga. Inst. Tech., Atlanta, 1984-2001, prof. emerita, 2001—; ret., 2001. Trustee Online Computer Libr. Ctr., Inc., 1978-84, chair, 1980-83; trustee Corp. for Rsch. and Edn. Networking, 1991-94, U.S. Depository Libr. Coun., 1991-94, Simmons Coll., 1999-2004; trustee, corporator adv. bd. Engring. Info., 1997—; trustee emerita Simmons Coll., 2004-; bd. dirs. Women's Commerce Club, 2005—. Author: User Fees: A Practical Perspective, 1981, Information Today, 2002; co-author: (with James Matarazzo) Information for Management, 1994; editor: Ency. Libr. Info. Sci., 2nd edit.; mem. editl. bd. Coll. and Rsch. Librs. Jour., 1985-90, Librs. and Microcomputers Jour., 1983-93, Sci. and Tech. Librs., 1989-98, Database, 1989-97; contbr. chpts. to books, articles to profl. jours. and trade mags. Recipient Alumni Achievement award Simmons Coll. Sch. Libr. and Info. Sci., 1985, Kent Meckler Media award U. Pitts., 1994. Fellow: Nat. Fedn. of Abstracting and Indexing Svs. (hon.); mem.: ALA (councilor at large 1985—89, Hugh Atkinson Meml. award 1992), Assn. Info. and Dissemination Ctrs. (pres. 2001—03), Spl. Librs. Assn. (pres.-elect 1992—93, pres. 1993—94, H.W. Wilson award 1983, John Cotton Dana award 2002), Am. Soc. Info. Sci., Am. Mgmt. Assn. Personal E-mail: mdrake@bellsouth.net. Business E-Mail: miriam.drake@library.gatech.edu.

DRAKE, MONICA PAJESTKA, human services manager; b. Belton, Tex., Mar. 11, 1956; d. Frank Emil Pajestka, Sr and Helen Ann Pajestka; m. Kenneth Lynn Drake, Sr, July 2, 1984; 1 child, Kenneth Lynn II; m. David Lee Ivicic, July 19, 1975 (div. Jan. 21, 1983); children: Monica Ann Weir, Michelle Lee Ivicic. BS, BA, Trinity So. U., 2002. Cert. coder Am. Acad. Profl. Coders, 2002. Patient svc. rep. Scott and White, Temple, Tex., 1983—97, clinic supr., 1997—2000, divsn. mgr., 2000—. Eucharistic min. Sacred Heart Cath. Ch., Lott, Tex., 2000—05. Mem.: Am. Acad. Profl. Coders (pres. elect 2005—), Assn. Dermatology Administrs. Mgrs., Am. Gastroenterology Assn. Office: Scott and White 2401 S 31st St Temple TX 76508 Office Phone: 254-724-2424. Office Fax: 254-724-6865. Personal E-mail: mdrake@swmail.sw.org.

DRAKE, PRISCILLA M., principal; b. Summerville, SC, Aug. 1, 1957; d. Malachi and Maggie Perry; m. Nathaniel L. Drake, Sr., Aug. 11, 1979; children: Nathaniel L. Jr., Mahlon M. MS, U. SC, 2000. Cert. ednl. adminstr. SC, bus. and consumer edn. tchr. SC. Tchr. Beaufort County Schools, Beaufort, SC, 1981, 1982—2000, prin., 2000—. Mem.: NEA, Alpha Kappa Alpha. Home: PO Box 100 St. Helena Island SC 29920 Office: Beaufort County Schs PO Drawer 309 Beaufort SC 29902 Office Phone: 843-322-3100. Home Fax: 843-322-3179; Office Fax: 843-322-3100. Personal E-mail: limsdrake@islc.net. E-mail: pd3684@beaufort.k12.sc.us.

DRAKE, RODMAN LELAND, investment company executive, consultant; b. Terre Haute, Ind., Feb. 2, 1943; s. Leland Rodman and Helen Virginia (Frederick) Drake; m. Lenir Leme-Lambert, July 26, 1975 (div. 1998); children: Stephan Rodman, Philip Lambert; m. Jacqueline B Weld, Dec. 18, 1998. BA, Yale U., 1965; MBA, Harvard U., 1969. Assoc. Cresap, McCormick & Paget, Inc., N.Y.C., 1969-70, Monterrey, Mexico, 1971-72, mng. ptnr. São Paulo, Brazil, 1972-77, v.p., bd. dirs. N.Y.C., 1977-81, mng. dir., CEO, 1981-90; pres. Mandrake Group, Inc., N.Y.C., 1993-97; pres., dir. Continuation Investments Group Inc., N.Y.C., 1997—2002; co-founder Baringo Capital LLC, 2002—. Lead dir. Parsons Brinckerhoff Inc.; bd. dirs. Excelsior Funds (sponsored by US Trust), Jackson Hewitt Tax Svc. Inc., Hyperion Strategic Mortgage Income Trust Inc., Crystal River Capital Inc.; chmn. Hyperion Total Return Fund Inc., Crystal River Capital Inc., Student Loan Corp.; co-chmn. KMR Power Corp., 1993—96. Bd. dirs. Animal Med. Ctr., Lebanese Am. U., 1983—88. With U.S. Army, 1965—67. Mem.: New Holland Soc., Waccabuc Club (NY), Banyan Golf Club (Fla.), River Club (NYC). E-mail: rdrake@cipmgmt.com.

DRAKE, SHOSHANAH WOLFE, music educator; b. Pa. MusB, U. Cin., 1992. Cert. levels I, II and III Am. Orff Schulwerk Assn. Music educator K-5 Burning Tree Elem. Sch., Bethesda, Md., 1997—. Pres. Mid. Atlantic Orff Schulwerk Assn. Home: 2 Canterfield Ct Germantown MD 20876 Office: Burning Tree Elem Sch 7900 Beech Tree Rd Bethesda MD 20817 Personal E-mail: thedrakeclan@comcast.net.

DRAKE, STEPHEN DOUGLAS, psychologist, health facility administrator; b. Iola, Kans., Sept. 8, 1947; s. Harry Francis and Emojean (Price) Drake; m. Rebecca Gonzalez, June 1, 1968; 1 child, Michael Paul. BA, U. Tex., 1970; PhD, U. North Tex., 1987. Diplomate Am. Bd. Forensic Examiners, lic. psychologist. Mental health worker Austin (Tex.) State Hosp., 1970-73; claims rep. Social Security Adminstrn., Galveston, Tex., 1974-77, ops. supr. Dallas, 1977-79, staff asst., 1979-80; clin. psychologist Terrell (Tex.) State Hosp., 1987-89, Austin State Hosp., 1989-90, program dir., 1990-92; cons. Tex. Rehab. Commn., 1992-98, chief mental med. cons., 1998—2003, med. adminstr., 2003—. Contbr. articles to profl. jours. Vice-chmn. bd. dirs. Galveston Island Mental Health/Mental Retardation Ctr., 1977. Recipient award, Nat. Assn. Disability Health Examiners, 2001, Commr.'s citation, Social Security Adminstrn., 2005. Mem.: APA, Assn. Advancement Behavior Therapy, Tex. Psychol. Assn., Mensa, Phi Kappa Phi. Avocations: Tae Kwon Do, weightlifting, eastern philosophy, languages, travel. Office: Tex Rehab Commn 6102 E Oltorf St Austin TX 78741

DRAKE, SYLVIE (JURRAS DRAKE), theater critic; b. Alexandria, Egypt, Dec. 18, 1930; arrived in U.S., 1949, naturalized, 1952; d. Robert and Simonette (Barda) Franco; m. Kenneth K. Drake, Apr. 29, 1952 (div. Dec. 1972); children: Jessica, Robert I.; m. Ty Jurras, June 16, 1973. M. Theater Arts, Pasadena Playhouse, 1969. Free-lance TV writer, 1962-68; theater critic Canyon Crier, L.A., 1968-72; theater critic, columnist L.A. Times, 1971-91, theater critic, 1991-93, theatre critic emeritus, 1993—; lit. dir. Denver Ctr. Theatre Co., 1985; pres. L.A. Drama Critics Circle, 1979-81, free lance travel writer, translator, book reviewer. Mem. Pulitzer Prize Drama Jury, 1994; adv. bd. Nat. Arts Journalism Program, 1994-97. Dir. pubs. Denver Ctr. for the Performing Arts, 1994—; artistic assoc. for spl. projects Denver Ctr. Theatre Co., 1994—. Mem.: Am. Theater Critics Assn. Office: Denver Ctr Performing Arts 1245 Champa St Denver CO 80204-2100 Office Phone: 303-893-4000. Business E-Mail: sdrake@dcpa.org.

DRAKE, THELMA DAY, congresswoman; b. Elyria, Ohio, Nov. 20, 1949; m. Ted Drake; 2 children. Grad. high sch. Realtor RE/MAX Allegiance Realty, Hampton Roads, Va.; mem. Va. State Legis., 1995—2004; chmn. Va. Housing Commn.; mem. U.S. Ho. Reps., 109th Congress, 2d Dist. Va., 2005—. Bd. mem. Va. Zoological Soc.; past mem. Chesapeake Bay Commn. Named Citizen of the Year, Va. Crime Prevention Assn., Legislator of the Year, YMCA, Commissioners of the Revenue, Va. Cable & Telecom. Assn.; named one of Outstanding Profl. Women of Hampton Roads; recipient John Marshall award, Va. Property Rights Coalition. Republican. United Church Of Christ. Office: 1208 Longworth House Office Bldg Washington DC 20515-4602 Office Phone: 202-225-4215.*

DRAKE, W. HOMER, JR., federal judge; b. 1932; AB, Mercer U., 1954, LLB, 1956. Law clk. to Hon. Lewis R. Morgan U.S. Dist. Ct. Ga., 1961-64; ptnr. Swift, Currie, McGhee & Hiers, 1976-79; judge U.S. Bankruptcy Ct., 1964-76, chief judge, 1968-76; bankruptcy judge U.S. Bankruptcy Ct. (no. dist.) Ga., 1979—. Adj. prof. U. Ga. Law Sch., 1971-72, Emory U. Law Sch., Atlanta, 1973-75. Author: Bankruptcy Practice for the General Practitioner, 3d edit., 1995; co-author: Chapter 13 Practice & Procedure, 1983, Chapter 11 Reorganizations, 2d edit., 1998. 1st lt. JAGC, U.S. Army, 1956-59. Recipient David W. Pollard Achievement award Atlanta Bar Assn., 1994; Walter Homer Drake professorship of bankruptcy law established at Walter F. George Sch. Law at Mercer U., 1996, Outstanding Alumnus award Mercer U. Sch. Law, 2003. Fellow: Am. Coll. Bankruptcy; mem.: Nat. Conf. Bankruptcy Judges (pres. 1972—73), Southeastern Bankruptcy Law Inst. (founder, advisor). Address: PO Box 1408 Newnan GA 30264-1408 Office: Lewis R Morgan Fed Bldg US Courthouse 18 Greenville St Newnan GA 30263-2602 Office Phone: 678-423-3080.

DRAKE, WILLIAM ALAN, art educator, minister; b. San Francisco, July 15, 1954; s. William Harrison and Doris Ames Drake; m. Deborah A. Drake, Mar. 3, 1979; children: Benjamin, Matthew. BSE, Ark. State U., 1976. Cert. tchr. K-12 art, K-12 phys. edn., advt. design, secondary tchr., health, day trade, comml. art. K-12 art and phys. edn. tchr. New Madrid County R-1, Parma, Mo., 1976-85; head coach, tchr. Semo Christian Acad., Sikeston, Mo., 1985-88; dist. mgr. World Book Ency., Paragould, Ark., 1985-89; pulpit min., youth dir. various chs., N.E. Ark., 1985—; art history instr. Crowley's Ridge Coll., Paragould, 1991-95; K-12 art, K-6 phys. edn. coach Jackson County Schs., Tuckerman, Ark., 1989-97; comml. art tchr. Area Tech. Ctr., Jonesboro, Ark., 1997—. Cons. advt. design, 1996—. Mem. Families First, Paragould, 1996—; state bd. dirs., sec. Skills USA/VICA, Little Rock, 1997—. Mem. Ark. Art Edn. Assn., Cmty. Tchrs. Assn., Ark. Skills USA/VICA (sec. 1996—, state bd. dirs. 1997—, Instr. of Yr. 1997). Avocations: computer work, comic book collecting, fishing, basketball.

DRAKE, WILLIAM FRANK, JR., lawyer; b. St. Louis, Mar. 29, 1932; s. William Frank and Beatrice Drake; m. Martha Minohr Mockbee. BA, Principia Coll., 1954; LLB, Yale U., 1957. Bar: Pa. 1958. Practice, Phila., 1958-68, 84—; mem. firm Montgomery, McCracken, Walker & Rhoads, 1958-68, 87-96, of counsel, 1984-87, 96—; sr. v.p., gen. counsel Alco Std. Corp., 1968-79, 96-98, sr. v.p. adminstrn., 1979-83; chmn., CEO Alco Health Svcs. Corp., 1983-84, vice chmn., 1984-98, also bd. dirs.; vice chmn., gen. counsel Alco Standard Corp. (now Ikon Office Solutions Inc.), 1996-98. Trustee Peoples Light & Theatre Co., Malvern, Pa. With U.S. Army, 1957-58. Mem. ABA, Phila. Bar Assn., Union League (Phila.), Roaring Fork Club (Basalt, Colo.), Wilmington (Del.) Country Club, First Troop, Phila. City Calvary. Office: Montgomery McCracken Walker & Rhoads 123 S Broad St Fl 24 Philadelphia PA 19109-1099

DRAKEMAN, DONALD LEE, biotechnologist, pharmaceutical executive; b. Camden, NJ, Oct. 21, 1953; s. Fred J. and Jean (Faucett) D.; m. Lisa Natale Drakeman, Aug. 23, 1975; children: Cynthia and Amy. BA magna cum laude, Dartmouth Coll., 1975; JD, Columbia U., 1979; MA, Princeton U., 1984, PhD, 1988. Bar: N.J. 1979; U.S. Dist. Ct. N.J. 1979, N.Y. 1980; U.S. Supreme Ct. 1984. Assoc. Milbank, Tweed, Hadley and McCloy, N.Y.C., 1979-82; gen. counsel Essex Chem. Corp., Clifton, NJ, 1982-89, v.p., 1987-89; pres. Essex Med. Products, Clifton, NJ, 1988-89; pres., CEO Medarex, Inc., Annandale, NJ, 1987—. Adj. prof. polit. sci. Montclair State Coll., NJ, 1984; rsch. cons. Lilly Found., Inc., 1989—90; lectr. politics dept. Princeton Univ., 1990—93, 1995—; chmn. adv. coun. James Madison Program in Am. Ideals and Instn., Princeton Univ., 2000—; co-chair adv. coun. religion dept. Princeton Univ.; mem. adv. coun. Index Ventures, Geneva, 2002—03; chmn. NJ Commn. Sci. and Tech., 2004—. Author: Church and State Constitutional Issues, 1990; co-editor Church and State in Am. History, 2d edit., 1986, 3d edit., 2003; contbg. articles to profl. journals. Chmn. Montclair bd. adjustment, 1984; trustee, chair Biotech. Coun. N.J., 1996-98; trustee, U. Charleston, 1999-2003, Drew U., 2002—; adv. coun. Rutgers Bus. Sch., 2002—; trustee, Woodrow Wilson Nat. Fellowship Found., 2003—. Harlan Fiske Stone Scholar, Columbia Univ., 1976-79; inducted N.J. High Tech Hall of Fame, 2000. Mem.: AAAS, ABA, John Maclean Soc., Assn. Bar City of N.Y., Yale Club, Princeton Club, Princeton Alumni Coun. Home: 49 Rolling Hill Rd Skillman NJ 08558-2319 Office: Medarex Inc 707 State Rd Princeton NJ 08540-1437 Business E-Mail: ddrakeman@medarex.com.

DRAKEMAN, LISA N., biotechnologist; b. Boston, Oct. 30, 1953; d. Paul and Josephine (Covino) Natale; m. Donald L. Drakeman, Aug. 23, 1975; children: Cynthia Leigh Drakeman, Amy Elizabeth Drakeman. BA, Mt. Holyoke Coll., 1975; MA, Rutgers U., 1983, Princeton U., 1986, PhD, 1988. Chair, v. chair Monclair (N.J.) Redevelopment Agy., 1981-84; vis. scholar Dartmouth Coll., 1988-89; lectr. Princeton U., 1989-92; asst. dir. Alumni Coun. of Princeton U., 1991; dir. administrn. Medarex, Inc., Princeton, N.J., 1991-94, v.p. adminstrn., 1994-96, v.p., 1996-98, sr. v.p., head bus. devel., 1998-2000; CEO Genmab A/S, 1999—. Faculty fellow Grad. Coll. Princeton U., 1991-93, mem. adv. coun. dept. religion, 1996—; bd. dirs. Medarex Europe, B.V., GenPharm. Internat., Inc., Biotech. Coun. NJ. Mem. biopharm. adv. coun. Tech. Coun. Greater Phila., 1993-96; mem. Gov.'s Biopharm. Task Force N.J. Econ. Master Plan Commn., Trenton, 1994-95; mem.biotech. adv. com. The Franklin Inst., Phila., 1994-96; commr. Prosperity N.J., 1995-2000; mem. Cancer Inst. N.J. Leadership Coun., 2004—; bd. mem. Biotechnology Coun. N.J., 2005—. Garden State grad. fellow State of N.J., 1981-85; named to N.J. High Tech. Hall of Fame, 2000. Mem. Soc. for Advancement of Women's Health Rsch. (steering com., corp. adv. coun. 1994-97), Biotech. Industry Orgn. (chair nat. capital formation task force 1995-98, Advocate of Yr. award 1995), Biotech. Coun. N.J. (v.p. 1996-2000, Outstanding Industry Woman of Yr. 1996), European Fedn. Pharm. Industries and Assns. (bd. dirs. emerging pharm. enterprises sect. 2004—, v.p. 2005). Home: 49 Rolling Hill Rd Skillman NJ 08558-2319 Office: 457 N Harrison St Princeton NJ 08540 also: Genmab A/S Toldbodgade 33 DK 1253 Copenhagen Denmark

DRAMIS, FRANCIS (FRAN) A., JR., communications company executive; m. Terri Dramis; children: Billy, Katelyn, Mollie, Jeni, Jimmy. BA, Rutgers U.; MS, Pace U. V.p., co-founder Am. Transtech; corp. exec. dir. data systems ops., exec. dir. MIS Bell Labs.; exec. dir. info. product mgmt. and automation AT&T; pres., COO TELIC Corp.; mng. dir. Salomon Bros. Inc., 1989-91; pres. Salomon Tech. Svcs., Inc.; pres., CEO Network Mgmt. Inc., Fairfax, Va., 1991-98; cons., transitional CIO CIO Strategy, Inc., Clifton, Va.; exec. v.p., CIO Bell South Corp., Atlanta, 1998—, eCommerce officer. Dir., chmn. BellSouth Tech. Svcs., Inc.; bd. dir. BellSouth Solutions Group, Inc., Internet Policy Inst., BellSouth Found. Avocations: golf, manages youth sports teams. Office: Bell South Corp 1155 Peachtree St NE Ste A Atlanta GA 30309-3610 Office Phone: 404-249-2000. Office Fax: 404-249-2071.

DRANCE, STEPHEN MICHAEL, ophthalmologist, educator; b. Bielsko, Poland, May 22, 1925; Can. citizen; MB,ChB, U. Edinburgh, Scotland, 1948, MD, 1949; Diploma in Ophthalmology, Royal Coll. Surgeons, London, 1953; LLD (hon.), Dalhousie U., Halifax, 1995; DSc (hon.), U. Oulu, Finland, 1998, U. B.C., Vancouver, 1998. Intern Western Gen. Hosp., Edinburgh, 1948-49; resident County Hosp., York, Eng., 1952-53, Edinburgh Royal Infirmary, 1953-55, Oxford Eye Hosp., Eng., 1955-57, Oxford U., 1955-57; asst. prof. and assoc. prof. medicine U. Sask., Saskatoon, Can., 1957-63; assoc. prof. ophthalmology U. B.C., Vancouver, Can., 1963-66, prof., 1966-90, dir. ophthalmologic research, 1967-73, head dept. ophthalmology, 1973-90. Cons., lectr. medicine; vis. prof., lectr. numerous univs. Author: (with H. Reed) The Essentials of Perimetry, 2d edit., 1971, (with A. Neufeld) Applied Pharmacology of Glaucoma, 1984, (with D.R. Anderson) Automatic Perimetry in Glaucoma, 1985, (with A. Neufeld, M. van Buskirk) Applied Pharmacology of Glaucoma, 1991; assoc. editor Am. Archives Ophthalmology, 1961-74; mem. editorial bd. Can. Jour. Ophthalmology, 1966; mng. editor Albrecht von Graefe's Archive for Clin. and Exptl. Ophthalmology, 1979-90; editl. bd. Am. Jour. Opthalmology, 1994-99; contbr. articles to profl. jours., chpts. to books Pres. Vancouver Summer Festivals Soc., 1997-2002. With RAF, 1949-51. Decorated officer Order of Can., 1987; recipient numerous awards and grants for excellence in medicine. Fellow Royal Australian Coll. Ophthalmologists U.K. (hon.), Coll. Ophthalmology U.K. (hon.), Royal Soc. Medicine, Royal Coll. Physicians and Surgeons Can. (sec. 1976-77), Royal Coll. Surgeons Eng.; mem. Can. Assn. Clin. Rsch., Assn. Ophthalmologic Rsch. (U.K.), Assn. for Rsch. in Vision and Ophthalmology, Can. Ophthalmol. Soc. (pres. 1974-75), B.C. Oto-Ophthalmol. Soc., Ophthal. Soc. U.K., Oxford Ophthalmol. Congress, Am. Acad. Ophthalmology (v.p. 1993), Can. Med. Assn., B.C. Med. Assn., Internat. Perimetric Soc. (pres. 1982-88), Glaucoma Soc. Internat. Congrss (pres. 1983-90), Pan-Am. Ophthalmol. Congress, Pan-Am. Glaucoma Soc., Pan-Am. Assn. Ophthalmology, Assn. N.Am. Glaucomatologists, N.Z. Ophthalmol. Soc. (hon.), Academia Ophthalmol. Internat., Internat. Congress Ophthalmology (pres. 1994), Concilium Ophthalmol. Univaersale (visual function com.) E-mail: smd@interchange.ubc.ca.

DRANGSHOLT, JAMES K., brother, educator; s. John T. and Dorothy Voth Drangsholt; m. John Drangsholt, Nov. 20, 1948 (dec.); children: William, James. Student, Chgo. Conservatory, 1969—71; BA, DePaul U., 1972, MA, 1975; diploma in theology, St. Mary's Sem., 1975; PhD, Franklin U., 1993. Cert. tchr. Iowa, Ill., Ind. Dir. music Old St. Mary's, Chgo., 1969—74; tchr., organist Holy Family/St. Anthonys, Davenport, Iowa, 1976—90; pastoral assoc., organist Sacred Heart Ch., Peoria, Ill., 1991—96; asst. prin., organist Queen All Sts., Michigan City, Ind., 1996—2000; tchr. Cardinal Ritter High Sch., Indpls., 2000—04, Am. Music, Orlando, Fla., 2004—05. Summer prin. Highwoods Learning Ctr., Washington, 1990—96. Composer: (piano & violin) Aria-Ave Maria, 1972. Mem.: Am. Soc. Composers, Authors and Pubs., Am. Guild Organists. Avocations: swimming, symphony, opera. Home: 228 N King St Xenia OH 45385

DRANITZKE, RICHARD J., surgeon; b. L.I., N.Y., 1940; MD, Columbia U., 1966. Diplomate Am. Bd. Surgery, Am. Bd. Thoracic Surgery. Intern Columbia-Presbyn. Hosp., N.Y.C., 1966-67; resident in surgery Bellevue Hosp. Ctr., N.Y.C., 1969-73; resident in cardiothoracic surgery Albany (N.Y.) Med. Ctr., 1973—75; chief thoracic and vascular surgery St. Charles Hosp., Port Jefferson, NY, 1991—, St. Charles and J.T. Mather Meml. Hosp., 1985—; clin. instr. dept. surgery Stony Brook U. Hosp., 1994—; chief vascular surgery Mather Hosp., 1991—. Mem. ACP, ACS, AMA, Soc. Thoracic Surgeons, Eastern Vascular Soc., N.Y. Soc. for Cardiovasc. Surgery. Office: 635 Belle Terre Rd Port Jefferson NY 11777 also: 286 Sills Rd Patchogue NY 11772-8810 Office Phone: 631-473-1602.

DRANOVE, DAVID STUART, business educator, consultant, economist; b. NYC, July 25, 1956; s. Alfred and Dorothy Dranove; m. Deborah Salgo, Aug. 21, 1983; children: Daniel, Michael. BA, Cornell U., 1977, MBA, 1979; PhD, Stanford U., 1983. Asst. prof. U. Chgo., 1983—91; Richard Paget disting. prof. strategy Northwestern U., Evanston, Ill., 1995—99, chmn. dept. mgmt. and strategy, 1996—2000, Walter McNerney disting. prof. of health industry mgmt., 2000—, founder, dir. Ctr. Health Industry Mkt. Econ., 2001—. Mem. adv. bd. Am. Assn. Nurse Anest., 1993—95, Beecken Petty, 1997—99, Clean Air Engineering, 1997—98; bd. dirs. Pediat. Faculty Found., Chgo., 2001—05; cons. U.S. FTC, U.S. DOJ. Author: How Hospitals Survived, 1999, Economic Evolution of American Health Care, 2001, Economics of Strategy 3d edit., 2003, What's Your Life Worth?, 2003, Kellogg on Strategy, 2005; contbr. articles to profl. jours., chapters to books. Adv. bd. Highland Park Dist., 1994—95; bd. trustees Roycemore Sch., 2005—. Recipient John Thompson prize, Assn. Univ. Programs Health Adminstrn., 1993, Rsch. prizes, Nat. Inst. Health Care Mgmt., 1998, 2003, Assn. Health Svcs. Rsch., 1999, Amer. Acad. Med Admin., 1993, 1996, 1999, Levy Teaching award, Kellogg, 2002, 2005, Reiter Rsch. prize. Mem.: Internat. Health Econ. Assn., Am. Econ. Assn., Beta Gamma Sigma (hon.). Achievements include research in breakthroughs in the study of competition in health care; development of bringing fundamental changes to business strategy education. Avocations: audiophile, sports enthusiast, fine dining enthusiast. Office: Kellogg Sch of Mgmt 2001 Sheridan Rd Evanston IL 60208 Home: 857 Highland Pl Highland Park IL 60035 Office Phone: 847-491-8682. Business E-Mail: d-dranove@northwestern.edu.

DRANSITE, BRIAN ROBERT, product engineer manager; b. Glen Cove, N.Y., Oct. 26, 1964; s. Robert Stanley and Jane Theresa (Reidy) D. AS in Engring. Sci. magna cum laude, Nassau C.C., Garden City, N.Y., 1984; BSEE, Rensselaer Poly. Inst., 1986; MBA in Mgmt., Hofstra U., 1995. Offset printer Plainview (N.Y.)-Old Bethpage Cen. Sch. Dist., 1980-84; project engr. Knogo Corp. (Sentry Technologies), Hauppauge, N.Y., 1987-91; sr. electronic design engr. Ultre divsn. Linotype-Hell (Heidelberg Publ. Svcs., Inc.), Melville, N.Y., 1991-96; sr. product mgr. Symbol Technologies, Holtsville, N.Y., 1996—. Mem. IEEE, MBA Assn. Hofstra U. (v.p. fin. 1994-95), Planetary Soc., Rensselaer Assn. Divers (equipment mgr. 1986-87), Phi Theta Kappa. Avocations: astronomy, numismatic research, photography, scuba diving, boating.

DRAPALIK, BETTY R., volunteer, artist, educator; b. Cicero, Ill., July 4, 1932; d. Henry William and Jennie Margaret (Robbins) Degen; m. Joseph James Drapalik, Oct. 30, 1951; children: Betty Jennifer Drapalik Coryell, Joseph Henry. Grad., HS, Cicero. Sec., clk. Gt. Lakes (Ill.) Naval Base, until 1982; sect. to asst. dir. Arden Shore Boys' Home, Lake Bluff, Ill., 1984-87; sub. tchr. art Visual Art Ctr., Waukegan, Ill. One-woman shows include Jack Benny Ctr. Arts, 1995—2004, Wauconda Area Pub. Libr., 1999, 2002, Invitational First Lady Hearts and Flowers Art Exhbn., Ill., 2001—05 (First Lady award, 2004), GreenBelt Cultural Art Ctr., North Chgo., 2003, Pikes Peak Watercolor Soc. Internat. Watermedia XIII/ Fine Art Ctr., Colo. Springs, 2003, St. Charles Nat. Juried Art Exhbn. and Music Festival, 2005, exhibited in group shows at Layson Gallery, Waukegan, Ill., 1993, Cmty. Gallery Art, Coll. Lake County, Grayslake, Ill., 1993—99, 2000—04, Women's Works,

Old Courthouse Art Ctr., Woodstock, Ill., 1994—2000, 2002, Anderson Art Ctr., Kenosha, Wis., 1994—2005, Hardy Gallery, Ephraim, Wis., 1996—2002 (Purchase award, 1998), North Point Marina, Winthrop Harbor, Ill., 1996—2003 (1st pl. watercolor, 1996, 1999, 2d pl. watercolor, 1997, 1998, Best of Show, 1996, 1997, award of Merit watercolor, 1998, award of Excellence, 1999, 3d pl., 2001, 3d pl. watercolor, 2002), Truman State U., Kirksville, Mo., 1997, Moorehead (Minn.) State U., 1997, Kenosha Art Assn. and Lake County Art League Combined Art Event, 1997 (Best of Show, 1997), David Adler Cultural Ctr., Libertyville, Ill., 1997—2002, Hawthorne Hollow Art Festival, Kenosha, 1997—98, Deer Path Art League Festival, Lake Forest, 1997, 1999, N.W. N.Mex Arts Coun., Farmington, 1997, Waukegan Visual Arts Ctr., 1998, Zion Chamber Orch. Concert and Art Contest, 1998 (Best of Show, 1st pl.), Kenosha Pub. Mus., 1998 (award of excellence), Spotlight Gallery, Kenosha, 1998—99, Monne's Gallery, 1998, Deilora A. Norris Cultural Ctr., St. Charles, Ill., 1998—2005, Clausen Art Shop, Wilmette, Ill., 1999, Gull Lake Gallery, Richland, Mich., 1999—2002, Nippersink Gallery, Richmond, Ill., 1999—2001, Deer Path Gallery, Lake Forest, 1999—2003, Wauconda Pub. Libr., 1999, Kenosha Art Assn. and Lake County Art League Combined Art Event, 2000 (Best of Show, 2001), Kenosha Art Assn. Art Event, 2001—05 (3d pl., 2002), Green Belt Cultural Ctr., North Chgo., 2000, 2005, City of Zion, Ill., 2001—02, Centennial Days Fine Art Show, 2001, Harring Galleries, Racine, Wis., 2001—05, Guenzel Gallery, Fish Creek, Wis., 2001—02, Wauconda Pub. Libr., 2002, Jack Benny Ctr. Arts, 2003—05, Colo. Fine Art Ctr., 2003, Cmty. Gallery Art, Coll. Lake County, 2001—05, Western Colo. Watercolor Soc. exhbn., 2004, William M. Scholl Coll. Pediat. Medicine, Rosalind Franklin U. Medicine and Sci., North Chicago, 2005 (2d pl., 2005), Art Wauk, Waukegan, Ill., 2005, traveling exhbn., America the Beautiful, 2001—03; work published in Celebrating Door Country's Wild Places, 2001. Former leader, mem. pub. rels. com. Girl Scouts U.S.; visual arts cons. Green Belt Cultural Ctr. Lake County Forest Preserve Dist.; organizer meml. svc. and exhbn. Phil Austin's Life, Waukegan, 2004; leader art program Walkerville (Mich.) Schs., 2003; mem. outreach and evangelism missions bd. First Presbyn. Ch. Waukegan, 2000—02. Recipient Purchase award, Coll. Lake County, Grayslake, 1994, numerous courtesy awards. Mem.: Nat. Mus. Women in the Arts (charter), Bloomin' Artists, N.W. Area Arts Coun., Kenosha Art Assn., Red River Watercolor Soc., Deerpath Art League, Lakes Region Watercolor Guild (past rec. sec., co-program chair, exhibit chair), Lake County Art League (resource person, past pres., various bd. positions, fine arts cons. Green Belt Cultural Ctr. Lake County Forest Preserve), Transparent Watercolor Soc. Am. (life), Internat. Starcraft Camper Club (Ill. chpt. sec./treas. 1975). Evangelical. Avocations: watercolor, photography, camping, gardening, hiking. Home: 2018 W Grove Ave Waukegan IL 60085-1607 Office Phone: 847-662-2617.

DRAPEAU, SUZANNE EVA, art educator; b. Montpelier, Vt., Apr. 8, 1954; d. Norman Emile and Lucille Lorretta (LaBelle) D.; m. Gary William Moylen, Feb. 28, 1976 (div.); 1 child, Benjamin Patrick; m. David Gewanter, Dec. 24, 1988. BA in Visual Studies, Columbia U., 1989; MA in Studio Art, NYU, 1997. Cert. tchr., Conn. Self-employed title abstractor, N.J., 1980-86; title officer Chgo. Title Ins. Co., N.J., 1987; sr. title office mgr. Mountainside, N.J., 1988; art tchr. Master's Sch., West Simsbury, Conn., 1989-93, Hartford (Conn.) Pub. Schs., 1993-95, Avon (Conn.) Pub. Schs., 1996—. Programming coord. Artworks Gallery, Hartford, 1999, pres., 2000—; resident Contemporary Artists Ctr., North Adams, Mass., 1997; workshop leader Avon Continuing Edn., 1999—; presenter in field. One-woman shows at Women's Ctr., U. Hartford, 1993, 80 Washington Sq. East Galleries, N.Y., 1996, Fourwinds Ctr., Farmington, Conn., 1997, Artworks Gallery, Hartford, 1999; exhibited in group shows at Slater Mus., Norwich, Conn., 1997, 98, L'Instituto Universitario d'Architettura di Venezia, Venice, Italy, 1993, 94, Nat. Arts Coun. at Hartford, 1993, Farmington Art Guild, 1994, Casa Italia Zerilli-Marimo, NYU, N.Y.C., 1997, 98, 2000, Artworks Gallery, 1997, 99, 2000, South Windsor (Conn.) Pub. Libr., 1999. Mem. NEA, Nat. Art Edn. Assn., Conn. Art Educators Assn., Conn. Edn. Assn., Internat. Sculpture Ctr., Coll. Art Assn. Home: 6 Tamarack Ln Simsbury CT 06070-2432 Office: Avon Pub Schs 34 Simsbury Rd Avon CT 06001-3714

DRAPER, DANIEL CLAY, retired lawyer; b. Boston, June 7, 1920; s. John W. and Lulu H. (Clay) D.; m. Marcia Humphreys, Nov. 25, 1989. BA, W.Va. U., 1940, MA, 1941; LLB, Harvard U., 1947. Assoc. Kelly, Drye & Warren, N.Y.C., 1947-55; ptnr. Cadwalader, Wickersham & Taft, N.Y.C., 1962-91, ret. Bd. dirs. Union Devel., Montclair, N.J.; adj. prof. history Bloomfield Coll., 1991. Contbr. articles to profl. jours. Mgr. campaign Montclair's Cmty. Com. Candidates, 1964; trustee Montclair Art Mus., 1966-71, Bloomfield Coll., 1974-81, 87-95. With USN, 1942-46. Decorated Bronze Star, European Service Ribbon (3 stars). Mem. N.Y. State Bar Assn. (chmn. banking com. 1981-85), N.Y. County Lawyers Assn. (sec. 1979-81, pres. 1984-87, chmn. banking com. 1968-78, housing and urban affairs and real property coms., chmn. investment com.), Harvard Club, N.Y.C. Episcopalian. Home: 115 Franklin St Vineyard Haven MA 02568-9999

DRAPER, DAVID STEWART, aerospace scientist; b. Westchester, Calif., Feb. 2, 1960; s. Harrison Scott and Rita Mae Draper; m. Cynthia Robyn Lohn, May 26, 2001. BS, Humboldt State U., 1985; PhD, U. Oreg., 1991. Macquarie u. rsch. fellow Macquarie U., Sydney, Australia, 1993—96; postdoctoral assoc. U. Bristol, England, 1992—93; rsch. scientist U. Tex., Richardson, 1996—98; project dir. NASA Johnson Space Ctr., Houston, 1999—2002; sr. rsch. scientist Inst. Meteoritics, Univ N.Mex, Albuquerque, 2002—. Dem. absentee ballot monitor, Albuquerque, 2004—04. Grantee, NSF, 1999—, NASA, 2000—. Mem.: Am. Geophys. Union. Liberal. Achievements include Authority on terrestrial and extraterrestrial igneous processes. Avocations: guitar, beer brewing. Office Phone: 505-277-1607.

DRAPER, EDGAR, psychiatrist; b. St. Louis, Feb. 5, 1926; s. Neal McLain and Florence Mabel (Meyers) D.; m. Norma Jane Alexander, Mar. 16, 1949; children: Sue Draper Masteller, Anne Draper Klevay, Neal Edgar. AB, Washington U., 1946, Duke Div. Sch., 1948; BD, Garrett Biblical Inst., 1949; MD, Washington U. Med. Sch., 1953; grad., Inst. for Psychoanalysis, Chgo., 1966. Diplomate Am. Bd. Psychiatry and Neurology; ordained deacon, elder Meth. Ch., 1946. Asst. pastor Edenton St. Meth. Ch., Raleigh, 1947; pastor Garden Prarie, Ill., 1949; intern Washington U. Svc. City Hosp., St. Louis, 1953-54; resident in psychiatry U. Cin., 1954-55, 57-59; sr. asst. surgeon USPHS, Ft. Worth, 1955-57; from instr. to assoc. prof. U. Chgo., 1959-68; co-dir. psychiat. outpatient dept., prof. psychiatry U. Mich., Ann Arbor, 1968, dir. psychiat. resident edn., 1968-74, prof. postgrad edn., 1970-75; prof., chmn. dept. psychiatry U. Miss. Med. Ctr., Jackson, 1975-93; prof. psychiatry U. Miss., Jackson, 1993-94; prof. emeritus, 1994—. Cons. in field. Contbr. numerous articles to profl. jours. Bd. dirs. Friends Libr. Named Vis. scholar U. Chgo., 1987, Fellow Soc. for Sci. Study of Religion, 1987, Man of Month Pastoral Psychology, 1970; recipient Physicians Recognition award, 1982-85, Cert. Appreciation Mental Health Assn. Hinds County, 1983, Plaque of Commendation Chgo. Acad. Religion and Mental Health, 1966-67. Fellow Am. Psychiat. Assn. (disting. life fellow), Am. Coll. Psychiatry (life), Am. Soc. Psychoanalytic Physicians, Soc. for Sci. Study of Religion (life), Am. Coll. Psychoanalysts (life, program chmn., bd. regents), So. Psychiat. Assn. (parlimentarian 1980—), Soc. for Study of Psychiatry and Culture; mem. Miss. Psychiat. Assn. (past pres., Disting. Svc. award 2001), Miss. State Med. Soc., Mich. Psychiat. Soc., Washtenaw County Med. Soc., Mich. State Med. Soc., So. Psychiat. Assn., Mich. Psychoanalytic Soc., Mental Health Assn. (bd. dirs. Jackson). Office Phone: 601-982-2176. E-mail: purpledoc@bellsouth.net.

DRAPER, E(RNEST) LINN, JR., retired electric utility executive; b. Houston, Feb. 6, 1942; s. Ernest Linn and Marcia L. (Saylor) D.; m. Mary Deborah Doyle, June 9, 1962; children: Susan Elizabeth, Robert Linn, Barbara Ann, David Doyle. Student, Williams Coll., 1960-62; BAChemE, Rice U., 1964, BSChemE, 1965; PhD in Nuclear Engring., Cornell U., 1970. Asst. prof. nuclear engring. U. Tex., Austin, 1969-72, assoc. prof., 1972-79; tech. asst. to CEO Gulf States Utilities Co., Beaumont, Tex., 1979, v.p. nuclear tech., 1980-81, sr. v.p. engring. tech. services, 1981-82, sr. v.p. external affairs, 1982-84, sr. v.p. external affairs and prodn., 1984-85, exec. v.p. external affairs and prodn., 1985-86, vice chmn., 1985-87, COO, 1986, pres., CEO, 1986-92, chmn. bd. dirs., 1987-92; pres. AEPCo., Inc.; pres., COO Am. Electric Power Svc. Corp., Columbus, Ohio, 1992-93; chmn., pres., CEO Am. Electric Power Co. and Svc. Corp., Columbus, 1993—2004. Bd. dirs. Sprint Corp., Temple Inland Corp., Alpha Natural Resources, North-Western Corp., Alliance Data Sys. Fellow NSF, 1965-66, AEC, 1967-68. Mem. NAE, Am. Nuclear Soc. (pres. 1984-85), Nuclear Energy Inst. (chmn. 1993-95), Edison Electric Inst. (chmn. 1996-97). E-mail: eldraper@aep.com.

DRAPER, GERALD LINDEN, retired lawyer; b. Oberlin, Ohio, July 14, 1941; s. Earl Linden and Mary Antoinette (Colloto) Draper; m. Barbara Jean Winter, Aug. 26, 1960; children: Melissa Leigh Price, Stephen Edward. BA, Muskingum Coll., 1963; JD, Northwestern U., 1966. Bar: Ohio 1966, US Dist Ct (so dist) Ohio 1966, US Ct Appeals (6th cir) 1975, US Supreme Ct 1980, US Dist Ct (no dist) Ohio 2000. Ptnr. Bricker & Eckler, Columbus, Ohio, 1966-88, Thompson, Hine & Flory, Columbus, 1989-95, Draper, Hollenbaugh, Briscoe, Yashko & Carmany, Columbus, 1996-99, Roetzel & Andress, Columbus, 1999—2004; ret. Trustee Ohio Bd. Bar Examiners, 1986—89; mem. Ohio Bd. Commn. on Unauthorized Practice of Law, 2002—, Ohio Med. Malpractice Commn., 2003—. Trustee, pres Wesley Glen Retirement Ctr, Columbus, Ohio, 1979—95; trustee Meth Elder Care Servs, Inc, 1995—, Muskingum Coll., New Concord, Ohio, 1988—92, Ohio, 1993—, vice chair, 1994—; trustee, pres Wesley Ridge Retirement Ctr, 1995—2000, treas, 2001—. Fellow: Am Bd Trial Advs (trustee Ohio chpt. 2001), Am Col Trial Lawyers; mem.: ABA (House Dels 1991—97, 1999—2001), Def Research Inst, Ohio Asn Hosp Attys, Ohio Continuing Legal Educ Inst (trustee 1992—98, chair 1997—98), Nat Conf Bar Found (trustee 1987—90, 1991—94), Columbus Bar Found (pres 1984—86), Columbus Bar Asn (pres 1982—83, Bar Serv Medal 1998), Ohio State Bar Found (trustee 1992—97), Ohio State Bar Asn (pres 1990—91). Avocations: travel, golf, photography.

DRAPER, JAMES DAVID, art museum curator; b. Lebanon, Mo., Mar. 6, 1943; s. John Hilton and Hazel (Berg) D. BA, U. Mo., 1965; MA, NYU, 1967, PhD, 1984. Curatorial asst. Met. Mus. Art, N.Y.C., 1969, various positions, 1969-84, dept. curator, 1984—, Henry R. Kravis curator, 1995—. Fellow J. Paul Getty Mus., Malibu, Calif., 1987; exec. dir. The Isaacson-Draper Found., 1999. Author: Bertoldo di Giovanni, Sculptor of the Medici Household, 1992; co-author: (exhbn. catalogs) Augustin Pajou, Royal Sculptor, 1998, La giovinezza di Michelangelo, 1999, Playing With Fire: European Terracotta Models, 1740-1840, 2004; editor: (rev. critical edit.) The Italian Bronze Statuettes of the Renaissance (W. von Bode), 1980. Decorated chevalier Order of Arts and Letters (France). Episcopalian. Office: Met Mus Art 1000 5th Ave New York NY 10028-0113 Business E-Mail: james.draper@metmuseum.org.

DRAPER, JAMES THOMAS, JR., (JIMMY DRAPER), clergyman; b. Hartford, Ark., Oct. 10, 1935; s. James T. Draper; m. Carol Ann Floyd, 1956; children: Randy, Bailey, Terri. BA, Baylor U., 1957; BD, MDiv, Southwestern Bapt. Theol. Sem.; DD (hon.), Howard Payne U., Brownwood, Tex.; DHum (hon.), Dallas Bapt. Coll.; DD (hon.), Campbell U., Buies Creek, N.C. Ordained to ministry Bapt. Ch. Pastor Steep Hollow Bapt. Ch., Bryan, Tex., Iredell (Tex.) Bapt. Ch., Temple Bapt. Ch., Tyler, Tex., Univ. Park Bapt. Ch., San Antonio, Red Bridge Bapt. Ch., Kansas City, Mo., First So. Bapt. Ch., Del City, Okla.; assoc. pastor First Bapt. Ch., Dallas, pastor Euless, Tex.; pres. Life Way Christian Resources of the So. Bapt. Convention, 1991—. Mem. adminstrv. com. Bapt. Gen. Conv., Tex., mem. exec. bd., mem. missions funding com., mem. exec. dir. search com.; pres. So. Bapt. Conv. (1982-84), So. Baptist Conv. Pastors Conf., 1979-80; trustee So. Bapt. Conv. Annuity Bd., 1974-82, Baylor U., Waco, Tex., 1974-83, Southwestern Bapt. Theol. Sem., 1984-91; preacher numerous convs., confs. Author 22 books; contbr. articles to religious jours. Office: Life Way Christian Resource Office of So Bapt Convention Office of the Pres 127 9th Ave S Nashville TN 37203-3802

DRAPER, JAMES WILSON, lawyer; b. Detroit, Dec. 26, 1926; s. Kenneth Draper and Dorothy (Wilson) Barker; m. Alice Patricia Sullivan, May 16, 1953; children: Catherine Draper Clain, Julie Draper Fazekas, James P., Martha Draper Grossman. BA, U. Mich., 1949, JD, 1951. Bar: Mich. 1951, U.S. Dist. Ct. (so. dist.) Mich. 1951, U.S. Ct. Appeals (6th cir.) 1951. Assoc. Dykema, Jones & Wheat and successor firms, Detroit, 1951-61; ptnr. Dykema Gossett, and predecessor firms, Detroit, 1961—. Past chmn. real property law sect. council State Bar Mich. Served with USN, 1944-46 Fellow Am. Coll. Real Estate Lawyers; mem. Mich. State Bar (past chmn. real property law sect., land title stds. com.), Detroit Club, Country Club Detroit (Grosse Point Farms, Mich.). Republican. Presbyterian. Home: 267 Hillcrest Ave Grosse Pointe Farms MI 48236-3622 Office: Dykema Gossett 400 Renaissance Ctr Detroit MI 48243-1603

DRAPER, J(OSIAH) EVERETT, artist, author, educator; b. East Orange, NJ, Oct. 17, 1915; s. Harold Walcott and Anna Frederika (Petersen) D.; m. Evelyn Ruth Wehlau, Sept. 25, 1943; children: Pamela Ruth Draper Whyte, Richard Everett. Grad. in Advt. Design, Pratt Inst., Bklyn.; student Illustration (Harvey Dunn), Grand Ctrl. Sch. of Art, N.Y.C. Art dir. Prudential Ins. Co., Newark and Jacksonville, N.J., Fla., 1935-72; pres. J.E. Draper AWS, Inc., Ponte Vedra, Fla., 1972—. Adj. instr. art and design Newark Sch. Fine and Indsl. Att, 1947-51; instr. water color workshops internationally, 1972—. Author: Putting People in Your Painting, 1986, People Painting Scrapbook, 1989; artist: paintings in many one man shows, over 400 corp., govt. and privat collections, permanent collections of several museums and univs.; twice seclected for Am. Watercolor Soc. travelling exhbns. Pres. St. Augustine (Fla.) Art Assn., 1973-76. Master sgt. U.S. Army Intelligence, 1941-45. Mem. Am. Watercolor Soc. (Carolyn Stern award 1967), Fla. Watercolor Soc. (past pres.), Salmagundi Club, Ponte Vedra Club, Whiskey Painters of Am. Episcopalian. Avocations: art, photography. Home and Office: JE Draper AWS Inc 20 Ponte Vedra Cir Ponte Vedra Beach FL 32082

DRAPER, NORMAN RICHARD, statistician, educator; b. Eng., Mar. 20, 1931; came to U.S., 1955; s. Norris and Helen (Draper). BA, Cambridge (Eng.) U., 1954, MA, 1958; PhD, U. N.C., 1958. Tech. officer, statistician plastics div. Imperial Chem. Industries, 1958-60; mem. Math. Rsch. Ctr., U. Wis., Madison, 1960-61, mem. faculty, 1961—, prof. statistics, 1966-99, prof. emeritus, 1999—, chmn., 1967-73, 94-97. Vis. prof. Imperial Coll., London, fall 1967, 68 Author: (with H. Smith) Applied Regression Analysis, 1966, 3d edit., 1998, (with G.E.P. Box) Evolutionary Operation, 1969, (with W. E. Lawrence) Probability: An Introductory Course, 1970, (with G.E.P. Box) Empirical Model Building and Response Surfaces, 1987. Recipient Max-Planck-Forschungs-Preis, Alexander von Humboldt-Stiftung, 1994. Fellow Royal Statis. Soc., Am. Statis. Assn., Inst. Math. Statistics, Am. Soc. Quality Control (lectr. 1963—); mem. Internat. Statis. Inst. Address: U Wis Dept Statistics 1300 University Ave Madison WI 53706-1532

DRAPER, STEPHEN ELLIOT, lawyer, engineer; b. Columbus, Ga., Mar. 17, 1942; s. Philip Henry and Ethel Illges (Woodruff) D.; m. Lucy Leila Hargrett, June 20, 1970; 1 child, Jessie Roxanne. BS, U.S. Mil. Acad., 1964; MBA, C.W. Post/L.I. U., 1976; JD, Ga. State U., 1992; MSCE, PhD, Ga. Inst. Tech., 1971, 81. Registered profl. engr., Ga., Fla. Commd. 2d. lt. U.S. Army, 1964, advanced through grades to col., retired, 1984; forensic engr. Atlanta, 1984-86; pres. and tech. dir. Draper Engring. Rsch., Atlanta, 1986-93, The Draper Group, Atlanta, 1993-98; mil. policy advisor, water policy advisor Gov. of Ga., Brig. Gen., 1999—2002. Apptd. mem. Clean Water Initiative, Met. Atlanta C. of C., 2000; rep. to gov. Ga. Joint Sturdy Com. Statewide Comprehensive Water Mgmt., 2001—02. Editor, prin. author: Model Water Sharing Agreements for the 21st Century, 2002; contbr. articles to profl. jours. Bd. dirs. J.W. & E.I. Woodruff Found., Columbus, Ga., 1991—, Met. Boys Club, Columbus, 1981-84; mem. long-range planning com. Atlanta Area Coun., Boys Scouts Am., 1972; trustee the Foxcroft Sch., Middleburg, Va., 1994; bd. visitors U. Ga. Libr., 1997—; mem. svc. acad. selection bd. U.S. Senate, 1998—. Decorated Gallantry Cross with Palm and Silver Star, Legion of Merit, Bronze Star (2), Soldier's medal, Purple Heart (3), Air medal (2), Army Commendation medal (4), others; recipient Am. Jurisprudence award Ga. State U., 1992, Spl. Actions award Women's Equity Action League, 1976. Mem. ABA, ASCE, NSPE, Am. Water Resources Assn., Nat. Acad. Forensic Engrs., Nature Conservancy of Ga. (bd. dirs. 1998—), Ga. Conservancy (bd. dirs. 1999—), Capital City Club, Commerce Club, Sea Island Beach Club. Avocations: travel, history, sports, exercise. Office: The Draper Group 1401 Peachtree St NE Ste 500 Atlanta GA 30309-3000

DRAPER, THOMAS B., lawyer; b. July 10, 1953; BA cum laude, Yale Univ., 1975; JD, Univ. Tex., 1979. Bar: Tex. 1979, Mass. 1980. Law clk. Judge Homer Thornberry, US Dist. Ct. 5th cir., 1979—80; assoc. Ropes & Gray, Boston, 1980—89, ptnr. corp. dept., 1989—, chmn. debt fin. practice group. Instr. Boston Univ. Sch. Law. Mem.: ABA, Boston Bar Assn. Office: Ropes & Gray 1 International Pl Boston MA 02110-2624 Office Phone: 617-951-7430. Office Fax: 617-951-7050. Business E-Mail: thomas.draper@ropesgray.com.

DRAPER, WILLIAM HENRY, III, venture capitalist; b. White Plains, N.Y., Jan. 1, 1928; s. William Henry and Katherine (Baum) Draper; m. Phyllis Culbertson, June 13, 1953; children: Rebecca, Polly, Timothy. BA, Yale U., 1950, MA (hon.), 1991; MBA, Harvard U., 1954; LLD (hon.), Southeastern U., 1985. With Inland Steel Co., Chgo., 1954-59, Draper, Gaither & Anderson, Palo Alto, Calif., 1959-62; pres. Draper & Johnson Investment Co., Palo Alto, 1962-65; founder, gen. ptnr. Sutter Hill Ventures, Palo Alto, 1965-81; pres., chmn. U.S. Export-Import Bank, Washington, 1981-86; adminstr., CEO, UN Devel. Programme, 1986-93; mng. dir. Draper Richards, San Francisco, 1994—, Draper Internat., San Francisco, 1994—. Bd. dirs. numerous cos. Nat. co-chmn. fin. com. George Bush for Pres., 1980; bd. dirs., former chmn. Rep. Alliance; chmn. bd. Am. Conservatory Theatre, 1980—81, bd. dirs., 1977—81; chmn. Internat. Inst. Edn. West, 1989—2000; vice chmn. Population Action Internat., 1993—; mem. adv. bd. Stanford Grad. Sch. Bus. Adminstrn., 1980—86; chmn. World Affairs Coun. No. Calif., 2000—02; trustee Yale U., 1991—98, George Bush Libr. Found., 1993—; bd. dirs. Population Crisis Com., 1976—81, Atlantic Coun., 1989—, World Rehab. Fund, 1988—92, Ctr. for Econ. Policy Rsch., Stanford U., 1988, Inst. Internat. Studies Stanford U., 1997—99, UN Assn.-USA, 2003—. With U.S. Army, 1946—48, with U.S. Army, 1951—52. Named one of U.S.'s 50 New Corp. Elite, Bus. Week mag., 1985; recipient Alumni Achievement award, Harvard Bus. Sch., 1982, medal of Honor, Ellis Island, 1992. Mem.: Overseas Devel. Coun., Coun. Fgn. Rels., River Club, Chevy Chase Club, Met. Club, Bohemian Club, Pacific Union Club. Home: 91 Tallwood Ct Atherton CA 94027-6431 Office: Draper Richards 50 California St Ste 2925 San Francisco CA 94111-4726 Office Phone: 415-616-4050. E-mail: bill@draperrichards.com.

DRAPKIN, DENNIS B., lawyer; b. NYC, Feb. 17, 1948; s. Eli and Ruth Drapkin; m. Adrienne Miller, June 30, 1974; children: Benjamin, Jennifer, Rebecca. AB summa cum laude, Dartmouth Coll., 1968, BE, 1969; JD, Yale U., 1972; LLM, London Sch. Econs., 1973. Bar: NY 1975, DC 1978, Tex. 1985. Assoc. Paul, Weiss, Rifkind, Wharton & Garrison, NYC, 1974—77; atty.-adv. to Tax Legis. Counsel, spl. asst. to asst. sec. tax policy Office of Tax Policy, U.S. Treasury Dept., 1977—80; assoc., ptnr. Cohen & Uretz, DC, 1980—83; ptnr. Jones Day, Dallas, 1984—. Mem. alumni coun. Dartmouth Coll., Hanover, NH, mem. nominating and alumni trustee search com., mem. joint com. alumni governance and trustee nominations, mem. com. trustees; mem. Exec. Com. Dartmouth Club of Dallas. Named one of the Top Tax Lawyers in US, Euromoney/Internat. Tax Rev., 1997—, Best Lawyers in Am., 1999—, Tex. Super Lawyers, 2003—. Mem.: ABA (former vice-chair profl. svcs., rep. to Nat. Conf. of Lawyers and CPAs, chair sect. of taxation), Am. Coll. Tax Counsel, Am. Law Inst. Office: Jones Day 2727 N Harwood St Dallas TX 75201-1515 Office Fax: 214-969-5100. Business E-Mail: dbdrapkin@jonesday.com.

DRASLER, GREGORY JOHN, artist; b. Waukegan, Ill., June 7, 1952; s. John W. and Patricia A. Drasler; m. Nancy B. Davidson, June 15, 1985. BFA, U. Ill., 1980, MFA, 1983. Tchr. Williams Coll., 1994, Princeton U., 1999—. One person shows include Marianne Deson Gallery, Chgo., 1988, R. C. Erpf Gallery, N.Y., 1986, 87, 88, Shea & Beker Gallery, N.Y., 1990, Ctr. for Contemporary Art, Chgo., 1990, Queens Mus., Bulova Ctr., N.Y., 1994, Generous Miracles Gallery, N.Y., 2000, Eyre Moore Gallery, Seattle, Wash., 2000, Van Brunt Gallery, N.Y., 2004, Calif. State Coll., Fullerton, 2005; exhibited in group shows New Mus. Contemporary Art, N.Y.C., 1983, 87, 92, 95, Germans Van Eck Gallery, N.Y., 1984, John Berggruen Gallery, San Francisco, 1985, Jack Tilton Gallery, N.Y.C., 1986, Wellesley (Mass.) Coll. Mus., 1986, Robeson Ctr. Gallery, Rutgers U., Newark, 1987, Ben Shahn Galleries, William Patterson Coll., Wayne, N.J., 1988, Three Rivers Arts Festival, Carnegie Mus. Art, Pitts., 1989, U. Art Mus., SUNY, Binghamton, N.Y., 1989, Artist Space, N.Y.C., 1990, Flint (Mich.) Inst. Arts, Philharm. Ctr. for Arts, Knoxville Mus. Art, 1991-92, Flint Inst. Arts, 1993; represented in permanent collections Dow Jones Inc., N.Y.C., Krannert Art Mus., Champaign, Ill., Sammuel Lindenbaum, Fisher Bros., U. Ill., Champaign, John W. Heckenger, Barbara Toll, Emily Landau, Henry Luce III Found., Sawyer Miller Group, N.Y.C.; featured in Flint Inst. Arts Cat., Art Press, 1991, Chgo. Tribune, 1990, Art in Am. mag., 1987, 90, N.Y. Times newspaper, 1987, 88, 91, The Independent Press newspaper, 1991, Ben Shahn Gallery cat., 1988, SUNY Binghamton U. Art Mus. cat., Carnegie Mus. Art cat., Artist Space cat., 1990, Mary C. MacLellan fellow, 1980; MacDowell Colony Residence fellow, 1986; art fellow N.Y. Found of Arts, 1991; Nat. Endowment of Arts fellow, 1993; Djerassi Resident Artist Program fellow, 1996.

DRASNER, FRED, newspaper publishing executive; b. Bklyn. m. Cynthia Drasner. JD, NYU. Commd. ensign USN; with J.K. Lasser and Co., N.Y.C.; real estate and tax lawyer Washington; pres., CEO US News and World Report, NYC, 1984—93; co-pub. NY Daily News, NYC, 1993—, CEO, 1993—99, co-chmn., 1998—; chmn., CEO, co-pub. Applied Graphics Techs., 1999—. Recipient Lifetime Achievement award, Guardian Angel, 2002. Office: New York Daily News 450 W 33rd St Fl 3 New York NY 10001-2681

DRAUT, ERIC J., insurance company executive; Degree, U. Ill., 1979; MBA, Kellogg Grad. Sch. Mgmt. Northwestern U., 1989. Controller Unitrin Corp., Chgo., 1990—97, treas., 1992—2002, v.p., 1997—99, CFO, 1997—, sr. v.p., 1999—2002, exec. v.p., dir., 2002—. Office: Unitrin Corp 1 E Wacker Dr Chicago IL 60601-1802

DRAWBAUGH, DANIEL, information technology executive, biomedical engineer; BS in Biomedical and Elec. Engring., Temple Univ., Phila.; MBA, Duquesne Univ. Dir. biomedical engring. Shadyside Hosp., Pitts., 1983—90, chief info. officer, 1990—97, Univ. Pitts. Med. Ctr., Pitts., 1997—; and pres. BioTronics Inc. (subs. UPMC), Pitts. Named one of top tech. innovators, Info Week mag., 2004. Office: Corporate Communications UPMC 200 Lothrop St Pittsburgh PA 15213-2582

DRAY, MARK S., lawyer; b. Alliance, Ohio, Feb. 8, 1943; s. Dwight Leroy and N. Pauline (Clark) Dray; m. Jonadell Pascoe, June 5, 1965; children: Melisa Louise, Justin Clark. BA, Mount Union Coll., Alliance, Ohio, 1965; JD, Coll. William and Mary, 1968, M in Law and Taxation, 1969. Bar: Va. 1968, U.S. Dist. Ct. (ea. dist.) Va. 1970, U.S. Tax Ct. 1971. Tax sr. Price Waterhouse, Washington, 1969-70; assoc. Hunton & Williams LLP, Richmond, Va., 1970-77, ptnr., 1977—. Mem. So. Employee Benefits Conf., 1974—; mem. adv. coun. William and Mary Tax Conf., 1980—88; trustee So. Fed. Tax Inst., 1989—, chair, 1997; spkr. in field. Contbr. articles to profl. jours. Fellow: Am. Bar Found., Va. Law Found., Am. Coll. Tax Counsel, Am. Coll. Employee Benefits Counsel (bd. govs., officer 2004—, charter); mem.: ABA (mem. com. employee benefits 1975—, mem. joint com. employee benefits 1988—91, chmn. 1989—90, 1990—91), Order of Coif, Richmond Bar Assn., Va. Bar Assn., Blue Key, Country Club Va. Episcopalian. Avocation: golf. Office: Hunton & Williams LLP Riverfront Plz East Tower 951 E Byrd St Richmond VA 23219-4074 Office Phone: 804-788-8408. Business E-Mail: mdray@hunton.com.

DRAY, PHILIP, history professor, writer; b. Chgo. Prof., African-Am. history The New Sch., NYC. Co-author (with Seth Cagin): We Are Not Afraid: The Story of Goodman, Schwerner, and Caney and the Civil Rights Campaign for Mississippi, 1988 (NY Times Notable Book, 1988); author: At the Hands of Persons Unknown: The Lynching of Black America, 2002 (Robert F. Kennedy Meml. Book Prize, 2003, So. Book Critics Circle award for nonfiction, Pulitzer Prize finalist, 2003), Stealing God's Thunder: Benjamin Franklin 's Lightning Rod & The Invention of America, 2005. Mailing: care Author Mail Random House 1745 Broadway New York NY 10019 Address: care Geri Thoma Elaine Markson Agy 44 Greenwich Ave New York NY 10011*

DRAY, WILLIAM HERBERT, philosophy educator; b. Montreal, June 23, 1921; s. William John and Florence Edith (Jones) D.; m. Doris Kathleen Best, Sept. 18, 1943; children: Christopher Reid, Jane Elizabeth. BA in History, U. Toronto, 1949; BA in Philosophy, Politics and Econs., Oxford U., 1951, MA, 1955, D.Phil., 1956; LLD (hon.), Trent U., 1987. Lectr. U. Toronto, 1953-55, asst. prof., asso. prof., 1956-63, prof., 1963-68, Trent U., 1968-76, chmn. dept. philosophy, 1968-73; prof. philosophy U. Ottawa, Ont., 1976-85, emeritus, 1986—. Author: Laws and Explanation in History, 1957, Philosophy of History, 1964, 2d edit., 1993, Perspectives on History, 1980, On History and Philosophers of History, 1989, History as Re-enactment, 1995; editor: Philosophical Analysis and History, 1966; co-editor: Substance and Form in History, 1981, Philosophie de l'histoire et la Pratique historienne d'aujourd'hui, 1982, The Principles of History, 1999. Served with RCAF, 1941-46, Active Res., 1956-66, wing comdr. ret. Am. Council Learned Socs. fellow, 1960-61; Can. Council fellow, 1971-72, 78-79; Killam research fellow, 1980-81; Nat. Humanities Ctr. fellow, 1983-84; recipient Can. Council Molson prize, 1986, Lifetime Achievement award Collingwood Soc., 2005. Fellow: Royal Soc. Can. Home: 818-32 Clarissa Dr Richmond Hill ON Canada L4C 9R7 Office: Dept Philosophy Univ of Ottawa Ottawa ON Canada K1N 6N5 Personal E-mail: whdray@aol.com.

DRAYER, BURTON PAUL, hospital administrator, neuroradiologist; b. N.Y.C., Mar. 19, 1946; s. Alexander and Marion Horowitz; m. Michaele Gerri Cohen, June 13, 1968; children: Aron Stuart, Alex Nathan. A.B., U. Pa., 1967; M.D., Chgo. Med. Sch., 1971. Diplomate Am. Bd. Psychiatry and Neurology, Am. Bd. Radiology. Intern, U. Vt. Med. Center, Burlington, 1971-72, resident in neurology, 1972-75; fellow, resident in radiology, U. Pitts. Health Center, 1975-78; asst. prof. neurology, U. Pitts., 1977-79, assoc. prof. radiology, 1978-79; dir. neuroradiology Children's Hosp. U. Pitts., 1978-79; assoc. prof. radiology and asst. prof. neurology, Duke U. Med. Center, Durham, N.C., 1979, chief sect. neuroradiology, 1981; dir. neuroradiol. rsch. Barrow Neurol. Inst.; Charles M. and Marilyn Newman Prof. and chmn. dept. radiology, Mt. Sinai Med. Sch., exec. v.p. hosp. and clinical affairs, Mt. Sinai Med. Ctr., pres., Mt. Sinai Hosp., 2004-. Past pres. Neuroradiology Edn. and Rsch. Found. Grantee, Squibb Research Inst., 1981-82, 82-83, Nat. Heart, Lung, and Blood Inst., 1983. Fellow Am. Acad. Neurology, Am. Coll. Radiology; mem. Am. Soc. Neuroradiology (past pres.), Soc. for Neuroscis., Am. Roentgen Ray Soc., Am. Heart Assn. (exec. com. stroke coun.), Radiol. Soc. N.Am. (bd. dirs. 2004—), Am. Acad. Neurology, Sigma Xi, Alpha Omega Alpha. Editor: Neuroimaging Clinics of N.Am.; mem. editl. bd. Neuroradiology; contbr. articles to books and jours. Office: Mt Sinai Med Ctr Dept Radiology One Gustave L Levy Pl Box 1234 New York NY 10029 Business E-Mail: Burton.Drayer@mountsinai.org.

DRAYTON, JOHN N., publishing executive; b. Adelaide, Australia, Mar. 6, 1944; m. Carol L. Pederson, 1972; 5 children. BA, Brigham Young U., 1969. Missionary Ch. of Jesus Christ of Latter-day Saints, Ctrl. Brit. Mission, 1963-65; mng. editor Brigham Young U. Press, Provo, Utah, 1972-80; asst. dir., editor-in-chief U. Okla. Press, Norman, 1981-97, dir., 1998—. Mem. faculty Denver U. Pub. Inst., 2004—05. Recipient award of merit, Western History Assn., 2002. Office: U Okla Press 2800 Venture Dr Norman OK 73069-8216 Office Phone: 405-325-3189. Business E-Mail: jdrayton@ou.edu.

DRAYTON, WILLIAM, social entrepreneur, lawyer, management consultant; b. NYC, June 15, 1943; s. William A. and Joan (Bergere) D. BA, Harvard U., 1965; MA, Oxford (Eng.) U., 1967; JD, Yale U., 1970. Bar: NY 1971, DC 1976. Cons. McKinsey and Co., Inc., N.Y.C., 1970-77, of counsel, 1981-87; vis. assoc. prof. law Stanford U., 1975-76; lectr. John F. Kennedy Sch. of Govt., Harvard U.; also dir. Harvard Regulatory and Mgmt. Group, 1976-77; cons. White House Domestic Policy Coun., 1977; asst. adminstr. for planning and mgmt. EPA, 1977-81; pres. Environ. Safety, Washington, 1981-89, chair, 1989—; pres., founder Ashoka: Innovators for the Pub., Arlington, Va., 1980-2001, chair, CEO, 2001—. Nat. staff mem. Hubert H. Humphrey Presdl. Campaign, Washington, 1968; dir. Corp. for Fiscal Policy, 1971-75; founder, chmn. Yale Legis. Svcs.; mem. adv. coun. Carnegie Commn. Sci., Tech. and Govt., 1990-96. Contbr. articles to profl. jours. Pres. Ams. in India for McGovern, 1972; mem. Carter-Mondale Policy Planning, 1976, Carter-Mondale Govt. Reorgn. Transition Group, 1976-77; dep. dir. for issues Mondale-Ferraro campaign, 1984; mem. energy and environment com. Dem. Nat. Com., 1982-86; bd. dirs. Oxfam Am., 1985-89, Appropriate Tech. Internat., 1988-97, chmn. bd. dirs., 1989-97; trustee Black Rock Forest (formerly Harvard Forest), N.Y.; chmn. bd. dirs. Youth Venture, 1994—; founder, chair Get Am. Working!, 1997—; pres. Save EPA, Washington, 1981-83; chair Cmty. Greens, 2000—; founder, dir. Social Entrepreneur Assocs., 1998—. Recipient Ann. award for Entrepreneurial Excellence Yale U. Sch. Mgmt., 1987, Nat. Pub. Svc. award Nat. Acad. Pub. Adminstrn. and Am. Soc. Pub. Adminstrn., 1995, Pub. Svc. Achievement award Common Cause, 1999, Vanguard Nonprofit Lawyers award ABA, 2002, Edward A. Smith Award for Excellence in Nonprofit Leadership, 2002, Fast Co. Fast 50 award, 2004, Nat. Conservation award Nat. Wildlife Fedn., 2005, Social Entrepreneur award The Skoll Found., 2005; Henry fellow, 1965-67, MacArthur Prize fellow, 1984-89. Mem. AAAS (com. on sci. pub. policy 1973-76), Assn. Bar City N.Y., Friends of India Soc. (chmn. 1974-75), Coun. Fgn. Rels., Nat. Acad. Pub. Adminstrn., Am. Acad. Arts and Scis., Asia Soc. (contemporary affairs com. 1987-2000), India Internat. Ctr. (New Delhi), Yale Club N.Y., Harvard Club N.Y., Phi Beta Kappa. Home: 1200 N Nash St Arlington VA 22209-3616 Office: 1700 N Moore St Ste 2000 Arlington VA 22209-1921

DRAZEN, JEFFREY MARK, medical educator; b. St. Louis, May 19, 1946; s. Yale and Sylvia (Wainer) D.; m. Erica Coburn Drazen, July 27, 1969; children: David, Daniel. BS, Tufts U., 1968; MD, Harvard U., 1972. Diplomate Am. Bd. Internal Medicine, Am. Bd. Pulmonary Medicine. Asst. prof. medicine Harvard U., Boston, 1977—81, assoc. prof. medicine, 1981—89, prof. medicine, 1989—90, Parker B. Francs prof. medicine, 1990—; asst. prof. physiology Harvard Sch. Pub. Health, 1980—81, assoc. prof. physiology, 1981—91, prof. physiology, 1991—; chief pulmonary and critical care medicine divsn. Brigham & Women's Hosps., Boston, 1985-2000; editor-in-chief New England Jour. of Medicine, 2000—. Mem. respiratory and applied physiology study sect. NIH, 1981-86, pulmonary disease adv. coun., 1988-92. NIH grantee, 1972—. Mem. Am. Soc. Clin. Investigation, Am. Thoracic Soc., Am. Physiology Soc., Am. Soc. Pharmacology and Exptl. Therapeutics, Assn. Am. Physicians, Inst. Medicine, 2004. Office: Brigham & Women's Hosp 75 Francis St Boston MA 02115-6106 also: New England Journal Medicine 10 Shattuck St Boston MA 02115 Office Phone: 781-434-7870. E-mail: jdrazen@rics.bwh.harvard.edu, jdrazen@nejm.org.

DRAZIN, DAVID BRADLEY, pianist; b. Cleve., Mar. 15, 1956; s. Sidney and Edith Drazin; m. Carol Lynn Wiggins, Jan. 26, 2002. MusB, Ohio State, 1978. Ballet class accompanist Ballet Metropolitan, Columbus, Ohio, 1980—82; pianist, composer Seeds of Fulfillment, Columbus, Ohio, 1978—82; ballet class accompanist Evanston Sch. of Ballet, Evanston, Ill., 1984—; silent film accompanist Gene Siskel, Chgo., 1985—; composer, writer, performer Famous in the Future, Chgo., 1989—2000; pianist Jesse Scinto and the Dignitaries, Chgo., 2000—; ballet class accompanist Northwestern U., Evanston, Ill., 2002—. Guest silent film accompanist Pordenone Silent Film Festival, Italy, 2003, Italy, 04. Mem.: Am. Recorded Sound Collections, Internat. Assn. of Jazz Record Collectors, Chgo. Fed. of Musicians. Avocation: collecting 78 rpm records. E-mail: carseymour@aol.com.

DRAZIN, LISA, real estate and corporate investment banker, financial consultant; b. Washington, Nov. 26, 1953; d. Sidney and Bernice Ann (Jeweler) D. AB with honors, Wellesley Coll., 1976; MBA, George Washington U., 1980. Chartered fin. analyst. Securities analyst Geico, Inc., Chevy Chase, Md., 1982; mng. prin. Jefferson Securities Ltd., Bethesda, Md., 1983; chmn., CEO Drazin & Co., Inc., Bethesda, 1983-89, Drazin Properties, Inc., Bethesda, 1985-89, Drazin Securities, Inc., Bethesda, 1985-88, Woodmont Asset Mgmt. Inc., 1989—. Affiliate Montgomery County Bd. Realtors; real estate investment banker Restructuring Fed. Deposit Ins. Corp. Founder Ivy Connection, Washington, 1982; bd. dirs. Friends of Tel Aviv U., actine planning com. Jewish Nat. Fund; active Nat. Truste for Historic Preservation, UJA Fedn. of Greater Washington (young leadership divsn., Ruth Heritage Forum), Am. Friends Hebrew U., Jewish Inst. for Nat. Security Affairs, The Israel Project, Nat. Kidney Found., Shakespeare Theatre Guild, Music Ctr. at Strathmere. Fellow Wexner Heritage Found., Renaissance Inst., Friends for Life Benefit, Whitman Walker Clinic, Spiritual Ctr. Am., Assn. for Investment Mgmt. and Rsch., Turnaround Mgmt. Assn.; mem. Nat. Assn. Realtors, Comml. Investment Real Estate Coun., Relators Nat. Mktg. Inst., Wash. Soc. Investment Analysts, Inc., Wellesley Club (interns coord., recent grads. rep. 1981-84, Washington), Ben Gurion Club, Beta Gamma Sigma, Tau Zeta Epsilon. Office: Woodmont Asset Mgmt Inc 6403 Kirby Rd Bethesda MD 20817-5523 Office Phone: 301-718-6400. Personal E-mail: lisa.drazin@verizon.net.

DRAZIN, MICHAEL PETER, mathematician, researcher; b. London, June 5, 1929; arrived in U.S.A., 1957; s. Isaac and Leah Drazin; m. Carol Margaret Vanstone, July 20, 1981 (div. Dec. 1994); m. Catherine Annabel Freeman, Oct. 26, 2001. BA with 1st class hons., Cambridge U., 1950, MA, PhD, Cambridge U., 1953. Scientific officer Royal Naval Scientific Svc., Teddington, England, 1953—55; rsch. fellow Trinity Coll., Cambridge, England, 1955—57; vis. lectr. N.W. Univ., Evanston, Ill., 1957—58; sr. scientist Rsch. Inst. Advanced Study, Balt., 1958—62; from assoc. prof. math. to prof. emeritus Purdue U., West Lafayette, Ind., 1962—99, prof. emeritus, 1999—. Hon. rsch. fellow U. Coll., London, 1987—; referee, reviewer NSF. Contbr. articles to profl. jours. Recipient Smith's prize, Cambridge U., 1952. Mem.: Soc. Indsl. & Applied Math., Am. Math. Soc. Achievements include discovery of Drazin inverse, 1958, and of the *-order for systems with involution; extension of Maschke's theorem from groups to semigroups; quasi-inverse; core-quasi-nilpotence. Avocations: photography, music, history of technology, squash. Office: Purdue Univ Math Dept W Lafayette IN 47907

DRAZKOWSKI, MARK, food products executive; b. Ironwood, Mich., 1949; BA in Acctg., U. Minn. Acct. Alexander Grant & Co.; internal audit mgr. Honeywell, Inc.; controller Reinhart Foods, 1976—77, gen. mgr., 1977—2004, chief operating officer, 2004—. Bd. dirs. All Kitchens; chmn. Markon; past chmn. DMA. Mem.: Internat. Food Svc. Distributors. Assn. Office: Reinhart Foods 1500 St James St La Crosse WI 54602

DRAZNIN, JULES NATHAN, journalist, educator, public relations executive, consultant; b. Chgo., May 14, 1923; s. Charles G. and Goldie (Malach) D.; m. Shirley Bernstein, Apr. 9, 1950; children: Dean, Jody, Michael. Student, Wright City Coll., Chgo., 1941; BA in Journalism, Calif. State U., Northridge, 1978, MA in Higher Edn., 1984. Various journalism positions City News Bur., Chgo. Am., Chgo., 1941; promotions and publicity Balaban & Katz Theaters, Chgo., 1942-43; asst. dir pub. rels. Combined Jewish Appeal, Chgo., 1944; prin. J.N. Draznin Assocs., Chgo., 1945-50; account supr. Olian & Bronner Advt. Agy., Chgo., 1951-53; dir. advt. Chgo. Defender, Robert S. Abbott Pub. Co., 1953-55; freelance cons. Chgo., 1955-60; v.p. pub. rels. Harshe-Rotman, Chgo., 1956; pub. rels. dir. Abel and Lamensdorf Properties, Chgo., 1960-62; editor-in-chief, assoc. pub. Indsl. News Bender Publs., Calif., 1962-64; labor editor, spl. features writer Valley News and Green Sheet, Calif., 1964; ind. ins. agt. Calif., 1965-74; lectr. pub. rels. UCLA and Calif. State U., L.A.; prof. journalism and pub. rels. L.A. Trade Tech. Coll., 1975-95, chmn. lang. arts dept., 1984-90, prof. emeritus, 2003—. Prof. journalism and pub. rels. LA City Coll., LA Pierce Coll., LA Southwest Coll., East LA Coll., LA Mission Coll.; guest lectr. Calif. State U., Northridge. Coord. Mass Media AARP/Grass Roots, 1996—2003; apptd. Calif. legis. adv. team AARP, 1998—99, spokesperson on social security and medicare; 1st v.p. L.A. County Commn. on Aging; adv. coun. L.A. (Calif.) County Agy. on Aging. Mem. Assn. for Edn. in Journalism and Mass Comm., Soc. Profl. Journalists. Avocations: classical music, travel. Personal E-mail: julesdraznin@msn.com.

DR. DRE, (ANDRE YOUNG), rapper, record producer; b. LA, Feb. 18, 1965; Co-founder Ruthless Records, 1987; founder Aftermath, 1996—. Albums include (with N.W.A.) Straight Outta Compton, 1989, 100 Miles and Runnin', 1990 (EP) Efil4zaggin, 1991, (solo) The Chronic, 1993 (Grammy award Best Pop Solo for "Let Me Ride" 1994), Concrete Roots, 1994, Back N The Day, 1994, First Round Knock Out, 1996, NWA Greatest Hits, 1996, Dr. Dre Presents the Aftermath, 1996, Dr. Dre 2001, 1999; prodr. Snoop Doggy Dog's album "Doggy Style", 1993, U Can't Cee Me and California Love singles, 1996; prodr. soundtrack albums Above the Rim, 1994, Murder Was the Case, 1994, Wild Wild West, 1999, The SLim SHady Lp, 1999, The Marshall Mathers LP, 2000, Death Row: Snoop Doggy Dogg at His Best, 2001, The Eminem Show, 2002; actor Who's The Man, 1993, Ride, 1998, Whiteboyz, 1999, The Wash, 2001, Training Day, 2001. Mailing: Aftermath Entertainment 10900 Wilshire Blvd Ste 1040 Los Angeles CA 90024-6501

DREBEN, RAYA SPIEGEL, judge; b. Vienna, Dec. 3, 1927; came to U.S., 1928, naturalized, 1936; d. Shalom and Rose (Goldschmiedt) Spiegel; children: Elizabeth, Jonathan. AB magna cum laude, Radcliffe Coll., 1949; LL.B. cum laude, Harvard U., 1954. Bar: Mass. 1957, U.S. Supreme Ct. 1960. Law clk. to Judge Bailey Aldrich, U.S. Dist. Ct. for Mass., 1954-55; Bigelow fellow and instr. U. Chgo. Law Sch., 1955-56; asso. Firm Palmer & Dodge, Boston, 1964-71, partner, 1971-79; assoc. justice Mass. Appeals Ct., Boston, 1979—. Lectr. in copyright Harvard U. Law Sch., 1973-76; mem. adv. com. on copyright registration and deposit Libr. of Congress, 1993. Trustee Radcliffe Coll., 1981-89. Recipient 1st prize Nathan Burkan competition Harvard U. Law Sch., 1954, nat. winner, 1954, Haskell Cohen award for disting. jud. svc. Boston Bar Assn., 2004. Mem. ABA (chmn. com. on authors 1977-79), Am. Law Inst. (adv. on restatement, property-donative transactions), Am. Bar Found., Copyright Soc. U.S.A. (trustee 1973-76, editl. bd. bull. 1974-85), Jud. Inst. Mass. Judiciary (chmn. adv. com. 1988-96). Office: Mass Appeals Ct John Adams Courthouse 1 Pemberton Sq Boston MA 02108 Office Phone: 617-725-8556.

DREBSKY, DENNIS JAY, lawyer; b. N.Y.C., Sept. 28, 1946; s. Benjamin and Ronnie (Penso) D.; m. Norma Louise Linschitz, Aug. 16, 1970; children: Richard Michael, Joshua William Evan. BBA magna cum laude, CCNY, 1967; JD, Cornell U., 1970. Bar: N.Y. 1971, U.S. Dist. Ct. (so. dist.) N.Y. 1972, U.S. Ct. Appeals (2d cir.) 1971, U.S. Ct. Appeals (5th cir.) 1980, U.S. Ct. Appeals (9th cir.) 1982, U.S. Ct. Appeals (1st cir.) 1981, U.S. Ct. Appeals (10th cir.) 1984, U.S. Ct. Appeals (4th cir.) 1986, U.S. Ct. Appeals (D.C. cir.) 1998. Assoc. Skadden, Arps, Slate, Meagher & Flom, N.Y.C., 1970-77, ptnr., 1978-91, Clifford, Chance, Rogers & Wells, 1991—2004, Nixon Peabody, LLP, 2004—. Trustee Community Law Offices, N.Y.C., 1980—. Mem. Assn. of Bar of City of N.Y. (mem. com. on corp. reorgn. 1985—). Jewish. Avocations: reading, jogging, theater. Home: 7 Glen Hill Ct Dix Hills NY 11746-8419 Office: Nixon Peabody LLP 437 Madison Ave New York NY 10022-0800 Office Phone: 212-940-3091. Business E-Mail: ddrebsky@nixonpeabody.com.

DRECHSLER, BEATRICE KRAIN, lawyer; BA magna cum laude, Barnard U., 1984; JD cum laude, Harvard U., 1987. Bar: NY 1988, NY 1988. Ptnr. Real Estate Dept. Kaye Scholer LLP, NYC. Mem.: Internat. Coun. of Shopping Ctrs., Estate Women - NY, Inc., NY Women Execs. in Real Estate. Office: Kaye Scholer LLP 425 Park Ave New York NY 10022 Office Phone: 212-836-8146. E-mail: bdrechsler@kayescholer.com.

DRECHSLER, THOMAS, lawyer; b. Flushing, N.Y., Mar. 15, 1953; s. Arthur John and Mary Krenicky) D. B of Engring., NYU, 1974; M of Engring., Polytech Inst. N.Y., 1975; JD, Boston Coll., 1978. Bar: Mass. 1978, U.S. Dist. Ct. Mass., U.S. Ct. Appeals (1st cir.). Law clk. Mass. Superior Ct., Boston, 1978-79; asst. dist. atty. Middlesex County Dist. Attys. Office, Cambridge, Mass., 1979-83, Essex County Dist. Attys. Office, Salem, Mass., 1983-85; of counsel Finneran & Byrne, Boston, 1985-87; ptnr. Finneran, Byrne, Drechsler & O'Brien, Boston, 1987—. Mem. Nat. Assn. Criminal Defense Lawyers, Mass. Assn. Criminal Defense Lawyers, Boston Yacht Club. Avocations: sailing, skiing. Office: Finneran Byrne Drechsler & O'Brien Ea Harbor Office Park 50 Redfield St Boston MA 02122-3630

DREEBEN, MICHAEL R., federal agency administrator; b. 1954; BA, U. Wis., Madison; MA, U. Chgo.; JD, Duke U., 1981. Bar: 1982. Law clk. to Judge Jerre S. Williams US Ct. Appeals (5th cir.); asst. to solicitor gen. Office of Solicitor Gen., US Dept. Justice, Washington, DC, 1988—95, dep. solicitor gen., 1995—. Lectr. Duke Law Sch., Mich. Law Sch., U. Tex. Law Sch.; adj. prof. law Georgetown U. Recipient Atty Gen.'s Award for Disting. Svc., 1998. Office: US Dept Justice 950 Pennsylvania Ave, NW Washington DC 20530

DREES, BASTIAAN MEIJER, entomologist; b. Amsterdam, Netherlands, June 28, 1952; s. Jan Meijer and Jacoba Meijer Drees; m. Carol Frost, Oct. 30, 1953; children: Carly Jobes, Erin Lien. BA in Biology, W.Va. U., 1974, MSc in Entomology, 1976; PhD in Entomology, Ohio State U., 1980. Diplomate Am. Bd. Entomology. Ext. entomologist Tex. Agrl. Ext. Svc., Coll. Sta., Tex., 1980—; prof. dept. entomology Tex. A&M U., Coll. Sta., 1993—, coord. Tex. imported fire ant rsch. and mgmt. project dept. entomology, 1997—2002, dir. Tex. imported fire ant rsch. and mgmt. project dept. entomology, 2002—03. Author: (book) A Field Guide to Common Tex. Insects, 1998 (Tex. Reference Source award, Tex. Libr. Assn., 2001); contbr. articles to profl. jour. Recipient Faculty Disting. Achievement award in ext., Assn. Former Students of Tex. A&M U., 1996, Disting. Achievement award in ext., Entomol. Soc. Am., 1997, award for rsch. excellence, Orkin, 2001; Regents fellow, Tex. A&M U., 1000. Mem.: Southwestern Entomol. Soc. (pres. 2002), Entomol. Soc. Am. (pres. S.W. br. 2005—). Avocations: photography, music, art. Office: Texas A&M U RM 412 Dept Entomology College Station TX 77843-2475 Office Phone: 979-845-7026. E-mail: b-drees@tamu.edu.

DREES, DAVID G., construction executive; Grad., Trinity Coll., 1982; MBA, Xavier U., 1984. Joined The Drees Co., Dallas, 1984, project mgr. comml. div. Ky., town home develop. mgr., v.p. Cin. region; pres. The Drees Co, Ft. Mitchell, Ky., 1994—, CEO, 2000—. Office: 211 Grandview Dr Fort Mitchell KY 41017-2755*

DREES, RALPH, construction executive; m. Irma Drees; 5 children. Joined The Drees Co., Dallas, 1984, CEO Ft. Mitchell, Ky., 1968—2000, chmn., 2000—. Mem. Erlanger City Coun., Ky., 1965—67, No. Ky. Area Planning Commn., Kenton County Airport Bd.; judge exec. Kenton County, 2004—. Named National Builder of the Year, Profl. Builder Mag., 1991, Northern Kentuckian of the Year, Covington Cath. HS Alumni Assn., 1993, Person of the Year, No. Ky. C. of C., 1999; named to Greater Cin. Bus. Hall of Fame, 2000. Office: 211 Grandview Dr Fort Mitchell KY 41017-2755*

DREHER, FRANK H., JR., retired optician; b. Phila., Sept. 21, 1923; s. Frank H. and Mary Catherine Dreher; m. Kathryn Marie Dreher, Aug. 27, 1955; children: Frank H. Dreher, III, George W. Modern Bus., Alexander Hamilton Inst., New York, New York, 1962; Optics and Math., Drexel Inst., Philadelphia, Pennsylvania, 1948. Real estate salesperson Craig J. Turnbull Atty., Camden, NJ, 1950—54; opthalmic dispenser Meserall Opticians, Haddonfield, NJ, 1969—77, hearing aid dispenser, 1974—77; opthalmic dispenser Cole Nat. Corp., Willingboro, NJ, 1977—87, Dr. David J. Mellish, O.D., Williamstown, NJ, 1987—98. Creative writing tchr. Salem C.C., Carneys Point, NJ, 1996—97. Contbr. articles to profl. mags. Scout master Boy Scouts of Am., Erial, NJ, 1949—51; sunday sch. supt. Episcopal churches, Clementon and Chews Landing, NJ, 1952—79. T/4 US Armed Forces, 1943—46, New Guinea and Luzon. Mem.: The Internat. Order of St. Luke the Physician. Independent. Episcopal Methodist. Avocations: writing, classical music, travel, cooking. Home: 248 Route 40 Lot F5 Newfield NJ 08344

DREHER, FREDERICK W., lawyer; b. Bryn Mawr, Pa., Aug. 21, 1940; AB, Princeton U., 1962; LLB, Harvard U., 1965. Bar: Pa. 1966, US Ct. Appeals 3rd Cir., US Dist. Ct. Ea. Dist. Pa. Assoc. Duane Morris LLP, Phila., 1965—70, ptnr., 1970—, chair corp. dept., 1982—98, mem. partners bd., mem. exec. com. Bd. dirs. Donegal Mutual Ins. Co., Marietta, Pa. Mem.: Pa. Bar Assn. (corp., banking and bus. law sect.). Office: Duane Morris LLP One Liberty Pl Philadelphia PA 19103-7396 Office Phone: 215-979-1234. Office Fax: 215-979-1020. Business E-Mail: fwdreher@duanemorris.com.

DREHER, MELANIE CREAGAN, dean, nursing educator; BSN magna cum laude, L.I. U.; D in Anthropology, Columbia U. Mem. faculty Columbia U., N.Y.C.; dean Sch. Nursing, William Ryan disting. prof. U. Miami; dean Sch. Nursing, prof. U. Mass., 1988—97; dean Coll. Nursing, prof. U. Iowa, 1997—2002; dean Univ. of Iowa Sch. of Nursing, 2002—. Mem. Council on Public Relations for the National Institutes of Health, Washington, 1999—2001. Mem. editl. bds. various profl. jours. Recipient May A. Brunson award, CASE award. Mem. Sigma Theta Tau (pres. Beta Zeta chpt. 1995). Office: U Iowa Office Dean 101F NB Iowa City IA 52242

DREIER, DAVID TIMOTHY, congressman; b. Kansas City, Mo., July 5, 1952; s. H. Edward and Joyce (Yeomans) D. BA cum laude, Claremont McKenna Coll., 1975; MA in Am. Govt., Claremont Grad. Sch., 1976. Dir. corp. rels. Claremont McKenna Coll., 1975-78; dir. mktg. and govt. rels. Indsl. Hydro, San Dimas, Calif., 1978-80; mem. U.S. Congress from 26th (formerly 33rd) Calif. dist., 1981—; v.p. Dreier Devel. Co., Kansas City, Mo., 1985—. Vice chmn. rules of the house com., 1995-99, chmn. rules com., 1999—; bd. dirs. Internat. Rep. Inst.; mem. spkrs. steering com. Recipient Golden Bulldog award Watchdogs of the Treasury, 1981-99, Taxpayers Friends award Nat. Taxpayers Union, 1981-99, Clean Air Champion award Sierra Club, 1988. Republican. Office: US Ho Reps 233 Cannon Ho Office Bldg Washington DC 20515-0001*

DREIER, KEITH LYNN, not-for-profit fundraiser; s. Thomas Bernard and Julia Lucille Dreier; m. Nancy Ellen Jackson, June 22, 1975; children: Sarah Lynn, Julie Marie. BS in Music Edn., S.W. Mo. State U., Springfield, 1973. Student dir. / band and choir S.W. Mo State U., Springfield, 1970—73; music tchr. Aurora Pub. Schools, Mo., 1973—86; fundraising salesperson Henco, Inc., Selmer, Tenn., 1986—91; music dept. chair Cmty. United Meth. Ch., Columbia, Mo., 2000—03; fundraising sales and svc. staff Stonebridge Fundraising, Columbia, Mo., 1991—. Product devel. adv. bd. Cherrydale Farms, Inc, Pennsburg, Pa., 1995—97; Mo. conv. coord. Cherrydale Farms, Allentown, Pa., 1998—; conf. worship com. mem. United Meth. Ch., Columbia, Mo., 2001—02. Dir. Cmty. United Meth. Youth choir. Sgt. first class Mo. Army N.G., 1970—2001, Springfield, Mo. Decorated Letter Of Commendation Mo Army N.G.; named one of Outstanding Young Men of Am., 1983; recipient Most Improved Salesman award, Cherrydale Farms, 1994. Mem.: Mo. N.G. Assn. (life), Music Educators Nat. Conf. (sw dist. pres. 1983—85). Home: 4413 Rockhampton Cir Columbia MO 65203 Office: Stonebridge Fundraising 4413 Rockampton Cir Columbia MO 65203

DREIER, R. CHAD, construction and mortgage company executive; BSBA, Loyola Marymount U., 1969. Exec. v.p. Golden West Holding Corp., L.A., 1979-80; v.p., dir. devel. Daon Corp., 1980-85; exec. v.p., CFO Kaufman and Broad Home Corp., 1986; chmn. Kaufman & Broad Mortgage Corp.; pres., CEO The Ryland Group, Inc., Woodland Hills, Calif., 1993—, chmn., 1994—. Bd. Occidental Petroleum Corp.; chmn. bd. trustees Loyola Marymount U.; adv. bd. Joint Ctr. Housing Studies, Harvard U. 1st lt. USAF, 1969—72. Avocation: sports. Office: Ryland Group Suite 400 24025 Park Sorrento Calabasas CA 91302*

DREIFKE, GERALD EDMOND, electrical engineering educator; b. St. Louis, June 21, 1918; s. Herman A. and Anna Margaret (Hollenbeck) D.; m. Lorraine Ann Feldhaus, June 9, 1951; children: Mark A., Matthew G., Laura Maria, Anne Marie. BS, MS, Washington U., 1948, DSc (NSF fellow), 1961. Registered profl. engr., Mo. Layout man Curtiss-Wright Co., St. Louis, 1936-39, design engr., 1939-44; layout man Douglas Aircraft Co., 1939; instr. engring. St. Louis U., 1948-50, asst. prof., 1950-54, assoc. prof. elec. engring., dir. grad. program elec. engring., 1954-61, prof. elec. engring., 1961-71; mgr. r & d Union Electric Co., 1971-77; cons., 1977—; vis. prof. physics U. Mo.-St. Louis, 1979-94. Cons. Emerson Electric Co., 1951-71, Monsanto Co., 1961-71; mem. tech. staff Bell Telephone Labs. NJ, summer 1963 Editor-in-chief: ISA Transactions, 1966-89; contbr. articles profl. jours. Mem. St. Louis County Bd. Elec. Examiners, Gov.'s Sci. Adv. Com. Mo. Served with USNR, 1944-45. Recipient cert. of merit WPB, 1942; rsch. grants NSF, 1964; rsch. grants NASA, 1965; rsch. grants Monsanto Co., 1965-69; Nancy McNair-Ring Outstanding Faculty award St. Louis U. chpt. Gamma Pi Epsilon, 1965-66 Fellow ISA; mem. Am. Soc. Engring. Edn. (past sec., com. chmn.), IEEE (past chmn. St. Louis sect.), Mo. Soc. Profl. Engrs. (past pres. St. Louis chpt., Engr. of Yr. St. Louis chpt. 1977), St. Louis Elec. Bd. Trade, Sigma Xi, Tau Beta Pi, Eta Kappa Nu, Pi Mu Epsilon, Phi Eta Sigma. Home and Office: 6 Westmoreland Pl Saint Louis MO 63108-1228 Office Phone: 314-361-2321.

DREILING, RICHARD, retail executive; b. 1953; Various mgmt. positions Safeway, Inc., 1969—97; pres. Vons (divsn. Safeway, Inc.), 1998—99; exec. v.p. mfg. and distbn. Safeway, Inc., 1999—2003; chief ops. officer, exec. v.p. Longs Drugs Stores Corp., 2003—. Office: Longs Drug Stores PO Box 5222 Walnut Creek CA 94596

DREIMANIS, ALEKSIS, emeritus geology educator; b. Valmiera, Latvia, Aug. 13, 1914; s. Peteris and Marta Eleonora (Leitis) D.; m. Anita Kana, Apr. 18, 1942; children: Mara Dreimanis Love, Aija Dreimanis Downing. Mag. rer. nat., U. Latvia, 1938; D.Sc. (hon.), U. Waterloo, Ont., Can., 1969, U. Western Ont., 1980; D Geography (hon.), U. Latvia, 1991, Habilitation, 1942. Asst. to pvt. docent U. Latvia, 1937-44; mil. geologist Latvian Legion, 1944-45; assoc. prof. geology Baltic U., Hamburg and Pinneberg, Germany, 1946-48; mem. faculty U. Western Ont., London, Can., 1948—, prof. geology, 1964-80, prof. emeritus, 1980—. Pres. Commn. on Genesis and Lithology of Quaternary Deposits, Internat. Union Quaternary Research, 1973-87; cons. in field. Assoc. editor Geosci. Can., 1976-78, Quaternary Sci. Revs., 1981-87, Tech. Rev. (in Latvian), 1978—, Latgeo (in Latvian), 1990-98, Geology Proc. Estonian Acad. Scis., 1991-97, Latvijas Geologijas Vestis, 2000—02; contbr. articles to profl. jours. Decorated officer Three Star Order of Latvia; recipient Centennial medal (Can.); Queen Elizabeth II 25th Anniversary medal; Centennial medal Geol. Survey of Finland, U. Helsinki medal; Albrecht Penck medal, teaching award Ont. Confedn. Univ. Faculty Assns., 1978. Fellow Royal Soc. Can. (Disting.), Geol. Assn. Can. (Logan medal 1978), Geol. Soc. Am. (Disting. Career award Quarternary geology and geomorphology divsn. 1987); mem. Swedish Geol. Soc. (hon. corr. mem.), Can. Quaternary Assn. (W.A. Johnston medal 1989), Am. Quarternary Assn. (pres. 1981-83), Assn. Advancement Baltic Studies, Internat. Union for Quaternary Rsch. (hon.), Latvian Nat. Fedn. Can. (chmn. coun. 1953-71, hon. mem.), Latvian Acad. Scis. (fgn. hon.), Latvian Cultural Found. (exec. com. 1973-77), London Latvian Soc. (pres. 1948—), Fraternity Lidums (pres. 1935-36, editor newsletter 1969—), Geol. Soc. Finland (hon. corr. mem.), Latvian Am. Assn. Univ. Profs. and Scientists (pres. 1983-85), Geog. Assn. Latvia (hon.), Assn. Latvian Geologists (hon.), Baltic Rsch. Inst. (hon. corr. mem.), Estonian Geol. Soc. (hon.). Home: 287 Neville Dr London ON Canada N6G 1C2 Office: U Western Ont Dept Earth Scis London ON Canada N6A 5B7

DREIMANN, LEONHARD, manufacturing executive; b. Riga, Latvia; D. in Mktg., Melbourne U., Australia. Pres. Salton Inc., a wholly-owned subs. SEVKO Inc., 1987—88; mng. dir. Salton Australia Pty. Ltd., 1988—93; founder Salton Inc., Lake Forest, Ill., 1988—, pres., 1988—98, CEO, 1988—, dir. Dir. Glacier Water Systems, 1987—93; officer, dir. Glacier Holdings Inc., 1988—93, Salton Time, 1989—93. Recipient Ernst & Young Entrepreneur Of The Year for Ill./North West Ind., 1999. Achievements include the successful mktg. of The George Foreman Grill, Breadman, Juiceman, Ingraham, Farberware and Toastmaster - growing the co. from $8 million to $1 billion in sales. Office: Salton Inc 1955 West Field Ct Lake Forest IL 60045*

DREISBACH, DANIEL LIVINGSTONE, lawyer, educator; b. Yadakunya, Nigeria, July 9, 1959; s. John Ardo and Bettie Short Dreisbach; m. Joyce Cowley, Sept. 5, 1987; children: Mollie Abigail, Moriah Esther. BA, U. S.C., 1981; DPhil, Oxford (Eng.) U., 1985; JD, U. Va., 1988. Jud. clk. U.S. Ct. Appeals (4th cir.), Columbia, S.C., 1988-89; pvt. practice Charlottesville, Va., 1989-91; prof. Am. U., Washington, 1991—. Author: Real Threat and Mere Shadow: Religious Liberty and the First Amendment, 1987, Thomas Jefferson and the Wall of Separation Between Church and State, 2002; editor: Religion and Politics in the Early Republic, 1996; co-editor: Religion and Political Culture in Jefferson's Virginia, 2000. Rhodes scholar, 1981-84; Andrew W. Mellon fellow, 1998-99. Mem. Am. Polit. Sci. Assn., Va. State Bar. Office: Am U Sch Pub Affairs 4400 Massachusetts Ave NW Washington DC 20016-8043 Office Fax: 202-885-2907.

DREISBACH, JOHN GUSTAVE, investment banker; b. Paterson, NJ, Apr. 24, 1939; s. Gustave John and Rose Catherine (Koehler) D.; m. Janice Lynn Petitjean; children: John Gustave Jr., Christopher Erik. BA, NYU, 1963. With Dreyfus & Co., 1959-62, Shields & Co., Inc., 1965-68, Model, Roland & Co., Inc., N.Y.C., 1968-72, F. Eberstadt & Co., Inc., N.Y.C., 1972-74; v.p., trust officer Bessemer Trust Co., 1974—76; pres. Cmty. Housing Capital, Inc., 1978-80; chmn., pres. John G. Dreisbach, Inc., Santa Fe, 1980—, JDG Housing Corp., 1982—, JGD Mgmt. Corp., 1996—. Gen. ptnr. numerous real estate ltd. partnerships; bd. dirs., pres. The Santa Fe Investment Conf., 1986—; assoc. Sta. KNME-TV. Mem. Santa Fe Cmty. Devel. Commn. with USAR, with USAFR, 1964. Mem. Internat. Assn. for Fin. Planning, Nat. Assn. Securities Dealers, Inc., NYU Alumni Assn., N.Mex. First, Friends of Vieilles Maisons Francaises Inc., Mensa, Santa Fe C. of C., Augustan Soc., St. Bartholomew's Cmty. Club, Essex Club, Hartford Club, Amigos del Alcalde Club. Republican. Mem. Episcopal Ch. Avocations: travel, art, architecture, classical music, shotokan karate (1st dan). Home: Elm Cottage Hemsford-Littlehempston Totnes Devon TQ9 6NE England Office: 369 Montezuma Ave No 215 Santa Fe NM 87501-2626 Home Fax: (01803) 762-322. Personal E-mail: john@dreisbach.freeserve.co.uk.

DRELL, LEA ARMSTRONG, lawyer; b. Chgo., Oct. 6, 1934; d. Sidney Citron and Mollie Rose Armstrong; m. Ronald Edward Drell, Mar. 28, 1953 (div. Mar. 28, 1978); children: Sydney Reiner, Michael, Murray; m. George McCarter Stuhr, Jan. 18, 1987. BA, Nat. Coll. Edn., 1970, MEd, 1978; JD, John Marshall Law Sch., 1985. Bar: Ill. 85. 7th grade sci. tchr. Wilmette (Ill.) Jr. H.S., 1975—76, 1977—85; 8th grade math. tchr. Red Oak Jr. H.S., Northbrook, Ill., 1976—77; assoc. Stuhr Law Offices, Joliet, Ill., 1985—86; ptnr. Stuhr & Drell, Joliet, 1986—. Bd. dirs. Will County Legal Assistance, Joliet. Bd. dirs. Joliet Jewish Congregation. Recipient Pro Bono award, Will County Legal Assistance, 1990, 2000. Office: Stuhr and Drell 54 N Ottawaw St Joliet IL 60432 E-mail: stuhr_drell@earthlink.net.

DRELL, PERSIS, physicist; B, Wellesley Coll.; PhD in Atomic Physics, U. Calif., Berkeley, 1983. Postdoctoral rsch. assoc. in high-energy physics Lawrence Berkeley Nat. Lab., 1983—88; asst. prof. physics Cornell U., 1988—97, prof. physics, 1997—, dep. dir., Lab. Nuclear Studies, chair, Synchrotron Radiation Com., Lab. Nuclear Studies; mem. program adv. com. Stanford Linear Accelerator Ctr. (SLAC), Menlo Park, Calif., 1993—95, assoc. dir., 2002—, current chair, scientific policy com. Leader of Cornell Group, Wilson Lab. CLEO (one of the world's most advanced particle detectors), 2000. Named One of the 50 Most Important Women in Science, Discover Mag., 2002. Office: Stanford Linear Accelerator Ctr 2575 Sand Hill Rd Menlo Park CA 94025 Address: Stanford Linear Accelerator Ctr PO Box 20450 Stanford CA 94309 Office Phone: 650-926-3300.

DRELL, SIDNEY DAVID, physicist, researcher; b. Atlantic City, N.J., Sept. 13, 1926; s. Tulla and Rose (White) D.; m. Harriet Stainback, Mar. 22, 1952; children: Daniel White, Persis Sydney, Joanna Harriet. AB, Princeton U., 1946; MA, U. Ill., 1947, PhD, 1949, DSc (hon.), 1981, Tel Aviv U., 2001, Weizman Inst. Sci., 2001. Rsch. assoc. U. Ill., 1949-50; instr. physics Stanford U., 1950-52, assoc. prof., 1956-60, prof., 1960-63, Lewis M. Terman prof. and fellow, 1979-84; co-dir. Stanford U. Ctr. for Internat. Security and Arms Control, 1983-89; prof. Stanford Linear Accelerator Ctr., 1963-98, dep. dir., 1969-98, exec. head theoretical physics, 1969-86, prof. emeritus, 1998—. Rsch. assoc. MIT, 1952-53, asst. prof., 1953-56, adv. bd. Lincoln Lab., 1985-90; vis. scientist Guggenheim fellow CERN Lab., Switzerland, 1961, U. Rome, 1972; vis. prof., Loeb lectr. Harvard U., 1962, 70; vis. Schrodinger prof. theoretical physics U. Vienna, 1975; vis. fellow All Souls Coll., Oxford, 1979; I.I. Rabi vis. prof. Columbia U., 1984; adj. prof. engring., pub. policy Carnegie Mellon U., 1989-96; cons. Office Sci. and Tech., 1960-73, Office Sci. and Tech. Policy, 1977-82, ACDA, 1969-81; adviser NSC, 1973-81, Office Tech. Assessment U.S. Congress, 1975-90, House Armed Svcs. Com., 1990-93, Senate Select Com. on Intelligence, 1990-93; founding mem. JASON, 1960—; mem. high energy physics adv. panel Dept. Energy, 1973-86, chmn., 1974-82, energy rsch. adv. bd., 1978-80; mem. Carnegie Commn. on Sci., Tech. and Govt., 1988-93, Pres.'s Fgn. Intelligence Adv. Bd., 1993-2001; Richtmyer lectr. to Am. Assn. Physics Tchrs., San Francisco, 1978; Danz lectr. U. Wash., 1983; Hans Bethe lectr. Cornell U., 1988; chmn. U.C. pres. coun. on nat. labs., 1992-99; chmn. internat. adv. bd. Inst. Global Conflict and Cooperation, U. Calif., 1990-93; mem. bd. dirs. Internat. Sci. Found., 1993-96; chair sr. rev. bd. Intelligence Tech. Innovation Ctr., 2001-02; mem. adv. com. Nat. Nuc. Secuirty Adminstrn., 2001-03; mem. sr. adv. group LANL, 2003—. Author: (books) Electromagnetic Structure of Nucleons, 1961, The Reagan Strategic Defense Initiative: a Technical, Political and Arms Control Assessment, 1985, In the Shadow of the bomb: Physics and Arms Control, 1993, The Gravest Danger: Nuclear Weapons, 2003, (book foreward) Explosion Aboard the Iowa, 2001; co-author (with Sergei P. Kapitza): (books) Sakharov Remembered: A Tribute by Friends and Colleagues, 1991; editor: The New Terror: Facing the Threat of Biological and Chemical Weapons, 1999, The Gravest Danger. Trustee Inst. Advanced Study, Princeton, 1974-83; bd. govs. Weizmann Inst. Sci., Rehovoth, Israel, 1970—; bd. dirs. Ann. Revs., Inc., 1976-97; mem. Pres. Sci. Adv. Com., 1966-70. Recipient Ernest Orlando Lawrence Meml. award and medal for rsch. in theoretical physics AEC, 1972, Alumni award for disting. svc. in engring. U. Ill., 1973, Alumni Achievement award, 1988, Hilliard Roderick prize in sci., arms. control and internat. security AAAS, 1993, Woodrow Wilson award Princeton U., 1994, Ettore Majorana-Erice Sci. for Peace prize, 1994, Gian Carlo Wick medal, 1996, Disting Assoc. award U.S. Dept. Environ., 1997, I. Pomeranchuk prize, 1998, Linus Pauling medal Stanford U., 1999-2000, Enrico Fermi award, 2000, Heinz R. Pagels Human Rights of Scientists award, 2001, Nat. Intelligence Disting. Svc. medal, 2001, William O. Baker award Security Affairs Support Assn., 2001, Heinz award for publlic policy, 2005, others; MacArthur fellow, 1984-89, Sr. fellow Hoover Instn., 1998—. Fellow Am. Phys. Soc. (pres. 1986, Leo Szilard award for physics in the pub. interest 1980); mem. AAAS, NAS, Am. Acad. Arts and Scis., Am. Philos. Soc., Arms Control Assn. (bd. dirs. 1978-93), Coun. on Fgn. Rels., Aspen Strategy Group (emeritus 1991), Academia Eruopea. Office: Stanford Linear Accelerator Ctr 2575 Sand Hill Rd MS 80 Menlo Park CA 94025-7015

DREMAN, DAVID NASANIEL, investment counselor, security analyst; b. Winnipeg, Man., Can., May 6, 1936; came to U.S., 1965; s. Joseph and Rae (Trone) D.; m. Holly Altner, Mar. 24, 1984; children: David Nasaniel Jr., Meredith Wakefield. B of Commerce, U. Man., 1957; postgrad. in Fin., Columbia U., 1958. Security analyst Dreman & Co., Winnipeg, 1958-64; sr. editor Value Line Investment Svc., N.Y.C., 1965-67; sr. investment officer J & W Seligman, N.Y.C., 1967-75; dir. N.Y. rsch. Rauscher Pierce Refsnes, N.Y.C., 1976-78; founder, pres. Dreman Value Mgmt. L.P., N.Y.C., 1978-91, chmn., chief investment officer, 1991-95; chmn. Dreman Value Advisors, Inc., 1995-97; founder, chmn., chief investment officer Dreman Value Mgmt., LLC, 1997—. Author: Psychology of the Stock Market, 1977, Contrarian Investment Strategy, 1979, The New Contrarian Investment Strategy, 1980; columnist Forbes mag., 1980—. Founder, pres. David N. Dreman Found., 1986—; bd. govs. India House. Mem. Fin. Analysts Fedn., N.Y. Soc. Security Analysts, N.Y. Stock Exch. Luncheon Club, Navesink Country Club (Middletown, N.J.), Seabright Lawn Tennis and Cricket Club (Rumson, N.J.), Monmouth Beach (N.J.) Bath and Tennis Club. Office: Dreman Value Mgmt LLC 3 Harding Rd Red Bank NJ 07701-2004

DRENGLER, WILLIAM ALLAN JOHN, lawyer; b. Shawano, Wis., Nov. 18, 1949; s. William J. and Vera J. (Simmonds) D.; m. Kathleen A. Hintz, June 18, 1983; children: Ryan, Jeffrey, Brittany. BA, Am. U., 1972; JD, Marquette U., 1976. Bar: Wis. 1976, U.S. Dist. Ct. (ea. and we. dists.) Wis. 1976. Assoc. Herrling, Swain & Drengler, Appleton, Wis., 1976-78; dist. atty. Outagamie County, Appleton, 1979-81; corp. counsel Marathon County, Wausau, Wis., 1981-96, Drengler Law Firm, Wausau, Wis., 1997—. Vice chmn. Wis. Equal Rights Coun., 1978-83, Wis. Coun. on Criminal Justice, Madison, 1983-87. Nat. pres. Future Bus. Leaders Am., 1967-68; mem. nat. Dem. delegation, 1974-76, Wis. Dem, Madison State Convention Del., 1972-, convention co-chair, 1980, convention parliamentarian, 1986-; mem. adminstrv. com. Wis. Dems., Madison, 1977-81, 86-88; chmn. local Selective Svc. Bd., Wausau, 1982-89; mem. adv. bd. Wausau Salvation Army, 1986—; judge adv. officer Wis. Army N.G., 1989-96; bd. dirs. Wausau Youth/Little League Baseball, 1988—, team mgr., 1994-2002; mem. Troop 453 com. troop 453 Samoset coun. Boy Scouts Am., 2000—. Mem. ABA (chair com. on govt. lawyers, sect. state and local govt. 1991-93, bylaws com. govt. and pub. sect. lawyers divsn. 1993-98), KC, Nat. Assn. County Civil Attys. (dir. 1986-88, v.p. 1988-91, pres. 1991-92), Nat. Assn. Counties (bd. dirs. 1991-92, taxation and fin. steering com. 1991-93, deferred compensation adv. com. 1993-95, justice and pub. safety steering com. 1993-94), State Bar Wis. (govt. lawyers divsn., bd. dirs. 1982-86, sec. 1986-87, pres. 1989-91, professionalism com. 1987-91, 92-2000, solo and small firm practice com. 2001--), Kiwanis (lt. gov. 1985-86, club pres. 1989-90, chair past lt. govs. coun. 1990-91), Wausau Elks (parliamentarian 2000-03), Kiwanis Internat. Found. (Hixon Fellowship Award 2001). Roman Catholic. Avocations: baseball, camping, fishing, tennis, golf. Office: PO Box 5152 609 Scott St Wausau WI 54402-5152

DRENKARD, KAREN NEIL, nursing administrator; b. Alexandria, La., Mar. 31, 1958; d. William John Jr. and Barbara (Light) Neil; m. Graham Drenkard, Dec. 6, 1980; children: Jennifer Lynn, Scott William, Mark Bradbury. BSN, Russell Sage Coll., 1980; MSN in Nursing Adminstrn., Marymount U., 1986. RN, Va.; cert. profl. in healthcare quality. Neurosurgery dir. Inova Fairfax (Va.) Hosp., 1987-88, patient care adminstr., adminstrn. dir., 1988—92; quality cons. Inova Health Sys., Falls Church, Va., 1992—98, dir. patient care delivery sys., 1999, chief nurse exec., 1999—. Mem. quality improvement com., documentation com., patient care com. Fairfax Hosp. Mem. Nat. Assn. Healthcare Profls., Sigma Theta Tau, Delta Epsilon Sigma. Home: 3114 Wynford Dr Fairfax VA 22031-2826

DRENNEN, EILEEN MOIRA, editor; b. Suffern, N.Y., May 27, 1956; d. D.A. and M. Eileen (Connolly) D. AA, Dutchess C.C., N.Y., 1978; BA in English, Fla. State U., 1983. Writer Fla. Flambeau, Tallahassee, 1980-84, editor, 1984-86; features editor Marietta (Ga.) Daily Jour., 1986-87; copy editor Atlanta Jour.-Constn., Atlanta, 1987-89, asst. arts editor, 1989-90, Leisure editor, 1990-93, Weekend Preview editor, asst. features editor, 1993-96, Dixie Living editor, 1997-2000; arts and entertainment editor Atlanta Jour.-Constn., Atlanta, 2000—, dep. features editor, 2001—. Recipient Hon. Mention award Fla. Press Club, 1982, Spotlight award Women in Comm., 1986; AAUW scholar, 1978. Office: Atlanta Jour-Constn Feature Desk 72 Marietta St NW Atlanta GA 30303-2804 Business E-Mail: edrennen@ajc.com.

DRENNEN, JEAN COBBLE, retired public relations executive, linguist; b. Rome, Ga., Sept. 30, 1924; d. James Ernest and Vorus Frost (Ware) Cobble; m. Gaston Cliff Drennen, Nov. 21, 1948 (dec. Sept. 1994); 1 child, Cheryl Jen. BA, U. Tenn., 1946, MA, 1965. Publicist Curt Weinberg Assoc., N.Y.C., 1946-47; freelance columnist N.Y.C., 1947-49; ad copywriter Miller's Inc., Knoxville, Tenn., 1949-51; pub. rels. dir. United Fund, Knoxville, Tenn., 1955-58; instr. dialect studies Knox County Schs., Knoxville, Tenn., 1961-66; copy dir. Lavidge Assocs., Knoxville, Tenn., 1967-73; program devel dir. Medic Regional Blood Ctr., Knoxville, Tenn., 1974-89. Author, prodr. (video, poster) What Good Is A Blood Donor, 1984 (10th anniversary choice of Am. Blood Commn. 1985); (book, audio tape) Speaking English: A Sound Approach, 1965; author book: The Company Blood Drive Coordinator's Guidebook, 1987; contbr. articles to profl. jours. Adv. United Way; mem. nat. pub. rels. bd. United Funds of Am., 1956—. Recipient 36 1st place awards for TV and newspaper ads Greater Knox Ad Club, 1970-73. Mem. Am. Assn. Blood Banks (nat. pub. rels. bd. 1985—). Avocations: travel, writing. Home: 8101 Elderberry Dr Knoxville TN 37919-7033

DRENNEN, WILLIAM MILLER, JR., cultural organization administrator, film producer, writer; b. Charleston, W.Va., Nov. 5, 1942; s. William Miller and Margaret (Morton) D.; m. Sarah Polk Wilson, Nov. 27, 1969; children: Zachary Polk, Samuel Boyd. BArch., Yale U., 1964; postgrad., George Washington U., 1977, U. Charleston, 1978, W.Va. Grad. Coll., 1989-92, MA in Humanities, 1993. Freelance writer, film maker, 1967-69; v.p. Communication Corps, Inc., Washington, 1969-79; pres. Briar Mountain Coal and Coke Co., Charleston, 1980-89; founder, pres. Max Media, Inc., Charleston, 1984-89; commr. W.Va. Culture and History Div., 1989—97; instr. history W.Va. State Coll., 1997—2001; freelance writer, prodr., cons., 2001—. Mng. gen. ptnr. C&D Enterprises, 1979—; pres. Cox Morton Co., 1980-89; past pres., founder W.Va. Internat. Film Festival, Charleston, 1986-89; owner, sec., real estate agt. Greg Didden Assocs., Shepherdstown, W.Va., 2003-. Author: One Kanawha Valley Bank, 2002, Red, White, Black, and Blue: A Dual Memoir of Race and Class in Appalachia, 2004; cameraman (film) Evolving Environment, 1972 (Cine Golden Eagle award); editor (film) River of Life, 1975 (U.S. Film Festival award); patentee computerized optical system. Founder, pres. W.Va. Youth Soccer Assn., 1979-84; bd. dirs. Sunrise Mus., Charleston, 1983-86, Renaissance Com., Charleston, 1984-89, Jefferson Co. Hist. Soc., 2002—, Contemporary Am. Theatre Festival, 2002—; mem. Pare Lorentz award panel Internat. Documentary Assn.; trustee U. Charleston, 1985-89; founder W.Va. Assn. Mus., 1990; v.p., sec. W.Va. History Film Project, Inc., 1991-97. Served in USN, 1964-67. Decorated Bronze Star; recipient 2 Cine Eagle awards, cert. Excellence for documentary film work, award Hist. Landmarks Commn. Kanawha County, Tele award, 1997. Mem. Film Arts Guild W.Va. (pres. 1981-87), Orgn. Am. Historians, Am. Hist. Assn., W.V. Hist. Soc., Shepherdstown Rotary, Cress Creek Golf and Country Club. Democrat. Episcopalian. Avocations: tennis, golf, mountain biking, jogging. Office Phone: 304-876-6400. Personal E-mail: bill@billdrennen.com. Business E-Mail: bill@gregdidden.com.

DRENSTEIN, MICHAEL (IAN ORENSTEIN), philatelic dealer, columnist; b. Bklyn., Jan. 6, 1939; s. Harry and Myra (Klein) Orenstein; m. Linda Turner, June 28, 1964; 1 child, Paul David Orenstein. BS, Clemson U., 1960; postgrad., U. Calif., Berkeley, 1960-61. Career regional mgr. Minkus Stamp & Pub. Co., Calif., 1964-70; mgr. stamp div. Superior Stamp & Coin Co., Inc., Beverly Hills, Calif., 1970-90; dir. stamp divsn. Superior Galleries, Beverly Hills, Calif., 1991-94; dir. space memorabilia Superior Stamp and Coin. Co., Inc., Beverly Hills, Calif., 1992-94; dir. stamp and space divsn. Superior Stamp & Coin an A-Mark Co., Beverly Hills, Calif., 1994-97; sr. buyer, appraiser Superior Stamp & Coin, Beverly Hills, Calif., 1997-2000; v.p., COO Superior Galleries, 2001; co-founder, ptnr., prin., pres. AuroraGalleries Internat., 2002—04. Cons. Office Insp. Gen. NASA, Nassau County Dist. Atty., NY. Columnist: L.A. Times, 1965—93; philatelic advisor/creator The Video Guide to Stamp Collecting, 1988; author: Stamp Collecting is Fun, 1990; contbr. articles to publs. With U.S. Army, 1962—64. Recipient medal of Yuri Gagarin, Fedn. Supporting Russian Cosmonauts, 2002. Mem.: AIAA, Internat. Soc. Appraisers: Stamps, Space Memorabilia, Internat. Fedn. Stamp Dealers, Am. Philatelic Soc. (writers unit 1975—80, 1989—93), Confederate Stamp Alliance, German Philatelic Soc., C. Z. Study Group, Am. Stamp Dealers Assn. Republican. Avocation: fishing. Address: 19546 Minnehaha Northridge CA 91326 Office Phone: 818-368-6888. Personal E-mail: rightstuf@verizon.net.

DREPAUL, LORIS OMESH, internist, infectious diseases physician; b. Georgetown, Guyana, Feb. 6, 1960; naturalized U.S. citizen; s. Frank Eric and Iris Ismay Etwaria (Masih-Das) D. BA (honors in philosophy)/BS, Bklyn. Coll., CUNY, 1985; MD, NYU, 1989. Diplomate Am. Bd. Internal Medicine. Intern St. Luke's Hosp.-Columbia U. Coll. Physicians and Surgeons, N.Y.C., 1989-90, resident in internal medicine, 1990-91, Booth Meml. Med. Ctr.-NYU Sch. Medicine, Queens, 1991-92; fellow in infectious diseases Bronx (N.Y.) VA Med. Ctr.-Mt. Sinai Sch. Medicine, 1992-94; attending in infectious diseases Mary Immaculate Hosp, Queens, Cath. Med. Ctr.-Albert Einstein Coll. Medicine, Bronx, 1995-96; mem. faculty, attending in infectious diseases Highland Hosp., Rochester, N.Y., 1997-98; pvt. practice, Rochester, 1997-98. Founder HIV/AIDS Bilingual Primary Care Outreach Program, Bridge Plaza Rehab. Clinic, Queens, N.Y., 1995-96; med. dir. Cmty. Health Network, Inc., Rochester, 1997-98. Mem. AMA, ACP, Med. Soc. State N.Y., Phi Beta Kappa. Avocations: music, bridge, chess, soccer, computers. Home: 952 E 214th St Bronx NY 10469 E-mail: drepaul@pol.net.

DRESBACH, MARY LOUISE, state educational administrator; b. St. Paul, Feb. 17, 1950; d. Ernest Joseph and Kathryn Marion (Lauer) Mathes; m. David Philip Dresbach, Nov. 29, 1980. BA, Coll. St. Catherine, 1972; postgrad., U. St. Thomas, 1979-80; MA, Coll. of St. Catherine, 1995. Tchr. St. Paul Pub. Schs., 1974-78; dir. cmty. outreach, human resources and agy. svcs. Minn. Office Higher Edn., St. Paul, 1978—. Speaker Minn. Quality Conf., 1994, chair, 1996. Contbg. author Leading Edge Newsletter. Mem. exec. steering com. Minn. Quality Coll., 1998. Mem.: Assn. for Psychol. Type, Internat. Pers. Mgmt. Assn. (Minn. chpt.), Minn. Coun. Mgrs. (chair 1998), Minn. Ctr. for Women in Govt., Dakota County Quality Initiative, Dakota County Quality Coun., Minn. Quality Initiative, Am. Soc. for Quality, Nat. Assn. Exec. Women, Am. Bus. Womens Assn. (sec. 1979—80), Citizens League-Minn., Met. Mus. Art, Mpls. Inst. Arts, AAUW, Pi Gamma Mu, Phi Beta Kappa.

DRESCH, STEPHEN PAUL, economist, state legislator; b. East St. Louis, Ill., Dec. 12, 1943; s. Lester Wilson Reuben and Leonore Marie (Steege) D.; m. Linda Carol Ness, May 18, 1963; children: Soren K., Stephanie Elizabeth, Phaedra Augusta, Karl Friedrick Johannes. AB Philosophy, Miami U., Oxford, Ohio, 1963; MPhil Econ., NSF fellow, Yale U., 1966, PhD, 1970. Mem. faculty dept. econs. Miami U., Oxford, Ohio, 1963-64; mem. Yale U., New Haven, Conn., 1966-67, South Conn. State Coll., New Haven, 1968-69, Rutgers U., New Brunswick, N.J., 1970; researcher Nat. Bur. Econ. Research, N.Y.C. and New Haven, 1969-77; cons. in residence Ford Found., N.Y.C., 1970-72; dir. reserch in econs. of higher edn. Yale U., 1972-75, chmn. Inst. for Demographic and Econ. Studies, 1975—; dean, prof. econs. and bus. Sch. Bus. and Engring. Adminstrn., Mich. Technol. U., 1985-90. Rsch. scholar Internat. Inst. Applied Systems Analysis, Austria, 1983-85; vis. scholar Inst. Econs. and Forecasting of Sci. and Technol. Progress, USSR Acad. of Scis., 1988; mem. from 110th dist. Mich. Ho. of Reps., Lansing, 1990-92. Author: Substituting a Value Added Tax for the Corporate Income Tax, 1977, Occupational Earnings, 1967-81, 86, The Economics of Foreign Students,

1987; contbr. articles to profl. jours. Bd. advisors MacKinac Ctr. for Pub. Policy Rsch., Rep. Liberty Caucus. Mem. AAAS, ACLU, Am. Econ. Assn., Fedn. of Am. Scientists, Assn. for Pub. Policy Analysis and Mgmt., Am. Statis. Assn., Sigma Xi. Libertarian. Home: 318 Cooper Ave Hancock MI 49930-2112

DRESCHER, FRAN, actress; b. Flushing, N.Y., Sept. 30, 1957; d. Mort and Sylvia D.; m. Peter Marc Jacobson, 1978. Co-creator, writer, prodr., actress in TV series The Nanny, 1993-99; appeared in feature films: Saturday Night Fever, 1977, American Hot Wax, 1978 (Five-Minute Oscar award Esquire mag.), Gorp, 1980, The Hollywood Knights, 1980, Ragtime, 1981, Young Lust, 1981, Dr. Detroit, 1983, This Is Spinal Tap, 1984, The Rosebud Beach Hotel, 1984, UHF, 1989, The Big Picture, 1989, It had to be You, 1989, Cadillac Man, 1990, Wedding Band, 1990, We're Talking Serious Money, 1992, Jack, 1996, Car 54, Where Are You:, 1996, The Beautician and the Beast, 1997 (also exec. prodr.), Picking Up the Pieces, 2000, Kid Quick, 2000; starred in TV series Charmed Lives, 1986, Princesses, 1991, Good Morning Miami, 2003-04; (TV film) Stranger in Our House, 1978, Rock 'n' Roll Mom, 1988, Love and Betrayal, 1989, What's Alan Watching?, 1989, Terror in the Towers, 1993, Beautiful Girl, 2003; actress, exec. prodr. (TV series) Living with Fran, 2005-; guest appearances on TV programs Civil Wars, Alf, Night Court, Nine to Five, Fame, The Tracy Ullman Show; Spokesperson: Old Navy; Author: Enter Whining, 1995, Cancer Schmancer, 2002. Office: Gersh Agy Inc 232 N Canon Dr Beverly Hills CA 90210-5302

DRESCHER, JOHN WEBB, lawyer; b. Norfolk, Va., May 13, 1948; s. Otto Charles and Anne Best (Webb) D.; m. Dale McKeithan Moore, June 13, 1970; 1 child, Ryan. BA, Hampden-Sydney Coll., 1970; JD, U. Richmond, 1973. Bar: Va. 1973, U.S. Supreme Ct. 1980, U.S. Ct. Appeals (4th cir.) 1985, U.S. Dist. Ct. (ea. dist.) Va. 1976. Assoc. Brydges, Hammers & Hudgins, Virginia Beach, 1973-74; asst. atty. Office of Commonwealth Atty., Virginia Beach, 1974-75; assoc. Pickett, Spain & Lyle, P.C., Virginia Beach, 1976-78; ptnr. Pickett, Lyle, Siegel, Drescher & Croshaw P.C., Virginia Beach, 1979-87, Breit, Drescher & Imprevento, P.C., Norfolk, 1988—. Trustee Hampden-Sydney Coll., 2003—. Named among best lawyers in Am. Naifch & Smith, 1995—. Fellow Am. Bd. Trial Advocates; mem. ATLA, Va. Trial Lawyers Assn. (bd. govs. 1990—), Am. Inns Ct., Norfolk-Portsmouth Bar Assn., Hampden-Sydney Coll. Alumni Assn. (pres. 1990), U. Richmond Law Sch. Alumni Assn., Virginia Beach Bar Assn. (pres. 1990). Democrat. Episcopalian. Avocations: physical fitness, golf. Home: 925 Holladay Pt Virginia Beach VA 23451-3912 Office: Breit Drescher & Imprevento 1000 Dominion Twr 999 Waterside Dr Ste 1000 Norfolk VA 23510-3304 Office Phone: 757-622-6000. Business E-Mail: jdrescher@breitdrescher.com.

DRESCHER, JUDITH ALTMAN, library director; b. Greensburg, Pa., July 6, 1946; d. Joseph Grier and Sarah Margaret (Hewitt) Altman; m. Robert A. Drescher, Aug. 10, 1968 (div. 1980); m. David G. Lindstrom, Jan. 10, 1981. AB, Grove City Coll., 1968; MLS, U. Pitts., 1971. Tchr. Hempfield Sch. Dist., Greensburg, 1968-71; children's libr. Cin. Pub. Libr., 1971-72, br. mgr., 1972-74; dir. Rolling Meadows (Ill.) Pub. Libr., 1974-79, Champaign (Ill.) Pub. Libr., 1979-85, Memphis/Shelby County Pub. Libr. and Info. Ctr., 1985—. Tenn. del. White House Conf. on Librs. and Info. Svcs. Task Force, 1991-92; mem. Tenn. Sec. of State's Commn. on Tech. and Resource Sharing, 1991, 93, steering com. Tenn. Info. and Infrastructure, 1994-97, nat. adv. panel for assessment of role of sch. and pub. librs. U.S. Dept. Edn., 1995-98. Commn. on 21st century Rhodes Coll., Memphis, 1986-88, presdl. adv. com., 1992-2000; active Leadership Memphis, 1987—, selection com., 1992-96; active Memphis Arts Coun., 1989-94; bd. dirs. Literacy Coun., 1986-91, Memphis NCCJ, 1989-93, Memphis Grants Info. Ctr., 1992-97, sec., 1993-95; bd. dirs. Memphis Literacy Found., 1988-92, v.p., 1989-90; bd. dirs. Goals for Memphis, 1988-93, chair edn. com., 1989-91, chair nominating com., 1992, leadership acad., 1999—; bd. dirs. U. Memphis Soc., 1998-2004; bd. dirs. Cmty. Svcs. Agy., 2002—, v.p., 2003—; exec. adv. bd. Children's Mus., 1988-94, exec. adv. coun. U. Memphis, 1989-99; allocations subcom. United Way, 1989-91, allocations com. Memphis Arts Coun., 100 for the Arts, 1989-91, Libr. Self-study Com. U. Memphis; pres. adv. coun. Lemoyne Coll.; search com. for dean librs. U. Memphis, 1999-2001; bd. mem. Cmty. Svcs. Agy., 2000—, fin. com., 2002, v.p., 2004—; adv. com. Memphis Symphony Orch., 2003—; v.p. Tennshare, 2004-05, pres., 2005—; bd. mem., treas. Mid South Reads, 2004-. Paul Harris fellow Rotary, Memphis, 2002; recipient Govt. Leader award U. Ill. YWCA, 1981, Communicator of Yr. award Pub. Rels. Soc. Am., 1992, Humanitarian award NCCJ, Memphis, 2003, Charlie Robinson award Pub. Libr. Assn., 2003; named Libr. Coun. Libr. of Yr., 2002-. Mem.: ALA (chmn. intellectual freedom com. 1985—87, mem. coun. 1992—99, mem. nominating com. 2001—02), Assn. Pub. Adminstrs. (mid-south chpt., Adminstr. of Yr. 2002), Pub. Libr. Assn. (v.p., pres. 1994—95), Memphis Libr. Coun., Urban Librs. Coun., Tenn. Libr. Assn., Rotary (bd. dirs. 1992—94, sec. 1993—94, chair membership devel. com. 1994—95, bd. dirs. 2004—), Beta Phi Mu. Home: 1505 Vance Ave Memphis TN 38104-3810 Office: Memphis Shelby County Pub Libr & Info Ctr 3030 Poplar Ave Memphis TN 38111 Office Phone: 901-415-2748.

DRESCHER, SEYMOUR, historian, educator, writer; b. NYC, Feb. 20, 1934; s. Sidney and Eva Rita (Levine) D.; m. Ruth Lieberman, June 19, 1955; children: Michael, Jonathan, Karen. BA, CCNY, 1955; MS, U. Wis., 1956, PhD, 1960. Instr. history Harvard U., 1960—62; asst. prof. U. Pitts., 1962—65, assoc. prof., 1965—69, prof., 1969—86, Univ. prof., 1986—, chmn., 1980—83; acad. dean. semester-at-sea, 1998, 2002. Vis. disting. prof. CUNY, 1987; Roger T. Anstey Meml. lectr., Canterbury, Eng., 1984; bd. advisors Slavery and Abolition, 1985—; George A. Miller lectr., 1987, Pa. Commonwealth Speakers Program, 1989-91, rsch. fellow Univ. Ctr. Internat. Studies, Pitts., 1992, 2000; C-SPAN adv. com., Tocqueville. Author: Tocqueville and England, 1964, Dilemmas of Democracy, 1968, Econocide, 1977, Capitalism and Antislavery, 1986, From Slavery to Freedom, 1999, The Mighty Experiment: Free Labor versus Slavery in British Emancipation, 2002 (Frederick Douglass Book prize 2004); co-author: The Abolition of Slavery and the Aftermath of Emancipation in Brazil, 1988; editor Jour. Contemporary History, 1991-99; editor: Tocqueville and Beaumont on Social Reform, 1968, Anti-Slavery, Religion and Reform, 1980, Political Symbolism in Modern Europe, 1982, The Meaning of Freedom, 1992, A Historical Guide to World Slavery, 1998, Slavery, 2001, Tocqueville's Memoir on Pauperism, 1997; contbr.: Fifty Years Later: Antislavery, Capitalism and Modernity in the Dutch Orbit, 1995, Is the Holocaust Unique?, 1996, Jews and the Expansion of Europe to the West, 2001, Freemasonry on both sides of the Atlantic, 2002, Slavery in the Development of the Americas, 2004, The Chattel Principle, 2004; creator film: Confrontation, Paris, 1968, 70. Recipient Pres.'s Rsch. award U. Pitts., 1992; Fulbright scholar, 1957-58; NEH fellow, 1973-74, Guggenheim Found. fellow, 1977-78, Resident fellow Bellagio Ctr. for Scholars, 1980, 90, Woodrow Wilson fellow, 1983-84, sec. European program Wilson Ctr., 1984-85. Mem. Am. Hist. Assn., Hist. Soc., Soc. for French Hist. Studies (v.p. 1978-79), N.Am. Conf. on Brit. Studies, Dutch Royal Inst. Linguistics and Anthropology, Fulbright Assn., Commn. Tocqueville (France). Home: 5550 Pocusset St Pittsburgh PA 15217-1913 Office: U Pitts Dept History Pittsburgh PA 15260 Office Phone: 412-648-7451. E-mail: syd@pitt.edu.

DRESCHHOFF, GISELA AUGUSTE MARIE, physicist, researcher; b. Moenchengladbach, Germany, Sept. 13, 1938; came to U.S., 1967, naturalized, 1976; d. Gustav Julius and Hildegard Friederike (Krug) D. PhD, Tech. U. Braunschweig (Ger.), 1972. Staff scientist Fed. Inst. Physics and Tech. Ger., 1965-67; research assoc. Kans. Geol. Survey, Lawrence, 1971-72; vis. asst. prof. physics U. Kans., 1972-74; dep. dir. radiation physics lab. Space Tech. Ctr., 1972-78, assoc. dir., 1979-84, co-dir., 1984-86, dir., 1996—; sr. sci. geology U. Kans., 1991, adj. assoc. prof. physics and astronomy, 1992. Assoc. program mgr. NSF, Washington, 1978-79. Patentee identification markings for gemstones and method of making selective conductive regions in diamond layers. Named to Women's Hall of Fame, U. Kans., 1978; recipient Antarctic Service medal U.S.A., 1979; recipient NASA Group Achievement award, 1983. Fellow Explorers Club; mem. AAAS, Am. Phys. Soc., Am. Geophys. Union, Am. Polar Soc. (pres. 2000-03), Antarctican Soc., Sigma Xi. Home: 2908 W 19th St Lawrence KS 66047-2301 Office: U Kans Dept Physics & Astronomy Lawrence KS 66045-7541 E-mail: giselad@ku.edu.

DRESDEN, JACOB A., headmaster; b. Netherlands; m. Patricia Markle. BA in Polit. Sci., MA in Internat. Polit., U. Penn. Various teaching & administrative positions including asst. headmaster William Penn Charter Sch., Phila., 1969—91; various teaching & administrative positions Abington Friends Sch.; head of sch. Collegiate Sch., NYC, 1991—99, Concord Acad., Concord, Mass., 2000—. Former teacher Columbia's Klingenstein Ctr. for Independent Edu. Mem.: Nat. Assn. of Principals of Schools for Girls. Office: Concord Acad 166 Main St Concord MA 01742*

DRESKIN, ERVING ARTHUR, pathologist, educator; b. Jan. 9, 1919; s. Harry and Sarah Molly (Krulvetsky) D.; m. Jeanet Irma Steckler, May 9, 1943; children: Richard Burgas, Stephen Charles, Jeanet Elizabeth, Rena Lynn. BS, Tulane U., 1940, MD, 1943. Diplomate Am. Bd. Pathology, sub-specialty blood banking. Intern Newark Beth Israel Hosp., 1943-44; resident in pathology, instr. pathology U. Ill. Coll. Medicine, Chgo., 1946-49, Am. Cancer Soc. fellow, 1949-50; assoc. pathologist Grant Hosp., Chgo., 1949-50; chief pathologist, dir. labs. and Blood Bank Greenville (S.C.) Hosp. Sys., 1950-85; med. dir. Carolina-Ga. Blood Ctr., 1980—2001. Cons. pathologist to hosps.; clin. prof. pathology Med. U. S.C.; past pres., chmn., exec. com. Pathology Assocs. Greenville, P.A.; bd. dirs. United Way Greenville County, 1973-76; treas. Greater Greenville Community Found., 1980-81, bd. dirs., 1980-83; pres. Temple of Israel, Greenville, 1966-68, Community Found. Greater Greenville, 1990-91, Greenville County Arts Commn., 1993, 95. Lt. M.C., USNR, 1944-46. Recipient SC Order of the Palmetto, 1992. Fellow Am. Soc. Clin. Pathologists, Coll. Am. Pathologists (S.C. regional commr. for lab. accreditation); mem. AMA, Am. Assn. Blood Banks (v.p. 1962, sec. 1963-65, pres. 1965-66), S.C. Soc. Pathologists (pres. 1957-59), S.C. Med. Assn., Alpha Omega Alpha, Rotary (Paul Harris fellow), Poinsett Club. Home: 60 Lake Forest Dr Greenville SC 29609-5038 Office: Carolina-Georga Blood Ctr 515 Grove Rd Greenville SC 29605-4206 Office Phone: 864-244-5630. E-mail: art@dreskin.net.

DRESSEL, HENRY FRANCIS, retired lawyer; b. Bklyn., Apr. 11, 1914; s. Henry Philip and Ernestine (Delmar) D.; m. Rose Marie Valentine, Nov. 24, 1937; 1 child, Diana (Mrs. Anthony P. Fradella). AB, Washington Square Coll., NYU, 1943, JD, 1949. Bar: N.Y. 1949. Clk. corp. law firm Chadbourne, Stanchfield & Levy (and its successors), N.Y.C., 1933-43; pvt. practice law N.Y.C., 1950-86; ptnr. Dressel & Altman, P.C.; of counsel Berger & Steingut, 1986-2000. Lt. USNR, 1943-46. Named hon. col. Okla., 1958, Okie, 1969. Mem. N.Y. State Bar Assn., Assn. Bar City of N.Y., Am. Judicature Soc., Justinian Soc., Internat. Footprint Assn., Phi Delta Phi. Democrat. Episcopalian. Office: Dressel & Hatab PC 18 E 50th St New York NY 10022-6817

DRESSEL, MARGARET JANE, artist, art educator; b. Brookline, Mass., Aug. 25, 1949; d. Chauncey Lovett Megargle and Esther Laura Field; m. Richard Dressel; children: Bethany, Keith. Student, Moore Coll. Art, 1967-68, Nat. Acad. Art, 1985-86; Assoc. in Occupl. Studies, Pratt Inst., 1985. Owner, artist Peggy Dressel Studio, Oakland, NJ, 1990—; graphic designer Intra Design Inc., Ramsey, NJ, 1990—94; illustrator, asst. Jacqui Morgan Studio, N.Y.C., 1986-90; painting instr. Ramsey Adult Sch., 1996—, Glen Rock (N.J.) Cmty. Sch., 1997—, Art Ctr. No. N.J., New Milford, 1999—2001, 2005—, Ridgewood Art Inst., 2002—. Founder Pastel Plus, N.J., pres., 1997—; mem. Blackwell St. Ctr. Arts; chmn. CAA Nat. Juried Exhbns., Ridgewood, N.J., 1993, 94, 95. One-woman shows include St. Peter's Ch., N.Y.C., 1992, Blackwell St. Gallery, Dover, N.J., 1994, Lena DiGangi Gallery, West Paterson, N.J., 1994, Ringwood Manor W. Wing Gallery, N.J. State Pk., 1994, ADP, Inc. Gallery, Roseland, N.J., 1995, Dow Jones & Co., S. Brunswick, N.J., 1994, 96; N.Y. Theol. Sem., N.Y.C., 1998, The Interch. Ctr., N.Y.C., 1998, Kurth Coll. Ridgewood, N.J., 2002; represented in numerous juried exhbns. and pvt. collections; illustrator mags., children's books, brochures, ads, posters; featured artist poster and calendar N.J. Fine Artist Collection, 1998. Recording sec. Oakland Libr. Bd., 1979-80, pres., 1980-82. Recipient Purchase award Degas Pastel Soc., 1992, Merit award Degas Pastel Soc., 1992, Cynthia Goodgal Meml., Ridgewood Art Inst., Nat. Bergen Mus., 1997, others; named Best in Show, Inserria Corp., 1992, Bergen Mus. Music & Art Festival, 2002. Mem. Cmty. Arts Assn. (pres. 1994-96), Southea. Pastel Soc. (signature mem.), Oreg. Pastel Soc. (signature mem.), Am. Artist Profl. League, Degas Pastel Soc. Democrat. Methodist. Avocations: art, music, travel, gardening. Office: Peggy Dressel Studio 11 Rockaway Ave Oakland NJ 07436-2122 Office Phone: 201-337-2143. E-mail: pegdartist@aol.com.

DRESSELHAUS, MILDRED SPIEWAK, physics and engineering educator; b. Bklyn., Nov. 11, 1930; d. Meyer and Ethel (Teichteil) Spiewak; m. Gene F. Dresselhaus, Aug. 25, 1958; children: Marianne Dresselhaus Cooper, Carl Eric, Paul David, Eliot Michael. BA, Hunter Coll., 1951; DSc (hon.), CUNY, 1982, Hunter Coll., 1982; Fulbright fellow, Cambridge (Eng.) U., 1951—52; MA, Radcliffe Coll., 1953; PhD in Physics, U. Chgo., 1958; D Engring. (hon.), Worcester Poly. Inst., 1976; DSc (hon.), Smith Coll., 1980, Hunter Coll., 1982, N.J. Inst. Tech., 1984; DHC (hon.), U. Catholique de Louvain, 1988; DSc (hon.), Rutgers U., 1989, U. Conn., 1992, U. Mass., Boston, 1992, Princeton U., 1992; DEngring, Colo. Sch. Mines, 1993; D (hon.), Technion, Israel Inst. Tech., Haifa, 1994; DHC (hon.), Johannes Kepler U., Linz, Austria, 1993; DSc (hon.), Harvard U., 1995, Ohio State U., 1998; PhD (hon.), U. Paris, Sorbonne, 1999; DSc (hon.), Columbia U., 1999; DHC (hon.), Cath. U. Louvain, 2000; DSc (hon.), Northwestern U., 2003, Weizmann Inst., Rehovot, Israel, 2003, U. Mich., 2005, George Washington U., 2005. NSF postdoctoral fellow Cornell U., 1958—60; mem. staff Lincoln Lab., MIT, Lexington, 1960—67; prof. elec. engring. MIT, Cambridge, 1968—, assoc. dept. head elec. engring., 1972—74, Abby Rockefeller Mauze chair, 1973—85, dir. Ctr. for Materials Sci. and Engring., 1977—83, prof. physics, 1983—, Inst. prof., 1985—; dir. Office of Science, U.S. Dept. of Energy, Washington, 2000—01. Vis. prof. dept. physics U. Campinas, Brazil, 1971, Technion, Israel, 1972, 90, Nihon and Aoyama Gakuin Univs., Tokyo, 1973, IVIC, Caracas, Venezuela, 1977; vis. prof. dept. elec. engring. U. Calif., Berkeley, 1983; Graffin lectr. Am. Carbon Soc., 1982; chmn. steering com. on evaluation panels Nat. Bur. Stds., 1978—83; mem. Energy Rsch. Adv. Bd., 1984—90; bd. dirs. Rogers Corp. Contbr. articles to profl. jours. Mem. governing bd. NRC, 1984—87, 1989—90, 1992—96; trustee Calif. Inst. Tech., 1993—2000; overseer Harvard U., 1997—2000; chmn. bd. Am. Inst. Physics, 2003—; bd. govs. Argonne Nat. Lab., 1986—89, Weizmann Inst., Rehovot, Israel, 1999—2000, 2001—. Named to Hunter Coll. Hall of Fame, 1972, Women in Tech. Internat. Hall of Fame, 1998; recipient Alumnae medal, Radcliffe Coll., 1973, Killian Faculty Achievement award, 1986—87, Nat. medal of Sci., 1990, Sigri Great Lakes Carbon award, 1997, Profl. Achievement award, Hunter Coll., CUNY, 1998, Nicholson medal, 2000, Karl T. Compton medal, 2001, Weizmann Woman and Sci. Millennial Lifetime Achievement award, 2000, Nat. Materials Advancement award, Fedn. Materials Socs., 2000, Heinz Award for Tech., the Economy and Employment, 2005. Fellow: AAAS (bd. dirs. 1985—89, pres. 1997—98, chair bd. dirs. 1998—99), IEEE (Founders medal 2004), Am. Carbon Soc. (Achievement medal carbon sci. and tech. 2001), Am. Acad. Arts and Scis., Am. Phys. Soc. (pres. 1984); mem.: NAS (coun. 1987—90, chmn. engring. sect. 1987—90, chmn. class III 1990—93, coun. 1992—96, treas. 1992—96), Am. Philos. Soc., Brazilian Acad. Sci. (corr.), Ioffe Inst., Russian Acad. Scis. (hon.), Engring. Acad. Japan (fgn. assoc. 1993—), Soc. Women Engrs. (Achievement award 1977), Nat. Acad. Engring. (coun. 1981—87). Office: MIT 77 Massachusetts Ave Rm 13-3005 Dept Elec Engring Cambridge MA 02139

DRESSLER, ALAN MICHAEL, astronomer; b. Cin., Mar. 23, 1948; s. Charles and Gay (Stein) Dressler. BA in Physics, U. Calif., Berkeley, 1970; PhD in Astronomy, U. Calif., Santa Cruz, 1976. Carnegie Instn. of Washington fellow Hale Obs., Pasadena, Calif., 1976-78, Las Campanas fellow, 1978-81; sci. staff Carnegie Obs. (formerly Mt. Wilson and Las Campanas Obs., formerly Hale Obs.), Pasadena, 1981—, acting assoc. dir., 1988-89. Chair origins subcomS NASA, 2000—03. Contbr. to sci. jours. Recipient Pub. Svcs. medal NASA 1999. Fellow Am. Acad. Arts and Scis.; mem. NAS, Am. Astron. Soc. (councilor 1989-91, Pierce prize 1983), Internat. Astron. Union. Office: Carnegie Obs 813 Santa Barbara St Pasadena CA 91101-1232

DRESSLER, DAVID CHARLES, retired aerospace transportation executive; b. Cleve., June 21, 1928; s. Walter Carl and Beatrice (Albin) D.; m. Dorothea Walker, Dec. 22, 1950; children: David Charles, Bradley, Christopher. BA, Yale U., 1950; grad., Advanced Mgmt. Program, Harvard Bus. Sch., 1973. With Armstrong Cork Co., 1950-51; with Martin Marietta Corp., 1953-92, pres. Master Builders div., 1977-80, pres. Martin Marietta Chem. Co., 1979-81, corp. v.p., 1979-83, sr. corp. v.p., 1983-92; pres. Master Builders Co. Ltd., Toronto, 1977-81, Martin Marietta Aluminum, 1982-85; chmn. bd. Internat. Light Metals, 1985-91; pres. Martin Marietta Materials, Bethesda, Md., 1985-91. Chmn. bd. Martin Marietta Ordnance Sys., 1985—87; chmn. corp. com. Corcoran Mus. Art, 1992; bd. dirs. Bowles Fluidics; pres. Dressler Corp.; ethics judge Nat. Capital Bus. Awards, 2003—05. Served to capt. USMCR, 1951-53. Mem.: Nat. Press Club, Harvard Bus. Sch. Club (pres. Washington club 1983, chmn. bd. dirs. 1984), Congl. Country Club (Washington) (bd. govs. 1990—96), Phi Beta Kappa. Episcopalian.

DRESSLER, MARK CHRISTOPHER, writer; b. Phila., Aug. 1, 1955; s. Bernard Michael and Dolores Marie D. BA, Temple U., 1980. Mideast-related writer, Washington, 1983—87; asst. news editor Castro Valley (Calif.) Forum, 1990-94; newspaper corr. King of Prussia (Pa.) Post, 1995-97; TV govt. corr. UMGA-TV, Montgomery County, Pa., 1997-98; writer Springfield Twp. Enterprise, Montgomery County, 1998—. Mem. Soc. of Profl. Journalists. Avocations: seeing movies, videos, music, conversation. Home: 69 Grove Ave Flourtown PA 19031 E-mail: M1C1D@aol.com.

DRESSLER, OSCAR H., music educator; b. Encarnacion, Itapua, Paraguay, Nov. 17, 1960; s. Reños Dressler and Ilsa Duré; m. Cristina O. Tinao, Apr. 25, 1987; children: Rocio Belen, Mathias Daniel. B in Ch. Music, Internat. Bapt. Theol. Sem., 1986; MusM, Southwestern Bapt. Theol. Sem., 1992, D of Musical Arts in Piano Performance, 1995. Cert. music tchr. Tex., 2001. Asst. prof. music Seminario Internacional Teologico Bautista, Buenos Aires, 1986—90, Ateneo Paraguayo Sch. of Music, Asuncion, Paraguay, 1996—97; tchr. music Steppingstone Christian Acad., Burleson, Tex., 1997—2000; head music dept. Hill Sch., Ft. Worth, 1999—; assoc. pastor music and worship Villa Morra Bapt. Ch., Asuncion, 1996—97. Adj. tchr. piano, artists-in-residence Tex. Wesleyan U./, Ft. Worth, 1998—2000; adj. tchr. piano Southwestern Bapt. Theol. Sem., 2000—02. Author: Teaching Piano to Students with Learning Disabilities. Assoc. min. of music and pianist First Bapt. Ch., Benbrook, Tex., 1997—2002. Recipient Wayne Polly McNeely Piano award, Southwestern Bapt. Theol. Sem., 1992, Academic Achievement award, 1992, 1995; fellow, 1991—95; scholar, U. Music Mozarteum of Salzburg, 1992, Southwestern Bapt. Theol. Sem., 1991, 1992, 1993, 1994, 1995. Mem.: Ft. Worth Music Tchrs. Assn., Tex. Music Tchrs. Assn., Music Tchrs. Nat. Assn., Music Educators Nat. Conf. Achievements include Introduction of piano studies as part of the music curriculum for students with learning disabilities at Hill School of Fort Worth; research in effects and impact on learning skills of piano instruction in students with learning disabilities. Home: 1413 High Ridge Rd Benbrook TX 76126 Office: Hill Sch Ft Worth 4817 Odessa Ave Fort Worth TX 76133 Personal E-mail: odressler@msn.com.

DRESSLER, ROBERT A., lawyer; b. Fort Lauderdale, Fla., Aug. 20, 1945; s. R. Philip and Elisabeth Dressler; children: James Philip, Kathryn S. AB cum laude, Dartmouth Coll., 1967; JD cum laude, Harvard U., 1973. Bar: Mass. 1973, Fla. 1974, D.C. 1980, U.S. Dist. Ct. (so. dist.) Fla., U.S. Dist. Ct. Mass., U.S. Ct. Appeals (1st cir.), U.S. Ct. Appeals (5th cir.), U.S. Supreme Ct. Assoc. Goodwin, Proctor & Hoar, Boston, 1973-75; ptnr. Dressler & Dressler, Ft. Lauderdale, 1975-82; mayor City of Ft. Lauderdale, 1982-86; pvt. practice law Ft. Lauderdale, 1982—. Bd. regents State Univ. System, 1987-93; mem. Estate Planning Coun. Broward County; adv. com. Fla. Atlantic U., Broward, 1989—; exec. com. Tchr. Edn. Alliance, 1991-2000. Capt USMC, 1969-72. Named Person of Yr. Fla. Atlantic U., 1993. Mem. Greater Ft. Lauderdale C.of C. (bd. govs. 1982-89), Broward County Bar Assn., Fla. Bar Assn., D.C. Bar Assn., Vietnam Vets. Am., Rotary Internat., Tower Forum (bd. govs. 1983-2005), Phi Beta Kappa. Presbyterian. Avocations: hiking, travel. Home: 1215 E Broward BlvdSuite 201 Fort Lauderdale FL 33301 Office: PO Box 2425 Fort Lauderdale FL 33303-2425 Office Phone: 954-523-9595. Business E-Mail: dresslerlaw@bellsouth.net.

DREVER, RICHARD ALSTON, JR., consulting architect; b. Kearny, N.J., Feb. 9, 1936; s. Richard A. and Dorothy L. (Farrer) D.; m. Ellen M. Cornell, Dec. 21, 1957 (div. Oct. 1978); children: Richard A. III, Diana J., Beverly K.; m. Jane L. Cash, June 1, 1981. AB, Columbia U., 1957, BArch, MArch, Columbia U., 1963. Registered architect, Calif., Alaska, Ariz., Nev., Nat. Coun. Archtl. Registration Bds. Intern Frederick, Frost & Assocs., N.Y.C., 1961, 63; with Allen-Drever-Lechowski, Architects, San Francisco, 1963-85, pres., 1983-85. Cons. architect in pvt. practice, 1985—; officer, dir. Medos Corp., San Francisco, 1979-81. Author profl. articles. Bd. dirs. Tamalpais Cmty. Svcs. dist., Marin County, Calif., 1970-75; mem. Tamalpais Parks and Recreation Commn., 1968-70. Lt. USNR, 1957-59. Mem.: AIA, Am. Coll. of Health Care Arch., Acad. Arch. for Health. Home and Office: 7576 Meadowlark Dr Sebastopol CA 95472-4434 Office Phone: 707-824-6920.

DREW, CLIFFORD JAMES, dean, psychologist, educator; b. Eugene, Oregon, Mar. 9, 1943; s. Albert C. and Violet M. (Caskey) D. BS magna cum laude, Ea. Oreg. Coll., 1965; EdM, U.Ill., 1966; PhD (hon.), U. Oreg., 1968. Asst. prof. edn. Kent State U., Ohio, 1968-69; asst. prof. dir. rsch. and spl. edn. U. Tex., Austin, 1969-71; assoc. prof. spl. edn. U. Utah, Salt Lake City, 1971-76, prof., 1977—, asst. dean Grad. Sch. Edn., 1974-77, assoc. dean, 1977-79, 89-95, prof. spl. edn., ednl. psychology, 1979—, coord. instrnl. tech., acad. v.p. office, 1995-97, assoc. acad. v.p., 1997—2004, assoc. dean Coll. Edn., 2004—. Cons. HEW, 1969-80; Bd. dir. Far West Lab. Ednl. Rsch. and Devel., San Francisco, 1974-80; mem. exec. bd. Salt Lake County Assn. Retarded Children, 1971-72; mem. adv. com. Mental Retardation Counseling Svc., Tex. Dept. Mental Health Mental Retardation, 1969-70. Author: Intro. to Designing Rsch. and Evaluation, 2d edit., 1976; co-author (with M. Hardman and H. Bluhm): Intellectual Disabilities across the Lifespa, 9th edit., 2004; author: Designing and Conducting Behavioral Rsch., 1985; co-author (with B. Wampold): Theory and Application of Stats., 1990; co-author: (with M. Hardman and A. Hart) Designing and Conducting Rsch.: Inquiry in Edn. and Social Sci., 1996; co-author: (with M. Hardman) Mental Retardation: A Life Cycle Approach, 2000, 8th edit., 2004; co-author: (with D. Gelfand) Understanding Child Behavior Disorders, 2003; co-author: (with M. Hardman) Mental Retardation: A Life Cycle Approach to People with Intellectual Disabilities, 8th edit., 2004, Intellectual Disabilites Across the Lifespan, 2005; contbr. numerous articles to profl. jours. NDEA fellow, 1965-66; U.S. Office Edn. fellow, 1966-68. Fellow Am. Assn. Mental Retardation; mem. Am. Psychol. Assn., Am. Ednl. Rsch. Assn. Office: U Utah Dean's Office 1705 Campus Center Dr Rm 225 Salt Lake City UT 84112-9007 Office Phone: 801-581-8221. Business E-Mail: cliff.drew@utah.edu.

DREW, DONALD ALLEN, mathematical sciences educator; b. Margaretville, NY, Sept. 11, 1945; s. Howard Charles and Marjorie Belle (Liddle) D.; m. Margaret Esther Miller, June 4, 1966; children— Elizabeth Margaret, Stacey Lynn BS in Math., Rensselaer Poly. Inst., 1967, MS, 1969, PhD, 1970. Instr. MIT, Cambridge, 1970-71; asst. prof. NYU, 1971-73; from asst. prof. math. to prof. Rensselaer Poly. Inst., Troy, NY, 1973—95, Ricketts prof., 1995—, chmn. Dept. Math. Sci., 2002—. Cons. Battelle, Richland, Wash., 1975-77, Chevron, 1996; mathematician U.S. Army Rsch. Office, Research Triangle Park, N.C., 1980-81; vis. assoc. prof. U. Wis.-Madison, 1981; summer faculty Sandia Nat. Labs., Albuquerque, 1984; vis. prof. theoretical and applied mechanics Math. Scis. Inst., Cornell U., 1988-89; assoc. dir. Ctr. Multiphase Rsch., 1987-94, dir., 1994-96; vis. faculty Centro Atomico, Bariloche, Argentina, 1997, Southampton (Eng.) U., 1997; vis. scientist Los Alamos (N.Mex.) Nat. Labs., 1997. Contbr. articles to profl. jours. Pres.

Faculty Senate, 1993-94. Mem. AAAS, Soc. Math. Biol., Soc. Indsl. and Applied Mathematics (edn. com. 1977-80), Soc. Engring. Sci., Soc. Natural Philosophy, Sigma Xi. Democrat. Home: 10 Eaton Rd Troy NY 12180-3603 Office: Rensselaer Poly Inst Dept Math Scis Troy NY 12180

DREW, ELIZABETH, commentator, journalist, writer; b. Cin., Nov. 16, 1935; d. William J. and Estelle (Jacobs) Brenner; m. J. Patterson Drew, Apr. 11, 1964 (dec. 1970); m. David Webster, Sept. 26, 1981 (dec. 2003); m. David Felton, Oct. 14, 2004. BA, Wellesley Coll., 1957; LHD, Hood Coll., 1976, Yale U., 1976, Trinity Coll., Washington, 1978, Reed Coll., 1979, Williams Coll., 1981, Georgetown U., 1981, George Washington U., 1994, Trinity Coll., Hartford, 2000. Writer, editor Congl. Quar., 1959-64; freelance writer, 1964-67; Washington editor Atlantic Monthly, 1967-73; host TV interview program Thirty Minutes With, 1971-73; commentator TV program Agronsky and Co. (now Inside Washington), 1973-92; Washington corr. New Yorker Mag., 1973-92; commentator Monitor Radio, 1992—95. Adv. bd. Shorenstein Ctr. on Press and Policies, Harvard U.; adv. coun. Bardeuas Ctr. for Study of Congress, NYU. Author: Washington Jour., 1975, Am. Jour., 1977, Senator, 1979, Portrait of an Election, 1981, Politics and Money, 1983, Campaign Jour., 1985, Election Jour., 1989, On the Edge: The Clinton Presidency, 1994, Showdown: The Struggle Between the Gingrich Congress and the Clinton White House, 1996, Whatever It Takes: The Real Struggle for Political Power in Am., 1997, The Corruption of Am. Politics, 1999, Citizen McCain, 2002; contbr. articles Washington Post, N.Y. Rev. of Books, jours. and periodicals. Recipient award for excellence Soc. Mag. Writers, 1971, Wellesley Alumnae Achievement award, 1973, DuPont award, 1973, Mo. medal, 1979, Sidney Hillman award, 1983, Amb. of Honor award Books Across the Sea, 1984, Lit. Lion award N.Y. Pub. Libr., 1985, Edward Weintal prize, 1988. Home and Office: NW #1121 700 New Hampshire Ave Washington DC 20037-2406 Office Phone: 202-298-6687.

DREW, ELIZABETH HEINEMAN, publishing executive; b. Evanston, Ill., Aug. 26, 1940; d. Ben Harlow and Marion Elizabeth (Heineman) D. BA, U. Wis., 1961. With Doubleday & Co., Inc., N.Y.C., 1961-84, prodn. asst., 1961-63, personal asst. to editor-in-chief, 1963-66, adminstrv. asst. to editor-in-chief, 1966-69, editl. asst. to editor-in-chief, 1969-71, assoc. editor, 1971-74, editor, 1974-77, sr. editor, 1977-79, exec. editor, editl. dir., 1979-84; v.p., sr. editor William Morrow and Co., N.Y.C., 1984-92; v.p., pub. Lisa Drew Books/Macmillan Pub. Co., N.Y.C., 1993-94; v.p. pub. Lisa Drew Books/Charles Scribner's Sons, N.Y.C., 1994—. Tchr. NYU Sch. Continuing Edn., 1981-82. Bd. dirs. Barbara Bush Found. Family Literacy, 1995—, Am. Booksellers Found. for Free Expression, 2004-. Mem.: PEN, Assn. Am. Pubs. (internat. freedom to pub. com. 1978—, freedom to read com. 1988—, chmn. 1990—93, 1994—98, 2004—), Nat. Press Club, Women's Media Group (treas. 1982—84, pres. 1985—86, bd. dirs. 2000—02), First City Club (Savannah, Ga.), Century Assn. (N.Y.). Democrat. Episcopalian.

DREW, FRASER BRAGG ROBERT, language educator; b. Randolph, Vt., June 23, 1913; s. George Albie and Hazel (Fraser) Drew. AB magna cum laude, U. Vt., 1933; MA, Duke U., 1935; PhD, U. Buffalo, 1952. Instr. Latin Green Mt. Coll., Poultney, Vt., 1936-39; grad. asst. English Syracuse U., 1939-41; instr. English Buffalo State Coll., 1945-47, asst. prof., 1947-52, prof., 1952-73, Disting. Tchg. prof., 1973-83. Author: (book) John Masefield's England, 1973; contbr. articles to profl. jours. Chmn. St. Patrick Scholarship Fund, Buffalo, 1969—79. Recipient Disting. Alumnus award, U. Vt., 1968, Irishman of the Yr. award, United Irish Socs. Western N.Y., 1970; grantee, SUNY Rsch. Found., 1960, 1967; St. Patrick scholar, 1967. Mem.: Robinson Jeffers Tor Ho. Found., Hemingway Soc., Boulder Soc., Wilbur Soc., Ira Allen Soc., John Masefield Soc., Housman Soc., Green Mountain Cir., Friends Duke U. Chapel, Duke U. Heritage Soc., Friends Bailey/Howe Libr., Friends Hemingway Collection John F. Kennedy Libr., Iron Dukes, Washington Duke Club, Phi Beta Kappa, Lambda Iota. Home: 33 Dante Ct Williamsville NY 14221

DREW, INA R., bank executive; BA, Johns Hopkins U., 1978; MA, Columbia U. Floor trader Bank of Tokyo, Manhattan, NY; with Chemical Bank, Springfield, NJ, 1982—96; mng. dir. Global Treasury Divsn. J.P. Morgan Chase & Co., N.Y.C., NY, 1996—. Mem. mgmt. com. J.P. Morgan Chase & Co., 1997—, mem. exec. com., 2003—. Named One of Most Powerful Women in Banking, U.S. Banker Mag., 2003. Office: JP Morgan Chase & Co 270 Park Ave New York NY 10017-2070

DREW, JODI HOFFMAN, music educator; b. St. Louis, Sept. 28, 1968; d. C. Phillip and Sue Elaine Hoffman; m. John Robert Drew, June 17, 1994; 1 child, Haley Nicole. BS in Music Edn., Fla. State U., 1990. Pks. and rec. music specialist Pks. Dept., Tallahassee, 1986—93; music dir. St. Paul's Ch., Tallahassee, 1989—93; choral dir. Cobb Mid. Sch., Tallahassee, 1990—; music dir. United Ch., Tallahassee, 1995—. Sponsor Nat. Beta Club, Tallahassee, 1999—; active United Sch., Tallahassee, 1995—. Mem.: Fla. Music Educators Assn., Fla. Vocal Assn. (dist. 3 chair 1999—, dist. 3 co-chair 1997—99, Secondary Enrollment award 1994, 1997, 2001). Avocations: piano, cooking, walking, movies. Office: Cobb Mid Sch 915 Hillcrest Ave Tallahassee FL 32308

DREW, JOHN ROBERT, music educator; b. Louisville, Feb. 12, 1951; s. John Oliver and Martha Marjorie Drew; m. Jodi Hoffman Drew, Sept. 28, 1968; 1 child, Haley Nicole. B of Music Edn., Ea. Ky. U., 1973, MusM, 1974; D of Music Adminstrn., U. Ky., 1978. With Transylvania U., Lexington, Ky., 1976—78, Asbury (Ky.) Coll., 1978, Fla. State U., Tallahassee, 1980—. Named to Music Hall of Fame, U. Ky., 2002; recipient Outstanding Alumnus award, Ea. Ky. U., 1986. Mem.: Internat. Trombone Assn. (pres. 2000—02). Home: 5325 Pembridge Pl Tallahassee FL 32309 Office: Fla State Univ Sch of Music Tallahassee FL 32306

DREW, KATHERINE FISCHER, history professor; b. Houston, Sept. 24, 1923; d. Herbert Herman and Martha (Holloway) Fischer; m. Ronald Farinton Drew, July 27, 1951. BA, Rice Inst., 1944, MA, 1945; PhD, Cornell U., 1950. Asst. history Cornell U., 1948-50; instr. history Rice U., 1946-48, mem. faculty, 1950—, prof. history, 1964—, Harris Masterson, Jr. prof. history, 1983-85, Lynette S. Autrey prof. history, 1985-96, prof. emeritus, 1996—, chmn. dept. history, 1970-80; editor Rice U. (Rice U. Studies), 1967-81, acting dean humanities and social scis., 1973, acting chmn. dept. art and art history, 1996-98. Author: The Burgundian Code, 1949, Studies in Lombard Institutions, 1956, The Lombard Laws, 1973, Law and Society in Early Medieval Europe, 1988, The Laws of the Salian Franks, 1991, Magna Carta, 2004, also articles; editor: Perspectives in Medieval History, 1963, The Barbarian Invasions, 1970; mem. bd. editors Am. Hist. Assn. Guide to Hist. Lit., 1987-94, Am. Hist. Rev. 1982-1985; contbr.: Life and Thought in the Middle Ages, 1967, Guggenheim fellow, 1959, Fulbright scholar, 1965, NEH sr. fellow, 1974—75. Fellow Mediaeval Acad. Am. (coun. 1974-77, 2d v.p. to pres. 1985-87, del. to Am. Coun. Learned Socs. 1977-81); mem. Am. Hist. Assn. (coun. 1983-86), Am. Soc. Legal History, So. Hist. Assn. (vice chair, chair European sect. 1986-88, exec. com. 1989-91), Phi Beta Kappa. Home: 9333 Memorial Dr # 306 Houston TX 77024-5739 Office: Rice U Dept History MS 42 PO Box 1892 Houston TX 77251-1892 E-mail: kdrew@rice.edu.

DREW, LAWRENCE JAMES, geologist, statistician; b. Dec. 18, 1940; s. James Joseph and Olive Virginia (McAfee) Drew; m. Sheila Moore Collins, Oct. 16, 1965; 1 child, Michael C. BS, U. N.H., 1962; MS, Pa. State U., 1964, PhD, 1966, postdoctoral studies, 1966—67; MS, VA. Polytech Inst., 1980. Statistician Geotech, Inc., Alexandria, Va., 1967—69; geologist Cities Svc. Oil Co., Tulsa, 1969—72, U.S. Geol. Survey, Reston, Va., 1972—, br. chief, 1982—87. Author: Recollections of a Forecaster, 1990, Undiscovered Petroleum and Mineral Resources in Assessment and Controversy, 1997; contbr. more than 100 articles to profl. jours., encys. Mem.: Am. Statis. Assn., Internat. Assn. Math. Geologists. Presbyterian. Avocation: gardening. Home: 12663 Magna Carta Rd Herndon VA 20171-2710 E-mail: ldrew@usgs.gov.

DREW, NANCY MCLAURIN SHANNON, counselor, consultant; b. Meridian, Miss., Apr. 29, 1934; d Julian Caldwell and Emma Katherine (Sanders) Shannon; m. Thomas Champion III, Feb. 11, 1956; children: Thomas Champion IV, Julian C. Shannon. BA, Furman U., 1956; MEd, N.C. State U., 1968. Cert. sch. counselor; cert. supr. curriculum and instrn., N.C. Rsch. asst. N.C. State U., Raleigh, 1957-59; tchr. English Raleigh City Schs., 1959-60; dir. guidance program Millbrook Sr. High/Wake County Schs., Raleigh, 1969-77; guidance chmn. Daniels Middle Sch./Wake County Schs., Raleigh, 1977-84, guidance info. specialist, 1984-85; guidance supr. Wake County Pub. Schs., Raleigh, 1985-88; coord. model dropout prevention program Wake County Pub. Sch./State Dept. Pub. Inst., Raleigh, 1985-88; counseling chmn. Garner Middle Sch., Raleigh, 1988-96. Presenter, cons. 1st and 2d Nat. Dropout Prevention Confs., Winston-Salem, N.C., 1986-87, Raleigh, 1986-88, N.C. Sch. Counselors Conf., Raleigh, 1986-88, Am. Pers. and Guidance Assn., 1976, N.C. Mid. Sch. Assn., 1987-88; presenter career workshops ParentScope 1996, speakers' staff ParentScope 1995-96. Contbr. articles to profl. jours. Vice chmn. bd. trustees Crossnore (N.C.) Sch., 1977—; mem. adv. bd. Tamassee DAR Sch., 1994—; sec., bd. dirs. Wake Teen Med. Svcs., Raleigh, 1978-88, Garner Edn. Found., 1991-95; mem. Wake County Bus. and Edn. Leadership Coun., 1992-96, L.L. Polk Found. Named Outstanding Sr. Citizen, Raleigh Jaycees, 1999. Mem. AACD, NEA, DAR (area rep. spkrs. staff N.C. 1995-98, chmn. state DAR sch. com. 1985-88, state editor DAR News 1989-91, 94-97, chpt. regent 1992-95, nat. house com. 1992-94, nat. vice chmn. spl. svcs., state officer 1989-91, dir. dist. VI N.C. State DAR 1992-99, N.C. Outstanding Jr. Mem. 1970, nat. vice chmn. membership 1996-98, nat. vice chmn. DAR sch. com. 1986-89, nat. vice chmn. mem. contest 1998-2001), N.C. Edn. Assn., Am. Sch. Counselors Assn., N.C. Sch. Counselors Assn., Phi Delta Kappa, Delta Kappa Gamma (pres. chpt. 1985-88, state chmn. 1991-93, state com. chmn. 1994-96). Republican. Methodist. Home: 6000 Winthrop Dr Raleigh NC 27612-2142

DREW, PAUL S., entrepreneur; b. Detroit, Mar. 10, 1935; s. Harry and Elizabeth (Schneider) Schlachman; m. Dove Ann Austin, Sept. 9, 1961. BA, Wayne State U., Detroit, 1957. Disc jockey, Port Huron, Mich. and Atlanta, 1955-67; program dir. Sta. WQXI, Atlanta, 1966-67, Sta. CKLW, Detroit, 1967-68; program cons. Storer Broadcasting Co., Phila., 1968-69; program dir. RKO Radio stas. in, Detroit, San Francisco, Washington and L.A., 1970-73; v.p. programming RKO Radio stas., 1973-77; pres. Paul Drew Enterprises, L.A., 1977—; dir. USIA-Radio Marti, 1984-85; pres. USA Japan Co., 1985—, The Mobotron Corp., Hollywood, Calif., 1988—, Fuzzmug Corp., 1991—, 2151 Corp., 1991—. Personal mgr. Pink Lady, outside Japan, 1978; ptnr. Teacup-Teaspoon Music Pub. Co., 1978; chmn. Billboard Internat. Programming Conf., 1976; commr. Calif. Motion Picture Coun., 1979-85. Del. Dem. Nat. Conv., 1976; mem. Dem. Nat. Com., Calif. Dem. Com., Dem. Nat. Fin. Council. Named DeeJay of Year Sixteen Mag., 1965; Program Dir. of Year Bill Gavin Report, 1967; recipient Superior Achievement award RKO Radio, 1973; also numerous gold records for contbs. toward million selling records. Mem. NARAS, Am. Advt. Fedn., Am. Film Inst., Hollywood Radio and TV Soc., L.A. World Affairs Coun., Town Hall Calif., Japan Am. Soc., Variety, Friars, Frat. of Friends, Music Ctr. Home and Office: 4155 Morningside Dr Cumming GA 30041-6609 *Don't make the same mistake once.*

DREW, PHILIP GARFIELD, retired engineering company executive, consultant; b. Dedham, Mass., Jan. 25, 1932; s. Garfield Albee and Katherine Marion (Dowling) D.; m. Anne Spengler, June 10, 1961 (div. 1972); children: Katherine, Philip Garfield; m. Patrice Anne Prall, May 20, 1978 (div. 1998); children: Evlyn Albee, Charles Prescott. BS, Carnegie-Mellon U., 1954; MS, Harvard U., 1959, PhD, 1964. Registered profl. engr., Mass. Staff Arthur D. Little, Inc., Cambridge, Mass., 1964-81; pres. Drew Cons., Inc., Carlisle, Mass., 1981—, Concord (Mass.) Cons. Group, 1996—97, 1999—2004, ret., 2004. Contbg. editor: Diagnostic Imaging, 1982—; assoc. sci. editor: Test and Measurement World, 1984-86; contbr. articles to profl. jours. Chmn. bd. overseers Bustins Island Village Corp., Freeport, Maine, 1981-84; pres. Savoyard Light Opera Co., 1988-90, Brown Bag Opera, 1993-2000. Served to 1st lt. AUS, 1954-58. Mem. IEEE, Soc. Photo-Optical Instrumentation Engrs., Soc. Computer Applications in Radiology (chmn. 1996), Harvard Club of Boston. Republican. Home and Office: 101 Bedford Rd Carlisle MA 01741-1817 Office Phone: 978-369-9276. Personal E-mail: pdrew@concordcg.com.

DREW, RICHARD ALLEN, retired electrical engineer; b. Milw., Jan. 10, 1941; s. Frank Emmons and Irene Louise Drew. BSEE, Milw. Sch. Engring., 1970. Registered profl. engr., Wis. Instrument engr. Nekoosa Papers Inc., Port Edwards, Wis., 1970—74, sr. instrument engr., 1974—85, Specialty Sys. Inc., Mosinee, Wis., 1985—87; chief elec. and instrument engr. Zimpro Environ. Inc., Rothschild, Wis., 1988—96, ret., 1997. With USAF, 1963—67. Recipient Outstanding Svc. award Pulp and Paper Industry Divsn., Instrument Soc. Am., 1983, Outstanding Alumnus award Milw. Sch. Engring., 1985. Mem. Instrument Soc. Am. (sr., chpt. pres. 1974-75), Am. Radio Relay League (life), Milw. Sch. Engring. Alumni Orgn. (chpt. pres. 1991-95). Achievements include research in pulp and paper industrial control systems and waste treatment control systems. Home: 5625 Sandpiper Dr Apt 301 Stevens Point WI 54481

DREW, THOMAS PAUL, chaplain; b. Harvey, Ill., May 19, 1930; s. Thomas Barnet Dorothy Emma D.; m. LorryJo Drew, May 1, 1954; children: Scott Thomas, Lori-Beth Jackson. BA, Bapt. Christian U., 1981, ThM, 1986; PhB in Philosophy, DePaul U., 1963; ThM, Internat. Bible Inst. and Sem., 1981; D Ministry, U. Biblical Studies, 1989. Underwriter America-Fore, Chgo., 1952-56; ins. broker Prudential, Chgo., 1956-86; chaplain, min., jail evangelist Huntsville (Ala.) Police Dept., 1970—. Counselor Huntsville, 1991—; stress counselor Internat. Critical Incident Stress Found., Huntsville. Author: Here's One Marine, 2000. State chaplain Marine Corps League, Ala., 1999—. Staff sgt. USMC, 1947-52. Independent. Avocations: lapidary, fishing. Home: PO Box 145 Union Grove AL 35175

DREW, WALTER HARLOW, retired paper industry executive; b. Chgo., Feb. 23, 1935; s. Ben Harlow and Marion Elizabeth (Heineman) D.; m. Gracia Ward McKenzie, June 27, 1959; children: Jeffrey, Martha. BS, U. Wis., 1957. With Kimberly-Clark Corp., 1959-88, exec. v.p., 1985-88; pres., CEO Menasha Corp., 1989-92. Bd. dirs. U. Wis. Found.; chmn. bd. visitors U. Wis. Bus. Sch., 1992—93. Lt. (jg.) USNR, 1957—63. Mem.: Ocean Club (amelia Island, Fla.), North Shore Golf Club (Menasha, Wis.) (pres. 1983—85).

DREWAL, HENRY JOHN, art historian, educator; b. Brooklyn, Mar. 11, 1943; BA, Hamilton Coll., 1964; MA, Columbia U., 1968, PhD, 1973. Asst. prof. art hist. Cleve. State U., 1973—77, prof., chairperson art dept., 1982—85, prof. art dept., 1982—90; Evjue-Bascom Prof. Art Hist. U. Wis.-Madison, Dept. Art Hist., 1990—. Vis. prof. art hist. SUNY Purchase, 1986, U. Calif., Santa Barbara, 1988. Fellow Guggenheim Meml. Found., 2004. Mem.: Wis. Acad. of Scis., Arts, and Letters, Midwest Art Soc., Congress on Rsch. in Dance, Coll. Art Assn., African Studies Assn. Office: Elvehjem Mus Art U Wis Madison WI 53706 Office Phone: 608-263-9362, 608-263-2340. E-mail: hjdrewal@wisc.edu.*

DREWES, ALFRED H., consumer products company executive; BSEE, U. Mass., 1978; MBA, Columbia U., 1982. Fin. analyst Pepsi Bottling Group, NJ, 1982; sr. v.p., CFO The Pepsi Bottling Group, Inc., Somers, NY, 2001—, Pepsi-Cola Internat., v.p. mfg. ops., 1991, v.p. bus. planning and new bus. devel., 1994, v.p., CFO Europe and Sub-Saharan Africa Bus. Unit London, 1996. Office: The Pepsi Bottling Group Inc One Pepsi Way Somers NY 10589-2201

DREWRY, DON NEAL, fire protection engineer; b. Chgo., Oct. 6, 1949; s. Ruben Neal and Vlasta A. (Waleck) D.; m. Patricia Ann English, Mar. 8, 1975; children: Neal Thomas, Michelle Lynn. BA, Govs. State U., 1978; BS in Engring., U. Hartford, 1984; MS in Fire Protection Engring., Worcester Polytech. Inst., 1986. Mfg. engring./NC programmer Bloomer-Fisk, Chgo., 1974-75; inspector, supr. Hartford Steam Boiler, Chgo., 1975-78; asst. mgr. quality assurance svc. Hartford Steam Boiler Inspection and Ins. Co., 1978-80, project engr., 1980-81, rsch. engr., 1982-84, fire protection cons., 1984-87, regional mgmt. property engr. Basking Ridge, N.J., 1987-92, regional manage ins. engr., 1992-94; br. mgr., property program mgr. power generation HSB Profl. Loss Control, Basking Ridge, 1994-97, v.p. industry svcs., 1997-99, v.p. loss control svcs., 1999—. Com. fire protection task force Edison Elec. Inst., Washington, 1995. With USN, 1970-74. Mem. ASME, Soc. Fire Protection Engrs., Nat. Fire Protection Assn. (com. NFPA-850 1985—), Nat. Bd. of Boiler and Pressure Vessel Inspectors. Home: 1401 Sycamore Ave Easton PA 18040-8106 Office: HSB Profl Loss Control 188 Mount Airy Rd Basking Ridge NJ 07920-2021

DREWS, JÜRGEN, pharmaceutical researcher; b. Berlin, Aug. 16, 1933; came to U.S., 1991; s. Walter and Charlotte (Schneider) D.; m. Helga Eberlein, July 26, 1963; children: Ulrike, Karoline, Bettina. MD, Free U. Berlin, 1959; Professorship, U. Heidelberg, Fed. Republic of Germany, 1973. Head chemotherapy Sandoz Rsch. Inst., Vienna, 1976-79, head of inst., 1979-82; head internat. pharm. rsch. and devel. Sandoz, Ltd., Basel, Switzerland, 1982-85; dir. pharm. rsch. F. Hoffmann-La Roche Ltd., Basel, 1985-86, chmn. rsch. bd., mem. exec. com., 1986-90; pres. internat. rsch. and devel., mem. exec. com. Hoffmann-La Roche Inc., Basel, 1991-97, pres. global rsch., mem. exec. com. Nutley, N.J., 1996-97; chmn. Internat. Biomedicine Mgmt. Ptnrs., Basel, 1998—2000; mng. ptnr. Bear Stearns Health Innoventures, N.Y.C., 2002—. Prof. medicine U. Heidelberg, 1973—; mem. sci. adv. bd. (jour.) Infection, München, Fed. Republic of Germany, 1973-95, Drug News & Perspectives, Barcelona, Spain, 1988—, Klinische Pharmakologie, München, 1989-2000; bd. dirs. Genentech, Inc., South San Francisco, 1990-97, Protein Design Labs., Mountain View, Calif., MorphoSys GmbH, Munich; bd. dirs., internat. bd. advisors Basel Inst. Immunology, 1986-97; mem. dean's coun. Yale U. Sch. Medicine, 1993-96, chmn. sci. panel inter-company collaboration for AIDS drug devel., 1993-96, chmn. bd. participants inter-company collaboration for AIDS drug devel., 1996-97; mem. adv. com. Mass. Gen. Hosp., Boston, 1994-98; chmn. steering com. Sr. Adv. Group Biotech., 1994-96; chmn. bd. mgmt. EuropaBio, 1997-98; bd. dirs. Human Genome Scis., Rockville, Md. Author: Chemotherapie: Grundlagen und Perspektiven, 1979, Immunpharmakologie, Grundlagen und Perspektiven, 1986, Immunopharmacology, Principles and Perspectives, 1990, In Quest of Tomorrow's Medicines, 1999; editor: (with others) Topics in Infectious Diseases, vol. 1, 1975, vol. 2, 1977; also over 250 articles. Personal E-mail: info@j_drews.de.

DREWS, RICHARD, tenor; b. Hebron, Nebr., Aug. 20, 1953; s. Raymond Herman and Naomi Dora (Schepker) D.; m. Mary Jane Means, July 20, 1985; 1 child, Emmet Lynn. EdB, U. Nebr., 1977, MusM, 1979. Instr. voice U. Wis., Eau Claire, 1980-85; mem. ensemble Lyric Opera Ensemble for Am. Artists, Chgo., 1986-87. Apprentice singer Santa Fe Opera, summers 1979, 80. Operatic debut as Alfredo in La Traviata, Edmonton (B.C., Can.) Opera, 1987; Am. debut as Rodolfo in La Boheme, Opera/Omaha, 1988; Met. Opera debut as Alfred Die Fledermaus, Jan. 1990, Washington Opera, Mar. 1990; appeared in Faust, Va. Opera, Norfolk, 1988, as Alfredo in La Traviata, Santa Fe (N.Mex.) Opera, 1989; Carnegie Hall debut in Nabucco, 1989 Recitalist in benefit for Blue Valley Nursing Home, Hebron, 1988. Winner Illinois Opera Guild Audition-on-the-Air, Chgo., 1987; regional winner Met. Opera Auditions, Chgo., 1987, nat. winner, 1988; William M. Sullivan grantee Nat. Inst. Am. Theatre, 1986 Mem. Nat. Assn. Tchrs. of Singing, 1980, Am. Guild Mus. Artists, Can. Actors Equity. Lutheran. Avocations: cooking, record collecting, antique furniture restoration. Office: care IMG 22 E 71st St New York NY 10021-4975

DREXEL, BARON JEROME, lawyer; b. Miami Beach, Fla., Sept. 3, 1954; s. Gustave L. and Dorris J. (Haas) D. AA, U. Fla., 1973; BA, U. Calif. Berkeley, 1979; MA in Econs., U. Miami, 1983, JD cum laude, 1985. Bar: Fla. 1985, Calif. 1987, U.S. Ct. Appeals (9th cir.) 1987, U.S. Ct. Appeals (11th cir.) 1989, U.S. dist. Ct. (no. dist.) Calif. 1986, U.S. Dist. Ct. (ctrl. dist.) Calif. 1987, U.S. Dist. Ct. (so. dist.) Calif. 1988. Survey crew mem. U.S. Forest Svc., Hayfork, Calif., 1979; sales rep. real estate Allen Morris Co., Miami, Fla., 1981-82; assoc. Shutts & Bowen, Miami, 1985-88, Lasky, Haas, Cohler & Munter, San Francisco, 1988-89, Aiken, Kramer & Cummings, Oakland, Calif., 1989-92, Bostwick & Tehin, San Francisco, 1992-95; pvt. practice Oakland, 1995—. Recipient J.B. Spence award U. Miami Law Rev. Mem. Order of Coif. Achievements include co-trial couns. for $15.4 million verdict. Office: Ste 1750 1 Kaiser Plz Oakland CA 94612-3688

DREXLER, KENNETH, lawyer; b. Aug. 2, 1941; s. Fred and Martha Jane (Cunningham) D. BA, Stanford U., 1963; JD, UCLA, 1969. Bar: Calif. 1970. Assoc. David S. Smith, Beverly Hills, Calif., 1970, McCutchen, Doyle, Brown and Enersen, San Francisco, Calif., 1970-77, Chickering & Gregory, San Francisco, Calif., 1977-80, ptnr., 1980-82, Drexler & Leach, San Rafael, Calif., 1982—. Served with AUS, 1964-66. Mem. Calif. State Bar (resolutions com. conf. of dels. 1979-83, chmn. 1982-83, adminstrn. justice com. 1983-89, chmn. 1987-88, adv. mem. 1990-2000), Marin County Bar Assn. (bd. dirs. 1985-87), Bar Assn. San Francisco (bd. dirs. 1980-81), San Francisco Barristers Club (pres. 1976, dir. 1975-76), Marin Conservation League (bd. dirs. 1985-97, 98—, treas. 2001—). Office: 1330 Lincoln Ave Ste 300 San Rafael CA 94901-2143 Office Phone: 415-485-1330. E-mail: kdrexler@svn.net.

DREXLER, MILLARD S., retail executive; b. Bronx, NY, 1944; married. Pres., CEO Ann Taylor Co., New York, NY, 1980—83; exec. v.p. merchandising, pres. Gap Stores div. Gap Inc., San Bruno, Calif., 1983—87; pres. The Gap Inc., San Bruno, 1987—95, pres., CEO San Francisco, 1995—2002; chmn., CEO J. Crew Group, Inc., New York, NY, 2003—. Office: J Crew Group Inc 770 Broadway New York NY 10003

DREXLER, RICHARD ALLAN, manufacturing executive; b. Chgo., May 14, 1947; s. Lloyd A. and Evelyn Violet (Kovaloff) D.; m. Clare F. Stunkel, Aug. 24, 1990; children by previous marriage: Dan Lloyd, Jason Ian. BS, Northwestern U., 1968, MBA, 1969. Staff v.p. Allied Products Corp., Chgo., 1971-75, sr. v.p. adminstrn., 1975-79, exec. v.p., COO, CFO, 1979-82, pres., COO, 1982-86, pres., CEO, 1986-93, chmn., pres., CEO, 1993—.

DREXLER, RUDY MATTHEW, JR., professional law enforcement dog trainer; b. Elkhart, Ind., Jan. 16, 1941; s. Rudy Matthew Sr. and Elaine Irene (Hardman) D.; m. Patricia Ann Overmyer, Apr. 4, 1981; children: Scott M., Tina S. Thode. Student, Purdue U., 1960-63. V.p. Custom Booth Mfg. Corp., Elkhart, Ind., 1962-80; pres. Orchard Kennels, Elkhart, Ind., 1964-79; pres., treas. Rudy Drexler's Sch. for Dogs, Inc., Elkhart, Ind., 1980—. Lectr. civic orgns.; instr. U. Del. Continuing Edn., Wilmington, 1978. Named to Honorable Order of Ky. Colonels, 1989; named hon. dep. Middlesex County Sheriff's Dept., New Brunswick, N.J., 1984, Daviess County Sheriff's Dept., Owensboro, Ky., 1988, Fairfield County Sheriff's Dept., Lancaster, Ohio, 1982. Mem. Midwest Police K-9 Assn. (founder 1984, tng. dir. 1984-87), Am. Soc. Law Enforcement Trainers (charter mem.), Internat. Narcotics Enforcement Officers Assn. (assoc. mem.), Can. Police K-9 Assn. (assoc. mem.), Nat. Police Res. Officers Assn. (hon. mem.), Moose. Office: Rudy Drexler's Sch for Dogs 50947 County Road 7 Elkhart IN 46514-8853 Office Phone: 574-264-7518. Business E-Mail: rudydrexler@aol.com.

DREYER, ALEC GILBERT, electric power industry executive; b. Murphysboro, Ill., Mar. 15, 1958; s. Gilbert Dean and Norma Mae (Cluster) D.; m. Sheri L. Snider, July 26, 1980; children: Hillary Christine, Ahren Grant. BA in Polit. Sci. and Acctg., U. Ill., 1980; MBA with honors, Washington U., 1987. CPA, Ill., Mo. Staff acct. Price Waterhouse, St. Louis, 1980-82, sr. acct., 1982-85, mgr., 1985-88, sr. mgr., 1988-92; contr. Ill. Power Co., Decatur, 1992-94, treas., contr., 1994-95, sr. v.p., 1999-2000; pres. Illinova Generating Co., Decatur, 1995-2000; sr. v.p. Illinova Corp., Decatur, 1999-2000; pres. Generation Dynegy, Inc., 2000—. Asst. treas. Com. To Expand Cervantes Conv. Ctr., St. Louis, 1987-88; mem. Citizens Adv. Coun., Edwardsville, Ill.,

1990-91; chmn. pers. svcs. divsn. United Way Macon County, Ill., 1994, bd. dirs., 1995-99, co-chmn. campaign drive, 1995, chmn. campaign drive, 1996, vice chmn. bd. dirs., 1997-98, chmn. bd. dirs., 1999; mem. Cmty. Leaders Coun. United Way Tex. Gulf Coast, 2001—. Mem. AICPA, Ill. Soc. CPAs, Phi Beta Kappa, Beta Gamma Sigma. Republican. Baptist. Avocations: golf, computing, in-line skating, reading. Home: 2631 Tangley St Houston TX 77005-2456 E-mail: alec.dreyer@dynegy.com.

DREYFOOS, ALEXANDER W., JR., investor, research scientist; b. 1932; m. Renate Dreyfoos; 1 child, Cathy; 1 child, Robert. BS, MIT, 1954; MBA, Harvard U., 1958; DSc (hon.), Lynn U., 1999. Chmn., chief rschr. The Dreyfoos Group, West Palm Beach, Fla. Lifetime trustee MIT Corp.; chmn. Raymond F. Kravis Ctr. for Performing Arts; bd. trustees Scripps Rsch. Inst., 2004—. Recipient Marshall B. Dalton Award, MIT, 1997, Bronze Beaver Award, 1997. Fellow: Am. Acad. Arts and Scis.; mem.: Sailfish Club of Fla., Beach Club, Harvard Club of N.Y.C., N.Y. Yacht Club. Avocations: yachting, flying, photography, scuba diving, fishing. Office: Scripps Rsch Inst 10550 N Torrey Pines Rd La Jolla CA 92037*

DREYFUSS, ERIC MARTIN, allergist; b. Bad Homburg, Germany, July 11, 1930; came to U.S., 1934; s. Walter and Hedwig (Herz) D.; m. Sandra Dale Gasul, June 16, 1957; children: Peter, Lisa. AB, Cornell U., 1953; MD, Chgo. Med. Sch., 1957. Diplomat Am. Bd. Allergy and Immunology. Intern Beth Israel Hosp., N.Y.C., 1957-58; resident in pediats. SUNY, Syracuse, 1958-60; fellow in allergy Rochester, N.Y., 1962-64; allergist Allergy Assocs. Rochester, 1964—. Asst. clin. prof. U. Rochester Sch. Medicine and Dentistry, 1970—. Capt. U.S. Army, 1960-62. Fellow Am. Acad. Allergy and Immunology, Am. Coll. Allergists, Am. Acad. Pediatrics. Office: Allergy Assocs Rochester 300 Goodman St S Rochester NY 14607-3105 Office Phone: 585-271-2755.

DREYFUSS, M(AX) PETER, research chemist, educator; b. Frankfurt, Germany, Sept. 24, 1932; came to U.S., 1938; s. Fritz David and Charlotte Pauline Dreyfuss; m. Patricia Marie Gajewski, Jan. 30, 1954; children: David Daniel, Simeon Karl. BS, Union Coll., 1952; PhD, Cornell U., 1957. Postdoctoral fellow U. Liverpool, Eng., 1963-65; sr. rsch. chemist B.F. Goodrich Co., Brecksville, Ohio, 1956-63, rsch. assoc., 1965-73, sr. rsch. assoc., 1973-81, sr. R&D assoc. Avon Lake, Ohio, 1982-84; sr. rsch. scientist, rsch. prof. Mich. Molecular Inst., Midland, 1984-90, adj. prof., 1986-92, Mich. Technol. U., Houghton, 1986-91, Cen. Mich. U., Mt. Pleasant, 1987-96. Vis. prof. Polish Acad. Scis., Poland, 1974; cons. in field. Contbr. over 25 articles to profl. jours., books. Leader Boy Scouts Am., Akron, Ohio, 1965-70, explorer advisor, 1970-81 Mem. Am. Chem. Soc. (treas. Akron ch. 1981, chmn. Midland ch. 1991), Phi Beta Kappa. Achievements include 5 patents in field; development of living oxonium ion polymerization. Home and Office: 3980 E Old Pine Trl Midland MI 48642-8891

DREYFUSS, RICHARD STEPHAN, actor; b. N.Y.C., Oct. 29, 1947; s. Norman and Gerry Dreyfuss; m. Jeramie Dreyfuss, 1983; children: Emily, Benjamin, Harry. Student, San Fernando Valley State Coll., 1965-67. Motion picture appearances include American Graffiti, 1973, Dillinger, 1973, The Apprenticeship of Duddy Kravitz, 1974, Jaws, 1975, Inserts, 1975, Close Encounters of the Third Kind, 1977, The Goodbye Girl, 1977, The Competition, 1980, Whose Life Is It Anyway?, 1981, Down and Out in Beverly Hills, 1986, Stand By Me, 1986, Tin Men, 1987, Stakeout, 1987, Nuts, 1987, Moon Over Parador, 1988, Let It Ride, 1989, Always, 1989, Postcards from the Edge 1990, What About Bob?, 1991, Once Around, 1991, Rosencrantz and Guildenstern Are Dead, 1991, Lost in Yonkers, 1993, Another Stakeout, 1993, Silent Fall, 1994, Mr. Holland's Opus, 1995 (Acad. award nominee for best actor 1996), The American President, 1995, Mad Dog Time, 1996, James and the Giant Peach, 1996, Night Falls on Manhattan, 1997, Krippendorf's Tribe, 1998, A Fine and Private Place, 1998, The Crew, 2000, The Old Man Who Read Love Stories, 2000, Who Is Cletis Tout?, 2001, Rudolph the Red-Nosed Reindeer and the Island of Misfit Toys (voice), 2001, Silver City, 2004; theatrical appearances include: Julius Caesar, 1978, Othello, 1979, Total Abandon, 1983, Death and the Maiden, 1992; actor, producer: The Big Fix, 1978; actor, TV movies: Two For The Money, 1972, Victory at Entebbe, 1976, The Call of the Wild (voice), 1997, Lansky, 1999, The Day Reagan Was Shot, 2001, producer Quiz Show, 1994, (TV movie) Oliver Twist, 1997; host TV series The Class of the 20th Century, 1991; actor, producer TV series The Education of Max Bickford, 2001-2002. Participant civil rights marches, lobbying for amnesty bills. Served alt. mil. duty Los Angeles County Gen. Hosp., 1969-71. Recipient Golden Globe award, 1978; Academy award as best actor in The Goodbye Girl, 1978 Mem. ACLU, Screen Actors Guild, Equity Assn., AFTRA, Motion Picture Acad. Arts and Scis. Office: William Morris Agy 151 S El Camino Dr Beverly Hills CA 90212-2775

DREYFUSS, ROCHELLE COOPER, law educator; b. 1947; BA, Wellesley Coll., 1968; MS, U. Calif., Berkeley, 1970; JD, Columbia U., 1981. Bar: NY 1982. Rsch. chemist Vanderbilt U. Med. Sch., Albert Einstein Med. Sch., Ciba Geigy Corp., 1970—78; law clk. to Hon. Wilfred Feinberg US Ct. Appeals 2nd Cir., NYC, 1981-82; law clk. to Chief Justice Warren E. Burger US Supreme Ct., Washington, 1982-83; asst. prof. NYU Sch. Law, 1983-86, assoc. prof., 1986-88, prof., 1988—, now Pauline Newman prof. law. Cons. Presdl. Commn. on Catastrophic Nuclear Accidents, 1989-90; vis. prof. U. Chgo., 1991; disting. vis. prof. U. Wash., Seattle, 2001. Mem. Am. Law Inst., Phi Beta Kappa, Sigma Xi. Office: NYU Sch Law Vanderbilt Hall Rm 308 40 Washington Sq S New York NY 10012-1099 Office Phone: 212-998-6258. E-mail: dreyfussr@juris.law.nyu.edu.*

DREYFUSS, STEPHEN LAWRENCE, lawyer; b. N.Y.C., May 28, 1949; s. Joseph David and Janet Roslyn (Schuman) D.; m. Lillian Francine Pliner, June 24, 1984; children: Katherine Marielle, Caroline Pliner. Student U. Paris, 1969-70; AB magna cum laude, Princeton U., 1971; JD (Harlan Fiske Stone scholar), Columbia U., 1974. Bar: N.J. 1974, N.Y. 1975, D.C. 1976. Law clk. to U.S. Dist. Judge, U.S. Dist. Ct., Newark, 1974-76; asst. dist. atty., N.Y. County, N.Y., 1976-79; assoc. Hellring, Lindeman, Goldstein, & Siegal, Newark, 1979-82, ptnr., 1983—. Mem. adv. com. dept. Romance langs. and Lits. Princeton U., 1989—, chmn., 1997—2002; chmn. adv. com. Dept. French and Italian, Princeton U., 2002—. Bd. dirs. French-Am. C. of C., N.Y.C., 1985—, nat. sec., 1987-90, v.p., 1991—98, exec. v.p. and legal counsel, 1998—. Co-author: (handbook) Special Considerations in Cases Involving Foreign Parties, 1992. Mem. N.J. State Bar Assn. (vice chair internat. law and orgns. sect. 1992—2001, chair com. on transnational litigation and arbitration 1992-93, vice chair antitrust law com. 1993-97, chair Com. on Internat. Trade and Investment, 1995), Assn. Fed. Bar State N.J., Union Internat. des Avocats (mem. bd. gov. U.S. nat. com., 1994—, del. gen. assembly, 1994—, conseiller du pres. 1997—98, regional sec. for N.Am., 1998—), Europe/USA 2000, Ivy Club. Home: 47 Cayuga Way Short Hills NJ 07078-1202 Office: Hellring Lindeman Goldstein & Siegal One Gateway Ctr Newark NJ 07102-5386 E-mail: sldreyfuss@hlgslaw.com.

DREZ, DAVID JACOB, JR., orthopedic surgeon, educator; b. Lake Charles, La., Aug. 21, 1938; s. David Jacob and Hester Adele (Bingham) D.; m. Judith Diane Wolfe, June 5, 1963; children: Susan, Catherine Ann Self, David Jacob III. BS, Tulane U., 1959, MD, 1963. Diplomate Am. Bd. Surgery, Am. Bd. Orthopaedic Surgery. Intern Charity Hosp., New Orleans, 1963-64, resident in gen. surgery, 1964-68, resident in orthopaedic surgery, 1968-71; resident Scottish Rite Hosp., Atlanta, 1969, USPHS Hosp., New Orleans, 1970; pvt. practice Orthopaedic Assocs., Lake Charles, 1971-82; pvt. practice Orthopaedic and Sports Injury Clinic Knee and Sports Medicine Ctr., Lake Charles, 1982-94; pvt. practice Ctr. for Orthopaedics, Lake Charles, 1994—. Staff Lake Charles Meml. Hosp., 1973—, bd. trustees, 1973, 80-82, sec.-treas., 1977, pres., 1981, chief surgery, 1984, 85; med. staff dept. orthopaedics Children's Hosp., New Orleans, 1988; La. state chmn. Orthopaedic Rsch. and Edn. Found., 1987, 90-92; network of orthopedic surgeons U.S. Gymnastics Fedn., 1988—; physician U.S. Soccer Assn., 1988—; examiner Am. Bd. Orthopaedic Surgery, 1989, 91, 92, bd. dirs.; vis. prof. numerous hosps. and univs.; speaker in field. Author: (with R. D'Ambrosia) Prevention and Treatment of Running Injuries, 1982, Prevention and Treatment of Running Injuries, 2d edit., 1989, (with D.W. Jackson) The Anterior Cruciate Deficient Knee-New Concepts in Ligament Repair, 1986, Orthopaedic Sports Medicine: Principles and Practice, 1994 (with Jesse DeLee); author 8 chpts. in books; editor Am. Jour. Sports Medicine, 1988—, Jour. Orthopaedic Techniques, 1993—; co-editor Operative Techniques in Sports Medicine jour., 1993—; mem. editorial bd. Orthopaedics, 1983—, Arthroscopy, 1984-89, Sports Medicine News, 1989—; author 5 video tapes, audio tape; mem. adv. bd. Clin. Update, Sports Medicine, 1983—, Clin. Orthopaedics and Related Rsch., 1987-93; con. rev. bd. Jour. Bone and Joint Surgeons, 1989—; contbr. over 35 articles to profl. jours. Team orthopaedist athletic dept. McNeese State U., Lake Charles, 1974—, pres. 100 Club, 1979; co-dir. Runner's Clinic, La. State U. Sch. Medicine, New Orleans, 1978-81; chief physician NAAU Boxing Championship, Lake Charles, 1979; mem. Gov.'s Coun. on Phys. Fitness and Sports, 1981; bd. dirs. Lake Area Runners, 1989-92. Maj. La. N.G., 1963-71. Named to La. Athletic Trainers Assn. Hall of Fame, 1989, McNeese State U. Hall of Honors, 1990. Mem. Acad. Orthopaedic Soc., Am. Acad. Orthopaedic Surgeons, Am. Acad. Sports Physicians, Am. Coll. Sports Medicine, Am. Coll. Surgeons, Am. Orthopaedic Assn., Am. Orthopaedic Foot Soc., Am. Orthopaedic Foot and Ankle Soc., Am. Orthopaedic Soc. Sports Medicine, Arthroscopy Assn. N.Am., Assn. Bone and Joint Surgeons, Assn. Sports Medicine Fellowship Dirs., Mid. Am. Orthopaedic Assn., Assn. Arthritic Hip and Knee Surgery, Australian-Am. Orthopaedic Soc., Calcasieu Parish Med. Soc., Clin. Orthopaedic Soc., European Soc. Knee Surgery and Arthroscopy, Herodicus Sports Medicine Soc. (past sec., v.p., pres.), Internat. Arthroscopy Assn., Internat. Soc. Knee, La. Orthopaedic Assn. (pres. 1992), La. State Med. Assn., Oscar Creech Surg. Soc., Orthopaedic Rsch. Soc., Soc. Internat. Chirurgie Orthopedique Traumatologie, Soc. Internat. Recherche Orthopedique Tramatologie. Avocations: reading, jogging, travel, family activities. Office: Ctr for Orthopedics 1717 Oak Park Blvd 3d Fl Lake Charles LA 70601-8990

DRIES, WILLIAM, III, human services manager, musician, educator; b. Allentown, Pa., Apr. 12, 1966; s. William Elijah and Karoline; m. Rochelle Leigh Prewitt, Dec. 18, 1999; 1 adopted child. BS in Music Edn., West Cheoler U., 1988. Band dir. Northwestern Lehigh Sch. Dist., Pa., 1988—90, Tamagua Area Sch. Dist., Pa., 1990—93, Upper Perkiomen Sch. Dist., Pennsburg, Pa., 1993—98, South Columbus Sch. Dist., Tabor City, NC, 1998—99, New Hanover Sch. Dist., Wilmington, NC, 1999—2003; human resources mgr. Custom Metal Products, Wilmington, NC, 2003—. Musician (trumpet): Wilmington Symphony, Long Bay Symphony, (Broadway plays) Chicago. Avocations: travel, sports. Home: 5007 Brenwood Ct Wilmington NC 28409 Office: Custom Metal Products 150 Division Dr Wilmington NC 28401 Business E-Mail: billd@custommetalproducts.bz.

DRIESSEN, CHRISTINE F., broadcast executive; m. Terry Driessen; 2 children. Contr. ESPN, 1985—90, v.p. fin. and planning, 1990—95, sr. v.p. and CFO, 1995—98, exec. v.p. and CFO Bristol, Conn., 1998—. Named one of Top 25 Women in Sports, St. & Smith's Sports Bus. Jour., 1999, Wonder Women in media, Multichannel News, 2003. Office: ESPN 935 Middle St Bristol CT 06010

DRIETZ, AMY MARIE GOLBERG, special education educator; d. Adrian Carl and Judith Ann Golberg; m. John Leonard Drietz, May 13, 2000; 1 child, Grace. BA in elem. and spl. edn., Augustana Coll., 1993—97; MSc in ednl. leadership, SW State U., 2001—03. Ld/ebd tchr. Canby Elem. Sch., Canby, Minn., 1997—; girl's basketball coach Canby H.S., Canby, Minn., 2002—04, volleyball coach, 1999—2003. Office Phone: 507-223-2003.

DRIGALENKO, EUGENE IVAN, geneticist, researcher; b. Tomsk, Russia, Mar. 20, 1953; arrived in U.S., 1995; s. Ivan Pavlovich and Tatiana Gavrilovna Drigalenko; m. Irina Yurii Radygina, Sept. 7, 1983; children: Polina Eugene, Alina Eugene. M, Tomsk State U., Tomsk, Russia, 1975; PhD, Med. Genetics Rsch. Inst., Moscow, 1989. Rsch. assoc. Siberian Physics-Technical Inst., Tomsk, Russia, 1975—80, Siberian Med. U., Tomsk, Russia, 1980—82, Siberian Br. of Moscow Psychiat. Inst., Tomsk, Russia, 1982—86, Med. Genetics Rsch. Inst., Tomsk, Russia, 1986—89; sr. rsch. assoc. Mental Health Rsch. Inst., Tomsk, Russia, 1989—93; sr. lectr. Tomsk State Acad. of Control Systems and Radioelectronics, Tomsk, Russia, 1993—95; sr. rsch. assoc. Case Western Res. U., Cleve., 1995—99; asst. prof. Tex. Tech U. Health Scis. Ctr., Lubbock, Tex., 1999—. Grantee, Fogarty Internat. Ctr. (Nat. Inst. of Health), 1996-1998. Mem.: Internat. Genetic Epidemiology Soc., Am. Soc. of Human Genetics. Achievements include research in More than 30 pub. papers. Home: 4830 72nd St Lubbock TX 79424-2102 Office: Texas Tech Univ Health Scis Ctr 3601 4th St Lubbock TX 79430-8321 Office Fax: 806-743-2698. Personal E-mail: eugeneid@lycos.com. Business E-Mail: eugene.drigalenko@ttuhsc.edu.

DRIGGS, CHARLES MULFORD, lawyer; b. East Cleveland, Ohio, Jan. 26, 1924; s. Karl Holcomb and Lila Vandeveer (Wilson) D.; children: Ruth, Rachel, Carrie, Karl H., Charles M.; m. Ann Eileen Zargari, Oct. 25, 1991. BS, Yale U., 1947, JD, 1950. Bar: Ohio 1951. Assoc. Squire, Sanders & Dempsey, Cleve., 1950-64, ptnr., 1964-88, of counsel, 1988-91; pvt. practice civil law Cleve., 1991-95; ptnr. Driggs, Lucas, Brubaker & Hogg Co., LPA, Willoughby Hills, Ohio, 1995—. Pres. Bratenahl (Ohio) Sch. Bd., 1958—62; mem. adv. coun. Cleve. Ctr. for Theol. Edn., 1978—. Mem. ABA, Ohio Bar Assn., Lake County Bar Assn., Cleve. Bar Assn., Greater Cleve. Growth Assn., Cleve. Law Libr. Assn. (trustee 1977-91), Ct. Nisi Prius (judge 2000), Citizens League Greater Cleve., Geauga County Bar Assn., Phi Delta Phi, Tau Beta Pi, Phi Gamma Delta. Home: 8011 Eagle Rd Kirtland OH 44094 Office: 38500 Chardon Rd Willoughby OH 44094 Office Phone: 440-391-5100. E-mail: charles@driggslaw.com. *Any success I may have achieved I attribute to my continuing attempt to live and conduct my affairs in a manner that my family and friends may later reflect upon with pride.*

DRIGGS, MARGARET, private school educator; b. Kansas City, Kans., June 30, 1909; d. William Foster and Lillian Edith (Landers) Brazier; m. J.W. Quarrier, Nov. 26, 1933 (div. July 1945); children: John Chilton, Philip Harrington, Camille Elizabeth; m. Howard R. Driggs, Sept. 26, 1948 (dec.). AB, U. Kans., 1930; postgrad., Hofstra Coll., 1960, Grad. Sch. Libr. Sci., Pratt Inst., 1964-65. Adminstrv. asst. to sec., dir. pub. rels. Hofstra Coll., 1956-61, staff adivser Nexus (yrbook.), 1961; mem. faculty Westover Sch., Middlebury, Conn., 1964-65; dir. devel. pub. rels., asst. to dean Cathedral Sch. of St. Mary, Garden City, N.Y., 1965, also yrbook adviser. Nat. dir. pub. rels. Am. Pioneer Trails Assn., 1948; chmn. pub. rels. NYU Faculty Women's Club, 1950-54; nat. 1st v.p. Assn. parents and Friends Kings Point, 1957-58; judge Nat. Svc. Acad. Debate Tournament, 1956; hostess Kings Point Congl. com., 1957; installed Duchess of Richelieu collection St. Mary's Libr., 1973; co-chmn. Guides N.J. Gov.'s Mansion Morven, 1975-82. Contbr. Kansas City Star and Johnson County (Kans.) Herald, 1930-33; editor Am. Trails Series filmstrips; curator Driggs Collection of Americana; represented in Native N. Am. Women Exhbn., Skillman Libr., Lafayette Coll., 1992; editor: New Light on Old Glory, 1950, Pitch Pine Tales, 1951, Nick Wilson, 1951, George, The Handcart Boy, 1952,The Old West Speaks, 1956, When Grandfather was a Boy and Western Cowkid, 1957 (all by Howard R. Driggs); contbg. editor Nat. Assn. Ind. Schs. Archives, Harvard, 1965; editor and photographer Vive Rochambeau, Vive Washington. Chmn. docents N.J. Hist. Soc. at Morven, Princeton, 1982-86; mem. women's coun. Hofstra Coll., 1959-60; mem. U.S. Com. for UN Children's Fund, 1957; mem. Friends of Princeton U. Libr., 1975, Friends of the Winston Churchill Meml. and Libr., Westminster Coll., 1989; mem. Princeton Med. Ctr. Aux.; chmn. Civilian Hostesses 15th Ann. U. S. Army Mus. Conf., Princeton, 1986, Salute to Hall of Fame Ceremony the Voice of Am. Broadcast, Gould Meml. Libr., NYU, 1953; mem. Am. Farm Trust, 1992; mem. Denver Pub. Libr. Friends Found. Recipient Disting. Svc. Citatin Am. Pioneer Trails Assn., 1943, Columbia Scholastic Press Assn. medal, 1970, pin for vol. work in Princeton, 1976, French-Am Alliance medal, cert. and hist. house tile award N.J. Hist. Soc., 1984; Margaret Brazier Driggs Collection of Americana established at U. Kans., 1953, Hofstra Coll., 1961. Mem. Hist. Soc. Gov.'s Mansion Guides, Internat. Platform Assn., Assn. Coll. and Rsch. Librs., Hist. Soc. Princeton, Nat. Trust Hist. Preservation, Smithsonian Assocs., Nat. Parks and Conservatin Assn., Women's Bd. N.J. Hist. Soc., Smithsonian Nat. Mus. of Am. Indian (charter 1999), Met. Mus. Art, Women's Coll. Club Princeton, Woodrow Wilson Internat. Ctr. for Scholars (assoc. 1999), Amiga of Orgn. of Am. States, NYU Faculty Club (hon., life), Libr. of Congress (charter assoc. 1994), Present Day Club (Princeton), Gold Medal Club, Learned Club, Pi Delta Epsilon (grand councilman 1960-61). Home: 11515 Quivas Way Denver CO 80234-2622 Personal E-mail: mdriggs@driggsfoundation.org.

DRIKER, EUGENE, lawyer; b. Detroit, Feb. 24, 1937; s. Charles and Frances (Hoffman) D.; m. Elaine Carol Zeidman, June 17, 1959; children: Elissa Ruth, Stephen Joel. AB, Wayne State U., 1958, JD, 1961; LL.M., George Washington U., 1962; LLD (hon.), Wayne State U., 2002. Bar: Mich. 1962, U.S. Ct. Appeals (5th and 6th cirs.), U.S. Supreme Ct. Trial atty. antitrust div. U.S. Dept. Justice, Washington, 1961-64; ptnr. Friedman, Meyers & Keys, Detroit, 1964-68, Barris, Sott, Denn & Driker, Detroit, 1968—. Lectr. law Wayne State U., Detroit, 1964-68; lectr. in field; arbitrator Am. Arbitration Assn. Commr. City of Detroit Bldg. Authority, 1974-79; mem. City of Detroit Bd. Police Commrs., 1979-83; chmn. Wayne State U. Law Sch. Fund, 1972-74, 87-88; bd. dirs. Jewish Vocat. Sch., 1983-92, pres., 1993-95; bd. dirs. Detroit Symphony Orch. Hall, Inc., 1983-2000; v.p. Am. Jewish Com., Detroit, 1988-90; bd. govs. Wayne State U., 2002—. Fellow Am. Coll. Trial Lawyers, Internat. Acad. Trial Lawyers, Am. Bar Found.; mem. Wayne State Law Sch. Alumni Assn. (pres. 1971-72), Am. Law Inst., Order of Coif, Detroit Club, Renaissance Club. Democrat. Jewish. Avocations: biking, reading, walking. Office: Barris Sott Denn & Driker 211 W Fort St 15th Fl Detroit MI 48226-3244 Office Phone: 313-596-9303. Business E-Mail: edriker@bsdd.com.

DRILLINGER, DAVID W., music educator; b. Springfield, Ill., Oct. 31, 1952; s. Fred E and Mary Ruth Drillinger; m. Gail F Plassman, July 10, 1954; children: Eric T, Claire E. MA, Ea. Ill. U., Charleston, 1975. Cert. K-12 spl. music tchr. Ill., 1974. Dir. of bands Centralia H.S., Centralia, Ill., 1975—86, Alton Cmty. Unit Sch. Dist. #11, Alton, Ill., 1986—; dir. of jazz bands Kaskaskia Coll., Centralia, Ill., 1977—78; dir. of cmty. bands Lewis & Clark C.C., Godfrey, Ill., 1996—2001. Music dir. Alton Mcpl. Band, 1987—; fin. advisor Alton Band and Orch. Builders, 1986—; bd. of dirs. Alton Symphony Orch., 1990—96. Music arranger (band music) Villanelle, Nathan's Song, Piano Concerto #1; musician: (trumpet soloist) Concerto, by Arutunian, Concerto, by Haydn. Named Hometown Hero in Edn., City on a Hill, Alton, Ill., 2002; recipient Educator of the Yr., Centralia H.S., 1984—85, Cmty. Builders award, Masons, 1996, Those Who Excel Award of Spl. Recognition, Ill. State Bd. of Edn., 1998—99, Cert. of Appreciation, USMC, 2003. Mem.: Am. Sch. Band Directors Assn., Nat. Band Assn. (ill. state chair 1991—2001), Internat. Trumpet Guild, Ill. Music Educators Assn. (dist. vi pres. 1991—2005), Music Educators Nat. Conf., Kappa Kappa Psi. Methodist. Avocations: reading, computers, music. Home: PO Box 502 Godfrey IL 62035 Office: Alton High School 2200 College Ave Alton IL 62002 Fax: 618 463 2018. Office Phone: 618 474 2700 x725. Personal E-mail: bach37@charter.net. E-mail: ddrillinger@alton.madison.k12.il.us.

DRINAN, ROBERT FREDERICK, law educator; b. Boston, Nov. 15, 1920; s. James Joseph and Ann Mary (Flanagan) D. AB, Boston Coll., 1942, MA, 1947; LL.B., Georgetown U., 1949, LL.M., 1950; Th.D., Gregorian U., Rome, 1954; study, Florence, Italy, 1954-55; LL.D. (hon.), Worcester State Coll., 1970, L.I. U., 1970, R.I. Coll., 1971, St. Joseph's Coll., Phila., 1975, Syracuse U., 1977, Villanova U., 1977, Framingham (Mass.) State Coll., 1978, U. Santa Clara, 1980, Kenyon Coll., 1981, Lowell U., 1981, U. Bridgeport, 1981, Loyola U., Chgo., 1981, Gonzaga U., 1981, Curry Coll., 1982, De Paul U., 1984, U. San Diego, 1984, Mt. St. Mary Coll., 1985, Hebrew Coll., 1987, Notre Dame Coll., Manchester, N.H., 1989, Walsh Coll., Ohio, 1990, Georgetown U., 1991; LLD (hon.), Trinity Coll., 1998, Brandeis U., 2002, CUNY, 2003. Bar: D.C. 1950, Mass. 1956, U.S. Supreme Ct. 1955; ordained priest Roman Cath. Ch., 1953. Asst. dean Boston Coll. Law Sch., 1955-56, dean, 1956-70; vis. prof. U. Tex. Law Sch., 1966-67; mem. 92d-96th Congresses from 4th Mass. dist.; mem. jud. com., govt. ops. com., house select com. on aging, chmn. subcom. on criminal justice; columnist Nat. Cath. Reporter, 1980; prof., Sch. of Law Georgetown U., Washington, 1980—. Chmn. adv. com. Mass. U.S. Civil Rights, 1962-70; mem. vis. com. Div. Sch., Harvard U., 1975-78; bd. dirs. Bread for the World; founder Nat. Interreligious Task Force on Soviet Jewry.; mem. exec. com. Assn. Am. Law Schs.; vis. lectr. Oxford U., Eng, 1988; vis. prof. U. Heidelberg, Germany, 2003. Author: Religion, the Courts and Public Policy, 1963, Democracy, Dissent and Disorder, 1969, Vietnam and Armageddon, 1970, Honor the Promise, America's Commitment to Israel, 1977, Beyond the Nuclear Freeze, 1983; editor: The Right To Be Educated, 1968, God and Caesar on the Potomac, 1985, Cry of the Oppressed: The History and Hope of the Human Rights Revolution, 1987, Stories from the American Soul, 1990, The Fractured Dream, 1991, The Mobilization of Shame--A World View of Human Richts, 2001, Can God & Caesar Coexist? Balancing Religious Freedom and International Law, 2004; editor in chief Family Law Quar., 1967-70; contbr. editor: nat. Cath. weekly America, 1958-70. Contbr. articles to jours. of opinion. Pres. Ams. for Dem. Action, 1981-84. Recipient Freedom of Worship medal, Roosevelt Inst., 2003. Fellow Am. Acad. Arts and Scis.; mem. ABA (chmn. sect. individual rights and responsibilities 1990-91, bd. dels. 1996-99, chmn. standing com. professionalism 1996—, ABA medal 2004), NCCJ (nat. trustee), Am. Law Inst., Common Cause (nat. governing bd. 1984-87, 96-99), Mass. Bar Assn. (v.p. 1961), Boston Bar Assn. Office: Georgetown U Law Ctr 600 New Jersey Ave NW Washington DC 20001-2022 Office Phone: 202-662-9073, 202-662-9073. Office Fax: 202-662-9412. Business E-Mail: drinan@law.georgetown.edu.

DRINFELD, VLADIMIR GERSHONOVICH, mathematician, educator; b. Kharkov, Ukraine, 1954; Grad., Moscow U., 1974, PhD, 1978. With B. Verkin Inst. Low Temperature Physics, Acad. Scis. Ukraine, 1981-98; prof. Bashkir U., Ufa, Russia, Ukrain Kharkav U.; sr. prof. dept math. U. Chgo., 1998—, Harry Pratt Judson Disting. Svc. Prof. in math. Recipient Fields medal Internat. Congress Mathematicians, Kyoto, Japan, 1990. Mem.: Acad. Scis. Ukraine. Achievements include research on quantum groups and number theory; proff. of the langlands conjecture for GL (2) over a functional field. Office: U Chgo Dept Math 5734 S University Ave Chicago IL 60637-1514

DRINKO, JOHN DEAVER, lawyer; b. St. Marys, W.Va., June 17, 1921; s. Emery J. and Hazel (White) D.; m. Elizabeth Gibson, May 14, 1946; children: Elizabeth Lee Sullivan, Diana Lynn Drinko, John Randall, Jay Deaver. AB, Marshall U., 1942; JD, Ohio State U., 1944; postgrad., U. Tex. Sch. Law, 1944; LLD (hon.), Marshall U., 1980, Ohio State U., 1986, John Carroll U., 1987, Capital U., 1988, Cleve. State U., 1990; DHL (hon.), David N. Myers Coll., 1990, U. N.H., 1992, Baldwin-Wallace Coll., 1993, Ursuline Coll., 1994, Notre Dame Coll., 1997, U. Rio Grande, 1999, Marietta Coll., 2001. Bar: Ohio 1945, D.C 1946, U.S. Dist. Ct. (no. dist.) Ohio 1958. Assoc. Baker & Hostetler, Cleve., 1945-55, ptnr., 1955-69, mng. ptnr., from 1969, sr. adviser to mng. com. Chmn. bd. Cleve. Inst. Electronics Inc., Double D Ranch Inc., Ohio; bd. dirs. Cloyes Gear and Products Inc., Orvis Co. Inc., Preformed Line Products Inc. Trustee Elizabeth G. and John D. Drinko Charitable Found., Orvis-Perkins Found., Thomas F. Peterson Found., Mellen Found., The Cloyes-Myers Found., Marshall U. Found.; founder Consortium of Multiple Sclerosis Ctrs., Mellen Conf. on Acute and Critical Care Nursing, Case Western Res. U. Disting. fellow Cleve. Clinc Found., 1991; Ohio State Law Sch. Bldg. named in his honor, 1995, libr. at Marshall U. named in his honor, 1997; inducted into Bus. Hall of Fame, Marshall Univ., 1996. Mem. ABA, Am. Jud. Assn., Bar Assn. Greater Cleve., Greater Cleve. Growth Assn., Ohio State Bar Assn., Jud. Conf. 8th Jud. Dist. (life), Soc. Benchers, Case Western Res. U. Law Sch. Assn., Cleve. Play House, Cleve. Civil War Round-table, Mayfield Country Club, Union Club, The Club at Soc. Ctr., O'Donnell Golf Club, Order of Coif, 33o Scottish Rite Mason, Knight Templar, York Rite, Euclid Blue Lodge No. 599 (Jesters, Shrine, Grotto). Republican. Presbyterian. Home: 4891 Middledale Rd Cleveland OH 44124-2522 also: 1245 Otono Dr Palm Springs CA 92264-8445 Office: Baker & Hostetler LLP 1900 E 9th St Ste 3200 Cleveland OH 44114-3485

DRINKWARD, CECIL, construction company executive; m. Sally Drinkward. BS in Engring., Calif. Tech. With Del E. Webb Corp., Phoenix; joined as exec. v.p., gen. mgr. Hoffman Corp., 1967; pres.; CEO Hoffman Corp., Portland, Oreg. Pres., mem. bd. trustees Oregon State U. Found.; mem. Oregon State U. Coun. Regents. Office: Hoffman Construction Co 805 SW Broadway Ste 2100 Portland OR 97205-3361*

DRINNON, JANIS BOLTON, artist, poet, volunteer; b. Pineville, Ky., July 28, 1922; d. Clyde Herman and Violet Ethiele (Hendrickson) Bolton; m. Kenneth Cleveland Drinnon, June 13, 1948; 1 child, Dena Daryl. Student, Lincoln Meml. U., Harrogate, Tenn., 1947-48, Newspaper Inst. Am.; comml. art cert., Art Instrn. Sch., Mpls., 1968. Author: (poems) In HIS Care: A Book of Inspirational Poetry, 1998. Organizer, prodr., dir. religious plays drama dept. Alice Bell Bapt. Ch., Knoxville, Tenn.; mem. New Hopewell Bapt. Ch., Knoxville. Named to Internat. Poetry Hall of Fame, 1996; recipient Editors Choice award, Nat. Libr. Poetry. Mem.: Internat. Soc. Poets (disting. mem.). Republican. Avocations: arts, crafts, painting, composing poetry. Home: 7342 Hodges Ferry Rd Knoxville TN 37920-9732 E-mail: kcdrinnon@aol.com.

DRINNON, RICHARD, retired historian; b. Portland, Oreg., Jan. 4, 1925; s. John Henry and Emma (Tweed) D.; m. Anna Maria Faulise, Oct. 20, 1945; children: Donna Elizabeth, Jon Tweed. BA summa cum laude, Willamette U., 1950; MA, U. Minn., 1951, PhD, 1957. Instr. humanities U. Minn., 1952-53, social sci., 1955-57; instr. Am. history U. Calif., 1957-58, asst. prof., 1958-61; Bruern fellow in Am. studies U. Leeds, 1961-63; faculty research fellow Social Sci. Research Council, 1963-64; asso. prof. history Hobart and William Smith Colls., 1964-66; chmn. dept. history Bucknell U., 1966-74, prof. history, 1974-87, prof. emeritus, 1987—. Vis. prof. U. Paris, 1975 Author: Rebel in Paradise: a Biography of Emma Goldman, 1961, White Savage: The Case of John Dunn Hunter, 1972, Facing West: The Metaphysics of Indian-Hating and Empire-Building, 1980, 90, 97, Keeper of Concentration Camps: Dillon S. Myer and American Racism, 1987; co-editor: Nowhere at Home: Letters from Exile of Emma Goldman and Alexander Berkman, 1974; contbr. articles and revs. to profl. jours. and mags. Served with USNR, 1942-46. NEH sr. fellow, 1980-81 Office: PO Box 1001 Port Orford OR 97465-1001

DRISCOLL, CHARLES FREDERICK, physicist, educator; b. Tucson, Feb. 28, 1950; s. John Raymond Gozzi and Barbara Jean (Hamilton) Driscoll; m. Suzan C. Bain, Dec. 30, 1972; children: Thomas A., Robert A. BA in Physics summa cum laude, Cornell U., 1969; MS, U. Calif. San Diego, La Jolla, 1972, PhD, 1976. Staff scientist Gen. Atomics, San Diego, 1969; rsch. asst. U. Calif. San Diego, La Jolla, 1971-76, rsch. physicist, sr. lectr., 1976-96, prof. physics, 1996—, assoc. dir. Inst. for Pure and Applied Scis., 1998—. Cons. Sci. Applications, Inc., 1980-81; staff physicist, cons. Molecular Biosystems, Inc., 1981-82. Editor: Non-Neutral Plasma Physics, 1988; contbr. numerous articles to sci. jours. Fellow NSF, 1969-71. Fellow Am. Phys. Soc. (Excellence in Plasma Physics Rsch. award 1991, Disting. Lectr. divsn. plasma physics 1999-2000); mem. AAAS, Math. Assn. Am., Phi Beta Kappa. Achievements include development of quantitative analysis of magnetic targeting of microspheres in capillaries, experiments and theory on magnetized electron plasmas, new camera-diagnosed electron plasma apparatus, new laser-diagnosed ion plasma apparatus for in-situ transport measurements; establishment of magnetic containment characteristics of unneutralized plasmas; measurement of collisional transport of heat and particles to thermal equilibrium; observation of new 2D fluid instability and relaxation of 2D turbulence to vortex crystal states. Office: U Calif San Diego Dept Physics 0319 9500 Gilman Dr Dept 0319 La Jolla CA 92093-5004 E-mail: fdriscoll@ucsd.edu.

DRISCOLL, DAVID LEE, chiropractor; b. Storm Lake, Iowa, Aug. 3, 1954; s. Glenn Francis and Jeannine Ann (Layer) D.; m. Joan Marie Valle, Sept. 8, 1973; children: Jennifer Marie, Matthew Bryan. D Chiropractic, Logan Coll. Chiropractic, Chesterfield, Mo., 1978. Pvt. practice, Colorado Springs, 1978—. Fellow Internat. Biocranial Acad. (assoc. instr., ednl. dir.), Internat. Acad. Clin. Acupuncture; mem. Am. Chiropractic Assn., Colo. Chiropractic Assn., El Paso County Chiropractic Assn., Internat. Biocranial Acad. (ednl. dir.). Republican. Roman Catholic. Avocations: volleyball, golf, reading. Home: 813 Crown Ridge Dr Colorado Springs CO 80904-1731 Office: Driscoll Chiropractic 1819 W Colorado Ave Colorado Springs CO 80904-3836 Office Phone: 719-635-3555. Business E-Mail: driscollbct@aol.com.

DRISCOLL, DAVID P., school system administrator; BA, Boston Coll.; PhD in Ednl. Adminstrn., Boston Coll; MA in Ednl. Adminstrn., Salem State Coll. Math. tchr. Jr. HS, Somerville, Mass., Sr. H.S., Melrose, Mass.; supt. schs. Melrose, 1984—93; dep. commr. schs. State of Mass., 1993—99; commr. of edn. Mass. Dept. Edn., 1999—. Prin. investigator in Mass. NSF Math. and Sci. Program; co-developer five year master plan Mass. Dept. Edn., 1995; mem. oversight bds. School to Work Initiative, Mass.; chmn. Mass. Tchrs. Retirement Bd., 1998—. Mem.: Coun. Chief State Sch. Officers (pres.). Office: Mass Dept Edn 350 Main St Malden MA 02148-5023 Mailing: Council of Chief State Sch Officers One Massachusetts Ave NW Ste 700 Washington DC 20001-1431 Office Phone: 202-336-7000. Office Fax: 202-408-8072.

DRISCOLL, GARRETT BATES, retired telecommunications executive; b. Terre Haute, Ind., July 10, 1932; s. James Edgar and Lorraine Emma (Simmons) D.; m. Suzanne Keder O'Reilly, Apr. 30, 1960 (div. Sept. 1984); children: Garrett Edward, Lorraine Elizabeth Driscoll Veltri; m. Ivy Juanita Bryant, Sept. 24, 1985 (div. Aug. 1995); children: Jennifer Louise, Caroline Margaret; m. Janice Patterson Buckalew, Oct. 25, 1996. AA, Broward C.C., Ft. Lauderdale, Fla., 1973; BA, Fla. Atlantic U., Boca Raton, 1979. Tech. supr. TRT Telecom. Corp., Ft. Lauderdale, 1972-80, asst. mgr. N.Y. ops. N.Y.C., 1980-82; asst. v.p. telecom. 1st Am. Bank, Lake Worth, Fla., 1983-86; dir. telecom. R&D John Alden Sys. Co., Miami, Fla., 1986-97; advisor Jan Gar Enterprises, Lake Wales, Fla., 1997—98; ret., 1998. Lectr. U. Miami, 1988-97. With USAF, 1951-71. Lutheran. Avocations: reading, woodworking, exercise. Business E-Mail: garrettjanice@msn.com.

DRISCOLL, JAMES S., entrepreneurial strategist; b. Boston, Apr. 8, 1966; s. James A. and Edna L. (Rust) Driscoll. BA, Stanford (Calif.) U., 1988; MA, Harvard U., 1995, postgrad., 1995—. Assoc. cons. Braxton Assocs., Boston, 1988-90; mgr. Deloitte & Touche, Moscow, 1990-92; ptnr. IMA Consulting, Boston, 1992-94; dir. consulting Cambridge (Mass.) Interactive Internet Pub., 1994-95; sr. cons. Denneen and Co., Boston, 1997—, of counsel, 1996—. Founder, editor Techne: Jour. Tech., Stanford, 1987-88, Release Mag., Stanford, 1988. Mellon fellow Andrew J. Mellon Found., Princeton, N.J., 1994, Packard fellow Harvard U., 1999. Mem. MLA, Am. Conf. Irish Studies, Cumann na Gaeilge im Boston, Soc. for Crit. Exch. Office: 401 Commonwealth Ave Boston MA 02215-2317

DRISCOLL, KIMBERLEE MARIE, lawyer; b. Binghamton, N.Y., July 17, 1961; d. Patrick Donald and Diane Cecile (Richmond) Lake; m. Matthew Victor Driscoll, Aug. 6, 1983; children: John Patrick, Bennett George. BA, Colgate U., 1983; JD, Union U., 1986. Bar: N.Y. 1987, Mass. 1988. Asst. gen. counsel Oxbow Corp., Dedham, Mass., 1987-90; corp. counsel, sec. Putnam, Hayes & Bartlett, Inc., Cambridge, Mass., 1990-92; v.p., gen. counsel Merrill Internat. Ltd., Cambridge, 1992—2000; gen. counsel Arthur D. Little, Inc., Cambridge, 2000—01; pres. Resolutions Mgmt. Ltd., Houston, 2001—. Mem. ABA (vice chair spl. com. internat. energy law 1993—), Mass. Bar Assn., N.Y. Bar Assn., Turnaround Mgmt. Assn. Office Phone: 781-929-6919. Business E-Mail: kmdriscoll@resolutionsmanagement.com.

DRISCOLL, MATTHEW J., mayor, real estate developer, small business owner; b. 1958; married; 3 children. 2d dist. councilor Syracuse Common Coun., 1987—89, 3d dist. councilor, 1995, pres., 1998—2001; mayor City of Syracuse, 2001—; prin., owner Restaurant. Office: 203 City Hall Syracuse NY 13202-1473

DRISCOLL, MICHAEL THOMAS, music educator, conductor; b. Portland, Maine, Mar. 6, 1975; BSEE, Worcester (Mass.) Poly. Inst., 1997, MSEE, 1999; MM in Choral Conducting, New Eng. Conservatory, Boston, 2003. Sr. software engr. Data Transl., Inc., Marlboro, Mass., 1999—2001; asst. dir. Masterworks Chorale, Belmont, Mass., 2000—04; music dir. Saengerfest Men's Chorus, Weston, Mass., 2001—; choral dir., tchr. Brookline (Mass.) H.S., 2003—; dir. choirs U. Mass., Dartmouth, 2004—. Mem.: Conductor's Guild, Chorus Am., Music Educators Nat. Conf., Am. Choral Directors Assn.

DRISCOLL, VIRGILYN MAE (SCHAETZEL), retired art educator, artist, consultant; b. Fond du Lac, Wis., May 14, 1932; d. Edward William and Louise (Heider) Schaetzel; m. Patrick A. Driscoll, Aug. 13, 1955; children: Mark P., Craig A., Chris T. BS in Art Edn., Wis. State Coll., 1954; MS in Art, U. Wis., Milw., 1973. Tchr. elem. art Green Bay (Wis.) Pub. Schs., 1954-55, Elm-Brook Pub. Schs., Elm Grove, Brookfield, Wis., 1955-58, supr. elem. art, 1958-66; tchr. secondary art, dept. chair Greendale (Wis.) Pub. Schs., 1967—93; exec. dir. Wis. Alliance Arts Edn., 1993—2000; dir., co-founder Wis. Champions for Arts Edn. Bus. and Cmty. Advs., Inc., 2002—. Arts Edn. Cons., 2000—; art curriculum task force Wis. Dept. Pub. Instrn., 1981—85; mem. task force Wis. Plan Arts Edn., Arts in Sch.s Basic Edn. Grant, 1986—88; mem. State Supts. Commn. Arts Edn., 1988—89; coord. Student Art Exhibit Wis. Assn. Sch. Bd. Joint Conv., 1988—; mem. steering com. arts edn. Wis. Arts Bd., Wis. Alliance Arts Edn., Dept. Pub. Instrn., 1992—; chmn. Wis. Challenging Content Stds. in Arts, 1994—96; coord., facilitator State Supt.'s Blue Ribbon Commn. Arts Edn., 1999—2000; mem. task force Wis. Dept. Pub. Instrn. Integrated Curriculum Guide, 1999—2000; hon. bd. dirs. Wis. Alliance Arts Edn., 2000—. Mem. editl. bd. Spectrum: Jour. Wis. Art Edn., 1986—87, 1988—90; author: (handbook) National Year of Secondary Art, 1990. Named Educator of the Yr., Beloit (Wis.) Coll., 1986, Wis. Rep. Tchr. Inst., 50th Ann. Nat. Gallery Art, Washington, 1991; recipient Excellence in the Arts award, 2000, cert. of Recognition in the Arts and Art Edn., 2000, Disting. Alumnus award, U. Wis., 2001, Distinction award for Dance Edn., 2002. Mem.: NEA, Milw. Area Tchrs. Art (pres. 1982—83), Wis. Painters and Sculptors, Wis. Alliance Art Edn. (pres. 1991—, bd. dirs.), Wis. Art Edn. Assn. (mem. adv. bd. Young Artists Workshop 1982—99, pres. 1985—87, 1987—89, mem. coun., Wis. Art Educator of the Yr. 1989, Career award 2000—), Nat. Art Edn. Assn. (bd. dirs. 1984—89, secondary divsn. dir., mem. exec. com. 1989—91, We. Region Art Educator of Yr. 1990), U. Wis. Milw. Alumni Assn. (1st v.p. 1966—73, pres. 1968—69, pres., emeritus bd. trustee 1996—2000, emeritus trustee 2000—, co-chair Chancellor's Soc. 2000—03, bd. dirs. womens alumni). Avocation: running. Home: 1161 N Lost Woods Rd Oconomowoc WI 53066-8790

DRISKELL, LUCILE G., artist; b. N.Y.C., Dec. 20, 1924; d. Charles Albert and Clarice Dorothy (Jung) Gall; m. Richard O. Driskell, Sept. 4, 1946; children: Douglas G., Donald A., David O. AA, Finch Coll., 1945; student, La Jolla Art Ctr., Calif., 1956-63, Fratelli Da Prato Foundry, Pietra Santa, Italy, 1973-78, Art Students League, N.Y.C., 1984-88. Artist, San Diego, 1950-63, Cin., 1963-67, Aspen, Colo., 1967-72, Greve in Chianti, Italy, 1972-79, Wellsboro, Pa., 1979—, Phila., 1985—. Represented by Environment Gallery, N.Y.C., 1968—84, Rodger Lapelle Gallery, Phila., 1984—, Agora Gallery, NY, 1993—2002, Amsterdam Whitney Internat. Fine Arts, N.Y.C., 2002—. Sculptures, 1960—, wall reliefs, 1988—, prints, 1956—. Represented in permanent collections Woodmere Art Mus., Phila. Recipient Purchase award, Exxon, N.Y.C., 1978, Wachovia Bank, Wilmington, Del., 1996, Macy's, Washington, 1989, SAS Inst., Inc., Cary, N.C., 2001. Mem.: Nas. Assn. Women Artists, Washington Sculpture Group, Internat. Sculpture Ctr., Art Students League (life). Avocations: hiking, photography, travel. Home: 389 Fischler St Ext Wellsboro PA 16901-8925 E-mail: drisk@epix.net.

DRISKILL, JAMES LAWRENCE, minister; b. Rustburg, Va., Aug. 18, 1920; s. Elijah Hudnall and Annie Pharr (Carwile) D.; m. Ethel Lillian Cassel, May 28, 1949; children: Edward Lawrence, Mary Lillian. BA, Pa. State U., 1946; BD, San Francisco Theol. Sem., 1949; ThM, Princeton Sem., 1957; S.T.D., San Francisco Theol. Sem., 1969. Ordained minister in Presbyn. Ch. 1949. Missionary Presbyn. Ch. USA, Japan, 1949-72; stated supply pastor Madison Square Presbyn. Ch., San Antonio, 1973; minister Highland Presbyn. Ch., Maryville, Tenn., 1973-82; supply pastor of Japanese-Am. chs. Presbyn. Ch. USA, Long Beach, Calif., Hollywood, Calif., Altadena, Calif., 1984-99. Vis. prof. religion dept. Trinity U., 1972-73. Author: Adventures in Senior Living, 1997, Christmas Stories from Around the World, 1997, Worldwide Mission Stories for Young People, 1996, Cross-Cultural Marriages and the Church, 1995, Mission Stories from Around the World, 1994, Japan Diary, 1993, Mission Adventures in Many Lands, 1992; contbr. articles to profl. jours. Mem. Sierra Club, Calif., 1988—; trustee Osaka (Japan) Girls Sch., 1952-65, Seikyo Gakuen Christian Sch., Japan, 1953-92. With USN, 1943-46. Mem. Am. Acad. Religion, Presbyn. Writers Guild. Democrat. Presbyterian. Home and Office: 1420 Santo Domingo Ave Duarte CA 91010-2698 *Experience has taught me that, ultimately, the meaning and value of a person's life is determined by the quality of one's personal relationships, especially by the quality of one's relationship to God.*

DRISKO, CONNIE LEE HASTINGS, dental educator, dean; Degree, Caruth Sch. Dentistry, Baylor Coll. Dentistry, 1961; BS, Baylor Coll. Dentistry, 1975; DDS, U. Mo., Kansas City, 1980. Cert. in periodontics Dept. Vet. Affairs Med. Ctr. Pvt. practice dental hygienist; prof. periodontics U. Louisville Sch. Dentistry, assoc. dean for academic planning, faculty devel., dir. clin. rsch.; dean, Merritt prof. of periodontics Sch. Dentistry, Med. Coll. Ga., 2003—. Fellow: Exec. Leadership in Acad. Med. Program for Women, Am. Coll. Dentists. Office: Med Coll Ga Sch Dentistry 1120 15th St Augusta GA 30912

DRIVER, JOE L., state legislator, consultant, insurance agent; b. Rockwall, Tex., Sept. 29, 1946; s. Marshall Laguin and Alice Elizabeth (Patillo) D.; m. S. DeAnne Browning, Nov. 20, 1993; stepchildren: Eric Browning, Lynsey Browning. BBA, U. North Tex., 1971; grad., Garland Citizen's Police Acad., 1993. With Steak & Ale Restaurants, Dallas, 1971—73; instr. Garland (Tex.) Ind. Sch. Dist., 1972; mgr. Marshall Driver Ins., Garland, 1972-73; owner, agt. Joe Driver Ins.-State Farm, Garland, 1973—; mem. Tex. Ho. of Reps., 1993—, mem. energy resources com., 1993—95, 1997—2003, mem. ins. com., 1993-97, mem. pub. safety com., 1995—2003, vice chmn. pub. safety com., 1997-99, chmn. select com. constitutional revision Tex. constitution, 1999—2003, chmn. law enforcement com., 2003—, mem. environ. regulations com., 2003—, mem. licensing and adminstrv. procedures com., 2003—05. Pres. Christian Singles Unltd., Garland, 1979; bd. dirs. First United Meth. Ch., Garland, 1979-81, Garland Econ. and Devel. Authority, 1986, Garland Crimestoppers, 1985-88, 93—, Am. Heart Assn., 1991-93; bd. dirs. New Beginning Family and Violence Prevention Ctr., 1988-91, v.p., 1990-91; chmn. SITE Found. of Garland, Inc., 1991-92; mem. bd. mgmt. Garland YMCA, 1983-85; fundraising chmn. YWCA, 1992; mem. long-range planning com. City of Garland, 1986-88; mem. devel. coun. Baylor Med. Ctr., Garland, 1991—; mem. Downtown Citizen Rev. Com., 1991-92; active Tex. Conservative Coalition, 1993—, Rep. Caucus Tex. Ho. of Reps., 1993—. Recipient Human Rels. award Dale Carnegie Cos., 1978. Mem. Nat. Assn. Life Underwriters (Nat. Quality award 1978-83, 86-92, 2002), Dallas Assn. Life Underwriters, Garland C. of C. (bd. dirs. 1983-87, chmn. 1986, corp. coun. 1988-90), Rowlett C. of C., Sachse C. of C., Tex. Dist. Exch. Clubs (dist. dir. 1984, Outstanding Dist. Dir. award 1985, Pres.'s award 1986), Noon Exch. Club Garland (bd. dirs. 1982-86, 90-91, pres. 1983, 90, Outstanding Svc. award 1986-87), Leadership Garland Alumni Assn. (bd. dirs. 1990-91), U. North Tex. Alumni Assn. (bd. dirs. 2001-), Lambda Chi Alpha (pres. 1971), Environ. Regulation Com. Avocations: golf, weight training. Office: 201 S Glenbrook Dr Garland TX 75040-6227

DRIVER, MARTHA WESTCOTT, English language educator, writer, researcher; b. N.Y.C., Oct. 24; d. Albert Westcott and Martha Louise (Miller) D.; m. Thomas Edward Earl Rhodes, Aug. 4, 2001. BA, Vassar Coll., 1974; MA, U. Pa., 1975, PhD, 1980. Lectr. English Vassar Coll., N.Y.C., 1980-81; from asst. prof. to assoc. prof. Pace U., N.Y.C., 1981-95, prof. English, 1995—2003, Disting. prof. English, 2003—, dir. honors program, 1998-2000. Cons. N.Y. Pub. Libr., 1984; seminar participant Folger Inst., Folger Shakespeare Libr., 1994. Editor: Jour. of the Early Book Soc., 1998—2005; guest editor: Film & History: The Middle Ages, 1998—99, Literary and Linguistic Computing, 1999; editor: The Medieval Hero on Screen, 2004; author: The Image in Print, 2004; contbr. 37 articles to profl. jours. Mem., lectr. St. John the Divine, N.Y.C., 1995. Recipient Dyson Achievement award, 2003; grantee Rsch. tools grantee, NEH, 1995, travel grantee, Am. Coun. Learned Socs., 1995, NSF, 2001—;, Houghton Libr. Harvard U. fellow, 1996—97. Mem. Early Book Soc. (chair 1988—), Coll. Art Assn., Medieval Acad. Am., Modern Humanities Rsch. Assn. (U.K.), Medieval Club of N.Y. (conf. coord. 1989-94. pres. 1987-89), Internat. Ctr. Medieval Art, Internat. Arthurian Soc., Medieval Feminist Art History Project, New Chaucer Soc. Episcopalian. Avocations: dance, museums, theater, concerts. Office: Pace U English Dept 41 Park Row New York NY 10038-1508 Office Phone: 212-346-1672. Business E-Mail: mdriver@pace.edu.

DRIVER, MICHAEL J., lawyer; b. Highland Park, Ill., Dec. 4, 1944; BA, Amherst Coll., 1967; JD, Univ. Denver, 1974. Bar: Colo. 1974. Ptnr., Public Policy, Legis. Affairs, Environ. Health & Safety practices, mem. exec. com. Patton Boggs LLP, Denver. Mem. Clinton for Pres. Nat. Exec. Com., Clinton Nat. Fin. Com., Pres. Inaugural Com., Clinton Transition Team Nat. Resources sect. Mem. Native Am. Rights Fund Nat. Sponsorship Com., John F. Kennedy Ctr for Performing Arts Adv. Com. on the Arts. Mem.: ABA, Colo. Bar Assn., Denver Bar Assn. Office: Patton Boggs LLP Suite 1900 1660 Lincoln St Denver CO 80264-1901 Office Phone: 303-830-1776. Office Fax: 303-894-9239. Business E-Mail: mdriver@pattonboggs.com.

DRIVER, MINNIE, actress; b. London, Jan. 31, 1970; d. Ronnie and Gaynor Driver. Actress (films) Circle of Friends, 1995, GoldenEye, 1995, Sleepers, 1996, Big Night, 1996, Grosse Pointe Blank, 1997, Mononoke Hime, 1997, Good Will Hunting, 1997, The Governess, 1998, At Sachem Farm, 1998, Hard Rain, 1998, Slow Burn, 1999, An Ideal Husband, 1999, Tarzan, 1999, South Park: Bigger, Longer and Uncut, 1999, Return to Me, 2000, Beautiful, 2000, High Heels and Low Lifes, 2001, Owning Mahowny, 2003, Hope Springs, 2003, Ella Enchanted, 2004, The Phantom of the Opera, 2004; TV appearances include God on the Rocks, 1990, That Sunday, 1994, Cruel Train, 1995; (TV mini-series) Mr. Wroe's Virgins, 1993, The Politician's Wife, 1995; prodr. At Sachem Farm, 1998; TV guest appearances include Lovejoy, 1986, Casualty, 1986, Murder Most Horrid, 1991, Peak Practice, 1993, The Day Today, 1994, Knowing Me, Knowing You with Alan Partridge, 1994, Will & Grace, 2003, 04; Musician (albums) Everything I've Got in My Pocket, 2004. ShoWest Female Star of Tomorrow award, 1998. Office: c/o Endeavor 9701 Wilshire Blvd Beverly Hills CA 90212 Fax: 310-205-0879.

DRIVER, ROBERT BAYLOR, JR., opera company administrator; b. Sao Paolo, Brazil, Aug. 26, 1942; came to U.S., 1949, naturalized, 1960; s. Robert Baylor and Mary Louise (Riechman) D.; m. Monica B. Macrae, 1968; 1 child, Katharine. BA, U. Va., 1964; MA, Middlebury (Vt.) Coll., 1971; postgrad., Johns Hopkins U. Asst. stage dir. Die Bayerische Staatsoper, 1966-68; asst. dir. Ky. Opera Assn., 1968-71; assoc. dir. Kansas City Lyric Opera, 1974-75; artistic dir. Opera Theatre, Syracuse, N.Y., 1975-87, Indpls. Opera, 1981-91, Opera Co. Phila., 1991—. Sec. Opera Memphis, Tenn., 1984-91. Mem.: OPERA Am. (bd. dirs.). Office: Opera Co of Philadelphia 1420 Locust St Ste 210 Philadelphia PA 19102-3601*

DRIVER, RODNEY DAVID, mathematics professor, retired state legislator; b. London, July 1, 1932; came to U.S., 1945; s. William T. and Marjorie E. (Carter) D.; m. Carole J. Frandsen, Sept. 4, 1955; children: David M., Karen L., Bruce K. BSEE, U. Minn., 1953, PhD in Math., 1960. Postdoctoral fellow Rsch. Inst. for Advanced Studies, Balt., 1960-61; staff mem. Math. Rsch. Ctr., Madison, Wis., 1961-62, Sandia Labs., Albuquerque, 1962-69; assoc. prof. math. U. R.I., Kingston, 1969-74, prof., 1974-98; mem. R.I. Ho. of Reps., 1987-94. Exec. dir. Govt. Accountability Project, 1995. Author: Ordinary and Delay Differential Equations, 1977, Introduction to Ordinary Differential Equations, 1978, Why Math?, 1984; contbr. articles on functional differential equations to math. jours. Del. R.I. Constnl. Conv., 1986. Mem. Am. Math. Soc., Math. Assn. Am., Amnesty Internat., Greenpeace. Home: PO Box 156 West Kingston RI 02892-0156 Office: U RI Math Dept Kingston RI 02881

DRIVER, THEODORE BRUCE, music educator; b. Winston Salem, NC, Feb. 15, 1954; s. Charles M. and Jewel U. Driver; m. Dianne Watson, Sept. 4, 1954; children: Laura Michele, Rebecca Dianne. MusB, NC Sch. Arts, 1976. Cert. Music Edn. K-12 NC, 1978. Performer Winston Salem Symphony, NC, 1974—76; tchr. Winthrop U., Rock Hill, SC, 1976—78; band dir. Newton Conover H.S., NC, 1978—84, River Bend Mid. Sch., Claremont, NC, 1984—. Recipient Tchr. Yr., Catawba County Schs., 1988, 1990, 2000. Mem.: MENC (assoc.), Nat. Mid. Sch. Assn., NC Music Educators Assn. (assoc.). Avocations: woodworking, antique restoration. Home: 303 11th St NW Conover NC 28613 Office: River Bend Mid Sch 4670 Oxford School Rd Claremont NC 28610

DRIVER, TOM FAW, theologian, writer, advocate; b. Johnson City, Tenn., May 31, 1925; s. Leslie Rowles and Sarah (Broyles) D.; m. Anne L. Barstow, June 7, 1952; children: Katharine Anne, Paul Barstow, Susannah Ambrose. AB, Duke U., 1950; M.Div., Union Theol. Sem., 1953; PhD, Columbia U., 1957; D.Litt., Denison U., 1970. Ordained to ministry United Meth. Ch., 1951. Dir. youth work Riverside Ch., N.Y.C., 1955-56; faculty Union Theol. Sem., N.Y.C., 1956-93, Paul J. Tillich prof. theology and culture, 1973-93, emeritus, 1993—. Drama critic Christian Century, 1956-62, Sta. WBAI-FM, 1960-61, The Reporter, 1963-64; vis. assoc. prof. English Columbia U., 1964-65; vis. assoc. prof. religion Barnard Coll., 1965-66, Fordham U., 1967; cons. humanities and arts Coll. Old Westbury (N.Y.), 1970; William Evans vis. prof. religion U. Otago, N.Z., 1976; vis. prof. religion Vassar Coll., 1978, Montclair State Coll., 1981; vis. prof. English lit. Doshisha U., Kyoto, Japan, 1983. Author: libretto for oratorio The Invisible Fire, 1958; The Sense of History in Greek and Shakespearean Drama, 1960, Jean Genet, 1966, Romantic Quest and Modern Query: A History of The Modern Theater, 1970, Patterns of Grace: Human Experience as Word of God, 1977, Christ in a Changing World: Toward an Ethical Christology, 1981, The Magic of Ritual: Our Need for Liberating Rites that Transform Our Lives and Our Communities, 1991, Liberating Rites: Understanding the Transformative Power of Ritual, 1998; editor: (with Robert Pack) Poems of Doubt and Belief, 1964; prodr., photographer (video, with Anne Barstow): Colombia: The Next Vietnam?, 2001, Colombians Speak Out about Violence and U.S. Policy, 2003, also articles. Bd. dirs. dept. worship and arts Nat. Council Chs., 1958-63, Found. for Arts, Religion and Culture, 1963-67. Served with AUS, 1943-46. Kent fellow, 1953; Guggenheim fellow, 1962-63 Mem. ACLU, Am. Acad. Religion, New Haven Theol. Group, Soc. Values in Higher Edn., Presbyn. Peace Fellowship, Witness for Peace, Vets. for Peace, Soc. of Arts, Religion & Contemporary Culture, Presbyterian Church, Phi Beta Kappa, Omicron Delta Kappa. Mem. United Methodist Ch. Home: 501 W 123rd St Apt 14G New York NY 10027-5010 E-mail: tfd3@columbia.edu.

DRIVER, WALTER W., JR., lawyer; b. El Paso, Tex., Apr. 10, 1945; s. Walter Williamson and Carolyn Bonds (Mayfield) D.; m. Bettie Townsend Willerson, Dec. 27, 1970; children: Eleanor, Anna, Walter III. AB, Stanford U., 1967; JD, U. Tex., 1970. Bar: Ga. 1970. Assoc. King & Spalding, LLP, Atlanta, 1970—76, ptnr., 1976—, chmn. policy com., 1992-94, 98-99, mng. ptnr., chmn., 1999—. Bd. dir. Total Systems Services, Inc., Old Mutual Advisors Funds. Mem. exec. com. Children's Mus. Atlanta, 1990-95; bd. dirs. Ctrl. Atlanta Progress, 1993—; chair Celebration of Life Cancer Soc., 1993. Mem. ABA, State Bar Ga., U.S. Golf Assn. (gen. counsel 1997-99, mem. exec. com. 1999—, treas. 2000-01, v.p. 2001—), Ga. State Golf Assn. (gen. coun., exec. com. 1988-97), Atlanta C. of C. (exec. com., bd. dirs.), Piedmont Driving Club, Peachtree Golf Club (bd. dirs.). Office: King & Spalding LLP 191 Peachtree St Atlanta GA 30303-1763 Office Fax: 404-572-5100. Business E-Mail: wdriver@kslaw.com.

DRIZIN, STEVEN A., law educator, lawyer; BA, Haverford Coll., 1983; JD, Northwestern U., 1986. Law clk. to Hon. Ilana D. Rovner US Dist. Ct. (no. dist.) Ill., 1988—89; litig. assoc. Sachnoff & Weaver Ltd., Chgo., 1986—88, 1989—91; supervising atty. Children and Family Justice Ctr., 1993—; clin. prof. law Northwestern U. Sch. Law, 2001—, asst. dir. Bluhm Legal Clinic, 2001—, legal dir. Ctr. on Wrongful Convictions. Contbr. articles to profl. jours. Policy com. mem. Ill. Coun. for prevention of violence, 1996—. Recipient PASS Award, Nat. Coun. Crime & Delinquency, 1999, Juvenile Defender Leadership Award, Nat. Juvenile Defender Ctr., 2000. Mem.: Chgo. Bar Assn. Office: Northwestern U Sch Law 357 E Chicago Ave Chicago IL 60611 E-mail: s-drizin@law.northwestern.edu.*

DRNEVICH, VINCENT PAUL, engineering educator; b. Wilkinsburg, Pa., Aug. 6, 1940; s. Louis B. and Mary (Kutcel) D.; m. Roxanne M. Hosier, Aug. 20, 1966; children: Paul, Julie, Jenny, Marisa. BSCE, U. Notre Dame, 1962, MSCE, 1964; PhD, U. Mich., 1967. Registered profl. engr., Ky., Ind. Asst. prof. civil engring. U. Ky., Lexington, 1967-73, assoc. prof., 1973-78, prof., 1978-91; chmn. civil engring., 1980-84; acting dean engring. U. Ky., Lexington, 1989-90; prof., head Sch. Civil Engring. Purdue U., West Lafayette, Ind., 1991-2000. Dir. joint hwy. rsch. project Purdue U., 1991-95; pres. Soil Dynamics, Instruments, Inc., West Lafayette, 1974—. Inventor in field. Fellow ASCE (chmn. dept. heads coun. exec. com. 1996-2000, vice chmn. com. on edn.-practitioner interface, 1994-98, Norman medal 1973, Huber Rsch. prize 1980), ASTM (exec. com., tech. editor Geotech. Testing Jour. 1985-89, C.A. Hogentogler award 1979, Merit award 1993, Woodland Shockley award 1996); mem. NSPE, Am. Soc. Engring. Edn. (sec./treas. civil engring. divsn. 1995-98, dir. 1999—, vice chair 2002-03, chair 2003—), Transp. Rsch. Bd., Earthquake Engring. Rsch. Inst., Ind. Soc. Profl. Engrs. (pres. A.A. Potter chpt.), Chi Epsilon (Harold T. Larson award 1985, James M. Robbins award 1989). Roman Catholic. Avocations: golf, fishing. Office: Purdue U 550 Stadium Mall Dr West Lafayette IN 47907-2051

DRNJEVIC, JONATHAN MARK, language educator; b. Phoenix, Dec. 20, 1959; s. Mirko and Ruth Drnjevic. PhD, Ariz. State U., 1997. Instr. English dept. Ariz. State U., Tempe, Ariz., 2004—. Mem.: MLA. Lutheran. Home: 4032 E St Joseph Way Phoenix AZ 85018-1102 Personal E-mail: jmd@asu.edu.

DROBENA, THOMAS JOHN, minister, educator; b. Chgo., Aug. 23, 1934; s. Thomas and Suzanne (Durec) D.; m. Wilma S. Kucharek, Dec. 27, 1980; children: Thomas Samuel, Joshua Michael. BA, Valparaiso U., 1964; ThB, Concordia Theol. Sem., 1961, MDiv, 1974; MA, Hebrew U., Jerusalem, 1968; PhD, Calif. Grad. Sch. Theology, 1975; STM, Luth. Theol. Sem., 1986; DSc (hon.), London U. Ordained to ministry Evang. Luth. Ch. in Am., 1962. English pastor Redeemer Luth. Ch., Jerusalem, 1967-68; prin. St. Mark's Luth. Ch., Bklyn., 1968-69; pastor Ascension Luth. Ch., Binghamton, 1969-78, Holy Emmanuel, Mahoney City, Pa., 1981-86, St. John, St. Clair, Pa., 1981-86, Nanticoke, Pa., 1981-86; co-pastor Holy Trinity Luth. Ch., Torrington, Conn., 1986—. Adj. prof. SUNY, Binghamton, 1975-77; chairperson Global Missions, Evang. Luth. Ch. in Am., Chgo., 1985—; rsch. scholar, Slavic Heritage Inst., Torrington, 1964-, v.p., treas., 1965—. Co-author: Heritage of the Slavs, 1976; editor The Zion, 1995—, Slovo, 1998—; contbr. articles to profl. jours. Chaplain Civil Air Patrol USAFA, 1964—; bd. dirs. ARC, 1986-1999; pres. Crimestoppers, 1988—, New Eng. Hist. Soc., 1990—; chair internat. rels. com. ELCA-Slovak Zion Synod, 1995, adminstrv. asst. to the bishop, 2002-. Grantee U.S. State Dept., Jerusalem, 1967-68, U. Ill. Russian and East European Ctr., Urbana, 1980—. Fellow Istituto Slovacco; mem. Am. Assn. for the Advancement of Slavic Studies, Am. Assn. of Tchrs. of Slavic and East European Langs., Czechoslovak Soc. for the Arts and Scis., New Eng. Luth. Hist. Soc. (pres. 1990—, editor Jour. New Eng. Luth. Hist. Soc. 1995—). Office: Slavic Heritage Inst PO Box 1003 Torrington CT 06790-1003

DROBNICKI, JOHN ARTHUR, librarian, educator; b. N.Y. AA Liberal Arts, St. John's U., 1983, BA in History, 1986, MA in History, 1988; MLS in Libr. Sci., CUNY, 1992. Cert. pub. libr. N.Y. State Edn. Dept., 1993. Adj. instr. of history St. John's U., Jamaica, NY, 1989—89; libr. Queens Borough Pub. Libr., Jamaica, 1990—95; asst. prof. of libr. svcs. York Coll. CUNY, Jamaica, 1995—2000, assoc. prof. of libr. svcs. York Coll., 2001—03, prof. of libr. svcs. York Coll., 2003—. Exec. bd. York Coll. Chpt. Profl. Staff Congress of CUNY, 2002—05. Contbr. articles to profl. jours., book reviews to profl. jours. Recipient David Cohen Multicultural award, Queens Coll. Grad. Sch. of Libr. and Info. Studies, 1993. Mem.: Polish Inst. Arts Sci. Am., Polish Geneal. Soc. of Am., Polish Am. Hist. Assn. Episc. Avocations: pipes, genealogy. Office: York College CUNY 94 20 Guy R Brewer Blvd Jamaica NY 11451 E-mail: drobnicki@york.cuny.edu.

DROE, MICHAEL GLENN, information technology executive, educator; s. Les and Donna Droe; m. Adela Franco; children: Leslie Helen, Laura Michelle. BS, Calif. State U., 1991. Systems programmer, analyst Hacienda La Puente Unified Sch. Dist., City of Industry, Calif., 1988—90, dir. of networks & computer services, 1990—2000, chief tech. officer, 2000—. Cons. SOS Computer Cons., Long Beach, Calif., 1988—90, Apple Computer, Irvine, Calif., 1991—93, Sacramento (Calif.) County Office of Edn., 1993—94. Bd. edn. Christ Luth. Ch., West Covina, Calif., 1994—96. Recipient John Philip Sousa award, Instrumentalist, 1981, Computerworld Smithsonian award, Smithsonian Inst., 1997; Ready To Teach Fed. grant, US Dept. Edn., 2002—05. Mem.: Alliance for Cmty. Media, Consortium for Sch. Networking, Calif. Ednl. Tech. Professionals Assn. (sec. 2004). Republican. Lutheran. Avocations: baseball, golf, travel. Office: Hacienda La Puente Unified Sch Dist 15959 East Gale Ave City Of Industry CA 91745 Office Phone: 626-934-4820. Business E-Mail: mdroe@hlpusd.k12.ca.us.

DROEGE, MARK E., telecommunications industry executive; b. Chgo. BA in Math., Carleton Coll., 1975; MBA in Fin., U. Mich., 1977; grad. Exec. Program, Stanford U. CFA. With Internat. Thomson, Harris Corp., BellSouth Corp., Atlanta, 1986—, pres. Interactive Media Svcs., CFO Dataserv, dir. investor rels., mgr. fin. analysis corp. hqrs., exec. dir. fin. and bus. planning, v.p. fin. mgmt., treas., v.p., CFO Latin Am. Group, 2000—04, v.p., treas., 2005—. Mem.: Fin. Execs. Internat. (Atlanta chpt. pres.). Office: BellSouth Corp 1155 Peachtree St NE Atlanta GA 30309-3610 Office Phone: 404-249-5200. Business E-Mail: mark.droege@bellsouth.com.

DROEGEMEIER, KELVIN K., meteorologist, educator; b. Ellsworth, Kans., Aug. 23, 1958; m. Lisa Roevekamp, Sept. 27, 1983. BS in meteorology with spl. distinction, U. Okla., 1980; MS in atmospheric sci., U. Ill., 1982, PhD in atmospheric sci., 1985. Meteorol. aide Nat. Severe Storms Lab., 1976—78, meteorol. technician, 1978—80; grad. rsch. asst. U. Ill., 1980—85; asst. prof., sch. meteorology U. Okla., 1985—91, co-founder, dep. dir. rsch. Ctr. Analysis and Prediction of Storms, 1989—92, dir. Ctr. Analysis and Predictions of Storms, 1989—, assoc. prof., sch. meteorology, 1991—98, prof., sch. meteorology, 1998—2001, regents' prof., sch. meteorology, 2001—, Roger and Sherry Teigen presdl. prof., 2004—; founder, dir. Environ. Computing Applications System Rsch. and Ednl. Superconducting Ctr., 1996—2001; dep. dir. Engring. Rsch. Ctr. Collaborative Adaptive Sensing Atmosphere, NSF, 2003—. Bd. dirs. Nat. Sci. Bd.; cons. Sperry Comml. Flight Systems Group, Honeywell Corp., 1989—92, Climatol. Cons. Corp., 1997, Am. Airlines, 1997, 1999—, Nat. Transportation Safety Bd., 1997—98; chair SoM Undergraduate Studies Com. U. Okla., 2001—, mem. Williams Chair Search Com., 2001—; mem. bd. advisors Supercomputing Ctr. Edn. and Rsch., 2001—; mem. patent adv. com. U. Okla., 2003—; spkr. in field; fellow NOAA Cooperative Inst. Mesoscale Meteorol. Studies, 1987—. Contbr. articles to profl. jours., chapters to books. Bd. dirs. Norman, Okla. C. of C., 2003—; chmn. Weather and Climate Team, Okla. Econ. Devel. Generating Excellence (EDGE) Gov. Task Force, 2003; deacon Riverside Ch., Norman, 2003—. Recipient Pioneer award, NSF, 2001, Excellence in Aviation award, Fedn. Aviation Adminstrn., 2002. Fellow: Am. Meteorol. Soc.; mem.: Phi Kappa Phi. Office: U Okla Ctr Analysis and Prediction of Storms Sarkeys Energy Ctr Rm 1110 100 E Boyd Norman OK 73019 Office Phone: 405-325-0453. Business E-Mail: kdroege@tornado.gcn.uoknor.edu, kkd@ou.edu.

DROGIN, ROBERT L., journalist; b. Jersey City, Mar. 29, 1952; s. Morris and Samantha Drogin. BA, Oberlin (Ohio) Coll., 1973; MS, Columbia U., 1976. Programme assoc. UNICEF Indonesia, Jakarta, 1973-75; investigative reporter Charlotte (N.C.) Observer, 1977-80; programme officer UNICEF, Thai/Cambodian border, 1980; environ. reporter Phila. Inquirer, 1981-83; nat. corres. N.Y. Bur. of L.A. Times, 1983-89; Manila bur. chief L.A. Times, Philippines, 1989-93, Johannesburg bur. chief, 1993-97, Washington corr., 1998—; Knight fellow Stanford U., 1997-98. Recipient Pulitzer Prize for meritorious pub. svc., 1981, Robert F. Kennedy Grand prize, 1981. Office: 1875 I St NW Ste 1100 Washington DC 20006

DROLL, RUTH LUCILLE, missionary pastor; b. Peoria, Ill., Mar. 13, 1941; d. Elisha John Droll and Beulah Lorene West-Droll; 1 child, Ruth Lucille. BA in bible theology, Nc. Ctrl. Mpls., 1963. Missionary pastor Assemblies of God, Ariz., 1963—2003. Home: PO Box 3742 Milan NM 87021 Office: Assembly of God PO Box 402 Prewitt NM 87045-0402

DROMM, DANIEL PATRICK, elementary school educator; b. Bklyn., Nov. 27, 1955; s. Warren William Dromm and Mary Audrey Gallagher. BA, Marist Coll., 1973—77; MS in edn., City Coll., 1978—81. Asst. dir. Grant DayCare Ctr., 1978—84; tchr. P.S. 199Q, LI, NY, 1984—. Mem. Jackson Hts. Beautification Group of Queens, 2002—; founder New Visions Dem. Club, 2002—; del. Dem. Nat. Convention, 2000; dem. dist. leader Queens County Dem. Org., 2002—; founder Queens Lesbian and Gay Pride, 1992—; co-founder Lesbian and Gay Dem. Club, 1994—, Generation Q. Youth Svcs. Program, Astoria, NY, 2000—. Recipient award, New Visions Dem. Club, 2004, Puerto Rican Soc. of Queens Annual award, 1998, Aaron Weiss Humanitarian award, 1994. Mem.: United Fedn. of Tchr. Union Rep. (Trachtenberg award 2000), Lesbian and Gay Tchrs. Assn. Democrat. Office: PS 199Q 39-20 48th Ave Long Island City NY 11104 Office Phone: 718-784-3431. Personal E-mail: ddromm@aol.com.

DROMS, WILLIAM GEORGE, finance educator, investment advisor; b. Schenectady, Aug. 20, 1944; s. George William and Frances (Maguire) D.; m. JoAnn Gilberti, June 17, 1967; children: Courtney, Justin. AB, Brown U., 1966; MBA, George Washington U., 1971, DBA, 1975. Chartered financial analyst. Prof. Georgetown U., Washington, 1973—, John J. Powers Jr. Chair prof., 1990—, assoc. dean, faculty chair Sch. Bus., 1978-81, 87-89, 92-94, 98-99. Pres. Droms Strauss Advisors, Inc., 1994—. Author: Finance and Accounting for Nonfinancial Managers, 1979, 5th edit., 2003, Dow Jones-Irwin No-Load Mutual Funds, 1984, 85, 86; author: (with others) The Dow Jones Irwin Guide to Personal Financial Planning, 1982, 86, Personal Financial Management, 1982, 86, The Life Insurance Investment Advisor, 1988, Investment Fundamentals, 1994; editor: Asset Allocation for Individual Investors, 1987, Managing a Global Investment Program, 1991; contbr. articles to profl. jours. Lt. USN, 1966-70. Mem. Am. Fin. Assn., Chartered Fin. Analyst Inst., Fin. Mgmt. Assn., DC Soc. Investment Analysts, Cosmos Club. Republican. Roman Catholic. Avocations: tennis, golf. Office: Georgetown U Sch Bus Washington DC 20057-0001 Office Phone: 202-687-3820. Business E-Mail: dromsw@msb.edu.

DRONEY, CHRISTOPHER F., judge; b. June 22, 1954; m. Elizabeth Kelly, Oct. 13, 1979. BA, Coll. Holy Cross, 1976; JD, U. Conn., 1979. Ptnr. Reid & Riege, P.C., Hartford, Conn., 1983-93; U.S. atty. for dist. of Conn. U.S. Dept. Justice, New Haven, 1993-97; judge U.S. Dist. Ct., Conn., 1997—. Notes and comments editor Conn. Law Rev., 1978-79. Mem. U.S. atty. gen. adv. com., 1996-97. Office: 450 Main St Hartford CT 06103-3022 Office Phone: 860-240-2635.

DROOYAN, JOHN NEAL, visual artist, photographer, fine artist; b. Glendale, Ariz., Sept. 29, 1952; s. Irving and Gertrude (Sommers) D. BS in Biology, Stanford U., 1974; MFA in Photography, San Francisco Art Inst., 1988. Photographer, asst. editor Dellen Pub. Co., San Francisco, 1978-84; freelance photographer San Francisco and L.A., 1984—; photographer United Photog. Industries, Galion, Ohio, 1996—, Event Photography Internat., Miami, Fla., 1996—. Tchr. color photography A.S.U.C. Studio, U. Calif., Berkeley, 1982-86, San Francisco Art Inst., 1987-90. Solo exhbns. include Union Gallery/U. Calif., Davis, San Jose State U. Union Gallery, San Francisco Mus. Modern Rental Gallery, Sierra Arts Found., Reno, Nev., Brand Art Gallery, Glendale, Calif.; exhibited in grop shows at Spectrum Gallery, San Francisco, Ventura Coll. New Media Gallery, Downey Mus. Art, numerous others. Recipient Gold award for mixed-media art Art of Calif. Mag., 1992. Mem. L.A. Ctr. for Exhbns., Santa Monica Mus. Art, Richmond Art Ctr., Mus. Contemporary Art, L.A. Artcore. E-mail: jduisart@yahoo.com.

DROSDICK, JOHN GIRARD, oil company executive; b. Hazelton, Pa., Aug. 9, 1943; m. Gloria J. Shenosky, May 10, 1944; children: Scott E., Candice M., Courtney J., Brooke K. BSChemE, Villanova U., 1965; MSChemE, U. Mass., 1968. Crude oil coordinator Exxon USA, Houston, 1973—74, marine planning mgr., 1974—76, corp. analysis mgr., 1978—81, facilities devel. dept. head Baton Rouge, 1976—78, refinery ops mgr., 1981—83; v.p. refining Tosco Corp., Santa Monica, Calif., 1983—85, sr. v.p. refining, 1985—86, exec. v.p., 1986—87, pres., COO, 1987—89, also bd. dirs.; pres., CEO Tosco Refining Co., Santa Monica, Calif., 1989—92, Ultramar, Inc., Long Beach, 1992—96; pres., COO Sunoco, Inc., Phila., 1996—2000, chmn., pres., CEO, 2000—. Mem.: Am. Petroleum Petroleum Refiners Assn. (bd. dirs. 1985—87), Nat. Petroleum Refiners Assn. (bd. dirs. 1985—), Jonathan Wilshire. Roman Catholic. Avocations: running, skiing, tennis, golf. Office: Sunoco Inc 10 Penn Ctr 1801 Market St Philadelphia PA 19103-1699

DROSSEL, NORLEN ELTOFT, lawyer; b. San Mateo, Calif., Jan. 8, 1944; d. Norman J. and Helen (Eltoft) D.; m. Robert P. Anderson, Nov. 22, 1977; children: Signe Anderssel, Jared Anderssel. AB, U. Calif., Berkeley, 1965; JD, San Francisco Law Sch., 1979; LLM, Golden Gate U., 1985. Bar: Calif. 1979. Law clk. to superior ct. judge, San Francisco, 1978-79; ptnr. Law Offices Anderson & Drossel, Berkeley, 1980—; judge/referee pro tem Alameda County Superior Ct., Oakland, Calif., 1988-93. Panel mem. Ct. Appointed Atty. Juvenile Ct., Berkeley, 1980-88; bd. dirs. Donald McCullum Youth Ct., Child Assault Prevention. Bd. dirs., cons. editor Calif. Conservatorships and Guardians, 1990, Calif. Will Drafting Practice, 1992. Bd. dirs. ARC, Oakland, 1985-91; mem. com. Alta Bates Hosp., Berkeley, 1988-91. Mem. Calif. Women Lawyers Assn., Berkeley-Albany Bar Assn., Alameda County Bar Assn., Women Lawyers Alameda County (past bd. dirs., editor newsletter 1981-83). Democrat. Home: 1149 Euclid Ave Berkeley CA 94708-1602 Office: 2041 Bancroft Way Ste 207 Berkeley CA 94704-1406 Fax: (510) 845-6419. E-mail: ndrossel@andersondrossel.com.

DROST, MARIANNE, lawyer; b. Waterbury, Conn., Feb. 21, 1950; d. Albin Joseph and Henrietta Jean (Kremski) D. BA, Conn. Coll., 1972; JD, U. Conn., 1975. Bar: Conn. 1975. Assoc. Ritter, Tapper & Totten, Hartford, Conn., 1975-77; sr. atty. GTE Svc. Corp., Stamford, Conn., 1977-84, Chesebrough-Pond's Inc., Greenwich, Conn., 1984-85; corp. sec. GTE Corp., Stamford, Conn., 1985—91; v.p., assoc. gen. counsel fin. GTE Svc. Corp., Stamford, Conn., 1991-97, v.p., dep. gen. counsel, 1997-2000; sr. v.p., dep. gen. counsel, corp. sec. Verizon Comm. Inc., NYC, 2000—. Tutor Lit. Vols., Stamford, 1985-90, bd. dirs. Lit. Vols. Am., 1988-94. Mem. ABA, Am. Soc. Corp. Secs. (former pres., bd. dirs. Fairfield-Westchester chpt.).

DROUILHET, PAUL RAYMOND, JR., retired science administrator, electrical engineer; b. San Pedro, Calif., Mar. 11, 1933; s. Paul R. and Elizabeth (Moffatt) D.; m. Betty Bratton; children: Ann, Stephen, Susan. BS, MS in Elec. Engring., MIT, 1955, EE, 1957. Various positions MIT Lincoln Lab., Lexington, 1959-81, div. head, 1981-85, asst. dir., 1985-93; fed. aviation adminstr. Chi Sci. for GPS/CNS, 1994-95, spl. asst. to dir. aviation rsch., 1996; cons. to dir. MIT Lincoln Lab., 1997—. Contbr. articles to profl. jours.; patentee in field. 1st lt. USAF, 1957-59. Fellow IEEE. Avocations: tennis, sailing, travel. Office: MIT Lincoln Lab 244 Wood St Lexington MA 02420-6426 E-mail: drouilhet@ll.mit.edu.

DROUIN, JACQUELINE SCHMIDT, physical therapist, educator; b. Hamtramck, Mich., July 29, 1948; d. Richard and Helen Schmidt; m. Joseph Frances Drouin, June 18, 1970; children: Jonathan Joseph, Christopher Joseph. BS in Phys. Therapy, Oakland U., 1985, MS in Exercise Sci., 1988; PhD in Ednl. Evaluation and Rsch., Wayne State U., 2002. Lic. phys. therapist Mich. Phys. therapist William Beaumont Hosp., Troy, Mich., 1985, Sportopaedics, Inc., Madison Hts., Mich., 1985—87, Lifespan Health Cons., Madison Hts., 1987—89; acute care phys. therapy supr. Wayne State U., Detroit, 1989—93, 1996—2000; asst. prof. U. Mich., Flint, 2000—. Co-chair cancer spl. interest group Am. Coll. Sports Medicine, 2002—03. Mem. editl. bd.: Rehabilitation Oncology; contbr. articles to profl. jours. Founder, dir. Troy (Mich.) Youth Soccer Ability League, 1997—98. Recipient Spl. Tribute award, State of Mich., 1990, Tchg. Excellence award, Wayne State U., 2000, Mable Holton Outstanding Scholarly Achievement award, Mich. Phys. Therapy Assn., 2004. Mem.: Internat. Soc. Exercise and Immunology, Am. Coll. Sports Medicine, Am. Phys. Therapy Assn. Roman Catholic. Avocations: bicycling, cross country skiing, kayaking, gardening. Home: 303 E Kearsley Flint MI 48502 Office: Univ Mich 303 E Kearsley St Flint MI 48502-1907

DROUIN, JOE, automotive executive; b. Memphis; B in Mgmt. Info. Sys., U. Memphis, 1990. With Electronic Data Sys. Corp. GM, Detroit; with Perot Sys. Corp.; IS dir. TRW Chassis Sys. Europe TRW, Germany, 1998—2002; v.p., CIO global info. sys. TRW Automotive, Livonia, Mich., 2002—. Bd. dirs. Automotive Industry Action Group; mem. Covisint Global Customer Adv. Coun. Office: TRW Automotive 12025 Tech Center Dr Livonia MI 48150

DROWOTA, FRANK F., III, retired state supreme court justice; b. Williamsburg, Ky., July 7, 1938; married; 2 children. BA, Vanderbilt U., 1960, JD, 1965. Bar: Tenn. 1965, U.S. Dist. Ct. Tenn. 1965. Pvt. practice, 1965-70; chancellor Tenn. Chancery Ct. Div. 7, 1970-74; judge Tenn. Ct. Appeals, Middle Tenn. Div., 1974-80; assoc. justice Tenn. Supreme Ct., Nashville, 1980-89, chief justice, 1989-93, 2001—05; assoc. justice Tenn. Supreme Ct., Nashville, 1993-2001; ret. Former pres. Nashville Am. Red Cross, Nashville Rotary Club; mem. exec. com. YMCA of Nashville and Middle Tenn., Cumberland Museum & Sci. Ctr., NCCJ, Bill Wilkerson Speech & Hearing Ctr. Served with USN, 1960—62. Mem.: Tenn. Bar Assn. Office: Tenn Supreme Ct 318 Supreme Ct Bldg 401 7th Ave N Nashville TN 37219

DROZD, LESZEK STANISLAW, composer, performer; b. Warsaw, May 23, 1969; arrived in US, 1994; s. Hanna Eugenia Drozd. Student, Weryho-Radziwillowiczowej, Warsaw, 1991-93; grad., Sch. Music of Fryderyk Chopin. Music composer Sta. WPNA-AM, WSBS-AM, Chgo., 1995-97; music composer, performer STYOPA Productions, Calif., 1998; pres. Hanna's Employment Agy., Inc., 2001; CEO, founder, prodr., dir. Story Tellers Prodns., Inc., 2005—. Soloist, mem. numerous symphonic orchs., bands, choirs; pres. Hannah's Employment Agy. Composer (and performer): (films) (soundtrack) The Innocents, 2000 (Film winner of 3 awards in Nat., Internat. film festivals.); composer: (documentary for Time Warner cable) Short Impression About Isolation, 2002. Mem. Nat. Campaign for Tolerance, 2005; ednl. videos prodr., spl. edn. music composer for films. E-mail: info@storytellersfilms.com.

DROZD, PHYLLIS ANN, agricultural products supplier; b. Allegan, Mich., July 26, 1932; d. Edward and Wilma (Busfield) Moored; m. Thomas Drozd, June 20, 1953; children: Julie, T. Jon, Jay H. Sec. Cresent Machine Co., Allegan, Mich., 1949-55; farmer Tom & Phyllis Drozd, Allegan, Mich., 1953-85; co-owner Drozd Seed, Inc., Allegan, Mich., 1953—. Pres. Allegan County Sch. Dist., 1978—; treas., 1965-78; sec.-treas. Allegan County Sch. Bds. Assn., 1991-92; pres. Allegan Bus. & Profl. Women, 1986-87, 91-92, 1st sr. v.p., 1984-85; bd. dirs. Mich. Assn. Sch. Bds., 1993—, v.p., 1999-2000, pres.-elect, 2000-01, pres., 2001—; mem. various ednl. coms. Avocations: reading, collecting antiques, walking, travel. Home and Office: 537 32nd St # M40 Allegan MI 49010-9763 E-mail: pdrozd@accn.org.

DROZDOWSKI, MARK JOHN, director, writer, educator; b. Holyoke, Mass., Sept. 22, 1966; s. Mitchell John and Elaine Ann Drozdowski; m. Kristen Anne Forslind, Oct. 11, 1997; children: Julia Anne, Sara May, Adam John. BA, U. Pa., 1990; M in Edn., Harvard U., 1991, EdD, 2001. Dir. corp., found. and govt. rels. Franklin Pierce Coll., Rindge, NH, 2001—. Author: The Insider's Guide to Graduate Programs in Education; columnist Chronicle of Higher Edn., writer N.Y. Times, contbg. editor Adj. Advocate. Mem.: Am. Assn. for Higher Edn., Coun. for Advancement and Support of Edn. Office Phone: 603-899-4032.

DROZDZIEL, MARION JOHN, aeronautical engineer; b. Dunkirk, N.Y., Dec. 21, 1924; s. Steven and Veronica (Wilk) D.; m. Rita L. Korwek, Aug. 30, 1952; 1 child, Eric A. BS in Aero. Engring., Tri State U., 1947, BSME, 1948; postgrad., Ohio State U., 1948, Niagara U., 1949-51, U. Buffalo, 1951-52. Stress analyst Curtiss Wright Corp., Columbus, Ohio, 1948; project engr. weight analysis Bell Aerospace Textron, Buffalo, 1949-52, stress analyst, 1952-60, asst. supr. stress analysis, 1960-64, chief stress analysis propulsion, 1964-79, chief engr. stress and weights, 1979-84, staff scientist, 1984-85, cons. structures and fractures mechanics, 1985—. Del. Internat. Citizens Ambassador Program; active Buffalo Fine Arts Acad., N.Y. Acad. Scis.; mem. Tech. Socs. Coun. of the Niagara Frontier. With U.S. Army, 1944-47. Recipient cert. of achievement NASA-Apollo, 1972, Wisdom award Wisdom Soc. for Advancement of Knowledge, Learning and Rsch. in Edn., 2000; cert. commendation U.K. NATO program, 1982; named to Wisdom Hall of Fame, Wisdom Soc. for Advancement of Knowledge, Learning and Rsch. in Edn., 2000. Mem. AAAS, AIAA (Mem. Chmn.'s award 1988-90, 92-93), Soc. Reliability Engrs. (bd. dirs. 1998-2005), U.S. Naval Inst., Am. Space Found., Nat. Conservancy, Nat. Audubon Soc., Sierra Club, Am. Acad. Polit. and Social Sci., Acad. Polit. Sci., Union Concerned Scientists, Air Force Assn., Nat. Space Soc., Soc. Allied Weight Engrs., Planetary Soc., Am. Mgmt. Assn.,Bibl. Archeology Soc., Archeol. Inst. Am., Cousteau Soc., Smithsonian Assocs., Buffalo Audubon Soc., Bell Mgmt. Club, Natural History Mus., Internat. Hypersonic Rsch., Disabled Am. Vets, Kosciuszko Found., Polish Arts Club Buffalo, Exch. Club of Tonawandas (sec. 1996-98, bd. dirs. 1999-2000), Nat. Exch. Club (Disting. Sec. award 1996-99). Republican. Roman Catholic. Achievements include development of criteria and methods of structural analysis extending analyses into the plastic and creep ranges for titanium and columbium rocket nozzle extensions; of criteria and methods of structural analysis for extendable rocket nozzle extensions, including rapid nozzle deployment involving plasticity; of methods of structural analysis for low strength, high ductility steels, aluminums, and teflons as positive expulsion devices for zero gravity application in propellant tanks including bellows, reversing heads, rolling diaphragms devices and collapsing or folding concepts; structural analysis on "X" series of aircraft, on Mercury, Gemini, and Apollo spacecraft reaction control and propulsion systems; structural and weight analysis of programs involving rocket engines, propulsion systems, aircraft, air cushion vehicles, surface-effect ships, laser systems avionics, airborne and ground antennae, Army tanks and fighting vehicles. Home and Office: 152 Linwood Ave Tonawanda NY 14150-4020 Office Phone: 716-693-6250.

DRUCK, KALMAN BRESCHEL, public relations counselor; b. Scranton, Pa., Dec. 6, 1914; s. Jacob L. and Mabelle (Breschel) D.; m. Pearl Spiro, Nov. 26, 1936; children: Ellen Druck Mirtz, Nancy Druck Brassem. BS in Journalism, magna cum laude, Syracuse U., 1936. With Hearst Enterprises, 1936-39, Carl Byoir & Assos., 1939-59; pres., vice chmn. Harshe-Rotman &

Druck, Inc., N.Y.C., 1960-81; prin. Kalman B. Druck, Inc., 1981—. Supr. courses pub. rels. Baruch Sch. Bus., CCNY, 1939-55; mem. adv. com. schs. communications Syracuse U., Boston U.; adj. prof. Grad. Sch. Communication, Fairfield (Conn.) U., 1987-88. Pub. Public Relations Career Guide, Impact of High Technology on Public Relations. Bd. dirs. Union Am. Hebrew Congregations, 1956-71, N.Y. Fedn. Jewish Philanthropies, 1957-72, Am. Jewish Com., 1979-87; hon. bd. dirs. Palm Beach Civic Assn.; v.p. Palm Beach Com. for Good Govt.; past chmn. civilian pub. affairs adv. com. U.S. Mil. Acad., West Point, N.Y. Recipient Disting. Alumnus Centennial medal Syracuse U., 1970 Mem. Pub. Rels. Soc. Am. (pres. N.Y. chpt. 1953-55, nat. chmn. 1972, chmn. com. on profl. devel. 1979-80, trustee Found. for Pub. Rels. Rsch. and Edn. 1981-86, Gold Anvil award 1966, named Pub. Rels. Profl. of Yr. 1966). Home: 1208 Devonshire Way Palm Beach Gardens FL 33418-6864 E-mail: kalpearl@aol.com.

DRUCKENMILLER, ROBERT THOMPSON, public relations executive; b. Bethlehem, Pa., Mar. 15, 1942; BA in Econs., Colgate U., 1964; MBA, U. Pa., 1966. Account rep. J. Walter Thompson, N.Y.C., 1966—71; advt. dir. Peace Corps/Action, Washington, 1971—72; media dir. Henry J. Kaufman, Washington, 1972—73; ptnr. Porter/Novelli, N.Y.C., 1973—80, sr. v.p., 1980—86, exec. v.p., gen. mgr. D.C. bd., 1986—92, pres., 1992—97, CEO, 1997—. E-mail: bdruckenmiller@porternovelli.com.

DRUCKER, ALAN STEVEN, mechanical engineer; b. Boston, Apr. 22, 1948; s. Eugene Elias and Corrine Ruth (Mintzer) D.; m. Patricia Ellen Sori, Aug. 10, 1974; children: Aaron, Zachary. BS, Cornell U., 1970. Jr. devel. engr. Carrier, Syracuse, N.Y., 1972-78, sr. devel. engr., 1978-82, program mgr., 1982-85, staff engr., 1985-94, sr. staff engr., 1994—2000, prin. engr., 2000—. Inventor, patentee in field. Democrat. Jewish. Avocations: diving, scuba, gardening, tennis. Office: Carrier Corp Carrier Pkwy Syracuse NY 13221 Office Phone: 315-432-6307. E-mail: al.drucker@carrier.utc.com.

DRUCKER, ANA BUENO, healthcare marketing and public relations executive, writer; b. NYC, Apr. 27, 1952; m. David M. Kreitzer, June, 1973 (div. Feb. 1979); 1 child, Anatol C. Kreitzer. Sr. writer healthcare Integral Sys., Inc., Walnut Creek, Calif., 1986-88; freelance writer L.A., 1989-92; cons. mktg. Health Net, L.A., 1992-96; pres. Bueno Healthcare Mktg., L.A., 1996-98; assoc. v.p. mktg. and creative svcs. City of Hope Cancer Ctr., L.A., 1998—2005; v.p. mktg. and devel. Santa Barbara (Calif.) Clinic, 2005—. Spkr. on branding and healthcare. Author: Special Olympics: The First 25 Years, 1994; contbr. articles to profl. jours. Sponsor, vol. Spl. Olympics, Calif., 1988-96. Recipient Disting. Vol. Svc. award Spl. Olympics, 1992. Mem. AAUW. Jewish. Avocation: art collector.

DRUCKER, MIRIAM KOONTZ, psychologist, educator; b. Mechanicsburg, Pa., Feb. 3, 1925; married AB, Dickinson Coll., 1947; MA, Emory U., 1948; PhD, Peabody Coll., 1955. Counselor psychology Millsaps Coll., 1949-51; instr. Monticello Coll., 1951-52; asst. prof. psychology Agnes Scott Coll., Decatur, Ga., 1955-58, assoc. prof., 1958-62, prof., 1962-80, Charles A. Dana prof. psychology, 1981-90, prof. emeritus, 1990—, former chmn. dept. psychology. Mem. Am. Psychol. Assn. Home: 425 Winn Way Apt 226 Decatur GA 30030-1734

DRUCKER, MORT, commercial artist; b. Bklyn., Mar. 22, 1929; s. Edward and Sarah (Spielvogel) D.; m. Barbara Hellerman, Aug. 28, 1948; children: Laurie Drucker Bachner, Melanie Drucker Amsterdam. Student public schs.; DFA (hon.), Art Inst. Boston, 1995. Staff artist Nat. Periodicals, N.Y.C., 1948-50; freelance artist, 1951—. Contbg. artist Mad mag., 1956—. Covers for Time mag; also nat. advt. agencies, TV commls. and movie posters; author: (with Paul Laikin) JFK Coloring Book, 1961, Mort Drucker's Showstoppers, 1985, (with Laikin) Ollie North Coloring Book, 1987, (David Duncan with Mort Drucker) Familiar Faces: The Art of Mort Drucker, 1988, (with Laikin) Farewell Tribute to Ronald Reagan Coloring Book, 1988, (with Lee J. Ames) Draw Fifty Famous Caricatures, 1990; illustrator: Whitefish Will Rides Again!, 1994, Tomatoes from Mars, 1996; co-author: (with Jerry Dumas) "Benchley" comic strip, 1984-86. Recipient cert. merit Art Dirs. Club N.Y., 1968, San Francisco Soc. Communicating Arts award of excellence, 1973, Cert. Merit Soc. Ill. 1991, Gold award, 1980, Booth Newspaper award of excellence Advertising Club of New York, 1981, Andy award Art Directors Show for Consumer Advertising, 1983, Showtime award Rochester Soc. Communicating Arts, 1983, Internat. Comic award Barcelona, Spain, 1985, Best in Spl. Features award Nat. Cartoonist Soc., 1986, 87, 88, 89, Reuben award outstanding cartoonist of the year, 1987, Best Cartoonist award Nat. Cartoonist Soc., 1988, Merit cert. Soc. Ill., 1991, Ink Pot award, 1996. Mem. Graphic Artists Guild, Soc. Illustrators. Time covers in Nat. Portrait Gallery, Smithsonian Instn. Office: care Mad Mag 1700 Broadway New York NY 10019-5905

DRUCKER, PETER FERDINAND, writer, consultant, language educator; b. Vienna, Nov. 19, 1909; came to U.S., 1937, naturalized, 1943; s. Adolph Bertram and Caroline D.; m. Doris Schmitz, Jan. 16, 1937; children: Kathleen Romola, J. Vincent, Cecily Anne, Joan Agatha. Grad., Gymnasium, Vienna, 1927; LLD, U. Frankfurt, 1931; 25 hon. doctorates. Economist London Banking House, 1933-37; Am. adviser for Brit. banks, Am. corr. Brit. newspapers, 1937-42; cons. maj. bus. corps., 1940—; prof. philosophy, politics Bennington Coll., 1942-49; prof. mgmt. NYU, 1950-72, chmn. mgmt. area, 1957-62; Clarke prof. social sci. Claremont Grad. U. (Calif.), 1971—2002; prof. dept. art Pomona Coll., Calif., 1979-85. Author: The End of Economic Man, 1939, new edit. 1995, The Future of Industrial Man, 1941, new edit. 1995, Concept of the Corporation, 1946, new edit., 1993, The New Society, 1950, new edit., 1993, The Practice of Management, 1954, new edit., 2004, America's Next Twenty Years, 1957, The Landmarks of Tomorrow, 1959, new edit., 1996, Managing for Results, 1964, new edit., 1993, The Effective Executive, 1966, new edit., 2002, The Age of Discontinuity, 1969, new edit., 1996, Technology; Management and Society, 1970, Men, Ideas and Politics, 1971, Management: Tasks, Responsibilities, Practices, 1974, new edit., 1993, The Unseen Revolution: How Pension Fund Socialism Came to America, 1976, new edit. (new title: The Pension Fund Revolution, 1996), Adventures of a Bystander, 1979, new. edit., 1998, Managing in Turbulent Times, 1980, new edit., 1993, Toward the Next Economics and Other Essays, 1981, (essays) The Changing World of the Executive, 1982, Innovation and Entrepreneurship, 1985, new edit., 1993, (essays) The Frontiers of Management, 1986, 8th edit., 2000, The New Realities, 1989, new edit., 2003, Managing the Non-Profit Organization, 1990, (essays) Managing for the Future, 1992, 7th edit., 2000, (essays) The Ecological Vision, 1992, new edit., 1997, Post Capitalist Society, 1993, (essays) Managing in a Time of Great Change, 1995, Drucker on Asia: A Dialogue With Isao Nagauchi, 1997, (essays) Drucker on the Profession of Management, 1998, Management Challenges for the 21st Century, 1999, (anthologies) The Essential Drucker on Management, 2001, (essays) Managing in the Next Society, 2002, A Functioning Society, 2003, The Daily Drucker, 2004; (fiction) The Last of All Possible Worlds, 1982, The Temptation to Do Good, 1984; co-author: The Song of the Brush: Japanese paintings, 1979; producer: movie series The Effective Executive, 1969, Managing Discontinuity, 1971, The Manager and the Organization, 1977, Managing for Tomorrow, 1981, The Future of Manufacturing, 2000; producer 25 audiocassette series The Non-Profit Drucker, 1988, 5 Online Teaching Devices on Managing Yourself, 2000, 5 Online Teaching Devices on Business Strategies, 2000, 3 Online Teaching Devices on Managing Change, 2003. Recipient gold medal Internat. U. Social Studies, Rome, 1957, Wallace Clark Internat. Mgmt. medal, 1963, Taylor Key Soc. for Advancement Mgmt., 1967, Presdl. citation NYU, 1969, CIOS Internat. Mgmt. gold medal, 1972, Chancellor's medal Internat. Acad. Mgmt., 1987, Evangeline Booth award Salvation Army, 2001, Disting. Leadership medal Nat. Acad. Mgmt., 2001, Presdl. Medal of Freedom, 2002. Fellow AAAS (council), Internat., Am., Irish Acads. Mgmt., Brit. Inst. Mgmt. (hon.), Am. Acad. Arts and Scis.; mem. Soc. for History Tech. (pres. 1965-66), Nat. Acad. Pub. Adminstrn. (hon.).

DRUCKER, RICHARD ALLEN, lawyer; b. NYC, Mar. 30, 1952; s. Charles and Bette Drucker; m. Jeanmarie Hamilton, Sept. 30, 1989; children: Richard Allen Jr., Hamilton Charles. BA, U. Vt., 1974; JD, U. Va., 1977. Bar: N.Y. 1978. Law clk. to Hon. William H. Webster, U.S. Ct. Appeals for 8th Cir., St. Louis, 1977-78; ptnr. Davis Polk & Wardwell, N.Y.C., 1978—. Contbr. articles to profl. jours. Mem. ABA, NY State Bar Assn., Assn. Bar City NY (Asian affairs com. 1998-99, securities regulation com. 2000-03, fin. reporting com. 2004—), Coun. Fgn. Rels. Avocations: golf, running, classical music. Office: Davis Polk & Wardwell 450 Lexington Ave Fl 31 New York NY 10017-3982 Office Phone: 212-450-4745. E-mail: drucker@dpw.com.

DRUCKER, RICHARD M., educational consultant, communications educator; b. Phila., Pa., Oct. 13, 1946; s. Jerome J Drucker and Ellen H Sand; m. Dianne C Ashton, Oct. 23, 1988. BS, West Chester U., 1986, MA, 1990. Dir. edn. Cmty. Occupational Readiness Placement Program, 1988—98; workforce coord. Dist. 1199 Union, Phila., 1999—2001; employer rep. Marriot Found. Bridges Program, Phila., 2001—. Adv. bd. Phila. Mayor's Commn. on Literacy, 1992—96; adj. instr. Camden County Coll., Peirce Coll. Co-author: (handbook) Collaborative Education: An Alternative Approach to Adult Literacy Instruction, 1993. Fundraiser Am. Heart Assn., 1998—. Avocations: gardening, weightlifting, travel. Home: 1121 Crane Dr Cherry Hill NJ 08003 Office: Marriot Found Bridges Program 100 South Broad St Ste 1117 Philadelphia PA 19110 Office Phone: 215-564-0327 13.

DRUCKER, SHELDON MAURICE, lawyer; b. Boston, Nov. 25, 1945; s. Myer and Mary (Hurwitz) D.; m. Harriet Avroch, Aug. 17, 1969 (div. July 21, 1992). BBA, U. Mass., 1967; JD, Suffolk U., 1970. Bar: Mass., 1970, U.S. Dist. Ct. Mass. 1971, U.S. Ct. Appeals (1st cir.) 1971. Asst. corp. counsel law dept. City of Boston, 1970-73; ptnr. Brown, Rudnick, Freed & Gesmer, Boston, 1973-91; pvt. practice Boston, 1991—. Pres., trustee Brookline (Mass.) Hosp., 1975-90; mem. adv. coun. Sch. Mgmt. U. Mass., Amherst, 1990—, chancellor's coun., 1991—; chairperson Newton (Mass.) Hist. Commn., 1973-79, Newton Upper Falls Hist. Dist. Commn., 1973-79. Mem. ABA, Mass. Bar Assn., Boston Bar Assn. Office: One Bowdoin Sq Ste 300 Boston MA 02114 Office Phone: 617-720-2027. Business E-Mail: relaw.bostn@verizon.net.

DRUCKMAN, DANIEL, social sciences educator, consultant, researcher; b. N.Y.C., Dec. 14, 1939; s. Irving and Gladys (Marcus) D.; m. Marjorie Kahn, July 22, 1962; children: Kathy Lee Berggren, James N. BA with honors, Mich. State U., 1961; student, Duke U., 1961-62; MS, Northwestern U., 1965, PhD, 1966. Sr. rsch. scientist Inst. Juvenile Rsch., Chgo., 1966-72, program dir., 1972-75; sr. rsch. analyst Mathematica, Inc., Bethesda, Md., 1975-79, math. tech. scientist, 1979-82; sr. scientist, program mgr. Booz-Allen & Hamilton, Bethesda, 1982-85; prin. study dir. Nat. Acad. Scis., Washington, 1985-97; Vernon M. and Minnie I. Lynch prof. conflict resolution George Mason U., Fairfax, Va., 2001, dir. doctoral program, 1997—2002. Vis. faculty IIS Inst. Mgmt., Cochin, India, 1998—; vis. scientist Internat. Inst. Applied Sys. Analysis, Vienna, Austria, 1991-92; cons. Nat. Rsch. Coun., Washington, 1997-2000. Mem. editl. bd. Jour. Conflict Resolution, 1990—, Am. Behavioral Scientist, others; assoc. editor, Negotiation Jour., Simulation & Games, Group Decision and Negotiation, editor spl. issue Annals of Am. Acad. Polit. and Social Sci., 1995; contbr. over 140 articles to sci. jours.; author, editor 12 books. Active Nat. Charity Campaigns, Tennis Profls. Tournament Wash. Tennis Patrons, 1990—; coach Montgomery Soccer, Inc., Md., 1979-87. Recipient award U.S. Inst. of Peace, Washington, 1992-93, 96-97, award for enhancing human performance U.S. Army Rsch. Inst., Alexandria, Va., 1986-97, Tchg. Excellence award, George Mason U., 1998. Fellow Soc. Psychol. Study of Social Issues (Otto Klineberg Intercultural and Internat. Rels. award 1995), Soc. Exptl. Social Psychology, Internat. Studies Assn., Internat. Assn. Conflict Mgmt. (Lifetime Achievement award 2003), Sigma Xi. Achievements included research in studies of negotiation and nationalism. Home: 10509 Gainsborough Rd Potomac MD 20854-4045 Office: Inst Conflict Analysis and Resolution George Mason U 4260 Chain Bridge Rd Fairfax VA 22030-4297 Fax: 703-993-1302.

DRUCKMAN, JOEL ISADORE, musician, educator; b. LA, Apr. 27, 1947; s. Jacob Storper Druckman and Margaret Shari Erhlich; children from previous marriage: Alexandra, Aaron. BA in Music History, U. So. Calif., 1974; MA in Music Performance, Calif. State U., LA, 1976. Instr. music Oxnard (Calif.) Coll., 2000—; lectr. Santa Monica (Calif.) Coll., 2000—. Musician: Culver City (Calif.) Orch., 2004—, (albums) Bonzo Dog Band, John Fahay, John Cale, others. Avocation: surfing. Office: Oxnard Coll 4000 S Rose Ave Oxnard CA 93033 Office Phone: 310-980-6351.

DRUDGE, MATT, journalist; b. Oct. 27, 1967; s. Bob Drudge. Gift shop mgr. CBS-TV, LA; founder, editor The Drudge Report website, 1995—; host TV show Drudge, 1998—99; host radio show ABC Network, 1999—2000, Premiere Radio Networks. Inc., 2001—. Author: Drudge Manifesto, 2000. Office: Premiere Radio Networks Inc 15260 Ventura Blvd 5th Fl Sherman Oaks CA 91403 Office Phone: 818-377-5300. Office Fax: 818-377-5333.

DRUE, KERRY ERICA, attorney general; b. Saint Thomas, V.I., Mar. 15, 1966; d. Ive Arlington Swan and Gertrude Maria (Niles) Drue Swan. BA, Princeton U., 1988; JD, Harvard U., 1991. Bar: Fla. 1991, D.C. 1992, U.S. Dist. Ct. (mid. dist.) Fla. 1992. Assoc. Steel, Hector & Davis, Miami, Fla., 1991-92; jud. clk. V.I. Territorial Ct., Saint Thomas, 1992-93; assoc. Steel, Hector & Davis, Miami, Fla., 1993; asst. atty. gen. V.I., acting atty gen., 2005—. Vol. lawyer Guardian Ad Litem Program, Miami, 1991. Mem. ABA, Fla. Assn. Women Lawyers, Black Lawyers Assn., Nat. Bar Assn., Harvard Club Miami, Japanese Cultural Soc. Avocations: travel, martial arts, politics. Office: Dept Justice GERS Complex 48B-50C Kronprinsdens Gade St Thomas VI 00802*

DRUKER, BRIAN JAY, medical educator, researcher; b. St. Paul, Apr. 30, 1955; s. Jean S. Druker. MD, U. Calif.-San Diego, La Jolla, 1981. Internship and residency in internal medicine Barnes Hosp., Washington Sch. of Medicine, St. Louis; trained in oncology Harvard's Dana-Farber Cancer Inst.; prof. medicine Oreg. Health & Sci. U., Portland, 1993—2001, JELD-WEN chair, dir., leukemia ctr. Recipient medal of honor, Am. Cancer Soc., 2001, AACR-Richard and Hinda Rosenthal award, 2001, Dameshak prize, Am. Soc. Hematology, 2001, Warren Alpert Found. award, Harvard Med. Sch., 2001, John J. Kenney award, Leukemia and Lymphoma Soc., 2000, Brupbacher Found. Cancer Rsch. award, 2001, Emil J. Freireich award for clin. rsch., MD Anderson Cancer Ctr., 2001, Charles F. Kettering prize, GM Cancer Rsch. Found., 2002, Pioneer Survivorship award, Lance Armstrong Found., 2002. Mem.: Inst. Medicine, 2004. Avocations: running, bicycling. Office: Oreg Health and Sci U 3181 SW Sam Jackson Park Rd Portland OR 97201

DRULINER, MARCIA MARIE, education educator; b. Dec. 18, 1946; M in Secondary Edn., U. Nebr., 1974; PhD, Marquette U., 1992. Assoc. prof. edn. Concordia Coll., Bronxville, N.Y., 1993-95; asst. prof. edn. Northwestern Coll., Orange City, Iowa, 1998-2000; instr. Spanish, Gretna (Nebr.) Pub. Schs., 2000—. Home: 20184 Glenmore Dr Apt 76 Gretna NE 68028 E-mail: mdruliner@cox.net.

DRULLINGER, LEONA PEARL BLAIR, obstetrics nurse; b. Norton, Kans., Aug. 10, 1962; d. Floyd Allen and Frances Marie (Redfield) Blair; m. Richard Lee Drullinger, Aug. 2, 1981; children: Richard Jr., Charity, Kelsy, Brandon. AD in Practical Nursing, Colby C.C., Kans., 1985; ADN, Garden City (C.C., Kans., 1987; BSN, Creighton U., 2003. RN; cert. BLS, ACLS, neonatal advanced life support, inpatient obstetrics. LPN Citizens Med. Ctr., Colby, Kans., 1985—86, Nursing Home, Lakin, Kans., 1986—87; RN labor and delivery staff nurse St. Catherine's Hosp., Garden City, Kans., 1987—88; acting head nurse VA Med. Ctr., Lincoln, Nebr., 1988—90; telemetry nurse Bryan Meml. Hosp., Lincoln, 1990—92; relief staff nurse Nurse Finders, Omaha, 1990—92; contract charge obstetric nurse Hunter Med. Inc., Offutt AFB Hosp., Bellvue, Nebr., 1992—94, Med. Nat. Inc., Offutt AFB Hosp., Bellvue, Nebr., 1994—96; staff nurse Brodstone Meml. Nuckolls County Hosp., Superior, Nebr., 1996—97, Cambridge Meml. Hosp., Nebr., 1997—98; staff relief nurse Olston-KQC Staffing, 1996—; dir. nursing svc. Good Samaritan Ctr., Arapahoe, Nebr., 1998—99; nursing svcs. program coord. Mid-Plains C.C., McCook, Nebr., 2000—02. Relief nurse Olston-KQC Staffing, 1996-2000. Mem. ANA, Nebr. Nurses Assn. Republican. Avocations: reading, crocheting, camping, cooking, sewing. Home: 5521 Spruce St Lincoln NE 68516-1347 E-mail: angelwings32@yahoo.com.

DRUM, ALICE, academic administrator, educator; b. Gettysburg, Pa., June 22, 1935; d. David Wentz and Charlotte Rebecca (Kinzey) McDannell; m. D. Richard Guise, June 15, 1957 (div. Aug. 1975); children: Gregory, Brent, Richard, Robert, Clay; m. Ray Kenneth Drum, Mar. 2, 1979; 1 child, Trevor. BA magna cum laude, Wilson Coll., 1957; PhD, Am. U., 1976. Adj. prof. gen. studies Antioch U., Columbia, Md., 1976-78; adj. asst. prof. English Gettysburg Coll., 1977-80; lectr. gen. studies Georgetown U., Washington, 1980-81; lectr. gen. honors U. Md., College Park, 1980-83; asst. prof. English Hood Coll., Frederick, Md., 1981-85, coord. writing program, 1981-83, assoc. dean acad. affairs, 1983-85; dean freshmen Franklin and Marshall Coll., Lancaster, Pa., 1985-88, v.p., 1988-2001, prof., chair women's studies, 2001—. Team mem. Mid. States Accreditation Assn., 1989-2003; cons. in field. Co-author: Funding A College Education, 1996; contbr. chpts. to books, articles and book revs. to profl. jours. Chair Lancaster County DA Commn., Lancaster, 1990-91; mem. Lancaster County Commn. on Youth Violence, Lancaster, 1990-91; bd. trustees Wilson Coll., 1997—, YWCA, Lancaster. Mellon grantee, 1979; Davison Foreman fellow, 1975-76. Mem. MLA, N.E. MLA, Deans (pres. 1988-89), Coll. English Assn., Phi Beta Kappa (pres. chpt. 1990-91), Phi Kappa Phi. Democrat. Episcopalian. Avocations: hiking, reading, visiting art museums. Office Phone: 717-291-3980. Business E-Mail: alicedrum@fandm.edu.

DRUM, SYDNEY MARIA, artist; b. Calgary, Alta., Can., Nov. 20, 1952; d. Ian Mondelet and Dorothy Mary (Weaver) D.; m. Frank DeSalvo, Nov. 7, 1987; 1 child, Christopher. BFA with distinction in art, U. Calgary, 1974; MFA, York U., 1976. Tchr. U. Ill., 1978-83, Govs. State U., 1983-84, Rutgers U., 1984-87. One-woman and 2 person exhibits include Art Gallery Ont., 1978, Condeso/Lawler Gallery, N.Y., 1981, Gallery Pascal, 1983, U. Pitts., 1984, Bau-Xi Gallery, Toronto, 1987, 90, 92, 95, 55 Mercer Gallery, N.Y., 1993, 96, 98, 2000, 2002, 2004, Mus. am Ostwall, Dortmund, Germany, 1994, Hart House-U. Toronto, 1995, Robert Birch Gallery, Toronto, 1999, 2002, Gallery Surge, Tokyo, 1999, Kunsturein Alle Fuerwache, Dresden, 2002, Optisches Mus., Jena, Germany, 2004; represented in pub. collections Can. Coun. Art Bank, U. Toronto, Toronto-Dominion Bank, Petro Can., Mus. Modern Art, N.Y., Phila. Mus. Art, Robert McLaughlin Gallery, Oshawa; commissions include Pope, Ballard, Shepard & Fowle, Chgo., 1983, Zimmerli Mus., Rutgers U., 1990; reviewer art exhibits New Art Examiner, Chgo., 1983-84. Can. Coun. grantee, 1978. Home: 138 W 120th St New York NY 10027-6401

DRUMBORE, BRIAN ALLEN, music educator; b. Seaford, Del., June 14, 1974; s. Sharon Laub and Ralph Drumbore, John George Laub (Stepfather); m. Julia Jean Morgan, Jan. 27, 1996; 1 child, Isabella Morgan. BS Music Edn., W. Chester U. Pa., W. Chester, Pa., 1996; MA Music History, West Chester U. of Pa., W. Chester, Pa., 2005. Cert. IB Music Internat. Baccalaureate Orgn., 2003, AP Music Theory The Coll. Bd., 2004. Instrumental music educator Mt. Pleasant H.S., Wilmington, Del., 1996—. Co-dir. Diamond State Concert Band, Wilmington, Del., 2001—. Editor: DMEA Notes. Mem.: Am. Musicological Soc., Del. Music Educators Assn. (editor 2004—05), Nat. Assn. for Music Edn.(MENC). Office: Mount Pleasant HS 5201 Wash St Ext Wilmington DE 19809 Office Phone: 302-762-7125. Office Fax: 302-762-7042. Business E-Mail: brian.drumbore@bsd.k12.de.us.

DRUMHELLER, JANET LOUISE, librarian; b. Walton, W. Va., June 23, 1951; d. Nathan Earl and Edna Osial (Dye) Vineyard; m. Fred John Drumheller, Apr. 11, 1971; 1 child, Stephanie Katarina. BS in History, U. Tenn., 1974, MS in Libr. and Info. Scis., 1977. Mgr. Farragut br. Knox County Pub. Librs., Knoxville, Tenn., 1977—81, reference libr., 1983—96, reference svcs. mgr., 1996—. Mem. East Tenn. Homeless Coalition; pres. alumni bd. U. Tenn. Sch. Info. Scis. Mem.: East Tenn. Libr. Assn., Tenn. Libr. Assn. Office: Knox County Libr System 500 W Church Ave Knoxville TN 37902

DRUMMER, DONALD RAYMOND, diversified financial services company executive, educator; b. Binghamton, NY, Oct. 10, 1941; s. Donald Joseph and Louise Frances (Campbell) D.; m. Rita Kovac, May 22, 1965; children: Shelley Rita, Adam Donn. BS, U. Colo., 1972; MBA, Regis U., 1981. With Lincoln First Bank, Binghamton, 1962-69; asst. comptr. Adams & Horne, Denver, 1969; with Colo. State Bank, Denver, 1969-87, v.p., 1972-81, comptr., 1972-87, sr. v.p., 1981-87; sr. v.p., CFO Wyo. Nat. Bancorp. (formerly Affiliated Bank Corp. of Wyo.), Casper, 1987-91, Wyo. Nat. Bank, Casper, Cheyenne, 1987—91; v.p., contr. Crop Hail Mgmt., Kalispell, Mont., 1991—92; sr. v.p. fin. Am. Nat. Bank, Cheyenne, 1993—95; v.p. Cmty. First Bancorp, Inc., 1994—95, cons., 1995—2001; sr. v.p., CFO Citizens Bank Oviedo, 2001—. Bd. dirs. Wyo. Nat. Bank, Lovell and Kemmerer, 1987-88; corp. sec. Wyo. Nat. Bancorp. (formerly Affiliated Bank Corp. of Wyo.), 1987-91; bd. dirs. Wheatland Ins. Agency, 1989-91; CFO, exec. com. Am. Bankers Assn., 1989-91; adj. faculty Regis U., mem. grad. edn. task force, 1986-87. Editor: Chronicle, 1980—81. Bd. dirs. Girls Club of Casper, 1988. Mem. Inst. Mgmt. Accts. (dir. 1975-79, v.p. 1977-79), Am. Acctg. Assn., Am. Taxation Assn., Denver Sertoma Club (past pres.), City Club (v.p., dir. 1979-83). Office: Citizens Bank Oviedo PO Box 620729 Oviedo FL 32762-0729 Office Phone: 407-365-6611. E-mail: don@cboviedo.com.

DRUMMOND, ADAM DAVID, elementary school educator; b. Huntington, Ind., Apr. 19, 1980; s. Daniel Michael and Barbara Jeanne Drummond; m. Tiffanney Michelle Day, June 15, 2002; 1 child, Chase Travis. BS in Elem. Edn., Ball State U., 2002, MA in Student Affairs Adminstrn. in Higher Edn., 2005. Elem. educator Huntington County Cmty. Sch. Corp., Ind., 2002—; mid. sch./H.S. youth dir. Evang. United Meth. Ch., Huntington, Ind., 2003—. Mem. LaFontaine Arts Coun., Huntington, Ind., 2004—05. Recipient Tchr. of the Yr. award, Wal-Mart, 2003, Showcase Program award, NODA Region VII, 2005. Mem.: Little Turtle Reading Coun. (treas. 2003—04), Nat. Orientation Dir.'s Assn., Phi Gamma Delta (life; bd. of chpt. advisor's dir. 2004—05). Methodist. Avocations: running, reading, softball. Home: 3025 Trappers Cove Huntington IN 46750 Office Phone: 260-356-7812. Personal E-mail: adamandtiff@yahoo.com.

DRUMMOND, DAVID C., information technology executive, lawyer; BA in history, Santa Clara U; JD, Stanford Law Sch., 1989. Former ptnr. corp. transactions group Wilson, Sonsini, Goodrich, & Rosati, 1998; exec. v.p. fin., CFO CBT Group PLC, 1999, SmartForce; v.p. corp. devel. Google Inc., Mountain View, Calif., 2002—, gen. counsel, 2002—, sec., 2002—. Office: Google Inc 1600 Amphitheatre Pky Mountain View CA 94043 Office Phone: 650-623-4000. Office Fax: 650-618-1499.

DRUMMOND, DOROTHY WEITZ, geography education consultant, educator, author; b. San Diego, Dec. 19, 1928; d. Frederick W. and Dora (Weidenhofer) Weitz; m. Robert R. Drummond, Sept. 5, 1953 (dec. June 1982); children: Kathleen, Gael, Martha. AB, Valparaiso U., 1949; MA, Northwestern U., 1951. Cert. tchr., Ind. Tchr. social studies Woodrow Wilson Jr. H.S., Oxnard, Calif., 1949—50; editl. asst. Am. Geog. Soc., N.Y.C., 1951—53; substitute tchr. Vigo County Sch. Corp., Terre Haute, Ind., 1960—67; tchr. social studies Ind. State U. Lab. Sch., Terre Haute, 1963—64. Geog. edn. cons., author, workshop presenter, Terre Haute, 1953—; adj. asst. prof. geography Saint Mary-of-the-Woods (Ind.) Coll., 1967-99, Ind. State U., Terre Haute, 1990—; dir. project GEO, Ind. State U., 1992-96; cons. McGraw-Hill, Scott-Foresman, Agy. for Instrnl. Tech., Hudson Inst.; grant developer GIS for the Twenty-First Century, Ind. State U., 1996-98. Author: People on Earth, 3d edit., 1988, Thinking Geographically: All Things Considered, 1990, 1998, Holy Land, Whose Land?, 2002, 2d edit., 2004; co-author: The World Today, 3d edit., 1971, World Geography, 1989; contbr.

numerous articles to profl. jours. Organizer, leader ednl. tours to China, Australia, New Zealand, Peru, Ecuador, 1986—2004; bd. dirs. United Campus Ministries, Terre Haute, 1991—94, 2003—. Fulbright scholar, Burma, 1957-58; grantee Geography Educators Network Ind., 1988-96, Ind. Commn. Higher Edn., 1990, 92, 94, 96, NSF, 1993, 95, 96, 97, U.S. Dept. Edn., 1992-96. Mem.: Assn. Am. Geographers, Am. Geog. Soc., Ind. Coun. Social Studies, Geography Educators Network Ind., Nat. Coun. Geog. Edn. (pres. 1990), Nat. Coun. Social Studies. Personal E-mail: dd2@indstate.edu.

DRUMMOND, JAMES EVERMAN, information technology executive, retired military officer; b. Stillwater, Okla., July 13, 1932; s. Garrett Bartlett and Frances Elizabeth (Rigdon) Drummond; m. Helen Wesley Hillman, Dec. 29, 1958 (dec. Aug. 2001); children: James Everman, Sarah Elizabeth; m. Jeanne Frances Leighton, Dec. 4, 2004. BS, U.S. Mil. Acad., 1955; MS, U. Ariz., 1962; postgrad., Army War Coll., 1975; MA, Central Mich. U., 1982. Commd. 2d lt. U.S. Army, 1955, advanced through grades to maj. gen., served in Europe, Vietnam, Korea, comdr. III Corps Arty., 1979-81, dep. dir. Material Systems Analysis Activity, 1981-82; comdr. TCATA Ft. Hood, Tex., 1983-86; comdr. OTEA Falls Ch., Va., 1986-88; v.p. BDM Corp, Norfolk, Va., 1988-90; pvt. practice cons., 1990-92; v.p. Coe-Truman Tech. Inc., Hampton, Va., 1992-96. Asst. prof. U.S. Mil. Acad., 1962-65 Decorated D.S.M., Legion of Merit with 2 oak leaf clusters, Bronze Star, Air medal, others. Mem. Assn. U.S. Army, Soc. Am. Mil. Engrs., Mil. Order World Wars, Assn. Grads. U.S. Mil. Acad., Internat. Test and Evaluation Assn., Co. of Mil. Historians, Sigma Alpha Epsilon, Masons, Kiwanis. Presbyterian. Home: 2510 Wildwood Dr Montgomery AL 36111 Personal E-mail: drummond55@aol.com.

DRUMMOND, LACREDA RENEE, journalist; b. Washington, Nov. 6, 1966; d. Percy Eugene and Rosa (Ross) D. BS in Journalism, U. Md., 1988. Wire editor WMUC AM 65/FM 88 Radio Stas., College Park, Md., 1986-87; TV prodn. asst. Strong Points, Hollywood, Md., 1986-87; TV producer The Quill Report, College Park, 1987; chyron operator Maryland Coaches' Corner, College Park, 1987-88; staff writer Diamondback newspaper, College Park, 1987-88; TV field reporter, tech. dir. Tuesday Weekly, Hollywood, Md., 1988; freelance sound tech. Image TV Co., Washington, 1993—; TV prodn. asst. USO World Headquarters, Washington, 1993; on-line asst. editor Henninger Video, Arlington, Va., 1997; assoc. prodr. WJLA-TV, Washington, 1997—. Mem. Soc. Profl. Journalists, (chpt. pres. 186-87). Home: 5491 Bluecoat Ln Columbia MD 21045-2227

DRUMMOND, MARSHALL EDWARD (MARK DRUMMON), academic administrator; b. Stanford, Calif., Sept. 14, 1941; s. Kirk Isaac and Fern Venice (McDeritt) D.; 2 children. BS, San Jose State U., 1964, MBA, 1969; EdD, U. San Francisco, 1979. Adj. prof. bus. and edn. U. San Francisco, 1975-81; adj. prof. bus. and info. systems San Francisco State U., 1981-82; prof. MIS, Ea. Wash. U., Cheney, 1985—98, exec. dir. info. resources, 1988, assoc. v.p. adminstrv. svcs., chief info. officer, 1988-89, v.p. adminstrv. svcs., 1989-90, exec. v.p., 1990, pres., 1990-98; chancellor L.A. C.C. Dist., 1999—2004, Calif. C.C. sys., 2004—. Cons. Sch. Bus., Harvard Coll., U. Ariz. Contbg. editor Diebold Series; contbr. articles to profl. jours. Democrat. Avocations: horse breeding and traing, equestrian sports. Office: Calif Cmty Colls Chancellor's Office 1102 Q St Sacramento CA 95814-6511 Office Phone: 916-322-4005. Business E-Mail: mdrummond@cccco.edu.

DRUMMOND, SALLY HAZELET, artist; b. Evanston, Ill., June 4, 1924; d. Craig Potter and Frances (Gillam) Hazlet; m. F. Weichel Drummond, Mar. 25, 1961; 1 child, Craig Potter. Student, Rollins Coll., 1942-44; BS, Columbia U., 1946, postgrad., 1946-48, Inst. Design, Chgo., 1949-50; MA, U. Louisville, 1952. Instr. Skowhegan Sch. Art, 1973. Exhibited in one-man shows at, Hadley Gallery, Louisville, 1952, Tanager Gallery, N.Y.C., 1955, 57, 60, Green Gallery, N.Y.C., 1962, Fischbach Gallery, N.Y.C., 1978, Aldrich Mus., Ridgefield, Conn., 1981, Merida Galleries, Louisville, 1982, Artists Space, N.Y.C., 1984, "Surface and Proportion", Margaret Roeder Gallery, N.Y. 1990, Cornell Fine Arts Ctr., Rollins Coll., Winter Park, Fla., 1989, Louisville Visual Arts Assn., 1990, Mitchell Algus Gallery, N.Y.C., 2003; exhibited in group shows at, Am. embassy, Rome, 1953, Fgn. Artists Invitational, Bordighiera, Italy, 1953, Am. Artists Ann., 1960, Whitney Mus., N.Y.C., 1958-59, 64, Green Gallery, 1961, Mus. Modern Art, N.Y.C., 1963, Am. Inst. Arts and Letters, N.Y.C., 1982, L.I. City, N.Y., 1987, Owensboro (Ky.) Mus. Art, 1987; 2 person exhbn.: Springfield (Ohio) Art Ctr., 1988, Urban Callery, N.Y.C., 1989, Hunter Coll., N.Y.C., 2003; retrospective exhbn. at Corcoran Gallery, Washington, 1972; rep. permanent collections at, Mus. Modern Art, Whitney Mus., Met. Mus. Art, N.Y.C., Chase Manhattan Bank, N.Y.C., Ciba-Geigy Corp., Speed Mus., Louisville, U. Iowa Mus. Art, Iowa City, Hirshorn Mus. Art, Washington, Greenwich, Conn., Hudsons Dept. Store, Detroit, AVCO Corp., Citizens Fidelity Bank and Trust Co., Louisville. Recipient Fulbright grant to Venice, 1952-53, Guggenheim grant to France, 1967-68

DRUMMOND, WILLA HENDRICKS, physiology and medical educator; b. Harrisburg, Pa., Dec. 5, 1945; d. George Edson and Leah Clementine (Connelly) Hendricks; m. Thomas Weston Drummond, June 1966 (div. 1978). BA cum laude, Brown U., 1966; MD, U. Pa., 1970; MS in Med. Informatics, U. Utah, 1999. Resident in pediat. Children's Hosp. Phila., 1970-72, cardiology fellow, 1972-74; instr. pediat. U. Pa., Phila., 1973-74; rsch. fellow perinatology U. Oreg., Portland, 1974-75; staff pediatrician Kaiser-Permanente Clinics, Portland, 1975-76; instr. neonatology, fellow Cardiovasc. Rsch. Inst.-U. Calif., San Francisco, 1976-78; asst. prof. pediat. U. Fla., Gainesville, 1978-82, asst. prof. pediat. and physiology, 1981-82, assoc. prof. pediat. physiology and vet. med. scis., 1982-88, prof., 1988—. Cons. Baxter-Travenol Labs., Deerfield, Ill., 1986-88; co-chair Equine Neonatology Study Group, Gainesville, 1981-91; dir. Neonatology Fellowship Program U. Fla., Gainesville, 1981-85; cons., chief med. officer, ICU DataSys., Inc., Gainesville, 2001-04, interim CEO, exec. v.p. for med. affairs, 2004—. Contbr. numerous rsch. papers and abstracts to profl. jours.; poet: Carousel of Progress, 1979. Rsch. grantee (25) including Am. Heart Assn., NIH, Dept. of Def., 1976—; sr. fellow Med. Informatics, 1997-99; named Best Dr. in USA, Best Doctors, Inc., 2005 Mem. Am. Physiologic Soc., Soc. for Pediat. Rsch., Am. Pediat. Soc., Am. Acad. Pediat., Am. Med. Informatics Assn., Am. Heart Assn., So. Soc. Pediat. Rsch., Internat. Soc. Vet. Perinatology (bd. dirs., pres. 1995-97), Internat. Physicians for Prevention of Nuc. War (collective Nobel Peace Prize 1985), Concerned Scientists, NOW, Sierra Club, other environ., women's, peace orgns. and archeologic conservancy. Democrat. Office: U Fla Coll Medicine PO Box 100296 Gainesville FL 32610-0296 Office Phone: 352-392-4195. Business E-Mail: DrWilla@peds.ufl.edu.

DRUMMOND, WINSLOW, lawyer; b. Phila., Jan. 29, 1933; s. Winslow Shaw and Dorothy (Moore) D.; m. Katherine Pace, June 18, 1983; children: Judith L., Kathryn W., Winslow Shaw II. AB, Coll. of Wooster, Ohio, 1954; LLB, Duke U., 1957. Bar: Ark. 1957, U.S. Dist. Ct. Ark. 1957, U.S. Ct. Appeals (8th cir.) 1958, U.S. Supreme Ct. 1992; diplomate Am. Bd. Trial Advs. Mem. firm Wright, Lindsey & Jennings, Little Rock, 1957-82, ptnr., 1962-82, McMath Woods P.A., Little Rock, 1982—. Mem. faculty Coll. Advocacy, Hastings Coll. Law, 1974-89, Nat. Inst. Trial Advocacy, 1979-92; chmn. com. on jury instrns. Ark. Supreme Ct., 1980-89. Co-author: Arkansas Model Jury Instructions-Civil, 1965, 3d edit., 1989. Pres., bd. dirs. Urban League Greater Little Rock; bd. dirs. Little Rock Sch. Dist; trustee U. Ozarks, 1991-99. With U.S. Army, 1957-58. Named Outstanding Lawyer, Pulaski County Bar Assn., 1998, Ark. Bar Assn., 1999. Fellow Am. Coll. Trial Lawyers, Am. Bar Found., Ark. Bar Found., ABOTA Found; mem. ABA, ATLA, Ark. Bar Assn. (past chmn. exec. com., ho. of dels.), Pulaski County Bar Assn., Am. Judicature Soc., Ark. Trial Lawyers Assn. (pres. 1985-86), Am. Inn of Ct. (master of the bench), Order of Coif, Phi Alpha Theta. Democrat. Presbyterian. Home: 1 Tree Tops Ln Little Rock AR 72202-1676 Office: McMath Woods PA 711 W 3rd St Little Rock AR 72201-2201 Office Phone: 501-396-5400. Business E-Mail: winslow@mcmathlaw.com.

DRUMMOND BORG, LESLEY MARGARET, geneticist; b. Wellington, New Zealand, Oct. 26, 1948; arrived in U.S., 1986; d. Grant Allen and Yolanda Drummond; m. Kenneth Irvin Borg; children: Marc Borg, Kyle Borg. MBChB, Otago Med. Sch., New Zealand, 1971, MD, 1983; BSc, Auckland U., New Zealand, 1976. Diplomate Am. Bd. Pediatrics, Am. Bd. Med. Genetics, cert. clin. geneticist. Fellow in clin. genetics U. Auckland Med. Sch., 1974-77, med. geneticist, 1977-79; pediatric resident Hosp. Sick Children, Toronto, Canada, 1980-82; gen. practitioner ARAMCO, Saudi Arabia, 1983-86; sr. fellow in med. genetics U. Wash., Seattle, 1986-88; clin. geneticist Genetic Screening and Counseling Svc., Denton, Tex., 1988-95; dir. genetics divsn. Tex. Dept. Health, Austin, 1995—2004; mgr. health screening br. Tex. Dept. State Health Svcs., Austin, 2004—. Clin. asst. prof. Tex. A&M U., College Station, 1991—98; cons. staff Odessa (Tex.) Women's Children's Hosp., 1991—96, Cook/Ft. Worth Children's Med. Ctr., 1991—98. Contbr. articles to profl. jours. Fellow: Am. Coll. Med. Genetics (founder), Am. Acad. Pediat.; mem.: AMA, Am. Soc. Human Genetics. Avocations: jogging, swimming, hiking. Office: Dept State Health Svcs Health Screening Br 1100 W 49th St Austin TX 78756-3160

DRUNGOLE, PAULA ELAINE, lawyer; b. Starkville, Miss., Mar. 29, 1963; m. George W. Ellis; three children. BS, Rust Coll., 1983; JD, U. Kans., 1986. Bar: Miss. 1986, U.S. Dist. Ct. (no. and so. dists.) Miss. 1986, U.S. Ct. Appeals (5th cir.) 1986, U.S. Supreme Ct. 1986. Legal intern, supr. Kans. Defender Project, Lawrence, 1984-86; assoc. Jackson M. Brown Law Firm, Starkville, 1987-93; sole practice Starkville, 1993—. Prof. Miss. State U., Starkville, 1987—. Bd. dirs. Judicare, Inc., Columbus, Miss. Methodist Leadership grantee, 1982. Mem. Assn. Trial Lawyers Am., Miss. Trial Lawyers Assn., Miss. Women Lawyers Assn., Bus & Profl. Women, Rust Alumni Club (sec. Starkville chpt. 1986—), Zeta Phi Beta. Methodist. Office: PO Box 186 Starkville MS 39760-0186

DRURY, CHARLES LOUIS, JR., hotel executive; b. Cape Girardeau, Mo., Nov. 4, 1955; s. Charles Louis Sr. and Shirley Jean (Luebbers) D.; m. Michelle Marguerite Swenson, Apr. 28, 1979; children: Charles L. III, Thomas Michael. BSBA, St. John's U., Collegeville, Minn., 1978. Gen. mgr. Drury Inns, Inc., St. Louis, 1978-79, regional mgr., 1979-81, v.p. ops., 1981-85, pres., 1985—, chief exec. officer, 1988—, also bd. dirs. Bd. dirs. Drury Industries, Inc., Cape Girardeau, Drury Displays, Inc., St. Louis, Druco, Inc., St. Louis; mem. exec. bd. Enterprise Bank, St. Louis, 1989— Bd. dirs. Dismas House of St. Louis, 1987—, Cardinal Glennon Children's Hosp. Devel. Bd. Mem. Pres. Assn., Am. Mgmt. Assn. Roman Catholic. Office: 721 Emerson Rd #400 Saint Louis MO 63141-6770

DRURY, CHRIS, professional hockey player; b. Trumbull, Conn., Aug. 20, 1976; Degree, Boston (Mass.) U. Hockey player Colo. Avalanche, 1998—2002, Calgary Flames, 2002—03, Buffalo (N.Y.) Sabres, 2003—. Mem. U.S.A. Olympic Hockey Team, 2002, Team U.S.A., World Cup of Hockey, 2004. Recipient Hober Baker award, 1998, Calder Meml. trophy, 1999. Mailing: 1 Seymour H Knox III Plaza Buffalo NY 14203

DRURY, JOHN R., retail executive; B, Fla. State U. Former CFO 3three Advt.; co-founder Harris Drury Cohen, Fla., 1980—97; sr. v.p. mktg. AutoNation, Inc., Ft. Lauderdale, Fla., 1997—. Past pres. Advt. Fedn. Greater Ft. Lauderdale. Office: AutoNation Inc 110 SE 6th St Fort Lauderdale FL 33301

DRURY, KENNETH CLAYTON, biologist; b. Madera, Calif., Mar. 27, 1945; s. Carma and Alice (Zollinger) D.; m. Sandra Rosemary hanlon, Apr. 28, 1972; children: Allison Hanlon, Vanessa Laura. BA, Westmont Coll., 1967; PhD, U. Geneva, Switzerland, 1979. Cert. in andrology and embryology high complexity lab. dir. Am. Bd. Bioanalysts. NIH fellow U. Calif., Berkeley, 1979-82; rsch. scientist Codon Corp., South San Francisco, Calif., 1982-84; sr. scientist Microgenics Corp., Concord, Calif., 1984-86; dir. U. Louisville, 1986-92, In Vitro Fertilization and Gamete Physiology Labs. U. Fla., 1992—. Contbr. articles to profl. jours. 1st Lt. US Army, 1969-72, Vietnam. Mem. Am. Fertility Soc., Am. Coll. Reproductive Biology, Am. Soc. Reproductive Medicine. Achievements include first investigator to directly implicate phosphorylation in mechanism of action of maturation promoting factor; one of first investigators to obtain a human live birth after ultra rapid freezing of embryos; successfully performed preimplantation genetic diagnosis to eliminate inherited genetic disease in pregnancy. Office: Univ Fla Dept Ob-Gyn Division Reproductive Endocrinology PO Box 100294 Gainesville FL 32610-0294 E-mail: druryk@obgyn.ufl.edu.

DRURY, LEONARD LEROY, retired oil company executive; b. Gillespie, Ill., Nov. 5, 1928; s. Roy August and Regina Loretta (Finnegan) D.; m. Myra Lee Klunk, June 30, 1951; 1 child, Marilyn Jo Drury Chandler. BS in Indsl. Mgmt., St. Louis U., 1950; MBA in Mgmt., U. Houston, 1957. Mgr. systems program info. and computer services Shell Oil Co., N.Y.C., 1966-68, mgr. data processing info. and computer services Menlo Park, Calif., 1968, mgr. acctg. info. and computer services, 1968-69, mgr. MTM bus. systems div. info. and computer services N.Y.C. and Houston, 1969-71, mgr. planning Houston, 1971-73, mgr. planning and tech. info. and computer services, 1973-75, asst. treas. fin., 1975-77, gen. mgr. info. and computer services, 1977-80, liaison Shell Ctr. London, 1980-81, gen. mgr. products fin. Houston, 1981-83, v.p. purchasing and adminstrv. services, 1983-86, v.p. info. and computer services, 1986-89, ret., 1989. Mem. United Way, Houston, 1982-89; bd. dirs. South Main Ctr. Assn., Houston, 1986-89. Mem.: Am. Petroleum Inst., Fin. Execs. Inst., Houston Bus. Coun. (pres. 1985—86), West Houston Assn. (bd. dirs. 1984—88), The Houstonian Club, Sigma Iota Epsilon. Roman Catholic. Home: 11711 Flintwood Dr Houston TX 77024-5110 E-mail: lldhouston@aol.com.

DRURY, RAYMOND W., JR., music educator; b. Springfield, Mass., July 11, 1956; s. Raymond W. and Jacqueline P. Drury; m. Nancy J. Herbst, Dec. 23, 1978; children: Bryan children: Sara, Colin. AA in Music Edn., Holyoke C.C., 1976; BA in Music Edn., Westfield State Coll., 1978, MA in Edn., 1991. Cert. Music Teacher K-12 Mass., 1978. Music tchr. Thornton Burgess Intermediate Sch., Hampden, Mass., 1978—85; condr./artistic dir. Wilbraham Choral Soc., Mass., 1993—; music dir./choirmaster Faith United Ch., Springfield; fine arts chair/choral dir. Minnechaug Regional H.S., Wilbraham, 1985—. Condr. Western Jr. Dist. Chorus, West Springfield, Mass., 1995—95, Northeastern Dist. Girl's Chorus, Wenham, Mass., 1998—98. Mem.: Mass. Music Educators Assn., Music Educators Nat. Conf., Am. Choral Directors Assn. Avocation: weight lifting, walking, cruising. Home: 1 Eastwood Dr Wilbraham MA 01095 Office: Minnechaug Regional HS 621 Main St Wilbraham MA 01095 E-mail: rdrury@hwrsd.org.

DRUSHAL, MARY ELLEN, education educator, former academic administrator; b. Peru, Ind., Oct. 24, 1945; d. Herrell Lee and Opal Marie (Boone) Waters; m. J. Michael Drushal, June 12, 1966; children: Lori, Jeff. B of Music Edn., Ashland Coll., 1969; MS, Peabody Coll., 1981; PhD, Vanderbilt U., 1986. Dir. music and spl. ednl. projects Smithville (Ohio) Brethren Ch., 1969-74; tchr. music Orrville (Ohio) Pub. Schs., 1969—70; seminar leader Internat. Ctr. for Learning, Glendale, Calif., 1974-76; dir. Christian edn. First Presbyn. and Christ Presbyn. Ch., Nashville, 1976-84; assoc. prof. Ashland (Ohio) Theol. Sem., 1984-91, acad. dean, 1991-95; provost Ashland U., 1995—2001, prof. edn., 2001—. Cons. in strategic planning for not-for-profit orgns. Author: On Tablets of Human Hearts: Christian Education with Children, 1991; co-author: Spiritual Formation: A Personal Walk Toward Emmaus, 1990; contbr. articles to profl. jours. Trustee Brethren Care Found., Ashland, 1989-99, Ashland Symphony Orch., 1986-87; pres., fundraiser Habitat for Humanity, Ashland, 1990-94; bd. dirs. JOY Day Care Ctr., 1988-90. Grantee Lilly Endowment Inc., 1991, 93, Brethren Ch. Found., 1989, 90. Mem. Assn. Theol. Schs. (com. under-represented constituencies 1994-96), Am. Assn. for Higher Edn., Nat. Assn. Ch. Bus. Adminstrs., N.Am. Assn. Profs. of Christian Edn., Assn. Profs. and Rschrs. in Religious Edn., Nat. Assn. Evangelicals, Nat. Assn. Black Evangelical Assns., Epiphany Assn. (bd. dirs. 1994-98). Republican. Presbyterian. Avocations: reading, needlepoint. Address: 20041 Sanibel View Cir # 102 Fort Myers FL 33908-6991 Office Phone: 419-289-5192. Business E-Mail: medrushal@sanibelviewfl.com.

DRUSIN, LEWIS MARTIN, physician, educator; b. N.Y.C., Sept. 25, 1939; s. David and Gladys Margaret (Apfel) D. BS, Union Coll., 1960; MD, Cornell U., 1964; MPH, Columbia U., 1974. Med. intern 2nd medicine Bellevue Hosp., N.Y.C., 1964-65; jr. asst. resident in medicine Med. Ctr. Hosp. of Vt., Burlington, 1965-66; sr. asst. resident N.Y. Hosp., N.Y.C., 1968-69; fellow in medicine divsn. allergy and infectious diseases Cornell U. Med. Coll., N.Y.C., 1969-70; asst. prof. pub. health Cornell U., N.Y.C., 1970-77, asst. prof. medicine, 1972-79, assoc. prof. pub. health, 1977-84, assoc. prof. clin. medicine, 1979-98, prof. clin. medicine, 1998—, prof. clin. pub. health, 1984—; dir. dept. epidemiology N.Y. Presbyn. Hosp./Cornell Ctr., N.Y.C., 1970—, assoc. attending physician, 1979-98, attending physician, 1998—. Cons. The Rockefeller Univ. Hosp., N.Y.C., 1981—; regional dir. for N.Am. Internat. Union Against Venereal Diseases and Treponematoses, Leeds, Eng., 1986-95; liaison officer, UN for IUSTI, 1995—. Contbr. book chpts., articles. Task Force Syphilis, N.Y. State Dept. Health, 1990-91. Sr. surgeon USPHS, 1966-68. Fellow ACP, Am. Coll. Preventive Medicine, Infectious Disease Soc. Am., N.Y. Acad. Medicine, Royal Soc. Medicine, Royal Soc. Tropical Medicine and Hygiene, Royal Coll. Physicians, Soc. Healthcare Epidemiology Am.; mem. Am. STD Assn. (pres. 1982), Brit. Assn. for Sexual Health and HIV (hon. life), Phi Beta Kappa, Sigma Xi, Alpha Omega Alpha. Office: NY Presbyn Hosp Cornell Med Ctr 525 E 68th St New York NY 10021-4885 E-mail: ldrusin@nyp.org.

DRUSKOFF, BARBARA THERESE, elementary school educator; d. Edward Francis and Helen Sullivan; children: Jennifer Bernier, Mark. Student, Calif. State U., Long Beach, 1980, San Diego State U., 1986; BS in Edn., CUNY, 1966; MEd, Azusa (Calif.) Pacific U., 1994. Tchr. 1st grade Matawan Sch. Dist., NJ, 1966—67; tchr. elem. sch. Newston Sch. Dist., NJ, 1968—69, Bainbridge Unified Sch. Dist., NY, 1972—74, Lake Elsinore Unified Sch. Dist., Calif., 1987—. Co-chair visual and performing arts Luiseno Elem., Corona, Calif., 1992—, chair math field day, 1999—, provider beginning tchr. support and assessment, 2001—03. Sculpture in Paper, 1966; contbr. poetry to anthologies. Mem. Habitat for Humanity, 2003—. Named Tchr. of Yr., Luiseno Elem. and Lake Elsinore Sch. Dist., 1994—95; recipient Best Actress awards, North County Comty. Theater, 1983—86, N.Y. Regents scholarship, 1961. Mem.: AAUW (past membership chair 1982—, Scholarship established in her name 1987), Art and Cultural Soc. Fallbrook, Nat. Assn. Educators Am., Nat. Women's History Mus., Mission Conservation Dist. Avocations: acting, the arts, antiques, reading, gardening. Office: Lake Elsinore Unified Sch Dist 545 Chanly st Lake Elsinore CA 92530 Office Phone: 951-674-0750.

DRUTCHAS, GEOFFREY GILBERT, minister, historian, writer; b. Detroit, Sept. 18, 1952; s. Gilbert Henry and Elaine Marie Drutchas; m. Eileen Vernor, Apr. 10, 1982; 1 child, Griffin Vernor. BA with high honors, Mich. State U., 1974; MDiv, Harvard U., 1982; D in Ministry in Christian Ethics, Lancaster Theol. Sem., 1996. Ordained Unitarian-Universalist Assn., 1982, ordained ministerial standing United Ch. of Christ, 1988, basic cert. clin. pastoral edn. Andover-Newton Theol. Sch., 1980, Andover-Newton Theol. Sch., 1982; cert. med. ethics Mich. State U., 1991. Dir. chaplaincy Tufts U., Medford, Mass., 1981—84; ext. min. Harford-York (Pa.) Ministerial Com., 1984—88; sr. pastor St. Paul United Ch. of Christ, Taylor, Mich., 1988—; exec. dir. ChristNet Emergency Shelter, Taylor, 2000—01. Co-convener econs. and clergy conf. Lincoln Filene Ctr. for Citizenship, Tufts U., Medford, 1983; co-convener continental campus ministry conf. Unitarian-Universalist Assn., Boston, 1984; founder, pres., cons. ChristNet Emergency Shelter, Taylor, 1993—; chair Rotating Shelter Roundtable Southeastern Mich., Detroit, 2000—. Author: (book) Is Life Sacred?, 1998 (Reinhold Niebuhr Min. and Scholar award, 1998); contbr. articles to profl. jours. Chair York County United Way Strengthen the Family Task Force, 1987—88, Harford County Food and Nutrition Com., Bel Air, Md., 1986—88; dir. Elisabeth Peabody Settlement Ho., Somerville, Mass. John Haynes Holmes fellow, Cmty. Ch. N.Y., 1981, St. Lawrence fellow, Unitarian Universalist Assn., 1982, Louisville Inst. fellow, Louisville Inst., Louisville Presbyn. Sem., 2001. Mem.: Soc. Christian Ethics (assoc.), Harvard Club Ea. Mich. (v.p. 1997—2001, pres. 2001—03), Phi Beta Kappa. United Church Of Christ. Achievements include discovery of authenticated artist for Michigan State Capitol rotunda; development of founding of county emergency shelter; authored first extensive history of Sanctity of Life concept in Christian ethics. Avocations: art and architectural history research, travel. Home: 24136 Goddard Rd Taylor MI 48180 Office: St Paul United Church of Christ 24158 Goddard Rd Taylor MI 48180

DRUTCHAS, GREGORY G., lawyer; b. Detroit, June 2, 1949; s. Gilbert Henry and Elaine Marie (Rutkowski) D.; m. Cheryl Aline June 9, 1973; children— Gillian Aline, Gregory Ryan, Allison Elaine, Ethan Charles. A.B., U. Mich., 1970; J.D., Duke U., 1973. Bar: Mich. 1973, U.S. Dist. Ct. (ea. dist.) Mich. 1974, U.S. Ct. Appeals (6th cir.) 1978, U.S. Dist. Ct. (we. dist.) Mich. 1983, U.S. Supreme Ct. 1984. Assoc. Kitch & Suhrheinrich, P.C. (now Kitch, Saurbier, Drutchas, Wagner & Kenney, P.C.), Detroit, 1973-78, prin., 1978—; lectr., seminar presenter on med. profl. liability. Served to capt., USAFR, 1972-82. Mem. State Bar Mich., Detroit Bar Assn., Oakland County Bar Assn., Mich. Defense Trial Counsel, Mich. Soc. Hosp. Attys., Am. Acad. Hosp. Attys. Republican. Unitarian. Club: Birmingham Country Club. Author: (with others) Michigan Court of Appeals Practice: A Primer, 1981; contbr. articles to profl. publs. Home: 485 Wishbone Dr Bloomfield Hills MI 48304-2352 Office: Kitch Saurbier Drutchas Wagner & Kenney PC 3002 W Big Beaver Rd Ste 200 Troy MI 48084

DRUTZ, JAN EDWIN, pediatrics educator; b. Louisville, Jan. 8, 1942; s. Abe Morris and Lillian (Billig) D.; m. Anne Edwina Sussman, June 7, 1965; children: Jeffrey Benjamin, Lisa Michele, Dana Nicole. BA, U. Louisville, 1964, MD, 1968. Pvt. practice, Houston, 1973-87; intern, then resident Baylor Coll. Medicine, Houston, 1968-71, from clin. asst. prof. to assoc. prof. pediat., 1973—2002, dir. pediat. continuity clinic, 1987—, prof. pediat., 2002—; pres. med. staff Tex. Children's Hosp., 1995, prof. pediats., 2002—. Maj. U.S. Army, 1971-73. Mem. AMA, Harris County Med. Soc., Tex. Pediat. Soc. (adv. com., mem. student preceptorship program 1995-96), Houston Pediat. Soc. (sec. 1984-85, pres. 1988-89), Ambulatory Pediat. Assn. (chmn. continuity clinic spl. interest group 1990-95, edn. com. 1993—). Office: Tex Children Hosp Clin Care Ctr Ste 1540-00 6701 Fannin St Houston TX 77030 Office Phone: 832-822-3441. Business E-Mail: jdrutz@bcm.fmc.edu.

DRUZDZEL, MAREK JOZEF, information systems educator, researcher; b. Radom, Poland, Oct. 7, 1957; s. Edward and Regina (Szymczak) D.; children: Marcin, Stefan, Roman, Julian. MS in Computer Sci. with distinction, Delft U. Tech., 1985, MSEE with distinction, 1987; PhD, Carnegie Mellon U., 1992. Vis. scientist Thomas J. Watson Rsch. Ctr. IBM, Yorktown Heights, NY, 1987—88; rsch. asst., adj. prof. Carnegie Mellon U., Pitts., 1988—91, rschr. assoc., 1993; rschr. Rockwell Internat. Sci. Ctr., Palo Alto, Calif., 1993; rsch. assoc. Inst. for Decision Sys. Rsch., Palo Alto, 1993; assoc. prof. intelligent sys. Sch. Info. Scis. U. Pitts., 1993—. Lectr. U. Pitts., Carnegie Mellon U., Imperial Cancer Rsch. Fund, London, U. Utrecht, The Netherlands, Delft U. of Tech., The Netherlands, Free U. of Amsterdam, Rockwell Internat., many others. Contbr. articles to profl. jours. Recipient Career award, NSF. Mem. IEEE, Am. Assn. for Artificial Intelligence, Inst. for Ops. Rsch. and Mgmt. Sci., Assn. for Uncertainty in Artificial Intelligence, European Assn. for Decision Making, Sigma Xi. Office: Univ Pitts Dept Info Sci Pittsburgh PA 15260 E-mail: marek@sis.pitt.edu.

DRUZHNIKOV, YURI ILYA, literature educator, writer; b. Moscow, Apr. 17, 1933; m. Valerie Linetsky, June 3, 1983; children: Elena, Ilya. B in History, Latvian U., Riga, 1953; MD, Moscow Pedagogy U., 1955; PhD, History and Theory Edn. Inst., Moscow, 1960. Prof. U. Tex., Austin, 1987—88, U. Calif., Davis, 1988—. Author: Informer 001, 1996, Prisoner of Russia, 1999, Angels on the Head of a Pin, 2003, Passport to Yesterday, 2004, Madonna from Russia, 2005. Named Best Russian Writer of 1998, City of Moscow, 1998; named to the "Author of 10 Best Russian Novels of the XXC"

List, U. Warsaw, 1998; recipient Dostoyevsky Prize, Writer's Union of Poland, 2001. Mem.: Internat. Pen Club (v.p. 1993—). Office: German & Russian Dept Univ Calif Davis CA 95616

DRVOTA, MOJMIR, retired cinema educator, author; b. Prague, Czechoslovakia, Jan. 13, 1923; came to U.S., 1958, naturalized, 1963; s. Jan and Zdenka (Krejcikova) D.; m. Jana Kratochvilova, May 18, 1957; 1 child, Monica. Student, Charles U., 1945-48; PhD, Palacky U., 1953; MS, Columbia U., 1961. Stage dir. state theaters, Czechoslovakia, 1952-56; libr. Bklyn. Pub. Libr., 1958-62; asst. prof. dramatic arts Columbia U., N.Y.C., 1962-69; assoc. prof. cinema NYU, N.Y.C., 1969-72; prof. cinema Ohio State U., Columbus, 1972-92, prof. emeritus, 1992—; ret., 1992. Script writer Czechoslovak State Film, Prague, 1948-52; author: Short Stories, 1946, Boarding House for Artists, 1947, Solitaire, 1974, Triptych, 1980, Solitaire, Triptych in Czech, 1993; The Constituents of Film Theory, 1973, in Czech, 1994, How Many ANgels Can Dance on the Tip of a Needle?, in Czech, 2002. Mem. Univ. Film Assn., AAUP, Phi Kappa Phi. Home: 3541 Prestwick Ct Columbus OH 43220-5097 *Everything I stood for was defeated, everything I longed for remained unfulfilled, everything I loved passed beyond reach. In the chasm thus rent I captured a glimpse of what is real and what only is, of what is an act of becoming and what is a mere activity. Henceforth, I made it my task to share in the linking effort of those individuals who communicate in the services of reality: the reality screened by objects into which we are situated.*

DRY, MARSHA G., librarian; b. Monahans, Tex., May 15, 1950; d. Buck N. and Jewel I. (Luxton) Miller; m. William C. Dry, Sept. 19, 1970. BS, Sul Ross State U., 1971; MLS, Tex. Woman's U., 1982. Cert. elem. edn., learning resource specialist, supr.; tech. applications cert. High sch. libr. Alpine (Tex.) Ind. Sch. Dist.; libr. Ector County Ind. Sch. Dist., Odessa, Tex. Mem. PTA (life), ATPE, Tex. Library Assn., Delta Kappa Gamma. Home: 22 Kahala Dr Odessa TX 79762 Office Phone: 432-368-3284. E-mail: mgdry@cableone.net.

DRYDEN, ROBERT EUGENE, lawyer; b. Chanute, Kans., Aug. 20, 1927; s. Calvin William and Mary Alfreda (Foley) D.; m. Jetta Rae Burger, Dec. 19, 1953; children: Lynn Marie, Thomas Calvin. AA, City Coll., San Francisco, 1947; BS, U. San Francisco, 1951, JD, 1954. Bar: Calif. 1955; diplomate Am. Bd. Trial Advocates (pres. San Francisco chpt. 1997). Assoc. Barfield, Dryden & Ruane (and predecessor firm), San Francisco, 1954-60, jr. ptnr., 1960-65, gen. ptnr., 1965-89; sr. ptnr. Dryden, Margoles, Schimaneck & Wertz, San Francisco, 1989—. Lectr. continuing edn. of the bar, 1971-77; evaluator U.S. Dist. Ct. (no. dist.) Calif. Early Neutral Evaluation Program; master atty. San Francisco Am. Inn of Ct. Mem. bd. counsellors U. San Francisco, 1993—. With USMCR, 1945-46. Fellow Am. Coll. Trial Lawyers, Am. Bar Found., Internat. Acad. Trial Lawyers; mem. ABA, San Francisco Bar Assn., Assn. Def. Counsel (bd. dirs. 1968-71), Def. Rsch. Inst., Internat. Assn. Ins. Counsel, Fedn. Ins. Counsel, U. San Francisco Law Soc. (mem. exec. com. 1970-72), U. San Francisco Alumni Assn. (mem. bd. govs. 1977), Phi Alpha Delta. Home: 1320 Lasuen Dr Millbrae CA 94030-2846 Office: Dryden Margoles Schimaneck & Wertz 101 California St Ste 2050 San Francisco CA 94111-5427

DRYDEN, WOODSON E., lawyer; b. Anadarko, Okla., Dec. 21, 1924; s. Harry Ernest and Ruth Sally (Woodson) D.; divorced; children: Judith, Carol, Kim, Christine, Erich. BBA, Kans. U., 1948; LLB, Tex. U., 1951. Sole practice, Beaumont, Tex., 1951—. With USNR, 1942-46. Mem. Tex. Trial Lawyers Assn. (pres. 1972-73). Democrat. Episcopalian. Home: 6625 Windwood Ln Beaumont TX 77706-4239

DRYER, MURRAY, physicist, educator; b. Bridgeport, Conn., Nov. 4, 1925; s. Sol and Sarah (Shapiro) D.; m. Geraldine Gray Goodsell, May 12, 1955; children: Steven Michael, Lisa Dryer Travis. Student, U. Conn., 1943-44; BS, Stanford U., 1949, MS, 1950; PhD, Tel-Aviv U., 1971. Research asst. NACA-NASA Ames Research Ctr., Calif., 1949; aero. research scientist NACA-NASA Lewis Research Ctr., Cleve., 1950-59; assoc. research scientist Martin Marietta Corp., Denver, 1959-65; chief interplanetary physics Space Environ. Lab., NOAA Environ. Research Labs., Boulder, Colo., 1965-94, guest worker emeritus, 1994—; sr. scientist Coop. Inst. for Rsch. in Environ. Scis., U. Colo., Boulder, 1994-96; cons. Exploration Physics Internat., Inc., 1996—, Geophysical Inst. U., Fairbanks, Ala., 2001—. Lectr. dept. aerospace engring. scis. U. Colo., 1963-76, dept. astrogeophysics, 1978; vis. assoc. prof. dept. mech. engring. Colo. State U., 1966-67; mem. com. solar terrestrial rsch. NAS, 1976-80, 84-91, com. geophys. data NAS, 1987-93. Author: (with others) Solar-Terrestrial Physics in the 1980's, 1981; editor: (with others) Solar Observations and Predictions of Solar Activity, 1972, Exploration of the Outer Solar System, 1976, Solar and Interplanetary Dynamics, 1980, Advances in Solar Connection wirh Interplanetary Phenomena, 1998; spl. issue editor Space Sci. Revs., 1976; contbr. articles to profl. jours. With U.S. Navy, 1944-46. Mem. Am. Phys. Soc., Am. Geophys. Union, AAAS, Sci. Com. Solar-Terrestrial Physics, Internat. Astron. Union, Com. Space Research, AIAA (Space Sci. award 1975), Sigma Xi Office: Space Environment Ctr NOAA NCEP NWS Mail Code R-E-SE Boulder CO 80305-3328 Office Phone: 303-497-3978. Personal E-mail: murraydryer@msn.com. Business E-Mail: murray.dryer@noaa.gov.

DRYFOOS, WALTER GALLATIN, academic administrator; s. David Michael and Jeanne Gallatin Dryfoos; m. Barbara Diane Enoch, Feb. 14, 1988; 1 child, David Jacob. AB in Rhetoric, U. Calif., 1983, MA in Sociology, 1986; MA in Counseling, St. Mary's Coll., 1988. Psychiatric Technician Lic., Bd. of Vocat. Nurse and Psychiat. Technician Examiners, Calif., 1975; Clear, Lifetime Credentials Calif. state CC Sys., 1986. Lic. psychiat. technician Camarillo State Hosp., Calif., 1975—78; rsch. and records mgr. U. of Calif. Coll. of Engring., Berkeley, Calif., 1981—89; external sys. mgr., ctrl. devel. office U. Calif., Berkeley, 1989—90; dir. of advancement svcs. Wash. State U., Pullman, 1990—2002; assoc. v.p. advancement svcs. U. Wash., Seattle, 2002—. Instr. St. Mary's Coll., Moraga, Calif., 1982—89. Bd. mem., chmn. bd. Neill Pub. Libr., Pullman, Wash., 1995—2002; mem. N.W. Pub. Radio Cmty. Adv. Bd., 1993—99. Mem.: Coun. for Advancement and Support of Edn., Iron Butt Assn. (Saddlesore 1000 2000), Harley Owners Group, Vintage Motorcycle Enthusiasts, Antique Motorcycle Club of Am. Avocation: motorcycling. Office: 1200 Fifth Ave #520 Seattle WA 98101-1116 Office Phone: 206-685-9530. E-mail: tamecat@u.washington.edu.

DRYMALSKI, RAYMOND HIBNER, lawyer, banker; b. Chgo., June 1, 1936; s. Raymond P. and Alice H. (Hibner) D.; m. Sarah Fickes, Apr. 1, 1967; children: Robert, Paige. BA, Georgetown U., 1958; JD, U. Mich., 1961. Bar: Ill. 1962. Lawyer Chgo. Title & Trust Co., 1963-65; asst. sec., atty. No. Trust Co., Chgo., 1965-68; ptnr. Boodell, Sears, Giambalvo & Crowley, Chgo., 1968-87; mem. Bell Boyd & Lloyd LLC, Chgo., 1987—. Contbr. articles to profl. jours. Chmn. Northwestern Meml. Healthcare, 2000—04; bd. dirs. Northwestern Meml. Hosp., Chgo., 1978—, chmn., 2000—04; bd. dirs. Northwestern Meml. HealthCare, 1987—, vice chmn., sec., 1998—99, chmn., 2000—04; bd. dirs. McGaw Med. Ctr. of Northwestern U., 2000—04, Lincoln Park Zool. Soc., 1972—, pres., 1980—84; bd. dirs., officer Offield Family Found., 1990—; mem. coun. govs. Northwestern Healthcare Network, 1990—, bd. dirs., 1999. Mem. ABA, Econ. Club Chgo. Roman Catholic. Home: 443 W Eugenie St Chicago IL 60614-5674 Office: Bell Boyd & Lloyd LLC 70 W Madison St Ste 3100 Chicago IL 60602-4244 E-mail: rdrymalski@bellboyd.com.

DRYMAN, AMY, epidemiologist; d. Sylvia and Irving Armin Dryman. BA, Yale U., 1977—81; postgrad., Columbia U., 1981—82; DSc, Johns Hopkins U., Sch. of Hygiene and Pub. Health, 1982—87. Rsch. scientist, rsch. assoc. Johns Hopkins U. Sch. Hygiene and Pub. Health, Balt., 1987—88; cons. Pfizer, Inc., NYC, 1993, project leader, 1993—99, asst. dir., 1999—2001, mgr., 2001—04. Contbr. articles to profl. jours. Personal E-mail: amydryscd@aol.com.

DRYOVAGE, MARY MARGARET, lawyer; b. Dearborn, Mich., May 14, 1954; d. Henry John and Kathleen T. Dryovage; m. Robert P. Carasik, Dec. 29, 1983, 1 child, Nora. BA in History, U. Mich., 1975; JD, Wayne State U., 1978. Bar: Mich. 1979, U.S. Dist. Ct. (ea. dist.) Mich. 1979, U.S. Dist. Ct. (no. dist.) Calif. 1981, Calif. 1984, U.S. Ct. Appeals (9th cir.) 1985, U.S. Dist. Ct. (cen. and ea. dists.) Calif. 1986, U.S. Ct. Appeals (fed. cir.) 1987, U.S. Supreme Ct. 1987. Hearing officer Mich. Employment Relations Commn., Detroit, 1978-81; trial counsel Fed. Labor Relations Authority, San Francisco, 1981-82; sole practice San Francisco, 1984—. Prof. Wayne State U., Detroit, 1980; instr. labor studies program San Francisco Community Coll., 1982-90. Contbr. articles to profl. jours. Mem. ATLA (vice chmn. sect. leaders coun., 2004—, chair employment rights sect. 2005—), San Francisco Trial Lawyers Assn., Nat. Lawyers Guild, NOW, Nat. Employment Lawyers Assn., Nat. Employment Lawyers Assn. (chair fed. employee rights com.), Calif. Employment Lawyers Assn. (chair 1995-96), Consumer Attys. Calif. Office: 600 Harrison St Ste 120 San Francisco CA 94107 Office Phone: 415-593-0095. Business E-Mail: mdryovage@igc.org.

DRYSDALE, JOHN EDWIN, retired music educator, performing arts association administrator, director; b. Lodi, Calif., Mar. 11, 1925; s. Joseph Harry Drysdale and Frances Salome Maiden-Goodenough; m. Betty Lou Walder, June 13, 1948; children: Robert Joseph, Christine Ellen. BS, U. Oreg., 1950, MusM, 1965; cert. in Supr., So. Oreg. State Coll., 1976. Tchr. Yoncalla (Oreg.) Grade Sch., 1949—50, Klamath Falls (Oreg.) HS, 1950—52, Oreg. Tech. Inst., Klamath Falls, 1951—52, Redmond (Oreg.) HS, 1952—53; from tchr. orch. to asst. to supt. Medford (Oreg.) HS, 1953—82, asst. to supt., 1982—83, ret., 1983; dir. So. Oreg. Concert Band, Inc., 1990—. Instr. h.s. music summer session U. Oreg., 1955—64; dir. Episc. Ch. Choir, Medford, 1955—65; guest condr. Concertmaster Rogue Valley Symphony, 1963—74. With USN, 1943—46, Atlantic, Pacific and Mediterranean. Named to Wall of Fame, Sunnyside HS, 1992; recipient Disting. Music Educator award, N.W. Bandmasters Assn., 1978. Mem.: VFW, Oreg. Music Educator's Assn., Music Educator's Nat. Conf. Avocations: music, writing, TV, band directing. Home: 417 Eastwood Drive Medford OR 97504

D'SOUZA, GERARD EUGENE, economist, educator; b. Feb. 20, 1956; s. George I. and Bernadette S. (Coelho) D'S. BS, U. Agrl. Scis., Bangalore, India, 1977; MS, Miss. State U., 1980, PhD, 1983. Rsch. asst. Miss. State U., 1978-84; asst. prof. agrl. econs. W.Va. U., Morgantown, 1984-92, assoc. prof., 1992—99, prof., 1999—. Cons. TVA, Muscle Shoals, Ala., 1983-84; vis. scholar Inst. for Alterative Agr., Greenbelt, Md., 1991. Mem. editorial bd. Agrl. and Resource Econs. Rev.; contbr. articles to profl. jours. Mem. Am. Agrl. Econs. Assn., European Cmty.-Pacific Region Agr. Project Data Working Group, Gamma Sigma Delta. Avocations: computers, sports, reading. Office: WVa U PO Box 6108 Morgantown WV 26506-6108

DUAN, JIWEN, chemical engineer; b. Taoyuan, Hunan, China, 1954; s. Zishen Duan and Yuanying Chen; m. Xueping Sherry Zhang, May 23, 1990; children: Lucia Y., Jessie J. BS, S. China Inst. Tech., 1982; MS, U. Mich., 1985, PhD, 1990. Rsch. engr. E.I. Du Pont, Kinston, NC, 1990—91, sr. engr., 1991—96, sr. rschr. engr., 1996—2001, rsch. assoc., 2001—02; tech. dir. Glysil Chem. Inc., Cary, NC, 2002—. Achievements include patents in field. Office: Glysil Chem Inc 207 Gingergate Dr Cary NC 27519

DUAN, XIAODONG, engineer; b. Beijing, Jan. 7, 1968; s. Tingyi Duan and Huifen Zhao; m. Wen Wu; children: Shawn children: Xinyu. BS, Tsinghua U., Beijing, China, 1991; MS, Tsinghua U., Beijing,China, 1996; PhD, U. Ctrl. Fla., 2000. Asst. prof. Tsinghua U., 1991—93; rsch. & develop. engr. Beijing Solar Energy Inst., 1996—97; sr. rsch. & develop. engr. Avanex, Corp., Richardson, Tex., 2001—. Tech. referee Optics & Laser Tech., Bournemouth, Dorset, 2001—, Jour. of Physics, 2002—. Contbr. invention new mica electrorheological fluid", articles and papers to profl. jours.; referee: Measurement Sci. and Tech., 2002—. Recipient New Young Scientist award, Inst. Sci. and Tech., Beijing, 1996. Mem.: AAAS, IEEE, Am. Physics Soc. Achievements include invention of apparatus and methods for channel monitoring in a hybrid distributed Raman/EDFA optical amplifier. Office: Avanex Corp 40919 Encyclopedia Cir Fremont CA 94538 Home: 38000 Camden St Apt 56 Fremont CA 94536-5152 Office Phone: 510-897-4355. Home Fax: 469-241-9633, 510-794-4105; Office Fax: 510-897-4293. Personal E-mail: wuwen99@hotmail.com. Business E-Mail: xiaodong_duan@avanex.com.

DUAN, ZHONG-HUI, education educator, researcher; b. Zhangzhou, Fujian, China, Nov. 30, 1962; arrived in U.S., 1991; d. Tao Duan and GuiLan Xing; m. Ting Shi, Jan. 30, 1988; 1 child, Ivy Shi. MS geo math., Chinese Acad. of Geol. Sci., Beijing, China, 1988; geol. and geophysics, Yale Univ., New Haven, Conn., 1992; MS, PhD, Fla. State Univ., Tallahassee, 1997. Rsch. scientist Anhui Inst. of Geology, Hefei, China, 1982—85, Beijing Computation Inst., Beijing, 1988—91; tchg. asst. Fla. State Univ., Tallahassee, 1992—97; asst. prof. Univ. Mich., Ann Arbor, Mich., 1997—2001, Univ. Akron, Akron, Ohio, 2001—. Referee Jour. of Computational Chemistry, Biophysical Jour. Contbr. scientific papers to profl. jour. Recipient Sci. Achievement award, Min. of Geology and Mineral Resources, China, 1986, 1991; Rackham Faculty Fellowship, Univ. Mich., 1999. Office: Dept Computer Sci Univ Akron Akron OH 44325

DUANE, JEANNINE MORRISSEY, retired elementary school educator; b. Lancaster, Pa., Dec. 4, 1932; d. Frank Morrissey and Elsie Ebersole; m. W. Richard G. Duane, Jr., Apr. 15, 1963 (dec. 1996). BS in Elem. Edn., Millersville State U., 1954; MEd, Lehigh U., 1979, EdD, 1989. Cert. tchr. N.J., Pa., Hawaii, supr. N.J., supr. elem. tchr. Pa. Supr. elem. tchr. interns Lehigh U., Bethlehem, Pa.; tchr. Global Assocs., Kwajalein, Micronesia, U.S. Dept. Def., Bermuda, Chester (N.J.) Bd. Edn. Mem. Washington Twp. N.J. Bd. Edn., 1979—; edn. cons. EdPro Consulting; lectr. NASA, Delta Kappa Gamma Soc. Internat. workshop; rschr. in field. Author: (book) English-Marshallese Cookbook, Marshallese-English Phrase Book, The Education of Gifted Children, British and American Schools. Active CAP. Named N.J. nat. Finalist Tchr. in Space, Morris County N.J. Woman of the Yr., 1988. Mem.: NJSBA, ASCD, NEA, N.J. Edn. Assn., N.J. Reading Assn., Challenger Ctr., World Space Found., Lunar Planetary Inst., Phi Delta Kappa. Home: 390 Naughright Rd Long Valley NJ 07853-3847

DUANGPLOY, ORAPIN, accounting educator; b. Bangkok, June 18, 1946; married BA in Acctg., Stephens Coll., 1971; MS in Acctg., U. Mo., 1972, PhD in Acctg., 1977. CPA, Kans., Tex. Staff acct. Harry Winfrey, CPA, 1973; chief acct. OATS, Inc., Columbia, Mo., 1973-74; lectr. Nat. Inst. Devel. and Administrn., Bangkok, 1976-77; asst. prof. acctg. U. Wis., Oshkosh, 1977-78; asst. v.p. dept. planning, systems, research Bangkok Bank, Ltd., 1978-80; spl. lectr. Thammasat U., Bangkok, 1979-80; asst. prof. Pittsburg (Kans.) State U., 1980-81, assoc. prof., 1984-87; prof. U. Houston Downtown, 1987—; acctg. area coord., 1988-89; cons. Office Extended Edn. Calif. State U., Fullerton, 1981-83; faculty devel. coord., 1991-92; asst. chair dept. fin., acctg. and computer info. sys., 1992-94; assoc. prof. Calif. State U., Fullerton, 1981-84; treas. Amarin, Inc., 1989—; Fiesta chair prof. acctg. U. Houston Downtown, 2003—. Advisor to treas. divsn. Bangkok Bank Pub. co., Ltd., 1994; participant Touche Ross-Trueblood Seminar. Author: (software and user's manual) Interactive Intermediate Accouting II Templates, 1985, Interactive Advanced Accounting Templates, 1986; (with others) (workbook) TRICALC: Integrated Microcomputer Applications for Principles of Accounting, 1987; contbr. articles to profl. jours. Recipient Hunt-Wesson Manuscript award Orange County chpt. Nat. Assn. Accts., Faculty Achievement award El Paso Found., 1999-2000; Sch. Bus. Adminstrn. and Econs. Calif. State U. grantee, 1983, U. Houston-Downtown Organized Rsch. grantee, 1987-90, 92, 94, 96, 98, 2002; Price Waterhouse Faculty fellow; Sasakawa fellow, 2000. Mem. Am. Acctg. Assn. (moderator Western Regional Ann. Meeting 1982, reviewer 1987-90, 1995-96, chmn. Calif. membership com. 1982-83, mem. notable contbns. to lit. nominations com. 1982-83, presenter Nat. Regional Ann. Meeting, 1985, 87-91, 93-94, named one of Outstanding Membership Com. Mems. 1982-83), AICPA, Am. Women's Soc. Women Accts., Beta Alpha Psi, Beta Gamma Sigma, Phi Kappa Phi Home: 4903 Cedar St Bellaire TX 77401-4020 Office: U Houston Downtown One Main St Houston TX 77002

DUARTE, FRANCISCO JAVIER, physicist, researcher; b. Santiago, Chile, Sept. 1, 1954; came to U.S., 1983; s. Luis Enrique and Ruth Virginia (Valenzuela) D. BA with honors, Macquarie U., Sydney, Australia, 1978, PhD in Physics, 1982. Postdoctoral fellow U. NSW, Sydney, 1981-82, Macquarie U., Sydney, 1982-83; asst. prof. physics U. Ala., University, 1983-85; sr. rsch. physicist Eastman Kodak Co., Rochester, NY, 1985—2002, rsch. assoc., 2002—. Analyst U.S. Army Missile Command Redstone Arsenal, Ala., 1985-97, Aviation and Missile Command, 2001-02. Author, co-editor: Dye Laser Principles, 1990; author, editor: High Power Dye Lasers, 1991, Tunable Laser Applications, 1995, Tunable Lasers Handbook, 1995; editor: Selected Papers on Dye Lasers, 1992; topical editor Applied Optics, 1990-96; adv. editor Optics Letters, 1999-2004, Optics and Photonics News, 2001—03; author: Tunable Laser Optics, 2003; contbr. numerous articles to profl. jours. Fellow Australian Inst. Physics, 1987, Optical Soc. Am., 1993, recipient Engineering Excellence Award, Optical Soc. Am., 1995; recipient Commonwealth postgrad. rsch. award Govt. of Australia, 1979. Achievements include rsch. in physics and technology of narrow-linewidth dispersive tunable laser oscillators and interferometric instrumentation; author of generalized multiple-prism dispersion theory; applied Dirac's notation to the description of classical optics; inventions in the fields of optics and lasers. Office: PO Box 26592 Rochester NY 14626 E-mail: fjduarte@kodak.com.

DUARTE, PROSPERO VILLACIN, retired entrepreneur; arrived in U.S., 1973, naturalized, 1979; s. Rizalino Batiancila and Rebecca Villacin Duarte; m. Anita Tobes Duarte, June 23, 1973; children: Maria Theresa, Alyssa Ann. BSBA, U. Philippines, Diliman, Quezon City, 1963; postgrad., Wayne State U., Detroit, 1978. Data processing mgr. D. W. Hacker Co., Detroit, 1976—78; sr. programmer/analyst State of Mich., Detroit, 1978—85; systems engr. Electronic Data Sys. Corp., Troy, 1985—87; pres. Azpen Inc., Troy, Mich., 1986—. Contbr. poem (Editors Award, 1998); author: (poem) A Vision Is Born (Best Poems in Am. finalist, 2000); editor: (newsletter) Cosmo Kiwanis; contbr. articles to profl. mags. Pres. Kiwanis Club of Cosmopolitan Detroit, Southfield, Mich., 1999—2000; cmty. rep. Filipino Am. Cmty. Coun., Southfield, 1999—2001; mem. - bd. of directors Filipino Am. Polit. Assn. of Mich., Southfield, 1997—2001; mem. & bd. of directors U. Philippines Alumni Assn. of Mich., Troy, 1990—2001; mem. Toastmasters Club, Birmingham, Mich., 1999—2000. Grantee, Tidewater Oil Corp., 1960—61. Roman Catholic. Avocations: writing, singing, gardening, reading, fishing.

DUATO, ARLENE CHANA LEAH, special education educator, consultant; b. Boston, Apr. 13, 1946; d. Menachem Mendel and Lillian Leiba Greece; 1 child, Yisroel Peter E. BA in Sociology, U. Mass., 1972; MS in Elem. Edn. and Spl. Edn., Adelphi U., 1985. Day care tchr. Headstart, Boston, 1970; social worker Dept. Pub. Welfare, Boston, 1970—78; spl. edn.tchr. Bd. Edn., Bklyn., 1985—97, clinician, evaluator, 1997—. Contbr. articles to profl. jours.; author poems. Pres. parent group WDCC (Wesley Day Care Ctr.), Boston, 1970—72; co-chairwoman mivtzayim N'shei Chabad, Bklyn., 1985—2001. Avocations: photography, theater, swimming, travel, antiques. Office: PS 289 SBST RM 144 900 St Marks Ave Brooklyn NY 11213

DUAX, WILLIAM LEO, biologist, researcher; b. Chgo., Apr. 18, 1939; s. William Joseph and Alice B. (Joyce) D.; m. Caroline Townsend Dowell, May 6, 1966; children: Julia, Sarah, William, Stephen. BA, St. Ambrose Coll., 1961; PhD, U. Iowa, 1967; DSc (hon.), U. Lodz, 1999. Postdoctoral research fellow Ohio U., Athens, 1967-68; rsch. assoc. Hauptman-Woodward Med. Rsch. Inst. (formerly Med. Found.), Buffalo, 1968-69; head crystallography dept. Med. Found. Buffalo, 1969-70, head molecular biophysics dept., 1970-88, assoc. dir. research, 1983-88, research dir., 1988-93, exec v.p. rsch., 1993-99, v.p., 1998-99, H.A. Hauptman Disting. Scientist, 2000—. Adj. assoc. prof. dept. medicinal chemistry SUNY, Buffalo, 1973—, assoc. rsch. prof. dept. biochemistry, 1981—, prof. dept. structural biology, 2001-; dir. distbn. Cambridge Database in U.S., Buffalo, 1983-99; lectr. various internat. confs. Editor: Atlas of Steroid Structure Vol. I, 1975, Vol. II, 1984, Molecular Structure and Biological Activity, 1982, Molecular Structure and Biological Activity of Steriods, 1992, Internat. Union of Crystallography Newsletter, 1993—. Mem. Am. Field Service, Amherst, N.Y. Served with USAR, 1961-67. Fulbright scholar Coun. for Internat. Exchange, 1987; grantee NIH, 1971—; recipient Spl. Merit award Inst. Arthritis and Metabolic Diseases NIH, 1987—, Disting. Alumni award, St. Ambrose Coll., 1983, Clin. Ligand Assay Soc. Disting. Scientist award, 1994. Mem. AAAS, Am. Crystallographic Assn. (v.p. 1985, pres. 1986, exec. officer 1988—, Am. Chem. Soc., Am. Cancer Soc., Biophys. Soc., Endocrine Soc., Peptide Soc., Protein Soc., Internat. Union Crystallography (charter mem., sec. com. on small molecules 1984-90, exec. com. 1999—, pres. 2002-), Am. Inst. Physics (bd. govs. 1987-94, exec. com. 1992), Coun. Sci. Soc. Pres. (govt. and pub. affairs com. 1987), Saturn Club (Buffalo). Democrat. Roman Catholic. Office: Hauptman Woodward Med Rsch Inst Inc 700 Ellicott St Buffalo NY 14203-1102 Office Fax: 716-852-6086. Business E-Mail: duax@hwi.buffalo.edu.

DUBACK, SALLY WOOD, artist, educator; b. St. Paul, Jan. 19, 1946; d. Thurston and Jane (Washburn) W.; m. Steven Rahr Duback, Aug. 6, 1966 (div. Dec. 1986); children: David, Peter, Andrew. Student, Vassar Coll., 1964; postgrad., U. Wis., Milw., 1969-75; BA, U. Mich., 1968. Tchr. U. Sch. Milw., 1988-93; owner, artist Spectrum 305 Studio, Grafton, Wis., 1983—. Designer, puppetmaster Marquette U. Theatre, Milw., 2000-01; tchr., artist-in-residence Milw. Pub. Schs., 1999-2000; theatrical designer Theatre X, Milw., 1996-98, Bialystock and Bloom, Milw., 1997-98. Author: Hand Papermaking, 1997; artist hand paper sculpture. Founder, The Truck Studio, Artists Working in Edn., Milw., 1999 (bd. dirs., co-pres., 2002-04); bd. dirs., officer Wild Space Dance Co., Milw., 1994-2000, Print Forum Milw. Art Mus., 1993-2002; bd. dirs., past pres. Theatre X, Milw., 1993-2002, bd. dirs. Riveredge Nature Ctr., 2003-; mem. North Suburban YMCA. Fellow Vt. Studio Ctr., 2001, 2002, 2004; recipient award Pub. Arts Commn., Wis. Arts Bd., 1996, Gov.'s award for Arts Artists Working in Edn., 2002. Mem. Wis. Acad. Scis., Arts and Letters, Cedarbury Artists Guild. Unitarian Universalist. Avocations: gardening, photography, writing, swimming, music. Office: Spectrum 305 Studio 1350 14th Ave Grafton WI 53024 E-mail: sally@sallyduback.com.

DUBACK, STEVEN RAHR, lawyer; b. Washington, Sept. 4, 1944; s. Paul Hewitt and Natalie (Rahr) D.; children: David, Peter, Andrew. BA, Princeton U., 1966; JD, U. Mich., 1969. Bar: Wis. 1969, U.S. Dist. Ct. (ea. dist.) Wis. 1969, U.S. Ct. Claims 1969, U.S. Tax Ct. 1969. Ptnr. Quarles & Brady LLP, Milw., 1969—. Bd. dirs. Oshkosh (Wis.) B'Gosh, Inc., Commerce Indsl. Chems., Inc. Dir. Ctr. for the Deaf and Hard of Hearing. Mem.: Am. Soc. Corp. Secs., Estate Counselors Forum, Milw. Estate Planning Coun., Wis. State and Local Tax Club, Town Club, Milw. Athletic Club, Rotary Club of Milw., Phi Beta Kappa, Order of Coif. Avocations: golf, tennis. Office: Quarles & Brady LLP 411 E Wisconsin Ave Ste 2550 Milwaukee WI 53202-4497 Office Phone: 414-277-5883. Personal E-mail: srd@quarles.com.

DUBANEVICH, KEITH SCOTT, lawyer; b. Springfield, Vt., Nov. 19, 1957; S. Walter Joseph and Sylvia Beatrice (Ward) D. BS, Northeastern U., 1980; JD, Tulane U., 1983. Bar: Tex. 1983, Mass. 1988, Oreg. 1997, U.S. Dist. Ct. (ea. and so. dists.) Tex. 1983, U.S. Ct. Appeals (5th cir.) 1984, U.S. Ct. Appeals (9th cir.) 2001, U.S. Dist. Ct. (we. dist.) Wis. 1989, U.S. Dist. Ct. Oreg. 1998, U.S. Supreme Ct. 1997. Assoc. Fulbright and Jaworski, Houston, 1983-87, jr. ptnr., 1987-88, 89-91, ptnr., 1992-98; assoc. Hale and Dorr, Boston, 1988-89; exec. com. Garvey Schubert Barer, Portland, Oreg., 1998—. Contbr. articles to profl. jours. Recipient La. Trial Lawyers award, 1983. Mem. ABA, Oreg. Assn. Def. Counsel, Order of Barristers, Multnomah Bar Assn. (domestic violence project), Owen M. Panner Am. Inn of Ct., Oreg. State Bar (exec. com. mem. bus. litig. sect.). Avocations: skiing, mountain climbing, American history. Home: 2953 NW Imperial Ter Portland OR 97210-3318 Office: Garvey Schubert Barer 11th Fl 121 SW Morrison St Portland OR 97204-3117 Office Phone: 503-228-3939. Business E-Mail: kdubanevich@gsblaw.com.

DUBASKY, VALENTINA, artist; b. Washington, Mar. 1, 1951; d. Alexander Cosmo and Mayo (Griggs) D. BA, Goddard Coll., 1974, MFA, 1977. Tchr. Pratt Inst., N.Y.C., 1989; vis. artist Skidmore Coll., 1986, L.I. U., 1996, Sch. Visual Arts, N.Y.C., 1994, Fashion Inst. Tech., N.Y.C., 1993. One women shows include Cheryl Pelavin Fine Art, N.Y.C., 1998, Hodges Taylor Gallery, Charlotte, N.C., 1997, Rena Haveson Gallery, Pitts., 1995, Robert L. Kidd Gallery, Detroit, 1983, 85, Van Straaten Gallery, Chgo., 1985, Oscarsson Hood Gallery, N.Y.C., 1981, 83, 85, Gloria Luria Gallery, Miami, Fla., 1985, Hodges Banks Gallery, Seattle, 1986, Ruth Siegel Gallery, N.Y.C., 1990, Oscarsson-Siegeltuch Gallery, N.Y.C., 1989, Semaphore Gallery, N.Y.C., 1981; exhibited in Weatherspoon Mus., Greensboro, N.C., 1983, Aldrich Mus. Contemporary Art, Ridgefield, Conn., 1985, Newark Mus., 1986, Albright Knox Mus., Buffalo, N.Y., 1983, 87, Jane Voorhees Zimmerli Art Mus., Rutgers, 1989, Nat. Mus. Women in the Arts, Washington, 1996, Art in Embassy Exhbns., Amman, Jordan and Muscat, Oman, 1995; contbr. etchings and monotypes to publ. Recipient Pollock-Krasner Found. award, 1987; Mixed Media grantee Ariana Found., 1986, Artist in Residence grantee Mid Atlantic States Consortium, 1987. Buddhist. Avocation: travel. Home: 463 West St Apt G111 New York NY 10014-2029

DUBBER, MARKUS DIRK, law educator; AB, Harvard Univ., 1988; JD, Stanford Univ., 1991. Law clk. U.S. Ct. Appeals Eleventh cir., Atlanta, 1991—92; lectr. Univ. Chgo. Law Sch., 1992—93; assoc. prof. SUNY Buffalo Sch. Law, 1993—99, prof., 1999—; dir. Buffalo Criminal Law Ctr., 1996—. Humboldt Rsch. Fellow Inst. Legal Phil., Ludwig Maximilians Universität, Munich, 2000—01; vis. prof. Univ. Mich. Law Sch., 2001. Editor: Buffalo Criminal Law Rev., 1996—; mem. bd. editors Law & History Rev., 2001—; contbr. articles to profl. jour. Mem.: Assn. Am. Law Sch. (chmn., comparative law sec.), Am. Law Inst. Office: School of Law SUNY Buffalo 712 O'Brian Hall Buffalo NY 14260

DUBÉ, CYNTHIA CHRISTINE, physics educator, consultant, video producer; b. Bridgeport, Conn., July 17, 1943; d. Charles Stuart and Marie (Fagan) D. AB, Emmanuel Coll., 1971; MA, Fairfield U., 1982; profl. diploma, DeVry Inst. Tech., 1977, Nat. Tech. Schs., 1978. Tchr. physics pvt. edn., Mass., Conn., R.I., 1965-77, pub. edn., Conn., 1977-91. Cons. Saturday Sci. Acad., Norwalk, Conn., 1976. Author: (textbook) Physics, 1986, (manual) Thinking Your Way Through Physics, 1986, (video series) The Magic of Physics, 1990, Smile! I Love You, Love, God, 2005, I Want To Walk With You, Love, God, 2004, Mystery, Myth, Mysticism and Miracles, 2004, Physics Guide to Fundamentals of Physics, 2005; producer, dir. videos Making Physics Fun, The Art of Teaching, Teaching Science Research Skills. Cons. State Conn. Dept. Edn., Hartford, 1989-90. Bell & Howell fellow, 1976. Mem. Am. Phys. Soc., Am. Assn. Physics Tchrs. (Metrologic Innovative Exptl. award 1984), N.Y. Acad. Scis., Conn. Assn. Physics. Tchrs. (exec. bd. 1987-90). Roman Catholic. Home: 53 Mountain Rd West Hartford CT 06107-2917

DUBE, MONTE I., lawyer; b. Jan. 20, 1956; AB, Boston U., 1977; JD, Benjamin N. Cardozo Sch. Law, 1981. Lic.: Ill. Supreme Ct., U.S. Dist. Ct. N. Dist. Ill., U.S. Ct. Appeals. Third Cir. Ptnr., chmn. firm health law dept. McDermott Will & Emery LLP, Chgo. Lectr. & Bigelow Teaching Fellow U. Chgo. Sch. Law, 1981—82. Mem.: ABA, Chgo. Bar Assn., Ill. Bar Assn., Ill. Supreme Ct. Office: McDermott Will & Emery LLP 227 W Monroe St Chicago IL 60606-5055 Office Phone: 312-984-7549. Office Fax: 312-984-7700. Business E-Mail: mdube@mwe.com.

DUBÉ, RONALD NORMAN, elementary school educator; b. Nashua, N.H., July 13, 1942; s. Norman Francis and Cecile (Soucy) D.; m. Roseanna Dougherty, Oct. 7, 1971; children: John, Ben, Luke. BA, U. N.H., 1964; MS, River Coll., 1976. Cert. tchr., N.H. Zookeeper Benson's Animal Farm, Hudson, N.H., 1963-75; vol. Peace Corps, Niger, Africa, 1964-66; sci. tchr. Salem (N.H.) Sch. Dist., 1967-68, Milford (N.H.) Sch. Dist., 1969-70, Nashua (N.H.) Sch. Dist., 1970-79, North Middlesex Sch. Dist., Townsend, Mass., 1979—, co-chair social studies curriculum, 1996-98. Contbr. articles to profl. publs. Mem. conservation com. Town of Mason, N.H., 1974-76; scoutmaster Boy Scouts Am., 1994—. Mem. Am. Can. Geneol. Soc., Acadian Cultural Soc. Roman Catholic. Avocations: reading, movies, walking, cutting wood.

DUBERMAN, MARTIN, historian, educator; b. N.Y.C., Aug. 6, 1930; s. Joseph M. and Josephine (Bauml) D. BA, Yale U., 1952; MA, Harvard U., 1953, PhD, 1957. Teaching fellow Harvard U., 1955-57; instr. history Yale U., 1957-61; Morse fellow, 1961-62; bicentennial preceptor, asst. prof. Princeton U., 1962-65, asso. prof., 1965-67, prof., 1967-71; Distinguished prof. Lehman Coll., City U. N.Y., 1971—. Founder Ctr. for Gay and Lesbian Studies, Grad. Ctr. CUNY, 1991, dir., 1986-96; mem. founding bd. Queer Econ. Justice, 2002—. Author: Charles Frances Adams, 1807-1886, 1961 (Bancroft prize 1962), In White America (Vernon Rice award 1963-64), James Russell Lowell, 1966 (finalist Nat. Book award 1966), The Uncompleted Past, 1969, Black Mountain: An Exploration in Community, 1972, revised edit., 1993, About Time: Exploring the Gay Past, 1986, rev. edit., 1991, Paul Robeson, 1989, 2d edit., 1996, Cures: A Gay Man's Odyssey, 1991, reissued with new afterword, 2002, Stonewall, 1993, Midlife Queer, 1996, Left Out: The Politics of Exclusion, 1999, reissued, expanded and revised, 2002, Haymarket: a novel, 2003; editor, contbr.: Antislavery Vanguard, 1965, Hidden From History: Reclaiming the Gay and Lesbian Past, 1989, A Queer World, 1997, Queer Representations, 1997; contbr.: (plays) Metaphors in Collision Course, 1968, The Memory Bank, 1970, The Recorder (in the Best Short Plays of 1970), 1971, The Colonial Dudes (in the Best Short Plays of 1972), 1973, Male Armor (Selected Plays 1968-74), 1976, Visions of Kerouac, 1977, Mother Earth: An Epic Drama of Emma Goldman's Life, 1991. Mem. ACLU (bd. dirs. N.Y. chpt. 1982-88), Phi Beta Kappa. Address: 475 W 22nd St New York NY 10011-2549

DUBERSTEIN, JOEL LAWRENCE, internist, pulmonologist, educator; b. Bklyn., Jan. 8, 1937; m. Judith Schwartz; children: Laura, Amy. AB, Princeton U., 1957; MD, Columbia U., 1961. Diplomate Am. Bd. Internal Medicine, Am. Bd. Pulmonary Diseases. Intern Mt. Sinai Hosp., N.Y.C., 1961-62, rsch. fellow in medicine, 1962, 65, asst. med. resident, 1963, chief med. resident, 1964, clin. asst., rsch. fellow, 1965-67; asst. chief medicine, chief pulmonary diseases Morrisania Hosp., Montefiore-Morrisania Affiliation, Bronx, N.Y., 1969-71; attending physician dept. medicine Overlook Hosp., Summit, N.J., 1971—, chmn. pulmonary sect., ICU com., med. dir. ICU, 1985-97, divsn. chief pulmonary disease dept. internal medicine; assoc. clin. prof. medicine Columbia U., 1998—. Assoc. vis. physician Morrisania City Hosp., Bronx, 1969-71; mem. staff Morristown Meml. Hosp., 1972—, med. co-dir. respiratory svcs., 1977-82; attending phsician dept. medicine St. Barnabas Med. Ctr., Livingston, N.J., 1971-89, past chmn. pulmonary sect.; mem. staff Newark Beth Israel Med. Ctr., 1971-82; spkr. in field; mem. Essex County Med. Soc. TB Control. Contbr. articles to profl. jours. Maj. U.S. Army, 1967-69. Recipient Recognition award Soc. N.J.'s Physicians. Fellow ACP, Am. Coll. Chest Physicians; mem. AMA (Physician's Recognition award), N.J. Med. Soc., Essex Thoracic Soc., N.J. Acad. Medicine. Office: 315 E Northfield Rd Ste 1D Livingston NJ 07039-4800 Office Phone: 973-994-1144.

DUBIE, BRIAN E., lieutenant governor; b. Burlington, Vt., Mar. 9, 1959; m. Penny Bolio; 4 children. Student, USAF Acad., 1977—80; BS in Mech. Engring., U. Vt., 1982. Aerospace industry project mgr. B.F. Goodrich, Vergennes; capt. Am. Airlines, 1988; lt.gov. State of Vt., 2003—. Emergency preparedness officer Nat. Security Emergency Preparedness Agy.; bd. dirs. Vt. Sys., Inc. Active Essex Junction Sch. Bd., 1995—2000, chair, 1996—2000, sch. dist. moderator, 2000—; active Essex Junction Cmty. Drug Awareness Com., 1993—95; asst. coach Youth Football and Little League. Lt. col. Vt. Air Nat. Guard, col. USAF, 1998. Decorated Meritorious Svc. medal with oak leaf cluster. Republican. Office: 115 State St Montpelier VT 05633-5401

DUBIN, ARTHUR DETMERS, architect; b. Chgo., Mar. 14, 1923; s. Henry and Anne (Green) D.; m. Lois Amtman, Mar. 10, 1951 (dec. Sept. 1980); children: Peter Arthur, Polly Louise (Mrs. Scott Pollak); m. Phyllis Vollen Burman, Nov. 27, 1981; stepchildren: Garry Arthur, Jill Meredyth, David Yale, Eric Vollen. Student, Lake Forest Coll., 1943-44; B.Arch., U. Mich., 1949. Architect, partner Dubin & Dubin (architects and engrs.), Chgo., 1950-65, Dubin, Dubin & Black (architects and engrs.), 1965-66, Dubin, Dubin, Black & Moutoussamy, 1966-78, Dubin, Dubin & Moutoussamy, 1978-93. V.p., dir. 7337 South Shore Dr. Corp., 1958—81, 7345 South Shore Dr. Corp., 1962—86; gen. ptnr. 340 Wellington Assocs., 1962—73; mem. adv. bd. Amtrak, 1972—95; v.p. DDBM, Inc., 1975—85; hon. rsch. assoc. Smithsonian Instn., 1975; tech. cons. Paramount Pictures, 1991, TV, 1998—2001; spkr. on confs., U.S. and France. Author: Some Classic Trains, 1964, More Classic Trains, 1974, Pullman Paint and Lettering Notebook, 1997; author: (editor for N.Am.) The Great Trains, 1973; contbr. articles to mags.; archtl. works include govt. bldgs., rail transit stas. and transp. facilities, mil. installations, banks, indsl. plants, schs. and colls., hosps., housing and urban renewal planning. Chmn. Civic Beautification Com., Highland Park, Ill., 1965—74; mem. Bicentennial Commn., Highland Park, 1974—76, Ill. Commn. on High Speed Rail Transit, 1966—68, Met. Housing and Planning Coun., Chgo., Nat. Coun. Archtl. Registration Bds., 1971—; trustee NORTRAN, Des Plaines, Ill., 1980—91; trustee emeritus George Krambles Transit Scholarship Fund, 1985—, John W. Barriger III Nat. R.R. Libr., St. Louis, 1989—; life mem., friend Art Inst. Chgo. With inf. U.S. Army, 1943—46. Decorated Bronze Star with cluster, Purple Heart; recipient award Gen. Svcs. Adminstrn. for U.S. Custom House, Chgo., 1993. Mem.: AIA (emeritus), Am. Pub. Transit Assn., Railway and Locomotive Hist. Soc. (bd. dirs. 1960—93, hon. life dir. 1993, Sr. Achievement award 2004, 2004), Train Collectors Assn., Steamship Hist. Soc. Am., Cliff Dwellers Club (bd. dirs. 1972—75, emeritus), Builders Club (pres. 1970—71, bd. dirs. 1970—80), Arts Club (Chgo.). Home: 229 Park Ave Highland Park IL 60035-2523

DUBIN, CHARLES LEONARD, lawyer; s. Harry and Ethel D.; m. Anne Ruth, 1951. BA, U. Toronto, Ont., 1941; LL.B., Osgoode Hall Law Sch., 1944. Bar: Ont. 1944, appointed Queen's Counsel 1952. Practiced in, Toronto, 1945-73; judge Ont. Supreme Ct. Appeal, Toronto, 1973—; chief justice Ont. Ct. Appeal, Toronto, 1990-96; counsel Torys LLP (formerly Tory Tory Des Lauriers & Binnington Barristers), Toronto, 1996—; dir. Can. Steamship Lines, 2003—. Royal Commr. to inquire into air safety in Can., 1979; Head of Inquiry into the practices and procedures of Hosp.for Sick Children, 1983; Royal Commr. to inquire into use of drugs and banned practices in athletics, 1988; apptd. to Bd. of Canadian Centre for Ethics in Sport, 2000-03, hon. counsel, 2003; lectr. Osgoode Hall Law Sch., 1945-48; bd. dirs. Can. Steamship Lines. Mem. York Club, Toronto Hunt Club, Toronto Club. Home: 619 Avenue Rd Apt 1702 Toronto ON Canada M4V 2K6 Office: Torys Barristers Toronto Dominion Ctr PO Box 270 #3000 Toronto ON Canada M5K 1N2

DUBIN, DAVID MEYER, lawyer, educator; b. Denver, Oct. 19, 1956; s. Gene and June (Wolf) D. AB, Colgate U., 1978; JD, Tulane U., 1982. Bar: N.Y. 1983, La. 1984, U.S. Dist. Ct. (so. and ea. dists.) N.Y. 1983, U.S. Dist. Ct. (ea. and mid. dists.) La. 1985, U.S. Ct. Appeals (2d cir.) 1984, U.S. Ct. Appeals (5th cir.) 1985, U.S. Supreme Ct. 1988. Assoc. Mudge Rose Guthrie Alexander & Ferdon, N.Y.C., 1982-84, Jones Walker Waechter Poitevent Carrere & Denegre, New Orleans, 1984-88; ptnr. Twomey Latham Shea, Kelley, Dubin, Reale and Quartararo, LLP, Riverhead, NY, 1988—. Adj. prof. Long Island U., Southampton, N.Y., 1989—. Office Phone: 631-727-2180. Business E-Mail: ddubin@suffolklaw.com.

DUBIN, HOWARD VICTOR, dermatologist; b. N.Y.C., Mar. 28, 1938; s. Meyer and Blanche D.; m. Patricia Sue Tucker, June 10, 1962; children—Douglas Scott, Kathryn Sue, David Andrew, Michael Stonier. AB, Columbia U., 1958, MD, 1962. Diplomate: Am. Bd. Dermatology, Am. Bd. Internal Medicine. Intern U. Mich., 1962-63, resident in internal medicine, 1963-64, resident in dermatology, 1968-70, asst. prof., 1970-72, asso. prof., 1972-75, clin. asso. prof., 1975-77, clin. prof., 1977—. Resident in internal medicine Columbia-Presbyn. Med. Center, N.Y.C., 1966-68; practice medicine specializing in dermatology, Ann Arbor, Mich., 1970—2003. Contbr. articles to profl. jours. Trustee Greenhills Sch., Ann Arbor, 1979-87, pres. bd. trustees, 1981-84. Served with U.S. Army, 1964-66. Fellow ACP; mem. Am. Acad. Dermatology, Am. Dermatol. Assn., Soc. Investigative Dermatology, Dermatology Found. (mem. exec. com. 1987-2001, sec.-treas. 1988-91, pres. 1991-98), Mich. Dermatol. Soc. (pres. 1985-87), AMA, Mich. Med. Soc., Washtenaw County Med. Soc., Rotary.

DUBIN, JAMES MICHAEL, lawyer; b. NYC, Aug. 20, 1946; s. Benjamin and Irene (Wasserman) D.; m. Susan Hope Schraub, Mar. 15, 1981; children: Alexander Philip, Elizabeth Joy. BA, U. Pa., 1968; JD, Columbia U., 1974. Bar: N.Y. 1975, D.C. 1984, U.S. Dist. Ct. (so. and ea. dists.) N.Y. 1975, U.S. Ct. Appeals (2d cir.) 1975. Assoc. Paul, Weiss, Rifkind, Wharton & Garrison, LLP, N.Y.C., 1974-82, ptnr., 1982—, chmn. corp. dept., 1995—2005. Bd. dirs. Conair Corp., Carnival Corp.; internat. bd. govs. Tel-Aviv U., 2001—; chmn. bd. govs. Tel-Aviv U. Law Sch., 2001—04. Mem. editl. bd.: Columbia Law Rev., 1973—74. Trustee Solomon Schechter Sch. Westchester, 1991—, vice chmn., 1997—; bd. dirs. Nat. Found. Advancement in Arts, 1991—, vice chmn., 1994—; bd. dirs. Jewish Guild for the Blind, 1989—, chmn., 1995—99, chmn. exec. com., 2000—; bd. dirs. YM-YWHA of Mid-Westchester, Scarsdale, NY, 1983—86. With U.S. Army, 1969—71. Mem.: ABA, Am. Arbitration Assn. (comml. panel arbitrators 1989—), Assn. Bar City N.Y., Drones Club, Colony Club, Queenwood Golf Club, Sunningdale Country Club (bd. govs. 1989—2004, pres. 2000—04), Indian Harbor Yacht Club, The Dukes Golf Club, Snowmass Club, Phi Delta Phi. Office: Paul Weiss Rifkind Wharton & Garrison LLP 1285 Avenue Of The Americas New York NY 10019-6064 Office Phone: 212-373-3026. Business E-Mail: jdubin@paulweiss.com.

DUBIN, LEONARD, lawyer; b. Trenton, N.J., July 30, 1934; s. Isadore and Selma (Lotman) D.; m. Marlene B. Bronstein, July 12, 1962; children: Elisa K., David I., Michael B. BS, Temple U., 1956, LLB, 1961. Bar: Pa. 1962. Law clk. Ct. Common Pleas, Phila., 1961-62; assoc. Blank Rome Comisky & McCauley LLP, Phila., 1962-69; ptnr. Blank Rome LLP and predecessor cos., Phila., 1969—. Contbr. articles to profl. jours. Bd. dirs. Juvenile Diabetes Found., 1974-95. 1st lt. U.S. Army, 1956-58. Fellow Am. Bar Found., Pa. Bar Found., Am. Coll. Trial Lawyers, Am. Acad. Matrimonial Lawyers; mem. ABA (ho. of dels. 1988-96), Pa. Bar Assn. (house of dels. 1977—, bd. govs. 1981-84, v.p. 1987-88, pres.-elect 1988-89, pres. 1989-90, chair family law sect. 1991-92), Phila. Bar Assn. (bd. govs. 1975-77). Democrat. Jewish. Office: Blank Rome LLP One Logan Sq Philadelphia PA 19103 Office Phone: 215-569-5602. E-mail: dubin@blankrome.com.

DUBIN, MARK WILLIAM, neuroscientist, educator, academic administrator; b. N.Y.C., Aug. 30, 1942; s. Sidney Stanley and Dorothy (Cirinsky) D.; m. Alma Hermine Heller, June 27, 1964; children: Lila Rachel, Miriam Rebecca AB in Biophysics, Amherst Coll., 1964; PhD in Biophysics, Johns Hopkins U., 1969. Research fellow Australian Nat. U., Canberra, 1969-71; asst. prof. dept. molecular, cellular and devel. biology U. Colo., Boulder, 1971-77, assoc. prof., 1977-82, prof., 1982—87, chmn. dept., 1983-87, assoc. chmn. dept., 2000—, assoc. vice chancellor for acad. affairs, 1988-97, chief info. officer, 1996-97, faculty fellow info. tech. svcs., 1997-98, dir. acad. devel. BP Ctr. for Visualization, 2003—05. Sci. cons. Wills Found., 1981-91; cons., mem. bd. sci. advisors Columbine Venture Fund, Denver, 1984-94, Photometrics, Tucson, 1987-89; owner MWm Crafts, 1996—; mem. acad. adv. bd. higher edn. Apple Computing, 1997-98. Author: How the Brain Works; contbr. articles to profl. jours. Bd. dirs. Congregation Har Ha-Shem, Boulder, 1976-80, pres., 1978, 79, Cmty. Access TV of Boulder, 1996-97. Grantee NIH-Nat. Eye Inst., 1972-90, NSF, 1976-83, March of Dimes Found., 1982-83; Fight for Sight fellow Australian Nat. U., 1969-71 Mem. AAAS, AAUP, Soc. Neurosci., Sigma Xi. Democrat. Jewish. Avocation: woodworking. Home: 1010 Grape Ave Boulder CO 80304-2129 Office: Univ Colo Dept Molecular Cellular Biology PO Box 347 Boulder CO 80309-0347 Office Phone: 303-250-6668. Business E-Mail: dubin@colorado.edu.

DUBIN, MARTIN STEVEN, principal; b. Queens, N.Y., July 1, 1950; s. Herman and Fay Dubin; m. Ellen Marlene Kohn, Aug. 18, 1973; children: Rachel Fay, David Isaac. BA, Hofstra U., 1972, MS in Edn. with univ. honors, 1974; D of Edn., Vanderbilt U., 1981. Cert. nursery, kindergarten, grades 1-6, social studies 7-9, spl. classes for emotionally disturbed K-12, Va.; kindergarten, elem. 1-7, spl. edn. for emotional disturbance and learning disabilities, elem. prin., secondary prin. Tchr. emotionally disturbed Mt. Vernon Ctr., Alexandria, Va., 1974—76; head tchr. emotionally disturbed Riverside Elem., Alexandria, 1976—77; resource tchr. emotionally disturbed Franconia Ctr., Alexandria, 1977—81; dept. chmn. learning disabled Robinson Secondary, Fairfax, Va., 1981—83; LD/MMR secondary specialist Area IV, Fairfax, Va., 1983—88; prin. Armstrong Ctr., Reston, Va., 1988—90, Franconia Ctr., Alexandria, 1990—97, Crestwood Elem., Springfield, Va., 1997—98; adminstrv. prin. Hayfield Secondary, Alexandria, 1998—2005. Adj. prof. George Mason U., Fairfax, 1988-93, 2005—; learning disabilities/mild mental retardation specialist Area IV Adminstrv. Office, Fairfax, 1983-88; grant evaluator U.S. Office of Edn., Washington, spring 1991, 93, 95. Pres. Adat Reyim, Springfield, Va., 1997-99; mem. Springfield Coalition, 1997-98. U.S. Office of Edn. rsch. grantee, 1979. Mem. CEC, Nat. Assn. Elem. Sch. Prins., Phi Delta Kappa. Achievements include study in how attitudes of non-disabled students influence the integration and mainstreaming of emotionally disabled students. Office: Hayfield Secondary Sch 7630 Telegraph Rd Alexandria VA 22315-3898 Personal E-mail: 4dubins@verizon.net. Business E-Mail: martin.dubin@fcps.edu.

DUBIN, MORTON DONALD, II, lawyer; BA in Polit. Sci., Columbia U., 1993; JD cum laude, U. Mich. Law Sch., 1995. Bar: NY 1997, US Dist. Ct., NY (So. & Ea. Dist.) 1998. Law clerk to Judge Sidney Fitzwater US Dist. Ct., Tex. No. Dist., 1996—97; assoc. then ptnr., general commercial, products liability, mass tort and employment litigation Orrick, Herrington & Sutcliffe LLP, NYC, 1998—. Mem.: NY State Bar Assn. Office: Orrick, Herrington & Sutcliffe LLP 666 Fifth Ave New York NY 10103-0001 Office Phone: 212-506-5000. Office Fax: 212-506-5151. Business E-Mail: mdubin@orrick.com.

DUBIN, STEPHEN VICTOR, lawyer; b. Bklyn., June 17, 1938; s. Herman E. and Rhoda (Fogel) D.; m. Paula L. Dubin, June 28, 1959; children: Jeffrey D., Michelle L. BA, CUNY, 1961; JD, Boston U., 1961. Bar: N.Y. 1961, Ill. 1975, Pa. 1984, U.S. Dist. Ct. (so. and ea. dists.) N.Y. 1966, U.S. Dist. Ct. (no. dist.) Ill. 1975, U.S. Ct. Appeals (2d cir.) 1975, U.S. Supreme Ct. 1970, U.S. Dist. Ct. (ea. dist.) Pa. 1993, U.S. Ct. Appeals (3d cir.) 1993. Assoc. Kronish, Lieb, Weiner & Hellman, N.Y.C., 1965-67; counsel corp. sec Seligman & Latz, N.Y.C., 1967-72; gen. atty. Montgomery Ward & Co., Inc., N.Y.C., 1972-75, regional counsel, asst. sec. Chgo., 1975-78; gen. counsel, exec. v.p., dir. CSS Industries, Inc., Phila., 1978—. Lectr. consumer law Am. Mgmt. Assn., 1974, 79, 81, Practicing Law Inst., 1982, 88. Nassau County Dem. committeeman, 1967-75, mem. county jud. screening com., 1972-75, del. Nat. Dem. Issues Conv., 1974; pres. Phila. chpt. Am. Jewish Com., 1995-97, chmn. 1997-99, nat bd. govs., 1997—, nat. v.p., 2002-05. Capt. JAGC USAR, 1961-65. Mem. ABA, N.Y. State Bar Assn., Pa. Bar Assn., Ill. Bar Assn., Chgo. Bar Assn., Phila. Bar Assn., Bar Assn. Nassau County, N.Y. County Lawyers Assn., Am. Soc. Corp. Secs., Masons (master 1982). Office: CSS Industries Inc 1845 Walnut St Philadelphia PA 19103-4708 Business E-Mail: steve.dub@cssindustries.com.

DUBINA, JOEL FREDRICK, federal judge; b. Elkhart, IN, Oct. 26, 1947; BS, U. Ala., 1970; JD, Cumberland Sch. Law, 1973. Pvt. practice law Jones, Murray, Stewart & Yarbrough, 1974—83; law clk. to Hon. Robert E. Varner U.S. Dist. Ct. (mid. dist.) Ala., Montgomery, 1973—74, U.S. magistrate, 1983—86, U.S. Dist. judge, 1986—90; judge U.S. Ct. Appeals (11th cir.), 1990—. Mem.: FBA (pres. Montgomery chpt. 1982—83), appellate ct. advisory com., U.S. ct., Montgomery County Bar Assn. (chmn. Law Day com. 1975, constrn. and bylaws com. 1977—80, grievance com. 1981—83), 11th Cir. Hist. Soc., Ala. State Bar Assn., Supreme Ct. Hist. Soc., Fed. Judges Assn., Nat. Coun. U.S. Magistrate Judges, Cumberland Sch. Law Alumni Assn., Am. Inn of Cts. (pres. Montgomery chpt. 1993—94), Lions, Phi Delta Phi. Office: US Cir Ct Appeals 11th Cir PO Box 867 Montgomery AL 36101-0867 also: US Courthouse Ste C5 1 Church St Montgomery AL 36104

DUBINER, MICHAEL, lawyer; b. N.Y.C., Jan. 9, 1954; s. Morris and Ann D.; m. Nancy Susan Tilles, May 31, 1975; children: David, Jeannie. BA, CUNY, 1975; JD, U. Miami, 1978. Bar: Fla. 1978, U.S. Dist. Ct. (so. dist.), U.S. Supreme Ct. 1983. Atty. PB County Pub. Defenders Office, West Palm Beach, Fla., 1978-81, Dubiner & Blumberg, PA, Boynton Beach, Fla., 1981-95; pvt. practice West Palm Beach, 1995-97; atty. Dubiner & Wilensky, P.A., West Palm Beach, 1997—. Founding chmn. Domestic Violence Counsel Palm Beach County, 1995-97. Recipient Fla. Bar Pres. Pro Bono award Fla. Bar Assn., 1985. Office: Dubiner & Wilensky LLC 515 N Flagler Dr Ste 325 West Palm Beach FL 33401-4349 E-mail: duby@adelphia.net.

DUBINETS, ELENA ALEXANDROVNA, musicologist; b. Moscow, July 27, 1969; arrived in US, 1996; d. Alexander and Margarita Frenkel; m. Sergey Dubinets, Oct. 13, 1990; children: Maria, Lev. BA, Moscow (Russia) Tchaikovsky Conservatory Music Coll., 1988; MA, Moscow (Russia) Tchaikovsky Conservatory, 1993, PhD, 1996. Artistic adviser Seattle (Wash.) Chamber Players, 2001—; music rsch. coord. Seattle (Wash.) Symphony, 2003—. Pres. DoubleSharp, Seattle, 2004—; artistic curator festival Icebreaker I and II, Seattle, 2002—04, Wired Strings, San Francisco, 2003. Author: Signs of Sounds: Contemporary Music Notation, 1999, Music is What Sounds Around, 2005; translator: Standing Room Only: Strategies for marketing the performing arts, 2004. Bd. dirs. Seattle (Wash.) Chamber Players, 2002—. Grantee, The Soros Cultural Initiative, 1993, Nuffic Found., Netherlands, 1995, Soc. Am. Music, 2002; scholar, Paul Sacher Found., Switzerland, 2002. Mem.: Am. Musicological Soc. Home: 1225 151st ave SE Bellevue WA 98007 Office: Seattle Symphony PO Box 21906 Seattle WA 98111 E-mail: dubinets@yahoo.com.

DUBLAC, ROBERT REVAK, artist; b. Hartford, Conn., Nov. 28, 1938; s. Andrew Francis and Mary Catherine (Revak) D'Lubac. BFA in Painting with honors, U. Hartford, 1963; postgrad., Yale U., Rome, 1967, Temple U., 1968-69. Cert. tchr., Conn. Art dept. chmn. Avon (Conn.) H.S., 1965-67; adj. prof. U. Conn., Avon, 1967; art dept. chmn. Litchfield (Conn.) H.S., 1969-80; co-dir. Fortman Studio, Florence, Italy, 1977-78. Resident at The Millay Colony For The Arts, Inc., Steepletop, Austerlitz, N.Y., 1989. Exhibited in group shows at Nat. Acad. Design, N.Y.C., 1963, Nat. Soc. Painters, N.Y.C., 1969, Nat. Water Color Soc., N.Y.C., 1969, New Britain Mus. Am. Art, Conn., 1969, The Springfield (Mass.) Mus., 1970, Signature Gallery, Canton, Conn., 1970-80, The Conn. Watercolor Soc., 1977, Beverly Gallery, Dallas, 1979, Up-River Gallery, Hadlyme, Conn., 1980, Slater Meml. Mus., Norwich, Conn., 1997, Berkshire Mus., Mass., 1998, others; one-man shows include Images Gallery, Toledo, 1989, Unionville Mus., 1988, Saugatuck Gallery, Westport, Conn., 1986, Chase/Freedman Gallery, West Hartford, Conn., 1997, Hurlbutt Gallery, Greenwch, Conn., 1996; represented in permanent collections; ltd. ed. "Summer Morning 2". Grantee Adolph & Esther Gorrieb Found., 1990, Elizabeth Found., NYC, 1995, Pollock-Krasner Found., 1999, 2004, Gottlieb Found., 2003, 2004, Puffin Found., 2003; recipient Best in Show award, Gallery on the Green, Canton, Conn., 1964, The Margaret Cooper Meml. Prize, Conn. Acad. Fine Arts, Hartford, 1971, North Adams (Mass.) St. Coll. Purchase award, Berkshire Art Assn., 1977, Top award, Conn. Watercolor Soc., Hartford, 1986-87, scholarship, Hartford Art Sch., U. Hartford, 1958-63 others. Mem. Conn. Acad. Fine Arts (monetary award 1971), Conn. Watercolor Soc. (monetary award 1986-87) Nat. Artists Equity. Avocation: gardening and garden design. Home: Brookside 62 Cottage St Unionville CT 06085-1108 Office Phone: 860-673-0175. E-mail: revak@usadatanet.net.

DUBLIN, THOMAS DAVID, retired preventive medicine physician; b. NYC, Jan. 18, 1912; s. Louis I. and Augusta (Salik) D.; m. Christina Macdonald Carlyle, June 3, 1939 (dec. Sept. 1997); children: Sarah Carlyle Dublin Slenczka, Barbara Dublin Van Cleve. AB, Dartmouth Coll., 1932; MD, Harvard U., 1936; M.P.H., Johns Hopkins U., 1940, Dr.P.H., 1941. Diplomate Nat Bd. Med. Examiners, Am. Bd. Preventive Medicine (dir. 1961-71, vice. chmn. for gen. preventive medicine 1965-71). Intern 2d Harvard med. service Boston City Hosp., 1936-38; asst. resident physician Hosp. Rockefeller Inst. for Med. Research, N.Y.C., 1938-39; epidemiologist-in-tng. N.Y. State Dept. Health, 1939-40, asst. dist. health officer, 1940, epidemiologist, 1941-42; instr. preventive medicine Johns Hopkins U. Med. Sch., 1940-41; instr. preventive medicine and public health Albany Med. Coll., 1942; lectr. epidemiology DeLamar Inst. Pub. Health, Coll. Physicians and Surgeons, Columbia U., 1942-45; assoc. prof., 1942-43; prof., exec. officer dept. preventive medicine/cmty. health L.I. Coll. Medicine, Bklyn., 1943-48; epidemiologist Kingston Ave. Hosp., Bklyn., 1943-48; exec. dir. Nat. Health Council, 1948-53; med. cons. Nat. Found. for Infantile Paralysis, 1953-55; med. dir. USPHS, 1955-76, Community Services Programs, Office of Dir., NIH, Bethesda, Md., 1955-60; chief epidemiology and biometry br. Nat. Inst. Arthritis and Metabolic Diseases, Bethesda, 1960-66; research adviser, health service Office Tech. Coop. and Research, AID, 1966-68; dir. Office Health Manpower, HEW, 1968-70; program planning officer Bur. Health Manpower, Health Resources Adminstrn., 1970-72, spl. asst. dep. dir. bur., 1972-76; cons. health manpower supply and edn., 1976-78; cons. div. med. edn. AMA and Coordinating Council on Med. Edn., 1976-78; cons. research and devel. Ednl. Commn. for Fgn. Med. Grads., 1978-86. Mem. expert adv. panel pub. health adminstrn. WHO, 1954-80; mem. Nat. Adv. Com. Epidemiology and Biometry, 1956-60; chmn. com. on cert. Am. Bd. Med. Specialists, 1972-77 Contbr. articles on internat. health and health manpower to profl. publs. Fellow Am. Pub. Health Assn. (governing council 1954-60, chmn. research policy com. 1957-60), Am. Coll. Preventive Medicine (regent 1973-76), N.Y. Acad. Medicine; mem. AMA, AAAS, Am. Epidemiol. Soc., Assn. Tchrs. Preventive Medicine (sec. 1944-48), Internat. Epidemiol. Assn., Delta Omega. Home: 4901 Connecticut Ave NW Washington DC 20008

DUBLON, DINA, former bank executive; b. Brazil, Aug. 1953; BA in Econs. and Math., Hebrew U.; MS, Carnegie Mellon U. Exec. v.p. corp. planning Chase Manhattan Corp., N.Y.C., 1996—2000; CFO, exec. v.p. J.P. Morgan Chase & Co., N.Y.C., 2000—04. Bd. dirs. Accenture, PepsiCo, Inc., Microsoft, 2005—. Trustee Carnegie Mellon U., Global Fund for Women, The Women's Commn. for Refugee Women and Children, Worldlinks. Named Woman of the Year, The Fin. Women's Assn., 2004.

DUBNAU, JENNY, artist; BA, Barnard Coll., 1985; MFA, Yale U., 1996. One-man shows include Clifford-Smith Gallery, Boston, 2000, 2002, The Dealership, Brooklyn, 2002, Bucheon Gallery, San Francisco, 2003, Black & White Gallery, Brooklyn, 2003, exhibited in group shows at The MMC Gallery, NYC, 1989, Women View Women, Brooklyn YMCA, 1991, Hot, K&E Gallery, 1995, Heads, 1996, Portraits, Graham Modern Gallery, 1996, Little, Jeffrey Coploff Gallery, 1998, !Go! Figure, Clifford-Smith Gallery, 1999, Winter White, 2004, Six Degrees of Separation, Forrest-Scott Gallery, 1999, Where are All the People, DeChiara Stewart Gallery, 2000, Smile, H.E.R.E., 2001, Artists to Artists, Ace Gallery, 2002, Sympathetic Nerves, Capsule, 2004, Portraits, Esso, 2004, Open House: Working in Brooklyn, Brooklyn Mus. Art, 2004, Head Games, Revolution Gallery, 2004. Grantee Louis Comfort Tiffany Found., 2002, Rema Hort Mann Found., 2002, Pollock-Krasner Grant, 2004, Guggenheim Found. Fellowship, 2004. Office: Black & White Gallery 483 Driggs Ave Brooklyn NY 11211 E-mail: jdubnau@verizon.net.*

DUBNER, DANIEL WILLIAM, pediatrician; b. Newark, Apr. 18, 1947; s. Nathan M. and Sara K. (Kuskin) D.; m. Janet Lee, Oct. 5, 1975; children: Sarah, Jeffrey, Emily. BS, Rutgers U., 1969; MD, U. Pa., 1973. Intern, resident Childrens Hosp. Phila., 1973-76; pediatrician Med. Assoc., Chelmsford, Mass., 1978-88, Greater Lowell (Mass.) Pediatrics, 1988—. Author: The Pediatricians' Best Baby Planner for the First Year of Life, 1994. Behavioral Pediatrics fellow U. Wash., Seattle, 1976-77, genetic counseling and birth defect edn. fellow Tufts U., Boston, 1977-78. Fellow Am. Acad. Pediatrics; mem. Mass. Med. Soc. Avocations: running, biking, travel. Office: Greater Lowell Pediatrics 33 Bartlett St Ste 306 Lowell MA 01852-1318 also: 504 Groton Rd Westford MA 01886-1151

DU BOFF, MICHAEL H(AROLD), lawyer; b. N.Y.C., June 27, 1945; s. Rubin Robert and Millicent Barbara (Pollack) Du B.; widowed; children: Jill Bonnie, Robert Evan. BBA, Pace U., 1967; JD, Bklyn. Law Sch., 1970. Bar: N.Y. 1971, U.S. Dist. Ct. (so. and ea. dists.) N.Y. 1972, U.S. Supreme Ct. 1974, U.S. Tax Ct. 1973, U.S. Ct. Internat. Trade 1973. Sr. trial asst. dist. atty. Bronx County, N.Y.C., 1970—73; ptnr. Gainesburg, Gottlieb, Levitan & Cole, N.Y.C., 1974—81; counsel Hahn & Hessen, N.Y.C., 1981-84; ptnr. Salon, Marrow & Dyckman, N.Y.C., 1985-97, Davidoff, Malito & Hutcher LLP, N.Y.C., 1997—2005, Snow Becker Krauss PC, 2005—. Dir., cons. Harwell Group, Inc., N.Y.C., 1982—; mem. panel of arbitrators NASD, 1991--, N.Y. Stock Exch., 1991--; v.p. Classic Antique & Restored Spls., Ltd., N.Y.C., 1980—; bd. trustees, gen. coun. Soundview Preporatory Acad., 1993—; bd. trustees The Harvey Sch. 1997—. Contbr. article to Bklyn. Law Sch. Law Review, 1969, Patron Children's Art Workshop, Mamaroneck, N.Y., 1979—. Sponsor Children's Med. Ctr., Lake Success, N.Y., 1979—; mem. Westchester Coun. Arts., N.Y., 1980—; assoc. chmn. fin. industries div. Nat. Asthma Ctr., Denver, 1981. Recipient award for disting. svc. Bronx Dist. Atty., 1973. Mem. ABA, Am. Arbitration Assn. (panel of arbitrators 1979—, guest spkr. 1983), Assn. Bar City of N.Y. (com. uniform state laws 1972-81), Fed. Bar Coun., N.Y. State Bar Assn. (arbitration com.), Lawyers Assn. Textile and Apparel Industries (pres.), Alpha Phi Omega (v.p. N.Y.C. chpt. 1964-67). Home: 7 Mckenna Pl Mamaroneck NY 10543-2112 Office Phone: 212-455-0322. Business E-Mail: mduboff@sbklaw.com.

DUBOIS, ALAN BEEKMAN, art museum curator; b. Forest Glen, N.Y., Dec. 14, 1935; s. Raymond Van Orden and Florence (Beekman) DuB.; m. Joan Edna Burger, Apr. 25, 1959; children: Dean, Ronald, Douglas, Jonathan. BS in Art Edn., SUNY-New Paltz, 1958; MFA in Photography and Related Arts, Ind. U., 1966. Dir. Washington County Mus. Fine Arts, Hagerstown, Md., 1964-66; asst. dir. Mus. Fine Arts, St. Petersburg, Fla., 1966-84, Orlando (Fla.) Mus. Art, 1984-89; curator decorative arts Ark. Arts Ctr., Little Rock, 1989—2004, ret., 2004. Nat. Endowment Arts fellow, 1972, 75. Office Phone: 501-939-9836. Personal E-mail: tetedubois@aol.com.

DUBOIS, ARTHUR BROOKS, physiologist, educator; b. N.Y.C., Nov. 21, 1923; s. Eugene Floyd and Rebeckah (Rutter) DuB.; m. Roberdeau Callery, June 21, 1950; children: Anne R., Brooks, James E.F. Student, Harvard U., 1941-43; MD, Cornell U., 1946. Intern in medicine N.Y. Hosp., 1946-47; med. research fellow U. Rochester, 1949-51; asst. resident Peter Bent Brigham Hosp., Boston, 1951-52; asst. prof. to prof. physiology and medicine U. Pa., 1952-74; prof. epidemiology and physiology Yale U., 1974—. Dir. John B. Pierce Found. Lab., 1974-88. Author: The Lung, 3d ed. 1986, Body Plethysmography, 1969; contbr. articles to profl. jours. Served with USNR, 1947-49. Recipient Rsch. Career award NIH, 1963-74; Edward Livingston Trudeau medal Am. Lung Assn., 1989. Mem. Am. Physiol. Soc., Am. Soc. Clin. Investigation, Assn. Am. Physicians, Undersea Med. Soc. Clubs: Harvard, Cosmos. Democrat. Home: 370 Livingston St New Haven CT 06511-1336 Office: 290 Congress Ave New Haven CT 06519-1403 Office Phone: 203-562-9901. E-mail: adubois@jbpierce.org.

DUBOIS, DIANE LOUISE, elementary school educator; d. Robert Dean (Stepfather) and Margaret Lucille Ellis; children: John Gaylon, Robert Brian. BA, Morningside Coll., Sioux City, Iowa, 1968; MA in Curriculum and Instrn., Nat. Louis U., Evanston, Ill., 1994; MA in Ednl. Leadership, No. Ill. U., DeKalb, 2001. Cert. self-contained gen. edn. K-9 Ill., 1969. Elem. tchr. Sioux City Pub. Schs., Iowa, 1968—69, Cmty. Unit Sch. Dist. 300, Carpentersville, Ill., 1969—70; k-8 substitute tchr. Elgin Sch. Dist. U-46, 1984—90, elem. tchr., 1990—94; elem. and mid. sch. tchr. Cmty. Unit Sch. Dist. 220, Barrington, 1994—98; mid. sch. tchr. Cmty. Consol. Sch. Dist. 15, Palatine, 1999—. Lang. arts dist. com. Cmty. Consol. Sch. Dist. 15, Palatine, Ill., 1999—, sch. improvement plan com. team rep., 2000—, yearbook advisor, 2002—, chair English dept., 2003—, bldg. leadership team, 2003—, new tchr. mentor, 2004—, mem. PBIS yellow team, 2004—; Ill. lang. arts tchrs. bd. Prentice-Hall Inc., Upper Saddle River, NJ, 2004—. Chairperson winter games vols. Northeastern Ill. Spl. Olympics, St. Charles, 1982—2005; founding mem. Living Lord Luth. Ch., Bartlett, ch. coun., 1971—, organist, choir mem. Mem.: ASCD, NEA, Internat. Reading Assn., Nat. Coun. Tchrs. English, Ill. Assn. Gifted Children, Ill. Edn. Assn., Kappa Delta Pi. Independent. Lutheran. Avocations: reading, walking, theater, concerts, travel. Office: Cmty Consol Sch Dist 15 900 E Palatine Rd Palatine IL 60074 Office Phone: 847-963-7536. Business E-Mail: duboisd@ccsd15.net.

DUBOIS, GUY, software company executive; MS in Engring., Lille Bus. Mgmt. Sch., France. Dep. mng. dir. Digital Equipment Corp., France; v.p. So. Europe Sybase Inc., 1994—95, v.p., gen. mgr. Europe, Mid. East, Africa Ops., 1995—99; exec. v.p., gen. mgr. The Vantive Corp., 1999—2000; exec. v.p. internat. ops. PeopleSoft Inc., Pleasonton, Calif., 2000—. Office: PeopleSoft Inc 4460 Hacienda Dr Pleasanton CA 94588

DUBOIS, JAN ELY, federal judge; b. Phila., Jan. 17, 1931; s. M. Norman and Syd (Stern) DuB.; m. Ruth Harberg, Aug. 19, 1956; children: Marc Norman, Jon Stuart, Peter Andrew, Pamela Sue. BS, U. Pa., 1952; LLB, Yale U., 1957. Law clk. civil div. U.S. Dept. of Justice, Washington, 1956; law clk. to Hon. Harry E. Kalodner Phila., 1957-58; atty. White and Williams, Phila., 1958-64, ptnr., 1964-88; judge U.S. Dist. Ct. (ea. dist.) Pa., Phila., 1988—2002, sr. judge, 2002—. Trustee Phila. Bar Found., 1981-89. pres. 1987; trustee Reform Congregation Keneseth Israel, Elkins Park, Pa., pres., 1985-87. 1st lt. U.S. Army. 1952-54, cpt. U.S.A.R., ret. Recipient John Currier Gallagher prize Yale U., 1957. Mem. ABA, Pa. Bar Assn., Phila. Bar Assn. (chmn. medico-legal com. 1981), Yale Law Sch. Assn. of Phila. (past pres.), Yale Club. Office: US Dist Ct 12613 US Courthouse 601 Market St Philadelphia PA 19106-1713 E-mail: Chambers_of_Judge_Jan_E_DuBois@paed.uscourts.gov.

DU BOIS, MAY M., music educator, humanities educator; b. Hong Kong, Dec. 25, 1942; arrived in US, 1957; d. Yuk Mann and Grace (Tai) Leung; children: Renard, Paul. MusM in Piano Performance, U. So. Calif., 1965. Faculty West LA Coll., Culver City, Calif., 1997—. Mem.: Honors Transfer Coun. Calif. (dir. honors program), Music Tchrs. Assn. Calif. (br. sec.). Avocation: running. Office: West LA Coll 9000 Overland Ave Culver City CA 90230 Office Phone: 310-287-4209. Business E-Mail: duboism@wlac.edu.

DUBOIS, MICHEL, anesthesiologist; s. Yvon and Renee Dubois; m. Judith Ray Jamison-Dubois, June 25, 1976; children: Marie-Laure, Matthieu. MD, Paris Sch. Medicine, 1968. Diplomate Am. Bd. Anesthesiology, Am. Bd. Pain Medicine, Am. Bd. Pain Mgmt., French Nat. Bd. Anesthesiology, lic. practitioner Gen. Med. Coun., London. Staff anesthesiologist Hopital Henri Mondor, Creteil, France, 1972—74; lectr. in anaesthesia The London Hosp. Med. Sch., 1974—76, sr. lectr. in anaesthesia, 1976—78; instr. anesthesiology Georgetown U. Sch. Medicine, Washington, 1978—80, asst. prof. anesthesiology, 1980—85, assoc. prof. anesthesiology, 1985—92, prof. anesthesiology, 1992—94, NYU Sch. Medicine, 1996—; dir. NYU Pain Program, 1996—. Staff attending NYU Med. Ctr., 1996—; chmn. instl. rev. bd. Georgetown U. Sch. Medicine, 1990—94; dir. clin. investigation unit, dir. pain mgmt. svcs. dept. anesthesia Georgetown U. Hosp., 1988—93; hon. cons. The London Hosp., 1976—77. Editor: Ethics Forum. Mem.: Ea. Pain Assn. (chmn. nomination com. 2002—, pres. 2001—02), France-USA Pain Assn. (pres., founder 1993—95), Am. Acad. Pain Medicine (chmn. ethics com. 1998—2003), Am. Soc. Anesthesiolologists (pain therapy com. 1993—94). Avocations: reading, petanque. Office: NYU Pain Mgmt Ctr 317 E 34th St Ste 902 New York NY 10016

DUBOIS, PHILIP LEON, academic administrator, political scientist, educator; b. Oakland, Calif., Oct. 17, 1950; s. Fernand Edmond and Germaine (Goodrich) D.; m. Lisa Lewis, Aug. 28, 1976; 3 children. AB in Polit. Sci. with highest honors, U. Calif., Davis, 1972; MA in Polit. Sci., U. Wis., 1974, PhD in Polit. Sci., 1978. Asst. prof. polit. sci. U. Calif., Davis, 1976—82, faculty asst. to vice chancellors, 1982—83, assoc. prof., 1982—87, asst. prof. to assoc. prof., vice chancellor, 1983—90, exec. assoc. dean letters and sci., 1990—91, prof., 1987—91; vice chancellor acad. affairs, provost U. NC, Charlotte, 1991—97, chancellor, 2005—; pres. U. Wyo., 1997—2005. Author (with Floyd Feeney): Lawmaking by Initiative, 1998; author: From Ballot to Bench: Judicial Elections and the Quest for Accountability, 1980; editor: The Analysis of Judicial Reform, 1982, The Politics of Judicial Reform, 1982; contbr. numerous articles, book revs. to law revs. and jours., other profl. pubs.; cons. (profl. jours., comml. book pubs.). Scholar, U. Wis., Madison; Ford Found. fellow, Jud. fellow, U.S. Supreme Ct., 1979—80. Mem.: Am. Assn. for Higher Edn., Am. Polit. Sci. Assn. (Edward S. Corwin award 1978), Phi Beta Kappa, Phi Kappa Phi. Democrat. Office: Univ NC Charlotte office Chancellor 9201 Univ City Blvd Charlotte NC 28223 Office Phone: 704-687-2201. Business E-Mail: pdubois@uncc.edu.

DUBOIS, RAYMOND FRANCIS, JR., civilian military employee, former marketing professional; b. Washington, June 5, 1947; married; 2 children. AB in Politics and Econs., Princeton U., 1972; postgrad., Columbia U., 1977-79. Rep. Smith, Barney and Co., N.Y.C., 1972-73; staff asst. to Sec. of Def. US Dept. Def., Washington, 1973-75; dep. under sec. US Army, Washington, 1975-77; pvt. cons. N.Y.C., 1978-80; management consultant Alexander Proudfoot Co. and Affiliates, 1980-84; pvt. cons. Washington, 1984-85; prin. Carre, Orban and Ptnrs. Internat., Brussels, 1985-86; dir. govt. affairs, mng. dir. fed. systems divsn. Nat. Edn. Corp. and Applied Learning Internat., Washington, 1987-90; dir. strategic initiatives U.S. govt. systems group Digital Equipment Corp., Washington, 1990-91, dir. strategic plans and policies, 1991-93, dir. def. industries mktg., 1993-95; mng. ptnr. Flint Hill Comm., Washington, 1995—2002; dep. under sec. installations & environments US Dept. Def., Washigton, DC, 2001—05, dir. adminstrn. & mgmt., Office of Sec. Washingto, DC, 2001—05, spl. asst. to sec. Dept. Army Washington, 2005—. Sr. counselor The Potomac Rsch. Group, Washington, 1995—. Mem. com. on internat. investment, tech. and devel. Dept. of State, Washington, 1982-88; rsch. asst. to chief economist U.S. C. of C., Washington, 1971. Sgt. U.S. Army, 1967-69. Kneller Found. grantee, 1970. Mem. Nat. Security Industry Assn., Assn. of U.S. Army, Armed Forces Comms. and Electroncis Assn., Mil. Order of Carabao (exec. com.). Office: US Army 102 Army Pentagon Washington DC 20310*

DUBOIS, RAYMOND N., medical educator, researcher; BS in biochemistry, Tex. A&M U.; PhD in biochemistry, Tex. SW Med. Sch.; MD, U. Tex. Health Sci. Ctr. Osler medicine intern, resident John Hopkins Hosp., Balt.; with Vanderbilt U. Med. Ctr., 1991—, head divsn. gastroenterology, hepatology, and nutrition Nashville, 1998—2003, Mina. C. Wallace prof. medicine and cell biology, 1998—2003, prof. medicine, cancer biology, cell and devel. biology, 2003—; dir. Vanderbilt Digestive Disease Rsch. Ctr., 1999—; Hortnse B. Ingram prof. molecular oncology Vanderbilt-Ingram Cancer Ctr., Vanderbilt U. Med. Ctr., 2004, dir. cancer prevention program. Sci. med. adv. bd. Nat. Colorectal Cancer Rsch. Alliance Found.; adv. bd. Nat. Cancer Inst., Nat. Inst. Diabetes and Digestive and Kidney Diseases, NIH; chmn. bd. dirs. Keystone Symposia on Molecular and Cellular Biology. Assoc. editor Gasteroenterology and Cancer Rsch.; contbr. articles to profl. jour. Recipient Outstanding Investigator award, AFMR, 2000, Disting. Achievement award, AGA, 2004. Mem.: Am. Assn. Cancer Rsch. (Dorothy P. Landon prize translational cancer rsch. 2004, Richard and Hinda Rosenthal award 2002), Am. Soc. Clin. Investigation, Am. Assn. Physicians, Royal Coll. Physicians. Achievements include first to report the link between cyclooxygenase-2 (COX-2) enzyme and colon cancer. Office: Vanderbilt U Med Ctr 694 Preston Rsch Bldg Nashville TN 37232-6838 Office Phone: 615-343-0527. Business E-Mail: raymond.dubois@vanderbilt.edu.

DUBOIS, SCOTT W., web site design company executive; b. New Bedford, Mass., Feb. 23, 1981; s. Wayne F. and Judith A. Dubois. MIS dir. Reynolds DeWalt Printing, Inc., New Bedford, 1998—99; pres. NDC Tech., New Bedford, 1999—. Mass. rep. Bus. Adv. Coun., Washington, 2001—03. Republican. Avocations: percussion, golf. Office: NDC Tech 1 Welby Rd New Bedford MA 02745 Business E-Mail: sdubois@ndctech.com.

DUBOSE, CHARLES WILSON, lawyer; b. Sumter, S.C., Mar. 2, 1949; s. Frank Elsivan and Fannie Louise (Wilson) DuB.; m. Patricia Holman Rayle, Dec. 5, 1987; children: Charles Wilson Jr., Margaret Louise Rayle, Frank Elsivan IV. AB magna cum laude, Harvard U., 1971; JD, U. Va., 1974. Bar: Ga. 1974, S.C. 1992, U.S. Dist. Ct. (no. dist.) Ga. 1974, U.S. Ct. Appeals (5th cir.) 1976, U.S. Ct. Appeals (4th cir.) 1978, U.S. Supreme Ct. 1979, U.S. Ct. Appeals (11th cir.) 1981, U.S. Dist. Ct. (mid. dist.) Ga. 1982, U.S. Dist. Ct. S.C. 2000. Assoc. Kutak, Rock & Huie and predecessor firms, Atlanta, 1974-79; ptnr. Kutak, Rock & Huie, Atlanta, 1979-84; of counsel Griffin, Cochrane & Marshall, P.C., Atlanta, 1985-86, ptnr., 1986-89, mng. ptnr., 1989-92; ptnr. Schnader, Harrison, Segal & Lewis, Atlanta, 1992—2000, Atlanta mng. ptnr., 1995-2000; ptnr. Winkler, DuBose & Davis LLC, Atlanta and Madison, Ga., 2000—. Mem. Chief Justice's Commn. on Indigent Def., 2000—; vice chmn. Ga. Pub. Defenders Stds. Coun., 2003-; mem. mediation and arbitration panels Closure Group ADR. Elder Peachtree Presbyn. Ch., Atlanta, Madison (Ga.) Presbyn. Ch.; mem. adv. bd. Atlanta's Table, 1991—, chmn., 1995; exec. vice chmn. Atlanta Billy Graham Crusade. Fellow Lawyers Found. Ga.; mem. ABA (ho. of dels. 2000—), Am. Law Inst., State Bar Ga. (bd. govs. 1998—, chair ind. def. com. 1997—), Atlanta Bar Assn. (bd. dirs. 1992-97, 2000—, sec. 1993-94, v.p., pres.-elect 1994-95, pres. 1995-96, bd. dirs. litig. sect. 1988-94, chmn. litig. sect. 1992-93), Lawyers Com. for Civil Rights Under Law (Atlanta steering com.), Atlanta Bar Found. (bd. dirs. 1995-96, 2000—), Atlanta Vol. Lawyers Found. (bd. dirs. 1995-96), Inst. Continuing Legal Edn. in Ga. (bd. trustees 1995-96), Am. Arbitration Assn. (comml. arbitration panel, constrn. industry arbitration panel), Lawyers Club Atlanta, World Trade Ctr. Atlanta. Avocations: photography, piano, architecture, historic preservation. Home: 1050 East Ave Madison GA 30650-1467 Office: 300 Hancock St Madison GA 30650-1380 also: 260 Peachtree St NE Ste 2000 Atlanta GA 30308-3263 Office Phone: 706-342-7900. Business E-Mail: wdubose@wddlaw.com.

DUBOSE, ELIZABETH (BETTYE DUBOSE), community health nurse; b. Ozark, Ala., Nov. 11, 1930; d. Samuel D. and Mattie Victoria (Harrell) Preston; m. Charles Raymond Hudson, July 31, 1949; 1 child, Julianne Schenker Adams; m. Frederick William Schenker, Jr., Dec. 15, 1962; m. John Calvin DuBose, July 15, 1978. ADN, Columbus State U., 1973, BSN, 1977. Lab tech. II Ala. Bureau of Labs., Dothan, Ala., 1951-62; student nurse CCU St. Francis Hosp., Columbus, Ga., 1972-73; charge nurse The Med. Ctr., Columbus, 1973-75, infection control nurse, 1975-78; charge nurse The Bradley Ctr., Columbus, Ga., 1974-78; clin. instr. nursing Columbus State U., 1977-78; dir. nursing Oakview Manor Nursing Home, Ozark, Ala., 1979-84; patient care coord. Wiregrass Home Health Agy., 13 Counties in SE Ala., 1984-86; home health coord. Ala. Pub. Health Dept., Abbeville, Ala., 1986-90; home health nurse Dale Co. Health Dept., Ozark, Ala., 1990—2002. Libr. com. mem. The Medical Ctr., Columbus, Ga., 1974-77; chmn. adv bd. Oakview Manor, Ozark, 1980-84. Mem. adv. bd. Henry Co. Health Dept., Abbeville, 1986-88, chmn. adv. bd., 1988-90. Republican. Protestant. Avocations: music, theater, chess. Home: Box 784 Co Rd 122 Ariton AL 36311-9718 Office: Ala State Health Dept Dale Co Ala Home Health Andrews Ave Ozark AL 36360

DUBOSE, GAYLAN RAY, elementary school educator, musician, writer; b. Pearsall, Tex., Oct. 4, 1941; s. Austin Gay and Luning Inez (Hull) DuBose. BA, North Tex. State U., 1964; MA in Classics, U. Minn., 1970. Tchr. Grapevine H.S., Tex., 1964—67, John Jay H.S., San Antonio, 1967—69, 1971—73, Escobar Jr. H.S., San Antonio, 1970, Travis H.S., Austin, Tex., 1973—86, Westwood H.S., Austin, 1986—97, Fulmore Mid. Sch., Austin, 1998—2000, St. Andrew Episcopal Sch., Austin, 2001—05. Author: Farrago Latina, 1997; co-author: Excelability, 2003. Co-chair Tex. State Jr. Classical League, Austin, 1988—99, Dist. Adv. Com., Round Rock, Tex., 1996—97; acad. contest chair Nat. Jr. Classical League, Oxford, Ohio, 1996—2005; organist St. Augustine's Orthodox Ch. and Procathedral, Pflugerville, Tex., 1998—2005. Named Tchr. of Yr., Travis H.S., 1979, 1983, Westwood H.S., 1996, Hon. Ky. Col., 2002. Office: St Andrew's Episcopal Sch 1112 West 31st St Austin TX 78705 Office Phone: 512-299-9895. Personal E-mail: gaylan1004@yahoo.com.

DUBOSE, GUY STEVEN, lawyer; b. Hollywood, Calif., June 12, 1954; s. Donald Thomas DuBose and Normalee Carol (Johnson) Farris. AB, U. So. Calif., 1976; JD, Whittier Coll., 1979; LLM, Cambridge U., Eng., 1981; cert., The Hague Acad. Internat. Law, The Netherlands, 1981. Bar: Calif. 1979, U.S. Dist. Ct. (cen. dist.) Calif. 1979. In house counsel Di-Line Corp., Orange, Calif., 1980-82; project contract adminstr. Rockwell Internat., Los Angeles, 1982-84; corp. counsel So. Calif. Savs., Beverly Hills, Calif., 1984-87; sr. v.p. gen. counsel Mercury Savs., Huntington Beach, Calif., 1987-91; COO, gen. counsel Guardian Fed., Huntington Beach, Calif., 1991-92; sr. v.p., assoc. gen. counsel Westcorp (Western Fin.), Irvine, Calif., 1992—. Mem. Orange County Bar Assn., Oxford and Cambridge Club (L.A.), L.A. Adventures Club. Avocation: world travel. Home: 2410 Naples Newport Beach CA 92660-3260 Office: Westcorp 23 Pasteur Irvine CA 92618-3816

DUBOSE, JAMES DAULTON, dentist; b. Turbeville, S.C., July 14, 1938; s. Robert Alvin and Olive (Dennis) DuB.; m. Kathy Elizabeth Johnson, Mar. 14, 1974; chldren: Olive Elizabeth, Dixie Dawn. BS, U. S.C., 1961; DMD, U. Louisville, 1965. Practice dentistry, Bishopville, S.C., 1965-70, Aiken, S.C., 1970-72, Manning, Aiken, 1972—. Mem. staff Clarendon Meml. Hosp., Manning; pres. D.M.D. Enterprises; owner Bluff Plantation, Colleton County, S.C.; v.p. R.A. DuBose, Inc.; pres. Best Western Inn, Three D. Inc., Santee, S.C. Chmn. Heart Fund, Lee County, S.C., 1966; trustee, deacon Summerton Bapt. Ch., Clarendon Hall Sch. Mem. ADA, Am. Soc. Dentistry for Children, Augusta Dental Soc., Pee-Dee Dist. Dental Soc., Century Club (Columbia, S.C.), Sertoma, Lions, Delta Sigma Delta. Home: 215 Cooper Dr Santee SC 29142-9319

DUBOSE, MICHAEL T., manufacturing executive; MS in Mgmt., Stanford U. With Gen. Electric Co.; sr. v.p. SAI Corp., 1993—95; with Gen. Instrument; chmn., CEO Grimes Aerospace Co., 1995—97; cons. Aurora Capital Group, 1997—98; pres. Aftermarket Tech. Corp., Westmont, Ill., 1998—, CEO, 1998—, chmn. bd. Office: Aftermarket Technology Corp 1 Oak Hill Ctr Ste 400 Westmont IL 60559

DUBOSE, MIKE STANLEY, ethnic studies educator; b. Fort Dix, NJ, Mar. 1, 1971; s. Edward Earl and Glenda Mary DuBose; m. Lori Ann Lamb, Jan. 24, 2003. PhD, Bowling Green State U., 2003. Part time instr. Bowling Green State U., Bowling Green, Ohio, 1998—, U. Toledo, 2003—05.

DUBOSE, SANDRA LYNN, finance educator; b. Waxahachie, Tex., July 28, 1946; d. Richard Lewis and Mary Evelyn Proffitt; m. Pete Brown, Oct. 18, 1997 (div.); children: Kirk Garrett, Keri Nicole. B in Bus. Edn., U. North Tex., 68; M in Bus. Edn., U. North Tex., 1970. Tchr. Dallas (Tex.) Ind. Sch. Dist., 1968—73, Duncanville (Tex.) Ind. Sch. Dist., 1973—2002; cons. Prentice Hall - DDC Pub., Coppell, Tex., 2002—04; instr. Tex. St. Tech. Coll., Breckenridge, Tex., 2005—. Trainee DDC Tng. Svcs., N.Y., 1999—; presenter in field. Author: Mous/Mos Correlations, 2000; editor: Bus. Edn. Tips: Tricks, 1998, TBTED Planner, 2004. Mem.: Assn. Career and Tech. Edn. (pres. 2001—03, Outstanding Svc. award 1998, named Outstanding Reg IV Bus. Edn. Tchr. 1999), Am. Career and Tech. Edn. Assn., Tex. Career and Tech. Coun. (chmn. 1994—95, 2005—), Tex. Bus. and Tech. Educators (pres. 1998—99, 2002—03, named Tchr. of Yr. 1999). Republican. Baptist. Home: 5311 FM 576E Breckenridge TX 76424 Office: Prentice Hall DDc Pub Co 600 Freeport Pkwy Ste 140 Coppell TX 75019

DUBOVI, TIMOTHY, elementary school educator; s. Joseph Paul Dubovi Jr. and Frances Jeanne Dubovi; m. Carol Lynn Banta; children: Lauren, Louis, Natalie, Josiah. BS in Elem. Edn., Lock Haven U., 1989. 2d gr. tchr. Mars (Pa.) Area Sch. Dist., 1989—90; 3th and 4th gr. tchr. Seneca Valley Sch. Dist., Harmony, Pa., 1990—2005. Asst. football coach h.s. Mars Area Sch. Dist., 1989—90, Seneca Valley Sch. Dist., 1990—2002. Sunday sch. tchr. St. John's Burry's Ch., Rochester, Pa., 2000—04, Sunday sch. supt., 2002—05, deacon; read-a-thon organizer Am. Heart Assn., 1999—2004. Recipient Friends of Edn. award, Robinson Industries, 2004. Mem.: Nat. Edn. Assn., Slovak Gymnastic Union. Republican. Avocations: hunting, fishing, football. Home: 129 Woodrow St New Brighton PA 15066

DUBOW, CRAIG A., publishing executive; b. Oct. 26, 1954; m. Denise Dubow; 3 children. BS in radio/TV/film, U. Tex., Austin, 1977. Various positions Gannett Co. Inc., 1981—, gen. sales mgr. KVUE-TV Austin, Tex., 1987—88, v.p. sta. mgr. KVUE-TV, 1988, v.p., gen. mgr. KVUE-TV, 1988—90, pres., gen. mgr. KVUE-TV, 1990—92, pres., gen. mgr. WXIA-TV Atlanta, 1992—2000, exec. v.p. Gannett TV, 1996—2000, pres. Gannett Broadcasting, 2000—05, CEO Gannett Broadcasting, 2001—05, pres., CEO, 2005—, bd. dir., 2005—. Bd. dir. Nat. Assn. Broadcasters, Assn. Maximum Svc. TV Inc., BMI. Office: Gannett Co Inc 7950 Jones Branch Dr Mc Lean VA 22107

DUBOWSKI, KURT MAX, toxicologist, educator, consultant; b. Berlin, Nov. 21, 1921; came to U.S., 1935; s. Jacques Dubowski and Gertrud (Baron) Steinberg. AB, NYU, 1946; MSc, Ohio State U., 1947, PhD, 1949; LLD (hon.), Capital U., 1984. Diplomate Am. Bd. Clin. Chemistry (pres. emeritus, sec.-treas. emeritus), Am. Bd. of Forensic Toxicology (founding pres., past pres.). Biochemist, asst. dir. labs. Norwalk (Conn.) Hosp., 1950-53; dir. chemistry Iowa Meth. Hosp., Des Moines, 1953-58; state criminalist State of Iowa Divsn. of Criminal Investigation, Des Moines, 1954-58; assoc. prof. clin. chemistry and toxicology U. Fla., Gainesville, 1958-61; George Lynn Cross disting. prof. medicine U. Okla., Oklahoma City, 1961-98, prof. surgery, prof. pathology, dir. toxicology labs., dir. forensic sci. labs. health scis. ctr., mem. clin. staff Univ. Hosps., 1961-2001, emeritus prof., 1998—. Cons. clin. chemistry and toxicology Dept. Vets. Affairs Med. Ctr., Oklahoma City, 1962-2001; cons. lab. medicine Okla. Med. Rsch. Found., Oklahoma City, 1967-2001; state dir. tests for alcohol and drug influence, State of Okla., 1967-97, state dir. emeritus, 1997—; chmn. emeritus Bd. Tests for Alcohol and Drug Influence, State of Okla., 2000—; sci. dir. Okla. Dept. Pub. Safety; ret. criminalist Okla. Dept. Pub. Safety/Okla. Hwy. Patrol, Okla. State Bur. Investigation, Oklahoma City Police Dept.; mem. sci. adv. bd. Armed Forces Inst. Pathology, U.S. Dept. Def., 1991-97; mem. Internat. Coun. Alcohol, Drugs and Traffic Safety; mem. exec. bd., co-chair subcom. alcohol pharmacology, toxicology and tech. com. on alcohol and other drugs Nat. Safety Coun.; past advisor subcom. urine drug testing NCCLS; toxicologist advisor DEC program Nat. Hwy. Traffic Safety Adminstrn., U.S. Dept. Transp.; cons. in field; mem. various fed. adv. groups; vis. lectr. and prof. various colls. and univs.; expert witness in forensic sci. matters. Author numerous books; contbr. chpts. to books and articles to profl. jours.; mem. editl. bd. Jour. Forensic Scis., Therapeutic Drug Monitoring, Forensic Sci. Rev.; past mem. editl. bd. Am. Jour. Forensic Medicine and Pathology, Clin. Chemistry, Internat. Microform Jour. Legal Medicine, Jour. Analytical Toxicology. 1st lt. U.S. Army, 1942-55. Recipient Widmark award Internat. Coun. Alcohol, Drugs and Traffic Safety, 1980, CIIT award Chem. Industry Inst. Toxicology, 1983, Cert. of Merit Forensic Scis. Found., 1984, Robert F. Borkenstein award Nat. Safety Coun., 1992, Disting. Svc. to Safety award NSC, 1995, Outstanding Contbn. to Clin. Chemistry award Am. Assn. for Clin. Chemistry, 1996; numerous others; named Disting. Alumnus Ohio State U., 1994; Nat. Rsch. Coun. fellow in phys. scis. Ohio State U., 1948-49. Fellow Am. Acad. Forensic Scis. (founding fellow, disting. fellow, past pres., editor procs., Award of Merit 1980, Rolla N. Harger award 1983), Am. Inst. Chemists (life), Assn. Clin. Scientists (emeritus), Am. Coll. Forensic Examiners (life, Golden Eagle award 1996); mem. AMA, Am. Chem. Soc. (sr., emeritus mem. com. clin. chemistry), Am. Conf. Govtl. Indsl. Hygienists (emeritus), Am. Assn. Clin. Chemistry (emeritus; past pres., chmn. com. constitution & bylaws, assn. parliamentarian, Outstanding Clin. Chemist award Tex. sect. 1981, Past Pres.'s award 1986, Presdl. citation 1992, award for outstanding contbn. to clin. chemistry 1996), Indian Acad. Forensic Scis. (hon. life), Southwestern Assn. Forensic Scientists (charter, emeritus), Internat. Assn. Forensic Toxicologists (founding), Internat. Assn. of Chiefs of Police (life), Internat. Assn. Forensic Scis. (charter), Internat. Soc. Clin. Forensic Medicine (founding), Acad. Clin. Lab. Physicians and Scientists (emeritus), Biomed. Engring. Soc. (founding/emeritus), Rsch. Soc. Alcoholism (emeritus), Soc. Forensic Toxicologists (charter, emeritus), Soc. Toxicology (emeritus), U. Okla. Univ. Club, Ind. Univ. Club, Phi Lambda Upsilon, Sigma Xi. Avocations: horology, photography, music, travel. Office: PO Box 7245 Oklahoma City OK 73153-1245 Office Phone: 405-799-6066. Business E-Mail: kurt-dubowski@ouhsc.edu.

DUBRIN, ANDREW JOHN, organizational behavior management educator, writer; b. NYC, Mar. 3, 1935; s. Albert Edward and Louise Theresa (Walsh) D.; m. Drew, Douglas, Melanie. AB, Hunter Coll., 1956; MS, Purdue U., 1957; PhD, Mich. State U., 1960. Diplomate: Am. Bd. Profl. Psychology; cert. psychologist N.Y. state. Psychologist Data Systems div. IBM, Kingston, N.Y., 1962-63; teaching asst., part-time instr. Purdue U., West Lafayette, Ind., 1956-57; psychol. cons. Clark, Cooper, Field & Wohl, N.Y.C., 1963-64, Rohrer, Hibler & Replogle, N.Y.C., 1964-70, ptnr., 1964-70; assoc. prof. Rochester (N.Y.) Inst. Tech., 1970-72, prof. behavioral sci., 1972—, dept. head mgmt., 1982-84, prof. mgmt., 1984—. Mem. N.Y. State Bd. Psychology, 1979-94; cons. lectr. in field Author: The Practice of Managerial Psychology, 1972, Women in Transition, 1972, The Singles Game, 1973, Fundamentals of Organization Behavior: An Applied Perspective, 1974, Survival in the Sexist Jungle, 1974, The New Husbands and How to Become One, 1976, Casebook of Organizational Behavior, 1979, Human Relations: A Job Oriented Approach, 1978, 8th edit., 2004, Fundamentals of Organizational Behavior: An Applied Perspective, 2d edit., 1978, Winning at Office Politics, 1979, Contemporary Applied Management, 1982, 4th edit., 1994, Essentials of Management, 1986, 7th edit., 2005, The Last Straw, 1987, Human Relations for Career and Personal Success, 3d edit., 1992, 7th edit., 2005, Management and Organization, 1989, 2d edit., 1992, Effective Business Psychology, 1980, 6th edit., 2004, Winning Office Politics: DuBrin's Guide for the '90s, 1990, Bouncing Back: How to Overcome Adversity in the Workplace, 1992, Your Own Worst Enemy: How to Prevent Career Self-Sabotage, 1992, Stand Out! 330 Ways to Gain the Edge with Superiors, Subordinates, Co-workers, and Customers, 1993, Getting It Done: The Transforming Power of Self-Discipline, 1995, The Reengineering Survival Guide, 1995, The Breakthrough Team Player, 1995, Leadership: Research Findings, Practice and Skill, 1995, 98, 2001, 03, Human Relations: Job-Oriented Interpersonal Skills, 2000, 2d edit., 2003, Fundamentals of Organizational Behavior, 1998, 3d edit., 2004, The 10-Min. Guide to Effective Leadership, Personal Magnetism, 1997, Complete Idiot's Guide to Leadership, 1998, 2000, Looking Around Corners, 1999, The Active Manager, 2000. Capt. U.S. Army, 1960-62. Mem. Am. Psychol. Assn., Am. Mgmt. Assn., Acad. of Mgmt. Home: 192 Barclay Square Dr Rochester NY 14618-3140 Office: 192 Barclay Square Dr Rochester NY 14618 Office Phone: 585-442-0484. Personal E-mail: ajdubrin@frontiernet.net. Business E-Mail: ajdbbu@rit.edu.

DUBROFF, HENRY ALLEN, editor, journalist; b. Neptune, N.J., Nov. 28, 1950; s. Sol and Gilda (Burdman) D.; married, 1980 (div. 1986). AB in History and Lit., Lafayette Coll., 1972; MS in Journalism, Columbia U., 1982. Program analyst Dept. Health and Human Svcs., Washington, 1972-73; tchr. English Holyoke (Mass.) St. Sch., 1974-78; employment & tng. program mgr. Knoxville (Tenn.)-Knox CY Community Action, 1978-81; bus. writer, columnist Springfield (Mass.) Newspapers, 1982-85, The Denver Post, 1985-88, bus. editor, 1988-95; editor Denver Bus. Jour., 1995-99; founder, editor, pub. Pacific Coast Bus. Times, 1999—. Contbg. writer CFO Mag., Boston, 1985-90; guest lectr. U. Wis., Madison, Calif. State U., Channel Islands, U. Colo., Denver. Contbr. articles to N.Y. Times, 1982-89. Vol. Russian Resettlement Program Jewish Family & Children's Svcs., Denver, 1989—90; mem. bd. United Way, 2005—; chmn. Santa Barbara County United Way Campaign, 2004—; bd. dirs. Ventura County Econ. Devel. Assn., U. Calif. Santa Barbara Econ. Forecast Project, Ptnrs. in Edn., Santa Barbara, Jewish Fedn. Santa Barbara. Recipient N.Y. Fin. Writers Assn. scholarship, 1982, Morton Margolin prize U. Denver, 1988, Bus. Story of Yr. award AP, 1989, Gen. Excellence award Am. City Bus. Jour., 1996, 97, Human Svc. award Am. Jewish Com., 1999; named Small Bus. Journalist of Yr., L.A. dist. U.S. SBA, 2004. Mem. Soc. Am. Bus. Editors and Writers (past pres., bd. govs., Best in Bus. award 1995, 96, 98, 2000). Avocations: writing, golf, restoring 1975 Porsche. Office: 14 E Carrillo St Ste A Santa Barbara CA 93101 Home (Summer): 1125 Vine St Denver CO 80206 Office Phone: 805-560-6950 222. E-mail: hadubroff@aol.com.

DUBROVIN, VIVIAN, writer; d. Ross Herr and Emilie Robert; m. Kenneth P. Dubrovin, Sept. 5, 1954; children: Kenneth R., Darryl, Diana, Laura, Barbara. BS in Journalism, U. Ill., 1953. Editor Cuneo Press, Chgo., 1953; staff writer US Savings & Loan, Chgo., 1954; editor U. Wis. Press, Madison, 1955—56; freelance writer, 1971—; mng.dir. Storycraft Pub., Masonville, Colo., 1993—, editor, jr. storyteller, 1994—, editor the kids storytelling club website, 1996—. Author: The Magic Bowling Ball, 1974, Rescue On Skies, 1974, Baseball Just For Fun, 1974, The Track Trophy, 1974, A Better Bit and Bridle, 1975, Trailering Troubles, 1975, Open The Gate, 1975, A Chance to Win, 1975, Write Your Own Story, 1984, Running A School Newspaper, 1985, Creative Word Processing, 1987, Guide to Alternative Education and Training, 1988, The ABC's of The New Print Shop, 1990, Storytelling For The Fun of It: A Handbook for Children, 1994 (Pegasus award, 2001), rev. edit., 1999, Create Your Own Storytelling Stories, 1995, Storytelling Adventures: Stories Kids Can Tell, 1997, Tradin' Tales With Grandpa: A Kid's Guide for Intergenerational Storytelling, 2000 (Pegasus award, 2001), Storytelling Discoveries: Favorite Activities for Young Tellers, 2002 (Parents' Choice Recommended award, 2002, Creative Child Mag. Preferred Choice award, 2003), (booklet) How to Write a Handbook for Children, 1994, Opportunities in Writing Fiction for Children, 1994, Opportunities in Writing Nonfiction for Children, 1994, Creating Books for Young Readers, 1999; contbr. articles to mags. Mem.: Soc. Childrens Book Writers and Illustrators, Nat. Storytelling Network. Office: Storycraft Pub PO Box 205 Masonville CO 80541 Business E-Mail: vivian@storycraft.com.

DUBROVSKY, GERTRUDE WISHNICK, journalist, researcher; b. NYC, Mar. 10, 1926; d. Benjamin and Esther Raisa (Katz) Wishnick; m. Jack Dubrovsky, Feb. 24, 1946 (div. Sept. 1975); children: Richard, Steven, Benjamin; m. Sidney Gray, June 13, 1976 (div. June 1997). AB, Georgian Ct. Coll., 1956; MA, Rutgers U., 1959; EdD, Columbia U., 1974. Tchr. Keyport (N.J.) grammar sch., 1956-57, Point Pleasant (N.J.) H.S., 1959-61; asst. prof. Trenton (N.J.) State Coll., 1964-66; program dir. YIVO Inst. for Jewish Rsch., N.Y.C., 1975-81; freelance journalist, writer N.Y. Times, N.Y.C., 1979—; ind. scholar, rschr. Princeton, 1980—; rschr., writer,asst. to pres. Carnegie Found. for the Advancement of Tchg., Princeton, NJ, 1982-85; Yiddish instr. Ctr. Jewish Life Princeton U., 1974-95. Pres. Documentary III, Princeton, 1980—; specialist in field of Am. Jewish rural history. Author: The Land Was Theirs: Jewish Farmers in the Garden State, 1992, Six From Leipzig, 2004; Editor newsletter: Rural Roots: Jewish Farm History, 1988-95; translator: (poems) Kentucky, 1990 (Jewish Book Club selection); prodr., dir. documentary The Land Was Theirs, 1993 (1st Pl. award Berkeley Film Festival, 1994). Mcpl. committeeperson Dem. Party, Princeton, 1980—, chair, 1982-84; mem. Commn. on Aging, Princeton, 1980—, chair, 1991-93 Fellow Meml. Found. for Jewish Culture, 1975, Oxford (Eng.) Ctr. Hebrew and Jewish Studies, 1994; NEH grantee, 1976, 78; fellow, life mem. Clare Hall, Cambridge U., 2000-01. Mem. Assn. for Jewish Studies, Am. Jewish Hist. Soc., Am. Jewish Archives, Princeton Rsch. Forum. Avocations: swimming, walking, bridge, Scrabble, poetry reading. Home and Office: 244 Hawthorne Ave Princeton NJ 08540-3826 Office Phone: 609-924-7527. E-mail: gdubrovsky@aol.com.

DUBROW, HEATHER, literature educator; b. San Antonio, Mar. 5, 1945; d. Hilliard and Helen (Volk) D.; m. Ian Ousby, June 21, 1969 (div. Dec. 1979). BA summa cum laude, Harvard/Radcliffe, 1966; PhD, Harvard U., 1972. Asst. prof. U. Mass., Boston, 1972-73; Leverhulme vis. fellowship U. Kent, Canterbury, Eng., 1973-74; lectr. U. Sussex, Brighton, Eng., 1974-75; from vis. asst. prof. to asst. prof. U. Md., College Park, 1975-80; from assoc. to prof. Carleton Coll., Northfield, Minn., 1980-90; from prof. to John Bascom prof. and Tighe-Evans prof. U. Wis., Madison, 1990—. External rev. team Oberlin Coll., Bryn Mawr Coll. Author: Genre, 1982, Captive Victors, 1987, A Happier Eden, 1990, Echoes of Desire, 1995, Transformation and Repetition, 1997, Shakespeare and Domestic Loss, 1999, Border Crossings, 2001; contbr. articles to profl. jours. Recipient Capt. Jonathan Fay award, Radcliffe Coll., 1966; sr. fellow Nat. Endowment for the Humanities, 1987—88, 2003—04, Guggenheim fellow, 2004. Mem. MLA (mem. editl. bd., exec. coun. 1996-2000), Milton Soc. of Am. (exec. com. 1997-99), Renaissance Soc. Am. (disciplinary rep. 2001-03), Spenser Soc., Phi Beta Kappa. Democrat. Avocations: architecture, art, cooking. Office: U Wis Dept of English 600 N Park St Madison WI 53706-1403 Office Phone: 608-263-2913. Business E-Mail: hdubrow@wisc.edu.

DUBROW, JOHN, artist; b. Salem, Mass., Oct. 14, 1958; s. Jerome David and Sally Ann (Grover) D.; m. Linda M. Morgenstern, July 6, 1986. BFA, San Francisco Art Inst., 1979-80, MFA, 1981-83. Prof. N.Y. Studio School of Drawing, Painting, and Sculpture. One man shows include Forum Gallery, N.Y.C., 1985, 87, 90; exhibited in group shows Am. Acad. Arts and Letters, Nat. Acad. Design, N.Y. Studio School, Hackett Freedman Gallery; represented in public collection Met. Mus. Art, N.Y.C.; permanent collections, Salander-O'Reilly Galleries. Recipient Pollock Krasner Found. award, 1986-87. Office: Forum Gallery 1018 Madison Ave New York NY 10021-0113*

DUBS, GLORIA L., artist, realtor; b. Hammond, Ind. d. Joseph and Mayme Gish; m. Jack H. Dubs, 1951; children: Jack R., David, Gary. BS, Purdue U., 1951. Lic. realtor, travel agt. Realtor Prudential Realty/Northside Realty, Atlanta. Exhibitions include Ocee Art Ctr., Duluth, Ga., 2001, 2002, 2003. Mem.: Ashford Club. Office Phone: 770-605-2046.

DUBUC, CARROLL EDWARD, lawyer; b. Burlington, Vt., May 6, 1933; s. Jerome Joachim and Rose (Bessette) D.; m. Mary Jane Lowe, Aug. 3, 1963; children: Andrew, Steven, Matthew. BS in Acctg., Cornell U., 1955; LLB, Boston Coll., 1962; postgrad., NYU, 1963-64. Bar: N.Y. 1963, D.C. 1972, Va. 1999; U.S. Dist. Ct. (so. and ea. dists.) N.Y. 1964, U.S. Ct. Appeals (2d cir.) 1965, U.S. Supreme Ct. 1970, D.C. 1972, U.S. Ct. Appeals (D.C. cir.) 1972, U.S. Dist. Ct. D.C. 1973, U.S. Ct. Claims 1975, U.S. Ct. Appeals (4th cir.) 1977, U.S. Ct. Appeals (7th cir.) 1984, U.S. Ct. Appeals (9th cir.) 1985, U.S. Ct. Appeals (5th cir.) 1986, U.S. Ct. Appeals (fed. cir.) 1988, U.S. Ct. Internat. Trade 1988, U.S. Ct. Appeals (6th cir.) 1989, Va. 1999; cert. ct. mediator 1998. Assoc. Haight, Gardner, Poor & Havens, N.Y.C., 1962-70, ptnr., 1970-75; resident ptnr. Finley Kumble Wagner Heine Underberg Manley Myerson & Casey, Washington, 1983-87, Laxalt, Washington, Perito & Dubuc, Washington, 1988-90, Washington, Perito & Dubuc, 1990-91; ptnr. Graham & James, 1991-95, of counsel, 1996-98, Cohen Gettings & Dunham, 1998—2003, Dubuc & Assocs. PC, 2003—. Capt. AC USN, 1954-59, Res. 1959-79. Mem.: ABA (vice chmn. ins. com. 1982—84, chmn. aviation and space law com. 1985—86, subcom. aviation ins., subcom. internat. practice 1985—87, vice chmn. alternative resolution com., mktg. legal svcs. com. 1991—92), ATLA, Internat. Soc. Air Safety Investigators, Internat. Bar Assn. (vice chmn. travel and tourism com. 1998—), Def. Rsch. Inst. (chair alternative dispute resolution com. 2003—), Fed. Ins. and Corp. Counsel (chmn. alternative dispute resolution sect. 1996—99, aviation transp. 1996—), Internat. Assn. Def. Counsel (past chmn. alternative dispute resolution com.), Maritime Law Assn. U.S., Fed. Bar Coun., Fed. Cir. Bar Assn., Assn. Bar of City of N.Y. (aeroav. com.), Va. Bar Assn., D.C. Bar Assn., N.Y. State Bar Assn. (past chmn. aviation law com.), French-Am. C. of C., Nat. AEro. Assn., Boston Coll. Law Sch. Alumni (pres. Washington chpt. 1992—96), Naval Aviation Command (vice comdr.), Congrl. Country Club, Internat. Aviation Club, Washington chpt. Aero Club, Wings Club, Cornell Club, Sigma Chi. Office Phone: 703-639-1643. Business E-Mail: dubucpc@vacoxmail.com.

DU BUSKE, LAWRENCE MICHAEL, immunologist, rheumatologist; b. Jersey City, Oct. 16, 1954; BS, Northwestern U., 1976, MD, 1978; diploma (hon.), Polish Allergy Soc., 2001; diploma in medicine (hon.), Crimean Med. U., 2001; diploma (hon.), Belarussian Inst. Epidemiology and Microbiology, Minsk, Belarus, 2001, Ukrainian Med. U., Ukraine, 2001, Russian Fed. Inst. Immunology, Moscow, 2002. Diplomate Am. Bd. Allergy and Immunology, Am. Bd. Internal Medicine, Am. Bd. Rheumatology. Dir. Allergy and Arthritis Family Treatment Ctr., Gardner, Mass., 1984—, Immunology Rsch. Inst. New England, Fitchburg, Mass., 1990—; dir.Immunology Ednl. Inst. New Eng., 1999—2003. Clin. instr. Harvard Med. Sch., Boston, 1984—; co-dir. allergy fellow tng. program Brigham and Women's Hosp., Boston, 1994—98; adv. bd. Hycor Biomedical, Garden Grove, Calif., 1995—97; hon. prof. Crimean Med. U., 2001, Inst. Immunology, Ministry of Health of Russia, Russia, 2002; cons. Schering Plough, Kenilworth, NJ, 1994—, Hoechst Marion Roussel Pharms., Kansas City, Kans., 1995—97, Hycor Biomedical, Garden Grove, 1995—97, Upjohn Pharms., Mich., 1997, Novartis Pharm., East Hanover, NJ, 2002, Aventis Pasteur Inc., Swiftwater, Pa., 2002—, Genentech, San Francisco, 2002—, Allergy Theraputics, 2004—05. Contbg. editor: Asthma & Allergy Procs., 1994—, Jour. Allergy & Clin. Immunology Supplement, 1996—97, Internat. Allergology Rev., 1997—, Internat. Jour. Immune Rehab., 1998—, Am. Jour. Respiratory Medicine, 2001—; mem. editl. bd. Balkan Allergy Jour., 2002—, Allergy, Hypersensitivity, Asthma; contbr. chapters to books, articles Exercise Induced Allergy Syndromes. Fellow: ACAAI, ACR, ACP, Am. Acad. Asthma, Allergy and Immunology (chmn. practice and therapeutics com. 1996—2000, chmn. practice stds. coun. 1999—2000); mem.: Am. Assn. Cert. Allergists (pres.-elect, pres. 2004—05), Alpha Omega Alipha (pres. northwestern chptr. 1977—78). Office: Immunology Rsch Inst New Eng 358 Elm St Gardner MA 01440-3926

DUCANTO, JOSEPH NUNZIO, lawyer, educator; b. Utica, NY, Mar. 18, 1927; s. Joseph and Martha (Purchine) D'Acunto; m. Connie Davis (div. May 1990); children: Anthony D. DuCanto, James C. DuCanto; m. Patricia Naegle, 1995; children: 1 adopted child, William P. Heiman-DuCanto BA, Antioch Coll., 1952; JD, U. Chgo., 1955. Bar: Ill. 1955, U.S. Tax Ct. 1960, U.S. Ct. Mil. Appeals 1960, U.S. Supreme Ct. 1960. Rsch. asst. Law and Behavioral Sci. Rsch. Project U. Chgo., 1955—62; assoc. Cotton, Fruchtman & Watt, Chgo., 1962—80; ptnr. Bentley, Campbell, DuCanto & Silvestri, Chgo., 1962—81; prin. Schiller, DuCanto & Fleck, Ltd., Chgo., 1981—; chmn. bd. Securatex, 1982—. Adj. prof. family law Loyola U., Chgo., 1968—2005, vis. prof., 2003; lectr. on family law, taxation, fin. planning and estate planning in connection with divorce. Author: Tax Aspects of Litigation, 1979; contbr. articles to profl. jours.; editor, pub. Tax, Fin. and Estate Planning Devels. in Connection with Divorce and Family Law, 1970-85. Served with USMCR, 1944-47, PTO, Guam, Iwo Jima, China. Fellow Am. Acad. Matrimonial Lawyers (nat. pres. 1977-79, chmn.-dir. Inst. Matrimonial Law 1976-85); mem. Ill. State Bar Assn. (bd. govs. 1983-89, Laureate 2003), Scribes, Cliff Dwellers Club, Union League Club. Republican. Unitarian Universalist. Office: 200 N LaSalle St 30th Fl Chicago IL 60601-1089 Office Phone: 312-609-5505. Business E-Mail: jducanto@sdflaw.com.

DUCASSE, ALAIN, chef; b. Castelsarrazin, France, Sept. 13, 1956; Trained with Alain Chapel. Chef L'Amandier, Mougins, France, 1980—87; chef, owner Le Louis XV, Hôtel Paris, Monaco, 1987—, Alain Ducasse, Paris, 1997—, Spoon, Food & Wine, Paris, 1998—, Alain Ducasse at the Essex House, NYC, 2000—, MIX, Las Vegas, Beige, Tokyo, 2004—, tamaris, Beirut; chmn. Châteaux et Hôtels Indépendents, 1999; owner La Bastide de Moustiers, France, L'Hostellerie de l'Abbaye de la Celle, L'Andana, Italy, 2004—, Ostape, 2004—. Author: Spoon Cook Book, 2004. Achievements include induction into the James Beard Found. for Alain Ducasse at the Essex House, 2002. Office: Alain Ducasse 155 W 58th St New York NY 10019-1530*

DUCAT, SUZANNE BASHA, communications executive, television producer; b. N.Y.C., Apr. 10, 1953; d. Josef Bert and Ellen Ruth (Wolff) Ducat; m. Stanley M. Cohen, June 26, 1988; 1 child, Hannah Elizabeth. BA, Mount Holyoke Coll., 1975; MA in Comm., U. Pa., 1984. Prodn. asst. Today in Del. WHYY-TV, Wilmington, Del., Phila., 1979-80; rsch. asst. Washington Week in Rev. WETA-TV, Washington, 1981-83, assoc. prodr., 1983-85, prodr., 1986-96, prodr. PBS sp. events coverage, 1987-96, exec.-in-chg. Talking with David Frost, 1990-96, sr. prodr., polit. dir. news and pub. affairs, 1990-96; dir. media rels. The Hawthorn Group, Alexandria, Va., 1996-98; dir. comm. and pub. affairs Coun. for Excellence in Govt., Washington, 1998. Prodr. numerous news spls., documentaries including: Summer of Judgement: The Impeachment Hearings, 1984, On the Air: The United States Senate, 1986, Wartime in Washington, 1985, Dateline Freedom: Civil Rights and the Press, 1988, Caring for Tomorrow's Children, 1989, Headline series, 1989-90, The changing of the Guard, 1993, The Challengers '96: A Washington Week in Review Special, 1995, others. Bd. dirs. Anne Frank House, Washington, 1990—; mem. media adv. com. Inst. for Mental Health, Washington, 1993—, World Child, Inc., Silver Spring, Md., 1996—, Rollingwood Citizens Assn., Chevy Chase, Md., 1996—. Recipient Individual Achievement award (as program rschr.) The Washington Area Emmy awards, 1983 (for Power and the Glory), Silver medal for best analysis, interpretation or commentary Internat. Film and TV Festival of N.Y., 1987, 88, Silver Gavel award (for coverage of Clarence Thomas Confirmation hearings) ABA, 1992, Nat. News and Documentary Emmy awrd NATAS, 1985. Mem. Nat. Press Club. Office: Coun for Excellence in Govt 1301 K St NW Ste 450 West Washington DC 20005 E-mail: sducat@excelgov.org.

DUCATMAN, ALAN MARC, physician; b. Plainfield, N.J., July 19, 1950; s. Fred Paul and Shirley (Buchman) D.; m. Barbara Steinmetz, June 18, 1978; children: Joseph, David, Samuel. BA, Columbia U., N.Y.C., 1972; MSc, CUNY, 1974; MD, Wayne State U., Detroit, 1978. Resident, fellow Mayo Clinic, Rochester, Minn., 1979-82; dir. occupational health Columbia Park Med., Mpls., 1982-83; dir. Environ. Med. Svcs. MIT, 1986-92; prof., dir. Inst. Occupational and Environ. Health W.Va. U., Morgantown, 1992-97, chair dept. cmty. medicine, 1996—. Adj. assoc. prof. Boston U. Sch. Medicine, 1990-92, U. Miss. Sch. Medicine, 1991—; adj. prof. medicine Med. U. S.C., 1994; trustee Am. Bd. Preventive Medicine, 1994—. Contbr. articles to profl. jours. Cmdr. USNR, 1983-86. Fellow ACP, Am. Coll. Occup. and Environ. Medicine (chmn. toxicology com. 1987-92, Adolph G. Kammer Merit Authorship award 1993, Harriet Hardy award 1997). Office: Inst Occupl & Environ Health WVa U/Sch Medicine Morgantown WV 26506-9190 Office Phone: 304-293-3693.

DUCE, ROBERT ARTHUR, atmospheric chemist, oceanographer, educator; b. Midland, Ont., Can., Apr. 9, 1935; s. Leonard Arthur and Irma Harriet (Gynn) D.; m. Mary Elizabeth Untz, June 8, 1968; children: Patricia Jean, David Robert. BA cum laude, Baylor U., 1957; postgrad., U. Colo., 1954; PhD in Inorganic and Nuclear Chemistry, MIT, 1964. Teaching asst. dept. chemistry MIT, Cambridge, Mass., 1961-62, rsch. asst. in geochemistry, 1962-63, USPHS predoctoral fellow in air pollution, 1963-64, rsch. assoc. dept. geology and geophysics, 1964-65; from asst. prof. to assoc. prof. chemistry U. Hawaii, Honolulu, 1965-70; assoc. prof. oceanography U. R.I., Kingston, 1970-73, prof. oceanography, 1973-91, dir. Ctr. for Atmospheric Chemistry Studies, 1981-91, dean Grad. Sch. Oceanography, vice provost marine affairs, 1987-91; prof. oceanography and atmospheric scis. Tex. A&M U., College Station, 1991—2004, disting. prof. oceanography and atmospheric scis., 2004—, dean coll. geosciences and maritime studies, 1991-97. Vis. prof. Inst. Marine Scis., U. Tex., Pt. Aransas, summer 1975, U. East Anglia, Norwich, Eng., 1997-98; vis. scientist aeronomy lab. NOAA Environ. Rsch. Labs., Boulder, Colo., 1977; collaborateur etranger CFR/Nat. Ctr. Sci. Rsch., Gif-sur-Yvette, France, 1976-77; William Evans vis. prof. chemistry U. Otago, Dunedin, New Zealand, 1983; participant disting. lecture series in USSR, U.S.-USSR Joint Working Group on Effects of Marine Pollution,

1974; mem. bd. atmospheric scis. and climate NAS/NRC, 1982-86, 89-93, mem. com. atmospheric chemistry, 1987-90, chmn. com. haze in nat. pks. and wilderness areas, 1990-93; chair NAS/NRC Panel on Global Tropospheric Chemistry, 1982-85; sr. vis. fellow Nat. Environ. Rsch. Coun., Gt. Britain, 1984; mem. UN Group on Experts on the Sci. Aspects of Marine Environ. Protection, 1986—, chmn., 2000-03, vice chmn., 2003—, mem. sci. com. Internat. Geopsphere-Biosphere program bd. govs. Joint Oceanographic Insts., 1987-97, vice chair, 1990-91, Consortium for Oceanographic Rsch. and Edn., 1994-97, vice chair, 1994-96; trustee Univ. Corp. Atmospheric Rsch., 1986-93; mem. exec. com. Ocean Drilling Program, 1987-97; mem. exec. com. Nat. Assn. State Univs. and Land Grant Colls. Bd. Oceans and Atmospheres, 1993-97; mem. adv. com. geosciences NSF, 1994-97; pres. Internat. Assn. of Meteorogy and Atmosphere Scis., 1995-99; vis. pro. environ. scis. U. E. Anglia, Eng., 1997-98; mem. Nat. Sea Grant Review Panel, 2000—; mem. NAS/NRC Ocean Studies Bd., 2001—. Contbr. articles to profl. jours. Capt. USAF, 1957-61. Fellow AAAS (chmn. sect. atmospheric and hydrospheric scis. 1987-88, mem. coun. 1990-93), Am. Meteorol. Soc. (mem. coun. 1988-91), Am. Geophys. Union; mem. ICSU (pres. sci. com. on oceanic rsch. 2000-04, past pres. 2004—), Oceanography Soc. (pres. 1996-98), Am. Chem. Soc. (chmn.-elect Hawaiian sect. 1969), Geochem. Soc., Am. Geol. Inst., Internat. Coun. for Sci., Sigma Xi, Alpha Chi. Avocations: travel, collecting single malt scotch. Home: 4708 Scrimshaw Ln College Station TX 77845-9399 Office: Tex A&M U Dept Oceanography College Station TX 77843-3146 Office Phone: 979-845-5756. Business E-Mail: rduce@ocean.tamu.edu.

DUCH, STEPHEN, corporate financial executive; b. Rochester, NY, Aug. 26, 1952; s. Michal and Johanna (Langer) Duch; m. Kathleen Ann Haberer, June 21, 1980; children: Sarah, Eric. BS, Cornell U., 1974, MBA, 1975. Fin. analyst Chase Manhattan Bank, N.Y.C., 1975-79, fin. mgr. Europe Inst., 1979-81, v.p., fin. mgr. Internat. Inst., 1981-84, v.p., fin. mgr. Global Electronic Banking, 1984-88, v.p., fin. contr. InfoServ Ops. and Sys., 1988-92, v.p., fin. contr. Retail Banking Tech. Svc. Ctr., 1992-93, v.p., product mgr. Bklyn., 1993-2000; product mgr. J.P.Morgan Chase, 2001—02; fin. mgr. Meml. Sloan Kettering Cancer Ctr., 2003—. Avocations: canoeing, nordic skiing, woodworking. Office: Meml SloanKettering Cancer Ctr 633 3d Ave New York NY 10017 Business E-Mail: stephen.duch@duchgroup.biz.

DUCHARME, NANCY SUE, elementary school educator; b. Streator, Ill., June 16, 1964; d. Bernard Paul and Carol Ann Beoletto; m. Leslie D. DuCharme, July 20, 1991; children: Garrett, Elliott. B, Ill. State U., 1986; M, Olivet NAzarene U., 1991. Tchr. jr. high math. Grant Park Elem. Sch., Ill., 1986—87; Montessoir tchr. 2d & 3d grades Kankakee Sch. Dist. #11, 1987—89; tchr. 3d grade Bourbonnais Sch. Dist. #53, 1989—. Mem.: NEA, Bourbonnais Elem. Assn. (bldg. rep.). Avocations: gardening, swimming, reading, hiking, drawing. Office: Vourbonnais Sch Dist #53 321 N Conrent Bourbonnais IL 60914

DUCHENE, TODD MICHAEL, lawyer; b. Akron, Ohio, June 19, 1963; s. Glenn Robert DuChene and Judith Ann (Dipnall) Kehoe; m. Jennifer Lee Belt, May 25, 1990; children: Elizabeth, Margaret, Emily. BA in polit. sci. with honors, Coll. Wooster, 1985; JD, U. Mich., 1988. Bar: Ohio 1988. Assoc. Baker & Hostetler, Cleve., 1985-93; v.p., gen. counsel, asst. sec. Office Max, Inc., Shaker Heights, Ohio, 1994—95, sr. v.p., gen. counsel, sec., 1995—96; v.p., gen. counsel, sec. Fisher Sci. Internat. Inc., Hampton, NH, 1996—. Mem.: New England Law Found., Ohio State Bar Assn. Office: Fisher Sci Internat Inc 1 Liberty Ln Hampton NH 03842*

DUCHIN, PETER OELRICHS, musician; b. N.Y.C., July 28, 1937; s. Edwin Frank and Marjorie (Oelrichs) D.; m. Cheray Zauderer, June 22, 1964 (div. 1982); children: Jason Edwin, Courtnay Oelrichs, Colin Zauderer; m. Brooke Hayward, Dec. 24, 1985. BAU, Yale U., 1958; student polit. scis. and music conservatory, Paris, 1957. Pres. Peter Duchin Orchs., 1963—. Bd. dirs. Chamber Music Soc., Lincoln Ctr., Ballet Theater Found., Citizens Com. for N.Y.C., Inc., N.Y. Found. for the Arts, World Policy Inst., Nat. Jazz Svc. Orgn.; mem. adv. bd. Congl. Arts Caucus Ednl. Program, Planned Parenthood, Musicians Emergency Fund. Mem. Am. Ctr. (bd. dirs.), N.Y. State Coun. on Arts. Clubs: Yale (N.Y.C.); Racquet and Tennis, Century Assn. Office: Peter Duchin Orchs Inc 305 Madison Ave Rm 755 New York NY 10165-0006 Office Phone: 212-972-2260. Personal E-mail: pdomessages@att.net.

DUCHOSSOIS, CRAIG J., manufacturing executive; m. Janet Duchossois; 2 children. BA, MBA, So. Meth. U., Dallas. Joined Duchossois Industries, 1971—, CEO, pres. Elmhurst, Ill. Vice chmn. bd. trustees Ill. Inst. Tech.; chmn. bd. dirs. Thrall Car Mfg. Co.; bd. dirs. Churchill Downs Inc., LaSalle Nat. Bank, Trinity Industries, Inc., 2002—. Trustee Culver Educational Found., Ill. Inst. Tech., Kellogg Grad. Sch. Mgmt., U. of Chicago. Officer USMC, 1968—71. Recipient Disting. Alumni, So. Meth. U., 2002. Office: Duchossois Industries 845 N Larch Ave Elmhurst IL 60126

DUCHOVNY, DAVID, actor; b. Aug. 7, 1960; s. Amram and Meg Duchovny; m. Tea Leoni, May 6, 1997; children: Madeline West, Kyd Miller. Student, Yale U.; grad., Princeton U. Actor: (TV series) Red Shoe Diaries, 1992, The X-Files, 1993—2002 (Golden Globe for best actor in drama series, 1996), Larry Sanders Show, 1996, Fraiser, The Simpsons, Dr. Katz, Professional Therapist; (TV films) Baby Snatcher, 1992; (films) Working Girl, 1988, New Year's Day, 1989, Bad Influence, 1990, Julia Has Two Lovers, 1991, The Rapture, 1991, Don't Tell Mom the Babysitter's Dead, 1991, Venice/Venice, 1992, Ruby, 1992, Chaplin, 1992, Beethoven, 1992, Kalifornia, 1993, Playing God, 1997, The X-Files, 1998, Return to Me, 2000, Evolution, 2001, Full Frontal, 2002, Connie and Carla, 2004; actor, dir., writer: House of D, 2004; actor: (TV series, guest appearance) Twin Peaks, 1990, 1991, (voice) Eek! The Cat, 1995, Duckman, 1996; (TV series) Frasier, 1996; (TV series, guest appearance) Space: Above and Beyond, 1996, (voice) The Simpsons, 1997; (TV series) The Lone Gunmen, 2001, Life with Bonnie, 2002, Sex and the City, 2003. Office: Creative Artists Agy 9830 Wilshire Blvd Beverly Hills CA 90212*

DUCK, PATRICIA MARY, librarian; b. Bklyn., Jan. 22, 1951; d. Warren James and Virginia Susan (Noonan) Johnson; m. John Jacob Duck, Feb. 2, 1973; children: Michael, Jennifer, Matthew. BA, George Washington U., 1974; MLS, U. Pitts., 1980, PhD in Libr. Sci., 1992. Libr., serials cataloger U. Pitts., 1980-84, libr., coord., 1984-85, libr., project supr., 1985-86; dir. libr. U. Pitts. Greensburg, 1986—. Facilitator region 10 Gov.'s Conf. Libr. and Info. Svcs., Pitts., 1990. Contbr. articles to profl. jours. Leader troop 47 Girl Scouts U.S., 1990-91; trustee Penn Area Libr., Level Green, Pa., 1989-91. Mem. ALA, Beta Phi Mu. E-mail: pmd1@pitt.edu Avocation: art. Office: U Pitts Greensburg Campus 1150 Mount Pleasant Rd Greensburg PA 15601-5860

DUCK, VAUGHN MICHAEL, software company executive; b. Rockford, Ill., Sept. 13, 1943; s. Vaughn Victor and Virginia Stella (Cielisz) D.; m. Sandra Jean Carlstrom, Jan. 27, 1968; children: Kirsten Lee, Kendra Edith. Assocs., Inst. Automation, Chgo., 1963. Dir. MIS G.C. Electronics, Rockford, 1964-67; gen. mgr., v.p. Computer Svcs. Ctr., Rockford, 1968-79; pres. Integrated Micro Systems, Rockford, 1980-82, Govtl. Data Systems, Rockford, 1983-85; exec. v.p. Bus. Records Corp., Dallas, 1986-87; pres. Interactive Software Products, Rockford, 1988—; v.p. Tyler Techs., Inc., Dallas, 2000—. Developer: (software) Election Mgmt. System, 1984, Retail Operations System Exec., Rose, 1988, Unix Retail POS System, UX/POS, 1991; Inventor election ballot processor, PEPS, 1980. Republican. Avocations: golf, reading, travel. Office: Interactive Software Products 2704 Broadway Rockford IL 61108-5800

DUCKER, BRUCE, writer, lawyer; b. N.Y.C., Aug. 10, 1938; s. Allen and Lillian Ducker; m. Jaren Jones, Sept. 1, 1962; children: Foster, Penelope, John. AB, Dartmouth Coll., 1960; MA, Columbia U., 1963, LLB, 1964. Bar: Colo. 1964, U.S. Dist. Ct. Colo. 1964, U.S. Ct. Appeals (10th cir.) 1964. Gen. counsel Great Western United Corp., Denver, 1972-73; pres., chmn. bd. dirs. Great Western Cities Inc., Denver, 1974-75; pres. Ducker, Montgomery, Aronstein & Bess P.C., Denver, 1979—97, of counsel, 1998—. Author: (novels) Rule by Proxy, 1976, Failure at the Mission Trust, 1986, Bankroll, 1989, Marital Assets, 1993, Lead Us Not Into Penn Station, 1994, Bloodlines, 2000, Mooney in Flight, 2003; contbr. articles, poetry and short stories to lit. jours. Former trustee Legal Aid Found. of Colo., Denver Symphony Assn., Kent Denver Country Day Sch. Recipient Colo. Book award, Macallan Story Prize. Mem. ABA, PEN/America, Authors' Guild, Poetry Soc. Am., Denver Club, Cactus Club. Office: Ducker Montgomery et al 1560 Broadway Ste 1400 Denver CO 80202-5151 Office Phone: 303-861-2828. Business E-Mail: bducker@duckerlaw.com.

DUCKETT, CATHERINE NATALIA, entomologist, educator; b. Ithaca, N.Y., 1961; m. David Hunter, Mar. 18, 2000. BA with honors, Brown Univ., 1983; PhD, Cornell U., 1993. Fellow Fulbright-Hayes /USIA, Maracay, Venezuela, 1989—90; postdoctoral fellow Mombusho/Toyama (Japan) U./NSF, 1993; assoc. prof. biology U. P.R., Rio Piedras, San Juan, 1994—2002; NSF advance fellow Smithsonian Instn., Washington, 2002—. Contbr. articles to profl. jours. Grantee, NSF, 1999—2002; Rsch. Planning grantee, 1997—98. Mem.: Entomol. Soc. Am., Zootaxa (Coleoptera co-editor 2005), N.Y. Entomol. Soc. (life). Achievements include research in phylogenetic analysis of the flea beeltes (Coleoptera:Chrysomelidae). Avocations: gardening, cooking, travel. Office: Smithsonian Instn Natural History 10th and Constitution Ave Washington DC 20560 Personal E-mail: catherineduckett@hotmail.com. E-mail: duckette@siu.edu.

DUCKETT, COLIN STEPHEN, molecular biologist; b. Surbiton, Surrey, Eng., July 11, 1965; s. Thomas Hugh and Joan Mary Duckett; m. Susan E. Lyons, June 12, 1994; children: Peter B., Rachel A. BSc in Molecular Biology with honors, U. London, Queen Mary Coll., 1989; PhD in Biochemistry, U. London, St. George's Hosp., 1993. Sr. investigator NIH, Bethesda, Md., 1997—2001; assoc. prof. depts. pathology and internal medicine U. Mich., Ann Arbor, 2002—. Office: U Mich 1301 Catherine Med Sci I Rm 5315 Ann Arbor MI 48109-0602 Office Phone: 1-734-615-6414.

DUCKETT, LILA WHEELER, retired language educator, writer; b. N.Y.C., Jan. 6, 1935; d. DePriest Edward Wheeler and Lila Sylvia Hollowell; m. Philip Chandler Duckett, June 13, 1959; children: John Chandler, Dawn Christine, Anais Court. BS in Edn., CCNY, 1958. Tchr. N.Y. Pub. Schs., N.Y.C., 1958—65; reading tchr. Beersley Reading Academy, Flushing, NY, 1965—86; ESL tchr. Japanese Sch. of N.Y., Flushing, 1986—90, Greenwich (Conn.) Japanese Sch., 1990—96. Lectr. in field; coord. Freedom Schs., Jamaica, NY. Author: Sun Soul Child Speaks. Panelist Queens Coun.on the Arts, 1993, 1994; pres. Fresh Meadows Poets, Flushing, 1995—97, chmn. judging com., 1992—94; judge First Poet Laureate of Queens, 1995; mistress of ceremonies, presenter awards Fresh Meadows Poets 18th Open Poetry Contest for Teens, 2004. Mem.: Svcs. to Parents of Exceptional Asian Children. Avocations: writing, poetry, jewelry design. Home: 196 05 B 65th Crescent Fresh Meadows NY 11365 Personal E-mail: sunsoulchild@juno.com.

DUCKRO, REBECCA SUE, literature educator; b. Sidney, Ohio, July 11, 1942; d. Jack Byron Duckro, Virginia Mae (Wical) Duckro. BS in Edn., Bowling Green U., 1969, MS in Edn., 1984. Tchr. English Bowling Green Jr. H.S., Bowling Green, Ohio, 1969—79; tchr. English, writing Bowling Green H.S., Bowling Green, 1979—97. Cons. Bowling Green U., 1982—90. Author: The Last Coffin, 2001; author: (poetry) The Cup, 1980. Vol. Wood Ct. Humane Soc., Bowling Green, 1993, Am. Heart Assn., Bowling Green, 1994, Am. Cancer Soc., Bowling Green, 1995. Scholar Jennings, 1978. Mem.: Mystery Writers Am., Nature Conservancy. Democrat. Lutheran. Avocations: fishing, travel, writing. Home: 54 Aynsley Lndg Bowling Green OH 43402-9381 Home Fax: rduckro@wcnet.org.

DUCKWORTH, JERRELL JAMES, electrical engineer; b. Ft. Payne, Ala., July 22, 1940; s. James K. and Maggie Lee (Hartline) D.; m. Yvonne Cheryl Jones, Nov. 2, 1974; one child, Shelby Elizabeth. AAS in Elec. Engring., DeVry Inst. Tech., 1963. Gen. engr. McDonnell Aircraft Corp., St. Louis, 1963-66; sr. assoc. engr. IBM Corp. Space Sys. Ctr., Huntsville, Ala., 1966-72; chief engr. Electric Sys. Inc., Chattanooga, 1972-80; dir. elec. engring. Chattanooga Corp., 1980-91; dir. engring. Chattanooga Group Inc., 1991-95; v.p. of engring. GoPro, Inc., Hendersonville, Tenn., 1995-2000; program mgr. ISC, Inc., Hendersonville, 2000—01; cons., 2001—. Served with US Army, 1958-61. Recipient Apollo 8 medallion NASA, 1968, Apollo 11 medallion, 1969, Apollo Achievement award, 1970. Mem. IEEE, Engring. Medicine Biology Soc., Assn. Advancement Med. Instrumentation, Instrument Soc. Am., US Space Found. Mem. Ch. of God. Achievements include development of the Recent History Storage Unit used to locate both hardware and software faults, AC and DC drive systems and a therapeutic ultrasound generator with a multiple-frequency transducer. Home and Office: 7916 Shallowmeade Ln Chattanooga TN 37421-1930 E-mail: jduckworth6@comcast.net.

DUCKWORTH, TARA ANN, insurance company executive; b. Seattle, June 7, 1956; d. Leonard Douglas and Audrey Lee (Limbeck) Hill; m. Mark L. Duckworth, May 16, 1981; children: Harrison Lee III, Andrew James, Kathryn Anne. AAS, Highline C.C., Seattle, 1976. From acctg. clk. to info. sys. supr. SAFECO Ins. Co., Seattle, 1977-90, rate sys. mgr., 1990-94; sys. mgr. SAFECO Mut. Funds, SAFECO Credit, PNMR, Seattle, 1994-97, mktg. comm. and incentives, quality assurance mgr., 1997-98, dir. comml. lines sys., 1998—2001, dir. quality assurance, 2001—03, dir. personal policy sys., 2003—. Mem. tech adv. com. for the computer info. svcs. program North Seattle Community Coll., 1984-96, chairperson tech. adv. com., 1988-90. Mem. Star Lake Improvement Club, 1988-94; mem. fellowship com. St. Lukes Luth. Ch., 1986—; mem. Boy Scouts Am., 1996-2003. Mem. NAFE, Nat. Assn. for Ins. Women, Soc. for State Filers, Nat. PTA. Office: SAFECO Ins Co Safeco Plz Seattle WA 98185-0001

DUCKWORTH, WINSTON HOWARD, retired ceramics engineer; b. Greenfield, Ohio, Oct. 15, 1918; s. Benton Raymond and Carrie Lois (Schrock) D.; m. Clara Elizabeth Ayres, Dec. 15, 1941 (dec. July 1999); children— Winston (dec.), Christopher. BChemE, Ohio State U., 1940, MS, 1941. Registered profl. engr., Ohio. With Battelle Meml. Inst., Columbus, Ohio, 1946-94, research engr., 1946-48, asst. chief ceramic research, 1948-52, chief ceramic research, 1952-66, fellow, 1966—; dir. Battelle Meml. Inst. (Def. Ceramic Info. Center), 1967-71, mem. research council, 1979-85. Mem. Engrs. Joint Council, 1968-78, trustee, 1975-77 Author: Engineering Properties of Ceramics; also numerous articles. With AUS, 1941-46; lt. col. USAF; Ret. Fellow Am. Ceramic Soc. (Cramer award 1974, trustee 1968-74, v.p. 1976, disting. life mem. 1985); mem. Nat. Inst. Ceramic Engrs. (pres. 1964, trustee 1963-74, permanent sec. 1978-91, Greaves-Walker award 1987), Can. Ceramic Soc., AAAS, Ohio Acad. Sci., Keramos, Sigma Xi. Home: 63 Brevoort Rd Columbus OH 43214-3823 Office Phone: 614-267-6502.

DUDA, JOHN LARRY, chemical engineering educator; b. Donora, Pa., May 11, 1936; s. John Jr. and Nellie (Tihanski) D.; m. Margaret K. Barbalich, Jan. 27, 1962; children: John Eric, David Andrew, Paul Laurence, Laura Margaret. BSChemE, Case Inst. Tech., Cleve., 1958; MSChemE, U. Del., 1961, PhD in Chem. Engring., 1963. Chem. engr. Dow Chem. Co., Midland, Mich., 1963-64, rsch. engr., 1964-69, sr. rsch. engr., 1969-71; assoc. prof. chem. engring. Pa. State U., University Park, 1971-75, prof., 1975—, head dept., 1983-2000. Contbr. articles to profl. jours. Fellow AIChE (co-recipient William H. Walker award 1981, Charles Stine award 1989, dir. materials divsn. 1990—, mem. coun. 1996—, dir. nat. 1996—); mem. Am. Chem. Soc. (E.V. Murphree award, 2000), Am. Soc. Engring. Edn. (Lectureship award 1989, NAE (W.K. Lewis award 1994), Soc. Petroleum Engrs., Soc. Plastic Engrs., Soc. Tribology and Lubrication Engrs. Home: 602 Holmes St State College PA 16803-3619 Office: Pa State U Dept Chem Engring 160 Fenske Lab University Park PA 16802-4400 Office Phone: 814-865-1640. Business E-Mail: jld@psu.edu.

DUDA, RICHARD FRANK, architect, engineering executive; b. New York, Sept. 23, 1923; s. Frank and Emma Louise Duda; m. Wynema Jane Bond, May 3, 1945 (dec. Jan. 2001); children: Wynema Jane, Richard Frank, Lesley June, Desiree Joan. Cert. in Meteorology, NYU, 1944; BS in Chem. Engring., Rensselaer Poly. Inst., 1948. Registered profl. engr., NY. Project engr. Kellex-Vitro Engring. Co., NYC, 1948-54; project mgr. Vitro Engring. Co., NYC, 1954-62, chief process engr., mgr. chem. programs, 1962-67; project mgr. Parsons-Jurden, NYC, 1967-68; project dir. Nuc. Materials and Equipment Co., Apollo, Pa., 1968-70; mgr. facilities design and constrn. nuc. fuel divsn. Westinghouse Power Sys., Monroeville, Pa., 1970-73, engring. mgr. Recycle Fuels Group, nuc. fuel divsn., 1973—79, mgr. fuel cycle planning Advanced Energy Sys. divsn., 1980-84; cons. Fuel Cycle Svc. Inc., Greensburg, Pa., 1984-85; project mgr. Ralph M. Parsons Co., Pasadena, Calif., 1985-90, v.p., 1990-94; cons. Westinghouse-Savannah River, Aiken, SC, 1994-99, SC&A Inc., McLean, Va., 1994-99. Liaison chmn. industry interface State Dept. and Arms Control Agy., 1983-84; nuclear industry expert US Internat. Nuclear Fuel Cycle Evaln. Asst. scoutmaster Boy Scouts Am., Paramus, NJ, 1960-62, cubmaster, 1960. 1st lt. USAF, 1943-46. Mem. ASTM, Am. Nuc. Soc. (mem. com. 1981-82, mem. std. N287 cirteria for design of mixed oxide fuel plants com. 1982-83, mem. com. fuel cycle and waste mgmt. divsn. 1982-84, tech. reviewer Nuc. Tech. 1983-85), ASTM (chmn. std. E909-83 1983), Inst. Nuc. Materials Mgmt. (mem. exec. com. 1983-84, chmn. sub-com. govt. liason 1984) Republican. Presbyterian. Achievements include project engineering for 1st Pu reprocessing plant, for first nerve gas plant, for many first-of-a-kind plants. Avocations: gardening, reading. Home: 3822 Coconut Palm Cir Oviedo FL 32765

DUDAREV, ARTEM, physicist; b. Donetsk, Ukraine, Aug. 7, 1978; BSc, Moscow Inst. Physics Tech., 1999. Grad. rsch. asst. U. Tex. Austin, 1999—. Achievements include research in Research in quantum dynamics of ultracold atoms. Avocations: swimming, photography. Office Phone: 1-512-475-6770.

DUDAS, JONATHAN W., federal agency administrator; married; 4 children. BS summa cum laude, U. Ill.; JD with honors, U. Chgo. Bar: Ill., U.S. Dist. Ct. Ill. (no. dist.). Atty. Neal Gerber & Eisenberg; counsel to subcommitte on Courts and Intellectual Property U.S. Ho. of Reps., Washington, dep. gen. counsel com. on judiciary, sr. floor asst. Office of Speaker; dep. under sec. Intellectual Property US Dept. Commerce, Washington, 2002—04, dep. dir. U.S. Patent and Trademark Office, 2002—04, under sec. for intellectual property, 2004—, dir. U.S. Patent and Trademark Office, 2004—. Office: US Dept Commerce Crystal Park Bldg 2 2121 Crystal Dr Rm 906 Arlington VA 22202 Office Phone: 703-305-8600.*

DUDDEN, ALEXIS, history professor; b. Bryn Mawr, Pa., May 26, 1969; d. Arthur Power and Adrianne Onderdonk Dudden; m. Robert Julian Gay, May 29, 2004; 1 child, Julian Onderdont Gay. BA, Columbia U., 1991; MA, U. Chgo., 1993, PhD, 1998. Asst. prof. Conn. Coll., New London, Conn., 1998—2004, assoc. prof., 2004—. Author: Japan's Colonization of Korea, 2004. Recipient Fulbright award, Seoul, 2002—03, Tokyo, 1995—96, ACLS award, 2001, Japan Found. award, 2001—02. Mem.: Assn. Asian Studies, Am. Hist. Assn. Democrat. Office: Conn Coll 270 Mohegan Ave New London CT 06320

DUDDEN, ARTHUR POWER, historian, educator; b. Cleve., Oct. 26, 1921; s. Arthur Clifford and Kathleen (Bray) D.; m. Adrianne Churchill Onderdonk, June 5, 1965; 1 child, Alexis Dudden; children by previous marriage: Kathleen Dudden Rowlands, Candace L. Dudden (Schweitzer). AB, Wayne State U., 1942; A.M., U. Mich., 1947, PhD, 1950. Faculty Bryn Mawr Coll., 1950—, prof. history, 1965-92, Fairbank prof. humanities, 1989-92, Katharine E. McBride prof. history, 1992-95, 98-99, prof. emeritus history and Fairbank prof. emeritus humanities, 1992—; rsch. prof., 2004—. Instr. CCNY, summer 1950; vis. asst. prof. Am. civilization U. Pa., 1953-54, ednl. coord. spl. program Am. civilization, 1956, mem. faculty Inst. Humanistic Studies for Execs., 1953-59, vis. assoc. prof. history, summers, 1958, 62-65, vis. prof. history, 1965-68; vis. assoc. prof. Princeton (N.J.) U., 1958-59, Haverford Coll., 1962-63; vis. prof. Trinity Coll., summer 1965; cons. Peace Corps, 1962-66; mem. Bicentennial Com. on Internat. Confs. of Americanists, 1973-76; founding pres. Fulbright Assn. of Alumni, 1976—, exec. dir., 1980-84; cons. Nat. Archives, 1993-95; adj. prof. history Lehigh U., 1993-95. Author: Teachers Manual to the American Republic, vols. I and II, 1959, 60, 70, Understanding the American Republic, vols. I and II, 1961, 70, Objective Tests, The American Republic, 1962, The Assault of Laughter, 1962, The United States of America: A Syllabus of American Studies, 2 vols, 1963, The Instructor's Guide to the United States, 3d edit, 1972, The Student's Guide to the United States, 2d edit, 1967, Joseph Fels and the Single Tax Movement, 1971, Pardon Us, Mr. President!, 1975, The Fulbright Experience, 1946-1986, 1987, American Humor, 1987, The American Pacific, 1992, paperback edit., 1993; editor: Woodrow Wilson and the World of Today, 1957, The Logbook of the Captain's Clerk, 1995; compiler: International Directory of Specialists in American Studies, 1975; contbr. Ency. Am. Social History, 1993, Ency. U.S. Fgn. Rels., 1997, American Empire in the Pacific, 2004. Served with USNR, 1942-45. Sr. Fulbright scholar Denmark, 1959-60 and West Europe, 1992. Mem. Fellows Am. Studies (sec.-treas. 1957-59, pres. 1960-61), Am. Studies Assn. (treas. 1968, 72, exec. sec. 1969-72, Bode-Pearson prize 1991), Am. Hist. Assn., Orgn. Am. Historians (local arrangements chmn. Phila. 1969), Harriton Assn. (bd. dirs. 1962—), Hist. Soc. of Pa. (trustee 1993-99). Home: 829 Old Gulph Rd Bryn Mawr PA 19010-2910 Office Phone: 610-525-6584. Personal E-mail: adudden@brynmawr.edu.

DUDDLES, CHARLES WELLER, food company executive; b. Cadillac, Mich., Mar. 31, 1940; s. Dwight Irving and Bertha (Taylor) D.; m. Judith Marie Robinson, June 23, 1962; children: Paul, Steven, Lisa. BS, Ferris State U., 1961. C.P.A. Mich., Mo. Audit mgr. Price Waterhouse & Co., Battle Creek, Mich., 1961-72; mgr. gen. acctg. Ralston Purina Co., St. Louis, 1973-77, dir. spl. acctg. svcs., 1977-79; v.p., contr. Jack in the Box, Inc., San Diego, 1979-81; sr. v.p. fin. and adminstrn., CFO Foodmaker, Inc., San Diego, 1981-87, sr. v.p., CFO, 1988, exec. v.p., CFO, chief adminstrv. officer, dir., 1988—. Chmn. ARC, San Diego; bd. dirs. Imperial County. Mem. Fin. Execs. Inst., Nat. Assn. Accts., Am. Inst. C.P.A.s Lodges: Rotary (San Diego). Republican. Presbyterian. Office: Jack in the Box Inc 9330 Balboa Ave San Diego CA 92123-1516

DUDEK, RICHARD ALBERT, engineering educator; b. Clarkson, Nebr., Sept. 3, 1926; s. Emil E. and Jennie (Indra) D.; m. Helen M. Staver, Dec. 19, 1954; children: Richard Emil, Rustin Max. BS in Mech. Engring., U. Nebr., 1950; MS in Indsl. Engring., U. Iowa, 1951, PhD, 1956. Plant indsl. engr. Fairmont Foods Co., Sioux City, Iowa, 1951-52, divsn. indsl. engr. Omaha, 1952-53; research asst. U. Iowa, 1953-54; asst. prof. mech. engring. U. Nebr., 1954-56; research assoc. Sch. of Health Professions, also asso. prof. indsl. engring. U. Pitts., 1956-58; prof., head dept. indsl. engring. Tex. Tech U., Lubbock, 1958-86; dir. Ctr. of Biotech. and Human Performance, 1969-74, P.W. Horn prof., 1970-92, P.W. Horn prof. emeritus, 1992—. Tech. cons. industry, instns., religious orgns., hosps., 1951—; instr. TV courses; dir. Found. Internat. Rsch. and Devel., Lubbock, 1960-65, MASET, Inc., Lubbock, 1974-85, Jay Bee Mfg. Inc., Tyler, Tex., 1984-86, Cellular Tech., Inc., Lubbock, 1984-88, Rowden Gas Inc., Lubbock, 1986-92, Sone Energy, Inc., Dallas, 1988-94. Mem. editl. bd. Engring. Costs and Prodn. Econs., 1980-94; contbr. articles to profl. jours. Bd. dirs. South Plains chpt. Muscular Dystrophy Assn. Am., 1966-76, campaign chmn., 1968. Recipient Faculty Recognition award, 1978, Disting. Scientist award Achievement Rewards for Coll. Scientists, 1984, award of Excellence Halliburton Edn. Found., 1987; named South Plains Engr. of Yr. Tex. Soc. Profl. Engrs., 1986. Fellow Am. Inst. Indsl. Engrs. (pres. Great Plains chpt. 1960-61, chmn. nat. student chpt. 1961-63, ECPD guidance rep. 1965-68, research com. 1967-69, regional v.p. 1969-71, Appreciation award 1970, spl. service award 1971); mem. Council Indsl. Engring. Acad. Dept. Heads (asst. sec. 1980, sec. 1981-82, vice chmn. 1982-83, chmn. 1983-84), Am. Soc. Engring. Edn. (editor indsl. engring. div. 1965-66, sec. indsl. engring. div. 1966-67, vice chmn. 1967-68, chmn. 1968-69, chmn. planning com. of council of tech. divs. 1970-71, sec. council 1972-73), Inst. Mgmt. Sci., ASME, Human Factors Soc., Tech. Assessment

Soc., Sigma Xi (pres. Tex. Tech. chpt. 1971-72), Tex. Tech. Acad. Indsl. Engrs., Phi Kappa Phi (chpt. pres. 1967), Pi Mu Epsilon, Pi Tau Sigma, Alpha Pi Mu, Tau Beta Pi, Phi Beta Delta. Home: 3707 46th St Lubbock TX 79413-3446 E-mail: kgric@ttacs.ttu.edu.

DUDERSTADT, JAMES JOHNSON, academic administrator, engineering educator; b. Ft. Madison, Iowa, Dec. 5, 1942; s. Mack Henry and Katharine Sydney (Johnson) D.; m. Anne Marie, June 24, 1964; children: Susan Kay, Katharine Anne. B in Engrng. with highest honors, Yale U., 1964; MS in Engrng. Sci, Calif. Inst. Tech., 1965, PhD in Engrng. Sci. and Physics, 1967. From asst. prof. nuclear engrng. to pres. U. Mich., 1969—88, pres. univ., 1988—96, pres. emeritus, prof. sci. engrng., 1996—. Dir. Millennium Project, 1996—. AEC fellow, 1964-68; recipient E. O. Lawrence award U.S. Dept. Energy, 1986, Nat. medal of Tech., 1991; named Nat. Engr. of Yr., NSPE, 1991. Fellow Am. Nuclear Soc. (Mark Mills award 1968, Arthur Holly Compton award 1985); mem. NAE (coun.), Am. Phys. Soc., Nat. Sci. Bd. (chair 1991-94), Am. Acad. Arts & Scis., Sigma Xi, Tau Beta Pi, Phi Beta Kappa. Office Phone: 734-647-7300. Business E-Mail: jjd@umich.edu.

DUDEWICZ, EDWARD JOHN, statistician, educator; b. N.Y.C., Apr. 24, 1942; s. Edward George and Adele (Drula) D.; m. Patricia Anne Scott, July 6, 1963; children: Douglas, Robert, Carolyn. SB, MIT, 1963; MS, Cornell U., 1966, PhD, 1969. Engrng. rsch. asst. AVCO Rsch. and Advanced Devel., 1962; asst. engr. AVCO Corp., Wilmington, Mass., 1963; asst. prof. stats. U. Rochester, 1967-72, asst. prof. biostats., 1971-72; assoc. prof. stats. Ohio State U., 1972-77, prof., 1977-82, chmn. grad. com. stats. and biostats., 1973-75, 78-80; prof. dept. math. Syracuse (N.Y.) U., 1982—, chmn. univ. stats. council, 1982—. Chief statistician NIH Resource for Multi-Nuclei Nuclear Magnetic Resonance and Data Processing, 1984-87; vis scholar, vis. assoc. prof. Stanford U., 1976; vis. prof. U. Louvain, Belgium, 1979, 81, 85-86, 93-94; vis. prof. faculty sci. Sci. U. Tokyo, 1989, 93; vis. Disting. prof. Clemson U., 1991; prof. titular exclusiva Nat. U. Comahue, Argentina, 1994; prof. postgrad. seminar Nat. U. Tucuman, Argentina, 1994; external PhD examiner Indian Inst. Tech., 1989-91, 2003, Panjab U., Chandigarh, India, 1989, 94, Cath. U. Brabant, Netherlands, 1990; co-organizer confs.; NSF Ala. EPSCoR lectr., 1994; external project dir. Nat. U. Comahue, Argentina, 1994-98; keynote spkr. at confs. Author: Introduction to Statistics and Probability, 1976, Solutions in Statistics and Probability, 1980, 2d edit., 1993, The Handbook of Random Number Generation and Testing, 1981, The Complete Categorized Guide to Statistical Selection and Ranking Procedures, 1982; Modern Design and Analysis of Discrete-Event Computer Simulations, 1985, Modern Mathematical Statistics, 1988, Modern Elementary Probability and Statistics, With Statistical Programming in SAS, MINITAB & BMDP, 1989, Modern Statistical, Systems, and GPSS Simulation: The First Course, 1991, 2d edit., 1999, Fitting Statistical Distributions: The Generalized Lambda Distribution and Generalized Bootstrap Methods, 2000; editor Statis. Theory and Method Abstracts, 1975-81, Am. Soc. Quality Basic References in Quality Control: Statis. Techniques, 1975-80, Am. Jour. Math. and Mgmt. Scis, 1979—, Stats. and Decisions, An Internat. Math. Jour. for Stochastic Methods and Models, 1982-2002, Info. Sys. Frontiers, 1998—; contbr. articles to profl. jours. Recipient Jacob Wolfowitz prize, 1984, chancellor's citation Syracuse U., 1985, Thomas L. Saaty prize for applied advances, 1990, 99, Seal of Banares Hindu U., 1997; NSF fellow, 1966-67; grantee Office Naval Rsch., 1967-72, 79-82, U.S. Army, 1972-74, NATO, 1978-86, 93—, Nat. Cancer Inst., 1979-83, NSF, 1989-90; Fulbright scholar; holder Internat. Francqui chair in exact scis., 1999. Fellow AAAS, N.Y. Acad. Scis., Inst. Math. Stats., Am. Statis. Assn., Am. Soc. Quality Control (Jack Youden prize 1981, Testimonial award 2001); mem. AAUP, Internat. Statis. Inst., Math. Assn. Am., Japan Statis. Soc., Sigma Xi (rsch. award Ohio State U. chpt. 1977), Phi Kappa Phi. Office: Syracuse Univ 215 Carnegie Hall Dept Math Syracuse NY 13244-1150 *When searching to make significant contributions to the theory of the field of mathematical statistics, look among the ideas and principles which are "self-evident" and accepted; there a wealth of substantial improvement is possible.*

DUDGEON, RALPH T., music educator; b. McKeesport, Pa., Nov. 8, 1948; s. Ralph S. and Genevieve M. Dudgeon; m. Virginia Britten Dudgeon, Apr. 15, 1973; children: Miles G., Calder M. BA in music edn., San Diego State U., 1970, MA in trumpet performance, 1972; PhD in musicology, U. Calif., 1980. Music tchr. San Dieguito HS, Encinitas, Calif., 1971—74; trumpet instr. Point Loma Coll., San Diego, 1976—77; dir., early music ensemble Mira Costa Coll., Oceanside, Calif., 1976—77; music dept. chair Torrey Pines HS, Del Mar, Calif., 1974—81; asst. prof. music U. Tex., Dallas, 1981—85; assoc. prof. music SUNY, NY, 1985—93; acting dir. Streitwieser Found. Trumpet Mus., Pottstown, Pa., 1993—94; affiliate artist Syracuse U., NY, 1998—99; chair Cortland Coll., Dept. Performing Arts, NY, 1997—2000; prof. music SUNY, 1994—. Contbr. articles various profl. jours. Recipient Chancellor's Rsch. Recognition award, 2005; European Union and German Gov. grant, Studie alter Handwerkstechniken anhand der, Indivdual Devel. Awards Program grant, State of NY, 2002, Mus. Assessment Program grant, Am. Assn. of Mus., 1994, Crystal Trust grant, Adminstrn. Streitwieser Found., 1993—94. Mem.: Internat. Trumpet Guild, Hist. Brass Soc., Coll. Music Soc., Am. Musicological Soc., Am. Musical Instruct Soc., Am. Fed. Musicians, Phi Kappa Phi. Democrat. Cath. Home: 5745 US Rt 11 Homer NY 13077 Office: State U of NY Cortland Box 2000 Homer NY 13077 Office Phone: 607-753-5721. Office Fax: 607-753-5728. E-mail: dudgeonr@cortland.edu.

DUDHIA, JIMY, atmospheric scientist; b. London, Sept. 20, 1957; s. Maneklal Laxmanbhai and Armi Sointu Haijele Dudhia. BSc with Honors, Imperial Coll., London U., 1979, MSc in Atmospheric Physics and Dynamics, 1980, PhD, 1984. Rsch. asst. Imperial Coll., London, 1984—85; rsch. assoc. Pa. State U., State Coll., 1985—89; vis. scientist Nat. Ctr. for Atmospheric Rsch., Boulder, Colo., 1989—93, assoc. scientist, 1993, project scientist, 1993—. Fellow: Royal Meteorol. Soc.; mem.: Am. Meteorol. Soc. Achievements include development of high-resolution numerical weather prediction models. Office: Nat Ctr for Atmospheric Rsch PO Box 3000 Boulder CO 80307-3000 Personal E-mail: dudhia@msn.com. Business E-Mail: dudhia@ucar.edu.

DUDICK, MICHAEL JOSEPH, retired bishop; b. St. Clair, Pa., Feb. 24, 1917; s. John and Mary (Jurick) D. BA, Ill. Benedictine Coll., Lisle, 1943; postgrad., St. Procopius Sem., Lisle, 1943—45; HHD (hon.), Kings Coll., 1987; DD (hon.), Scranton U., 1989. Ordained priest Roman Cath. Ch., 1945. Vice chancellor Exarchate of Pitts., 1946—55; chancellor Diocese of Passaic, NJ, 1963—68, bishop, 1968—96; ret., 1996. Mem. N.J. Coalition of Religious Leaders; cons. ecumenical and interreligious com. Nat. Conf. Cath. Bishops, 1986—96. Bd. regents Seton Hall U. Seton Hall U., 1968—96. Roman Catholic.*

DUDICK, STEPHEN T., plastic surgeon; b. Elizabeth, N.J. s. Thomas S. and Anne Dudick; m. Cathy A. Buletza, July 15, 2000; children: Christopher, Colin, Caitlin. BA, U. Cin., 1970; MD, Autonoma U. Guadlajara, Mex., 1975. Surg. intern, resident St. Vincent's Hosp. & Med. Ctr., N.Y.C., 1976—81; plastic surgery resident Ind. U. Med. Ctr., Indpls., 1981—83; plastic surgeon pvt. practice, Red Bank, NJ, 1983—. Med. missionary N.E. Med. Missions, Holmdel, NJ, 1993—, Aloha Med. Missions, Honolulu, 1993—. Fellow: ACS; mem.: Am. Soc. Plastic Surgery. Roman Catholic. Avocations: baseball, golf. Office: Stephen T Dudick MD 252 Broad St Red Bank NJ 07701

DUDLEY, CRAIG JAMES, retired executive recruiter; b. Pendleton, Oreg., July 19, 1930; s. Craig James and Elizabeth (Thieman) Dudley; m. Alta Mae McKelvey, June 21, 1952 (div. Nov. 1974); children: Erin Maureen, Craig James; m. Grace Vota, May 30, 1975. BS, U. Oreg., 1955; B in Fgn. Trade, Am. Inst. Fgn. Trade, 1958. Counselor Marion County Juvenile Dept., Salem, Oreg., 1955-57; v.p., gen. mgr. ESB Inc., Phila., Monterrey, Mex., 1958-69; v.p. Boydon Latin Am., Mexico City, 1970-75; pres., ptnr. Conrey-Paul Ray, Mexico City, 1975—2002; ret., 2002. Bd. dirs. Ray & Berndtson Internat. Chmn. United Way, Mexico City, 1987, 1988. With U.S. Army, 1952—54. Named one of Am.'s Top 150 Exec. Recruiters, Career Makers, 1994—. Mem.: Am. C. of C. Mex. (bd. dirs. 1983—85, 1987), Am. Soc. Mex. (pres. 1989, 1990), Club Indsl.-Mex. Republican. Avocations: hiking, golf, fishing.

DUDLEY, DENNIS MICHAEL, lawyer; b. Kalamazoo, Mich., Dec. 24, 1949; s. Arthur Kenneth and Marcia Louise (Rapaport) D.; m. Elizabeth Jane Mann Dudley, Apr. 17, 1971; children: Jennifer Elizabeth, Ruth Ellen. BA, Western Mich. U., 1971; JD, U. Cin., 1975. Bar: Mich. 1975, Minn. 1983, U.S. Dist. Ct. (ea. and we. dists.) Mich. 1975, U.S. Ct. Appeals (6th cir.) 1976, U.S. Supreme Ct. 1998. Assoc. Sablich, Ryan, Dudley & Rapaport, Lansing, Mich., 1975-79; shareholder, dir., v.p. Farhat, Story & Kraus, PC, East Lansing, Mich., 1979-90; assoc. Church, Kritselis & Wyble, Lansing, Mich., 1990-95; pvt. practice East Lansing, Mich., 1995-2000; pres. Dudley, Panek & Assocs., P.C., East Lansing, 2000—. Author: Michigan Medical Malpractice Cases Annotated, 1981; (with others) Michigan Medical Malpractices Cases Annotated, Part II, 1984. Mem. Ingham County (Mich.) Bd. Canvassers, 1989-91; chair 3d Congressional Dist. Democratic Party, Lansing, Mich., 1986-88; co-chair Fiscal Needs Com., Lansing Sch. Dist., 1989. Mem. Mich. Bar Assn. (representative assembly mem., 1989-92, 96-97), Mich. Trial Lawyers Assn. (bd. mem., 1981-87), Ingham County Bar Assn., Civitan Club Lansing (pres. 1990-91). Democrat. Jewish. Avocations: outdoor, wildlife photography, political memorabilia. Home: 317 John R St East Lansing MI 48823-4703 Office: 4572 S Hagadorn Rd Ste 1C East Lansing MI 48823-5385 E-mail: dmdudley_law@msn.com.

DUDLEY, DORIS S., music educator, small business owner; b. Honolulu, July 11, 1931; d. Matsutaro and Yoshiko Kamioka; m. Michael Kioni Dudley, Aug. 22, 1981; children from previous marriage: Luis Kazuo San Miguel, Daniel Kenji San Miguel. At, Oberlin Conservatory of Music, Ohio, 1949—52, Geneva Conservatory of Music, Switzerland, 1951; MusB in edn., U. Colo., Boulder, 1953. Cert. profl. in music edn. Hawaii, 1965. Sch. music specialist Dept. of Edn., Honolulu, 1967—80, dist. resource music tchr., 1981—83, sch. music specialist, 1983—87; instr. keyboard and piano Leeward CC, Pearl City, Hawaii, 1988—92, Spl. Sr. Program, Pearl City, Hawaii, 1988—2003, self-employed, Kapolei, 2000—; piano tchr. Barbers Pt. Elem. Sch., Kapolei, 2000—; piano instr. Kapolei Cmty. Sch. Adults, 2000—. Adjudicator Leeward dist. Spring Festival Dept. of Edn., Honolulu, 1981—87; adjudicator Sterling award Brigham Young U., Laie, 1983—84; condr. Pianomania at Neal Blaisdell Concert Hall, Honolulu, 2002. Dist. 20 chmn. Rep. Party of Hawaii, 1997—99; bd. sec. Palehua Vista Assn., Kapolei, 2000—02. Recipient Tchr. of the Yr., Maili Elem. Sch., 1979. Mem.: Hawaii Music Tchrs. Assn. Avocations: musical activities, exercise, plants, church choir and accompanist. Home: 92-1365 Hauone St Kapolei HI 96707

DUDLEY, EARL C., JR., law educator; b. Manila, Philippines, 1941; BA, Amherst Coll., 1961; LLB, U. Va., 1967. Bar: Va. 1967, DC 1969. Woodrow Wilson fellow Harvard U., 1961—62; law clk. to Justice Stanley Reed US Supreme Ct., law clk. to Chief Justice Earl Warren; atty. Williams & Connolly, Washington, 1969—75; gen. counsel com. on judiciary US Ho. of Reps., 1975—77; ptnr. Seymour & Dudley, Washington, 1977—81, Nussbaum, Owen & Webster, Washington, 1981—89; lectr. U. Va. Sch. Law, 1981—89, assoc. prof., 1989—94, prof., 1994—. Office: U Va Sch Law 580 Massie Rd Charlottesville VA 22903-1789 Office Phone: 434-924-8813. E-mail: ecd3u@virginia.edu.

DUDLEY, EVERETT HASKELL, JR., lawyer; b. Fitchburg, Mass., June 2, 1930; s. Everett H. Sr. and Marguerite I. (Connors) D.; m. Joyce Pettapiece, Aug. 23, 1952; children: Everett H. III, Lisa R.Rentz. AA, Boston U., 1950, BS, 1954; JD, U. Miami, 1960. Bar: Mass. 1961, Fla. 1960, U.S. Dist. Ct. (so. dist.) Fla. 1961, U.S. Supreme Ct. 1964. Assoc. Sams, Anderson, Alper, Meadows & Spencer, Miami, Fla., 1960-61; ptnr. Stamey, Kravitz & Dudley, Hialeah, Fla., 1961-63, Kravitz, Dudley & Dean, Hialeah, Fla., 1963-69, Kravitz, Dudley & Duckworth, Hialeah, Fla., 1972-79, Weinbtraub, Weintraub, Seiden, Dudley & Press, Miami, Fla., 1979-85; judge Dade County Criminal Ct. of Record, Miami, Fla., 1969-71, City of Miami Springs, Fla., 1971-73; pres., prin. Everett H. Dudley Jr., P.A., Ft. Lauderdale, Fla., 1985-89; ptnr. Keeley, Hayes, Dudley, Johnson, Roberts, Keeley, Hayes & Dudley, Boca Raton, Fla., 1989-95, Keeley, Hayes, Dudley, Garrett & Mahle, Boca Raton, 1995—. Founder, pres. Coun. on Drug Edn., Miami, 1970-72; chmn. Nat. Cancer Cytology Ctr., 1961-79, Miami Springs Charter Bd., 1974, Miami Springs Code Rev. Bd., 1975; cons. Dade County Drug Abuse Adv. Bd., 1971-75; mem. Dade County Secretariat on Crime and Law Enforcement, 1971-72; bd. dirs. Dade County Crime Commn., 1971-81. With USMC, 1953-56. Recipient Citizen of Yr. award Op. Self-Help, 1970, Disting. Svc. award City of Miami Springs, 1974; commd. Ky. Col., Commonwealth of Ky., 1990. Mem. ABA, Assn. Trial Lawyers Am., Am. Judicature Soc., Mass. Bar Assn., Fla. Bar Assn., Am. Arbitration Assn., Navy League of U.S. (judge adv. Delray Beach coun. 1990—), Am. Legion, Masons, Shriners, Delta Theta Phi, Sigma Alpha Epsilon. Office: Keeley Hayes Dudley Garrett & Mahle 2424 N Federal Hwy Boca Raton FL 33431-7735

DUDLEY, GARY EDWARD, clinical psychologist; b. Columbus, Ohio, July 19, 1947; s. Ray Leonard and Mary Virginia (Russi) D.; m. Linda Jean Patterson, June 21, 1969; children: Michelle Denise, Karen Elizabeth. BS, Ohio State U., 1969; MS, U. Miami, 1972, PhD, 1975. Lic. psychologist, Ga., Fla. Tchr. Columbus Pub. Schs., 1969—70; intern in clin. psychology Mt. Zion Hosp. and Med. Ctr., San Francisco, 1972—73; clin. psychologist Met. Dade County Jail, Miami, Fla., 1974—76, Southeast Inst. Criminal Justice, Miami, 1974—76, Ga. So. U., Statesboro, 1976—80; pvt. practice Marietta, Ga., 1980—. Cons. Child Devel. Ctr., Ga. Psycho-Ednl. Network, Atlanta; bd. dirs. svcs. Atlanta Area Psychol. Assocs., PC; pres. Accurate Assessment Svcs. Atlanta. Contbr. articles to profl. jours. NIMH fellow, 1971, 73, VA fellow, 1971. Mem. APA, Nat. Acad. Neuropsychologists, Am. Bd. Med. Psychotherapists, Southeastern Psychol. Assn., Ga. Psychol. Assn., Nat. Honor Soc. Psychology, Sigma Xi. Office: Doctors Bldg/Windy Hill 2520 Windy Hill Rd Ste 203 Marietta GA 30067-8650 E-mail: ged69@hotmail.com.

DUDLEY, GEORGE ELLSWORTH, lawyer; b. Earlington, Ky., July 14, 1922; s. Ralph Emerson and Camille (Lackey) D.; m. Barbara J. Muir, June 28, 1950 (dec. Feb. 1995); children: Bruce K., Camille Dudley McNutt, Nancy S., Elizabeth Dudley Stephens. BS in Commerce, U. Ky., 1947; JD, U. Mich., 1950. Bar: Ky. 1950, D.C. 1951, U.S. Dist. Ct. (we. dist.) Ky. 1962, U.S. Ct. Appeals (6th cir.) 1987. Assoc. Gordon, Gordon & Moore, Madisonville, Ky., 1950-51; pvt. practice law Louisville, 1952-59; ptnr. Brown, Ardery, Todd & Dudley, Louisville, 1959-72, Brown, Todd & Heyburn, Louisville, 1972-92, of counsel, 1992—, mem. mgmt. com., 1972-90, chmn., 1989-90. Pres. Ky. Easter Seal Soc., Louisville, 1971-72; treas. Ky. Dem. Party, Frankfort, 1971-74; bd. dirs. Alliant Adult Health Svcs., Louisville, 1976—; 1st v.p. Nat. Easter Seal Soc., Chgo., 1981. Capt. inf. U.S. Army, 1943-46, ETO; capt. JAGC, U.S. Army, 1951-52. Mem. ABA, Ky. Bar Assn., Louisville Bar Assn., U.S. 6th Cir. Jud. Conf. (life), Harmony Landing Country Club (pres. 1978-79), Barristers Soc., Omicron Delta Kappa. Presbyterian. Avocations: golf, tennis, travel, sports spectator. Home: 1905 Crossgate Ln Louisville KY 40222-6405 Office: Frost Brown Todd 3200 Aegon Ctr Louisville KY 40202

DUDLEY, GEORGE H.T., real estate company executive; B, George Washington U.; JD, Villanova U. Bar: V.I., Pa. Co-chmn. bd., co-CEO, mem. exec. com. Lockhart Cos., Inc., St. Thomas, 1987—; co-chmn. Lockhart Ins. and Lock Fin. Svcs.; dir. Lockhart Real Estate and Lockhart Ventures, Inc.; founder, mng. ptnr. Dudley, Topper and Feuerzeig. Named Chevelier (Knight), King Belgium. Mem.: Am. Law Inst. (governing coun., membership com.). Office: PO Box 7020 St Thomas VI 00801

DUDLEY, JOHN HENRY, JR., lawyer; b. Lansing, Mich., June 22, 1941; s. John Henry and Elizabeth (Dean) D.; m. Elizabeth Merrill Casgrain, Dec. 27, 1975; 1 child, John. BA, Denison U., 1963; LLB, Stanford U., 1966; MA, U. Mich., 1968. Bar: Mich. 1968, U.S. Ct. Appeals (6th cir.) 1972, U.S. Ct. Appeals (2d cir.) 1987. Assoc. Devine & Devine, Ann Arbor, Mich., 1968-69; ptnr. Butzel Long, Detroit, 1969—. Adj. prof. law sch. U. Detroit, 1991. Chair, bd. dirs. Ann Arbor YMCA, 1997-99. Named Master of Bench U. Detroit-Mercy. Fellow Mich. State Bar Found.; mem. ABA (litig. sect.), Mich. State Bar Assn. (rep. assembly 1974-77), Detroit Bar Assn. (vol. lawyers com. 1989—), Washtenaw County Bar Assn., Am. Inn of Ct. Office: Butzel Long 150 W Jefferson Ave Fl 9th Detroit MI 48226-4430 Office Phone: 313-225-7012.

DUDLEY, KENNETH EUGENE, manufacturing executive; b. Bellville, Ohio, Nov. 26, 1937; s. Kenneth Olin and Ethel Elizabeth (Poorman) D.; m. Judith Ann Brown, Apr. 15, 1972; children: Camaron J. McCluggage, Kenneth Alan. Inventory control mgr. Gorman-Rupp Industries, Bellville, 1958-67, prodn. mgr., 1967-69, mgr. data processing, 1969-74, cost mgr., 1974-78, contr., 1978-82; treas., chief fin. officer Gorman-Rupp Co., Mansfield, Ohio, 1982—2002; ret., 2002. With USAF, 1962-63. Republican. Lutheran. Home: 18203 Millspring Dr Foley AL 36535-5095

DUDLEY, RICHARD MANSFIELD, mathematician, educator; b. East Cleveland, Ohio, July 28, 1938; s. Winston Mansfield and Charlotte Mae (Wheaton) D.; m. Elizabeth Allen Martin, June 3, 1978. AB, Harvard U., 1959; PhD, Princeton U., 1962. Asst. prof. math. U. Calif., Berkeley, 1963-66; asso. prof. MIT, 1967-72, prof., 1972—. Author: Real Analysis and Probability, 1989, 2d edit., 2002, Uniform Central Limit Theorems, 1999; editor: White Mountain Guide, 1979, Annals of Probability, 1979—81. Alfred P. Sloan Found. fellow, 1966-68, Guggenheim Found. fellow, 1991. Fellow AAAS, Am. Statis. Assn., Inst. Math. Stats.; mem. APHA, Am. Math. Soc., Bernoulli Soc., Internat. Statis. Inst. Democrat. Home: 92 Lewis St Newton MA 02458-1840 Office: MIT 77 Massachusetts Ave Rm 2-245 Cambridge MA 02139-4307 Office Phone: 617-253-7567.

DUDLEY, RICK (RICHARD C. DUDLEY), professional sports team executive; b. Jan. 31, 1949; m. Ja-Hee Dudley. Player Am. Hockey League, Internat. Hockey League, World Hockey Assn., Cleve., Cin., 1969-79, Buffalo Sabres, NHL, 1972—81, Winnipeg Jets, NHL, 1981; head coach Carolina Thunderbirds, ECHL, 1981—86, New Haven Nighthawks, AHL, 1988—89, Flint Spirits, IHL, 1986—88, Buffalo Sabres, NHL, 1989—92, San Diego Gulls, IHL, 1992—93, Phoenix Roadrunners, IHL, 1993—94; head coach, gen. mgr. Detroit Vipers, IHL, 1994—96; v.p., gen mgr Ottawa Senators, 1996-99; gen. mgr., v.p. Tampa Bay Lightning, 1999—2002; gen. mgr. Fla. Panthers, Sunrise, 2002—04, head coach, 2003—04; consultant, hockey operations Chicago Blackhawks, 2005—. Office: 1901 W Madison St Chicago IL 60612

DUDLEY, WILLIAM SHELDON, historian; b. Bklyn., July 14, 1936; s. William Henry and Dorothy (Lawson) D.; m. Julia Bartel, Aug. 21, 1965 (dec.); children: Jennifer Bee, Mary Megan; m. Donna Tully, Feb. 20, 2001 BA, Williams Coll., 1958; MA, Columbia U., 1966, PhD, 1972. History tchr. Poly. Prep. County Day Sch., Bklyn., 1963-66; asst. prof. History So. Meth. U., Dallas, 1970-77; supervisory historian Naval Hist. Ctr., Washington, 1977-82, head early history br., 1982-90, sr. historian, 1990-95, dir., sr. exec. svc., 1995—2004. Editor: Naval War of 1812, vol. 1, 1985, vol. 2, 1992, vol. 3, 2002. Dir. Naval Hist. Found., 2005—. Lt. USNR, 1959—63. Recipient Samuel Eliot Morison award USS Constitution Mus., 1993, Nat. Trust for Historic Preservation, Nat. Pres. awards U.S.S. Constn., 1997, H.L. Hunley Recovery, 2002, Navy Superior Civilian Svc. award, 2004, Spl. Recognition award Surface Navy Assn., 2005, K. Jack Bauer award Nasoh, 2005 Mem. Am. Revolution Roundtable (pres. 1987), Soc. History in the Fed. Govt. (pres. 1989-90, Thomas Jefferson prize 1993), Md. Hist. Soc. (maritime com. 1994—), N.Am. Soc. Oceanic History (pres. 1999—2003), Mass. Hist. Soc. (corr. mem.), Annapolis Maritime Mus. (dir.), Md. Adv. Com. Archeology. Avocations: sailing, gardening, choral music. Home: 4420 Cobalt Dr Harwood MD 20776

DUDLEY-ESHBACH, JANET, university president; b. Balt. m. Joseph Eshbach; two children. BA in Spanish and Latin Am. Studies, Ind. U.; PhD in Latin Am. Lit., El Colegio de Mexico, Mexico City. Mem. faculty, instr. Spanish Allegheny Coll., Meadville, Pa., 1978-79; asst. prof., then assoc. prof. Spanish and Latin Am. Studies Goucher Coll., Towson, Md., 1979-88; chmn. dept. Modern Langs., then assoc. v.p. Acad. Affairs SUNY, Potsdam, 1988-92, dean Sch. Arts and Scis., then provost, 1992-96; pres. Fairmont (W.Va.) State Coll., 1996—. Mem. Sen. Jay Rockefeller's Trade Mission to Taiwan and Japan, 1997. Mem. MLA, Am. Assn. Higher Edn., Am. Assn. State Colls. and Univs. (internat. studies com.), N.Y. State Assn. Women in Higher Edn., Coun. Colls. of Arts and Scis., Latin Am. Studies Assn., Marion County C. of C., Phi Delta Kappa, Phi Beta Kappa Office: Fairmont State Coll Office of Pres 1201 Locust Ave Fairmont WV 26554-2451

DUDMAN, RICHARD BEEBE, journalist; b. Centerville, Iowa, May 3, 1918; s. Virgil Ernest and Wilma (Beebe) D.; m. Helen Sloane, Mar. 14, 1946; children: Iris Janet Sloane, Martha Tod. BA, Stanford U., 1940; LLD (hon.), U. Mo., St. Louis, 1979. Reporter, photographer Oroville (Calif.) Mercury-Register, 1937; reporter Denver Post, 1945-49, St. Louis Post-Dispatch, 1949-53, Washington corr., 1954-68, bur. chief, 1969-81; chmn. bd., treas. Dudman Communications Corp., Ellsworth, Maine, 1981-92, chmn. emeritus, 1992-99. Mem. adv. com. Nieman Found. for Journalism, 1977-81; trustee South-North News Svc., 1985-95, pres., 1987-90, mng. editor, 1987-95; cons. to Washington Bur., St. Louis Post Dispatch, 1997; editl. writer Bangor (Maine) Daily News, 2000--. Author: Men of the Far Right, 1962, 40 Days with the Enemy, 1971, also articles. Trustee Washington Journalism Ctr., 1974-92, Inst. Current World Affairs, 1983-89, 95-98; bd. dirs. Downeast Family YMCA, Ellsworth, 1987-91; pub. mem. Maine Lobster Promotion Coun., 1991-2000. With USNR, 1942-45. Recipient award Asia Overseas Press Club, 1972, Edward Weintal award, 1979, Mo. medal U. Mo., 1981, George Polk Career award, 1993; Nieman fellow Harvard U., 1953-54, Knight Internat. Press fellow, South Africa, 1994, 96. Mem. Nat. Assn. Broadcasters (First Amendment com. 1985-89). Clubs: Gridiron (Washington). Lodges: Rotary. Avocations: sailing, boat building. Office Phone: 207-667-9557.

DUDRAK, KIMBERLY AMATRUDA, physician assistant; b. New Haven, Apr. 29, 1964; d. Joseph Vincent and Marie Perrelli Amatruda; m. Richard Anthony Dudrak II, June 25, 1988 (div. Dec. 2000); children: Stephanie, Richard. BS in Elem. Edn., So. Conn. State U., 1988; MS in Elem. Edn., Nazareth Coll., 1990; BS in Physician Asst., RIT, 1997. Cert. physician asst. Physician asst. in occupl. medicine CoMed Customized Health Svc., Rochester, NY, 1997—98; physician asst. in family medicine Farmington Family Practice, NY, 1998—2004; physician asst. in pediat. Arnold H. Matlin, MD, Geneseo, NY, 1998—. Clin. adj. faculty RIT, Rochester, 1999—; med. dir. Camp SOAR, Rochester, 2003—. Troop leader Girl Scouts U.S.A., Henrietta, NY, 2000—; den leader Cub Scouts Am., Henrietta, 2002—. Fellow: Am. Acad. Physician Asst. Roman Catholic. Avocations: music, art, crafts, dance. Home: 2 Yarrow Hill West Henrietta NY 14586 Office: David H Breen MD 3889 North Rd Geneseo NY 14454 E-mail: kimdiva@mail2mom.com.

DUDRICK, STANLEY JOHN, surgeon, research scientist, educator; b. Nanticoke, Pa., Apr. 9, 1935; s. Stanley Francis and Stephania Mary (Jachimczak) D.; m. Theresa M. Keen, June 14, 1958; children: Susan Marie, Paul Stanley, Carolyn Mary, Stanley Jonathan, Holly Anne, Anne Theresa. BS cum laude, Franklin and Marshall Coll., 1957; MD, U. Pa., 1961; MA (hon.), Yale U., 1999. Diplomate Am. Bd. Surgery. Intern Hosp. of U. Pa., Phila., 1961-62, resident in gen. surgery, 1962-67; acad. practice specializing in surgery Phila., 1967-72, 88-90, Houston, 1972-88, 90-94, Waterbury, New Haven, 1994—2000, 2002—, Bridgeport, 2002; chief surg. svcs. Hermann Hosp., Houston, 1972-80, surgeon in chief, dir. Ctr. Cardiovascular Disease, dir. nutritional support svcs., dir. Nutritional Sci. Ctr., 1990-94; prof. surgery U. Tex. Med. Sch., Houston, 1972-82, clin. prof. surgery, 1982-95, chmn. dept. surgery, 1972-80. Cons. in surgery M.D. Anderson Hosp. and Tumor Inst., 1973-88, clin. prof. surgery, cons. to pres., 1982-88; sr. cons. surgery and medicine Tex. Inst. for Rehab. and Rsch., 1974-88; mem. Anat. Bd., State of Tex., 1973-78; examiner Am. Bd. Surgery, 1974-78, bd. dirs., 1978-84, sr. mem. 1984-2000, also mem. and chmn. various coms.; chmn. sci. adv. com. Tex. Med. Ctr. Libr., 1974; mem. food and nutrition bd. NRC-Nat. Acad. Scis., 1973-75; mem. sci. adv. com. Nat. Found. for Ileitis and Colitis; mem. surgery, anesthesia and trauma study sect. NIH, 1982-86; chmn. dept. surgery Pa. Hosp., Phila., 1988-90, surgeon in chief, 1988-91, hon. surgery staff, 1991—; clin. prof. surgery U. Pa., 1988-93; assoc. chmn. dept. surgery, 1994-2000, 02-04, chmn. dept. surgery, 2004—, dir. surgery program, 1994-2000, 02—, dir. Med. Edn., 1995-2000, 02—, St. Mary's Hosp., Waterbury, Conn.; clin. prof. surgery, Yale U., New Haven, Conn., 1995-99, prof. surgery, 1999—; chmn. dept. surgery, dir. surg. edn. Bridgeport Hosp.-Yale U. New Haven Health Sys., 2000-02; adj. prof. surgery Quinnipiac U., 1996—. Editor: Manual of Surgical Nutrition, 1975, Manual of Preoperative and Postoperative Care, 1983, Current Strategies in Surgical Nutrition, 1991, Practical Handbook of Nutrition in Clinical Practice, 1994, Surgical Nutrition: Strategies in Critically Ill Patients, 1995; assoc. editor Nutrition in Medicine, 1975—; editorial bd. Annals of Surgery, 1975—, Infusion, 1978—, Nutrition and Cancer, 1980-2000, Nutrition Support Services, 1980-86, Jour. Clin. Surgery, 1980-83, Nutrition Research, 1981—, Intermed. Communications Nursing Services, 1981—, Postgraduate General Surgery, 1992—; others; contbr. chpts. to books, articles to profl. jours.; inventor of new technique of intravenous feeding and anti-cholesterol therapy. Bd. dirs. Found. for Children, Houston, Harris County unit Am. Cancer Soc., Phila. chpt., 1988-90; trustee Franklin and Marshall Coll., 1985—, mem. student life, art collection, and trusteeship coms., 1986-2002, mem. overseers bd., 1986-2002, exec. com. 1986-2002, alumni programs and devel. com., 1991-2002, pres. regional adv. coun., 1992-94, vice chmn. 1994-2002, John Marshall Soc., 1993—; founder Benjamin Rush Soc., 1987, hon. chmn., 1999—, campaign nat. chmn., 1995-2002, chmn. campaign exec. com., 1995-2002, mem. bldgs. and grounds com., 2002—, academic investments com., 2002—, campaign nat. vice chmn., 2002—. Decorated knight Order St. John of Jerusalem Knights Hopitalier; recipient VA citation for significant contbn. to med. care, 1970; Mead Johnson award for rsch. in hosp. pharmacy, 1972; Seale Harris medal So. Med. Assn., 1973; AMA-Brookdale award in medicine, 1975; Great Texan award Nat. Found. Ileitis and Colitis, 1975; Modern Medicine award, 1977; Disting. Alumnus citation Franklin and Marshall Coll., 1980; WHO, Houston, 1980; Stinchfield award Am. Acad. Orthopedic Surgery, 1981; Bernstein award Med. Soc. State of N.Y., 1986, Alumni Svc. award U. Pa. Med. Sch., 1996, Excellence in Surgery Tchg. award Mary's Hosp., 1999, Roswell Park award Buffalo Surgery Soc., 2000, Alumni medal Franklin and Marshall Coll., 2002, Nos Magni Nominis Umbra tchg. and rsch. award Yale Gen. Surgery Residents, 2000, others; Stanley J. Dudrick MD Surg. Edn. and Rsch. Fund named in his honor, 2003. Fellow ACS (vice chmn. pre and post operative com. 1975, gov. 1979-85, com. on med. motion pictures 1981-90, SESAP com. 1990-94, co-chmn. multiple choice com. 1993-94, mem. Conn. chpt., recipient Jacobson Innovation award 2005), Philippine Coll. Surgeons (hon.), Coll. Medicine and Surgery of Costa Rica (hon.), Am. Coll. Nutrition (Grace A. Goldsmith award 1982), Phi Beta Kappa; mem. AMA (coun. on food and nutrition 1971-76, exec. com. 1975-76, council on sci. affairs 1976-81, Goldberger award in clin. nutrition 1970), AAAS, AAUP, Am. Surg. Assn. (Flance-Karl award 1997), Am. Acad. Pediatrics (hon., Ladd medal 1988), Am. Pediatric Surg. Assn. (hon.), Am. Soc. Nutritional Support Services (bd. dirs. 1982-87, pres. 1984, Outstanding Humanitarian award 1984) Soc. Univ. Surgeons (exec. coun. 1974-78), Assn. for Acad. Surgery (founders group), Internat. Soc. Surg., Internat. Fedn. Surg. Colls., Internat. Soc. Parenteral Nutrition (exec. coun. 1975-81, pres. 1978-81), Internat. Fedn. Surgery Soc., So. Med. Assn. (chmn. surgery sect. 1984-85), Houston Gastroent. Soc., Houston Surg. Soc., Tex. Surg. Soc., Tex. Med. Assn. (com. nutrition and food resources), Tex. Med. Found., Harris County Med. Soc., New Haven (Conn.) County Med. Soc., Conn. Soc. Am. Bd. Surgeons, New England Surg. Soc., L.A. Surg. Soc. (hon.), Am. Radium Soc., Am. Soc. Clin. Oncology, Am. Soc. Parenteral and Enteral Nutrition (pres. 1977, bd. advs. 1978—, chmn. bd. advisers 1978, Vars award 1982, Rhoads lectr. 1985, 2005, Dudrick Rsch. Scholar award named in his honor), Penn. Nutritionists Soc. (pres. 1985), Am. Gastroent. Assn., Soc. Surg. Oncology, L.A. Surg. Soc. (hon.), James Ewing Soc., Ravdin-Rhoads Surg. Assn., Excelsior Surg. Soc. (Edward D. Churchill lectr. 1981), Soc. Laparoendoscopic Surgery, Soc. Surg. Chairmen, So. Surg. Assn., Southwestern Surg. Congress, Southeastern Surg. Congress, Surg. Biology Club II, Surg. Infection Soc. (chmn. membership com. 1987-90), Western Surg. Soc., Halsted Soc., Allen O. Whipple Surg. Soc., Am. Inst. Nutrition, Soc. Clin. Surgery, Am. Soc. Clin. Investigation, Soc. for Surgery of Alimentary Tract, Am. Trauma Soc. (founders group), Am. Assn. for Surgery of Trauma, Soc. Clin. Surgery, Am. Soc. Clin. Nutrition, Fedn. Am. Soc. Exp. Biology, Am. Burn Assn., Assn. Program Dirs. Surgery (bd. dirs. 1998—), John Marshall Soc., Coll. Physicians Phila., Phila. Acad. Surgeons, George Hermann Soc., Polish Soc. Parental and Enteral Nutrition (hon.), Union League Phila., L.A. Surg. Soc. (hon.), Med. Club Phila., Franklin Club Phila., Houston Doctors Club (gov. 1973-76), Nat. Alumni Coun. U. Pa. Med. Sch. (chmn. 1994-2001), Conn. United for Rsch. Excellence (bd. dirs. 1995-2001), Waterbury Symphony Orch. (bd. dirs. 1999—, chmn. endowment com. 2002—), Cosmos Club, Athenaeum, The Penn Club (charter), Phi Beta Kappa Assocs., Sigma Xi, Alpha Omega Alpha. (sec.-treas. Houston chpt. 1982-83), Fellows Leadership Soc. (life). Home: 40 Beecher St Naugatuck CT 06770-2721 Office: St Mary's Hosp 56 Franklin St Waterbury CT 06706 Office Phone: 203-709-6479. Business E-Mail: sdudrick@stmh.org.

DUDUIT, MICHAEL, editor, academic administrator; b. Sandwich, Ill., Aug. 18, 1954; s. James Loren and Sarah Lee (Baker) D.; m. Laura Ann Niemann, Aug. 10, 1959; 1 child, James Robert. BA in Speech, Stetson U., 1975; MDiv, So. Bapt. Sem., Louisville, 1979; PhD in Humanities, Fla. State U., 1983. Ordained to ministry Bapt. Ch., 1977. News dir. So. Bapt. Sem., Louisville, 1975-77; dir. pub. affairs Palm Beach Atlantic Coll., West Palm Beach, Fla., 1977-80; asst. to pres. Cuneo Advt., Tallahassee, 1980-81; assoc. pastor Immanuel Bapt. Ch., Tallahassee, 1981-84; dir. comms .So. Bapt. Sem., 1984-87; dir. devel. Samford U., Birmingham, Ala., 1987-93; exec. v.p. Union U., Jackson, Tenn., 1996—2001; pres., CEO Am. Ministry Resources LLC, Franklin, 2002—; editor Preaching Mag., 1985—. Author: Joy in Ministry, 1991; editor: Handbook of Contemporary Preaching, 1993, Abingdon Preaching Annual, 1995, 96, 97, 98, 99, Communicate with Power, 1996. Mem. Bapt. Communicators Assn. (pres. 1994-95), Acad. of Homiletics, Evang. Homiletics Soc. E-mail: duduit@gmail.com.

DUDUKOVIC, MILORAD P., chemical engineering educator, consultant; b. Beograd, Yugoslavia, Mar. 25, 1944; arrived in U.S., 1968; s. Predrag R. and Melita Maria Dudukovic; m. Judith Ann Reiff, Dec. 27, 1969; children: Aleksandra Anne, Nicole Maria. BS in Engring., U. Beograd, 1967; MS, Ill. Inst. Tech., 1970, PhD, 1972. Rsch. engr. Process Design Inst., Beograd, 1967-68; instr. Ill. Inst. Tech., Chgo., 1970-72; asst. prof. Ohio U., Athens, 1972-74; assoc. prof. Washington U., St. Louis, 1974-80, prof., dir., 1980—, Laura and William Jens prof. environ. engring., 1993—, chmn. dept. chem. engring., 1998—. Cons. in field. Assoc. editor: Indsl. and Engineering Chemistry Research, 1991—; contbr. articles to profl. jours. Recipient Burlington No. Found. Tchg. award, 1986, Nat. Catalyst award Chem. Mfrs. Assn., 1988, St. Louis award ACS, 1995, Malcolm E. Pruitt award Coun. Chem. Rsch., 1999; 2 NASA certs. of recognition and citations; Fulbright scholar Inst. for Higher Edn., 1968. Fellow AIChE (R.H. Wilhelm award 1994), St. Louis Acad. Scis.; mem. AAAS, Am. Chem. Soc., Am. Assn. Engring. Edn., Yugoslav Acad. Engring. (fgn. mem.), Sigma Xi, Century Club (St. Louis). Achievements include pioneering work on trickle bed reactors, bubble columns; research in Czochralski crystal growth, novel experimental techniques for multiphase reactors; environmentally benign processing. Office: Washington U Dept Chem Engring Campus Box 1198 One Brookings Dr Saint Louis MO 63130-4899 Business E-Mail: dudu@wustl.edu.

DUDZIAK, DONALD JOHN, nuclear engineer, educator; b. Alden, N.Y., Jan. 6, 1935; s. Joseph and Josephine Mary (Ratajczak) D.; m. Judith Ann Staib, Aug. 22, 1959; children: Alan Joseph, Matthew John, Karin Marie. BS in Marine Engring., U.S. Mcht. Marine Acad., 1956; MS in Radiation Biology/Radiol. Physics, U. Rochester, 1957; PhD in Applied Math., U. Pitts., 1963. Registered profl. engr., Calif., USCG lic. engr. steam & diesel 1956-92. Commd. ensign USN, 1956, advanced through grades to capt.; sr. engr. Bettis Atomic Power Lab., Pitts., 1957-65; staff mem. U. Calif.-Los Alamos (N.Mex.) Nat. Lab., 1965-68, 69-74, assoc. and alt. group leader, 1974-78, group leader, 1978-82, theoretical divsn. tech. advisor, 1982, dep. group leader, sect. leader, 1983—88, lab. fellow, 1988—; ret. USN, 1995; prof., head dept. nuclear engring. N.C. State U., Raleigh, 1990—2001; pres. Pinorealosa Corp, 1989-90. Vis. prof. U. Va., Charlottesville, 1968-69; adj. prof. U. N.Mex., 1966, Kans. State U., 1989-90; guest scientist Swiss Fed. Inst. Reactor Rsch., Wuerenlingen, 1981-82; mem. lab. microfusion facility steering com. U.S. Dept. Energy, 1986-90, inertial confinement fusion adv. com., 1992-96; vice-chair accelerator prodn. of tritium rev. panel Los Alamos Nat. Lab., 1995-98; chmn. fusion tech. working group Neutronics, Brookhaven, N.Y., 1975; mem. Nat. Nuc. Accrediting Bd., Nat. Acad. Nuc. Tng., 1998-2004; cons. nuclear power schs. USN, 1962-65; cons. Oak Ridge Nat. Lab., 1993-96, TSI Rsch. Co., 1992-, U.S. Nuclear Regulatory Commn., 1997, Am. Coun. on Edn., 1995-, Duke U., 1997-98. Editor: Reactor Principles, 1964, Radiation Shielding, 1964, Progress in Nuclear Energy, 1992—; contbr. editor Fusion Tech., 1987-2001; contbr. articles to profl. jours. Vice-chmn. Los Alamos County Planning and Zoning Commn., 1969-74. Fellow Am. Nuclear Soc. (divsn. chair 1972-73, 77-78, 92-93, gen. chair fusion energy divsn. nat. meeting 1994); mem. Am. Soc. Engring. Edn., U.S. Naval Inst., Los Alamos Sunrise Kiwanis (treas. 1987-89), Sigma Xi, Phi Kappa Phi. Libertarian. Avocations: hunting, hiking, skeet shooting, rifle shooting, pistol shooting. Office: Los Alamos Nat Lab Tech Assessment Group D-2 MS F609 Los Alamos NM 87545 Business E-Mail: dudziak@lanl.gov.

DUDZIAK, EMMA M., cardiac sonographer; b. Buffalo, N.Y., July 27, 1957; d. Norman P. Koneski and Geraldine E. Jans (Queeno); m. Gregory D. Dudziak, Sept. 15, 1979; children: Keith G., Scott G. Diploma, Bryant & Stratton Bus. Inst., Buffalo, N.Y. Registered Diagnostic Cardiac Sonographer Am. Registry of Diagnostic Med. Sonographers, Rockville, Md., 2002. Supr., echo, stress, holter & EKG lab Erie County Med. Ctr., Buffalo, 1982—97; sr. cardiac sonographer Buffalo Heart Group, 1997—. Mem.: Am. Inst. of Ultrasound in Medicine, Soc. of Diagnostic Med. Sonography, ARDMS (assoc.). Roman Catholic. Avocations: travel, bowling, needlepoint, sewing, knitting. Office: Buffalo Heart Group 3435 Bailey Ave Buffalo NY 14215 Office Phone: 716-835-2966. Personal E-mail: thedudz@hotmail.com.

DUDZIAK, MARY LOUISE, law educator; b. Oakland, Calif., June 15, 1956; d. Walter F. Dudziak and Barbara Ann Campbell; 1 child, Alicia. AB in Sociology with highest honors, U. Calif., Berkeley, 1978; JD, Yale Law Sch., 1984; MA, MPhil in Am. Studies, Yale U., 1986, PhD in Am. Studies, 1992. Adminstrv. asst. to dep. dir. Ctr. Ind. Living, Berkeley, 1978-80; law clk., nat. legal staff ACLU, N.Y.C., 1983; law clk. Judge Sam J. Ervin, III Fourth Cir. Ct. Appeals, Morganton, N.C., 1984-85; assoc. prof. coll. law U. Iowa, Iowa City, 1986-90, prof. coll. law, 1990-98. Vis. prof. U. So. Calif., 1997-98, Harvard Law Sch., 2005-; prof. U. So. Calif., 1998-2002, Judge Edward J. and Ruey L. Guirado prof. law and history, 2002-; mem. faculty senate task force on faculty devel. U. Iowa, 1989-90, mem. faculty welfare com., 1990-92, mem. faculty senate task force on faculty spouses and ptnrs., 1991-92, mem. presdl. lecture com., 1992-95; v.p. rsch. adv. com. in social scis., 1992-94; fellow law and pub. affairs program Princeton U., 2002; presenter in field. Author: Cold War Civil Rights: Race and the Image of American Democracy, 2000; editor, co-author: September 11 in History: A Watershed Moment?, 2003; mem. bd. mng. editors Am. Quar., 2003—; contbr. articles to profl. jours. Bd. dirs. Iowa Civil Liberties Union, 1987-88; chairperson office svcs. for persons with disabilities program rev. com., U. Iowa, 1987-88, law sch. ombudsperson, 1991. Charlotte W. Newcombe Doctoral Dissertation fellow Woodrow Wilson Fellowship Found., 1985-86; Old Gold fellow U. Iowa, 1987, 88, 89, Moody Grant Lyndon Baines Johnson Fdn., 1998, Theodore C. Sorenson Fell., JFK Libr. Fdn., 1997, Orgn. Am. Historians-Japanese Assn. for Am. Studies fellow 2000; travel grantee Eisenhower World Affairs Inst., 1993; recipient Scholars Devel. award Harry S. Truman Libr. Inst., 1990. Mem. Am. Soc. Legal History (mem. com. on documentary preservation 1988-2000, mem. program com. for 1988 conf., mem. exec. com., bd. dirs. 1990-92, 95-97, chairperson program com. 1993, mem. nominating com. 1999-2001, chair nominating com. 2001), Am. Hist. Assn. (Littleton-Griswold rsch. grantee 1987), Am. Studies Assn. (mem. nominating com. 1999-2002, chair nominating com. 2002), Assn. Am. Law Schs. (sec.-treas. legal history sect. 1987, vice chair 1988, chair 1989), Law and Soc. Assn. (mem. Hurst prize com. 1992), Orgn. Am. Historians, Soc. Am. Law Tchrs., Soc. for Historians Am. Fgn. Rels. Democrat. Office: U So Calif Law Sch Los Angeles CA 90089-0001

DUE, JEAN MARGARET, agricultural economist, educator; b. Peterborough, Ont., Can., Sept. 19, 1921; d. Allan B. and Katherine Jean (Calder) Mann; m. John F. Due, Aug. 18, 1950; children— Allan Malcolm, Kevin John Burritt. B.Com., U. Toronto, 1946; MS, U. Ill., 1950, PhD, 1953. Economist Dept. Agr., Ottawa, Ont., 1946-49; research asso. in home econs. U. Ill., 1959-61, vis. prof., 1965-70, prof. dept. agr. econs., 1970-90. Contbr. articles to profl. jours. Mem. African Studies Assn., Am. Econ. Assn., Am. Agrl. Econs. Assn., Internat. Assn. Agrl. Econs., Assn. Women Internat. Devel. Home: 1208 Clark Lindsey Village 101 W Windsor Rd Urbana IL 61802-6663 Office: Univ Illinois 305MH 1301 W Gregory Dr # 305mh Urbana IL 61801-9015 E-mail: jdue@uiuc.edu.

DUE, JOHN FITZGERALD, economist, educator; b. Hayward, Calif., July 11, 1915; s. Jackson Angelo and Emmarene (Hurd) D.; m. Margaret Jean Mann, Aug. 18, 1950; children: Nancy, Allan, Kevin. AB, U. Calif.-Berkeley, 1935, PhD, 1939; A.M., George Washington U., 1936. Instr. U. Utah, 1939-42, asst. prof., 1945-48; economist Treasury Dept., 1942; faculty U. Ill., 1948-86, prof. econs., 1951-86, prof. emeritus, 1986—, chmn. dept. econs., 1963-67, 71-72; acting dean Coll. Commerce U. Ill., 1976, 85-86. Author: Taxation and Economic Development in Tropical Africa, 1963, Indirect Taxation in Developing Economies, 2d edit., 1988; co-author: Sales Taxation: State and Local Structure and Operation, 1983, rev., 1994, The Electric Interurban Railway in America, 1960, Rails to The Ochoco Country-The City of Prineville Railway, 1968, Government Finance, 7th edit, 1981, Rails to the Mid Columbia Wheatlands, 1979, Roads and Rails South from the Columbia, 1991. Served with USMCR, 1942-45. Mem. Am. Econ. Assn., Nat. Tax Assn., Phi Beta Kappa. Home: 101 W Windsor Rd Apt 1208 Urbana IL 61802-6663 Office: Univ Ill Wohlers Hall 1206 S 6th St Champaign IL 61820-6978 Business E-Mail: jdue@uiuc.edu.

DUEL, WARD CALVIN, retired health care consultant; b. Fond du Lac, Wis., Mar. 13, 1924; s. Myrton M. and Matie Rose (Tidyman) D.; m. Madelyn Mae Kressin, Oct. 1, 1950; children: Ward Rick, Christine Selma, Roxanne Matie, Beth Dawn. BS, U. Wis., 1950; postgrad., Marquette U., 1955-57; MPH, U. Calif., Berkeley, 1959. Registered environ. health specialist, Calif., Nat. Environ. Health Assn. Sanitarian City of Kenosha (Wis.), 1951-59; br. office mgr. Lake County Health Dept., Waukegan, Ill., 1959-65; dir. health Skokie (Ill.) Dept. Health, 1965-68; dir. McHenry County Health Dept., Woodstock, Ill., 1968-70; asst. dir. pub. and environ. health AMA, Chgo., 1971-81; chief environ. health City of Chgo., 1981-82; dir. Mid-Ohio Valley Dept. Health, Parkersburg, W.Va., 1982-83; dir. environ. health, pub. and mental health Choctaw Indians, Philadelphia, Miss., 1984—2005; cons. on environ. health to prisons, juv. detention ctrs. and mental hosps. in 44 states and D.C., 1995—2002; ret., 2002. Active Nat. Com. on Correctional Health Care; capt. U.S. Pub. Health Svc. Commn. Corps Res., 1958—; cons. in field; lectr. in field. Co-editor: Clinical Implications of Air Pollution Research; author monographs: Physicians Guide to Solid Waste, 1975, Physicians Guide to Air Pollution, 1973-80, Flood Area Health Guide, 1961; contbr. articles to profl. jours. Served in U.S. Army, 1944-45. Decorated 3 Battle Stars and Bronze Star for heroism; recipient Theta award Defenders, 1969, Samuel J. Crumbine award Single Svc. Inst., 1963, Walter S. Mangold award Nat. Environ. Health Assn., 1978, Outstanding Citizen award Ill. Dept. Edn., 1984, Jour. Environ. Health Editors award, 1979, Pres. Vol. Svc. award, 2005. Fellow Am. Pub. Health Assn. (task force correctional stds., Disting. Svc. award 2002); mem. Nat. Environ. Health Assn. (pres. 1967-68), Wis. Environ. Health Assn. (pres. 1957-58), Ill. Environ. Health Assn. (pres. 1964-65), Am. Correctional Assn., Am. Jail Assn. (nat. stds. com. 1993—). Lutheran. Home and Office: 4907 N West St Mchenry IL 60050-7968

DUELFER, CHARLES A., weapons inspector; b. Stamford, Conn., Sept. 18, 1952; s. Charles A. and Grace H. Duelfer. BA, U. Conn., 1974; MS, MIT, 1977. Nat. security analyst Office of Mgmt. and Budget, Washington, 1977—82; polit.-mil. affairs officer U.S. State Dept., Washington, 1982—85; dir. Office of Internat. Security Policy U.S. Dept. State, Washington, 1985—90, dep. to asst. sec. of state, 1990—93; dep. chmn. UN spl. commn. on Iraq UN, N.Y.C., 1993—2000; dir. Iraq Survey Group, 2004—. Polit.-mil. expert various TV and radio programs, 2000—; vis. scholar Ctr. for Strategic and Internat. Studies, Washington, 2000—. Contbr. articles to profl. jours., 2000. Mem.: Coun. Fgn. Rels. Avocations: skydiving, ice hockey, painting.

DUEMLING, ROBERT WERNER, diplomat, museum director; b. Ann Arbor, Mich., Feb. 8, 1929; s. Werner William and Anne (Lindemulder) D.; m. Louisa duPont Copeland, May 15, 1982. BA, Yale U., 1950, MA, 1953; student, Cambridge U., Eng., 1950-51. Joined fgn. service Dept. State, Washington, 1957, with, 1957-60, 66-70, Am. embassy, Rome, 1960-63, Kuala Lumpur, 1963-65, Tokyo, 1970-74; U.S. consul Kuching, Malaysia, 1965-66; exec. asst. to dep. sec. state Dept. State, Washington, 1974-76; dep. chief of mission with rank of minister Am. embassy, Ottawa, Ont., Can., 1976-80; chief Fgn. Contingents, Multinat. Force and Observers, Sinai, 1981-82; U.S. ambassador to Suriname, to Paramaribo, 1982-84; dir. Nicaraguan Humanitarian Assistance Office, Dept. State, 1985-87; pres., dir. Nat. Bldg. Mus., Washington, 1987-94. Sr. fellow Washington Coll., 1983—, adj. prof., 2000—. Trustee Cafritz Found., Washington Nat. Monument Assn., Nat. Gallery of Art, Soc. Archtl. Historians. Served in U.S. Navy, 1953-57. Henry fellow, 1950-51; decorated Order of the Palm (Suriname). Fellow Royal Soc. for Arts (U.K.); mem. Washington Inst. Fgn. Affairs, Met. Club (trustee), Century Assn., Alibi Club. Home: 2950 University Ter NW Washington DC 20016-3461

DUENSING, DOROTHY JEAN, music educator, vocalist; d. George Prescott Duensing I and Patricia Ann (dec.) Gasthoff-Duensing, Catherine Dew-Duensing (Stepmother); m. Michael William Miller, Nov. 9, 1997 (div. Nov. 18, 2004); m. Thomas Andrew Cormie, Oct. 10, 1987 (div. Oct. 3, 1996); 1 child, Mason Andrew Cormie. MusB, Ind. U., 1984; MusM, U. of Mich., 1990. Orff Schulwerk Music-Level I Madonna U., Livonia, Mich., 2001, Orff Schulwerk Music-Level II Madonna U., Livonia, Mich., 2002, Orff Schulwerk Music-Level III Madonna U., Livonia, Mich., 2003. Adj. prof. voice Wayne State U. Dept. Music, Detroit, 1999—; educator, primary music dir. Acad. Sacred Heart, Bloomfield Hills, Mich., 2000—03; dir. mid. sch. vocal music Sherman Mid. Sch., 2004—, Richter Intermediate Sch. Holly Area Schs., Holly, Mich., 2004—. Soprano soloist, sect. leader Christ Episcopal Ch., Dearborn, Mich., 1986—94; part-time voice faculty Ctr. for Creative Studies' Inst. of Music and Dance, Detroit, 1990—2000; alto soloist, sect. leader Temple Israel, West Bloomfield, Mich., 1991—97; artist-in-residence Toledo Opera Co., 1991—99; performing artist Omni Arts in Edn., Southfield, Mich., 1992—; full-time vocal music substitute U. Liggett Mid. and Upper Schools, Grosse Pointe Farms, Mich., 1996; part-time voice, piano faculty Ward Church's Christian Sch. of Fine and Performing Arts, Northville Twp., Mich., 1998—2002; adj. prof. voice William Tyndale Coll., Farmington Hills, Mich., 2001—02; alto soloist, sect. leader Met. United Meth. Ch., Detroit, 2001—02, First Presbyn. Ch., Royal Oak, Mich., 2002—. Choral music dir. Music Study Club, Detroit, 1995—96, Bel Canto Choral Group, Southfield, Mich., 1998—2001; deacon Faith Cmty. Presbyn. Ch., Novi, Mich., 1998—2000; teen choir dir. Faith Cmty. Presbyn., Novi, Mich., 1999—2000. Recipient Hazel Mueller Meml. award, Interlochen Ctr. for the Performing Arts, 1979, 1980, First Pl. Vocalist in the State of Mich., Mich. Schs. Vocal Music Assn., 1980, Dist. Finalist, Met. Opera Assn. (Midwest Dist.), 1991, Second Pl. Winner, Harold Haugh Light Opera Vocal Competition, Ann Arbor, MI, 2001; scholar Interlochen Alumnae Scholarship for Half Tuition at Nat. Music Camp, Interlochen Ctr. for the Performing Arts, 1979, Scholarship, Iota Epsilon Patroness Chpt., Bloomington, IN, 1983, Patricia Brinton-Becirovic Meml. Scholarship, Am. Inst. of Musical Studies, Austria, 1989. Mem.: Livonia Area Piano Tchrs. Forum, Mich. Music Tchrs. Assn., Music Tchrs. Nat. Assn., Detroit Orff Schulwerk Assn., Nat. Orff Schulwerk Assn., Nat. Assn. Tchrs. Singing, Nat. Fedn. Music Clubs' Tuesday Musicale Detroit, PEO Sisterhood, Chpt. FE, Novi, MI (life; chaplain 2001—02), Sigma Alpha Iota (life; Detroit Alumnae chptr. v.p. mem. 2002—). Office: Wayne State U Dept of Music 1321 Old Main Bldg Studio #2315 Detroit MI 48202 Home: 21724 Sunflower Rd Novi MI 48375 Mailing: PO Box 107 Novi MI 48376-0107 Personal E-mail: Divaduensing@aol.com.

DUER, ELLEN ANN DAGON, anesthesiologist, general practitioner; b. Balt., Feb. 3, 1936; d. Emmett Paul and Annie (Sollers) Dagon; m. Lyle Jordan Millan IV, Dec. 21, 1963; children: Lyle Jordan V, Elizabeth Lyle, Ann Sheridan Worthington.; m. T. Marshall Duer, Jr., Aug. 23, 1985. AB, George Washington U., 1959; MD, U. Md., 1964; postgrad., Johns Hopkins U., 1965—68. Intern Union Meml. Hosp., Balt., 1964-65; resident in anesthesiology Johns Hopkins Hosp., Balt., 1965-68, fellow in surgery, 1965-68; practice medicine specializing in anesthesiology Balt., 1968—; faculty Ch. Home and Hosp., Balt., 1969—; attending staff Union Meml. Hosp., Ch. Home and Hosp., Franklin Sq. Hosp., Children's Hosp., James Lawrence Kernan Hosp., Balt., 1982-94; co-chief anesthesiology James Kernan Hosp., 1983-94, med. dir. out-patient surgery dept., 1987-94. Affiliate cons. emergency room Ch. Home and Hosp., Balt., 1969—, med. audit and utilizaions com., 1970-72, mem. emergency and ambulatory care com., 1973-74, chief emergency dept., 1973-74; cons. anesthesiologist Md. State Penitentiary, 1971; fellow in critical care medicine Md. Inst. Emergency Medicine, 1975-76; infection control com. U. Md. Hosp., 1975—; instr. anesthesiology U. Md. Sch. Medicine, 1975—; staff anesthesiologist Mercy Hosp., 1978—, audit com., 1979-80, 82; asst. prof. anesthegiology U. Md. Med. Sch., 1989-94; med. exec. com. Kernan Hosp., 1990-94, v.p. 1990, chief of staff, 1992—; active Tappahannock Family Practice, 1994-96, Rappahannock Gen. Hosp. Family Practice, 1996—, Rappahannock Gen. Hosp., 1996—, ethics com., 1997—; med. examiner No. Neck of Va., 1996—; active Commonwealth of Va. Med. Bd. Mem. AMA, Am. Coll. Emergency Physicians, Am. Acad. Gen. Practitioners, Met. Emergency Dept. Heads Am., Md. Soc. Anesthesiologists, Balt. County Med. Soc., Mid. Peninsula Med. Soc., No. Neck Med. Soc., Med. Soc. Va., Med. and Choir Faculty Med., Chirurg. Soc., Internat. Congress Anaesthesiologists, Internat. Anesthesia Rsch. Soc., Am. L'Hirondelle Club, Annapolis Yacht Club, Chesapeake Bay Yacht Racing Assn., Rappahannock River Yacht Club. Anglican. Address: PO Box 347 White Stone VA 22578-2021 Office Phone: 804-462-5155.

DUERINCK, LOUIS T., retired rail transportation executive, lawyer; b. Chgo., Aug. 1, 1929; s. Aloys L. and Thais E. (De Backer) D.; m. Patricia A. Bird, June 27, 1953; children: Louis M., Kathleen M. Lutgen, Kevin F., Mark V., Lynn P. Dressel, Brian T., Paul S. Student, U. Notre Dame, 1947-48; JD, DePaul U., Chgo., 1952. Bar: Ill. 1952. Commerce atty. N.Y. Cen. R.R., Chgo., 1955-65; gen. atty. Nat. Ry. Labor Conf., Chgo., 1967-68; with C&NW Ry. Co., Chgo., 1965-67, 68-89; sr. v.p. law and real estate C&NW Transp. Co., 1979-83, sr. v.p. traffic, 1983-88, sr. v.p., 1988-89, also bd. dirs. Served with AUS, 1952—55. Mem. ABA, Assn. Transportation Law Profls., Ill. Bar Assn., Glen Oak Country Club, Wyndemere Country Club (Naples). Roman Catholic. Home and Office: 718 Midwest Club Pky Oak Brook IL 60523-2531

DUERKSEN, CHRISTOPHER JAMES, lawyer, municipal official; b. Newton, Kans., July 25, 1948; s. Benjamin F. and Dorothy (Brown) D.; m. Janice Louise Duerksen, Feb. 6, 1971 (div.); children: Benjamin, Matthew. BA, Kans. State Coll., 1970; JD, U. Chgo., 1974. Bar: Ill. 1975. Assoc. Ross & Hardies, Chgo., 1974-78; sr. assoc. The Conservation Found., Washington, 1978-87; dir. resource devel. and pub. policy The Enterprise Found.,

Columbia, Md., 1987-88; dir. Gateway/Stapleton Devel. Office, Denver, 1988-91; mng. dir. Clarion Assocs., Denver, 1991—. Author: Environmental Regulation of Industrial Plant Siting, 1984 (Best Acad. Book award 1984), Handbook on Historic Preservation Law, 1983, Dow v. California, 1984, (with others) National Parks for a New Generation, 1986. Mem. Fredericksburg (Va.) City Coun., 1984-87, Va. Waste Mgmt. Bd., Richmond, 1986-87, TrueWest, 2004, Nature-Friendly Communities, 2005; founder Friends of Rappahannock, Fredericksburg, 1986; bd. dirs. Preservation Action, 1986-89, Scenic Am., 1987—, Air and Space West, Inc., 1989-91. Mem. ABA (chmn. com. on land use sect. on urban, state and local govt. law 1984-86, coun. 1986-88). Democrat. Mem. Mennonite Ch. Office: Clarion Assocs 1700 Broadway Ste 400 Denver CO 80290-1700 Office Phone: 303-830-2890. Business E-Mail: c.duerksen@clarionassociates.com.

DUERKSEN, GEORGE LOUIS, music educator, music therapist; b. St. Joseph, Mo., Oct. 29, 1934; s. George Herbert and Louise May (Dalke) D.; m. Patricia Gay Beers, June 3, 1961; children— Mark Jeffrey, Joseph Scott, Cynthia Elizabeth Student, Tabor Coll., 1951-52; BMusEdn, U. Kans., 1955, MMusEdn, 1956, PhD, 1967. Cert. music educator Kans., Mo., registered music therapist Nat. Assn. Music Therapy, bd. cert. music therapist Cert. Bd. Music Therapists. Tchr. music Tonganoxie High Sch., Kans., 1955-56, Stafford Jr. and Sr. High Sch., Kans., 1959-60, Labette County High Sch., Altamont, Kans., 1960-62, Shawnee Mission (Kans.) North High Sch., 1962-63; asst. prof., dir. psychology of music lab. Mich. State U., East Lansing, 1965-69; prof., chmn. dept. art and music edn. and music therapy U. Kans., Lawrence, 1969-93, dir. Singing Jayhawks, 1979-83, prof., dir. music edn. and music therapy divsn., 1993—2004, prof., interim chair dept. music and dance, 2000-01, dir. Ctr. for Rsch. on Music Behavior, 2001—; assoc. dir. Kans. North Ctrl. Assn. Colls. and Schs., 1992-2000. Cons., vis. prof. U. Hawaii, Honolulu, summer 1978; cons., vis. prof. U. Melbourne, Australia, summer 1981; cons., lectr. N.Z. Soc. for Music Therapy, Wellington, 1983, Ctr. for Contemporary Music Rsch., Athens, 1991, U. Thessaloniki, Greece, 1993, Korean Assn. for Music Therapy, 1994, 97, Sook Myung U., Seoul, 1997; cons. functional music applications, 1967—, Deakin U., Geelong, Victoria, Australia, 1990. Author: (monograph) Teaching Instrumental Music, 1973; Music for Exceptional Children, 1981; contbr. articles to profl. jours. Fulbright scholar Inst. for Internat. Edn., Australia, 1956-57; U.Kans. fellow, Lawrence, 1963-64; U.S. Office Edn. grantee, 1966-67, 73-75, 78-81. Mem. AAAS, Music Educators Nat. Conf., Am. Music Therapy Assn.(award of merit, 2000), Music Edn. Rsch. Coun. (chmn. 1980-82), Brit. Soc. for Music Therapy, Coun. for Rsch. in Music Edn., Pi Kappa Lambda, Phi Mu Alpha, Phi Delta Kappa. Avocations: photography, boating, travel. Office Phone: 785-864-9632. E-mail: gduerksen@ku.edu.

DUERR, DAVID, civil engineer; b. Newark, July 4, 1953; s. Warren August and Dorothy (Lanzillo) D.; m. Roberta Kay Apolant, Oct. 12, 1991. B of Engring., Pratt Inst., 1975; MS, U. Houston, 1985. Registered profl. engr. Project engr. Hoffman Internat., Pt. Newark, N.J., 1974-76; chief engr. Williams Crane & Rigging, Richmond, Va., 1976-79; sr. structural engr. Hudson Engring. Corp., Houston, 1980-86; pres. 2DM Assocs., Inc., Houston, 1986—. Frequent lectr. constrn. industry seminars. Contbr. tech. papers to profl. jours. Mem.: ASME (mem. BTH stds. com. on below-the-hook lifting devices), ASCE, Specialized Carriers and Rigging Assn., Soc. Naval Archs. and Marine Engrs., Soc. Automotive Engrs., Am. Coun. Engring. Cos. Achievements include research in the design of pinned connections and development of standards for the design of telescopic hydraulic gantries. Office: 2DM Assocs Inc 9235 Katy Freeway Ste 350 Houston TX 77024-1526

DUERR, HERMAN GEORGE, retired publishing executive; b. Nagold, Germany, June 24, 1931; came to U.S., 1949, naturalized, 1975; s. Adolf Gustav and Wilhelmine Dorothea (Walz) Durr; m. Shirley Yvonne Jones, June 29, 1957; children: Suzanne, Steffan, Krista. B.F.A., Wayne State U., 1958. Publs. designer Ceco Comm. Inc., Warren, Mich., 1958-60; art dir. Am. Youth mag., 1960-67, Friends mag., 1967-86, exec. editor, 1978-87; v.p. Ceco Comm., Inc., 1981-91; dir. mktg. prodn. Ceco Pub. Co., 1987-91; publ. cons. Harrison, Mich., 1991—. Adj. faculty Mid Mich. C.C., 1991—. Served with U.S. Army, 1952-55.

DUERST, ANDREAS, information technology executive; Mng. dir. Ctrl. and Ea. Europe Lucent Tech., 1995—2000; mng. dir. Swiss ops. Tech Data Corp., Clearwater, Fla., 2000—03, sr. v.p. Ctrl. Europe, 2003—. Office: Tech Data Corp 5350 Tech Data Dr Clearwater FL 33760-3122

DUES, ANTONETTE Y., art educator; d. Mildred and William Victor; 1 child, Tajz William Armand. BA, Seton Hill Coll., 1978—82. Instructional 2 Commonwealth of Pa., 2003. Art tchr. Connellsville Sch. Dist., Pa., 1998—; christian dance instr. Morningstar Ministries, Scottdale, Pa., 2003—. Sponsor, co-sponsor Art/Multicultural Clubs, Connellsville, Pa., 2000—. Christian. Avocations: art, dance, travel, reading. Office: Connellsville Senior High 201 Falcon Dr Connellsville PA 15425 Office Phone: 724-628-1350 1134.

DUESBERRY, JOELLYN TOLER, artist; b. Richmond, Va., June 30, 1944; d. Arthur Reginald and Joellyn Dean (Toler) D.; m. Dr. Ira Kowal; stepchildren: Rebekah, Jessica. Student, U. Va., 1962-64; BA with distinction, Smith Coll., 1966; MA, NYU, 1967; postgrad., Dartmouth Coll., 1967-68. Instr. in landscape painting Art Students League of Denver, 1989—. One woman shows include Tatistcheff Gallery, N.Y.C., 1979, 81, 83, 85, Gerald Peters Gallery, N.Mex., 1986-2000, Graham Modern Gallery, N.Y.C., 1989-2004, Denver Art Mus., 1992; numerous exhbns.; traveling monotype exhbn. Va. Mus. Fine Arts, 1998-2005, Tremaine Gallery, Hotchkiss, 2005—. Woodrow Wilson fellow NYU Inst. Fine Arts, 1966-67; NEA grantee, 1985. Mem. Phi Beta Kappa. Avocations: helicopter skiing, gardening, xeriscape. Home: 2800 E Willamette Ln Greenwood Village CO 80121-1615 Office: 35 Thimble House Trail Millbrook NY 12545 Office Phone: 303-770-3716.

DUESENBERG, RICHARD WILLIAM, lawyer; b. St. Louis, Dec. 10, 1930; s. (John August) Hugo and Edna Marie (Warmann) D.; m. Phyllis Evelyn Buehner, Aug. 7, 1955; children: Karen, Daryl, Mark, David. BA, Valparaiso U., 1951, JD, 1953, LLD, 2001; LLM, Yale U., 1956. Bar: Mo. 1953. Prof. law NYU, N.Y.C., 1956-62, dir. law ctr. publs., 1960-62; sr. atty. Monsanto Co., St. Louis, 1963-70, asst. gen. counsel, asst. sec., 1975-77, sr. v.p., sec., gen. counsel, 1977-96. Dir. law Monsanto Textiles Co., St. Louis, 1971-75; corp. sec. Fisher Controls Co., Marshalltown, Iowa, 1969-71, Olympia Industries, Spartanburg, S.C., 1974-75; vis. prof. law U. Mo., 1970-71; faculty Banking Sch. South, La. State U., 1967-83; vis. scholar Cambridge U., England, 1996; vis. prof. law St. Louis U., 1997-98. Author: (with Lawrence P. King) Sales and Bulk Transfers Under the Uniform Commercial Code, 2 vols, 1966, rev., 1984, New York Law of Contracts, 3 vols, 1964, Missouri Forms and Practice Under the Uniform Commercial Code, 2 vols, 1966; editor: Ann. Survey of Am. Law, NYU, 1961-62; mem. bd. contbg. editors and advisors: Corp. Law Rev, 1977-86; contbr. articles to law revs., jours. Mem. lawyers adv. coun. NAM, Washington, 1980, Adminstrv. Conf. U.S., 1980-86, legal adv. com. N.Y. Stock Exch., 1983-87, corp. law dept. adv. coun. Practising Law Inst., 1982; bd. dirs. Bach Soc., St. Louis, 1985-86, pres., 1973-77; bd. dirs. Valparaiso U., 1977—, chmn. bd. visitors law sch., 1966—, Luth. Charities Assn., 1984-87, vice chmn., 1986-87; bd. dirs. Luth. Med. Ctr., St. Louis, 1973-82, vice chmn., 1975-80; bd. dirs. Nat. Jud. Coll., 1984-90, St. Louis Symphony, 1988-2002, Opera Theatre St. Louis, 1988—, Luth. Brotherhood, Mpls., 1992-2000, Liberty Fund, Inc., Indpls., 1997—. Served with U.S. Army, 1953-55. Decorated officer's cross Order of Merit (Germany); named Disting. Alumnus, Valparaiso U., 1976. Fellow Am. Bar Found.; mem. ABA (chmn. com. uniform comml. code 1976-79, coun. sect. corp., banking and bus. law 1979-83, sec. 1983-84, chmn. 1986-87), Mo. Bar Assn., Am. Law Inst., Mont Pelerin Soc., Nat. Jud. Coll. (bd. dirs. 1984-90), Order of Coif, Bach Soc., Am. Soc. Corp. Sec. (bd. chmn. 1987-88), Assn. Gen. Coun., Am. Arbitration Assn., St. Louis Club. Home: 1 Indian Creek Ln Saint Louis MO 63131-3333 Personal E-mail: rwduesenberg@worldnet.att.net.

DUESENBERG, ROBERT H., retired lawyer; b. St. Louis, Dec. 10, 1930; s. Hugo John August and Edna Marie (Warmann) D.; m. Lorraine Freda Hall, July 23, 1938; children: Lynda Renee, Kirsten Lynn, John Robert. BA, Valparaiso (Ind.) U., 1951, LLB, 1953; LLM, Harvard U., 1956. Bar: Mo. 1953, U.S. Supreme Ct. 1981, Va. 1993. Pvt. practice, St. Louis, 1956-58; atty. Wabash R.R. Co., St. Louis, 1958-65, Norfolk & Western Ry. Co., St. Louis, 1962-65; atty., assoc. gen. counsel Pet Inc., St. Louis, 1965-77, v.p., assoc. gen. counsel, 1977-80, v.p., gen. counsel, 1980-83, Gen. Dynamics Corp., Falls Church, Va., 1984-91, sr. v.p. and gen. counsel, 1991-93; ret., 1993. Bd. dirs. Valparaiso (Ind.) U., QuidTech Marine, Inc.; adv. bd. ELawForum, Inc., Washington. Contbr. numerous articles to profl. jours. Sec., treas., legal advisor Am. Kantorei, St. Louis, 1970-75; mem. Coun. on World Affairs, St. Louis, 1975—, Mo. Coordinating Bd. for Higher Edn., Jefferson City, 1976-83, chmn., 1978-81; mem. pres.'s coun. Valparaiso (Ind.) U., 1979—, bd. dirs., 1995—; bd. dirs. Higher Edn. Loan Authority, 1982-84; mem. adv. bd. Northwestern U. Corp. Counsel Ctr., 1988—, chmn. adv. bd., 1992; bd. dirs. Opera Theatre of St. Louis, 1988—; bd. dirs. Luther Inst., Washington, 1999—, chair, 2000-03; mem. adv. bd. ELawForum, Washington. Cpl. U.S. Army, 1953-55. Recipient Disting. Alumnus award Valparaiso U., 1982. Mem. ABA, Va. Bar Assn., Mo. Bar Assn., St. Louis Bar Assn. (chmn. antitrust com. 1971-73, v.p. bus. law sect. 1972-73, chmn. 1973-74), Am. Law Inst., Gen. Counsels Assn., Machine and Allied Products Inst. (legal counsel 1986—), Am. Corp. Counsel Assn., S.W. Legal Found. (adv. bd.), Aerospace Industry Assn. (legal com. 1981-88), Bach Soc. of St. Louis (bd. dirs.). Republican. Lutheran. Home: 10171 Castlewood Ln Oakton VA 22124-3027 E-mail: rhduesenberg@earthlink.net.

DUFAULT, MARY LOUISE SELKER, lawyer; b. Clarion, Pa., May 9, 1937; d. Ambrose John and Mary Elizabeth (Meisinger) Selker; m. Larry Bernard Dufault, June 22, 1963; children: Michael, Jacqueline. BS, Ind. State Tchrs. Coll., 1959; MS, Pa. State U., 1962; MA, U. Conn., 1974; JD, Franklin Pierce Law Ctr., 1980. Tchr. Carlisle Pub. Schs., Pa., 1959-61; asst. prof. Juniata Coll., Huntingdon, Pa., 1962-69, Colby Coll., New London, N.H., 1975-77; ptnr. Dufault & Dufault, New London, 1980—. Trustee New London Hosp., 1983-93; mem. stewardship com. St. Andrew's Ch., New London, 1982-84, budget com. Town of New London, 1982-86. Ind. State Tchrs. Coll. scholar, 1955-59. Mem. ABA, N.H. Bar Assn. (econs. of law com. 1984-86, long range planning com. 1983-86, 88-89, vice-chair family law sect. 1993—, women in the profession com. 1991—), New London Bar Assn. (co-pres. 1993), New London C. of C. (dir. 1981-88), LWV, NOW, Kappa Delta Pi, Kappa Omicron Phi. Clubs: Lake Sunapee Yacht, New London Garden, New London Outing. Democrat. Episcopalian. Home: Woodland Way PO Box 851 New London NH 03257-0851

DUFF, ERNEST ARTHUR, political scientist, educator; b. Charlottesville, Va., Dec. 27, 1929; s. Ernest Ragland and Emma Ruth (Bennett) D.; m. Barbara Ellen Jones, Aug. 30, 1955; children: Ernest A. Jr., Melanie Duff Badesch, Cameron John, Valerie Duff-Strautmann. BA, U. Va., 1952, MA, 1957, PhD, 1964. Fgn. svc. officer Dept. of State, Havana, Cuba, 1957-60, Washington, 1960-62, Bogota, Colombia, 1962-63; prof. Randolph-Macon Woman's Coll., Lynchburg, Va., 1964-97, Charles Dana prof., 1986, prof. emeritus, 1997—. Spl. field rep. Rockefeller Found., Cali, Colombia, 1966-67; vis. Fulbright prof. U. Mexico, Mexico City, 1979-80. Author: Agrarian Reform in Colombia, 1968, Violence and Repression in Latin America, 1974, Leader and Party in Latin America, 1984; reviewer Choice mag. Am. Libr. Assn. Polit. analyst WSET-TV, Lynchburg, Va., 1987—. Lt. USN, 1952-55, Korea. NROTC scholar USN and U. Va., 1948-52; Helen Wessell fellow, U. Va., 1963-64, NEH fellow, Brown U., Providence, 1990. Mem. Latin Am. Studies Assn., So. Polit. Sci. Assn., Southeastern Coun. Latin Am. Studies, Va. Polit. Sci. Assn. Baptist. Avocations: tennis, gardening. Home: 1633 Dogwood Ln Lynchburg VA 24503-1923 Personal E-mail: ebdu@earthlink.net.

DUFF, GILL, advertising executive; married; 4 children. BA, Univ. Tenn. Sr. acct. positions Young & Rubicam, D'Arcy, Leo Burnett, Foote Cone & Belding; worldwide sr. acct. dir. BBDO; pres., CEO NY office Publicis Groupe's Publicis USA, 2004—. Bd. dir. Advt. Week, 2005—. Office: Publicis NY 4 Herald Sq 950 Sixth Ave New York NY 10001 Office Phone: 212-279-5550. Office Fax: 212-279-5560.*

DUFF, HILARY ANN, actress, singer; b. Houston, Sept. 28, 1987; d. Bob and Susan Duff. Released own product line Stuff by Hilary Duff. Actor: (TV films) True Women, 1997, Soul Collector, 1999; (TV series) Lizzie McGuire, 2001—03; (films) Human Nature, 2001, Cadet Kelly, 2002, Agent Cody Banks, 2003, The Lizzie McGuire Movie, 2003, Cheaper by the Dozen, 2003, A Cinderella Story, 2004, Raise Your Voice, 2004, The Perfect Man, 2005, (guest appearances on): (TV series) Chicago Hope, 2000, George Lopez, 2003, American Dreams, 2003, Frasier (voice), 2004; singer: (albums) Lizzie McGuire Television Soundtrack, 2001, Santa Claus Lane, 2002, The Lizzie McGuire Movie Soundtrack, 2003, Hilary Duff, 2004, (debut solo album) Metamorphosis, 2003 (charted #2 on Billboard 200 first week of release). Internat. spokesperson Kids With A Cause, 1999—. Recipient Nickelodeon Kids Choice Award for Favorite Female Singer, 2004. Office: c/o PMK Public Relations 650 Fifth Ave 33rd Fl New York NY 10019*

DUFF, JAMES GEORGE, finance company executive, retired automotive executive; b. Pittsburg, Kans., Jan. 27, 1938; s. James George and Camilla Matilda (Vinardi) D.; m. Linda Louise Beeman, June 24, 1961 (div.); children: Michele, Mark, Melissa; m. Beverly L. Pool, Nov. 16, 1984. BS with distinction, U. Kans., 1960, MBA, 1961. With Ford Motor Co., Dearborn, Mich., 1962-97, various positions fin. staff, 1962-71; dir. product, profit, price, warranty Ford of Europe, 1972-74; controller Ford Div., 1974-76, controller car ops., 1976, controller car product devel., 1976-80; exec. v.p. Ford Motor Credit Co., 1980-88, bd. dirs.; pres., COO U.S. Leasing Internat. Inc., San Francisco, 1988-89, pres., CEO, 1990-91; chmn., CEO USL Capital (formally U.S. Leasing Internat. Inc.), San Francisco, 1991-97, also bd. dirs. Bd. dirs. Boulder Total Return Fund, 1997-99; mem. Conf. Bd., 1990-97. Mem. adv. bd. U. Kans. Sch. Bus., 1980-98; bd. dirs. Bay Area Coun., 1990-97; trustee San Francisco Mus. Modern Art, 1990-97; chmn. bus. devel. unit Detroit United Fund, 1980-85, chmn. edn. and local govt. unit Detroit United Fund, 1986-88. Sunray Mid-Continent scholar, Bankers scholar, to 1960. Mem. San Francisco C. of C. (bd. dirs. 1990-91). Home: 7544 S Dunns Farm Rd Maple City MI 49664-8718 also: 1 The Courtyard 65 Old Church St London SW3 5BS England Personal E-mail: onmyduff@msn.com.

DUFF, JAMES HENRY, museum director, environmental services administrator; b. Pitts., Oct. 11, 1943; s. James Sylvester and Virginia (Henry) D.; m. Sally Kathryn Tredwell, Sept. 14, 1963; children: Abigail Margaret, Jessica Lauren. BA, Washington and Jefferson Coll., 1965; MA, U. Mass., 1970. Teaching asst. U. Mass., Amherst, 1965-66; dir. Mus. of Hudson Highlands, Cornwall-on-Hudson, N.Y., 1966-73, Brandywine River Mus., Chadds Ford, Pa., 1973—; exec. dir. Brandywine Conservancy, Chadds Ford, 1976—. Cons. N.Y. State Coun. on Arts, 1970-72; panel mem. Pa. Coun. on Arts, 1976-79, 83-85; mem. adv. coun. Nat. Mus. Act, 1982-85; mem. Nat. Mus. Svcs. Bd., 1986-95. Author: The Western World of N. C. Wyeth, 1980, Landscapes, Still Lifes and Portraits by N. C. Wyeth, 1982, An American Vision, 1987; contbr. articles on mus. programs to profl. jours. Trustee Wyeth Endowment for Am. Art, 1986-95, Am. Arts Alliance, 1995-96, Greater Phila. Cultural Alliance (trustee 2001—). With U.S. Army, 1967-69. Mem. Mid-Atlantic Assn. Mus. (pres. 1983-85, The Katherine Coffey award 1992), Assn. Art Mus. Dirs. (trustee 1993-98, 2001—04, v.p. 1995-96, pres. 1996-97), Am. Assn. Mus. (trustee 1983-88). Home: PO Box 297 Chadds Ford PA 19317-0297 Office: Brandywine River Mus Brandywine Conservancy PO Box 141 Chadds Ford PA 19317-0141 Office Phone: 610-388-2700. Business E-Mail: jduff@brandywine.org.

DUFF, JOHN A., law educator; BS, Univ. Lowell; JD, Suffolk Univ.; LLM, Univ. Wash.; MA, Univ. Miss. Dir. Miss./Ala. Sea Grant Legal Prog., Univ. Miss., 1995—99; assoc. rsch. prof. Univ. Maine Sch. Law, 1999—, dir., Marine Law Inst. Vis. instr. Univ. Victoria, BC, Canada, 1998; mem. sci. team NOAA vessel Ron Brown, VENTS expdn., 1998; mem. United Nations Environment Programme, Nairobi, Kenya. Mem. Submerged Lands Adv. Bd., Maine, 2001. Mem.: Coastal Soc. (pres. 2003—). Office: Marine Law Institute University of Maine School of Law 246 Deering Ave Portland ME 04102

DUFF, JOHN EWING, sculptor; b. Lafayette, Ind., Dec. 2, 1943; s. John Ewing and Ruth (Miller) D. B.F.A., San Francisco Art Inst., 1967. One man shows include: Margo Leavin Gallery, L.A., 1981, Blum-Helman Gallery, N.Y.C., 1985-90, L.A., 1987, 91, San Jose (Calif.) Mus. Art, 1991, Gallery 57, Madrid, 1992, Salama Caro Gallery, London, 1992, David McKee Gallery, 1995, Johnson County C.C. Gallery Art, 1995, Knoedler Gallery, N.Y.C., 1997, 2001, 04, Hill Gallery, Birmingham, Mich., 1999, Brantley Gallery, Scottsdale, Ariz., 1999, Ingred Rabb Gallery, Berlin, 1999, Manfred Baumgartner Gallery, N.Y.C. 2001 (recent work), Weatherspoon Art Mus., Greensboro, N.C., 2005; two-person show at Hill Gallery, Birmingham, Mich., 1996; group exhbns. include Whitney Mus., N.Y.C., 1969, 81, David Whitney Gallery, N.Y.C., 1970, 71, Irving Blum Gallery, L.A., 1972, John Bernard Meyers Gallery, N.Y.C., 1972, 73, Willard Gallery, N.Y.C., 1975-78, Whitney Mus. Equitable Ctr., 1987, The Edward R. Broida Collection, Orlando Mus. of Art, 1998, Anderson Gallery, Va. Commonwealth U., 2000, Am. Acad. Invitational Exhbn. of Painting and Sculpture, 2002; represented in public collections Kaiser Wilhelm Mus., Krefeld, Fed. Republic Germany, Mus. Modern Art, N.Y.C., Walker Art Ctr., Mpls., Met. Mus. Art, N.Y.C., Solomon R. Guggenheim Mus., N.Y.C., L.A. Mus. Contemporary Art, Mus. Contemporary Art, Chgo. Recipient Theodoren award Guggenheim Mus., 1977, award Am. Acad. and Inst. Arts and Letters, 1981, John Simon Guggenheim fellowship, 1979-80, Brandeis U. Creative Arts award Citation in Sculpture, 1987. Home and Office: 7 Doyers St New York NY 10013-5112

DUFF, MICHAEL JAMES, physicist; b. Manchester, Jan. 28, 1949; s. Edward and Elizabeth (Kaylor) D.; m. Lesley Yearling, 1984; children: Jessica, Matthew. BS, Queen Mary Coll., U. London, 1969; PhD, Imperial Coll., U. London, 1972. Postdoctoral fellow in theoretical physics Internat. Ctr. Theoretical Physics, Trieste, Italy, Oxford (Eng.) U., U. London, Brandeis U., Waltham, Mass., 1972-79; faculty mem. Imperial Coll., 1979-88; sr. physicist CERN, Geneva, 1984-87; prof. physics Tex. A&M U., College Station, 1988-92, Disting. prof. physics, 1992-99; Oskar Klein prof. physics U. Mich., Ann Arbor, 1999—; dir. Mich. Ctr. for Theoretical Physics, 2000—; prof. physics and prin. faculty physical scis. Imperial Coll., London, 2005—. Contbr. articles to profl. jours. Recipient Meeting Gold medal, El Colegio Nacional, Mex., 2004. Fellow Am. Phys. Soc., Inst. Physics U.K. Avocations: water colors, golf. Home: 846 Arboretum Dr Saline MI 48176-1354 Office: U Mich Dept Physics 3425 Randall Lab Ann Arbor MI 48109-1120

DUFF, PATRICIA, civic activist; b. L.A., Apr. 12, 1954; d. Robert Orr and Mary Williamson; 1 child, Caleigh Sophia Perelman. Student, Internat. Sch. Brussels, 1971, Barnard Coll.; BS in Internat. Econs., Georgetown U., 1976. Spl. asst. to chief counsel house select com. on assassinations U.S. Ho. of Reps., Washington, 1976-78; prodr., writer, researcher John McLaughlin Show-NBC Radio, Washington, 1979-80; asst. rsch. dir. Dem. Nat. Com., Washington, 1980; v.p. Patrick Caddell and Assocs., Washington, 1980-82, Squier, Eskew Assoc., 1982-84; with Mondale for Pres., L.A., 1984, Americans for Hart, L.A., 1984; ind. producer Columbia Pictures, Burbank, Calif.; pres. Revlon Found., 1995-97. Assoc. producer Dem. Nat. Conv., Atlanta, 1988; mem. nat. media adv. bd. Hart for Pres., L.A., 1988; polit. talk show host Plum TV; guest co-host Sta. WABC-Radio. Contbg. editor Vogue Mag., 1989; editor at large Premier Mag., 1995-97; host Duff Talk. Founder Am. Spirit Awards, 1992; chair N.Y. Gov.'s Task Force on Teen Pregnancy, 1994—95, Women Vote Campaign of Emily's List, 1996, Saves Women's Leadership Coun., 1999—2004; mem. platform com. Dem. Nat. Conv., 1984, 1992; mem. Hollywood Women's Polit. Com., 1986; co-chair N.Y. fin. com. Clinton for Pres., 1996; bd. dirs. People for the Am. Way, 1996—2002; mem. bd. councilors Ascus sch. pub. policy and adminstrn. U. So. Calif.; founder, chair bd. dirs. Show Coalition The Common Good, L.A., 1988—; mem. bd. visitors Sch. Fgn. Svc. Georgetown U., 1988—; mem. pvt. sector adv. bd. Inter Am. Devel. Bank; bd. trustees Save the Children; bd. dirs. L.A. Colors United, Summer of Svc., Nat. Svc., 1993, L.A. Commn. on Status of Women, 1994—96, Women in Film, 1990—, Lincoln Ctr. Film Soc., 1995—2000; trustee Nat. Pub. Radio, Am. Ballet Theatre, 1995—96; mem. Presdl. Commn. on Libr. of Congress Trust Fund, 1994—2000; founder Families for Justice, 2004. Named one of Rising Young Stars L.A. Times, 1989; named Dem. of Yr. L.A. County, 1989; recipient Women We Love award for polit. activism Esquire Mag., 1990, Women in Film award Women in Film, 1995, Citizen's Achievement award NDD, 1998. Office Phone: 212-722-6390.

DUFF, WILLIAM GRIERSON, electrical engineer, educator; b. Alexandria, Va., Dec. 16, 1936; s. Johnnie Douglas and Annetta Osceola (Rind) D.; m. Sandra K. Via, June 25, 1983; children: Warren David, Valerie Lynn, Dawn Elizabeth, Deborah Arleen, Kelly Juanita. BEE, George Washington U., 1959, postgrad., 1959-72; MS, Syracuse U., 1969; DSc in Elec. Engring., Clayton U., 1977. Pres. SEMTAS, Fairfax, Va., 1959—. Asst. prof. Capitol Inst. Tech., Greenbelt, Md., 1972—; instr. Interference Control Technologies, Don White Cons., Inc., Gainesville, Va. Author: EMI Handbook, vol. 5, EMI Prediction and Analysis Techniques, 1972, Mobile Communications, 1976, Fundamentals of EMC, 1988, EMC in Telecommunications, 1988; contbr. articles to profl. jours. Counselor Meth. Sr. High Youth Group, 1965-73. Recipient Good Citizenship award DAR, 1955, Math. award George Washington H.S., Alexandria, 1955. Fellow IEEE (pres. EMC Soc., assoc. editor group newsletter 1970—); mem. AIEE (Best Paper award 1961), George Washington U. Engring. Alumni Assn. (pres. 1963-64, Engring. Alumni Svc. award 1980), Springfield Golf and Country Club, Occoquan Water Ski Club (pres. 1976), Sigma Tau, Theta Tau. Home: 7601 S Valley Dr Fairfax VA 22039-2965 Office: Sentel 7601 S Valley Dr Fairfax Station VA 22039 Office Phone: 703-239-0429. Personal E-mail: wmduff@cox.net.

DUFF, WILLIAM LEROY, JR., university dean emeritus, business educator; b. Oakland, Calif., Sept. 14, 1938; s. William Leroy and Edna Francis (Gunderson) D.; m. Arline M. Wight, Sept. 1, 1962; children— Susan M., William Leroy III. BA, Calif. State U.-, San Francisco, 1963, postgrad., 1963-64; MSSc., Nat. Econs. Inst., U. Stockholm, 1965; PhD, UCLA, 1969. Research assoc. C.F. Kettering Found., 1967-69; asst. JOBS program Nat. Alliance Businessmen, 1969-70; prof. U. No. Colo., Greeley, 1970—, dir. Sch Bus., Bur Bus. and Pub. Research, 1972-75, dean Coll. Bus. Adminstrn., 1984—, interim v.p. acad. affairs, 1987, chmn. faculty senate, 1981-82. On leave as UN adviser to Govt. of Swaziland, 1975-77; cons. in field. Contbr. articles to profl. jours. Mem. Greeley Planning Commn., 1972-75, chmn., 1974-75; trustee U. No. Colo., 1983; mem. Greeley Water and Sewer Bd., 1994-98, Greeley City Coun., 2000; bd. dirs. Centennial Svcs., 2003, United Way of Weld County, 2003, exec. bd. and investment com., UNC Found., 2003. With U.S. Army, 1958-60. Mem. Greeley Rotary Club (bd. dirs.), Greeley Area C. of C. (bd. dirs.). Home: 1614 Lakeside Dr Greeley CO 80631-5343 Office: U No Colo Coll Bus Adminstrn Kepner Greeley CO 80639-0001

DUFFEE, BEVERLY ANN, secondary school educator; b. Sharon, Pa., Apr. 18, 1946; d. Kenneth Ira and Edith Belle (Farringer) Duffee. BA, Roberts Wesleyan Coll., 1968; MA, Calif. State U., 1973. Pers. adminstr./programmer Newport Electronics, Santa Ana, Calif., 1973—77; pers. counselor Dennis & Dennis Pers. Svcs., Santa Ana, 1978; sales sec. Auto Battery Divsn. Gould Inc., Irvine, Calif., 1979—81; chmn. dept. English, tchr. music, art, drama, bible Leffingwell Christian Jr./Sr. H.S., Norwalk, Calif., 1981—90; tchr. lang. arts, forensic coach John H. Glenn H.S., Norwalk, 1990—. Instr. English Biola U., La Mirada, Calif., 1984—85; vocal dir., instr. Puente Project, 1990—. Mem.: World Gospel Mission, Alpha Kappa Sigma. Republican. Methodist. Home: 8811 Park St Space 98 Bellflower CA 90706 Office: 13520 Shoemaker Ave Norwalk CA 90650-4521 Office Phone: 562-868-0431.

DUFFEY, JOSEPH DANIEL, academic administrator; b. Huntington, W.Va., July 1, 1932; s. Joseph I. and Ruth (Wilson) Duffey; m. Anne Wexler, 1974; children: Michael, David, Danny Wexler, David Wexler. BA, Marshall U., 1954; STM, Yale U., 1963; BD, Andover Newton Theol. Sch., 1958; PhD, Hartford Sem. Found., 1969; LHD, CUNY, 1978, U. Cin., 1978, U. Mass., 1991; LittD, Dickinson Coll., Pa., 1978, Centre Coll., Ky., 1977, Gonzaga U., Wash., 1980, Monmouth Coll., 1980, CCNY; LLD, Amherst Coll., Bethany Coll., Austin Coll., Ritsuimaneu U., Kyoto, Japan, 1993; LittD, Alderson-Broadus Coll., Adelphi U., Central Fla. Asst. prof. Hartford (Conn.) Sem., 1960—63; assoc. prof., dir. Ctr. Urban Studies, 1965—70; fellow Harvard U. Kennedy Sch. Govt., 1971; adj. prof. and fellow Calhoun Coll., Yale U., 1971—73; exec. officer AAUP, 1974—77; asst. sec. for edn. and cultural affairs Dept. State, 1977; chmn. NEH, 1978—81; chancellor U. Mass., Amherst, 1982—, pres., 1990—91, Am. U., Washington, 1991—93; dir. U.S. Info. Agy., Washington, 1993—98; sr. exec., chmn. internat. univ. project Sylvan Learning Sys., Washington, 1999—. Mem. U.S. dept. 20th and 21st gen. confs. UNESCO, 1978, 80; mem. exec. com. Nat. Coun. Competitiveness Govt. and Industry Univ. Panel Nat. Acad. Scis.; bd. dirs. Bay Bank, Springfield, Mass. Contbr. articles to profl. jours. Bd. dirs. Woodrow Wilson Internat. Ctr. Scholars, East-West Ctr., Western Mass. Area Devel. Corp., Jewish Theol. Sem. Libr., Springfield Symphony. Decorated Order of The Crown Belgium; recipient Tree of Life award, Nat. Jewish Fund, 1987; scholar, Rockefeller Found., 1966—68. Mem.: Century Assn., Coun. Fgn. Rels., Cosmos Club. Office: Laureate Learning Sys 2801 New Mexico Ave NW Apt 311 Washington DC 20007-3913 Office Phone: 202-965-1044. Personal E-mail: jduffey@earthlink.net.

DUFFEY, WILLIAM SIMON, JR., federal judge, former prosecutor; b. Phila., May 9, 1952; s. William Simon and Elinor (Daniluk) D.; m. Betsy Byars, Dec. 17, 1977; children: Charles, Scott. BA in English, honors, Drake U., 1973; JD cum laude, U. S.C., 1977. Bar: S.C. 1977, Ga. 1982, U.S. Dist. Ct. (no., mid. and so. dists.) Ga. 1982, U.S. Ct. Appeals (llth cir.) 1983, U.S. Supreme Ct., 1992. Atty. Nexson, Pruet, Jacobs & Pollard, Columbia, S.C., 1977-78; assoc. King & Spalding, LLP, Atlanta, 1981—87, ptnr., 1987—94, 1995—2001; dep. ind. counsel Office of the Ind. Counsel, Little Rock, 1994-95; U.S. Atty. (No. dist.) Ga. US Dept. Justice, Atlanta, 2002—04; judge U.S. Dist. Ct. (No. dist) Ga, 2004—. Adj. prof. U. S.C. Law Sch., 2000—01. Articles editor S.C. Lawyer, 1990-94. Pres. Pine Hills Civic Assn., Atlanta, 1984-88; trustee Drake U.; Ga. Rep. Found., Leadership Atlanta; bd. dirs. Ga. Wilderness Inst., 1992-2001; mem. Peachtree Rd. Race Com., 1993—, chmn. Ga. Good Govt. Com., 1995-2001; chmn. bd. advisors Coverdell Leadership Inst., 1995-2002; bd. mem. North Ga. Walk to Emmaus, 1999-2001; founder New Century Forum. Asst. staff judge advocate USAF, 1978—81. Mem. Altanta Bar Assn. (chmn. alt. dispute resolution com. 1984-88), Lawyers Club, Atlanta Track Club (gen. counsel 1993-2001). Republican. Avocations: running, cooking, woodturning. Office: US Courthouse 75 Spring St SW Atlanta GA 30303-3361 Office Phone: 404-215-1480. Personal E-mail: billduffey@bellsouth.net.

DUFFIE, L. TRAYWICK, lawyer; b. Augusta, Ga., Feb. 13, 1947; BA, Wofford Coll., 1969; JD, Univ. SC, 1972. Bar: SC 1972, Fla. 1975, Ga. 1977. Ptnr., co-head, labor, employment Hunton & Williams LLP, Atlanta. Mem. Magistrate Judge Merit Selection Panel, 1998—2000. Named a Top 100 Georgia Super Lawyer, Atlanta Mag., 2004; named an Employment Litig. Super Lawyer, Georgia Super Lawyers Mag., 2005; named one of Georgia's 2004 Legal Elite, Georgia Trend Mag., 2004. Mem.: Phi Delta Phi. Office: Hunton & Williams Bank of Am Plz Ste 4100 600 Peachtree St NE Atlanta GA 30308-2216 Office Phone: 404-888-4004. Office Fax: 404-888-4190. Business E-Mail: tduffie@hunton.com.

DUFFIÉ, MARY KATHARINE, anthropologist, researcher, educator; b. Phila., June 23, 1963; d. Claire Alfred Pelton III and Nikki Joan (Newcomb) D. BA, U. Ariz., 1985, MA, 1989; PhD, Wash. State U., Pullman, 1994. Asst. prof. Mont. State U., Bozeman, 1995-97; asst. prof. anthropology UCLA, 1997—. Prin. investigator UCLA/Calif. Dept. Health Svcs., 1997-98, CDC, Atlanta, 1996-97, Ariz. Humanities Coun., Tucson, 1989-90. Author: Heeni: A Tainui Elder Remembers, 1997, Through the Eye of the Needle: A Maori Elder Remembers, 2001. Chair So. Calif., Am. Indian Health Working Group, L.A., 1997—; vol. Together, Inc., Glassboro, NJ, 1976-81, Hospice, Tucson, 1987-89. Recipient W.H.R. Rivers award Soc. for Med. Anthropology, 1993; book recognized among top 20 titles for 1997 Listener Women's Book Festival, Auckland, New Zealand, 1997; nominated Victor Turner award Am. Anthropology Assn., 2001. Democrat. Presbyterian. Avocations: reading, writing, horseback riding, hiking. Home: 8050 Lupine Ln Bozeman MT 59718 E-mail: mkduffie@aol.com.

DUFFIELD, DAVID A., former computer software company executive; b. Shaker Heights, OH, Sept. 1940; m. Cheryl Duffield. BS in Elec. Engring., MBA, Cornell U. Mktg. rep., sys. engr. IBM, 1964—69; co-founder Info. Assocs.; founder, chmn. Integral Systems Inc., Walnut Creek, Calif., 1972—87, PeopleSoft Inc., Pleasanton, Calif., 1987—2004, pres., 1987—99, CEO, 1987—99, dir., bd. chmn., CEO, 2004. Co-founder Maddie's Fund, Alameda, Calif., 1999.

DUFFIELD-MYERS, ARLENE ANNA, elementary school educator; b. Camden, N.J., Nov. 3, 1936; d. Herbert and Hilda (Hurst) Duffield; m. Benjamin Frank Myers, July 15, 1959 (dec. 1984); children: Benjamin Frank Jr., Janet Lorraine Bennett. BA cum laude, Glassboro State Coll., 1973, MA summa cum laude, 1976; postgrad., Rutgers U., 1980-81, Rowan U., 1983-88. Cert. prin./supr., student personnel svcs., elem. educator. Tchr. 3rd grade Woodbury (N.J.) Pub. Schs., 1974-84, tchr. 5th grade, 1984—, elem. enrichment tchr., 1990-91, chair site-based com., 1994-96. Advisor N.J. Math. Computer Sci. Instrl. Improvement Program, Rowan U., 1988-90, adj. faculty, 1990-92; grad. degree com. Antioch U., Yellow Springs, Ohio, 1989-92. Author: The Effects of Token Payment Upon Standardized Achievement Test Scores, 1988-89, Teaching Time to Developmentally Delayed Children, 1980, Drug and Alcohol Addiction Prevention for Primary Grades, 1979. Resource mem. N.J. Supreme Ct. Jud. Conf., 1990; mem. N.J. Gov.'s Coun. on Alcoholism and Drug Abuse, 1991-97, 2d vice chmn., 1992-94, chmn. alliance com., 1993; chmn. state edn. com. N.J. Gov.'s Coun., 1991, 2d vice-chmn., 1993, 94. Recipient Rowan Summer Inst. award for Dedication to Children of N.J., 1993; named Gloucester County Women of Yr., 1993. Mem. ASCD, NEA, N.J. Edn. Assn., Woodbury Edn. Assn. (pres. 1979-81, v.p. 1984-85), Rotary Internat. (mem. cmty.!it! involvement com. 1990, dir. youth svcs. 1992-93, mem. dist. vocations com. 1993, chair dist. 4-way test com. 1994, mem. dist. interact com. 1994, Outstanding Vocat. award 1993, Paul Harris fellow). Avocations: reading, writing, international travel. Home: 5 Bittersweet Pl Mount Laurel NJ 08054-4977 Office: Woodbury Pub Schs Jackson St Woodbury NJ 08096

DUFFNER, LEE R., ophthalmologist; b. June 3, 1936; m. Alvina Bross, Aug. 31, 1957; children: Fay, Rachel, Tamar. BS Engring., Purdue U., 1957; MS Physiology, Marquette U., 1961; MD, Med. Coll. Wis., 1962. Diplomate Am. Bd. Ophthalmology. Intern Stanford U., 1962—63; resident U. Miami, Fla., 1966—69; practice medicine specializing in ophthalmology Hollywood, Fla., 1969—; clin. prof. ophthalmology U. Miami Sch. Medicine, 1969—; dir. Am. Bd. Ophthalmology, 1995—2002, chmn., 2002. Pres. town coun. Town of Golden Beach, Fla., 1983—95. Capt. USAF, 1963—66. Fellow: ACS, Am. Acad. Ophthalmology; mem.: Miami Ophthal. Soc. (pres. 1983—84). Avocation: racewalking. Home: 185 Ocean Blvd Golden Beach FL 33160-2208 Office: 2740 Hollywood Blvd Hollywood FL 33020-4826 Office Phone: 954-925-2740.

DUFFY, BRIAN P., editor; Investigative editor Wall St. Jour., 1996—98; nat. editor US News & World Report, Washington, 1996—2001, exec. editor, 1998—2000, editor, 2001—. Office: US News & World Report 1050 Thomas Jefferson St NW Washington DC 20007 Office Phone: 202-955-2000. Office Fax: 202-955-2049. E-mail: bduffy@usnews.com.*

DUFFY, CHERYL HOFSTETTER, language educator; b. Hill City, Kans., June 23, 1959; d. Paul Louis and Deloris Luhman Hofstetter; m. Robert Edward Duffy, June 5, 1999; m. John Oliver Towns, Aug. 17, 1978 (dec. June 18, 1995); 1 child, Anna Marie Towns. At, Colby CC, Kans., 1977—78; BSE in English, Emporia State U., Kans., 1981; MA in English, Fort Hays, Kans., 1984; PhD in English, U. Kans., Lawrence, 1996. Writing ctr. tutor Emporia State U., 1978—80; English instr. Colby CC, 1981—86; disabled student svcs. coord. Ft. Hays State U., 1986—88, English instr., 1988—89; curriculum writing specialist Kans. State Dept. Edn., Topeka, 1989—90; gta U. Kans., 1991—92; assoc. prof. English Ft. Hays State U., 1992—, chair English dept., 2004—. Svc.-learning faculty cons. comty. svc. program Kans. State U., 2002—. Contbr. articles to profl. jours. Mem.: Nat. Coun. of Tchrs. of English. Office: Fort Hays State U English Dept 600 Park St Hays KS 67601

DUFFY, DAN, computer company executive; BA, Ind. Kelley Sch. Bus.; MBA, Northwestern Kellogg Sch. Bus. Sr. exec. Ernst & Young LLP; CFO, chief devel. officer MachineWeb; CEO ePartners, 2000—. Office: ePartners 1304 W Walnut Hill Ln Irving TX 75038

DUFFY, EARL GAVIN, hotel executive; b. Boston, Oct. 11, 1926; s. William Emmett and Mary Irene (Costello) D.; m. Bernice Rose MacMaster, Feb. 14, 1948; children— Earl Gavin, Joan Irene, Mark Charles, Neil William, Lynn Anne. Student public schs., Boston. In various hotel positions, Boston, 1941-52; sales mgr. Somerset Hotel, Boston, 1952-56; eastern sales mgr. Hotel Corp. Am., Boston, 1956-59, asst. nat. sales mgr., 1959-61, nat. sales mgr., 1961-64; v.p., gen. mgr. Hotel America, Houston, 1964-67, Hartford, Conn., 1967-69, Royal Sonesta Hotel, New Orleans, 1969-71, Soneta Beach Hotel, Key Biscayne, Fla., 1971-76, Boston Park Plaza Hotel, 1977-80; pres. Earl G. Duffy & Assos., 1981—. Guest lectr. Cornell U., 1961, U. Houston, 1965, Wash. State U., 1966, Fla. Internat. U., 1971-76; pres. Greater Hartford Conv. and Visitor's Bur., 1969 Chmn. div. bus. and industry Harris County (Tex.) March of Dimes, 1964-67; pres. New Orleans Jazz Festival, 1970-71. Served with USN, 1943-46. Recipient Golden Host award Wash. State U., 1964 Mem. Skal Club, Am. Hotel and Motel Assn., Hotel Sales Mgmt. Assn. Internat., Greater Boston Hotel and Motor Inn Assn., Mass. Hotel and Motel Assn., New Eng. Innkeepers Assn., Boston Exec. Club. Clubs: Rotary. Roman Catholic. Home and Office: 600 Three Islands Blvd 1503 Hallandale Beach FL 33009 *There is no question in my mind that anyone who wants to "make it" in America can do so.*

DUFFY, EDMUND CHARLES, lawyer; b. N.Y.C., Jan. 16, 1942; s. Thomas and Helen (Fisher) D.; m. Terry L. Davis, Oct. 21, 1973; children: Elisabeth, Margot. AB in Eng., Boston Coll., 1963; LLB, Columbia U., 1966. Bar: N.Y. 1967. Assoc. Cravath, Swaine & Moore, N.Y.C., 1968-77; from assoc. to ptnr. Skadden, Arps, Slate, Meagher & Flom, N.Y.C., 1977—. Served to capt. U.S. Army, 1966-68, Vietnam. Mem. ABA, N.Y. State Bar Assn. Office: Skadden Arps Slate Meagher & Flom LLP 4 Times Sq New York NY 10036-6595 Office Phone: 212-735-3950. E-mail: eduffy@skadden.com.

DUFFY, JAMES EARL, JR., state supreme court justice; b. St. Paul, June 4, 1942; s. James Earl and Mary Elizabeth (Westbrook) Duffy; m. Jeanne Marie Ghiardi; children: Jennifer, Jessica. BA, Coll. St. Thomas, 1965; JD, Marquette U., 1968. Bar: Wis. 1968, Hawaii 1969. Assoc. Cobb & Gould, Honolulu, 1968—71, Chuck & Fujiyama, Honolulu, 1972—74; partner Fujiyama, Duffy & Fujiyama, Honolulu, 1975—2003; assoc. justice Hawaii Supreme Ct., 2003—. Mem. Am. Bd. Trial Advocates, med. ethical resources com. Kapiolani Children's Med. Ctr., 1984—. recipient Lifetime Achievement award, Consumer Lawyers of Hawaii, John S. Edmunds award for Civility & Vigorous Advocacy. mem. Hawaii Bar Found. (bd. dirs. 1984—), Hawaii Bar Assn. (pres. 1982, Lifetime Achievement award), Hawaii Trial Lawyers Assn. (pres. 1981), Hawaii Supreme Ct. Jud. Coun., Trial Lawyers Assn. Am. (bd. govs. 1982-85), Hawaii Acad. Plaintiff's Attys. (pres. 1986-93), Am. Inns of Court IV. Office: Ali'iolani Hale 417 S King St Honolulu HI 96813-2902*

DUFFY, JAMES FRANCIS, III, lawyer; b. Providence, Jan. 28, 1956; s. James Francis Jr. and Eileen (Barry) D.; m. Catherine Anne Barrett, Oct. 20, 2001; 1 child, Mary Margaret. BA, U. R.I., 1978; JD, Harvard U., 1981. Bar: Mass. 1981, U.S. Dist. Ct. Mass. 1982. Assoc. Peabody & Brown, Boston, 1981-89, ptnr., 1989-99, Nixon Peabody LLP, Boston, 1999—. Mem. ABA, Boston Bar Assn. (real estate steering com. 1991-93, chmn. equity fin. com. of real estate sect. 1991-93), Mass. Bar Assn. Home: 17 Jackson Rd Somerville MA 02145-2908 Office: Nixon Peabody LLP 100 Summer St Fl 24 Boston MA 02110-2131 Office Phone: 617-345-1129. E-mail: jduffy@nixonpeabody.com, james.f.duffy@verizon.net.

DUFFY, JAMES HENRY, writer, retired lawyer; b. Lowville, N.Y., Feb. 3, 1934; s. William Christopher and Phyllis Catherine (Rofinot) D.; m. Martha McDowell, May 25, 1968 (dec. 1997). AB, Princeton U., 1956; LLB, Harvard U., 1959. Bar: N.Y. 1960. Assoc. Cravath, Swaine & Moore, N.Y.C., 1959-67, ptnr., 1968-88. Bd. dirs. Albanian-Am. Enterprise Fund, Am. Bank of Albania. Author: Domestic Affairs: American Programs and Priorities, 1979, Dog Bites Man: City Shocked, 2001, (under pseudonym Haughton Murphy) Murder for Lunch, 1986, Murder Takes a Partner, 1987, Murders and Acquisitions, 1988, Murder Keeps a Secret, 1989, Murder Times Two, 1990, Murder Saves Face, 1991, A Very Venetian Murder, 1992. Mem. Mayor's Commn. Cultural Affairs, 1981-91; bd. dirs. Nat. Corp. Fund for Dance, Inc., 1981-88, Sch. Am. Ballet, Paul Taylor Dance Found., Baryshnikov Dance Found., Commonweal Mag., Alliance for the Arts, N.Y.C.; trustee N.Y.Pub. Libr. Mem. Assn. of Bar of City of N.Y., Coun. Fgn. Rels., Mystery Writers Am. (bd. dirs. 1986-92, treas. 1992), Authors Guild (mem. coun. 1993—), Crime Writers Assn. (U.K.), Century Assn. Democrat. Roman Catholic. Address: 116 E 68th St New York NY 10021-5955 E-mail: jduffy@attglobal.net.

DUFFY, JAMES RAYMOND, lawyer; b. N.Y.C., July 22, 1936; s. Terence Patrick and Roasleen (Layden) D.; m. Mary Ellen Powers, Aug. 29, 1959; children: Terence, James Jr., Sean, Michael, Mary Ellen. BBA, St. John's U., N.Y.C., 1961; LLB, Bklyn. Coll. Law, 1965. Bar: N.Y. Ptnr. Kramer Dillof Tessel Duffy & Moore, N.Y.C., 1971-2000; sr. ptnr. Duffy, Duffy & Burdo, Uniondale, N.Y., 2001—. Author: Who Killed JFK?, 1988, Lone Crazed Gunman?, 2004 Recipient Martin Luther King Legal Svcs. award Congress of Racial Equality, 1995. Mem. N.Y. State Acad. Trial Lawyers (founding. mem. 2004). Office: Duffy Duffy & Burdo EAB Plz Uniondale NY 11556-1370 E-mail: xxexam@aol.com.

DUFFY, JAN, lawyer; b. Wichita, Kans., Apr. 27, 1950; d. Dwight C. and Helen J. Hornberger; AB, Stanford U., 1972; JD, Case Western Res. U., 1976. Bar: Ohio 1976, Calif. 1978. Assoc. Jones Day Reavis & Pogue, Cleve., 1976-77, Orrick, Herrington & Sutcliffe, San Francisco, 1978-80; prof. Calif. Poly. State U., San Luis Obispo, 1980-98; of counsel Sinsheimer, Schiebelhut & Baggett, San Luis Obispo, 1983-91; prin. Mgmt. Practices Group, Inc., 1998—. Contbr. articles to legal jours. Chair Calif. Minimum Wage Bd., 1984. Mem. ABA (co-chair workplace privacy subcom. 1981-94, co-chair employee rights and responsibilities com. 1994-97, co-chair technology com. 2000-03), Calif. Women Lawyers, XBHR (founding mem.). Democrat. Office: Ste 207 355 Bryant St San Francisco CA 94107-4141 E-mail: janduffy@managementpractices.com.

DUFFY, JOHN CHARLES, psychiatrist, educator, consultant; b. Cleve., June 19, 1934; s. John Joseph and Hannah (McIllwee) D.; m. Francoise C. Antonini; children: Charles, Robert, John. Grad., Boston Coll., 1956; MD, N.Y. Med. Coll., 1960. Intern Henry Ford Hosp., Detroit, 1960-61; resident Mayo Clinic, Rochester, Minn., 1963-67; exec. dir. Tucson Child Guidance Ctr., 1971-74; commd. med. officer USPHS, 1974; prof., assoc. chmn. Uniformed Svcs. U. Sch. Medicine, Bethesda, Md., 1974-81; assoc. commr. health affairs FDA, cons. Surgeon Gen., Rockville, Md., 1981-88; asst. surgeon gen. USPHS, 1983-92, chief physician officer, 1983-88; dir. C. Everett Koop Inst. Dartmouth Coll., Hanover, N.H., 1992-94; prof. psychiatry Uniformed Svcs. U. Sch. Medicine, Bethesda, 1981-94, clin. prof., 1994—. Nat. and internat. surveyor Joint Commn. on Accreditation of Healthcare Orgns., 1998—; founder Integrative Healthcare Solutions. Author: Psychiatric Morbidity of Physicians, 1964, Psychiatric Issues in the Lives of Physicians, 1966, Child Psychiatry, 1972, 86, Psychiatric Reviews, 1976; founding editor-in-chief Child Psychiatry and Human Devel., 1970-83; editor: Ship's Medical Chest, 1984; editor-in-chief Mil. Medicine; mem. editl. bd. MD mag., 1976—. Recipient OutstandingSvc. medal Bd. Regents Uniformed Svcs. U., 1981, Surgeon Gen.'s medallion. Fellow Am. Psychiat. Assn. (life), Aerospace Med. Assn. (assoc.; Longacre medal); mem. Assn. Mil. Surgeons U.S., Sigma Xi. Roman Catholic. Home: 2402 Golf Vista Blvd Viera FL 32955 Office Phone: 312-626-9373. E-mail: jduffy@pol.net.

DUFFY, JOHN JOSEPH, retired academic administrator, historian, educator; b. Charleston, S.C., Apr. 25, 1931; s. John Joseph and Mary (McMahon) D.; m. Marcia Fletcher Tinkham, Aug. 15, 1959; children: Katharine, John Joseph, Eleanor. BA in History, Coll. Charleston, 1952; MA in History, U. S.C., 1955, PhD in History, 1963. Dir. U. S.C., Beaufort, 1959-66, assoc. prof. history Columbia, 1964-98, acad. coord. Coll. Gen. Studies, 1966-67, asst. provost regional campuses, 1967-68, assoc. provost regional campuses, 1968-72, assoc. v.p. regional campuses, 1972-77, system v.p. univ. campuses and continuing edn., 1977-88, chancellor univ. campuses and continuing edn., 1988-91; vice provost for regional campuses and continuing edn., 1991-92; vice provost, exec. dean regional campuses/continuing edn. U. S.C., Columbia, 1992-98; ret., 1998. Author: (radio script) Secession Convention of 1860, 1960; (pamphlet) A Short History of Beaufort County, 1975, also articles. Dist. chmn. Midlands coun. Boy Scouts Am., 1969-71; sustaining mem. S.C. Dem. Party. Recipient Disting. Svc. award Garnet and Black of U. S.C., 1969, Outstanding Edn. Profl. award S.C. Assn. Higher Continuing Edn., 1983, Disting. Svc. award Ednl. Found. U. S.C., 1989; named Young Man of Yr. Jaycees, Beaufort County, S.C., 1964 Mem. So. History Assn., S.C. History Assn., Nat. Univ. Continuing Edn. Assn. (chair region III 1980-82), Nat. Assn. State Univs. and Land Grant Colls., Rotary, Phi Beta Kappa Roman Catholic. Avocations: reading, music.

DUFFY, JOHN LEONARD, lawyer; b. Oelwein, Iowa, Feb. 8, 1947; s. Leonard Francis and Margaret Elizabeth (Miller) D.; m. Paula Ann Rundle, June 7, l969; children: Adam, Bridget, Alex. BA maxima cum laude, Loras Coll, l969; JD with distinction, U. Iowa, l973. Bar: Iowa l973, U.S. Dist. Ct. (no. and so. dists.) Iowa l973, U.S. Ct. Appeals (8th cir.) l985. Mem. Heiny, McManigal, Duffy, Stambaugh & Anderson, P.L.C., Mason City, Iowa, 1973—. Author: (with others) Iowa Land Title Standards, l984. Bd. dirs. North Iowa Area Community Coll. Found., Mason City, 1977-83, Mason City Devel. Assn., 1983-; pres. YMCA, Mason City, 1980; pres. Newman High Sch. Bd. Edn., Mason City, 1990-91. With U.S. Army, 1970-71. Mem. Iowa Bar Assn., VFW, K.C. Roman Catholic. Avocations: racquetball, golf, bicycling, baseball, photography. Office: Heiny McManigal Duffy Stambaugh & Anderson PLC 11 Fourth St NE Mason City IA 50401-3252 Office Phone: 641-423-5154.

DUFFY, JOHN LEWIS, retired Latin, English and reading educator; b. Whittemore, Iowa, Oct. 6, 1934; s. Lewis A. and Dorothy (Bestenlehner) D.; m. Anne O'Brien, July 19, 1958; children: Jane, Paul, Sarah, Steven. BA, Loras Coll., 1956; MS Edn., Creighton U., 1961; student, U. Minn., 1967. Tchr. jr. and sr. H.S., coach Presentation Acad., Whittemore, Iowa, 1957—58; H.S. tchr. Clear Lake Cmty. Schs., Iowa, 1958—61; tchg. asst. U. Iowa, Iowa City, 1961—62; tchr. Latin Larkin H.S., Elgin, Ill., 1962—96, students' coun. advisor, 1965—71, chmn. English and fgn. langs., 1969—77, chmn. English and reading divsn., 1977—96. Tchr. prep. courses for ACT, PSAT and SAT Elgin YWCA and Larkin H.S., Elgin, 1977-96. Summer chef's asst. The Frugal Gourmet, WTTW-TV, Chgo., 1983. Bd. trustees Elgin Cmty., 1975—, chmn., 1980-81, 85-87, 97-2001, vice-chmn., 1981-84, 94-95; bd. dirs. Elgin Area Cath. Social Svcs., 1981-90, pres., 1986-88; mem. St. Laurence Parish Bd., 1974-79, Edn. Commn., 1972-79, chmn. Edn. Commn., 1974-79; state advisor Iowa Jr. Classical League, 1960-61 Named Kane County Disting. Educator of Yr., 1982, Outstanding Young Men in Am., 1970; recipient Outstanding Young Educator award Elgin Jaycees, 1969. Mem.: Am. Assn. Cmty. and Jr. Colls., Ill. Coun. Tchrs. English, Nat. Coun. Tchrs. English, Ill. Classical League, Am. Classical League, Elgin Assn. Sch. Adminstrs., Elgin Tchrs. Assn. (welfare chmn. and chief negotiator 1963—65, pres. 1966—67), Ill. Edn. Assn. (legis., chmn. northeastern divsn. 1968—71, chmn. ad hoc com. on tchr. tenure 1972—73), Ill. C.C. Trustees Assn. (exec. com. 1981—84, chmn. west suburban region 1981—84, chmn. fed. rels. com. 1982—87, bd. rep. 1986—95, 1997—, exec. com. 1998—2000, chmn. west suburban region 1998—2000, exec. com. 2002—04, chmn. west suburban region 2002—04, Trustee of Yr. award 2002), Am. Assn. C.C. (bd. dirs. 1990—93), Assn. C.C. Trustees (chmn. ctrl. region nominating com. 1981—82, sgt.-at-arms ann. conv. 1982, mem. com. on internat. rels. 1983—84, bd. dirs. 1983—89, chmn. future directions com. 1984—86, fed. rels. commn. 1985—93, chmn. ctrl. region, vice-chmn. fed. rels. commn. 1987—88, chmn. fed. rels. commn. 1988—89, chmn. ctrl. region nominating com. 1992—93, select com. 2001—, Ctrl. Region Trustee of Yr. award 1991, 2002). Home (Winter): 4840 Heron Run Cir Leesburg FL 34748-7819 Home (Summer): 192 Kathleen Dr Elgin IL 60123-5914 Fax: 352-323-1827; Home Fax: 847-429-0408.

DUFFY, KEVIN THOMAS, federal judge; b. N.Y.C., Jan. 10, 1933; s. Patrick John and Mary (McGarrell) D.; m. Irene Krumeich, Nov. 9, 1957; children: Kevin Thomas, Irene Moira, Gavin Edward, Patrick Giles. AB, Fordham Coll., 1954, LLB, 1958. Bar: N.Y. 1958. Clk. to chief circuit judge, N.Y.C., 1955-58; asst. chief criminal div. U.S. Atty.'s Office, N.Y.C., 1958-61; assoc. Whitman, Ransom & Coulson, N.Y.C., 1961-66; ptnr. Gordon & Gordon, N.Y.C., 1966-69; regional adminstr. SEC, N.Y.C., 1969-72; judge U.S. Dist. Ct. (So. Dist.), NY, 1972—, sr. judge, 1997—. Adj. prof. securities law Bklyn. Law Sch., 1975-80; prof. trial advocacy NYU, 1982-84, Pace Law Sch., 1984-85, Fordham Law Sch., 1993—. Author: Cross-Examination of Witnesses: The Litigator's Puzzle, 1990, Impeachment of Witnesses, 1990. Recipient Achievement in Law award Fordham Coll. Alumni Assn., 1976, Alumni Gold medal Fordham Law Sch., 1984, Kupferman's award Laymen's Nat. Bible Assn., 1992, Disting. Pub. Svc. award N.Y. County Lawyers' Assn., Lifetime Achievement award SEC, 1995. Mem. ABA, Am. Bar Assn., N.Y. State County Bar Assn., Westchester County Bar Assn., Assn. of Bar of City of N.Y., Fed. Bar Council (trustee 1970-72), Fordham Law Sch. Alumni Assn. (trustee 1969—, v.p.). Clubs: Merchants (N.Y.C.). Office: US Dist Ct US Courthouse 40 Centre St Room 2104 New York NY 10007-1502*

DUFFY, LAWRENCE KEVIN, biochemist, educator; b. Bklyn., Feb. 1, 1948; s. Michael and Anne (Browne) D.; m. Geraldine Antoinette Sheridan, Nov. 10, 1972; children: Anne Marie, Kevin Michael, Ryan Sheridan. BS, Fordham U., 1969; MS, U. Alaska, 1972, PhD, 1977. Tchg. asst. dept. chemistry U. Alaska, 1969-71, rsch. asst. Inst. Arctic Biology, 1974-77; postdoctoral fellow Boston U., 1977-78, Roche Inst. Molecular Biology, 1978-80; rsch. asst. prof. U. Tex. Med. Br., Galveston, 1980-82; asst. prof. neurology (biol. chemistry) Med. Sch. Harvard U., Boston, 1982-87, adv. biochemistry instr. Med. Sch., 1983-87; instr. gen. and organic chemistry Roxbury C.C., 1984-87; prof. chemistry and biochemistry U. Alaska, Fairbanks, 1992—, head dept. chemistry and biochemistry, 1994-99; assoc. dean for grad. studies and outreach Coll. Sci. Engring. and Math., U. Alaska, Fairbanks, 2000—. Coord. program biochemistry and molecular biology for summer undergrad. rsch., 1987-96; dir. Alaska Basic Neuroscience Program, 2000-04; pres. U. Alaska Fairbanks Faculty Senate, 2000-01; curriculum adv. bd. N. Star Sch. Sys., 2002-04, pollution ctrl. commn. 2004. Mem. editl. bd. Sci. of Total Environment. Pres., bd. dirs. Alzheimer Disease Assn. of Alaska, 1994-95; mem. instnl. rev. bd. Fairbanks Meml. Hosp., 1990; sci. adv. bd. Am. Fedn. Aging Rsch, 1994-95. Lt. USNR, 1971-73. NSF trainee, 1971; J.W. McLaughlin fellow, 1981; W.F. Milton scholar, 1983; recipient Alzheimer's Disease and Related Disorders Assoc. Faculty Scholar award, 1987; Carol Fiest Outstanding Advisor award, 1994, 97, 2005, Nat. Inst. Deafness

& Commn. Disorders, NIH Cert. of Merit for mentoring, 1996, North Star Bough Sch. Dist. Svc. award, 1998, Alumni Achievement award for profl. activity U. Alaska-Fairbanks, 1999, Usibelli award for rsch., 2002. Fellow: Am. Inst. Chemists (bd. dirs. 2002—, sec. bd. dirs. 2003, pres.-eclect 2004, pres. 2005—, cert. profl. chemist); mem.: AAAS (arctic divsn. exec. dir.), Am. Soc. Circumpolar Health (bd. dirs. 2003—04), Am. Chem. Soc. (Analytical Chemistry award 1969), N.Y. Acad. Scis., Am. Soc. Biol. Chemists, Am. Soc. Neurochemists, Sigma Xi (assoc. regional dir. 2000—02, pres. 1991 Alaska club, nominating com.), Phi Lambda Upsilon. Roman Catholic. Office: U Alaska Fairbanks Box 756160 Fairbanks AK 99775 Office Phone: 907-474-7525. Personal E-mail: duffy@gci.net. Business E-Mail: fychem@uaf.edu.

DUFFY, MARTIN EDWARD, management consultant, economist; b. Fall River, Mass., May 24, 1940; s. Arthur Louis and Edna Marie (Cunneen) D.; m. Irene Patricia Daley, Aug. 24, 1968 (div. Jan. 1980); 1 child, Kathryn; m. Priscilla Claire Stieff, May 14, 1988; 1 child, Brianna. BS in History, BSEE, Tufts U., 1963; MBA, U. Pa., 1967. Asst. dean U. Pa., 1967-71; asst. dir. Fels Ctr., U. Pa., 1971-73; v.p. Data Resources, Lexington, Mass., 1975-84; v.p., gen. mgr. MRCA Info. Svcs., Cambridge, 1984-86; pres. The Perseus Group/RCG, Boston, 1986—; co-founder AllSeasons Investments, 1999—. Planning com. White Ho. Conf. on Aging, Washington, 1981; cons. La in 2001, Baton Rouge, 1982; lectr. in field; adj. prof. mgmt. Emmanuel Coll., Suffolk U.; conf. leader Presdl. Summit for Am.'s Future, 1997. Author: The Elderly in Future Economy, 1981. Lt. USN, 1963-65. Mem. Am. Econs. Assn., Nat. Assn. Forensic Economists, Cambridge Sports Union, Tufts U. Alumni Assn. (pres. 1985, exec. com. 1982-87, mem. coun. 1978—), Nat. Bus. Travelers Assn. (bd. dirs. ednl. com. 1988-93). Roman Catholic. Avocations: running marathons, mountain climbing, biking. *A career is an unfolding process, like the gradual opening of an exotic design, demanding only our presence, attention and determination to do well.*

DUFFY, MARTIN PATRICK, lawyer; b. Louisville, Feb. 2, 1942; s. Martin Joseph and Elsie (Shrader) D.; m. Virginia Schoo, Mar. 20, 1970; children: Timothy Brian, Kathleen Kelly. AB in English, U. Notre Dame, 1964; JD, U. Louisville, 1975. Bar: Ky. 1975, U.S. Tax Ct. 1980. Ptnr. Olson, Baker, Henriksen & Duffy, Louisville, 1978-79, Wyatt, Tarrant & Combs, Louisville, 1979–. Bd. dirs. Bellarmine Coll. Overseers, Louisville, 1974-80; trustee St. Mary & Elizabeth Hosp., Louisville, 1980-86, chmn. bd. 1982-85. With U.S. Army, 1964-65, 68-69. Mem. ABA, Ky. Bar Assn., Louisville Bar Assn. Democrat. Roman Catholic. Avocations: running, golf. Office: Wyatt Tarrant & Combs 2700 Citizens Plz Louisville KY 40202 Fax: 502-589-0309. Office Phone: 502-562-7564. E-mail: pduffy@wyattfirm.com.

DUFFY, MARY KATHLEEN, neonatal nurse; b. Oak Park, Ill., Aug. 10, 1949; d. William F. and Mary F. (Lang) D. ADN, Triton Coll., 1975; BSN with honors, Ill. Benedictine Coll., 1986. Cert. neonatal intensive care nurse, Nat. Cert. Corp. Obstetric, Gynecologic and Neonatal Nursing Specialties, 2004. Staff nurse gen. med./surg. unit MacNeal Hosp., Berwyn, Ill., 1976—80, staff nurse, level II nursery, 1980—86; staff nurse, neonatal intermediate intensive care nursery DeKalb Gen. Hosp., Decatur, Ga., 1986—87; staff nurse level II nursery MacNeal Hosp., Berwyn, 1987—88; staff nurse level III neonatal intensive care unit Good Samaritan Hosp., Downers Grove, Ill., 1988—. Mem. Nat. Assn. Neonatal Nurses, Sigma Theta Tau. Personal E-mail: mkd50@earthlink.net.

DUFFY, MAURA YVONNE, conservator; b. Point Pleasant, Nj, Dec. 7, 1958; d. Bernardine and John Beauvais Duffy; m. Antonio Vergari, Oct. 29, 1998; 1 child, Tony Joseph Vergari. Cert. Painting Conservation, Il Istituto Per L'Arte e Il Restauro, Florence, Italy, 1986. Head painting conservator Maura Duffy Mural Painting Conservation, Point Pleasant Beach, 1986—; sr. painting conservator Huston Olin Conservation, Great Falls, Va., 1998—. Mem.: Am. Inst. Conservation (assoc.). Home: 718 McLean Ave Point Pleasant Beach NJ 08742

DUFFY, MICHAEL F., commissioner; BA, Catholic U. Am., 1971; JD, George Washington U., Nat. Law Ctr., 1976. Bar: Am., DC. Atty. Fed. Mine Safety Health Rev. Commn., 1977—79; sr. counsel Am. Mining Congress, 1979—87; counsel to chmn. Fed. Mine Safety Health Rev. Commn., 1987—93; dep. gen. counsel Nat. Mining Assn., 1993—2002; commr. Fed. Mine Safety Health Rev. Commn., 2002—, chmn., 2003. Author: Resolution of MSHA Disputes The Need for Change and Suggestions for a More Productive Approach, 1993, Safety and Health Beyond the Gates The Overlap of EPA and MSHA Standards on Explosives: A Case Study, 1994, Prometheus Re-Bound: How Adoption of the Kyoto Protocol on Climate Change Would Devastate the Western U.S. Coal Industry, 1999. Office: Fed Mine Safety Health Rev Commn 601 New Jersey Ave Washington DC 20001 Office Phone: 202-434-9900. Business E-Mail: mduffy@fmshrc.gov.

DUFFY, MICHAEL JAMES, IV, librarian; s. Michael James Duffy, Jr. and Julia Elizabeth Duffy; m. Kristin Clark, June 24, 2000. MusB, Western Mich. U., 1997; MusM, Northwestern U., 2002; M of Libr. and Info. Sci., Dominican U., 2002. Asst. prof., music libr. No. Ill. U., DeKalb, 2002—. Book rev. editor Music Reference Services Quar., 2004—. Mem.: Music OCLC Users Group, Music Libr. Assn. (midwest chpt. sec.-treas. 2003—, Kevin Freeman Travel grantee 2002). Office Phone: 815-753-9839.

DUFFY, NANCY KEOGH, newscaster, broadcast executive; b. Washington, Nov. 24, 1947; d. William Francis and Gertrude K. (Keogh) D.; divorced; children: Peter Patrick, Matthew Michael. Student, St. Mary of the Woods Coll.; AB, Marywood Coll., 1967. News reporter Sta. WHEN TV and Radio, Syracuse, N.Y., 1967-70; press sec. City of Syracuse, 1970; news reporter Sta. WTVH, Syracuse, 1971-77; news anchorperson Sta. WIXT-TV, Syracuse, 1977—. Talk show host Syracuse New Channels, 1986-87; talk show host, producer Community Connections, 1987-89; instr. Syracuse U. Prodr. TV series Duffy's People, With Steve on Sunday. Founder Syracuse St. Patrick's Parade, 1983, pres., organizer, 1983-2001, hon. pres., 2002-; organizer Cooperstown 50th Ann. Baseball Hall of Fame Parade, 1989, opening ceremonies Empire State Games, 1990; co-organizer Save Our Syracuse Symphony, 1984—; organizer Bark-Out Against Rabies Paws Parade, 1995-98, Artist Eagle Faces Exhibits, 1999-2003; bd. dirs. Syracuse Symphony, 1992-98, The Media Unit, 1977-97; active Project children, Syracuse, YMCA; telethon hostess Muscular Dystrophy Assn.; organizer poetry workshops for children, 1995—; mem. Onondaga County Traffic Safety Bd., 1977-2002, Le Moyne Coll. Pres. Assocs.; honorary chair, Civil War Weekend, Peterborough, NY.; bd. dirs. Native Am. Svc. Agy., 2002. Recipient Nat. Angel award Best Spl. Religion in Media, Post Std. Woman of Achievement award, 1st Downtown award for excellence, 1986, Mayor's Achievement award, 1985, Humanitarian award Project Children, 1993, N.Y. State Senate commendation, 1995; named Woman of Achievement N.Y. State Fair, 1994, YWCA Acad. Diversity Achievers, 2004. Mem. Am. Women in Radio and TV (nat. award 1973), Women in Comms. (Outstanding Communicator award 1985), Syracuse Press Club (bd. dirs. 1987—, v.p. 1990, 97, 98, pres. 1991-92, Bernard and Dorothy Newer Svc. award 1995, lifetime achievement award 2000), Syracuse Rotary (pub. rels. 1989-92), Am. Heart Assn. (hon. co-chair Ctrl. N.Y. 1997). Roman Catholic. Office: Sta WIXT-TV 5904 Bridge St East Syracuse NY 13057-2941 Office Phone: 315-446-9999.

DUFFY, RICHARD JOSEPH, lawyer; b. Tarrytown, N.Y., Nov. 29, 1947; children: Christine, Brian. BA, Marietta (Ohio) Coll., 1969; JD, Case Western Res. U., 1972. Bar: N.Y. 1973, Fla. 1978. Assoc., ptnr. Rockwood, Edelstein & Duffy, White Plains, N.Y., 1973-84; ptnr. Duffy & Watkins, White Plains, 1984-93; of counsel Epstein Becker & Green, P.C., N.Y.C., 1993-96; ptnr. Putney, Twombly, Hall & Hirson, N.Y.C., 1996-2001, Wolf, Block, Schorr and Solis-Cohen, LLP, N.Y.C., 2001—. Spkr. on estate planning. Contbr. articles to profl. jours. Advisor to various not-for-profit corps. and assns. and family founds., 1984—. Office: Wolf Block Schorr and Solis-Cohen LLP 250 Park Ave New York NY 10177 E-mail: rduffy@wolfblock.com.

DUFFY, ROBERT ALOYSIUS, aeronautical engineer; b. Buck Run, Pa., Sept. 9, 1921; s. Joseph Albert and Jane Veronica (Archer) D.; m. Elizabeth Reed Orr, Aug. 19, 1945 (dec.); children: Michael Gordon, Barclay Robert (dec.), Marian Orr (dec.), Judith Elizabeth Parsons, Patricia Archer; m. Jenifer Williams Pickett, Nov. 28, 1992. BS in Aero. Engring., Ga. Inst. Tech., 1951. Commd. 2d lt. U.S. Army, 1942; commd. U.S. Air Force, advanced through grades to brig. gen., 1967; vice comdr. USAF Space and Missile Systems Orgn., L.A., 1970-71; ret., 1971; v.p., dir. Draper Lab. div. MIT, Cambridge, Mass., 1971-73; pres., chief exec. officer Charles Stark Draper Lab., Inc., 1973-87, dir., 1973-91, dir. emeritus, 1991—. Contbr. articles to profl. jours. Decorated Disting. Svc. medal, Legion of Merit; recipient Thomas D. White award Nat. Geog. Soc., 1970; named to Ga. Tech. Engring. Hall of Fame, 1994. Fellow AIAA; mem. NAE, Internat. Acad. Astronautics, Inst. Navigation (Thurlow award 1964, pres. 1976-77), Air Force Assn., Tau Beta Pi. Home: 1001 Arbor Lake Dr #1108 Naples FL 34110 Office: Charles Stark Draper Lab 555 Technology Sq Cambridge MA 02139-3539 Personal E-mail: fortressd@aol.com.

DUFFY, SEAMUS C., lawyer; b. Phila., 1961; BA, Villanova Univ., 1984, JD summa cum laude, 1987. Bar: Pa. 1988. Clerk US Dist Ct., Phila., 1987—88; joined Drinker Biddle & Reath LLP, Phila., 1988, ptnr., litig., and mem., mgmt. com. Bd. dir. Leadership, Inc. Lectr. in field. Office: Drinker Biddle & Reath LLP One Logan Sq 18th & Cherry Sts Philadelphia PA 19103-6996 Office Phone: 215-988-2440. Office Fax: 215-988-2757. Business E-Mail: seamus.duffy@dbr.com.

DUFFY, SIMON, telecommunications industry executive; MA, Oxford (Engl.) U.; MBA, Harvard U. Dir. ops. United Distillers, Guinness plc, dir. corp. fin.; dep. chmn., group fin. dir. EMI Group; group fin. dir. THORN EMI EMI Group plc; dep. chmn., CEO World Online Internat. NV; CEO End2End, 2001; CFO Orange SA; COO NTL Europe, 2003; CEO NTL Inc., N.Y., 2003—. Office: NTL Inc 110 East 59th St New York NY 10022 also: NTL Europe Inc 22 Suffolk St London SW1Y 4HG England

DUFFY, TERRENCE A., futures and options exchange executive; BSBA, U. Wis., Whitewater, 1980. Pres. TDA Trading, Inc., 1981—; mem. Chgo. Merc. Exch. Inc., 1981—, vice chmn., 1998—2002, chmn. bd., 2002—, Chgo. Merc. Exch. Holdings Inc., 2002—. Office: Chgo Merc Exch 20 S Wacker Dr Chicago IL 60606

DUFFY, THOMAS M., transportation services executive, lawyer; b. 1961; BBA, JD, U. Ga. Bar: 1986. Assoc. Peterson Dillard Young Asselin & Powell LLP, 1986—94, ptnr., 1994—97, Troutman Sanders LLP, Atlanta, 1997—98; v.p. Allied Holdings, Inc., Decatur, Ga., 1998—2000, gen. counsel, 1998—, sec., 1998—, sr. v.p., 2000—04, exec. v.p., 2004—. Office: Allied Holdings Inc Ste 200 160 Clairemont Ave Decatur GA 30030 Office Phone: 404-373-4285. Office Fax: 404-370-4206.

DUFFY, W. LESLIE, lawyer; b. NYC, Dec. 31, 1939; s. William L. and Edna (Torseillo) D.; 1 child, Alexander Durand. BA, U. Notre Dame, 1961; LLB, Columbia U., 1964; LLM, NYU, 1967. Assoc. Cahill, Gordon & Reindel, N.Y.C., 1965-73, ptnr., 1973—. Bd. dirs. various pub. cos. Contbr. articles to profl. jours. Served to lt. USNR. Mem. ABA, N.Y. State Bar Assn. Office: Cahill Gordon & Reindel LLC 80 Pine St Fl 17 New York NY 10005-1790 Business E-Mail: wduffy@cahill.com.

DUFFY, WILLIAM EDWARD, JR., retired education educator; b. Fostoria, Ohio, Aug. 30, 1931; s. William Edward and Margaret Louise (Drew) D.; m. Sally King Wolfe, Nov. 21, 1958 (div. 1978). BS, Wayne State U., 1958, MEd, 1960; PhD, Northwestern U., 1967. Tchr. social studies Detroit Pub. Schs., 1957-61; instr. Northwestern U., Evanston, Ill., 1961-65; asst. prof. gen. edn. U. Iowa, Iowa City, 1965-70, assoc. prof., 1970-94, coord. Soc. Found. Edn. program, 1978-93, chmn. divsn. founds., postsecondary edn., 1981-88; ret., 1994. Lectr. in field. Mem. editl. bd. Ednl. Philosophy Theory, 1969-71; contbr. book revs. and articles to profl. jours. With USAF, 1951-54. Fellow John Dewey Soc., Philosophy Edn. Soc.; mem. Am. Ednl. Rsch. Assn. Home: 376 Samoa Pl Iowa City IA 52246-3632

DUFFY, WILLIAM J., lawyer; b. Allentown, Pa., Nov. 25, 1954; s. James Edward and Shirley Ritter Duffy; m. Teri S. Anderson, Aug. 30, 1986; children: Lucas James, Katherine Jeanne. BS, U. Del., 1976; MS, Pa. State U., 1983; JD, U. Denver, 1986. Bar: Colo. 1986, U.S. Dist. Ct. (D.C. dist.), U.S. Ct. Appeals (10th cir.). Assoc. Kelly Standsfield/O'Donnel, Denver, 1986-89; dir. Parcel Mauro Hultin & Spaanstra, Denver, 1989-98, Parcel Mauro, PC, Denver, 1998—; ptnr. Davis Graham & Stubbs, LLC, Denver, 1999—. Office: Davis Graham & Stubbs 1550 17th St Ste 500 Denver CO 80202-1500 E-mail: william.duffy@dgslaw.com.

DUFFY-KING, JAN (JOHN MITCHELL MAVER WALLACE), journalist, media consultant; b. Edinburgh, Scotland, July 21, 1965; came to U.S., 1991; s. John and Annie Elizabeth (Devine) Wallace; 1 child, Shelley (dec.); m. Laurie Meredith Haughton. BA with honors, U. Oxford, Eng., 1987. Journalist Mirror Group Newspapers, London, 1987-90, editor Amsterdam, 1990-91; author JWE Internat., N.Y.C., 1991-93; info. architect eurotrash-.com., N.Y.C., also Cologne and Edinburgh, 1993—. Bd. dirs. Johnboy Records, London, eurotrash.com Inc., NYC, eurotrash.com Ltd., Eng., perfectit.com Ltd., NY, Edinburgh, perfectit.com GmbH, Cologne, JWE Internat., Edinburgh, Brian Roache Archtl.Svcs.; chmn. Consili Ltd., Edinburgh; e-bus. advisor Scottish Parliament. Author: Zuid-Amerikaanse Reis Gids, 1993, Knowledge Management for E-Business Performance, 2001, e-Initiatives for Europe 2005, 2003, Information Architecture, Its Place in the Business Plan, 2002, (with Laurie Haughton) Search Engine Optimization, 2001. Lt. Dutch Army, 1983-87. Named Journalist of Yr., Nat. Union Journalists, 1990. Avocations: flying helicopters, free-fall parachuting, travel. Office: 20 River Rd New York NY 10044-1100 also: 107 Magdalene Gardens Edinburgh EH15 3DS Scotland E-mail: jan@eurotrash.com.

DUFKA, CORINNE, human rights activist; BA in Social Work, San Francisco State U., 1979; MSW, U. Calif., Berkeley, 1984. Soc. worker, El Salvador; photojournalist Reuters, 1989—99; rschr. Human Rights Watch, Sierra Leone, 1999—2003; rsch. and cons. Chief Investigators and the Prosecutor on the UN-backed Spl. Ct. for Sierra Leone, 2003—; mem. African Div. of Human Rights Watch. Fellow MacArthur Found., 2003. Office: 350 Fifth Ave 34th flr New York NY 10118

DUFNER, EDWARD JOSEPH, editor; b. Reading, Pa., May 26, 1960; s. Edward J. Sr. and Marcia (Keiser) D.; m. Connie Elizabeth Pryzant, July 29, 1984; children: Elena Miriam, Adam Joseph. BS in Journalism, Northwestern U., 1982. Reporter, asst. regional editor Abilene (Tex.) Reporter-News, 1982-83; news editor/editor Arlington (Tex.) Daily News, 1983—84, editor, 1984; copy editor The Dallas Morning News, 1984-86, asst. nat. editor, 1986-89, nat. editor, 1990-91, 93-95, polit. editor, 1992, 96, bus. reporter, 1997-99, bus. editor, 1999—2004, asst. mng. editor, 2004—. Trustee Temple Emanu-El, Dallas, 1996-2000. Mem. Soc. Am. Bus. Editors and Writers. Jewish. Avocations: running, swimming, piano, history. Office: The Dallas Morning News Comms Ctr PO Box 655237 Dallas TX 75265-5237

DUFORD, STACEY, reporter, writer; b. Flint, Mich., Mar. 18, 1964; d. Norman O. and Margaret A. Duford; m. Elliot G. Lerner, July 3, 1993; children: Alicia Margaret Lerner, Beau William Lerner. BA in English, Albion Coll., 1986. Morning show personality Sta. WNIC Radio, Dearborn, Mich., 1990—2001; freelance reporter Sta. WXYZ-Ch. 7, Detroit, 1999—. Author: (children's book) The Fairy Painting. Mem.: Mich. Reading Assn., Girls Scouts of Am. (assoc.). Personal E-mail: sduford@aol.com.

DUFOUR, JEAN-MARIE, economist, statistician, educator; b. Montreal, Que., Can., Dec. 27, 1949; s. Jean-Marie Dessureault and Bella Dufour. BA, U. Montreal, 1969; BSc in Math. with hon., McGill U., Montreal, 1971; MSc in Stats., U. Montreal, 1973; MA in Econs., Concordia U., 1974, U. Chgo., 1978, PhD in Econs., 1979. Lectr. stats. U. Que., Trois-Rivières, 1972-73; prof. math. Coll. Édouard-Montpetit, Montreal, 1973-75; rsch. assoc. Inst. Applied Econ. Rsch. Concordia U., 1978-79; lectr. econs. U. Montreal, 1978-79, mem. rsch. staff ctr., 1979—85, sr. mem. rsch. staff, dir. rsch. program in econometrics and macroecons. ctr. de recherche et développement en économique, 1985-90, asst. prof., 1979-83, assoc. prof., 1983-88, prof., 1988—, dir. ctr. recherche et développment en économique, 1988—95, 1997—98, chmn. dept. econs., 1995—97, Can. rsch. chair in econometrics, 2001—. Vis. scholar MIT, 1980, Queen's U., 1986, CEPREMAP, Paris, 1986, U. Libre de Bruxelles, 1988, 89, 90, 91, 93, 95, Ecole Nat. des Stats. et l'Adminstrn. Economique, Paris, 1990, 91, 93, 95, 2000, 2001, 2004, U. Scis. Sociales de Toulouse, France, 1992, 94, 2002, Humboldt U. Berlin, 1994, Deutsche Bundesbank, Frankfurt, 2001-04; cons. Econ. Coun. Can., 1981, Office de Planification et Devel. economique du Que., 1982, Royal Commn. Econ. Union and Devel. prospects for Can., 1983-84; invited prof. U. de Toulouse I, 1983, 94, 2002, U. Pa., 1992, U. Lausanne, 1995; rsch. fellow Ctr. Ops. Rsch. and Econometrics U. Cath. de Louvain, 1985-86; bd. dirs. Soc. Can. de Sci. Economique, 1984-87; Benjamin Meaker chair, U. Bristol, 1993, 99; vis. prof. Stanford U., 1999, Tilburg U., 2000, Technische U. Dresden, 2000, U. Amsterdam, 2003-04, Inst. Fur Wirtschaftsforschung Halle, Germany, 2005. Assoc. editor Econometrica, 1996—2002, Jour. Econometrics, 1994—, Empirical Econs., 1994—, Econometric Theory, 1991-93, Econometric Reviews, 1991-96, 98—, Annales d'Économie et de Statistique, 1990—, Cahiers de Centre d'Études de Recherche Opérationnelle, 1989—95, Can. Jour. Econs., 1984-88; guest editor Jour. Econometrics, 1992-93, Empirical Econs., 1993—; contbr. 100 articles to profl. jours. Recipient Excellence in Rsch. award Soc. Can. de Sci. Économique, 1988, 2000, Leave fellowship Social Scis. and Humanities Rsch. Coun. Can., 1985-86, Doctoral fellowship Can. Coun., 1975-78, Doctoral fellowship Govt. Que., 1975-78, Scholarship, U. Montreal, 1971-72; rsch. grantee Ministry Edn. Que., 1979-80, 80-81, 81-82, Social Scis. and Humanities Rsch. Coun. Can., 1980-81, 83, 83-85, 87-89, 89-91, 91-94, 94-97, 97—, U. Montreal 1979-80, Econ. Coun. Can., 1981, Govt. Que., 1982-83, 83-84, 84-85, 85-86, 86-87, 87-90, 90-93, 96-96, 96—, Royal Commn. on Econ. Union and Devel. Prospects per Can., 1983-84, Natural Scis. and Engring. Rsch. Coun. Can., 1983-86, 87-90, 89-91, 91-94, 94-97, 97—, Govt. Que. and Communauté française de Belgique, 1989-90, Govt. Que. and Govt. France, 1990-92, Can. Internat. Devel. Agy., 1991-93, Marcel-Vincent prize, Assn. Francophone Pour Le Savior, 2005. Fellow: CIRANO, Am. Statis. Assn., Jour. Econometrics, Econometric Soc., Am. Statis. Assn., Royal Soc. Can.; mem.: Can. Econ. Assn. (pres. 2002—03), Société canadienne de sci. économique (bd. dirs. 1984—87, pres. 1998—2001), Inst. Mathematical Stats., Econometric Soc., Internat. Statis. Inst., Can. Econometric Study Group Bd. (dir. 2002—, dir. 2002—), Statis. Soc. Can. (rsch. com. 1988—), Can. Econs. Assn. (John Rae prize 1994, spl. prize outstanding rsch. 1994), Am. Econ. Assn. Achievements include research in statistical methodology in econometrics, exacr distribution-free and parametric methods, time series analysis, casuality analysis, and statistical inference in weakly identified models; macroeconomics, finance, public finance, development. Avocations: philosophy, history, movies, art. Home: 1060 Ave Bernard Apt 5 Outremont PQ Canada H2V 1V2 Office Phone: 514-343-2400. Business E-Mail: jean.marie.dufour@umontreal.ca.

DUFRESNE, ARMAND FREDERICK, management and engineering consultant; b. Manila, Aug. 10, 1917; s. Ernest Faustine and Maude (McClellan) DuF.; m. Theo Rutledge Schaefer, Aug. 24, 1940 (dec. Oct. 1996); children: Lorna DuFresne Turnier, Peter; m. Lois Burrell Klosterman, Feb. 21, 1987. BS, Calif. Inst. Tech., 1938. Dir. quality control, chief product engr. Consol. Electrodynamics Corp., Pasadena, Calif., 1945-61; pres., dir. DUPACO, Inc., Arcadia, Calif., 1961-68; v.p., dir. ORMCO Corp., Glendora, Calif., 1966-68; mgmt., engring. cons. Duarte and Cambria, Calif., 1968—. Dir., v.p., sec. Tavis Corp., Mariposa, Calif., 1968-79; dir. Denram Corp., Monrovia, Calif., 1968-70, interim pres., 1970; dir., chmn. bd. RCV Corp., El Monte, Calif., 1968-70; owner DUFCO, Cambria, 1971-82; pres. DUFCO Electronics, Inc., Cambria, Calif., 1982-86, chmn. bd. 1982-92; pres. Freedom Designs, Inc., Simi Valley, Calif., 1982-86, chmn. bd. dirs., 1982-97; owner DuFresne Consulting, 1992—; chmn. bd., pres. DUMEDCO,Inc., 1993-95. Patentee in field. Bd. dirs. Arcadia Bus. Assn., 1965-69; bd. dirs. Cambria Community Services Dist., 1976, pres., 1977-80; mem., chmn. San Luis Obispo County Airport Land Use Commn., 1972-75. Served to capt. Signal Corps, AUS, 1942-45. Decorated Bronze Star. Mem. Instrument Soc. Am. (life), Arcadia (dir. 1965-69), Cambria (dir. 1974-75), C. of C., Tau Beta Pi. Home: 61 Broad St Apt 211 San Luis Obispo CA 93405-1772

DUFRESNE, ELIZABETH JAMISON, retired lawyer; b. Winter Haven, Fla., July 29, 1942; d. John W. and Thelma M. (Kinney) Jamison; 1 child, Brennan. BA, Vanderbilt U., 1964; JD, U. Fla., 1966. Bar: U.S. Dist. Ct. (so. dist.) Fla. 1967, U.S. Dist. Ct. (mid. dist.) Fla. 1968, U.S. Ct. Appeals (5th cir.) 1968, U.S. Supreme Ct. 1969, U.S. Ct. Appeals (11th cir.) 1981. Atty. So. Fla. Migrant Legal Svc., Miami, 1967-69; law reform chief Greater Miami Legal Svc., Miami, 1969-71; assoc. Tobias Simon P.A., Miami, 1971; ptnr. Tobias Simon & Elizabeth duFresne, P.A., Miami, 1971-77; sr. ptnr. duFresne & duFresne, P.A., Miami, 1977-82, duFresne & Bradley, P.A., Miami, 1982-86; equity ptnr. Steel, Hector & Davis, Miami, 1986—2000, bd. dirs., chmn. labor law divsn., ret., 2000. Adj. prof. law U. Miami, Coral Gables, Fla., 1977-93; mem. Civil Justice Adv. Group USDC, S.D. Fla., 1990-2000. Recipient Award of Honor ACLU, Dade, 1969, Award of Merit ACLU, Fla., 1970, 73. Mem. ABA, Fla. Bar Assn. (Pioneer award 1977), Dade County Bar Assn., Fed. Bar Assn., Assn. Trial Lawyers Am., Assn. Trial Lawyers Fla., Fla. Assn. Women Lawyers. Democrat. Roman Catholic. Avocations: cooking, reading, racquetball, bicycling, sailing.

DUGAN, CHARLES CLARK, physician, surgeon; b. Penn Yan, N.Y., Jan. 24, 1921; s. Charles Emanual and Wilhemia May (Clark) D.; m. Eugenie Alice Pounds, Aug. 12, 1944 (div. 1963); children: Charles Clark II, Douglas Craig, Timothy Gene; m. Ruth Louise Fugh, Dec. 3, 1965 (dec. 1983); adopted children: Dain Walters, Carl Jay. AA, Wentworth Mil. Jr. Coll., 1940; AB, Cornell U., 1942; MD, Jefferson Med. Coll., 1946; MPH, Naval Med. Sch. and Johns Hopkins U., 1956. Diplomate Am. Bd. Dermatology, Am. Bd. Allergy and Immunology, Spl. Bd. Dermatopathology, Am. Bd. Cosmetic Plastic Surgery, Am. Bd. Preventive Medicine, Aviation Medicine and Pub. Health, Nat. Bd. Med. Examiners. Resident in psychiatry Pa. Psychiat. Hosp., Phila., 1945-46; rotating intern extended in gen. surgery Harrisburg (Pa.) Gen. Hosp., 1946-47; resident in dermatology U. Colo. Med. Ctr., Denver, 1956-57; resident in dermatology and allergy Henry Ford Hosp., Detroit, 1957-59; pvt. practice dermatology, allergy, cosmetic plastic surgery West Palm Beach, Fla., 1959—. Physician mem. bd. Palm Beach County Environ. Control Hearing Bd., West Palm Beach, 1981-94; active staff Palm Beach Gardens (Fla.) Cmty. Hosp., Good Samaritan Hosp., West Palm Beach, St. Mary's Hosp., West Palm Beach; mem. Wellington Regional Med. Ctr., West Palm Beach; active staff Good Samaritan Hosp., West Palm Beach. Contbr. articles to profl. jours. Lt. col., pilot/flight surgeon USAF, 1947—56. Recipient Cert. of Svc., Am. Cancer Soc., West Palm Beach, 1961; named Surgeon of Yr., Fla. Soc. Dematol. Surgeons, 199r4 Fellow AMA, FMA, PBCOMS, Am. Acad. Dermatology, Am. Coll. Preventive Medicine, Am. Coll. Allergy, Asthma and Immunology, Am. Acad. Allergy, Asthma and Immunology, Internat. Acad. Cosmetic Surgery, Am. Acad. Facial Plastic and Reconstructive Surgery, Am. Acad. Cosmetic Surgery, Am. Soc. Dermatol. Surgery (bd. dirs. 1980-83), Am. Soc. Dematopathology, Am. Soc. Cryosurgeons, Am. Soc. Cert. Allergists, Internat. Soc. Dematopathology, Fla. Soc. Dermatology (pres. 1973-74, Practitioner of Yr. award 1990-91), Fla. Soc. Dermatol. Surgeons (pres. 1980-83, Lifetime Achievement award, 2005), numerous others; mem. Noah Worcester Dermatologic Soc. Republican. Presbyterian. Avocations: swimming, scuba diving, tennis, stamp collecting/philately, coin collecting/numismatics. Personal E-mail: ccdugan554@aol.com.

DUGAN, FORTUNE ANTHONY, cardiologist, consultant; b. Dallas, Aug. 31, 1944; s. Albert Francis and Ruth (Welsch) D.; m. Sandra Mary Duracher, 1968; children: Fortune Anthony, Bridget Ann. BS cum laude, La. State U.,

New Orleans, 1966, MD, 1968. Diplomate in internal medicine and cardiovascular disease Am. Bd. Internal Medicine; bd. cert. in interventional cardiology. Straight med. intern La. State U. divsn. Charity Hosp. of La., New Orleans, 1968-69, resident in medicine, 1969-71; fellow in cardioloy Duke U. Med. Ctr., Durham, N.C., 1973-75; chief cardiovascular lab. Vets. Hosp., Durham, 1975-76; assoc. in medicine, dept. int. medicine Duke U. Med. Ctr., Durham, 1975-76; mem. staff dept. cardiology East Jefferson Gen. Hosp., Metairie, La., 1979—; clin. assoc. prof. dept. medicine Tulane U. Sch. medicine, New Orleans, 1979—, med. dir. cardiology, 1998—, med. dir. cardiac catheterization lab., 1998—. Vis. staff Chairty Hosp., New Orleans, 1979—. Contbr. articles to profl. jours. Named Top cardiologist New Orleans Mag., 1994; recipient Bel award, 1968, Outstanding Alumnus award U. New Orleans Col. Scis., 1997. Fellow ACP, Am. Coll. Chest Physicians, Am. Coll. Cardiology (v.p. La. chpt. 1991, pres. 1993-96, gov. 1993-96), Soc. for Cardiovasc. Angiography and Interventions, Internat. Soc. Cardiovasc. Interventionists; mem. AMA, Am. Heart Assn. (fellow coun. on clin. cardiology, Silver Torch award 1994), New Orleans Acad. Internal Medicine (pres. 1989-90), Am. Coll. Sports Medicine, Am. Soc. Internal Medicine, Alpha Omega Alpha, Omicron Delta Kappa, Phi Kappa Phi. Avocation: exercise. Home: 3009 Palm Vista Dr Kenner LA 70065-1560 Office: East Jefferson Gen Hosp 4200 Houma Blvd Metairie LA 70006-2996 E-mail: fdoc@msn.com.

DUGAN, GERALD F., physicist, educator; b. New York, NY, Dec. 3, 1945; s. Francis Dugan and Veronica Bogue; m. Edna R Haley, Aug. 10, 1969. PhD, Columbia U., 1967—73. Prof. of physics Cornell U., Ithaca, NY, 1995—; assoc. dir. Superconducting Super Collider Lab., Dallas, 1991—94; scientist Fermilab, Batavia, Ill., 1982—91; asst. prof. of physics Columbia U., New York, 1976—82, rsch. assoc., 1972—76. Fellow: Am. Phys. Soc., Divsn. of Physics of Beams (vice chair, chair-elect, chair 2004—). Achievements include contributions to the design of international linear collider; design of contributions to the conceptual design of a post-LHC hadron collider; accelerator physics design of the SSC collider and high energy booster; development of leadership of the fermilab accelerator division; leadership of the Tevatron Collider to achieve desugn luminosity; research in design, fabrication and commissioning of the Fermilab lithium lens; measurement of the residual polarization of the muonic He-3 atom; high precision measurements of the mass and magnetic moments of elementary particles. Avocations: photography, hiking. Office Phone: 607-255-5744.

DUGAN, JEAN BRODSHAUG, public relations executive; b. Fargo, N.D., Oct. 11, 1959; d. Robert L. and Jacqueline Adelle (Qualley) Brodshaug; m. Joseph Robert Dugan, Sept. 14, 1991; children: Patrick Robert, Brian Joseph. BA, BS, U. N.D., 1981; MS, Boston U., 1984. Sr. copy editor Viewdata Corp., Miami, Fla., 1983-85; press sec. U.S. Senator Quentin Burdick, Washington, 1985-92, U.S. Senator Jocelyn Burdick, Washington, 1992-93; cons. Nat. Women's Polit. Caucus, Washington, 1993-96; comms. dir., dep. campaign mgr. Joan Kelly Horn for Congress, 1996—; sr. pub. rels. mgr. Osborn & Barr Comms., 1998—2002; instr. comm. U. Phoenix, 2001—; pub. rels. supr. Brighton, St. Louis, 2004—05. Author: Campaigning to Win, 1993. Chair Metro St. Louis Women's Polit. Caucus, 1997-98. Lutheran. Home and Office: 316 Oak Manor Ln Saint Louis MO 63119-1542 E-mail: jbdugan@aol.com.

DUGAN, JOHN CUNNINGHAM, federal official, lawyer; b. June 3, 1955; BA in English Lit, with high distinction, U. Mich., 1977; JD cum laude, Harvard U., 1981. Bar: DC 1981. Minority gen. counsel US Senate Com. Banking, Housing & Urban Affairs, 1987—89; asst. sec. treasury domestic fin. to Pres. George HW Bush The White House, Washington; dep. asst. sec. Fin. Inst. Policy US Dept. Treasury, Washington, 1989—92, asst. sec. domestic fin., 1992—93, comptroller of the currency, 2005—; ptnr. Covington & Burling, Washington, 1993—2005, coord., Fin. Inst. Practice Group. Office: US Dept Treasury Independence Sq 250 E St SW Mail Stop 9-1 Washington DC 20220

DUGAN, JOHN F., lawyer; b. Phila., May 25, 1935; s. Albert C. and Helen Josephine (Pritchard) D.; m. Colette Gregory, Jan. 18, 1987. AB, U. Pa., 1956, LLD, 1960. Bar: Pa. 1961, U.S. Ct. Appeals (3d cir.) 1961, Va. 1966, U.S. Supreme Ct. 1967. Assoc. Obermayer Rebmann Maxwell & Hippel, Phila., 1960-66; of counsel Reynolds Metals Co., Richmond, Va., 1966-69, Pennwalt Corp., Phila., 1969-71; ptnr. Berkman Ruslander, Pitts., 1971-85, Kirkpatrick & Lockhart, Pitts., 1985—. Labor rels. law rep. mgmt., Kirkpatrick & Lockhart. Mem. Pitts. Field Club, Duquesne Club, Order of the Coif, Phi Beta Kappa. Republican. Office: Kirkpatrick & Lockhart 1500 Oliver Building Pittsburgh PA 15222-2312

DUGAN, JOHN LESLIE, JR., foundation executive; b. Phila., Nov. 6, 1921; s. John Leslie and Ellen May (Reid) D.; m. Barbara McClelland Day, Dec. 21, 1946; children: Barbara Nicholas, Geoffrey McClelland, Sara Ellen. BS, Swarthmore Coll., 1943; postgrad., Harvard U., 1947-48; MBA, U. Pa., 1950. Instr. Swarthmore Coll., 1946-47, U. Pa., 1948-50; cons. Booz, Allen and Hamilton, 1951-55; asst. to pres. Grace Nat. Bank, N.Y.C., 1955-58; treas. Underwood Corp., N.Y.C., 1958-60; v.p. fin. Chicopee div. Johnson & Johnson, New Brunswick, N.J., 1960-75; dir., adminstr. Robert Wood Johnson Found., Princeton, N.J., 1975-77; exec. v.p. Am. Diabetes Assn., Inc., N.Y.C., 1977-80; exec. dir. Fin. Analysts Fedn., N.Y.C., 1981-84; pres. The Greenwall Found., N.Y.C., 1981-90; founder, pres. Buck Hill Conservation Found., 1992-97, trustee, 1992-99. Adj. prof. mgmt. St. Peter's Coll., 1975-81 Committeeman Millburn Twp., N.J., 1975-79, commr. fin. and welfare, 1976-79; vestryman, warden, lay reader Christ Ch. in Short Hills, N.J. Served to lt. comdr. USNR, 1942-61. Mem. Tau Beta Pi. Clubs: Baltusrol Golf, Short Hills, Ozone, Buck Hill Golf. Republican. Home: PO Box 851 New Vernon NJ 07976-0851 E-mail: j09dg@aol.com.

DUGAN, JOHN VINCENT, JR., legislative affairs specialist, educator, researcher; b. Lost Creek, Pa., Oct. 22, 1936; s. John Vincent and May Ann (Curley) D.; m. Joan Elaine Thomas, Dec. 26, 1964; children: John Edward, Paul Michael, Michael Thomas, Erin Elaine (dec.). BA in Chemistry, Lasalle Coll., 1957; PhD in Phys. Chemistry, U. Notre Dame, 1965. Scientist, adminstr. NASA Lewis Rsch. Ctr., Cleve., 1961—75; congressional staff US House of Reps., Majority & Minority, 1975—88; prof. Space Aviation Environ. and Energy, 1975—81; staff dir. Energy Rsch. and Devel., 1981—88; dir. Washington ops. Cortana Corp., Falls Church, Va., 1988-92; sr. phys. scientist ozone depletion, atmospheric chemistry Tech. Assessment Systems, Inc., Washington, 1992; v.p. congl. affairs Gen. Dynamics Space Systems Divsn., 1992—94; v.p. govt. affairs Martin Marietta Corp., 1994—95; dir. for energy, environ. and space legis. affairs Lockeed-Martin Co., Arlington, Va., 1995—99, cons. energy, sci. and tech., pub. policy, 1999—. Vis. prof. U. Notre Dame, 2004. Author: (with John L. Magee) Dynamics of Ion Molecule Collisions, 1971; contbr. more than 50 tech. papers and articles to profl. jours. Head physics judge Fairfax County Sci. Fairs, Va., 1985-92; mem. adv. bd. Fairfax County Com. on Exceptional Children, 1977-79. Named Man of the Yr., Shenandoah (Pa.) C. of C., 1982. Mem. E.F. Sorin Soc. (Founder's Cir. U. Notre Dame), Founders Club (LaSalle Coll.), Sigma Xi. Roman Catholic. Achievements include first analytical and computer studies of directional forces in dynamics of ion-molecule collisions and predicted formation of long-lived collision complexes; development of computer movies of ion-molecule collisions involving orientation dependent forces; advanced research in concept integration, hydrodynamics, advanced materials and automation. Home and Office: 8301 Miss Anne Ln Annandale VA 22003-4619 Office Phone: 703-801-7033. E-mail: jackdugan@cox.net.

DUGAN, MICHAEL JOSEPH, former career officer, health agency executive; b. Albany, N.Y., Feb. 22, 1937; s. D. Joseph and Dorothy M. (Krebs) D.; m. Grace A. Robinson, Aug. 9, 1958; children: Colleen, Erin, Mike, Sean, Kathleen, Kevin. BS, U.S. Mil. Acad., 1958; MBA, U.Colo., 1972. Commd. officer USAF, 1958, advanced through grades to gen.; comdr.-in-chief U.S. Air Forces Europe, 1989-90; comdr. Allied Air Forces Cen. Europe, 1989-90; chief of staff USAF, 1990, ret., 1991; lectr. in strategic studies Johns Hopkins U., Washington, 1991-92; pres., CEO Nat. Multiple Sclerosis Soc., N.Y.C., 1992—. Decorated three D.S.M., Silver Star, two Legion of Merit, D.F.C., Purple Heart; Knight's Cross (Germany). Home: 36 James Ct Dillon CO 80435 Office: NMSS 700 S Broadway Ste 810 Denver CO 80203-3442 E-mail: mike.dugan@nmss.org.

DUGAN, MICHAEL T., communications executive; AA in elec. engring., Pa. State DuBois, 1968; BS in elec. engring., Rochester Inst. Tech., 1978. Former v.p. engring. Tandon Corp., dir. product mktg. and dir. engring.; several positions held with Xerox Corp.; pres., COO EchoStar Communications. Named Alumni fellow by the Pa. State Alumni Assn., 2001, Rochester Inst. Tech. Alumni of the Yr., Coll. of Applied Sci. and Tech., 2003. Office: EchoStar Communications 5701 S Santa Fe Dr Littleton CO 80120

DUGAN, PATRICK J., lawyer; b. Lima, Ohio, 1957; BSBA cum laude, Bowling Green State U., 1979; JD with honors, Ohio State U., 1981. Bar: Ohio 1982. Ptnr. Squire, Sanders & Dempsey LLP, Columbus & Cleve., co-chmn., Corp. Practice Group, 2002—05, chmn., Fin. Services Practice Group, 2005—. Bd. trustees Raymond E. Mason Found.; bd. dir. Ariel Corp.; mem. exec. com. Columbus Venture Network. Named an Ohio Super Lawyer mergers & acquisition, Law & Polit. Media, Inc., 2004, 2005; named one of 100 Leaders for New Millennium, Columbus Smart Bus. News, 2000, Columbus Power 100, 2002, 2003, 2004, 2005. Mem.: Beta Alpha Psi, Order of Coif. Office: Squire Sanders & Dempsey LLP 4900 Key Tower 127 Public Sq Cleveland OH 44114-1304 also: Squire Sanders & Dempsey LLP 1300 Huntington Ctr 41 South High St Columbus OH 43215-6197 Office Phone: 216-479-8500, 614-365-2709. Office Fax: 216-479-8780, 614-365-2499. Business E-Mail: pdugan@ssd.com.

DUGAN, PATRICK RAYMOND, microbiologist, educator, dean; b. Syracuse, N.Y., Dec. 14, 1931; s. Francis Patrick and Joan Irma (Clause) D.; m. Patricia Ann Murray, Sept. 22, 1956; children: Susan Eileen, Craig Patrick, Wendy Shawn, Carolyn Paige. BS, Syracuse U., 1956, MS, 1959, PhD, 1964. Assoc. rsch. scientist Syracuse U. Rsch. Corp., 1956-63; mem. faculty Ohio State U., Columbus, 1964—, asso. prof., 1968-70, prof., chmn. dept. microbiology, 1970-73; acting dean Ohio State U. (Coll. Biol. Scis.), 1978-79, dean, 1979-85; prin. scientist EG&G Idaho Nat. Engring. and Environ. Lab. (now Idaho Nat. Lab.), Idaho Falls, 1987-91, sci. and engring. fellow, 1991-94, dir. Ctr. for Bioprocessing Tech., 1987-94; ret., 1994—. Cons., 1994—. Author: Biochemical Ecology of Water Pollution, 1972. Trustee Columbus Zool. Assn. and Zoo, 1982—87. Fellow Am. Acad. Microbiology; mem. AAAS, Am. Soc. Microbiology (Ohio pres. 1968-70), Soc. Indsl. Microbiology, Am. Chem. Soc. Personal E-mail: pdugan1@swfla.rr.com.

DUGAN, ROBERT PERRY, JR., retired minister, religious organization administrator; b. Morristown, N.J., Jan. 19, 1932; s. Robert P. and Marion Frances (Sahrbeck) D.; m. Marilyn I. Wertz, Aug. 8, 1953; children: Robert Perry III, Cheryl. AB, Wheaton Coll., 1953; MDiv, Fuller Theol. Sem., 1956; DD, Denver Conservative Bapt. Sem., 1985; LHD, Geneva Coll., 1985; LLD, Roberts Wesleyan Coll., 1990. Ordained to ministry Conservative Bapt. Assn. Am. 1957. Postgrad. teaching fellow in Hebrew Fuller Theol. Sem., 1954-57; minister of youth ch. Bloomfield, N.J., 1957-58; pastor Rochester, N.H., 1959-63, Elmhurst, Ill., 1963-69, Trinity Baptist Ch., Wheat Ridge, Colo., 1970-75; chaplain Senate of State of Colo., 1974-75; pres. Conservative Baptist Assn. Am., 1973-76; v.p. Rockmont Coll., Lakewood, Colo., 1976-78; dir. Office of Pub. Affairs, Nat. Assn. Evangelicals, Washington, 1978-96; v.p. governmental affairs Nat. Assn. Evangelicals, Washington, 1996-98; ret., 1999. Bd. dirs. Denver Sem., chmn., 1998-2001; Staley disting. Christian scholar lectr., 1973, 82, 84, 86, 88, 94; participant Internat. Congress on World Evangelism, Lausanne, Switzerland, 1974. Author: Winning the New Civil War: Recapturing America's Values, 1991, Stand and Be Counted: A Washington Insider Tells How to Preserve America's Liberties for You and Your Children, 1995; editor monthly newsletter NAE Washington Insight, 1979-97. Candidate for U.S. Congress, 1976; mem. ethics adv. bd. USIA, 1982-84; bd. dirs. Justice Fellowship, 1983-91, Transformation Internat., 1987-91; bd. trustees Williamsburg Charter Found., 1988-89. Home: 37784 Pineknoll Ave Palm Desert CA 92211-2128 E-mail: RPDuganJr@aol.com.

DUGAS, DAVID ROY, prosecutor, lawyer; b. New Iberia, La., July 4, 1953; s. Claude Anthony and Gladys Marie (Hippler) D.; m. Dolores Ann Broussard, Mar. 22, 1974; children: Brandy Nicole, Kelly Ann, Mary Katherine. JD, La. State U., 1978. Bar: La. 1978, U.S. Dist. Ct. (mid. dist.) La. 1978, U.S. Dist. Ct. (we. dist.) 1980, U.S. Ct. Appeals (5th cir.) 1981, U.S. Dist. Ct. (ea. dist.) 1984. Assoc. Sanders, Downing, Kean & Cazedessus, Baton Rouge, 1978-80; from assoc. to ptnr. Caffery, Oubre, Dugas & Campbell, New Iberia, 1980—2000; US atty. (mid. dist.) La. U.S. Dept. of Justice, 2001—. Editor La. State U. Law Rev., 1977. Chmn. Iberia Parish Reps., 1984, Dist. H delegation to Rep. State Convention, 1984. Mem. ABA, La. Bar Assn., Iberia Parish Bar Assn., La. Assn. Def. Counsel (bd. dirs. 1985—), Order of Coif, Phi Kappa Phi, Omicron Delta Kappa. Lodges: Kiwanis. Republican. Roman Catholic. Avocations: golf, sailing. Office: 777 Florida St Ste 208 Baton Rouge LA 70801

DUGAS, DONNA, conductor, music educator; d. Irving and Patricia Sills; m. David Rene' Dugas; children: David, Danielle. BA, La. Tech U., 1978; MA, La. Tech. U., 1979. Music tchr. Bossier (La.) Parish, 1983—86; founder, condr. Masterworks Singers, Monroe, La., 1987—. Music asst. N. Monroe Bapt. Ch., La., 1988—91; music tchr. River Oaks Sch., Monroe, La., 1989—91; guest dir. St. Andrew's Children's Choir, Ft. Worth. V.p. Jr. League, Monroe; mem. River Oaks Sch., Monroe. Recipient Gold medal, Heritage Festivals, 1994—2004. Mem.: Am. Choral Directors Assn. (life), Ouachita Parish Med. Soc. Alliance (pres.), Monroe Surg. Hosp. Ambassadors (sec.). Home: 1155 Finks Hideaway Rd Monroe LA 71203

DUGAS, RICHARD J., JR., construction executive; Degree, La. State U. Various positions in mktg., retail and customer svc. Exxon, 1986—89; various positions in process improvement and plant operational efficiency Pepsico, 1990—94; joined Pulte Homes Inc., Bloomfield Hills, Mich., 1994—, v.p., process improvement, city pres. and market mgr. for Atlanta div., coastal region pres., exec. v.p., COO, 2002—03, pres., CEO, 2003—. Office: Pulte Homes 100 Bloomfield Hills Parkway Bloomfield Hills MI 48304-2946*

DUGGAN, DENNIS MICHAEL, newspaper editor; b. Detroit, Oct. 12, 1927; s. Michael and Anne (Judge) D.; divorced; 1 child, Nancy Ellen. AB, Wayne U., Detroit, 1952. Wall St. columnist N.Y. Herald Tribune, 1960-61; asst. real estate editor N.Y. Times, 1961-62; fin. writer N.Y. Daily News, 1967; sr. editor, N.Y. bur. chief Newsday, 1973-83; columnist, 1983—. Recipient Meyer Berger award Columbia U. Grad. Sch. Journalism, 1987; co-recipient Pulitzer prize N.Y. Newsday, 1991. Mem. Inner Circle, Soc. Silurians (pres., Peter Kihss award), Dutch Treat Club. Home: 235 W 11th St New York NY 10014-2277 Office: 780 3rd Ave New York NY 10017-2024 Office Phone: 718-575-2564. Personal E-mail: dinkydiz@aol.com.

DUGGAN, JAMES E., JR., state supreme court justice; b. 1942; Grad., Georgetown U., Wash., D.C., Georgetown U. Law Ctr. Prof. Franklin Pierce Law Ctr., 1977—2001, interim dean, 1997—99; chief appellate defender State of NH, 1981—2001; assoc. justice NH Supreme Ct., 2001—. Chair N.H. Bd. of Claims. Supervises production Annual Survey N.H. Law. Named Merrimack County Lawyer of the Yr., 1991. Mem.: N.H. Bar Found., Am. Coll. Trial Lawyers Assn. (bar examiner, bd. mem.), Am. Acad. of Appellate Lawyers, N.H. Bar Assn. (mem. bd. govs.). Office: Supreme Ct Bldg One Noble Dr Concord NH 03301-6160

DUGGAN, JAMES EDGAR, law librarian; b. Roanoke, Va., Mar. 24, 1961; s. Daniel David Sr. and Margaret Candler (Mallonee) D. BA, Va. Tech., 1983; JD, U. Miss., 1986; MLIS, La. State U., 1987. Bar: Miss. 1987, U.S. Dist. Ct. (so. dist.) Miss., U.S. Ct. Appeals (5th cir.). From asst. prof. to assoc. prof. So. Ill. U. Sch. Law, Carbondale, 1988-98, prof., 1998—. Ref. libr. So. Ill. U. Sch. Law, Carbondale, 1988—90, computer svcs. libr., 1990—98, dir. info. tech., 1998—; mem. faculty senate So. Ill. U., Carbondale, 2001—, pres. faculty senate, 2004—05. Del. Synergy, The Ill. Libr. Leadership Initiative, 2005; pres. bd. trustees Carbondale Pub. Libr., 2001—, trustee, 1998—; trustees Shawnee Libr. Sys., 2001—, pres. bd. trustees, 2003—. Scholar West Pub. Co., 1987. Mem. Miss. State Bar Assn., Am. Assn. of Law Librs. (grant 1987, grant New Orleans chpt. 1987, Call for Papers Competition award 1990, chair coun. chpt. pres. 1999, exec. bd. 2001-04), Mid-Am. Assn. of Law Librs. (pres. 1997-98), Phi Alpha Delta, Pi Kappa Delta, Beta Phi Mu. Roman Catholic. Home: PO Box 605 Carbondale IL 62903-0605 Office: So Ill U Law Sch Carbondale IL 62901 E-mail: duggan@siu.edu.

DUGGAN, JOHN DAVID, JR., computer technician; b. Battleboro, Vt., Nov. 21, 1972; s. John David and Martha Jane Duggan; m. Sara Ruth Wardell, Sept. 18, 1999; children: John David III, Charles Barry. BS in Biology, Salve Regina U., 1995. Velidonan specialist Glaxo Welcome, West Greenwich, RI, 1996—98; sr. velidanon engr. VelSource, Inc., Downingtown, Pa., 1998—2000; assoc. mgr. computer velidonan Amgen, Inc., West Greenwich, 2000—. Mem.: Inst. Validanon Tech., Parenal Drug Assn. Democrat. Unitarian. Office: Amgen Corp 40 Tech Way West Greenwich RI 02817 E-mail: dugganj@amgen.com.

DUGGAN, MICHAEL E., health facility administrator; Diploma, U. Mich. Lawyer pvt. practice; dep. county exec. Wayne County, Mich.; elected Wayne County prosecutor, 2000; pres., CEO Rehab. Inst. Mich. (Detroit Med. Ctr. and Wayne State U.), Detroit, 2004—. Bd. chair Health Choice, 1995—2000. Founder, former pres. Wayne County Kidspace, Inc. Achievements include work to pass legislation a "plus card" system, a health assistance program that put 50,000 unemployed poor people into a Wayne County system allowing local HMOs to bid for their business in 1987; efforts to establish another county health program called Health Choice in 1995. Office: Rehab Inst Mich 261 Mack Blvd Detroit MI 48201-1203

DUGGAN, THOMAS PATRICK, management consultant; b. Hartford, Conn., Mar. 17, 1946; s. Edward O. and Mildred B. (Balf) Duggan; m. Marcia McCormack, Aug. 31, 1968 (div. 1978); children: Mary Christina, T. Patrick; m. Ann Hailey, Sept. 21, 1985; 1 child, Christopher T. AB, Providence Coll., 1968; postgrad. studies in Mgmt., We. N. Eng. Coll., 1969-71. Mgr. Travelers Mgmt. Svcs., Hartford, Conn., 1968—75; mgr. mgmt. cons. svcs. Coopers & Lybrand, N.Y.C., 1975-79; prin., dir. ins. mgmt., cons. svcs. Hay Assocs., N.Y.C., 1979-84; exec. v.p., nat. dir. bus. strategy cons. group Alexander & Alexander Mgmt. Cons. Svcs., N.Y.C., 1984; pres. Duggan Cons. Assocs., New Albany, Ohio, 1984—. 1st lt. USAR, 1968-75. Mem. Human Resource Planning Soc., Am. Mgmt. Assn., Ins. Acctg. and Statis. Assn. (session chmn. 1975-79), New Albany Country Club. Home: 7531 Ehret Round New Albany OH 43054-8926 Personal E-mail: tpatrickduggan@insight.rr.com.

DUGONI, ARTHUR A., orthodontics educator, dean; b. San Francisco, June 29, 1925; s. Arthur B. and Lina Marie (Bianco) D.; m. Katherine Agnes Groo, Feb. 5, 1949; children: Steven, Michael, Russell, Mary, Diane, Arthur, James. DDS, Coll. Physicians and Surgeons, San Francisco, 1948; MSD, U. Wash., 1963; BS, Gonzaga U., 1986; DHL honoris causa, U. Detroit, 1997. Diplomate Am. Bd. Orthodontics (bd. dirs., pres. 1979-86). Clin. instr. operative dentistry Coll. Physicians and Surgeons, San Francisco, 1951-55, asst. clin. prof. operative dentistry, 1955-60, asst. clin. prof. orthodontics, 1963-64, chair dept. orthodontics, 1963-67; assoc. prof. orthodontics U. Pacific, San Francisco, 1966-77, prof., 1977—, dean Sch. Dentistry, 1978—. Chair coun. deans Am. Assn. Dental Schs., 1985; active Pew Commn. for the Health Professions, 1993-96. Recipient Disting. Svc. award San Mateo County Dental Soc., 1971, 1990, Disting. Svc. award Pacific Coast Soc. Orthodontists, 1976, Merit award, 1976, 2001, Disting. Practitioner award Nat. Acads. Practice Press Club, 1987, Hinman medallion, 1989, medallion of distinction U. Pacific, 1989, Orthodontic Edn. and Rsch. Found. disting. merit award, 1993, Albert H. Ketcham award Am. Bd. Orthodontics, 1994, Chmn.'s award Am. Dental Trade Assn., 1994, Dr. Irving E. Gruber award, 1997, List of Honor of FDI World Dental Fedn., 1998; named Person of Yr., South San Francisco, 1960, Alumnus of Yr., U. Pacific Sch. Dentistry, 1983, U. Wash., 1984, U. San Francisco, 1988, Gonzaga U., 1992, Gold medal Pierre Fauchard Acad., 1996, Callahan Internat. award Ohio Dental Assn., 1999, William J. Gies award Am. Coll. Dentists, 2001, Excellence in Dentistry award 13th Dist.'s Internat. Coll. Dentists, 2002, Willard C. Fleming Meritorious Svc. award No. Calif. sect. Am. Coll. Dentists, 2003. Fellow Pierre Fauchard Acad., Acad. Dentistry Internat., Acad. Gen. Dentistry (hon.); mem. ADA (trustee 1984-87, treas. 1987-88, pres. 1988-89, Found. pres., Pres.'s citation 1994, 99, Disting. Svc. award 1995), Fedn. Dentaire Internat. (councilor 1989-98, treas. 1992-98, List of Honour 1999), Am. Assn. Dental Schs. (pres. 1995, Disting. Svc. award 2000), Calif. Dental Assn. (pres. 1982-83, Dist. Svc. award, 1978, Dale F. Redig Dist. Svc. award, 2003), Am. Dental Assn. (foundation pres. 2003-), Concordia-Argonaut Club, Peninsula Golf and Country Club, Phi Kappa Phi, Omicron Kappa Upsilon, Tau Kappa Omega, Xi Psi Phi. Republican. Roman Catholic. Avocation: golf. Office: U Pacific 2155 Webster St San Francisco CA 94115-2333 Business E-Mail: adugoni@pacific.edu.

DUGOSH, JEREMY W., medical editor, writer; b. Jourdanton, Tex., Aug. 15, 1972; s. Alfred A. and Deborah L. Dugosh; m. Karen Leggett, Apr. 4, 1998; 1 child, Ezra W. BA summa cum laude, Tex. A&M U., 1995; MS, U. Tex. Arlington, 1998, PhD, 2001. Rsch. asst. U. Tex., Arlington, 1995—98, rsch. assoc., 1998—2001; editor Am. Bd. Internal Medicine, Phila., 2001—05, sr. editor, 2005—. Contbr. articles to profl. jours. Mem.: Am. Ednl. Rsch. Assn., Nat. Coun. Measurement Edn., Am. Med. Writers Assn. Green Party. Avocations: fly fishing, hiking, art, mountain biking. Home: 413 S Iseminger St Philadelphia PA 19147 Office: Am Bd Internal Medicine 510 Walnut St Ste 1700 Philadelphia PA 19016

DUGUID, DOROTHY ANN RAMSEYER, artist; b. Bloomington, Ill., Nov. 8, 1924; d. Roy Arthur and Ruth Frances (Bodell) Ramseyer; m. James Mitchell Duguid, mar. 31, 1947; children: John Robinson, Robert Mitchell, Carol D. Hootman, Barbara P. Ungs. Student, U. Ill., Champaign, Coe Coll., Ill. Wesleyan U., Chgo. Art Inst. Cert. tchr. Tchr. Jr. High Sch., San Antonio, Tex., Albuquerque, Urbana (Ill.) Jr. High; substitute tchr. Bloomington H.S. Mem. McLean County Weavers Guild, Bloomington - Normal Artists Guild, PEO, Margaret Fuller Club, Epsilon chpt. Kappa Kappa Gamma. Republican. Presbyterian. Avocation: piano.

DUGUNDJI, JOHN, aeronautical engineer; b. N.Y.C., Oct. 25, 1925; s. Basile and Rosa (Finale) D.; m. Wraye Polkey, July 25, 1965; children: Elenna Rose, Elisa Anthe. BAE, NYU, 1944; MS in Aero. Engring, MIT, 1948, Sc.D. in Aero. Engring, 1951. Research engr. Grumman Aircraft Co., Bethpage, N.Y., 1948-49; dynamics engr. Republic Aviation Corp., Farmingdale, N.Y., 1951-56; research asso. M.I.T., 1956-57, asst. prof. aero. engring., 1957-62, asso. prof., 1962-70, prof., 1970-93, sr. lectr., 1993-2001. Served with USN, 1944-46. Mem. AIAA, Sigma Xi, Tau Beta Pi. Greek Orthodox. Home: 39 Albert Ave Belmont MA 02478-4203 Office: MIT Dept Aeros & Astronautics Cambridge MA 02139

DUHAIME, NINA LEE, energy executive, research and development company executive; Founder, exec. v.p., treas., dir. Atom, Inc., Santa Fe, 1968—81; owner-broker Sun Mountain Agy., Santa Fe, 1964—84; owner, rancher, farmer, operator Bar V Ranch, N.Mex.; tech. writer and journalist R.W. Byram Co., Austin, Tex., 1966—78; owner, broker Sun Mountain Real Estate Agy. Contbr. columns and articles to newspapers, trade, and profl. jours. Mem.: N.Y. Acad. of Sci. Achievements include U.S. presdl. fitness award, 1973. Address: Santa Fe NM

DUHAMEL, JUDITH REEDU OLSON, public information officer, former state senator; b. Mitchell, S.D., June 24, 1939; d. John Marvin and Camille (Murphy) Reedy; m. Robert George Olson, Aug. 5, 1961; children: Jeffrey, Jennifer, Jon, Jaime, Jason, Jeremy; m. William F. Duhamel, Aug. 3, 2003. EdB, U. Ariz., Tucson, 1961; MEd, S.D. State U., 1984; postgrad., U. S.D.,

1985—. Cert. secondary tchr., edn. adminstrn. Tchr. jr. high sch. Mpls. Pub. Schs., 1961-63; mem. State Bd. Edn., S.D., 1972-83, pres., 1975-78; dir. S.D. Edn. Policy Seminar, 1975-79; substitute tchr. Rapid City (S.D.) Schs., 1979-81, tchr. adult basic edn., 1979-81, supr. community relations, 1981-88, supr. community edn., pub. info., 1988—95; senator S.D. Legis. (dist. 33), Pierre, SD, 1989—93; edn. dir. Career Learning Center of the Black Hills. Speaker, cons. sch. bds., adminstrs., tchrs., sch. dists., pub. relations, various states, 1972—. Bd. dirs. Black Hills Symphony, 1987—; chair S.D. State Dem. Party, 1998—. Mem. AAUW (Women of Worth award), Rotary, PEO, Delta Kappa Gamma. Democrat. Roman Catholic. Avocations: reading, spectator sports. Office: South Dakota Democratic Party 207 East Capitol Pierre SD 57501-2724 Home: 1106 Hyland Dr Rapid City SD 57701-4456

DUHE, JOHN MALCOLM, JR., federal judge; b. Iberia Parish, La., Apr. 7, 1933; s. J. Malcolm and Rita (Arnandez) D.; children: Kim Duhe Holleman, Jeanne Duhe Sinitier, Edward M., M. Bofill. Student Washington and Lee U., 1951-53, BBA, Tulane U., 1955, LLB, 1957. Atty. Helm, Simon, Caffery & Duhe, New Iberia, La., 1957-78; dist. judge State of La., New Iberia, 1979-84; judge U.S. Dist. Ct. (we. dist.) La., Lafayette, 1984-88; judge, U.S. Ct. Appeals (5th cir.), Lafayette, 1988-99, sr. judge, 1999—. Assoc. editor Tulane Law Rev., 1956, editor-in-chief, 1967. Mem. Order Coif, Omicron Delta Kappa, Kappa Delta Phi. Office: US Ct Appeals 800 Lafayette St Ste 5200 Lafayette LA 70501-6865*

DUHL, LEONARD J., psychiatrist, educator; b. NYC, May 24, 1926; s. Louis and Rose (Josefsberg) D.; m. Lisa Shippee; children: Pamela, Nina, David, Susan, Aurora. BA, Columbia U., 1945; MD, Albany Med. Coll., 1948; postgrad., Menninger Sch. Psychiatry, 1949—54. Diplomate Am. Bd. Psychiatry and Neurology (examiner 1977, 85); cert. in psychoanalysis Wash. Psychoanalytic Inst., 1964. With USPHS, 1951-53, 54-72, med. dir., 1954-72; fellow Menninger Sch. Psychiatry Menninger Sch. Psychiatry, Winter VA Hosp., Topeka, 1949-51, resident psychiatry, 1953-54; asst. health officer Contra Costa County (Calif.) Health Dept., 1951-53; with USPHS, 1949-51, 53-54; psychiatrist profl. svcs. br., chief office planning NIMH, 1954-66; spl. asst. to sec. HUD, 1966-68; cons. Peace Corps, 1961-68; assoc. psychiatry George Washington Med. Sch., 1961-63, asst. clin. prof., 1963-68, assoc. prof., 1966-68; prof. public health Sch. Pub. Health U. Calif., Berkeley, 1968—93; prof. city planning Coll. Environ. Design U. Calif., Berkeley, 1968-92; dir. dual degree program in health and med. scis. U. Calif., Berkeley, 1971-77, clin. prof. psychiatry San Francisco, 1969—; pvt. practice psychiatry Berkeley. Sci. adv. coun. Calif. Legis., 1970-73, sr. cons. Assembly Office of Rsch., 1981-85; cons. Health Cities Program, Environ. Health, WHO, UNICEF, ICDC, Florence, Global Forum of Parliamentarians and Spiritual Leaders, 1989-98, Ctr. for Fgn. Journalists, 1987-90, Am. Hosp. Assn. Health Rsch. and Edn. Trust, 1995—. Author: Approaches to Research in Mental Retardation, 1959, The Urban Condition, 1963, (with R.L. Leopold) Mental Health and Urban Social Policy, 1969, Health Planning and Social Change, 1986, Social Entrepreneurship of Change, 1990, 1995, Health and the City, 1993; bd. editors Jour. Community Psychology, 1974, Jour. Cmty. Mental Health, 1974—, Jour. Mental Health Consultation and Edn., 1978—, Jour. Prevention, 1978—, Nat. Civic Rev., 1991—; contbr. articles to tech. lit. Trustee Robert F. Kennedy Found., 1971-83; bd. dirs. Citizens Policy Ctr., San Francisco, 1975-85, New World Alliance, 1980-84, Calif. Inst. for Integral Studies, 1991-95, Ptnrs. for Dem. Change, 1990-2002; chair First Internat. Healthy Cities Conf., San Francisco, 1993; exec. trustee Nat. Inst. for Citizen Participation and Negotiation, 1988-90; trustee Menninger Found., Topeka, Houston, 1994—, bd. dirs., 1995—; bd. dirs. Louis August Jonas Found. (Camp Rising Sun), 1990—, Ctr. for Transcultural Studies, 1996—; exec. dir. Internat. Healthy Cities Found., 1993—. Med. dir. USPHS, 1950—72. Recipient Albert Deutsh award, 1957, World Health Day award, WHO, 1996, Health Cities award for Coalition of Healthier Cities and Cmtys., 1999, A. Horwitz award Pan Am. Health Orgn., 2002. Fellow Am. Psychiat. Assn. (life), Am. Coll. Psychiatry (life), No. Calif. Psychiat. Soc. (disting. life), Group for Advancement in Psychiatry (chmn. com. preventive psychiatry 1962-66), APHA. Democrat. Jewish. Avocations: photography, woodcarving, snorkeling, painting, reading. Home and Office: 639 Cragmont Ave Berkeley CA 94708-1329 Business E-Mail: lduhl@berkeley.edu.

DUHL, MICHAEL FOSTER, lawyer; b. Chgo., July 12, 1944; s. Samuel Harold and Gertrude (Crodgen) D.; m. Judith Ann Currie, Jan. 30, 1970; children: Emilie Ann, Benjamin Currie. BBA, U. Mich., 1966; JD magna cum laude, Harvard U., 1969. Bar: Ill. 1969; CPA, Ill. Law clk. to presiding justice Ill. Supreme Ct., Chgo., 1969-70; assoc. Hopkins & Sutter, Chgo., 1971-75, ptnr., 1976-96; prin. Deloitte & Touche, L.L.P., Chgo., 1997—. Bd. editors Harvard Law Rev., 1967-69. Treas. Winnetka (Ill.) Pub. Libr. Dist. Bd., 1980-85; bd. dirs. Winnetka Hist. Soc., 1990-94, Winnetka Landmark Preservation Commn., 1992-96; bd. trustees Village of Winnetka, 1996-2000, pres., 2001—. Mem. ABA, Univ. Club Chgo. Jewish. Office: Deloitte & Touche LLP 2 Prudential Plz 180 N Stetson Ave Fl 19 Chicago IL 60601-6779

DUHL, OLGA ANNA, literature educator, researcher; arrived in U.S., 1984; d. Emeric and Olga Kiss; m. Joseph Samuel Duhl, Oct. 17, 1981; 1 child, Esther Annamaria. MA, U. Cluj-Napoca, Romania, 1979; PhD, Rutgers U., 1992. Instr. Barnard Coll., N.Y.C., 1991; French lit. cons. Jane Voorhees Zimmerli Art Mus., New Brunswick, NJ, 1991; head tchg. asst. Rutgers U., New Brunswick, NJ, 1991; vis. prof. Eotvos Lorand U., Budapest, Hungary, 1998; adj. asst. prof. Columbia U., N.Y.C., 1999; instr. Lafayette Coll., Easton, Pa., 1992—93, asst. prof., 1993—2000, assoc. prof., 2000—. Mem. U. Burgundy Rsch. Ctr., 1998—. Author: Folie et Rhétorique Dans la Sottie, 1994, Geneva Droz, 2004, Sotise a huit personnaiges (Le Nouveau Monde), 2005; editor: Le Théâtre Français Des Années 1450-1550, 2002, Quêtes spirituelles et actualités contemporaines dans le théâtre de Marguerite de Navarre, Renaissance et Reformation, Special Issue, 2002; editl. bd. (other) Revue d'Etudes Françaises, 1998—; contbr. articles to profl. jours.; reviewer: Renaissance and Reformation/Renaissance et Réforme. Grantee, The Renaissance Soc. Am., 2003. Mem.: MLA. Avocations: music, theater.

DUHME, CAROL MCCARTHY, civic worker; b. St. Louis, Apr. 13, 1917; d. Eugene Ross and Louise (Roblee) McCarthy; m. Sheldon Ware, June 12, 1941 (dec. 1944); 1 child, David; m. H. Richard Duhme, Jr., Apr. 9, 1947; children: Benton (dec.), Ann, Warren (dec.). AB, Vassar Coll., 1939; DHL (hon.), Eden Theol. Sem., 2002. Tchr. elem. sch., 1939-41, 42-44; moderator St. Louis Assn. Congl. Chs., 1959—62; trustee 1st Congl. Ch., 1964—66; mem. ch. coun. St. Louis Assn. Congl. Ch., 1974-75, 84-85, 87-89, bd. deaconesses, 1978-81, bd. deacons 1982-85, 92-95, chmn. bd. Christian Edn., 1987-88. Former bd. dirs. Community Music Schs., St. Louis, Community Sch., Ch. Women United, John Burroughs Sch., St. Louis Bicentennial Women's Com., St. Louis Jr. League; pres. St. Louis Vassar Club; pres., bd. dirs. YWCA, St. Louis, 1973-76, chmn. ann. fund, 1989-90; bd. dirs. North Side Team Ministry, 1968-84, Chautauqua (N.Y.) Instn., 1971-79, mem. adv. coun. to bd., 1987—. Mem. adv. coun. Mo. Bapt. Hosp., 1973—89; mem. exec. com. bd. dirs. Eden Theol. Sem., 1981—95, presdl. search com., 1986—87, 1992—93, v.p., bd. dirs., 1991, chmn. 150th ann. com., 1996—2000; sec. bd. dirs. UN Assn., St. Louis, 1976—84, coun. advisors, 1993—, nat. coun., 1995—2001; mem. nat. coun. UN-USA, 1995—2001; pres. bd. dirs. Family and Children's Svc. Greater St. Louis, 1977—79; mem. chancellor's long range planning com. Wash. U., 1980—81, mem. Nat. Coun., Sch. Social Work, 1987—; chmn. Benton Roblee Duhme Scholar Fund; trustee Joseph H. and Florence A. Roblee Found., St. Louis, 1984—, pres., 1984—90; bd. dirs.; chmn. Chautauqua Bell Tower Scholar Fund, 1961—; bd. dirs. Nat. Inland Waterways Libr., St. Louis Merc Libr.; mem. corp. assembly Blue Cross Hosp. Svc. Mo., 1978—86; pres. Joseph H. and Florance A. Roblee Found., 2002. Recipient Mary Alice Messerley award for volunteerism Health and Welfare Coun. St. Louis, 1971, Vol. of Yr. award, YWCA, 1976, Woman of Achievement award St. Louis Globe Democrat, 1980, Outstanding Lay Women nomination Mo. United Ch. of Christ, 1991, Outstanding Alumna award John Burroughs Sch., 1992, Humanitarian award Planned Parenthood St. Louis, 2000. Home: 8 Edgewood Rd Saint Louis MO 63124-1817

DUHME, H(ERMAN) RICHARD, JR., sculptor, educator; b. St. Louis, May 31, 1914; s. Herman Richard and Ruth Frances (Leggat) Duhme; m. Carol Louise McCarthy, Apr. 9, 1947; children: David W., Benton Roblee(dec.), Ann Duhme Nelson, Warren L.(dec.). Student, Pa. Acad. Fine Arts, 1932-38, U. Pa., 1934, Am. Sch. Classical Studies, Athens, Greece, 1951; B.F.A., Washington U., St. Louis, 1953. Prof. sculpture Washington U., St. Louis, 1947-82, prof. emeritus, 1982—2005; head sculpture dept. Chautauqua Instn. Summer Sch., 1953-85, Syracuse U. Chautauqua Center, 1953-69. Numerous sculpture commns. including St. Martin and the Beggar, Episcopal Cathedral, Erie, Pa., Lion Cub Fountain, Mycenae, Greece, Bears, Washington U., St. Louis, fountain Boy with Recorder, Chautauqua, NY, Pettus Meml. Fountain in Mo. Bot. Garden, St. Louis, Busts, John Horan, Merck Chem. Co., Rahway, N.J., George Kassabaum, St. Louis, Dr. Koici Iwadare, Tokyo, Dr. William H. Danforth, St. Louis, others. Served with USAAF, 1942-46. Decorated Bronze Stars; designed medals Shepherd's award Nat. Coun. Chs., Mo. Sesquicentennial, Chatutauqua Centennial, Dr. Evarts A Graham medal, Christi Vivit medal Concordia Sem., others. Fellow Nat. Sculpture Soc.; mem. Allied Artists Am., Lauderdale Yacht Club, Town Club (Jamestown, N.Y.), St. Louis Country Club, Univ. Club St. Louis. Home: Saint Louis, Mo. *I feel that an artist's life and work is of no importance unless it touches those around him and gives pleasure, help, or increased knowledge and enrichment in so doing. I have tried to remember this in creating my sculpture and in my contacts with my students.* Died Mar. 24, 2005.

DUJACK, STEPHEN RAYMOND, editor; b. N.Y.C., Apr. 7, 1953; s. Raymond Leon and Inge (Wassermann) D. BA, Princeton U., 1976. Assoc. editor Princeton (N.J.) Alumni Weekly, 1976-80; graphic artist Forte, Inc., Alexandria, Va., 1980-81; editor Fgn. Svc. Jour., dir. comms. Am. Fgn. Svc. Assn., Washington, 1981-88; dir. comms. Worldwatch Inst., Washington, 1988-90. Lectr. George Washington U., Washington, 1983-88. Editor: The Environ. Forum, 1990—; contbr. articles on pub. policy to The Washington Post, The L.A. Times, The New Republic, The Christian Sci. Monitor, Gannett Syndicate, L.A. Times Syndicate. Recipient Allen Furniss award Daily Princetonian, Princeton, 1976; Best Feature Article, Soc. Nat. Assn. Publs., 1983, Best Spl Issue, 1983, Most Improved Mag., 1992, Best Ann. Report, 1994, 96, 98, 99, 1st pl. Master's Divsn., TriAtlantic Biathlon Series, 1994, 3d pl. 45-49 divsn., 1998, 1st pl., 2000. Office: Environ Law Inst 2600 L St NW Ste 620 Washington DC 20036 Office Phone: 703-824-0854. E-mail: dujack@eli.org. *Honor is the central principle of a moral life.*

DUJARDIN, RICHARD CHARLES, journalist; b. Queens, N.Y., Dec. 20, 1944; s. Julien Camille and Veronica (Venesoen) D.; m. Rosemarie Catherine Levesque, Jan. 20, 1947; children: Julianne, Peter, Philip, Joelle, Jean-Paul, Jeffrey. BA in Comm. Arts, Fordham U., 1966. Reporter Providence Jour.-Bulletin, 1966-68, 71-75, bur. mgr., 1975-77, religion writer, 1977—. V.p. Action for Franco-Ams. in N.E., 1991-93, dir., 1986-94; dist. pres. Union St. Jean Baptiste, 1990-94. Lt. (j.g.) USN, 1968-71. Recipient Wilbur award Religious Pub. Rels. Coun., 1986, 91, 95. Mem. Religion Newswriters Assn. (treas. 1989-90, v.p. 1990-94, pres. 1994-96, Supple Meml. award 1986, Templeton Reporter of Yr. award 1991). Roman Catholic. Home: 129 Hillside Ave Providence RI 02906-2900 Office: Providence Jour Bull 75 Fountain St Providence RI 02902-0050 Office Phone: 401-277-7384. E-mail: rdujardi@projo.com, rcdujardin@cox.net.

DUJON, DIANE MARIE, director, activist; b. Boston, Dec. 29, 1946; d. Alfred and Agnes C. (Hall) White; 1 child, Lisa M. Dujon. BA, U. Mass., 1983, MS, 1996. Asst. dir. assessment Coll. Pub. and Cmty. Svc. U. Mass., Boston, 1984-93, co-dir. assessment Coll. Pub. and Cmty. Svc., 1993-97, dir. experiential learning Coll. Pub. and Cmty. Svc., 1997—. Co-editor: For Crying Out Loud: Women's Poverty in U.S., 1996 (Myers Ctr. for the Study of Human Rights in N.Am. Outstanding Book award 1997); prodr. (radio documentary) Workfare: Anatomy of a Policy, 1982 (Alice award 1982), Nat. Commn. on Working Women; alternative radio (NPR) recorded speech, Women, Welfare and Poverty, 1998. V.p. Survivors, Inc., Boston, 1986—. Recipient Earl Douglas award City Mission Soc., 1987, Taking a Stand award Boston Women's Fund, 2004; named Unsung Heroine Rosie's Place, 1997. Mem. Nat. Welfare Rights Union, Mass. AFL-CIO (mem. exec. women's com. 1997-2001), U. Mass. Profl. Staff Union (bd. mem. chpt. Svc. Employees Internat. Union, Local 888), Golden Key Internat. Hon. Soc Baptist. Office: U Mass/Boston 100 Morrissey Blvd Boston MA 02125-3300 Office Phone: 617-287-7126. Business E-Mail: diane.dujon@umb.edu.

DUKAKIS, OLYMPIA, actress; b. Lowell, Mass., June 20, 1931; d. Constantine S. and Alexandra (Christos) D.; m. Louis Zorich; children: Christina, Peter, Stefan. BS, Boston U., 1952, MFA, 1957. Co-founder, artistic dir. Whole Theatre, Montclair, N.J., 1970-90; co-founder Charles Playhouse, Boston; master tchr. NYU, 1970-85. Appeared in over 125 prodns. for regional theatres, N.Y. Shakespeare Theatre, Circle Repertory Theatre, American Place Theatre and numerous Off-Broadway theatres; appearances on stage include A Mother, Mother Courage, The Rose Tattoo, The Cherry Orchard, Three Sisters, The Sea Gull, Long Day's Journey Into Night, Iphegenia in Aulis, Othello, Miss Julie, A Streetcar Named Desire, The Night of the Iguana, King of America, Social Security, Rose, 2005; appearances in film include Lilith, 1964, Twice a Man, 1964, John and Mary, 1969, Made for Each Other, 1971, Death Wish, 1974, Rich Kids, 1979, The Wanderers, 1979, The Idolmaker, 1980, National Lampoon Goes to the Movies, 1982, Flanagan, 1985, Moonstruck, 1988 (Golden Globe, Academy Award Suppporting Actress), Working Girl, 1988, Steel Magnolias, 1988, Look Who's Talking, 1988, Dad, 1989, In the Spirit, 1990, Look Who's Talking II, 1990, Over the Hill, 1992, Look Who's Talking Now, 1993, The Cemetery Club, 1993, I Love Trouble, 1994, Digger, 1994, Jeffrey, 1995, Mighty Aphrodite, 1995, Mr. Holland's Opus, 1996, Dead Badge, 1995, Picture Perfect, 1997, Never Too Late, 1997, Jane Austen's Mafia!, 1998, A Life for a Life, 1998, Better Living, 2000, Brooklyn Sonnet, 2000, The Intended, 2002, The Event, 2003, Charlie's War, 2003, Jesus, Mary and Joey, 2003, The Great New Wonderful, 2005; (TV movies) Nicky's World, 1974, The Neighborhood, 1982, The Last Act is a Solo, 1990 (Ace award), Lucky Day, 1991, Fire in the Dark, 1991, Sinatra: The Mini-Series, 1992, Armistead Maupin's Tales of the City, 1994, A Century of Women, 1994, Young at Heart, 1995, A Match Made in Heaven, 1997, Scattering Dad, 1998, The Pentagon Wars, 1998, More Tales of the City (mini-series), 1998, Joan of Arc, 1999, Last of the Blonde Bombshells, 2000, And Never Let Her Go, 2001, Ladies and the Champ, 2001, Further Tales of the City (mini-series), 2001, My Beautiful Son, 2001, Guilty Hearts (mini-series), 2002, Mafia Doctor, 2003, Babycakes, 2003; (TV series) Center of the Universe, 2004. Del. Dem. Nat. Convention, 1988. Recipient 2 Obie awards, Los Angeles Film Critics award, 1988. Mem. Actor's Equity Assn., Screen Actors Guild, Am. Fedn. TV and Radio Artists. Office: William Morris Agy care Parseghian 1325 Avenue Of The Americas Fl 32 New York NY 10019-4702*

DUKE, ANDREA K., music educator; b. Jacksonville, Fla., Mar. 5, 1968; d. Earl F. and Janet S. Knight; m. Mark P. Duke, Apr. 4, 1992. MusB in Edn., Jacksonville U., 1990. Music educator Suzuki Talent Edn., Orange Park, Fla., 1989—95, The Bolles Sch., Jacksonville, Fla., 1992—. Lower sch. music dir. The Bolles Sch., Jacksonville, Fla., 1999—. Composer: (songs) (grade-level plays and performances) Balles Sch. Sec./treas. Corner Oaks Owners Assn., Inc, Jacksonville, Fla., 1999—2005. Mem.: Pi Kappa Lambda. Republican. Avocations: playing musical instruments, composing music, decorating, swimming, landscaping. Home: 12118 Corner Oaks Dr Jacksonville FL 32223 Office: 7400 San Jose Blvd Jacksonville FL 32217 Personal E-mail: dia1@comcast.net.

DUKE, ANTHONY DREXEL, retired sociologist, educator, philanthropist; b. NYC, July 28, 1918; s. Angier Buchanan and Cordelia (Biddle) D.; children by previous marriage: Anthony D. Jr., Nicholas R., Cordelia Duke Jung, Josephine Duke Brown, December Duke McSherry, John O., Douglas D.; m. Maria Luly de Lourdes Alcebo, Sept. 27, 1975; children: Lulita C., Washington A., James B. Student, Princeton U., 1941; DHL (hon.), Adelphi Coll., 1957, L.I. U., 1988, Drexel U., 1991. With Import Export Co., 1946-50; prin. A.D. Duke Realty, Inc., 1955-65. Chmn. bd. dirs., pres., founder Boys Harbor Inc., 1937—. Trustee Big Brother Movement, 1951-63; past trustee Henry St. Settlement, N.Y.C.; del. Internat. Conf. Pvt. Sector Initiatives, 1986; hon. commr. Manhattan Borough Projects, 1954-57, Civic Affairs and Pub. Events, N.Y.C.; mem. N.Y.C. Youth Bd., 1955-58; rep. Internat. Rescue Com., Vietnam War, Meriel refugee crisis Cuba, 1983; active Save the Children, Pomfret Sch., Duke U., U.S. Naval Acad. Lt. comdr. USNR, 1941-46, PTO, ATO, ETO. Decorated Bronze Star. Recipient Town and Country Most Generous Am. award 1988, Save the Children award, 1977; Presdl. citation for pvt. sector commendation, 1986, Citation for Promotion of Human Welfare Commonwealth of Mass., 1987. Mem. Bodman and Achelis Found., Nat. Com. on Am. Fgn. Policy, Maidstone Club (former gov.), Piping Rock (former gov.), River Club, Racquet and Tennis Club, Beaver Dam Club. Home: PO Box 177 East Hampton NY 11937-0177 Office: Boys Harbor Inc PO Box 3000 New York NY 10029-0300

DUKE, CHARLES BRYAN, electronics executive, physicist, educator; b. Richmond, Va., Mar. 13, 1938; s. Charles Joseph Jr. and Virginia (Welton) Duke; m. Ann Evans, July 1, 1961; children: Amy Dickerson, Emily Elizabeth. BS in Math., Duke U., 1959; PhD in Physics, Princeton U., 1963. Staff corp. rsch. GE, Schenectady, N.Y., 1963-69, cons., 1969-72; prof. physics U. Ill., Urbana, 1969-72; mgr., sr. fellow Xerox Corp., Webster, NY, 1972-88, sr. rsch. fellow, 1989-96, v.p., sr. rsch. fellow, 1996—; dep. dir., chief scientist Battelle Pacific Northwest Div., Richland, Wash., 1988-89. Bd. govs. Am. Inst. Physics, N.Y.C., 1976—82, N.Y.C., 1984—87; adj. prof. physics U. Rochester, NY, 1972—88; affiliate prof. physics U. Wash., Seattle, 1988—89; gen. chmn. Phys. Electronics Conf., 1997—2000. Author: Tunneling in Solids, 1969, Surface Science: The First Thirty Years, 1994, Color Systems Integration, 1998, Frontiers in Surface and Interface Science, 2002; editor-in-chief: Jour. Materials Rsch., 1985—86, Surface Sci., 1992—2001; contbr. articles to profl. jours. Named one of 1000 Most Cited Scientists, Inst. Sci. Info., 1981. Fellow: IEEE, Am. Phys. Soc. (councillor 1995—98, exec. bd. 1997—98), Am. Vacuum Soc. (hon.; bd. dirs. 1973—76, pres. 1979, trustee 2003—05, M. W. Welch award in vacuum sci. and tech. 1977); mem.: NAS, NAE, Materials Rsch. Soc. (councillor 1988—90, treas. 1991—92, councillor 1995—97). Office: Xerox Wilson Ctr for R & T 800 Phillips Rd # 114-38D Webster NY 14580-9720 Office Phone: 585-422-2106. Business E-Mail: charles.duke@xeroxlabs.com.

DUKE, CHARLES RICHARD, academic dean; b. West Stewartstown, N.H., July 6, 1940; s. George Tunicliffe and Evelyn Agnes (Murray) D.; m. Leona Ruth Hubbard, June 1, 1983. BE, Plymouth (N.H.) State Coll., 1962; MA, Middlebury (Vt.) Coll., 1968; PhD, Duke U., 1972. Tchr. English, head dept. Sunapee (N.H.) H.S., 1962-68; prof. English Plymouth State Coll., 1968-78, Murray (Ky.) State U., 1978-84; prof., head dept. secondary edn. Utah State U., Logan, 1984-89; dean Coll. Edn. and Human Svcs. Clarion (Pa.) U., 1989-94; dean Coll. Edn. Appalachian State U., Boone, NC, 1995—. Dir. West Ky. Writing Project, 1980-84; co-dir. Utah Writing Project, 1984-89, Clarion U. Student Literacy Corps, 1990-94. Author: Creative Dramatics and English Teaching, 1974, Writing Through Sequence, 1983, Strategies for teaching, 1987; contbr. articles to profl. jours; editor: Exercise Exchange, 1979—2001, Poets Perspectives, 1992, American Overseas Education, 2000, Assessing Writing Across the Curriculum, 2001. Am. Studies fellow Coe Found., 1964; recipient Alumni Outstanding Svc. award Plymouth State Coll., 1977. Mem. ASCD, Internat. Reading Assn., Nat. Coun. Tchrs. English, Am. Assn. Colls. Tchr. Edn., Assn. Tchr. Educators, Phi Delta Kappa. Office: Appalachian State U 222 Duncan Hall PO Box 32038 Boone NC 28608-2038 Business E-Mail: dukecr@appstate.edu.

DUKE, DONALD NORMAN, publishing executive; b. LA, Apr. 1, 1929; s. Roger V. and Mabel (Weineger) D. BA in Ednl. Psychology, Colo. Coll., 0951. Comml. photographer, Colorado Springs, Colo., 1951-53; pub. rels. Gen. Petroleum, LA, 1954-55; agt. Gen. S.S. Corp., Ltd., 1956-57; asst. mgr. retail advt., sales promotion Mobil Oil Co., 1958-63; pub. Golden West Books, Alhambra, Calif., 1964—. Dir. Pacific R.R. Publs., Inc., Athletic Press; pub. rels. cons. Santa Fe Rlwy., 1960-70. Author: The Pacific Electric: A History of Southern California Railroading, 1958, Southern Pacific Steam Locomotives, 1962, Santa Fe...Steel Rails to California, 1963, Night Train, 1961, American Narrow Gauge, 1978, RDC: the Budd Rail Diesel Car, 1989, The Brown Derby, 1990, Camp Cajon, 1991, Fred Harvey: Civilizer of the American West, 1994, editor: Water Trails West, 1977, Branding Iron, 1988-91, Santa Fe...The Railroad Gateway to the American West, Vol. 1, 1995, Vol. 2, 1997, Incline Railways of Los Angeles and Southern California, 1998, Electric Railroads of San Francisco Bay, Vols. 1 and 2, 1999, Pacific Electric Railway (The No. Divsn.), vol. 1, 2001, Pacific Electric Railway (The Ea. Divsn.), vol. 2, 2002, Pacific Electric Railway (The So. Divsn.), vol. 3, 2003, Pacific Electric Railway (The We. Divsn.), vol. 4, 2004, The Union Pacific in Southern California. Recipient Spur award for Trails of the Iron Horse Western Writers Am., 1975. Mem. Rlwy. and Locomotive Hist. Soc. (dir. 1944-98), Western History Assn., Newcomen Soc., Lexington Group of Transp. History, Western Writers Am., PEN Internat. (v.p. 1975-77), Authors Guild Am., Book Pubs. Assn. So. Calif. (dir. 1968-77), Calif. Writers Guild (dir. 1976-77), Calif. Book Pubs. Assn. (dir. 1976-77), Westerners Internat. (hon., editor Branding Iron 1971-80, 88-91), Hist. Soc. So. Calif. (dir. 1972-75), Henry E./Arabella Huntington Soc., Kappa Sigma (lit. editor Caduceus 1968-80). Home: PO Box 80250 San Marino CA 91118-8250 Office: Golden West Books 525 N Electric Ave Alhambra CA 91801-2032 Office Phone: 626-458-8148. E-mail: trainbook@earthlink.net.

DUKE, ELIZABETH (BETSY) A., bank executive; b. July 1952; BFA U. NC, Chapel Hill; MBA, Old Dominion U., Norfolk, VA; grad., Stonier Grad. Sch. Banking, Am. Bankers Assn. Sch. of Bank Investments, Va. Bankers Assn. Sch. Bank Mgmt. Pres., CEO Bank of Tidewater, 1991—2001; sr. v.p. govt. rels. SouthTrust Corp., Va. Beach, Va., 2001—03, exec. v.p. cmty. bank devel., 2003—. Nat. adv. coun. Fannie Mae, 2004—. Named One of 25 Women to Watch, U.S. Banker Mag., 2003. Mem.: Am. Bankers Assn. (chmn.-elect 2003—). Home: 301 Booty Lane Virginia Beach VA 23451-2030

DUKE, ELIZABETH M., health facility administrator; B Polit. Sci., M Polit. Sci., Rutgers U.; M African Studies, Northwestern U.; PhD, George Washington U. Dir. gov. affairs inst. office exec. and mgmt. devel. Health Resources and Svcs. Adminstrn., HHS, 1978—84; dep. asst. dir., dir. policy and sys. office tng. and devel. U.S. Office Pers. Mgmt., 1984—86; dep. asst. sec. adminstrn. Adminstrn. Children and Families U.S. Dept. Health and Human Svs., 1997—2001, CFO, mgmt. control officer, chief grants officer, chief info. officer Adminstrn. Children and Families, head grants policy, fin. mgmt. internal and state sys., human resources, other adminstrv. duties Adminstrn. Children and Families; acting adminstr. Health Resources and Svcs. Adminstrn., HHS, 2001—02; adminstr. Health Resources and Svs. Adminstrn., HHS, 2002—. Rsch. writer Congressional Quarterly. Office: Health Resources and Svs Adminstrn US Dept Health & Human Svcs Parklawn Bld 5600 Fishers Ln Rockville MD 20857

DUKE, JAMES T, art educator, consumer products company executive; b. Chicago, Ill., Feb. 21, 1937; s. James E. and Anna M. Duke. Owner, operator Duke Sign, Chicago, Ill., 2000—02; sign co. exec. U.S.A. Sign, Fort Lauderdale, Fla., 2002—; pub. sch. educator Broward County, Fort Lauderdale, Fla., 2002—. Specialist 4 class US Army. Avocations: martial arts, fine art, commercial art, gourmet cooking. Home: 609 NE 14th Place Fort Lauderdale FL 33304 Office: Duke Sign 609 NE 14th Place Fort Lauderdale FL 33304

DUKE, MARGARET JOYCE, sound recordist, broadcast engineer; b. Baton Rouge, La., Nov. 18, 1945; d. James Henry and Joyce Olga (Boyd) D.; children: Diane Alana, Julie Rene, Richard Mark. BFA, La. State U., 1980. Sound recordist (films) John Huston and the Dubliners, The Wild West, Comic Strip Live, Sledgehammer, Destined to Live, Diabetes Camp, Prisoners of Wedlock, It Was a Wonderful Life, Labours of Eve, Wise Women, Science, Math and Middleschool Girls, The Desert is No Lady, Far Out Man, Galaxies Are Colliding, Bang, Street Pirates, George Shdanoff and Hollywood, Your Children, The Thistle Hotel; broadcast engr. tV: The View, General Hosp., Port Charles. Mem. Women in Film, Cinewomen. Avocations: photography, gardening, art, antiques. Office: 17160 Avenida De Santa Ynez Pacific Palisades CA 90272-2133

DUKE, MICHAEL, retail executive; m. Susan Duke; 3 children. Bachelor's in Indsl. Engring., Ga. Tech. With Federated Dept. Stores, May Dept. Stores, Venture Stores; sr. v.p. logistics Wal-Mart Stores, Inc., 1995—2000, sr. v.p. distbn., exec. v.p. logistics, 2000, exec. v.p. adminstrn., 2000—03, exec. v.p., 2003—, exec. v.p. and pres. Wal-Mart Stores div., 2003—. Mem. adv. bd. Ga. Tech; bd. dirs. Arvest-Bank of Bentonville. Mem.: Internat. Mass Retail Assn. (bd. dirs.). Office: Wal-Mart Stores Inc 702 SW Eighth St Bentonville AR 72716*

DUKE, PHYLLIS LOUISE KELLOGG HENRY, school administrator, consultant; b. Mason City, Iowa, May 3, 1932; d. Wilbur Rhode and Dorothy Margaret (Bauer) Kellogg; children— Curtis Dean Henry, Catherine Rose Henry Jones, David Russell Henry. A.A. in Elem. Teaching, U. No. Iowa, 1953; B.A. Calif. State U.-Los Angeles, 1963, M.A., 1968. Cert. elem. tchr., cert. reading specialist, sch. adminstrn. credential. Tchr., Arlington pub. schs., Iowa, 1951-52, St. Louis Park pub. schs., Minn., 1953-55; tchr., supr. ABC Sch. Dist., Cerritos, Calif., 1963-69; cons. in reading State Dept. of Calif., Sacramento, 1969-70; cons. in edn. Orange County Dept. Edn., Santa Ana, Calif., 1970-75; sch. adminstr. Oakwood Acad., Long Beach, Calif., 1975—, 5 other pvt. elem. and pre-schs.; chmn. bd. dirs. New City Bank, Orange, Calif.; cons. in field. Author: Song of Sounds, 3d edit., 2002, Beginnings for Christian Schools, 1976, Destined to Live 9 Lives, 2005. Conf. coordinator State Dept. Edn., Calif., Sacramento, Santa Barbara, 1970 (Outstanding Leadership award 1974-75). Mem. Nat. Ind. Pvt. Sch. (v.p. 1982-83, dir. seminars 1983), Pre-Sch. Assn. Calif. (legis. chair 1978-84), Reading Specialists Calif. (pres. 1970-73). Republican. Avocations: skiing; scuba diving; painting; photography; travel. Home: 1208 S Lemon Ave Walnut CA 91789-4822 Office: Oakwood Acad 2951 N Long Beach Blvd Long Beach CA 90806-1532 Office Phone: 562-424-4816.

DUKE, ROBERT DOMINICK, lawyer; b. Goshen, N.Y., Oct. 14, 1928; s. Robert DeWitt and Elma Christina (Dominick) D.; m. Jeannette Parham, Apr. 24, 1954; children: Katherine Campbell, Robert Dominick, Peter Benjamin DeWitt, Lois Christina. BA, Va. Mil. Inst., 1947; LL.B., Yale U., 1950; MBA, U. Pa., 1952. Bar: N.Y. 1950, Conn. 1989. With Cravath, Swaine & Moore, N.Y.C., 1951-52, 54-64, Freeport-McMoRan Inc. and predecessors, N.Y.C., 1964-84, gen. counsel, 1970-84, sr. v.p., 1973-84; sr. v.p., gen. counsel The Pittston Co., Stamford, Conn., 1984-93, sr. counsel, 1993—2002, also bd. dirs., 1991-93. Served as 1st lt. JAGC, U.S. Army, 1952-54. Mem.: ABA, Assn. Bar City NY, Silver Spring Golf Club, Silvermine Golf Club, Yale Club (N.Y.C.). Presbyterian. Home: 67 Ridgefield Rd Wilton CT 06897-3006

DUKE, ROBIN CHANDLER TIPPETT, retired public relations executive; b. Balt., Oct. 13, 1923; d. Richard Edgar and Esther (Chandler) Tippett; m. Angier Biddle Duke, May 1962; children: Jeffrey R. Lynn, Letitia Lynn, Angier Biddle Jr. Fashion editor N.Y. Jour. Am., N.Y.C., 1944-46; freelance writer N.Y.C., 1946-50; rep. Orvis Bros., N.Y.C., 1953-58; mem. pub. rels. staff Pepsi Cola Co., Internat., N.Y.C., 1958-62; amb. to UNESCO, Belgrade, 1980; amb. U.S. to Norway, 2000—01. Bd. dirs. Am. Home Products, N.Y.C., Internat. Flavors & Fragrances, N.Y.C., East River Bank, New Rochelle, NY; bd. dirs. emeritus Inst. Internat. Edn.; dir. Rockwell Corp., 1977—95. Co-chmn. Population Action Internat., N.Y.C., 1975-96; Met. Club Washington; bd. dirs. David Packard Found., U.S. Japan Found. Recipient Albert and Mary Lasker Social Svc. award, 1991, Margaret Sanger Woman of Yr. Valor award, 1995. Mem. Coun. on Fgn. Rels., Acad. Arts & Scis., World Affairs Coun. L.I. (co-chmn.), Colony Club, River Club. Democrat. Avocations: skiing, swimming. Home: 435 E 52nd St New York NY 10022-6445

DUKE, STEPHEN OSCAR, physiologist, research scientist, educator; b. Battle Creek, Mich., Oct. 9, 1944; s. Oscar and Azalee Rosa (Tallant) D.; m. Barbara Alice Rowe, June 2, 1967 (div. Dec. 1993); children: Gregory Ivan, Robin Anne. BS, Henderson State U., 1966; MS, U. Ark., 1969; PhD, Duke U., 1975. Plant physiologist So. Weed Sci. Lab., USDA, Stoneville, Miss., 1975-84, rsch. leader, 1984-87, lab. dir., 1987-96, rsch. leader Oxford, Miss., 1996—. Adj. prof. U. Miss., Oxford, 1996—. Co-author: Physiology of Herbicide Action, 1993; editor: Weed Physiology, 2 vols., 1985, Pest Control with Enhanced Environmental Safety, 1993, Porphyric Pesticides, 1994, Herbicide Resistant Crops, 1995; contbr. articles to profl. jours. Head referee Greenville Youth Soccer Assn. (Miss.), 1982-96; soccer coach Washington Sch., Greenville, 1986-88. Lt. U.S. Army, 1968—70, Vietnam. Decorated Bronze Star; recipient Edminster award USDA, 1986, Disting. Alumnus award Henderson State U., 1989, CIBA-GEIGY/Weed Sci. Soc. Am. award CIBA-GEIGY Corp., 1990, Outstanding Sr. Scientist award USDA, Agr. Rsch. Svc., 2001, Extraordinary Prof. award U. Pretoria RSA, 2002-, Molisch award Internat. Allelopathy Soc.; elected Henderson State U. Acad., 2001. Fellow AAAS, Weed Sci. Soc. Am. (assoc. editor 1978-83, pres. 1996, Outstanding Young Scientist award 1984, Outstanding Article award 1984, Rsch. award 1990); mem. Am. Soc. Plant Physiology (chmn. so. sect. 1985-86), Coun. for Agrl. Sci. and Tech. (bd. dirs. 1993-94), Am. Chem. Soc.(Internat. Rsch. award agrochem. divsn. 2004), So. Weed Soc. (pres. 1995, disting. svc. award 1998), Internat. Weed Sci. Soc. (pres. 2000-04). Avocations: gardening, writing. Home: 9 Private Rd 3078 Oxford MS 38655 Mailing: PO Box 3964 University MS 38677 Business E-Mail: sduke@olemiss.edu.

DUKE, STEVEN BARRY, law educator; b. Mesa, Ariz., July 31, 1934; s. Alton and Elaine (Altman) D.; m. Janet Truax, 1956 (div. 1971); children: Glenn, Warren, Alison, Sally; m. Margaret Munson, 1984 (div. 1999); children: Jennifer, Lauren. BS, Ariz. State U., 1956; JD, U. Ariz., 1959; LL.M., Yale U., 1961. Bar: Ariz. 1959. Law clk. to Supreme Ct. Justice Douglas, 1959; grad. fellow Yale Law Sch., 1960, mem. faculty, 1961—, prof. law, 1966—81, 1999—, Law of Sci. and Tech. prof., 1982—99. Vis. prof. U. Calif.-Berkeley, 1965, Hastings Coll. Law, 1981, Ariz. State U., 1986; Bd. dirs. New Haven Legal Assistance Assn., 1968-70; cons. Commn. to Revise Fed. Criminal Code; mem. Conn. Commn. on Medicolegal Investigations, 1976—; bd. visitors Fordham U. Law Sch., 1986-1999. Author: (with A. Gross) America's Longest War: Rethinking Our Tragic Crusade Against Drugs, 1993; editor-in-chief Ariz. Law Rev.; contbr. articles to profl. jours. Mem. Woodbridge (Conn.) Bd. Edn., 1970-72; mem. Woodbridge Democratic Town Com., 1967-72. Mem. Nat. Assn. Criminal Def. Lawyers, Am. Trial Lawyers, ACLU, Phi Kappa Phi, Alpha Tau Omega. Home: 250 Grandview Ave Hamden CT 06514-3028 Office: Yale Law Sch PO Box 208215 New Haven CT 06520-8215

DUKE, WILLIAM EDWARD, public affairs executive; b. Bklyn., July 18, 1932; m. Leilani Kamp Lattin. BS, Fordham U., 1954. City editor Middletown (N.Y.) Record, 1956—60; asst. state editor Washington Star, 1961—63; exec. asst. U.S. Sen. Jacob K. Javits, Washington, 1963—69; dir. pub. affairs Corp. Pub. Broadcasting, Washington, 1969—72; dir. fed. govt. rels. Atlantic Richfield Co., Washington, 1973—78, mgr. pub. affairs L.A., 1978—91; mgr. external affairs We. States Petroleum Assn., 1993—95; pres. W.E. Duke and Co., 1996—. Lectr. U. So. Calif. Grad. Sch. Journalism, 1988—; cons. in field. Fellow: Pub. Rels. Soc. Am., Nat. Press Club. Office Phone: 310-454-3480.

DUKE DE LEONEDES OF SPAIN SICILY GREECE, HIS ROYAL HIGHNESS See SANCHEZ, LEONEDES MONARRIZE WORTHINGTON

DUKERT, BETTY COLE, television producer; b. Muskogee, Okla., May 9, 1927; d. Irvan Dill and Ione (Bowman) Cole; m. Joseph M. Dukert, May 19, 1968 Student, Lindenwood Coll., St. Charles, Mo., 1945-46, Drury Coll., Springfield, Mo., 1946-47; B.J., U. Mo., 1949. With Sta. KICK, Springfield, Mo., 1949-50; adminstrv. asst. Juvenile Office, Green County, Mo., 1950-52; with Sta. WRC-TV-NBC, Washington, 1952-56; assoc. producer Meet the Press, NBC, Washington, 1956-75, producer, 1975—92; sr. producer Meet the Press, NBC News, 1992—. Mem. Robert F. Kennedy Journalism Awards Com., 1978-82, exec. producer, 1997—. Trustee Drury Coll., Springfield, Mo., 1984— Recipient Disting. Alumna award Drury Coll., 1975, Disting. Alumni award U Mo., 1978, Ted Yates award Washington chpt. Nat. Acad. TV Arts and Scis., 1979, Pub. Rels. award for pub. svc. Am. Legion Nat. Comdrs., 1981, Internat. Disting. Svc. Journalism medal U. Mo. Sch. Journalism, 1993, Peter Hackes Meml. award Washington D.C. chpt. Radio/TV News Dirs. Assn., 1995. Mem. Am. Women in Radio and TV, Am. News Women's Club, Radio/TV Corrs. Assn., Women's Forum Washington, Soc. Profl. Journalists (dir. 1983-84, inducted into Hall of Fame 1991), Silver Circle Broadcasting, Nat. Acad. TV Arts and Scis., Nat. Press Club. Office: NBC News 4001 Nebraska Ave NW Washington DC 20016-2733

DUKES, VANESSA JOHNSON, dietician; b. Charleston, S.C., Aug. 4, 1955; d. Rubin and Christena (Weston) Johnson; m. Warren L. Dukes, May 21, 1983. BS, S.C. State U., 1977, MEd, 1979. Registered and lic. dietitian. Grad. asst. in home econs. S.C. State Coll., Orangeburg, 1977-79; nutritionist Services Council Day Care Ctr., Aiken, S.C., 1980-83; food service supr. III S.C. Dept. Correction, Ridgeville, 1987—; tchr. emotionally handicapped Charleston County Sch. Dist., 1987-97; diet technician, dietitian Sodexho, Des Moines, 1997—; food svc. supr., diet tech., Mariott, Des Moines, 1997—. Dietary asst. S.C. Dept. Health and Environ. Control, Columbia, 1978; substitute tchr. Charleston County Sch. Dist., 1985—; nutritionist Franklin C. Fetter Health Clinic, Charleston, 1988—; companion, homemaker Med. Pers. Pool, Des Moines; asst. food svc. mgr. Fountain West Health Care Ctr., Des Moines, 1995—; hospitality coord. Dietary Dept. BMC, 2004—. Vol. Meals on Wheels, Aiken, 1976, Mercy House Diabetic Clinic, 1999—2004; vol. Project NOW Broadlawns Med. Ctr., 2001; alt. del. S.C. Dem. conv., 1980; voter registrar Aiken, SC, 1980—82. Recipient John H. Cromer Meml. scholarship S.C. Dietetic Assn., 1977. Mem. Am. Dietetic Assn., Ctrl. Iowa Dietetic Assn., Iowa Dietetic Assn., Kappa Omicron Phi. Avocations: reading, creative cooking, gardening, crafts. Home: 4046 Plainview Dr Des Moines IA 50311

DUKMEJIAN, MICHAEL, publishing executive; Advt. mgr., mgr. bus. devel. Time Mag., 1980—93; dir. sales devel. Sports Illustrated, 1993—98; pub. Mut. Funds Mag., 1999—2002, Money Mag., N.Y.C., 2002—. Office: Money Mag 1271 Avenue of the Americas New York NY 10020-1300 Office Phone: 212-522-2824. Office Fax: 212-467-1178.*

DUKORE, MARGARET MITCHELL, writer; b. Honolulu, Sept. 27, 1950; d. Donald Dean and Winifred Ann Mitchell; m. Bernard Frank Dukore, Nov. 13, 1974 (div. Feb. 1982); m. Gary B. Lisman, Aug. 31, 1997; children: Joan Dukore, Kristine Lisman. BA, Lewis & Clark Coll., 1972. Editor Ideafishers, Honolulu, Irvine, Calif. Author: (play) Move, 1981, (novels) A Novel Called Heritage, 1982 (Maxwell Perkins prize 1982), Bloom, 1985. Fundraiser Ballet Hawaii, Honolulu, 1987-91, Hoo-mana-o-lana AIDS Housing, Honolulu, 1992-95; rschr. Hawaii State Senate, Honolulu, 1991-95. Lit. grantee Nat. Endowment for the Arts, 1982. Mem. SAG. Democrat. Avocation: horseback riding. Home: 5030 Firwood Rd Lake Oswego OR 97035 E-mail: mdukore@aol.com.

DUL, JOHN A., lawyer, electronics executive; b. 1961; BBA, U. Miami; JD, Northwestern U. Bar: Ill., 1986. Assoc. gen. counsel. Anixter Inc. (subsidiary of Anixter Internat.), 1990—96, sec., gen. counsel, 1996—; v.p., gen. counsel Anixter Internat., Skokie, Ill., 1998—, sec., 2002—. Office: Anixter Internat Inc 2301 Patriot Blvd Glenview IL 60025-8020

DULAC, CATHERINE, biology professor, researcher; Grad., Ecole Normale Supérieure de la rue d'Ulm, Paris; PhD, U. Paris. Rschr. Institut d'Embryologie du Collège de France; postdoctoral fellow Columbia U.; asst. prof. molecular & cellular biology dept. Harvard U., 1996—2000; asst. investigator Howard Hughes Med. Inst., 1997—2002; assoc. prof. molecular & cellular biology dept. Harvard U., 2000—01, prof. molecular & cellular biology, 2001—; investigator Howard Hughes Medical Inst., 2002—. Mem. scientific advisory bd. Senomyx, Inc., Allen Brain Atlas, Max Planck Inst., Friedrich Miescher Inst. Fellow: AAAS. Achievements include discovery of genes encoding families of pheromone receptors in mammals. Office: Harvard U Rm 4017 16 Divinity Ave Cambridge MA 02138 also: Harvard Univ Rm 4017 16 Divinity ave Cambridge MA 02138

DULAINE, PIERRE, ballroom dancer; Became ptnr. to Yvonne Marceau, 1976; founder Am. Ballroom Theatre, N.Y.C., 1984—; faculty mem. Sch. of Am. Ballet, 1986—, The Juilliard Sch., 1992—. Guest tchr. Sch. Am. Ballet, N.Y.C., The Juilliard Sch., N.Y.C. Appearances include Smithsonian Inst., Washington, JFK Ctr. Performing Arts, Washington, White House, 1992, (Broadway and London show) Grand Hotel, 1989-92; toured with Yvonne Marceau and Am. Ballroom Theatre numerous internat. locations. Recipient Brit. Theatrical Arts Championships 4 times, Spl. Astaire award, Dance Educator awards, Outstanding Achievement in Dance award Nat. Dance Coun. Am., 1992, Dance Mag. award, 1993, Dance Educators of Am. award, 1990. Office: Pierre Dulaine Dance Club 25 W 31st St Fl 4 New York NY 10001-4413 Fax: 212-244-9299. Office Phone: 212-244-9442. E-mail: pdulaine@msn.com.

DULANY, DONELSON EDWIN, JR., psychology professor; b. Shreveport, La., Dec. 9, 1928; s. Donelson Edwin and LaVera (Jackson) D.; m. Elizabeth Carolyn Gjelsness, Mar. 19, 1955; 1 child, Christopher Daniel. AB, U. Tenn., 1948; PhD, U. Mich., 1955. Rockefeller rsch. fellow in philosophy U. Mich., Ann Arbor, 1951-52, instr. psychology, 1952—54; rsch. fellow Harvard U., Cambridge, Mass., 1958; asst. prof. psychology U. Ill., Urbana-Champaign, 1956-59, assoc. prof., 1959-64, prof. psychology, 1964-98, prof. emeritus, 1998—. Inst. affiliate Beckman Inst., U. Ill., 1990—. Co-author: A Method for Teaching English to Spanish Speaking Military Personnel, 1956; editor: Contributions to Modern Psychology, 1963; editor Am. Jour. Psychology, 1988—; contbr. articles to profl. publs. With U.S. Army, 1954—56. Grantee NSF, NIH. Fellow APA (chmn. com. on equal opportunity and condtions of employment 1970), Am. Psychol. Soc, Psychonomic Soc., Assn. Sci. Study Consciousness. Avocations: reading, photography, travel, music. Office: U Ill Dept Psychology 603 E Daniel St Champaign IL 61820-6232

DULANY, ELIZABETH GJELSNESS, editor; b. Charleston, SC, Mar. 11, 1931; d. Rudolph Hjalmar and Ruth Elizabeth (Weaver) Gjelsness; m. Donelson Edwin Dulany, Mar. 19, 1955; 1 son, Christopher Daniel. BA, Bryn Mawr Coll., 1952. Editor, R.R. Bowker Co., 1948-52; med. editor U. Mich. Hosp., Ann Arbor, 1953-54; editorial asst. E.P. Dutton & Co., N.Y.C., 1954-55, U. Ill. Press, Champaign, 1956-59, asst. editor, 1959-67, assoc. editor, 1967-72, mng. editor, 1972-90, asst. dir., 1983-90, assoc. dir., 1990—98, editor, 1998—. Democrat. Episcopalian. Home: 73 Greencroft Dr Champaign IL 61821-5112 Office: U Ill Press 1325 S Oak St Champaign IL 61820-6903 Office Phone: 217-244-0158. Business E-Mail: edulany@uillinois.edu.

DULANY, WILLIAM BEVARD, lawyer; b. Sykesville, Md., Sept. 4, 1927; s. William Washington and Helen Marie (Bevard) D.; m. Anna Winifred Spencer, Aug. 16, 1952; children: William Bryant, Thomas Patrick, Anne French. AB, McDaniel Coll., 1950, LLD (hon.), 1989; postgrad., U. Mich., 1950—51; JD, U. Md., 1953. Bar: Md. 1953, U.S. Dist. Ct. Md. 1954, U.S. Tax Ct. 1979, U.S. Supreme Ct. 1990. Assoc. Baldwin, Jarman & Norris, Balt., 1953-59; sr. ptnr. Dulany, Leahy, Curtis & Williams, LLP, Westminster, Md., 1959—. Mem. character com. Md. Ct. Appeals, Annapolis, 1974—93. Mem. Md. Ho. of Dels., Annapolis, 1962-66, Md. Constl. Conv., Annapolis, 1967-68, Md. Regional Planning Coun., 1964-66; chmn. Md. Fair Campaign Practices Commn., 1975-78; chmn. adv. com. Carroll County C.C., 1976; trustee McDaniel Coll., Westminster, Md., 1976—; bd. dirs. nat. office Am. Heart Assn., Dallas, 1982-89, chmn., 1987-88; bd. dirs. Episcopal Ministries to Aging, Inc., Fairhaven, 1982-2005, chmn., 1986-2005; former commr. Md. Human Rels. Commn.; vice chmn. Md. Spl. Com. on Gen. Equality, 1989-91; mem. commn. on Racial and Ethnicity Fairness in Judicial Process, 2002-04; trustee Md. Hist. Soc., 1991-01; past pres. Hist. Soc. Carroll County; former mem. Vestry Ascension Episc. Ch. Named one of Outstanding Young Men of Am., Westminster chpt. Jaycees, 1961, Alumnus of Yr., McDaniel Coll., 1986; recipient Outstanding Citizen award Westminster chpt. Rotary, 1985, Trustee of Yr. award Am. Assn. Homes and Svcs. for the Aging, 2002. Fellow Md. Bar Found. (pres. 1986-88, bd. dirs.); mem. ABA, Md. Bar Assn. (v.p. 1970-71), Carroll County Bar Assn. (pres. 1966-67), Am. Judicature Soc., Am. Bar Found., Bachelor's Cotillon Club (Balt.), Phi Alpha Delta. Avocations: travel, volunteer work in non-profit organizations. Home: 1167 Old Taneytown Rd Westminster MD 21158-3605 Office: Dulany Leahy Curtis & Williams LLP 127 E Main St Westminster MD 21157-5012 Office Phone: 410-876-2117. Business E-Mail: dulany@dulany.com.

DULBECCO, RENATO, biologist, educator; b. Catanzaro, Italy, Feb. 22, 1914; arrived in U.S., 1947, naturalized, 1953; s. Leonardo and Maria (Virdia) D.; m. Gulseppina Salvo, June 1, 1940 (div. 1963); children: Peter Leonard (dec.), Maria Vittoria; m. Maureen Rutherford Muir; 1 child, Fiona Linsey. MD, U. Torino, Italy, 1936; DSc (hon.), Yale U., 1968; LL.D., U. Glasgow, Scotland, 1970; DSc (hon.), Vrije Universiteit, Brussels, 1978, Ind. U., 1984, U. Bologna, 1988. Asst. U. Torino, 1940-47; research asso. Ind. U., 1947-49; sr. research fellow Calif. Inst. Tech., 1949-52, asso. prof., then prof. biology, 1952-63; sr. fellow Salk Inst. Biol. Studies, San Diego, 1963-71; asst. dir. research Imperial Cancer Research Fund, London, 1971-74, dep. dir. research, 1974-77; disting. research prof. Salk Inst., La Jolla, Calif., 1977—, pres., 1989-92, pres. emeritus, 1993—; prof. pathology and medicine U. Calif. at San Diego Med. Sch., La Jolla, 1977-81, mem. Cancer Ctr.; with Nat. Rsch. Coun. Milan. Vis. prof. Royal Soc. G.B., 1963—64; Leeuwenhoek lectr., 1974; Clowes Meml. lectr., Atlantic City, 61; Harvey lectr. Harvey Soc., 1967; Dunham lectr. Harvard U., 1972; 11th Marjory Stephenson Meml. lectr., London, 73; Harden lectr., Wye, England, 73; Am. Soc. for Microbiology lectr., L.A., 79; mem. Calif. Cancr Adv. Coun., 1963—67; mem. vis. com. Case Western Res. Sch. Medicine; adv. bd. Roche Inst., 1968—71, Inst. Immunology, Basel, Switzerland; esperto Italian Nat. Rsch. Coun.; trustee Am.-Italian Fedn. for Cancer Rsch.; bd. dirs. Scientific Counselors Dept. Etiology NCI; cons. Nat. Rsch. Coun. ESPERTO, 1994—. Trustee La Jolla Country Day Sch., Am.-Italian Fedn. for Cancer Rsch.; bd. mem. sci. counselors dept. etiology Nat. Cancer Inst. Decorated grand ufficiale Italian Republic; co-recipient (with David Baltimore and Howard Martin Temin) Nobel prize in medicine, 1975; named Man of Yr., London, 1975, Italian Am. of Yr., San Diego County, 1978, hon. citizen, City of Imperia (Italy), 1983, City of Arezzo, City of Sommariva Perno, City of Catanzaro, City of Torino, hon. founder, Hebrew U., 1981; recipient John Scott award City Phila., 1958, Kimball award Conf. Pub. Health Lab. Dirs., 1959, Albert and Mary Lasker Basic Med. Rsch. award, 1964, Howard Taylor Ricketts award, 1965, Paul Ehrlich-Ludwig Darmstaedter prize, 1967, Horwitz prize, Columbia U., 1973, Targa d'oro Villa San Giovanni, 1978, Mandel Gold medal, Czechoslovak Acad. Scis., 1982, Via de Condotti prize, 1990, Cavaliere di Gran Croce Italian Rep., 1991, Natale Di Roma prize, 1993, Columbus prize, 1993, Spl. Oscar of Italian TV, 1999; fellow Guggenheim and Fulbright fellow, 1957—58. Mem.: NAS, Am. Acad. Arts and Scis., Fedn. Am. Scientists, Royal Soc. (fgn.), Academia Nazionale del Lincel (fgn.), Am. Philos. Assn., Internat. Physicians for Prevention Nuclear War, Am. Assn. Cancer Rsch., Comitato di Collaborazione Culturale (hon.), Academia Ligure di Scienze e Lettre (hon.), Alpha Omega Alpha. Office: Salk Inst PO Box 85800 San Diego CA 92186-5800*

DULCHINOS, PETER, lawyer; b. Chicopee Falls, Mass., Feb. 2, 1935; s. George and Angeline D.; children: Matthew George, Paul Constantine, Gregory Peter. BSEE, MIT, 1956, MSEE, 1957; MS in Engring. Mgmt., Northeastern U., 1965; JD, Suffolk U., 1984. Bar: Mass. 1984, U.S. Dist. Ct. (Mass.) 1984, U.S. Ct. Appeals (1st cir.) 1985, U.S. Supreme Ct. 1988, U.S. Patent and Trademark Office 1989, U.S. Claims Ct. 1989. With Sylvania Co., Waltham, Mass., 1957-61, Needham, Mass., 1963-66, Tech Ops, Burlington, Mass., 1961, RCA, Burlington, 1962-63, Raytheon Co., Lexington, Mass., 1966—. Computer ops. mgr. tactical software devel. facility Patriot Ground Computer System, 1977-86, intellectual property mgr., 1986—; lectr. Fitchburg State Coll., 1985-90; corporator Ctrl. Savs. Bank, Lowell, Mass., 1980-92; sec.-treas. U. Lowell Bldg. Authority, 1974-85; mem. statewide adv. coun. Dept. Mental Health, 1996—. Mem. statewide adv. coun. Dept. Mental Retardation, 1993-96; mem. human studies subcom. Bedford VA Hosp., 1987-90; pres. Chelmsford Rep. Club, 1964-70; chmn. Chelmsford Rep. Town Com., 1972-76, 80—, chmn., 2000-04; Rep. state committeeman, 2004—; assoc. town counsel Tyngsborough, Mass., 1985-87; mem., chmn. Chelmsford Bd. Health, 1972-87, 93—; mem. Nashoba Tech. High Sch. Com., 1970-71; trustee, chmn. Medfield State Hosp., 1993-2003; trustee Westborough State Hosp., 2003—; v.p. Greater Lowell Comprehensive Cmty. Support Systems Bd. Dept. Mental Health, 1994-99; mem. State Mental Health Planning Coun., 1999—. 2d lt. U.S. Army, 1957-58; corporator Lowell Gen. Hosp., 2005— Mem. Mass. Bar Assn., Boston Patent Law Assn., Raytheon Employees Profl. Assn. (treas. 1998, pres. 1999). Republican. Greek Orthodox. Home: 17 Spaulding Rd Chelmsford MA 01824-1021 Office: Raytheon Co 870 Winter St Waltham MA 02451-1449 Office Phone: 781-522-3041. Business E-Mail: peter_dulchinos@raytheon.com.

DULIN, MAURINE STUART, volunteer; b. Lonerock, Iowa, Feb. 16, 1919; d. Frank Meagher and Fern Adrienne (Wetzel) Stuart; m. William Carter Dulin, Oct. 5, 1940; children: Jacquelyn Dulin Wilson, Patricia F., Stuart M. AB in Polit. Sci./Econs., Coll. of William and Mary, 1939. Coll. cons. Woodward and Lothrop, Washington, 1939-40; adminstv. asst. Sightler and Cox, Washington, 1942-43; acctg. dept. asst. Am. U., Washington, 1964-69; corp. sec. Bittinger and Dulin, Arlington, Va., 1949-73; ptnr. 41 Ltd. Partnership, Bethesda, Md., 1979—, Montrose-270 Ltd. Partnership, Bethesda, 1979—. Mem. Rock Creek Womens Rep. Club, Bethesda, 1951-57; sgt.-at-arms Montgomery County Fed. of Rep. Women, Bethesda, 1952-53, State Fedn. of Womens Rep. Club, 1953-54; charter mem., com. chmn. Nat. Mus. of Women in the Arts; women's bd. Cathedral Choral Soc. 1975—, com. chmn., 1988-90; women's bd. George Washington U. Hosp., 1970—, Save Our Seminary at Forest Glen, Md., 1989—. Mem. The Town Club (pres. 1958-59), Pi Beta Phi (nat. com. chmn. 1971-75, province officer 1967-71). Episcopalian. Home: 9707 Old Georgetown Rd Apt 1416 Bethesda MD 20814

DULIT, EVERETT PAUL, psychiatrist, educator; b. Bklyn., May 2, 1929; s. Benjamin and Florence Dulit; m. Elinor Greenspun, Sept. 12, 1954; children: Rebecca, Kathryn, Alan. BS, MIT, 1950, PhD in Physics, 1957; MD, U. Minn., 1958; grad., N.Y. Psychoanalytic Inst., 1968. Intern Kaiser Found. Hosp., San Francisco, 1958—59; resident in psychiatry Bronx Mcpl. Hosp. Ctr., 1959—61, chief resident dept. psychiatry, 1961—62; rsch. fellow Albert Einstein Coll. Medicine, 1962—65, instr. in psychiatry, 1965—68, asst. clin. prof. psychiatry, 1968—74, assoc. clin. prof. psychiatry, 1974—76, 1980—2000, dir. overall divsn. child and adolescent psychiatry, 1984—87, assoc. clin. profl. pediat., 1988—2000, assoc. clin. prof. emeritus, 2000—; assoc. clin. prof. psychiatry Cornell Med. Coll., 1976—80; psychiat. cons. divsn. adolescent medicine Montefiore Med. Ctr., 1980—2000, acting dir. child and adolescent psychiatry, 1983—84, dir., 1984—87, psychiat. cons. child protective svcs., 1991—95, psychiat. cons. dept. pediat., 1994—2000; psychiat. cons. Westchester Family Svc., White Plains, NY, 1997—. Dir. sch. consultation svc. Bronx H.S. Sci., 1963—76; overall dir. h.s. consultation project Albert Einstein Coll. Medicine and N.Y.C. Bd. Edn., 1965—76; fellow in child psychiatry Albert Einstein Coll. Medicine, 1966—70, dir. ann. Ed Hornick Meml. lecture, 1985—, dir. child psychiatry Ground Rounds series, 1987—2000; dir. divsn. adolescent psychiatry Albert Einstein Coll. Medicine-Bronx. Mcpl. Hosp. Ctr., 1969—76, acting dir., 1971—72, 1974—75, assoc. dir., 1971—75; dir. adolescent psychiatry Westchester divsn. N.Y. Hosp. Cornell Med. Sch., 1976—80, coord., moderator Grand Rounds vis. lecture series, 1977—80; vis. prof. numerous hosps. and univs.; spkr. numerous confs.; lectr. in field, 1967—89. Author: (chpt.) Personality Development and Deviation, 1975, Clinical Update in Adolescent Psychiatry, 1983; contbr.

articles and book revs. to profl. jours. Named Shell fellow in Physics, MIT Grad. Sch., 1951—52, Sol Ginsberg fellow, Group for Advancement Psychiatry, 1961—62; recipient Rsch. Career Devel. award, NIMH, 1962—67. Fellow: APA (task force preparing DSM3 1976—80, com. on childhood and adolescence 1976—80, com. on DSM3 ASAP 1976—80); mem.: Am. Bd. Adolescent Psychiatry (founding mem.), Am. Soc. Adolescent Psychiatry, Sigma Xi. Avocations: jazz, clarinet, saxophone, skiing. Home and Office: 16 Sage Terr Scarsdale NY 10583

DULL, CLIFFORD JOHN, religious organization administrator; b. Richland Ctr., Wis., Jan. 11, 1946; s. Clifford LaVerne and Olive Clare (McKittrick) D.; m Helen Marie Kirkpatrick, June 12, 1970. BA in History, Milligan Coll., 1968; MA in Classics, U. Wis., 1970, PhD in History, 1975; Cert. in Book Pub., NYU, 1980. Vis. asst. prof. U. Colo., Boulder, 1975-76; faculty mem. Roanoke Bible Coll., Elizabeth City, N.C., 1976-77; lectr. Carthage Coll., Kenosha, Wis., 1977-78; editorial cons. Standard Pub., Cin., 1978-79; lectr. U. Wis.-Washington County, West Bend, 1980; computer specialist Def. Logistics Agy., Columbus, Ohio, 1980—. Contbr. articles and book revs. to profl. jours. and articles to books. Elder Upper Arlington Christian Ch., Columbus, 1983—. Mem. Assn. Ancient Historians, Am. Inst. Archaeology, Disciples of Christ Hist. Soc., Am. Soc. Ch. History, State Hist. Soc. Wis. Avocations: playing organ and piano, wallyball, collecting videos of b-movies, attending operas, visiting turreted victorian homes. Home: 225 Tibet Rd Columbus OH 43202-1439 E-mail: cjdullrm@cs.com.

DULL, DAVID A., lawyer; b. 1949; BA with honors in Am. Studies, Yale U., 1971, JD, 1982. Staff mem. UN Assn. U.S.A.; ptnr. Irell & Manella LLP, Century City, Silcon Valley, Calif., 1985—98; v.p. bus. affairs, gen. counsel Broadcom, Irvine, Calif., 1998—. Bd. dirs. Magfusion. Office: Broadcom Corp 16215 Alton Pkwy Irvine CA 92618 Office Phone: 949-450-8700. Office Fax: 949-450-8710.

DULL, WILLIAM MARTIN, retired engineering executive; b. Buchanan, Mich., June 24, 1924; s. Curtis Frank and Daisy Julia (Sharp) D.; m. Margaret Ann McMillan, Apr. 10, 1976; children: Richard William, Beverly Ann, William McMillan. BSME, U. Mich., 1945. Registered profl. engr., Mich. Dir. tech. staff Detroit Edison, 1951-66, asst. gen. supt. cen. plants, 1966-70, gen. supt. underground lines, 1970-71, mgr. employee relations, 1971-74, mgr. orgn. planning and devel., 1974-89; pres. Charleston Engring. Cons., 1990-92; ret., 1992. Chmn. Charleston Engrs. Joint Coun., 1991—, chmn. 1993-94. Bd. dirs. World Med. Relief, Detroit, 1971-90, chmn., 1988-90; bd. dirs. Jr. Achivement, Southeastern Mich., 1971-90; trustee Detroit Sci. Ctr., Inc., 1979-85. Served to lt. (s.g.) USN, 1942-51, PTO. Recipient Gold Leadership award Jr. Achievement, 1985. Fellow Engrng. Soc. Detroit (pres. 1970-71, Disting. Svc. 1980, life); mem. ASHRAE (pres. 1964-65, Outstanding Engr. award 1965, life), ASME (life), IEEE (chmn. nat. conf. 1971), NSPE (life), Architects, Engrs., Surveyors Registration Coun. (chmn. 1968-69), Mich. Soc. Profl. Engrs. (bd. dirs. 1973-75, Disting. Engr. 1980), S.C. Soc. Profl. Engrs. (bd. dirs. 1994-95), Charleston Engrs. Joint Coun. (chmn. 1993-94), U. Mich. Alumni Assn. (v.p., bd. dirs. 1964-71, Disting. Svc. award 1970), Charleston Navy League (v.p., bd. dirs. 1993—), Detroit Yacht Club. Republican. Methodist. Office Phone: 843-849-8213. Personal E-mail: mwmdull@aol.com.

DULLES, AVERY, cardinal, theologian; b. Auburn, NY, Aug. 24, 1918; s. John Foster and Janet Pomeroy (Avery) D. AB, Harvard U., 1940, postgrad. in law, 1940—41; PhL, Woodstock Coll., 1951, STL, 1957; STD, Pontifical Gregorian U., Rome, 1960; LLD (hon.), St. Joseph's Coll., Phila., 1969; LHD (hon.), Georgetown U., 1977; ThD (hon.), U. Detroit, 1978; LLD (hon.), Iona Coll., New Rochelle, N.Y., 1980; DD (hon.), St. Anselm Coll., Manchester, N.H., 1981; LHD (hon.), Creighton U., 1983; DD (hon.), Jesuit Sch. Theology, Berkeley, Calif., 1984, Protestant Episcopal Theol. Sem., Alexandria, Va., 1986; LHD (hon.), Seton Hall U., 1989, Stonehill Coll., 1990, Loyola U., Chgo., 1990; STD (hon.), Providence Coll., 1991; DD (hon.), Carthage Coll., Kenosha, Wis., 1991; ThD (hon.), U. Dayton, 1992; LHD (hon.), Christ the King Seminary, East Aurora, N.Y., 1994; DD (hon.), Nashotah (Wis.) House, 1996; LittD (hon.), Fordham U., 1996; DD (hon.), John Carroll U., Cleveland, Ohio, 1997; LLD (hon.), U. Mass., Boston, 1998; LHD (hon.), St. Francis Coll., Bklyn., 1999; ThD (hon.), Theol. Faculty Paderborn, Germany, 2000; LLD (hon.), U. Notre Dame, 2001; LHD (hon.), LeMoyne Coll., Syracuse, NY, 2001, Univ. St Thomas, Miami, 2001, Seminary St. Charles Borromeo, Overbrook, Pa., 2002, Univ. St. Thomas, St. Paul, Minn., 2002; DD (hon.), Univ. Scranton, Pa., 2002; STD (hon.), Franciscan Univ., Steubenville, Ohio, 2002; LHD (hon.), St. Joseph's Coll., Rensselaer, Ind., 2003, Christendom Coll. Front Royal, Va., 2003, Coll. of the Holy Cross, Worcester, Mass., 2003; STD (hon.), Siena Coll., Londonville, NY, 2003, Coll. New Rochelle, 2003, Bobolanum, Warsaw, Poland, 2003; DD (hon.), Heythrop Coll., London, 2003; LHD (hon.), Ohio State U., 2004. Joined S.J., Roman Cath. Ch., 1946, ordained priest, Soc. of Jesus, 1956, created cardinal, 2001. Instr. philosophy Fordham U., 1951-53, vis. lectr., 1970, Laurence J. McGinley prof. religion and society, 1988—; mem. faculty Woodstock Coll., NYC, 1960-74, prof. theology, 1969-74, Cath. U. Am., Washington, 1974-88; Gasson prof. theology Boston Coll., Boston, 1981-82; prof. emeritus Cath. U. Am., Washington, 1988—. Vis. lectr. Weston Coll., 1971, Union Theol. Sem., 1971-74, Princeton Theol. Sem., 1972, Pontifical Gregorian U., 1973, 90, 93, Episcopal Theol. Sem., 1975, Luth. Sem. Pa., 1978; Martin C. D'Arcy lectr. Campion Hall, Oxford (Eng.) U., 1983; vis. John A. O'Brien prof. theology Notre Dame U., 1985; vis. prof. theology Cath. U. of Leuven, 1992; vis. prof. religious studies Yale U., New Haven, 1996; fellow Woodrow Wilson Internat. Ctr. for Scholars, 1977; mem. Commn. on Christian Unity, Archdiocese of Balt., 1962-70, Cath. Bishops' Adv. Coun., 1969-75; consultor to Papal Secretariat for Dialogue with Non-Believers, 1966-73, mem. USA Luth.-Cath. Dialogue, 1972-92; cons. to Com. on Doctrine, Nat. Conf. Cath. Bishops, 1991—; mem. Internat. Theol. Com., 1992-97; mem. Luth.-Roman Cath. Coord. Com., 1994-96. Author: Princeps Concordiae, 1941, A Testimonial to Grace, 1946, (with others) Introductory Metaphysics, 1955, Apologetics and the Biblical Christ, 1963, The Dimensions of the Church, 1967, Revelation and the Quest for Unity, 1968, Revelation Theology: A History, 1969, (with others) Spirit, Faith and Church, 1970, The Survival of Dogma, 1971 (Christopher award 1972), A History of Apologetics, 1971, 2d edit., 2005, Models of the Church, 1974, 3d rev. edit., 2002, Church Membership as a Catholic and Ecumenical Problem, 1974, The Resilient Church, 1977, A Church to Believe In, 1982, Models of Revelation, 1983, 2d rev. edit., 1992, (with Patrick Granfield) The Church: A Bibliography, 1985, The Reshaping of Catholicism, 1988, The Craft of Theology, 1992, expanded edit., 1995 (Best Book in Theology Cath. Press Assn. 1993), The Assurance of Things Hoped For, 1994, A Testimonial to Grace and Reflections on a Theological Journey, 1996, The Priestly Office, 1997, (with Patrick Granfield) The Theology of the Church: A Bibliography, 1999, The Splendor of Faith: The Theological Vision of Pope John Paul II, 1999, rev. edit., 2003, The New World of Faith, 2000, Newman, 2002; assoc. editor for ecumenism Concilium, 1963-70, adv. editl. bd., 1970-92; adv. editl. bd. Midstream: An Ecumenical Jour., 1974—; mem. editl. bd. Logos: A Jour. of Cath. Thought and Culture, 1997—; contbr. column to Theology for Today, America, 1967-68; contbg. editor New Oxford Rev., 1990-2001; cons. Theology Digest, 1985—; mem. adv. coun. Pro Ecclesia, 1991—; contbr. articles to theol. publ. Bd. dirs. Georgetown U., 1966-68, Woodstock Theol. Ctr., 1974-79; trustee Fordham U., 1969-72, St. Mary's Sem. and Univ., Balt., 1992-98; acad. coun. Irish Sch. Ecumenics, 1971-78. Served to lt. USNR, 1942-46. Decorated Croix de Guerre with silver star (France), 1945; scholar-in-residence St. Joseph's Sem., Dunwoodie, NY, 1996; recipient Cardinal Spellman award for disting. achievement in theology, 1970, Religious Edn. Forum award Nat. Cath. Edn. Assn., 1988, Campion award Cath. Book Club, NY, 1989, F. Sadlier Dinger award, 1994, Choate Alumni Seal prize Choate Rosemary Hall, 1995, Christus Magister medal U. Portland, 2001, James Cardinal Gibbons medal Cath. U. Am., Washington, 2001, Gold Medal award Nat. Inst. Social Sci., N.Y.C., 2001, John Henry Newman award Cardinal Newman Soc., 2001, John Carroll Soc. Medal, Washington, 2002, John Paul II award Inst. for Social Sci., Arlington, Va., 2002, Jerome award Cath. Libr. Assoc., 2002, Hall of Fame, NY Mil. ROTC, 2004, Newman medal Loyola Coll., Md., 2004, Saint Thomas Aquinas medallion Saint Thomas Aquinas Coll., Santa Paula, Calif., 2005. Mem. Cath. Theol. Soc. Am. (bd. dir. 1970-72, 74-77, v.p. 1974-75, pres. 1975-76), Am. Theol. Soc. (v.p. 1977-78, pres. 1978-79), Cath. Commn. on Intellectual and Cultural Affairs (exec. com. 1991-94), Phi Beta Kappa. Roman Catholic. Office: Fordham U Faber 255 Bronx NY 10458 Office Phone: 718-817-4747. Business E-Mail: mcgchair@fordham.edu.

DULLES, FREDERICK HENDRIK, lawyer; b. N.Y.C., Mar. 12, 1942; s. William Winslow and Joanna (deLeu) D.; m. Martine Pred'homme, Aug. 26, 1977; 1 child, Emilie Pred'homme. AB cum laude, Harvard U., 1964; JD, MBA, Columbia U., 1968. Bar: D.C. 1971, N.Y. 1972. Assoc. Shearman & Sterling, N.Y.C. and Paris, 1971-80; counsel Philip Morris Inc., N.Y.C., 1980, asst. gen. counsel, 1981-83; dir. regional counsel EFTA-Eastern Europe-Middle East-Africa region, Lausanne, Switzerland, 1983-92; counsel Pirenne Python Schifferli Peter & Ptnrs., Geneva, 1993-94; ptnr. McDermott, Will & Emery, Chgo., 1994-96; of counsel Jackson & Nash, LLP, N.Y.C., 2000; ptnr. McFadden, Pilkington & Ward, LLP, London, N.Y.C., 1997—2003, Ten State St. LLP, Charleston, SC, 2003—05. Adj. prof., The Citadel Sch. of Bus. Admnstrn., 2003-; trustee Mass. Fin. Svcs.-Sun Life Compass mut. funds, 2001-; internat. exec. Assn. Internat. des Etudiants en Sciences Economiques et Commerciales, 1961-66, U.S. gen. counsel, 1977-80. Trustee Am. U. of Paris, 2001-2004. Lt. Security Group Command, USNR, 1968-71. Decorated Navy Achievement medal. Mem. ABA, Assn. Bar City N.Y., Swiss Arbitration Assn., Am. Mgmt. Assn., Internat. Bar Assn., Nat. Assn. Corp. Dirs., Harvard Club (N.Y.C., Boston), Rotary Club of Charleston. Republican. Office: 180 E Bay St Charleston SC 29401-2123 Business E-Mail: fhd@fhdulles.com.

DULLES, JOHN WATSON FOSTER, history professor; b. Auburn, N.Y., May 20, 1913; s. John Foster and Janet Pomeroy (Avery) D.; m. Eleanor Foster Ritter, June 15, 1940; children: Edith, John, Ellen, Avery. AB, Princeton U., 1935; MBA, Harvard U., 1937; BS in Metall. Engring., U. Ariz., 1943, Metall. Engr., 1951. Clk. The Bank of N.Y., N.Y.C., 1937-38; miner Callahan Zinc-Lead Co., Patagonia, Ariz., 1938-41; head ore dept., smelter operator Cia Minera de Peñoles, S.A., Monterrey, Mex., 1943-49, head comml. divsn., 1949-51, asst. gen. mgr., 1951-59, exec. v.p., 1959; v.p. Cia Mineração Novalimense, Belo Horizonte, Brazil, 1959-62; prof. history U. Ariz., Tucson, 1966-91; univ. prof. L.Am. studies U. Tex., Austin, 1962—. Advisor to U.S. delegation to OAS Conf., Vina Del Mar, Chile, 1967; cons. U.S. Dept. State, Bur. Intelligence and Rsch., 1968-72. Author: Yesterday in Mexico, 1961, Vargas of Brazil, 1967, Unrest in Brazil, 1970, Anarchists and Communists in Brazil, 1973, Castello Branco: The Making of a Brazilian President, 1978, President Castello Branco, 1980, Brazilian Communism, 1935-1945, 1983, The São Paulo Law School, 1986, Carlos Lacerda: Brazilian crusader, Vol. 1, 1991, Vol. 2, 1996 (Brazilian Union Writers and Carioca Acad. Leters prize 2000), Sobral Pinto: The Conscience of Brazil, 2002. Pres. exec. bd. Union Ch. Monterrey, Mexico, 1948—49, elder, 1957—59. Recipient Achievement medal, U. Ariz., 1960, Ptnrs. of the Alliance Medal, Brazilian Govt., 1966. Fellow Calif. Inst. Internat. Studies; mem. The Am. Soc. of the Most Venerable Order of the Hosp. of St. John of Jerusalem (knight), Am. Hist. Assn., Tex. Inst. of Letters, Theta Tau (Alumni Hall of Fame), Inst. History and Geography Brasil. Avocation: tennis. Office: U Texas PO Box 7934 Austin TX 78713-7934 Office Phone: 512-505-2705. E-mail: dulles@mail.utexas.edu.

DUMA, RICHARD JOSEPH, epidemiologist, microbiologist, educator, pathologist, researcher, physician; b. Bethlehem, Pa., Apr. 2, 1933; s. Joseph Anthony and Helen Veronica (Bartek) D.; m. Mary Alyce Fridley, Apr. 18, 1957; 1 child, Scott. BA, Va. Poly. Inst., 1955; MD, U. Va., 1959; PhD, Va. Commonwealth U.-Med. Coll. Va., 1978. Diplomate Am. Bd. Internal Medicine; lic. physician, Fla., Va.; lic. pvt. pilot. Intern, then resident in medicine U. Ala. Med. Center, Birmingham, 1959-60, 62-65; research fellow Harvard U. Med. Sch.-Mass. Gen. Hosp., 1965-67; mem. faculty Med. Coll. Va., Richmond, 1967-91, chmn. div. infectious diseases, 1974-92, prof. medicine and pathology, 1975-92, prof. microbiology, 1977-92. Mem. U. S. Pharmacopeia Adv. Panel on Hosp. Practices, 1971-82, chmn. subcom. rsch., 1976-82, clin. prof. medicine and infectious diseases Med. Coll. Richmond, 1992—; exec. dir. Nat. Found. for Infectious Diseases, 1991-94, v.p. bd. dirs., 1973-75, pres., 1975-91, trustee, 1994-2003, bd. dirs., 2004—; chmn. Nat. Coalition for Adult Immunization, 1988-94; didr. infectious diseases Halifax Med. Ctr., Daytona Beach, Fla., 1995—. Mem. bd. visitors Embry-Riddle Aero. U., 1999—. Served with M.C., USNR, 1960-62. Fellow ACP, Infectious Disease Soc. Am., Royal Soc. Tropical Medicine and Hygiene, Am. Soc. Tropical Medicine and Hygiene, Am. Soc. Rickettsiology, Fla. Infectious Disease Soc. (pres. 1997-99, bd. dirs. 1997-); mem. AAAS, Am. Fedn. Clin. Rsch., Am. Soc. Microbiology, Va. Soc. Microbiology, Am. Soc. Internal Medicine, Va. Soc. Internal Medicine, Richmond Soc. Internal Medicine, So. Soc. Clin. Investigation, Am. Thoracic Soc., Royal Soc. Medicine, Med. Soc. Va., Richmond Acad. Medicine, Acad. of Medicine, Washington, Med. Assn. Fla., Volusia Med. Soc., Sigma Xi, Tau Beta Pi. Home: 1 Capri Ct Palm Coast FL 32137- Office: Halifax Medical Ctr 303 N Clyde Morris Blvd Daytona Beach FL 32114-2700 Office Phone: 386-258-4871.

DUMANOSKI, DIANNE, journalist, writer; b. 1998; BA, Vassar Coll.; MA, Yale U. Prodr. WGBH-TV, Boston; staff writer The Boston Phoenix; with Boston Globe, 1979—, environ. journalist, 1983—93. Lectr. in field; bd. dirs. Environ. Media Svcs.; mem. Ted Scripps Fellowships adv. bd. Author (with Theo Colborn and Pete Myers): (book) Our Stolen Future: How Man-Made Chemicals are Threatening Our Fertility, Intelligence and Survival, 1996. Fellow Ctr. Environ. Journalism, U. Colo., Knight Fellow in Sci. Journalism, 1983—84. E-mail: ddumanoski@earthlink.net.

DUMARS, JOE, III, retired professional basketball player; b. Shreveport, La., May 24, 1963; m. Debbie Nelson, 1989; 1 child, Jordan. Grad. in bus. mgmt., McNeese State U., 1985. With Detroit Pistons, 1985—99. Mem. NBA Championship team, 1989, 90, Dream Team II, 1994. Named Most Valuable Player, NBA Finals, 1989; named to NCAA All-Am. 2d team, Sporting News, 1985, NBA All-Rookie team, 1986, NBA All-Defensive 1st team, 1989—90, All-NBA 3d team, 1990, NBA All-Star team, 1990—93, All-NBA 3d team, 1991, NBA All-Defensive 2d team, 1991, NBA All-Defensive 1st team, 1992, 1993, NBA All-Defensive 2d team, 1993; recipient Citizenship award, 1994. Office: Detroit Pistons 2 Championship Dr Auburn Hills MI 48326-1753

DUMAS, LAWRENCE B., academic administrator; BA in Biochemistry with high honors, Mich. State U., 1963; MA in Biochemistry, U. Wis., 1965, PhD in Biochemistry, 1968. Faculty mem. Northwestern U., Evanston, Ill., 1970—, assoc. prof., 1975—80, prof. biochemistry, molecular biology and cell biology, 1980—95, provost, 1995—. Recipient Career Devel. award, USPHS, 1974—79, John Boezi award for outstanding molecular biology rsch., Mich. State U., 1987. Mem.: AAAS, Am. Soc. for Microbiology, Am. Soc. Biol. Chemists. Office: Office of the Provost Northwestern Univ Rebecca Crown Ctr 633 Clark St Evanston IL 60208-1101

DUMAS, MICHAEL GODFREY JOSEPH, artist; b. Whitney, Ont., Can., Sept. 20, 1950; s. Alphyr Adrian and Caroline Anna (Cenzura) D.; m. Ellen Kocsis, July 19, 1975; 1 child, Shae Shannon-Mae. Student, Art Instrn. Sch., Mpls., 1968, Humber Coll., 1970, postgrad., 1971, Cornell U., 1984. Apprentice to his. painter Lewis Parker Lazare & Parker Studios, 1971-72. Mem. adv. bd. Art Impressions mag., 1993—97. Major exhibits include Nat. Mus. Nat. Sci., Ottawa, Ont., 1977, Theodore Roosevelt Inaugural Nat. Hist. Site, Buffalo, 1977, McMichael Can. Coll., Kleinburg, Ont., 1981, Royal Bot. Gardens, Hamilton, 1985, R.O.M., 1987-88, Yamanaakako-Takamura Mus. Art, 1991-2001, Mitsukoshi Galleries, Tokyo, 1994-2003, Algonquin Gallery, Algonquin Park, Ont., 1995-2002, 05, Suntory Mus. Art, Osaka, 1995, Suntory Mus. Art, Tokyo, 1996, Matsuya Gallery, Tokyo, 1997, Sogo Gallery, Osaka, 1997, Yumehodaka Mus., Nagano, 1997, Spanierman Gallery, NY, 1998, Mitsukoshi Gallery, Sendai, 1999-2004, Arai Gallery, Tokyo, 2002-04, Cedar Ridge Creative Ctr., Scarborough, 1999, Fukuyu Gallery, Hiroshima, Japan, Buckingham Gallery, Uxbridge, Ont., Can., 2003; represented in permanent collections including Internat. Mus. Art Inspired By Nature, Gloucester, Eng., Yamanakako-Takamura Mus. Art, Japan, Imaoka Collection, Japan, Ont. Provincial Collection, Queen's Park, Ont. Binghamton U. Art Mus.; major conservation events include The Spirit of the Wild fundraiser and exhibit, 1982, Kenya Wild Elephant fundraiser, Toronto, 1987, 91, Bird Preservation fundraiser, Osaka, Japan, 1990, Save the Rhino Trust, Namibia, 1998; commd. to design four coins for Royal Can. Mint, 1994, commd. to design Can. commemorative postage stamps; author: Nature in Art, 1991; columnist Angler & Hunter, 1976-83; contbr. articles to mag Recipient Waterfowl Art award Ducks Unltd., 1983-84, Carling-O'Keefe Profl. Conservation award, 1986, Wildlife Conservation award Ont. Min. Natural Resources, 1987, Bronze Teal Conservation award Ducks Unltd., 1989; named Artist of the Yr., Can. Collector's Clubs, 1987, first winner by competion Wildlife Habitat Can., 1990, Internat. Flyway Artist, Ducks Unltd., Inc., 1992, Artist of the Yr., Ont. Fedn. Anglers and Hunters, 1993-2004, Outdoor Card Program award Ont. Ministry of Natural Resources, 1998, Peterborough Pathway to Fame award, 2004, Master Palette award Masterworks in Miniature, Gallery One, 2005. Fellow Internat. Biog. Assn. (Eng., life); mem. Soc. Animal Artists, Soc. Wildlife Art of the Nations (charter). Avocations: travel, photography, camping. Address: PO Box 8314 RR 1 Peterborough ON Canada K9J 6X2 E-mail: natures.studio.inc@sympatico.ca.

DUMAS, RHETAUGH ETHELDRA GRAVES, university official; b. Natchez, Miss., Nov. 26, 1928; d. Rhetaugh Graves and Josephine (Clemmons) Graves Bell; m. A.W. Dumas, Jr., Dec. 25, 1950; 1 child, Adrienne. BS in Nursing, Dillard U., 1951; MS in Psychiat. Nursing, Yale U., 1961; PhD in Social Psychology, Union Grad. Sch., Union for Experimenting Colls. and Univs., Cinn., 1975; also various other courses; D Pub. Svc. (hon.), Simmons Coll., 1976, U. Cin., 1981; LHD (hon.), Yale U., 1989; LLD (hon.), Dillard U., 1990; LHD (hon.), U. San Diego, 1993, Georgetown U., 1996, U. Mass, 1997, Regis Coll., 2002; DPub. Svc., Fla. Internat. U., Miami, 1996; DSc (hon.), Ind. U., Gary, 1996; JD (hon.), Bethune-Cookman Coll., 1997. Instr. Dillard U., 1957-59, 61; research asst., instr. Sch. Nursing Yale U., 1962-65, from asst. prof. nursing to assoc. prof., 1965-72, chmn. dept. psychiat. nursing, 1972; dir. nursing Conn. Mental Health Ctr., Yale-New Haven Med. Ctr., 1966-72; chief psychiat. nursing edn. br. Div. Manpower and Tng. Programs, NIMH, Rockville, Md., 1972-76; dep. dir. Div. Manpower and Tng. Programs NIMH, 1976-79, dep. dir. alcohol, drug abuse and mental health adminstrn., 1979-81; dean, prof. U. Mich. Sch. Nursing, 1981-94; vice provost health affairs U. Mich., 1994-97, Lucille Cole prof. sch. nursing, 1994—, vice provost emerita, 1997—, dean emerita, 1997—. Dir. Group Rels. Confs. in Tavistock Model; cons., speaker, panelist in field; fellow Helen Hadley Hall, Yale U., 1972, Branford Coll., 1972; dir. Community Health Care Ctr. Plan, New Haven, 1969-72; mem. U.S. Assessment Team, cons. to Fed. Ministry Health, Nigeria, 1982; mem. adv. com. Health Policy Agenda for the Am. People, AMA, 1983-86; cons. NIH Task Force on Nursing Rsch., 1984; mem. Nat. Commn. on Unemployment and Mental Health, Nat. Mental Health Assn., 1984-85; mem. com. to plan maj. study of nat. long-term care policy Inst. Medicine, 1985; mem. adv. com. to dir. NIH, 1986-87; mem. Sec.'s Nat. Commn. on Future Structure of VA Health Care System, 1990-91; mem. coun. on grad. med. edn. Nat. Adv. Coun. on Nurse Edn. and Practice Workgroup on Primary Care Workforce Projection, Divsn. Nursing, 1994; mem. com. to rev. breast cancer rsch. program U.S. Army Med. Rsch. and Material Command, Inst. of Medicine, 1996-97; mem. Pres.'s Nat. Bioethics Adv. Commn., 1996—. Author profl. monographs; contbr. over 40 articles to profl. publs.; mem. editorial bd. Community Mental Health Rev., 1977-79, Jour. Personality and Social Systems, 1978-81, Advances in Psychiat. Mental Health Nursing, 1981. Bd. dirs. Afro Am. Ctr., Yale U., 1968-72; mem. New Haven Bd. Edn., 1968-71, New Haven City Demonstrations Agy., 1968-70, Human Rels. Coun. New Haven, 1961-63, Nat. Neural Circuitry Database Com., Inst. Medicine, Nat. Acad. Scis., mem. bd. scientific advisors, 1985—; mem. commn. on future structure of vets. health care U.S. Dept. Vets. Affairs, 1990; mem. Pres. Clinton's Nat. Bioethics Adv. Commn., 1996-01. Named Disting. Alumna, Dillard U., 1966; recipient various awards, including cert. Honor NAACP, 1970, Disting. Alumnae award Yale U. Sch. Nursing, 1976, award for outstanding achievement and service in field mental health D.C. chpt. Assn. Black Psychologists, 1980, Pres. 21st Century award The Nat. Women's Hall of Fame, 1994, Lifetime Achievement award, nat. Black Nurses Assn., 2000—. Fellow A.K. Rice Inst., Am. Coll. Mental Health Adminstrs. (founding), Am. Acad. Nursing (charter, pres. 1987-89); mem. Inst. Medicine NAS, Am. Nurses Assn., Nat. Black Nurses Assn., Am. Assn. Colls. Nursing (govtl. affairs com. 1990-93), Am. Pub. Health Assn., Nat. League Nursing (pres. 1997-99), Nat. Bioethics Adv. Commn., Sigma Theta Tau Internat. (mentor award 1989), Delta Sigma Theta. Business E-Mail: rhetaugh@umich.edu.

DUMBLETON, DUANE DEAN, college president, educator; b. Shiocton, Wis., May 30, 1939; s. Reginald William and Marguerite Eva (Testin) D.; m. Nancy M. Cavins; children: Laura Layli, Mary Bahiyyih, Rama Ali Sequoyah, Nuriyyih Alexandra, Benjamin Idal. BS, U. Wis., 1962; MA, Syracuse (N.Y.) U., 1969; EdD, U. Ga., 1973. Tchr. geography Hillsborough County Pub. Schs., Tampa, Fla., 1962-63; tchr. English, Geneva (N.Y.) Pub. Schs., 1964-65; tchr. world culture Onondoga County Pub. Schs., Syracuse, 1965-70; tchr. English, Clarke County Pub. Schs., Athens, Ga., 1970-71; mem. faculty Fla. C.C., Jacksonville, 1973—, div. chmn. humanities dept., prof. Asian humanities, edn., 1978-83; campus pres. Fla. Community Coll., Jacksonville, 1988—, dir. staff develop., 1984—87, asst. to pres., 1987—88. Author: Education for American Indians, 1973; contbr. articles to profl. jours. Mem. Jacksonville Cmty. Coun., Inc., 1986—; mem. com. Pine Castle, Inc., 1994—99, Sister Cities Assn., Jacksonville, 1989—92, Urban Core Citizens Planning Adv. Com.; mem. com., bd. pres. Interfaith Coun., Jacksonville, 1989—; mem. com. Spiritual Assembly of Bahais of Jacksonville, 1974—2000; mem., chair Spiritual Assembly of the Bahais of Clay County, 2001—. Recipient Svc. award Jacksonville Jaycees, 1978, Clay County Bahai Community, 2000—. Mem. Cmty. Colls. for Internat. Devel. (bd. dirs., sec. 1988-92), Assn. Bahai's Studies, Fla. Assn. Community Colls., Leadership Jacksonville Alumni Assn., Urban League (bd. dirs.), Learn to Read (bd. dirs. 2000-04), Nat. Conf. of Cmty. and Justice (bd. dirs. 1998-, chmn. 2004-05). Avocations: writing poetry and essays, public speaking. Home: 526 Los Palmas Dr Orange Park FL 32003-8207 Office: Fla CC 3939 Roosevelt Blvd Jacksonville FL 32205-8945 Office Phone: 904-381-3534. E-mail: ddumbltn@fccj.edu.

DUMENCI, LEVENT, psychologist, educator; arrived in U.S., 1987; s. Adem and Muserref Dumenci; m. Frances Hagen, June 16, 1996. BS in Psychology, Hacettepe U., Ankara, 1986; MS in Psychology, Iowa State U., 1989, PhD in Psychology, 1993. Rsch. assoc. Rsch. Inst. Addictions, Buffalo, 1994—97; asst. prof. U. Ark. Med. Scis., Little Rock, 1997—98, rsch. asst. prof., 1998—99, U. Vt., Burlington, Vt., 1999—. Contbr. chpt. to book, article to profl. publs.; mem. editl. bd.: Turkish Jour. Psychology. Recipient award, NIMH, 2003. Mem.: APA, Am. Statis. Assn. Avocation: bridge. Office: U VCt UHC Arnold 6 Burlington VT 05401 Business E-Mail: Levent-Dumenci@uvm.edu.

DUMERER, LORRAINE JOANNE LORI, secondary school educator, consultant; b. Providence, July 10, 1946; d. John and Edith (Flippin) Florio; m. James Edward Dumerer, Nov. 23, 1966; children: James, Marc, Jennifer, Matthew, Paul. Student, Seton Hill Coll., 1964-66, St. Louis U., 1966; AB, U. Ill., 1969, MAT, 1972; postgrad., Tex. Women's U., 1987-88, U. Tex., Dallas, 1993, So. Meth. U., 1999-2001. Cert. social studies tchr. talented and gifted Tex., coll. bd. endorsed Advanced Placement cons. Tchr. Dayton (Ohio) Pub. Schs., 1970—71, St. Benedicts Sch., San Antonio, 1979—80, Incarnate World H.S., San Antonio, 1980—81, Diocese of Dallas, 1981—88, Dallas Ind. Sch. Dist., 1988—97; tchr., chmn. social studies dept., dean of faculty Long Trail Sch., Dorset, Vt., 1997—98; tchr. AP govt. and politics, AP macro and microecons., law studies Carrollton-Farmer's Branch Ind. Sch. Dist., 1998—; owner LJD Edn. Connection. Coach Fed Challenge econs. competition, 1998-2001, North Dallas H.S. CIS-site based team, 1996-97; mem. R.L. Turner H.S. CIC-site based team, 1999-2004; coach model UN teams, 2000-; clinician Acad. Clin. Svc., Dallas, 1985-; coord. nat. history day

Diocese of Dallas, 1985-87; coord. Jane Goodall CHIMP project, 1991; chmn. dept. social studies, student coun. advisor North Dallas H.S., 1993-97; ednl. cons., presenter Specialty Limited English Proficient Integration, 1990-96, Tex. Coun. Social Studies, Advanced Placement Reading Strategies, Cross-grade Level Curriculum Integration; Creating an Inclusive AP and Pre-AP Program, Integrating State Mandates in Pre-AP and AP Programs, Nat. Coun. for the Social Studies, AP Econ. Strategies, AP Govt., presenter AP Nat. Conf., 2003—, others; participant NEH Inst., 1995, Woodrow Wilson Inst., U. Tex., Dallas, 1993-1995, Nat. Coun. for Econ. Edn. ann. conf. presenter, 2005, Congress in the Classroom Dirkson Ctr., Ill., 2003, 05, Econs. for Leaders Found. for Tchg. Econs., So. Meth. U., 2000, Economic Forces in American History, Found. for Tchg. Econs.; reader Coll. Bd. Am. Govt., 2001-05, instr.; nat. endorsed Coll. Bd. cons.; selected for Tng. of Writers Project, Nat. Coun. Econ. Edn., U.S. Depts. of State and Edn., Bucharest, Romania, 2003; curriculum writer Dallas Pub. Schs., 1995-1997, Carrollton Farmers Br. Ind. Sch. Dist., 2002-2005, econs., 2004-05; advanced placement instr. Summer Inst. U.S. Govt., U. Ark., Fayetteville, Ark., 2005; presenter in field Author: (essays) The Dilemma of Ethical Citizenship and the Political Outsider, 1995, numerous poems; contbr. chapters to books. Referee coord. N.E. Youth Soccer Assn., 1979-80, coach, 1979-80; coach, referee Mesquite Soccer Assn., 1981-86, referee liaison, 1981-82, sec., 1982-83, commr. of coaches, 1982-83. Mellon grantee, 1994; named Tchr. of Yr. Dallas Coun. for Social Studies, 1996, Outstanding HS Social Studies Tchr. of Yr., Tex. Coun. for Social Studies, 2002; named one of 50 Elite Tchrs., Nat. Coun. Econ. Edn. Tex. Coun. Econ. Edn., 2001. Mem. Nat. Coun. Social Studies, Tex. Coun. for Social Studies (sec. Peter's Colony Coun. for social studies 1998-99, v.p. 2000, pres. 2001-03, programs chair 2004—), Global Assn. for Tchrs. of Econs., North Tex. Women's Soccer Assn. (capt. 1989-95), Ctr. for Applied Linguistics (cons. World Culture Project 1996) Avocations: writing, soccer, travel. Home: 3535 Misty Meadow Dr Dallas TX 75287-6027 Office Phone: 972-389-3850. E-mail: dumererl@cfbisd.edu, dumererl@earthlink.net.

DUMINUCO, VINCENT JOSEPH, academic administrator, educator; b. Bronx, N.Y., Jan. 13, 1934; s. Joseph S. Duminuco and Mary Dora Morreale. BA, Fordham U., 1957; degree in Sacred Theology, Woodstock Coll., 1965; MA, Stanford U., 1966, PhD, 1969. Headmaster Xavier H.S., N.Y., 1969—74; dir. rsch. U.S. Jesuit Conf., Washington, 1974—77; pres. Jesuit Secondary Edn. Assn., Washington, 1977—86; sec. edn. Soc. Jesus, Rome, 1987—97; rector Jesuit Cmty. Fordham U., Bronx, 2001—. Dir. worldwide Internat. Jesuit Leadership Program, Rome, 1996—; dir. Joseph O'Hare Jesuit Tchr. Leadership Program, N.Y., 2003—; bd. dirs. St. Barnabus Hosp., Bronx; bd. trustees Fordham U., Loyola U., New Orleans, 1976—92; bd. adv. H.K. Internat. Inst. Ednl. Leadership, Hong Kong, 1998—; mem. pontifical coun. interreligious dialogue, Rome, 1990—96. Author: Ingantian Pedagogy: A Practical Approach, 1993; editor: The Jesuit Ratio, 2000; co-author: Catholic Education: Inside Out, Outside In, 1999. Recipient The Guerra award, Nat. Cath. Edn. Assn., 2003; fellow, Stanford U., 1967—69, 1969. Mem.: Nat. Cath. Ednl. Assn. (pres. 1983—86, sec. sch. dept. 1983—86), N.Y. Botanical Gardens. Independent. Roman Catholic. Avocations: bonsai, fishing, gardening, swimming. Office: Fordham Univ 113 West 60th St Rm 1024 New York NY 10023

DUMITRAS, ADRIANA, computer scientist; d. Ioan and Ghizela Dumitras. MSc, Poly. U., 1988, PhD, 1996, U. B.C., 1999. R & D tech. staff mem. Peripheral Equipment Co., Bucharest, 1988—91; tchg. asst. Poly. U., Bucharest, 1991—96, asst. prof., 1996—2001, assoc. prof., 2001—02; rsch. asst. U. B.C., Vancouver, Canada, 1997—99; rsch. assoc. NRC of Can., Vancouver, 1997—99; sr. tech. staff mem. AT&T Laboratories - Rsch., Middletown, NJ, 2001—02; sr. scientist Apple Computer, Cupertino, Calif., 2002—. Mem. faculty bd. electronics and telecom. dept. Poly. U., 1996—2000; head Can. del. ISO/IEC JTC 1/SC 29/WG 11 (MPEG) standardization group, 1998—99; voting mem. Can. Del. to Internat. Standardization Orgn. ISO/IEC JTC 1/SC 29, 1998—2000. TEMPUS-JEP European Union fellow, U. Denmark, 1993, postdoctoral fellow, Nat. Scis. and Engring. Rsch. Coun. of Can., 2000—01. Mem.: IEEE (sr.; reviewer IEEE Transactions on Image Processing 1998—, IEEE Transactions on Circuits and Systems II 2000—02, IEEE Transactions on Multimedia 2000—, session chair internat. conf. on image processing 2001, tech. program chair internat. conf. on image processing 2001—04, session chair internat. conf. on image processing 2002, tech. program com. internat. workshop on multimedia signal processing 2002, internat. symposium on circuits and systems 2002, internat. conf. on acoustics, speech and signal pro 2002—05, track chair internat. conf. on multimedia and expo 2003, area chair internat. conf. on multimedia and expo 2004, tech. program com. internat. workshop on multimedia signal processing 2004, tech. program com. internat. symposium on circuits and systems 2004, multimedia signal processing tech. com. of Signal Processing Soc. 2004—, multimedia systems & applications tech. com. Circuits and Systems Soc. 2004—, sub-track chair internat. symposium on circuits and systems 2005, tech. program com. internat. conf. on multimedia and expo 2005, internat. workshop on multimedia signal processing 2005). Achievements include development of algorithms for Apple's QuickTime H.264/AVC content-based video codec. Office Phone: 408-974-6337. E-mail: adrianad@ieee.org.

DUMITRESCU, CRISTINA M., intensive care nurse; b. Bucharest, Romania, Mar. 5, 1960; d. Mircea and Margareta Ispas; m. Gabriel N None, June 6, 1989. Degree in Biochem. Rsch. Mgmt., C.A. Rosetti, Bucharest, Romania, 1980, BSc in Biochemistry, 1981; ADN, Walla Walla C.C., 1986; BS, U. Wash., 1988, studies in Psychiat. Social Nursing, 1987, studies in Family Analysis, studies in Cmty. Health Care Sys., U. Wash., 1988. RN Wash., 1986, lic. advance cardiac life support, Medic 7 Dist. Snohomish County, 1996. Biochem. rschr. Pharm. Co. Bucharest, Romania, 1981—82; registry relief nurse Kimberly Quality Care, Seattle, 1986—92; RN/charge nurse Swedish Med. Ctr., Seattle, 1988—93; home care ventilator nurse Nurse's Ho. Call, Seattle, 1989—94; registry relief nurse Amserv Western Med., Seattle, 1990—95; case mgr./mktg. dir. Vis. Nurse Svcs., Seattle, 1991—96; ICCU/CO RN Stevens Med. Ctr., Edmonds, Wash., 1996—. Marketer Vis. Nurse, Seattle, 1991—96; cmty. health care cons. Walla Walla DSHS, 1986; exec. sec./office mgr. Musica Romanica Inc., Seattle, 2000—; property mgmt. Dumitrescu Fourplex, Kent, Wash., 2002—; cmty. svc. dir. Seventh Day Adventist Ch., Seattle, 1992—. Contbr. articles to profl. jours. Dir. allocation of cmty. resources Cmty. Services Ctr., Seattle, 1992; project mgr. Helping Hands of Am., Seattle, 1993—94, Cmty. Services SDA, Snohomish, Wash., 1994—95. Mem.: NAFE (Excellence in Nursing award 2001), Walla Walla Businesswoman's Assn., U. Wash. Alumni Assn., Sigma Theta Tau Internat. Office: Musica Romanica Inc PO Box 5037 Kent WA 98064 Office Phone: 253-859-2870. Office Fax: 253-859-2873. Personal E-mail: musirom@earthlink.net.

DUMITRESCU, DOMNITA, Spanish language educator, researcher; b. Bucharest, Romania; came to U.S., 1984; d. Ion and Angela (Barzotescu) D. Diploma, U. Bucharest, 1966; MA, U. So. Calif., 1987, PhD, 1990. Asst. prof. U. Bucharest, 1966-74, assoc. prof., 1974-84; asst. prof. Spanish Calif. State U., L.A., 1987-90, assoc. prof., 1990-94, prof., 1995—. Author: Gramatica Limbii Spaniole, 1976, (with Dan Munteanu) Indreptar Pentru Traducerea Din Limba Romana in Limba Spaniola, 1980; translator from Spanish to Romanian; assoc. editor: Hispania, 1996-2000, S.W. Jour. Linguistics, 2000-05; contbr. articles to profl. jours. Recipient Outstanding Prof. award Calif. State U., L.A., 2003-04; Fulbright scholar, 1993—. Mem. MLA, Linguistic Soc. Am., Internat. Assn. Hispanists, Linguistic Assn. S.W. (pres. 2005, Am. Assn. Tchrs. Spanish and Portuguese (past pres. So. Calif. chpt., Tchr. of Yr. award 2000), Sigma Delta Pi (v.p. West 1996—). Office: Calif State U 5151 State University Dr Los Angeles CA 90032-4226 Business E-Mail: ddumitr@exchange.calstatela.edu.

DUMITRU, DANIEL, physiatrist; b. Massillon, Ohio; MD, U. Cin., 1980. Diplomate Am. Bd. Phys. Medicine and Rehab. Resident phys. medicine and rehab. VA Hosp., San Antonio, 1980—83; prof. U. Tex. Health Sci. Ctr., San Antonio, 1983—. Attending physician Audie Murphy Vets. Hosp., San Antonio. Mem.: ASIA, AANEM, Am. Acad. Phys. Medicine & Rehab. (pres.-elect 2002—). Office: U Tex Health Sci Ctr Dept RM/PMR 7703 Floyd Curl Dr San Antonio TX 78229-3900

DUMITRU, MIRELA, accountant; b. Constanta, Romania, Dec. 3, 1959; d. Nicolae and Lucia Bradeanu; 1 child, Corina-Luiza. BS, St. Francis Coll., 2003. Acct. Robert Half Internat., Inc., N.Y.C., 1998—2002; acctg. supr. DSi Group, Maspeth, NY, 2002—. Cons. Descendent of Holy Spirit, Ridgewood, NY, 1991—2003. Scholar, St. Francis Coll., 2000. Christian Orthodox. Office: Display Sys Inc 57-13 49th Pl Maspeth NY 11378-2020 Office Phone: 718-628-2617. Personal E-mail: mireladtru@aol.com. Business E-Mail: mirela@displaysystemsinc.com.

DUMKE, MELVIN PHILIP, dentist; b. Sleepy Eye, Minn., Jan. 23, 1920; s. Herman Gustav and Else Ida (Battig) D.; m. Phyllis Lorraine Steuck, June 25, 1950; children: Pamela, Bruce, Shari. DDS, U. Minn., 1943. Practice dentistry, Sleepy Eye, 1946-50, Morgan, Minn., 1950-66, Mankato, Minn., 1966—. Lectr. dental assts. Mankato State Coll., 1967-69. Mem. Town Coun., Morgan, 1960-65; bd. control Martin Luther Acad., New Ulm, Minn., 1965-79; bd. dirs. The Luth. Home, Belle Plaine, Minn., 1981-96, Orgn. Wis. Luth. Svcs.; pres. Luth. Congregation, 1970, 86-87. Served to capt., Dental Corps, AUS, 1943-46. Fellow Royal Soc. Health, Internat. Coll. Dentists, Am. Coll. Dentists, Pierre Fouchard Acad.; mem. ADA (ho. of dels. 1977-87), Minn. Dental Assn. (chmn. peer rev. com. 1973-79, mem. ho. of del. 1978-89, pres. 1983-84, guest of honor 1993), So. Dist. Dental Soc. (exec. coun., trustee 1988-89, guest of honor 1986), South Cen. Dental Study Club (pres. 1970), Fedn. Dentaire Internationale, U. Minn. Alumni Assn., VFW (Disting. Svc. award 1966, comdr. 1965), Am. Legion, Lions (pres. 1965, 74, zone chmn. 1975, Melvin Jones fellow 1999), Mankato Golf Club, St. Paul U. Club, U. Minn. Sch. Dentistry Century Club, Psi Omega. Home: 364 Carol Ct Mankato MN 56003-3300 Office: 430 S Broad St Mankato MN 56001-3703 Personal E-mail: dumkes@hickorytech.net.

DUMLER, RICHARD J., venture capitalist; BA in Econs., Georgetown U., 1964; MBA, U. Mich., 1968. Jr. analyst to mng. dir. venture capital divsn. Allstate Ins. Co., 1968—79; gen. ptnr. Bessemer Venture Ptnrs., 1979—82; ptnr. Lambda Funds, 1982—2001; 1 v.p. Drexel, Burnham, Lambert, Inc., 1983—90; gen. ptnr. Milestone Venture Ptnrs., 2002—. Mem. bd. Kronos Inc., 1982—. Office: Milestone Venture Ptnrs 551 Madison Ave 7th Fl New York NY 10022 Office Fax: 212-223-0315. E-mail: rjd@milestonevp.com.

DUMM, ROBERT WAYNE, musician, educator, writer; b. East McKeesport, Pa., May 21, 1928; s. Claude Alvin and Garnet Sarah (Weaver) D.; m. Mary Elizabeth Covert, Dec. 24, 1952 (div. June, 1981); children: Dexter Hearn, Claudia Ann. MusB with honors, U. Mich., 1949, MusM in Piano and Theory, 1952, postgrad., 1953—57. Tchr. piano, Ann Arbor, Mich.; dean Boston Conservatory, 1958—68; editor Boston Music Co., 1958—68; critic Christian Sci. Monitor; prof. piano, head piano pedagogy Cath. U., Washington, 1968—79. Tchr. music courses Ann Arbor Adult Edn. Program, 1950-57; condr. combined piano ensembles Nat. Music Camp, Interlochen, Mich., 1956-57; founder libr. concerts Twinbrook Lib., Rockville, Md., 1979-81; tchr. courses Elderhostel, Shenandoah U., Winchester, Va., 1995-98; judge numerous competitions; founder, dir. numerous music workshops; conducted 500 taped interviews with pianists for Internat. Piano Archive, U. Md. Author: Adult Piano Course, 1981, Instead of Scales, 2001, Pumping Ivory, 1989; contbg. editor Clavier mag., 2000—. (also cover photo feature); author technique column Piano Today, 1979—, Sheet Music Mag., 1982—; contbr. articles to profl. jours. Mem. Am. Liszt Soc. (founder), Music Tchrs. Nat. Assn. (lifetime cert.), Phi Beta Kappa, Phi Sigma Phi Democrat. Presbyterian. Avocations: gardening, walking, wide reading. Home: 123 Milton Rd Daytona Beach FL 32118 Office Phone: 386-255-6210. E-mail: pianoman84@bellsouth.net.

DUMMER, J. STEPHEN, physician; b. Danville, Pa., Oct. 9, 1943; s. Richard S. and Ida S. (Schorr) D.; m. Kathleen L. Dowd, Apr. 30, 1977; children: Jessica A., Christopher J. BA, Wesleyan U., Middletown, Conn., 1966; MD, U. Pitts., 1977. Asst. prof. U. Pitts., 1984-88, assoc. prof., 1989-90, Vanderbilt U., Nashville, 1990-97, prof. medicine, 1997—; dir. transplant infectious diseases Vanderbilt Med. Ctr., Nashville, 1990—. Contbr. over 100 articles to profl. jours., chpts. to books.; editl. bd. Transplantation, 1993-99. Fellow Infectious Disease Soc. Am.; mem. Am. Soc. Transplant Physicians (infectious disease com. 1996—), Internat. Heart Lung Soc., Am. Soc. Microbiology, Phi Beta Kappa, Alpha Omega Alpha Avocations: reading, classical music, golf, languages. Office: 911 Oxford House 1313 21st Ave S Nashville TN 37232-0001 E-mail: stephen.dummer@vanderbilt.edu.

DUMMETT, CLIFTON ORRIN, dentist, educator; b. Georgetown, British Guiana, May 20, 1919; s. Alexander Adolphus and Eglantine Annabella (Johnson) Dummett; m. Lois Maxine Doyle, Mar. 6, 1943; 1 child, Clifton Orrin Jr. BS in Psychology, Roosevelt U., Chgo., 1941; DDS, Northwestern U., 1941, MScD, 1942, DSc (hon.), 1976; MPH, U. Mich., 1947; ScD (hon.), U. Pa., 1978; DSc (hon.), Meharry Med. Coll., 2004. Diplomate Am. Bd. Periodontology, Am. Bd. Oral Medicine. Dean, prof. periodontology Meharry Med. Coll., Nashville, 1945-49; chief dental service VA Hosp., Tuskegee, Ala., 1949-65, assoc. chief staff for rsch. and edn., 1958-65, chief dental service Chgo., 1965-66; dental dir., dir. ctr. Watts Health Ctr., L.A., 1966-69; assoc. dean, chmn. dept. cmty. dentistry U. So. Calif. Sch. Dentistry, L.A., 1969-75, prof., 1969-89, prof. emeritus, 1989-96, disting. emeritus prof., 1997—. Adj. prof. Northwestern U. Dental Sch., 1989; vis. prof., cons. Sch. Vet. Medicine Tuskegee Inst., 1962—65; vis. prof. Meharry Med. Coll., 1989—; trustee Am. Fund Dental Health, Chgo., 1968—78; chem. devel. component rev. panel Calif. Regional Med. Programs, L.A., 1975—77; mem. Pres.'s Com. on Nat. Health Ins., 1977; sr. reviewer U.S. Surgeon Gen. Report on Oral Health, 2000. Author: Community Dentistry, 1974, Afro-Americans in Dentistry: Sequence and Consequence of Events, 1977, Charles Edwin Bentley, 1982, Dental Education at Meharry Medical College: Origin and Odyssey, 1992, Culture and Education in Dentistry at Northwestern University, 1993, NDA.II The Story of America's Second National Dental Association, 2000, (editl.) Nor Yet the Last, 1962 (W.J. Gies award, 1963), The Hillenbrand Era, 1986; editor: Nat. Dental Assn., 1953—75; contbr. chapters to books, more than 300 articles to profl. jours. Chmn. adv. bd. Econ. and Youth Opportunity Agy. Project Head Start, Tuskegee, Ala., 1964—65; mem. spl. health adv. com. Calif. Bd. Edn., L.A., 1972—74; mem. L.A. regional hearing planning coun. Pres.'s Com. on Health Edn., L.A., 1973—74. Lt. col. USAF, 1955—58. Named to, U. So. Calif. Dental Hall of Fame, 1997; recipient Alumni Merit award, Northwestern U., 1971, Fones Gold medal, Conn. Dental Assn., 1976, Pierre Fauchard Gold medal, Pierre Fauchard Acad., 1980, John R. Callahan award, Ohio Dental Assn., 2003. Fellow: AAAS (chmn. dental sect. 1975—76, 1987—88), APHA (v.p. for U.S. 1995—96, John W. Knutson Disting. Svc. award 1992), Am. Acad. History of Dentistry (pres. 1982—83, Hayden and Harris award 1987), Internat. Coll. Dentists; mem.: ADA (hon.), Am. Dental Edn. Assn. (Presdl. citation 2003), Inst. Medicine of NAS (sr. mem.), Nat. Acads. Practice (Disting. Practitioner 1987), Am. Assn. Dental Editors (editor 1963—72, pres. 1974—75, Disting. Svc. medal 1976), Assn. Mil. Surgeons (life), Internat. Assn. Dental Rsch. (pres. 1969—70), Am. Coll. Dentists (Wm. J. Gies award 1992), Sigma Xi, Omicron Kappa Upsilon (pres., founder Nashville chpt. 1947—49), Delta Omega, Alpha Phi Alpha, Sigma Pi Phi. Democrat. Episcopalian. Avocations: music, politics, track. Home: 5344 Highlight Pl Los Angeles CA 90016-5119 Office: U So Calif Sch Dentistry PO Box 77006 Los Angeles CA 90007-0006

DUMOND, ROBERT WILFRED, clinical mental health consultant, lay pastoral worker; b. Lawrence, Mass., Nov. 1, 1952; s. Wilfred Albert and Claire Marie (Dumas) D.; m. Doris Ann Cocchiaro, May 1, 1976; children: Amy Marie, Matthew Christian, Claire Elizabeth. BA in Psychology, U. Mass., 1974; MA in Counseling Psychology, Assumption Coll., Worcester, Mass., 1982. Lic. cert. social worker, Mass.; lic. mental health counselor, Mass.; cert. rape investigator, Mass.; lic. clin. mental health counselor, N.H.; lic. marriage and family therapist, Mass.; lic. rehab. counselor, Mass.; cert. justice of peace, N.H., 1988—; nat. cert. counselor Am. Acad. Cert. Clin. Mental Health Counselors; cert. trainer prison fellowship, 1998—; diplomate clin. forensic counseling Am. Coll. Cert. Forensic Counselors. Child care counselor St. Anne's Home, Inc., Methuen, Mass., 1971-74; dir. region IV The Key Program, Inc. (formerly Cmty. Advancement Program), Lawrence, 1974-79; dir. victim/witness assistance program Commonwealth of Mass., Essex County Dist. Atty's Office, Lawrence, 1979-83, Haverhill, 1983-87; mem. continuing edn. faculty Franklin Pierce Coll., Salem, N.H., 1984—; prin. psychologist Commonwealth of Mass. Dept. Correction, Concord, 1987-91; mental health clinician EMSA Correctional Care, Inc., various cities, Mass., 1992-94; mental health adminstr. Correctional Med. Svcs., Inc., Gardner, Mass., 1994-95; vol. mental health cons., educator Roman Cath. Diocese of Manchester, N.H., 1997—, State of N.H., Concord, 1997—. Pastoral/correctional liaison Roman Cath. Diocese of Manchester and State of N.H. Dept. of Corrections, 1997-99; v.p., bd. dirs. C'ESTA, Inc., Manchester, 1995-2000; cons. Safer Soc. Program and Press, Orwell, Vt., 1992-94, Fed. Emergency Mgmt. Agy., Boston, 1991-92; mem., provider Dept. Mental Health, Cmty. Mental Health and Retardation Area Bd., Lawrence, 1981-83; cons., faculty mem. Nat. Coun. on Crime and Delinquency, Hackensack, N.J., 1980-82; cons. City of Hartford, Conn., 1976; gov.'s appointee N.H. State Rehab. Coun., Concord, 1998—; mem. N.H. HIV Prevention Cmty. Planning Group, Concord, 1998-2000; sr. lectr. divsn. Grad. and Profl. Studies Franklin Pierce Coll., N.H., 1998—; invited witness, presenter U.S. Senate Judiciary Com., Washington, Prison Rape Reduction Act of 2002, 2002; invited participant 1st Nat. Conf. on Prison Rape, Washington, 2002, U.S. Atty. Gen.'s Symposium on Child Molestation, Washington, 1984; invited witness Pres.'s Task Force on Crime Victims, Boston, 1982; cons., author, 1999—. Manuscript reviewer: Trauma, Violence & Abuse: A Review Journal, 2002—; contbr. articles to profl. jours. and tng. manuals; contbg. author manuals, resource handbooks, ednl. audiotapes. Pastoral care vol. St. Joseph's Hosp., Nashua, N.H., 1997-99; bd. dirs. Lazarus Ho. Ministries, Inc., Lawrence, 1986-89, Family Svcs. Assn. Greater Lawrence, Inc., 1982-84, Mental Health and Retardation Svcs., Inc., Lawrence, 1981-83, N.H. Brain Injury Assn., 1997-2000; mem. human rights com. Area Agy. for Developmental Disability, Nashua, 1997-2000; disability rights advocate U. N.H. Inst. Disabilities, Concord, 1997—; mem. steering com. Citizens for Discipline in the Schs., Hudson, N.H., 1995-97; participant, panelist, profl. expert various confs., commns., and pub. hearings, in areas of juvenile justice, prison sexual assault, prison conditions, child abuse, and violent crime; mem. No. Essex (N.H.) Com. Against Sexual Assault, 1985-87, co-chair, 1986-87; pres. Mass. Dept. Social Svcs. Area Bd. #12, 1980-81; mem. Mass. Office for Children Statewide Adv. Coun., 1975-77; pres. Greater Lawrence Coun. for Children, 1975-76; vol. coord. prison ministries Roman Cath. Diocese Manchester, N.H., 1998—; gov. appointee N.H. Dept. Corrections, Citizen's Adv. Bd. Exec. Com., Concord, 2001—, N.H. State Prison-Men, 2000—; bd. advisers Stop Prisoner Rape, L.A., 2002—; mem. prison rape steering com. Hudson Inst., Inst. on Civil Justice Reform, Washington, 2000—; mem. Diocesan Prison Ministries com. Diocese of Manchester, 2000—, mem. pub. policy com., 1998—; founding mem. Prison Ministries Assn. N.H., Manchester, 1998—. Recipient Beyond Excellence Recognition award, Commr. Mass. Dept. Correction, Boston, 1990, Liberty Bell award for Outstanding Cmty. Svc., Lawrence Bar Assn., 1976, Stephen Donaldson award Stop Prisoner Rape, 2002. Mem. APA (assoc. mem., chair symposium 103rd conf. and session 98th conf. 1990 divsn. 18 criminal justice sect.), Nat. Assn. Cath. Chaplains (student mem.), Acad. Criminal Justice Scis. (roundtable convenor 1995, workshop panelist 1992), Am. Acad. Psychiatric Svcs. to Children (presenter 36th and 37th Ann. Confs., 1985, 86), Nat. Orgn. Victim Assistance (presenter Ann. Conf. 1981, nominated to U.S. Dept. Justice Symposium 1984), The Perspectives Network, Inc., New England Assn. Child Care (presenter 1975 spring and fall meetings), Knights of Columbus (Grand Knight 2001-2002, coun. 5162, officer 1998—, 4th degree mem., youth dir. 1997—, Knight of Yr. 1997). Roman Catholic. Avocations: playing guitar, biblical archeology, antiquarian books, on-line computing, writing. Home: 27 Baker St Hudson NH 03051-3606 E-mail: rwdumond@aol.com.

DUMONT, ALLAN ELIOT, retired physician, educator; b. N.Y.C., Oct. 8, 1924; m. Joan Auerbach, Oct. 1, 1949; children: Mark E., James A., David H. BA, Hobart Coll., 1945; MD, NYU, 1948. Diplomate Am. Bd. Surgery. Intern Bellevue Hosp., N.Y.C., 1948-49, resident, 1949-51, 53-54, chief resident, 1954-55; instr. surgery NYU, 1955-59, asst. attending surgeon Univ. Hosp., asst. vis. surgeon 3d and 4th surg. divs. Bellevue, 1955-60, asst. prof. surgery, 1959-62, assoc. vis. surgeon 3d and 4th surg. div. Bellvue, 1961-65; attending surgeon Manhattan VA Hosp., N.Y.C., 1958-67, cons. surgeon, 1967-90; assoc. attending surgeon Univ. Hosp. NYU, 1961-68, attending surgeon, 1968-90, assoc. prof. surgery, 1962-68, prof. surgery, 1968-73, Jules Leonard Whitehill prof. surgery, 1973-90, prof. emeritus, 1990—; clin. prof. surgery U. Conn. Sch. Medicine, 1991. Career scientist N.Y.C. Health Research Council, 1959-62; univ. senate NYU, 1966-69; vis. surgeon Bellevue Hosp., 1965-90, assoc. dir. surg. service, 1975-90; cons. surgeon St. Francis Hosp., Hartford, 1990—. Editor: Lymphology. 1974-84. Served to lt (j.g.) USN, 1951-53. Recipient Research Career Devel. award USPHS, 1961-71, Purkinje medal, Czechoslovakia, 1977. Mem. Am. Coll. Surgeons, New Eng. Surg. Soc., Harvey Soc., N.Y. Surg. Soc. (pres. 1987-88), Am. Physiol. Soc., Soc. Univ. Surgeons, Soc. for Surgery Alimentary Tract, Internat. Soc. Lymphology (pres. 1979-83), Am. Surg. Assn.

DUMONT, EDWARD ABDO, architect, interior designer; b. Bklyn., July 4, 1961; AA, Miami Dade Community Coll.; BArch, U. Fla., 1984. With Paul, Paul and Madrid Archs., Houston, 1984—87, William Crosskey and Assocs. Archs., Hartford, Conn., 1987—89, Brand Allen Archs., Houston, 1989—98, Gensler-Houston, 1998—99, Gotsdiner Archs., Houston, 1999—2001, Morris Archs., Houston, 2001—04, Studio Red Archs., Houston, 2004—. Mem. Rice Design Alliance, Tex. Soc. Interior Designers, IIDA, Mus. Fine Arts Houston, U. Fla. Nat. Alumni Assn. Avocations: art, photography, furniture design. Home: 4412 Effie St Bellaire TX 77401-5617 Office: Studio Red Archs 3465A W Alabama Houston TX 77027 Business E-Mail: dumont@studioredarchitects.com.

DUMONT, JAMES KELTON, JR., actor, theater producer; b. Chgo., Aug. 12, 1965; s. James Kelton and Judith Katherine (Johnson) DuMont; m. Wendell Faith Hall, Dec. 14, 1968; children: Sinclair Marie, Kelton Hall. Student, Boston U., 1983-85. Field recruiter Nat. Rsch. Group, Hollywood, Calif., 1993-2000; pres., CEO DuMont Entertainment Group, Hollywood, 1994—; v.p. sales and mktg. PACE Am., Hollywood, 2000—04, website, 2005—. Mem. Ensemble Studio Theatre, N.Y.C., 1989—, co-artistic dir. L.A. Project, 1996. Actor: (Broadway plays) Six Degrees of Separation, 1990—93, (off-Broadway play) Tony & Tina's Wedding, 1989—90; (films) Speed, 1993, Combination Platter, 1993, Bombshell, 1996, The Peacemaker, 1996, Primary Colors, 1996, Erasable You, 1997, In Quiet Night, 1997, Bellyfruit, 1998, Love & Basketball, 1999, Catch Me if You Can, 2002, S.W.A.T., 2003, Seabiscuit, 2003, Along Came Polly, 2003, Miss Congeniality 2, 2004, Dating Games People Play, 2004, War of the Worlds, 2005, Statistics, 2005, Lost Dogs, 2005; (TV series) NYPD Blue, 1995, Lois & Clark, 1996, Chgo. Sons, 1996, Tracy Takes on, 1995, Fallen Angels, 1995, The Client, 1995, Sweet Justice, 1995, Can't Hurry Love, 1995, Arliss, 1998, Then Came You, 1999, The West Wing, 2000, Becker, 2000, Titus, 2001, That's Life, 2001, That Was Then, 2002, Cold Case, 2003, C.S.I., 2003, ER, 2004, Joan of Arcadia, 2005; (TV films) Pentagon Wars, 1998, Winchell, 1999, Gotta Kick It Up, 2001; prodr., actor: (films) The Confession, 1996. Democrat. Buddhist. Avocation: writing prose and short stories, plays and screenplays. Office: Ensemble Studio Theatre 137 N Larchmont Blvd # 134 Los Angeles CA 90004-3704 E-mail: dumontentgrp@earthlink.net.

DU MONT, NICOLAS, psychiatrist, educator; b. San Juan, PR, Dec. 22, 1954; s. Joseph Henri and Isabel (Solano) Du M. Postgrad. adult psychiatry, Columbia U., 1990; MD, U. P.R., 1986; postgrad. child, adolescent psychiatry, Columbia U., 1992, postgrad. pub. cmty. psychiatry, 1993. Assoc. prof. Polytech. U., San Juan, 1984-88, InterAm. U., San Juan, P.R., 1986-87; med. dir. Holistic Med. Ctr., N.Y.C., 1993-94; asst. prof. Albert Einstein Coll. of

Medicine, N.Y.C., 1991-96, Mt. Sinai Sch. of Medicine, N.Y.C., 1993-96, Columbia Physicians and Surgeons Coll. Medicine, N.Y.C., 1997—; asst. attending physician Elmhurst Med. Ctr., N.Y.C., 1993-94; asst. physician Mt. Sinai Med. Ctr., N.Y.C., 1993-96; v.p., CEO Engring. Med. Support, Inc., N.Y.C., 1992—; asst. prof. Columbia Physicians and Surgeons Coll. Medicine, N.Y.C., 1997—. Attending physician Westchester Jewish Med. Svcs., Hartsdale, N.Y., 1990-95, Montefiore Med. Ctr., N.Y.C., 1991-96, Albert Einstein Coll. Medicine, 1991-96, Puerto Rican Family Inst., 1994—; asst. attending physician and med. dir. Tavares Hispanic Mental Health Clin. at Columbia Presbyn. Med. Ctr., 1997—. Mem. editl. bd.: Jour. Pagan Studies, NY edit., 1990—. Vis. fellow N.Y. State Psychiat. Inst., 1992-93. Mem. Assn. Hispanic Mental Health Profls. (exec. bd. dirs. 1999-2003, sr. advisor, 2003—, treas.). Office: Engring Med Support Inc 200 W 70th St Ste 8F New York NY 10023-4326 Business E-Mail: info@dumont.org.

DUMOUCHELLE, ERNEST J., art appraiser; s. Joseph N. DuMouchelle and Charlotte D.; m. Lucy DuMouchelle. BA, Univ. Detroit Coll.; student, Wayne State Univ., Gemological Inst. Cert. appraiser. V.p. DuMouchelle Art Gallery Co., Detroit. Appraiser Antiques Roadshow, WGBH-PBS. Mem.: Am. Gemological Inst., Am. Soc. Appraisers. Office: DuMouchelle Gallery 409 E Jefferson Detroit MI 48226 Office Phone: 313-963-6255. Office Fax: 313-963-8199. Business E-Mail: bobdumo@dumouchelle.com.*

DUMOUCHELLE, LAWRENCE F., art appraiser; s. Joseph N. DuMouchelle and Charlotte D.; married. CEO DuMouchelle Art Galleries, Detroit, 1957—. Past. pres. Founders' Soc., Jr. Coun., Detroit Inst. for Arts; past pres. Detroit & Canada Tunnel Corp.; appraiser Antiques Roadshow, WGBH-PBS. Past pres. St. Paul's Parish Coun. Mem.: Internat. Soc. Appraisers, Nat. Auctioneers Assn., Mich. Auctioneers Assn., Am. Soc. Appraisers, Appraiser's Assn. Am., Meadowbrook Arts Commn. Office: DuMouchelle Gallery 409 E Jefferson Ave Detroit MI 48226 Office Phone: 313-963-6255. Office Fax: 313-963-8199. Business E-Mail: bobdumo@dumouchelles.com.*

DUMOULIN, DIANA CRISTAUDO, small business owner, writer, musician; b. Washington, Jan. 5, 1939; d. Emanuel A. and Angela E. (Cogliano) Cristaudo; m. Philip DuMoulin, May 30, 1964; children: Joanmarie Patricia, John Philip. MA, U. Wis., 1967; BA, Rosary Coll., 1961; cert. in Creative Writing, Piano, Phoenix Coll., 2002. Project mgr. IDC Cons. Group, Framingham, Mass., 1982-84; sr. market analyst Cullinet, Inc., Westwood, Mass., 1984-86; prof. assoc. Ledgeway Group, Lexington, Mass., 1988—93; prin. Customer Mktg. Specialist, Brookline, Mass., 1994—2000; pres. Customer Solutions Internat., Phoenix, 1994—. Adj. faculty Ulster County C.C. Stone Ridge, N.Y., 1967-74; lectr. Boston Coll., Chestnut Hill, Mass., 1976. Author:The Love Pad Dream Journal, 1996, Ourselves in the Garden, 1998; contbr. articles to profl. jours., mags., poetry jours. Pres. LWV, Kingston, N.Y., 1973-74. Recipient Svc. to Young Adults award 70001 Career Assn., 1977, Honorable Mention award Writers Digest Writing Competition, 1996, 98; faculty fellow U. Wis., 1964-66 Mem. Am. Marketing Assn., Nat. Writers Union. Office: Create Music Poetry 8441 N 1st Dr Phoenix AZ 85021-5515 Office Phone: 602-371-0804. E-mail: dianadumoulin@yahoo.com.

DUMOVICH, LORETTA, retired real estate and transportation company executive; b. Kansas City, Kans., Sept. 29, 1930; d. Michael Nicholas and Frances Barbara (Horvat) D. Student public schs., Kansas City. Lic. real estate broker, Kans., Mo. Corp. sec., dir. Riss Internat. Corp., 1950-86, Riss Intermodal Corp., 1969-86, World Leasing Corp., 1969-86; pres., dir. Columbia Properties, Inc., 1969-86; v.p., dir. Republic Industries, 1969-86; corp. sec., dir. Comml. Equipment Co. Inc., Charlotte, N.C., 1980-93; v.p., corp. sec. Commonwealth Gen. Ins. Co., Kansas City, Mo., 1986-93, Heart of Am. Fire & Casualty Co., Kansas City, 1986-93, ret., 1993. Mem. Kansas City (Mo.) Real Estate Bd., Bldg. Owners and Mgrs. Assn. of Kansas City (Mo.), Terminal Properties Exchange (founding mem.), Am. Royal Assn. (gov.) Office: 215 W Pershing Rd Kansas City MO 64108-4317

DUMVILLE, JOHN P., historic site director; b. Hanover, N.H., Feb. 17, 1950; BA, U. Vt., 1972, MA, 1976. Tchr. Turnbridge (Vt.) Sch. Sys., 1974-75; arch. historian State of Vt., 1976-79; dir. Vt. State Historic Sites, Montpelier, 1979—. Trustee Vt. Hist. Soc., 1976-82, 86-92, Royalton Meml. Libr., 1969-97; selectboard Town of Royalton, Vt., 1994—. Office: Historic Preservation Nat Life Bldg Drawer 20 Montpelier VT 05620-0001 Office Phone: 802-828-3051. Business E-Mail: John.Dumville@state.vt.us.

DUNAGAN, WALTER BENTON, lawyer, educator; b. Midland, Tex., Dec. 11, 1937; s. Clinton McCormick and Allie Mae (Stout) D.; m. Tera Childress, Feb. 1, 1969; children: Elysha, Sandi. BA, U. Tex., 1963, JD, 1965, postgrad., 1965-68. Bar: Tex. 1965, Fla. 1970, U.S. Dist. Ct. (mid. dist.) Fla. 1971, U.S. Ct. Appeals (11th cir.) 1982. Corp. atty. Gulf Oil, New Orleans, 1968-69, Getty Oil Co., L.A., 1969—, Westinghouse/Econocar, Internat., Daytona Beach, Fla., 1969-72; assoc. Becks & Becks, Daytona Beach, 1973-75; prin. Walter B. Dunagan, Daytona Beach, 1975—. Cons. Bermuda Villas Motel, Daytona Beach, Buccaneer Motel, Daytona Beach, Pelican Cove West Homeowners Assn., Edgewater, Fla. Organizer Interfaith Coffee House, New Orleans; tchr., song leader various chs.; chief Indian guide/princess program YMCA, Daytona Beach; bd. dirs. Legal Aid, Daytona Beach. Lance cpl. USMC. Mem. Volusia County Bar Assn., Lawyers Title Guaranty Fund, Phi Delta Phi. Avocations: reading, languages. Office: 110 Live Oak St New Smyrna Beach FL 32168-7114 Fax: 386-409-3710. E-mail: wbdunfla@msn.com.

DUNAIF, ANDREA ELIZABETH, endocrinologist; b. N.Y.C., Feb. 26, 1952; d. Samuel Lewis and Nancy Marie (Peters) D. BA, Sarah Lawrence Coll., 1973; MD, Columbia U., 1977. Diplomate Am. Bd. Internal Medicine, Am. Bd. Endocrinology, Diabetes and Metabolism. Intern, resident in medicine Presbyn. Hosp., N.Y.C., 1977-80; clin. and rsch. fellow in endocrinology Mass. Gen. Hosp., Boston, 1980-81, clin. and rsch. fellow in medicine and gynecology, 1981-82; instr. in ob-gyn., reproductive sci. and medicine Mt. Sinai Sch. Medicine, N.Y.C., 1982-88, asst. prof. medicine, ob-gyn., reproductive sci., 1985-88, assoc. program dir. clin. rsch. ctr., assoc. prof. medicine, 1988-91, assoc. prof. ob-gyn. and reproductive scis., 1989-91; prof. medicine and cellular and molecular physiology Pa. State Coll., Hershey, 1991-96, program dir. gen. clin. rsch. ctr., 1995-96, dean's lectr., 1995; assoc. dir. Nat. Ctr. for Infertility Rsch. Brigham and Women's Hosp., Boston, 1996—, dir. and chief medicine and ob-gyn divsn. women's health, 1997-2001, sr. physician, 1997—; dir. Nat. Ctr. Excellence in Women's Health Harvard Med. Sch., 1998-2001; chief divsn. of endocrinology metabolism/molecular medicine, Charles F. Kettering prof. medicine Northwestern U. Med. Sch., Chgo., 2001—. Asst, attending physician Mt. Sinai Hosp., N.Y.C., 1982-88, assoc. attending physician, 1988-91; attending physician medicine Hershey (Pa.) Med. Ctr., 1992-96; sr. dir. Diabetes, Med. and Sci. Affairs, Parke-Davis, Morris Plains, N.J., 1996-97. Editor (with others, book) The Polycystic Ovary Syndrome, 1992; assoc. editor Jour. Clin. Endocrinology and Metabolism, 1993-2000; contbr. numerous articles to profl. jours, also abstracts and revs.; mem. editl. bd. Molecular and Cellular Endocrinology. Named Kelly West lectr., U. Okla., Okla. City, 1995; recipient Sinsheimer Scholar award, 1986—89, Pennsylvanians of Vision award, Tri-County chpt. Am. Diabetes Assn., Pa. affil., 1995, Citation for alumnae achievement, Sarah Lawrence Coll., 1996, Woman of Achievement award, Big Sister Assn. Greater Boston, 1999; fellow Charles H. Revson fellow, 1983—85; grantee NIH, 1985—2002, others. Mem.: Assn. Am. Physicians, Am. Soc. Clin. Investigation, Am. Fedn. Med. Rsch. (future directions com. 1997), Endocrine Soc. (mem. clin. initiatives com. 1992—94, steering com. recent progress in hormone meeting 1995—97, mem. coun. 1998—2001), Am. Diabetes Assn. (chair 1992—93, liason com. with endocrine soc.), Women in Endocrinology (chair program com. 1990—94). Avocation: opera. Office: Northwestern U Med Sch Tarry 15-709 303 E Chicago Ave Chicago IL 60611-3008 E-mail: a-dunaif@northwestern.edu.

DUNAR, ANDREW J., historian, educator; b. Milw., Jan. 25, 1946; s. Andrew and Marion Dunar; m. Catherine A. Chrzan, Dec. 28, 1968; children: James A., Michael P., Kimberly E. BA, Northwestern U., Evanston, IL, 1968; MA, UCLA, 1974; PhD, U. So. Calif., LA, 1981. Asst. prof. history Manchester Coll., North Manchester, Ind., 1983; vis. asst. prof. history Union Coll., Schenectady, NY, 1983—84; prof. history U. of Ala., Huntsville, Ala., 1984—. Editor Oral History Rev. Oral History Assn., 1999—. Author: The Truman Scandals and the Politics of Morality, 1984; co-author: Bldg. Hoover Dam: An Oral History of the Gt. Depression, 1993, Power to Explore: A History of Marshall Space Flight Ctr., 1960-1990, 1999 (AIAA History Book award, 2001). Lt. supply corps USN, 1968—72. Mem.: Am. Hist. Assn., Orgn. of Am. Historians, Oral History Assn. Office: Univ AL Huntsville History Dept 301 Sparkman Dr NW Huntsville AL 35899 Office Fax: 256-824-6477. E-mail: dunara@uah.edu.

DUNATHAN, HARMON CRAIG, college dean; b. Celina, Ohio, July 25, 1932; s. Harry V. and Mildred B. (Greek) D.; m. Katy Mary Dragati, Mar. 15, 1956 (div. July 1990); children: Christine, Susan, Amy, Andrea; m. Mary Frances Pitts, Sept. 29, 1990. BA, Ohio Wesleyan U., 1954; MS, Yale U., 1956, PhD, 1958. Mem. faculty Haverford (Pa.) Coll., 1957-75, assoc. prof. chemistry, 1964-70, prof., 1970-75; provost, dean faculty Hobart and William Smith Colls., Geneva, N.Y., 1975-84, acting pres., 1978-79; dean faculty Hampshire Coll., 1984-87; dean acad. affairs Rhodes Coll., Memphis, 1987-93; prof. chemistry, dir. rsch. and sponsored programs LeMoyne-Owen Coll., Memphis, 1993-95, prof. chemistry, interim v.p. instl. advancement, 1996-97, 00-01, prof. chemistry, dir. internat. rsch. and planning, 1997—. Home: 2014 Hallwood Dr Memphis TN 38107-4703

DUNAWAY, CAROLYN BENNETT, retired sociology professor; b. Atlanta, Mar. 3, 1943; d. Clarence Rhodes and Gay (McKenzie) Bennett; m. William Preston Dunaway, Aug. 26, 1967; 1 child, Robert Bennett Dunaway. BA in Social Scis., Auburn U., 1966, EdD, 1983; MA in Sociology, U. Ala., Tuscaloosa, 1967. Instr. sociology Jefferson State C.C., Birmingham, Ala., 1967-69; prof. Auburn U., Montgomery, Ala., 1970-71; prof. sociology and gerontology dept. Jacksonville (Ala.) State U., 1971-95, prof. emeritus, 1999—. Student counselor Jacksonville State U., Ala., 1971—. Contbd. articles to profl. jours. Cons., trainer Calhoun County Hospice Anniston, Ala., 1983—; presenter Calhoun County Gerontology, Anniston, 1985—; officer Jacksonville Book Club, Ala., 1984; elder, tchr. First Presbyn. Ch., Jacksonville, 1993. Recipient 100 Most Outstanding Women Alumna award Auburn U., 1991, U. Rsch. award Jacksonville State U., 1989. Mem. Ala.-Miss. Sociol. Assn. (v.p. 1975-76, Sociology Club, Inter-Se Study Club, Ala. Fedn. Womens Club (dist. sect.), Phi Kappa Phi, Kappa Delta Pi, Delta Delta Delta, Phi Delta Kappa. Democrat. Presbyn. Avocations: flower arranging, gardening, reading. Home: 902 11th St NE Jacksonville AL 36265-1230 Office Phone: 256-435-3231.

DUNAWAY, FAYE (DOROTHY DUNAWAY), actress; b. Bascom, Fla., Jan. 14, 1941; d. John and Grace D.; m. Peter Wolf, Aug. 7, 1974 (div. 1979); m. Terrence O'Neill, 1983 (div. 1987); 1 child, O'Neill. Student, U. Fla., Boston U. Appearances include as original mem. Lincoln Ctr. Repertory Co., N.Y.C., off-Broadway in Hogan's Goat; also in (play) Curse of the Aching Heart, 1982; motion picture appearances include Bonnie and Clyde, 1967, Hurry Sundown, 1967, Puzzle of a Downfall Child, The Happening, 1967, The Thomas Crown Affair, 1968, A Place For Lovers, 1969, The Arrangement, 1969, The Extraordinary Seaman, 1969, Little Big Man, 1970, The Puzzle of a Downfall Child, 1970, Doc, 1971, La Maison Sous les Arbres, 1971, Oklahoma Crude, 1973, The Three Musketeers, 1973, Chinatown, 1974, The Towering Inferno, 1974, The Four Musketeers, 1975, Three Days of the Condor, 1975, Network, 1976 (Acad. award for Best Actress), The Voyage of the Damned, 1976, The Eyes of Laura Mars, 1978, The Champ, 1979, The First Deadly Sin, 1980, Mommie Dearest, 1981, The Wicked Lady, 1982, Ordeal by Innocence, 1984, Supergirl, 1984, Barfly, 1987, Burning Secret, 1988, La Partita, 1988, Midnight Crossing, 1988, The Gamble, 1989, On a Moonlit Night, 1989, Wait Until Spring, Bandini, 1989, The Handmaid's Tale, 1990, Three Weeks in Jerusalem, 1990, Scorchers, 1990, Arrowtooth Waltz, 1991, Double Edge, 1992, Arizona Dream, 1993, The Temp, 1993, Even Cowgirls Get the Blues, 1994, Don Juan DeMarco, 1995, En brazos de la mujer madura, 1996, The Chamber, 1996, Albino Alligator, 1996, Dunston Checks In, 1996, Twilight of the Golds, 1997, Drunks, 1997, Fanny Hill, 1998 Love Lies Bleeding, 1999, The Messenger: The Story of Joan of Arc, 1999, The Thomas Crown Affair, 1999, The Yards, 2000, Stanley's Gig, 2000, Changing Hearts, 2002, The Rules of Attraction, 2002, Mid-Century, 2002, The Calling, 2002, Blind Horizon, 2004, The Last Goodbye, 2004, El Padrino, 2004, Jennifer's Shadow, 2004, Ghosts Never Sleep, 2004, Love Hollywood Style, 2005; TV movies: Hogan's Goat, 1971, The Woman I Love, 1972, After the Fall, 1974, The Disappearance of Aimee, 1976, Evita Peron, 1981, The Country Girl, 1982, 13 at Dinner, 1985, Beverly Hills Madame, 1986, Raspberry Ripple, 1986, Casanova, 1987, Cold Sassy Tree, (co-exec. prodr.), 1989, Silhouette, 1990 (co-exec. prodr.), Columbo: It's All in the Game (Emmy award for Guest Actress in Drama 1994), Mother Love, 1995, A Family Divided, 1995, The People Next Door, 1996, Rebecca, 1997, Twilight of the Golds, 1997, Gia, 1998, A Will of Their Own, 1998, Running Mates, 2000, The Biographer, 2002, Anonymous Rex, 2004, Back When We Were Grownups, 2004; TV appearances: Seaway, 1965, The Trials of O'Brien, 1966, Road to Avonlea, 1995, Touched By An Angel, 2001, Soul Food, 2002, Alias, 2002, 03; TV miniseries: Ellis Island, 1984, Christopher Columbus, 1985; TV series: It Had To Be You, 1993, A Will of Their Own, 1998, Starlet, 2005-; Acted, dir, prodr. (films): The Yellow Bird, 2001; Author: Looking for Gatsby: My Life, 1995. Recipient Most Promising Newcomer Award Brit. Film Acad., 1968*

DUNAWAY, LEAH DECKER, training specialist; b. Repton, Ala., Aug. 6, 1940; d. John Benjamin and Mildren (Jennings) Brown; children: Andrea, Caroline. BS, U. Houston, 1961, MS, 1970, EdD, 1983, postgrad. in Indsl.-Orgnl. Psychology, 1987—. Tchr. Tex. Pub. Schs., 1961-70; asst. editor, Darien (Conn.) News, 1971-72; ednl. cons. State of Tex., Houston, 1979-82; instructional technologist NL Petroleum Services, Houston, 1982-83; sr. tng. analyst Exxon Prodn. Research, Houston, 1983—. Writer, editor, cons. for various tech. tng. manuals for petroleum industry, 1982—. Vol. St. Luke's Emergency Room, Houston, 1980, St. Joseph Hosp., Houston, 1978; mem. Tex. Sesquicentennial Com. Mem. Am. Soc. Tng. and Devel. (pres.-elect Houston chpt. 1988), Jr. League Houston, Nat. Soc. for Performance and Instrn. (pres. 1987), Park People. Avocations: social systems, travel, ecology, archeology, restorations of homes and furniture. Office: Exxon Prodn Research Co PO Box 2189 Houston TX 77252-2189

DUNAWAY, WILLIAM PRESTON, retired school system administrator; b. Lineville, Ala., June 30, 1936; s. Robert Johnson and Zylpha Mae (Preston) D.; m. Carolyn Bennett, Mar. 3, 1943; 1 child, Robert Bennett. BS, Jacksonville (Ala.) State U., 1959; MEd, Auburn (Ala.) U., 1966; AA, U. Ala., 1972; EdD, U. Miss., 1974. Tchr. math. Clay County High Sch., Ashland, Ala., 1960-61, Benjamin Russell High Sch., Alexander City, Ala., 1961-65; asst. supt. Alexander City Bd. Edn., 1965-67; asst. prin. Erwin High Sch., Birmingham, Ala., 1967-70; headmaster St. James Sch., Montgomery, Ala., 1970-71; prin. Anniston (Ala.) High Sch., 1971-73; prof. Sch. Adminstrn. Jacksonville (Ala.) State U., 1974-91, prof. emeritus, 1993—. Cons. in field; computer edn. dir. Jacksonville State U., 1983-91. Contbr. articles to profl. jours. Boy scout and cub scout master, bd. dirs. coun. Boy Scouts Am., Anniston, contbr. Handicapped Scouting Manual 1980; officer, tchr., First Presbyn. Ch., Jacksonville, 1975—; mem. Jacksonville Housing Authority Commn., 1992—, vice chair, 1993—; founding mem. Nat. Campaign for Tolerance, Wall of Tolerance. Capt. U.S. Army Res. and N.G., 1954-68. Recipient Jacksonville State U. Research award, 1988, Citizen of Yr. award, 1984; grantee Ala. Commn. on Higher Edn., 1986, ROTC Alumni Civilian Excellence award, 2004. Mem. Nat. Assn. Secondary Sch. Prins., Am. Assn. Sch. Adminstrs., Coun. for Computer Edn., Assn. Pub. Housing and Devel., Kiwanis, Sierra Club, Kappa Delta Pi, Phi Delta Kappa. Democrat. Avocations: computer enthusiast, landscape gardening, environmental issues, church and civic activities. Home and Office: 902 11th St NE Jacksonville AL 36265-1230

DUNBACK, M. KATHLEEN MEYER, literature and language educator; b. Kansas City, Feb. 24, 1948; d. Arthur Hopkins and Mary Sue (Abell) Meyer; m. Steven J. Dunback, Dec. 27, 1972; children: Kimberly Dunback Bentrott, Christopher. BA in Modern Langs., Kans. State U., 1970. Tchr. French, English Belleville High Sch., Kans., 1970—71, 1972—74; tchg. asst. Kans. State U., Manhattan, 1971—72; founder, dir. Belleville Area Free U., 1974—81; tchr. secondary sch. French, English, drama C-H-B Schs., Chester, Nebr., 1984—2001; tchr. secondary sch. English, world langs., drama Thayer Ctrl. Cmty. Schs., Hebron, 2001—. Dir. state qualifying drama teams C-H-B High Sch., 1989—2000. Co-founder Thayer Ctrl. Mid. Sch. Core Curriculum, 2001—02; fundraiser UNICEF, NYC, 1971. Mem.: NEA, Nebr. State Edn. Assn. (negotiatoe 1997—99, 2000—, sec. 1993—95). Democrat. Methodist. Avocations: writing, drawing, travel, Celtic heritage, classical music. Office: Thayer Ctrl High Sch PO Box 9 Hebron NE 68370-0009

DUNBAR, BONNIE J., engineer, astronaut; b. Sunnyside, Wash., Mar. 3, 1949; d. Robert Dunbar; m. Ronald M. Sega. BS in Ceramic Engring., U. Wash., 1971, MS in Ceramic Engring. cum laude, 1975; PhD in Biomed. Engring., U. Houston, 1983. With Boeing Computer Svcs., 1971-73; sr. rsch. engr. space div. Rockwell Internat., Downey, Calif.; with NASA, 1978—, astronaut, 1981—, mission specialist flight STS 61-8, 1985, mission specialist flight STS-32, 1990, payload commander Shuttle Columbia Flight, 1992, spl. asst. to dep. assoc. adminstr. Washington, 1993, with mission STS-71 Shuttle Atlanis, 1995, with mssion STS-89 Shuttle Endeavour, 1998, asst. dir. univ. rsch. Johnson Space Ctr. Vis. scientist Harwell Labs., Oxford, Eng., 1975; adj. asst. prof. mech. engring. U. Houston, mem. bioengring. adv. group; adj. prof. mech. engring. U. Houston.; bd. dirs. Arnold Air Soc., Angel Flight, Internat. Acad. Astronautics, Exptl. Aircraft Assn., Soc. Women Engrs. Recipient Nat. Engring. award Am. Assn. Engring. Socs., 1992, Engring. Achievement award Design News, 1993, Judith Resnik award IEEE, 1993, Resnik Challenger Medal Soc. Women Engrs., 1993; named to Hall of Fame Women in Tech. Internat., 2000. Mem. AAAS, NSF (engring. adv. bd. 1993-), NAE, Am. Ceramics Soc. (life, Greaves-Walker award 1985, Schwalt Zwalder PACE award 1990, James I. Mueller award, 2000), Soc. Biomed. Engring., Materials Rsch. Soc., Nat. Inst. Ceramic Engrs., Arnold Air Soc. and Angel Flight (bd. dirs.), Keramos, Tau Beta Pi. Achievements include research in ceramics that played a key role in developing the ceramic tiles used in the space shuttle's thermal protection system; first woman assigned to a laboratory mission to operate the Spacelab, its subsystems and experiments.

DUNBAR, HOLLY JEAN, communications executive, public relations executive; b. Plainfield, N.J., May 15, 1960; d. Robert Kenneth and Marian (DuBets) D. BA, Rutgers U., 1982. Graphic designer Chubb & Son, Inc., Warren, N.J., 1983-86; freelance writer, 1984—; pub. rels. rep., archivist AT&T Bell Labs., Warren, 1987; self-employed graphic designer North Plainfield, N.J., 1987-88; direct response mktg. coord. U.S. and Can. Beneficial Mgmt. Corp. of Am., Peapack, NJ, 1988-94; internal comms. mgr. Beneficial Mgmt. Corp., Peapack, NJ, 1994—98; dir. comms. and mktg. Somerset County United Way, Somerville, NJ, 1998—. Photographer: (survey) Tark Farm Site Monmouth Battlefield, 1982, Ellis Island Restoration, 1988-92; designer: Official Logo and Slogan of Somerset County, N.J., 1985 (Winning entry). Recipient Photography awards Cook Coll., New Brunswick, N.J., 1981, Chubb & Son, Inc., Warren, 1984, N.J. Agrl. Fair, 1994; Outstanding Svc. to 4-H award Somerset County 4-H, Somerville, 1996, Outstanding Alumna, Somerset Co. 4-H, 1999, Outstanding Vol., 2000; cited for Distinctive Contbr. N.J. Culture and History Am. Studies Dept., Douglass Coll., New Brunswick, 1982, numerous others; recognized for vol. efforts and participation Somerset County Bd. Chosen Freeholders, Somerville, N.J., 1996, 2003. Mem. DAR (nat. vice chmn. pub. rels.-print media 2001-2004, dep. rep. Nat. Soc to Vet. Affairs Vol. Svc., 1983-92, state chmn. Am. Heritage-Art N.J. Soc. 1989-92, state chmn. N.J. Jr. Mem. Centennial Project N.J. Soc. 1991-92, nat. and N.J. state page 1983-2000, regent Elizabeth Snyder chpt. 1992-95, registrar, 1991-92, Continental Congress Thatcher award 1992, state chmn. DAR Mag. Advt. N.J. Soc. 1992-95, Ad Excellence award, 1993, 94, state corr. sec. N.J. soc. 1995-98, state chmn. Conservation N.J. Soc., 1998—, Outstanding Jr. Mem. N.J. Soc. 1996), N.J. Audubon Soc., Internat. Assn. Bus. Communicators, Douglass Coll. Alumnae Assn., Somerset County 4-H Assn. (4-H fair publicity com.), Am. Birding Assn., Clan Dunbar. Avocations: history of New Jersey, genealogy, liturgical art, birdwatching, travel. Home: 725 Ayres Ave North Plainfield NJ 07063-1607

DUNBAR, LEILA, antiques appraiser, auction house executive; Graduate in Journalism and Spanish, U. N.C., 1983. Appraiser Dunbar's Gallery, Milford, Mass., 1984—91, pres., 1991—99; regular featured appraiser PBS' Antiques Roadshow, 1996—; sr. v.p., dir. collectibles dept., global dir. online collectibles auctions Sotheby's, N.Y.C., 1999—. Jazz staff mem. WGBH-FM, Boston. Contbr. Downbeat Mag., Reuters News Svc., profl. pubs. including USA Today, AP, N.Y. Times, GQ, N.Y. Daily News, London Standard, New Orleans Picayune, Chgo. Sun-Times, Auction Universe, others; author: Motorcycle Collectibles, 1996, More Motorcycle Collectibles, 1997, Automobilia, 1998. Office: Global Dir Online Collectibles Auctions Sothebys 1334 York Ave New York NY 10021

DUNBAR, LESLIE WALLACE, writer, consultant; b. Lewisburg, W.Va., Jan. 27, 1921; s. Morrison Leslie and Minnie (Crickenberger) Lee; m. Peggy Rawls, July 5, 1942; 1 foster child, Nha Van children: Linda Dunbar Knox, Anthony Paul. MA, Cornell U., 1946, PhD, 1948. Asst. prof. polit. sci. Emory U., Atlanta, 1948-51; chief community affairs Savannah River plant AEC, Aiken, S.C., 1951-54; asst. prof. polit. sci. Mt. Holyoke Coll., 1955-58; dir. research So. Regional Council, Atlanta, 1958-61, exec. dir., 1961-65; exec. dir., sec. Field Found., N.Y.C., 1965-80; vis. prof. polit. sci. U. Ariz., 1981. Cons. Fund for Peace, Nat. Urban League, 1981-84; sr. project assoc. social welfare policy, 1985-87, Ford Found.; guardian ad litem State of N.C., 1993-2001. Author: A Republic of Equals, 1966, The Common Interest, 1988, Reclaiming Liberalism, 1990, The Shame of Southern Politics, 2002; co-author: Where We Stand, 2004; co-author, editor: Minority Report, 1984; book rev. editor So. Changes, 1989-93. Deacon Watts St. Bapt. Ch., Durham, 1998—2001; bd. dirs. Nation Inst., 1980—86, pres., 1980—84; bd. dirs. Village of Pelham Libr. Bd., 1980—84, pres., 1982—84; bd. dirs. Children's Found., 1980—86, pres., 1982—84, Franklin and Eleanor Roosevelt Inst., 1987—2001, v.p., 1987—92; bd. dirs. Eleanor Roosevelt Inst., 1976—87, Field Found., 1978—80, Minority Rights Group, N.Y.C, 1980—85, Ctr. Nat. Security Studies, 1980—87, Amnesty Internat./U.S.A., 1984—86, Winston Found. for World Peace, 1985—89, Voter Edn. Project, 1987—90, N.C. Coun. Chs., 1991—93, Southeastern Efforts Developing Sustainable Staples, Inc., 1998—2001, Ruth Mott Fund, 1988—99, chair, 1992—94; bd. dirs., mem. selection com. Windcall REsident Program, 1990—94. Guggenheim fellow, 1954-55; United Negro Coll. Fund scholar-at-large, 1984-85. Fellow So. Regional Coun. (life). Home: 3050 Military Rd NW Washington DC 20015 E-mail: lesdunbar@earthlink.net.

DUNBAR, MARY ASMUNDSON, communications executive, public information officer, consultant, investor; b. Sacramento, Calif., Feb. 6, 1942; d. Vigfus Samundur and Aline Mary (McGrath) Asmundson; m. Robert Copeland Dunbar, June 21, 1969; children: Geoffrey Townsend, William Asmundson. BA in English Lit., Smith Coll., 1964; MA in Comm., Stanford U., 1967; MBA in Fin., Case Western Res. U., 1985. Cert. pub. rels. profl. Tchr. Peace Corps, Cameroun, Africa, 1964-66; writer, editor Ednl. Devel. Corp., Palo Alto, Calif., 1967-68, Addison-Wesley, Menlo Park, Calif., 1969-70; freelance writer, editor various cos., Cleve., 1970-85; account exec. Edward Howard & Co., Cleve., 1985-87, Dix & Eaton, Inc., Cleve., 1987-89, sr. account exec., 1990-92, v.p., 1992-96, sr. v.p., 1997—. Author publs. in field. Trustee Cleve. Coun. World Affairs, 1994—99. Smith Coll. scholar, Northampton, Mass., 1960-64; fellowship Stanford Univ., Palo Alto, Calif., 1967; recipient Internat. Assn. Bus. Comm. award, 1987, Women in Comm.

award, 1987, Arthur Page award, 1990. Mem. Smith Coll. Club Cleve., Pub. Rels. Soc. Am. (Silver Anvil award 1997), Nat. Investor Rels. Inst. (past pres. Cleve.-No. Ohio chpt., nat. bd. dirs. 2002, chmn. bd. 2005—), CFA Soc. Cleve. Republican. Episcopalian. Avocations: yoga, music. Home: 2880 Fairfax Rd Cleveland OH 44118-4014 Office: Dix & Eaton Inc 200 Public Square Ste 1400 Cleveland OH 44114-2316 Office Phone: 216-241-4601. Business E-Mail: mdunbar@dix-eaton.com.

DUNBAR, MAURICE VICTOR, English language educator; b. Banner, Okla., May 24, 1928; s. Moyer Haywood and Louise Edna (Curry) D.; m. Carol Ann Cline, July 28, 1948 (div. 1963); children: Kurt, Karl, Karla, Karen, Kristen. AA, Compton Jr. Coll., 1948; BA, U. Calif., Berkeley, 1952; MA, Calif. State U., Sacramento, 1965. Elem. tchr. Lone Tree Sch., Beale AFB, Calif., 1962-64; tchr. Anna McKenney Jr. H.S., Marysville, Calif., 1964-66, Yuba City (Calif.) H.S., 1966-67; instr. Foothill Coll. Jr. Coll., Los Altos Hills, Calif., 1967-82; prof. English, De Anza Coll., Cupertino, Calif., 1982-98; ret., 1998. Author: Fundamentals of Book Collecting, 1976, Books and Collectors, 1980, Collecting Steinbeck, 1983, Hooked on Books, 1997; contbr. articles to profl. jours. With U.S. Army, 1948-58, PTO. Mem. Masons, Shriners (orator, libr. 1982—), B'nai B'rith. Avocations: book collecting, reading, travel, visiting university campuses.

DUNBAR, PRESCOTT NELSON, investment company executive; b. New Orleans, Feb. 22, 1942; s. Lewis D. Prescott and Eleanor (Nelson) D.; m. Sarah W. Blodgett, Feb. 10, 1969; children: P. Hayden, Lander G. BA, U. of South, 1964; MA, La. State U., 1967; MA (Ford fellow), Harvard U., 1969. Financier, New Orleans. Author: History of the New Orleans Museum of Art: The First 75 Years, 1990, The History of the Normans, 2004. Trustee New Orleans Mus. Art, 1974-93, 97-2000, chmn. of accessions, 1977, 98-99, 01, treas., 1978, 1st v.p., 1979, sec. 1982, 86, 2d v.p. 1984-85; pres. of fellows, 1993, 96-97, v.p. 2001, hon. life trustee 2002—; trustee New Orleans Ballet, 1983-87, English Speaking Union New Orleans, 1986—, Friends of French Market, 1984, pres. 1985, U. of the South, 1989-91; bd. dirs. Save Our Cemeteries, 1975-86, Anglo-Am. Mus. Friends, 1985, La. Soc. Prevention of Cruelty to Animals, 1981-84, Friends of Stage Harbor Waterways, 1982—; adv. bd. Newcomb Coll. Art Gallery, 2000—; trustee New Orleans Internat. Ballet Conf., Inc., 1999, v.p., 2000; co-chmn. Ballet Russes Celebration Gala, 2000. Mem. SAR, La. Hist. Soc., Friends of Cabildo, Friends of Winterthur, Provincetown Art Assn., Am. Assn. Mus. Trustees, Royal Order of Soc. St. George, Stage Harbor Yacht Club, Chatham Beach and Tennis Club, Harvard Club of N.Y., New Orleans Country Club, Internat. House Club, Internat. Dendrology Soc. Democrat. Episcopalian. Home and Office: 2423 Prytania St New Orleans LA 70130

DUNBAR, ROBERT EVERETT, writer, educator; b. Quincy, Mass., Nov. 24, 1926; s. Charles Wheeler Dunbar and Eva Emma Duquette; m. Thelma Rose Arseneault, June 26, 1954 (div. Apr. 1986); children: Yvette Maria Dunbar Orsini, Jesse Robert. BA, Marietta Coll., 1951; MS, Northwestern U., 1954. Asst. editor publs. Continental Assurance Co., Chgo., 1954—57; dir. comm. Jr. Achievement, Chgo., 1957—58; editor Nat. Sporting Goods Assn., Chgo., 1958—67; dir. comm. Am. Soc. Anesthesiologists, Park Ridge, Ill., 1967—70; dir. pub. info. divsn. Am. Fund for Dental Health, Chgo., 1970—74; owner Dunbar Editl., Nobleboro and Gardiner, Maine, 1974—; internet bookseller Christie Books, Gardiner, Maine, 2004—. Instr. U. Health Sci., Chgo. Med. Sch., 1973—74, adj. asst. prof., 1974—75. Columnist: Maine Life Mag., 1981—86; author: Learning How to Cope with Arthritis, Rheumatism, and Gout, 1973 (Beth Fonda award for Excellence, Chgo. area chpt., Am. Med. Writers Assn., 1974), How to Debate, 1987, (15 books including) Homosexuality, 1996 (named one of the Notable Books of 1996, Nat. Coun. Social Studies and Children's Books Coun.), (books for musicals) Vaudeville Gold, 1987, Friends and Lovers, 1988, Folk and Fancy, 1991; co-author: (stage adaptation) It's A Wonderful Life, 1986. Pres. Saint Andrew's Soc. Maine, 1980—81; first selectman Nobleboro, Maine, 1977—78. With USN, 1944—45. Fellow: Am. Med. Writers Assn. (pres. Chgo. area chpt. 1970—71, gen. chmn. ann. meeting 1971, nat. co-chmn. 1971—75, edn. com. 1971—75, founder, chmn. organizing com. New Eng. chpt. 1975—76, treas. New Eng. chpt. 1976—77, Judith Linn mem. award com. 2001—); mem.: Thoreau Soc., Authors Guild, New Eng. Sci. Writers, Nobleboro Hist. Soc. (pres. 1978—79), Gaslight Theater. Republican. Roman Catholic. Achievements include design of two courses in sci. writing, one basic, one advanced, for Sch. Related Health Scis., U. Health Sci., Chgo. Med. Sch. Avocations: singing, acting. Address: 830 Water St Gardiner ME 04345 Office Phone: 207-588-2065. Personal E-mail: robbiedun@yahoo.com.

DUNCAN, A. BAKER, investment banker; b. Waco, Tex., Dec. 29, 1927; s. A. Baker and Frances (Higginbotham) Duncan; m. Sally P Witt, Jan. 31, 1953; children: Addison Baker III, Richard Witt, Andrew Prescott. Grad., Woodberry Forest (Va.) Sch., 1945; BA, Yale U., 1949; MA, U. Tex., 1952. Master Hill Sch., Pottstown, Pa., 1949-51; ptnr. Rotan Mosle & Co. (investment bankers), Houston, 1953—61; headmaster Woodberry Forest Sch., 1962-70; sr. v.p., dir. Rotan Mosle Inc., 1970-78; chmn. Duncan-Smith Co., 1978—. Bd dirs SW Research Inst; gov emeritus Tex Mil Inst; chmn. devel. com. Episcopal Diocese W. Tex. Mem.: Chi Psi. Democrat. Episcopalian. Home: 610 Garraty Rd San Antonio TX 78209-6149 Office: 711 Navarro Ste 740 San Antonio TX 78205-1786 Office Phone: 210-223-9807. E-mail: mvaaler@duncansmith.com.

DUNCAN, ALLYSON K., federal judge; b. Durham, NC, Sept. 5, 1951; BA, Hampton U., 1972; JD, Duke U., 1975. Bar: N.C. 1975, D.C. 1977. Assoc. editor Lawyers Coop. Publ. Co., 1976—77; law clk. to Hon. Julia Cooper Mack DC Ct. Appeals, 1977—78; appellate atty., asst. to dep. gen. counsel, asst. to chmn. EEOC, 1978—86; assoc. prof. NC Ctrl. U. Sch. Law, 1986—90; assoc. judge NC Ct. Appeals, 1990; commr. NC Utilities Commn., 1991—98; ptnr. Kilpatrick Stockton LLP, Raleigh, NC, 1998—2003; judge US Ct. Appeals (4th cir.), 2003—. Mem.: Wake County Bar Assn. (pres. 2002—03), N.C. Bar Assn. (pres.-elect 2002). Office: Kilpatrick Stockton LLP Ste 400 3737 Glenwood Ave Raleigh NC 27612*

DUNCAN, BRUCE W., real estate company executive, hotel executive; BS in Econ., Kenyon Coll., 1973; MBA, U. Chgo., 1975. Various positions JMB Instl. Realty Corp., Chgo., 1978—92, pres., co-CEO, 1992—94; chmn., pres., CEO Cadillac Fairview Corp., Toronto, Canada, 1995—2000; pres. Equity Residential, Chgo., 2002—03, pres., CEO, 2003—; dir. Starwood Hotels & Resorts Worldwide, 1999—, chmn., 2005—. Trustee Amresco Capital Trust; mem., partnership com. Rubenstein Co. LP, 2001—; bd. trustees Equity Residential, Chgo., 2002—. Office: Equity Residential 2 N Riverside Plaza Chicago IL 60606*

DUNCAN, CHARLES WILLIAM, JR., investor, retired federal official; b. Houston, Sept. 9, 1926; s. Charles William and Mary Lillian (House) D.; m. Thetis Anne Smith, June 10, 1957; children: Charles William III, Mary Anne. BSChemE, Rice U., 1947; postgrad. mgmt., U. Tex., 1948-49. Roustabout, chem. engr. Humble Oil & Refining Co., 1947; with Duncan Foods Co., Houston, 1948-64, adminstrv. v.p., 1957-58, pres., chmn. adv. bd., 1958-64; pres. Coca-Cola Co. Food Div., Houston, 1964-67; chmn. Coca-Cola Europe, 1967-70; exec. v.p. Coca-Cola Co., Atlanta, 1970-71, pres., 1971-74; chmn. bd., dir. Rotan Mosle Fin. Corp., Houston, 1974-77; dep. sec. Dept. Def., Washington, 1977-79; sec. Dept. Energy, Washington, 1979-81. Trustee emeritus, past chmn. Rice U.; bd. dirs. The Meth. Hosp.; treas. The Meth. Hosp. With USAAF, 1944-46. Mem. Coun. Fgn. Rels., Houston Country Club, River Oaks Country Club, Allegro Club, Sigma Alpha Epsilon, Sigma Iota Epsilon. Methodist. Home: 2 Briarwood Ct Houston TX 77019-5801 Office: 600 Travis St Ste 6100 Houston TX 77002-3007

DUNCAN, CHRISTOPHER, information technology executive; Global leader e-comm. tech. The Dow Chem. Co., Midland, Mich. Named one of premier 100 IT leaders, Computer World, 2003. Office: The Dow Chem Co 2030 Dow Ctr Midland MI 48674

DUNCAN, CONSTANCE CATHARINE, psychologist, educator, researcher; b. Watertown, Wis., Nov. 2, 1948; d. Howard Burton and Mary Elizabeth (Fagan) Duncan; m. R.E. Johnson, Jr., 1974 (div. 1984); m. Allan Franklin Mirsky, July 4, 1986. BA, Northwestern U., 1970; AM, U. Ill., 1973, PhD, 1978. Sr. rsch. analyst Adolf Meyer Mental Health Ctr., Decatur, Ill., 1971-73; asst. in rsch. and tchg. dept. psychology U. Ill., Champaign, 1974-78; NIMH postdoctoral fellow in neurosis. Stanford U. Sch. Medicine, Palo Alto, Calif., 1978-81; rsch. psychologist VA Med. Ctr., Palo Alto, 1978-81; sr. staff fellow Lab. Psychology and Psychopathology, NIMH, 1981-88; chief unit on psychophysiology NIMH, Bethesda, Md., 1982-89, rsch. psychologist, 1988-89, rsch. specialist, 1989-93; pvt. practice Bethesda, Md., 1981—. Adj. assoc. prof. Johns Hopkins Sch. Hygiene and Pub. Health, Balt., 1987—; guest rschr. Lab. Psychology and Psychopathology NIMH, 1993—97, Sect. on Clin. and Exptl. Neuropsychology NIMH, 1997—; rsch. assoc. prof. Uniformed Svc. Univ. Health Sci., 1993—. Assoc. editor Psychophysiology, 1987-91; mem. editl. bd. Internat. Jour. Psychophysiology, 2002—; cons. editor numerous sci. jour.; contbr. articles to profl. jour., chpt. to books. Found. assoc. Nat. Women's Econ. Alliance; mem. NIMH/NINCDS Assembly of Sci. Coun., 1982-84. Recipient Nat. Rsch. Svc. award, NIMH, 1978-81, Golden Anniversary Scholarship award, AAUW, 1974; NIMH fellow, 1970-74. Fellow: APA (mem. awards com. 2001—), Internat. Orgn. Psychophysiology (mem. world congress com. 2004—, mem. working com. learning disabilities and attentional disorders 2005—), Am. Psychol. Soc.; mem.: EEG and Clin. Neurosci. Soc., Am. Psychopathol. Assn., Internat-.Neuropsychol. Soc., Soc. for Neurosci., Soc. for Rsch. in Psychopathology (bd. dir. 1986—88, membership com. 1987—88), Soc. for Psychophysiol. Rsch. (program com. 1979, 1980, nominating com. 1981, chmn. early career award com. 1981—84, program com. 1982, bd. dir. 1982—85, nominating com. 1983, chmn. conv. com. 1983—87, program com. 1986, chmn. program com. 1987, program com. 1988, nominating com. 1989, Blue Ribbon Panel on state of soc. in Yr. 2000 1990—93, chmn. enhancement com. 1992—93, chmn. early career award com. 1994—96, conv. com., sec.-treas. 1996—99, com. governance and ops. 2000—01, program com. 2001, sr. award com. 2001—04, chair sr. award com. 2002—03, pres. 2002—03, chair student award com. 2003—04, chair nominations com. 2004—05, chair nominating com. 2004—05, Early Career Contbn. award 1980), Phi Beta Kappa, Pi Mu Epsilon, Alpha Lambda Delta, Phi Kappa Phi, Sigma Xi, Shi-Ai, Mortar Bd. Achievements include electrophysiological and neuropsychological research on normal and disordered attn. and cognition. Office: Uniformed Svcs U Health Sci Dept Psychiatry Clin Psychophysiology & Psychopharm Lab 5502 Spruce Tree Ave Bethesda MD 20814-1623 Business E-Mail: connieduncan@mail.nih.gov.

DUNCAN, DAN L., gas company executive; With Wanda Petroleum, 1957—69; prin. EPCO Inc., Houston, 1969—70, pres., 1970—79, CEO, 1970—95, chmn., 1979—; chmn. & dir. Enterprise Products GP LLC Gen. Ptnr., Houston, 1998—. Bd. trustees Baylor Medical Coll. Office: Enterprise Products Ptnrs LP 2727 N Loop W Ste 700 Houston TX 77008-1037*

DUNCAN, DAVID EWING, editor, writer; Contbg. editor, writer Wired, Discover, Harper's, Atlantic Monthly, Smithsonian, Outside, NY Times, San Francisco Chronicle. Founder, editl. dir. BioAgenda; commentator Morning Edit. Nat. Pub. Radio; tchr. in field. Author: (book) Pedaling the Ends of the Earth, 1985, Calendar: Humanity's Epic Struggle to Determine a True and Accurate Year, 1998, Hernando de Soto: A Savage Quest in the Americas, 1996, Residents: The Perils and Promise of Educating Young Doctors, 1996, The Geneticist Who Played Hoops With My DNA, 2005; dir.: Grotto Nights; spl. corr., prodr. (television) Nightline ABC, 20/20; prodr.: (television) Discovery TV; corr., writer (television) ScienceNow PBS Nova sci. mag. program, founder, editl. dir. BioAgenda. Office: D2 Productions The Grotto 26 Fell St San Francisco CA 94102 Office Phone: 415-861-3795. E-mail: deduncan@literati.net.*

DUNCAN, DIANNE WALKER, elementary school educator; b. Altavista, Va., Nov. 15, 1954; d. Robert and Catherine Forte. BS in History and Govt., Longwood Coll., 1977; MEd in Curriculum and Instrn., Va. Commonwealth U., 1993. Cert. tchr. social studies. Social studies tchr. Stonewall Jackson Mid. Sch., Mechanicsville, Va., 1977—98; civics tchr. John Witherspoon Mid. Sch., Princeton, NJ. Cmty. svc. coach John Witherspoon Mid. Sch. Do Something, N.Y.C.; mem. Character Edn. Partnership, Washington, DC; character edn., citizenship presenter N.J. Edn. Assn. Conf., Atlantic City, 2001; mentor jr. level presvc. tchrs. Rider U., Lawrenceville, NJ, Princeton U., NJ. Mem. So. Poverty Law Ctr., Mont., Ala., 2001—; sponsor, coord. of food dr. John Witherspoon and Crisis Ministry Trenton and Princeton, 1999—2003; sponsor, supervise mid. sch. tutors Princeton Young Achievers After Sch. Programs, Princeton, 2000—03; mem. People to People Amb. Programs' Social Studies Edn. Del. to South Africa, 2004. Recipient John Marshall award for excellence in tchg. the Constn., Va. Ctrl. Region, 1995, Best Practices award in citizenship, character edn., N.J., 2000. Mem.: N.J. Edn. Assn., N.J. Coun. Social Studies, Nat. Coun. Social Studies, Assn. Supervision and Curriculum Devel. D-Liberal. Avocations: gardening, reading. Office: Princeton Regional Schs 217 Walnut Ln Princeton NJ 08540 Office Phone: 609-806-4270.

DUNCAN, DONALD WILLIAM, lawyer; b. Baldwin, Md., May 18, 1932; s. William Rush and Mary Alice (MacBlane); children: David (dec.), Lisa; m. Auria Adorno Duncan; 1 child, Roberto Millan. AA, U. Balt., 1956, JD, 1960. Bar: Md. 1960, Fla. 1992. Asso. Haynie & McFerrin, C.P.A., Balt., 1956-61; controller H.C. Weiskettel Co., Balt., 1961-62; v.p., counsel, sec., Balt. Aircoil Co., Inc., 1962-87; pvt. practice Palm Coast, Fla., 1987—. Mem. Md. Bar Assn., Fla. Bar. Republican. Presbyterian. Office: Donald W Duncan PA PO Box 352411 Palm Coast FL 32135-2411 Office Phone: 386-445-0500. E-mail: dwduncan@bellsouth.net.

DUNCAN, DONNA, artist; b. Oakland, Calif., May 5, 1952; d. Wiliam E. and Lucille A. Ward; m. Jeré Laurence Fournier, June 1970; 1 child, William F. Fournier; m. James Steven Duncan, Jan. 1976 (div. June 1984); children: Mary E. Duncan, Susan R. Duncan. AA in Arts and Scis., Sinte Gleska U., Rosebud, S.D., 1995; AA in Lakota Studies, Sinte Gleska U., 1998; BS in Interdisciplinary Studies, Sinte Gleska U., Rosebud, S.D., 1999; student, U. S.D. Layout/pasteup Fran's Printshop, Cottonwood, Ariz., 1990-91; illustration, freelance art Concord Calif., 1987-90; artist Mission, S.D., 1997—. Student exhbn. include Cottonwood, Ariz., 1991, Beresford, SD, 2001; one-woman shows include Coffee Shop Gallery, Vermillion, 2001, 03, Vermillion Arts Coun. Bldg., 2002; also group exhbn. Mem. Assn. Colored Pencil Assn. Am., Local C. of C. Democrat. Home: 501 W Cedar St Vermillion SD 57069-1906 Office: 501 W Cedar St Vermillion SD 57069-1906 E-mail: djduncan@peoplepc.com.

DUNCAN, DORIS GOTTSCHALK, information systems educator; b. Seattle, Nov. 19, 1944; d. Raymond Robert and Marian (Onstad) D.; m. Robert George Gottschalk, Sept. 12, 1971 (div. Dec. 1983). BA, U. Wash., Seattle, 1967, MBA, 1968; PhD, Golden Gate U., 1978. Cert. data processor, systems profl., computer profl., data educator. Comm. cons. Pacific N.W. Bell Tel. Co., Seattle, 1968-71; mktg. supr. AT&T, San Francisco, 1971-73; sr. cons., project leader Quantum Sci. Corp., Palo Alto, Calif., 1973-75; dir. co. analysis program Input Inc., Palo Alto, 1975-76; lectr. acctg. and info. systems Calif. State U., East Bay Hayward, Calif., 1976-78, assoc. prof. Hayward, 1978-85, prof., 1985—, coord. computer info. sys., 1994-97; dir. info. sci. dept. Golden Gate U., San Francisco, 1982-83, mem. info. systems adv. bd., 1983-85, co-advisor grad. program Computer Inf. Sys., e-bus. programs, 1999—. Vis. prof. U. Wash., Seattle, 1997-98; spkr., cons. in field. Author: Computers and Remote Computing Services, 1983; contbr. articles to profl. jours.; mem. editl. bd. Jour. Info. Sys. Edn., 1992-97, Jur. Info. Tech. Edn., Jour. Informatics Edn. Rsch., 2000-02, assoc. editor, 2003--. Loaned exec. United Good Neighbors, Seattle, 1969; nat. com. woman bd. dirs. Young Reps., Wash., 1970-71; advisor Jr. Achievement, San Francisco, 1971-72; nat. bd. Inst. for Certification of Computer Profls. Edn. Found., 1990-93; bd. dirs. Computer Repair Svcs., 1992-94, adv. bd. Ximnet Corp., 2000-02; mem. College Park Redistricting Commn., 2003. Recipient Disting. Rsch. award Allied Acads., 1999; named Computer Educator of Yr., Internat. Assn. Computer Info. Systems, 1997. Mem. Data Processing Mgmt. Assn. (Meritorious Svc. award, Bronze award 1984, Silver award 1986, Gold award 1988, Emerald award 1992, Diamond award 1994, Double Diamond award 1999, Triple Diamond award 2001, Nat. grantee, 1984, dir. edn. chmn. San Francisco chpt. 1984-85, sec. and v.p. 1985, pres. 1986, assn. dir. 1987, by-laws chmn. 1987, chair awards com. 1992-95, nat. bd. dirs. spl. interest group in edn. 1985-87), Soc. Profl. Journalists, Soc. Profl. Journalism., Am. Inst. Decision Scis., Western Assn. Schs. and Colls. (accreditation evaluation team 1984-85), Assn. Computing Machinery, Investigative Reporters and Editors, Assn. Edn. in Jurnalism and Mass Comm., Ea. Comm. Assn., Internat. Listening Assn., Jr. Club Seattle (Beautiful Home award Foster City 1994, 95, winner Tournament of Christmas Lights 1996, 2003), Bus. Honor Soc., Beta Gamma Sigma. Achievements include development of info. systems (info. science), curriculum development, professional certification, industry standards, computer literacy and user education, system analysis and design, design of databases and data banks, electronic commerce. Office: Calif State U East Bay Coll Bus and Econs Hayward CA 94542

DUNCAN, ED EUGENE, lawyer; b. Gary, Ind., Dec. 10, 1948; s. Attwood and Freddie Leon (Ballard) D.; m. Patricia Louise Revado, Sept. 8, 1973 (div.); children: Kristin, Anika, Gregory. BA, Oberlin Coll., 1970; JD, Northwestern U., 1974. Bar: Ohio 1974, U.S. Dist. Ct. (no. dist.) Ohio 1977, U.S. Supreme Ct. 1977. Assoc. Arter & Hadden, Cleve., 1974-82, ptnr., 1982—2003, Tucker Ellis & West, Cleve., 2003—. Bd. mem. Glenville br. YMCA, Cleve., 1979—, Ohio Bd. of Bldg. Standards, Columbus, 1986-89; trustee Legal Aid Soc., Cleve., 1990-91. Mem.: Cleve. Bar Assn., Ohio Bar Assn. Avocations: writing, reading. Home: 935 Roland Rd Cleveland OH 44124-1033 Office: Tucker Ellis & West 925 Euclid Ave Ste 1150 Cleveland OH 44115-1475 Office Phone: 216-696-2862. E-mail: EDuncan@TuckerEllis.com.

DUNCAN, FRANCES MURPHY, retired special education educator; b. Utica, NY, June 23, 1920; d. Edward Simon and Elizabeth Myers (Stack) Murphy; m. Lee C. Duncan, June 23, 1947 (div. June 1969); children: Lee C., Edward M., Paul H., Elizabeth B., Nancy R., Frances B.(dec.), Richard L.(dec.). BA, Columbia U., 1942; MEd, Auburn U., 1963, EdD, 1969. Head sci. dept. Arnold Jr. H.S., Columbus, Ga., 1960-63; tchr. physiology, Spanish Jordan H.S., Columbus, Ga., 1963-64; tchr. spl. edn. mentally retarded Muscogee County Sch. Sys., Columbus, Ga., 1964-65; instr. spl. edn. Auburn (Ala.) U., 1966-69; assoc. dir. Douglas Sch. for Learning Disabilities, Columbus, 1969-70; prof. edn. and spl. edn. Columbus Coll., 1970-85, ret., 1985. Past dir. Columbus Devel. Ctr.; past sec. exec. bd. Muscular Dystrophy Assn., 1968-70; 73-74; mem. Gov.'s Commn. on Disabled Georgians; past trustee Listening Eyes Sch. for Deaf; past mem. Mayor's Com. on Handicapped; mem. team for evaluation and placement of exceptional children Columbus Pub. Schs.; pres., Aux., Columbus Med. Ctr. Vol. Med. Ctr. Columbus Regional Healthcare Sys., Ga. Fellow Am. Assn. Mental Retardation; mem. AAUP, AAUW (pres. 1973-75, divsn. rec. sec. 1975—), Coun. Exceptional Children (legis. chmn. 1973-74), Psi Chi, Phi Delta Kappa. Roman Catholic. Home: 655 Spring Harbor Dr Columbus GA 31904 E-mail: duncanf@knology.com.

DUNCAN, FRANCIS, historian, retired government official; b. Oak Park, Ill., July 12, 1922; s. Fred B. and Olive (Whitney) Duncan; m. Frances M. Mergus, Aug. 16, 1947 (dec. June 2002); children: Evan, April. BA, Ohio Wesleyan U., 1944; MA, U. Chgo., 1947, PhD, 1954. Instr. history Wayne State U., Detroit, 1947-50; civilian employee Office of Intelligence, USAF, Washington, 1950-57; analyst Office of Controller, AEC, Washington, 1957-62, asst. historian, 1962-74; asso. historian div. naval reactors ERDA, 1974-77; historian div. naval reactors Dept. Energy, 1977-86, cons. hist. divsn., 1986-96. Author: Rickover and the Nuclear Navy, the Discipline of Technology, 1990, Rickover: The Struggle for Excellence, 2001; author: (with Richard G. Hewlett) Atomic Shield, 1969, Nuclear Navy 1946-1962, 1974; contbr. articles on naval history to profl. jours. Served with USNR, 1943-46. Recipient David D. Lloyd Prize in History 1970, Theodore and Franklin D. Roosevelt Naval History Prize, 1991. Mem. AAAS, U.S. Naval Inst., Naval Hist. Found., Nat. Coun. on Pub. History. Home: 9209 Ewing Dr Bethesda MD 20817-3313 E-mail: frncdunc9@aol.com.

DUNCAN, JOHN ALEXANDER, lawyer; b. Seattle, May 5, 1937; s. John A. Sr. and Elizabeth M. Duncan. BA in Econs., U. Wash., 1960; JD, U. Calif., San Francisco, 1963. Bar: Calif. 1964. Sole practice, Santa Ana, Calif., 1968-76, Newport Beach, Calif., 1976-93, Orange, Calif., 1993—. Lectr. estate and trust litigation Calif. Continuing Edn. of Bar, 1986—. Contbg. author: Estate and Trust Litigation, 2005. Fellow Am. Coll. Trust and Estate Counsel; mem. Orange County Bar Assn., Orange County Estate Planning Coun. (chair probate trust law sect. 1996). Office: 333 City Blvd W Ste 1420 Orange CA 92868-2992

DUNCAN, JOHN J., JR., congressman; b. Lebanon, Tenn., July 21, 1947; m. Lynn Hawkins; children: Tara, Whitney, John J. III, Zane. BS in Journalism, U. Tenn., 1969; JD, George Washington U., 1973. Bar: Tenn. 1973. Pvt. practice, Knoxville, Tenn., 1973-81; state trial judge, 1981-88; mem. U.S. Congress from 2nd Tenn. dist., Washington, 1989—; mem. transp. and infrastructure com., resources com., govt. reform com. Bd. dirs. or past bd. dirs. ARC, YWCA, Sunshine Ctr. for Mentally Retarded, Beck Black Heritage Ctr., Knoxville Union Rescue Mission, St. Citizens Home Aid Svc., Knoxville Girls Club, others; active elder Eastminster Presbyn. Ch. Capt. U.S. N.G. and Res. Named One of Top 5 Most Fiscally Conservative Mems. of House and Senate, Nat. Taxpayers Union; recipient Super Hero award Citizens Against Govt. Waste, Golden Bulldog award Watchdogs of Treasury, Inc., Hartranft award Airline Operators and Pilots Assn., 1998; honored by Ams. for Tax Reform, Nat. Fefn. Ind. Bus., Concord Coalition, U.S. C. of C., Citizens for Sound Economy. Mem. Am. Legion, Elks, Sertoma Club, 40&8, Masons, Shriners. Republican. Office: US Ho of Reps 2267 Rayburn House Office Bldg Washington DC 20515-4202*

DUNCAN, JOHN PATRICK CAVANAUGH, lawyer; b. Kalamazoo, Mich., Jan. 25, 1949; s. James H. and Colleen Patricia (Cloney) D.; children: Sarah Ellen, James Patrick Cloney. BA cum laude, Yale U., 1971; JD, U. Chgo., 1974. Bar: Ill. 1974, U.S. Dist. Ct. (no. dist.) Ill. 1974, U.S. Ct. Appeals (7th cir.) 1975, U.S. Supreme Ct. 1979, trial bar U.S. Dist. Ct. Assoc. firm Holleb & Coff, Chgo., 1974-79; mem., 1979-87; ptnr. Jones Day, Chgo., 1987-99; leader banking and investment practice area Jones, Day, Reavis & Pogue, Chgo., 1996-99; prin. Duncan Assocs., 2000—; founder Pvt. Trust Assn., 2000. Adj. prof. IIT Chgo.-Kent Coll. Law Fin. Svcs. LLM Program, 1988—; mem. Fulbright Vis. Scholar Adv. Bd., 1995—98; mem. Chgo. com. Chgo. Coun. on Fgn. Rels., 1998—2000; author fed. and state trust co. laws. Contbr. articles to profl. jours. Fellow NSF, 1970. Fellow: Ill. Bar Found.; mem.: ABA (chmn. securities activities banks subcom. 1995—98, privacy task force 1998—2001, banking com.), Ill. Bankers Assn. (legal affairs com. 1986—87), Chgo. Bar Assn. (chmn. fin. insts. com. 1985—86), Yale Club (Chgo., N.Y.). Home: 3814 N Paulina St Chicago IL 60613-2716 Office: Duncan Assocs 180 N LaSalle Ste 2410 Chicago IL 60601-3850 Office Phone: 312-580-4949. Business E-Mail: jpcd@jpcdlaw.com.

DUNCAN, LELAND RAY, retired mission administrator; b. Bee Branch, Ark., Nov. 9, 1929; s. Enoch R. and Julia C. (Lane) D.; m. M. Ruth Tindall, May 28, 1952; children: Wallace L., Gregory A. BA, Oakland City U., 1962; postgrad., So. Theol. Sem., 1966-67; DD, Oakland City U., 1974. Owner, oper. Twin City Radio & TV, North Little Rock, Ark., 1956-59; pastor Gen. Bapt. Chs., Ind., Ark., Ky. & Mo., 1959-71; exec. dir. Gen. Bapt. Home Missions, Poplar Bluff, Mo., 1972-97, pres., until 1997; ret., 1997. Chmn. com. to revise Gen. Bapt. Statements of Faith, 1968-71; founder Gen. Bapt. Investment Fund, Popular Bluff, 1974, pres., 1974—; chmn. nominating com. N.Am. Bapt. Fellowship, Washington, 1978, chmn. cons. on ch. planting, 1979; mem. Connect Mo., Jefferson City, 1994. Mem. Poplar BLuff PTA,

1969-73; pres. Poplar BLuff Min.'s Assn., 1971. With 7th infantry divns. U.S. Army, 1951-52, Korea. Mem. VFW, Am. Legion, Am. Woodcarvers Assn. Avocations: wood carving, gardening, walking, reading. Home: 3643 Mclane Dr Poplar Bluff MO 63901-8752

DUNCAN, LINDA M., elementary school educator; b. Dixon, Ill., July 23, 1946; d. Robert Lyle and Evelyn Marie Brown; m. Dan Curtis Duncan, Aug. 13, 1966; children: Douglas Allen, Darren Curtis. BS, Wis. State U., 1969; postgrad., No. Ill. U., Ill. State U.; postgrad. in Leadership, DePaul U., 2000—05. Tchr. Pecatonica Schs., 1975—. Chair sci. curriculum Pecatonica Elem. Sch., 2003—05; gifted coord. Pecatonica Schs., 1989—2004; coord. Pecatonica Invention Conv. Program, 1985—2005, Pecatonica Youth Authors, 1984—2005. Mem. adv. bd. Boone-Winnegabo Regional Office Edn., 1995—97, pres., 1996—97. Mem.: ASCD, Ill. Edn. Orgn., Ill. Sci. Tchrs. Assn. (bd. dirs. 1990—91), Kappa Delta Pi. Home: 482 Marstonmoor Rd Davis IL 61019 Office: Pecatonica Schs Dist 321 721 Reed St Pecatonica IL 61063

DUNCAN, LINDSAY VERE, actress; b. Edinburgh, Scotland, Nov. 7, 1950; m. Hilton McRae; 1 child, Cal. Attended, Ctrl. Sch. Speech and Drama, London. Actor: (films) Loose Connections, 1983, Prick Up Your Ears, 1987, Manifesto, 1988, Body Parts, 1991, The Reflecting Skin, 1991, A Midsummer Night's Dream, 1996, City Hall, 1996, An Ideal Husband, 1999, Mansfield Park, 1999, Star Wars: Episode 1 - The Phantom Menace, 1999, Under the Tuscan Sun, 2003, Afterlife, 2004 (Best Actress award, Bratislava Film Festival, Best Actress, Bownore Scottish Screen Awards); (TV series) Just William, 1977—78, Ace of Spies, 1983, Dead Head, 1986, Traffik, 1989 (FIPA Golden award, Cannes Internat. Film Festival, 1990), Jake's Progress, 1995, Get Real, 1998; (TV miniseries) G.B.H., 1991, A Year in Provence, 1993, The Rectors Wife, 1994, The History of Tom Jones, 1997, Oliver Twist, 1999, Shooting the Past, Perfect Strangers; (Broadway plays) Les Liaisons Dangereuses (Tony award nomination, 1987, Theatre World award, 1987), Top Girls (Obie award, 1982), A Midsummer Night's Dream, Ashes to Ashes (Drama Desk nomination), Celebration, The Room, Private Lives (winner Tony award for Best Performance by a Leading Actress in a Play, 2002, Drama Desk Best Actress award, 2002). Office: ICM Oxford House 76 Oxford St London W1D 1B5 England

DUNCAN, LIONEL SEBASTIAN, artist, educator; b. Cristobal, Canal Zone, Panama, Oct. 24, 1929; s. Lionel Joseph and Ruby Veronica Duncan; children: Valerie Babb, Joseph, Damaris, Zena. Lic. Physics, U. Argentina, 1965; MFA Painting, Towson State U., 1998; PhD Edn., U. So. Calif., 1971. Cert. Sch. Adminstr., L.A, 1973. Prof. edn. Morgan State U., Balt., 1971—, dir. distance edn., 1995—2001. Cons. US Agencies of Ed. Devel., Washington. Exhbn., Howard County of the Arts Exhibiton, 1997 (Honarary Mention, 1997). Bd. dirs. Internat. Associaton Knowledge Engrs., Washington. Grantee UN Fellowship to Argentina, Unesco, 1963—65. Mem.: Fulbright Alumni Assn. (life Fulbright Fellow 1976, 1985, 1998). Green Party. Roman Catholic. Avocation: travel. Home: 1444E Baltimore St Ste 2A Baltimore MD 21231 Office: Morgan State U 1700 E Cold Spring Ln Baltimore MD 21251 Office Phone: 443 885 3500. Fax: 410 319 3698. Personal E-mail: lionelsduncan@aol.com. Business E-Mail: lduncan@moac.morgan.edu.

DUNCAN, LYN M., pathology educator; MD, Washington U., 1986. Bd. cert. pathology, dermatopathology. Resident anatomic pathology Barnes Hosp., 1990; fellow dermatopathology Mass. Gen. Hosp., 1991; clin. faculty anatomic pathology; asst. prof. pathology, dir. dermatopathology tng. Harvard Med. Sch. Achievements include research in melanoma, lymphoma, pregnancy associated skin disease, pigmented lesions. Office: Mass Gen Hosp WRN 827 55 Fruit St Boston MA 02114-2696 Fax: 617-726-8711. E-mail: duncan@helix.mgh.harvard.edu.

DUNCAN, MARGARET CARLISLE, physical education educator; b. Norwalk, Conn., May 22, 1951; d. Hugh Scott and Jean Shepherd Duncan; m. Alan Aycock, Dec. 3, 1994; m. Barry Scott Brummett, July 7, 1973 (div.); children: Elizabeth Brummett, Katharine Duncan Brummett. BA, Macalester Coll., 1973; PhD, Purdue U., 1984. Asst. prof. U. Wis., Milw., 1985—91, assoc. prof., 1992—98, prof., 1998—. Editor: Play & Culture, 1991—92. Fellow: Am. Acad. Kinesiology and Phys. Edn.; mem.: Assn. Study Play (pres. 1994—95), N.Am. Soc. Sociology Sport (pres. 1995—96). Office: U of WI-Milwaukee Dept of HMS PO Box 413 Milwaukee WI 53201 Office Phone: 414-229-5341.

DUNCAN, MARGARET CAROLINE, physician; b. Salt Lake City, June 9, 1930; d. Donald and Margaret Aileen (Eberts) D.; m. N. Paul Arceneaux, Dec. 26, 1958; children: David Paul, Eleanor Anne, Stephen Louis, Andre. BA, U. Tex., 1952, MD, 1955. Intern Kings County Hosp., Seattle, 1955-56; resident in pediat. John Sealy Hosp., Galveston, Tex., 1956-58; resident in neurology Charity Hosp., New Orleans, 1958-60; fellow child neurology Johns Hopkins Hosp., Balt., 1960-61; mem. faculty La. State U. Med. Ctr., New Orleans, 1961—, prof. neurology and pediat., 1973-2000, prof. neurology emeritus, 2000—. Chmn. La. Com. Epilespy and Cerebral Palsy, 1976-79. Fellow Am. Acad. Neurology, Am. Acad. Pediat.; mem. Child Neurology Soc., Profs. Child Neurology, Alpha Omega Alpha. Episcopalian. Office: 1542 Tulane Ave New Orleans LA 70112-2825

DUNCAN, MARK, district attorney; b. Philadelphia, Miss. m. Joni Duncan; 1 child, Ben. BA in Banking and Finance, U. Miss., 1981; JD. Solo practice, Philadelphia, Miss., 1983; part time public defender, 1984—88; asst. dist. atty., 1988—2004; dist. atty. 8th Judicial Dist., 2004—. Achievements include prosecuted (with Atty. Gen. Jim Hood) Edgar Ray Killen for the 1964 triple murders of civil rights workers Andrew Goodman, James Chaney and Michael Schwerner, June 2005. Avocations: gourmet cooking, golf. Office: P O Box 603 Philadelphia MS 39350 Office Phone: 601-656-1991. Office Fax: 601-656-2287.*

DUNCAN, MARY ELLEN, academic administrator; b. N.Y.C., NY, Aug. 29, 1941; d. Harry and Mary (Laveglia) Fielder; 1 child, Kathryn Mary Dickens. BS, St. John's U., 1963; MA, U. Conn., 1973, PhD, 1982. Grad. rsch. asst. U. Conn., Storrs, 1971-75; instr. English and Latin West Islip Pub. Schs., N.Y.C., 1963-71; instr. Tri-County Tech. Coll., Pendleton, S.C., 1975-76, instrnl. assoc. ACCTion Ctr., 1976-82, dir. ea. region, 1980-82, dir. instnl. devel., 1982-83, dean, 1987-88; dean planning and devel. Catonsville Community Coll., Balt., 1988-89, 90-91, interim pres., 1989-90; pres. Tech. Coll. SUNY, Delhi, 1991—. Author: Indicators of Institutional Effectiveness, 1989. Recipient Merit award S.C. women in Higher Edn., 1985. Mem. Am. Assn. Community and Jr. Colls. (fed. rels. task force 1990-91, Merit award 1982, John Fry award 1981), Am. Assn. Women Community and Jr. Colls., Nat. Coun. Resource Devel. (legis. liaison 1990—). Avocation: golf. Home: 1236 Crows Foot Rd Marriottsville MD 21104-1445 Office: SUNY Coll Tech Delhi Delhi NY 13753

DUNCAN, MICHAEL CLARKE, actor; b. Chgo., Dec. 10, 1957; Actor, 1987—. Actor: (TV series) The Bold and the Beautirul, 1992—94, Skwids, 1996; (films) Friday, 1995, Back in Business, 1997, Caught Up, 1998, The Players Club, 1998, Bulworth, 1998, Armageddon, 1998, A Night at the Roxbury, 1998, Breakfast of Champions, 1999, The Green Mile, 1999, The Underground Comedy Movie, 1999, The Whole Nine Yards, 2000, Wrestlemania 2000, 2000, Soldier of Fortune, 2000, See Spot Run, 2001, The Immigrant Garden, 2001, Cats & Dogs, 2001, Planet of the Apes, 2001, They Call Me Sirr, 2001, Hollywood Digital Diaries, 2001, The Scorpion King, 2002, Daredevil, 2003, George and the Dragon, 2004, Pursued, 2004, (voice) Dinotopia: Curse of the Ruby Sunstone, 2004, Racing Stripes, 2005, The Island, 2005, numerous TV guest appearances. Office: Dolores Robinson Ent 9250 Wilshire Blvd Ste 220 Beverly Hills CA 90212-3344*

DUNCAN, PATRICIA DUBOSE, artist; b. Nashville, Aug. 16, 1932; d. Robert William and Edith Crump DuBose; m. Herbert Ewing Duncan Jr., July 10, 1954; children: David Ewing, Donald DuBose. Student, Phila. Mus. Sch., 1944; BFA, Washington U., St. Louis, 1954; postgrad., Kansas City Art Inst., 1967-71. Cons., lectr. in field; appeared on various radio and TV programs, including all Things Considered/Nat. Pub. Radio, 1977, Today Show/NBC, 1973, 75. One-woman shows include Smithsonian Instn., 1976—86, Stuhr Mus., Grand Island, Nebr., 1977, So. Ill., U., Carbondale, Ill., 1977, The Octagon, Washington, 1977, Union Carbide, N.Y.C., 1977, Aspen (Colo.) Inst., 1978, Sears Bldg., Chgo., 1979, Nikon House, N.Y.C., 1980, Albrecht Art Mus., St. Joseph, Mo., 1980, Kans. U. Regents Ctr., Kansas City, Mo., 1981, Ctrl. Exch., Kansas City, 1985, Ann Weber Gallery, Gerogetown, Maine, 1990, Unity (Maine) Coll., 1988, Soc. Contemporary Photography Gallery, Kansas City, 1989, U. So. Maine, Portland, 1990, Caldbeck Gallery, Rockland, Maine, 1990, Leedy-Voukos Gallery, Kansas City, 1991, The Writers' Place, 1995, Maine Coast Artists, Rockport, 50 Year Retrospective: Taking Root, Beach Mus. Art, Kans. State U., 2001, exhibited in group shows at U. N.Mex., 1987—88, Dean Valentgas Gallery, Portland, 1989, Kansas City Artists Coalition, 1990, Farnsworth Mus., Rockland, 1990, U. Wis., Green Bay, 1990—91, Kultur Huse, Stockholm, 1991, Portland Sch. Art, 1991, 1991, exhibited in group shows, Kansas City, 1993, exhibited in group shows, Spencer Mus. of Art, Kans. U., Lawrence, 1994, Maine Coast Artists, Rockport, 1995, Represented in permanent collections Smithsonian Instn., Washington, Nelson-Atkins Mus. Art, Farnsworth Mus. Art, Spencer Mus. of Art, Albrecht Kemper Mus. Art, Washington U., Kans. State U., Manhattan, Kauffman Mus., Bethel Coll., Hallmark Cards, Inc., Crown Ctr. Corp., Kansas City, Hyatt Regency Hotels, Mercantile Bank, Kansas City, others; author, artist: Seewaw, 1964, Tallgrass Prairie: The Inland Sea, 1979. Founder Save the Tallgrass Prairie, Inc., 1973, Grassland Heritage Found., 1976; mem. Kansas City Mcpl. Art Commn., 1980-87; trustee emeritus Nature Conservancy, 1980—; bd. dirs. Soc. for Contemporary Photography, 1985-88, Grantee USN, 1956, Kansas City Trusts and Founds., 1971, Am. the Beautiful Fund, 1971, EPA, 1974, Hallmark Cards, Inc., 1974-75, Smithsonian Instn., 1975-76; recipient award Chgo. Artists Guild, 1969, Silver medal Soc. Publ. Designers, 1977, award of merit Soc. Publ. Designers, 1978, spl. recognition award Kappa Alpha Theta, 1979, Disting. Alumni award Washington U., 1979, 1st pl. award Tri Delta Exhbn., 1981, 87, active sponsor award Mid-Four Exhbn., 1987; resident Cité Internat. des Arts, Paris, 1992. Home: 221 W 48th St Apt 907 Kansas City MO 64112-3163

DUNCAN, PRISCILLA BLACK, lawyer; b. Centerville, Ind., Oct. 18, 1948; d. Paul Herbert and Bonnie (Clevenger) Hedges; m. Charles Le Roy Black,Jr., Nov. 7, 1975 (dec. Oct. 1982); m. Donald Arthur Duncan (dec. Dec. 2003). BA, DePauw U., 1970; JD, U. Ala., 1997. Bar: Ala. 1997, U.S. Dist. Ct. (mid. dist.) Ala. 1997. Asst. libr. Centerville (Ind.) Twp. Libr., 1968-70; newswriter Palladium Item, Richmond, Ind., 1970-74, AP, Atlanta, 1974; editor, columnist Columbus (Ga.) Ledger-Enquirer, 1974-92; dir. consumer affairs Ala. Office of Atty. Gen., Montgomery, 1993-97; assoc. Taber, Rountree, Singleton & Lyons, Montgomery, 1997-98; ptnr. P.B. Duncan & Assocs., Montgomery, 1998—. Pres. Ala. Solution, Montgomery; mem. exec com. Montgomery County Dems., 1998—; mem. Good Govt., Montgomery, 1997—. Mem.: ATLA, Ala. Bar Assn., Montgomery County Trial Lawyers Assn., Ala. Trial Lawyers Assn. Episcopalian. Avocations: politics, reading. Office: PB Duncan & Assocs 472 S Lawrence St Ste 204 Montgomery AL 36104-4261

DUNCAN, RICHARD FREDRICK, JR., secondary school educator, consultant; b. Millry, Ala., July 12, 1947; s. Richard F. and Claire Louise (Wood) D.; m. Rebecca Susan Davis, July 14, 1973. AA, Okaloosa-Walton Jr. Coll., 1967; BS, Fla. State U., 1969, MS, 1971; postgrad., Ore. State U., 1981-82. Tchr. Gadsden County Sch. Bd., Quincy, Fla., 1970-71, Leon County Sch. Bd., Tallahassee, Fla., 1972-73, Beaverton (Oreg.) Sch. Dist. No. 48, 1973—. Microbiologist Washington County, Hillsboro, Ore., 1971-72; cons. on sci. edn. Northwest Regional Ednl. Lab., Portland, Ore., 1978-79; cons. on marine edn. Ore. Dept. Edn., Salem, 1980-81. Recipient award for excellence in sci. teaching Ore. Mus. Sci. and Industry, Portland, 1984, Psdl. award, 1984. Mem. Assn. Presdl. Awardees in Sci. Teaching (nat. pres. 1987-88), Nat. Assn.Biology Tchrs. (Ore. Biology Tchr. of Year award 1981), Nat. Sci. Tchrs. Assn. (Presdl. award for excellence in sci. teaching, 1983, Sheldon award 1993, Nat. Disting. Svc. to Sci. award 2001), Oreg. Sci. Tchrs. Assn. (pres. 1980-81, Oreg. Jr. High Tchr. of Yr. award 1982), North Assn. Marine Educators (state dir. 1978-80), Masons, Shriners. Democrat. Avocations: sports, photography, sailing, scuba diving, camping. Office: Beaverton Sch Dist # 48 PO Box 200 Beaverton OR 97075-0200 Home: 1035 Northshore Pl Lake Oswego OR 97034-3722

DUNCAN, ROBERT, real estate company executive; BBA, MBA, LLB, U. Tex. With Trammell Crow Co., Dallas; founder, chmn. Transwestern Comml. Svcs., Inc., Houston, 1978—. Founding mem. adv. coun. U. Tex. Real Estate Ctr.; dir. Greater Houston Cmty. Found., Greater Houston YMCA. Mem.: Urban Land Inst., World Pres. Orgn. Office: Transwestern Comml Svcs Ste 1300 1900 W Loop S Houston TX 77027

DUNCAN, ROBERT BANNERMAN, dean, strategy and organizations educator; b. Milw., July 4, 1942; s. Robert Lynn and Irene (Hoenig) D.; m. Susan Jean Phillips, June 12, 1965; children: Stephanie Olcott, Christopher Robert. BA, Ind. U., 1964, MA, 1966; PhD, Yale U., 1971. From asst. prof. to prof. Kellogg Grad. Sch. Mgmt. Northwestern U., Evanston, Ill., 1970—96, prof. leadership orgnl. change, 1996—2002, provost, 1987—91; Eli and Edythe L. Broad dean Eli Broad Coll. Bus. Mich. State U., East Lansing, 2002—. Co-author: Innovations and Organizations, 1973, Strategies for Planned Change, 1977; also numerous articles in profl. jours. Fellow Acad. Mgmt. (chair nat. program 1980-81, pres. 1983-84). Avocation: sailing.

DUNCAN, ROBERT MICHAEL, lawyer, political organization administrator; b. Oneida, Tenn., Apr. 14, 1951; s. Robert C. and Barbara (Taylor) D.; m. Joanne Kirk, June 3, 1972; children: Robert Michael. BA, Cumberland Coll., 1971; JD, U. Ky., 1974; postgrad., U. Wis., 1977-80; LLD (hon.), Cumberland Coll., 1990; D Pub. Svc. (hon.), Coll. of Ozarks, 1992. Cert. lener-bus. banking, 1994. V.p. Inez (Ky.) Deposit Bank, 1974—77, exec. v.p., 1977—81, chmn., 1981—, Cmty. Holding Co., Inez, 1983—; with First Nat. Bank (now Inez Deposit Bank FSB), Louisa, Ky., 1984—; gen. counsel Rep Nat Com, Washington, 2002—. Dir. Cin. Br. of Cleve. Fed. Res. Bank, 1987-90; chmn. Morehead State U., 1985-86; trustee, chmn. Alice Lloyd Coll., Pippa Passes, Ky., 1978—, acting pres., 1993-94; mem. class XX Pres.'s Commn. on Exec. Exch. assigned to White House Office Pub. Liaison as asst. dir.; dir. Christian Appalachian Project, 1995—; mem. Pres.'s Commn. on White House Fellows, 2001—; polit. commentator WYMT-TV, 1999—; chmn.transition team Gov.-elect Fletcher, 2003-04; acting sec. revenue, State of Ky. Del. Rep. Nat. Conv., 1972, 76, 92, 96, 2000, 2004, chair contest com. 2000 conv.; nat. committeeman for Ky., 1992-, Rep. Nat. Com., vice chmn. so. region, 1992-2001, treas., 2001-02, gen. counsel, 2002-, exec. com., 1996; chmn. Ky. Rep. Com., 1995; trustee Highlands Regional Med. Ctr., 1977—, sec., 1994; active Govt. Rels. Coun., White House Conf. on Small Bus., 1995; chmn. Govs. Scholars, 1995—, bd. dirs. 1996—; chmn. East Ky. Corp., 1996, vice chmn. Ctr. Econ. Devel.; chmn. Bunning for U.S. Senate campaign, 1998; midwest regional chmn. Bush Presdl. campaign, 1999. Named Cumberland Coll. Outstanding Alumnus, 1976, Outstanding Young Man, Ky. Jaycees, 1982; U. Ky. fellow, 1978, White House fellow finalist, 1989; recipient Cmty. Leadership award McConnell Scholars U. Louisville, Cmty. Leadership award, 1999, Vic Hellard award Pub. Svc., 2003; named to U. Ky. Coll. of Law Hall of Fame, 2002. Mem. Am. Bankers Assn., Ky. Bankers Assn. (pres. 1985-86, dir.), Ky. Bar Assn., Ky. C. of C. (dir.), Kiwanis (lt. gov. 1983-84). Baptist. Office: Rep Nat Com 310 First St SE Washington DC 20003 Office Phone: 606-298-3511. E-mail: mduncan@inezdepositbank.com.

DUNCAN, SAM K., retail executive; b. Blytheville, Ark. Joined as courtesy clerk Albertson's Inc., 1969, numerous mgmt. positions, 1969—91; dir. operations Albertson's, 1991—92; v.p. grocery dept. Fred Meyer, Inc., 1992—97, exec. v.p. food divsn., 1997—98, pres., 2001—02, Ralph's Supermarkets, 1998—2001; pres., CEO ShopKo Stores Inc., 2002—05; pres., CEO, chmn. OfficeMax Inc., Itasca, Ill., 2005—. Office: OfficeMax Inc 150 E Pierce Rd Itasca IL 60143*

DUNCAN, STEPHEN ROBERT, elementary school educator; b. Lancaster, Pa., June 23, 1950; s. Robert L. Duncan and Joan L. (McLaughlin) Turns; m. Deborah R. Jakubik, June 30, 1973; children: Rhiannon Alissa, Teague Stephen. BS in Edn., California U. of Pa., 1972; MEd, Coll. N.J., 1977, postgrad. Cert. elem. tchr., sch. program specialist, Pa. 5th grade tchr. Council Rock Sch. Dist., Richboro, Pa., 1972-83, 85-90, 2d grade tchr., 1983-85, math./tech. integration specialist, 1990—, staff computer instr., 1982—, bldg. lead tchr., 2001—; dist. staff math. resource, 1995—. Chmn. Newtown (Pa.) Twp. Youth Aid Panel, 1987—97; presenter NCTM Nat. Convention, Anaheim, Calif., 2005. Recipient Outstanding Svc. award Bucks County Juvenile Cts., 1991; Council Rock Found. technology grantee, 1998. Mem. NEA, Nat. Coun. Tchrs. Math., Pa. State Edn. Assn., Coun. Rock Edn. Assn. (building rep. 2002-2006). Avocations: golf, tennis, computers. Office: Newtown Elem Sch 1 Wrights Rd Newtown PA 18940-1336 Office Phone: 215-968-7040. E-mail: sduncan@crsd.org.

DUNCAN, TIM, professional basketball player; b. Apr. 25, 1976; m. Amy Duncan, 2001. BA Psychology, Wake Forest, 1997. Center San Antonio Spurs, 1997—. Mem. U.S. Olympic Basketball Team, Athens, 2004. Founder, Executive Vice Pres. Tim Duncan Foundation. Named MVP, NBA Finals, 1999, 2003, 2005, NBA, 2002, 2003, Co-MVP, NBA All-star game, 2000; named to NBA All-star game, 1997, 1998, 2000—05, All-NBA team, 1997—2003, USA Basketball Men's Sr. Nat. team, 2003, NBA All-Defensive Team, 1999—2003; recipient Naismith award, 1996, Rookie of the Year, 1998. Achievements include mem. NBA Champion San Antonio Spurs, 1999, 2003, 2005. Office: 100 Montana St San Antonio TX 78203-1033

DUNCOMBE, PATRICIA WARBURTON, retired social worker; b. London, Jan. 30, 1925; came to U.S., 1940. d. P.G. Eliot and Mary Louise (Thompson) Warburton; m. David S. Duncombe, July 11, 1947 (dec. Apr. 1976); children: Elizabeth, Mari, Edward, David, Peter. BA, Barnard Coll., 1944; MS in Social Work, Columbia U., 1947. Cert. social worker. Social worker YWCA, Chgo., Evanston, Ill., 1947-50, B.I.A., Elko, Nev., 1966-67, Nev. State Welfare Div., Elko, Nev., 1967-69; dir. St. Michael's Youth Residence, Ethete, Wyo., 1970-76; asst. prof. U. Wyo., Laramie, 1976-83; program dir. St. Jude's Ranch, Boulder City, Nev., 1983-85; med. social worker home health agys., Las Vegas, Nev., 1985-95; retired. Mem. Wyo. Commn. for Women, 1971-83, chmn., 1975-77; bd. dirs. SE Wyo. Mental Health, 1980-83; founder Lend-A-Hand Program, Boulder City, 1989 (awarded 700th Point of Light, 1992). Recipient Gov.'s award, 2000. Mem. NASW (chpt. pres. 1979, 81, commn. on women 1977-79, exec. dir. Nev. chpt. 1985-90, Social Work of Yr. award Wyo. chpt. 1980, Nev. chpt. 1989, lifetime achievement award 1992), AAUW (nat. bd. dirs. 1983-85), Mesquite Club (Las Vegas, pres. 1998-99), Phi Theta Kappa. Democrat. Episcopalian. Avocations: gardening, travel, reading, art. Home: 3890 N Buffalo Dr Unit 264 Las Vegas NV 89129-8818

DUNCOMBE, RAYNOR BAILEY, lawyer; b. Washington, July 17, 1942; s. Raynor Lockwood and Avis Ethel (Bailey) D.; m. Janice Assunta Rini, Apr. 12, 1969; children: Christina Luccioni, Raynor Luccioni. AB, Franklin and Marshall Coll., 1965; JD, Syracuse U., 1968. Bar: N.Y. 1972, U.S. Dist. Ct. (no. dist.) N.Y. 1972. Staff atty. State of N.Y., Albany, 1968-70; mgmt. trainee State Bank Albany, 1970-72; staff atty. Vibbard, Donaghy & Wright, Schoharie, N.Y., 1972-73, F. Walter Bliss, Esq., Schoharie, 1973-74; pvt. practice Schoharie, 1974—. Chmn. bd. dirs. Fulmont Mut. Ins. Co., Mohawk Minden Ins. Co.; town atty. seven towns two villages and one water dist. in Schoharie County, 1975—; adminstr. Assigned Counsel Program, 1975—; sch. atty. Middleburgh (N.Y.) Schs., 1981—85, 1997—; atty. Schoharie County, 1982—87, 1990—91, Schoharie County Hist. Soc., 1975—; mem. Tax Cons. Tech. Adv. Group Catskill Watershed Corp., 1998—. Dist. commr. Boy Scouts Am., 1987—92, asst. scoutmaster, 1988—91, Explorer advisor, 1991—99, dist. chmn., 1992—95, asst. coun. commr., 1995—96, coun. commr., 1996—99, coun. pres., 1999—2002, cub master, 2004—; mem. Area 3 commn., 2002—03; Rep. committeeman Schoharie county, 1984—92; chmn. Middleburgh Rep. Town Com., 1995—2000; elder Presbyn. Ch., 1992—98, 2001—; mem. pers. com. Albany Presbytery of Presbyn. Ch., 1998—2001. Mem. ABA, N.Y. State Bar Assn., Schoharie County Bar Assn. (sec.-treas. 1975—), Rotary (past pres.), Masons (past master), Lions. Avocations: camping, cross country skiing, collecting stamps. Home: 190 Main St Middleburgh NY 12122-9415 Office: PO Box 490 283 Main St Schoharie NY 12157 Office Phone: 518-295-7515.

DUNCOMBE, RAYNOR LOCKWOOD, astronomer; b. Bronxville, N.Y., Mar. 3, 1917; s. Frederic Howe and Mabel Louise (Taylor) D.; m. Julena Theodora Steinheider, Jan. 29, 1948; 1 son, Raynor B. BA, Wesleyan U., Middletown, Conn., 1940; MA, U. Iowa, 1941; PhD, Yale U., 1956. Astronomer U.S. Naval Obs., Washington, 1942-62; dir. Nautical Almanac Office, 1963-75; prof. aerospace sci. U. Tex., Austin, 1976—. Research assoc. Yale U. Obs., 1948-49; lectr. dynamical astronomy U. Md., 1963, Yale Summer Inst., 1959-70, Office Naval Research Summer Inst. in Orbital Mechanics, 1971, NATO Advanced Study Inst., 1972; cons. orbital mechanics Projects Vanguard, Mercury, Gemini, Apollo, USN Space Surveillance System; mem. NASA space scis. steering com., NASA research adv. panel in applied math., 1967; adviser Internat. Com. on Weights and Measures, Internat. Radio Consultative Com., Internat. Telecommunications Union; mem. NAS-NRC astronomy survey com., 1970-72, Hubble Space Telescope Astrometry Team, 1976—. Author: Motion of Venus, 1958, Coordinates of Ceres, Pallas, Juno and Vesta, 1969; editor: (with V.G. Szebehely) Methods in Celestial Mechanics, 1966, Dynamics of the Solar System, 1979; (with D. Dvorak and P.J. Message) The Stability of Planetary Systems, 1984; assoc. editor: Fundamentals of Cosmic Physics, 1971; exec. editor: Celestial Mechanics, 1977-85; contbr. articles to profl. jours. Fellow Royal Astron. Soc., AAAS (sect. chmn.); assoc. fellow AIAA; mem. Internat. Astron. Union (pres. com. on ephemerides), Minor Planet 3368 named Duncombe, 1988), Am. Astron. Soc. (chmn. div. dynamical astronomy 1970), Inst. Navigation (councillor 1960-64, v.p. 1964-66, pres. 1966-67, Superior Achievement award 1967, Hays award 1975), ASME (sponsor applied mechanics div. 1968-70), Internat. Assn. Insts. Nav. (v.p.), Assn. Computing Machinery, Sigma Xi. Home: 1804 Vance Cir Austin TX 78701-1035 Office: U Tex Dept Aerospace Engring Austin TX 78712 Business E-Mail: duncombe@csr.utexas.edu.

DUNDAS, PHILIP BLAIR, JR., lawyer; b. Middletown, Conn., Apr. 29, 1948; s. Philip Blair and Madolyn Margaret Dundas; m. Elizabeth Anne Adorno, Aug. 9, 1969; children: Philip Blair III, Chapman P. BA, Wesleyan U., Conn., 1970; JD, Washington and Lee U., 1973. Bar: N.Y. 1974. Assoc. Shearman & Sterling, N.Y.C., 1973-81, ptnr., 1981—, ptnr. in charge of Abu Dhabi, United Arab Emirates Office, 1981—. Mem. ABA, Internat. Bar Assn., N.Y. State Bar Assn., Clinton Country Club. Home: 599 Lexington Ave New York NY 10022-6030

DUNDON, MARGO ELAINE, museum director; b. Cleve., July 3, 1950; d. Elmer Edward and Ruth Ann (Dreger) Buckeye. BS in Comm. cum laude, Ohio U., 1972; postgrad. in Mus. Studies, U. Okla, 1987. Mem. gen. staff Grout Mus. History and Sci., Waterloo, Iowa, 1974—75, coord. edn., 1976—78, co-dir., 1979—87, dir., 1988—90; exec. dir. Mus. Sci. and History, Jacksonville, Fla., 1990—99, pres., 1999—. Apptd. grievance com. Fla. Bar 4th Jud. Cir., 2002—05. Chairperson Waterloo Hist. Preservation Commn., 1987—88; cultural com. Visitors and Conv. Bur., Waterloo, 1988—90, My Waterloo Days, 1982, 1983; mem. Jacksonville Women's Network, Non-Profit Execs. Round Table, 1990—95; bd. dirs. Resource Plus, Waterloo-Cedar Falls, Iowa, 1986—88, CJI, Girls Inc. of Jacksonville, 1994—95, Ritz Theater & LaVilla Mus., 1998—2000, Jacksonville and the Beaches Conv. and Vis. Bur., 2001—. Am. Law Inst.-ABA scholar, 1979, 86; recipient Mayor's Vol. Performance award, Waterloo, 1983, Vol. award Gov. of Iowa,

1990. Mem.: Iowa Mus. Assn. (pres. 1984—86), Fla. Attractions Assn. (bd. dirs. 1997—98), Fla. Assn. Mus. (pres. 1995—96), Southeast Mus. Conf., Midwest Mus. Conf. (pres. 1988—90), Am. Assn. Mus. (site surveyor mus. assessment program 1982—, site examiner mus. accreditation commn. 1987—, regional councilor 1988—90, Peer Reviewer award 2000), Jacksonville C. of C., Quota Club (pres. 1982), Rotary. Avocations: snorkeling, scuba diving, travel, gardening. Office: Mus Sci & History 1025 Museum Cir Jacksonville FL 32207-9053 Office Phone: 904-396-7062. E-mail: director@themosh.com. *Share your life with a cat. When life is cold and hard edged, a cat is warm and soft. Cats do not fawn over our successes or judge us lacking for our failures. Cats remind us of the importance of life's simple gifts: a good meal, a warm nap, a relaxing bath, and an interesting bird at the window. For balance, there is nothing like living with a cat.*

DUNE, STEVE CHARLES, retired lawyer; b. Vithkuqi, Korca, Albania, June 15, 1931; s. Costa Pappas and Evanthia (Vangel) D.; m. Irene Duff Boudreau, Sept. 4, 1955; children: Michelle Dune Gesky, Christopher Michael. AB, Clark U., 1953; JD, NYU, 1956. Bar: N.Y. 1957. Law clk. U.S. Ct. Appeals 1st Cir., 1956-57; from assoc. to ptnr. Cadwalader, Wickersham & Taft, N.Y.C., 1957-95; counsel Albanian-Am. Enterpise Fund, 1995-96. Trustee Clark U., Worcester, Mass., 1974-86, 93-97, hon. trustee, 1997-2001, vice-chmn. bd. dirs., 1980-84, chmn. bd. dirs., 1984-86, chmn. presdl. search com., 1983-84, mem. pres.'s coun., 1987-90; dir. Albanian Children Fund, 1998-2002, chmn. Albanian-Am. C. of C., 1995-96. Recipient Disting. Svc. award, Clark U. Alumni Assn., 2003; Root-Tilden scholar, NYU Law, 1953—56. Mem.: ABA (divsn. sr. lawyers), Assn. Bar City NY, NY State Bar Assn. (com. on Ea. European affairs 1992—95, admiralty com. 1976—79, 1987—90), India House, Phi Beta Kappa. Home and Office: PO Box 456 98 Barrett Hill Rd Brooklyn CT 06234-1500 Personal E-mail: scdune@snet.net. *Commitment, determination and perseverance are a person's best allies in solving any problem, meeting any challenge and realizing upon any opportunity of life.*

DUNEA, GEORGE, nephrologist, educator; b. Craiova, Rumania, June 1, 1933; came to U.S., 1964; s. Charles L. and Gerda (Low) D.; 1 dau., Melanie. MD, U. Sydney, Australia, 1957. Diplomate Am. Bd. Internal Medicine, Am. Bd. Nephrology. Intern Royal North Shore Hosp., Sydney, 1958—59; resident internal medicine Australia, 1959—63, 1959—63; fellow in nephrology Cleve. Clinic, Presbyn.-St. Luke's Hosp., Chgo., 1964—66; practice internal medicine specializing in nephrology Chgo., 1972—; attending physician Cook County Hosp., Chgo., 1966—, dir. dept. nephrology-hypertension, 1969—; prof. medicine U. Ill., Chgo., 1986—; pres., CEO Hektoen Inst. of Med. Rsch., Chgo., 1991—. Vis. prof. medicine Rush Med. Sch., Chgo., 1976—. Contbr. chpts. to books, articles to profl. publs. Fellow A.C.P., Royal Coll. Physicians (London, Edinburgh); mem. AMA, Am. Soc. Nephrology, Brit. Med. Assn., Soc. Med. History. Home: 222 E Chestnut St Chicago IL 60611-2360 Office: 1835 W Harrison St Chicago IL 60612-3701 Office Phone: 312-864-4603. Personal E-mail: gdu222@yahoo.com.

DUNFEE, THOMAS WYLIE, law educator; b. Huntington, W.Va., Nov. 15, 1941; s. Wylie Ray and Chloe Edith (Wylie) D.; m. Dorothy Jane Taylor, Aug. 26, 1967; children: John Wylie, Jennifer Sue, Shannon Elizabeth. AB, Marshall U., 1963; JD, NYU, 1966, LLM, 1969. Instr. N.Y. Inst. Tech., 1965-68; asst. prof. Ill. State U., Normal, 1968-70, Ohio State U., Columbus, 1970-72, assoc. prof., 1972-74; assoc. prof. legal studies Wharton Sch., U. Pa., Phila., 1974-79, prof., 1979—, Kolodny prof. social responsiblity, 1982—, chmn. dept. legal studies and bus. ethics, 1980—84, 1987—91, 2005—, dir. Wharton ethics program, 1995-96, dir. Zicklin Ctr. for Bus. Ethics Rsch., 1997—2000, vice dean, 2000—03. Vis. prof. U. Fla., 1989, U. Newcastle, Australia, 1981, 85, Georgetown U., 1994, U. Mich., 2000; cons. United Way of Am., McGraw-Hill, Ind. Stds. Bd., Citibank, GM, Honda, GlaxoSmithKline, AT&T. Author: Business and Its Legal Environment, 1992, Modern Business Law, 1996; co-editor: Business Ethics: Japan and the Global Economy, 1993; co-author: (with Thomas Donaldson) Ethics in Business and Economics, 2 vols., 1997, Ties That Bind: A Social Contracts Approach to Business Ethics, 1999; editor-in-chief Am. Bus. Law Jour., 1976-79; contbr. articles to profl. jours. Grantee Exxon Found., 1985-86, Kemper Found., 1993. Mem. Acad. Legal Studies in Bus. (pres. 1989-90, Disting. Sr. Faculty award for Excellence 1991), Soc. Bus. Ethics (pres. 1995-96). Office Phone: 215-898-7691. Business E-Mail: dunfeet@wharton.upenn.edu.

DUNGAN, JOHN RUSSELL, JR., (12TH VISCOUNT DUNGAN OF CLANE, HEREDITARY PRINCE OF FERMOY AND ARRA), anesthesiologist, health facility administrator; b. Boston, Dec. 12, 1953; s. John Russell and Nancy Pauline (Beaton) Dungan; m. Nancy Elizabeth Perkins, July 12, 1986 (div. 1997); children: Elizabeth Adelaide, Thayer Warren, Eleanor Grace Appleton. AB magna cum laude, Harvard U., 1977, EdM, 1978; DDS, Baylor U., 1984; MD cum laude, Creighton U., 1989. Diplomate Nat. Bd. Anesthesiology (dir. 1989-92, 97-, v.p. 1997-), Am. Acad. Pain Mgmt. Instr. anesthesiology Boston U. Sch. Medicine, 1986-89; attending staff anesthesiologist, residency instr. Boston City Hosp., 1986-89; anesthesiologist, chief Tobey Hosp., Wareham, Mass., 1989-91; chief anesthesia Mary Lanning Hosp., Hastings, Nebr., 1991—, chief surgery, 1995, 2001; pres. Hastings Anesthesiology Assocs., 1992—; med. dir. Hastings Surg. Ctr., 2005—. Author: (books) The Kings of the Picts and Dál Riads, 1976, The Beatons, 1976, Angus MacDonald, 1977; contbr. articles to profl. jours. Rschr. nat. trust Restoration of Celbridge Chapel and Cemetery, Kildare, Ireland, 1995. Named to, Honorable Order Ky. Cols.; 13th head and comdr., Mil. Order Knights of Leinster (estab. 1645), John Eliot scholar, 1967, Nat. Merit scholar, 1971, Harvard Coll. scholar, 1975—77, John Harvard scholar, 1976. Mem.: Soc. Interventional Pain Physicians (pres. 2003—), Adams County Med. Soc. (pres. 2001—), Nebr. Soc. Anesthesiologists, Am. Soc. Anesthesiologists, Cum Laude Soc. (Tabor chpt.), United Empire Loyalists Assn. (Can.), New Eng. Hist. Geneal. Soc., N.Y. Irish History Roundtable, English-Speaking Union U.S. (internat. fellow 1971—72), N.Y. Biog. and Geneal. Soc., Harvard Club Nebr., Clan Dungan (clan chief, pres. 1998—), Wild Geese, Old Tonbridgian Soc., Hasty Pudding Inst. 1770, Phi Beta Kappa. Republican. Episcopalian. Avocations: medieval and Jacobean British history research, family history. Home: Heartwell Park 923 N Elm Ave Hastings NE 68901-4021 Office: Hastings Anesthesiology Ste 101 420 W 5th St Hastings NE 68901-7551 Office Phone: 402-463-9841. Business E-Mail: jdungan@inebraska.com.

DUNGEY, CHANNING NICOLE, broadcast executive; d. Donald Maurice and Judith Ann Dungey. BA in Theater, Film and TV magna cum laude, UCLA, 1991. Story editor Steamroller Productions, Warner Bros. Features, Burbank, Calif., 1991—93; creative exec. feature film divsn. Warner Bros., Burbank, 1993—95, prodn. exec. feature film divsn., 1995—98, sr. v.p. material Warner Bros. Features, 1998—2000, pres. material Warner Bros. Features, 2000—02; prodr./ptnr. Dexterity Pictures, Santa Monica, Calif., 2003—04; v.p. drama series Touchstone TV, Burbank, 2004—. Founding bd. mem., com. chair Step Up Women's Network, L.A., 1998—2004. Mem.: Phi Beta Kappa. Avocations: travel, writing, languages, yoga, bicycling, accordion. Office: Touchstone Television 500 S Buena Vista Old Animation #1A-1 Burbank CA 91521 Office Phone: 818-560-8690. Business E-Mail: channing.dungey@abc.com.

DUNGY, KATHRYN R., humanities educator; b. Stanford, Calif., Sept. 21, 1969; d. Claibourne I. and Madgetta Thornton Dungy; life ptnr. Timothy Voigt. BA magna cum laude, Spelman Coll., Atlanta, 1991; MA, Duke U., 1993, PhD, 2000. Vis. lectr. U. of Vt., Burlington, 1999—2000, asst. prof. Latin Am. and Caribbean history, 2000—04; asst. prof. Latin Am. and Caribbean studies New Coll., Fla., 2004—. Contbg. author: Black Students and Overseas Programs: Broadening the Base of Participation; biographical compiler To Conserve a Legacy: American Art from Historically Black Colleges and Universities; contbr. articles to The So. Friend, Jour. of the N.C. Friends Hist. Soc. Caribbean Studies. Co-chair Pres.'s Coun. on Racial Equality, 2000—02. Internat. Student Identity Card scholar, CIEE, 1989—90, Fgn. Study scholar, Spelman Coll./Charles A. Merrill Found., 1989—90, Minority fellow, Dana Found., 1989—91, Ford Found. Predoctoral fellow for Minorities, 1991—94, Tinker Found. Summer Rsch. grantee, Duke U., 1993, Latin Am. Studies fellow, 1994—96, George Washington Henderson fellow, U. Vt., 1998—99, Travel grantee, Women's Studies Program, U. Vt., 2001. Mem.: Am. Hist. Assn., Caribbean Studies Assn., Assn. Caribbean Historians, Mortar Bd., Sigma Delta Epsilon (v.p. chpt. 1990—91), Phi Alpha Theta (pres. chpt. 1990—91), Delta Sigma Theta. Avocations: photography, travel. Office: New Coll 5700 N Tamiami Tr Sarasota FL 34243 Personal E-mail: kdungy@ncf.edu.

DUNGY, TONY, professional football coach; b. Jackson, Mich., Oct. 6, 1955; Def. asst. Pitts. Steelers, 1981-83, def. back coach, 1982-83, def. coord., 1984-88; def. backs coach Kansas City Chiefs, 1989-91; def. coord. Minn. Vikings, 1992-95; head coach Tampa Bay (Fla.) Buccaneers, 1996—2001, Indpls. Colts, 2002—. Mem. Super Bowl Championship Team, 1978. Office: Indianapolis Colts 7001 West 56th Street Indianapolis IN 46254*

DUNHAM, ARCHIE WALLACE, petroleum and chemical products company executive; b. 1938; m. Linda Dunham; 3 children. BS, MBA, U. Okla. Assoc. engr. Conoco Inc., 1966—73, mgr. gas prodn., 1978—81, v.p. logistics and downstream planning, 1981—83, v.p. transp. natural gas, gas products, 1983—85, exec. v.p. div., 1985, pres., CEO Houston, 1996—, chmn., 1999—; exec. v.p. Douglas Oil Co., 1976—79, pres., 1979; group v.p. chems. and pigments E.I. du Pont de Nemours & Co., Wilmington, Del., 1987—96; v.p. Exploration Products, Houston, 1992—96. Bd. dirs. LA Pacific Corp., Phelps Dodge Corp., Union Pacific Corp., API, Energy Inst. Ams., Meml. Hermann Healthcare System; served on Commn. Nat. Energy Policy, Nat. Infrastructure Advisory Coun.; chmn. NAM; past chmn. US Energy Assn., Nat. Petroleum Coun.; exec. com. and bd. dirs. US-Russia Bus. Coun.; mem. Bus. Round Table, Bus. Coun.; mem. exec. com. and bd. dirs. Greater Houston Partnership; bd. gov. Houston Forum. Bd. dirs. Smithsonian Inst.; trustee George Bush Presdl. Libr. Found.; mem. Marine Corps Heritage Found., Bretton Woods Com., Beta Gamma Sigma Dir. Table, 2003—; trustee Houston Symphony, United Way Tex. Gulf Coast; bd. dirs. Horatio Alger Assn. Disting. Am.; sr. mem. bd. visitors M.D. Anderson Cancer Ctr.; sr. chmn. Houston Grand Opera, past pres. Capt. USMC, 1960—64. Recipient Father Yr., Houston, 1998, inducted into Okla. Hall of Fame, 1998, CEO Yr. for Global Vision in Energy, 2000, Internat. Achievement award, 2000, Horatio Alger award, 2001, Ellis Island Medal Honor, 2001, Legend of the Industry, A&D Summit, 2002, Houston's Internat. Citizen Yr., World Affairs Coun. Office: ConocoPhillips 600 N Dairy Ashford St Houston TX 77079-1175

DUNHAM, BENJAMIN STARR, editor, art association administrator; b. N.Y.C., Sept. 19, 1944; s. George Roscoe and Portia Elizabeth (Playfair) Dunham; m. Wendy H. Rolfe, Apr. 12, 1986; 1 child, Samuel Edward Rolfe; m. Mimi Cox, Sept. 9, 1978 (div.). BA, Harvard U., 1966; postgrad., Boston U., 1970, Cath. U., 1971-73. Asst. editor Music Educators Jour., Washington, 1967-70; editor Symphony News, Vienna, 1971-78; dir. spl. projects Chamber Music Soc. Lincoln Ctr., N.Y.C., 1982; exec. dir. Chamber Music Am., N.Y.C., 1978-82, Am. Symphony Orch., N.Y.C., 1982-84; exec. v.p. Nat. Music Coun., N.Y.C., 1984-90; editor Am. Recorder, 1990—2002, Early Music Am. Mag., 2002—. Cons. to TV, fundraising and mktg. in chamber music, pubs. and rsch.; pvt. tchr. recorder, 1971—78; mem. music faculty Trinity Coll., Washington, 1973—75; pvt. tchr. recorder MusiCo-op, Wareham, Mass., 1986—92, Cranberry Concerts, 1993—; cons. on period instrument orch. program Andrew W. Mellon Found., 1989—91; lectr. in field. Contbr. articles to profl. jours.; prin. recorder performer: Handel Festival Orch., 1977—78. Mem. Wareham Arts and Humanities Coun., 1986—90, 1992—94; Hist. Dist. Commn. Wareham, 1986—97; bd. dirs. Marion Art Ctr., 1996—99; Sippican Elem. Sch. Coun., 1998—2001. Named Arts Adminstr. of the Yr., Arts Mgmt. Mag., N.Y.C., 1981. Mem.: Am. Recorder Soc. (bd. dirs. 1984—89), Nat. Guild Cmty. Schs. Art (trustee 1982—87), Early Music Am. (bd. dirs. 1988—92, 1993—99, 2000—02, treas. 1993—95). E-mail: dunhamb@post.harvard.edu.

DUNHAM, CHRISTOPHER COOPER, lawyer; b. N.Y.C., Jan. 29, 1937; s. Robert Secrest and Elizabeth Walls (Cooper) D.; m. Marjorie Jean Corliss, June 14, 1958; children: Douglas Webber, William Sigler, Anne Corliss. BA, Wesleyan U., 1958; JD, Columbia U., 1961. Bar: N.Y. 1961, U.S. Dist. Cts. (so. and ea. dists.) N.Y. 1963, U.S. Patent and Trademark Office 1964, U.S. Ct. Appeals (2d cir.) 1964. Assoc. Cooper, Dunham, Dearborn & Henninger, N.Y.C., 1961-68; ptnr. Cooper & Dunham LLP and predecessor firms, N.Y.C., 1968—. Chmn. Westport Democratic Town Com., Conn., 1965-66, 67-70, 80-86; mem. Conn. Dem. Ctrl. Com., 1978-80; del. Conn. Dem. Conv., Conn., 1966, 68, 74, 80, 82, 84, 90, 98; alt. Westport Planning and Zoning Com., 1965; mem. Westport Bd. Fin., 1975, Conn. Safety Commn., 1977-78, Westport Rep. Town Meeting, 1986-93. Mem. N.Y. Intellectual Property Law Assn., Gamma Psi, Phi Beta Kappa. Congregationalist. Home: 277 Compo Rd S Westport CT 06880-6513 Office: Cooper and Dunham 1185 Ave of the Americas New York NY 10036 Office Phone: 212-278-0419. E-mail: cdunham@cooperdunham.com.

DUNHAM, CHRISTOPHER SCOTT, librarian; b. Balt., Mar. 12, 1964; s. Curtis Lee and Susan Ingrid (Meyer) D.; m. Colleen Marie Davis, Nov. 16, 1997 (div. Apr. 2002). BA, Rutgers U., 1986, MLS, 1994. Dist. exec. Boy Scouts of Am., Denville, N.J., 1987-91; trips dir. Citta Scout Reservation at Brookville, Barnegat, N.J., 1991, aquatics dir., asst. camp dir., 1992; info. supr. Rutgers U., New Brunswick, NJ, 1992-94, reference libr., 1993-95, Sussex County C.C., Newton, N.J., 1993-97, Montclair State U., Upper Montclair, N.J., 1994-95; electronic resources libr. Passaic County C.C., Paterson, N.J., 1995-97; reference and interlibr. svcs. libr. Fairfield (Conn.) U., 1997—. Mem. ALA, Rutgers U. Sch. Comm. Info. and Libr. Studies Alumni Assn. (exec. com. 1995-99), N.J. Recreation and Park Assn. (conf. com. 1992-98), N.J. Forest Fire Svc. (sect. sec. 1992-99), Boy Scouts Am. Avocations: travel, outdoor adventure, theater, aquatics, music. Office: Fairfield U/DiMenna-Nyselius Libr 1073 N Benson Rd Fairfield CT 06824-5195 Office Phone: 203-254-4206. Business E-Mail: cdunham@mail.fairfield.edu.

DUNHAM, DANIEL PATRICK, internal medicine physician; b. Chgo., Ill., May 27, 1963; s. John Edward and Geraldine Ann Dunham; m. Jennifer Eden Lim, June 18, 1988; children: Theresa Brigid, Caitlin Miranda, Conor Patrick. BS, U. Ill., 1981—85; MD, U.Chgo., 1985—89; MPH, U. Ill., 1992—95. Bd. cert. Am. Bd. of Internal Medicine, 2003. Asst. prof. medicine Northwestern U., Feinberg Sch. of Medicine, Chgo., 1999—2004; dir. quality improvement Northwestern Med. Faculty Found., Divsn. Gen. Internal Medicine, 2001—04; clin. practice dir. Northwestern Med. Faculty Found, 2001—04; head girls basketball coach St. Mary Sch., Riverside, 2002—04; assoc. chief, divsn. of gen. internal medicine Northwestern U., Feinberg Sch. of Medicine, 2002—; asst. track coach St. Mary Sch., 2003—04. Contbr. articles to jours. Mem. sch. bd. St. Mary Sch., Riverside, 2000—03. Scholar, Ill. Dept. of Health, 1985—89. Fellow: Am. Coll. Physicians. Labor. Roman Catholic. Avocations: bodhran playing, trumpet, solitaire. Office: Northwestern Univ Feinberg Sch 675 N St Clair 18-200 Chicago IL 60611 Office Phone: 312-695-8630.

DUNHAM, JOAN ROBERTS, administrative assistant; b. Dayton, Ohio, Jan. 25, 1933; d. Harold Hathaway and Lydia Roberts Dunham. BA, U. Colo., 1954; postgrad., U. Pa., 1959-65, U. Chgo., 1971-72. Office clk. Daniels & Fisher Stores, Denver, 1954-56; clk., stenographer Dept. of State, Madras, India, 1957-59; clk. admissions office Temple Buell Coll., Denver, 1969—71; typist, adminstrv. clk. State of Colo., Denver, 1987-99; ret., 1999. Fgn. lang. fellow U.S. Dept. Health, Edn. and Welfare, U. Pa., 1961-62. Republican. Christian Scientist. Home: 1350 Josephine St Unit 210 Denver CO 80206-2243

DUNHAM, JOHN L., retail company executive; m. Mary Jane Beadles. BA in Engring., U.S. Air Force Acad., 1968. Divisional v.p. merchandise processing Ohio divsn. May Dept. Stores Co., St. Louis, 1976-78, v.p. ops. D&F divsn., 1978-83, sr. v.p. ops. Calif. divsn., 1983-87, chmn. Sibley's divsn., 1987-89, chmn. G. Fox divsn., 1989-93, chmn. merchandising co., 1993-96, exec. v.p., CFO, 1996—2001, also bd. dirs., 1997—, vice chmn., 1999—2001, pres., 2001—, acting CEO & chmn., 2005—. Bd. dirs. YMCA of Greater St. Louis. Office: May Department Stores Co 611 Olive St Saint Louis MO 63101-1721*

DUNHAM, KATHERINE, choreographer, anthropologist, dancer; b. Glen Ellyn, Ill., June 22, 1909; d. Albert Millard and Fanny June (Taylor) Dunham; m. Jordis McCoo (div.); m. John Thomas Pratt, July 10, 1941 (dec. Jan. 1986); 1 child, Marie Christine Pratt. BA in Anthropology, U. Chgo., 1936, MS; PhD, Northwestern U.; LhD (hon.), MacMurray Coll., 1972. Dir., tchr. of own schs. of dance, theatre and cultural arts, Chgo., N.Y.C., Haiti, Stockholm and Paris, from 1931; profl. dancer, from 1934; choreographer for theatre, opera, motion pictures and TV; mem. Chgo. Opera Co., 1935-36; supv. Chgo. City Theatre Project on cultural studies, 1939; dance dir. Labor Stage, 1939-40; prodr., dir. Katherine Dunham Dance Co., from 1945; established dance sch. Port-au-Prince, Haiti, 1961; advisor to First World Festival on Negro Art U.S. Dept. State, 1966; artistic and tech. advisor to Pres. of Senegal, 1966-67; cultural counselor and dir. Performing Arts Tng. Ctr., So. Ill. U., East St. Louis, from 1967; prof. So. Ill. U., Edwardsville, from 1968. Choreographer concerts Tropics, 1937, Schulhoff Tango, 1937, Madame Christoff, 1937, Primitive Rhythms, 1937, Biguine-Beguine, 1937, Florida Swamp Shimmy, 1937, Lotus Eaters, 1937, Haitian Suite, 1937, Peruvienne, 1938, Le Jazz Hot (Boogie-Woogie), 1938, Saludade da Brazil, 1938, Spanish Earth Suite, 1938, Island Songs, 1938, Mexican Rhumba, 1938, L'Ag'Ya, 1938, A Las Montanas, 1938, Bre'r Rabbit an' de Tah Baby, 1938, Bahiana, 1939, Cuidad Maravillosa, 1939, Concert Rhumba, 1939, Cumbancha, 1939, Plantation Dances, 1940, Babalu, 1941, Haitian Suite II, 1941, Honky-Tonk Train (added to Le Hot Jazz), 1941, Rites de Passage, 1941, Tropical Revue, 1943, Callaco, 1944, Choros Nos. 1-5, 1944, Flaming Youth 1927, 1944, Para Que Tu Veas, 1944, Havana 1910/1919, 1944, Carib Song, 1945, Bal Negro, 1946, Motivos, 1946, Haitian Roadside, 1946, Nostalgia (Ragtime), 1946, Batacada, 1947, Bolero, 1947, C'Est Lui, 1947, Rhumba Trio, 1947, Floor Exercises, 1947, La Valise, 1947, Octaroon Ball, 1947, Angelique, 1948, Blues Trio, 1948, Macumba, 1948, Missouri Waltz, 1948, Street Scene, 1948, Veracruzana, 1948, Adeus Terras, 1949, Afrique, 1949, Jazz in Five Movements, 1949, Brazilian Suite, 1950, Los Indios, 1950, Frevo, 1951, Rhumba Jive, 1951, Rhumba Suite, 1951, Spirituals, 1951, Caymmi, 1952, Ramona, 1952, La Blanchisseuse, 1952, Southland, 1952, Afrique du Nord, 1953, Samba, 1953, Cumbia, 1953, Dora, 1953, Honey in the Honeycomb, 1953, Incantation, 1953, Carnaval, 1955, Floy'd Guitar Blues, 1955, Jazz Finale, 1955, Just Wild About Harry, 1955, New Love, 1955, Banana Boat, 1957, Plating Rice, 1957, Sister Kate, 1957, Ti'Cocomaque, 1957, A Touch of Innocence, 1959, Bamboche, 1962, Diamond Thief, 1962, Anabacoa, 1963, theatre The Emperor Jones, 1939, with George Balanchine Cabin in the Sky, 1941, theatre Pins and Needles, 1940, Tropical Pinafore, 1939, Les Deux Anges, 1965, (films) Carnaval of Rhythum, 1939, Pardon My Sarong, 1942, Star Spangled Rhythum, 1942, Stormy Weather, 1943, Casbah, 1948, Boote e Risposta, 1950, Mambo, 1954, Green Mansions, 1958, The Bible, 1966, (Operas) Aida, 1963; author: Katherine Dunham's Journey to Accompong, 1946, Katherine Dunham's Journey to Accompong, rev. edit., 1972; author: (autobiography) A Touch of Innocence, 1959, A Touch of Innocence, rev. edit., 1980; author: Island Possessed, 1969, Kasamance: A Fantasy, 1974; co-author: (plays) Ode to Taylor Jones, 1967—68; author: TV scripts, produced in Mexico, Australia, France, Eng., Italy; contbr. short stories sometimes under pseudonym Kaye Dunn to mags. Pres. Dunham Fund for Rsch. and Devel. Cultural Arts Inc.; founder Found. Study of Arts and Scis. of Vodun; v.p. Found. Devel. and Preservation Cultural Arts Inc.; bd. dirs. Nat. Inst. Aging, Ill. Arts Coun.; mem. Ill. com. JFK Ctr. Alliance Arts Edn., Am. Coun. Arts in Edn., Arts Worth/Intercultural Coun.; cons. Interamerican Inst. Ethnomusicology and Folklore, Caracas, Venezuela, NEH; mem. rev. com. OAS; mem. adv. bd. Modern Orgn. Dance Evolvement. Decorated Legion of Honor Haiti; named Cmdr., Grand Officer, Hon. Citizen, Port-au-Prince, Haiti, 1957; recipient Merit Chevalier, Haiti, Dance Mag. award, 1968, Eight Lively Arts award, 1969, Disting. Svc. award, So. Ill. U., 1970, East St. Louis Monitor award, 1970, Dance Divsn. Heritage award, AAH-PERD, 1972, Nat. Ctr. Afro-Am. Artists award, 1972, Black Merit Acad. award, 1972, Am. Dance Guild award, 1975, 6th Kennedy Ctr. Honors award, 1983, Profl. Achievement award, U. Chgo., Samuel M. Scripps/Am. Dance Festival award, 1986, Nat. Medal Arts, 1989, Capezio Dance award, 1991, Key to City, East St. Louis, Ill., 1968; Julius Rosenfeld Travel fellow, 1936—37, Fulbright fellow, State Dept. Internat. Edn., Mather scholar, Case We. Res. U., 1973. Mem.: AEA, SAG, ASCAP, Lincoln Acad., Royal Anthrop. Soc., Negro Actors Guild, Inst. Black World (bd. dirs.), Black Acad. Arts and Scis., Writers Guild, Am. Fedn. Radio Artists, Am. Guild Music Artists, Am. Guild Variety Artists (bd. govs. 1943—49), Sigma Epsilon. Avocations: horseback riding, cooking, painting, walking, steam baths. Office: Katherine Dunham Mus 532 N 10th St East Saint Louis IL 62201-1946*

DUNHAM, LAURA, elementary school educator; b. Highland Park, Mich., June 2, 1947; d. Clement and Joy C. Harland; m. Roger W. Dunham, Feb. 14, 1969; children: Chad Roger, Craig William. B in Music Edn. cum laude, U. Miami, 1969; BA in Edn. magna cum laude, Fla. Atlantic U., 1979, MEd in Sch. Guidance and Counseling, 2004. Music tchr. grades K-5 Hollywood (Fla.) Park Elem., 1969-70; substitute tchr. grades K-5 Otis AFB Elem. Sch., Falmouth, Mass., 1970-71; music tchr. grades 6-9 Olsen Mid. Sch., Dania, Fla., 1971—74; music tchr. grades 6-12 Westminster Acad., Ft. Lauderdale, Fla., 1979-83; art tchr. Ft. Lauderdale Christian Sch., 1983—2002, chmn. developing tchr. program for new educators, 1993—2002; art tchr. Sunrise Mid. Sch., 2002—03; guidance counselor Broadview Elem. Sch., 2004—. Cons. scholarship and award writer graduating srs. Ft. Lauderdale Christian Sch., 1993-95; sponsor Nat. Art Honor Soc. at Ft. Lauderdale Christian Sch., 1995-2002, Nat. Honor Soc., 2001-02; host Internat. Children's Art Exhbn., 1996; entourage mem. Broward County Ctr. for the Performing Arts, 1996—; com. mem. Broward County Nat. Week of the Ocean, 1996-2002; nat. mem. The Smithsonian Instn., 1998-99; presenter Christian Schs. Fla. Seminar, 1999. Profl. flautist, 1969—. Vol. hosp. surg. suite; Sunday sch. tchr., mem. ch. choirs, handbell choirs, vacation Bible sch. tchr., vol. classroom arts and crafts, deacon, pastor nominating com.; vol. for badges, cub scout leader Boy Scouts Am., 1984—, Habitat for Humanity, 2001-03; active Fla. Rep. Party, 1993—. Named H.S. Tchr. of Yr., Broward County Fair, 1996. Mem. ACA, Nat. Art Edn. Assn., Fla. Art Edn. Assn., Nat. Mus. Women in the Arts, Assn. Ind. Schs. Fla. (accreditation team 1999), Am. Assn. Christian Counselors, Am. Sch. Counseling Assn., U. Miami Alumnae Assn., U. Miami Band of the Hour Club, Mortar Bd., Alpha Tau Omega (little sister), Delta Zeta (alumnae pres., Woman of Yr. Broward County Gold Coast Area Alumnae 1996), U. Miami Alumnae Delta Zeta (area chair), Rho Lambda, Chi Sigma Iota (sec.), Tau Beta Sigma, Alpha Theta Kappa, Sigma Alpha Iota (pres., Province award), Phi Delta Kappa, Phi Kappa Phi, Kappa Delta Pi. Republican. Methodist. Home: 301 Lake Dr Coconut Creek FL 33066-1840 Office: Broadview Elem Sch 1800 SW 62d Ave North Lauderdale FL 33068

DUNHAM, MICHAEL HERMAN, human services executive; b. Dayton, Ohio, Mar. 30, 1951; s. Robert Fredrick and Marjory Katherine (Fortune) D.; m. Nancy Lynn Cross, July 2, 1977; children: Lisa Yandow Olson, A. Richard Yandow. Student, Kent State U., 1970-72, U. Vt., 1975-77; BA in sociology, U. Wis., 1980. Rsch. assoc. U. Wis., Madison, 1977-84; dir. managed care Univ. Health Care, Inc., Madison, 1984-86; dir. fiscal affairs Health & Hosps. Corp., N.Y.C., 1986-88; CEO Total Health HMO, Inc., N.Y.C., 1988-89; pres., CEO Practice Mgmt., Inc., Madison, 1989-92, Cmty. Care Mgmt., Inc., Madison, 1992—. Faculty mem. CASSP Inst., Georgetown U., Washington, 1992-96. Contbr. chpts. to books, articles to profl. jours. Mental health Interagy. Coun. State Wis., Madison, 1992-94, grad. med. edn. rev. commn.,

1986, cert. need adv. com., 1984-86. Mem. N.Y. State HMO Coun. (exec. bd. 1988), Wis. Assn. Family & Children's Agys. Office: Cmty Care Mgmt Inc 16 N Carroll St Ste 640 Madison WI 53703-2756

DUNHAM, PHILIP BIGELOW, biology professor, physiologist; b. Columbus, Ohio, Apr. 26, 1937; s. T. Chadbourne and Margaret (Bigelow) D.; m. Gudrun Bjarnarson, Mar. 9, 1985 BA, Swarthmore Coll., 1958; PhD, U. Chgo., 1962. USPHS postdoctoral fellow Carlsberg Found., Copenhagen, 1962-63; asst. prof. zoology Syracuse U., 1963-67, assoc. prof., 1967-71, prof. biology, 1971—2004, prof. emeritus, 2004—. Rsch. prof. pharm. SUNY Health Sci. Ctr., Syracuse, 1990—; vis. assoc. prof. physiology Yale U. Sch. Medicine, 1968-70, vis. prof., 1986; vis. prof. medicine U. N.C., 1993-94; vis. scientist physiol. lab. Cambridge (Eng.) U., 1979, August Krogh Inst., Copenhagen, 1985-87; vis. prof. biochemistry U. Copenhagen, 1994; vis. honors examiner Swarthmore Coll., 1966-67, 74-76, mem. alumni coun., 1971-73; mem. exec. com. bd. trustees Marine Biol. Lab., Woods Hole, Mass., 1972-76; mem. physiology study sect. NIH, 1986-89; mem. review panel Am. Heart Assn., 1994-97, co-chair, 1995, 97. Assoc. editor Am. Jour. Physiology, 1984-87; contbr. over 100 rsch. publs. in field. Rsch. grantee NSF, 1963-65, NIH, 1965—, MERIT grantee NIH, 1996-2004; recipient Chancellor's Citation for Exceptional Acad. Excellence, Syracuse U., 1994-95. Mem. Soc. Gen. Physiologists (council 1967-69), Am. Physiol. Soc., Biophys. Soc. Home: 6402 Terese Ter Jamesville NY 13078-9430 Office: Syracuse U 130 College Pl Syracuse NY 13210-2819 Business E-Mail: pbdunham@syr.edu.

DUNHAM, SCOTT H., lawyer; b. Seattle, May 7, 1950; BA with highest honors, Wash. State U., 1972; JD, U. Wash., 1975. Bar: Calif. 1975, U.S. Dist. Ct. (ctrl. dist.) Calif. 1976, U.S. Supreme Ct. 1977. Mem. O'Melveny & Myers, LLP, L.A. Author: Avoiding and Defending Wrongful Discharge Claims, 1987, Designing an Effective Fair Hiring and Termination Compliance Program, 1992; contbr. chpts. to books; editor-in-chief Wash. Law Rev., 1974-75. Mem. ABA (mem. com. occupational safety and health labor and employment law sect.), L.A. County Bar Assn. (tchr., lectr. Calif. Bus. Law Inst., ABA nat. Inst., Pers. and Indsl. Rels. Assn., Japan Bus. Assn., Inst. Applied Mgmt. and Law, Inc., Calif. Continuing Edn. Bar and various other employer assns.), Order of Coif, Phi Beta Kappa, Phi Kappa Phi, Omicron Delta Kappa, Phi Delta Phi (magister Ballinger inn chpt. 1974). Office: O'Melveny & Myers LLP 400 S Hope St Los Angeles CA 90071-2899

DUNHAM, STEPHEN SAMPSON, lawyer; b. Bloomington, Ind., Oct. 19, 1945; s. Allison and Anne Campbell (Toll) Dunham; m. Victoria Baldwin Cass, May 24, 1969; children: Sarah W., Isaac P. BA, Princeton U., 1966; JD, Yale U., 1969. Bar: Calif. 1970, U.S. Dist. Ct. (no. dist.) Calif. 1972, U.S. Ct. Appeals (9th cir.) 1972, U.S. Dist. Ct. (ctrl. dist.) Calif. 1973, U.S. Supreme Ct. 1978, Minn. 1979, U.S. Dist. Ct. Minn. 1982, U.S. Ct. Appeals (8th cir.) 1983, Colo. 1988, U.S. Ct. Appeals (10th cir.) 1990. Law clk to Judge Stanley A. Weigel U.S. Dist. Ct. Calif., San Francisco, 1969-70; acting prof. law U. Calif., Davis, 1970-71; vis. assoc. prof. law Nat. Chengchi U., Taipei, 1971-72; assoc. Morrison & Foerster, San Francisco, 1972-76, ptnr., 1976-79; assoc. prof. law U. Minn., Mpls., 1979-82, gen. counsel, 1982-85, v.p., gen. counsel, 1985-88; ptnr. Morrison & Foerster, Denver, 1988—, mem. exec. com. Instr. Nat. Inst. Trial Advocacy, Boulder, Colo., 1980, Boulder, 83, Harvard U. Law Sch., Cambridge, Mass., 1985. Mem.: Colo. Lawyers Com. (bd. dirs. 1989—), Nat. Assn. Coll. and Univ. Attys. (bd. dirs. 1986—88), Calif. State Bar (chari com. on legal svcs. 1978). Home: 650 Emerson St Denver CO 80218-3217 Office: Morrison & Foerster 5200 Republic Plaza 370 17th St Denver CO 80202-1370 Office Phone: 303-592-2251. Office Fax: 303-592-1510. Business E-Mail: sdunham@mofo.com.*

DUNHAM, WOLCOTT BALESTIER, JR., lawyer; b. NYC, Sept. 14, 1943; s. Wolcott Balestier and Isabel Caroline (Bosworth) D.; m. Joan Scott Findlay, Jan. 26, 1974; children: Mary Findlay, James Wolcott. AB magna cum laude, Harvard U., 1965, LLB cum laude, 1968. Bar: N.Y. 1969. Vol. VISTA, 1968-69; assoc. Debevoise & Plimpton LLP and predecessor Debevoise, Plimpton, Lyons & Gates, N.Y.C., 1969-76, ptnr., 1977—. Exec. dir. N.Y. State Exec. Adv. Commn. on Ins. Industry Regulatory Reform, 1982; spkr. in field. Co-author: Insurance M&A, 1997—; contbr. articles to profl. jours.; gen. editor and chpt. author, New York Insurance Law, 1991, and ann. supplements. Treas., trustee Fund for Astrophys. Rsch., N.Y.C., 1970—, sec., 1970-84, pres., 1984—; bd. dirs. UN Assn., N.Y.C., 1973-79, vice chmn., 1975-79, adv. coun., 1992-2000; vestry mem. St. James's Ch., N.Y.C., 1987-93, clk., 1988-93, jr. warden, 1993-94, sr. warden, 1994-95, chancellor, 1994—; bd. dirs. Neighborhood Coalition for Shelter, Inc., 1983—; pres., bd. dirs. East Side Cmty. Ctr., Inc., 1988—; bd. dirs. Dutchess Land Conservancy, 1996—; bd. mgrs. Shekomeko Valley Farm Assn., LLC, 1996-2003; bd. dir. Episcopal Charities of the Diocese of N.Y., 2005-. Fellow Am. Coll. Investment Counsel; mem. ABA (chmn. com. on ins. sect. adminstrv. law 1979-83), Assn. Bar City N.Y. (com. on ins. 1981-87, chmn. com. 1984-87), Assn. Life Ins. Counsel, Union Internationale des Avocats, Am. Soc. Internat. Law, Harvard Law Sch. Assn. N.Y.C. (dir. 1978-81). Episcopalian. Office: Debevoise & Plimpton LLP 919 Third Ave New York NY 10022-3904

DUNHILL, ROBERT, advertising direct mail executive; b. L.A., Sept. 28, 1929; s. Herbert G. and Irma (Meyer) Odza; m. Joan Scheer, Dec. 19, 1952; children: Andrew, Candy, Cindy. BS, Adelphi Coll., 1952; MBA, NYU, 1954. Prin. Dunhill Internat. List Co., Inc., N.Y.C., 1952—, pres., chmn., 1975—. With USNR, 1955-57. Mem. Chgo. Assn. of Direct Mktg., Widener U. Alumni Assn., Direct Mktg. Assn., Fla. Direct Mktg. Assn. (chmn.). Republican. Home: 6711 North Ocean Blvd #32 Ocean Ridge FL 33435 Office: 621 NW 53rd St Ste 200 Boca Raton FL 33487-8239 Business E-Mail: robert@dunhills.com.

DUNIGAN, DENNIS WAYNE, real estate executive; b. Cin., Apr. 28, 1952; s. Park George and Hazel Edna (Hines) D. AA, U. Cin., 1974, BBA, 1975. Salesman Comey and Shepherd, Inc., Cin., 1978—79; property mgr. Dunigan Properties, Cin., 1980—; assoc. T.J. Carter Realty, Cin., 1984—. Contbr. articles to profl. jours. Chmn. trans. com. Reagan for Pres. Cin., 1980--; active Cin. Hist. Soc., Mus. Nat. Hist., 1987--, Cin. Zoo, 1987--, Contemporary Arts Ctr., Cin., 1988--, The Taft Mus., 1988--; contbg. mem. Cin. Art Mus., 1987—Mem. Supreme Ct. Hist. Soc. (contbg.), U. Cin. Alumni Assn., Ohio Assn. Realtors, Cin. Bd. Realtors, Nat. Baseball Hall of Fame and Mus., Greater Cin. Tennis Assn., U.S. Tennis Assn., U.S. Golf Assn., PGA Tour Ptnrs., UCats Club, Gold Bearcats. Republican. Avocations: golf, tennis, reading, stamp and coin collecting, baseball, football. Home: 6022 Saint Regis Dr Cincinnati OH 45236-4218

DUNION, CELESTE MOGAB, municipal official, consultant, foundation administrator; b. Atlantic City, Mar. 6, 1932; d. Cyril Joseph and Lavina Edna (Bolen) Mogab; m. John Joseph Dunion, May 8, 1954 (dec. Apr. 1978); children: Dana, John, Robert, Denise. Tech. degree, Am. Acad. Dramatic Arts, N.Y.C., 1951; grad. advanced govt. fin. inst., Georgetown U., 1986. Cert. govt. fin. mgr.; lic. notary pub., Pa. Asst. to bus. mgr. Rose Tree Media Sch. Dist., Media, Pa., 1969-78; dir. fin., tax collector, treas. Twp. of Middletown, Glen Riddle, Pa., 1978-98; bus. mgr. Rocky Run YMCA, 2003—. Profl. model, NYC, Phila., Atlantic City; mem. Christy Modeling Agy., Phila. Models Guild, Atlantic City Models Guild, Atlantic City Press Bur.; cons. in fin. mgmt. peer-to-peer program Pa. Dept. Cmty. Affairs, Harrisburg, 1988-96; treas., bd. dir. Pa. Mcpl. Investment Program, 1990-98. Past sec. Wyncroft Civic Assn.; former committeewoman Middletown Twp; treas. Middletown Rep. Women, 1998-2003; treas. Rep. Women of Western Delaware County, 2003-; bd. dirs. Darlington Woods, 2001—. Recipient Dedicated Pumper award Lenni Fire Co., 1983, Pres.'s award Lima Fire Co., 1985, Outstanding Leadership award Pa. East Govt. Fin. Officers Assn., 1986, Cmty. Svc. award Middletown Fire Co., 1996. Mem. Govt. Fin. Officers Assn. (Pa. rep., nat. cash mgmt. com., women's fin. network, Mid-Atlantic rep.), Assn. Govt. Acct., Pa. Govt. Fin. Officers Assn. (past pres., sec., S.E. bd.), MidAtlantic Govt. Fin. Officers Assn. (Pa. rep., mem. legis. com.), Women's Fin. Officers Network (chmn. membership), Delaware County Tax Collectors Assn. (v.p. 1984-85, pres. 1986), Pa. Tax Collectors Assn., Pa. Assn. Notaries. Republican. Roman Catholic. Avocations: silk flower arranging, tap dancing, country western dancing, poetry, cooking. Office: CMD/CGFM Darlington Woods 153 Kingswood Ct Glen Mills PA 19342-2016 also: Rocky Run YMCA 1299 W Baltimore Pike Media PA 19063 E-mail: cmdcgfm@msn.com.

DUNIPACE, IAN DOUGLAS, lawyer; b. Tucson, Dec. 18, 1939; s. William Smith and Esther Morvyth (McGeorge) D.; m. Janet Mae Dailey, June 9, 1963; children: Kenneth Mark, Leslie Amanda. BA magna cum laude, U. Ariz., 1961, JD cum laude, 1966. Bar: Ariz. 1966, U.S. Supreme Ct. 1972, Nev. 1994, Colo. 1996. Reporter, critic Long Branch (N.J.) Daily Record, 1963; assoc. firm Jennings, Strouss, Salmon & Trask, Phoenix, 1966-69; assoc. Jennings, Strouss & Salmon, PLC, Phoenix, 1969-70, ptnr., 1971-93, mem., 1993—2003, chmn. comml. practice dept., 1998—2001; mem. I. Douglas Dunipace, PLC, Phoenix, 2004—. Comments editor Ariz. Law Rev., 1965-66. Reporter Phoenix Forward Edn. Com., 1969-70; mem. Phoenix Arts Commn., 1990-93, chmn., 1992-93; bd. mgmt. Downtown Phoenix YMCA, 1973-80, chmn. 1977-78; bd. dirs. Phoenix Met. YMCA, 1976-87, 1988-2005, chmn. 1984-85; bd. mgmt. Paradise Valley YMCA, 1979-82, chmn. 1980-81; bd. mgmt. Scottsdale/Paradise Valley YMCA, 1983, mem. legal affairs com. Pacific Region YMCA, 1978-81; chmn. YMCA Ariz. State Youth and Govt. Com., 1989-95, cmty. resource bd., 2005—; bd. dirs. The Schoolhouse Found. 1990-96, pres. 1990-94, Kids Voting, 1990-94, Beaver Valley Improvement Assn. 1977-79, Pi Kappa Alpha Holding Corp., 1968-72, The Heard Mus. 1993-94, Ariz. Bar Found., 1996-2003, pres., 2001-02, Phoenix Kiwanis Charitable Found, 2001—, Phoenix Ctr. Cmty. Devel., 2002-04; trustee Paradise Valley Unified Dist. Employee Benefit Trust, 1980-93, chmn. 1987-93, Sch. Theology, Claremont, Calif. 1994—, chmn., 2004-; bd. mgrs. Desert Schs. Fin. Svcs., 2003—; trustee First Meth. Found. of Phoenix, 1984-93, 99—, pres., 2002-04; mem. Greater Paradise Valley Cmty. Coun., 1985-87; bd. dirs. Heard Mus. Coun., 1990-95, pres. 1993-94; mem. Ariz. Venture Capital Conf. Planning Com., 1994-2003, mem. exec. com. 1997-2003, chmn., 2000; mem. Assn. for Corp. Growth, 1995-96, Ariz. Bus. Leadership Assn., 1996—, bd. dirs., 2001-04, sec.-treas., 2002-04, Ariz. Town Hall, 2003—; bd. visitors U. Ariz. Law Coll., 1996-2003; mem. met. Phoenix commn., Meth. Ch., 1968-71, lay leader, 1975-78, trustee, 1979-81, pres., 1981; mem. Pacific S.W. ann. Meth. Conf., 1969-79, lawyer commn., 1980-85, chancellor Desert S.W. ann. conf. 1985—2005. Capt. AUS, 1961-63. Mem. State Bar Ariz. (securities regulation sect. 1970-2004, chmn. 1991-92, mem. com. unauthorized practice of law 1972-84, chmn. 1975-83, mem. bus. law sect. 1981—, chmn. 1984-85), State Bar Nev., State Bar Colo., Am., Fed. (pres. Ariz. chpt. 1980-81), Maricopa County Bar Assns. (bd. dirs. Corp. Coun. divsn. 1996-99), U. Ariz. Law Coll. Assn. (bd. dirs. 1983-90, pres. 1985-86), U. Ariz. Alumni Assn. (bd. dirs. 1985-86), Orange Tree Club, Masons, Kiwanis (pres. Phoenix 1984-85, disting. lt. gov. 1986-87, S.W. dist. cmty. svc. chmn. 1987-88, dist. activity com. coord. 1988-89, dist. laws and regulation chmn. 1989-90, 92-93, 95-96, 2002—, asst. to dist. gov. for club svcs. 1990-91, field dir. 1991-92, dist. conv. chmn. 1993-94, pub. rels. chmn. 1996-98, mem. internat. com. on Project 39, 1988-89, internat. com. On to Anaheim 1990-91, internat. com. on leadership tng. and devel. 1991-92, 93-94, trustee SW dist. found. 1987-92, 1st v.p. 1990-92)), Phi Beta Kappa, Phi Kappa Phi, Phi Delta Phi, Phi Alpha Theta, Sigma Delta Pi, Phi Eta Sigma, Pi Kappa Alpha (nat. counsel 1968-72). Democrat. Methodist. Home: 2527 E Vogel Ave Phoenix AZ 85028-4729 Office: I Douglas Dunipace PLC 3116 E Shea Blvd # 251 Phoenix AZ 85028 Office Phone: 602-370-6895. Personal E-mail: dunipaceplc@cox.net.

DUNIPHAN, J. P., state legislator, small business owner; b. Aug. 31, 1946; Mem. SD Ho. of Reps., Pierre, 1995—2002, mem. commerce com., judiciary com., chair local govt. com., 1995—2002; mem. SD State Senate, Dist. 33, 2002—. Ptnr. Elks II, 1993—, Quad Investments, 1993—. Republican. Fax: 605-342-6399.*

DUNKELMAN, LORETTA, artist; b. Paterson, N.J., June 29, 1937; d. Samuel and Rae (Gutkind) Dunkelman. BA, Rutgers U., 1958; MA, Hunter Coll., 1966. Lectr. Hunter Coll., N.Y.C., 1966-67; vis. artist U. Cin., 1974; asst. prof. U. R.I., Kingston, 1974-75, Cornell U., Ithaca, N.Y., 1977-80; vis. artist Ohio State U., Columbus, 1984; asst. prof. Va. Commonwealth Univ., Richmond, 1986-88; vis. artist The Sch. of the Art Inst. of Chgo., 1990; vis. prof. art U. Calif., Berkeley, 1993-94. One woman shows include A.I.R. Gallery, N.Y., 1973-74, 78, 81, 83, 87, Douglass Coll., New Brunswick, 1973, U. Cin., 1974, U. R.I., Kingston, 1975, 1708 E. Main Gallery, Richmond, 1987; exhibited in group shows at Whitney Mus. Am. Art, N.Y., 1973, N.Y. Cultural Ctr., N.Y., 1973, Newark Mus., 1973, Cranbrook Acad. Art Mus., Bloomfield Hills, Mich., 1974, Grand Rapids (Mich.) Art Mus., 1974, Johnson Mus., Cornell U., Ithaca, N.Y., 1977, Inst. Art and Urban Resources, Pub. Sch. 1, N.Y.C., 1978, McIntosh/Drysdale Gallery, Washington, 1980, Douglass Coll., Rutgers U., New Brunswick, NJ, 1981, Kulturhuset, Stockholm and Lunds Konsthall, Sweden, 1981-82, Picker Art Gallery, Colgate U., Hamilton, N.Y., 1983, Hopkins Hall Gallery, The Ohio State U., 1984, Kenkeleba Gallery, N.Y., 1985, A.I.R. Gallery, 1985, 91, Bernice Steinbaum Gallery, N.Y., 1986, Anderson Gallery, Va. Commonwealth U., Richmond, Va., 1987, Rabbet Gallery, New Brunswick, N.J., 1989, Michael Walls Gallery, 1989, 148 Duane St., N.Y.C., 1992, Contemporary Art Inst., N.Y.C., 1994, Mason Gross Sch. of the Arts Galleries, Rutgers U., New Brunswick, N.J., 1996, A.I.R. Gallery, N.Y.C., 1997, Kingsborough C.C., Bklyn., 1998, Yaddo Centennial Arts Festival, N.Y.C., 2000, Mabel Smith Douglass Libr., Rutgers U., New Brunswick, 2005; represented in permanent collections Bellevue Med. Ctr., N.Y.C., The Chase Manhattan Bank, N.Y.C., City Univ. Grad. Ctr., N.Y.C., The Picker Art Gallery, Dana Art Ctr., Colgate U., Hamilton, N.Y., U. Cin., Gene Swenson Collection at U. Kansas Art Mus., Lawrence, Bristol-Myers, Squibb, Lawrenceville, N.J., Hunter Coll., N.Y.C. CAPS fellow N.Y. State Coun. Arts, 1975; Visual artist fellow Nat. Endowment for the Arts, 1975, 82, 93, AAUW fellow, 1976-77, Artist fellow N.Y. Found. for the Arts, 1991; grantee Adolph & Esther Gottlieb Found., 1991. Home and Office: 151 Canal St New York NY 10002-5033

DUNKERLY, ROBERT MATTHEW, historian; b. Lewisburg, Pa., Jan. 8, 1973; s. Robert Edward Dunkerly, Mary O'Neil. BA in history, St. Vincent Coll., 1995; MA in historic preservation, Middle Tenn. State U., 1998. Archaeologist Assn. for the Preservation of Va. Antiquities, Jamestown, Va., 1997—98; pk. ranger Colonial Nat. Hist. Pk., Jamestown, 1997—98; interpreter Colonial Williamsburg Found., 1998; pk. ranger George Washington Birthplace Nat. Monument, 1999, Kings Mountain Nat. Mil. Pk., Blacksburg, SC, 1999—. Spkr. in field. Author: (book) More than Roman Valor: The Revolutionary War Fact Book, 2003, Kings Mountain Walking Tour Guide, 2003; contbr. articles. Mem.: Civil War Preservation Trust, Coun. on America's Mil. Past, Am. Assn. for State and Local History. Avocations: painting, photography, camping. Office: Kings Mountain Nat Mil Pk 2625 Park Rd Blacksburg SC 29702 Home: 28 New River Terr Lake Wylie SC 29710 Office Phone: 864-936-7921.

DUNKLAU, RUPERT LOUIS, financial planner, consultant; b. Arlington, Nebr., May 19, 1927; s. Louis Z. and Amelia S. (Gnuse) Dunklau; m. Ruth Eggert, June 4, 1950 (dec. Nov. 1998); children: Paul, Janet; m. Ruth King, Sept. 3, 2000. BS, U. Nebr., 1950; LittD (hon.), Concordia Coll., St. Paul, 1982; LLD (hon.), Midland Luth. Coll., Fremont, Nebr., 1985, Valparaiso U., 2005. Exec. v.p. Valmont Industries, Inc., Valley, Nebr., 1950-73; dir. Fremont Nat. Bank, Nebr., 1968-2000. Bd. dirs. Midland Luth. Coll., Cmty. Chest Fremont; bd. dirs. Concordia Pub. House Valparaiso (Ind.) U.; chmn. bd. dirs. Meml. Hosp. Dodge County; bd. dirs. Luth. Ch.-Mo. Synod, St. Louis. With USNR, 1945. Mem.: Rotary Club. Republican. Home: 2948 Deer Ln Fremont NE 68025 Office: PO Box 1558 Fremont NE 68026-1558 Office Phone: 402-721-6046.

DUNKLE, KEITH ALLEN, military officer; b. Waverly, Mo., Feb. 2, 1968; s. Elden Thomas Dunkle and Margaret Alice Petet; m. Brenda Ann Dulle, Oct. 8, 1994; children: Sophia Athena, Isabella Alexandra. BS, BA, Cen. Mo. State U., 1990; MA, Kings Coll., London, 2003. Commd. 2d lt. U.S. Army, 1990, advanced through grades to maj., 2002; security officer nuclear weapons detachment 558th U.S. Field Arty., Perivolaki, Greece, 1991-92; field arty. officer 41st Field Arty. Regiment, Ft. Stewart, Ga., 1992-95; spl. forces operational detachment A comdr. 7th Spl. Forces Group, Ft. Bragg, NC, 1996—99; aide-de-camp U.S. Army South, P.R., 1999-2000; spl. forces operational detachment A comdr. 7th Spl. Forces Group, PR, 2000—02, Brit. Joint Command and Staff Coll., Watchfield, England, 2002—03; pres. spl. forces operational detachment B comdr. 1st Spl. Forces Group, Okinawa, Japan, 2003—. Avocations: chess, reading, outdoor sports. Home: PSC 560 Box 342 Apo AP 96376 E-mail: keithdunkle@hotmail.com.

DUNKLY, JAMES WARREN, theological librarian; b. Alexandria, La., Aug. 1, 1942; s. James Warren and Frances Estelle (Jones) D. BA, Tex. Christian U., 1963; diploma in Theology, Oxford U., Eng., 1964; MA, Vanderbilt U., 1968, PhD, 1982. Grad. fellow, tutor Episcopal Theol. Sch., Cambridge, Mass., 1969-71; libr. Nashotah (Wis.) House, 1975-83; dir. librs. Episcopal Div. Sch., Weston Sch. Theology, Cambridge, 1983-92; libr. Sch. Theology U. of the South, Sewanee, Tenn., 1993—; assoc. libr. U. of the South, Sewanee, 1995—. Instr. Inst. Christian Studies, Milw., 1975-83, Wis.; lectr. New Testament U. of the South, 1993—. Asst. editor N.T. Abstracts, 1971-72, mng. editor, 1972-75; mem. corp. for Anglican Theol. Rev., 1976-95, asst. editor for N.T., 1976-84, editor, 1984-88; mem. bd. Sewanee Theol. Rev., 1994—, book rev. editor, 2000—; contbr. articles to profl. jours. Conant Fund grantee, Episcopal Ch., 1981-82; Henry fellow, Oxford U., 1963-64, Vanderbilt U. teaching fellow, 1967-69, Rockefeller doctoral fellow, 1969-70; Vanderbilt U. scholar, 1966-67. Mem. Am. Theol. Libr. Assn. (publs. com. 1977-83, bd. dirs. 1980-83, task force on structure, 1981, index bd. 1985-89, exec. com. index and preservation bds. 1988-89, v.p. 1989-90, pres. 1990-92). Home: PO Box 3206 Sewanee TN 37375-3206 Office: U of the South Du Pont Libr Sewanee TN 37383-1000 E-mail: jdunkly@sewanee.edu.

DUNLAP, BENJAMIN BERNARD, academic administrator; b. Columbia, S.C. m. Anne Dunlap, 1963; children: Boykin Dunlap Bell, Susannah, Ben. Grad. summa cum laude, U. of the South, 1959; BA with honors, Oxford (Eng.) U., 1962, MA, 1966; PhD in English Lang. and Lit., Harvard U., 1967. Mem. faculty Harvard U.; Carolina rsch. prof., prof. English, adj. prof. anthropology U. S.C., SC, 1968—93; Chapman Family prof. humanities Wofford Coll., Spartanburg, SC, 1993—2000, pres., 2000—. Moderator Exec. and CEO Seminars Aspen (Colo.) Inst.; lectr. in field. Writer, prodr. (over 200 programs for pub. television). Named Sr. Fulbright lectr., Chulalongkorn U., Bangkok, Chiang Mai U., Thailand; Rhodes scholar, Oxford U., 1959—62, U.S.-Japan Leadership fellow, Japan Soc. N.Y. and Tokyo, 1984—85. Office: Wofford Coll 429 N Church St Spartanburg SC 29303

DUNLAP, CONNIE, librarian; b. Lansing, Mich., Sept. 9, 1924; d. Frederick Arthur and Laura May (Robinson) Robson; m. Robert Bruce Dunlap, Aug. 9, 1947. AB, U. Mich., 1946, AM in Libr. Sci., 1952. Head acquisitions dept., then head grad. library U. Mich. Libr., 1961-75, dep. assoc. dir., 1972-75; univ. libr. Duke U., 1975-80; cons., 1981—. Contbr. articles to publs. in field, chpts. in books. Forewoman Grand Jury U.S. Dist. Ct. 13th Dist. Mich., 1967-68; bd. dirs. U. Mich. Libr. Friends, v.p., 1997-2000, officer at large, 2000-02, bd. dirs. A.B. Bach, 1999—, v.p., 2002, chair, 2003—; treas. Ann Arbor Hist. Found., 1998—. Recipient Disting. Alumnus award U. Mich. Sch Libr. Sci., 1977 Mem. ALA (mem. coun. 1974-83, mem. exec. bd. 1978-83, pres. resources and tech. svcs. divsn. 1972-73), AAUP, Assn. Coll. and Rsch. Librs. (bd. dirs. 1975-78, pres. 1976-77), Assn. Rsch. Librs. (bd. dirs. 1976-80, pres. 1979-80). Address: 1570 Westfield Ave Ann Arbor MI 48103-5740

DUNLAP, ELLEN S., library administrator; b. Nashville, Oct. 12, 1951; d. Arthur Wallace and Elizabeth (Majers) Smith; m. Arthur H. Dunlap, Jr., Dec. 27, 1972 (dec. 1977); m. Frank Armstrong, May 11, 1979; 1 child, Libbie Sarah. BA, U. Tex., Austin, 1972, MLS, 1974. Rsch. assoc. Humanities Rsch. Ctr. U. Tex., Austin, 1973-76, rsch. libr., 1976-83; exec. dir. Rosenbach Mus. and Library, Phila., 1983-92; pres. Am. Antiquarian Soc., Worcester, Mass., 1992—. Dir. 18th Century Short Title Catalogue/N.Am., 1992—. Dir. Worcester Mcpl. Rsch. Bur., 1993—; mem. fin. com. Town of West Boylston, Mass., 1997—, chmn., 2001—; bd. dirs. Greater Worcester Cmty. Found., Mass., 2004—, clerk, 2005—; bd. dirs. Mass. Found. for Humanities, 1996—2004, pres., 2002—04; bd. dirs. Rare Books Sch., U. Va., 1994—. Mem. Am. Antiquarian Soc., Mass. Hist. Soc., Colonial Soc. Mass., Grolier Club (N.Y.C.), Worcester Club. Office: Am Antiquarian Soc 185 Salisbury St Worcester MA 01609-1636

DUNLAP, F. THOMAS, JR., lawyer, retired electronics executive; b. Pitts., Feb. 7, 1951; s. Francis Thomas and Margaret (Hubert) D.; m. Kathy Dunlap; children: Bridgette, Katie. BSE.E., U. Cin., 1974; JD, U. Santa Clara, Calif., 1979. Bar: Calif., 1979, U.S. Dist. Ct. (no. dist.) Calif. 1979. Mgr. engring. Intel Corp., Santa Clara, Calif., 1974-78, adminstr. tech. exchange, 1978-80, European counsel, 1980-81, sr. atty., 1981-83, gen. counsel, sec., 1983-87, v.p., gen. counsel, sec., 1987—2001, sr. v.p., gen. counsel, 2001—04. Drafter, lobbyist Semiconductor Chip Protection Act, 1984 Republican. Roman Catholic. Avocation: jogging. Office: Intel Corp 2200 Mission College Blvd Ste 4 Santa Clara CA 95054-1549

DUNLAP, JAMES, poet, writer; b. Keokuk, Iowa, Jan. 3, 1945; s. Arthur E. and Gladys Irene Dunlap. Author: (chapbook) Entwined in Wonder, 1996; co-author: Five Gates; newsletter editor Des Moines Area Writers' Network; contbr. over 600 poems and short stories to varous publs. in U.S., Can., Eng., France, Switzerland. Named One of Top 100 in rhymed verse and lit. short story Writers' Digest, 1994, in unrhymed verse, 1995. Democrat. E-mail: ecrivain01@yahoo.com.

DUNLAP, JEFFREY LEE, minister, educator; b. Washington Courthouse, Ohio, Dec. 7, 1955; s. Orville Ray and Carolyn Sue (Merritt) D. BA in Christian Ministries, Lincoln Christian Coll., 1980. Cert. tchr., adminstrn., supervision, Ohio. Youth min. First Christian Ch., Washington Courthouse, 1975—76; intern Westside Christian Ch., Springfield, Ill., 1978; youth min. Christian Ch., Kenosha, Wis., 1981—83; dir. cmty. edn. Washington Courthouse City/Miami Trace Local Schs., Fayette County, 1987—89; substitute tchr. various Ohio Pub. Schs., 1990—91; vocat. counselor Pvt. Industry Coun., Circleville, Ohio, 1991—; dir. Christian edn. South Side Ch. of Christ, Washington Courthouse, 1996—. Counselor youth and adult ministry First Christian Ch., 1985—, grant writer, cons., 1986-89. Assoc. United Way, Washington Courthouse, 1986-89, Am. Heart Assn., Columbus, 1986-89; program coord. community edn. County of Fayette, Washington Courthouse, 1986-89; health coord. Fayette County Health Dept., Washington Courthouse, 1986-89. Named One of Outstanding Young Men of Am., 1987. Avocations: tennis, basketball, golf, baseball, photography. Home: 316 E Elm St Washington Court House OH 43160-2521

DUNLAP, KAREN F. BROWN, academic administrator; BA, Mich. State U.; MS, Tenn. State U.; PhD Mass Comm., U. Tenn. Dean reporting, writing and editing faculty The Poynter Inst., St. Petersburg, Fla., pres., 2003—. Bd. trustees Poynter; reporter Nashville Banner, Macon News, St. Petersburg Times. Co-author: The Effective Editor: How to Lead Your Staff to Better Writing and Better Teamwork, The Editorial Eye. Office: The Poynter Inst 801 3rd St S Saint Petersburg FL 33701

DUNLAP, MATTHEW GORDON, state official, former state legislator; b. Ellsworth, Maine, Nov. 26, 1964; s. Robert Gordon and Susan Perkins Dunlap; m. Michelle Ann Dunphy, Dec. 22, 1996; 1 child, Emily Charlotte. BA in Roman History, U. Maine, 1987, MA in English Lit., 1994; postgrad., Harvard U., 2000. Finish sewer Dunlap Weavers, Bar Harbor, Maine, 1974—89; cook, bartender various, Orono, Bangor, Maine, 1986—2003; asst. editor Nat. Poetry Found., Orono, 1987—89; mem. Maine Ho. Reps., Augusta, 1996—2004, chair fish and wildlife com., 1998—2004, mem. ho. elections com., 2002—03, chair govt. oversight com., 2003; sec. state State of Maine, Augusta, 2005—. Columnist: Northwoods Sporting Jour., 1999—, assessing editor: Jour. Mind and Behavior, 1997—; contbr. articles to profl.

jours. Chair Maine Citizens Commn. on Wildlife, Augusta, 1999—2001, Old Town (Maine) Dem. Com., 1998—, Marsh Island Deer Com., Old Town, 2002—; bd. mem. Grad. M-Club, Orono, 1995—; bd. mem., founder Maine Youth Fish and Game, 2001—. Recipient Govt. Svc. award, Maine Merchants Assn., 2003; fellow, Flemming Fellows/Ctr. for Policy Alts., 1997; grantee, Am. Coun. Young Polit. Leaders, Russia, 2002. Mem.: Maine Profl. Guides Assn., Friends Maine Track (v.p. 1994—98), Old Town Grange. Democrat. Episcopalian. Avocations: hunting, fishing, writing, chess, books and antiquities. Office: Office Sec State Nash School Bldg 148 State House Station Augusta ME 04333*

DUNLAP, PATRICIA C., state legislator; b. Rochester, N.H., Nov. 6, 1926; Grad. h.s. Mem. N.H. Ho. of Reps., mem. comm., small bus., consumer affairs, econ. devel. coms., also mem. com. environment and agr. Ward clk., Rochester, NH, 1991—92; supr. checklist, 1992; bank customer rels. rep., 90. Treas. Gafney Home for Aged Mgmt. Bd., 1992—; asst. treas. 1st Ch. Congl., 1992-95, fin. sec., 1996—. Mem. DAR (asst. treas. Mary Torr chpt. 1992-94), OWLS (treas. 2001—).

DUNLAP, PAUL EDWARD, secondary school educator, writer; 1 child, Gwendolyn Sophia. BA, Cal Poly SLO, 1988—93; MFA, San Jose State U., 2004. Single Subject Credential Cal Poly SLO, 1994. Tchr. Henry M. Gunn Sr. H.S., Palo Alto, 1994—, instrnl. supr., 2001—. Cooperating tchr. Stanford U., Palo Alto, Calif., 1996, San Jose State U., San Jose, 1996, Stanford U., SJSU, Palo Alto, San Jose, 2000, Stanford U., 1998, San Jose State U., San Jose, 1998. Author: (poems) English Jour., Image: A Jour. of Arts and Religion, The Montserrat Rev., The Greensboro Rev., Proposing on the Bklyn. Bridge: Poems about Marriage. Recipient Best Educator award, Sylvan Learning Ctr., 2003, Principal's Cup for Excellence in Tchrg., 2004. Mem.: NCTE (assoc.), MLA (assoc.). Avocations: writing, drawing, languages, running, travel. Office Phone: 650-354-8238. E-mail: pdunlap@pausd.org.

DUNLAP, WILLIAM, artist, art educator, art critic, lecturer; MFA, U. Miss. Prof. Appalachian State U., NC, 1970—79, Memphis State U., 1979—80; art commentator, "Around Town" WETA-TV, Arlington, Va. Spkr. in field; lectr. on art related subjects at colleges, universities, institutions and profl. confs. Represented in permanent collections, Met. Mus. Art, Corcoran Gallery Art, Lauren Rogers Mus., Mobil Corp., Riggs Bank, IBM Corp., Fed. Express, Equitable Collection, Ark. Art Ctr., U.S. State Dept., U.S. Embassies throughout the world, Rogers Ogden Collection, one-man shows include, Corcoran Gallery Art, Nat. Acad. Sci., Aspen Mus. Art, Southeastern Ctr. Contemporary Art, Mus. Western Va., Albany Mus. Art, Cheekwood Fine Arts Ctr., Mint Mus. Art, Miss. Mus. Art, Contemporary Art Ctr., New Orleans, exhibitions include Reconstructed Recollections, Inaugural Exhibition: Story of South, Ogden Mus. Southern Art, New Orleans, 2003—04, What Boys Draw & Other Works, Soren Christensen Gallery, New Orleans, 2004, Panorama Am. Landscape, Gibbes Mus. Art, Charleston, S. C., 2004—05, In Spirit of the Land; co-curator (exhibitions) Winding River: Contemporary Painting from Vietnam, Meridian Internat. Ctr., Washington D.C., 1997—98, Outward Bound: Am. Art Brink of 21st Century, writer Art & Antiques, Washingtonian, Arts Review. Office: WETA TV 2775 South Quincy St Arlington VA 22206 Office Phone: 703-998-2600. Office Fax: 703-998-3401. E-mail: bill@williamdunlap.com.*

DUNLAP, WILLIAM CRAWFORD, physicist; b. Denver, July 21, 1918; s. William Crawford and Helen (Kiester) D.; m. Ellen Hebrew, Mar. 22, 1940; 1 dau., Nancy. BS, U. N.M., 1938; PhD, U. Calif. at Berkeley, 1943. Asst. physicist Dept. Agr., 1942-45; research asso., research lab. Gen. Electric Co., 1945-55, cons. physicist electronics lab., 1955-56; supr. solid state research, research lab. Bendix Corp., 1956-58; dir. solid state electronic research Raytheon Co., 1958-64; asst. dir. electronic components research Electronics Research Center, NASA, Cambridge, Mass., 1964-68, dir. research, 1968-70; sci. adviser to dir. U.S. Transp. Systems Center, Cambridge, 1970-75; pres. W.C. Dunlap & Co., 1975—. Author: An Introduction to Semiconductors, 1957; founding editor, editor-in-chief Solid State Electronics, 1959-94. Fellow IEEE (dir. 1966-68, dir. region I 1966-68), Am. Phys. Soc., AIAA (assoc.). Achievements include special research transistor production techniques in alloying, diffusion, epitaxy. Home and Office: 126 Prince St Newton MA 02465-2604 E-mail: crawdunlap@comcast.net.

DUNLAP, WILLIAM DEWAYNE, JR., advertising agency executive; b. Austin, Minn., Apr. 8, 1938; s. William D. and Evelyn (Hummel) D.; m. Lois Mary Apple, Sept. 23, 1961; children: Kristin, Leslie, Brenda. BA, Carleton Coll., 1960. Brand mgr. soap Procter & Gamble, Cin., 1960-69; asst. postmaster gen. U.S. Postal Svc., Washington, 1970-75, chmn. postmaster gen.'s customer coun., 1971-75, chmn. stamp adv. coun., 1972-75; pres. MCA Advt., Westport, Conn., 1976-81, Campbell-Mithun Esty, Mpls., 1981—2003, CEO, 1983—2003, chmn., 1994—2003, Petters Consumer Brands, Mpls., 2004—. Bd. dirs. Operation Smile Internat. Lutheran. Office: Petters Consumer Brands 4400 Baker Rd Hopkins MN 55343-8684 Office Phone: 952-934-9918.*

DUNLEAVY, MICHAEL JOSEPH, professional basketball coach; b. Brooklyn, NY, Mar. 21, 1954; m. Emily Dunleavy; children: Michael, William Baker, James. Ed., Univ. S.C. Player Phila. 76ers, NBA, 1976-77; former player-coach Carolina Lightning, All-Am. Basketball Alliance; player Houston Rockets, NBA, 1978-83, San Antonio Spurs, NBA, 1982, Milw. Bucks, 1984, asst. coach, to 1990; head coach L.A. Lakers, 1990-92, Milw. Bucks, 1992-93, gen. mgr., v.p. basketball ops., 1993-96; head coach Portland (Oreg.) Trailblazers, 1997—2001, LA Clippers, 2003—. Office: Portland Trailblazers One Center Ct Ste 200 Portland OR 97227

DUNLEAVY, MIKE, SR., professional basketball coach; 1 child, Mike Jr. Grad., U. S.C., 1976. Profl. basketball player Phila. 76'ers, 1976—78, Houston Rockets, 1978—82, San Antonio Spurs, 1982—83, Milw. Bucks, 1983—85, 1988—90, asst. coach, 1986—87, 1989—90; profl. basketball coach L.A. Lakers, 1990—91, Milw. Bucks, 1992—95, Portland Trailblazers, 1997—2001, L.A. Clippers, 2003—. Named NBA Coach of Yr., 1989. Office: Staples Ctr Ste 1100 1111 S Figueroa St Los Angeles CA 90015

DUNLEVIE, STEVEN S., lawyer; b. Atlanta, Ga., Apr. 24, 1948; BA, U. NC, Chapel Hill, 1970; JD, Emory U., 1973. Bar: Ga. 1973, admitted to practice: All Ga. Trial and Appellate Cts., US Dist. Ct. (No. Dist. Ga.). Atty. Office of Judge Advocate, US Navy, Charleston, SC, 1973; assoc. atty. Hule, Stern, Brown & Ide (formerly known as Ware & Sterne), Atlanta, 1973—77; ptnr. Ware, Hopkins, Dunlevie & McNairy, Atlanta, 1977—80, Parker, Johnson, Cook & Dunlevie, Atlanta, 1981—96; mem. mgmt. com. Womble Carlyle Sandridge & Rice, PLLC, Atlanta, 1996—, mng. mem. Lt. USNR, 1970—73. Mem.: Ga. State Bar, Internat. Assn. of Attys. and Execs. in Corp. Real Estate, Ga. Bankers Assn. (mem. bank counsel sect.), Am. Judicature Soc., ABA (mem. real property, probate & trust law sect., mem. brokers & brokerage and conveyancing Committees), Atlanta Bar Assn. (mem. corp., banking & real property law sect.). Office: Womble Carlyle Snadridge & Rice PLLC One Atlantic Ctr Ste 3500 1201 West Peachtree St Atlanta GA 30339 Office Phone: 404-888-7401. Office Fax: 404-870-4828. Business E-Mail: sdunlevie@wcsr.com.

DUNLEVY, WILLIAM SARGENT, lawyer; b. Burbank, Calif., June 5, 1952; s. Roy William and Zella LaVerne (Singleton) D.; m. Margaret Joy Lehman Dunlevy, June 22, 1974; children: Thomas William, Gregory Michael. BA, U. Calif., Davis, 1974; JD, UCLA, 1977. Bar: Calif. 1977. Lawyer Law office of Robert Silver, Ventura, Calif., 1977-80, Taylor, Churchman & Lingl, Camarillo, Calif., 1980-84, Liebmann & Dunlevy, Camarillo, Calif., 1984-88, James P. Lingl & Assoc., Camarillo, Calif., 1988-97, Knopfler & Robertson, Camarillo, Calif., 1998-2001; pvt. practice, 2001—. Editor Inst. Channel Islands chpt. Cmty. Assn., Ventura, Calif., 1984—, pres., 1986-87. Pres. Ventura (Calif.) Downtown Lions Club, 1985-86; bd. mem. Am. Youth Soccer Orgn., Ventura, Calif., 1986-88, 90-96. Mem. Community Assn. Inst., Poinsetta Lodge. Republican. Baptist. Avocations: photography, hiking. Office: Law Offices William S Dunlevy 1200 Paseo Camarillo Ste 255 Camarillo CA 93010-6085 Fax: 805-383-6227. E-mail: dunlevylaw@aol.com.

DUNLOP, DAVID JOHN, geophysics educator, researcher; b. Toronto, Ont., Can., Jan. 30, 1941; s. Harry John Ewart and Mary Scott Dunlop; children: Lisa Karen, Jennifer Michelle; m. Özden Özdemir, June 2, 1987. BSc, U. Toronto, 1963, MA, 1964, PhD, 1968. Postdoctoral studies U. Tokyo, 1968-69; rsch. fellow Université de Paris VI, 1969-70; asst. prof. U. Toronto, 1970-73, assoc. prof., 1973-78, prof., 1978—. Vis. scientist NASA Johnson Space Ctr., Houston, 1972; sr. vis. scientist CSIRO, Sydney, Australia, 1992; assoc. prof. U. Montpellier, France, 1997; vis. prof. U. Paris VII, 2004. Editor: Origin of Thermomagnetism, 1977; assoc. editor Can. Jour. Earth Scis., 1983-94; co-author: Rock Magnetism Fundamentals and Frontiers, 1997, 2d edit., 2001. Killam Found. fellow, Can. Coun., 1983-85, USSR Acad. Scis. fellow, 1988, Sr. Rsch. fellow Tokyo Inst. Tech., 1988-89, DAAD rsch. fellow Munich, 1990; sr. rsch. fellow Kyoto (Japan) U., 1997, 2003; recipient Louis Néel medal European Geophys. Soc., 1999. Fellow Royal Soc. Can., Am. Geophys. Union (sect. pres. 1992-94), Geol. Assn. Can. (councillor 1985-87); mem. Can. Geophys. Union (pres. 1985-87, Tuzo Wilson medal 1999). Avocations: canoeing, hiking, lepidoptera, photography, restoring old houses. Office: U Toronto Dept Physics Toronto ON Canada M5S 1A7

DUNLOP, EDWARD ARTHUR, computer company executive; b. Wilmington, Del., 1951; s. Edward C. and Eleanor (Smith) D.; m. Gladys Englehart, July 21, 1984; 1 child, Elizabeth. BS, U. Del., 1978, postgrad., 1978-79. Rsch. asst., cons. U. Del., Newark, 1972-78; pres. Technology Logistics, Newark, 1978-85, West Chester, Pa., 1989—; asst. to v.p. Continental Ins. Co., Neptune, N.J., 1985-88; sr. project mgr., asst. to vice chmn. Roy F. Weston Inc., West Chester, 1988-89. Voting mem. Nat. Standards com. on Local and Metro. Area Networks, 1994—; advisor Nat. Computer Security Ctr., Nat. Security Agy., Nat. Inst. Stds. and Tech., U.S. Govt., 1985-2001. Mem. Coun. on Environ Control State of Del., 1975-81. Univ. fellow bus. and govt. ethics U. Del., 1983-85. Mem. IEEE, IEEE Computer Soc., Assn. for Computing Machinery, Ea. Tech. Coun. Office: Technology Logistics 1265 Estate Dr West Chester PA 19380-1258 E-mail: ed@computer.org.

DUNLOP, FRED HURSTON, lawyer; b. Clarksville, Tenn., May 3, 1946; s. William Barrett and Nelle Major (Hurston) D.; m. Jacqueline Rae Thompson, Aug. 17, 1968; children: Holt McKinney, Lindsay Barrett. BA, Vanderbilt U., 1968, JD, 1971. Bar: Tenn. 1971, Tex. 1972; comml. mediator, arbitration cert. Internat. Ctrs. Arbitration. Assoc. Baker Botts LLP, Houston, 1972—78, ptnr., 1979—. 1st lt. U.S. Army, 1971-72. Fellow Tex. Bar Found.; mem. ABA, Am. Coll. Real Estate Lawyers, State Bar Tex., Houston Bar Assn., Houston Real Estate Lawyers Coun., Coll. of State Bar of Tex. Avocations: golf, hunting, skiing. Home: 5609 Tupper Lake Dr Houston TX 77056-1628 Office: Baker Botts LLP 1 Shell Pla 910 Louisiana St Ste 3100 Houston TX 77002-4916 E-mail: fred.dunlop@bakerbotts.com.

DUNLOP, GEORGE RODGERS, retired surgeon; b. St. Peter, Minn., Mar. 31, 1906; s. George Crawford and Pearl (Rodgers) D.; m. Barbara Wallace, Apr. 3, 1939; children: Susan Dunlop Roberts, Madora Howell. BS, U. Cin., 1927; MD, Harvard U., 1931. Diplomate Am. Bd. Surgery. Intern Cin. Gen. Hosp., 1931-32; asst. resident in surgery N.Y. Hosp.-Cornell Med. Ctr., 1932-35; resident in surgery Worcester (Mass.) City Hosp., 1935-36; practice medicine specializing in surgery, 1935-82; sr. surgeon, past chief surgery Worcester Meml. Hosp. Prof. surgery emeritus U. Mass. Med. Sch.; dir., past chmn. Mass. Blue Shield; bd. dirs., past chmn. bd. Nat. Assn. Blue Shield Plans; past dir. Med. Indemnity Am.; bd. commrs. Joint Commn. Accreditation Hosps., chmn. bd. coms.; mem. Pres.'s Commn. for Study of Ethical Problems in Medicine and Biomed. and Behavioral Rsch. Bd. dirs. Meml. Hosp. Found.; bd. dirs., past chmn. Mass. divsn. Am. Cancer Soc., also, Worcester Found. Exptl. Biology; bd. dirs. U. Mass. Med. Sch. Found., Meml. Health Care Found.; past bd. dirs. Bancroft Sch., Worcester Boys' Club, Cmty. Chest. Served to lt. comdr. M.C. USNR, 1942-45. Fellow ACS (past pres.), Royal Australasian Coll. Surgeons (hon.); mem. AMA, New Eng. Surg. Soc. (past pres.), New Eng. Cancer Soc., Northwestern Med. Soc. (past pres.), Am. Surg. Assn., Boston Surg. Soc., Soc. Surgery Alimentary Tract (founder), Pan Am. Med. Assn. Clubs: Worcester. Home: 54 Massachusetts Ave Worcester MA 01602-2139 Office: 340 Main St Ste 356 Worcester MA 01608-1606

DUNLOP, KAREN OWEN, lawyer; b. 1966; BS, Georgetown U., 1987; MA, U. Va., 1989, JD, 1992. Bar: Ill. 1992. With Sidley Austin Brown & Wood, Chgo., 1992—, ptnr., 2001—. Mem.: Am. Health Lawyers Assn. (vice chair health sys. transactions com.). Office: Sidley Austin Brown and Wood Bank One Plz 10 S Dearborn St Chicago IL 60603

DUNLOP, MARIANNE, retired language educator; b. Niobrara, Nebr, Mar. 14, 1933; d. Harvey Wesley LaBranche and Karen Sanna Arneson; m. Richard Campbell Dunlop, Apr. 26, 1959; 1 child, Christopher Campbell. BA, Vt. Coll., 1985, MA, 1989. Bd. dir./bd. mem. The Sargent House Mus., Gloucester, Mass., 1992-96; ESL educator Penasquitos Laubach Literacy Ctr., San Diego, 1999—2002; ret., 2002. Author: (book) Judith Sargent Murray: Champion of Social Justice, 1993; editor: (book) Judith Sargent Murray: Her First 100 Letters, 1995; writer, contbr.: (book) Standing Before Us: Unitarian Universalist Women and Social Reform 1776-1936, 1999; spkr., contbr. (documentary) Judith Sargent Murray: 18th Century Feminist. Officer, bd. dirs. Sargent House Mus., Gloucester, Mass., 1992—96, mem. adv. bd., 1996—; ESL educator Penasquitos Laubach Literacy Ctr., San Diego, 1999—2002; mem. Sargent House Mus. Mem. Virginia Woolf's Outsider Soc. Unitarian Universalist. Avocation: honoring otherness. Home: 11032 Ipai Ct San Diego CA 92127-1382

DUNLOP, SCOTT GRAHAM, lawyer; b. Honolulu, Oct. 5, 1958; s. R. Graham Dunlop and Martha J. (Bloomstrand) Solomon; m. Katherine A. Sherry, Oct. 4, 1986; children: Hannah Sherry, Samuel Graham, Molly Katherine. BA in History, BSBA Bus. Mgmt., W.Va. U., 1981; JD, U. Pitts., 1984. Bar: Pa. 1984, U.S. Dist. Ct. (we. dist.) Pa. 1985, U.S. Supreme Ct. 1988, U.S. Ct. Appeals (3d cir.) 1994. Law clk. to Honorable John F. Rauhauser Jr. York (Pa.) County Ct. Common Pleas, 1984-85; assoc. Gaitens Tucceri & Nicholas P.C., Pitts., 1985-88, Zimmer Kunz P.C., Pitts., 1988-93, Marshall Dennehey Warner Coleman & Goggin, Pitts., 1993-94, shareholder, br. office mgr., 1995—, sr. v.p., bd. dirs., 2004—. Mem. Allegheny County Bar Assn. Office: Marshall Dennehey Warner Coleman & Goggin PC 600 Grant St Ste 2900 Pittsburgh PA 15219-2713

DUNN, ANNE EWALD NEFFLEN, retired elementary school educator; b. Elkins, W.Va., Feb. 9, 1935; d. Edgar Lantz and May (Bradley) Nefflen; m. Delma Douglas Dunn, July 20, 1961; children: Susan Bradley Dunn, Robert Cameron, Richard Tullos. BS in Home Econs., U. Md., 1956; student, U. Miami, 1953-54, San Diego State Coll., 1958-60; MEd, U. Ark., 1985. Cert. elem. tchr., reading specialist, gifted and talented, Ark. Tchr. 2d grade San Diego City Schs., 1958-61, Oak Harbor (Wash.) Schs., 1961-63; tchr. 2d and 3d grades Albuquerque Pub. Schs., 1963-65; tchr. 3d grade Prairie Grove (Ark.) Sch. Dist., 1978-85, tchr. gifted and talented, coord., 1985-88, tchr. remedial reading and math., 1988-92, tchr., coord. At-Risk Alternative Edn. 1st grade, 1992-94, chpt. I reading specialist, reading tchr., 1994—2003; ret. Interviewer Navy Relief Soc., Whidbey Island, Wash., 1961-63. Leader 4-H Horse Club, Whidbey Island, 1961-63, 4-H Club, Prairie Grove, 1979-81; leader, trainer Girl Scouts U.S., Prairie Grove, 1975-78; mem. Prairie Grove Libr. Bd., 1980-82; show sec. Nat. Arabian Horse Assn. Show, Albuquerque, 1965. Mem. Phi Delta Kappa. Presbyterian. Avocations: sewing, reading, horseback riding. Home: 22530 Cove Crk S Prairie Grove AR 72753-9230 Office: Prairie Grove Elem Sch 824 N Mock St Prairie Grove AR 72753-2610

DUNN, ARNOLD SAMUEL, biochemistry educator; b. Rochester, N.Y., Jan. 31, 1929; s. Alexander and Dora (Cohen) D.; m. Doris Ruth Frankel, Sept. 14, 1952; children: Jonathan Alexander, David Hillel. BS, George Washington U., 1950; PhD, U. Pa., 1955; LHD (hon.), Hebrew Union Coll., 1995. Research assoc. Michael Reese Hosp. Research Inst., Chgo., 1955-56; asst. prof. NYU Sch. Medicine, N.Y.C., 1956-62; vis. prof. Weizmann Inst. Sci., Rehovot, Israel, 1972-73, 83-84, Hebrew U., Jerusalem, 1972-73; prof. molecular biology U. So. Calif., Los Angeles, 1962—, dir. molecular biology L.A., 1982-90, assoc. dean, 1990-92; vis. fellow history sci. Princeton U., 1993. Contbr. articles to profl. jours.; mem. editorial bd.: Am. Jour. Physiology, 1979-, Analytical Biochemistry, 1980-. UPSHS fellow, 1972, 83; Meyerhoff fellow Weizmann Inst. Sci., 1983. MEm. Am. Physiol. Soc., Am. Soc. Biol. Chemists, Endocrine Soc., Phi Beta Kappa, Sigma Xi, Phi Kappa Phi, Golden Key. Office: U So Calif University Park Los Angeles CA 90089-0001 Office Phone: 213-740-8230. E-mail: arnolddu@usc.edu.

DUNN, BERNARD DANIEL, former naval officer, consultant; b. Providence, Feb. 10, 1934; s. Alexander Gerard and Mary Alice (Fitzpatrick) D.; m. Hilda Hughes Tunney, Jan. 4, 1958; children: Bernard Daniel Jr., Brian Lindsay, Mary Catherine, J. Alexander. BS in Econs., Villanova U., 1956; MBA in Transp., Mich. State U., 1971. Commd. ensign USN, 1956, advanced through grades to capt.; asst. supply and disbursing officer USS Rushmore, Little Creek, Va., 1957-58; asst. material divsn. officer, stock control divsn. officer Sub Base New London, Groton, Conn., 1958-61; material and fiscal divsn. supt. Ship Repair Facility, Guam, 1961-63; nuclear weapons material divsn. officer Naval Supply Ctr., Oakland, Calif., 1963-64; supply ops. officer Nuc. Weapons Supply Annex, Oakland, Calif., 1964-65; commn. supply officer USS Fox, 1965-68; project officer Naval Supply Sys. Command, Washington, 1968-70; asst. for sea transp. Office Chief Naval Ops., Washington, 1971-73; sr. mem. Mobile Tng. Team to Colombian Navy, Bogota, Colombia, 1973; dir. warehousing, chief transp. office Def. Depot, Tracy, Calif., 1973-76; dep. project mgr., Navy rep. Joint Container Steering Group Office of Sec. of Def., Washington, 1976-77; dir. transp. field ops. divsn. Naval Supply Sys. Command, Washington, 1977-78; head transp. mgmt. and policy br. Office Chief Naval Ops., Washington, 1978-83; comptr./dir. supply Naval Edn. and Tng. Command, Newport, R.I., 1983-85; A-76 program officer Mil. Sealift Command, Washington, 1985; acting dir./chief staff commn. on Merchant Marine and Def., Alexandria, Va., 1985-88; bd. dirs., corp. sec. Greenwich Ctr., Inc., East Greenwich, RI, 1988—2002. Cons., Alexandria, Va., 1988-91; chief program analyst Resource Cons., Inc., Vienna, Va., 1991-94, sr. supply specialist, 91-98. Life mem. East Greenwich (R.I.) Fire Dept., 1953—. Decorated Def. Meritorious Svc. medal, Meritorious Svc. medal, Joint Svc. Commendation medal with oak leaf cluster, Navy Meritorious Unit commendation, Air Force Outstanding Unit award, Humanitarian medal, Nat. Def. Svc. medal, Vietnam Svc. medal with one bronze star, Rep. of Vietnam Campaign medal. Mem. U.S. Naval Inst., Nat. Def. Transp. Assn. (pres. San Joaquin chpt. 1974-75), USCG Acad. Found., East Greenwich Vets. firemen Assn., Mil. Officers Assn., Washington Area Navy Supply Corps Assn., Naval Submarine League, USS Rushmore Assn. (founder and charter mem., assoc. treas.1995-2001, 1st v.p. 2003-). Roman Catholic. Avocations: stamp collecting/philately, ice hockey, running, volunteer fireman, golf. Home: 5817 Shalott Ct Alexandria VA 22310-1427 E-mail: bddunn@erols.com.

DUNN, BRUCE SIDNEY, materials science educator; m. Wendy Joan Rader, 1970; 1 child. BS in Ceramic Engrng., Rutgers U., 1970; MS in Materials Sci., UCLA, 1972, PhD in Materials Sci., 1974. Staff scientist GE, Schenectady, N.Y., 1976-80; assoc. prof. materials sci. UCLA, 1981-85, prof., 1985—, Nippon Sheet Glass chair materials sci., 2003. Cons. to numerous corps.; invited prof. U. Paris, 1986, 91, 92, 93, 98, U. Bordeaux, 2000 Contbr. articles to profl. jours. Fulbright fellow, 1985-86. Fellow Am. Ceramic Soc.; mem. Electrochem. Soc., Materials Rsch. Soc. Achievements include patents in field. Office: UCLA Dept Materials Scis & Engring 6532 Boelter Hl Los Angeles CA 90095-0001

DUNN, CHARLES DEWITT, academic administrator; b. Magnolia, Ark., Dec. 2, 1945; s. Charles Edward and Nora Lucille (Bailey) D.; m. Donna Jane Parsons, Apr. 9, 1966; children: Aimee, James, Joseph, Mary Elizabeth. BA, So. Ark. U., 1967; MA, North Tex. State U., 1970; PhD, So. Ill. U., 1973; cert. inst. ednl. mgmt., Harvard U., 1991. Instr. polit. sci. U. Ark., Monticello, 1969-72, asst. prof., 1972-75; assoc. prof. U. Ctrl. Ark., Conway, 1975-80, prof., 1980—, chmn. dept. polit. sci., 1976-82, dir. govt. rels., 1982-86; pres. Henderson State U., Arkadelphia, Ark., 1986—. Chmn. Commn. Ark.'s Future, 1989-93; chmn. Ark. Higher Edn. Coun., 1992-96; chmn. fin. com. Ark. Cmty. Found. Bd. Dirs., v.p., 2000-02, pres., 2002-03; active Blue Ribbon Commn. Pub. Edn., 2001-02, Ark. Commn. Coordination Edn., 2004-; bd. dirs. Meth. Children's Home, 2003-. Mem. Am. Assn. State Coll. and Univs., NCAA (pres.'s commn. 1996-97, pres.' coun. 1997-2001, pres. Gulf South conf. 1998-2000), Ark. Polit. Sci. Assn. (pres. 1976-77), Conway C. of C. (bd. dirs. 1984-85, v.p. 1985-86), Arkadelphia C. of C. (bd. dirs. 1987-91), Rotary. Methodist. Office: Henderson State U PO Box 7532 1100 Henderson St Arkadelphia AR 71999-0001 Office Phone: 870-230-5091. Business E-Mail: cddunn@hsu.edu.

DUNN, CHRISTOPHER JOSEPH, public affairs consultant; b. Oak Park, Ill., June 20, 1952; s. Paul Joseph and Kathryn Dooley Dunn; m. Elizabeth Catherine Hanley; children: Christopher Patrick children: John Fitzgerald. BA, U. Ill., Chgo., 1974; MA, U. Chgo., 1976; JD, DePaul U., 1982. Bar: Ill. 1982, U.S. Dist. Ct. (no. dist.) Ill. 1982. Cen. states regional dir. external affairs AT&T Wireless, Chgo., 1995—2005; exec. asst. to adminstr./White House liaison NASA, Washington, 1993—95; search mgr. Office of Presdl. Pers. The White House, Washington, 1993—93; spl. asst. to adminstr./White House liaison U.S. Gen. Svcs. Adminstrn., Washington, 1993—93; dir. state regulatory affairs City of Chgo., 1991—93; gen. counsel U.S. Sen. Paul Simon U.S. Senate, Washington, 1989—91; counsel subcom. on Constn., minority counsel subcom. on juvenile justice U.S. Senate Com. on the Judiciary, Washington, 1985—89; atty. Law Offices Gerhard E. W. Kelter, Jr., Chgo., 1982—85; environmentalist U.S. Dept. Commerce - Econ. Devel. Adminstrn., Chgo., 1977—80; sr. v.p. The Dunn Group, LLC. Chmn. bd. police and fire commrs. Village of Wilmette, Ill., 1999—; chmn. Govt. Assistance Program DePaul U., Chgo., 1999—; alt. del. to Dem. Nat. Conv. Ill.'s 10th Congl. Dist., L.A., 2000—00; standing com. on rules Dem. Nat. Conv., Chgo., 1996—96. Roman Catholic. Avocations: travel, reading. Home: 1616 Highland Ave Wilmette IL 60091 Office: AT&T Wireless Ste 400 227 W Monroe Chicago IL 60606

DUNN, CRAIG ANDREW, entertainer, conductor, writer, composer, educator; b. Point Pleasant, N.J., Nov. 11, 1947; s. Andrew Robert and Ruth Agnes (Schott) D.; m. Crystal Lynn Kesler, May 26, 1970. MusB, U. Cin., 1972; MusM, Ohio U., 1973; EdD, Nova Southeastern U., 1996. Cert. tchr., Fla. Dir. bands Greenville (S.C.) Sr. H.S., 1973-74, Bayonne (N.J.) H.S., 1974-75; studio instr. Buddy Rogers Music Studios, Inc., Cin., 1975-78; music specialist, music dir. Diocese of St. Petersburg, Fla., 1979-88; music specialist Sch. Dist. of Hillsborough County, Tampa, Fla., 1988—; performing artist, entertainer, 1972—; mem. faculty music St. Petersburg Coll., Fla., 2001—. Mem. adv. bd. Am. Youth Symphony Band and Chorus, Pitts., 1980-85, artistic advisor, coach, 1980, 83, 85; dir. sch. dance and choral ensembles Fla. State Fair, 1992—. Composer: The Devil's Jester, 1971, Come to Me, 1971, Fishers of Men, 1976, The One-Hundred Fiftieth Psalm, 1976, A Mass for the Feast of the Triumph of the Cross, 1981; contbr. articles to profl. jours. Mem. Music Educators Nat. Conf., Fla. Music Educators Assn., Nat. Acad. Songwriters (pub. composer, author). Avocations: orchestrating, writing, reading. Home: 11800 4th St E Isle of Capri Treasure Island FL 33706

DUNN, DAVID BENJAMIN, II, music educator; b. Dothan, Ala., Oct. 22, 1970; s. David Benjamin and Beulah Mae Dunn; m. Delila Ann Cuthriell, Oct. 4, 2003. B in music edn., Auburn U., 1997; M in counselling psychology, Troy U., 2005. Band dir. Phillips H.S., Bear Creek, Ala., 1998—99, Graceville H.S., Fla., 1999—2000; ptnr. Winding Oaks Drafting, Georgetown, Ga., 2000—02; band dir. Samson H.S., Ala., 2002—04; tchr. Laurel Oaks Behavior Clinic, Dothan, Ala., 2004—. Judge Honor Band, Geneva, 2002. Mem.: Chi Sigma Iotu, Phi Mu Alpha. Avocations: reading, boating, swimming, video games, walking. Home: 102 Leafwood Circle Enterprise AL 36330

DUNN, DAVID E., university dean; b. Dallas, Oct. 13, 1935; s. Nelson E. and Lemoine (Kellett) Dunn Neal; m. Gretchen Yost, Jan. 24, 1958 (dec. 1987); children: Dusty, Peter; m. Sarah Sue Holmes, Dec. 25, 1990. BS in Geology, So. Meth. U., 1957, MS, 1959; PhD, U. Tex., 1964. Cert. profl. geologist. Instr. geology U. Tex., Austin, 1960-61; asst. prof. geology Tex. Tech. Inst., Lubbock, 1962-63, U. N.C., Chapel Hill, 1963-66, assoc. prof., 1967-73, prof., 1973-79; dean coll. sci. U. New Orleans, 1979-84; dean Sch. Natural Sci. and Math. U. Tex.-Dallas, 1984-97, prof., dean emeritus, 1998—. Cons. various legal firms, N.C., 1967-79, Pennzoil, Houston, 1980-87, Amoco, Houston, 1982-89. Oryx. 1991-92; chmn. La. Univs. Marine Consortium, Baton Rouge, 1981-83; chmn. bd. dirs. Drilling, Observation and Sampling of Earth's Continental Crust Inc. 1991-93; chmn. steering com. VIIth Internat. Symposium on Continental Sci. Drilling, 1994. Co-author: A Characterization of Faults in the Appalachian Foldbelt, 1980; contbr. chpt. to book, articles to sci. jours. Fund-raiser numerous candidates, Chapel Hill, 1969-75. Fellow Geol. Soc. Am. (chmn. structure and tectonics div. 1983, councilor 1985-87, 92-2001, treas. 1992-2001, Disting. Svc. award 2002); mem. AAAS, Am. Geophys. Union, Am. Inst. Profl. Geologists, Geol. Soc. Am. Found. (trustee 2001—), Carolina Geol. Soc. (chmn. 1968-69). Home: 6 Crown Pl Richardson TX 75080-1603 Office: Univ of Tex at Dallas Dept Geoscis PO Box 688 Richardson TX 75083-0688 Office Phone: 972-883-4044. Business E-Mail: ddunn@utdallas.edu.

DUNN, DAVID JOSEPH, investment company executive; b. Bklyn., July 30, 1930; s. David Joseph and Rose Marie (McLaughlon) Dunn; m. Marilyn Percaccia, June 1955 (div.); children: Susan, Steven, Linda; m. Marilyn Bell, Apr. 1994. BS, U.S. Naval Acad., 1955; MBA, Harvard U., 1961. Investment banker G.H. Walker & Co., N.Y.C., 1961-62; ptnr. J.H. Whitney & Co., N.Y.C., 1962-70; mng. ptnr. Idanta Ptnrs., San Diego, 1971—. Chmn. bd. dirs. FORT Properties Inc., Munchkin, Inc.; bd. dirs. Engineous Software, NanoNexus. With USMC, 1950—51, with USMC, 1955—59. Mem.: Glenwild Country Club, Del Mar Country Club, Vintage Club, La Jolla Country Club, Univ. Club (N.Y.C.). Office: Idanta Ptnrs 12526 High Bluff Dr Ste 160 San Diego CA 92130

DUNN, DAVID L., sales executive; b. Washington, Pa., Jan. 19, 1938; s. Herbert M. and Dorothy L. Dunn; m. Diana DeBlander (div.); children: Mark David, Brent Allan; m. Deborah M. Juras. Attended, Muskingum Coll., New Concord, OH, 1955—59; student in Dentistry, U. Pitts., 1960—61. Divsn. sales mgr. World Book Ency., Pitts., 1966—75, Phoenix, 1975—81, western US and Can. sales mgr. Chgo., 1981—93, dir. sch., libr. sales, 1993—95; dir. sch. sales Baker & Taylor, Bridgewater, NJ; nat. sales mgr. Millbrook Press, Brookfield, Conn., 1997—2003, Bearport Pub. Co., NYC, 2004—. Mem. Rotary Internat., Pitts., 1967—75, Willow Creek Cmty. Ch., S. Barrington, Ill., 1997—. Protestant. Avocations: golf, exercise, reading.

DUNN, DEBRA L., computer company executive; B.Comparative Econs., Brown U., Providence; M.Bus., Harvard U. Exec. devel. mgr. corp. tng. divsn. Hewlett-Packard Co., Palo Alto, Calif., 1983—86, various devel. and mfg. mgmt. positions, 1986—92, mfg. mgr., 1992—93, mktg. mgr., 1993—96, gen. mgr. video comm. divsn., 1996—98, gen. mgr. exec. com., 1998, v.p., 1999—2000, v.p. strategy and corp. ops., 2000—02, sr. v.p. corp. affairs, 2002—. Mem. UN Info. and Comm. Tech. Task Force; bd. dirs. Opportunities Industrialization Ctr. West, BayCat. Office: Hewlett Packard Co 3000 Hanover St Palo Alto CA 94304

DUNN, DELMER DELANO, political science professor; b. Sentinel, Okla., Oct. 31, 1941; s. Robert Patrick and Mildred Marion D.; m. Ann Gregg Swinford, May 15, 1971; children: John Swinford, Kielly McKee BA, Okla. State U., 1963; MS, U. Wis., 1964, PhD, 1967. Asst. prof. polit. sci. U. Ga., Athens, 1967-71, assoc. prof., 1971-77, prof., 1977-82, Regents prof., 1982—, dir. Inst. Govt., 1973-82, acting head dept. polit. sci., 1987-88, assoc. v.p. acad. affairs, 1988-91, dir. Inst. Higher Edn., 2001—02, v.p. instrn., 2002—; rsch. assoc. The Brookings Instn., Washington, 1969-70. Vis. fellow dept. polit. sci. faculty of arts Australian Nat. U., Canberra, 1992. Author: Public Officials and the Press, 1969, Financing Presidential Campaigns, 1972, Politics and Adminstration at the Top: Lessons from Down Under, 1997 (Charles Levine Book award 1998); mem. editl. bd. Social Sci. quar., 1988-94; contbr. articles to profl. jours. Trustee Leadership Ga., 1976-82; pres. Clarke/Oconee unit Am. Cancer Soc., 1981-82, chmn., 1982-83. Mem. AAAS, Am. Polit. Sci. Assn. (Congl. fellow, 1968-69), Nat. Assn. Schs. of Pub. Affairs and Adminstrn. (pres. 1987-88), Am. Soc. Pub. Adminstrn., Pi Alpha Alpha (nat. pres. 1983-85). Presbyterian. Office: Univ Ga Sch Pub and Internat Affairs Athens GA 30602 Business E-Mail: ddunn@uga.edu.

DUNN, DONALD JACK, law librarian, educator, dean, lawyer; b. Tyler, Tex., Nov. 9, 1945; s. Loren Jack and Clara Inez (Milam) Dunn; m. Cheryl Jean Sims, Nov. 24, 1967; 1 child, Kevin. BA., U. Tex.-Austin, 1969, MLS, 1972; JD, Western New Eng. Coll., 1983. Asst. to law libr. U. Tex., 1969-72, supervising libr. Criminal Justice Reference Libr., 1972-73; law libr., prof. law Western New Eng. Coll., Springfield, Mass., 1973-96, interim dean, 1996-98, dean, 1998—2001, assoc. dean for libr. and info. resources, prof. law, 2002—03; dean, prof. law U. La Verne Coll. Law, Ontario, Calif., 2003—. Editor (with Flynn): Immigration and Nationality Law Rev., vols. 3-7, 1979—84; editor: (with Mersky) Fundamentals of Legal Research, 8th edit., 2002. Bd. dirs. Pioneer Valley chpt. ARC. Fellow: Am. Bar Found.; mem.: ABA (chair law librs. com. 1988—92), ALA, Am. Law Inst., Law Librs. New Eng. (pres. 1982—83), Spl. Libr. Assn., Am. Assn. Law Librs. (chair acad. law librs. spl. interest sect. 1989—90), Scribes. Democrat. Episcopalian. Office: U La Verne Coll Law 320 East D St Ontario CA 91764 Office Phone: 909-460-2020. Business E-Mail: dunnd@ulv.edu.

DUNN, DORIS, retired critical care nurse, artist, rancher; b. Enid, Okla., June 13, 1935; d. Glen Olen Powell and Emma Jean Anderson; m. Lynn E. Dunn, Sept. 13, 1989 (dec. Sept. 17, 1993); m. Leroy George Doerfler, Sept. 7, 1961 (div. Apr. 1971); children: James G., Deborah, Mitchell, Christopher, Vicki. At, Enid Bus. Coll., 1959; AT in Nursing, Barton County CC, Great Bend, Kans., 1969. RN. Charge nurse CCU/ICU, Great Bend, Kans.; head nurse GYN Wesley Med. Ctr., Wichita, Kans., 1973—90, charge CCRN, 1973—90; CCRN St. Francis Med. Ctr., Wichita, 1975—87; horse breeder, 1987—. Lectr. Life Ins. Joint Member, Wichita, 1994—95; instr. Steve Colgate's Offshore Sailing Sch., Tortola, British Virgin Islands, 1989. Author: Painting Your First Portrait - For the Beginner, 2001. Vol. RN to Guatemala; career counselor U.S. Coast Guard Acad. Mem.: Coast Guard Aux. Divsn. 31 (vice capt. 1987—, vessel examiner, staff officer, coxswain-career, Outstanding Individual 1996, Outstanding Divsn. staff officer 1995—96). Democrat. Avocations: painting, horseback riding, sailing. Home: 4135 E Blaney Rd Peyton CO 80831

DUNN, DORIS MARJORY, retired secondary school educator, volunteer; b. Chgo., Jan. 7, 1921; d. William Christian and Mary Esther (Hoffman) Rose; m. Jack Harold Wheeler Dunn, Sept. 19, 1945 (dec. June 1978); children: Randall L., Jon G., Bonham. BS in Edn., Ind. U., 1942; postgrad., Northwestern U., 1943-44; MS, Valparaiso U., 1973. Life lic. in teaching, Ind. Tchr. Crown Point (Ind.) High Sch., 1963-74, Lowell (Ind.) High Sch., 1942-45; sch. tchr., jr. coll. tchr., 1976-78. Asst. to engring.libr. U. Tex., Austin, 1947-49. Pres. LWV, Crown Point, 1974; pres.-elect Good Samaritan Hosp. Aux., v.p., 1988-89, pres., 1989-90; buyer Good Samaritan Gift Shop, 1989—; chmn. ways and means Assistance League, 1988-89, regional coun. rep., 1990-91, mem. resource devel. nat. bd., 1991-98; pres. Luckiamute Water Bd., 1988—; mem. Republican Senatorial Inner Circle, State of Oreg., 1997-98. Mem. P.E.O. (pres. 1989-90), Corvallis Country Club. Ladies Orgn. (pres. 1989-90), Kappa Kappa Kappa (pres. 1975), Delta Kappa Gamma. Methodist. Avocations: wood carving, golf, flying, stained glass creation, travel. Home: 12260 Rolling Hills Rd Monmouth OR 97361-9758

DUNN, DURWOOD, historian, educator; b. Chickamanga, Ga., Nov. 30, 1943; s. Charles Snider and Lucille (Oliver) Dunn. BA, U. Tenn., Knoxville, 1965, MA, 1968, PhD, 1976. Instr. Hiwassee Coll., Madisonville, Tenn., 1970—74; prof. Tenn. Wesleyan Coll., Athens, 1975—, chair dept. history, 1976—. Danforth assoc., 1977—79. Author: (Book) Cades Cove: The Life and Death of a Southern Appalachian Community, 1818-1937, 1988 (Thomas Wolfe Literary award, 1988), An Abolitionist in the Appalachian South, 1997; editor: (Reprint Series) Appalachian Echoes, 1998—. Fellow Woodrow Wilson Nat. fellowship, 1965, Nat. Endowment for Humanities, 1978—79, 1992—93. Mem.: Phi Beta Kappa, Phi Kappa Phi. Methodist. Home: PO Box 1041 Athens TN 37371-1041

DUNN, DWAYNE EARLE, music educator; b. Joplin, Mo., Mar. 7, 1962; s. Lloyd Wayne and Dorothy Sue Dunn, Kay (Francis) Dunn (Stepmother); m. Cynthia Melissa Colwell, Mar. 11, 1996; m. Donna Lee Wilson, May 21, 1983 (div. Mar. 18, 1992); children: Danielle Sue, Bryce Colwell Cahoon, Cuyler Timothy, Cassidy Lisle. MusB in Edn., Tex. Christian U., 1984; MusM in Performance, SW Tex. State U., 1992; PhD in Music Edn., La. State U., 1995. Dir. choral activities Olathe East H.S., Olathe, Kans., 2001—; dir. music grades 5-12 Barstow Sch., Kansas City, Mo., 2000—01; asst. prof. music edn. U. Ariz., Tucson, 1995—2000; asst. dir. choral activities Harlingen Consol. Ind. Sch. Dist., Tex., 1988—91. Musical dir., accompanist Barn Players, Shawnee-Mission, Kans., 2001—03; musical dir., accompanyist Jewish Cmty. Ctr. of Kans. Ct. Theater, 2002—04. Dir., founder (performing ensemble) U. Airz. H.S Outreach Choir (Dean's Fund for Excellence Grant, 1996); contbr. articles to profl. jours. Sr. city counselor Tex. Am. Legion Boys State, Austin, Tex., 1989—2000; elder Lawrence Heights Christian Ch., 2003—. Alumni fellow for doctoral study, La. State U., 1992—95. Mem.: Kans. Choral Dir.'s Assn., Am. Choral Directors Assn., Music Educators Nat. Conf. (ariz. state chairperson: nat. menc collegiate adv. coun. 1995—2000, Chairperson Ariz. chpt., Collegiate adv. coun. 1995—2000), Ariz. Collegiate Music Educators (pres. 1999—2000, pres. 1999—2000), Ariz. Music Educators Assn. (music tchr. edn. chair 1997—99, George C. Wilson Leadership, Svc. award 2000, chair Music Tchr. Edn. 1997—99), Kans. Music Educators Assn., Pi Kappa Lambda, Phi Mu Alpha (chpt. pres. 1982—83, Louden Meml. Scholarship 1983, chpt. pres. 1982—83). Avocations: piano, reading, golf. Office: Olathe East High School 14545 W 127th St Olathe KS 66062 Office Phone: 913-780-7120. Business E-Mail: ddunnoe@olatherschools.com.

DUNN, EDWIN RYDELL, lawyer; b. Boston, July 24, 1942; s. Richard Joseph and Clara Hudson (Rydell) Dunn; m. Kathleen Lynch, July 23, 1966; children: Jeanne, Kathleen, Anne, Daniel. BA U. Notre Dame, 1964; JD cum laude, Northwestern U., Chgo., 1967. Bar: Ill. 1967. Assoc. Baker & McKenzie, Chgo., 1967—73, ptnr., 1973—. Mem. law bd. Northwestern U. Law Sch., 1996—, chmn., 2004—; bd. dirs. Nr. West Side Cmty. Devel. Corp., 1991—. Mem. bd. advisors Cath. Charities, Chgo., 1999—. Mem.: ABA, Ill. Bar Assn., Chgo. Bar Assn. Office: Baker & McKenzie 1 Prudential Pla 130 E Randolph Dr Ste 3900 Chicago IL 60601-6342 Office Phone: 312-861-2864. Business E-Mail: edwin.r.dunn@bakernet.com.

DUNN, FLOYD, biophysics professor, biomedical engineering educator; b. Kansas City, Mo., Apr. 14, 1924; s. Louis and Ida (Leibtag) Dunn; m. Elsa Tanya Levine, June 11, 1950; children: Andrea Susan, Louis Brook. Student, Kansas City Jr. Coll., 1941-42, Tex. A&M U., 1943; BS, U. Ill., Urbana, 1949, MS, 1951, PhD, 1956. Rsch. assoc. elec. engring. U. Ill., Urbana, 1954-57, rsch. asst. prof. elec. engring., 1957-61, assoc. prof. elec. engring. and biophysics, 1961-65, prof., 1965—95, prof. elec. engring., biophysics and bioengring., 1972-95, faculty mem. Beckman Inst. Advanced Sci. and Tech., prof. emeritus, 1995—, dir. bioacoustics rsch. lab., 1976-95, chmn. bioengring. faculty, 1978-82. Vis. prof. U. Coll., Cardiff, Wales, 1968—69, Inst. Chest Diseases and Cancer, Tohoku U., Sendai, Japan, 1982, Sendai, 1989—90, U. Nanjing, China, 1983; mem. bioengirng., radiation and diagnostic radiology study sects. NIH, 1970—81; steering com. workshop interaction ultrasound and biol. tissues NSF, 1971—72; vis. sr. scientist Inst. Cancer Rsch., Sutton, Surrey, England, 1975—76, Sutton, 1982—83, Sutton, 1990; chmn. working group health aspects exposure to ultrasound radiation WHO, London, 1976; mem. tech.-elec. products radiation stds. com. FDA, 1974—76; adj. prof. radiation oncology U. Ariz., Tucson, 1996—; mem. Nat. Coun. Radiation Protection and Measurement, 1980—2003; treas. Interscience Rsch. Inst., Champaign, Ill., 1957—58. Mem. editl. bd. Jour. Acoustical Soc. Am., 1968—, Ultrasound Medicine and Biology, 1981—, Ultrasonics, 1981—2003, Encyclopedia of Acoustics, 1981—97, Encyclopedia of Applied Physics, 1981—, Am. Inst. Physics Series Modern Acoustics and Signal Processing, 1990—97; contbr. articles to profl. jours. Trustee Hensley Twp., Ill., 1980—81. With AUS, 1943—46. Recipient Spl. Merit medal, Acoustical Soc. Japan, 1988, History Med. Ultrasound Pioneer award, AIUM/WFUMB, 1988; fellow, Nat. Coun. Radiation Protection and Measurement, 2003—; Spl. Rsch. fellow, NIH, 1968—69, Eleanor Roosevelt-Internat. Cancer fellow, Am. Cancer Soc., 1975—76, 1982—83, Fulbright fellow, 1982—83, Japan Soc. Promotion Sci. fellow, 1982, 1996, Fogarty Internat. fellow, 1990. Fellow: AAAS, IEEE (life), Inst. Acoustics (U.K.), Am. Inst. Ultrasound in Medicine (William J. Fry meml. award 1984, Joseph H. Holmes Basic Sci. Pioneer award 1990), Acoustical Soc. Am. (assoc. editor Jour. 1968-, exec. coun. 1977-80, v.p. 1980-81, pres. 1985-86, chmn. pub. policy com. 1994-, Silver medal 1989, Gold medal 1998), Am. Inst. Med. Biol. Engring. (IEEE Engring. Medicine and Biology Soc. Career Achievement award 1995, Edison medal 1996), Internat. Acad. Med. Biol. Engring.; mem.: NAE, NAS, Biophys. Soc., Rochester Soc. Biomed. Ultrasound (hon.), Japan Soc. Ultrasound in Medicine (hon.), Am. Inst. Physics (mem. editl. bd. series in modern acoustics and signal processing 1990—97, publs. policy com. 1992—2000), NCRP Alumni Assn., NIH Alumni Assn., Sigma Xi, Phi Sigma Phi, Phi Sigma, Pi Mu Epsilon, Tau Beta Pi, Eta Kappa Nu, Sigma Tau. Home: 2631 E Avenida de Maria Tucson AZ 85718-3081 Personal E-mail: floyd@ece.arizona.edu. *Excellent, dedicated and understanding teachers, bright and energetic students, and a single-mindedness to see a problem to solution are the ingredients for a modest success.*

DUNN, GORDON HAROLD, physicist, researcher; b. Montpelier, Idaho, Oct. 11, 1932; s. Jesse Harold and Winifred Roma (Williams) D.; m. Donetta Dayton, Sept. 25, 1952; children: Jesse Lamont, Randall Dayton, Michael Scott, Brian Eugene, David Edward, Susan, Harold Paul, Richard Elzo. BS in Physics, U. Wash., 1954, PhD in Physics, 1961. NRC postdoctoral rsch. assoc. Nat. Bur. Standards, Washington, 1961-62; physicist Nat. Bur. Standards/Join Inst. for Lab. Astrophysics, Boulder, Colo., 1962-77, chief quantum physics divsn., 1977-85; sr. scientist and fellow Nat. Inst. Standards/Joint Inst. for Lab. Astrophysics, Boulder, 1985—2002. Lectr. dept. physics U. Colo., Boulder, 1964-74, adj. prof., 1974—; commerce sci. fellow Com. on Sci. & Tech., U.S. Ho. of Reps., Washington, 1975-76; chmn. com. on atomic molecular & optical sci. NRC, Washington, 1990-92, vice-chair, 1989-90, mem. com., 1983-86; mem. NRC Panel on Instruments and Facilities, Washington, 1983-84, NRC Panel on Ion Storage Rings for Atomic Physics, 1985-88; chmn. Internat. Conf. on Physics of Electron & Atomic Collisions, 1995-97, vice chair, 1993-95, exec. com., 1991-93, 97-99, gen. com., 1969-73, program com., 1974-75; chmn. Gaseous Electronics Conf., 1968-69, com. mem., 1966-70, sec., 1967-68; chmn. Atomic Processes in High Temperature Plasmas, 1980-81, com. mem., 1977-81, co-sec., 1978-79; co-organizer NATO Advanced Study Inst., 1984-85, U.S.-Japan Workshop, 1985-86; bd. editors Jour. Phys. & Chem. Reference Data, 1990—. Editor, author: Electron-Impact Ionization, 1985; contbr. more than 170 articles to profl. jours. Scoutmaster Boy Scouts Am., Boulder, 1967-72, 87-88; coach, league pres. Little League, Boulder, 1966-71, 76-77; pres. Parent-Tchr. Orgns., Boulder, 1973, 75; bishop LDS Ch., Boulder, 1977-82; trainer family history missionaries Family History Libr., Salt Lake City, 1999-2000. Recipient Gold medal U.S. Dept. Commerce, 1970. Fellow Am. Phys. Soc. (chmn. div. atomic & molecular physics 1989-90, vice-chair 1988-89, exec. com. 1969, 85-88, 91, counsilor 1995-99, audit com. 1996-97, com. constitution & by-laws 1997-99, task force governance 1998-99, panel pub. affairs, Davisson-Germer prize 1984), Joint Inst. for Lab. Astrophysics. Avocations: jogging, skiing, dance, hunting, camping. E-mail: dunn9307@msn.com.

DUNN, H. STEWART, JR., lawyer; b. Pitts., July 9, 1929; s. H. Stewart and Marie (Galvin) D.; m. Martha J. Hoovler (dec. Sept. 1975); children—Christopher T., Anthony S., Timothy P.; m. Loti Kennedy, Aug. 3, 1978. AB, Yale U., 1951; LL.B. magna cum laude, Harvard U., 1954. Bar: D.C. 1954, U.S. Supreme Ct. 1960. Assoc. firm Ivins, Phillips & Barker, Washington, 1957-61, ptnr., 1962—. Bd. dirs. Wilmington Trust Co.; adj. prof. Georgetown U. Law Ctr.; mem. U.S. Com. Selection Jud. Officers, 1977-79, chmn., 1979-81; lectr. Harvard Law Sch., 1986. Bd. editors: Harvard Law Rev, 1953-54. Fellow Am. Bar Found., Am. Coll. Trust and Estate Counsel; mem. ABA (vice chmn. sect. taxation 1970-73), Coll. Tax Counsel, Am. Law Inst. Office: 1700 Pennsylvania Ave NW Washington DC 20006-4704 Office Phone: 702-393-7600.

DUNN, HELEN ELIZABETH, retired secondary school educator; b. Peoria, Ill., July 14, 1930; d. Albert Edward and Corinne Ada (Rudel) Joos; m. Harry Christie Dunn, Feb. 4, 1951; children: Pamela Elizabeth Dunn Baumann, Patricia Louise Dunn Workley. BS in Edn., Bradley U., 1951, MA in Guidance/Counseling, 1969. Tchr. Pub. Schs. of Hawaii, Lanai City, 1951-54, Ulupalakua, 1954-56, Pub. Schs. of Peoria, 1956-69; English LaSalle (Ill.)-Peru H.S., 1970-71; counselor, tchr. Peru (Ill.) Pub. Schs., 1971-89; ret., 1989. Author: This Life I Love, 2005, numerous poems. Presenter programs on Hawaii, Peoria. Mem.: PEO, LWV (bd. dirs. 1973—89, treas. 1982—89), NEA (del. 1951—56, rep. 1957—69), Ret. Tchrs. Assn. (legis. com. 1991—98), Peoria Area Ret. Tchrs. Assn. (sec. 2001—02), Peoria Women's Club Chorus, Peoria Women's Club (corr. sec. 2000—05), Phi Lambda Theta, Sigma Kappa (alumni chpt., pres. 1962, 1991), Delta Kappa Gamma (pres. 1968—70, 1978—80, 1992—94). Methodist. Avocations: poetry, tennis, dance, reading, singing.

DUNN, HOLLAND, banker; b. Charlotte, NC, Mar. 7, 1975; d. Jackson Thomas Dunn, Jr. and Mary Miller Dunn; m. Geoffrey David Farrar, July 19, 2003. BA in Journalism and Mass Comm., U. Ga., 1997; M in Govt. Rels., Harvard U., 2003. Govt. affairs mgr. Am. C. of C., Singapore, 2003—04; assoc. NY Pvt. Bank and Trust, NYC, 2005—. Mgr. patron and programs Boston Lyric Opera, 1999—2002; forum series mgr. JFK Presdl. Libr., Boston, 2002—03; vol. NY Jr. League, 2005—; liason to nat. dir. Dem. Nat. Com., Washington, 1996; event dir., liason Presdl. Inaugural Com., Washington, 1997; event dir. Robert F. Kennedy Meml., Washington, 1997—99. D-Liberal. Catholic. Avocations: international travel, marathons, volunteering. Home: 514 West 114th St #4D New York NY 10025 Office: NY Private Bank and Trust 6 East 43rd St New York NY 10017 Office Phone: 212-850-4079. Personal E-mail: holland_dunn@yahoo.com. E-mail: dunnh@nypbt.com.

DUNN, HORTON, JR., organic chemist; b. Coleman, Tex., Sept. 3, 1929; s. Horton and Lora Dean (Bryant) D. BA summa cum laude, Hardin-Simmons U., 1951; MS, Case Western Res. U., 1975, PhD, 1979. Instr. chemistry Hardin-Simmons U., 1951; ONR fellow Ohio State U., Columbus, 1951-52; teaching fellow in chemistry Purdue U., Lafayette, Ind., 1952-53; rsch. chemist Lubrizol Corp., Cleve., 1953-70, dir. tech. info. ctr., 1970-79, supr. rsch. divsn., 1980-98; pvt. practice Cleve., 1998—. Chmn. bd., bus. mgr. Isotopics, Cleve., 1964-67, editor, 1961-63, supr. rsch. divsn., 1989-97, cons. in field Contbr. articles to profl. jours.; patentee in field. Treas. Cleve. Cir. Decorative Arts Trust, 1990-91, 93—, v.p., 1992-93; bd. mgrs. One Bratenahl Place, 2001—; active Cleve. Art Assn., Rock and Roll Hall of Fame, Mus. Founders Club.; mem., vol. Great Lakes Sci. Ctr., Cleve. Mus. Natural History; mem. Cleve. Bot. Garden, Condr.'s Cir. of Cleve. Orch. Fellow Am. Inst. Chemists; mem. AAAS, SAR (life), Am. Chem. Soc. (treas. Cleve. chpt. 1968-70, chmn. 1987, bd. dirs. 1990—), Am. Soc. for Info. Sci. (chpt. pres. 1973-74), Royal Soc. Chemistry (life), Soc. Tribologists and Lubrication Engrs., Nat. Coun. Met. Opera, Royal Oak Soc. (life), Cleve. Tech. Soc. Coun. (treas. 1987), Cleve. Art Assn., Univ. Club, Cleve. Club, Cleve. Play House Club, Rock and Roll Hall of Fame Mus. Founders Club (charter), English Speaking Union (bd. dirs. Cleve. br. 2005—), Trideca Soc. of Cleve. Mus. Art, Cleve. Skating Club. Home and Office: 1 Bratenahl Pl Apt 103 Bratenahl OH 44108-1152

DUNN, JACKSON THOMAS, JR., lawyer, educator; b. Charlotte, NC, Nov. 30, 1943; s. Jackson Thomas and Dorothy Holland (Schweiger) D.; m. Mary Louise Miller, Apr. 23, 1944; children: Jackson Thomas, Michael Lansing, Mary Katharine Holland. AB, Belmont Abbey Coll., 1965; JD, U. N.C., 1968. Bar: N.C. 1968, U.S. Dist. Ct. (mid. dist.) N.C. 1977, U.S. Dist. Ct. (we. dist.) N.C. 1974, U.S. Supreme Ct. 1982. Asst. prof. East Carolina U., Greenville, N.C., 1968-69, U. Ga., Athens, 1969-75; ptnr. Edwards & Dunn, Charlotte, N.C., 1975; counsel The Ervin Co., Charlotte, N.C., 1976; v.p., sr. counsel Northwestern Fin. Corp./Northwestern Bank, North Wilkesboro, N.C., 1976-85; sr. v.p., dep. gen. counsel 1st Union Corp./1st Union Nat. Bank, Charlotte, 1985-2000; ptnr. Moore & Van Allen PLLC, Charlotte, 2000—. Instr. NC Bankers Assn. Seminars. Contbr. articles to profl. jours. Bd. govs. U. N.C. Law Sch. Alumni Assn.; mem. bd. advisors U. N.C. Law Sch. Banking Inst. Mem.: ABA, N.C. Bankers Assn., Am. Law Inst., N.C. Carolina Bar Assn., N.C. Bar Assn. (chmn. fin. Instns. com., chmn. bank counsel com., bus. law coun.). Democrat. Office: Moore & Van Allen PLLC 100 N Tryon St Ste 4700 Charlotte NC 28202 Office Phone: 704-331-3535. Business E-Mail: tomdunn@mvalaw.com.

DUNN, JAMES DAVID, language educator; b. Sacramento, Oct. 13, 1947; s. James Howard and Bonita Reed Dunn; m. Gwendalynn Dee Gohlke, Aug. 25, 1971; children: Michael Edward, Heidi Marie. BA cum laude, U. Tex., 1972; MA, Tex. Tech. U., 1974. Commd. 2d lt. USAF, 1975, major, 1986, ret., 1992; nat. intelligence officer Nat. Security Agy., Ft. Meade, Md., 1989—92; tchr. Ashcroft High Sch., Luton, England, 1992—97; prof. fgn. langs. San Antonio Coll., 1997—. Sst. prof. aerospace studies Tex. A&M U., College Station, 1986—89. Decorated Meritorious Svc. medal (2 oak leaf clusters, . Home: 425 Drift Wind San Antonio TX 78239 Office: San Antonio Coll 1300 San Pedro Ave San Antonio TX 78212 Business E-Mail: jadunn@accd.edu.

DUNN, JAMES MILTON, religious organization administrator; b. Ft. Worth, Tex., June 17, 1932; s. William Thomas and Edith (Campbell) Dunn; m. Marilyn McNeely, Dec. 19, 1958. BA, Tex. Wesleyan Coll., 1953; BD, Southwestern Bapt. Theol. Sem., 1957, ThD, 1966, PhD, 1978; LLD, Alderson-Broaddus Coll., William Jewell Coll.; DHL, Linfield Coll.; DD, Ctrl. Bapt. Theol. Sem., Furman U.; DD (hon.), Franklin Coll., 2004. Ordained to ministry So. Bapt. Conv. and Am. Bapt. Ch. in U.S.A., 1955. Assoc. pastor First Bapt. Ch., Weatherford, Tex., 1955-57; pastor Emmanuel Bapt. Ch., Weatherford, 1957-61; religion instr., campus minister W. Tex. State U., Canyon, 1961-66; dir. christian life commn. Bapt. Gen. Conv. Tex., Dallas, 1967-80; exec. dir. Bapt. Joint Com. on Pub. Affairs, Washington, 1981-99, pres. endowment, 1999—; prof. Christianity and pub. policy Wake Forest U. Div. Sch., 1999—. Sec. bd. Ams. United for Separation of Ch. and State, 1978-88; bd. dirs. Bread for the World, Washington, pres., 1987; chmn. ethics commn. Bapt. World Alliance, McLean, Va., 1975-80; chmn. adv. bd. ProVision Asia, 1985—; bd. dirs. Ch.'s Ctr. for Theology and Pub. Policy, Washington, 1993—; vis. prof. Wake Forest Div. Sch., 1999—. Editor, co-author: Politics a Guidebook for Christians, 1970, Endangered Species, 1976; co-author: An Approach to Christian Ethics, 1979, Teacher Renewal, 1987; author: (with others) Equal Separation, 1990, The Fundamentalist Phenomenon, 1990, Defining Baptist Convictions, 1996, Proclaiming the Baptist Vision, Religious Liberty, 1997, Why I Am a Baptist, 1999, Baptists in the Balance, 1997, Soul Freedom: Baptist Battle Cry, 2000. Sec. Anti-Crime Coun. Tex., Dallas, 1968-80; founding mem. Dallas Dem. Forum, 1976-80, People for the Am. Way; mem. Fair Campaign Practices Com., Dallas, 1972-76, Gov.'s Juvenile Justice Coun., State of Tex., Austin, 1976-77; pres. Whitsitt Hist. Soc., 2003-04. Recipient Disting. Svc. award Christian Life Commn. of So. Bapt. Conv., 1979, Moore-Bowman Award of

Excellence, Tex. Coun. on Family Relations, 1979, Disting. Svc. award Chs. Ctr. for Theology and Pub. Policy, 1993, T.B. Maston Christian Ethics award, 1995, Abner V. McCall Religious Liberty award Baylor U., 1998, Disting. Svc. award Christian Life Commn. Bapt. Gen. Conv. Tex., 1998, Madison-Jefferson award Americans United, 1999, Disting. Svc. medal Colgate Rochester Div. Sch., 2000. Mem. Soc. for the Sci. Study of Religion, Hymn Soc. US. and Can. Baptist. Avocation: music. Office: Baptist Joint Com 200 Maryland Ave NE Ste 302 Washington DC 20002-5797 Business E-Mail: dunnj@wfu.edu. *All freedom is rooted in our being made in the image of God and is one aspect of the two-sided coin of freedom and responsibility. The two go together inextricably.*

DUNN, JEFFREY A., lawyer; b. E. Orange, NJ, July 26, 1951; BA cum laude, U. Kansas, 1973; JD, Georgetown U., 1976. Bar: Mo. 1976, Md. 1984, DC 1984, US Dist. Ct., DC & Md., US Supreme Ct. Ptnr., intellectual property litigation, commercial litigation, public contract law Venable LLP, Balt. Mem.: ABA, Md. Assn. of Defense Trial Counsel, Md. State Bar Assn., Balt. Bar Assn., DC Bar Assn. Avocation: flying. Office: Venable LLP 2 Hopkins Plaza 1800 Mercantile Bank & Trust Bldg Baltimore MD 21201 Office Phone: 410-244-7400. Office Fax: 410-244-7742. Business E-Mail: jadunn@venable.com.

DUNN, JEFFREY EDWARD, neurologist; b. Shaker Heights, Ohio, Nov. 27, 1960; s. John Kenneth and Mary Margaret (O'Neill) D.; m. Sandra Lee Judy, Feb. 3, 1990; children: Caitlin Irene, Bronwyn Leigh, Colin John Donald. BA in French Lit., Haverford (Pa.) Coll., 1983; MD, Temple U., 1989. Diplomate Am. Bd. Psychiatry and Neurology. Molecular immunologist Fox Chase Cancer Ctr., Phila., 1984-85; intern Ea. Va. Grad. Sch., Norfolk, 1989-90; resident in neurology U. Wash., Seattle, 1990-93; attending physician Neurol. Assocs. Wash., Bellevue, 1993—; clin. asst. prof. neurology U. Wash., Seattle, 1993—; founder, med. dir. Overlake Multiple Sclerosis Ctr., Bellevue, Wash., 1996—. Pres. MS Hub Med. Group, Seattle, 2004—. Guest physician TV: MS Update, Denver, 1994, ALS Update, Seattle, 1995, MS Ctr. Vision, Seattle, 2001, PBS Documentary on MS, 2005. Recipient Cert. of Excellence in MS Rx, Prodigy Online Com., 1995; named to Outstanding Young Men of Am., 1996. Fellow Royal Soc. Medicine; mem. Am. Acad. Neurology, Am. Neurol. Assn., World Congress Neurology, North Pacific Soc. of Psychiatry and Neurology, Pacific N.W. Alliance of MS Ctrs. Avocations: golf, skiing, camping, outdoor recreation. Office: MS Hub Med Group 1100 Olive Way 150 Seattle WA 98101

DUNN, JEFFREY T., food products executive; Grad., U. Ga.; MBA, Pepperdine U. So. Calif. mkt. mgr. The Wine Spectrum divsn. The Coca-Cola Co., 1981—82, region mgr., 1982—83, nat. account exec., mgmt. supr. Coca-Cola Fountain, 1985—87, dir. Hardee's account team, 1987—90, v.p. presence mktg., 1990—94, v.p. mktg. Fountain Dept., 1994—96, v.p. field sales and mktg. Coca-Cola USA Fountain, 1996—98, v.p., gen. mgr. Coca-Cola USA Fountain, 1998, sr. v.p. Coca-Cola USA Fountain, 1998—2000, sr. v.p. Coca-Cola N.Am. mktg. divsn., 2000—01, pres., COO Coca-Cola Ams., 2001—; divsn. mgr. Seagram, 1983—85. Trustee Ga. Alliance for Children, Atlanta Dogwood Festival. Office: The Coca-Cola Co PO Box 1734 Atlanta GA 30301

DUNN, JENNIFER BLACKBURN, former congresswoman; b. Seattle, Wash., July 29, 1941; d. John Charles and Helen (Gorton) Blackburn; div.; children: Bryant, Reagan. Student, U. Wash., 1960-62; BA in English Lit., Stanford U., 1963. Sys. engr. IBM, 1964-69; with King County Dept. of Assessments, 1979-80; former chmn. Rep. Party State of Wash., 1981-92; mem. U.S. Congress from 8th Wash. dist., Washington, 1993—2005. Bd. dirs. Nat. Endowment Democracy; mem. ways and means com., homeland sec. com., econ. com.; mem. adv. bd. Internat. Rep. Inst.; participant Preparatory Commn. World Conf. Status of Women, Nairobi, 1985, World Econ. Forum, Davos, Switzerland, 2000. Del. Rep. Nat. Conv., 1980, 84, 88; presdl. apptd. adv. coun. Historic Preservation, adv. coun. volunteerism SBA; apptd. presdl. commn. on debates; N.W. Regional Dir. Met. Operal Regional Auditions; mem. Jr. League of Seattle Named one of 25 Smartest Women in Am., Mirabella mag., one of 10 Most Powerful Women in Wash., Washington Law and Politics mag. Mem. Internat. Women's Forum (Wash. chpt.), Gamma Phi Beta. Republican.

DUNN, JERI R., food products executive; Grad., Edinboro State U. With Parker White Metal Co., Curtis Industries; assoc. dir. application systems Stouffer's Hotels; asst. v.p. tech. and standards Nestle SA, Switzerland; v.p., chief info. officer Nestle USA; with Tyson Foods, Inc., Springdale, Ark., 2001—02, sr. v.p., chief info. officer, 2002—. Office: Tyson Foods Inc 2210 W Oaklawn Dr Springdale AR 72762-6999

DUNN, JOHN CLINTON, writer, editor, organization executive; b. Little Rock, Mar. 12, 1942; s. Eugene William and Clara Ava (Samuel) D.; m. Wanda Padgett, Aug. 29, 1970; children: Jonathan Victor, Gene Stephen, Samuel Padgett. Student, U. Ala., 1961-64; BA in English, Columbus (Ga.) State U., 1974. Reporter, city editor, state editor The Columbus Enquirer, 1967-75; dir. pub. rels. LaGrange (Ga.) Coll., 1975-78; editor News/Daily of Clayton County, Jonesboro, Ga., 1978-80; asst. exec. dir. Ga. Tech. Alumni Assn., Atlanta, 1980—. Editor Ga. Tech. Alumni Mag., Tech. Topics alumni newspaper. With U.S. Army, 1964-67. Avocations: gardening, tennis, reading, travel. Home: 9450 Brown Rd Jonesboro GA 30238-5962 Office: Georgia Tech Alumni Assn 225 North Ave NW Atlanta GA 30332-0001

DUNN, JOHN FRANCIS, lawyer, state representative; b. Logansport, Ind., Dec. 24, 1936; s. John Francis and Bertha (Newman) D.; m. Barbara Burke, Feb. 10, 1962; children: John F. III, Robert E., William M., Nancy L. BS in Chem. Engring., U. Notre Dame, 1958, JD, 1961. Bar: Ill. 1961, Ind. 1961, U.S. Dist. Ct. (so. dist.) Ill. 1961, U.S. Ct. Appeals (4th cir.) 1962. Atty. Standard Oil Ind. (now Amoco), Chgo., 1961-64; assoc. Morey and Dunn, Attys., Decatur, Ill., 1964-74; ptnr. Dunn and Fichter, Attys., Decatur, Ill., 1975-85; pvt. practice Decatur, Ill., 1986—. State rep. Ill. Gen. Assembly, Springfield, 1974-94, asst. majority leader; city councilman City of Decatur, 1971-74. Democrat. Roman Catholic. Avocations: bicycling, jogging. Office: 301 Millikin Ct Decatur IL 62523-1399

DUNN, JOHN RAYMOND, JR., stockbroker; b. Pittsfield, Mass., Aug. 24, 1937; s. John Raymond and Margaret Mary (Coyne) D.; 1 child, John Raymond III. AB, Boston Coll., 1960. Ins. agt. John Hancock Ins. Co., Boston, 1964-67; dist. mgr. Nat. Life Ins. Co., Montpelier, Vt., 1967-74; gen. agt. United Life & Accident Ins. Co., Concord, N.H., 1974—; stockbroker, regional mgr. Cornerstone Fin. Svcs., Inc., Boston, 1974-80; stockbroker, br. mgr. Weinrich, Zitzman, Whitehead Fin. Svcs., Inc., St. Louis, 1980—; pres. Dunn Assocs., Amherst, Mass., 1965—; br. mgr. Jefferson Pilot Securities Corp., 1998—. Field adv. mem. Pres. Adv. Coun. CFS-Div. Weinrich, Zitzman, Whitehead, Inc., 1982—; named to gen. agts. adv. com. Chubb Life Am./Chubb Securities Corp., 1988-89; dist. mgr. Chubb Securities Leaders' Club; lectr. in field. Author seminar: Let's Make Money; freelance writer Investment Dealer Digest, 1980; film prodr. Ernest Hemingway documentary. Dir. Parents and Tchrs. for Social Responsibility, Moretown, Vt., 1982-85. Mem. White Mountain Club (Club award 1984-92), Summit Club, Life U.S.A. Club, Chmns. Club., Pres. Club. Roman Catholic. Fax: 413-253-9356.

DUNN, JON MICHAEL, logician, dean; b. Ft. Wayne, Ind., June 19, 1941; s. Jon Hardin and Philomena Elizabeth (Lauer) D.; m. Sarah Jane Hutchison, Aug. 8, 1964; children— Jon William, Jennifer Anne AB, Oberlin Coll., 1963; PhD, U. Pitts., 1966. Asst. prof. philosophy Wayne State U., Detroit, 1966-69; vis. asst. prof. philosophy Yale U., New Haven, 1968-69; assoc. prof. philosophy Ind. U., Bloomington, 1969-76, prof., 1976—, Oscar Ewing prof. philosophy, 1989—, chmn. dept. philosophy, 1980-84, 94-97, adj. prof. computer sci., 1987-89, prof., 1989—, assoc. dean Coll. Arts and Scis., 1988-91, exec. assoc. dean, 1991-93, dean. Sch. Informatics, 2000—, prof. informatics, 2002—. Vis. fellow Inst. Advanced Studies, Australian Nat. U., Canberra, 1975-76; sr. visitor Math. Inst., U. Oxford, Eng., 1978; faculties vis. scholar U. Melbourne, Australia, 1983; fellow Ind. U. Inst. for Advanced Study, 1984; sr. visitor Ctr. for Philosophy of Sci., U. Pitts., Nov. 1984; adj. prof. U. Mass., Amherst, spring 1985. Author: (with G. Hardegree) Algebraic Methods in Philosophical Logic, 2001; contbg. author: Entailment, Vol. I, 1975, co-author Vol. II, 1992; editor: (with A. Gupta) Truth of Consequences: Essays in Honor of Nuel Belnap, 1990, (with G. Epstein) Modern Uses of Multiple-Valued Logic, 1975, (with G. Hardegree) Algebraic Methods in Philosophical Logic, 2001; editor Jour. Symbolic Logic, 1982-87; chief editor Jour. Philos. Logic, 1987-95; N.Am. editor Bull. Logic Sect., Polish Acad. Scis.; mem. editl. bds. Jour. Philos. Logic, 1979-87, Nous, 1968—, Studia Logica, 1978-2000, Jour. Non-Classical Logic, 1985-91, Annals of Math., Computing and Teleinformatics, Logic and Logical Philosophy, 1993—. Am. Council Learned Socs. fellow, 1984-85; NSF prin. investigator, 1969-74; Fulbright-Hays rsch. sr. scholar, 1975-76 Mem. Assn. Symbolic Logic (exec. com. 1978-81, coun. 1982—), Soc. Exact Philosophy (treas. 1982-84, v.p. 1986-88, pres. 1988-90), Am. Philos. Assn. (com. rsch. and publs. 1985-88), Computing Rsch. Assn. (vice chair IT deans group 2004—). Office: Ind U Sch Informatics 901 E 10th St Bloomington IN 47408

DUNN, KEITH A., government agency administrator, consultant; b. Cape Girardeau, Mo., Feb. 13, 1948; s. Lyman Hamby Dunn, Louise Pender Dunn; m. Terry Kelly Dunn, Sept. 6, 1975; children: Chris Vile, Drew. MA, U. Mo., 1971, PhD History, 1973. Sr. policy analyst, polit. scientist Strategic Studies Inst., U.S. Army War College, Carlisle Barracks, Va., 1977—85; sr. fellow Inst. Nat. Strategic Studies, Nat. Def. U., Washington, 1985—90; dir. def. plans divsn. U.S. Mission to NATO, 1990—95, dep. def. advisor, 1995—96; prin. dir. Inter-Am. Affairs Office of the Sec. Def., Washington, 1997—98; sec. def. rep. U.S. Commn. Nat. Security/21st Century, Arlington, Va., 1998—2001; staff mem. Bush-Cheney Transition Nat. Security Coun., Washington, 2001, office of sec. def. enduring freedom coalition coord., 2001—, office of sec. def. Iraqi freedom, 2003—04; prin., dir. tidewater ops. DFI-Internat., Washington, 2003—; dir. coalition & interagy. programs Whitney, Bradley & Brown, Vienna, Va., 2004—. Author: (book) In Defense of NATO: The Alliance's Enduring Value, 1990, The Strategic Implications of the Continental-Maritime Strategy Debate, 1984; editor: NATO's Fifth Decade, 1990, Military Strategy and Conflict Termination: Persuasion, Coercion and War, 1987, Alternative Military Strategies for the Future, 1985, Military Strategy in Transition--Defense and Deterrence in the 1990s, 1984; contbr. articles to profl. jours. Capt. U.S. Army, 1973—77. Presbyterian. Avocation: golf. Home: 153 John Browning Williamsburg VA 23185 Office: Whitney Bradley & Brown Hampton VA 23666 E-mail: kdunn@wbbinc.com.

DUNN, KENNETH B., dean; b. Ohio, Nov. 2, 1951; m. Pamela Dunn; children: Brett, Amy. B in bus. adminstrn., Ohio State U., 1974, MBA, 1976; PhD indsl. adminstrn., Purdue U., 1979. Asst. prof. indsl. adminstrn. Carnegie Mellon U., 1979, prof. fin. and econ., 1987—89; dean Kepper Sch. Bus., Carnegie Mellon U., 2002—; Leslie Wong disting. prof. U. British Columbia, 1986; joined Miller Anderson & Sherrerd, 1987; named ptnr. Miller Anderson & Sherrerd (acquired by Morgan Stanley 1996), 1989; mng. dir. Morgan Stanley Investment Mgmt.; co-dir. US Core Fixed Income Team and Morgan Stanley's Mortgage Team. Assoc. editor: Jour. Fixed Income. Trustee Friends' Ctrl. Sch., Phila., chair investment com.; trustee Ardmore United Meth. Ch., Pa. Office: Dean's Office Carnegie Mellon Univ Tepper Sch Bus 5000 Forbes Ave Pittsburgh PA 15213-3890 Office Phone: 412-268-2265. Office Fax: 412-268-8163. Business E-Mail: kbdunn@andrew.cmu.edu.

DUNN, LEO JAMES, obstetrician, gynecologist, educator; b. Trenton, N.J., May 23, 1931; s. Augustine Leo and Molly (McDaid) Dunn; m. Betty Beatrice Buchanan, Aug. 28, 1954; children: Laurie, Cary. AB, Hofstra U., 1952; MD, Columbia U., 1956. Diplomate Am. Bd. Ob-Gyn., Am. Bd. Gyn. Oncology. Intern Cin. Gen. Hosp., 1956—57; resident Sloane Hosp for Women, Columbia-Presbyn. Med. Ctr., 1957—62; asst. prof. ob-gyn U. Iowa Coll. Medicine, Iowa City, 1962—65, assoc. prof. ob-gyn, 1965—67; prof., former chmn. dept. Med. Coll. Va., Richmond, 1967—, interim dean, chmn. of dept. Ob-Gyn., 1983—85, prof. emeritus; pres. Am. Bd. Med. Specialties, 1998—2000. Bd. dirs. Am. Bd. Ob-Gyn, 1975—, pres., 1982—; mem. Nat. Bd. Med. Examiners, 1979—83. Recipient Silver medal as disting. alumnus, Columbia U. Coll. Physicians and Surgeons, 1967; scholar Markle, 1963. Fellow: ACOG (dist. v.p. 1976—78); mem.: Va. Ob-Gyn. Soc. (pres. 1981—82), Am. Assn. Ob-Gyn. (coun. 1975—79, pres. found. 1980—82, trustee 1975—82), Soc. Gynecol. Oncology (chmn. program com., v.p.), Phi Beta Kappa. Office: Med Coll Va MCV Station PO Box 980034 Richmond VA 23298-0034

DUNN, LINDA KAY, physician; b. Grand Rapids, Mich., Jan. 11, 1947; d. Roger John and Mary Kathryn (Bouwer) Kloote; m. Jeffrey Marc Dunn, June 3, 1972; children: David Alan, Kathryn Ann. AB in Chemistry, Hope Coll., 1968; MD, U. Mich., 1972. Diplomate Am. Bd. Ob-Gyn, Am. Bd. Maternal-Fetal Medicine, Am. Bd. Med. Genetics. Resident in ob-gyn U. Mich., Ann Arbor, 1972-75, fellow in maternal-fetal medicine, 1975-77; hon. rsch. registrar St. Mary's Hosp., London, 1977-78; dir. of perinatology Temple U. Sch. Medicine, Phila., 1978-79, assoc. prof. ob-gyn, 1991-97; dir. subsect. on genetics Pa. Hosp., Phila., 1980-90; pres Medigen, Inc., Phila., 1987-90; dir. maternal-fetal medicine and genetics Abington (Pa.) Meml. Hosp., 1991-97. Med. dir. Comprehensive Maternal and Infant Svcs., Phila., 1987-90; pres. Abington Perinatal Assocs., P.C., 1993-97; dir. maternal-fetal medicine, chair dept. ob-gyn. Allegheny U., 1997-99; pres., CEO Allegheny U. Hosp. at City Ave.; chair dept. ob-gyn. Chestnut Hill Hosp., Phila., 1999—. Fellow Am. Coll. Ob-Gyn.; mem. AMA, Soc. Maternal Fetal Medicine, Am. Soc. Human Genetics, Am. Coll. Med. Genetics, Pa. State Med. Soc., Phila. Obstet. Soc., U. Mich. Med. Ctr. Alumni Soc. (chair 1996), Norman Miller Gynecologic Soc. (pres. 1996). Mem. Soc. Of Friends. Avocations: travel, piano. Office: Chestnut Hill Hosp 8835 Germantown Ave Philadelphia PA 19118-2765 Office Phone: 215-248-8492. Business E-Mail: dunnl@chh.org.

DUNN, MARVIN IRVIN, physician; b. Topeka, Dec. 21, 1927; s. Louis and Ida (Leibtag) D.; m. Maureen Cohen, Mar. 10, 1956 (dec. Nov. 1988); children: Jonathan Louis, Marilyn Paulette. BA, U. Kans., 1950, MD, 1954. Intern USPHS, San Francisco, 1954-55; resident U. Kans., 1955-58, fellow, 1958-59, instr. medicine, 1958-60, assoc. in medicine, 1960-62, asst. prof. medicine, 1962-65, assoc. prof., 1965-70, prof., 1970-2000, prof. emeritus, 2001—, Franklin E. Murphy Disting. prof., 1978-2000, dir. Cardiovascular Lab., head sect. Cardiovascular Disease Med. Center, 1963-92, dean Sch. of Medicine, 1979-84. Cons. USAF, 1971-95; spl. cons. to fed. air surgeon of FAA, 1990—. Author: Home Study Course: Difficult EKG Diagnosis, 1969, Translator Deductive and Polyparametric Electrocardiography, 1970; (with others) Clinical Vectorcardiography and Electrocardiography, 2d edit., 1977, Clinical Electrocardiography, 8th edit., 1989; editor in chief Cardiovascular Perspectives, 1985-89; mem. editl. bd. Am. Jour. Cardiology, 1970-75, Catheterization and Cardiovascular Diagnosis, 1980-87, AMA Archives Internal Medicine, 1984-94, Jour. Am. Coll. Cardiology, 1983-89, Biomedicine and Pharmacotherapy, 1985-90, Am. Jour. Noninvasive Cardiology, 1985-89, Chest, 1984-89, 94-98, Practical Cardiology, 1980-88, Heart and Lung, 1986-88, Bd.-Advanced in Therapy, 1992, Slovak Jour. Noninvasive Cardiology, 1993, Griffith Resource Libr., 1980-90, Am. Heart Jour., Jour. Acoustical Soc.; mem. internat. sci. bd. Italian Heart Jour., 2005—. Bd. dirs. Hebrew Acad. Jewish Geriatric and Convalescent Center, Beth Shalom Synagogue. Served with AUS, 1946-47. Recipient Alumnus of Yr. award U. Kansas Sch. Medicine, 1987, silver medal U. Socrates, Thessaloniki, Greece, 1992. Master Am. Coll. Chest Physicians (mem. bd. regents, pres. 1988-89, gov. State of Kans.); fellow ACP (Laureate award 1990), Am. Coll. Cardiology (trustee), Am. Heart Assn., Royal Acad. Medicine (Ireland), Royal Coll. Physicians (Valencia, Spain); mem. Am. Physicians Fellowship (dir.), Univ. Cardiologists, Alpha Omega Alpha, Phi Chi (cited Best Doctors in Am., 1998). Home: 3205 Tomahawk Rd Shawnee Mission KS 66208-1861 Office: U Kans Hosp 3901 Rainbow Blvd Kansas City KS 66160-0001 *My small modicum of success was achieved by hard work, dedication to a single goal, and an application of total energy in achieving this goal. Open-mindedness, imaginativeness, and fair play have helped to make the road easier.*

DUNN, MARY MAPLES, former university dean; b. Sturgeon Bay, Wis., Apr. 6, 1931; d. Frederic Arthur and Eva (Moore) Maples; m. Richard S. Dunn, Sept. 3, 1960; children— Rebecca Cofrin, Cecilia Elizabeth. BA, Coll. William and Mary, 1954, LHD (hon.), 1989; MA, Bryn Mawr Coll., 1956, PhD, 1959; LLD (hon.), Marietta Coll., 1987, Amherst Coll., 1987, Brown U., 1989; LittD (hon.), Lafayette Coll., 1988, Haverford Coll., 1991; LHD (hon.), Transylvania U., 1991, U. Pa., 1995, Mt. Holyok Coll., 1996, Smith Coll., 1998, U. Mass., 1998, U. South, 1999. Faculty Bryn Mawr Coll., 1958-85, prof. history, 1974-85; acting dean Undergrad. Coll. Bryn Mawr (Pa.) Coll., 1978-79, dean, 1980-85; pres. Smith Coll., Northampton, Mass., 1985-95; Carl and Lily Pforzheimer Found. dir. Arthur and Elizabeth Libr. Radcliffe Coll., 1995-99; acting pres., acting dean Inst. for Advanced Study Harvard U., 1999—2000. Author: William Penn: Politics and Conscience, 1967; editor: Political Essay on the Kingdom of New Spain (Alexander von Humboldt), 1972, rev., 1988, (with Richard S. Dunn) Papers of William Penn, vols. I-IV, 1979-87. Trustee The Clark Sch. for the Deaf, 1988-95, Acad. Mus., 1985-95, Hist. Deerfield, Inc., 1986—, Bingham Fund for Teaching Excellence at Transylvania U., 1987—, John Carter Brown Libr., 1994-99, NOW/Legal Def. and Edn. Fund., 1996—, Marlboro Music, 1996—. Recipient Disting. Tchg. award Lindbeck Found., 1969, Radcliffe medal Radcliffe Assn., 2001; fellow Inst. Advanced Study Princeton U., 1974. Mem. Berkshire Conf. Women Historians (pres. 1973-75), Coordinating Com. Women Hist. Profession (pres. 1975-77), Am. Hist. Assn., Am. Philos. Soc. (co-exec. officer 2001—), Inst. Early Am. History and Culture (chmn. adv. council 1977-80), Mass. Hist. Soc., Phi Beta Kappa. Office: American Philosophical Society Exec Office 104 S Fifth St Philadelphia PA 19106-3287

DUNN, MAUREEN H., lawyer; b. Minneola, NY, Aug. 17, 1949; BA, LeMoyne Coll., 1971; JD, Cath. U., 1974. Bar: Tenn., DC. Atty. Tenn. Valley Authority (TVA), Knoxville, 1978—86, asst. gen. counsel, 1986—2001, exec. v.p., gen. counsel, 2001—. Office: Tenn Valley Authority 400 W Summit Hill Dr Knoxville TN 37902-1499 Office Phone: 865-632-2101.

DUNN, MICHAEL CHALMER, management consultant; b. L.A., Mar. 31, 1949; s. Beverly Nathan and Robyn E. Dunn; children: Lorn Christopher, Jennipher S., Garth Carson. AS in Sci., Rio Hondo Coll., 1972; BA, U. Redlands, 1974; MA, Cambridge (Eng.) U., 1991, MPhil in Polar Studies, 1992. Fire safety/crash-rescue tech. NASA Goldstone Complex, Barstow, Calif., 1973—75; faculty test pilot Ultraist Products, Rancho California, Calif., 1976; sr. mgmt. analyst State of Nev., Carson City, 1977—79; sr. expedition mgr./founding ptnr. Adventure Network Internat., 1980—95; ret., 1996; part-time mgmt. cons., 1996—. Author: The Forever Rainbow Boy, 1999, Stone Pigeons, 2002; contbr. articles to profl. jours. Sgt. U.S. Army, 1970—72. Achievements include organizer/expedition leader 1985 Sir Edmund Hillary-Neil Armstrong North Pole Expedition; organizer/expedition leader 1989 Mt. Everest International Goodwill Expedition, Tibet, China. Avocations: chess, music, flying, sailing, languages. Home: 201 Sierra Nevada Ln Carson City NV 89706 Office Phone: 775-450-8448. E-mail: mdunny632@springpcs.com.

DUNN, MICHAEL J., dean; m. Patricia O'Reilly; 5 children. MD, Med. Coll. of Wisconsin, 1962. Intern Johns Hopkins Hosp, Baltimore, 1962—63, resident, 1963—65; asst. prof. & co-dir., nephrology unit U. Vermont Coll. Medicine, 1969—77; various pos. Case Western Reserve, 1977—95; dean, prof. of med. and exec v.p. Med. Coll. Wis., Milw., 1995—. Grantee Fogarty Senior International Fellow. Mem.: Am. Soc. Nephrology (pres. 1989—90). Office: Med Coll Wis Office of the Dean 8701 W Watertown Plank Rd Milwaukee WI 53226-3548

DUNN, MICHAEL M., academic administrator, career military officer; BS in Astrodynamics, USAF Acad., 1972; grad., Squadron Officer Sch., 1976; MS in Sys. Mgmt., U. So. Calif., 1981; grad., Air Command & Staff Coll., 1983; nat. security mgmt. course, 1984; grad., Air War Coll., 1986. Commd. 2d lt. USAF, 1972, advanced through grades to lt. gen., 2003; student pilot training Moody AFB, Ga., 1972—73; student F-106 Tyndall AFB, Fla., 1973—74; instr. pilot, standardization & evaluating officer & weapons officer 84th Fighter Interceptor Squad, 1974—78; action officer Air Staff tng. program, sec. Air Force legis. liaison, Washington, 1978-79; instr. pilot, chief of tactics, R&D Interceptor Weapons Sch., Tyndall AFB, Fla., 1979-82; F-15 pilot, chief plans, programs, spl. projects 18th Tactical Fighter Wing, Kadena Air Base, Japan, 1983-85; F-15 pilot, dir. fighter ops. Hdqs. 5th Air Force, Yokota Air Base, Japan, 1985—88; div. chief Pacific East divsn., dir. plans, dep. chief staff Hdqs. USAF, Washington, 1989-90, dep. asst. dir. Joint Nat. Security Coun. Matters, 1991, exec. asst. to dep. chief of staff, plans and ops., 1991-92; comdr. 1st Ops. Group 1st Fighter Wing, Langley AFB, Va., 1992-93; divsn. chief strategy, resources, legis. affairs divsn. U.S. European Command, Stuttgart, Germany, 1993-94, exec. officer to dep. comdr. in chief, 1994-95; sr. mil. fellow Coun. on Fgn. Rels., N.Y.C., 1995-96; sr. mil. asst. to dep. sec. US Dept. Def., Washington, 1996-97; dir. plans and programs Hdqs. Pacific Air Forces, Hickam AFB, Hawaii, 1997-99; dep. chief staff UN Command and Forces Korea Youngsan Army Garrison, Seoul, Republic of Korea, 1999—2001; vice dir. strategic plans & policy, The Joint Staff The Pentagon, Washington, 2001—03; pres. Nat. Def. U., Washington, 2003—. Decorated Def. Disting. Svc. medal with oak leaf cluster, Def. Superior Svc. medal, Legion of Merit, Meritorious Svc. medal with 3 oak leaf clusters, Air Force Commendation medal with two oak leaf clusters. Office: Nat Def U Ft Lesley J McNair Washington DC 20319*

DUNN, M(ORRIS) DOUGLAS, lawyer; b. Ionia, Mich., Nov. 1, 1944; s. Morris Frederick and Lola Adella (Gee) D.; m. Jill Lynn Fasbender, July 22, 1967; children: Brooks, Gillian, Joshua. BSME, U. Mich., 1967; JD, Vanderbilt U., 1970. Bar: U.S. Dist. Ct. (so. dist.) N.Y. 1972, U.S. Ct. Appeals (2d cir.) 1973, U.S. Supreme Ct. 1978. Assoc. Winthrop Stimson, Putnam & Roberts, N.Y.C., 1970-78, ptnr., 1978-84; sr. v.p., mng. dir. Shearson Lehman Bros., Inc., N.Y.C., 1984-85; ptnr. Milbank, Tweed, Hadley & McCloy, N.Y.C, 1985—. Contbr. articles to profl. jours. Fellow: Am. Bar Found.; mem.: ABA (fed. regulation of securities com. bus. law sect. 1981—, chair pub. utility, comms. and transp. law sect. 1997—98, bd.govs. 1998—2001), Internat. Bar Assn. (com. chmn. 1990—94), Assn. Bar City NY, Grey Oaks Country Club, Canoe Brook Country Club, Down Town Assn. Office: Milbank Tweed Hadley & McCloy LLP 1 Chase Manhattan Plz Fl 47 New York NY 10005-1413 Office Phone: 212-530-5062. Business E-Mail: mdunn@milbank.com.

DUNN, NORMAN SAMUEL, plastics and textiles company executive; b. Woonsocket, R.I., Sept. 17, 1921; s. Israel M. and Ida (Mayerson) D.; m. Mildred M. Michaels, Aug. 31, 1975; 1 son, by previous marriage, Jeffrey Mark. Ph.B. cum laude, Providence Coll., 1942. Purchasing agt. Uniroyal Inc., Conn., 1942-48; pres. Emerson Textile Co., Chelsea, Mass., 1948-64; exec. v.p., treas. Chelsea Industries Inc., 1948-84, officer, bd. dirs., 1948—; chmn. bd. Am. Shacks Inc., 1982—. Dir. NFA Corp. Trustee Combined Jewish Philanthropies; overseer Beth Israel/Deaconess Hosp., Boston; past chmn. 330 Beacon St. Condominium Trust; hon. trustee The Rehab. Ctr. for the Aged, Boston. Mem. Two Ten Nat. Found., Rockrimmon Country Club. Home: Bayberry Way Pound Ridge NY 10576 Office: 42B Cherry Hill Dr Danvers MA 01923

DUNN, PATRICIA C., investment company executive; AB in Journalism and Econ., U. Calif., Berkeley. With Barclays Global Investors, N.A., San Francisco, 1976—, co-chmn., CEO, 1995—2002, vice chmn. San Francisco, 2002—; non-exec. chmn. Hewlett-Packard Co., Palo Alto, Calif., 2005—. Bd. dirs. Hewlett-Packard Co. 1998- Contbr. articles to profl. jours. Mem. new media bd., U. Calif. Sch. Journalism, Berkeley. Named one of Most Powerful Women, Forbes mag., 2005. Office: Barclays Global Investors 45 Fremont St San Francisco CA 94105-2204*

DUNN, RANDALL LAWSON, judge; b. Gary, Ind., May 28, 1950; s. Jack Harold Wheeler and Doris Marjorie (Rose) D.; m. Laurie Marie Loomis, Sept. 17, 1954; children: Jonathan Loomis, Andrew Jack. BA with honors,

Northwestern U., Evanston, Ill., 1972; JD, Stanford U., 1975. Bar: Oreg., Wash., U.S. Dist.Ct. Oreg., U.S. Dist. Ct. Utah, U.S. Ct. Appeals (9th and 10th cirs.), U.S. Dist. Ct. (ea. and we. dists.) Wash. Law clk. Hon. James J. Richards Chief Judge Superior Ct. Lake County, Hammond, Ind., 1973-74; assoc. Berman & Giauque, Salt Lake City, 1975-76; assoc., ptnr. to mng. ptnr. Copeland, Landye, Bennett & Wolf, Portland, Oreg., 1977—98; apptd. bankruptcy judge US Dist. Ct. Oreg., 1998—. Articles editor Stanford Law Rev., 1974-75; editor-in-chief Bankruptcy Briefs, 1991-95; cons. editor Fed. Bar News and Jour., 1994; editor-in-chief, author Oreg. Debtor Creditor Newsletter, 1988-95. Pres., treas., bd. dirs. Beaverton (Oreg.) Arts. Commn., 1986-92; pres., bd. dirs. Portland Festival Symphony, 1985—; chmn. West Sylvan Mid. Sch. Funding Com., Portland, 1993. Mem. ABA (sects. on antitrust, corp. banking and bus. law), Oreg. State Bar Assn. (sects. on antitrust, debtor/creditor, treas. exec. com.), Fed. Bar Assn. (chmn. exec. com. bankruptcy sect. 1994-95), Wash. State Bar Assn. (sects. on creditor, debtor, corp., bus. and banking law), Am. Fedn. Musicians. Avocations: playing the clarinet, running, weightlifting, reading, gardening. Office: 1001 SW 5th Ave Ste 700 Portland OR 97204-1141

DUNN, RANDY J., school system administrator; b. Aledo, Ill., July 5, 1958; s. Charles A. and Shirley A. (Forrest) D.; m. Laurie R. Waltrip, Dec. 17, 1977; children: Lindsey S., Erin L. BS in Edn., Ill. State U., 1980, MS in Edn., 1983; EdD, U. Ill., 1991. Tchr. Gibson City Schs., Ill., 1980-83; prin. Lee Ctr. Schs., Paw Paw, Ill., 1983-84, Roanoke Benson Schs., Ill., 1984-89; supt. Argenta Oreana Schs., Ill., 1989-91, Chester Pub. Schs., Ill., 1991; chair Dept. of Ednl. Adminstrn. and Higher Edn. So. Ill. U., Carbondale, 1995—2004; interim supt. edn. State of Ill., 2004—. Cons. Ednl. Svc., Ottawa, Ill., 1991—; trainer Ctr. #9 Administrs.' Acad. Contbr. articles to profl. jours. Chair United Way, Decatur, Ill., 1989; active Argenta Civic Club, 1989-91, Macon County Rural Leaders, Decatur, 1990-91, Chester Mcpl. Band, Chester, 1992—. Rsch. grantee Ill. Assn. Sch. Bds., Springfield, 1991. Mem. ASCD, Am. Assn. Sch. Adminstrs., Ill. Assn. Sch. Adminstrs., Univ. Ill. Ednl. Adminstrn. Alumni Assn. Avocations: travel, reading. Office: Ill Dept Edn 100 N St Springfield IL 62701-5042*

DUNN, REBECCA M., telecommunications industry executive; b. Selma, Ala. BS in Math., Auburn U., 1970. Asst. engr. South Ctrl. Bell, 1970, engring. assoc., staff engr., asst. engring. mgr. costs, dist. mgr. capital recovery, 1975, ops. mgr. regulatory, asst. v.p. pub. affairs, 1984, gen. mgr. bus. mktg. for Ala. and Miss. ops., 1987—89; v.p. corp. affairs BellSouth Corp., Atlanta, 1989—91, v.p. human resources and corp. svcs., 1991—99, v.p. shared svcs., sr. v.p. corp. compliance, corp. sec., 2001—. Mem. adv. coun. Coll. of Bus., Auburn U.; vol. United Way; bd. dirs. Atlanta History Ctr., Homeward Inc., Ctrl. Atlanta Progress. Office: BellSouth Corp 1155 Peachtree St NE Atlanta GA 30309-3610

DUNN, RICHARD JOSEPH, retired investment banker; b. Chgo., Apr. 5, 1924; s. Richard Joseph and Margaret Mary (Jennett) Dunn; m. Marygrace Calhoun, Oct. 13, 1951 (dec. May 2000); children: Richard, Robert(dec.), Marianne, Anthony, Gregory, Noelle. AB, Yale U., 1948; LLB, Harvard U., 1951; MBA, Stanford U., 1956. Bar: Tex. 1952. Mem. Carrington, Gowan, Johnson & Walker, Dallas, 1951-54; investment counselor Scudder, Stevens & Clark, San Francisco, 1956-84, gen. ptnr., 1974-84, ret., 1984. Mem. Sovereign Coun., Rome, 1999—2004. With AUS U.S. Army, 1943—46, Japan. Decorated Combat Infantry Badge, Purple Heart, Bronze Star, knight comdr. with star Papal Order St. George; recipient Bailiff Grand Cross Hon. and Devotion Obedience Sovereign Mil. Hospitaller award, Order St. John Jersusalem Rhodes and Malta. Roman Catholic.

DUNN, ROBERT GIDDINGS, writer, educator; b. Santa Monica, Calif., Nov. 16, 1950; s. Gerald Rohrer and Mary Benjamin Dunn; m. Patricia Woodbridge. AB, U. Calif., Berkeley, 1973. Pub. Coral Press, N.Y.C., 2001—; writing prof. The New Sch., N.Y.C., 1986—. Copyreader Sports Illustrated, N.Y.C., 1984—; writing prof. Dickinson Coll., Carlisle, Pa., 1982—83; editl. asst. New Yorker Mag., N.Y.C., 1976—82. Author: The Sting Rays, 2000, Pink Cadillac, 2001, Cutting Time, 2003, Soul Cavalcade, 2005; musician: (compact disc) Thin Wild Mercury, 2005. Recipient O. Henry Prize Short Story, Doubleday, 1980. Office Phone: 212-522-4475. Personal E-mail: rgdunn@aol.com.

DUNN, ROBERT LAWRENCE, lawyer; b. Westerly, RI, Jan. 2, 1938; m. Sammie Louise Sanford (dec. Sept. 1999); children: Christopher Jon, Geoffrey Robert; m. Linda Elizabeth Barry, 2003. BA, Cornell U., 1958; JD magna cum laude, Harvard U., 1962. Bar: N.Y. 1962, Calif. 1966, U.S. Dist. Ct. (no. dist.) Calif. 1966, U.S. Ct. Appeals (9th cir.) 1966, U.S. Dist. Ct. (ea. dist.) Calif. 1970, U.S. Supreme Ct. 1984, U.S. Dist. Ct. (cen. dist.) Calif. 1987. Law clk. to cir. judge U.S. Cir. Ct., Hartford, Conn., 1962-63; assoc. Paul, Weiss, Rifkind, Wharton & Garrison, N.Y.C., 1963-65, Bancroft, Avery & McAlister, San Francisco, 1965-71; ptnr. Bancroft & McAlister, San Francisco, 1971-93, Cooper, White & Cooper, San Francisco, 1993-99; corp. counsel Real Restaurants, Sausalito, Calif., 1999—. Author: Recovery of Damages for Lost Profits, 1978, rev. edit., 2005, Recovery of Damages for Fraud, rev. edit., 2004, Expert Witnesses: Law and Practice, 1996, Winning with Expert Witnesses in Commercial Litigation, 2003; contbr. articles to profl. jours. Planning commn. Town of Corte Madera, Calif. 1974-78, town coun., 1978-84, mayor, 1979, 82; bd. dirs. Merola Opera Program, 1995—, Philharmonia Baroque Orch., San Francisco, 1991-94. 1st lt. U.S. Army, 1958-59. Avocations: travel, opera, literature. E-mail: attydunn@earthlink.net.

DUNN, RONALD HOLLAND, civil engineer, management executive, consultant; b. Balt., Sept. 15, 1937; s. Delmas Joseph and Edna Grace (Holland) D.; m. Verona Lucille Lambert, Aug. 17, 1958; children: Ronald H., Jr. (dec.), David R., Brian W. BS in Engring., Johns Hopkins U., 1969. Registered profl. engr., Va., D.C.; diplomate forensic engring. Field engr. Balt. & Ohio R.R., Balt., 1958-66; chief engr. yards, shops, trackwork DeLeuw, Cather & Co., Washington, 1966-73; mgr. engring. support Parsons-Brinckerhoff-Tudor-Bechtel, Atlanta, 1973-76; dir. railroad engring. Morrison-Knudsen Co., Inc., Boise, Idaho, 1976-78; v.p. Parsons-Brinckerhoff-Centec, Inc., McLean, Va., 1978-83; v.p., area mgr., tech. dir. railway engring., profl. assoc. Parsons Brinckerhoff Quade & Douglas, Inc., McLean and Pitts., 1983-84; dir. transp. engring. R.L. Banks & Assocs., Inc., Washington, 1984; pres. R.H. Dunn & Assocs., Inc., Fairfax, Va., 1984-91, Williamsburg, Va., 1991—. Insp., rail transit facilities, Europe, 1980, 82, 84, 99, China and Hong Kong, 1985; involved in engring. of 18 railroads and 17 rail transit systems throughout N.Am.; guest Japan Railway Civil Engring. Assn., 1972, French Nat. Railroads and Paris Transport Authority, 1988; adv. com. track engrs. U.S. Dept. Transp., 1968-71. Pack chmn. Boy Scouts Am., 1972-73, committeeman, 1973-75, troop committeeman, 1979-85. Fellow ASCE, Inst. Transp. Engrs., Nat. Acad. Forensic Engrs.; mem. NSPE, NAS (mem. select panel), Am. Arbitration Assn., Mgmt. Assn., Am. Rlwy. Engring. Assn. (life), Am. Pub. Transit Assn., Soc. Am. Mil. Engrs., Roadmasters and Maintenance of Way Assn. Am., Am. Rlwy. Bridge and Bldg. Assn., Constrn. Specifications Inst., Transp. Rsch. Bd., Nat. Assn. R.R. Safety Cons. and Investigators, Can. Soc. Civil Engring (life), Va. Soc. Profl. Engrs., Can. Urban Transit Assn., Rlwy. Tie Assn., Inst. Rapid Transit, Phi Kappa Sigma. Methodist. Office: PO Box 3106 Williamsburg VA 23187-3106

DUNN, RONNIE GENE, musician; b. Coleman, Tex., June 1, 1953; div.; children: Whitney, Jesse Wayne; m. Janine Dunn. With Brooks & Dunn, 1988—; recording artist Artista, 1991—. Singer: (albums) (with Kix Brooks) Brand New Man, 1991 (Acad. Country Music award Album of Yr., 1992), Hard Workin' Man, 1993 (Grammy award Best Country Vocal Performance by Duo or Group for "Hard Workin' Man", 1993), Waitin' on Sundown, 1994, Borderline, 1996 (Grammy award Best Country Vocal Performance by Duo or Group for "My Maria", 1996), Greatest Hits Collection, 1997, If You See Her, 1998, Tight Rope, 1999, Super Hits, 1999, Steers and Stripes, 2001, It Won't Be Christmas Without You, 2002, Red Dirt Road, 2003, Greatest Hits Collection: Volume II, 2004, (singles) Boot Scootin' Boogie, 1992, We'll Burn That Bridge, 1993, Rock My World (Little Country Girl), 1993, (songs) (8 Seconds soundtrack) Ride 'Em High, Ride 'Em Low, 1994, (with Hank Thompson) Hooked on Honky Tonk, 1997, (with Reba McEntire) If You See Him, If You See Her, 1998; background vocals, chorus: albums T-r-o-u-b-l-e (Travis Tritt), 1992, appears on: albums Common Thread: The Songs of the Eagles, 1994 (Country Music Assn. Album of Yr., 1994). Named Top New Vocal Duo or Group, Acad. Country Music, 1991, Entertainer of Yr., 1995, 1996, 2001, Top Vocal Duo, 1991—97, 2000—03, 2005, Country Music Assn., 1992—99, 2001—03, Vocal Group of Yr., 2004, Entertainer of Yr., 1996, Favorite Band, Duo or Group-Country Music, Am. Music Awards, 2004. Office: Brooks and Dunn PO Box 120669 Nashville TN 37212-0669

DUNN, SUSAN DAICOFF See DAICOFF, SUSAN

DUNN, THOMAS E., lawyer; b. Salem, Oreg., June 17, 1966; BA, Coll. William & Mary, 1987; JD, Duke Univ., 1992. Bar: NY 1993. Assoc. Cravath Swaine & Moore LLP, NYC, 1992—2000, ptnr., corp., 2000—. Mem.: ABA, Assn. of Bar of City of NY. Office: Cravath Swaine & Moore LLP Worldwide Plz 825 Eighth Ave New York NY 10019-7475 Office Phone: 212-474-1108. Office Fax: 212-474-3700. Business E-Mail: tdunn@cravath.com.

DUNN, VINCENT, lawyer; b. Queens, NY, Aug. 18, 1964; BS with honors, SUNY, Buffalo, 1986; JD, SUNY Sch. Law, Buffalo, 1989. Bar: NY 1989, NJ 1990. Ptnr., corp. dept. Chadbourne & Parke LLP, NYC, chmn. recruitment com. Head note and comment editor Buffalo Law Review. Named one of Am. Top Black Atty., Black Enterprise, 2003. Office: Chadbourne & Parke LLP 30 Rockefeller Plz New York NY 10112 Office Phone: 212-408-1064. Office Fax: 212-541-5369. Business E-Mail: vdunn@chadbourne.com.

DUNN, VIRGINIA, artist; b. Long Island, N.Y., Dec. 11, 1951; d. James Joseph and Margaret Virginia Dunn. Student, Lynn U., 1970—71, SUNY, Purchase, 1972-75, Propersie Sch. of Art, 1975-76, Lynn U., Boca Raton, Fla. Nurse's aide St. Joseph's Hosp., Stamford, Conn., 1967-70; with advt. dept. Cuisinart, Greenwich, Conn., 1977-89. One-woman shows include Greenwich Hosp., 2002, Garden Cafe, Greenwich, 2002, Nathaniel Witheral, exhibitions include Hurlbutt Gallery, Greenwich (Conn.) Libr., various yrs., Gertrude White Gallery, Greenwich, 1998—2002, Greenwich Garden Ctr., Cos Cob, Conn., 1989—2002 (honorable mention, 2002, 2d place, 2 honorable mentions), Ferguson Libr., Stamford, Conn., 1993—2002 (Koi Fish Chinese Hon Mention, 3d Pl. award, 2001, 2002, 2002, 2003), Hammond Mus. & Japanese Stroll Garden, North Salem, N.Y., 1993—2001, Whitby Sch., Greenwich, 1994, Rush-Holley House, Cos Cob, 1994, Wilton (Conn.) Libr., 1995—96, E.C. Potter Gallery, Greenwich, 1996—2002, The Coffee Shoppe, Greenwich Hosp., 1997, Stamford Art Assn., 1999 (3d Pl. award, 2000), Greenwichart, Stamford, 1999, Art Soc. Old Greenwich Sidewalk Shows, 1999—2003, Stamford Art Assn., 2001, Westfield Ct., 2001, Greenwich Libr., Flinn Gallery, 2001, 2002, Landson Park, Katona, N.Y., 2001—04, Flynn Gallery, Greenwich Libr., 2001—02, Landson Park, Katona, N.Y., 2002, St. Raphael's Hosp., New Haven, 2002, Hammond Mus., 2002, Circe d'Art Gallery, Rowayton Art Ctr., Hammond Mus., 2002—03, Greenwich Libr., 2003. Recipient Honorable Mention award Greenwich Art Soc., 1999, other awards for art. Mem. Oriental Brush Artist Guild (mailing com. 1993-2002), Eastern Arts Connection, The Greenwich Art Soc. (mailing com. 1988-89, Second Place award 2000), The Art Soc. of Old Greenwich (hostess 1988-89, 2d place award 2002, numerous honorable mentions), Conn. Graphic Art Ctr., Greenwich Arts Coun., The Stamford Art Assn., The Hammond Mus., Women in the Arts, Rowayton Art Assn. Avocations: music, travel, cats, Bluegrass banjo music. Home: 12 Newton Rd Gaylordsville CT 06755

DUNN, WALTER SCOTT, JR., writer, museum director, consultant; b. Detroit, Apr. 5, 1928; s. Walter Scott and Minnie (Van Lahr) D.; m. Jean Wendeberg, July 11, 1959. BA, U. Durham, Eng., 1951; MA, Wayne State U., 1953; PhD, U. Wis., 1971. Curator indsl. history Detroit Hist. Mus., 1952-56; chief curator State Hist. Soc. Wis., Madison, 1956-63; mus. cons., 1962—; dir. Buffalo and Erie County Hist. Soc., 1963-78, Des Moines Ctr. Sci. and Industry, 1978-84, Nat. Mus. Transport, St. Louis, 1984-86, Dog Mus., St. Louis, 1987-89. Author: Western Commerce, 1760-1774, 1971, Second Front Now, 1943, 80, Hitler's Nemesis: The Red Army, 1994, The Soviet Economy and the Red Army 1930-1945, 1995, Kursk: Hitler's Gamble, 1943, 1997, Frontier Profit and Loss, 1760-1764, 1998, Views of America: Walworth County, 1998, Soviet Blitzkrieg, 2000, The New Imperial Economy, 2000, Opening New Markets, 2002, Heroes or Traitors, 2003, People on the Frontier, 2005; host several Pub. TV series on mil. history, Madison, Wis. and Buffalo, 1959-78. Served with AUS, 1946-47. Mem. Walworth County Hist. Soc. (pres. 1996). Home: N6539 Peck Station Rd Elkhorn WI 53121-3246 Office Phone: 262-642-9771. E-mail: peterjolly@elknet.net. *Human progress can be achieved only through constant questioning of the past and innovative action to solve the problems of the future.*

DUNN, WILLIAM BRADLEY, lawyer; b. Newark, Dec. 2, 1939; s. Ernest William and Ruth Harriet (Bradley) D.; m. Judy Ann Shepherd, Aug. 2, 1988; children: John, Peter, Brian, Kelly. AB, Muskingum Coll., 1961; JD, U. Mich., 1964. Bar: Mich. 1964. Mem. Clark Hill PLC (formerly Clark, Klein & Beaumont), Detroit, 1964—. Mem. com. profl. ethics State Bar of Mich., 2002—; lectr. in field. Contbr. articles to legal jours. Mem.: ABA (chair sect. real property, probate and trust law 1989—90, mem. Ho. dels. 1990—98, mem. standing com. on professionalism 1993—96, mem. standing com. on ethics and profl. responsibility 1998—2001, spl. adv. standing com. on ethics and profl. responsibility 2001—02, mem. standing com. on ethics and profl. responsibility 2003—, chmn. standing com. ethics and profl. responsibility 2005—), Internat. Assn. Attys. and Exec. Corp. Real Estate, Am. Coll. Real Estate Lawyers (pres. 1983—84). Episcopalian. Home: 6398 Catalpa Ct Troy MI 48098-2231 Office: Clark Hill PLC 500 Woodward Ave Ste 3500 Detroit MI 48226-3435 Office Phone: 313-965-8511. Business E-Mail: wdunn@clarkhill.com.

DUNN, WILLIAM BRUNA, III, journalist; b. Streator, Ill., Jan. 26, 1947; s. William Bruna and Mary Elizabeth (Allgaier) D.; m. Sandra Lee Ann Klein, Aug. 23, 1969; 1 child, William IV. BS in Journalism, U. Fla., 1969. Reporter Orlando (Fla.) Sentinel, 1967-69, mag. editor, 1970-80, dep. mng. editor, 1979-81, mng. editor, 1981-91, assoc. mng. editor, photos, graphics and design, 1991-2001; design editor Orlando (Fla.) Sentinel, 2001—02. Author: Kidding Around, 1973; editor: SHAQ! That Magical Rookie Season, 1993; editor: Martin Andersen: Editor, Publisher, Galley Boy, 1996. Recipient Silver Gavel award ABA, 1974; Gold and Silver medals Soc. News Design, 1984. Mem. Nat. Press Photographers Assn., Soc. Profl. Journalists (past pres. Cen. Fla. chpt.), Soc. of News Design. Roman Catholic. Home: 4 E Vanderbilt St Orlando FL 32804-5925

DUNN, WILLIAM JACKSON, dental educator, researcher; b. Ozark, Ala., Oct. 13, 1959; s. Leo Miner and Sue Dunn; m. Betsy Diane Eberly, Apr. 18, 1987; children: Thomas Destin, William Jackson, Darien James. BA, Tex. Tech U., 1981; DDS, U. Tex., Houston, 1986. Diplomate Fed. Services Bd. Dentistry, Am. Bd. of Dentistry. Comdr. 320 Aeromedical Dental Squadron, Seeb Air Base; dir. of rsch. 59 Dental Squadron, Lackland AFB, Tex., 2000—; chair med. bioethics Wilford Hall Med. Ctr., Lackland AFB, Tex., 2001—. Cons. to surgeon gen. USAF, Washington, 2000—; alt. chair Instl. Rev. Bd., Wilford Hall Medical Center, Tex., 2000—; del. ADA, Chgo., 1998—; dep. regent Internat. Coll. of Dentists, San Antonio, 2002—. Author: (scientific research) Journal of the American Dental Association, American Journal of Dentistry, Journal of Prosthodontics, American Journal of Orthodontics. Lt. col. USAF, 1987—2002. Decorated Meritorious Svc. medal USAF; recipient Fellow award, Internat. Coll. of Dentists, 2001, Peirre Fauchard Honor Acad., 1998. Fellow: Am. Coll. of Dentists; mem.: ADA (del. Chgo. 1998—2002), Lion's Club Internat. (life; del. 1998—2002, Life award 2002). Conservative. Presbyterian. Achievements include research in Polymer Chemistry/Dental; Orthodontic Bonding; Light-Emitting Diodes. Avocations: golf, tennis, running. Home: 9406 Tranquil Park Dr San Antonio TX 78254 Office: 59 DS/MRDGB 1615 Truemper St Lackland A F B TX 78236-5551 Personal E-mail: wjdarkhorse@aol.com. E-mail: william.dunn@lackland.af.mil.

DUNNE, DIANE C., marketing professional; b. Milw. d. Francis and Ruth (Borman) Cantine; 1 child, Dana Philip. BS, Marquette U.; MBA, NYU, 1985. Mgr. advt. NBC, N.Y.C., 1975-77; dir. mktg. CBS, N.Y.C., 1977-80; dir. funding Bloomingdale's, N.Y.C., 1980—; sr. assoc. Corcoran Group; cons. Am. Express, DuPont de Nemours. Dir. Women's Econ. Round Table, 1988—, 750 Park Ave. Corp., N.Y.C., 1999—. Author: Guidelines to Advertising All News Radio, 1976, Guidelines for Catalogues Copywriters, 1985; assoc. editor: Am. Cancer Soc., Gourmet Guide for Busy People by Famous People, 1985, International Directory of Distinguished Leadership, columnist: N.Y. Sun; contbr. articles to profl. jours. Mem. Am. Cancer Soc., N.Y.C., 1980—; chair Feed the Homeless com. St. James Ch., N.Y.C., 1984—87; mem. pastoral and cmty. ministry com. St. James Altar Guild. Recipient Contribution honor, Oxford U. Mem.: NYU Exec. MBA Assn., Women's Econ. Roundtable (bd. dirs. 1988), Fashion Group (co-chair regional com.), Oxford U. Alumni Assn. N.Y. (v.p. events, bd. dirs. 1993—), Corcoran's Multi-Million Dollar Club. Episcopalian. Avocations: opera, jogging, skiing, rollerblading. Home: 750 Park Ave New York NY 10021-4252

DUNNE, DONALD REDMOND, military officer; b. Toms River, N.J., July 16, 1959; s. Donald James and Jane Irene Dunne; m. Mi Suk Kim, Mar. 17, 1987; children: Morgan, Jacqulaine, Brittany, Megan. BA in Polit. sci., SUNY, Geneseo, 1981; MA in Nat. Security studies, Calif. State U., San Bernardino, 2003. Commd. 2d lt. U.S. Army, advanced through grades to maj., 1997; nuclear weapons platoon leader 27th U.S. Army Field Arty. Detachment, Turkey, 1987—88, 6-37 Field Arty. Bn., Uijongbu, Republic of Korea, 1988—89; all source intelligence officer 4-21 Infantry Bn., Ft. Ord, Calif., 1990—91; intelligence tng. officer 7th Infantry Divsn. (Light), 1991—92; signals intelligence officer 122d Signal Bn., Tongduchon, Republic of Korea, 1992—93; asst. intelligence ops. officer 102d Mil. Intelligence Bn., 1993—94, all source intelligence co. comdr., 1994—95; intelligence adminstrn. exec. officer 372d Mil. Intelligence Bn., Oakland, Calif., 1995—96; fin. planner Am. Express, San Rafael, 1996—97; asst. chief counterterrorism analyst 7th Army Chief of Staff Intelligence, Heidelberg, Germany, 1997; lang. bn. ops. officer 372d Mil. Intelligence Bn., Bell, Calif., 1997—99; detailed insp. gen. 63d Regional Support Command, Los Alamitos, 1999—. Recipient Knowlton award Mil. Intelligence Corps Assn., 1997. Mem. Turkish-Am. Soc. Roman Catholic. Home: 13363 Rusty Fig Cir Cerritos CA 90703-1311 Office: 63 Regional Support Command 4235 Yorktown Ave Los Alamitos CA 90720 Office Fax: 562 795 2269. E-mail: donald.dunne@usarc-emh2.army.mil.

DUNNE, GERARD FRANCIS, lawyer; b. Huntington, N.Y., Aug. 23, 1947; s. Frank and Adele A. (Malerba) D.; m. Judith Ellen Gordon, Dec. 5, 1976; 1 child, Heather Chelsey. B in Engring., Manhattan Coll., 1969; JD, U. Balt., 1974. Bar: D.C. 1974, N.Y. 1974, U.S. Patent Office, U.S. Dist. Ct. (ea. and so. dists.) N.Y. 1976, U.S. Ct. Appeals (fed. cir.) 1982, U.S. Ct. Appeals (2d, 3d, 8th, 9th and Fed. cirs.), U.S. Supreme Ct. 1987. Examiner patents U.S. Patent Office, Washington, 1969-74; assoc. Law Offices of Albert C. Johnston P.C., N.Y.C., 1974-76, Wyatt, Gerber, Burke & Badie, N.Y.C., 1976-82, ptnr., 1982-94; sole practice law N.Y.C., 1995—. Mem. ABA, Assn. of Bar of City of N.Y., Fed. Bar Council, Am. Intellectual Property Law Assn. Home: 89-04 63rd Ave Rego Park NY 11374-2815 Office: 156 5th Ave Ste 1223 New York NY 10010-7002 E-mail: gfdunne@rcn.com.

DUNNE, KEVIN JOSEPH, lawyer; b. Pitts., Sept. 22, 1941; s. Matthew S. and Marjorie (Whelan) D.; m. Heather Wright Dunne, Sept. 27, 1963; children: Erin, Kevin Jr., Patrick, Sean. BA, U. Conn., 1963; JD, Georgetown U., 1966. Bar: Calif. 1967, U.S. Dist. Ct. (no. dist.) Calif., 1967, U.S. Dist. Ct. (ea. dist.) Calif. 1969, U.S. Dist. Ct. (ctrl. dist.) Calif. 1971, U.S. Ct. Appeals (9th cir.) 1971. Assoc. Sedgwick, Detert, Moran & Arnold, San Francisco, 1968-75, ptnr., 1975—, chmn., 2001—. Adj. prof. U. San Francisco Sch. Law, 1980-86; bd. editorial advisors Bender's Drug Product Liability Reporter, 1988-92. Author: Dunne on Depositions, 1995; contbr. articles to profl. jours. Capt. U.S. Army, 1966-68, Vietnam. Recipient Bronze Star, Army Commendation medal; recipient Exceptional Performance award Def. Rsch. Inst., 1988. Fellow: Am. Coll. Trial Lawyers, Internat. Acad. Trial Lawyers; mem.: Lawyers for Civil Justice (pres. 1998—2000), Am. Bd. Trial Advocates, Internat. Assn. Def. Counsel (pres. 1994—95), No Calif. Assn. Def. Counsel (pres. 1987—88). Roman Catholic. Avocation: golf. Office: Sedgwick Detert Moran & Arnold 1 Embarcadero Ctr Ste 1600 San Francisco CA 94111-3716 Office Phone: 415-627-1475.

DUNNE, MARY MAGUIRE, federal agency administrator, lawyer; BA, Coll. of New Rochelle, 1963; JD, St. John's U., Jamaica, N.Y., 1966. From asst. U.S. atty. to spl. asst. U.S. atty. So. Dist. N.Y. Dept. Justice, Bklyn., 1966-67, chief atty. examiner bd. immigration rev. Falls Church, Va., 1977-95, vice chmn. bd. immigration appeals, 1995—; dep. assoc. adminstr. for major sys. and policy Ofice Mgmt. and Budget, Washington, 1980-82. Editor St. John's Law Rev., 1965-66.

DUNNE, MYRA SCHLEY, nurse, consultant; b. Stamford, Conn., June 10, 1950; d. Charles Henry and Myra Catherine Schley; m. Frank Edward Dunne, May 22, 1981 (div. Sept. 23, 1997); children: Elizabeth Anne, Michael Edward. BSN, Sacred Heart U., 1972, MBA, 1989. Cert. case mgr. Commn. for Case Mgr. Cert., Rolling Meadows, Ill., 1997, legal nurse consultant Am. Legal Nurse Cert. Bd., Chgo., 2001. Nurse case mgr. CNA Ins., Quincy, Mass., 1996—2000; med. cons. Encompass Ins., Quincy, 2000—05; with Blue Cross Blue Shield Mass., Rockland, Mass., 2005—. Trainer Encompass Ins., Quincy, 2003—. Vol. Boston Rescue Mission, 2004—. Mem.: Am. Assn. Legal Nurse Cons. (assoc.). Democrat. Roman Catholic. Avocations: walking, yoga, weightlifting. Home: 23 Smith Rd Hingham MA 02043 Office: Blue Cross Blue Shield 1030 Hingham St Rockland MA 02370 Office Phone: 617-246-5822. Business E-Mail: myra.dunne@bcbsma.com.

DUNNE, NANCY ANNE, retired social services administrator; b. Ionia, Mich., Aug. 5, 1929; d. Warner Kingsley and Hazel Fern (Alliason) McSween; m. James Robert, Oct. 28, 1952; children: James Robert Jr., Stephen Michael. BA, Albion (Mich.) Coll., 1951. Tchr. Oakdale Elem., Grand Rapids, Mich., 1951-53, Lakeside Sch., East Grand Rapids, Mich., 1953; clk. Office of Naval Rsch., Washington, 1954-55; dir. pub. rels. Diocesan Office Health and Social Svcs., Albany, N.Y., 1971-74; dir. vol. action dept. Coun. of Human Resources, Schenectady, N.Y., 1974-76; pers. asst. Am. Soc. Assn. Execs., Washington, 1977-78; adminstrv. asst. N.Y. Soc. Cons. Engrs., N.Y.C., 1978-79, Assessment Designs, Inc., Orlando, Fla., 1980-82, Catholic Social Svcs., Orlando, Fla., 1982-84, ret., 1984. Active NY State Comm. Cultural Resources, Albany, 1970-73, Anna Maria Island Cmty. Ctr., 2000-01; bd. dirs. Coalition for the Homeless, Orlando, 1983-87; tutor Anna Maria Island Elem. Sch., Fla.; vol. Blake Hosp., Bradenton, Fla., 1999-2003, Imagine Manatee Task Force, Bradenton, 2003; 1st v.p. Performing arts Downtown Manatee County, Inc., 2003; tutor Anna Maria Island Elem. Sch. Mem. AAUW (pres. Manatee County br. 2001-03), Jr. League of Schenectady (Vol. of Yr. award 1965-66), Schenectady Symphony Orch. (pres. 1969-70), Ladies of Charity (pres. Albany chpt. 1970-72, pres. Orlando chpt. 1984-86, nat. pres. 1990-94, nat. bd. dirs. 2001-02, v.p. internat. 1990-94, bd. dirs. 1994-2000), Women's Club Anna Maria Island (1st v.p. 2004—, pres. 2005-06). Roman Catholic. Avocations: reading, travel, golf, bridge, entertaining friends. Home: 6400 Flotilla Dr Apt 31 Holmes Beach FL 34217-1425

DUNNE, PATRICK W., military officer, academic administrator; BS, U.S. Naval Acad., Annapolis, 1972; MS, Naval Postgraduate Sch. Commd. ensign USN, advanced through grades to rear adm., 1972—; served at sea USS Nathanael Greene (SSBN 636), USS Batfish (SSN 681), USS Baton Rouge (SSN 689); comdr. USS Baltimore (SSN 704), USS Frank Cable (AS40);

material officer Submarine Squadron Eight; naval aide to U.S. Pres. Ronald Reagan; spl. asst. to CNO for Joint Chiefs of Staff Matters; congl. liaison officer for submarine programs; dir. naval programs; dep. chief legis. affairs; U.S. Pacific Command rep. & comdr. U.S. Naval Forces Marianas, 2001—03; pres. Naval Postgraduate Sch., Monterey, Calif., 2003—. Decorated Def. Superior Svc. medal (2 awards), Legion of Merit (4 awards), Meritorious Svc. award (2 awards), Navy Commendation medal (5 awards), Navy Achievement medal (2 awards), Humanitarian Svc. medal. Office: Naval Postgraduate School Office of the President 1 University Pl Monterey CA 93943*

DUNNE, THOMAS, geology educator; b. Prestbury, U.K., Apr. 21, 1943; arrived in U.S., 1964; s. Thomas and Monica Mary (Whitter) D. BA with honors, Cambridge (Eng.) U., 1964; PhD, Johns Hopkins U., 1969. Rsch. assoc. USDA-Agrl. Rsch. Svc., Danville, Vt., 1966—68; rsch. hydrologist U.S. Geol. Survey, Washington, 1969; asst. prof. McGill U., Montreal, Canada, 1969—73; from asst. prof. to prof. U. Wash., Seattle, 1973—95, chmn. dept., 1984—89; prof. Sch. Environ. Scis. & Mgmt. U. Calif., Santa Barbara, 1995—. Vis. prof. U. Nairobi, Kenya, 1969—71; cons. in field, 1970—. Author (with L.B. Leopold) Water in Environmental Planning; (with L.M. Reid) Rapid Evaluation of Sediment Budgets, 1996. Fulbright scholar 1984; grantee NSF, NASA, Rockefeller Found., 1969—; Guggenheim fellow, 1989-90. Fellow AAAS, Am. Acad. Arts and Scis., Am. Geophys. Union (Robert E. Horton award 1987, Langbein lectr. 2003), Calif. Acad. Scis.; mem. NAS (G.K. Warren prize in Fluviatile Geology 1998), Geol. Soc. Am. (Easterbrook Disting. Scientist award 2003), Sigma Xi. Office: U Calif Donald Bren Sch Environ Scis & Mgmt 3510 Bren Hall Santa Barbara CA 93106 Business E-Mail: tdunne@bren.ucsb.edu.

DUNNER, DAVID LOUIS, medical educator; b. Bklyn., May 27, 1940; s. Edward and Reichel (Connor) D.; m. Peggy Jane Zolbert, Dec. 27, 1964; children: Laura Louise, Jonathan Michael. AA, George Washington U., 1960; MD, Washington U., St. Louis, 1965. Diplomate Am. Bd. Psychiatry and Neurology. Intern Phila. Gen. Hosp., 1965-66; resident in psychiatry Barnes Renard Hosp. of Washington U., St. Louis, 1966-69; research psychiatrist N.Y. State Psychiat. Inst., N.Y.C., 1971-79; from asst. prof. to assoc. prof. clin. psychiatry Columbia U., N.Y.C., 1972-79; chief psychiatry Harborview Med. Ctr., Seattle, 1979-89, dir. outpatient psychiatry, 1989-97; prof. psychiatry and behavioral scis. U. Wash., Seattle, 1979—, vice chmn. clin. svcs., 1989-97; dir. Ctr. for Anxiety & Depression, 1997—. Cons. Found. for Depression and Manic Depression, N.Y.C., 1974—. Editor-in-chief Comprehensive Psychiatry, 1997—; contbr. articles to profl. jours. Served to lt. comdr. USPHS, 1969-71. Fellow Am. Psychiat. Assn., Am. Psychopathol. Assn. (pres. 1986), Am. Coll. Neuropsychopharmacology, West Coast Coll. Biol. Psychiatry (charter, pres. 1987); mem. Psychiat. Research Soc. (pres. 1984). Office: Ctr for Anxiety & Depression 4225 Roosevelt Way NE Ste 306C Seattle WA 98105-6099 Office Phone: 206-543-6768. Personal E-mail: dldunner@comcast.net. Business E-Mail: ddunner@u.washington.edu.

DUNNER, DONALD ROBERT, lawyer; b. Bklyn., 1931; s. Edward Dunner and Mollie Friedman; m. Jenny Sue Dailey, 1957; children: Jennifer D. Weaver, Lisa A. BSChemE, Purdue U., 1953; JD, Georgetown U., 1958. Bar: D.C. 1958, U.S. Supreme Ct. 1963, U.S. Ct. Appeals (fed. cir.) 1982. Patent examiner U.S. Patent & Trademark Office, Washington, 1955-56; law clk. U.S. Ct. Customs and Patent Appeals, Washington, 1956-58; assoc. Strauch, Nolan & Neale, Washington, 1958-60; assoc., ptnr. Diggins & Le Blanc, Washington, 1960-62; ptnr. Lane, Aitken, Dunner & Ziems, Washington, 1962-78; of counsel Finnegan, Henderson, Farabow & Garrett, Washington, 1978-79; ptnr. Finnegan, Henderson, Farabow, Garrett & Dunner, Washington, 1979—. Mem. Pres. Adv. Com. on Indsl. Innovation, 1978-79; professorial lectr. in law George Washington Law Ctr., 1969-82; adj. prof. Washington Coll. of Law, Am. U., 1992-99. Co-author: Patent Law Perspectives, 1970-89, Court Review of Patent Office Decisions: CCPA, 1973, Court of Appeals for the Federal Circuit: Practice and Procedure, 1985. Chmn. Fed. Cir. Adv. Com., 1982-92; mem. adv. commn. on Patent Law Reform, 1991-92. With U.S. Army, 1953-55. Recipient Best Article of Yr. award Patent Office Soc., 1980, award Patent Resources Group, 1980, named one of 100 most influential lawyers, Nat. Law Jour., 2000, named one of best lawyers in intellectual property law, Best Lawyers in Am., 2005. Fellow Am. Coll. Trial Lawyers; mem. ABA (chair intellectual property law sect. 1995-96, ho. of dels. 2002—), Am. Intellectual Property Law Assn. (pres. 1979-80), D.C. Bar Assn. (chmn. patent, trademark and copyright law sect. 1964-65), D.C. Bar (chair patent, trademark and copyright law sect. 1976-77), Fed. Cir. Bar Assn. (bd. dirs. 1999-2002), Am. Inn of Ct. (pres. Giles S. Rich Inn 1994-95), Cosmos Club. Avocations: tennis, skiing, sailing. Office: Finnegan Henderson Farabow Garrett & Dunner LLP 901 New York Ave NW Washington DC 20001-3315 E-mail: dunnerd@finnegan.com.

DUNNETT, DENNIS GEORGE, retired state official; b. Auburn, Calif., Aug. 5, 1939; s. George DeHaven and Elizabeth Grace (Sullivan) D. AA in Elec. Engring., Sierra Coll., 1959; AB in Econs., Sacramento State Coll., 1966. Engring. technician State of Calif., Marysville, 1961-62, data processing technician Sacramento, 1962-67, EDP programmer and analyst, 1967-74, staff services mgr. and contract adminstr., 1974-76, hardware acquisition mgr., 1976-86, support services br. mgr., information security officer, 1986-90, chief Office Security and Operational Recovery, 1990-92, spl. projects mgr., 1992-93, customer support ctr. mgr., 1994, procurement mgr., 1994-97, chief bur. adminstrn., 1997-2000, ret., 2000—. Patron San Francisco Opera, TV Sta. KVIE. Mem. AARP, IEEE, ACLU, IEEE Computer Soc., Fine Arts Mus. of San Francisco, Crocker Art Mus., Calif. State U.-Sacramento Alumni Assn. (life). Home: 729 Blackmer Cir Sacramento CA 95825-4704 Personal E-mail: dpdennis39@comcast.net.

DUNNIGAN, BRIAN LEIGH, historian, curator; b. Detroit, July 11, 1949; s. James Patrick and Dorothy Jane (McKay) D.; m. Carol Lynn Fredriksen, Sept. 21, 1974 (div. Oct. 1988); m. Candice Maria Cain, Apr. 22, 1989; children: James Cain, Claire Beausom. BA in History, U. Mich., 1971, MA in History, 1973; MA in History and Museum Studies, Cooperstown Grad. Programs, 1979. Curator Mackinac Island (Mich.) State Park Commn., 1971-74; mng. dir. Historic Fort Wayne, Ind., 1974-79; exec. dir. Old Fort Niagara Assn., Youngstown, N.Y., 1979-96; curator of maps William L. Clements Libr. U. Mich., Ann Arbor, 1996—. Author: History and Guide to Old Fort Niagara, 1985, Siege-1759, 1986, rev. edit., 1996, Glorious Old Relic, 1987, Forts Within A Fort, 1989, Old Fort Niagara in Four Centuries, 1991; editor: Pouchot's Memoirs on the Late War in North America, 1994, Niagara, 1796, 1996, Frontier Metropolis, 2001. Fellow Co. Mil. Historians. Home: 4531 Maute Rd Grass Lake MI 49240 Office: William L Clements Libr 909 S University Ave Ann Arbor MI 48109-1190 Office Phone: 734-764-2347. Business E-Mail: briand@umich.edu.

DUNNIGAN, T. KEVIN, electrical and electronics manufacturing company executive; b. Montreal, Que., Can., Jan. 31, 1938; s. John George and Olive Mary (Brophy) D.; m. Beverley Alice Laramee, Apr. 11, 1960 (div. June 1980); children: David, Kathleen; m. Leah Anne Merlo. BA in Commerce, Loyola U., 1971. With Can. Elec. Distbg. Co., prior to 1962; salesman No. Telecom, Montreal, 1956-60; purchasing agt. Black-MacDonald, Montreal, 1960-62; salesman Thomas & Betts Corp., Iberville, Que., 1962-67, v.p. sales, 1967-70, pres., 1970-73, div. pres. Bridgewater, N.J., 1974-78, corp. exec. v.p. electronics, 1978-80, pres., 1980—, chief oper. officer, 1980-85, chief exec. officer, 1985-97, chmn. bd. Memphis, 1992—. Bd. dirs. C.R. Bard Inc., Deere & Co., Imagistics Inc., Pro-Mach, Inc. Office: Thomas & Betts Corp 8155 T&B Blvd Memphis TN 38125

DUNNING, JEAN, artist; b. Granby, Conn., 1960; MFA, Sch. Art Inst. Chgo., 1985. One-woman shows include, Feature, Chgo., 1987, 1988, Hirshhorn Mus., Washington, 1994, Mus. Contemporary Art, Chgo., 1994, Richard Telles Fine Art, LA, 1995, Galerie Massimo de Carlo, Milan, 1995, Feigen Inc., Chgo., 1996, Feigen Contemporary, 1997, Galleria Massimo de Carlo, Milan, 1998, Malmö Konstmuseum, Sweden, 1999, James Harris Gallery, Seattle, 2000, Bodybuilder & Sportsman Gallery, Chgo., 2001, exhibited in group shows at Changing Views, Feigen Inc., Chgo., 1994, Traces; Body in Contemporary Photog., Bronx Mus. Art, NYC, 1995, Wallflower, Randolph St. Gallery, Chgo., 1995, Up Close & Personal, Phila. Mus. Art, 1996, Slad, Apex Art, NYC, 1997, New Photog. 14, Mus. Modern Art, NYC, 1998, Rapture, MassArt, Boston, 2000, Wanderings of the Mind's Eye: Photographs by Ill. Artists, Mus. Contemporary Art, Chgo., 2004. Grantee, Louis Comfort Tiffany Found., 1993; Individual Artist Fellowship, Ill. Arts Coun., 1992, 1991, Cmty. Arts Assistance Grant, Chgo. Office Fine Arts, 1989, Spl. Assistance Grant, Ill. Art Coun., 1987. Mailing: c/o Museum Contemporary Art 220 East Chicago Ave Chicago IL 60611*

DUNNING, JEREMY DAVID, application developer, dean, educator; b. Washington, Feb. 15, 1951; s. John Laurance and Jacquelin (Creamer) D.; m. Deborah Humeler, June 3, 1972; children: Katherine, Nicholas, Abigail. BA in Geology with honors, Colgate U., 1973; MS, Rutgers U., 1975; PhD, U. N.C., 1978. Asst. prof. Oreg. State U., Corvallis, 1978-79, Ind. U., Bloomington, 1979-84, assoc. prof., 1984—94, full prof., 1994—, assoc. dean Bloomington, 1985—, dir. indsl. rsch. liaison program, 1986—. Hearst disting. lectr. U. Calif., Berekely, 1986; advisor Nat. Acad. Sci.; pres. ArJung Multimedia; cons. in field. Contbr. articles to profl. jours. Mem. bd. advisors NASA/USRA, nationwide, 1987—; mem. nat. adv. bd. Gov.'s Tech. Assessment, Ind., 1989-90; mem. Gov.'s Modernization Bd., Ind., 1990; dir. Ind. Univ. Res. Park, 1993-96; dean Sch. of Continued Studies, 1996-2003. Recipient Sloan C. Effective Practices award, 2003, Best Paper award, EISTA, 2003, Gold Medal, ICI, 2003, Novel Use of Technology award, ACHE, 2004. Mem. Am. Geophys. Union, Econ. Devel. Assn., NAMTAC. Office: Ind U Dept Geology Rm 121 Bloomington IN 47401 Business E-Mail: dunning@indiana.edu.

DUNNING, RICHARD L., health products executive; MBA, U. Del., 1971. With DuPont Co., 1968; exec. v.p., CFO DuPont Merck Pharm. Co., 1991—96; CEO Nexell Therapeutics, Irvine, Calif., 1996—, chmn. bd. dirs., 1999—. Office: Nexell Therapeutics Inc 280 Shuman Blvd Ste 170 Naperville IL 60563-2500

DUNPHY, EDWARD JAMES, science educator, crop science extension specialist; b. Frederick, Md., Nov. 14, 1940; s. Edward John and Marie W. (Barlow) D.; m. Judith Kay Mitchell, Aug. 18, 1962; children: Kevin James, Brian Patrick, Cory Edward. MS, U. Ill., 1964; PhD, Iowa State U., 1972. Rsch. asst. U. Ill., Urbana, 1962-64; agronomist Dunphy's Feed & Fertilizer, Sullivan, Ill., 1964-66; rsch. asst. Iowa State U., Ames, 1969-72, crop prodn. specialist Des Moines, 1972-75; extension specialist soybeans N.C. State U., Raleigh, 1975—, prof. crop sci., 1986—. Instr. soybean prodn. N.C., 1975—; mem. N.C. Land Use Value Adv. Bd., Raleigh, 1987—. Author 4 computer programs; contbr. numerous articles to profl. jours. Cubmaster Boy Scouts Am., Raleigh, 1976-81, troop com. chair, 1979-98; officer Athens Dr. Band Boosters, Raleigh, 1983-90. Sgt. U.S. Army, 1966-69. Recipient Meritorious Svc. award N.C. Soybean Producers. Fellow Am. Soc. Agronomy (bd. mem., com. chair, Agronomic Extension Edn. award); mem.Crop and Soil Sci. Socs. Am., Am. Soybean Assn. (Ext. Edn. award, mem. S.Am. soybean mission), Coun. Agrl. Sci. and Tech., Internat. Cert. Crop Advisers (bd. mem., com. chair), Alpha Zeta, Epsilon Sigma Phi, Gamma Sigma Delta, Phi Eta Sigma, Phi Kappa Phi, Sigma Xi. Achievements include research on soybean varieties, production, management and econ. Home: 3708 Swift Dr Raleigh NC 27606-2572 Office: NC State U Box 7620 Raleigh NC 27695-7620 Office Phone: 919-515-5813. E-mail: jim_dunphy@ncsu.edu.

DUNSAY, CHARLES WILLIAM, elementary school educator; b. Buffalo, N.Y., Nov. 11, 1943; s. Solomon Herzel and Elizabeth Lillian Dunsay; m. Bernadette (Carina) Rosemarie Curcio, Jan. 16, 1970; 1 child, Emily Mae. BS Secondary Edn., SUNY, New Paltz, N.Y., 1965. Cert. Instrnl. Tech. Proficiency Framingham State Coll., Mass., 2002. Grade 4 tchr. Webatuck Ctrl. Sch. Dist., Amenia, NY, 1965—66, New Rochelle Pub. Sch. Dist., New Rochelle, NY, 1966—74; grade 2-3 tchr. So. Berkshire Regional Sch. Dist.Sheffield, Mass., 1974—, k-5 math tchr. leader, 2003—. Contbr. conf. presentor (3 person team). Office: New Marlborough Ctrl Schl 44 Hartsville Mill River Rd Mill River MA 01244 Office Phone: 413-229-8867.

DUNSCOMBE, EDWARD ANDREW, library director, librarian; b. Bklyn, NY, Nov. 8, 1954; s. Edward and Edith Jean (Schweikert) Dunscombe; m. Sharon Misura; children: Andrew Edward, Hannah Rose. BA, State U. Coll., 1972—76; MLS, Sch. of Libr. and Info. Sci., 1977—78. Cert. Pub. Libr. NY State Edn. Dept., 1978. Records analyst City of Rochester, NY, 1978—79; reference libr. Vestal Pub. Libr., Vestal, NY, 1980; adult services libr. George F. Johnson Meml. Libr., Endicott, NY, 1980—2003, libr. dir., 1990—91, 2003—. Site dir. and pub. rels. So. Tier SeniorNet, Endicott, NY, 2003—05. Democrat-Npl. Lutheran. Avocations: genealogy, sports. Home: 302 E Edwards St Endicott NY 13760 Office: George F Johnson Meml Libr 1001 Park St Endicott NY 13760 Office Phone: 607-757-2415. Office Fax: 607-757-2491. Personal E-mail: edunscombe@stny.rr.com. E-mail: en.ed@4cls.org.

DUNSIRE, P(ETER) KENNETH, insurance company executive; b. Spearhill, Man., Can., Mar. 1, 1932; came to U.S., 1969; s. Robert Anderson and Margaret (Kinnear) D.; m. Lily Martha Bell (div. Nov. 1971); children: Robert K., Barbara L. Dunsire Belanger; m. Stephanie Alice Mooradian. Student, U. B.C., Can., 1949-50, U. Alta., 1955-56. V.p. Avco Fin. Services, Newport Beach, Calif., 1961-71; exec. v.p. Carte Blanche, Los Angeles, 1971-74, pres., 1974-78; chmn. Am. Benefit Plan Adminstrn., Los Angeles, 1978-80; exec. v.p. Paul Revere Life Ins. Co., Worcester, Mass., 1980-84, Lincoln Nat. Life Ins. Co., Ft. Wayne, Ind., 1984-86, also bd. dirs.; exec. v.p. Lincoln Nat. Corp., Ft. Wayne, Ind., 1986-95, ret., 1995. Bd. dirs. Ft. Wayne Med. Soc. Found., Ft. Wayne C. of C. Found., Nat. Auto & Truck Mus.; chmn. Cannon Lincoln Plc., London, 1984-90, chmn. bd., 1992-95. Chmn. bd. Sta. WFWA-TV, Ft. Wayne, 1985-91, Auburn Cord Duesenberg Mus., Ind., 1986-2001, Ft. Wayne Civic Theater, 1985-86. Mem. Ft. Wayne C. of C. (vice-chmn. 1989-91, chmn. 1991-92). Republican. Avocation: automobile collecting. Home: 8140 Auburn Rd Fort Wayne IN 46825-3016 E-mail: pkdunsire@aol.com.

DUNSKER, STEWART B., neurosurgeon; b. Cin. s. Shiel and Tillie Dunsker; m. Ellen Lothian Treiman, July 2, 1966. BA, Harvard U., 1956; MD, U. Cin., 1960. Diplomate Am. Bd. Neurol. Surgery (pres.). Intern U. Ill., Chgo., 1960-61; resident in internal medicine U. Cin., 1961-62, resident in gen. surgery, 1964-65; resident in neurol. surgery Washington U., St. Louis, 1965-69; prof. clin. neurosurgery U. Cin.; treas. Mayfield Clinic, Cin. Capt. U.S. Army, 1962-64. Fellow: ACS; mem.: Am. Bd. Neurol. Surgeons (vice chair), Am. Acad. Neurol. Surgeons (v.p.), Am. Assn. Neurol. Surgeons (pres., Harvey Cushing medal 2003), Ohio State Neurosurg. Soc. (pres.), Soc. Univ. Neurosurgeons (pres.), Ohio State Med. Assn. (pres., Ohio Neurosurgeon of Yr. 1992, Evans award 1998). Office: Mayfield Clinic 2123 Auburn Ave # 441 Cincinnati OH 45219-2906

DUNSKY, MENAHEM, retired advertising executive, communications executive, consultant, painter; b. Montreal, Que., Can., July 5, 1930; s. Shimson D. and Esther Dunsky; children: Ron Abraham, Ilan Isaac, Dan David Gil. Teaching diploma, Jewish Tchrs. Sem., Montreal, 1948; BA, Concordia U., Montreal, 1952; MA, NYU, 1954; hons. diploma, Parsons Sch. Design, 1956. Tchr. Jewish People's Schs., Montreal, 1948-52; asst. art dir. L.W. Frohlich Advt., N.Y.C., 1956-58; creative dir. Gordon, Lewinson Advt., Tel Aviv, 1958-59; founding mem. Com. for Planning Saidye Bronfman Cultural Ctr., 1962; lectr. art history Saidye Bronfman Cultural Centre, Montreal, 1960-63; founder, pres. Dunsky Advt. Ltd., Westmount, Que., Can., 1960-87. Cons. Govt. of Man., Winnipeg, 1970-77, Govt. of Sask., Regina, 1971-82, Govt. of B.C., Victoria, 1972-75; panelist pub. symposium Politics and the Media, 1980 Published Jewish Iconography, 1961; paintings exhibited at Jewish Pub. Libr., Montreal, 1964; retrospective Le Waldorf, Montreal, 2002. Chmn. bd. Saidye Bronfman Cultural Centre, 1969-70; officer Jewish People's Sch. System, Montreal, 1982-85; chmn. edn. com. Bialik High Sch., Montreal, 1981-85, chmn. personnel com., 1983-85; exec. mem. YM/YWHA, Montreal, 1969-71; chmn. nat. edn. com. Can. Zionist Fedn., 1984-88; mem. nat. exec. com., 1985-88; bd. dirs. Jewish Edn. Coun., 1986-88; chmn. pub. rels. com. Can. Ben Gurion Centennial Celebration, 1986-87. Mem. Trans Can. Advt. Agy. Network-Toronto (founding mem.), Trans. Can. Advt. Agy. Network-Toronto (bd. dir. 1962-87), Trans Can. Advt. Agy. Network-Toronto (pres. 1965), Inst. Can. Advt.-Toronto (dir. 1972-75), Inst. Can. Advt. (chmn. profl. com. 1974-75), Advt. Agy. Coun. Que. (founding mem., exec. com. 1969-75) Jewish. E-mail: emdunsky@videotron.ca. *The extent to which one manages to meld the pursuit of one's career interests with considerations of a broader social and cultural nature has always served me as a principal concern. As well, I have kept career considerations from diminishing the time and quality of attention which family and self deserve and require.*

DUNSON, WILLIAM ALBERT, biology professor, ecological consultant; b. Cedartown, Ga., Dec. 17, 1941; s. James Blake and Eleanor (Adams) D.; m. Margaret E. Kvashay, Aug. 19, 1963; children: Mary Elizabeth, William Albert, David Brian. BS in Zoology with honors, Yale U., 1962; MS, U. Mich., 1964, PhD, 1965. Teaching fellow U. Mich., Ann Arbor, 1962-63; mem. faculty Pa. State U., University Park, 1965—, prof. biology, 1974-97, prof. emeritus, 1997—; environ. scientist Seminole Tribe Fla., 1997—2002. Adj. prof. biology U. Miami, Old Dominion U., Fla., Atlantic U.; chief scientist various internat. oceanographic expdns.; collaborator Everglades Nat. Park Author: The Biology of Sea Snakes, 1975; contbr. over 140 articles to profl. jours. Queens marine sci. fellow, 1972, hon. Fulbright fellow, 1972; grantee NSF, U.S. Dept. Interior, U.S. Geol. Survey, U.S. EPA. Mem. Soc. for Study Amphibians and Reptiles (jour. edit. bd.). Achievements include study of ecotoxicology, physiological ecology and wetlands ecology. Office: 577 State Shd Ln Galax VA 24333 Business E-Mail: wad4@psu.edu.

DUNST, KIRSTEN, actress; b. Point Pleasant, N.J., Apr. 30, 1982; d. Klaus and Inez Dunst. Appeared in films Bonfire of the Vanities, 1990, High Strung, 1991, Greedy, 1994, Interview with the Vampire, 1994, Little Women, 1994, Jumanji, 1995, Wag the Dog, 1997, (voice) Anastasia, 1997, Drop Dead Gorgeous, 1999, Dick, 1999, The Virgin Suicides, 1999, Bring It On, 2000, crazy/beautiful, 2001, The Cat's Meow, 2001, Spider-Man, 2002, Levity, 2003, Mona Lisa Smile, 2003, Eternal Sunshine on the Spotless Mind, 2004, Spider-Man 2, 2004, Wimbledon, 2004; appeared on TV in Storytime, 1994, Darkness before Dawn, 1993, Saturday Night Live, others. Recipient Golden Globe Award nomination for best supporting actress, 1995, Boston Soc. of Film Critics Award for best supporting actress, 1994, Chicago Film Critics Assn. Award for most promising actress, 1994. Office: c/o Iris Burton Agy 8916 Ashcrof Ave Los Angeles CA 90069-1327

DUNST, LAURENCE DAVID, advertising executive; b. N.Y.C., Feb. 21, 1941; s. Philip R. and Mae (Fruchthendler) D.; m. Diane Gordon, Dec. 22, 1962; children: Lee Gordon, Melissa Susan. BA, Syracuse U., 1961. Advt. copywriter R.H. Macy & Co., 1961-63; with Daniel & Charles, N.Y.C., from 1963; pres. Laurence, Charles, Free & Lawson, Inc., N.Y.C., 1969-86, chmn., 1986-91, pres., CEO, 1991-95; chmn, CEO Gotham Inc., N.Y.C., 1995—. Mem. Young Pres.'s Orgn., The Met. Club. Home: 900 Fifth Ave New York NY 10021 Office: Gotham Inc 930 Fifth Ave Fl 16 New York NY 10011-6996

DUNTON, CHARLES JOSEPH, gynecologist, oncologist; b. Phila., Oct. 21, 1952; s. Joseph and Margaret Dunton; m. Karen Crane; children: Brittany, McCrea. MD, Jefferson Med. Coll., Phila., 1980. Diplomate Am. Bd. Ob-Gyn, Am. Bd. Gynecol. Oncology. Intern Lankenau Hosp., 1980—81, resident ob/gyn, 1981—84; physician USPHS, Chester, Pa., 1984—86; fellow in gynecologic oncology Hosp. U. Pa., 1987—89; active staff Med. Coll. Pa., Phila., 1989—91, Thomas Jefferson U. Hosp., Phila., 1991—2002, Albert Einstein Med. Ctr., Phila., 2002—04. Active staff Main Line Health Sys., Wynnewood, Pa., 1985—; cons. Fitzgerald Mercy Hosp., Darby, Pa., 1986—96, Frankford-Torresdale Hosp., Phila., 1989—91, Mercer Med. Ctr., Trenton, NJ, 1992—94, Meth. Hosp., Phila., 1993—2001, Riddle Meml. Hosp., Media, Pa., 1997—; prof. ob-gyn. Jefferson Med. Coll., Phila., 1999—; assoc. staff Thomas Jefferson U. Hosp., Phila., 2002—05; dir. divsn. gyn. oncology Albert Einstein Med. Ctr., Phila., 2002—04; dir,. divsn. gyn. oncology Lankenau Hosp., Wynnewood, 2005—. Prin. investigator Gyn. Oncology Group, Phila., 1994—97. Recipient Nat. Faculty award, ACOG, 2003, Searle prize, 1990, Abbott award, Assn. Profs. Gyn.-Ob., 1990, Excellence in Tchg. award. Fellow: ACS; mem.: Phila. Ob. Soc. (vice chmn. 1998—99), Internat. Gyn. Cancer Soc. (corr.), Am. Soc. Colposcopy and Cervical Pathology (assoc. Merit award 1996), Soc. Gyn. Oncologists (assoc.), Am. Soc. Clin. Oncology (assoc.), Phila. Colposcopy Soc. (pres. 1996—98). Office: Main Line Health Med Bldg East Ste 661 100 Lancaster Ave Wynnewood PA 19096 Office Phone: 610-649-8085. E-mail: duntonc@mlhs.org.

DUNTON, GARY C., insurance company executive; Attended, Northeastern U.; MBA, Harvard Grad. Sch. Bus. Adminstrn. Cert. Fin. Analyst, Chartered Property Casualty Underwriter. In sr. positions Aetna Life & Casualty Co., 1980s; pres. Family and Bus. Ins. Group, USF&G Ins., 1997—; with MBIA Inc., Armonk, NY, 1998—, pres., dir., 1999—, COO, 2000—04, CEO, 2004—, also bd. dirs. Office: MBIA Ins Inc 113 King St Armonk NY 10504-1610

DUNTON, JAMES RAYNOR, publisher; b. Wilmington, Del., June 17, 1955; s. Guthrie Raynor III and Jane (Hill) D. BA, U. Va., 1977; MBA, Boston U., 1981. Editor Quorum Books, Westport, Conn., 1984-87; sr. editor Praeger Pubs., N.Y.C., 1987-91, editor-in-chief, 1991-94; pub. acad. and trade Greenwood Pub. Group, Westport, 1994-96; dir. publs. Ctr. for Strategic and Internat. Studies, Washington, 1996—; consulting editor Praeger Pubs., Washington, 1996—, Brassey's, Inc., Washington, 2003—. Mem.: Washington Book Pubs., Soc. for Scholarly Pub., English-Speaking Union, Va. Club of N.Y. Home: 1520 16th St NW Apt 704 Washington DC 20036-1448 Office: Ctr for Strategic and Internat Studies 1800 K St NW Washington DC 20006-2202 Office Phone: 202-775-3160. Business E-Mail: jdunton@csis.org.

DUNWODY, EUGENE COX, architect; b. Macon, Ga., July 19, 1933; s. William Elliott and Mary Bennet (Cox) D.; m. Susan Howe Foxworth, June 15, 1957; children: Susan, Eugene Jr., George, Mary Bennet. BS, Ga. Inst. Tech., 1955, BArch, 1956. Registered architect, Ga., Fla. V.p., treas. W. Elliott Dunwody Jr., Macon, 1959-69; pres. Dunwody and Co., Macon, 1969-81, Dunwody, Beeland and Henderson Architects Inc., Macon, 1981-97, Dunwody, Beeland, Azar, Walsh, and Matthews, Architects Inc., Macon, 1997-2000, Dunwody/Beeland, Archs., 2000—. Pres. Rotary, Macon, 1974, City Coun., Macon, 1975-87, C. of C., Macon, 1977; dir. Ga. Mcpl. Assn., Atlanta, 1982-83, Nat. League Cities, Washington, 1985-87; chmn. Macon-Bibb County Indsl. Authority, 1992-93, 99, 2000, Macon Econ. Devel. Commn., 1992-93, 99, 2000; pres. Macon Symphony Orch., 2000-2002; deacon Presbyn. Ch. Named Community leader of Yr. Robins Air Logistics Ctr., Warner Robins, Ga., 1987; recipient Motie Wiggins award for Outstanding elected ofcl. Ga. Mcpl. Assn., Atlanta, 1987, Ga. Tech.'s Dean Griffin Cmty. Svc. award, 2000, Macon Arts Alliance Cultural award, 2002. Fellow AIA; mem. Middle Ga. chpt. AIA (pres. 1993), Ga. Assn. AIA (dir. 1992-93). Democrat. Presbyterian. Avocations: golf, piano, choir. Office: Dunwody/Beeland 484 Mulberry St Ste 220 Macon GA 31201-7922 Office Phone: 478-742-5321. E-mail: ccd@dbdgn.com.

DUNWOODY, KENNETH REED, magazine and book editor; b. Washington, Iowa, Oct. 1, 1953; s. Kenneth W. and Marilyn Jane (Green) D.; m. Patricia P. Seale, July 7, 1990 BS in Journalism with honors, U. Ill., 1976. Sports announcer Sta. WPGU, Champaign, Ill., 1972-75; sports editor Free Press Newspaper Group, Carpentersville, Ill., 1976-79, Daily Crystal Lake Herald, Ill., 1979-82; mag. editor Fur-Fish-Game mag. A.R. Harding Pub. Co., Columbus, Ohio, 1982-86, art dir., 1982-86; mag. editor Game & Fish Pub., Marietta, Ga., 1986-88, editorial dir., 1989—. Contbr. articles to mags. Recipient Journalist of Yr. award Free Press Newspapers, 1977, 79, Sports Photography award Ill. Press Assn., 1978, Best Sports Writing award UPI, Ill. Press Assn., 1979, 80, Best Sports Column award UPI, 1979, 80, 81 Mem.

Outdoor Writers Assn. Am. Avocations: photography, writing, fishing, baseball. Home: 2381 N Forest Dr Marietta GA 30062-6553 Office: Game & Fish Pub 2250 New Market Pkwy SE Ste 110 Marietta GA 30067-9394 E-mail: kdunwoody@cowles.com, pdunwood@mindspring.com.

DUNYE, CHERYL, artist, filmmaker; b. Phila. BA, Temple U.; MFA, Rutgers U. Part-time instr. dept. media studies Pitzer Coll., Calif. Film maker (short film films) Greetings from Africa, 1994, (video films) The Potluck and the Passion, creator (films) The Watermelon Woman, contbr. articles to profl. jours. Recipient Major Artists award, MARMAF Pa., 1993; fellow, Rutgers U., 1990, 1991, Art Matters, Inc., 1992, grantee, Astrea Found., 1992, Frameline, 1992, NEA, 1995. Office: c/o Media Studies Pitzer Coll Scott Hall Basement 1050 N Mills Ave Claremont CA 91711-3908

DUONG, JOHN QUOC, real estate developer; b. Saigon, 1973; arrived in US, 1982; Grad., U. Calif., Davis. Various positions including dep. dir. Govs. Office of Community Relations, Calif, Calif.; founder Q-Strategies, 1999—; v.p. Bridgecreek Develop., Calif.; exec. dir. White House Initiative on Asian Am. and Pacific Islanders, 2001—04. Mem. President's Advisory Commn. on Asian Am. and Pacific Islanders. Mem. Contra Costa Coll. Found., Contra Costa County Workforce Develop. Bd., Am. Viet League, Vietnamese Am. Council, Commonwealth Club of Calif., Richmond-San Pablo Exchange Club, Vietnamese Am. Public Affairs Com. Office: Bridgecreek Develop 8907 Warner Ave Huntington Beach CA 92647*

DUONG, TIMOTHY, medical educator; b. Saigon, Vietnam, June 3, 1972; PhD, Wash. U., 1998. Rsch. scientist U. Minn., Mpls., 1998—2001; dir., asst. prof. U. Mass. Med Sch, Worcester, Mass., 2001—. Grantee, Nat. Inst. of Health, AMA, Whitaker Found., 1999, 2001, 2004, 2004, 2004. Office: Emory U Yerkes Rsch Ctr 954 Gatewood Rd Atlanta GA 30329

DUPIES, DONALD ALBERT, retired civil engineer; b. Waukegan, Ill., Apr. 17, 1934; s. Renie Bernard and Catherine Marie (Dowe) D.; m. Margaret T. McKibbin, Sept. 29, 1962; children: Mark, Patrick, Peggy, Colleen. BCE, Marquette U., 1957. With Howard, Needles, Tammen & Bergendoff, Milw., 1959—, office engr., 1969-71, engr. in charge, 1971-74, assoc., 1974-79, cons. engr., ptnr., 1980-95. Pres. Great Lakes divsn. HNTB Corp., ret., 1995. Bd. dirs. Centurions of St. Joseph Hosp., Milw., 1971-76; cubmaster Milw. County coun. Boy Scouts Am., 1973-75; mem. Bd. Appeals, Town of Delafield, Wis., 1996-2002. Served with C.E. U.S. Army, 1957-59. Mem. ASCE (nat. dir. 1982-85), Internat. Inst. of Transportation Engrs., Marquette Club of Milwaukee, Marquette U. Engring. Alumni Assn. (dir. Milw. 1976-83pres. 1981-82), Tau Beta Pi, Chi Epsilon. Roman Catholic. Home: 1480 Fairways Cir Oconomowoc WI 53066

DUPILL, DANIEL NORMAN, librarian; b. Fitchburg, Mass., Dec. 9, 1946; s. Norman Albert Dupill and Maxine Pratt; m. Christine Joan Bocek, Aug. 10, 1989; children: Cassie Toni Camille Chow, Eli Stephenson Bocek-Rivele, Max Daniel. BS Secondary Edn., Fitchburg State Coll., Fitchburg, Mass., 1968; MLS, U. So. Calif., L.A., Calif., 1982. Cert. English, History, Social Studies Tchg. Credential Mass., 1968. Mgr., kettering music rm. Pitkin County Libr., Aspen, Colo., 1976—80; asst. br. mgr. Harris County Libr., Houston, 1983—84; libr., fiction dept. L.A. Pub. Libr., Calif., 1984—86, sr. libr., ctrl. libr. L.A., 1986—95, mgr., mid -valley regional br. & valley bookmobile L.A., Calif., 1995—2000, dept. mgr., art/music/rare books; edn. developer Burroughs Corp., El Monte, Calif., 1981—82. Fiction editor Aspen Leaves Lit. Mag., Aspen, Colo., 1979—80. Mem./pres. Bd. of Libr. Trustees, Alhambra, Calif., 1995—2003; mem. CALTAC, Calif., 1995—2003. Scholar R. Cracchi Meml. Scholarship, Slim. U.S.C., 1982. Mem.: LA Preservation Network (steering com. 2000—05), ALA, Beta Phi Mu (life). Office: LA Pub Libr 630 W Fifth St Los Angeles CA 90071 Office Phone: 213-228-7241. Office Fax: 213-228-7239. Business E-Mail: ddupill@lapl.org.

DUPLANTIER, ADRIAN GUY, federal judge; b. New Orleans, Mar. 5, 1929; s. F. Robert and Amelie (Rivet) D.; m. Sally Thomas, July 15, 1951; children: Adrian G., David L., Thomas, Jeanne M., Louise M., John C. JD cum laude, Loyola U., New Orleans, 1949; LLD, Loyola U., 1993; LLM, U. Va., 1988. Bar: La. 1950, U.S. Supreme Ct. 1954. Pvt. practice law, New Orleans, 1950-74; judge Civil Dist. Ct. Parish of Orleans, 1974-78, U.S. Dist. Ct., New Orleans, 1978-94, sr. judge, 1994—. Part-time prof. code of civil procedure Loyola U., 1951—, lectr. dental jurisprudence, 1960-67, lectr. English dept., 1948-50, chmn. law sch. vis. com., 1995-97, adj. prof. law, 1952—; prof. summer sch. abroad Tulane Law Sch., Rhodes, Greece, 1992, Cambridge, England, 1993, Loyola Law Sch., Vienna, Austria, 1996; mem. La. State Senate, 1960-74; 1st asst. dist. atty. New Orleans, 1954-56; mem. Jud. Conf. of U.S. Bankruptcy Rules Adv. Com., 1994-96, chmn. 1997—; elected La. State Senate, 1960-74; 5th cir. dist. judge rep. Jud. Conf. U.S., 1993-94, com. bicentennial of constn., 1986-91; chmn. Bill of Rights Bicentennial Conf. Fed. Judges, 1991. Editorial bd.: Loyola Law Rev, 1947-48; editor-in-chief, 1948-49. Del. Democratic Nat. Conv., 1964; pres. Associated Cath. Charities New Orleans, Social Welfare Planning Council Greater New Orleans; mem. adv. bd. St. Mary's Dominican Coll., 1970-71, Ursuline Acad., 1968-73, Mt. Carmel Acad., 1965-69; chmn. pres.'s adv. coun. Jesuit H.S., 1980-81, mem., 1976—; chmn. bd. dirs. Boys Hope, 1980—, nat. bd. dirs., 1982-92, coun., 1992—; active Assn. Retarded Children. Recipient Meritorious award New Orleans Assn. Retarded Children, 1965, Gov.'s Cert. of Merit, 1970, Outstanding Alumnus award Loyola U., 1985, Vol. Activist award Outstanding Vol. Svc., 1986. Mem. ABA (award 1960), La. Bar Assn., New Orleans Bar Assn., Loyola Law Sch. Vis. Com. (chmn. 1993-96), Jud. Conf. of U.S., Loyola Law Sch. Alumni Assn. (St. Ives award 1998), U.S. Adv. Com. (jud. conf. on bankruptcy rules 1993—, chmn. 1996—), Order of Coif, Alpha Sigma Nu. Office: US Dist Ct C-205 US Courthouse 500 Camp St New Orleans LA 70130-3313

DUPLESSIS, AUDREY JOSEPH, school system administrator; b. New Orleans, June 23, 1920; d. Louis Joseph and Sidonie Josephine (DeLaRose) Boyer; m. Norwood Jerome Duplessis, Sr., June 27, 1984. B in Vocat. Edn., So. U., Baton Rouge, 1942; BA, Calif. State U., 1959, MA, 1966. Tchr., dir. Tri State Coll., New Orleans, 1948-50; from elem. tchr. to dir. Magnet Sch. L.A. Unified Schs., 1954—2002, dir. Magnet Sch., 2002—. Playground L.A. Unified Schs., 1956-59, reading resource tchr., 1965-70, curriculum coord., 1972-78, dir. L.A. Unified Magnet Sch., 1978-02; reading tchr. Calif. Lutheran Coll., Thousand Oaks, 1968-70. Mem. United Tchrs. PAC, L.A., 1980-88. Recipient svc. award Congress of Parents, L.A., 1988, spl. recognition U.S. Congress, 1988. Mem. Internat. Assn. Childhood Edn. (state pres. 1987-89, appreciation award 1989), St. Brigid Edn. Com., Delta Sigma Theta. Democrat. Roman Catholic. Avocations: reading, sewing, travel, opera, listening to music.

DU PLESSIS, ERIC, literature educator, language educator; b. Albertville, France, Sept. 19, 1950; s. Jean-Pierre Leopold and Simone Jeanne Babu; children: Harrison Asher, Miriam Isabelle, Carey Jennifer Benton, David Lindsey Bendiksen, Kenneth Jean-Pierre Bendiksen. Student, Univ. Paris; BA, Va. Commonwealth U., 1973; MA, Univ. of Richmond, 1975; PhD, Univ. of Va., Charlottesville, 1979. Asst. prof. Tex. A&M U., 1979—87; prof. Radford U., Va., 1987—. Translator: Balzac's Wann-Chlore, Balzac's The Last Fay, The Nightcharmer and other Tales of Claude Seignolle; author: Nietzsche in France, 1892-1915; contbr. European Studies Jour., Poe Studies, World Education Encyclopedia, World Press Encyclopedia, Revue De Litterature Comparee; translator: Honore de Balzac's Wann-Chlore; contbr. Dalhousie French Studies. Independent. Roman Catholic. Avocations: aikijitsu, flying, photography, hiking. Home: 523 Maple St Dublin VA 24084 Office: Radford U Box 6937 Radford VA 24142-6937 Office Phone: 540-831-5120. Business E-Mail: ehduples@radford.edu.

DUPLESSIS, SANDRA WALSH, librarian, educator; b. N.Y.C., Mar. 14, 1945; d. Maurice David and Helen Rose (Flynn) Walsh; m. Dwight Charles Duplessis, July 11, 1970; children: Anton, Laura, James. BA in Edn., U. La., Monroe, 1966; MLS with honors, La. State U., 1984. Libr., tchr. Chapelle H.S., Metairie, La., West Jefferson H.S., Harvey, La.; libr., cataloger Jefferson Pub. Libr., Metairie, La.; libr., tchr. St. Rita Sch., Harahan, La. Chair Regina Medal Selection Com. Recipient Sister Mary Aquin award/Libr. of the Yr. Mem.: ALA, Greater New Orleans Libr. Assn., La. Libr. Assn., Greater New Orleans Cath. Libr. Assn. (v.p., pres., newsletter editor), Cath. Libr. Assn. (children's sect., mem. at large, sec., v.p., pres.), Beta Phi Mu. Home: 138 Miami Pl Kenner LA 70065

DUPLESSY, JEAN CLAUDE, research scientist; b. Paris, Oct. 3, 1942; s. Andre and Lucette (Fauvet) D.; m. Sylwia Kowalska, Sept. 21, 1968; children: Jacques-Eric, Catherine. Agrégation Physics, Ecole Normale Sup., Paris, 1967; D. Geology, U. Paris, 1967, D. Scis./Physics, 1972; D. (hon.), Univ. Kiel, 2003. Rsch. intern Ctr. Natl. de la Recherche Scientifique, Gif Sur Yvette, France, 1967-68, rsch. attaché, 1968-73, rsch. asst., 1973-76, rsch. master, 1976-84, dir. rsch., 1984-91, dir. rsch.-exceptional class, 1991—. Dir. Ctr. des Faibles Radioactivites, Gif Sur Yvette, 1985-96. Co-Author: Gros Temps Sur la Planete, 1990; co-editor: (2 book series) Nato, 1989-94. Recipient prix Aime Berthe, French Acad. Sci., 1987, Milankovitch medal European Geophys. Soc., 1995, prix Dolomieu, French Acad. Scis., 2004, prix. Louis D. Inst. France, 2005. Mem. Acad. Europaea. Office: Lab des Scis Climat et L'environnement Parc Du CNRS 91198 Gif-sur-Yvette France Office Phone: 33169823526. Business E-Mail: jean.claude.duplessy@lsce.cnrs-gif.fr.

DUPONT, AUGUSTUS IRÉNÉE, lawyer; b. N.Y.C., Oct. 18, 1951; s. Francis I. and Rosamont S. (Lee) duP.; m. Jill Greenwood, June 23, 1979; children: Jessie G., John W., Hilary G. AB, Stanford U., 1975; JD, U. Chgo., 1978. Bar: Mass. 1978, N.Y. 1980. Assoc. Skadden, Arps, Slate, Meagher & Flom, N.Y.C., 1978-84; assoc. counsel The Penn Cen. Corp., Greenwich, Conn., 1984-86, asst. gen. counsel, 1986-87; v.p., gen. counsel, sec. Sprague Techs., Inc., Stamford, Conn., 1987—93; v.p., gen. counsel Reeves Industries, Inc., 1994—95; v.p., sec., gen. counsel Crane Co., Stamford, Conn., 1996—. Mem. ABA, Am. Corp. Counsel Assn. Home: 346 North St Greenwich CT 06830-3930 Office: Crane Co 100 First Stamford Pl Stamford CT 06902 Office Phone: 203-363-7223. Office Fax: 203-363-7295. E-mail: adupont@craneco.com.

DUPONT, HERBERT LANCASHIRE, medical educator, researcher; b. Toledo, Nov. 12, 1938; s. Robert L. and Martha (Lancashire) DuP.; m. Margaret Wright, June 9, 1963; children: Denise Lorraine, Andrew Wright BA, Ohio Wesleyan U., 1961; MD, Emory U., 1965; doctorate (hon.), U. Zurich, 2004. Diplomate Am. Bd. Internal Medicine. Resident U. Minn. Med. Ctr., Mpls., 1965-67; officer epidemic intelligence svc. CDC Atlanta, infectious disease fellow U. Md. Sch. Medicine, Balt., 1967-69; faculty, prof., dir. Ctr. for Infectious Diseases U. Tex., Houston, 1973-94, prof. Sch. Pub. Health, 1975—, prof. medicine M.D. Anderson Cancer Ctr., 1988—, Mary W. Kelsey chmn. med. sci., 1988—, interim chmn. dept. internal medicine, 1987-89; chief internal medicine svc. and vice chmn. dept. medicine, H. Irving Schweppe chair St. Luke's Episcopal Hosp. and Baylor Coll. Medicine, Houston, 1995—; clin. prof. dept. medicine Baylor Coll. Medicine, Houston, 1995—; dir., ctr. for infectious diseases, prof. epidemology U. Tex. Sch. Pub. Health, 2002—. Clin. prof. dept. medicine and adj. prof. dept. microbiology and immunology Baylor Coll. Medicine, Houston, 1995—; vaccines and related biologic products adv. com. U.S. FDA, 1989—93; sci. adv. com. Inst. Medicine, NAS, 1989—94; bd. sci. counselors Nat. Ctr. for Infectious Diseases, CDC, 1992—96; mem. standing sci. adv. com. Thrasher Rsch. Fund, 1993—96; bd. mem. Kelsey Rsch. Found., 2001—. Author various med. books; assoc. editor: Am. Jour. Epidemiology, 1978—81, Jour. Infectious Diseases, 1983—88; mem. editl. bd. Clin. Infectious Diseases, 1990—95, Infectious Diseases in Clin. Practice, 1992—, Jour. of Infection, 1997—, dep. editor Jour. of Travel Medicine, 2003—; contbr. articles to profl. jours. Lt. comdr. USAF, 1967—69. Rsch. grant NIH, 1975-97. Fellow ACP (regional gov.-elect 2002-03, gov. 2003-04); mem. Am. Soc. Clin. Investigation, Infectious Diseases Soc. Am. (counselor 1978-81, sec. 1982-87, pres. 1989-90), Nat. Found. Infectious Diseases (bd. dirs. 1981-2002, v.p. 1994-97, pres. 1997-99), Am. Clin. and Climatol. Assn. (recorder, coun. mem. 2000—), Am. Epidemiology Soc., Assn. Am. Physicians, U.S. Mex. Found. Sci. and Tech. (com. chair health 1994-99), Tex. Acad. Internal Medicine (bd. dirs.), Internat. Soc. Travel Medicine (pres. 1991-93), Am. Coll. Physicians (bd. dirs. 2001-), Alpha Omega Alpha. Republican. Methodist. Home: 1111 Hermann Dr Apt 19F Houston TX 77004-6931 Office: St Luke's Episcopal Hosp # MC 1-164 6720 Bertner St Houston TX 77030-2697 E-mail: hdupont@sleh.com.

DUPONT, NICOLE, artist; b. Wilmington, Del., July 24, 1957; d. Henry E.I. duPont and Deborah (Eldredge) duPont Hogan. Artist, CEO Visionary Art Studios, Novato, Calif., 1989-93, Creative Light Prodns., Kapa'a, Hawaii, 1993—. Artist; creator Hawaiian Legend Leis; leis collected in museums including Bishop Mus., Honolulu. Adminstrv. for cmty. classes in Hawaiian culture, Kapa'a, 1994-95. Winner 1st Place award Mokihana Festival Lei Contest, 1997, 98. Mem. Kaua'i Soc. Artists, Garden Island Arts Coun., Kaua'i C. of C. Office: Creative Light Prodns 1191 Kuhio Hwy 116 Kapaa HI 96746 E-mail: hnd@aloha.net.

DU PONT, PIERRE SAMUEL, IV, lawyer, former governor of Delaware; b. Wilmington, Del., Jan. 22, 1935; s. Pierre Samuel and Jane (Holcomb) du P.; m. Elise Ravenel Wood, 1957; children: Elise, Pierre, Benjamin, Eleuthere. Grad., Phillips Exeter Acad., 1952; BS M.E., Princeton U., 1956; LL.B., Harvard U., 1963. Bar: Del. 1964. Mem. staff Photo Products Dept., E.I. duPont Co.; mem. Del. Ho. of Reps., 1968-70; mem.-at-large 92d to 94th congresses from Del., Washington; gov. State of Del., State of Del., 1977-85; mem. Richards, Layton and Finger, Wilmington, 1985—. Served with USNR, 1957-60. Republican. Office: Richards Layton and Finger 1 Rodney Sq Wilmington DE 19801-3305 E-mail: petedupont@att.net.

DUPONT, RALPH PAUL, lawyer, educator; b. Fall River, Mass., May 21, 1929; s. Michael William and Gertrude (Murphy) Dupont; children: Ellen O'Neill, Antonia Chafee, William Albert, Christien Paul. AB in Am. Civilization cum laude with highest honors, Brown U., 1951; JD cum laude, Harvard U., 1956. Bar: Conn. 1956, U.S. Supreme Ct. 1967, diplomate: Nat. Bd. Trial Advocacy, cert.: Conn. (civil trial specialist). Assoc. Davies, Hardy & Schenck, N.Y.C., 1956-57; ptnr. Copp & Dupont, New London, Conn., 1957-60; mem. Suisman, Shapiro & Wool, New London, 1961-63; ptnr. Dupont & Dupont (and successor firms), New London, 1963-91; of counsel Durant, Nichols, Houston, Mitchell & Sheahan, Bridgeport, Conn., 1992-97; ptnr. Dupont and Radlauer LLP, New London, Stamford, 1997—. Instr. Am. history and bus. law Mitchell Coll., New London, 1955, New London, 1957—58, trustee, 1991—94; vis. prof. Northeastern U. Sch. Law, 1977—78; lectr.-on-law U. Conn. Sch. Law, 1980—86; mem. adv. coun. Conn. Legal Svcs., 1980—82; trustee Anne S. K. Brown Mil. Collection Brown U., 1988—94, presiding trustee, 1990—92; vis. prof. law Bridgeport Law Sch. Quinnipiac Coll., 1991—92, mem. exec. bd., adj. prof. Sch. Law, Hamden, Conn., 1994—96; vis. prof. We. New Eng. Coll. Law, 1992—94; instr. bus. law U. New Haven, 1998. Author: (book) Litigation in 1 Attorney's Desk Library, 1994, Dupont on Connecticut Civil Practice, 2003. Mem. New London Bd. Edn., 1959—61; Dem. candidate Conn. Senate, 1960; trustee U.S. Atlantic Tuna Tournament, 1984—93, pres., 1988—90, chmn., 1991—92. Lt. (j.g.) USNR, 1951—53. Named Outstanding Young Man of the Yr., Conn. Jr. C. of C., 1960; recipient Disting. Svc. award, Greater New London Jr. C. of C., 1960. Fellow: Am. Coll. Trust and Estate Coun.; mem.: ABA, Internat. Acad. Estate and Trust Law, Conn. Bar Found. (bd. dirs. 1975—79), Conn. Bar Assn., Harvard U. Law Sch. Assn., Harvard Club, Kappa Sigma, Delta Sigma Rho. Roman Catholic. Home: 6770 Hawaii Kai Dr apt PH 9 Honolulu HI 96825 Office Phone: 203-321-2176. E-mail: radlaw2001@aol.com.

DUPONT, ROBERT LOUIS, psychiatrist, physician; b. Toledo, Mar. 25, 1936; s. Robert Louis and Martha Ireton (Lancashire) DuP.; m. Helen Gayden Spink, July 14, 1962; children: Elizabeth, Caroline. BA, Emory U., 1958; MD, Harvard U., 1963. Diplomate in psychiatry and addiction psychiatry Am. Bd. Psychiatry and Neurology; cert. med. rev. officer. Intern Western Res. U., 1963-64; resident in psychiatry Harvard Med. Sch., 1964-66; clin. assoc. NIH, 1966-68; research psychiatrist, acting assoc. dir. for community services D.C. Dept. Corrections, Washington, 1968-70; practice medicine specializing in psychiatry, 1968—. Adminstr. Narcotics Treatment Adminstrn., D.C. Dept. Human Resources, 1970—73; acting adminstr. Alcohol, Drug Abuse and Mental Health Adminstrn., HEW, Rockville, Md., 1974; dir. Nat. Inst. on Drug Abuse, HEW, Rockville, 1973—78, Spl. Action Office for Drug Abuse Prevention, Exec. Office Pres., Washington, 1973—75; pres. Inst. for Behavior and Health Inc., 1978—, Am. Coun. Drug Edn., 1980—85; U.S. del. UN Commn. on Narcotic Drugs, 1973—78; mem. Coordinating Coun. on Juvenile Justice and Delinquency Prevention, Dept. Justice, 1974—76; assoc. clin. prof. psychiatry and behavioral scis. George Washington Med. Sch., 1972—80; clin. prof. psychiatry Georgetown U. Med. Sch., 1980—; vis. assoc. clin. prof. psychiatry Harvard U. Med. Sch., 1978—84; chmn. Ctr. Behavioral Medicine, 1978—89; v.p. Bensinger, DuPont Assocs., Inc., 1982—; chair Prescription Drug Rsch. Ctr., 2004—. Author: The Selfish Brain, 2000, The Anxiety Cure, 2003, The Anxiety Cure for Kids, 2003, Drug Testing in Treatment Settings, 2005, Drug Testing in Schools, 2005; contbr. articles in fields of drug abuse, criminology and mental health to profl. jours.; appeared on Good Morning Am., ABC-TV, 1978—80. Bd. dirs. Washington Soc. for Performing Arts, 1972-76; mem. adv. com. Washington Jr. League, 1972-76. Served to surgeon (maj.) USPHS, 1966-68. Fellow: Am. Soc. Addiction Medicine (life; diplomate), Am. Psychiat. Assn. (life); mem.: Anxiety Disorders Assn. Am. (pres. 1982—85), Washington Psychiat. Soc. Home: 8708 Susanna Ln Chevy Chase MD 20815-4714 Office: 6191 Executive Blvd Rockville MD 20852-3901 Office Phone: 301-231-9010. Personal E-mail: bobdupont@aol.com. *As a practicing physician dealing with addiction and anxiety disorders, I have seen first-hand the intense suffering experienced by those afflicted and by those who love them. As a public health practitioner, I have seen the immense cost of these disorders. The miracle of recovery has been the inspiration of my career.*

DUPONT, TODD F., mathematics professor; b. Houston, Aug. 29, 1942; s. T.F. and Nan G. D.; m. Judy Smith, Aug. 20, 1964; children: Michelle, Todd K. BA, Rice U., 1963, PhD, 1968. Research mathematician Esso Prodn. Research, Houston, 1968; instr. U. Chgo., 1968-69, asst. prof., 1969-72, assoc. prof., 1972-75, prof. math., 1975—, prof. computer sci., 1985—, chmn. computer sci., 1994-97. Prin., officer, past bd. dirs. DREM (formerly Dupont-Rachford Engring. Math. Co.), Houston, 1969-92; prin. tech. adv. Advantica, Stoner Software, 1992—. Assoc. editor Math. of Computation, 1977—84, SIAM Jour., 1976—86. Home: 1335 E Park Pl Chicago IL 60637-1767 Office: Univ Chgo Dept Computer Sci 1100 E 58th St Chicago IL 60637-1588

DUPONT, WILLIAM DUDLEY, biostatistician, educator; b. Montreal, Que., Can., Nov. 6, 1946; came to U.S., 1971; s. Charles Thomas and Jean (White) Dupont; m. Susan Miller McChesney, July 20, 1974; children: Charles Thomas, Peter William. BSc, McGill U., 1969, MSc, 1971; PhD, Johns Hopkins U., 1976. Lectr. U. Md., Balt., 1976-77; asst. prof. biostats. Vanderbilt U. Sch. Medicine, Nashville, 1977-85, assoc. prof., 1986-92, prof., 1992—, dir. divsn. biostats., 1989—2003. Nat. Cancer Inst. grantee, 1980—. Mem. AAAS, Am. Statis. Assn., Biometric Soc., Soc. Clin. Trials, Soc. Epidemiol. Rsch. Office: Vanderbilt U Sch Medicine Dept Biostats 1161 21st Ave S S-2323 MCN Nashville TN 37232-2158 E-mail: william.dupont@vanderbilt.edu.

DUPRE, FELIX, career military officer; BS, USAF Acad., Colorado Springs, 1972; M in Mgmt. & Human Rels., Webster Coll., 1978. Commd. 2d lt. USAF, 1972, advanced through grades to col., 1994; instr. pilot 71st Flying Tng. Squadron, Moody AFB, Ga., 1974-75, 560th Flying Tng. Squadron, Randolph AFB, Tex., 1975-78; F-15 fighter lead-in Holloman AFB, N.Mex., 1978; asst. flight comdr. 71st Tactical Fighter Squadron, Langley AFB, Va., 1979-82; wing flight examiner 21st Tactical Fighter Wing, Elmendorf AFB, Alaska, 1982-85; test mgr. global position sys. initial operational test Air Force Operational Test & Evaluation Ctr., Kirtland AFB, N.Mex., 1985-88; air liaison officer Korean First Army, Wonju, 1988-89; asst. ops. officer 58th Tactial Fighter Squadron, Eglin AFB, Fla., 1990-91; comdr. 60th Fighter Squadron, Eglin AFB, Fla., 1992-93; chief exercises divsn., chief tactical evaluation divsn. 5th Allied Tactical Air Force, Vicenza, Italy, 1993-95; vice comdr. 1st Fighter Wing, Langley AFB, 1995-96; dir. staff Air Combat Command, Langley AFB, 1996-97; comdr. 33d Fighter Wing, Eglin AFB, 1997-99; comdr., 1st Fighter Wing Langley Air Force Base, Va., 1999—. Office: 1 FW/CC 159 Sweeney Blvd Ste 200 Langley Afb VA 23665-2207

DUPRE, LONNIE, arctic explorer, writer, photographer; b. 1961; m. Kelly Dupre. Author: (books) Greenland Expedition - Where Ice is Born, 2000. Named a laureate, Rolex for Enterprise award, 2004; named Fellow Nat. of the Explorers Club, 1996; recipient Soviet Sportsman Medal for Arctic exploration, 1989. Achievements include numerous polar expeditions including circumnativation of Greenland, Northwest Passage Expedition, Bering bridge expedition, Brooks Range Alaska. Home and Office: PO Box 940 Grand Marais MN 55604 Business E-Mail: dupre@boreal.org.

DUPRÉ, LOUIS, retired philosopher, educator; b. Veerle, Belgium; arrived in U.S., 1958, naturalized, 1966; s. Clement and Francisca (Verlinden) D. PhD, U. Louvain, Belgium; PhD (hon.), Loyola Coll., 1989, Sacred Heart U., 1992, Georgetown U., 1996, Siena Coll., 1997, Regis Coll., U. Toronto, 1998, St. Michael's Coll., 2002. From asst. prof. to prof. philosophy Georgetown U., Washington, 1959-73; T. Lawrason Riggs prof. philosophy of religion Yale U., New Haven, 1973-98. Author: Kierkegaard as Theologian (also in Dutch), 1963, The Philosophical Foundations of Marxism, 1966, Dutch edit., 1970, Korean edit., 1982, The Other Dimension, 1972, French edit., 1977, Chinese edit., 1986, Polish edit., 1990, Dutch edit., 1991, Korean edit., 1995, Spanish edit., 1999, Transcendent Selfhood, 1976, Dutch edit., 1981, A Dubious Heritage, 1979, The Deeper Life, 1981, Polish edit., 1994, German edit., 2002, Marx's Social Critique of Culture, 1983, The Common Life, 1984, Polish edit., 1994, Passage to Modernity, 1993, Metaphysics and Culture, 1994, Religious Mystery and Rational Reflection, 1997, Symbols of the Sacred, 2000, The Enlightenment and the Intellectual Foundations of Modern Culture, 2004; editor: Faith and Reflection, 1968; co-editor: Light from Light, 1987, 2d edit., 2001; contbr. articles to profl. jours. Recipient Phi Beta Kappa medal as Tchr. of Yr. at Yale U., 1996, Aquinas medal, Am. Cath. Philos. Assn., 1997. Mem. Am. Cath. Philos. Assn. (pres. 1971), Hegel Soc. Am. (pres. 1972-73), Am. Acad. Arts and Scis., Belgian Acad. Letters, Arts, & Scis. Roman Catholic. Home: 67 N Racebrook Rd Woodbridge CT 06525-1407 Business E-Mail: louis.dupre@yale.edu.

DUPREE, CLIFFORD H. R., lawyer; b. Phila., Sept. 11, 1950; s. Frederick Douglass and Dorothy Olivia (Rylander) DuP. AB, Princeton U., 1972; JD, Harvard U., 1975. Bar: N.Y. 1976. Assoc. Chadbourne, Parke et al, N.Y.C., 1976-83; v.p., assoc. gen. counsel, sec. Inspiration Resources Corp., N.Y.C., 1983-92; assoc. gen. counsel, asst. sec. Reader's Digest Assn., Pleasantville, N.Y., 1992-97, v.p., assoc. gen. counsel, sec., 1997—. Mem. ABA, N.Y. Bar Assn., Am. Soc. Corp. Secs. Office: Readers Digest Assn Inc Readers Digest Rd Pleasantville NY 10570

DUPREE, NATHALIE, chef, television personality, writer; b. Dec. 23, 1939; m. Jack Bass. Advanced Cert., Cordon Bleu; D of Culinary Arts, Johnson-Wales U., 2004. Founder Rich's Cooking Sch., Atlanta, 1975; guest PM Mag., Atlanta; host New So. Cooking with Nathalie Dupree, 1986—. Bd. dirs. So. Foodways Alliance, 2000—02. Author: Cooking of the South, 1984, New Southern Cooking, 1986, Nathalie Dupree Cooks for Family and Friends, 1988, Nathalie Dupree's Matters of Taste, 1990, Nathalie Dupree Cooks for Family and Friends, 1992, Nathalie Duprees Southern Memorie, 1994 (James Beard award, 1995), Nathalie Dupree Cooks Great Meals for Busy Days, 1994, Nathalie Dupree Cooks Everyday Meals from a Well-Stocked Pantry, 1995, Nathalie Dupree's Quick Meals, 1996, Nathalie Dupree's Comfortable Entertaining: At Home with Ease and Grace, 1998 (James Beard award, 1999). Founder Internat. Assn. Cultural Sch. Recipient Tastemaker award.

Fellow: Internat. Assn. Culinary Profls.; mem.: Womens Forum (pres. Atlanta chpt.). Office: 100 Queen St Charleston SC 29401 Office Phone: 843-958-8806. Personal E-mail: nathalieonly@aol.com.

DUPREE, SHERRY SHERROD, reference librarian, historian, religion consultant, writer; b. Raleigh, N.C., Nov. 25, 1946; d. Matthew Needham and Mary Elouise (Heartley) Sherrod; m. Herbert Clarence DuPree, Jan. 11, 1975; children: Amil, André, Andrew. BS, N.C. Ctrl. U., 1968, MA, 1969; MLS, U. Mich., 1974, EdS, 1978. Media specialist Ann Arbor (Mich.) Pub. Schs., 1970-77; assoc. ref. libr. U. Fla. Librs., Gainesville, 1977-83; ref. libr. Santa Fe C.C. Libr., Gainesville, 1983—. Project dir. Inst. Black Culture U. Fla., Gainesville, 1982—; vis. prof. Ea. Mich. U., Ypsilanti, 1975; prof. edn. Bethume Cookman Coll., Daytona Beach, Fla., 1984-88. Author: Displays for Schools: An Avenue of Communication, 1976, rev. edit., 1979, Busy Bookworm: Good Conduct, 1980, Mini Course in Library Skills, 1983, Bible Lessons for Youth, 1987, What You Always Wanted to Know About the Card Catalog But Were Afraid to Ask, 1988, Biographical Dictionary of African Americn Holiness--Pentacostals: 1880-1990, 1989, African American Pentecostals: Sourcebook, 1992, Exposed! Federal Bureau of Investigation (FBI) Unclassified Reports on Chruchs and Church Leaders, 1993, African-American Goods News (Gospel) Music, 1993, African-American Holiness Pentecostal Movement: An Annotated Bibiography, 1996, The Rosewood Massacre At A Glance, 1997; designer, dir. Gospel Music Travel Exhibit, 1995, Rosewood Traveling Exhibit, 1999. Chair Rosewood Massacre Forum; archivist for Gospel Music Hall of Fame and Mus., Detroit. Vis. fellow Smithsonian Instn., 1987; recipient Gov.'s Achievement award State of Fla., 1986, Black Achievers award in religion Fla. conf. Black State Legislators, 1997; rsch. grants Nat. Coun. Chs., 1983, Gatorade Found., 1987, 88, 90; travel grants NEH, 1983, So. Regional Edn. Bd., 1987, 88, 89, 90; grant-in-aid fellow Bd. Regents, State of Fla., 1980-81, Horace H. Rackham's Opportunity grant, 1975-76, OEG Libr. Sci. grant U. Mich., 1973-74, grad. fellow N.C. Cen. U., 1968-69; recipient Sojourner Truth award, 1995, Resources to Religion award Fla. Libr. Assn., 1997, Alpha Phi Alpha award, 1997, Zeta Phi Beta award, 1998, Humanitarian of Yr. award Marion County Teen Ct., Fla., 1999, others; grantee Fla. Humanities Coun., 1999, others. Mem. ALA, NAACP, Soc. Pentacostal Studies, Soc. Am. Archivists, Alachua Libr. League, Fla. Libr. Assn. (chair resources to religions caucus 1994-96), Fla. C.C. Assn., League Innovations. Democrat. Mem. Ch. of God in Christ. Avocation: reading. Office: Santa Fe C C Libr 3000 NW 83rd St Bldg S Rm 212 Gainesville FL 32606-6210

DUPRI, JERMAINE, recording industry executive, music producer; b. Asheville, N.C., Sept. 23, 1973; s. Michael and Tina Mauldin; 1 child, Shaniah. Prodr., 1987—; founder, CEO So So Def Prodns., Atlanta, 1989—; solo artist, 1998—; sr. v.p. Arista Records, 2003—05; pres. Virgin Records Urban Music, 2005—. Singer, songwriter (albums) Jermaine Dupri Presents: Life in 1472, 1998, Jermaine Dupri Presents: 12 Soulful Nights, 1998, Instructions, 2001, Green Light, 2004, prodr. for artists including Aaliyah, Destiny's Child, Da Brat, Warren G, Aretha Franklin, Dru Hill, Jay-Z, Alicia Keys, Lil' Kim, Elton John, Kris Kross, Run DMC, Whodini, Usher, Funkmaster Flex, Johnny Gill, Murphy Lee, Ludacris, MC Lyte, Master P., Monica, Chante' Moore, Nelly, New Edition, TLC, Tamia, Tyrese, Lil' Bow Wow, and others. Recipient Songwriter of Yr., ASCAP, 1999. Achievements include making it to #1 on Top R&B/Hip Hop Chart and #3 on the Billboard 200 for "Jermaine Dupri Presents: Life in 1472" in 1998.

DUPRIEST, DOUGLAS MILLHOLLEN, lawyer; b. Ft. Riley, Kans., Dec. 28, 1951; s. Robert White and Barbara Nadine (Millhollen) DuP. AB in Philosophy with high honors, Oberlin Coll., 1974; JD, U. Oreg., 1977. Bar: Oreg. 1977, U.S. Dist. Ct. Oreg. 1977, U.S. Ct. Appeals (9th cir.) 1977. Assoc. Coons & Anderson and predecessors, Eugene, Oreg., 1977—81, Hutchinson, Harrell et al, 1981; ptnr. Hutchinson, Cox, Coons, DuPriest, Orr, and Sherlock and predecessors, 1982—. Adj. prof. sch. law U. Oreg., 1986; mem. task forces Wetlands Mgmt., 1988-89, 92-93. Author: (with others) Land Use, 1982, 2000, Administrative Law, 1985; contbg. editor Real Estate & Land Use Digest, 1983-86; articles editor, mng. bd. mem. U. Oreg. Law Rev., 1976-77. Bd. dirs. Home Health Agy., Eugene, 1977-79, pres., 1978-79; bd. dirs. Oreg. Environ. Coun., Portland, 1979-84, pres., 1980-81, McKenzie River Trust, 1998—; chair voters pamphlet com. Eugene City Club, 1993. Recipient Disting. Svc. award Oreg. Environ. Coun., 1988. Mem. Oreg. Bar Assn. (exec. com. real estate and land use sect. 1978-81). Home: 225 Dartmoor Dr Eugene OR 97401-6620 Office: Hutchinson Cox Coons Du-Priest Orr & Sherlock 777 High St Ste 200 Eugene OR 97401-2750 Office Phone: 541-686-9160. Business E-Mail: dupriest@engene-law.com.

DUPUIS, RUSSELL DEAN, electrical engineer, research scientist; b. Kankakee, Ill., July 9, 1947; s. Rudolph William and Evelyn Marie (Hoevet) D.; m. Dana Elizabeth Gammage, Nov. 19, 1973; 1 child, Elizabeth Anne. BSEE, U. Ill., 1970, MSEE, 1971, PhD in Elec. Engring., 1973. Lic. profl. engr., Tex., 2001. Mem. tech. staff Tex. Instruments Corp., Dallas, 1973—75, Rockwell Internat. Corp., Anaheim, Calif., 1975-79, AT&T Bell Labs., Murray Hill, N.J., 1979-85, disting. tech. staff mem., 1985-89; prof. and Judson S. Swearingen Regents Chair in Engring. Dept. Elec. and Computer Engring U. Tex., Austin, 1989—2003; prof. Ga. Inst. Tech., Atlanta, 2003—. Contbr. articles to profl. jours. Recipient Disting. MTS award AT&T-Bell Labs., 1985, Nat. Acad. Engring, 1989, Young Scientist award GaAs Symposium, 1986, Disting. Alumnus award U. Ill., 1987, Nat. Medal Tech., US Dept. Commerce, 2002, John Bardeen award, Minerals and Metals Soc., 2004. Fellow IEEE (Morris Liebmann award 1985), Optical Soc. Am.; mem. NAE, Lasers and Electro-Optics Soc. of IEEE (bd. govs. 1989, tech. achievement award 1995), Am. Phys. Soc., Electrochem. Soc., Electronics Materials Com. Achievements include first to use Metalorganic Chemical Vapor Deposition (MOCVD) to grow high quality thin films and devices; demonstrate room temperature continuous wave operation of AlGaAs-GaAs quantum well injection lasers establishing that these lasers were reliable enough for practical use. Avocation: genealogy.

DUPUIS, VICTOR LIONEL, retired curriculum and instruction educator; b. Chgo., Oct. 30, 1934; s. Edward G. and LaVerne Ann (Brown) D.; m. Mary Jean Miles, Aug. 11, 1956; children: Mary Catherine, Victor Edward, Elizabeth Ann. BS, Northwestern U., 1956; MA, Am. U., 1961; PhD, Purdue U., 1965. Tchr. jr. high sch., Arlington, Va., 1956-61; tchr. Klondike Sch. Dist., West Lafayette, Ind., 1961-63, curriculum dir., 1962-63; grad. instr. Purdue U., West Lafayette, 1963—65; asst. prof. Pa. State U., University Park, 1967—70, assoc. prof. curriculum, 1970—74, prof., chmn. curriculum and supervision, 1974—91, prof. edn. curriculum and instrn., 1989-91, Waterbury prof. secondary edn., 1990-92, chmn. curriculum and suprvision, 1991, prof. emeritus curriculum and instrn., 1992—; CEO Dupuis Assocs., 1985—. Cons. to various pvt. and public schs., state depts. edn. Native Am. programs. Author: Resource Booklet and Overhead Transparency Masters for Foundation of American Education, 1966, (education texts) Introductory Readings in the Foundation of American Education, 1966, (education textbook) An Introduction to the Foundations of American Education, 1969, 12th edit., 2004; author: (with others) (education texts) Introduction to the Foundations of American Education, 1966; author: Foundation of American Education: Readings, 1969, 1985, Issues in Education, 1991, Resource Booklet: Foundations of American Education, 2002. Chmn. Patton Twp. (Pa.) Park Bd., 1969-70, Patton Twp. Planning Commn., 1971-73; Democratic precinct committeeman Patton Twp., 1971-76, chmn., twp. supr., 1973-92. Served to 2d lt. inf. U.S. Army, 1957-59. Mem. ASCD, Am. Ednl. Rsch. Assn., Nat. Staff Devel. Coun., Pa. Assn. for Supervision and Curriculum Devel., Phi Delta Kappa. Home: 3203 Buffalo Run Rd Bellefonte PA 16823-9027

DUPUY, BOB (ROBERT A. DUPUY), major league baseball executive; AB, Dartmouth Coll., 1968; JD, Cornell U., 1973. With Foley and Lardner, 1973—89, ptnr., 1980—89; legal counsel Major League Baseball, NYC, 1989—92, prin. outside counsel to commr. and exec. coun., 1992—98, exec. v.p. adminstrn., chief legal officer, 1998—2002, pres., COO, 2002—. Lectr. Northwestern U., U. Wis., Marquette U.; facutly mem. Nat. Inst. Trial Advocacy. With U.S. Army, 1968—70, served with 504th Military Police Battalion. Decorated Army Commendation Medal. Mem.: State Bar Wis. (past chmn.). Office: Major League Baseball 245 Park Ave New York NY 10167*

DUQUETTE, DIANE RHEA, library director; b. Springfield, Mass., Dec. 15, 1951; d. Gerard Lawrence and Helen Yvette (St. Marie) Morneau; m. Thomas Frederick Duquette Jr., Mar. 17, 1973. BS in Sociology, Springfield Coll., 1975; MLS, Simmons Coll., 1978. Libr. asst. Springfield City Libr., 1975-78; reference libr. U. Mass., Amherst, 1978-81; head libr. Hopkins Acad., Hadley, Mass., 1980; instr. Colo. Mountain Coll., Steamboat Springs, 1981-83; libr. dir. East Routt Libr. Dist., Steamboat Springs, 1981-84; agy. head Solono County Libr., Vallejo, Calif., 1984; dir. libr. svcs. Shasta County Libr., Redding, Calif., 1984-87; dir. librs. Kern County Libr., Bakersfield, Calif., 1987—. Chmn. San Joaquin Valley Libr. Sys., 1988. Contbr. articles to profl. jours. Recipient John Cotton Dana Spl. Pub. Rels. award, H.W. Wilson and ALA, 1989, 2d ann. Pub. Libr. Mgmt. award of excellence, Urban Librs. Coun./LSSI, 2002. Mem. ALA, Calif. Libr. Assn. (mem. coun. 1987—), Calif. County Librs. Assn. (pres. 1990). Democrat. Roman Catholic. Avocations: golf, skiing, bicycling, reading, gardening. Home: Pine Mountain Club PO Box 6595 Frazier Park CA 93222-6595 Office: Kern County Libr 701 Truxtun Ave Bakersfield CA 93301-4800 Office Phone: 661-868-0789. Business E-Mail: duquette@kerncountylibrary.org.

DUQUETTE, DONALD NORMAN, law educator; b. Manistique, Mich., Apr. 3, 1947; s. Donald Francis and Martha Adeline (Rice) D.; m. Kathy Jo Loudenbeck, June 17, 1967; 1 child, Gail Jean. BA, Mich. State U., 1969; JD, U. Mich., 1974. Bar: Mich. 1975. Children's caseworker Mich. Dept. Social Svcs., Muskegon, 1969-72; asst. prof. pediatrics and human devel. Mich. State U. Coll. Human Medicine, East Lansing, 1975-76; clin. prof., dir. child advocacy law clinic U. Mich., Ann Arbor, 1976—, co-dir. interdisciplinary project on child abuse and neglect, 1979-89, dir. permanency planning legal svcs., 1984—90, dir. interdisciplinary grad. edn. in child abuse-neglect, 1986-92, dir. Kellogg child welfare law program, 1995-98, clin. prof., dir. child advocacy law clinic, 1976—, dir. mediation clinic, 2004—. Bd. visitors U. Ariz. Sch. of Law, 1995—99; legal cons. U.S. Children's Bur., Pres. Clinton's Initiative on Adoption and Foster Care, 1997—98; bd. dirs. Nat. Assn. Counsel for Children, 1999—. Author: (non-fiction) Advocating for the Child, 1990, Michigan Child Welfare Law, 1990, Michigan Child Welfare Law, rev. edit., 2000; editor (mem. editl. bd.): (jour.) Child Abuse and Neglect Internat. Jour., 1985—90; editor: Child Welfare Law and Practice: Representing Children, Parents, and State Agencies in Abuse, Neglect, and Dependency Cases, 2005; contbr.: articles to profl. jours. Mem. Washtenaw County Bd. Commrs., 1981-88; bd. dirs. Children's Trust Fund for Prevention of Child Abuse, 1983-85; mem. Permanency Planning Com. Mich. Supreme Ct., 1982-85, Probate Ct. Task Force, 1986-87, Govs. Task Force on Children's Justice, 1992—; trustee Bay Vierw Assn., 1998--. Named Citizen of Yr. Huron Valley NASW, Ann Arbor, 1985; recipient Rsch. in Advocacy award Nat. Ct. Apptd. Spl. Advocate Assn., Seattle, 1985, Outstanding Legal Advocacy award Nat. Assn. of Counsel for Children, 1996, Hicks Child Welfare Leadership award Mich. Fedn. Children's Agys., 1998. Mem.: Mich. State Bar (co-chair Children's Task Force 1993—95), Am. Profl. Soc. on Abuse of Children. Democrat. Unitarian Universalist. Avocations: piano, sailing. Home: 1510 Linwood Ave Ann Arbor MI 48103-3659 Office: U Mich Sch Law Child Advocacy Law Clinic 625 S State St Ann Arbor MI 48109-1215 Office Phone: 734-763-5000. Business E-Mail: duquette@umich.edu.

DUQUETTE, JEAN-PIERRE, retired French language and literature educator; b. Valleyfield, Que., Can., June 27, 1939; s. J.-Armand and Marguerite (Besner) D. BA, Université de Montréal, Can., 1960, L ès L, 1963; Doctorat 3e cycle, Paris X, France, 1969. Asst. prof. French McGill U., Montréal, 1969-73, assoc. prof. French, 1973-83, prof. French, 1983—2004; ret., 2004. Author: Flaubert, 1972, Germaine Guèvremont, 1973, Fernand Leduc, 1980, Colette, 1984, L'Espace du regard, 1994. Decorated chevalier Order Nat. de Que. Mem. Acad. of Letters of Que., Internat. PEN Que., McGill U. Faculty Club. Office: McGill U Dept of French Lang 3460 McTavish St Montreal PQ Canada H3A 1X9 Business E-Mail: jean.duquette@mcgill.ca.

DUQUETTE, JIM, professional sports team executive; m. Pam Duquette; children: Lauren, Lindsey, Matthew. Grad., Williams Coll., 1988. Asst. Mets Minor League and Scouting Dept. N.Y. Mets, 1991—96; dir. player devel. Houston Astros, 1996—97; dir. player pers. N.Y. Mets, 1997—98, asst. gen. mgr., 1998—2000, sr. asst. gen. mgr., 2000—03, gen. mgr. Flushing, 2003—04; sr. v.p., baseball operations New York Mets, 2004—. Office: NY Mets 123-01 Roosevelt Ave Flushing NY 11368

DUR, PHILIP ALPHONSE, defense aerospace executive, retired military officer; b. Bethesda, Md., June 22, 1944; s. Philip Francis and Elena (Delgado) D.; m. Kathleen Mary Donovan, June 6, 1966; children: Courtney Morris, Philip Ralston. BA, U. Notre Dame, 1965, AM, 1966; MPA, Harvard U., 1973, PhD, 1976. Commd. ensign USN, 1965, advanced through grades to rear adm., 1991, strategic planner Office of the Chief Naval Ops. Washington, 1977-79, mil. asst. Office of Sec. Def., 1979-80, dir. polit. mil. affairs Nat. Sec. Coun., 1982-84, exec. asst. Chief Naval Ops. plans, policy, ops., 1984-86, exec. asst. sec. of navy, 1988-89, commanding officer USS Comte De Grasse Norfolk, Va., 1980-82, commanding officer USS Yorktown, 1986-88, 91-93; U.S. def. attache Am. embassy Paris, 1989—91; comdr. Cruiser Destroyer Group Eight, 1991-93; dir. strategy and policy Office of the Chief Naval Ops., Washington, 1993—94, dep. asst. CNO plans, policy and ops., 1994—95; retired USN, 1995; v.p. Tenneco Inc., Houston, 1995-96; exec. v.p. Walker-Gillet Europe, Edenkoben, Germany, 1996-97; v.p. worldwide bus. devel. & strategy Tenneco, Inc., Lake Forest, IL, 1997-2000; v.p. program ops. Northrop Grumman, Balt., 2000—01; pres. Northrop Grumman Ship Sys., 2001—. Scoutmaster Boy Scouts Am., Gaeta, Italy, 1967. Decorated Def. Disting. Svc. medal, Navy Disting. Svc. medal, Def. Superior Svc. medal, Legion of Merit; comdr. Ordre Nat. du Merite (France). Mem. U.S. Naval Inst. Found., Coun. on Fgn. Rels., Cercle de l'Union Interallice, Surface Navy Assn., Marine Acad. (France), Nat. Eagle Scouts Assn., Notre Dame Alumni Club, Army-Navy Club, Harvard Club. Avocations: history, golf, foreign languages. Office: Northrop Grumman Ship Sys PO Box 149 Pascagoula MS 39568 Office Phone: 228-935-8034. Business E-Mail: phil.dur@ngc.com.

DUR, PHILIP FRANCIS, political scientist, educator, retired diplomat; b. St. Louis, June 30, 1914; s. Alphonse and Sarah (Ralston) D.; m. Elena Delgado, June 30, 1942; children: Elena (Mrs. Philip A. Morris), Philip, Stansbury, Carmen (Mrs. Norman B. Conley, Jr.), Jacqueline (Mrs. James Chase Sheppard), John. AB, Harvard U., 1935, PhD, 1941; postgrad., Fgn. Service Inst., 1961. Consul, pub. affairs officer, Lyon, France, 1948-51; chief Office Pub. Affairs, Office U.S. High Commr. for Germany, Bonn, 1951-52; consul, exec. officer Am. Consulate Gen., Bremen, Germany, 1952—53; comml. controls officer Mil. Security Bd., Coblenz, Germany, 1953-54; consul Colon, Panama, 1954-55, Yokohama, Japan, 1954—58; pub. affairs adviser Dept. State, 1958-61; consul Nagoya, Japan, 1961—65; Jefferson Caffery prof. polit. sci. U. Southwestern La., Lafayette, 1965-84, prof. emeritus, 1984—, faculty senate, 1969-84. Adviser Council for Devel. of French in La., 1968—; mem. U. Southwestern La. Found., 1969-71; pres. France-Amerique de la Louisiane Acadienne, 1970-72; resident dir. La. Consortium Colls. and Univs., Montpellier, France, 1976-77; organizer, exchange prof. La. Ctr. for Studies, U. Paul Valéry, Montpellier. Served to lt. comdr. USNR, 1942-46. Decorated Acad. Palms (France); recipient Nat. Medal of Honor, DAR, 1983, 1st prize French poetry Deep South Writers Conf., 1995. Mem. Am. Fgn. Service Assn., La. Historical Assn., Phi Beta Kappa. Home: 517 Woodvale Ave Lafayette LA 70503-3435 E-mail: pfd2009@louisiana.edu, dur@bellsouth.net.

DURAN, CHARLES DANA, music educator; s. Charles D and Dorothy H. Duran; m. Eva F. Bato, June 7, 1986. BS in Music Bus., Jacksonville U., 1985; Fla. tchg. cert., U. North Fla., Jacksonville, 1986. Profl. educator's cert. State of Fla. Dept. of Edn., 1998, clin. educator tng. Duval County Pub. Schools, 1999. Profl. musician (cornet) St. John's River City Brass Band, Jacksonville, 1984—2001; dir. of instrumental music duPont Mid. Sch., Jacksonville, 1995—. Ch. musician Sunrise Cmty. Ch., Atlantic Beach, Fla., 1995—. Mem. Town Ctr. Green Market, Neptune Beach, Fla., 2003—05. Named Tchr. of Yr., duPont Mid. Sch.; recipient Future Leaders, Fla. Bandmasters Assoiaition, 2004-2005. Mem.: Fla. Bandmasters Assn., Fla. Music Educators Assn. Republican. Avocations: surfing, gardening. Office: duPont Middle School 2710 duPont Avenue Jacksonville FL 32217 Office Phone: 904-739-5200. Office Fax: 904-739-5321. Personal E-mail: chuckandeva@prodigy.net. E-mail: duranc@educationcentral.org.

DURAN, MATIAS MARTIN, adult education educator; b. Valladolid, Yucatan, Mexico, Feb. 24, 1922; s. Marcelo Duran, Aureliana Martin; m. Faasoa Togiaso Duran, Nov. 15, 1980; children: Mary F., Martin T., Marcelo, Matthias. Aa, Riverside City Coll., Calif., 1970; BA, U. Calif., Riverside, 1974; MA, U. Dominguez Hills, Long Beach, Calif., 1988. Psychiat. technician Met. State Hosp., Norwalk, Calif., 1965; correctional officer Calif. Rehab. Ctr., Norco, 1966—72; probation officer Riverside County Probation, Blythe, Calif., 1975—77; ESL tchr./bilingual crosscultural instr. Compton Unified Sch. Dist., Calif., 1977—93; ret., 1993. Mem.: K.C. (warden of coun. 1999—). Home: 140 W Barclay St Long Beach CA 90805-2108 Office Phone: 310-639-1958.

DURAND, JOËL-FRANÇOIS, music educator, composer; b. Orléans, France, Sept. 17, 1954; arrived in US, 1984; s. Marcelle Durand; m. Melanie Jane Shapiro, May 21, 1988; children: Nicholas Pierre, Sophia Helena. PhD Composition, SUNY, Stony Brook, N.Y., 1988. Vis. asst. prof. U. Calif., San Diego, 1994—94; asst. prof. Sch. of Music, U. Wash., Seattle, 1991—96; assoc. prof. Sch. of Music, U. Wash., Seattle, 1996—2002, prof., 2002—. Assoc. dir. academic affairs Sch. of Music, U. Wash., Seattle, 2002—. Composer: (songs) Ombre/Miroir, for flute and ensemble, Au-delà, Cinq Etudes pour piccolo, for solo piccolo, Par le feu recueilli, for flute, Les raisons des forces mouvantes, for organ, Un chant lointain, for electronic carillon, Le chemin, for piano, Concerto for piano and orchestra, B.F., Ein Mittelpunkt, for ensemble, La mesure des choses I. La mesure de l'air, for clarinet, Un feu distinct, for five instruments, L'exil du feu, for ensemble and electronics, In the Mirror Land, for flute and oboe, Die innere Grenze, for string sextet, Lichtung, for ensemble, Trois Mélodies, for mezzo soprano and ensemble, So er, for ensemble, .D'asiles Déchirés., For Piano, Roman, for violin, String Trio, La mesure des choses II. La mesure de la mer, for piano, Athanor for Orch., Tiodhlac, for clarinet, Cinq Duos, for violin and viola, La mesure des choses III. La mesure de la terre et du feu, for oboe and viola, La terre et le feu, for oboe and ensemble, She or not, for solo baritone, Five Musical Tales, for orchestra. Adv. bd. mem. Wash. Composers Forum, Seattle, 2000—05. Recipient Kranichsteiner Musikpreis, Internationalen Ferienkurse für Neue Musik Darmstadt (Germany), 1990, Donald E. Petersen Endowded Professorship, U. Wash., 2003-2006, Composition Award, Third Stockhausen Composition, Brescia (Italy), 1983, Scholarship Preis, Internat. Ferienkurse für Neue Musik Darmstadt (Germany), 1982; grantee Royalty Rsch. Fund Recipient, U. Wash., 1994, 2002; scholar Ministry of Culture Scholarship, French Ministry of Culture, 1985-86, Fulbright Scholarship, Fulbright Found., 1984-85, Scholarship, Deutsche Akademische Austauschdienst (Germany), 1982-83. Mem.: Am. Music Ctr. Home: 15533 Densmore Ave N Seattle WA 98133 Office: Univ Wash Sch of Music Box 353450 Seattle WA 98195-3450 Office Phone: 206-543-1229. Personal E-mail: music@joelfdurand.com. Business E-Mail: jdurand@u.washington.edu.

DURANG, CHRISTOPHER, actor, playwright; b. Montclair, NJ, Jan. 2, 1949; s. Francis Ferdinand and Patricia Durang. BA, Harvard U., 1971; MFA, Yale U., 1974. Playwright: The Nature and Purpose of the Universe, 1971, 75, 'dentity Crisis, 1971, 75, Better Dead than Sorry, 1972, 75 (with Albert Innaurato) I Don't Generally Like Poetry but Have You Read 'Trees'?, 1972, 73, The Life Story of Mitzi Gaynor, or Gyp, 1973, The Marriage of Bette and Boo, 1973, revised 1979, 85, (with Albert Innaurato) The Idiots Karamazov, 1974, Titanic, 1974, 76, Death Comes to Us All, Mary Agnes, 1975, (with Wendy Wasserstein) When Dinah Shore Ruled the Earth, 1975, Das Lusitania Songspiel, 1976, 80, Sex and Longing, The Vietnamization of New Jersey, 1977, 78, Sister Mary Ignatius Explains it All For You, 1982 (Obie award 1984), The Actor's Nightmare, 1982, Beyond Therapy, 1982, 83, Baby with the Bath Water, 1983-84, Adrift in Macao, Mrs. Bob Cratchit's Wild Christmas Binge, 2004, Miss Witherspoon, 2005; actor: (stage prodns.) Hotel Play, 1981, The Birthday Present, 1983, Putting It Together, 1993, Laughing Wild, 1987, 2005. Recipient Kenyon Festival Playwriting award, 1983; CBS fellow, 1975, Guggenheim playwriting fellow, 1979; Rockefeller grantee, 1976. Mem. Dramatists Guild, Writers Guild, Actors' Equity Assn., ASCAP. Office: care Helen Merrill Helen Merrill Agy 337 W 22nd St New York NY 10011-2607 also: Creative Artists Agy 9830 Wilshire Blvd Beverly Hills CA 90212-1804*

DURANT, FREDERICK CLARK, III, aerospace history and space art consultant; b. Ardmore, Pa., Dec. 31, 1916; s. Frederick Clark, Jr. and Cornelia Allen (Howel) D.; m. Carolyn Griscom Jones, Oct. 4, 1947 (dec.); children: Derek C. (dec.), Carolyn M., William C. (dec.), Stephen H. BSChemE, Lehigh U., 1939; postgrad., Phila. Mus. Sch. Indsl. Arts, 1946-47. Registered profl. engr., D.C., Mass. Engr. E.I. duPont de Nemours & Co., Inc., 1939-41; rocket engr. Bell Aircraft Corp., 1947-48; dir. engring. Naval Air Rocket Test Sta., 1948-51; cons. Washington, 1952-53; mem. sr. staff Arthur D. Little, Inc., 1954-57; dir. Maynard Ordnance Test Sta., 1954-55; exec. asst. to dir. Avco-Everett Rsch. Lab., 1957-59; dir. pub. and govt. rels., rsch. and advanced devel. divsn. Avco Corp., Wilmington, Mass., 1959-61; sr. rep. Bell Aerosys., Washington, 1961-64; asst. dir. and head astronautics dept. Nat. Air and Space Mus., Smithsonian Instn., Washington, 1964-80; cons., 1980—; dir. Nat. Space Soc., Washington, 1982-88; conservator Bonestell Space Art and Space Art Internat.; dir. Arthur C. Clarke Found. U.S. Inc. Cons. space mus. Nippon Steel Corp., Japan, 1989—; participant ann. congresses Internat. Astron. Fedn., 1951—, pres., 1953-56; mem. organizing com. Project Orbiter, 1954; cons. Astro Assocs., Space Art Internat. Author: First Steps toward Space, 1975, Worlds Beyond, 1983, The Art of Chesley Bonestell, 2001; Contbg. editor Missiles and Rockets, 1956-58; contbr. to Ency. Brit., 1958-96, Funk & Wagnalls Year Book; contbr. space terms to Am. Heritage Dictionary. Comdr. as naval aviator USNR, 1941-46,48-52. Recipient spl. medal L'Assn. Pour l'Encouragement de l'Aeronautique et de l'Astronautique, 1963, Charles A. Lindbergh award Smithsonian Instn., 1976, hon. 6 Dan Karate-Do, Japan, 1978, Rathbone Alumni Achievement award Lehigh U., 1989, Lucien Rudaux Meml. award, Internat. Assn. Astron. Artists, 2000. Fellow Am. Astronautical Soc., AIAA, Am. Rocket Soc. (pres. 1953); mem. Internat. Acad. Astronautics (co-chmn. history com. 1981-89), Nat. Space Club (gov. 1961), Nat. Space Club (Disting. Svc. award 1982), hon. fellow or mem. numerous fgn. rocket and space flight socs., Cosmos Club. Home and Office: 2440 Springmoor Cir Raleigh NC 27615-5724

DURANT, JOHN RIDGEWAY, retired oncologist, health facility administrator, consultant; b. Ann Arbor, Mich., July 29, 1930; s. Thomas Morton and Jean Margaret (deVries) D.; m. Mary Sue Avery Dillon, Jan. 13, 1990; children by previous marriage: Christine Joy, Thomas Arthur (dec.), Michele Grace, Jennifer Margaret. BA, Swarthmore (Pa.) Coll., 1952; MD, Temple U., Phila., 1956; hon. degree, U. Ala., 1993. Diplomate: Am. Bd. Internal Medicine. Intern, then jr. asst. resident in medicine Hartford (Conn.) Hosp., 1956-58; resident in medicine Temple U. Med. Center, 1960-62; spl. fellow med. neoplasia Meml. Hosp. for Cancer and Allied Diseases, N.Y.C., 1962-63; Am. Cancer Soc. advanced clin. fellow Temple U. Health Scis. Center, 1964-67, instr., then asst. prof. medicine, 1963-67; clin. assoc. chemotherapy Moss Rehab. Hosp., Phila., 1964-67; research assoc. Fels Research Inst., Phila., 1965-67; mem. faculty U. Ala. Med. Center, Birmingham, 1968-82, prof. medicine, dir. comprehensive cancer center, 1970-82, prof. radiation oncology, 1978-82, chmn. Southeastern coop. cancer study group at univ., 1975-82, Disting. faculty lectr., 1980; pres. Fox Chase Cancer Ctr., Phila., 1982-88; sr. v.p. health affairs and dir. med. ctr. U. Ala., Birmingham, 1988-95; exec. v.p. Am. Soc. Clin. Oncology, Alexandria, Va.,

1995-2000; cons. med. dir. Walther Cancer Inst., Indpls., 2000—; cons. Baptist Health Sys., Birmingham, Ala., 2000—. Chmn. coop. group exec. com. Nat. Cancer Inst., NIH, 1977-82, chmn. coop. group chairmen, 1979-82; cons. VA Hosp., Tuskegee, Ala., 1970-82; exec. com. Birmingham chpt. ARC, 1972-77; mem. Nat. Cancer Adv. Bd., 1986-92. Mem. editorial bd. Cancer Clin. Trials, 1979-82, assoc. editor, 1982—; editorial bd. Med. and Pediatric Oncology News, 1975-90; assoc. editor Cancer, 1984-92; contbr. numerous articles to med. jours. Mem. adv. coun. for sci. Notre Dame U., 2002—. Served as officer M.C. USNR, 1958-60. Recipient Oncologist of Yr. award So. Oncology Assn., 1999; named Temple U. Med. Sch. Alumnus Yr., 1982, Cancer Fighter of Yr., Cancer Fighter Awards Trust, 2000. Fellow ACP, Coll. Physicians Phila.; mem. Am. Cancer Soc. (vice chmn. advanced clin. fellowship com. 1974-76, 85-87, mem. instl. rsch. grant com. 1979-82, pres. Ala. divsn. 1973-75, 77-79, mem. blue ribbon com. to rev. nat. rsch. program 1994-95), Am. Assn. Cancer Rsch., Am. Radium Soc. (pres. 1984), Am. Bd. Int. Med. Oncology (subcom. 1979-85, chmn. 1983-85), Assn. Am. Cancer Insts. (dir. 1978—, pres. 1982-83), Assn. Cmty. Cancer Ctrs. (dir. 1979-81), Am. Soc. Clin. Oncology (chmn. pub. rels. com. 1976-79, bd. dirs. 1979-82, 84-87, pres. 1985-86, Spl. Recognition award 1999), others. Baptist.

DURANT, SAM, artist; b. Seattle, 1961; BFA, Mass. Coll. Art, Boston; MFA, Calif. Inst. Arts. Artist-in-residence Walker Art Ctr., Mpls., 2003. One-man shows include Pardon Our Appearance, Bliss Gallery, Calif., 1992, Tomio Koyama Gallery, Tokyo, 2000, Blum & Poe, Santa Monica, 2000, Emi Fontana Gallery, Milan, 2001, Mus. Contemporary Art, LA, 2002, Wadsworth Atheneum, Hartford, 2002, Project Row Houses, Houston, 2003, Kunstverein Dusseldorf, 2003, Smak, Ghent, 2004, The Suburban, Oak Park, 2004, Paula Cooper Gallery, NY, 2005, exhibited in group shows at Thanks, Three Day Weekend, LA, 1994, Places that are elsewhere, David Zwirner, NY, 1997, Other Narratives: Fifteen Years, Contemporary Arts Mus., Houston, 1999, Archtl. Uncanny, Mus. Contemporary Art, Chgo., 2001, Artists Imagine Architecture, Inst. Contemporary Art, Boston, 2002, Break It Fix It, Secession, Vienna, 2003, Baja to Calif., Seattle Mus. Art, 2003, Venice Biennale, 2003, Whitney Biennial, Whitney Mus. Am. Art, 2004, Faces in Crowd, White Chapel, London, 2004, Brown vs. Bd. Edn., Calif. Afrian-Am. Mus., LA, 2004, Moscow Biennale, 2005, Monuments to U.S.A., CCA, San Francisco, 2005. Mailing: c/o Blum & Poe 2745 South La Cienega Blvd Los Angeles CA 90034

DURANTE, THOMAS, music educator; b. Bklyn., 1958; s. Michael J. and Audrey Durante; m. Bridget M. Gates, 1989; children: Adam, Andrew. B in Music Edn., U. Tex., 1983. Arts edn. supr. Arlington (Va.) Pub. Schs., 1997—2000; dir. bands Prince George' Ct., Md., 2000—. Home: 4816 Bradford Dr Annandale VA 22003

DURBIN, DEAN D., corporate financial executive; Acctg. supr. McGraw-Hill Cos., v.p., group controller constrn. info. group; v.p., chief fin. officer Thomson Profl. Pub.; sr. v.p., chief fin. officer TC Advt. (not Vertis), 1997—2000; chief fin. officer Vertis, 2000—. Mem.: Balt. Mus. Industry. Office: Vertis 250 W Pratt St Baltimore MD 21201 Office Phone: 410-361-8367. Business E-Mail: ddurbin@vertisine.com.

DURBIN, DICK (RICHARD JOSEPH DURBIN), senator; b. East St. Louis, Ill., Nov. 21, 1944; s. William and Ann D.; m. Loretta Schaefer, June 24, 1967; children: Christine, Paul, Jennifer. BS in Econs., Georgetown U., 1966, JD, 1969. Bar: Ill. 1969. Chief legal counsel to Lt. Gov. Paul Simon State of Ill., 1969—72; parliamentarian Ill. Senate, 1969-77, mem. staff minority leader, 1972-77; assoc. prof. med. humanities So. Ill. U., 1978—; ptnr. Durbin & Lestikow, Springfield, Ill., 1979—82; mem. 98th-104th Congresses from 20th Dist. Ill., 1983-97; U.S. senator from Ill., 1997—; asst. minority leader, 2004—; mem. judiciary com., govtl. affairs com., budget com. Mem. appropriations com., subcoms. on agriculture, rural devel. and related agys., def., legis. br., and D.C. (ranking mem.), 1999—; mem. budget com.; mem. govt. affairs com. subcom. on oversight of govt. mgmt., restructuring and the D.C., 1999—, and permanent subcom. on investigations, 1997—; mem. select com. on ethics, 1999—; asst. Dem. fl. leader. Campaign worker Sen. Paul Douglas of Ill., 1966; staff Office Ill. Dept. Bus. and Econ. Devel., Washington; candidate for Ill. Lt. Gov., 1978; staff alt. Pres.'s State Planning Council, 1980; advisor Am. Council Young Polit. Leaders, 1981; mem. YMCA Ann. Membership Roundup, YMCA Bldg. Drive, Pony World Series; bd. dirs. Cath. Charities, United Way of Springfield, Old Capitol Art Fair, Springfield Youth Soccer; mem. Sch. Dist. 1986 Referendum Com., Springfield NAACP. Democrat. Roman Catholic. Office: US Senate 332 Dirksen Sen Office Bldg Washington DC 20510-0001*

DURBIN, MARGOT JANE, librarian; b. Memphis, July 15, 1958; d. Richard Louis and Carolyn (Bohrer) D.; children: Carolyn Eileen Morris, Robert Benson Morris. BA, Marshall U., 1992; MLIS, U. S.C., 1995. Coord. lit. Hamlin-Lincoln County Pub. Libr., W.Va., 1992—95; supr. audiovisual Cabell County Pub. Libr., Huntington, W.Va., 1995—97, coord. popular svcs., 1997—2004, chief devel. officer, 2004—. Bd. dirs. Appalread, Logan, W.Va., 1999—, Barnett Child Care Ctr., Huntington, W.Va., 1999—. Editor Forum newsletter, 1996-2005 Mem. ALA, W.Va. Libr. Assn. Office: Cabell County Pub Libr 455 9th St Huntington WV 25701-1417 E-mail: mdurbin@cabell.lib.wv.us.

DURBIN, RICHARD LOUIS, SR., health facility administrator, consultant; b. Millersport, Ohio, Aug. 28, 1928; s. Clark Babe and Mabel (Bushee) Durbin; m. Carolyn Bohrer, Mar. 18, 1955; children: Richard Louis, Margot Jane, Melissa Bushee. BA, Ohio State U., 1949; MBA, U. Chgo., 1956; MPA, U. Ariz., 1969; postgrad., Pace Coll., 1973; MPH, U. Tex. Sch. Pub. Health, 1992, postgrad, 1999—. Cert. govt. fin. mgr., Assn. Govt. Accts.; profl. sanitarian. Research chemist Battelle Meml. Inst., Columbus, Ohio, 1949—50; sales rep. Am. Cyanamid Co., N.Y.C., 1953—54; adminstrv. asst. Lancaster (Ohio)-Fairfield Hosp., 1954; with Bus. Devel. Outreach Helath, Austin, 1995—; asst. adminstr. City of Memphis Hosps., 1956—58, assoc. adminstr., 1958—60; dir. outpatient and profl. services Presbyn.-St. Luke's Hosp., Chgo., 1960—61; assoc. dir. grad. program in hosp. adminstrn., faculty U. Chgo. Grad. Sch. Bus., 1961—62; exec. sec. Am. Assn. Univ. Programs in Hosp. Adminstrn., 1960—62; assoc. prof. bus. adminstrn. Temple U., 1967—69, prof. mgmt., 1969—70; exec. dir. Lubbock (Tex.) County Dist. Hosp., 1970—71; v.p. Coll. Medicine and Dentistry N.J., 1971—75; also v.p. Acad. Health Center; asst. prof. N.J. Med. Sch., 1973—75; pres., CEO Harris County Hosp. Dist., Houston, 1975—89; asst. regional dir. region #6 Tex. State Dept. Health, 1989—92; adminstr. Tex. Alcoholic Beverage Commn., Austin, 1992—93; pres., CEO Durbin Internat., San Marcos, Tex., 1993—; health dir. Cameron County Health Dept., San Benito, Tex., 1995—; CEO/dir. Maverick County Hosp. Dist., Eagle Pass, Tex.; dir. Maverick County Health Dist., Eagle Pass; pres. Health Edn. Found. for Deserving Students, Eagle Pass; CEO, Montgomery County Hosp. Dist.; pres. Vineyard Inc., Houston, 2003—. Founder, dir. grad. program in health care adminstrn., 1967—70; exec. dir., 1966—70; cons. in field; pres. D&H Enterprises, Durbin Internat., CIA, 1967—71; project dirl., chief planner, exec. dir. Newark Comprehensive Health Plan, 1974; cons. divsn. hosp. and med. facilities HEW, 1967—; design adv. group, nat. rev. com., cons. exptl. health systems, 1971—73; cons. Nat. Commn. on Productivity, U.S. Bur. Prisons, 1968—; mem. Hosp. Devel., Inc. N.J. Gov.'s Correctional Health Svc. Investigations Com.; mem. adv. bd. Comprenetics, Inc., 1967—; steering com. Tucson Hosp. and Health Planning Commn., 1962—, Assoc. Hosp. Svcs. Ariz., 1963—64; treas. Ariz. League Nursing, 1963—64; adj. assoc. prof. Tex. Woman's U.; mem. coordinating coun. Tex. Health and Human Svcs., 1986—; appraisal rev. bd. Travis Ctrl. Appraisal Dist., 1994—; dir. bus. devel. Outreach Health Svcs., 1995—; adj. assoc. prof. U. Tex. Sch. Pub. Health, 1996—2003; med. adv. com. Tex. Workman's Compensation Commn.; lectr. informal classes U. Tex., Mexico, 1994—. Author: A Statistical Methodology of Evaluating a Medical Staff, 1961, New Ideas and Concepts in Outpatient Management, 1963; author: (with others) Ivory Tower to Workshop, 1964; author: Ambulatory Care Development, 1966; author: (with W.H. Springall) Organization and Administration of Health Care, 1974; author: (with Springall, P. High) Manual for Hospital Program and Performance Budgeting at the Operating Level, 1968; author: (with G. Connor) Design of a City-Wide HMO, 1974; author: Border Issues, 2000; cons. editor Hosp. Topics, editor The Forum, What's Going On: Hospital Topics, mem. editl. bd. Physician Weekly; contbr. articles to profl. jours. Mem. Phila. Crime Commn., 1967—, Tex. Indigent Care Task Force; chmn. Harris County Jail com., 1987—88, Health Svcs. com. AIDS panel; ch. deacon; bd. dirs. Ariz. Blue Cross, Mexic-Arte Mus., 1994—. Lt. USNR, 1945—46, lt. USNR, 1950—53. Recipient Editl. award, Hosp. Mgmt. mag., 1961, 1963, 1965, cert. of merit, Gov. Ariz., 1967, 1968, Silver medal (DeBakey) award, Baylor Coll. of Medicine, 1986. Fellow: Am. Coll. Hosp. Adminstrs. (cert.); mem.: AAUP, Tex. Pub. Health Assn., Am. Coll. Managed Care Adminstrs., Am. Coll. Healthcare Assn. (chmn. book award com. 1983, membership com. 1986), Am. Mgmt. Assn. (Excellence award 1968), Internat. Hosp. Fedn., Am. Inst. Mgmt., Am. Soc. Pub. Adminstrn., Am. Criminology Soc., So. Ariz. Hosp. Coun. (pres. 1963), Tex. Hosp. Assn. (bd. dirs., mem. exec. com. 1987—88), Pa. Hosp. Assn., Am. Hosp. Assn. (coun. pub. hosps.), Nat. Assn. Clinic Mgrs., Am. Chem. Soc., Nat. Assn. Pub. Hosps. (dir., founder), Blanton Art Mus., Texans Standing Tall, U. Tex. Recreational Sports (life), Tucson Press Club (life), U. Tex. Faculty Ctr., Quadrangle Club (U. Chgo.), Midway Club (Chgo.), Buckeye Lake Yacht Club, Columbian Yacht Club (Chgo.), Pa. Soc. Club, Army-Navy Capitol Hill Club (Washington), Houston Yacht Club, Headliners Club (Austin, Tex.), Hillcrest Country Club, Rotary, Houston C. of C. (health com.), Sigma Xi, Sigma Alpha Epsilon. Presbyterian. Home: 505 W 7th St Apt 319 Austin TX 78701-2836 Office: 9415 Burnet Rd Ste 300 Austin TX 78758-5266 Office Phone: 512-477-1147.

DURCHSLAG, STEPHEN P., lawyer; b. Chgo., May 20, 1940; s. Milton Lewis and Elizabeth (Potovsky) D.; m. Ruth Florence Mayer, Nov. 21, 1976; children: Rachel Beth, Danielle Leah. BS, U. Wis., 1963; LLB, Harvard U., 1966. Bar: Ill. 1966. Assoc. Sidley & Austin, Chgo., 1966-72, ptnr., 1972-89, Winston & Strawn, Chgo., 1989—. Contbr. articles to profl. jours. Trustee Nathan Cummings Found., 1996—, Anshe Emet, Chgo., 1983—, pres., 2000—02. Mem. ABA (AAF legal com.), Promotion Mktg. Assn. (bd. dirs.), Am. Standard Club, East Bank Club. Jewish. Avocations: skiing, running, tennis, rare books. Office: Winston & Strawn 35 W Wacker Dr Ste 3600 Chicago IL 60601-1695 Office Phone: 312-558-5288. Business E-Mail: sdurchsl@winston.com.

DURDEN, JULIE MARIANN, music educator; b. Cleveland, Ga., Dec. 21, 1979; d. William Edward and Louise (Adams) Thomas; m. Robert Lewis Durden, Jan. 15, 2005. A in Music, Truett McConnell Coll., Cleveland, Ga., 1999; BA in Music Edn., Piedmont Coll., Demorest, Ga., 2001, MA in Music Edn., 2002. Elem. music tchr. Long Branch Elem., Dahlonega, Ga., 2001—. Mem.: Ga. Music Educators Assn., Phi Theta Kappa. Baptist. Avocations: piano, violin. Home: 120 Adams Rd Cleveland GA 30528

DURDEN, ROME L., aircraft manufacturing company executive; b. L.A., Apr. 5, 1935; s. Rome and Hortense (Anderson) D.; m. Priscilla Louise Bibby, Oct. 27, 1962; children: Suzette, Steven. B of Laws, La Salle Extension U., 1971; DD (hon.), Universal Life, Modesto, Calif., 1980. Tech. writer Hughes Aircraft Co., Culver City, Calif., 1962-72, sr. tech. editor, 1972-79, sr. mgmt. systems specialist, 1979-89. Author: (Manuals) Guide for Drafting Procedure, 1981, Simplified Drawing Substitutions, 1984. Treas. Marysville United Meth. Ch., 1997-99; mem. Lake Stevens Governance Coun., 1999, 2000. Recipient Presentation gavel Ramona Park Adv. Coun., Long Beach, Calif., 1971. Mem. Harmony Woods Homeowners Assn. (bd. dirs., treas. 1996-99, v.p. 2000-02). Home: PO Box 1322 Lake Stevens WA 98258-1322

DURDEN, WILLIAM G., academic administrator; Grad., Dickinson Coll., 1971; MA in German Lit. and Lang., PhD in German Lit. and Lang., Johns Hopkins U.; postgrad., U. Freiburg, Germany, U. Münster, U. Basle, Switzerland. Exec. dir. Inst. for the Acad. Advancement of Youth; faculty mem. German dept. Johns Hopkins U.; pres. Sylvan Acad., Sylvan Learning Sys. Inc., Dickinson Coll., Carlisle, Pa., 1999—. Sr. edn. cons. US Dept. State, chair adv. com. exceptional children and youths; mem., adv. bd. Ctr. for Internat. Exchange of Scholars, Fulbright Scholar Program. Actor: (books); contbr. articles to prof. jours. Recipient Klingenstein award, Tchrs. Coll., Columbua U.; fellow Klingenstein fellow, Wis. Policy Rsch. Inst.; grantee, Am. Coun. Learned Socs., Volkswagen Found., German Soc. Md.; scholar, Fulbright. Office: Dickinson Coll PO Box 1773 Carlisle PA 17013-2896 Fax: 717-245-1457.

DUREK, DOROTHY MARY, retired language educator; b. Pitts., Jan. 23, 1926; d. Joseph Adam and Helen Barbara (Ondich) D. BS in Edn., Youngstown State U., 1962; MS in Edn., Westminster Coll., 1969. Cert. English tchr., Ohio, comprehensive English cert., Pa. Tchr. English Brookfield (Ohio) Schs., 1962-64, Sharon (Pa.) City Schs., 1964-88. Mem., pres. Coll. Club Sharon, 1993-94. Charter mem., bd. dirs. LWV Mercer County, Pa., 1993—97; docent Butler Inst. Am. Art, Youngstown, 1988—2004; mem. Shenango Valley Women's Interfaith Coun., Jewish-Christian Dialogue Group, Sharon; charter mem. Mus. Women's Art, Washington, Nat. Mus. of the Am. Indian, Washington; mem., bd. dirs. Christian Assocs. Shenango Valley. Mem.: AAUW, NEA, Read and Discuss Group, Sharon Lifelong Learning Coun. (bd. dirs. 1995), Cath. Collegiate Assn., Sharon Tchrs. Assn., Pa. State Educators Assn., Prospect Heights Lit. Club. Roman Catholic. E-mail: dorothy_durek@yahoo.com.

DURELL, JACK, psychiatrist; b. NYC, July 5, 1928; s. Sam and Helen (Schwartzman) D.; m. Viviane M. diGioja, May 19, 1955. BA summa cum laude, Harvard U., 1949; MD cum laude, Yale U., 1953. Rsch. biochemist NIMH, Bethesda, Md., 1954-57, chief, sect. of psychiatry, 1963-67; v.p. med. affairs, clin. dir. The Psychiat. Inst., Washington, 1967-72, pres., med. dir., 1972-78; assoc. dir. sci. Nat. Inst. Drug Abuse, Rockville, Md., 1979-86; med. dir. clin. affairs div. Ea. Va. Med. Authority, Norfolk, 1986-87; chmn. dept. psychiatry Mercy Cath. Med. Ctr., Phila., 1987-92; prof. psychiatry U. Pa., Phila., 1987—. Exec. dir. Treatment Rsch. Inst., 1992—; pres. Delta Metrics, 1994—; pres. The Psychiat. Inst. Found., Washington, 1973-78; trustee Phila. Mental Health Care Connection, 1987-89. Editor: The Changing Clinical Picture of Schizophrenia, 1977; asst. editor-in-chief Jour. Psychiat. Rsch., 1966-82, mem. editorial bd., 1982—; contbr. to numerous med. publs. With USPHS, 1953-86. Fellow Am. Psychiat. Assn.; mem. Am. Acad. Psychiatrists in Alcoholism and Addictions (sec.-treas. 1985-93), Am. Psychopathological Assn., Am. Coll. Neuropsychopharmacology. Personal E-mail: jadurell@aol.com. Business E-Mail: jdurell@deltametrics.com.

DUREN, BRAD L., social studies educator; b. Duncan, Okla., July 22, 1968; s. Robert L. and Frankie L. Duren; m. Amy Lynn Mueller, May 13, 1967; children: Benjamin Robert, Joseph Ryan. ABD, Okla. State U., 2004; MA, U. of Ctrl. Okla., 1994; MusB, B, Okla. City U., 1990. Asst. prof. of history Okla. Panhandle State U., Goodwell, Okla., 1999—. Governing bd. mem. Am. Culture Assn., 2001—; pres. Tex. Popular Culture Assn., 2002—, v.p., 2000—02. Historical consultant (television documentary) Kent State: The Day the War Came Home (Emmy Award, Outstanding Documentary for TV, 2001). Parish coun. St. Peter's Cath. Ch., Guymon, Okla., 2003—04, instr., 2001—04, Rite of Cath. Initiation for Adults. Fellow Dr. John Hampton Disting. Grad. Fellowship, Okla. State U., 1997-2000. Mem.: Film and History League, Okla. Assn. of Profl. Historians, Am. Culture Assn. (governing bd. 2001—), Orgn. of Am. Historians, Phi Alpha Theta, Phi Kappa Phi, Sigma Theta Epsilon (life), Kappa Alpha Order (life; pres.gamma kappa chpt. 1988—90). Independent. Roman Catholic. Avocations: travel, music, movies, reading. Office: Oklahoma Panhandle State University PO Box 430 Goodwell OK 73939 Office Phone: 580-349-1498. Personal E-mail: uriah768@aol.com.

DUREN, MELISSA ANNE, music educator; b. Sikeston, Mo., Jan. 23, 1974; d. Danny R. and Juletta S. Carnell; m. Wayne M. Duren, Nov. 9, 1996; children: Spencer, Madeline. B in Music Edn., Ctrl. Meth. U., Fayette, Mo., 1996; MEd in Adminstrn., William Woods U., Fulton, Mo., 2004. Cert. tchr. Mo. Tchr. music K-12 Brunswick (Mo.) R-II Sch., 1996—99; vocal/instrumental music tchr. grades 6-12 New Franklin (Mo.) R-II Sch., 1999—. V.p. elem. Mo. Music Educators Assn., 2002—05. Music dir. Faith Family Fellowship, Fayette, Mo., 2004—. Mem.: Cmty. Tchrs. Assn. (legis. chairperson 2001—05, chairperson Am. edn. week 2002—04, Mo. Kids 1st campaign coord. 2004), Mo. State Tchrs. Assn. (leadership tng. 2002—05, exec. com. 2004—05, Mo. Cmty. Tchrs. Assn. mem. of yr. 2004), Fayette R-II PTA (membership chair 2004—05, family night coord. 2003—04), Delta Kappa Gamma. Avocations: piano, singing, scrapbooks, home remodeling.

DUREN, STEPHEN D., artist; b. Fairfield, Calif., Apr. 8, 1948; s. Donald and Ruth Lenore (Alley) D.; m. Maureen Jo Dozeman, Nov. 11, 1972 (div. Aug. 1986); children: Adelle Meadow, Havalah Rose; m. Victoria S. Peabody, Aug. 25, 1995; 1 child, Lindsey McNeil. Diploma, Def. Info. Sch., Indpls., 1970; BFA, San Francisco Art Inst., 1974; MA, Calif. State U., Sacramento, 1977. Asst. prof. Kendall Coll. Art and Design, Grand Rapids, Mich., 1979-84; artist-in-residence Oxbow Art Camp, Saugatuck, Mich., 1984, Niangua Colony, Mo., 1986, Ucross Found., Wyo., 1988, Shoreline Arts Project, Muskegon, Mich., 1989. Adj. artist William James Coll., Allendale, Mich., 1978, Muskegon C.C., 1978, Grand Valley State U., Allendale, Mich., 1984, 86. One-person shows include Grand Rapids Art Mus., 1994, Dennos Mus. Ctr., Traverse City, Mich., 1995, Midland Art Ctr., Mich., 1995, Krasl Art Ctr., St. Joseph, Mich., 1995, Patricia Carlisle Fine Art, Santa Fe, N.Mex., 1999, Urban Inst. Contemporary Art, Grand Rapids, 2000, Byron Roche Gallery, Chgo., 2000. Spkr. Grand Valley State U., Allendale, 1981, Muskegon Mus. of Art, 1984, Acquinas Coll., Grand Rapids, 1992, Grand Rapids Art Mus., 1994. With USN, 1968-72. Recipient Best of Show Mich. Found./Arts, Battle Creek Art Ctr., Mich., 1984, 88, 1st prize Grand Rapids Arts Coun., 1986, CAA Drawing award Nat. Exhibit, Am. Art, Chautauqua, N.Y., 1987. Avocations: black and white photography, gardening. Home: 6087 100th St SE Caledonia MI 49316-9431 Business E-Mail: dur@duren.info.

DURFEE, HERBERT ASHLEY, JR., medical educator; b. Burlington, Vt., Nov. 5, 1924; s. Herbert Ashley and Margaret Elizabeth (Spaulding) D.; m. Elizabeth Lea Dole, Sept. 18, 1947; children: Herbert Ashley III, Eleazer Lea Dole. BS, Yale U., 1948; MD, U. Vt., 1948. Diplomate Am. Bd. Ob-Gyn. Intern Lenox Hill Hosp., N.Y.C., 1948-50; fellow in pathology Free Hosp. Women, Brookline, Mass., 1950; resident in obstetrics Boston Lying-In Hosp., 1951; resident in surgery Faulkner Hosp., Jamaica Plain, Mass., 1953; resident in ob-gyn. Boston Lying-In Hosp. and Free Hosp. Women, Brookline and Boston, 1954-57; from instr. to assoc. prof. ob-gyn. U. Vt., Burlington, 1957-70, prof. ob-gyn., 1970-90, prof. emeritus ob-gyn., 1990—. Assoc. chmn. Dept. Ob-Gyn., U. Vt., Burlington, 1965-90, acting chmn., 1961, 69, 76, 85; pres. med. staff Med. Ctr. Hosp. Vt., Burlington, 1985, 89, chmn. various coms. Capt. USAF, 1951-53. Mem. AMA, Am. Coll. Ob-Gyn. (Vt. sect. past vice-chmn., chmn.), N.Am. Ob-Gyn. Soc. (sec.-treas., 1980-90), Vt. State Med. Soc., N.E. Med. Assn., Baker-Channing Soc. Republican. Home: 25 Woodcrest Ln Burlington VT 05401-4151

DURFEE, KEVIN LEE, music educator; b. Fairfield, Iowa, Nov. 1, 1972; s. George K and Sharon S Durfee; m. Kiersa D Durfee, Apr. 1, 2000; 1 child, Kaleb L. BME, Butler U., 1993—95; MS, So. Oreg. U., 1999—2001. Music Education Ind., 1996. Tchr. Perry Meridian H.S., Ind., 1996—2004, Tempe Prep Acad., Ariz., 2005—. E-mail: kevindurfee@yahoo.com.

DURGIN, DIANE, arbitrator, lawyer, mediator; b. Albany, N.Y., May 17, 1946; BA, Wellesley Coll., 1970; JD magna cum laude, Boston Coll., 1974. Assoc. Shearman & Sterling, N.Y.C., 1974-83; corp. sec. Ga.-Pacific Corp., Atlanta, 1983-92, v.p. law, dep. gen. counsel, 1986-89, sr. v.p. law, gen. counsel, 1989-93; arbitrator, mediator Atlanta, 1993—; dep. exec. dir. legal and non-profit affairs Atlanta Housing Authority, 1994-98. Bd. dirs. Atlanta Symphony Orch., 1991-97, Am. Arbitration Assn., 1991-97, Met. Atlanta chpt. ARC, 1988-94, Actor's Express, 2000—, Atlanta Women's Found., 1999—; bd. dirs., mem. exec. com. Alliance Theatre Co., 1985-97; mem. bd. sponsors Georgian Chamber Players, Inc., 1986-92, 97-2002. Mem.: ABA, Am. Law Inst., Ga. State Bar, Bd. Dirs. Network, Nature Conservancy (bd. dirs. Ga. chpt. 1989—96), 191 Club, Order of Coif.

DURHAM, CHRISTINE MEADERS, state supreme court chief justice; b. L.A., Aug. 3, 1945; d. William Anderson and Louise (Christensen) Meaders; m. George Homer Durham II, Dec. 29, 1966; children: Jennifer, Meghan, Troy, Melinda, Isaac. AB, Wellesley Coll., 1967; JD, Duke U., 1971. Bar: N.C. 1971, Utah 1974. Sole practice law, Durham, N.C., 1971-73; instr. legal medicine Duke U., Durham, 1971-73; adj. prof. law Brigham Young U., Provo, Utah, 1973-78; ptnr. Johnson, Durham & Moxley, Salt Lake City, 1974-78; judge Utah Dist. Ct., 1978-82; assoc. justice Utah Supreme Ct., 1982—2002, chief justice, 2002—. Pres. Women Judges Fund for Justice, 1987-88. Fellow Am. Bar Found.; mem. ABA (edn. com. appellate judges' conf.), Nat. Assn. Women Judges (pres. 1986-87), Utah Bar Assn., Am. Law Inst. (coun. mem.), Nat. Ctr. State Courts (bd. dirs.), Am. Inns of Ct. Found. (trustee). Office: Utah Supreme Ct PO Box 140210 Salt Lake City UT 84114-0210

DURHAM, FLOYD WESLEY, JR., economist, educator; b. Yuma, Ariz., Feb. 9, 1930; s. Floyd Wesley and Inez (Irvin) D.; BA, North Tex. State U., 1951, MA, 1952; PhD, U. Okla., 1963; m. Patricia Keehan, May 24, 1973; children— Mark Kipling, Ronald Chappell. Claimsman, Liberty Mutual Ins. Co., Boston and Ft. Worth, 1955-58; mem. faculty dept. econs. Tex. Christian U., Ft. Worth, 1960—, prof., 1971—; cons., 1964— . Pres., Suicide Prevention Tarrant County, 1968-69. Bd. dirs. Ft. Worth Literacy Council, 1963-70, Cen. Tax Authority, Parker County, Tex. Served with AUS, 1953-55. Danforth Found. grantee, 1969-70. Mem. AAUP, Am. So. Econ. Assns., Southwestern and Western Social Sci. Assns., Western Writers Am., Beta Gamma Sigma, Omicron Delta Epsilon, Lambda Chi Alpha. Author: A Pilot Methodological Study to Determine Dibilitating Conditions, 1967; The Trinity River Paradox; Flood and Famine, 1976. Contbr. articles to profl. jours. Home: 6025 Wrigley Way Fort Worth TX 76133-3535 Office Phone: 817-257-7230. E-mail: durham8@charter.net.

DURHAM, HARRY BLAINE, III, lawyer; b. Denver, Sept. 16, 1946; s. Harry Blaine and Mary Frances (Oliver) Durham; m. Lynda L. Durham, Aug. 4, 1973; children: Christopher B., Laurel A. BA cum laude, Colo. Coll., 1969; JD, U. Colo., 1973. Bar: Wyo. 1973, U.S. Tax Ct. 1974, U.S. Ct. Appeals (10th cir.) 1976. Assoc. Brown, Drew, Apostolos, Massey & Sullivan, Casper, Wyo., 1973-77; ptnr. Brown & Drew, Casper, 1977-98, Brown, Drew & Massey, LLP, Casper, 1998—. Articles editor: U. Colo. Law Rev., 1972—73. Bd. dirs. Natrona County United Way, 1974—76, pres., 1975—76; mem. City of Casper Pks. and Recreation Commn., 1985—94, vice chmn., 1987—94; Rep. precinct committeeman, 1999—2002; Wyo. editor of 50 State Lien and Bond Law, 2003—; bd. dirs. Casper Symphony Assn., 1974—88, vice chmn., 1979—82, pres., 1983—87. Named Permanent Class Pres., Class of 1969, Colo. Coll., Mem. Nat. Alumni Coun.; recipient State Heroes award, Sporting Goods Mfg. Assn., 1997. Mem.: Nat. Assn. R.R. Trial Counsel, Natrona County Bar Assn., Wyo. Bar Assn. (Wyo. editor fifty state constrn. lien and bond law), Wyo. Amateur Hockey Assn. (bd. dirs., sec. 1974—85, pres. 1985—88), Casper Amateur Hockey Club (bd. dirs. 1970—77, sec. 1974—77), Phi Beta Kappa. Home: 3101 Hawthorne Ave Casper WY 82604-4975 Office: 159 N Wolcott St Ste 200 Casper WY 82601-7009 Office Phone: 307-234-1000.

DURHAM, HARVEY RALPH, academic administrator; BS, Wake Forest U., 1959; MA, U. Ga., 1962, PhD in Math., 1965. Asst. prof. math. Appalachian State U., Boone, NC, 1965-67, assoc. prof., chair dept. math., 1967-71, prof. math., 1971-74, assoc. dean faculty, 1971-74, assoc. vice chancellor for acad. affairs, 1974-79, acting vice chancellor for acad. affairs, 1979-80, vice chancellor for acad. affairs, 1980-89, provost, exec. vice chancellor, 1989—2003, interim chancellor, 2003—. Office: Appalachian State U Chancellor's Office Boone NC 28608-0001 E-mail: durhamhr@appstate.edu.

DURHAM, JAMES W., lawyer; b. Nov. 18, 1937; m. Kathleen B. Wollman; children: Linda, Cynthia, Andrea. BSBA, Pa. State U., 1959; MBA in Bus. Adminstrn., U. Portland, 1962; JD, Pa. State U., 1965. Bar: Oreg. 1965, U.S. Dist. Ct. Oreg., U.S. Ct. Appeals (9th cir.), U.S. Supreme Ct. Assoc. Davies, Biggs, Strayer, Stoel & Boley, Portland, Oreg., 1965—68; ptnr. Durham, Smith, Todd & Ball, Portland, 1968—70; atty. Oreg. Dept. Justice, Salem, Oreg., 1970—78; sr. v.p., gen. counsel, sec. Portland Gen. Electric Co., 1978—87; sr. v.p., gen. counsel Phila. Electric Co. (now Exelon Corp.), Phila., 1988—2001, mediator, arbitrator, 2001—. Chmn. bd. dir. Oreg. Pub. Broadcasting Found., 1984—88; chmn. Oreg. Pub. Defender Com., 1984—85. Chmn., bd. dir. Columbia-Willamette YMCA; bd. dir., trustee Franklin Inst., 1991—2001; bd. dir. Del. Valley Citizens Crime Commn., vice chmn., 2000—02, chmn., 2002—04; mem. legal adv. com. Rep. Com. Oreg., 1984—86. Mem.: ABA, Phila. Bar Found. (trustee 1991—94), Del. Valley Corp. Counsel Assn. (bd. dir. 1989—, pres. 1998), Phila. Bar Assn., Pa. Electric Assn. (chmn. 1993—94), Pa. Bar Assn., Oreg. Law Found. (bd. dir. 1986—88, pres. 1988), Oreg. State Bar (bd. govs. 1983—86, pres. 1985—86), Rotary, Tau Kappa Epsilon (fraternity alumnus of yr. 1987). Office: 2620 N Providence Rd Media PA 19063 Office Phone: 610-566-6608. Personal E-mail: durhamjw@aol.com.

DURHAM, JEANETTE RANDALL, artist, educator; b. Plainfield, NJ, June 17, 1945; d. F. Gilbert and Alice (Petricek) Randall; m. Ormonde G. Durham III, June 26, 1971; 1 child, O. Ethan. BA in Fine Arts, Montclair State U., 1967; postgrad., Art Students League, 1970, 71, 72, Westchester Art Workshop, 1980-81; MS in Edn., SUNY, Oneonta, 1991. Cert. art tchr. N.Y., N.J., reading tchr. N.Y. Art instr. Mohawk Valley Ctr. Arts, Little Falls, N.Y., 1983, Owen D. Young Cen. Sch., Van Hornesville, N.Y., 1987-92; adj. humanities instr. Herkimer County C.C., 1998—. Mem. decentralization grants panel Ctrl. NY Cmty. Arts Coun., Utica, 1999—2001, mem. exhbn. coms., 2001—04; mem. exhbn. com. Mohawk Valley Ctr. for the Arts, 1995—. One woman shows include Gallery 57, Cambridge (Mass.) Arts Coun., 1984, Gannett Gallery, SUNY Tech., Utica, NY, 1988, South Shore Arts, Little Falls, N.Y., 1991, Pleiades Gallery, NYC, 1993, Mohawk Valley Ctr. for Arts, Little Falls, 1994, 2004, Rensselaer Poly. Inst., Troy, 1997, Herkimer County C.C., 1997, Arts Ctr. Old Forge, NY, 1998; two-person show at Cazenovia (NY) Coll., 2001, Mohawk Valley Ctr. for Arts, Little Falls, 2004; exhibited in group shows at Art of N.E. U.S.A., Silvermine, New Canaan, Conn., 1986, 98 (award), NY State Mus., Albany, 1988, Cooperstown Art Assn., 1991, 94, 97, 99, Butler Inst. Am. Art, 1992, Albany Inst. History and Art, 1993, 96 (award), Arts Coun. Ctrl. NY, Utica, 1994, 2001, Pleiades Gallery, NYC, 1991-2004, Schweinfurth Art Ctr., 1998, Albany Ctr. Galleries, 1999, Gallery 210, Syracuse, 1999, South Shore Art Gallery, Little Falls, NY, 1987-2001, Tex. A&M, Coll. Sta., 2004 SOS grantee N.Y. Found. for Arts, 1997. Mem. Nat. Assn. Women Artists (William Meyerowitz Meml. award 1991, Florence Andreson award 1998), N.Y. Artist Equity, Coll. Art Assn. Home: 111 Hoke Rd Jordanville NY 13361-2017 Business E-Mail: durhamjr@hccc.suny.edu.

DURHAM, NANCY RUTH, elementary school educator, music educator; b. Cushing, Okla., Aug. 28, 1947; d. Edward Fowler and Margaret Mailine Albritton; m. Dale Leonard Durham, Aug. 8, 1970. B in Music Edn., Okla. State U., 1969. Vocal music tchr. grades 3-12 Okeene (Okla.) Pub. Schs., 1969—70; elem. music tchr. grades K-6 Choctaw (Okla.) Pub. Schs., 1970—76; pvt. bus. owner Mayo-Durham Clothing, Wagoner, Okla., 1977—86; bus. owner Bartlesville/Tulsa, Okla., 1986—88; elem. music tchr. Wagoner Pub. Schs., 1988—. Sec. Wagoner Assn. Classroom Tchrs., 1991—93, bldg. rep., 1994—95. Christmas parade chmn. Wagoner C. of C., 1979—80, v.p., 1979—81, pres., 1982; chmn./co-chmn. Tartan Day Celebration State of Okla., 2000—01. Mem.: Okla. Music Educators Assn. (choir dir. grades 5 and 6 elem. choir state honor group 1974, 1976), United Scottish Clans Okla., Scottish Club Tulsa (sec. 1997—2000). Republican. Mem. Ch. Of Christ. Avocations: sewing, embroidery, gardening, exercise, Scottish heritage activities. Home: 1505 Berkley Wagoner OK 74467

DURHAM, OLGA KALAPACA, retired art educator, civic volunteer; b. Chgo., Aug. 11, 1927; d. John and Anna (Bojkowicz) Kalapaca; m. Leonard Durham, June 12, 1948; children: Leonard David, Lynn Ellen, James Scott, Lawrence Bruce. BFA with high honors, U. Ill., 1949; MA in Art with distinction, Ea. Ill. U., 1974. Cartographer argonomy dept. U. Ill., Urbana, 1948-49, artist Univ. Press, 1950-52; artist/designer Our Wonderful World, Spencer Press, Champaign, Ill., 1953-54; instr. art dept. Ea. Ill. U., Charleston, 1957-76, Lake Land Jr. Coll., Mattoon, Ill., 1957-74; dir. community club awards program Sta. WEIC-AM-FM, Charleston, 1975-79; commr. City of Charleston, 1977-85; energy coord. Ret. Sr. Vol. Program, Coles County, Ill., 1981-86. Chmn. Coles County chpt. ARC, 1981-88; bd. dirs. Coles County Emergency Food and Shelter Com., 1983-91; chmn. corp. bd. East Ctrl. Ill. Area Agy. on Aging, Bloomington, 1987-92; active pub. rels. com. Charleston Area Arts Coun., 1988-89; bd. dirs., Rotonda West Property Owners Assn., 1992-94, East Ctrl. Ill. Older Ams. P.O.A. Resources Corp., 1992—1993. Rotonda West Assn., Inc., 1993-2005; pres., 2000, 2002-04 Recipient adminstrn. award Ill. ARC, St. Louis, 1988, Arthur A. Larsen Leadership award, 1991. Mem. Panther Club of Ea. Ill. (Rookie award 1982, Vets. award 1989), LWV (v.p. Coles County chpt. 1987-89, Outstanding Civic Participation award 1977), Zonta Club. Democrat. Presbyterian. Avocations: golf, bowling, reading, art activities. Home: 11 Oakland Hills Pl Rotonda West FL 33947-2234 E-mail: bulldurham@ewol.com.

DURHAM, ROBERT DONALD, JR., state supreme court justice; b. Lynwood, Calif., May 10, 1947; s. Robert Donald Durham and Rosemary Constance (Brennan) McKelvey; m. Linda Jo Rollins, Aug. 29, 1970; children: Melissa Brennan, Amy Elizabeth. BA, Whittier Coll., 1969; JD, U. Santa Clara, 1972; LLM in the Jud. Process, U. Va., 1998. Bar: Oreg. 1972, Calif. 1973, U.S. Dist. Ct. Oreg. 1974, U.S. Ct. Appeals (9th cir.) 1980, U.S. Supreme Ct. 1987. Law clk. Oreg. Supreme Ct., Salem, 1972-74; ptnr. Bennett & Durham, Portland, Oreg., 1974-91; assoc. judge Oreg. Ct. Appeals, Salem, 1991-94; assoc. justice Oreg. Supreme Ct., Salem, 1994—. Adv. com. Joint Interim Judiciary Com., 1984-86; chmn. Oreg. Commn. on Adminstrv. Hearings, 1988-89; faculty Nat. Jud. Coll., Reno, Nev., 1992; mem. Case Disposition Benchmarks Com., 1992-93, Coun. on Ct. Procedures, 1992-93, 95—; mem. Oreg. Rules of Appellate Procedure Com., 1998-2002; bd. dirs. Oreg. Law Inst.; chmn. commn. on jud. rule 4 Oreg. Supreme Ct., 1995-97, 2002—. Mem. ACLU Lawyer's Com., Eugene and Portland, Oreg., 1978-91. Recipient award for civil rights litig. ACLU of Oreg., 1988, Ed Elliott Human Rights award Oreg. Edn. Assn., Portland, 1990. Mem. Am. Acad. Appellate Lawyers (ninth cir. screening com. 1991—, rules com. 1994, co-chair appellate cts. liaison com. 1994), Oreg. Appellate Judges Assn. (pres. 1996-97), Oreg. State Bar (chair labor law sect. 1983-84, adminstrv. law com. govt. law sect. 1986), Willamette Valley Inns of Ct. (master of bench, team leader 1994—). Office: Oreg Supreme Ct 1163 State St Salem OR 97310-1331 Office Phone: 503-986-5725. Business E-Mail: robert.d.durham@ojd.state.or.us.

DURHAM, RONALD DALE, lawyer; b. Jan. 25, 1953; s. Billie Jack Durham and Annie Liberia (Ward) Burham; m. Joy Lynn Miller, Sept. 4, 1976; children: Christopher Eric, DeAnna Marie(dec.), Cassandra Nicole. Student, U.S. Coast Guard Acad., 1971—73; BA, Okla. Bapt. U., 1976; JD, U. Tulsa, 1977—81. Bar: Okla. 1981, U.S. Dist. Ct. (ea., we. and no. dists.) Okla. 1982, U.S. Ct. Appeals (10th cir.) 1982, Colo. 1988, U.S. Dist. Ct. Colo. 1988. Staff law libr. U. Tulsa, 1977—81; assoc. Jones, Gungoll, Jackson, Collins & Dodd, Enid, Okla., 1981—83; ptnr. Jones, McNaughton & Blakely, Enid, Okla., 1983—85; sr. assoc. Jones & Jennings, Enid, 1985—86; prin. Durham Law Offices, Norman, Okla., 1986—87; mng. bankruptcy atty. Hyatt Legal Svcs., Denver, 1987; assoc. J.E. Lasavio, Jr., Pueblo, Colo., 1987—91; sr. editor, project mgr. Lexis Nexis, 1991—. Author (with others): (book) The Surface Damages Act After Davis Oil Company vs Cloud, 1987. Co-counsel Okla. State Rep. Com., 1985—86. With USCG, 1971—73. Mem.: ABA (mineral, banking law sect.). Home: 2445 Norwich Dr Colorado Springs CO 80920-5336

DURHAM, SUSAN K., research scientist; b. Stafford, Kans., May 18, 1957; d. Rolla Evern and Betty Florence Durham. BS, Kans. State U., 1979, MS, 1981; PhD, Iowa State U., 1991. Postdoctoral fellow Mayo Clinic, Rochester, Minn., 1991-94, Baylor Coll. Medicine, Houston, 1994-98, rsch. assoc., 1998—; tech. svcs. coord. Diagnostic Systems Lab. Inc., Webster, Tex., 1999—. Mem. Endocrine Soc., Women in Endocrinology (travel award 1993), Am. Soc. Animal Sci. Avocations: reading, antiques, animals. Office: Baylor Coll Medicine 6621 Fannin St Houston TX 77030

DURHAM, THENA MONTS, microbiologist, researcher, management executive; b. Bradenton, Fla., July 10, 1945; d. Turner and Silverrene (Taylor) M.; m. Millard Durham, Aug. 30, 1969 (div. 2001); children: Bryce Vincent-Barnard, Brittanie Yvonne. BS, Fisk U., 1966; MS, Purdue U., 1968. Rsch. microbiologist Ctrs. for Disease Control, Atlanta, 1968-86, assoc. dir. for programs Nat. Ctr. for Prevention Svcs., 1988-95; program analyst Office Dir. Ctr. for Health Promotion and Edn., 1986-88; dir. exec. secretariat Ctrs. for Dis. Control and Prevention, Atlanta, 1995—2001; dep. dir. for policy Nat. Ctr. for HIV, STD, and TB Prevention for CDC, Atlanta, 2001—05; ret., 2005. Cons. FDA; mem. Purdue U. Dept. Biological Scis., alumnae advisory com., pres. coun. Author numerous tech. papers; contrb. articles to profl. jours. Mem. NAACP, Neighborhood Planning Unit, SCLC/Women Adv. Coun.; bd. dirs. Cmty. Advanced Practices Nurses. Recipient Sec.'s award for Disting. Svc. Dept. HHS, 2001. Mem. AAAS, Sci. Rsch. Soc., Am. Soc. Microbiologists, CDC Assn. Exec. Women (founder, co-chmn.), Women in Sci. and Engring., Alumni Adv. Com., Sigma Xi. Democrat. Office Phone: 678-613-6265. Personal E-mail: thena1@bellsouth.net.

DURHAM, WALTER THOMAS, historian, researcher; b. Nashville, Oct. 7, 1924; s. George Franklin and Celeste McAlister Durham; m. Anna Armstrong Coile, Apr. 23, 1949; children: Anna Durham Windrow, Robert, James F., Elizabeth Durham Lindsey. BA, Vanderbilt U., 1948, MA, 1953. Mng. ptnr. Durham Mfg. Co., Gallatin, Tenn., 1948—63, chmn., prin. owner, 1972—98; sec. Gallatin Aluminum Products Co., 1958—63, pres., CEO, 1963—72; pres., prin. owner Wholesale Plumbing and Electric, Gallatin, 1975—93; chmn. bd. First and People's Nat. Bank, Gallatin, 1976—87; state historian State of Tenn., Nashville, 2001—. Mem. bd., v.p. Tenn. Bldg. Material Soc., Nashville, 1948—64; mem. bd., treas. Archtl. Alumni Mfg. Assn., Chgo., 1966—72; mem. adv. bd., chair AmSouth Bank, Gallatin, 1995—2001. Author (with James W. Thomas): A Pictorial History of Sumner County, Tennessee, 1796-1986, 1986; author: Before Tennessee: The Southwest Territory, 1990, Wynnewood, Bledsoe's Lick, Castalian Springs, Tennessee, 1994; author: (with James W. Thomas and John F. Creasy) A Celebration of Houses Built Before 1900 in Sumner County, Tennessee, 1995; author: Volunteer Forty-Niners: Tennesseans and the California Gold Rush, 1997, The Life of William Trousdale, Soldier, Statesman, Diplomat, 2001; author: (with Glenda Milliken) Gallatin 200, A Time Line History Celebrating the Bicentennial of Gallatin, Tennessee, 2002; author: Josephus Conn Guild and Rosemont: Politics and Plantation in Nineteenth Century Tennessee, 2002, Balie Peyton of Tennessee: Nineteenth Century Politics and Thoroughbreds, 2004; contbr. essays to ency., chapters to books, articles to profl. jours.; consulting editor, mem. editl. com., contbr. Tennessee Encyclopedia of History and Culture, 1998. Sgt. Army Air Force, 1943—46, Italy, Africa. Mem.: Tenn. Hist. Soc. (mem. bd., past pres. 1973), Fairview Plantation, Lions Internat. (various local positions, Melvin Jones fellow 1949—2003). Democrat. Methodist. Avocations: watching spectator sports, travel, music, reading. Office: Office State Historian State Tenn 1010 Durham Dr Gallatin TN 37066 Office Phone: 615-452-3201. Office Fax: 615-452-3251.

DURIG, JAMES ROBERT, chemistry professor; b. Washington, Pa., Apr. 30, 1935; s. and Roberta Wilda Mounts; m. Kathryn Marlene Sprowls, Sept. 1, 1955; children: Douglas Tybor, Bryan Robert, Stacey Ann. BA, Washington and Jefferson Coll., 1958, D.Sc. (hon.), 1979; PhD, M.I.T., 1962. Asst. prof. chemistry U. S.C., Columbia, 1962-65, asso. prof., 1965-68, prof., 1968-93, Ednl. Found. prof. chemistry, 1970-73, dean Coll. Sci. and Math., 1973-93; dean Coll. Arts and Scis., U. Mo., Kansas City, 1993—2000, Curators' prof. chemistry and geosci., 1993—. Editor: Vibrational Spectra and Structure, 24 vols., 1972—, Jour. Raman Spectroscopy, 1979-94; mem. editl. bd. Jour. Molecular Structure, 1972—; contbr. articles to profl. jours. Served with Chem. Corps U.S. Army, 1963-64. Recipient Russell award U.S.C., 1968; Alexander von Humboldt Sr. Scientist award W. Ger., 1976; award Spectroscopy Soc. of Pitts., 1981; U. S.C. Ednl. Found. award, 1984 Mem. Am. Chem. Soc. (So. Chemist award Memphis sect. 1976, Charles A. Stone award S.E. Piedmont sect. 1975), Am. Phys. Soc., Soc. for Applied Spectroscopy (Pitts. sect. award 1981), Coblentz Soc. (mem. governing bd. 1972-76, pres. 1974-76, award for outstanding rsch. in molecular spectroscopy 1970), Internat. Union Pure and Applied Chemistry (chmn. sub-commn. on infrared and Raman spectroscopy 1975-95, mem. commn. molecular spectra and structure 1978-89, sec. 1981-83, chmn. 1983-89, editor Spectrochimica Acta 1999—), Blue Key Soc., Phi Beta Kappa (pres. chpt. 1970), Sigma Xi, Phi Lambda Upsilon, Phi Kappa Phi. Presbyterian. Home: 1213 W 64th Ter Kansas City MO 64113-1516 Office: Univ Mo 410 RHFH Kansas City MO 64110 Office Phone: 816-235-6038. Business E-Mail: durigj@umkc.edu. *Everything has a lighthearted side which is sometimes difficult to recognize. Never lose your sense of humor.*

DURINGER, DAVID ROBERT, lawyer; b. Coronado, Calif., June 28, 1964; m. Lena Nicolaevna Duringer; 1 child, Ayn. BA in Econs., U. Calif., San Diego, 1986; JD, U. Calif., San Francisco, 1989. Bar: Calif. 1989, Wash. 1997; lic. real estate broker, Calif. Sole practice, Orange County, Calif., 1989-95; owner, broker Adv. Realty Mgmt., Vancouver, Wash., 1995-97; gen. counsel Genisys Fin. Corp., San Diego, 1997—2001; atty., pres. Law News.TV, P.C., Carlsbad, Calif., 1999—. Mem. Calif. Bar Assn. (estate planning, trust and probate sect.), Wash. State Bar Assn., Federalist Soc., Nat. Eagle Scout Assn., Calif. Rifle and Pistol Assn. (NRA pistol instr.). Republican. Office: PMB 630 27762 Antonio Pkwy Ste L-1 Ladera Ranch CA 92694 E-mail: info@lawnews.tv.

DURKEE, JACKSON LELAND, civil engineer; b. Tatanagar, India, Sept. 20, 1922; s. E. Leland and Bernice J. (Jackson) D.; m. Marian H. Carty, Feb. 20, 1943; children: Janice D. Parry, Judith D. Burton, Christine D. Simpson. BSCE, Worcester Poly. Inst., 1943, CE, 1951; MCE, Cornell U., 1947. Registered profl. engr., Calif., Conn., N.Y., Pa.; chartered engr., U.K. Designer Douglas Aircraft Co., 1943-44; various engring. positions Fabricated Steel Constrn. div. Bethlehem Steel Corp., 1947-65, chief bridge engr., 1965-76; vis. prof. structural engring. Cornell U., 1976; ptnr. Modjeski and Masters, cons. engrs., Harrisburg, Pa., 1977-78; cons. structural engr. Bethlehem, Pa., 1978—. Mem. numerous tech. and profl. coms. Contbr. chapters to books, articles on bridge and structural engring. to profl. jours. Served to lt. USNR, 1944-46, PTO. Recipient constrn. industry citation Engring. News-Record, 1968, Robert H. Goddard award Worcester Poly. Inst., 1998, John A. Roebling medal Engrs. Soc. Western Pa., 2002. Fellow ASCE (Ernest E. Howard award 1982, hon. mem. 1996), Instn. Civil Engrs. (U.K.), Instn. Structural Engrs. (U.K.); mem. Nat. Soc. Profl. Engrs., Am. Ry. Engring. and Maintenance-of-Way Assn., Am. Welding Soc., Structural Stability Rsch. Coun., Internat. Assn. for Bridge and Structural Engring., Nat. Acad. Engring. (cited for origination and devel. of innovations in fabrication and erection engring. of longspan bridges), Tau Beta Pi, Sigma Xi. Republican. Mem. Moravian Ch. Clubs: Silver Creek Country (Hellertown, Pa.); Cosmos (Washington); St. Andrews Golf, New Golf (St. Andrews, Scotland). Achievements include patents for shop-fabricated parallel-wire-strand method for construction of suspension bridge cables, and for pipe-assembly anchorage method and plastic-type weather protection system for such cables. Home and Office: 217 Pine Top Trl Bethlehem PA 18017-1729 Office Phone: 610-868-1614.

DURKEE, WILLIAM ROBERT, retired internist; b. Kansas City, Mo., Apr. 12, 1923; s. Dwight and Bessie Deane (Williams) D.; m. Billie Maxine Schreiner, Sept. 19, 1946; m. Jeanne Elizabeth Wells, June 7, 1975; children— Bruce William, Ellen Jeanne AA, Kansas City Jr. Coll., 1941; student, U. Chgo., 1941-42; MD, U. Kans., 1945. Diplomate Am. Bd. Internal Medicine. Intern U. Kans. Med. Ctr., Kansas City, 1945-46, resident, 1948-51; practice medicine specializing in internal medicine Manhattan, Kans., 1951-91; ptnr. Ball Meml. Clinic, 1951-76, Drs. Durkee and Boese, 1976-91; med. dir. Kans. Farm Bur. Life Ins. Co., Manhattan, 1963-91; ret., 1991. Mem. staff Mercy Health Ctr.; trustee Meml. Hosp., Manhattan, Kans., 1994-03, chmn. 2001-03. Bd. dirs. Friends of McCain, 1988-95, Sunset Zoo Wildlife Conservation Trust, Manhattan, 1995-2002, pres., 1998; mem. adv. bd. Friends of Libr., Kans. State U., 1993-2002. Capt. U.S. Army, 1943-48. Fellow ACP, Am. Coll. Cardiology (assoc.); mem. AMA, Riley County Med. Soc., Kans. Med. Soc., Am. Soc. Internal Medicine, Manhattan C. of C., Pres.'s Club Kans. State U., Manhattan Country Club, Rotary. Republican. Methodist. Home: 440 Oakdale Dr Manhattan KS 66502-3736

DURKIN, DOROTHY ANGELA, university official; b. Glen Cove, NY, June 23, 1945; d. Frank Vincent and Rose Marie Durkin; 1 child, David Francis. BA, SUNY, Stony Brook, 1968; MA, NYU, 1974. Adminstrv. asst. SUNY, Stony Brook, 1965-67; prodn. editor Holt, Rhinehart & Winston, Inc., Stony Brook, 1967-69; editor Hill & Wang Pub., Inc., NYC, 1969-70; asst. dir. pub. info. NYU Sch. Continuing Edn., 1970-72; assoc. dean pub. affairs and student svc. Sch. Continuing and Profl. Studies NYU Sch. Continuing Edn. and Profl. Studies, 1983—2002, assoc. dean strategic devel., 2002—05; co-acting dean NYU Sch. Continuing and Profl. Studies, 2005—. Cons. NYC Ctr. for Lifelong Learning, 1974; producer TV series Continuum, Sta. WNYC, 1974. Editor: NSF student mag., 1961. Recipient Merit award Andy Advt., 1972, Art Dirs. Club, 1980, Soc. Illustrators, 1980, Big Apple award NY Radio Broadcasters Assn., 1985, Admissions Mktg. Report awards, 1987-88, 98-2001, Catalog Age awards, 1988, 93, Silver and Bronze award in Print Advt., 2004, Gold and Silver award in Print Pub., 2004. Mem. Univ. Continuing Edn. Assn. (chair info. svc. 1980-81, nat. award chair, chair mktg. adv. com. 1989-98, group leader Learn From Success series 1989-90, bd. dir. 1991-93, membership com. 1994-95, mktg. conf. planning com. 1993-00, presenter, Bronze, Silver and Gold awards 1978, 81-2002, Internat. Leadership in Continuing Edn. award 1999, Gold award in publications, 2002, Gold and Bronze award in Electronic Marketing Communications, 2002, Silver award in Mixed Media: Publications, Advertising, PR and Web), Am. Coll. Pub. Rels. Assn. (nat. award 1973), Coun. for Advancement and Support of Edn. (awards 1982-83, 85-87, 89-90, 92-94), Women in Comms. (job chair), Pub. Rels. Soc. Am. (Am. demographics adv. bd. 1989-90), Direct Mktg. Assn. (Echo Leadership award 1987, 88), Internat. Direct Mktg. Assn., SUNY Alumni Assn. (bd. dir.), The College Bd. (speaker, cons.), Learning Resources Network. Office: NYU Sch Continuing Edn 25 W 4th St Rm 203 New York NY 10003-4475 Business E-Mail: dorothy.durkin@nyu.edu.

DURKIN, G. MICHAEL, food products executive; BS in mktg. fin., U. RI; MBA, Pace U. Fin. oper. PepsiCo, Inc., 1981; v.p., customer devel. PepsiCo Inc., Heartland Bus. Unit (acquired by Whitman 1999); sr. v.p., gen. mgr. Whitman Corp., Eastern Group (prior to merger with PepsiAmericas); sr. v.p., CFO PepsiAmericas, Mpls., 2002—. Office: PepsiAmericas 4000 Dain Rauscher Plz 60 S Sixth St Minneapolis MN 55402

DURKIN, KEVIN P., lawyer; b. Chgo., July 22, 1955; BS, U. Ill., 1977; JD, DePaul U., 1980. Bar: Ill. 1980, U.S. Dist. Ct., No. & Ctrl. Ill. 1980, U.S. Dist. Ct., We. Mich. 1980, U.S. Ct. Appeals, 7th cir. 1980. Asst. state atty. Cook County, Ill., 1980—88; ptnr. Clifford Law Offices, Chgo., 1988—. Adj. Prof. DePaul U. Mem.: ABA (mem. sect. Litigation 1992—, mem. sect. Tort & Ins. Practice 1992—, mem. Aviation Litigation comm. 1992—, mem. Aviation & Space Law comm. 1992—, co-chair, Aviation Litigation comm. 2000—), Chgo. Bar Assn. (bd. mgr. 1998—2000, chmn. Hearing div. 1995—97, gen. chmn. 1997—98, chmn. Jud. Evaluation comm. 1995—97, treas. 2002—), Ill. Trial Lawyers Assn. (bd. advocates 1993—2001, bd. mgrs. 2001—), Assn. Trial Lawyers Am., Nat. Coll. Dist. Attys. Assn., Trial Lawyers Club Chgo., Chgo. Bar Found. Achievements include obtained the largest personal verdict of the year involving a motor vehicle accident, 2004. Office: Clifford Law Offices 31st Fl 120 N LaSalle St Chicago IL 60602

DURLAND, JACK RAYMOND, retired lawyer; b. Taylor, Tex., Sept. 21, 1916; s. Den D. and Percy (Langrill) D.; m. June Kathryn Cain, Feb. 5, 1937; children: Jack Raymond, Diane Elizabeth. LLB, U. Okla., 1941. Bar: Okla. 1941. Spl. agt. FBI, 1942-46; sole law practice Oklahoma City, 1946-50; asst. to pres. Cain's Coffee Co., Oklahoma City, 1950-52, pres., 1952-82, Gallery at Nichols Hills Inc., Oklahoma City, 1982-87; ret. Chmn. bd. Nat. Coffee Assn., 1961-62 Bd. dirs. Met. YMCA, Oklahoma City. Mem. ABA, Okla. Bar Assn., World Pres. Orgn. Home: 1620 Queenstown Rd Oklahoma City OK 73116-5523

DURN, RAYMOND JOSEPH, lawyer; b. Cleve., Nov. 28, 1925; s. Joseph Frank and Mary (Spenko) D.; m. Emmy Reboly, June 5, 1954; children: David, Sarah, Tamara. BA, Harvard U., 1950, LL.B., 1953. Bar: Ohio 1953, U.S. Dist. Ct. Ohio 1954, U.S. Ct. Appeals 6th cir. 1974. Assoc. Jones, Day, Reavis & Pogue, Cleve., 1953-60, ptnr., 1960-89; acting gen. counsel Univ. Hosps., Cleve., 1989-91, sr. counsel, 1991-93; v.p., gen. counsel Bravo Devel., Inc., 1998—. Trustee Cleve. Neighborhood Health Svcs., Inc., 1969-93, pres., 1987-89; trustee Chester Twp., Ohio, 1972-75; mem. Chester Twp. Bd. Zoning Appeals, 1969-72, Chester Twp. Zoning Commn., 1985-91. Served with USAAF, 1944-46. Mem. Ohio Bar Assn., Cleve. Bar Assn. Democrat. Unitarian Universalist. Home: 13088 W Geauga Trl Chesterland OH 44026-2830 E-mail: raydurn@earthlink.net.

DURNBAUGH, DONALD FLOYD, church history educator, researcher; b. Detroit, Nov. 16, 1927; s. Floyd Devon and Ruth Elsie (Tombaugh) D.; m. Hedwig Therese Raschka, July 10, 1952; children: Paul D., Christopher S., Renate E. BA, Manchester Coll., Ind., 1949, LHD (hon.), 1980; MA, U. Mich., 1953; PhD, U. Pa., 1960; LHD (hon.), Juniata Coll., Pa., 2003. Dir. program Brethren Svc. Commn., Austria, 1953-56; asst. prof. history Juniata Coll., Huntingdon, Pa., 1958-62, J. Omar Good disting. prof. evang. Christianity, 1988-89, archivist, 1992—; assoc. prof. ch. history Bethany Theol. Sem., Oak Brook, Ill., 1962-69, prof. ch. history, 1970-88; Carl W. Zeigler prof. religion and history Elizabethtown (Pa.) Coll., 1989-93; dir. in Europe Brethren Colls. Abroad, France, Germany, 1964-65. Cons. Brethren Hist. Com., Elgin, Ill., 1982—; moderator Ch. of the Brethren, 1985-86 Author: European Origins of the Brethren, 1958, 4th edit., 1986, The Brethren in Colonial America, 1967, 3rd edit., 1996, Guide to Research in Brethren History, 1968, The Believers' Church: The History and Character of Radical Protestantism, 1968, 2nd edit., 1985, Every Need Supplied: Mutual Aid and Christian Community in the Free Churches, 1525-1675, 1974, Pragmatic Prophet: The Life of M.R. Zigler, 1989, Brethren Beginnings: The Origin of the Church of the Brethren in Early Eighteenth-Century Europe, 1992, Fruit of the Vine: A History of the Brethren, 1708-1995, 1997; editor: Die Kirche der Brueder: Vergangenheit und Gegenwart, 1971, The Church of the Brethren: Past and Present, 1971, To Serve the Present Age: The Brethren Service Story, 1975, On Earth Peace: Discussion on War/Peace Issues Between Friends, Mennonites, Brethren and European Churches, 1935-1975, 1978, Church of the Brethren: Yesterday and Today, 1986; editor-in-chief The Brethren Ency., Inc., 1978-84; contbr. articles, book revs. to scholarly jours., periodicals. Alternative svc. as conscientious objector, 1953-56. U. Pa. Scholar, 1956-57, fellow, 1957-58; NEH sr. fellow, 1976-77; fellow Assn. Theol. Schs., 1986-87; recipient Alumni award Manchester Coll., 1978. Fellow Young Ctr. for Study of Anabaptist and Pietist Groups; assoc. Inst. of Mennonite Studies; mem. Am. Soc. Ch. History, Brethren Jour. Assn., Soc. German Am. Studies, Communal Studies Assn., Pa. German Soc. Mem. Ch. Of The Brethren. Home: PO Box 484 James Creek PA 16657-0484 Office: Juniata Coll PO Box 948 Huntingdon PA 16652-0948 Office Phone: 814-641-3484. Business E-Mail: durnbaughd@juniata.edu.

DURNELL, LAURA, writer, educator; b. Melrose Park, Ill., Aug. 3, 1971; d. Gladys Joyce (Carlson) and William Joseph Durnell; m. William Thomas Hincks, Apr. 8, 2000. BA in Journalism cum laude, Ea. Ill. U., 1993; MFA in writing, Sch. of Art Inst. Chgo., 1998. Adj. English instr. Roosevelt U., Chgo., 1999—2002; part-time English lectr. DePaul U., Chgo., 2000—. Editl. intern Time mag., N.Y.C., 1992—92; features corr. The Times of N.W. Ind.,

Munster, Ind., 2003—. Author: (short stories) Judgment (Mary Roberts Rinehart award, 2004), Needs - ACM, Regina Leigh - Room of One's Own (Notorious Fellow for Lit. Fiction, 2004, Third Prize, Playboy Coll. Fiction Contest, 1998, Samuel Ostrowsky Humanities award, Roosevelt U., 2001); contbr. Facts on File Guide to the Am. Novel. Recipient First Prize, Issues Relevant to Women, Chgo. Women in Pub., 1995; fellow, Ragdale Found. and Union League Club of Chgo., 2000; grantee Cmty. Arts Assistance Program grant, Chgo. Dept. of Cultural Affairs, 2002;, 2003, 2004, Spec. Assistance grant, Ill. Arts Coun., 2004, Ludwig Vogenstein Found. grant, 2005. Mem.: Teachers & Writers Collaborative, Assn. Writers and Writing Programs, Authors Guild. Independent. Roman Catholic. Avocations: swimming, music. Business E-Mail: ldurnell@depaul.edu.

DURNEY, MICHAEL CAVALIER, lawyer; b. Piedmont, Calif., May 20, 1943; s. James Joseph and Camille (Cavalier) D.; m. Ann E. Belanger, Nov. 27, 1971 (dec. Oct. 2001); 1 child, Christine Cavalier; m. Carla Voetsch, June 6, 2002; 1 child, James McIvor. BA, U. Calif., Berkeley, 1965; JD, U. Calif.-Hastings Coll. of Law, 1968. Bar: Calif. 1969, DC 1972, admitted to practice: US Supreme Ct. 1972. Trial atty. Tax div. Dept. Justice, Washington, 1968-72, dep. asst. atty. gen. Tax div., acting asst. atty. gen., 1986-88; assoc. Hamel and Park, Washington, 1972-78, ptnr., 1978-86, Myerson, Kuhn & Sterrett, Washington, 1988-89, Law Offices of Michael C. Durney, Washington, 1990—. Chmn. bd. trustees St. Patrick's Episcopal Day Sch., Washington, 1989—92. Named one of 75 Best Lawyers in Washington, Washingtonian mag., 2002. Mem. ABA (tax and litigation sects.), Fed. Bar Assn. (chmn. tax sect. 1982-84), Calif. Bar Assn., D.C. Bar Assn. Clubs: Metropolitan (Washington), Burning Tree. Republican. Episcopalian. Avocation: golf. Home: 6732 Selkirk Dr Bethesda MD 20817-4955 Office: 1072 Thomas Jefferson St NW Washington DC 20007-3832 Office Phone: 202-965-7744. E-mail: mcd@mdurney.com.

DURNIN, RICHARD GERRY, education educator; b. Haverhill, Mass., Mar. 9, 1920; s. William Edward and Ethel (Millett) Durnin. BS, Columbia U., 1947; MEd, Harvard U., 1950; postgrad. summers, U. Nottingham, 1950, U. Oxford, 1956; EdD, U. Pa., 1968. Tchr. pub. schs. N.J., Mass., 1946-49; instr. State Coll. at Fitchburg (Mass.), 1949-51; dir. Antioch Sch., Yellow Springs, Ohio, 1951-52; asst. prof. SUNY, Buffalo, 1952-58; vis. lectr. edn. Tufts U., spring 1957; dir. Smith Coll. Day Sch., 1958-59; asst. prof. edn. Rutgers U., 1959-65; prof. social and hist. founds. of edn. CCNY, 1965-90, prof. emeritus, 1990—. Instr. U. Nev., U. N.H., Coll. William and Mary, Johns Hopkins U., 1951—68. Author: (book) American Education: A Guide to Information Sources, 1982; contbr. articles to profl. jours. Mem. nat. coun. Travelers Aid Internat. Social Svc., 1972—77; mem. coun. Middlesex County (N.J.) Cultural and Heritage Commn., 1976—95; mem. adv. commn. Mercer County (N.J.) C.C., 1980—87; Rep. committeeman Middlesex County, 1992—; bd. dirs. Internat. Social Svc.-WAIF; trustee Proprietary Ho. Assn., NJ, 1977—97; mem. adv. com. Old Barracks, Trenton, NJ, 1982—88, trustee, 1992—98. 1st lt. USAF, 1942—46. Mem.: SAR, Sons of the Revolution, Soc. Colonial Wars, Jamestowne Soc., Soc. War of 1812, N.J. Hist. Soc., Nat. R.R. Hist. Soc., New Brunswick Hist. Soc. (pres. 1969—71), History Edn. Soc., New Eng. Soc. N.Y., St. George Soc. N.Y., Mil. Order Fgn. Wars U.S., English-Speaking Union (pres. New Brunswick br. 1991—93), Soc. Mayflower Descs., Joyce Kilmer Centennial Comm. (v.p. 1986—), Colonial Order Acorn, Phi Delta Kappa, Kappa Delta Pi. Episcopalian. Home: 50 Chester Cir New Brunswick NJ 08901-1526 E-mail: durnin@megalink.net.

DURNING, STEVEN JAMES, internist, educator; b. Neptune, nj, Aug. 31, 1968; s. James Charles Durning and Judy Davis; m. Kristen L. Durning, June 8, 1991; children: Andrew Steven, Daniel Richard. BS, Pa. State U., 1991; MD, U. Pitts., Sch. of Medicine, 1995. Resident, 1995—98; clerkship dir., staff internist Wright Patterson Med. Ctr., Dayton, 1998—2002; course dir., staff internist Uniformed Svcs U., Bethesda, Md., 2002—. Reviewer Intersite Consistency As A Measurement of Programmatic Evaluation (New Investigator Award, Rsch. In Med. Edn. Meeting, 2004). Bd. govs. Soc. of Air Force Physicians, San Antonio, 2002—; chair, med. student com. Am. Coll. Physicians, Washington, 2003—. Maj. USAF, 2002—, Uniformed Svcs. U. Decorated Meritorious Svc. medal USAF, Joint Svc. Commondation medal; recipient William P. Clements award, Excellence in Edn., Uniformed Svcs U., 2001, Inaugeral Waxman award, Nat. Am. Coll. Physicians. Fellow: Am. Coll. Physicians (bd. gov. DC chpt.). Home: 19800 Fawn Vista Way Montgomery Village MD 20886

DUROCHER, DANIEL LEONARD, lawyer; b. Houghton, Mich., Sept. 27, 1948; s. Marshall Vincent and Mary Rose (Hornick) D.; children: Amy Rebecca, Melanie Kay; m. Diane Lorene Coleman, Oct. 7, 1991. BS in Biology, Baylor U., 1970; MBA (honors), Oklahoma City U., 1979, JD, 1983. Bar: Okla. 1984, U.S. Dist. Ct. (we. dist.) Okla. 1984, U.S. Ct. Appeals (10th cir.) 1984, U.S. Ct. Mil. Appeals 1987. Atty. Lee, Buford & Durocher, Oklahoma City, 1983-86; prin. Daniel Durocher, Inc., Oklahoma City, 1986—; ptnr. Lee, Durocher, Stratton & Mauritson and predecessor, Oklahoma City, 1987—; private practice Daniel Durocher, Inc., 1999—; judge Okla. county, 2002—. Deacons First So. Bapt. Ch., Del City, Okla., 1978—. Capt. USAF, 1970-82, col judge adv. USAFR, 1987-2002. Mem. Assn. Trial Lawyers Am., Okla. Trial Lawyers Assn. Republican. Baptist. Avocation: music. E-mail: dandlaw@direcway.com.

DUROCHER, VERNLE C. (SKIP), JR., lawyer; b. Menominee, Mich., Aug. 9, 1961; s. Vernle Charles and Judith Ann (Stodola) D.; m. Ann M. Novacheck, Sept. 13, 1986; children: Tyler, Justin, Kelsey. BA in Polit. sci., Marquette U., Milw., 1983; JD, U. Wis., 1986. Law clk. U.S. Dist. Ct. (no. dist.) Tex., Dallas, 1986-87; assoc. Kirkland & Ellis, Chgo., 1987-90, Dorsey & Whitney, Mpls., 1990-95, ptnr., trial dept., chmn., ins. law, 1995—. Adj. prof. Hamline U., St. Paul, 1992-96. Note and Comment editor U. Wis., 1986. Mem. Minn. State Bar Assn. (investigator Hennepin County ethics panel 1992—), Order of the Coif. Avocations: basketball, fishing, skiing. Office: Dorsey & Whitney Ste 1500 50 S 6th St Minneapolis MN 55402-1498 Office Phone: 612-390-7855. Office Fax: 612-340-2868. Business E-Mail: durocher.skip@dorsey.com.

DUROSE, STANLEY CHARLES, JR., insurance executive; b. Joliet, MT, Oct. 26, 1923; s. Stanley Charles and Wilhelmena Amelia (Zwicky) DuR.; m. Lorraine Homan, May 27, 1977. BS, U. Wis., 1948. Various positions Wis. Dept. Ins., Madison, 1948-65; dep. commr. ins. State of Wis., Madison, 1965-69, commr. ins., 1969-75; v.p. govt. rels. Cuna Mut. Ins., Madison, 1976-80; sr. v.p. adminstrn. Cumis Ins. Soc., 1980-86, sr. v.p. reinsurance, 1986-88; dep. commr. of ins. State of Wis., 1989-91; ret., 1991. Contbr. articles to profl. pubs. With USAF, 1943-45, 51-52. Mem. Casualty Actuarial Soc., Am. Acad. Actuaries. Home: 201 Durose Ter Madison WI 53705-3322

DUROST, BARBARA JEANNE, music educator; d. Walter Irving and Margaret Lorraine Durost. MusB, Anna Maria Coll., 1975; MusM, Cath. U., 1979; MusD, Claremont Grad. U., 1997. Mem. faculty Claremont (Calif.) Cmty. Sch. Music, 1993—. Adj. faculty Claremont (Calif.) Grad. U., 1999—, Claremont (Calif.) Sch. Theology, 1999—, Calif. State U., San Bernardino, Calif., 2003—; artistic dir. Youth Theatre Works, Claremont, 2002—; cons. in field. Author (editor): Sacred and Court Odes of William Craft, 1997. Dir. music Claremont (Calif.) United Meth. Ch., 1996—. Mem.: Handel Soc.

DURR, JANICE LORRAINE HOWARD, art educator, painter; b. Dublin, Ga., Jan. 24, 1946; d. Willie Griffin and Pinkie Elizabeth Rice; m. Frederick Durr, Oct. 0, 1968 (dec.); 1 child, Kiera Nicole. BFA, Montclair State U., Upper Montclair, N.J., 1967, MFA, 1981. Cert. tchg./std. N.J., 1967. Tchr. art Maple Ave. Sch., Newark, 1967—68, F.V. Evans Sch., Marlton Evesham Twp., 1969—71, Barringer H.S., Newark, 1972—92, Arts H.S., 1992—. Developer art curriculum Newark City Schs. Exhibitions include, prin. works include Masai Sambura Dream, Jazz Portraits for Spelman Alumni of N.J. Choir mem. St. John's Bapt. Ch., Newark, 1975—2004. Grantee, Newark Edn. Coun., 1993—94, Michael Jordan grant, Nat. Assn. Improvement of Edn., 2001. Mem.: Nat. Conf. Artists, Newark Art Tchrs. Assn., Nat. Art Edn. Assn., N.J. Art Edn. Assn. Independent. Baptist. Avocations: reading, guitar, swimming, dancing, poetry. Office: Arts HS 550 Martin Luther King Blvd Newark NJ 07102 Office Phone: 973-733-7391. Office Fax: 973-733-7395.

DURR, ROBERT JOSEPH, construction executive, mechanical engineer; b. N.Y.C., June 25, 1932; s. Otto and Veronica U. (Quinlan) D.; m. Julia Loretta, Apr. 16, 1955; children— Kathryn A., Robert J. Jr., Kenneth A., Jennifer L. BBA, Iona Coll., 1954; Cert. in Mech. Engring., NYU, 1957. Mem. staff Courter & Co., Inc., N.Y.C., 1955-60, mgr., 1960-71, v.p., 1971-81, pres. Secaucus, NJ, 1981-85, Durr Mech. Constrn., Inc., N.Y.C., 1986-98, chmn., 1998—. Chmn. Nat. Joint Steamfitter Apprenticeship Com., Washington, 1980-84; trustees Nat. Cert. Pipe Welding Bur., Washington, 1983—. Recipient Recognition award Nat. Cert. Pipe Welding Bur., 1980 Mem. Subcontractors Trade Assn., Mech. Contractors Assn. Am. (bd. dirs. 1989—, mem. exec. bd. 1993, pres. 1996), Mech. Contractors Assn. N.Y. (bd. dirs., pres. 1976-82, Appreciation award 1982), N.Y. Bldg. Congress (bd. govs. 1978-84), Bldg. Trade Employers Assn. N.Y. (Greater N.y. welding chpt. 1975-88, chmn. 1979-88), Upper Montclair (N.J.) Country Club. Roman Catholic. Avocations: golf, swimming, sailing. Business E-Mail: rdurrsr@durrmech.com.

DURRANI, SAJJAD HAIDAR, aerospace engineer, consultant, communications engineer; b. Pakistan, Aug. 27, 1928; came to U.S., 1959, naturalized, 1966; s. Inayat Ullah and Hameedah Khanum D.; m. Brita Katarina Yasmin Portin, May 21, 1959; children: Zarina, Amina, Arif. BA, Govt. Coll., Lahore, Pakistan, 1946; BSc in Elec. Engring. with honors, Engring. Coll. Lahore, 1949; MScTech, Coll. Tech., Manchester, Eng., 1953; ScD, U. N.Mex., 1962. Lectr., asst. prof. Engring. Coll., Lahore, 1949-59; instr., research assoc. U. N.Mex., Albuquerque, 1959-62; sr. engr. Gen. Electric Co., Lynchburg, Va., 1962-64; prof., chmn. dept. elec. engring. Engring. U. Lahore, 1964-65; assoc. prof. Kans. State U., Manhattan, 1965-66; sr. engr. RCA Space Center, Hightstown, N.J., 1966-68; staff scientist, br. mgr. COMSAT Labs., Clarksburg, Md., 1968-73; sr. scientist Ops. Research, Inc., Silver Spring, Md., 1973-74; sr. engr. NASA-Goddard Space Flight Center, Greenbelt, Md., 1974-79; chief communications scientist NASA Hdqrs., Washington, 1979-81; mgr. for system planning, tracking and data relay satellite system NASA-GSFC, 1981-84; mgr. research and planning NASA Communications Div., 1984-88; program mgr., Advanced Systems Office NASA Hdqrs., Washington, 1988-92; consulting engr. Computer Scis. Corp., Beltsville and Seabrook, Md., 1992-98; ret., 1998. Vis. prof. U. Md., 1972, adj. prof. Univ. Coll., 1997—,; adj. prof. George Washington U., 1980-82, 86, 87, rsch. prof., 1993-97; mem. Engring. Manpower Commn., Am. Assn. Engring. Socs., 1981; exec. fellow, tech. advisor Fed. Comm. Commn., 2000-01, fellow, tech. advisor State Dept., 2004-05. Mem. editorial bd.: COMSAT Tech. Rev., 1972, IEEE Spectrum, 1975-78, IEEE Procs., 1988-92. Pres. Muslim Cmty. Ctr., Silver Spring, Md., 1976-82, trustee, 1989-94, 95-2000, chmn., 1998-2000. Recipient spl. achievement award NASA, 1977, 78, 90, Amb. award Computer Scis. Corp., 1996. Fellow: IEEE (bd. govs. aerospace and electronic sys. soc. 1977—93, pres. 1982—83, dir. Divsn. IX 1984, 1985, publs. bd. 1986, 1987, 1991, bd. dirs. nat. telesys. conf. 1991—94, publs. bd. 1992, bd. govs. aerospace and electronic sys. soc. 1997—2003, Citation of Honor U.S. Activties Bd. 1980, Outstanding Mem. Region 2 1982, Meritorious Achievement in Continuing Edn. award 1994, Millennium medal 2000, Profl. Activities award 2001, Centennial medal 1984), AIAA (assoc.), Wash. Acad. Scis. (v.p. adminstrn. 2001—04); mem.: D.C. Coun. Engring. Archtl. Socs. (v.p. 2005—06). Personal E-mail: s.durrani@ieee.org.

DURRANT, GEOFFREY HUGH, retired language educator; b. Pilsley, Eng., July 27, 1913; s. John and Charlotte (Atkinson) D.; m. Barbara Joan Altson, June 2, 1942; children: John Guy, Catherine Jane. BA, Cambridge (Eng.) U., 1932-35; diploma in edn., London U., 1935-36; student, Tuebingen (W. Ger.) U., 1937-39. Prof., English U. Natal, South Africa, 1945-60, head dept. English; prof. U. Man., Winnipeg, Can., 1961-66; now prof. emeritus U. B.C., Vancouver, Can., master tchr., 1973. Author: William Wordsworth, 1969, Wordsworth and the Great System, 1970. Served with South African Armed Forces, 1940-44. Carnegie fellow, 1960; Killam sr. fellow, 1976 Fellow Royal Soc. Can.; mem. Assn. Can. Univ. Tchrs. English. Anglican. Home: 10-4388 Moncton St Richmond BC Canada V7E 6R9

DURRANT, M. PATRICIA, diplomat; BA, Diploma in Internat. Rels., U. W.I.; Diploma in Overseas Devel. Studies, U. Cambridge, Eng. With Jamaica Fgn. Svc., 1971—, minister, dep. permanent rep. to UN, 1983—87, amb. to Germany, 1987—92, non-resident amb. to Israel, the Netherlands, Switzerland and the Holy See, 1987—92; dir.-gen. Min. of Fgn. Affairs and Fgn. Trade, 1992—95, permanent rep. of Jamaica to UN N.Y.C., 1995—, rep. for Jamaica on Security Coun. UN, 2000—01, vice chair Open-Ended Working Group on the Reform of UN Security Coun.; ombudsman United Nations, N.Y.C. Chair consultative com. UN Devel. Fund for Women; pres. High Level Com. on Tech. Coop. Among Developing Countries, 1999—2001; vice chair preparatory com. spl. session on population and devel. UN Gen. Assembly, 1999. Named Disting. Grad., U. W.I., 1998; recipient Order of Distinction in the rank of Comdr., 1992, Order of Jamaica, 2000, Disting. Achievement award, World Assn. of Former UN Interns and Fellows. Office: Permanent Mission of Jamaica to UN 767 Third Ave 9th Flr New York NY 10017*

DURRANT, MATTHEW B., state supreme court justice; JD, Harvard U., 1984. Adj. prof. Brigham Young U., Salt Lake City; law clerk U.S. Supreme Ct. Appeals (10th cir.), Salt Lake City; shareholder Parr, Waddoups, Brown & Gee, Salt Lake City; judge Third Dist. Ct., Salt Lake City, 1997-2000; justice Utah Supreme Ct., 2000—. Founding chair Supreme Ct. Professionalism Com.; former chair Judicial Council Technology Com. Office: Utah Supreme Ct PO Box 140210 Salt Lake City UT 84114-0210

DURRENBERGER, CHRISTOPHER, music educator, musician; b. Manchester, Conn., Dec. 29, 1965; s. Corie Durrenberger; m. Peng-Hsin Chen, May 20, 1995; children: Isabelle, Leon. MusB, Oberlin Coll. Conservatory of Music, Ohio, 1988; MusM, U. So. Calif., LA, 1991, D in Musical Arts, 1996. Asst. piano technician U. So. Calif., 1994—97; assoc. prof. music Taipei City Mcpl. Teachers Coll., Taiwan, 1997—99, Wittenberg U., Springfield, Ohio, 1999—. Artist faculty Internat. Inst. Young Musicians, Santa Barbara, Calif., 1998—99; music dir. Christ Episcopal Ch., Springfield, Ohio, 2001—; conf. presentor World Piano Pedagogy Conf., Orlando, Fla., 2001—02, Ohio Music Teachers Nat. Assn., Dayton, 2004; music critic Chamber Music Yellow Springs, Ohio, 2004—. Musician (concert pianist): (soloist) Rhapsody in Blue, Poulenc Concerto for Two Pianos, Beethoven Triple Concerto; musician: (chamber musician) (collaboration) Brahms Piano Quintet; contbr. articles to profl. reviews and jour. Recipient First Prize, Ohio Music Tchrs. Nat. Assn. Nat. Piano Competition, 1985, Fourth prize, Young Keyboard Artists Assn. Internat. Piano Competition, 1986, Chamber Music Rural Residency, Nat. Endowment for the Arts, 1992 - 1993, Florence Allen Award, Carmel Nat. Chamber Music Competition, 1992; grantee East Asian Traditional Music rsch. in Japan and Taiwan, Freeman Found., 2002, Masterclass Tour and East Asian Traditional Music rsch. in Taipei, Hong Kong, Shanghai, Shenyang, Beijing and Tokyo, 2004; scholar Merit Scholarship, Oberlin Conservatory, 1984 - 1988;, U. So. Calif. Sch. Music, 1989 - 1991. Mem.: Coll. Music Soc., Music Teachers Nat. Assn. D-Liberal. Episcopal. Avocations: rebuilding pianos, scuba diving, golf. Office: Wittenberg Univ PO Box 720 Springfield OH 45501-0720 Office Phone: 937-327-7371. Office Fax: 937-327-7347. Business E-Mail: cdurrenberger@wittenberg.edu.

DURRETT, JAMES FRAZER, JR., retired lawyer; b. Atlanta, Mar. 23, 1931; s. James Frazer and Cora Frazer (Morton) D.; m. Lucretia McPherson, June 9, 1956; children: James Frazer III, William McPherson, Lucretia Heston Miller, Thomas Ratcliffe. AB, Emory U., 1952; postgrad., Princeton U., 1952-53; LLB cum laude, Harvard U., 1956. Bar: Ga. 1955. Ptnr. Alston & Bird (and predecessor firm), Atlanta, 1956-97, retired, 1997. Adj. prof. Emory U. Law Sch., 1961—77. Trustee emeritus Student Aid Found., The Howard Sch. Mem. Am. Law Inst. (life, adv. estate and gift tax project, restatement, second. property, Fed. Income Tax project), Capital City Club, Harvard Club (Atlanta). Presbyterian. Home: 2734 Peachtree Rd NW C 302 Atlanta GA 30305-2944 Office: Alston & Bird 1 Atlantic Ctr Atlanta GA 30309-3400

DURST, ROBERT JOSEPH, II, lawyer; b. Pitts., Jan. 23, 1943; s. Robert J. and Catherine (Thomas) D.; m. Sandra A. Cattani; children: Thomas Sandberg, Eric Francis. BA, Gettysburg Coll., 1964; JD, Villanova U., 1967. Bar: Pa. 1967, N.J. 1968, U.S. Dist. Ct. (we. dist.) Pa. 1967, U.S. Dist. Ct. (N.J.) 1968, U.S. Supreme Ct. 1973. Corp. staff atty. Alcoa, Pitts., 1967; assoc. Herr & Fisher, Flemington, N.J., 1967-76; ptnr. Bernhard, Durst & Dilts, Flemington, 1976-89, Stark & Stark, Princeton, N.J., 1989—. Board cert. matrimonial atty. N.J. Supreme Ct., 1982—; lectr., author on divorce and family law. With USMC, 1960—64. Fellow Am. Acad. Matrimonial Lawyers (pres. N.J. chpt. 1998-99); mem. ABA, Am. Trial Lawyers Assn., N.J. Bar Assn. (mem. exec. com. family law sect., Saul Tiscu;er award Lifetime Contbn. Family Law 2003), Hunterdon County Bar Assn., Mercer County Bar Assns., Am. Coll. Family Trial Lawyers (diplomate). Home: 28 Marvin Ct Lawrenceville NJ 08648-2112 Office: Stark & Stark PO Box 5315 Princeton NJ 08543-5315

DURSUN, DERYA, environmental engineer, researcher; d. Iffet and Abidin Dursun. MSc (hon.), Dokuz Eylul U., Izmir, Turkey, 2001. Rsch. and tchg. asst. Akdeniz U., Antalya, Turkey, 2000—02; rsch. asst. U. Del., Newark, 2002—. Mem. Women in Engring., Newark, Del., 2004—05. Rsch. grant, NSF. Mem.: Air and Waste Mgmt. Assn., Internat. Water Assn. Home: 138L Chestnut Crossing Dr Newark DE 19713 Office: Univ Del Dupont Hall #160 Newark DE 19716 Office Phone: 1-302-831 6936.

DURYEE, HAROLD TAYLOR, insurance consultant; b. Willoughby, Ohio, Feb. 11, 1930; s. Gerald Fancher and Margaret Grace (Taylor) D.; m. Phyllis Annette Painter, June 18, 1966. AB, Kenyon Coll., 1951. Field rep. Mahoning Valley Coun., Boy Scouts Am., Youngstown, Ohio, 1951-56; mgr. claims svcs. Nationwide Ins. Cos., Canton, 1956-65; legis. and field dir. Ohio Rep. Party, Columbus, 1965-70, exec. dir., 1970-77, cons., 1980-81; dep. adminstr. Ohio Bur. Workers' Compensation, Columbus, 1977-84; exec. dep. adminstr. Fed. Ins. Adminstrn., Washington, 1984-86; adminstr. fed. ins. Fed. Emergency Mgmt. Agy., Washington, 1986-90; dir. Ohio Dept. Ins., 1991-99; sr. advisor Internat. Ins. Found., 1999—. Trustee, exec. com. Griffith Found. for Ins. Edn.; mem. Ohio Elections Commn., 1980-84. Vice chmn. North Canton City Planning Commn., 1958-67; precinct committeeman Stark County Cen. Com., 1958-72; organizer North Canton Rep. Com., 1958, chmn., 1960-72; sec. North Canton Area Devel. Com., 1959-64; chmn. North Canton City Charter Commn., 1960; campaign mgr. U.S. Rep. Frank T. Bow, 1962, Oliver P. Bolton for U.S. Congress, 1964, Clarence J. Brown, Jr. for U.S. Congress, 1965; state chmn. Ohio League Young Rep. Clubs, 1962-63; nat. vice chmn. Young Rep. Nat. Fedn., 1963-65; former chmn. bd. trustees Nat. Assn. Ins. Commrs. Edn. and Rsch. Found.; former trustee ASFPM Edn. and Rsch. Found. Recipient Disting. Svc. award Jaycees, 1961, Civic Affairs award Rotary, 1964, Meritorious Svc. award Fed. Emergency Mgmt. Agy., 1989, Disting. Civilian Svc. medal, Fed. Emergency Mgmt. Agy., 1990. Mem. Acad. Polit. Sci. Episcopalian. Avocation: genealogy. Home: 925 City Park Ave Columbus OH 43206-2511 Office Phone: 614-443-8285. Personal E-mail: hduryee@columbus.rr.com.

DUSANSKY, RICHARD, economist, educator; b. Bklyn., Dec. 23, 1942; s. Abraham and Mary (Strawitz) D.; m. Abigail November, July 3, 1965; children: Eric, Deborah. BA cum laude, Bklyn. Coll., 1964; PhD in Econs., Brown U., 1969. Asst. prof. econs. SUNY, Stony Brook, 1968-72, assoc. prof, 1972-74, prof., 1974-84, dir. Econ. Rsch. Bur., 1977-82; prof., head dept. econs. U. Ga., 1984-89; Powell Centennial prof. dept. econs. U. Tex., Austin, 1989-91, Richard Gonzalez Regents Chair prof. econs., 1991—, chmn., 1989-97,98-2000, dir. Ctr. for Applied Rsch. in Econs., 1999—2004. Vis. scholar dept. econs. U. Calif., Berkeley, 1973, 78, 96; vis. prof. dept. econs. U. Wis., Madison, 1974-75. Contbr. articles on econs. to profl. jours. Ford Found. fellow, 1967-68. Mem. Am. Econs. Assn., Econometric Soc. Office: U Tex Dept Econ Austin TX 78712 Office Phone: 512-471-3664. E-mail: dusansky@eco.utexas.edu.

DUSCHA, JULIUS CARL, journalist; b. St. Paul, Nov. 4, 1924; s. Julius William and Anna (Perlowski) D.; m. Priscilla Ann McBride, Aug. 17, 1946 (dec. Sept. 1992); children: Fred C., Steve D., Suzanne, Sally Jean; m. Suzanne Van Den Heurk, June 21, 1997. Student, U. Minn., 1943—47; AB, Am. U., 1951; postgrad., Harvard Coll., 1955—56. Reporter St. Paul Pioneer Press, 1943-47, Congl. Quar., 1947—48; publicist Dem. Nat. Com., 1948, 52; writer Labor's League for Polit. Edn., AFL, 1949-52, Internat. Assn. Machinist, 1952-53; editl. writer Lindsay-Schaub Newspapers, Ill., 1954-58; nat. affairs reporter Washington Post, 1958-66; assoc. dir. profl. journalism fellowships program Stanford (Calif.) U., 1966-68; dir. Washington Journalism Ctr., 1968-90; columnist, freelance journalist, West Coast corr. Presstime mag., San Francisco, 1990-99; sr. corr. News Inc., San Francisco, 1998—. Author: Taxpayer's Hayride: The Farm Problem from the New Deal to the Billie Sol Estes Case, 1964, Arms, Money and Politics, 1965, The Campus Press, 1973; editor: Defense Conversion Advisory; contbr. articles to mags., including Washingtonian, N.Y. Times Mag., Changing Times, Harper's, Reporter, Progressive, New Leader. Recipient award for Disting. Washington corr. Sigma Delta Chi, 1961 Mem.: Cosmos Club (Washington), Kappa Sigma. Home: 2200 Pacific Ave Apt 7D San Francisco CA 94115-1412 Personal E-mail: juliusduscha@aol.com.

DUSENBERRY, PHILIP BERNARD, advertising executive; b. Bklyn., Apr. 28, 1936; s. Harry Augustus and Margaret Maria (Shaw) D. Student, Emory and Henry Coll., 1955. Copywriter Batten, Barton, Durstine & Osborne, Inc., N.Y.C., 1962-65, creative supr., 1965-67, v.p., 1967-69, assoc. creative dir., sr. v.p., dir., 1977-78, creative dir., 1978-80, exec. creative dir., exec. v.p., mem. exec. com., 1980-86, later vice chmn., exec. creative dir.; vice chmn. BBDO Worldwide, 1986, also bd. dirs.; former chmn. bd. BBDO N.Y.; retired, 2002. Owner Dusenberry-Ruriani-Kornhauser, N.Y.C., 1969-73, Clyne-Dusenberry, 1973-76. Author: (motion picture) (with Larry Spiegel) Hail to the Chief, 1973, (screenplay, with Roger Towne) The Natural, 1975, (with Norman Cohen) August Strangers, 1977, Then We Set His Hair on Fire: Insights and Accidents from a Hall-of-Fame Career in Advertising, 2005. Served with USNG, 1960-61. Named Advt. Exec. Yr., AdWeek, 1986; named one of the 100 most influential people in advt. during the last century, Advt. Age, 1999; named to Am. Advt. Fedn. Hall of Fame, 2003. Mem.: Am. Assn. Advt. Agencies (chmn. 2000—01).*

DUSENBERY, WALTER CONDIT, sculptor; b. Alameda, Calif., Sept. 21, 1939; s. Walter A. and Allegra V. (McIlrath) D.; m. Irene McManus, Jan. 25, 1986. Student, San Francisco Art Inst., 1961; M.F.A., Calif. Coll. Arts and Crafts, Oakland, 1969. Instr. U. Calif. Extension-San Francisco, 1967-69; vis. sculptor Grad. Sch. Design-Harvard U., Cambridge, Mass., 1979—; dir. Stone divsn. Johnson Atelier, 1996—2003; chmn. bd. Digital Stone Project, Mercerville, NJ, 2003—. Exhibitor one-man shows, Laumeir Internat. Sculpture Park, St. Louis, 1983, Va. Commonwealth U., Richmond, 1983, Harvard U. Grad. Sch. Design, 1982, Nassau County Mus. Fine Art, Roslyn, N.Y., 1981, Hamilton Gallery Contemporary Art, N.Y.C., 1978, 80, Fendrick Gallery, Washington, 1986, 88; represented in permanent collections, Carnegie Inst., Pitts., Columbus (Ohio) Mus. Art, Commune of Glostrup, Denmark, Solomon R. Guggenheim Mus., N.Y.C., Huntington (W. Va.) Galleries, Met. Mus. Art, N.Y.C., San Francisco Mus. Modern Art, U. N.Mex. Mus., Albuquerque, Jerusalem Found, Israel, City of Portland Oreg., U. No. Iowa, Cedar Falls, Rainier Bank, Seattle; author: The Story of the Bed, 1970. Recipient Meml. prize Augustus St. Gaudens Found.; fellow Creative Artists Program Svc., N.Y.C., 1980, Nat. Endowment for Arts, 1980. Home: PO Box 144 Fly Creek NY 13337 Office Phone: 607-547-8431. E-mail: wdusenbery@stny.rr.com.

DUSOLD, LAURENCE RICHARD, chemist, computer specialist; b. Chgo., Nov. 15, 1944; s. Henry E. and Colette M. Dusold; m. Karen A. Marsh, Aug. 29, 1970; children: Amy, Lauren, Patricia, Amanda. BS in Chemistry, Purdue U., 1966; MS, U. N.C., 1969; postgrad., Wayne State U., 1969-71. Rsch. chemist, residue analysis and methods investigation br. Bur. Foods FDA, Washington, 1971—75, chemist, computer specialist, div. chemistry and physics, 1975—81, sr. chemist, computer specialist, div. of chemistry and physics, 1981—86, chief telecomms. and sci. computer support, 1986—2003, dep. info. tech. dir. sci. computing, 2004—. Faculty, evening divsn. U. Md., 1973-2000; fed. engring. planning group Dept. HHS, 1990-95. Mem. editl. bd. Sci. Computing and Automation, 1990-2003; contbr. articles to profl. jours., chpts. to books. Mem. AAUP, Am. Chem. Soc., Internet Soc., IEEE, IEEE Computer Soc., Assn. Computing Machinery (chmn. SIGAPL, D.C. chpt. 1978-91, vice chmn. Potomac chpt. 1993-96), Greater Washington Fed. Agy. APL Users Group (co-chmn. 1977-87), Alpha Chi Sigma, Phi Lambda Upsilon. Republican. Roman Catholic. Office: FDA 5100 Paint Branch Pky College Park MD 20740-3835 Office Phone: 301-436-1481. Business E-Mail: laurence.dusold@fda.hhs.gov.

DUSSAULT, NANCY, actress, singer; b. Pensacola, Fla., June 30, 1936; d. George Adrian and Sarah Isabel (Seitz) D.; m. James D. Travis, Oct. 4, 1958. MusB, Northwestern U., 1957; studies with Alvina Kraus, Lotte Lehmann. Actress: (stage prodns.) Guys and Dolls, 1955, Street Scene, 1959, The Mikado, 1959, The Cradle Will Rock, 1960, Do Re Mi, 1960 (Theatre World award 1960), The Sound of Music, 1962 (Kit Kat Club award), Apollo and Miss Agnes, 1963, What Makes Sammy Run, 1964, Phoebe, 1965, Carousel, 1966, Finian's Rainbow, 1967, Fiorello!, 1968, On a Clear Day You Can See Forever, 1968, South Pacific, 1969, Trelawny of the Wells, 1970, The Last of the Red Hot Lovers, 1972, Detective Story, 1973, Irene, 1975, Winter Interludes, 1976, Side by Side by Sondheim, 1977, (TV series) The New Dick Van Dyke Show, 1971, Too Close for Comfort, 1980-83, (TV spls.) Alan King Looks Back in Anger: A Review of 1972, 1973, Burt and the Girls, 1973, The Many Faces of Comedy, 1973, The Lily Tomlin show, 1973, Night of 100 Stars, II, 1985; solo vocalist Chgo. Symphony Orch., 1957 (Young Artists award Soc. Am. Musicians 1957); other mus. performances include Broadway Answers Selma, 1965, ASCAP Salute, 1967, The Magic of Cole Porter, 1967, The Heyday of Rodgers and Hart, 1969, A Salute of Rudolph Friml, 1969, A Hammerstein Salute, 1972, The Revue of Revues, 1973, A Salute to Jules Styne, 1974; host Good Morning, America, 1975, The Shape of Things, 1982; guest various talk shows including The Tonight Show, The Mike Douglas Show, The Merv Griffin Show. Mem. Actors' Equity Assn., AFTRA, Screen Actors Guild, Am. Guild Mus. Artists, AGVA, Delta Delta Delta. Avocations: needlecrafts, cooking, reading, music.

DUSSAULT, WILLIAM LEONARD ERNEST, lawyer; b. New Westminster, B.C., Can., May 9, 1947; came to U.S., 1960; s. Eugene Leo and Louise (Hobbs) D.; m. Kate Stitt, Jan. 19, 1999; 1 child, Amy Louise. BA, U. Wash., 1969, JD, 1972. Bar: Wash. 1972, U.S. Dist. Ct. (we. dist.) Wash. 1973, U.S. Supreme Ct. 1982. Ptnr., prin. Dussault Lawgroup, Seattle, 1972—. Adj. prof. U. Wash. Sch. Law, dept. spl. edn. Cen. Wash. U.; mem. faculty U. Wash. Sch. Nursing; guest lectr. U. Oreg., Seattle U.; cons. Guardian, Advocacy and Protective Services Program, Oreg., supt. of pub. instruction, devel. disabilities planning council, protection and advocacy agy., Assn. for Retarded Citizens, Devel. Diabilities Residential Service Assn., Coalition for Spl. Edn. State of Wash., Assn. Retarded Citizens, div. mental health State of Oreg., Devel. Disabilities Council State of Mont., Dept. Edn. States of N.D. and Kans., Protection Advocacy Agy. State of Tenn., Northwest Assn. Rehab. Industries; past president Wash. Ch, Nat. Assn. Elder Law Attys. Mem. Editorial bd. The Assn. for the Severely Handicapped; author: drafted legislation concerning edn. rights of the handicapped; conbr. articles to profl. jours. Bd. dirs., trustee Found. for the Handicapped; former mem. Wash. Spl. Edn. Commn., Wash. State Legis. Rev. Com. Spl. Edn., Gov.'s Com. on Employment of the Handicapped, Wash. State Human Rights Commn. Adv. Council for the Physically, Mentally and Sensory Handicapped; vol. atty. Wash. Assn. for Persons with Disabilities; vol. Wash. State Spl. Olympics; bd. dirs. Wash. State Disabilities Polit. Action Com.; bd. dirs., officer Coun. Parent Advocates and Attys. Served to capt. USAR, 1967-75. Mem. ABA (family law com. on mental disability, cons. to guardianship/limited guardianship report 1981), Wash. Bar Assn. (civil rights com.), Seattle-King County Bar Assn., Brain Injury Assn. Am. (bd. dirs., officer). Office: 219 E Galer St Seattle WA 98102-3794 E-mail: Billd@Dussaultlaw.com.

DUST, MARGARET CECILE, psychology professor; b. East Chicago, Ind., Aug. 1, 1947; d. Isidor Gerhardt and Nettie Zelenda (Klingspor) D. BA in Polit. Sci., Loyola U., Chgo., 1969; postgrad., John Marshal Law Sch., 1970-71; BA in Psychology, Purdue U. Calumet, 1977; MS in Indsl. Psychology, Ill. Inst. Tech., 1985; PhD in Ednl. Psychology and Stats., Andrews U., 1995. Lic. secondary sch. tchr., Ind. Field worker ARC, Vietnam, 1969-70; coord. of advising Purdue U. Calumet, Hammond, Ind., 1978-82, instr. psychology, 1978-88, asst. prof. psychology, 1988-90; assoc. prof. psychology Chgo. State U., 1990—. Assessment cons. Calumet Coll., Whiting, Ind., 1999-2000; mem. Ill. State Steering Panel; co-chair Behavioral Sci. Panel, State of Ill.; chair, Coll. Arts and Sci. curriculum,; mem. U. Strategic Planning, faculty senator, Chgo. State U., coord., dept. team, undergrad. com. psychology, grad. com. psychology; presenter in field Contbr. articles to profl. jours. Grantee for data analyis NSF, San Francisco, 1994; grantee for rsch. tng. and minority students Corp. for Tng. Minority Students, Chgo., 1998, 99. Mem. APA, Soc. for Computers in Tech., Ind. Coun. for the Humanities, Vietnam Vets. Am. (post traumatic stress disorder chair chpt. 285). Avocations: photography, gardening, world traveling. Home: 215 Greiving St Dyer IN 46311-1810 Office: Chgo State Univ 9501 S King Dr Chicago IL 60628-1501 Office Phone: 773-995-2227. E-mail: mdust@csu.edu.

DUSTMAN, PATRICIA (JO) ALLEN, public school educator, educational consultant, researcher; b. Salem, Ohio, Mar. 22, 1947; d. Alton Davis Allen and Mary Evaline Allen (Iler); m. George Bird Dustman, June 10, 1972; 1 child, Mary Elizabeth Wastchak. BS, Kent State U., 1967—69, MA, 1970—71; EdD, Ariz. State U., 1998. Cert. Teacher AZ. Tchr. Ashtabula City, Ravenna City, N. Ridgeville City Sch. Districts, Ohio, 1969—75; prin. North Ridgeville City Schools, Ohio, 1975—80; asst. supt. Madison Local Schools, Ohio, 1980—82; supt. of schools St. Clairsville-Richland City Schools, Ohio, 1982—85; dist. and bldg. adminstr. Scottsdale Pub. Schools, Ariz., 1985—94; supt. of schools Queen Creek Unified Sch. Dist., Ariz., 1994—98; rschr., cons. SW Interdisciplinary Rsch. Consortium, Ariz. State U., Tempe, Ariz., 1999—; ednl. cons. The Dustman Group, Scottsdale, Ariz., 1999—. Mem. Bel-Tech Adv. Bd., St. Clairsville, Ohio, 1982—85; academic standards design team mem. Ariz. Dept. of Edn., Phoenix, 1996—98; mem. East Valley Think Tank, Mesa, Ariz., 1994—98, Mesa C.C. Adv. Bd., Ariz., 1997—98; mentor SPR-Early Career Preventionist Network, Washington, 2003—; mem., cmty. adv. bd. for student services Osborn Elem. Sch. Dist., Phoenix, 2000—; mem., acad. profls. Sch. of Social Work, Ariz. State U., 2003—. Contbr. articles to profl. jours. Mem. C. of C., St. Clairsville, Ohio, 1982—85; founding mem. and chair Scottsdale Prevention Inst., Ariz., 1985—87; mem. Scottsdale Ednl. Enrichment Services, Ariz., 1985—2003; donor Kent State U. Alumni Assn., The Wilson Conf. of the Coll. of Edn., The Bowman Fellowship Fund, Ariz. State U. Alumni Assn. Founders' Day, 1990—2003. Recipient Key to the City, Mayor and City Coun. of St. Clairsville Ohio, 1985; grantee Key Pers.: Devel. and Implementation Dir.: SW Interdisciplinary Rsch. Consortium, NIH/NIDA, 2002; Tech. grant, Olin Charitable Trust, 1995—98, Saturday Sch., Rural Metro Corp., 1998, Summer Acad. scholarships, MGC Pure Chemicals Am., 1997—98, grant, Key Pers.: Drug Resistance Strategies Project, NIH/NIDA, 1999—. Mem.: Belmont- Harrison Superintendents' Assn. (chair 1983—85), Soc. for Prevention Rsch., Ariz. Sch. Administrators (life), Phi Delta Kappa (program chair 1978—80). Avocations: reading, writing, travel, skiing. Office: Southwest Interdisciplinary Research Con P O Box 873711 Tempe AZ 85287-3711 Office Phone: 480-945-5485. Personal E-mail: dustmangroup@yahoo.com. Business E-Mail: patricia.dustman@asu.edu.

DUSZAK, ROBERT S., optometrist; b. Abington, Pa., May 4, 1976; s. Richard L. and Mary Ellen Duszak; m. Carey G. Duszak, June 7, 2003. OD, Pa. Coll. Optometry, 2002. Resident Primary Care Optometry, The Eye Inst., Phila., 2002—03; staff optometrist Phila. Veterans Affairs Med. Ctr., 2003—, Nemours Health Clinic, Wilmington, 2003—; optometrist Del. Ophthalmology Cons., Wilmington, 2003—. Adj. prof. optometry Pa. Coll. Optometry, Elkins Pk., 2003—; cons. The Eye Inst., Phila., 2003—; academic referee Jour. Am. Optometric Assn.; presenter Clin. Grand Rounds The Eye Inst. Author: various opthalmic and optometry jours. Mem.: Nat. Assn. VA Optometrists, Am. Geriatrics Soc., Pa. Optometric Assn., Am. Acad. Optometry, Am. Optometric Assn., Lions Club. Office: Phila VAMC 38th and Woodland Ave Philadelphia PA 19104 Home: 2112 Pine St Apt 2 Philadelphia PA 19103

DUTCHER, JANICE JEAN PHILLIPS, oncologist; b. Bend, Oreg., Nov. 10, 1950; d. Charles Glen and MayBelle (Fluit) Phillips; m. John Dutcher, Sept. 8, 1971 (div. 1980). BA with honors, U. Utah, 1971; MD, U. Calif., Davis, 1975. Diplomate Am. Bd. Internal Medicine, Am. Bd. Med. Oncology. Intern Rush-Presbyn. St. Luke's Hosp., Chgo., 1975-76, resident, 1976-78; clin. assoc. Balt. Cancer Rsch., Nat. Cancer Inst., 1978-81, sr. investigator, 1981-82; asst. prof. U. Md., Balt., 1982, Albert Einstein Coll. Medicine, N.Y.C., 1983-86, assoc. prof., 1986-92, prof., 1992-98, course co-dir. Advances in Cancer Treatment Rsch. Manhattan, 1984-96; prof. medicine N.Y. Med. Coll., 1998—; assoc. dir. for clin. affairs Comprehensive Cancer Ctr., Our Lady of Mercy Med. Ctr., 1998—. Chmn. biol. response mod. com. Ea. Coop. Oncology Group, Madison, Wis., 1989-95, mem. exec. com., 1995-97, chair renal subcom., 1998—; mem. data safety com. Nat. Heart Lung Blood Inst., Bethesda, Md., 1990-95; mem. biologic response modifier study sect. Nat. Cancer Inst., Bethesda, 1988, 90, 94, 96; mem. NIH Consensus Panel on Early Melanoma, 1992; mem. FDA Oncology Drug Adv. Bd., 1995-99, chair FDA-ODAC, 1996-99, NCI subcom. D for program project rev., 1995-98, mem. subsplty. med. oncology bd. Am. Bd. Internal Medicine, 1997-2003; mem. NCI subcom. A for Cancer Ctrs., 1998-2002; mem. faculty AACR/ASCO Workshop on Clin. Trials Devel., 1996-2002, NIH Progress Rev. Group on Kidney Cancer, 2001. Editor: Handbook of Hematology/Oncology Emergencies, 1987, Modern Transfusion Therapy, 1990; sect. editor: Neoplastic Diseases of the Blood, 3d edit., 1996, 4th edit., 2003; mem. editl. bd. Jour. Immunotherapy, Med. Oncology, Jour. Clin. Oncology, Jour. Clin. Pharm., Ann. Intern. Med.; sect. editor Current Treatment Options in Oncology, 2000-, Chronic Leukemia, 2000—; contbr. articles to Blood, Leukemia, Jour. Clin. Oncology, Jour. Immunotherapy, Clin. Cancer Rsch., Soc. Am. Cancer Jour. Recipient Beecham award in Hematology So. Blood Club, 1983, Henry C. Moses Clin. Rsch. award Montefiore Med. Ctr., 1989, Outstanding Alumnus award U. Calif., Davis, 1989; named Outstanding Young Investigator Ea. Coop. Oncology Group, 1993; recipient numerous grants. Internat. Soc. Biol. Therapy (exec. com.). Achievements include findings related to management of alloimmunization to platelet transfusions, intensive maintenance of patients with acute leukemia, studies of new biologic response modifiers as antitumor drugs, management of renal cell cancer, melanoma and breast cancer, study and treatment with biologic antitumor agents. Address: Our Lady of Mercy Med Ctr Comprehensive Cancer Ctr 600 E 233rd St Bronx NY 10466-2604 Office Phone: 718-304-7200. E-mail: jpd4401@aol.com.

DUTCHER, JUDI, state auditor; b. MI, Nov. 27, 1962; married; two children. BA, U. of MN, 1984, JD, 1987. Asst. atty. City of Minneapolis, MN, 1987-88; atty. Lang, Pauly & Gregerson, Ltd, Minneapolis, MN, 1988-94; state auditor Minn. State, Saint Paul, 1995—. Bd. dirs. State Bd. of Investment, State Exec. Coun., Land Exch. Bd., Pub. Employees Retirement Assoc. Bd., MN Housing Fin. Agy., Rural Fin. Adminstrn. Bd., Bd. of Govt. Innovation and Cooperation.

DUTIKOW, IRENE VLADIMIROVNA, librarian; b. Tallinn, Estonia, Russia, Nov. 7, 1938; arrived in US, 1951; d. Vladimir A. and Ludmilla P. (Minjaev) Vekshin; m. Wsewolod M. Dutikow, July 26, 1959; children: Ekateriana, Larissa. BA, Hunter Coll., 1970; MLS, Queens Coll., 1975; MA, Hunter Coll., 1980. Cert. Libr. NY. Tech. asst. NYC Pub. Libr., 1970-78, libr., 1978-80; reference libr., head libr. Radio Free Europe-Radio Liberty, Inc., 1980-94; archivist Synod Bishops, 1994—2003; adminstr. Russian Orthodox Youth Com., Inc., Astoria, NY, 1995—. Author: K.I. Chukovsky, 1975, 2d edit., 1979; contbr. to profl. publs.; compiler scrapbooks on Greek and Brit. royal families. Mem. ALA, Am. Assn. Advancement of Slavic Studies, Spl. Library Assn., Congress Russian Ams. (pres. Flushing chpt. 1978-86), Slavic Heritage Council Am. (bd.dirs. 1979-85). Republican. Russian Orthodox. Avocations: collecting romonov dynasty items, miniature books, russian art and fiction. Home and Office: Russian Orthodox Youth Com Inc 25-36 37th St Astoria NY 11103-4228 Personal E-mail: dutikow@juno.com.

DUTILE, FERNAND NEVILLE, law educator; b. Lewiston, Maine, Feb. 15, 1940; s. Wilfred Joseph and Lauretta Blanche (Cote) D.; m. Brigid Dooley, Apr. 4, 1964; children: Daniel, Patricia. AB, Assumption Coll., 1962; JD, U. Notre Dame. 1965. Bar: Maine 1965. Atty. U.S. Dept. Justice, Washington, 1965-66; prof. law Cath. U. Am., Washington, 1966-71, U. Notre Dame Law Sch., Ind., 1971—. Bd. dirs. Ind. Lawyers Commn., Indpls., 1975-85, Legal Svcs. No. Ind., South Bend, 1975-83; dir. South Bend Work Release Ctr., 1973-75, Ind. Criminal Law Study Commn., 1991-99. Editor: Legal Education and Lawyer Competency, 1981; author: Sex, Schools and the Law, 1986; co-editor: Early Childhood Intervention and Juvenile Delinquency, 1982, The Prediction of Criminal Violence, 1987; co-author: State and Campus, 1984. Mem.: Athletics Reps. Assn. (exec. com. 2004—). Democrat. Roman Catholic.

DUTILE, ROBERT ARTHUR, executive management consultant; b. Stoneham, Mass., Dec. 26, 1959; s. Robert Arthur and Mary-Helene (Revane) D.; m. Ellen R. Ahearn, June 9, 1995. BS, Boston Coll., 1981. Cons. Monchik-Weber, Boston, 1981-83, Gately, Glew & Co., Wellesley, Mass., 1983-84; dir. MIS Reebok Internat., Ltd., Stoughton, Mass., 1984-91; sr. cons. Grant Thornton, LLP, Boston, 1992, mgr., 1992-95, sr. mgr., 1995-97, prin., 1997-99, Value Edge, 2005—; exec. v.p. Key Corp., Cleve., 1999—. Author: The Benchmarking Course, 1993. Mem. Am. Soc. Quality Control, Am. Mgmt. Assn., Am. Prodn. & Inventory Control Soc., Am. Mountain Guides Assn., Am. Alpine Club (life), Two/Ten Found, (life.). Avocations: writing, rock climbing, mountain climbing, golf. Office: Value Edge 36043 Heather Ln Solon OH 44139 Office Phone: 216-410-0359. Business E-Mail: robert_dutile@keybank.com, dutile@ameritech.net.

DUTRO, JOHN THOMAS, JR., geologist, paleontologist; b. Columbus, Ohio, May 20, 1923; s. John Thomas and Dorothy Durstine (Smith) D.; m. Nancy Ann Pence, Jan. 2, 1948; children: Sarah Dutro Cormier, Christopher, Susan Dutro Hultman. BA, Oberlin Coll., 1948; MS, Yale U., 1950, PhD, 1953; DSc, Denison U., 1993. Geologist, U.S. Geol. Survey, 1948-94, chief paleontology and stratigraphy br., 1962-68, mem. geologic names com., 1962-83; ret., 1994; emeritus vol. U.S. Geol. Survey, 1994—; rsch. assoc. Smithsonian Instn., 1962—. Vis. lectr. Am. U., 1957-59, George Washington U., 1962-63; mem. geology panel Bd. Civil Svc. Examiners, 1958-65; dir., field trip chmn. 9th Internat. Carboniferous Congress, 1979. Active area PTA, 1959-69, Boy Scouts Am., 1963-66, Fairlington Players, 1965-75. With Army Air Corps, 1943-46. Recipient Meritorious Svc. award U.S. Dept. Interior, 1983, Disting. Svc. award, 1996; Sterling fellow, 1949. Fellow AAAS (sec. sect. E 1981-85, Pacific divsn. pres. 1996-97), Arctic Inst. N.Am., Geol. Soc. London, Geol. Soc. Am. (assoc. editor 1974-82); mem. Am. Geol. Inst. (vis. geoscientist 1961-67, bd. dirs., sec.-treas. 1965-71), Paleontol. Soc. (tech. editor 1991), Palaeontol. Assn., Paleontol. Rsch. Inst. (trustee 1986—, v.p. 1990-91, pres. 1992-94), Internat. Paleontol. Assn., Paleontol. Soc. Washington (pres. 1955-56, 2003-04), Geol. Soc. Washington (sec. 1959-60, pres. 1978), Assn. Earth Sci. Editors (pres. 1989-90), Am. Polar Soc., Alaska Geol. Soc., Sigma Xi, Pick and Hammer Club, Cosmos Club, Yale Club (Washington). Democrat. Achievements include research in brachiopoda, Paleozoic biostratigraphy and biogeography of Arctic regions and western hemisphere, biostratigraphy of east Asia, and history of paleontology. Home: 5173 Fulton St NW Washington DC 20016-3448 Office: US Nat Mus Natural History Washington DC 20560-0137 Office Phone: 202-633-1322. Office Fax: 202-786-2832. Business E-Mail: dutro.tom@si.edu.

DUTSON, THAYNE R., university dean; b. Idaho Falls, Oct. 3, 1942; s. Rollo and Thelma (Fugal) D.; m. Joyce Cook, Dec. 19, 1962 (div. 1980); 1 child, Bradley; m. Margaret McCallum, June 23, 1989; children: Taylor, Alexandra. BS, Utah State U., 1966; MS, Mich. State U., 1969, PhD, 1971. Postdoctoral fellow U. Nottingham, Sutton Bonnington, Eng., 1971-72; prof. Tex. A&M U., College Station, 1972-83; dept. head Mich. State U., East Lansing, Mich., 1983-87; dir. agrl. exptl. sta. Oreg. State U., Corvallis, 1987-93, dean, dir. Coll. Agrl. Sci., 1993—. Editor: Advances in Meat Research (11 vols.) 1985-97; contbr. articles to profl. jours. Scoutmaster Boy Scouts Am., Mich., 1966-71. Fellow Inst. Food Technologists; mem. Am. Meat Sci. Assn. (bd. dirs. 1979-81, Disting. Rsch. award 1985), Am. Soc. Animal Sci. (Meat Rsch. award 1981), Coun. for Agr. Sci. and Tech. (pres. 1988), Phi Kappa Phi, Sigma Xi. Avocations: skiing, running, exercise, golf.

DUTT, KAMLA, medical educator; b. Lahore, Punjab, India; came to U.S., 1969; d. Gulzari Lal and Raj Bansi Dutt. BS with honors, Panjab U., Chandigarh, India, 1961, MS in Zoology with honors, 1962, PhD, 1970. Rsch. assoc. Harvard Med. Sch. Sidney Farber Cancer Ctr., Boston, 1972-76; rsch. assoc. Eye Inst. Retinal Fedn., Boston, 1977-80; sr. rsch. assoc. Yale Med. Ctr., New Haven, 1980-81, Emory U., Atlanta, 1981-82; asst. prof. Morehouse Sch. Medicine, Atlanta, 1983-89, assoc. prof., 1989—2001, prof., 2001—. Sci. adv. bd. Fernbank Sci. Ctr., Atlanta. Contbr. numerous articles to sci. jours.; author short stories (in Hindi); prodr., actor 3 maj. plays, Atlanta; actor 11 maj. plays, India. Bd. dirs. VSEI (vol. fundraising orgn. for edn. in India), 1973-78; v.p. Indian Am. Cultural Assn., 1985; podium spkr., participant King Week, 1990, 91, 93; spkr. Gandhi Day Celebration, 1984, 85; key participant Intercultural Conf., 1990; main participant joint document Women's Perspective; active human rights issues; stake holder Vision 20/20 Collaborative State of Ga., diversity and edn. coms., 1995. Hindu. Achievements include establishment of human ocular cell lines by gene trasfaction, used as model for study of eye diseases and tissue engineering. Office: Morehouse Sch Medicine 720 Westview Dr SW Atlanta GA 30310-1458 Office Phone: 404-752-1769. Business E-Mail: kdutt@msm.edu.

DUTTA, HIRAN MOYEE, biologist, educator; b. Patna, Bihar, India; came to the U.S., 1966; s. Trailokha N. and Sarujobala (Dutta) D.; m. Ashok K. Dutt, Jan. 19, 1958; children: Rinku Dutt, Jhumku D. Kohtz. PhD, Leiden U., 1968. Asst. prof., chmn. dept. sci. N.H. Coll., Manchester, 1966-68; asst. prof., chmn. dept. biology Walsh Coll., North Canton, Ohio, 1968-70; vis. asst. prof. Kent (Ohio) State U., 1970-75, asst. prof., 1975-80, assoc. prof., 1981-89, prof., 1990—. Dir. exchange student program Kent State U. and Leiden U. (The Netherlands), 1978—; vis. prof. Inst. Zoology Jagellonian U., Krakow, Poland, 1987, Polish Acad. Scis. Inst. Zoology, 1989, Paradenia U., Sri Lanka, 1991; invited spkr. ann. conf. India Sci. Congress Assn., 1994, 2001, India Inst. Sci., 1995, Internat. Symposium on Water/Air Transitions in Biology, 1996. Author: Functional Morphology of the Head of Anabas testudineus, 1968; editor: Fish Morphology Horizon of New Research, 1996, Vertebrate Functional Morphology: Horizon of Research in the 21st Century, 2001; editor (book series) Biological Systems in Vertebrates 2002...Continued; contbr. chpts. to books, articles to profl. jours. Faculty advisor Kent State Indian Assn., 1976-82, Kent State U. Bangladesh Student Assn., 1983-89. Fulbright lecturing/rsch. fellow, 1991; Smithsonian Instn. grantee, 1990-93. Mem. AAAS, Indian Assn. Freshwater Biology (mem. editorial bd.), Ichthologists and Herpetologists, Ohio Acad. Sci., Soc. Environ. Toxicology & Chemistry, Soc. for Integrative and Comparative Biology, Indian Assn. Greater Ak ron (v.p. 1979, pres. 1980), Cleve. Bengali Cultural Soc. (bd. trustees 1998—). Avocations: music, travel. Office: Kent State U Dept Biology 256 Cunningham Hl Kent OH 44242-0001 Fax: 330-672-3713. Office Phone: 330-672-3613. Business E-Mail: hdutta@kent.edu.

DUTTA, MANORANJAN, economics professor; b. India, Oct. 1, 1925; naturalized, U.S., 1972; m. Kanak Dutta; 1 child, Kavery Dutta Kaul. PhD, U. Pa., 1962. Asst. prof. econs. Rutgers U., New Brunswick, N.J., 1962-64, assoc. prof. econs., 1964-76, prof. econs., 1976—. Hon. rsch. prof. Shanghai Acad. Social Scis., 1988; vis. scholar Japan Ministry Fin., De Nederlandsche Bank, Der Deutsche Bundesbank, Banque de France, 2000; lectr., asst. prof. various colls. W. Bengal Edn. Svc. affiliated to U. Calcutta, 1951—58; cons. Mathematica, Princeton, NJ, 1969—70; adj. prof. Pace U., NY, 1975; dir., pres. bd. trustees Am. Com. Asian Econ. Studies; dir. Coun. State Econ. Studies; chmn. Nat. Adv. Coun. S. Asian Affairs; spkr., presenter and vis. lectr.in field at various univs. in Europe, N.Am., Asia, Australia, New Zealand. Editor: Jour. of Asian Economics, 1990—; contbr. articles to profl. jours. and books; author, co-author, editor, co-editor: Econometric Methods, 1976, Economic Regionalization in the Asia-Pacific, 1999; editor: (jour.) Rsch. Asian Econ. Studies, 1985—2002. 1980 census adv. com. for Asia-Pacific Ams. Recipient cert. of Appreciation, Bur. Census U.S. Dept. Commerce, 1982, Honor award, Assn. Asian Indians in Am., 1986, Honored Am. award, Congl. resolution signed by Pres. Reagan, 1986; fellow Fulbright-Smith-Mundt, 1958, 1959, Faculty Rsch., Rutgers U., 1967, 1987, Nat. Sci. Found., 1973, 1976; grantee, U.S. Dept. Labor, 1978, Rutgers U. Rsch. Coun., 1979, N.J. State Dept. Industry and Labor, 1979, Ford Found., 1980, 1981, Port Authority N.Y. and N.J., 1981, 1985, AT&T, 1981, John D. and Catherine T. MacArthur Found., 1988, USAID, 1994, U.N. Devel. Program, 1996, Asia Devel. Bank, 1998. Mem.: AAUP, AAAS, Fulbright Sr. Specialists' Program, Calif. Inst. Internat. Studies, N.Y. Acad. Scis., Econometric Soc., Ea. Econ. Assn., Am. Com. Asian Econ. Studies, Assn. Indian Econ. Studies, Asia Soc. N.Y., Am. Assn. Asian Studies, Am. Statis. Assn., Am. Econ. Assn. Office: Rutgers U Faculty Arts and Scis 75 Hamilton St New Brunswick NJ 08901-1248 Fax: 732-932-1558. Office Phone: 732-932-7054. E-mail: mdutta@rci.rutgers.edu.

DUTTA, MITRA, physicist, educator; b. Patna, Bihar, India, July 3, 1953; came to U.S., 1976; d. Dhiren N. and Aruna (Ray) D.; m. Sudhin Datta, Apr. 26, 1983. BS, U. Delhi (India), MSc, 1973; PhD, U. Cin., 1981. Lectr. Coll. Arts, Sci. and Tech., Kingston, Jamaica, 1973-76, U. West Indies, Kingston, 1973-76; rsch. assoc. Purdue U., West Lafayette, Ind., 1981-83; sr. rsch. assoc. CCNY, N.Y.C., 1983-86; rsch. engr. Systematic Gen. Corp., Eatontown, N.J., 1986-88; rsch. physicist and leader optoelectronics team Army Rsch. Lab. Electronics and Power Sources Directorate, Ft. Monmouth, NJ, 1988—2001, coord. NSF, 1990—2001; prof. U. Ill., Chgo., 2001—, head, electrical & computer engring. dept., 2001—. Mem. JDL Reliance Sub-Sub Panel on Photonic Devices, 1991—, tech. adv. com. on narotechnology Univ. Rsch. Iniative, 1992—, condensed matter adv. group, ARO, 1993—. Contbr. approximately 60 articles to Phys. Rev., Applied Physics Letters, IEEE Jour. Quantum Electronics. Nat. Merit scholar Govt. of India, 1968-71, Univ. Grants scholar Univ. Grants Commn., Delhi, India, 1971-73, R & D Achievement award, U.S. Army, 1990, 92, 94, ETDL Narold Jacobs award, 1991, Nat. Achievement award, Soc. for Women Engrs., 2003. Mem. IEEE (sr. mem.), Am. Phys. Soc., Optical Soc. Am., Sigma Xi. Achievements include 2 patents in field. Office: U Ill at Chgo 851 S Morgan M/C 154 Chicago IL 60607 E-mail: dutta@ece.uic.edu.

DUTTA, RAJIV, Internet company executive; BA with hons. in Econs., Delhi (India) U.; MBA, Claremont (Calif.) U. With Bio-Rad Labs., Inc., 1988—98; controller worldwide sales KLA-Tencor, 1998; fin. dir. eBay Inc., San Jose, Calif., 1998—99, v.p. fin., investor rels., 1999—2001, sr. v.p., CFO, 2001—. Bd. dir. Jamadat Mobile Inc. Office: eBay Inc 2145 Hamilton Ave San Jose CA 95125-5905*

DUTTA, SISIR K., molecular biologist, researcher; b. Rajshahi, India, Aug. 28, 1928; s. Krishna K. and Satyabati Dutta; m. Minati Dutta, July 1, 1955; children: Mahasweta, Basabi Dipanla. BS in Plant Genetics and Breeding, Dacca U., 1949; MS in Biochem. Genetics, Kans. State U., 1958, PhD in Biochem. Genetics, 1960. Rsch. scientist, dept. genetics & breeding Dept. Agriculture, Govt. of W. Bengal, India, 1949—53; dir., chief resident officer Malaysian Pineapple Industry Bd., 1961—64; asst. prof., biology Tex. So. U.,

Houston, 1965—66; chmn., dept. sci. & math., assoc. prof., biology Jarvis Christian Coll., Tex., 1966—67; vis. scientist, biochem. genetics lab. Rockefeller U., NY, 1968—69; vis. scientist Pasteur Inst., Paris, 1974—75; faculty fellow, molecular genetics lab. NIH, Bethesda, Md., 1977—78; prof, dept. biology Howard U., Washington, 1967—; specialist in biotech. UN, 1981—82; collaborator U.S. Dept. Agriculture, Beltsville, Md., 1985—. Spkr. in field. Mem.: AAAS, U.S. Bioelectromagnetic Soc., Nat. Inst. Sci., Mycological Soc. Am., Tex. Acad. Sci., Am. Inst. Biol. Scis., Am. Horticultural Soc., Am. Soc. Phytopathology, Am. Botanical Soc., Am. Soc. Eniron. Mutagens, Internat. Inst. Microwave Power, Genetics Soc. Am., Indian Sci. Congress (life), Beta Kappa Chi. Home: 5505 Thornbush Ct Bethesda MD 20814 Office: Howard Univ Dept Biology 415 College St NW Washington DC 20059

DUTTON, DIANA CHERYL, lawyer; b. Sherman, Tex., June 27, 1944; d. Roy G. and Monett D.; m. Anthony R. Grindl, July 8, 1974. BS, Georgetown U., 1967; JD, U. Tex., 1971. Bar: Tex. 1971. Regional counsel U.S. EPA, Dallas, 1975-79, dir. enforcement div., 1979-81; ptnr., head firm-wide environ. practice, mem. Dallas practice com. Akin, Gump, Strauss, Hauer & Feld, L.L.P., Dallas, 1981—. Bd. dirs. Girls Inc., 2004—, Mental Health Assn. Dallas, 2005—; chair Greater Dallas Chamber Environ. Com., 2001. Named a Tex. Super Lawyer, Tex. Monthly Mag., 2003, 2004; named one of Best Lawyers in Dallas, D Mag., 2001—04, Ams. Leading Bus. Lawyers, Chambers USA, 2003—05, Top 50 Tex. Women Attys., Tex. Monthly Mag., 2003. Mem. ABA, Tex. Bar Assn. (chmn. environ. and natural resources law sect. 1985-86), Dallas Bar Assn. (chmn. environ. law sect. 1984), Dallas Bar Found., Mental Health Assn. Dallas (bd.dirs. 2005—). Episcopalian. Office: Akin Gump Strauss Hauer & Feld LLP 1700 Pacific Ave Ste 4100 Dallas TX 75201-4675 Office Phone: 214-969-2855. Office Fax: 214-969-4343. E-mail: ddutton@akingump.com.

DUTTON, FRANK ELROY, data processing executive, writer; b. Warren, Ohio, Nov. 16, 1946; s. Robert Wade and Ann Victoria (Sessions) D.; m. Nancy June Gephart, Nov. 6, 1965 (div. 1981); children: Cynthia, Frank, Robert; m. Margaret Elizabeth Sessions, Dec. 16, 1981 (div. Dec. 1987); m. Paula Kay Gately, Feb. 14, 1992 (div. Sept. 1994). With sales dept. Zylco Cutlery Rena Ware Distrs., Warren, 1964-68; advt. salesman Directory Dept. Ohio Bell Telephone Co., Cuyahoga Falls, 1968-69; pvt. practice residential constrn. Warren and Hammond (La.), 1970-74; technician J. Ray McDermott & Co., New Orleans, 1974-83, McDermott Internat., Antwerp, Belgium, 1975, McDermott SE Asia, Singapore, 1981-83; owner Computer Time, Inc., Hammond, 1983-85; mgr. tech. services Industry Programs, Inc., Houston, 1985-86; owner Affordable Automation, Houston, 1987-89; program, analyst The Phillips Group, Stafford, Tex., 1989-92; owner software and hardware integrator IHMS Software Support, Many, La., 1992—; owner computer software, internet web site design hosting Fred Software, Many, 1998—. Cons. in computer communications Southmark Industries, Houston, 1986-87, Crown Broadcasting, Hammond, La., 1987-89, Bee-Line Delivery Svc., Houston, 1986-89. Author, designer various computer games, utility software programs, computer software for radio stas., computer software for retail furniture stores, Turbo Pascal Toolbox, 1988 (award of disting. tech. communication 1989, award of excellence Internat. Soc. Tech. Communication 1989), French transl., 1988, Portuguese trans., 1990, French trans., 1990; contbr. articles to profl. jours. Served with USAR, 1966—72. Recipient semi-finalist award, Global Info. Infrastructure, 1999. Mem.: Am. Mensa Soc. Avocation: photography. Home and Office: 80 Anna St Many LA 71449

DUTTON, JOHN ALTNOW, meteorologist, educator; b. Detroit, Sept. 11, 1936; s. Carl Evans and Velma (Altnow) D.; m. Frances Elizabeth (Andrews), Jan. 13, 1962; children: Christopher Evan, John Andrews, Jan Frederik. BS, U. Wis., 1958; MS, 1959, PhD, 1962. Mem. faculty Pa. State U., Univ. Pk., 1965—2002, assoc. prof. meteorology, 1968—71, prof., 1971—2002, head dept. meteorology, 1981—86, dean Coll. Earth and Mineral Sci., 1986—2002; chmn. Weather Ventures Ltd., 2000—, pres., 2005—. Expert aero. sys. div. USAF, 1965-71; vis. scientist Riso Rsch. Establishment, Roskilde, Denmark, 1971-72, summer 1975, 78-79; vis. prof. Tech. U., Denmark, 1978-79; v.p. UCAR Found., 1986-87, pres., 1987-95, chmn. bd. dirs., 1995-2001; trustee Mt. Nittany Med. Ctr., 1996—, mem. exec. com., 1999—. Author: The Ceaseless Wind: An Intro. to the Theory of Atmospheric Motion, 1976, 2d edit., 1986 (reprinted as Dynamics of Atmospheric Motion, 1995); (with H.A. Panofsky) Atmospheric Turbulence: Models and Methods for Engring. Applications, 1984; assoc. editor: Meteorol. Monographs, 1973-79, editor, 1979-84; contbg. articles to profl. journals. Trustee Univ. Corp. for Atmospheric Rsch., 1974-81, sec., 1977, treas., 1978-79, vice-chmn., 1980-84, chmn. unidata steering com., 1982-86, chmn. unidata policy com., 1986-88; chmn. long range planning com. NSF, Univ. Corp. for Atmospheric Rsch., 1986-87; mem. bd. atmospheric sci. and climate NRC, 1982-83, 88-97, chmn. bd., 1989-97, mem. internat. space yr. planning com., 1986-89, panel of experts on earth sci. and tech. Internat. Space Yr. 1992, 1989-92, space sci. bd. com. on earth sci., 1987-89, mem. space studies bd., 1989-93, chmn. task group priorities space rsch. of space studies bd., 1989-94, mem. nat. weather svc. modernization com., 1989-95; mem. Nat. Aviation Weather Svc. Com., 1994-95; mem. com. long term retention sci. and tech. records of fed. govt., 1993-95; ex-officio mem. Com. on Global Change Rsch., 1995-97, chmn. com. on aeronautics rsch. and tech. for environ. compatibility, 2000-02; mem. space and earth sci. adv. com. NASA, 1982-86, earth system sci. com., 1983-87, ctr. sci. assessment team, 1986-88. 1st lt. USAF, 1962-65. Fellow AAAS (sect. atmospheric and hydrospheric sci.), fellow, Am. Meteorol. Soc. (councillor 1986-88, chmn. publ. commn. 1984-85); mem. Math. Assn. Am., Soc. Indsl. and Applied Math., Sigma Xi, Phi Kappa Phi, Theta Delta Chi. Home: 240 Mt Pleasant Dr Boalsburg PA 16827-1810 Office: Pa State U 508 Walker Bldg University Park PA 16802-2710

DUTTON, LESLIE RUTH, music educator; b. Odessa, Tex., Dec. 1, 1968; d. Tommy Joe and Esther Ruth Dutton; m. Bryan Allen, June 11, 1988 (div. May 11, 1999). MusB, East Tex. State U., 1992, MusM, 1994. Voice instr. Panola Coll., Carthage, Tex., 1994-96; choir dir. Covenant Presbyn. Ch., Lubbock, Tex., 1996—; assoc. dir. orgnl. mgmt. Lubbock Christian U., 1996-99. Mem. Nat. Assn. Tchrs. Singing, Nat. Music Tchrs. Assn., Sigma Alpha Iota. Lutheran. Home: 53 Linwood Dr Marshall TX 75672-2383

DUTTON, ROBERT D., state official; b. Lincoln, Nebr., Oct. 13, 1950; m. Andrea Dutton; 1 child, Kara. AA, L.A. Valley Coll., 1972. Pres., CEO property mgmt. co., 1972—; pres., CEO Dutton & Assocs., Inc., 1992—; mem. Calif. Rep. Party, 1990—; state assembly mem. Dist. 63 Calif. State Assembly, 2002—. Mem. health com.; mem. ins. com.; vice chair VA com.; commr. Rancho Cucamonga Pub. Safety Commn., San Bernardino County Econ. and Cmty. Devel., Inland Empire of Calif., 1998—; mem. Calif. Rep. Party, 1990—. Mem. San Bernardino County Sheriff's Coun., 1990—; chair West End and Rancho Cucamonga Family YMCA. Sgt. USAR, 1969—74. Mem.: Rancho Cucamonga C. of C. (past pres. 1982—), Calif. State Chamber Small Bus. Com., Rep. Nat. Com. (life). Republican. Roman Catholic. Mailing: Rm 3149 PO Box 942849 Sacramento CA 94249 Office: Ste 210 8577 Haven Ave Rancho Cucamonga CA 91730 Office Phone: 916-651-4031.

DUTTON, STEPHEN JAMES, lawyer; b. Chgo., Sept. 20, 1942; S. James H. and Marjorie C. (Smith) D.; m. Ellen W. Lee; children: Patrick, Mark. BS, Ill. Inst. Tech., 1965; JD, Ind. U., 1969. Bar: Ind. 1969, U.S. Dist. Ct. (so. dist.) Ind. 1969, U.S. Ct. Appeals (7th cir.) 1972, U.S. Ct. Appeals (D.C. cir.) 1980, U.S. Supreme Ct. 1978. With McHale, Cook & Welch, P.C., Indpls., 1969-86, Dutton & Overman, P.C., 1986-91, Dutton & Bailey, P.C., 1991-94, Locke, Reynolds, Boyd & Weisell, 1994-99, Leagre Chandler & Millard LLP, Indpls., 1999—2003, Barnes & Thorburg, Indpls., 2003—. Mem. Com. on Law of Cyberspace Bus. Law Sect.; chair TechPoint, Inc., 2005—. Mem. ABA. Office: 11 S Meridian St Indianapolis IN 46208 Office Phone: 317-231-7542. Business E-Mail: sdutton@btlaw.com.

DUTZ-KOHOUT, ELFRIEDE, physician, educator; b. Vienna, June 23, 1926; came to U.S., 1974; d. Leopold and Valerie (Schiffer) Kohout; children: Peter, Michael. MD, U. Vienna, 1952. Intern Miseri Cordia Hosp., Edmonton, Alta., Can., 1954-55; resident Nassau County Hosp., L.I., N.Y., 1956-58, Delafield Hosp., N.Y., 1958-59; fellow Columbia U., N.Y., 1959-60, Mt. Sinai Hosp.; from asst. prof. to prof. clin. pathology Pahlavi U., Shiraz, Iran, 1960-76; prof. pathology Med. Coll. Va., Richmond, 1974-94. Grantee NIH, 1964. Fellow Royal Soc. Pathology, Am. Soc. Pathology, Am. Soc. Clin. Pathology, Am. Soc. Microbiology, Am. Soc. Tropical Medicine. Avocations: antiques, music, archeology, travel, paintings. Home: 111 N 28th St Richmond VA 23223-7325

DUUS, PETER, retired historian; b. Wilmington, Del., Dec. 27, 1933; s. Hans Christian and Mary Anita (Pennypacker) D.; m. Masayo Umezawa, Nov. 25, 1964; 1 child, Erik. AB magna cum laude, Harvard U., 1955, PhD, 1965; MA, U. Mich., 1959. Asst. prof. history Washington U., St. Louis, 1964-66, Harvard U., Cambridge, Mass., 1966-70; assoc. prof. history Claremont (Calif.) Grad. Sch., 1970-73, Stanford (Calif.) U., 1973-78, prof., 1978—2003, ret., 2003. Author: Party Rivalry and Political Change in Taishó Japan, 1968, Feudalism in Japan, 1969, The Rise of Modern Japan, 1976, The Cambridge History of Japan, Vol. 6: The Twentieth Century, 1989, The Japanese Informal Empire in China, 1989, The Abacus and the Sword: The Japanese Penetration of Korea, 1995, The Japanese Discovery of America, 1996, Modern Japan, 1997. Exec. sec. Inter-Univ. for Japanese Lang. Studies, Tokyo, 1974-90; bd. dirs. Com. for Internat. Exch. of Scholars, Washington, 1987-91. Served with U.S. Army, 1955-57. NEH sr. fellow, 1972-73, Japan Found. postdoctoral fellow, 1976-77, Fulbright rsch. fellow, 1981-82, 94-95, Japan Found. rsch. fellow, 1986-87. Fellow AAAS, mem. Assn. for Asian Studies (bd. dirs. 1972-75, nominating com. 1983, v.p. 1999-2000, pres. 2000-01), Am. Hist. Assn. (bd. editors 1984-87). Home: 818 Esplanada Way Palo Alto CA 94305-1015 Office: Stanford U History Dept Stanford CA 94305 Business E-Mail: pduus@leland.stanford.edu.

DUVAL, DANIEL WEBSTER, manufacturing executive; b. Cin., May 27, 1936; s. Harry A. and Wilda (Webster) V.; m. Sue Ann Howard, July 20, 1962; children: Laurie Ann, Paula Lee, Christopher Webster. BA, U. Cin., 1960. V.p. staff elec. products div. Midland-Ross, Cleve., 1976-78, group v.p., 1979-81, exec. v.p., 1981-83, pres., chief operating officer, 1983-86; pres., chief exec. officer Robbins & Myers Inc., Dayton, Ohio, 1986-98, also bd. dirs., ret. vice chmn., bd. dirs., 1999. Bd. dirs. Arrow Electronics, Gosiger, Inc., Dayton, The Manitowac Co., Wis.; chmn. Arrow Electronics, Inc., N.Y.C., 2002—. Patentee container coupling mechanism. Bd. trustees Wright State U., 1991-2000, Wright State U. Found.; pres. Civitan Found., Ariz., 1973-74, Dayton Ballet Assn., 1990-93; participant Leadership Cleve.; bd. dirs. U.S. Air and Trade Show; intern, pres. and CEO Robbins & Myers, Inc., Dayton, Ohio., 2003-2004. Mem. Dayton Racquet Club. Republican. Roman Catholic. Home: 829 Timberlake Ct Kettering OH 45429 Office: 1480 Kettering Tower Dayton OH 45423-1001

DUVAL, DAVID ROBERT, professional golfer; b. Jacksonville, Fla., Nov. 9, 1971; Student, Ga. Inst. Tech. Profl. golfer PGA, 1993—. Mem. Walker Cup team, 1991, Presidents Cup team, 1996, 98, Ryder Cup Team, 1999. Winner Nike Wichita Open, 1993, Nike Tour Championship, 1993, Michelob Championship at Kingsmill, 1997, Walt Disney World/Oldsmobile Classic, 1997, The Tour Championship, 1997, Tucson Chrysler Classic, 1998, Shell Houston Open, 1998, NEC World Series of Golf, 1998, Michelob Championship at Kingsmill, 1998, Mercedes Championship, 1999, Bob Hope Chrysler Classic, 1999, The Players Championship, 1999, Bell South Classic, 1999, Ryder Cup, 1999; recipient Dave Williams award, 1993, Jasper award, Jacksonville, 1996; named Collegiate Player of Yr., 1993. Avocations: reading, fly fishing, surfing, skiing, baseball. Office: PGA of Am Box 109601 100 Ave of Champions Palm Beach Gardens FL 33410

DUVAL, STANWOOD RICHARDSON, JR., judge; b. New Orleans, Feb. 8, 1942; BA, La. State U., 1964, JD, 1966. Ptnr. Duval, Arceneaux & Lewis, 1966-94, Duval, Funderburk, Sundberry & Lovell, L.L.P., 1966-94; asst. city atty. Terrebonne Parish Consol. Govt., 1970-72, parish atty., 1988-92; dist. judge U.S. Dist. Ct. (ea. dist.), New Orleans, 1994—. Mem. Indigent Def. Bd., 1976-82; elected La. Constnl. Conv., 1973, mem. exec. br. com., com. to write rules of procedure. Mem. Terrebone Parish. Mem. ABA (adv. com. appellate rules 1997-2003), La. Law Inst. (coun. 1996-2001), Tulane Inns Ct. (pres. 2001-04). Avocations: travel, scuba diving, fishing, performing arts. Office: US Dist Ct Ea Dist 500 Poydras St New Orleans LA 70130 Office Phone: 504-589-7540.

DUVAL-CARRIÉ, EDOUARD, artist; b. Haiti, 1954; Student, Ecole Nat. Superieure des Beaux Arts, Paris, 1988—89; BA, U. Loyola Montreal, 1978; student, McGill U., U. Montreal. Resident Arts Internat., Found. Claude Monet, Giverny, France, 1998. One-man shows include Art Ctr., Port-au-Prince, Haiti, 1980, Franz Bader Gallery, Washington, 1982, Paul Waggoner Gallery, Chgo., 1983, Anderson Gallery, Va. Commonwealth U., Richmond, 1986, Brent Gallery, Houston, 1987, Nicole Gallery, Chgo., 1987, Malraux Gallery, L.A., 1991, Armand Gallery, Paris, 1991, Mus. de Arte Contemporaneo de Monterrey, Mex., 1992, Porter Randall Gallery, San Diego, 1994, Lakaye Gallery, L.A., 1994, 1998, Galeria Fernando Quintana, Bogota, Colombia, 1994, Gutierez Fine Arts, Miami Beach, Fla., 1994, Mus. du Coll. St. Pierre, Port-au-Prince, 1996, Polk Mus. Art, Lakeland, Fla., 1997, Quintana Gallery, Miami, 1997, David Beitzel Gallery, Project Room, N.Y.C., 1997, exhibited in group shows at Southeastern Ctr. Contemporary Art, Winston-Salem, 1997, Palacio del Segundo Cabo, Havana, Cuba, 1997, Mus. African Am. Art, Tampa, Fla., 1998, Internat. Arts Club, Chgo., 1973, Ramscale Gallery, N.Y.C., 1998, Taller Boricua Gallery, Julia de Burgos Cultural Ctr., 1998, Miami-Dade Cultural Ctr., 1999, Miami Art Mus., 2000, New Work Gallery, 2000, Bernice Steinbaum Gallery, Miami, 2002, numerous others, Represented in permanent collections; illustrator Imagen mag., 1995; illustrator Cantos to Blood and Honey, 1997, numerous others; contbr. articles to profl. jours. South Fla. Cultural Consortium Visual Art fellow, 1995, So. Arts Fedn. Visual Art fellow, 1996. E-mail: duvalcarrie@bellsouth.net.

DUVALL, CHARLES PATTON, retired internist, retired oncologist; b. Evanston, Ill., June 16, 1936; s. Charles Fleming and Edith (Osgood) Duvall; m. Nancy Ash, June 21, 1958; children: Lawrence Charles, Stephen Rogers, Doulgas Patton, Lauren Duvall Meacham. AB, Cornell U., 1958; MD, U. Rochester, N.Y., 1962. Diplomate Am. Bd. Internal Medicine, Am. Bd. Med. Oncology. Intern Yale New Haven Med. Ctr., 1962-63; resident in internal medicine U. Rochester, 1963-64; clin. assoc. Nat. Cancer Inst., NIH, Bethesda, Md., 1964-66; resident in medicine Georgetown U. Hosp., Washington, 1966-67, USPHS spl. fellow in hematology, 1967-68; physician Foxhall Internists, Washington, 1968-2000; ret., 2000. Clin. prof. medicine Georgetown U. Hosp., Washington, 1968—2000; vice chmn. dept. medicine Sibley Hosp., Washington, 1987—90, chmn., 1990—91; mem. emeritus staff Washington Hosp. Ctr., 1988—. Contbr. articles to profl. jours. Chmn. bd. dirs. Blue Cross Blue Shield Nat. Capital area, Washington, 1986—94, Group Hospitalization Med. Svcs., Inc., Washington, 1986—94; vice chmn., trustee Vols. Medicine Inst., Hilton Head Island, 1998—2002; elder Bradley Hills Presbyn. Ch., Hilton Head Island, SC, 2003—05, v.p. men of ch.; deacon 1st Presbyn. Ch., pres., mem., 2005—. Lt. comdr. USPHS, 1964—66. Recipient 5 Yr. Svc. award, Am. Cancer Soc., 1978, President Emeritus hon. designation, ACP, 2005. Master: ACP (Outpatient Tchg. award 1998, Laureate award 2000); mem.: AMA (del. 1988—93, coun. legis. 1991—2000, coun. legis. chmn. 1996—97), Clin. Pathologic Soc. (pres. 1995—96), Osler Soc. DC (pres. 1978—79), Sect. Coun. Internal Medicine (chmn. 1987—88), Spltys. and Svcs. Soc. (pres. 1990—91, sect. coun. IM), Am. Soc. Internal Medicine (pres. DC chpt. 1977, pres. rsch. found. 1987—88, pres.-elect 1988—89, pres. 1989—90, spkr. ho. of dels. 1991—95, chmn. federated coun. internal medicine 1989—90, Spl. Recognition award 1979), Bear Creek Club (pres. S.C.), Country Club Hilton Head, Congl. Country Club, Sigma Chi, Alpha Omega Alpha. Republican. Presbyterian. Avocations: golf, skiing, photography, painting. Home: 316 Seabrook Dr Hilton Head Island SC 29926-1979

DUVALL, DEBRA, school system administrator; Asst. supt. elem. edn. Mesa Pub. Sch., Ariz., 1987—95, asst. supt. curriculum and instrn., 1987—95, acting assoc. supt., 1995—2000, supt., 2000—. Chair Mesa Cmty. Coll. Commn. on Excellence in Edn., 2001—03. Recipient Disting. Adminstr. award (Supt. Divsn.), Ariz. Sch. Adminstrs. Assn., 2003. Office: Mesa Pub Sch #101 63 E Main St Mesa AZ 85201-7400 Office Phone: 480-472-0000. E-mail: dlduvall@mpsaz.org.

DUVALL, HOLLIE JEAN, music educator; b. Greensburg, Pa., Dec. 8, 1953; d. William Gilbert Smail and Betty Jane Rygiel; m. Charles Timothy Duvall, Feb. 18, 1977; children: Charles Timothy, Renee Jean. B in Music Edn., Seton Hill Coll., 1995; MA, Ind. U. of Pa., 1997. Pa. instrnl. cert. in music edn. Music dir. Ch. of God (Holiness), Greensburg, Pa., 1970—; wedding and fashion show cons. Greensburg, 1982-98; interior designer, 1982—; freelance pianist, 1985—; instr. piano and voice Pvt. Studio, Greensburg, 1985—; prof. music Westmoreland County C.C., Youngwood, Pa., 1996—, music coord., 1998—; prof. music C.C. of Allegheny County, West Mifflin, Pa., 1999—, Pa. State U., Fayette, Pa., 2002—. Judge-fine arts Keystone Christian Edn. Assn., Pa., 1989—, Ea. Nazarene Regional Div., Greensburg, Pa., 1990, Am. Fedn. Women's Clubs, Greensburg, 1995-97; choral clinician Pa. State Cooperative Ext., 2004. Reviewer in field. Sunday sch. tchr. Ch. of God (Holiness), Greensburg, 1975—. Scholar, AAUW, 1993, PEO Sisterhood, 1994. Mem. Profl. Music Educator's Assn., Alpha Sigma Lambda (Scholarship award 1992). Republican. Avocations: reading, floral arranging, decorating. Office: Westmoreland County CC 400 Armbrust Rd Youngwood PA 15697-1801 Personal E-mail: hollie_duvall@yahoo.com. Business E-Mail: hjd11@psu.edu.

DUVALL, JOHN EDWARD, law librarian; b. Washington, July 18, 1947; s. John Bernard and Barbara Annette (Bangham) D. BA in French, U. Md., 1970, MA in French, 1972, MLS, 1974. Bibliographic searcher George Washington U. Library, Washington, 1975; libr. Nat. Press Club, Washington, 1975-77, Washington Met. Area Transit Authority, 1975-79; adminstrv. analyst Hogan & Hartson, Washington, 1979—. Mem. ALA, Spl. Librs. Assn., Phi Beta Kappa, Kappa Delta Pi. Republican. Methodist. Home: 14605 Dowling Dr Burtonsville MD 20866-1711 Office: Hogan & Hartson 555 13th St NW Washington DC 20004-1109 Office Phone: 202-637-8713. Business E-Mail: jeduvall@hhlaw.com.

DUVALL, LAWRENCE DELBERT, insurance company executive; b. Jacobsburg, Ohio, Mar. 5, 1942; s. Lawrence and Lillian Elizabeth (Brocklehurst) D.; m. Sandra Lee Parrish, May 16, 1970. BS in Indsl. Mgmt., Ohio State U., 1964; MBA, Columbia U., 1976; BS in Meterology, Northwestern U., 1966. Cert. constrn. engr., NY. Exec. mgmt. trainee Crum & Forster, NYC, 1967-69; inland marine underwriter, mgr. Am. Home Assurance Co., Constrn. Divsn., NYC, 1969-73; southwestern regional property mgr. Nat. Union Fire Ins. Co., Dallas, 1973-76, Am. Home Assurance Co., Dallas, 1973-76; mgr. Ins. Co. of the State Pa., 1976-82; atty.-in-fact A. I. Lloyds Ins. Co., 1976-82; v.p. A.I. G. Energy Inc., NYC, 1982-86; sr. v.p. Starr Tech. Risk Agy., Inc., NYC, 1986—94; dir. Worldwide Utilities, NYC, 1994—2002; v.p. Am. Internat. Underwriters, NYC, 1994—2002; pres. EuroAm Group, Colorado Springs, 2002—. Bd. dirs. USMC Dependent Scholarship Fund, 1987—. With USMC, 1963-67, Vietnam Decorated Silver Star, Purple Heart with gold star; Medal of Merit (Vietnam); named Constrn. Cons. of Yr., U. Wis., 1971. Mem. Soc. Petroleum Engrs., Conf. Spl. Risk Underwriters, Tex. Ins. Adv. Assn. Avocations: automobile racing, flying. Home: 390 Paisley Dr Colorado Springs CO 80906-8251 Office: Ste 155 445c E Cheyenne Mountain Blvd Colorado Springs CO 80906 Office Phone: 719-338-2029. Personal E-mail: deldf4e@aol.com.

DUVALL, MARJORIE L., English and foreign language educator; b. Lehighton, Pa., Dec. 2, 1958; d. Charles Jacque and Carole Faye (Eckhart) Lusch; m. Glenn Edward Duvall, July 26, 1954. BA in German, Lafayette Coll., 1980; MA in German, U. Fla., 1998; postgrad., East Stroudsburg U., 1982, Ga. So. U., Middlebury Coll., 1988, Augusta State U., U. Pa., 1994, U. S.C., 1993; student, Goethe-Inst., Germany, 2003, Accord Lang. Sch., Paris, France, 2003. German and French tchr. Evans (Ga.) Mid. Sch., 1987-89, Harlem (Ga.) Mid. Sch., 1989-92; ESOL tchr. Lakeside Mid. and H.S.'s, Evans, Ga., 1992-97; ESL tchr. Davidson & Murphy H.S.'s, Mobile, Ala., 1997-99; German tchr. Brookwood H.S., Snellville, Ga., 1999-00; tchr. ESOL and lang. arts for gifted Freedom Middle Sch., Stone Mountain, Ga., 2000—03; tchr. English, mem. sch. coun. Dunwoody H.S., Ga., 2003—. Mem. sch. coun. Dunwoody H.S. Contbr. articles to profl. jours. Recipient scholarship Profl. Assn. Ga. Educators, 1994. Mem.: TESOL, Fgn. Lang. Assn. Ga., Ga. Assn. Gifted Children, Nat. Coun. Tchrs. English, Am. Assn. Tchrs. of French, Am. Assn. Tchrs. of German, Friends of Goethe, DeKalb County Supporters of the Gifted, Mensa (coord. gifted children Ga. chpt.). Lutheran. Avocations: choral music, piano, swimming, baton twirling, dance. Home: 1587 Old Spring House Lane Dunwoody GA 30338 Office: Dunwoody HS 5035 Vermack Rd Dunwoody GA 30338 Office Phone: 678-874-8574. Personal E-mail: pardette80@aol.com.

DUVALL, ROBERT, actor; b. San Diego, Calif., Jan. 5, 1931; s. William Howard Duvall; m. Barbara Benjamin, 1964 (div. 1975); m. Gail Youngs, Aug. 1982 (div. 1986); m. Sharon Brophy, May 1, 1991 (div. 1996). Grad., Principia Coll., Ill.; student, Neighborhood Playhouse, N.Y. Film appearances include To Kill a Mockingbird, 1963, Captain Newman, M.D., 1964, The Chase, 1965, Countdown, 1968, The Detective, 1968, Bullitt, 1968, True Grit, 1969, The Rain People, 1969, M*A*S*H, 1970, The Revolutionary, 1970, THX-1138, 1971, Lawman, 1971, The Godfather, 1972 (N.Y. Film Critics award for best supporting actor 1972, Acad. award nominee for best supporting actor), Tomorrow, 1972, The Great Northfield, Minnesota Raid, 1972, Joe Kidd, 1972, Lady Ice, 1973, Badge 373, 1973, The Outfit, 1974, The Conversation, 1974, The Godfather Part II, 1974, Breakout, 1975, The Killer Elite, 1975, Network, 1976, The Seven Per Cent Solution, 1976, The Eagle Has Landed, 1977, The Greatest, 1977, The Betsy, 1978, Apocalypse Now, 1979 (Acad. award nominee for best supporting actor), The Great Santini, 1980 (Acad. award nominee for best actor 1981), True Confessions, 1981, The Pursuit of D.B. Cooper, 1981, Tender Mercies, 1983 (Acad. award for best actor 1984), The Stone Boy, 1984, The Natural, 1984, The Lightship, 1986, Let's Get Harry, 1986, Belizaire the Cajun, 1986, Colors, 1988, Convicts, Roots in a Parched Ground, The Handmaid's Tale, 1990, A Show of Force, 1990, Days of Thunder, 1990, Rambling Rose, 1991, Newsies, 1992, Falling Down, 1993, Geronimo, 1993, Wrestling Ernest Hemingway, 1993, The Paper, 1994, The Stars Fell on Henrietta, 1995, The Scarlet Letter, 1995, Sling Blade, 1996, Phenomenon, 1996, A Family Thing, 1996, Gingerbread Man, 1997, The Apostle, 1997 (also prodr., dir., writer) (nominated Oscar for best actor), Deep Impact, 1998, A Civil Action, 1999, Gone in Sixty Seconds, 2000, A Shot at Glory, 2000 (also prodr.), The Sixth Day, 2000, John Q, 2002, Assassination Tango, 2002 (also prodr., dir., writer), Gods and Generals, 2003, Open Range, 2003, Secondhand Lions, 2003, Kicking & Screaming, 2005; TV movies include Fame is the Name of the Game, 1966, The Terry Fox Story, 1983, Stalin, 1992 (Emmy nomination, Lead actor-Miniseries, 1993), The Man Who Captured Eichmann, 1996; plays including A View From the Bridge, 1965 (Obie award), Wait Until Dark, 1966, American Buffalo, 1977; TV miniseries include Ike, 1979, Lonesome Dove, 1989; dir.: film We're Not the Jet Set; actor, dir. film: Angelo My Love, 1983; rec. artist: Triad Records. With U.S. Army, 1953—54. Recipient Golden Globe award, Brit. Acad. award, Nat. Assn. Theatre Owners award; decorated Nat. Def. Svc. Medal. Office: William Morris Agy 151 El Camino Dr Beverly Hills CA 90212-2775*

DUVALL, SHELLEY, actress; b. Houston, July 7, 1949; d. Robert Duvall and Bobbie Crawford. Founder Armadillo Prodns. Actress: films (debut) Brewster McCloud, 1970, McCabe and Mrs. Miller, 1971, Thieves Like Us, 1974, Nashville, 1975, Buffalo Bill and the Indians, 1976, Three Women, 1977 (Cannes Film Festival Best Actress award, L.A. Film Critics' Best Actress award, 2d pl. N.Y. Film Critics), Annie Hall, 1977, Popeye, 1981, The Shining, 1981, Time Bandits, 1981, Roxanne, 1987, Suburban Commando, 1991, Changing Habits, 1996, The Portrait of a Lady, 1996, Alone, 1997,

Home Fries, 1997, Space Cadet, 1997, Tale of the Mummy, 1998, Big Monster on Campus, 2000, Dreams in the Attic, 2000, Manna From Heaven, 2003, (TV movies) Bernice Bobs Her Hair, 1977, Lily, 1986, (TV episode) Twilight Zone, 1986; creator, exec. producer, on-camera host Faerie Tale Theatre; exec. producer: video and pay TV series Faerie Tale Theatre, (Peabody award, Golden Ace award, others), Shelley Duvall's Bedtime Stories, Shelley Duvall's Tall Tales and Legends, The Strange Case of Dr. Jekyll and Mr. Hyde, 13 episode children's series Mrs. Piggle-Wiggle. Founder, Think Entertainment prodn. co., 1988. Mem. Nat. Acad. Cable Programming (bd. govs.). Office: care The Gersh Agency 232 N Canon Dr Beverly Hills CA 90210-5302

DUVALL, WILLIAM (BILL) C., real estate company executive; b. 1948; married; 5 children. Student, U. Tex. Sr. v.p. Lincoln Property Co., Dallas, pres. Ea. region, pres., CEO comml. divsn. Mem.: Tex. Cowboys Alumni Assn. Office: Lincoln Property Co Comml Inc 3300 Lincoln Plaza 500 N Akard St Dallas TX 75201

DUVA-MIKHAIL, DONNA MARIE, financial executive; b. Paterson, N.J., June 28, 1956; d. Alfred Dominick and Frances P. (D'Andrea) D. AAS, Bergen Community Coll., 1976; BS in Acctg., Ramapo Coll., 1985. Bookkeeper Passaic County Treas. Office, Paterson, 1973-77; acctg. tutor Bergen Community Coll., Paramus, N.J., 1974-76; full charge bookkeeper Weisz Supermarket, Inc., Clifton, N.J., 1977-79; acct. Beecham, Inc., Clifton, 1980-85; CFO, contr. Al Duva Enterprises, Inc., Paterson, 1976—98, Power Battery Corp., Paterson, 1986-96, Atlantic Battery Corp., 1986-96, Power Auto & Truck Parts of Fla., 1986-96, Power Battery & Truck Parts of Vt., 1986-96; pvt. practice, 1997—2002; CFO Consolidated Mortgage, Las Vegas, 2003—. Author newspaper editorials Paterson Evening News, 1976. Mem. Ramapo Coll. Alumni Assn., Bergen Community Coll. Alumni Assn., Nat. Assn. Female Execs. Democrat. Roman Catholic. Avocations: games of chance, bowling, tennis, travel. Home: 8284 Orange Vale Ave Las Vegas NV 89131 Office Phone: 702-739-9090. E-mail: dmikhail@cmclu.com.

DUVICK, DONALD NELSON, plant breeder; b. Sandwich, Ill., Dec. 18, 1924; s. Nelson Daniel and Florence Henrietta (Appel) D.; m. Selma Elizabeth Nelson, Sept. 10, 1950; children: Daniel, Jonathan, Randa. BS, U. Ill., 1948; PhD, Washington U., St. Louis, 1951. With Pioneer Hi-Bred Internat., Inc., Johnston, Iowa, 1951-90, corn breeding coordinator Ea. and So. div., 1965-71, dir. corn breeding dept., 1971-75, dir. plant breeding div., 1975-85, v.p. research, 1985-86, sr. v.p. research, 1986-90, co. dir., 1982-90; affiliate prof. Iowa State U., 1990—. Chmn. nat. plant genetic resources bd. USDA, 1990-91, vice-chmn. nat. genetic resources adv. com., 1992-93; trustee Internat. Ctr. for Maize and Wheat Improvement, 1988-94, trustee Internat. Rice Rsch. Inst., 1996-98; lectr. in field. Assoc. editor: Plant Physiology Jour., 1977-78; contbr. articles to profl. jours. on genetics and plant breeding, devel. anatomy and cytology, cytoplasmic inheritance, quantititive genetics and biodiversity. Pres. Johnston Consol. Sch. Bd., 1965-67. Served with AUS, 1943-46. Pioneer Hi-Bred fellow U. London, 1968; Disting. fellow Iowa Acad. Sci. Fellow AAAS, Crop Sci. Soc. Am. (pres. 1986), Am. Soc. Agronomy (pres. 1992), Iowa Acad. Sci.; mem. NAS, Coun. Agrl. Sci. and Tech. (bd. dirs. 1987-90), The Nature Conservancy (chair bd. trustees Iowa chpt. 1994). Democrat. Mem. United Ch. Christ. Achievements include identification of intra cellular site of zein storage in maize endosperm; research in maize cytoplasmic male sterility, in plant breeding's effects on crop plant genetic diversity, in changes in productivity of hybrid maize since 1930. Office: 6837 NW Beaver Dr Johnston IA 50131-0446 Office Phone: 515-278-0861. Personal E-mail: dnd307@aol.com. *Love science and humanity with equal fervor. Pursue knowledge for its own sake but also seek to apply it to useful ends.*

DUVIN, ROBERT PHILLIP, lawyer; b. Evansville, Ind., May 18, 1937; s. Louis and Henrietta (Hamburg) D.; m. Darlene Chmiel, Aug. 23, 1961; children: Scott A., Marc A., Louis A. BA with honors, Ind. U., 1958, JD with highest honors, 1961; LLM with highest honors, Columbia U., 1963. Bar: Ohio 1964. Since practiced in, Cleve.; pres. Duvin, Cahn & Hutton, 1972—. Lectr. law schs.; labor adviser corps., cities and hosps. Contbr. to books and legal jours.; bd. editors: Ind. Law Jour., 1961, Columbia Law Rev., 1963. Served with AUS, 1961-62. Mem. ABA, FBA, Ohio Bar Assn., Cleve. Bar Assn., Cleve. Racquet Club, Beechmont Country Club, Soc. Club, Canterbury Golf Club, Sanctuary Golf Club. Jewish. Home: 2775 S Park Blvd Cleveland OH 44120-1669 Office: Duvin Cahn & Hutton Erieview Tower 1301 E 9th St Ste 2000 Cleveland OH 44114-1886 Office Phone: 216-696-7600. E-mail: rduvin@duvin.com.

DUVIVIER, KATHARINE KEYES, lawyer, educator; b. Alton, Ill., Jan. 1, 1953; d. Edward Keyes and Marjorie (Attebery) DuVivier; m. James Wesley Perl, Mar. 30, 1985 (dec. Feb. 2002); children: Alice Katharine, Emmett Edward Perl. BA in Geology and English cum laude, Williams Coll., 1975; JD, U. Denver, 1982. Bar: Colo. 1982, U.S. Dist. Ct. Colo. 1982, U.S. Ct. Appeals (10th cir.) 1982. Intern-curator Hudson River Mus., Yonkers, N.Y., 1975; geologist French Am. Metals Corp., Lakewood, Colo., 1976-79; assoc. Sherman & Howard, Denver, 1982-84, Arnold & Porter, Denver, 1984-87; atty. Office of City Atty., Denver, 1987-90; sr. instr. sch. law Univ. Colo., 1990-00; reporter of decisions Colo. Ct. of Appeals, Denver, 2000; asst. prof., dir. Lawyering Process Program U. Denver Coll. Law, 2000—. Chair Appellate Practice Subcom., 1998—2000, vice-chmn., 1996—98, 2000—04. Contbr. articles to profl. jours. Mem. Denver Botanic Gardens, 1981—88, Denver Mus. Nature and Sci., 1982—; vol. Outdoor Colo., Denver, 1985—87, 1998—. Mem.: ABA (vice chmn. subcom. 1985—91), Boulder Women's Bar Assn. (pres. 1991—93), Colo. Bar Assn., Alliance Profl. Women (bd. dirs. 1985—90, pres. 1988—89), Work and Family Consortium (bd. dirs. 1988—90), St. Ives, William Coll. Alumni Assn. (co-pres. Colo. chpt. 1984—86), Phi Beta Kappa. Avocations: geology, skiing, swimming, dance. Office: D U Coll Law 2255 E Evans Ave Denver CO 80208 Home: 1960 S Gilpin St Denver CO 80210 Office Phone: 303-871-6281. Business E-Mail: kkduvivier@law.du.edu.

DUVOISIN, CATHY LYNN, elementary school educator; d. Andrew and Gladys Dankovich; m. Bob DuVoisin, June 23, 1979; children: Jessica, Andrew. BS in Elem. Edn., U. Ill., 1978; MA in Early Childhood Edn., Govs. State U., 1981, MA in Ednl. Adminstrn., 1997. 5th grade tchr. Limestone Grade Sch., Kankakee, 6th grade tchr. Active Jr. League. Office: Limestone Elem Sch 963 N 5000 W Rd Kankakee IL 60901-8272

DUXBURY, THOMAS CARL, planetary scientist; s. John Lawrence and Justine Agnus (Jaron) D.; m. Natalia Duxbury, Nov. 8, 1990; children: Brett Harding, Katerina. BSEE, Purdue U., 1965, MSEE, 1966. Planetary scientist Jet Propulsion Lab., Pasadena, Calif., 1966—. Participant Soviet PHOBOS Mission to Mars Dept. Def., 1988—89, Clementing sci. team for lunar exploration, 1992—94, Russian Mars, 1994—96, mission sci. team, 1992—97, project mgr. NASA STARDUST mission, scientist Mars Global Surveyor mission, 1996—, interdisciplinary scientist European Space Agy. Mars Express mission, 1999—; sci. definition team dep. leader USAF/NASA, 1997—98. Co-author: Television Investigations of Phobos, 1994. Recipient Sci. Achievement medal NASA, Washington, 1972, Space Mission Svc. medal Russian Lavochkin Assn., The Hague, The Netherlands, 1991, Burka award Inst. of Navigation, 1973, Achievement awards NASA, 1980, 82. Mem. Am. Geophysical Union, 1978—, Am. Astronomical Soc., 1980—, Russian Assn. for Space Sci. & Tech., 1993—. Achievements include prodn. of first map of another planet's moon; discovery of the Groove Network on Phobos (Mars moon); co-discovery of the Rings of Jupiter, of the Jupiter Lightning. Office: Jet Propulsion Lab 4800 Oak Grove Dr # 264-379 Pasadena CA 91109-8099 Office Phone: 818-354-4301. Business E-Mail: tduxbury@jpl.nasa.gov.

DUZY, MERRILYN JEANNE, artist, educator; b. L.A., Mar. 29, 1946; d. Berton John and Marva Lorinne (Barrow) D.; m. Howard Bentkower, Sept. 28, 1974. BA, Calif. State U., Northridge, 1974; MFA, Otis Art Inst., L.A., 1988. Tchr. L.A. H.S. for Arts, 1988-90, The Atelier, Chatsworth, Calif. Pvt. tchr., lectr., West Hills, 1991-93; creator slide lecture Walking Through History: Women Artists Past and Present, 1982—; curator Autobiographies, 1977, Erotica '88, 1988, Angeles, Ancestors and Spirit Guides, 1994, Closure invitational Artspace Gallery, 1994, Quarks to Quasars, 1997, Merrilyn Duzy: twenty five years, Mt. San Jacinto Coll., 1998. Lecture, Sex in History: A Pictorial View, 2004. Founder Artists Networking, Woodland Hills, Calif., 1992-93. Mem. Coll. Art Assn., Women's Caucus for Art (pres. So. Calif. chpt. 1980-82, founder, pres. Fla. West Coast chpt. 1983-84, mem. nat. adv. bd.), Group Nine. Home: 8356 Capistrano Ave West Hills CA 91304-3319

DVORAK, ALLEN DALE, radiologist; b. Dodge, Nebr., Mar. 13, 1943; s. Rudolph Charles and Mildred B. (Misek) D.; m. Carol Ann Cockson, July 22, 1967; children: Kristin Ann, Andrea Marie, Ryan Allen. Grad., Creighton Coll. Arts and Scis., 1961-64; MD, Creighton Sch. Medicine, 1969. Intern Creighton Meml. St. Joseph Hosp., Omaha, 1969-70; resident Ind. U. Med. Ctr., Indpls., 1970-73, chief resident, 1972—73; asst. prof. radiology Creighton U. Sch. Medicine, Omaha, 1973-83; diagnostic radiologist Nebr.-Iowa Radiology Cons., Papillion, Nebr., 1983—, mng. ptnr., 1987—, pres., 2004—. Staff radiologist Alegent Midlands Cmty. Hosp., Papillion, 1983—, med. staff exec. bd., 1996—, pres. med. staff, 2001-02; mem. Nebr. Bd. Health, 1995-2000; bd. dirs. Blue Cross Blue Shield Nebr., 2000—, bd. dirs. PRIME Therapeutics, Inc., 2002-04. Author: (chpt.) Ultrasound, 1981; contbr. articles to profl. jours. Chmn. Midlands Area Health Adv. cuon., State of Nebr., 1982-86; trustee Duchesne Acad., 1988-91, Boys Town Nat. Coun. Friends, 1989—; bd. dirs. Safety and health Coun. of Greater Omaha, 1990-91; mem. Gov.'s Blue Ribbon Coalition to Study Health Care in Nebr., 1991-98; mem. Creighton Med. Sch. Alumni Adv. Bd., 1993—, pres., 1998-2000; trustee Western Conf. Prepaid Med. Svc. Plans, 2004—. Fellow Am. Coll. Radiology; mem. AMA (alt. del. 1992-98, del. 1999-2000), Nebr. Radiol. Soc. (pres. 1980-81), Omaha Midwest Clin. Soc. (pres. 1982), Nebr. Assn. Nuclear Physicians (pres. 1976-78, del. 1984-94), Met. Omaha Med. Soc. (exec. com. 1980-2000, pres. 1990), Nebr. Med. Assn. (del. 1986—, pres. 1997-98), Regency Lake and Tennis Club (bd. dirs. 1981-85, chmn. bd. 1983-85), Happy Hollow Country Club. Avocations: golf, gardening. Home: 9733 Brentwood Rd Omaha NE 68114-4970 Office: Nebr-Iowa Radiology Cons Mng Ptnr 401 E Gold Coast Rd Ste 102 Papillion NE 68046-4194 Office Phone: 402-339-8991.

DVORAK, DELYLE DENNIS, music educator, consultant, early childhood educator; b. Olivet, S.D., Nov. 13, 1941; s. Alvin John and Frieda K. (Rembold) Dvorak; m. Patricia Ann Dunlap, May 11, 1979; children: Lori Michele, Debra Jean Baker, Jeff Michael. BS, U. S.D., Springfield, 1959—62; MusM, U. S.D., Vermillion, 1963—65; EdD, Ariz. State U., Tempe, 1969—73. Dir., bands & choral music Delmont Pub. Schs., SD, 1961—62, Armour Pub. Schs., SD, 1962—64; dir., bands Chamberlain H.S., SD, 1964—66; asst. dir., bands Minot State Coll., ND, 1966—67; dir., bands Palo Verde Unified Sch. Dist., Blythe, Calif., 1967—69; grad. tchg. asst. Ariz. State U., Tempe, 1969—72; dir., bands, acting dept. chmn. William Penn Coll., Oskaloosa, Iowa, 1972—75; asst. prof., music Southwestern Okla. State U., Weatherford, 1975—76; dir., bands Mt. San Jacinto CC, Calif., 1976—81; music dept. program leader, dir. bands Jefferson Sch. Performing Arts, Portland, Oreg., 1982—85; french horn instr. Colo. State U., Fort Collins, 1988—90; owner Dvorak Assocs., Loveland, Colo., 1988—92, Dvorak Enterprises, Las Vegas, 1992—; educator CCSD, Las Vegas, Nev., 1995—. Asst. musical condr. Douglas County Bi-Centennial, Corsica, SD, 1961—61; dir., bands Minot State Coll. Model Sch., Minot, ND, 1966—67; dean, students Internat. Peace Garden Music Camp, Dunseith, ND, 1967, guest band condr., 76; state chmn. Nat. Band Assn., Ariz., 1970—72, Iowa, 1972—74. Contbr. articles to profl. jours. Ch. organist & vocal soloist St. John's Luth. Ch., Kaylor, SD, 1953—59; choir dir. Redeemer Luth. Ch., Armour, SD, 1962—64; choir dir. & organist Zion Luth. Ch., Chamberlain, SD, 1964—66; organist, confirmation tchr. Zion Luth., Blythe, Calif., 1967—69; choir dir. Luth. Ch., Knoxville, Iowa, 1973—74; Ariz. State U. rsch. rep. Music Educator's Nat. Conf., Atlanta, 1970. Recipient Outstanding Educator of Am., 1974—75. Mem.: Music Educator's Conf. (life). Conservative. Lutheran. Avocations: photography, travel, computers, golf. Home: 4917 Pounding Surf Ave Las Vegas NV 89131 Office: CCSD 400 Sky Rd Indian Springs NV 89018 Office Phone: 702-799-0932. Personal E-mail: drddd@cox.net. E-mail: drdddla@yahoo.com.

DVORAK, GEORGE J., mechanics and materials engineering educator; came to U.S., 1964; Degree in Civil Engring., Czech Technol. U., Prague, 1956, DSc (hon.), 1997; C.Sc., Czechoslovak Acad. Sci., Prague, 1964; PhD, Brown U., 1968. Rsch. assoc. divsn. engring. Brown U., 1964-67; with civil engring. and biomedical engring. dept. Duke U., Durham, NC, 1967-79; prof., chmn. civil engring., prof. materials sci. U. Utah, Salt Lake City, 1979-84; prof., chmn. dept. civil and environ. engring. Rensselaer Poly. Inst., Troy, NY, 1984—95, prof. mech. engring., aero. engring. and mechanics, chmn. civil and environ. engring., William Howard Hart prof. mechanics, 1995—. Sr. vis. fellow Brit. sci. rsch. coun. Cambridge U., Eng.; vis. fellow Clare Hall, Cambridge, 1975-76; vis. prof. Politecnico di Milano, Milan, Italy; with inst. ctr. composite materials and structures Rensselaer Poly. Inst., dir. univ. rsch. initiative Dept. Def. Assoc. editor Internat. Jour. Plasticity, 1984-2001, Mech. Composite Mater Structures, 1993—, Jour. Applied Mechanics, 1989-95, Applied Mechanics Revs., 1989-95, Jour. Composite Materials, 2000--. Recipient Citations for Accomplishment of Spl. Merit, Army Rsch. Office, 1977, 79; Fulbright fellow Tech. U. Denmark, 1995, Brown Engring. Alumni medal Brown U., 1999. Fellow ASME (founding chmn. com. composite materials applied mechanics divsn., Arpard L. Nadai award 1992, Daniel C. Drucker medal 2002), ASCE, Am. Acad. Mechanics, Soc. Engring. Sci. (William Prager medal in mechanics of solids 1994), Nat. Acad. Engring. Achievements include research in mechanics, physics of solids, micromechanics of heterogeneous media, mechanical behavior of composite materials. Office: Dept Mech & Aero Engring and Mechanics Jonsson Engring Ctr 5003 Rensselaer Polytech Inst Troy NY 12180 Business E-Mail: dvorak@rpi.edu.

DVORAK, HAROLD FISHER, pathologist, educator; b. Milw., June 20, 1937; s. Harold J. and Laura (Fisher) D.; m. Ann Marie Tompkins, June 13, 1962; children: John, Laura, Jane. AB, Princeton U., 1958; MD, Harvard U., 1963. Diplomate: Am. Bd. Pathology. Practice medicine specializing in pathology, Boston; asst. prof. pathology Harvard Med. Sch., Boston, assoc. prof., prof., Mallinckrodt prof. pathology, 1979—; mem. staff Mass. Gen. Hosp., asst. pathologist, 1969-75, assoc. pathologist, 1975-78, head immunopathology unit, 1976-80; chief dept. pathology Beth Israel Hosp., Boston, 1979-96, Beth Israel Deaconess Med. Ctr., Boston, 1996—. Mem. study sect. pathology B NIH, 1978-82, Am. Cancer Soc., N.Y.C., 1982-86; chmn. merit rev. bd. immunology VA, Washington, 1982-84. Served to lt. comdr. USPHS, 1965-67. Mem. Am. Assn. Immunologists, Am. Soc. Investigative Pathology (v.p. 1996, pres.-elect), Internat. Acad. Pathology, Pluto Club, Collegium Internat. Allergologicum, Phi Beta Kappa, Sigma Xi, Alpha Omega Alpha Office: Beth Israel Deaconess Med Ctr 330 Brookline Ave Boston MA 02215-5400 E-mail: hdvorak@bidmc.harvard.edu.

DVORAK, MARK ANTHONY, music educator; b. Ft. Worth, July 30, 1958; s. Thomas Earl and Bobbie Sue (Coulson) D.; m. Ann Dvorak, Sept. 29, 1989; 1 child, Jody Collins. MusB, U. Tex., Arlington, 1983, MEd in Tchg., 1998. Cert. educator Tex. Min. of music St. George Cath. Ch., Ft. Worth, 1984—2001; tchr. elem. music Holiday Heights Elem., North Richland Hills, Tex., 1991—. Acad. dir. Coll. Edn. U. Tex., Arlington, 2002—; mem. PTA exec. bd. Holiday Heights Elem., North Richland Hills, 2003—. Contbr. articles to profl. jours. Named Birdville Ind. Sch. Dist. Elem. Tchr. of Yr., 1999, Holiday Heights Elem. Tchr. of Yr., 1999, N.E. Tarrant Star Tchr., 1999; recipient Disting. Alumni award, U. Tex. Arlington Sch. Edn., 1999, N.E. Tarrant Chamber Golden Apple award, 1999. Mem.: PTA (life), Tex. Music Educators Assn., Tex. Classroom Tchrs. Assn., Music Educators Nat. Conf., Tex. PTA (life), Kappa Delta Pi, Phi Mu Alpha, Phi Delta Kappa. Roman Catholic. Avocations: music, reading. Home: 8620 Brookridge Dr North Richland Hills TX 76180 Office: Holida Heights Elem 5221 Susan Lee Ln North Richland Hills TX 76180

DVORAK, ROGER GRAN, health facility executive; b. St. Paul, Aug. 30, 1934; s. William Anthony and Evelyn Carolyn (Gran) D.; m. Gail Ann Peterson, Dec. 30, 1960; children: Karen, Mark. BBA, U. Minn., 1955, MHA, 1957. Asst. adminstr. Glenwood Hills Hosp., Mpls., 1958-61; asst. hosp. adminstrv. svcs. dir. Phila. Gen. Hosp., 1961-65; asst. dir. Presbyn. U. Pa. Med. Ctr., Phila., 1965-67, assoc. dir., 1967-72; adminstr. Symmes Hosp., Arlington, Mass., 1972-78; exec. dir. Lawrence Hosp., Bronxville, N.Y., 1978-86, pres., 1986-2000; ret., 2000. Fellow Am. Coll. Healthcare Execs. Presbyterian. Avocations: painting, music. Home: 8167 Galway Cir Woodbury MN 55125

DVORNEK, LINDA SMITH, chemist; b. Stamford, Conn., Nov. 11, 1951; d. Thomas I. and Marguerite A. (Tiani) Smith; m. Jerome Dvornek, June 26, 1982; children: Jeffrey, Allison. BS, Sacred Heart U., Fairfield, Conn., 1973; MS, U. Bridgeport, 1986. Chemist R.T. Vanderbilt Co., Norwalk, Conn., 1973-79, sr. chemist, 1979-87, rsch. assoc., 1987-90, mgr. analytical dept., 1990-92, dir. analytical svcs., 1992—98, v.p. R&D, 1998—. Mem.: STLE, AIChE, ASTM, Am. Chem. Soc. Republican. Roman Catholic. Avocations: travel, learning to play golf. Office: R T Vanderbilt Co 30 Winfield St Norwalk CT 06855-1329 Office Phone: 203-853-1400. E-mail: ldvornek@rtvanderbilt.com.

DWAN, DENNIS EDWIN, broadcast executive, photographer; b. St. Joseph, Mich., Oct. 6, 1958; s. Edwin O. and Elizabeth L. (Miller) D.; m. Tami L. Nixon, Oct. 13, 1984; children: Megan, Kaitlyn. BA, Mich. State U., 1981. Photographer Sta. WJIM-TV, Lansing, Mich., 1981-83, Sta. KAYU, Spokane, Wash., 1984-86, Sta. KREM-TV, Spokane, 1984-87; ops. mgr. Sta. KOMO-TV, Seattle, 1987—. Mem. Nat. Press Photographers Assn. E-mail: DennisD@Komotv.com.

DWEIK, RAED A., physician, researcher, educator; b. Hebron, Jordan, Aug. 20, 1964; came to U.S., 1990; s. Abdul-Rahim a. and Fikrat (Salhi) D.; m. Erin Makley, Sept. 23, 1995; children: Zayn, Sana, Qyce. MB BS, U. Jordan, 1988. Diplomate Am. Bd. Internal Medicine, Am. Bd. Pulmonary Disease, Am. Bd. Critical Care Medicine. Resident Wright State U., Dayton, Ohio, 1990-93; fellow Cleve. Clinic Found., 1993-96; staff physician Cleve. Clinic, 1996—. Contbr. aticles to profl. jours. Fellow ACP, Am. Coll. Chest Physicians, Royal Coll. Physicians and Surgeons; mem. AMA, AAAS, Am. Thoracic Soc., Soc. Critical Care Medicine. mem. Am. Physiol. Soc., Am. Fed. for Med. Rsch. Achievements include investigating regulation of nitric oxide production in the lungs by oxygen and the role of nitric oxide in lung physiology and pathology. Office: Cleve Clinic Found A-90 9500 Euclid Ave Cleveland OH 44195-0001

DWEK, CYRIL S., bank executive; b. Kobe, Japan, Nov. 9, 1936; s. Nessim S. and Alice (Stambouli) Dwek; children: Nevil, Alicia. BS, U. Pa., 1958. With Trade Devel. Bank, Geneva, 1962-65; with Republic Nat. Bank of N.Y., 1966-99, dir., 1967—, exec. v.p., 1973—, vice chmn., 1983-99; dir. Republic N.Y. Corp., 1974—, vice chmn., 1983-99; chmn. HSBC Republic Adv. Bd., N.Y.C., 2000—. Bd. dirs. HSBC Republic, France, dir., vice chmn., Monaco. Mem.: Racing Club de France (Paris). Office: HSBC USA 2nd Flr 452 5th Ave New York NY 10018-2706 Office Phone: 212-525-6416.

DWIGGINS, CLAUDIUS WILLIAM, JR., chemist; b. Amity, Ark., May 11, 1933; s. Claudius William and Lillian (Scott) D. BS, U. Ark., 1954, MS, 1956, PhD, 1958. With U.S. Dept. of Energy Bartlesville Tech. Ctr., Okla., 1958-83, chemist, 1958-60, project leader surface physics project, 1960-65, project leader petroleum composition rsch. project, 1965-80, supervisory rsch. chemist, thermodynamics divsn., 1980-83; sr. chemist Nat. Inst. Petroleum and Energy Rsch., 1983-84, cons., 1984—. Contbr. articles to profl. jours. Am. Oil Co. fellow, Coulter-Jones scholar Mem. Am. Chem. Soc., N.Y. Acad. Scis., AAAS, Am. Crystallographic Assn., Am. Inst. Physics, Sigma Xi (sec. 1966-67), Alpha Chi Sigma, Delta Sigma Phi (treas. 1952). Home: 1211 S Keeler Ave Bartlesville OK 74003-4756

DWIGHT, ANNETTE B., music educator, administrative assistant; b. Cherokee County, S.C., Sept. 25, 1940; d. John Bonner Blanton and Sarah Maude McDaniel-Blanton; m. Sidney Thornton Zemp, Jr. (div.); children: Pamela, Sidney Thornton III 5 stepchildren; m. Francis Marion Dwight, Feb. 9, 1976. BA, Carson Newman Coll., 1962. Pvt. practice music educator, Bamberg, SC, 1963—. Author: Making a Living on Making a Life, 2004. Musician First Bapt. Ch., Bamberg, 1970—. Mem.: Nat. Guild Piano Tchrs. (chmn. Bamberg (S.C.) chpt. 1964—, named to Hall Fame 1984), Nat. Fedn. Music Clubs (life Rose Fay Thomas fellow 2003), S.C. Fedn. Music Clubs (pres. 2001—), Delta Kappa Gamma. Avocations: gardening, entertaining. Home: PO Box 455 Bamberg SC 29003

DWIGHT, DONALD RATHBUN, publishing executive, corporate communications specialist; b. Holyoke, Mass., Mar. 26, 1931; s. William and Dorothy Elizabeth (Rathbun) D.; m. Susan Newton Russell, Aug. 9, 1952 (div. Aug. 1982); children: Dorothy Campbell, Laura Newton, Eleanor Addison, Arthur Ryan, Stuart Russell.; m. Nancy John Sinnott, Dec. 18, 1982; children: Christopher Sinnott, Helen Rathbun. AB, Princeton U., 1953; DSc (hon.), U. Mass., Lowell, 1974. Reporter, asst. to pub. Holyoke (Mass.) Transcript-Telegram, 1955-63, assoc. pub., 1966-69; assoc. commr. Mass. Dept. Pub. Works, Boston, 1963-66; commr. adminstrn. Commonwealth Mass., Boston, 1969-70, lt. gov., 1971-75; assoc. pub., v.p. Mpls. Star and Tribune, 1975-76, pub., sr. v.p., 1976-81; pres., pub. Star & Tribune Newspapers, Mpls., 1981-82; exec. v.p., dir. Cowles Media Co., 1981-82; chmn. Newspapers of New Eng., Inc., 1982-98, chmn. emeritus, 1999—; assoc. The Prospect Group, N.Y.C., 1983-88; chmn., mng. ptnr. Clark, Dwight & Assocs., Inc., 1988-90; pres. Dwight Ptnrs., Inc., Lyme, N.H., 1988—. V.p. Wood River Capital Corp., 1984—88; exec. v.p. Entretech Inc., 1988—90; trustee Eaton Vance Mut. Funds, Boston, 1986—2003, The Royce Funds, NYC, 1998—. Mem. Town Meeting, South Hadley, Mass., 1957-69; bd. dirs. Mpls. Soc. Fine Arts, 1976-82; trustee Twin Cities Pub. TV, 1976-82; chmn. bd. Guthrie Theater Found., 1978-81; v.p., dir. Nat. Corp. Theatre Fund, 1985-88; dir. Joint Action in Cmty. Svc., Washington, 1989-92, Lyme (NH) Found., Inc., 1994-98; trustee Trust Funds, Lyme, NH, 1997-00, Lyme Planning Bd., NH, 2005-; mem. vestry St. Thomas Episcopal Ch., Hanover, NH, 1998-01; bd. dirs. The Josiah Bartlett Ctr. Pub. Policy, Concord, NH. 1st lt. USMCR, 1953-55. Mem. Newspaper Assn. Am., Knickerbocker Club, Round Hill Club, Somerset Club, Hillsboro Club. Republican. Episcopalian. Home and Office: 92 Shoestrap Rd Lyme NH 03768-3301 Office Phone: 603-795-2800. Business E-Mail: dwight.partners@valley.net.

DWIGHT, REGINALD KENNETH See SIR JOHN, ELTON

DWINELL, ANN JONES, retired special education educator; b. Lowell, Mass., Oct. 28, 1934; d. George Hubert and Bridget Jones; m. Roland A. Dwinell, Dec. 23, 1956; children: Theresa, Joseph, Richard, John. BA, Framingham State Coll., 1972; MEd, Lesley Coll., 1974; PhD, Boston Coll., 1991. Cert. Eng. tchr., moderate spl. needs instr., Mass., adminstr., supt., spl. edn. adminstr., R.I. Spl. edn. tchr., adminstr. Marlborough (Mass.) Pub. Schs., 1972-78; core chairperson Malden (Mass.) Pub. Schs., 1978-80, spl. edn. specialist, 1980—2001. Contbr. articles to profl. jours. Mem. NEA, Mass. Tchrs. Assn. (rep. 1983-85, liaison 1987—), Phi Delta Kappa. Roman Catholic. Avocations: dance, music, boating, reading.

DWIVEDI, YOGESH, science educator; b. Gorakhpur, India, Apr. 22, 1965; PhD, CDNI, India, 1992. Asst. prof. U. Ill., Chgo., 2003—. Treas. UP Assn., Chgo., 1998—99. Recipient Young Investigator award, Am. Found. Suicide Prevention, 2002—04, Internat. Congress Biol. Psychiatry, 2003, Nat. Inst. Mental Health, 2004—; CNIP fellowship, Collegium Internationale Neuropsychopharmacology, 2000. Office: Univ Illinois 1601 W Taylor St Chicago IL 60612 Office Fax: 312-355-3857. Business E-Mail: ydwivedi@psych.uic.edu.

DWON, LARRY, retired electrical engineer, educator, consultant; b. N.Y.C., May 2, 1913; s. Lucas and Mary (Woytowich) Dzwonczyk; m. Mary Jean Skala, Feb. 14, 1941; children: Lawrence A. Dwon, Roger R. Dzwonczyk. D in Electrical Engring., Cornell U., 1935; MBA, NYU, 1954. Registered profl. engr., N.Y., N.C. Engr. Diehl Mfg. Co., Elizabethport, N.J., 1935-37, Holophane Lighting, Inc., Newark, Ohio, 1937-38; mem. tech. staff Office Sci. and Rsch. Devel. Harvard Radio Rsch. Lab., Bell Telephone Labs., NYC, 1942-45; engr. Am. Electric Power Svc. Corp., NYC, 1938-45, sr. engr., 1945-52, operating sponsor (reporting to operating exec. v.p.), 1952-55, adminstrv. asst. to exec. v.p. ops., 1955-57, mgr. engring. manpower, 1957-78, ret., 1978—. Cons., cons. instr. N.C. State U., Raleigh, 1978—, N.C. State U. Coll. Engring., 1979—; self-employed cons., Apex, N.C., 1978—. Author: History of Eta Kappa Nu, 1976; contbr. over 200 tech. and profl. papers to many profl. jours. Recipient Plummer lecture medal, Am. Welding Soc., 1975, Disting. Svc. award, Power Engring. Edn. Com., 1977, Spl. Citation, Edison Elec. Inst., 1977, Disting. Svc. award, 1976, Cert. of Distinction, Assn. of Coll. Honor Socs., 2001, IEEE-USA Bd. recognition for SPAC founder and yrs. of leadership, 2002. Fellow IEEE (chmn. various coms. from 1969, U.S. Activities Bd. award 1982, Centennial medal 1984, Lit. Contbns. award 1988); mem. Am. Assn. Concerned Engrs. (bd. dirs.), Cornell Engring. Soc., Eta Kappa Nu (v.p. 1958, pres. 1959, eminent mem. 1984, Disting. Svc. award 1976). Avocations: classical music, writing, speaking. Home and Office: PO Box 216 West Kill NY 12492-0216 Personal E-mail: l.dwon@att.net.

DWORETZKY, JOSEPH ANTHONY, lawyer, city manager; b. N.Y.C., Sept. 17, 1951; s. Lawrence H. and Grace W. (Jackson) D.; m. Amy L. Banse; children: Lydia Light, Adam Eliot, Alex John, Anna Grace. BA with distinction, Purdue U., 1972; JD summa cum laude, Villanova U., 1977. Bar: Pa. 1977, D.C. 1978. Law clk. to judge U.S. Ct. Appeals 2d Cir., N.Y.C., 1977-78; assoc. Drinker Biddle & Reath, Phila., 1978-84, ptnr., 1984-93, mng. ptnr., 1992-93; chmn. corp. group law dept. City of Phila., 1993, city solicitor, 1994-96; shareholder Hangley Aronchick Segal & Pudlin, 1997—, exec. com., 1998—. Adj. prof. Rutgers U. Sch. Law, Camden, 1986-93. V.p., bd. dirs. Phila. Vol. Lawyers for Arts, 1981-84, Phila. Bd. Pensions, 1994-96, Phila. Indsl. Devel. Corp., 1994-96, Phila. Theatre Co., 1998-2000, William Penn Found., 2001—, Moore Coll. Art and Design, 2003-, Pa. Energy Devel. Authority; bd. dir., Penn. Energy Develop. Authority, 2004-; sec.-treas., bd. dirs. Consumer Bankruptcy Assistance Project, 1992—, Acad. for Law, Pub. Adminstrn. and Criminal Justice, 1995-98; chair East Dist. Pa. Bankruptcy Conf., 2001. Fellow Am. Coll. Bankruptcy (3d cir. regent); mem. ABA, Pa. Bar Assn., Phila. Bar Assn., Order of Coif, Phi Beta Kappa. Home: 7801 Huron St Philadelphia PA 19118-4218 Office Phone: 215-496-7014. Business E-Mail: jad@hangley.com.

DWORETZKY, MURRAY, retired physician, educator; b. N.Y.C., Aug. 18, 1917; s. Samuel and Frieda (Newhoff) D.; m. Barbara Ratner, June 11, 1943; children: Thomas Alan, Joan Mara. BA, U. Pa., 1938; MD, SUNY, Coll. Medicine, N.Y.C., 1942; MS in Medicine, U. Minn., 1950. Diplomate: Am. Bd. Internal Medicine (examiner allergy subbd. 1967-71), Am. Bd. Allergy and Immunology (founding mem., dir. 1971-74), Pan Am. Med. Assn. Intern City Hosp., N.Y.C., 1942-43, asst. resident pathology, 1943, fellow in pathology, 1946-47; resident pathology U. Chgo., 1947-48; fellow in medicine Mayo Found., Rochester, Minn., 1948-50; practice medicine, specializing in internal medicine, allergy and clin. immunology N.Y.C., 1951—; asst. physician N.Y. Hosp., 1951, physician, 1951-56, asst. attending physician, 1956-61, assoc. attending, 1961-66, attending physician, 1966—2005, physician-in-charge Allergy Clinic, 1961-88; asst. in medicine Cornell U. Med. Coll., 1951-52, instr. medicine, 1952-56, clin. asst. prof., 1956-61, clin. asst. prof. pub. health, 1957-62, clin. assoc. prof. medicine, 1961-66, dir. tng. program div. allergy and immunology, 1961-88, clin. prof. medicine, 1966—2005, emeritus prof. medicine, 2005—; attending physician Manhattan Eye, Ear and Throat Hosp., 1953-62; ret., 2005. Med. dir.-at-large Asthma-Allergy Found. Am., 1963-64, bd. dirs., 1964-78, mem. exec. com., 1964-77; founding mem. bd. dirs. Am. Bd. Allergy and Immunology, 1971-74; examiner sub-bd. allergy Am. Bd. Internal Medicine, 1967-71. Co-editor Allergy Archives, Jour. Allergy and Clin. Immunology, 2001-04; contbr. articles to profl. jours. Served to capt., M.C. AUS, 1943-46. Recipient Frank L. Babbott M.D. Meml. award Alumni Assn. Coll. Med. SUNY, 1992. Fellow: ACP, N.Y. Acad. Medicine, Am. Acad. Allergy and Immunology (past pres. 1968, Disting. Svc. award 1989, Spl. Achievement award 2002); mem.: AMA (chmn. allergy sect. coun. 1974—77, residency rev. com. for allergy and immunology 1980—85), Am. Assn. Immunologists, Am. Fedn. Clin. Rsch., Harvey Soc., Soc. Exptl. Biology and Medicine, N.Y. Allergy Soc. (past pres., exec. com. 1958—94, tchg. day dedicated in his honor 1995), N.Y. County Med. Soc., Sigma Xi. Home: 21 E 87th St New York NY 10128-0506 Office: 115 E 61st St New York NY 10021-8183 Office Phone: 212-838-3421. Personal E-mail: mbjdwor@aol.com.

DWORIN, MICKI (MAXINE DWORIN), automobile dealership executive; widowed; children: Judy, Diane. V.p. Dworin Chevrolet, Inc., East Harford, Conn., 1955-83, Dworin Auto Leasing. Pres. Eastern Auto Ins., Conn. Chevrolet Dealers Assn., Tarrytown Zone Dealer Coun., Atlantic Coast Region Dealer Coun., Boulevard, Inc. Sec. BBB, Hartford, Conn.; vol. coord. Vol. Broward, 1998-99, Children's Diagnostic and Treatment Ctr., 1996-98, Am. Cancer Soc., 1994-96, Kids in Distress, 1991-95; hon. trustee Hartford Coll. for Women; sec., bd. govs. Point of Am. Condominium; coord. Trinity Coll.; bd. dirs. Combined Health Appeals; chmn. King David Soc., 1995-96. Mem. Advt. Assn. Grtr. Hartford. Fax: 954-522-6770. E-mail: volbrow@safari.net.

DWORKIN, GARY STEVEN, insurance company executive; b. NYC, July 7, 1947; s. Irving Milton and Grace Wilhelmina (Korn) D.; student Hofstra U., 1965-68, NYU, 1969-71; m. Linda Lee Fuchs, Aug. 28, 1970; children: Robert Benjamin, Alexandra Tenille. Sales mgr. Chatham Blankets, NYC, 1968-70; ins. agt. Travelers Ins. Co., Hartford, Conn., 1970-74; broker Dworkin Assos., Rochester, NH, 1974-76; pres. Dworkin Assos., Inc. (DAI), Rochester, 1976—. Registered health underwriter; chartered life underwriter. Mem. Nat. Assn. Ins. Fin. Advisors, Life, Inc., Lifemark Ptnrs. Inc., Home Office Life Underwriters Assn., NH NAIFA, New Eng. Forum, Nat. Assn. Health Underwriters, Am. Risk and Ins. Assn., Risk Appraisal Forum, Nat. Assn. Ind. Life Brokerage Agys. (charter, bd. dirs.), Soc. Fin. Svcs. Profls. Republican Office: PO Box 2000 Rochester NH 03866-2000 Office Phone: 800-777-0061. E-mail: gsd@dworkin.com.

DWORKIN, HOWARD JERRY, nuclear medicine physician, educator; b. Bklyn., Oct. 29, 1932; s. Joseph Henry and Mollie M. (Hodas) Dworkin; m. Gina Gora; children: Rhonda Fran, Steven Irving, Paul J., Edward Joshua, Joseph Jacob. BSChemE, Worcester Poly. Inst., 1955; MD, Albany Med. Coll., 1959; MS in Radiation Biology, U. Mich., 1965. Diplomate Am. Bd. Internal Medicine, Am. Bd. Nuclear Medicine. Intern Albany Hosp., NY, 1959-60; resident Rochester (N.Y.) Gen. Hosp., 1960-62, U. Mich. Hosps., 1962-65, asst. coord. nuclear medicine unit, 1963-66, instr., 1965-66; asst. prof. medicine U. Toronto, Canada, 1966, assoc. prof., 1967; head dept. nuclear medicine Princess Margaret Hosp., Toronto, 1967; head nuclear medicine sect., radiology Nat. Naval Med. Ctr., Bethesda, Md., 1967-69; dir. sch. nuclear medicine tech. William Beaumont Hosp., Royal Oak, Mich., 1969—, chief dept. nuclear medicine, 1969—2002, dir. nuclear medicine resident tng. program, 1970—, chmn. CME com., 1993—. Clin. asst. prof. dept. medicine Wayne State U. Med. Sch., Detroit, 1970—; clin. assoc. prof. dept. radiology Mich. State U., East Lansing, 1976—; clin. prof. med. physics Ctr. Health Scis. Oakland U., Rochester, Mich., 1977—; adj. prof. radiology U. Mich., 2003—. Author (with N. Aspin and R. G. Baker): (book) Use of Isotopes in the Physics of Radiology, 1969, Part Two, Clinical Procedures in Radioisotope Laboratory Procedures, 1969; contbr. articles and chpts. to med. jours. and texts. With USN, 1967—69. Mem.: AMA, Mich. State Med. Soc. (chmn. continuing med. edn. com. 1999—), Am. Coll. Nuc. Physicians (sec. 1974—75, pres. 1978—79), Endocrine Soc., Am. Thyroid Assn., Soc. Nuc. Medicine (trustee 1973—81, v.p. 1982, pres. 1986—87), Am. Bd. Nuc. Medicine (treas. 1982—84), Accrediation Coun. Continuing Med. Edn. (chmn. 1998). Achievements include patents for in radioactive labeled protein material process and apparatus. Office: William Beaumont Hosp Dept Nuclear Medicine Royal Oak MI 48073 Office Phone: 248-898-4128. E-mail: hdworkin@beaumont.edu.

DWORKIN, MARTIN, microbiologist, educator; b. NYC, Dec. 3, 1927; s. Hyman Bernard and Pauline (Herstein) D.; m. Nomi Rees Buda, Feb. 2, 1957; children: Jessica Sarah, Hanna Beth. BA, Ind. U., 1951; PhD (NSF predoctoral fellow), U. Tex., Austin, 1955. NIH research fellow U. Calif., Berkeley, 1955-57, vis. prof., summers 1958-60; asst. prof. microbiology Ind. U. Med. Sch., 1957-61, assoc. prof., 1961-62, U. Minn., 1962-69, dir. MD/PhD tng. program, 1990-97, prof., 1969—. Vis. prof. U. Wash., 1965, Stanford U., 1978-79; vis. scholar Oxford (Eng.) U., 1970-71; Found. for Microbiology lectr., 1973-74, 76-77, 81-82; Sackler scholar Tel Aviv U., 1992. Author: Developmental Biology of the Bacteria, 1985, Microbial Cell-Cell Interactions, 1991; contbr. numerous articles, revs. to profl. publs.; mem. editorial bd. Jour. Bacteriology, 1967-74, 86-88, Ann. Revs. Microbiology, 1975-79, The Prokaryotes, 2d edit., editor-in-chief 3d edit. Alt. del. Democratic Nat. Conv., 1968; mem. Minn. Dem. Farm Labor Central Com., 1969-70. Served with U.S. Army, 1946-48. Recipient Career Devel. award NIH, 1963-73; John Simon Guggenheim fellow, 1978-79 Fellow Am. Acad. Arts and Scis. (chmn. Midwest ctr., v.p., 2002); mem. Am. Soc. Microbiology (vice chmn. div. gen. microbiology 1977-78, chmn. 1978-79, div. councillor 1980-82), Soc. Gen. Microbiology (Eng.). Home: 2123 Hoyt Ave W Saint Paul MN 55108-1314 Office: U Minn Dept Microbiology Minneapolis MN 55455 Office Phone: 612-624-5634. Business E-Mail: martin@lenti.med.umn.edu.

DWORKIN, PAUL HOWARD, pediatrician; b. Paterson, NJ, Oct. 22, 1947; s. Bernard and Ruth (Steinhauer) D.; m. Sheila Ann Maher, Oct. 7, 1979; children: Molly Maher, Eamon Timothy. AB, Rutgers U., 1969; MD, Johns Hopkins U., 1973. Diplomate Am. Bd. Pediatrics. Pediatric registrar Paddington Green Children's Hosp./St. Mary's Med. Sch., London, 1976; resident in pediatrics Children's Hosp., Boston, 1973-75, fellow in ambulatory pediatrics, 1976-78; asst. prof. pediatrics W.Va. U. Sch. Medicine, Morgantown, 1978-81; prof./asso. chair pediats., head div. gen. peds., asst. dean U. Conn. Sch. Medicine, Farmington, 1981-98, prof./chair pediats., 1998—. Dir., chair pediats. St. Francis Hosp. and Med. Ctr., Hartford, Conn., 1992-03; physician-in-chief Conn. Children's Med. Ctr., Hartford, 1998-04, v.p., chief med. officer, 2005-. Author: Learning and Behavior Problems of Schoolchildren, 1985; editor: Pediatrics: National Medical Series for Independent Study, 1987, 4th edit., 2000; editor Jour. Devel. & Behavioral Pediats., 1996-2002; editl. bd. Pediats., 1991-98, Ambulatory Child Health, Current Pediatrics, 1991—. Vol. Salvation Army Shelter Pediat. Clinic, Hartford, 1991—. Fellow: Am. Acad. Pediats. (chair com. on sci. mtgs. 1994—96); mem.: Soc. Devel. and Behavioral Pediats. (pres. 2005—), Ambulatory Pediat. Assn. Office: Conn Children's Med Ctr 282 Washington St Hartford CT 06106-3322

DWORKIN, RONALD MYLES, law educator; b. Worcester, Mass., Dec. 11, 1931; s. David and Madeline (Taber) D.; m. Betsy Ross, July 18, 1958; children: Anthony Ross, Jennifer. BA, Harvard U., 1953, LLB, 1957; BA, Oxford U., 1955; MA; LLB (hon.), Yale U., 1965. Bar: N.Y. 1959. Law clk. to Judge Learned Hand, 1957-58; assoc. firm Sullivan & Cromwell, 1958-62; faculty Yale Law Sch., 1962-69, master Trumbull Coll., 1966-69, Hohfeld prof. jurisprudence, 1968-69, Oxford, England, 1969-98; Quain prof. jurisprudence Univ. Coll., London, 1998—2004, Bentham prof. juris prudence, 2004—; prof. law NYU, 1975—. Prof.-at-large Cornell U., 1976—; vis. prof. philosophy Princeton (N.J.) U., 1963, 74-75, Gauss seminarian, 1966; vis. prof. law Stanford U., 1967; vis. prof. law and philosophy Harvard U., Cambridge, Mass., 1977, vis. prof. philosophy, 1979; acad. freedom lectr. U. Witwatersrand, 1976. Author: Taking Rights Seriously, 1977, A Matter of Principle, 1985, Law's Empire, 1986, A Bill of Rights for Britain, 1990, Life's Domain, 1993, Freedom's Law, 1996, Sovereign Virtue, 2000; editor: Philosophy of Law, 1977, A Badly Flawed Election, 2002; contbr. articles to profl. jours. Chmn. Dems. Abroad, 1972-74; del. Dem. Nat. Conv., 1972, 76; mem. Dem. Charter Commn., 1974. Fellow Brit. Acad., Am. Acad. Arts and Scis. Office: NYU Law Sch 40 Washington Sq S New York NY 10012-1099

DWORS, ROBERT F., retail executive; BA, Bowling Green (Ohio) State U.; MBA, Ohio State U., 1967. Sr. v.p. corp. real estate svcs. AutoNation, Inc., Ft. Lauderdale, Fla., 1996—. Office: AutoNation Inc 110 SE 6th St Fort Lauderdale FL 33301

DWORSKY, CLARA WEINER, lawyer, brokerage house executive; b. NYC, Apr. 28, 1918; d. Charles and Rebecca (Becker) Weiner; m. Bernard Ezra Dworsky, Jan. 2, 1944; 1 child, Barbara G. Goodman. BS, St. John's U., N.Y.C., 1937, LLB, 1939, JD, 1968. Bar: N.Y. 1939, U.S. Dist. Ct. (ea. dist.) N.Y. 1942, U.S. Dist. Ct. (so. dist.) Tex. 1993, U.S. Ct. Appeals (9th cir.) 1994, U.S. Ct. Appeals (5th cir.) 1995, U.S. Supreme Ct. 2003. Pvt. practice, N.Y.C., 1939-51; assoc. Bessie Farberman, N.Y.C., 1942; clk., sec. U.S. Armed Forces, Camp Carson, Colo., Camp Claiborne, La., 1944-45; abstractor, dir. Realty Title, Rockville, Md., 1954-55; v.p. Kelley & Dworsky Inc., Houston, 1960—. Appeals agt. Gasoline Rationing Appeals Bd., NYC, 1942; bd. dirs. Southlan Sales Assocs., Houston. Vol. ARC, N.Y.C.; vice chmn. War Bond pledge drive, Bklyn.; vol. Houston Legal Found., 1972-73; pres. Women's Aux. Washington Hebrew Acad., 1958-60, v.p. bd. trustees, 1959-60; co-founder, v.p. S. Tex. Hebrew Acad. (now Beren Acad.), Houston, 1970-75, hon. pres. women's divsn., 1973. Recipient Cert. award Treas. of U.S., 1943; Commendation Office of Chief Magistrate of City N.Y., 1948; Pietas medal St. Johns U., 1985. Mem.: ABA (chmn. social security com., sr. lawyers divsn. 1989—93, mem. sr. lawyers divsn. coun. 1989—95, chairsubcom. 1993—95, chmn. social security com., sr. lawyers divsn. 1995—, mem. editl. bd. sr. lawyers divsn. pub. Experience), Nat. Assn. Women Lawyers (chmn. organizer Juvenile Delinquency Clinic N.Y. 1948—51), Houston Bar Assn. (sec. social secutiry sect. 1995—96), Fed. Bar Assn. (vice chair programs, sr. lawyers divsn. 1994—96, dep. chair 1996—97, chmn. 1997—98, chair sr. lawyers com. south Tex. chpt. bd. 1998—, co-editor sr. citizens handbook, 2d printing 2002—03, chmn. soc. sec. com., sen. lawyers divsn.), N.Y. State Bar Assn., St. Johns U. Alumni Assn. (coord. Houston chpt. 1983—, pres. 1986), Amit Women Club, Delphians Past Pres.'s Club, Hadassah. Jewish. Home: 9726 Cliffwood Dr Houston TX 77096-4406 Office Phone: 713-523-3332.

DWORSKY, DANIEL LEONARD, architect, educator; b. Mpls., Oct. 4, 1927; s. Lewis and Ida (Fineberg) D.; m. Sylvia Ann Taylor, Aug. 10, 1957; children: Douglas, Laurie, Nancy. BArch, U. Mich., 1950. Practice architecture as Dworsky Assocs., LA, 1953-2000, Cannon Dworsky, LA, 2000—03; design critic, lectr. architecture U. So. Calif., 1983—84, U. Mich., 1983—84, UCLA, 1983—84. Chmn. archtl. rev. panel Fed. Res. Bank. Recipient Design citation Progressive Arch. mag. 1967, Gov. Calif. award 1966, 3 LA Grand Prix awards So. Calif. AIA and City of LA 1967; prin. works include Angelus Plz. Elderly Housing, LA, 1981, Ontario (Calif.) City Hall, 1980, CBS Exec. Office Bldg., North Hollywood, Calif., 1970, UCLA Stadium, 1969, Fed. Res. Bank Bldg., LA, 1987, U. Mich. Crisler Arena at Ann Arbor, 1966, Dominguez Hills State U. Theatre, 1977, Ventura County Govt. Ctr., 1979, Northrop Electronics Hdqrs., LA, 1983, Hewlett-Packard Region Office, North Hollywood, 1984, LA County Mcpl. Cts. Bldg., 1985, Tom Bradley Internat. Terminal LA Airport, 1984, City Tower, Orange, Calif., 1988, Fed. Office Bldg., Long Beach, Calif., 1992, Las Vegas Fed. Cts. Bldg., 2000. Disting. Alumnus award U. Mich. Architecture Sch., 2005. Fellow AIA (more than 100 awards including 24 awards Calif. chpts., Nat. Honor award 1974, 68-69, Firm award Calif. chpt. 1985, L.A. Gold Medal award 1994, State of Calif. Lifetime Achievement award 2004). Home: 9225 Nightingale Dr Los Angeles CA 90069-1117 Office Phone: 310-271-2106. Business E-Mail: dandworsky@mac.com.

DWORSKY, MARY, interior designer; b. Mpls., Feb. 17, 1948; d. Zollie and Lucille Dworsky. Attended, U. Minn., 1966-71. Cert. interior designer Minn. Interior designer Creative Furniture, Mpls., 1974-79, Mr. Furniture, Mpls., 1980-82, Dorothy Collins Interiors, Edina, Minn., 1982-89, Interior Design Ptnrs., Edina, 1989-92, The Design Studio of Gabberts, Edina, 1992-2000, Mary Dworsky Interior Design Ltd., Mpls. Decorations chair Mpls. Crisis Nursery, 1996, chair Showcase House Cmty. Svc. Mem.: ASID (Minn. chpt. pres. 2000—01, pres. 2000—01, dir., sec., Presdl. Citation 1994, 1996, 1999, 2000, 2002, 2003, 2004), Quota Club Mlps. (bd.mem., v.p.), Rotary (com. chair 1991—99). Home: #121 3720 Independence Ave S Minneapolis MN 55426-3781 Office: Mary Dworsky Interior Design Ltd 275 Market St Ste 451 Minneapolis MN 55405

DWORZAN, HELENE LIBERMAN, novelist, poet, playwright; b. Paris, France, Mar. 13, 1925; d. Ansjel and Rebecca (Weiripp) Liberman; came to U.S., 1950, naturalized, 1952; student Lycee Victor Hugo, Paris, 1937-43, New Sch. for Social Research, 1952-53; BA, Richmond Coll., 1974; m. George R. Dworzan; 1 son, Patrice Olivier; m. 2d, Donald H. Reiman, 1975. Translator, Robin Internat./Cinerama, N.Y.C., 1954-59; freelance translator NBC, 1962-72; assoc. editor Chelsea, lit. rev., 1970-81; tchr. French, Lang. Inst., N.Y.C., 1970-73, Riverdale Country Sch., N.Y.C., 1973-86; founder, dir. Continuum, poetry and fiction readings, 1970-76. Recipient novel grant Material Jewish Claims against Germany, 1961, Short Story award Dial Press, 1953; Prairie Schooner prize for fiction, 1978. Mem. Authors League Am., Dramatists Guild. Author: (novel) Le Temps de la Chrysalide, 1957; editor: (with Donald H. Reiman) Shelley's Last Notebook, 1990; also short stories and poems in various publs. Address: 907 Aster Ave Newark DE 19711-2631

DWYER, CARRIE ELIZABETH, lawyer; b. San Mateo, Calif., Dec. 19, 1950; d. Robert Harold and Alice Marian (Daley) Dwyer; m. Richard M. Konecky, Feb. 12, 1977; children: Rachel Anne, Philip. BA in English, U. Santa Clara, 1973, JD, 1976. Bar: Calif., NY. Staff atty. Am. Stock Exchange, NYC, 1977-79, exec. asst. to exec. v.p. legal and regulatory affairs, 1979—81, asst. v.p., exec. asst. to pres., 1981—83, v.p., exec. asst. to pres., 1983—85, v.p., assoc. gen. counsel, 1985—87, sr. v.p., gen. counsel, 1987—89; contract lawyer Milbank, Tweed, Hadley & McCoy, NYC; sr. counsel to chmn. Arthur Levitt SEC, 1993—96; exec. v.p. corp. oversight The Charles Schwab Corp., San Francisco, 1996—, gen. counsel, 1998—. Mem. ABA, The Assn. of Bar of City of NY, NY State Bar Assn., Investment Assn. Office: The Charles Schwab Corp 101 Montgomery St San Francisco CA 94104*

DWYER, CORNELIUS J., JR., lawyer; b. New Rochelle, N.Y., Sept. 3, 1943; s. Cornelius John and Mary Cecelia (McDonough) D.; m. June Forsythe Sonnekalb, Sept. 14, 1968; children: Cornelius William, Colin Micheal. BA, Yale U., 1965; LLB, Harvard U., 1968. Bar: N.Y. 1968, U.S. Dist. Ct. N.Y. 1969. Assoc. Shearman & Sterling, N.Y.C., 1968-76, ptnr., 1976—. Democrat. Roman Catholic. Office: Shearman & Sterling 599 Lexington Ave Fl C2 New York NY 10022-6069 E-mail: cdwyer@sharman.com.

DWYER, DARRELL JAMES, finance company executive; b. Vermillion, S.D., Nov. 27, 1946; s. Michael Leroy and Faye Awilda (Hansen) Dwyer; m. Helen K. Howard, 1989; 1 child, Sean Patrick. BS, Minn. State U., 1977; MBA, U. Calif., Berkeley, 1978. CPA, cert. mgmt. acct., internal auditor; data processor. Acct. Touche Ross & Co., Salem, Oreg., 1978-79; cons. Arthur, Persons Co., Salem, 1980-82; v.p. fin. Evergreen Internat. Airlines Inc, McMinnville, Oreg., 1982-87; CFO Erickson Group Ltd., Medford, Oreg., 1987-89; sr. v.p., corp. sec. Evergreen Internat. Aviation, Inc., McMinnville, 1989-90; pres., CEO Dwyer Co., Rocklin, Calif., 1990—. Recipient award of merit, Evergreen Internat. Aviation, McMinnville, 1984; Calif. State scholar. Mem.: Inst. Cert. Mgmt. Accts., Calif. Soc. CPA. Republican. Episcopalian. Avocations: skiing, tennis, travel. Office: Dwyer Co 3111 Sunset Blvd Rocklin CA 95677 Personal E-mail: djdwyer@pacbell.net.

DWYER, DENNIS D., information technology executive; b. Oak Park, Ill., July 19, 1943; s. John J. and Jessie M. Dwyer; m. Carolyn R. Schultz, Apr. 29, 1967; children: David, Julianne. Various positions Harris Bank, Chgo., 1967-83, mgr. info. tech. planning, 1983-86, v.p. tech. facilitation, 1986—. Resolutions chmn. Cooperating Users of Burroughs Equipment, Detroit, 1978-82; cons. Unisys mainframe computers. Pres. Hunting Ridge Homeowners Assn., 1983-85; mem. Palatine Plan Commn., 1984—, chmn., 1989—. Recipient Tom Grier award for Excellence Unisys Users Group, 1988. Home: 1032 Raven Ln Palatine IL 60067-6649 Office: Harris Bank PO Box 755 Chicago IL 60690-0755 Office Phone: 312-461-6941. Business E-Mail: dennis.dwyer@harrisbank.com. E-mail: dennis-carolyn@ravenlane.com.

DWYER, GARY JOSEPH, lawyer; b. Yonkers, N.Y., Dec. 5, 1958; s. Donald A. and Josephine (Heller) D.; m. Magdalen Marton, Sept. 14, 1985; children: Kevin John, Donald Patrick, Ryan Joseph. BA magna cum laude, Fordham U., 1980; JD cum laude, Bklyn. Law Sch., 1983. Bar: N.Y. 1984, U.S. Dist. Ct. (ea. and so. dists.) N.Y. 1984. Assoc. Morris, Duffy, Alonso & Marulli, N.Y.C., 1983-94; ptnr. Dwyer & Taglia, N.Y.C., 1994—. Mem. ABA, N.Y. State Bar Assn. Republican. Roman Catholic. Office: Dwyer & Taglia 111 John St New York NY 10038-3101

DWYER, GERALD PAUL, JR., economist, bank executive; b. Pittsfield, Mass., July 9, 1947; s. Gerald Paul and Mary Frances (Weir) Dwyer; m. Katherine Marie Lepiane, Jan. 15, 1966; children: Tamara K., Gerald P. III, Angela M., Michael J. L., Terence F. BBA, U. Wash., 1969; MA in Econs., U. Tenn., 1973; PhD in Econs., U. Chgo., 1979. Economist Fed. Res. Bank, St. Louis, 1972-74, Chgo., 1976-77, asst. v.p. Atlanta, 1997-98, v.p., 1998—; asst. prof. Tex. A&M U., College Station, 1977-81, Emory U., Atlanta, 1981-84, sr. rsch. assoc. Law and Econ. Ctr., 1982-84; assoc. prof. U. Houston, 1984-89; prof. Clemson (S.C.) U., 1989-99, acting head dept. econ., 1992-93. Cons. Arthur Bros., Corpus Christi, Tex., 1980—81, FTC, Washington, 1983—84, Amerigas, Houston, 1985, We. Container Corp., 1987, Metrica, Inc., Bryan, Tex., 1989—93; vis. scholar Fed. Res. Bank, Atlanta, 1982—84, St. Louis, 1987—89, Atlanta, 1994—97, Mpls., 1995; vis. fin. economist Commodity Futures Trading Commn., Washington, 1990; vis. faculty Ga. State U., 1997, U. Ga., 1999—2000, 2003—, Univ. Rome, 2000—04, U. Carlos III, Madrid, 2005—. Contbr. articles to profl. jours. Fellow, Earhart Found., 1975—77; Weaver fellow, Intercollegiate Studies Inst., 1974—75, Rsch. grantee, Earhart Found., NSF. Mem.: Western Econ. Assn. (exec. com. 2005—), Assn. of Pvt. Enterprise Edn. (exec. com. 2002—), Soc. Nonlinear Dynamics and Econometrics (treas. 1997—2003, pres. 2003—05), Am. Fin. Assn., Am. Econ. Assn., Phi Kappa Phi, Beta Gamma Sigma. Avocation: sailing.

DWYER, JOHANNA TODD, nutritionist, educator; b. Syracuse, NY, Oct. 20, 1938; d. M. Harold and Frances (Markey) D. BS with distinction, Cornell U., 1960; MSc, U. Wis., 1962; MS, Harvard Sch. Pub. Health, Boston, 1965, DSc, 1969. Asst. prof. Harvard Sch. Pub. Health, 1969-73; home economist Procter & Gamble, Cin., 1962-64; rsch. asst. U. Wis., Madison, 1960-62; assoc. prof. Tufts Med. Sch., 1974, prof. medicine and nutrition, 1984—; sr. scientist human nutrition rsch. USDA, Boston, 1988—, asst. adminstr. for human nutrition Agrl. Rsch. Svc. Washington, 2001—02; sr. nutrition rsch. scientist Office of Dietary Supplements, NIH, 2004—. Dir. Frances Stern Nutrition Ctr., New Eng. Med. Ctr., Boston, 1974—; adj. prof. Harvard Sch. Pub. Health, 1988—. Author 3 books, 1979, 83; editor Nutrition Today, 1995—; contbr. over 300 articles to profl. jours. Mem. Mass. Nutrition Bd., Boston, 1980—; cons. Exec. Office of Pres., Washington, 1976; mem. bd. sci. counselors Nat. Cancer Inst., 1985-89; com. mem. and nuitrition work study Am. Cancer Soc., 1990-94. Robert Wood Johnson Health Policy fellow, 1980-81, John Stalker award Am. Sch. Food Svc. Assn., 1990, Alumni Merit award Harvand Sch. Pub. Health, 2004. Fellow: Am. Soc. Nutrition Scis. (Conrad Elvejhem award for pub. svc. 2005), Am. Inst. Nutrition (pres. 1994—95, bd. dirs.), Am. Soc. Clin. Nutrition (sec. 1990—93), Soc. for Nutrition Edn. (bd. dirs. 1975—77, J. Harvey Wiley award 1983); mem.: APHA (program devel. bd. 1990—92), Dannon Inst. (sci. adv. bd. 2003—), Internat. Life Scis. Inst. (bd. dirs. 1999—), Food and Drug Law Inst. (bd. dirs. 1980—95), Am. Inst. Food and Wine (bd. dirs. 1991—95), Nutrition Screening Initiative (tech. and sci. rev. com. 1990—2004), Inst. Medicine of NAS (food and nutrition bd. 1990—2000, councilor 2001—03), Am. Dietetic

Assn. (legis. and pub. policy com. 1998—2004, sec. found. 2005—, lectr., Medallion award 2002, Found. award 2004, Lenna Frances Cooper award), Am. Soc. Parenteral and Enteral Nutrition (adv. bd. 1978—). Office: Tufts New Eng Med Ctr 750 Washington St PO Box 783 Boston MA 02102-0783 Office Phone: 617-636-5273. Personal E-mail: toddyd@msn.com. Business E-Mail: dwyerj1@od.nih.gov.

DWYER, JOHN M., mathematician, statistician, computer scientist; b. Ann Arbor, Mich., June 8, 1937; s. Paul Sumner and Florence Baylis (Brown) D.; children: Anne Louise, Laura Beth. BA, U. Mich., 1959, MS, 1965; PhD, Tex A&M U., 1971. Asst. prof. stats. U. Wyo., Laramie, 1962-66; asst. prof. math. U. Detroit, 1969-73, assoc. prof. math., 1974—, chair, 1974-77, interim chair, 1989-91. Vis. assoc. prof. dept. mgmt. and mktg. Northern Mich. U., Marquette, 1983-84; dir. rsch. Detroit Inst. Abuse Rsch. and Tng., 1973-74; cons. Detroit Tax Assessor's Office, 1971; expert witness Focus: HOPE, Detroit, 1981-86; panelist "Ask the Professor" radio show U. Detroit, 1977-83. Mem.: AAAS, Computer Profls. for Social Responsibility (co-founder Mich. chpt. 1997, chair 1998—2001, bd. dirs. 2001—, treas. 2002), Assn. Computing Machinery, Union of Concerned Scientists, Math. Assn. Am. Office: U Detroit Mercy Dept Math and Computer Sci 4001 W McMichaels Detroit MI 48222 Office Phone: 313-993-1061. Business E-Mail: dwyerjm@udmercy.edu.

DWYER, JOHN P., law educator; b. 1951; BA DePauw U.; PhD, Calif. Inst. Tech., 1978; JD, U. Calif., Berkeley, 1980. Bar: D.C. 1981, Calif. 1982. Law clk. to Hon. Harry T. Edwards U.S. Ct. Appeals (D.C. cir.), Washington, 1980-81; law clk. to Hon. Sandra O'Connor U.S. Supreme Ct., Washington, 1981-82; staff atty. D.C. Pub. Defender Svc., 1982-84; prof. U. Calif. Berkeley, 1984—2002, dean, 2000—02, John H. Boalt Prof. Law, Emeritus, 2002—. Visiting prof. Harvard Law Sch., Vrije Universiteit, Amsterdam.

DWYER, MAUREEN ELLEN, lawyer; BA, Smith Coll., 1973; JD, Cath. U. Am. Columbus Sch. Law, 1978. Bar: DC 1979, US Dist. Ct. (DC), US Ct. Appeals (DC cir.), US Supreme Ct. Shareholder Wilkes Artis, Wash., DC; ptnr. real estate group Pillsbury Winthrop Shaw Pittman, Wash., DC. Adj. prof. American Univ. Chmn. adv. bd. Salvation Army; past chmn. Eugene & Agnes Meyer Found. Named one of 100 Most Powerful Women in Wash., Washingtonian mag., 2001. Mem.: Comml. Real Estate Women (past pres.), Fed. City Council, DC C. of C., Urban Land Inst., Greater Wash. Bd. Trade, DC Bldg. Industry Assn., Economic Club. Office: Pillsbury Winthrop Shaw Pittman 2300 N St NW Washington DC 20037-1128 Office Phone: 202-663-8834. Office Fax: 202-663-8007. Business E-Mail: maureen.dwyer@pillsburylaw.com.

DWYER, WILLIAM H., real estate company executive; b. Milw., Sept. 6, 1950; s. Thomas H. and Eileen M. Dwyer; m. Sue D., Sept. 6, 1980; 2 children. BS, U. We. Wis., 1973. Cert. property mgr.; accredited resident mgr. Real estate broker Dwyer/Kloce Realtor, 1972—80; pres. Premier Real Estate Mgmt., LLC (formerly Calvin Akin), Brookfield, Wis., 1990—2003; v.p. Bartlein & Co., Inc., 1980—90. Mem.: Notary. Office: Premier Real Estate Mgmt LLC 12630 W North Ave Brookfield WI 53005-4626

DWYER, WILLIAM MICHAEL, health care company marketing executive; b. Sparta, Wis., Sept. 7, 1952; s. William Ambrose and Beatrice Helen (Kopenhafer) D.; m. Ruth Elaine Heitzman, Feb. 21, 1976; children: Meghan Ruth, Gretchen Mary, William Theodore, Michelle Elizabeth. BA in adolescent psychology, U. Minn., Mpls., 1974; MBA in marketing, health svs. mgmt., gen. mgmt., Northwestern U., Evanston, Ill., 1989. Psychiat. technician Mounds Park Hosp., St. Paul, 1974-77; hosp. sales rep. Abbott Labs., Rochester, Minn., 1977-81, profl. sales specialist Houston, 1981-83, sr. market rsch. analyst Abbott Park, Ill., 1983—85, mgr. major market planning, 1985-88, dir. major market planning, 1988-90, dir. corp. account devel., 1990-94, sr. dir. strategic mtkg., 1994—2000; divisional v.p. Abbott Labs. Strategic Mktg., Abbott Park, 2000—04; sr. v.p. Cerner Corp., Kansas City, Mo., 2004—. Mem. payment adv. bd. Health Industry Mfrs. Assn., Washington, 1994—, Patient Safety Task Force (chmn. 2000-03); bd. dirs. Nat. Com. Quality Health Care, Washington, 1990—, chmn., 1996, Nat. Ctr. for Healthcare Leadership, Health Rsch. & Ednl. Trust, Nat. Com. Quality Health Care, Medical Clin. Affairs Com. Advocate HealthCare, Banner Health Systems; mentor, preceptor J.L. Kellogg Program Health Adminstrn., Evanston, Ill., 1995-96; corp. liaison Healthcare R&D Inst., 1988—. Contbg. author: Reinventing Health Care: Revolution At Hand, 1992, Total Quality Management: Health Care Pioneers, 1992, Medical Group Practices Face Uncertain Future, 1995, Enhancing Physician Performance, 2000, Careers in Healthcare Management, 2002, Hospital of the Future: A Leaders' Perspective, 2003. Pres. Tullamore Home Assn., Mundelein, Ill., 1990; deacon Calvary Bapt. Ch., Mundelein, 1992-94; state del. Rep. Party, State of Minn., 1972 Recipient scholarship Stout Meml. Found., 1970, A.B. Dick Trustee Forum award Lake Forest (Ill.) Hosp., 1991, Laura G. Jackson Disting. Alumnus award Health Svcs. Mgmt., J.L. Kellogg Grad. Sch. Mgmt., Northwestern U., 1998, Marshall A. Faulk, M.D. Disting. Lectureship Finch Univ. Health Scis., 2001, Edward John Noble Lecture Greenwhich Hosp., 2003, Disting. Svc. award, Ohio State Univ., 2003. Mem. Am. Hosp. Assn./Soc. Hosp. Plan and Mktg., Am. Coll. Healthcare Execs. (mem. leadership adv. bd. 1994-97), Beta Gamma Sigma. Avocations: skiing, fly fishing, wilderness canoeing. Office: 2800 Rockcreek Pkwy Kansas City MO 64117-2551 Home: 4315 N Hickory Ln Kansas City MO 64116 Office Phone: 816-201-4267.

DWYER SOUTHERN, KATHY, museum administrator; m. Hugh Southern; 1 child. BA in Mktg., U. Wis., 1968, MA in Arts Adminstrn., 1972. Exec. dir. Nat. Cultural Alliance, 1990—94, Montpelier, Va., 1994—96; pres., CEO Port Discovery, Balt., 1996—2001, Nat. Children's Mus., 2001—. Arts mgmt. prof. Am. U., Va. Commonwealth U., Shenandoah Conservatory Music; bd. dirs. Am. Assn. Mus., Coun. Children's Mus. Office: Nat Children's Mus 955 L'Enfant Plaza N Ste 5100 Washington DC 20024-2103 Office Phone: 202-675-4120. Business E-Mail: ksouthern@ncm.museum.org.

DWYRE, WILLIAM PATRICK, journalist; b. Sheboygan, Wis., Apr. 7, 1944; s. George Leo and Mary Veronica (O'Brien) D.; m. Jill Ethlyn Jarvis, July 30, 1966; children— Amy, Patrick BA, U. Notre Dame, Ind. Sports copy editor Des Moines Register, 1966-68; sports writer, asst. sports editor, sports editor Milw. Jour., 1968-81; asst. sports editor, sports editor Los Angeles Times, 1981—. Columnist Referee Mag., 1977-02; voting mem., bd. dirs. Amateur Athletic Found. Nat. Sports Hall of Fame, 1981—. Bd. dirs. Honda-Brockerick Cup Women's Collegiate Athlete of Yr.; bd. dirs. Casa Colina Hosp. Rehab., Pomona. Named Sportswriter of Yr., Wis. Nat. Sportscasters and Sportswriters Assn., 1980; Nat. Editor of Yr., Nat. Press Found., 1985; recipient award for Sustained Excellence by Individual, L.A. Times, 1985, Red Smith award AP sports Editors, 1996, Acad Literary award, 2004, Los Angeles Sports and Entertainment Commn. Ambassador award, 2005. Mem. Nat. Sportscasters and Sportswriters Assn. (bd. dirs., Powerade Sport Story of Yr. award 1999), Assoc. Press Sports Editors (pres. 1989), LA Sports and Entertainment Comm. Amb. award, 2005, Subiaco (Ark.). Avocation: tennis. Office: Los Angeles Times Times Mirror Sq Los Angeles CA 90012 E-mail: bill.dwyre@latimes.com.

DYAR, KATHRYN WILKIN, pediatrician; b. Colquitt, Ga., Feb. 20, 1945; d. Patrick McWhorter and Virginia (Wilkin) Dyar; m. James Ansley Patten, Jan. 1, 1985. BS in Biology, Emory U., Decatur, Ga., 1966; MD, Med. Coll. Ga., Augusta, 1970. Resident in pediatrics Eugene Talmadge Meml. Hosp., Augusta, Ga., 1970-72, Georgetown U. Hosp., Washington, 1972-73; pediatrician Children's Clinic, Tifton, Ga., 1973-74, Children and Youth Project, Norfolk, Va., 1974-83, 90-95, dir., 1990-94; pediatrician Hampton (Va.) Health Dept., 1983-90. Fellow: Am. Acad. Pediatrics.

DYAS, DONNA F., elementary school educator; b. Artesia, N.Mex., Oct. 7, 1955; d. Warren Thomas Johnston and Norma Shirleen Campbell; children: Allyson, Amy, Adam. BA in Edn., N.Mex. State U., 1977; MA in Elem. Edn., No. Ariz. U., 2003. Tchr. 1st grade Gilbert Pub. Schs., Ariz., 1989—2005. Peer mentor Gilbert Pub. Schs., 2004—05, grade level choir, 2003—05. So. Baptist. Avocations: quilting, porcelain dolls. Home: 927 E Constitution Gilbert AZ 85296

DYBEK, STUART, language educator, writer; b. Chgo., Apr. 10, 1942; s. Stanley and Adeline (Sala) S.; m. Caren Bassett, Feb. 7, 1967; children: Anne, Nicholas. BS, Loyola U., Chgo., 1964, MA, 1967; MFA, U. Iowa, 1973. Tchr. U.S. V.I. Sch., St. Thomas, 1968-70, U. Iowa, Iowa City, 1970-73; prof. English Western Mich. U., Kalamazoo, 1973—. Vis. prof. creative writing Princeton (N.J.) U., 1991, U. Calif., Irvine, 1995, U. Iowa, 1998, Northwestern U., 2001. Author: (poetry) Brass Knuckles, 1979, Streets In Their Own Ink, 2004; (fiction) Childhood and Other Neighborhoods, 1980, The Coast of Chicago, 1990, I Sailed With Magellan, 2003. Guggenheim fellow, 1982; recipient Whiting Writers award, 1985, O. Henry first prize, 1985, Acad. award in fiction Am. Acad. Arts and Letters, 1994, PEN/Malamud award, 1995, Lannan Lit. prize, 1998. Mem. PEN. Home: 320 Monroe St Kalamazoo MI 49006-4436 Office: Western Michigan U Dept English Kalamazoo MI 49008 also: care Amanda Urban Intl Creative Mgt 40 W 57th St New York NY 10019-4001 Personal E-mail: sdybek@earthlink.net.

DYCHE, DAVID BENNETT, JR., retired management consultant; b. Port Chester, N.Y., July 23, 1932; s. David B. and Julia H. D.; m. Mary J. Moorman, Apr. 28, 1956; children— David B. III, Williard H. AB, Dartmouth Coll., 1954; MBA, U. Pa., 1958. Chartered fin. analyst. With J.P. Morgan & Co., and Morgan Guaranty Trust Co., N.Y.C., 1958-81; dir. fin. industries Arthur D. Little, Inc., 1981-98; mgr. North Creek Cons. LLC. Chmn., commr. Boca Grande Fire Control Dist., 2000-04. With U.S. Army, 1954-56. Mem. Assn. Investment Mgmt. Rsch., N.Y. Soc. Security Analysts. Home: 61 Bayhead Ln Osprey FL 34229-8992

DYCK, DENNIS G., psychologist, educator; b. Abbotsford, British Columbia, Canada, Feb. 18, 1946; s. Benjamin E. Dyck and Anne Quiring; m. Susan Jean Goodman, Jan. 24, 1949; children: Benjamin Joseph, Joshua Jay. BA, Fresno Pacific U., 1969; MA, Pepperdine U., 1970; PhD, U. Okla., 1973. Lic. Psychologist Wash., 1992. Dir. Health Rsch. and Edn. Ctr., Spokane, Wash., 1991—2002; prof. Wash. State U., Spokane, 1991—, vice chancellor, 1991—. Mem.: APA (licentiate). Protestant. Achievements include research in clinical psychology and neurosciences. Avocations: running, travel, music. Office: Washington State U Health Scis Bldg Rm 320 NPO Box 1495 Spokane WA 99210-1495 Home Fax: (509) 358-7627. Personal E-mail: dyck@wsu.edu.

DYCK, MARTIN, literary agent, mathematician; b. Grünfeld, Ukraine, Jan. 16, 1927; came to U.S., 1956; s. Martin and Helene (Peters) Sommer D.; m. Marie Wiens, June 12, 1949 (div. 1983); children: Vernon, Victor, Martin Christopher Columbus and Ingrid Rose Marie (twins). BA German and Pure Math. (double hons.), U. Manitoba, Can., 1953, MA in German and Math., 1954; PhD in German Lit., U. Cin., 1956. Grad. asst. math. U. Manitoba, 1952-53, sessional lectr. in Germn, 1953-54; Taft Meml. fellow U. Cin., 1954-56; asst. prof. German and Russian MIT, Cambridge, 1956-58, prof. German and humanities, 1965-87, prof. emeritus, 1987—; from asst. to prof. German U. Mich., Ann Arbor, 1958-65. Author: Goethe und die Mathematik, 1954, Novalis and Mathematics, 1960, 70, Die Gedichte Schillers, 1967; mem. editorial bd. Historia Mathematica, 1972-76; contbr. articles to profl. jours. and book chpts. Fellow Guggenheim, 1961-62, Am. Coun. Learned Socs., 1961-62; grantee Am. Philos. Soc., 1969. Mem. MLA (del. assembly 1979-81), Modern Humanities Rsch. Assn., Assn. Lit. Scholars and Critics, History of Sci. Soc., Lessing Soc., Am. Soc. for Eighteenth Century Studies, Am. Assn. Tchrs. German, German Studies, Assn., N.E. MLA. Avocations: mountain climbing, walking, reading. Home: PO Box 1179 Lincoln NH 03251-1179 Office: MIT 77 Massachusetts Ave Rm E38-277 Cambridge MA 02139-4307 *I have striven to test and taste the poetry, comedy, and mathematics of man against matter and nothingness.*

DYCK, PETER, neurosurgeon, educator; b. Neuhalbstadt, Russia, June 16, 1935; came to the U.S., 1962; s. Peter Dueck and Margaret Derksen; m. Barbara Ann Keenan, 1959 (div. 1964); children: Deborah Nailon, Carrie Froese; m. Carole Jean Cassetto, Oct. 30, 1964; children: Christopher, Michelle. MD, U. B.C., Vancouver, Can., 1961. Intern, Youngstown, Ohio, 1961-62; resident in neurosurgery U. So. Calif./Los Angeles County Med. Ctr., 1962-66; pvt. practice Calif., 1962-98; clin. prof. neurosurgery U. So. Calif., L.A., 1998—. Clin. prof. neurosurgery U. So. Calif., L.A. Editor: 2 books, 1984, 89; contbr. chpts. to books and articles to profl. jours. Elder First Hollywood Presbyn. Ch. Fellow ACS; mem. AMA, Internat. Soc. for Study of the Lumbar Spine, Royal Coll. Medicine, Western Neurosurg. Soc., Congress Neurol. Surgeons, Calif. Assn. Neurol. Surgeons, Calif. Assn. Neurol. Surgeons (pres. 1997-98), Calif. Med. Assn., L.A. County Med. Assn. Republican. Avocations: golf, reading, poetry, fishing. Home: 484 Starlight Crest Dr La Canada Flintridge CA 91011-2853 Office: Univ So Calif 2750 E Washington Blvd Ste 130 Pasadena CA 91107-1449 also: 1510 San Pablo St Ste 268 Los Angeles CA 90089-0113

DYCK, WALTER PETER, gastroenterologist, educator, academic administrator; b. Winkler, Man., Can., 1935; MD, U. Kans., 1961. Diplomate Am. Bd. Internal Medicine, Am. Bd. Gastroenterology. Intern Henry Ford Hosp., Detroit, 1961—62, resident in internal medicine, 1962-63, 65-66; rsch. fellow gastroenterology U. Zurich, Switzerland, 1963—64; fellow enzymology rsch. U. Toronto, Canada, 1964—65; fellow gastroenterology Mt. Sinai Sch. Medicine, N.Y.C., 1966—68; mem. sr. staff Scott and White Clinic, Temple, Tex., 1968—, chmn. dept. rsch., 1969—72, dir. divsn. gastroenterology, 1972—96; prof. medicine, dir. divsn. gastroenterology Tex. A&M Coll. Medicine, 1978—96; adminstrv. dir. rsch. and edn. divsn., chief acad. officer Scott and White Meml. Hosp., Temple, 1996—; sr. assoc. dean Tex. A&M Coll. Medicine, 1996—2003, exec. assoc. dean, 2003—. Mem. gen. medicine study sect. A NIH, 1973-77. Fellow ACP, Am. Coll. Gastroenterology; mem. AMA, Am. Fedn. Clin. Rsch., Am. Gastroenterology Assn., Am. Physiol. Soc., So. Soc. Clin. Investigation, Soc. for Exptl. Biology and Medicine, Am. Pancreatic Assn., N.Y. Acad. Scis. Office: Scott and White Hosp 2401 S 31st St Temple TX 76508-0002 Office Phone: 254-724-2368. Business E-Mail: wdyck@swmail.sw.org.

DYCKMAN, THOMAS RICHARD, accountant, educator; b. Detroit, Feb. 25, 1932; s. Clovis E. and Wildarene A. (Andrus) Dyckman; m. Alice Ann Pletta, Nov. 4, 1955; children: Daniel, James, Linda, David. BA, U. Mich., 1954, MBA, 1955, PhD, 1961. Asst. prof. acctg. U. Calif., Berkeley, 1961-64; assoc. prof. Cornell U., Ithaca, NY, 1964-68, prof., 1968—, Ann Whitney Olin prof. bus., 1978—, assoc. dean Johnson Grad. Sch. Mgmt., 1985-95, acting dean, 1996-97, acting v.p. for info. tech., 1998-99. Cons. IBM, GTE, SNET, Fin. Acctg. Stds. Bd., mem. adv. com., 1984—88; chair audit com. bd. dirs. Galaxy Nutritional Foods, 2002—. Author: (book) Topics in Cost Accounting and Decisions, 1963, Statistical Decision Theory, 1968, Algebra and Calculus for Business, 1975, Managerial Cost Accounting, 1971, 2d edit., 1976, Fundamental Statistics for Business and Economics, 1977, Efficient Capital Markets, 1975, 2d edit., 1986, Cases in Financial Accounting, 1987, 3d edit., 1989, Cost Accounting: Concepts and Managerial Applications, 1990, 2d edit., 1994, Intermediate Accounting, rev. edit., 1992, 5th edit., 2001. Mem. adv. com. Fin. Acctg. Found., 1990—93. With USNR, 1955—58. Recipient Gold medal award, AICPA, 1968, 1976. Mem.: Am. Acctg. Assn. (pres. 1981—82, dir. rsch. 1976—78, Outstanding Acctg. Educator award 1987). Home: 135 Eastlake Rd Ithaca NY 14850-9700 Office: Cornell U Sage Hall Ithaca NY 14853 Business E-Mail: trd2@cornell.edu.

DYCUS, ELIZABETH RASMUSSEN, academic administrator; d. John Juergen Rasmussen and Elise Louise Leinhardt; m. J. Stephen Dycus, Sept. 21, 1968; children: Jamie Stephen, Anne Lee Dycus Shapiro. BA, So. Meth. U., 1962. Staff asst. Congressman Speedy O. Long, Washington, 1966—68; itinerary sec. Senator Elect Lloyd Bentsen, Houston, 1970; asst. to chair Three Mile Island Commn., Hanover, Washington, 1979; asst. to the pres. Dartmouth Coll., Hanover, NH, 1980—83; dir. external rels. CLIPP, Dartmouth Coll., Hanover, NH, 1988—95; asst. dir. for recruitment IDE, Dartmouth Coll., Hanover, NH, 1999—2003; sr. assoc. Kornferry Internat., Strafford, Vt., 2003—. Mem., chair Vt. State Bd. of Health, Burlington, 1988—2004; mem. exec. com. Vt. State Dem. Party, 1985—91. Democrat. Congregationalist.

DYCUS, STEPHEN, law educator; b. Dallas, Nov. 13, 1941; m. Elizabeth Rasmussen, Sept. 21, 1968; children: Jamie S., Anne Lee. BA, So. Meth. U., 1963, LLB, 1965; LLM, Harvard U., 1976. Bar: Tex. 1965, Vt. 1980. Trust officer Oak Cliff Bank & Trust Co., Dallas, 1965-66, Tex. Comm. Bank, Houston, 1966-72; asst. dean Law Sch. So. Meth. U., Dallas, 1972-75; prof. Vt. Law Sch., South Royalton, 1976—. Vis. scholar Law Sch., U. Calif., Berkeley, 1983-84, Nat. Resources Def. Coun., Washington, 1991; vis. prof. U.S. Mil. Acad., West Point, N.Y., 1991-92; mem. Vt. Water Resources Bd., Montpelier, 1993-97. Co-author: National Security Law, 1990, 3d edit., 2002; author: National Defense and the Environment, 1996; co-editor: Jour. Nat. Security Law and Policy, 2004—. Mem. Lawyers Alliance for World Security (bd. dirs. 1986—), Am. Law Inst. Democrat. Congregationalist. Home: 215 Justin Morrill Mem Hwy Strafford VT 05072-7703 Office: Vt Law Sch South Royalton VT 05068 Office Phone: 802-831-1292. Business E-Mail: sdycus@vermontlaw.edu.

DYE, ANNE C., management consultant; BA in Interdisciplinary Studies, Western Wash. U., 1981; M of Health Svcs. Adminstrn., George Washington U., 1992. Counselor, exec. asst. KHI Svcs., Inc., Md., 1983—86; adminstr. Cmty. Clinic, Inc., 1986—89; adminstrv. resident Nat. Lutheran Home for the Aged, 1991—92; pres. Mirror Lake Assoc., 1992—96; from orgnl. devel. specialist to dir. bus. ops. Vitas Health Care Corp, Fla., 1992—95; from adminstr. to regional dir. bus. devel. Interim Health Care South Fla., 1995—96; mgr. CAP Gemini/Ernst & Young, 1996—2001; sr. mgr. V4 Cons., LLP, 2001; v.p. corp. svcs. TBN of TN, Inc., 2001—02; dir. client svcs. Pricewaterhousecooper's, 2002—. Spkr. in field. Bd. v.p., bd. liaison for capital campaign Hillsborough Assn. for Retarded Citizens; com. chair ann. night at the circus Tampa (Fla.) Gen. Hosp. Found., 2003, com. chair ann. gala, 2004. Mem.: Healthcare Fin. Mgmt. Assn., Am. Coll. Health Care Execs. Home: 4706 W Leona St Tampa FL 33629

DYE, H. MICHAEL, marketing professional; b. Parkersburg, W.Va., Jan. 21, 1941; s. Max D. and Pauline (Gygax) D.; m. Carolyn A. Moore, Apr. 30, 1964; children: M. Andrew, Elizabeth Anne. BA in Econs., U. Charleston, 1966; MPA in Polit. Adminstrn., Fla. State U., 1978. Spl. asst. Nat. Govs. Conf., Washington, 1970-73; state-fed. programs coord. Fla. Dept. Transp., Tallahassee, 1973-76; regional mgr. Tallahassee office Post, Buckley, Schuh & Jernigan, Inc., 1976-83, v.p., dir. mktg., 1983-88, sr. v.p., dir. mktg., 1988-90, exec. v.p., dir. adminstrv. svcs., 1989-90, pres., COO Miami, 1991-96, pres., CEO, 1996-2000, chmn. bd., CEO, 2000—, The PBSJ Corp., 2001—. Adv. bd. NationsBank South Fla., 1998—. Trustee Fla. State U. Found., 1994—; mem. adv. bd. St. Thomas U., Miami, Enterprise Fla. Inc., Internat. Trade Econ. Devel, Orange Bowl Com., 1996—; exec. com. Floridians for Better Transp. Mem. Pres., Fla. C. of C. (bd. dirs. 1989—, chmn. 1991-92), Fla. Chamber Found., Greater Miami C. of C. (bd. govs., bd. trustees 1993—). Avocations: tennis, travel. Office: The PBSJ Corporation 2001 NW 107th Ave Miami FL 33172-2507

DYE, JAMES LOUIS, chemistry professor; b. Soudan, Minn., July 18, 1927; s. Ray Ashley and Hildur Ameda Dye; m. Angeline Rosalie Medure, June 10, 1948; children: Roberta Rae, Thomas Anthony, Brenda Lee. AA, Virginia (Minn.) Jr. Coll., 1948; BA, Gustavus Adolphus Coll., 1949; PhD, Iowa State U., 1953; DSc (hon.), No. Mich. U., 1992. Rsch. assoc. Iowa State U., Ames, 1953; asst. prof. chemistry Mich. State U., East Lansing, 1953-60, assoc. prof., 1960-63, prof., 1963-94, chmn. dept. chemistry, 1986-90, prof. emeritus, 1994—. Vis. scientist Ohio State U., Columbus, 1968-69; cons. AT&T Bell Labs., Murray Hill, N.J., 1982-83. Author: Thermodynamics and Equilibrium, 1978; contbr. more than 220 articles to profl. jours. With U.S. Army, 1945-46. NSF fellow, 1961-62, Guggenheim fellow, 1975-76, 90-91, Fulbright scholar, 1975-76; recipient Disting. Alumni award Gustavus Adolphus Coll., 1969. Fellow AAAS; mem. NAS, Am. Acad. Arts and Scis., Am. Chem. Soc. (Inorganic Chemistry award 1997), Am. Inst. Chemists (Chem. Pioneer award 1990), Am. Phys. Soc., Materials Rsch. Soc., Phi Kappa Phi, Sigma Xi (rsch. awards 1968, 87), Golden Key (teaching award 1986). Lutheran. Avocations: fishing, golf. Home: 2698 Roseland Ave East Lansing MI 48823-3847 Office: Mich State Univ Dept Of Chemistry East Lansing MI 48824 Office Phone: 517-355-9715 ext. 288. Business E-Mail: dye@msu.edu.

DYE, JERMAINE, professional baseball player; b. Overland, Kansas, Jan. 28, 1974; Student, Cosumnes River C.C. Player Atlanta Braves, 1996-97, Kansas City Royals, 1997—2001, Oakland A's, 2001—04, Chicago White Sox, 2004—. Named to Am. League All-Star Team, MLB, 2000. Office: Chicago White Sox 333 W 35th St Chicago IL 60616

DYE, NANCY SCHROM, academic administrator, historian, educator; b. Columbia, Mo., Mar. 11, 1947; d. Ned Stuart and Andrea Elizabeth (Ahrens) Schrom; m. Griffith R. Dye, Aug. 21, 1972; children: Molly, Michael. AB, Vassar Coll., 1969; MA, U. Wis., 1971, PhD, 1974; LittD (hon.), Obirin U., 2005. Asst. prof. U. Ky., Lexington, 1974—80, assoc. prof., 1980—88, prof., 1988, assoc. dean arts and scis., 1984—88; dean faculty Vassar Coll., Poughkeepsie, NY, 1988—92, acting pres., 1992—94; pres. Oberlin Coll., Oberlin, Ohio, 1994—. Author: As Equals And As Sisters, 1981; contbr. articles to profl. jours. Bd. mem. Pomona Coll. Mem.: Coun. Colls. of Art and Scis. (bd. dirs. 1980—91). Office: Oberlin Coll Cox Admin Bldg, Room 201 70 N Professor St Oberlin OH 44074-1090

DYE, RALPH DEAN, JR., lawyer; b. Zanesville, Ohio, Sept. 10, 1931; s. Ralph Dean Sr. and Mary Elizabeth (Coulson) D. BSBA, Ohio State U., 1953; LLB, Youngstown (Ohio) U., 1958. Bar: Ohio 1958. Mgmt. trainee, cost acct. U.S. Steel Corp., Youngstown, 1953-58; pvt. practice McConnelsville, Ohio. Republican. Methodist. Avocations: collecting banks, hunting, fishing. Office: PO Box 178 Mc Connelsville OH 43756-0178

DYE, REBECCA FEEMSTER, commissioner; b. Charlotte, N.C., May 8, 1952; BA, U. N.C., 1974, JD, 1977. Spl. counsel Broughton (N.C.) Psychiat. Hosp., 1977-78; atty. project coord. Legal Svcs. N.C., 1978-79; atty. office of chief counsel USCG, 1979-83; law instr. USCG Acad., 1983-85; atty. office of chief counsel Fed. Maritime Adminstrn., 1985-87; minority counsel Com. Merchant Marine & Fisheries, Washington, 1987—95; counsel Coast Guard & Maritime Transp. Subcommittee, Com. on Transp. & Infrastructure, US Ho. Reps., Washington, 1995—2002; commr. Fed. Maritime Commn., Washington, 2002—. Office: Fed Maritime Commn 800 N Capitol St NW Rm 1038 Washington DC 20573 E-mail: rdye@fmc.gov.*

DYE, ROBERT HARRIS, retired manufacturing company executive; b. N.Y.C., Feb. 22, 1918; s. Abatha Agusta and Julia (Harris) D.; m. Tereseua Vergine, May 13, 1950; 1 child, Leslie Julie. BSEE, Purdue U., 1942. Engr. Gen. Elec. Co., Schenectady, 1942-43, 46-47, mgr. field engr. test group Key West, Fla., 1947-49, prog. mgr. Schenectady, 1949-53; divsn. chief guidance and control Dept. of Navy, Newport, R.I., 1953-56; sect. mgr. Gen. Precision Co., Little Falls, N.J., 1956-60; prog. mgr. missile Gen. Precision Co./Singer, Little Falls, 1960-87; ret. Author: Post-WWII ComSun Pac Training Doctrine. Lt. USNR, 1942—46. Mem. IEEE, Submarine Vet. WWII, NRA, Am. Legion. Republican. Achievements include development of procedures for mine field penetration by submarine; wrote post-WWII ComSun Pac Training Doctrine.

DYE, SALLY ANN, middle school educator; b. Cleve., June 3, 1947; d. Chester James and Sarah Ellen (Harris) Ullom; children: Tammy Dye Anderson, Terry Dye. BS in Elem. Edn., Ohio State U., 1979, MA in Edn., 1986. Social studies and reading tchr. 6th grade Cardington (Ohio) Lincoln Mid. Sch., 1980—. Sunday sch. tchr. Ctr. United Meth. Ch., 1978—, mem.

adminstrv. bd., 1991—, sec. pastor parish rels. com., 1996—, United Meth. Ministries of So. Morrow County Coun., sec., 1996—, Sunday sch. treas., 1997—. Mem. AAUW (pres. Morrow County br. 1991-93, 99-2001, Ohio dist. coord. 1993-98, Ohio v.p. membership 1998-2000, program v.p. 2000-02, diversity chair 2002—), NEA, Ohio Edn. Assn., Internat. Reading Assn. (also Ohio Coun. and Morrow County Coun.), Ohio Coun. Tchrs. English Lang. Arts, Ohio State U. Alumni, Reveille Club (treas., 1998-2000, program v.p. 2001-03, pres. 2003), Delta Kappa Gamma Soc. (pres. chpt. 1996-98, treas. 2003—), Phi Delta Kappa. Avocations: reading, sports. Home: 157 S 3rd St Cardington OH 43315-1046 Office: Cardington Lincoln Mid Sch 349 Chesterville Ave Cardington OH 43315-9217

DYE, STUART S., lawyer; b. Ogden, Utah, 1939; BS cum laude with honors, U. Utah, 1961; LLB, U.Va., 1967. Bar: Va. 1967, D.C. 1967. Sec. Navy staff Deep Submergence Sys. Rev. Group Office of Legis. Affairs, 1963-64; spl. asst. on Law of the Sea matters internat. law divsn. Office of Judge Adv. Gen., 1965-66; ptnr. Holland & Knight, Washington. Adv. bd. Latin Am. Law and Bus. Report, 1994—. Mem. editl. bd. Va. Jour. Internat. Law, 1966-67; contbg. editor Oil and Gas Regulations Analyst, 1976-82. Mem. nat. adv. coun. U. Utah, 2001--. Lt. comdr. USNR. Mem. ABA (natural resources law sect., adminstrv. law sect.), Maritime Law Assn. (exec. com.), U.S., Maritime Adminstrv. Bar Assn., U.S.-Mex. C. of C. (chmn., bd. dirs. 1998-2004, chmn. transp. task force), Caribbean-Ctrl. Am. Action (bd. trustees, sec. 2003-), Phi Alpha Delta. Office: Holland & Knight LLP 2099 Pennsylvania Ave NW Washington DC 20006-6801 Office Phone: 202-457-7074. Business E-Mail: stuart.dye@hklaw.com.

DYE, THOMAS ROY, political science professor; b. Pitts., Dec. 16, 1935; s. James Clair and Marguerite Ann (Dewan) D.; m. Joan Grace Wohleber, June 29, 1957; children: Roy Thomas, Cheryl Price. BA, Pa. State U., 1957, MA, 1959; PhD, U. Pa., 1961. Asst. prof. polit. sci. U. Wis., Madison, 1962-63; asso. prof., head dept. polit. sci. U. Ga., Athens, 1963-68; prof., chmn. dept. govt. Fla. State U., Tallahassee, 1968-72, dir. policy scis., 1978-91, McKenzie prof. govt., 1991—98, prof. emeritus of polit. sci., 1998—. Vis. prof. polit. studies Bar Ilan U., Israel, 1972, U. Ariz., 1976 Author: Politics, Economics and the Public, 1966, Politics in States and Communities, 1969, 11th edit., 2003, The Irony of Democracy, 1970, 13th edit., 2005, The Politics of Equality, 1971, Understanding Public Policy, 1972, 11th edit., 2004, Power and Society, 1975, 10th edit., 2005, Who's Running America, 1976, Policy Analysis, 1976, Who's Running America-The Carter Years, 1979, Determinants of Public Policy, 1980, Who's Running America-The Reagan Years, 1983, Politics in the Media Age, 1983, 5th edit., 2003, Who's Running America-The Conservative Years, 1986, Power Elites and Organizations, 1987, Who's Running America-The Bush Era, 1990, American Federalism: Competition Among Governments, 1990, Politics in America, 1994, 6th edit., 2005, Who's Running America-The Clinton Years, 1994, Politics in Florida, 1998, Top Down Policymaking, 2000, Who's Running America: The Bush Restoration, 2002; co-dir.:. 1st lt. USAF, 1961—62. Mem. Am. Polit. Sci. Assn. (sec. 1969-72), So. Polit. Sci. Assn. (v.p. 1974-75, pres. 1976-77), Phi Beta Kappa, Omicron Delta Kappa. Home: 690 Fern St West Palm Beach FL 33401-5712 Personal E-mail: tomrdye@aol.com.

DYEN, ISIDORE, linguistic scientist, educator; b. Phila., Aug. 16, 1913; s. Jacob and Dena (Bryzell) D.; m. Edith Brenner, June 11, 1939 (dec. 1976); children— Doris Jane, Mark Ross. BA, U. Pa., 1933, MA, 1934, PhD in Indo-European Linguistics, 1939; postgrad. Slavic, Columbia, 1938-39, Yale, 1939-40. Faculty Yale U., 1942-84, prof. Malayan langs., 1957-58, prof. Malayopolynesian and comparative linguistics, 1958-73, prof. comparative linguistics and Austronesian langs., 1973-84, prof. emeritus, 1984—, dir. grad. studies Indic and Far Eastern langs. and lit., 1960-62, Indic and Southeast Asia, 1960-66, dir. grad. studies linguistics, 1966-68; adj. prof. linguistics U. Hawaii, 1985-89; linguist Coordinated Investigation Micronesian Anthropology, Truk, 1947, Sci. Investigation Micronesia, Yap, 1949. Vis. prof. U. Padjadjaran, Bandung, 1960-61, U. Auckland, summer 1969, Australian Nat. U., fall 1971, U. Philippines, spring 1972, Inst. Study of Langs. and Cultures of Asia and Africa, Tokyo U. for Fgn. Langs., 1982-83; coordinator linguistics sect. 10th Pacific Sci. Congress, Honolulu, 1961; asso. prof. U. Chgo. and Linguistic Soc. Am. Summer Inst., 1955; prof. U. Mich. and Linguistic Soc. Am. Summer Inst., 1957; dir. SE Asia Linguistics Program, 28th Internat. Congress Orientalists, Canberra, 1971; organizing com. Conf. Genetic Lexicostatistics, New Haven, 1971; organizer 1st Eastern Conf. Austronesian Linguistics, New Haven, 1973; adv. com. 1st Internat. Conf. Comparative Austronesian Linguistics, Honolulu, 1974; mem. adv. bd. Oceanic Linguistics. Author: Spoken Malay, 2 vols., 1945, The Proto-Malayo-Polynesian Laryngeals, 1953, A Lexicostatistical Classification of the Austronesian Languages, 1965, A Sketch of Trukese Grammar, 1965, A Descriptive Indonesian Grammar, 1967, Beginning Indonesian, 4 vols., 1967, Lexicostatistics in Genetic Linguistics: Proc. of Yale Conf., 1973, (with David Aberle) Lexical Reconstruction: The Case of the Athapaskan Kinship System, 1974, Linguistic Subgrouping and Lexicostatistics, 1975, (with Guy Jucquois) Lexicostatistics in Genetic Linguistics II, 1976, (with Joseph B. Kruskal and Paul Black) An Indoeuropean Classification: A Lexicostatistical Experiment, 1992. Research fellow Slavic Am. Council Learned Socs., 1938-40; Guggenheim fellow, 1949, 64; Tri-Instl. Pacific Program grantee, 1956-57; NSF grantee, 1960-77 Mem. Linguistic Soc. Am., Am. Oriental Soc. (v.p. 1965-66), Am. Anthrop. Assn., Current Anthropology, Société de Linguistique de Paris, Koninklijk Instituut voor Taal-, Land-, en Volkenkunde, New Haven Oriental Club (pres. 1963-64, 74-76) Office: Univ Hawaii Manoa Dept Linguistics Honolulu HI 96822 also: Yale U Dept Linguistics Hall Grad Studies New Haven CT 06520 *My aim has been to further linguistic science, particularly in comparative linguistics, by research in both Austronesian and Indoeuropean languages. In large part my work has been devoted to combining traditional and mathematico-statistical methods to improve subgrouping procedures. The different interlocking roles of theory, hypothesis, and methodology have been kept to the fore throughout. I hope my research will develop strong evidence regarding the Austronesian homeland.*

DYER, ALLAN M., medical association administrator; b. Toronto, Can., Aug. 23, 1923; s. Dyer and Mabel Brandow; m. Natalie M. Staron Dyer, May 19, 1965; children: Lawrence, Brandon, Cherie, Cinda. PhmB, U. Toronto, 1949, PhD in Pharmacology, 1955; MD, 1967; BSc in Pharmacy, U. Buffalo. Lic. Nat. Bd. Med. Examiners, Coll. Physicians and Surgeons, Ont., Coll. Pharmacy, Ont. Dir. pharm. rsch. and quality control Connaught Med. Rsch. Labs., 1955—63; pres. interns and residents Toronto We. Hosp., 1967—68; dir. drugs and therapeutics br. Ministry Health, Ont., 1968—77, exec. chmn. Dist. Health Coun. Program, 1977—78, asst. dep. minister, 1978—81, assoc. dept. minister, 1981—84; dep. minister Ministry Environ., Ont., 1984—85, Ministry Health, Ont., 1985—88; pres. VAT-TECH, Inc., 1988—96, Vax-D Med. Techs., L.L.C., Ont., 1996—. Office: VAX-D Med Techs LLC 310 Mears Blvd Oldsmar FL 34677 Address: Vat-Tech Can In PO Box 279 135 Muskoka Rd N Gravenhurst ON P1P 1T7 Canada Office Phone: 813-343-5000.

DYER, BARBARA F., retired accountant, writer; b. Rockland, Maine, May 19, 1924; d. Milton Earl and Elizabeth Ayoube Dyer. Grad., LaSalle Ext. U., 1967; student, U. Maine, Thomaston, 2001. Office mgr., acct. Camden Shipbuilding Co., 1942—86; tchr. Adult Edn. Sch. Adminstrv. Dist. #28, Camden, 1987—93; freelance writer Camden, 1984—. Hist. lectr., 1984, 2004—; writer Village Soup.com, Village Soup Times, 1999—. Author: Grog Ho, 1984, Vintage Views, 1987, History 1st Congregational Church, 1991, Images Camden-Rockport, 1995, Home Sweet Home, 1996, Vessels of Camden, 1998, More Memories of Camden, 1997; contbr. articles to publs. Bd. selectmen Town of Camden, 1992—95; ind. commr. Camden Pub. Libr., 1998—2002; mem. Camden War Meml. Com., 2003—; budget com. Town of Camden, 2003—; bd. mem. Camden Area History Ctr., 2004—; deacon First Congl. Ch., Camden, 1970—74, historian, 1985—2002, 2003—, 200th ann. com., 2003—. Named Paul Harris fellow, Rotary Internat., Camden, 1995, Townsperson of Yr., Camden, Lincolnville, Rockport C. of C., Camden, 1996; recipient Disting. Personal Enrichment award, Maine Adult Edn. Assn., 1993, first place/weekly award, Maine Press Assn., 1993. Mem.: Camden H.S. Alumni Assn. (com.), Camden Women's Club (charter, past pres.), Phi Theta Kappa. Republican. Avocations: knitting, crocheting, painting, swimming, dancing. Home: 11 Highland Ave Camden ME 04843-2119 Personal E-mail: bdyer88921@aol.com.

DYER, CHARLES RICHARD, law librarian, law educator; b. Richmond Heights, Mo., Aug. 20, 1947; s. Helmuth Kinner and Sue Anne (Stone) D.; m. Cecelia Ann Duncan, Dec. 20, 1969 (div. June 1982); m. Roberta Sharlyn Monroe, June 2, 1984; 1 child, Christina L. Floyd. BA, U. Tex., 1969, JD, 1974, MLS, 1975; MA, Northwestern U., 1971. Bar: Tex. 1974. Assoc. law libr., asst. prof. law St. Louis U., 1975-77; law libr., assoc. prof. U. Mo., Kansas City, 1977-87; dir. librs. San Diego County Pub. Law Libr., 1987—. Cons. in field. Editor Law Libr. Jour., 1972-74. Centre City adv. com. City of San Diego, 2000—02; chair relocation appeal bd. City of San Diego Redevel. Agy., 2001—05. Mem. Am. Assn. Law Librs., Mid-Am. Assn. Law Librs (sec.-treas. 1976-78), Southwestern Assn. Law Librs. (v.p. 1981-82, pres. 1982-83), So. Calif. Assn. Law Librs. (mem. exec. bd. 1991-93), Coun. Calif. County Law Librs. (pres. 1998-2000). Democrat. Unitarian Universalist. Home: 2323 Montclair St San Diego CA 92104-5344 Office: San Diego County Pub Law Libr 1105 Front St San Diego CA 92101-3904 Office Phone: 619-531-3904. Business E-Mail: cdyer@sdcpll.org.

DYER, CROMWELL ADAIR, JR., lawyer, legal association administrator; b. St. Louis, Sept. 9, 1932; (parents Am. citizens); s. Adair and Tompie Leora (Giles) Dyer; m. Margaret Copeland Peickert, June 12, 1958 (div. Aug. 1976); children: Gretchen, Jack, Julie, Stephen; m. Susan Aynesworth, Aug. 20, 1977; stepchildren: Carol Godso, Amanda McDonough, Donnella Railsback. BA, U. Tex., 1954; JD, 1961; LLM, Harvard U., 1971. Bar: Tex. 1961, U.S. Dist. Ct. (no. dist.) Tex. 1965, U.S. Ct. Appeals (5th cir.) 1965, U.S. Dist. Ct. (ea. dist.) Tex. 1966, U.S. Ct. Appeals (11th cir.) 1982, U.S. Ct. Appeals (9th cir.) 1999, U.S. Dist. Ct. (we. dist.) Tex. 2003. Law clk. FTC, Washington, 1960; assoc. Branscomb, Gary, Thomasson & Hall, Corpus Christi, Tex., 1961-62; staff atty. So. Union Gas Co., Dallas, 1962-64; assoc. Dedman & May, Dallas, 1964-65, White, McElroy & White, Dallas, 1965-67; pvt. practice, 1967-73, 1997—; sec. Hague (The Netherlands) Conf. Pvt. Internat. Law, 1973-78, 1st sec., 1978-93, dep. sec. gen., 1993-97; observer, cons. to intergovtl. orgns., 1976-97. Lectr. Asser Coll. Europe, 1992—96, Sch. Law U. Calif., Davis, Brigitte M. Bodenheimer Meml. Lecture Family, 1996; moderator Common Law Jud. Conf. Internat. Child Custody, Washington, 2000; condr. seminars. Honoree of symposium Globalization of Child Law The Role of the Hague Conventions, 1999; co-author: Report on Trusts and Analogous Institutions, 1982; contbr. articles to profl. jours. Mem. adv. com., faculty internat. kidnapping program Nat. Jud. Coll., Reno, 2003; faculty mem. Internat. Parental Abduction Course, Reno, 2004; juror award diploma in internat. law Hague Acad., 1980, 1984—87, 1991, 1994—96, dir. studies, 1985, instr. unfair competition in pvt. internat. law, 1988. Ensign USN, 1954, lt. (j.g.) USNR, 1957. Named hon. mem., Mexican Acad. Pvt. Internat. and Comparative Law; recipient Leonard J. Theberge award. Mem.: ABA (chair com. on internat. family law 2002—03, co-chair 2003—04, law sect. internat. law and practice 2000—, Leonard J. Theberge award for pvt. internat. law), Internat. Law Assn. (Am. br.), Inter-Am. Bar Assn., Internat. Bar Assn., Assn. Louis Chatin pour la Def. des Droits de l'Enfant (Paris), Internat. Soc. Family Law, Dallas Bar Assn., Austin Bar Assn., Am. Fgn. Law Assn., Acad. Mexicana de Derecho Internacional Privado y Comparado (hon.), Club du jeudi (The Hague) (pres. 1983—85). Office: PO Box 30020 Austin TX 78755-3020 Office Phone: 512-343-7899. Personal E-mail: adairdyer@austin.rr.com.

DYER, DAVID F., apparel company executive; B in Engring., Vanderbilt U. Various Burdines, Miami, 1972-89; from mng. dir. coming home catalog to v. chmn. merchandising Lands' End, Inc., Dodgeville, Wis., 1989-93, v. chmn. merchandising and sales, 1993-94, pres., CEO, 1998—2002; pres., COO Home Shopping Network, 1994-97; catalog/retail cons. Tex. Pacific Group, San Francisco, 1997—98, J. Crew Group, N.Y.C., 1997; CEO Lands' End, 1998—2003; pres., CEO Tommy Hilfiger Corp., 2003—. Dir. ADVO, Inc.; bd. dirs. Lands' End. Office: Tommy Hilfiger Corp 9 F Novel Industrial Bldg 850-870 Lai Chi Kok Rd Cheung Sha Wan Hong Kong Address: Tommy Hilfiger Corp 25 W 39th St New York NY 10018 Office Phone: 212-840-8888, 852 2216 0668.

DYER, EDWARD JAMES, public utilities commissioner; b. St. Joseph, Mo., Dec. 9, 1937; m. Shari Dyer; children: Jim, Andy, Matt. BA in English, Benedictine Coll., 1959; BA in Career Counseling, Fort Lewis Coll., 1986. Commd. ensign USN, 1959; transfer to USMC, 1964, advanced through grades to Lt. Col., 1975, served in Vietnam 3yrs, commd. field artillery battery and battalion, 1979, ret.; sales mgr. Power Motive Corp., 1979—86; rep. Colo. House Rep., 1986—98; Colo. Senate, 1999—2001; commr. Colo. Dept. Regulatory Agys., Denver, 2001—. Mem. various coms. Colo. House Rep.; chmn. Senate Agrl. Natural Resources Com. Coach Youth Soccer, Youth Baseball; active local campaigns. Decorated 3 Bronze Stars with V USMC, Soldier's medal; Toll fellow, 1988. Avocations: reading, walking, crossword puzzles. Office: Colo Dept Regulatory Agencies PUC 1580 Logan St OL2 Denver CO 80203

DYER, IRA, ocean engineering educator, consultant; b. N.Y.C., June 14, 1925; s. Charles and Frieda (Griffman) D.; m. Betty Ruth Schanberg, Sept. 4, 1949; children: Samuel S., Debora J. SB, MIT, 1949, SM, 1951, PhD, 1954. V.p. Bolt Beranek & Newman Inc., Cambridge, Mass., 1951-70; prof. ocean engring. MIT, Cambridge, 1971-89, Weber Shaughness prof., 1989-96, head dept., 1971-81, dir. MIT Sea Grant program, 1973-75, Robert Bruce Wallace lectr., 1982-83, emeritus prof., 1996—. Vis. fellow Cambridge (Eng.) U., 1979-80; cons. Oasis Inc., Lexington, Mass., 1988—; advisor U.S. Dept. Def., Washington, 1988—, Am. Inst. Physics, N.Y.C., 1988-91 Contbr. over 100 articles to sci. jours. With USAAF, 1944-45. Recipient Meritorious Pub. Svc. award USCG, 1979. Fellow AAAS, IEEE (disting. tech. award 1982), ASME (Per Bruel gold medal 2002), Acoustical Soc. Am. (pres. 1986-87, Lindsay award 1960, gold medal 1996); mem. NAE, Marblehead Yacht Club Avocation: sailing.

DYER, JAMES HAROLD, JR., language educator; b. Christiansburg, Va., Mar. 23, 1946; s. James Harold and Dorothy Louise (Bennett) Dyer. BA in English, Augusta Coll., 1970; MEd in English Edn., Ga. State U., 1975, EdS in English Edn., 1978; PhD in Brit. Lit., U. S.C., 1992. Cert. secondary sch. tchr. S.C. English tchr. Aiken (S.C.) HS, 1975-79; prof. English Ga. Mil. Coll., Ft. Gordon, 1979—2000; prof. grad. English, grad. English MEd program coord. Troy State U., Augusta, Ga., 2002—. Grad. tchg. asst. U. S.C., Columbia, 1982—83. Mem.: MLA, The Acad. Am. Poets, Children's Lit. Assn., Dickens Fellowship, Acad. Am. Poets, Lambda Iota Tau (Saul Bellow hon. pres.). Avocations: book collecting, chess, golf. Office: Troy State U Dept Grad English 2743 Perimeter Pky Ste 201 Augusta GA 30909 Office Phone: 866-557-8617. Personal E-mail: jimdyer2@netzero.net.

DYER, JAMES MASON, JR., investment company executive; b. Corsicana, Tex., Sept. 22, 1928; s. James Mason Sr. and Tabby (Jackson) D.; m. Lorelle Wright, Dec. 29, 1954; children: James Mason IV, Diane Dyer Campbell. BBA, U. Tex., 1950. V.p. J. M. Dyer Co., Corsicana, 1954-77, pres., 1978-87; nmg. ptnr. J.M. Dyer Co., Corsicana, 1987—; pres. The Piccolo Co., Corsicana, 1988—. 1st lt. U.S. Army, 1952—54, ETO. Episcopalian. Office: JM Dyer Co PO Box 620 Corsicana TX 75151-0620 Office Phone: 903-874-4735.

DYER, JOSEPH WENDELL, retired naval officer; b. Murphy, NC, Mar. 2, 1947; s. Joseph Wendell Sr. and Margaret (Kale) D. BSChemE, N.C. State U., Raleigh, 1969; MS in Fin. Mgmt., Naval Post Grad. Sch., Monterey, Calif., 1981. Commd. ensign USN, 1969, advanced through grades to vice admiral, 2000; test pilot USN Naval Air Test Ctr, Patuxent River, Md., 1976-80; sys. integrator USN, China Lake, Calif., 1982-84, Commanding Officer Plant Rep. Office Melbourne, Australia, 1984-87, dep. program mgr. F/A-18 program Washington, 1988-90, AX airplane chief engr., 1990-91, exec. asst. to comdr. naval air sys. command, 1991-92, navy's chief test pilot Patuxent, Md., 1992-93, mgr. F/A 18 program Washington, 1993-97; comdr. Naval Air Warfare Ctr., Aircraft Divsn., 1997—2000; asst. comdr. for rsch. and engring. Naval Air Sys. Command, 1997-2000, comdr. naval air sys. command, 2000—03; ret. USN, 2003; gen. mgr., exec. v.p. govt. and indsl. divsn. iRobot Corp., Burlington, Mass., 2003—. Chair aeroispace safety adv. panel NASA. Contbr. articles to profl. jours. Decorated Disting. Svc. medal US Navy; recipient Acquisition Excellence award, US Dept. Def., J.H. Doolittle award for outstanding tech./engring. achievement in aerospace tech., 2001. Fellow Soc. Exptl. Test Pilots, Nat. Acad. Pub. Adminstrn. Achievements include leading DOD's first counter stealth, tactical data-fusion effort. Avocation: sailing. Office: iRobot 63 South Ave Burlington MA 01803 Personal E-mail: dyerjoseph2@aol.com. Business E-Mail: jdyer@irobot.com.

DYER, NANCY JOE, foreign language educator, consultant; b. Navasota, Tex., Apr. 15; d. Onis E. and Josephine Mims (Greenwood) D.; m. Steven M. Hodge, June 18, 1977; children: Josephine Jane, Mary Priscilla. BA, Tex. Tech U., 1964; MA, Tulane U., 1968; PhD, U. Pa., 1975. Asst. lectr. U. Tex., Austin, 1968-70; asst. prof. UCLA, 1974-75, U. Houston, 1975-77, Tex. A&M U., College Station, 1977-81, assoc. prof., 1981—97, prof., 1997—. Cons. dept. of higher edn. State of N.J., 1986; cons. U. Ky. Press, Lexington, 1991, Ednl. Testing Svc., Princeton, N.J., 1991—. Author: El PMC Taller Alfonsi, 1993, Memoriales de Motolinia, 1993; contbr. articles to profl. jours., chpts. to books. Volunteer College Station Ind. Schs., 1985—; coord. Am. Cancer Soc., College Station, 1986, Neighborhood Watch Program, College Station, 1991. NEH grantee, 1982, Am. Coun. Learned Socs. grantee, 1984, Spanish Ministry of Culture grantee, 1991. Mem. Am. Assn. Tchrs. of Spanish and Portuguese, Assn. Historians of Medieval Spain, Soc. of the Cantigueiros of Santa Maria, Medieval Acad. Am., Asociacion Internacional de Hispanistas, Alfonsine Soc. of Am. (adv. bd. 1990—), Modern Lang. Assn. (chair romance lang. sect. 1982, co-chair scholarly edits. 2005—). Presbyterian. Avocation: gardening. Office: Tex A&M U Dept Hispanic Studies College Station TX 77840-4238

DYER, NATALIE MARY, health products executive, physician; b. Loniow, Kielce, Poland, Dec. 21, 1924; arrived in Can., 1930; came to U.S., 1996; d. Nicholas and Katherine (Szkutnicka) Staron; m. Allan Edwin Dyer, May 19, 1965; children: Lawrence, Brandon, Cherie, Cinda. MD, U. Toronto, Ont., Can., 1947. Jr. intern St. Michael's Hosp., 1947-48; resident anesthesiology Women's Coll. Hosp., Hosp. for Sick Children, 1949-50; resident in anesthesiology Toronto Western Hosp., 1950-51; anesthesiologist Humber Meml. Hosp., Weston, Ont., 1951-75; med. dir. birth control ctrs. Etobicoke (Ont.) Health Dept., 1975-80, Physicians Weight Control Ctrs., Toronto, 1980-85; v.p., med. dir. Vat-Tech Inc., Toronto, 1985-96, Vax-D Internat., Palm Harbor, Fla., 1996—. Contbr. articles to med. jours., including Can. Jour. Biochemistry and Physiology. Mem.: AMA, N.Y. Acad. Scis., Ont. Med. Assn., Coll. Physicians and Surgeons Ont., Can. Med. Assn., Can. Anesthesiologists Soc. Avocations: cooking, crafts, boating, skiing, snowmobiling. Office Phone: 813-343-5000. E-mail: vaxdcapo@vaxd.com, vaxdmd@vaxd.com.

DYER, VICTOR EUGENE, II, library administrator; b. Laconia, N.H., Jan. 26, 1950; s. Victor Eugene and Pauline Lucille (Truchon) D. BA, Boston Coll., 1972; MA, U. Chgo., 1975; cert. spl. studies in adminstrn. & mgmt., Harvard U., 1991. Cert. profl. libr. and sch. libr., Mass. Editor, searcher U. Chgo. Libr., 1974-76; cataloger Mcpl. Reference Libr., Chgo., 1976-77; libr. II Chgo. Pub. Libr., 1978-79; asst. dir. Abbot Pub. Libr., Marblehead, Mass., 1979-99; dir. Ipswich (Mass.) Pub. Libr., 1999—. Pres. Essex County Coop. Librs., Beverly, Mass., 1986-87, 88-89, 92-93; sec. Merrimack Valley Libr. Consortium, Andover, Mass., 2000—. Author: Prairie Avenue: An Annotated Bibliography, 1977. Vol. guide and rschr. Chgo. Archtl. Found., 1976-79; vol. guide Peabody Mus., Salem, Mass., 1984-91; vol. Brigham and Women's Hosp., Boston, 1996—. Mem. ALA, Pub. Libr. Assn., Mass. Libr. Assn., New Eng. Libr. Assn., Marblehead Hist. Soc. (dir. 1987-92, 94-98), Hyde Park Hist. Soc. (dir. 1978-79), Phi Beta Kappa. Democrat. Roman Catholic. Avocations: travel, reading, hiking, architecture. Home: 16 Pleasant St Hamilton MA 01982-4401 Office: Ipswich Pub Libr 25 N Main St Ipswich MA 01938-2287 Office Phone: 978-356-6649. E-mail: victordyer@worldnet.att.net.

DYER, WAYNE WALTER, psychologist, writer, radio and television personality; b. Detroit, May 10, 1940; s. Melvin L. and Hazel I. (Vollick) D.; m. Marcelene Louise Dyer; children: Tracy, Stephanie, Skye, Sommer, Serena, Sands Jay, Saje Eykis. BS, Wayne State U., 1965, MS in Counseling and Ednl. Psychology, 1966, EdD in Counseling and Psychology, 1970. Tchr. and counselor Pershing H.S., Detroit, 1965-67; instr. counselor edn. Wayne State U., Detroit, summer, 1970, 71, 72, 73; dir. guidance and counseling Mercy H.S., Farmington, Mich., 1967-71; staff cons. and trainer guidance and sch. psychol. personnel Half Hollow Sch. Dist., Huntington, N.Y., 1973-75; staff cons. Drug Info. and Svc. Ctr., N.Y., 1972-74, Herman Kiefer Hosp., Detroit, 1974-75; mem. tchg. faculty North Shore U. Hosp. divsn. Cornell U. Med. Coll., Manhasset, N.Y., 1974-75; pvt. practice counseling and psychotherapy Huntington, N.Y., 1973—; asst. prof. counselor edn. St. John's U., Jamaica, N.Y., 1971-74; assoc. prof., 1974-77. Over 4000 appearances on TV and radio shows and programs including Phil Donohue Show, Tonight Show, Dinah Shore Show, Merv Griffin Show, Mike Douglas Show, Good Morning America, Canada A.M., Oprah Winfrey Show, numerous other talk shows in every state; radio host for: Kathryn Crosby Show, San Francisco, At Your Service program, Sta. KMOX, St. Louis.; Author: (with John Vriend) Counseling Effectively in Groups, 1973, Counseling Techniques That Work, 1974, 2d edit., 1977, Group Counseling for Personal Mastery, 1980, Your Erroneous Zones, 1976 (Literary Guild selection, Psychology Today Book Club selection, also 4 others), Pulling Your Own Strings, 1977, 1978 (Lit. Guild main selection, also 6 others), The Sky's the Limit, 1980 (Lit. Guild selection); novel Gifts from Eykis, 1983, What Do You Really Want for Your Children?, 1985, Happy Holidays, 1986, You'll See It When You Believe It, 1988, Real Magic, 1992, Everyday Wisdom, 1994, Your Sacred Self, 1995, Staying on the Path, 1995, A Promise is a Promise, 1996, Manifest Your Destiny, 1997, Wisdom of the Ages, There's A Spiritual Solution To Every Problem, 2000, The Power of Intention: Learning to Co-create Your World Your Way, 2004; cassette tape series The Wit & Wisdom of Dr. Wayne W. Dyer, 1977, How To Be a No-Limit Person, 1981, Secrets of the Universe, Choosing Your Own Greatness, What Do You Really Want for Your Children?, Transformation: You'll See It When You Believe It, The Awakened Life, others; contbr. chpts. on counseling to books on psychology, numerous articles on psychology to popular mags. and articles on counseling to profl. jours.; producer tape recordings on counseling techniques; audio cassette program Secrets of the Universe. Served with USN, 1958-62. Named Disting. Alumni of Yr., Wayne State U., 1980; recipient Golden Gavel award Internat. Toastmasters, 1987.

DYER, WILLIAM EARL, JR., retired newspaper editor; b. Kearney, Nebr., May 15, 1927; s. William Earl and Hazel Maud (Hosfelt) D.; m. Betty M. Meisinger, June 26, 1967; children: Lee Michael, Scott William. BA, U. Nebr., 1949. Reporter Nebr. City Daily News Press, 1943-44; reporter, copy editor The Lincoln Star, Nebr., 1948-50, city editor, 1951-60, exec. editor, 1960-92. Pres. Nebr. AP Editors, 1964. Author: Headline: Starkweather, 1993. Pres. Lincoln Unitarian Ch., 1962-63; state chmn. Nebr. We Shake Hands Indian Project, 1958-60; mem. Nebr. Adv. Com. on Indian Law Enforcement, 1960-62; mem. State Adv. Com. to Welfare Dept., 1970-73, 80-84. With AUS, 1945-46. Named hon. mem. Omaha Indian Tribe. Mem. Open Forum Club, Phi Beta Kappa, Sigma Delta Chi. Democrat. Home: 247 N 56th St West Lincoln NE 68504 Office: Jour-Star Printing Co PO Box 81609 926 P St Lincoln NE 68508-3615 E-mail: dyers@inebraska.com.

DYER-RAFFLER, JOY ANN, special education diagnostician, educator; b. Stiltner, W.Va., Aug. 10, 1935; d. Ralph William and Hazel (Terry) Dyer; m. John William Raffler, Sr., Jan. 1, 1993; 1 child from a previous marriage, Keith Brian DeArmond. BA, U. N.C., 1969; MEd in Secondary Edn., U. Ariz., 1974, MEd in Spl. Edn., 1976. Cert. spl. edn.-learning disabilities, art edn., spl. edn.-emotionally handicapped. Art educator Tucson Unified Sch. Dist., Tucson, 1970-75; tchr. spl. edn. Tucson (Ariz.) Unified Sch. Dist., 1975-89, diagnostician spl. edn., 1989—2003; tchr. exceptional edn. Tucson Unified Sch. Dist., 2003—05. Den mother Cub Scouts Am., Raleigh, N.C., 1968-69. Recipient grant Tucson Unified Sch. Dist., 1977. Mem. CEC, Ariz. Edn. Assn., Learning Disabilities Assn. Avocations: painting, skiing, bird watching, weightlifting, jogging. Home: 1781 S Desert Vista Dr Tucson AZ 85748

DYER-SMITH, DARLENE, minister; b. Phila., Jan. 1, 1953; d. John Booker Dyer and Pearl Arlene Rucker; m. Andrew Tyrone Smith, Apr. 11, 1981. Student, Crusaders for Christ Bible Inst., Phila., 1995. Traveling evangelist Crusaders for Christ, Phila., 1974—90, ch. elder, 1990—95; sr. pastor, founder and CEO Branches of Christ Ministries, Inc., Phila., 1995—. Traveling evangelist U.S., P.R., Korea, Africa, Japan, Can.; lectr. in field; sem. tchr. Song of Solomon, Ghana, 1986. Author: His Banner Over Me is Love, 2001, Yellow Roses, 2001, A Loving Caress, 2001. Named Poet of the Yr., Internat. Soc. of Poets, 2001; recipient Award ofHonor, Bridgeton Crusaders for Christ, 1980. Avocations: travel, poetry writing, crafts, reading, angel collecting. Home: 6902 Paschall Ave Philadelphia PA 19142 Office: Branches of Christ Ministries 6900 Woodland Ave Philadelphia PA 19142

DYESS, BOBBY DALE, lawyer; b. Waxahachie, Tex., Jan. 27, 1935; s. Robert Olin and Rubie Lee (Odom) D.; m. Janet Lee Hassell, Jan. 30, 1960 (dec. 1973); children: Robert Dale, Jonathan David, Julianna Whitfield; m. Sharon Erwin Saylor, June 6, 1974. BA, U. N. Tex., Denton, 1956; JD, So. Meth. U., 1959. Bar: Tex. 1959. Ptnr. Elliott, Churchill, Hansen, Dyess & Maxfield, 1965-82, DeHay & Blanchard, 1983-92, Payne & Blanchard, Dallas, 1992—. Chmn. bd. Rainbow Sound, Inc., 1975-85; dir. edn. found. Waxahechie Ind. Sch. Dist., 2004—. Editor: Bests, Life and Health Ins. Edit., 1973-85. Mem. bd. mgmt. East Dallas YMCA, 1970, 1976, campaign chmn., 1976, chmn. bd. mgmt., 1977—79; chief Indian Guides, 1971; chmn. Cub Scout pack com. Boy Scouts Am., 1970; trustee Baylor Med. Ctr., Waxahachie, Tex., 2002—, vice chair, 2004—05, chair bd. trustees, 2005—; bd. dirs. Waxahachie Found., 1999—2003, Ednl. Found., 2004—. Mem.: Am. Counsel Assn. (membership chmn. 1976, pres. 1979—80, sec.-treas. 1984—87, membership chmn. 1996—98), Coll. State Bar Tex. (dir. 1996—, chmn. 1999—2001), Scribes (bd. dirs. 1976), Am. Soc. Legal Writers, Dallas Bar Found. (charter), Tex. Bar Assn. Presbyterian. Home: 110 Magnolia Dr Waxahachie TX 75165 Office: Payne and Blanchard 500 N Tower Plz of America Dallas TX 75201 Office Phone: 972-938-1181. Personal E-mail: bdyess@msn.com.

DYK, TIMOTHY BELCHER, federal judge; b. Boston, Feb. 14, 1937; s. Walter and Ruth (Belcher) Dyk; m. Inga Shirer, June 18, 1960 (div. 1970); children: Deirdre, Caitlin; m. Sally Katzen, Oct. 31, 1981; 1 child, Abraham Benjamin. AB, Harvard U., 1958, LLB magna cum laude, 1961. Bar: DC, NY. Law clk. to Justices Reed and Burton U.S. Supreme Ct., Washington, 1961—62, law clk. to Chief Justice Earl Warren, 1962—63; spl. asst. to asst. atty. gen. U.S. Dept. Justice, Washington, 1963—64; assoc. Wilmer Cutler & Pickering, Washington, 1964—69, ptnr., 1969—90, Jones, Day, Reavis and Pogue, Washington, 1990—2000; cir. ct. judge U.S. Ct. of Appeals Fed. Cir., 2000—. Adj. prof. Georgetown U. Law Ctr., Washington, 1983, Washington, 86, Washington, 89, Washington, 91, U. Va. Law Sch., Charlottesville, 1984—85, Charlottesville, 1987—88, Yale U. Law Sch., 1986—87, 1989; pres. The Edward Coke Appellate Inn of Ct., 2000—02. Mem.: Harvard Law Rev., 1959—61; contbr. articles to profl. jours. Office: US Court Appeals Fed Cir 717 Madison Pl NW Ste 915 Washington DC 20439 Office Phone: 202-633-8200.

DYKE, CHARLES WILLIAM, retired army officer; b. Covington, Ga., July 28, 1935; s. John William and Chessie Belle (Burke) D.; m. Hedwig Friederike Adam, Dec. 1958 (div. 1979); children: Michael Alexander, Eva Joyce, Charles Martin, Robert William; m. Nancy Jeanne Bearg, June 22, 1980 (div. 2002); children: Sarah Claire, Rachel Anne; m. Ann Stouffer Bisconti, Oct. 13, 2002. BA in History, U. So. Miss., 1963; MMil Arts and Sci., U.S. Army Command and Gen. Staff Coll., 1967; MA in Internat. Rels., George Washington U., 1968; postgrad., U.S. Army War Coll., 1970—71; postgrad. in polit. sci., Shippensburg State Coll., 1970—71. Enlisted U.S. Army, 1954-55, commd. 2d lt., 1955, advanced through grades to lt. gen., 1985, exec. officer 1st Brigade, 101st Airborne Divsn., 1968, comdr. 2d Bn., 327th Inf., 1968-69, G1, later G3, 101st Airborne Divsn., 1969-70, exec. asst. Ops. Directorate J3 Orgn. Joint Chiefs of Staff Washington, 1971-72, asst. sec. of gen. staff Office Chief of Staff, 1972-73, mil. asst., later exec. to sec. of army The Pentagon, 1973-75, comdr. 1st Brigade, 101st Airborne Divsn. Ft. Campbell, Ky., 1975-76, asst. divsn. comdr. 3d Inf. Divsn. Germany, 1976, exec. to supreme allied comdr. Europe, 1977-78, dir. internat. standardization for NATO Hdqs. Dept Army Washington, 1978-79, vice dir. J3, later vice dir. joint staff Orgn. Joint Chiefs of Staff, The Pentagon, 1979-82, dep. chief staff for ops. Europe, 1982-83, comdg. gen. 8th Inf. Divsn. (Mech), 1983-85, comdr. Japan/IX Corps, 1985-88, ret., 1988; exec. advisor Aerospace divsn. Mitsubishi Corp., Tokyo, 1988—; chmn., CEO Internat. Tech. and Trade Assocs. Inc., Washington, 1989—. Mem. NATO Indsl. adv. group, 1999—2004, vice chmn., 2001—04. Decorated D.S.M. with oak leaf cluster, Silver Star with oak leaf cluster, Def. Superior Svc. medal, Legion of Merit with 3 oak leaf clusters, Soldiers medal, Bronze Star with V device and 2 oak leaf clusters, Joint Svc. Commendation medal, Army Commendation medal with 4 oak leaf clusters, Air medal (19), Purple Heart, U.S. Presdl. Unit citation, Joint Chiefs of Staff and Army Gen. Staff indentification badges, Combat Infantry Badge, others, also various fgn. decorations including Japanese Order of Rising Sun (2d class) with gold and silver stars. Mem. Assn. U.S. Army, 101st Airborne Divsn. Assn., Army Aviation Assn., Nat. Def. Indsl. Assn., USAF Assn., Armed Forces Comm. and Electronics Assn., Pen and Sword Assn., Nat. Beta Club, Pi Gamma Mu, Phi Alpha Theta. Office: Internat Tech and Trade Assocs Inc 1330 Connecticut Ave NW Ste 210 Washington DC 20036-1726 Office Phone: 202-828-2614. Business E-Mail: cdyke@itta.com.

DYKEMAN, WILMA, writer, lecturer; b. Asheville, N.C., May 20, 1920; d. Willard J. and Bonnie (Cole) Dykeman; m. James R. Stokely Jr., Oct. 12, 1940; children: Dykeman Cole, James R. III. BS inSpeech, Northwestern U., 1940; LittD, Maryville Coll., 1974; LHD, Tenn. Wesleyan Coll., 1978; DHL (hon.), U. N.C., Asheville, 1997. Lectr. English dept. U. Tenn., Knoxville, 1975-95, adj. prof., 1985-95; now writer, lectr. Columnist Knoxville News-Sentinel, 1962-99; historian State of Tenn., 1980—; nat. lectr. in field. Author 18 books including: The French Broad: A Rivers of America Volume, 1955, The Tall Woman, 1962, Seeds of Southern Change, 1962, The Far Family, 1966, Return the Innocent Earth, 1973; co-author: Neither Black Nor White, 1957, Tennessee: A Bicentennial History, 1976, Tennessee Women: An Infinite Variety, 1993, Explorations, a collection of essays, 1984, others; contbr. articles to nat. mags. and Ency. Brit. Trustee Berea Coll., 1971-95, Phelps Stokes Fund, 1981-91, U. N.C.-Asheville, 1985-91; active Friends of Great Smokies Nat. Park. Guggenheim fellow, 1956-57, NEH fellow, 1976-77; recipient Hillman award, 1957, Disting. So. Writers award So. Festival of Books, 1989; N.C. Gold medal for Contbn. to Am. letters, 1985. Mem. PEN, Authors Guild, So. Hist. Assn., Cosmos Club, Phi Beta Kappa, Delta Kappa Gamma. Home: 282 Clifton Heights Rd Newport TN 37821-2402 also: 189 Lynn Cove Rd Asheville NC 28804-1910

DYKEN, MARK LEWIS, JR., neurologist, educator; b. Laramie, Wyo., Aug. 26, 1928; s. Mark L. and Thelma Violet (Achenbach) D.; m. Beverly All, June 8, 1951; children: Betsy Lynn, Mark Eric, Julie Suzanne, Amy Luise, Andrew Christopher, Gregory Allen. BS in Anatomy and Physiology, Ind. U., 1951, MD, 1954. Diplomate Am. Bd. Psychiatry and Neurology. Intern Indpls. Gen. Hosp., 1954-55; resident in neurology Ind. U. Med. Ctr., 1955-58; clin. dir., dir. rsch. New Castle (Ind.) State Hosp., 1958-61; asst. dept. neurology Ind. U., 1958-61, assoc. prof. neurology, 1964-69, prof., 1969—, chmn. dept. neurology, 1971-94, prof. emeritus, 1994—. Chmn. profl. adv. coun. Nat. Easter Seal Soc., 1974-82; cons., chmn. panel on rev. neurol. devices subcom. FDA, 1979-83; bd. dirs. Am. Bd. Psychiatry and Neurology, 1988-96, pres., 1995. Editor-in-chief Stroke, 1992-2000; contbr. numerous articles on topics including cerebral vascular disease, blood flow, epilepsy, electroencephalography, muscle disease, to profl. jours. With U.S. Army, 1946-48. Recipient numerous grants in cerebrovascular disease. Fellow ACP; mem. AMA, Am. Assn. Univ. Profs. Neurology (pres. 1986-88), Epilepsy Found. Am., Am. Heart Assn (chmn. stroke coun. 1984-86, v.p. for sci. couns. 1988-89), Ind. Neurol. Assn. (charter pres. 1966-68), Am. Acad. Neurology, Am. Neurol. Assn., Sigma Xi, Alpha Omega Alpha. Home: 7406 W 92nd St Zionsville IN 46077-9103 Office: Ind U Med Ctr Neurol Dept 545 Barnhill Dr EM124 Indianapolis IN 46202 Office Phone: 317-278-2340. E-mail: mdyken@aol.com.

DYKES, ARCHIE REECE, finance company executive; b. Rogersville, Tenn., Jan. 20, 1931; s. Claude Reed and Rose (Quillen) Dykes; m. Nancy Jane Haun, May 29, 1953; children: John Reece, Thomas Mack. BS cum laude, East Tenn. State U., 1952, MA, 1956; EdD, U. Tenn., 1959. Prin., Church Hill (Tenn.) HS, 1955-58; supt. Greeneville (Tenn.) Schs., 1959-62; prof. edn., dir. Ctr. Advanced Grad. Study Edn. U. Tenn., 1962-66, chancellor Martin, 1967-71, Knoxville, 1971-73, U. Kans., 1973-80; chmn., pres., CEO Security Benefit Group Cos., Topeka, 1980-88; chmn. Capital City Holdings Inc., 1988—. Chmn. bd., CEO, Fleming Cos., Inc., Dallas; chmn. bd. dirs. Pepsi Ams., Inc.; bd. dirs. Raytech Corp., Midas, Inc.; trustee Keene Industries Trust, N.Y.C., Kans. U. Endowment Assn., Raytech Corp. Trust, N.Y.C. Author: School Board and Superintendent, 1965, Faculty Participation in Academic Decision Making, 1968. Vice chmn. Commn. Operation U.S. Senate, 1975—76; mem. Nat. Adv. Coun. Edn. Professions Devel., 1975—76; trustee Truman Libr. Inst., 1973—80, Nelson Art Gallery, 1973—80, Menninger Found., 1982—88, Dole Found., William Allen White Found.; mem. bd. regents State of Kans., 1982—86; mem. adv. commn. U.S. Army Command and Gen. Staff Coll., 1974—79, chmn., 1978—79; chmn. bd. trustees U. Mid.-Am., 1978—79; mem. consultative bd. regents U. Qatar, 1979—80. Named Outstanding Alumnus, E. Tenn. State U., 1970; Ford Found. fellow, 1957—59, Am. Coun. Edn. Postdoctoral fellow, U. Ill., 1966—67. Mem.: Kans. Assn. Commerce and Industry (bd. dirs. 1975—82), Nat. Assn. State Univs. and Land Grant Colls. (coun. pres. 1971—80), Am. Coun. Life Ins. (bd. dirs. 1981—86), Tenn. Coll. Assn. (pres. 1969—70), Newcomen Soc. N.Am., Phi Kappa Phi. Home: 2102 W 116TH St Leawood KS 66211-2953

DYKES, OSBORNE JEFFERSON, III, lawyer; b. LA, Dec. 3, 1944; s. Osborne J. Jr. and Frances (Fox) D.; m. Ann Dennis, Dec. 29, 1973; children: Barbara Nell, Osborne J. IV. BA, Stanford U., 1966, MA, 1968; JD, U. Tex., 1972. Bar: Tex. 1973, U.S. Supreme Ct. 1977, U.S. Ct. Appeals (5th cir.) 1973, U.S. Ct. Appeals (11th cir.) 1981, U.S. Dist. Ct. (so. dist.) Tex. 1975, U.S. Dist. Ct. (ea. dist.) Tex. 1976, U.S. Dist. Ct. (no. dist.) Tex. 1994. Law clk. to Hon. Homer Thornberry U.S. Ct. Appeals 5th Cir., Austin, Tex., 1972-73; ptnr. Fulbright & Jaworski, Houston, 1973—. Contbr. articles to profl. publs. With U.S. Army, 1969-71. Fellow Am. Bar Found., Tex. Bar Found. (life), Houston Bar Found. (life); mem. ABA (chmn. property ins. law com. 1983-84, tort and ins. practice sect.), Fed. Bar Assn. (sec. South Tex. chpt. 2005), Energy Bar Assn., Bar Assn. of Fifth Fed. Cir., Am. Bd. Trial Advs., Tex. Assn. Civil and Appellate Trial Specialists (pres. 2002-2003). Republican. Episcopalian. Avocation: bicycling. Home: 5135 Holly Terrace Dr Houston TX 77056-2125 Office: Fulbright & Jaworski 1301 Mckinney St Houston TX 77010-3031 E-mail: jdykes@fulbright.com.

DYKES, RONALD MITCHELL, telecommunications executive; BSEE, Auburn U., 1969; MBA, Emory U., 1981; MS in Mgmt., Stanford U., 1986. With Southern Bell, Atlanta, 1971-83; dir. fin. mgmt. BellSouth Corp., Atlanta, 1983-85; asst. to the pres., dir. bus. and fin. planning BellSouth Ent., Atlanta, 1986-88, v.p. fin., 1988-93; v.p., contr. BellSouth Corp., Atlanta, 1993-95, CFO, 1995—; dir. Cingular Wireless. Trustee St. Joseph's Health Sys. With Signal Corps. U.S. Army, 1969—71. Sloan fellow Stanford U., 1985-86 Office: Bellsouth Corp 1155 Peachtree St NE Ste 2008 Atlanta GA 30309-3610 E-mail: ron.dykes@bellsouth.com.

DYKEWICZ, MARK STEVEN, physician; b. Flint, Mich., May 21, 1955; s. Richard Alfred and Evelyn Ellen Dykewicz; m. Lenora-Marya Anop, June 19, 2004. BS, U. Mich., 1977; MD, St. Louis U., 1981. Resident medicine Northwestern U. Med. Sch., Chgo., 1981-84, fellow allergy-immunology, 1984-86, asst. prof. medicine, 1986-90; asst. prof. internal medicine St. Louis U. Med. Sch., 1990—94, assoc. prof., 1994—2002, prof., 2002—, dir. allergy immunology postgrad. tng. program. Mem. pulmonary allergy drug adv. com. FDA, 1999—2003, chmn., 2001—03. Lead editor: Joint Task Force Practice Parameters on Rhinitis, 1998—. Recipient Disting. Svc. award, Am. Coll. Allergy, Asthma and Immunology, 1999. Fellow ACP, Am. Coll. Chest Physicians, Am. Acad. Allergy-Immunology; mem. Am. Thoracic Soc., Am. Acad. Allergy, Asthma and Imunology (chmn. com. on occupl. lung disease 1998-2000, chmn. com. on adverse reactions to drugs and biols. 2001-03, chmn. com. on rhinitis 2004—, Spl. Recognition award 1999) Office: St Louis U Med Sch 1402 S Grand Blvd #R209 Saint Louis MO 63104-1004 Office Phone: 314-977-8827. Business E-Mail: dykewicz@slu.edu.

DYKSTRA, DANIEL D., lawyer; b. Patterson, N.J., Oct. 29, 1955; s. H. Allan and Evelyn M. (Brown) D.; m. Sharon R. Leensvaart, June 4, 1976; children: Josiah, Jesse, Jordan, Shantelle. BA, Dordt Coll., 1977; JD with distinction, U. Iowa, 1980. Bar: Iowa 1980, U.S. Dist. Ct. (no. dist.) Iowa 1980. Assoc. Gleysteen, Harper, Eidsmoe, Heidman & Redmond, Sioux City, Iowa, 1980-83; ptnr. Heidman, Redmond, Fredregill, Patterson, Plaza, Dykstra & Prahl LLP, Sioux City, 1983—. Adj. prof. bus. law Dordt Coll., 1990—93; lectr. various orgns. Author: Practical Financial Stewardship Handbook, 2000. Mem. Siouxland Com. for Handicapped, Sioux City, 1980-98; mem. subcom. on governance State of Iowa Edn. Task Force, 1988-90; mem. funds allocation com. Siouxland United Way, 1988-92; mem. cmty. rels. com. Marion Health Ctr., 1987-90; elder, past v.p. Sunnybrook Cmty. Ch.; pres., dir. G.I.F.T.S. Found., 1988-94; mem. Siouxland Regional Cancer Ctr. Found., 2000—; bd. dirs. Sioux City Symphony, 2002—; mem. planned giving com. St. Luke's Health Found. Recipient Gov's. Disting. Svc. award Siouxland Com. for Handicapped, 1990. Mem. ABA (real property probate and trust div.), Iowa Bar Assn. (chair legal forms com. 1991-93, real estate practice manual com., profl. corps. com.), Woodbury County Bar Assn. (probate com.), Estate Planning Coun. Greater Siouxland Inc. (pres.), Planned Giving Coun. of Siouxland (pres.), Dordt Coll. Alumni Assn. (coord. 1985-2000, pres. 1994-97). Mem. Reformed Ch. Am. Avocations: gardening, photography, travel, drama. Home: 2515 Mcdonald St Sioux City IA 51104-3740 Office: Heidman Redmond Fredregill Plaza Dykstra & Prahl LLP PO Box 3086 Sioux City IA 51102-3086 Office Phone: 712-255-8838.

DYKSTRA, DAVID ALLEN, real estate company executive; b. Kalamazoo, Feb. 5, 1938; s. Alle and Elizabeth (VanderHorst) D. m. Kathryn Ann DeNio, Aug. 4, 1962 (div. Nov. 1985); children: Brian Thayer, Kristen Lee, Holly Beth. BBA, Western Mich. U., 1966. Pres. Dyco Corp., Portage, Mich., 1970—; realtor Crossroads Real Estate, Kalamazoo, 1994-96, Callander Woollam & Britigan Comml. Realtors, Portage, Mich., 1996-2000, Exit Gulder Real Estate, Naples, Fla., 2000—02, VR Bus. Brokers, Naples, 2002—. Cons. Waste Industry, Mich., 1976-82; owner Dairy World Yogurt Shops. Bd. dirs. Portage C. of C., 1980-83, econ. devel. com.; alt. del. Rep. Conv., Mich., 1984; adv. bd. Naples Christian Chamber; exec. bd. dirs. Parkinson Assn. SW Fla. Mem.: Beacon Club, Safari Club Internat. (bd. dirs. Ft. Myers/Naples chpt.). Republican. Avocations: big game hunting, golf. Home: 2068 Crestview Way Naples FL 34119-3306 Office: 5629 Strand Blvd Naples FL 34110 Office Phone: 239-261-1111. Personal E-mail: naplesdavid@earthlink.net.

DYKSTRA, DAVID CHARLES, management executive, consultant, accountant, author, educator; b. Des Moines, July 10, 1941; s. Orville Linden and Ermina (Dunn) Dykstra; m. Susan Ogden, Aug. 18, 2001; children from previous marriage: Suzanne, Karin, David S. BSChemE, U. Calif., Berkeley, 1963; MBA, Harvard U., 1966. CPA, Calif. Corp. controller Recreation Environs., Newport Beach, Calif., 1970-71, Hydro Conduit Corp., Newport Beach, 1971-78; v.p. fin. and adminstrn. Tree-Sweet Products, Santa Ana, Calif., 1978-80; pres., owner Dykstra Cons., Irvine, Calif., 1980-88, Marcer Island, Wash., 1998—. Pres. Easy Data Corp., 1981-88; pub. Easy Data Computer Comparisons, 1982-87; sr. mgr. Deloitte & Touche, Costa Mesa, Calif., 1988-90; prof. mgmt. info. sys. Nat. U., Irvine, 1984-90; pub. Dykstra's Computer Digest, 1984-90; pres., owner Golden West Pers., Long Beach, Wash., 1992-93; exec. v.p. Tegris Corp., Bellevue, Wash., 1994-98. Author: Manager's Guide to Business Computer Terms, 1981, Computers for Profit, 1983; contbr. articles to profl. jours. Chmn. 40th Congl. Dist. Tax Reform Immediately, 1977-80; mem. nat. com. Rep. Com.; vice-chmn. Orange County Calif. Rep. Assembly, 1979-80; bd. dirs. Corona Del Mar Rep. Assembly, 1980-94, v.p., 1980-87, pres., 1987-89; mem. Mercer Island Presbyn. Ch., 1998—. Mem. AICPA, Am. Mgmt. Assn., Calif. Soc. CPAs, Data Processing Mgmt. Assn., Am. Prodn. and Inventory Control Soc., Ind. Computer Cons. Assn., Internat. Platform Assn., Data Processing Mgmt. Assn., Orange County C. of C., Newport Beach C. of C., Harvard U. Bus. Sch. Assn. Orange County (bd. dirs. 1984-90, v.p. 1984-86, 87-88, pres. 1986-87, 91-92, chmn. 1993-94), Harvard U. Bus. Sch. Assn. So. Calif. (bd. dirs. 1986-87, 91-92, v.p. 1992-93), Harvard U. Bus. Sch. Assn. Puget Sound, Town Hall, Mercer Island Presbyn. Ch., Mercer Island Country Club, John Wayne Tennis Club, S. Cowichan Lawn Tennis Club, Lido Sailing Club, Columbia Tower Club, Rotary (bd. dirs. 1984-86). Home and Office: 3465 W Mercer Way Mercer Island WA 98040-3355

DYKSTRA, DENNIS DALE, physiatrist; b. Lakewood, Ohio, Feb. 21, 1950; s. Gerald and Grace Maire (Thomas) D.; m. Mary Louise Kerker, May 16, 1992; children: Dorothy, Perry, Caitlin, Patrick. AB in Zoology summa cum laude, Ohio U., 1972; MD, U. Cin., 1976; PhD, U. Minn., 1988, M in Health Adminstrn., 1999. Diplomate Am. Bd. Pediatrics, Am. Bd. Phys. Medicine and Rehab. Intern/resident Cin. Children's Hosp., 1976-81; instr. U. Minn., Mpls., 1981-88, asst. prof., 1988-92, assoc. prof. phys. medicine/rehab./pediatrics/urol. surgery, 1992—, head dept. phys. medicine/rehab., 1992—; assoc. chief staff for rehab. VA Med. Ctr., Mpls., 1994-97. Author: Krusen's Handbook of Phys. Medicine and Rehabilitation, 1991; contbr. articles to profl. jours. Med. advisor Minn. Spasmodic Torticolits Soc., Duluth, Minn., 1991—. Recipient Phys. Med. and Rehab. Investigator award Phys. Med. and Rehab. Rsch. Found., 1984, 85; Spinal Cord Soc. grantee, 1990. Fellow Am. Acad. Phys. Med. and Rehab. (chair edn. com. 1996—), Am. Acad. Pediatrics, Am. Assn. Electrodiagnostic Medicine. Achievements include 2 patents on method of apparatus for mechanical stimulation of nerves, method and device for pharmacological control of spascitity. Office: Univ Minn 420 Delaware St SE Box 297 Mayor Bldg Minneapolis MN 55455 Office Phone: 612-626-5399.

DYKSTRA, PAUL HOPKINS, lawyer; b. Chgo., July 13, 1943; s. Paul C. and Frances Marie (Hopkins) D. Student, Exeter Coll. Oxford U., Eng., 1964; AB, Princeton U., 1965; LLB, Yale U., 1968. Bar: Ill. 1968, D.C. 1977. Assoc. Gardner, Carton & Douglas, Chgo., 1968-74, ptnr., 1975—2003, ptnr. Washington office, 1977-79, fin. ptnr., 1985-89, chmn., 1989-95; mem. Bell, Boyd & Lloyd LLC, Chgo., 2003—. Adj. prof. law Northwestern U. Sch. Law, 2001—. Contbr. articles to profl. jours. Trustee Chgo. Theatre Group, Inc. (Goodman Theatre), 1975—, pres., 1983-85, vice chmn., 1988-92, pres., 1992-97; mem. aux. bd. Art Inst. Chgo., 1973-77, 79-88, exec. com., 1976-77, 82-87, 2000—; chmn. Orange and Black Club of Princeton Club of Chgo., 1987-90; chmn. maj. gifts Princeton U. Class of 1965, 1982-85; mem. cultural affairs adv. bd. City of Chgo., 1990-2003, Blue Skies for Kids, Chgo. Cmty. Trust, Chgo. Pub. Libr. Bd., 1991-97, chmn. adminstrn. and fin. com., 1996—; trustee Chgo. Pub. Libr. Found., 1999—. Mem. ABA (fed. and regulation of securities com.), Chgo. Bar Assn. (sec. 1976-77), Chgo. Hist. Soc. (trustee 1999—, mem. Making History awards com. 1994—, chmn. 2000-2002), Econ. Club of Chgo. (reception com. 1982-85), Legal Club of Chgo., Law Club Chgo., Racquet Club of Chgo. (bd. govs., vice chmn. membership com. 1980-83), Chgo. Club (bd. dirs., sec. 1996-2000), Shoreacres, Chgo. Commonwealth Club, The Comml. Club of Chgo. (sec., mem. exec. com. 2001-03), Chgo. Coun. Fgn. Rels. (Chgo. com.). Episcopalian. Avocations: travel, golf, bicycling. Office: Gardner Carton Douglas 191 N Wacker Dr Chicago IL 60606-1698 Office Phone: 312-781-6029. E-mail: pdykstra@bellboyd.com.

DYKSTRA, ROBERT, retired education educator; b. Vesper, Wis., Feb. 26, 1930; s. John and Anna (Holstein) D.; m. Lou Ann Conselman, Oct. 6, 1956; children: S. Kim, Paul, Randall. BS in Elem. Edn., U. Wis., River Falls, 1957; MA in Ednl. Psychology, U. Minn., 1959, PhD in Ednl. Psychology, 1962. Cert. elem. edn. Elem. tchr. Cedar Grove (Wis.) Pub. Sch., 1954-55; asst. prof. U. Minn., Mpls., 1962-64, assoc. prof., 1965-69, prof., 1970-73, chair dept. curriculum and instrn., 1974-85, prof., 1986-93, ret., 1993. Co-author: Teaching Reading, 1974, Language Arts: Teaching and Learning Effective Use of Language, 1988; contbr. articles to profl. jours. With U.S. Army, 1952—54. Recipient Disting. Alumnus award U. Wis./River Falls, 1998; elected to Reading Hall of Fame, 1996; U.S. Office Edn. rsch. grantee, 1963, 65. Mem. Nat. Coun. Tchrs. of English (mem. exec. com. 1969-71), Nat. Conf. on Rsch. in English (pres. 1984-85), Twin City Area Reading Coun. (pres. 1990-91), Internat. Reading Assn. (mem. pub. com. 1975-77), Nat. Reading Conf. (mem. pub. com. 1978-80). Lutheran. Avocations: barbershop quartet singing, reading, golf. Home: 1998 16th St NW Saint Paul MN 55112-5555 E-mail: bolo19@netzero.com.

DYKSTRA, WILLIAM DWIGHT, management executive, consultant; b. Grand Rapids, Mich., June 15, 1927; s. John Albert and Irene (Staplekamp) D.; m. Ann McGuiness, Nov. 2, 1957 (dec. 1988); children: William Hugh, Mary Irene. AB, Hope Coll., 1949; MBA, Ind. U., 1951. Asst. mgr. Ply-Curves, Inc., 1950; originator magnesium metal furniture, 1951; pres. Dwignt Corp., 1952-56, W.D. Dykstra Group, Grand Rapids, 1956—. Pres. Burton L. Norton Co., 1990, Tie Life Care, Inc.; bd. dirs. Sheldon Co., Orchard Machine Co. Author: Management and the 4th Estate, New Profits for Management. George F. Baker Scholar selector; elder Dutch Ref. Ch. Recipient Outstanding Furniture Merit award, 1955, Vehicle Color Design award, 1967, P.I.A. Graphic award, 1971, Am. Advt. Fedn. award, 1971, 73, 76, Disting. Entrepreneur Alumnus award Ind. U., 1983. Mem. Am. Econs. Assn., Am. Inst. Graphic Arts (Packaging award 1965, 67), Acad. Polit. Sci., Am. Mktg. Assn. (Mktg. Man of Yr. 1981), Engring. Soc. of Detroit, Soc. Packaging and Handling Engrs., Rotary, Phi Kappa Psi, Pi Kappa Delta. Republican. Home: 1145 Edison Ave NW Grand Rapids MI 49504-3919 Office: Old Tallmadge Grange Hall 01845 Leonard St NW Grand Rapids MI 49544-9510

DYKSTRA LYNCH, MARY ELIZABETH, library and information scientist, educator; b. Phila., May 21, 1939; arrived in Canada, 1964; d. Edward and Marietta R. (Kuiper) Heerema: m. Michael F. Lynch, Aug. 12, 1995; children from previous marriage: Mark Edward, Jeffrey Garth. BA, Calvin Coll., 1960; MLS, Dalhousie U., Halifax, N.S., 1970; PhD, Sheffield (Eng.) U., 1986. Head cataloguer Dalhousie U. Libr., 1970-74; asst. prof. Sch. Libr. Svc. Dalhousie U., 1974-78, assoc. prof., 1978-82, assoc. prof. Sch. Libr. and Info. Studies, 1983-86, prof., 1987-97, prof. emeritus, 1997—, dir. Sch. Libr. and Info. Studies, 1986-95. Sr. audiovisual libr. Nat. Film Bd. of Can., Montreal, 1982-83, cons. 1977-83; cons. Coun. Mins. Edn., Toronto, Ont., 1984-85, art history info. program J. Paul Getty Trust, Williamstown, Mass., 1988-94; mem. adv. bd. Sch. Health Records Sci., Halifax Infirmary, 1984-97, Libr. Technician Programme, Kings Regional Vocat. Sch., N.S., 1987-90; mem. Can. Commn. on Cataloguing, 1986-94; mem. working group on stds. for subject access Nat. Archives of Can., 1987-93; mem. Can. Adv. Com. for Internat. Orgn. for Standardization, Tech. Commn., Info. and Documentation, 1991—; mem. nat. info. highway adv. coun. of Can., 1994-95, 96-97; rsch. officer U. Sheffield (Eng.), 1996-97. Author: Access to Film Information, 1977, Precis: A Primer, 1985; editor 2 books, several film catalogues; editl. bd. Film Canadiana, 1982-84, Cataloging and Classification Quar., 1980-86, Expert Sys. for Info. Mgmt., 1990-93, Libr. and Info. Sci. Rsch., 1992-96; series editor, occasional papers Sch. Libr. and Info. Studies Dalhousie U., 1986-94; contbr. articles to profl. jours. Pres. Citadel North Neighbourhood Assn., Halifax, 1988; bd. dirs. CANARIE (Canadian Network for Advancement of Rsch., Industry & Edn.), 1996-98, internat. consultants com. World Info. and Comm. Report, UNESCO, Paris, 1998-99, Biblioteca nazionale centrale, Florence, Italy, 2001. Rsch. grantee Dalhousie U., 1976, 80, 90, 96, Social Scis. and Humanities Rsch. Coun., Ottawa, 1987-90. Mem. Can. Libr. Assn. (rep. Can. com. on cataloguing 1986-94), Nova Knowledge, Internat. Soc. for Knowledge Orgn. Office: Dalhousie Univ Sch Libr & Info Studies Halifax NS Canada B3H 4H8 E-mail: m.lynch@sheffield.ac.uk.

DYLAN, BOB (ROBERT ALLEN ZIMMERMAN), singer, composer; b. Duluth, Minn., May 24, 1941; s. Abe Zimmerman and Beatrice Rutman; m. Sara Rowndes, Nov. 22, 1965 (div. June 19, 1977); children: Jakob, Jesse, Samuel, Anna, Maria; m. Carolyn Y. Dennis, June 4, 1986 (div. Oct. 1992); 1 child, Desiree Gabrielle. Self-taught on guitar, piano, autoharp, harmonica; student, U. Minn., 1960; Mus D (hon.), Princeton U., 1970. Performer numerous tours and concerts, 1960—. Musician: (albums) Bob Dylan, 1962, The Freewheelin' Bob Dylan, 1963, The Times They Are A-Changin', 1964, Another Side of Bob Dylan, 1964, Bringing It All Back Home, 1965, Highway 61 Revisited, 1965, Blonde on Blonde, 1966, John Wesley Harding, 1967, Bob Dylan's Greatest Hits, 1967, Nashville Skyline, 1969, Self Portrait, 1970, New Morning, 1970, Bob Dylan's Greatest Hits, Vol. 2, 1971, Dylan, 1973, (soundtrack) Pat Garrett and Billy the Kid, 1973, Planet Waves, 1974, Blood on Tracks, 1975, Desire, 1976, Hard Rain, 1976, Street Legal, 1978, Masterpieces, 1978, Slow Train Coming, 1979, At Budokan, 1979, Saved, 1980, Shot of Love, 1981, Infidels, 1983, Real Live, 1984, Empire Burlesque, 1985, Biograph, 1985, Knocked Out Loaded, 1986, Down In The Groove, 1988, Oh Mercy, 1989, Under the Red Sky, 1990, The Bootleg Series, Vols. 1-3, 1991, Good as I Been to You, 1992, World Gone Wrong, 1993 (Grammy Award for Best Traditional Folk Album, 1994), Greatest Hits, Vol. 3, 1994, Unplugged, 1995, Time Out of Mind, 1997 (Grammy Award for Album of Yr., 1998, Grammy Award for Best Contemporary Folk Album, 1998), The Best of Bob Dylan, 1997, The Bootleg Series, Vol. 4: The Royal Albert Hall Concert, 1998, Essential Bob Dylan, 2000, The Best of Bob Dylan, Vol. 2, 2000, The Very Best of Bob Dylan, 2000, Love and Theft, 2001 (Grammy Award for Best Contemporary Folk Album, 2002), The Bootleg Series, Vol. 5, Live 1975, 2002, (soundtrack) Masked and Anonymous, 2003, Bootleg Series, Vol. 6 Live 1964, 2004; musician: (with various artists) The Concert for Bangladesh, 1971 (Grammy Award for Album of Yr., 1973), (soundtrack) The Last Waltz, 1976, Bob Dylan 30th Anniversary Concert Celebration, 1993; musician: (with The Band) Before the Flood, 1974, The Basement Tapes, 1976; musician: (with Traveling Wilburys) Traveling Wilburys Vol. 1, 1988 (Grammy Award for Best Rock Performance by a Duo or Group with Vocal, 1990), Traveling Wilburys Vol. 3, 1990; musician: (with Grateful Dead) Dylan and the Dead, 1988; composer: (songs) Blowin' in the Wind, Like a Rolling Stone (Named Greatest Rock 'n' Roll song of All Time Rolling Stone mag., 2004), Lay, Lady, Lay, Subterranean Homesick Blues, Forever Young, Gotta Serve Somebody, Don't Think Twice, It's Alright, A Hard Rain's A-Gonna Fall, The Times They are A-Changin', Just Like a Woman, I'll Be Your Baby Tonight, I Shall Be Released, Mr. Tambourine Man, Tangled Up In Blue, others; dir., editor (films) Eat the Document, 1972; appeared in: (documentaries) Don't Look Back, 1967; actor: (TV films) The Madhouse on Castle Street, 1963; (films) Pat Garret and Billy the Kid, 1973, Hearts of Fire, 1987; actor, composer, dir., editor, writer (films) Renaldo and Clara, 1978, actor, composer, writer Masked and Anonymous, 2003, Songs appear in films including Easy Rider, 1969, In the Name of the Father, 1993, Jerry Maguire, 1996, The Big Lebowski, 1997, American Beauty, 1999, The Hurricane, 1999, Girl Interrupted, 1999, Wonder Boys, 2000 (Acad. Award for best original song for Things Have Changed, 2001), High Fidelity, 2000, Blow, 2001, Monster's Ball, 2001, Vanilla Sky, 2001, Gods and Generals, 2003, The Hunted, 2003, and many others; author: Tarantula, 1971, Writings and Drawings, 1973, Tarantula: Poems, 1994, (book of sketches) Drawn Blank, 1994, (memoirs) Chronicles, Vol. 1, 2004. Named to Rock and Roll Hall of Fame, 1988; recipient GrammyAward for Best Male Rock Vocal Performance, (for Gotta Serve Somebody), 1980, Lifetime Achievement Award, Grammy Awards, 1991, Grammy nomination for Best Rock Performance by a Duo or Group, (with Roger McGuinn, Tom Petty, Neil Young, Eric Clapton, and George Harrison for My Back Pages), 1997, Grammy Award for Best Male Rock Vocal Performance, (for Cold Irons Bound), 1998. Achievements include devising and popularizing folk-rock. Office: Columbia Records 550 Madison Ave New York NY 10022-3211

DY-LIACCO, GABRIEL S., psychotherapist; AB in Psychology, Ateneo de Manila U., Quezon City, Philippines, 1993; MS in Pastoral Counseling, Loyola Coll., 1999, PhD in Pastoral Counseling, 2005. Cert. Nat. Bd. of Cert. Counselors, 1999, lic. clin. profl. counselor Md. Bd. of Profl. Counselors and Therapists, 2001. Adult and adolescent psychotherapist Key Point Health Svcs., Inc., Catonsville, Md., 1999—2004; doctral rsch. fellow dept. pastoral counseling Loyola Coll., Columbia, Md., 2002—03, tchg. asst. dept. pastoral counseling, 2003—04, rsch. asst. dept. psychology, 2004—05; asst. prof. Sch. Psychology and Counseling Regent U. Grad. Ctr., Alexandria, Va., 2005—. Patient care monitor Key Point Health Svcs., Inc., Catonsville, Md., 2003—04, clin. peer trainer, 2003—04, clin. internship supr., 2002—03; individual clin. supr. Pastoral Counseling Dept., Loyola Coll. in Md., Columbia, Md., 2002—03. Contbr. articles and revs. to profl. jours.; translator: (Tagalog version) Spiritual Transcendence Scale. Vol. Parish Pastoral Coun. for Responsible Voting, Quezon City, Philippines, 1992, SJ Prison Ministry, Muntinlupa, Philippines, 1989—90; mem. Arvisu Ho. SJ Prenovitiate, Quezon City, Philippines, 1989—91. Mem.: APA (student mem.), Am. Mental Health Counselors Assn. (clin. mem.), Profl. Assn. Diving Instrs. (life; dive master (inactive) 1989—2003), Chi Sigma Iota, Alpha Sigma Nu. Avocations: scuba diving, travel. Personal E-mail: gdyliacco@regent.edu.

DYM, CLIVE LIONEL, engineering educator; b. Leeds, Eng., July 15, 1942; came to U.S., 1949, naturalized, 1954; s. Isaac and Anna (Hochmann) D.; children: Jordana, Miriam; m. Joan Dym, June 28, 1998. BCE, Cooper Union, 1962; MS, Poly. Inst. Bklyn., 1964; PhD, Stanford U., 1967. Asst. prof. SUNY, Buffalo, 1966-69; assoc. professorial lectr. George Washington U., Washington, 1969; research staff Inst. Def. Analyses, Arlington, Va., 1969-70; assoc. prof. Carnegie-Mellon U., Pitts., 1970-74; vis. assoc. prof. TECHNION, Israel, 1971; sr. scientist Bolt Beranek and Newman, Inc., Cambridge, Mass., 1974-77; prof. U. Mass., Amherst, 1977-91, head dept. civil engring., 1977-85; Fletcher Jones prof. engring. design Harvey Mudd Coll., Claremont, Calif., 1991—, dir. Ctr. Design Edn., 1995—, chair dept. engring., 1999—2002. Vis. sr. rsch. fellow Inst. Sound and Vibration Rsch., U. Southampton, Eng., 1973; vis. scientist Xerox PARC, 1983-84; vis. prof. civil engring. Stanford U., 1983-84, Carnegie Mellon U., 1990; Eshbach vis. prof. Northwestern U., 1997-98; cons. Bell Aerospace Co., 1967-69, Dravo Corp., 1970-71, Salem Corp., 1972, Gen. Analytics Inc., 1972, ORI, Inc., 1979, BBN Inc., 1979, Avco, 1981-83, 85-86, TASC, 1985-86, D.H. Brown Assocs., 1991, Johnson Controls, 1996; vice chmn. adv. bd. Amerinex Artificial Intelligence, 1986-88. Author: (with I.H. Shames) Solid Mechanics: A Variational Approach, 1973, Introduction to the Theory of Shells, rev. edit. 1990, Stability Theory and Its Applications to Structural Mechanics, 1974, 2002, (with E.S. Ivey) Principles of Mathematical Modeling, 1980, (with I.H. Shames) Energy and Finite Element Methods in Structural Mechanics, 1985, (with R.E. Levitt) Knowledge-Based Systems in Engineering, 1990, Engineering Design: A Synthesis of Views, 1994, Structural Modeling and Analysis, 1997, (with P. Little) Engineering Design: A Project-Based Introduction, 1999, 2d edit., 2004, (with P.D. Cha and J.J. Rosenberg), Fundamentals of Modeling and Analyzing Engineering Systems, 2000, Principles of Mathematical Modeling, 2nd edit., 2004; editor: (with A. Kalnins) Vibration: Beams, Plates, and Shells, 1977, Applications of Knowledge-Based Systems to Engineering Analysis and Design, 1985, Computing Futures in Engineering Design, 1997, Designing Design Education for the 21st Century, 1999, (with L. Winner) Social Dimensions of Engineering Design, 2001, Designing Engineering Education, 2003, Artificial Intelligence for Engring. Design Analysis and Mfg., 1986-96; contbr. articles and tech. reports to profl. publs. NATO sr. fellow in sci., 1973; Boeing Outstanding Engring. Educator award (first-runnerup), 2001. Fellow Acoustical Soc. Am., ASME (Ruth and Joel Spira Outstanding Design Educator award 2004), ASCE (Walter L. Huber rsch. prize 1980); mem. Am. Assn. for Artificial Intelligence, Computer Soc. of IEEE, ASEE (Western Electric Fund award 1983, Fred Merryfield Design award 2002). Jewish. Office: Harvey Mudd Coll Engring Dept 301 E 12th St Claremont CA 91711-5901 Office Phone: 909-621-8853.

DYMALLY, MERVYN MALCOLM, retired congressman; b. Cedros, Trinidad, W.I., May 12, 1926; s. Hamid A. and Andreid S. (Richardson) D.; m. Alice M. Gueno; children: Mark, Lynn. BA in Edn., Calif. State U., 1954; MA in Govt., Calif. State U., Sacramento, 1970; PhD in Human Behavior, U.S. Internat. U., 1978; JD (hon.), Lincoln U., Sacramento, 1975; LLD (hon., U. W. L.A., 1970, Calif. Coll. Law, L.A., City U., L.A., 1976, Fla. Meml. Coll., 1987, Lincoln U., San Francisco, 1984; HLD (hon.), Shaw U., N.C., 1981; PHD (hon.), Calif. Western. U., 1982. Cert. elem., secondary and exceptional children tchr. Tchr. L.A. City Schs., 1955-61; coord. Calif. Disaster Office, 1961-62; mem. Calif. Assembly, 1962-66, 2002—, Calif. Senate, 1967-74; lt. gov. Calif., 1975-79; mem. 97th-102nd Congresses from 31st Calif. dist., 1981-92; pres. Dymally Internat. Group Inc., Inglewood, Calif., 1992—. Mem. Com. on Fgn. Affairs and its subcoms. on Internat. Ops., chmn. subcom. on Africa, 1989-92; mem. Com. on D.C. and chmn. subcom. on judiciary and edn., 1981-92; chmn. Congl. Task Force on Minority Set Asides, 1987-92; chmn. Senate Majority Caucus, Senate Select Com. on Children and Youth; chmn. Senate coms. on mil. and vets. affairs, social welfare, elections and reapportionment, subcom. on med. edn. and health needs; chmn. joint coms. on legal equality for women, on revision of election code; chmn. assembly com. on indsl. rels.; current mem. Congl. Hispanic Caucus, Congl. Caucus Women's Issues, Congl. Human Rights Caucus, Congl. Black Caucus and chmn. of its task force on Caribbean; chmn. Caribbean Action Lobby, Caribbean Am. Rsch. Inst.; founder Congl. Inst. for Space, Sci. and Tech., chmn. adv. bd.; past chmn. Calif. Commn. Econ. Devel., Commn. of Califs. (U.S., Baja Calif., Calif. Sur, Mex.); past vice chmn., Nat. Conf. Lt. Govs.; former Gov.'s designee U.S. Border States Commn.; past mem. State Lands Commn., others; lectr. Claremont (Calif.) Grad. Sch., Golden Gate U., Sacramento, Pepperdine U., L.A., Pomona (Calif.) Coll., U. Calif., Davis, Irvine, Whittier (Calif.) Coll., Shaw U., Raleigh, N.C.; Disting. prof. Ctrl. State U.; mem. faculty Drew U. Medicine and Sci.; adj. prof. Compton Coll.; cons. to chancellor L.A. C.C. Author: The Black Politician-His Struggle for Power, 1971; co-auhtor: (with Dr. Jeffrey Elliot) Fidel Castro: Nothing Can Stop the Course of History, 1986, also articles; former editor:The Black Politician (quar.) Mem. L.A. County Water Appeals Bd.; advisor to Calif. Assembly Spkr. for Cmty. Congress; chmn. Calif. Black Leadership Roundtable, Caribbean Am. Coalition; chair select com. cmty. colls. Prof. Charles R. Drew U. Medicine Sci.; mem. Calif. Assembly, 2003—. Recipient numerous awards including Chaconia Gold medal Govt. Trinidad and Tobago, Adam Clayton Powell award Congl. Black Caucus, Dr. Solomon P. Fuller award Black Psychiatrists of Am., others from Golden State Med. Assn., United Tchrs. L.A., Bd. Suprs. L.A., L.A. City Coun., various univs., colls., orgns. Mem. AAUP, NAACP, Am. Acad. Polit. Sci., Am. Polit. Sci. Assn., Am. Acad. Polit. and Social Sci., ACLU, Urban League, Phi Kappa Phi, Kappa Alpha Psi Democrat. Office: Calif Assembly 322 W Compton Blvd # 100 Compton CA 90220 Home: 223 S Acacia Ave # 206 Compton CA 90220 Office Phone: 310-223-1201. Business E-Mail: mervyn.dymally@asm.ca.gov.

DYMAN, JENNI L., author; b. Oklahoma City, Aug. 10, 1941; d. Ernest F. Hiser and Jennie M. (Bick) Hiser Moore; m. James E. Caldwell, Jan. 26, 1962 (div. Sept. 1967); m. Thaddeus S. Dyman, Apr. 11, 1987; 1 child, Ken C. BA, U. Denver, 1963; MA, U. Okla., 1968; PhD, U. Colo., 1990. Tchr. Arapahoe C.C., Littleton, Colo., 1969-96, dept. chmn., 1980-82, 91-96. Author: Lurking Feminism: The Ghost Stories of Edith Wharton, 1996. English-Speaking Union scholar, 1979. Mem. MLA, Edith Wharton Soc., Edith Wharton Restoration Soc. Democrat. Unitarian Universalist. Home: 524 S Ogden St Denver CO 80209-4418

DYMIOTIS-WELLINGTON, CHRISTIANA, structural engineer, educator; b. Limassol, Cyprus, Jan. 18, 1974; d. Antonios and Niki Dymiotis; m. Gregory R.W. Wellington, July 6, 2003; 1 child, Nicola Joanna Wellington. BEng (Hons) Civil Engring., City U., London, 1995; MSc Earthquake Engring. and Structural Dynamics, Imperial Coll. Sci., Tech. and Medicine, London, 1996; PhD Structural Engring., Imperial Coll. Sci., Tech. and Medicine, London, 1999—99; postgrad. in Acad. Practice, Heriot-Watt U., Edinburgh, Scotland, 2002. Lectr. Heriot-Watt U., Edinburgh, Scotland, 1999—2003; rsch. fellow Sch. Engring. and Math. Sci. City U., London, 2003—. Contbr. scientific papers to profl. jours. and confs. Orthodox Christian. Avocations: classical music, tennis, donkeys. Home: 94 Arlington Rd Southgate London N14 5 AT England Office: Sch Engring and Math Scis City U Northampton Square London EC1V 0HB England Office Phone: 020 7040 3623. Office Fax: 020 7040 8566. Personal E-mail: c_dymiotis@hotmail.com. Business E-Mail: c.dymiotis-wellington@city.ac.uk.

DYMOND, LEWIS WANDELL, lawyer, educator; b. Lansing, Mich., June 28, 1920; s. Lewis Wandell and Irene (Parker) D.; m. Betty Louise Blood, Sept. 6, 1942; children: Lewis W., Jean Ann; m. Joann Surrey, Sept. 3, 1966; 1 son, Steven Henry. JD cum laude, U. Miami, 1956. Bar: Fla. 1957; cert. ct. mediator, Fla. With Nat. Airlines, Inc., Miami, Fla., 1938-62, mechanic, agt., sta. mgr., flight dispatcher, ops. mgr., pilot, v.p. ops., maintenance and engring., 1955-62; pres., chief exec. officer, dir. Frontier Airlines, 1962-79. Adj. prof. Sch. Bus. U. Miami, Coral Gables, Fla. Mem. U. Miami Alumni Club, Union League, Surf Club, Masons, Shriners, Phi Kappa Phi, Phi Alpha Delta. Home and Office: 6 E Belleview Way Greenwood Village CO 80121-1408

DYNACK, DAVID M., theater educator; BA in English, Mich. State U., 1968, MA in Ednl. Founds., 1972, PhD in Theatre, 1994. Instr. Lansing (Mich.) C.C., 1972—75; tchr. St. Ignace, Mich., 1975—78, Cheboygan, Mich., 1978—80; dir. CETA Learning Ctr., Cheboygan, 1980—82; tchr. DoDDS, Wiesbaden, Germany, 1982—86, Augsburg, Germany, 1988—91; instr. Mich. State U., E. Lansing, Mich., 1986—88, Kalamazoo (Mich.) Coll., 1991—93; asst. prof., dir. Integrated Creative Arts Minor We. Mich. U., Kalamazoo, 1993—97; from asst. prof., head Theater Edn. Programs to assoc. prof. U. Utah, Salt Lake City, 1997—2004, assoc. prof., 2004—, dir. Grad. Studies, 2004—, head Theatre Edn., 2004—. Presenter in field; dramaturg Pioneer Theatre Co., 2001—; mem. adminstrv. staff Sundance Theatre Lab., 1997—; cons. in field; artistic dir. various prodns., 1993—. Contbr. articles to profl. jours.; dir.: (plays) U. Utah, 1998—2005, We. Mich. U., Augsburg Am. Schs., Mich. State U., Wiesbaden Am. Schs., Cheboygan (Mich.) Area Schs.; actor(dir.): (plays) Northland Players; editor: Reading Horizens; mem. editl. bd.: Youth Theatre Jour., 2000, 2001. Dramaturg Pioneer Theatre Co., 2001—; judge Desert News, 2000—; adjudicator Am. Coll. Theatre Festival Utah State U., 1998; bd. dirs. Imagination Celebration Ky. Ctr., Salt Lake City, 2000. Recipient Dean's Adminstrv. Merit award, We. Mich. U., 1995, Dept. Merit award, 1995—96, Spirit award, 1997, Excellence in Tchg., Rsch. and Svc. award, Coll. Fine Arts, U. Utah, 2000; grantee, Mich. Pub. Theatre, 1991—94, Kalamazoo (Mich.) Valley Intermediate Sch. Dist., 1995, We. Mich. U., 1996, Utah Arts Coun. and Utah State Office Edn., 1999—2002, U.S. Dept. Edn. and Mariner S. Eccles Found., 2001, Utah Arts Coun., 2003, U. Rsch. Instrumentation Fund, 2003, U. CF&R Com., 2003, The Dana Found., 2005; At-Risk Ctr. scholar, We. Mich. U., 1996—97. Mem.: Utah Theatre Assn. (bd. dirs. 1997—), Theatre Alliance Mich. (steering com. 1995—96), Nat. Assn. Schs. Theatre, Literary Mgrs. and Dramaturgs Am., Internat. Schs. Theatre Assn. (exec. coun. 1990—94, treas. 1993—94), Assn. Tchr. Educators (reviewer 1996—97), Assn. Theatre Higher Edn., Am. Ednl. Rsch. Assn. (editl. rev. bd. Arts and Learning Jour. 1996—97), Am. Alliance Theatre and Edn. (co-chmn. higher edn. network 1994—95, chmn. pubs. com. 1995—97, mem. strategic action planning com. 1995—97, mem. rsch. com. 1997—, editl. rev. bd. 1999—, co-editor Stage of Art 2003—, coord. conf. facilities 2004, Presdl. citation 1996, Disting. Dissertation award 1996, Presdl. citation 1995, 1997, 2004), Internat. Thespian Soc., Kappa Delta Pi. Home: 7405 Stagecoach Dr Park City UT 84098-5333

DYNES, ROBERT C., academic administrator, physicist; b. London, Ont., Can., Nov. 8, 1942; m. Frances Dynes Hellman. BS of Math. & Physics, U. Western Ont., 1964; MS of Physics, McMaster U., 1965, PhD of Phys., 1968. Postdoctoral fellow AT&T Bell Labs, Murray Hill, NJ, 1968—70, mem., technical staff, 1970—74, dept. head, semiconductor & chem. physics rsch., 1974—81, dept. head, solid state & physics of materials rsch., 1981—83, dir., chem. physics rsch., 1983—90; physics prof. U. Calif., San Diego, 1991—; chair, dept. physics U. Calif, San Diego, 1994—95; sr. vice chancellor, acad. affairs U. Calif., 1995—96, chancellor, 1996—2003; pres. U. Calif. Sys., Oakland, 2003—. Founding mem. San Diego Sci. and Tech. Coun.; adv. bd. Tex. Ctr. Superconductivity U. Houston; spkr. in field. Contbr. articles to profl. jours. Dir. Calif. C. of C.; mem. Calif. Commn. Jobs and Econ. Growth. Recipient Fritz London award Low Temp. Physics, 1990. Fellow: Can. Inst. Advances Rsch., Am. Phys. Soc.; mem.: NAS, Am. Acad. Arts & Scis. Office: Office of Pres Univ Calif 1111 Franklin St Oakland CA 94607-5200

DYNKIN, EUGENE B., mathematics professor; b. Leningrad, USSR, May 11, 1924; came to U.S., 1977, naturalized, 1983; s. Boris and Rebecca (Sheindlin) D.; m. Irene Pakshver, June 2, 1959; 1 child, Olga. BA, Moscow U., 1945, PhD, 1948, D.Sc., 1951; D Honoris Causa, U. Pierre and Marie Curie, Paris, 1997, Ind. Moscow U., U. Warwick, U.K., 2003. Asst. prof. Moscow U., 1948-49, assoc. prof., 1949-54, prof., 1954-68; sr. research scholar Central Inst. Math. Econ. Acad. of Sci., Moscow, 1968-76; prof. math. Cornell U., Ithaca, N.Y., 1977—. Author: Theory of Markov Processes, 1960, Mathematical Conversations, 1963, Markov Processes, 1965, Mathematicl Problems, 1969, Markov Processes-Theorems and Problems, 1969, Controlled Markov Processes, 1979, Markov Processes and Related Problems of Analysis, 1982, An Introduction to Branching Measure-Valued Processes, 1994, Biography and Bibliography in the Dynkin Festschrift, Markov Processes and Their Applications, 1994, Selected Papers of E.B. Dynkin, 2000, Diffusion, Superdiffusions and Partial Differential Equations, 2002, Superdiffusions and Positive Solutions of Nonlinear Partial Differentiae Equations, 2004. Fellow: AAAS, Inst. Math. Stats.; mem.: NAS, Bernoulli Soc. Math. Stats. and Probability, Moscow Math. Soc. (hon. prize 1951), Am. Math. Soc. (Leroy P. Steele prize 1993). Home: 107 Lake St Ithaca NY 14850-3855 Office: Cornell U Dept Math Malott Hall Ithaca NY 14853 E-mail: ebd1@cornell.edu.

DYNNER, ALAN ROY, lawyer; BA, Dartmouth Coll., 1962; LLB, Yale U., 1965. Bar: U.S. Dist. Ct. D.C. 1966, U.S. Dist. Ct. N.Y. 1966. Ptnr. Kirkpatrick & Lockhart LLP, Washington, 1965—93; exec. v.p. Neuberger Berman Mgmt., N.Y.C., 1994—96; v.p., chief legal officer Eaton Vance Corp., Boston, 1996—. Bd. overseers Boston Symphony Orch., 2002—, New Eng. Aquarium, Boston, 2003—. Mem.: Harvard Musical Assn., The Badminton & Tennis Club, Longwood Cricket Club. Office: Eaton Vance Corp 255 State St Boston MA 02109 Office Phone: 617-598-8180.

DYREGROV, MICHAEL See BAKER, JOHN

DYRENFURTH, MICHAEL JOHN, education educator, academic administrator; b. Schlitz, Fed. Republic Germany, June 16, 1946; came to U.S., 1970; m. Mary Belle Gullekson, June, 1967; children: Walter John, Michelle Lee, Grant Michael. EdB, U. Alta., Can., 1968, MEd, 1970; PhD, Bowling Green (Ohio) State U., 1973. Cert. tchr., Alta. Tchr. indsl. arts pub. schs., Alta., 1967—69; asst. prof., chmn. dept. indsl. edn. Valley City (N.D.) State Coll., ND, 1972—75; assoc. prof. indsl. edn. Montclair (N.J.) State Coll., 1975—78; prof. tech. and industry, practical arts, vocat. tech. edn. U. Mo., Columbia, 1978—98; prof., grad. coord. dept. indsl. edn. and tech. Iowa State U., Ames, 1998—2001; asst. dean, grad. & internat. Sch. Tech., Purdue U., 2001—. Pres. Applied Expertise Assocs.; chair World Coun. Assns. Tech. Edn. Contbr. articles to profl. jours. Mem. Internat. Tech. Edn. Assn. (Outstanding Young Leader award 1985), Internat. Vocat. Edn. and Tng. Assn., Am. Vocat. Assn. (Svc. award 1983, IAD Profl. Leadership award 1986), Coun. Tech. Tchr. Edn., Nat. Assn. Indsl. and Tech. Tchr. Edn. (pres.), Indsl. Tech. Edn. Assn. Mo., Mo. Vocat. Assn. (Outstanding Svc. award 1985), Phi Delta Kappa, Kappa Delta Phi, Epsilon Pi Tau (Disting. Svc. Laureate Citation 1996). Office: Purdue Univ Coll Tech Knoy 150 West Lafayette IN 47907-1410 Office Phone: 765-496-1203.

DYSART, BENJAMIN CLAY, III, conservationist, consultant, engineer; b. Columbia, Tenn., Feb. 12, 1940; s. Benjamin Clay and Kathryne Virginia (Thompson) D.; m. Betty Blanche Walthall, June 7, 2005. BE, Vanderbilt U., 1961, MS in San. Engring., 1964; PhD in Civil Engring., Ga. Inst. Tech., 1969. Staff engr. Union Carbide Corp., 1961-62, 64-65; from asst. prof. to prof. Clemson U., 1968-90, McQueen Quattlebaum prof. engring., 1982-83, dir. S.C. Water Resources Rsch. Inst., 1968-75, dir. water resources engring. grad. program, 1972-75, adj. prof., 1990-93; facility devel. mgr. Chem. Waste Mgmt., Inc., Marietta, Ga., 1990-91, regional facility devel. mgr. Memphis, 1991; dir. project planning and integration Waste Mgmt., Inc., Washington, 1991-92; pres. Dysart & Assocs., Inc., Nashville, 1992—. Sci. advisor Office Sec. of Army, Washington, 1975-76; mem. EPA Sci. Adv. Bd., 1983-, Reinvention Cuitevia Com., NACEPT, US EPA, 1998-2000; sr. fellow The Conservation Found., 1985-90; mem. adv. coun. Electric Power Rsch. Inst., 1989-95; mem., chief of engrs. environ. adv. bd. U.S. Army Corps Engrs., 1988-92; mem. Glacier Nat. Park Sci. Coun., Nat. Park Svc., 1988-91; mem. S.C. Gov.'s Wetlands Forum, 1989-90; sec. appointee Outer Continental Shelf Adv. Bd. and OCS Sci. Com. Dept. Interior, 1979-82; mem. S.C. Environ. Quality Control Adv. Com., 1980-90, chmn., 1980-81; mem. Sci. Panel to Rev. Interagy. Rsch. on Impact of Oil Pollution NOAA, Dept. Commerce, 1980; mem. Nuclear Energy Ctr. Environ. Task Force Dept. Energy-So. States Energy Bd., 1978-81; mem. Nonpoint Source Pollutant Task Force EPA, 1979-80; mem. civil works adv. com. Office Sec. Army-Young Pres.'s Orgn., 1975-76; mem. S.C. Heritage Adv. Bd., 1974-76; mem. Pangue Project, ind. review panel, World Bank, 1996-97; chmn. Ga. Erosion & Sedimentation Control Tech. Study Com., 1996-2001; cons. on effective stakeholder engagement, value adding corp. social responsibility and pub. accountability matters to corp., internat. inst., & govt.; sr. assoc. Internat. Council Mining & Metals, London, 2001-02; leader Ind. Review on Compliance Advisor Ombudsman Office, World Bank, 2003. Editor: (with Marion Clawson) Managing Public Lands in the Public Interest, 1988, Public Interest in the Use of Private Lands, 1989; contbr. articles on math. modeling in water quality and environ. mgmt. and pub. involvement to profl. jours.; author numerous profl. papers, reports. Trustee Rene Dubos Ctr. for Human Environs., 1985-94, vice chmn., mem. exec. com., 1988-94; trustee Issue Mgmt. Coun., 1997-2003, 2005-; bd. visitors Kanuga Episcopal Conf. Ctr., 1988—. Recipient Tribute of Appreciation for Disting. Svc. EPA, 1981, 86, McQueen Quattlebaum Engring. Faculty Achievement award Clemson U., 1982, Order of Palmetto Gov. S.C., 1984; named Hon. Ky. Col., 1976. Mem. Trout Unltd. (trustee 1990-94), Nat. Wildlife Fedn. (bd. dirs. 1974-90, v.p. 1978-83, pres., chmn. bd. dirs. 1983-85), Assn. Environ. Engring. Profs. (bd. dirs. 1978-83, pres., chmn. bd. dirs. 1981-82), Water Environ. Fedn. (hon., bd. dirs. Rsch. Found. 1989-91), S.C. Wildlife Fedn. (bd. dirs. 1969—, pres., chmn. bd. dirs. 1973-74, S.C. Wildlife Conservationist Yr.), The Ga. Conservancy (bd. trustees 1994-97), Cosmos Club (Washington), Sigma Xi, Tau Beta Pi, Phi Kappa Phi, Chi Epsilon, Omega Rho, Sigma Nu. Episcopalian.

DYSART, RICHARD A., retired actor; b. Brighton, Mass., Mar. 30, 1929; m. Kathryn Jacobi. BS, Emerson Coll., 1956, MS, 1983, LLD (hon.), 1988; PhD (hon.), U. Maine, 1992. Appeared off Broadway in Our Town, Six Characters in Search of an Author; on Broadway in A Man for All Seasons, The Little Foxes, A Place Without Doors, That Championship Season, Another Part of the Forest; (feature films) Petulia, The Lost Man, The Sporting Club, The Hospital, The Terminal Man, The Day of the Locust, The Hindenberg, Prophecy, Meteor, Being There, An Enemy of the People, The Thing, The Falcon and the Snowman, Mask, Pale Rider, Wall Street, Back to the Future Part III, Hard Rain; (TV movies) The Autobiography of Miss Jane Pittman, It Happened One Christmas, First You Cry, Bogie, The Ordeal of Dr. Mudd, Churchill and the Generals (BBC), Sandburg's Lincoln, People Vs. Jean Harris, Bitter Harvest, Last Days of Patton, Malice in Wonderland, Day One, Truman; (series) L.A. Law, 1986-94 (Supporting Actor TV-Series Emmy award 1992), L.A. Law Reunion Movie, 2002; (PBS spl.) Concealed Enemies; (mini-series) War and Remembrance. Trustee Gallaudet U., Washington, 1990-2003, trustee emeritus, 2004—, Gould Acad., Bethel, Maine; founding mem. Am. Conservatory Theatre, San Francisco; active Native Am. Rights Fund, 1978—. Sgt. USAF, 1951—55. Mem.: Am. Judicature Soc. (bd. dirs., nat. exec. com. 1998—). E-mail: homerpilgrim@adelphia.net.

DYSINGER, PAUL WILLIAM, preventive medicine physician, educator; b. Burns, Tenn., May 24, 1927; s. Paul Clair and Mary Edith (Martin) D.; m. Yvonne Minchin, May 11, 1958; children: Edwin, Wayne, John, Janelle. BA, So. Missionary Coll., 1951; MD, Loma Linda U., 1955; M.P.H., Harvard, 1962. Diplomate Nat. Bd. Med. Examiners, Am. Bd. Preventive Medicine. Intern, Washington, 1955-56; sr. asst. surgeon USPHS; with Blackfeet Indians in Mont., Navajos of Ariz., 1956-58; physician, med. adviser Am. embassy, PhnomPenh, Cambodia, 1958-60; rsch. assoc. dept. preventive medicine Loma Linda (Calif.) U. (formerly Coll. Med. Evangelists), 1960-62, dir. field sta. Western Tanganyika, 1962-64, adminstrv. asst. div. pub. health, 1964-67, asst. to dean, chmn. dept. tropical health Sch. Pub. Health, 1967-69, asst. dean for acad. affairs and internat. health Sch. Pub. Health, 1969-71, assoc. dean for acad. affairs, 1971-79, assoc. dean emeritus, sch. public health, dir. preventive med. residency Sch. of Medicine, 1983-88, clin. prof. emeritus, preventive medicine; pres. Devel. Svc. Internat., Williamsport, Tenn., Tenn., 1992—. Med. cons. dept. Vocat. Rehab., Riverside, Calif., 1964-88; mother and child health cons. Ministry of Health, Tanzania, 1978-80; med. dir. Village Health Program, Punjab, Pakistan, 1980-81, tchr., cons., S.Am. and Caribbean, 1981-83; chief preventive medicine Pettis Meml. VA Hosp., Loma Linda, 1986-88; sr. health advisor Adventist Devel. and Relief Agy., 1988-92; country dir. ADRA, Yemen, 1998-99. Contbr. articles to med. publs. WHO fellow, Somalia, Ethiopia, India, Nepal and Burma, 1969. Fellow Royal Soc. Tropical Medicine and Hygiene, Am. Pub. Health Assn., Am. Coll. Preventive Medicine, Internat. Health Soc. (pres.); mem. AMA, Global Health Coun., Adventist Internat. Med. Soc. (pres. 1983-84), Delta Omega (nat. pres. 1977-78). Adventist. Home and Office: 684 Dry Prong Rd PO Box 210 Williamsport TN 38487-0210 Office Phone: 931-583-2792. Personal E-mail: pwdys@bellsouth.net.

DYSON, ALLAN JUDGE, retired librarian; b. Lawrence, Mass., Mar. 28, 1942; s. Raymond Magan and Hilda D.; m. Susan Cooper, 1987; 1 child, Brenna Ruth. BA in Govt., Harvard U., 1964; MSLS, Simmons Coll., 1968. Asst. to dir. Columbia U. Librs., N.Y.C., 1968-71; head Moffitt Undergrad. Libr. U. Calif., Berkeley, 1971-79, univ. libr. Santa Cruz, 1979—2003, ret., 2003. Editor Coll. and Rsch. Librs. News, 1973-74; chmn. editl. bd. Choice mag., 1978-80, Am. Librs., 1986-89. CFO Cabrillo (Calif.) Music Festival, 1985-86; chmn. No. Calif. Regional Libr. Bd., 1986-88, 94-98, U. Calif. Librs. Group, 1998-2001. Lt. U.S. Army, 1964-66. Decorated Army Commendation medal; Coun. on Libr. Resources fellow, 1973-74. Mem. ALA, ACLU, Librs. Assn. U. Calif. (pres. 1976), Sierra Club.

DYSON, ESTHER, publisher, editor; b. Zurich, Switzerland, July 14, 1951; d. Freeman John and Verena Esther (Huber) D. BA in economics, Harvard U., 1972. Reporter Forbes Mag., N.Y.C., 1974-77, columnist, 1987—; v.p. New Ct. Securities, N.Y.C., 1977-80, Oppenheimer & Co., N.Y.C., 1980-82; editor Rosen Electronics Letter, 1982; founder, owner, chmn. EDventure Holdings, Inc. (acquired by CNET Networks 2004), 1983—. Founder, past chmn. ICANN; past dir. Electronic Frontier Found. Author: Release 2.0: A Design for Living in the Digital Age, 1997; columnist Release 3.0, N.Y. Times syndicate; moderator ann. Personal Computer Forum; contbr. articles to profl. jours. Mem. Women's Forum N.Y., Assn. Data Processing Svc. Orgns., Software Pubs. Assn. Avocation: swimming. Office: EDventure Holdings 104 5th Ave Fl 20 New York NY 10011-6987

DYSON, FREEMAN JOHN, physicist, educator; b. Crowthorne, Eng., Dec. 15, 1923; s. George and Mildred Lucy (Atkey) D.; m. Verena Haefeli-Huber, Aug. 11, 1950 (div. 1958); children: Esther, George; m. Imme Jung, Nov. 21, 1958; children: Dorothy, Emily, Mia, Rebecca. BA, Cambridge U., 1945. Operations research RAF Bomber Command, 1943-45; fellow Trinity Coll., Cambridge U., Eng., 1946-49; Commonwealth fellow Cornell U., Princeton, 1947-49; prof. physics Cornell U., 1951-53; prof. Inst. Advanced Study, Princeton, 1953-94; prof. emeritus, 1994—. Author: Disturbing the Universe, 1979, Weapons and Hope, 1984, Origins of Life, 1986, Infinite in all Directions, 1988, From Eros to Gaia, 1992, Imagined Worlds, 1997, The Sun, the Genome and the Internet, 1999. Recipient Enrico Fermi award U.S. Dept. of Energy, 1995, Templeton prize for Progress in Religion, 2000. Fellow Royal Soc. London; mem. NAS, Am. Phys. Soc. Home: 105 Battle Road Cir Princeton NJ 08540-4904 Office Phone: 609-734-8055. Business E-Mail: dyson@ias.edu.

DYSON, TIM, public relations executive; Student, Loughborough U., Eng. CEO Next Fifteen Comm. Group plc, parent co. of Text 100, San Francisco. Bd. dir. Text 100; advisory bd. Biz360, Ketera. Mem. U.K. Inst. Dirs., Inst. Pub. Rels., Pub. Rels. Soc. Am., Washington Software Assn. and Digital Media Alliance, Seattle C. of C. Office: Next Fifteen plc Power Rd Studios 114a Power Rd Chiswick London W4 5PY England Office Fax: +44(0)20 8996 1200.

DYSON, WILLIAM R., state legislator, educator; b. Waycross, Ga., July 12, 1940; s. Edward James Jr. and Lula Lorene (William) D.; m. Rebecca Johnson, 1964; children: Sonia, Wilfred, Erick, Michael. BA, Morris Coll., 1962; postgrad., NYU, 1963-66, Howard U., 1970; MA, So. Conn. State U., 1976, diploma, 1981. Alderman, New Haven, Conn., 1976; mem. Dist. 94 Conn. Ho. of Reps., 1977—, asst. minority leader, mem. edn. com., chmn. appropriations com., mem. gov.'s child care study com.; tchr. Blackshear, Ga., 1967, Douglas, Ga., 1968-69, New Haven, Conn., 1970—. Mem. NEA, Conn. Edn. Assn., New Haven Edn. Assn., Masons. Address: 196 Mansfield St New Haven CT 06511-3539

DYSONWILLIAMS, BARBARA LEIGH, restaurant owner, writer; b. Balt., June 25, 1946; d. Murrel Franklin and Erline Frances Williams; 1 child, Joseph Galvan. BA in Art and Journalism, George Peabody Coll., 1968; M. Ea. N.Mex. U., 1980; cert., Radio and TV Sch., Nashville, 1982. Exec. sec. Tenn. Legis., Nashville, 1985—87; disc jockey County Radio Sta., Nashville, 1987—88; office mgr. Vanderbilt Hosp., Nashville, 1988—96, U. N.Mex. Hosp., Albuquerque, 1996—2000; owner The Tex. Rose Restaurant, San Saba, Tex., 2000—. Author: Enter Justice, 2000, Road of Silk, 2004. Office: The Texas Rose San Saba TX 76877

DYYON, MARIO (LEROY FRAZIER), artist; b. Fort Myers, Fla., May 2, 1946; s. Sallie Frazier. Lectr., Westside Community Ctr., N.Y.C., 1971, Case Western Res. U., 1983. Group exhbns. include Cleve. Top Artists, Intown Club, Cleve., 1969, Art Inst. Akron, 1969-70, Mus. Modern Art, N.Y.C., 1970, Whitney Mus. Ann., 1972, Mus. Contemporary Hispanic Art, 1985; one-man show at Case Western Res. U., 1983; represented in permanent collections Mus. Modern Art, N.Y.C., Whitney Mus. Am. Art, N.Y.C., Case Western Res. U., Larry Aldrich Mus., Conn., various pvt. collections. Printmaker's Workshop scholar, 1982. Roman Catholic. Address: 155 W 73rd St New York NY 10023-2921 *Success is a love for your work. This may be too broad. Let me put a fine point on it. How to be successful really? In all your deeds, and in your dreams, try to make God smile. So, throw your vanity out the window and get to work. Be as the commen tern, on the move.*

DZAU, VICTOR JOSEPH, cardiologist, director, researcher; b. Shanghai, Oct. 23, 1946; MD, McGill U., 1972. Cert. in internal medicine, subspecialty in cardiovasc. disease. Intern N.Y. Hosp., 1972-73; resident in medicine Peter Bent Brigham Hosp., Boston, 1974-76, chief resident, 1976-78; fellow in rsch. Mass. Gen. Hosp., Boston, 1976-78, fellow in cardiology, 1979-80; chief divsn. vascular medicine and atherosclerosis Brigham & Women's Hosp., 1984-90; chief divsn. cardiovasc. medicine Stanford U. Sch. Medicine, 1990-96, dir. cardiovasc. rsch. ctr., assoc. chmn. dept. medicine, 1993-96, chmn. dept. medicine, 1995-96; dir. Am. Heart Assn.-Bugher Found. Ctr. for Molecular Biology, 1991-96; chmn. dept. med., dir. rsch. Brigham & Women's Hosp., 1996—2004; chancellor Duke U., 2004—; pres., CEO Duke U. Health Sys., 2004—. From asst. prof. medicine to assoc. prof. medicine Harvard Med. Sch., 1980-90; William G. Irvin prof. medicine Stanford U. Sch. Medicine, 1990-96, Arthur L. Bloomfield prof., chmn. medicine, 1995-96; Hersey prof. theory and practice of medicine Harvard Med. Sch., 1996-2004; James B. Duke prof. medicine Duke U., 2004—. Office: Duke U Med Ctr 1 Davison Blvd Box 3701 Durham NC 27710 Office Phone: 919-684-2255. Business E-Mail: victor.dzau@duke.edu.

DZIEWANOWSKA, ZOFIA ELIZABETH, pharmaceutical executive; b. Warsaw, Nov. 17, 1939; came to U.S., 1972; d. Stanislaw Kazimierz Dziewanowski and Zofia Danuta (Mieczkowska) Rudowska; m. Krzysztof A. Kunert, Sept. 1, 1961 (div. 1971); 1 child, Martin. MD, U. Warsaw, 1963; PhD, Polish Acad. Sci., 1970. MD recert. U.K., 1972, U.S., 1973. Asst. prof. psychiatry U. Warsaw Med. Sch., 1969—71; sr. house officer St. George's Hosp., U. London, 1971—72; assoc. dir. Merck Sharp & Dohme, Rahway, NJ, 1972—76; vis. assoc. physician Rockefeller U. Hosp., N.Y.C., 1975—76; adj. asst. prof. psychiatry Cornell U. Med. Ctr., N.Y.C., 1978—; v.p., global med. dir. Hoffmann-La Roche, Inc., Nutley, NJ, 1976—94; sr. v.p., dir. global med. affairs Genta Inc., San Diego, 1994—97; sr. v.p. drug devel. and regulatory Cypros Pharms. Corp., Carlsbad, Calif., 1997—99; pres., med. dir. New Drug Assocs., La Jolla, Calif., 1999—; sr. v.p. clin. and regulatory Maxia Pharms, San Diego, 2001—02; v.p. clin. rsch. Ligand Pharm, Inc., San Diego, 2002—. Lectr. in field. Contbr. articles to profl. publs. Bd. dirs Royal Soc. Medicine Found.; mem. alumni coun. Cornell U. Med. Ctr. Recipient TWIN Honoree award for Outstanding Women in Mgmt., Ridgewood (N.J.) YWCA, 1984. Mem. AMA, AAAS, Am. Soc. Pharmacology and Therapeutics, Am. Coll. Neuropsychopharmacology, N.Y. Acad. Scis., PhRMA. (vice chmn. steering com. med. sect., chmn. internat. med. affairs com., head biotech. working group), Royal Soc. Medicine (U.K.), Drug Info. Assn. (Woman of Yr. award 1994), Am. Assn. Pharm. Physicians. Roman Catholic. Achievements include original research on the role of the nervous system in the regulation of respiratory functions, research and development and therapeutic uses of many new drugs, pharmaceutical medicine and biotechnology; molecular biology derived as well as conventional products including antisense, interferon efficacy in cancer, virology and AIDS and drugs useful in cardiovascular, immunological, neuropsychiatric, infectious diseases, and others; impact of different cultures on medical practices and clinical research; drug evaluation and development management strategies of pharmaceutical industries; treatments against cardiac and brain ischemia, cytoprotection; speaker in field.

DZIEZAK, JUDIE D., lawyer; d. Martin and Martha Dziezak; m. John Smith, Aug. 9, 1980. BS in Chemistry and Biology, Marian Coll., 1977; MS, Purdue U., 1980; JD, Loyola U., 1994. Bar: Ill. 1994, U.S. Dist. Ct. (no. dist.) Ill. 1994, U.S. Patent and Trademark Office 1997, Can. Patent Office 2004, DuPage County (Cert. Arbitrator, 18th jud. cir.) 1997. Lab. technician, endocrinology dept. Ind. U. Sch. Medicine, Indpls., 1976—77; chemist Morton Chem. Co., Woodstock, Ill., 1981; assoc. scientist The Quaker Oats Co., Barrington, Ill., 1981—85; assoc. editor, Food Tech. Inst. of Food Technologists, Chgo., 1985—91; tech. asst. Loyola U. Sch. of Law, Chgo., 1993—94, contract atty., 1993—94; assoc. atty. Kostow & Daar, P.C., Chgo., 1995—96, Knight, Hoppe, Fanning & Knight, Des Plaines, Ill., 1996—98, Ryndak & Lyerla, Chgo., 1998—2000, Wildman Harrold Allen & Dixon, Chgo., 2000—01; sr. assoc. atty. Wallenstein & Wagner, Chgo., 2001—02; pvt. practice Hoffman Estates, Ill., 2003—. Cons. to food and chem. industries, Hoffman Estates, 1991—92, 1994—95. Faculty (seminar) Mining Patent Portfolios; contbr. over 80 articles to profl. pubs.; speaker (Chgo. Section meeting of Inst. of Food Technologists), (12th World Congress, Food Sci. & Tech.), (symposium, society of cosmetic chemists) Overview of Patents, Trademarks and Copyrights, (seminar on agricultural biotechnology) Ag-Biotech Food Forum, (presentation) Chicago Section meeting of American Chemical Society, Meeting of the American Association of Confectionary Technologists, author (article on food labeling) Prepared Foods. Clin. assoc. Crisis and Suicide Intervention Svc., Indianapolis, Ind., 1974—77; vol. classroom asst. - worked with children with autism and down's syndrome Noble I Ctr. for Retarded Children, Indianapolis, Ind., 1973—77; chair, legislative com. AAUW, Schaumburg, Ill., 1984—85. Recipient Three awards for excellence in writing - one from Society's nat. competition, two from the Chgo. Chpt.'s regional competitions, Am. Soc. Bus. Press Editors, 1989—90, Am. Jurisprudence Awards for Moot Ct., Legal Writing, and Advanced Legal Bibliography, Loyola U. Sch. of Law, 1992—94, Leadership and Svc. Award, 1993; fellow, NIH, 1977; Newman Scholarship, Marian Coll., 1973—77, Sixth Armored Divsn. Scholarship, 1973—77, Williams Fellowship, Loyola U. Sch. of Law, 1993. Mem.: ABA, Licensing Executives Soc., Inst. Food Technologists, Chgo. Bar Assn., Am. Intellectual Property Law Assn., Am. Chem. Soc., Kappa Gamma Pi, Pi Tau Sigma, Iota Sigma Pi. Avocations: running, gourmet cooking, landscape architecture and gardening, writing. Office: Dziezak Law Firm PC 2300 N Barrington Rd Hoffman Estates IL 60195 Office Phone: 847-490-5370.

DZINDOLET, MARY TERESA, psychology professor; b. Framingham, Mass., July 16, 1962; d. Ricahrd Joseph and Patricia (Dowd) D.; m. George Lewis Porter, Aug. 9, 1987; children: Patricia, George. PhD, U. Tex., Arlington, 1992. Asst. prof. psychology Cameron U., Lawton, 1994-2001; prin. investigator Army Rsch. Lab., Ft. Sill, Okla., 1999—. Contbr. chpt. to book. Mem. APA. Fax: (580) 581-2623. E-mail: maryd@cameron.edu.

DZIORDZ, WALTER MICHAEL, priest; b. New Bedford, Mass., Oct. 20, 1951; s. Michael Raphael and Jane (Szczepanik) D. BA, U. Mass., 1977; MDiv, Washington Theol. Union, Silver Spring, Md., 1984; cert., Salem Inst., 1988; postgrad., Oblate Sch. Theology. Joined Soc. Marians, Roman Cath. Ch.; ordained priest; cert. in reality therapy. Asst. pastor St. Joseph's Cath. Ch., Pittsfield, Mass., 1984-85; pastor Our Lady of Grace Cath. Ch., Greensboro, N.C., 1988—; dir. vocation Marian Fathers-Province of St. Stanislaus Kostka, Stockbridge, Mass., 1986-87; dir. of resident/non resident candidates Marian Fathers Scholasticate, Washington, 1987-88, councilor 1st house, 1987-88. Superior local house Marian Community for Our Lady of Grace Parish, Greensboro, 1988—; 3d provincial councilor Congregation of Marians, Stockbridge, Mass., 1989—; del. provincial chpt. Marian Province of St. Stanislaus Kostka, Stockbridge, 1984, 90, elected provincial superior, 1993; chaplain pilgrimage Marian Helpers Ctr., Stockbridge, 1990. Sgt. U.S. Army, 1970-73; N.G., 1973-74. Mem. Washington Theol. Union Alumni Assn., KC (chaplain Greensboro chpt. 1988—, cert. appreciation 1989, 90). Republican. Home: 201 S Chapman St Greensboro NC 27403-1611 Office: Our Lady of Grace Cath Ch 2205 W Market St Greensboro NC 27403-1515

DZIUK, PHILIP JOHN, retired animal scientist, educator; b. Foley, Minn., Mar. 24, 1926; s. Edmund William and Ellen Catherine (Carlin) Dziuk; m. Patricia Rosemary Weber, Sept. 29, 1951; children: Corinne, Constance, Rita, Catherine, Kenneth, Ronald, Carl. BS, U. Minn., 1950, MS, 1952, PhD, 1955. From rsch. asst. to rsch. assoc. U. Minn., Mpls., 1950-55; from asst. prof. to prof. U. Ill., Urbana, 1955-88, prof. emeritus, 1988, ret., 1988. Cons. Upjohn, Abbott, Eli Lilly, Am. Cyanamid, Schering, Batelle, Advisys; reviewer grants NIH, Bethesda, Md., 1982—86, USDA, Beltsville, Md., 1983—89. Contbr. articles to profl. jours. With USN, 1945—46. Recipient Achievement in Rsch. award, Am. Fertility Soc., 1970, Sr. Scientist award, Alexander von Humboldt Found., 1981, Pioneer award, Internat. Embryo Transfer Soc., 2001, Outstanding Achievement award, U. Minn., 2002; fellow, Lalor Found., 1958, 1961, Pig Industry Devel. Authority, Eng., 1961. Mem.: AAAS, Soc. Study Reproduction (dir., pres. 1987—88, Disting. Svc. award 1989), Soc. Study Fertility, Am. Soc. Animal Scis. (fellow 1987, Rsch. in Physiology award 1971), Am. Assn. Anatomist, Farm House, Lions (pres., sec. 1992—94), KC, Sigma Xi, Alpha Zeta, Gamma Sigma Delta, Phi Zeta, Phi Kappa Phi, Gamma Alpha. Avocations: woodworking, gardening, racquetball. Office: U Ill Dept Animal Scis 1207 W Gregory Dr Urbana IL 61801-4733 Office Phone: 217-333-2901. Business E-Mail: p_dziuk@uiuc.edu.

DZOMBAK, AGNES MARIE (JO), secondary school educator; b. Chgo., Feb. 17, 1931; d. Joseph John and Agnes Ann (Szymanski) Reiter; m. William Charles Dzombak, Nov. 28, 1953; children: Deborah, David, Laura, Ivan, Stefanie. BA magna cum laude, Mundelein Coll., Chgo., 1952; postgrad., U. Chgo., 1952-53, Pa. State U., 1973-83, U. Pitts., 1987. Tchr. Chgo. Pub. Schs., 1952-53; secondary tchr. devel. reading Greater Latrobe (Pa.) Sch. Dist., 1972-96. Presenter in field. Mem. Western Pa. Conservancy, 1986—, Phipps Conservatory; lifetime mem. Lincoln Forum; bd. dirs. Loyalhanna Watershed Assn., Ligonier, Pa., 1988-99. Western Pa. Writing Project fellow U. Pitts. Mem. NEA, Pa. State Edn. Assn., Pitts. Poetry Soc., Abraham Lincoln Assn., Lincoln Group N.Y. Democrat. Roman Catholic. Avocations: Lincoln studies, poetry, writing, travel.

DZOMBAK, DAVID ADAM, environmental engineering educator; b. Latrobe, Pa., Apr. 17, 1957; s. William Charles and Agnes Marie (Reiter) D.; m. Carolyn Jane Menard, Oct. 6, 1984; children: Daniel Charles, William Gerard, Rachel Victoria. BA in Math., St. Vincent Coll., Latrobe, 1979; BSCE, Carnegie Mellon U., 1979, MS in Civil-Environ. Engring., 1981; PhD in Civil-Environ. Engring., MIT, 1986. Registered profl. engr., Pa.; diplomate Am. Acad. Environ. Engrs. Rsch. asst. Carnegie Mellon U., Pitts., 1979-81, MIT, Cambridge, 1981-86; sr. staff cons. Paul C. Rizzo Assocs., Monroeville, Pa., 1986-88; asst. prof. environ. engring. Carnegie Mellon U., Pitts., 1989-93, assoc. prof., 1994-97, prof., 1998—. Author: (with others) Surface Complexation Modeling: Hydrous Ferric Oxide, 1990; contbr. articles to profl. jours. Mem. EPA Sci. Adv. Bd., 2002—; mem. environ. tech. subcom. EPA NACEPT, 2004—. Recipient Presdl. Young Investigator award, NSF, 1991; Aldo Leopold Leadership Program fellow, Ecol. Soc. Am., 2000. Fellow ASCE (Walter L. Huber Civil Engring. Rsch. prize 1997, chmn. EWRI/EMMC awards com. 1999-02); mem. Am. Acad. Environ. Engrs. (chmn. publs. com. 2000-04), Am. Chem. Soc. (assoc. editor ES&T 2005-; ES&T Excellence in Rev. award 2003), Am. Geophys. Union, Am. Water Works Assn., Nat. Ground Water Assn. (mem. editl. bd. jour. 1990-93), Assn. Environ. Engring. and Sci. Profs. (bd. dirs. 1996-99, Doctoral Thesis award 1987, Dist. Svc. award 1999, chmn. strategic planning com. 2001-03), Soc. Environ. Toxicology and Chemistry, Water Environ. Fedn. (chmn. ground water com. 1993-96, mem. editl. bd. jour. 1993-98, H.P. Eddy medal 1993, J.E. McKee medal 2000, WEA of Pa. Profl. Rsch. award 2002). Home: 6929 Rosewood St Pittsburgh PA 15208-2638 Office: Carnegie Mellon Univ Dept Civil/Environ Engring Pittsburgh PA 15213-3890 Office Phone: 412-268-2946. Business E-Mail: dzombak@cmu.edu.

DZURIS, LINDA, music educator, musician; b. Mich., 1970; MusB, U. Mich., 1992, MusM, 1993, AMusD, 1998. Cert. carillonneur Guild of Carillonneurs N.Am. Univ. carillonneur, asst. prof. music Clemson (S.C.) U., 1999—; organist, choir dir. Ch. of Redeemer Episc. Ch., Greenville, SC, 1999—. Chair pub. rels. com. Guild Carillonneurs N.Am., 2000—, exam. com. adjudicator, 2004—; bd. dirs. Alain Assn. Am. Musician: solo carillion performances; contbr. articles to profl. jours. Achievements include research in models of cognition and music; development of digital portfolio curriculum. Office: Clemson U Box 340525 210 Brooks Ctr Clemson SC 29634-0525 Office Phone: 864-656-6366. Office Fax: 864-656-1013. E-mail: ldzuris@clemson.edu.

DZYALOSHINSKII, IGOR EKHIELIEVICH, physicist; b. Moscow, Feb. 1, 1931; s. Ekhiel Moiseevich and Maria Semionovna (Aseeva) D.; m. Elena Aronovna Lebedeva, Dec. 2, 1960; 1 child, Elena. MA in Physics, Moscow State U., 1953; PhD in Physics, Inst. for Phys. Problems, Moscow, 1957, DSc in Physics, 1962. Sr. rschr. Inst. for Phys. Problems, Moscow, 1957—65; head dept. magnetism Landau Inst. for Theoretical Physics, Moscow, 1965—91; prof. physics U. Calif., Irvine, 1992—2004, prof. emeritus, 2004—. Author: Methods of Quantum Field, Theory in Statistical Physics (in Russian, English, Japanese and Chinese), 1962, 3d edit., 1975, 2d Russian edit., 1998. Decorated Order of Red Banner of Labour, Order of Honor, Medal of Vet. of Labour, Govt. of Russia; recipient State prize Govt. USSR, 1984. Fellow AAAS, Am. Phys. Soc.; mem. Russian Acad. Scis. (Lomonosov prize 1962, Landau prize 1989), Am. Acad. Art and Scis. (hon. fgn. mem.). Achievements include research in theory of weak ferromagnetism; theory of van der Waals forces in condensed media; theory of one-dimensional metals. Office: Univ Calif Dept Physics Irvine CA 92697-0001

EACHEMPATI, SOUMITRA R., surgeon; b. Hyderabad, India, Jan. 2, 1966; s. Rama and Uma Eachempati. MD, Northwestern U., Chgo., 1991. Assoc. prof. of surgery Weill Med. Coll. of Cornell U., N.Y.C., 2002—. Fellow: Am. Coll. Surgeons; mem.: Soc. of Univ. of Surgeons. Office Phone: 212-746-5312.

EADE, GEORGE JAMES, retired military officer, researcher; b. Lockney, Tex., Oct. 27, 1921; s. George William and Isabel Theresa (Barnd) E.; m. Colette Eliane Cachelin, May 18, 1946 (dec. 1994); children: George Walter, Helen Marie-Louise (Mrs. Jean Oesch), Anne Catherine Eade Berry, Christine Colette, Dominique Frances. Commd. 2d lt. USAAF, 1942; advanced through grades to gen. USAF; pilot 37 combat missions in Europe World War II, 1942-46; pilot, squadron comdr., B-52 wing comdr.; airborne emergency action officer, sr. staff officer Strategic Air Command, Nat. Strategic Target Planning Staff, 1947-70; dep. chief of staff plans and ops. Hdqrs. USAF, Washington, 1971—72; dep. comdr.-in-chief U.S. Forces Europe, 1972-75; ret., 1975. Pres. Cath. Edn. Assn., Omaha, 1968—70. Decorated DSM with two oak leaf clusters, Legion of Merit, DFC, Air medal with five oak leaf clusters, Air Force Commendation medal with two oak leaf clusters; Order of Merit (France). Home: 1131 Sunnyside Dr Healdsburg CA 95448-3536 *Establish some general goals and lay plans to reach them. Neither be capricious nor struggle doggedly toward a goal no longer of interest. Above all follow your own plan, not what someone plans for you. The ultimate objective is to make a contribution to mankind and be happy in the process of so doing. Putting the two together is to discover the art of living and the meaning of life.*

EADE, MICHAEL GREGORY, painter; b. Portland, Feb. 26, 1957; s. Robert Allen Eade and Barbara Lee Lengacher. BA, Oreg. State U., 1980; postgrad., NYU, 1983—85. Asst. Louise Nevelson, sculptor, N.Y.C., 1983—84. Exhibited in group shows at Cheryl Pelavin Gallery, 2003, Aljira Ctr. Contemporary Art, 2003, Wave Hill Glyndor Gallery, 2003, Lexington Arts and Cultural Coun., Lexington, Ky., 2004, one-man shows include Nicholas Davies, N.Y.C., 1996, Triangle Gallery, Sinclair Coll., Dayton, Ohio, 2001, Cheryl Pelavin Gallery, 2005. Recipient Grand Prize winner, AT&T Art and Appreciation Sculpture Contest, 2004; grantee, Artists' Fellowship Inc., N.Y.C., 1999; Printmaking scholar, Oreg. State U., Corvallis, 1980. Home: 445 W 49th St #A New York NY 10019 E-mail: michael_eade@att.net.

EADIE, JOHN WILLIAM, historian, educator; b. Ft. Smith, Ark., Dec. 18, 1935; s. William Robert and Helen (Montgomery) B.; m. Joan Holt, Aug. 18, 1957; children: Robin, Christopher. BA with honors, U. Ark., 1957; MA, U. Chgo., 1959; PhD, Univ. Coll., London, 1962. Asst. prof. Ripon Coll., Wis., 1962-63; asst. prof. history U. Mich., Ann Arbor, 1963-67, assoc. prof., 1967-73, prof., 1973-86, assoc. chmn. dept. history, 1970-71, humanities-arts advisor Office V.p. for Research, 1974-86, assoc. dean Rackham Sch. Grad. Studies, 1984-86; prof. history, dean Coll. Arts and Letters Mich. State U., East Lansing, 1996—97, sr. advisor to provost, 1997—2000, prof. and dean emeritus, 2002—. Dir. Consortium for Inter-Instnl. Collaboration in African and L.Am. Studies, 1989-2000, chmn. liberal arts and scis. dean Consortium for Instnl. Collaboration, 1991-94, bd. mem. Santa Fe Coun. Internat. Rels. Author: The Breviarium of Festus: A critical-Edition with Historical Commentary, 1967, The Conversion of Constantine, 1971, (with others) Western Civilization, 1975; editor: Classical traditions in Early America, 1976; co-editor The Craft of the Ancient Historian, 1985, Urban Centers and Rural Contexts in Late Antiquity, 2001. Chmn. Mich. Council for Humanities, E. Lansing, Mich., 1977-80, Mich. Alliance for Conservation Cultural Heritage, 1988-90. Marshall scholar Brit. Marshall Commn. Univ. Coll., London,

1960-62; recipient Disting. Service award Mich. Council Humanities, 1980, Ralph Smucker award for advancing internat. programs, 2001. Mem.: Archaeol Inst. Am., Soc. Promotion Roman Studies. Democrat. Presbyterian. E-mail: jweadie@msu.edu.

EADS, ALBERT E., JR., school system administrator; b. Chgo., Aug. 30, 1937; s. Albert E. and Pauline (White) E.; m. Margaret Oliver, Dec. 31, 1957; children: Rosemarie, Albert E. III, Randy, David, Ellen. BS, The Citadel, Charleston, S.C., 1959; MEd, Duke U., 1964; advanced cert., U. S.C., 1973, PhD, 1974. Cert. English, social sudies, gen. sci., elem. reading tchr., reading supr., elem. and secondary prin., supt., S.C. Prin. Riverland Terr. Elem. Sch., 1960-63, Stiles Point Elem. Sch., Charleston, S.C., 1963-66, St. John's High Sch., Darlington, S.C., 1976-84, Gaffney (S.C.) High Sch., 1984-86; supt. schs. Hampton Dist. 2, Estill, S.C., 1988-96; exec. dir. S.C. Assn. for Rural Edn., St. George, SC, 1996—2002; pres. Nat. Rural Edn. Assn., 2002—. Contbr. articles to profl. publs. Recipient numerous civic awards; fellow NDEA. Mem. ASCD, Am. Assn. Sch. Adminstrs. (S.C. Supt. Yr. 1994), Nat. Assn. Secondary Sch. Prins., Internat. Reading Assn., S.C. Optimists (past gov.), Phi Delta Kappa, Kappa Delta Pi.

EADS, GEORGE CURTIS, economic consultant; b. Clarkesville, Tex., Aug. 20, 1942; s. Delbert Curtis and Eliza Mae (Hicks) E.; m. Margaret Helen Hall, Nov. 17, 1973; children: Geoffrey Thomas, Katherine Elizabeth. BA, U. Colo., 1964; MA, Yale U., 1965, MPhil, 1967, PhD, 1968. Asst. prof. econs. Harvard U., Cambridge, Mass., 1968-69, Princeton (NJ) U., 1969-71; spl. asst. antitrust divsn. Dept. Justice, Washington, 1971-72; assoc. prof. George Washington U., Washington, 1972-74; asst. dir. Coun. Wage and Price Stability, Washington, 1974-75; exec. dir. Nat. Commn. Supplies and Shortages, Washington, 1975-77; economist, rsch. program dir. Rand Corp., Santa Monica, Calif., 1977-79, 81; mem. Pres.'s Coun. Advisors, Washington, 1979-81; prof. Sch. Pub. Affairs, U. Md., College Park, 1981-85, dean Sch. Pub. Affairs, 1985-86; v.p., chief economist GM, 1986-95; v.p. Charles River Assocs., Washington, 1995—. Mem. com. on consequences on uninsurance Inst. Medicine, 2000—04; lead cons. sustainable mobility project World Bus. Coun. Sustainable Devel., 2002—04. Author: The Local Service Airline Experiment, 1972, Relief or Reform? Reagan's Regulatory Strategies, 1984. Mem. Am. Econ. Assn. Democrat. Home: 3718 Harrison St NW Washington DC 20015-1816 Office: Charles River Assoc Ste 700 1201 F St SW Washington DC 20004-1204 E-mail: geads@crai.com.

EADS, JOHN WILLIAM, lawyer, state representative; b. Princeton, Ind., Apr. 24, 1952; m. Patsy Ford. BA, US Naval Acad., 1974; MA, U.S. Naval War Coll., Salve Regina U.; JD, U. Miss. Aviator USN, 1974—94; lawyer Oxford, Miss.; rep. Ho. of Reps State of Miss., Jackson, 1999. Mem. Constitution, Edn., Ins., Mil. Affairs, Judiciary A coms. Miss. Ho. Reps., Jackson, 1999—. Bd. mem. Oxford City Sch. Bd., Miss. Mem.: N. Miss. Bd. Realtors, Lafayette County Bar Assn., Miss. Bar Assn., Am. Legion, Oxford C. of C., Rotary Club. Democrat. Presbyn. Home: PO Box 793 Oxford MS 38655 Office: Ho of Reps PO Box 1018 Jackson MS 39215-1018 E-mail: jeads@mail.house.state.ms.us.

EADS, ORA WILBERT, clergyman, church official; b. Mill Spring, Mo., Jan. 2, 1914; s. John Harrison and Effie Ellen (Borders) E.; m. Mary Ivaree Cochran, Mar. 25, 1944; children— Ora Wilbert, Wayne B., Carol Vernice, Janet Karen and Janice Inez (twins). JD, John Marshall Law Sch., Atlanta, 1940, LL.M., 1941; postgrad., Sch. Theology, St. Lawrence U., Canton, N.Y., 1947-48. Bar: Ga. bar 1940. Practiced in, Atlanta, 1940-46; ordained to ministry Christian Congregation, Inc., 1946; parish minister Sampson County, N.C., 1948-52; evangelist Charlotte, N.C., 1952-61; gen. supt. Christian Congregation, Inc., 1961—. Author numerous books of poetry, 1967— . Mem. Christian Congregation Ch. Home and Office: Christian Congregation Inc 812 W Hemlock St La Follette TN 37766 *A high school teacher asked her class, "What is our purpose on earth? Why are we here?" We students didn't know the answer. I now believe, some 70 years later, that the highest responsibility of any individual is to achieve his best potential.*

EADS, PENNI DAUN, music educator; b. Montpelier, Idaho, Oct. 29, 1960; d. Donald J. and Wanda Beth (Densley) Sparks; m. Thomas Andrew Eads, Dec. 21, 1984; children: Michael, Perry, Malena, James, Autumn, Reina, Rey, Joseph, Benjamin, Hyrum, Jonathan. AAS, Ricks Coll., 1981; BMus in Piano Performance, Utah State U., 1983. Piano instr. Ricks Coll., Rexburg, Idaho, 1979-81, Utah State U. Youth Conservatory, Logan, 1981—83; pvt. practice, 1984—; vocal, dance and performance dir. Sunshine Generation, Inc., Dayton, Ohio, 1996—99. Advisor skin, hair care and cosmetics, dir. nutrition and house cleaning products Sunrider Internat., 1987— Missionary LDS Ch., Minn., 1983-84. Scholar Ricks Coll., 1979-81, Utah State U., 1981-83. Mem. Music Tchrs. Nat. Assn., Relief Soc. (tchr. 1979—, pianist 1979—). Avocations: nutrition, reading, walking, gardening, water and dance aerobics. Home: 203 E 1400 S Kaysville UT 84037 Personal E-mail: tomandpenni.eads@juno.com.

EAGAN, DAVID EUGENE, lawyer; b. Oil City, Pa., June 23, 1956; s. Robert Francis Eagan and Margaret Agnes Kirshner; m. Mary Ann McCaffrey, May 16, 1980. BA with History magna cum laude, SUNY, Geneseo, 1979; JD cum laude, SUNY, Buffalo, 1982. Bar: N.Y. 1983. Assoc. Chadbourne & Parke LLP, N.Y.C., 1982—94; ptnr. Bittle, Fouler LLP, N.Y.C., 1994—2000, Fulbrith & Jaworski LLP, N.Y.C., 2000—. Mem. Wainscott Citizens Adv. Com. Sea Grant Law scholar, 1981. Mem.: Met. Club, N.Y. Athletic Club (mem. law com.). Avocation: horse farm. Home: PO Box 249 Roosevelt NY 11575 Office: Fulbrigh and Jaworski LLP 666 5th Ave Fl 31 New York NY 10103-0001 Business E-Mail: degan@fulbright.com.

EAGAN, SHERMAN G., producer, communications executive; b. Peoria, Ill., Feb. 12, 1942; s. Joseph K. and Gracia (Sherman) E.; m. Paige Mannelly, Aug. 13, 1966; children: S. Joseph, Shannon Colleen. BA, U. N.Mex., 1967; postgrad., Northwestern U., 1967-68. Mgr. sales adminstrn. NBC-TV, Chgo., 1967-68; copywriter, producer D'Arcy Advt., St. Louis, 1968-69, Ad Com div. Quaker Oats, Chgo., 1969-71; writer CBS TV, Chgo., 1971-75; producer CBS News, N.Y.C., 1975-79; producer, dir. CBS Sports, N.Y.C., 1979-84; pres. Conn. Yankee Internat., Darien, 1984—. Cons. Tokyo Broadcasting Co., 1976-84. Producer, dir. U.S. Open Tennis, 1980-90, Daytona: Drama, Danger, Dedication, 1991; producer, dir. Daytona 500, 1992, producer, 1994; dir., writer Battle of the NASCAR Legends, CBS, 1991; dir. Internat. Emmy Presentation, 1989, supervising producer The Winners, 1991; exec. producer IBM TV, 1993, 94; producer NFL Sunday, Fox Sports, 1995-98; editor: Aerodynamic Trading, 1995. Recipient Emmy award NATAS, 1984, 86, Telly award, 1995, 96, 97, 98, Exec. Prodr. and Dir. Entrepreneur of Yr. awards CNBC, 1996, 97, field producer Fox Superbowl Sunday, 1997; 1st Classic Telly award for Best Bus. Video of Last 20 Yrs.; named one of Am.'s Top 100 Prodrs., Prodr. mag., 2000, 2001. Mem. Dirs. Guild Am. Office: Conn Yankee Intl Inc 737 Canal St #35A Stamford CT 06902-5930 E-mail: rlmotto@aol.com.

EAGAN, WILLIAM LEON, lawyer; b. Tampa, Fla., Feb. 10, 1928; s. John Robert and Margaret (Williams) E.; m. Marjorie Young, Mar. 6, 1949; children: Barbara Anne, Rebecca Elizabeth, Laurel Lea. Student, U. Tampa, 1959; LLB, JD with honors, U. Fla., 1961. Bar: Fla. 1961, U.S. Dist. Ct. (mid. dist.) Fla. 1959, U.S. Dist. Ct. (so. dist.) Fla. 1962, U.S. Ct. Appeals (5th cir.) 1972; bd. cert. civil trial lawyer, Fla., 1984. Assoc. Dexter, Conlee & Bissell, Sarasota, Fla., 1961-62; ptnr., v.p. Arnold, Matheny & Eagan, P.A., Orlando, 1962—2004, of counsel, 2004—. Mem. Fla. Bar Ninth Circuit Grievance Com., 1982-84; mediator Family Law Mediation Program. Articles editor U. Fla. Law Rev., 1961. Chmn. bd. trustees First Bapt. Ch., Winter Park, Fla., 1970-72, chmn. bd. deacons, 1967-69; active Indsl. Devel. Commn. Mid-Fla., Orlando, 1979-84. Served to seaman 2d class USN, 1945-46. Mem. Atty.'s Title Ins. Fund Inc., Orange County Bar Assn. (exec. coun.), Univ. Club, Order of Coif, Phi Alpha Delta, Phi Kappa Phi. Republican. Baptist and Methodist. Office: Arnold Matheny & Eagan PA 605 E Robinson St Ste 730 Orlando FL 32801 Office Phone: 407-841-1550. E-mail: Weagan@ameorl.com.

EAGAR, THOMAS WADDY, metallurgist, educator; b. Chattanooga, Jan. 9, 1950; s. Harry Douglas Sr. and Emily Clarkson (Thompson) E.; m. Pamela Dozier Garrett, Apr. 17, 1973; children: Matthew, Rebekah, Linda, Karen, James, Anna, Thomas. BS in Metallurgy, MIT, 1972, ScD in Metallurgy, 1975, postgrad., 1988, Lehigh U., 1975-76. Registered profl. engr., Mass. Rsch. engr. Homer Rsch. Labs. Bethlehem (Pa.) Steel Corp., 1974-76; asst. prof. materials engring. MIT, Cambridge, 1976-80, assoc. prof., 1980-87, prof., 1987—, acting dept. head, 1989, Richard P. Simmons prof. materials engring., 1990-93, Posco prof. materials engring., 1993-99, Thomas Lord prof. engring. systems, 2001—, dir. Materials Processing Ctr., 1990-93, dir. mfg. program, 1993-95, dept. head, 1995—2000. Liaison Scientist U.S. Office Naval Rsch., Tokyo, 1984-85; dir. metall. engring. Simpson, Gumpertz and Heger, Inc., 1994; adv. bd. Edison Welding Inst., Columbus, Ohio, 1989-95; unit mfg. process rsch. com. Nat. Rsch. Coun., Washington, 1990-94, mem. nat. materials adv. bd., 1998-2003, mem. mfg. and engring. design bd., 2003—; tech. rev. bd. U.S. Army Rsch. Labs., 1993-95; cons. metallurgy and metall. failure analysis, 1976—; presenter and lectr. in field. Mem. adv. and tech. rev. bds. Materials Tech.; key reader Welding Jour.; contbr. over 200 articles to tech. publs.; patentee method of resistance welding, non-hygroscopic welding flux binders, large diameter stud and method and apparatus for welding same, laser instrument, age-hardenable sterling silver, emissivity independent multi-wavelength pyrometry, silver alloys of exceptional and reversilbe hardness; wear-resistant bond for abrasive tools, abrasive tool containing coated abrasive grain. Named Internat. Jr. Civitan of Yr., 1968; Dennison K. Bullens scholar, 1969-71, Foundry Edn. Fund scholar, 1970-71; grad. fellow NSF, 1972-74, Creativity Ext. award, 1988-90. Fellow AAAS, Am. Soc. Metals (Henry Marion Howe medal 1992), Am. Welding Soc. (hon. mem. Adams membership award 1979-83, Warren F. Savage award 1990, 96, Williams Sparagen award 1991, 94, Comfort A. Adams lectr., 1992, Charles H. Jennings Meml. medal 1983, 91, 2003, William Irrgang award 1993, Silver Quill award 2002); mem. AIME (metallurgy and metals prize Boston sect. 1972, Champion H. Mathewson Gold medal 1987, Henry Krumb lectr. 1987), Nat. Acad. Engring., ASTM, ASME, Am. Ceramic Soc., Materials Rsch. Soc., Soc. Automotive Engrs., Soc. Mfg. Engrs., Welding Rsch. Coun. Internat. Inst. Welding (Am. coun. Houdremont lectr. 1990), Tau Beta Pi (bd. dirs. New England dist. 1977-80, chief advisor MIT chpt., disting. svc. award 1980), Phi Lambda Epsilon. Mem. Lds Ch. Office: MIT Rm 4-136 77 Massachusetts Ave Cambridge MA 02139-4307

EAGER, GEORGE SIDNEY, JR., electrical engineer, engineering executive; b. Balt., Sept. 5, 1915; s. George S. and Ada Elizabeth (Heinz) E.; m. Ruth Duff, Oct. 13, 1945; children: Robert W., John W., George S. III. BEE, Johns Hopkins U., 1936, PhD in Engring., 1941. Rsch. supr., asst. dir., assoc. dir. to dir. rsch. Gen. Cable Corp., Edison, N.J., 1945-80; pres. Barr Duff Corp., Upper Montclair, NJ, 1998—. Contbr. numerous articles to profl. jours. Author 35 patents elec. wires and cables. Lt. col. Signal Corps, U.S. Army, 1941-45, ETO. Fellow IEEE, Montclair Golf Club. Republican. Congregationalist. Home: 14 Bellegrove Dr Montclair NJ 07043-2527 E-mail: geager@earthlink.net.

EAGLE, KIM ALLEN, cardiologist; m. Darlene Eagle; 1 child, Taylor. MD, Tufts U. Sch. of Medicine, Boston, 1979. Intern, resident Yale New Haven Hosp., 1979—82, chief resident, 1982—83; cardiology fellow Mass. Gen. Hosp., Boston, 1983, instr., 1986—88, asst. prof., 1988—94, assoc. prof., 1994; prof. medicine U. of Mich., Ann Arbor, 1994—. Editor: (book) Practice of Cardiology, Practical Cardiology, 100 Years of Cardiology, (jour.) Current Jour. Rev. Fellow: Am. Coll. of Cardiology (life). Office: Univ of Mich Cardiovascular Ctr 300 N Ingalls 8B02 Ann Arbor MI 48109-0477

EAGLEBURGER, LAWRENCE SIDNEY, former secretary of state; b. Milw., Aug. 1, 1930; s. Leon Sidney and Helen (Van Ornum) E.; m. Marlene Ann Heinemann, Apr. 23, 1966; 1 son by previous marriage, Lawrence Scott; children: Lawrence Andrew, Lawrence Jason. Student, Cen. State Coll., Stevens Point, Wis., 1948-50; BS, U. Wis., 1952, MS, 1957; LLD (hon.), U. S.C., 1985, George Washington U., 1986. Teaching asst. U. Wis., 1956-57; joined U.S. Fgn. Service, 1957; 3d sec. Tegucigalpa, Honduras, 1957-59; assigned US Dept. State, 1959-62, 65-66; 2d sec. Belgrade, Yugoslavia, 1962-65; mem. staff NSC, 1966-67; spl. asst. under sec. US Dept. State, 1967-69; exec. asst. to asst. to Pres. for nat. security affairs The White House, 1969; polit. adviser, counselor for polit. affairs U.S. Mission to NATO, Brussels, 1969-71; dep. asst. sec. US Dept. Def., 1971-73, dep. asst. to Pres. for nat. security ops., 1973, exec. asst. to sec., 1973-75; dep. under sec. state for mgmt., exec. asst. to sec. US Dept. State, 1975-77, US amb. to Yugoslavia Belgrade, 1977-81, asst. sec. for European affairs, 1981-82, undersec. for polit. affairs, 1982-84, dep. sec., 1989—92, acting sec., 1992, sec., 1992-93; pres. Kissinger Assocs., Inc., N.Y.C., 1984—89; sr. pub. policy advisor Baker, Donelson, Bearrnan and Caldwell, Washington, 1993—. Bd. dirs. ITT Corp., Josephson Internat., Inc., Phillips Petroleum Co., Halliburton Co., Universal Corp.; trustee Mutual of N.Y. Vice chmn. 7th Dist. Young Republicans Wis., 1950-51; mem. Wis. Young Rep. Exec. Com., 1949-51. Served to 1st lt. AUS, 1952-54. Recipient Disting. Civilian Service medal US Dept. Def., 1973; President's award for Disting. Fed. Civilian Svc., 1977, William J. Carr award, US Dept. State, 1984, Presdl. Citizen's medal by Pres., 1991, Disting. Svc. award, US Dept. State, 1992; awarded honorary knighthood by Britain, 1995; named ARC internat. amb.-at-large. Mem. Alpha Sigma Phi. Republican. Lutheran. Mailing: Baker Donelson Bearman & Caldwell 555 11th St NW Washington DC 20004 E-mail: leagleburger@bakerdonelson.com.*

EAGLES, SIDNEY SMITH, JR., judge; b. Asheville, NC, Aug. 5, 1939; s. Sidney Smith Sr. and Mildred Truman (Brite) E.; m. Rachel Phillips, May 22, 1965; children: Virginia Brite, Margaret Phillips. BA, Wake Forest U., 1961, JD, 1964. Bar: N.C. 1964. Revisor Gen. Statutes Commn., Raleigh, N.C., 1967-70; asst. atty. gen. legis. drafting service Office Atty. Gen. N.C., Raleigh, 1970-74, dep. atty. gen. spl. prosecution divsn., 1974-76; counsel to speaker N.C. State Legislature, Raleigh, 1976-80; ptnr. Eagles Hafer & Hall, Raleigh, 1977-82; judge N.C. Ct. Appeals, Raleigh, 1983—2004, chief judge, 1998—2004; of counsel Smith Moore LLP, 2004—. Adj. prof. Campbell U. Sch. Law, 1977—; chmn. N.C. Jud. Stds. Commn., 1994—96; mem. faculty Appellate Judges Sch. Law Sch. NYU, N.Y.C., 1993—99; mem. Uniform Laws Conf., 1968—83, 1992—, life mem., 2000. Co-author: North Carolina Criminal Procedure Forms, 1975, 3d edit., 1989; contbr. articles to profl. jours. V.p. Raleigh Jaycees, 1972-73; mem. Senatorial Dist. Dem. Com., 1979-81; bd. dirs. Wake County (N.C.) Symphony Soc., 1980-81, Women's Aid of Wake County, 1978—, Carolinas Dist. Kiwanis Found, 2004—.; bd. elders, bd. deacons, trustee, tchr. Sunday sch. Hillyer Meml. Christian Ch., 1980—, chmn bd., 1989; bd. visitors Wake Forest U. Sch. Law; vice chair bd. trustees Barton Coll., 1999, chair, 2002—. Served to capt. USAF, 1964-67; col., ret. 1991. Named Disting. Law Alumnus, Wake Forest U., 1981; N.C. Justice Found. fellow, 1972. Mem. ABA (chmn. appellate judges conf. 1993-94, mem. appellate jud. edn. com. 1994-98, ho. of dels. 1992-, mem. legal edn. 2002—), Am. Law Inst. (life), N.C. Bar Assn. (v.p. 1989-90), Wake County Bar Assn. (chmn. exec. com. 1975, pres.-elect 2005-), N.C. State Bar, Execs. Club (pres. 1985), Kiwanis (disting. pres. Raleigh 1986-87, disting. lt. gov. 1995, Kiwanian of Yr. award 1989), Phi Delta Phi, Phi Alpha Delta (James Iredell award 1990). Avocations: politics, reading. Office: Smith Moore LLP PO Box 27525 Raleigh NC 27611 Business E-Mail: sid.eagles@smithmoorelaw.com.

EAGLES, STUART ERNEST, real estate company officer; b. Saint John, N.B., Can., July 29, 1929; s. Ernest Lyle and Evelyn Gertrude (Feltmate) E.; m. Margaret Anne Gulliver, Sept. 30, 1952; children: James Stuart, Patricia Anne, Mark Edward. B.Sc., Acadia U., 1949, D.C.L. (hon.), 1992. Pres. Aegean Devel. Inc., Toronto, 1988—. Bd. dirs. AGF Trust Co., AGF Mgmt. Ltd., Hardit Corp., OPB Realty Inc.; past trustee, dir. Internat. Coun. Shopping Ctrs.; past pres. and dir. Can. Inst. Pub. Real Estate Cos. Gov. Jr. Achievement Can. Mem. Nat. Club (past pres.), Can. Club, Empire Club. Home: 24 Garfield Ave Toronto ON Canada M4T 1E7 Office Phone: 416-601-3925. Business E-Mail: stuart.eagles@opb.on.ca.

EAGLESON, PETER STURGES, civil engineer, environmental engineer, educator; b. Phila., Feb. 27, 1928; s. William Boal and Helen (Sturges) E.; m. Marguerite Anne Partridge, May 28, 1949 (div.); children: Helen Marie, Peter Sturges, Jeffrey Partridge; m. Beverly Grossmann Rich, Dec. 27, 1974. BS in Civil Engring, Lehigh U., 1949, MS, 1952; Sc.D., MIT, 1956; D of Engring. (hon.), Lehigh U., 1998. Jr. engr. George B. Mebus (cons. engr.), Glenside, Pa., 1950-51; teaching asst. Lehigh U., 1951-52; research asst. Mass. Inst. Tech., 1952-54; mem. faculty MIT, 1954-93, prof. civil engring., 1965-93, head dept. civil engring., 1970-75, emeritus prof. civil and environ. engring., 1993—. Vis. asso. Calif. Inst. Tech., 1975-76; Fulbright sr. research scholar Commonwealth Sci. and Indsl. Research Orgn., Canberra, Australia, 1966-67 Author: (with others) Estuary and Coastline Hydrodynamics, 1966, Dynamic Hydrology, 1970, Ecohydrology, 2002. Served to 2d lt. C.E. AUS, 1949-50. Recipient Desmond Fitzgerald medal, 1959, Clemens Herschel prize, 1965 both Boston Soc. Civil Engrs., rsch. prize ASCE, 1963, William Bowie medal Am. Geophysical Union, 1994, Stockholm Water prize Stockholm Water Found., 1997. Fellow AAAS, Am. Meteorol. Soc. (hon.), Am. Geophys. Union (Robert E. Horton award 1979, Robert E. Horton medal 1988, pres. 1986-88, William Bowie medal 1994), Internat. Assn. Hydrological Scis. (Internat. Hydrology prize 1991); mem. NAE, European Geophys. Soc. (John Dalton medal 1999). Office: MIT Dept Civil & Environ Engring Room 48-325 Cambridge MA 02139 Office Phone: 617-253-2725.

EAGLET, ROBERT DANTON, electrical engineer, aerospace scientist, consultant, retired military officer; b. Cleve., Mar. 2, 1934; s. Albert Rudy and Dorothy Margaret (Beamer) E.; m. Sally Perry; children: Suzanne Carolyn, Allison Leigh, Kevin Robert. BSEE, U. Ariz., 1962; MSEE, U. So. Calif., 1968, PhD in Elec. Engring. and Physics, 1970. Commd. 2d lt. USAF, 1956, advanced through grades to maj. gen., 1986, forward air contr. in Vietnam, 1965-66, chief, classified program, space div. L.A., 1966-68, chief strategic def. div. hdqrs. Washington, 1970-74, mil. asst. to dep. undersec. def., 1974-75; dep. gen. mgr. NATO airborne early warning program Brussels, 1975-79; dep. chief of staff devel. planning, sys. command USAF, Andrews AFB, Md., 1979-84, dep. comdr. armament divsn. Eglin AFB, Fla., 1984-86, dir. F-16 multinat. fighter program Wright Patterson AFB, Ohio, 1986-89; dep. asst. sec. of Air Force Pentagon, Washington, 1989-91; ret. USAF, 1991; pres. Eaglet Internat. Assocs., McLean, Va., 1992—. Decorated Disting. Svc. medal with oak leaf cluster, Legion of Merit with oak leaf cluster, Silver star, Disting. Flying Cross with oak leaf cluster, Bronze star with Valor device, Air medal with 24 oak leaf clusters, Purple Heart; named Outstanding Alumnus U. So. Calif. Mem. Air Force Assn., Nat.Security Indsl. Assn., Assn. Old Crows, Assn. U.S. Army, Navy League, Belgian-Am. Assn. (bd. dirs.), French Am. Assn. Republican. Avocation: wind surfing. Office Phone: 703-538-2778. Business E-Mail: eaglet@compuserve.com.

EAGLETON, EDWARD JOHN, lawyer; b. Tulsa, Jan. 22, 1932; s. William L. and Pauline (Dellinger) E.; m. Norma Lee, Oct. 6, 1956; children: Courtney Jean, Richard John. BA, Okla. U., 1954, JD, 1956. Bar: Okla. 1955, U.S. Dist. Ct. (ea., we. and no. dists.) Okla. 1956, U.S. Tax Ct. 1958, U.S. Supreme Ct. 1964; CPA, Tex., Okla. Acct. Peat Marwick Mitchell, Dallas, 1956-58; with IRS, Dallas and New Orleans, 1958-62; assoc. Houston & Klein, Tulsa, 1962-65; ptnr. Kothe & Eagleton, Tulsa, 1965-74, Houston & Klein Inc., Tulsa, 1974-94, Eagleton Eagleton & Harrison Inc., Tulsa, 1994—. Served with U.S. Army, 1956. Named one of Best Tax Lawyers in Am., Bar Register of Preeminent Lawyers, 1983—2005. Republican. Unitarian Universalist. Home: 3210 E 65th St Tulsa OK 74136-1225 Office: Eagleton, Eagleton & Harrison Inc 320 S Boston Ave Ste 1700 Tulsa OK 74103-4706

EAGLETON, THOMAS FRANCIS, lawyer, former senator; b. St. Louis, Sept. 4, 1929; s. Mark David and Zitta Louise (Swanson) E.; m. Barbara Ann Smith, Jan. 20, 1956; children: Terence, Christin. BA cum laude, Amherst Coll., 1950; LL.B. cum laude, Harvard U., 1953; doctorate (hon.), Amherst Coll., Culver-Stockton Coll., Northeastern U., U. Mo., Wash. U., Westminster Coll., others. Bar: Mo. 1953. Ptnr. Eagleton & Eagleton; circuit atty. St. Louis, 1957-60; atty. gen. State of Mo., 1961—64, lt. gov., 1965—68; U.S. senator, 1968—87; ptnr. Thompson & Mitchell (now Thompson Coburn LLP), St. Louis, 1987—. Prof. pub. affairs Wash. U., 1987-99; mem. Pres.'s Fng. Intelligence Adv. Bd., 1993—98. Author: War and Presidential Power, 1974, Our Constitution and What It Means, 1987, Issues on Business and Government, 1990. Served with USNR, 1948-49. Recipient Pres.'s award, Mo. Bar Assn., Disting. Lawyer award, Bar. Assn. Met. St. Louis. Office: Thompson Coburn LLP One US Bank Plaza Saint Louis MO 63101-1693 Office Phone: 314-552-6030, 314-552-7030. E-mail: teagleton@ThompsonCoburn.com.

EAGLY, ALICE HENDRICKSON, social psychology educator; b. L.A., Dec. 25, 1938; d. Harold Martin and Josara Alberta (Whyers) Hendrickson; m. Robert Victor Eagly, Sept. 8, 1962; children: Ingrid Victoria, Ursula Elizabeth. BA, Radcliffe Coll., 1960; MA, U. Mich., 1963, PhD, 1965. Asst. prof. Mich. State U., East Lansing, 1965-67; asst. to assoc. to full prof. U. Mass., Amherst, 1967-80; vis. asst. prof. U. Ill., Champaign, 1970-71; vis. assoc. prof. Harvard U., Cambridge, Mass., 1974-75; prof. social psychology Purdue U., West Lafayette, Ind., 1980-95, Northwestern U., Evanston, Ill., 1995—. MacEachern Meml. lectr. U. Alta., 1985; vis. prof. U. Tuebingen (Germany), 1991-92; vis. scholar Murray Rsch. Ctr., 1998-99, vis. rsch. prof. U Amsterdam, 2005- Author: Sex Differences in Social Behavior: A Social Role Interpretation, 1987, (with Shelly Chaiken) The Psychology of Attitudes, 1993; cons. editor Jour. Personality and Social Psychology: Attitudes and Social Cognition, 1979—, mem. editorial bd., 1983—; cons. editor Psychology of Women Quar., 1978-86, also others; contbr. articles to profl. jours. Recipient Gordon Allport Intergroup Rels. prize Soc. Psychol. Study Social Issues, 1976, Disting. Pub. award Assn. for Women in Psychology, 1978, Cattell Sabbatical award Soc. for Psychology of Women, 2000, Carolyn Wood Sherif award 2005; Nat. Merit scholar, 1956-60, Fulbright fellow, 1960-61, Woodrow Wilson fellow, 1961-62, NSF fellow, 1962-65; various rsch. grants. Mem. APA (citation as disting. leader for women in psychology com. on women in psychology), Soc. Personality and Social Psychology (pres. 1981, Donald Campbell award for disting. contbn. to social psychology 1994), Soc. for Exptl. Social Psychology (exec. com. 1973-76, 81-83, Disting. Sci. Contbn. award), Midwestern Psychol. Assn. (pres. 1998-99), Am. Psychol. Soc., Phi Beta Kappa, Sigma Xi. Office: Northwestern U Dept Psychology Swift Hall 2029 Sheridan Rd Evanston IL 60208-0828

EAKELEY, DOUGLAS SCOTT, lawyer; b. Morristown, NJ, Mar. 2, 1946; m. Priscilla Van Tassel, June 2, 1973. BA, Yale U., 1968, JD, 1972; BA in Jurisprudence, MA in Jurisprudence, Oxford (England) U., 1970. Bar: NY 1973, US Ct. Appeals (2nd cir.) 1974, NJ 1978, US Ct. Appeals (3rd cir.) 1980, US Supreme Ct. 1981. Law clk. judge Harold R. Tyler, Jr. US Dist. Ct. (so. dist.) NY, NYC, 1972-73; assoc. Debevoise, Plimpton, NYC, 1973-80; ptnr. Riker, Danzig, Scherer, Hyland & Perretti, Newark, Morristown, NJ, 1980-90, 91-94; first asst. atty. gen. State NJ, 1990-91; ptnr. Lowenstein Sandler, PC, Roseland, NJ, 1994—. Chmn. Legal Svcs. NJ, North Brunswick, 1981-90, Legal Svcs. Corp., Washington, 1993-2003; pres. Legal Svc. Found. Essex County, Newark, 1981-90; chmn. NJ Sentencing Policy Study Commn., 1992-93; trustee Practising Law Inst., NYC, 1994—; trustee Boys Girls Clubs Newark, 1993-2003. Chmn. bd. editors NJ Law Jour., 1984-90. Trustee NJ Network Found., 1994—, NJ Inst. Social Justice, 1996—; pres. NJ Shakespeare Festival, Madison, 1982-86. Rhodes scholar Oxford U., 1968. Fellow Am. Bar Found.; mem. ABA (John Minor Wisdom award, litigation sect. 1997), NJ Bar Assn., Essex County Bar Assn., Fed. Bar Assn. NJ (v.p. 1983-90), Urban League Essex County (trustee 1987-88), Assn. Am. Rhodes Scholars (bd. dirs. 1995-2002), Phi Beta Kappa. Democrat. Office: Lowenstein Sandler PC 65 Livingston Ave Roseland NJ 07068-1791 Office Phone: 973-597-2348. Business E-Mail: deakeley@lowenstein.com.

EAKER, CHARLES WILLIAM, chemistry educator; b. St. Louis, May 25, 1949; s. Charles Mayfield and Mildred Catherine (Staples) E.; m. Mary Alice Eisenmann, July 6, 1974; children: Stephanie Eisenmann Eaker, Sara Marie. BS, Mich. State U., 1971; PhD, U. Chgo., 1974. Instr. U. Dallas, Irving, Tex., 1976-78, asst. prof., 1978-81, assoc. prof., 1981-89, prof., 1989—; dean Constantin Coll., 2005—. Contbr. articles to profl. jours. Rsch. grantee Robert A. Welch Found., 1984, faculty devel. grantee Arthur Vining Davis, 1980, NSF equipment grantee 1997; recipient Presdl. award U. Dallas, 1987, 91, 95, 96, 98. Mem. Am. Chem. Soc. (rsch. grantee 1978, 88), Sigma Xi. Office: U Dallas 1845 E Northgate Dr Irving TX 75062-4736 E-mail: eaker@udallas.edu.

EAKER, SHERRY ELLEN, editor; b. NYC, Nov. 30, 1949; d. Ira and Lee (Eisenberg) Eaker. BA, Queens Coll., 1971, MS, 1976. Tchr. art, English N.Y.C. Bd. Edn., 1971-76; editor-in-chief Back Stage, The Performing Arts Weekly, N.Y.C., 1977—. Editor, compiler Handbook for Performing Artists: The How-to and Who-to-Contact Reference for Actors, Singers, Dancers, 1989, rev. edit., 1991, 1995, 2004, The Cabaret Artist's Handbook-Creating Your Own Act in Today's Liveliest Theatre Setting, 2000. Mem. Drama Desk (sec. 1984-87, v.p. 1987-91), Am. Theatre Critics Assn., Nat. Theatre Conf., League Profl. Theatre Women, N.Y. Coalition Profl. Women in Arts and Media (spl. adv.), Inst. of Outdoor Drama (adv. coun.), Manhattan Assn. Cabarets, NY Women in Film and TV. Avocations: theater, cabaret. Office: Back Stage 770 Broadway New York NY 10003-9595

EAKIN, J. MICHAEL, state supreme court justice; b. Mechanicsburg, Pa., Nov. 18, 1948; m. Heidi Eakin; children: Michael, Zachary, Chase. BA in Govt., Franklin & Marshall Coll., 1970; JD, Pa. State U., 1975. Asst. dist. atty. Cumberland County, 1975—83, dist. atty., 1984—95; pvt. practice, 1980—83; judge Pa. Superior Ct., 1995—2001; justice Pa. Supreme Ct., 2001—. Lectr. Nat. Coll. Dist. Attys. Contbr. articles to profl. jours. With Pa. Army N.G., 1971—77. Recipient Sweetheart of the Yr. award, MADD, 1988, Best Catch award, Mid-Penn Anglers, 1991, Career Achievement award, Dickinson Sch. Law, 2000. Mem.: ABA, Pa. Dist. Atty.'s Inst. (bd. dirs. 1987—95, pres. 1994—95), Pa. Dist. Atty.'s Assn. (mem. exec. com., chmn. edn. 1987—95, pres. 1992—93), Pa. Bar Inst. (faculty, mem. criminal law sympmosium planning com.), Am. Inns Ct., Cumberland County Bar Assn., Dauphin County Bar Assn., Lancaster County Bar Assn., Pa. Bar Assn. (mem. plain English com.), Am. Judges Assn., Brehon Soc. Office: Pa State Supreme Ct 4720 Old Gettysburg Rd #405 Mechanicsburg PA 17055

EAKIN, MARGARETTA MORGAN, lawyer; b. Ft. Smith, Ark., Aug. 27, 1941; d. Ariel Thomas and Oma (Thomas) Morgan; m. Harry D. Eakin, June 7, 1959; 1 child, Margaretta E. BA with honors, U. Oreg., 1969, JD, 1971. Bar: Oreg. 1971, U.S. Dist. Ct. Oreg. 1973, U.S. Ct. Appeals (9th cir.) 1977. Law clk. to chief justice Oreg. Supreme Ct, Salem, 1971-72; Reginald Heber Smith Law Reform fellow, 1962-73; house counsel Hyster Co., 1973-75; assoc. N. Robert Stoll, 1975-77; pvt. practice, Margaretta Eakin, P.C., Portland, Oreg., 1977—. Tchr. bus. law Portland State U., 1979-80; spkr.; mem. bd. profl. responsibility Oreg. State Bar, 1979-82; mem. bd. visitors U. Oreg. Sch. Law, 1986-93, vice chair, 1989-91, chair, 1992-93; mem. Oreg. State. Bar Com. on Uniform State Laws, 1989-93; vol. lawyer Fed. Emergency Mgmt. Assn., 1995—. Mem. ann. fund com. Oreg. Episcopal Sch., 1981; chmn. subcom county fair, 1981; sec. bd. Parent Club St. Mary's Acad., 1987. Paul Patterson fellow. Mem. ABA, ATLA, Oreg. Trial Lawyers Assn., Oreg. State Bar Assn. (bus. law sect., bus. litig. sect., civil rights, computer and internat. law, constrn. law, litig., intellectual property, sole and small firm practitioners, constl. law, elder law, consumer law exec. com.), Multnomah County Bar Assn. (jud. selection com. 1992-94), Oreg. State Bar Consumer Law Exec. Com. Office: PO Box 25523 Portland OR 97298 Office Phone: 503-244-1077, 503-227-1811. Personal E-mail: ME71051@aol.com.

EAKIN, RICHARD RONALD, academic administrator, mathematics educator; b. New Castle, Pa., Aug. 6, 1938; s. Everett Glenn and Mildred May (Hammerschmidt) E.; m. Jo Ann McGeehan, Aug. 23, 1960; children: Matthew Glenn, Maridy Lynn. AB in Math., Geneva Coll., Beaver Falls, Pa., 1960; MA in Math., Washington State U., 1962, PhD in Math., 1964. Asst. prof. math. Bowling Green (Ohio) State U., 1964-68, assoc. prof. math., 1968-87, asst. dean grad. sch., 1969-72, vice-provost student affairs, 1972-80, vice-provost instl. planning, 1979-80, exec. vice-provost budgeting and planning, 1980-83, v.p. budgeting and planning, 1983-87; chancellor, prof. math. East Carolina U., Greenville, 1987—2001, prof. ednl. leadership., 2001—. Editor revs. and evaluations sect. (jour.) The Math. Tchr., 1968-70. V.p. and mem. bd. dirs. Nat. Hemophilia Found., N.Y.C., 1983-84, chmn. bd., v.p. adminstrn. and fin., 1984-87; mem. bd. dirs. Ednl. Commn. for Fgn. Med. Grads., 2002—. NDEA fellow Wash. State U., Pullman, 1960-63, NSF fellow, 1963-64. Mem. Math. Assn. Am., So. Assn. Colls. and Schs. (commn. on colls.), Phi Kappa Phi, Omicron Delta Kappa. Office: East Carolina U Ragsdale Bldg Rm 217 Greenville NC 27858 E-mail: eakinr@mail.ecu.edu.

EAKIN, THOMAS CAPPER, sports promotion executive; b. New Castle, Pa., Dec. 16, 1933; s. Frederick William and Beatrice (Capper) E.; m. Brenda Lee Andrews, Oct. 21, 1961; children: Thomas Andrews, Scott Frederick. BA in History, Denison U., 1956. Life ins. cons. Northwestern Mut. Life Ins. Co., Cleve., 1959-67; dist. mgr. Putman Pub. Co., Cleve., 1968-69; regional bus. mgr. Chilton Pub. Co., Cleve., 1969-70; dist. mgr. Hitchcock Pub. Co., Cleve., 1970-72; founder, pres. Golf Internat. 100 Club, Shaker Heights, Ohio, 1970—; pres TCE Enterprises, Shaker Heights, 1973—. Founder, pres. Ohio Humanitarian Hall of Fame, 2000—, Internat. Humanitarian Hall of Fame, 2004—, US Humanitarian Hall of Fame, 2004—, Ohio Pacesetters Hall of Fame, 2004—. Ohio Baseball Hall of Fame and Mus., 1976, Ohio Youth Sports Hall of Fame, 1996—, Tuscarawas County Sports Promotions Enterprises, 1987—, Ohio Sports Promotions Co., 1989, Ohio Sports Hall of Fame Promotional Enterprises, 1990—, Summit County Sports Promotion Enterprises, 1990—, Geauga County Hist. and Sports Traditions Enterprises, 1990—, Licking County Sports Stars Enterprises, 1990—, Lake County Cmty. Promotions Enterprises, 1990—, Trumbull County Sports Stars Publs., 1990—, Portage County Hist. and Sports Publs., 1990—, Cuyahoga County Promotion Co., 1990—, Ashtabula County Hist. and Sports Publs., 1990—, Ohio Pride in Cmty. Publs., 1990—, Mahoning County Sports Headlines Publs., 1990—, Ohio Fire Dept. Promotional Publs., 1990—, Ohio Law Enforcement Cmty. Publs., 1990—, Erie County Excellence in H.S. Sports Publs., 1990—, Ohio Sports Logo Creations, 1991—, Ohio Sports Stars Enterprises, 1991—, Ohio Sports Licensing Enterprise, 1991—, Huron County Sports Pub., 1995, Lucas County Baseball Pub., 1995, Winners of Wood County Pub., 1995, Harrison County Baseball Digest, 1998—, Belmont County Baseball League, 1998—, Ohio Promotions For Sports, 2000—, Ohio Baseball Digest Harrison County, 1998—; founder, chmn. Twinsburg (Ohio) Cmty. Heritage Pubs., Garrettsville (Ohio) Cmty. Svc. Publ., lectr. series Catch The Spirit, 2000—; founder, pub. Touching All the Bases, 1991; bd. dirs. New Hope Records, Hit and Run Records, Red Hour Records, Nat. William "Dummy" Hoy Baseball Com., 1995—; founder, dir. Cy Young Mus., 1975; mem. adv. bd. Sportsbeat, 1985—, sch. Calendar Co., Inc., 1984, 89, D & D Sports Prodn. and Mktg. Creations, 1990—, Damascus Steel Casting Co., 1987—, Advantage Sports Co., 1989—, Base Sports Co., 1989, M & M Publs., 1987—; founder, pres. Ohio Baseball Assocs., 2005—. Founder, pres., dir. Cy Young Mus., 1975-80, Ohio Baseball Hall of Fame, 1976—, Ohio Baseball Hall of Fame and Mus., 1980—, celebration, 1977-79, golf invitational, 1980—; founder, pres. Ohio Sports Hall of Fame, 1985—, Shaker Hts Sports Hall of Fame, 1989—, Ohio Sports Legends Found., 1991—, Toledo Baseball Bluecoats, 1984—, Tuscarawas County Sports Hall of Fame, 1980—, Tuscarawas County Am. Revolution Bicentennial Commn., exec. com. 1974-1976, Tuscarawas Valley Tourist Assn., 1979-81, Buckeye Baseball Lecture Series, 1989—, Cleve. Baseball Old Timers Assn., Ohio Sports Celebrity Golf Invitational, 1991—, 1991—, Midwest Sports Coun., Chesterland (Ohio) Hist. Found. Enhancement Fund, 1989—, Berea (Ohio) Hist. and Sports Fund, 1984—, Windham (Ohio) Cmty. Svc. Found., 1990—, Jefferson Hist. and Sports Found., 1986—, Ohio Sports Ednl. Coun., 1991—, Youth in Cmty. Svc. and Vols. are Winners Lecture Series, 1991—, Ohio Minor League Baseball Hall of Fame Assn., 1992—, U.S. Sports Hall of Fame, 1989—, Ohio Founders League, 1990—, Ohio Negro Baseball Hall of Fame Vets. Coun., 1991—, Ohio Women's Baseball Hall of Fame, 1998—, Alta Weiss Meml. award, 1998—, Ohio Baseball History Mus, 2002—; founder, nat. chmn. Cy Young Centennial, 1967, Cy Young Golf Invitational; founder, chmn. Streetsboro (Ohio) Athletic Found., 1989—, Wickliffe (Ohio) Cmty. and Sports Fund, Madison (Ohio) Village Hist. Preservation Fund, Middlefield (Ohio) Fire Dept. Cmty. Promotions Fund, Burton Athletic Enhancement Fund, Fairview Pk. (Ohio) Cmty. Svc. Fund, Bath-Richfield Ohio Cmty. Fund, Independence Freedom Fund, 1988—, Aurora Hist. Preservation Fund, 1988—, Conneaut (Ohio) Cmty. Promotional Fund, 1991—; founder, dir. Target/Reach Youth, 1971—; pres. Tuscarawas County Old Timers Baseball Assn., 1985—; trustee Hiram House, 1989—, Nat. Jr. Tennis League, 1985—; hon. bd. dirs. Chautaugua Sports Hall of Fame, 1982—; bd. dirs. Greater Toledo Sports Hall of Fame; exec. sponsor, Ohio chmn. World Golf Hall of Fame, Pinehurst, NC, 1979—; founder Famous Ohioans in Print Hall of Fame, 1994; adv. bd. Portage County Sports Hall of Fame, 1983—, Cuyahoga Hills Boys Sch., Warrensville Hts., Ohio, 1971—, Camp Hope, Warrensville Hts., 1973—, Cleve. Sports Legend Found., 1988—, Great Ohioans Hall of Fame, 1988—, Solon Cmty. Promotional Fund, 1989—; disting. citizens adv. bd. Am. Police Hall of Fame and Mus., 1987—; career adv. bd. Denison U., 1990—; nom. com. Ohio Profl. and Amateur Athlete of Yr. Awards, 1990—; active Geauga County Hist. Soc., Summit County Sports Hall of Fame, Dunham Tavern Mus.; founder, chmn. Shaker Hts. Youth Hall of Fame, 1996; chmn. Ray Chapman Meml. com., 2000, others; assoc. Merrick Art Gallery; bd. trustees Great Expectations Ltn., 2004—. Served in AUS, 1956-58. Named to Order of Long Leaf Pine, NC State Senate, 1984, Sch. Calendar Co., 1985, Hon. Order of Ky. Cols., 1986, Venerable Order Michael the Archangel, Am. Police Hall of Fame, 1989; named Hon. Citizen, City of Memphis, 1986, City of Little Rock, 1986, Ohio Baseball Man of Yr., 1991; named to Ohio Baseball Hall of Fame, World Biog. Hall of Fame, 1984, Wis. Baseball Hall of Fame, 1998; recipient Disting. Svc. award Hubbard, Ohio, 1986, Vermilion Kiwanis, 1996, Internat Friendship award Premier Ont., Can., 1985, Commr.'s award Trumbull County, 1985, Gov.'s citation State of Md., 1987, Hon. West Virginian award, 1987, J. Edgar Hoover award Am. Police Hall of Fame, 1991, Humanitarian award City of Cleve., 1991, Mayor's Volunteerism award, 1991, Vol. of Yr. award No. Ohio Live, 1991, Ohio Govs. award, 1978, Ohio Govs. award Cmty. Action, 1974, Sports Achievement award Dapper Dan Club of Upper Ohio Valley, 1993, Ohio Baseball Man of Yr. award Greater Youngstown Baseball Old Timers Assn., 1991, Sports Hero award Am. Athletic Assn. of Deaf, Inc., 1992, Ohio Profl. and Athlete of Yr. award, 1995, Lifetime Achievement award, 1995, 20th Century award Achievement Nat. Assn. Chiefs Police, 1998, A Spl. Friend award Blair County Spl. Olympics, 1998, Lifetime Achievement award Lake County Hist. Soc., 1998, Disting. Svc. award Rotary, Twinsburg, Ohio, 1998, Cmty. Svc. award Ohio Dr. Martin Luther King, Jr. Holiday Commn., 1999, Cmty. Builders award Flushing Ohio Masonic Lodge No. 298, 1998, Disting. Svc. award Solon Ohio Rotary Club, 1999, Cmty. Svc. award Middlefield Fire Dept., 1999, Disting. Comty. Svc. award Lorain County Assn. Township Trustees and Clks., 2001; commendation State of NC Senate, 1984, State of Pa. Senate, 1984, State of La., State of Ohio Senate and Reps., Greater Stark County Baseball Hall of Fame, 1994; Columbus (Ohio) City Coun., 1985, Cleve. City Coun., 1989; Thomas C. Eakin Day declared City of Cleve., 1974, N.Mex., 1987, others; world record holder Guinness Book of World Records, 1991; inducted into Cy Young Tuscarawas County Old Timers Baseball Assn. Hall of Fame, 1993, Am. Athletic Assn. of Deaf Hall of Fame, 1992, Sports Hero Award, 1992, Chautauqua Sports Hall of Fame, 1983, City of Cleve. Vol. Hall of Fame, 1991, Ohio Record Holders Hall of Fame, 1989, Greater Akron Baseball Hall of Fame, 1993, Ohio Sr. Citizens Hall of Fame, 1995, Ohio Vets Hall of Fame, 1995, Old Time Ball Players Assn. of Wis. Hall of Fame, 1998, Rufus Putnam Disting. Svc. award Ohio Masons, 1999, medal of Honor DAR, 2000, Trumbull County Baseball Commendation Mahoning Valley Profl. Baseball Assn., 2000; named Trustee of Yr. Nat. Jr. Tennis League, Cleve., 1996, Disting. Svc. award, Solon Ohio Rotary, 1999, Cmty. Svc. award, Middlefield Fire Dept., 1999, Paul Harris fellow Rotary Internat., 1999, Disting. Cmty. Svc. award, Lorain County Assn. Township Trustees and Clks., 2001, Ravenna Kiwanis Club honor award, 2001, Munroe Falls Kiwanis Club honor award, 2001, Commendation award Mahoning Valley Profl. Baseball Assn., 2002, Ellis Island Medal of Honor, 2002, Am. Spirit award, 2002, U.S. Marine Corps. Commendation, 2002, Cmty. Svc. award Copley Ohio Hist. Soc., 2002, Outstanding Spkr. award Stow-Munroe Falls Ohio C. of C., 2002, The Golden Legion of Phi Delta Theta, 2003, Baseball Achievement award, Greater Youngstown Old Timers Assn., 2003, Cmty. Svc. award Wellington Kiwanis Club, 2003, Liberty Bell Hist. award Independence Hist. Soc., 2004, Summit County Svc. award N.W. Summit Country Rotary Club, 2004, Hist. Merit award Aurora Hist. Soc., 2004, others. Mem. White House Hist. Assn. (charter), U.S. Assn. Sports Halls of Fame, U.S. Hist. Soc., Soc. Am. Baseball Rsch., Nat. Trust Hist. Preservation, Ohio Hist. Soc., Ohio Assn. Sports Halls of Fame, Ohio Baseball Roundtable (founder, pres. 1991—), Ohio Assn. Old Time Baseball Players (founder, pres. 1990—), Ohio Racquetball Assn. (adv. bd. 1981-82), Old Time Ball Players Assn. Wis., Western Pa. Sports Hall of Fame, North Ohio Old Time Baseball Players Club (adv. bd. 1978—), Tuscarawas County Old Timers Baseball Assn. (hon. dir. 1972—, commendation 1970), Tuscarawas County Hist. Soc. (trustee 1978-81), Lawrence County Hist. Soc., Greater Youngstown Old Timers Baseball Assn. (inductee Hall of Fame 1994, King of the Realm award 2004), Madison Hist. Soc., Middlefield Hist. Soc. (adv. bd. 1986—), Clinton Hist. Soc. (hon. trustee 1987—), Windsor Hist. Soc. (adv. bd. 1987—), Solon Hist. Soc., Newcomerstown Hist. Soc., Shaker Hist. Soc. (trustee 1980-82), Greater Canton Amateur Sports Hall of Fame Assn. (commendation 1994), Barberton Sports Hall of Fame (founder, chmn. publs. 1989—), Holloway Old Timers Baseball Club (adv. bd. 1990—), Temperance House Mus., Negro Leagues Baseball Mus., Internat. Platform Assn., English Speaking Union (trustee 1994—), Denison U. Cleve. Men's Club, Gustave Courbet Soc., Western Res. Hist. Soc., Interact Club (adv. bd. Twinsburg chpt. 1981—, founder, dir. Shaker Heights chpt. 1971—), Exec. Club (Woodmere, Ohio chpt., Hall of Fame 1990), Univ. Sch. Tennis Club, Grandview Golf Club, PGA Nat. Golf Club (internat. mem.), Legend Lake Golf Club, Beachwood Athletic Club, Rotary (Svc. Above Self award Wickliffe chpt. 1991, Disting. Svc. award Swanton chpt. 1991, Outstanding Sports and Civic Svc. award Bellevue chpt. 1990, Spirit of Twinsburg award Twinsburg chpt. 1991, pres. Shaker Heights chpt. 1970-71), The Order of St. George (named Knight Comdr., 1994), Phi Delta Theta (exec. com. nat. Lou Gehrig award com. 1975—, charter mem. trustees roundtable 2003, charter inductee Ohio Iota Hall of Fame 1989, Outstanding Alumnus award 1989, Cleve. pres. 1970, Hall of Fame 1975, Disting. Alumnus award 1997, named to Internat. Fraternity Hall of Fame 1997, Mr. Ohio Iota award 2004), Ray Chapman Meml. Com. (chmn. 2000), Merrick Art Gallery (assoc.), Ohio Patriots Assn. (founder, pres. 2004), Masons, Scottish Rite, Brunswick Rotary Club (County Svc. award, 2005). Address: 2729 Shelley Rd Shaker Heights OH 44122

EAKINS, WILLIAM SHANNON, lawyer; b. Glen Cove, NY, July 22, 1951; s. William Shannon and Jean (Pickup) E.; 1 child, Amelia Moore. BA, Yale U., 1974; JD, Cornell U., 1977. Lawyer, trust adminstr. J.P. Morgan Bank, NYC, 1977-81; counsel com. on taxation, investigations & govt. ops. NY State Senate, Albany, 1981-84; assoc. Gelberg & Abrams, NYC, 1981-84, Phillips, Nizer, Benjamin, Krim & Ballon, NYC, 1984-88, ptnr., 1989-92; ptnr., chmn. dept. trusts and estates Olshan, Grundman, Frome & Rosenzweig, NYC, 1993—98, Patton, Eakins, Lipsett, Holbrook & Savage (formerly Forsythe, Patton, Ellis, Lipsett & Savage), NYC, 1998—. Bd. dirs. Asphalt Green Inc.; mem. estate planning com. Arthritis Found. Contbr. articles to profl. jours. Vice-chmn. NY Rep. County Com., NYC, 1985-89, exec. com., 1979-87, dist. leader, 1979-87; vice-chmn. Manhattan Cmty. Bd. #8, NYC, 1980-84, 93-97; Rep., Ind. Neighbors and Conservative candidate for NY State Assembly, 1992; bd. dirs. Homecrest Cmty. Svcs., Inc., NY Found. Sr. Citizens, 1981-93; sec. Hellgate Hill-Highgate Cmty. Assn.; elder, mem. session, chmn. planned giving com., chmn. Mission Outreach, Brick Presbyn. Ch., 2005—; mem. NY Presbyn.-Jewish Dialogue Steering Com., Am. Jewish Com. and Auburn Theolog. Seminary Com. on Jewish-Presbyn. rels. Mem. NY State Bar Assn., Assn. Bar City NY (com. on estate and gift taxation, com. on NY state legislation), Yale Club, St. Andrews Soc. State of NY (bd. mgrs. 2003-04). Republican. Presbyterian. Office: Patton Eakins Lipsett Holbrook & Savage 420 Lexington Ave New York NY 10170-0002 E-mail: wmeakins@rcn.com.

EAKLE, ARLENE HASLAM, genealogist; b. Salt Lake City, July 19, 1936; d. Thomas E. and Margaret Haslam; m. Alma D. Eakle, Jr., Feb. 8, 1957; children: JoAnn, Richard, Linda, John. ADN, Weber State U.; MA in English history, PhD of English history, U. Utah. Author: (with Linda Brinkerhoff) Genealogy in Scotland: Jurisdictional Approach, 2004, Family History for Fun and Profit-The Genealogy Research Process, 30th anniversary edit., 2003, Genealogy in Land Records, 1998, Migration Patterns of American Families, 1999, (with Johni Cerny) The Source: A Guidebook for American Genealogy, 1984, Ancestry's Guide to Research, 1985; editor: Research News, Immigration Digest; editor: Virginia Notebooks, N.Y. Rsch. Fellow Utah Geneal. Assn., 1987; recipient Award of Merit Fedn. Geneal. Soc., 1984, Julian Bickersteth medal Inst. Heraldic and Geneal. Studies, Eng., 1988, Gold and VIP awards Kennedy Inner Cir., 2002-05. Mem. Am. Family Records Assn. (bd. dirs. 1990-2004), Assn. Profl. Genealogists (pres. 1980-82, Grahame Thomas Smallwood Jr. Award of Merit 1984), Md. Geneal. Soc., West Fla. Geneal. Soc. Office: Genealogical Inst 56 W Main St PO Box 129 Tremonton UT 84337-0129 Office Phone: 800-377-6058. Business E-Mail: genealogy@utahlinx.com.

EALY, CYNTHIA PIKE, artist, real estate agent; b. Eveleth, Minn., Apr. 13, 1932; d. Robert Sheldon Pike and Lila Mary Saari; m. Donald Rae Ealy, Dec. 14, 1952; children: Elizabeth, Dennis, Jonathan, Richard. Student, Coll. of Ams., Mexico City, 1950-52, U. So. Calif., 1952-53. Actress, Mexico City, 1950-52; owner Woodland World Travel, Tarzana, Calif., 1965-70; decorator Ridgewood, N.J., 1970-71; artist, 1972—; realtor, 1987—. Bd. dirs., pres. Rep. Women's club, Woodland Hills, Calif., 1964-69; active Internat. Sch. of Brussels, 1975-80; co-chmn. Reps. Abroad, Europe, 1978-82. Recipient Outstanding Svc. award Am. Women's Club of Brussels, 1984. Mem. Sierra Artists Network, Niguel Art Assn. of Orange County. Avocation: instructing french language and cuisine. also: 27142 Paseo Del Este San Juan Capistrano CA 92675-4927

EALY, JONATHAN BRUCE, lawyer; b. L.A., Apr. 20, 1960; s. Donald Rae and Cynthia Howland (Pike) E. AB cum laude, Harvard U., 1982; JD, Duke U., 1985. Bar: Alaska 1986, U.S. Ct. Appeals (9th cir.) 1986. Clk. judge Karen Hunt Alaska Superior Ct., Anchorage, 1985-86; assoc. Taylor & Hintz, Anchorage, 1986-89, Heller, Ehrman, White & McAuliffe, Anchorage, 1989-93; gen. counsel Borisovich Internat., Inc., Anchorage, 1993—; of counsel Partnow, Sharrock & Tindall, Anchorage, 1995-2000; spl. counsel Heller Ehrman White and McAuliffe, Anchorage, 2000—03, Tindall Bennett & Shoup, Anchorage, 2003—. Bd. dirs. Borealis Brewing Co.; prin. Na'au, Inc., 1998—. Author: Third Story, 1998, What, If Anything, Is an E-mail, 2002. Pres. Anchorage Youth Ct., 1993-94, legal advisor, 1989-92; bd. dirs. Kids Voting Alaska, Anchorage, 1993, Alzheimer's Disease Resource Agy. of Alaska, 2003—, v.p., 2004— Mem. Anchorage Bar Assn. (pres. 1994, v.p. 1993, pres. young lawyers sect. 1988-90). Office: 508 W 2d Ave 3d Fl Anchorage AK 99501

EARHART, EILEEN MAGIE, retired child and family life educator; b. Hamilton, Ohio, Oct. 21, 1928; d. Andrew J. and Martha (Waldorf) Magie; m. Paul G. Earhart; children: Anthony G., Bruce P., Daniel T. BS, Miami U., Oxford, Ohio, 1950; MA in Adminstrn. and Ednl. Services, Mich. State U., 1962, PhD in Edn., 1969; H.H.D. (hon.), Miami U., Oxford, Ohio, 1980. Tchr. home econs. W. Alexandria (Ohio) Schs., 1950-51; elementary tchr. Waterford Twp. Schs., Pontiac, Mich., 1958-65, reading specialist, 1965-67; prof., chmn. family and child ecology dept. Mich. State U., East Lansing, 1968-84; prof., head dept. home and family life Fla. State U., Tallahassee, 1984-89; ret., 1989. Author: Attention and Classification Training Curriculum; co-editor spl. issue of Family Relations, 1984; contbr. chpts. to profl. jours., books. Mem. adv. bd. Lansing Com. on Children's TV, Family/Sch./Cmty. Partnership Project, Tallahassee; bd. dirs. Women's Resource Ctr., Grand Rapids, Mich., Wesley Found., Fla. State U., 1989-99; mem. campus ministries bd. Fla. A&M U., 1995-98; Sunday sch. tchr. Haines City United Meth. Ch., 2001--; mem. Mich. Gov.'s Task Force on Youth. Mem. Nat. Coun. Family Rels. (pres. Assn. of Couns. 1987-88, bd. dirs. 1986-88, chair nat. meeting local arrangements 1992), Fla. Coun. Family Rels. (pres. elect 1985-86, pres. 1986-87), Nat. Assn. Edn. Young Children, Assn. Childhood Edn. Internat., Am. Home Econs. Assn. (named AHEA leader at 75th Ann. of Assn. 1984), Internat. Fedn. Home Econs., Mich. Home Econs. Assn. (pres. 1980-82), Fla. Home Econs. Assn. (chmn. scholarship com. 1986-88, dist. chmn. 1990-91, chmn. nominating com. 1991-92, co-chair ann. meeting 1995), Ednl. Rsch. Assn., Killearn United Meth. Ch., United Meth. Women (cir. chair 1993-97, pres. 1994), Phi Kappa Phi (pres. Fla State U. chpt. 1988-89), Delta Kappa Gamma, Omicron Nu, others. Home (Summer): 22 Oak Tree Ct Franklin NC 28734 Home: 2973 Chickasaw Dr Haines City FL 33844-8419 E-mail: emearhart@aol.com.

EARL, ANTHONY SCULLY, retired governor, lawyer; b. Lansing, Mich., Apr. 12, 1936; s. Russell K. and Ethlynne Julia (Scully) E.; children: Julia, Anne, Mary, Catherine. BS, Mich. State U.; JD, U. Chgo. Bar: Wis., Minn. Asst. dist. atty. Marathon County, Wausau, Wis., 1965-66; city atty. City of Wausau, 1966-69; mem. Wis. Assembly, Madison, 1969-74; mem. firm Crooks, Low & Earl, 1969-74; sec. Wis. Dept. Adminstrn., Madison, 1974-75, Dept. Nat. Resources, Madison, 1975-80; v.p. firm Foley & Lardner, Madison, 1980-82; gov. State of Wis., Madison, 1983-87; ptnr. Quarles and Brady, Madison, 1987—. Served as lt. USN, 1962-65. Democrat. Roman Catholic. Office: Quarles & Brady 1 S Pinckney St PO Box 2113 Madison WI 53701-2113 also: 360 W Washington Ave Unit 1007 Madison WI 53703-2766 Office Phone: 608-283-2471. Business E-Mail: ase@quarlet.com.

EARL, CHRISTOPHER D., health products executive; BA in Biology, U. Pa.; PhD in Cellular and Developmental Biology, Harvard U. Gen. ptnr. Plant Resources Venture Funds; pres., CEO Avitech Diagnostics, Inc.; mng. dir. Perseus-Soros Biopharm. Fund, LP; chmn. bd. GeneFormatics, Inc. Mem. Com. for Econ. Devel.; trustee The Nutre Conservancy of Pa. Address: Perseus-Soros Biopharm Fund 29th Fl 888 7th Ave New York NY 10106 Office: 10929 Technology PL San Diego CA 92127-1811

EARL, LEWIS HAROLD, economist, consultant, lawyer; b. Guthrie, Tex., Dec. 17, 1918; s. Henry W. and Ruth (O'Neal) E.; m. Patricia Miller, Mar. 5, 1943 (dec. 1973); children: William Lee, Patricia Lewise, Robert Charles, James Michael; m. Meade Randolph Loomis, July 1, 1977 (div. 1979); m. Maxine Durrett Marks, Jan. 31, 1981. BA, Tex. Technol. Coll., 1939; student, U. Tex., 1939-40, Am. U., 1941-42, George Washington U., 1942-62; JD, Georgetown U., 1950. Bar: D.C. 1950, U.S. Supreme Ct. 1972, Tex. 1983. With Bur. Labor Stats., Dept. Labor, 1940-42, 46-51; industry, commodity economist NPA Dept. Commerce, 1951-53; productivity specialist, economist, program analyst, asst. program officer U.S. Tech. Cooperation Program in Brazil, 1953—57; program officer U.S. Ops. Missions in Argentina and El Salvador, 1957—61; internat. rels. officer U.S. AID, Washington, 1961-63; chief internat. rsch. Office of Manpower Automation and Tng., U.S. Dept. Labor, Washington, 1963-65; chief fgn. manpower program staff Office Manpower Policy, Evaluation and Rsch., Dept. Labor, 1965-70; U.S. del. 8th meeting Am. mem. states ILO, Ottawa, Canada, 1966, U.S. del. to chem. industries com. Geneva, 1969; tech. dir. Seminar for Ministry Labor Tng. Coordinators, OAS, Mexico City, 1970; asst. dir. for program devel. Ctr. for Human Resources U. Houston, 1970-75; manpower planning officer Gulf Coast CAMPS Secretariat, Mayor's Office, City of Houston, 1970-74; cons. Tex. Gov.'s Office Policy Coordination, Austin, 1974; asso. dir. human resources program, instr. econs. U. Mo.-Columbia, 1975-78; expert cons. Human Resources Devel., Bur. Internat. Labor Affairs, U.S. Dept. Labor and UN Devel. Program for Egypt, 1978-80; staff adv. Am. Productivity Center, Houston, 1980. Expert cons. UN Indsl. Devel. Orgn., Cairo, Egypt, 1981; lectr. Coll. Bus. Adminstrn. Tex. Tech U., 1982-83; mgr. Post C. of C., 1984-87. Sec.-treas. Post Econ. Devel. Corp., 1984-90; bd. dirs. Tex.

Common Cause, 1987—, legis. liaison, 1991, 93; mem. Lubbock-Garza County Pvt. Industry Coun., 1986-92, Friends of the Libr., Tex. Tech. U., Tex. Indsl. Devel. Coun.; chmn. Garza County Dem. Com., 1986-87, 91—; bd. dirs. Tex. Alliance for Edn. and the Arts, 1991-97, Maxine Durrett Earl Charitable Found., 1994—; founder Lewis and Maxine Earl Survey Rsch. Lab., Tex. Tech U., 2001; del. Dem. Nat. Conv., Chgo., 1996. With USNR, 1942—46, lt. comdr. ret. USNR. Mem. ASTD, VFW, South Plain Assn. Govt. (vol. ombudsman), Am. Statis. Assn., Am. Acad. Polit. and Social Ssis., Acad. Polit. Sci., Tex. Hist. Assn., Houston Pers. Assn., South Plains Cmty. Action Assn., Soc. Internat. Devel., Nat. Planning Assn., Indsl. Rels. Rsch. Assn., Nat. Economist Club, Caprock Fin. (capital fin. com.), Garza County Trail Blazers (pres. 1994-97), Rotary, Lions (pres. 1996-97, 2001-02), Alpha Chi, Omicron Delta Epsilon, Pi Sigma Alpha, Sigma Iota Epsilon. Methodist. Home: 1929 Stoney Brook Houston TX 77063-1809 Office: PO Box 580 Post TX 79356-0580 E-mail: 1hearl@arh.net. *I believe that individuals will make the right decisions if they have full and adequate information and facts, and therefore, I have sought to find the truth that will make men free.*

EARL, MARTHA FRANCES, librarian, researcher; b. Washington, Aug. 18, 1956; d. Jefferson Davis Earl, Ruby Smith; m. Walter Robert Gawryla; 1 child, Frank Gawryla; m. Stephen Jack Cobert (div. Aug. 6, 1984). BS, U. Tenn., 1978, MS in Libr. Sci., 1985. Cert. seconary edn. Sci. tchr. First Assembly Christian Sch., Memphis, 1979—80; libr. clk. Memphis State U., 1980—81; sr. libr. asst. U. Tenn., Knoxville, 1981—87; reference libr. Meharry Med. Coll., Nashville, 1987—90; head of reference East Tenn. State U., Coll. Medicine Libr., Johnson City, Tenn., 1990—97; reference coord. U. Tenn. Grad. Sch. Med., Knoxville, 1997—. Cons. Indian Path Hosp., Kingsport, 1990—94, N.E. Tenn. Rehab. Hosp., Johnson City, 1992—97, Morristown Hamblen Hosp., 1993—97, N.E. Tenn. Area Health Edn. Ctr., Greeneville, 1994—98, East Tenn. State U., Johnson City, 2001—; mem. adv. bd. Tenn. Adv. Coun. on Librs., Nashville, 1998—99. Author: (book) Bibkit #9: Managed Care: A Guide to Information Sources, 2000; contbr. chapters to books, revs. to publs., articles to profl. jours. Organizer Tenn. Libr. Legislative Day, 1999—2001; historian Alpha Phi Omega Svc. Fraternity, Knoxville, 1976—78; comm. team Ebenezer United Meth. Ch., Knoxville, 1998—2001; libr. First United Meth. Ch., Bristol, 1994—97, Holston Chapel United Meth. Ch., Knoxville, 1973—78, Sunday sch. tchr., 1972—78. Grantee Grateful Med. Outreach grant, Nat. Libr. Medicine, 1990—92, Exhibit grant, Nat. Network Librs. Medicine, 1994, 1996, 2003—05, Internet Tng. grant, Nat. Libr. Medicine, 1997—98, Access to Electronic Info. for the Pub. grant, NIH, 2001—02, Physicians Med. Edn. Resource Fund, 2001—04; scholar Nat. Alumni scholar, U. Tenn. Nat. Alumni Found., 1974—78, Roddy Mfg., 1974, 1978. Mem.: ALA (chpt. rels. coun. 1998—99), LMS (task force chpt. level programming 2004—05), Med. Libr. Assn. (Brodman com. for excellence in acad. health scis. libr. 1995—97, So. chpt. rsch. com. chair 1997—98, So. chpt. sec. 1999—2000, program com. leadership and mgmt. sect. 2000—01, R&D and demonstration project jury chair 2000—01, Kronick jury chair 2001—02, So. chpt. comm. com. 2001—05, Rsch. award South Ctrl. chpt. 2001, 2004, Chpt. award 2004—05), Assn. Coll. and Rsch. Librs. (state affiliate chair 1995—96), Knoxville Area Health Scis. Librs. Consortium (pres. 2001—02), East Tenn. Libr. Assn. (pres. 2003—), Tenn. Adv. Coun. on Librs. (electronic libr. subcom. 1998—99), Tenn. Health Scis. Librs. Assn. (membership chair 1998—2000), Tri-Cities Health Scis. Librs. Consortium (chair 1994), Tenn. Libr. Assn. (coll. and univ. librs. sect. chair 1996—97, libr. editl. rev. bd. 1996—2000, pres. 1998—99, conf. com. program chair 1998—2000, assoc. pres. 1999, ad hoc com. on staffing 2000—01, chair strategic planning 2000—03, publs. bd. chair 2003—, Appreciation award 1999, 2002, Centennial award 2002), Tennshare (chmn. long range planning 2002—, TELII steering com. 2002—04), U. Tenn. Sch. Info. Sci. Alumni Bd. (mentoring subcom. and mem.-at-large 2001—03), Pi Lambda Theta, Gamma Beta Phi. Methodist. Avocations: reading, walking, swimming, movies, travel. Office: Univ Tenn Grad Sch Medicine 1924 Alcoa Hwy Knoxville TN 37920 Office Phone: 865-544-9525. Office Fax: 865-544-9527. Personal E-mail: earlmartha@yahoo.com. Business E-Mail: mearl@utk.edu.

EARL, SISTER PATRICIA HELENE, religious school administrator, educator, consultant; b. Cleve. d. Warren and Helen McLauglin Earl. BA, Dunbarton Coll. of Holy Cross, Washington, D.C., 1970; MA, Villanova Univ., Villanova, Pa., 1980; PhD, George Mason Univ., Fairfax, Va., 2003. Cert. Advanced Catehist Diocese of Arlington, basic in Catehetics Notre Dame Inst., Arlington, Va.; lic. Supr. Commonwealth of Va., profl. elem. prin., sec. prin., elem. grades pk-8, English7-12 Commonwealth of Va., Instrl. II Pa. Mem. religious cmty. Sisters, Servants of the Immaculate Heart of Mary, Immaculata, Pa., 1974—; dir. religious edn. Our Lady of Lourdes Parish, Arlington, Va., 1983—85; elem. religion, English tchr. Archdiocese of Phila., Diocese of Arlington, Diocese of Allentown, Pa.; asst. supt. of schs. Diocese of Arlington, Arlington, Va., 1990—2003; asst. prof., dir. Cath. sch. leadership program Marymount Univ., Arlington, Va., 2003—. Mem. prin. search com. Diocese of Arlington, 1990—2003; mem. Arlington Diocesan Sch. Bd., 1990—2003, Notre Dame Acad. Sch. Bd., Middleburg, Va., 1990—2003; dir. Cath. Diocesan partnership adv. bd. Marymount Univ., Arlington, 2004—; mem. vis. team-rep. of Va. dept Edn. Mary Washington Coll., Fredericksburg, Va., 2005; speaker in field. Reader for the Prin. of the Yr. award Pvt. Sch. Divsn., Washington Metropolitan area, 1999, 2002. Mem.: Nat. Cath. Edn. Assn., Assn. for Supervision and Curriculm Devel., Nat. Assn. of Secondary Sch. Prin., Nat. Assn. of Elem. Sch. Prin. Roman Cath. Avocations: piano, guitar, reading, writing. Home: 101 N Spring St Falls Church VA 22046 Office: Marymount Univ 2807 N Globe Rd Arlington VA 22207 Office Phone: 703-284-1517. Office Fax: 703-284-1631. Business E-Mail: patricia.earl@marymount.edu.

EARLE, ARTHUR PERCIVAL, textiles executive, airport executive; b. Montreal, Que., Can., Apr. 23, 1922; s. Arthur Percival and Bernadette (Gosselin) E.; m. Muriel Elizabeth Vining, June 1, 1946; children: Arthur Percival, Richard John, Janet Elizabeth. BEE, McGill U., Montreal, 1949; MMP, Harvard U., 1957. Registered profl. engr., Que., Ont. With Shawinigan Water & Power Co., 1949-63, asst. mgr. prodn. and plant; with Dominion Textile Inc., Montreal, 1963-90, chief engr., then group v.p. subs., 1970-78, sr. v.p. ops. svcs., 1978-87, sr. v.p., 1987-88, cons. corp. affairs, 1988-90. Bd. dirs. Stella Jones Inc., chmn., 1993; bd. dirs. Shermag Inc.; past pres. Lana Knit Ltd., Fireside Fabrics Ltd., Fiber-World Ltd., Elpee Yarns Ltd., Jaro Ltd., Esmond Mills Ltd., 1972-78; past chmn. Pemans Ltd., 1972-78, Foresbec Inc., 1989-91; chmn. Aeroport de Montreal, 1989-96, bd. dirs., 1989-96, pres., 1989-90. Bd. dirs. Ecole de Technologie Superieure, U. Que., 1978-85, mem. exec. com., 1981-85; pres. Montreal Bd. Trade, 1980-81, chmn. bd. dirs., 1981-82; pres., exec. com. Phoenix Found., 1985-89; bd. dirs. Lakeshore Gen. Hosp., Pointe Claire, Que., 1987-94, vice chmn., 1989-94; chmn., Les Mercuriades Bus. Awards, 1985; chmn., bd. dirs. Aeroport De Montreal, 1989-96, pres., 1989-90; founding chmn. Can. Airports Coun., 1990-93, bd. dirs., 1990-96; chmn., pres. La Societe De Promotion Des Aeroport De Montrèal, 1987-96; hon. chmn. bd. Phoenix Ctr., 1991-96; bd. dirs. Griffith McConnell Residence, 1997-2005, first hon. dir., 2005. Pilot RCAF, 1941-45. Named to Order of Can., 1996; recipient Award of Distinction, Concordia U., 1989, 125th Anniversary Can. Commemorative medal, 1992, Queen Elizabeth Jubilee medal, 2002. Fellow Engring. Inst. Can. (hon. treas. 1986-88, sr. v.p. 1988-89, pres. 1989-90); mem. IEEE (past sect. chmn.), Am. Textile Managerial Engring. Soc., Que. C. of C. (pres. 1983-84, chmn., 1984-85), Royal Montreal Golf Club. Anglican. E-mail: apearle@sympatico.ca.

EARLE, CLIFFORD JOHN, JR., mathematician; b. Racine, Wis., Nov. 3, 1935; s. Clifford John and Anne Elizabeth (Griffith) E.; m. Elizabeth Joan Deutsch, Dec. 27, 1960; children— Rebecca Ann, Susan Deborah. BA, Swarthmore Coll., 1957; MA, Harvard U., 1958, PhD, 1962. Instr. Harvard U., 1962-63, vis. lectr., 1968-69; mem. Inst. for Advanced Study, Princeton, N.J., 1963-65, 81; asst. prof. Cornell U., Ithaca, N.Y., 1965-66, assoc. prof., 1966-69, prof., 1969—2004, prof. emeritus, 2005—, chmn. dept. math., 1976-79; vis. prof. U. Warwick, 1967; vis. lectr. Inst. Mittag-Leffler, 1972. Mem. geometric function theory program, Math. Scis. Rsch. Inst., Berkeley, Calif., 1986; hon. prof. U. Warwick, 1999—. Assoc. editor Duke Math. Jour., 1973-79; contbr. articles to math. rsch. jours. John Simon Guggenheim Meml. fellow, 1974-75 Mem. Am. Math. Soc. (editor Proc. 1989-97, mng. editor 1997-2001). Home: 314 Elmwood Ave Ithaca NY 14850-4812 Office: Cornell U Dept Math Ithaca NY 14853-4201 Business E-Mail: cliff@math.cornell.edu.

EARLE, EUGENIA, music educator; b. Birmingham, Ala., May 2, 1922; d. Paul Hamilton Earle and Rosa Munger; m. Jere Butler Faison, Nov. 26, 1969 (dec.). BA, Birmingham So. Coll., 1943; MA, Columbia U., 1956, PhD, 1979. Instr. Mannes Coll. Music, N.Y.C., 1946—63, Union Theol. Sem. Sch. Sacred Music, N.Y.C., 1963—73, Manhattan Sch. Music, N.Y.C., 1963—73; adj. assoc. prof. Columbia U. Tchrs. Coll., N.Y.C., 1969—. Harpsichordist concerts throughout U.S. Composer: Conversation Pieces, 1972, 18th Century Dances: How to Add Melodic Ornamentation, 1973. Mem.: Coll. Music Soc., Am. Bach Soc., Am. Musicol. Soc. Democrat. Presbyterian. Avocations: hiking, attending concerts, theater. Home: 15 W 84st (9D) New York NY 10024

EARLE, JEAN BUIST, finance company executive, computer company executive; b. Newton, N.J., Oct. 5, 1951; d. Richardson and Jean (Mackerly) Buist; m. Terry Dean Earle, Mar. 4, 1989; children: Morgan, Abigail. AB, Cornell U., 1973; MEd, Coll. William and Mary, 1974; MBA, U. Pa., 1987. Mgr. The Korman Corp., Jenkintown, Pa., 1975-77; v.p. ops. Community Assn. Mgmt. Co., Havertown, Pa., 1977-78; adminstrv. asst. Albert Einstein Med. Ctr., Phila., 1978-83; assoc. adminstr. Meml. Hosp. Burlington County, Mt. Holly, NJ, 1983-87; v.p. Overlook Hosp., Summit, NJ, 1987-95; exec. dir. Summit (N.J.) Child Care Ctrs., Inc., 1995-96; owner, ptnr. Computer Edn. Inst., Chatham, NJ, 1996—; CFO ECLC of N.J., Chatham, 1998—. Past pres. Family Link of Union and Essex Counties, 1994—96; chmn. Kirby Ctr. YMCA Family Coun., 1996—98. Fellow Am. Coll. Healthcare Execs; mem. AICPA, Am. Hosp. Assn., U. Pa. Wharton Sch. Alumni Assn., Cornell Club, Ctr. for Enabling Tech. (trustee 1997-2004, treas. 1999-2004). Home: 37 Rose Ter Chatham NJ 07928-1826 Office: ECLC NJ 21 Lum Ave Chatham NJ 07928 Office Phone: 973-635-1705. E-mail: jbearle@hotmail.com.

EARLE, SYLVIA ALICE, research biologist, oceanographer; b. Gibbstown, N.J., Aug. 30, 1935; d. Lewis Reade and Alice Freas (Richie) E. BS, Fla. State U., 1955; MA, Duke U., 1956, PhD, 1966, PhD (hon.), 1993, Monterey Inst. Internat. Studies, 1990, Ball State U., 1991, George Washington U., 1992, U. R.I., 1996, Plymouth State Coll., 1996; DSc (hon.), Ripon Coll., 1994, U. Conn., 1994. Resident dir. Cape Haze Marine Lab., Sarasota, Fla., 1966-67; research scholar Radcliffe Inst., 1967-69; research fellow Farlow Herbarium, Harvard U., 1967-75, researcher, 1975—; research assoc. in botany Natural History Mus. Los Angeles County, 1970-75; research biologist, curator Calif. Acad. Scis., San Francisco, from 1976; research assoc. U. Calif., Berkeley, 1969-75; fellow in botany Natural History Mus., 1989—; chief scientist U.S. NOAA, Washington, 1990-92, advisor to the adminstr., 1992-93; founder, pres., CEO, bd. dirs. Deep Ocean Engrs., Inc., Oakland, Calif., 1981-90; founder, chmn., CEO Deep Ocean Exploration and Rsch., Oakland, 1992—, bd. dirs., 1992—; advisor SeaWeb, 1996—. Bd. dirs. Dresser Industries, Oryx Energy, Inc.; explorer-in-residence Nat. Geog., 1998; dir., Natl. Geographic Suatainable Seas Expedition, 1998—. Author: Exploring the Deep Frontier, 1980, Sea Change, 1995; editor: Scientific Results of the Tektite II Project, 1972-75; contbr. 100 articles to profl. jours. Trustee World Wildlife Fund U.S., 1976-82, mem. coun., 1984—; trustee World Wildlife Fund Internat., 1979-81, mem. coun., 1981-95; trustee Charles A. Lindbergh Fund, pres., 1990-95; trustee Ctr. Marine Conservation, 1992—, Perry Found., chmn., 1993-95; mem. coun. Internat. Union for Conservation of Nature, 1979-81; corp. mem. Woods Hole Oceanographic Inst., trustee, 1996—; mem. Nat. Adv. Com. on Oceans and Atmosphere, 1980-94. Recipient Conservation Svc. award U.S. Dept. Interior, 1970, Boston Sea Rovers award, 1972, 79, Nogi award Underwater Soc. Am., 1976, Conservation Svc. award Calif. Acad. Sci., 1979, Order of Golden Ark Prince Netherlands, 1980, David B. Stone medal New Eng. Aquarium, 1989, Gold medal Soc. Women Geographers, medal Radcliffe Coll., 1990, Pacon Internat. award, 1992, Dirs. award Natural Resources Coun. Am., 1992, Washburn award Boston Mus. Sci., 1995, Charles A. and Ann Morrow Lindbergh award, 1996, Julius Stratton Leadership award, 1997, Kilby award, 1997, Bal de la Mar Found. Sea Keeper award, 1997, Sea Space Environment award, 1997; Environmental Global Zoo Awd., 1998; U.S. Environmental Hew Awd., 1998; named Woman of Yr. L.A. Times, 1970, Scientist of Yr., Calif. Mus. Sci. and Industry, 1981. National Women's Hall of Fame, 2000. Fellow AAAS, Marine Tech. Soc. (Compass award 1997), Calif. Acad. Scis., Calif. Acad. Sci., Explorers Club (hon., bd. dirs. 1989-94, Lowell Thomas award 1980, Explorers medal 1996); mem. Internat. Phycological Soc. (sec. 1974-80), Phycological Soc. Am., Am. Soc. Ichthyologists and Herpetologists, Am. Inst. Biol. Scis., Brit. Phycological Soc., Ecol. Soc. Am., Internat. Soc. Plant Taxonomists. Planted a flag in the seafloor off Hawaii to mark the first solo dive to 1,250 feet without a support vessel, wearing hardened diving suit "JIM"; Set and still holds the depth record for women's solo dive:3,300 feet; designed a manned sub capable of diving to 36,000 feet; lived for two weeks underwater with an all-female crew to test the effects of prolonged subsea habitation. Home and Office: 12812 Skyline Blvd Oakland CA 94619-3125

EARLE, TIMOTHY KEESE, anthropology educator; b. New Bedford, Mass., Aug. 10, 1946; s. Osborne and Eleanor (Clark) E.; m. Eliza Howe, June 14, 1969; children: Caroline, Hester. BA summa cum laude, Harvard U., 1969; MA, U. Mich., 1971, PhD, 1973. Rsch. archaeologist Bishop Mus., Honolulu, 1971-72; prof. anthropology UCLA, 1973-95, dir. Inst. of Archaeology, 1987-92; prof. anthropology Northwestern U., Evanston, Ill., 1995—, chair dept., 1995-2000. Author: Bronze Age Economics, 2002, How Chiefs Come to Power, 1997; co-author: Evolution of Human Society, 1987, 2nd edit., 2000; editor: Exchange Systems in Prehistory, 1977, Contexts for Prehistoric Exchange, 1982, Chiefdoms, 1991. Mem.: Soc. Econ. Anthrop., Soc. Am. Archaeology, Am. Anthrop. Assn. (pres. archaeology divsn. 1995—97, exec. bd. 1999—2002), Phi Beta Kappa. E-mail: tke299@northwestern.edu.

EARLE, VICTOR MONTAGNE, III, lawyer; b. NYC, June 13, 1933; s. Victor Montagne and Marian Jeanette (Litonius) E.; m. Lois MacKennan, Dec. 28, 1955 (div. Jan. 1980); children: Jane Stewart, Susan Elizabeth, Anne McCallum; m. Karen Peterson Howard, Aug. 24, 1985. AB, Williams Coll., 1954; LLB, Columbia U., 1959. Bar: NY 1960, US Supreme Ct. 1963. Law clk. to Hon. Leonard Moore, US Ct. Appeals (2nd cir.), 1959-60; assoc. Cravath, Swaine & Moore, NYC, 1960-68; gen. counsel KPMG, NYC, 1968-86, Peat, Marwick Internat., 1978-86; ptnr. Cahill, Gordon & Reindel, NYC, 1986-89; sr. v.p., gen. counsel Minet, NYC, 1989-93; gen. counsel KWELM Co. and KWELM Holdings, London, 1993—98, KWELM Co. and KWELM Holdings Ltd., NYC, 1993-98, sr. counsel, 1998-2000; of counsel O'Melveny & Myers, NYC, 2000—. Lectr. constl. and corp. law issues, U.S. and abroad. Contbr. articles to profl. jour. and popular mag. With US Army, 1954-56. Recipient Constitutional Law prize Columbia U. Assn. of Bar of City of NY (judiciary com. 1983-86), Am. Law Inst. (life), Legal Aid Soc. (bd. dir. 1980-86), Fund for Modern Ct. (bd. dir.), Columbia U. Alumni Assn. (bd. dir. 1982-87). Office: O'Melveny & Myers Times Sq Tower 7 Times Sq New York NY 10036 E-mail: vearle@omm.com.

EARLEY, ANTHONY F., JR., utilities executive; BS in Physics, MS in Engring, JD, U. Notre Dame. Ptnr. Hunton & Williams; exec. v.p., gen. counsel L.I. Lighting Co., 1985—89, pres., COO, 1989—94, Detroit Edison (now DTE Energy), Detroit, 1994—2000, chmn., CEO, 2001—. Bd. dirs. Mut. Am. Capital Mgmt. Corp., Comerica Bank, Henry Ford Health Sys. Mem. adv. coun. Coll. Engring. U. Notre Dame; mem. bd. coun. Loyola H.S.; exec. bd. Cornerstone Schs.; bd. dirs. Detroit Renaissance, New Detroit, United Way Cmty. Svcs. Officer USN. Office: 2000 2d Ave Detroit MI 48226-1279*

EARLEY, LAURENCE ELLIOTT, retired medical educator; b. Ahoskie, N.C., Jan. 23, 1931; s. Frank Claxton and Eleanor (Dilday) Earley; m. Joanne Frances Sinclair, Sept. 5, 1953; children: Laurence Elliott Earley Jr., Peter Hunter Earley. BS, U. N.C., 1953, MD, 1956; MA (hon.), U. Pa., 1978. Diplomate Am. Bd. Internal Medicine . Asst. prof. Harvard Med. Sch., Boston, 1967—68; assoc. prof. U. Calif. Sch. Medicine, San Francisco, 1968—69, prof., 1969—73, chief of nephrology, 1968—73; prof., chmn. dept. medicine U. Tex. Health Sci. Ctr., San Antonio, 1973—77; chmn. dept. medicine, Frank Wister Thomas Prof. U. Pa., Phila., 1977—90, chmn. dept. phys. medicine & rehab., 1987—90, Francis C. Wood prof., 1983—95, sr. assoc. dean., 1992—95; clin. prof. medicine U. N.C., Chapel Hill, 1995—2000; ret., 2001. Study sect. NIH, Bethesda, Md., 1969—77; chmn. Am. Bd. Internal Medicine, 1987—88. Editor: Diseases of The Kidney; contbr. articles to profl. jours. Chmn. sci. adv. bd. Nat. Kidney Found., N.Y.C., 1973—74. Sr. asst. surgeon USPHS, 1959—61. Recipient Kaiser award, U. Calif., 1972, Disting. Svc. award, U. N.C., 1976. Master: ACP; mem.: Assn. Am. Physicians (pres. 1988—89), Inst. Medicine, Am. Soc. Nephrology (pres. 1977—78), Am. Soc. for Clin. Investigation (pres. 1975—76), Assn. Profs. Medicine (pres. 1983—84), Alpha Omega Alpha, Phi Beta Kappa. Achievements include research in kidney disease, physiology. Avocations: photography, woodwork. Home: 10 Gevrey Arbordeau Devon PA 19333 Personal E-mail: jseleech@aol.com.

EARLL, JERRY MILLER, internist, educator, endocrinologist; b. Hawarden, Iowa, Aug. 15, 1928; s. Harry Ezra and Magdalene Anna (Miller) E.; m. Faith Anne Allbaugh, Sept. 14, 1956; children: Leslie Anne, Nikki Lee, Holly Magdalene. BS, U. Nebr., 1950; MD, U. Iowa, 1958; postgrad., U. Calif., 1965-66. Diplomate Am. Bd. Internal Medicine, Am. Bd. Endocrinology, Am. Bd. Nuc. Medicine, Am. Bd. Geriat. Commd. 2d lt. U.S. Army, 1951, advanced through grades to col., 1972; intern Letterman Gen. Hosp., San Francisco, 1958, resident in internal medicine, 1959-62; chief endocrinology and metabolism William Beaumont Gen. Hosp., El Paso, 1963-65, Tripler Gen. Hosp., Honolulu, 1965-69, Walter Reed Army Inst. Rsch. and Walter Reed Army Hosp., Washington, 1969-76; chief dept. medicine Walter Reed Army Hosp., 1976-79; cons. endocrinology Office Surgeon Gen.; assoc. prof. medicine U. Hawaii, 1967—69; clin. prof. medicine Georgetown U., Washington, 1976—79, prof., 1979—, chief divsn. internal medicine, 1979—94, dir. geriatrics svc. dept. medicine, 1993—2000; prof. medicine, vice chmn. dept. medicine Uniformed Svcs. U. Health Scis., Washington, 1977-79; med. dir. to v.p. med. affairs Washington Home, 1996, 97—. Decorated Legion of Merit, Army Commendation medal, Meritorious Service medal. Fellow ACP (regional laureate); mem. Am. Med. Dirs. Assn., Endocrine Soc., Am. Geriatric Soc. (Clinician of Yr. 2002, 03), Assn. Mil. Surgeons, Acad. Medicine of Washington, Physicians for Nat. Health Program (spkr.). Achievements include research and publs. on pituitary and thyroid physiology. Home: 313 6200 Oregon Ave Washington DC 20015 Office: Georgetown U Hosp 3800 Reservoir Rd NW Washington DC 20007-2113 Office Phone: 202-895-0122. Business E-Mail: jearll@thewashingtonhome.org.

EARLS, KEVIN GERARD, insurance company executive; b. NYC, Mar. 24, 1952; s. Kevin Gerard and Geraldine Earls; m. Juliet Posner, Jan. 21, 1989; children: Tara, Sean. BS, Fordham U., 1974; MS, Columbia U., 1980. ChFC, CLU. Sales rep. Phoenix Home Life, N.Y.C., 1982-85, sales supr., 1985-87, asst. gen. mgr., 1987-90, assoc. gen. mgr., 1990-98; pres. Kevin G. Earls & Assocs., 1990-98; sr. v.p. fin. svcs. Hilb, Rogal & Hamilton Inc., N.Y.C., 1998—. Pres. HRH Securities Inc., 2000—. Contbg. author, illustrator: New Techniques in Rehabilitation, 1982. Mem. Nat. Assn. Life Underwriters, Am. Soc. Fin. Svcs. Profls., U.S. Judo Assn., U.S. Judo Fedn., Gen. Agts. and Mgrs. Assn. (bd. dirs. NYC), Am. Soc. Fin. Svc. Profls., U.S. Judo Inc., NY Athletic Club (judo chmn. 1991-01, bd. govs. 2001—, chmn. athletics 2001—). Avocations: Judo, art, reading. Office: Hilb Rogal & Hamilton Inc 1211 Ave of Americas Fl 27 New York NY 10036-8701 E-mail: earls@hrh.com.

EARLY, BERT HYLTON, lawyer, consultant; b. Kimball, W.Va., July 17, 1922; s. Robert Terry and Sue Keister (Hylton) E.; m. Elizabeth Henry, June 24, 1950; children— Bert Hylton, Robert Christian, Mark Randolph, Philip Henry, Peter St. Clair Student, Marshall U., 1940-42; AB, Duke U., 1946; JD, Harvard U., 1949. Bar: W.Va. 1949, Ill. 1963, Fla. 1981. Assoc. Fitzpatrick, Marshall, Huddleston & Bolen, Huntington, W.Va., 1949-57; asst. counsel Island Creek Coal Co., Huntington, W.Va., 1957-60, assoc. gen. counsel, 1960-62; dep. exec. dir. ABA, Chgo., 1962-64, exec. dir., 1964-81; sr. v.p. Wells Internat., Chgo., 1981-83, pres., 1983-85, Bert H. Early Assocs. Inc., Chgo., 1985-94, Early Cochran & Olson, Chgo., 1994-98, of counsel, 1999—2004. Dir. Am. Bar Found., Chgo., 1993-95; instr. Marshall U., Huntington, W.Va., 1950-53; legal search cons. and lectr. in field. Bd. dirs. Morris Meml. Hosp. for Crippled Children, 1954-60, Huntington Pub. Libr., 1951-60, W.Va. Tax Inst., 1961-62, Huntington Mus. Art, 1961-62; mem. W.Va. Jud. Coun., 1960-62, Huntington City Coun., 1961-62; bd. dirs. Cmty. Renewal Soc., Chgo., 1965-76, United Charities Chgo., 1972-80, Hinsdale (Ill.) Hosp. Found., 1987-93, Internat. Bar Assn. Found., 1987-89; bd. dirs. Am. Bar Endowment, 1983-95, sec., 1987-89, treas., 1989-91, v.p., 1991-93, pres., 1993-95, dir. emeritus, 1995-2000; mem. vis. com. U. Chgo. Law Sch., 1975-78; trustee Davis and Elkins Coll., 1960-63; mem. Hinsdale Plan Commn., 1982-85. 1st lt. AC, U.S. Army, 1943-45. Fellow Am. Bar Found., Ill. Bar Found. (charter); mem. ABA (ho. of dels. 1958-59, 84-93, chmn. young lawyers divsn. 1957-58, Disting. Svc. award young lawyers divsn. 1983), Am. Law Inst. (life), Internat. Bar Assn. (asst. sec. gen. 1967-82), Nat. Legal Aid and Defender Assn., Legal Aid Soc. Chgo., Am. Judicature Soc. (bd. dirs. 1981-84), Fla. Bar, W.Va. Bar Assn. Presbyterian.

EARLY, BONNIE JEAN, voice educator; b. Wahoo, Nebr., July 2, 1937; d. Edwin Nels and Emily Helen Sorenson; m. Valrey W. Early, Jr., Jan. 1, 1959; children: Valrey W. III, Cara Lynne. MusB, Princeton U., 1958; MusM, U. So. Miss., 1965. Choral dir. Robert E. Lee HS, Stauton, Va., 1959—60, Davidson HS, Mobile, Ala., 1960—64; instr. Mobile (Ala.) Coll., 1966—76; instr. voice U. So. Ala., Mobile, 1978—. Founder, condr. Mobile's Singing Children, 1977—2005; min. music Dauphin Way Meth. Ch., Mobile, 1967—90, Ctrl. Presbyn. Ch., Mobile, Spring Hill Presbyn. Ch., Mobile, 1990—2000; interim choir dir. Fairhope (Ala.) United Meth. Ch., 2004—. Mem.: Nat. Assn. Tchrs. Singing, Am. Choral Dirs. Assn. Avocations: embroidery, sewing, drawing. Office: U So Ala LPSC 1072 Mobile AL 36688-0001

EARLY, DELOREESE PATRICIA **See REESE, DELLA**

EARLY, JACK JONES, foundation executive; b. Corbin, Ky., Apr. 12, 1925; s. Joseph M. and Lela (Jones) E.; m. Nancye Bruce Whaley, June 1, 1952; children: Lela Katherine, Judith Ann, Laura Hattie. AB, Union Coll., Barbourville, Ky., 1948; MA, U. Ky., 1953, Ed.D. (So. scholar 1955-56), 1956; B.D., Coll. of Bible, Lexington, Ky., 1956; D.D., Wesley Coll., Grand Forks, N.D., 1961; LL.D., Parsons Coll., 1962, Iowa Wesleyan Coll., 1972; Litt.D., Dakota Wesleyan U., 1969; L.H.D., Union Coll., Barbourville, Ky., 1979; D.Adminstrn., Cumberland Coll., 1981. Ordained to ministry Methodist Ch., 1954; pastor Rockhold Circuit, Ky., 1943-44, Craig's Chapel and Laurel Circuit, London, Ky., 1944-47, Trinity Ch., Oak Ridge, summer 1945, Hindman Ch., Ky., 1947-52; dean of men Hindman Settlement Sch., 1948-51; assoc. pastor Park Ch., Lexington, Ky., 1952-54; asst. to pres., dean Athens Coll., Ala., 1954- 55; v.p., dean of coll. Iowa Wesleyan Coll., Mount Pleasant, 1956-58; pres. Dakota Wesleyan U., 1958-69, Pfeiffer Coll., Misenheimer, N.C., 1969-71; exec. dir. Am. Bankers Assn., Washington, 1971-73; pres. Limestone Coll., Gaffney, S.C., 1973-79; exec. dir. edn. Combined Ins. Co. Am., Chgo., 1979-82, v.p., exec. dir. edn. and communications, 1982-84; pres. Ky. Ind. Coll. Fund, Louisville, 1984-93, pres. emeritus, 1993—; dir. edn., con. Napoleon Hill Found., Northbrook, Ill., 1997—. Pres. W. Clement Stone PMA Communications, Inc., Chgo., 1987—. Active Boy Scouts Am.; mem. pres. adv. coun. North Pk. Coll.; mem. Felician adv. bd. Felician Coll.; mem. Ky. Ho. of Reps., 1952-54; bd. dirs. S.D. Found. Pvt. Colls., S.D. Meth. Found., Nat. Coun. on Youth Leadership, Ctr. for Citizenship Edn., YMCA, Motivational Inst., Mid-Am. chpt. ARC, 1980—, W. Clement and Jessie V. Stone Found., Northbrook Symphony Orch., Ky. Mountain Laurel Festival, 1990—, Internat. Coun. on Edn. for Teaching, 1990—; chmn. bd. Religious Heritage Am., 1989-92, Internat. Leadership Network, 1991—; Rep. nominee for Metro Mayor, Louisville, 2002. Recipient Spoke award Mitchell Jr. C. of C., 1959, Disting. Svc. award, 1960, Disting. Svc. award S.D. Jr. C. of C.,

1960, Gaffney Jaycees, 1979, Chief Iron Eyes Cody medal of Peace, 1987, Outstanding Kentuckian award O'Tucks, 1990; named Outstanding Former Kentuckian, 1963; hon. fellow Wroxton Coll., Oxfordshire, Eng.; named to Disting. Alumni Hall of Fame, U. Ky., 1965, Union Coll. Hall of Fame, 2000. Mem. Am. Soc. Assn. Execs., Louisville C. of C., Blue Key, Masons (33d degree, chaplain Valley of Louisville chpt. 1990—), Rotary (pres. Louisville 1992-93, dist. 6710 gov. 1996—), Ky. Soc. Sons of the Am. Revolution (pres. 1998—), Order of Founders and Patriots of Am. (gov. Ky. chpt. 2003—, dep. chaplain gen.), Soc. War of 1812 in the Commonwealth of Ky. (pres. 1997—), Huguenot Soc. of Ky. (pres. 1999—), Huguenot Soc.-Soc. of Manakin (Ky. br. pres. 1999—), Nat. Soc. Sons and Daus. of Pilgrims (gov. Ky. br. 2000—), Gen. for Pub. Rels.-Gen. Soc. of the War of 1812 (v.p. 1998—), Del. State Soc. of Cin., Gen. Soc. Sons of Reolution (gen. chmn.), Nat. Sojourners Camp #134, Heroes of '76 (E.B. Jones Camp), Jamestowne Soc., Kappa Delta Pi, Phi Delta Kappa (bd. dirs. Northwestern U. chpt. 1980—), Kappa Phi Kappa, Alpha Psi Omega, Theta Phi, Pi Tau Chi, Sigma Beta Delta. Republican. Home: 9002 Hurstwood Ct Louisville KY 40222-5716 Office Phone: 502-426-6078.

EARLY, JAMES DONALD, language educator; b. Schenectady, NY, July 3, 1938; s. Joseph Anthony Early and Catherine Loretto Powers; m. Helen Katherine Clark, June 24, 1967; children: Grace Elizabeth, Mary Ellen, Jane Frances, Margaret Helen, Kathleen Loretto. BA, St. Bernard's, 1959; MA, Coll. of St. Rose, 1965. Instr. to prof. Hudson Valley Cmty. Coll., 1967—99; music min. St. Joseph's Ch., Troy, NY, 1997—. Home: 33 Washington Ave Waterford NY 12188

EARLY, JAMES H., JR., lawyer; b. Henderson, N.C., May 6, 1939; s. James Howard and Nettie Anna (Hicks) E.; children from previous marriage: James H. III, Anna Elizabeth, Mary Elizabeth. AA, Mars Hill Coll., 1960; BA, Wake Forest U., 1962, LLB, 1964, JD, 1970. Bar: N.C. 1964, U.S. Dist. Ct. (mid. dist.) N.C. 1970, U.S. Ct. Appeals (4th cir.) 1995; cert. mediator Superior Cts. of N.C., 1992. Pvt. practice, Winston-Salem, 1964—; mediator Adminstrv. Office of the Cts. of N.C., 1992—. Mediator Am. Arbitration Assn., 1992—. Author: The Best Tar Heel Barbecue Manfeo to Murphy, 2000, Jim Early's Reflections The Memiors and Recipes of a Southern Cook, 2005; contbr. articles pub. to profl. jours. With U.S. Army, 1957. Chmn. fundraising Cub Scouts/Boy Scouts Am., Little League, Pop Warner, Indian Guides, March of Dimes, others. Mem. ABA, ATLA, N.C. Bar Assn. (chmn. continuing legal edn. subcom., mem. effectiveness and quality of life com., moderator skills course com.), Forsyth County Bar Assn. (sec. 1970-71), N.C. Acad. Trial Lawyers, Phi Alpha Delta (alumni advisor 1969-84, Outstanding Alumnus award 1967), Kiwanis (pres. 1989-90, 91-92), Masons. Baptist. Avocations: hunting, fishing, walking horses, bird dogs, racing. Home: 144 Sterling Pt Ct Winston Salem NC 27104 Office: 1320 Westgate Center Dr Winston Salem NC 27103-2933

EARLY, TERI WILSON (DENISE WILSON), elementary school educator, educator; b. Jacksonville, Ill., Sept. 3, 1952; d. Arthur Amos and LaVada Inez (Norton) Wilson (dec.); 1 child, Bill Duane (dec.). BS, No. Ill. U., 1973, MS, 1974. Tng. and tech. grad. asst. Head Start/No. Ill. U., DeKalb, 1973-74; tchr. 2d grade North Chicago (Ill.) Dist. 64, 1974-75; Head Start site adminstr. Archdiocese Bd. Edn., Chgo., 1975-76; Head Start tchr. Denver Pub. Schs., 1976-77; tchr., dir. day care lab. Met. State Coll., Denver, 1977; instr. Community Coll., Denver, 1980; toddler day-care dir. Denver Pub. Schs., 1977-80, tchr. 4th grade, 1980-81, kindergarten tchr., 1981-85; fin. rep. Equitable Fin. Svcs., 1985-86; Kindergarten tchr. San Diego Unified Sch. Dist., 1986-89; resource CRISD tchr., 1989-90, race and human rels. facilitator, 1991-92; project resource tchr. Keiller Mid. Sch., 1992-93; v.p. Garfield H.S., 1993-95. V.p. spl. assignment Sch. Cmty. Safety Network, grant coord. Race Human Rels. and Guidance Program, 1995-96; pres. African Am. Educators, 1997-98; v.p. Freese Elem. Sch., 1997-99; prin. Birney Elem. Sch., 1999—2002; del. People-to-People, China, 2001. Mem. Gov.'s Subcom. on Infants and Toddlers, State of Colo., 1979-80; bd. dirs. Big Sisters League, San Diego, 1994-96; grant resource tchr. Valencia Pk., 2002—. Fellow San Diego Area Writing Project, 1987, Sci. Tchrs. Inst. U. Calif.-San Diego, 1988-90, Future Adminstrs. Academy-San Diego County; mem. Nat. Sci. Tchrs. Assn., Nat. Assn. Edn. Young Children, African Am. Educators, Nat. Coun. Negro Women, Assn. Calif. Sch. Adminstrs., ASCD, Alpha Kappa Alpha, Pi Lamba Theta, Phi Delta Kappa. Mem. African Methodist Episcopalian Ch. Home: 4937 Brighton Ave San Diego CA 92107-2519 Office: Valencia Park Elem 5880 Skyline Drive San Diego CA 92114 Personal E-mail: teridenet@yahoo.com.

EARLY, WILLIAM TRACY, journalist; b. Scurry County, Tex., Feb. 20, 1934; s. Willis Worley Jr. and Lillian Marian (Walton) E. BA, Baylor U., 1954; BDiv, Southeastern Bapt. Sem., 1958; ThD, Union Theol. Sem., 1963. Ordained minister So. Bapt. Conv, 1957. Pastor Urbanna (Va.) Bapt. Ch., 1964-68; editl. asst. World Coun. Chs., N.Y.C., 1968-69; freelance journalist N.Y.C., 1969—. Author: Simply Sharing, 1980. 1st lt., chaplain U.S. Army, 1957-59. Democrat. Home: 102 W 80th St Apt 31 New York NY 10024-6304

EARNER, WILLIAM ANTHONY, JR., naval officer; b. Pitts., Nov. 2, 1941; s. William Anthony and Marie Veronica (Ward) E.; m. Jennifer Elizabeth Laurence, Dec. 11, 1971; children: William Andrew, John Laurence. BS, U.S. Naval Acad., 1963; MS, U.S. Naval Postgrad. Sch., 1969; DBA, Harvard U., 1973. Commd. ensign USN, 1963, advanced through grades to vice adm., 1994, 1st lt. USS Blue Yokosuka, Japan, 1963-65, weapons officer USS Black San Diego, 1965-67, ops. officer River Sect. 534 Vietnam, 1967-68, weapons officer USS Dale Mayport, Fla., 1973-75, exec. officer USS Luce, 1975-77, prof. Naval War Coll. Newport, R.I., 1977-78, fellow strategic studies group, 1987-88, with Office Chief Naval Ops. Washington, 1978-81, comdg. officer USS Deyo, 1981-83, mil. asst. to dir. NET assesment Office of Sec. Def. Washington, 1983-85, comptr. naval air systems, 1988-90, comdr. Destroyer Squadron Four Charleston, S.C., 1985-87, comdr. naval Surface Group Mid-Pacific Pearl Harbor, Hawaii, 1990-92; budget officer Dept. Navy, 1992-94, dep. chief naval ops. (logistics), 1994—96, exec. v.p. Navy Fed. Credit Union Merrifield, Va., 1996—97, sr. exec. v.p. Navy Fed. Credit Union, 1998—2003, COO, Navy Fed. Credit Union, 2003—. Instr. Harvard Grad. Sch. Edn., Cambridge, Mass., 1972-73; adj. prof. Bryant Coll., Smithfield, R.I., 1977-78; COO Navy Fed. Credit Union, 1998—; bd. dirs. Service Source, Inc. Chmn. George Mason dist. Boy Scouts Am., 2000—02; mem. supervisory com. Wescorp Fed. Credit Union, 2004—. Decorated D.S.M., Legion of Merit, Bronze Star with V device. Mem. U.S. Naval Inst., Am. Soc. Mil. Comptrs., Credit Union Exec. Soc., U.S. Naval Acad. Alumni Assn., CUNA Govt. Affairs Com. Avocations: running, gardening. Office: Navy Fed Credit Union PO Box 3000 Merrifield VA 22119-3000 Business E-Mail: william_earner@navyfederal.org.

EARNEST, MELISSA WEBB, education educator; d. John Richard and Janet French Webb; m. John Walter Earnest, June 20, 1981; 1 child, Amanda Jo. BS, Austin Peay State U., 1982, MA in Edn., 1994. Adj. prof. Hopkinsville C.C., Ky., 1993—; tchr. Caldwell County H.S., Princeton, Ky., 1998—. Mem. coun. Caldwell County H.S. Sch.-Based Decision Making Coun., Princeton, 2002—. Musician: (organist) First Christian Church (Disciples of Christ), (accompanist advanced choir) Caldwell County H.S.; mem. editl. adv. bd. N.Y. Times Upfront, 2001—05. Leader Girl Scouts USA, Princeton, Ky., 1983—2005; mem. com. Caldwell County H.S. Tech. Com., Princeton, Ky., 1998—2005; deacon First Christian Ch. (Disciples of Christ), Dawson Springs, Ky., 1997—2004, elder, 2005—. Mem.: NEA, ASCD (assoc.), Caldwell County Edn. Assn. (v.p. 2004—), Ky. Edn. Assn., Family, Career & Cmty. Leaders Am. (hon.), Kappa Delta Pi, Tri-M Music Honor Soc. (life). Mem. Christian Ch. Avocation: music. Office: Caldwell County HS 350 Beckner Ln Princeton KY 42445-5002 Office Phone: 270-365-8000. E-mail: mearnest@caldwell.k12.ky.us.

EARNEST, NASH, JR., minister; b. Dewitt, Ark., Jan. 29, 1969; s. Earnest Nash, Sr. and Cora Lee Nash; m. Marshall Lynn Anderson, Aug. 20, 1994; children: Jazzmin Kesha Nash, Julia Kay Nash, Jazzmin Kesha Nash, Julia Kay Nash, Jhansi Karol Nash, Earnest Jeremiah Nash. BA, U. Ark., Pine Bluff, 1995; diploma, U.S. Army Chaplain Sch., 2000; grad. Delta Regional Leadership Sch., Ark. State U., 2000; grad. Fast Track Bus. Program, U. Ark., 2000; BA, Morris Booker Meml. Coll., 2003. Cert. tchr. Nat. Bapt. Conv. USA, Inc., 2001; clin. pastoral edn. Jefferson Hosp. and Assn. Pastoral Edn., Ark., 1999. Vista vol. Americorps Vista, Memphis, 1997—98; chaplain Jefferson Hosp., Pine Bluff, Ark., 1998—99; employee recruiter U.S. Census Bur., Pine Bluff, 1999—2000; pastor Union Grove Missionary Bapt. Ch., Gould, Ark., 1999—; substance abuse prevention coord./educator Desha County Cmty. Svcs., Dumas, Ark., 2001—02; chief clk. of the ct. Gould City Ct., Gould, 2003—. Vol. recruiter U. Ark., Pine Bluff, 1993—95, vol. substance abuse prevention, intervention, edn. counselor, 1993—95; founder May on Main St. Gould C. of C., 2004; alderman City of Gould, 1999—2000; vice-moderator Big Creek and Reedville Bapt. Assn., Gould, 2002—03; chaplain 3rd of the 153rd Inf. Balt., Southeast Arkansas, Ark., 1999—2002. 2nd lt. USAR, 1998—2003. Master: Prince Hall Grand Lodge (worshipful master 1998—2002). Independent. Home: PO Box 552 Gould AR 71643 Office: Union Grove MB Church Highway 65 South Gould AR 71643 Office Phone: 870-263-4126. Personal E-mail: revnash@yahoo.com.

EARNEST, OLA MAY, curator; b. Montrose, Mo., Apr. 5, 1934; d. Marion Leslie Callahan and Bianna Elizabeth Wallace; m. Jesse E. Earnest, Dec. 6, 1950; children: Jessel, Linda K., Billy J., Rodney G., Diana L. Attended in genealogy, Ft. Scott Cmty. Coll., 1974, Pitts. State U., Kans., 1974. V.p. Linn Co. Genealogical Soc., Pleasanton, Kans., 1975—78, pres., 1978—79; pres., curator Linn Co. Hist. Soc. Mus. and Libr., Pleasanton, 1980—. Author: 100 Cemetaries - Linn County, Kansas, 1987; editor (designer): (brochure) Bleeding Kansas, 2003. Mem. Linn Co. Rep. Women, Linn Co., Kans.; treas. Potosi Twp., Linn Co., Kans., 1992—; mem. South East Kans. Tourism, Kans., 1990—. Named Woman of Yr., Iota Phi Sorority, 1985; recipient Cmty. Svc. award, Beta Pi Sorority, 1989. Mem.: Kans. State Hist. Soc., Territorial Kans. Heritage Alliance, Nat. Soc. Daughters Am. Revolution, Nat. Soc. Wash. Family Descendants. Republican. Meth. Avocations: genealogy, gardening, reenactments. Home: 7535 White Rd Pleasanton KS 66075 Office: Linn County Hist Soc 307 E Park St Pleasanton KS 66075 Office Phone: 913-352-8739. Office Fax: 913-352-8739. E-mail: linncohist-gen@ckt.net.

EARNEY, MICHAEL PATRICK, artist; s. Sidney Arthur and Beatrice Edna Earney; children: Miles, Lucas. Student, Sutton & Cheam Sch. Art, Surrey, Eng. Studio asst. Pentagon Design Svc., London, 1952—53; painter Alick Jonson Theatrical, London, 1955—56; tchr. U. Leicester, 1964—65, Falmouth Sch. Art, 1965—66; filmmaker Blue Sky Prodns., Santa Fe, 1972—82; artist, pvt. practice Blanco, Tex., 1983—. Advisor Bi-centennial Com., Santa Fe, 1975—76; judge N.Mex. Arts Commn., Santa Fe, 1982. Co-author: (book) Land & Cattle, 1977; prodr., dir.: (film) Lifeways Series, 1975 (Bronze medal, 1983); book jackets, Tastes of Tex., Inns of Tex., 1986; contbr. writings and illustrations in books and mags.; various exhbns., Eng., U.S.A., Mex. AC Royal Airforce, 1954—57, Aden. Avocations: walking, swimming, yoga, tai chi, reading. Home and Office: 5303 N US Hwy 281 Blanco TX 78606 Office Phone: 830-833-5484. Personal E-mail: themichaelearney@yahoo.com.

EARNHARDT, DALE, JR., race car driver; b. Concord, N.C., Oct. 10, 1974; s. Dale Earnhardt. Co-owner, NASCAR Nextel Cup Series (formerly Winston Cup Series) No. 8 Budweiser-sponsored Chevrolet, 1998—; co-owner, driver Chance 2 Motorsports team, 2002—. Guest appearance (TV) 60 Minutes, 2004, The Tonight Show with Jay Leno, MTV Diary, VH1 Driven, 2003; author: (novels) Driver #8, 2002. Recipient Espy Award for Best Driver, 2004. Achievements include became the only third-generation NASCAR champion with Busch Series Championship, 1998, 1999; winner, Daytona 500, 2004; sponsors include Budweiser, Remington, Drakkar Noir, Enterprise Rent-a-car, Napa Auto Parts, Ritz, Gillette, Wrangler, Polaris; 12 career NASCAR victories. Avocations: water sports, computers. Office: Dale Earnhardt Inc 1675 Coddle Creek Hwy Mooresville NC 28115-8245

EARNHARDT, DAVID LU, retired literature and language educator, writer, musician; b. Denver, May 8, 1949; s. Albert Bain and Elaine Mae Earnhardt; m. Bonnie Jane Quinn, June 14, 1969; children: Christopher, Chelsea. AB in English, Wabash Coll., 1971; postgrad. in English, Ind. U., 1972—75; tchg. license credits, U. Colo., 1993—95, Met. State Coll. Denver, 1993—95. Lic. secondary tchr. Colo. Coord., libr. McData, 1st Interstate Bank, Denver, 1967—72; tech. writer tng. Diner's Club, Storagetech, IBM, Denver and Boulder, 1976—98; tchr. 11th grade English Eaglecrest H.S. Cherry Creek Sch. Dist., Englewood, Colo., 1996—97, tchr. English, summer sch., 1999—2003, tchr. English, 1996—2005; tchr. lit., composition and English Thunder Ridge H.S., Highlands Ranch, Colo., 1999—2000; tchr. 6th grade English Aurora (Colo.) Pub. Schs., 2003—04; ret., 2005. Tchr., tutor, mentor Colo. Outward Bound Met. State Coll. Denver, 1994—95; jazz pianist, co-founder Equinox Jazz Quartet, Denver, Blue Jazzman Quartet, Denver. Author: (poetry vol.) Wings of Silence, 1979, (novel) Salem Village on Trial: A Chronicle in the Diary of Reason, 2004; composer: (CD) Classically Blue; contbr. short stories and poems to numerous publs. Vol. March of Dimes, Denver, 1979. Mem.: Am. Soc. Poets, Beta Theta Pi. Avocations: Tae Kwon Do (3d degree black belt), running. Home: 17855 E Berry Dr Centennial CO 80015 Office: Poetry.com One Poetry Plz Owings Mills MD 21117

EARNS, LANE ROBERT, academic administrator, historian, educator; b. Flint, Mich., May 8, 1951; s. Robert Lewis Earns and Shirley M. Earns (nee Martin). BA, Mich. State U., 1973; MA, U. Hawaii, 1977, PhD, 1987. Lectr. Kwassui Women's Jr. Coll., Nagasaki, Japan, 1977—79, 1984—86; asst. prof. U. Wis., Oshkosh, 1987—93, assoc. prof. history, 1993—97, prof. history, 1997—, John M. Rosebush prof., 2000, assoc. vice chancellor, 2002—05, interim provost, vice chancellor, 2004—05, provost, 2005—, vice chancellor, 2005—. Co-founder, editor, writer Nagasaki Harbor Light, Nagasaki, 1985. Author: Nagasaki Kyoryuchi no seiyojin; co-author: Across the Gulf of Time: The International Cemeteries of Nagasaki; co-editor: Crossroads: A Jour. of Nagasaki History and Culture, 1993—98. Fellow, Fulbright Found., 1974—75; grantee, Japan Found., 1983, NE Asian Coun. Assn. Asian Studies, 1989, NEH, 1990—91. Mem.: Midwest Conf. Asian Affairs (program chair 1992), Midwest Japan Sem. (exec. bd. mem. 1989—92, chair 1992—94). Home: 1219 Merritt Ave Oshkosh WI 54901 Office: University of Wisconsin Oshkosh 800 Algoma Blvd Oshkosh WI 54901 E-mail: earns@uwosh.edu.

EASLEY, CHARLES D., JR., state supreme court justice; b. Port of Spain, Trinidad, 1949; (parents Am. citizens); s. Charles D. and Doris B. Easley; m. Pamela Easley; children: Christopher, Lindsey, Ali Mara. BBA, U. Miss., 1972; MBA, Miss. State U., 1976; JD, U. Miss., 1979; attended, Nat. Dist. Attorneys Coll., 1980; grad., Am. Acad. Jud. Ed. Asst. dist. atty. 3d Jud. Cir. Ct. Dist., 1980—83; pvt. practice Columbus, Miss., 1983—2000; prosecutor Caledonia, 1999, judge, 2000; assoc. justice Miss. Supreme Ct., 2001—. Bd. dirs. Big Brothers & Big Sisters of Miss., Am. Cancer Soc., Miss. Prosecutor's Assn. Mem.: AARP, ABA, Am. Judges Assn., Lowndes County Bar Assn., NRA, Masons, Shriners. Office: Miss Supreme Ct Gartin Justice Bldg 450 High St Jackson MS 39201 also: PO Box 249 Jackson MS 39205 Office Phone: 601-359-3697.

EASLEY, CHRISTA BIRGIT, nurse, researcher; b. Berlin, Apr. 30, 1941; came to U.S., 1966; d. Albert and Marianne (Uhlmann) Baldauf; m. Loyd Allen Easley, Oct. 23, 1964 (widowed Dec. 1993). Degree in nursing, Pawlow Coll. of Nursing, Aue, Fed. Republic of Germany, 1959; BS, NYU, Albany, 1978; MBA, Cen. Mich. U., 1979; EDS, Ctrl. Mo. U., 1983; PhD, Kensington U., Glensdale, Calif., 1983. With placement sect. Sembach, A.B., Germany, 1972-73, 1973-74; adminstrv. clk. Lajes Field, A.B., Terceira, Portugal, 1975-78, incentive awards and suggestion program mgr., 1978-79; intern Cen. Mo. State U., Warrensburg, 1980-81; instr. in bus. overseas campus Cen. Tex. Coll./Yokota, A.B., Japan, 1983; instr. Tokyo Ctr. for Lang. and Culture, 1981-83; tchr. dept. of def. Yokota Dept. of Def., Yokota AFB, Japan, 1981-84; tax examiner IRS, Austin, Tex., 1984-86; sr. clin. rsch. coord. HealthQuest Rsch., Austin, 1987-96; v.p. Austin Clin. Rsch., 1996—. Treas. Am. Sch. System PTA, Acores, 1978-79; precinct chmn. Austin Rep. Com., 1988-96. Mem. Am. Acad. Allergy & Immunology, Am. Assn. Translators, AAUW, Sigma Tau Delta. Methodist. Avocations: rock hunting, flower gardens. Home: 12422 Deer Trak Austin TX 78727-5746 Office: Austin Clin Rsch Inc 12885 Research Blvd # 109 Austin TX 78750-3220 Personal E-mail: christabeasley@yahoo.com.

EASLEY, DAVID, economics professor; b. Lexington, Ky., Nov. 3, 1952; s. Alan Eugene and Jean (Ogden) E.; m. Maureen O'Hara, July 13, 1977; children: Megan, Casey. BA, U. Ky., 1974; PhD, Northwestern U., 1979. Asst. prof. econs. Cornell U., Ithaca, N.Y., 1979-84, assoc. prof., 1984-88, prof., 1988—, chmn. econs. dept., 1988-93, Henry Scarborough prof. econs., 1996—. Vis. prof. Calif. Inst. Tech., Pasadena, 1985-86; Overseas fellow Churchill Coll., Cambridge U., 1993-94. Contbr. articles to profl. jours. Recipient numerous grants NSF. Fellow Econometric Soc. Office: Cornell U Dept Econ Uris Hall Ithaca NY 14853 Office Phone: 607-255-6283. E-mail: dae3@cornell.edu.

EASLEY, DAVID FUMITAKA, musician; b. Hilo, Hawaii, Oct. 4, 1958; s. John Allen and Elizabeth Fumiko Easley. Freelance rec. session musician, Ill., New Orleans, Calif., N.Y., 1980—; singer, songwriter, guitarist Heartifacts, New Orleans, S.E., Midwest, 1992—; blues pedal steel player Coco Robicheaux, New Orleans, Europe, 1996—; jazz pedal steel player 3 Now 4, New Orleans, Europe, 1996—, Brian Blade Fellowship, N.Y., Europe, 1998—2000, Dave Anderson, New Orleans, Southeast, East Coast, 2002—, George Mason Jazz Trio, 2004—. Songwriter, prodr., engr., musician, singer (record album) Boatmen Waiting on the Wind, 1999, The Icicle Man, 2002; musician: Reginald Sanders Jazz Combo, 2000, 2001, Coco Robicheaux, 2003. Named Best Emerging artist, Big Easy awards, 1998; recipient New Orleans Jazz All Star award, New Orleans mag., 2003. Mem.: Am. Fedn. Musicians. Achievements include 1st pedal steel guitar player to record on the Blue Note label known for recording many of the world's best jazz artists. Avocations: bicycling, poetry, gardening, reading, travel.

EASLEY, JUNE ELLEN PRICE, genealogist; b. Chgo., June 7, 1924; d. Fred E. and Bernadette (Mailloux) Price; m. Raymond Dale Easley, Dec. 24, 1945. Student, McCormack Sch. Commerce, Englewood Jr. Coll., Chgo. Lic. genealogist Assn. Profl. Genealogists. Statis. clk. Arthur Andersen & Co., Chgo., 1968-74; corr. sec. ICG R.R., Chgo., 1974-86; self-employed genealogist-computers Arlington Heights, Ill., 1986-94, Mountain Home, Ark., 1994—2001, Springfield, Mo., 2001—. Editor, typist genealogical books, 1996—. Contbr. religion articles to Daily Herald, 1991; editor romance stories, 1990—, genealogy books, 1996—. Sec. Citizens for Clean Water, Mountain Home, Ark., 1996-98. Mem. AARP (sec. 1997-98), DAR (auditor-treas. Chgo. chpt. 1981-82, rec. sec. Chgo. chpt. 1982-88, Mountain Home ROTC 1995-97, publicity chmn. 1996-97), Huguenot Soc., Nat. Soc. R.R. Bus. Women (newsletter editor 1991-2002), Northwest Suburban Coun. Genealogists (pres. 1988-90, corr. sec. 1990-94), Daus. of War 1812, Daus. of Union Vets. (Civil War). Republican. Avocations: genealogy, writing, antiques, computers, travel. Home and Office: 2315 E Lark St Springfield MO 65804 Office Phone: 417-823-3835. E-mail: juneeasley@alltel.net.

EASLEY, MICHAEL F., governor; b. Rocky Mount, N.C., 1950; m. Mary Pipines; 1 child, Michael F., Jr. BA in Polit. Sci. cum laude, U. N.C., 1972; JD cum laude, N.C. Ctrl. U. Dist. atty. 13th Dist., N.C., 1982-91; pvt. practice Southport, N.C., 1991-93; atty. gen. N.C., 1993-2000; gov. State of N.C., 2000—. Contbr. numerous articles in field. Recipient Pub. Svc. award U.S. Dept. Justice, 1984. Pres. N.C. Conf. Dist. Attys.; mem. N.C. Dist. Attys. Assn. (past pres., legis. chmn.). Democrat. Avocations: hunting, sailing, woodworking. Office: Office of the Gov 20301 Mail Service Ctr Raleigh NC 27699-0303 Office Phone: 919-733-4240. E-mail: governor.office@ncmail.net.

EASLEY-MCPHERSON, WILLIAM REEVES, computer technician; s. Joanna R. Easley and Kerry Patrick McPherson, William Glenn Easley; m. Hillarie L. Thompson, Sept. 5, 1998; 1 child, Jacob. B in Gen. studies, W. Tex. A&M U., Canyon, 1986—89. Mgr., software sys. Cal Farley's, Amarillo, Tex., 1999—. Vol. Boy Scouts of Am., Amarillo, Tex., 1983—, ARC, Amarillo, Tex., 1980—. Mem.: Nat. Coun. on Pub. History (corr.), Am. Hist. Assn. (corr.). Independent. Presbyterian. Avocation: history. Office: Cal Farley's 600 W 11th Amarillo TX 79101 Office Phone: 806-372-2341. Office Fax: 806-372-6638. E-mail: reasleymcpherson@calfarley.org.

EASON, MARCIA JEAN, lawyer; b. Dallas, Aug. 31, 1953; d. John Keller and Sara Marguerite (Prindle) McCarron; m. S. Lee Meredith, Sept. 12, 1981 (div. Oct. 1989); m. David O. Eason, Aug. 21, 1993; stepchildren: Chelsea, Shannon, Valerie. BA magna cum laude, Trinity U., 1975; JD, U. Houston, 1979. Bar: Tex. 1978, U.S. Dist. Ct. (so. dist.) Tex. 1978, U.S. Ct. Appeals (5th cir.) 1979, Tenn. 1985, U.S. Dist. Ct. (ea. dist.) Tenn. 1985, U.S. Supreme Ct. 1985, U.S. Ct. Appeals (6th cir.) 1986, U.S. Ct. Appeals (4th cir.) 1994. Ptnr. Byrnes & Martin, Houston, 1984-85, Miller & Martin, Chattanooga, 1987—. Pres., bd. dirs. Chattanooga's Kids on the Block, 1987-94; bd. dirs., chair AIM Ctr, Chattanooga, 1993-2005; campaign chair, attys. divsn. United Way, Chattanooga, 1994, leadership, campaign chair, 1998. Fellow: Am. Bar Found., Tenn. Bar Found.; mem. ABA, Tenn. Bar Assn. (v.p. 2005—), Chattanooga Bar Assn. (bd. govs. 2004-05), Tenn. Supreme Ct. Commn. (mem. racial and ethnic and gender fairness, mem. enhancing pub. trust in ct. sys.), Tenn. Lawyers Assn. for Women (co-chair com. 1994, treas. 1995-97, pres. 1998) Home: 33 Rock Crest Dr Signal Mountain TN 37377-2326 Office: Miller & Martin 832 Georgia Ave Ste 1000 Chattanooga TN 37402-2289 Office Phone: 423-785-8304. Business E-Mail: meason@millermartin.com.

EASON, WILLIAM EVERETTE, JR., lawyer; b. Elizabeth City, N.C., Jan. 20, 1943; s. William Everette and Helen (Mathews) E.; m. Mildred Judith Harris, Aug. 20, 1965; 1 child, Kimberly. AB, Duke U., 1965, JD, 1968. Bar: Ga. 1968. Sr. v.p., gen. counsel, sec. Scientific Atlanta, Inc., 1994—. Bd. dirs. Herty Found., Savannah, Ga., 1984-94, Families First, Atlanta, 1978-88, SciTrek Mus., Atlanta, 1995—; trustee, chmn. exec. com. Woodward Acad., Atlanta, 1987—; pres. North Atlanta Club Area Civic Assn., 1981-82; mem. Leadership Atlanta; gen. counsel Met. Atlanta Olympic Games Authority, 1989—. Mem. Ga. Bar Assn. (chmn. corp. and banking law sect. 1988-89, chmn. corp. counsel sect. 1996-97), Capital City Club, Georgian Club Atlanta (dir. 1987-90). Methodist. also: Sci-Atlanta Inc One Technology Pky S Norcross GA 30092

EASSON, WILLIAM MCALPINE, psychiatrist, educator; b. Evanston, Ill., July 3, 1931; s. Alexander and Anne Meldrum (Watson) E.; m. Gwendolyn Bowen, May 31, 1958; children: Anne, Jane, David, Michael. M.B., Ch.B., U. Aberdeen, Scotland, 1954, MD, 1967. Fellow in medicine and psychiatry Mayo Clinic, Rochester, Minn., 1956-59; resident in psychiatry U. Sask., 1959-60, instr. psychiatry, 1959-61; fellow in child psychiatry Menninger Clinic, Topeka, 1961-63, staff child psychiatrist, 1963-67; prof. psychiatry, chmn. dept. Med. Coll. Ohio, Toledo, 1967-72; prof., dir. div. child and adolescent psychiatry U. Minn. Med. Sch., Mpls., 1972-74; prof. psychiatry La. State U. Med. Ctr., New Orleans, 1974-96, head dept. psychiatry, 1974-82, prof. emeritus, 1996—. Vis. prof. psychiatry U. Garyounis Med. Sch., Benghazi, Libya, 1979; prof. grad. studies U. Riyadh, Saudi Arabia; U.S.-USSR health scientist, Moscow and Leningrad. Author: The Severely Disturbed Adolescent, 1969, The Dying Child, 2d edit., 1981, Psychiatry Exam. Rev., 5th edit., 1994, Psychiatry Patient Mgmt. Rev., 1977, (with N. Rock) Psychiatry Splty. Bd. Rev., 1991, The Management of the Severely Disturbed Adolscent, 1996; editor: Jour. Clin. Psychiatry, 1977-80. Carnegie fellow, 1956-58; Anderson fellow, 1956-58; WHO fellow, 1976 Fellow Am. Psychiat. Assn. (life). Home: 5218 Saint Charles Ave New Orleans LA 70115-4943

EAST, ERNEST EARL, lawyer, electric power industry executive; b. Vallejo, Calif., Oct. 17, 1942; s. Ernest Earl East Sr. and Evelyn E. (Pendergrass) Walworth. BA, U. Tulsa, 1965; JD, U. Ark., 1969. Bar: Ark. 1969, Tex. 1973, U.S. Supreme Ct. 1973. Atty. SEC, Washington, 1969-73;

assoc. Ritchie, Ritchie & Crosland, Dallas, 1973-74; assoc. gen. counsel Boise (Idaho) Cascade Corp., 1974-80, Ga. Pacific Corp., Atlanta, 1980-84; assoc. gen. counsel, asst. sec. Del Webb Corp., Phoenix, 1984-85, v.p., sec., gen. counsel, 1985—98; sr. v.p., gen. counsel, chief compliance officer Hyatt Gaming Mgmt., Inc., 1998—2003; v.p., gen. counsel, sec. Sierra Pacific Resources, Reno, 2003—. Pres. Idaho Human Rights Commn., Boise, 1976-80; bd. dirs. Ariz. Hist. Soc., Phoenix, 1987—. Mem. ABA, Am. Soc. Corp. Secs., Am. Corp. Counsel Assn., State Bar Tex., Plaza Club, Mansion Club. Office: Sierra Pacific Resources 6100 Neil Rd Reno NV 89511

EAST, JOHN, computer company executive; married. BSEE, MBA, U. Calif. Berkeley. Various mktg., engring. and mgmt. positions Fairchild Semiconductor; sr. v.p. AMD; joined Actel Corp., 1988, pres., CEO Sunnyvale, Calif. Bd. dirs. Adaptec Corp. Office: 2061 Stierlin CT Mountain View CA 94043-4698

EASTAUGH, ROBERT L., state supreme court justice; b. Seattle, Nov. 12, 1943; BA in English Literature, Yale U., 1965; JD, U. Mich., 1968. Bar: Alaska 1968. Asst. atty. gen. State of Alaska, 1968—69, asst. dist. atty., 1969—72; lawyer Delaney, Wiles, Hayes, Reitman & Brubaker, Inc., 1972—94; assoc. justice Alaska Supreme Ct., 1994—. Charter mem. Advisory Com. on Rules of Practice & Internal Operating Procedures, Alaska Ninth Circuit Ct., 1983—92; mem. Alaska Supreme Ct. Appellate Rules Com., 1985—; co-chair Alaska Supreme Ct. Fairness & Access Implementation Com., 1998—. Mem.: Alaska Bar Assoc. (bar examiner). Office: Alaska Supreme Ct 303 K St Anchorage AK 99501-2013*

EASTBURN, JOHN S., JR., venture capitalist; BA, Amherst Coll.; MBA, NYU. Pres., CEO Scovill Fasteners, Inc., 1989—93; COO Crystal Dynamics, Inc., 1993—96; founder, cons. JBX Eastburn, LLC, 1996—97; joined Kohlberg & Co., 1997, prin., 2002. Bd. dirs. BI Inc., Nancy's Specialty Foods, Inc., Thousand Trails, Inc. Office: Kohlberg & Co 111 Radio Cir Mount Kisco NY 10549 Office Phone: 914-241-7430. Office Fax: 914-241-7476.

EASTER, JEANMARIE, conservator; b. Syracuse, NY, May 11, 1956; d. Stanley Walter and Mary Bonita (Caraglin) Kalwara; m. Mark Richard Easter, June 15, 1990. A in Buying and Merchandising, Fashion Inst. Tech., NYC, 1988, BA Restoration of Decorative Objects, 1989. Frame conservator Indpls. Mus. Art, 1989—2001; owner Easter Conservation Svcs. Ltd., Indpls., 2001—. Contbr. article to profl. jour. Core mem. Meth. Hosp. Task Core, Indpls., 2000—04; bd. mem. Friends Herron Sch. Art, Indpls., 2000—, Meridian St. Found., Indpls., 2003—. Recipient Furniture in France award, Am. Inst. Hist. Artistic Works, France, 2004; Creative Renewal fellowship, Arts Coun. Indpls., London, 2000. Mem.: Contemporary Art Soc., Am. Inst. Conservation Hist. Artistic Works (assoc.; chmn. conservators in pvt. pracice 2003—04). Avocations: gardening, swimming, travel, painting. Office: Easter Conservation Services Ltd 644 E 52nd St Indianapolis IN 46205 Office Phone: 317-396-0885.

EASTER, MARK WAYNE, infomation technology director; b. Des Moines, Apr. 25, 1955; s. Wayne and Beverly Easter; m. Susan Lynn Gowans, Oct. 21, 1978; children: Stephanie, Chris, Brittany. Capt., battalion adjutant in honors JROTC Corps. USAF, 1972—73.

EASTER, STEPHEN SHERMAN, JR., biology professor; b. New Orleans, Feb. 12, 1938; s. Stephen Sherman and Myrtle Olivia (Bekkedahl) E.; m. Janine Eliane Piot, June 4, 1963; children: Michele, Kim BS, Yale U., 1960; postgrad., Harvard U., 1961; PhD, Johns Hopkins U., 1966. Postdoctoral fellow Cambridge U., Eng., 1967; postdoctoral U. Calif., Berkeley, 1968-69; asst. prof. biology U. Mich., Ann Arbor, 1970-74, assoc. prof., 1974-78, prof., 1978—, assoc. chmn., 1992-93, mem. Coll. Lit., Sci. and the Arts exec. com., 1993-96, dir. neurosci. program, 1984-88, Mathew Alpern Collegiate prof., 1998—. Vis. prof. U. Murcia, Spain, 1997, Ecole Normale Supérieure, Paris, 1997. Editor Vision Rsch., 1978-85, Jour. Neurosci., 1989-95, Visual Neurosci., 1990-92, Investigative Ophthalmology and Visual Sci., 1992-97, Jour. Comparative Neurology, 1994-99. Recipient Sokol award, 1998. Mem. Soc. Neurosci., Assn. Rsch. in Vision and Ophthalmology, Internat. Brain Rsch. Orgn., Soc. for Devel. Biology. Office: U Mich Dept Biology 3113 Natural Sci Bldg Ann Arbor MI 48109-1048 E-mail: sseaster@umich.edu.

EASTER, WILLIE, JR., artist, writer; b. York, S.C., Oct. 27, 1963; Author: (book) Dawn of a New Age (Copyright award, 1998), Dawn of a New Age II: The Dragon People (Copyright award, 1999), Combinations, 2005, (animated film) Dawn of a New Age: Conflict. Active connectional Lay Coun. Trinity A.M.E. Zion Ch., Gastonia, NC, 1991—92. Recipient Cert. Enrollment, Attendance, and Cooperation, Vocat. Bible Sch. Trinity A.M.E. Zion Ch., 1990. Mailing: 307 N Morris St Gastonia NC 28052 E-mail: easterone77@yahoo.com.

EASTERBROOK, FRANK HOOVER, federal judge; b. Buffalo, Sept. 3, 1948; s. George Edmund and Vimy (Hoover) E. BA, Swarthmore Coll., 1970; JD, U. Chgo., 1973. Bar: D.C. Law clk. to Hon. Levin H. Campbell U.S. Ct. Appeals (1st cir.), Boston, 1973-74; asst. to solicitor gen. U.S. Dept. Justice, Washington, 1974-77, dep. solicitor gen. of U.S., 1978-79; asst. prof. law U. Chgo., 1978-81, prof. law, 1981—85, Lee & Brena Freeman prof., 1984-85; prin. employee Lexecon Inc., Chgo., 1980-85; sr. lectr. U. Chgo., 1985—; judge U.S. Ct. Appeals (7th cir.), Chgo., 1985—. Mem. adv. com. on tender offers SEC, Washington, 1983 Author: (with Richard A. Posner) Antitrust, 1981, (with Daniel R. Fischel) The Economic Structure of Corporate Law, 1991; editor Jour. Law and Econs., Chgo., 1982-91; contbr. articles to profl. jours. Trustee James Madison Meml. Fellowship Found., 1988—. Recipient Prize for Disting. scholarship Emory U., Atlanta, 1981 Mem. AAAS, Am. Law Inst., Mont Pelerin Soc., Order of Coif, Phi Beta Kappa. Office: US Ct Appeals Everett McKinley Dirksen Fed Bldg 219 S Dearborn St Ste 2746 Chicago IL 60604-1803*

EASTERBROOK, GREGG EDMUND, writer; b. Buffalo, N.Y., Mar. 2, 1953; s. George Edmund and Vimy Roslyn (Hoover) Easterbrook; m. Nan Terese Kennelly, Jan. 1, 1988; 3 children. BA, Colo. Coll., 1976; MSJ, Northwestern U., 1977; LittD (hon.), Colo. Coll., 1992. Former contbg. editor Newsweek, Washington; contbg. editor The Washington Monthly, Washington, The Atlantic Monthly, Boston, 1980—; sr. editor The New Republic, 1998—, BeliefNet.com. Visiting fellow, economic studies Brookings Instn., 2000—; contr. Tuesday Morning Quarterback column Slate, 2000—02, ESPN.com, 2002—03, NFL.com, 2004—; commentator NFL Total Access, 2004—. Author: This Magic Moment, 1986, Surgeon Koop, 1991, A Moment on the Earth, 1995, Beside Still Waters, 1998, Tuesday Morning Quarterback, 2001, The Here and Now, 2002, The Progress Paradox, 2003. Recipient Investigative Reporters and Editors award (with Thomas Bethell), 1980, Investigative Reporters and Editors award, 1982, Livingston award, 1986; disting. fellow, Fullbright Found., 1996. Democrat. Office: The New Republic 1331 H St NW Ste 700 Washington DC 20005 Office Phone: 202-508-4444.

EASTERDAY, BERNARD CARLYLE, veterinary medicine educator; b. Hillsdale, Mich., Sept. 16, 1929; s. Harley B. and Alberta M. Easterday D.V.M., Mich. State U., 1952; MS, U. Wis., 1958, PhD, 1961. Diplomate Am. Coll. Veterinary Microbiologists. Pvt. practice veterinary medicine, Hillsdale, Mich., 1952; veterinarian U.S. Dept. Def., Frederick, Md., 1955-61; assoc. prof., then prof. veterinary sci. U. Wis., Madison, 1961-94, prof. emeritus, 1994—, dean Sch. Vet. Medicine, 1979-94, dean emeritus, prof emeritus Sch. Vet. Medicine, 1994—. Mem., chmn. com. animal health Nat. Acad. Sci.-NRC, Washington, 1980-83, mem. com. on sci. basis meat and poultry inspection program, 1984-85; mem. tech. adv. com. Binat. Agrl. Research and Devel., Bet-Degan, Israel, 1982-84; mem. expert adv. panel on zoonoses WHO, Geneva, 1978-94; mem. tech. adv. com. on avian influenza USDA, 1983-85; mem. sec. USDA adv. com. on fgn. animal and poultry diseases, 1991-96. 1st lt. V.C., U.S. Army, 1952-54. Recipient Disting. Alumnus award Coll. Vet. Medicine, Mich. State U., 1975, Disting. Alumni award Mich. State U., 1999, Disting. Alumni award U. Wis., Madison, 2003; named Wis. Veterinarian of Yr., Wis. Vet. Med. Assn., 1979. Mem. AVMA, Am. Assn. Vet. Med. Colls. (pres. 1975), Am. Assn. Avian Pathologists Office: U Wisconsin-Madison Sch Vet Medicine 2015 Linden Dr W Madison WI 53706-1100

EASTERDAY, TAMMY MORAN, literature educator; d. Dana Lou and Turle Ryan (Stepfather); m. William Vern Easterday, Aug. 11, 1984; 1 child, Marcus William. BS in elem. edn., Bob Jones U., 1980—84; M in reading and lang. arts, Furman U., 1994—96. Tchr. North Houston Bapt. Schools, Houston, 1984—87; kindergarten tchr. Paris Elem., Greenville, SC, 1988—89; first grade tchr. Southside Christian Sch., Greenville, 1993—97; reading recovery tchr. Langston Magnet Sch., Hot Springs, Ark., 1997—2002, literacy coach, 2002—. Sunday sch. tchr. Hot Springs Bapt. Ch., Ark., 2002—. Recipient Milken Nat. Educators award, Milken Family Found., 2004, Innovative Project award, Hot Springs Sch. Dist., 1997—98, Tchr. of the Month, 2002, Tchr. of the Yr., North Houston Bapt. Schools, 1987. Mem.: Internat. Reading Assn., Ark. Reading Assn., Tri Lakes Reading Assn., Alumni Assn. (licentiate). R-Consevative. Bapt. Avocations: camping, reading, swimming, scrapbooks, piano. Office: Langston Magnet Sch 120 Chestnut St Hot Springs AR 71901 Office Phone: 501-620-7821.

EASTERLING, DAVID ROYER, climatologist; b. Chapel Hill, N.C., Nov. 25, 1955; s. William Ewart Jr. and Ellyn (Royer) E.; m. Kimberly O'Daniel, May 23, 1981; children: Hannah Marie, Katherine Ann. BA, U. N.C., 1979, MA, 1984, PhD, 1987. Asst. prof. Ind. U., Bloomington, 1987-90; rsch. meteorologist NOAA, Nat. Climatic Data Ctr., Asheville, NC, 1990-98, prin. scientist, 1999—2002, chief scientific svcs. divsn., 2002—. Adj. prof. dept. atmospheric scis. U. N.C., Asheville, 1996—; contbr. Intergovtl. Panel on Climate Change, 1999—. Contbr. articles to profl. jours. Recipient bronze medal U.S. Dept. Commerce, 1996, 2001. Mem. Am. Meteorol. Soc. (chair com. on applied climatology 1999—, com. on probability and stats. 1995-97, program chair), Assn. Am. Geographers. Episcopalian. Avocations: competitive swimming, golf. Office: Nat Climatic Data Ctr 151 Patton Ave Ste 120 Asheville NC 28801-5001 E-mail: david.easterling@nasa.gov.

EASTERLY, DAVID EUGENE, communications executive; b. Denison, Tex., June 26, 1942; s. Claud Eugene and Ruth Eleanor (Davis) E.; children: Jennifer, Greg, Anne. BA in Polit. Sci., Austin Coll., 1965. Reporter Denison (Tex.) Herald, 1964-66; reporter, news editor San Angelo (Tex.) Standard-Times, 1967-68; asst. mng. editor Austin (Tex.) Am.-Statesman, 1968-70; pres. Dayton (Ohio) Newspapers, Inc., 1977-81, Atlanta Jour. and Constn., from 1982; former pres. Cox Newspapers; pres., COO Cox Enterprises, 1994—. Mem. AP, So. Newspaper Pubs. Assn. (bd. dirs.), Newspaper Assn. Am. Office: Cox Enterprises 1400 Lake Hearn Dr NE Atlanta GA 30319-1418

EASTERSON, SAM, artist; b. Hartford, Jan. 24, 1972; BFA, Cooper Union Sch., 1994; MS, U. Minn., 1999. Instr. Art Inst. Minn., 1998—. Exhibited in group shows at Whitney Mus. Am. Art, N.Y.C., 1997, Walker Art Ctr., Mpls., 1998, New Mus., N.Y.C., 1998, Sanburg Inst., Amsterdam, 1998, Williams Coll. Mus. Art, 2001, Palm Beach Inst. Contemporary Art, 2001, others, Mass. Coll. Art, Boston, 1995, Grinnell Coll., Iowa, 1997. Recipient Book prize, RISD, 1990, Louis Comfort Tiffany prize, 1999; Creative Capital grantee, 2001. Home: 4286 Tujunga Ave Studio City CA 91604-2746 E-mail: anivegvideo@hotmail.com.

EASTHAM, ALAN WALTER, JR., foreign service officer, lawyer; b. Dumas, Ark., Oct. 16, 1951; s. Alan Walter and Ruth E. (Clayton) E.; m. Carolyn Laux, Aug. 2, 1974; children: Mark A., Michael S.G. BA, Hendrix Coll., Ark., 1973; JD cum laude, Georgetown U., 1982. Bar: D.C. 1982. Mgr. KDDA-AM Radio, Dumas, Ark., 1973-74; vice consul Am. Embassy, Kathmandu, Nepal, 1975-78; info. officer Dept. State, Washington, 1978-80, staff mem. office for combatting terrorism, 1980-82, desk officer Sri Lanka and Maldives, 1982-83, polit. officer for India, 1983-84; prin. officer Am. consulate, Peshawar, Pakistan, 1984-87; spl. asst. to under sec. polit. affairs Dept. State, 1987-89; counselor Am. Embassy, Nairobi, Kenya, 1989-92, Kinshasa, Zaire, 1992-94; consul gen. Bordeaux, France, 1994-95; counselor Am. Embassy, New Delhi, 1995-97, dep. chief of mission Islamabad, Pakistan, 1997-99; dep. asst. sec. of state for South Asian affairs Dept. of State, Washington, 1999—2001, spl. negotiator for conflict diamonds, 2001—02, dir. Cen. African affairs, 2002—05, U.S. amb. to Republic of Malawi, 2005—. Methodist. Office: Am Embassy Ulongwa Malawi E-mail: easthamaw@state.gov.

EASTHAM, JOHN D., marketing executive; Profl. Degree, Burnley Sch., Seattle, 1967. Mng. ptnr. EMB Ptnrs., Seattle, 1994—2002, Eastham Hinton & Simpson LLC, 2002—. Recipient Clio awards, 1986, Effie, Am. Mktg. Assn., 1991, Totem awards Pub. Rels. Soc. Am., 1982. Office: Eastham Hinton & Simpson LLC 87 Wall St #2 Seattle WA 98121-1330*

EASTHAM, THOMAS, foundation administrator; b. Attelboro, Mass., Aug. 21, 1923; s. John M. and Margaret (Marsden) E.; m. Berenice J. Hirsch, Oct. 12, 1946; children: Scott Thomas, Todd Robert. Student English, Northwestern U., 1946-52. With Chgo. American, 1945-56, asst. Sunday editor, 1953-54, feature writer, 1954-56; news editor San Francisco Call Bull., 1956-62, exec. editor, 1962-65; exec. editor, then D.C. bur. chief San Francisco Examiner, 1965-82; dir. pub. info, press sec. to mayor of San Francisco, 1982-88; v.p., western dir. William Randolph Hearst Founds., 1988—. Active Nat. Trust Historic Preservation; mem. Pres.'s Roundtable, U. San Francisco. Pulitzer prize finalist, 1955, Disting Acheivement in Journalism award, Assn. Schs. of Journalism & Mass Comm., 1994. Mem. ACLU, Amnesty Internat., Am. Soc. Newspaper Editors, Inter-Am. Press Assn., Am., Internat. Press Insts., White House Corrs. Assn., Nat. Press Club, Ind. Sector, Coun. on Foundations, San Francisco Planning and Urban Rsch. Assn. Commonwealth Club, Marine Meml. Club, Peninsula Tennis Club, Sigma Delta Chi. Home: 1473 Bernal Ave Burlingame CA 94010-5559 Office: Hearst Found 90 New Montgomery St Ste 1212 San Francisco CA 94105-4596 E-mail: teastham@hearstfdn.com.

EASTIN, DELAINE ANDREE, education educator; b. San Diego, Aug. 20, 1947; d. Daniel Howard and Dorothy Barbara Eastin. BA in Polit. Sci., U. Calif., Davis, 1969; MA in Polit. Sci., U. Calif., Santa Barbara, 1971. Instr. Calif. Community Colls., various locations, 1971-79; acctg. mgr. Pacific Bell, San Francisco, 1979-84; corp. planner Pacific Telesis Group, San Francisco, 1984-86; assemblywoman Calif. State Legis., Sacramento, 1986-95; supt. of public instruction Calif. Edn. Dept., Sacramento, 1995—2003; exec. dir. Nat. Inst. Sch. Leadership, 2003—04; disting. prof. ednl. leadership Mills Coll., Oakland, Calif. Ex officio mem. bd. regents U. Calif., 1995—2003; ex officio mem. bd. trustees Calif. State U., 1995—2003. Bd. dirs. CEWAER, Sacramento, 1988-2003, Pence Gallery, 2003—, Internat. Assn. Fgn. Students Found., 2003—; commr. Commn. on Status of Women, Sacramento, 1990-2003; mem. coun. City of Union City, Calif., 1980-86; chair Alameda County Libr. Commn., Hayward, Calif., 1981-86; planning commr. City of Union City, 1976-80; mem., pres. Alameda County Solid Waste Mgmt. Authority, Oakland, Calif., 1980-86. Named Outstanding Pub. Ofcl. Calif. Tchrs. Assn., 1988, Cert. of Appreciation Calif. Assn. for Edn. of Young Children, 1988-92, Legislator of the Yr. Calif. Media Libr. Educators, 1991, Calif. Sch. Bd. Assn., 1991, 94, Ednl. Excellence award Calif. Assn. Counseling and Devel., 1992. Mem.: Am. Bus. Women's Assn. (Outstanding Bus. Woman 1988), The Internat. Alliance (21st Century award 1990), World Affairs Coun., Commonwealth Club. Democrat. Avocations: photography, hiking, reading, theater, travel. Home: 4228 Dogwood Pl Davis CA 95616-6066 Office Phone: 510-430-2365.

EASTIN, KEITH E., civilian military employee, lawyer; b. Lorain, Ohio, Jan. 16, 1940; s. Keith Ernest and Jane E. (Heimer) E. AB, U. Cin., 1963, MBA, 1964; JD, U. Chgo., 1967. Bar: Ill. 1967, Tex. 1974, Calif. 1975, U.S. Supreme Ct. 1975, D.C. 1983. Atty. Vedder, Price, Kaufman & Kammholz, Chgo., 1967-73; v.p., sec., gen. counsel Nat. Convenience Stores, Inc., Houston, 1973-79; ptnr. Payne, Eastin & Widmer, Houston, 1977-83; dep. under sec. U.S. Dept. Interior, 1983-86; prin. dep. asst. sec. USN, 1986-88; ptnr. Hopkins & Sutter, Washington, 1989-91; sr. v.p. Guy F. Atkinson Co., San Francisco, 1991-92; dir. environ. svcs. Deloitte & Touche, Washington, 1992-98, PricewaterhouseCoopers, 1998—2000; v.p., gen. counsel The Customer Co., 2000—03; sr. advisor Ministry of Environment, Baghdad, Iraq, 2004—05; asst. sec. for installations & environment, Dept. Army U.S. Dept. Def., Washington, 2005—. Bd. dirs. Pricewaterhouse Coopers. Bd. dirs. Theatre Under the Stars, Houston, Statue of Liberty-Ellis Island Found.; mem. exec. com. Harris County Republican Party, 1976-83. Mem. ABA, Ill. Bar Assn., Tex. Bar Assn., D.C. Bar Assn., State Bar Calif., Knights Templar, Met. Club (Washington, Capitol Hill Club (Washington), Beta Gamma Sigma, Phi Delta Phi, Beta Theta Pi. Office: Dept Army 110 Army Pentagon Rm 3E464 Washington DC 20310

EASTLAND, LARRY L., entertainment and theme park development executive; b. Nampa, Idaho, Mar. 16, 1943; s. Fred and Edla Jennett (Homer) E.; m. Beverly Ann Caulder, Jan. 19, 1971; children: Christopher, Rebekah, Justin, Ashley. BA, Brigham Young U., 1967; AM, U. So. Calif., 1973, PhD, 1976. Rsch. asst. in fgn. policy U.S. Senator Len B. Jordan, Washington, 1969-71; staff asst. Gerald R. Ford/The White House, Washington, 1974-77; pres. Lea Mgmt. Corp., Conn., Va., Idaho, 1977—; dir. ops. Summit of Industrialzed Nations, 1982-83; pres. Medtex Corp., Salt Lake City, 1994-96; chmn. bd. Northwest Parks LLC, Boise, Idaho, 1996—. Author: Harvesting Dollars, 1993. Bd. dirs. World Sports Humanitarian Hall of Fame, Boise, 1996—, Unruh Inst. Politics/U. So. Calif., 1978-92; mem. Pres.'s Dist. Export Coun., Boise, 1988-94; U.S. del. World Tourism Orgn., Sofia, Bulgaria, 1985; candidate for Gov., State of Idaho, 1994; chmn. Idahoans for Competitive Govt., 1991-92; fin. chair Idaho Rep. Party, Boise, 1989-90; mem. nat. fin. com. Bush-Quayle, 1992. Capt. USMCR, 1967-73, Vietnam. Decorated Bronze Star with V. Mem. Lds Ch. Avocations: teaching, music, writing, golf. Office: Northwest Parks LLC PO Box 1400 Boise ID 83701-1400 E-mail: swj@micron.net.

EASTMAN, CHARLES (CHUCK) M., architecture educator; BArch, U. Calif., Berkeley, 1964, MArch, 1966. Prof. arch. and computer sci. Carnegie-Mellon U., 1967—82, dir. Ctr. for Bldg. Sci. and Computer Graphics Lab., 1978—82; co-founder, pres. Formative Techs., Inc., Pitts., 1982—87; prof. arch., dir. Ctr. for Design and Computation UCLA, 1987—95; prof. Coll. Arch. and Computer Sci. Ga. Inst. Tech., Atlanta, dir. Coll. Arch. PhD program. Author: Building Product Models: Computer Environments Supporting Design and Construction, 1999. Mem.: Assn. for Computer-Aided Design in Arch. (founder, first pres.). Office: Ga Inst Tech Coll Arch Rm 219 247 4th St Atlanta GA 30332-0155 Office Phone: 404-894-3476.

EASTMAN, DEAN ERIC, physicist, researcher; b. Oxford, Wis., Jan. 20, 1940; m. Ella Mae Staley. BSEE, MIT, 1962, MSEE, 1963, PhDEE, 1965. Rsch. staff IBM T.J. Watson Rsch. Ctr., Yorktown Heights, N.Y., 1963-71, mgr. photoemission and surface physics group, 1971-81, mgr. lithography packaging and compound semicondr. tech., 1981-82, dir. Advanced Packaging Tech. Lab., 1983-85, rsch. v.p. system tech. and sci., 1986-94; dir. product devel. IBM Systems Tech. Div., Danbury, Conn., 1985-86; dir. hardware devel. reengring. IBM Corp., Armonk, N.Y., 1994-96; dir. Argonne Nat. Lab., 1996-98; prof. physics U. Chgo., 1998—. Prof. physics U. Chgo., 1998—. Contbr. over 180 articles to profl. jours. Recipient Oliver E. Buckley prize, 1980; IBM Corp. fellow, 1974. Fellow Am. Phys. Soc.; mem. NAS, NAE, Am. Acad. Arts and Scis. Office: University of Chicago JFI Box 15 RI 231 5640 S Ellis Ave Chicago IL 60637-1433

EASTMAN, DONNA KELLY, composer; b. Denver, Sept. 26, 1945; d. Donald Lewis and Frances Marie (Smith) Kelly; m. John Bernard Eastman, July 1, 1973; children: Jonathan Kelly, James Alan; stepchildren: Barbara Kathleen, Sally Toye. B in Music Edn., U. Colo., 1967; MA, U. Md., 1973, D in Mus. Arts, 1992. Pvt. studio tchr., coach, 1960—; choral dir. Dept. Def. Overseas Sch., Okinawa, Japan, 1970—72; dir. Choraleers Choral Ensemble, Stuttgart, Germany, 1974—76, Bangkok Music Soc. Ensemble and Madrigal Singers, 1982—84; instr. in music No. Va. C.C., Alexandria, 1986—89. Creator, pianist, vocalist Am. Music Programs for U.S. Mission, Thailand, 1981-84; vis. asst. prof. Ill. Wesleyan U., Bloomington, 1994; vis. composer Sweet Briar (Va.) Coll., 1998, Grinnell (Iowa) Coll., 1999. Composer choral, orchestral, opera, vocal/instrumental solo and chamber, and electronic works; recs. include Capstone Records-Soc. of Composers, Inc. Series CPS 8632, 1996, and New Music for Flute and Piano, CPS 8664, 1999; Living Artist Recs.-Music from the Setting Century Series, Vol. 2, 1996; New Ariel Recordings-Contemporary American Eclectic Music for the Piano Series, AE002, 1996; Columbine Chorale Recs.-European Tour, 1999, Blue House Productions-Alone Into the Crowd, 2002; contbr. to jours. Recipient 6 Internat. Composition awards, Composer Guild, 1991—, Internat. Piano Composition award, Roodeport Internat. Eisteddfod, South Africa, 1991, Glad-Robinson-Youse Composition award, Nat. Fedn. Music Clubs, 1992, Internat. Choral Composition award, Florilège Vocal Tours, France, 1995, Keyboard award, Delius Composition Competition, 1997, Margaret Fairbank Jory Copying Assistance award, Am. Music Ctr., 1999, Nat. Music Composition Competition award, Nat. League of Am. Pen Women, 2000, Miriam Gideon prize for New Music, 2002; fellow, Charles Ives Ctr. for Am. Music, 1990; grantee, 1993, Ragdale Found., 1991, Va. Ctr. for Creative Arts, 1991—2002. Mem. Soc. for Electro-Acoustic Music in the U.S., Internat. Alliance for Women in Music, Soc. of Composers, Inc. (life), Nat. Mus. Women in Arts (charter), Broadcast Music, Inc., Am. Composers Forum, Southeastern Composers League (past. pres.), Phi Kappa Phi, Pi Kappa Lambda, Sigma Alpha Iota. Avocations: travel, art glass work, photography. Home: 15253 W Morningtree Dr Surprise AZ 85374-4619 Personal E-mail: dkeastman@cox.net.

EASTMAN, FOREST DAVID, lawyer, educator; b. Iowa City, Mar. 30, 1950; s. Forest Emery and Wanda Mae (Lightner) E.; m. Susan Laurie Chenous, Jan. 4, 1975; children: Jeffrey David, Chad Ryan. BA, U. Wis., Plattville, 1975; JD, Washburn U., 1982. Bar: Iowa 1982, U.S. Dist. Ct. (no. dist.) Iowa 1982, U.S. Dist. Ct. (so. dist.) Iowa 1983. Pvt. practice, Mason City, Iowa, 1982-89, Clear Lake, Iowa, 1989—2003. Part time instr. North Iowa Area Community Coll., 1990-91, Buena Vista U., 1991—, Vol. Vol. Lawyers Project, 1986—. Served with U.S. Army, 1968-72. Mem. Iowa Bar Assn., Cerro Gordo County Bar Assn., Elks (inner guard, esquire 1986, esteemed lecturing knight 1987, esteemed loyal knight 1988, esteemed leading knight 1989). Republican. Avocations: racquetball, fishing, skiing, golf. Office: 914 N 8th St W Clear Lake IA 50428-1825

EASTMAN, HAROLD DWIGHT, retired social studies educator, journalist; b. Harbor Springs, Mich., Dec. 11, 1915; s. William Raymond and Edith Georgianna (Cross) Eastman; married, June 1, 1943; children: Danite Rae, Bruce Clyde, Jonathan Porter. BA, Sioux Falls Coll., 1941; MA, Coll. William and Mary, 1947; PhD, U. Iowa, 1954. Caseworker ARC, St. Paul, 1946-52; chief divsn. diagnosis and treatment Youth Conservation Commn., St. Paul, 1950-52; asst. prof. sociology Macalester Coll., St. Paul, 1947-50; assoc. prof. sociology Midland Coll., Fremont, Nebr., 1954-57; prof. sociology Carroll Coll., Waukesha, Wis., 1957-63; vis. prof. sociology U. Glasgow, Scotland, 1967-68; vis. lectr. Ottumwa Heights Coll., Ottumwa, Iowa, 1969-70; prof., head dept. sociology Parsons Coll., Fairfield, Iowa, 1963-71; head dept. sociology Truman State U., Kirksville, Mo., 1971-81, prof. emeritus Point Lookout, Mo., 1981—; guest prof. sociology Coll. of the Ozarks, Point Lookout, Mo., 1981-98, ret., 1998. Mem. Mayor's Com. Alcoholism, Mayor's Com. Juvenile Delinquency, Mayor's Com. Drug Abuse, 1963—70, Mayor's Study Com. Housing Needs for Impoverished Sr. Citizens, 1963—70. Contbr. articles to profl. jours., poems to lit. publs., including The Best Poems and POets of 2003. Hospice creator, Kirksville, Mo., 1975; transport provider for terminally ill patients Branson, Mo.; pres. Waukesha County Coun. Social Agys., 1957—63; provost marshal 84th Divsn. Tng., Milw., 1957—63; chmn., co-founder N.E. Mo. Hospice Com., 1979—81; vol. Ozark Mountain Hospice, Branson, 1983—; chair com. Election of Hubert Humphrey for U.S. Senate, St. Paul, 1950; elected mem. Waukesha County Bd. Suprs., 1957—63; elder United Presbyn. Ch., 1971—;

chmn. scholarship com. UNICO, Waukesha, 1957—63. Lt. col. U.S. Army, 1941—46. Mem.: Mark Twain Mental Health Assn. (bd. dirs. 1976—79), Am. Sociol. Assn., Am. Assn. Univ. and Coll. Profs., Ret. Officers Assn. (pres. 1987), Mo. Hospice Assn., Phi Kappa Phi, Kappa Delta Pi, Alpha Kappa Delta. Home: 15 Fleming Dr Columbia MO 65201-5418 E-mail: eastmanhar@aol.com.

EASTMAN, JOHN ROBERT, education educator; b. San Diego, June 30, 1945; s. John Henry and Theresa (Wimberger) E. BA, Va. Poly. Inst. and State U., 1968; PhD, Julius-Maximilians U., Wuerzburg, 1985. Cert. tchr., Va. Tchr. So. H.S., Harwood, Md., 1968-69; restoration worker Blersch-Lenz, Munich, 1971—75; instr. for English Dolmetscher Inst., Wuerzburg, 1976-83; bilingual tourist guide Arbeitsamt, Wuerzburg, 1976-85; summer sch. tchr. Archbishop Spalding H.S., Severn, Md., 1992; substitute tchr. Ft. Meade High Sch., 1990, Old Mill H.S., 1992, Anne Arundel Co., Md., 1987-97, Hampton (Va.) City Schs., 2001—; tchr. Peninsula Cath. H.S., Newport News, Va., 1997—2001; asst. prof. German Old Dominion U., Norfolk, Va., 2002—03; tchr. Walsingham Acad., Williamsburg, Va., 2003—05; adj. faculty history Christopher Newport U., Newport News, 2005—. Author: Papal Abdication in Later Medieval Thought, 1990; editor: Aegidius Romanus, De Renunciatione Pape, 1992; contbr. Internat. Medieval Bibliography, 1995—; contbr. articles to profl. jours. Mem. Am. Hist. Assn., Southeastern Medieval Assn., Nat. Coalition Ind. Scholars, Capital Area Ind. Scholars (sec.-treas. 1992-94, newsletter editor 1994-96), Am. Philol. Assn., Am. Cath. Hist. Assn., Am. Assn. Tchrs. German. Avocation: genealogy. Home: 11131 Winston Pl Apt 8 Newport News VA 23601-2238 Personal E-mail: jreastman@mycidco.com.

EASTMAN, LESTER FUESS, electrical engineer, educator; b. Utica, N.Y., May 21, 1928; s. Howard Socrates and Mayme Lois (Fuess) E.; m. Anne Marie Gardner, Dec. 22, 1948; children: David Joel, Daniel Gardner, Laurie Suzanne. BEE, Cornell U., 1953, MS, 1955, PhD, 1957. Instr. Cornell U., Ithaca, NY, 1954-56, asst. prof., 1957-60, assoc. prof., 1960-66, prof. elec. engring., 1966-84; John L. Given Found. Chair prof. elec. engring., 1985—; founder, dir. joint services electronics program and research lab., 1977-87. Founding mem. Nat. Rsch. and Resource Facility for Submicron Structures, 1977—; laborator Chalmers Tech. U., Gothenburg, Sweden, 1960—61; mem. tech. staff RCA Rsch. Lab., 1964—65; founder, pres. Cayuga Assoc., Ithaca, 1971—72; mem. tech. staff MIT, Lincoln Lab., Lexington, Mass., 1978—79; dir. Cornell Rsch. Found., 1974—86; mem. U.S. Adv. Group Election Devices, 1978—85, 1986—88; vis. scientist IBM Watson Rsch. Lab., 1985—86; founder, chmn. bd. dirs. N.E. Semicondr., Inc., 1987—93; chmn. sci. adv. bd. Nova Crystals, 1998—2003; mem. kuratorium, sr. advisory bd. Fraunhofer Applied Physics Inst., 1994—2000; cons. to industry. Guest editor IEEE transactions, 1967, 78; Contbr. articles to profl. jours.; patentee in field. Served with USN, 1946-48. Recipient Welker medal and award Internat. Symposium Gallium Arsenide and Related Compounds, 1991, Aldert Van Der Ziel award, 1995, Prof. William Gould Dow Lectureship award U. Mich., 2002; Sperry Gyroscope fellow, 1953-54, GE fellow, 1956-57, Humboldt Sr. fellow, 1994—. Fellow IEEE (Grad. Educator award 1999, Third Millenium Medal, 2000, J.J. Ebers award 2002, Lester F. Eastman Biennial conf., 2002—), Am. Phys. Soc.; mem. NAE, Electromagnetics Acad., Sigma Xi, Eta Kappa Nu, Tau Beta Pi, Phi Kappa Phi. Presbyterian. Home: 61 Burdick Hill Rd Ithaca NY 14850-9760 Office: Cornell U 425 Phillips Hall Ithaca NY 14853-5401 E-mail: lfe@iiiv.tn.cornell.edu. *As a professor, I believe that my life contribution is through giving many students the opportunity to reach their full potential in the highest technology available.*

EASTMAN, W. DEAN, secondary school educator; b. Lawrence, Mass., Feb. 22, 1948; s. Weston D. and Harriett R. Eastman. BS in Social Sci. Edn., Drake U., 1970; MS in Edn., Springfield (Mass.) Coll., 1976, cert. advanced grad. adminstrn. studies, 1977; M in Liberal Arts, Harvard U., 2000. Coach track and field Springfield Coll. and U. Mass., Lowell, 1970-81; tchr. social sci. Beverly (Mass.) H.S., 1970—. Vis. prof. edn. Drake U., 1994—95. Contbr. biography on Nathan Dane to Yale Biographical Dictionary of American Law, 2004; contbr. articles to publs. including Scholastic Coach, Track Technique, Jour. Phys. Edn. and Recreation, Harvard Newsletter: Civil Perspective, Local History Mag. Common-Place; featured in (book) I Am a Teacher, 1990, (mags.) Tchg. Tolerance, Boston Mag.; featured for work with homeless students Today Show, NBC-TV, 1991; host 10-part series on immigration Mass. Ednl. TV, 1992; features include (PBS series) Only a Teacher, 2001. Mem. ednl. steering com. Mass. Civil Liberties Union, Boston, 1990—; mem. PBS Tchg Adv. Bd., 2004—. Christa McAuliffe fellow Mass. Dept. Edn., 1989, resident fellow Mass. Hist. Soc., 2001; recipient Outstanding Tchr. award John F. Kennedy Presdl. Libr., 1989, Am. Tchr. award Disney Channel, 1991, Alumni Achievement award Drake U., 1991, Derek Bok prize Harvard U., 2000; named one of Outstanding Young Men of Am., 1982, Preserve Am. Mass. History Tchr. of the Yr., 2004. Mem. Nat. Assn. Scholars. Avocations: surf casting, poetry, harvard football games. Office: Beverly HS 100 Sohier Rd Beverly MA 01915-5533 Business E-Mail: wdeastman@post.harvard.edu.

EASTMENT, THOMAS JAMES, lawyer; b. N.Y.C., Mar. 3, 1950; s. George Thomas and Grace Anne Eastment. BChemE, Manhattan Coll., 1972; JD, U. Mich., 1975. Bar: N.Y. 1976, D.C. 1977. Assoc. Morton, Bernard, Brown, Washington, 1975-77, Baker Botts LLP, Washington, 1977-84, ptnr., 1985—. Mem. D.C. Bar Assn., Fed. Energy Bar Assn. Office: Baker Botts LLP The Warner 1299 Pennsylvania Ave NW Washington DC 20004-2400 Office Phone: 202-639-7717. Business E-Mail: Tom.Eastment@BakerBotts.com.

EASTMOND-ROBINSON, JUNE PATRICIA, nursing educator; b. N.Y.C., June 21, 1938; d. Claude T. Eastmond and Olivia G. DeBello; m. Maroa W. Gikuuri, 1968 (div. 1978); children: Maroa L., Nyahiri Gikuuri-Bandele; m. Arthur L. Robinson, May 16, 1981; 1 stepchild, Randall. RN, Kings County Hosp. Sch. Nursing, Bklyn., 1958; BSN, NYU, 1964; MS Cmty. Health, L.I. U., Bklyn., 1974; EdD, Fla. Atlantic U., 1999. RN Fla. Bd. Nursing, 1978; cert. healing touch IIB Fla. Ctr. for Healing Touch. Staff nurse Kings County Hosp., Bklyn., 1958—59, dir. patient rels., 1974—78; pub. health nurse Dept. Health, Bklyn., 1961—63; pub. health nurse for pregnant teens Project Teen Aid, Bklyn., 1968—72; in svc. edn. coord. Medgar Evers Coll., Bklyn., 1972—74; dir. nursing Fla. Cmty. Health Ctrs., West Palm Beach, 1978—80; assoc. prof. Indian River C.C., Fort Pierce, Fla., 1980—2001, ret., 2001. Co-chair State of Fla. Sci. Taskforce, 1980—86; test cons. Nat. Coun. State Bds. Nursing, Atlanta, 1994, Atlanta, 97. Co-author: (textbook) Nursing Assistant Fundamentals, 1998. Active, past pres., publicity chair African-Am. Cultural Exposition for the Arts, Fort Pierce, Fla., 1983—2002; treas., actor Faces and Voices of St. Lucie County Inc., 2001—03; mem. The Links Inc. Orlando chpt., 1996—; v.p. region III Fla. Spl. Needs Assn., 1986—89; bd. dirs. Big Bros. Big Sisters, Fort Pierce, Fla., 2001—03. Recipient cert. of appreciation, Nat. Coun. State Bd. Nursing, 1997, cert. acad. excellence award, Fla. Atlantic U., 1997. Mem.: NAACP, Fla. Nurse Assn. (treas. 2000—03), Caribbean Nurses Assn. (bd. dirs. 1999—2003, gratitude award 2000), Assn. Practical Nurse Educators (pres., treas., bd. dirs. 1991—2000), The Links Inc. Avocations: reading, exercising, organizing community activities, guest speaking on health issues, acting in community theater. Home: 14556 Lycastle Cir Orlando FL 32826-4212

EASTON, CHARLES CLEMENT, JR., corporate financial executive; b. Allentown, Pa., July 14, 1930; s. Charles Clement and Harriet Ida (Williamson) E.; m. Priscilla Emma Herbert, Dec. 26, 1954; children: Joanne, Charles III, June, Jennifer. BS in Econs., Wharton Sch., 1952; MBA, Harvard U., 1956. CFP. Asst. to treas. Inmont Corp., N.Y.C., 1956-62, asst. treas., 1962-67, treas., 1967-80, Inmont Div./United Technologies, Clifton, NJ, 1980-84; dir. fin. planning Coatings and Inks Div./BASF Corp., Clifton, 1984-88; sr. rep. Excel Comms., Inc., Boca Raton, Fla. and Short Hills, N.J., 1995—2004; mem. adv. bd. Cmty. Agys. Corp., Newark, 2005—. Trustee, bd. dirs. Comm. Agys. Corp., Newark, N.J., 1989-2004. 1st lt. USAF, 1952-54, Korea. Mem. Wyo. Club of Millburn, N.J., Racquets Club of Boca Raton, Alpha Chi Rho. Republican. Congregationalist. Avocations: tennis, bridge. E-mail: ceastonjr74@yahoo.com.

EASTON, GLENN HANSON, JR., management consultant, federal official, military officer; b. N.Y.C., Mar. 11; s. Glenn Herman and Cornelia Blanchard (Hanson) E.; m. Jeanne Milhall, June 15, 1944; children: Jeanne, Glenn Hanson III, Michelle, Carol. Assoc. in Bus. Adminstrn., U. Pa., 1949, BA in Econs., 1950; MBA, NYU, 1959. USCG lic. 3d asst. engr. steam vessels of any horsepower, 3d mate of steam and motor vessels of any gross tons upon the waters of oceans, Panamanian master; CLU. Various positions to asst. traffic mgr. Keystone Shipping Co., Phila., 1940—54, Phila. Jr. C. of C., 1946-54; various positions to mgr. transp. econs. div. Standard-Vacuum Oil Co., White Plains, N.Y., 1954-59; various positions to cons. to pres. S.R. Guggenheim Found., N.Y.C., 1959-84; pres. Glenn Easton & Assocs. (mgmt. and ins. cons.), Port Chester, N.Y., 1970—; emeritus spl. agent Northwestern Mutual Life Ins. Co., 1974—; polit. appointee U.S. Dept. Labor, Washington, 1982-88; emeritus spl. agt. Northwestern Mut. Life Ins. Co., 1974—. Assoc. prof. mgmt. LI U., Brookville, NY, 1971—72. Rep. candidate for congressman, N.Y., 1972, 74, 80; pres. local Rep. Club, 1973-74; mem. Westchester County Rep. Com., 1972-83; Rep., Conservative and Ind. candidate for supr. Town of Rye, N.Y., 1973, 75, 79, 81, Rep. Candidate for councilman, 1977; vice chmn. Ind. Conservative Caucus, Westchester, 1977-83; exec. v.p. bd. trustees N.Y.-Phoenix Schs. Design, 1968-74; Eagle Scout with 4 Silver Palms. With Maine N.G., 1936-38; served to comdr. USN, 1938-40, 43-46, 50-54, 70, PTO, ret., 1979. Mem. Soc. Naval Archs. and Marine Engrs. (life, Golden award), Navy Athletic Assn., Sr. Execs. Assn., Fed. Exec. Inst., Ret. Officers' Assn., C. of C., Am. Mgmt. Assn., Naval Res. Assn. (life, v.p. Westchester chpt.), Militia Assn. N.Y. (life), Westchester Organ Soc. (v.p.), Met. Organ Soc. Va., No. Va. Ragtime Soc., Am. Theatre Organ Soc., U.S. Capitol Hist. Soc., The Conservative Network (life), Am. Legion, Kiwanis, Elks, 32rd Degree Scotish Rite Freemason and Shriner, Club, Pi Gamma Mu, Sigma Kappa Phi, Phi Delta Theta (Golden Legionnaire) Avocations: swimming, reading, music, archery, coin collecting/numismatics. Home: 1385 Old Quincy Ln Reston VA 20194-1309 Office: 1537 Inlet Ct Reston VA 20190-4423 Office Phone: 703-437-1666. *Much hard work, a desire for knowledge, great integrity, persistence, enthusiasm, determination, and some vision are essential ingredients in the success formula. In addition, successful leaders must never shrink from responsibility! While it helps to be lucky, to have friends in the right places, or to be in the right place at the right time, it is more important in a man's quest for success to deal honestly and fairly with one's fellowman in order that when material success is achieved peace of mind and happiness come with it.*

EASTON, JILL JOHANNA, state official; b. Nassau County, N.Y., June 6, 1949; d. E. Paul and Thelma R. Easton. BA, U. So. Miss., 1971, MPA, 1986. Mgr. classified advt. Thibodeaux (La.) Daily Comet, 1971-73; on-air personality Sta. WNAT, Natchez, Miss., 1973-74; classified sales rep. Natchez Democrat, 1974; co-owner House of Pisces Pet Shop, Vidalia, La., 1974-75; employment interviewer Miss. Employment Svc., Gulfport, 1976-80; pub. relations rep. Miss. Dept. Health, Gulfport, 1980—2001, health program rep., vital records and child care lic., 1983-2000; COO Treble Hook Unltd.; free-lance outdoor writer, 2000—. Pres. J & K Ltd. Columnist: Sun Herald, contbg. writer: Today in Miss. Mem.: S.E. Outdoor Press Assn., Outdoor Writers of Am. Assn., So. Miss. Hist. and Geneal. Soc., Miss. Archaeology Assn. (bd. dirs.), Divers Alert Network. Lutheran. Avocations: scuba diving, hunting, fishing, painting, field archaeology. Home and Office: 206 Kuyrkendall Pl Long Beach MS 39560-3308 Office Phone: 870-297-4415. E-mail: jjeaston@worldnet.att.net.

EASTON, J(OHN) DONALD, neurologist, educator; b. Saskatoon, Sask., Can., Apr. 1, 1938; s. John and Winnifred J. (Small) E.; m. Carol Anne May, 1959 (div. 1984); children: Erin, John, Murray; m. K. Von Gunten, May 19, 1985; children: Andrew, Alexander. BS in Zoology, Wash. State U., 1960; MD, U. Wash., 1964. Cert. Am. Bd. Psychiatry and Neurology (examiner, dir. 1984-92). From asst. to assoc. prof. U. Calif., San Diego, 1970-73; from assoc. prof. to prof. So. Ill. U. Sch. Medicine, Springfield, 1974-77; prof., chair neurology dept. U. Mo. Sch. Medicine, Columbia, 1977-82, U. Tex. Health Sci. Ctr., San Antonio, 1982-86, Brown U. Sch. Medicine, Providence, 1986—. Pres. Neurology Found., Inc., Providence, 1990—. Author med. books; editor med. jours. Fellow Am. Heart Assn. Stroke Coun., 1971—, chmn., 1991-93, vol., Providence, 1986—. With USN, 1968-70. Fellow Am. Acad. Neurology; mem. Am. Neurol. Assn., Alpha Omega Alpha, Phi Beta Kappa. Presbyterian. Avocations: travel, computers, sports. Home: 7 Seaview Ave Jamestown RI 02835-1644 Office: RI Hosp Brown U 110 Lockwood St Providence RI 02903-4801 Office Phone: 401-444-8795. Business E-Mail: j_easton@brown.edu.

EASTON, JOHN JAY, JR., lawyer; b. San Francisco, June 16, 1943; s. John Jay and Julia (Crawford) Easton; m. Donna Cecilia Ringger Startzel, May 4, 1996. BS, U. Colo., 1964; JD, Georgetown U., 1970. Bar: Va. 1970, Vt. 1971. Mktg. rep. Gen. Dynamics Corp., Washington, 1968-70; assoc. Paterson, Gibson, Noble & Brownell, Montpelier, Vt., 1970-72; ptnr. Davison & Easton, Stowe, Vt., 1972-75; asst. atty. gen., chief consumer protection Office Vt. Atty. Gen., 1975-78; dir. div. rate setting Vt. Agy. Human Svcs., 1978-80; atty. gen. State of Vt., 1981-85; pvt. practice Burlington, Vt., 1985-86; v.p. Syn-Cronamics, Inc., Englewood Cliffs, NJ, 1986-87, Miller, Eggleston & Rosenberg, Ltd., 1987-89; asst. sec. Internat. Affairs and Energy Emergencies Dept. Energy, Washington, 1989-91, gen. counsel, 1991-92, asst. sec. Domestic and Internat. Energy Policy, 1992-93; pvt. practice, 1993-94; v.p. internat. programs Edison Elec. Inst., Washington, 1994—. Product safety adv. coun. U.S. Consumer Product Safety Com., 1977—79; industry sector adv. com. energy for trade policy matters, 1997—. Mem. Vt. Natural Resources Coun., 1976—89; Rep. nominee for gov. Vt., 1984. Served to capt. USAF, 1964—68. Mem.: VFW, ABA (ho. dels. 1979—84), Vt. Bar Assn. (del. 1980—84, chmn. coms. 1974—78, bd. mgrs. 1973—75), Am. Legion. Roman Catholic. Home: 5310 Saint Albans Way Baltimore MD 21212-3305 Office: Edison Elec Inst 701 Pennsylvania Ave NW Washington DC 20004-2696 Office Phone: 202-508-5633. E-mail: jeaston@eei.org.

EASTON, KENNETH GLENN, retired utilities executive; b. Mattoon, Ill., Jan. 7, 1923; s. Omer Otis Easton and Inza Burrage Reagin; m. Hazel Florence Duncan, Aug. 25, 1946. Diploma, Franklin Credit Sch., Va., 1949. Apprenticeship Local 489 I.B.E.W., 1955. Announcer Radio Sta. WLBH, Mattoon, Ill., 1948—51; owner Music Studio, Mattoon, Ill., 1948—60; pres. Local 489, Mattoon, Ill., 1961—73; gen. foreman Decatur Indsl. Electric, Decatur, Ill., 1961—71; br. mgr. Marion Electric Co., Chicago, Ill., 1971—74; supr. Comstock Electric, Chicago, Ill., 1975—88. Organist Matteson Lodge #175 A.F. & A.M., Joliet, Ill., 1990—2005. Author (editor): Richard Easton, Descendents and Allied Families. Constable Mattoon Twp., Coles County, Mattoon, Ill., 1948—56; republic precinct com. Mattoon, Ill., 1948—56. Technician 5th grade U.S. Army, 1942—46. Recipient Knight York Cross of Honor, Joliet Commandery #4, Joliet, IL, 1980, Order of the Purple Cross, York Rite Sovereign Coll. of N.Am., 2000, Coronated a 33rd Degree Mason, Ancient Accepted Scottish Rite, 1983. Mem.: Ancient Accepted Scottish Rite (mem. of speakers bur. for valley of danville and chgo.), Ill. Grand Lodge of Rsch. (corr.), Peotone Lodge # 636 (hon.), Elwood Lodge # 919 (hon.), Mt. Joliet Lodge # 42 (hon.), Matteson Lodge # 175 (hon.), Braidwood Lodge # 704 (hon.), East Ctrl. York Rite Coll. of Am. # 81, Ansar Shrine Temple. Achievements include initiated into Mattoon Lodge ancient free & accepted masons of Illinois; initiated into royal & select masters, council #82, Joliet, IL; served as thrice illustrious master of council #82; initiated into Joliet Commandery #4, Joliet, IL; served as eminent commander of commandery #4; elected to holy royal arch knight templar priests; served as Knight Commander, 1990; raised to sublime degree of Master Mason in Mattoon Lodge A.F. & A.M. in 1962; served as worshipful Master of Mattoon Lodge #260 A.F. & A.M. in 1970; commissioned as grand lecturer by the Grand Lodge in 1978; served as chairman of the edn. Com. of Grand Lodge of Ilinois 1992-1996; initiated into ancient accepted scottish rite, Valley of Danville in 1968, Received 32nd Degree; served as Most Wise Master of Rose Croix in 1983; initiated into Royal Arch Chapter #27, York Rite Masons at Joliet, IL; served as High Priest of Royal Arch Chapter #27. Home: 1012 John St Joliet IL 60435 Personal E-mail: easton8@juno.com.

EASTON, MARK, lawyer; b. Portland, Maine, 1963; BA, Swarthmore Coll., 1985; MPA, Princeton U., 1989; JD, Harvard U., 1992; Sanwa Bank Fellowship, Inter-U. Ctr. for Japanese Language Studies, Yokohama. Bar: Calif. 1993. Ptnr. mergers and acquisitions/private equity practice group O'Melveny & Myers LLP, LA, sec. policy com. Mng. editor Harvard Internat. Law Jour., 1991—92. Bd. advisors Harvard Law Sch., 1990—92. Mem.: Nat. Assn. Real Estate Investment Trusts, Calif. Society for Healthcare Atty., Am. Health Lawyers Assn., State Bar Calif. (Bus.Law Sect.). Office: O'Melveny & Myers LLP 400 S Hope St Los Angeles CA 90071-2899 Office Phone: 213-430-6549. Office Fax: 213-430-6407. Business E-Mail: measton@omm.com.

EASTON, MICHELLE, foundation executive; b. Phila., Aug. 12, 1950; d. Glenn H. Jr. and Jeanne (Mulhall) Easton; m. Ron Robinson, Sept. 14, 1974; children: Ronald Jr., Daniel, Thomas. AA, BA, Briarcliff Coll., 1972; JD, Am. U., Washington, 1980. Bar: Va. 1981. Asst. to exec. dir. Young Ams. for Freedom, Sterling, Va., 1973-78; asst. to dir. pub. rels. Nat. Right to Work Com., Springfield, Va., 1978; legal asst. Nat. Right to Work Legal Def. Found., 1979; transition team mem. Office of Pres.-Elect, Equal Employment Opportunity Commn., Washington, 1980-81; atty. U.S. Dept. Justice, Washington, 1981; spl. asst. to gen. counsel U.S. Dept. Edn., Washington, 1981-83; pvt. vol. orgns. liaison officer, Africa Bur. Agy. for Internat. Devel., 1984; dir. Missing Children's Program Office of Juvenile Justice and Delinquency Prevention, U.S. Dept. Justice, 1985-87; dir. intergovtl. affairs U.S. Dept. Edn., Washington, 1987-88, dep. under sec. for intergovtl. and interagy. affairs, 1988-91; dir. Office Pvt. Edn., Washington, 1991-93; pres. Clare Boothe Luce Policy Inst., 1993—. Apptd. by Gov. Allen to Va. State Bd. Edn., Richmond, 1994-98, bd. pres. 1996; bd. dirs. The Family Found., Richmond, Va., 1998-99; sec. Nat. Conservative Campaign Fund, 2000—. Mem.: Phila. Soc. (trustee 2000—02). Republican. Episcopalian.

EASTON, STEPHEN DOUGLAS, law educator, lawyer; b. Pasco, Wash., May 11, 1958; s. T. Alex and Zona Gayle (Walker) E.; m. Marivern Slaveck, July 12, 1986. AA, Northland Community Coll., Thief River Falls, Minn., 1978; BBA in Acctg., Dickinson (N.D.) State U., 1980; JD, Stanford U., 1983. Bar: N.D. 1983, U.S. Dist. Ct. N.D. 1984, U.S. Ct. Appeals (8th cir.) 1990, Mont. 1994, Mo. 1998. Aide Sen. Wendell R. Anderson, Washington, 1978; acct. Eide, Helmeke & Co., CPAs, Dickinson, 1980; law clk. N.D. Atty. Gen., Bismarck, 1981, U.S. Ct. Appeals (9th cir.), San Francisco, 1983-84; assoc. Pearce & Durick, Bismarck, 1984-88, 93-94, ptnr., 1988-90, 95-98; U.S. atty. Dist. of N.D., 1990-93; assoc. prof. Sch. Law U. Mo.-Columbia, 1998—. Pres. Stanford Law Forum, 1981-82. Author: How To Win Jury Trials: Building Credibility with Judges and Jurors, 1998; co-author: Problems, Cases and Materials in Professional Responsibility, 3d edit., 2004; assoc. mng. editor Stanford Law Rev., 1982-83; contbr. articles, columns to profl. publs. Del. N.D. State Republican Conv., 1980, 86, 88, 94, 96, Rep. Nat. Conv., 1996; Rep. nat. committeeman for N.D., 1996-98; chmn. N.D. Rep. Victory Club, Bismarck, 1986-90; candidate for state treas., N.D., 1988. Recipient 1st ann. Warren E. Burger prize, Am. Inns of Ct., 2004. Mem. The Mo. Bar, State Bar Mont., State Bar Assn. N.D., AICPA, N.D. Soc. CPAs. Roman Catholic. Avocations: golf, writing, bicycling. Office: Hulston Hall Sch Law U Mo-Columbia Columbia MO 65211 E-mail: eastons@missouri.edu.

EASTON, SUSAN DAWN, biochemist, educator; b. Harvey, Ill., Oct. 8, 1959; d. Dee Charles and Barbara Louise Shaffer. BS in Biol. Scis., Ill. State U., 1981. Med. rsch. technician Washington U. Sch. Medicine, St. Louis, 1981-83; biol. lab. technician VA Med. Ctr., Indpls., 1983-86; rsch. technician Ind. U., Bloomington, 1987-88, rsch. assoc., 1988-92; chemistry, microbiology, validation, document control, quality assurance mgr. Cook Imaging Corp., Bloomington, 1993-96, regulatory affairs mgr., 1996-99, tech. svcs., 1999—2001; tech. svcs. mgr. Baxter Pharm. Solutions, LLC, Bloomington, 2001—, mem. emergency response team, 2001—. Mem. emergency response team Cook Imaging Corp., Bloomington, 1995-2001; lectr. Ctr. Profl. Advancement, East Brunswick, N.J., 1996—, Internat. Soc. Pharm. Engrs., 2001—; lectr. Internat. Soc. for Pharm. Engrs., 2001. Author: Protein Expression and Purification, 1993. Named one of Outstanding Young Women of Am., 1983. Mem. Internat. Soc. Pharm. Engrs., Parenteral Drug Assn., Phi Sigma. Office: Baxter Pharm Solutions LLC PO Box 3068 Bloomington IN 47402-3068 Home: 3702 Stoney Brook Blvd Bloomington IN 47404 E-mail: susan_easton@baxter.com.

EASTWOOD, CLINT (CLINTON EASTWOOD JR.), actor, film director, film producer; b. San Francisco, May 31, 1930; s. Clinton and Ruth Eastwood; m. Maggie Johnson, Dec. 19, 1953 (div.); children: Kyle, Alison; m. Dina Ruiz, Mar. 31, 1996; 1 child, Morgan; children: Kimber Lynn, Scott, Kathryn, Francesca Ruth. Grad., Oakland Tech. High Sch., 1948; attended, LA City Coll. Worked as lumberjack in Oreg. before being drafted into the Army. Owner Malpaso Records Co., Mission Ranch Resort, Carmel, Calif., Tehama Golf Club, Carmel, Calif; co-founder, ptnr. Tehama Inc.; co-owner Pebble Beach Co. Starred in TV series Rawhide, 1959-1966; Motion pictures include: (actor) Revenge of the Creature, 1955, Francis in the Navy, 1955, Lady Godiva, 1955, Tarantula, 1955, Never Say Goodbye, 1956, The First Travelling Saleslady, 1956, Star in the Dust, 1956, Away All Boats, 1956, Escapade in Japan, 1957, Ambush at the Cimmaron Pass, 1958, Lafayette Escadrille, 1958, Ambush at Cimarron Pass, 1958, A Fistful of Dollars, 1964, For a Few Dollars More, 1965, The Good, the Bad and the Ugly, 1966, The Witches, 1967, Hang 'Em High, 1968, Coogan's Bluff, 1968, Where Eagles Dare, 1968, Paint Your Wagon, 1969, Two Mules for Sister Sara, 1970, Kelly's Heroes, 1970, The Beguiled, 1971, Dirty Harry, 1971, Joe Kidd, 1972, Magnum Force, 1973, Thunderbolt and Lightfoot, 1974, The Enforcer, 1976, Every Which Way But Loose, 1978, Escape from Alcatraz, 1979, Any Which Way You Can, 1980, The Dead Pool, 1988, Pink Cadillac, 1989, In the Line of Fire, 1993; (dir.) Breezy, 1973; (actor, dir.) Play Misty For Me, 1971, High Plains Drifter, 1973, The Eiger Sanction, 1975, The Outlaw Josey Wales, 1976, The Gauntlet, 1977, The Rookie, 1990; (actor, composer) City Heat, 1984; (prod.) The Stars Fell on Henrietta, 1995; (actor, prod.) Tightrope, 1984; (dir., prodr.) Bird, 1988, Midnight in the Garden of Good and Evil, 1997; (actor, dir., prodr.) Firefox, 1982, Honkytonk Man, 1982, Sudden Impact, 1983, Pale Rider, 1985, White Hunter Black Heart, 1990, Unforgiven, 1992 (Academy Award for best director, 1992, Golden Globe award for best director, 1993), A Perfect World, 1993, Blood Work, 2002, (actor, dir., composer) Bronco Billy, 1980; (dir., prodr., composer) Mystic River, 2003; (actor, dir., prodr., composer) Heartbreak Ridge, 1986, The Bridges of Madison County, 1995, Absolute Power, 1997, True Crime, 1999, Space Cowboys, 2000, Million Dollar Baby, 2004 (Golden Globe award for best director, 2005, Director's Guild award for best feature, 2005, Academy award for best director & best motion picture of yr., 2005); (exec. producer) Thelonious Monk-Straight, No Chaser, 1989; dir. (TV series) Amazing Stories - episode Vanessa in the Garden, 1985, (TV miniseries) The Blues - episode Piano Blues, 2003. Singer (singles) Unknown Girl, 1981, Rowdy, For You, For Me, For Evermore, Cowboy in a Three Piece Suit, 1981, (albums) Rawhide's Clint Eastwood Sings Cowboy Favorites, 1962, (appeared on soundtracks) Kelly's Heroes, Bronco Billy, Any Which Way You Can, Midnight in the Garden of Good and Evil, (appeared on country recordings) Make My Day with TG Sheppard, Smokin' the Hive with Randy Travis. Mem. Nat. Coun. Arts, 1972-78; mem. bd. Monterey Jazz Festival; chmn. Monterey Peninsula Found.; hon. bd. governors Entertainment Industry Found.; mayor Carmel, Calif., 1986-88; Calif. State Parks commr. for Carmel, 2002-; vice-chair Calif. State Parks & Recreation Commn.; nat. spokesman Take Pride in Am., 2005-. Named one of Time Mag. Most Influential People, 2005; recipient Golden Globe award for world film favorite, 1971, Cecil B. DeMille Award, 1988, Kennedy Ctr. Honors, John F. Kennedy Ctr. Performing Arts, 2000, Lifetime Achievement Award, Screen Actors Guild, 2002. Office: c/o Leonard Hirshan 1680 Clearview Dr Beverly Hills CA 90210*

EASTWOOD, DELYLE, chemist; b. Upper Darby, Pa., Nov. 19, 1932; d. Earl Vivian and Thelma Bernice Eastwood. MS in Phys. Chemistry, U. Chgo., 1955, PhD in Phys. Chemistry, 1964; MS in Mgmt. Sci., Rensselaer Poly. Inst., 1982. Postdoctoral rsch. fellow Harvard U., Cambridge, Mass., 1964-

66; rsch. assoc. U. Wash., Seattle, 1966-69, Northeastern U., Boston, 1970-71; sr. scientist Baird Atomic Corp., Bedford, Mass., 1971-72; project chemist Bendix Rsch. Ctr., Southfield, Mich., 1972-73; rsch. chemist USCG Rsch. and Devel. Ctr., Groton, Conn., 1974-81; sr. staff scientist Brookhaven Nat. Lab., Upton, N.Y., 1981-83; Nat. Superfund design ctr. chemist U.S. Army Corps Engrs., Omaha, 1983-88; sr. staff scientist Lockheed Environ. Sys. and Tech. Co., Las Vegas, Nev., 1988-95; consulting scientist, 1996; sr. rsch. assoc. dept. engring. physics Air Force Inst. Tech., Wright-Patterson AFB, Ohio, 1996-99; rsch. prof. dept. chemistry and biochemistry U. S.C., Columbia, 2000-01; rsch. chemist Western Regl. Rsch. Ctr., Agrl. Rsch. Svc., USDA, Albany, Calif., 2001—04; postdoctoral fellow nano technology dept. chemistry U. Idaho, Moscow, 2004—05. Adj. prof. physics U. Nev., Las Vegas, 1990-99. Editor books in field; contbr. articles to profl. publs., chpts. to books. Recipient Silver medal for Meritorious Svc. U.S. Dept. Transp., 1978. Fellow ASTM (chmn. subcom E13, exec. bd. 1983—, chmn. task force D19 1974—, E-13 Award of Merit, 1996, D-19 Stds. Devel. award 1991); mem. Soc. Applied Spectroscopy (chmn. Nev. chpt. 1988-90), Assn. Women in Sci. (facilitator, nat. contact So. Nev. chpt. 1989-94), Am. Chem. Soc., Am. Phys. Soc., Soc. of Photo Optical Instrumentation Engrs. Office: U Idaho Dept Chemistry PO Box 442343 Moscow ID 83844-2343 Office Phone: 208-885-7785. Business E-Mail: delyle@uidaho.edu.

EASTWOOD, GREGORY LINDSAY, academic administrator; b. Detroit, July 28, 1940; s. William Inwood and Kathryn (Bradley) E.; m. Lynn Marshall, June 19, 1964; children: Kristen, Lauren, Kara. AB, Albion Coll., 1962; MD, Case-Western Res. U., 1966. Diplomate: Am. Bd. Internal Medicine, Am. Bd. Gastroenterology. Resident in internal medicine Hosp. U. Pa., 1966—70; asst. prof. medicine Harvard U., Boston, 1974-77; assoc. prof. medicine U. Mass., Worcester, 1977-82, prof., 1982—89, dir. gastroenterology, 1977-89; dean Sch. Medicine Med. Coll. Ga., Augusta, 1989—92; pres. SUNY Upstate Med. U., Syracuse, 1993—. Chair biodef. coun., past chair bd. dirs. Assn. Acad. Health Ctrs. Fellow ACP. Office: SUNY Upstate Med U 750 E Adams St Syracuse NY 13210

EASUM, DONALD BOYD, consultant, educator, former institute executive, diplomat; b. Ind., Aug. 27, 1923; m. Augusta Pentecost (dec.). BA, U. Wis., 1947; MPA, MA, Princeton U., 1950, PhD, 1953. With USAF, 1943—45; tchr., 1947-48; newspaper reporter, 1949; ind. rschr. London and Buenos Aires, 1950—52; with U.S. Dept. of State, 1953-79; pers. officer Washington, 1953-54; econ.-labor officer, Nicaragua Nicaragua, 1955—57; cons., econ. officer, Indonesia, 1957—59; exec. secretariat Washington, 1959—61; exec. sec. ICA, 1961, AID, 1962-63; polit. officer Senegal, Gambia, Port Guinea, 1963-66; dep. chief mission Niger, 1966—68; sr. sem. in fgn. policy Fgn. Svc. Inst., Washington, 1968-69, staff dir. NSC interdepartmental group for Latin Am., 1969—71; amb. to Upper Volta, 1971-74; asst. sec. state for African affairs, 1974-75; amb. to Nigeria, 1975-79; pres. African-Am. Inst., N.Y.C., 1980-88. Lectr. Princeton (N.J.) U., 1991; dir. World Space Found., Washington, 1997-98; bd. dirs. Vols. in Tech. Assistance, 1988-90. Trustee The Rothko Chapel, Houston, Am. Sch. of Tangier; v.p. Global Bus. Access, Ltd., Washington; mem. Corp. Coun. for Africa, Washington; v.p. Coun. on Fgn. Rels., River Blindness Found., 1991-1995. Woodrow Wilson Nat. fellow, 1988—90, Stimson fellow, Yale U., 1999—2004. Mem.: Am. Acad. Diplomacy, Rotary Internat. (Paul Harris fellow 1995). Address: 801 W End Ave Apt 3A New York NY 10025-5361 Office Phone: 212-666-9609.

EATMAN, LOUIS PERKINS, lawyer; b. Montgomery, Ala., Nov. 16, 1948; s. Jack Bernard and Margaret Worthington (Perkins) E. BS in Fgn. Svc., Georgetown U., 1970; MBA, JD, Stanford U., 1974. Bar: Calif. 1974. Ptnr. Loeb and Loeb, LA, 1974—94, Mayer, Brown, Rowe & Maw LLP, LA, 1994—, co-adminstr., nat. real estate practice group, 1994—96, ptnr.-in-charge, LA office, 1996—, co-leader global real estate practice group, 2002—04; pres. Constitutional Rights Found., 2004—. Mem. Los Angeles County Bar Assn., Internat. Coun. Shopping Ctrs., Riviera Country Club, City Club on Bunker Hill. Phi Beta Kappa. Avocations: golf, fly fishing. Office: Mayer Brown Rowe & Maw LLP 25th Fl 350 S Grand Ave Los Angeles CA 90071-1503 Office Phone: 213-229-5144. Business E-Mail: leatman@malyerbrownrowe.com.

EATON, ALVIN RALPH, aeronautical engineer, electronics executive, systems engineer; b. Mar. 13, 1920; s. Alvin Ralph and Katherine (Hasel) E., m. Kathleen Steiner, Aug. 15, 1942 (div.); children: Eric Lloyd, Alan Ralph; m. Ellen Griffiths Phillips, Oct. 3, 1970. AB in Physics, Oberlin Coll., 1941; MS in Aero. Engring., Calif. Inst. Tech., 1943. Rsch. asst. Calif. Inst. Tech., 1941-44; engr. So. Calif. Co-op Wind Tunnel, Pasadena, 1944-45; with The Johns Hopkins U. Applied Physics Lab., Silver Spring, Md., 1945-75, Laurel, Md., 1975—, mem. prin. profl. staff, 1950—, supr. aerodynamics, dynamics and guidance analysis groups, 1949-54, program supr. supersonic missile and weapon sys. programs, 1954-64, supr. missile sys. divsn., 1964-73, faculty evening coll. grad. sch., 1973-75, supr. fleet sys. dept., 1973-83, asst. dir. for tactical sys. Applied Physics Lab., 1973-79, asst. dir., 1979-86, assoc. dir., 1986-89, dir. spl. programs, 1989-2000, sr. fellow, 1989—. Mem. Johns Hopkins U. adv. bd. for Applied Physics Lab., 1963, 69-70, 73-89; chmn. Def. Sci. Bd. Task Force on Patriot Air Def. Sys., 1977-78, mem. task forces, 1979-83; cons. to under sec. def. for rsch. and engring., 1977-83, chmn. and mem. spl. NATO and U.S. task forces, 1977-92, mem. under sec. def. high energy laser rev. group, 1981-83, mem. under sec. def. durability of electronic countermeasures rev. group, 1983-86; mem. Navy planning and steering adv. Group for Surface Ship Security, 1979-82, chmn. and mem. subgroups, 1979-82; cons. to Asst. Sec. of Army for rsch., devel., and acquisition, 1969-74, 80-86, 2005, chmn., Asst. Sec. of Army ind. rev. panel for Patriot air def. sys., 1980-86; mem. Army Sci. Bd., 1980-86, 89-95; chmn. panel on adv. sys. test, 1980-81; dep. chmn. summer studies on sci. and engring. pers. and future devel. goals, 1982-83, mem. subgroup on ballistic missile def., 1984-86, 89; chmn. atmospheric scis. lab. effectiveness rev., 1985, chmn. panel on electromagnetic/electrothermal gun tech. devel., 1989-92; chmn. subgroup on Army tactical space sys., 1991-92; mem. rsch. and new initiatives issue group, 1991-95; mem. ad hoc study group on space sys. and airland ops., 1992; mem. summer study on future army missile programs, 1993; mem. ad hoc study group missile tech. shelf life, 1994; cons. army sci. bd., 2002-04, mem.summer studies on future Army combat systems, 2002, 2003; chmn., asst. sec. army rsch., devel. and acquisition ind. rev. panel for anti-tactical missile programs, 1986-2002; chmn. high altitude theater missile def. sensor panel Army Strategic Def. Command, 1992-93; dep. chmn., exec. bd. Air Armaments Sys. Divsn. of Am. Def. Preparedness Assn., 1984-90 (life mem.). Mem. editl. bd. Jour. Def. Rsch., 1988-92, Johns Hopkins APL Tech. Digest, 1995—; inventor in field; contbr. articles to profl. jours. Trustee Howard County (Md.) Gen. Hosp., 1977-85, chmn. fin. com., treas., 1979-81, vice-chmn., 1981-83, chmn., 1983-85, chmn. Cmty. Rels. Coun., 1988-94. Recipient Meritorious Pub. Svc. award USN, 1957, Disting. Pub. Svc. award, 1975, Gov. Md. citation for leadership of Howard County (Md.) Gen. Hosp. Cmty. Rels. Coun., 1994, Patriotic Civilian Svc. award U.S. Army, 1995, 2005, Disting. Alumni award Morrison R. Waite H.S., Toledo, Ohio, 1995. Fellow Explorers Club; mem. Balt. Coun. on Fgn. Affairs, Rotary, Cosmos Club (Washington), Country Club of Hilton Head, Sons of Am. Revolution (Hilton Head Island Chapter), Sigma Xi, Phi Beta Kappa. Methodist. Office: Johns Hopkins Rd Laurel MD 20723-6099 Office Phone: 240-228-5058. Business E-Mail: alvin.eaton@jhuapl.edu.

EATON, CHARLES EDWARD, language educator, writer; b. Winston-Salem, NC, June 25, 1916; s. Oscar Benjamin and Mary Gaston (Hough) E.; m. Isabel Patterson, Aug. 16, 1950. Student, Duke U., 1932-33; AB, U. N.C., 1936; postgrad., Princeton, 1936-37; MA, Harvard, 1940; DLitt (hon.), St. Andrews Coll., N.C., 1998. Instr. English U. Mo., 1940-42; prof. creative writing U. N.C., 1946-51; Am. vice-consul Rio de Janeiro, Brazil, 1942-46. Fellow Bread Loaf Writers Conf., 1941, Boulder Writers Conf., 1942. Author: (poems) The Bright Plain, 1942, The Shadow of the Swimmer, 1951, The Greenhouse in the Garden, 1956, Countermoves, 1963, On the Edge of the Knife, 1970, Colophon of the Rover, 1980, The Thing King, 1983, The Work of the Wrench, 1985, New and Selected Poems, 1942-87, 1985, New and Selected Poems, 1992, 2002, 2003, A Guest on Mild Evenings, 1991, The Work of the Sun: New and Selected Poems, 1991—2002, 2004, The Labyrinth, 1995, (poems) The Country of the Blue, 1994, The Fox and I, 1996, The Scout in Summer, 1999, The Jogger By the Sea, 2000, Between the Devil and the Deep Blue Sea, 2002, (art criticisms) Karl Knaths: Five Decades of Painting, 1973, Robert Broderson: Paintings and Graphics, 1975, (short stories) Write Me From Rio, 1959, The Girl from Ipanema, 1972, The Case of the Missing Photographs, 1978, New and Selected Stories: 1959-89, 1989, (novels) A Lady of Pleasure, 1993, (essays) The Man from Buena Vista. Selected Nonfiction, 1944-2000, 2001; contbr. anthologies including Best American Short Stories, 1952, American Literature: Readings and Critiques, 1961, Epoch Anthology, 1968, Best Poems of the Year, 1955-65, Best Poems of the Year, 1968-70, Best Poems of the Year, 1974-75, O. Henry Prize Stories, 1972, New Southern Poets, 1974, The Poet in Washington, 1977, Contemporary Poetry of North Carolina, 1977, Contemporary Southern Poetry, 1979, Anthology of Magazine Verse, 1980-81, Anthology of Magazine Verse, 1981, Anthology of Magazine Verse, 1985, 1980 Arvon Poetry Competition Anthology, The Direction of Poetry, 1988, 1988, The Courage to Grow Old, 1989, The Rough Ride Home, 1992, N.C. Poetry Soc. Anthology, 1992, Contemporary Authors Autobiographical Series, 1994, Anthology of Magazine Verse, 1997, anthologies Voices from Home, 1997, anthologies The Zeppelin Reader, 1998, anthologies Word and Witness: 100 Years of North Carolina Poetry, 1999, autobiographical/critical essays The Man from Buena Vista: Selected Nonfiction, 1999, New and Selected Nonfiction, 1999-2001. Mem. vis. com. Ackland Mus., U. N.C., 1987-98. Recipient Ridgely Torrence Meml. award, 1951, Gertrude Boatwright Harris award, 1955, Ariz. Quar. award, 1955, 56, 82, Roanoke-Chowan Poetry Cup, 1970, Oscar Arnold Young Meml. award, 1971, Golden Rose award New Eng. Poetry Club, 1972, Alice Fay di Castagnola award Poetry Soc. Am., 1974, Ariz. Quar. award, 1977, 79, Arvon Found. award London, 1980, Brockman award N.C. Poetry Soc., 1984, 86, Hollins Critic award, 1984, Roanoke-Chowan Poetry award, 1987, 91, Fiction award Kans. Quar./Kans. Art Commn., 1987, N.C. award for lit., 1988, Fortner award, 1993. Mem. Am. Acad. Poets, Poetry Soc. Am., New Eng. Poetry Club, N.C. Poetry Soc., N.C. Art Soc., North Caroliniana Soc., Phi Beta Kappa, Sigma Nu. Clubs: Harvard U.; Chancellors U. N.C. Address: 808 Greenwood Rd Chapel Hill NC 27514-3908 *I believe in the world seen through a temperament, and I am certain that it is always the main task of the writer to give us his personal vision of reality, objectively and subjectively explored.*

EATON, CLARA BARBOUR, retired librarian; b. Cleve., Oct. 24, 1930; d. George Willis and Lena Logan (Dulaney) Barbour; m. James Marvin Eaton, July 5, 1952 (div. July 1975); children: Jeffery George, Gary Lee. BS, Western Ky. U., 1952. Cert. librarian, Ky. Librarian Woodford County Schs., Versailles, Ky., 1952, Nortonville (Ky.) Sch., 1952-53, Anton (Ky.) Sch., 1953-54, Ea. Jr. High Sch., Owensboro, Ky., 1962-65, Emerson Elem. Sch., Owensboro, 1968-70, Owensboro Pub. Library, 1975-95. Mem. Ky. Libr. Assn., Green River Libr. Group (pres. 1984-86). Democrat. Episcopalian. Home: 621 Owen Ct Owensboro KY 42301-3641

EATON, CURTIS HOWARTH, banker, lawyer; b. Twin Falls, Idaho, Sept. 3, 1945; s. Curtis Turner and Wilma (Howarth)E.; m. Mardo Ohisson, Aug. 2, 1969; 1 child, Dylan Alexander. BA, Stanford U., 1969; MPA, Johns Hopkins U., 1971; JD, U. Idaho, 1974. Bar: Idaho 1974. Atty. Idaho Atty. Gen.'s Office, Boise, 1974-76; ptnr. Stephan, Slavin, Eaton, Twin Falls, 1975-82; exec. v.p. Twin Falls Bank & Trust, 1982-84, area pres., from 1984, also bd. dirs., from 1984; former v.p., bd. dirs. 1st Security Bank at Idaho, Twin Falls, pres., 1992—. Bd. dirs. San Francisco Fed. Res. Bank, Salt Lake City. Bd. dirs. United Way Magic Falley, 1978—, Sr. Citizens, 1978-82; mem. Idaho Bd. Edn., 1993—, now pres.; trustee YFCA, 1981—; pres. Coll. So. Idaho Found., 1986-88. Mem. ATLA, Idaho Bar Assn.

EATON, DORLA DEAN See KEMPER, DORLA DEAN EATON

EATON, GARETH RICHARD, chemistry professor, dean; b. Lockport, N.Y., Nov. 3, 1940; s. Mark Dutcher and Ruth Emma (Ruston) E.; m. Sandra Shaw, Mar. 29, 1969. BA, Harvard U., 1962; PhD, MIT, 1972. Asst. prof. chemistry U. Denver, 1972-76, assoc. prof., 1976-80, prof., 1980-97, dean natural scis., 1984-88, vice provost for rsch., 1988-89, John Evans prof., 1997—. Organizer Internat. Electron-Paramagnetic Resonance Symposium. Author, editor: 7 books, mem. editl. bd.: 4 jours.; contbr. articles to profl. jours. Lt. USN, 1962-67. Mem. AAAS, Am. Chem. Soc., Royal Soc. Chemistry (London), Internat. Soc. Magnetic Resonance, Soc. Applied Spectroscopy, Am. Phys. Soc., Internat. Electron Paramagnetic Resonance Soc. Office: U Denver Dept Chem/Biochem Denver CO 80208 Office Phone: 303-871-2980. Business E-Mail: geaton@du.edu.

EATON, GEORGE WESLEY, JR., petroleum engineer, oil company executive; b. Searcy, Ark., Aug. 3, 1924; s. George Wesley and Inez (Roberson) E.; m. Adriana Amin, Oct. 28, 1971; 1 child, Andrew. BS in Petroleum Engring., U. Okla., 1948. Registered profl. engr. Tex., N.Mex. Petroleum engr. Amoco, Longview, Ft. Worth, Tex., 1948-54, engring. supr. Roswell, N.Mex., 1954-59, dist. engr. Farmington, N.Mex., 1959-70; constrn. mgr. Amoco Egypt Oil Co., Cairo, 1970-81; ops. mgr. Amoco Norway Oil Co., Stavanger, 1981-84; petroleum cons. G.W. Eaton Cons., Albuquerque, 1984-94. Adj. prof. San Juan Coll., Farmington, 1968-70. Bd. dirs. Paradise Hills Civic Assn., Albuquerque, 1986-89; elder Rio Grande Presbyn. Ch., Albuquerque, 1987-90; mem. Rep. Nat. Com., Washington, 1986-92. Mem. N.Mex. Soc. Profl. Engrs. (bd. dirs. 1967-70), Soc. Petroleum Engrs. (Legion of Honor), Egyptian Soc. Petroleum Engrs. (chmn. 1980-81). Home: 5116 Russell Dr NW Albuquerque NM 87114-4325

EATON, GORDON PRYOR, geologist, consultant; b. Dayton, Ohio, Mar. 9, 1929; s. Colman and Dorothy (Pryor) E.; m. Virginia Anne Gregory, June 12, 1951; children: Gretchen Maria, Gregory Mathieu. BA, Wesleyan U., 1951, Doctorate (hon.), 1995; MS, Calif. Inst. Tech., 1953, PhD, 1957; Doctorate (hon.), Colo. Sch. Mines, 2001. From instr. geology to asst. prof. Wesleyan U., Middletown, Conn., 1955-59; from asst. prof. to assoc. prof. U. Calif., Riverside, 1959-67, chmn. dept. geol. sci., 1965-67; with U.S. Geol. Survey, 1963-65, 67-81, 94-97; dep. chief Office Geochemistry and Geophysics, Washington, 1972-74; project chief geothermal geophysics Office Geochemistry Geophysics, Denver, 1974-76; scientist-in-charge Hawaiian Volcano Obs., 1976-78; assoc. chief geologist Reston, Va., 1978-81; dean Tex. A&M U. Coll. Geoscis., 1981-83; provost, v.p. acad. affairs Tex. A&M U., 1983-86, prof. emeritus, 2003—; pres. Iowa State U., Ames, 1986-90; dir. Lamont-Doherty Earth Obs. Columbia U., Palisades, NY, 1990-94, U.S. Geol. Survey, Reston, 1994-97. Former mem. Com. on Internat. Edn., Am. Coun. Edn.; mem. bd. earth scis. and resources; ocean studies bd., and com. on formation of nat. biol. survey NRC, also mem. geophysics study com.; bd. dirs. Midwest Resources, Inc., Bankers Trust; mem., chair adv. com. U.S. Army Command and Gen. Staff Coll.; adv. bd. Sandia Nat. Lab. Geoscis. & Environ. Ctr.; adv. bd. Ohio State U. Ctr. Mapping. Mem. editl. bd. Jour. Volcanology and Geothermal Rsch., 1976-78; contbr. articles to profl. jours. Trustee Wesleyan U., 1995-98, Geol. Soc. Am. Found., 1999-2003; pres., bd. dirs. Iowa 4-H Found., 1986-90; mem. adv. bd. Sch. Earth Sci. Stanford (Calif.) U., 1995-2000; mem. U.S. del. sci. and tech. com. Gore-Chernomyrdin Commn., 1996-97; mem. vis. com. Colo. Sch. Mines, 2002-04; mem. water res. adv. com. Island Co., 2001-03. Named Gordon P. Eaton Hall in his honor, Iowa State U., 2003; grantee, NSF, 1955—59; Standard Oil fellow, Calif. Inst. Tech., 1953. Fellow: AAAS, Geol. Soc. Am.; mem.: Am. Geophysical Union. Home: 201 Pershing Ave College Station TX 77840 Office: Tex A&M U Dept Geology & Geophysics College Station TX 77844 Personal E-mail: gordon.eaton@verizon.net.

EATON, HARVILL CARLTON, university administrator; b. Nashville, May 16, 1948; s. Robert Caldwell and Margaret Elizabeth (Stewart) E.; m. Lois Jean Acuff, June 28, 1969; children: Christopher Carlton, Mary Elizabeth. BS, Tenn. Tech. U., 1970, MS, 1972; PhD, Vanderbilt U., 1976. Asst. prof. of engring. sci. La. State U., Baton Rouge, 1976-78, assoc. prof., 1981-87, assoc. dean. engring., 1986-88, prof., 1988—97, vice chancellor for rsch., 1989—91; vice chancellor for rsch. and econ. devel., 1991; vice chancellor for corp. initiatives and pub. svc. La. State U., Baton Rouge, La.; asst. prof. Tenn. Tech. U., Cookeville, 1978-80; provost and sr. v.p. for acad. affairs Drexel U., Phila., 1997—2003; pres. Cumberland U., Lebanon, Tenn., 2004—. Bd. dirs. Baton Rouge Bank, La. Rsch. Pk. Corp.; tech. cons. La. Rsch. Pk. Corp. Contbr. articles to profl. jours. Bd. dirs. Boys and Girls Club, Baton Rouge, La. Arts and Sci. Ctr., Baton Rouge, Baton Rouge Urban League. Numerous rsch. grants 1976-92. Mem. Am. Soc. for Mechanical Engrs., Am. Ceramic Soc., Sigma Xi, Theta Tau (Hall of Fame 1992). Office: Cumberland U One Cumberland Sq Lebanon TN 37087-3408

EATON, JAMES ALONZA, humanities educator; b. Portsmouth, Va., Dec. 26, 1921; s. Lloyd Russell and Mary Louise Eaton; m. Bernice Freeman, Sept. 11, 1951 (div. Nov. 1955); 1 child, Christopher. AB, Va. State U., 1943; BD, Howard U., Washington, 1946; MA, Boston U., 1951; EdD, Columbia U., 1959. Acting chaplain Tuskegee (Ala.) Inst., 1955-56; asst. prof. psychology Ky. State Coll., Frankfort, 1957-58; prof. psychology Elizabeth City (N.C.) State Coll., 1959-63; program dir. Econ. Opportunity Authority, Savannah, Ga., 1965-67; dean grad. studies Savannah State U., 1968-81, prof. humanities, 1981-86, prof. emeritus, 1986—. Cons. Econ. Opportunity Authority, 1987—. Maj. U.S. Army, 1951-54, ETO. NEH fellow, 1980, 84. Mem. United Ch. of Christ. Avocations: photography, record collection.

EATON, JAMES COLEMAN, music educator, therapist; b. Frederick, Md., Nov. 18, 1949; s. Henry and Ethelene (Harper) E.; m. Sooki Ja Russin, Aug. 25, 1989. B Music Edn. and Music Therapy, Shenandoah U., 1979; MA in Spl. Edn., Hood Coll., 1984; MS in Music Edn., Towson State U., 1993. Cert. tchr., music and spl. edn. tchr., music therapist, reading specialist, Md. Music instr., therapist Daytona Beach (Fla.) C.C., 1980-81; music therapist Henryton Ctr. for Mental Retardation, Md., 1981—84; elem. music tchr., therapist Prince Georges County Pub. Schs., Upper Marlboro, Md., 1984—. Arranger music books: Memories in Melodies, 1981, Songs for Special Occasions, 1981, Happy Holidays Song Book, 1982. With USN, 1969-71, Vietnam. Mem. Music Educators Nat. Conf. (registered music educator), Coun. for Exceptional Children, Am. Music Therapy Assn. Avocation: ballroom dancing. Home: 11109 Luttrell Ln Silver Spring MD 20902-3556

EATON, JAMES DAVID, III, military officer; b. Rockville Center, N.Y., Dec. 14, 1965; s. James David, Jr. and Elin Yvonne Eaton; m. Kristin Jill Zelenak, Oct. 6, 1990; children: James David Eaton IV, Alexander Joseph. BS in Constrn. Mgmt., Colo. State U., Ft. Collins, 1983—87; MSA in Gen. Adminstrn., Ctrl. Mich. U., Grand Forks AFB, N.D., 1989—91. Dep. missile combat crew comdr. 448 Strategic Missile Squadron, Grand Forks AFB, ND, 1988—89, missile combat crew comdr., 1989—91. Missile combat crew comdr. instr. 321 Strategic Missile Wing, Grand Forks AFB, ND, 1991—92; project programmer 319 Civil Engr. Squadron, Grand Forks AFB, ND, 1992—93; chief of maintenance engring. 23 Civil Engr. Squadron, Pope AFB, NC, 1993—95, chief of base devel., 1995—96; comdr. 31 RED HORSE Flight, Leghorn Depot, Italy, 1996—99; program mgr. Hdqs., Air Edn. and Tng. Command, Plans and Programs Directorate, Randolph AFB, Tex., 1999—2002, chief of airborne systems, 2002—02; comdr. 380th Expeditionary Civil Engr. Squadron, Al Dhafra Airbase, United Arab Emirates, 2002—03; dep. comdr. 823rd RED HORSE Squadron, Hurlburt Field, Fla., 2003—. Contbr. articles to profl. jours. Lt. col. USAF. Decorated Bronze Star, Meritorious Svc. Medal, Air Force Commendation Medal, Air Force Achievement Medal, . Mem.: RED HORSE Assn., Soc. Am. Mil. Engrs. Conservative. Presbyterian. Office Phone: 850-881-2224. Personal E-mail: harryvaducci@msn.com.

EATON, JOE OSCAR, federal judge; b. Monticello, Fla., Apr. 2, 1920; s. Robert Lewis and Mamie (Gireadeau) E. AB, Presbyn. Coll., 1941, LLD (hon.), 1979; LLB, U. Fla., 1948. Pvt. practice law, Miami, Fla., 1948-51, 55-59; asst. state atty. Dade County, Fla., 1953; circuit judge Miami, 1954-55, 59-67; mem. Fla. Senate, 1956-59; mem. law firm Eaton & Achor, Miami, 1955-58, Sams, Anderson, Eaton & Alper, Miami, 1958-59; judge U.S. Dist. Ct. (so. dist.) Fla., 1967-83, chief judge, 1983-85, sr. judge, 1985—. Instr. law U. Miami Coll. Law, 1954-56 Served with USAAF, 1941-45; Served with USAF, 1951-52. Decorated D.F.C., Air medal. Mem.: Kiwanian. Methodist.

EATON, JOSEPH W., sociology educator; b. Nuremburg, Germany, Sept. 28, 1919; s. Jacob and Flora (Wechsler) E.; m. Helen Goodman, June 8, 1947; children: David, Seth, Debra, Jonathan. BS, Cornell U., 1940; PhD, Columbia U., 1948. Faculty Wayne State U., Detroit, 1947-56; lectr., then vis. prof. Sch. Social Welfare, U. Calif. at Los Angeles, 1956-60; prof. social work rsch. U. Pitts., 1960-70, dir. advanced program, 1966-69, prof. sociology in pub. health and social work research, 1970-73; prof. sociology in pub. health and social work rsch. Sch. Pub. and Internat. Affairs, 1974—, prof., later dir. program in econ. and social devel.; co-dir. U.S. Comparative Mgmt. Survey Title Ins., 1999—. Russell Sage Found. vis. prof. We. Res. U. (Med. Sch.), 1958-59; project dir. Conf. on Social Welfare Consequences of Migration and Residential Movement, 1969; dir. instn. bldg. program Interuniv. Rsch. Consortium, 1966-71; curriculum cons., later dir. social work and social adminstrn. program U. Haifa, Israel, 1970-74 USIA cons., lectr., Africa, 1979, Sweden, Fed. Republic Germany, 1982, 86, Romania, 1982, Abu Dhabi, Pakistan, Egypt, Sudan, Israel, 1986, Nepal, Pakistan, Egypt, Ethiopia, Iraq, 1988, Yugoslavia, USSR, 1989; Fulbright lectr. and cons., 1979, NAS. guest scholar in Poland and German Dem. Republic, 1980; co-dir. Jordan River Basin Water Resources Devel., U.S. Inst. Peace, 1992—; co-investigator search for inherited causes of schizophrenia in a genetically isolated cmty., 1997—; co-prin. investigator A Pub. Policy-Oriented Audit of Title Ins., 1999—. Author: (with Saul M. Katz) Research Guide on Cooperative Group Farming, 1942, Exploring Tomorrow's Agriculture, 1943, (with Albert Mayer) Man's Capacity to Reproduce, 1954, (with Robert J. Weil) Culture and Mental Disorders, 1955, (with Kenneth Polk) Measuring Delinquency, 1961, Stone Walls Not a Prison Make: The Anatomy of Planned Adminstrative Change, 1962, Prisons in Israel, 1964, (with Michael Chen) Influencing the Youth Culture: A Study of Youth Organization in Israel, 1970, The Rurban Village, 1980, Can Business Save South Africa, 1980, Card Carrying Americans: Security, Privacy and the National ID Card Controversy, 1986, (with Yuri Lvov) Capitalist Communism, 1991, The Privacy Card: A Low Cost Strategy to Combat Terrorism, 2003; also contbr. chpts. to books, articles to profl. jours.; editor: Institution Building and Development, 1972. Mem. cable svc. adv. com. City of Pitts. City Coun., 1994—, chmn., mem. cable comm. adv. com., 1996—. With AUS, 1941-46. Faculty Rsch. fellow, Social Sci. Rsch. Coun., 1962. Mem. NASW (chmn. rsch. coun. 1968-71), Internat. Assn. Social Psychiatry (coun. 1969-72). Home: 1008 Summerset Dr Pittsburgh PA 15217-2535

EATON, LARRY RALPH, lawyer; b. Quincy, Ill., Aug. 18, 1944; s. Roscoe Ralph and Velma Marie (Beckett) E.; m. Janet Claire Rosen, Oct. 28, 1978. BA, Western Ill. U., 1965; JD, U. Mich., 1968. Bar: Ill. 1968, U.S. Dist. Ct. (no. dist.) Ill. 1978, U.S. Ct. Appeals (D.C. cir.) 1984, U.S. Ct. Appeals (7th cir.) 1989, N.Y. 1997. Vol., instr. law U. Liberia Sch. Law, U.S. Peace Corps, Monrovia, 1968-70; lawyer Forest Park Found., Peoria Heights, Ill., 1970-71; asst. atty. gen. State of Ill., Springfield, 1971-75; ptnr. Peterson & Ross and predecessors, Chgo., 1975-94; founder Blatt, Hammesfahr & Eaton, Chgo., 1994-2000; sr. mem. Cozen O'Connor, Chgo., 2000—. Instr. environ. law Quincy Coll., Ill., 1973—75; contbg. writer Chgo. Daily Law Bull., 1975—77; field editor. Pollution Engring., 1976. Bd. dirs. Edgewater Cmty. Coun., Chgo., 2000—; pres. Lakewood Balmoral Residents' Coun., Chgo., 2000—02; bd. dirs. Near North Montessori Sch., 1989—95, vice chmn., 1992—95; bd. dirs. Edgewater Devel. Corp., 2000—, v.p., 2002—. Recipient Ill. Super Lawyer, 2005. Fellow: Ill. Bar Found. (charter); mem.: ABA (environ. ins. litig. task force 1990), Bar Assn. for 7th Jud. Cir., Chgo. Bar Assn., Ill. Bar Assn. (editor sect. newsletter 1972—77, coun. 1973—77, chmn. environ. control law sect. 1976—77, assembly 1980—86, 1989—92, coun. 1990—94, coun. jud. evaluation Cook County 2000—), Atticus Finch Inn of Ct., Lawyers Club Chgo. Office Phone: 312-382-3100. Business E-Mail: leaton@cozen.com.

EATON, LEONARD KIMBALL, retired architecture educator; b. Mpls., Feb. 3, 1922; s. Leo Kimball and Elizabeth (Barber) E.; m. Ann Valentine White, Dec. 24, 1979; children— Mark. R., Elisabeth K. BA, Williams Coll., 1943; MA, Harvard U., 1948, PhD, 1951. Mem. faculty U. Mich., Ann Arbor, 1950-89, prof. architecture, 1963-89. Author: New England Hospitals, 1790-1833, 1956, Landscape Artist in America, 1964, Two Chicago Architects and Their Clients, 1969, American Architecture Comes of Age, 1972, Gateway Cities and Other Essays, 1989, also numerous articles, revs.; book rev. editor Jour. Soc. Archtl. Historians, 1967-69 Democratic candidate for coun., City of Ann Arbor, 1957. With AUS, World War II, MTO. Decorated Bronze Star; recipient Finlandia award Finlandia Soc. Met. N.Y., 1965; Ford Found. faculty fellow, 1954-55 Mem. Soc. Archtl. Historians (bd. dirs. 1957-58), Phi Beta Kappa Clubs: Army-Navy (Washington). Home: PO Box 300 Otter Rock OR 97369-0300

EATON, MAJA CAMPBELL, lawyer; b. 1955; BA, U. Iowa, 1977, JD, 1984. Bar: Ill. 1984, U.S. Dist. Ct. (no. dist.) Ill. 1984, U.S. Dist. Ct. (no. dist.) Calif. 1993. With Sidley Austin Brown & Wood, Chgo., ptnr., 1993—. Former adj. prof. law Chgo.-Kent Coll. Law. Mem.: Def. Rsch. Inst. Office: Sidley Austin Brown and Wood Bank One Plz 10 S Dearborn St Chicago IL 60603

EATON, MICHAEL CHRISTOPHER, contractor; b. Columbus, Ohio, Aug. 8, 1959; s. Ronald Andrew and Rosaleen Ann (Murnane) E. AS, Burlington C.C., 1984. Contracting specialist Def. Supply Ctr., Columbus, 1996—2002. Active Feinstein Found. to Help Hunger. Sgt. USAF, 1980-86. Mem. K.C. (chancellor 1994—, 4th degree 1994, Dep. Grand Knight 1996-2000, Grand Knight 2001-01, Sir Knight), DAV (life), AMVETS (life), Am. Legion, Cath. War Vets. Republican. Roman Catholic. Home: 1103 Weybridge Rd Apt B Columbus OH 43220-2717

EATON, MICHAEL WILLIAM, lawyer, educator; b. Dallas, July 28, 1958; s. Charles H. and Helen Gilbough (Miller) E. BS in Polit. Sci., So. Meth. U., 1980, JD, 1984; postgrad., U. Tex., Dallas, 1997—. Bar: Tex. 1984, U.S. Dist. Ct. (no. dist.) Tex. 1985, U.S. Ct. Appeals (5th cir.) 1986, U.S. Supreme Ct. 1988. Asst. gen. counsel Kirby Oil Co., Inc., Dallas, 1984-85; ptnr. Leonard & Eaton, Dallas, 1985-86; assoc. Page & Addison, P.C., Dallas, 1986-87; pvt. practice Dallas, 1987; pres. San Jacinto Investments Group, 1992—2000; founding ptnr. Eaton, Deaguero & Bishop, LLP, Dallas, 2002—. Lectr. in econs. El Centro (Tex.) Coll., 1995—; lectr. in constl. law U. Tex., Dallas, 1996—; founder, dir. Tex. Jury Rsch. Inst., 1996—; founding ptnr. Affordable Housing Solutions, 1998—. Co-author: Expert Witnesses in The Courtroom, 1996; reviewer Am. Jour. of Polit. Sci., 1994—. Vol. Texans for Bush/Quayle, Dallas, 1988; del. John Connolly for Pres. Campaign, Dallas, New Orleans, 1980; north Tex. youth coord. William P. Clements for Gov. Campaign, Dallas, Ft. Worth, Denton, 1978; So. Meth. U. re-election chmn. John Tower for U.S. Senate Campaign, Dallas, 1978. Mem. Nat. Audubon Soc., Nature Conservancy, State Bar Tex., Assn. Trial Lawyers Am., Lawyers Concerned for Lawyers (officer Dallas Lawyers Concerned Lawyers 1996-97, 1997—), Smithsonian Instn. Nat. Arbor Day Found., Phi Alpha Delta, Ancient Order of Hibernians (pres. 1998-2000). Republican. Avocations: golf, gourmet cooking, travel. Office: Eaton Deaguero & Bishop LLP 1111 W Mockingbird Ste 1150 Dallas TX 75247

EATON, NANCY RUTH LINTON, librarian, dean; b. Berkeley, Calif., May 2, 1943; d. Don Thomas and Lena Ruth (McClellan) Linton; m. Edward Arthur Eaton III, June 19, 1965 (div. 1980) AB, Stanford U., 1965; MLS, U. Tex., 1968, postgrad., 1969. From cataloger to asst. to dir. U. Tex. Libr., Austin, 1968-74; automation libr. SUNY, Stony Brook, 1974-76; head tech. svcs. Atlanta Pub. Libr., 1976-82; dir. libr. U. Vt., Burlington, 1982-89; dean libr. svcs. Iowa State U., Ames, 1989-97; dean univ. librs. Pa. State U., University Park, Pa., 1997—. Bd. dirs. Ctr. for Rsch. Libr., 1988-92, chair, 1989-90; del. users coun., mem. exec. com. Online Computer Libr. Ctr., Inc., Dublin, Ohio, 1980-82, 86-88, trustee, 1987-2002, chair bd. trustees 1992-96; mgr. Nat. Agrl. Text Digitalizing Project, 1986-92; bd. dirs. New Eng. Libr. Network, 1987-89; chair steering com. Digital Libr. Fedn., 2000-2002; mem. adv. bd. Nat. Digital Info. Infrastructure and Preservation Program, 2001-2002; bd. dirs. Rsch. Librs. Group, 2004—. Co-author: Optical Information Systems: Implementation Issues for Libraries, 1988.; co-editor: A Cataloging Sampler, 1971, Book Selection Policies in American Libraries, 1972; contbr. articles to profl. jours. U.S. Office of Edn. post-master's fellow, 1969; Dept. Edn. Title II-C grantee, 1985, 87-88, Title II-D grantee, 1992-96. Mem. ALA, Libr. and Info. Tech. Assn. (pres. 1984-85, bd. dirs. 1980-86), Assn. Rsch. Librs. (bd. dirs. 1994-97), Digital Libr. Fedn. (exec. com. 1997-2003), Coalition for Networked Info. (steering com. 1999—), Rsch. Librs Group (bd. dirs. 2004—). Democrat. Avocations: tennis, walking. Home: 441 Homan Ave State College PA 16801-6337 Office: Pa State Univ 510 Paterno Library University Park PA 16802-1812 Office Phone: 814-865-0401. E-mail: neaton@psu.edu.

EATON, RICHARD KENYON, federal judge; b. Walton, NY, Aug. 22, 1948; s. Paul Francis and Frances Emmaretta E.; m. Susan Henshaw Jones, Sept. 26, 1981; children; Alice, Elizabeth. BA, Ithaca Coll., 1970; JD, Albany Law Sch., N.Y., 1974. Bar: N.Y. 1975. Chief of staff Senator Daniel Patrick Moynihan, Washington, 1983, 1991—93; assoc. Mudge Rose Guthrie Alexander & Ferdon, 1983—91, ptnr., 1993—95, Stroock & Stroock & Lavan, 1993—95; judge U.S. Ct. Internat. Trade, NYC, 2000—. Office: US Ct of Internat Trade 1 Federal Plaza New York NY 10278-0001

EATON, SABRINA CATHERINE ELIZABETH, journalist; b. N.Y.C., Mar. 5, 1965; d. Barton Denis and Anne Elizabeth (Schaeffer) Eaton; life ptnr. Wendy Ann Rodgers; children: Isaac Nicholas, Gillian Elizabeth Rodgers Eaton. BA, U. Pa., 1985. Correspondent The Record, Hackensack, N.J., 1985-87; reporter Daily Record, Morristown, N.J., 1987-88; Washington correspondent States News Svc., Washington, 1988-90; metro reporter The Plain Dealer, Cleve., 1990-94, Washington correspondent Washington, 1994—. Mem. DAR, Nat. Press Club, Nat. Lesbian and Gay Journalists Assn., Investigative Reporters and Editors. Episcopalian. Office: The Plain Dealer Wash Bur 930 National Press Building Washington DC 20045-1928

EATON, THOMAS R., state legislator; b. Keene, N.H., Nov. 23, 1949; children: Kristin, Tom Jr. Grad., New Eng. Inst. Anatomy. Pres., treas. Fletcher Funeral Home, Keene; mem. N.H. Senate from 10th Dist., Concord, 2000—, dep. majority leader, chmn. trans. com., 2000—, mem. fin., ways and means, environment coms., 2000—, mem. wildlife and recreation coms., 2000—, pres., 2002—. Bd. trustees Cheshire Med. Ctr., Cedarcrest, the Home Health & Cmty. Svcs. Bd., Cheshire County chpt. ARC, Cheshire County Crimestoppers; active Keene Family YMCA. Mem. Greater Keene C. of C., Lions, Elks, Masons, Shriner, Old Homestead Garden Club. Republican. E-mail: senate10Ajuno.com. Home: 27 Pheasant Hill Rd Keene NH 03431 Office: State House Rm 302 State House Bldg Concord NH 03301*

EATON, WILLIAM A., federal agency administrator; Degree magna cum laude, U. Va., 1978. Polit. and consular officer U.S. Dept. of State, Georgetown, Guyana, 1979—81, gen. svcs. officer Moscow, 1982—84; spl. asst. to asst. sec. adminstrn. U.S. Dept of State, 1984; spl. asst. to asst. sec. for diplomatic security U.S. Dept. of State, 1985—86; spl. asst. to under sec. state for mgmt. U.S. Dept. of State, 1986—87, adminstrv. officer Istanbul, Turkey, 1988—89, coord. in office of dep. sec. state, 1992—94, adminstrv. officer Milan, 1993—94, adminstrv. counselor Ankara, Turkey, 1994—98, exec. dir. of bus. European affairs, 1998—2000, sr. adviser to under sec. for mgmt., 2001; asst. sec. state for adminstrn. U.S. Dept. State, Washington, 2001—; dir. internat. ops. Young Pres. Orgn., 1989—90, exec. dir., 1991—92. Former reporter, news editor Shenandoah Valley Herald, Woodstock, Va. Recipient Va. Press Assn. award. Office: US Dept of State Adminstrn 2201 C St NW Washington DC 20520-6310

EAVES, ALLEN CHARLES EDWARD, hematologist, health facility administrator; b. Ottawa, Ont., Can., Feb. 19, 1941; s. Charles and Margaret E.; m. Connie Jean Halperin, July 1, 1975; children: Neil, Rene, David, Sara. BSc, Acadia U., Wolfville, N.S., Can., 1962; MSc, Dalhousie U., Halifax, N.S., 1964, MD, 1969; PhD, U. Toronto, Ont., Can., 1974. Intern Dalhousie U., Halifax, N.S., Can., 1968-69; resident in internal medicine Sunnybrook Hosp., Toronto, 1974-75, Vancouver Gen. Hosp., 1975-79; dir. Terry Fox Lab., Cancer Control Agy. B.C., Vancouver, Can., 1980—; asst. prof. medicine U. B.C., 1979-83, assoc. prof., 1983-88, head div. hematology, 1985—2003, prof., 1988—; pres. StemCell Technologies Inc., Vancouver, 1993—, Malachite Mgmt. Inc., 1996—, StemSoft Software Inc., 2000—. Treas. Found. for Accreditation of Hematopoetic Cell Therapy, 1995-2002. Fellow Royal Coll. Physicians (Can.), ACP; mem. Internat. Soc. Hematotherapy and Graft Engring. (pres. 1995-97), Am. Soc. Blood and Marrow Transplantation (pres. elect 1998-99, pres. 1999-2000). Home: 2705 W 31st Ave Vancouver BC Canada V6L 1Z9 Office: Terry Fox Lab 601 W 10th Ave Vancouver BC Canada V5Z 1L3 Office Phone: 604-877-6070. E-mail: aeaves@bccrc.ca.

EAVES, GEORGE NEWTON, science foundation director, educator; b. Athens, Tenn., Mar. 12, 1935; s. Felmont Farrell and Margaret Isobel (Dobson) E. BA, U. Chattanooga, 1957; MS, U. Tenn., 1959; PhD, Wayne State U. Sch. Medicine, 1962. Postdoctoral fellow Bryn Mawr Coll., Pa., 1963-65; postdoctoral fellow, guest investigator The Rockefeller U., N.Y.C., 1970-71; exec. sec. molecular biology study sect. NIH, Bethesda, Md., 1967-73; exec. sect. Nat. Heart and Lung Adv. Coun., NIH, Bethesda, 1973-74; assoc. staff dir. Pres.'s Biomed. Rsch. Panel, Washington, 1974-76; dep. dir. Divsn. Blood Diseases and Resources, NIH, Bethesda, 1976-83, dep. dir. Divsn. of Stroke and Trauma, 1983-94. Lectr. on tech. writing, grant applications and peer rev.; bd. dirs. Cyclotec Med. Industries, Inc.; asst. prof. Washington and Jefferson Coll., 1962-63. Cons. editor Procs. NAS, 1973-76; mem. editl. bd. Grants Mag., 1978-81, Nonprofit Mgmt. and Fin., 1981—; contbr. articles to tech. jours. and chpts. to sci. books. Mem. adv. coun. Park and Tree Commn., City of Savannah, 1994—. Recipient Citation for Profl. Achievement, McDonnell Douglas Corp., 1968, NIH Dir.'s award, 1976, 86, Sustained High Quality Performance award NIH, 1970, 74, 79, Spl. Achievement award HHS, 1989, Spl. Recognition award Pub. Health Svc., 1990. Mem. Sigma Xi. Republican. Anglican. Avocation: church organist. Home: 110 W Gordon St Savannah GA 31401-4909

EAVES, MARIA PERRY, realtor; b. Cluj, Romania; d. Nicholas Brudan and Ema (Filipescu) Perry; m. John Eaves, June 16, 1951; children: Bryan Perry, Susan Eaves Clark. BA, MA, UCLA, 1945; postgrad., Columbia U., 1947-51, U. London, 1953-54. Lic. realtor, Md., Va.; rev. appraiser. Advt. and market analyst Foote, Cone & Belding, N.Y.C., 1948-49; fgn. affairs officer U.S. Dept. State, N.Y.C., 1950-53; dir. rsch. Radio Free Europe Press, N.Y.C., 1955-56; info. officer, media reaction analyst USIA, Washington, 1956-58, rsch. cons., 1958-61; market and pub. opinion cons., Washington, 1969-72; realtor Colquitt Carruthers Inc., Bethesda, Md., 1972-81, Long & Foster Real Estate Inc., Potomac, Md. and McLean, Va., 1982—. One-woman paintings show at Nicosia, Cyprus; group shows include New Delhi (India), White Plains, N.Y., Bethesda, Md.; also pvt. collections. Vol. Gov. Nelson Rockefeller's Com. to Welcome UN Diplomats, N.Y.C., 1968, 69; mem. World Affairs Coun. Washington; Woodrow Wilson Info. Ctr. for Scholars, Washington; charter mem. Nat. Mus. Women in the Arts, Washington, Nat. Mus. Am. Indian. Mem. NAFE, LWV, AAUW, NARFE, FIAPCI, Internat. Fedn. Realtors, Internat. Real Estate Inst. (registered), Nat. Assn. Realtors, Nat. Assn. Rev. Appraisers and Mortgage Underwriters, Md. Assn. Realtors, No. Va. Assn. Realtors, Women's Coun. Realtors, Greater Capital Area Assn. Realtors, Woman's Nat. Dem. Club (Washington), Tournament Players Club (Potomac, Md.), Diplomatic and Officers Club Ret., Columbia U. Club (Wash.), Mil. Dist. of Washington Club. Democrat. Episcopalian. Avocations: bridge, painting, classical music, reading, computers. Home: 11312 Coral Gables Dr North Potomac MD 20878-3803 Office: Long & Foster Realtors 9812 Falls Rd Potomac MD 20854-3996

EAVES, MORRIS EMERY, English language educator; b. Monroe, La., May 12, 1944; s. Archie Harmon and Mary Louise (Morris) E.; m. Georgia Ann Butler, Dec. 24, 1963; children: Obadiah, Dashiell. BA, L.I. U., 1966; PhD, Tulane U., 1972. Asst. prof. English U. N.Mex., Albuquerque, 1970-74, assoc. prof. English, 1974-82, prof. English, 1982-86, U. Rochester, N.Y., 1986—, chmn. dept., 1988—. Presdl. prof. U. N.Mex., 1985-86. Author: William Blake's Theory of Art, 1982, The Counter-Arts Conspiracy: Art and Industry in the Age of Blake, 1992; editor: Romantic Texts, Romantic Times, 1982, Romanticism and Contemporary Criticism, 1986, William Blake: The Early Illuminated Books, 1993, Cambridge Companion to William Blake, 2002; editor: Blake/An Illustrated Quar., 1970—; co-editor: William Blake Archive, 1995—. Nat. Humanities Ctr. fellow Research Triangle Park, N.C., 1984-85; Guggenheim fellow, 1997. Mem. MLA (William Riley Parker prize, 1977-78). Democrat. Office: U Rochester Dept English Arts & Scis River Campus Rochester NY 14627

EAVES, STEPHEN DOUGLAS, high school and vocational administrator, educator, consultant; b. Honolulu, Aug. 30, 1944; s. Alfred Aldee and Phyllis Clarissa (Esty) E.; m. Sally Ann Winslow, Apr. 27, 1974; children: Trevor Bernard, Lindsay Douglas, Christian Francis. BA in Polit. Sci., U. Hawaii, 1967; MS in Bus. Mgmt., U. Ark., 1974; PhD in Edn. Adminstrn., Colo. State U., 1997. Cert. secondary tchr., prin., vocat. dir., post secondary bus. tchr., Colo. Commd. 2d lt. USAF, 1967, advanced through grades to lt. col., ret., 1989; aerospace sci. tchr. Adams County Sch. Dist. 50, Westminster, Colo., 1989-94, vocat. dir./prin., 1994—2003; asst. prin. Westminster HS, 2003—. Cons. Dept. of Edn., Colo., 1993—. Eucharistic min. Spirit of Christ Cath. Ch., Arvada, Colo., 1989—. Decorated Silver Star, DFC, Air medals, Commendation medals, Air Force Achievement medal; named Outstanding Tchr. Focus on Excellence Program, 1992, Outstanding Nat. Aerospace Sci. Tchr., 1994. Mem. Colo. Assn. Sch. Execs., Am. Nat. Rose Soc., Royal Nat. Rose Soc., Lions (sec. Adams Centennial chpt. 1991-92, Lion of Yr. 1992), Elks, Phi Delta Kappa, Omicron Tau Delta. Avocations: skiing, rose gardening. Home: 8708 Independence Way Arvada CO 80005-1247 Office: Westminster High Sch Westminster CO 80030

EAVES, STEPHEN R., music educator; b. Nashville, Tenn., Aug. 9, 1963; s. Calvin Denton and Jo Ellen Eaves; m. Linda L. Stover, Jan. 6, 1996; children: Sam, Holly. B Music Edn., Union U., 1986; MusM, U. Miss., 1990; D of Conducting, U. S.C., 1999. Choral dir. Fayette-Ware H.S., Somerville, Tenn., 1986—88, Morton H.S., Morton, Miss., 1990—92; dir. choral activities Roane State C.C., Harriman, Tenn., 1992—99, McMurry U., Abilene, Tex., 1999—2005, Henderson State U., Arkadelphia, Ark., 2005—. Vol. YWCA, Abilene, 1999—, Zion Luth. Ch., Abilene, 1999—. Mem.: Tex. Music Educators Assn., Am. Choral Dirs. Assn. Avocations: travel, reading. Office: McMurry Univ S 14th St & Sayles Ave Abilene TX 79697

EBATA, MASAKO, artist; b. Mito, Ibaraki, Japan; d. Yoshimi and Yukie Ebata; m. Naoki Muramatsu, June 24, 1998. BA, Ibaraki U., 1985; MFA, Sch. Visual Arts, N.Y.C., 1991. Illustrator, art dir., graphic designer, web designer. Recipient awards Am. Illustration, Tokyo Art Dirs. Club, Clio Awards. Personal E-mail: info@ebata.com.

EBB, PETER L., lawyer; BA, Harvard Univ., 1984; JD, Boston Univ., 1990. Bar: Mass. 1990, US Dist. Ct. (Mass.). Law clk. Justice Herbert P. Wilkins, Supreme Judicial Ct. Mass.; rsch. dir. Mass. Legislature Joint Com. on Pub. Svc.; ptnr. labor & employment dept. Ropes & Gray, Boston. Trustee Urban Coll., Boston. Mem.: ABA. Office: Ropes & Gray 1 International Pl Boston MA 02110-2624 Office Phone: 617-951-7457. Office Fax: 617-951-7050. Business E-Mail: peter.ebb@ropesgray.com.

EBBELS, BRUCE JEFFERY, retired physician, health facility administrator; b. NYC, Dec. 26, 1924; s. Walter Jeffery and Mildred Christiana (Bruce) E.; m. Shirley Marie Cooley, July 3, 1950; children: Bruce Jeffery Jr., Cynthia, Stephanie, Leslie, David. Student, Colgate U., 1943-44; MD, N.Y. Med. Coll., 1948. Intern Hurley Med. Ctr., Flint, Mich., 1948-49; staff Mercy Hosp., Watertown, NY, 1954—88, House of the Good Samaritan, Watertown, 1954—88; resident in internal medicine VA Hosp., Richmond, Va., 1951—54; pvt. practice gastroenterology and internal medicine Watertown, N.Y., 1954-90; med. dir. N.Y. Air Brake Co., Watertown, 1992-94; med. coord. VA Clinic, Watertown, N.Y., 1994-97; staff Genesis Healthcare, Watertown, NY, 1998-99; med. advisor Credo Cmty. Ctr. Addictions, Carthage, NY, 1992—. Chief medicine Mercy Hosp., Watertown, N.Y., 1975-78, House of the Good Samaritan Hosp., Watertown, 1978-83, pres. med. staff, 1978; cons. in internal medicine E.J. Noble Hosp., 1960-88, Lewis County Gen. Hosp., 1960-88, Carthage Area Hosp., 1966-88; cons. in field. Contbr. chapters to books. Pres. Jefferson County Assn. for Mental Health, Watertown, 1969-70; bd. trustees Watertown (N.Y.) Savs. Bank, 1971—; bd. vestry Trinity Ch., Watertown, 1972-78, 2000—; med. advisor Credo-Cmty. Ctr. for Addicitons, 1992—. Capt. USNR, 1979—. Recipient John Philips Rice Svc. award Jefferson County Assn. for Mental Health, Watertown, 1970, Disting. Svc. award Jefferson County divsn. Am. Heart Assn. Fellow ACP (life), Am. Coll. Gastroenterology (sr.); mem. AMA (life), Med. Soc. State N.Y. (life), Med. Soc. Jefferson County (life; pres. 1979-80), Staplin Creek Soc. (past pres.). Republican. Episcopalian. Avocations: aquatic sports, scuba diving, writing, lecturing. Home: 1200 Jewell Dr Apt 205 Watertown NY 13601 Office: Credo Cmty Ctr Addictions 410 State St Carthage NY 13619

EBBERS, LARRY HAROLD, education educator; b. Rockwell, Iowa, June 17, 1941; s. Harold Theodore and Gertrude Eleanor (Robeoltmann) E.; m. Barbara Ellen Smith, June 17, 1962; children: Lori Ann, Kimberly Jo. BS, Iowa State U., 1962, MS, 1968, PhD, 1971. Vocat. agrl. instr. Iowa Falls (Iowa) Sch., 1962-63, Spencer (Iowa) Schs., 1963-65; asst. dir. residences Iowa State U., Ames, 1965-72, asst. prof., 1972-75, assoc. prof., 1975-80, prof. edn., 1981—, disting. Univ. prof., 2004—, dept. chair, prof. studies in edn., 1983-93, asst. to dean Coll. Edn., 1972-76, asst. dean Coll. Edn., 1976-83, assoc. dean, 1996-2000, prof., 2004—. Contbr. articles to profl. jours. Bd. dirs. Ames Parks and Recreation Commn., 1983-86, Iowa State U. Meml. Union, 1989-94; pres. Ctrl. Iowa Regional Substance Abuse Ctr., Ames, 1984-85, Meeker Sch. PTO, Ames, 1975-76; mem. task force on campus ministry Am. Luth. Ch., Des Moines, 1979-84; bd. regents Waldorf Coll., Iowa, 1999—, vice chair, 2005—. Recipient Outstanding Young Alumnus award, 1976, Outstanding Acad. Adv. award, 1977, Human Rels. award Human Rels. Commn., 1984, Human rels. award Student Affairs Divsn., 1985, Outstanding Faculty Citation award, 1991, Cardinal Key Leadership Hon., 1995, Golden Key Honor Soc., 1996, Pres.'s Disting. Svc. award, 1999, Regents award for faculty excellence, 2001, all from Iowa State U.; Rotary Found. fellow, Brazil, 1977; Fulbright scholar, Germany, 2000. Mem. Nat. Assn. Student Pers. Adminstrs. (dir. rsch. and program devel. 1979-81, chmn. Am. Coun. on Edn. Inst. 1984-86, editor jour. 1981-84, pres. 1987-88, v.p. Found. 1989-92, Disting. Svc. award 1990, Fred Turner award 1991, nat. conf. program chair 1992, chair Acad. Leadership & Exec. Effectivness, dir. acad. leadership & exec. effectiveness, 2002-04, Robert Shaffer award for academic excellence as a grad. faculty mem. 1996), Kiwanis (Ames pres. 1977-78), Phi Delta Kappa, Phi Kappa Phi (pres. 1977-79, centennial medalist 1997). Lutheran. Avocations: sports, jogging, farming. Home: 220 24th St Ames IA 50010-4832 Office: Iowa State U N226 N Lagomarcino Hl Ames IA 50011-0001 Business E-Mail: lebbers@iastate.edu.

EBBS, GEORGE HEBERLING, JR., university executive; b. Sewickley, Pa., Sept. 20, 1942; s. George Heberling and Mae Isabelle (Miller) E.; m. Agnes Rak, 1989; children: Stacey Kirsten, Cynthia Lynn, George Heberling III, Alexandra Christine. BS in Engring., Purdue U., 1964; MBA, U. Wash., 1966; PhD in Bus., Columbia U., 1970. Sr. engr. Boeing Co., Seattle, 1966; assoc. Booz Allen & Hamilton, N.Y.C., 1969—72, sr. v.p., 1974—86; v.p. Fry Cons., 1973; chmn. and pres. The Canaan Group, Park City, Utah, 1986—98; pres. Embry-Riddle Aeronautical U., Daytona Beach, Fla., 1998—. Bd. dirs. Pinnacle Bank; chmn. Southeast SATS Lab. Consortium; mem. Aerospace Edn. Found. Adv. Bd. Bronfman fellow. Fellow: Royal Aero. Soc.; mem.: AIAA, Air Force Assn., Nat. Bus. Aviation Assn. (assoc. mem. adv. coun.), Purdue Old Masters, Wings Club (bd. dirs.), Aero Club of Washington, Oceanside Country Club, Prestwick Country Club, Beta Gamma Sigma, Omicron Delta Kappa, Iron Key. Presbyterian. Office: Embry-Riddle Aeronautical U 600 S Clyde Morris Blvd Daytona Beach FL 32114-3966

EBEID, RUSSELL JOSEPH, glass manufacturing executive; b. Detroit, Feb. 9, 1940; s. Joseph Zahour and Theresa (Salamie) E.; m. Carolee M. Cram, Feb. 11, 1961; children: Kevin, Evon, Carrie, Scott. BEE, Kettering U., 1963; MS in Indsl. Engring., Wayne State U., 1969. Registered profl. engr., Mich. Sr. mech. engr. Gen. Motors Corp., Detroit, 1968-70; maintenance supt. Guardian Industries Corp., Carleton, Mich., 1970-71, plant engr., 1971-73, prodn. mgr., 1974-76, plant mgr. Kingsburg, Calif., 1977-80, group v.p., 1981-84, pres. glass div., dir., 1985—. Bd. dirs. Del Claux Cia S.A., Bilbao, Spain, Vidrierias de Llodio S.A., Llodio, Alava, Spain, Guardian Industries, Auburn Hills, Mich., Knight Industries, Toledo, Consol. Glass and Mirror, Galax, Va., Guardian Japan Ltd., Lift GmbH, Germany, Guardian de Venezuela, Monagas, Gulf Guard, Jubail, Saudi Arabia; chmn., mng. dir. Guardian Europe S.A., Luxembourg, Industries Covert Inc., Quebec City, Gujarat Guardian Ltd., India, Siam Guardian Glass Co. Ltd., Bangkok, Thailand; dir. Guardian Africa, Johannesburg, Guardian Flachglass Gmbh, Thalheim, Guardian Brazil, Resende, Egyptian Glass Co., 10th of Ramadan City, Egypt. Author: Instrumentation of Welding, 1963. Decorated knight Order of Merit (Luxembourg), Fed. Cross of Merit (Germany); recipient Employee of Yr. for Corp. award Guardian Industries Corp., 1979; named Nat. Arab Am. Businessman of Yr., Am. Arab C. of C., 2003. Roman Catholic. Office: Guardian Industries Corp 2300 Harmon Rd Auburn Hills MI 48326-1714

EBEL, DAVID M., federal judge; b. 1940; BA, Northwestern U., 1962; JD, U. Mich., 1965. Law clk. assoc. justice Byron White U.S. Supreme Ct., 1965—66; pvt. practice Davis, Graham & Stubbs, Denver, 1966—88; judge U.S. Ct. Appeals (10th cir.), Denver, 1988—. Adj. prof. law U. Denver Law Sch., 1987—89; sr. lectr. fellow Duke U. Law Sch., 1992—94. Mem.: Jud. Conf. U.S. (com. on codes of conduct 1991—98, co-chair 10th cir. gender bias task force 1994—99), Colo. Bar Assn. (v.p. 1982), Am. Coll. Trial Lawyers. Office: US Ct Appeals 1823 Stout St Rm 109L Denver CO 80257-1823 E-mail: david_m_ebel@ca10.uscourts.gov.

EBENSPERGER, MARVIN LEE, mathematics professor; b. Plum City, Wis., June 21, 1950; s. Richard Harry and Lorraine Fern (Weldon) E.; m. Margaret Frances Blaylock, July 7, 1979; children: Bradley, Rebecca. BS in Math., U. Wis., River Falls, 1972. Instr. math. Holy Trinity H.S., Winsted, Minn., 1975—. Active City Planning Commn., Winsted, 1984—. With U.S. Army, 1972-75. Roman Catholic. Avocations: golf, fishing. Home: 120 Fairlawn Ave E Winsted MN 55395-1057 Office: Holy Trinity High Sch 110 Winsted Ave W Winsted MN 55395

EBERBACH, STEVEN JOHN, retired electronics company executive; b. Ann Arbor, Mich., Apr. 30, 1943; s. Robert Ottmar and Marie (Eichelberger) E.; m. Mary Jean Head, Oct. 15, 1983; children: Amy Elizabeth, Michael James, Amanda Claire, Kathryn Louise. BSEE, MIT, 1965; MBA, U. Mich., 1967. Engr. U. Mich. Space Physics Rsch. Lab., Ann Arbor, 1967-73; founder, owner, engr., pres. and chmn. DCM Corp., Ann Arbor, 1974-99; ret., 1999. Inventor loudspeaker design. Mem. IEEE, IEEE Consumer Elect. Soc., IEEE Signal Processing Soc., Audio Engring. Soc., Foresight Inst. (sr. assoc.). Avocations: sailing, photography, computer science and financial software programming. Home and Office: 4455 E Loch Alpine Dr Ann Arbor MI 48103-9422 E-mail: Seberback@aol.com.

EBERHARD, FRANZ VALENTIN, retired educational association administrator; b. St. Johann, Carinthia, Austria, Feb. 1, 1947; s. Johann and Theresia (Krušic) E.; m. Irmgard Kothmaier, Aug. 4, 1968; children: Christoph, Stephan. LLD, U. Vienna, Austria, 1970; D of Polit. Sci., U. Paris, 1973.

Lectr. U. Vienna, 1970-82, U. Paris II, 1972-73; sec. Constl. Ct., Vienna, 1974-78; sec. gen. Austrian Rectors' Conf., 1978-82; dir. European Centre Higher Edn., UNESCO, Bucharest, Romania, 1982-86; sec. gen. Internat. Assn. U., Paris, 1987—2001; dir. Internat. U. Bur., UNESCO, Paris, 1987-2001, cons., 2001. Cons., 2002—. Editor in chief Higher Edn. in Europe, 1982-86; co-editor Adminstrv. Law and Adminstrv. Sci., 1976-82; pub. dir. Higher Edn. Policy, 1988-2001; contbr. articles to profl. jours.

EBERHARD, JEFFREY W., physicist, researcher; b. New Braunfels, Tex., Feb. 21, 1950; s. Leon and Laverne Hinman Eberhard; m. Patricia L. Maxwell, Sept. 15, 1979; children: Matthew J., Melissa A. BA, U. Tex., 1972; SM in Physics, U. Chgo., 1974, PhD in Physics, 1978. Imaging physicist GE Global Rsch., Niskayuna, NY, 1977—96, advanced applications imaging physicist, 1999—; mammography image quality architect GE Med. Systems, Paris, 1997—99. Tech. cons. Com. on Comml. Aviation Security, Nat. Rsch. Coun., 1991—93. Contbr. articles to profl. jours.; patentee in field. Bd. dirs. Lisha's Kill Reformed Ch., Colonie, NY, 2000—. Recipient Sylvia Sorkin Greenfield award for best paper published in Med. Physics, Am. Assn. Physicists in Medicine, 2004. Mem.: Am. Phys. Soc. Avocations: hiking, canoeing, classical music, French culture. Office: GE Global Rsch 1 Research Cir Bldg K10 Rm B320 Niskayuna NY 12309

EBERHARD, WILLIAM THOMAS, architect; b. St. Louis, Apr. 11, 1952; s. George Walter and Bettie Alma (Seilkop) E.; m. Cynthia Ann Hardy, Aug. 20, 1977 (div. 1981); m. Linda W. Bayer, Dec. 5, 1986; children: Elena Lynn, Alysse Marie. BArch, U. Cin., 1976; postgrad., Archtl. Assn., London, 1974. Registered arch. Ohio, Mich., Pa., Fla., D.C., Ill., Mo. V.p. Visnapuu & Assocs., Inc., Cleve., 1972-82; prin.-in-charge Oliver Design Group, Cleve., 1983—. V.p., prin.-in-charge Grubb & Ellis, Cleve., Detroit, Pitts., 1989-90, Grubb & Ellis Nat. Accounts Team, 1987-90. Author: Public Interiors, 1986, 2d edit., 1996, Professional Office Design, 1988, Docket, 1988, Facility Design & Management, 1990, 91, Interior Design, 1992, Contract Design, 1995, Architecture Record Lighting, 1996, Facility Management Journal, 1996; contbr. articles to profl. jours. Profl. team leader Inst. Urban Design, Cleve., 1983; mem. evangelism com. First Bapt. Ch. of Greater Cleve., 1990—. Recipient Best Comml. Interior Design Project award NAIOP, 1991-96, 2000, Best Office Interior Design Project award, 1992, Best Renovation Project, 1995, Design award Nat. Inst. Bus., 1992, 93, Best Comml. Space, 1993, NAIOP Design award Best Pub. Space, 1993, Best Comml. Interior Design, 1994, 95, 96, 97, 2000, Best Renovation Project, 1995, 1st Pl. award Build Ohio Competition, 1992, AIA, 1993, Cleve. Chpt. Design award AIA, 1993, 94, 99, Ohio Area Design awards AIA, 1994-95, Internat. Int. Design awards, 1992, 94, 95, Best of Show, First Place Large Corp. Category, Details Category, Award of Merit Details Category, Award of Merit Retail Category IIDA Regional Design Awards Program, 1998, Lignting Design award IIDA/IESNA, 2002, 03. Mem. AIA (chpt. sec. 1982-84, 2 Design awards 1993, 1 Design award 1994), Internat. Facility Mgrs. Assn., Cleve. Art Assn., Nat. Trust for Hist. Preservation, Inst. Urban Design, Am. Soc. Interior Designers (assoc.), Seminotic Soc. Am. (founding), Design Forum of Cleve. (founding 1990—, pres. 1991—), Club Soc. Ctr. (founding), Cleve. Design Task Force (founding pres. 1996—), Shaker Heights Country Club (house com., design com.), Union Club of Cleve, IIDA/IESNA Reginal Design awards, 2002, 03. Avocations: drawing, photography, tennis, snowmobiling, golf. Home: 2867 Torrington Rd Shaker Heights OH 44122-2555 Office: Oliver Design Group 1301 E 9th St Ste 2900 Cleveland OH 44114-1835 E-mail: wte@oliver-design.com.

EBERHARD-NEVEAUX, CHRISTINE, aviation and public relations executive; b. Fremont, Ohio, Jan. 12, 1951; d. Richard Lesley and Elva Lucille (Ransom) Eberhard; m. Michael Lee Neveaux, May 24, 1997; stepchildren: Jamie, Stephen, Sarah, Spencer. Student, U. Am., Cholula, Mex., 1972-73; BA in Internat. Studies, Ohio State U., 1973; postgrad., Pepperdine U., 1999. Cert. in dispute resolution; lic. helicopter pilot. Account exec. News-Times Pub. Co., Anaheim, Calif., 1975-77; asst. dir. pub. rels. and devel. Hawthorne Cmty. Hosp., 1977-80; dir. pub. rels. Presbyn. Intercmty. Hosp., Whittier, Calif., 1980-82; pres. CommuniQuest, Simi Valley, Calif., 1982—. Contracts with numerous airports and FAA including a contract to teach cmty. involvement course to FAA mgmt. Bd. dirs. L.A. South Bay-Harbor Industry Edn. Coun., 1978-81. Served with USAR, 1975-93. Mem. Res. Officers Assn. (Calif. Outstanding Jr. Officer 1983), Profl. Helicopter Pilots Assn. (past bd. dirs.), Publicity Club L.A., L.A. County Commn. on Local Govt. Svcs. (chair air svcs. com. 1994-99), Helicopter Assn. Internat. (past chair heliport promotion and devel. com., chair pub. rels. adv. coun., spl. advisor to bd. dirs.), L.A. Internat. Airport C. of C. (bd. dirs. 1983-86), Am. Assn. Airport Execs. (S.W. chpt. bd. dirs. 2002—, Corp. award Excellence, 2001), Internat. Assn. Pub. Participation Practitioners, Whirly-girl Number 766, So. Calif Mediation Assn, Ventura County Dispute Settlement Mediation Panel (mediator). Home: 2728 Bitternut Cir Simi Valley CA 93065-1315 Office: CommuniQuest 2728 Bitternut Cir Simi Valley CA 93065-1315 Office Phone: 805-577-0913.

EBERHARDT, ROBERT MICHAEL, diversified financial services company executive, sales executive; b. Hinsdale, Ill., Mar. 11, 1969; s. Robert James and Linda Mary Eberhardt; m. Kristen Lynn Swearingen, Apr. 12, 1971; children: Ryan Robert, Sara Kristen. BS in Fin., No. Ill. U., 1992. CFP CFP Bd. Stds., 1997. Investment officer Invest Fin. Corp., Hinsdale, 1994—96, FCNIS (now known as Bank One Securities), Bolingbrook, Ill., 1996—98, Harris Investors Direct, St. Charles, Ill., 1998—99, LaSalle Fin. Svcs., Lisle, Ill., 1999—2000; regional dir. sales Jackson Nat. Life, Seattle, 2000—00, Farmers Fin. Solutions, LLC, Oswego, Ill., 2000—. Contbr. articles to profl. jours. Mem.: Nat. Assn. Ins. and Finl. Advisors, Fin. Planning Assn. Achievements include patents for trademark for turnkey program in financial services. Avocations: golf, travel. Office: Farmers Finl Solutions LLC 338 Millstream Ln Oswego IL 60543 Office Phone: 630-554-6774. Personal E-mail: eberhardtcfp@yahoo.com.

EBERHART, RALPH E., retired military officer; BS in Polit. Sci., USAF Acad., 1968; grad., Squadron Officer Sch., 1973, Air Command and Staff Coll., 1974; MS in Polit. Sci., Troy State U., 1977; postgrad. studies, Nat. War Coll., Ft. Lesley J. McNair, Washington, 1987. Commd. 2d lt. USAF, 1968, advanced through grades to gen., 1997; forward air controller Tactical Air Support Squadron USAF, Plieka Air Base, S. Viet Nam, 1970; from instr. pilot to squadron hdqrs. comdr. 71st Flying Tng. Wing Air Tng. Command USAF, Vance AFB, Okla., 1970-74; flight commdr., instr. pilot 525th Tactical Fighter Squadron USAFs in Europe, Bitburg Air Base, Germany, 1975-77; instr. pilot. flight examiner, asst. chief evaluation 50th Tactical Fighter Wing, Hahn Air Base, Germany, 1977-78; action officer, chief exec. com. Air Force Budget team Hdqs. USAF, Washington, 1979-80; aide to comdr.-in-chief, comdr. Air Forces Ctrl. Europe USAF, Ramstein AFB, Germany, 1980-82; comdr. 10th tactical fighter squadron, asst. dep. comdr. ops. 50th tactical fighter wing USAF in Europe, Hahn Air Base, Germany, 1982—84; exec. officer to Air Force chief of staff Hdqs. USAF, Washington, 1984-86; vice comdr. to comdr. 363d tactical fighter wing Tactical Air Command USAF, Shaw AFB, S.C., 1987-90; dep. chief of staff, plans and ops. Hdqs. USAF, Washington, 1995-96; cmdr. U.S. Forces Japan, cmdr. 5th Air Force USAF, Yokota Air Base, Japan, 1996-97; vice chief of staff Hdqs. USAF, Washington, 1997—99; comdr. Air Combat Command, Langley AFB, Va., 1999—2000, Air Force Space Command, Peterson AFB, Colo., 2000—02; mgr. for manned space flight support ops. Dept. Def., Peterson AFB, Colo., 2000—02; comdr. in chief N.Am. Aerospace Def. Command and U.S. Space Command, Peterson AFB, Colo., 2000—04; comdr. U.S. Northern Command, Peterson AFB, Colo., 2002—04. Numerous decorations include: Legion of Merit with Oak Leaf cluster, Disting. Flying Cross, Air medal with 11 Oak Leaf clusters, Vietnam Svc. medal with 3 svc. stars, Humanitarian Svc. medal with svc. star, Republic of Vietnam Gallantry Cross with Palm, Republic of Vietnam Campaign medal, The Grand Cordon of the Order of the Sacred Treasure, Japan. and many others. Mem. Coun. of Fgn. Rels.*

EBERHART, ROBERT CLYDE, biomedical engineering educator, researcher; b. Oakland, Calif., Apr. 17, 1937; s. George Perrin and Roberta Eberhart; m. Carol Eberhart, Aug. 4, 1960; 3 children. AB in Applied Physics, Harvard U., 1958; MS in Mech. Engring., U. Calif., Berkeley, 1960, PhD, 1965. Staff scientist Inst. Med. Scis., San Francisco, 1964—70, sr. scientist, 1970—75; assoc. prof. mech. engring. U. Tex., Austin, Tex., 1975—76; assoc. prof. surgery U. Tex. So. Med. Ctr., Dallas, 1976—86; chmn. biomed. engring. U. Tex. So. Med. Ctr. and U. Tex.-Arlington, 1983—2001; prof. engring. in surgery U. Tex. So. Med. Ctr. and U. Tex., Arlington, 1984—. Bd. dirs. Advanced Neuromodulation Systems, Inc.; pres. Tex. Stent Tech., 2005—; bd. sci. advisors Andev, Inc.; founding fellow Am. Inst. Med. and Biol. Engring., 2000—03; cons. in field. Editor: Heat Transfer in Medicine and Biology, 1985; co-editor: Biomaterials-Living Sys. Interactions, 1993—98; mem. editl. bd.: Jour. Applied Biomaterials, Jour. Biomaterials Sci.; contbr. articles to profl. jours., chpts. in books. Recipient C.W. Hall Rsch. award So. Biomed. Engring. Conf., 1987, Career Achievement award Houston Symposium for Biomed. Engring., 1996. Fellow: ASME, Biomed. Engring. Soc., Am. Inst. Med. and Biol. Engring.; mem.: Biomaterials Soc., Soc. Critical Care Medicine (editl. bd. 1973—75), Am. Soc. Artificial Internal Organs (pres. 1994—95), Harvard Club. Achievements include patentee nonthrombogenic treatment for med. polymers 1985. Office: U Tex So Med Ctr Biomed Engring Program 5323 Harry Hines Blvd Dallas TX 75390-9130 E-mail: robert.eberhart@utsouthwestern.edu.

EBERL, JAMES JOSEPH, physical chemist, consultant; b. Dunkirk, N.Y., Oct. 7, 1916; s. George M. and Florence S. (Stedler) E.; m. Donna Davis, July 18, 1996. BA, U. Buffalo, 1938, PhD, 1941; AMP, Harvard U., 1955. Asst. prof. chemistry U. Del., Newark, 1941-42; mgr. rsch. Paper Chem. Divsn. Hercules Inc., Wilmington, Del., 1942-43; sr. fellow Mellon Inst. Indsl. Rsch., Pitts., 1943-44; dir. spl. prodn. rsch. Johnson and Johnson, New Brunswick, N.J., 1944-48; asst. corp. v.p. Scott Paper Co., Chester, Pa., 1948-70; pres., CEO Newbold Inc., Phila., 1970-72; cons. Moylan, Pa., 1972-2000; pres., CEO Eberl Group, 2000—, Ebersytes, LLC, 2002—. Contbr. articles to profl. jours. Trustee The Franklin Inst., Phila., 1960—, mem. sci. and arts com., 1987—; chmn. bd. dirs. rsch. fund Phila. Gen. Hosp., 1963-76; mem. adv. coun. Pa. Tech. Assistance program Pa. State U., 1965-71; mem. dean's adv. coun. U. Buffalo Coll. Arts and Scis., 2000—. Receipent Disting. Alumni award, U. Buffalo, 1999. Mem. Am. Chem. Soc., Am. Inst. Chem. Engrs., N.Y. Acad. Scis., Empire State Paper Rsch. Assn. (pres. 1965-71), Sigma Xi. Achievements include 50 patents for dusting powder for surgical rubber gloves that does not produce abdominal adhesions, single crystal whisker fibers, process for making hard coated plaster of Paris bandages, process for making high strength plaster of Paris, polystyrene foam sheet process, making soybean protein, bleaching process for groundwood pulp; for new chemical sterilization of microbes with epoxides, hemostatic agents, synthetic paper pulp fiberous extenders; process for the manufacture of Viva paper towel; novel dermal formutations; Dermatological Compositions Using Bio-Activating Organocatalysts. Home: 9 Wexford Dr Hilton Head Island SC 29928

EBERLE, WILLIAM DENMAN, international management consultant; b. Boise, Idaho, June 5, 1923; s. Julius Louis and Clare (Holcomb) E.; m. Jean Cilista Quick, Sept. 20, 1947; children— Jeffrey Louis, William David, Francis Quick, Cilista Clare. BA, Stanford U., 1945; MBA, Harvard U., 1947, JD, 1949; LLB (hon.), Gonzagua U., 1976. Bar: Idaho 1950. Ptnr. firm Richards, Haga & Eberle, Boise, 1950—57; mem. Idaho Ho. of Reps. from Ada County, 1953-61, majority leader, 1957, minority leader, 1959; dir., v.p. Boise Cascade Corp., 1959—70; speaker Idaho Ho. of Reps. from Ada County, 1961; chmn. Tertiary, Inc., Boise, 1965—66; pres., chmn., dir. Am. Standard, Inc., N.Y.C., 1965—71; U.S. trade rep., amb. Washington, 1971-75; exec. dir. Cabinet Council on Internat. Econ. Policy, 1974-75; mem. Pres.'s Econ. Policy Bd., 1974-75; pres., chief exec. officer Motor Vehicle Mfrs. Assn., 1975-77; chmn. Manchester Assocs. Ltd., Washington, 1977—. Bd. dirs. Ampco-Pitts. Corp., Am. Svc. Group; of counsel Kaye, Scholer, LLP, N.Y.C., Mid-States Plc. Chmn. Idaho Rep. Fin. Com., 1961-66; mem. nat. Rep. Fin. Com., 1968-80; trustee Stanford U., 1970-80, Com. for Econ. Devel., 1966-. Lt. USNR, 1942-46. Mem. ABA, Idaho Bar Assn., Coun. Fgn. Rels., Univ. Club (N.Y.C.), Met. Club (Washington). Episcopalian. Office: Manchester Assoc PO Box 1425 13 Garland Rd Concord MA 01742-2214 Office Phone: 978-287-1470. E-mail: wd.eberle@tertiaryinc.com.

EBERLEY, HELEN-KAY, opera singer, recording industry executive, poet; b. Sterling, Ill., Aug. 3, 1947; d. William Elliott and P. (Conneely) E. MusB, Northwestern U., 1970, MusM, 1971. Chmn., pres., artistic coord. Eberley Inc., Evanston, Ill., 1973-92; founder H.K.E. Enterprises, 1993—, pres., 1993—; circulation libr. Evanston Pub. Libr., 1995-98; prin., owner The Kidusche Eberley Trust. Founder EB-SKO Prodns., 1976-92, tchr., coach, 1976—; exec. dir., performance cons. E-S Mgmt., 1985-92; featured artist Honors Concert, Northwestern U., 1970, Alumni Concert, 1999, Master Class and guest lectr. various colls. and univs.; host Poetry in Process monthly seminar Barnes & Noble; music lectr. rep. Harvard Club, Chgo.; numerous TV and radio talk show appearances and interviews. Operatic debut in Peter Grimes, Lyric Opera, Chgo., 1974; starred in: Cosi Fan Tutte, Le Nozze Di Figaro, Dido and Aeneas, La Boheme, Faust, Tosca, La Traviata, Falstaff, Don Giovanni, Brigadoon, others; jazz appearances with Duke Ellington, Dave Brubeck and Robert Shaw; performing artist Oglebay Opera Inst., Wheeling, W.Va., 1968, WTTW TV/PBS, Chgo., 1968; solo star in: Continental Bank Concerts, 1981-89, United Airlines-Schubert, Schumann, Brahms, Mendelssohn, Faure, Mozart, Duparc/Wolf, Supersta. WFMT Radio, Chgo., 1982-90; featured artist with North Shore Concert Band, 1989; starring artist South Bend Symphony, 1990, Mo. Symphony Soc., 1990, Milw. Symphony, 1990; spl. guest artist New Studios Gala Sta. WFMT, 1995, West Valley Fine Arts Concert Series, Phoenix, 1999; prodr.-annotator Gentlemen Gypsy, 1978, Strauss and Szymanowski, 1979, One Sonata Each: Franck and Szymanowski, 1982; starring artist-exec. prodr. Separate But Equal, 1976, All Brahms, 1977, Opera Lady, 1978, Eberley Sings Strauss, 1980, Helen-Kay Eberley: American Girl, 1983, Helen-Kay Eberley: Opera Lady II, 1984; performed Am. and Can. nat. anthems for Chgo. Cubs Baseball Team, 1977-83, Chgo. Bears Football, 1977; also starred in numerous concert recital and symphony appearances, Europe, Can., U.S.; author: Angel's Song, 1994, The Magdaleva Poems, 1995, ChapelHeart, 1996, Desert Dancing, 1997, Canyon Ridge, 2000, Rivervoice, 2002. Docent, new mem. tour guide Art Inst. Chgo.; spl. events hotline vol. Art Inst. Chgo., Chgo. Christian Indsl. League, St. Joseph's Table of St. Peter's in the Loop, Chgo.; vol., facilitator City Yr. Chgo.-Urban Peace Corps; Chgo. Humanities Festival VIII of Ill. Humanities Coun., Evanston Shelter for Battered Women, Rape Victim Adv., Habitat for Humanity; Midwest Vol. Facilitator 1st Indsl. Realty Trust; mem. Mayor's founding com. Evanston Arts Coun., 1974-75; judge Ice-Skating Competition, Wilmette (Ill.) Park Dist., 1974-77, bd. dirs., 1973-77; bd. dirs. Ctr. for Voice, Chgo., 1994-96; vol. Saints-Usher Corps of Chgo., 1998-99. Recipient Creative and Performing Arts award Ind. Jr. Miss. and South Bend Jr. Miss, 1965, Milton J. Cross award Met. Opera Guild, 1968; prize winner Met. Opera. Nat. Auditions, 1968, 1st pl. prize for The Pond, Chicagoland Poetry Contest, 1997, 1st pl. prize and Best of the Best award for The Rose Garden, 1999; F.K. Weyerhauser scholar Met. Opera, 1967. Mem. People for Ethical Treatment of Animals, Am. Soc. for Prevention of Cruelty to Animals, Assisi Animal Found., Am. Guild Mus. Artists, Internat. Platform Assn., Whale Adoption Project, Amnesty Internat., Environ. Def. Fund, Doris Day Animal Found., Poets and Patrons, Humane Soc., Greenpeace, Physicians Com. for Responsible Medicine, Notre Dame Alumni Club, St. Mary's Acad. Alumnae Assn., Delta Gamma. Office: HKE Enterprises 1726 Sherman Ave Evanston IL 60201-5619

EBERLY, HARRY LANDIS, retired communications company executive; b. Lancaster, Pa., Nov. 1, 1924; s. Chester Landis and Nola Marie (Clark) E.; m. Marion Ruth Royer, May 26, 1951; children: Jenny Ellen Eberly Holmes, Susan Lynn Eberly Patrick. BS in Chem. Engring., Pa. State U., 1945; postgrad., Lehigh U., 1947-48, Franklin and Marshall Coll., 1949. Engr. We. Electric, N.Y.C., 1945-49; mfg. engr. RCA, Lancaster, Pa., 1949-51, product devel. Harrison, N.J., 1951-64, mgr. mfg. Somerville, N.J., 1964-66, plant mgr. Palm Beach Garden, Fla., 1996-68, mgr. purchasing Palm Beach Gardens, Fla., 1968-72; v.p. Telex Computer Products, Inc., Tulsa, 1972-76, sr. v.p., 1976-77, pres. Communication Products div. Raleigh, N.C., 1977-83, exec. v.p., 1983-88, mem. exec. com. Tulsa, 1984-88, dir., 1982-84; exec. v.p. Memorex Telex Corp., 1988-90; COO, Novatel Comm., Ltd., Calgary, Can., 1991-92. Mem. bd. assocs. Meridith Coll., Raleigh, 1981—98, presdl. adv. coun., 1999—2002; mem. bd. assocs. Barton Coll. Global Focus Program, 1988—97; bd. dirs. Wake Tech. Cmty. Coll. Found., Raleigh, 1982—97, chmn., 1990—94; mem. N.C. State U. Engring. Found., Raleigh, 1984—87; exec. com. Edn. and Psychology Found., 1990—95; vice-chmn. Triangle East N.C., 1986—90, chmn., 1990—92; regional maj., gifts chmn. Campaign for Pa. State, 1986—90; chair Pa. State Grand Destiny Campaign Coll. of Edn., 1999—2003; mem. presdl. adv. bd. Pa. State U.; bd. dirs., exec. com. Occoneechee Coun. Boy Scouts Am., 1989—95; bd. dirs. Raleigh Little Theatre, 1989—92, 1995—2003, Raleigh Housing Authority Scholarship Fund, 1993—98; bd. dirs., 1988 campaign chmn. United Way Wake County, 1980—89. Mem. IEEE (life), Wake County Edn. Found. (bd. dirs. 1990-92), Greater Raleigh C. of C. (bd. dirs. 1979-87), North Ridge Country Club, Masons, Shriners, Delta Gamma Delta. Methodist. Home: 7003 N Ridge Dr Raleigh NC 27615-7036

EBERLY, JOSEPH HENRY, physics professor, consultant, quantum optics scientist; b. Carlisle, Pa, Oct. 19, 1935; s. Norman McKinley and Mary Weigle (Keeny) E.; m. Shirley Warren Smith; children: Rebecca Leas, Virginia Westcott, Lynn Elizabeth. BS, Pa. State U., 1957; PhD, Stanford U., 1962. Prof. physics U. Rochester, NY, 1976-79, prof. physics and optics, 1979—; Andrew Carnegie prof. physics, 1996—; dir. Rochester Theory Ctr. for Optical Sci. and Engring., 1995—. Vis. fellow Joint Inst. for Lab. Astrophysics and Nat. Bur. Std., Boulder, Colo., 1977-78, sci. and engring. rsch. coun. physics dept. London Imperial Coll., 1983; vis. mem. Max-Planck Inst. Quantum Optics, Munich, 1985, 89, 95; adv. editor for physics John Wiley Publ., NYC, 1975—; cons. US Dept. Energy, 1974—, Battelle Labs., Durham, NC, 1974-84, Inst. Def. Analyses, 1986-94; mem. physics adv. com. Lawrence Livermore Nat. Lab., 1995-97; guest prof. Peking U., 2004—. Author: Lasers, 1988, Optical Resonance and Two-Level Atoms, 1975, Contemporary Physics, Laser Physics; editor: Multiphoton Bibliography, 1970—, Multiphoton Processes, 1978, Optics Express, 1996-2001. Recipient Alexander von Humboldt award, 1984, Marian Smoluchowski medal, 1987, Charles H. Townes award Optical Soc. Am., 1994, Disting. Alumni award Pa. State Coll. Sci., 1998. Fellow Optical Soc. Am. (bd. dir., chair, Bd. of Editors, 2002-04, v.p. 2005), Am. Phys. Soc. (chair divsn. laser sci. 1996-97, mem. of Coun., 2003-05); mem. C.V. Tummer Soc. (founding mem.), Acad. Sci. Poland (fgn. mem.), Inst. Theoretical Atomic, Molecular and Optical Physics Harvard-Smithsonian Obs. (mem. adv. bd. 2004-), Inst. Theoretical Physics UCSB (mem. adv. bd. 2001-03), Am. Inst. Physics (gov. bd. 2003-04, investment adv. com. 2004-).

EBERSBERGER, ARTHUR DARRYL, insurance company executive, consultant; b. Balt., June 18, 1946; s. George Henry and Althea Ebersberger; m. Judith Simison, Nov. 18, 1982; 1 child, Leonard Darryl. BS in Mktg. and Mgmt., Susquehanna U., 1968; MBA, Loyola Coll., Balt., 1985; postgrad., Am. Coll., Bryn Mawr, Pa. CLU, ChFC; cert. ins. counselor; mem. Md. Bd. Architects. Owner Ebersberger & Assocs., Inc., Severna Park, Md., 1968-2000; pres. Ebersberger Consulting Inc., Severna Park, Md., 1986—. Pres. Anne Arundel Trade Coun., 1995-96, chmn., 1996-97; mem. Md. Bus. and Econ. Devel. Commn., 1995-99; mem. Md. Bd. Architects, 1993-99. Pres. Sheltered Workshop of Anne Arundel County, Glen Burnie, Md., 1978; pres., founder Leadership Anne Arundel, Inc., 1993-95, bd. dirs., 1995-96, chmn., immediate past pres., 1995-96, chmn. Exec. Series Program, 1997-99; mem. Anne Arundel County Planning Adv. Bd., 1996-99; chmn. v.p. Md. Conf. on Sml. Bus., 1989-90; grad. Leadership Md., 1993; bd. dirs. Ginger Cover Retirement Cmty, 1994-99, ASPIRE, 1995-99; trustee Anne Arundel Health Sys., Inc., 1997—, Anne Arundel C.C., 1998—. With USNR, 1960-71, Vietnam. Named Small Bus. Advocate of Yr., SBA, 1993. Mem. U.S. Jaycees (adv. bd. 1982, Outstanding Young Man Am. 1980-81, pres. Severna Park br. 1976), Assoc. Builders and Contractors (pres. 1986), Anne Arundel Life Underwriters (pres. 1981, life mem.), Million Dollar Round Table, CLU's (bd. dirs. Balt. chpt. 1981-83), Md. C. of C. (chmn. 1999-2001), Safari Club Internat. (pres. Chesapeake chpt. 1998-99), Profl. Liability Agts. Network (pres. 1985-86, exec. com. 1986-98), Chartwell Golf and Country Club (bd. dirs. 1981-83). Republican. Lutheran. Avocations: golf, fly fishing, hunting, exercise, tennis. Home: 51 Boone Trl Severna Park MD 21146-4501 Address: PO Box 959 Severna Park MD 21146-0959

EBERSOL, DICK (DUNCAN DICKIE EBERSOL), television broadcasting executive; b. Torrington, Conn., July 28, 1947; s. Charles Ebersol; m. Susan Saint James; children: Charles Duncan, William James, Edward Bright(dec.) stepchildren: Sunshine, Harmony. Student, Yale U. Rschr. Grenoble Olympics, 1968; exec. asst. to Roone Arledge ABC Sports, 1974; sports prodr. ABC Wide World of Sports, 1974; dir. weekend late night programming NBC, NYC, 1974-75, v.p. late night programming, 1976-77, v.p. comedy, variety and event programming, 1977-81; co-creator Saturday Night Live, NYC, 1975, exec. prodr., 1981-85; founder No Sleep Prodns., 1983—; pres. NBC Sports, 1989-98; sr. v.p. NBC News, 1989; chmn. NBC Sports & NBC Olympics, 1998—2004, NBC Universal Sports & Olympics, 2004—. Creator: NBC's Friday Night Videos, 1983, Saturday Night's Main Event, 1985, Later with Bob Costas, 1988. Named Most Powerful Person in Sports, The Sporting News, 1996; named one of the 100 Most Powerful Sports Figures; recipient Olympic Order, Internat. Olympic Com., 1992, Corp. Leadership award, March of Dimes, 2000, Dick Schaap Lifetime Achievement award in Sports, Michael S. Modell Awards Dinner, 2003. Office: NBC Sports 30 Rockefeller Plz Fl 2 New York NY 10112-0036

EBERSOLE, CHRISTINE, actress; b. Chgo. m. Peter Bergman (div.). Student, McMurray Coll., Am. Acad. Dramatic Arts. Actress: (stage prodns.) Green Pond, 1978, On the Twentieth Century, 1978, Oklahoma!, 1979, The Three Sisters, 1982, Geniuses, 1983, Harrigan 'n Hart, 1985, Steel Magnolias, 2005 (feature films) Tootsie, 1982, Amadeus, 1984, Thief of Hearts, 1984, Mac and Me, 1988, (TV movies) The Doll Maker, 1984, Acceptable Risks, 1986, (TV series) The Cavanaughs, 1986; cast mem. Saturday Night Live. Office: William Morris Agy 1350 Avenue Of The Americas New York NY 10019-4702*

EBERSOLE, CURT, music educator; b. Lancaster, Pa., Feb. 2, 1958; s. John C. and Helen L. Ebersole. MusB in Edn., Northwestern U., 1980, MusM, 1981; MFA, SUNY, 1996. Dir. of bands No. Valley Regional HS, Old Tappan, NJ, 1982—. Founder & coord. Bergen County Wind Conducting Symposium, Old Tappan, NJ, 1987—94. Musician: (plays) West Side Story, 1997 (Outstanding Overal Prodn. of the Yr. award Paper Mill Playhouse Rising Star, 1997), Phantom, 1998 (Outstanding Overal Prodn. of the Yr. award Paper Mill Playhouse Rising Star, 1998), Big, 2000 (Outstanding Overal Prodn. of the Yr. award Paper Mill Playhouse Rising Star, 2000); prodr.: (commission) El Jardin de Esperanza, by Timothy Broege; condr.: commission El Jardin de Esperanza, by Timothy Broege, musician. Named a J. Curtis Ebersole Day, Old Tappan, NJ. Mayor and Coun., 2002. Mem.: North Jersey Band Festival (sec. 1998—2002), Music Educators of Bergen County (treas. 1985—87). Avocations: bicycling, exercise, travel, roller coasters. Home: 10 Stewart Place 2HE White Plains NY 10603 Office: Northern Valley Regional High School Central Avenue Old Tappan NJ 07675 Personal E-mail: jcebersole@ebernet.com. E-mail: ebersole@nvnet.org.

EBERSOLE, JODI KAY, lawyer; b. Pitts., Mar. 15, 1966; d. Denver J. Weigel and JoAnn Ramsey; m. Gary R. Ebersole, Nov. 3, 1990. BA in Social Work, Elizabethtown Coll., 1987; JD, Widener U., 1990. Bar: Md. 1990, D.C. 1991, U. S. Dist. Ct. Md. 1991, U.S. Ct. Appeals (4th cir.) 1991, U.S. Ct. Appeals (3d cir.) 1994. Assoc. Thieblot, Ryan, Martin & Ferguson, Balt., 1990-96, Ferguson, Schetelich & Heffernan, Balt., 1996-97, ptnr., 1997-99; sr. claim counsel St. Paul Fire & Marine Ins. Co., Balt., 1999-2000, regional group counsel, 2000—. Fellow Md. Bar Found., Balt. Bar Found. (trustee 1999—); mem. Md. State Bar Assn. (bd. govs. 2001—), Def. Rsch. Inst., Bar

Assn. Balt. City (chair young lawyers divsn. 2000—). Office: St Paul Fire & Marine Ins Co MC-31 Claim Legal Exposure Mgmt 5801 Smith Ave Baltimore MD 21209-3611 E-mail: jodi.ebersole@stpaul.com.

EBERSOLE, MARK CHESTER, emeritus college president; b. Hershey, Pa., Nov. 3, 1921; s. Benjamin W.S. and Mary (Patrick) E.; m. Dorothy Baugher, June 26, 1943; children— Philip B., Stephen B. BS, Elizabethtown (Pa.) Coll., 1943, LL.D., 1969; B.D., Crozer Theol. Sem., 1946; MA, U. Pa., 1948; PhD, Columbia, 1952. UNRRA relief adminstr., Europe, 1946-47; asst. prof. religion and philosophy Elmira Coll., 1952-53; faculty Bucknell U., 1953-69, prof. religion, chmn. dept., chaplain of univ., 1958-61, asst. dean univ., 1961; dean Coll. Arts and Scis., 1961-62, v.p. acad. affairs, 1961-68, univ. provost, 1968-69; project specialist, spl. projects in edn. Ford Found., 1967-69, program adviser, 1969-71; dean Grad. Sch.; assoc. v.p. for acad. affairs Temple U., 1971-77; pres. Elizabethtown (Pa.) Coll., 1977-85, pres. emeritus, 1985—. Bd. dirs. Educators Mutual Life Ins. Co.; interim pres. Maryville Coll., 1992-93; ednl. cons., 1987—. Author: Christian Faith and Man's Religion, 1961; editor: Hail to Thee, Okoboji U. A Humor Anthology on Higher Education, 1992; contbr. articles to profl. jours. Trustee Linden Hall Sch., 1992—. J.P. Crozer Found. fellow, 1949-51 Mem. Pa. Soc., Cliosophic Soc. Home: 3001 Lititz Pike PO Box 5093 Lancaster PA 17606-5093 Office Phone: 717-581-0980.

EBERSOLE, TODD MICHAEL, lawyer; b. San Bernardino, Calif., Sept. 23, 1966; s. Thomas Mark Ebersole and Linda Sue Curtis; m. Nori Noreen Kubota; children: Madison Noreen, Maison Victoria. BA Polit. Sci., Environ Sci., U.Southern Calif., 1991; JD, Southwestern U., 1994. CA Bar License: Calif. State Bar 1996. Corp. counsel, asst. sec. SafeGuard Health Enterprises, Aliso Viejo, Calif., 1996—99; sr. counsel CIGNA HealthCare, Glendale, Calif., 1999—. Presenter in field. Contbr. articles to profl. jours. Recipient Outstanding Young Men of Am., OYA Found., Wash., D.C., 1998. Mem.: ABA (chief editor, vice chmn. TIPS 2004—), America's Health Ins. Plans, State Bar Calif., Assn. Corp. Counsel, Am. Health Lawyers Assn. (vice chmn. 2005—). Avocations: swimming, hiking, football. Office: CIGNA HealthCare 400 North Brand Blvd Glendale CA 91203 Office Phone: 818-500-6220. Home Fax: 860-298-2383; Office Fax: 860-298-2383. Personal E-mail: tmeber@cox.net. E-mail: todd.ebersole@cigna.com.

EBERSTEIN, ARTHUR, former biomedical engineering educator, researcher; b. Chgo., Apr. 23, 1928; s. Nathan and Sara (Estes) E.; m. Marion Apfel, Aug. 1, 1961; children— Sharon, Laura BS, Ill. Inst. Tech., 1950; MS, U. Ill., 1951; PhD, Ohio State U., 1957. Asst. mem. Inst. for Muscle Disease, N.Y.C., 1959-61; sr. scientist Am. Bosch Arma Corp., 1961-63; dir. biomed. engrng. Lundy Electronics, Inc., Glen Head, N.Y., 1963-64; prof., dir. research dept. rehab. medicine NYU Med. Ctr, N.Y.C., 1964-96; rsch. coord. dept. rehab. medicine Kingsbrook Jewish Med. Ctr., Bklyn., 1997—2003. Co-author: Electrodiagnosis of Neuromuscular Disease, 1983 Served with U.S. Army, 1955-57 Fellow NSF, 1958, NIH, 1959 Mem. Am. Physiol. Soc., Biophys. Soc., Biomed. Engring. Soc. Am. Assn. Electrodiagnostic Medicine, Sigma Pi Sigma. Avocations: skiing, tennis.

EBERT, GERARD (GERRY EBERT), hypnotherapist, freelance/self-employed writer; b. Bklyn., June 14, 1956; s. George Thomas Ebert and Leonora Conway; m. Susan Anne Cabral-Ebert; 1 child, John. Cert. hypnotherapist, attention deficit disorder/attention defitit hyperactivity disorder. Price and order clk., sales mgr. D&S Chem. Co., 1982—89; with Hoffman LaRoche Maintenance, 0990—1992; hypnotherapist Belleville, NJ, 1993—98, Glendale, Calif., 1999—. Author: (poetry) Rage and Anger, 1998 (Achievement award, 1998), Little Girls, 1999 (Editors Choice award, 2000), Halloween Night, 2000 (Editors Choice award, 2000), The Hour is Late, 2000 (Achievement Award award, 2000), A Public Service Poem, 2001 (Poet of Merit award, 2002), Thoughts of a Man, 2002, (poetry) In a Potpourri of Poetry & Prose, 2004. Mem.: Acad. of Am. Poets (assoc.). Home: 3227 Cornwall Dr Glendale CA 91206-1420 Personal E-mail: GerryEbert@msn.com.

EBERT, LAWRENCE BURTON, lawyer; b. Bronxville, NY, Jan. 14, 1949; s. Burton Eidell and Mildred Elizabeth (Hearting) E.; m. Rebecca Ann Vares, Aug. 3, 1997. BS, U. Chgo., 1971, JD, 1993; PhD, Stanford U., 1975. Bar: N.Y. 1994, U.S. Dist. Ct. (ea. and so. dists.) N.Y. 1995, Fed. Cir. Ct. 1995, N.J. 2001. Staff scientist Exxon Corp. Rsch., Annandale, N.J., 1975-90; assoc. Pennie & Edmonds LLP, N.Y.C., 1993-98, Kenyon & Kenyon, N.Y.C., 1998—2000, Reed Smith LLP, Princeton, NJ, 2000—03, IPAnalytics/IPBiz/ipABC, Hamilton, NJ, 2004—. Contbr. articles to profl. jours. Fannie and John Hertz Found. fellow, 1971-75. Mem. ABA, Am. Phys. Soc., Am. Chem. Soc. Home: 390 Garretson Rd Bridgewater NJ 08807-1967 Office: IPAnalytics/IPBiz 1850 Greenwood Ave Hamilton NJ 08609-2332 Office Phone: 609-588-0660. Business E-Mail: lb_ebert@yahoo.com.

EBERT, LESLIE, artist; b. Oregon City, Oreg., Sept. 20, 1962; d. Larry Dwayne Ebert and Carol Kay Bino; m. Paul Ian Boundy, May 2, 1988. BArch, U. Oreg., 1987. Archtl. intern, Portland, Oreg., 1986; studio apprentice Debra Olsen, Portland, 1990—91; owner Leslie Ebert Studio, Portland, 1994—. Exhbn. artist Celebration of Am. Paper Arts, Crane Mus. Papermaking, Mass., 2003, Landmarks in Paper, Friends of Dard Hunter, St. Paul, 2003, Crossing Boundaries, Internat. Symposium of Print Arts, Portland, 2000. Contbr. artwork to book The Artful Greeting, 2003, artwork to mag. Somerset Studio, 2000, artwork Am. Mus. Papermaking, 2003; Represented in permanent collections Crane Papermaking Mus., exhibitions include Washington State U. Gallery, 2005, Nat. Coll. Soc. Small Works Exhibit, Cork Gallery, NYC, 2004, SLMM Nat. Exhbn., 2004; contbg. artist The Art of Layering: Making Connections, 2004. Founding bd. dirs. Art in the Pearl, Portland; mem. curatorial adv. bd. Am. Inst. Archs., Portland, 1992; publicity chair Waterstone Gallery, Portland, 1994; N.W. regional coord. Soc. Layerists in Multi-Media, 2004—. Mem.: Nat. Coll. Soc., Internat. Assn. of Papermakers, Friends of Dard Hunter, N.W. Print Coun., Soc. Layerists in Multimedia. Avocations: travel, photography, gardening, reading. Office: Leslie Ebert Studio PO Box 68604 Portland OR 97268 E-mail: leslie@leslieebert.com.

EBERT, ROBERT PETER, education educator; b. Mt. Vernon, N.Y., Aug. 5, 1944; s. Robert Frederick and Verna Marion (Lashier) E.; m. Martha Ann Epp, June 9, 1969; children: Peter, Margaret. AB, Union Coll., 1966; MA, U. Wis., 1968, PhD, 1972. Asst. prof. U. Chgo., 1972-79; assoc. prof. Princeton (N.J.) U., 1979-87, prof., 1987—. Vis. asst. prof. U. Calif., Berkeley, 1977-78. Author: Infinitival Complement Constructions in Early New High German, 1976, Historische Syntax des Deutschen, 1978; co-author: Frühneuhochdeutsche Grammatik, 1993. Mem. Linguistic Soc. Am., Phi Beta Kappa. Avocation: musician.

EBERT, ROBERT T., lawyer; BBA magna cum laude, U. Notre Dame, 1984; JD cum laude, U. Mo., 1987. Bar: Mo. 1987. Ptnr., mem. oper. group Bryan Cave LLP, St Louis. Mailing: One Metropolitan Square 211 N Broadway, Ste 3600 Saint Louis MO 63102 Office Phone: 314-259-2633. E-mail: rtebert@bryancave.com.

EBERT, ROGER JOSEPH, film critic; b. Urbana, Ill., June 18, 1942; s. Walter H. and Annabel (Stumm) E.; m. Chaz Hammelsmith, July 18, 1992. BS, U. Ill., 1964; postgrad., U. Cape Town, South Africa, 1965, U. Chgo., 1966-67; LHD (hon.), U. Colo., 1993. Editor Daily Illini, 1963-64; pres. U.S. Student Press Assn., 1963-64; staff writer News-Gazette, Champaign-Urbana, Ill., 1958-66; film critic Chgo. Sun-Times, 1967—, US mag., 1978-79, NBC-TV News, Chgo., 1980-83, ABC-TV News, Chgo., 1984—, N.Y. Post, N.Y.C., 1986-88, N.Y. Daily News, 1988-92, Compu Serve, 1991—; pres. Ebert Co., Ltd., 1981—; Microsoft Cinemania, 1994-97; columnist Yahoo Internet Life mag., 1997—. Instr. English Chgo. City Coll., 1967-68; lectr. film criticism, fine arts program U. Chgo., 1969-; Kluge fellow U. Va., 1995-96, adj. prof. U. Ill., 2000—; lectr. film Columbia Coll., Chgo., 1973-74, 77-80; cons. Nat. Endowments for Arts and Humanities, 1972-77; juror film festivals. Co-host (TV shows) Sneak Previews, PBS, 1976-82, At the Movies, syndicated, 1982-86, Siskel & Ebert (now Ebert & Roeper), syndicated, 1986—; broadcaster: Movie News, ABC Radio, 1982-85; author: An Illini Century, 1967, (screenplay) Beyond the Valley of the Dolls, 1970, Beyond Narrative: The Future of the Feature Film, 1978, A Kiss Is Still a Kiss, 1984, Roger Ebert's Movie Home Companion, 1986-93, Roger Ebert's Video Companion, 1994-98, (with Daniel Curley) The Perfect London Walk, 1986, Two Weeks in the Midday Sun, 1987, The Future of the Movies, 1991, Behind the Phantom's Mask, 1993, Ebert's Little Movie Glossary, 1994, Roger Ebert's Book of Film, 1996, Questions for the Movie Answer Man, 1997, Roger Ebert's Movie Yearbook, 1998, The Little Book of Hollywood Cliches, The Bigger Little Book of Hollywood Cliches, 1999, Ebert's Bigger Little Movie Glossary, 1999, I Hated, Hated, Hated This Movie, 2000, Great Movies I, 2002, Great Movies II, 2005; co-author: The Future of the Movies, The Computer Insectiary, 1994. Recipient Overseas Press club, 1963, award Chgo. Headline Club, 1963, award Chgo. Newspaper Guild, 1973, Pulitzer prize, 1975, Emmy award, 1979, Peter Lisagor award, 1998, Online Film Critics Soc. Best Movie Website award, 1999; inducted into Chgo. Journalism Hall of Fame, 1997; Rotary fellow, 1965, Kluge fellow in film studies U. Va., 1995-96. Mem. Newspaper Guild, Writers Guild Am. West, Nat. Soc. Film Critics, Acad. TV Arts and Scis., Arts Club of Chgo., Cliff Dwellers, Acad. Club (London), Sigma Delta Chi, Phi Delta Theta. Avocations: drawing, painting, art collecting. Office: Chgo Sun-Times Inc 401 N Wabash Ave Rm 110 Chicago IL 60611-5642

EBERT, VIOLA ROTH, neuropsychologist, entrepreneur; b. McAlester, Okla., Feb. 1, 1938; d. Johann Maria and Irene Turnbow Roth; m. Robert Oliver Ebert (div. Dec. 2, 1992); children: Adrienne Ebert-LeBlanc, Cecile'. BA, U. N.C., 1972; MA, Wake Forest U., 1976; PhD, Heed U., 1979. Psychol. asst. Iredell County Mental Health Ctr., Statesville, NC, 1972—74; psychol. assoc. Bowman Gray Sch. of Medicine, Winston-Salem, NC, 1976—79, assoc. faculty mem., 1979—82; pvt. practice Biofeedback and Pain Control Clinic, Statesville, 1982—86; lectr./workshop leader USNAH, Inc., Statesville, 1982—2002; writer under pen name T. F. Sisters, Hendersonville, Tenn., 1998—2002; inventor KAH, Inc., Mooresville, NC, 1999—2002; artist mgr. SEM, Inc., Hendersonville, 1992—2002. Author: (book) DEADLY BREW She Loved Him to Death, 2002. Mem.: Nat. Assn. Women Writers, N.C. Psychol. Assn., Spiritual Frontiers Fellowship (life; dir. 1986—90), Bluegrass Yacht and Country Club. Avocation: fishing, off-road trekking,painting, designing jewelry, photography.

EBIE, WILLIAM D., retired museum director; b. Akron, Ohio, Feb. 7, 1942; s. William P. and Mary Louise (Karam) E.; m. Gwyn Anne Schumacher, Apr. 11, 1968 (div. Jan. 1988); children: Jason William, Alexandra Anne; m. Mary Teresa Hayes, June 10, 1989. BFA, Akron Art Inst., 1964; MFA, Calif. Coll. of Arts and Crafts, 1968. Graphic artist Alameda County Health Dept., Oakland, Calif., 1967-68; instr. painting Fla. A&M U., Tallahassee, 1968-69; instr. photography Lawrence (Kans.) Adult Edn. Program, 1969-70; asst. dir. Roswell (N.Mex.) Mus. & Art Ctr., 1971-87, dir., 1987-98, Millicent Rogers Mus., Taos, N.Mex., 1998—2002. Juror various art exhbns., 1971—; panelist N.Mex. Arts Divsn., Santa Fe, 1983-87; field reviewer Inst. for Mus. Svcs., 1988-90; mem. State Capitol Renovation Art Selection Com., Santa Fe, 1991-92; bd. dirs. State Capitol Found., Santa Fe, 1992-2002. Bd. dirs. Helene Wurlitzer Found., Taos, N.Mex., 1999—. Mem. Am. Assn. of Mus., Mountain Plains Mus. Assn., N.Mex. Assn. of Mus. Democrat. Avocations: photography, carpentry. Personal E-mail: billebie@earthlink.net.

EBIEFUNG, ANIEKAN ASUKWO, mathematics professor, researcher; b. Nto Mbadum, Akwaibom State, Nigeria, Nov. 10, 1958; came to U.S., 1985; s. Asukwo Thomas and Florence Asukwo (Udofa) E.; m. Anne Aniekan Ekon, Jan. 2, 1989; children: Ediobong, Uduak, Mary Ann. BS in Math. and Statistics with honors, U. Calabar, Nigeria, 1982; MS in Math., Howard U., 1987; PhD in Math. Scis., Clemson U., 1991. Instr. math. Federal U. of tech., Owerri, Nigeria, 1982-83, U. Cross River State, Uyo, Nigeria, 1983-85, U. D.C. Lorton (Va.) Prison Coll. Program, 1987-88, Howard U., Washington, 1985-88; teaching asst. Clemson U., 1988-91; asst. prof. math. U. Tenn., Chattanooga, 1991-96, U.C. found. assoc. prof., 1996—2001, prof. math., 2001—. Lectr. in field; ctr. chmn. Tenn. Math. tchrs. Assn. state-wide math contest, U. Tenn., Chattanooga, 1992—. Contbr. articles to profl. jours.; editor NASM Bull., 1980-81. Grantee Ctr. of Excellence for Computer Applications, 1993, scholar, 1995-96, 98-99; grantee Oak Ridge Assoc. Univs., 1993, UC Found., 1993, Tenn. Higher Edn. Commn., 1994-95, 97-99. Mem. Math. Assn. Am., Am. Math. Soc., Ops. Rsch. Soc. Am., Chattanooga Area Math. Tchrs. Assn., Internat. Linear Algebra Soc. Avocations: writing, tennis, reading. Office: Univ of Tenn 615 Mccallie Ave Chattanooga TN 37403-2504

EBINER, ROBERT MAURICE, lawyer; b. LA, Sept. 2, 1927; s. Maurice and Virginia (Grand) E.; m. Paula H. Van Sluyters, June 16, 1951; children: John, Lawrence, Marie, Michael, Christopher, Joseph, Francis, Matthew, Therese, Kathleen, Eileen, Brian, Patricia, Elizabeth, Ann. JD, Loyola U., L.A., 1953. Bar: Calif. 1954, U.S. Dist. Ct. (cen. dist.) Calif. 1954. Pvt. practice, West Covina, Calif., 1954—. Judge pro tem L.A. Superior Ct., 1964-66, 90—, arbitrator, 1979—; arbitrator San Bernardino Superior Ct., 1990—; judge pro tem Citrus Mcpl. Ct., 1966-70, 1990—, El Monte Mcpl. Ct., 1998—, Whittier Mcpl. Ct., 2001—, mediator, 2000-; mem. disciplinary hearing panel Calif. State Bar, 1968-75. Bd. dirs. West Covina United Fund, 1958-61, chmn. budget com., 1960-61; organizer Joint United Funds East San Gabriel Valley, 1962, bd. dirs., 1961-68; bd. dirs. San Gabriel Valley Cath. Social Svcs., 1969—, pres., 1969-72; bd. dirs. Region II Cath. Social Svc., 1970—, pres., 1970-74; trustee LA Cath. Welfare Bur. (now Cath. Charities), 1978—; charter bd. dirs. East San Gabriel Valley Hot Line, 1969-74, sec., 1969-72; charter bd. dirs. N.E. LA County unit Am. Cancer Soc., 1973-78, chmn. by-laws com., 1973-78; bd. dirs. Queen of the Valley Hosp. Found., 1983-89; organizer West Covina Hist. Soc., 1982—; active Calif. State Dem. Cen. Com., 1963-68; mng. meet dir. Greater La Puente Valley Spl. Olympics, 1985-88, Bishop Amat Relays, 1981-96; mem. MSAC Relays Com., 1978—99; campaign mgr. Congressman Ronald B. Cameron, 1964; bd. dirs. Cal-Nev-Ha Found. 1986-98, pres. 1994-96. With U.S. Army, 1945-47. Recipient L.A. County Human Rels. Commn. Disting. Svc. award, 1978, Thomas A. Kiefer Humanitarian award, 1993; named West Covina Citizen of Yr., 1986, San Gabriel Valley Daily Tribune's Father of Yr., 1986. Mem. ABA, Calif. Bar Assn., L.A. County Bar Assn. (arbitrator 1975—), Fed. Ct. So. Dist. Calif. Assn., Consumer Attys. LA, Ea. Bar Assn. L.A. County (pres. Pomona Valley 1965-66), West Covina C. of C. (pres. 1960), Am. Arbitration Assn. (arbitrator 1965-98), KC, Bishop Amat H.S. Booster Club (bd. dirs. 1973-96, pres. 1978-80), Kiwanis (charter West Covina, pres. 1976-77, 2002-04, lt. gov. divsn. 35 1980-81, Kiwanian of Yr. 1978, 82, Disting. Lt. Gov. 1980-81, Disting. Pres., 2002-04) Avocation: collector western U.S. historical olympic and political memorabilia. Office: 100 N Citrus St Ste 520 West Covina CA 91791-1694 Office Phone: 626-918-9000.

EBITZ, DAVID MACKINNON, art historian, educator, museum director; b. Hyannis, Mass., Oct. 5, 1947; s. Robert White Creeley and Ann (MacKinnon) Kucera; m. Mary Ann Stankiewicz, Jan. 1, 1983; children: Rebecca Aemilia, Cecilia Charlotte. BA, Williams Coll., 1969; AM, Harvard U., 1973, PhD, 1979. Teaching fellow, then head teaching fellow dept. fine arts Harvard U., Cambridge, Mass., 1975-78; asst. prof., then assoc. prof. dept. art U. Maine, Orono, 1978-87, interim dir. galleries, curator univ. art collection, 1986-87; head dept. edn. and acad. affairs J. Paul Getty Mus., Santa Monica, Calif., 1987-92; dir. John and Mable Ringling Mus. Art, Sarasota, Fla., 1992-2000; assoc. prof. art and art edn. Pa. State U., University Park, 2000—. Vis. faculty Bangor (Maine) Theol. Sem., 1981; lectr. in field; presenter workshops. Author exhbn. revs., book revs.; contbr. articles to arts publs., exhbn. catalogues. Heritage Found. fellow, 1968. Mem. Coll. Art Assn., Nat. Art Edn. Assn., Am. Assn. Museums (mus. edn. com.), Mus. Edn. Roundtable, Internat. Ctr. Medieval Art, Phi Beta Kappa. Office: Pa State U 212 Arts Cottage University Park PA 16802 Office Phone: 814-863-1004. Business E-Mail: dme12@psu.edu.

EBNETER, STEWART DWIGHT, utility industry management consultant; b. Ledgewood, N.J., Oct. 10, 1933; s. William and Emily Ann (Burd) E.; m. Evadna Grace Custer, Dec. 28, 1957; children: Stewart D. Jr., Steven D., Scott D. BSEE, Tri-State U., 1959; MBA, Athens State Coll., 1971. Registered profl. engr., Calif. System engr. Boeing Co., Seattle, 1959-61; reliability dept. head Spaco, Inc., Huntsville, Ala., 1961-70, v.p. engring., 1971-73; div. dir. br. chief U.S. Nuclear Regulatory Commn., Atlanta, King of Prussia, Pa., 1973-87, dir. office spl. projects Washington, 1987-88, dir. div. radiation safety, regional adminstr. Atlanta, 1989-97; mgmt. cons. to utility industry, 1997—. Mem. allocation com. United Way, Huntsville, 1970-73; scout leader Boy Scouts Am., Huntsville, 1970-73. Sgt. USAF, 1953-57. Mem. Am. Soc. for Quality Control (sr.), Am. Nuclear Soc., Nat. Nuclear Accrediting Bd. Home and Office: 107 Whitfield Run Peachtree City GA 30269-3313 E-mail: s.ebneter@comcast.net.

EBOMOYI, WILLIAM EHIGIE, epidemiologist; b. Benin, Edo, Nigeria, Dec. 19, 1949; came to the U.S., 1971; s. James and Igbinowan Ebomoyi; m. Josephine I. Orobor, Aug. 1, 1984; children: Carolyn, Pat, Uyi, Nosa. BA, Western Ill. U., 1975, MS, 1976; PhD, U. Ill., 1981; post-doctorate cert., USPHS NIH, 1990. Intern Tulane U. Med. Sch.; intern, resident Fed. Ministry Health, Lagos, Nigeria, 1977; sr. lectr. U. Ilorin (Nigeria) Med. Sch., 1982-88; rsch. fellow Tulane U. Med. Ctr., New Orleans, 1988-90, adj. asst. prof. pediat., 1992-96; program evaluator Boston Med. Ctr., 1990-91; sci. faculty Concordia U., New Orleans, 1996; assoc. prof. U. No. Colo., Greeley, 1996—2001, prof., 2002—. Cons. APHA, 1980—, Appeal for Charities and Good Will, Inc., Chgo., 1980—, The World Bank, Washington, 1993—, Weld County Dept. Pub. Health, Greeley, 1997—, Colo. Pub. Health Assn., 1999; adv. bd. vice chmn. Air Quality and Natural Resources, Greeley, 1999—. Author: Community Medicine: A Global Perspective, 1998, International Health: A Multi-cultural Approach, Public Health and Sustainable Development; contbr. articles to profl. jours. V.p. Edo Club, New Orleans br., 1992-96. Rsch. fellow Fogarty Internat., Bethesda, Md., 1988, Leadership fellow AAAS, 1990. Mem. AAHPERD, Am. Inst. for Health Promotion, Planetary Soc., Legacy Internat. Inc. (pres.), New Eng. Regional Genetic Group, Fedn. Am. Scientists, Greeley Writers Club. Avocations: bird watching, poetry, soccer, softball, chess. Home: 1739 28th Ave Greeley CO 80634-5764 Office: Univ No Colo Gunter 2280 501 20th St Greeley CO 80639-0001 E-mail: Webomoyi@hhs.unco.edu.

EBONY, DAVID, editor, arts critic; Writer ArtNet Mag.; assoc. mng. editor, news editor Art in Am. Mag., now mng. editor. Author: Curve: The Female Nude Now, 2003, Carlo Maria Mariani, 2003, New York Top Ten. Office: Art in America Brant Art Publications 575 Broadway New York NY 10012 Office Phone: 212-941-2800. Office Fax: 212-941-8885.

EBOZUE, BENSON OBIAN, financial analyst; b. Onitsha, Anambra, Nigeria, Nov. 14, 1960; came to U.S., 1984; s. Benjamen A. Ebozue and Regina A. Abanafo; m. Comfort N. Ndubisi, Feb. 16, 1994; children: Benson Onyeka Jr., Jesse Mezue Nna. Diploma in acctg., Sch. of Accountancy & Mgmt., Aba, Imo, Nigeria, 1982; BBA, Dallas Bapt. U., 1991; cert., U. Tex., Arlington, 1992. CPA, Tex.; cert. adminstrv. acct., U.K. Tutor Sch. of Commerce, Onitsha, 1980—81; sr. acctg. asst. Ekwenibe & Sons Trading Co., Onitsha, 1982—84; accounts payable asst. Makai Bros., Orlando, Fla., 1984—88, CompUsa, Dallas, 1989; loan auditor Mortgage Bankers Cons., Dallas, 1991—92; acctg. analyst Sunbelt Nat. Mortgage, Dallas, 1992—; default auditor FTB Mortgage Svcs., Dallas, 1992—97; pres., CFO, Home Health Care Response, Dallas, 1997—98; mgr., owner Diamond Shamrock (BCE Mart), Dallas, 1998—99; sr acct. Fed. Mgmt. System, Inc., Washington, 2000—; owner Benson O. Ebozue CPA, Cedar Hill, Tex., 2001—. Staff auditor Logan & Assocs., CPA, Cedar Hill, Tex., 1999—. Tutor Dallas Ind. Sch. Dist., 1991-92; vol. Boys Brigade, Onitsha, 1971-76. Mem. AICPA, Tex. Soc. CPAs (cert.). Avocations: soccer, ping pong/table tennis. Home and Office: PO Box 4238 Cedar Hill TX 75106-4238 Mailing: 2504 Lost Mesa Grand Prairie TX 75052 Office Phone: 972-641-0699.

EBRAHEIM, NABIL ANWAR, orthopedist, surgeon; MD, Cairo U., 1975. Diplomate Am. Bd. Orthop. Surgery, 1987. Vice chmn. dept. orthop. surgery Med. Coll. Ohio, Toledo, 1985—97, acting chmn. dept. orthop. surgery, 1997—98, prof., chmn. dept. orthop. surgery, 1998—. Orthop. residency program dir. Med. Coll. Ohio, Toledo, dir. orthop. trauma fellowship program, chief divsn. orthop. trauma. Contbr. articles to profl. jours. Recipient Foot and Ankle Rsch. award, 1999. Home: 3065 Arlington Ave Toledo OH 43614 Personal E-mail: nebraheim@mco.edu.

EBRAHIMI, BAHMAN PAUL, finance educator; PhD, Ga. State U., 1984. Assoc. prof. Hong Kong (China) Bapt. U., 1995—99; assoc. prof. Daniels Coll. Bus. U Denver, 1999—. Asst. prof. U. North Tex., Denton, Tex., 1981—97. Author: Transfer Technology in the Global Economy, The Internal Environment of Global Business, International Business: Economics, Environements, and Strategies, The External Environment of Global Business; contbr. articles to profl. jours. Advisor Rockies Venture Club, Denver, Colo., 2001. Mem.: Acad. Internat. Bus., Acad. Mgmt. Achievements include research in global strategy, cross-cultural management, corporate entrepreneurship. Office: Daniels College of Bus Univ of Denver 2101 S University Blvd Denver CO 80208 Office Phone: 303-871-4576. Office Fax: 303-871-2294. E-mail: ebrahimi@du.edu.

EBRAHIMI, NERCY BOZORG, process engineer; b. Tehran, Iran, Feb. 24, 1963; s. Mostafa and Pari Bozorgebrahimi; m. Adonna May Ruff Ebrahimi, Aug. 6, 1991; children: Kyle, Ryan. BS in Physics with honors, U. Cinn., 1984, MSEE, 1987, PhD, 1991. Sr. process engr. Anadigics Inc., Warren, NJ, 1991—96, mgr. process engring., 1996—98, Rockwell Internat., Newbury Park, Calif., 1998—99, Conexant, Newbury Park, 1999—2000, dir. process engring., 2000—03, Skyworks Solutions, Inc., Newbury Park, 2003—. Presenter at confs. Contbr. articles to profl. jours. Achievements include patents for food distribution system for passenger aircraft. Avocations: astronomy, skiing, golf, hiking, exercise. Office: Skyworks Solutions Inc 2427 W Hillcrest Dr Newbury Park CA 91320

EBRAHIMPOUR, MALING, management consultant, educator; PhD, U. Nebr., Lincoln, 1986. Chair dept. mgmt. sci. and info. sys. U. R.I., Kingston, 1990—97, assoc. dean, 1997—2001. Contbr. articles to profl. jours. Bd. dirs. Wood River Health Svcs., Hopkinton, RI, 1993—2002. 2d lt. Iranian Army, 1976—78. Named to RI Quality Hall of Fame, RI Ctr. for Performance Excellence, 1999. Mem.: NE Decision Scis. Inst. (pres., v.p., procs. editor 1997—98, Disting. Svc. award 1999). Office: Roger Williams Univ One Old Ferry Rd Bristol RI 02809 Office Phone: 401-254-3218. E-mail: bizdean@rwu.edu.

EBRAHIM-SAID, FAWZY AHMED, psychologist, educator; arrived in U.S., 2000; s. Ahmed Ebrahim Said and Nagia Gabal Hussein; m. Zaineb Kamal Hanafy, May 19, 1980; children: Ghaidaa Fawzy Ahmed, Areej Fawzy Ahmed. BEd in Physics and Chemistry, South Valley U., Kena, Egypt, 1993; PhD, U. Ga., 2004, EdD, 2005—05. Cert. counselor gifted edn. Ga. Dept. Edn. Instr. Am. U., Cairo, 1998—2000; tchr. Barrow Elem. Sch., Athens, Ga., 2001—03; asst. prof. U. Ga., Athens, 2004—. Cons. Athens/Clarke County Schools, Athens. Assistant editor Jour. Tchg. Ednl. Psychology. Grantee, Ga. Dept. Edn., 2004. Mem.: Am. Ednl. Rsch. Assn. (assoc.). Achievements include research in increasing the underrepresentation of disabled children in gifted programs. Personal E-mail: febrahim@uga.edu.

EBSWORTH, BARNEY A., retired travel company executive; m. Pamela Ebsworth. Founder, chmn., pres., CEO INTRAV, 1959—99, Royal Cruise Line, 1972—86, Clipper Cruise Line, 1981—97; founder, chmn., CEO Windsor Inc., St. Louis, 1979—. Commr. Am. Art Mus., Smithsonian Inst.; dir. Build-A-Bear Workshop Inc., 2000—; trustee St. Louis Art Mus., Seattle

Art Mus., Nat. Gallery, co-chmn., 1996—. Stationed in Paris during Korean War. Named one of Top 200 Collectors, ARTnews Mag., 2004. Avocation: collector of Am. modern & contemporary art. Mailing: 13 Upper Ladue Saint Louis MO 63124*

EBSWORTH, WILLIAM ROBERT, investment company executive; m. Anandi Pratap. BA, Johns Hopkins U., 1980; MBA, Wharton Sch., 1984. Chartered fin. analyst. Chief investment officer Fidelity Investments, Hong Kong, 1991-97, officer, various fidelity funds, 1994—, dir. of rsch., 1997—. Bd. dirs. Stock Exch. Hong Kong Options Clearing House, H.K. Securities Clearing Co., China Securities Investment Trust, Taipei, Taiwan, Thailand Internat. Fund, London; v.p. Fidelity Advisor Korea Fund, N.Y.C., Emerging Asia Fund, N.Y.C. Mem. Boston Security Analysts Soc., Hong Kong Security Analysts Soc., Internat. Soc. Fin. Analysts Soc., Am. Club Hong Kong, China Club, Penn Club (N.Y.C.). Office: Fidelity Investments 82 Devonshire St Boston MA 02109-3605

EBY, CECIL DEGROTTE, language educator, writer; b. Charles Town, W.Va., Aug. 1, 1927; s. Cecil and Ellen (Turner) E.; children: Clare Virginia, Lillian Turner. AB, Shepherd Coll., 1950; MA, Northwestern U., 1951; PhD, U. Pa., 1958. Instr., then asst. prof. English High Point Coll., 1955-57; asst. prof., then asso. prof. Madison Coll., 1957-60; mem. faculty Washington and Lee U., 1960-65; prof. U. Mich., 1965—; prof. English, chmn. dept. U. Miss., University, 1975-76. Fulbright prof. Am. lit. U. Salamanca, Spain, 1962-63; Fulbright prof. Am. studies U. Valencia, 1967-68; Fulbright prof. Am. lit. U. Budapest, 1981; prof. U. Szeged, 1988-89. Author: Porte Crayon: The Life of David H. Strother, 1960, The Siege of the Alcazar, 1965, (translations in Italian, German, Finnish, Dutch, Portuguese) Between the Bullet and the Lie: American Volunteers in the Spanish Civil War, 1969 (transl. in Spanish), That Disgraceful Affair: The Black Hawk War, 1973, The Road to Armageddon: The Martial Spirit in English Popular Literature, 1987, The War in Hungary: Civilians and Soldiers in World War II, 1998 (Hungarian transl.); editor: The Old South Illustrated, 1959, A Virginia Yankee in the Civil War, 1961. Served with USNR, 1945-46. Episcopalian.

EBY, GARY MOORE, lawyer; b. Cin., Mar. 30, 1951; s. Vincent Vernon and Betty Lou (Moore) E.; m. Cornelia A. Matzkofz, July 3, 1982; 1 child, Victoria A. BA, U. Cin., 1973, JD, 1976, MAIR, 1984. Bar: Ohio 1976, D.C. 1990, Ky. 1992; U.S. Dist. Ct. (so. dist.) Ohio 1976, U.S. Dist. Ct. (ea. dist.) Ky. 1982; U.S. Ct. Appeals (6th cir.) 1977. Assoc. Latimer & Swing, Cin., 1976-78, Thomas F. Phalen, Cin., 1978-79, Kircher & Phalen, Cin., 1979-81, ptnr., 1981-90; pvt. practice Cin., 1991-98; of counsel Manley, Burke & Lipton, Cin., 1999—. Mem. AFL-CIO Lawyer Coord. Com., 1980—. Asst. editor: (book) The Developing Labor Law and Supplements, (3d edits.) 1990—. Mem. ABA, Ohio State Bar Assn. (labor and employment law cert. bd. 1999—), Ky. Bar Assn., Cin. Bar Assn., D.C. Bar. Home: 401 Lafayette Ave Cincinnati OH 45220-1078 E-mail: garyeby@mblclaw.com.

EBY, MICHAEL JOHN, marketing research and technology consultant; b. South Bend, Ind., Aug. 3, 1949; s. Robert T. and Eileen Patricia (Holmes) Eby; m. Judith Alyson Gaskell, May 17, 1980; children: Elizabeth, Katherine. Student, Harvey Mudd Coll., 1969-70; BS in Biochemistry with high honors, U. Md., 1972, MS in Chemistry, 1977; postgrad., IMEDE, Lausanne, Switzerland, 1984. Product mgr. LKB Instruments Inc., Rockville, Md., 1976-79; mktg. mgr. LKB-Produkter AB, Bromma, Sweden, 1979-87; strategic planning mgr. Pharmacia LKB Biotech. AB, Bromma, 1987-88; dir. mktg. Am. Bionetics, Hayward, Calif., 1988-89; pres. PhorTech Internat., San Carlos, Calif., 1989—. Author: The Electrophoresis Explosion, 1988, Electrophoresis in the Nineties, 1990, DNA Amplification, 1993, Blotting and Hybridization, 1993, Capillary Electrophoresis, 1993, Densitometers and Image Analysis, 1995, Visualization Reagents, 1995, U.S. Laboratory Product Usage, 1996, Cell Biology Reagent Systems, 1996, Centrifugation, 1996, Molecular Biology Reagent Systems, 1997, DNA Diagnostics, 1997, DNA Amplification in Europe, 1998, Recombinant Protein Expression Systems, 1998, DNA Sequencing in Europe, 1998, Molecular Biology Reagent Systems in the Far East, 1998, HPLC in the Life Sciences, 1998;: Cytokines and Growth Factors, 1998, Cell and Tissue Culture, 1998, Monoclonal Antibodies, 1999, Microplate Instrumentation in Europe, 1999, DNA Sequencing, 1999, 2000, Global Laboratory Product Usage, 2000, DNA Amplification, 2000, Electrophoretic Equipment and Reagents, 2001, Densitometers and Image Analysis in Europe, 2001, DNA Sequencing in the Far East, 2001, DNA Amplification Instrumentation, 2002, DNA Amplification Regents and Methodology, 2002, Microplate Readers and Equipment, 2002, Global Laboratory Product Usage, 2002, Proteomics Research, Vols. 1-2, 2003, Protein Expression Systems, 2003, Molecular Biology Reagent Systems, 2003, HPLC Columns in the Life Science, 2004, Electrophoresis Instruments & Reagents, 2004, Worldwide Directory of Life Science Distributors, 2005, Microarrays, Arrayers & Scanners in Europe, 2005, DNA Sequencing, 2005, others; contbr. articles to profl. jours. Mem.: AAAS, Am. Soc. Cell Biology, Am. Chem. Soc., Am. Philat. Soc., U. Md. Alumni Assn., Calif. Separation Sci. Soc., Am. Mensa. Episcopalian. Avocations: astronomy, cheesemaking, photography, travel. Office: PhorTech Internat 238 Crestview Dr San Carlos CA 94070-1503 E-mail: mikeby@phortech.com.

ECCLES, TOM, non-profit arts organization administrator; b. Cumbernauld, Glasgow, Scotland; arrived in US, 1993; m. Jennifer Eccles; 1 child, Rachel. MA in philosophy and Italian, Glasgow U., Scotland; studied for 2 years with Umberto Eco, Bologna U., Italy. Tchr. moral philosophy U. Glasgow, Scotland; tchr. critical theory Glasgow Arts Sch., Scotland, 1990—92; independent curator Glasgow, Scotland, 1989—92; devel. dir. Project Ability, Glasgow, Scotland; pub. art cons., project mgr. Art in Partnership, Edinburgh, Scotland; joined Pub. Art Fund, NYC, 1993, dir., 1996—, founder In the Pub. Realm program for emerging artists, founder Tuesday Night Talks lecture series. Lectr. on public art. Co-author: (book) Plop: Recent Projects of the Public Art Fund, 2004; Has written articles and reviews for Art in Am. Recipient Award for Best Show in an Alternative or Pub. Space as curator of Janet Cardiff: Her Long Black Hair, Internat. Assn. Art Critics/USA, 2005. Office: Pub Art Fund 1 E 53rd St New York NY 10022*

ECHELMAN, JANET, artist, educator; Student Honors Program, Internat. Sch. Am., 1985—86; AB Magna Cum Laude with highest honors, Harvard Coll. Harvard U., Cambridge, Mass., 1987; Grad. scholar, 1987—88; ind. studio program, N.Y. Sch. Visual Arts, 1991; MFA, Bard Coll., N.Y., 1995; MA Psychology, Lesley U. Grad. Sch. Arts and Scis., 1996. Art critic St. Petersburg Times, Fla., 1984—85; staff writer Tampa Tribune, Fla., 1984—85; regional coord. S.E. Asia Rauschenberg Overseas Culture Exchange, 1989—91; vis. faculty assoc. Harvard U. Grad. Sch. of Design, Cambridge, Mass., 1992—94, vis. faculty, 1994—96; Fulbright sr. lectr. Indian Nat. Inst. Design, 1997; sr. lectr. Grad. Sch. Arts and Scis., Lesley Coll., 1998—2001; dir. Adama Artspace and Studio Art Program Harvard Coll., Harvard U., 1993—2001; dir pub. art curriculum New Sch. U., N.Y.C., 2001—. One-woman shows include Paintings by Janet Echelman, Mather House Artium Gallery, Harvard U., 1985, Ctrl. Gallery, The Fringe Club, Hong Kong, 1988, BMPAH, Ft. Myers, Univ. South Fla., Tampa, Fine Arts Gallery, Hong Kong, 1989, one-woman shows include Acrylic-Batik-Crayon Works from Bali by Janet Echelman, 1990, one-woman shows include Recent Paintings from the Bali Studio, Nations Bank Plaza, 1991, New Vision, Tampa Mus. Art, Two Worlds, One Artist, Jakarta Cultural Torch Mus., 1993, Havard Sch. of Design Lobby Gallery, Josh Kligerman Gallery, San Miguel de Allende, Mex., 1994, Fogg Art Mus., Harvard, Adams Artspace Harvard Coll., 1995, Birla Mus., Calcutta, Birla Century Bhavan Gallery, Bombay Sculpture combining bronze and net, 1997, Fogg Art Mus., Harvard, Mus. of the Ctr. of Europe, Vilnius, Lithuania, 1998, Florence Lynch gallery Gravity's Angel, Chelsea N.Y., 2000, Florence Lynch gallery Target Swooping #3, Chelsea, N.Y., 2002, Casa De Cordon, Burgos, Spain, Swooping II, Arco Internat. Art Fair, Madrid, Target Ctyd. Juan Carlos I, Madrid, 2001, Florence Lynch Gallery One-person exhbn. Jan-Feb., N.Y.C., 2003, Art Rotterdam, Netherland Art Project in Port., Praca Cidade de Salvador, Portugal Sculpture 150ft by 150ft. on waterfront, 2004, Hoboken Meml. Island, Sept 11th Meml. in the Hudson River, 2004, exhibited in group shows at Carpenter Ctr., Main Gallery, Harvard U., 1987, Hong Kong, Kowloon and New Territories Sites, Modern Art Competition Winners, 1988, Tampa Mus. Art, Fla. State U. Mus. Art, U. Fla. Art Mus., Vero Beach Art Ctr., Daytona Beach Mus. Fine Art, 40th ann. Juried Exhibition Fla. Craftsmen, 1991—92, Harvard U. 30th Ann. Exbn. Alumni Works, 1993, De Cordova Mus. Sch. of Art Gallery, Faculty Exhbn. Inauguration., 1994, Fuller Art Mus. Outdoor Sculptue Exhbn., Brockton, Mass., 1994, Boston Sculptors at Chapel Gallery, Newton, Mass., 2000, Ctr. for Contemporary Non-Objective Art, Brussels, Belgium, 2004, Represented in permanent collections U.S. Ednl. Found. in India, New Delhi, The Fields Sculpture Park, Omi, N.Y., U.S. Consulate, Bombay, India, Hong Kong Univ. Collection, Tampa Mus. of Art, French Ambassador;s Residence, Jakarta, Mus. of the Ctr. of Europe, Vilnius, Lithuania, Harvard Library Collection, Kohler Factory Collection, Birla Acad Mus., Calcutta, India, Fung Ping Shan Mus. of Art, Hong Kong. Named to Pub. Art Network Nat. Coun., 2003—08; recipient 1st place piano Young Artists Concerto Competition, Fla. Orch., 1981, Fulbright Sr. lectureship in Visual Art to lecture in India, 1996—97, Award for Visual Art, Pollock-Krasner Found., N.Y.C., 1999, Award for 9-11 Meml. Design., City of Hoboken, N.J., 2003—04; grantee Finishing grant for 16 mm film, Harvard Film Archive, 1987, Muliple grants for art, Office for the Arts of Harvard-Radcliffe Coll., 1993—99, Grant for installation, Harvard U. Art Mus. Fogg Mus., 1995, Harvard U. Art Mus. Sackler Mus., 1996, Extension grant, Fulbright Trust, 1997—98, Grant for building permanent sculpture in South India, G.V. Meml. Trust, 1997—98, For Artist' s Residency in Spain, Found. Valparaiso, 1998, Grant for Residency and Perm. Sculpture, Mus. of Ctr. of Europe, 1998, For Mus. of Ctr. Europe Sculpture, Am. Ctr., Lithuania, 1998, Highest Level grant, Mass. Cultural Coun., 1999, Major Visual Artist Grant, Japan Found., 2001, Sr. Creative Artist grant, Am. Inst. Indian Studies, 2001; One Year Art Scholarship in Hong Kong, Rotary Internat. Found., 1987—88, MFA Program Scholarship, Bard Coll., Ammandale on Hudson, N.Y., 1993—94, Art/Omi Internat. Artists Residency, Omi, N.Y., 1999, Kohler Arts/Industry Fellowship, Kohler Inc., 2000, Residenccy in Genoa, Italy, Bogliasoco Found., 2001. Achievements include widespread acclaim in the world of art; reproductions of her work have appeared not only in many art museum catalogs but in numerous publications both professional and popular and international. Home: 175 Florence St Chestnut Hill MA 02467-2600

ECHEMPATI, RAGHU, mechanical engineering educator, consultant; came to U.S., 1979; naturalized. s. Raja Gopal and Subhadra (Prativadi) E.; m. Pankaja Karri, June 1, 1978; children: Sharwari, Aparna. BEng, Andhra U., Waltair, India, 1970; MTech, Indian Inst. Tech., Kharagpur, 1972, PhD, 1978. Registered profl. engr., Miss. Postdoctoral assoc. U. Fla., Gainesville, 1979-81; asst. prof. Indian Inst. Tech., New Delhi, 1977-87, Wash. State U., Pullman, 1988-90, Mich. Tech. U., Houghton, 1990-94, U. Miss., University, 1994-97; Bosch prof. Kettering U., Flint, Mich., 1997—2000, assoc. prof., 1997—. Cons. GM, Batesville (Miss.) Am., Indian Railways, Lucknow, India, 1978-82, Greneda (Miss.) Elem. Sch., 1995, CMI-Schneible, Holly, Mich., 1998; dir. Indus Industries, India, 1987-97. Reviewer: Mechanics of Materials, 1996; contbr. articles to profl. jours., book chpts. Sec. Tech. Apt., New Delhi, 1983-87. Recipient Young Scientist award Dept. Sci. & Tech., India, 1984. Fellow ASME (chmn. Saginaw (Mich.) Valley chpt.); mem. Soc. Mfg. Engrs., Assn. Machines & Mechanisms (life), Soc. Automobile Engrs., Am. Soc. Engring. Edn. Avocations: singing, tennis. Office: Kettering Univ Flint MI 48504 Office Phone: 810-762-7835.

ECHOHAWK, JOHN ERNEST, lawyer; b. Albuquerque, Aug. 11, 1945; s. Ernest V. and Emma Jane (Conrad) E.; m. Kathryn Suzanne Martin, Oct. 23, 1965; children: Christopher, Sarah. BA, U. N.Mex, 1967, JD, 1970. Bar: Colo. 1972, US Dist. Ct. Colo. 1972, US Appeals (8th Cir.) 1976, US Ct. Appeals (9th Cir.) 1980. Research assoc. Calif. Indian Legal Services, Escondido, 1970, Native Am. Rights Fund, Berkeley Calif. and Boulder, Colo., 1970-72, dep. dir. Boulder, 1972-73, 1975-77, exec. dir., 1973-75, 1977—. Mem. task force Am. Indian Policy Rev. Commn., US Senate, Washington, 1976-77; bd. dirs. Am. Indian Lawyer Tng. Program, Oakland, Calif., 1975—; bd. dirs. Assn. Am. Indian Affairs, 1980—, Nat. Com. Responsive Philanthropy, Washington, 1981-2000; mem. Clinton Adminstrn. Transition Team for Interior Dept., 1992-93. Presdl. appointee Western Water Policy Rev. Adv. Commn., 1995-97; Ind. Sector, Washington, 1986-92; mem. Natural Resources Def. Coun., NYC, 1988—; bd. dirs. Nat. Ctr. Enterprise Devel., 1988—, Keystone Ctr., 1993-99, Environ. and Energy Study Inst., 1994—. Recipient Disting. Service award Ams. For Indian Opportunity, 1982, Pres. Indian Service award Nat. Congress Am. Indians, 1984, Annual Indian Achievement award Indian Council Fire, 1987; named one of most influential attys. Nat. Law Jour., 1988, 91, 94, 97, 2000. Mem. Native Am. Bar Assn., Colo. Indian Bar Assn. Democrat. Avocations: fishing, skiing. Office: Native Am Rights Fund 1506 Broadway St Boulder CO 80302-6217 Office Phone: 303-447-8760. Office Fax: 303-443-7776.*

ECHOLS, IVOR TATUM, retired dean; b. Oklahoma City, Dec. 28, 1919; d. Israel E. and Katie (Bingley) Tatum AB, U. Kans., 1942; postgrad., U. Nebr., 1945-46; MS in Social Work, Columbia U., 1952; postgrad., U. So. Calif., 1961-62, DSW, 1968. Tchr. social studies h.s., Holdenville, Okla., 1942-43, Geary, Okla., 1943-45; caseworker ARC, Chgo., 1946-47; resident group worker Dosoris House for Teen-Age Girls Cmty. Svcs. Soc., N.Y.C., 1950-51; supr. group work Walnut Grove Ctr. Neighborhood Clubs, Oklahoma City, 1948-51; program dir. Camp Lookout YWCA, Denver, 1951; dir. program svcs. Presbyn. Neighborhood Svcs., Detroit, summer 1960; supr. group work Merrill-Palmer Inst., Detroit, 1951-70; asst. dir. Merrill-Palmer Camp, Dryden, Mich., 1951-59; prof. Sch. Social Work U. Conn., West Hartford, 1970-89, also asst. dean, ret., 1989. Del. Inter-Univ. Consortium of Social Devel., Nairobi, Kenya, 1974, Hong Kong, 1980; mem. Conn. adv. com. U.S. Commn. Civil Rights. Mem. ad hoc com. Citizens Concerned with Equal Ednl. Opportunity, Detroit, 1964—; cons. to NEA Conf. Family Camping Washington, 1959, ednl. film Scott Paper Co., Phila., 1963, 64; summer study skills project Presbyn. Ch. Bd. Nat. Missions, Knoxville, Tenn., 1965—; nat. sec. United Neighborhood Ctrs. Am., N.Y.C.; pres. Protestant Cmty. Svcs., Detroit, 1969-70; trustee Conn. Energy Found., 1987-92; commr. Conn. Hist. Commn., 1986-96, ret., 1996. ARC scholar; fellow Nat. Urban League, Porter R. Lee fellow, fellow NIMH; recipient Educator Human Rights award UN Assn., 1987, Sojourner Truth award Detroit chpt. Nat. Assn. Negro Bus. and Profl. Women, 1969, UN Assn. award for Edn. and Women's Rights, 1987, Maria R. Stewart Women's Rights award Conn. Women's Ednl. and Legal Found., 1991, Outstanding Women award U. Conn., 1991, Achievement award Assn. Advancement Soc. Groupwork, 1994, 1st Truth award Capitol C.C. Hartford, 1999; named Conn. Social Worker of Year NASW, 1979; Ivor J. Echols Endowment Fund named in her honor U. Conn. Found., 1990. Mem. Nat. Assn. Colored Women's Clubs (participant White House conf. on Children and Youth 1960), A.M.E. Ministers Wives, Acad. Certified Social Workers (hon.), Nat. Assn. Black Social Workers (honored as founding mem. 1968), Nat. Trust for Hist. Preservation, Delta Sigma Theta (Delta Dear recognition 1998). Mem. A.M.E. Ch. Office: U Conn 1798 Asylum Ave Ste 1 West Hartford CT 06117-2603

ECHOLS, MARY EVELYN, training services executive, writer; b. LaSalle, Ill., Apr. 5, 1915; d. Francis Ira and Mary Irene (Coleman) Bassett; m. David H. Echols, Aug. 31, 1951 (dec.); children: Susan Echols O'Donnell, William. Grad. St. Mary's Nursing Hosp., Chgo. Founder Internat. Travel Tng. Courses, Inc., Chgo., 1962—; pres. Evelyn Echols Cons. Ltd., 1998, Echols Comms. Ltd., 2004—. Author: Saying Yes to Life. Bd. dirs. Chgo. Conv. and Tourism Bur.; past pres. Pres. Reagan's Adv. Com. for Women's Bus. Ownership; v.p. United Cerebral Palsy Assn.; nat. spokesperson Prevent Blindness in Am.; bd. dirs. Am. Cancer Soc., Gus Giordiano Jazz Dance Chgo., Little Sisters of the Poor; mem. Women's Internat. Forum. Named Entrepreneur of Yr. Women Bus. Owners N.Y., 1985, Bus. Woman of Yr. Nat. Assn. Women Bus. Owners, 1985, Crain's Chgo. Bus., 1993; named to Chgo.'s Entrepreneurial Hall of Fame, 1992. Mem.: Soc. Am. Travel Agts., Acad. TV Arts and Scis., Chgo. Execs. Club. Office Phone: 773-348-1553. E-mail: evelyn@evelynechols.com.

ECHOLS, ROBERT L., federal judge; b. 1941; BA, Rhodes Coll., 1962; JD, U. Tenn., 1964. Law clk. to Hon. Marion S. Boyd US Dist. Ct. (we. dist.) Tenn., Nashville, 1965-66; legis. asst. Congressman Dan Kuykendall, 1967-69; ptnr. Baily, Ewing, Dale & Conner, Nashville, 1969-72, Dearborn & Ewing, Nashville, 1972-92; fed. judge US Dist. Ct. (mid. dist.) Tenn., Nashville, 1992—, chief judge, 1998—. Mem. Jud. Br. Com. US Jud. Conf., exec. com. 6th Cir. Jud. Coun., libr. com. 6th Cir. Ct. Appeals, ann. conf. planning com. 6th Cir., executive com. Federal Judges Assoc., Tenn. State-Fed. Jud. Count. With US Army, 1966; brig. gen. Tenn. Army N.G., 1969-2001 Mem. ABA, Am. Bar Found., Tenn. Bar Found., Tenn. Bar Assn., Nashville Bar Assn., Nashville Bar Found., Harry Phillips Am. Inn of Ct. Office: US Dist Ct 801 Broadway Ste 824 Nashville TN 37203-3868 Office Phone: 615-736-2774.

ECK, GEORGE GREGORY, lawyer; b. Evanston, Ill., Sept. 3, 1950; s. George F. and Dorothy E. (Frake) E.; m. Margaret K. Gorman, Sept. 1, 1973; children: Jessica Elizabeth, Michelle Margaret. BS, No. Ill. U., 1972; JD cum laude, U. Minn., 1977. Bar: Minn 1977, U.S. Dist. Ct. Minn. 1977, U.S. Ct. Appeals (8th cir.) 1977. Assoc. Dorsey & Whitney, Mpls., 1977-83, ptnr., 1983—. Mem. editorial bd. U. Minn. Law Rev., 1977. With U.S. Army, 1972—74. Home: 6413 Mendelssohn Ln Hopkins MN 55343-8424 Office: Dorsey & Whitney LLC 50 S 6th St Ste 1500 Minneapolis MN 55402-1498 E-mail: eck.george@dorsey.com.

ECK, ROBERT EDWIN, physicist; b. Ames, Iowa, Nov. 28, 1938; s. John Clifford and Helen (Behrendt) E.; m. Carolyn Jennie Vodicka, May 11, 1974; children: David Michael, Elizabeth Claire. BA in Physics, Rutgers U., 1960; MS in Physics, U. Pa., 1962, PhD in Physics, 1966; MA in Econs., U. Calif., Santa Barbara, 1973. Sr. rsch. scientist Ford Motor Co., Newport Beach, Calif., 1966-69; project engr. Santa Barbara Rsch. Ctr., Goleta, Calif., 1969-73, asst. mgr. infrared components, 1974-81, mgr. major program, 1982-84, dir. tech., 1985-88, dir./mgr. engring., 1989-95; new bus. devel. mgr. R.G. Hansen & Assocs., Santa Barbara, Calif., 1995-96; program mgr. Optoelectronics-Textron, Petaluma, 1996-2000; adminstrv. dir. Enhancement Inst., Houston, 2002—03. Bd. dirs. Goleta Edn. Found. Mem. Goleta Noontime Rotary Club (pres. 1989-90). Achievements include patents on superconductors, infrared detector testing and magnetoresistor sensors.

ECKARD, KEVIN BRUCE, music educator; b. Columbia, S.C., Apr. 28, 1971; s. Dianne Cheryl Rosenquist and Bruce Oliver Eckard; m. Laura Elizabeth Eagle, June 12, 1993. D in Musical Arts, U. S.C., 2002. Adj. faculty U. S.C., Columbia, 2003; asst. prof. voice U. Ctrl. Okla., Edmond, 2003—. Singer: (opera and oratorio) performances throughout U.S. and Europe. Grad. assistantship, Ind. U., 1993 - 1997. Mem.: Nat. Assn. Tchrs. of Singing. Achievements include Recording of contemporary work. Office: Univ Ctrl Okla 100 N University Dr Edmond OK 73034 Office Phone: 405-974-5171. Business E-Mail: keckard@ucok.edu.

ECKARDT, JASON, composer; b. Princeton, N.J., May 17, 1971; MA, Columbia U., N.Y.C., 1994; DMA, Columbia U., 1998. Co-dir. Ensemble 21 contemporary music performance group, N.Y.C., NY, 1992—; lectr. Northwestern U., Evanston, Ill., 2003—. Composer: (concerto for piano and four instruments) A Glimpse Retraced (Carnegie Hall commn.), (voice and ensemble) Tongues (Koussevitzky Found. commn.), (chamber ensemble) After Serra (Fromm Found. commn.), (percussion concerto) Reul na Coille (Evelyn Glennie commn.), (flute quartet) 16 (Brannen-Cooper commn.), (voice and piano) Performance (Guggenheim Mus. commn.). Recipient Symposium NRW prize, Stadt Wesel, Deutschen Musikrat, Nat. Composition prize, ISCM, Martirano prize, U. of Ill., Morton Gould prize, ASCAP; fellow Guggenheim Meml. fellow, John Simon Guggenheim Found., Bellagio fellow, Rockefeller Found. Personal E-mail: ping@ensemble21.com.

ECKAUS, RICHARD SAMUEL, economist, educator; b. Kansas City, Mo., Apr. 30, 1926; s. Julius and Bessie (Finklestein) E.; m. Patricia L. Meaney; 1 child, Susan L. BS, Iowa State Coll., 1946; MA, Washington U., St. Louis, 1948; PhD, MIT, 1954. Instr., asst. prof., assoc. prof. Brandeis U., 1951-62; rsch. assoc. Ctr. Internat. Studies MIT, Cambridge, 1954-61, from assoc. prof. to prof., 1962—96, Ford internat. prof., 1977-96, head dept. econs., 1987-90, emeritus prof., 1996—. Vis. scholar Roxbury C.C., 1996—2002; nat. adv. coun. for environ. and tech. policy EPA; joint program sci. and policy climate change; mem. Bd. Econ. Advisors to Gov. Mass., 1963—65; cons. ADB, OECD, AID, World Bank, govts. of Jamaica, Portugal, Egypt, Sri Lanka, Chile, China, Mexico. Author: (with K. Parikh) Planning for Growth, 1968; editor: (with J. Bhagwati) Foreign Aid, 1970, Development and Planning, 1973, Basic Economics, 1972, Estimating the Returns to Education, 1973, Appropriate Technologies for Developing Countries, 1976; contbr. articles to profl. jours. Served with USNR, 1944-46. Guggenheim and Social Sci. Rsch. Coun.fellow, 1962; Ford Found. Faculty fellow, 1965. Mem. Am. Econ. Assn. Home: 131 Sewall Ave Apt 72 Brookline MA 02446-5336 Office: MIT Dept Econs 50 Memorial Dr Cambridge MA 02142-1347 Office Phone: 617-253-3367. Business E-Mail: eckaus@mit.edu.

ECKEL, JAMES J., aerospace engineer; b. Newark, Oct. 26, 1949; s. John Joseph and Margaret Agnes (Ellison) E.; m. Barbara Ann Stout Keeley, Oct. 4, 1992. BEEE, Stevens Inst. Tech., 1971; MA, U. No. Colo., 1980. Officer USAF, 1972-80; asst. supt. Reynolds Elec. & Engring. Co., Las Vegas, 1980-84; sr. project engr. Northrop Grumman Corp., 1984—. Recipient nat. def. medal USAF, 1972, combat crew medal, 1979. Mem.: AIAA, Soc. Flight Test Engrs., Assn. of Old Crows. Republican. Roman Catholic. Avocations: racquetball, model railroading, soaring, horseback riding. Home: 4514 Ripon Rd Crystal Lake IL 60012-2026 Office: Northrop Grumman Corp 600 Hicks Rd Rolling Meadows IL 60008-1015 Office Phone: 847-259-9600. Business E-Mail: james.eckel@ngc.com.

ECKELMAN, RICHARD JOEL, engineering specialist; b. Bklyn., Mar. 25, 1951; s. Leon and Muriel (Brietbart) E.; m. Janet Louise Fenton, Mar. 21, 1978; children: Christie, Melanie, Erin Leigh, Alexandra. Student, Ariz. State U., 1988—. Sr. engr., group leader nondestructive testing Engring. Fluor Corp., Irvine, Calif., 1979-83; sr. engr. nondestructive testing McDonnell Douglas Helicopter Co., Mesa, Ariz., 1983-91; engring. specialist Convair div. Gen. Dynamics, San Diego, 1991-94; sr. tech. specialist McDonnell Douglas Techs., Inc., San Diego, 1994-96; scientist, engr. The Boeing Co., Mesa, Ariz., 1996-99, prin. engr., scientist Huntington Beach, Calif., 1999—. Mem. Am. Soc. Nondestructive Testing (nat. aerospace com. 1987—, sec. Ariz. chpt. 1987-88, treas. 1988—, sect. chmn. 1989—, sect. bd. dirs. 1990-91), Am. Soc. Quality Control, Soc. Mfg. Engrs., Lindbergh Yacht Club. Avocations: racquetball, sailing. Home: 3342 Hillrose Dr Los Alamitos CA 90720-4802

ECKENHOFF, EDWARD ALVIN, health facility administrator, educator; b. Durham, N.C., Mar. 4, 1943; s. James Edward and Bonnie Lee E.; m. Judi G. Vicich, May 27, 1978 BA, Transylvania U., 1966, PhD (hon.), 2000; MA, U. Ky., 1968; MHA, Washington U., 1974. V.p., adminstr. Rehab. Inst. Chgo., 1976-82; pres., chief exec. officer Nat. Rehab. Hosp., Washington, 1982—; asst. prof. dept. community and family practice Med. Sch., Georgetown U., Washington, 1983-94; v.p. Medlantic Healthcare Group, 1987-99. V.p. Medlantic Healthcare Group, 1987-98; pres. Nat. Rehab. Services Corp., 1987-92; chmn. bd. NASCOTT, IBIS; instr. Med. Sch., Northwestern U., preceptor Grad. Sch. Bus.; mem. Ill. Commn. on Health Assistance Programs; mem. Ill. adv. com., chmn. exec. com. Internat. Yr. of Disabled; surveyor Commn. on Accreditation of Rehab. Facilities, bd. dirs., 1980-82; bd. dirs. Nat. Assn. Rehab. Facilities, 1982-83; mem. com. on accreditation and edn. Am. Phys. Therapy Assn.; mem. Healthcare Rsch. Devel. Inst.; bd. dirs. Am. Med. Rehab. Provider Assn., chmn. bd. dirs., 2000-01 Contbr. articles to profl. jours. Bd. dirs. Am. Occupl. Therapy Found., Easter Seal Soc., Boy Scouts Am., Chgo. Area Coun., Nat. Area, 1987-87, Operation ABLE Chgo., Access Living of Met. Chgo., Am. Chamber Symphony, Chgo. Named Washingtonian of the Yr., Washingtonian Mag., 1989; recipient Citation for Disting. Svc., AMA, 1990, Ann. Healthcare Leader award B'nai B'rith, 2003. Fellow

Inst. Medicine Chgo., Am. Coll. Hosp. Execs.; mem. Am. Hosp. Assn. (chmn. governing coun. for rehab. hosps. 1985, trustee 1991-93, chmn. policy com. 1993, exec. com. 1993), Am. Congress Rehab. Medicine (chmn. policy and devel. com.), Chgo. Hosp. Coun. (chmn. com. rehab. 1978-82, exec. com. 1983), Healthcare Devel. and Rsch. Inst., Am. Med. Rehab. Providers Assn. (chmn. bd. dirs. 2000-01), Nat. Orgn. on Disability (Medicare Coverage adv. commn. 1999—), DC Hosp. Assn. (DCHA) (bd. dirs.). Episcopalian. Office: Nat Rehab Hosp 102 Irving St NW Washington DC 20010-2949

ECKER, ROBERT DONIGER, neurosurgeon; b. Boston, Apr. 6, 1972; s. Howard Malcolm and Wendy Lee Ecker; m. Lissa Diaz, Apr. 29, 2001; children: Emily Doniger, Alexander Diaz. AB, Harvard U., 1995; MD, Med. Coll. Va., 1999. Resident in neurol. surgery Mayo Clinic, Rochester, Minn., 1999—; endovascular fellow U. Buffalo, 2004—. Contbr. articles to profl. jours. Intern Office of Senator Albert Gore, Jr., Washington, 1990—91. Lt. comdr. USN, 1999—. U.S. Health Profl. scholar., USN, 1999—. Mem.: AMA (assoc.), Am. Assn. Neurol. Surgeons (assoc.), Congress Neurol. Surgeons (assoc.), Phi Kappa Phi, Alpha Omega Alpha. Avocations: scuba diving, triathalons. Office Phone: 716-200-8494.

ECKERSLEY, DENNIS LEE, former professional baseball player; b. Oakland, Calif., Oct. 3, 1954; m. Nancy O'Neill; 1 child, Mandee. Baseball player Cleve. Indians, 1974-78, Boston Red Sox, 1978-84, Chgo. Cubs, 1984-87, Oakland A's, 1987-95, St. Louis Cardinals, 1996-97, Boston Red Sox, 1997-98, ret., 1998. Named Am. League Champion Series MVP, 1988, Am. League MVP, 1992; named to Am. league All-Star Team, 1977, 1982, 1988, 1990—92; recipient Rolaids Relief Award, 1988, 1992, Am. League Cy Young Award, 1992. Achievements include mem. of World Series Championship Oakland A's, 1989; holds AL record for most games pitched (869), most saves (324), most consecutive errorless games (470); only pitcher in history with 100 complete games and 100 saves; inducted into Baseball Hall of Fame, Cooperstown, NY, 2004.

ECKERSLEY, RICHARD LAURENCE, accountant; b. Scranton, Pa., July 29, 1948; s. Robert Neal and Helen Elizabeth (Palmer) E.; m. Linda K. Forsythe, Feb. 11, 1967; children: Laura Lynnette, Tristan Dael, Travis Morgan. AB in English, U. Scranton, 1971, MA in History, 1993. CPA, Pa. Staff acct. Acctg. Svc. Assocs., Inc., Scranton, 1967-77; ptnr. Eckersley Acctg. Svc., Scranton, 1977-80; shareholder, pres. Eckersley and Eckersley, P.C., Scranton, 1980-86; ptnr. Eckersley and Ostrowski, LLP, Scranton, 1987—. Lectr. acctg. Keystone Jr. Coll., LaPlume, Pa., 1974-76. Asst. treas. The Real Bob Casey Com., Scranton, 1985-96; bd. dirs., officer Family Svc. Lackawanna County, Scranton, 1978-84, Planned Parenthood N.E. Pa., Trexlertown, Pa., 1981-86, 89-93; treas. Casey for Congress Com., 1998—. Mem. AICPA, Pa. Inst. Cert. Pub. Accts. Methodist. Avocations: reading, history, hunting, diving. Home: RR 3 Box 5 Dalton PA 18414-9528 Office: Eckersley and Ostrowski LLP 300 Gerard Bldg Scranton PA 18503

ECKERT, ALLAN WESLEY, writer; b. Buffalo, Jan. 30, 1931; s. Edward Russell and Ruth Rose (Roth) E.; m. Joan Dowling, 1955 (div.1975); children: Joseph Matthew, Julie Anne; m. Gail Greene, 1977 (div. 1978); m. Nancy Dent, 2005. Student, U. Dayton, 1951-52, Ohio State U., 1953-54; PhD (hon.), Bowling Green State U., 1985, Wright State U., 1998. Assoc. editor Nat. Cash Register Co. News, Dayton, Ohio, 1955-58; reporter, columnist Dayton Jour. Herald, Dayton, Ohio, 1958-60; free-lance writer, 1960—. Cons. LaSalle Extension U., Chgo. Writer over 200 TV scripts for NBC's Wild Kingdom; created courses article and short story writing Writer's Digest; author: The Great Auk, 1963, A Time of Terror, 1965, The Silent Sky, 1965, Wild Season, 1967, The Frontiersmen, 1967, Bayou Backwaters, 1967, The Dreaming Tree, 1967, The Crossbreed, 1968, Blue Jacket, 1968, The King Snake, 1968, Wilderness Empire, 1968, In Search of a Whale, 1969, The Conquerors, 1970, Incident at Hawk's Hill, 1971, The Court-Martial of Daniel Boone, 1973, The Owls of North America, 1973, The HAB Theory, 1976, The Wilderness War, 1978, The Wading Birds of North America, 1979, Savage Journey, 1979, Song of the Wild, 1980, Whattizzit?, 1981, Gateway to Empire, 1982, Johnny Logan: Shawnee Spy, 1982, The Dark Green Tunnel, 1983, The Wand, 1984, The Scarlet Mansion, 1985, Earth Treasures, 4 vols., 1987, Twilight of Empire, 1988, A Sorrow in Our Heart: The Life of Tecumseh, 1991, That Dark and Bloody River: Chronicles of the Ohio River Valley, 1995, The World of Opals, 1997, Return to Hawk's Hill, 1998, (outdoor drama) Tecumseh!, 1970, (screenplays) Kentucky Pioneers, 1969, The Legend of Koo-Tan, 1971, (playscript) Tecumseh!, 1974; editor: A Treasury of Tips for Writers, 1966; contbr. articles to popular and profl. publs. Trustee Dayton Museum Natural History, 1963-65; Founder, chmn. bd. Lemon Bay Conservancy, Englewood, Fla. Served with USAF, 1948-52. Recipient Ohioana Book award, 1968, Best Book award Friends of Am. Writers, 1968, Emmy award outstanding program achievement Nat. Acad. TV Arts and Scis., 1968-69, Newbury-Caldecott Honor Book award, 1972, George G. Stone/Claremont Colls. Recognition of Merit, 1974, Austrian Juvenile Book of Yr. award, 1976, Americanism award The Daniel Boone Found., 2d Ann. Silver Arrow Humanitarian award Scioto Soc., 1987, Internat. Readers Assn. Tchrs. Choice award, 1999; commd. Ky. Col. by Gov. State of Ky., 1987; finalist Spur award Western Writers Am., 1995; named Writer of Yr., Am. Culture Assn., 1997; nominated 7 times for Pulitzer prize; Allan W. Eckert Collection established at Howard Gotlieb Meml. Libr., Boston U., 1965, at the Filson Club Hist. Soc., Louisville, 1993, named by Citizens of Ohio as favorite Ohio writer of all time, Ohioana Libr. Assn., 1999; Allan W. Eckert Nature Trail, Scioto County Commrs., Riverside Park, 2001. Mem. Dayton Soc. Natural History (life), Am. Soc. of Gem Cutters, Mazon Creek Project (life). Office: care Russell Galen Scoville Chichak and Galen 381 Park Ave S Rm 1020 New York NY 10016-8806 Office Fax: 212-679-6710. Personal E-mail: allaneck@earthlink.net.

ECKERT, JEAN PATRICIA, elementary school educator; b. Pitts., July 22, 1935; d. Homer Michael and Berdena Leona (Kessler) Canel; m. William L. Eckert, June 13, 1959; 1 child, Suzanne Mary. *Jean has four grandchildren: William Cody, Robert Kentucky, Mari-Therese Suzanne, and Faith Melinda Burton. Jean's career is intertwined with Law Enforcement, and her husband, William L., served 40 years, with 20 as Chief of Police in Aspinwall, PA. Jean's uncle, Joseph A. Kessler, devoted 36 years with 28 as Chief of Police in Fox Chapel, PA.* BS, Indiana U. Pa., 1957; postgrad., U. Pitts., 1958-59, U. San Diego, 1981. Cert. pub. instrn., Pa. Elem. tchr. Pine-Richland Sch. Dist., Gibsonia, Pa., 1957—60, substitute tchr., 1963—65; elem. tchr. Shaler Twp. Sch. Dist., Glenshaw, Pa., 1965—66, St. Scholastica Sch., Diocese of Pitts., Aspinwall, Pa., 1966—91, substitute tchr., 1991—, tutor, 1991—. Judge election 4th dist. Rep. Party, Aspinwall, 1962-65, 91-98. Mem.: AAUW, Nat. Cath. Edn. Assn., Literacy Vols. Am., Ind. U. (Pa.) Alumni Assn., Delta Zeta (sec. 1955, pres. 1956). Roman Catholic. Avocations: travel, literature. Home: 210 12th St Pittsburgh PA 15215-1600

ECKERT, JOHN ANDREW, chemist, technical consultant; b. Rochester, N.Y., Apr. 12, 1941; BS with honors, Rochester Inst. Tech., 1964; PhD, MIT, 1970. Scientist Kodak, Rochester, N.Y., 1960-64; solar mgr. Exxon, Linden, N.J., 1970-79, sr. assoc. Clinton, N.J., 1982-86; rsch. mgr. Enlighten, Stewartsville, N.J., 1986—. Edn. dir. Exxon, Florham Park, N.J., 1979-82. Mem. editorial bd. Solar Energy Materials jour., 1979-80; editor Enlighten newsletter, 1991—. Recipient Indsl. Chemistry Affiliate award Am. Chem. Soc., 1960, 61. Mem. Water Gap Gliding Club (sec. 1987—). Achievements include patents for semi-conductor photogalvanic effects and anti-mist fuels. Office: Enlighten PO Box 313 Stewartsville NJ 08886-0313

ECKERT, LINDA O., physician; m. Buckley A. Eckert, June 25, 1987; children: Conor Jett, Shane O'Neal. MD, U. Calif., Sch. of Medicine, San Diego, Calif., 1987. Fellowship, Infectious Diseases U. Wash., Dept. of Medicine, 1996, Residency, Ob-gyn U.Tex. at Houston, 1992. Gynecology coord. Ctr. for Sexual Assault, Seattle, 1998—; gynecology tech. bulletins com. Am. Coll. of Ob-gyn., Washington, 2003—; asst. prof. Dept. of Ob-gyn., U. Wash., Seattle, 1996—2004, assoc. prof., 2004—. Vol. physician Kikuyu Hosp., Kikuyu, Kenya, 1992—92; ad hoc reviewer NIH Study Sect., Human Embryology and Devel.-1, Washington, 2003. Invited reviewer (peer review scientific articles) (Outstanding Reviewer for Quantity, Quality and Timeliness of Reviews, 2004); contbr. scientific papers (Best Abstract in Domestic Violence at the ann. meeting of the Am. Coll. of Obstetrics & Gynecology, 2001), articles pub. to profl. jour. Admissions com. U. Wash. Med. Sch.; elder Wallingford Presbyn. Ch., Seattle, 2005. Recipient Deans' List, Carleton Coll., 1979-1983, Distinction in Chemistry, 1983, APGO Solvay Nat. Award for Outstanding Med. Student Edn., 2004; scholar NCAA Scholar, NCAA, 1983. Fellow: Am. Coll. of Ob-gyn.; mem.: Infectious Diseases in Ob-gyn., Pacific Coast Obstet. & Gynecologic Soc., Phi Beta Kappa. Christain. Avocations: sports, outdoor activities. Office: Harborview Hosp 325 9th Ave Box 359865 Seattle WA 98104 Office Phone: 206-731-3319.

ECKERT, ROBERT A., consumer products company executive; m. Kathie Eckert; 4 children. BSBA, U. Ariz., 1976; MBA in Mktg. and Fin., Northwestern U., 1977. Various mktg. positions Kraft Foods, 1977-87, v.p. strategy and devel. grocery products divsn., 1987-89, v.p. mktg. refrigerated products, 1989-90, v.p., gen. mgr. cheese divsn., 1990-97, pres., CEO, 1997-2000; chmn. bd., CEO Mattel, Inc., 2000—. Bd. dirs. McDonalds Corp., 2003—; com. mem. Trilateral Commn. Active adv. bd. J.L. Kellogg Grad. Sch. Mgmt., Northwestern U.; bd. visitors, Anderson Sch., UCLA; bd. dirs., mem. exec. com. Met. Family Svcs.; trustee Ravinia Festival Assn., Art Inst. Chgo.; nat. trustee Lake Forest Coll. Bd. dirs., chmn. govt. affairs coun. Grocery Mfrs. Am.; bd. dirs. L.A. World Affairs Coun., Bus. Coun., Wash. D.C.; mem. Asia Society, Young Presidents' Org., L.A., Town Hall L.A. Office: Mattel Inc 333 Continental Blvd El Segundo CA 90245-5012 Fax: 310-252-2179.*

ECKHARDT, CRAIG JON, chemistry educator; b. Rapid City, S.D., June 26, 1940; s. Reuben H and Hilda W. (Craig) E. BA magna cum laude, U. Colo., 1962; MS, Yale U., 1964, PhD, 1967. Asst. prof. chemistry U. Nebr., Lincoln, 1967-72, assoc. prof., 1972-78, prof., 1978—, interim chmn. dept. chemistry, 1986-87, prof. physics, 1988—. Cons., mem. adv. panel, condensed matter scis. div. materials research NSF, 1976-79 NIH predoctoral fellow, 1964-67; Yale predoctoral fellow, 1967; John Simon Guggenheim fellow, 1979-80; German Acad. Exchange fellow; Grantee NSF, 1974-84, Dept. Energy, 1979-82, Petroleum Rsch. Fund-Am. Chem. Soc., 1968-72, Rsch. Corp., 1971-74, 3M Corp., 1983-89, Army Rsch. Office, 1989—. Mem. Am. Phys. Soc., Am. Assn. Physics Tchrs., Optical Soc. Am., Am. Chem. Soc., Royal Chemistry Soc., Phi Beta Kappa, Sigma Xi. Office: U Nebr Dept Chemistry Lincoln NE 68588

ECKHARDT, LAUREL ANN, biologist, researcher, educator; b. Palo Alto, Calif., Sept. 4, 1951; d. Joseph Carl Augustus Eckhardt and Ada Jane Williams Smith; m. Michael Warren Young, Dec. 27, 1978; children: Natalie Alice Eckhardt Young, Arissa Caroline Eckhardt Young. BA summa cum laude, U. Tex., 1974; PhD in Genetics, Stanford (Calif.) U., 1980. Damon Runyon-Walter Winchell postdoctoral fellow Albert Einstein Coll. Medicine, Bronx, 1980-83; asst. prof. Dept. Biol. Sci., Columbia U., N.Y.C., 1984-88, assoc. prof., 1989-92; prof. Dept. Biol. Sci., Hunter Coll. of CUNY, 1992—, Marie Hesselbach prof. biology, 1999—. Reviewer immunobiology study sect. Dept. Rsch. Grants, NIH, Bethesda, Md., 1993-96; reviewer grand rev. com. Am. Heart Assn., N.Y.C., 1990-93, sci. rev. Immunological Sciences peer rev. com., Dept. of Def. Breast Cancer Rsch. Program, 1998, 2000, 03, rev. panelist for rsch. tng. fellowships for med. students, Howard Hughes Med. Student, Howard Hughes Med. Inst., 2002-04. Assoc. editor Jour. Immunology, 1997-2001; contbr. articles to profl. jours. Rsch. grantee NIH-Inst. Allergy and Infectious Diseases, 1984-90, 90—, Am. Cancer Soc., 1990-95, NIH-Nat. Cancer Inst., 1994-99. Mem. Am. Assn. Immunologists (program com. mem. 1995-99), N.Y. Acad. Scis., Harvey Soc. Democrat. Avocations: tennis, gardening, dance. Office: Hunter College of CUNY Dept Biol Sci 695 Park Ave New York NY 10021-5085

ECKHART, MARYLOUISE CHRISTINE SANTILLI, pre-school educator; d. Richard William and Louise May Santilli; m. Jeffery Gene Eckhart, Sept. 4, 1983; children: Andrew William, Kyle Gene, Matthew Russell. BEd, U. Toledo, 1982; MEd, Ashland (Ohio) U., 1994. Cert. tchr. Ohio Dept. of Edn., 1982. Spl. edn. tchr. Anthony Wayne Local Schs., Ohio, 1982—85; from spl. edn. tchr. to early childhood intervention specialist Canton (Ohio) City Schs., 1985—2000, early childhood resource specialist, 2000—. Adj. instr. Ashland U., Massillon, Ohio, 2001—. Contbr. chpt. to book. Mem.: ASCD, Canton Area Assn. Edn. Young Children, Assn. Childhood Edn. Internat., Nat. Assn. Edn. Young Children. Avocations: travel, camping, reading, exercise, spending time with my family. Home: 6589 Dale St NW Massillon OH 44646 Office Phone: 330-580-3033 123. E-mail: eckhart_m@ccsdistrict.org.

ECKHART, MYRON, JR., (MAX ECKHART), retired marine engineer; b. South Bend, Ind., Mar. 29, 1923; s Myron Lester and Neva (Whitmer) E.; m. Joan Elizabeth Daniels, June 29, 1946; children: Joan Theresa, Michael Thomas, Jeri Anne. BS, U.S. Naval Acad., 1945; BSEE, MIT, 1949; MSEE, George Washington U., 1967. Commd. ensign USN, 1945, advanced through grades to capt., 1966; stationed at Norfolk Naval Shipyard, Va., 1950—56; project officer Underwater Sound Lab. Regulus Missile, 1955—60; chmn. elec. sci. U.S. Naval Acad., 1962—65; dir. ship design divsn. Hdqrs. USN, 1965—70; ret., 1970; mgr. advanced engring., chief scientist marine sys. divsn. Rockwell Internat., Anaheim, Calif., 1970—84, cons., 1985—. Contbr. articles to profl. jours. Mem. Soc. Naval Architects and Marine Engrs., Am. Soc. Naval Engrs., Am. Def. Preparedness Assn., U.S. Naval Inst. Achievements includes patent of fourier synthesis of complex waveforms; shipsinclude designs of Nimitz aircraft carriers, Trident strategic submarines, Los Angeles class submarines; prin. devel. roles include airborne radar to shipboard displays, radar-based landing control of aircraft, in-helmet radio communications link, REGULUS strategic missile guidance system. Home: 1211 Belle Vista Dr Alexandria VA 22307-2016 *Success depends upon figuring out the price associated with each of one's goals, and then being willing to pay that price with no assurance of reward.*

ECKHART, WALTER, molecular biologist, educator; b. Yonkers, N.Y., May 22, 1938; s. Walter and Jean E. BS, Yale U., 1960; postgrad., Cambridge U., Eng., 1960-61; PhD, U. Calif.-Berkeley, 1965. Postdoctoral fellow Salk Inst., San Diego, 1965-69, mem., 1970-73, assoc. prof. molecular biology, 1973-79, prof., 1979—, cancer ctr. dir., 1976—. Adj. prof. U. Calif.-San Diego, 1973-2003. Contbr. articles on molecular biology and virology to profl. jours. NIH research grantee, 1967—. Mem. AAAS, Am. Soc. Microbiology, Am. Soc. Virology Home: 951 Skylark Dr La Jolla CA 92037-7731 Office: Salk Inst PO Box 85800 San Diego CA 92186-5800 Office Phone: 858-453-4100 1386. Business E-Mail: eckhart@salk.edu.

ECKL, WILLIAM WRAY, lawyer; b. Florence, Ala., Dec. 2, 1936; s. Louis Arnold and Patricia Barclift (Dowd) E.; m. Mary Lynn McGough, June 29, 1963; children: Eric Dowd, Lynn Lacey. BA, U. Notre Dame, 1959; LLB, U. Va., 1962. Bar: Va. 1962, Ala. 1962, Ga. 1964. Law clk. Supreme Ct. of Ala., 1962; ptnr. Gambrell, Harlan, Russell & Moye, Atlanta, 1965-68, Swift, Currie, McGhee & Hiers, Atlanta, 1968-82, Drew, Eckl & Farnham, Atlanta, 1983—. Served to capt. JAGC USAR, 1962—65. Mem. Am. Bd. Trial Advocates, Trial Attys. Am., Lawyers Club of Atlanta, Brookwood Hills Club. Roman Catholic. Home: 348 Camden Rd NE Atlanta GA 30309-1513 Office: Drew Eckl & Farnham 880 W Peachtree St PO Box 7600 Atlanta GA 30357-0600 Office Phone: 404-885-6327. E-mail: weckl@deflaw.com.

ECKLAND, WILLIAM S, lawyer; b. 1954; BA, Univ. Md., 1976; JD with honors, George Washington Unv, 1979. Bar: DC 1979, NY 1989. Ptnr. fed. regulatory issues Sidley Austin Brown & Wood LLP, Washington, and mem. exec. com. Mem. George Washington Univ. Law Rev., 1979. Mem.: ABA, Order of Coif. Office: Sidley Austin Brown & Wood LLP 1501 K St NW Washington DC 20005 Office Phone: 202-736-8267. Office Fax: 202-736-8711. Business E-Mail: weckland@sidley.com.

ECKLEY, WILTON EARL, JR., humanities educator; b. Alliance, Ohio, June 25, 1929; s. Wilton Earl and Louise (Bert) E.; m. Grace Ester Williamson, Sept. 12, 1954; children: Douglas, Stephen, Timothy. BA, Mt. Union Coll., 1952; MA, Pa. State U., 1955; PhD, Case Western Reserve U., 1965; John Hay fellow, Yale U., 1961-62. Chmn. English Euclid (Ohio) Sr. High Sch., 1955-63; dir. tchr. tng. Hollins Coll., 1963-65; prof. English Drake U., 1965-84, chmn. dept. English, 1965-80; head dept. humanities and social scis. Colo. Sch. Mines, 1984-93, dir. honors program, 1989-92; prof. humanities Drake U., 1984—; prof. humanities and internat. studies Colo. Sch. Mines, 1994-99, prof. emeritus, 1999—. Fulbright prof. Am. lit. U., Ljubljana, Yugoslavia, 1972-73, U. Veliko, Turnovo, Bulgaria, 1981-82; vis. prof. Bilkent U., Ankara, Turkey, 1993-94. Chmn. bd. dirs. Colo. Endowment for the Humanities, 1989-91. Coe fellow Am. Studies, 1957— Mem. MLA, Circus Hist. Soc., AAUP, Phi Kappa Tau. Home: 636 Ridgeside Dr Golden CO 80401-5757

ECKLIN, ROBERT LUTHER, materials company executive; b. Lancaster, Pa., Sept. 26, 1938; s. Luther Joseph and Ella Frances (Smith) E.; m. Loretta Rohrer Stoner, Sept. 3, 1960; children: Robert Luther, Jr., Suzanne Beth, Kristina Ann, Stephanie Ann. B in Archtl. Engring., Chgo. Tech. Coll., 1961; postgrad., Dartmouth U., 1983, cert., 1984. With Corning Inc., N.Y.C., 1961—; pres. Corning Engring. Corning (N.Y.) Glass Works, 1982-86, corp. v.p. bus. devel., chmn. Corning Engring., 1986-88, sr. v.p., 1988-99, exec. v.p., 1999—. Chmn. Maklin Ltd., Stone-on-Trent, Eng., 1983-86; ptnr. Ecklin & Ecklin Investments, Lancaster, 1986—; bd. dirs. MacDermid, Inc., Waterbury, Conn., Alfred Ul. Tech. Resources, Pitts.-Corning Corp., Pitts.-Corning Europe, Cormetech, Infotonics, RPC Photonics. Chmn. Com. of 50, Corning, 1985—; mem. rsch. adv. bd. N.Y. State U.; pres. Univ. Industry Pub. Partnership for Econ. Growth. Mem. Corning C. of C. Republican. Methodist. Home: 248 Cedar St Corning NY 14830-3128 Office: Corning Inc MP HQ E2 Riverfront Plz Corning NY 14831-0001 E-mail: ecklinrl@corning.com.

ECKLUND, RALPH EARL, property manager; b. Seattle, Jan. 29, 1930; s. Earl Frank and Ruby Frances (Bradshaw) Ecklund. AB in Design/Arch., Harvard U., 1952; postgrad., U. Wash., 1955. Asst. mgr. Liberty Ct. Apts., Seattle, 1957—68; dir. Lockhaven Apts., Seattle, 1958—. Author: Ripples newsletter, 1970. Sgt. U.S. Army, 1952—55. Mem.: Seattle Rhododendron Soc. (life), Seattle Men's Garden Club (sec.-editor 1963—70). Republican. Congregationalist. Avocations: photography, reading, genealogy, rhododendrons, collecting books. Home: 8321 32d Ave NW Seattle WA 98117-3922 Office: Lockhaven Apts 3040 NW Market St Seattle WA 98107

ECKLUND-JOHNSON, ERIC PHILLIP, psychologist; b. Mpls., Minn., Jan. 30, 1970; s. Phillip Douglas and Sandra Joyce Johnson; m. Jennifer Ecklund, May 20, 1995; 1 child, Violet Iben. BA, North Park Coll., Chgo., 1992; MA, Loyola U., Chgo., 1996, PhD with distinction, 2002. Lic. psychologist Pa., Ill. Intern in neuropsychology U. Fla., Gainesville, 1999—2000, post doctoral assoc., 2000—02; post doctoral fellow Evanston Northwestern Healthcare, Ill., 2002—04; asst. dir. psychology Allied Svcs., Scranton, Pa., 2004—. Mem.: APA, Internat. Neuropsychology Soc., Alpha Sigma Nu. Mem. Evang. Covenant Ch.

ECKMAN, DAVID WALTER, lawyer; b. Ogden, Utah, Oct. 23, 1942; s. Walter and Ann-Marie Pauline Eckman; m. Laurie Alden Waters, Aug. 28, 1965. Student, Rice U., 1960-61; BA with honors, U. Tex., Austin, 1964, JD (Sam D. Hanna scholar), 1967. Bar: Tex. 1967, Calif. 1976, U.S Ct. Appeals (5th cir.) 1983. With Exxon Co., U.S.A. div. Exxon Corp., 1967-78, mem. Prudhoe Bay Law Task Force Houston and Los Angeles, 1974-75, counsel Pacific Region Los Angeles, 1975-77, counsel hdqrs. Houston, 1977-78; gen. counsel Natomas N.Am. Inc., Houston, 1978, v.p.-legal, corp. chief legal counsel, 1978-82; sole practice Houston, 1982—. Vestryman, dir. Christian edn. All Sts. Episcopal Ch., Corpus Christi, 1968-70; leader adult study St. Mark's Episcopal Ch., Houston, 1971-74; v.p. St. Mark's Sch. PTO, 1981-82; vol. Bible Study tchr., one-on-one counseling Tex. Dept. Criminal Justice, Houston, 1983-94; lay reader St. John the Divine Episc. Ch., Houston, 1982—, leader adult study, 1983-86, 94—; bd. mem. Rolling Waters (pro bono advocacy), 1999-2001; mem. St. Patrick's Sch. Bd., Thousand Oaks, Calif., 1976-77; pres. Houston Youth Soccer Assn., 1979-81, bd. dirs., 1979-83; pres. Neartown Soccer Club, 1980-83; v.p. Old Braeswood Civic Assn., 1982-85; bd. dirs. Friends of Pyramid House, Inc., 1985-95. Recipient Am. Jurisprudence award in antitrust law U. Tex., 1967 Mem. Tex. State Bar, Calif. State Bar, Houston Bar Assn., Full Gospel Bus. Men's Fellowship Internat. (v.p. downtown Houston chpt. 1985-89), Lambda Chi Alpha, Phi Delta Phi. Office: 3730 Kirby Dr Ste 1200 Houston TX 77098-3932 E-mail: davide@eckman-law.com.

ECKMAN, FERN MARJA, journalist; b. N.Y.C., Aug. 27; d. Isidor Peter and Zara Nettie (Sloate) Friedman; m. Irving Eckman, June 21, 1957. BA, N.Y. U., 1957. Reporter N.Y. Post, 1944-78; assigned to UN, 1945-49, 60-65. Author: The Furious Passage of James Baldwin, 1967; contbg. editor Working Mother, 1981-91; feature writer for nat. publs., 1965-90. Recipient George Polk Meml. award for distinguished met. reporting, 1951, 55; Page One award for community service N.Y. Newspaper Guild, 1955, for best feature reporting, 1961; citation for community service Council Puerto Rican and Spanish-Am. Orgns., 1955; Lasker award for med. journalism, 1960; Front Page award for distinguished feature writing, News Women's Club N.Y., 1949, 51, 56, 64; for distinguished series (co-recipient), 1970; Cultural News award Newspaper Reporters Assn., N.Y.C., 1967; Empire State award for excellence in med. reporting, 1968 Home: 749 W End Ave New York NY 10025-6224

ECKMANN, DOROTHY FLETCHER, fiber artist, art educator; b. Sacremento, Dec. 16, 1939; d. John Brewer and Helen Montana Fletcher; m. Michael Ralph Eckmann, Mar. 27, 1964 (div. Nov. 1992); children: April Eckmann Lange, Teresa Lynn. BA, U. of Wash., 1963. Part time instr. Atlantic Armstrong State U., Savannah, Ga., 1997—98, Augusta State U., Augusta, Ga., 2000—; program officer Morris Mus. of Art, Augusta, Ga., 1997—99; edn. dir. Gertrude Herbert Inst. of Art, Augusta, Ga., 1999—. Fiber arts, mixed-media, Two Woman Exhibition (Artist Initiated Grant; Cultural Affairs Bur., Savannah, GA, 1997), fiber arts one- woman exhibition, A Search for Center; dir.: (collaborative arts outreach program with) The Mural Project (Savannah Cultural Affairs Grant and SOSCO Olympic Endorsement, 1995); handwoven fiber art, Tidepools I (Purchase Award, High Mus. of Art, 1992), group exhibition; textile museum, d.c., Country of Origin, USA: A Decade of Comtenporary Rugs, exhibitions include in group and one woman shows. Mem.: Ga. Art Edn. Assn. (mus. divsn. rep. 2001—03, sec. 2003—, Mus. Educator of the Yr. 2003), Nat. Art Edn. Assn., Am. Craft Coun., Handweavers Guild of Am., Georgia-Carolina Toastmasters (pres., v p edn., vp membership, vp pub. rels. 1998—2005, dist. 14, divsn. F, area 56 2003—04). D-Liberal. Office: Gertrude Herbert Institute of Art 506 Telfair St Augusta GA 30901 Office Phone: 706-722-5495. Office Fax: 705-722-3670. Business E-Mail: deckmann@ghia.org.

ECKSTEIN, DAVID, professional baseball player; b. Sanford, Fla., Jan. 20, 1975; Attended Univ. Fla. Short stop Anaheim Angels, 2001—04, St. Louis Cardinals, 2004—. Named to Nat. League All-Star Team, 2005. Office: St Louis Cardinals 250 Stadium Plz Saint Louis MO 63102*

ECKSTEIN, JEROME, retired philosopher, educator; b. NYC, June 28, 1925; s. Marcus and Blanche (Wohlberg) E.; m. Kathleen Sharon Hoisington; 1 stepchild, Mari O'Donnell Midurski; children: Esther Schwartz, Sandra Bellehsen, Michael. Student, Rabbi Isaac Elchanan Theol. Sem., 1943-45; BA, Bklyn. Coll., 1949; postgrad., New Sch. Social Research, 1949-50; PhD, Columbia U., 1961. Buyer antique silverware Blanche Eckstein Silverware, Bklyn., 1945-53; dir. edn. and youth activities, various Hebrew congregations, 1950-61; lectr. philosophy CCNY, 1955-56, Bklyn. Coll., 1955-60; instr. contemporary civilization and philosophy Columbia U., N.Y.C., 1960-63; asst. prof., then assoc. prof. philosophy, coordinator div. humanities Adelphi Suffolk Coll., Adelphi U., 1963-66; prof. philosophy of edn.

SUNY-Albany, 1966-70, also first chmn. Judaic studies, 1970-74, prof. Judaic studies, 1970-97, prof. religious studies, 1990-97, prof. emeritus, 1997—. Participant Internat. Philosophy Yr., Brockport, N.Y., 1967, Conf. on Gerontology, U. Minn., 1978; vis. prof. philosophy Bar-Ilan U., Israel, 1978-79 Author: The Platonic Method: An Interpretation of the Dramatic-Philosophic Aspects of the Meno, 1968; The Deathday of Socrates, 1981, Metaphysical Drift: Love and Judaism, 1991, On Meanings or Life: Their Nature and Origin, 2002; contbr. articles to profl. jours. Fellow in logic CCNY, 1955-56; vis. scholar Va. Commonwealth U., Richmond, 1975; Am. Council Learned Socs. sr. fellow, 1973 Mem. Phi Beta Kappa

ECKSTEIN, JOHN WILLIAM, internist, educator, retired dean; b. Central City, Iowa, Nov. 23, 1923; s. John William and Alice (Ellsworth) Eckstein; m. Imogene O'Brien, June 16, 1947; children: John Alan, Charles William, Margaret Ann, Thomas Cody, Steven Gregory. BS, Loras Coll., 1946; MD, U. Iowa, 1950; DSc (hon.), Ind. U., 1995. Asst. prof. internal medicine U. Iowa, Iowa City, 1956—60, assoc. prof., 1960—65, prof., 1965—92, prof. emeritus, 1993; assoc. dean VA Hosp. affairs, 1969—70, dean coll. medicine, 1970-91, dean emeritus, 1993. Chmn. cardiovasc. study sect. NIH, 1970—72, Nat. Heart, Lung and Blood Adv. Coun., 1974—78; mem. adv. com. to dir. NIH, 1990—95. Author papers and abstracts. Mem. VA Manpower Study Group, 1988—92. Served with USAF, 1943—45, served with U.S. Army Med. Corps., 1950—51. Named established investigator, Am. Heart Assn., 1958—63, in his honor, Eckstein Med. Rsch. Bldg., U. Iowa, 1988; recipient Rsch. Career award, USPHS, 1963—70, Dist. Alumni Svc. award, U. Iowa, 1994, Disting. Physicians, Dept. Vets. Affairs, 1995—98; fellow postdoctoral, Rockefeller Found., 1953—54, Am. Heart Assn. Rsch., 1954—55, spl. rsch., Nat. Heart Inst., 1955—56. Mem.: Assn. Acad. Health Ctrs. (mem. sci. policy study group 1988—93), Inst. Medicine, Assn. Am. Med. Colls. (exec. coun. 1981—82, adminstrv. bd. 1980—82, 1985—86), Assn. Am. Physicians, Am. Clin. and Climatol. Assn., Am. Soc. Clin. Investigation, Ctrl. Soc. Clin. Rsch. (sec.-treas. 1965—70, pres. 1973—74), Am. Fedn. Clin. Rsch. (chmn. Midwestern sect. 1965), AMA (mem. health policy agenda panel 1982—86, mem. study sect. faculty and resh. 1985—86, governing. coun. sect. on med. schs. 1985—95, alt. del. Ho. of Dels. 1986—90, del. 1990—92, Disting. Svc. award 1992), Am. Heart Assn. (v.p. 1969, chmn. coun. on circulation 1969—71, pres. 1978—79). Home: 1415 William White Blvd Iowa City IA 52245-4443 Office: U Iowa Hosps & Clinics Iowa City IA 52242-1101 E-mail: john-eckstein@uiowa.edu.

ECKSTEIN, MARC, physician; BS, Cornell U., 1981—85; MD, Mt. Sinai Sch. of Medicine, 1985—89. Assoc. prof. of emergency medicine Keck Sch. of Medicine of the U. of So. Calif., Los Angeles, 1993—; med. dir. LA Fire Dept., 1996—. Medico-legal cons. self-employed, Los Angeles, Calif., 1993—; lectr./instr. - emergency medicine, emergency med. services, weapons of mass destruction Dept. of Emergency Medicine, Los Angeles, Calif., 1993—. Grant, Am. Heart Assn., 1999—2000, EMS Block grant, Calif. State EMS Authority, 1998—2000, grant, NIH, 2003—. Fellow: Am. Coll. of Emergency Physicians; mem.: Nat. Assn. of EMS Physicians. Office: Los Angeles County/USC Medical Center 1200 N State Str Room 1011 Los Angeles CA 90033 Office Phone: 213-978-3741. E-mail: eckstein@usc.edu.

ECKSTEIN, MAYA M., lawyer; b. Jerusalem, Aug. 2, 1969; d. Yoram and Yona Eckstein; m. Neil Robert Burton, Feb. 24, 2000; 1 child, Eitan Alexander Burton. JD, Syracuse U. Coll. of Law, 1992—95. Staff atty. US Ct. of Appeals for the Fourth Circuit, Richmond, Va., 1995—97; atty. Hunton & Williams, Richmond, Va., 1997—2001, 2001—; elbow clk. Hon. Roger L. Gregory, US Ct. of Appeals for the Fourth Circuit, Richmond, 2001. Bd. mem. Va. League for Planned Parenthood, 2000—04, Legal Services Corp. of Va., 2003—05, Ctrl. Va. Legal Services, 2005, Va. State Bar Young Lawyers Conf., 2001—05, Flagler Ho. at St. Joseph's Villa, Richmond, 2002—05. Recipient Sandra Day O'Connor award for Profl. Svc., Am. Inns of Ct., 2003, Inside Bus. Top 40 Under 40, Inside Bus. Mag., 2002, Outstanding Young Lawyer of the Yr., Va. State Bar Young Lawyers Conf., 1999. Mem.: Richmond Bar Assn., NY State Bar, Va. State Bar (pres.-elect young lawyers conf. 2005—), John Marshall Inn of Ct. Jewish. Office: Hunton & Williams 951 East Byrd St Richmond VA 23225 Office Phone: 804-788-8788. Office Fax: 804-343-4630. Personal E-mail: mayaeckstein@yahoo.com. E-mail: meckstein@hunton.com.

ECKSTEIN, MICHAEL LEHMAN, lawyer; b. New Orleans, June 18, 1954; s. Robert E. and Ernestine (Lehman) E. B in Gen. Studies, U. Ky., 1976; JD, Tulane U., 1979; LLM in Taxation, Georgetown U., 1980. Bar: U.S. Dist. Ct. (ea. dist.) La. 1979, U.S. Ct. Claims 1980, U.S. Tax Ct. 1980; cert. estate planning and adminstrn. specialist; cert. tax atty. Assoc., tax counsel Molony, Nolan, North & Riess, Metairie, La., 1980—84; pvt. practice New Orleans, 1984—86; tax counsel, head bus. sect. Gelpi, Sullivan, Carroll & Laborde, New Orleans, 1986—90; mng. ptnr. Eckstein Law Firm PC, New Orleans, 1990—. Contbr. articles to profl. jours. Fund raiser Boy Scouts Am., New Orleans, 1981, Children's Hosp., New Orleans, 1985, Rep. Nat. Conv.; vol. Ron Faucheaux Mayorial Campaign, New Orleans, 1982; bd. dirs. Big Brothers/Big Sisters S.E. La., past pres.; vol. La. Tax Free Shopping Program, Inc., Catholic Charities Archdiocese New Orleans, past pres. adv. bd. Mem. ABA (taxation, real property, probate, trust, corporations and business law sects., com. on depreciation and investment tax credit 1982—), New Orleans Bar Assn., Sports Lawyers Assn., Assn. Employee Benefit Planners of New Orleans, Estate Planning Coun., Tulane Alumni Assn. (past dir., past dir. Tulane Law Sch. CLE adv. bd.), New Orleans Lawn Tennis Club. Clubs: Audubon Tennis, World Trade Ctr. (New Orleans). Republican. Avocations: tennis, scuba diving, fishing, swimming, horses. Home: 7035 Birch St New Orleans LA 70118-5547 Office: 1515 Poydras St Ste 2195 New Orleans LA 70112-3753 Office Phone: 504-527-0701.

ECKSTEIN, RUTH, artist; b. Nuremberg, Germany, May 11, 1916; came to the U.S., 1939; d. Nathan and Ida (Schiffer) Friedmann; m. George Gunther Eckstein, May 16, 1935; children: Margaret E. Loble, Susan E. Student, Art Students League, N.Y.C., 1953-57, Pratt Graphic Art Ctr., 1957-58, 68. One woman shows include Nassau County Mus., Roslyn, N.Y., Elaine Benson Gallery, Bridgehampton, N.Y., 1976, 81, Silvermine Guild, New Canaan, Conn., 1984, Anita Shapolsky Gallery, N.Y.C., 1985, Discovery Gallery, Glen Cove, N.Y., 1985, 91, St. Peter's Ch., N.Y.C., 1986, Great Neck (N.Y.) Libr., 1988, Suzuki Gallery, N.Y.C., 1994, Nese Alpan Gallery, Roslyn, N.Y., 1996, 98, 99, Heckscher Mus. at Bryant Libr., Roslyn, N.Y., 1998-99, Art Ctr., Great Neck, N.Y., 2000, 2004, Kantar Fine Arts, Newton, Mass., 2004; exhibited in group shows at Neuberger Mus., Purchase, N.Y., 1989, Midge Karr Art Ctr., Old Westbury, N.Y., 1990, Andre Zarre Gallery, N.Y.C., 1991, Edwin Ulrich Mus. Art, Wichita, Kans., 1992, Silvermine Guild Galleries, New Canaan, Conn., 1992, 96, Suzuki Gallery, N.Y.C., 1993, Noyes Mus., Oceanville, N.J., 1994, Nassau C.C., Garden City, N.Y., 1994, S.W. Tex. State U., San Marcos, 1994, Nelson Atkins Mus. Art, Kansas City, Mo., 1995, James Howe Gallery, Keane Coll., Union, N.J., 1996, Westbeth Gallery, N.Y.C., 1996, Baruch Coll., N.Y.C., 1996, Nassau County Mus. Art, Roslyn, 1997, Fed. Res. Bank Hdqs., N.Y.C., 1997, Discovery Gallery, Sea Cliff, N.Y., 1998, Prince St. Gallery, N.Y.C., 1999, A.I.R. Gallery, N.Y.C., 2000, Hillwood Art Mus., L.I. U., Brookville, N.Y., 2000, Brooklyn Mus. of Art, Civic Ctr., Tulsa, Columbia U., Omni Gallery, Uniondale, N.Y., 2002, Martin Art Gallery, Muhlenberg Coll., Allentown, Pa., 2002, Swope Art Mus., Terre Haute, Ind., 2002. Recipient James R. Marsh award Audubon Artists, N.Y.C., 1977, Edna P. Stauffer award Audubon Artists, N.Y.C., 1978, Fairfield award Silvermine Guild, New Canaan, Conn., 1983, John Taylor Arms award Audubon Artists, N.Y.C., 1985. Mem. Silvermine Guild Artists (life), Am. Abstract Artists (hon.), Art Students League (life). Home: 60 Seminary Ave #171 Auburndale MA 02466-2671 Office Phone: 617-244-1861. E-mail: rutheckstein@webtv.net.

ECONOMAKI, CHRIS CONSTANTINE (CHRISTOPHER ECONOMAKI), publishing executive; b. Bklyn., Oct. 15, 1920; s. Christopher C. and Gladys Toomey (Burt) E.; m. Alvera H. Tomljanovic, May 29, 1946; children: Christine, Corinne. Student, Drake U. Sales rep. Divco Corp., 1946-49; editor, pub. emeritus Nat. Speed Sport News newspaper; pres. Kay Pub. Co., Harrisburg, N.C., 1949—; Color commentator Wide World of Sports ABC-TV, 1961-83, CBS-TV Sports, 1984-93. Served with AUS, 1942-46, ETO. Recipient Tom Marchese award for dedication to automobile racing, 1972, Henry McLemore award for excellence in broadcast journalism, 1973, Ken Purdy award Internat. Motor Press Assn., 1978, Ray Marquette Meml. award, 1981, Patrick Jacquemart award for service to motorsports, 1983, Dave Fritzlen Meml. award Outstanding Service to Chgo. Lathrop Boys Club, 1984, Walt Ader Meml. award, 1985, 1st Hugh Deery Meml. award for long service to automobile racing, 1985, Excellence award Nat. Assn. for Stock Car Auto Racing, 1990, Presdl. award U.S. Auto Club, 1992, Appreciation award svc. auto racing Charlotte, N.C. Motor Speedway, 1990, Chevy Proud award to Dean Am. Motorsports Journalism, 1990, Achievement award svc. racing Ford Motor Co., 1990, Dean Batchelor award Lifetime Achievement, 1996, Lifetime Media award NASCAR/ESPN, 1998; Economaki Award named in his honor Driver of Yr. Panel, 1991; Amb. Motorsports Time, Cleve., 1992; Lifetime Achievement award named in his honor; named to Stock Car Hall of Fame, Oceanside (Fla.) Rotary Club, 1993, Nat. Sprint Car Hall of Fame, Knoxville, Iowa, 1993, Motorsports Hall of Fame, 1994, Nebr. Auto Racing Hall of Fame, 1999,Indpls. Motor Speedway Hall of Fame, 2005; NASCAR's Buddy Shuman award for svc. to auto racing, 2000, Speedvision Lifetime Achievement award for motorsports journalism, 2000; recipient 12th ann. Good Scout award Great Sauk Trail Coun., Boy Scouts Am., 2002, Lifetime Achievement award Ea. Motorsports Press Assn., 2003; Mayor Indpls. pronounces May 2, 2002 Chris Economaki Day; Gov. Jeb Bush declares Sunday, February 20, 2005 Chris Economaki Day in Fla. Mem. Am. Assn. Auto Racing Writers and Broadcasters (pres. 1969-71, Angelo Angelopolous Meml. award 2000), Nat. Motorsports Press Assn., Ea. Motorsports Press Assn., Oceanside Rotary, Order of Long Leaf Pine. Home: Apt 314 The Kentshire 187 Paterson Ave Midland Park NJ 07432 Office: PO Box 1210 Harrisburg NC 28075-1210

ECONOMIDES, CHRISTOPHER GEORGE, pathologist; b. Alexandria, Egypt, Dec. 25, 1940; came to U.S., 1967; s. George and Tina E. MD, Alexandria U., 1966. Diplomate Am. Bd. Anatomic Pathology, Am. Bd. Clin. Pathology, Am. Bd. Cytopathology. Intern Alexandria U. Hosps., 1965-66, Balt. City Hosps., 1967-68; resident in anatomic pathology, then chief resident Jackson Meml. Hosp., U. Miami, Fla., 1968-70, resident in clin. pathology, 1970-71, 73-74, resident in ob-gyn., 1971-72, resident in anatomic pathology, 1972-73; pathologist Hialeah (Fla.) Hosp., 1974, chief dept. pathology, 1975—. Officer med. bd. Hialeah Hosp., 1975—, chief of staff, chmn. med. bd., 1980, 81, trustee, 1989-95, chmn. governing com., 1996—, mem. numerous coms.; med. and surg. clerkships Alexandria U. Hosp., Victoria Hosp., Scotland, Royal Salop Infirmary, England; mem. family planning program Broward County Health Dept., Fla., 1972-77; mem. courtesy staff North Shore Hosp., Miami, 1975, Palmetto Gen. Hosp., Hialeah, 1979-90; clin. asst. prof. pathology U. Miami, 1980-85; med. dir. SmithKline-Beechman Clin. Labs., 1983-99; bd. dirs. Immunopathology Labs., 1987-92, Ambulatory Ctr. of Hialeah, 1987-95, Dimension Health-PHO, 1993—. Trustee The Hialeah Found., 1989-91, Dade Community Found., 1992-94. Trustee The Hialeah Found., 1989-91, Dade Community Found., 1992—. Recipient Physician Recognition award AMA, 1971—, St. Marks Cross from His Holiness Patriarch Nicholaus I, 1981. Fellow Am. Soc. Clin. Pathologists, Coll. Am. Pathologists, Internat. Coll. Surgeons; mem. Am. Soc. Cytology, Internat. Acad. Pathology, Internat. Acad. Cytology, Fla. Med. Assn., Fla. Soc. Pathologists, South Fla. Soc. Pathology (pres. 1983, 84), Dade County Med. Assn., N.Y. Acad. Sci., Fisher Island Club (charter). Avocation: sailing. Office: Hialeah Hosp 651 E 25th St Hialeah FL 33013-3878

ECTON, DONNA R., business executive; b. Kansas City, Mo., May 10, 1947; d. Allen Howard and Marguerite (Page) E.; m. Victor H. Maragni, June 16, 1986; children: Mark, Gregory. BA (Durant Scholar), Wellesley Coll., 1969; MBA, Harvard U., 1971. V.p. Chem. Bank, N.Y.C., 1972-79, Citibank, N.A., N.Y.C., 1979-81; pres. MBA Resources, Inc., N.Y.C., 1981-83; v.p. adminstrn., officer Campbell Soup Co., Camden, N.J., 1983-89; chmn. Triangle Mfg. Corp. subs. Campbell Soup Co., Raleigh, N.C., 1984-87; sr. v.p., officer Nutri/System, Inc., Willow Grove, Pa., 1989-91; pres., CEO Van Houten N.Am., Delavan, Wis., 1991-94, Andes Candies Inc., Delavan, 1991-94; chmn., pres., CEO Bus. Mail Express, Inc., Malvern, Penn., 1995-96; bd. dirs. PETsMART, Inc., Phoenix, 1994—98, COO, 1996-98; chmn., pres., CEO EEI Inc., Phoenix, 1998—. Bd. dirs. H&R Block, Kansas City, Mo., Johns Hopkins PIEGO; commencement spkr. Pa. State U., 1987. Bd. Overseers Harvard U., 1984-90; mem. Coun. Fgn. Rels., N.Y.C., 1987—; trustee Inst. for Advancement of Health, 1988-92. Named One of 80 Women to Watch in the 80's, Ms. mag., 1980, One of All Time Top 10 of Last Decade, Glamour mag., 1984, One of 50 Women to Watch, Bus. Week mag., 1987, One of 100 Women to Watch, Bus. Month mag., 1989; recipient Wellesley Alumnae Achievement award, 1987; Fred Sheldon Fund fellow Harvard U., 1971-72; Margaret Rudkin scholar Harvard U., 1969-71. Mem. Harvard Bus. Sch. Assn. (pres. exec. council 1983-84), Harvard Bus. Sch. Club Greater N.Y. (pres. 1979-80, lifetime bd. dir.), Wellesley Coll. Nat. Alumnae Assn. (bd. dirs., 1st v.p. 1977-80). Avocations: public speaking, art, gardening, reading, bicycling.

EDBERG, JUDITH FLORENCE, music educator; b. Royal Oak, Mich., Apr. 13, 1933; d. DeWitt and Florence (Machris) Patterson; m. Hugo Charles Edberg; children: Charles Eric, Christine Elisabeth. B Music, Wayne State U., 1954, M Music, 1971. Tchr. Royal Oak Pub. Sch. Sys., 1952-54; pianist, artist tchr. Edberg Music Studio, Royal Oak, 1950-71; prof. music U. Tampa, Fla., 1972—, pre-coll. music program exec. dir., 1981—. Pre-concert lectr. Fla. Orchestra, 1990—, mem. edn. com., 1998—; co-dir. Nicaragua Music Edn. Project, 1998—. Pianist recording Piano Works of Clark Eastham, 1987. Mem. governing bd. Tampa Bay Youth Orch., Tampa, 1990—; bd. dirs. Sarasota Music Archives, Tampa, 1995-98. Grantee Dana Found., 1987, 95; named Outstanding Musical Artist, Tampa Bay Chamber Orch., 1996. Mem. Nat. Guild Piano Tchrs. (chmn. Tampa chpt. 1994—, adjudicator 1997—), Fla. Music Tchrs. Assn., Music Tchrs. Nat. Assn. Democrat. Avocations: herbalist, couture sewing, photography. Office: U Tampa Music Dept Tampa FL 33606 E-mail: jedberg@ut.edu.

EDDEY, GARY ERWIN, physician, administrator, educator; b. Englewood, N.J., Dec. 10, 1951; s. Erwin Carnes and Emma (Bogart) E.; m. Ilene N. Eddey, July 31, 1976 (div.); children: John, AnnMichele, Emily. BS, U. Md., 1976; ScM, U. Pitts., 1978; MD, Cornell U., 1983. Diplomate Am. Bd. Pediats. Intern U. N.C., Chapel Hill, 1983-84; resident N.Y. Hosp.--Cornell, N.Y.C., 1984; chief resident in pediats. N.Y. Hosp.-Cornell U., N.Y.C., 1984; asst. prof. pediats. Cornell Med. Coll., N.Y.C., 1986-88; clin. asst. prof. pediats. Columbia U., N.Y.C., 1986-88; from clin. assoc. prof. to assoc. prof. pediats. N.J. Med. Sch., Newark, 1997—; assoc. med. dir. Matheny Hosp., Peapack, N.J., 1990—, dir. comprehensive continuum of care, 2001; med. dir. Matheny Ctr. Medicine and Dentistry, Peapack, 2002—. Bd. dirs. Lesch-Nyhan Coun., Matheny. Contbr. articles to profl. jours. Recipient Outstanding Pediatrician award Morris County Office Hispanic Affairs, 1993. Mem. Am. Acad. Pediats., Am. Acad. Devel. Medicine. Unitarian Universalist/Methodist. Avocations: genealogy, history, creative writing, jazz, recording arts. Home: 22 Max Dr Apt 7A Morristown NJ 07960 Office: Matheny Hosp Main St Peapack NJ 07977 Office Phone: 908-234-0011. E-mail: GaryEddey@aol.com.

EDDINGTON, THOMAS L., human resources specialist, consultant; b. Westland, Mich., Mar. 10, 1960; s. William Thomas and Janet Lorraine (Woodard) E.; married; 2 children. BA in Bus. Psychology, Adrian Coll., 1982; MA in Orgnl. Dynamics, U. Pa., 1997. Employee benefits rep. Aetna Life Ins. Co., N.Y.C., 1982-84, Concord, N.H., 1984-86, account exec. Phila., 1986-90; mng. cons., owner Hewitt Assocs., Phila., 1990—98, mng. cons. St. Albano, 1998—2002, St. Albans, 1998—2002. Bd. dirs. Taproot Found. Mem. Pa. Employee Benefits Assn. Office: Hewitt Assoc Embarcadero Ctr #1 Ste 1400 San Francisco CA 94111

EDDINS, JAMES, JR., benefits compensation analyst, consultant; b. Athens, Ala., Oct. 17, 1936; s. James and Lottie (Smith) Eddins. BA in bus. mgmt., U. Dorchester, 1985, MBA (magna cum laude), 1990, PhD in bus. mgmt., 2003. Systems program mgr. U.S.A.F., Kadena Air Base, Japan, 1972—75, sr. enlisted advisor Los Angeles, Calif., 1976—78; hosp. admin. officer Dept. of Veterans Affairs, Loma Linda, Calif., 1981—83, med. admin. supr. St. Louis, 1984—86; comm. mgr. Dept. Vet. Affairs, LA, 1988—89; coll. program facilitator Sinclair Cmty. Coll., Dayton, Ohio, 1998—2001. Services supt. U.S. Air Force, Topeka, Japan, Los Angeles, 1972—79; EEO officer Dept. Vet. Affairs, Loma Linda, Calif., 1980—82; minority program adv. Dept. Vet. Affairs, Dayton, Ohio, 1997—99. With USAF, 1954—78, worldwide. Recipient 3d Degree Knight, Knights of Columbus, 1996, G.I.G. Hon. 33d Degree, U.S. C PHA, 1977. Office: Dr James Eddins Jr PO Box 13643 Dayton OH 45413 Personal E-mail: jjeddins@aol.com.

EDDLEMAN, FLOYD EUGENE, retired English language educator; b. Mena, Ark., Dec. 3, 1930; s. Floyd Newton and Ruby Kate (Cannon) E. BSE, U. Cen. Ark., 1951; MA, U. Ark., 1955, PhD, 1961. Teaching asst. U. Ark., Fayetteville, 1953-55, 56-58; instr. U. Colo., Boulder, 1955-56; instr. English, Tex. Tech U., Lubbock, 1958-62, asst. prof., 1962-65, assoc. prof., 1965-75, prof., 1975-90, prof. emeritus, 1991—. Author: American Drama Criticism, 1976, 79, 84, 89, 92; co-editor: Almayer's Folly in the Cambridge Edit. of the Works of Joseph Conrad, 1994; contbr. articles to profl. jours. Sgt. U.S. Army, 1951—53. Democrat. Mem. Christian Ch. (Disciples Of Christ). Avocations: travel, collecting bison art objects. Home: 1309 Cole Ave Mena AR 71953-3722

EDDLESTON, KIMBERLY ANN, management educator; b. Fall River, Mass., May 8, 1970; d. John George and Gloria Jean Rego; m. Robert Matthew Eddleston, Sept. 6, 1997; children: Evan Jay, Heidi Jeanne. BS, Bryant Coll., Smithfield, R.I., 1988—92; cert. in Hotel Mgmt., Swiss Internat. Tng. Ctr., Neuchatel, 1989—90; MBA, Cornell U., Ithaca, N.Y., 1993—95; PhD, U. Conn., Storrs, 1996—2001. Instr. U. Conn., Storrs, 1999—2001; asst. prof. Northeastern U., Boston, 2001—. Asst. dir., Wolff family program in entrepreneurship U. Conn., Storrs, 1996—2001. Contbr. articles to profl. jours. Editl. bd. Group & Orgn. Mgmt., 2001—04. Mem.: Cornell Soc. Hotelmen, Acad. Mgmt. Achievements include research in the studies on managerial & entrepreneurial careers. Office: Northeastern Univ 319 Hayden Hall Boston MA 02115-5000 Office Phone: 617-373-4014. Business E-Mail: k.eddleston@neu.edu.

EDDY, CHARLES ALAN, chiropractor; b. Kansas City, Mo., Feb. 20, 1948; s. Sam Albert and Ella Louise (Gani) E.; m. Donna Darlene Perry, Oct. 23, 1971. Student, U. Mo., Kansas City, 1967; D in Chiropractic, Cleveland Chiropractic, Kansas City, 1970. Diplomate Nat. Bd. Chiropractic Examiners. Pvt. practice, Kansas City, 1970—. Peer rev. bd. Blue Cross and Blue Shield, Kansas City, 1972; pres. hon. bd. govs. Bapt. Hosp., Kansas City, 1993-94; cons. Quality Corp., Overland Park, Kans., 1988. Leader, profl. musician Chuck Eddy Band, Kansas City, 1964—; res. officer Kansas City Police Dept., 1970-77, sgt., 1977-82, capt., 1982-94; vice chmn. Citizens Assn., 1995-98, candidate for City Coun., Kansas City, 1995; mem. pub. improvement adv. com. City of Kansas City, 1997-98; city councilperson 6th Dist., chmn. bd. Mid Am. Reg. Coun., Kansas City, Mo., 2003-2005, 1st v.p. 2001-02; bd. dirs. Econ. Devel. Coun., 1999—, 1st v.p. 2001-03, chair Mo. total transp. com. 2003—. Mem. Am. Chiropractic Assn., Mo. State Chriopractic Assn., Mo. Dist. II Chiropractic Assn. (bd. dirs., v.p. 1998-2003), Cleve. Chiropractic Coll. (trustee 1990, vice chmn. 1992-03, chmn. 2003—), Cleve. Chiropractic Alumni Assn. (v.p. 1995-97, pres. 1997-99, bd. dirs. 1990—, amb.'s soc. 1983—, chmn. 1990-96, 2001—, bd. mem. Truman Med. Ctr.), Optimist Club of Landing (pres. 1980, lt. gov. Mo. dist. 1982), South Kansas City C. of C. (Sml. Bus. of Yr. award 1998), Am. Lebanon Syrian Men's Club (pres. 1988-91, chmn. bd. 1992), St. Andrews Soc. (drummer in pipe band), DeMolay Legion Hon. (sec. 1988, treas. 1990, vice-dean 1991, dean 1992), Pipes and Drums of Ararat (treas. 1977-90, pres. 1985, dir. 1989, 90), Elks, Shriners (Potentate of Ararat shrine temple 1999, publicity chmn. 1991-92), Royal Order Jesters, Order Quetzalcoatl, Rotary Club (Paul Harris fellow). Episcopalian. Avocations: photography, guns, stereo and video entertainment. Home: 406 W 109th St Kansas City MO 64114-4910 Office: 8301 State Line Rd Ste 108 Kansas City MO 64114-2019 Personal E-mail: dr.eddy@juno.com.

EDDY, COLETTE ANN, aerial photography studio owner, photographer; b. Sept. 14, 1950; d. William F. and Jeanne (Valeski) Trump; m. Robert K. Eddy, Aug. 21, 1976 (div. Sept. 1992). AA, St. Petersburg (Fla.) Jr. Coll., 1970; BA, U. South Fla., 1973; MS, Nova U., 1988. Yacht caretaker The Sundowner, St. Petersburg, 1972-73; mgr. Aunt Hattie's Restaurant, St. Petersburg, 1973-79, Johnathan Jones, Inc., St. Petersburg, 1979-80; photographer, sales rep. Smith Aerial Photos, Tampa, Fla., 1980—; owner, aerial photographer Aerial Innovations, Inc., Tampa, 1987—; owner Havanna Connection Inc., Carribean. Mem. Tampa Mus. Art. Named Winner Tampa Chamber Small Bus. of Yr., 1998. Mem. Profl. Photographers Am. (30 Merit awards), Fla. Profl. Photographers (22 Merit awards 1987-90), Profl. Aerial Photographers Assn., Tampa C. of C., Emerging Bus. Coun. Republican. Home: 198 Ceylon Ave Tampa FL 33606-3330 Office: Aerial Innovations Inc 3703 W Azeele St Tampa FL 33609-2807

EDDY, DARLENE MATHIS, poet, educator; b. Elkhart, Ind., Mar. 19, 1937; d. William Eugene and Fern (Paulmer) Mathis; m. Spencer Livingston Eddy, Jr., May 23, 1964 (dec. May 1971). BA, Goshen Coll., 1959; MA, Rutgers U., 1961, PhD, 1967. Instr., lectr. Douglass Coll. and Rutgers U., 1962-64, 66-67; asst. prof. English Ball State U., Muncie, Ind., 1967-70, assoc. prof., 1971-75, prof., 1975-99, poet-in-residence, 1989-93, prof. emerita, 1999. Whitinger lectr. Honors Coll., 1998-99; adj. prof. core program and coll. seminar program U. Notre Dame, 2001-; adj. prof. Eng. Goshen Coll., 2002-; cons., presenter in field. Author: The Worlds of King Lear, 1968, Leaf Threads, Wind Rhymes, 1985, Weathering, 1991, Portraits, 1992; poetry editor Forum, 1985-89; contbg. editor Snowy Egret, 1988-89; cons. editor Blue Unicorn, 1995—; founding editor The Hedge Row Press, 1995; contbr. articles to English Lang. Notes, Am. Lit., others; author numerous poems. Mem. commn. on the status of women in the profession, Nat. Coun. of Teachers of English, 1976-79; coord. Women's Studies program, 1976-82. Woodrow Wilson Nat. fellow, 1959-62, Notable Woodrow Wilson fellow, 1991, Rutgers U. grad. honors fellow, 1964-65; recipient numerous rsch., creative teaching and creative arts grants. Mem. AAUW, DAR, Soc. Mayflower Descs., Nat. League Am. Pen Women, League Women Voters. Home: 1840 Cobblestone Blvd Elkhart IN 46514

EDDY, DAVID MAXON, health policy and management advisor; BA, Stanford (Calif.) U., 1964, PhD with great distinction, 1978; MD, U. Va., 1968. Gen. surg. intern Stanford U. Med. Ctr., 1968-69, resident, postdoct. fellow cardiovascular surgery, 1969-71, acting asst. prof., 1976-78; asst. prof. dept. engring.-econ. sys. Stanford U., 1978-80, prof., 1980-81; J. Alexander McMahon prof. health policy and mgmt. Duke U., 1986-90, prof. health policy and mgmt., 1980—95; dir. WHO Collaborating Ctr. for Rsch. in Cancer Policy, 1984-95. Sr. advisor health policy, mgmt. Kaiser Permanente So. Calif. Region, 1991—; columnist Jour. of the AMA, 1990—; spl. govt. employee Hillary Rodham Clinton's Health Care Task Force, 1993; expert adv. panel on cancer WHO, 1981-96; cons. numerous cos., orgns. and assns. Author: A Manual for Assessing Health Practices and Designing Practice Policies, 1992, FAST*PRO: Software for Meta-Analysis by the Confidence Profile Method, 1992, The Synthesis of Statistical Evidence: meta-Analysis by the Confidence Profile Method, 1992, Common Screening Tests, 1991, Screening for Cancer: Theory, Analysis and Design, 1980, (Lanchester Prize, 1981), Clinical Decision Making: From Theory to Practice, 1996; contbr. articles to profl. jours. Recipient Sci. and Technol. Achievement award EPA, 1993, FHP Prize Internat. Soc. of Tech. Assessment in Health Care, 1991, USQA Quality Algorithm award, 1995, Novartis Outcomes Leadership award, 1997, Founders award Am. Coll. Med. Quality, 1998. Mem. Inst. of Medicine, Nat. Acad. Scis.

EDDY, DON, artist; b. Long Beach, Calif., Nov. 4, 1944; s. Myron and Ruth (Chase) Eddy King; m. Nancy Walker, June 12, 1967 (div. 1976); 1 child, Sarah. B.F.A., U. Hawaii, 1967, M.F.A., 1969. Artist, N.Y.C. Subject of monographs: Don Eddy: The Resonance of Realism in the Art of Post War America, Virginia Anne Bonita, Internet Publ.; Conversations with Don Eddy, interviewer Lela Cempollin, Pub. Cleup Scarl, Padua, Italy; Don Eddy: The Art of Paradox, Donald Kuspit, 2002. One-man shows include Galerie Petit, Paris, 1973, Nancy Hoffman Gallery, NYC, 1974, 1976, 1979, 1983, 1986, 1990, 1992—94, 1996, 1998, 2000, 2002, 2005, Mitch Shaheen Gallery, Cleve., 1994, Molly Barnes Gallery, LA, 1970, 1971, French & Co., NYC, 1971, Huntington (W.Va.) Mus., 1996, Duke U. Mus. Art, 2000, Boca Raton Mus. Art, 2000, New Orleans Contemporary Art Ctr., 2000; exhibited in group shows U.S. and Europe; Represented in permanent collections Akron Art Inst., Cleve. Mus. Art, Fogg Art Mus., Harvard U., Utrecht Mus. Belgium, Whitney Mus. Am. Art, Met. Mus. Art, NYC, others. E-mail: doneddyart@aol.com.

EDDY, DONALD DAVIS, language educator; b. Norfolk, Va., Apr. 19, 1929; s. Clarence Ford and Rebekah (Proctor Davis) E.; m. Edith Ann Quattlebaum, Dec. 20, 1954; children: Edith Evelyn, Elizabeth Nelson. BA, Dartmouth Coll., 1951; MA, PhD, U. Chgo.; MA (Munby fellow), Cambridge (Eng.) U., 1978. Prof. English Cornell U., Ithaca, N.Y., 1961-96, head dept. rare books univ. libr., 1968-89, prof. emeritus, 1996—. Works include A Bibliography of John Brown, 1971, Samuel Johnson: Book Reviewer in the Literary Magazine, 1979, Samuel Johnson, LL.D., 1983, Bibliography of Richard Hurd, 1999; editor John Brown, Essays on the Characteristics, 1969, Samuel Johnson and Periodical Literature, 16 vols., 1978-79, Sale Catalogues of the Librs. of Samuel Johnson, Hester Lynch Thrale (Mrs. Piozzi) and James Boswell, 1993. Served with USN, 1952-55. Mem. MLA, Bibliog. Soc., Oxford Bibliog. Soc., Cambridge Bibliog. Soc., Bibliog. Soc. Am., Bibliog. Soc. U. Va. Clubs: Grolier; Athenaeum (London); The Johnsonians. Episcopalian. Home: 240 Renwick Dr Ithaca NY 14850-2142 E-mail: dde2@cornell.edu.

EDDY, JOHN JOSEPH, diplomat; b. Lakewood, Ohio, Jan. 8, 1933; s. John Ezekiel and Pauline Edna (Ryan) E.; m. Armonia Badenes, Feb. 14, 1967; children— John Louis, Christopher Robert, William Francis, Isabel Ann (dec.) AB, Boston Coll., 1960; MA, Fletcher Sch. of Law and Diplomacy, 1961; student, Nat. Def. U., 1979-80. Joined Fgn. Service, Dept. State, 1966; asst. comml. attache Am. Embassy, Caracas, Venezuela, 1966-69, comml. attache San Salvador, El Salvador, 1970-71, first sec., comml. attache Bogota, Colombia, 1971-74, counselor for econ. and comml. affairs Nairobi, Kenya, 1974-77, dep. chief of mission Bridgetown, Barbados, 1977-79; dir. Office Regional Econ. Policy, Bur. Inter-Am. Affairs, Dept. State, 1980-81; consul gen. Am. consulate gen., Dhahran, Saudi Arabia, 1983-87, Am. Consulate Gen., Bombay, 1987-90; sr. spl. asst. to dir. gen. Fgn. Svc., Dept. State, Washington, 1991-92; sr. insp. Dept. State, 1992-94, ret., 1994, cons., 1994—. Served with USAF, 1952-56, Korea. Roman Catholic. Office: Dept State Oig Isp Rm 6817 Washington DC 20520-0001

EDDY, ROGER L., state representative; b. Ottawa, Ill., May 8, 1958; m. Rebecca Eddy; children: Matt, Lisa, Brenda, Beth, Jessica. BA, Northern Ill. Univ., 1981; MA, Eastern Ill. Univ., 1986, Specialist, 1996. State Rep. House of Representitves, Dist. 109, Ill., 2002—; supt. Hutsonville Sch. Dist. #1, 1996—; prin. Watseka HS, 1991—96, Hutsonville HS, 1988—91, tchr., 1981—88. Mem. Local Town Bd., 1986—88. Mem.: Elem. & Secondary Ed. Comm., Legis. Comm., Ill. Assoc. of Sch. Admin., 1996-present, Computer Tech. Comm., Agr. & Conservation Comm., Appropriations: Elem., Secondary, Higher Ed., Elks, 1987-present. Republican. Efca. Office: Capitol 222-N Stratton Office Bldg Springfield IL 62706 also: District 108 South Main PO Box 125 Hutsonville IL 62433 Office Phone: 618-563-4128. Personal E-mail: reddyunit1@aol.com.

EDDY, VICTORIA LEE, military administrative assistant; b. Accra, Ghana, Dec. 15, 1970; m. Sterling Lee Eddy, Jan. 5, 2001; children: Solomon Sterlin, Isabella L. AS, Bronx CC, NY, 1999; student, Norfolk State U., 2001—. Adminstrv. asst. US Navy, Va., 1999—. Pres. NOI Charity Funds. Es USN, 1999—. Decorated Navy Achievement medal Naval Submarine Forces, Bravo Zuly plaque Vice Adm. Mid. Atlantic. Mem.: Nurses Svc. Orgn. Avocations: cooking, baking, travel.

EDDY-JOHNSON, DEANNA M., home health care advocate; b. Bklyn., Aug. 26, 1950; d. Charles Jess and Virginia Fern (Hoelscher) Deck; m. Dennis R. Eddy (div.); children: Denny R. Eddy, Ginger Deann Spillers; m. Jamie W. Johnson, Jan. 9, 1999. Degree in computer programming, Parkland Jr. Coll., Champaign, Ill., 1983; degree in real estate, Parkland Jr. Coll., 1985, nursing cert., 1990. CEO Jenn Swing Co., Urbana, Ill., 1993—97. Inventor Jenn Swing, 1st full body accessible swing, 1996, The Cubby, toddler swing, 2004; author: Idea to Financial Success, 2003, Patty Panda Joins the Circus, 2005; lyricist I Want to Rock with you Jesus, 2005. Recipient Sec. award, Ambucs Assn., Urbana, 1996. Republican. Baptist. Avocations: walking, bicycling, concerts, plays. Home: 306 Dodson Dr E Urbana IL 61802 E-mail: djohns306@insightBB.com.

EDELCUP, NORMAN SCOTT, management and financial consultant; b. Chgo., May 8, 1935; s. Irving L. and Pauline (Bolz) Edelcup. BS in Bus. Adminstrn, Northwestern U., 1957. CPA Fla., Ill. Sr. accountant Arthur Andersen & Co., Chgo., 1957-62; sec.-treas. Acme Printing Ink Co., Chgo., 1962-65; accountant, asst. to chmn. Commonwealth Edison Co., Chgo., 1965-68; sr. v.p., vice-chmn. bd. Keller Industries, Miami, Fla., 1968-76; v.p., treas. Avatar Holdings (formerly GAC Corp.), 1976-80, exec. v.p., treas., chief fin. officer, dir., mem. exec. com., 1980-83; pres., treas., dir. Avatar Properties Inc. (formerly GAC Properties, Inc.), 1976-83, Avatar Properties Credit (formerly GAC Properties Credit, Inc.), 1976-83; vice chmn., chief operating officer Nat. Banking Corp. Fla., Miami, 1983-84; chmn. treas. Scroll Casual Inc., 1983-84; chmn. Fla. Powder Coatings, Inc., Confidata Corp., 1983-87; chmn., treas. First United Leasing Corp., 1983-86; ptnr. E&H Assocs., 1983-91; chmn. Item Processing Am. Inc., Miami, 1987-98. Sr. v.p., dir. Fla. Savs. Bancorp, Pinecrest, Fla., 2001—; bd. dirs. Valhi Inc., Baron Asset Fund. Mayor City of Sunny Isles Beach, Fla., 2003; bd. dirs. Mt. Sinai Med. Ctr. Found., 2003. With AUS, 1958—60. Mem. Am. Inst. CPA's, Fla. Inst. CPA's, Ill. Inst. CPA's, Greater Miami C. of C. (trustee 1979-83). Lodges: Kiwanis. Home: 244 Atlantic Isle Sunny Isles Beach FL 33160 Office: Sunny Isles Beach City Hall 18070 N Collins Ave Sunny Isles Beach FL 33160 Office Phone: 305-947-0606. Personal E-mail: nsedelcup@aol.com.

EDELHEIT, LEWIS S., research physicist; b. Chgo., Aug. 24, 1942; m. Susan Wershkoff, 1965; children: David, Dena. BS in Engring. and Physics, U. Ill., 1964, MS in Physics, 1965, PhD in Physics, 1969. Physicist GE R&D Ctr., Schenectady, NY, 1969—76; mgr. Applied Sci. & Diagnostic Imaging Lab. GE Med. Sys., Milw., 1976—80; mgr. computed tomography prodn. engring. GE Corp. R&D, Schenectady, 1980—82, gen. mgr. dept. engring., 1982—83, gen. mgr. dept. computed tomography programs, 1983—86; pres., CEO Quantum Med. Sys., 1986—91; mgr. electronics sys. rsch. ctr. GE Corp. R&D, Schenectady, 1991—92, sr. v.p., 1992—2001; ret., 2001. Bd. dir. Silicon Graphics, Inc., Mountain View, Calif., 2002—, Sonic Innovations, Inc., Pacific Northwest Nat. Lab. Bd. trustees Rensselaer Polytechnic Inst., Troy, NY, 1995—2002; adv. bd. OVP Venture Partners. Fellow: Am. Physics Soc. (George E. Pake prize 2001); mem.: NAE, Indsl. Rsch. Inst. (named as the Medalist 2003), Sigma Xi. Achievements include research in medical imaging systems, computerized imaging systems. Office: GE Corp R&D Ctr Bldg K1 Rm 5A1 One Rsch Cir Niskayuna NY 12309

EDELIN, KENNETH CARLTON, physician; b. Washington, Mar. 31, 1939; s. Benedict and Ruby (Goodwin) E.; m. Barbara Evans, Aug. 5, 1978; children— Kenneth Carlton, Kimberly Cybele, Joseph Evans, Corrine Ruby-Elizabeth. B.A., Columbia Coll., 1961; M.D., Meharry Med. Coll., 1967. Intern, Wright-Patterson AFB Hosp., Ohio, 1967-68; resident Boston City Hosp., 1971-74; instr. ob-gyn sch. Medicine, Boston U., 1974-76, asst. prof., 1976, assoc. prof., 1977-78, prof. ob-gyn, dept. chmn., 1978—; asst. dir. ob-gyn Boston City Hosp., 1974-76, asso. dir., 1977-78, dir., 1978—; gynecologist-in-chief Univ. Hosp., 1978—; med. dir. Boston Family Planning Project; pres. Roxbury Comprehensive Community Health Ctr., Inc. Pres., New Eng. com. NAACP-Legal Def. Fund, Inc. Served to capt. USAF, 1968-71. Fellow Am. Coll. Obstetricians and Gynecologists, Obstetrical Soc. Boston; mem. Planned Parenthood Fedn. Am. (tru- stee), Nat. Med. Assn., New Eng. Med. Soc., Am. Fertility Soc., Assn. Profs. Ob-Gyn, Assn. Gynecologist Laparoscopists, Sigma Pi Phi. Office: 80 E Concord St Boston MA 02118-2307

EDELMAN, ALVIN, lawyer; b. Chgo., Dec. 12, 1916; m. Rose Marie Slossy, Sept. 22, 1940; children: Marilyn Frances Edelman Snyder, Stephen D., Leon F. BS in Law, Northwestern U., 1938, JD, 1940. Bar: Ill. 1940. Practiced in Chgo., 1940—; pres. Edelman & Edelman, Chartered and predecessors, 1973—; gen. counsel Internat. Coll. Surgeons. Lectr. Internat. Mus. Surg. Sci. and Hall of Fame; chmn. wills and gifts com. Medinah Temple of Masonic Shrine, Chgo., 1975-79; pres. Lawyers Shrine Club of Medinah Temple, 1971-73. Contbr. articles to profl. jours. Fellow Am. Coll. Trust and Estate Counsel; mem. ABA, Ill. Bar Assn., Chgo. Bar Assn. (chmn. grievance com. 1971-72), Phi Beta Kappa (pres. Chgo. area assn. 1975-85), Phi Beta Kappa Fellows (bd. dirs. 1985—, nat. v.p. 1986-95, nat. pres. 1996-2001), Elks (past exalted ruler). Office: 100 W Monroe St Chicago IL 60603-1967

EDELMAN, DANIEL JOSEPH, public relations executive; b. N.Y.C., July 3, 1920; s. Selig and Selma (Pfeiffer) Edelman; m. Ruth Rozumoff, Sept. 3, 1953; children: Richard, Renee, John. Grad., Columbia U., 1940; MS, 1941. Reporter Poughkeepsie (N.Y.) newspapers, UPI, 1941—42; news writer CBS, 1946—47; staff mem. Edward Gottlieb & Assocs., 1947; pub. rels. dir. Toni Co., Chgo., 1948—52; founder, chmn. 41 offices Daniel J. Edelman, Inc. (Edelman, Zeno, Blue Advt., Strategy One Rsch., Edelman Interactive Svcs.), Chgo., 1952—. Chmn. vis. com. U. Chgo. Libr., 1976; chmn. sustaining fellows individual campaign Chgo. Art Inst., 1982; bd. dirs. Lyric Opera, Chgo., 1995—2003; dir. Comm. for Econ. Growth of Israel, The Chgo. Project for Violence Prevention. With U.S. Army, 1942—46. Named Pub. Rels. Profl. of Yr., Pub. Rels. News, 1993; named to Chgo. Bus. Hall of Fame, Jr. Achievement, 1998, Entrepeneurship Hall of Fame, U. Ill., Chgo., 2001; recipient Disting. Alumnus award, Columbia U., 1988, John Jay award, 1990, Agy. of Yr., Inside PR Mag., 1993, Lifetime Achievement All-Star award, 1998, Tom Mosser award, St. Bonaventure U., 1998, First award, China Pub. Rels. Assn., 1999, First Lifetime Achievement award, Publicity Club Chgo., 2003, Atlas award for Internat. Pub. Rels., Pub. Res. Soc. Am., 2003, Agy. of the Yr. award, Holmes Report, 2003, 1st Annual Dean's Pub. Svc. award, Columbia U. Grad. Sch. Journalism, 2005. Fellow: Pub. Rels. Soc. Am. (past chmn., counselor sect., Top Gun Career Achievement award 1998, Gold Anvil award for outstanding contbns. to pub. rels. profession 1999, 35 Silver Anvil awards); mem.: Pub. Rels. Seminar, Arthur Page Soc. (Hall of Fame 1997), Chief Execs. Orgn., Young Pres. Orgn. (chmn. Chgo. chpt. 1963), Casino Club, Chgo. Club, Mid-Am. Club, Harmonie Club, Std. Club, Phi Beta Kappa (dir., Living Treasure award Chgo. area chpt. 2004). Jewish. Home: 1301 N Astor St Chicago IL 60610 Office: Edelman Aon Ctr 200 E Randolph Dr Chicago IL 60601-6436 Office Phone: 312-240-2600. Business E-Mail: dan.edelman@edelman.com.

EDELMAN, ERIC STEVEN, federal agency administrator, former ambassador; m. Patricia Davis; children: Alexander, Stephanie, Terrence, Robert. BA in History and Govt., Cornell U., 1972; PhD in U.S. Diplomatic History, Yale U., 1981. With U.S. Fgn. Svc., U.S. Middle East Delegation to West Bank/Gaza Autonomy Talks, 1980-81, watch officer State Dept. Ops. Ctr., 1981-82, staff officer Secretariat Staff, 1982, spl. asst. to Sec. of State George P. Shultz, 1982-84; mem. Office of Soviet Affairs U.S. Dept. of State, Moscow, 1984-86, head external polit. sect., 1987-89, spl. asst. to Under Sec. of State for Polit. Affairs, 1989-90; asst. dep. under sec. def. for Soviet/East European Affairs Office of Sec. of Def., 1990-93; dep. to Strobe Talbott, spl. advisor Sec. of State U.S. Dept. of State, 1993, dep. chief of mission Prague, Czech Republic, 1994-96; exec. asst. to dep. sec. U.S. Dept. State, Washington, 1996-98, US amb. to Finland Helsinki, 1998—2001; prin. dep. asst. to Vice Pres. Richard B. Cheney. for national security affairs The White House, Washington, 2001—03; U.S. amb. to Turkey U.S. Dept. State, Ankara, 2003—05; under sec. for policy US Dept. Def., Washington, 2005—. Recipient Sec. of Def. award for disting. Civilian Svc., 1993, Superior Honor award State Dept., 1989, 90, 95. Office: US Dept Def 2000 Def Pentagon Rm 4E830 Washington DC 20301

EDELMAN, GERALD MAURICE, biochemist, neuroscientist, educator; b. NYC, July 1, 1929; s. Edwin and Anna (Freedman) Edelman; m. Maxine Morrison, June 11, 1950; children: Eric, David, Judith. BS, Ursinus Coll., 1950, ScD, 1974; MD, U. Pa., 1954, DSc, 1973; PhD, Rockefeller U., 1960; MD (hon.), U. Siena, Italy, 1974; DSc (hon.), Gustavus Adolphus Coll., 1975, Williams Coll., 1976, U. Paris, 1989; LSc (hon.), U. Cagliari, 1989; DSc (hon.), Georgetown U., 1989, U. degli Studi di Napoli, 1990, Tulane U., 1991, U. Miami, 1995, Adelphi U., 1995, U. Bologna, 1998, U. Minn., 2000; MD (hon.), U de A Coruña, Spain, 2000. Med. house officer Mass. Gen. Hosp., 1954—55; asst. physician hosp. of Rockefeller U., 1957—60, mem. faculty, 1960—92, assoc. dean grad. studies, 1963—66, prof., 1966—74, Vincent Astor disting. prof., 1974—92; mem. faculty and chmn. dept. neurobiology Scripps Rsch. Inst., La Jolla, Calif., 1992—. Mem. biophysics and biophys. chemistry study sect. NIH, 1964—67; mem. Sci. Council Ctr. for Theoretical Studies, 1970—72, assoc., sci. chmn. Neurosciences Research Program, 1980—, dir. Neuroscis. Inst., 1981—; mem. adv. bd. Basel Inst. Immunology, 1970—77, chmn., 1975—77; non-resident fellow, trustee Salk Inst., 1973—85; bd. overseers Faculty Arts and Scis. U. Pa., 1976—83; trustee, mem. adv. com. Carnegie Inst., Washington, 1980—87; bd. govs. Weizman Inst. Sci., 1971—87, mem. emeritus; researcher structure of antibodies, molecular and devel. biology. Author: The Mindful Brain, 1978, Neural Darwinism, 1987, Topobiology, 1988, The Remembered Present, 1989, Bright Air, Brilliant Fire, 1992, A Universe of Consciousness: How Matter Becomes Imagination, 2000, Wider than the Sky: The Phenomenal Gift of Consciousness, 2004. Trustee Rockefeller Bros. Found., 1972—82. Capt. M.C. U.S. Army, 1955—57. Recipient Spencer Morris award U. Pa., U. Pa., 1954, Ann. Alumni award, Ursinus Coll., 1969, Nobel prize for physiology or medicine, 1972, Albert Einstein Commemorative award, Yeshiva U., 1974, Buchman Meml. award, Calif. Inst. Tech., 1975, Rabbi Shai Shacknai meml. prize, Hebrew U.-Hadassah Med. Sch., Jerusalem, 1977, Regents medal Excellence, N.Y. State, 1984, Hans Neurath prize, U. Wash., 1986, Sesquicentennial Commemorative award, Nat. Libr. Medicine, 1986, Cécile and Oskar Vogt award, U. Dusseldorf, 1988, Disting. Grad. award, U. Pa., 1990, Personnalité de l'année, Paris, 1990, Warren Triennial Prize award, Mass. Gen. Hosp., 1992, C.V. Ariens-Kappers medal, 1999, medal of the Presidency of the Italian Republic, 1999, medaille de la Ville de Paris, 2002, Cátedra Santiago Grisolia prize, Spain, 2003, Caianiello Internat. award, INNS, 2003, Calabria award, Italy, 2003. Fellow: AAAS, N.Y. Acad. Medicine, N.Y. Acad. Scis.; mem.: NAS, Am. Chem. Soc. (Eli Lilly award biol. chemistry 1965), Century Assn., Coun. Fgn. Rels., Soc. Developmental Biology, Acad. Scis. of Inst. France (fgn.), Am. Soc. Cell Biology, Japanese Biochem. Soc. (hon.), Pharm. Soc. Japan (hon.), Am. Acad. Arts and Scis., Harvey Soc. (pres. 1976—77), Genetics Soc. Am., Am. Assn. Immunologists, Am. Soc. Biol. Chemists, Am. Philos. Soc., Cosmos Club, Alpha Omega Alpha, Sigma Xi, Phi Beta Kappa. Office: Scripps Rsch Inst Dept Neurobiol SBR-14 10550 N Torrey Pines Rd La Jolla CA 92037-1000

EDELMAN, HENDRIK, library and information science professor; b. Wageningen, Netherlands, Nov. 27, 1937; came to U.S., 1967; s. Cornelis Hendrik and Johanna (van Werkhoven) E.; m. Antoinette M. Kania; children: Stijn Willem, Mark Bastiaan, Kees Maarten. MLS, George Peabody Coll., 1969. With Martinus Nijhoff (Pubs. & Booksellers), Netherlands, 1958-65, D. Reidel Pub. Co., Netherlands, 1965-67; bibliographer Vanderbilt U., 1967-70; asst. dir. Cornell U. Libraries, Ithaca, N.Y., 1970-78; libr. Rutgers-State U. N.J., New Brunswick, 1979-85, prof. libr. and info. sci., 1985—2000. Adj. prof. Palmer Sch. Libr. and Info. Sci., L.I. U., 2002—; chmn. bd. Ctr. Book Rsch., U. Scranton, 1983-88; chmn. bd. Rsch. Libr. Group, Inc., 1982-83; bd. dirs. Book Industry Study Group, 1977-84; USIA/ALA Libr./Book fellow, U. Surinam, 1992-93; editl. mktg. cons. Am. European pubs. (booksellers); acad. libr. cons.; chmn. edn. com. Netherland Am. Found., 1993-2002; chmn. adv. bd. Rutgers Inst. Jazz Studies, 2001—. Author: The Dutch Language Press in America, 1986, Libraries and Information Science in the Electronic Age, 1986, A History of Religious Publishing and Bookselling in the United States and Canada, 1640-1985, 1987, Marketing to Libraries for the New Millennium, 2002, The Netherland Club of New York, An Illustrated History, 2003; contbr. articles, revs. to profl. jours. Mem. ALA, Soc. for Scholarly Pub., Bibliog. Soc. Am., Am. Antiquarian Soc., Grolier Club, Beta Phi Mu. Office: 315 W 55th St New York NY 10019 Personal E-mail: edelman@earthlink.net.

EDELMAN, JACK ROBERT, science educator; b. Bklyn., July 8, 1953; s. Irving and Frances Edelman. BS, Bklyn. Coll., 1975; MS, Long Island U., 1978; MS in Edn., Pace U., 1984; MPhil, St. John's U., 1982, PhD, 1990; MS in Edn., Bklyn. Coll., 2001. Biology tchr. N.Y.C. Bd. Edn., Bklyn., 1978—; asst. sci. prof. Bourough Manhattan Cmty. Coll., N.Y.C., 1994—. Author: The Natural Classroom, 1996; contbr. articles various profl. jours.; radio DJ: NBS Radio Kaleidascope Program, 1977—79. Pythian knight Knights of Pythias, Bklyn., 1985. Summer fellowship, NEH, 1993. Mem.: NY Acad. Scis., Am. Federation TV and Radio Artists. Avocations: gardening, music, record collecting, scientific rsch on chromosomes. Office: Borough Manhattan Cmty Coll 199 Chambers St New York NY 10007 Personal E-mail: themadprofessor47@hotmail.com, thechromosomekid@37.com.

EDELMAN, JOEL, health facility administrator; b. Chgo., Mar. 24, 1931; s. Maurice B. and Ethel J. (Newman) E.; m. Beth L. Sommers, July 31, 1955; children: Peter J., Ann Elizabeth, Deborah S. BA in Spl. Edn., U. Mich., 1952; JD, DePaul U., 1960. Bar: Ill. 1961. Program dir. Chgo. Heart Assn., 1955-61; staff atty. Michael Reese Hosp. and Med. Center, Chgo., 1961-70, exec. v.p., 1971-73; dir. Ill. Dept. Pub. Aid, 1973-74; exec. dir. Ill. Legis. Adv. Com. on Pub. Aid, 1974-77; pres. Rose Med. Ctr., Denver, 1979-95; prin., sr. v.p. Frontier Holdings, Inc., Englewood, Colo., 1995—. Asst. prof. dept. preventive medicine U. Colo.; U.; dir. office legal affairs Am. Hosp. Assn., 1970 Contbr. articles to profl. jours. Served with AUS, 1955. Mem. Soc. Hosp. Attys. (charter) Home: 3156 S Hills Ct Denver CO 80210-6830

EDELMAN, JUDITH H., architect; b. Bklyn., Sept. 16, 1923; d. Abraham and Frances (Israel) Hochberg; m. Harold Edelman, Dec. 26, 1947; children: Marc, Joshua. Student, Conn. Coll., 1940—41, NYU, 1941—42; BArch, Columbia U., 1946. Designer, drafter Huson Jackson, N.Y.C., 1948-58; Schermerhorn traveling fellow, 1950; pvt. practice, 1958-60; ptnr. Edelman & Salzman, N.Y.C., 1960-79, Edelman Partnership (Archs.), N.Y.C., 1979—2002, Edelman, Sultan, Knox, Wood /Archs. LLP, N.Y.C., 2002—. Adj. prof. Sch. Architecture CUNY, 1972-76, vis. lectr. grad. program in environ. psychology, 1977, 77; vis. lectr. Washington U., St. Louis, 1974, U. Oreg., 1974, MIT, 1975, Pa. State U., 1977, Rensselaer Poly. Inst., 1977, Columbia U., 1979; First Claire Watson Forrest Meml. lectr. U. Oreg., U. Calif., Berkeley, U. So. Calif., 1982. Prin. works include Restoration of St. Mark's Ch. in the Bowery, N.Y.C., 1970-82, Two Bridges Urban Renewal Area Housing, 1970-96, Jennings Hall Sr. Citizens Housing, Bklyn., 1980, Goddard Riverside Elderly Housing and Cmty. Ctr., N.Y.C., 1983, Columbus Green Apartments, N.Y.C., 1987, Chung Pak Bldg., N.Y.C., 1992, Child Care Ctr., Queens, N.Y., 1999. Recipient Bard 1st honor award City Club N.Y., 1969, Bard award of merit, 1975, 82, award for design excellence HUD, 1970, 1st prize Nat. Trust for Hist. Preservation, 1983, award of merit Mcpl. Art Soc. N.Y., 1983, Pub. Svc. award Settlement Housing Fund, 1983, Women of Vision award NOW, 1989, 1st prize for design excellence C. of C., Borough of Queens, N.Y., 1989, Best in Srs.' Housing award Nat. Assn. Home Builders, 1993, Hamilton-Madison House Cmty. Svc. award, 1997. Fellow AIA (dir. N.Y. chpt., chmn. commn. on archtl. edn. 1971-73, chmn. nat. task force on women in architecture 1974-75, v.p. N.Y. chpt. 1975-77, chmn. ethics com. 1975-77, Residential design award 1969, Pioneer in Housing award 1990, N.Y. State Assn. Archs.-AIA Honor award 1975); mem. Alliance of Women in Architecture (founding, mem. steering com. 1972-74), Archs. for Social Responsibility (mem. exec. com. 1982-85), Columbia Archtl. Alumni Assn. (bd. dirs. 1968-71). Home: 37 W 12th St New York NY 10011-8502 Office: Edelman Sultan Knox Wood 100 Lafayette St Ste 204 New York NY 10013 Office Phone: 212-431-4901. Business E-Mail: jedelman@edelmansultan.com. E-mail: judithedelman@mac.com.

EDELMAN, LAUREN B., sociologist, law educator; d. Murray J. and Bacia Edelman. JD, Boalt Hall, 1986; PhD, Stanford U., 1986. Asst. to assoc. prof. U. Wis., Madison, 1986—96; prof. U. Calif., Berkeley, 1996—. Fellow, Guggenheim Found., 2000, Ctr. for Advanced Study in the Behavioral Scis., 2003—04. Mem.: Am. Sociol. Assn. (chair, sociology of law sect. 1993—94, Dist. Scholarship award 1995), Law and Soc. Assn. (pres. 2002—03). Achievements include research in analyses of relationship between employment law and organizational governance. Office: JSP Program/ UC Berkeley 2240 Piedmont Ave Berkeley CA 94720-2150 Office Phone: 510-642-4038. Business E-Mail: ledelman@law.berkeley.edu.

EDELMAN, MARIAN WRIGHT, not-for-profit organization administrator, lawyer; b. Bennettsville, S.C., June 6, 1939; d. Arthur J. and Maggie (Bowen) Wright; m. Peter B. Edelman, July 14, 1968; children: Joshua, Jonah, Ezra. Merrill scholar, Univs. Paris, Geneva, 1958-59; BA, Spelman Coll., 1960; LLB (J.H. Whitney fellow 1960-61), Yale U., 1963, LLD (hon.), Smith Coll., 1969, Lowell Tech. U., 1975, Williams Coll., 1978, Columbia U., U. Pa., Amherst Coll., St. Joseph's Coll.; DHL (hon.), Lesley Coll., 1975, Trinity Coll., Washington, Russell Sage Coll., 1978, Syracuse U., Coll. New Rochelle, 1979, Swarthmore Coll., 1980, SUNY Old Westbury, Northeastern U., 1981, Bard Coll., 1982, U. Mass., 1983, Hunter Coll., U. So. Maine, SUNY, Albany, 1984, Columbia U., U. Pa., Yale U., 1985, Rutgers U., Bates Coll., Maryville Coll., Bank St., 1986, Claremont Grad Sch., Lincoln U., Georgetown U., Chgo. Theol. Coll., 1987, Wheaton Coll., Tulane U., Grinnell Coll. Brandeis U., Wheelock Coll., Dartmouth Coll., U. S.C., U. N.C., Grad. Ctr. CUNY, U. Wis. Milw., 1988, Interdenom. Theol. Ctr., Hofstra U., Tufts U., Borough Manhattan Community Coll., Wesleyan U., Calif. State U. L.A., Dillard U., U. Md., U. Miami, 1989, Howard U., Beloit Coll., Queens Coll., Am. U., New Sch. of Social Rsch., Coll. of Notre Dame, DePaul U., 1990, Beaver Coll., Fordham U., Simmons Coll., Hamline U., Clark U., Harvard U., Union Coll., 1991, Tuskegee U., Washington U. St. Louis, Hood Coll., Duke U., Mercy Coll., 1992, Princeton U., U. Ill., Calif. State U. San Francisco, Wittenberg (Ohio) Coll., Shaw U., So. Meth. U., 1993, Brown U., U. Balt., Ea. Conn. State U., U. Notre Dame, 1994. Bar: D.C., Miss., Mass. Staff atty. NAACP Legal Def. and Ednl. Fund, Inc., N.Y.C., 1963-64, dir. Jackson, Miss., 1964-68; Congl. and fed. liaison Poor People's Campaign, summer 1968; partner Washington Research Project of So. Center for Pub. Policy, 1968-73; dir. Harvard U. Center for Law and Edn., 1971-73; pres., founder Children's Def. Fund, 1973—. Author: The Measure of Our Success: A Letter To My Children and Yours, 1992, Families in Peril, 1987. Mem. exec. com. Student Non-Violent Coordinating Com., 1961-63; mem. adv. coun. Martin Luther King Jr. Meml. Libr.; mem. adv. bd. Hampshire Coll.; mem. Presdl. Commn. on Missing in Action, 1977, Presdl. Commn. on Internat. Yr. of Child, 1979, Presdl. Commn. on Agenda for 80's, 1980; bd. dirs. NAACP Legal Def. and Ednl. Fund; trustee Spelman Coll., Carnegie Coun. on Children, 1972-77, Martin Luther King Jr. Meml. Ctr.; mem. Yale U. Corp., 1971-77, Aetna Found., Nat. Commn. on Children, 1989—; bd. dirs. Aetna Life Casualty Found., Citizens for Constitutional Concerns, US. com. UNICEF, Robin Hood Found., Aaron Diamond Found., Nat. Alliance Business, City Lights, Leadership Conf. Civil Rights, Skadden Fellowship Found., Parents as Tchrs. Nat. Ctr., Inc.; U.S. rep. UNICEF; active U.S. Olympic Com. Named one of Outstanding Young Women of Am., 1966; recipient Mademoiselle mag. award, 1965, Louise Waterman Wise award, 1970, Washington of Yr. award, 1979, Wilma M. Young award, 1979, Profl. of Yr. award Black Ent., 1979, Leadership award Nat. Women's Polit. Caucus, 1980, Black Womens Forum award, 1980, medal Columbia Tchrs.

Coll., Barnard Coll., 1984, Eliot award Am. Pub. Health Assn., John W. Gardner Leadership award of Ind. Sector, Pub. Svc. Achievement award Common Cause, Compostela award Cathedral St. James, 1987, MacArthur prize fellow, 1985, Albert Schweitzer Humanitarian prize Johns Hopkins U., 1987. Philip Hauge Ahelson award AAAS, 1988, Hubert Humphrey Civil Rights award, AFL-CIO award, 1989, Radcliffe Coll. medal, 1989, Fordham Stein prize, 1989, Gandhi Peace award, 1990, M. Carey Thomas award, Robie award for humanitarianism, Essence award, numerous others; hon. fellow U. Pa. Law Sch. Mem. Phi Beta Kappa (hon.), Inst. Medicine. Address: Children's Def Fund 25 E St NW Washington DC 20001-1522

EDELMAN, NORMAN HERMAN, dean, medical educator, academic administrator; b. NYC, May 21, 1937; s. Irving H. and Pearl Ruth (Solomon) E.; m. Ida Nadel, June 1959; children: David, Ruth, Deborah. AB, Bklyn. Coll., 1957; MD, NYU, 1961. Diplomate Am. Bd. Internal Medicine, Am. Bd. Pulmonary Diseases. Intern NYU Med. Sch., N.Y.C., 1961-62, resident, 1962-63; rsch. fellow NIH, Balt., 1963-65; vis. fellow Columbia U., Presbyn. Med. Ctr., N.Y.C., 1965-67; rsch. assoc. Michael Reese Med. Ctr., Chgo., 1967-69; asst. prof. medicine U. Pa. Sch. Medicine, Phila., 1969-72; prof. medicine, chief pulmonary medicine Robert Wood Johnson Med. Sch., U. Medicine and Dentistry of N.J., New Brunswick, N.J., 1972-95, dean, 1988-95; prof. medicine and physiology and biophysics SUNY, Stony Brook, 1996—, v.p. health sci. ctr., dean Sch. Medicine, 1996—. Cons. for sci. Am. Lung Assn., N.Y.C., 1984—; mem. pulmonary disease adv. com. NIH, 1984-88. Contbr. articles, abstracts to profl. jours., chpts. to med. textbooks; mem. editorial bd. Jour. Applied Physiol., Am. Rev. Respiratory Diseases. Served as surgeon USPHS, 1963-65. Fellow AAAS; mem. Assn. Am. Physicians, Am. Soc. Clin. Investigation, Am. Thoracic Soc., Am. Physiol. Soc. Office Phone: 631-444-2080. Business E-Mail: norman.edelman@stonybrook.edu.

EDELMAN, PAUL STERLING, lawyer; b. Bklyn., Jan. 2, 1926; s. Joseph E. and Rose (Kaminsky) Edelman; m. Rosemary Jacobs, June 15, 1951; children: Peter, Jeffrey. AB, Harvard U., 1946, JD, 1950. Bar: NY 1951, US Dist. Ct. (so. and ea. dists.) NY 1954, US Ct. Appeals (2d cir.) 1965, US Supreme Ct. 1967. Ptnr. Kreindler & Kreindler, NYC, 1953-95, counsel, 1996—. Legal advisor Andrea Doria TV show, 1984, QE2 TV show, 1995; cons. Slave Ship TV Program, April, 2001. Author: Maritime Injury and Death, 1960; editor: Maritime Law Reporter, 1987-99, Marine Laws, 1993, 94; columnist NY Law Jour.; contbr. 17 Causes of Action 2d on Personal Injury of Maritime Pers. With U.S. Army, 1944—46. Fellow NY Bar Found.; mem. ABA (past chmn. admiralty com., toxic hazardous substances litigation com., mem. long range planning com. 1982-84, mem. TIPS coun. 1984-88, Soviet-Am. lawyers conf. Moscow 1987, 94, TIPS lawyer conf. Russia 1993), ATLA (past chmn. admiralty coms.), Maritime Law Assn. (rep. law sea seminar Moscow 1994), NY State Bar Assn. (TICL award 1980, 90, 93, 2005, chmn. INCL sect. 1982-83, editor Ins. Jour. 1973—), Maritime Law Assn. (sec. maritime personnel com.), Hastings Hist. Soc., Oliver Wendell Holmes Soc. Harvard Law Sch., Supreme Ct. Hist. Soc., World Peace Through Law Ctr., Hudson Valley Tennis Club, Hastings Hudson (past chmn., planning bd.), Supreme Ct. Hist. Soc., Hastings Hist. Soc. Democrat. Jewish. Home: 57 Buena Vista Dr Hastings On Hudson NY 10706-1103 Office: 100 Park Ave New York NY 10017-5516 Office Phone: 212-687-8181. Business E-Mail: pedelman@kreindler.com.

EDELMAN, PETER BENJAMIN, lawyer, educator; b. Mpls., Jan. 9, 1938; s. Hyman and Miriam Hazel (Lieberman) E.; m. Marian Elizabeth Wright, July 14, 1968; children: Joshua, Jonah, Ezra. AB, Harvard U., 1958, LL.B., 1961. Bar: N.Y. 1962, D.C. 1979. Law clk. Judge Henry J. Friendly, N.Y.C., 1961-62, Justice Arthur J. Goldberg, Washington, 1962-63; spl. asst. to asst. atty. gen. John Douglas Dept. Justice, Washington, 1963-64; legis. asst. to Sen. Robert F. Kennedy, Washington, 1964-68; asso. dir. Robert F. Kennedy Meml., Washington, 1969-70; staff dir. Pres.'s Com. on the Future of U. Mass., Boston, 1971; v.p. univ. policy U. Mass., 1972-75; dir. N.Y. State Div. Youth, Albany, 1975-79; ptnr. Foley, Lardner, Hollabaugh & Jacobs, Washington, 1979-82; prof. law Georgetown U. Law Ctr., Washington, 1982-93, 96—, assoc. dean, 1989-92; counselor Sec. of Health and Human Svcs., Washington, 1993-95; asst. sec. for planning and evaluation Dept. of Health and Human Svcs., Washington, 1995-96. Lectr. MIT, 1972-75; issues dir. presdl. campaign Senator Edward M. Kennedy, 1980; co-dir. Justice Dept. Transition, 1992-93. Chmn. bd. New World Found., 1982-87; vice chmn. bd. Ctr. for Comty. Change, 1983-87, chmn., 1987-93, bd. dirs., 1996—; mem. exec. com. Washington Lawyers Com. for Civil Rights Under Law, 1981-93, 97—; bd. dirs. Ctr. for Nat. Policy, 1981-93; trustee U. D.C., 1984-90; bd. dirs. Food Rsch. and Action Ctr., 1988-93, Pub. Voice, 1988-93; mem. nat. gov. bd. Common Cause, 1989-93; chmn. bd. Fair Employment Coun. Greater Washington, 1990-93; co-chmn. Americans for Peace Now, 1990-93, bd. dirs., 1997—; bd. dirs. Pub. Welfare Found., 1994-95, 96—, New Israel Fund, 1997—, bd. pres. 2002—. Ctr. for Law and Social Policy, 1997—, Juvenile Law Ctr., 1997—, Nat. Ctr. for Youth Law, 1997—, bd. chair, 2004—, Chapin Hall Ctr. for Children, 1997-2005; chmn. Comn. Access to Justice, Washington, D.C., 2005—. With Air N.G., 1963. Ford Found. travel-study grantee, 1968; U.S.-Japan leadership program fellow, 1985; J. Skelly Wright Meml. fellow Yale Law Sch., 1991. Democrat. Jewish. Home: 3208 Newark St NW Washington DC 20008-3345 Office: Georgetown U Law Ctr Washington DC 20001 Office Phone: 202-662-9074. Business E-Mail: edelman@law.georgetown.edu.

EDELMAN, ROBERT, medical educator; m. Marge Edelman. MD cum laude, AB, Washington U., St. Louis, 1962. Instr. Case Western Res. U. Sch. of Medicine, Cleveland, Ohio, 1967—68; vis. lectr. Mahidol U., Bangkok, 1970—73; clin. assoc. prof. medicine Uniformed Services U. of the Health Sciences, 1978—84; clin. prof. medicine Uniformed Services U. of the Health Scis., 1984—88; prof. medicine U. Md. Sch. Medicine, Balt., 1988—, prof. pediat., 1990—; affiliate prof. U. Md. Sch. Pharmacy, Balt., 1997—. Capt., maj., and lt. col. Med. Rsch. and Devel. U.S. Army, 1968—76. Recipient Mosby Book award, 1962, U.S. Army Commendation medal, 1970, U.S. Army Meritorious Svc. medal, 1973, Commendation medal, USPHS, 1984. Mem.: Alpha Omega Alpha, Phi Beta Kappa. Office: U Md Sch Medicine 685 W Baltimore St Rm 480 Baltimore MD 21201 E-mail: redelman@medicine.umaryland.edu.

EDELMAN, SCOTT A., lawyer; b. Flushing, N.Y., 1963; BA summa cum laude, MA, Yale Univ., 1985; JD magna cum laude, Harvard Univ., 1988. Bar: N.Y. 1989. Assoc. Wachtell Lipton Rosen & Katz, NYC; asst. US atty. So. Dist. NY, US Dept. Justice; assoc. Milbank Tweed Hadley & McCloy, NYC, 1994—95, ptnr. Litigation Dept. & mem. global exec. com., 1995—. John Olin Fellow. Mem.: Phi Beta Kappa. Office: Milbank Tweed Hadley & McCloy 1 Chase Manhattan Plz New York NY 10005-1413 Office Phone: 212-530-5149. Office Fax: 212-530-5219. Business E-Mail: sedelman@milbank.com.

EDELMAN, STUART EDWARD, psychiatrist; b. N.Y.C., Mar. 14, 1947; s. Norman David and Mollie (Wollruch) E.; children: Joseph Jake, Kimberly Jean. BS cum laude, Trinity Coll., Hartford, Conn., 1968; MD, Columbia U., 1972. Diplomate Am. Bd. Psychiatry and Neurology. Resident in psychiatry Harvard U. Med. Sch., Boston, 1972—75; pvt. practice Wayland, Mass., 1975—; clin. instr. in psychiatry Harvard U. Med. Sch., Boston, 1975—2002; asst. clin. prof. psychiatry Sch. Medicine Boston U., 1993—. Staff psychiatrist Trinity Mental Health Ctr., Framingham, Mass., 1975-80; chief dept. psychiatry, med. dir. Eliot Cmty. Mental Health Ctr., Concord, Mass., 1980-90; supr. Erikson Ctr., Harvard U., Cambridge, Mass., 1982-90. Contbr. articles to med. jours. Mem. Am. Psychiat. Assn., Mass. Psychiat. Assn., New Eng. Soc. for Adolescent Psychiatry (v.p.), Phi Beta Kappa. Avocations: tennis, squash, skiing, painting. Office: 58 Glezen Ln Wayland MA 01778-1604

EDELMANN, JOHN FREDERICK, information technology manager, consultant; s. Paul Frederick and Martha Rose Edelmann; m. Ute Erika Edelmann, Nov. 20, 1993; 1 child, Erika Paula. BS, U. Dayton, 1984. Mgr. sys. and network Siemens Energy and Automation, Inc., Norwood, Ohio, 1991—95; tech. cons. Hewlett-Packard Co., Dayton, Ohio, 1995—. Dir. music St. Agnes Cath. Ch., Dayton, 1998—2002, The Ch. of Holy Angels, Dayton, 2003—. Composer: (miscellaneous musical instrumentals) Miscellaneous. Chmn. zoning commn. Clearcreek Twp., Warren County, Ohio, 2003—05. Recipient Computer Vagrancy award, U. Dayton, Computer Sci. Dept., 1984, Outstanding Accomplishment award, Compaq Computer Corp., 2002. Mem.: ASCAP, Nat. Eagle Scout Assn., Soc. of Mary (dir. music 2000—), Miami Valley Cath. Ch. Musicians (program coord. 2004—05, Tng. scholarship 2003), Order of Arrow (Vigil honor 1983), Boy Scouts Am. (Eagle Scout award 1979), Hon. Order Ky. Cols. (hon.). Republican. Roman Catholic. Avocations: wine making, meteorology, astronomy, weightlifting, music performance. Home: 2594 Pekin Rd Springboro OH 45066 Personal E-mail: edelmann@hcst.net.

EDELSBERG, SALLY COMINS, physical therapist, director, educator; b. Rowno, Poland, Aug. 6, 1939; came to U.S., 1949; d. Joseph Luria and Chana (Bebczuk) Comins; m. Warde C. Pierson, Oct. 8, 1968 (div. 1978); m. Paul Edelsberg, Feb. 2, 1979; 1 child, Tema. BS in Phys. Medicine, U. Wis., 1963; MS, Northwestern U., 1972. Lic. phys. therapist. Staff and supervisory phys. therapist Hines VA Hosp., Maywood, Ill., 1963-67; program dir. Health Careers Council of Ill., Chgo., 1967-70; instr., clin. edn. coord. Programs in Phys. Therapy, Northwestern U. Med. Sch., Chgo., 1970—72, dir., assoc. prof., 1972—99, dir. devel. and alumni rels., 1999—2003. Pres. Phys. Therapy Ltd., Chgo., 1986-95; v.p. World Confedn. Phys. Therapy, 1995-99, exec. com., 1991-95. Mem.: Am. Phys. Therapy Assn. (bd. dirs. 1975—78, 1979—82, Ill. pres. 1972—76, Catherine Worthingham fellow 1999). E-mail: s-edelsberg@northwestern.edu.

EDELSBRUNNER, HERBERT, computer scientist, educator, mathematician; b. Graz, Styria, Austria, Mar. 14, 1958; s. Herbert and Berta Edelsbrunner; m. Ping Fu, Nov. 14, 1991; children: Daniel, Xixi. MS in Tech. Math., Graz U. Tech., 1980, PhD in Tech. Math., 1982. Mem. faculty Graz U. Tech., 1981-85, Universitätsassistent Inst. Informationsverarbeitung, 1984-85; asst. prof. dept. computer sci. U. Ill., Urbana-Champaign, 1985-87, assoc. prof. dept. computer sci., 1987-90, prof. dept. computer sci., 1990-99; arts and scis. prof. computer sci. and math. Duke U., Durham, N.C., 1999—. Founder, dir. Raindrop Geomagic, 1996—. Author: Algorithms in Combinatorial Geometry, 1987, Geometry and Topology for Grid Generation, 2001. Recipient Alan T. Waterman award NSF, 1991. Mem.: AAAS. Achievements include research in data structures and algorithms, computational geometry, discrete geometry, combinatorial topology, computational biology, scientific computation. Office: Duke U Dept Computer Sci Durham NC 27708 Business E-Mail: edels@cs.duke.edu.

EDELSON, EDWARD HAROLD, research chemist; m. Judith Linda Miller, Mar. 28, 1970; children: Erica, Mindy. BS, CUNY, 1973; PhD, Rensselaer Poly. Inst., 1977. Rsch. assoc. Ames Rsch. Ctr. NASA, Moffet Field, Calif., 1977-79; instr., rsch. asst. U. So. Calif., L.A., 1979-80; rsch. chemist Exxon Rsch. and Engring. Co., Baytown, Tex., 1980-85; sr. rsch. chemist Mobil Rsch. and Devel. Corp., Paulsboro, N.J., 1985-93; analytical lab. mgr., quality sys. mgr. Anderol, Inc., East Hanover, NJ, 1993—. Author: (with others) COSPAR Life Sciences and Space Research, 1980, 1980 McGraw-Hill Yearbook of Science and Technology, 1980, Origin of Life, 1981; contbr. articles to profl. jours. Mem. SAE, ASTM, Am. Soc. for Quality, Am. Chem. Soc. (chmn. symposium 1978, 80), Soc. Tribologists and Lubrication Engrs. Avocations: classical guitar, photography. Office: Anderoi PO Box 518 East Hanover NJ 07936-0518 Office Phone: 973-887-7410. Business E-Mail: ehe@anderol.com.

EDELSON, GILBERT SEYMOUR, lawyer; b. N.Y.C., Sept. 15, 1928; s. Saul and Sarah (Sunshine) E.; m. Jane Barbara Levin, Sept. 6, 1953; children: Martha Jane, Paula Topal, Dorothy Rachel. BS, NYU, 1948; LLB, Columbia U., 1955. Bar: N.Y. 1955, U.S. Dist. Ct. (so. dist.) N.Y. 1959, U.S. Ct. Appeals (2nd cir.) 1959, U.S. Dist. Ct. (ea. dist.) N.Y. 1960, U.S. Ct. Appeals (9th cir.) 1995. Assoc. Rosenman Goldmark Colin & Kaye, N.Y.C., 1955-63; ptnr. Rosenman & Colin, N.Y.C., 1963-97, counsel, 1997—2002, Katten Muchin Rosenman, NYC, 2002—. Adminstrv. v.p., counsel Art Dealers Assn. Am., N.Y.C., 1985—. Editor Columbia Law Rev., 1955. Bd. dirs. Coll. Art Assn. Am., N.Y.C., 1969-88, High Five Tickets for the Arts, N.Y.C., 1999-2001; sec., trustee Am. Fedn. Arts, N.Y.C., 1984-94; trustee Internat. Found. for Art Rsch., 1986-99, N.Y. Studio Sch., 1989—, Archives Am. Art, N.Y.C., 1989—. With U.S. Army, 1950-52, JLC. Mem. ABA, N.Y. Bar Assn., Assn. Bar of N.Y.C. (chmn. com. on art law 1992-95), Columbia U. Law Sch. Alumni Assn. (bd. dirs. 1981-84), Century Assn. Jewish. Avocation: collecting art. Home: 580 W End Ave New York NY 10024-1723 Office: Katten Muchin Rosenman 575 Madison Ave New York NY 10022-2585 Office Phone: 212-940-7070. E-mail: gilbert.edelson@kattenlaw.com.

EDELSON, IRA J., venture capitalist, trade association administrator; b. Chgo., Dec. 30, 1946; s. Alvin L. and Naomi Edelson; m. Starr Gramaila, Feb. 11, 1973; children: Jason Avrum, Megan Anne. BS, DePaul U., 1968. Spl. advisor to chmn. Chgo. Housing Authority, 1983; acting dir. revenue City of Chgo., 1984; ptnr.-in-charge bus. svcs. dept. Deloitte, Haskins & Sells, Chgo., 1979-87; ptnr.-in-charge corp. fin. Deloitte & Touche-U.S. Partnership, Chgo., 1987-91; pres. Transcap Assocs. Inc., Northbrook, Ill., 1991—. Fin. and policy advisor to mayor City of Chgo., 1984-85; former instr. Northwestern Grad. Sch. Bus. (Kellogg); cons., speaker in field. Co-chmn. Chgo. Sports Stadium Commn., 1985. Mem.: AICPA, Fgn. Trade Assn., TMA (Turn Around Mgmt. Assn.), Nat. Contract Mgmt. Assn., Comml. Fin. Assn., Ill. Soc. CPAs. Office: Transcap Assocs Inc 900 Skokie Blvd Ste 210 Northbrook IL 60062-4031 Office Phone: 847-753-9600.

EDELSON, JAY PERES, lawyer; b. N.Y.C., Aug. 28, 1972; s. Rae Temkin Edelson and Peter Edward Gordon (Stepfather); m. Dana Peres Edelson, Jan. 4, 1997; 1 child, Leah Peres. BA in Philosophy, Brandeis U., 1996; JD, U. Mich., 1996. Bar: Ill. 1997. Assoc. Holleb & Coff, Chgo., 1997—99, Plotkin, Jacobs & Orlofsky, Ltd., Chgo., 1999—2001; mem. Blim & Edelson, LLC, Chgo., 2001—. Office: Blim & Edelson LLC Ste 1642 53 W Jackson Blvd Chicago IL 60604 Office Phone: 312-913-9400. Business E-Mail: jay@blimlaw.com.

EDELSON, MARY BETH, artist, educator; b. East Chgo. d. Albert Melvin and Mary Lou (Young) Johnson; children: Lynn Switzman, Nick. Student, Art Inst. Chgo.; BA, DePauw U., 1955; MA, NYU, 1959; DFA (hon.), DePauw U., 1993. Instr. Corcoran Sch. Art, Washington, 1970-75; artist in residence U. Ill., Chgo., 1982, 88, U. Tenn., Knoxville, 1983, Ohio U., Columbus, 1984, Md. Inst. Art, Balt., 1985, Kansas City Art Inst., Mo., 1986, Cleve. Art Inst., 1991, U. Colo., 1993, Clemson U., 1994, McMullen Mus. of Art, Boston Coll., 1997, Danish Royal Acad., Copenhagen, 2000—02, Art and Film Sch., Kabelvag, 2004. Lectr. at various art gatherings. Solo exhbns. include Nicole Klagsburn Gallery, N.Y.C., 1993, A/C Project Rm., N.Y.C., 1993, Creative Time, N.Y.C., 1994, Nicolai Wallner, Copenhagen, Denmark, 1996, Halle für Kunst, Berlin, 1997, Agency Gallery, London, 1998, Malmö Mus., Sweden, 2000, traveling solo exhbn. to 8 sites in U.S., 2000-2002 30 yr. survey of Edelson's work with 200 page book, full color book, The Art of Mary Beth Edelson; group exhbns. include Internat. Feministiche Kunst, Stichting de Appel, Amsterdam, The Netherlands, 1980, Mendel Gallery, Mus. du Que., Phillips Gallery, Can., 1986-88, Corcoran Gallery Art, Washington, 1989, Mus. Modern Art, N.Y.C., 1988-89, Walker Art Ctr., Mpls., 1989, W.P.A., Washington, 1989, A.C. Project Room, N.Y.C., 1991-97, Phillippe Rizzo, Paris, 1992, P.P.O.W., N.Y.C., 1992, Fawbush Gallery, N.Y.C., 1992, Amy Lipton Gallery, N.Y.C., 1992, David Zwirner Gallery, N.Y.C., 1993, Turner/Krail Galleries, L.A.,o1993, Mercer Union, Toronto, 1996, The Agency, London, 1995, Lombard/Freid, N.Y.C., 1995, Chaisse Post gallery, Atlanta, 1996, Linda Kirkland Gallery, N.Y.C., 1996, Boston Mus. Art, McMullen, 1997, Magasin Ctr. National D'Art Contemporain, Grenoble, France, 1997, Dorfman Projects, N.Y.C., 1998, Internat. Ctr. Photography, N.Y.C., 1997, Neuberger Mus., Purchase, N.Y., 1999, Nicolai Wallner, Copenhagen, 1999, Postmasters, N.Y.C., 1999, New Mus., N.Y.C., 2000, 2001, Tate Mus., London, 2001, Gallerie LeLong, N.Y.C., 2002, Guild Hall, East Hampton, 2002; Chelsea Mus., NYC, 2003; ShedHalle Space, Zurick, 2003, Mumok Museum, Vienna, 2003, Internat. Art Festival, Lofoten, Norway, 2004, Remy Toledo Gallery, NYC, 2005, Yaddo Residency, 2005; represented in permanent collections: Walker Art Ctr., Nat. Mus. Am. Art, Washington, Nat. Collection, Washington, Nat. Mus. Women in the Arts, Washington, Guggenheim Mus. Art, N.Y.C., Mus. Contemporary Art, Chgo., Malmo Mus., Sweden, and others; subject of 15-yr. retrospective travelling to numerous art and ednl. instns. throughout U.S., 1988-91, Survey of Edelson's Work Rescripting the Story, various locations, 2000-02; author: Seven Cycles: Public Rituals, 1981, To Dance: Painting with Performance in Mind, 1985, Seven Sites, 1988-90, Shape Shifter: Seven Mediums, 1990; author/photographer: Firsthand, 1993, The Art of Mary Beth Edelson, 2002; contbr. articles to profl. jours.; included numerous books including The Power of Feminist Art, 1994, Lone Visions, Crowder Frames, 1994, The Pink Glass Swan, 1995, Art and Propaganda, 1997, Saffrages and She-Devils, 1997, Where is Ana Mendiata, 1999, Picturing the Modern Amazon, 2000, Feminist Art-Theory; An Anthology, 1968-2000, Art and Feminism, 2001, The Artists Body, 2000, Sex Politik, 2001, Alternative Art N.Y., 2002, The Art of Marybeth Edelson, 2002, The End of Art, 2004. Recipient Visual Arts grant NEA, 1981, 2000, Creative Artists Pub. Svc. grant State of N.Y., 1982, Andy Warhol Found. grant NEA, Pollack/Krasner Found., Florsheim Found., 2000 Mem. Conf. Women in Visual Arts (founding mem.), Women's Action Coalition, Heresies Mag. Collective (founding mem.). Home: 110 Mercer St New York NY 10012-3865 E-mail: yourstory@earthlink.net.

EDELSON, RICHARD L., dermatology educator, director; b. Livingston, NJ, Dec. 19, 1944; s. Edmond and Merilyn Edelson; m. Ruth Cheris Edelson; children: Andrew, Ari. BS, Hamilton Coll., NY, 1966; MD, Yale U. Sch. Medicine, 1970. Intern U. Chgo., 1970-71; resident in dermatology Mass. Gen. Hosp., Boston, 1971-72; research assoc. in immunology NIH, Bethesda, Md., 1972-75; sr. resident in dermatology Columbia-Presbyn. Hosp., NYC, 1975-76; asst. prof. Columbia U. Coll. Physicians and Surgeons, NYC, 1976-78, assoc. prof., 1978-80, prof., assoc. dir. dermatol. rsch., 1980-85; head immunobiology group Comprehensive Cancer Ctr., Columbia U., assoc. dir., gen. clin. rsch. ctr.; prof., chmn. dept. Yale U. Sch. Medicine, New Haven, 1986—; deputy dean, clin. affairs Yale U. Sch. Medicine-Medical Center, 2000—, dir., cancer ctr. lymphoma rsch. program; dir. Yale Cancer Ctr., New Haven, 2003—. Editor: Antigen and Clone Specific Immunoregulation, 1991; contribr. to scientific papers; author and co-author review articles, book chpts., and books. Trustee Yale-New Haven Hosp., 1994—; bd. gov. Yale Med. Group Mem. Dermatology Found. (exec. com. 1990—), Am. Acad. Dermatology, Assn. Profs. Dermatology, Interurban Club, Am. Soc. for Clin. Investigation, Assn. Am. Physicians. Achievements include patents in field. Avocations: tennis, computer graphics, biking. Home: 75 Coleytown Rd Westport CT 06880-1529 Office: Cancer Ctr Yale Comprehensive Cancer Ctr 333 Cedar St New Haven CT 06510-3206

EDELSON, ZELDA SARAH TOLL, retired editor, artist; b. Phila., Oct. 18, 1929; d. Louis David and Rose (Eisenstein) Toll; m. Marshall Edelson, Dec. 27, 1952 (dec. Jan. 16, 2005); children: Jonathan Toll Edelson, Rebecca Jo Edelson, David Edelson Tolchinsky. BA, U. Chgo., 1949, postgrad., 1949-52. Editor-writer Consol. Book Pubs., Chgo., 1953-56; social worker Balt. City Dept. Pub. Welfare, 1956-57; pub. rels. writer Md. Dept. Employment Security, Balt., 1958-59; mus. editor Yale Peabody Mus., New Haven, 1970-76, head publs., 1976-95, editor mus.'s Discovery mag., 1983-95; lectr. in sci. writing Yale U., 1983—84. Author (and illustrator): Apologies for a Nightingale: Images of Turkey, 1997; editor: numerous publs. including The Great Dinosaur Mural at Yale: The Age of Reptiles, 1990. U. Chgo. scholar, 1947-51. E-mail: zeldaedelson@yahoo.com.

EDELSTEIN, BARBARA A., radiologist; b. N.Y.C., 1952; MD, NY Med. Coll., 1977. Cert. diagnostic radiology 1983. Intern Lenox Hill Hosp., N.Y.C., 1977—78; resident Montefiore Hosp., N.Y.C., 1979—82; radiologist Women's Radiology, N.Y.C., 1983—. Office: Womens Radiology 1045 Park Ave New York NY 10028-1030 Office Phone: 212-860-7700. Personal E-mail: b99xray@aol.com.

EDELSTEIN, JEAN, artist, performance artist; b. N.Y.C., Mar. 18, 1927; d. Jack Silvers and Sarah Glassman; m. Seymour Edelstein, June 23, 1949; children: Bruce, Barbara. Cert., Pratt Inst., 1947; student, Art Students League, 1947-48, UCLA, 1952. One-person shows include Laguna Beach (Calif.) Mus. Art, 1973, Jacqueline Anhalt Gallery, L.A., 1974, Bird's Eye View Gallery, Newport Beach, Calif., 1978, Karl Bornstein Gallery, Santa Monica, Calif., 1981, Gallery Newz, Tokyo, 1985, Ruth Bachofner Gallery, Santa Monica, 1985, 87, 89, Sherry Frumkin Gallery, Santa Monica, 1992, U. Judaism, L.A., 1993, Nemiroff-Deutsch Gallery, Santa Monica, 1994; exhibited in group shows Otis Art Inst., L.A., 1967, Mt. St. Mary's Coll., L.A., 1975, L.A. County Mus. Art, Rental Gallery, 1978, LACE Gallery, L.A., 1980, Eason Gallery, Santa Fe, 1983, San Francisco Mus. Art, 1985, Korean Cultural Gallery, L.A., 1989, Sherry Frumkin Gallery, Santa Monica, 1991, Valerie Miller Gallery, Palm Desert, Calif., 1992, Art Space Gallery, N.Y.C., 1992; represented in pub. collections and commns. Robert Civitas Pub., Sao Paolo, Brazil, Sheraton Inner Harbor Hotel, Balt., Focus Lexington Hotel, Tulsa, Lloyds Bank, L.A., Toyota Corp., Torrance, Calif., Revoltella Mus., Trieste, Italy; performances at Ruth Bachofner Gallery, L.A., 1985, 93, Pacific Asian Mus., Pasadena, Calif., 1990, Exploratorium Mus., San Francisco, 1992, Revoltella Mus., Trieste, 1993, Nat. Mus. Women in Arts, Washington, 1994; works published in L.A. Times, Artweek, Images and Issues, ArtScene, Visions Mag., Flash Art. Recipient scholarship Art Students League, 1947, fellowship NEA Midatlantic, 1996. Home: # 5A 48 Brooks Ave Venice CA 90291-3226 Office Phone: 310-399-3592.

EDELSTEIN, MARK S., lawyer; BA summa cum laude, CUNY, 1979; JD magna cum laude, Yeshiva U., Benjamin N. Cardozo Sch. Law, 1982. Bar: N.Y. 1983. Ptnr. Milbank, Tweed, Hadley & McCloy, 1992—99, Morrison& Foerster LLP, N.Y.C., 1999—, mem. exec. com. Contbr. articles to profl. jours. Mem.: Real Estate & Construction Coun., Lincoln Ctr., Real Estate Board N.Y., Mortgage Bankers Assn., Urban Land Inst., N.Y. Lawyers Assn., ABA, N.Y. State Bar Assn., Assn. Bar City N.Y. Office: Morrison & Foerster LLP 1290 Avenue of Americas New York NY 10104-0185 Office Phone: 212-468-8273. Office Fax: 212-468-7900. Business E-Mail: medelstein@mofo.com.

EDELSTEIN, MELVIN, education educator; b. NY, NY, May 23, 1939; s. Samuel and Selma (Tarnower) Edelstein; m. Marilyn Manera Edelstein, June 7, 1969; 1 child, Elizabeth Manera. BA, U. Chgo., 1956—60; MA, Princeton U., 1960—62, PhD, 1965. Instr. Stanford U., Stanford, Calif., 1964—67; asst. prof. Herbert H. Lehman Coll. of CUNY, Bronx, 1967—73; assoc. prof. William Paterson Coll. of N.J., Wayne, 1973—79, prof., 1979—. Chair, history dept. William Paterson Coll. of N.J., 1981—87, chair, faculty senate, 2001—03. Author: (book) La Feuille Villageoise: Communication et Modernisation dans les Regions Rurales pendant la Revolution, 1977. Recipient NEH summer stipend, 1989; grantee, Am. Philos. Soc., 1969, 1975, 1990, 1994, 1999; Fulbright fellowship for rsch. in France, Wash., D.C., 1995—96. Mem.: Societe des Etudes robespierristes, Soc. for French Hist. Studies, Am. Hist. Assn. Democrat. Jewish. Avocations: travel, photography, cultural activities. Home: 444 East 82d St New York NY 10028 Office: William Paterson Univ 300 Pompton Rd Wayne NJ 07470 Office Phone: 973-720-2324.

EDELSTEIN, ROSEMARIE (ROSEMARIE HUBLOU), medical/surgical nurse, educator, geriatrics nurse; b. Drake, ND, Mar. 3, 1935; d. Francis Jerome and Myrtle Josephine (Merbach); m. Harry George Edelstein, June 22, 1957 (div.); children: Julie, Lori, Lynn, Toni Anne. BSN, St. Teresa of Avila Coll., Winona, Minn., 1956; MA in Edn., Holy Names Coll., Oakland, Calif., 1977; EdD, U. San Francisco, 1982, postgrad., 1987, U. Ariz., 1985—; cert. pub. health nurse, U. Calif., Berkeley, 1972. Dir., clin. supr. San Francisco Sch. for Health Professions, 1971-74, Rancho Arroyo Sch. of Vocat. Nursing, Sacramento, 1974-75; intensive care nurse Kaiser-Permanente Hosp., San

Rafael, 1976-77; dir. insvc. edn. Ross Hosp., 1977-78; dir. nursing edn. St. Francis Meml. Hosp., San Francisco, 1978-85; med.-surg. staff nurse met. hosps., San Francisco, 1985-90; med.-legal nursing cons., med.-surg. staff nurse St. Luke's Hosp., Duluth, Minn., 1990-91, St. Charles Hosp., New Orleans, 1992, U. Tex. Med. Br., Galveston, Tex., 1992—94; staff nurse St. Anthony of Padua Hosp., Oklahoma City, 1994—95, med.-surg. nurse, 1994-95; nurse Northgate Conv. Hosp., San Rafael, Calif., 1995—, Idaho Falls Care Ctr., 2003—04, Minidoka Mem. Hosp. Extended Care Facility, 2004—05. Night charge nurse Creekside Conv. Hosp., Santa Rosa, Calif., 1996; charge nurse medications, treatment and Alzheimer's Unit Fallon Conv. Ctr., Nev., 1996; charge nurse Medicare unit White Pine Conv. Ctr., Ely, Nev., 1997; emergency rm., ICU nurse Battle Mt. Gen. Hosp., Nev., 1997; nurse supr. Medicare-Med. Seaview Care Ctr. Sun Corp., Eureka, Calif., 1997—98; mem. staff Walker Post Manor Oxford, NE Lantis Corp., 1998, The Lincoln Ambassador, 1999, Rapid City (S.D.) Care Ctr. Beverly Enterprises, 2000—01, Houghton County Med. Care Facility, Hancock, Mich., 2000—, Norlite Nursing Ctr., Marquette, Mich., 2001—02; mem. staff Medicare unit Everett (Wash.) Rehab. and Care Ctr., 2001—02; mem. staff Whidbey Island Manor, Oak Harbor, Wash.; staff medicare unit St. Joseph Care Ctr., Spokane, 2003; invited mem. people to people nursing edn. and adminstrn. delegation to Japan, Hong Kong, and China Eisenhower Found. Wayne State U., 1985. Author: The Influence of Motivator and Hygiene Factors in Job Changes by Graduate Registered Nurses, 1977; Effects of Two Educational Methods Upon Retention of Knowledge in Pharmacology, 1981; co-author: (with Jane F. Lee) Acupunture Atlas, 1974. Candidate U.S. Senate Inner Circle, 1988, 89. Lt. col. USAR Med. Res. Mem. Am. Heart Assn., Calif. Nurses Assn., Sigma Theta Tau. Roman Catholic.

EDELSTEIN, TERI J., art educator, art director, consultant; b. Johnstown, Pa., June 23, 1951; d. Robert Morten and Hulda Lois (Friedhoff) E. BA, U. Pa., 1972, MA, 1977, PhD, 1979; cert., NYU, 1984. Lectr. U. Guelph, Ont., 1977-79; asst. dir. for acad. programs Yale Ctr. Brit. Art, New Haven, 1979-83; dir. Mt. Holyoke Coll. Art Mus., South Hadley, Mass., 1983-90, Skinner Mus., 1983-90, mem. faculty dept. art., 1983-90; dir. Smart Mus. Art U. Chgo., 1990-92, sr. lectr. dept. art, 1990-2000; prin., owner Teri J. Edelstein Assocs., Chgo., 1999—. Dep. dir. Art Inst. Chgo., 1992—99; pres. Teri J. Edelstein Assocs. Museum Strategies, 1999—; mem. adv. bd. Sculpture Chgo., 1991—96, Mus. Loan Network, Knight and Pew Founds., 1994—96. Office: 1648 E 50th St # 6B Chicago IL 60615-3207 Fax: 773-241-9992. Office Phone: 773-241-9991. Business E-Mail: tedelstein@tedelstein.com.

EDELSTEIN, TILDEN GERALD, academic administrator, historian, educator; b. N.Y.C., June 11, 1931; s. Theodore and Nettie (Strusser) Edelstein; m. Marjorie Sukoff, June 17, 1955 (div. July 1970); m. Rose Ann Stargardter, Nov. 1, 1970; children: Jordan, Russell. BS, U. Wis., 1953; PhD, Johns Hopkins U., 1961. From instr. to assoc. prof. Simmons Coll., Boston, 1957-67; from adj. assoc. prof. to prof. history Rutgers U., New Brunswick, N.J., 1967-89, chmn. history dept., grad. dir., 1974-81, assoc. dean social sci. and humanities, faculty personnel, 1981-84, dean faculty arts and scis., 1984-89; prof. history, provost, acad. v.p. SUNY, Stony Brook, 1989-93, prof. history, provost, exec. v.p. for academic affairs, 1992-94; v.p. for acad. affairs Wayne State U., Detroit, 1995-98, prof. history, 1998—2003. Hist. cons. Columbia Pictures, Hollywood, Calif., 1978-80, NBC, N.Y.C., 1980-89; chair Sponsors Bd. The Thomas A. Edison Papers Project, 1980-89. Author: Strange Enthusiasm, 1968, 2d edit., 1970; co-editor: The Black Americans, 1975. Commr. Housing Authority, Highland Park, N.J., 1977-89; Einstein Archives Adv. Com. Hebrew U., 1993-94; mem. adv. bd. Cohen/Haddow Ctr. for Jewish Studies, Mich. Civil War Regimental Round Table. Mem.: Prismatic Club Detroit. Office: Wayne State U Coll Liberal Arts & Scis Dept of History Detroit MI 48202 E-mail: aa1768@wayne.edu.

EDEN, ALVIN NOAM, pediatrician, writer; b. Bklyn., Mar. 21, 1926; s. Emanuel M. and Rae (Taran) Edelstein; m. Elaine R. Jaffe, Nov. 20, 1952; children: Robert, Elizabeth. BA, Columbia Coll., 1948; MD, Boston U., 1952. Intern Bellevue Hosp., N.Y.C., 1952-53; resident in pediat. Univ. Hosp., N.Y.C., 1953-55; pvt. practice specializing in pediat. Forest Hills, N.Y., 1955—. Assoc. clin. prof. pediat. NYU Sch. Medicine, 1960-84; chmn., dir. dept. pediat. Wyckoff Heights Med. Ctr., Bklyn., 1959—; lectr. SUNY-Downstate Med. Ctr., Bklyn., 1984-86, assoc. clin. prof. pediat., 1986-90; assoc. clin. prof. pediat. Cornell Med. Coll., 1990-99, clin. prof., 1999—. Author: Growing Up Thin, 1975, Handbook for New Parents, 1978, Positive Parenting, 1980, Dr. Eden's Healthy Kids, 1987; contbr. articles to profl. jours.; author text and reference materials. Mem. med. adv. com. YMCA of U.S., 1987—2003. With USMC, 1944-46. Mem. N.Y. Pediatric Soc. (pres. 1980-81), Queens Pediatric Soc. (pres. 1972-73), N.Y. Acad. Medicine (chmn. pediatric sect. 1985-89), Am. Acad. Pediatrics (chmn. nutrition com. chpt. 2 1985-89). Avocation: tennis. Home: 710 Park Ave New York NY 10021-4944 Office: 10721 Queens Blvd Forest Hills NY 11375-4451 Office Phone: 718-261-8989. Personal E-mail: babydoceden@hotmail.com.

EDEN, BARBARA JANIECE, commercial and residential interior designer; b. Inpls., Oct. 14, 1951; d. Justin January and Marjorie May (Miller) E.; m. Stephen A. Bowman, Oct. 25, 1975; children: Christopher Eden Bowman, Jessica Eden Bowman. BA, Purdue U., 1973. Interior design dir. Bohlen, Meyer, Gibson & Assoc., Indpls., 1973-78; interior designer, sole propr. Barbara Eden Design, Indpls., 1978-85; pres., prin. designer Eden Design Assocs., Inc., Carmel, Ind., 1985-97, Carson Design Assocs. Design/Project Mgmt./ Mktg., Carmel, Ind., 1997—. Past mem. accreditation team Found. for Interior Design Edn. Rsch. (FIDER); past mem. adv. bd. Purdue U. Interior Design Dept.; bd. dirs. Hamilton County Intercultural Svcs. Prin. projects include wheelchair accessible bathroom Kohler (Wis.) Design Ctr., United Airlines, Indpls. Maintenance Ctr., N.Am. hdqrs. Brightpoint, Inc., Plainfield, Ind., Peabody Retirement Ctr., North Manchester, Ind., Oakwood Inn, Syracuse, Ind., Resort Condominiums, Internat., Carmel, Ind., Merchants' Pointe, Carmel, restaurant, retail & office devel., arch., interior design; also corp., healthcare, schs., univs., librs., sr. living and residential interior design, space planning and project mgmt. Mem. Internat. Facility Mgrs. Assn., Internat. Interior Design Assn., Illuminating Engring. Soc., Carmel Clay C. of C. (mem. exec. bd., chair edn. com., Small Bus. Person of Yr. 1993). Avocations: hiking, horseback riding, travel. Office: Carson Design Assocs 2325 Pointe Pkwy 200 Carmel IN 46032-3283 E-mail: edenbj@carsondesign.com.

EDEN, F. BROWN, artist; b. Jericho Center, Vt., Oct. 10, 1916; d. Arthur Castle and Eva Merita (Lowrey) Brown; m. Edwin Winfield Eden, Sept. 4, 1937; m. Allan L. Day, July 11, 1994 (dec.); children: Donna Jean, Sandra Elizabeth, Kathy Lynn. Student, U. Fla. Extension, 1955—59, U. Mich., 1963. Art instr. Ann Arbor (Mich.) City Club, 1962-63; tchr., oil painting, printmaking Jacksonville (Fla.) Art Mus., 1963-68. One-woman shows include The Fox Galleries, Atlanta, 1986, Harmon Galleries, Sarasota, 1987, 1989—90, 1992—93, Gallery Contemporanea, Jacksonville, Artist Assocs. Gallery, Atlanta, 1965—90, The Hodgell Gallery, Sarasota, 1997—2002, The Center, Ponte Vedra, Fla., 1998, Kent Campus Gallery, Fla. C.C., Jacksonville, 1999, Represented in permanent collections Fed. Res. Bank Atlanta, Bank Am., Coca-Cola, So. Bell, Sheraton Corp., AT&T, Trust Co. Ga., Shell Oil Co., Touche Ross, Cooper and Lybrand, Delta Airlines "Crown Rm.", 5th Dist. Ct. Appeals Bldg., Daytona Beach, Fla., Edwin and Ruth Kennedy Mus. Am. Art, U. Ohio, Athens, exhibited in group shows at Ala. Nat. Watercolors, Fla., Ga., nationally, exhibitions include Am. Painters in Paris, 1975—76, Painters in Casein and Acrylics, N.Y.C. Chmn. area VI Fla. Artist Group, Jacksonville Mus. Art, 1979—89. Recipient Painting of Yr. award, Mead Co., 1962—63, First award, Fla. Artist Group, 1971, 1979, Fla. Artists, 1969, The Painting award, Maj. Fla. Artists, 1979, others. Mem.: Fla. Crown Treasures, Fla. Artists Jacksonville, Jackson Coalition of Visual Artists, Ala. Watercolor Soc., Ga. Watercolor Soc., Fla. Watercolor Soc. (Signature artist), So. Watercolor Soc., Nat. Mus. of Women in Arts (charter), Am. Women Artists. Avocation: playing organ. Home: 5375 Sanders Rd Jacksonville FL 32277-1333

EDEN, GREGORY, musician, educator; BA, UCLA, 1994; JD, U. San Francisco, 1997; MusM, Johns Hopkins U., 2003. Grad. instr. U. Minn., Mpls., 2003—. Musician: (recital) Guitar Recital of Works by Bach, Villa-Lobos, Granados, and Sor, 1997, Guitar Recital of Works by Bach, Torroba, Dowland, Martin, and Barrios, 2002, Guitar Recital of Works by Sor, Berkeley, Turina, Argento, and Albeniz, 2003, Guitar Recital of Works by Bach, Barrios, and Ponce, 2004. Recipient Music History award, U. Nebr., Omaha, 2000; Peabody grantee, Peabody Inst. of Johns Hopkins U., 2003. Mem.: Minn. Guitar Soc. Avocations: art, travel, movies. Office: U Minn 2106 4th St S Minneapolis MN 55455 Office Phone: 612-624-5740. Personal E-mail: eden0015@umn.edu.

EDEN, JAMES GARY, electrical engineer, educator, physicist, researcher; b. Washington, Oct. 11, 1950; s. Robert Otis and Joyce (West) Eden; m. Carolyn Sue Thomas, June 10, 1972; children: Robert Douglas, Laura Ann, Katherine Joy. BS, U. Md., 1972; MS, U. Ill., 1973, PhD, 1976. Rsch. asst. U. Ill., Urbana, 1972—75, asst. prof. elec. engring. dept., 1979—81, assoc. prof., 1981—83, prof. elec. engring. dept. and rsch. prof. Coordinated Sci. Lab, 1983—, rsch. prof. Micro and Nanotech. Lab., 2000—, dir. Lab. for Optical Physics and Engring., 1995—, affiliate faculty materials sci. and engring., assoc. vice-chancellor rsch., 2000—03, asst. dean Coll. Engring., 1992—93, assoc. dean. Grad. Coll., 1994—96; postdoctoral rsch. assoc. NRC, Washington, 1975—76; rsch. physicist U.S. Naval Rsch. Lab., Washington, 1976—79. Mem. tech. adv. bd. Anvik Corp., Hawthorne, NY, Caviton, Inc., Urbana; assoc. mem. Ctr. Advanced Study U. Ill., 1987—88; mem. program com. Conf. Lasers and Electro-Optics, 1982, 83, 88, 89, 1994—97; co-founder, chmn. Conf. Ultraviolet Lasers Engring. Found., 1987, co-chair Conf. Ultraviolet Lasers, 90, 94; program chair annual meeting IEEE Lasers and Electro-Optics Soc., 1990, conf. chair, 92, mem. program com., 1988—2005; mem. adv. bd. Chem. Vapor Deposition, 1995—2003, CRC Handbook Series Laser Sci. and Tech., 1996—; cons. Wilson, Sonsini, Goodrich, and Rosati, Palo Alto, Calif., 1996—2003, Morrison & Foerster, Palo Alto, 1998—2000, Alexandria, Va., 2003—04, San Francisco, 2003—04, Smart and Biggar, Ottawa, Canada, 1999—2000; program chair Interdisciplinary Laser Sci. Conf., 1990, conf. chair, 92. Author: Photochemical Vapor Deposition, 1992, Gas Laser Technology, 2000; editor: IEEE Jour. Quantum Electronics, 1996—2002; assoc. editor: Photonics Tech. Letters, 1988—94; contbr. chapters to books, more than 200 articles to profl. jours. Recipient Rsch. Publ. award, Naval Rsch. Lab., 1978, Beckman Rsch. award, U. Ill., 1988, IBM Rsch. award, 1994, Faculty Outstanding Tchg. award, Dept. Elec. and Computer Engring., U. Ill., 2000; James F. Towey Univ. scholar, U. Ill., 1996—99. Fellow: IEEE (3d Millennium medal 2000), Am. Phys. Soc., Optical Soc. Am.; mem.: IEEE Lasers and Electro-Optic Soc. (bd. govs. 1991—93, v.p. tech. affairs 1993—95, pres. 1998, Disting. Svc. award 1996, Disting. Lectr. 2003—05, Aron Kressel award 2005), Phi Kappa Phi, Eta Kappa Nu, Tau Beta Pi, Sigma Xi. Achievements include patents for 22 inventions. Home: 314 County Rd 2650 N Mahomet IL 61853-9579 Office: U Ill Everitt Lab 1406 W Green St Urbana IL 61801-2918 Office Phone: 217-333-4157. Business E-Mail: jgeden@uiuc.edu.

EDEN, MURRAY, electrical engineer, emeritus educator; b. Bklyn., Aug. 17, 1920; s. Emanuel and Rae (Taran) Edelstein; m. Patricia Warnock, Sept. 16, 1962; stepchildren: Shirley Hartle McDaniel, John W. Hartle; children by previous marriage: Abigail, Susanna, Mark D. BS, CCNY, 1939; MS, U. Md., 1944, PhD, 1951. Phys. chemist Nat. Bur. Stds., 1943-49; biophysicist Nat. Cancer Inst., 1949-53; spl. fellow math. USPHS, Princeton U., 1953-55; biophysicist Nat. Heart Inst., 1955-59; prof. elec. engring. MIT, Cambridge, 1959-79, prof. emeritus, 1979—; adj. prof. elec. engring. Johns Hopkins U., Balt., 1979-81; guest prof. Ecole Polytechnique Federale de Lausanne (Switzerland), 1983, 87; dir. bioengring. and instrumentation program NIH, 1976-94, scientist emeritus, 1994—. Lectr. preventive medicine Harvard Med. Sch., 1960-74, Am. U., 1949-50; adj. prof. environ. health Sch. Pub. Health, Boston U., 1999—; cons. for rsch. to dir. gen. WHO, 1963-74. Author: (with David Rutstein) Engineering and Living Systems, 1970; editor: (with Paul Kolers) Recognizing Patterns, 1968, (with Henry S. Eden) Microcomputers in Patient Care, 1981, (with John W. Boretos) Contemporary Biomaterials for Clinical Care, 1983, (with Leonid Yaroslavsky) Fundamentals of Digital Optics, 1996; editor-in-chief: Information and Control, 1961-84; editor: Methods of Information in Medicine, 1961-82; mem. editl. bd.: Med. Rsch. Engring., 1964-80, Internat. Jour. Health Care Tech. Assessment, 1986-92, Real Time Imaging, 1994-2000; adv. editl. bd.: Linguistic Inquiry, 1970-85. Chmn. U.S. Nat. Com. Engring. in Medicine and Biology, 1967-73. Recipient Med. Soc. medal WHO, 1983, Dirs. award NIH, 1993. Fellow IEEE (chmn. adminstrv. com. group engring. in medicine and biology 1964-66, 87-90, mem. editl. bd. Spectrum 1990-92, mem. press bd. 1993-2001, mem. publs. adv. bd. 1998-2003, Centennial medal 1984), AAAS, Am. Inst. for Med. Biol. Engring. (founding fellow); mem. Am. Physiol. Soc., Biophys. Soc., Am. Soc. for Engring. Edn., Cosmos Club, Sigma Xi, Tau Beta Pi.

EDENFIELD, BERRY AVANT, federal judge; b. Bulloch County, Ga., Aug. 2, 1934; s. Perry and Vera E.; m. Vida Melvis Bryant, Aug. 3, 1963. BBA U. Ga, 1956, LL.B., 1958. Bar: Ga. 1958. Partner firm Allen, Edenfield, Brown & Wright (and predecessors), Statesboro, Ga., 1958-78; judge U.S. Dist. Ct. (so. dist.) Ga., Savannah, 1978-90, chief judge, 1990-97, judge, 1997—. Mem. Ga. Senate, 1965-66. Office: US Dist Ct PO Box 9865 Savannah GA 31412-0065

EDENS, BETTY JOYCE, reading recovery educator; b. Hillsboro, Tex., Oct. 20, 1944; d. Edward Alton and Mary Alma (Pendley) Harbin; m. Eugene Cliett Edens, May 29, 1964; children: Michael Eugene, Anne-Marie DeWitt, Kristen Babovec. BEd, Ind. U., 1985; MS, Tex. A&M of Commerce, 1995. Cert. elem. tchr., reading tchr., Tex. 1st grade tchr. Monday Primary, Kaufman, Tex., 1986-93, Franklin Elem., Hillsboro, Tex., 1993-96, reading recovery tchr., 1994-98, 99-00, 2nd grade tchr., 1998-99; reading recovery tchr. Hillsboro Elem. Sch., 1999—2005, reading specialist 2d and 3d grades, 2005—. Mem. early literacy com. TSRA, 1998, Susan G. Komen Found. Mem. Reading Recovery Coun. of N.Am., Internat. Reading Assn., Tex. Reading Assn., Heritage League hillsboro. Republican. Mem. Ch. of Christ. Avocations: recreational reading, walking, computers. E-mail: edens@hillsboro.net.

EDENS, GARY DENTON, broadcast executive; b. Asheville, N.C., Jan. 6, 1942; s. James Edwin and Pauline Amanda (New) E.; m. Hannah Suellen Walter, Aug. 21, 1965; children: Ashley Elizabeth, Emily Blair. BS, U. N.C., 1964. Account exec. PAMS Prodns., Dallas, 1965-67, Sta. WKIX, Raleigh, N.C., 1967-69; gen. mgr. Sta. KOY, Phoenix, 1970-81; sr. v.p. Harte-Hanks Raido, Inc., Phoenix, 1978-81, pres., CEO, 1981-84; chmn., CEO Edens Broadcasting, Inc., 1984-95. Dir. Citibank Ariz., 1986—, Inter-Tel, Inc., 1994—; chmn. The Hanover Cos., Inc., 1995—; chair fin. seminar Chief Execs. Orgn./World Pres. Orgn., N.Y.C., 1998. Bd. dirs. Valley Big Bros., 1972-80, Ariz. State U. Found., 1979—, COMPAS, 1979—, Men's Arts Coun., 1975-78. Named one of Three Outstanding Young Men, Phoenix Jaycees, 1973; entrepreneurial fellow U. Ariz., 1989; inducted into Ariz. Broadcasters Assn. Hall of Fame, 2000. Mem. Phoenix Execs. Club (pres. 1976), Nat. Radio Broadcasters Assn. (dir. 1981-86), Radio Advt. Bur. (dir. 1981—), Young Pres. Orgn. (chmn. Ariz. chpt. 1989-90), Chief Execs. Orgn., Ariz. Pres. Orgn. Republican. Methodist. Office: 5112 N 40th St Ste 102 Phoenix AZ 85018-2142 E-mail: edens@hanover.com.

EDGAR, HAROLD SIMMONS HULL, legal educator; b. 1942; AB, Harvard U., 1964; LLB, Columbia U., 1967. Bar: N.Y. 1968. Law clk. to judge U.S. Ct. Appeals (D.C. cir.), 1967—68; asst. prof. Columbia U., NYC, 1968—73; Julius Silver prof. law, sci. and tech. Columbia U. Sch. Law, NYC, dir. program in law, sci. and tech., 1985—. Rapporteur UNESCO Internat. Com. on Bioethics, 1992—96; chmn. bd. The Hastings Ctr., 2004—; comdr. Nat. Order Merit, France, 2004. Office: Columbia U Law Sch 435 W 116th St New York NY 10027-7201 Office Phone: 212-854-5059. Business E-Mail: hedgar@law.columbia.edu.

EDGAR, JAMES MACMILLAN, JR., management consultant; b. NYC, Nov. 7, 1936; s. James Macmillan Edgar and Lilyan (McCann) E.; m. Judith Frances Storey, June 28, 1958; children: Suzanne Lynn Randolph, James Macmillan III, Gordon Stuart. B in Chem. Engring., Cornell U., 1959, MBA with distinction, 1960. CPA; cert. mgmt. cons. New product rep. E.I. duPont Nemours, Wilmington, Del., 1960-63, mktg. svcs. rep., 1963-64; with Touche Ross & Co., 1964-78, mgr. Detroit, 1966-68, ptnr. in charge, mgt. svcs. ops. for No. Calif. and Hawaii San Francisco, 1971-78, ptnr. Western regional mgmt. svcs., 1978; sr. ptnr. Edgar, Dunn & Co., San Francisco, 1978-2000; ind. mgmt. cons., 2000—. Bd. dirs. Assoc. Oreg. Industries Svcs. Corp.; ptnr. Global Brand Positioning LLC, 2001—; owner Western Sport Shop, San Rafael, Calif., Santa Rosa, Calif. Patentee nonwoven fabrice. Active San Francisco Mayor's Fin. Adv. Com., 1976-2001, exec. com., 1978-2001, Blue Ribbon com. for Bus., 1987-88, Alumnae Resources adv. bd., 1986-94, San Francisco Planning and Urban Rsch. Bd., 1986-89, adv. bd., 1989-93; alumni exec. coun. Johnson Grad. Sch. Mgmt. Cornell U., Cornell Coun., 1970-73; steering com. Bay Area Coun., 1989-95, program adv. com., 1996-2001, bd. dirs., 1999-2001; chmn. San Francisco Libr. Found., 1989-96; bd. dirs. Rosenberg Found., 1996-2004, chmn. bd. dirs., 2001-02; bd. dirs. Harding Lawson Assoc. Group, 1996-2000, Golden Gate U., 1997-99; mem. San Francisco Com. on Jobs, 1994-2000. Recipient Merit award for outstanding pub. svc. City and County of San Francisco, 1978, Honor award for outstanding contbns. to profl. mgmt. Johnson Grad. Sch. Mgmt., Cornell U., 1978. Mem. AICPA, Assn. Corp. Growth (v.p. membership San Francisco chpt. 1979-81, v.p. programs 1981-82, pres. 1982-83, nat. bd. dirs. 1983-86), Calif. Soc. CPAs, Inst. Mgmt. Cons. (regional v.p. 1973-80, bd. dirs. 1975-77, v.p. 1977-80), San Francisco C. of C. (bd. dirs. 1987-89, 1991-2003, mem. exec. com. 1988-89, 91-95, chmn. mktg. San Francisco program 1991-92, membership devel. 1993, chmn. bd. dirs. 1994, dir. emeritus 1995-2003), Pacific Union Club, Marin Rod and Gun Club, Tau Beta Pi. Home: 10 Buckeye Way San Rafael CA 94904-2602 Office: James Edgar Mgmt Cons 10 Buckeye Way Kentfield CA 94904-2602 Office Phone: 415-279-4107. Personal E-mail: jedgarconsulting@aol.com, jedgar7777@aol.com.

EDGAR, JANELLE DIANE WARD, financial services executive; b. Albany, Ga., Aug. 27, 1955; d. John David and Margaret Irene (Curtis) Ward; m. James Curtis Edgar, July 7, 1973; children: Lauren Marie, William Robert. BA, Marymount U., 1989. Treas. specialist Fed. Home Loan Mortgage Corp., Washington, 1977-81; mgr. cash acctg. Pentagon Fed. Credit Union, Alexandria, Va., 1981-84; mgr. bus. devel. Fin. Technologies, Inc., Alexandria, 1984-85; v.p. ops. Continental Fed. Savs. Bank, Fairfax, Va., 1985-88; v.p. corp. ops. and info. svcs. Md. Nat. Bank/Am. Security Bank, Washington, 1988-89; dir. mktg. NRC, McLean, Va., 1990-91; dir. mktg. cash mgmt. div. Fin. Mgmt. Svcs. Dept. U.S. Treasury, 1991-98; dir. bus. devel. Diversinet Corp., McLean, Va., 1998—2000; v.p. Sun Trust Bank, 2000—03, Nat. City Bank, 2003—. Mem. tech. and ops. com. Internet, Inc., Reston, Va., 1986-88. Adv. The Women's Ctr. of No. Va., Vienna, 1987; deacon Little Falls Presbyn. Ch. Mem. Washington Cash Mgmt. Assn., Mid-Atlantic Clearing House Assn. (rep. Va. League Savs. to bd. dirs. 1987-88), Bank Adminstrn. Inst. (bd. dirs. 1989-90), Nat. Corp. Cash Mgmt. Assn., Nat. Automated Clearing House Assn. (rules and ops. com.). Republican. Presbyterian. Avocations: ice skating, reading, kayaking, kick-boxing. Office: Nat City Bank 20 Stanwix St Pittsburgh PA 15222 also: 322 6th St Oakmont PA 15139-1715

EDGAR, JIM, former governor; b. Vinita, Okla., July 22, 1946; m. Brenda Smith; children: Brad, Elizabeth. Grad., Eastern Ill. U., 1968; postgrad., U. Ill., Sangamon State U., 1971-74. Legis. intern pres. pro tem Ill. Senate, 1968; key asst. to speaker ho. Ill. Ho. of Reps., 1972-73; aide to pres. Ill. Senate, 1974, to ho. minority leader, 1976; mem. Ill. Ho. of Reps., 1977-79; dir. legis. affairs Ill. Gov., 1979-80; sec. state State of Ill., 1981-91; gov. State of Ill., 1991-98; disting. fellow Inst. Govt. and Publs. U. Ill., Urbana, 1999—. Co-lead gov. Nat. Gov.'s Assn. Transp. Com., 1995-96; chair Edn. Commn. of States, 1993-94; chair Nat. Gov.'s Assn. Com. on Econ. Devel. and Commerce, 1992-93; pres. Coun. State Govts., 1992-93; chair Gov.'s Ethanol Coalition, 1992-93; chair Nat. Gov.'s Assn. Com. on Econ. Devel. and Tech. Innovation, 1991-92. Precinct committeeman, treas. Coles County Rep. Com., 1974; dir. state svc. Nat. Conf. State Legislatures, 1975, 76; mem. campaign com. Ill. Ho. of Reps.; pres. Nat. Assn. Secs. of State, 1988; exec. com. Coun. State Govts., 1988, v.p. exec. com., 1991, pres., 1992-93; bd. dirs. Nat. Commn. Against Drunk Driving, 1989; chmn. Ill. Literacy Coun., 1989; chmn. Edn. Commn. of the States, 1993-94; chmn. Gov.'s Ethanol Coalition, 1992-93; pres. Bd. Coun. State Govts. Mem. Nat. Govs. Assn. (chmn. econ. devel. and commerce com. 1992-93, strategic planning rev. task force 1991—, past chmn. task force on edn., mem. edn. goals panel, chair com. econ. devel. and technol. innovation 1991-92, edn. commn. of states 1993-94, co-lead gov. transp. com. 1995-96), Coles County Hist. Soc. (pres. 1976-79). Baptist. Office: U Ill Inst Govt and Pub Affairs 1007 W Nevada St # MC-037 Urbana IL 61801-3812*

EDGAR, REBECCA SUE, English language educator; b. Flint, Mich., Jan. 19, 1977; d. Charles Hubert Roy and Judith Ann Cole; m. Kenneth Allen Edgar, Jr., Aug. 14, 1999; 1 child, Lucas Allen. BA, U. Mich., 2000, M of Reading, 2004. Tchr. English Flint Cen. H.S. Flint Comty. Schs., 2000—. Adviser Student Coun., Flint, 2000—. Recipient grad. scholarship, U. Mich., 2003. Mem.: NEA, Mich. Edn. Assn. Avocations: running, travel, writing, camping, reading.

EDGAR, R(OBERT) ALLAN, federal judge; b. Munising, Mich., Oct. 6, 1940; s. Robert Richard and Jean Lillian (Hansen) E.; m. Frances Gail Martin, Mar. 30, 1968; children: Amy Elizabeth, Laura Anne. BA, Davidson Coll., 1962; LLB, Duke U., 1965. Bar: Tenn. 1965. From assoc. to ptnr. Miller & Martin, Chattanooga, 1967-85; judge US Dist. Ct. (ea. dist.) Tenn., Chattanooga, 1985—, chief judge, 1999—. Mem. Tenn. Ho. of Reps., Nashville, 1970-72, Tenn. Wildlife Resources Commn., Nashville, 1979-85. Served to capt. U.S. Army, 1966-67, Vietnam. Decorated Bronze Star, 1967. Mem. Fed. Bar Assn., Chattanooga Bar Assn. Episcopalian. Office: US Dist Ct PO Box 1748 960 Georgia Ave Chattanooga TN 37402-2220

EDGAR, RUTH R., retired elementary school educator; b. Great Falls, S.C., Jan. 7, 1930; d. Robert Hamer and Clara Elizabeth (Ellenberg) Rogers. AA, Stephens Coll., Columbia, Mo., 1949; BS, So. Meth. U., 1951; MA, Appalachian State U., Boone, N.C., 1977; postgrad., Limestone Coll., Gaffney, S.C., 1971. Lic. real estate salesman, broker. Home economist Lone Star Gas Co., Dallas, 1951-53, So. Union Gas Co., Austin, Tex., 1953-56, Southwestern Pub. Svc. Co., Amarillo, Tex., 1956-57; with Peeler Real Estate, 1970-71, Burns High Sch., Lawndale, N.C., 1971-73, Cen. Cleveland Mid. Sch., Lawndale, 1973-77, Burns Jr. High Sch., Lawndale, 1977-88; resource tchr. South Cleveland Elem. Sch., Shelby, N.C., 1988-90, Elizabeth Elem. Sch., Shelby, 1990-94, Washington Elem. Sch., Waco, N.C., 1990-92; ret., 1994. Mem. supts. adv. coun., Cleveland County, 1971-75, Cleveland County Art Soc., 1972-73, Cen. United Meth. Ch. Home: 401 Forest Hill Dr Shelby NC 28150-5520

EDGAR, THOMAS FLYNN, chemical engineering professor; b. Bartlesville, Okla., Apr. 17, 1945; s. Maurice Russell and Natalie (Flynn) E.; m. Donna Jean Proffitt, July 15, 1967; children: Rebecca, Jeffrey. BS in Chem. Engring., U. Kans., 1967; PhD in Chem. Engring., Princeton U., 1971. Registered profl. engr., Tex. Process engr. Conoco, Balt., 1968-69; prof. chem. engring. U. Tex., Austin, 1971—, chmn. dept., 1985-93, Abell chair, 1991—, assoc. dean engring., 1993-96, assoc. v.p. acad. computing, 1996-2001; prof. chem. engring. U. Calif., Berkeley, 1978. Pres. CACHE Corp., Austin, Tex., 1981-84, exec. officer, 2000-; pres. Am. Automatic Control Coun., Chgo., 1990-91; chair Coun. for Chem. Rsch., Washington, 1992-93. Author: Coal Processing and Pollution Control, 1983; co-author: Real Time Computing, 1982, Optimization of Chemical Processes, 1988, 2d edit., 2001, Process Dynamics and Control, 1989, 2d edit., 2004; editor: Chemical Process Control, 1981, In Situ (Marcel Dekker), 1977-89; also jours. Recipient Edn. award Am. Automatic Control Coun., 1992, IFAC Control Engring. prize, 2005. Fellow AIChE (Outstanding Counselor award 1975, Colburn award 1980, Computing in Chem. Engring. award 1995, editl. bd.

jour. 1983-85, 03-, chmn. cast divsn. 1986, bd. dirs. 1989-92, v.p. 1996, pres. 1997, chair bd. dirs. Found. 2000—); mem. Am. Soc. Engring. Edn. (Westinghouse award 1988, Meriam-Wiley Disting. Author 1990, Chem. Engring. Divsn. Leadership award 1996, fellow 2005), Instrument Soc. Am. (Eckman Edn. award 1993), Am. Chem. Soc., Tau Beta Pi, Phi Lambda Upsilon, Omicron Delta Kappa, Phi Kappa Phi (Joe King award U. Tex. 1989, U. Kans. Disting. Engring. Svc. award 1990). Democrat. Methodist.

EDGAR, WALTER BELLINGRATH, historian, educator; b. Mobile, Ala., Dec. 10, 1943; s. Ernest, Jr. and Amelia E.; m. Elizabeth Giles, Aug. 6, 1966; children: Eliza, Amelia. AB, Davidson Coll., (N.C.), 1965; MA, U. S.C., 1967, PhD, 1969; LLD (hon.), Coker Coll., 1999; HLD (hon.), Coastal Carolina U., 2001; LLD (hon.), Davidson Coll., 2003. From asst. prof. to prof. history U. S.C., Columbia, 1974—, dir. Inst. So. Studies, 1980—, Neuffer prof. so. studies, 1995—, George Washington Disting. prof. history, 1999—. Author: History of Santee Cooper, 1984, South Carolina in the Modern Age, 1992, South Carolina: A History, 1998, Partisans and Redcoats, 2001; editor: The Letterbook of Robert Pringle, 1972, A Southern Renascence Man: Views of Robert Penn Warren, 1984. Served to capt. U.S. Army, 1969-71; col. Res. Decorated Bronze Star, Legion of Merit; Nat. Hist. Publs. Commn. fellow, 1971-72. Mem. The Hist. Soc., So. Hist. Assn., SC Hist. Assn. (pres. 1982-83), SC Hist. Soc. (bd. mgrs. 2000—, pres. 2005-), South Caroliniana Soc. (pres. 1984-87), Blue Key, Omicron Delta Kappa, Phi Alpha Theta. Home: 1731 Hollywood Dr Columbia SC 29205-3215 Office: U SC Inst So Studies Columbia SC 29208-0001 Office Phone: 803-777-2340.

EDGE, JAMES EDWARD, health care administrator; b. Anacortes, Wash., Apr. 29, 1948; s. Edward and Carol Marie (Lian) E.; m. Nellie Ruth Horton, Mar. 21, 1970; children: Elissa Marie, Gina Dawn. BS in Pharmacy, U. Wash., 1971; MPH, U. Hawaii, 1979. Registered pharmacist. Commd. USPHS, 1969-2000, advanced through grades to capt.; staff pharmacist USPHS Indian Hosp., Albuquerque, 1971-73; chief pharmacy, lab/x-ray S.W. Indian Poly. Inst., Albuquerque, 1972-73, Neah Bay Indian Health Ctr., Wash., 1973-75; svc. unit dir. Neah Bay Svc. Unit, Indian Health Svc., 1975-78, Western Oreg. Service Unit, Indian Health Svc., Salem, 1980-2000; mgr. policy unit Office of Med. Assistance Programs, State of Oreg., Salem, 2000—02; dep. state Medicaid dir. State of Oreg., 2003—. Cons. in field. Active Combined Fed. Campaign, Salem, 1985-2000. John Quick Pharmacy scholar, U. Wash., 1967, Health Professions scholar, 1969. Mem. APHA, Am. Coll. Healthcare Adminstrs., Am. Acad. Med. Adminstrs., Assn. Mil. Surgeons U.S., Mensa, Res. Officers Assn., Commd. Officer USPHS, Wash. Pharm. Assn., nat. Coun. Svc. Unit Dirs. (chmn. 1986-88). Avocations: running, sculling. Office: PO Box 932 Salem OR 97308 Personal E-mail: jeedge@aol.com.

EDGE, JOE D., lawyer; b. Birmingham, Ala., 1948; BSEE, Auburn Univ., 1970; JD, Univ. Ala., 1973; LLM, George Washington Univ., 1976. Bar: Ala. 1973, DC 1975. Trial atty. FCC, 1974—75; gen. counsel General Communication, Inc., Alaska, 1985—88; ptnr., bus., fin. dept. Drinker Biddle & Reath LLP, Washington, and head, comm. law practice group. Mem.: Am. Econ. Assn., IEEE. Office: Drinker Biddle & Reath LLP Ste 1100 1500 K St NW Washington DC 20005-1209 Office Phone: 202-842-8809. Office Fax: 202-842-8465. Business E-Mail: joe.edge@dbr.com.

EDGE, KATHRYN REED, lawyer; b. Birmingham, Ala., Feb. 15, 1946; d. William Alvin and Charlotte Rowena (Rickles) Reed; m. Michael Wayne Edge, Aug. 18, 1967 (div. 1979); 1 child: Michael Lawrence. BA, Peabody Coll., 1967; JD, Nashville Sch. Law, 1983. Bar: Tenn. 1983. Staff atty. Tenn. Dept. Fin. Instns., Nashville, 1983—, gen. counsel/asst. commr., dep. commr.; ptnr. Miller & Martin, Nashville, 1994—. Instr. law Nashville Sch. Law, 1995—; co-chair Tenn. Supreme Ct. Commn. on Gender Fairness, 1994—; past mem. adv. bd. So. Banking Law Conf. Contbr. articles to profl. jours. Mem. Tenn. Dem. Party Compliance Counsel, 1998—; mem. bd. trustees W. End United Meth.; mem. Nashville Sch. Law fundraising com., Tenn. Bankers Assn. lawyers com., 1997—, govt. rels. com., 1997—; mem. bd. Ctr. for Non-Profit Mgmt., Legal Aid Soc. of Mid. Tenn. and the Cumberlands; mem. chmn. bd. Neighborhood Justice Ctr. Recipient cert. of appreciation Tenn. Supreme Ct., 1996. Mem. ABA (mem. bus. law sect., banking law com., former chair subcom. on state banking law devels.; mem. commn. on pub. understanding about the law, Achievement award young lawyers divsn. 1992-93), Am. Bar Found., Tenn. Bar Assn. (pres. 2000-01, bd. govs. 1993—, mem. exec. com., v.p. 1993—, mem. editl. bd. TBALink 1996—, mem. publs. com. 1996—, fin. com. 1993—, treas. 1993-97, mid. Tenn. gov. 1997-98, chair bar ctr. and capital campaign com. 1998-99, chair drafting com. on policy on response to unjust criticism of the judiciary 1997-98, chair commn. on women and minorities in the profn. 1992-93, mem. 1993-97, mem. pub. edn. about judiciary com., participant Tenn. Conclave on Legal Edn. 1997, Pres.'s award for svc. 1996), Tenn. Lawyers Assn. for Women (charter mem., pres. 1990-91, editor IN RE TLAW 1997), Nashville Bar Assn. (past chair Nashville lawyers concerned for lawyers com., mem. bar mentoring com. 1995-98, chair 1997-98), Lawyers Assn. for Women, (Marion Griffin chpt., Nashville; pres. 1987-88), Tenn. Bar Found., Nashville Bar Found. (mem. grant rev. com. 1995-98, mem. history project com. 1998—), Harry Phillips Am. Inn of Ct. Democrat. United Methodist. Avocations: reading poetry, photography, dogs. Office: Miller & Martin LLP One Nashville Pl 150 4th Ave N Nashville TN 37219 E-mail: kedge@millermartin.com.

EDGE, RONALD DOVASTON, physics professor; b. Bolton, Eng., Feb. 3, 1929; arrived in U.S., 1958, naturalized, 1968; s. James and Mildred (Davies) E.; m. Margaret Skulina, Aug. 14, 1956 (div. 1989); children: Christopher James, Michael Dovaston; m. Gertrude Hansen, Dec. 31, 1992. BA, Cambridge U., 1950, MA, 1952, PhD, 1956. Rsch. fellow Australian Nat. U., Canberra, 1954-58; asst. then assoc. prof. physics U. S.C., Columbia, 1958-63, prof., 1964-94, disting. prof. emeritus, 1994—. Rsch. assoc. Yale U., New Haven, 1963-64; vis. prof. Stanford U., Calif. Tech. Inst., U. Munich, U. Sussex, U. Witwatersrand, U. Aarhus, Oak Ridge Nat. Lab., Los Alamos Nat. Lab.; leader 1st Am. team Internat. Physics Olympiad, 1986; judge Internat. Young Physicists Tournament, 1999, 2001. Author: Physics in the Arts, 1973, String and Sticky Tape Experiments, 1978; contbr. articles to profl. jours. Recipient Russell award U. S.C., Guy And Rebecca Forman award tchg. Physics, Vanderbilt U., 1998. Fellow Am. Phys. Soc. (James B. Pegram award 1979), Am. Assn. Physics Tchrs. (apparatus award 1973, v.p. 1995, pres. elect 1996, pres. 1997). Unitarian (past pres. Columbia fellowship) Home: 220 Jadetree Dr Hopkins SC 29061-9347 Office: U SC Physics Dept Columbia SC 29208-0001 Personal E-mail: redge@sc.rr.com.

EDGEIN, DANIEL R., social studies educator; s. Rennie C. and Elaine M. Edgein; m. Ali Edgein, July 5, 2003. BS in Edn., Kent State U. Tchr. social studies Tuslaw Local Schs., Massillon, Ohio, 1995—. V.p. planning & zoning commn. City of Louisville, Ohio, 2003—; mem. Louisville YMCA Facilities Commn. Mem.: Leopard Touchdown Club. Home: 822 Overlook St Louisville OH 44641 Office: Tuslaw Local Schs 1847 Manchester Ave Massillon OH 44647

EDGERLY, WILLIAM SKELTON, banker; b. Lewiston, Maine, Feb. 18, 1927; s. Stuart and Florence (Skelton) E.; m. Lois Stiles, June 12, 1948; children: Leonard Stuart, Stephanie Lois. BS in Econs. and Engring., MIT, 1949; MBA, Harvard U., 1955. With Eastman Kodak Co., 1949-50; with Cabot Corp., Boston, 1952-75, fin. v.p., 1969-75, also dir.; chief exec. officer State St. Corp., 1975-91, chmn., 1992, chmn. emeritus, 1993—. Bd. dirs., former chmn. Met. Boston Housing Partnership, Fed. Res. Bank Boston, Depository Trust Co., N.Y.C., Arkwright-Boston Ins. Co.; life mem. emeritus MIT Corp. Bd. fellows Harvard Med. Sch.; bd. dirs. Jobs for Mass., former pres.; dir. Boston Pvt. Industry Coun., former chmn.; bd. dirs. Inst. for Fgn. Policy Analysis and Pioneer Inst.; trustee Com. Econ. Devel., The Gen. Hosp. Corp.; former mem. fed. adv. coun. Fed. Res. Bd., Washington. With USNR, 1945-46, 50-52. Fellow Am. Acad. Arts and Scis.; mem. MIT Alumni Assn. (pres. 1973-74), Harvard Bus. Sch. Assn., Assn. Res. City Bankers, Boston Econ. Club, Somerset Club, Cambridge Boat Club. Office: 124 Mount Auburn St Cambridge MA 02138-5758

EDGERTON, BRADFORD WHEATLY, plastic surgeon; b. Phila., May 8, 1947; s. Milton Thomas and Patricia Jane (Jones) E.; children: Bradford Wheatly Jr., Lauren Harrington; m. Louise Dungan Edgerton; stepchildren: Catherine Kelleher, Robert Kelleher. BA in Chemistry, Vanderbilt U., 1969, MD, 1973. Diplomate Am. Bd. Plastic Surgery, Am. Bd. Hand Surgery. Intern U. Calif., San Francisco, 1973-74; resident U. Va., Charlottesville, 1974-78; resident in plastic surgery Columbia-Presbyn., N.Y., 1979-81; fellow in hand surgery NYU, 1981-82, clin. instr. plastic surgery, 1981-89; ptnr. So. Calif. Permanente Med. Group, L.A., 1989—; assoc. prof. clin. plastic surgery U. So. Calif., L.A., 1989—. Mem. Pacific Coun. Internat. Policy. Trustee Harvard-Westlake Sch., L.A., 2001—; pres. Edgerton Found., Beverly Hills, Calif, 2001-. Mem. Am. Assn. Hand Surgery, Am. Soc. Plastic and Reconstructive Surgery, Am. Soc. Surgery of Hand, L.A. (Calif.) Tennis Club, L.A. (Calif.) Country Club Episcopal. Home: 494 S Spalding Dr Beverly Hills CA 90212-4104 Office: 6041 Cadillac Ave Los Angeles CA 90034-1702

EDGERTON, DEBRA, artist, educator; b. Junction City, Kans., Mar. 15, 1958; d. Hughes and Tamie E.; m. Terry Baxter, Apr. 13, 1991; children: Noah Hunter, Jesse Dylan. Student, Am. Acad. Art, Chgo., 1979; BFA, U. Kans., 1980; MFA, Vermont Coll., 2003. Artist Hallmark Cards, Kansas City, Mo., 1981-86; freelance artist Flagstaff, Ariz., 1986—. Instr's. asst in printmaking U. Kans., Lawrence, 1987, instr. painting Lawrence Art Ctr., 1991-93, Sr. Citizen Ctr., Lawrence, 1992, No. Ariz. U., Flagstaff, 1993—. Exhibited in group shows Tex. Watercolor Soc., Ann. Allied Artists of Am. 86th Ann. Exhbn., Midwest Watercolor Soc. Ann. Transparent Exhbn., Am. Watercolor Soc.'s Ann. Exhbn., Nat. Watercolor Soc.'s Ann. Exhbn. Mem. Round Table for Arts, Lawrence, 1991-92; mayoral appointee Lawrence Art Commn., 1992-93; pres. Lawrence Art Guild Assn., 1992. Recipient Excellence award Geary County Sch. Dist., 1991, Merit award Ariz. Aqueous, 1994; Profl. Devel. grantee Kans. Art Commn., 1992, Tech. Asst. grantee Lawrence Arts Commn., 1992; Dolan Found. scholar, 2001; San Francisco Art Inst. Grad. fellow, 2001. Mem. Am. Watercolor Soc., Nat. Watercolor Soc., Allied Artists Am., Midwest Watercolor Soc. (life). Office: No Ariz U PO Box 6020 Flagstaff AZ 86011-0001

EDGERTON, ROBERT BRECKENRIDGE, anthropologist, educator; b. Maywood, Ill., Nov. 28, 1931; s. Robert Alfred and Marjorie Adelaide (Close) E.; m. Karen Ito. PhD, UCLA, 1960. Faculty dept. psychiatry UCLA, 1962—, prof., 1996—. Author: The Cloak of Competence, 1967, Rules, Exceptions and Social Order, 1985, Sick Societies, 1992, Death or Glory, 1999, Hidden Heroism, 2001, Remember the Maine: To Hell with Spain, 2004. Sgt. USAF, 1951-54. Am. Assn. on Mental Deficiency Rsch. awardee, 1976; recipient Career Rsch. award Acad. Mental Retardation, 1995. Fellow AAAS, Am. Assn. Arts and Scis.; mem. Soc. for Med. Anthropology (pres. 1976-77), Soc. for Psychol. Anthropology (pres. 1985-86). Office: UCLA Dept Psychiatry Los Angeles CA 90024 Office Phone: 301-794-3754.

EDGERTON, WINFIELD DOW, retired gynecologist; b. Caruthersville, Mo., Nov. 8, 1924; s. Winfield Dow and Anna Kathryn (Hale) E.; m. Rose Marie Cahill, June 24, 1945; 1 child, Winfield Dow Student, Central Coll., Fayette, Mo., 1942-44; MD, Washington U., St. Louis, 1947. Intern St. Luke's Hosp., St. Louis, 1947-48; resident Chgo. Lying-In Hosp., 1948-49, Free Hosp. for Women, Brookline, Mass., 1951, U.S. Naval Hosp., Chelsea, Mass., 1951-53; practice medicine specializing in obstetrics and gynecology Davenport, Iowa, 1955-87; clin. asst. prof. obstetrics and gynecology U. Iowa Coll. Medicine, 1971-78, clin. assoc. prof., 1979-82, clin. prof., 1982—; ret., 2000. Mem. staff, med. dir. Maternal Health Ctr. St. Luke's Hosp. (name changed to Edgerton Women's Health Ctr.), 1972-2000. Contbr. articles to med. jours. and texts Served to lt. M.C., USN, 1949-55 Fellow Am. Coll. Obstetricians and Gynecologists (past chmn. Iowa sect.), Royal Soc. Medicine; mem. Central Assn. Obstetricians and Gynecologists, Am. Fertility Soc., Am. Assn. Gynecologic Laparoscopists (past trustee), Gynecologic Laser Soc., AMA, Iowa Med. Soc., Scott County Med. Soc. (past pres.) Republican. Congregationalist. Home: 4 Lombard Ct Davenport IA 52803-2348

EDGETT, WILLIAM MALOY, lawyer, arbitrator; b. Balt., Feb. 26, 1927; s. Eugene Albert and Priscilla Ruff (Streett) E.; m. Bronwen Winifred Reese, Nov. 25, 1950. AA, Towson State Coll., 1949; BA, U. Md., 1951, JD, 1959; LL.M., Georgetown U., 1970. Bar: Md. bar 1959. Asst. personnel mgr. Am. Sugar Refining Co., Balt., 1951-55; supr. indsl. relations Westinghouse Electric Co., Balt., 1955-61; sr. labor relations specialist Martin Co., Balt., 1961-64; asst. mgr. indsl. relations Md. Shipbuilding and Drydock Co., Balt., 1964-67; pvt. practice law, 1967—. Asst. prof. Towson State U., 1971-72 Mem. Md. Commn. Nursing, 1974-76; chmn. pub. law bds. Nat. Mediation Bd., 1971—; neutral mem. Nat. R.R. Adjustment Bd., 1971— . Served to staff sgt. USAAF, 1944-46. Mem. ABA. Nat. Acad. Arbitrators, Am. Arbitration Assn., Am., Roster Arbitrators Fed. Mediation and Conciliation Service. Home and Office: 200 Hampton Cir Bluffton SC 29909-5018

EDGHILL, VERNESE ELAINE, director; b. St Michael, Barbados, Barbados, June 16, 1965; d. Clifford Arthur and Grace Vernese Alexandria Edghill. BA, Bucknell U., Lewisburg, Pa, 1987; M of Edn., U. of Del., 1992. Minority student advisor Franklin and Marshall Coll., Lancaster, Pa., 1987—88; asst. dean and dir. of ctr. for black culture U. of Del., Newark, Del., 1988—2000; dir. for diversity Georgetown Day Sch., Washington, 2000—03; grad. assisant Howard U., Washington, 2003. Edni. cons. East Ed Ednl. Svcs., Washington, 2002—03. Chair of the edn. ministry and sch. New Destiny Fellowship, Wilmington, 1995—2000; mem. Christina Cultural Arts Ctr., Wilmington, Del., 1997—99; bd. mem. Lancaster Urban League, Lancaster, Pa., 1987—88. Recipient Del. YMCA Black Achievers award, YMCA, 1995; fellow Grad. Assistantship, Howard U., 2003—. Mem.: Assn. of Coll. Unions Internat. (conf. planning comm. mem. & chair, comm. on minority programs 1988—2004), Assn. of Black Cultural Ctrs. (bd. mem. 1990—92), Nat. Assn. for Student Pers. Assn., Am. Colllege Pers. Assn., Assn.Black Sociologist. Home and Office: 6100 Westchester Pk Dr Apt 901 College Park MD 20740 Home Fax: 301-474-0155. Personal E-mail: vee616@yahoo.com.

EDGINGTON, THOMAS S., pathologist, educator, molecular biologist, vascular biologist; b. LA, Feb. 10, 1932; BA in Biol. Scis., Stanford U., 1953, MD, 1957. Diplomate Am. Bd. Pathology, spl. cert. immunopathology. Intern Hosp. Univ. Pa., Phila., 1957—58; resident Ctr. Health Scis. UCLA, 1958—60; sr. postdoctoral fellow immunology Scripps Clinic & Rsch. Found., La Jolla, Calif., 1965—68, assoc. mem. dept. exptl. pathology, 1968—71; founder, head dept. anatomic pathology and lab. medicine Scripps Clinic and Rsch. Found., La Jolla, 1968—74, prof. depts. immunology and vascular biology, 1971—; asst. prof., surg. pathologist dept. pathology UCLA Sch. Medicine, 1962—65; assoc. adj. prof. pathology U. Calif., San Diego, La Jolla, 1968—75, adj. prof., 1975—. Cons. Centocor, 1993—95, Eli Lilly, 1982—85, Becton-Dickinson, 1977—80; founder, bd. dirs. Corvas Internat., NuVas. Contbr. numerous articles to profl. jours. Recipient Coll. de France medal, 1981, John A. Lynch Molecular Biology award, U. Notre Dame, 1992, Rous-Whipple prize, Am. Soc. Investigative Pathology, 1995, Disting. Career award, Internat. Soc. Thrombosis and Hemostatis, 1995. Fellow: AAAS; mem.: Inst. of Medicine of NAS, Thrombosis Inst. (bd. sci. govs. 1995—), Internat. Soc. Thrombosis and Hemostatis, Fedn. Am. Socs. Exptl. Biology (pres. 1990—91, chmn. bd. 1990—91). Office: The Scripps Rsch Inst C-204 10550 N Torrey Pines Rd # C204 La Jolla CA 92037-1000 E-mail: tsedgington@hotmail.com.*

EDGINTON, JOHN ARTHUR, lawyer; b. Kingsburg, Calif., July 23, 1935; s. Arthur George and Pochantas Clementina (Ball) E.; m. Jane Ann Simmons, June 25, 1960. AA, U. Calif., Berkeley, 1955, AB in Econs., 1957, JD, 1963. Bar: Calif. 1964, No. Marianas 1969, U.S. Ct. Claims 1969, U.S. Ct. Appeals (9th cir.) 1969, U.S. Supreme Ct. 1969. Assoc. Graham & James, San Francisco, 1964-71, ptnr., 1971-94, Dezurick Edginton & Harrington LLP, Emeryville, Calif., 1994-98, Booth Banning LLP, San Francisco, 1999-2000; pvt. practice Point Richmond, Calif., 2000—. Author: Maritime Bankruptcy, 1989, Benedict on Admiralty, vol. 3B and 3C; editor-in-chief Maritime Practice and Procedure, vol. 29 Moore's Federal Practice, 1997, Benedict's Maritime Bull., 2003; editor Maritime Desk Reference, Benedict on Admiralty, vol. 8, 2001; contbr. articles to profl. jours. Bd. dirs., v.p. Richmond Conv. and Visitors Bur., 2004—, pres., 2005—. With USN, 1957—60. Disting. U. Calif. alumni Order of Golden Bear. Mem.: Richmond Conv. and Vis. Bur. (dir., v.p. 1994—, pres. 2005—), East Bay Model Engrs. Soc. (bd. dirs. 1996—2002, pres. 2000—02), Swedish-Am. C. of C. (bd. dirs. 1971—, pres. Western Nat. 1988—90, nat. vice chmn. 1988—90, pres. Western Nat. 1998—2000, bd. dirs. 1998—2003, CFO 1999—2000, corp. sec. 2000—03), Maritime Law Assn. (chmn. practice and procedure com. 1991—95, bd. dirs. 1993—96), Golden State Model R.R. Mus. (corp. sec., bd. dirs. 1995—), Sierra Club (nat. outing com. 1964—, chmn. ins. com. 1991—, internat. trips 1992—95, outing governance com. 1992—). Democrat. Methodist. Avocations: mountain climbing, hiking, photography, model railroads. Office: Law Office of John A Edginton 124 Washington Ave Ste A-1 Point Richmond CA 94801-3979 Office Phone: 510-232-7180. Business E-Mail: jedginton@edglaw.com.

EDGREN, GRETCHEN GRONDAHL, magazine editor; b. Portland, Oreg., Mar. 17, 1931; d. Jack W. and Alice Belle (Wells) Grondahl; m. James McNeese, Oct. 22, 1955 (div. Nov. 1974); children: Amy, Terence James; m. Alvin H. Edgren, Dec. 14, 1984. BJ, U. Oreg., 1952. Staff writer The Oregonian, Portland, 1952-61; editor Sunday mag. The San Juan (P.R.) Star, 1963-65; inventory and info. specialist USAF and U.S. Army Recruiting Command, San Antonio and Chgo., 1965-67; assoc. editor VIP mag. Playboy Clubs, Chgo., 1967-69, mng. editor, 1969-70; assoc. editor Playboy mag., Chgo., 1970-74, sr. editor, 1974-92, contbg. editor, 1992—. Author: The Playboy Book: 40 Years, 1994, The Playboy Book: 50 Years, 2005, The Playmate Book, 1996, Inside the Playboy Mansion, 1998; editor: New Credit Rights for Women, 1976; contbr. articles to mags. Adv. bd. Old Oreg. Alumni mag. U. Oreg., Eugene, 1988-96; bd. dirs. Civic Arts Coun., Oak Park, Ill., 1976-84, pres., 1979-80, Village Players, Oak Park-River Forest (Ill.) Symphony Assn., Oak Park Concert chorale, 1975-91, All Island Denominations, 2004—; mem. Oak Park Cable TV Commn., 1984-86; active Anna Maria Island (Fla.) Cmty. Chorus, 1992—, Anna Maria Island Turtle Watch, 1992—. Mem. Confrerie des Vignerons de St. Vincent Mâcon (maitresse du chpt. 1988-92, bd. all-island denom. 2004—), Webfoot Soc. U. Oreg., Phi Beta Kappa, Delta Delta Delta. Episcopalian. Avocations: singing, travel, loggerhead turtle rescue, wines. E-mail: aedgren@tampabay.rr.com.

EDIGER, JUSTIN DEAN, music educator; b. Beaver, Okla., Feb. 13, 1971; s. Bobby Eugene and Renita Ethel Ediger; m. Amy Lou Shilling, May 15, 1993; children: Anna Lou, Andrew Carson. MusB in Edn., Southwestern Okla. State U., Weatherford, 1993, MusM, 2001. Cert. secondary vocal music Okla., 1993. Vocal music instr. Purcell (Okla.) Pub. Schs., 1995—96, Elk City (Okla.) Pub. Schs., 1996—. Sports broadcaster Paragon Comms., 1996—. Named Teacher of Yr., Elk City H.S., 2000—01;, Edn. Leadership Okla., 2003—04. Mem.: Okla. Choral Dirs. Assn. (exec. bd. mem. 2004—), Western Okla. Choral Dirs. Assn. (pres. 1998—99, vocal dir. of distinction), Okla. Music Educato's Assn. Republican. Baptist. Avocations: travel, hunting, fishing, golf, sports. Office: Elk City Public Schools 222 West Broadway Elk City OK 73644 Office Phone: 580-225-1357. Office Fax: 580-225-1359. E-mail: jde_sing@itlnet.net.

EDIGER, MARLOW, education educator; b. Inman, Kans., Oct. 10, 1927; BS in Edn., Kans. State Tchrs. Coll., 1958, MS in Edn., 1960; EdD, U. Denver, 1963. Tchr. Sandcreek Sch., rural Newton, Kans., 1951-52; English tchr. Mennonite Sch., Jericho, 1952-53; tchr. English and geography Friends Boys Sch., Ramallah, Jordan, 1953-54; tchr. Countryside Sch., Lehigh, Kans., 1955-57; tchr., prin. Lincolnville Grade Sch., Kans., 1957-61; prof. edn. Truman State U., Kirksville, 1962—92. Spkr. in field at over 200 nat., internat. tchr. edn. convs.; evaluator over 147 PhD theses at numerous univs. in India including Kerala U., Mother Theresa U., U. Madras, Utkal U., Sambalpur U., Alagappa U.; evaluator Annamalia U., St. Xavier Coll. Edn.; mem. editl. bd. Experiments in Edn. Jour., India, Jour. Kamataka Sate Edn. Fedn., India, Reading Improvement, Edn., Jour. English Lang. Tchg. in India, The Progress of Edn. in India, Edutracks (India), Jour. of Rsch. in Edn.; v.p. NMSU-AAUP, 1974—75, pres., 1975—76. Author: Relevancy in the Elem. Curriculum, 1975, Relevancy in the Elem. Curriculum, 2nd edit., 1991, Relevancy in the Elem. Curriculum, 3rd edit., 2004, The Elem. Curriculum, A Handbook, 1977, The Elem. Curriculum, A Handbook, 2nd edit., 1988, Social Studies Curriculum in the Elem. Sch., 5th edit., 2000, Lang. Arts Curriculum in the Elem. Sch., 1983, 1992, Lang. Arts Curriculum in the Elem. Sch., 2nd edit., 1988, Lang. Arts Curriculum in the Elem. Sch., rev., 1994, The Modern Elem. Sch., 1997, Tchg. Math in the Elem. Sch., 1997, Improving the Tchg. of Elem. Sch. Math., 1999, The Holy Land, 1998, Tchg. Sci. in the Elem. Sch., 2nd edit., 2000; co-author: Tchg. Reading Successfully, 2000; author: Tchg. Sci. Successfully, 2001, Tchg. Social Studies Successfully, 2001; mem. editl. bd.: The Edn. Rev., The Math Tchr., Jour. English Lang. Tchg., also Edn., publ.: more than 2,400 manuscripts on six continents; co-author: Tchg. Math. Successfully, 2000, Lang. Arts Curriculum, 2003, Improving Sch. Admin., 2003, Elem. Curriculum, 2003, Organizing Schools, 2004, Issues in School Education, 2005; co-editor: Quality in Schol Education, 2005, co-author. Treas. Marion County Kans. Tchrs. Assn., 1958-59, pres., 1959-60; mem. adv. coun. Himalayan Jour. Ednl. R&D, India; mem. nat. coun. social studies com. Religion in the Schs.; chmn. Marion County Curriculum Com., 1960-61tchr. Sunday sch., 1950-52, 54-58, 64-99. Mem. ASCD, NSTA (com. tchr. edn.), NEA (life, Mo. chpt., core competencies and key skills com., higher edn. com., com. on pub. rels. 2000-01), Internat. Reading Assn. (sub com. evaluating literacy standards, com. mem.), Nat. Coun. Social Studies (adv. coun. rural schs. and social studies, ethics com., pub. rels. curriculum com., archives com., com. on acad. freedom, tenure and ethics), Nat. Coun. Tchrs. English (vice chmn. rural lang. arts com., lang. and learning across the curriculum com., tracking in the pub. schs. com.), Mo. Coun. Social Studies (bd. control), Sci. Tchrs. Mo. (bd. dirs.), Mo. Geog. Alliance, Critical Perspectives in Reading, Phi Delta Kappa. Office: 201 W 22nd PO Box 417 North Newton KS 67117-0417 Personal E-mail: mediger2@cox.net.

EDINGER, LEWIS JOACHIM, political science professor; b. Frankfort, Germany, Feb. 1, 1922; U.S., 1936; s. Mark A. and Dora (Meyer) E.; m. Hanni Blumenfeld, Sept. 11, 1950; children: Monica Ruth, Susan Yvonne. AB, Wabash Coll., 1943; PhD, Columbia U., 1951. Instr. NYU, 1947-49; vis. asst. prof. Sweet Briar Coll., 1950-51; vis. lectr. Vassar Coll., 1951-52; vis. asst. prof. U. N.C., 1952-53; assoc. prof. Air War Coll., 1953-57; asst. prof.to prof. Mich. State U., East Lansing, 1957-63; Fulbright prof. Free U. Berlin, 1959-60; prof. Washington U., St. Louis, 1963-67; Fulbright prof. U. Bonn, 1964-65; prof. govt. Columbia U., N.Y.C., 1967-92, prof. emeritus, 1992. Co-adj. prof. Rutgers U., 1975; vis. Fulbright prof. U. Bonn, Fed. Republic Germany, 1980-81; vis. fellow Nuffield Coll., Oxford U., 1981; vis. prof. U. Bonn, 1988, U. Florence, Italy, 1989. Author or co-author: West German Armament, 1955, German Exile Politics, 1956, Germany Rejoins the Powers, 1959, 73, Kurt Schumacher: A Study in Personality and Political Behavior, 1965, France, Germany, and the Western Alliance, 1967, Political Leadership in Industrialized Societies, 1967, 76, Politics in Germany, 1968, Politics in West Germany, 1977, West German Politics, 1986, From Bonn to Berlin: German Politics in Transition, 1998. Ford Found. fellow, 1956-57; Social Sci. Research Council grantee, 1958, 59-63; NSF grantee, 1971-73; Guggenheim Found. fellow, 1973-74 Mem.: Compassion and Choices. Office: 420 W 118th St New York NY 10027-7213 Office Phone: 212-854-1401.

EDINGER, STANLEY EVAN, clinical chemist; b. Bklyn., Aug. 9, 1943; s. Louis and Lenore (Danenberg) E. BS in Chemistry cum laude, CUNY, 1964; MS in Phys. Chemistry, NYU, 1969, PhD in Phys. Chemistry, 1970. Lic. clin. chemistry lab. dir. N.Y.C., N.Y. State; cert. chemist, Nat. Cert. Commn. for Chemists and Chem. Engrs. From tchg. fellow to asst. rsch. N.Y.U., 1964-70; translator, editor N.Y.C., 1970-71; clin. chemist Mt. Sinai Med. Ctr., N.Y.C., 1971-76; sr. scientist bur. quality assurance USPHS, 1976-78; sr. scientist health standard and quality bureau U.S. Health Care Fin. Adminstrn., Balt., 1978-86, scientist dir., asst. to dir. OSC, 1986-87; scientist dir. Nat. Inst. on Drug Abuse, Pres. Initiative on Drug Testing in Work Place, Rockville, Md.; scientist dir. Office Program Assessment and Info. U.S. Health Care Fin.

Adminstrn., Rockville, Md., 1988; USPHS rep. to com. on energy and commerce, Congl. fellow U.S. Ho. of Reps., Washington, 1989; sr. health policy analyst Agy. for Health Care Policy and rsch. office of forum for quality and effectiveness in health care USPHS, Rockville, 1990-93; spl. asst., chmn. subcom. on oversight and investigation U.S. Ho. of Reps. Com. on Energy & Commerce, Washington, 1991-94; sr. legis., adv., adminstr. Agy. for Healthcare Policy and Rsch., 1993-94, sr. sci. advisor Ctr. Info. Tech., 1994-98, sr. sci. advisor Ctr. Quality Measurement and Improvement, 1998-99; sr. sci. advisor Agy. for Health Care Rsch. and Quality Ctr. for Quality Improvement and Patient Safety, 2000—. Sr. legis. advisor Office of Surgeon Gen., 1995—96; project office HHS, Washington, 1977—80; sr. scientist bur. com. health svcs. and delivery systems, 1989—90; mem. U.S. Surgeon Gen.'s Scientist Profl. Adv. Com., Rockville, 1986—90, adv. com., 1984—87; commr. Nat. Cert. Commn. Chemistry and Chem. Engring., Bethesda, Md., 1987—; mem. U.S. Health Care Fin. Adminstrn. AIDS Task Force, Washington, 1986—90, Profl. Exam. Svc., Inc., N.Y.C., 1974—76, Nat. Com. Clin. Lab. Stds. subcom. on cost acctg. and wellness testing and com. on quality of care, materials coms. on computer record sys., med. records and clin. lab. data sys.; chief staffer for quality work group Nat. Ctr. for Vital Health Stats., 1999—2003, mem. staff for quality workgroup and populations subcom., 2003—; mem. mentor program NYU; mem. Nat. Cert. Commn. in Chemistry and Chem. Engring., 1986—; lead staff for health U.S. Quality Interagy. Com., 2004—. Author: The Chemistry of Gypsum and its Dehydration Products, 1975, Infection Control As Health Care Facilities, 1977, Statistics for Laboratory Surveyors; co-author: The Federal Regulation of Clinical Laboratories Quality Assurance Standards and Technological Change, 1986; contbr. articles to profl. jours. Sr. scientist USPHS, 1976-77, comdr., 1976-86, capt., 1986—. N.Y. State Regents scholar, 1960-64, N.Y. State Scholar Incentive award, 1964-68. Fellow Am. Inst. Chemists (chmn. membership com. N.Y. sect. 1974-76, chmn. nat. coun. for health lab. svcs., 1988-92, govt. affairs com. 1993—, bd. dirs. 1996-98, 2000—), D.C. Inst. of Chem.(pres. 2004—) fellow Wash. Acad. of Sci., Royal Inst. of Health, 2003, Washington Acad. Scis.; mem. ASTM (com. computer records sys., med. records, clin. lab. data), Am. Assn. for Clin. Chemists (legis. com. 1989, advisor to legis. com. 1990—), Am. Chem. Soc., N.Y. Acad. Scis., Assn. of Mil. Surgeons U.S., Soc. Armed Forces Mil. Lab. Scientists, Commd. Officers Assn. U.S., APHA (lab. sect. legis. com., chmn. membership com., planning com., action bd. 1984-96, joint policy com. 1993-96), U.S. Naval Sailing Assn., Annapolis Naval Acad. Sailing Assn., Bklyn. Coll. Chemistry Alumni (dir. 1970-86), Bklyn. Coll. Alumni Assn., NYU Alumni Assn., Sigma Xi. Clubs: Washington Ski. Democrat. Jewish. Achievements include development of legislation and regulations to assure quality of clinical laboratory and drug abuse testing, oversight legislative initiatives to improve quality, access and financing of American health care system. Home: 5901 Montrose Rd 1400 South Rockville MD 20852 Office: Agy for Health Care Rsch and Quality Ctr for Qual Improvement/Patient Safety 540 Gaither Rd Ste 3000 Rockville MD 20852 Office Phone: 301-427-1334. Business E-Mail: sedinger@arhq.gov. E-mail: stanedinger@earthlink.net.

EDIRISOORIYA, GUNAPALA, finance educator; s. Sadiris A. P. Edirisooriya and Abanchihamy K. Hennedige; m. Ariyamala W. Edirisooriya, Sept. 13, 1948; children: Milinda C. P., Sithari P. BCom, U. of Ceylon, Peradeniya, Sri Lanka, 1967; MLitt, U. of Glasgow, 1974; MA, U. Del., Newark, 1988, PhD, 1990. Asst. lectr., dept. of economics U. of Colombo, Colombo, Sri Lanka, 1968—77, lectr., dept. of econs., 1977—80, sr. lectr., dept. of econs., 1980—81; inaugural chair, dept. of econs. and commerce Ruhuna U., Matara, Sri Lanka, 1978—79; grade one lectr. U. of Nigeria, Enugu, Nigeria, 1981—84; rsch. asst. / temp. lectr. / merit grad. fellow / tchg. asst. U. of Del., Newark, 1984—90; rsch. and evaluation specialist Balt. City Pub. Schools, 1990—94; prof. East Tenn. State U., Johnson City, 1995—2002, assoc. dean, coll. of edn., 1998—2002; prof. Youngstown State U., Youngstown, Ohio, 2002—. Cons. on ednl. restructuring project Ministry of Edn., Govt. of Sri Lanka, Colombo, Sri Lanka, 1999. Cons. reviewer (jour. manuscript reviewer) Educational Rschr. jour. Maj. benefactor / founding chair Edirisooriya Found., Tangalle, Sri Lanka, 2001—05. Recipient British Coun. Overseas Students award, U. Glasgow, 1973—74; scholar, U. Colombo, 1970—73. Mem.: Am. Ednl. Rsch. Assn. (co-chair, best paper award comm.; judge, nominating comm. 1992—2005, web mgr. SIG-SRE chair 1997—2002, chair SIG on survey rsch. in edn. 1999—2002, web mgr. SIG-SRE chair 2004—05), Phi Kappa Phi. Achievements include research in evolution of the American higher education sector; doctoral research that laid the groundwork for Delaware Cost Study (estimation of institutional cost in higher education); complexity of state-university relationship; Attitude formation as the basis for attitude measurement: A new approach; development of SAS programming for graphical presentation of survey data. Avocations: jogging, travel. Office: Youngstown State Univ EARF BCOE One University Plz Youngstown OH 44555-0001 Office Phone: 330-941-1571. Office Fax: 330-941-3034. E-mail: gedirisooriya@ysu.edu.

EDIS, GLORIA TOBY, pediatrician; b. N.Y.C., Dec. 6, 1939; d. Murray Alvin and Anna G. (Goldstein) E.; m. Myron Royal Schoenfeld, June 14, 1959; children: Bradley, Glenn, Dawn, Melody. BA, Cornell U., 1960; MD, NYU, 1963. Intern Montefiore Hosp., N.Y.C., 1963-64; pediatric resident Columbia Presbyn. Med. Ctr., N.Y.C., 1966-68; pediatrician Scarsdale (N.Y.) Pediatric Assocs., 1977—; pediatric attending Albert Einstein Med. Coll., Bronx, 1968-70; pediatrician Barsky Med. Group, N.Y.C., 1970-80. Fellow Am. Acad. Pediatrics; mem. AMA, Westchester County Med. Soc., Cornell Alumni Assn. Avocations: hiking, bicycling, reading, weight training, theater. Office: Scarsdale Pediatric Assn 2 Overhill Rd Scarsdale NY 10583-5323 Office Phone: 914-725-0800.

EDISEN, CLAYTON BYRON, physician; b. Chgo. s. Byron Parker and Elsie Elinor (Mielkie) E.; m. Adele Uskali, 1948 (div. 1968); children: Laura, Glenn, Lynn; m. Barbara S., Dec. 1968 (dec. 2000). PhB, U. Chgo., 1949, MD, 1953. Diplomate Am. Bd. Neurology and Psychiatry. Various positions in field to psychiatrist The Monroe (La.) Area Guidance Ctr., 1956-58, med. dir., psychiatrist, 1957-58; instr. psychiatry Tulane U. Sch. Medicine, New Orleans, 1956-57; staff cons. Children's Bur., New Orleans, 1958-60; staff psychiatrist The Guidance Ctr., New Orleans, 1957-59; staff cons. Crippled Children's Divsn./La. State Dept. Health, 1959; with New Orleans Psychoanalytic Tng. Ctr., 1958-61; pvt. practice New Orleans, 1957—; apptd. in psychiatry De Paul Hosp., New Orleans, 1957—. Adj. full prof. exptl. comms. design, Tulane U., New Orleans, 1973-74; courtesy staff Coliseum Med. Ctr., New Orleans, 1974—; fellow Scientific Coun. of the Internat. Coll. of Angiology, 1972; del. Internat. Congress on Drug Edn., Montreux, Switzerland/World Psychiat. Assn., 1973, others; vis. faculty lectr. Sch. of Social Work, Tulane U., 1958-60; asst. vis. physician Charity Hosp. of La., New Orleans, 1954-56; vis. staff psychiatrist Touro Infirmary, New Orleans, 1958-72; temporary dir. De Paul Hosp., New Orleans, 1960; lectr. to Annual Life Inst., Jewish Fedn. New Orleans, 1961, others; panelist/lectr. in field. Contbr. numerous articles to profl. jours. and publs. Sgt. U.S. Army, 1945-47, ETO. Fellow Am. Geriatric Soc., Interam. Coll. Physicians and Surgeons, Royal Soc. Health/London; mem. AMA (Physicians Recognition awards), Am. Group Psychotherapy Assn., La. Group Psychotherapy Soc. and Inst., La. State Med. Soc. (numerous offices), Orleans Parish Med. Soc., Am. Psychiat. Assn., So. Med. Assn., New Orleans Psychiat. Forum, 2nd Dist. Med. Soc., La. Dist. Br. APA, New Orleans Area Psychiat. Soc., La. Psychiat. Assn., Pan Am. Med. Assn., World Psychiatric Assn., Assn. Am. Physicians and Surgeons, Am. Heart Assn., N.Y. Acad. Scis., Sigma Xi, others. Republican. Avocations: golf, bridge. Office: 2900 Hessmer Ave Metairie LA 70002-5820 Personal E-mail: cedisenmd@aol.com.

EDISON, ALLEN RAY, electrical engineer, educator; b. Plainview, Nebr., Sept. 21, 1926; s. Arthur and Lela (Johnson) E.; m. Betty Jean Broer, Dec. 27, 1949; children— Karl Arthur, Kathryn Johannah. BS, U. Nebr., 1950, MS, 1957; D.Sc., U. N.M., 1962. Engr. Silas Mason Co., Burlington, Iowa, 1950-53; instr. U. Nebr., Lincoln, 1953-57, prof. elec. engring., 1957-89, prof. emeritus, 1989—, chmn. dept. elec. engring., 1964-70. Served with USNR, 1944-46. Mem. I.E.E.E. (past sect. chmn.), Sigma Xi, Sigma Tau, Eta Kappa Nu. Home: 511 S 54th St Lincoln NE 68510-2006 E-mail: aedison@alltel.net.

EDISON, BERNARD ALAN, retired apparel executive; b. Atlanta, 1928; s. Irving and Beatrice (Chanin) Edison; m. Marilyn S Wewers, Apr. 26, 1975. BA, Harvard U., 1949, MBA, 1951. With Edison Bros. Stores Inc., St. Louis, 1951—, asst. v.p., 1957-58, v.p. leased depts., 1958-67, v.p., asst. treas., 1967-68, pres., 1968-87, chmn. fin. com., 1987-89, dir. emeritus, 1989-96. Office: Edison Founds 220 N Fourth St Ste A Saint Louis MO 63102

EDLAVITCH, SUSAN T., lawyer; b. Washington, Sept. 29, 1948; BS, Washington U., 1970; JD, Indiana U., 1976; LLM in Taxation with high honors, George Washington U., 1990. Bar: Indiana 1976, DC 1991, Md. 1991, US Tax Ct., US Ct. of Appeals, Fourth Circuit, US Supreme Ct. Law clerk to Judge V. Sue Shields and Judge Patrick D. Sullivan Indiana Ct. of Appeals, 1976—79; atty. Office of Gen. Counsel, FCC, 1980—88, Office of Chief Counsel, IRS, 1988—96; assoc. Venable LLP, Washington, ptnr., federal taxation law, 2000—. Mem. Thompson West Tax Advisory Bd. Author: Tax Management Memorandum, Journal of Real Estate Taxation. Mem.: ABA (mem. tax section, mem. corp. tax and partnership tax com.), DC Women's Bar Assn., Md. State Bar Assn., DC Bar Assn. (mem. corp. tax com.). Office: Venable LLP 575 7th St NW Washington DC 20004 Office Phone: 202-344-4000. Office Fax: 202-344-8300. Business E-Mail: stedlavitch@venable.com.

EDLES, GARY JOEL, lawyer, law educator; b. N.Y.C., Feb. 27, 1941; s. Allen Irving and Helen (Hurowitz) E.; m. Nadine Cohen, Feb. 15, 1973. BA, Queens Coll., 1962; JD, NYU, 1965; LLM, George Washington U., 1966, DJuridical Sci., 1975. Bar: N.Y. 1966, U.S. Ct. Appeals (D.C. cir.) 1970. Staff atty. Civil Aeronautics Bd., Washington, 1967-75, assoc. gen. coun., 1975-77, dep. gen. coun., 1977-80; dir. office of procs. Interstate Commerce Commn., Washington, 1980-81; adminstrv. appeals judge Nuclear Regulatory Commn., Washington, 1981-87; gen. coun. Administrv. Conf. U.S., Washington, 1987-95; fellow Am. U., 1995—. Faculty Dept. Justice Legal Edn. Inst., 1982-97; vis. prof. U. Sheffield, Eng., 1994, U. Hull, Eng., 1997—. Co-author: Federal Regulatory Process, 2d edit., 1989; contbr. articles to profl. jours. Mem. ABA, Fed. Bar Assn. (chmn. administrv. law sect. (1989-91). Home: 10 Keldgate Beverley HU17 8HY England Office Phone: 202-274-4186. E-mail: G.J.Edles@hull.ac.uk, Gedles@wcl.american.edu.

EDLEY, CHRISTOPHER F., JR., dean, law educator; b. 1953; m. Maria Echaveste. BA, Swarthmore Coll., 1973; JD, MPP, Harvard U., 1978. Bar: D.C. 1980. Asst. dir. White House Domestic Policy Staff, D.C., 1978-79; spl. asst. sec. Dept. Health Edn. and Welfare, Washington, 1979-80; assoc. asst. to the Pres. White House Office of the Chief of Staff, Washington, 1980; asst. prof. Harvard U. Law Sch., Cambridge, Mass., 1981-87, prof., 1987—; assoc. dir. Office of Mgmt. & Budget, Washington, 1993—95; dean, prof. law U. Calif., Boalt Hall Law Sch., Berkeley, 2004—. Mem. U.S. Civil Rights Commn., Nat. Commn. on Fed. Election Reform. Editor and officer Harvard Law Review; author: Not All Black and White: Affirmative Action, Race and American Values, Administrative Law: Rethinking Judicial Control of Bureaucracy. Nat. issues dir. Dukakis for Pres. Campaign, Boston, 1987-88; co-founder, Civil Rights Project, 1996-; spl. consultant to Pres. Clinton on Race Initiative, 1997-99. Office: The Civil Rights Project 125 Mt Auburn St 3rd Fl Cambridge MA 02138 also: U Calif 215 Boalt Hall Berkeley CA 94720-7200 Office Phone: 510-642-6483. E-mail: edley@law.berkeley.edu.*

EDLICH, RICHARD FRENCH, biomedical engineering educator; b. N.Y.C., Jan. 19, 1939; MD, NYU, 1962; PhD, U. Minn., 1973. From instr. to assoc. prof. U. Va. Sch. Medicine, Charlottesville, 1971-76, prof. plastic surgery and biomed. engring., dist. prof. emergency medicine, 1976-82, disting. prof. plastic and maxillofacial surgery and biomed. engring., 1983-96, Raymoon F. Morgan prof. plastic surgery and disting. prof. biomed. engring., 1996—2001; dir. Trauma Prevention, Rsch. and Edn. Trauma Specialist LLP of Legacy Emanuel Hosp., Portland, 2004—. Founder dept. emergency medicine U. Va., 1973, Pegasus Air Med. Transp. Sys., 1984, DeCamp Burn and Wound Healing Ctr., 1986; dir. Emergency Med. Svc. and Burn Ctr., 1974-85; physician tech. adviser Bur. Emergency Svc., HEW, 1974-79; cons. Divsn. Health Manpower and Nat. Ctr. Health Svc. Rsch., 1977-79. Editor-in-chief: Jour. Long-Term Effects of Med. Implants, 2000—. Recipient Disting. Pub. Svc. aweard for contbns. to emergency medicine USPHS, 1979, Outstanding teaching award U. Va., 1989, Thomas Jefferson award, 1991, outstanding faculty award Commonwealth of Va. Coun. Higher Edn., 1989, 5th Ann. David Boyd Lectr. in Emergency Medicine, 2001, Dist. Alumni award U. Minn. Med. Alumni Assn., 2005 Mem. ACS, Soc. Univ. Surgeons, Am. Assn. Surg. Trauma, Am. Burn Assn. (Harvey Stuart Allen award 2000), Univ. Assn. Emergency Medicine, Am. Soc. Plastic and Reconstructive Surgeons, Soc. of Acad. Emergency Medicine, Coll. Emergency Physicians, Am. Surg. Assn., Alpha Omega Alpha. Achievements include research in biology of wound repair and infection, systems approach to emergency medical and trauma care; development of Edlich Gastric Lavage, 1971; Reinforced Steri-Strip, 1975; CSM Gram Stain Procedure, 1975; Shur-Clens, 1984; Stabilized Topical Pharmaceutical Preperations, 1997. Home and Office: 22500 NE 128th Cir Brush Prairie WA 98606 Office Phone: 360-944-7641. Fax: 360-944-7612. E-mail: richardedlichmd@gmail.com.

EDLIN, RICHARD A., lawyer; b. Rantoul, Ill., July 21, 1960; BA magna cum laude, Tufts Univ., 1982; JD, Columbia Univ., 1985. Bar: NJ 1985, NY 1986, US Supreme Ct., US Ct. of Appeal (2nd, 3rd, 7th, fed. cir.), US Tax Ct. Law clk. Hon. Lee P. Gagliardi US Dist. Ct. (so. dist.) NY, 1985—86; shareholder corp. and securities litig., co-chair nat. life sciences practice Greenberg Traurig LLP, NYC. Bd. dir. Firebrand Fin. Group. Bd. dir. Youth Edn. Through Sports Inc; adv. bd. mem. Entrepreneurship Inst.; bd. govs. Hackensack U. Med. Ctr.; mem. judiciary com. Fedn. Internationale du Sport Universitaire. Mem.: Bar Assn. NYC, Internat. Bar Assn. Office: Greenberg Traurig LLP MetLife Bldg 200 Park Ave New York NY 10166-1400 Office Phone: 212-801-6528. Office Fax: 212-805-5528. Business E-Mail: edlinr@gtlaw.com.

EDLING, LYNN M., financial analyst; d. Joyce Edling. BA, Westminster Coll., New Wilmington, Pa., 1980; MDiv, Union Theol. Sem., N.Y.C., 1985. Libr. systems adminstr./electronic resources libr. Latham & Watkins, LLP, N.Y.C., 1997—2000, knowledge mgmt. analyst, 2000—. Lectr. Practicing Law Inst., N.Y.C., 2003. Author: (treaties) Globally Distributed Information: Virtual Library from Behind the Scenes to the Desktop. Mem.: Am. Assn. of Law Librs., Spl. Librs. Assn. Achievements include development/design of Intranet web site for attorney work product and information distribution; development of a blog for internal use by attorney - probably first in any law firm. Office: Latham & Watkins LLP 885 Third Ave New York NY 10022-4802 Office Phone: 212-906-3066. Office Fax: 212-751-4864. Business E-Mail: lynn.edling@lw.com.

EDLIS, STEFAN T., plastics company executive; m. Gael Neeson. Pres. Apollo Plastics Corp., Chgo. Trustee Mus. Modern Art, NYC. Named one of Top 200 Collectors, ARTnews Mag., 2004. Mem.: Whitney Mus. Am. Art (nat. com.). Avocation: collector of contemporary art. Office: Apollo Plastics 5333 N Elston Ave Chicago IL 60630 Address: 96 Ute Pl Aspen CO 81611-2162*

EDLOW, KENNETH LEWIS, security firm executive; b. Washington, July 27, 1941; s. Ellis and Leonora (Kraft) Edlow; m. Mary Glanzrock, Dec. 19, 1970; children: E. Fielding, Brian. BS in Econ., U. Pa., 1963. Stockbroker Ferris & Co., Washington, 1963-69; various positions Bear, Stearns & Co., Inc., N.Y.C., 1969—; corp. sec. Bear Stearns Cos. Inc., 1987—. Pres Monterey Fund Inc; vpres, secy Edlow Family Fund, Inc. Trustee Congregation Emanu-El, New York, NY, 1994—. Mem.: Am Numismatic Soc (trustee 1993—). Avocations: fishing, numismatics. Home: 35 E 85th St New York NY 10028-0954 Office: Bear Stearns & Co Inc 383 Madison Ave New York NY 10179 Office Phone: 212-272-4394. Business E-Mail: kedlow@bear.com.

EDMANDS, SUSAN BANKS, consulting company executive; b. New Rochelle, N.Y., Oct. 7, 1944; d. George Dixon and Marian (Lepied) Banks; children: Whatleigh Winthrop, Benjamin Bruce II. BS, Boston U., 1966; cert. in libr. sci., Northeastern U., Boston, 1974. Tchr. project head start Office Econ. Opportunity, Washington, 1966; English tchr. Wattana Sch., Bangkok, 1969-71; market researcher Pauline Rendell Assocs., Somerville, Mass., 1971-72; food info. specialist FIND/SVP Inc., N.Y.C., 1977-80; mgr. tech. and indsl. group Find/SVP, Inc., N.Y.C., 1980-90, dir. consulting svcs. divsn., 1990—2003, v.p. corp. quality svcs., 2003—. Pres. Packer Collegiate Parents Orgn., Bklyn. Heights, N.Y., 1987-89, trustee, 1987-89. Mem. Soc. Chimie Industrielle (v.p. Am. sect. 1985-93), Chemists Club (trustee 1984-93), Am. Soc. Info. Sci., Spl. Librs. Assn. Avocations: antique collecting and restoration, travel, cooking, bicycling, gardening. Home: PO Box 1655 New Canaan CT 06840 Office: Find/SVP Inc 625 Avenue Of The Americas New York NY 10011-2095

EDMARK, DAVID STANLEY, communications director; b. Oklahoma City, Aug. 2, 1951; s. Carl Bernard and Dorothy (Stacy) E. BJ, U. Mo., 1973; MA, U. Ark., 1993. Reporter Springdale (Ark.) News, 1974-78, State Jour.-Register, Springfield, Ill., 1978-79, Ark. Gazette, Little Rock, 1979-81; asst. dir. info. U. Ark., Fayetteville, 1981-84; city editor The Morning News, Springdale, Ark., 1984-95; comm. dir. Food Safety Consortium, U. Ark., 1995—. Mem. Coun. for Advancement and Support of Edn., 1981-84; bd. dirs. Fayetteville Open Channel TV, 1986-90, pres. bd., 1988. Named Ark. Journalist of Yr., Council for Advancement and Support of Edn., 1989. Mem. Sigma Delta Chi Soc. Profl. Journalists (pres. Ozarks chpt. 1977. 82), Assn. for Commn. Excellence, Pub. Rels. Soc. Am. (N.W. Ark. chpt. bd. dirs., accredited), Fayetteville Evening Lions Club. Presbyterian. Avocations: travel, reading, golf. Home: 220 E Cleburn St Fayetteville AR 72701-2109 Office: U Ark 110 Agriculture Bldg Fayetteville AR 72701 Business E-Mail: dedmark@uark.edu.

EDMISTON, MARK MORTON, publishing company executive; b. Yonkers, N.Y., July 9, 1943; s. Marcus Morton and Josephine (Brown) E.; m. Lisa Mary Pustorino, Aug. 28, 1965; children: Ann Kathleen, Laura Mary. BA, Wesleyan U., 1966. Circulation mgr. Life mag., N.Y.C., until 1969, circulation and mktg. dir. Tokyo, 1969-70; circulation dir. Saturday Rev., Inc., 1971-73; circulation dir. internat. edits. Newsweek, Inc., 1973-76, pub., 1976-78, pres., 1978-79, corp. exec. v.p., 1979-81, chmn. and pres., 1981-86; pres. TVSM Inc., N.Y.C., 1987-91; exec. v.p. Times Mirror Mag., N.Y.C., 1991-92; co-chmn. The Jordan Edmiston Group Inc., N.Y.C., 1992—99; mng. dir. Admedia Ptnrs., Inc., N.Y.C., 1998—. Bd. dirs., mem. governing bd. for pub. Am. Chem. Soc., Washington. Founder Civilization: The Mag. of the Libr. of Congress, Univ. Bus. Mag. Trustee emeritus Wesleyan U.; trustee Children's Aid Soc. of N.Y., Cmty. Svc. Soc. N.Y. Office: Admedia Ptnrs 444 Madison Ave New York NY 10022-6903 Business E-Mail: medmiston@admediapartners.com.

EDMISTON, SCOTT, academic administrator, educator; Artistic assoc. Huntington Theatre Co., Boston; asst. prof. - dramatic lit. Boston U. Coll. Fine Arts, chmn. MFA Directing Program; dir. office of arts Brandeis U., 2003—. Dir.: (plays) Harold Pinter's Betrayal, 2003 (Elliot Norton Award Outstanding Production, 2003), Brian Friel's Molly Sweeney, 1998 (Elliot Norton Award Outstanding Dir.), Jacques Brel is Alive & Well & Living in Paris, 2003. Named one of region's ten best theatre dir., Boston Herald. Mem.: Alliance Boston Theatre Artists & Producers (pres. bd., StageSource 1998—). Office: Dir Office of Arts Brandeis University MS 051 Waltham MA 02454 Office Phone: 781-736-2027. E-mail: scotted@brandeis.edu.*

EDMONDS, ALBERT J., career officer; b. Columbus, Ga., Jan. 17, 1942; m. Jacquelyn Y. McDaniel; children: Gia, Sheri, Alicia. BS Chemistry, Morris Brown Coll., 1964; MA Counseling Psychology, Hampton U., 1969; grad., Air War Coll., 1980; completed, Harvard U. Nat. Security Program; DSc (hon.), Morris Brown Coll., 1990. Entered Air Force, 1964; data systems officer, tactical comm. area Keesler AFB, Miss., 1966; inspection team chief, dir. emergency mission support Pacific Comm. Area Hickam AFB, Hawaii, 1969; chief ops. 2083rd Comm. Squadron, Takhli Royal Thai AFB, Thailand, 1969-72; action officer Directorate Command, Control and Comm. Hdqs. USAF, Washington, 1973; head Commercial Comm. Policy Office Defense Comm. Agy., Washington, 1975; dir. comm. electronics Strategic Air Command's 3rd Air divsn., commander 27th comm. squadron Andersen AFB (Guam), 1977; chief joint matters group, Directorate Command, Control, Telecom., Office Dep. Chief Staff Plans and Ops. Hdqs. USAF, Washington, 1980-83, dir. plans and prgrams for asst. chief info. systems, 1983; asst. dep. chief staff comm. and electronics, vice commander Tactical Comm. divsn. Hdqs. Tactical Air Command Langley AFB, 1983-84; dep. chief staff comm.-computer systems, commander Tactical Comm. divsn. AF Comm. Command Langley AFB, 1985-88; dir. Command and Control, Comm. and Computer Systems Directorate, US Ctrl. Command MacDill AFB, Fla., 1988—89; asst. chief staff, systems for command, control, comm. and computers AF Hdqs., Washington, 1989-90, dep. chief staff, command, control, comm. and computers, 1990-91, vice dir. command, control, comm. and computer systems directorate, dep. dir. Defense-Wide C4 support, 1991; lt. gen., dir. command, control, comm., computer systems directorate Joint Staff Dept. Defense, Washington, 1993; dir. Def. Information Sys. Agy., 1994—97; mgr. Nat. Comm. Sys., Arlington, Va.; dir. President's Nat. Security Telecommunications Adv. Com.; pres. TRI-COR Industries; v.p., COO Electronic Data Systems Federal, 1998—99; v.p. global sales and client solutions, US Gov. Electronic Data Systems, Plano, Tex., pres. US Gov. accounts, Information Solutions, 2001; sr. advisor, technology Dimensions Internat., Inc., Va., 2004—. Dir. comm.-electronics Strategic Air Command Third Air Divsn., comdr., 27th Comm. Squadron; mem. Nat. Infrastructure Adv. Coun., 2002. Recipient Disting. Svc. medal, Defense Superior Svc. medal, Legion of Merit, Meritorious Svc. medal with two oak leaf clusters, AF Commendation medal with three oak leaf clusters. Life Mem. Kappa Alpha Psi, Kappa Delta Pi, Armed Forces Comm. and Electronics Assn. (chmn.). Office: Dimension Internat Inc 2800 Eisenhower Ave Ste 300 Alexandria VA 22314 Office Phone: 703-998-0098. Office Fax: 703-379-1695.

EDMONDS, ANNE CAREY, librarian; b. Penang, Malaysia, Dec. 19, 1924; d. William John and Neil (Carey) E. Student, U. Reading, England, 1942-44; BA, Barnard Coll., 1948; MSLS, Columbia U., 1950; MA, Johns Hopkins U., 1959; postgrad., Western Res. U., 1960-61; LHD, Mount Holyoke Coll., 1994. With War Damage Commn., London, 1944-46; children's asst. Enoch Pratt Free Libr., Balt., 1948-49; reference libr. Sch. Bus. Adminstrn., CCNY, 1950-51; reference libr. then asst. libr. readers' svcs. Goucher Coll., Balt., 1951-60; exchange reference libr. European svcs. libr. BBS, London, 1955; instr. Sch. L.S., Syracuse U., summer 1960; libr. Douglass Coll., Rutgers U., New Brunswick, N.J., 1961-64, instr., summer 1962, fall 1963; libr. Mt. Holyoke Coll., 1964-94. Vis. libr. U. North, Turfloop, South Africa, 1976-77; mem. libr. vis. com. Wheaton Coll., Norton, Mass., 1978-92; mem. local systems adv. group Online Computer Libr. Ctr., Inc., 1984-87, mem. adv. com. on coll. and univ. librs., 1988-89. Author: A Memory Book: Mount Holyoke College, 1834-1987, 1988 (with Gai Carpenter and others) Computing Strategies in Liberal Arts Colleges, 1992. Mem. South Hadley (Mass.) Bicentennial Com., 1975—76; mem. accreditation teams Middle State Assn. Colls. and Secondary Schs., 1963—94, New Eng. Assn. Schs. and Colls., 1986—94; exec. com. New Eng. Libr. Info. Network, 1974—76, 1979—85, chmn., 1982—84; mem. Adv. Commn. Historic Deerfield, 1975—81, 1986—94; trustee Ctr. for Maine Contemporary Art, Rockport, Maine, 2001—; bd. dirs. U.S. Book Exch., 1973—76, 1980—83, Maine Grand Opera, Camden, Conservancy for Camden Harbor Park and Amphitheatre. Mem. AAUW (bd. dirs. main chpt. 1998—), ALA, Assn. Coll. Rsch. Librs. (pres. 1970-71, chmn. constn. and bylaws com. New Eng. chpt. 1975-76, pres. New Eng. chpt. 1983-84). E-mail: ACE13@midcoast.com.

EDMONDS, BETH, state legislator, lieutenant governor; m. Dan Nickerson. BA, Clark U., 1972; MA, Goddard Coll., 1974. Children's libr. Freeport Cmty. Libr., 1988—; mem. Maine Senate from 23d Dist., Augusta, 2001—, chair labor com., 2001—, mem. marine resources com., 2001—. Mem. Freeport Housing Trust, 1987-95, chair, 1991-95; chair Freeport Mcpl.

Employee Labor Com., 1996-97. Democrat. Home: 122 Hunter Rd Freeport ME 04032 Office: State House 3 State House Sta Augusta ME 04333 Office Phone: 207-287-1500. Office Fax: (207) 287-1585. E-mail: edmonds@gwi.net.

EDMONDS, DEAN STOCKETT, JR., physicist, educator, director; b. N.Y.C., Dec. 24, 1924; s. Dean Stockett and Mary Watkins (Arms) Edmonds; m. Mary Louise Wilson, July 28, 1951 (dec. May 1978); children: Dean Stockett III, Louis Round Wilson, Ann Helene Edmonds Mahoney, Elizabeth V. Casey; m. Wendy Nickerson Adams, Nov. 7, 1993. BS, MIT, 1950, PhD, 1958; MA, Princeton U., 1952. Co-founder, v.p., dir. Nuclide Corp., 1958—65; asst. prof. physics Coll. Liberal Arts Boston U., 1961—67, assoc. prof. physics, 1967—83, prof. physics, 1983—91, prof. emeritus, 1991—; co-founder, pres., chmn. Tachisto Laser Sys., Inc., 1971—85; dir., chief sci. adv. bd. Gen. Ionex Inc., 1974—85; regional v.p., dir. Nat. Aeronautic Assn., 1988—. Vis prof physics Univ Western Ont, London, 1972—74; research fellow Harvard Univ, Cambridge, Mass., 1959—61; guest physics dept MIT, Cambridge, Mass., 1959—61. Author: (book) Novel Experiments in Physics II, 1975; author: (with B Cioffari) Experiments in College Physics, 6th ed, 1978, Cioffari's Experiments in College Physics, 7th ed, 1983, Cioffari's Experiments in College Physics, 10th ed, 1997; co-editor: Experiments in Physics for General Physics Courses Without Calculus, 1968, Experiments in Physics for General Physics Courses With Calculus, 1968; contbr. articles to profl jours. Master sgt U.S. Army, 1943—47, ETO, PTO. Mem.: IEEE, Am. Assn. Physics Tchrs. (Spec Merit Award), Am Phys. Soc. Achievements include research in molecular beams leading to cesium atomic clock, the present internat. time standard; development of of the racetrack microtron accelerator for cancer therapy. Avocations: amateur radio, restoring antique aircraft and sports cars, sport flying, opera, building high fidelity systems. Home: 1019 Spyglass Ln Naples FL 34102-7734 Office: Boston U Dept Physics 590 Commonwealth Ave Boston MA 02215-2521 Office Phone: 617-353-2612.

EDMONDS, IVY GORDON, retired writer; b. Frost, Tex., Feb. 15, 1917; s. Ivy Gordon and Delia Louella (Shumate) E.; m. Reiko Mimura, July 12, 1956; 1 dau., Annette. Student pub. schs. Pub. rels. mgr. Northrop Corp., Anaheim, Calif., 1968-79, indsl. editor, Hawthorne, Calif., 1979-86. Freelance writer; author books including: Solomon In Kimono, 1957, Ooka the Wise, 1961, The Bounty's Boy, 1963, Hollywood RIP, 1963, Joel of the Hanging Gardens, 1966, Trickster Tales, 1966, Taiwan-the Other China, 1971, The Possible Impossibles of Ikkyo The Wise, 1971, The Magic Man, 1972, Mao's Long March, 1973, Motorcycling for Beginners, 1973, China's Red Rebel: Mao Tse-Tung, 1973, Micronesia, 1974, Pakistan, Land of Mystery, Tragedy and Courage, 1974, Automotive Tuneups for Beginners, 1974, Ethiopia, 1975, The Magic Makers, 1976, The Shah of Iran, 1976, Allah's Oil: Mid-East Petroleum, 1976, Second Sight, 1977, Motorcycle Racing for Beginners, 1977, Islam, 1977, The Mysteries of Troy, 1977, Big U Universal in the Silent Days, Buddhism, 1978, D.D. Home, 1978, Bicycle Motocross, 1979, Hinduism, 1979, Girls Who Talked to Ghosts, 1979, The Magic Brothers, 1979, (with William H. Gebhardt) Broadcasting for Beginners, 1980, (with Reiko Mimura) The Oscar Directors, 1980, The Mysteries of Homer's Greeks, 1981, The Kings of Black Magic, 1981, Funny Car Racing for Beginners, 1982, The Magic Dog, 1982; author textbooks: (with Ronald Gonzales) Understanding Your Car, 1975, Introduction to Welding, 1975; also author pulp and soft cover fiction and nonfiction under names of Gene Cross and Gary Gordon and publishers house names. With USAAF, 1940-45, USAF, 1946-63. Decorated D.F.C., Air medals, Bronze Star. Home: 5801 Shirl St Cypress CA 90630-3326

EDMONDS, JAMES PATRICK (JIM EDMONDS), professional baseball player; b. Fullerton, Calif., June 27, 1970; Grad., H.S., Calif. Outfielder Calif. Angels (now Anaheim Angels), 1993—99, St. Louis Cardinals, 2000—. Named to All-Star Team, Am. League, 1995, Nat. League All-Star Team, 2000, 2003, Nat. League All-Star Game, 2005; recipient Am. League Gold Glove Award, 1997, 1998, Nat. League Gold Glove Award, 2000—04. Office: St Louis Cardinals 250 Stadium Plz Saint Louis MO 63102-1722*

EDMONDS, NICK, sculptor; b. 1937; Student, Ogunquit School of Painting and Sculpture, 1953—56; grad. with honors, Boston Museum School, 1961. Prof., sculpture Museum School and Milton Acad., 1962—65, Boston U., 1965—2003, prof. emeritus, 2003—. Exhibitions include, Sullivan Goss, 808 Gallery, Saint Gaudens Historic Site, New Britain Museum of Am. Art, U. Art Gallery, NorthEastern U., Copley Soc. of Boston, Represented in permanent collections, Nat. Acad. of Design, N.Y., New Britain Museum of Am. Art, Tufts U., Wiggen Gallery, Saint Anselm College, State U. of N.Y., College at Cortland. Named Nat. Academician, Nat. Acad. of Design, 1994; recipient Blanche E. Colman Award, 1973, first prize for sculpture, 171st Annual Exhibition, Nat. Acad. of Design, 1996, Orville Lance Prize for sculpture, 176th Annual Exhibition, Nat. Acad. of Design, 2001, Harry Watroos prize and medal, Nat. Acad. Design, 2005; fellow Saint Gaudens Fellowship, 1981; grantee Fullbright grant (Japan), 1975—76, Mass. Council for the Arts and Humanities, 1977. Office: PO Box 86 Sharon MA 02067 Office Phone: 781-784-4531.

EDMONDS, THOMAS ANDREW, legal association administrator; b. Jackson, Miss., July 5, 1938; BA, Miss. Coll., 1962; LL.B., Duke U., 1965. Bar: Fla. 1965, Va. 1981. Pvt. practice law, Orlando, Fla., 1965-66; assoc. prof. law U. Miss., Oxford, 1966-70; assoc. prof.law Fla. State U., Tallahassee, 1970-74, prof., 1974-77; dean Sch. Law, U. Richmond (Va.), 1977-87, U. Miss. Sch. Law, University, 1987-89; exec. dir. Va. State Bar, Richmond, 1989—. Vis. assoc. prof. Duke U., 1968-69; vis. prof. McGeorge Sch. Law of the Univ. of the Pacific, 1975-76. Served with USMC, 1957-60. Office: VA State Bar 707 E Main St Ste 1500 Richmond VA 23219-2800

EDMONDS, VELMA MCINNIS, nursing educator; b. N.Y.C., Feb. 17, 1940; d. Walter Lee and Eva Doris (Grant) McInnis; children: Stephen Clay, Michelle Louise. Diploma, Charity Hosp. Sch. Nursing, New Orleans, 1961; BSN, Med. Coll. Ga., 1968; MSN, U. Ala., Birmingham, 1980; D of Nursing Sci., La. State U., 2001. Staff nurse Ochsner Found. Hosp., New Orleans, 1961—63, 1987—2002, clin. educator, 1987-89; staff nurse Suburban Hosp., Bethesda, Md., 1963-65; asst. DON svc., dir. staff devel. Providence Hosp., Mobile, Ala., 1967-70; staff nurse MICU U. So. Ala. Med. Ctr., Mobile, 1980-82, clin. nurse specialist, nutrition/metabolic support, 1982-84; instr., coord., BSN completion program Northwestern State U. Coll. Nursing, Pineville, La., 1984-86; head nurse So. Bapt. Hosp., New Orleans, 1986-87; instr. nursing La. State U. Health Sci. Ctr., New Orleans, 1989-91, asst. prof. nursing, 1991—2002; clin. coord. Transitional Hosp. Corp., 1994-95; cons., vis. prof. U. Guam Coll. Nursing and Health Scis., 2002—03. Gov.-apptd. mem. La. Bd. Examiners in Dietetics and Nutrition, 1990—98, sec.-treas., 1996—97; cons. on internat. health and nursing edn., 1992—; cons., faculty U. Guam, 2002—; co-prin. investigator, project dir. The Recruitment and Retention of Hispanic Nursing Students, U. Tex. El Paso; rschr. with recently immigrated Honduran women; rschr. with recently immigrated Mex. women, 2004; presenter in field. Author: publs. in field. Advisor Hispanic C. of C., New Orleans; adv. bd. Cmty. Vietnamese Outreach Program, Meth. Hosp., New Orleans; chmn. Silent Auction, New Orleans Dollars for Scholars Found., 2000; founding bd. dirs., edn. coord. Orgn. Health and Med. Profession Women. Recipient Excellence in Nursing group award Ochsner Fedn. Hosp., New Orleans, 1987, cert. Merit Tb Assn. Greater New Orleans, 1961; USDA fellow, 2004; fellow Rsch. Inst. U. Pa., 2005—. Mem. ANA, Nat. Soc. Nutrition Edn., La. State Nurses' Assn. (dist. 7), Am. Soc. Parenteral and Enteral Nutrition, La. State Soc. Parenteral and Enteral Nutrition (program and edn. coms.), Mobile Area Nonvolitional Nutrition Support Assn. (past pres.), Transcultural Nursing Soc., Soc. Nutrition Edn., Orgn. Health & Med. Profl. Women (Guam & We. Pacific region founding bd. dirs., edn. coord.), Sigma Theta Tau. Office: U Tex at El Paso Coll Health Scis 1100 N Campbell St El Paso TX 79902 Office Phone: 915-747-7261. Personal E-mail: vmedmonds@hotmail.com. Business E-Mail: vedmonds@utep.edu.

EDMONDSON, DAVID J., retail executive; b. 1959; Degree, Pacific Coast Bapt. Coll.; degree in Mgmt., Harvard U. With ADVO Inc., 1982—93; from v.p. mktg. to pres., COO RadioShack Corp., Fort Worth, Tex., 1994—2000, pres., 2000—, COO, 2000—05, CEO, 2005—, also chmn. Bd. dir. Van Cliburn Found. Bd. dir. Women's Ctr., Ft. Worth. Office: RadioShack Corp 100 Throckmarton Ste 1900 Fort Worth TX 76102*

EDMONDSON, DREW (WILLIAM ANDREW EDMONDSON), state attorney general; b. Washington, D.C., Oct. 12, 1946; m. Linda Larason; children: Mary Elizabeth, Robert Andrew. BA in Speech Edn., Northeastern State U., Tahlequah, Okla., 1968; JD, U. Tulsa, 1978. Mem. Okla. Legislature, 1974—76; intern Office Dist. Atty., Muskogee, Okla., 1978—, asst. dist. atty., 1979, chief prosecutor, 1982—, dist. atty., 1982—92; pvt. practice atty. Muskogee, 1979—82, Green & Edmondson, 1992—94; atty. gen. State of Okla., 1994—. With USN, 1968—72. Named Outstanding Dist. Atty., State of Okla., 1985. Mem.: Nat. Assn. Attys. Gen. (pres. 2002—03), Okla. Dist. Attys. Assn. (pres. 1983—85), Okla. Bar Assn. Democrat. Office: Office Atty Gen 2300 N Lincoln Blvd Rm 112 Oklahoma City OK 73105-4894

EDMONDSON, EARNEST EUGENE, secondary school educator; b. Greensboro, Ga., Jan. 12, 1953; s. James and Eissie Mae Edmondson; m. Eugenia Richards Edmondson, Sept. 16, 1996; 1 child, Mary Christa Williams. BS, Morris Brown Coll., 1976; MA, Ga. State U., 1987. Cert. tchr. Ga., L.A. Evaluator So. Accreditation Colls. and Schs., 1990. Usher Met. Opera, N.Y.C., 1971—73. Recipient nat. music grant, Ga. State U., 1978. Mem.: Ga. Music Educators Assn., Music Educators Nat. Conf., Phi Mu Alpha. Baptist. Avocations: music, reading, sports. Home: 578 Sunnyhill Dr Jonesboro GA 30238 Office: Atlanta Pub Sch Atlanta GA

EDMONDSON, FRANK KELLEY, retired astronomer; b. Milw., Aug. 1, 1912; s. Clarence Edward and Marie (Kelley) E.; m. Margaret Russell, Nov. 24, 1934 (dec. Jan. 1999); children: Margaret Jean Olson, Frank K. Jr. AB, Ind. U., 1933, A.M., 1934; PhD, Harvard U., 1937. Lawrence fellow Lowell Obs., 1933-34, research asst., 1934-35; Agassiz fellow Harvard Obs., 1935-36, asst., 1936-37; instr. astronomy Ind. U., Bloomington, 1937-4O, asst. prof., 1940-45, assoc. prof., 1945-48, prof., 1949-83, prof. emeritus, 1983—, dir. Kirkwood Obs., 1945-78; dir. Goethe Link Obs., 1948-78, chmn. astronomy dept., 1944-78; research asso. McDonald Obs., 1944-83. Observations of asteroids in cooperation with Internat. Astron. Union's Minor Planet Ctr.; statistical adviser to Prof. Alfred Kinsey for gall wasp and human sex behaviour rsch., 1939-56; program dir. for astronomy NSF, 1956-57; acting dir. Cerro Tololo Inter-Am. Obs., 1966; lectr. astron. socs.; mem. adv. bd. Lowell Obs., 1988-2000. Author: AURA and its US National Observatories, 1997; contbr. numerous papers to Am., Brit., German astron. jours. Decorated Order of Merit Chile, 1964; recipient Meritorious Pub. Svc. award NSF, 1983, Disting. Alumni Svc. award Ind. U., 1997; honored with Daniel Kirkwood (1814-95) in Ho. Resolution No. 58 adopted by Ind. 109th Gen. Assembly, First Session, 1995. Fellow AAAS (chmn. sect. D, v.p. 1962); mem. Assn. Univs. Rsch. in Astronomy (v.p. 1957-61, pres. 1962-65, dir. 1957-83, cons./historian 1983—2003, historian emeritus 2003—), Can. Astron. Soc., Am. Astron. Soc. (treas. 1954-75, 70 yr. attendence award 2001), Astron. Soc. Pacific, Internat. Astron. Union (chmn. U.S. nat. com. 1963-64, v.p. commn. minor planets, comets and satellites 1967-70, pres. 1970-73), Ind. Acad. Sci. (named Disting. Scholar 2004), Am. Mus. Natural History (corr. mem.), Friends of Ctr. for History of Physics (exec. com. 2001—), Explorers Club, Phi Beta Kappa, Sigma Xi. Home: 716 S Woodlawn Ave Bloomington IN 47401-4936 Office: Ind U Dept Astronomy 319 Swain Hall West 727 E 3rd St Bloomington IN 47405-7105 Office Phone: 812-855-6912. *President Calvin Coolidge was right when he said: "Nothing in the world can take the place of persistence".*

EDMONDSON, FRANK KELLEY, JR., lawyer, legal administrator; b. Newport, R.I., Aug. 27, 1936; s. Frank Kelley Sr. and Margaret (Russell) E.; m. Christiane Semirot, Mar. 5, 1959 (div. Sept. 1969); children: Mylene Anne, Yvonne Marie, Catherine May; m. Elaine Sueko Kaneshiro, Aug. 17, 1970 (div. June 1992); m. Karen Louise Bishop, Feb. 27, 1993 (div. Feb. 1996). BBA, Ind. U., 1958; MBA, So. Ill. U., 1978; JD, U. Puget Sound, 1982. Bar: Wash. 1982, U.S. Dist. Ct. (we. dist.) Wash. 1983. Commd. 2d lt. USAF, 1959, advanced through grades to maj., 1969, ret., 1979; contracts specialist Wash. State Lottery, Olympia, 1982-85, asst. contracts adminstr., 1985-87; contracts officer 1989 Washington Centennial Commn., 1987-90; fin. svc. officer Office of the Adminstr. for the Cts., 1990-92; contracts officer, office of adminstr. for the cts. State of Wash. Supreme Ct., Olympia, 1992-99. Mem. scholarship com. Wash. State Employees Credit Union, 1995-2001. Bd. dirs. Friends of Chambers Creek, Tacoma, 1981-90; mem. pro bono panel Puget Sound Legal Assistance Found., Olympia, 1985-90; mock trial program com. Youth and Govt. YMCA, 1994-96. Mem. Wash. State Bar Assn. (spl. dist. counsel 1993-95), Thurston County Bar Assn., Ind. U. Soc. Advanced Study, Govt. Lawyers Bar Assn. (sec. 1985-86, 1st v.p. 1986-87, pres. 1987-89, liaison to Wash. State Bar Assn. 1989-93), Coll. Club, Seattle U. Sch. Law Alumni Soc. (nat. coun. 1997-2003), Beta Gamma Sigma. Home: 6600 Miner Dr SW Tumwater WA 98512-7282 E-mail: fkedmon@aol.com.

EDMONDSON, JAMES E., state supreme court justice; b. Kansas City, Mo., 1945; m. Suzanne Edmondson; 2 children. BA, Northeastern State U., Tahlequah, 1967; JD, Georgetown Law Sch., 1973. Asst. dist. atty. Muskogee County, Okla., 1976—78; asst. U.S. atty., 1978—80; acting U.S. atty., 1980—81; prtnr. Edmondson Law Office, 1981—83; judge Okla. Dist. Ct., 1983—2003; justice Okla. Supreme Ct., 2003—. Served in USN, 1967—69. Mem.: Okla. Bar Assn. Office: Okla Supreme Ct Rm 202 State Capitol Bldg Oklahoma City OK 73105

EDMONDSON, J.L. (JAMES LARRY EDMONDSON), federal judge; b. Jasper, Ga., July 14, 1947; s. James George and Betty Ruth (Holcomb) Edmondson; m. Eugenia Dettelbach (div. 1992); children: Kelley Eugenia, Alexandra Lisa. BA, Emory U., 1968; JD, U. Ga., 1971; LLM in Jud. Process, U. Va., 1990. Bar: Ga. 1971. Law clk. to Hon. Sidney O. Smith U.S. Dist. Ct. (no. dist.), Gainesville, Ga., 1971—73; assoc. Webb, Fowler, Tanner & Edmondson, Lawrenceville, Ga., 1973—76, ptnr., 1976—81; mem. Tennant, Davidson & Edmondson, PC, Lawrenceville, 1982—86; judge U.S. Ct. Appeals (11th cir.), Atlanta, 1986—, chief judge, 2002—. Instr. U. Ga. Sch. Law, 1975—84. Contbr. articles to profl. jours. Trustee Inst. Continuing Legal Edn., 1980—84. Mem.: Lawyers Club Am., ABA, Fellows Ga. Bar Found. (charter), Gwinnett County Bar Assn. (pres. 1980—81), State Bar Ga. (bd. govs. 1982—86), Old War Horse Lawyers Club, Order of Barristers, Pi Sigma Alpha. Episcopalian. Office: US Ct Appeals 11th Circuit 56 Forsyth St NW Rm 416 Atlanta GA 30303-2205*

EDMONDSON, REBECCA LOG, secondary school educator; b. Oswego, Kans., Mar. 12, 1948; d. Roy and Anna Marie (Cunningham) Stice; m. Ted David Edmondson, Aug. 11, 1968; children: Amenda Ann Lacy, Christopher David. BS in Secondary Edn., Kans. State U., 1970. Cert. vocat. tchr. Tchr. bus. Oswego HS, 1971—74, S.E. Kans. Vocat.-Tech. Sch., Columbus, 1989—91, Columbus (Kans.) HS, 1991—. Mem.: Bus. Profls. Am. (advisor 1990—), PEO, C. of C. Republican. Methodist. Avocations: reading, computers, cooking, walking. Home: 4730 SW Cheneyville Rd Columbus KS 66725 Office: Colubmus Unifed HS 124 S High School Ave Columbus KS 66725

EDMONDSON, ROBERT CAMPBELL, retired hematologist, oncologist, internal medicine educator; b. Waukesha, Wis., Feb. 16, 1930; BA, U. Wis., 1951, MD, 1954. Diplomate of Am. Bd. Internal Medicine, Am. Bd. Med. Oncology, Am. Bd. Hematology. Intern Phila. Gen. Hosp., 1954-55; resident in pathology Boston City Hosp., 1957-58; resident in internal medicine Cleve. Clinic, 1958-60; fellow in hematology U. Utah, Salt Lake City, 1960-61; mem. staff Woodland (Calif.) Meml. Hosp., 1961-95; ret., 1995. Clin. prof. internal medicine U. Calif., Davis. Fellow ACP; mem. AMA, Am. Soc. Clin. Oncology, Am. Soc. Hematology, Western Trauma Assn. E-mail: edsmails@earthlink.net.

EDMONDSON, WILLIAM BROCKWAY, retired foreign service officer; b. St. Joseph, Mo., Feb. 6, 1927; s. Harold and Anna Laura (Sherman) E.; m. Donna Elizabeth Kiechel, Oct. 6, 1951; children: Barbara Elizabeth Edmondson Schneider, Paul William. AB with high distinction, U. Nebr., 1950; MA, Fletcher Sch. Law and Diplomacy, 1951; student African area studies, Northwestern U., 1957-58. Joined U.S. Fgn. Service, 1952; fgn. affairs officer Bur. UN Affairs, State Dept., 1951-52; adviser U.S. delegation 11th session UN Trusteeship Council, 1952; vice consul Dar es Salaam, Tanganyika, 1952-55; 3d sec., then 2d sec. embassy Bern, Switzerland, 1955-57; research analyst, then acting chief W. Africa div. Office Research and Analysis for Africa, State Dept., 1958-61; 2d sec., then 1st sec. and consul, polit. sect. chief Am. embassy, Accra, Ghana, 1961-64; officer charge Ghanaian affairs Bur. African Affairs, State Dept., 1964-65; counselor of embassy, dep. chief of mission Lusaka, Zambia, 1965-68; chargé d'affaires ad interim, 1968-69; assigned Nat. War Coll., 1969-70; dep. dir. African programs Bur. Ednl. and Cultural Affairs, Dept. State, 1970, dir. Office African Programs, 1971-74; minister-counselor, dep. chief mission Am. embassy, Pretoria, South Africa, 1974-76; dep. asst. sec. for African affairs State Dept., 1976-78; ambassador to South Africa Pretoria, 1978-81; sr. fgn. service insp., 1981-82; dep. insp. gen., 1982-86. Served to 1st lt. AUS, 1944-48. Mem. Am. Fgn. Svc. Assn. Diplomatic and Consular Officers Ret. (past pres., hon. life gov.), DACOR Bacon House Found. (past pres., trustee), Phi Beta Kappa. Address: 4900 28th St N Arlington VA 22207-2712 E-mail: wbedmondson@aol.com. *Persistent hard work, sincerity, broad intellectual curiosity and a strong touch of idealism in striving for a better world are qualities I admire and try to emulate.*

EDMONSON, PHYLLIS DENTY, artist; b. Hope, Ark., Feb. 27, 1935; d. Nathaniel Wynne and Dell (McRae) Denty; m. Frank Alonzo Edmonson, Jan. 29, 1956; children: Frank Jr., Kathryn Dell BS in Edn., Henderson State U., 1956. Exhibitions include Mid-Southern Watercolorists Ann. Exhbn., 1999, 2001, 2005, Houston Ann. Internat. Exhbn. Watercolor Art Soc., 2001, Hilton Head Art League An. Nat. Exhbn., 2001, Fort Smith (Ark.) 51st Ann. Art Competition, 2001, North East Watercolor Soc. 25th Ann. Internat. Exhbn., 2001, Audubon Artist, Inc. 59th Ann. Exhbn. Salamagundi Club, N.Y.C., 2001, Southwestern Watercolor Soc. 39th Ann. Exhbn., 2002, 2004, Internat. Soc. Exptl. Artists Ann. Exhbn., 2000, 2002, Nat. Watercolor Okla. Ann. Exhbn., 2000, 2002, 2003, Tom Peyton Meml. Arts Festival, Alexandria, La., 2003, 2004, 2005, Art Ctr. of the Ozarks, Springdale, Ark., 2002, Ga. Ann. Nat. Exhbn., 2002, 2003, Watercolor, Houston, 2003, Western Fedn. 27th Ann. Watercolor Soc., 2002, 2003—04, We. Colo. Watercoloer Soc., 2004, Soc. Watercolor Arists 23d Ann. Exhbn., Ft. Worth, 2004, Tex. and Neighbors Annual Exhibn., 2004, Adirondacks Nat. Exhbn. Am. Watercolors, 2004, San Diego Internat. Ann. Exhbn., 2004, 2005, Ala. Watercolor Soc. Ann. Nat. Exhbn., 2005, one-woman shows include Southwestern Elec. Power Co. Bldg., Texarkana, 1992, Cantrell Art Gallery, Little Rock, 1994, 1998, exhibited in group shows, Little Rock, Ark., 2004, one-woman shows include Texarkana Regional Arts and Humanities Coun. Mus., 1999, exhibited in group shows at Cantrell Art Gallery, Little Rock, Ark., 2002, Sen. Blanche Lincoln's Little Rock Offices, 2003—, others, Mo. Watercolor Soc. Ann. Nat. Exhbn., 2005, Represented in permanent collections Ark. Arts Ctr., Little Rock, Southeast Ark. Arts and Sci. Ctr. Recipient 2d pl. award Texarkana Regional Arts and Humanities Coun. Ann. Exhbn., 1995, Purchase award, Ark. Arts. Coun., 1996, Corp. Purchase award, Henderson State U., 1996, First Place Mid-So. Watercolorists, Little Rock, 1997, Finalist The Artist's Mag. Art Competition, 1999, Merit award Tom Peyton Meml. Arts Festival, 2001, 02, 04, Neiman Marcus award Ga. Watersolor Soc. XXIII Exhbn., 2002, Merchandise award, Nat. Watercolor Okla. 28th Ann. Exhbn., 2002. Mem.: Ala. Watercolor Soc., Little River Arts Coun., Mo. Watercolor Soc., Nat. Collage Soc., Audubon Artist, Inc., Southwestern Watercolor Soc. (signature mem. 2004), Ark. Arts Ctr., Internat. Soc. Exptl. Artists, Nat. Mus. Women in the Arts, Texarkana Regional Arts and Humanities Coun., Mid-So. Watercolorists, PEO Internat. Sisterhood (treas. 1980—82, v.p. 1982—83, chaplain 1988—90, corr. sec. 1996—98). Baptist. Avocation: photography. Home: 210 Highway 32 West Ashdown AR 71822-8792 Office: The Carousel Studio 410 W Main St Ashdown AR 71822-2752

EDMONSTON, WILLIAM EDWARD, JR., publishing executive, writer, retired psychology professor; b. Balt., Nov. 20, 1931; s. William Edward and Helen (Mallonee) E.; m. Nellie Jane Kerley, Aug. 3, 1957; children: Kathryn Nell, Rebecca Jane, Owen William. BA, Johns Hopkins U., 1952; MA, U. Ala., 1956; PhD, U. Ky., 1960. Diplomate: Am. Bd. Psychol. Hypnosis. Instr., asst. prof. Washington U., St. Louis, 1960-64; mem. faculty Colgate U., Hamilton, N.Y., 1964-93, dir. neurosci. program, 1972-93, prof. psychology, 1973-93, prof. emeritus, 1993—, chmn. dept. psychology, 1971-81; Gast prof. U. Erlanger, Nürnberg, Fed. Republic Germany, 1982. Pub. Edmonston Pub., Inc., Hamilton Author: Hypnosis and Relaxation: Modern Verification of an Old Equation, 1981, The Induction of Hypnosis, 1986, Unfurl the Flags: Remembrances of the American Civil War, 1989, The Strange Case of Mr. Nobody, 2000; editor: Am. Jour. Clin. Hypnosis, 1968-76; contbr. articles to profl. jours. Served with U.S. Army, 1952-54. Sloan Found. fellow, 1967, 69, Fulbright Found. fellow, 1982, U. Wash. sr. fellow, 1971; recipient Bernard E. Gorton award, 1961, grant USPHS, 1964-65, Prof. of Yr. award CASE N.Y. State, 1988. Mem. Sigma Xi. Home: 1841 Preston Hill Rd Hamilton NY 13346-9522 *By being born to intelligent parents, I started with the genetic potential for success and was reared in a social atmosphere in which hard work, honesty, thrift and accomplishment were highly regarded. I later recognized perseverance, even in the face of apparent failure, and a compulsive attention to (but not an obsession with) details as fundamental to accomplishment. Perseverance is by far the most regnant, for without tenacity one's genetic potential and early social learnings will lie fallow. There is a time for action and a time for reflection. Choosing the appropriate time for each is the secret of happiness and success.*

EDMUND, DAVID C., music educator, musician; b. Davenport, Iowa, Aug. 13, 1970; s. William C. Edmund and Cheri D. Salisbury. MusB in Music Edn., U. Fla., 1993; MusM in Edn., U. North Tex., 1996; postgrad., U. Fla., 2005—. Cert. tchr. music K-12 Fla. Dept. Edn., 1996. Trumpet player U. North Tex. One o' Clock Lab Band, Denton, 1995—96; tchr. elem. sch. music Ruskin Elem., Hillsborough County Schs., Fla., 1996—; instr. trumpet Manatee C.C., Bradenton, Fla., 2000—01. Instr. jazz band U. North Tex. Six o' Clock Lab Band, 1995—96. Musician: (jazz band tour) U. North Texas One o' Clock Lab Band. Founder, tchr. Ruskin Elem. Band Program, 1999—2005. Fellow, U. Fla., 2005—. Mem.: Fla. Music Educator's Assn. (assoc.). Avocations: sports, jazz performance, video editing, sound recording collections.

EDMUND, NORMAN WILSON, educational researcher; b. Feb. 27, 1916; Cert., U. Pa., 1939. Founder, pres. Edmund Sci. Co., Barrington, N.J., 1942-75; ednl. rschr. Ft. Lauderdale, Fla., 1989—. Author: The General Pattern of the Scientific Method, 1994, The Scientific Method Today, 2000, End the Biggest Educational and Intellectual Blunder in History, 2005. Office: 407 NE 3rd Ave Fort Lauderdale FL 33301-3233 E-mail: nwe@scientificmethod.com.

EDMUNDS, JANE CLARA, media consultant; b. Chgo., Mar. 16, 1922; d. John Carson and Clara (Kummerow) Carrigan; m. William T. Dean, Aug. 30, 1947 (div. 1953; dec. July 1984); 1 son, John Charles; Edmund S. Kopacz, Sept. 24, 1955 (div. 1973); children: Christine Ellen, Jan Carson. Student in chemistry and math., Northwestern U. Chemist Mars Inc., Oak Park, Ill., 1942-47; with Cons. Engr. Mag., Maujer Pub. Co., St. Joseph, Mich., 1953-58, 69-74; sr. editor Cons. Engr. Mag. Tech. Pub. Co., Barrington, Ill., 1975-77, exec. editor, 1977-82, editorial dir., 1983-86; asst. editor women's pages rewrite desk News-Palladium, Benton Harbor, Mich., 1967-68; freelance journalist St. Joseph, 1959-68; communications cons. Schaumburg, Ill., 1987—. Chmn. Berrien County (Mich.) Nat. Found. March of Dimes, 1968; mem. campaign com. Rep. Party, 1954. Recipient award Bausch & Lomb, 1940, award Nat. Found. Service, 1969, Silver Hat award Constrn. Writers Assn., 1986, honor mem. 2000, Chmn.'s award Profl. Engrs. in Pvt. Practice div. NSPE, 1987; grantee AID, 1979 Assoc. fellow Soc. Tech.

Communication (chmn. St. Joseph chpt. 1972 Disting. Tech. Communication awards); mem. Am. Soc. Bus. Press Editors (past bd. mem.), Constrn. Writers Assn., Smithsonian Instn., Chgo. Art Inst. Assocs., Field Mus. Assocs. Republican. Episcopalian.

EDMUNDS, JEFFREY GARTH, librarian; b. Scottsbluff, Nebr., Sept. 11, 1953; s. Lafe Rees and June LaFawn (Law) E.; m. Rachel Jeanette Hughes, July 17, 1982; children: Jeffrey Garth Jr., Gavin Nathaniel. BA, U. Va., 1975; MLS, Fla. State U., 1976; JD, George Mason U., 1986. Bar: Va. 1986, U.S. Ct. Appeals (4th cir.) 1986. Reference librarian J. Sargeant Reynolds Community Coll., Richmond, Va., 1976-78; spl. instr. U.S. Navy Program for Afloat Coll. Edn., Naples, Italy, 1978-79; devel. rsch. assoc. Georgetown U., Washington, 1979-84; law clk. U.S. Atty.'s Office for Ea. Dist. Va., Alexandria, 1985, U.S. Dept. Labor, Washington, 1985-86; asst. Commonwealth's atty. Pulaski County, Va., 1986-87, City of Petersburg, Va., 1988-89, City of Fredericksburg, Va., 1989-96; atty. pvt. practice, Fredericksburg, 1996—99; reference libr. Ctrl. Rappahannock Regional Libr., Fredericksburg, Va., 1999—. Sec., dir. FIMC & 3d Virginia Regiment, Inc., Fredericksburg, Va., 2000—04; v.p., dir. Fredericksburg Masonic Mus. Found., 2003—. Mem. editorial bd., bus. mgr. Essays in History mag., 1973-75. Vestryman, St. George's Episcopal Ch., 1990-92; bd. dirs. Legal Aid Soc. New River Valley, Christiansburg, Va., 1986-87. Mem. Welsh Soc. Fredericksburg (pres. 1990-92), Masons, Delta Theta Phi. Home: 3524 Waverly Dr Fredericksburg VA 22407-6849 Office: 1201 Caroline St Fredericksburg VA 22401

EDMUNDS, JOHN SANFORD, lawyer; b. L.A., Jan. 3, 1943; s. Arthur Edmunds and Sarah Bernadine (Miles) E.; m. Virginia Maejan Ching, Nov. 30, 1975; children: Laura, Shauna. AB, Stanford U., 1964; JD, U. So. Calif., 1967. Bar: Hawaii 1972, U.S. Dist. Ct. Hawaii, U.S. Ct. Appeals (9th cir.), U.S. Supreme Ct. Chief dep. pub. defender State of Hawaii, 1970-72, spl. dep. atty. gen., 1974-75; acting chief justice Supreme Ct., Republic of Marshall Islands, 1980-81; ptnr. Edmunds & Verga, Honolulu, 1981-97, Edmunds, Maki, Versa and Thorn, Honolulu, 1997—. Adj. prof. law U. Hawaii, 1976-77, 85-89; counsel Hemmeter Investment Co., Obayashi Corp., Shell Oil Co., Nestle, U.S.A., Inc., Bank of Am. Bd. dirs. Legal Aid Soc. Hawaii, 1974-75; vice-chair selection commn. Hawaii State Jud., 2000-. Fellow Internat. Acad. Trial Lawyers, Am. Coll. Trial Lawyers (state chmn. 1991-92, nat. com. legal ethics and profl. responsibility 1994), Internat. Soc. Barristers, Am. Bar Found.; mem. ABA, ACLU (bd. dirs. 1969-73, pres. 1971-73, adv. counsel 1974-75), Hawaii Bar Assn., Assn. Trial Lawyers Am., Hawaii Acad. Plaintiffs Attys (bd. govs. 1995—), Master of Bench, Am. Inns. of Ct. Office: Edmunds Maki Verga & Thorn 841 Bishop St Ste 2104 Honolulu HI 96813-3921 E-mail: jedmunds@emut.com.

EDMUNDS, NANCY GARLOCK, federal judge; b. Detroit, July 10, 1947; m. William C. Edmunds, 1977. BA cum laude, Cornell U., 1969; MA in Teaching, U. Chgo., 1971; JD summa cum laude, Wayne U., 1976. Bar: Mich. 1976. With Plymouth Canton Public Schools, 1971-73; law clk. Barris, Sott, Denn & Driker, 1973-75; law clk. to Hon. Ralph Freeman U.S. Dist. Ct. (ea. dist.) Mich., 1976-78; with Dykema Gossett, Detroit, 1978-84, ptnr. litigation sect., 1984-92; apptd. judge U.S. Dist. Ct. (ea. dist.) Mich., 1992—. Commr. 21st Century Commn. on Cts., 1990; mem. faculty, bd. mem. Fed. Advocacy Inst., 1983-91. Editor in chief Wayne Law Review. Mem. com. of visitors Wayne Law Sch., Detroit; bd. dirs. Mich. Mems. of Stratford Festival; bd. trustees Stratford Shakespearean Festival of Am., Temple Beth El, 1990-97, Hist. Soc. U.S. Dist. Ct. (ea. dist.) Mich., 1993-98. Mem. ABA, FBA (exec. bd. dirs. 1989-92), Am. Judicature Soc., Fed. Judges Assn., State Bar Mich. (chair U.S. cts. com. 1990-91). Avocation: reading. Office: US Dist Ct US Courthouse #211 231 W Lafayette Blvd Detroit MI 48226-2700 E-mail: karen_hillebrand@mied.uscourts.gov.

EDMUNDS, ROBERT HOLT, JR., state supreme court justice; b. Danville, Va., Apr. 17, 1949; s. Robert Holt and Mary (Rucker) Edmunds; m. Linda M. Edmunds; 2 children. Student, Williams Coll., Williamstown, Mass., 1967—69; BA in English, Vassar Coll., 1971; JD, U. NC, Chapel Hill, 1975. Bar: NC 1975, Va. 1977. Asst. dist. atty. 18th Judicial Dist., Guilford County, NC, 1978—82; asst. U.S. atty. Mid. Dist. N.C. U.S. Dept. Justice, Greensboro, 1982—86, US atty. Mid. Dist. NC, 1986—93; ptnr. Stern & Klepfer, 1993—98; assoc. judge NC Ct. Appeals, 1999—2001; assoc. justice NC Supreme Ct., 2001—. Mem. Atty. Gen. Advisory Subcom. on Guideline Sentencing, 1987—93, chair, 1991—93; mem. Atty. Gen. Subcom. on Controlled Substances, 1987—93. Contbr. articles to profl. jours. Served in USN, 1975—77. Mem.: Greensboro Criminal Defense Lawyers Assn., Guilford Inn of Ct., Nat. Assn. of Former US Attorneys, Greensboro Bar Assn. Office: NC Supreme Ct PO Box 2170 Raleigh NC 27602

EDMUNDSON, LORNA DUPHINEY, academic administrator; b. Sept. 6, 1942; MEd, Boston Coll., 1969; EdD, Columbia U. Tchrs. Coll., 1975. Continuing edn. program dir. Am. U. Paris, 1976-77; asst. dean dir. Columbia U., New York, N.Y., 1978-84; acad. v.p. Marymount Coll., Tarrytown, N.Y., 1984-92; acting pres. v.p. Colby Sawyer Coll., New London, N.H., 1993-96; pres. Trinity Coll. Vt., Burlington, Vt., 1996-98, Assoc. Vt. Colls., Shelburne, Vt., 1998—.

E'DRIE, LORRAINE, artist; b. L.A. d. Frank G. Steiner and Leona E'drie; m. Russell C. Murphy, Sept. 26, 1948; children: Stephen Murphy, Paula Murphy Hinz. Lifetime tchg. credential, Calif. Exhibited at Salmagundi Club, N.Y., Nat. Art Club Gallery, N.Y., L.A. Artcore, Laguna Art Mus., San Bernardino Mus., Riverside Art Mus., Columbia River Maritime Mus., Oreg., San Juan Capistrano Mission Mus., Art-A-Fair Festival, 1978-2004, Cove Gallery, Laguna Beach, Calif., Judith Hale Gallery, Los Olivos, Calif.; works featured in books including Yacht Portraits, Artists of Southern California Fine Arts, A Gallery of Marine Art. Mem. Nat. Watercolor Soc. (assoc.), Am. Watercolor Soc. (assoc.), Am. Soc. Marine Artists, Internat. Soc. Marine Artists, Watercolor West (asso. juried mem.), Catherine Lorillard Wolfe Art Club, Salmagundi Club (N.Y.). Home: 1809 1/2 W Bay Ave Newport Beach CA 92663-4516

EDSALL, THOMAS BYRNE, reporter; b. Cambridge, Mass, Aug. 22, 1941; s. Richard Linn and Katharine (Byrne) E.; m. Mary Deutsch, Aug. 22, 1965; 1 child, Alexandra Tileston Victor Edsall. BA, Boston U., 1966. Reporter Providence Jour., 1965; vol. VISTA, Balt., 1966-67; reporter Balt. Sun, 1967-81, Washington Post, 1981—. Regents lectr. U. Calif., San Diego, 1991; lectr. Nutfield Coll. Oxford U., 1995. Author: The New Politics of Inequality, 1984, Power and Money, 1988, (with Mary D. Edsall) Chain Reaction: The Impact of Race, Rights and Taxes on American Politics, 1991; co-editor: The Reagan Legacy, 1988; contbr. articles to NY Rev. of Books, Atlantic, Am. Prospect, popular jour. Chmn. Standing Com. of Corr. US Congress, 1982. Recipient Front Page award, Bill Pryor Meml. award Washington-Balt. Newspaper Guild, 1981, Carey McWilliams award Am. Polit. Sci. Assn., 1994; finalist Pulitzer prize for general non-fiction, 1992; Woodrow Wilson found. fellow, 1996-97, Hoover Instn. media fellow, Stanford U., 1997, 2001, 03, 05. Home: 19 2nd St NE Washington DC 20002-7301 Office: Washington Post 1150 15th St NW Washington DC 20071-0002 Office Phone: 202-334-6703. Business E-Mail: edsallt@washpost.com.

EDSBERG, LAURA E., research scientist, consultant; b. Rochester, N.Y., Jan. 3, 1964; d. Robert L. and Amina Edsberg. BS, Cornell U., 1986; MS, PhD, SUNY, Buffalo, 1994. Dir. biomed. rsch. lab. Sisters of Charity Hosp., Buffalo, 1995—98; dir. Natural and Health Scis. Rsch. Ctr. Daemen Coll., Amherst, NY, 1998—; dir. Ctr. for Wound Healing Rsch., 2005—. Contbr. articles to profl. jours. Mem.: Wound Healing Soc. Office: Daemen Coll 4380 Main St Amherst NY 14226 Office Phone: 716-839-8351. Personal E-mail: leedsberg@aol.com.

EDSON, ANDREW STEPHEN, public relations executive; b. N.Y.C., Jan. 8, 1946; s. Herbert and Frances (Bauling) E.; m. Marilyn Borer, July 22, 1972; children: Garrett Matthew, Gregory Todd. BA, Fairleigh Dickinson U., 1967; MA, Memphis State U., 1969. Staff writer Memphis Press-Scimitar, 1968-69; account exec. Harshe-Rotman & Druck, Inc., Memphis, 1969-70, Ruder & Finn, Inc., N.Y.C., 1970-73; asst. dir. corp. pub. relations Anaconda Co., N.Y.C., 1973-74; pub. affairs mgr. Citicorp, N.Y.C., 1974-78; sr. account exec. Padilla & Speer Inc., N.Y.C., 1978-79, v.p., 1979-86, sr. v.p., 1986, Padilla Speer Beardsley Inc., N.Y.C., 1986-94; pres., COO Anreder and Co., N.Y.C., 1994-96; pres. Andrew Edson & Assocs., Inc., N.Y.C., 1996—; sr. counselor, corp. and fin. rels. Manning, Selvage & Lee, Inc., N.Y.C., 1996-2001. Adj. asst. prof. NYU, 1983-87; sec., bd. dirs. The Worldcom. Group, Inc., N.Y., 1988-96; pres. bd. dirs. Finch Apt Corp., N.Y.C. Mem.: LI Capital Alliance, Nat. Investor Rels. Inst., Jericho Pub. Libr. (trustee 1998—99). Republican. Avocations: tennis, skiing, bicycling, golf. Office: Andrew Edson and Assoc 1675 Broadway 10th Fl New York NY 10019 Office Phone: 631-468-5546. E-mail: andrew@edsonpr.com.

EDSON, CHARLES LOUIS, lawyer, educator; b. St. Louis, Dec. 14, 1934; s. Harry G. and Mildred (Solomon) E.; m. Susan Kramer, Mar. 29, 1959; children: Richard, Nancy, Margaret. AB, Harvard U., 1956, LLB, 1959. Bar: Mo. 1959, U.S. Supreme Ct. 1966, D.C. 1967. Assoc. Lewis, Rice, Tucker, Allen & Chubb, St. Louis, 1959-65; chief ops. officer Legal Svc. Program, OEO, Washington, 1966-67; gen. counsel Pres.'s Commn. on Postal Orgn., Washington, 1967-68; chief pub. housing sect. Officer of Gen. Counsel, HUD, Washington, 1968-70; ptnr. Lane and Edson, P.C., Washington, 1970-89, Kelley, Drye & Warren, Washington, 1989-93, Peabody & Brown, Washington, 1993-99, Nixon Peabody LLP, Washington, 1999—, ptnr., sr. counsel, 2002—. Adj. prof. law Georgetown U. Law Sch., Washington, 1970-76, 2000—; HUD coord. Pres. Carter's Transition Staff, 1976-77. Co-author: A Practical Guide to Low and Moderate Income Housing, 1972, A Leased Housing Primer, 1975, A Section 8 Deskbook, 1976, Guide to Federal Housing Programs, 1982, Secondary Mortgage Market Guide, 1985, HDR Affordable Seniors Housing Handbook, 2005. Councilman Town of Somerset, Md., 1976-78; trustee Md. Hist. Trust, 1995—, vice chair, 2000—. With USNR, 1953-61. Alt. White House fellow, 1965. Mem. ABA (chmn. forum com. on affordable housing and comm. devel. 1991-93, chmn. spl. housing and urban devel. 1987-90), Harvard U. Law Sch. Assn. D.C. (pres. 1972-73), Cosmos Club (Washington). Home: 5802 Surrey St Chevy Chase MD 20815-5419 Office: 401 9th St NW Ste 900 Washington DC 20004-2134 E-mail: cedson@nixonpeabody.com, granchuck@aol.com.

EDSON, EVELYN, history professor, writer; b. Oklahoma City, Nov. 28, 1940; d. Arthur Lewis Edson and Margery Huff Edson-Gould; m. Andrew Austin Wilson, Aug. 15, 1976; children: Meredith Swan Cole, Benjamin Andrew Wilson. BA, Swarthmore Coll., Pa., 1962; MA, U. Chgo., 1965, PhD, 1972. Tchr. HS Oakwood Sch., Poughkeepsie, NY, 1962—64; lectr. western civilization U. Chgo., 1966—69; vis. asst. prof. history Roosevelt U., Chgo., 1970—71, assoc. dean continuing edn., 1971—72; prof. Piedmont Va. CC, Charlottesville, 1972—. Coll. rep. Chancellor's adv. coun. Va. CC Sys., Richmond, 1983—88; co-chair joint com. transfer students State Coun. Higher Edn. Va., Richmond, 1990—91; mem. adv. bd. western tradition telecourse WGBH, Boston, 1986—88; coun. mem. Nat. Coun. Humanities, Washington, 2000—04. Author: Mapping Time and Space: How Medieval Mapmakers Viewed Their World, 1997; co-author (with E. Savage-Smith): Medieval Views of the Cosmos, 2004; contbr. articles to profl. jours. Pres. Southside Fellowship, Scottsville, Va., 1990—2004, sec., v.p.; pres. James River Book Club, Scottsville, 1977—2004, sec.; bd. dirs. Tandem Sch., Charlottesville, 1990—93, Va. Women's Forum, Charlottesville, 1990—2000, Scottsville Mus., 2004—. Named Disting. Humanities Educator, C.C. Humanities Assn., 1993; recipient Outstanding Faculty award, State Coun. of Higher Edn., Va., 1990, Eugene Asher Disting. Tchg. award, Am. Hist. Soc. and Soc. for History Edn., 2003; fellow summer program India, Fulbright Found., 1980, Nat. Endowment for the Humanities, 1999, Am. Coun. of Learned Societies, 2003—04. Mem.: Va. C.C. Assn., Wash. Map Soc., C.C. Humanities Assn., Medieval Acad., Am. Hist. Assn. (nominating com. 1992—94, program com. 2004). Avocations: reading, gardening, music, hiking, socializing. Office: Piedmont Va CC 501 College Dr Charlottesville VA 22902 Office Phone: 434-961-5384.

EDSON, HERBERT ROBBINS, retired foundation and hospital executive, retired military officer; b. Upper Darby, Pa., Dec. 26, 1931; s. Merritt Austin and Ethel Winifred (Robbins) E.; m. Constance Anne Lowell, May 20, 1961 (div. Nov. 8, 1967); m. Rose Anne McGowan, July 25, 1970; children: Patricia Anne, David William, Merritt Austin III, Herbert Robbins Jr. BA, Tufts U., 1955; MBA, U. Pa., 1972. Commd. 2d lt. USMC, 1955, advanced through grades to major, 1967, adminstr., mgr., supr. various orgns., 1955-72, controller III Marine Amphibious Force and 3d Marine Div. Camp Butler, Japan, 1972-73, dir. acctg. Marine Corps Supply Activity Phila., 1973-75, ret., 1975; cons. acctg. Ardmore, Pa., 1975-77; CFO Mercy Meml. Hosp. Corp., Monroe, Mich., 1977-92, Mercy Meml. Hosp. Found., Monroe, 1986-92, Monroe Health Ventures Inc., 1986-92, Monroe Cmty. Health Svcs., 1989-92, Byerly Hosp., Hartsville, SC, 1992-95, Byerly Found., Hartsville, 1995-97; ret., 1997. Assoc. Quorum Health Resources, Inc., Brentwood, Tenn., 1992-95. Bd. dirs., treas. Foxchase Subdivsn. Homeowners' Assn., Inc., Parrish, Fla., 2003—; co-pres. Custer Elem. Sch. Parent Tchr. Orgn., Monroe, 1985-87; v.p., trustee Christ Evang. Luth. Ch., Monroe, 1981-86; dir. Monroe County C. of C., 1982-84; treas., chmn. Taylor Endowment Fund com. St. Paul's Evang. Luth. Ch., Ardmore, Pa., 1974-76, trustee, chmn. property com., 1976. Decorated Purple Heart, Navy Commendation medal, Combat Action ribbon. Mem. NRA (life), U.S. Naval Inst. (life), Marine Corps Assn. (life), 1st Marine Divsn. Assn. (life), Edson's Raiders Assn. (hon. life 1st Marine Raider Bn.), Mil. Officers Assn. Am. (life), Am. Assn. Ret. Persons, Nat. Geog. Soc., Edson Geneal. Assn Democrat. Lutheran. Home: PO Box 569 Ellenton FL 34222-0569

EDSON, MARGARET, playwright; b. Washington, July 4, 1961; life ptnr. Linda Merrill. BA, Smith Coll., 1983; MA, Georgetown U., 1992. Tchr., elementary D.C. public schools, 1992—98; tchr. kindergarten John Hope Elem. Sch., Atlanta, 1998—. Author: (play) Wit, 1999. Recipient Drama League of NY playwright award, 1993, LA Drama Critics Circle award, 1996, Berrilla Kerr Found. playwrights award, 1998, Fellowship of Southern Writers drama award, 1999, Pulitzer prize for drama, 1999. Home: 6201 Trolley Sq Xing NE Atlanta GA 30306-3791

EDSON, WILLIAM ALDEN, retired electrical engineer, researcher; b. Burchard, Nebr., Oct. 30, 1912; s. William Henry and Pearl (Montgomery) E.; m. Saralou Peterson, Aug. 23, 1942; children: Judith Lynne, Margaret Jane, Carolyn Louise. BS (Summerfield scholar), U. Kans., 1934, MS, 1935; D.Sc. (Gordon McKay scholar), Harvard U., 1937. Mem. tech. staff Bell Telephone Labs., Inc., N.Y.C., 1937-41, supr., 1943-45; asst. prof. elec. engring. Ill. Inst. Tech., Chgo., 1941-43; prof. physics Ga. Inst. Tech., Atlanta, 1945-46, prof. elec. engring., 1946-51, dir. sch. elec. engring., 1951-52; vis. prof., research assoc. Stanford U., 1952-56, cons. prof., 1956; mgr. Klystron sub-sect. Gen. Electric Microwave Lab., Palo Alto, Calif., 1955-61; v.p., dir. research Electromagnetic Tech. Corp., Palo Alto, 1961-62, pres., 1962-70; sr. scientist Vidar Corp., Mountain View, Calif., 1970— 71; asst. dir. Radio Physics Lab., SRI Internat., Menlo Park, Calif., 1971-77; sr. prin. engr. Geosci. and Engring. Ctr., SRI Internat., 1977-2001; ret., 2001. Cons. high frequency sect. Nat. Bur. Standards, 1951-64; dir. Western Electronic Show and Conv., 1975-79 Author: (with Robert I. Sarbacher) Hyper and Ultra-High Frequency Engineering, 1943, Vacuum-Tube Oscillators, 1953. Life fellow IEEE (chmn. San Francisco sect. 1963-64, com. standards piezoelectricity 1950-67); mem. Am. Phys. Soc., Sigma Xi, Tau Beta Pi, Sigma Tau, Phi Kappa Phi, Eta Kappa Nu, Pi Mu Epsilon. Home: 23350 Sereno Ct Unit 29 Cupertino CA 95014-6543 Personal E-mail: wedson6418@aol.com.

EDWALL, DENNIS, physicist, researcher; b. Houston, July 26, 1948; s. Harold and Leticia Edwall; children: Heather, Kara. BS, Iowa State U., 1970; MS, Cornell U., 1972. Sr. scientist Rockwell Sci., Camarillo, Calif., 1975—. Libertarian. Office: Rockwell Sci 5212 Verdugo Way Camarillo CA 93012 Office Phone: 805-373-4260. E-mail: dedwall@rwsc.com.

EDWARD, DEEPAK P., ophthalmologist, researcher; s. John Chinayya and Premalatha Edward; m. Catherine S. Ayappa, May 20, 1985; children: Neeraj John, Nikhil Benjamin, Priya Rachael. MD, St Johns Med. Coll., Bangalore, India, 1980; MBBS, Bangalore (India) U., 1981; MS, Punjab (India) U., 1985. Lic. ophthalmologist. Resident U. Ill., Chgo., 1985, fellow ophthal. pathology, 1989, rsch. asst prof. ophthalmology, 1989—91, assoc. prof. ophthalmology, 1999—; fellow in glaucoma Wash. U., St. Louis, 1986; asst prof. St Johns Med. Coll., Bangalore, India, 1986—87. Dir. glaucoma svc. U. Ill., 2004—; dir. glaucoma svc., assoc. dir. rsch. King Khaled Eye Specialist Hosp., Riyadh, Saudi Arabia, 2000—01. Recipient Golden Apple award, U. Ill., 1990, 1997, 2004, John Nuveen Internat. Devel. award, 2000. Fellow: ACS; mem.: Am. Assn. Ophthalmic Pathologists (sec., treas. 2004—, bd. dirs. 2002—), Am. Acad. of Ophthalmology (Achievement award 2004), Am. Glaucoma Soc. (life Rsch. award 1996), Verhoeff-Zimmerman Ophthalmic Pathology Soc. (life), St. Johns Med. Coll. Alumni Assn. (pres. N.Am. chpt. 2004—). Achievements include research in pathophysiology of light induced retinal degeneration; optic nerve changes in glaucoma, pathophysiology of congenital glaucoma. Office: Univ Illinois at Chicago 1855 W Taylor Chicago IL 60612 Office Phone: 312-996-6504. Business E-Mail: deepedwa@uic.edu.

EDWARDS, ANN CONCETTA, human resources director; b. Bklyn., Feb. 15, 1941; d. Joseph T. and Anna R. Lazzarino; m. Andrew F. Edwards, Jan 14, 1967; children: Alison, Jacqueline. BA, U. S.C., 1961; MA, St. John's U., Jamaica, N.Y., 1963. Cert. sr. profl. human resources. From asst. to mgr. human resources Lab-Volt Sys., Inc., Wall Township, N.J., 1982-97, human resources mgr., 1997—2001, human resources dir., 2002—. Writer Shore News, Sea Girt, N.J., 1970-75; cons. Edwards Assocs., Sea Girt, 1975-82. Recipient Govs. Certificate of Achievement award N.J. Sch. to Careers Sys., 1997-98. Mem.: NAFE, Jersey Shore Assn. Human Resources (area 1 rep. 1990—92), Soc. for Human Resource Mgmt. (dir. 1994—, found. chair 1997—2001, high tech. net 1998—, workforce readiness dir. 2002—, trustee Garden State coun.). Avocation: writing. Office: Lab-Volt Systems Inc PO Box 686 Farmingdale NJ 07727-0686 Office Phone: 732-938-2000. E-mail: aedwards@labvolt.com.

EDWARDS, ANTHONY, actor; b. Santa Barbara, CA, July 19, 1962; Student, Royal Acad. of Dramatic Art, London, 1980. Films include: Fast Times at Ridgemont High, 1982, Heart Like a Wheel, 1982, Revenge of the Nerds, 1984, The Sure Thing, 1985, Gotcha!, 1985, Top Gun, 1985, Summer Heat, 1987, Revenge of the Nerds II: Nerds in Paradise, 1987, Mr. North, 1988, Miracle Mile, 1989, How I Got Into College, 1989, Hawks, 1989, Downtown, 1990, Pet Sematary II, 1992, The Client, 1994, Playing by Heart, 1998, Northfork, 2003, Thunderbirds, 2004, The Forgotten, 2004; television movies include: The Killing of Randy Webster, 1981, High School U.S.A., 1983, Going for the Gold: The Bill Johnson Story, 1985, El Diablo, 1990, Hometown Boy Makes Good, 1990, In Cold Blood (TV), 1996, Playing by Heart, 1998, Don't Go Breaking My Heart (also prodr.), 1998, Jackpot, 2001, Northfork, 2003; series include: It Takes Two, 1982-83, Northern Exposure, 1992-93, ER, 1994-2002, Rock Story, 2000; dir. (TV series) ER, 1996, 98, Charlies Ghose Story, 1994; prodr. Us Begins with You, 1998; guest appearance Monday Nigh Clive, 1999, Strangers, 1996; producer of film Die, Mommie, Die, 2003, (TV films) Border Line, 1999, N.Y.H.C., 1999, My Louisiana Sky, 2001. Recipient SAG award, 1996, 98, 99, Golden Globe, 1998.

EDWARDS, ARDIS LAVONNE QUAM, retired elementary education educator; b. Sioux Falls, S.D., July 30, 1930; d. Norman and Dorothy (Cade) Quam; m. Paul Edwards, Apr. 18, 1953 (dec. Sept. 1988); children: Kevin (dec. 1980), Kendall, Erin, Sally, Kristin, Keely. Tchg. credentials, Augustana Luth. Coll., Sioux Falls, 1949; provisional tchg. credentials, San Jose State Coll., 1953, student, 1953-57. Lic. pvt. pilot, FAA, 1984. Mgr. The Cottage Restaurant, Sioux Falls, 1943-50; one-room sch. tchr. Whaley Sch., Colman, S.D., 1949-50; one-room sch. tchr. 8 grades East Sioux Sch., Sioux Falls, 1950-51; recreation dir. City of Albany, Calif., 1951-52; first grade tchr. Decoto (Calif.) Sch. Dist., 1952-58; ret., 1958. Author Health Instrn. Unit Study Packet for Tchrs. Treas. PTA, Hayward, Calif., 1959; chmn. Our Savior Luth. Ch. Blood Bank, 1968—; officer Healthy Cmtys., Healthy Youth; mem. Am. Heart Assn., March of Dimes, Am. Cancer Soc., Arthritis Found.; rm. mother Chadbourne Grammar Sch.; team mother Fremont Little League; Brownie leader, den mother; bible sch. tchr., Sunday sch. tchr. East Side Luth. Ch., Sioux Falls, SD, 1945—51; charter mem. Our Savior Luth. Ch., Fremont, Calif., 1964—, mem. choir, transition task force, Christian Week Day Sch. tchr., 1970, 1987, ch. historian, 1986—; other offices; pres. Luth. Women's Missionary League, 1976; edn. officer, fraternal communicator, respecteen officer Luth. Brotherhood; youth dir. Thrivent Fin. for Luth. Recipient Spl. Svc. award Girl Scouts U.S., 1971, Arthritis Found., Fremont, 1974-75, Spl. Commendation March Fong Eu, 1954. Mem. NAFE, AARP, Republic Airlines Ret. Pilots Assn., Ret. Airline Pilots Assn., N.W. Airlines Ret. Pilots Assn., Aircraft Owners and Pilots Assn., S.W. Airways Pilots Wives Assn., Concerned Women for Am., World Affairs Coun., Philomathian Lit. Soc., Tri-Cities Assn. Evangelicals, Washington Twp. Hist. Soc., Mission Highlands Swim Club. Republican. Avocations: bible study, flying, history, antiques. *My greatest sense of fulfillment is in being a Christian, wife, mother, teacher and writer...in that order.*

EDWARDS, BARRY L., leasing company executive; BS in Fin. and Econs., Lehigh U., 1969; MBA, U. Va., 1972. V.p., treas. Liberty Corp., 1978—94; exec. v.p., CFO AMRESCO, 1994—2000, Sourcecorp Inc., Dallas, 2000—. Bd. dirs. Ryan's Family Steakhouses, Robert Harris Homes. Office: Sourcecorp Inc Ste 1000 3232 McKinney Ave Dallas TX 75204

EDWARDS, BERT TVEDT, accountant; b. Washington, Aug. 23, 1937; s. Archie Campbell and Geniana (Rasmussen) Edwards; m. Susan Elizabeth Dye, July 18, 1964; children: Christopher Andrew, Stacey E. Leonard. BA, Wesleyan U., 1959; MBA, Stanford U., 1961. CPA D.C. With Arthur Andersen LLP, Washington, 1961-69, 70-94, mgr., 1965-69, 70-71, ptnr., 1971-94, cons., 1994—98, 2001, ret. ptnr., 1994—; fin. v.p. Leisure Time Industries, Inc., 1969-70; CFO, asst. sec. U.S. Dept. State, 1998-2001; exec. dir. office hist. trust acctg. U.S. Dept. Interior, 2001—. Mem. U.S. Comptr. Gen. Auditing Stds. Adv. Coun., 1985—88, 1999—2002; chmn. audit com. U.S. Dept. Air Force, 2004—. Mem. spl. adv. commn. for indsl. and comml. devel. D.C. City Coun., 1972—74; mem. D.C. Mayor's Commn. Budget and Fiscal Priorities, 1989—91, 1993—95, D.C. Tax Rev. Commn., 1996—98; bd. dirs. Children's Nat. Med. Ctr. Rsch. Inst., 2002—, Com. Capital City, 1995—98, 2001—02; trustee Barker Found., 1968—78, 1994—96, treas., 1968—71, 1st v.p., 1971—72, pres., 1972—75; trustee, treas. Population Reference Bur., Inc., 1975—98, 2001—, vice chmn., 1993—94; bd. dirs. Jr. Achievement Met. Washington, Inc., 1973—87, treas., 1973—74, 2d v.p., 1974—75, 1st v.p., 1975—77, pres., 1977—78, chmn., 1978—80; bd. dirs., treas. Heritage Walk Homes Corp., 1975—80; chmn. JA Nat. Bus. Leadership Conf., 1978, Boys and Girls Clubs Greater Washington Ann. Congl. Dinner, 1993, dinner com. mem., 1992—98, found. bd., treas., 1995—; mem. Nat. Com. Pub. Employees Pension Sys., 1993—98, treas., 1995—98; bd. dirs., treas. Bethany West Recreation Assn., 1994—98; bd. dirs. D.C. Appleseed Found. Ctr. Law and Justice, 1995—98, 2001—, treas., 1998; mem. cmty. rels. bd. Sta. WAMU, 1994—97, CFO coun., chmn. stds. com., 1998—2001. Mem.: AICPA (govt. acctg. and auditing com. 1981—84, fed. govt. audit subcom. 1981—84, ad hoc task force univ. audit 1985—87, govt. acctg. and auditing com. 1985—88, author single audit course 1985—96, task force on quality of govt. audits 1986—87, govt. acctg. and auditing com. 1989—92, task force on quality of fed. program audits 1991—94), Govt. Fin. Officers Assn. Met. Washington (co-founder, bd. dirs. 1984—91, Outstanding Svc. award 1993), Assn. Govt. Accts. (Andy Barr Lifetime Achievement award 1993, Frank Greathouse award 2004), Md. Govt. Fin. Officers Assn. (bd. dirs. 1992—94), Orgn. Am. States (chmn. bd. external auditors 2000—02), Govt. Fin. Officers Assn. (co-chmn. ann. conf. 1987), Am. Acctg. Assn. (vice chair govt. nonprofit sect. 1993—94), Inst. Mgmt. Accts., Va. Soc. CPAs, Assn. Govt. Accts. Edn. and Rsch. Found. (chmn. bd. dirs. 1993—95), Greater Washington Soc. CPAs (chmn. membership com. 1973—74, chmn. SEC com. 1974—75, chmn. govt. acctg. com. 1979—81, chmn. rels. with D.C. govt.

com. 1995—98, bd. govs. 2002—05, Lifetime Pub. Svc. award 1997), Hist. Soc. Washington (bd. dirs. 2002—, chmn. fin. com. 2003—, treas. 2003—), Univ. Club (mem. bd. admissions 1976—82, chmn. 1980—82, bd. govs. 1982—85), Wesleyan U. Alumni Club Washington (pres. 1969—71). Methodist. Home: 309 Casey Ln Rockville MD 20850-4733 Personal E-mail: berttedwards@aol.com.

EDWARDS, BETH YARNELLE, artist, photographer; b. Johnstown, Pa., Aug. 16, 1950; d. Arthur Lee and Dolores Marie (Yacos) Yarnelle; m. John Gregory Edwards, Aug. 18, 1973; 1 child, Gregory Arthur. AB, UCLA, 1972; MA, San Francisco State U., 1980, MFA, 1998. One-woman shows include Southern Light Gallery, Amarillo, Tex., 1996, Workspace Gallery, U. Colo., Boulder, 1997, Exit Gallery, U. Nev., Reno, 1997, Firehouse Gallery, Grants Pass, Oreg., 1997, UCB Extension, San Francisco, 1997, SRO Gallery Tex. Tech. U., Lubbock, 1998, Davis (Calif.) Art Gallery, 1998, CEPA Gallery Satellite, Buffalo, N.Y., 1998, San Francisco Art Commn. Gallery, 1998, Recontres Internationales de la Photographie, Arles, France, 1999, The Fringe Festival, 1999, Centro Colombo Americano, Medellin, Colombia, 1999, Silver Eye Ctr. for Photography, Pitts., 1999, Photographic Ctr. Northwest, Seattle, 1999, Photographic Image Gallery, Portland, Oreg., 1999, City of Las Vegas Cultural Affairs, 1999, Ctr. for Photography at Woodstock, N.Y., 2001; exhibited in group show at Soc. Contemporary Photography, Kansas City, Mo., 1998, Cambridge (Mass.) Art Assn. Nat. Prize show, 1999, The Alternative Mus., N.Y.C., 1999, San Francisco Camerawork, 1999, Haydon Gallery, Lincoln, Nebr., 2000, Longview (Tex.) Mus. Fine Arts, 2000, Musee de la Photographie, Charleroi, Belgium, 2000, Salon Internationale de la Recherche Photographique de Royan, 2000 (grand prize); represented in permanent collections Musee de la Photographie Charleroi, Musset for Fotokunst, Odense, Denmark, San Francisco Mus. Modern Art, L.A. County Mus. Art, Mus. Fine Arts, Santa Fe, Mus. Fine Arts Houston, Harry Ransom Collection, Austin, Tex. Recipient First place and Purchase award Fine Arts Ctr., Lubbock, 1997, First place Santa Fe (N.Mex.) Ctr. for Visual Arts Project Competition, 1999. E-mail: byedwards@aol.com.

EDWARDS, BLAKE, film director; b. Tulsa, July 26, 1922; m. Julie Andrews. Ed. high sch. Writer, prodr., actor: Panhandle, 1947; writer, producer Stampede, 1948, Soldier in the Rain, 1963, The Pink Panther, 1963; writer: Sound Off, 1952, Rainbow 'Round My Shoulder, 1952, All Ashore, 1953, Cruisin' Down the River, 1953, Drive a Cooked Road, 1954, My Sister Eileen, 1955, Operation Mad Ball, 1957, The Notorious Landlady, 1962; writer radio shows Line-Up; writer-creator radio show Richard Diamond; creator TV show Mr. Lucky; writer, dir. Bring Your Smile Along, 1955, He Laughed Last, 1955, Mr. Cory, 1956, This Happy Feeling, 1958, The Perfect Furlough, 1958, The Great Race, 1964, The Tamarind Seed, 1973, A Fine Mess, 1985, That's Life, 1985, Sunset, 1987, Justin Case, 1988, Skin Deep, 1989, Peter Gunn, 1989, Switch, 1991, Son of the Pink Panther, 1993; writer, prodr., dir.: A Shot in the Dark, 1964, What Did You Do in the War, Daddy?, 1966, Gunn, 1967, The Party, 1968, Darling Lili, 1969, Wild Rovers, 1971, The Return of the Pink Panther, 1975, The Pink Panther Strikes Again, 1976, Revenge of the Pink Panther, 1978, 10, 1979, S.O.B., 1980, Victor/Victoria, 1981, Trail of the Pink Panther, 1982, Curse of the Pink Panther, 1982, The Man Who Loved Women, 1983; dir.: Operation Petticoat, 1959, High Time, 1960, Breakfast at Tiffany's, 1961, Days of Wine and Roses, 1962, The Carey Treatment, 1972, Micki and Maude, 1984, Blind Date, 1986; prodr.: Waterhole No. Three, 1967; writer, prodr., dir. (Broadway) Victor/Victoria, 1995. Served with USCGR, World War II. also: Creative Artists Agy 9830 Wilshire Blvd Beverly Hills CA 90212-1804 Office: 11948 Saltair Ter Los Angeles CA 90049-4137*

EDWARDS, BOYKIN, JR., lawyer; b. Atlanta, Mar. 10, 1950; m. Jean Elizabeth Henderson, June 28, 1975; children: Rachelle, Tonya. BBA, Morris Brown Coll., 1972; JD, John Marshall Law Sch., Atlanta, 1985. Bar: Ga. 1987, U.S. Dist. Ct. (no. dist.) Ga. 1987. Claims rep. Liberty Mut. Ins. Co., Atlanta, 1972-75; spl. claims rep. Nationwide Ins. Co., Atlanta, 1975-87; sole practice Decatur, Ga., 1987—. Appointed spl. master Supreme Ct. of Ga., 1999; appointed judge DeKalb Recorder's Ct., 2000. Mem. bd. stewards St. Philip A.M.E. Ch., Atlanta, 1987—. Mem. ABA, State Bar of Ga. Avocations: spectator sports, bowling, jazz. Office: 3951 Snapfinger Pkwy Decatur GA 30035-3203

EDWARDS, BRIAN FRANCIS PEREGRINE, science educator; b. Kamloops, B.C., Can., Jan. 4, 1947; m. Lana Lee; children: David, Sarah. BS, U. B.C., 1969; AM, Harvard U., 1971, PhD, 1975. Rsch. assoc. U. Alberta, Edmonton, 1975-77, profl. assoc., 1977-80; asst. prof. to prof. Wayne State U., Detroit, 1980-89, prof., 1989—. Mem. Am. Chem. Soc., Can. Fedn. Biol. Socs., Am. Cystallographic Assn., Biophys. Soc., Am. Soc. Biochemistry and Molecular Biology, Protein Soc. Office: Wayne State U Biochemistry 540 E Canfield St Detroit MI 48201-1928 Office Phone: 313-577-5107.

EDWARDS, C. WEBB, bank executive; b. Tenn. Grad., U. Tenn., Harvard U. Exec. v.p., gen. mgr. info. svcs. 1st Interstate Bancorp, 1984—95; exec. v.p. Norwest, 1995—98; exec. v.p. tech. and ops. group Wells Fargo & Co., 1998—. Office: Wells Fargo & Co 420 Montgomery St San Francisco CA 94163

EDWARDS, CHARLE MUNDY, III, financial consultant; b. N.Y.C., Jan. 30, 1935; s. Charles Mundy Jr. and Nancy Blow (Rawls) E.; m. Janice Elaine Petty, Oct. 22, 1966; children: Melanie LeMoyne, Meghan Elizabeth Adams. AB, Princeton U., 1957; postgrad., NYU, 1959-63. With Shearson Lehman Bros., Inc., N.Y.C., 1959-85, assoc., asst. v.p., v.p., sr. v.p.; prin. Grumman Hill Assocs., Inc., Westport, Conn., 1985—. Cons. Lynch & Mayer, Inc., N.Y.C., 1994; bd. dirs. EOMG, Inc., Virginia Beach, Va. Treas. fund for Ednl. Advancement, Newark, 1985-87, pres., 1988-90, v.p., 1990-97, trustee, 1985—; trustee Family Svc. Assn. of Summit, 1987-91; pres., adminstrv. bd. United Meth. Ch., Summit, 1987-94, trustee, 1990-94; mem. City Planning Bd., Summit, 1989-91; mem. adminstrv. bd. Mt. Bethel United Meth. Ch., Marietta, Ga., 1995—, mem. fin. com., 1995-2004, chmn. endowment com., 1997—; bd. advisors Thurston Arthritis Rsch. Ctr., Chapel Hill, N.C., 1999-2002. 1st lt. USMCR, 1957-59. Mem. Princeton Quadrangle Club, Beacon Hill Club (pres. 1987-88, v.p. 1986-87, treas. 1985-86), Chattahoochee Plantation Tennis Club. Republican. Methodist. Home: 495 Atlanta Country Club Dr Marietta GA 30067-4684 Personal E-mail: charlieandjanice@bellsouth.net.

EDWARDS, CHARLES, neuroscientist, educator; b. Washington, Sept. 22, 1925; s. James Moses and Lola (Rosenthal) Edlavitch; m. Lois Bender, Aug. 12, 1951; children: Jan, James, Sally, David. AB, Johns Hopkins U., 1945, MA, 1948, PhD, 1953. Found. Infantile Paralysis postdoctoral fellow, asst. lectr. Univ. Coll., London, 1953-55; instr., asst. prof. physiol. optics Johns Hopkins U., Balt., 1955-58; asst. prof. physiology U. Utah, Salt Lake City, 1958-60; assoc. prof. physiology U. Minn., Mpls., 1960-65, prof., 1965-67; prof. biol. scis., dir. neurobiology rsch. ctr. SUNY, Albany, 1967-84, prof. emeritus biol. sci., 1986—; spl. asst. to sci. dir. Nat. Inst. Diabetes and Digestive and Kidney Diseases, NIH, 1984-88; prof. physiology, assoc. dean rsch. and grad. affairs U. South Fla. Coll. Medicine, Tampa, 1988-91. Grass lectr. CIEA del IPN, Mexico City, 1966; vis. prof. Karolinska Inst., 1975, 79, 84; mem. physiology study sect. NIH, 1971-75. Mem. editorial bd. Am. Jour. Physiology, 1967-73, Gen. Physiology Biophysics, 1983-95, Neurosci., 1979-92, Neurosci. Rsch., 1984-94. Mem. ACLU, Md. chpt., 1956-58, Utah chpt., 1959-60; mem. citizen adv. com. Sarasota Bay Nat. Estuary Program, 1994—. Lalor fellow, 1957, Lederle fellow, 1959-60; Nat. Acad. Scis. Czechoslovak Acad. Sci. Exchange fellow, 1980, 82, 84, 87, Japan Soc. Promotion of Sci. fellow, 1981, Naito Found.fellow, 1985; named to Johns Hopkins Univ. Soc. Scholars, 1987. Fellow AAAS; mem. AAUP (mem. coun. 1972-75), Am. Physiol. Soc., Marine Biol. Lab., Biophys. Soc., Physiol. Soc. Japan (hon.), Soc. Gen. Physiology (sec. 1971-73), Neurosci. Soc.

EDWARDS, CHARLES ARCHIBALD, lawyer; b. Lumberton, NC, Sept. 19, 1945; s. Charles Edwin and Elizabeth Gertrude (Gooden) E.; m. Judy Carol Griffin, Aug. 14, 1966; children: Lee McNeill, Caroline Averitt Clark. AB, Davidson Coll., 1967; JD, U. N.C., 1970. Bar: Ga. 1970, U.S. Supreme Ct. 1974, D.C. 1981, N.C. 1987. Assoc. Connerat, Dunn, Hunter, Houlihan, Maclean & Exley, Savannah, Ga., 1970-71, ptnr., 1972-76, Constangy, Brooks & Smith, Atlanta, 1976-82, Greene, Buckley, Derieux & Jones, Atlanta, 1982-86, Graham & James, Raleigh, NC, 1986-94, Womble Carlyle Sandridge & Rice, PLLC, Raleigh, 1994—, labor & employment practice group leader. Author: Georgia Employment Law, 1983; contbr. articles to profl. publs. Mem. Warrenton Town Council, 2001—. Mem. ABA, N.C. Bar Assn., State Bar Ga., Atlanta Bar Assn. (chmn. labor law sect. 1983-84). Republican. Episcopalian. Office: Womble Carlyle Sandridge & Rice PO Box 831 2100 1st Union Capitol Ctr Raleigh NC 27602 Office Phone: 919-755-2184. Office Fax: 919-755-6047. Business E-Mail: cedwards@wcsr.com.

EDWARDS, CHARLES CORNELL, surgeon, medical association administrator; b. Overton, Nebr., Sept. 16, 1923; s. Charles Busby and Lillian Margaret (Arendt) Edwards; m. Sue Cowles Kruidenier, June 24, 1945; children: Timothy, Charles Cornell, Nancy, David. Student, Princeton U., 1941—43; BA, U. Colo., 1945, MD, 1948; MS, U. Minn., 1956; LLD (hon.), Phila. Coll. Pharmacy and Sci.; LHD (hon.), Pa. Coll. Podiatry; LHD (hon.), U. Colo., 1993. Diplomate Am. Bd. Surgery. Intern St. Mary's Hosp., Mpls., 1948—49; resident surgery Mayo Found., 1950—56; pvt. practice medicine specializing in surgery Des Moines, 1956—61; mem. surg. staff Georgetown U., Washington, 1961—62; also cons. USPHS; dir. div. socio-econ. activities AMA, Chgo., 1963—67; v.p., mng. officer health and sci. affairs Booz, Allen & Hamilton, 1967—69; commr. FDA, Washington, 1969—73; asst. sec. for health HEW, Washington, 1973—75; sr. v.p., dir. Becton, Dickinson & Co., 1975—77; pres. Scripps Clinic and Research Found., La Jolla, Calif., 1977—91; pres., CEO Scripps Insts. Medicine and Sci., La Jolla, 1991—93. Bd. dirs. Bergen Brunswig Corp., No. Trust Bank, IDEC Pharms., Materia, Inc., Scripps Health Sys. Bd. regents Nat. Libr. Medicine, 1981—85; mem. Nat. Leadership Commn. on Health Care, 1986—; bd. govs. Hosp. Corp. Am., 1986—89; trustee Scripps Insts. Medicine & Sci., Scripps Found.; Scripps Rsch. Inst.; chmn. bd. dirs., trustee San Diego Hospice; trustee San Diego, YMCA. Lt. M.C. USNR, 1942—46. Recipient Disting. Svc. award, HEW, Disting. Alumnus award, Mayo Found., 1986, Humanity award, Nat. Conf., 1994, Lifetime Achievement in Corp. Governancy award, Corp. Dirs. Forum, 2001. Mem.: Nat. Acad. Scis., Inst. Medicine, Am. Hosp. Assn. (hon.), La Jolla Beach and Tennis Club, La Jolla Country Club, Princeton Club. Office: Scripps Rsch Inst 10666 N Torrey Pines Rd La Jolla CA 92037-1027 Business E-Mail: c.edward@ix.netcom.com.

EDWARDS, CHARLES HENRY, JR., surgeon, educator; b. Goldsboro, N.C., Dec. 22, 1920; s. Charles Henry and Lillie Estelle (Thornton) E.; m. Betty Shea, Mar. 11, 1950; children: Charles Henry, Christopher G. BA, U. N.C., 1940, postgrad. in Medicine, 1942; MD, Thomas Jefferson U., 1944. Diplomate Am. Bd. Surgery. Intern Pa. Hosp., Phila., 1944; resident in gen. surgery Halloran VA Hosp., S.I., 1947—51; surg. resident Martland Hosp., Newark, 1951—52; practice gen. and vascular surgery Newark, 1951—55, Glen Ridge, NJ, 1955—71, Montclair, NJ, 1971—. Mem. surg. staff St. Barnabas Hosp., St. James Hosp.; med. dir. Riverside Hospice, Boonton, N.J., 1976-78; clin. asst. prof. surgery N.J. Coll. Medicine and Dentistry, Newark, 1966—; med. dir. Individual Freedom Found. Ednl. Trust, 1976— Bd. dirs. Citizens Freedom Found. N.Y./N.J. Served to capt., M.C., U.S. Army, 1944-47. Fellow ACS; mem. AMA, N.J. State Med. Soc., Essex County Med. Soc., Mason (32 deg.), Shriners. Office: 5 Roosevelt Pl Montclair NJ 07042-3366 Office Phone: 973-748-5357.

EDWARDS, CHARLES LLOYD, lawyer; b. Chgo., July 2, 1940; s. Ed and Anita (Sopkin) E.; m. Lois S. Levine, Apr. 5, 1970; children: Laura, Karen. BBA with highest honors, U. Wis., 1962; JD, U. Chgo., 1965. Bar: Ill. 1965. Assoc. Aaron, Aaron, Schimberg & Hess, Chgo., 1965-67; ptnr., sr. counsel, Real Estate Practice DLA Piper Rudnick Gray Cary, Chgo., 1968—. Adj. prof. John Marshall Law Sch., 1997—98. Mem. ABA, Ill. State Bar Assn., Chgo. Bar Assn. (chmn. subcom. real property fin. 1986-88, vice chmn. real property continuing legal edn. 1989-91, vice chmn. real property 1991-92, chmn. real property 1992-93), Lawyers Club Chgo., Am. Coll. Mortgage Attorneys, Am. Coll. Real Estate Lawyers, Phi Beta Kappa, Beta Gamma Sigma. Avocations: classic music, collecting art, fishing, driving. Office: DLA Piper Rudnick Gray Cary Suite 1900 203 N La Salle St Chicago IL 60601-1293 Office Phone: 312-368-4010. Office Fax: 312-236-7516. Business E-Mail: charles.edwards@dlapiper.com.

EDWARDS, CHET (THOMAS CHESTER EDWARDS), congressman; b. Corpus Christi, Tex., Nov. 24, 1951; m. Lea Ann Wood. BA, Tex. A&M U., 1974; MBA, Harvard U., 1981. Legislative and dist. aide to Rep. Teague, 1974-77; assoc. Trammell Crow Ptnrs., 1981—85; pres. Edwards Communications Corp.; state senator, 1983—91; chmn. Tex. Sunset Commn.; mem. U.S. Congress from 11th Tex. dist., Washington, 1991—; Dem. chief dep. whip; mem. appropriations and policy coms., co-chmn. house army caucus and impact aid coalition. Mem. Nat. Security Com., ranking min. mem. vets. affrs. subcom. on hosp. and health care. Democrat. Office: US House of Reps 2459 Rayburn HOB Washington DC 20515-0001*

EDWARDS, CHRISTINE ANNETTE, lawyer; b. Ft. Monmouth, N.J., Aug. 30, 1952; d. Harry W. Jr. and Elizabeth Power; m. John H. Edwards, Aug. 24, 1974; children: Lindsey, John. BA, U. Md., College Park, 1974; JD with honors, U. Md., Balt., 1983. Bar: Md. 1983, D.C. 1984, Ill 1990. With Sears, Roebuck and Co., Md., 1971-81, sr. paralegal, staff asst. Washington, 1981-83, atty. govt. affairs, 1983-87; asst. v.p., dir. govt. affairs Dean Witter Fin. Svcs. Group, Washington, 1987-88, v.p., gen. counsel Lincolnshire, Ill., 1988-89, sr. v.p., 1989-91, exec. v.p., sec., chief legal officer NYC, 1991-97; exec. v.p., chief legal officer, corp. sec. Morgan Stanley Dean Witter & Co. (merger Dean Witter Discover & Co. with Morgan Stanley & Co. Inc.), NYC, 1997—99; legal dept. ABN AMRO, 1999—2000; v.p., gen. counsel Bank One Corp., 2000—03; ptnr. Winston & Strawn LP, Chgo., 2003—. Mem. bd. Fin. Svcs. Coun., Washington, 1990—; bd. trustees Nat. Found. for Consumer Credit Counseling Svcs., Silver Spring, Md., 1990-92; mem. Women in Housing and Fin., Washington, 1982—, SAI Letigation Com., 1995—, N.Y. Stock Exchange Legal Adv. Com., 1992-95; bd. dirs. Chgo. Bd. of Options Exchange, SPS Transaction Svcs. Inc.; exec. v.p., chief legal officer, corp. sec. CLO Roundtable, 1995—. Recipient Disting. Mem. award Women in Housing and Fin., Washington, 1988; named 1 of 50 Top Women Lawyers Nat. Law Journal, 1998. Mem. ABA, Securities Industry Assn. (mem. fed. regulation com. 1990—). Home: 70 Sequoia Ct Lake Forest IL 60045-2827 Office: Winston & Strawn LP 35 W Wacker Dr Chicago IL 60601-9703

EDWARDS, CHRISTOPHER LEVON, medical association administrator; PhD, U. Ky., 1997. Dir. Duke U. Med. Ctr., Chronic Pain Mgmt. Program, Durham, NC, 2001—03. Dir. Duke U. Med. Ctr., Neurobehavioral Cognitive Assessment Lab., 2001—. Orgnl. devel. Bridges Point Found., Inc., Durham, 2000—03. Grantee Fin., Nat. Alliance for Rsch. on Schizophrenia and Depression, 1. Mem.: APA (assoc.), Soc. of Behavioral Medicine. Achievements include research in race and pain; race and diabetes; prostate cancer and african am. men; Alzheimer's Disease and african ams; genetics and Alzheimer's Disease. Office: Duke U Med Ctr 932 Morreene Rd Rm 170 Durham NC 27705 Office Phone: 919-684-6908. E-mail: christopher.edwards@duke.edu.

EDWARDS, CLIFFORD HENRY COAD, law educator; b. Jamalpur, Bihar, India, Nov. 8, 1924; s. George Henry Probyn and Constance Ivy (Coad) E.; m. Kathleen Mary Faber, Jan. 6, 1951; children: Jeanette Marie, John Philip, Michael Hugh, Margaret Susan. LLB with 1st class honors, U. London, 1945. Sr. lectr. Kumasi Coll., Chana, 1956-58; assoc. prof. law U. Man., Winnipeg, 1958-64, prof., dean Sch. Law, 1964-79, dean emeritus, 1986—; pres. Man. Law Reform Commn., 1979—. Queen's coun., 1980. Recipient Stanton Tchg. Award for Excellence, U. Man., 1994. Mem. Soc. Internat. Ministries (chmn. 1984-90), Can. Bar Assn., Man. Bar Assn. (Disting. Svc. award 1995). Mem. Anglican Ch. Office: Univ of Manitoba Fort Garry Campus Robson Hall Winnipeg MB Canada R3T 2N2 Office Phone: 204-474-6138.

EDWARDS, D. M., retail executive, wholesale distribution executive, real estate company executive; b. Tyler, Tex., Apr. 12, 1953; s. Welby Clell and Davida (Mount) E.; m. Susan Alicia Pappas, 1984 (div. 1986). AA cum laude, Tyler Jr. Coll., 1974; BBA, Baylor U., 1976. Ordained deacon Bapt. Ch. Corp. coord. Dillard Dept. Stores, Inc., Ft. Worth, 1976-77; exec. v.p. W.C. Supply Co., Tyler, 1977-83; pres., owner Walker Auto Spring, Inc., Shreveport, La., 1978-88, Edwards & Assocs., Inc., 1984—96; v.p. W.C. Square, Inc., 1976-92; CEO, chmn. bd. dirs. Pruitt Co. Inc., Houston, 1988—; chmn. bd., CEO Odessa Spring Brake & Axle, Inc., 1991—; pres., owner Shreveport Spring, Brake & Axle, Inc., 1998—; v.p. CountryMedic, Inc., Ft. Worth, 2001—03. Comml. real estate investor, Shreveport, La., Houston, Odessa, and Tyler, Tex.; gen. ptnr. ESE Properties, Tyler, 1991—; mng. gen. ptrn. Heritage Dr. Plz. Office Stes., 1992-95. Mem. planning com. Tyler Heritage Tour, 1982-83; originator Designer Show-Case, Tyler, 1983; founder, chmn. Rose Garden Trust Fund, 1981-87; bd. dirs. Carnegie History Ctr., 1984-85; chmn. merger com. Smith County Hist. Soc. and Carnegie History Ctr. merger, 1993-94; pres. Smith County Youth Found., 1986-87, mem., bd. dirs., 1984-91; pres. East Tex. State Fair, 1991-94; bd. assocs. East Tex. Bapt. U., Marshall, 1988—, v.p. bd. assocs., 1990-91, pres. bd. assocs., 1991-93; mem. exec. com. bd. trustees, vice chmn. bd. trustees, 2001-2003, chair bd. trustees, 2003-2005; mem. exec. com. East Tex. State Fair, 1990—; v.p. Camp Fannin Assoc., 1992-97, Tyler, 1992—; trustee Timberline Bapt. Camp and Conf. Ctr., 1987-90, 2001-04, treas., 1989-90; mem. Smith County Hist. Commn., 1984-85, 1991-94; chmn. stewardship com. First Bapt. Ch., Tyler, 1995-96, mem. fin. com., 1987-2001, mem. long range planning com., 1999-2003; v.p. Camp Fannin Assn., 2001—; treas. Timberline Bapt. Camp and Conf. Ctr., 2002-03. Mem. Tyler Area C. of C., Smith County Hist. Soc. (chmn. bd. govs. 1984-85, 87-88, pres. 1984-85, bd. govs. 1991-94), Hist. Tyler, Inc., Tyler Jaycees (v.p. 1982-83, bd. dirs. 1982-85), Nat Trust for Hist. Preservation, SCV (treas. camp 124, 1979-83), Rotary Club of Tyler (bd. dirs. 1998—, pres. 2000—, pres. found. 2002—), Rotary Internat. (Paul Harris fellow 1998), Willow Brook Country Club (stockholder), Hollytree Country Club, East Tex. Baylor Club (chair scholarship com. 1997—, pres. 2001-05), Camp Ford Hist. Assn. (bd. dirs. 1999—, v.p. 2000, pres. 2001-03). Baptist. Home: 3600 Jill Cir Tyler TX 75701-8619 Office: PO Box 929 Tyler TX 75710-0929 also: Mountwood Ranch 7596 CR 1143 Tyler TX 75704-9817

EDWARDS, DANIEL PAUL, lawyer; educator; b. Enid, Okla., Apr. 15, 1940; s. Daniel Paul and Joye Virginia (van Horn) E.; m. Virginia Lee Kidd, Mar. 27, 1976; children: Austin Daniel, David Paul, Anne Marie. BA, U. Okla., 1962; JD, Harvard Law Sch., 1965. Bar: Colo. 1965, Hawaii, 1987, Ariz. 1988. Ptnr. Beltz, Edwards & Sabo, Colorado Springs; lectr. law Colo. Coll., 1976-87. Pres. Springs Area Beautiful Assn., 1978. Mem. ABA, Colo., Ariz. and Hawaii Bar Assn., Harvard Law Sch. Assn. Colo. (pres. 1986-87), El Paso Club, Broadmoor Golf Club, Cheyenne Mt. Club, Garden of the Gods Club, Kapalua Tennis Club, Phi Beta Kappa, Phi Delta Theta. Republican. Presbyterian. E-mail: dpedwards@bestlawllp.com.

EDWARDS, DARREL, psychologist; b. San Francisco, July 9, 1943; s. Darrus and Rose Pearl (Sannar) E.; children: Alexander Hugh, Peter David, James Royce. BS in Psychology and Philosophy, Brigham Young U., 1965, MS in Psychology and Philosophy, 1967, PhD in Clin. Psychology and Philosophy, 1968. Diplomate Am. Bd. Profl. Psychology. Postdoctoral fellow in psycholinguistics Pa. State U., 1969; commd. lt. (j.g.) USN, 1970, advanced through grades to lt. comdr., 1978; dir. psychologist Tri Community Svc. Systems, San Diego, 1973-78; prof. Calif. Sch. Profl. Psychology, San Diego, 1971-78; dir. Grid Rsch., San Diego, 1978-83; pres. The Edwards Assoc., San Diego, 1983—. Pres. Strategic Vision, 1987—; founder Inst. for Value-Centered Life, 1999; adv. Marriott Sch. Bus., Brigham Young U., 2004; cons. in field. Co-inventor in field; contbr. articles to profl. jours. Mem. adv. bd. Marriott Sch. Bus., Brigham Young U. Fellow: Am. Soc. Clin. Psychology, Am. Acad. Clin. Psychology; mem.: APA. Achievements include devel. of total quality measures for the automotive industry; development: Infinite Learning: a computer program fpr academic success.; inventor of Shadows: a value centered game for life. Office: The Edwards Assocs PO Box 420429 San Diego CA 92142-0429 Office Phone: 858-576-7141. Personal E-mail: drdarrele@aol.com.

EDWARDS, DONALD MERVIN, systems engineer, educator, dean; b. Tracy, Minn., Apr. 16, 1938; s. Mervin B. and Helen L. (Halstenrud) E.; m. Judith Lee Wilson, Aug. 8, 1964; children: John, Joel, Jeffrey, Mary. BS, S.D. State U., 1960, MS, 1961; PhD in Agrl. Engring, Purdue U., 1966. Registered profl. engr. With soil conservation svc. U.S. Dept. Agr., Marshall, Minn., 1957-62; teaching, rsch. asst. S.D. State U. and Purdue U., 1960-66; assoc. prof. agrl. engring. U. Nebr., Lincoln, 1966-71, prof., 1971-80, asst. dean Coll. Engring and Architecture, 1970-73, assoc. dean, dir. Engring Rsch. Ctr., Coll. Engring and Tech., 1973-80, dir. Energy Rsch and Devel. Ctr., 1976-80; prof. and chmn. dept. agrl. engring Mich. State U., East Lansing, 1980-89; prof. biol. systems engring., dean Coll. Agrl. Scis. and Natural Resources U. Nebr., Lincoln, 1989-00, spl. projects, 2000-01, emeritus prof. biol. sys. engring., 2001—, emeritus dean Coll. Agrl. Scis. and Natural Resources, 2001—. Mem. Engring. Accreditation Bd. Engring. and Tech.; collaborator, cons. to numerous industries and agys., 1966—. Contbr. numerous articles on irrigation, water pollution, remote sensing, energy, agrl., natural resources and engring. edn. to profl. jours. Past bd. dirs. Nat. Safety Coun.; past chmn. bd. dirs. Lincoln Transp. System. Recipient Massey-Furguson award Am. Soc of Agriculture Engineers, 1994, Outstanding Tchr. award U. Nebr. Fellow Am. Soc. Engring. Edn., Am. Soc. Agrl. Engrs., NSPE (nat. bd. dirs., nat. v.p.); mem. AAAS, Profl. Engrs. Nebr., Mich. Soc. Profl. Engrs., Coun. for Agrl. Sci. and Tech., Farmhouse Fraternity, Sigma Xi, Alpha Gamma Rho, Triangle. Home: 11420 Wenzel Dr Lincoln NE 68527-9484 E-mail: dedwards1@unl.edu.

EDWARDS, DORIS PORTER, computer specialist; b. Lambert, Miss., Jan. 18, 1962; d. Willie Morris and Carrie Mae (Tillman) E.; 1 child, Stacy Nicole. AA in Computer Sci., Draughons Coll., Memphis, 1981. Counselor French Riviera Spa, Memphis, 1989-90; pvt. practice, computer application developer Memphis, 1990—; owner, fin. cons., fund locator Developing Processing in Comm., Memphis, 1998—. Bus. owner Developing Processing in Comms.; fin. cons., cream developer. Developer cosmetic cream. Jehovah's Witness. Avocations: mathematics, reading. Home and Office: 5429 Kindle Creek Dr Memphis TN 38141-0543 E-mail: easibis@aol.com.

EDWARDS, E. STEPHEN, retired pediatrician; b. Spring Hope, N.C. m. Sylvia Edwards; 3 children. Postgrad., Davidson Coll., Duke U. Sch. Medicine, Emory U. Former pres. Rex Hosp. Med. Staff; former mng. prtnr., pediat. practice Raleigh Children and Adolescent Medicine; clin. prof., pediat. U.N.C. Co-author: Signs of Safety: A Solution and Safety Oriented Approach to Child Protection Casework, 1999. Former chair Wake County Drug Awareness Com. Fellow: Am. Acad. of Pediatrics (bd. mem., former v.p. & pres.). Avocations: golf, poker.

EDWARDS, EDITH MARTHA, lawyer; b. Great Neck, NY, Mar. 7, 1945; d. Paul Walter and Alice Matilda (Hansen) Steen; m. Thomas Murray Edwards Sr., Dec. 27, 1966; children: Janice Audrey, Thomas Murray Jr. BS, Coker Coll., 1967; JD, Olgethorpe U., 1981. Bar: Ga. 1982, U.S. Dist. Ct. (no. dist.) Ga. 1983, U.S. Supreme Ct. 1986. Atty. Ga. Legal Svcs., Nashville, 1983-84; asst. dist. atty. Alapaha Cir., Ga., 1984-86; asst. dist. Cherokee Jud. Cir., Ga., 1987; atty. pvt. practice, Valdosta, Ga., 1988—. Mem.: AAUW. Republican. Episcopalian. Avocation: art. Home and Office: 508 Gornto Rd Valdosta GA 31602-1602 Office Phone: 229-244-7993. Personal E-mail: emelegalart@hotmail.com.

EDWARDS, FRANKLIN R., economist, educator, consultant; b. Palmerton, Pa., May 5, 1937; s. Franklin Richard and Mary Edytha (Morgan) E.; m. Linda Nasif, June 9, 1968; children— Rebecca, Jarett BA in Econs., Bucknell U., 1958, MA in Econs., 1960; PhD in Econs., Harvard U., 1964; JD, NYU, 1968. Economist Bankers Trust Co., N.Y.C., 1961; economist Fed. Res. Bd., Washington, 1962, 63-64; sr. economist Office of Comptroller of Currency, Washington, 1964-66; asst. prof. Bus. Sch. Columbia U., N.Y.C., 1966-68, assoc. prof. Bus. Sch., 1968-74, prof. Bus. Sch., 1974—, vice dean acad. affairs, 1979-81, dir., prof. Columbia Futures Ctr., 1980—. Vis. scholar Am. Enterprise Inst., Washington, 1994-95; vis. prof. Inst. des Sci. Economique, Ctr. Rsch. Interdisciplinaires Droit-Economie, U. Cath., Louvain, Belgium, 1969-70. Assoc. editor Jour. of Futures Markets; editor Jour. Fin. Svcs.; contbr. articles to profl. jours. Mem. adv. bd. Futures Industry Assn. Bd., 1981-88; nominating com. Am. Stock Exchange, 1988-90; mem. bus. conduct com. N.Y. Merc. Exchange, 1989-92. Mem. Am. Econ. Assn., Am. Fin. Assn., Soc. Royale D'Economie Politique Belgique (hon.), Shadow Fin. Regulations Com., Fin. Economists Roundtable. Home: 25 Fairview Rd Scarsdale NY 10583-2137 Office: Columbia U Dept Fin Uris Hall 625 3022 Broadway New York NY 10027-6945

EDWARDS, GEOFFREY HARTLEY, newspaper publisher; b. Liverpool, Eng., Mar. 28, 1936; s. James S. and Edith (Ellison) E.; m. Pamela Duncan, Oct. 9, 1965; children: Robert James, Alistair Duncan. HNC Mech. Engring., Merseyside Tech. Coll., Birkenhead. Plant mgr. Inverest Paper Group, Derbyshire, Eng., 1962-65; gen. mgr. Liverpool Web Offset Ltd., 1965-68; asst. gen. mgr. Liverpool Daily Post & Echo, 1968-71, dir., gen. mgr., 1971-77; pub. Jour. Newspapers, Inc., Washington, 1977-91, Army Times, Washington, 1991-93; pub., CEO Current Newspapers, Washington, 1993-94; v.p. Washington Times, 1994—. Bd. dirs. Greter Washington Bd. Trade, Cultural Alliance Greater Washington, pres., 1984-86; mem. kennedy Ctr. Cmty. & Friend Bd., 1987—; campaign chmn. United Way of Nat. Capital Area, 1989, pres., 1998-2000. Mem. Brit. Newspaper Soc. (coun. 1974-77), Indsl. Rels. Newspaper Soc. (vice chmn. 1974-77).

EDWARDS, GLENN THOMAS, history educator; b. Portland, Oreg., June 14, 1931; s. Glenn Thomas E. and Marie Ann (Cheska) McMullen; m. Nannette Wilhelmina McAndie, June 15, 1957; children: Randall Thomas, Stephanie Lynn. BA, Willamette U., 1953; MA, U. Oreg., 1960, PhD, 1963. Asst. prof. San Jose State U., 1962-64, Whitman Coll., Walla Walla, Wash., 1964-68, assoc. prof., 1968-75, prof., 1976-98, ret., 1998. Cons. TV documentary Yakima Valley Mus. on William O. Douglas, Yakima, Wash., 1981-82; trustee Wash. Commn. of Humanities, Olympia, 1980-86. Author: Sowing Good Seeds: The Northwest Suffrage Campaigns of Susan B. Anthony, 1990, The Triumph of Tradition: The Emergence of Whitman College, 1859-1924, 1992; co-editor: Experiences in a Promised Land: Essays on Pacific Northwest History, 1986; contbr. articles to profl. jours. Mem. pub. edn. adv. com. State Supt. of Pub. Instrn., Olympia, 1975-78; mem. bd. trustees Wash. State Hist. Soc., 1983-92, Wash. Commn. for Humanities. Served with U.S. Army, 1954-56. Grantee Am Philos. Soc., 1971 Mem. Orgn. Am. Historians, Western History Assn., Oreg. Hist. Soc., Washington Hist. Soc. (photography cons. 1980). Congregationalist. Office: Whitman Coll Dept History Walla Walla WA 99362 E-mail: tomed@spiretech.edu.

EDWARDS, GREY HOLT, JR., academic administrator, adult education educator; b. Camp Rucker, Ala., Aug. 17, 1945; s. Grey Holt and Margaret Maddox Edwards. BA, Frederick Coll., 1967; MS, Longwood Coll., 1970; CAGS, Boston (Mass.) U., 1974; EdD, Nova Southeastern U., 1992. Cert. counselor Nat. Bd. Cert. Counselors, 1984. Tchr. Va. Beach (Va.) Pub. Schs.; prin. Charlotte (S.C.) County Pub. Schs., 1970—72; regional adminstr. Ctrl. Tex. Coll., Frankfurt, Germany, 1972—78; officer edn. svcs. U.S. Army Continuing Edn., Hanau, Germany, 1978—94; mgr. edn. U.S. Army Edn., Ft Hood, 1994—96; dir. edn. Dept. Army Edn., Giessen, Germany, 1996—. Pres. Commn. Mil. Edn., Alexandria, Va., 2001—05; bd. dirs. Assn. of Adult Edn., Washington. Prodr.: (films) Pride of Broken Arrow; contbr. articles to profl. jours. Avocations: travel, attending olympics, baseball, hiking. Home: 3 Unter Den Linden Obbornhofen 35410 Germany Office: Department of Army Education Giessen Education Center Apo Ae 09045 Germany Fax: 49-641-402-6875. Office Phone: 49-641-402-7494. Personal E-mail: grey_edwards@hotmail.com. E-mail: grey.edwards@us.army.mil.

EDWARDS, HAROLD MORTIMER, mathematics professor; b. Champaign, Ill., Aug. 6, 1936; s. Harold Mortimer and Marian Bell (Scarlett) E.; m. Betty Rollin, Jan. 21, 1979. BA, U. Wis., 1956; MA, Columbia U., 1957; PhD, Harvard U., 1961. Instr. Harvard U., 1961-62; rsch. assoc. Columbia U., 1962-63, asst. prof., 1963-66, N.Y. U., N.Y.C., 1966-69, assoc. prof., 1969-79, prof. math., 1979—2002, prof. emeritus, 2002—. Vis. sr. lectr. Australian Nat. U., 1971. Author: Advanced Calculus, 1969, Riemann's Zeta Function, 1974, Fermat's Last Theorem, 1977, Galois Theory, 1984, Divisor Theory, 1990, Linear Algebra, 1995, Essays in Constructive Mathematics, 2005. Guggenheim fellow, 1981-82 Mem. Am. Math. Soc. (Steele prize 1980, Whiteman prize 2005), Math. Assn. Am., N.Y. Acad. Scis. Home: 67 Park Ave New York NY 10016-2557 Office: 251 Mercer St New York NY 10012-1110 Office Phone: 212-998-3168. Business E-Mail: edwards@cims.nyu.edu.

EDWARDS, HARRY LAFOY, lawyer; b. Greenville, SC, July 29, 1936; s. George Belton and Mary Olive (Jones) E.; m. Suzanne Copeland, June 16, 1956; 1 child, Margaret Peden. *Third Great Grandfather, Judge Thomas Edwards, Revolutionary War soldier with Washington at Yorktown, Probate, County and District Judge and Member of South Carolina Legislature from Greenville County, married Mary Ann McClanahan, niece of Mary Marshall, Aunt of Chief Justice John Marshall. Great Great Grandfather, Francis, Edwards, War of 1812 soldier, married Laodicea, daughter of Captain Daniel Bailey, Revolutionary war solder at Kings Mountain and Cowpens. Great Grandfather, Thomas Edwards, was with Lee at Appomattox. Grandfather William Francis Edwards was a farmer. Father was President of the family real estate company. Mother was a descendant of the Aiken and Peden families.* LLB, U. S.C., 1963, JD, 1970. Bar: S.C. 1963, U.S. Dist. Ct. S.C. 1975, U.S. Ct. Appeals (4th cir.) 1974. Assoc. Edwards and Edmunds, Greenville, 1963; v.p., sec., dir. Edwards Co., Inc., Greenville, 1963-65; atty. investment legal dept. Liberty Life Ins. Co., Greenville, 1965-67, asst. sec., asst. v.p., head investment legal dept., 1967-70; asst. sec. Liberty Corp., 1970-75; asst. v.p. Liberty Life Ins. Co., 1970-75; sec. Bent Tree Corp., CEL, Inc., 1970-75; sec., dir. Westchester Mall, Inc., 1970-75; asst. sect. Libco, Inc., Liberty Properties, Inc., 1970-75; pvt. practice, Greenville, 1975—. Editor U. S.C. Law Rev., 1963. Com. mem. Hipp Fund Spl. Edn., Greenville County Sch. Sys.; mem. Boyd C. Hipp II Scholarship Com., Wofford Coll. Spartanburg, S.C.; scholarship com. Liberty Scholars, U. S.C., 1984, 86-2005. With USAFR, 1957-63. Mem.: ABA, Greenville Lawyers, Greenville County Bar Assn., S.C. Bar Assn., Soc. Descs. of Knights of the Garter/Windsor Castle, Magna Charta Barons (Somerset chpt.), Poinsett Club (Greenville), Phi Delta Phi. Baptist. Home: 106 Ridgeland Dr Greenville SC 29601-3017 Office: PO Box 10350 Greenville SC 29603-0350 E-mail: harryedwards106@bellsouth.net.

EDWARDS, HARRY THOMAS, federal judge; b. NYC, Nov. 3, 1940; s. George H. Edwards and Arline Ross Lyle; m. Pamela Carrington; children: Brent, Michelle. BS, Cornell U., 1962; JD, U. Mich., 1965. Assoc. firm Seyfarth, Shaw, Fairweather & Geraldson, Chgo., 1965—70; prof. law U. Mich., 1970—75; vis. prof. Free U. Brussels, 1974; vis. prof. law Harvard U., 1975—76, prof., 1976—77; prof. law U. Mich., 1977—80; dir. AMTRAK, 1977—80, chmn. bd., 1979—80; judge U.S. Ct. Appeals (D.C. cir.), Washington, 1980—, chief judge, 1994—2001; disting. lectr. law Duke U., 1983—89; lectr. law Georgetown Law Ctr., 1985—86. Neutral arbitrator, 1970—80; mem. Adminstrv. Conf. of U.S., 1976—80; faculty mem. Inst. for Ednl. Mgmt., Harvard U., 1976—82; lectr. in law Pa. Law Sch., 1981—82; lectr. Harvard Law Sch., 1982—88, Mich. Law Sch., 1988—89; adj. prof. law NYU Law Sch., 1989—; mem. Judicial Conf. of the US, 1994—2001; vis. prof. Cornell Sch. Indsl. & Labor Relations, 2002. Co-author: Labor Relations Law in the Public Sector, 1974, 1979, 1985, Lawyer as a Negotiator, 1977, Collective Bargaining and Labor Arbitration, 1979, Higher Education and the Law, 1979; editl. and adv. bds. West Publishing Co., 1978—80. Chmn. Ann Arbor Model Cities Legal Svcs. Ctr., Inc., 1971—72; mentor Unique Learning Ctr., Washington. Mem.: ABA (sec. sect. labor law 1976—77), Supreme Court Hist. Soc., Fed. Judges Assn., Assn. Am. Law Sch., Am. Soc. Internat. Law, Am. Judicature Soc., Am. Bar Found., Am. Law Inst., Am. Arbitration Assn. (dir. 1979—80), Am. Acad. Arts and Scis., Nat. Acad. Arbitrators (dir. 1975—80, v.p. 1978—80), Order of Coif. Office: US Ct Appeals 333 Constitution Ave NW Washington DC 20001-2805

EDWARDS, HELEN THOM, physicist; b. Detroit, May 27, 1936; d. Edgar Robertson and Mary (Milner) Thom; m. Donald A. Edwards. BS in Physics, Cornell U., 1957, MA in Physics, 1963, PhD in Physics, 1966. Rsch. assoc. Cornell U., Ithaca, NY, 1966-70; assoc. head booster Fermi Nat. Accelerator Lab., Batavia, Ill., 1970-71, staff physicist, M.R., 1971-75, head switchyard extraction group, 1975-78, leader tevatron design group, 1978-79, dep. head saver div., 1980-81, dep. head accelerator div., 1981-86, head accelerator div., 1987-88, guest scientist, 1992—; head accelerator constrn. div. SSC/URA, Dallas, 1989-90, tech. dir., 1990—92. Recipient Achievement in Accelerator Physics and Tech. U.S. Summer Sch. on Particle Accelerator Prize, 1985, Ernest O. Lawrence award Dept. of Energy, 1986, Nat. Medal Tech., 1989; MacArthur Found. Chgo. fellow, 1988. Fellow Am. Phys. Soc.; mem. NAE.

EDWARDS, HERMAN, professional football coach; b. Monmouth, N.J., Apr. 27, 1954; m. Lia Edwards; 1 child, Gabrielle Lee; 1 child, Marcus. Student, U. Calif., 1972, student, 1974, Monterrey Peninsula J.C., 1973; BA in Criminial Justice, San Diego State, 1976. Profl. football player Phila. Eagles, 1977—85, L.A. Rams, 1986, Atlanta Falcons, 1986; defensive backs coach San Jose State, 1987—89; scout, asst. coach Kansas City Chiefs, 1990—95, 1995, defensive backs coach, 1992—94; asst. head coach, defensive backs coach Tampa Bay Buccaneers, 1996—2000; head coach N.Y. Jets, 2001—. Co-author (with Shelly Smith): You Play to Win the Game: Lessons for Success On and Off the Field, 2004. Office: NY Jets Ticket Office 1000 Fulton Ave Hempstead NY 11550-1099

EDWARDS, HOWARD LEE, retired gas industry executive, lawyer; b. Baker City, Oreg., June 10, 1931; s. Elmer L. and Bernice (Stringham) E.; m. Carolyn Bagley, Mar. 19, 1954; children: Bryant B., H. McKay, Mitchell L., Paul S. BS, Brigham Young U., 1955; postgrad., Stanford U., 1955-56, U. Utah, 1956-57; JD, George Washington U., 1959. Bar: Utah 1959, Colo. 1981, Alaska 1982, Calif. 1987. Legal asst., atty. US Dept. Interior, Washington and Salt Lake City, 1957-61; ptnr. Van Cott, Bagley, Cornwall & McCarthy, Salt Lake City, 1961-68; asst. gen. counsel Anaconda Co., NYC, 1968, asst. to chmn. bd., 1969, v.p., sec., 1970-77; gen. atty. Denver, 1977-82, Anchorage, 1982-83; corp. sec. Atlantic Richfield Co., LA, 1984-95; ret., 1995. Bd. dirs. Dynatronics Corp., 1996—. Trustee Rocky Mountain Mineral Law Found., 1968-87; mem. nat. adv. coun. Brigham Young U. Sch. Mgmt., 1972-85; mem. nat. adv. coun. Dixie State Coll., St. George, Utah, 1987—, chmn., 1994-95; bd. visitors J. Reuben Clark Law Sch., 1980-83; bd. dir. LA region NCCJ, 1987-94, Ettie Lee Homes for Youth, 1989-96, Kostopoulos Dream Found., 1997-2002, Deseret Found.; chmn. cmty. adv. coun. Heart and Lung Rsch. Found.; mem. exec. bd. Verdugo Hills coun. Boy Scouts Am., 1992-95, Verdugo Hills Hosp. Found., 1992-95; honorary bd. Utah Symphony and Opera, 2002—. Recipient Disting. Citizen award, Dixie State Coll., St. George, Utah, 2000. Mem. Am. Mining Congress (chmn. pub. lands com. 1970-84, Disting. Svc. award 1983), Coun. on Fgn. Rels., Pacific Coun. on Internat. Policy, Brigham Young U. Alumni Assn. (bd. dir. 1974-83, pres. 1980-81), Econ. Round Table, Rotary. Republican. Mem. Lds Ch. Home: PO Box 680934 Park City UT 84068-0934 E-mail: howardledwards@hotmail.com.

EDWARDS, IRENE ELIZABETH (LIBBY EDWARDS), dermatologist, educator, medical researcher; b. Winston-Salem, N.C., Mar. 17, 1950; d. Robert Dixon Edwards and Irene Octavia (Temple) Fisher; m. Clayton Samuel Owens, Apr. 19, 1985; 1 child, Sarah Tay. BS magna cum laude, Wake Forest U., 1972; MD, Bowman Gray Sch. Medicine, 1976; postgrad., N.C. Bapt. Hosp., 1979, U. Ariz., 1981, 84. Diplomate Nat. Bd. Med. Examiners, Am. Bd. Internal Medicine, Am. Bd. Pediatrics, Am. Bd. Dermatology. Intern N.C. Bapt. Hosp., Winston-Salem, 1976-78, resident in pediatrics, 1978-79; resident in internal medicine U. Ariz. Health Scis. Ctr., Tucson, 1979-81, resident in dermatology, 1982-84; instr. dermatology U. Ariz. Coll. Medicine, Tucson, 1984-85, asst. prof. dermatology, 1985-90; clin. rschr., chief sect. dermatology Tucson VA Med. Ctr., 1984-90; chief dermatology Carolinas Med. Ctr., Charlotte, N.C., 1990—; clin. assoc. prof. dermatology, clin. rschr. Wake Forest U., Winston-Salem, 1993—, U. N.C., Chapel Hill, 1993—. Nat. lectr. in field. Author: Dermatology in Emergency Care, 1997; co-author: Genital Dermatology, 1994; editor: Genital Dermatology Atlas, 2004; contbr. chpts. to books, numerous articles to profl. jours. Reynolds scholar, 1969-72, Fellow Am. Acad. Dermatology, Am. Acad. Pediatrics; mem. Soc. Pediatric Dermatology, Internat. Soc. Tropical Dermatology, Women's Dermatologic Soc., Internat. Soc. for Study of Vulvovaginal Disease (pres.-elect), Charlotte Dermatological Soc., Phi Beta Kappa, Alpha Epsilon Delta. Home: 2409 Cuthbertson Rd Waxhaw NC 28173-8110 Office Phone: 704-367-9777.

EDWARDS, JACK, congressman, lawyer; b. Birmingham, Ala., Sept. 20, 1928; s. William Jackson and Sue (Fuhrman) E.; m. Jolane Vander Sys, Jan. 30, 1954; children: Mrs. Richard Weavil, Richard Arnold. BS in Commerce and Bus. Adminstrn., U. Ala., 1952, LLB, 1954. Bar: Ala. 1954, D.C. 1983. Practice, Mobile, 1954-64; mem. 89th-98th Congresses from 1st Dist. Ala., 1965-85; mem. com. appropriations; mem. def. and transp. subcom.; vice chmn. Ho. Rep. Conf.; with Hand Arendall L.L.C., Mobile, Ala., 1985—. Bd. dirs. ret. The Southern Co., Holnam Inc., Northrop Grumman Corp., Aerospace Corp., Dravo Corp., QMS, Inc. Trustee U. Ala. Served with USMC, 1946-48, 50-51. Mem. ABA, Ala. Bar Assn., Mobile Bar Assn. (sec. 1956), Mobile Jr. Bar Assn. (pres. 1957), D.C. Bar Assn., Mobile Area C. of C. (chmn. bd. 1986), Kappa Alpha (pres. 1951-53), Omicron Delta Kappa. Presbyterian. (elder). Office: Am South Bank Bldg 107 Saint Francis St Ste 3000 Mobile AL 36602-3330 Office Phone: 251-694-6234. Business E-Mail: jedwards@handarendall.com.

EDWARDS, JAMES ALFRED, lawyer; b. Orlando, Fla., Feb. 18, 1954; BA in Psychology with high honors, Auburn U., 1976; JD with high honors, U. Fla., 1979. Bar: Fla. 1979, U.S. Dist. Ct. (no. dist.) Fla. 1979, U.S. Dist. Ct. (mid. and so. dists.) Fla. 1981, U.S. Ct. Appeals (5th cir.) 1979, U.S. Ct. Appeals (11th cir.) 1982, U.S. Supreme Ct. 1984; bd. cert. civil trial lawyer Fla. Bar Assn.; cert. mediator cir., dist. and ct. of appeals. Ptnr. Rumberger, Kirk & Caldwell, Orlando, Fla., 1979-89, Roth, Edwards & Smith, P.A., Orlando, Fla., 1989-2000, Cabaniss, Conroy & McDonald, LLP, Orlando, 2000, Law Office James A. Edwards, PA, Maitland, Fla., 2001—. Mem. Fla. Bar Assn. (cert. civil trial lawyer, mem. trial lawyers, appellate practice sects., com. on professionalism), Orange County Bar Assn. (mem. jud. rels. com.), Coastal Conservation Assn. (Fla. state bd. mem.). Avocations: fishing, water-skiing, skiing. Office: 100 E Sybelia Ave # 375 Maitland FL 32751 Fax: 407-647-9735. Office Phone: 407-647-9733. Business E-Mail: JEdwards@bigfishlaw.com.

EDWARDS, JAMES D., accounting company executive; b. Cleve., Nov. 4, 1943; s. James D. and Elizabeth (Reynolds) E.; m. Sharon E. Bordelon, May 2, 1968; 1 child, David. BS in Acctg., Bob Jones U., 1964. CPA, Ga. From staff acct. to ptnr. Arthur Andersen & Co., Atlanta, 1964-73, mng. ptnr. Atlanta office, 1979-87, mng. ptnr. Americas N.Y.C., 1987—. Bd. dirs., exec. com. Atlanta C. of C., 1982-85, Woodruff Arts Ctr., Atlanta, 1986-87; chmn. Cen. Atlanta Progress, 1986-87. Mem. Board Room (N.Y.C.),d The Stanwich Club (Greenwich, Ct.) Atlanta Country Club. Office: Arthur Andersen 33 W Monroe St Chicago IL 60603-5300

EDWARDS, JAMES DALLAS, III, consulting company executive; b. Harriman, Tenn., Aug. 9, 1937; s. James Dallas Jr. and Helen Louise (Milburn) E.; m. Louisa Diane Fultz, July 15, 1961. BBA, U. Tenn., 1959. Customer service supr. Aluminum Co. Am., Alcoa, Tenn., 1964-67, staff product planner Pitts., 1967-70, traffic mgr., 1970-74; plant mgr. Soundesign Corp., Santa Claus, Ind., 1974-78; v.p., gen. mgr. Thermwood Corp., Dale, Ind., 1978-81; pres., chief exec. officer Spencer Plastic Products Corp. (name now Spencer Industries), Dale, 1981-92, also bd. dirs.; pres. Edwards & Assocs., Santa Claus, Ind., 1992—. Chmn. bd. dirs. So. Ind. Rehab. Services, Boonville, 1977-82; bd. dirs. Southwest Ind. Pvt. Industry Coun., 1989—, Ind. Small Bus. Coun.; mem. Santa Claus Indsl. Park Bd., Santa Claus, 1978—; pres. Licolnland Econ. Devel. Corp. Named Ind. Small Bus. Person of Yr., 1989, Ind. Entrepeneur of Yr., 1989, recipient Ind. Global Competitiveness award, 1989. Mem. Am. Prodn. and Inventory Control Soc. (bd. dirs. 1970-72), Soc. Plastics Engrs., Soc. Mfg. Engrs., Naval Res. Assn. (pres. 1967-71), SBA (Ind. adv. coun. 1989—), Res. Officers Assn., Ind. C. of C. (dir.), Dale C. of C., Rolling Hills Country Club, Kiwanis, Elks, Optimist. Presbyterian. Avocations: golf, reading. Home: 826 Balthazar Dr Santa Claus IN 47579 Office: PO Box 372 Santa Claus IN 47579-0372 Office Phone: 812-544-2276. Business E-Mail: jdedwards@psci.net.

EDWARDS, JAMES FRANK, artist, educator; b. N.Y.C., July 25, 1948; s. J. Frank and Norma M. Edwards. BA, U. Calif., Santa Barbara, 1970, MFA, 1972. Instr. dept. art U. S.C., Columbia, 1972-75, asst. prof., 1975-80, assoc. prof., 1980-90, prof. dept. art, 1990—, acting assoc. head dept. art, 1989, chair art studio div. dept. art, 1984-94. Lectr., presenter, workshop facilitator. Works exhibited in one-person shows including Greenville County Mus. Art, Greenville, S.C., 1976, Calif. State U., Stanislaus, 1980, Hodges Taylor Gallery, Charlotte, N.C., 1986, The Upstairs, Tryon, N.C., 1989, Meteor, Columbia, S.C., 1992; group shows include Atlanta Festival of Art, 1989, S.C. State Mus., 1989, 90, 92, Rowe Art Ctr. Gallery, U. N.C., Charlotte, 1990, Gibbes Mus. Art, Charleston, S.C., 1992-93; executed mural Playhouses, Atlanta Legal Aid Bldg, 1988; represented in permanent collections including Atlanta Newspapers, 1979, Ala. Power Co., 1987, U.S. State Dept., 1988, Nations Bank Corp. Hdqrs., Charlotte, 1992; contbr. articles to profl. jours.; featured in mag. articles. Office: U SC Dept Art Columbia SC 29208-0001

EDWARDS, JAMES ROBERT, minister, educator; b. Colorado Springs, Oct. 28, 1945; s. Robert Emery and Mary Eleanor (Callison) E.; m. Mary Jane Pryor, June 22, 1968; children: Corrie, Mark. BA, Whitworth Coll., Spokane, Wash., 1967; MDiv, Princeton Sem., 1970; PhD, Fuller Sem., Pasadena, Calif., 1978. Youth min. First Presbyn. Ch., Colorado Springs, 1971-78; prof. religion Jamestown (N.D.) Coll., 1978—97, Whitworth Coll., Spokane, Wash., 1997—. Mem. spkrs. bur. N.D. Humanities Coun., 1983-84; rsch. scholar U. Tuebingen, Germany, 1988, Tyndale Ho., Cambridge, England, 2000; spkr. in field. Author: (with others) The Layman's Overview of the Bible, 1987, Commentary on Romans, 1992, The Divine Intruder, 2000, Commentary on Gospel of Mark, 2002, Is Jesus the Only Savior?, 2005; contbg. editor Christianity Today, 1993—; contbr. articles to profl. jours. Recipient several tchg. awards; Templeton grantee in sci. and religion, 1996; scholar German Acad. Exch., 1993 Mem. Soc. Bibl. Lit. Office: Whitworth College Dept Theology Spokane WA 99251 Business E-Mail: jedwards@whitworth.edu.

EDWARDS, JEFFREY ALAN, economics professor; s. John A and Ann P Edwards; m. Catherine Stasser Edwards, 2002. BA, U. NC at Chapel Hill, 1996; MA, Va. Tech., 2001, PhD, 2002. Econ. prof. Tex. Tech. U., 2003—. Asst. editor Jour. Econ., 2004—; contbr. articles. Mem.: Internat. Atlantic Econ. Assn., Mo. Valley Econ. Assn., Internat. Water Resources Assn. Republican. Office: Tex Tech U Dept Econ Box 41014 Lubbock TX 79409

EDWARDS, JEROME, retired lawyer; b. N.Y.C., July 5, 1912; s. Philip and Anna (Hollinger) E.; m. Mildred Kahn, Dec. 7, 1941 (dec.); children: Susan, Bruce (dec.). BS, NYU, 1931, JD, 1933. Bar: N.Y. State 1934, Calif. 1975. Asso. firm T.J. Lesser, 1934-36; pvt. practice N.Y.C., 1936-42; sr. partner Phillips, Nizer, Benjamin, Krim & Ballon, N.Y.C., 1942-62; v.p., gen. counsel 20th Century Fox Film Corp., N.Y.C. and Los Angeles, 1962-77; of counsel Kaplan, Livingston, Goodwin, Berkowitz & Selvin, Beverly Hills, Calif., 1977-81, Musick, Peeler & Garrett, Los Angeles, 1982-83, Phillips, Nizer, Benjamin, Krim & Ballon, Los Angeles, 1985-89. Mem. ABA, Am. Film Mktg. Assn. (arbitrator panel), Am. Arbitration Assn. (nat. pnel neutral arbitrators 1960-2000). Address: 5370 Yolanda Ave Tarzana CA 91356-3322

EDWARDS, JESSE EFREM, pathologist, educator; b. Hyde Park, Mass., July 14, 1911; s. Max and Nellie (Gordon) E.; m. Marjorie Helen Brooks, Nov. 12, 1952; children— Ellen Ann Villa, Brooks Sayre. BS, Tufts Coll., 1932, MD, 1935; DSc (hon.), Georgetown U., 1990. Diplomate Am. Bd. Med. Examiners, Am. Bd. Pathology. Resident Mallory Inst. Pathology, Boston, 1935-36, asst., 1937-40; intern Albany (N.Y.) Hosp., 1936-37; instr. pathology Boston U., 1938; instr. pathology, bacteriology, surgery Tufts Med. Coll., 1939-40; research fellow Nat. Cancer Inst. USPHS, 1940-42; cons. sect. pathologic anatomy Mayo Clinic, 1946-60; asst. prof. grad. sch. U. Minn., 1946-51, asso. prof., 1951-54, prof. pathologic anatomy, clin. prof. med. sch., prof. pathology grad. sch., 1960—96; chief pathologist United Hosp. (formerly Chas. T. Miller Hosp.), St. Paul, 1960-80; cons. pathologist Hennepin County Hosp., Mpls., 1964—; cons. dept. pathology Mpls. Vets. Hosp., 1966—90; cons. pathologist St. Paul Ramsey Hosp., 1967-80; dir. registry of cardiovascular disease United Hosp., St. Paul, 1980-87, sr. cons. registry of cardiovascular disease, 1987—, also sr. cons. Jesse E. Edwards Registry of Cardiovascular Disease, 1987—. Pres. World Congress Pediatric Cardiology, 1980; mem. pathology study sect. USPHS, 1957-62; civilian cons. surgeon gen. AUS, 1947-69 Author: Atlas Acquired Diseases of Heart and Great Vessels, 1961, (with T.J. Dry and others) Congenital Anomalies of the Heart and Great Vessels, 1948, (with others) An Atlas of Congenital Anomalies of the Heart and Great Vessels, 1954, (with R.S. Fontana) Congenital Cardiac Disease, 1962, (with J.R. Stewart, O. Kincaid) An Atlas of Vascular Rings and Related Malformations of the Aortic System, 1963, (with C.A. Wagenvoort, D. Heath) Pathology of Pulmonary Vasculature, 1963, (with others) Correlation of Pathologic Anatomy and Angiocardiography, 1965, Coronary Arterial Variations in the Normal Heart and in Congenital Heart Disease, 1975, Coronary Heart Disease, 1976, (with Brooks S. Edwards) Jesse E. Edwards Synopsis of Congenital Heart Disease, 2000; Editor: (with others) Circulation; Contbr. (with others) articles to profl. jours. Served from capt. to lt. col. M.C. AUS, 1942-46. Recipient Distinguished Tchr. award Minn. Med. Found., 1974; Gold Heart award Am. Heart Assn., 1970; Gifted Tchr. award Am. Coll. Cardiology, 1977 Mem. AMA, Minn. Med. Assn., Soc. Exptl. Biology and Medicine, Am. Heart Assn. (pres. 1967-68), Minn. Heart Assn. (pres. 1962-63), Internat. Acad. Pathology (pres. 1955-56), Am. Assn. Pathologists and Bacteriologists, World Congress Pediat. Cardiology, Coll. Am. Pathologists, Am. Soc. Exptl. Pathology, Sigma Xi, Alpha Omega Alpha. Home: 1565 Edgcumbe Rd Saint Paul MN 55116-2304 Office: United Hosp Saint Paul MN 55102 E-mail: doctorjee@aol.com.

EDWARDS, JOHN CARVER, retired archivist; b. Charleston, S.C., Dec. 8, 1939; s. John Pelham and Elizabeth Carver Edwards; m. Judith Brina Task, Jan. 29, 2002; children: Leigh Carver, John Spann, Liam Morgan Quinlan, Kelly Harris Quinlan. BA with honors, Wofford Coll., 1964; MA, U. Ga., 1966, PhD, 1975. Head, manuscripts divsn. Ga. Dept. of Archives and History, Atlanta, 1970—72; records officer U. Ga., Athens, 1972—77, archivist, 1977—93, spl. projects archivist, 1993—2000, emeritus, 2000—. Program co-director, exhibit preparator conf. and exhibit Deliver Them From Evil: A Commemoration of America's Role in the Global War Against Fascism, 1941-1945, 1994; regular history and biography book reviewer Libr. Jour., N.Y.C., 1996—. Author: (books) Patriots In Pinstripe: Men Of The National Security League, 1982, Berlin Calling: American Broadcasters in Service to the Third Reich, 1991, Airmen Without Portfolio: U.S. Mercenaries In Civil War Spain, 1997, Flying For Orville: Howard Rinehart's Life of Adventure, 2004; contbr. 3 essays Encyclopedia Of World War I, two one hour radio broadcasts Berlin Calling, Nat. Pub. Radio (Best Documentary award Soc. of Profl. Journalists, The Pub. Radio News Directors Inc., Ga. Assn. of Broadcasters, 1994), Flyers Of Fortune, Nat. Pub. Radio (Hon. Mention award, 1999), articles to profl. publs. Active various polit. campaigns, Cleveland, Ga., 2002—03. Mem.: Acad. Cert. Archivists (cert., charter mem.), Soc. Am. Archivists, Delta Tau Kappa (assoc.), Pi Gamma Mu (assoc.), Phi Alpha Theta (assoc.), Phi Kappa Phi (assoc.). Independent. Episcopalian. Avocations: military modeling, reading, walking, baseball, fishing. Home: 1475 Highway 255 South Cleveland GA 30528 E-mail: jedwards@uga.edu.

EDWARDS, JOHN RALPH, retired chemist, educator; b. Streator, Ill., Feb. 27, 1937; s. Ralph E. and Ruth M. Edwards; m. Margaret E. Smith, July 15, 1961; children: Peter J., Sharon E., Susan D. BS, Ill. Wesleyan U., 1959; PhD, U. Ill., 1964. NIH postdoctoral fellow Tufts U., Boston, 1964-66; asst. prof. chemistry Villanova (Pa.) U., 1966-73, assoc. prof., 1973-80, prof., 1980—, chmn. dept. chemistry, 1980-90, asst. chmn., 1996—2002, ret., 2002. Contbr. articles to profl. jours. Grantee, NIH, 1970—76. Mem. Am. Soc. Biochemistry and Molecular Biology, Am. Chem. Soc., U.S. Orienteering Fedn., Sigma Xi, Phi Kappa Phi Office: Villanova U Dept Chemistry Villanova PA 19085 Business E-Mail: John.Edwards@Villanova.edu.

EDWARDS, JOHN REID, former senator, lawyer; b. Seneca, SC, June 10, 1953; s. Wallace R. and Catherine (Bobbie) Edwards; m. Mary Elizabeth Anania, July 30, 1977; children: Lucius Wade (dec. 1996), Catharine, Emma Claire, Jack Atticus. Student Clemson U., 1971; BS with high honors in textile mgmt., NC State U., 1974; JD with honors, U. NC, 1977. Bar: NC 1977, Tenn. 1978, US Dist. Ct. (ea. dist.) NC. Law clk. to Hon. Franklin T. Dupree US Dist. Ct. (ea. dist.) NC, 1977—78; assoc. Dearborn & Ewing, Nashville, 1978-81, Tharrington Smith & Hargrove, Raleigh, NC, 1981-83, ptnr., 1984-92; founder, ptnr. Edwards & Kirby, LLP, Raleigh, NC, 1993-99; US senator from NC, 1999—2005; dir. Ctr. on Poverty, Work, and Opportunity, U. NC, Chapel Hill, 2005—. Co-author (with John Auchard): Four Trials, 2004. Bd. dirs. Urban Ministries, Raleigh, 1996—97; soccer coach Capital Area Soccer League, Raleigh, 1985—97; v.p. Challenge Soccer League, Raleigh; youth basketball coach YMCA Salvation Army, Raleigh; founding trustee Wade Edwards Found., 1996—; mem. adv. bd. Frank Porter Graham Child Devel. Ctr., Chapel Hill, 2000—; visionary com. Edenton St. United Meth. Ch. Recipient Steven J. Sharp Pub. Svc. award Assn. Trial Lawyers Am., 1997; named Lawyer of Yr. Lawyers Weekly, 1996. Fellow Am. Coll. Trial Lawyers; mem. NC Law Review, 1976-77, ABA, ATLA, Inner Circle of Advocates, Am. Bd. Trial Advocacy, Chief Justice Susie M. Sharp Inns of Ct. (master), NC Acad. Trial Lawyers (v.p., bd. govs.), NC Bar Assn., Tenn. Bar Assn., So. Trial Lawyers Assn., U. NC Law Sch. Alumni Assn. (bd. dirs. 1993-99), Order of Coif, Phi Kappa Phi. Democrat. Meth. Achievements include winning the largest personal injury settlement in NC history, 1987; Democratic candidate for Vice Pres. of the US, 2004. Office: U NC 250 E Franklin St Chapel Hill NC 27599

EDWARDS, JOHN WESLEY, JR., urologist; b. Ferndale, Mich., Apr. 9, 1933; s. John W. and Josephine (Wood) E.; m. Ella Marie Law, Dec. 25, 1954; children: Joella, John III. Student, Alma Coll., 1949-50; BS, U. Mich., 1954; postgrad., Wayne State U., 1954-56; MD, Howard U., 1960. Internship Walter Reed Gen. Hosp., 1960-61, surg. resident, 1962-63, urol. resident, 1963-66; asst. chief urology Tripler Army Med. Ctr., 1966-69; comdr. 4th Med. Battalion, 4th Infantry Div., Vietnam, 1969; chief profl. svcs., urology 91st Evacuation Hosp., Vietnam, 1969-70; urologist Straub Clinic, Inc., 1970-74; pvt. practice, 1974-97; v.p. med. staff svcs. Queen's Med. Ctr., Honolulu, 1993-94; v.p. physician rels. Queen's Health Sys., Honolulu, 1994-96; acting adminstr. Diagnostic Lab. Svcs., Inc., Honolulu, 1995-96, pres., 1996—. Chief dept. surgery Straub Clinic and Hosp., 1973; asst. chief dept. srgery Queen's Med. Ctr., 1977-79, chief, 1989-93; cons. in urology; chief det. cln. svcs. Kapiolani Women's and Children's Med. Ctr., 1981-83; clin. assoc. prof. U. Hawaii Sch. of Medicine; chmn. task force on phys. hosp. collaboration The Queens Health System, 1993—. Contbr. articles to profl. jours. Bd. dirs. Hawaii Med. Svc. Assn., Honolulu, 1979—85, Hawaii Heart Assn., Honolulu, 1977—79, Hawaii Assn. for Physician's Indemnification, Honolulu, 1980—86; commr. City and County of Honolulu, Honolulu, 1990—91; Bd. dirs. Mediation Ctr. of the Pacific, Inc., 1995—2001, Queens Devel. Corp., 1999—2000, Kahala Sr. Living Cmty., Inc., 2000—01. Recipient Howard O. Gray award for Professionalism, 1988, Leaders of Hawaii award, 1983; named Hawaii African-Am. Humanitarian of the Yr. by Hawaii chpt. Links, Inc., 1991. Fellow: ACS (gov. at large from Hawaii 1986—92, sec.-treas. Hawaii chpt. 1991); mem.: NAACP, AMA, Surgicare of Hawaii (v.p. 1983—86), Hawaii Med. Assn., Hawaii Urol. Assn., Am. Urol. Assn. (gen. chmn. Western sect. 56th ann. meeting 1980, exec. com. 1983—84, del. dist. 1 1985—86, gen. chmn. 63d ann. meeting 1987, pres. 1989—90, nom. com. 1990—93, alt. del. Western sect. 1991—92, chmn. nom. 1992—93), Alpha Omega Alpha, Chi Delta Mu, Alpha Phi Alpha. Office: Diagnostic Lab Svcs 650 Iwilei Rd Ste 300 Honolulu HI 96817-5319 E-mail: jedwards@dls.queens.org.

EDWARDS, JOHN WESLEY, II, lawyer; b. Williamsport, Pa., Nov. 29, 1948; s. Robert Wesley Edwards and Jean Eleanor (Seitzer) Leprohon; m. Lee Ellen Berliner, May 22, 1971; children: Wesley David, Katherine Lee, Meredith Jean. BA, Colgate U., 1970; JD, Duke U., 1974. Bar: Ohio 1974, Calif. 2001, U.S. Dist. Ct. (no. dist.) Ohio 1974, U.S. Dist. Ct. (no. dist.) Calif. 2001, U.S. Ct. Appeals (6th cir.) 1974, U.S. Ct. Appeals (9th cir.) 2001. Assoc. Jones, Day, Reavis & Pogue, Cleve., 1974-82, ptnr., 1982—. Served to cpl. USMCR, 1970-76. Mem. Cleve. Bar Assn. (Fed. ct. com.), Order of Coif, Phi Beta Kappa. Clubs: Mayfield Country (Lyndhurst, Ohio). Republican. Presbyterian. Office: Jones Day 2882 Sand Hill Rd Ste 240 Menlo Park CA 94025 Home: 1272 San Raymundo Rd Hillsborough CA 94010-6653

EDWARDS, JORDAN TUCKER, music educator; b. Richmond, Va. s. John Allen and Sharron Anne Edwards. B of music, Longwood U., 1999—2003. Music tchr. Bensley, Hopkins and Wells Elementary Sch., Chesterfield, Va., 2003—04, Evergreen, Watkins, Chesterfield, Va., 2004—05. Mem.: Phi Kappa Phi, Phi Mu Alpha. United Meth.

EDWARDS, JOYCE PERRY, language educator; b. Durham, NC, Dec. 24, 1944; d. Lawrence Pryor and Artelia Marsh Perry; m. Murray L. Edwards, Mar. 12, 1988. BA, NC Coll., Durham, 1966; MA, NC Ctrl. U., 1978; MEd, NC State U., 1971, PhD, 1983. Cert. tchr. NC, curriculum specialist NC, prin. NC, supt. NC. English tchr. Somerset County Schs., Princess Anne, Lynchburg (Va.) City Schools, 1966—68; sch. counselor Wake County Pub. Sch. Sys., Raleigh, NC, 1971—76, guidance supr., 1976—81, asst. supt., 1981—86; exec. dir. of student services and instrn. Durham (NC) City Schools, 1988—91, supt. of schools, 1991—92, assoc. supt., 1992—93; asst. supt. Edgcombe County Schools, Tarboro, NC, 1993—96; assoc. prin. for instrn. Moore County Schools, Southern Pines, NC, 1996—99, prin. Southern PInes, NC, 1999—2001; assoc. prof. of edn. Pfeiffer U., Misenheimer-Charlotte, NC, 2001—; supt. of schools Halifax County Schools, Halifax, NC. Workshop leader, adminstr. in Cchristian edn. AME Zion Ch., NC, 1990—2003. Named Outstanding Black North Carolinian, Ea. Region of Zeta Phi Beta Sorority, Inc., 1987, Citizen of Yr., Tau Beta Beta chpt., Omega Psi Phi Frat., 1987, Woman of the Yr., Durham chpt., Nat. Coun. of Negro Women, 1992; recipient Outstanding Svc. award, Nat. Coun. of Negro Women, 1984, Citizen of Yr., James E. Shepard Sertoma Club of Durham, 1992; Action Rsch./ Edn. of the Learning Disabled grantee, U.S. Dept. of Edn., 1986. Mem.: NC ASCD, ASCD. African Methodist Episcopal Zion. Office: Pfeiffer U US Hwy 52N Misenheimer NC 28109 E-mail: jedwards@pfeiffer.edu.

EDWARDS, JUDITH ELIZABETH, advertising executive; b. St. Louis, May 22, 1933; d. Archie Earl and Ivy Elizabeth (Jones) Hector; m. George N. LaMont Jr., Jan. 9, 1960 (div. Oct. 1965); m. Gary W. Edwards, Nov. 25, 1966 (dec. Feb. 14, 2001); stepchildren: Michael Brent, David Reed. Grad. high sch., St. Louis, 1951; student, Brown's Bus. Coll., St. Louis. Exec. sec., asst. to chmn. Rep. Nat. Com., Washington, 1958-60; dep. to county clk. Vanderburgh County, Evansville, Ind., 1972-76; sec.-treas. Edwards Outdoor Advtg., Carmi, Ill., 1979-2000, ret., 2000. Mem. Evansville Health Planning Coun., 1974-76. Pres. White County Rep. Women's Club, Carmi, 1989—, White County Hosp. Aux. Named Ky. Col. Mem. Carmi Bus. and Profl. Women's Club (past pres.), Carmi C. of C., Kiwanis, Order Ea. Star, Sigma Alpha. Methodist. Avocation: music. Home: PO Box 260214 Saint Louis MO 63126-8214 Personal E-mail: stlouiswoman@sbcglobal.net.

EDWARDS, KENNETH NEIL, chemical engineering executive; b. Hollywood, Calif., June 8, 1932; s. Arthur Carl and Ann Vera (Gomez) E.; children: Neil James, Peter Graham, John Evan. BA in Chemistry, Occidental Coll., 1954; MS in Chem. and Metall. Engring., U. Mich., 1955. Prin. chemist Battelle Meml. Inst., Columbus, Ohio, 1955-58; dir. new products rsch. and devel. Dunn-Edwards Corp., L.A., 1958-72; sr. lectr. organic coatings and pigments dept. chem. engring. U. So. Calif., L.A., 1976-80; CEO Dunn-Edwards Corp., 2001—. Bd. dirs. Dunn-Edwards Corp., L.A.; co-chair indsl. adv. coun., mem. pres.'s cir. Calif. Poly. U., San Luis Obispo. Contbr. articles to sci. jours. Recipient Judo Masters belt (6th dan), Korean Judo Assn., 2000, 38th Western Regional Indsl. Innovations award, 2003. Mem. Am. Chem. Soc. (chmn. divisional activities 1988-89, exec. com. divsn. polymeric materials sci. and engring. 1963—, chair divsn. 1970, mem. devel. adv. com. 1996-99, Disting. Svc. award 1996, chair Disting. Svc. award selection 1997—, chair So. Calif. local sect. 1999), Alpha Chi Sigma (chmn. L.A. profl. chpt. 1962, counselor Pacific dist. 1967-70, grand profl. alchemist nat. v.p. 1970-76, grand master alchemist nat. pres. 1976-78, nat. adv. com. 1978—). Achievements include patents for air-dried polyester coatings and application, for process and apparatus for dispensing liquid colorants into a paint can, fluidic fillers, and for mechanical mixers. Home: Bottle Bay Rd Sagle ID 83860 also: 2926 Graceland Way Glendale CA 91206-1331 Office: Dunn Edwards Corp 136 W Walnut Ave Monrovia CA 91016-3444 Personal E-mail: kneatde@aol.com.

EDWARDS, LARRY DAVID, internist, educator, dean; b. Macomb, Ill., June 20, 1937; s. Richard Marshall and Anna Louise (Hare) Edwards; m. Ann Leanor Will, Mar. 31, 1959; children: Elliott, Sharon, Beth. Pre-Med, U. Ill., 1961, MD, 1965. Diplomate Am. Bd. Internal Medicine, Am. Bd. Infectious Disease, Nat. Bd. Med. Examiners, Am. Bd. Med. Mgmt., Am. Coll. Healthcare Execs; cert. physician exec., healthcare exec. Rotating intern USPHS Hosp., Staten Island, N.Y., 1965-66, resident in internal medicine, 1966-68; fellow in infectious diseases Rush-Presbyn.-St. Luke's Med. Ctr., Chgo., 1968-70; instr. dept. internal medicine U. Ill. Coll. Medicine, Chgo., 1968-70; asst. prof. depts. internal medicine, preventive medicine, microbiology Rush Med. Coll., Chgo., 1972-74; assoc. prof. internal medicine U. Ill. Coll. Medicine, Rockford, 1974-80, prof., 1980-81; prof. internal medicine Oral Roberts U. Sch. Medicine, Tulsa, 1981-90; dir. div. infectious diseases Rockford Sch. Medicine, 1974-81, dep. head dept. biomed. scis., 1980-81; prof. internal medicine U. Va., Charlottesville, 1991-92; chief of staff VA Med. Ctr., Salem, Va., 1990-92; assoc. dean for acad. affairs VA, U. Va., Charlottesville, 1991-92. Adj. assoc. prof. epidemiology U. Ill. Sch. Pub. Health, 1977—81; affiliate dept. medicine Abraham Lincoln Sch. Medicine, U. Ill., Chgo., 1977—81; dir. divsn. infectious diseases Oral Roberts U., 1981—84; assoc. dean clin. affairs Oral Roberts Sch. Medicine, 1981, 84, vice chmn. dept. internal medicine, 1981—83, chmn., 1983—86, chmn. preventive and internat. medicine, 1987—88, dean, 1984—90, v.p. for health affairs, 1987—90; COO City of Faith Med. & Rsch. Ctr., 1989—90; med. dir. Cen. Bapt. Home for Aged, Norridge, Ill., 1968—74, Columbia County Homes, Wyocena, Wis., 1974—80; asst. dir. infectious diseases, hosp. epidemiologist, dir. infectious disease research Rush-Presbyn.-St. Luke's Hosp., Chgo., 1972—74, asst. sci. dept. microbiology, 1970—74; asst. med. dir. Mcpl. Contagious Disease Hosp., Chgo., 1970—74; cons. infectious diseases numerous other hosps. and med. ctrs.; med. dir. City of Faith Hosp., Tulsa, 1984—87, chmn. bd., 1989—90; bd. dirs. City of Faith Clinic, Tulsa, 1985—87; pres. Infectious Diseases Cons. Svcs., Inc., Barnhart, Mo., 1993—2001. Contbr. numerous articles to med. jours. Advisor resource com. Sch. Health Coalition of N.W. Ill., 1979-81; med. adv. com. State of Ill. Refugee Health Services Program, 1980-81; Ill. health svcs. task force State Ill. Dept. Pub. Health, 1980-81; infectious disease adv. com. Tulsa City-County Health Dept., 1981-88; physician manpower adv. com. Okla. Bd. Regents, 1984-88; Titan scholarship bd. Oral Roberts U., 1985-87; v.p. World-Wide Med. Missions, Oral Roberts Evangelistic Assn., 1986-88, pres. 1989-90; active Leadership Roanoke Valley, 1991-92; dir. Strategic Tchg. and Reaping; med. dir. Bible Basics Internat.; Bible tchr., missionary in Russia, Dominican Republic, Chile, Honduras. With U.S. Army, 1955-58, with USPHS, 1965-70, lt. col. USAR, 1985, col. 1990-97, ret., 1997. Smith, Kline and French fellow for study in Ethiopia, 1964; named Outstanding Faculty Mem. of Yr. Oral Roberts U. Sch. Medicine, 1982-83. Fellow: ACP, Am. Coll. Healthcare Execs. (ret.), Am. Coll. Physician Execs., Infectious Diseases Soc. Am. (emeritus). Avocations: reading, writing.

EDWARDS, LOUIS MARCELLUS, retired mathematics professor; b. Stuart, Fla., Aug. 29, 1928; s. William Dennis Edwards and Lota Mary Riles; m. Margaret Jean Call, Feb. 16, 1952; children: David Louis, Brenda Jean Edwards Mires. BS in Math., U. Fla., 1950, M in Math. Edn., 1953; Ednl. Specialist degree, Fla. State U., 1978. Edn. instr. U.S. Airforce, Tex. and Calif., 1951—55; math tchr. Edgewater H.S., Orlando, Fla., 1955—61; county math supr. Orange County Schs., Orlando, 1961—67; math prof. Valencia C.C., Orlando, 1967—92, dept. dean math, 1969—92; dir. ext. ctr. Luther Rice Bible Coll., Orlando, 1993—2005. Adj. prof. Valencia C.C., 1993—2005. Mem.: Math. Assn., Nat. Coun. Tchrs. Math. Republican. Baptist. Avocation: hiking. Home: 1521 E Spring Ridge Cir Winter Garden FL 34787 Office: 1st Bapt Ch Ctrl Fla 800 N Pine Hills Rd Orlando FL 32808 Office Phone: 407-293-4571.

EDWARDS, MARIE D., social services administrator; b. Cin., Sept. 17, 1943; d. George Junior Denning and Lola Dortheia Jackson; children: Daniel J., Grayson G.; m. Terrance Anthoney Edwards Sr., July 24, 1982; stepchildren: Terrance A. Edwards, Troy Edwards, Heather Kraus. Owner, mgr. Greendale Grill, Lawrenceburg, Ind., 1980-86, M.E. & Assocs. Realtors, Vevay, Ind., 1986-93; mgr. Coldwell Banker, Lawrenceburg, 1993-98; exec. dir. Dearborn Adult Ctr., Lawrenceburg, 1998—. Bd. dirs. Southea. Ind. Econ. Opportunity Ctr., 1995—, Hist. Landmarks; chairperson I Love Lawrenceburg com., 1999-2000, 2001, 2002, 2003, Bicentennial City of Lawrenceburg, 2001—; chairperson Lawrenceburg Gateway Project, Gateway Ctr. Project. Named Cmty. Leader 2000, Lawrenceburg C. of C., 2001, Cmty. Leader, 2002, 2003, Ofcl. Bell Ringer, City of Lawrenceburg; recipient Dearborn County award for svc. and humanitarian effort, 2001. Mem. Dearborn County C. of C. (gov.'s com. transp., Southea. Women's Network, pres. 2000-2001), Southea. Bd. Realtors (treas. 1990), Order Ea. Star (assoc. matron). Democrat. Methodist. Avocation: gardening. Office: Dearborn Adult Ctr Inc 311 W Tate St Lawrenceburg IN 47025 E-mail: maedwards@seidata.com.

EDWARDS, MARK E., lawyer; b. Iowa City, Iowa, July 25, 1950; BBA, U. Iowa, 1972; JD, Vanderbilt U., 1975. Assoc. Fisher & Phillips, 1979-86; ptnr. Ford & Harrison, 1986-90; labor counsel Hosp. Corp. Am., 1990-94; v.p., chief labor employment counsel HCA/ The Healthcare Co., Nashville, 1994-2000, v.p., chief labor counsel, 2000—. Capt. USAF, 1975-79. Mem. ABA, Ga. Bar Assn., Iowa Bar Assn., Tenn. Bar Assn. Office: HCA/The Healthcare Co 2501 Park Plz Nashville TN 37203-1512

EDWARDS, MARK U., JR., academic administrator, history professor, writer; b. Oakland, Calif., June 2, 1946; s. Mark U. and Margaret Edwards; m. Linda Johnson, Mar. 1968; 1 child, Teon. BA in Psychology, Stanford U., 1968, MA in History, 1969, PhD in History, 1974. Jr. fellow U. Mich., 1971-74; asst. prof. history Wellesley (Mass.) Coll., 1974-80; asst. prof. Purdue U., West Lafayette, Ind., 1980-83, assoc. prof., 1983-86, prof. history, 1986-87; prof. christianity Harvard U., Cambridge, Mass., 1987-94; pres. St. Olaf Coll., Northfield, Minn., 1994—2000; assoc. dean for academic affairs and spl. programs Harvard Div. Sch., 2003—. Founder, v.p. ELK Software Devel. Corp., 1985—; pres. Sixteenth Century Studies Conf., 1987-88; chair continuing com. Internat. Congress for Luther Rsch., 1988-94; bd. dirs. Wittenberg U., 1985—. Author: Luther and the False Brethren, 1975, Luther's Last Battles, 1983, Printing, Propaganda and Martin Luther, 1994; co-author: Luther, A Reformer for Churches, 1983; mem. editl. bd. The Ency. of the Reformation, 1989—. Bd. dirs. Holden Village, 1993-94, 96—. Mem. Am. Norwegian Hist. Assn. Office: St Olaf Coll 1520 Saint Olaf Ave Northfield MN 55057-1574

EDWARDS, MARTIN, real estate company executive; Degree, Memphis (Tenn.) State U. Cert. comml. investment mem. Nat. Assn. Realtors. Realtor, 1965; ptnr., broker Colliers Wilkinson & Snowden, 1999—; prin., owner Edwards Mgmt. Inc. Mem. nat. adv. bd. dirs. Fed. Nat. Mortgage; mem. Pres. George W. Bush Transition Team on Housing and HUD Policy; trustee Memphis (Tenn.) State U. Edn. Found.; assoc. prof. Continuing Edn. Dept. Memphis (Tenn.) State U.; sr. instr. Comml. Investment Inst. Named Realtor of Yr., Tenn., 1989; recipient Cert. Recognition Outstanding Cmty. Svc., City of Memphis, 1990, 1994, Excellencein Real Estate Edn. award, Tenn. Real Estate Commn., 1999. Mem.: Memphis (Tenn.) Area Assn. Realtors, Nat. Assn. Realtors (pres. 2002, treas., CFO 1996—97). Office: Colliers Wilkinson & Snowden 3644 Winchester Rd Ste 101 Memphis TN 38118

EDWARDS, MARVIN RAYMOND, investment counselor, economical consultant; b. N.Y.C., June 29, 1921; s. Albert H. and Blanche (Gans) E.; m. Helene C. Sirota, Mar. 20, 1955; children: Jeffrey Randall, Douglas Lee, Carolyn Beth. BS, NYU, 1947. Pres. White Star Sales Corp., Jacksonville, Fla., 1947-58; pres. Edwards & Edwards, Inc., Jacksonville, 1958—. Interviews on investments and the economy have appeared in numerous publs. including Bus. Week, Scrap Age, Miami Herald, Tampa Tribune, The Market Chronicle, Fla. Trend Mag., others; polit. columnist Folio Weekly, 1996—; subject of interview ABC World News Tonight, 1993, 94, 2002. Exec. v.p., bd. dirs. Greater Jacksonville Taxpayers Assn., 1965-71; pres., bd. dirs. Better Schs. Citizens Com, Jacksonville, 1959-65, Community Service Planning Council, Jacksonville, 1955-58; v.p., b.d dirs. Jacksonville Humane Soc., 1953-56, Jacksonville Safety Council, 1948-50; bd. dirs. North East Fla. Kidney Found., Jacksonville, 1971-73; mem. Office Strategic Svcs. Lt. USAF, 1943-46, ETO. Decorated Air medal; recipient Outspoken Citizen's award Jacksonville Southside Bus. Men's Club, 1993, Cert. of Appreciation for Disting. Svc. and Dedication, Econ. Roundtable Jacksonville, 2005. Mem. CFA Jacksonville (pres., bd. dirs. 1977-78, 87-88), Econ. Roundtable Jacksonville (pres., bd. dirs. 1975-77, 90-91, 95—), CFA Inst., Nat. Assn. Bus. Economists, Nat. Economists Club, Soc. Profl. Journalists, Nat. Press Club of Washington, The O.S.S. Soc., Inc., Mosquito Aircrew Assn. Eng., Smithsonian Nat. Air and Space Mus., Am. Mus. Natural History, Nat. Space Soc., Planetary Soc. Office: Edwards & Edwards Inc 1345 Riverbirch Ln Jacksonville FL 32207-7540 Office Phone: 904-737-8688. E-mail: eandeinc@earthlink.net.

EDWARDS, MARY LEE, retired secondary vocational and home economics educator; b. Mc Cune, Kans., Sept. 27, 1939; d. John Wesley and Mamie Delores (Parsons) Justice; m. Justice Edwards; children: William Dietrich, Jeffrey Jonathan. BS in Edn., Pittsburg (Kans.) State U., 1961, MS with honors, 1980, EdS, 1986. Jr. asst. home econs. agt. Kans. State U., Manhattan, summer 1959, county agr. extension home economist Yates Center, 1961-72; sec. housing dept. Pitts. State U., 1960-61; tchr. vocat. home econs. Unified Sch. Dist. 366, Yates Center, 1978—2004; ret., 2004. Recipient Kans. Vocat. Tchr. of Yr. award, 1991, Tchr. of Yr. award Region V Am. Vocat. Assn., 1992, Regional Kans. Tchr. of Yr. award, 1998. Democrat. Methodist. Avocations: movies and videos, sewing, needlecrafts, reading, fishing. Home: 1714 Grouse Rd Yates Center KS 66783-9803 Office Phone: 620-625-2609. Personal E-mail: edwardsranch@yatescenterks.net.

EDWARDS, MATTHEW E., physicist, educator; b. Snow Hill, N.C., Mar. 3, 1947; s. Offie Collin and Calena Edwards; m. Glenda R. Edwards, Dec. 29, 2001; m. Mary E. Ferrell, June 10, 1966 (div.); m. Cheri Y. White, July 17, 1993 (div.); children: Natasha M., Matthew E. Jr. BS in Engring Physics, N.C. State U., 1969; MS in Physics, Howard U., 1975, PhD in Physics, 1977. Lectr. D.C. Tchrs. Coll., 1975—77; asst. prof. physics Howard U., 1977; assoc. prof. physics U. Ark., Pine Bluff, 1977—81; assoc. prof. physics, dir. MBRS program Fayetteville State U., NC, 1981—96; assoc. prof. physics, dir. IDS course Spelman Coll., Atlanta, 1996—2001; prof. physics Ala. A & M U., Normal, 2002—. Adj. prof. physics U. Pitts., 1992—94, vis. rsch. prof., 1995—2001, co-founder rsch. for undergrads. program; vis. rsch. prof. Spelman Coll., 2002—. Contbr. articles to profl. jours. Recipient Presdl. award Excellence Tchg., Spelman Coll., 2001; grantee, NASA Goddard Space Flight Ctr., 2002—, NSF, 2002—. Fellow: AICE (assoc.); mem.: Soc. Indsl. and Applied Math., Soc. Photo-Optical Instrumentation Engrs., Nat. Soc. Black Physcists (assoc.), Am. Math. Soc. (assoc.), Am. Phys. Soc. (assoc.), Sigma Pi Sigma Physics (life). Home: 156 RiverWalk Trail New Market AL 35761 Office: Ala A & M U PO Box 1268 Normal AL 35762 Personal E-mail: edwar4@aol.com. E-mail: edwardsm@aamu.edu.

EDWARDS, MICHAEL GERARD, physician; b. Duluth, Minn., Apr. 27, 1956; s. Charles and Cecelia Edwards; m. Patricia Ann Roedl; children: Matthew, Conor, Anne. BA, U. Notre Dame, 1978; MD, Creighton U., 1982. Resident in radiology SUNY, Buffalo, 1983-86; fellow William Beaumont Hosp., Royal Oak, Mich., 1986-87, staff radiologist, 1987-92, Providence Hosp., Southfield, Mich., 1992—, St. John Macomb Hosp., Warren, 2004—. Address: 1825 Pine St Birmingham MI 48009 E-mail: medwards02@comcast.net.

EDWARDS, OTIS CARL, JR., theology studies educator; b. Bienville, La., June 15, 1928; s. Otis Carl and Margaret Lee (Hutchinson) E.; m. Jane Hanna Trufant, Feb. 19, 1957; children: Carl Lee, Samuel Adams Trufant, Louise Reynes BA, Centenary Coll., 1949; postgrad., Duke U., 1949-51; STB, Gen. Theol. Sem., 1952; postgrad., Westcott House, Cambridge, Eng., 1952-53; STM, So. Meth. U., 1962; MA, U. Chgo., 1963, PhD, 1971; DD, Nashotah House, 1976. Ordained priest Episcopal Ch., 1954. Curate Episcopal Ch., Baton Rouge, 1953-54, vicar Abbeville, La., 1954-57, Waxahachie, Tex., 1960-61, rector Morgan City, La., 1957-60, priest in charge Chgo., 1961-63; instr. Wabash Coll., 1963-64; asst. prof. Nashotah House, Wis., 1964-69, assoc. prof., 1969-72, prof., 1972-74, sub-dean, 1973-74, acting dean, 1973-74; dean Seabury-Western Theol. Sem., Evanston, Ill., 1974-83, prof., 1983-93, prof. emeritus, 1996; chaplain, scholar in residence Coll. Preachers. Chmn. Coun. for Devel. of Ministry, Episcopal Ch., Coun. Sem. Deans; mem. Bd. for Theol. Edn.; mem. Gen. Bd. Examining Chaplains; vis. prof. Notre Dame, 1986—, Duke U., 1996; rsch. assoc. The Newberry Libr.; interim priest Episcopal Ch., Asheville, N.C. Author: How It All Began, 1973, The Living and Active Word, 1975 (with Robert Bennett) The Bible for Today's Church, 1979, Luke's Story of Jesus, 1981, (with John Westerhoff) A Faithful Church: Issues in the History of Catechesis, 1981, Elements of Homiletic, 1982, How Holy Writ Was Written, 1989, A History of Preaching, 2004; book rev. editor Anglican Theol. Rev., 1971-76, v.p. of corp., 1975-85; chair editl. bd. Sewanee Theol. Rev., 2002-; contbr. articles and book revs. to various jours. and mags. Chmn. campus affairs com.; trustee Kendall Coll.; sec., co-chair Commn. on Faith and Order Nat. Coun. Chs.; bd. dirs., Native Am. Theol. Assn., U. N.C. at Asheville Found.; exec. com., Nat. Coun. Chs. in the USA; v.p. bd. dirs. Coll. for Srs./U. N.C., Asheville; program com. Kanuga Confs., Inc., Friends of St. Benedict. Recipient Spl. award Mystery Writers Am., 1965; grantee The Conant Fund, Pew Foun., St. Paul's Ministry and Mission Found., Indpls. Mem. Soc. Bibl. Lit., Cath. Bibl. Assn., Am. Acad. Religion, Chgo. Soc. Bibl. Rsch., Acad. Homiletics, (pres.), Societas Homiletica (exec. coun., treas.), Coll. of Preachers (long-range planning com.), Mystery Writers of Am. Democrat. Home: 115 Murphy Hill Rd Weaverville NC 28787-8630 Personal E-mail: janeoce@aol.com.

EDWARDS, PATRICK ROSS, retail executive, lawyer, management consultant; b. Montreal, Que., Can., Mar. 17, 1940; came to U.S., 1952; s. Claude Victor and Edith May Peace (Wyatt) E.; m. Gracelyn Regina LaSala, July 2, 1961; children— Pamela Lynn, Jennifer Anne BA, Kenyon Coll., 1962; JD, Columbia U., 1965. Bar: N.Y. 1967. Staff atty. Allied Stores Corp., N.Y.C., 1965-69, asst. to pres., 1970-74, v.p. adminstrn., 1974-83, sr. v.p. ops. and adminstrn., 1983-85; pres., chief operating officer Genovese Drug Stores, Inc., Melville, N.Y., 1985-86; exec. v.p., chief operating officer Am. Trim

Products, Inc., 1987-88, pres., chief exec. officer, 1988-89; prin. The Rosse Co., 1990—. Sr. v.p. sys. svcs. North Shore--L.I. Jewish Health Sys., 1996-2000. Trustee Northshore U. Hosp., Manhasset, N.Y., 1984-93, spl. asst. to pres., 1993-96; mem. exec. coun. Inner City Scholarship Fund, N.Y.C., 1983-93; mem. deans adv. coun. SUNY Sch. Bus., Albany, 1984-86; mem. Ea. regional panel Pres.'s Commn. on White House Fellowships, N.Y.C., 1984-86. Mem. Kenyon Coll. Alumni Assn. Clubs: Strathmore Vanderbilt Country (Manhasset). Roman Catholic.

EDWARDS, PAUL BEVERLY, retired science and engineering educator; b. Ridge Spring, S.C., Nov. 12, 1915; s. Paul Bee and Chloe Agnes (Watson) E.; m. Sarah Dee Barnes, Apr. 10, 1943 (dec. July 1999); 1 child, Susan Dee Edwards Von Suskil. BS, U. Tampa, 1937; EdM, Harvard U., 1958; EdD, George Washington U., 1972. Owner, operator Edwards' Hobbies, Tampa, Fla., 1938-54; tchr. math. Hillsborough High Sch., Tampa, 1955-60; head dept. math. King High Sch., Tampa, 1960-63; coord. Grad. Ctr., supr. edn. and tng. Johns Hopkins U. and Applied Physics Lab., Balt. and Laurel, Md., 1963-75, dir. Grad. Ctr., supr. edn. and tng., 1975-81. Contbr. articles to profl. jours. Mem. Sun City Ctr. Voters League, 1989—, Community Assn., Sun City Ctr., 1987—; mem. Greenbriar Property Owners Assn., Sun City Ctr., 1987—. Lt. comdr. USNR, 1942-46. Named Meritorious Tchr., State of Fla., 1962; recipient various fellowships. Mem. Ret. Officers Assn., Naval Res. Assn., Golf and Racquet Club. Avocations: swimming, computing, photography. Home: 1843 Wolf Laurel Dr Sun City Center FL 33573-6422

EDWARDS, PETER S., management and computer consultant; b. Staten Island, N.Y., June 7, 1966; s. Theodore Peter and Gertrude Edwards; m. Teresa S. Robinson, Aug. 28, 1993; children: Tess, Will children: Ben. BS in computer sci., Villanova U., 1985—89. Sr. mgmt. Application Consulting Group, Morristown, NJ, 1990—2000, ceo, 2001—. Mem.: Data Warehousing Inst. (assoc.). Home: 15 Stonehenge Rd Morristown NJ 07960 Office: Application Consulting Group 121 Headquarters Plaza Morristown NJ 07960 E-mail: pedwards@acgi.com.

EDWARDS, PHILLIP MILTON, retired import/export company executive; b. Borger, Tex., Feb. 24, 1933; s. Aaron Moses and Ada Elsie (Feist) E.; m. Mildred M. L. Weber, Aug. 18, 1956 (dec. Sept. 2001); m. Arlene Irvine Davis, Jan. 4, 2002. BA, Okla. U., 1958. Polit. officer U.S. Embassy, Jedda, Saudi Arabia, 1961-64; vice consul U.S. Consulate Gen., Dhahran, Saudi Arabia, 1965-67; sr. advisor Dept. of Army, Vinh Long, Vietnam, 1968-70; publs. mgr. DOT Systems, Incorp., Vienna, Va., 1971-77; v.p. Transcontinental Trade Corp., Washington, 1978-81; sr. writer, editor Sci. Applications Internat. Corp., McLean, Va., 1981-87; v.p. Security Support Svcs., Washington, 1981-92; mem. profl. staff Alderson Reporting Co., Washington, 1992-97; ret., 1997. Freelance writer, editor, 1997—. Contbr. articles to profl. jours. Recipient Silver medal SAR, 1979. Presbyterian. Avocations: flying, photography, mountain climbing, tennis. Home: 1917 Aubrey Place Ct Vienna VA 22182-1976 E-mail: pedwa666@aol.com.

EDWARDS, PRISCILLA ANN, small business owner; b. Orlando, Fla., Sept. 28, 1947; d. William Granville and Bernice Royster; m. Charles R. King, Apr. 4, 1981. Paralegal cert., U. Calif., Berkeley, 1994. Paralegal Charles R. Garry Esquire, San Francisco, 1989-90; owner, mgr. Fed. Legal Resources, San Francisco, 1991—2004; prin., owner SunWest Pub. Co., LLC, San Francisco, 2003—. Speaker Sonoma State U., Santa Rosa, Calif., 1993. Publisher: (book) Zero Weather, 1981; author (as Una King): Tiny Tug's Adventures On San Francisco Bay, 2003. Recipient Wiley W. Manuel award for pro bono legal svcs. Bd. Govs. State Bar of Calif., 1994, 95, 96, 97, 98. Episcopalian. Avocations: horseback riding, mountain biking.

EDWARDS, RALPH M., librarian; b. Shelley, Idaho, Apr. 17, 1933; s. Edward William and Maude Estella (Munsee) E.; m. Winifred Wylie, Dec. 25, 1969; children: Dylan, Nathan, Stephen. BA, U. Wash., 1957, MLS, 1960; DLS, U. Calif.-Berkeley, 1971. Libr. NY Pub. Libr., NYC, 1960-61; catalog libr. U. Ill. Libr., Urbana, 1961-62; br. libr. Multnomah County Libr., Portland, Oreg., 1964-67; asst. prof. Western Mich. U., Kalamazoo, 1970-74; chief Ctl. Libr. Dallas Pub. Libr., 1975-81; city libr. Phoenix Pub. Libr., 1981-95, ret., 1996—. Author: Role of the Beginning Librarian in University Libraries, 1975. U. Calif. doctoral fellow, 1967-70; library mgmt. internship Council on Library Resources, 1974-75 Mem. ALA, Pub. Library Assn. Democrat. Home: 2884 Spring Blvd Eugene OR 97403-1662 E-mail: wedwards@efn.org.

EDWARDS, RHONDA STRICKLAND, elementary school educator; b. Wilmington, N.C., Nov. 26, 1958; d. Priscilla Currie Ward; m. Ricky D. Edwards, June 9, 1979; 1 child, Ricky D. Edwards, Jr. BS in Elem. Edn., Coll. Charleston, 1994. Cert. tchr. Nat. Bd. Certification for Tchrs., 2004. 3d grade tchr. WB Goodwin Elem. Sch., North Charleston, SC, 1994—. Author: (poem) Gentle Summer Breeze (Pub. in The Nat. Libr. of Poetry). Recipient SC Finalist for Presdl. Award for Excellence in Math and Sci., NSF, 2002, 1st pl. Finalist Charleston County Disting. Reading Tchr., Charleston County Reading Assn., 2003. Fellow: Charleston Writing Project; mem.: NEA (S.C. br.), Charleston Tchr. Alliance, Nat. Coun. of Tchrs. of English, Sc 2, Internat. Reading Assn. Home: 5234 Dorchester Rd North Charleston SC 29418 Office: WB Goodwin Elem Sch 5501 Dorchester Rd North Charleston SC 29418 Office Phone: 843-767-5911. Personal E-mail: rhondae362@aol.com.

EDWARDS, RICHARD ALAN, retired lawyer; b. Portland, Oreg., June 28, 1938; s. Howard A. and Kay E. (Sheldon) E.; m. Renee Rosier, June 18, 1960; children: Teri Edwards Obye, Lisa Edwards Smith, Steve. BS, Oreg. State U., 1960; JD summa cum laude, Willamette U., 1968. Bar: Oreg. 1968, U.S. Dist. Ct. Oreg. 1968, U.S. Ct. Appeals (9th cir.) 1969. Various positions 1st Interstate Bank of Oreg., Portland, 1960-65; assoc. Miller, Nash, Wiener, Hager & Carlsen, Portland, 1968-74, ptnr., 1974—99, mng. ptnr., 1991-96. Editor Willamette Law Jour., 1967-68. Mem. ABA (litig. sect. 1972), Oreg. State Bar (chairperson debtor-creditor sect. 1981-82, mem. various coms.). Republican. Presbyterian.

EDWARDS, RICHARD CLAIRE, retired speech educator; b. Muncie, Ind., May 17, 1930; s. Richard Claire and Helen Mae Edwards; m. Nancy Sonia Baspiñeiro, May 20, 1962; 1 child, Richard Carlton. BA in Eng., Olivet Nazarene U., 1955; MA in Cultural Studies, Govs. State U., 1973. Lic. tchr. State Tchr. Cert. Bd. Ill., 1957. Eng. tchr., dir. dramatics Thornton Fractional North H.S., Calumet City, Ill., 1957—60; ESL tchr., supr. Eng. instrn. Anglo-American Sch., Oruro, Bolivia, 1960—64; Eng. tchr., dir. dramatics Thornton Fractional North H.S., Calumet City, 1964—66; Eng., speech, theatre tchr., fine arts dept. chair Westview H.S., Kankakee, Ill., 1966—90; prof. speech Kankakee C.C., 1990—2001, speech prof. emeritus, 2001—. Accredited speech and theatre judge Ill. H.S. Assn., Springfield, 1965—90; coll. rep. on speech panel Ill. Articulation Com., Springfield, 1995—2001; coord. working adult bus. degree program Kankakee C.C., 1997—2001. Contbr. poetry to anthologies; actor: The IChing; dir.: The King and I, My Fair Lady, A Man Called Peter. Pres. Kankakee Cmty. Arts Coun., 1988—89; docent Kankakee County Hist. Mus.; state dir. Internat. Thespian Soc., Ill., 1975—77. With U.S. Army, 1955—57. Named Outstanding Leaders in Elem. & Secondary Edn., 1976; recipient Poet of Merit, Internat. Soc. Poets, 1995, Diamond Homer award, Famous Poets Soc., 1999. Mem.: Acad. Am. Poets, Poetry Soc. Am., State Univs. Annuitants Assn. (chpt. v.p. 2003—), Kankakee County Hist. Soc., Gretchen Charlton Art Gallery. Avocations: gardening, poetry & short story writing, theater. Home: 860 S Wildwood Ave Kankakee IL 60901-5371 Personal E-mail: redwardsii@aol.com.

EDWARDS, RICHARD LAWRENCE, geology educator; b. Boston, Mar. 14, 1953; s. Richard and Vee-tsung (Ling) E.; m. Melissa Ann McDonald, m. Sept. 24, 1988. SB, MIT, 1976; MS, U. Mich., 1986; PhD, Calif. Inst. Tech., 1988. Asst. prof. U. Minn., 1988-90, McKnight land-grant prof., 1990—. Dir. Minn. Isotope Lab., Mpls., 1988—. Contbr. more than 20 articles to profl. jours. Recipient Taylor Disting. Rsch. award, 1995. Fellow: Am. Acad. Arts & Sci.; mem.: AAAS, Geochem. Soc., Am. Geophys. Union, Geol. Soc. Am. Office: U Minn Dept Geol and Geophysics 310 Pillsbury Dr SE Minneapolis MN 55455-0219

EDWARDS, RICHARD LEROY, dean, social sciences educator, management consultant; b. Rahway, N.J., Aug. 9, 1943; s. Richard Lorraine and Norma (Higley) E.; children: Jeffrey, Julia, Jennifer. BA, Augustana Coll., Rock Island, Ill., 1965; MA, U. Chgo., 1967; PhD with distinction, SUNY, Albany, 1986. Social worker Ill. State Psychiat. Inst., Chgo., 1967-70; asst. prof. Augustana Coll., 1970-74; staff assoc. Nat. Assn. Social Workers, Washington, 1974-78; assoc. dir. continuing social work edn. U. Tenn., Knoxville, 1978-80; assoc. prof., assoc. dean SUNY, Albany, 1980-88; prof., dean Mandel Sch. Applied Social Scis. Case Western Res. U., Cleve., 1988-92; dean sch. social work U. N.C., Chapel Hill, 1992—2000, interim provost, 2000—01, alumni disting. prof., 2001—. Editor: Skills for Effective Human Services Management, 1991, Skills for Effective Managementof non-Profit Organizations, 1996; editor-in-chief Ency. of Social Work, 1995; contbr. numerous articles to profl. jours.; chpts. to book. Elected mem. Bd. Edn., Davenport, Iowa, 1972-74; trustee numerous non-profit agy. bds. Recipient Achievement in Edn. award No. Ohio Live Mag., 1991. Mem. Acad. Cert. Social Workers, Nat. Assn. Social Workers (Social Worker of Yr. award N.Y. chpt. 1987, pres. 1989-91), Coun. on Social Work Edn. Avocation: golf. Office: U NC Sch of Social Work 301 Pittsboro St Chapel Hill NC 27599-3550 Home: 1010 Chancellors Ridge Dr Durham NC 27713

EDWARDS, ROBERT HAZARD, retired college president; b. London, May 26, 1935; s. Arthur Robinson and Marjorie Hazard (Mayes) E. (father Am. citizen); m. Blythe Morton Bickel, Nov. 5, 1988; children from previous marriage: Elizabeth, Daphne, Nicholas. AB, Princeton U., 1957; BA, Cambridge (Eng.) U., 1959, MA (hon.), 1977; LLB, Harvard U., 1961; LHD (hon.), Carleton Coll., 1986, Bowdoin Coll., Colby Coll., 2001. Bar: Fed. 1961. Fellow Ford Found., 1961—63; with UN polit. affairs Dept. State, 1963—65, Ford Found., 1965—77; rep. for Pakistan, 1968—72; head Middle East and Africa, 1973—77; pres. Carleton Coll., Northfield, Minn., 1977—86; head social welfare dept. Secretariat of the Aga Khan, Paris, 1986—90; pres. Bowdoin Coll., Brunswick, Maine, 1990—2001. Mem. bd. visitors U. Maine; trustee Aga Khan U. Mem. Coun. on Fgn. Rels., Am. Acad. Arts and Sci.

EDWARDS, ROBERT L., corporate financial executive; BA, MBA, Brigham Young U. Various exec. positions Santa Fe Pacific Corp.; sr. v.p., CFO, chief adminstrv. officer Imation Corp., 1998—2003; exec. v.p., CFO Maxtor, Milipitas, Calif., 2003—04, Safeway Inc., 2004—. Office: Safeway Inc 5918 Stoneridge Mall Rd Pleasanton CA 94588

EDWARDS, ROBIN MORSE, lawyer; b. Glens Falls, NY, Dec. 9, 1947; d. Daniel and Harriet Morse; m. Richard Charles Edwards, Aug. 30, 1970; children: Michael Alan, Jonathan Philip. BA, Mt. Holyoke Coll., 1969; JD, U. Calif., Berkeley, 1972. Bar: Calif. 1972. Assoc. Donahue, Gallagher, Thomas & Woods, Oakland, Calif., 1972—77, ptnr., 1977—89, Sonnenschein, Nath & Rosenthal, San Francisco, 1989—, mgmt. com., 1998—. Bd. dirs. Temple Sinai, 1997-2002. Mem. ABA, Calif. Bar Assn., Alameda County Bar Assn. (bd. dirs. 1978-84, v.p. 1982, pres. 1983), Alameda County Bar Found. (bd. dirs. 1998-2000). Jewish. Avocations: skiing, cooking. Office: Sonnenschein Nath Rosenthal 685 Market St 6th Fl San Francisco CA 94105-4202 Business E-Mail: redwards@sonnenschein.com.

EDWARDS, RYAN HAYES, baritone; b. Columbia, S.C. m. Leila Scelonge. MusB, U. Tex.; MusM, Tex. Christian U. Artistic cons. Marquee Theatre Co., Evanston, Ill., Internat. Opera Acad., Rome, master tchr. Scholar Julliard Am. Opera Ctr., N.Y.C., debut, N.Y.C. Opera, Hollywood Bowl, N.Y. Philharm., L.A. Philharm., Chgo. Symphony, London Symphony, Boston Symphony, San Francisco Opera Co., Teatro del Liceo, Barcelona, Royal Festival Hall, London, Metropolitan Opera; radio debut, O.R.T.F., Paris; films and recs. include Caterina Cornaro, I Pagliacci, Maid of Orleans, Mahler Symphony No. 8 others; author: The Verdi Baritone: Studies in Development of Dramatic Character, Verdi & Puccini Heroines: Dramatic Characterization in Great Soprano Roles, A.K.A. Doc: Oral History of a New Orleans Street Musician. Named awardee Nat. Opera Inst.; Rockefeller grantee, Nat. Opera Inst. grantee, Edwin H. Mosler Found. grantee, William Mathews Sullivan Mus. Found. grantee. Mem. Nat. Opera Assn. (past pres.), Am. Guild Musical Artists, Actors Equity, Phi Mu Alpha, Lambda Chi Alpha, Pi Kappa Lambda. Achievements include winning San Angelo Symphony competition, Nat. Radio Auditions for Acad. Vocal Arts, Phila., Internat. Verdi competition, Busseto, Italy. *I was a totally American trained and prepared artist. Hopefully this fact will be of inspiration to other young American singers who, for too many years, have had to try to impress European smaller companies before becoming worthy to have any sort of career here in their own country. America is finally coming to acknowledge its own native operatic talent.*

EDWARDS, SIR SAMUEL FREDERICK, physicist, researcher; b. Swansea, Wales, Feb. 1, 1928; m. Merriell Bland, 1953; 4 children. Ed., Cambridge U., Harvard U.; DSc (hon.), U. Bath, U. Edinburgh, U. Loughborough, U. Salford, U. Birmingham, 1976, U. Strasbourg, 1986, U. Wales, 1987, U. Sheffield, 1989, U. Dublin, 1991, U. Leeds, U. Swansea, 1994, East Anglia, 1995, U. Cambridge, Eng., 2001; DSc (hon.), U. Mainz, 2002. Mem. Inst. Advanced Study, Princeton, N.J.; rsch. fellow U. Birmingham; prof. U. Manchester; emeritus Cavendish prof. physics Cavendish Lab.; pro vice chancellor Cambridge U., 1992-95; fellow, pres. Gonville and Caius Coll. Vis. prof. U. Calif., San Diego, 1980-81; dir. Lucas Industries, 1981-93; chmn. Sci. Rsch. Coun. U.K., 1973-77, Def. Sci. Adv. Coun., 1977-80; chief sci. advisor U.K. Dept. Energy, 1983-88; program dir. ITP U. Calif., Santa Barbara, 1997; hon. prof. chemistry Beijing U., Peking U. Contbr. articles to profl. jours. Recipient Sci. pour l'Art prize Louis Vuitton Moet Hennessy, 1993, Boltzmann medal Internat. Union Pure and Applied Physics, 1995. Fellow Royal Soc. (Davy medal 1985, Royal medal 2001), Inst. Physics (Maxwell medal, Guthrie medal, Keller Meml. Polymer medal 2001), Royal Soc. Chemistry, Inst. Math. (Gold medal 1986), Am. Phys. Soc. (High Polymer Physics prize), Brit. Assn. Advancement of Sci. (chmn. 1977-82, pres. 1988-89), Brit. Soc. Rheology (Gold medal 1991), French Acad. Scis. (fgn. assoc.), NAS (fgn. assoc.), French Phys. Soc. (hon.), European Phys. Soc. (hon.); mem. Athenaeum Club. Home: 7 Penarth Pl Cambridge CB3 9LU England Office: Cavendish Lab Cambridge CB3 OHE England Office Phone: (44)1223337259. Business E-Mail: sfe11@phy.cam.ac.uk.

EDWARDS, SAMUEL ROGER, internist; b. Santa Barbara, Calif., Aug. 11, 1937; s. Harold S. and Margaret (Spaulding) E.; m. Marcia Elizabeth Dutton, June 17, 1961; children: Harold S. II, Charles Dutton. BA, Harvard U., 1960; MD, U. So. Calif., 1964. Intern Presbyn. Hosp., Phila., 1964-65; resident in internal medicine U Calif., San Francisco, 1968-70; fellow in cardiology Pacific Presbyn. Med. Ctr., San Francisco, 1970; pvt. practice specializing in internal medicine Santa Paula, Calif., 1971-94; med. dir. Santa Paula Convalescent, Twin Pines Convalescent Hosps., 1974-95; pres. med. staff Ventura (Calif.) County Med. Ctr., 1979-80, med. dir., 1983-95, hosp. adminstr., 1995—2002. Mem. clin. faculty UCLA Sch. Medicine, 1980—95; chmn. Citizens State Bank of Santa Paula, 1994—97; bd. dirs. Limoneira Co., chmn., 2003—04; bd. dirs. Santa Barbara Bank and Trust; chief dept. medicine Ventura County Gen. Hosp., 1975; chief med. staff Santa Paula Meml. Hosp., 1977. Lt. comdr. USNR, 1966-68. Recipient Disting. Svc. award Ventura County Heart Assn., 1974. Fellow: ACP; mem.: AMA, Am. Coll. Hosp. Execs. Episcopalian. Home: 19789 E Telegraph Rd Santa Paula CA 93060-9693 Office: 243 March St Santa Paula CA 93060-2511

EDWARDS, SARAH ANNE, social worker, psychologist; b. Tulsa, Jan. 7, 1943; d. Clyde Elton and Virginia Elizabeth Glandon; m. Paul Robert Edwards, Apr. 24, 1965; 1 son, Jon Scott. BA with distinction, U. Mo., Kansas City, 1965; MSW, U. Kans., 1974. LCSW; cert. ecopsychologist. Cmty. rep. OEO, Kans. City Regional Office, 1966-68; social svc./parent involvement and resource specialist Office of Child Devel., HEW, Kansas City, Kans., 1968-73; dir. tng. social svcs. dept., children's rehab. unit U. Affiliated Facility, U. Kans. Med. Ctr., Kansas City, 1975-76; co-dir. Cathexis Inst. S., Glendale, Calif., 1976-77; pvt. practice psychotherapy, tng. and cons. personal and interpersonal, orgnl. behavior, Sierra Madre, Calif., 1973-80; sys. operator CompuServe Info. Svc., 1983-98; faculty mem. grad. dept. applied ecopsychology Inst. Global Edn., 2005—; NGO cons. UNESCO, 2005—. Prodr., co-host radio show Working From Home, on Bus. Talk Radio, 1988-01; co-host radio show Entrepeneur's Home Business Edition, 2003—co-host cable show Working from Home Scripp's Howard Home and Garden Cable TV Network, 1995-97; commentator CNBC, 1996-99, NPR Marketplace, 1996-97; co-host Entrepreneurs Home Bus. Show, WS Radio, 2000—. Columnist for Home Office Computing Mag., 1988-97, Your Home Office, L.A. Times Syndicate, 1997-99, Entrepreneur's Home Office, 1998—, Price CostCo Connection, 1994—, Inc-Com., 2000—; co-author: How to Make Money with Your Personal Computer, 1997, Getting Business to Come to You, 1998, Working From Home, rev. edit., 1999, Secrets of Self-Employment, 1996, Finding Your Perfect Work, 1996, Teaming Up, 1997, Home Businesses You Can Buy, 1997, Cool Careers for Dummies, 1998, Making Money in Cyberspace, 1998, Best Home Business for the 21st Century, 1999, Working From Home, 1999, The Practical Dreamer's Handbook, 2000, Home-Based Business for Dummies, 2000, Changing Directions without Losing Your Way, 2001, Entrepreneurial Parent, 2002, Sitting with the Enemy, A Novel, 2002, Why Aren't You Your Own Boss?, 2003, Best Home Business for People 50+, 2004; mem. editl. bd. Jour. Applied Ecopsychology, 2005—. Dir. nature-guided counseling programs, career and life coach Pine Mountain Inst., 2001. Address: Box 6775 2624 Teakwood Ct Frazier Park CA 93222 Business E-Mail: sedwards@frazmtn.com. E-mail: sarahecopsych@aol.com.

EDWARDS, SHARON MARIE, minister, educator; b. Akron, Ohio, Jan. 28, 1944; d. Michael Robert Batche and Kathleen Marie Austin; m. Ronald Payne Edwards, Apr. 4, 1970; children: Carrie JoAnn, Suzanne Kathleen. BA, Malone U., 1971. Lic. pastor Ohio, 1977, minister Abundant Life Ministries. Pastor Abundant Life Ministries, Akron, Ohio, 1977—78; founder and sr. pastor Harvest Christian Ctrs., Internat., North Canton, Ohio, 1978—. Adv. bd. Living Water Tchg., Internat., Caddo Mills, Tex.; fin. sec. Living Water Ch., Akron; mem. fin. bd. Sherwood Pk. Baptist, Akron; spkr. in field. Author bible studies materials, (corr. course) Foundations Series, 1999—2003. Recipient Voices award, Nat. Campaign Influential Women USA, 2003. Mem.: Women's Missionary Union (mem. state bd. 1972—74). Avocations: travel, bible studies. Office: Harvest Christian Ctrs Internat 116 9th St NW North Canton OH 44720 Office Phone: 330-499-5683.

EDWARDS, STEPHEN ALLEN, lawyer; b. Battle Creek, Mich., July 12, 1953; s. Louis Ward and Elizabeth Yvonne (Stahl) E.; m. Alice Veronica; children: Amelia Hatfield, Nathaniel Gordon. BA with high honors, U. Mich., 1975, JD cum laude, 1978. Bar: Wis. 1978, U.S. Dist. Ct. (ea. and we. dists.) Wis. 1978, Mich. 1980, Pa. 1980, Ga. 1999. Assoc. Godfrey & Kahn S.C., Milw., 1978-80, Pepper, Hamilton & Scheetz, Phila., 1980-82, Morgan, Lewis & Bockius, Phila., 1982-87, ptnr., 1987-98, Kilpatrick Stockton LLP, Altanta, 1998—. Author: Arbitrage, 1990; exec. editor: The Issuer's Guide to Tax-Exempt Finance, 1994, Municipal Leasing, 2002. Mem. ABA (tax sect.), Wis. Bar Assn., Mich. Bar Assn., Ga. Bar Assn., Phila. Bar Assn., Pa. Bar Assn., Nat. Assn. Bond Lawyers (chmn. arbitrage seminar 1990, edn. com. 1990-91, bd. dirs. 1991-94, treas. 1994-95), Bond Attys. Workshop (panelist 1984-95, steering com., chmn. arbitrage 1986-87), Pa. Soc. SR (bd. dirs. 1991-94), Phila. Club. Episcopalian. Avocation: bicycling. Home: 360 Cannady Ct Atlanta GA 30350-5622 Office Phone: 404-815-6278. Business E-Mail: sedwards@kilpatrickstockton.com.

EDWARDS, STEVEN CHARLES, musician, music educator; b. Racine, Wis., Apr. 18, 1957; s. Charles and Mary Spillane Edwards; m. Marta L. Jurjevich, Dec. 27, 1981; children: Madeleine J., Mark J., Vera J., Thomas J., Mary Rose. BA in Music summa cum laude, U. Wis.-Parkside, Kenosha, 1978; MusM in Musicology, U. Ill., 1982, postgrad., 1981—. Lectr. program ch. music St. Joseph's Coll., Rensellaer, Ind., 1981—89; dir. choral activities No. Mich. U., Marquette, 1982—86; Dana prof. Am. music and dir. choral activities Franklin & Marshall Coll., Lancaster, Pa., 1986—90; music dir. Symphony Chorus New Orleans, 1990—; dir. choral activities Loyola U., New Orleans, 1990—97; dir. music ministries Most Holy Name of Jesus Cath. Ch., New Orleans, 1994—; prof. music, coord. music and music bus. Delgado C.C., New Orleans, 1997—. Music dir. Superior Festival Orch. and Chorus, Marquette, Mich., 1986—; guest condr. in field. Chorus master: musical performance, CD, DVD A Creole Mass CD/DVD/Live Performance (Tribute to the Classical Arts Best New Classical Music Performance 2001, 2001), chorus master Symphony Chorus New Orleans: musical performance Carmina Burana (Orff) (Tribute to the Classical Arts Best Choral Arts Presentation 2002, 2002), Verdi Requiem (Tribute to the Classical Arts Best Choral Arts Presentation 1999, 1999), chorus master: musical performance Poulenc Gloria (Tribute to the Classical Arts Best Choral Arts Presentation 2001, 2001). Mem. adv. bd. Greater New Orleans Youth Orch., 2002. Mem.: Nat. Assn. Pastoral Musicians, Condrs. Guild (newsletter editor 1988—92), Chorus Am., Am. Choral Dirs. Assn. (la repertoire and standards chair for two yr. coll. choirs 2002). Office: Delgado Community College 615 City Park Ave New Orleans LA 70119 Office Phone: 504-483-4168. Business E-Mail: sedwar@dcc.edu.

EDWARDS, STEVEN MARK, lawyer; b. New Haven, Mar. 20, 1947; s. J. Richard and Lillian S. (Solomon) E.; m. Robin E. Randall, June 1, 1975; children: Mark, Elisabeth, William. BA, U. Iowa, 1969; postgrad., U. Oxford, Eng., 1969; JD, U. Va., 1972. Bar: N.Y. 1973, U.S. Dist. Ct. (So. dist.) N.Y. 1973, U.S. Ct. Appeals (2d cir.) 1973, U.S. Supreme Ct. 1980. Assoc. Cravath, Swaine & Moore, N.Y.C., 1972-80; ptnr. Davis, Scott, Weber & Edwards, N.Y.C., 1980—, Hogan & Hartson LLP, N.Y.C., dir. litig. practice group. Notes editor U. Va. Law Rev., 1971-72. Pres. Nazareth Housing; treas. Welfare Law Ctr. Mem. ABA (Clayton Act com.), Assn. of Bar of City of NY, NY State Bar Assn. (chmn. antitrust sect. 2003), Fed. Bar Coun. (pres. 1998-2000). Office: Hogan & Hartson LLP 875 Third Ave New York NY 10022 Office Phone: 212-918-3506. Office Fax: 212-918-3100. Business E-Mail: smedwards@hhlaw.com.

EDWARDS, SYLVIA ANN, artist; b. Boston, Jan. 30, 1937; d. Junius Griffiths and Sylvia Emma (Mailloux) E.; m. Sadredin M. Golestaneh (div.); children: Shirin, Nader, Leila. Diploma, Mass. Coll. of Art, Boston, 1957, Boston Mus. of Fine Arts, 1958; postgrad., Modern Art Studies, London, 1980-81. One-woman shows include CCA Gallery, Oxford, Eng., 1996, Munson Gallery, Chatham, Mass., 1992, Jaeshke Gallery, Braunschweig, Germany, 1991, Natalie Knight Gallery, Johannesburg, South Africa, 1991, Bankamura, Tokyo, 1991, Gallery K. Hyazaki Perfecture, 1991, The Berkeley Sq. Gallery, London, 1991, CCA Gallery, 2003, numerous others, exhibited in group shows at Cadogan Contemporary Art, London, 1996, Berkeley Sq. Gallery, Korea Art Expo, Seoul, 1996, 2002, N.Y. Art Expo, N.Y.C., 1994, Lond Internat. Contemporary Art Fair, 1989, The Bath Arts Festival, Eng., 1988, Paris Art Salon, 1986, 1987, 1988, Sarasota Visual Art Ctr., numerous others, Represented in permanent collections Nat. Mus. for Women in the Arts, Washington, Boston U. Spl. Collections, Cape Mus Fine Arts, Dennis, Mass, Mus. Fine Arts, Alexandria, Egypt, Governorate of Alexandria, Mass. Gen. Hosp., Boston, Chelsea Westminster Hosp., London, Midwest Mus. Am. Art, Elkhart, Ind., Tate Gallery, London, publs., Valley of Sils, Lithograph, 1982, N.Mex. Watch, lithograph, 1982, covers, Arts Rev., 1982, 1985, others, numerous, UNICEF cards, Greenpeace publs., World Wildlife/U.K., book covers, reference and art books, others, monograph, Pallas Athere, London, 2003. Mem. U.K. UNICEF Com. Mem. London Royal Acad., World Watercolor Soc., Chelsea Arts Club/London. Avocations: writing, theater, travel, swimming, reading. Studio: 14 Cadogan Square London SW1X 0JU England

EDWARDS, TERRI LYN WILMOTH, education educator; b. Bremerton, Wash., June 18, 1959; d. Marvin Earl and Beverly Joanne Wilmoth; m. Eddie Lee Edwards, Sr., Nov. 4, 1988; children: Eddie Lee Jr., Clint, Sparky, Jaime. AAS, Rogers State Coll., Claremore, Okla., 1986; BABS in Edn., Langston U., 1988; MEdn., Northeastern State U., Tahlequah, Okla., 1996; postgrad. in Edn. Psychology PhD program, Okla. State U., Stillwater, 1996—. Nat. Bd. Cert. Tchr. Elementary sch. tchr. Coweta (Okla.) Pub. Schs., 1988—2001; Great Expectations instr. Northeastern State U., Tahlequah, 1999—; prof. edn. U. Phoenix, Tulsa, 1999—; instr. COE Northeastern State U., Tahlequah, Okla., 2001—. Spkr. Shurley English, Ark., 1998—2001, Nat. Bd. Profl. Tchg. Stds., 1999—. Named State Sci. Tchr. of Yr., Nat. Conservation Dists., Oklahoma City, 2000; recipient Fulbright Found. award, 2000. Mem.: ACEI, ASCD, Nat. Bd. Profl. Tchg. Stds., Delta Kappa Gamma. Democrat. Baptist. Avocations: continued learning, golf. Home: PO Box 215 Ft Gibson OK 74434 Office: Northeastern State Univ 500 N Grand Tahlequah OK 74464 Office Phone: 918-456-5511 3757. Business E-Mail: edward22@nsu.edu. E-mail: terriee_1999@yahoo.com.

EDWARDS, VICKI ANN, director; b. Fremont, Nebr., Dec. 19, 1947; d. Howard Carl and Donna Marie (Earleywine) Schneider; m. Charles Douglas Edwards, May 27, 1977; 1 child, Janci. BS in Edn., Midland Luth. Coll., Fremont, 1972; MA in Edn., Ariz. State U., 1979, No. Ariz. U., 1986, EdD in Curriculum and Instrn., 1988. Lang. arts tchr. Arlington (Nebr.) Pub. Schs., 1972-76, Glendale (Ariz.) Elem. Sch. Dist., 1977-80; from reading specialist to prin. Deer Valley Sch. Dist., Phoenix, 1980—2004, dir. assessment, 2004—. Mentor tchr. Midland Luth. Coll., 2004. Recipient award of achievement U.S. West Comm., Ariz., 1992, Mountain Shadows PTSA Outstanding Educator award, 2001. Mem. Internat. Reading Assn., Assn. for Supervision and Curriculum Devel. Nat. Coun. Tchrs. English, Ariz. Sch. Adminstrs., Phi Kappa Phi, Phi Delta Kappa. Democrat. Avocations: reading, needlecrafts, music. Home: 2336 W Laurel Ln Phoenix AZ 85029-3423 Office: Deer Valley Unified Sch Dist 20402 N 15th Ave Glendale AZ 85027-3699 Business E-Mail: vicki.edwards@dvusd.org.

EDWARDS, VICTOR HENRY, chemical engineer; b. Galveston, Tex., Oct. 17, 1940; s. Philip Lacey and Margaret Ruth (Hopkins) E.; m. Mary Margaret Litzmann, June 10, 1963; children: Henry L., Mary E. BA, Rice U., 1962; PhD in Chem. Engring., U. Calif., Berkeley, 1967. Registered profl. engr., Tex. Asst. prof. chem. engring. Cornell U., Ithaca, NY, 1967-73; mgr. adv. tech. U.S. Nat. Sci. Found., Washington, 1971-72; rsch. fellow Merck, Sharp, Dohme Rsch., Rahway, NJ, 1973-76; supr. rsch. engring. United Energy Resources, Houston, 1976-79; vis. prof. environ. engring. Rice U., Houston, 1979-80; sr. process engr. Fluor Engrs. and Constructors, Houston, 1980-82; southwest editor Plant Services mag., Chgo., 1982-85; project engr. Allstates/BE&K, Inc., Houston, 1984-90, lead process engr., 1990-93, process engring. mgr., 1993-94, prin. engr. process and environ., 1994-95; process dir. Aker Kvaerner, Houston, 1995—. Tech. adv. com. Mary Kay O'Connor Process Safety Ctr., Tex. A&M U., 1995—, chmn., 2005— Mem. editl. bd. Chem. Processing mag., 2003-; contbr. articles to profl. jours. Organizing com. Woodlands (Tex.) Harvest Festival, 1979-86; chmn. industry adv. coun. dept. chem. engring. Prairie View A&M U., 1991-94. Recipient Disting. Svc. award Prairie View A&M U., 1992, 94, Shield of Irenee award E.I. duPont de Nemours & Co., 1994, 98, 2001, Environ. Excellence award, 1994, Safety, Health, and Environ. Excellence award, 1996, Svc. award Mary Kay O'Connor Process Safety Ctr., 2002. Fellow: AIChE (chmn. Process Plant Safety Symposium 1992, exec. position 1 1993, program co-chmn. 1994, chmn. 1995, South Tex. sect. chmn. 2nd internat. plant ops. and design conf. 1997, Disting. Svc. award 1991); mem.: Nat. Fire Protection Assn., NSPE, AAAS, Engrs. Coun. Houston (councilor 1987—92), Rice U. Alumni Assn. (class of '62 reunion com. 1982, 1987, 1992, 1997, co-chmn. fundraising drive 1998, class of '62 reunion com. 2002), Am. Chem. Soc. (chmn. Ithaca sect. 1969, councilor divsn. biochem. and microbial tech. 1970—77), N.Y. Acad. Scis. (life). Methodist. Avocations: reading, tennis, sailing, golf. Office Phone: 713-270-2817. Business E-Mail: vic.edwards@akerkvaerner.com.

EDWARDS, WALLACE WINFIELD, retired automotive executive; b. Pontiac, Mich., May 9, 1922; s. David W. and Ruby M. (Nutting) E.; m. Jean Austin Wolfe, Aug. 24, 1944; children: Ronald W., Gary R., Ann E. BS in Mech. Engring, Gen. Motors Inst., 1949; MBA, Mich. State U., 1966. With GMC Truck & Coach div. Gen. Motors Corp., Pontiac, Mich., 1940-78, truck service mgr., 1961-62, head engine design, 1962-64, dir. reliability, 1964-66, dir. prodn. control and purchasing, 1966-70, dir. engring., 1970-78; dir. Worldwide Truck Project Center, Warren, Mich., 1978-80; gen. dir. Worldwide Truck and Transp. Sys. Center, 1980-81; v.p. G.M.O.D.C., 1980-81; group mgr. small and light truck and van ops. Truck and Bus. Group, Gen. Motors Corp., 1981-82, mgr. internat. staff, 1982-84, gen. dir. mil. vehicle ops. Power Products and Def. Group, 1984-86. Bd. dirs. Crystal Mountain Resort, Thompsonville, Mich., 1991-2003. Past pres., mem. exec. com. Clinton Valley coun. Boy Scouts Am.; dir. Grand Traverse Regional Land Conservancy, 1991-2003, chmn. 1996-98; regent Nat. Eagle Scout Assn. (life). Served with USNR, 1944-46. Mem. Soc. Automotive Engrs., U.S. Navy League, Tau Beta Pi, Beta Gamma Sigma. Office: 5089 Crystal Dr Beulah MI 49617-9617

EDWARDS, WARREN CHAPPELLE, military career officer; b. Franklin, Va., June 3, 1947; m. Diane Dorsey; 1 child, Joel. BS in English, U. Richmond; MA in Nat. Security, U.S. Naval War Coll.; M in Mil. Arts and Scis., U.S. Army Command & Gen. Coll.; grad., Army Command & Gen. Staff Col., Naval War Coll. Commd. 2nd lt. U.S. Army, advanced through grades to maj. gen., 1998, comdr. 4th Squadron, 7th Cavalry, comdr. 5th Squadron, 17th Cavalry, 2nd Infantry Divsn., comdr. 10th Aviation Brigade, 10th Mountain Divsn., chief ops. divsn., ops. directorate Office Joint Chiefs; chief of staff U.S. Army Aviation Ctr., Ft. Rucker, Ala.; asst. divsn. comdr. 2nd Infantry Divsn. U.S. Army, Korea; dep. commanding gen. Fifth U.S. Army, 1997-99, Third U.S. Army, 1999—. Decorated Def. Superior Svc. medal, Legion of Merit with 2 oak leaf clusters, Meritorious Svc. medal with oak leaf cluster, 10 air medals, Army Commendation medal.

EDWARDS, WARREN D., computer company executive; married; 2 children. BBA, Tex. Tech U. CPA. Former v.p. purchasing and v.p. trading ops. Foxmeyer Health Corp.; formerly with PriceWaterhouseCoopers; sr. v.p. fin. and acctg. Affiliated Computer Svcs., Inc., Dallas, 1996—2001, exec. v.p., CFO, 2001—. Office: Affiliated Computer Svcs Inc 2828 N Haskell Bldg 1 Dallas TX 75204

EDWARDS, WILLIAM T. (BILLY EDWARDS), information technology executive; BA in Biomed. Engring.; BA, MD, PhD in Materials Sci. Engring., Vanderbilt U. With Tech. Assocs., Inc., 1979—86, Boston Consulting Group, 1986—93; v.p., dir. corp. strategy Motorola, 1993—97, sr. v.p., dir. strategic mgmt. semiconductor product sector, 1997—2000, sr. v.p., gen. mgr., 2000—01; CEO Hesson Labs., Inc., 2001—02; v.p., gen. mgr. personal connectivity solutions group Advanced Micro Devices, Sunnyvale, Calif., 2002—04, chief strategy officer, 2004—. Office: Advanced Micro Devices One AMD Pl PO Box 3453 Sunnyvale CA 94088-3453

EDWARDS-LEBOEUF, RENEE CAMILLE, public relations executive, protective services official; b. Falls Church, Va., Aug. 6, 1961; d. Walter Thomas and Elizabeth Ann Holt. BS, George Mason U., Fairfax, 1983; MS, Central Mich. U., Merrifield, 1988; grad. program mgmt. course, Def. Systems Mgmt. Coll., 1990. Cert. contracting officer's rep. Logistics analyst The BDM Corp., McLean, Va., 1983-85; deputy program mgr. COMARCO/IBS, Arlington, Va., 1985-88; logistics mgr., speaker, briefer SWL, Inc., Arlington, Va., 1988-89; mem. profl. staff Def. Systems Mgmt. Coll., Ft. Belvoir, Va., 1989-92; dir. computer-aided acquisition and logistics support tng. and edn. Office Asst. Sec. of Def. Prodn. and Logistics, Falls Church, Va., 1992-93; dir. pub. affairs U.S. Dept. Commerce, Nat. Tech. Info. Svc., Springfield, Va., 1993—. Co-chmn. computer aided acquisition Logistics Systems Rsch. Group. Contbr. articles to profl. jours. Bd. dirs. Woodwalk Condominium, Burke, Va., 1987-96, mem. indsl. tech. adv. com., 1997-99. Named Best Speaker Toastmasters, McLean, 1985, Best Evaluator Toastmasters, McLean, 1985; recipient Excellence award Dept. Def., 1993, Outstanding Svc. award Dept. Commerce, 1996. Mem. Soc. of Logistics Engrs., Pub. Rels. Soc. Am. Republican. Avocations: racquetball, bicycling, embroidery, guitar. Office: US Dept Commerce NTIS 5285 Port Royal Rd Springfield VA 22161-0001

EDWARDS-MITCHUM, LILLIAN (RED THE POET), secondary school educator, writer; d. Richard and Kathrine Edwards; m. Lawrence Joseph Mitchum, Apr. 11, 1977 (div. 1993); children: Lawrence Joseph Mitchum Jr., Lance Alexander Mitchum. AAS, Harold Washington, Chgo., 1990; BS in Behavioral Sci., Nat. Louis U., Chgo., 2000. Cert. tchr. Ill. Adminstr. Cook County Hosp., Chgo., 1972—2002; tchr. Bd. Edn., Chgo., 2003—. Author: Bold From the Soul Spiritual Healing, 2003; contbr. poetry to anthology. Domestic violence advocate Chgo. Woman Abuse, 2001—02; mem. bldg. and ground com. Deliverance Bapt. Ch., Chgo., 2003.

EDWARDSON, JOHN ALBERT, security firm executive; b. Terre Haute, Ind., July 23, 1949; s. John Albert and Mildred Ruth (Anderson) E.; m. Catharine Orr, June 11, 1971; children: Laura, Anne, Shelley. BS in Indsl. Engring., Purdue U., 1971; MBA in Fin. and Internat. Bus., U. Chgo., 1972. Comml. banking officer First Bank-St. Paul, 1972-77; v.p., treas. Ferrell Cos. Inc., Kansas City, Mo., 1977-83, sr. v.p. fin. services group, 1983-85; exec. v.p. fin., chief fin. officer Northwest Airlines Inc. and NWA Inc., St. Paul, 1985-88; exec. v.p., chief fin. and adminstrv. officer Internat. Minerals and Chems. Corp., Northbrook, Ill., 1988-90; chief fin. officer United Airlines Employees Acquisition Corp., Chgo., 1990; exec. v.p., chief fin. officer Ameritech, Chgo., 1991-94; pres., COO UAL Corp., Elk Grove Village, Ill., 1994—; chmn., pres. & CEO Burns Internat. Svcs Corp, Chgo., 1999—2000; chmn., CEO CDW, Vernon Hills, Ill., 2001—. Trustee, pres. Ravina Festival Assn., Highland Park, Ill., bd. trustees Art Inst. Chgo. Recipient Disting. Engring. Alumnus award Purdue U., 1988. Presbyterian. Avocations: sailing, hiking, bicycling. Office: CDW 200 N Milwaukee Ave Vernon Hills IL 60061

EDWARDSON, SANDRA, dean, nursing educator; BSN, St. Olaf Coll., Minn., 1963; MN in Maternal and Child Nursing, U. of Wash., 1964; PhD, U. of Minn., 1980. Dean Sch. Nursing, U. Minn., Mpls. Office: U Minn Twin Cities Sch Nursing 6-101 Weaver-Densford Hall 308 Harvard St SE Minneapolis MN 55455-0353

EEKMAN, THOMAS ADAM, Slavic languages educator; b. Middelharnis, Holland, May 20, 1923; came to U.S., 1966; s. Thomas Adam and Anna (de Kruyff) Eekman; m. Tine de Jong, May 2, 1946 (dec. Feb. 2001); children: Menno, Roeland, Ivo (dec.), Milja. MA, U. Amsterdam, 1946, PhD, 1951. Research asst. Russian Inst., Amsterdam U., 1948-55, lectr. Slavic langs. at univ., 1955-60, asst. prof., 1960-66; vis. prof. UCLA, 1960-61, prof. Slavic langs., 1966-90, chmn. dept., 1968-72; ret., 1990. Author: The Realm of Rime, A Study of Rime in the Poetry of the Slavs, 1974, Thirty Years of Yugoslav Literataure, 1945-75, 1978; editor: Anton Cechov, 1860-1960, (with A. Kadic) Juraj Krizanic (1618-1683) Russophile and Ecumenic Visionary, 1976, (with P. Debreczeny) Chekhov's Art of Writing, 1977, (with H Birnbaum) Fiction and Drama in Eastern Europe, Evolution and Experiment in the Postwar Period, 1980, Calif. Slavic Studies, 1972-92, (with D.S. Worth) Russian Poetics, 1983; Critical Essays on Chekhov, 1989; contbr. articles to profl. jours. Decorated Order Yugoslav Flag, 1964; recipient Martinus Nijhoff prize, 1981 Mem. Am. Assn. Advancement Slavic Studies, Bulgarian Studies Assn., Philol. Assn. Pacific Coast (pres. 1971), N.Am. Soc. Serbian Studies, N.Am. Chekhov Soc. Unitarian Universalist. Address: 334 Santa Margarita Dr San Rafael CA 94901-1640 also: Esseboom 2 1251 CP Laren Netherlands E-mail: t.eekman@hetnet.nl.

EELLS, WILLIAM HASTINGS, retired automobile company executive; b. Princeton, Mar. 30, 1924; s. Hastings and Amy (Titus) E.; 1 child, Jonathan William. BA, Ohio Wesleyan U., 1946; MA, Ohio State U., 1950; DHL (hon.), Kent State U., 1983; D of Pub. Svc., Bowling Green State U., 1983; D in Comm. (hon.), Franklin U., 2005. Asst. to dir. Inst. Practical Politics Ohio Wesleyan U., 1948-50, dir., 1953-57, instr. dept. polit. sci., 1952-59; instr. polit. sci. Mt. Union Coll., 1950-51; mem. Ohio Gov.'s Cabinet, 1957-59; coord. Atomic Devel. Activities State of Ohio, 1957-59; Midwest regional mgr. civic and govtl. affairs Ford Motor Co., Columbus, 1959-87. Author: Your Ohio Government, 1953 (6 edits.); contbr. articles to profl. jours. Mem. Nat. Coun. on Arts, NEA, 1976-82; chmn. bd. Blue Cross of Northeast Ohio, 1963-72, Blossom Music Ctr., Cleve., 1968—; chmn. bd. govs. Gov.'s Coun. on Rehab., 1966-68; mem. exec. com. Met. Opera's Nat. Coun., 1967-81; pres. Nat. Coun. High Blood Pressure Rsch., 1974-79; chmn. Ohio Pub. Expenditure Coun., 1981-84, Gov.'s Task Force on State Ops., 1984-85; vice chmn. Ohio Northwest Bicentennial Com., 1986-87; bd. dirs. Am. Heart Assn., 1974-79, Columbus Mus. Art, 1982-88, Opera/Columbus, 1984-86, Columbus Ballet, 1985-86, Nat. Coun. French Am. Scholarship Found., 1985-87; trustee Cleve. Orch., 1964—, Hist. Morven Found., Princeton, N.J., 1988-96, Ednl. TV, Cleve., 1965-75, Cleve. Playhouse, 1965-82, Cleve. Ballet, Cleve. Zoo, 1965-76, Ohio Arts Coun., Columbus Symphony, Cleve. Luth. Hosp., 1966-76, Mt. Union Coll., 1984—, Ohio Wesleyan U., 1988—; trustee Franklin U., 1987—, Columbus Assn. Performing Arts, 1978—, Ohio Found. Ind. Colls., 1986—, Grady Meml. Hosp., 1987-94, Riverside Hosp. Found., 1990-96; hon. chmn. Del. Arts Ctr., 1989—; life trustee Fairview Health Cleve., 1980—; trustee, v.p. Oak Grove Cemetery, 1983—; chmn. Ohio Commn. for Son of Heaven Imperial Arts of China, 1988; mem. Ohio Humanities Coun., 1993-95; patron Morgan Libr., N.Y.C., 1995—; trustee Del. County Dist. Libr. Bd., 1994—; mem. Ohio Bicentennial Commn., 1997—; trustee Columbus Zoo Assn., 1998—; mem. Friends Princeton U. Libr., 1997—. Recipient USCG Disting. award, 1965, Silver medal Royal Life Saving Soc., Ohio State U. Devel. award, 1967, award for disting. svc. Am. Heart Assn., 1979, Ohio Arts Coun. award, 1979, Ohio Theatre Alliance award, 1981, Gov. award, 1985, Alumni Achievement award Ohio State U., 1987, Silver medal Japanese Red Cross Soc. Republican. Presbyterian (elder). Home: Honeystone 54 Elmwood Dr Delaware OH 43015-1617 *Parents, teachers and friends can do just so much, you have to do the rest. God helps those who help themselves, and being in the right place at the right time does help.*

EERNISSE, GLENN P., music educator; b. Sheboygan, Wis., Feb. 2, 1957; s. Jess Earl and June Josephine Eernisse; m. Florence Susan Freeman, Aug. 26, 1976; children: Melody, Jessica. A in Fine Arts, Anderson Coll., 1977; MusB, Berry Coll., 1979; M of Ch. Music, So. Bapt. Theol. Sem., 1981, D of Music Ministry, 1994. Min. of music Northside Bapt. Ch., Ruskin, Fla., 1981—83, Brunswick, Ga., 1983—87, First Bapt. Ch., Cedartown, Ga., 1987—95; prof. Brewton-Parker Coll., Mt. Vernon, Ga., 1995—. Bd. dirs. Creator Mag., Healdsburg, Calif. Contbr. articles to profl. jours.; composer: numerous songs. Mem.: ASCAP (Std. award 2001—04), Internat. Trombone Assn., Mus. Educators Nat. Conf. Office: Brewton-Parker Coll Hwy 280 Mount Vernon GA 30445 Office Phone: 912-583-3131. Business E-Mail: geernisse@bpc.edu.

EFFEL, LAURA, lawyer; b. Dallas, May 9, 1945; d. Louis E. and Fay (Lee) Ray; m. Marc J. Patterson, Sept. 19, 1992 (dec. July 30, 2002); 1 child, Stephen Patterson. BA, U. Calif., Berkeley, 1971; JD, U. Md., 1975. Bar: N.Y. 1976, U.S. Dist. Ct. (so. and ea. dists.) N.Y. 1976, U.S. Ct. Appeals (2d cir.) 1980, U.S. Supreme Ct. 1980, D.C. 1993, N.C. 1998, Va. 2001; cert. mediator Judicial Coun. Va., 2004. Assoc. Burns Jackson Miller Summit & Jacoby, N.Y.C., 1975-78, Pincus Munzer Bizar & D'Alessandro, N.Y.C., 1978-80; v.p., sr. assoc. counsel Chase Manhattan Bank, N.A., N.Y.C., 1980-96; counsel Baker & McKenzie, N.Y.C., 1996-99; gen. counsel Garban Cos., 1999-2000; counsel LeClair Ryan Flippin Densmore, Roanoke, Va., 2000—02, ptnr., 2002—. Bd. dirs. Blue Ridge Pub. TV, 2001—. Mem. Workforce Devel. Com., New Century Tech. Coun.; bd. dirs. Bklyn. Legal Svcs. Corp. A, 1992-2000. Named one of Best Lawyers in Am., 2005. Mem.: ABA (com. pretrial practice 2000—03, litig. sect. co-chair, subcom. atty. client privilege), Roanoke Bar Assn., Va. Bar Assn., NC Bar Assn., Am. Corp. Counsel Assn. (dir. emeritus, pro bono svc. award 1989). Office: LeClair Ryan Flippin Densmore Drawer 1200 Roanoke VA 24006 Office Phone: 540-510-3026. Business E-Mail: laura.effel@leclairryan.com.

EFFORD, R. JOHN, Canadian government official; b. Port de Frave, Newfoundland and Labrador, Can., Jan. 6, 1944; m. Madonna Efford; 3 children. Mem. Newfoundland and Labrador Ho. of Legis. Assembly, 1985—2000, Can. Parliament, 2002—; min. natural resources Govt. Can., 2003—. Office: Ho of Commons Ottawa ON Canada K1A 0A6 also: Sir William Logan Bldg 21st Fl 580 Booth St Ottawa ON Canada K1A 0E4

EFFREN, GARY ROSS, financial executive; b. Jersey City, Feb. 27, 1956; s. Ronald Lewis and Ethel Frances (Ross) E.; m. Francine Oberfest, May 24, 1980; children: Jessica Leigh, Jenna Ashlee. BS summa cum laude, Rider Coll., 1978; postgrad., U. Miami, Coral Gables, Fla., 1984-89. CPA, Fla. Sr. auditor Peat, Marwick, Mitchell & Co., Miami, 1978—80; sr. fin. acct. Knight-Ridder, Inc., Miami, Fla., 1980—82, mgr. fin. reporting, 1982—84, dir. corp. acctg., 1986—88, asst. to v.p./finance, 1988—95; bus. mgr. Viewdata Corp. Am., Miami Beach, Fla., 1984—86; v.p., contr. Knight Ridder, Inc., San Jose, Calif., 1995—2001, sr. v.p. fin., CFO, 2001—04, v.p. fin., 2004—. Mem. Am. Inst. CPA's, Fla. Inst. CPA's. Jewish. Avocations: guitar playing, racquetball. Office: Knight-Ridder Inc 50 W San Fernando St San Jose CA 95113-2413 E-mail: geffren@knightridder.com.

EFFRON, ANDREW S., federal judge; b. Stamford, Conn., 1948; BA, Harvard U., 1970, JD, 1975; student, JAG's Sch. US Army, 1976, student, 1984. Intermittent legis. aide to Rep. William A. Steiger US Ho. Reps., Washington, 1970-76; with Office of staff Judge Adv., Ft. McClellan, Ala., 1976-77; atty.-advisor Office of Gen. Counsel US Dept. Def., Washington, 1977-87; counsel Senate Armed Svcs. Com., Washington, 1987—88, gen. counsel, 1988—95, minority counsel, 1995—96; judge US Ct. Appeals for the Armed Forces, Washington, 1996—. Office: US Ct Appeals Armed Forces 405 E St NW Washington DC 20442-0001

EFFRON, DAVID LOUIS, conductor, performing company executive; b. Cin., July 28, 1938; s. Sigmund and Babette Jane (Holstein) E.; children: Michael, Daniel. MusB, U. Mich., 1960; MusM, Ind. U., 1962. Asst. condr., condr. N.Y.C. Opera, 1964-82; asst. condr. Nat. Ballet, Washington, 1969-70; music dir. Central City (Colo.) Opera, 1972-76; condr. Curtis Inst. Music, Phila., 1970-77; music dir. Eastman Philharm., Eastman Sch., Rochester, NY, 1977-98, Youngstown (Ohio) Symphony Orch., 1987-96, Heidelberg (Fed. Republic Germany) Castle Festival, 1980-92, Chautaugua Instn. Music Sch. Festival Orch., 1990-96; artistic dir., prin. condr. Brevard (N.C.) Music Ctr., 1996—; prof. instrumental conducting Ind. U., Bloomington, 1998—. Guest condr. numerous assignments Europe, Far East, U.S. Condr. recs. Schwantner Aftertones, 1983, Schuman Judith, 1984, Benita Valente, 1986, Mahler & Berlioz with Jan deGaetani, 1989. Recipient Grammy award, 1984, Best Contemporary Rec. award Ovation Mag., 1988, Musician of Yr. award Nat. Fedn. Music Clubs, 2003. Office: Brevard Music Center PO Box 312 Brevard NC 28712-0312 Office Phone: 828-862-2100. E-mail: deffron@indiana.edu.

EFFRON, SETH ALAN, editor, journalist; b. July 23, 1952; m. Nancy G. Thomas; children: Rebecca, Eve. BA in Polit. Sci. with honors, U. N.C., 1974. Asst. to editor Fayetteville (N.C.) Times (now Fayetteville Observer), 1974—75, reporter, 1975—77, Tallahassee Dem., 1977—80, Wichita (Kans.) Eagle-Beacon (now Wichita Eagle), 1980—82, 1983—85, coord. legis. coverage, 1982; state govt. and polit. reporter Greensboro (N.C.) News & Record, 1985—93; editor, founder the insider, N.C. State Govt. News Svc., Raleigh, 1993—96; exec. editor on-line content Nando Media, Nando Times, Raleigh, 1996—99; account exec. Capital Strategies, Raleigh, 2000—01; dep. curator Nieman Found. for Journalism, 2001—02, spl. projects dir., 2002—04; exec. editor State Govt. Radio, Curtis Media Group, Raleigh, 2004—. NEH summer fellow Williams Coll., 1979; lectr. Freedom Forum Media Studies Ctr. Columbia U., N.Y.C., 1995; lectr. Annenberg Washington program Northwest U., 1995; lectr. Ctr. for Pub. TV U. N.C., fellow, 1993; lect. Inst. for Polit. Leadership, 1994; lectr. Salzburg (Austria) Seminar, 1994, Human Svcs. Automation Conf., 1994. Author: 100 Proof Pure Old Jess: Jesse Helms Quoted, 1993, Coachspeak: Triangle ACC Men's Basketball Coaches Quoted, 1995, North Carolina Almanac of Government and Politics, 1995—96; contbr. articles contributed articles to popular publs., including LA Herald-Examiner, Des Moines Register, Christian Science Monitor, 1995. Mem. adv. panel Z. Smith Reynolds Found., 1988—91; mem. area edn. adv. bd. Broughton HS, 1996—2001; v.p. Fred A. Olds Elem. Sch. PTA, 1994—95, pres., 1995—96; bd. dirs. Edenton St. United Meth. Ch. Child Devel. Ctr., 1986—88, 1993—94. Recipient Nieman fellow, Harvard U., 1991—92, Cert. of Merit, Am. Acad. Trial Lawyers, 1975, Pub. Svc. award, N.C. Press Assn., 1976, News Enterprise award, William Allen White Found., 1985, 2nd Pl. awards, N.C. Press Assn., 1987, 1989, 3rd Pl. awards, 1990. Home: 3613 Eden Ct Raleigh NC 27612 Office: State Govt Radio 3012 Highwoods Blvd Raleigh NC 27604 Office Phone: 919-882-3782. Business E-Mail: seffron@curtismedia.com.

EFIRD, JIMMY THOMAS, statistician; BA, UCLA, Los Angeles, CA, 1979; MSC, Calif. State U., Hayward, 1985; PhD, Stanford Sch. of Medicine, Palo Alto, CA, 2003. Pres. Applied Stats. Corp., Palo Alto, Calif., 1986—2002. Mem.: Am. Statis. Assn., Bay Area SAS Users Group (chmn.), Disting. Statistician Filming Com. E-mail: jimy.efird@stanfordalumni.org.

EFRON, BRADLEY, statistician, educator; b. St. Paul, May 24, 1938; s. Miles Jack and Esther (Kaufman) Efron; m. Gael Guerin, July 1969 (div.); 1 child, Miles James; m. Nancy Troup, June 1986 (div.). BS in Math., Calif. Inst. Tech., 1960; PhD, Stanford U., 1964; DSc (hon.), U. Chgo., 1995; D (hon.), U. Carlos III de Madrid, 1998; DSc (hon.), U. Oslo, 2002. Asst. and assoc. prof. stats. Stanford (Calif.) U., 1965-72, chmn. dept. stats., 1976-79, 1991-1994, chmn. math. scis., 1981—, prof. stats., 1974—, assoc. dean humanities and scis., 1987-90, endowed chair Max H. Stein prof. humanities and scis., 1991-94. Statis. cons. Alza Corp., 1971—, Rand Corp., 1962—. Author: Bootstrap Methods, 1979, Biostatistics Casebook, 1980. MacArthur Found. fellow, 1983; named Outstanding Statistician of Yr. Chgo. Statis. Assn., 1981; Wald and Rietz Lectr. Inst. Math. Stats., 1977, 81; recipient Fisher award, Chgo., 1996, Parzen prize for statis. innovation, 1998, Rao prize, 2003. Fellow Inst. Math. Stats. (pres. 1987), Am. Statis. Assn. (pres. 2004, Wilks medal 1990); mem. NAS, Am. Acad. Arts and Scis., Internat. Statis. Assn. Office: Stanford U Dept Stats Sequoia Hall Stanford CA 94305

EFROS, ELLEN ANN, lawyer; b. N.Y.C., Jan. 18, 1950; d. Edwin David and Judith (Breitman) E.; m. Fritz R. Kahn, June 26, 1983. BA, Case Western Res. U., 1971; MA, St. John's U., 1973; JD, Hofstra U., 1978. Bar: D.C. 1978, N.Y. 1979, Md. 1990, U.S. Ct. Appeals (5th cir.) 1978, U.S. Ct. Appeals (2d, 7th and D.C. cirs.) 1979, U.S. Ct. Appeals (Fed. cir.) 1993, U.S. Dist. Ct. D.C. 1981, U.S. Ct. Claims 1986, U.S. Supreme Ct. 1989. Trial atty. ICC Gen. Counsel, Washington, 1978-79; assoc. Verner & Liipfert, Washington, 1979-81; ptnr. Vorys, Sater, Seymour & Pease, Washington, 1981-97; hearing officer, office dispute resolution NASD Regulation, Inc., Washington, 1997-2000; ptnr. Rader, Fishman & Grauer, Washington, 2000—. Asst. editor Antitrust Law Jour., 1987-90. Mem. ABA (sects. intellectual property and litigation), D.C. Bar Assn., N.Y. Bar Assn., Md. Bar Assn. Office: Rader Fishman & Grauer 1233 20th St NW Ste 501 Washington DC 20036-2365 Office Phone: 202-955-8779. Business E-Mail: eae@raderfishman.com.

EFRUSSY, ALAN MAURICE, urban planner; b. Chgo., May 6, 1937; s. Benjamin and Rose E.; m. Linda Louise, Mar. 25, 1973; children: Joel Brian, Jill Ellen. BA in Liberal Arts and Scis., U. Ill., 1959; MA in Urban Studies with honors, Roosevelt U., 1973. Chief planner Freese & Nichols, Austin, Tex., 1983-84; coord. comprehensive planning program City of Richardson, Tex., 1984-87; dir. planning, cmty. devel. City of McKinney, 1987-94, City of Rowlett, Tex., 1994—. Contbg. author: Guide to Urban Planning in Texas

Communities, 2000. With U.S. Navy, 1960-62. Recipient Profl. Merit award Am. Planning Assn., 1984-85, 90. Mem. Am. Inst. Cert. Planners (charter). Avocations: fly fishing, model trains. Office: Planning Dept City of Rowlett 3901 Main St Rowlett TX 75088

EFSTRATIADES, ANASTASIUS, lawyer; b. Athens, Greece, July 17, 1951; BA, Villanova U., 1972, MA, 1974, JD, 1976. Bar: Pa. 1976, D.C. 1978, N.J. 1984, U.S. Dist. Ct. N.J., U.S. Dist. Ct. (ea. dist.) Pa., U.S. Tax Ct., U.S. Ct. Appeals (3d cir.). Ptnr., mem. mgmt. com. Obermayer, Rebmann, Maxwell & Hippel LLP, Phila., 1988—. Chmn. N.J. Commn. on Internat. Trade, 1992—95; mem. N.J. Assembly Task Force on Bus. Retention and Export Opportunities, 1994—2001, N.J. Econ. Devel. Authority, 1990—92, NJ Health Care Adminstrn. Bd., 2002—. Contbr. articles to profl. jours. Vice-pres. Fedn. Am. Hellenic Socs. Delaware Valley, 1980-81, 86-87; pres. Phila. chpt. Am. Hellenic Ednl. Progressive Assn., 1980-81. Mem. Greek Am. C. of C. (pres. NJ chpt. 1993-95, Achievement award 1996). Office: Obermayer Rebmann Maxwell & Hippell LLP 1 Penn Ctr 1617 JFK Blvd Philadelphia PA 19103 also: 20 Brace Rd Cherry Hill NJ 08034 Office Phone: 215-665-3030. Business E-Mail: tassos@obermayer.com.

EFSTRATION, GARY GERASIMOS, lawyer; b. Drexel Hill, Pa., Nov. 18, 1963; s. Michael and Mary Efstration; m. Angela Tsoflias, May 25, 1991; children: Michael, Kalliopi. BA in Econs., Villanova U., 1989; JD, Widener U., Harrisburg, Pa. and Del., 1992. Bar: Pa. 1992. Law clk. to Hon. Wayne G. Hummer, Lancaster, Pa., 1992-93; assoc. Pyfer & Reese, Lancaster, 1993-96; pvt. practice, Lancaster, 1996—. Mem.: Am. Hellenic Ednl. and Progressive Assn. (chpt. 71 pres. 1998—2000). Office: 232 E Orange St Lancaster PA 17602-2851 E-mail: tlwgge@aol.com.

EFTEKHARI, NASSER, physiatrist; b. Aug. 15, 1940; MD, U. Tehran, 1965. Diplomate Am. Bd. Phys. Medicine and Rehab. Intern Greater Balt. Med. Ctr., 1967-68; resident in phys. medicine and rehab. Temple U. Sch. Med., Phila., 1968-70, Hahneman Med. U., Phila., 1970-71; rsch. fellow SUNY, Bklyn., 1971-72; chief dept. phys. medicine and rehab. Shafa Rehab. Hosp., Tehran, Iran, 1973-75; dean Coll. of Rehab. Scis., Tehran, 1973-79; phys. med. and rehab. cons. Golestan Clinic, Mehr Hosp., Tehran, 1980-84; staff physician VA Hosp., Miami, Fla., 1985—, Mercy Hosp., 1989—, Cedars Med. Ctr., 1989—, Bapt. Health Sys. Hosp. South Fla., Miami, 1996—; chief phys. med. and rehab. svc. VA Hosp., Miami, 1997—. Clin. prof. rehab. medicine U. Miami Sch. Med., 2003—. Fellow Am. Assn. Electrodiagnostic Medicine; mem. Fla. Soc. Phys. Medicine and Rehab., AMA, Am. Acad. Phys. Medicine and Rehab. Office: 8600 SW 92 St Ste 201 Miami FL 33156

EFTHEMIS, TRACY ANN, literature and language educator; d. Paul Merle and Bonnie Jean FitzSimmons; m. John Nicholas Efthemis, Jan. 2, 2004; children: Samuel Paul, Allyse Katherine. MS, Canisius Coll., 2000. Cert. tchr. NY. Tchr. English Lancaster (NY) H.S., 1995—.

EFTHIMIOU, COSTAS JOHN, physicist, educator, physicist, researcher; s. John and Maria Efthimiou. BSc, U. Athens; MSc, PhD, Cornell U. Vis. scientist Cornell/Columbia U., Ithaca, NY, N.Y.C., Harvard U., Cambridge, Mass.; rsch. assoc. Tel Aviv U.; lectr. Cornell U., Ithaca, NY; asst. prof. U. Ctrl. Fla. Editor (with B. Greene): Fields, Strings and Dualities, 1997. Mem.: Campus Freethought Alliance, U. Ctrl. Fla., Soc. Physics Students U. Ctrl. Fla., Am. Phys. Soc., Math. Assn. Am., Am. Assn. Physics Tchrs., Soc. Physics Students, Sigma Pi Sigma. Office: Dept Physics Univ Ctrl Fla Orlando FL 32816

EFTIMOFF, ANITA KENDALL, educational consultant; b. Granite City, Ill., May 3, 1927; d. David Harlow and Ollie Lorena (Galloway) Kendall; m. Vasil Eftimoff, June 14, 1959; 1 child, James Kendall. BA, Washington U., St. Louis, 1949; MA, So. Ill. U., Edwardsville, 1978, EdD, 1983. Cert. in multiple gen. edn., spl. edn., Ill. Spl. edn. instr. Community Unit 9, Granite City, 1968-83; ednl. cons. Efti Enterprises, Granite City, 1982—; program dir. At-Risk Presch. Grant, Granite City, 1986—. Del. NDEA Conf. Ea. Mich. U., Ypsilanti, 1968, Gifted Edn. Conf. Ill. Office of Edn., Springfield, 1975-77; adminstrv. intern Ill. State Bd. Edn., Springfield, 1981. Editor: Symphony Youth Orch. Newsletter, 1991—, Symphony Vol. Key Notes Newsletter, 1991-93. Bd. dirs. Ill. Gov.'s Adv. Coun. on Women's Affairs, Springfield, Rape Crisis and Sexual Abuse Ctr., So. Ill. U., 1978—, Family Resource Ctr.; chmn. adopt-a-friend St. Louis Ambs., 1982-84, co-chmn. Vets. Day, 1984-86; chmn. St. Louis Symphony Youth Orch., 1985—, St. Louis Symphony Young Artists Competitions, 1993—; mem. aux. St. Louis Children's Hosp., 1980; v.p. mus. activities St. Louis Symphony Vol. Assn.; bd. pres. Ill. Ctr. for Autism, 1993. At-risk presch. grantee Ill. Bd. Edn., 1986—. Mem. AAUW, World Coun. for Gifted and Talented Children, Nat. Assn. for Gifted Children, Assn. for the Gifted, Ill. Council for the Gifted, Asthma and Allergy Found. Southeastern Mo., Am. Lung Assn. St. Louis, Women's Assn. (bd. dirs. 1961—, pres. 1989-91), St. Louis Symphony Women's Assn., St. Louis Art Access (bd. dirs. 2003-04), St. Louis Artist Guild, Nev. Women's Lobby, League of Women Woters No. Nev., Progression Leadership Alliance Nev., Washoe County Alliance, Delta Kappa Gamma, Phi Delta Kappa. Lodges: Daus. of Nile, Rotary-Anns. Avocations: performing arts, classical music. Home: 205 E Coyote Dr Carson City NV 89704 Office: At-Risk Presch Program 2300 W 25th St Granite City IL 62040-2025

EGAN, BYRON F., lawyer; b. Dallas, Feb. 1, 1943; s. Joseph M. and Mae Rene (Flanary) E.; m. Nancy Dean; children: Elizabeth, Katherine, Mary. BA, U. Tex., 1965, JD, 1968. Bar: Tex. 1968. Law clk. to Hon. Irving L. Goldberg, U.S. Ct. Appeals 5th Cir., Dallas, 1968-69; ptnr. Ritchie, Crosland & Egan, Dallas, 1969-82, Andrews & Kurth LLP, Dallas, 1982-92, Cohan, Simpson, Cowlishaw & Wulff, LLP, Dallas, 1992-95, Jackson Walker LLP, Dallas, 1996—. Chmn., mem. exec. com., bd. dirs. Tex. Bus. Law Found., Dallas, 1991-94; chmn. bus. law sect. State Bar Tex., 1991-92; exec. com. chancellor's coun. U. Tex., 2005—. Contbr. numerous articles to legal jours. Bd. dirs. Dallas Symphony Assn., 1996—; mem. exec. com. U. Tex. Chancellor's Coun., 2005—. Recipient award for best law jour. article Tex. Bar Found., 1992, Burton award, 2005 Mem. ABA (vice chmn. negotiated acquistions com.), Am. Law Inst., Dallas Country Club, Dallas Petroleum Club, Dallas Gun Club, City Club. Republican. Presbyterian. Avocations: jogging, skeet shooting. Office: Jackson Walker LLP 901 Main St Ste 6000 Dallas TX 75202-3797 Office Phone: 214-953-5727. Business E-Mail: began@jw.com.

EGAN, CHARLES JOSEPH, JR., lawyer, consumer products company executive; b. Cambridge, Mass., Aug. 11, 1932; s. Charles Joseph and Alice Claire (Ball) E.; m. Mary Bowersox, Aug. 6, 1955; children: Timothy, Sean, Peter, James. AB, Harvard U., 1954; LLB, Columbia U., 1959. Bar: N.Y. 1960, Mo. 1973. Assoc. Donovan, Leisure, Newton & Irvine, N.Y.C., 1959-62; ptnr. Hall, McNicol, Marett & Hamilton, N.Y.C., 1962-68; v.p., gen. counsel Thomson & McKinnon Securities, N.Y.C., 1969-70, Hallmark Cards, Inc., Kansas City, Mo., 1972—. Bd. dirs. Am. Multi Cinema, Inc., Kansas City, Mo. Trustee Notre Dame de Sion Sch., Kansas City, 1973-77, Pembroke Country Day Sch., Kansas City, 1976-82, Kansas City Art Inst., 1995—; bd. dirs. Kansas City YMCA, 1976-80; mem. dean's coun. Columbia Law Sch., 1991—; vice chmn. Harvard Coll. Fund, 1994-99, co-chmn., 2000-03; sole trustee Stanley H. Durwood Found. Served to 1st lt. USMC, 1954-56. Mem. Mo. Bar Assn., Kansas City Lawyers Assn., Harvard Alumni Assn. (pres. 1989-90, exec. com. 1987-2003), Century Assn., Somerset Club, Harvard Club of N.Y., Harvard Club of Kansas City (pres. 1985-87). Roman Catholic. Office: Hallmark Cards Inc 2501 Mcgee St Kansas City MO 64108-2600 Office Phone: 816-274-4687.

EGAN, EDWARD MICHAEL CARDINAL, archbishop, cardinal; b. Oak Park, Ill., Apr. 2, 1932; s. Thomas J. and Genevieve (Costello) Egan. PhB, St. Mary of Lake, 1954; STL, Gregorian U., 1958, JCD, 1963; PhD (hon.), St. John's U., Thomas More Coll., Western Conn. State U., Fordham U., Manhattan Coll., U. Lublin; PhD Cardinal Wyszynski U. (hon.), Warsaw. Ordained priest Roman Catholic Ch., 1957. Sec. to Albert Cardinal Meyer Archdiocese of Chgo., 1958—60, sec. to John Cardinal Cody, 1966—68, co-chancellor, 1969—72; faculty Pontifical N.Am. Coll., Vatican City, 1960—65; judge Sacred Roman Rota, Vatican City, 1972—85; aux. bishop, vicar for edn. Archdiocese of N.Y., N.Y.C., 1985—88; bishop of Bridgeport Conn., 1988—2000; archbishop of N.Y. N.Y.C., 2000—; cardinal Roman Cath. Ch., 2001—. Mem. Pontifical Coun. for the Family and Pontifical Coun. for Fin. and Adminstrv. Affairs of the Holy See, 2000—; chmn. bd. Bishop Curtis Homes, Fairfield County, Conn., 1988—2000; adminstrv. bd. U.S. Cath. Conf., 1991—94, 1996—99; chmn. bd. govs. Pontifical N.Am. Coll., Vatican City, 1991—95; mem. Supreme Tribunal of the Apostolic Signatura, 2002—, Coun. of Cardinals for the Study of Orgnl. and Econ. Problems of the Apostolic See, 2001—, Pontifical Coun. of the Family, 2001—, Prefecture of the Econ. Affairs of the Holy See, 2002—, Pontifical Commn. for the Cultural Goods of the Ch., 2002—; chmn. com. sci. and human values Nat. Conf. Cath. Bishops, com. Canonical Affairs, com. nat. collections, com. edn., com. nominations. Trustee Cath. U. Am., Washington, 2000—; bd. trustees Ratisbonne Inst., Jerusalem, 2000—, Thomas More Coll., Merrimack, NH, 1995—, Nat. Shrine Immaculate Conception, Washington, Cath. U. Am., Washington, Ave Maria Sch. Law, Ann Arbor, Mich.; chmn. bd. trustees St. Joseph Med. Ctr., Stamford, Conn., 1988—96; chmn. Inner-City Found. for Edn. and Charity, Fairfield County, Conn., 1992—2000; chmn. bd. trustees Sacred Heart U., Fairfield, Conn., 1988—2000, bd. trustees. Mem.: Cath. Neareast Welfare Assn. (chmn. 2000—). Roman Catholic.

EGAN, JOHN FREDERICK, retired electronics executive; b. Council Bluffs, Iowa, Feb. 25, 1935; s. Frederick Emerson and Ruth Pauline (Russell) E.; m. Anne B. Patterson, June 14, 1958; children: John Jr., James Michael. BA in Physics with honors, Grinnell Coll., 1957; MSEE, Northwestern U., 1958, PhD in Elec. Engring., 1961. Tech. dir. computer systems, Electronics Systems div. USAF, Bedford, Mass., 1964-67; sr. staff specialist intelligence Office Dir. Def., Research and Engring., Washington, 1967-71; chief scientist command support Office Chief Naval Ops., Washington, 1971-73; group dir. fed. systems Sanders Assocs., Inc., Nashua, N.H., 1973-77; v.p. Sanders Assoc., Inc., Nashua, N.H., 1977-87; group v.p. Lockheed Corp., 1987-93; corp. v.p. corp. devel. Lockheed Martin Corp., Bethesda, Md., 1993-98. Mem. exec. panel Chief Naval Ops., Washington, 1971—; mem. naval studies bd. NRC, 1990-98, 2004, chair 2005-. Trustee Grinnell Coll., 2002—, Hunt Cmty., 2002—, Daniel Webster Coll., 1998—, chair 2003-. Officer USAF, 1961—64. Mem. IEEE, AIAA, AAAS, Sigma Xi, Rotary Internat. Home: 7 Beverlee Dr Nashua NH 03064-1674 E-mail: ergwatt@hotmail.com.

EGAN, KAREN ESTHER, elementary school educator; b. Elmhurst, Ill., Mar. 2, 1955; d. Lester and Elaine Victoria (Nelson) Madsen; m. Patrick Nelson Egan, June 27, 1987. BA, Luther Coll., 1977; MAT, Nat.-Louis U., 1991. Cert. tchr., Ill. Tchr. elem. phys. edn. Sch. Dist. 44, Lombard, Ill., 1978—92, tchr. elem., 1992—. Coord. jump rope for heart Am. Heart Assn., Lombard, 1978-92; speaker Ill. Kindergarten Conf., 1985, 87, 88, 5th Great Lakes Rd. Coun., 1983. Mem. AAHPERD, NEA, Ill. Edn. Assn., Lombard Edn. Assn., Ill. Reading Coun., Ill. AHPERD (Tchr. of Yr. 1988, speaker convn. 1987). Republican. Lutheran. Avocations: reading, cooking, sewing, crafts, running. Home: 267 N Charlotte St Lombard IL 60148-2035 Office: Hammerschmidt 617 Hammerschmidt Ave Lombard IL 60148-3498 Office Phone: 630-827-4211.

EGAN, KENNETH J., dermatologist; b. N.Y.C., Feb. 2, 1956; m. Marcia Beth Robins, May 23, 1982; children: Heather, Daniel, Brian. BA, Franklin and Marshall Coll., 1978; MD, N.Y. Med. Coll., 1982. Bd. cert. Am. Acad. Dermatology. Resident internal medicine North Shore Univ. Hosp./Meml. Sloan-Kettering Hosp., Manhasset, N.Y., 1982-85; resident dermatology Albert Einsten Coll. Medicine, N.Y.C., 1985-88; pvt. practice Ridgefield, Conn., 1988—. Fellow Am. Acad. Dermatology; mem. AMA, Am. Soc. for Laser Medicine, Fairfield County Med. Assn. Avocation: golf. Office: 38B Grove St Ridgefield CT 06877-4667 Office Phone: 203-438-4111.

EGAN, KEVIN JAMES, lawyer; b. Chgo., June 24, 1950; s. Raymond Basil and Harriet Olene (Landbo) E.; children: Ryan, Daniel. BA, U. Ill., 1972; JD, Northwestern U., 1975. Bar: Ill. 1975, U.S. Dist. Ct. (no. dist.) Ill. 1975, U.S. Ct. Appeals (7th cir.) 1976, U.S. Ct. of Customs and Patent Appeals 1978. Law clk. to judge U.S. Dist. Ct. (no. dist.) Ill., Chgo., 1975-77; assoc. Pattishall, McAuliffe & Hofstetter, Chgo., 1977-78; asst. U.S. atty. No. Dist. of Ill., 1978-82; assoc. Winston & Strawn, Chgo., 1982-84, ptnr., 1984-93, Sonnenschein, Nath & Rosenthal, Chgo., 1993-98, Foley & Lardner, Chgo., 1998—. Article editor Jour. Criminal Law and Criminology, 1974-75. Bd. trustees Village of Frankfort, 1991—. Mem. ABA, Chgo. Bar Assn. (com. mem.), Bar Assn. of 7th Cir., Prestwick Country Club (Frankfort, Ill.). Roman Catholic. Avocation: hockey. Home: 904 Huntsmoor Dr Frankfort IL 60423-8747 Office: Foley & Lardner 321 N Clark St Ste 2800 Chicago IL 60610 Office Phone: 312-832-4500. E-mail: kegan@foley.com.

EGAN, MICHAEL JOSEPH, retired lawyer, state legislator; b. Savannah, Ga., Aug. 8, 1926; s. Michael Joseph and Elise (Robider) E.; m. Donna Cole, Apr. 14, 1951; children: Moira Elizabeth, Michael Joseph, Donna, Cole, Roby, John Patrick. BA, Yale U., 1950; LL.B., Harvard U., 1955. Bar: Ga., D.C. Assoc. Sutherland, Asbill & Brennan, Atlanta, 1955-61, ptnr., 1961-77, 79-97, ret. ptnr., 1998; mem. Ga. Ho. of Reps., 1966-77, minority leader, 1971-77; assoc. atty. gen. U.S. Dept. Justice, Washington, 1977-79; mem. Ga. Senate, 1989-2001. Served with U.S. Army, 1945-47, 50-52. Mem. ABA, Atlanta Bar Assn., State Bar Ga., Am. Law Inst. Republican. Roman Catholic. Home: 3145 Argonne Dr NW Atlanta GA 30305-1949 Office: Sutherland Asbill & Brennan 999 Peachtree St NE Atlanta GA 30309-3915 also: 1275 Pennsylvania Ave NW Washington DC 20004-2404 Office Phone: 404-853-8056.

EGAN, MOIRA, poet, educator; b. Baltimore, Md., July 21, 1962; d. Michael and Betty Egan. B.A., Bryn Mawr Coll., 1980—85; M.A., Johns Hopkins U., 1993—94; M.F.A., Columbia U., 1990—92. Tchr., english & creative writing Catonsville H.S., Catonsville, Md., 2002—; lectr. in english Morgan State U., Balt., 2002—02, Towson U., Towson, Md., 2001—01; instr., ib english Anatolia Coll., Thessaloniki, Greece, 1998—2001; cmty. rels. mgr. Barnes & Noble, NYC, 1997—98; cons. curricular outreach U. Md. Ctr. Visual Arts and Culture, 2003—. Poetry editor Link: A Critical Jour. on the Arts, Balt., 2002—; host, readings for reading benefit series The Learning Bank, Balt., 2002; mem.; contbr. to pedagogical papers sessions Associated Writing Programs, 2001—. Author: (poems) The Garden of Her Choosing (Spl. Merit award, Mayor's Adv. Com. on Arts & Culture, 1994), Poetry, Boulevard, American Letters & Commentary, Laurel Review, Smartish Pace, West Branch, Poems & Plays, Poet Lore, and in numerous other journals., nominated for the Pushcart Prize, 1994, 2002, anthology, Kindled Terraces: American Poets in Greece, Cleave (First Book award, 2004); multi-media visual piece, Elegy. Vol. Com. to Re-elect the Mayor, Balt., 2003. Recipient David Craig Austin Prize, The Writing Divsn., Columbia U., 1992, Campbell Corner Poetry Prize, 2nd Pl., Campbell Corner, 2002; Grad. Writing fellowship, Columbia U., 1990—92, Grad. Tchg. fellowship, Johns Hopkins U., 1993—94. Mem.: Assoc. Writing Programs. Avocations: yoga, travel, reading. Personal E-mail: moirae333@earthlink.net.

EGAN, PATRICIA JANE, foundation administrator, retired director; b. San Francisco, Aug. 7, 1951; m. Paul Max Payton, Dec. 27, 2003; 1 child, Kathryn Michele. AB, U. Calif., Berkeley, 1978; postgrad., N.J. Inst. Tech., 1996—. Cert. fund raising exec. Grants officer Mus. Modern Art, N.Y.C., 1979—81; assoc. devel. officer grants Whitney Mus. Am. Art, N.Y.C., 1981—84; assoc. dir. devel. Columbia Bus. Sch., Columbia U., N.Y.C., 1984—86; mgr. major gifts New York Bot. Garden, N.Y.C., 1987—88; dir. devel. N.Y.C. Partnership, 1989—91; dir. devel. Cal Performances U. Calif., Berkeley, 1991—92, instr. bus. and engring. ext. svcs., 2004—. Cons. various cultural and environ. orgns., NY; co-prodr. distance learning course proposal writing N.J. Inst. Tech., 1997—. Prodr., program host Terpischore, Sta. KUSF-FM, 1978—79. Bd. dirs. Universala Esperanto Asocio, NY, 1980—83, Dance Perspectives Found., N.Y.C., 1985—2002, Shakespeare for Kids, 2005—; treas. Dance Perspectives Found., N.Y.C., 1987—91, found. officer, treas.; trustee Riverside Ch., N.Y.C., 1986—87. Fellow, Nat. Endowment Arts, 1977. Mem.: Internat. Assn. Bus. Communicators, Women in Comm., Soc. Tech. Comm. (Bernard J. Goodman Meml. award N.Y. Metro chpt. 1998), Mensa, Esperanto League N.Am., Jr. League San Francisco, Churchill Club, Alpha Epsilon Lambda. Avocations: art and technology, ballet, modern dance, martial arts. Office: PO Box 194391 San Francisco CA 94119-4391

EGAN, ROBERT THOMAS, lawyer; b. Bklyn., Sept. 4, 1952; s. Thomas Edward and Gloria Elise (Rudolph) E.; children: Timothy, Mary. BA in Polit. Sci. summa cum laude, U. Conn., 1974; JD, U. Pa., 1977. Bar: N.J. 1977, U.S. Dist. Ct. N.J. 1977, U.S. Ct. Appeals (3d cir.) 1990. Assoc. Archer & Greiner, Haddonfield, N.J., 1977-84, ptnr., 1984—. Com. on complimentary dispute resolution N.J. Supreme Ct., 1995-98; vis. lectr. in pretrial advocacy Rutgers U. Sch. Law, Camden, 1992. Chmn. activities com. Kings Grant Open Space Assn., Evesham Twp., N.J., 1982-86. Mem.: ABA, Camden County Bar Assn., N.J. Bar Assn., Phi Beta Kappa. Avocations: softball, ice hockey, golf, boxing, furniture restoration and refinishing. Home: 9 Corlen Ct Medford NJ 08055-2358 Office: Archer & Greiner 1 Centennial Sq Haddonfield NJ 08033-2328 E-mail: regan@archerlaw.com.

EGAN, RON, corporate financial executive; BA in Acctg. and Mgmt. first in class, MBA in Fin. and IT magna cum laude, U. Utah, Salt Lake City. CPA. Staff acct. Arthur Andersen, Salt Lake City, 1980—82; sr. fin. analysy Am. Express Corp., N.Y.C., 1982—85; mgr. fin. and acctg. Kenway Eaton Corp., Salt Lake City, 1985—94, mgr. strategic and fin. planning Cutler Hammer Pitts., 1994—97, group contr. Oxford Automotive Ontario, Canada and Troy, Mich., 1997—99; v.p. global fin. and corp. contr. Eagle Ottawa Automotive/Woodbridge, Rochester Hills, 1999—. Bd. dir. Voyager Fin. Co.; course instr. U. Utah, Salt Lake City; instr. and trainer Internat. Divsn. Contr.; instr. ISO 9000 audit stds. Quality Inst. Mem. Boy Scouts Am.; tchr. and cons. applied econ. Jr. Achievement. Named Outstanding Exec. Advisor, Jr. Achievement Assn., QS 9000 Quality Sys. Internal Audit Champion. Mem.: Fin. Execs. Internat., Phi Kappa Phi. Address: 13887 Woodsett Ct Utica MI 48315

EGAN, SHIRLEY ANNE, retired nursing educator; b. Haverill, Mass. d. Rush B. and Beatrice (Bengle) Willard Diploma, St. Joseph's Hosp. Sch. Nursing, Nashua, N.H., 1945; BS in Nursing Edn., Boston U., 1949, MS, 1954. Instr. sci. Sturdy Meml. Hosp. Sch. Nursing, Attleboro, Mass., 1949-51, Peter Bent Brigham Hosp. Sch. Nursing, Boston, 1951-53, ednl. dir., 1953-55, assoc. dir. Sch. Nursing, 1955-59, med. surg. coord., 1971-73, assoc. dir. Sch. Nursing, 1973-79, dir., 1979-85; cons. North Country Hosp., Newport, Vt., 1985-86; infection control practitioner, 1986-87; contract instr. Natchitohes Area Tech. Inst., 1988-90, Sabine Valley Tech Inst., 1990-91; coord. quality assurance Evangeline Health Care Ctr., 1991-92, asst. dir. nursing, 1992-93, coord. quality assurance Natchitoches, La., 1994-96, retired, 1996. Nurse edn. adviser AID (formerly ICA), Karachi, Pakistan, 1959-67; prin. Coll. Nursing, Karachi, 1959-67; dir. Vis. Nurse Service, Nashua, N.H., 1967-70; cons. nursing edn. Pakistan Ministry of Health, Labour and Social Welfare, 1959-67; adviser to editor Pakistan Nursing and Health Rev., 1959-67; exec. bd. Nat. Health Edn. Com., Pakistan; WHO short-term cons. U. W.I., Jamaica, 1970-71; mem. Greater Nashua Health Planning Council. Contbr. articles to profl. publs. Bd. dirs. Matthew Thornton health Ctr., Nashua, Nashua Child Care Ctr.; vol. ombudsman N.H. Council on Aging; mem. Nashua Service League. Served as 1st lt., Army Nurse Corps., 1945-47. Mem. Trained Nurses Assn. Pakistan, Nat. League for Nursing, Assn. for Preservation Hist. Natchitoches, St. Joseph's Sch. Nursing Alumnae Assn., Boston U. Alumnae Assn., Brit. Soc. Health Edn., Cath. Daus. Am. (vice regent ct. Bishop Malloy), Statis. Study Grads. Karachi Coll. Nursing, Sigma Theta Tau. Home: 729 Royal St Natchitoches LA 71457-5716

EGAN, SUSAN CHAN, securities analyst, writer; b. Manila, Feb. 11, 1946; came to U.S., 1969; d. Mariano Sui Ming and Rita Patricia (Quejong) Chan; m. Ronald Christopher Egan, Mar. 22, 1971; 1 child, Louisa. BA in Chinese Lang. and Lit., U. Wash., 1970; MBA, Boston U., 1981; MA in Comparative Lit., U. Wash., 1971. Chartered Fin. Analyst. Bus. counselor Local Devel. Corp. of South End, Boston, 1973-74; cons. Boston, 1974-76; dir. edn. and tng. Mass. Dept. Commerce and Devel., Boston, 1976-79, program devel. cons., 1979-81; trust investment officer State St. Bank and Trust Co., Boston, 1981-83, sr. trust investment officer, 1983-86, v.p., 1986-87, Scudder, Stevens & Clark, L.A., 1987-98; pres. Pacific Trade Winds Co., Santa Barbara, Calif., 1998—. Author: Coping With Utility Bills and Other Energy Costs, 1971, How to Do Business with the State, 1980, New Business, 1981, A Latterday Confucian, 1987, Hung Yeh Chuan, 1992, An Introduction to Securities Markets, 1997. Mem. Assn. for Investment Mgmt. and Rsch. Home: 921 W Campus Pt Santa Barbara CA 93117-4341 Office Phone: 805-680-5492.

EGAN, WESLEY WILLIAM, former ambassador; b. Madison, Wis., Jan. 21, 1946; s. Wesley William and Ruth (Skeuse) E.; m. Virginia Warren, Aug. 15, 1967; children: Wesley Matthew, Kimberly Katherine. BA with honors, U. N.C., 1968. Vice consul Am. Consulate Gen., Durban, South Africa, 1972-74; spl. asst. to sec. state Dept. State Washington, 1974-77; 1st sec. Am. embassy, Portugal, 1977-79, dep. chief mission, 1979-82; ambassador to Republic of Guinea-Bissau, 1983-85, Chief of Staff to Dep. Sec. of State, 1985-87; Dep. Chief of Mission Am. Embassy, Lisbon, Portugal, 1987-90, Cairo, 1990-93; ambassador to Hashemite Kingdom of Jordan, 1994-98; dep. insp. gen. Dept. of State, Washington, 1998-2000. Chmn. bd., pres. Petra Nat. Found. (USA), Washington, 2003—. Mem.: Assn. for Diplomatic Studies and Tng. (bd. dirs.), Middle East Inst., Washington Inst. Fgn. Affairs (bd. dirs.). Episcopalian.

EGAS, ERIC, artist; b. N.Y.C., July 27, 1944; s. Camilo Egas and Alice Lindsay; m. Edith Smith Egas, Sept. 1, 1966 (div. Oct. 1968); 1 child, Emile; m. Carolyn Marie Parry, Feb. 15, 1974; 1 child, Ean. Student, Pratt Inst., 1961—65, New Sch. for Social Rsch., 1965, Kunstfacskolan, Stockholm, Sweden, 1966. Asst. film maker Arnold Eagle Prodns., N.Y.C., 1965—66; supr. film and media N.Y. State Mus., Albany, 1967—78; artist Cairo, NY, 1978—80; exec. dir. Greene County Coun. on Arts, Catskill, NY, 1980—82; artist Greenville, NY, 1982—90; dir., CEO Advanced Graphics Rsch. Inc., Greenville, 1990—99; artist Viegues, PR, 1999—, NY, 1999—. Bd. dirs. Art Awareness Inc., Lexington, NY, 1986—90; visual arts panelist N.Y. State Coun. on Arts, N.Y.C., 1983—86. Grantee Creative Artist Pub. Svc. grantee, N.Y. Found. for Art, 1979; Media grantee, Haleakela Found., 1980—82, Sponsored Project grantee, N.Y. state Coun. on Arts, 1984. Atheist. Achievements include one of the earliest developers of Raster to vector conversion software; development of unique methodology for making anaglyphic (3D) photographs using the dye transfer process. Avocations: solar energy, architecture.

EGBERT, EMERSON CHARLES, retired publisher; b. Los Angeles, Nov. 30, 1924; s. Charles Barnes and Ethel Annette (Feader) E.; m. Kathryn Eleanor Tressel, Apr. 6, 1947; children— Susan Ann, John Charles, James Emerson, Michael Warren, Patricia Ann. Ed., Pasadena Jr. Coll., Woodbury Bus. Coll. Distbn. mgr. Newsstand Distbrs., 1947-49; dist. sales mgr. So. Calif., Pocket Books, Inc., 1949-59, sales mgr. Eastern div., 1959-61, v.p., circulation dir., 1961-71; pres. Pocket Books Distbn. Corp., N.Y.C., 1971-81; sr. v.p. Silhouette Books div. Simon & Schuster, 1981-85, sr. v.p. trade pub. group, 1985-89; ret., 1989; pres. B/K Book Cons. Svcs. Inc., Rockville Ctr., N.Y., 1990-93, Madison, Conn., 1993-97; ret., 1997. Past dist. commr. Boy Scouts Am.; bd. dirs. 25 Yr. Club; bd. dirs. YMCA, Westbrook, Conn.; mem. vestry com. St. Andrew's Episcopal Ch., Madison. With USNR, 1942-45. Decorated D.F.C., Air Medal with 4 oak leaf clusters. Mem. Ind. Newsstand Circulation Execs. Assn. (past chmn.), Internat. Periodical Distbrs. Am. (chmn.), Bur. Ind. Pubs. and Distbrs. (past chmn. book com.), Anti-Defamation League. Republican. Home: 287 Legend Hill Rd Madison CT 06443-1864

EGBERT, PETER ROY, ophthalmologist, educator; b. Indpls., Dec. 6, 1941; BA magna cum laude, DePauw U., Greencastle, Ind., 1963; MD, Yale U., 1967. Diplomate Nat. Bd. Med. Examiners, Am. Bd. Ophthalmology.

Intern Cleve. Met. Gen. Hosp., 1967—68; resident in ophthalmology Yale U., New Haven, 1968—69; acting asst. prof. surgery (ophthalmology Stanford (Calif.) U., 1973—74, dir. Ophthalmic Pathology Lab., 1973—, asst. prof. surgery, 1974—81; acting head divsn. ophthalmology Stanford U. Med. Ctr., 1980—82, assoc. prof. surgery, 1981—88, prof. ophthalmology, 1988—, chmn. dept. ophthalmology, 1992—97; resident in ophthalmology Yale U., New Haven, 1971—73. Vis. prof. ophthalmology Govt. Hosp., San Pedro Sula, Honduras, 1974, Noor Eye Hosp., Kabul, Afghanistan, 1975, U. West Indies Med. Sch., Kingston, Jamaica, 1976, Princess Marina Hosp.-The Ctrl. Govt. Hosp., Gadorone, Botswana, 1978, Grenfell Regional Health Avcs., St. Nathony, Nfld., Canada, 1981, Govt. Hosp. Western Samoa, 1982, Project Orbis, Ismir, Turkey, 1985, Bamako, Mali, 1983, San Jose, Costa Rica, 1986, Port-au-Prince, Haiti, 1987, King Khaled Eye Hosp., Rihayd, Saudi Arabia, 1985, Korle-bu Tchg. Hosp., U. Ghana, Accra, 1987—2002, Leicester Royal Infirmary, England, 1987, Esperanca Hosp., Santarem, Brazil, 1987, Chinese Med. Sch., Hong Kong, 1988, Inst. Ophthalmology, Canton, 1988, Peking Med. Coll., Beijing, 1988, Nepal-Trilovan Tchg. Hosp., 1990; vis. prof. ophthamology COVA Eye Hosp., Tegucigalna, Honduras, 2000—. Recipient Bordon prize, DePauw U., 1960. Mem.: Verhoeff Ophthalmic Pathology Soc., Peninsula Eye Soc., Michael Hogan Eye Pathology Soc., Am. Intra-Ocular Implant Soc., Am. Assn. Ophthalmic Pathologists, Am. Acad. Ophthalmology, Phi Beta Kappa, Alpha Omega Alpha. Office: Stanford U Sch Medicine 300 Pasteur Dr Stanford CA 94305-5308

EGBERT, RICHARD MICHAEL, lawyer; b. Newton, Mass., Feb. 13, 1947; s. Marcus Manuel and Annette Honey (Segal) E.; children: Shea N., Danielle F., Manuel R. BBA, U. Mass., 1969; JD, Northeastern U., 1972. Bar: Mass. 1972, U.S. Dist. Ct. Mass. 1973, U.S. Ct. Appeals (1st cir.) 1974, U.S. Supreme Ct. 1980. Founder Law Offices of Richard M. Egbert, Boston, 1972—. Lectr. Mass. CLE. Dir. Nat. Coun. Northeastern U., Boston, 1996—; mem. Chancellors Coun., U. Mass., Amherst, 1993—. Named one of top Boston lawyers, Boston Mag., 2004. Fellow Internat. Acad. Trial Lawyers; mem. ABA, Boston Bar Assn., Mass. Bar Assn., Nat. Assn. Criminal Def. Lawyers, Mass. Assn. Criminal Def. Lawyers (pres. 1999-2000), Mass. Acad. Trial Lawyers. Office: 99 Summer St Ste 1800 Boston MA 02110-1213 Office Phone: 617-737-8222. Office Fax: 617-737-8223.

EGDAHL, RICHARD HARRISON, surgeon, educator, health science association administrator; b. Eau Claire, Wis., Dec. 13, 1926; s. Harry I. and Rebecca (Ball) Egdahl; m. Cynthia Taft, Apr. 1983; children from previous marriage: Scott, David, Bruce, Julie. MD, Harvard U., 1950; PhD, U. Minn., 1957. Intern U. Minn. Hosp., 1950—51, resident, 1956—57; prof. surgery Med. Coll. Va., 1957—64; prof., chmn. surgery Boston U. Med. Ctr., 1964—73, dir., 1973—96, Health Policy Inst., Boston U.; Alexander Graham Bell prof. health care entrepreneurship Boston U. Trustee Pioneer Family of Mut. Funds. Past mem. editl. bd.: Am. Jour. Surgery, New Eng. Jour. Medicine. Trustee Boston Med. Ctr. Lt. USNR, 1952—55. Mem.: ACS, Am. Soc. for Clin. Investigation, Internat. Assn. Endocrine Surgeons (pres. 1981—83), Inst. Medicine NAS, Endocrine Soc. (CIBA award 1961), Soc. Med. Adminstrs., Boston Surg. Soc. (pres. 1977), Am. Surg. Assn. (1st v.p. 1980), Soc. Univ. Surgeons (pres. 1970—71), The Registry Resort, Badminton and Tennis Club, Algonquin Club, Brookline Country Club, Comml. Club, Alpha Omega Alpha, Phi Beta Kappa. Office: Boston U Healthcare Entrepreneurship program 53 Bay State Rd Boston MA 02215-2101 Office Phone: 617-353-4525. Business E-Mail: regdahl@bu.edu.

EGE, HANS ALSNES, securities company executive; b. Haugesund, Norway, Jan. 31, 1924; came to U.S. 1953; naturalized, 1961; s. Sigvald Svendsen and Hilda Svendsen (Hansen) E.; m. Else Mathea Lindstrom, July 11, 1953; children: Elisabeth, Anne Christine. Bus. degree, Oslo Handelsgymnasium, 1946; student spl. bus. courses, City of London Coll., 1947; MBA, Drexel U., 1950. Analyst Alderson & Sessions, Mgmt. & Mktg. Cons., Phila., 1950-51; exec. asst. to U.S. ambassador to Norway Oslo, 1951-53; asst. to pres., asst. v.p. corp. sec. A.M. Kidder & Co., Inc., N.Y.C., 1953-64; stockbroker Reynolds Securities Inc., N.Y.C., 1964-65; mgr. Ridgewood (N.J.) Office, 1965-71; mgr. and resident officer, 1971-77; resident v.p., mgr. Dean Witter Reynolds, Inc., Ridgewood, 1978-82, v.p. investments, 1983—. Trustee, v.p. The Bay Found., N.Y.C., Josephine Bay-Paul & C. Michael Paul Found., N.Y.C. Trustee The Norwegian Seamen's Ch., N.Y.C., Norwegian Immigration Assn., N.Y.C.; mem. Pres.'s Club Drexel U. Served with Norwegian Underground, 1942-45. Decorated War medal. Mem. Am. Scandinaian Found., Norwegian Am. C. of C., Joe Jefferson Club (pres. 1969-70), Saddle River (N.J.) Club, Norwegian Club (N.Y.C.), Tau Kappa Epsilon. Home: 220 Bush Ln Apple Ridge Mahwah NJ 07430 Office: 1200 E Ridgewood Ave Ridgewood NJ 07450-3937

EGELAND, JAN, international organization official; married; 2 children. MA in Polit. Sci., U. Oslo. Head of devel. studies Henry Dunant Inst.; dir. Internat. Dept. Norwegian Red Cross; state sec. Norwegian Min. Fgn. Affairs, 1990—97; sec.- gen. spl adv. UN, Colombia, 1999—2002; sec. gen Norwegian Red Cross; under sec. gen. for humanitarian affairs and emergency relief coord. UN, 2003—. Chair Amnesty Internat., Norway; vice-chair Internat. Exec. Com. of Amnesty Internat.; active participant in a number of peace processes.; co-initiated and co-organized the Norwegian channel between Israel and the Palestine Liberation Orgn. (PLO), 1992; dir. Norwegian facilitation of the UN-led peace talks leading up to ceasefire agreement between Govt. Guatemala and the Unidad Revolucionaria Nacional Guatemalteca guerillas signed in Oslo, 1997. Published (a number of reports, studies and articles on conflict resolution, humanitarian affairs and human rights.). Chmn. Amnesty Internat., Norway; vice chmn Internat. Exec. Com. of Amnesty Internat. Fellow, Internat. Peace Rsch. Inst., Oslo, Truman Inst. for the Advancement for Peace, Jerusalem; Fulbright Scholar, U. of Calif. Office: Un Hdqs First Ave at 46th St New York NY 10017

EGELI, CEDRIC B., artist, educator; b. Shady Side, Md., Aug. 10, 1936; s. Herbjorn Peter and Lois Baldwin Egeli; m. Joanette Astrid Hoffmann, Mar. 18, 1962; children: Matthew Alfred, Arthur Bjorn, Anastasia Hoffmann, Ingrid Baldwin. A, Principia Coll., 1955. Artist-in-residence U. Del., Newark, 1963—64. Presenter in field. Represented in permanent collections Pentagon, U.S. Dist. Ct., CIA, Johns Hopkins Hosp., Md. State Archives, Duke U., Brandeis U., U. Del., Md. Hist. Soc., Notre Dame Coll. Balt, St. Mary's Sem., Balt. With U.S. Army, 1959—61. Recipient Grand prize, Nat. Protrait Soc., N.Y.C., 1979, Annie award, Cultural Arts Found., 2001. Mem.: Md. Portrait Soc. (pres. 1979—83), Am. Artist Profl. League (Gold medal 1980), Beach Combers Club. Home: 111 Fiddlers Hill Rd Edgewater MD 21037 Office Phone: 410-703-5567. E-mail: cedric@egelistudio.com.

EGELSON, PAULINE C., educational association administrator, researcher; b. Geneva, Ill., June 27, 1953; d. Donald and Pauline Wiese Ericson; m. Robert Louis Egelson, Sept. 1, 1979; children: Daniel, Benjamin. BA in Child Devel., Rockford Coll., 1975; MA in Reading Edn., Western Carolina U., 1982; EdD in Ednl. Leadership, U. NC, Greensboro, 1993. Cert. tchr. NC, prin. K-12 superintendency NC. Cmty. organizer United Meth. Ch., Asheville, NC, 1975—77; tchr. K-8 Diocese of Charlotte, Asheville, 1977—81; sales staff Dancer's Place, Asheville, 1981—84; reading clinician Western Carolina U., Oteen, NC, 1982—84; tchr. reading Buncombe County Schs., Asheville, 1983—90; ednl. rschr. SERVE, Greensboro, NC, 1991—2002, program dir., 2002—. Co-author: Formative Teacher Evaluation: Models and Current Findings, 1998, How Class Size Makes a Difference, 2002, Life at Draper Elementary: Taking Small Classes One Step Further, 2002, A Compedium of Senior Project Research, 2003, Preliminary Findings: Professional Learning Teams in Elementary Schools, 2004; co-devel. (video) The Senior Project: Student Work for the Real World, 1999. Mem. com. Boy Scouts Am., Greensboro, 1992—; precinct coord. Guilford County Kids Voting, Greensboro, 1998—. Named Blue Ribbon Schs. panelist, U.S. Dept. Edn., 2000, 2002; Dropout Prevention grantee, NEA/NFIE, 1989. Mem.: Internat. Reading Assn., Am. Ednl. Rsch. Assn., Jt. Com. Stds. for Evaluation (exec. com. 2001—). Avocations: photography, travel. Office: SERVE 915 Northridge St Greensboro NC 27403

EGEN, MAUREEN MAHON, publishing executive; BA, Trinity Coll., 1964. Editl. trainee and numerous other positions Doubleday & Co., Inc., 1964; mng. dir. Doubleday Book Clubs, 1979, pub., editl. dir., 1981; editor-in-chief Warner Hardcover Books Time Warner Book Group, 1990—98, pres., chief oper. officer N.Y.C., 1998—. Co-chair ann. book fair Goddard Riverside Cmty. Ctr.; mem. diversity steering com. Time Warner Book Group. Bd. dirs. The Ctr. Ind. of Disabled, N.Y.C. Mem.: Assn. Am. Pubs. (mem. freedom to read com.), Women's Media Group. Office: Time Warner Book Group 1271 Ave of Ams New York NY 10020

EGER, JOSEPH, conductor; b. Hartford, Conn., July 9, 1925; s. Abraham and Clara (Ellovich) E. Grad., Curtis Inst., Berkshire Music Ctr.; studied with, Monteux, Stokowski, Steinberg, Lert, Rudolf, Kahne. Faculty Aspen (Colo.) Music Festival, 1952-57; mem. faculty Peabody Conservatory, 1962-65, New Sch., 1971-72; condr. Greater Hollywood Philharm., 2001—03; lectr. Fla. Atlantic U., 2003, U. NC, Asheville, 2004—. Creator Harlem Music Project (pub. by Schirmer's, Consol. Music Pubs.); condr. seminar Smithsonian Instn., 1979; faculty, dir. internat. concert/seminar Salzburg Seminars, 1980; lectr. Nova Southeastern U. First horn N.Y. Philharm., L.A. Philharm., Israel Philharm., other major orchs.; solo rec. artist: RCA Victor, (albums) Joseph Eger Retrospective Series, 1978, also for motion picture, TV and radio; French horn soloist world concert tours, 1956; lectr., music dir. Eger Players; founder, condr. Camera Concerti Chamber Orch., 1958, Westside Symphony Orch., 1961, N.Y. Orch. Soc., 1963-73; condr. Midland (Mich.) Symphony, 1962-64, Town Hall series, 1962-63, Carnegie Hall, 1964-71, Philharm. Hall, 1965-72, Athens Festival, young people and teenage concerts, (concert series) UN, 1980, N. Miami Beach Symphony, 1997; guest condr. Royal Philharm., London Philharm., Moscow State Symphony, Lithuania State Symphony, New Philharmonia, Sinfonia of London, Pitts. Symphony Orch., Dallas Symphony, Cin. Symphony Orch., Balt. Symphony Orch., Am. Symphony Orch., Vienna Radio Orch., Dessoff Choir, Haifa, Nat. Symphony Costa Rica, Shanghai Philharm. Orch., Nat. Symphony Cuba, Nat. Symphony South Africa, Bucharest Philharm. Orch., 1997, Romanian Orch., 1997, others; assoc. condr. to Leopold Stokowski, 1967-70; composer: (recs.) Life mag., 1966, Westminster Record Co., 1967; (film score) Carolina, 1970, Hidden Fears; music dir. Indian Hill, 1967, N.Y. Symphony Premiere Performance, 1968, N.Y. Concertante, Symphony for UN, 1975—, UN Singers, 1975, Bklyn. Heights Symphony, 1978-82, S.W. Fla. Symphony, 1986-90, Champlain Islands Symphony, 1988—; founder, music dir. Symphony of N.Y., Aware, N.Y., 1971-74, Internat. Yoga Symphony, Can. and N.Y., 1973; founder Crossover; apptd. prin. guest condr. Ctrl. Symphony, Beijing, People's Republic of China; contbg. author: UNESCO Cultures; author: (guest editls.) Newsweek mag., 1980, Christian Sci. Monitor, 1981, N.Y. Times, 1982; editor: Citibank AWARE Playbill; exec. prodr.: (TV film/music video) Ode to Joy, 1988; author: Einstein's Violin: A Conductor's Notes on Music, Physics and Social Change, 2005. Chmn. UN Coord. Com. for Nongovtl. Orgns., 1990—; elected chmn. cultural com. City of Pompano Beach, 1999. Served to staff sgt. USAAF. Recipient Eleanor Roosevelt Man of Vision award, 1994, N.Y.C. Mayor's award, 1975, Internat. Music Therapist award, 1993; Maestro Joseph Eger Day named in his honor, Pompano Beach, 1999. Mem. Nat. Assn. Am. Condrs. and Composers (program chmn. 1965-67), Acad. Ind. Scholars. Personal E-mail: suneger@bellsouth.net.

EGERTON, CHARLES PICKFORD, anatomy and physiology educator; b. Toronto, Ont., Can., Mar. 17, 1939; (parents Am. citizens); s. Matthew Davis and Margaret Swain (Pickford) E.; m. Carol Anne Carlson, Dec. 16, 1976; children: Matthew, Andrew, Victoria. BA in Zoology, Duke U., 1962; BS in Medicine, U. Okla., Oklahoma City, 1978; MS in Sci. Edn., U. So. Miss., 1981, PhD in Sci. Edn., 1991, MPH in Health Edn., 1994. Cert. physician asst. Nat. Commn. on Cert. Physician Assts. Commd. 2d lt. USAF, 1962, advanced through grades to maj., 1980, ops. officer, 1962-76, primary care med. officer Keesler AFB, Miss., 1978-88; ret., 1988; instr. anatomy and physiology Miss. Gulf Coast C.C., Gautier, 1992—. Mem. Miss. Health Adv. Coun., Jackson, 1990—; guest lectr. dept. physician asst. studies U. South Ala. Author: Student Study Guide for Anatomy and Physiology; editor: Physician Assistant Handbook, 1995, Principles of Anatomy and Physiology, 9th edit., 2000; contbr. articles to profl. jours. Lectr. Miss. Inst. Drug-Free Sch., Hattiesburg, 1992; lectr. single parent-displaced spouse, Guatier, 1994-97; dir. smoking cessation Keesler AFB Med. Ctr., 1986-88; lay reader St. Luke's Anglican Ch., Gulfport, Miss., 1986-94. Mem. Am. Assn. Anatomists, Am. Acad. Physician Assts., Human Anatomy and Physiology Soc., Miss. Acad. Scis., Miss. Sci. Tchrs. Assn., Phi Delta Kappa, Eta Sigma Gamma. Democrat. Avocation: boating. Home: 6008 E Moreton Pl Ocean Springs MS 39564-2725 Office: Miss Gulf Coast CC PO Box 100 Gautier MS 39553-0100 Office Phone: 228-497-7783. E-mail: charles.egerton@mgccc.edu, egerton@cableone.net.

EGGEBRAATEN, DORIS ALPHILD, elementary educator; b. Fortuna, ND, Mar. 9, 1926; d. Hans Osborneson and Nellie (Nelson) Sather; m. Claude Julian Eggebraaten, June 25, 1947; children: Sonja Mae, Ronald John. Diploma, Itasca Jr. Coll., Coleraine, Minn., 1946; BEd, Sacramento (Calif.) State U., 1959. Cert. kindergarten, primary tchr., Calif. Dep. supt. Placer County Supt. Schs., Auburn, Calif., 1948-52; tchr. Rocklin (Calif.) Elem. Sch., 1952-53, Placer Hills Elem. Sch., Meadow Vista, Calif., 1954-61, Alta Vista Elem. Sch., Auburn, 1971-86. Kindergarten assessment com. Auburn Union Elem. Sch., 1987-92. Recipient Elda Goff Annual award Auburn Union Sch. Dist., 1984-85. Mem. Calif. Tchrs. Assn., Auburn Unions Tchrs. Assn. (Dist. Svc. award 1986). Republican. Lutheran. Avocation: travel. Home: 208 Fulweiler Ave Auburn CA 95603-4509

EGGENBERGER, ANDREW JON, federal agency administrator; b. Harlowton, Mont., May 8, 1938; s. Andrew D. and Gladys E. Eggenberger. BS, Carnegie Mellon U., 1961, PhD, 1967; MS, Ohio State U., 1963. Prof. U. S.C., Columbia, 1967-72; project mgr. D'Appolonia Cons. Engrs., Pitts., 1972-84; program dir. NSF, Washington, 1984-89; chmn. Def. Nuclear Facilities Safety Bd., Washington, 1989—. Fellow Marshall Space Flight Ctr., Huntsville, Ala., 1969, Lewis Rsch. Ctr., Cleve., 1967, 68; rsch. engr. Boeing Co., Seattle, 1961-63. Recipient Ralph R. Teetor award Soc. Automotive Engrs., 1968. Mem. AIAA, Am. Nuclear Soc., Earthquake Engring. Rsch. Inst., Sigma Alpha Epsilon. Lutheran. Avocations: auto racing, flying. Office: Def Nuclear Facilities Safety Bd 625 Indiana Ave NW Ste 700 Washington DC 20004-2901

EGGERS, GEORGE WILLIAM NORDHOLTZ, JR., anesthesiologist, educator; b. Galveston, Tex., Feb. 22, 1929; s. George William Nordholtz and Edith (Sykes) E.; m. Mary Futrell, Dec. 30, 1955; children: Carol Ann, George William. BA, Rice U., Tex., 1949; MD, U. Tex., Galveston, Tex., 1953. Diplomate Am. Bd. Anesthesiology. Instr. dept. anesthesiology, U. Tex., Galveston, Tex., 1956-59; asst. prof. dept. anesthesiology, U. Tex., Galveston, Tex., 1959-61; assoc. prof. dept. anesthesiology, U. Mo., 1961-67; prof. dept anesthesiology U. Mo., 1967—94, acting chmn. dept. anesthesiology, 1969, chmn. dept. anesthesiology, 1970-94, prof. emeritus, 1994—2001. Vis. instr. USAF Hosp., Lackland AFB, San Antonio, 1956-61; vis. rsch. prof. dept. anesthesiology Northwestern U. Med. Sch., Chgo., 1968-69; rsch. assoc. Space Sci. Rsch. Ctr., U. Mo., 1965-66. Contbr. over 50 articles to profl. jours. Recipient Ashbel Smith Disting. Alumnus Award U. Tex., 1993. Mem. Am. Soc. Anesthesiology (bd. dirs. 1979-86, v.p. 1986-89, 1st v.p. 1990, pres. elect 1991, pres. 1992), Am. Coll. Anesthesiology (bd. govs., 1965-74, chmn. bd. govs., 1973), Soc. Acad. Anesthesiology Chmn. (pres. 1971), Assn. Am. Med. Colls. (adminstrv. bd. coun. acad. socs. 1976-79), Mo. Soc. Anesthesiologists (pres. 1970, Disting. Svc. Award 2001), Tex. Gulf Coast Anesthesiology Soc. (v.p. 1960), Boone County Med. Soc. (pres. 1988), Am. Bd. Anesthesiology (assoc. examiner 1968, joint coun. with Am. Soc. Anesthesiology on in-tng. exams.), Acad. Anesthesiology (pres. 1995, Citation of Merit 1997), Accreditation Coun. Grad. Med. Edn. (mem. residency rev. com. for anesthesiology 1989-94), Anesthesia Found. (trustee 1993-2003), Jefferson Club of U. Mo., Alpha Omega Alpha, Mu Delta, Sigma Xi. Republican. Roman Catholic. Avocations: hunting, astronomy, magic, photography, shooting. Home: 1509 Woodrail Ave Columbia MO 65203-0931 Office: U Mo Dept Anesthesiology 1 Hospital Dr Dept Columbia MO 65201-5276 E-mail: nordholtz@aol.com.

EGGERS, JAMES WESLEY, executive search consultant; b. Des Moines, Feb. 7, 1925; s. Paul William and Opal Imo (Cardiff) E.; m. Marjorie Mardell Freel, Aug. 2, 1947; children: James S., Barbara Bucher, Mark D. Grad., Knoxville High Sch., 1943. Farmer, Knoxville, Iowa, 1948-55; sales rep. Iowa Power & Light Co., Des Moines, 1953-60, Cedar Rapids, Iowa, 1960-62; sales exec. Thomas D. Murphy Co., Red Oak, Iowa, 1962-67; pres., owner Eggers Cos., Omaha, 1967—. Bd. dirs. Nebr. State Bank, Omaha; owner, mgr. Exec. Realty and Mgmt. Co., Omaha, 1979—. Bd. dirs. local Meth. Ch., Nebr. Meth. Hosp. Found.; chmn. local dist. George Bush for Pres. campaign, Nebr., 1988; chmn. State of Nebr. Merit Coun., Lincoln, 1979-83; mem. nat. adv. cabinet Guideposts, Pawling, N.Y.; chmn. and mem. various civic bds. Mem. Nebr. Assn. Pers. Cons. (pres. 1974-75), Nat. Assn. Pers. Cons. (mem. nat. com. 1979-83, cert.), Omaha C. of C. (bd. dirs. 1980-83), Rotary (bd. dirs. Omaha chpt. 1983—, sgt.-at-arms 1986-90), Masons, Shriners. Republican. Avocations: reading, travel, religious study, walking. Office: Eggers Cons Co Inc Eggers Plz 11272 Elm St Omaha NE 68144-4788 Office Phone: 402-333-3480. Business E-Mail: jamese@eggersconsulting.com.

EGGERS, WILLIAM D., manufacturing executive, lawyer; b. Ft. Wayne, Ind., Apr. 9, 1944; BA, Yale U., 1966; JD, U. Pa., 1969. Bar: N.Y. 1970. Ptnr. Nixon Hargrave Devans & Doyle LLP, Rochester, NY, 1971-97; v.p., dep. gen. counsel Conring Inc., NY, 1997—98, gen. counsel, sr. v.p., 1998—. Mem. bd. dirs. Chemung Canal Trust Co., Chemung Financial Corp. Mem.: ABA. Office: Corning Inc 1 Riverfront Plz Corning NY 14831-0002

EGGERSMAN, DENISE, computer engineer, educator; b. Orange, Calif., Feb. 22, 1954; d. Arthur Fred and Margaret Frances Eggersman. BS, Kennesaw State U., 1998; MS, U. Phoenix, Ariz., 2002; PhD, U. Phoenix, 2002—. Systems adminstrn. Smallwood, Reynolds, Stewart & Stewart, Atlanta, 1983—89; trainer/adminstr. Ctrl. Health, Atlanta, 1989—91; cons. Software Assist, Duluth, Ga., 1991—97; LAN adminstrn. IBM, Atlanta, 1997; project mgmt. Hewlett-Packard, Atlanta, 1998; sales/network engr. Verizon Comm., Alpharetta, Ga., 1999—2001; prof. Chattahoochee Tech. Coll., Marietta, Ga., 2003, Capella U., Mpls., 2003—, S. Univ. Online, 2004—. Vol. Hands on Atlanta, 2003. Mem.: IEEE (assoc.), Assn. Computing Machinery. Home: PO Box 965452 Marietta GA 30066 Office: Chattahoochee Tech Coll 980 South Cobb Dr Marietta GA 30066 also: Grad Sch of Tech Capella Univ Minneapolis MN 55402 Office Phone: 770-528-4400. Personal E-mail: deggersman@prodigy.net. E-mail: deggersman@chat.tec.com.

EGGERT, ROBERT JOHN, SR., economist; b. Little Rock, Dec. 11, 1913; s. John and Eleanora (Fritz) Lapp; m. Elizabeth Bauer, Nov. 28, 1935 (dec. Dec. 1991); children: Robert John, Richard F., James E.; m. Annamarie Hayes, Mar. 19, 1994. BS, U. Ill., 1935, MS, 1936; candidate in philosophy, U. Minn., 1938; LHD (hon.), Ariz. State U., 1988; D Econ. Forecast, Lincoln Coll., 2002. Research analyst Bur. Agrl. Econs., U.S. Dept. Agr., Urbana, Ill., 1935; sec. War Meat Bd., Chgo., 1942-45, prin. marketing specialist, 1943; rsch. analyst U. Ill., 1935-36, U. Minn., 1936-38; asst. prof. econs. Kans. State Coll., 1938-41; asst. dir. mktg. Am. Meat Inst., Chgo., 1941-43, economist, assoc. dir., 1943-50; mgr. dept. mktg. rsch. Ford divsn. Ford Motor Co., Dearborn, Mich., 1951-53, mgr. program planning, 1953-54, mgr. bus. rsch., 1954-57, mgr. mktg. rsch. mktg. staff, 1957-61, mgr. mktg. rsch., mem. div. op. com., 1961-64, mgr. internat. mktg. rsch. mktg. staff, 1964-65, mgr. overseas mktg. rsch. planning, 1965-66, mgr. mktg. rsch. Lincoln-Mercury div., 1966-67; dir. and founder first agribus. programs Mich. State U., 1967-68; staff v.p. econ. and mktg. rsch. RCA Corp., N.Y.C., 1968-76; pres., chief economist Eggert Econ. Enterprises, Inc., Sedona, Ariz., 1976—. Founder, editor emeritus Blue Chip Econs. Ind.; lectr. mktg. U. Chgo., 1947-49; chmn. Fed. Statistics Users Conf., 1960-61; adj. prof. bus. forecasting No. Ariz., 1976-79; mem. econ. adv. bd. U.S. Dept. Commerce, 1969-71, mem. census adv. com., 1975-78; mem. panel econ. advisers Congl. Budget Office, 1975-76; interim dir. Econ. Outlook Ctr. Coll. Bus. Adminstrn. Ariz. State U., Tempe, 1985-86, cons., 1985—; mem. Econ. Estimates Commn. Ariz., 1979-03; apptd. Ariz. Gov.'s Commn. Econ. Devel., 1991-95, vice chmn. investment adv. coun. Ariz. State Retirement System, 1993-98; trustee Marcus J. Lawrence Med. Ctr. Found., 1992-96, Flagstaff Inst.; chmn. market rsch. com. Gov.'s Strategic Partnership for Econ. Devel.; co-chmn. Ariz. Sr. Industries Cluster, 1995-97. Contbr. articles to profl. lit.; founder, editor emeritus: monthly Blue Chip Econ. Indicators, 1976—; exec. editor Ariz. Blue Chip, 1984—, Western Blue Chip Econ. Forecast, 1986—, Blue Chip Job Growth Update, 1990—, Mexico Consensus Econ. Forecast, 1993—, Red Rock Sales Tax Collections, 1998—, National Consensus Forecast of Labor Employment, Compensation and Productivity, 2000-01; guest appearances on CNN, Wall Street Week, NBC's Today show. Mem. fin. com. Sedona Libr., 2002—; mem. long range planning com. Ch. of Red Rocks, 1998—2001. Recipient Econ. Forecast award Chgo. chpt. Am. Statis. Assn., 1950, 60, 68; Seer of Yr. award Harvard Bus. Sch. Indsl. Econ., 1973, Golden Gloves Boxing award, U. Ill., 1935, Participation in Genetics of Human Longevity Study, 2002, Proclamation signed by Gov. Ariz., 2003. Fellow Am. Statis. Assn. (chmn. bus. and econ. stats sect. 1957—, pres. Chgo. chpt. 1948-49), Nat. Assn. Bus. Economists (coun. 1969-72); mem. Coun. Internat. Mktg. Rsch. and Planning Dirs. (chmn. 1965-66), Am. Mktg. Assn. (dir., v.p. mktg. mgmt. divsn. 1972-73, nat. pres. 1974-75), Fed. Stats. Users Conf. (chmn. trustees 1960-61), Conf. Bus. Economists (chmn. 1972-73), Am. Quarter Horse Assn. (dir. 1966-73), Ariz. Econ. Roundtable, Am. Econs. Assn., Phoenix Econ. Club (hon.), Ariz. C. of C. (bd. dirs. 1991-95), Alpha Zeta. *I have always strived to be a person of greater value. My modest success has resulted largely from the manifold contribution of others. For example, my AG teacher, Ralph K. Morray at Lincoln, Ill., obtained a four year scholarship for me at the University of Illinois in 1931. In fact, the only true measure of my accomplishments will unfold in the future. What the future will be is difficult to foretell, but it always has been a challenge to maximize productivity and to look ahead, and to dream of things that never were and say—why not? My motto is "Aiming for Excellence in Economic Forecasting".*

EGGERT, RUSSELL RAYMOND, lawyer; b. Chgo., July 28, 1948; s. Ralph A. and Alice M. (Nischwitz) E.; m. Patricia Anne Alegre, 1998. AB, U. Ill., 1970, JD, 1973; postgrad., Hague Acad. Internat. Law, The Netherlands, 1972. Bar: Ill. 1973, U.S. Supreme Ct. 1979. Assoc. U. Ill., Champaign, 1973-74; asst. atty. gen. State of Ill., Chgo., 1974-79; assoc. O'Conor, Karaganis & Gail, Chgo., 1979-83; legal counsel to Ill. atty. gen., Chgo., 1983-87; ptnr. Mayer, Brown, Rowe & Maw, LLP, Chgo., 1987—. Contbr. articles to profl. jours. Mem. ABA. Democrat. Office: Mayer Brown Rowe & Maw LLP 71 S Wacker Dr Chicago IL 60606 Office Phone: 312-701-7350. Business E-Mail: reggert@mayerbrownrowe.com.

EGGERTSEN, JOHN HALE, lawyer; b. Ann Arbor, Mich., Jan. 7, 1947; s. Claude Andrew and Nita (Wakefield) E.; m. Claire Chenoweth, July 19, 1969 (div. 1987); children: Melissa Anne, Helen Emma; m. Sharon Ingram, June 13, 1987 (div. 1994); children: Alexandria, Andrea; m. Robin Rich, Sept. 23, 1995; 1 child, Brendon Hale. BA, U. Mich., 1968; JD cum laude, U. Toledo, 1974; LLM in Taxation, NYU, 1975. Bar: Ohio 1974, Mich. 1975. Instr. Highland Park (Mich.) Sch. Dist., 1968; claims adjuster State Farm Mutual Ins. Co., Ann Arbor, Mich., 1968-70; ptnr. Honigman Miller Schwartz and Cohn, Detroit, 1975-2000. Adj. prof. Wayne State U. Law Sch., Detroit, 1980-94; active Mich. Employee Benefits Conf., Detroit, 1980—. Contbr. articles to profl. jours. Bd. dirs. Neighborhood Svcs. Orgn., Detroit, 1992-2000, pres., 1994-97. Rsch. grantee NYU, 1974-75; Gerald Wallace scholar NYU, 1974-75. Mem. ABA (taxation sect., employee benefits com.), State Bar Ohio, State Bar Mich. Democrat. Mem. Lds Ch. Avocations: softball, bowling, reading. Home: 6369 Munger Ypsilanti MI 48197 Office: Eggertsen & Assocs PC Ste 107 5340 Plymouth Rd Ann Arbor MI 48105 Business E-Mail: john@jhelaw.com.

EGGINTON, EVERETT, educational administrator; b. N.Y.C., Apr. 6, 1943; s. Hersey Benner and Mary Florence (Twining) Egginton; m. Wynn Meagher, Sept. 27, 1986; 1 child from previous marriage, William Everett. BA in Econs., Colgate U., 1965, MA in Social Sci. Edn., 1968; MS in Comparative Edn., Syracuse U., 1971, PhD in Edn. Founds., 1974; EdD (hon.), U. Francisco Gavidia, San Salvador, El Salvador, 1990. Asst. prof. U. Louisville, 1974-78, acting dir. Internat. Ctr., 1978-79, assoc. prof., 1978-84, prof. edn., 1984—2002, dir. L.Am. Edn. Ctr., 1986—2002, chair ednl. founds., 1989-2000, dir. Internat. Ctr., 1996—2002; vice provost Internat. and U.S.-Mex. Border Programs N.Mex. State U., Las Cruces, N.Mex., 2003—. Sr. policy analyst U.S. Dept. Health and Human Svcs., Washington, 1980—81; pres. Consortium of Ctrl. Am. Univs., 1990—96, sec.-gen., 1991—98; cons. Ministry of Edn. El Salvador and Honduras; cons. World Bank, U.S. AID, 1992—; mem. exec. com. Commn. on Internat. Programs Nat. Assn. State Univs. and Land Grant Colls., 2000—. Contbg. editor: U.S. Libr. of Congress, 1980—88, Handbook of Latin Am. Studies; contbr. revs. and articles to profl. publs. and encys. Recipient Fulbright Rsch./Lectr. award, El Salvadaor, 1999—2000; Fulbright/Hays fellow, 1973—74, Fulbright/Stanford fellow, U. Santiago Compostela Spain, 1977, HEW fellow, 1979—80. Home: 5371 Redman Rd Las Cruces NM 88011 Office: New Mexico State Univ MSC 3567 PO Box 30001 Las Cruces NM 88003-8001 Office Phone: 505-646-7506. Business E-Mail: eegginton@nssu.edu.

EGGLESTON, DIANE PALAZZI, elementary school educator; b. Springfield, Mass., May 30, 1965; d. Richard R. Palazzi and Rose J. (Amato) Palazzi; m. Robert L. Eggleston, June 17, 1988. BS, U. Conn., 1987; MEd, Westfield State Coll., 1991. Tchr. 5th grade Suffield (Conn.) Pub. Schs., 1988-92, reading cons., grades 5-8, 1992—. Home: 37 Edward St Agawam MA 01001-2613

EGGLETON, ARTHUR C., former Canadian government official, member of Parliament; b. Toronto, Ont., Can., Sept. 29, 1943; 1 child, Stephanie. Acct., up to 1969; mem. Toronto City Coun., Met. Toronto Coun., 1969-91, city budget chief, 1973-80; mayor City of Toronto, 1980-91; mem. from York Centre in City of North York Parliament of Can., 1993—, pres. treasury bd., minister for infrastructure, 1993-96; min. international trade Can., 1996-97, min. nat. def., 1997—2002. Mem. Bd. Fedn. Can. Mcpls.; chmn. Internat. Programs Com.; co-chmn. Nat. Action Com. Race Rels., apptd. Minister for Internatl. Trade, 1996, apptd. pres. of treas. bd. and Minister, Infrastructure, 1993, appointed Minister of Natl. Defense, 1997, vice chmn. of cabinet com. on Econ. Policy. Mem. Met. Toronto Police Commn., Bd. Can. Nat. Exhbn. Recipient Civic Award of Merit, City of Toronto, 1992. Mem. York Centre for City of Toronto. Office: York Centre 845 Wilson Ave M3K1E6 Downsview ON Canada also: House of Commons 365 W Block Ottawa OT Canada

EGGMANN, WALTER G., supervisor, educator; s. Joseph Jacob and Anna Maria Eggmann. BA in French, St. Francis Coll., Bklyn., 1965; MS in French, St. John's U., Jamaica, NY, 1969, PhD, 1975. Spanish cert. NYU, German cert. Rockland CC. French tchr. Edmund J. Reilly HS, Fresh Meadows, NY, 1965—75; French, Spanish tchr. Paramus Cath. HS, NJ, 1975—78, Lincoln Sq. Acad., NYC, 1978—80, Hasbrouck Heights HS, NJ, 1981—98; dist. world lang. coord. Hasbrouck Heights Sch. Dist, 1995—2001, dist. supr. world lang., 2002—. Mentor Dodge Found., 1998; Friends of Lincoln Ctr. NYC, 2002—; Friends of NY Philharmonic. Recipient NJ Pub. Schs. Govs. award, 1996. Mem.: ACTFL, AATF, NWELL, FLENT, NYSALFT, Met. Opera Guild, Rockland Ctr. for the Arts. Avocations: piano, music, opera. Office: Hasbrouck Heights HS 365 Boulevard Hasbrouck Heights NJ 07604 E-mail: waltereggmann@prodigy.net.

EGHBAL, MORAD, geologist, lawyer; b. Tehran, Iran, June 7, 1952; s. Mohammad Ali and Fari Eghbal; m. Niloofar Sadjadi, July 17, 1983; children: Elaheh, Aria. BA, George Washington U., 1975, MA, 1977; JD, Howard U., 1989; LLM, U. Pacific, 1991. Asst. George Washington U., Washington, 1972; asst. to dir. Smithsonian Instn., Washington, 1972-75; spl. advisor to dir. Georgetown U., Washington, 1975; cons. Leo A Daly, Washington, 1975, Kodak, Rochester, N.Y., 1976; ofcl. del. 2d Circum-Pacific Energy and Mineral Resources conf., Honolulu, 1978; CEO MERE Enterprises, Washington, 1976—87; fgn. assoc. Pestalozzi, Gmuer & Heiz, Zurich, 1989; law clk. to Hon. William B. Bryant, US Dist. Ct. DC, Washington, 1990-91; trustee, CFO Riess Inst., Washington, 1983—. Dir., pres. The Grail Corp., 1983—; dir., v.p. exploration GASCO, Inc.; adj. prof. legal and ethical studies U. Balt., 1994—95, adj. prof. law, 1995—99, adj. prof. internat. mgmt., 1998—99, vis. asst. prof. law, internat. mgmt. and legal, ethical and hist. studies, 1999—2001, asst. dir. Ctr. for Internat. and Comparative Law, 2000—03, dep. dir., 2003—, vis. assoc. prof. law, 2001—04, dir. LLM in Law of U.S.; mng. editor Ius Gentium, 2003—, Internt. Legal Theory, 2003—; past mem. bd. dirs. Internat. Law Students Assn., judge oral arguments and memls. regional and internat. semi-finals, finals Jessup competition, 1990—2005; vice chmn. Md. Baltic European Coun., 2004—. Rschr. The Divining Hand (E.P. Dutton), 1973-79; keynote spkr. symposium Dickinson Sch. Law, Carlisle, Pa., 1991, 1st Conf. Expeditionary Learning/Outward Bound, Greenbelt, Md., 2000; author: 1995 Philip C. Jessup Internat. Law Moot Ct. Competition Problem, 1995. Trustee Capital City Pub. Charter Sch., 2000—03; bd. dirs., pres. Md. Baltic Ednl. Consortium, 2003—04; chair Baltic Am. Inst., 2004—. Recipient Cert. Achievement, Circum-Pacific Energy & Mineral Resources conf., 1978, Ga. U., 1980, 2d Place Nat. Roscoe Hogan Environ. Law Essay contest award ATLA, 1988, Outstanding Student Adv. award Met. Trial Lawyers Assn., 1989, Citizen Citation City and mayor of Balt., 2000, Spirit of Excellence award U. Balt. Alumni Assn., 2002, John May Award for Teaching Excellence and Svc. to the Univ., SBA- Univ. of Balt., 2003, Lifetime Achievement award Cert. Merit, U. Balt., 2005 Mem. ABA, Nat. Bar Assn., Internat. Law Assn., Am. Assn. Petroleum Geologists (founding mem. energy minerals divsn.), Geol. Soc. Am., Soc. Econ. Paleontologists and Mineralogists, Potomac Appalachian Trails Club, Nat. Capital Area Paralegal Assn., Internat. Law Students Assn. (past mem. bd. dir.), Nat. Lawyers Club, US Japan Trade Coun., Am. Inns Ct. (Prettyman/Leventhal chpt.), Phi Delta Phi. Office: Riess Inst 9555 Friendship Station Washington DC 20016-9555 E-mail: eghbal@riess.org.

EGIELSKI, RICHARD, illustrator; b. N.Y.C., July 16, 1952; s. Joseph and Caroline (Rzepny) Egielski; m. Denise Saldutti, May 8, 1977. Student, Pratt Inst., Bklyn., 1970—71, Parsons Sch. Design, N.Y.C., 1971—74. Illustrator (children's books) Moonguitars, 1974, The Porcelain Pagoda, 1976, The Letter, the Witch and the Ring, 1976, I Should Worry, I Should Care, 1979, Finders Weepers, 1980, Louis the Fish, 1980, Getting Even, 1982, It Happened in Pinsk, 1983 (Plaque award, 1985), Lower! Higher! You're a Liar!, 1984, The Little Father, 1985, Amy's Eyes, 1985, Hey, Al, 1986 (Caldecott medal, 1987), Friends Forever, 1988, Bravo Minski, 1988, The Tub People, 1989, Oh, Brother, 1989, A Telling of Tales: Five Stories, 1990, Christmas in July, 1991, The Lost Sailor, 1992, Ugh, 1992, The Tub Grandfather, 1993, Fire! Fire! Said Mrs. McGuire, 1995, Call Me Ahnighito, 1995, Buz, 1995 (Best Illustrated Book of 1995 by N.Y. Times), The Gingerbread Boy, 1997. Recipient Cert. of Merit, Soc. of Illustrators, N.Y.C., 1978, 1981, 1984, 1985. Avocation: playing the mandolin. Office: care Farrar Straus & Giroux 19 Union Sq W New York NY 10003-3304*

EGILMEZ, NEJAT K., science educator; b. Istanbul, Turkey, Feb. 23, 1958; arrived in U.S., 1976; s. Ahmet Nurettin and Sukran Egilmez; m. Samina Z. Raza-Egilmez, June 24, 1988; 1 child, Aral. BS, U. Minn., 1980; MA, SUNY, Buffalo, 1983, PhD, 1986. Post-doctoral fellow La. State U. Med. Ctr., New Orleans, 1986—88; asst. prof. Bogazici U., Istanbul, 1989—93; cancer rsch. scientist Roswell Park Cancer Inst., Buffalo, 1994—2001; asst. prof. SUNY, Buffalo, 2001—03; asst. prof. J.G. Brown Cancer Ctr. U. Louisville, 2003—. V.p. Therapyx, Inc., Buffalo, 2001—. Contbr. articles to profl. jours. Grantee, NIH, 2000—03, 2001, 2002, Nat. Cancer Inst., 2001, DOD Breast Cancer Program, 2001—. Mem.: AAAS, Soc. for Biol. Therapy. Achievements include patents pending for methods and products for tumor immunotherapy. Office: U Louisville J G Brown Cancer Ctr 580 S Preston 119C Louisville KY 40202

EGINTON, WARREN WILLIAM, federal judge; b. Bklyn., Feb. 16, 1924; AB, Princeton U., 1948; LLB, Yale U., 1951. Bar: N.Y. 1952, Conn. 1954. Assoc. Davis Polk & Wardwell, N.Y.C., 1951-53; ptnr. Cummings & Lockwood, Stamford, Conn., 1954-79; judge U.S. Dist. Ct., Bridgeport, Conn., 1979—. Editor-in-chief Products Liability Law Jour., 1988-93. Mem. ABA, Am. Judicature Soc., Am. Bar Found., Am. Law Inst., Conn. Bar Assn., Fed. Bar Coun., Fed. Bar Assn., Ins. Jud. Adminstrn., Jud. Leadership Devel. Coun., Internat. Jud. Acad., Fgn. Policy Assn., Raymond E. Baldwin Am. Inn of Ct. (founder, pres.). Office: US Dist Ct 915 Lafayette Blvd Ste 335 Bridgeport CT 06604-4765 Office Phone: 203-579-5819.

EGLEE, CHARLES HAMILTON, scriptwriter, film producer; b. Boston, Nov. 27, 1951; s. Donald Read and Nancy (Hamilton) E.; m. Madeline Dalton, Feb. 29, 1984; children: Blythe Dalton, Eli Hamilton. BA in English, Yale U., 1974. Teaching asst. Yale U., New Haven, 1976; producer, writer for film Deadly Eyes Warner Bros., L.A., 1982; story editor for TV series St. Elsewhere MTM Prodns., Studio City, Calif., 1984-86; exec. story cons. for TV series Moonlighting ABC Circle Films, L.A., 1986-87, prodr. for TV series Moonlighting, 1987-89; prodr. 20th Century Fox TV, 1989-91; writer, co-exec. producer "Civil Wars" Steven Bochco Prodns., 1991-93; writer L.A. Law, 1992; co-creator, exec. producer The Byrds of Paradise (Steven Bochco Prodns.), 1993-94; co-exec. producer N.Y.P.D. Blue (Steven Bochco Prodns.), 1994-95; co-creator, exec. prodr. Murder One (Steven Bochco Prodns.), 1995-97, Total Security (Steven Bochco Prodns.), 1997-98; co-creator, exec. prodr. TV series Dark Angel Cameron-Eglee Prodns., 1999—2002; writer, exec. prodr. The Shield, FX, 2003—. Story editor (St. Elsewhere episode) Bye George, 1985 (Humanitas prize); co-writer (St. Elsewhere episode) Haunted, 1986 (Emmy nomination, Salute to Excellence Award nominee NAACP 1986), (Moonlighting episode) I Am Curious, Maddie, 1987 (Emmy nomination), N.Y.P.D. Blue, 1994 (Emmy award for best drama), Murder One, 1996 (People's Choice award for best new drama, Emmy nomination, best writing in one hour drama, pilot episode 1996, Golden Globe nomination 1996, best fgn. drama Brit. Acad. Film and TV, 1996), Dark Angel, 2001 (People's Choice award for best new drama 2001). Nominee Best Drama award Writers Guild Am., 1996. Mem. Acad. TV Arts and Scis., Writers Guild Am., Yale U. Alumni Fund, Mory's Assn. (New Haven). Democrat. Avocations: sailing, skiing, pottery, gardening, hip-hop.

EGLER, STEVEN LENHART, music educator; b. Dixon, Ill., June 18, 1949; Floyd Jr. and Phyllis Irene (Lenhart) E. BMus, U. Mich., 1971, MMus, 1974, AMusD, 1981. Organist Rosedale Gardens United Presbyn. Ch., Livonia, Mich., 1969-74; minister of music First Presbyn. Ch., Detroit, 1974-76, dir. music, organist Mt. Pleasant, 1976—; prof. music Cen. Mich. U., Mt. Pleasant, 1976—. Concert organist, accompanist, clinician, 1968—. Mem. Am. Guild Organists (coord. edn. region V 1990-97, dean Saginaw Valley chpt. 1987-89, co-dean 2000, councillor region V 2000—). Home: 2221 Pinehurst Ct Midland MI 48640-4190 Office: Cen Mich U Sch of Music Mount Pleasant MI 48859-0001 Office Phone: 989-774-3326. E-mail: egler1s@cmich.edu.

EGLIN, JOHN ARTHUR, historian, educator; b. Santa Monica, Calif., Apr. 26, 1962; s. Stuart Baker Eglin and Paula Louise Garrison. BA, Davidson Coll., 1984; MA, U. Ga., 1989; PhD, Yale U., 1996. Asst. prof. U. Mont., Missoula, 1996—2001, assoc. prof., 2001—. Author: Venice Transfigured, 2001, The Imaginary Autocrat: Beau Nash and the Inveition of Bath, 2005. Fellow, NEH, 2003. Fellow: Royal Hist. Soc.; mem.: Am. Soc. 18th Century Studies, N.Am. Coun. Brit. Studies, Am. Hist. Assn. Episcopalian. Avocations: reading, exercise. Office: U Mont Dept History Missoula MT 59812 Office Phone: 406-243-6755. Office Fax: 406-243-4076. Business E-Mail: je168477c@mail1.umt.edu.

EGNER, DAVID OWEN, foundation administrator; b. East St. Louis, Ill., Mar. 1, 1962; s. James E. and Mary Ann (Rankin) E.; m. Tamatha Lee Heard, June 21, 1986; children: Alexandria, Daniel, Morgan, Madeline. BA, Westminster Coll., 1984; MBA, Western Mich. U., 1993. Dir. sales Holiday Inn, South Bend, Ind., 1985; membership rep. St. Louis Regional Commerce and Growth Assn., 1985-86; pres. Jr. Achievement Springfield & Sangamon Viley, Inc., Springfield, Ill., 1986-88; dir. ops. Jr. Achievement, Inc., St. Louis, 1988-89; exec. asst. to chmn. and CEO W.K. Kellogg Found., Battle Creek, Mich., 1989-93; pres., CEO Mich. Nonprofit Assn., East Lansing, 1993-97, Hudson-Webber Found., Detroit, 1997—. Chair Detroit Cmty. Devel. Funders Collaborative, 1998-2004; bd. dirs. Coun. Mich. Founds., Grand Haven, Detroit Local Initiative Support Corp., 2004—. Bd. dirs. Boys Hope/Girls Hope Detroit, 1998—; bd. dirs., vice chair Arts Centered Edn., Detroit, 1997—; trustee Leadership Detroit, 1999—; advisor cabinet ArtServe Mich., 1999; bd. dirs. Mich. Pub. Policy Inst., 1998—, Mich. Future, Inc., 2001—; coun. mem. Mich. Coun. for Arts and Cultural Affairs. Recipient Dream Maker award Detroit Hispanic Devel. Corp., 1999; named to Crain's Detroit Bus. 40 Under 40, 1999. Mem. Assn. Child Devel. (bd. dirs., chair 1996—). Avocation: golf. Office: Hudson-Webber Found 333 W Fort St Ste 1310 Detroit MI 48226-3149

EGNER, JOHN DAVID, electrical engineer; b. New Castle, Pa., June 30, 1957; s. John David Enger and Ann Irene (Nevin) Parta; m. Ann E. Willgrube, Dec. 21, 2001; 1 child, Travis J. BS in Elec. Engring., U. Vt., 1979. Devel. engr. Hewlett-Packard Co., Sunnyvale, Calif., 1979—82, Apple Computer, Inc., Cupertino, Calif., 1982—86; analog engr. Next Computer, Inc., Redwood City, Calif., 1986—93; compliance engring. mgr. Fire Power Sys., Inc., Menlo Park, Calif., 1993—96; sr. sys. engr. Microsoft, Inc., Redmond, Wash., 1996—. Mem.: IEEE, Tau Beta Pi. Home: 22109 NE 27th Pl Sammamish WA 98074 Office: Microsoft Inc One Microsoft Way Redmond WA 98052-6399 Office Phone: 425-722-2464. Business E-Mail: degner@microsoft.com.

EGOLF, JAMES EDWARD, history educator; b. Lewistown, Pa. s. John LeRoy and Anna Barbara E.; m. Aileen Janice, June 6, 1966 (div. Feb. 1982); children: James E. Jr., Sonya L. Jordan; m. Dolores T. Starnes, Nov. 13, 1984. BEd, Clarion State Coll., 1966; MA, Duquesne U., 1970. Cert. secondary sch. tchr., Fla. Grad. tchg. asst. Duquesne U., Pitts., 1967-69; instr. history South Coll. (Patrick Henry), Monroeville, Ala., 1975-83; tchr. Christian Bros., Kansas City, Mo., 1983-84; tchr. history Okeechobee (Fla.) High Sch., 1990—; instr. history Indian River C.C., Ft. Pierce and Okeechobee, Fla., 1986—. Mem. Kiwanis (adv. Key Club 1990-95, 99—, 5-yr. plaque 1995). Home: 9730 NE 16th St Okeechobee FL 34974-8268 Office: Indian River C C 2229 NW 9th Ave Okeechobee FL 34972-4342

EGOYAN, ATOM, film director; b. Cairo, July 19, 1960; arrived in Can., 1962; s. Joseph and Shushan (Devletian) E.; m. Arsinee Khanjian; 1 child, Arshile. BA in Internat. Rels. with honours, U. Toronto, Ont., Can., 1982; Phd (hon.), Trinity Coll., U. Toronto and U. Victoria. Dir. Ego Film Arts, Toronto, 1982—. Films shown at internat. film festivals of Sydney, Birmingham, Melbourne, Valladolid, Picadilly, Cleve., Berlin, Hong Kong, Locarno, Melbourne, Jerusalem, London, LA, Miami, Turin, Cairo, Antwerp, Montreal, Uppsala, Ghent, Chgo., Chgo., Sao Paulo, NYC, Edinburgh, San Francisco, Rotterdam, also others. Writer, dir., prodr. (feature films) Next of Kin, 1984 (Gold Ducat award Mannheim Internat. Film Week 1984), Family Viewing, 1987 (Internat. Critics award 1988, Best Feature Film award Uppsala, Priz Alcan, Festival du Nouveau Cinema, Montreal), Speaking Parts, 1989 (best screenplay prize Vancouver Internat. Film Festival), The Adjuster, 1991 (spl. prize of jury Moscow Film Festival, Golden Spike award Valladolid Film Festival), Calendar, 1993 (prix Berlin Internat. Film Festival), Exotica, 1994 (Internat. Film Critics award Cannes Film Festival 1994, Prix de la Critique award for best foreign film 1994, Acad. award nominee), Salome Canadian Opera Co., 1996, 2002, Houston Grand Opera, 1997, The Sweet Hereafter, 1997 (Grand Prix, Internat. Critics prize Cannes Film Festival 1997, Acad. award nominee), Elsewhereless, 1998, Dr. Ox's Experiment, 1998, Felicia's Journey, 1999, Ararat, 2002, Special Recognition for freedom expression, Nat. Bd. of Rev., 2002; Genie for Best Motion Picture, Acad. Can. Cinema and TV, 2002; Samuel Beckett's Krapp's Last Tape, 2000; Die Walkure/Wagner's Der Ring des Nibelungen, Can. Opera Co., 2004 (Golden Apricot Grand Prix 2004). Recipient Officer Order Can., other numerous awards and nominations for awards. Avocation: classical guitar. Office: Ego Film Arts 80 Niagara St Toronto ON Canada M5V 1C5 E-mail: questions@egofilmarts.com.

EGUCHI, YASU, artist; b. Japan, Nov. 30, 1938; came to U.S., 1967; s. Chihaku and Kiku (Koga) E.; m. Anita Phillips, Feb. 24, 1968. Student, Horie Art Acad., Japan, 1958-65. Exhibited exhbns., Tokyo Mus. Art, 1963, 66, Santa Barbara Mus. Art, Calif., 1972-74, 85, Everson Mus. Art, Syracuse, N.Y., 1980, Nat. Acad. Art, N.Y.C., 1980—; one-man shows include Austin Gallery, Scottsdale, Ariz., 1968-87, Joy Tash Gallery, Scottsdale, 1989-99, Greystone Galleries, Cambria, Calif., 1969, 70, 72, Copenhagen Galleries, Calif., 1970-78, Charles and Emma Frye Art Mus., Seattle, 1974, 84, 98, Hammer Galleries, N.Y.C., 1977, 79, 81, 93, 2001, 2002, City of Heidenheim, Germany, 1980, Artique Ltd., Anchorage, 1981—, Heidenheim Mus. Art, 2000; pub. and pvt. collections, Voith Gmbh, Germany, City of Giengen and City of Heidenheim, Germany, represented, Deer Valley, Utah, Hunter Resources, Santa Barbara, Am. Embassy, Paris, Charles and Emma Frye Art Mus., Seattle, Nat. Acad. Art; author: Der Brenz Entlang, 1980; author: Yasu Eguchi, Kunstmuseum Heidenheim, 2000; contbr. to jours in field. Active Guide Dogs for the Blind, San Raphael, Calif., 1976, City of Santa Barbara Arts Coun., 1979, The Eye Bank for Sight Restoration, NY, 1981, Anchorage Arts Coun., 1981, Santa Barbara Mus. Natural History, 1989, Kinder & Kunst Artist Projecti, Heidenheim. Recipient Selective Artist award Yokohama Citizen Gallery, 1965; recipient Artist of Yr. award Santa Barbara Arts Council, 1979, Hon. Citizen award City of Heidenheim, 1980, The Adolph and Clara Obrig prize NAD, 1983, Cert. of Merit NAD, 1985, 87. Home: PO Box 30206 Santa Barbara CA 93130-0206

EGUCHI-DONOVAN, YUKIE, foreign language educator; b. Nakatsu, Oita, Japan, Mar. 9, 1962; came to U.S., 1991; d. Shoji and Fukami Eguchi; m. Craig Thomas Donovan, Dec. 4, 1999. BA, Doshisha Women's Coll., Kyoto, Japan, 1984; MA, NYU, 1997, MA, 1999. Lectr. Japanese Mary Baldwin Coll., Staunton, Va., 1991-94; adj. instr. Japanese NYU, N.Y.C., 1997, New Sch. U., N.Y.C., 1999; adj. instr. Japanese Fashion Inst. Tech. SUNY, N.Y.C., 2000—, adj. instr. Cooper Union for the Advancement of Sci. and Art, 2000—01. Area expert Cendant Internat., Chgo., 1999—; country presenter Japan Berlitz Cross-Cultural, Princeton, N.J., 1999—; cross-cultural cons. Across Frontiers, N.Y.C., 1999. Cultural editor (CD-ROM) Global Country Series, 1999. Mem. Assn. Asian Studies, Assn. Tchrs. Japanese, N.Y. State Comm. Assn., Pi Lambda Theta. E-mail: eguchidonovan@earthlink.net.

EHDE, AVA LOUISE, librarian, educator; b. Buffalo, Feb. 11, 1963; d. Louise and Robert Andrew Kinn (Stepfather), Henry Emil Nonnenberg. BA in History and German cum laude, SUNY, Buffalo, 1995, MLS, 1997. Cert. pub. libr. N.Y. Intern libr. Niagara Falls (N.Y.) Pub. Libr., 1996—97, local history libr., 1997—98; reference libr. Trocaire Coll., Buffalo, 1998—99, libr. dir., 1999; libr. Buffalo & Erie County Pub. Libr., 1999—2002; head reference, sys. coord. D'Youville Coll. Libr., Buffalo, 1999—2002; adj. faculty SUNY Sch. Informatics, Buffalo, 2001—; is. br. supr. Manatee County Pub. Libr. Sys., Bradenton, Fla., 2002—. Co-chair Western N.Y. Reference Discussion Group, Buffalo, 2000—02; mem. Regional Automation Com., Buffalo, 2000—02, TBLC Continuing Edn. Com., 2003—. Co-author: (workshop) Networking and Operating Systems for Librarians, 2001—; author: Implementing New Libr. Technologies, 2003—; book reviewer: Voice o Youth Advocates, 2004—. Reader Niagara Frontier Radio Reading Svc., Cheektowaga, NY, 1999—2002; reviewer Voice of Youth Advocates, 2004—. Recipient Dr. Marie Ross Wolcott Meml. award, Sch. Info. and Libr. Studies, 1997, yearlong award, Sunshine State Libr. Leadership Inst., 2004—05; grantee, NYLA Reference and Adult Svcs. Sect. Continuing Edn., 2002; Alberta Riggs Meml. scholar, Sch. Info. and Libr. Studies, 1997, Profl. Devel. grantee, Western N.Y. Libr. Resources Coun., 2001, 2002. Mem.: AAUP (v.p., exec. com. 2001—02), ALA, Manatee Young Profls. (amb.), Assn. Coll. and Rsch. Librs., Libr. and Info. Tech. Assn., Beta Phi Mu. Avocations: bicycling, hiking, reading, scuba diving, cooking. Home: 401 Clark Ln Holmes Beach FL 34217 Office: Island Br Libr 5701 Marina Dr Holmes Beach FL 34217 Office Phone: 941-778-1721. Personal E-mail: librarianava@hotmail.com. Business E-Mail: ava.ehde@co.manatee.fl.us.

EHLE, JOHN MARSDEN, JR., writer; b. Asheville, N.C., Dec. 13, 1925; s. John M. and Gladys (Starnes) E.; m. Gail Oliver, Aug. 30, 1952 (div. Apr. 1967); m. Rosemary Harris, Oct. 22, 1967; 1 child, Jennifer Anne. BA, U. N.C., 1949; DFA (hon.), N.C. Sch. Arts, 1981; LHD (hon.), Berea Coll., 1986, U. N.C., Asheville, 1987; DLitt (hon.), U. N.C., Chapel Hill, 1990. Faculty U. N.C., Chapel Hill, 1951-63; spl. asst. to Gov. Terry Sanford, Raleigh, N.C., 1963-64; program officer Ford Found., N.Y.C., 1964-65. Spl. cons. Duke U., 1976-80; co-founder N.C. Gov.'s Sch., N.C. Sch. Arts, N.C. Sch. Sci. and Maths. Author: (novels) Move Over, Mountain, 1957, Kingstree Island, 1959, Lion on the Hearth, 1961, The Land Breakers, 1964, The Road, 1967, Time of Drums, 1970, The Journey of August King, 1971, The Changing of the Guard, 1975, The Winter People, 1981, Last One Home, 1983, The Widows Trial, 1989, (biographies) The Free Men, 1965 (Mayflower Soc. cup), The Survivor, 1968, Shepherd of the Streets, 1960, Dr. Frank, Living with Frank Porter Graham, 1993, (non-fiction) The Cheeses and Wines of England and France, with Notes on Irish Whiskey, 1972, Trail of Tears: The Rise and Fall of the Cherokee Nation, 1988; pub. also in several fgn. countries; (screenplay) The Journey of August King, 1996. Apptd. by Pres. Johnson to White House Group for Domestic Affairs, 1964-66, Nat. Coun. Humanities, 1966-70; mem. exec. com. Nat. Book Com., N.Y.C., 1972-75, N.C. Sch. Arts Found., Winston-Salem, 1970-75; mem. awards commn. State of N.C., 1982-93, Mary Reynolds Babcock Found., Winston-Salem, 1985-89; pres. Anne C. Stouffer Found., 1970-80; pres. Awards Com. Edn., 1980-90. With AUS, 1944-46. Recipient Walter Raleigh prize for fiction N.C. Dept. Cultural Affairs, 1964, 67, 70, 75, 84, State of N.C. award for Lit., 1972, Gov.'s award for Disting. Meritorious Svc., 1978, Lillian Smith prize Southern Regional Coun., 1982, Disting. Alumnus award U N.C., Chapel Hill, 1984, Thomas Wolfe Meml. award Western N.C. Hist. Assn., 1984, W.D. Weatherford award Berea Coll., 1985, Caldwell award N.C. Humanities Coun., 1995; named to N.C. Lit. Hall of Fame, 1997. Mem. PEN, Authors League, Century Club (N.Y.C.). Democrat. Methodist. Home: 125 Westview Dr NW Winston Salem NC 27104

EHLERMAN, PAUL MICHAEL, motorcycle and recreational batteries manufacturing company executive; b. Montgomery, Ala., 1938; BBA, U. Notre Dame, 1960. With GE, 1960-65, U.S. Gypsum, Chgo., 1965-68, Northwest, Inc., Chgo., 1968-75, Gen. Battery, Exide Corp., Reading, Pa., 1975-91; vice chmn., CEO Yuasa, Inc., Reading, 1991-2000; chmn. Yuasa Battery, Inc., 2000—. Mem. exec. com., bd. dirs. Greater Berks Devel. Fund; bd. dirs. Sovereign Bancorp and Sovereign Bank; mem. Berks Econ. Partnership Bd., Our City Reading Bd. Bd. dirs., chmn. Berks County Conv. Ctr. Authority; bd. dirs. Reading Hosp. and Med. Ctr., Berks County Cmty. Found. Office: Yuasa Battery Inc PO Box 14715 Reading PA 19612-4715

EHLERS, DEBORAH LAYNE, theater director; b. Lincoln, Nebr., Dec. 29, 1950; d. Joseph Buddy Plessel and Ellen Janet (McDonald) Lesoing; m. Christian H. Ehlers, Apr. 7, 1973; children: Jeff, Matt, Brian, Zack. BA, Nebr. Wesleyan U., 1973; MA, U. Nebr., 1987, PhD, 1995. Instr. U. Northern Iowa, Cedar Falls, 1988; grad. tchr. asst. U. Nebr., Lincoln, 1986-92, adj. instr., 1993-96, dir. theatre camp, 1995-97; dir. theatre, asst. prof. Bethany (W.Va.) Coll., 1997—2001, Bacone Coll., Okla., 2001—, chmn. Divsn. Humanities, 2003—, chmn. divsn. arts & scis., 2004—. Investigator opera houses Nebr. State Hist. Soc., Lincoln, 1987-88; news letter editor Assn. for Theatre in Higher Edn., 1987-94; festival coord. Region V Kennedy Ctr. Am. Coll. Theater Festival, 1990-91, 94-95, mem. selection com., 1996, 1999-2000, region II preliminaries judge, 1999; focus group conf. planner Playwrights Program, 2003—, focus group rep, 2004—. Workshop developer A Little Feelgood Magic, 1987; makeup designer A Little Night Music, 1988; playwright Harry's Bar, 1989 (crawford hon. mention); dir. Blind Harassment, 1999, The Futz Theatre, 1996, Muskogee Little Theatre, 2002—(Newcomer of Yr. award 2002-03), Brooke Hills Playhouse, 1999-2000,

Inherit The Wind Show of the Yr., 2002-03; editl. adv. bd. Collegiate Press, 1999.; contbr. to articles to profl. jours. Den leader Cub Scouts, 1989; merit badge counselor Boy Scouts, 1994-1997; children's coord. Calvary United Meth., Lincoln, 1987-91; Saratoga Sch. Parents Orgn. Travel grant rsch. Day Found., U. Nebr., 1990, 91. Mem.: Nebr. Masquers, Pi Kappa Delta, Theta Alpha Phi, Alpha Psi Omega. Avocations: trivia, movies. Home: 219 North P St Muskogee OK 74403 Office: Bacone Coll 214 Barnett 2299 Old Bacone Rd Muskogee OK 74403

EHLERS, KATHRYN HAWES (MRS. JAMES D. GABLER), physician; b. Richmond Hill, NY, Aug. 22, 1931; d. Albert and Edna (Hawes) E.; m. James D. Gabler, Dec. 5, 1959; children— Jennifer K., Emily E. AB, Bryn Mawr Coll., 1953; MD, Cornell U.; MD (Hannah E. Longshore Meml. Med. scholar 1953-57, Elsie Strang L'Esperance scholar 1956-57), 1957. Diplomate: Am. Bd. Pediatrics, Am. Bd. Pediatric Cardiology. Intern N.Y. Hosp., 1957-58, asst. resident pediatrics, 1958-60; fellow in pediatric cardiology Cornell U. Med. Coll., N.Y.C., 1960-64, instr. pediatrics, 1964-66, asst. prof., 1966-70, asso. prof. pediatrics, 1970-75, prof., 1975-96, prof. emeritus, 1996—, vice-chmn. pediat., 1988-96; practice medicine specializing in pediat. cardiology N.Y.C., 1958-96. Contbr. articles to profl. jours. Research trainee N.Y. Heart Assn., 1960-62, Am. Heart Assn., 1962-64. Fellow Am. Coll. Cardiology; mem. N.Y. Heart Assn., Am. Heart Assn., Harvey Soc., Am. Pediatric Soc., Am. Acad. Pediatrics, Alpha Omega Alpha. Home: Apt 1117 102 Wilderness Dr Naples FL 34105-2603

EHLERS, VERNON JAMES, congressman; b. Pipestone, Minn., Feb. 6, 1934; m. Johanna Meulink, 1958; children: Heidi, Brian, Marla, Todd. Student, Calvin Coll.; AB, U. Calif., Berkeley, 1956, PhD in Physics, 1960. Tchg. asst. U. Calif., Berkeley, 1956-57, rsch. asst., 1957-60, lectr. in physics, 1960-66; prof. physics Calvin Coll., 1966-83; mem. Mich. State Ho. of Reps., 1983-85, Mich. State Senate, 1985-94, pres. pro tem, 1991-94; mem. U.S. Congress from 3d Mich. dist., 1994—; chmn. Joint Com. Libr. Congress; mem. transp. and infrastructure com., sci. com., edn. and workforce com., house adminstrn. com. Mem. Gov. Milliken's Task Force on Environ. Problems, 1977, Kent County Rep. Exec. Com., Kent County Bd. Commrs., 1975-83, chmn., 1979-82, Mich. Toxic Substance Control Commn., 1982; asst. floor leader Mich. State Ho. of Reps., 1983-85 Contbr. NATO Rsch. fellow U. Heidelberg, Germany, 1961-62, Sci. Faculty fellow NSF, Joint Insts. for Lab. Astrophysics, U. Colo. 1971-72, fellow Calvin Coll. Ctr. for Christian Scholar, 1977-78. Mem.: Am. Assn. Phys. Tchrs., Am. Phys. Soc., AAAS. Mem. Christian Reformed Ch. Home: 1848 Morningside Dr SE Grand Rapids MI 49506-5121 Office: 1714 Longworth House Ofc Bldg Washington DC 20515-2203 also: Federal Bldg 110 Michigan St Grand Rapids MI 49503-2313*

EHLIG-ECONOMIDES, CHRISTINE A., petroleum engineer; BA cum laude, Rice U., 1971; MAT, U. Kans., 1974, MS in chem. engring., 1976; PhD in petroleum engring., 1979. Rsch. asst. petroleum engring. dept. Stanford U., 1976—78, prog. mgr. geothermal prog., 1979—80, acting asst. prof. petroleum engring, 1979—80; head petroleum engring. dept. U. Alaska, Fairbanks, 1981—83; section head dynamic reservoir description Flopetrol Johnston Schlumberger, Melun, France, 1983—86; section head layered reservoir testing Schlumberger Perforating and Testing, Houston, 1986—88; section mgr. reservoir engring. Schlumberger Well Service, 1988—90; project leader reservoir dynamics Etudes et Productions, Schlumberger, Clamart, France, 1990—92; tech. advisor Schulumberger Internat. Coordination, Houston, 1993—95, Anadrill Schulumberger, Sugar Land, Tex., 1995—96; tech. and mktg. mgr., production enhancement Schulumberger Oilfield Services, 1996—97; area mgr. Latin Am. North Schulumberger Reservoir Tech., Caracas, Venezuela, 1997—99; global account mgr. Schulumberger Global Client Accounts, Houston, 1999—; adj. prof. U. Houston, 2000—. Vis. prof. U. Houston, 1994, Stanford U., 1995. Grantee Standard Oil of Calif. Fellowship, Stanford U. Mem. Soc. Petroleum Engrs. (disting., Europe steering com. 1992, chmn. cultural diversity com. 1993-95, Disting. Achievement award for Petroleum Engring. Faculty, 1982, Formation Evaluation award 1995, Lester C. Uren award 1997, disting. lectr. 1997-98), Phi Kappa Phi, Sigma Xi. Achievements include contributions to analytical models for well-test analysis; development of practical methodology for well-test interpretation, design of testing procedures; evaluation of testing hardware and pressure-transient data quality. Office: Dept Chem Engring U Houston 4800 Calhoun Ave Houston TX 77204-4004 E-mail: ceconomides@uh.edu.

EHLINGER, RALPH JEROME, lawyer; b. Oconto, Wis., Mar. 22, 1941; s. Jerome Nicholas and Margaret Ann (Otradovec) E.; m. Nancy L. McKinley, Dec. 26, 1966 (div. Oct. 1986); children: Nicholas Joseph, Martha Johanna; m. Mary Verstegen, Sept. 25, 1987; children: Autumn V., Andrea V., Jessa V., Jenna V. BA in Philosophy, St. Paul Sem., 1963; JD, Georgetown U., 1968. Bar: Wis. 1968, D.C. 1988, U.S. Dist. Ct. (ea. dist.) Wis. 1969, U.S. Dist. Ct. (we. dist.) Wis. 1977, U.S. Ct. Appeals (7th cir.) 1983, U.S. Supreme Ct. 1986, U.S. Ct. Appeals (4th cir.) 1988. Ptnr. Meissner, Tierney, Ehlinger & Whipp, Milw., 1968-86; pvt. practice Milw., 1986-87; counsel Casson, Harkins & LaPallo, Washington, 1987-88; pres. Ehlinger & Krill, SC, Milw., 1988-99, Ehlinger Law Office, Milw., 2000—; adj. prof. law Marquette U. Law Sch., 1999—. Articles editor: The Georgetown Law Jour., 1967-68 (Outstanding Editor 1968); editor-in-chief: The Milwaukee Lawyer, 1982-84. Trustee Wis. Sch. Profl. Psychology, Milw., 1990-93; bd. pres. Grand Ave Club, Milw., 1990-92, Mental Health Assn., Milw., 1992-93; dir. Centro Legal Por Derechos Humanos, 1996-2001; mem. planning commn. Town of Richfield, 2002-, chmn. 2004-05. Mem. ABA, Milw. Bar Assn. Found. (pres. 1994-97), Nordic Ski Club (life), Milw. Bar Assn. (bd. dirs. 1990-93, Lawyer of Yr. award 1997), Washington County Bar Assn. Democrat. Roman Catholic. Avocations: instrumental and vocal music, cross country skiing, backpacking, canoeing, poetry. Office: Ehlinger Law Office W175 N 11117 Stonewood Dr Germantown WI 53022 Office Phone: 262-255-5060. Business E-Mail: ehlinger@execpc.com.

EHMANN, ANTHONY VALENTINE, lawyer; b. Chgo., Sept. 5, 1935; s. Anthony E. and Frances (Verweil) E.; m. Alice A. Avina, Nov. 27, 1959; children: Ann, Thomas, Jerome, Gregory, Rose, Robert. BS, Ariz. State U., 1957; JD, U. Ariz., 1960. Bar: Ariz. 1960, U.S. Tax Ct. 1960, U.S. Supreme Ct. 1968; CPA, Ariz.; cert. tax specialist, trusts and estates specialist. Spl. asst. atty. gen., 1961-68; mem. Ehmann and Hiller, Phoenix, 1969—2004, Fennemore Craig, Phoenix, 2004—. Rep. dist. chmn. Ariz., 1964; pres. Grand Canyon coun. Boy Scouts Am., 1987-89, mem. exec. com., 1981—, v.p. western region, 1991-99; bd. dirs. Nat. Cath. Com. on Scouting, 1995—. Recipient Silver Beaver award Boy Scouts Am., 1982, Bronze Pelican award Cath. Com. on Scouting, 1981, Silver Antelope award Boy Scouts Am., 1994. Fellow Am. Coll. Trusts and Estate Counsel; mem. State Bar Ariz. (chmn. tax sect. 1968, 69), Ctrl. Ariz. Estate Planning Coun. (pres. 1968, 69), Rotary Club, KC (grand knight Glendale, Ariz. 1964, 65), Serra Internat. (pres. Phoenix 1992-93, dist. gov. ariz. 1993-95), Knight of Holy Sepulchre, Knight of Malta, Legatus. Republican. Roman Catholic. Office: Fennemore Craig 3003 N Central Ste 2600 Phoenix AZ 85012 Office Phone: 602-916-5416. Business E-Mail: ehmann@fclaw.com.

EHMANN, WILLIAM DONALD, chemistry professor; b. Madison, Wis., Feb. 7, 1931; s. William F. and Victoria V. (Koperski) E.; m. Nancy M. Gallagher, July 16, 1955; children: William J., John M., James T., Kathleen E. BS, U. Wis., 1952, MS, 1954; PhD, Carnegie Inst. Tech., 1957. NRC-NSF rsch. assoc. Argonne Nat. Lab., Ill., 1957-58; mem. faculty U. Ky., Lexington, 1958—, asst. prof., 1958-63, assoc. prof. chemistry, 1963-66, prof., 1966-95, chmn. dept., dir. grad. studies, 1972-76, Coll. Arts and Scis. Disting. prof., 1968-69, univ. rsch. prof., 1977-78, assoc. dean for rsch. Grad. Sch., 1980-84, prof. emeritus, 1995—. Vis. prof. Ariz. State U., Tempe, 1969, Fla. State U., Tallahassee, 1972; cons. Argonne Nat. Lab., 1958-67; rsch. dir. project AEC, 1960-71, Agr. Dept., 1968-70, NASA, 1968-77, NIH, 1977-80, 84-98, DOE, 1983-85, NSF EPSCOR, 1986-91, NIST, 1993-94 Author: Radiochemistry and Nuclear Methods of Analysis, 1991; contbr. articles to profl. jours. Hon. assoc. Sanders-Brown Ctr. on Aging, 1988-95; bd. dirs. U. Ky. Rsch. Found., 1991-93; bd. dirs., exec. com. Alzheimer's Disease Rsch. Ctr., U. Ky., 1990. Recipient William D. Ehmann award Am. Nuclear Soc., 1996, Sturgill award U. Ky., 1987; Fulbright scholar; hon. fellow Australian Nat. U. Inst. Advanced Studies, Canberra, 1964-65. Fellow AAAS, Meteoritical Soc.; mem. Am. Chem. Soc. (chmn. Lexington sect. 1963-64, Herty medal for career achievements 1994, nat. award in nuclear chemistry 1996), Ky. Acad. Scis. (bd. dirs. 1964-67, Disting. Ky. Scientist award 1982), Sigma Xi, Phi Lambda Upsilon, Phi Eta Sigma, Phi Theta Kappa. Roman Catholic. Achievements include first analysis (with others) of Apollo Mission lunar samples; research on the chemistry of meteorites, lunar samples and trace elements involvement in neurological diseases; on the etiology of Alzheimer's Disease. Home: 769 Zandale Dr Lexington KY 40502-3371 Office: U Ky 312 Chem Physics Bldg Lexington KY 40506-0055 E-mail: wdehmann@att.net.

EHREN, CHARLES ALEXANDER, JR., lawyer, educator; b. NYC, Dec. 13, 1932; s. Charles Alexander and Alma Elise (Holmstrom) E.; m. Joan Anne Bansemer, Sept. 4, 1954. AB, Columbia U., 1954, JD, 1956. Bar: N.Y. bar 1956. Asso. firm LeBoeuf, Lamb and Leiby, N.Y.C., 1958-67; Reginald Heber Smith fellow U. Pa. Sch. Law at Legal Aid Soc. of Westchester County (N.Y.), White Plains, 1967-68, dir. soc., 1975-77; dir. curriculum Nat. Inst. Edn. in Law and Poverty, Northwestern U., 1968-70; asso. prof. law U. Denver, 1970-74, prof., 1974-75; dean, prof. Pace U. Sch. Law, 1975-76; vis. scholar Columbia U. Sch. Law, 1976-77; dean Valparaiso U. Sch. Law, 1977-82, prof., 1977-96, prof. emeritus, 1996—. Trustee Ind. Continuing Legal Edn. Found., Ind. Bar Found., 1977-82; dir. Westchester Legal Services, 1975-77 Author: (with others) Electricity and the Environment, The Reform of Legal Institutions, 1972. Served with U.S. Army, 1956-58. Mem. Ind. State Bar Assn. (ho. of dels. 1977-82), Assn. Bar City N.Y. (exec. dir. spl. com. on electric power and environment 1971-73), ABA, N.Y. State Bar Assn., Fed. Energy Bar Assn., Soc. Am. Law Tchrs. Democrat. Lutheran. Home: 16 High Point Rd East Hampton NY 11937-1059

EHRENBARD, ROBERT, lawyer; b. N.Y.C., Aug. 20, 1925; m. Lila T. Ehrenbard, Apr. 17, 1949; children— Richard, Dan. LL.B. cum laude, Harvard U., 1951. Bar: N.Y. 1951, U.S. Dist. Ct. (so. dist.) N.Y. 1952, U.S. Ct. Appeals (2d cir.) 1952, U.S. Ct. Appeals (3d cir.) 1971, U.S. Ct. Appeals (7th cir.) 1976, U.S. Ct. Appeals (D.C. cir.) 1982, U.S. Ct. Appeals (11th cir.) 1982, U.S. Ct. Appeals (9th cir.) 1984, U.S. Supreme Ct. 1969. Law clk. U.S. Dist. Ct. (so. dist.) N.Y. 1951-53, U.S. Dist. Ct. (so. dist.) N.Y. 1954; sr. litigation ptnr. Kelley Drye & Warren, N.Y.C., 1961— . Author: Interrogatories And Document Requests, 1983. Served to lt. (j.g.) USN, 1943-46; PTO. Mem. Lawyer's Com. for Civil Rights Under Law, ABA, N.Y. State Bar Assn., Assn. Bar City N.Y. Home: 239 Central Park W New York NY 10024-6038 Office: Kelley Drye & Warren 101 Park Ave Fl 30 New York NY 10178-0062

EHRENFELD, DAVID WILLIAM, biology professor, writer; b. N.Y.C., Jan. 15, 1938; s. Irving and Anne Ehrenfeld; m. Joan Gardner, June 28, 1970; children: Kate, Jane, Jonathan, Samuel. BA, Harvard Coll., 1959; MD, Harvard Med. Sch., 1963; PhD, U. Fla., 1966. From asst. prof. biology to assoc. prof. biology Barnard Coll. Columbia U., N.Y.C., 1967-74; prof. biology Cook Coll. Rutgers U., New Brunswick, N.J., 1974—. Author: Biological Conservation, 1970, Conserving Life on Earth, 1972, The Arrogance of Humanism, 1978, Beginning Again: People and Nature in the New Millennium, 1993, 1995, Swimming Lessons: Keeping Afloat in the Age of Technology, 2002; co-author (with C.K. Mack): (novels) The Chameleon Variant, 1980; founder, editor Conservation Biology, 1987—93, consulting editor, 1994—, bd. editors Ecosys. Health, 1994—, mem. adv. bd. Conservation and Society, 2002—, mem. editl. adv. bd. Conservation in Practice, 1999—2005, contbg. editor, 2005, columnist (mag.) Orion, 1989—2002; contbg. editor: (mag.) Orion, 2003—; contbr. articles to profl. and popular publs. Trustee E.F. Schumacher Soc., Great Barrington, Mass., 1979-2002, bd. founders, 2003—; bd. trustees Caribbean Conservation Corp., Gainesville, Fla., 1980—, Ednl. Found. Am., Westport, Conn., 1987-93, 98-2002. Fellow AAAS; mem. Ecol. Soc. Am., Internat. Union for the Conservation of Nature, Marine Turtle Specialist Group. Jewish. Home: 44 N 7th Ave Highland Park NJ 08904-2931 Office: Rutgers U Cook Coll New Brunswick NJ 08901-8551 Office Phone: 732-932-9553.

EHRENFELD, ELLIE (ELVERA EHRENFELD), biologist, researcher; b. Phila., Mar. 1, 1942; m. Donald F. Summers. BA cum laude, Brandeis U., 1962; PhD in Biochemistry, U. Fla., 1967; postdoctoral student, Albert Einstein Coll. Medicine, 1967—74. Asst. to assoc. prof. dept. cell biology Albert Einstein Coll. Med.; from assoc. prof.to prof. biochemistry and biology U. Utah, 1974—92; dean sch. biol. scis. U. Calif., Irvine, 1992—97; dir. Center for Scientific Review, NIH, Bethesda, Md., 1997—2003; chief picornavirus replication, Laboratory of Infectious Diseases NIH, Bethesda, Md., 1997—. Mem. various coms. including rsch. adv. panel Walter Reed Army Inst. Rsch., exptl. virology study sect. NIH; mem. bd. sci. counselors Nat. Inst. Allergy and Infectious Diseases; cons. immunopathology lab. Scripps Inst. Med. Rsch. Recipient Bill Joklik Lectureship award, Am. Soc. Virology; scholar Nat. Sci., Brandeis U. Office: NIAID MSC 6612 6610 Rockledge Dr Bethesda MD 20892-6612

EHRENHAFT, PETER DAVID, lawyer; b. Vienna, Aug. 16, 1933; came to U.S., 1940, naturalized, 1945; s. Bruno B. and Ann J. (Polacek) E.; m. Charlotte Kennedy, May 4, 1958; children: Elizabeth Ann, James Bruno, Daniel Parker. AB with honors, Columbia Coll., 1954; LLB, M Internat. Affairs with honors, Columbia U., 1957. Bar: (N.Y.) 1958, (D.C.) 1961. Motions law clk. to U.S. Ct. Appeals (D.C. cir.), 1957—58; sr. law clk. to Chief Justice U.S. Supreme Ct., 1961—62; assoc. Cox, Langford & Brown, Washington, 1962—66, ptnr., 1966—68, Fried, Frank, Harris, Shriver & Kampelman, Washington, 1968—77; dep. asst. sec., spl. counsel tariff affairs U.S. Dept. Treasury, Washington, 1977—79; ptnr. Hughes Hubbard & Reed, Washington, 1980—83, Bryan Cave, Washington, 1984—95; mem. Ablondi, Foster, Sobin & Davidow, P.C., Washington, 1995—2001, Miller & Chevalier, Chartered, Washington, 2001—03, of counsel, 2004—. Professorial lectr. law George Washington U., 1965-72, U. Pa., 1980-85; mem. faculty Salzburg (Austria) Seminar in Am. Studies Law Session, 1973; mem. Fed. Jud. Ctr. Study Group on Workload of Supreme Ct., 1971-74; mem. adv. com. U.S. Ct. Appeals (fed. cir.), 1992-96; mem. industry trade adv. com. on svcs. Dept. Commerce and U.S. Trade Rep., 1999—. Contbr. articles and revs., primarily on internat. trade, to law jours.; mem. adv. bd. Georgetown Internat. Law Jour., 1967—, Patent, Trademark and Copyright Jour., 1970—; mem. editl. bd. Internat. Legal Materials, 1977-87. Pres. bd. trustees Nat. Child Rsch. Ctr., Washington, 1976-77; mem. adv. coun. George Washington U. Med. Ctr., 1990-96. With USAF, 1958-61, USAFR, 1962-88; judge Ct. Mil. Rev., 1987-88. Mem.: ABA (mem. coun. internat. law sect. 1983—85, 1989—97, chmn. task force on legal svcs. in Japan 1991—98, liaison to Gen. Agreement on Tariffs and Trade 1992—94, vice chair 1993—94, internat. legal scholar 1994—97, vice chair transnat. practice com. 1998—, commn. on multijurisdictional practice 2000—02, mem. GATS Task Force 2004—, mem. coun. internat. law sect. 2003—), Am. Arbitration Assn. (internat. arbitration com. 1993—, panel internat. arbitrators 1994—), Washington Fgn. Law Soc. (bd. govs. 1982—92, pres. 1986—87), Am. Soc. Internat. Law, Am. Law Inst. (mem. various cons. coms.). Home: 2510 Virginia Ave NW Washington DC 20037-1904 Office: Miller & Chevalier Chartered 655 15th St NW Washington DC 20005-5701 Office Phone: 202-626-5915. Business E-Mail: pehrenhaft@milchev.com.

EHRENKRANZ, JOEL S., lawyer; b. Newark, Mar. 25, 1935; s. George J. and Hilda (Schreiber) Ehrenkranz; m. Anne B. Bick, June 9, 1963; children: Alissa, John, Jeanne. BS in Econs., U. Pa., 1956, MBA, 1957; LLB, NYU, 1961, LLM in Taxation, 1964. CPA NY; bar: NY 1961. Acct. Peat, Marwick, Mitchell & Co., NYC, 1957-62; sr. ptnr. Ehrenkranz & Ehrenkranz, NYC, 1962—. Trustee, distbn. com. Fedn. Jewish Philanthropies, N.Y.C., 1979—83, United Jewish Appeal/Fedn. Jewish Philanthropies, N.Y.C., 1982—92, pres., 1987—92; trustee Archives Am. Art, 1973—, pres., 1984—86; trustee Whitney Mus. Am. Art, 1973—; adv. bd. Wheelchair Found.; v.p. Whitney Mus. Am. Art, 1973—2002, pres., 1998—2002; trustee NYU Law Sch., 1992—, chmn. investment com., 2003—05; grad. bd. Wharton Sch. U. Pa., 1985—2004; trustee, vice chmn., mem. exec. com. Mt. Sinai Med. Ctr., NYC, 1987—92; trustee NYU, 1998—2001, 2003—; bd. overseers Calif. Inst. Arts, 2001—; trustee Archives Am. Art, 1973, pres., 1984—86; trustee, treas. Blythedale Children's Hosp., 1966—74. Named one of Top 200 Collectors, ARTnews Mag., 2004. Mem.: Century Club (White Plains, NY). Avocation: collector of contemporary art. Office: 375 Park Ave New York NY 10152-0002 also: Keeler Ln North Salem NY 10560 also: Mayfly Dr Wilson WY 83014

EHRENKRANZ, RICHARD ALLAN, pediatrician; b. Newark, July 28, 1946; s. Robert and Miriam (Wiskind) Ehrenkranz; married, 2000. BS in Life Scis., MIT, 1968; MD cum laude, SUNY Downstate Med. Ctr., 1972. Diplomate Nat. Bd. Med. Examiners, Am. Bd. Pediatrics. Intern in pediatrics Yale-New Haven Med. Ctr., 1972-73, resident in pediatrics, 1973-74; rsch. assoc. pregnancy rsch. br. Nat. Inst. Child Health and Human Devel., NIH, Bethesda, Md., 1974-76; fellow in neonatology divsn. perinatal medicine Yale U. Sch. Medicine, New Haven, 1976-78, asst. prof. pediatrics, 1978-82, asst. prof. ob-gyn, 1979-82, assoc. prof. pediatrics and ob-gyn, 1982-88, prof. pediatrics and ob-gyn, 1988—; attending physician pediatrics Yale-New Haven Hosp., 1978—, clin. dir. newborn spl. care unit, 1982—2005, med. dir. newborn spl. care unit, 2005—. Mem. NIH pulmonary SCOR grant site visit, dept. pediatrics Vanderbilt U. Sch. Medicine, Nashville, 1981; mem. adv. com. perinatal medicine seminars Ross Labs., 1985-89; mem. ad hoc study sect. multictr. trial of cryotherapy for retinopathy of prematurity NEI, 1985, mem. ad hoc rev. group planning grants for retinopathy of prematurity trials, 1989; mem. adv. com. perinatal and devel. medicine symposium Mead Johnson, 1995-2000; prin. investigator NICHD Neonatal Rsch. Network, 1991—; mem. initial rev. group Maternal and Child Health Rsch. Subcom., NICHD, 2001--. Author book chpts., articles, abstracts, procs. in field. Lt. comdr. USPHS, 1974-76. Fellow: Am. Coll. Nutrition; mem.: AAAS, New Eng. Perinatal Soc., Am. Acad. Pediat., Am. Soc. Clin. Nutrition, Am. Pediatric Soc., Soc. for Pediatric Rsch., Alpha Omega Alpha, Sigma Xi. Office: Yale U Sch Medicine 333 Cedar St PO Box 208064 New Haven CT 06520-8064 Home: 25 Kildeer Rd Hamden CT 06517 Office Phone: 203-688-2320. Personal E-mail: richard.ehrenkranz@yale.edu.

EHRENREICH, BARBARA, writer; b. Butte, Mont., Aug. 26, 1941; d. Ben Howes and Isabelle (Oxley) Alexander; m. John H. Ehrenreich, Aug. 6, 1966; children: Rosa, Benjamin; m. Gary Stevenson, Dec. 10, 1983 BA in Chem. Physics, Reed Coll., 1963; PhD in Biology, Rockefeller U., 1968; D (hon.), Reed College, SUNY, Old Westbury, College of Wooster, Ohio, John Jay College, UMass-Lowell, La Trobe University, Melbourne, Australia. Editor Health Policy Adv. Ctr., NYC, 1969-70; asst. prof. SUNY-Old Westbury, 1971-74; free-lance writer, lectr.; fellow NY Inst. Humanities, NYC, 1980, Inst. Policy Studios, Washington, 1982—; editor Seven Days mag., 1974; columnist Mother Jones mag., 1986-89; essayist Time mag., 1991—97; columnist The Guardian, United Kingdom, 1992—. Author: For Her Own Good: 150 Years of the Experts' Advice to Women, 1978, (with Deirdre English) The American Health Empire, 1970, (with John Ehrenreich) Witches, Midwives and Nurses: A History of Women Healers, 1972, (with D. English) Complaints and Disorders: The Sexual Politics of Sickness, 1973, The Hearts of Men: American Dreams and the Flight from Commitment, (with E. Hess & G. Jacobs) Re-Making Love: The Feminization of Sex, 1986, (with others) The Mean Season: The Attack on the Welfare State, 1987, Fear of Falling: The Inner Life of the Middle Class, 1989, The Worst Years of Our Lives: Irreverent Notes From An Age of Greed, 1990, Kipper's Game, 1993, Blood Rites: Origins and History of the Passions of War, 1997, Nickeled and Dimed, 2001 (Christoper award, 2002, LA Times Book award, 2002, NY Times Bestseller list), Bait and Switch, 2005; contbg. editor: Ms mag., 1981—, Mother Jones mag., 1988—, Leavs mag., 1988—. Recipient Nat. Mag. award, 1980, Ford Found. award for Humanistic Perspectives on Contemporary Issues, 1981; Guggenheim fellow, 1987, Sydney Hillman award for Journalism.*

EHRENREICH, HENRY, physicist, researcher; b. Frankfurt, Germany, May 11, 1928; came to U.S., 1940, naturalized, 1945; s. Nathan and Frieda (Rosenstein) E.; m. Tema P. Hasnas, Feb. 1, 1953; children: Paul, Beth Herst, Robert. Student, Columbia U., 1950-51; BA, Cornell U., 1950, PhD, 1955; MA (hon.), Harvard U., 1963. Theoretical physicist Gen. Electric Research Lab., Schenectady, N.Y., 1955-63; vis. lectr. Harvard U., 1960-61, Gordon McKay prof. applied physics, 1963-82, Clowes prof. sci., 1982—2001, Clowes rsch. prof., 2001—02; vis. prof. Brandeis U., 1969, U. Paris, 1969, U. Pa., 1976; univ. ombudsman Harvard Univ., Cambridge, Mass., 2002—. Mem. def. scis. rsch. coun. Advanced Rsch. Projects Agy., U.S. Dept. Def., 1972-2002; sec. solid state commn. Internat. Union Pure and Applied Physics, 1978-81; mem. solar photovoltaic energy adv. com. Dept. Energy, 1980-83; dir. Harvard Materials Rsch. Lab., 1982-90; cons. White House Office Sci. and Tech., 1991. Contbr. articles to profl. jours.; bd. editors Phys. Rev. 1965-67; co-editor: Solid State Physics, 1966—; asst. editor Annals of Phys., 1984-2002. Trustee Dibner Inst. for History of Sci. and Tech., 1992-98; cons. Wolf Found., 1997-99. Fellow AAAS, Am. Acad. Arts and Scis., Am. Phys. Soc. (chmn. div. solid state physics 1969, chmn. study group on solar energy 1977-81, chmn. panel on pub. affairs 1990-91); mem. Phi Beta Kappa, Sigma Xi. Office: Harvard U Divsn Engring and Applied Scis and Physics Dept Cambridge MA 02138 Office Phone: 617-495-3213. E-mail: ehrenreich@deas.harvard.edu.

EHRENSTEIN, GERALD, retired biophysicist; b. N.Y.C., Sept. 27, 1931; s. Irving and Adele (Holzer) E.; m. Deborah Ploscowe, Dec. 17, 1960; children: Ruth, David, Steven. BEE, Cooper Union, 1952; MA, Columbia U., 1958, PhD, 1962. Engr., Arma Corp., N.Y.C., 1952; rsch. physicist, NIH, Bethesda, Md., 1962-75, chief biophysics sect., 1975—2002, ret., 2002. Corp. mem. Marine Biol. labs., Woods Hole, Mass., 1970-86 . Mem. editl. bd. Biophys. Jour., 1980-83; editor Methods of Exptl. Physics-Biophysics, 1982. Lt. (j.g.) USCG, 1952-54. Mem. Biophys. Soc. (mem. program com. 1981-84, 1992-93, coun. mem. 1992-95, mem. pub. policy com. 1991-96), Am. Phys. Soc., Sigma Xi. Avocation: birdwatching. E-mail: debandger@earthlink.net. Home: 7502 Nevis Rd Bethesda MD 20817-4742 E-mail: debandger@earthlink.net.

EHRENWERTH, DAVID HARRY, lawyer; b. Pitts., Apr. 22, 1947; s. Ben and Beatrice Lee (Schwartz) E.; m. Judith B. Ehrenwerth; children: Justin Reid, Lindsey Royce. BA, U. Pitts., 1969; JD, Harvard U., 1972. Bar: Pa. 1972, U.S. Dist. Ct. (we. dist.) Pa. 1972, U.S. Ct. Appeals (3d cir.) 1976. Asst. atty. gen. Commonwealth of Pa., Pitts., 1972-74; assoc. Kirkpatrick & Lockhart LLP, Pitts., 1974-79, ptnr., 1979—; adminstrv. ptnr., mem. mgmt. com. Kirkpatrick & Lockhart Nicholson Graham LLP, Pitts., 1988—. Pres. Pitts. chpt. Am. Jewish Com., 1988-90, nat. bd. govs., 1991-95, 01-, chmn. Pitts. chpt., 1996-98; mem. nat. adv. coun. Fed. Nat. Mortgage Assn., 1984-85; bd. dirs. Pa. Bd. Vocat. Rehab., Harrisburg, 1983-88, United Jewish Fedn., Pitts., 1991-93, Presbyn. U. Hosp., Pitts., 1993-94, Riverview Ctr. Jewish Srs., 1991-93, U. Pitts. Cancer Inst., 1995-99, Pitts. Symphony, 2001-; bd. mem. Am. Israel Pub. Affairs Com., 1995-99, 01-04; bd. dir. Montefiore Hosp., Pitts., 1985-93, treas., 1989, vice chmn., 1990-92, chmn., 1992-93; bd. govs. Pa. Econ. League, Western Region, 1999—. Recipient Human Rels. award Am. Jewish Com., 1999, Bonds award State Israel, 2004; named Pittsburgher to Watch Pitts. Mag., 1980, Pa. Super Lawyer, 2004, 05. Mem. Pa. Bar Assn. (chmn. real estate fin. com. 1985-87), Allegheny County Bar Assn. (Bar fellow, 2000—, chmn. real property sect. 1989), Harvard U. Law Alumni Assn. Western Pa. (pres. 1986-87), Concordia Club, Westmoreland Country Club, Heinz Fifty-Seven Club (chmn. 1974-91), Duquesne Club, Phi Beta Kappa. Jewish. Home: 413 Windmere Dr Pittsburgh PA 15238-2440 Office: Kirkpatrick & Lockhart Nicholson Graham LLP 1500 Oliver Building Bldg Pittsburgh PA 15222-2312 Office Phone: 412-355-6532. Office Fax: 412-355-6501. Business E-Mail: dehrenwerth@klng.com.

EHRET, JOSEPHINE MARY, microbiologist, researcher; b. Roswell, N.Mex., Feb. 26, 1934; d. Edward and Glenna (Memmer) E. BS, U. N.Mex., 1955. Med. technologist U. Colo. Health Scis. Ctr., Denver, 1956-75, rsch.

microbiologist, 1956—, Denver Dept. Health and Hosps., 1980—2004; instr. Sch. Medicine, U. Colo., 1985—. Contbr. articles to profl. publs. Mem. Am. Soc. for Microbiology, Am. Soc. Med. Technologists (cert.), Am. Venereal Disease Assn., Calif. Assn. Continuing Med. Lab. Edn. Democrat. Avocations: reading, birding. Home: 1344 S Eudora St Denver CO 80222-3526 Office: U Colo Sch Medicine Div Inf Dis B168 Dept Medicine 4200 E 9th Ave Denver CO 80262 E-mail: JsphnEhret@aol.com.

EHRHARDT, ANJA, biochemist, researcher; b. Stade, Germany, May 6, 1971; arrived in U.S., 1999; d. Klaus and Anke Ehrhardt. Student, U. Gottingen, Germany, 1992; diploma in biochemistry, U. Hamburg, Germany, 1995, PhD, 1999. Postdoctoral fellow Stanford (Calif.) U., 1999—2004, rsch. scientist, 2004—. Cons. in field. Contbr. articles to profl. jours. Recipient Excellence in Rsch. award, Boston, 2003. Mem.: Am. Soc. Gene Therapy. Achievements include patents in field. Business E-Mail: anja3@stanford.edu.

EHRHART, JOSEPH EDWARD, retired broadcast technician; b. Monterey Park, Calif., Dec. 27, 1933; s. Theophile George and Catherine Louise (Spaulding) E.; m. Mary Frances Bos, Nov. 30, 1957; children: James Edward and Teresa Louise. AA in Electronics, Pasadena City Coll., 1954. 1st class lic. radiotelephone, FCC. Child actor MGM, RKO, United Artists, Republic, Warner Bros., 20th Century Fox, Universal, Hollywood, Calif., 1939-54; TV broadcast engr. Sta. KOAT-TV, Albuquerque, 1957, Sta. KOB-TV, Albuquerque, 1958, Sta. KHJ-TV, Hollywood, Calif., 1959, ABC, Hollywood, 1960-93; videotape supr. Sta. KABC-TV, Hollywood, 1987-93, ret., 1993. Scoutmaster Boy Scouts of Am., Montrose, Calif., 1970-72; choir dir., Holy Redeemer Cath. Ch., Montrose, 1967-75, mem. Am. Assn. of Variable Star Observers, 1973-78; inspector County of San Diego Registrar of Voters, 1998—. Served in USNR, 1954-56. Mem. Soc. Motion Picture and TV Engrs., Cath. Press Coun., Mensa, Pacific Pioneer Broadcasters, Soc. for Preservation and Encouragement of Barber Shop Quartet Singing in Am., L.A. Astron. Soc., Am. Legion. Lodges: KC, Order of the Alhambra Illustrious Supreme Vizier, 2003-2005). Avocations: church choir, instrumental music. Home: Apt 333 1255 N Broadway Escondido CA 92026-2865

EHRHORN, RICHARD WILLIAM, electronics company executive; b. Marshalltown, Iowa, Jan. 21, 1934; s. Theodore Raymond and Zelda Elizabeth (Axtell) E.; m. Marilyn Patrick, Aug. 1, 1959; children: Scott Patrick, Kimberlee Dawn. BSEE, U. Minn., 1955; MSEE, Calif. Inst. Tech., 1958. Sr. engr. Gen. Dynamics Corp., Pomona, Calif., 1956-60; sr. rsch. engr. Calif. Inst. Tech. Jet Propulsion Lab., Pasedena, 1960-63; mgr. advanced devel. lab. Electronic Communications Inc., St. Petersburg, Fla., 1963-68; gen. mgr. Signal/One div., 1968-70; chmn., CEO Ehrhorn Tech. Ops., Inc., Colorado Springs, Colo., 1970-95; vice chmn. ASTeX/ETO, Inc., Colorado Springs, 1996-99; regent Liberty U., 1995—; chmn., CEO Alpha/Power, Inc., Longmont, Colo., 1996-2000; ptnr. Alpha Radio Products, LLC, Boulder, Colo., 2005—. Author: (with others) Principles of Electronic Warfare, 1959; patentee in field. Mem.: IEEE (sr. life), Am. Radio Relay League (life). Home and Office: PO Box 6249 Breckenridge CO 80424-6249 Personal E-mail: w4eto@comcast.net.

EHRLICH, AMY, editor, writer; b. N.Y.C., July 24, 1942; d. Max and Doris (Rubenstein) E.; m. Henry A. Ingraham; 1 son, Joss. Student, Bennington Coll., 1960-63, 64-65. Roving editor Family Cir. Mag., N.Y.C., 1975-76; sr. editor Dial Books for Young Readers, N.Y.C., 1977-82, exec. editor, 1982-85; v.p., editor-in-chief Candlewick Press, Cambridge, Mass., 1991-95, editor at large, 1996—. Author: children's book Zeek Silver Moon, 1972 (named Best Book of Yr. 1972), Leo, Zack and Emmie (named booklist reviewers choice Sch. Libr. Jour. 1981), Leo, Zack and Emmie Together Again, The Snow Queen, 1982, The Random House Book of Fairy Tales, others, (novel) Where It Stops, Nobody Knows, 1988 (ALA booklist Best of the Decade 1989, Dorothy Canfield Fisher award), The Story of Hannukah, Leo Zack and Emmie Together Again, Pome and Peel, 1990, The Dark Card, 1991, Lucy's Winter Tale, 1992, Parents in the Pigpen, Pigs in the Tub, 1993 (Best Youth Picture Book award Booklist 1993), Maggie and Silky and Joe, 1994; editor: When I Was Your Age: Original Stories of Growing Up, Vol. 1, 1996, Vol. 2, 1999, Rachel: The Story of Rachel Carson, 2003.

EHRLICH, AVA, television executive; b. St. Louis, Aug. 14, 1950; d. Norman and Lillian (Gellman) Ehrlich; m. Barry K. Freedman, Mar. 31, 1979; children: Alexander Zev, Maxwell Samuel. BJ, Northwestern U., 1972, MJ, 1973; MA, Occidental Coll., 1976. Reporter, asst. mng. editor Lerner Newspapers, Chgo., 1974-75; reporter, news editor Sta. KMOX, St. Louis, 1976-79; producer Sta. WXYZ, Detroit, 1979-85; exec. producer Sta. KSDK-TV, St. Louis, 1985—. Guest editor Mademoiselle mag., N.Y.C., 1971; freelance writer, coll. prof. Detroit, Chgo., St. Louis, 1987; adj. faculty mem. Washington U., St. Louis, 1994—. Trustee CORO Found., St. Louis, 1976-77, 86—, St. Louis Jewish Light, 1999—, Crown Ctr., 2000; bd. dirs. Nat. Kidney Found., St. Louis, 1987, Crowne Ctr., 2000—. Named Outstanding Woman in Broadcasting, Am. Women in Radio & TV, 1983, Among 18 Most Influential Women in the Region St. Louis Dispatch, 2000; recipient Journalism award Am. Chiropractic Assn., 1989, AP award Ill. UPI, 1989, Illuminator award AMC Cancer Rsch., 1994, Women in Comms. Nat. award, 1988, Emmy award, 1995, Virginia Betts award for Contbns. in Journalism, 1999; CORO Found. fellow in pub. affairs, 1975-76. Mem. NATAS (com. mem. 1986—, bd. dirs. 1994—, 18 local Emmy awards 1986—), Women in Comms., Inc. (sec. 1978-79, Clarion award 1989, Best in Midwest Feature award 1989), Soc. Profl. Journalists. Democrat. Jewish. Home: 8002 Walinca Ter Saint Louis MO 63105-2565 Office: Sta KSDK-TV 1000 Market St Saint Louis MO 63101-2011 Office Phone: 314-444-5120. Business E-Mail: aehrlich@ksdk.gannett.com.

EHRLICH, BERNARD HERBERT, lawyer, trade association administrator; b. Washington, Apr. 3, 1927; s. Samuel Zachary and Elsie (Klein) E.; m. Edna Kraft, June 17, 1951 (div.); children— Vivian Rose, Beverly Denise, Brenda Susan, Lisa Jean. AB, George Washington U., 1946, LLB, 1949, MA, JD, 1950. Bar: D.C. 1949. Pvt. practice, Washington; gen. counsel numerous corps., industries, 1947-89; mgr., gen. counsel Inst. Indsl. Launderers, Washington, 1947-89; counsel KEX Nat. Assn., 1960-94. Counsel Nat. Home Study Coun., 1947-89, Nat. Assn. Cosmetology Schs., 1967-83; mem. adv. panel employee recruitment and job devel. U.S. C. of C., 1967-84; mem. Pres.'s Com. on Employing the Handicapped, 1975—; gen. counsel KEX Nat. Assn., 1960-95; Accrediting Bur. Health Edn. Schs., 1965-92, Commn. Accredited Truck Driving Schs., 1985-92, Nat. Assn. Trade and Tech. Schs., 1968-86. Bd. dirs. Washington B'nai B'rith Hillel Found., 1997-2000; bd. trustees Temple Emanu-or, Sarasota, Fla., 2005—. With USN, 1943-45. Recipient svc. plaque Am. Inst. Launderers, 1966, svc. plaque Nat. Assn. Trade and Tech. Schs., 1967, svc. plaque Nat. Home Study Coun., 1970, svc. plaque Accrediting Bureau of Health Edn. Schs., 1992, svc. plaque Commn. Accredited Truck Driving Schs., 1992, N.F. Cimaglia award Melody Pub. Co., 1985. Mem. ABA, Bar Assn. D.C., Am. Soc. Internat. Law, Am. Hist. Assn., Am. Soc. Assn. Execs., Soc. Am. Travel Writers, Am. Polit. Sci. Assn., Nat. Assn. Trade and Tech. Schs. (hon.), KEX Nat. Assn. (hon.), Inst. Indsl. Launderers (hon.), Am. Forestry Assn. (life), Phi Beta Kappa, Nu Beta Epsilon, Phi Delt Pi. Jewish. Home and Office: 4907 Lakescene Pl Sarasota FL 34243 Office Phone: 941-351-8341.

EHRLICH, CHARLES DAVID, physicist; b. Miami, Fla., Sept. 10, 1951; s. Maurice Lee and Bena Zeva (Shechtman) E.; m. Susan Rae Morris, June 2, 1974; children: Rebecca, Gabriel. BS, U. Miami, 1973; PhD, U. Pa., 1979. Physicist R&D Varian Assocs. Extrion Div., Gloucester, Mass., 1979-83, mgr. batch process product devel., 1984; staff physicist Nat. Bureau of Standards, Gaithersburg, Md., 1984-87; group leader, pressure group Nat. Inst. Standards & Tech., Gaithersburg, Md., 1987-94, program analyst, 1994-95, sr. program analyst, 1995-96, dep. chief, tech. stds. activities program, 1996-99, nat. measurement and stds. needs assessment coord., 1999-2000, chief tech. stds. activities program, 2000—01, leader Internat. Legal Metrology Group, 2002—. U.S. rep. Internat. Orgn. Legal Metrology, 2000—; workshop organizer Nat. Inst. Stds. and Tech., 1987-89; instr. 1990-94; co-chmn. to Internat. Sts. Orgn. Tech. Adv. Group 4 on Metrology; invited conf. procs. author Proceedings of 4th Italy-U.S. Bilateral Seminar, 1992. Contbr. articles to profl. jours. Boy scout asst. patrol leader Boy Scouts Am., Gaithersburg, 1991-94, cub scout den leader Cub Scouts Am., Gaithersburg, 1989-91. Recipient Bronze Medal award U.S. Dept. Commerce, 1992, Best Paper award Nat. Conf. Standards Labs., 1997, Andrew J. Woodington award for Professionalism in Metrology Measurement Sci. Conf., 1999. Mem.: Am. Nat. Stds. Inst. Exec. Stds. Coun., Internat. Joint Com. Guides for Metrology, Intrinsic Derived Sts. Com., Nat. Conf. Stds. Labs. (chmn. 1989—98), Internat. Bur. Weights and Measures, Am. Vacuum Soc., Am. Soc. Testing & Materials (vice chmn 1986—90), Internat. Orgn. Legal Metrology (U.S. rep.), Sigma Xi (NIST chpt. pres.-elect 2002—03, pres. 2003—04). Achievements include invited keynote speaker IMEKO World Congress, Turin, Italy, 1994; invited speaker Shanghai and Beijing, China, 1994, Bratislava, Slovakia, 1991 explained measured equilibration time constants in helium permeation leaks. Milestones in Metrology Congress, Maastricht, The Netherlands, 2003. Home: 9804 Darcy Forest Dr Silver Spring MD 20910-1176 Office Phone: 301-975-4834. E-mail: charles.ehrlich@nist.gov.

EHRLICH, CHARLES GORDON, insurance company executive, lawyer; b. London, Apr. 3, 1949; came to U.S., 1953; s. Josef and Lotte (Engel) E.; m. Ann Curry, Dec. 16, 1978; children: Lisa, Jennifer. AB, U. Calif., Berkeley, 1970, JD, 1973. Bar: Calif. 1973, Ill. 1995. Assoc. Lawler, Felix & Hall, L.A., 1974-79, Pettit & Martin, San Francisco, 1979-80, ptnr., 1981-94; v.p., dep. gen. counsel Internat. Ins. Co., Chgo., 1994-96, acting gen. counsel, 1996-97, sr. v.p., 1997—2002, also bd. dirs.; sr. v.p., gen. counsel, sec., bd. dirs. TIG Ins. Group: TIG Ins. Holdings, Manchester, NH, 2002—. Editl. cons. Calif. Forms of Jury Instruction, Matthew Bender, 1985, Proof in Competitive Bus. Practices Litigation, Calif. Continuing Edn. of Bar, 1993; bd. dirs. Resolution Group, Chgo., RiverStone Holdings Ltd., TIG Ins. Co., RiverStone Ins. UK, River Stone Ins. UK, Sphere Drake Ins., Ltd.; arbitrator San Francisco Superior Ct., 1987-94, US Dist. Ct. No. Dist. Calif., San Francisco, 1989-94. Contbr. articles to profl. jours., local newspapers. Founder, bd. dirs. Legal Cmty. Against Violence, San Francisco, 1993-95. Recipient award of merit Bar Assn. San Francisco, 1993. Mem. ABA (co-chmn. sect. ligitation, corp. counsel com. regional workshop programs 1993—, vice chmn. sect. on tort and ins. practice 1995—, program chmn. sect. on litigation 1997), State Bar Calif. (com. on adminstrn. of justice 1992-94). Avocations: sports car racing, travel. Office: RiverStone Resources 250 Commercial St Manchester NH 03101 Office Phone: 603-656-2456. Business E-Mail: charles_ehrlich@trg.com.

EHRLICH, CLIFFORD JOHN, Internet company executive; b. N.Y.C., Nov. 17, 1938; s. Joseph George and Eugenia Marie (Rybacky) E.; m. Patricia Marie Stankunas, June 20, 1964; children: Susan, Brian, Scott. BA in Econs., Brown U., 1960; JD, Boston Coll., 1965; H.H.D. (hon.), Bethany Coll., 1986. With Monsanto Co., 1960-73; dir. labor relations, then v.p. employee relations Marriott Corp., Washington, 1973-78; sr. v.p. human resources Marriott Internat., 1978-97; chmn. bd. Alexus Internat., 1997—. Chmn. Employment Policy Found., 1995-97. Fellow Nat. Acad. Human Resources; Pers. Roundtable (chmn. 1993-95), Bus. Roundtable (chmn. employee rels. com. 1990-91), Labor Policy Assn. (vice chmn. 1994-97). Clubs: Congl. Country. Office: Alexus Internat Ste 480 555 Quince Orchard Rd Gaithersburg MD 20878-1437 Home: PO Box 385 Oakville CA 94562-0385

EHRLICH, DAVID GORDON, film director, educator; b. Elizabeth, N.J., Oct. 14, 1941; s. Max and Jeannette (Gordon) E.; m. Marcela Josepha Rydlova, July 17, 1975. BA in Govt., Cornell U., 1963; sculpture cert., Madras Sch. Fine Arts, India, 1964; MA in Dramatic Art, U. Calif., Berkeley, 1966; MFA in Film, Columbia U., 1975. Artist-in-residence Vt. Coun. on Arts, Montpelier, Vt., 1978—, N.H. Coun. on Arts, Concord, N.H., 1986—; vis. prof. film studies Dartmouth Coll., Hanover, N.H., 1993—. Lectr. art U. Vt., 1977-82; adj. asst. prof. interdisciplinary arts SUNY, Purchase, 1971-75; instr. animation summer session U. Calif., Berkeley, yearly 1988-93, summer session U. Hawaii, Honolulu, yearly 1991-98, Mongolia Coll. Art, Ulan, Baatar, Mongolia, CAS Sch., Karachi, Pakistan, 1993; mem. adv. bd. ADA Animation Inst., Shanghai, 1988—; vis. prof. film MRDH Coll., Volda, Norway, 1990-91; art therapy cons. Manhattan State Hosp., 1975-76; hon. pres. Ottawa Internat. Animation Festival, 2002; presenter various internat. confs. and festivals. Author: The Bowel Book, 1981, chpts. to Chinese, Mongolian and Japanese animation Animation in Asia and the Pacific, 2001; dir., animator: (animated short films) Metamorphosis, 1975, Album Leaf, 1976, Vermont Etude, 1977, Robot, 1977, Vermont Etude, No. 2, 1979, Robot Two, 1979, Precious Metal, 1980, Fantasies: Animation of Vermont Schoolchildren, 1981, Dissipative Dialogues, 1982, Precious Metal Variations, 1983, Point, 1984, Dissipative Fantasies, 1986, Pixel, 1987, Dryads, 1988, Academy Leader Variations, 1987, Animated Self-Portraits, 1989, A Child's Dream, 1990, Dance of Nature, 1991, Genghiz Khan, 1993, Etude, 1994, Interstitial Wavescapes, 1995, Robot Rerun, 1996, Asifa Variations, 1997, Radiant Flux, 1999, Color Run, 2001, Taking Color for a Walk, 2001, Current Events, 2002; mem. editl. bd. Animation Jour., 1991—, Cartoons, 2005—; contbr. articles to profl. jours.; films in collections at MOMA, Pacific Film Archive, Berlin ASIFA Animation Archive, Tokyo Internat. Animation Libr., Montreal Cinematheque Quebecoise, Moscow Film Archive; film retrospectives include Ottawa Internat. Animation Festival, 2002, Ballargues Animation Festival, France, 1998, Balt. Film Forum, Cinanima Animation Festival, Portugal, 1990, N.W. Film & Video Study Ctr., 1989, Pacific Film Archives, Shanghai Animation Festival, 1988, Mus. Modern Art, Varna World Animation Festival, Bulgaria, Belgrade Film Inst., Yugoslavia, 1987, Sinking Creek Film Celebration, Vienna Art Acad., 1986, Mus. Moving Image, 1985, Turin (Italy) City Hall, Cakovec Cultural Ctr., Yugoslavia, 1984, SUNY at Plattsburgh, Bradford Coll., 1982, Animators Gallery, N.Y.C., 1982, BVAU Gallery, Boston, Umwelt Galerie, Stuttgart, Germany, 1979; subject of book David Ehrlich: Citizen of the World, 2002. Recipient awards Cannes Film Festival, Chg. Film Festival, San Francisco Film Festival, Am. Film Festival, Krakow Film Festival, Cinanima Film Festival, Houston Film Festival, WorldFest, Charleston Film Festival, Roshd Film Festival, Iran, Murcia Film Festival, Spain, ASIFA-East Animation Festival, Sinking Creek Film Celebration, Black Maria Film Festival, N.Y. Filmakers' Expo, Athens Film Festival, New Eng. Film Festival, ASIFA Spl. award, 2002; travel grantee Arts Internat., N.Y.C., 1992-93, Am. Film Inst. grantee, 1988, Holographic Film Found grantee, 1978, 83, 84; Fulbright fellow, 1963-64. Mem. Nat. Expressive Therapy Assn. (cert. expressive therapist), Internat. Animation Assn. (exec. bd. 1988-2000, v.p. 1991-97), Soc. Animation Studies (mem. steering com. 1999-2000), Asian Cinema Studies Soc., Vt. Coun. on Arts (filmmaking grantee 1978, 79, 84, 86, 89, 90, 91), Mongolia Soc., Miagmar Animation Workshop (bd. dirs. 1992—). Avocations: composing music, painting, sculpture, dance, travel. Office: Dartmouth Coll Film Studies Wilson Hall Hanover NH 03755

EHRLICH, GARTH DAVID, molecular biologist; b. Plattsburgh, N.Y., July 9, 1956; s. Robert Elias and Evelyn Gertrude (Talvitie) E.; children: Ian S.G., Nathan E.G. BA, Alfred U., 1977; PhD, Syracuse U., 1987. Rsch. microbiologist Bethesda Rsch. Labs., Md., 1980-81; rsch. specialist Syracuse U., NY, 1981-83; rsch. scientist C indsl. divsn. Bristol Meyers, 1981-83, rsch. scientist B, 1983-84; tech. specialist I SUNY Health Sci. Ctr., Syracuse, NY, 1984-86, rsch. instr., 1988-89, rsch. asst. prof., 1989-90; tech. specialist II SUNY Rsch. Found., Syracuse, NY, 1986-88; asst. prof., dir. PCR facility U. Pitts., Pa., 1990-97; chief microbiology, virology and infectious diseases sect. molecular diogostics divsn. U. Pitts. Med. Ctr., Pa., assoc. prof., 1995-97; vis. prof. Cleve. Clin., 1992. Cons. Teltech, Inc., 1990—, Kodak, Rochester, NY, 1991-95, Oncogenetics, Phoenix, 1993-95; Visible Genetics, 1997-99, CL Sci., 1997-99, Quest Diagnostics, 1998-99; invited participant NCI Symposia, 1989, NMMS Symposia, 1989, NIAID Symposia, 1991, NILD Coun., 1995, NILC Symposiun, 2000; adj. mem. Ctrl. Blood Bank Pitts., 1992—; lectr. Heritage Found. Cross Cancer Ctr., Edmonton, Can.; Feinstein lectr. Alfred U., 1995; invited participant Internat. Chromosome 10 Workshop, Crete, Greece; invited guest spkr. Mexican Infection Disease Soc. Ann. Meeting, 1995; exec. dir. Ctr. for Genomic Sci., Allegheny Singer Rsch. Inst., 1997—; prof. microbiology, immunology, otolaryngology and human genetics Drexel Univ. Coll. of Med., vice-chmn. dept. human genetics, 1998—; hon. prof. med. genetics West China U. of Med. Sci., Chengdu, Sichuan, 1999—; invited spkr. World Congress of Pediat. Infectious Disease, Acapulco, Mex., 1996, Bicor Conf. on Antiinfective Agents, Leipzig, Germany, 1996, Case Western Res. U., 1997, others; lectr. Kaiyuon Bioengring., Xian, China, 1997, Chinese U. Hong Kong, 1999; hon. lectr. West China U. Med. Sci., 1999; vis. prof. Shantou U. Med. Coll., China, 2001; mem. adv. com. Med. Biofilms, Tokyo, 2002, Extraordinary Meeting on Ohh's Media, Amsterdam, 2005; organizer symposia in field, 1995-1997, 2000, 2003; mem. numerous NIH grant rev. coms. Author, editor: PCR-Based Diagnostics in Infectious Disease, 1994; contbr. 200 articles to profl. jours., chpts. to books, editls. to med. jours. Mem. gifted edn. adv. bd. Syracuse City Sch. Dist., 1989-90; lectr. on AIDS to secondary sch. children, sci. to elem. sch. children, 1989—. Recipient Disting. Alumni citation Alfred U., 1995, Feinstein Lectureship Alfred U., 1995, 4 NIH grants, 2000. Mem. Soc. for Leukocyte Biology, Assn. for Rsch. in Otolaryngology, Assn. Med. Lab. Immunologists, Acad. Clin. Lab. Physicians and Scientists, Am. Soc. for Microbiology, Assn. Molecular Pathology (co-chair infectious diseases sect.), Sigma Xi, Phi Kappa Phi. Address: Allegheny Singer Rsch Inst Ctr Genomic Sci 320 E North Ave Pittsburgh PA 15212-4756 Office Phone: 412-359-8169. E-mail: gehrlich@wpahs.org.

EHRLICH, GENYA S., retired writer; b. Odessa, Ukraine, Sept. 22, 1927; 1 child, Evelina. Degree, U. Odessa, 1945. Tchrs. diploma. Sr. tchr. conversational english Odessa State Courses for Adults, 1959—89. Author books and poetry. Bd. dirs. Senior Action Network, San Francisco, 1993—2000, promoter, 2001. Mem.: Creative Writing Class. Jewish. Avocation: performing. Home: Apt 4-O 711 Eddy San Francisco CA 94109

EHRLICH, GEORGE EDWARD, rheumatologist, pharmacologist, consultant; b. Vienna, July 18, 1928; came to U.S., 1938, naturalized, 1944; s. Edward and Irene (Elling) E.; m. Gail S. Abrams, Mar. 30, 1968; children: Charles Edward, Steven L. Abrams, Rebecca Sayles. AB cum laude, Harvard U., 1948; MB, MD, Chgo. Med. Sch., 1952. Intern Michael Reese Hosp., Chgo., 1952; resident Francis Delafield Hosp., N.Y.C., 1955, Beth Israel Hosp., Boston, 1956, New Eng. Center Hosp., Boston, 1957; fellow rheumatology NIH, Bethesda, Md., 1958, Hosp. for Spl. Surgery, N.Y.C., 1959-61, asst. attending physician, 1960-64; spl. fellow Sloan Kettering Inst., 1960-61; instr. medicine Cornell U., 1960-64; dir. Arthritis Center, chief rheumatology Albert Einstein Med. Center and Moss Rehab. Hosp., Phila., 1964-80; asst. prof. medicine Temple U., 1964-67, asso. prof. medicine, 1967-72, prof. medicine, 1972-80, asso. prof. rehab. medicine, 1964-74, prof., 1974-80; vis. lectr. U. Pa., 1964-80; prof. medicine, dir. div. rheumatology Hahnemann U., Phila., 1980-83; v.p. Anti-Inflammatory/Endocrine CIBA-Geigy Pharmaceuticals, Summit, N.J., 1983-86; head med. affairs CIBA-Geigy Ltd., Switzerland, 1987-88; pres. George E. Ehrlich Assocs., pharmaceutical cons. Adj. prof. clin. medicine NYU Med. Ctr., 1984—; lectr. medicine U. Pa., 1989-91, adj. prof. medicine, 1992—; expert advisor, cons. Diabetes and Other Noncommunicable Diseases unit WHO, 1990-98, Chronic Disease Mgmt., 1998—; chmn. Internat. Low Back Pain Initiative; rep. of pres. Internat. League Assns. Rheumatology for Soft Tissue Rheumatisms, 1993-97, exec. com.; liaison to WHO, 1997—; mem. arthritis adv. com. FDA, 1993-96, chmn., 1993-96; expert, FDA, 1997-99; mem. coun. Chairs, FDA, 1996—; chmn. sci. adv. bd. Hochrheininstitut (Rheumatic Disease and Rehab. Rsch. Inst. of Upper Rhine in Germany, France and Switzerland for Treatment, Tchg., and Rsch.), 1993—; bd. dirs. Greenwich Inst. Am. Edn.; chmn., U.S. mem. Expert Adv. Panel on Chronic Degenerative Diseases, WHO, 1996—. Author: Differential Diagnosis of Rheumatoid Arthritis, 1972, Oculocutaneous Manifestations of Rheumatic Diseases, 1973; editor: Total Management of the Arthritic Patient, 1973, Rehabilitation Management of Rheumatic Conditions, 1980, 2d edit., 1986; editor: (with J. Fries) Prognosis, 1981; editor: (with H.E. Paulus) Controversies in the Clinical Evaluation of Analgesic-Anti-Inflammatory-Antirheumatic Drugs, 1981; editor: (with P. Utsinger, N. Zvaifler) Rheumatoid Arthritis, 1985; editor: (with W. Simon) Medicolegal Consequences of Trauma, 1992; editor: (with N. Khaltaev) Low Back Pain, 2000; editor: (with W. Simon A. Sadwin) Conquering Chronic Pain After Injury, 2002; editor: Jour. Albert Einstein Med. Ctr., 1966—71, Arthritis and Rheumatic Diseases Abstracts, 1968—71; mem. editl. bd.: Inflammation, 1974—88, Psychosomatics, 1977—83, Sexual Medicine Today, 1977—84, Jour. Rheumatology, 1982—, Internat. Jour. Immunotherapy, 1984—, Immunopharmacology, 1985—. Med. Problems Performing Artists, 1985—92, Brazilian Jour. Rheumatology, 1992, 1996—99, Italian Jour. Rheumatic Diseases, 1999—; contbr. articles to profl. jours. Pres. Ea. Pa. chpt. Arthritis Found., 1970-72; mem. Phila. Mayor's Sci. and Tech. Adv. Coun., 1972-81; chmn. ad hoc adv. com. Bur. Drugs, FDA, 1971; subcom. on redefinition of disability Social Security Adminstrn., 1982-86. Served to comdr. M.C. USNR, 1953-55; Res. to 1975, ret. Decorated Cavaliere Order of Star of Italian Solidarity; recipient citations, City Phila., 1969, 1974, Distinguished Alumnus award, Chgo. Med. Sch., 1969, Dr. Joseph Lee Hollander award, Ea. Pa. chpt., Arthritis Found., 2004. Fellow ACP, Royal Coll. Physicians Edinburgh, Phila. Coll. Physicians, Am. Coll. Rheumatology (elected master, 1994, com. for publ. Arthritis and Rheumatism, 1977-79, mem. editl. bd. 1980-83), Rheumatism Socs. Ecuador, India (hon.); mem. AMA (editl. bd. Jour. 1972-82), Am. Soc. Clin. Pharmacology and Therapeutics, Assn. Mil. Surgeons (Philip Hench award 1971), Brit. Assn. Rheumatology and Rehab. (overseas mem., editl. bd. 1979-82), Internat. Soc. for Behcet's Disease (hon. life pres.), Harvard Club (Boston, N.Y.C.), Alpha Omega Alpha. Office: 1 Independence Pl Ste 1101 241 S Sixth St Philadelphia PA 19106-3731 Personal E-mail: ge2@mindspring.com. *Respect for the ideas of others, but ultimately responsible for my own ideas, thus, a liberal philosophy in a conservative setting. Like Brecht's Galileo, I should like to be remembered as a lover of old wines and new ideas.*

EHRLICH, GERALDINE ELIZABETH, management consultant; d. Joseph Vincent and Agnes Barbara (Campbell) McKenna; m. S. Paul Ehrlich, Jr.; children: Susan Patricia, Paula Jeanne, Jill Marie. BS, Drexel Inst. Tech. Nutrition cons. hypertension rsch. team U. Calif. Micronesia, 1970; regional sales mgr. Marriott Corp., Bethesda, Md., 1976-78; dir. sales and profl. svcs. Coll. and Health Care divsn. Macke Co., Cheverly, Md., 1978-79, v.p. ops. divsn., 1979-80, pres. Health Care divsn., 1980-81; regional v.p. Custom Mgmt. Corp., Alexandria, Va., 1981-83, v.p. mktg., 1983-87; v.p. mktg. and healthcare sales Morrison's Custom Mgmt., Mobile, Ala., 1987-88; v.p. sales ARA Svcs., Phila., 1988-93; v.p. bus. devel. ARAMARK, Phila., 1993-95; exec. dir. The Resource Group, Phila., 1995—2001; healthcare mktg. cons., 2001—. Cons. mktg. The Green House, Tokyo, 1987-88; chmn. bd. Mktg. Matrix, Falls Church, Va., 1984—. Mem. Health Systems Agy. No. Va., 1976-77; chmn. Health Care Adv. Bd., Fairfax County, Va., 1973-77; vice chmn. Fairfax County Cmty. Action Com., 1973-77; treas. Fairfax County Dem. Com., 1969-73; trustee Fairfax Hosp., 1973-77; bd. dirs. Tennis Patrons, Washington, 1984-88, Phila. Singers, 1993-98, Physicians for Peace, 1993-98; mem. adv. bd. Nat. Mus. Women in the Arts, 2000—, mem. bd. Fla. State Com., 2005—. Mem. NAFE, AAUW, Internat. Women's Assn., Am. Mgmt. Assn., Soc. Mktg. Profls., Gulfstream Club, Rotary Club. Home: 1132 Seaspray Ave Delray Beach FL 33483 Office Phone: 561-573-2492. E-mail: gehrlich@profserve.com.

EHRLICH, GERT, science educator, researcher; b. Vienna, June 22, 1926; arrived in U.S., 1939; s. Leopold and Paula Maria (Kucera) Ehrlich; m. Anne Vogdes Alger, Apr. 27, 1957. AB with honors in Chemistry, Columbia U., 1948; AM, Harvard U., 1950, PhD, 1952. NIH postdoctoral fellow Harvard U., Cambridge, Mass., 1951-52; research assoc. dept. physics U. Mich., Ann Arbor, 1952-53; mem. rsch. staff GE Rsch. Lab., Schenectady, NY, 1953-68; prof. materials sci. Coordinated Sci. Lab. U. Ill., Urbana-Champaign, 1968—. Former mem. editl. adv. bd. Chem. Physics Letters, Jour. Chem. Physics, Jour. Vacuum Sci. & Tech., Surface & Colloid Sci., Progress in Surface & Membrance Sci.; contbr. articles to profl. jours. With U.S. Army, 1945—47, ETO. Guggenheim fellow, 1985. Fellow: N.Y. Acad. Scis., Am. Phys. Soc.; mem.: Am. Vacuum Soc. (Medard W. Welch award 1979), Am. Chem. Soc.

(Kendall award 1982), Nat. Acad. Scis., Alexander von Humboldt Found. (Humboldt-Preis 1992), Sigma Xi. Office: U Ill Materials Rsch Lab 104 S Goodwin Ave Urbana IL 61801-2985 Office Phone: 217-333-6448. Business E-Mail: ehrlich@mrl.uiuc.edu.

EHRLICH, HENRY LUTZ, biology professor; b. Stettin, Pommerania, Germany, Aug. 31, 1925; came to U.S., 1940; s. Max and Gerda (Tannenwald) E. BS cum laude, Harvard Coll., 1948; MS, U. Wis., 1949, PhD, 1951. From asst. prof. to prof. biology Rensselaer Poly. Inst., Troy, N.Y., 1951-94; prof. emeritus, 1994. Cons. in field. Author: Geomicrobiology, 1996, 3d edit., 1995, 4th edit., 2002; author, co-editor: Workshop on Biotechnology for the Mining, Metal Refining and Fossil Fuel Processing Industries, 1986; co-author, co-editor: Microbial Mineral Recovery, 1990; editor-in-chief Geomicrobiology Jour., 1983-95; mem. editl. bd. Applied and environ. Microbiology, Applied Microbiology and Biotech. Mem. interdisciplinary com. World Cultural Coun., Monterrey, Mex. Am. Acad. Microbiology fellow. Fellow AAAS; mem. Symposia for Environ. Biogeochemistry (former v.p., treas.), Am. Soc. Microbiology, Soc. Indsl. Microbiology, Am. Inst. Biol. Scis., Sigma Xi. Jewish. Achievements include research on microbial manganese oxidation and reduction; microbial chromate reduction; microbial bauxite weathering; bioleaching. Home: 2423 21st St 3 Troy NY 12180-1826 Office: Rensselaer Polytech Inst Biology Dept 110 8th St Troy NY 12180-3590 Office Phone: 518-276-8428. Business E-Mail: ehrlih@rpi.edu.

EHRLICH, IRA ROBERT, mechanical engineering consultant; b. Washington, Sept. 1, 1926; s. Abraham Moses and Anna (Garonzik) E.; m. Sheila Lenor Kaminsky, June 11, 1950; children: Richard Mark, Heather Maureen Ehrlich Reiser BS, U.S. Mil. Acad., 1950; MS, Purdue U., 1956; PhD, U. Mich., 1960; MS (hon.), Stevens Inst. Tech., 1982. Registered profl. engr., Mich., N.J. Supr. ITT, Paramus, N.J., 1960-62; mgr. transp. research group Stevens Inst. Tech., Hoboken, N.J., 1962-74, dean research, 1974-83, head dept. mech. engring., 1979-83, v.p. research, 1983-85, v.p. acad. affairs, 1984-85, prof. emeritus, 1988—; pres. I. Robert Ehrlich P.A., Teaneck, N.J., 1988—. Chmn. sci. adv. com. U.S. Army Tank-Automotive Rsch. and Devel. Command, 1970-77; cons. to industry; mem. N.J. Motor Vehicle Insp. Sta. Rev. Commn., chmn. safety com., 1977-80. Asso. editor Tire Sci. and Tech, 1972-80. Served to capt. U.S. Army, 1950-60. Themis grantee, 1967-72 Fellow Soc. Automotive Engrs., Internat. Soc. Terrain-Vehicle Systems (gen. sec. 1967-78, v.p. 1978-81, pres. 1981-84); mem. ASME, NSPE, ASTM, Nat. Safety Coun., Nat. Assn. Profl. Accident Reconstructionists (bd. dirs. 1997-99), B'nai Brith (chpt. pres. 1967-68). Jewish. Home and Office: 859 Columbus Dr Teaneck NJ 07666-6612 Office Phone: 201-833-8316. Personal E-mail: irehrlich@verizon.net. *Make the most of your scraps of time.*

EHRLICH, JERROLD IVAN, lawyer; b. Bklyn., Jan. 21, 1934; s. Harvey B. and Belle R. (Crames) E.; m. Elaine J. Bergman, Dec. 26, 1954 (div. Jan. 1976); children: Mark S., Bruce D., Alan M., Philip L.; m. Vivian R. Fenster, June 27, 1976; children: Laurie B., Joshua B. AB, Oberlin Coll., 1955; LLB, Yale U., 1958. Bar: N.Y. 1958, U.S. Dist. Ct. (so. dist.) N.Y. 1961, U.S. Dist. Ct. (ea. dist.) N.Y. 1962, U.S. Supreme Ct. 1967, U.S. Ct. Appeals (2d cir.) 1968, N.J. 1969. Assoc. Law Office Harold Sylvan, N.Y.C., 1958-59, Burke & Groh, Jamaica, N.Y., 1959-66; asst. dist. atty. Queens County, N.Y., 1967; assoc. Law Office Harry Lipsig, N.Y.C., 1968-71; sole practice N.Y.C., 1971-73; asst. counsel Empire Blue Cross and Blue Shield, N.Y.C., 1973-82, assoc. gen. counsel, 1982—. Bd. dirs., sec. Access Am. Inc., N.Y.C., 1985-90. Sec. Beacon Corp. Benefit Services, 1987—, W. 91st St. Block Assn., N.Y.C., 1982—; bd. dirs., sec. Riverside Park Fund Inc., 1986—, Westside Yiddish Assn., 1986—. Mem. ABA, Am. Corp. Counsel Assn., N.Y. State Bar Assn. (sec., mem. exec. com. corp. counsel sect.), Nat. Health Lawyers Assn, N.Y. County Lawyers Assn. Democrat. Jewish. Home: 186 Riverside Dr New York NY 10024-1007 Office: Empire Blue Cross & Blue Shield 622 3rd Ave Fl 9 New York NY 10017-6707

EHRLICH, JOHN GUNTHER, writer; b. Berlin, Apr. 6, 1930; s. Walter Frederick and Henrietta (Fletch) E.; m. Frances Hendrika Vernon, Nov. 17, 1952 (div. Nov. 1978); children: Timothy Walter, Lisa Frances Gaffney; m. Karen Ann Carr, Dec. 31, 1982. BJ, Syracuse U., 1952; JD, Bklyn. Law Sch., 1962. Bar: N.Y. 1962; Federal, 1962; U.S. Dist. Ct. (so. dist., ea. dist.), 1962. Reporter Newsday, Huntington, N.Y., 1955-60; exec. asst. Suffolk County Rep. Com., Blue Point, N.Y., 1960-63; bur. chief Suffolk County Dist. Atty., Hauppauge, N.Y., 1963-90; writer Little River, S.C., 1990—. Author: (as Jack Ehrlich) Revenge, 1959, Court Martial, 1960, Parole, 1961, Slow Burn, 1961, Cry, Baby, 1962, The Girl Cage, 1967, Close Combat, 1969, The Drowning, 1970, The Chatham Killing, 1976, The Fastest Gun in the Pulpit, (German, French, Swedish transl., movie script from novel), 1972, Bloody Vengeance, 1973, The Laramie River Crossing, 1973, Rebellion at Cripple Creek, 1979, Command Influence, 2000; contbr. short stories, non-fiction articles to mags. Capt. USAF, 1952-54. Recipient Investigative Reporting award Nat. Home Builders, 1958, Edgar Allan Poe award Mystery Writers, N.Y.C., 1970, Cert. Appreciation, Suffolk County Police Benevolent Assn., 1989. Republican. Episcopalian. Avocations: golf, gardening, music, horseback riding. Office: PO Box 62 Little River SC 29566-0062 also: Theron Raines 103 Kenyon Rd Medusa NY 12120-2507

EHRLICH, M. GORDON, lawyer; b. Springfield, Mass., Sept. 28, 1930; s. Robert and Ida (Gordon) E.; m. Eleanor Fradkin, Sept. 1, 1956; children: Kenneth, Virginia, Sarah, Alexandra. BS, Yale U., 1951; LLB, Harvard U., 1954. Bar: Mass. 1954. Atty. Bingham, McCutchen, Boston, 1957—. Former chmn. Boston Tax Forum; chmn. Boston Estate and Bus. Planning Coun.; lectr. Harvard U. Law Sch. Contbr. articles to profl. jours. Former pres. Chestnut Hill Assn.; bd. overseers Beth Israel Deaconess Hosp., Boston. Mem. ABA (tax sect.), Am. Law Inst. Office: Bingham McCutchen 150 Federal St Fl 14 Boston MA 02110-1745

EHRLICH, MORTON, finance company executive; b. N.Y.C., Dec. 1, 1944; s. Milton and Anne (Tannenbaum) E.; children from previous marriage: Bruce, Ellen, Wendy; m. Paula Ehrlich, Feb. 25, 1991. BBA cum laude, CCNY, 1960; PhD in Econs. (Ford Found. fellow), Brown U., 1965. Economist Fed. Res. Bank of N.Y., 1965-67, Nat. Indsl. Conf. Bd., N.Y.C., 1967-68; v.p. Eastern Airlines, Miami, 1968-76, sr. v.p. planning, 1976-85; exec. v.p. Transworld Airlines, N.Y., 1985-88; also bd. dirs.; pres. LIFECO Svcs. Corp., 1988—91; chmn., CEO Integrated Mgmt. Corp., 1991—96; CEO A Privileged Lifestyle, Inc., 1996—. Trustee AETNA Mut. Funds; bd. dirs. Nat. Bur. Econ. Rsch., IBM/AFEC. Author: Discretionary Income, 1967, A Weekly Index of Business Activity, 1967, U.S. Foreign Trade, 1968, Computer Application in the Allocation of Airline Resources, 1975, An Integrated System for Airline Planning and Management Information, 1977, An Integrated Strategic Plan for Network Marketing, 1996, Paradigm Shift Syndrome, 1997. With U.S. Army, 1953-56. Mem. Am. Econ. Assn., Nat. Assn. Bus. Economists, U.S. C. of C. Office: A Privileged Lifestyle Inc 1000 Venetian Way Ste 1702 Miami FL 33139-1009 Office Phone: 305-530-8011. Personal E-mail: lifestyle2@bigplanet.com.

EHRLICH, PAUL RALPH, biology professor; b. Phila., May 29, 1932; s. William and Ruth (Rosenberg) E.; m. Anne Fitzhugh Howland, Dec. 18, 1954; 1 child, Lisa Marie. AB, U. Pa., 1953; AM, U. Kans., 1955, PhD, 1957. Research assoc. U. Kans., Lawrence, 1958—59; asst. prof. biol. scis. Stanford U., 1959—62, assoc. prof., 1962—66, prof., 1966—, Bing prof. population studies, 1976—, dir. grad. study dept. biol. scis., 1966—69, pres. Ctr. for Conservation Biology, 1988—, dir. grad. study dept. biol. scis., 1974—76. Cons. Behavioral Rsch. Labs., 1963—67; corr. NBC News, 1989—92. Author: How to Know the Butterflies, 1961, Process of Evolution, 1963, Principles of Modern Biology, 1968, Population Bomb, 1968, Population Bomb, 2d edit., 1971, Population, Resources, Environment: Issues in Human Ecology, 1970, Population, Resources, Environment: Issues in Human Ecology, 2d edit, 1972, How to Be a Survivor, 1971, Global Ecology: Readings Toward a Rational Strategy for Man, 1971, Man and the Ecosphere, 1971, Introductory Biology, 1973, Human Ecology: Problems and Solutions, 1973, Ark II: Social Response to Environmental Imperatives, 1974, The End of Affluence: A Blueprint for the Future, 1974, Biology and Society, 1976, Race Bomb, 1977, Ecoscience: Population, Resources, Environment, 1977, Insect Biology, 1978, The Golden Door: International Migration, Mexico, and the U.S., 1979, Extinction: The Causes and Consequences of the Disappearance of Species, 1981, The Machinery of Nature, 1986, Earth, 1987, The Science of Ecology, 1987, The Birder's Handbook, 1988, New World/New Mind, 1989, The Population Explosion, 1990, Healing the Planet, 1991, Birds in Jeopardy, 1992, The Birdwatchers Handbook, 1994, The Stork & the Plow, 1995, Betrayal of Science and Reason, 1996, World of Wounds, 1997, Human Natures, 2000, Wild Solutions, 2001, Butterflies: Ecology and Evolution Taking Flight, 2003, On the Wings of Checkerspots, 2004, One with Nineveh, 2004; contbr. articles to profl. jours. Co-recipient Crafoord prize in population biology and conservation biol. diversity, 1990; recipient World Wildlife Fedn. medal, 1987, Volvo Environ. prize, 1993, World Ecology medal, Internat. Ctr. Tropical Ecology, 1993, UN Sasakawa Environ. prize, 1994, Heinz prize for the environment, 1995, Tyler Environ. prize, 1998, Heineken prize for environ. sci., 1998, Blue Plant prize, 1999, Disting. Achievement award, Kansas U. Alumni, 2003; fellow MacArthur Prize fellow, 1990—95. Fellow: AAAS, Entomology Soc. Am., Am. Philos. Soc., Am. Acad. Arts and Scis., Calif. Acad. Scis. (Fellows medal 2003); mem.: NAS, Lepidopterists Soc., Am. Mus. Natural History (hon.), Am. Mus. Natural History (life), Brit. Ecol. Soc. (hon.), Am. Soc. Naturalists, Soc. Systematic Biology, Soc. for Study of Evolution, Ecol. Soc. Am. (Eminent Ecologist award 2001). Office: Stanford U Dept Biol Scis Stanford CA 94305

EHRLICH, ROBERT L., JR., governor, former congressman; b. Arbutus, MD, Nov. 25, 1957; Law clk. to H. Russell Smouse, 1981; assoc. Ober, Kaler, Grimes, and Shriver, 1982-92, of counsel, 1992-94; mem. Md. Ho. of Dels., 1987-94, mem. Ho. Jud. Com., Joint Legis. Ethics Com., Gov.'s Coun. Child Abuse & Neglect, Gov.'s Adv. Panel for Justice Adminstrn., mem. Gov.'s Select Panel on Drug-Addicted Newborns, Gov.'s Select Panel on the Hickey Sch., also Ho. co-chmn. Joint Com. on Md.'s Procurement Laws; mem. U.S. Ho. of Reps., Washington, 1995—2003, mem. commerce com., subcom. finance & hazardous waste, energy & power, telecomm., trade & consumer protection, mem. budget com., mem. Banking & Fin. Svcs. Com., subcoms. Fin. Insts. and Commercial Credit, Housing and Fin. Svcs., Spkrs. Spl. Adv. Com. on Corrections, asst. majority whip, Nat. Security Working Group, House Commerce Com.; gov. State of Md., Annapolis. Mem. house com. on energy and commerce, subcom. on environ. and hazardous waste, subcom. on telecomm. and internet, subcom. on health; co-chair congressional biotech. caucus, 2000-03. Named Guardian of Small Bus. Nat. Fedn. Ind. Bus., 1987-90, Legislator of Yr. Md. State's Attys. Assn., 1989, Fraternal Order of Police Md. State Lodge, 1994, Nat. Conf. for Prevention of Child Abuse, 1994, Outstanding Young Marylander Md. Jaycees, 1995, Outstanding Rep. Male Md. Rep. State Ctrl. Com., 1995, Disting. Svc. award German Soc. Md., 1997, Legislator of Yr. Nat. Assn. Mortgage Brokers, 1997; recipient Spirit of Enterprise award U.S. C. of C., 1996, 97, Thomas Jefferson award Food Distbrs. Internat., 1996, Congl. Tax Fighter award Nat. Tax Limitation Com., 1996, Taxpayer Hero award Citizens Against Govt. Waste, 1997. Republican. Office: Office of the Gov 100 State Circle Annapolis MD 21401 Office Phone: 410-974-3591. Business E-Mail: governor@gov.state.md.us.

EHRLICH, SUSAN PATRICIA, bank executive; b. Long Beach, Calif., July 23, 1966; d. Clifford John and Patricia Marie E. BA, Brown U., 1988; MBA, Harvard U., 1993. Asst. v.p. Citibank NA, N.Y.C., 1995-97, Citibank Mastercard/Visa, Long Island City, N.Y., 1997-2000; v.p., dir. electronic bill payment c2it by Citibank, N.Y.C., 2000—. Mem. Congl. Country Club, Harvard Club. Roman Catholic. Avocations: golf, travel, sailing, wine. Office: 2140 Pacific Ave Apt 601 San Francisco CA 94115-1589 E-mail: susan.ehrlich@citicorp.com.

EHRLICH, THOMAS, law educator; b. Cambridge, Massachusetts, Mar. 4, 1934; s. William and Evelyn (Seltzer) E.; m. Ellen (Rome), June 18, 1957; children, David, Elizabeth, Paul. AB, Harvard U., Cambridge, Mass., 1956, LLB, 1959; LLD (hon.), Villanova U., 1979, Notre Dame U., 1980, Pa. State U., 1987. Bar: Wis., 1959. Law clk. Judge Learned Hand U.S. Ct. Appeals 2d. Cir., 1959-60; spl. asst. to legal adviser U.S. State Dept., 1962-64, spl. asst. to under-sec., 1964-65; assoc. prof. law Stanford U., Stanford, Calif., 1965-68; prof. Stanford U., Stanford, Calif., 1968-75; dean Stanford U., Stanford, Calif., 1971-75, Richard E. Lang dean and prof., 1973-75; pres. Legal Services Corp., Washington, 1976-79; dir. Internat. Devel. Coop. Agy., Washington, 1979-81; provost, prof. law U. Penn., Phila., 1981-87; pres., prof. law Ind. U., Bloomington and Indpls., Ind., 1987-94; vis. prof. Duke U., Durham, NC, 1994; disting. Univ. scholar U. Calif., San Francisco, 1995-2000. Vis. prof. Stanford Law Sch., 1994-99; sr. scholar, Carnegie Found. for Advancement of Tchg., 1997—. Author: (with Abram Chayes and Andreas F. Lowenfeld) The Internat. Legal Process, 3 vols., 1968; (with Herbert L. Packer) New Directions in Legal Edn., 1972, Internat. Crises and the Role of Law, Cyprus, 1958-67, 1974; editor: (with Geoffrey C. Hazard Jr.) Going to Law School?, 1975; (with Mary Ellen O'Connell) Internat. Law and the Use of Force, 1993, The Courage to Inquire, 1995, Philanthropy and the Nonprofit Sector in a Changing Am., 1998, Civic Responsibility and Higher Edn., 2000; (with Jane V. Wellman) How the Student Hour Shapes Higher Education: The Tie that Binds, 2003; (with others) Educating Citizens: Preparing America's Undergraduates for Lives of Moral and Civic Responsibility, 2003. Office: Carnegie Found Advancement Tchg 51 Vista Ln Stanford CA 94305-8703 Office Phone: 650-566-5137. E-mail: ehrlich@carnegiefoundation.org.

EHRLICHMAN, NEIL R., sales executive; A in Bus. Mgmt., Nassau C.C., N.Y. Supr. Steve's Ho. of Electronics, East Meadow, NY, 1978—85; cargo agt. to supr. Air France Cargo, JFK Internat. Airport, 1990—96, regional cargo ops. and sales mgr. N.J. mgmt. Newark Internat. Airport, 1996—2001; dist. sales mgr. internat. Airborne Express (now DHL), Phila. Internat. Airport, 2001—03; mgr. multinational customer bus. devel. DHL Danzas Air and Ocean, Phila., 2003—. Address: 4307 N Church St Whitehall PA 18052

EHRMAN, DAVID L., music educator; b. Franklin Furnace, Ohio, Nov. 30, 1946; s. David Lee Ehrman and Clara Helen Waddell, Ehrman; m. Lisa Ann Stark, June 28, 1984; children: Brett Taylor children: David Lee, Claire Elise. MusM, Cin. Conservatory, 1968. Cert. Ohio Dept. Edn., 1973. Prof. piano Liberty U., Lynchburg, Va., 1976—, artist in residence, 1977—2005. Musician: (concerts) Concert Pianist. Orch. pianist Timberlake Bapt. Ch., Lynchburg, 2000—05. Mem.: Phi Kappa Lambda (hon.). Conservative. Baptist. Avocations: hiking, home remodeling. Office: Liberty U 1971 Univ Blvd Lynchburg VA 24502 Office Phone: 434-582-2215. Personal E-mail: dehrman@liberty.edu.

EHRMAN, LEE, geneticist, educator; b. NYC, May 25, 1935; m. Richard Ehrman, 1955; children: Esther, Judith. BS, Queens Coll., 1956; MS, Columbia U., 1957, PhD in Genetics, 1959; DSc (hon.), CUNY, 1989. Mem. faculty Barnard Coll., 1956-58; postdoctoral fellow in genetics Columbia U., N.Y.C., 1959-61, assoc. seminar on population biology, 1981—; mem. faculty SUNY-Purchase, 1970—, prof. div. natural scis., 1972—; Disting. prof. biology SUNY, Purchase, 1995—; mem. spl. study sect. NIH, NIMH, 1979-80. Vis. disting. prof. U. Miami, Coral Gables, Fla., 1981; vis. lectr. U. Puerto Rico, Rio Piedras, 1987; coordinator, panelist workshops, programs in field; mem. panels NIH, 2003—. Author: Behavior Genetics and Evolution, 2nd edit., 1981; assoc. editor Evolution; assoc. editor for genetics and cytology Am. Midland Naturalist; co-editor: Behavior Genetics; assoc. editor, exec. com. Soc. Am. Naturalists, 1977-85, pres.-elect 1990; contbr. more than 500 articles to profl. jours. Recipient Lit. Soc. Found. medal in German, 1956; Shirley Farr postdoctoral fellow, 1961-62; USPHS postdoctoral fellow, 1959-61; faculty exch. scholar, 1974—; NSF grantee, 1979-84; Sr. Scientist awardee Whitehall Found., 1987, 93; NIH gen. med. scis. grantee, 1987—; SUNY travel grantee, 1988, 93, 96; Merck rsch. support grantee, 2000—. Fellow AAAS (Rsch. Support award Merck/AAAS, 2001), Inst. Soc. Ethics and Life Scis; mem. AAUW (life), Am. Soc. Naturalists (pres. 1990), Behavior Genetics Assn. (pres. 1978, Dobzhansky award for lifetime resch. 1988), Soc. for Study of Evolution (exec. council 1986), Phi Beta Kappa, Sigma Xi Home: 2 Jennifer Ln Rye Brook NY 10573-1916 Office: SUNY Div Natural Scis Purchase NY 10577 Office Phone: 914-251-6671. Office Fax: 914-251-6635.

EHRNSCHWENDER, ARTHUR ROBERT, former utility company executive; b. Cin., Oct. 3, 1922; s. Arthur Michael and Lydia Carol (Widmer) E.; m. Grace Scholl Popplewell, Oct. 19, 1950 (dec. Apr. 2004); children: Barry N., Scott A. ME, U. Cin., 1948, BS in Commerce, 1959; MBA, Xavier U., 1959; D in Tech. Letters (hon.), Cin. Tech. Coll., 1980. Registered profl. engr., Ohio, Ky. Field engr. SKF Bearing Co., Cin., 1948-49; Chevrolet field rep. GM, Cin., 1949-50; with Cin. Gas and Electric Co., 1952-84, former sr. v.p. Bd. dirs. Porter Precision Products, Cin.; vice chmn., bd. dirs. OKI Supply Co., Cin.; past chmn. The Hwy. Rental Co., Cin. Electric Co. Past pres. Goodwill Industries, Cin., 1961-85; trustee emeritus Cin. Assn. for Blind, 1965—, Deaconess Hosp., Cin., 1970—, Hamilton County YMCA, 1974—. Capt. U.S. Army, 1943-46, 1950-52. Decorated Bronze Star, 1952; named Disting. Alumnus U. Cin., 1974, Xavier U. Mem. Soc. Automotive Engrs. (sect. chmn.), Engring. Soc. Cin., Edison Electric Inst. (divsn. chmn.), Am. Gas Assn. (sect. chmn.), Univ. Club Cin., Cin. Country Club, The Club Pelican Bay, Naples Yacht Club, Stumps Boat Club, Masons (hon. 33d degree). Republican. Presbyterian. Home: 1201 Edgecliff Pl Apt 1083 Cincinnati OH 45206-2853

EHSANI, MEHRDAD (MARK EHSANI), electrical engineering educator, consultant; naturalized, 1980; s. Heshmat and Didar (Ahmadi) Ehsani; m. Zohreh Khadem; children: Evan Mancil, Nathaniel William. MS, U. Tex., 1974; PhD, U. Wis., 1981. Registered profl. engr., Tex. Rsch. engr. Fusion Rsch. Ctr. U. Tex., Austin, 1974-77; rsch. engr. Argonne (Ill.) Nat. Lab., 1977-81; prof. elec. engring. Tex. A&M U., College Station, 1981, Halliburton prof. elec. engring., 1992, Dress Industries prof., 1994, dir. Tex. Applied Power Electronics Ctr., 1999, dir. advanced vehicle systems rsch. program, Dow Chem. fellow Coll. Engring., 2001—02, Robert M. Kennedy endowed chair prof. elec. engring., 2004—. Lectr. in field. Author: Converter Circuits for Superconductive Magnetic Energy Storage, 1988, Modern Electrical Drives, 2000; co-author: ANSI/IEEE Standards 936, 1987, Vehicular Power Systems: Land, Sea, Air and Space, 2003, Modern Electric, Hybrid Electric and Fuel Cell Vehicles: Fundamentals, Theory and Design, 2004; contbr. over 300 articles to profl. jours.; 23 patents in field. Named Outstanding Young Engr., Tex. Soc. Profl. Engrs., 1984, Disting. Lectr., IEEE-Industry Applications Soc., Inds. Elecs. Soc., Dow Chem. fellow, Coll. Engring., Tex. A&M U., 2001. Fellow IEEE (Field award in undergrad. tchg. 2003), Soc. Automotive Engrs. (SAE), 2005; mem. Power Electronics Soc. of IEEE (adminstrv. com. 1990-96), Industry Applications Soc. of IEEE (exec. coun. 1989-93, Disting. lectr.), IEEE Vehicular Tech. Soc. (bd. govs., bd. dirs., assoc. editor, James R. Evans Avant Garde award, 2001). Baha'I. Office: Tex A&M U Dept Elec Engring College Station TX 77843-0001 Office Phone: 979-845-7582. Business E-Mail: ehsani@ee.tamu.edu.

EIBEN, ROBERT MICHAEL, pediatric neurologist, educator; b. Cleve., July 12, 1922; s. Michael Albert and Frances Carlysle (Gedeon) E.; m. Anne F. Eiben; children: Daniel F., Christopher J., Thomas M., Mary, Charles G., Elizabeth A. BS, Western Res. U., 1944, MD, 1946. Diplomate Am. Bd. Pediatrics. Intern medicine Univ. Hosp., Cleve., 1946-47; asst. resident pediatrics and contagious diseases City Hosp., Cleve., 1947; asst. resident pediatrics Babies and Children's Hosp., Cleve., 1948, clin. fellow pediatrics, 1948-49; clin. instr. pediatrics Western Res. U., 1949-50; asst. med. dir. div. contagious diseases City Hosp., 1949-50, visitant in pediatrics, 1949-50; practice medicine specializing in pediatrics Cleve., 1949-90; acting dir. dept. pediatrics and contagious diseases City Hosp., 1950-52; asst. dir. dept. pediatrics and contagious diseases Cleve. Met. Gen. Hosp., 1952-60; med. dir. Respiratory Care and Rehab. Center, 1954-60, pres. med. staff, 1958-60; USPHS fellow in neurology U. Wash., 1960-63; pediatric neurologist Cleve. (Ohio) Met. Gen. Hosp., 1963—90, acting med. dir. comprehensive care program, 1966-67, med. dir., 1968-73, mem. med. exec. com., 1974-76; acting chief, sect. on clin. investigations and therapeutics Developmental and Metabolic Neurology br. Nat. Inst. Neurol. and Communicative Disorders and Strokes, NIH, Bethesda, Md., 1976-77; acting dir. dept. pediatrics Metro Health Med. Ctr., 1979-80; from instr. pediatrics to prof. emeritus Western Res. U., 1950—91, prof. emeritus pediatric neurology, 1991—. Cons., project site visitor Nat. Found. Birth Defects Center Programs, 1961-66; mem. adv. com. on grants to train dentists to care for handicapped Robert Wood Johnson Found., 1975-80; marshall emeritus faculty Case Western Res. U., 1994—, mem. regional leadership coun., 2003—. Mem. coun. Bratenahl Village-County of Cuyahoga, 1982-98. Recipient Presdl. award Internat. Poliomyelitis Congress, Geneva, 1957, Clifford J. Vogt Alumni Svc. award Case Western Res. U., Cleve., 1985; established Annual Robert M. Eiben, M.D. vis. professorship in child neurology MetroHealth Med. Ctr. Dept. Pediat., 1991. Mem.: Child Neurology Soc. (chmn. tng. program com. 1976—77, sec.-treas. 1978—81, pres. 1983—85, Lifetime Career Achievement award 2005), Innominatum Soc., No. Ohio Pediat. Soc., Am. Epilepsy Soc., Am. Pediat. Soc., Am. Soc. Human Genetics, Am. Acad. Neurology (chmn. residence exam. com. 1989—93), Am. Acad. Pediat., Case Western Res. U. Med. Alumni Assn. (pres. 1979, bd. of trustees 2002—), Pasteur Club. Home: 2 Oakshore Dr Bratenahl OH 44108-1118 Office: MetroHealth Med Ctr 2500 Metrohealth Dr Cleveland OH 44109-1900

EIBENSTEINER, RON, political organization administrator, venture capitalist; Co-founder, CFO Arden Med. Sys., 1983-87; pres., CEO, chmn. Mirror Techs., Inc., 1988-92, 94—, chmn., 1992-94; pres. Wyncrest Captial; dir. IntraNet Solutions, Inc., 2003—; chmn. OneLink Comm., Inc., 2003—, KidsFirst Scholarship Fund Minn., Inc., 2003—; dir. Ctr. Am. Experiment, 2003—. Co-founder Diametrics, OnHealth Network; chmn. Prodea Software. Chmn. Minn. Reps., 1999—; chair Minn. Rep. Party, 1999-. Mem.: Republican Nat. Conv. (com. on call 2000), Midwestern State Chmn.'s Assn. Office: Republican Party Minn Ste 250 525 Park St Saint Paul MN 55103-2145

EIBERGER, CARL FREDERICK, lawyer; b. Denver, Jan. 17, 1931; s. Carl Frederick and Madeleine Anastasia (Ries) E.; children: Eileen, Carl III, Mary, James. BS in Chemistry magna cum laude, U. Notre Dame, 1952, JD magna cum laude, 1954; MBA, Denver U., 1959. Sole practice, 1954-55; ptnr. Rovira, DeMuth & Eiberger, Denver, 1957—79, Eiberger, Stacy, Smith & Martin, Denver, 1979-96; prin. Carl F. Eiberger & Assocs., Denver, 1996—. Chmn. CBA/DBA/Econs. of Law Practice Coms.; co-founder CBA/Steering Com. Labor Law Com., Denver; arbitrator Am. Arbitration Assn.; asst. bar examiner, 1963-68; lectr. on continuing legal edn. Contbr. articles to legal jours. Bd. dirs. Colo. Assn. Commerce and Industry; pres. Prospect Recreation and Park Dist.; founder Applewood Athletic Club, Jefferson County; gen. counsel Denver Symphony Orch. Recipient merit award Jefferson County Commrs., merit cert. Jefferson County Homeowners, McCafferty Disting Svc. award U. Notre Dame Law Sch.; named Man of the Yr. Notre Dame Club of Denver, Vol. of Yr. Channel 9TV, Denver., Citizen of Yr., Lions Club Internat; Prospect Dist. Pk. named in his honor. Mem. ABA, Colo. Bar Assn. (bd. govs.), Denver Bar Assn. (nominated pres.), Notre Dame Law Assn. (bd. dirs. 1965—, exec. com. 1998—), Gov. Adv. Coun. to Colo dept. of labor, Notre Dame Club (pres., bd. dirs.), Athletic Club (Denver). Roman Catholic. Home and Office: 14330 Fairview Ln Golden CO 80401-2050 Office Phone: 303-278-0707. Fax: 303-278-0113.

EICHBERG, RODOLFO DAVID, physiatrist, educator; b. Pforzheim, Germany, July 26, 1937; came to the U.S., 1965; s. Julio and Ilse (Schonfarber) E.; m. Yvette Salama, May 21, 1965; children: William Amadeo, Matias David. Baccalaureate, St. Andrews Scots Sch., Argentina, 1955; MD, U. Buenos Aires, 1963. Diplomate Am Bd Phys Medicine and Rejab, cert. ind. med. examiner Am. Acad. Disability Evaluating Physicians, ringside physician Am. Assn. Profl. Ringside Physicians. Intern, resident Grace Hosp. Wayne State U., Detroit, 1965-67; orthopedic surgeon Mar Del Plata, Argentina, 1968-73; resident physical medicine NYU, 1973-75; pvt. practice Rehab. and Electro Diagnosis Assocs., P.C., Tampa, 1975-96, 98—; asst. prof. U. So. Fla., Tampa, 1975-93, clin. assoc. prof., 1994—; chief spinal cord injury rehab. Tampa Gen. Hosp., 1984-96; chief phys. medicine & rehab. VA Med. Ctr., New Orleans, 1997-98; med. dir. Meml. Hosp. Ctr. for Comprehensive Rehab., 1998—2004. Mem. state adv. coun. Head Spinal Cord Injuries, Tallahassee, 1976-96; clin. assoc. prof. La. State U. Sch. Medicine, 1997-98; physician advisor State of Fla. Athletic Commn., 1998-99; mem. advisor State of Fla. Agy. for Healthcare Adminstrn., 2001—; cons. MetLife Ins. Co., 2003-. Contbr. articles to profl. jours. Bd. trustees Congregation Schaaraizedek, Tampa, 1980-82. Recipient Honors award City of La Paz, Bolivia, 1994, Physician of Yr. award Tampa Bay Latin Am. Med. Soc., 1997. Mem. AMA, Am. Acad. Phys. Medicine and Rehab. (health policy legis. com. 1990-95), Am. Spinal Injury Assn. (internat. rels. rep. S.C. 1990-95), Assn. Med. Latino Americana de Rehab., Colombian Phys. Medicine Rehab. Soc. (corr.), Argentine Soc. Rehab. Medicine (corr.), Fla. Med. Assn., Fla. Soc. Phys. Medicine Rehab. (pres. 1994-96), Hillsborough County Med. Assn. (exec. coun. 2001-03), So. Soc. Phys. Medicine and Rehab. (pres. 1999-2000). Jewish. Avocations: boating, travel, aerobics. Office: Rehab and Electro Diag Assocs PA 2914 N Boulevard Tampa FL 33602-1208 Office Phone: 813-228-7696. Personal E-mail: eichberg@tampabay.rr.com.

EICHEL, EDWARD WILLIAM, psychotherapist, painter; b. Bklyn., June 8, 1932; s. Martin and Elizabeth (Shapiro) Eichelbaum. BFA, Sch. Art Inst. Chgo., 1958; MA, NYU, 1984; LHD (hon.), Med. U. of Americas, Nevis, W.I., 2003. Cert. experiential psychotherapist. Psychotherapist in pvt. practice, N.Y.C., 1969—; group therapy leader Aureon Inst., N.Y.C., 1968-70; founder, dir. Creativity Labs., Inc., 1971-84; pres. Marriage Sci., Inc., N.Y.C., 2001—. Instr. art Ea. Mich. U., Ypsilanti, 1965-66, Queens (N.Y.) Coll., 1966, L.I. U., Bklyn., 1967, St. Vincent's Hosp., N.Y.C., 1967-69, Hartford (Conn.) Art Sch., 1981-83; health educator Medgar Evers Coll., Bklyn., 1984, Flushing (N.Y.) Boys Club, 1985-86; counselor AIDS Hotline, N.Y.C. Health Dept., 1990; faculty 1995 Nat. Clin. Conf., Am. Acad. Clin. Sexologists. Artist: The Glass Cage: The Jerusalem Trial (of Adolf Eichmann), 1962 (original drawings on loan to Dallas Meml. Ctr. for Holocaust Studies), Israel Sketchbook, 1962, The Beast Book (by Jan Wahl), 1964; author: Kinsey, Sex and Fraud: The Indoctrination of a People, 1990, The Perfect Fit: How to Achieve Mutual Fulfillment, 1992; prodr. (video) The Coital Alignment Technique, version 1.1, 2002; contbr. articles to profl. jours. With USCG, 1951-54. Recipient award Oskar Kokoschka Acad., Salzburg, Austria, 1959, medal of merit Painters and Sculptors Soc. N.J., 1968; Louis Comfort Tiffany Fond. grantee for painting, 1967; George D. and Isabella A. Brown Fgn. Travel fellow, 1958. Mem. Soc. for Sci. Study of Sex (com. on sci. and profl. affairs 1986-87), Am. Assn. Sex Educators, Counselors and Therapists, Fedn. Modern Painters and Sculptors (v.p.), Nat. Expressive Therapy Assn. (hon. life; bd. dirs. 1979-83). Office Phone: 212-989-1826. E-mail: eichel@marriagescience.com.

EICHELBERGER, CHARLES BELL, retired career officer; b. LaGrange, Ga., Nov. 19, 1934; s. Charlie Wirt and Sybil Peavy (Johnson) E.; m. Jaqueline Ann Wood, July 17, 1955; children: Susan Christie Eichelberger Benator, Terrie Lynn Eichelberger Safranca. Cert. in Liberal Arts, Ga. Mil. Coll., 1955; BS in Law Enforcement, U. Nebr., 1971; MEd, Pepperdine U., 1977. Commd. 2d lt. U.S. Army, 1957, advanced through grades to lt. gen., 1989; comdr. U.S. Army Field Station, Berlin, 1978-80; div. chief Reconnaissance, Intelligence, Surveillance and Electronic Warfare Div., dep. chief of staff for ops. and plans, Dept. of Army, Washington, 1980-82; dep. comdt. U.S. Army Intelligence Ctr. and Sch., Ft. Huachuca, Ariz., 1982-84; dir. of intelligence (J-2) U.S. Cen. Command, MacDill AFB, Fla., 1984-86; dep. chief of staff for intelligence U.S. Army Europe, Heidelberg, Fed. Republic Germany, 1986-88, Dept. of Army, Washington, 1988-91; ret., 1991. Contbr. articles to profl. jours. Decorated D.S.M. with oak leaf cluster, Nat. Intelligence D.S.M. (CIA), Master Parachutist badge. Mem. Assn. Old Crows, Assn. U.S. Army, Ret. Officers' Assn. Home: 7121 Bailey Rd Sachse TX 75048-2542 E-mail: gen.ike@verizon.net.

EICHEN, JEFFREY L., lawyer; b. Rochester, NY; BSE cum laude, U. Penn., Wharton Sch. of Bus., 1987; JD cum laude, Georgetown U., 1990. Bar: NJ 1990, NY 1991, Fla. 1991, Pa. 1991, US Ct. of Appeals, Second, Third & Ninth Circuits, US Dist. Ct., NJ, NY (Ea. & So. Dist.), Pa. (Ea. Dist.), US Patent and Trademark Office. Ptnr. Schnader, Harrison, Segal & Lewis, Phila.; ptnr., intellectual property litigation Venable LLP, Washington, 2004—. Adjunct prof., intellectual property law Peirce Coll., Phila. Mem.: ABA, Bucks County Bar Assn., Pa. Bar Assn., NYC Bar Assn., AIPLA. Office: Venable LLP 575 7th St NW Washington DC 20004 Office Phone: 202-344-4985. Office Fax: 202-344-5775. Business E-Mail: jeichen@venable.com.

EICHENBERG, PETER THOMPSON, retired criminal investigator; s. Paul Lawrence Eichenberg and Patricia Ann Thompson; married, June 2, 1982; children: Cory Franklyn, Pete L. AS, BS, U. Albuquerque, 1986. Juvenile probation officer 2d Jud. Dist. Ct., 1974—75; security officer Fed. Protection Svc., 1975—76; fraud investigator, owner Albuquerque Investigation Svc., 1977—91; patrol operator, owner Peter Thompson & Assoc., 1978—80; recreation aide KAFB Youth Ctr., N.Mex., 1980—82, asst. dir., 1982—84; spl. dep. Sandoval County Sheriff's Dept., 1983—84; investigator litigation unit City Atty.'s Office, 1985—86; fraud investigator N.Mex. Workers' Compensation Adminstrn., 1991—2000; cons. Peter Eichenberg & Assocs., 2000—02; gaming auditor N.Mex. Gaming Control Bd., N.Mex., 2002—04. Instr., coach Youth Sports Assn., 1981—; dir. N.Mex. Respite Assn., Inc., 2001—04. Contbr. articles to profl. jours. Driver Catholic Charities of N.Mex.; sponsor Christian Found. for Children and Aging, Kansas City, Kans. With U.S. Army, 1965—71. John Robert Meml. scholar, 1986. Mem.: VFW, Nat. Notary Assn., Nat. Police and Firefighters Assn., Delta Epsilon Sigma. Democrat. Roman Catholic. Avocations: reading, fishing, softball, running. Mailing: PO Box 11671 Albuquerque NM 87192 Office: News in NMex Albuquerque NM 87192

EICHENWALD, HEINZ FELIX, physician; b. Switzerland, Mar. 3, 1926; came to U.S., 1936, naturalized, 1945; s. Ernst M. and Stella E.; m. Linda E. Moragné, July 20, 1995; children: Kathryn S., Eric C., Kurt A., Michael M. BA in Biochem. Scis. magna cum laude, Harvard U., 1946; MD, Cornell U., 1950. Intern, sr. asst. resident, sr. resident pediatrician N.Y. Hosp., 1950-51; asst. in pediat. Cornell U. Med. Sch., 1951-53, instr., then asst. prof., 1955-58, assoc. prof., then prof. pediat., 1958-64; USPHS instr. pediat. Emory U. Med. Sch., 1953-55; also vis. physician Grady and Crawford Long hosps., Atlanta; mem. staff N.Y. Hosp., 1958-65, attending pediatrician, 1963-65; vis. asst. prof. Albert Einstein Med. Sch., 1956-58; cons. Hosp. Spl. Surgery, N.Y.C., 1956-64, Patterson (N.J.) Gen. Hosp., 1958-64; prof. pediat., chmn. dept. U. Tex. Southwestern Med. Sch., Dallas, 1964-83; chief-of-staff Children's Med. Ctr., Dallas, 1964—; chief pediat. Parkland Meml. Hosp., Dallas, 1964—. Cons. St. Paul, Irving Cmty., Presbyn. Hosps., Dallas; chief hepatitis investigation unit, epidemiology br. USPHS, 1954-55; Richard Bruce Miller lectr. Harvard U. Med. Sch., 1960; lectr. Columbia U. Tchrs. Coll., 1960-64; chmn. Internat. Rsch. Confs. Mental Retardation, 1965-66; chmn. panel anti-infectives NAS-NRC, 1966-69; vis. prof. U. Saigon Med. Sch., 1968-72; Vanuxem lectr. Princeton U., 1970; bd. dirs. Dallas Free Clinic, 1970-74, Children's Devel. Ctr., Dallas, 1974—; mem. bd. maternal and child health NIH, 1974-78; cons. in field, mem. numerous profl. coms. Assoc. editor Pediatric Therapy, 1974; editor Practical Pediatric Therapy, 1985, Current Therapy in Pediatrics, 1989, Pediatric Therapy, 1993; mem. editorial bd. profl. jours.; contbr. numerous articles in profl. publs. Bd. dirs., chmn. exec. com. Lamplighter Sch., Dallas, 1971—; bd. dirs. Winston Sch., 1974. Recipient Career Rsch. award NIH, 1963-65, Alexander von Humboldt prize Govt. of Germany (then Fed. Republic Germany), 1979, Weinstein-Goldeson award United Cerebral Palsy Found., 1980; Markle scholar med. sci., 1953. Mem. Harvey Soc., Soc. Pediatric Rsch., Am. Pediatric Soc., Infectious Disease Soc. Am., N.Y. Acad. Scis., Tex. Pediatric Soc., Phi Beta Kappa, Sigma Xi, Alpha Omega Alpha. Office: 5323 Harry Hines Blvd Dallas TX 75390-9063 Personal E-mail: echo18@swbell.net.

EICHENWALD, KURT, writer; married; 3 children. B in Polit Sci, Swarthmore, 1983. Speechwriter Walter Mondale presidential campaign; bus. writer NY Times, NYC & Dallas, 1987—. Author: (non-fiction) Serpent on the Rock, 1995, The Informant, 2000 (Business Week bestseller), Conspiracy of Fools, 2005 (NY Times bestseller, Publishers Weekly bestseller). Finalist Pulitzer Prize, twice; recipient two George Polk awards.*

EICHHORN, FREDERICK FOLTZ, JR., retired lawyer; b. Gary, Ind., Oct. 16, 1930; s. Frederick Foltz and Adele D. (DeLano) E.; m. Julia Abel, Aug. 27, 1955; children: Jill, Thomas, Timothy, Linda. BS, Ind. U., 1952, JD, 1957. Bar: Ind. 1957, U.S. Ct. Appeals (7th cir.) 1957, U.S. Dist. Ct. (no dist.) Ind. 1957, U.S. Supreme Ct. 1973. Assoc. Gavit, Eichhorn, Gary, 1957-62; ptnr. Eichhorn, Eichhorn & Link, and predecessor firm, 1963-76; sr. ptnr. Eichhorn, Eichhorn & Link and predecessor firm, 1977-96; ret., 1996. Mem. Ind. Sesquicentennial Commn.; chmn. Lake County Cmty. Devel. Com., 1984; commr. Conf. Uniform State Law; bd. dirs. Gary Housing Authority, 1972—75, Planned Parenthood, Gary Police Civil Svc. Commn., 1975—82; bd. dirs., founder Miller Citizens Corp., 1971; bd. dirs. N.W. Ind. Symphony; trustee Ind. U., 1990—, bd. pres., 2002—; chmn. N.W. Ind. Forum, World Affairs Coun., Gary Regional Airport Task Force, 1989—94. With USAF, 1952—54. Fellow: Ind. Bar Found. (pres. 1985—86), Am. Bar Found.; mem.: ABA (membership chmn. for Ind. ho. of dels.), Ind. Soc. Chgo. (trustee 1989—92), Midwest Gas Assn. (legal affairs sect. 1982), Am. Gas Assn. (state rate litigation com. 1982, regulation of gas supplies com., state regulatory matters com.), Ind. Bar Assn. (treas. 1977—78, inst. chmn. white collar crime 1979, bd. mgr. 1979—80, v.p. 1983—84), Delta Tau Delta, Phi Delta Phi.

EICHHORN, GUNTHER LOUIS, chemist, researcher; b. Frankfurt am Main, Germany, Feb. 8, 1927; s. Fritz David and Else Regina (Weiss) E.; m. Lotti Neuhaus, June 25, 1964; children: David Mark, Sharon Julie. AB in Chemistry, U. Louisville, 1947; MS, U. Ill., 1948, PhD, 1950. From asst. prof. to assoc. prof. chemistry La. State U., 1950-57; commd. officer USPHS, 1954-57; assoc. prof. chemistry Georgetown U., 1957-58; guest scientist Naval Med. Rsch. Inst., 1957-58; chief sect. molecular biology Gerontology Rsch., NIH, Balt., 1958-78, chief lab. cellular and molecular biology and head sect. inorganic biochemistry, 1978-94; scientist emeritus NIH, 1994—. Counsellor La. State U. Hillel Found., 1952—54; pres. Nat. Inst. Child Health and Human Devel. Assembly of Scientists, 1972—73; mem. panel nickel NRC, 1974; organizer Am. Chem. Soc. Symposium on Function of Metal Ions in Biol. Processes, NY, 1961; disting. lectr. Mich. State U., 1972; lectr. Internat. Conf. on Biology and the Future of Mankind, Paris, 1974, Internat. Conf. on Coord. Chemistry, São Paulo, Brazil, 1977, Symposium on Coord. Chemistry and Cancer Chemotherapy, Toulouse, France, 1978; Watkins vis. prof. Wichita State U., 1983; organizer symposium Internat. Conf. Bioinorganic Chemistry, Netherlands, 1987; lectr. Internat. Conf. Molecular Mechanisms of Metal Toxicity and Carcinogenicity, Urbino, Italy, 1988, Bailar Symposium, Houston, 1992, G.L. Eichhorn Symposium on Metals, Nucleic Acids, Transcription and Aging, 1995; acting sci. dir. Nat. Inst. Aging, 1988; Henry Lardy lectr. S.D. U.; lectr. Metal Ion Nucleic Acid Interactions Conf., Amsterdam, 1991; organizer, presenter and lectr. in field; lectr. Internat. Conf. on Coord. Chemistry, Sao Paulo, Brazil, 1997, Internat. Symposium on Biomolecular Structure, Bangalore, India, 1984, Internat. Conf. on Coord. Chemistry, Athens, Greece, 1986. Editor: Inorganic Biochemistry, 1973; co-editor: Advances in Inorganic Biochemistry, 1978—; contbr. numerous articles to profl. jours. Gen. Aniline and Film Co. grantee, 1949; Ohio State U. fellow, summers 1951-52; recipient Woodcock medal U. Louisville, 1947, Md. Chemist of Yr. award, 1978, NIH Dir.'s award, 1979, Sr. Exec. Svc. bonus award, 1982, 88. Fellow AAAS, Am. Inst. Chemists, Gerontol. Soc. (fin. com. 1980-82, research and edn. com. 1982-83); mem. Am. Chem. Soc., N.Y. Acad. Scis., Am. Inst. Biol. Chemists, Biophys. Soc. Achievements include reseach in metal-ion induced stabilization and destabilization of DNA double helix, mechanism of RNA degradation by metal ions, nucleic acid conformational changes induced by metal ions; structural basis by which RNA polymerase produces fidelity in transcription (of DNA to RNA), catalysis of double bond cleavage by metal ions, discovery of Schiff base tautomers in vitamin B6-metal complexes; molecular age changes involving metal ions, proteins and nucleic acids. Home: 10500 Rockville Pike Rockville MD 20852-3350 Office: NIH NIA Gerontology Rsch Ctr 5600 Nathan Shock Dr Baltimore MD 21224-6825 Personal E-mail: eichhorngl@juno.com.

EICHINGER, MARILYNNE HILDEGARDE, museum administrator; children: Ryan, Kara, Julia, Jessica, Talik. BA in Anthropology and Sociology magna cum laude, Boston U., 1965; MA, Mich. State U., 1971. With emergency and outpatient staff Ingham County Mental Health Ctr., 1972; founder, pres., exec. dir. Impression 5 Sci. and Art Mus., Lansing, Mich., 1973-85; pres. Oreg. Mus. Sci. and Industry, Portland, 1985-95; bd. dirs. Portland Visitors Assn., 1985-95; pres. Informal Edn. Products Ltd., 1995—, Portland, 1995—. Bd. dirs. N.W. Regional Edn. Labs., 1991-97; instr. Lansing (Mich.) C.C., 1978; ptnr. Eyrie Studio, 1982-85; condr. numerous workshops in interactive exhibit design, adminstrn. and fund devel. for schs., orgns., profl. socs. Author: (with Jane Mack) Lexington Montessori School Survey, 1969, Manual on the Five Senses, 1974; pub. Mich. edit. Boing mag. Founder Cambridge Montessori Sch., 1964; bd. dirs. Lexington Montessori Sch., 1969, Mid-Mich. South Health Sys. Agy., 1978-81, Cmty. Referral Ctr., 1981-85, Sta. WKAR, 1981-85; active Lansing "Riverfest" Lighted Boat Parade, 1980; mem. state Health Coordinating Coun., 1980-82; mem. pres.'s adv. coun. Portland State U., 1986—90, mem. pres.' adv. bd., 1987-91; bd. dirs. Portland Visitors Assn., 1994-97, Friends of Tryon Creek State Pk., 2001—. Recipient Diana Cert. Leadership, YWCA, 1976-77, Woman of Achievement award, 1991, Cmty. Svc. award Portland State U., 1992, Cataloguer of Yr. award Catalog Success, 2005. Mem. Am. Assn. Mus., Oreg. Mus. Assn., Assn. Sci. and Tech. Ctrs. (bd. dirs. 1980-84, 88-93), Mus. Store Assn., Direct Mktg. Assn., Zonta Lodge (founder, bd. dirs. East Lansing club 1978), Internat. Women's Forum, Portland C. of C. Office: Informal Edn Products Ltd 2517 SE Mailwell Dr Milwaukie OR 97222 Office Phone: 503-794-7100. Business E-Mail: sales@museumtour.com.

EICHMAN, CHARLES MELVIN, school counselor, career assessment educator; b. Ft. Hays, Kans., June 16, 1950; s. Melvin Joseph and Barbara Ann (Bennett) E. BA, U. No. Colo., 1972; MA, Fuller Theol. Sem., 1974; cert., U. Mo., 1991, Idaho State U., 2002. Cert. vocat. evaluator, career guidance specialist, sch. counselor, job devel. specialist, secondary sch. tchr, sch. admin. K-12, vocational admin. Coord. youth activity YMCA, Glendale, Calif., 1972—74; counselor U. Colo., Colorado Springs, 1975—76; resident hall advisor U. No. Colo., Greeley, 1976—77; secondary tchr., coach Jefferson County Dist. R-1, Lakewood, Colo., 1978—80; pres., owner Big Sky C.F.M. and Mgmt. Resources, Rock Springs, Wyo., 1980—85; secondary tchr. Boulder Valley Dist. RE-2, Colo., 1986—88; vocat. evaluator and dir. Vocat. Evaluation Ctr. Platte County Dist. RE-111, Platte City, Mo., 1988—92; pres., owner Career Assessment Svcs., Arvada, Colo., 1992—94; sch. counselor, head dist. elem. at-risk student program Albany Schs. Re-1, Laramie, Wyo., 1993—94; sch. counselor, dir. dist. model Kids at Risk program Franklin Jr. H.S. and New Horizons Alt. H.S., Pocatello, 1994—; developer counseling program New Horizons Alt. H.S., Pocatello, 1994—. Affiliate faculty and site supr. Idaho State U., 2001—. Contbr. articles to profl. jours. Bd. dirs. YMCA, Pocatello, Idaho. Mem. ACA (one of 25 nat. legis. inst. participants 2000), NEA, Am. Vocat. Assn., Nat. Assn. Vocat. Edn. Spl. Needs Pers. (region III com. chair 1989-90, cert. of recognition 1990), Am. Sch. Counselors Assn., Am. Assn. Marriage and Family Therapy, Vocat. Evaluation and Work Adjustment Assn. (Wyo. rep. 1993-94, conf. presenter 1991), Mo. Vocat. Spl. Needs Assn. (exec. v.p. 1990-92, spkr. 1989-92, Outstanding Achievement award 1990-91, certs. of appreciation 1988-91), Mo. Sch. Counselors Assn. (spkr. 1989-91), Mo. Vocat. Assn. (spkr. 1992), Idaho Edn. Assn. (assembly del. 2001-03, state legis. del. 2002-05), Idaho Sch. Counseling Assn., Idaho Counseling Assn. (chair pub. policy and legis. com. 1999-2002, conf. presentor, exec. bd. dirs. legis. bill writing), Idaho Assn. Marriage and Family Therapy, Idaho Vocat. Guidance Assn. (com. chair 1997), Idaho Assn. Career Devel., Kiwanis. Avocations: handball, skiing, outdoor adventure, creative arts, swimming. Office: PO Box 4931 Pocatello ID 83205-4931 E-mail: CMEichman@aol.com.

EICHMAN, JOHN C., lawyer; b. Atlanta, Aug. 14, 1957; AB magna cum laude, Georgetown U., 1979; JD, U. Chgo., 1982. Bar: Tex. 1982, US Ct. Appeals 5th Cir., US Ct. Appeals 9th Cir., US Dist. Ct. No., Ea., We. & So. Districts Tex. Shareholder, litig. practice group Jenkens & Gilchrist, P.C., Dallas, firm v.p. bd. dirs. Mem.: ABA, Tex. Bar Found., Dallas Bar Assn. Office: Jenkens & Gilchrist PC Ste 3200 1445 Ross Ave Dallas TX 75202-2799 Office Phone: 214-855-4372. Office Fax: 214-855-4300. Business E-Mail: jeichman@jenkens.com.

EICHOLD, SAMUEL, internal medicine educator, curator; b. Mobile, Ala., May 27, 1916; s. Bernard H. and Myra (Solomon) E.; m. Charlotte Hartsig, Feb. 26, 1943; children: Beth, Alice, Bert. BS, Tulane U., 1937, MD, 1940; LLD (hon.), Spring Hill Coll., 1991. Intern Touro Infirmary, 1941; resident in internal medicine City Hosp. Mobile, 1941; pvt. practice medicine specializing in internal medicine Mobile, 1946-72; prof. medicine dept. internal medicine U. South Ala., Mobile, 1973-84, prof. emeritus, 1984—; hon. prof. Universidad Francisco Marroquin, 1985—; dir. continuing edn. U. South Ala., Mobile, 1975-82, perceptor history of medicine, 1976, perceptor rural and tropical medicine in developing nation, 1976—; med. dir. Central Plaza Towers Med. Ctr., 1981-98, Allen Meml. Home, 1973—2002, Cogburn Nursing Home, 1975-81, Hillhaven-Mobile, 1980-85, Mercy Med. Hosp., 1985-94; med. advisor Ala. Dept. Corrections, 1987—. Bd. dirs. Mercy Med., 1989-98, vice chmn. Old Mobile Restoration; bd. trustees Spring Hill Coll., 1991-2000, emeritus, 2001; pres. Mobile Revolving Fund for Hist. Properties, 1992-96. Author: Without Malice-100 Year History of Comic Cowboys of Mobile; mem. editorial bd. ADA Forecast mag., 1987-91, Ala. Treasure Forest Gulf Coast Hist. rev.; contbr. articles to profl. jours. Asst. county health officer Mobile County; bd dir. Preventable Disease, 1974-75; active Josiah C. Nott Found., 1980; founder, curator Heustis Med. Mus.; established Camp Seale Harris for Diabetic Children, 1947; sec./treas. Mobile Imfirmary, 1967-68; officer Mobile Tree Commn., 1968-73, chmn., 1973; bd. dirs. Mobile Symphony, Mobile Chamber Music Soc., Inc., 1952-75, Mobile Opera Assn., Hist. Mobile Preservation, 1977-84, Mobile chpt. ARC, 1951, Fine Arts Mus. of South, 1975-81, Mobile Mus., 1975-81, Mobile Hist. Mus., 1994—, Mobile Mus. Art, 1995—, Cmty. Found. S.W. Ala., 1998—, Friends Magnolia Cemetery, 1999—; active adv. bd. Ala. Hist. Commn., 1974—; pres. Mobile Hist. Devel. Found., 1973-75, bd. dirs., 1973-76; mem. council, chmn. regents Spring Hill Coll., 1984, trustee, 1991—. With USNR, 1941-69, comdr. ret. Recipient M.O. Beale Scroll of Merit award, 1951, 56, 59, Doc E award ADA, 1975, Ruth E. Hanson award 1978, Dept. Internal Medicine Faculty award, 1979, Comic Cowboy of Yr. award, 1982, Joe Treadwell award Ala. affiliate ADA, 1990; named Hon. Fellow Mobile Coll., 1977, Lifetime Achievement award Ala. Hist. Commn, 2004; named Mobilian of Yr. Mobile Civitan Club, 1989. Mem. AMA, ACP, Am. Assn. Diabetes Educators, Med. Soc. Mobile County (recognition award 1975), So. Med. Assn., Am. Diabetes Assn. (citation Mobile chpt. 1980, Becton Dickinson award 1981), Am. Soc. Internal Medicine, Ala. Diabetes Assn., Mobile County Physicians, Franklin Soc. (pres. 1975), Mobile Area C. of C. Clubs: Country of Mobile, Mobile Yacht. Lodges: Masons, Shriners, Kiwanis. Republican. Jewish. Home: 300 Chatham St Mobile AL 36604-3107 Personal E-mail: seicholdii@comcast.net.

EICKHOFF, THEODORE CARL, epidemiologist; b. Cleve., Sept. 13, 1931; s. Theodore Henry and Clara (Strasen) E.; m. Margaret Heinecke, Aug. 24, 1952; children: Stephen, Mark, Philip. BA, Valparaiso U., 1953; MD, Case Western Res. U., 1957. Diplomate Am. Bd. Internal Medicine. Intern, then resident Harvard Med. Svcs., Boston City Hosp., 1957-59; fellow in medicine Harvard Med. Sch.-Boston City Hosp., 1961-64; epidemiologist Ctr. for Disease Control, 1964-67; prof. medicine U. Colo. Med. Ctr., 1975—2003, prof. emeritus, 2003—, head divsn. infectious disease, 1967-80, vice chmn. dept. medicine, 1976-81; dir. medicine Denver Gen. Hosp., 1978-81; dir. internal medicine Presbyn./St. Luke's Med. Ctr., 1981-92. Cons. FDA, Ctrs. for Disease Control, Am. Hosp. Assn.; mem. nat. commn. orphan diseases HHS, 1986-90, mem. vaccines adv. com., 1995-99. Contbr. articles to med. jours. Served with USPHS, 1959-67. Recipient Commr.'s Spl. Citation, FDA, 1990, Trustee's award Am. Hosp. Assn., 1993. Mem. ACP (Disting. Internist award Colo. chpt. 1995), Am. Fedn. Clin. Rsch., Am. Soc. Clin. Investigation, Assn. Am. Physicians, Infectious Diseases Soc. Am. (sec. 1978-82, pres. 1983-84, Finland Lectureship award 1995), Am. Epidemiol. Soc. (pres. 1985-86). Home: 15 S Franklin Cir Greenwood Village CO 80121-1245 Office: Univ Colo Health Sci Ctr Div Infectious Disease B 168 Denver CO 80262-0001 Office Phone: 303-315-3052. Business E-Mail: theodore.eickhoff@uchsc.edu.

EIDE, HANS A., physicist, educator; b. Stavanger, Norway, Aug. 20, 1968; arrived in US, 1995; PhD in Atmospheric sci., U. of Alaska, Fairbanks, 2000; MS in Physics, U. of Bergen, Norway, 1993, BS in sci., 1990. Postdoctorate Stevens Inst. of Tech., Hoboken, NJ, 2000—02, rsch. asst. prof., 2003—. Mem. Dept. Energy/ARM (Atmospheric Radiation Program) Sci. Team, 1996—2001; participant SHEBA (Surface Heat Budget Artic Ocean) Ice Camp Experiment, Arctic Ocean, 1997—98. Contbr. articles to sci. jours. Cpl. NODECA, 1993—94, Norway. Mem.: Soc. Photo-Optical Instrumentation Engrs., Am. Geophys. Union. Office: Stevens Inst Tech Castle Point on Hudson Hoboken NJ 07030 E-mail: heide@stevens.edu.

EIDE, JOEL SYLVESTER, art consultant, appraiser; Dir. No. Ariz. U. Art Mus. and Galleries, 1975-98; prof. fine art No. Ariz. U., Flagstaff, 1970—98; fine art cons. Clarkdale, Ariz., 1999—. Home: 1926 N Crescent Dr Flagstaff AZ 86001-1114 Office: PO Box 82 Sycamore Canyon Rd Clarkdale AZ 86324 E-mail: eideart@bmol.com.

EIDSON, JAMES ANTHONY, lawyer; b. Atlanta, June 3, 1952; s. Howard Curtis and Emma Delores (Wilson) E.; m. Dianne Claudia Chesslock, Jan. 9, 1982. BS in Psychology cum laude, Ga. State U., 1977; JD cum laude, Mercer U., Macon, Ga., 1980. Bar: Ga. 1980; U.S. Ct. Appeals (11th cir.) 1984, U.S. Dist. Ct. (no. dist.) 1981, U.S. Dist. Ct. (mid. dist.) 1982, U.S. Dist. Ct. (so. dist.) 1982, U.S. Ct. Appeals (5th cir.) 1981. Assoc. atty. Powell, Goldstein, Frazier and Murphy, Atlanta, 1980-83; ptnr. Eidson & Assocs., P.C., Atlanta, 1983—. City atty. City of East Point, Ga., 1983-90, City of Fairburn, Ga., 1986-96; dir. First Bank of Ga., East Point, 1988—, First Bankshares, Inc., Hapeville, Ga., 1994—. Author: (Jour.) Mercer Law Review, 1978. Lt. USMC, 1969-80. Mem. Atlanta Lawyers Club, 191 Club. Republican. Methodist. Avocations: sailing, hunting. Home: 2515 Habersham Rd NW Atlanta GA 30305-3557 Office: Eidson & Assocs PC 600 S Central Ave Atlanta GA 30354-1928

EIFERMAN, JACK A., lawyer; b. Bklyn., Sept. 12, 1951; s. Irving and Deborah Eiferman; m. Fern Fisher. BA, SUNY, Albany, 1972; MPH, Yale U., 1975; JD, Rutgers U., 1980. Bar: N.J. 1980, N.Y. 1981, Mass. 1984. Legis./health cons. Citizens' Conf./Johnson Found., Hartford, Conn., 1974-77; assoc. Epstein, Becker & Green, N.Y.C., 1980-83; dep. gen. counsel Mass. Dept. Pub. Health, Boston, 1983-86; assoc. Goulston & Storrs, Boston, 1986-90, ptnr., 1991—. Chairperson of bd. Germaine Lawrence Sch., Arlington, Mass., 1997-99. Mem. Am. Health Lawyers Assn., Boston Bar Assn. (non-profit corp. statute revision com. 1986-87, 2000-01, chair, Tax Exempt Com. 2003-2005, Maguire Pro Bono award 1996). Office: Goulston & Storrs 400 Atlantic Ave Boston MA 02110-3333 Office Phone: 617-574-4074. E-mail: jeiferman@goulstonstorrs.com.

EIFLER, MARK ANTHONY, historian, educator; b. Louisville, Jan. 30, 1956; s. Waller Davenport and Virginia Marie (Livingston) Judy; m. Karen Elizabeth Perlenfein, Oct. 10, 1987; 1 child, Conor. PhD, U of CA, Berkeley, CA, 1985—92. Asst. prof. U of NE, Kearney, Nebr., 1992—98; assoc. prof. U of Portland, Portland, Oreg., 2000—. Author: (novels) (history) Gold Rush Capitalists. Office: U of Portland 5000 N Willamette Blvd Portland OR 97203-7803 Home: 4902 N Amherst Portland OR 97203 Office Phone: 503-943-7346. E-mail: eiflerm@up.edu.

EIGEL, EDWIN GEORGE, JR., mathematics professor, retired university president; b. St. Louis, June 4, 1932; s. Edwin George and Catherine (Rohan) E.; m. Marcia Jeanne Duffy, May 30, 1959; children: Edwin George III, Mary Marcia. BS, MIT, 1954; postgrad., U. Marburg, Germany, 1954-55; PhD, St. Louis U., 1961; DHL (hon.), U. Bridgeport, 1999. Lectr. math. George Washington U., 1961; asst. prof. math. St. Louis U., 1961-64, assoc. prof., 1964-69, asst. to dean Grad. Sch., 1965-67, prof., 1969-79, dean Grad. Sch., 1967-71, assoc. acad. v.p., 1971-72, acad. v.p., 1972-79, exec. v.p., 1973; assoc. prof. math. U. Bridgeport, Conn., 1979-82, prof., 1982—, Univ. prof., 1995—, v.p. acad. affairs, 1979-91, provost, 1981-91; pres., 1991-95; pres. emeritus U. Bridgeport, Conn., 1995—. Mem. adv. com. on accreditation Conn. Dept. Higher Edn., 1989—92. Commr. McDonnell Planetarium, St. Louis, 1972-79; mem. Conn. Disting. Citizens Task Force on Quality Tchg., 1982-83; acting exec. dir. Bridgeport Area Consortium Colls. and Univs., 1989; bd. dirs. Bridgeport Pub. Edn. Fund, 1993-97, Bridgeport Regional Bus. Coun., 1994-95, United Way Ea. Fairfield County, 1994-98, Univ. Bridgeport, 1995—. Capt. U.S. Army, 1959—61. Mem. Am. Math. Soc., Math. Assn. Am., Rotary (bd. dirs. Bridgeport 1994-97), Rotary Internat. (Paul Harris fellow), Phi Beta Kappa, Phi Beta Kappa Fellows, Sigma Xi, Pi Mu Epsilon, Phi Kappa Phi, Beta Gamma Sigma, Upsilon Pi Epsilon, Sigma Beta Delta. Achievements include: research in math. applications of computers. Home: 33 Pepperbush Ln Fairfield CT 06824-4036 E-mail: egeorgee@optonline.net.

EIGEN, HOWARD, pediatrician, educator; b. N.Y.C., Sept. 8, 1942; s. Jay and Libbie (Kantrowitz) E.; children: Sarah Elizabeth, Lauren Michelle. BS, Queens Coll., 1964; MD, Upstate N.Y. Med. Ctr., Syracuse, 1968. Diplomate Am. Bd. Pediatrics, Am. Bd. Pediatric Pulmonology, Am. Bd. Critical Care Medicine, Nat. Bd. Med. Examiners (mem. pediatric test com. 1986-90). Resident in pediatrics Upstate Med. Ctr., Syracuse, 1968-71; fellow in pediatric pulmonology Tulane U., New Orleans, 1973-76; asst. prof. pediatrics Ind. U., Indpls., 1976-84, prof., 1984-96, Billie Lou Wood Prof. pediatrics, 1996—. Assoc. chmn. of Pediatrics for Clin. Affairs, dir. pediatric intensive care, pulmonology sect. Riley Hosp. for Children, med. dir. ambulatory care, 1989— Co-editor: Respiratory Disease in Children: Diagnosis and Management; assoc. editor Pediatric Pulmonology, 1984-91; contbr. articles to profl. jours. Served to maj. U.S. Army, 1971-73. Fellow Am. Acad. Pediatrics (pres. chest sect. 1983-85, pulmonology 1986—), Am. Thoracic Soc., Am. Bd. Pediatrics, Am. Lung Assn. (pres. Ind. 1984-85). Avocation: tennis. Office: Ind U Dept Pediatrics 702 Barnhill Dr Rm 2750 Indianapolis IN 46202-5128

EIGER, RICHARD WILLIAM, retired publisher; b. N.Y.C., May 11, 1933; s. William and Helen M. (Fetten) E.; m. Ruth B. Engelke; 1 child, Keith R. BFA, Pratt Inst., 1955; MBA, NYU, 1960. With Western Pub. Co., N.Y.C., 1958-80, pub. dir., 1968-74, v.p. pub., 1975-80; pres. Macmillan Ednl. Co., N.Y.C., 1980-91; sr. v.p. Macmillan Pub. Co., N.Y.C., 1980-91; v.p. K-III Reference Corp. (now PRIMEDIA Reference Corp.), Mahwah, N.J., 1991-93; pub. The World Almanac, 1993-98; ret., 1998. Cons. Langenscheidt Pub. Co., 2002—, VirtuelEd., Inc., 2000—; prof. pub. Pratt Inst. Sch. Info. and Libr. Sci., 2003—; advisor Bearport Pub. Co., 2003—. Bd. dirs. alumni bd. The Pratt Inst., N.Y.C., 1986—, trustee, 1992—, mem. exec. com., 1995—, sec. 1996—, chmn. devel. com., 1997—; mem. pub. com. Brandeis U., Waltham, Mass., 1993-2000; trustee The Katharine Gibbs Sch., Montclair, N.J., 1995-2001, Piscataway, N.J., 1996-2001, Hist. Soc. Princeton, NJ, 2002—, Del. Coll. Art and Design, Wilmington, 2004—. Lt. U.S. Army, 1956-57. Home: 6 Otter Creek Rd Skillman NJ 08558-2364 E-mail: dickeiger@aol.com.

EIGLER, DONALD MARK, physicist; b. L.A., Mar. 23, 1953; s. Irving Baer and Evelin Muriel (Baker) E.; m. Roslyn Winifred Rubesin, Nov. 2, 1986. BA, U. Calif., San Diego, 1975, PhD in Physics, 1984; D (hon.), Delft U. Tech., 2002. Rsch. assoc. U. Köln (Fed. Republic Germany), 1975-76, U. Calif., San Diego, 1977-84, postdoctoral rsch. assoc., 1984, assoc. rsch. physicist dept. physics, 1986; postdoctoral mem. tech. staff AT&T Bell Labs., Murray Hill, N.J., 1984-86; rsch. staff mem. IBM, San Jose, Calif., 1986-93, IBM fellow, 1993—. Alexander M. Cruickshank lectr. in phys. sci. (Gordon Rsch. Confs.), 1994; Alvin Weinberg lectr. Oak Ridge (Tenn.) Nat. Labs., 2001; Regents lectr. UCLA, 2001; Hubert James lectr. Purdue U., 2002; conf. chmn. Gordon Rsch. Conf. on Chemistry & Physics of Nanostructure Fabrication, 2004. Co-winner 1993-94 Newcomb Cleveland prize AAAS; recipient Dannie Heineman prize Göttingen Acad. Scis., 1995, Outstanding Alumnus award U. Calif. San Diego alumni Assn., 1998, Nanoscience prize Conf. on Atomically Controlled Interfaces and Surfaces, 1999. Fellow AAAS, Am. Phys. Soc. (Davisson-Germer prize 2001), Max Planck Soc. Office: IBM Almaden Rsch Ctr 650 Harry Rd San Jose CA 95120-6099

EIGNER, RICHARD MARTIN, lawyer; b. Swampscott, Mass., July 7, 1929; s. Israel and Bessie (Polansky) E.; m. Beverly Israel, Dec. 26, 1964; children: David, Danielle. AB, Dartmouth Coll., 1951; LLB, Harvard U., 1954. Bar: Calif. 1955, Mass. 1956. Ptnr. Pillsbury Winthrop, San Francisco, 1965—. Cons. Internat. Tax Project, Am. Law Inst., 1981-86. Mem. Internat. Tax Planning Assn., Internat. Fiscal Assn., Phi Beta Kappa. Jewish. Home: 2955 Piedmont Ave Berkeley CA 94705-2342 Office: Pillsbury Winthrop 50 Fremont St Fl 9 San Francisco CA 94105 E-mail: reigner@pillsburywinthrop.com.

EIGNER, WILLIAM WHITLING, lawyer; b. Dover, Ohio, Feb. 4, 1959; s. Stanley Spencer and Jeraldine (Lippy) E.; m. Jeanne Beach, May 24, 1987. BA, Stanford U., 1981; JD, U. Va., 1986. Bar: Calif. 1986, U.S. Dist. Ct. (so. dist.) Calif. 1986. Jud. intern U.S. Supreme Ct., Washington, 1981; assoc. Higgs, Fletcher & Mack, San Diego, 1986-89, Procopio, Cory, Hargreaves & Savitch, LLP, San Diego, 1989-95, ptnr., 1995—. Bd. dirs. Concerto Networks, Inc., Mundoval Fund; mem. bd. advisors QuantumThink Group, Inc. (QThink), Skyriver Comms., Inc., Bioelectric Med. Solutions, Inc., Am. Eco-Energy, Mobile DataComm; mem. San Diego Venture Group; mem. San Diego Telecom Coun. and chmn. policy com. Contbr. articles to profl. jours. Trustee, La Jolla (Calif.) Town Coun., 1988-92, chmn. land use com., 1988-90; trustee La Jolla Country Day Sch. Recipient spl. commendation San Diego City Coun., Vol. Advocate of Yr., San Diego Regional C. of C., 2004. Mem. ABA, State Bar Calif., San Diego County Bar Assn. (bus. sects.), San Diego Regional C. of C. (bd. dirs. 1998-2001, 03—, chmn. bus. recognition and awards com. 1989-98, chmn. emerging bus. com. 1998-2000, pub. policy com.). Republican. Jewish. Avocations: tennis, Civil War history. Office: Procopio Cory Hargreaves & Savitch LLP 530 B St Ste 2100 San Diego CA 92101-4496 Office Phone: 619-515-3210. Business E-Mail: wwe@procopio.com.

EIGSTI, ROGER HARRY, retired insurance company executive; b. Vancouver, Wash., Apr. 17, 1942; s. Harry A. and Alice E. (Huber) E.; m. Mary Lou Nelson, June 8, 1963; children: Gregory, Ann. BS, Linfield Coll., 1964. CPA, Oreg., Wash. Staff CPA Touche Ross and Co., Portland, Oreg., 1964-72; asst. to controller Safeco Corp., Seattle, 1972-78, controller, 1980, Safeco Life Ins. Co., Seattle, 1978-80; pres. Safeco Credit Co., Seattle, 1980-81, Safeco Life Ins. Co., Seattle, 1981-85; exec. v.p., CFO Safeco Corp., Seattle, 1985, CEO, chmn., 1985-2001. Bd. dirs. Ind. Colls. of Wash., Seattle, 1981-87, bus. dir. Seattle Repertory Theatre, 1981—, bd. dirs. 1981—. Mem. Am. Inst. CPA's, Life Office Mgmt. Assn. (bd. dirs. 1983—), Seattle C. of C. (chmn. metro budget rev. com. 1984—). Clubs: Mercer Island (Wash.) Country (treas., bd. dirs. 1981-84); Central Park Tennis. Republican. Home: 1503 Parkside Dr E Seattle WA 98112-3719

EIKENBERRY, JILL, actress; b. New Haven, Jan. 21, 1947; m. Michael Tucker; 1 stepchild. Student, Yale U. Actress stage prodns. Saints, 1976, Uncommon Women and Others, 1977, Watch on the Rhine, 1980, Onward Victoria, 1980, Holiday, 1982, Porch, 1984, Fine Line, 1984, Life Under Water, 1985, A Picasso, 2005; feature film appearances include Between the Lines, 1977, An Unmarried Woman, 1977, The End of the World in Our Ususal Bed in a Night Full of Rain, 1978, Rich Kids, 1979, Butch and Sundance: The Early Days, 1979, Hide in Plain Sight, 1980, Arthur, 1981, Grace Quigley, 1985, The Manhattan Project, 1986; TV movie appearances include The Deadliest Season, 1977, Orphan Train, 1979, Swan Song, 1980, Sessions, 1983, Kane and Abel, 1985, Assault and Matrimony, 1987, Family Sins, 1987, A Stoning in Fulham County, 1988, My Boyfriend's Back, 1989, The Diane Martin Story, The Secret Life of Archie's Wife, 1990, An Inconvenient Woman, 1991, Living A Lie, 1991, Doc: The Dennis Littky Story, 1992, Chantilly Lace, 1993, Parallel Lives, 1994, The Other Woman, 1995, My Very Best Friend, 1996, Gone in a Heartbeat, 1996; teleplay Uncommon Women and Others, 1978; regular (TV series) L.A. Law, 1986-94 (Emmy nomination, Supporting Actress - Drama Series, 1994). Office: care William Morris Agency 151 S El Camino Dr Beverly Hills CA 90212-2704*

EIKENBERRY, KARL W., career military officer; BS, U.S. Mil. Acad.; MS in East Asian Studies, fellow in Nat. Security, Harvard U.; PhD in Polit. Sci., Stanford U. Commd. 2d lt. U.S. Army, advanced through grades to lt. gen., 2005; def. attaché Def. Intelligence Agy., Beijing, 1997—2000; asst. divsn. comdr. 25th Infantry Divsn. U.S. Army, Schofield Barracks, Hawaii, 2000—01, dep. dir. chief Strategy, Plans & Policy Directorate Washington, 2001—02; chief, Office of Mil Cooperation U.S. Embassy, Kabul, Afghanistan, 2002—03; dir. J-5 US Pacific Command, Camp H.M. Smith, Hawaii, 2003—05; comdr. Combined Forces Command, Afghanistan, 2005—. Decorated Def. Superior Svc. medal, Legion of Merit award with oak leaf cluster, Def. Meritorious Svc. medal with oak leaf cluster, Meritorious Svc. medal with 5 oak leaf clusters, Joint. Svc. Commendation medal, Army Commendation medal with 4 oak leaf clusters, Army Achievement medal with oak leaf cluster. Office: US Ctrl Command 7115 S Boundary Boulevard Macdill Afb FL 33608*

EIKNER, TOD BAYARD, lawyer; b. Ft. Lauderdale, Fla., Sept. 8, 1967; s. Charles Buford and Jacqueline (Tod) E. JD, Mercer U., 1994. Bar: Fla. 1994, Ga. 1994, U.S. Dist. Ct. (mid. dist.) Fla. 1994, U.S. Dist. Ct. (so. dist.) Ga. 1994. Atty. Cole, Stone, Stoudemire, Morgan & Dore, P.A., Jacksonville, Fla., 1994-2001; ptnr. Eraclides, Johns, Hall, Gelman, Eikner & Johanneson, Jacksonville, 2001—. Mem. Jacksonville Claims Assn. (membership chmn., bd. dirs. 1994-98). Office: 4811 Atlantic Blvd Jacksonville FL 32207 Home: 2203 Miller Oaks Ct Jacksonville FL 32217-3506 E-mail: teikner@insdefense.net.

EILER, GERTRUDE S., writer; b. Syracuse, N.Y., July 7, 1914; d. Edward Franklin and Gertrude (Van Duyn) Southworth; m. George Phelps, Jan. 4, 1935 (div. 1950); children: William Henry Phelps, George Phelps, James Phelps; m. Edward S. Jay, Dec. 18, 1954 (dec. Aug. 1962); m. George R. Eiler, Aug. 24, 1963 (dec. May 1984); stepchildren: Larry Eiler, Roger Eiler. Student, Wellesley Coll., 1932-33. Asst. sec., treas., v.p. Iroquois Pub. Co., Inc., Syracuse, 1950-60; salesperson Roney Realty Co., Syracuse, 1960-62; registrar Onondaga C.C., Syracuse, 1962-64; asst. editor Singer Pub. Co., 1966-67; propr. Log Cabin Gift Shop, Cuyler, N,Y., 1968-76; freelance editor, typist Syracuse, 1980-90; owner, editor Pine Grove Press, Syracuse, 1990—2002. Mem. Social Art Club Syracuse (sec. 1983-). Avocation: writing. Home: 1290 Boyce Rd Apt A311 Pittsburgh PA 15241

EILER, HENRY PHILIP (HARRY EILER), foundation administrator; b. N.Y.C., May 2, 1929; s. Philip Louis and Elsie Marie (Staubach) Eiler; m. Alice Jezek. BA in History, Wagner Coll., 1950; PhD in Music, Stanford U., 2004. Pub., owner Artel Publs. Inc., Studio City, Calif., 1960—80; hotelier Admiralty Club, Jamaica, 1980—85; chmn. Eiler Found., Encinitas, Calif., 2004—. Bd. dirs. Wave Link, Inc. Composer: Orfeo Suite, Rubaiyat Suite, Caribe, Sonata in G Major. Bd. dirs. Either/Or Ensemble, N.Y.C., 2005—. Sgt. USAF, 1951—55. Grantee, Encinitas Commn. Arts, 2005. Mem.: Am. Composers (pres. 2004), Rotary (hon.). Republican. Lutheran. Avocations: orchidist, lecturing in music.

EILERS, MARLENE ANNA LOUISE, librarian, royal genealogist; b. Teaneck, NJ, June 14, 1954; d. Thomas Theodore and Gertrude Clara (Last) E.; m. William Allen Koenig, Nov. 25, 1995. BA in Eng., William Paterson Coll. of N.J., 1976; MLS, SUNY, Albany, 1981. News libr. Assoc. Press, N.Y.C., 1981-89; libr. mgr. CNN, Washington, 1989-94; rschr. Daily Telegraph, 1999—2001; libr. Am. Soc. Landscape Architects, 2002—. Author: Queen Victoria's Descendants, 1987, 3d edit. 2004, A Grand Alliance, 2004; co-editor: A Romanov Diary, 1989; pub. Royal Book News, 1985—; contbr. articles to mags. Republican. Lutheran. Home: 5590 Jowett Ct Alexandria VA 22315-5542

EILTS, HERMANN FREDERICK, international relations educator, retired diplomat; b. Weissenfels Saale, Germany, Mar. 23, 1922; came to U.S., 1926; naturalized, 1930; s. Friedrich Alex and Meta Dorothea (Pruser) E.; m. Helen Josephine Brew, June 12, 1948; children: Conrad Marshall, Frederick Lowell. BA, Ursinus Coll., 1942, LLD, 1960; MA, Johns Hopkins U., 1947; postgrad., U. Pa., 1950-51. Joined Fgn. Svc., Dept. State, 1947; 3d sec., vice consul Tehran, Iran, 1947-48, Jidda, Saudi Arabia, 1948-50; consul prin. officer Aden, 1951-53; 2d sec., consul Taiz, Yemen, 1951-53; 2d sec., consul, chief polit. sect. Bahdad, Iraq, 1954-56; officer in charge Baghdad Pact affairs Dept. State, Washington, 1957-59, officer in charge Arabian Peninsula affairs, 1959-61; 1st sec. Am. Embassy, London, 1962-64, counsellor, dep. chief of mission Tripoli, Libya, 1964-65; amb. to Saudi Arabia, 1965-70; dep. commandant for internat. affairs, diplomatic adviser U.S. Army War Coll., Carlisle Barracks, Pa., 1970-73; amb. to Egypt Cairo, 1973-79; Disting. Univ. prof. internat. rels. Boston U., 1979—, chmn. dept. polit. sci., 1982-87, chmn. dept. internat. rels., 1989-93, acad. coord., mil. edn. div., 1990-93, prof. emeritus, 1993—. 1st lt. M.I., AUS, 1942-45. Decorated Purple Heart, Bronze Star; recipient Arthur Flemming award, 1958, Disting. Civilian Honor award Dept. Army, 1973, Disting. Honor award Dept. State, 1979, Joseph C. Wilson award, 1979, Disting. Alumnus award Johns Hopkins U., 1980, All-Pa. Coll. Alumni Assn. citation, 1987, Am. Foreign Svc. cup Dept. State, 1992; named Disting. Fellow U.S. Army War Coll., 1991. Fellow Royal Geog. Soc., Royal Asiatic Soc.; mem. Am. Fgn. Svc. Assn., Middle East Inst., Royal Cen. Asian Soc. Mem. Evang. Reformed Ch. Address: 67 Cleveland Rd Wellesley MA 02481-2434

EILTS, SUSANNE ELIZABETH, physician; b. Council Bluffs, Iowa, Oct. 12, 1955; d. Ervin Edwin and Mary Margaret (Leonard) E. BS, Nebr. Wesleyan U., 1976; MD, U. Iowa, 1980; M of Pub. Health, Johns Hopkins U., 2004. Diplomate Am. Bd. Internal Medicine. Intern, resident U. Nebr. Med. Ctr., Omaha, 1980-83; pvt. practice, Omaha, 1983—. Clin. instr. internal medicine U. Nebr., Omaha, 1983-2001, asst. prof., 2001—; med. dir. Amb. Nursing Home, Omaha, 1990-92; quality assurance reviewer Sunderbruch Corp. Nebr., Lincoln, 1990-92; v.p. quality assurance Internal Med. Assocs., 1993-95, bd. dirs.; chmn. dept. medicine Clarkson Hosp., 1994-95, sec.-treas. med. staff, 1996-98, mem. staff exec. com., 1994-98, med. outcomes coun., 1994-96; v.p. pvt. practice category Nebr. Health Sys., 1998-99, pres., 2000; bd. examiners in medicine and surgery Nebr. State Dept. Health, 1996-2001, chair, 2000, sec., 1998, vice chair, 1999; mem. Nebr. Health Care Facility Licensure Reform Rationale Task Force, 1997, Health Professions Licensure Sys. Reengring., 1998; bd. dirs. Clarkson Regional Health Svcs., Pvt. Practice Assocs. LLC, chmn. enrollment com. Mem. ACP, Am. Geriatric Soc., Nebr. Med. Assn. (alt. del. 1990-91, del. 1992, young physician com. 1989-93, com. health care reform 1993-94, legis. com. 1993—, legis. subcom. for HMO/PPO policy statement 1995-96, chmn. advocacy com. 1998-2000, spkr. ho. of dels. 2000-2004), Am. Women's Med. Assn. Nebr. (sec. 1987), Nebr. Soc. Internal Medicine (bd. dirs. 1994-98), Beta Beta Beta, Phi Kappa Phi, Phi Lambda Upsilon. Avocations: bicycling, playing the pennywhistle. Office: Westroads Med Group 10170 Nicholas St Omaha NE 68114

EIMER, NATHAN PHILIP, lawyer; b. Chgo., June 26, 1949; s. Irving A. and Charlotte Eimer; m. Lisa S. Eimer; children: Micah Jacob, Noah Joseph, Daniel Jordan, Anna Beatrice. AB in Econs. magna cum laude, U. Ill., 1970; JD cum laude, Northwestern U., 1973. Bar: Ill. 1973, U.S. Supreme Ct. 1978, N.Y. 1985, Tex. 1998. Assoc. Sidley & Austin, Chgo., 1973-80, ptnr., 1980—2000, mem. exec. com., 1999; founding ptnr. Eimer Stahl Klevorn & Solberg, Chgo., 2000—. Adj. prof. Law Sch., Northwestern U., Chgo., 1989-96. Note and comment editor Northwestern U. Law Rev., 1972-73. Bd. dirs. Chgo. Lawyers Com. for Civil Rights, 1991—, pres., 1993-94; bd. dirs. UNICEF, 1992-93, Infant Welfare Soc., Chgo., exec. v.p., 1992-96, pres., 1996-98; mem. adv. bd. Children & Family Justice Ctr., Northwestern U. Legal Clinic, 1996—. Mem. ABA, Univ. Club. Office: Eimer Stahl Klevorn & Solberg LLP Ste 1100 224 S Michigan Ave Chicago IL 60604 Office Phone: 312-660-7601. Business E-Mail: neimer@eimerstahl.com.

EIN, DANIEL, allergist; b. Liege, Belgium, Nov. 26, 1938; arrived in U.S., 1941; s. Max Motel and Sabine (Toeman) E.; m. Marion Hess, June 25, 1961 (div. 1978); children: Mark David, Jon Spencer; m. Marina Wallach, Apr. 10, 1988; stepchildren: Jacqueline A. Newmyer, Tory Newmyer. AB, Columbia U., 1959; MD, Albert Einstein Coll. Medicine, 1964. Diplomate Am. Bd. Internal Medicine, Am. Bd. Allergy and Immunology. Intern Bronx Mcpl. Hosp., N.Y.C., 1964—65; staff assoc. Nat. Cancer Inst., Washington, 1965—67, clin. assoc., 1967—68; asst. resident Mass. Gen. Hosp., Boston, 1968—69; sr. investigator Nat. Cancer Inst., Washington, 1969—71; pvt. practice Washington, 1971—2005. Clin. prof. medicine George Washington U., Washington, 1984—, chief divsn. allergy, 2005—; founder, pres. Capital Physicians Network, 1994-99. Contbr. articles to profl. jours. and newspapers. Fellow ACP, Am. Acad. Allergy (AMA del. 1994), Am. Coll. Allergy (bd. dirs. 2000-03, v.p. 2004); mem. Joint Coun. of Allergy (pres. 1998-2000), Med. Soc. of D.C. (pres. 1991), Greater Washington Allergy Soc. (pres. 1979), Cosmos Club. Jewish. Achievements include discovery of OZ factors on human immunoglobulin light chains. Home: 4636 Kenmore Dr NW Washington DC 20007-1924 Office Phone: 202-785-0668. Personal E-mail: dein1@bellatlantic.net.

EINAUDI, LUIGI ROBERTO, international organization official, diplomat; b. Cambridge, Mass., Mar. 1, 1936; s. Mario and Manon (Michels) E.; m. Carol Peacock, Aug. 26, 1958; children: Maria, Elisabeth, Mario, Peter. AB cum laude, Harvard Coll., 1957; postgrad., Harvard U., 1959-61, PhD, 1966. Tchg. fellow Harvard U., 1960-61; instr. Wesleyan U., 1961-62; with social sci. dept. Rand Corp., 1962-73; vis. prof. U. Calif., L.A., 1964-73; mem. policy planning staff US Dept. State, Washington, 1974-77, dir. inter-Am. regional planning office, 1977-89, sr. adviser policy planning staff, 1993-97, acting dir., 1994; U.S. rep. with rank of amb. OAS, Washington, 1989-93, spl. rep. of sec. gen. for Honduras and Nicaragua, 1999-2000, asst. sec. gen., 2000—, acting sec. gen., 2004—. Mem. Coun. on Fgn. Rels.; mem. internat. coun. Inst. Conflict Analysis and Resolution, George Mason U., 1991—; U.S. spl. envoy for Ecuador-Peru peace talks, 1995-98; mem. sci. com. Luigi Einaudi Found., Turin, Italy, 1995—; sr. fellow multilateral govt. and conflict resolution Inter-Am. Dialogue, Washington, 1997-2000; adj. prof. Georgetown U., 1998, 99; mem. edn. adv. bd. U.S. Army, 1998-2000. Author: Beyond Cuba, 1974; contbr. numerous articles to profl. jours. With U.S. Army, 1957-59. Bartels World Affairs fellow Cornell U., 1993; recipient Disting. Exec. Presdl. Rank award, 1987, Robert C. Frasure Meml. award, 1997, Disting. Honor award Sec. of State, 1997, Gran Cruz, Orden "el Sol del Peru", 1999, Gran Cruz, Orden "Nacional al Merito", Ecuador, 1999. Mem. Acad. Am. Diplomacy. Office: OAS 17th St and Constitution Ave NW Washington DC 20006

EINFINGER, CARMEN MIRANDA, artist, computer graphics designer; b. Nottingham, Eng., Apr. 26, 1950; came to U.S., 1980; m. Michael Ayers, Aug. 1975 (div. 1978). BA in Painting, SUNY, Buffalo, 1984; MA in Portuguese and Brazilian Studies, Brown U., 1989. Moderator discussion panel Soho Photo Gallery, N.Y.C., 1990; co-dir. Czech-Mate Prodns., N.y.C., 1991. One-woman shows Essex Gallery, Buffalo, 1985, List Art Ctr., Brown U., Providence, 1989, Nada Gallery, N.Y.C., 1991, Ridge Street Gallery, N.Y.C., 1993; exhibited in group shows Contemporary Arts Ctr., Buffalo, 1984, 85, Barbara Schuller Gallery, Buffalo, 1990, Albright-Knox Gallery, Buffalo, 1990, Home for Contemporary Theater and Art Gallery, N.Y.C., 1991, R&J Fine Art, N.Y.C., 1995, also others; represented in pvt. collections; work reviewed in various publs. Am. liaison Pan-European Cultural Event. 1990. Scholar Brown U., 1987; Andrew Mellon fellow, 1987; grantee Artists Space, N.Y.C., 1991.

EINHORN, DAVID ALLEN, lawyer; b. Bklyn., Dec. 11, 1961; s. Harold and Jane Ellen (Wiener) Einhorn. BA in Computer Sci. magna cum laude, Columbia U., 1983, JD, 1986. Bar: N.Y. 1987, DC 1988, U.S. Dist. Ct. (so. and ea. dists.) N.Y. 1989, U.S. Ct. Appeal (fed. cir.) 1992, U.S. Dist. Ct. (no. dist.) Calif. 1994, U.S. Dist. Ct. Conn. 2003. Assoc. Kaye, Scholer, Fierman, Hays & Handler, N.Y.C., 1986-89; ptnr. Anderson Kill & Olick, PC, N.Y.C., 1989—. Lectr. Am. Conf. Inst.; arbitrator Nat. Arbitration Forum, 2002—. Co-author: (2-vol. treatise) Patent Licensing Transactions; editor-in-chief: Intellectual Property for the New Millenium, 1997—; contbr. articles to profl. jours. Lt. col. JAGC, Army Divsn. N.Y. Guard, 1987—. Named to Order of Merit, Les Amis du Vin, 1982; recipient Nat. prize, Nathan Burkan Copyright Essay Competition, 1985, Off Off Broadway Rev. award for producing Ionesco Fest.; Harlan Fiske Stone scholar, Columbia U., 1985. Mem.: ABA (chmn. software patent subcom. 1988—91, software licensing subcom. 1991—95, software copyright subcom. 1995—96, chmn. broadcasting, sound recordings, and performing artists com. 2000—02, chmn. com. online trademark issues 2002—, chmn. com. online copyright issues 2004—), Licensing Execs. Soc. (lectr.), DC Bar Assn. (computer law sect.), Internat. Trademark Assn., N.Y. Intellectual Property Law Assn., Am. Intellectual Property Law Assn. (chmn. software copyright subcom. 1999—), Intellectual Property Owners Assn. (chmn. cybersquatting com. 2003—), Untitled Theater Co. #61, Ltd. (chmn. bd. dirs., producing dir., treas. 1994—), Tasters Guild (v.p., bd. dirs. 1997—), N.Y. Soc. Mil. and Naval Officers (v.p. 1995—). Democrat. Jewish. Avocations: tennis, wine tasting, theater. Office: Anderson Kill & Olick PC 1251 Ave of the Americas New York NY 10020-1182 Home: 36 Sutton Pl S Apt 7-A New York NY 10022 Office Phone: 212-278-1359. Business E-Mail: deinhorn@andersonkill.com.

EINHORN, JERZY, internist, endocrinologist, consultant; b. Sosnowiec, Poland, Mar. 17, 1919; s. Oskar Einhorn and Karola (Birman) Mazurkiewicz; m. Jadwiga Piaskowski, Mar. 17, 1946 (div. Apr. 1968); children: Janusz Richard, Robert Krzysztof (dec.), Ewa Krystyna; m. Ruth Mary Gregor, May 23, 1968; 1 child, Edward William. MD, Poznan Med. Acad., 1951; PhD, Silesia Med. Acad., 1963. Dir. State Endocrinology Consulting Ctr., Katowice, 1954—66; assoc. prof. 3d Dept. Internal Medicine, Katowice, 1962—66; endocrine rschr. Royal Postgrad. Med. Sch., London, 1965; assoc. prof. U. Pitts. Med. Sch., 1971—94; dir. Hazelwood & Greenfield Cmty. Health Ctrs., Pitts., 1971—84; dir. thyroid screening program U. Pitts. Med. Sch., 1976—93; endocrine rschr. Royal Postgrad. Med. Sch., London, 1967. Author: Recollections of the End of an Era, 2000; contbr. over 35 rsch. articles to profl. jours. With Polish Light Horse Artillery, 1939, with Polish Underground Army, 1940—44, with Warsaw Uprising, 1944. Recipient Silver Cross of Merit, 1957, Endocrine rsch. awards Polish Endocrine Soc., 1962, 63, 1st Class prize Min. Health, 1967; recipient mil. awards Virtuti Militari, 1939, Cross of Valour, 1944, Cross of the Warsaw Uprising, 1944. Avocations: woodworking, photography, horseback riding. Home: 415 Summit Dr Pittsburgh PA 15228-2617

EINHORN, LAWRENCE HENRY, medical educator; b. Dayton, Ohio, 1942; MD, U. Iowa, 1967. Diplomate Am. Bd. Internal Medicine, Am. Bd. Oncology. Med. intern Ind. U. Hosp., Indpls., 1967—68; resident in medicine Ind. U., 1968—69, fellow in hematology and oncology, 1972—72, assoc. prof. medicine, clin. oncology and hematology, 1973—; now Disting. prof. medicine Ind. U.- Purdue U., Indpls.; fellow in oncology M.D. Anderson Hosp. and Tumor Inst., 1972—73. Capt. Med. Corps USAF, 1969—72. Office: Ind U Sch Med 550 University Blvd Rm 1730 Indianapolis IN 46202-5149

EINHORN, MARTIN B., physicist, educator; b. Dayton, Ohio, Aug. 14, 1942; s. Aaron Howard and Rosalind (Rosen) E.; m. Vibeke Gjoe Geleff, Feb. 18, 1967; children: Michael, Linda. BS (hons.), Calif. Inst. Tech., 1965; PhD, Princeton U., 1968. Post-doctoral fellow Stanford (Calif.) Linear Accelerator

Ctr., 1968-70, Lawrence Berkeley (Calif.) Lab., 1970-72, Fermi Nat. Accelerator Lab., Batavia, Ill., 1972-73, staff physicist, 1973-76; assoc. rsch. scientist U. Mich., Ann Arbor, 1976-79, assoc. prof., 1979-83, prof. physics, 1983—. Chair adv. bd. Theoretical Advanced Study Inst., Boulder, Colo., 1984-91, dep. dir. Inst. for Theoretical Physics, U. Calif., Santa Barbara, 1990-92. Contbr. 75 articles to profl. jours. Mem. high energy physics adv. panel Dept. of Energy, Washington, 1983-87. John Simon Guggenheim Meml. Found. fellow, 2003—. Fellow Am. Phys. Soc.; mem. AAUP, AAAS.

EINIGER, CAROL BLUM, investment company executive; b. Nov. 30, 1949; d. Bernard Michael and Bella (Karff) Blum; m. Roger William Einiger, Dec. 21, 1969; 1 child. BA, U. Pa., 1970; MBA, Columbia U., 1973. With Conde Nast Publs., N.Y.C., 1970-71, Goldman, Sachs & Co., N.Y.C., 1971-72, 1st Boston Corp., N.Y.C., 1973-88, mng. dir., 1982-88, head short-term fin. dept., 1983-88, head capital markets dept., 1985-88; vis. prof., exec.-in-residence Columbia U. Bus. Sch., N.Y.C., 1988-89; mng. dir. Wasserstein Perella & Co. Inc., N.Y.C., 1989-92; CFO, acting pres. Edna McConnell Clark Found., NYC, 1992—96; chief investment officer Rockefeller U., N.Y.C., 1996—. Trustee Horace Mann Sch., 1988-94, U. Pa., 1989-99, mem. audit, budget and fin., investment, external affairs, and student life coms.; bd. overseers Columbia U. Bus. Sch., 1988-, nominating com.; vice chair investment com. Mus. Modern Art, 1994-; mem. adv. bd. Blackstone Alternative Asset Mgmt., 1999-; bd. dirs. Credit Suisse First Boston (U.S.A.), Inc., 2001-02, Boston Properties, Inc., 2004-. Office: Rockefeller Univ 1230 York Ave New York NY 10021-6399

EINISMAN, MYRON SACHAR, publisher; b. Chgo., Mar. 13, 1940; s. William and Ada Joyce (Brenner) E.; m. Margaret Movius Boland, Sept. 26, 1977. BA in Liberal Arts, U. Chgo. Coll., 1962; MBA, U. Chgo., 1963; JD, U. Louisville, 1966. Atty. NLRB, L.A., 1966-67; devel. officer U. Chgo., 1967-71; cons. Charles R. Feldstein & Co., Chgo., 1971-73; dir. devel. and pub. rels. United Charities of Chgo., 1973-76; chief cons. I.D.C. Corp., Chgo., 1976-82; v.p. mktg. OMG/Publs., Chgo., 1982-94; pres., pub. OMG/Philanthropy Publ. Founding chmn. student/alumni theatre com. U. Chgo., 1992-96. Author syndicated articles on charitable fin. planning, 1990—; pub., project editor: (audiotapes) Masterpieces of Legal Fiction, 1997; co-pub. reprints of artists' drawings used in origianl Sherlock Holmes mag. stories, 1988. Student editor, chmn. U. Louisville Law Sch. Brandeis Lecture Series, 1963-65; paid con. to variety of charitable groups in health, edn., arts, 1967-86; cons., advisor Recovery, Inc., 1986-87; coll. reunion co-chmn. U. Chgo. Coll., 1992; donated major audiotape collectionto Union League Libr., 1997; chmn. Friends of Union League. Recipient Outstanding Alumni Svc. award U. Chgo. Theatre Alumni, Chgo., 1994. Mem. Union League Club of Chgo., Club of Chgo. Libr. Avocations: collector of autographed mystery books, mystery writing, admirer of wife's gardening, sports. Home: 477 Green Bay Rd Highland Park IL 60035-4935

EINODER, CAMILLE ELIZABETH, retired secondary school educator; b. Chgo., June 15, 1937; d. Isadore and Elizabeth T. (Czerwinski) Popowski; m. Joseph X. Einoder, Aug. 5, 1978; children: Carl Frank, Mark Frank, Vivian Einoder, Joe Einoder, Tim Einoder, Sheila Einoder, Jude Einoder. Student, Fox Bus. Coll., 1954; BEd in Biology, Chgo. Tchrs. Coll., 1964; MA in Analytical Chemistry, Gov.'s State U., 1977; MA in Adminstrn. and Supervision, Roosevelt U., 1986; postgrad., 1992—. Sec., Chgo., 1955-64; tchr. biology Chgo. Bd. Edn., 1964-1975, tchr. biology and agr., 1975-81, tchr. biology, agr. and chemistry, 1981-2000, ret., 2000. Human rels. coord. Morgan Park High Sch., Chgo., 1980—, tchr. biology Internat. Studies Sch., 1983—, adv. bd., 1989—; owner Einoder Masonry, 1997—, Einoder Antiques, 1996—; career devel. cons. for agr. related curriculum; internat. baccalaureate tchr., Chgo. pub. schs. consulting tchr., 1997; edn. cons. Neighborhood Coun., 1974; rep. Chgo. Tchrs. Union, 1969; exec. bd. dir. The Lira Ensemble, 1996—; mem. Renaissance Circle, DePaul U.; edn. com. Polish-Am. Initiative of Chgo. Cmty. Trust, 1999—; owner Einoder Masonry, 1986—; antique dealer, 1995—. Bd. dirs., founding mem., author constn. Cmty. Coun., 1970—; bd. dirs., edn. cons. Neighborhood Coun., 1974; rep. Chgo. Tchrs. Union, 1969; exec. bd. dirs. The Lira Ensemble, 1996—; mem. Chums Giving Club Com.; charter mem. Humanists Cir. Chgo. Humanities Festival, 2003—. Mem. AAAS, NSTA, Polish Inst. for Arts and Sci., Am. Chem. Soc., Am. Biology Tchrs. Assn., Nat. Assn. Women Bus. Owners, Found. Women Contractors, Copernicus Found., Kosciuszko Soc., Polish Arts Club, Phi Delta Kappa, Iota Sigma Pi. Office Phone: 773-445-6210. E-mail: camilleein@aol.com, camilleein@rcn.com.

EINS, STEFAN, artist; b. Prague, Bohemia; came to U.S., 1967; s. Stefan and Daisy (Ganghofer) Schmid. MA in Theology, U. Vienna, 1965; BA in Sculpture, Akad. Bildenen Kuenste, Vienna, 1967. Founder, exec. dir. 3 Mercer St, N.Y.C., 1972-79, Fashion Moda, N.Y.C., 1978-84, 88-93; painter, 1980—. Sculptor: prin. works include Variables, 1966, Liquid Steel/Life, NYC, 1972, Project Vertebrae, Austria, 1994. Co-founder chpt. The Audubon Soc., N.Y.C., 1979. Grantee, NEA, 1980, 1987, NY Found. for the Arts, 2002, Adolph and Esther Gottlieb Found., 2004. Mem. Collaborative Projects, Inc. (pres. 1988-89, 2001—). Achievements include research on liquids formation; discovery of formation process of vertebrae, 1985; uncovered stone age artifacts in Austria, 1987-94; research on creating life through conditions inherent in the sun; research on living forever and physics law necessity. Home: PO Box 33 New York NY 10013-0033 Office Phone: 917-605-0974, 212-987-9749. E-mail: einsoneuno@aol.com.

EINSEL, DAVID WILLIAM, JR., retired army officer, consultant; b. Tiffin, Ohio, Nov. 4, 1928; s. David William and Naomi Dorothy (Williams) E.; m. Elva yates Aylor, June 16, 1956; children: Susan Vagnier, Mary Kost. BA, MA in Chemistry, Ohio State U., 1950; MSc, U. Va., 1956. Commd. 2d lt. U.S. Army, 1950, advanced through grades to maj. gen., 1980; staff officer Orgn. of the Joint Chiefs of Staff, Washington, 1968-70; comdr. Harry Diamond Labs., Adelphi, Md., 1970-75; chief nuclear-chem. officer hdqrs. Dept. of the Army, Washington, 1975-76; dep. commanding gen. U.S. Army Armament R&D Command Picatinny (N.J.) Arsenal, 1976-80; asst. to sec. of def. Office of the Sec. of Def., Washington, 1980-85; officer Nat. Intelligence Coun., Washington, 1985-89; ret. U.S. Army, 1985; cons. Tiffin, Ohio, 1989—. Author: International Military Encyclopedia, 1991; contbr. article to Jour. Analytical Chemistry. Decorated Silver Star, Bronze Star, Purple Heart; named to U.S. Army Chem. Corps Hall of Fame, 1993; recipient Profl. Achievement award, Ohio State U., 1998, Disting. Citizenship award, Tiffin (Ohio) Area C. of C., 2004. Mem. AAAS, Assn. of the U.S. Army, Am. Def. Preparedness Assn., Kiwanis, Masons (33d degree), Phi Beta Kappa, Sigma Xi. Republican. Methodist. Achievements include patent in automatic electrolytic apparatus for determining acid prodn. rates. Home and Office: 594 S Washington St Tiffin OH 44883-3320 Personal E-mail: einseld@bright.net.

EINSPRUCH, BURTON CYRIL, psychiatrist; b. N.Y.C., June 27, 1935; s. Adolph and Mala (Goldblatt) E.; m. Barbara Standen Traeger, Oct. 9, 1960; children: Julia E. Lewis, Alexander Louis, Robert Sands. BA, So. Meth. U., 1956, ScB, 1958; MD, Southwestern Med. Sch., Dallas, 1960. Diplomate Am. Bd. Psychiatry and Neurology (examiner 1974—). Intern Montefiore Hosp., N.Y.C., 1960-61; resident Nat. Hosp. Inst. Neurology, London, 1962; resident, fellow U. Tex., Dallas, 1961—64; chief resident Parkland Meml. Hosp., Dallas, 1964; instr. psychiatry U. Pa., 1964-66; pvt. practice psychiatry Dallas, 1966—. Staff Presbyn. and Parkland Hosps., Timberlawn Psychiat. Hosp.; clin. asst. prof. U. Tex., Health Sci. Center, Dallas, 1966-70, dir. Southwestern Adult Psychiat. Clinic, Dallas, 1966-74; dir. psychiat. service Dallas Geriatric Research Inst., 1974-80; adj. prof. sociology U. North Tex., Denton, 1975-82; cons. staff Baylor U. Hosp., Golden Acres Hosp.; clin. assoc. prof. psychiatry U. Tex. Health Scis. Ctr., Dallas, 1971—; prof. psychiatry U. Tex. Southwestern Med. Ctr., Dallas, 1971—; bd. dirs., founder Dallas Nat. Bank; clin. assoc. prof. psychiatry NYU Med. Ctr., N.Y.C., 1990; adj. prof. Dept. Occupl. and Environ. Med. U. Tex. Med. Ctr., Tyler, Tex., cognitive and neuroscience, U. Tex., Dallas; chmn. bd. dirs. Planned Behavioral Health Care, Inc., Dallas; affiliate Tex. Inst. Rsch. and Edn. on Aging, Health Sci. Ctr. Fort Worth; bd. dirs. Am. Svc. Group. Contbr. articles to profl. jours.; mem. editl. bd.: Tex. Medicine Bd., 1991—2002. Trustee Evans Fedn., N.Y.C., 1986-94, U. Tex., Dallas, 1987—, St. Mark's Sch. Tex., 1987-94, chmn. holocaust studies program bd., 1998—; mem. exec. bd. libr. So. Meth. U., 1992-97; adv. dir. Leonhardt Fedn., N.Y.C., 1990, Children of Alcoholics Fedn., 1991, 1995; arbitrator, N.Y. and Am. Exchs., N.Y.C., 1984; bd. dirs. Wyndham Internat., 1997-2000; dir. Dallas Mus. Natural History, Belief Found., Coll. First Found., Dallas, Tex. Lt. comdr. M.C., USNR, 1964-66. Fellow Am. Psychiat. Assn. (disting. life, Am. Coll. Psychiatrists, Am. Soc. Adolescent Psychiatry, N. Tex. Soc. Adolescent Psychiatry (past pres.); mem. Royal Coll. Psychiatry London, AMA, Tex. Med. Assn. Home: 3505 Lindenwood Ave Dallas TX 75205-3229 Office: 8330 Meadow Rd Ste 117 Dallas TX 75231-3750 Office Phone: 214-369-1636. Personal E-mail: einspruch@charter.net.

EINSPRUCH, NORMAN GERALD, physicist, engineering educator; b. NYC, June 27, 1932; s. Adolph and Mala (Goldblatt) E.; m. Edith Melnick, Dec. 20, 1953; children: Eric, Andrew, Franklin. BA in Physics, Rice U., 1953; MS in Physics, U. Colo., 1955; PhD in Applied Math, Brown U., 1959. Mem. tech. staff, central research labs. Tex. Instruments, Inc., Dallas, 1959-62, mgr. electron transport physics br., central research labs., 1962-68, dir. advanced tech. lab., central research labs., 1968-69, dir. tech., chem. materials div., 1969-72, dir. central research labs., 1972-75, asst. v.p., 1975-77, mgr. corp. devel., 1975-76, mgr. tech. and planning consumer products, 1976-77; prof. dept. elec. and computer engring. Coll. Engring. U. Miami, Coral Gables, Fla., 1977—, dean Coll. Engring., 1977-90, sr. fellow in sci. and tech., 1990—, chmn. dept. indsl. engring., 1994-99. Vis. prof. Rensselaer Poly. Inst., 2001-02; chmn. panel on thin film microstructure sci. and tech. NRC, 1978-79, mem. panel on impact of DoD very high speed integrated circuits program, 1980-81, panel on edn. and utilization of the engr., 1981-82; bd. dirs. Zinc Matrix Power, Inc. Author: Electronic Genie: The Tangled History of Silicon, 1998 editor: (series) VLSI Electronics: Microstructure Science, 24 vols., VLSI Handbook, 1985; contbr. articles to profl. jours. Recipient George Washington Honor medal Freedoms Found. Valley Forge. Fellow Am. Phys. Soc., Acoustical Soc. Am., IEEE, AAAS; mem. Golden Key, Iron Arrow, Sigma Xi, Omicron Delta Kappa, Tau Beta Pi, Eta Kappa Nu, Phi Kappa Phi, Alpha Pi Mu, Tau Sigma Delta. Home: 1415 Trillo Ave Miami FL 33146-2312 Office: U Miami Coll Engring PO Box 248581 Coral Gables FL 33124-8581 Office Phone: 305-284-3812. Business E-Mail: neinspruch@miami.edu.

EINSTEIN, ALBERT See BROOKS, ALBERT

EINSTEIN, CLIFFORD JAY, advertising executive; b. LA, May 4, 1939; s. Harry and Thelma (Bernstein) E.; m. Madeline Mandel, Jan. 28, 1962; children: Harold Jay, Karen Holly. BA in English, UCLA, 1961; PhD, DFA, Otis Coll. Art and Design, 2002. Writer Norman, Craig and Kummel, N.Y.C., 1961-62, Foote, Cone and Belding, L.A., 1962-64; ptnr. Silverman and Einstein, L.A., 1965-67; pres., creative dir. Dailey and Assos., L.A., 1968-93, chmn., 1994—, also bd dirs. Dir. Campaign '80, advt. agy. Reagan for Pres., 1980; lectr. various colls.; founder First Coastal Bank; bd. dirs. The Jewish Cmty. Found. Contbr. articles to Advertising Age; prodr.: (play) Whatever Happened to Georgie Tapps, L.A. and San Francisco, 1980; film appearances include Real Life, Modern Romance, Defending Your Life, Face/Off, 1997; T.V. appearance in Bizarre, Super Dave Show. Bd. dirs. Rape Treatment Ctr., Santa Monica Med. Ctr., Discovery Fund for Eye Rsch.; chmn. bd. Mus. Contemporary Art, L.A.; trustee Otis Coll Art & Design. With U.S. Army, 1957. Recipient Am. Advt. award, 1968, 73, 79, Clio award, 1973, Internat. Broadcast Pub. Svc. award, 1970, 85, Nat. Addy award, 1979, Gov.'s award, 1987; named Creative Dir. of the West, Adweek Poll, 1982, Exec. of West, 1986, Western States Assn. Advt. Agys. Leader of Yr., 1992, Leader of the West, Am. Advt. Fedn., 2002. Mem. AFTRA, ASCAP, SAG, Dirs. Guild Am., Hillcrest Country Club, Calif. Club. Office: Dailey & Assocs 8687 Melrose Ave West Hollywood CA 90069-5701

EINSTEIN, STEPHEN JAN, rabbi; b. LA, Nov. 15, 1945; s. Syd C. and Selma (Rothenberg) E.; m. Robin Susan Kessler, Sept. 9, 1967; children: Rebecca Yael, Jennifer Melissa, Heath Isaac, Zachary Shane. AB, UCLA, 1967; BHL, Hebrew Union Coll., L.A., 1968, DHL, 1995, DD (hon.), 1996; MAHL, Hebrew Union Coll., Cin., 1971. Ordained rabbi. Rabbi Temple Beth Am, Parsippany, NJ, 1971-74, Temple Beth David, Westminster, Calif., 1974-76, Congregation B'nai Tzedek, Fountain Valley, Calif., 1976—. Lectr. Calif. State U., Fullerton. Co-author: Every Person's Guide to Judaism, 1989; co-editor: Introduction to Judaism, 1983. Pres., trustee Fountain Valley (Calif.) Sch. Bd., 1984—90; chmn. pers. commn. Fountain Valley Sch. Dist., 1991—; pres. Retinoblatoma Internat., 2000—01; chaplain Fountain Valley Police Dept.; pres. Greater Huntington Beach Inter-Faith Coun., 2001—02; active Anti Defamation League, Am. Jewish Com.; co-chmn. Commn. on Outreach and Synagogue Cmty., 1999—; regional bd. dirs. Nat. Conf. Cmty. and Justice, 2001—. Recipient Micah Award for Interfaith Activities, Am. Jewish Com., 1988. Mem.: Inst. for Character Edn. (exec. adv. bd.), Clergy for Choice, Orange County Bur. Jewish Edn. (v.p. 1982—84, 1992—94, pres. 1994—97, honored for Maj. Contbns. to Jewish Learning 1986), Jewish Educators Assn. Orange County (pres. 1979—81), Orange County Bd. Rabbis (pres. 1976—79, 1997—98), Pacific Assn. Reform Rabbis (exec. bd. 1987—91, 1998—2002, pres. 2002—03), Ctrl. Conf. Am. Rabbis (exec. bd. 1989—91, ethics com. 1993—98), Alzheimers Assn. (religious adv. com.), Am. Cancer Soc. (v.p. West Orange County dist. 1994—98), Phi Beta Kappa. Democrat. Office: Congregation Bnai Tzedek 9669 Talbert Ave Fountain Valley CA 92708 Office Phone: 714-963-4611. E-mail: rebgiraffe@aol.com.

EINSTEIN, STEVEN HENRY, lawyer, investment banker; b. N.Y.C., Aug. 14, 1954; s. Ralph Gunther and Beatrice (Katz) E.; children: Theodore Aaron, Peter Raymond, Hannah Louise. BS, Lehigh U., 1976; JD, Seton Hall U., 1979; LLM in Taxation, NYU, 1985. Lic. CPA, N.Y., N.J.; Bar: N.J. 1979, N.Y. 1985, U.S. Dist. Ct. N.J. 1979, U.S. Tax Ct. 1982, U.S. Ct. Appeals (3d cir.) 1983, U.S. Supreme Ct. 1985. Judicial law clk. to presiding justice Superior Ct., Hackensack, NJ, 1979—80; assoc. Wacks, Hirsch, Ramsey & Berman Esqs., Morristown, NJ, 1980—81; sr. tax mgr. Touche Ross & Co., Newark, 1981—86; v.p., investment banking, mergers & acquisitions dept. PaineWebber Capital Mkts., N.Y.C., 1986—88; v.p., merchant banking/pvt. equity Kluge, Subotnick, Perkowski & Co., N.Y.C., 1988—90; mng. dir. Price WaterhouseCoopers Corp. Fin. Group, N.Y.C., 1991—98; ptnr. & mng. dir. PricewaterhouseCoopers Securities LLP, N.Y.C., 1998—99, ptnr., chmn.'s office, global leader, corp. devel., 1999—. Mem. editl. bd. Corp. Taxation Mag.; contbr. articles to profl. jours. Mem. ABA, AICPAs, N.J. State Bar Assn., N.Y. State Bar Assn., Essex County Bar Assn. (taxation divsn.), N.J. Soc. CPAs, Beta Gamma Sigma, Phi Eta Sigma. Jewish. Office: PricewaterhouseCoopers LLP 1177 Avenue of the Americas New York NY 10036-2714 Home: PO Box 403 New Canaan CT 06840-0403

EINZIG, STANLEY, pediatric cardiologist, researcher; b. Bklyn., July 25, 1942; s. Louis and Sally (Weiser) E.; m. Gloria Einzig (div.); children: Deborah, Dana, David. MD, UCLA, 1967; PhD, U. Minn., 1977. Diplomate Am. Bd. Pediatrics, sub.-bd. Pediatric Cardiology. Intern, then resident dept. pediatrics U. Minn., Mpls., 1967-70, from instr. to assoc. prof., 1977-90; prof. physiology and pediatrics, chief pediatric cardiology W.Va. U., Morgantown, 1990—2001; with children's cardiac ctr. Newark Beth Israel Md. Ctr., 2001—. Contbr. numerous articles to profl. jours. Lt. comdr. USN, 1971-73. NIH fellow, 1974, 75. Fellow Am. Coll. Cardiology; mem. Am. Phys. Soc., Soc. for Pediatric Rsch., Alpha Omega Alpha. Achievements include discovery of blood flow and antioxidant effects of anisodamine. Office: Childrens Cardiac Ctr 201Lyons Ave at Osborne Terr Newark NJ 07112 Office Phone: 973-926-3582. E-mail: seinzig@sbhcs.com.

EIRE, CARLOS, historian, educator, writer; b. Havana, Cuba; BA, Loyola U., 1973; MA, Yale U., 1974, MPhil, 1976, PhD, 1979. Lectr. Albertus Magnus Coll., New Haven, 1978; asst. prof. St. John's U., Collegeville, Minn., 1979—81, U. Va., Dept. Religious Studies, 1981—87, assoc. prof., 1987—94, U. Va., Dept. Hist., 1989—94; prof. U. Va., Dept. Hist. and Religious Studies, 1994—96, Yale U., Dept. History and Religious Studies, 1996—2000; seminar leader Folger Inst., Folger Shakespeare Libr., 2000; chair Yale U., Dept. Religious Studies, 1999—2002; T. Lawrason Riggs prof. of hist. and religious studies Yale U., 2000—. Mem. Sch. of Hist. Studies, Inst. for Advanced Studies, Princeton, NJ, 1986—87; vis. Sch. of Hist. Studies, Inst. for Advanced Study, Princeton, NJ, 1992—93; mem. Ctr. for Advanced Studies, U. Va., 1992—93. Author: (book) War Against the Idols: The Reformation of Worship from Erasmus to Calvin, 1986, From Madrid to Purgatory: The Art and Craft of Dying in Sixteenth Century Spain, 1995; author: (with J. Corrigan, M. Jaffee, F. Denny) Jews, Christians, Muslims: A Comparative Introduction to Monotheistic Religions, 1997; author: Waiting for Snow in Havana: Confessions of a Cuban Boy, 2003 (Nat. Book award, 2003). Recipient U. Va. Alumni Bd. Trustees Tchg. award, 1990; Fulbright Program Fellowship for Rsch. in Spain, 1984, Exxon Edn. Found. Fellowship, Ctr. for Renaissance Studies. Office Phone: 203-432-1357.

EIS, TERRY FLORA, secondary school educator; b. Tacoma, Wash., Oct. 7, 1954; d. Kenneth E. and Hazel L. (Stork) Flora; div., 1991; children: Ashley K., Erikn K. BA, Friends U., Wichita, Kans., 1977; MA, Southwestern Coll., Winfield, Kans., 1991. Cert. secondary sch. tchr., lang. arts, social sci., Kans. Lang. arts instr. Arkansas (Kans.) City H.S., 1977-79; social sci., lang. arts tchr. Winfield (Kans.) H.S., 1979—. Bus. cons., writing, ethics, Winfield, 1995—. Mem. Kans. Edn. Assn. (polit. action rep. 1995—), Nat. Coun. Tchrs. of English, Kans. Staff Devel. Coun., Profl. Devel. Coun. (chairperson 1994—). Office: Winfield HS 300 N Viking Blvd Winfield KS 67156-2508

EISCH, AMELIA JOAN, neuroscientist, researcher; b. Silver Spring, Md., Jan. 4, 1968; d. John Joseph and Joan Scheuerell Eisch; m. Shae Buckley Padrick, June 22, 2002; 1 child, Zachary Eisch Padrick. BA, Yale U., 1990; PhD, U. Calif., 1997. Asst. prof. UT Southwestern Med. Ctr., Dallas, Tex., 2000—. Office: UT Southwestern Medical Center 5323 Harry Hines Blvd Dallas TX 75390-9070 Office Phone: 214-648-5549.

EISCH, JOHN JOSEPH, chemist, educator, writer, consultant; b. Milw., Nov. 5, 1930; s. Frank Joseph and Gladys (Riordan) E.; m. Joan Terese Scheuerell, Sept. 5, 1953; children: Margaret (dec.), Karla, Paula, Joseph, Amelia. BS summa cum laude, Marquette U., 1952, PhD, 1956; P&G fellow, Iowa State U., 1956; DS honoris causa (hon.), Marquette U., 2002. Postdoctoral Union Carbide fellow Max Planck Inst. für Kohlenforschung, Mülheim, Germany, 1956-57; rsch. assoc. European Rsch. Assocs., Brussels, 1957; mem. faculty St. Louis U., 1957-59; faculty U. Mich., 1959-63, Cath. U. Am., Washington, 1963-72; chmn. dept. chemistry SUNY, Binghamton, 1972-78, prof., 1972—, disting. prof., 1983—. Sr. rsch. fellow Japan Soc. for Promotion of Sci., 1979, Alexander von Humboldt Found., Germany, 1993-96; cons. in field, 1957—; legal expert witness. Author: The Chemistry of Organometallic Compounds, 1967, (with R. B. King) Organometallic Syntheses, Vol. I, 1965, Vol. II, 1981, Vol. III, 1986, Vol. IV, 1988; contbr. over 350 articles to profl. publs.; patentee in field. Mem. Am. Chem. Soc., Am. Inst. Chemists, Sigma Xi, Phi Lambda Upsilon, Phi Kappa Phi. Republican. Roman Catholic. Achievements include research and publs. on the synthesis and properties of organometallic compounds (those with carbon-metal bonds) and heterocycles, with emphasis on the kinetics and stereochemistry of carbon-metal bond and hydrogen-metal bond additions to olefins, acetylenes; radical-anion, nonbenzenoid aromatic studies, photochemistry of organometallics; catalytic processes of carbocyclization, oligomerization and polymerization of carbon pi-bonded molecules and prebiotic organic synthesis of sugars. Home: 212 Sheedy Rd Vestal NY 13850-5905 Office: SUNY Binghamton Dept Chemistry Binghamton NY 13902-6000 Office Phone: 607-777-4261. Office Fax: 607-777-4865. Business E-Mail: jjeisch@binghamton.edu.

EISCHEN, DONALD F., psychologist, educator; s. Joseph Francis Eoscjem and Emily Elizabeth White-Eischen; m. Jennie Capriola (dec. Aug. 1999); children: Donna-Marie, Emily A. Kamansky. BA, Calif. State U., 1949; MA, Columbia U., 1951; PhD, Stanford U., 2002, Madison U., 2004. Psychologist pvt. practice, Santa Cruz, Calif. Camp counselor Calif. State U., Fresno, 1959—60, supr., master tchr., 1960—85. Author: Mirror Up to Nature, 2002, Love Against Hate as it Relates to Gays, Lesbians, Bisexual Transgender in the 21st Century, 2004. Vol. Cmty. Bridges, Santa Cruz, 1991—2005; flutist St. Joseph Ch., Capitola, Calif. Recipient Outstanding Tchr., Fresno, 1988. Fellow: Elks (greeter, treas. 1994—2005); mem.: Sons of Italy (treas. 1991—95), Italian Cath. Fedn. (sec., orator 1975—2005), KC (sir knight, faithful navigator 1976—82, Grand Knight 1976—80, Sir Knight 1976—82). Roman Catholic. Avocations: antiques, swimming, dance, walking, travel. Home and Office: 219 Woodrow Ave Santa Cruz CA 95060 Office Phone: 831-469-3487.

EISDORFER, CARL, psychiatrist, health facility administrator; b. Bronx, NY, June 20, 1930; BA, NYU, 1951, MA, 1953, PhD, 1959; MD, Duke U., 1964; postgrad. in health systems mgmt., Harvard U., 1981. Lectr. in psychology Duke U. Med. Ctr., Durham, N.C., 1959-72, intern in medicine, 1964-65, psychiat. trainee, 1964-67, dir. tng., research coordinator Ctr. for Study Aging and Human Devel., 1965-70, prof. psychiatry and med. psychology, 1968-72, dir. med. studies behavioral scis. program, 1970-72, head div. med. psychology dept. psychiatry, 1970-72, dir. Ctr. for Study Aging and Human Devel., 1970-72; founding dir. Inst. on Aging, U. Wash., Seattle, 1977-79, prof., chmn. dept. psychiatry and behavioral scis. Sch. of Medicine, adj. prof. psychology, 1972-81; sr. scholar in residence Inst. Medicine, Nat. Acad. Scis., Washington, 1979-80; prof. psychiatry and neurosci. Albert Einstein Coll. Medicine, N.Y.C., 1981-85; chief exec. officer Montefiore Med. Ctr., N.Y.C., 1981-85; prof., chmn. dept. psychiatry U. Miami, Fla., 1986—2005, dir. Ctr. on Aging, 1986—, Knight profl, spl. asst. to pres., 2004—; chief div. mental health Jackson Meml. Med. Ctr., 1986—. Coordinator Community Mental Health Services, Halifax County N.C., 1969-70; vis. prof. architeture U. Calif.-Berkeley, 1969-70; H.T. Dozer vis. prof. geriatrics and psychiatry Ben Gurion U., Negev, Israel, 1980; cons. NIH, Bethesda, Md., Robert Wood Johnson Found., numerous others. Editor in chief Ann. Rev. Gerontology and Geriatrics, 1978; mem. editl. bd. Alzheimers Disease and Related Disorders-Internat. Jour., Aging and Human Devel., Western Jour. Medicine, Neurobiology of Aging: Exptl. and Clin. Rsch.; contbr. articles to profl. jours and books. Served with U.S. Army, 1954-56 Recipient Kesten award Ethel Percy Andrus Gerontology Ctr., U. So. Calif., 1976, Potamkin prize, 1982, Disting. Alumnus award Duke U. Sch. of Medicine, 1985, Allid Signal award, 1991. Fellow Soc. Behavioral Medicine, N.Y. Acad. Medicine, Am. Psychol. Assn. (chmn. div. adult devel. and aging 1970-71, task force on aging 1971-73, award for disting. contbns. 1981, award for contbns. on aging research 1985), Gerontol. Soc. Am. (pres. 1971-72, Robert W. Kleemeier award 1969, Donald P. Kent award, 2002, Joseph Freeman award div. clin. medicine 1979), Am. Geriatrics Soc. (Edward B. Allen award 1974, Edward Henderson Meml. award 1988), Am. Psychiat. Assn. (Jack Weinberg Meml. award 1984), Am. Coll. Psychiatrists, Am. Coll. Physicians (Menninger award 1990), AAAS; mem. Am. Soc. Aging (pres. 1980-82), Am. Fed. Aging Res. (pres. 1986-88), Sigma Xi, Alpha Omega Alpha, Phi Beta Kappa. Office: U Miami Sch Medicine Dept Psychiatry D-28 PO Box 16960 Miami FL 33101-6960 Office Phone: 305-355-9040. E-mail: ceisdorf@med.miami.edu.

EISELE, FRED LOUIS, atmospheric chemist; b. N.Y.C., May 14, 1947; s. Louis Fred and Lottie May Eisele; m. Carolyn Jean Sleeper, June 28, 1975; children: Jason Thomas, Prescott Lawrence. BS in Physics, Rensselaer Poly. Inst., 1970; PhD in Physics, U. Vt., 1975. Rsch. assoc. U. Ga., Athens, 1975—76; postdoctoral fellow Ga. Inst. Tech., Atlanta, 1976—78, rsch. scientist II, 1978—82, sr. rsch. scientist, 1982—87, prin. rsch. scientist, 1987—2004; sr. rsch. assoc. Nat. Ctr. for Atmospheric Rsch., Boulder, Colo., 1993—. Contbr. articles to profl. jours., chapters to books. 30 rsch. grants, various U.S. govt. agencies, 1978—. Mem.: Am. Geophys. Union, Am. Phys. Soc., Sigma Xi. Achievements include patents for high pressure selected ion chemical interface for connecting a sample source to an analysis device; Ion source and sample introduction method and apparatus using two stage ionization for producing sample gas ions; research in several first time measurements of ions and gas phase compounds in the atmosphere. Office: National Center for Atmospheric Research 1850 Table Mesa Dr Boulder CO 80305 Office Phone: 303-497-1483. Office Fax: 303-497-1400. Business E-Mail: eisele@ucar.edu.

EISEMAN, TIMOTHY WILLIAM, art and history educator; b. Ann Arbor, Mich., Feb. 5, 1950; s. Alfred F. and Marian J. (Fischer) E.; m. Irene A. Pengrin, Dec. 30, 1978. Assoc. Architecture, Washtenaw C.C., 1970; B Art Edn., Ea. Mich. U., 1974, MA, 1978, MA, 1998. Cert. elem. and secondary art tchr., Mich. High sch. art tchr. Chelsea (Mich.) Pub. Schs., 1975; art tchr. Ann Arbor Pub. Schs., 1975-87, 88, art coord., 1988, mem. visual arts curriculum team, 1978-95. Mem. curriculum arts and editorial panel Mich. State Bd. Edn., Lansing, 1987-88. Recipient Tech. in Edn., Gov. of Mich., 1990. Mem. NEA, Mich. Edn. Assn., Mich. Alliance for Arts in Edn., Nat. Art Edn. Assn., Mich. Art Edn. Assn. Avocations: fine arts, architecture, outdoor recreation, motorcycle touring and travel. Office: Slauson Mid Sch 1019 W Washington St Ann Arbor MI 48103-4241

EISEN, ERIC ANSHEL, lawyer; b. N.Y.C., Apr. 9, 1950; s. Morton and Victoria (Goldstein) E.; m. Claire L. Shapiro, Jan. 6, 1979; children: Rebecca, Jennifer, Melissa. AB, U. Mich., 1971, JD magna cum laude, 1975. Bar: Alaska 1976, D.C. 1977, Md. 1988. Law clk. to presiding justice Alaska Supreme Ct., Fairbanks, 1975-76; assoc. Covington & Burling, Washington, 1976-81, Birch, Horton, Bittner, Washington, 1981-85, ptnr., 1985-93, Eisen Law Offices, Bethesda, Md., 1993—. Prin. speaker various seminars and colloquia on energy and bus. matters. Contbr. articles to legal publs. Pres. Wildwood Hills Citizens Assn., Bethesda, Md., 1987—; sec. N. Bethesda Cong. Citizens Assns., 1989-90. Mem. ATLA, Energy Bar Assn. (antitrust com.), D.C. Bar Assn., Montgomery County Bar Assn. (chmn. bus. sect., mem. intellectual property and litig. sects.), Toastmasters, Order of Coif. Avocation: woodworking. Office: Eisen Law Offices 10028 Woodhill Rd Bethesda MD 20817-1218 also: 1101 30th St NW Ste 500 Washington DC 20007-3708

EISEN, HERMAN NATHANIEL, immunology researcher, medical educator; b. Bklyn., Oct. 15, 1918; m. Natalie Aronson, 1948; 5 children. AB, NYU, 1939, MD, 1943; ScD (hon.), Washington U., St. Louis, 2003. Asst. in pathology Coll. Physicians and Surgeons, Columbia U., N.Y.C., 1944—46; NIH fellow Coll. Medicine, NYU, 1947—48, fellow in chemistry, 1948—49, asst. prof. indsl. medicine, 1949—53, assoc. prof., 1953—55; prof. medicine Sch. Medicine, Washington U., St. Louis, 1955—61; dermatologist-in-chief Barnes Hosp., St. Louis, 1955—61; prof. microbiology, head dept. Sch. Medicine Washington U., St. Louis, 1961—73; prof. MIT, Cambridge, 1973—82, Whitehead Inst. prof. immunology, 1982—89; prof. emeritus, 1989—. Mem. adv. bd. Mass. Gen Hosp., Yale Med. Sch., Harvard Sch. Pub. Health, Children's Hosp., Boston, Merck, Sharpe, Dohme Rsch. Labs., Roche Inst. for Molecular Biology, Howard Hughes Med. Inst.; chmn. Nat. Inst. Health Study, 1962—66; bd. of sci. counselors Nat. Inst. of Arthritis and Metabolic Dis., 1971—75; chmn. World Health Orgn. Sci. Group on Regulation of Immune Responses, 1969; lectr. Harvey Soc., N.Y., 1964; Phillips lectr. Haverford Coll., 1971; Burroughs & Wellcome vis. lectr. Med. Coll. So. Carolina, 1979; Culpepper Found. lectr. State Univ. of N.Y., Stonybrook, 1981; Lowry lectr. Washington Univ., St. Louis, 1989. Recipient Med. Sci. Achievement award, NYU, 1978, Outstanding Investigator award, Nat. Cancer Inst., NIH, 1986—93, Dupont award, Clin. Ligand Soc., 1987, Behring-Heidelberger award, 1993. Mem.: Am. Soc. for Clin. Investigation (v.p. 1965), Am. Assn. Immunologists (pres. 1968), Am. Acad. Arts and Scis., Inst. Medicine, Am. Assn. Physicians, Nat. Acad. Sci. (editl. bd. Procs. of the NAS 1994—2004). Office: MIT Ctr Cancer Rsch E17-128 77 Massachusetts Ave Cambridge MA 02139-4307 E-mail: hneisen@mit.edu.

EISEN, HOWARD JOEL, internist, researcher; b. Forest Hills, N.Y., May 25, 1956; s. Ezra Michael and Gertrude Margaret (Schmidt) Eisen; m. Judith Ellen Wolf, June 26, 1983; children: Jonathan Ezra, Miriam Sarah. BA in Biology, Cornell U., 1977; MD, U. Pa., 1981. Diplomate Am. Bd. Med. Examiners, Am. Bd Internal Medicine, Am. Bd. Cardiovascular Diseases. Med. intern Hosp. U. Pa., Phila., 1981—82, resident in medicine, 1982—84; fellow in cardiology Washington U. Sch. Medicine-Barnes Hosp., St. Louis, 1984—87; asst. prof. medicine U. Pa., Phila., 1990—93; assoc. prof. medicine and physiology Temple U., Phila., 1993—97, prof. medicine and physiology, 1997—2004, dir. heart failure care unit, 1993—99, med. dir. cardiac transplant program, 1999—2004, assoc. dir. Gen. Clin. Rsch. Ctr., 1995—2002, med. dir. Cardiomyopathy and Transplant Ctr., 1999—2002, med. dir. advanced heart failure and transplant program, 1999—2004; Thomas J. Vischer prof. medicine Drexel U. Coll. Medicine, 2004—, dir., Ctr. Advanced Heart Failure Care at Hahnemann, chief, divsn. cardiology, dir. Ctr. for Cardiovascular Disorders. Mem. cryptosporidiosis adv. com. Dept. Pub. Health, Phila., 1995—2000. Fellow: Am. Heart Assn. (clin. coun. 1995—, mem. rsch. com. 1995—, chmn. peer-review com. 1996—, established investigatorship award 1996—), Am. Coll. Cardiology, ACP; mem.: Internat. Soc. Heart and Lung Transportation, Am. Fedn. Clin. Rsch (mem. nat. coun. 1992—95, H. Christian award 1993), Phi Beta Kappa, Alpha Omega Alpha. Avocations: reading, rowing, classical music, running, e-mail. Home: 507 Shortridge Dr Wynnewood PA 19096-1609 Office: Drexel Univ Coll Medicine Mail Stop 1012 245 N 15th St Philadelphia PA 19102 Office Phone: 215-762-3829. Business E-Mail: heisen@drexelmed.edu.

EISEN, JONATHAN A., research scientist; AB in Biology cum laude, Harvard Coll., 1990; PhD in Biol. Scis., Stanford U., 1998. Field asst. Rocky Mountain Biol. Lab., Crested Butte, Colo., 1988, 1991; rsch. asst. Harvard U., Cambridge, Mass., 1989, 1990—91; predoctoral fellow NSF, 1991—94; Centennial tchg. asst. Stanford U., 1993, 1997; asst. investigator dept. microbial genomics Inst. for Genomic Rsch., Rockville, Md., 1998—, investigator dept. microbial genomics, 2002—. Adj. asst. prof. biology dept. Johns Hopkins U., Balt., 2000—; mem. sci. adv. bd. Geneformatics, Inc., 2000—. Mem. editl. bd.: Genome Rsch., 1999—, Microbiology, 2001; contbr. articles to profl. jours. Named one of Best and Brightest, Esquire Mag., 2002; Martin Rodbell fellow, Inst. for Genomic Rsch., 1999. Achievements include research in phylogenomics; genome evolution; DNA repair; endosymbionts; extremophiles; microbial evolution. Office: Inst for Genomic Rsch 9712 Medical Center Dr Rockville MD 20850

EISEN, LIZABETHANN R., lawyer; b. Portland, Oreg., June 14, 1972; BA magna cum laude, Cornell Univ., 1994; JD, Univ. Pa., 1997. Bar: NY 1998. Assoc. Cravath Swaine & Moore LLP, NYC, 1997—2005, ptnr., corp., 2005—. Office: Cravath Swaine & Moore LLP Worldwide Plz 825 Eighth Ave New York NY 10019-7475 Office Phone: 212-474-1930. Office Fax: 212-474-3700. Business E-Mail: leisen@cravath.com.

EISEN, ROBERT L., lawyer; b. Bklyn., Mar. 26, 1947; BA, Queens Coll., 1967; JD, NYU, 1970. Asst. chief counsel NY Customs, 1970—80; ptnr., head Global Customs & Internat. Trade practice Coudert Bros., NYC. Contbr. articles to profl. jours. Mem. adv. bd. Fashion Inst. of Tech., NYC. Mem.: ABA, NY State Bar Assn., Am. Assn. Exporters & Importers (bd. mem.), Customs & Internat. Trade Bar Assn. Office: Coudert Bros LLP 1114 Ave of the Americas New York NY 10036 Office Phone: 212-626-4492. Office Fax: 212-626-4120. Business E-Mail: eisenr@coudert.com.

EISEN, STEVEN LESLIE, neurologist; b. N.Y.C., July 15, 1940; s. Sidney and Bernice Leffert E.; m. Emily Littman, July 23, 1967; 1 child, Andrew Wallace. BS, Union Coll., 1962; MD, Albany Med. Coll., 1966. Intern Montefiore Hosp., Bronx, N.Y., 1966-67; resident Albert Einstein Coll. Medicine, Bronx, 1967-70; attendint neurologist Waterbury (Conn.) Hosp., 1970—, St. Mary's Hosp., Waterbury, 1970—. Chief staff Waterbury Hosp., 1999, chief medicine, 1988-94. Chmn. Planning Commn., Bethlehem, Conn., 1976-79. Avocations: fishing, sailing. Office: 1211 W Main St Waterbury CT 06708-3106

EISENBERG, ADI, chemist; b. Breslau, Germany, Feb. 18, 1935; emigrated to U.S., 1951; s. Oscar and Helene E.; m. Sandra M. Kloner, June 9, 1957 (div. 1985); 1 son, Elliot; m. Katia Chantal Wegliszewski, Sept. 1, 2002; 3 children by previous marriage. BSc, Worcester Poly. Inst., 1957; MA, Princeton U., 1959, PhD, 1960. Postdoctoral fellow U. Basel, Switzerland, 1961-62; asst. prof. chemistry UCLA, 1962-67; assoc. prof. chemistry McGill U., Montreal, Que., Can., 1967-74, prof., 1975—; dir. Polymer McGill, 1991-99, Otto Maass Prof. Chemistry, 1993—. Cons. in field. Author 7 books in field; contbr. articles to profl. jours. NATO fellow, 1961-62; Killam Research fellow, 1987-88; recipient E.W.R. Steacie award, 1998, Prix Urgel Archambault, 2004. Fellow Royal Soc. Can., Am. Phys. Soc. (chmn. div. high polymer physics 1975-76), Chem. Inst. Can. (Macromolecular Sci. and Engrng.-Dunlop award 1988, E.W.R. Steacie award 1998); mem. Am. Chem. Soc. Achievements include patents in field. Office: McGill University 801 Sherbrooke St W Montreal PQ Canada H3A 2K6 Business E-Mail: adi.eisenberg@mcgill.ca.

EISENBERG, ALAN, professional society administrator; b. N.Y.C., Apr. 15, 1935; s. Arthur and Mollie (Novak) E.; m. Claire Copley, May 23, 1982; children: Mollie Copley, Emma Copley. AB, U. Mich., 1956; LLB, NYU, 1959. Bar: N.Y., Va., D.C. Assoc. Booth. Lipton & Lipton, N.Y.C., 1960, Hirson & Bertini, N.Y.C., 1960-64; atty. NLRB, Washington and Chgo., 1964-68; assoc. Seligman & Seligman, N.Y.C., 1968-72; ptnr. Eisenberg & Paul, Arlington, Va., 1972-81; exec. dir. Actors' Equity Assn., N.Y.C., 1981—. Vis. prof. theatre adminstrn. Yale U. Sch. Drama, New Haven, 1982—; adj. faculty Sch. of Arts Columbia U., 1995-98. Gen. v.p. dept. for profl. employees AFL-CIO; dir. Actor's Equity Found., Non Traditional Casting Project, Inc., Career Transition for Dancers, Times Square Bus. Improvement Dist.; trustee Equity League Pension and Health Funds, Actors' Fund of Am.; trustee, v.p. Broadway Cares, Equity Fights AIDS. Office: Actors' Equity Assn 165 W 46th St Fl 15 New York NY 10036-2500 Office Phone: 212-869-8530. E-mail: aeisenberg@actorsequity.org.

EISENBERG, BARBARA ANNE K., lawyer; b. NYC, Oct. 7, 1945; d. Jerome Comet and Joy Klein; m. Edward Eisenberg, Oct. 20, 1974; 1 child. BA with distinction, Barnard Coll., 1967; JD cum laude, Columbia U., 1970. Bar: N.Y. Assoc. Kaye, Scholer, Fierman, Hays & Handler, 1970—77; v.p., gen. counsel, corp. sec. Pantasote Inc., Greenwich, Conn., 1978-86; asst. gen. counsel Burlington Industries, Inc., N.Y.C., 1986-88, v.p., assoc. gen. counsel, asst. sec., 1988-93, v.p., assoc. gen. counsel, corp. sec., 1993—98; sr. v.p., gen. counsel, corp. sec. J. Crew Group, Inc., 1998—2001; sr. v.p., gen. counsel, sec. Ann Taylor Stores Corp., N.Y.C., 2001—05, exec. v.p., gen. counsel, corp. sec., 2005—. Pres. Columbia Law Sch. Assn., 2000—02; mem. bd. visitors Columbia Law Sch., 2002—, bd. dirs., Maidenform Brands, 2005—; first v.p. Columbia Law Sch. Assn., 1998—2000; mem. Info. Tech. Law Commn., 2000—01. Mem. ABA, Assn. of Bar of City of N.Y., Corp. Bar Assn. (bd. dirs. 1986-88, vice chmn. SEC-fin. com. 1984-85, chmn. 1985-86), Am. Soc. Corr. Secs. Office: Ann Taylor Stores Corp 142 W 57th St New York NY 10019 Office Phone: 212-536-4229. Office Fax: 212-536-4412. E-mail: barbara_eisenberg@anntaylor.com.

EISENBERG, BRUCE ALAN, lawyer; b. Balt., Dec. 3, 1952; s. Leonard E. and Elaine Bondy Eisenberg; m. Doreen E. Caplan, Aug. 30, 1977; children: Brett H., Lindsay A. BA, Yale U., 1974; JD, U. Pa., 1977. Bar: Pa. 1977, D.C. 1979, Md. 1979. Assoc. Pepper Hamilton & Scheetz, Phila., 1977-78; law clk. to Hon. Raymond Broderick, U.S. Dist. Ct. for Ea. Dist. Pa., Phila., 1978-79; ptnr. Cohen Snyder Eisenberg & Katzenberg, Balt., 1979—. Avocations: softball, soccer, racquetball. Home: 2103 Burdock Rd Baltimore MD 21209-1001 Office: Cohen Snyder Et Al 347 N Charles St Baltimore MD 21201-4307

EISENBERG, CAROLA, psychiatrist, educator; b. Buenos Aires, Sept. 15, 1917; came to U.S., 1945; d. Bernardo and Teodora (Kahan) Blitzman; m. Manfred Guttmacher, Oct. 11, 1946 (dec. 1966); m. Leon Eisenberg, Aug. 31, 1967; children: Laurence, Alan. M of Social Work, Liceo de Senoritas; MD, U. Buenos Aires, 1945. Resident in psychiatry U. Md., 1946-48; fellow in child psychiatry Johns Hopkins Hosp., 1948-50, asst. prof. psychiatry and pediatrics Balt., 1960-67; psychiatrist MIT, Boston, 1967-72, dean of students, 1972-78; dean student affairs Harvard Med. Sch., Boston, 1978-90, dir. internat. programs for students, 1990-92, lectr. psychiatry, 1970-92, lectr. social medicine, 1992—. Co-chmn. women in biomed. careers workshop Office on Women's Health, NIH, 1992, mem. adv. com. on rsch. and women's health, 1995-98; mem. com. on human rights ACP; mem. com. on women in sci. and engrng. NAS, 1992-95. V.p. Physicians for Human Rights, Boston, 1987-, pres. 1993-2000. Recipient Morani Renaissance Woman award, Found. for History of Women in Medicine, 2003. Fellow Am. Psychiat. Assn. (Disting. life fellow 2003, mem. Coun. Internat. Affairs, com. on human rights, Human Rights award 2005), Am. Orthopsychiat. Assn. (life); mem. AAUP. Avocations: travel, music, reading. Home and Office: 9 Clement Cir Cambridge MA 02138-2205 Office Phone: 617-868-0112. Business E-Mail: carola_eisenberg@hms.harvard.edu.

EISENBERG, DANIEL, filmmaker; Instr. in film Collective For Living Cinema, NY, 1978, Boston Film/Video Found., 1979; asst. prof. film Mass. Coll. Art, Boston, 1979—82, 1993—94, instr. video, 1987; spl. instr. in film and photography U. R.I., Kingston, 1984; vis. artist in film San Francisco Art Inst., 1993; asst. prof. film, chair dept. filmmaking Sch. Art Inst. Chgo., 1994—97, assoc. prof. film, chair dept. filmmaking, 1998—2000, prof. film, video, new media, 2001. Editor various works WGBH, Boston, 1981—90; presenter in field. One-man shows include Collective for Living Cinema, NYC, 1981, 1989, MIT, Cambridge, 1984, Sch. Mus. Fine Arts, Boston, 1986, Boston Film/Video Found., 1987, Montserrat Sch. Art, Beverly, Mass., 1987, Brattle Theatre, Cambridge, 1988, Art Cinema, Binghamton, N.Y., 1988, Mass. Coll. Art, Boston, 1988, San Francisco Cinematheque, San Francisco, 1988, Pacific Film Archive, Berkeley, 1988, Kino Arsenal, Berlin, 1988, 1991, Am. Mus. Moving Image, NY, 1988, Inst. Contemporary Arts, Boston, 1989, Mus. Modern Art, Cineprobe, NY, 1989, 1998, Harvard U., Grad. Sch. Design, 1990, Boston Film/Video Found., 1991, London Filmmakers Coop, 1991, Hochschule der Kunst, Berlin, 1991, Braunschweig, 1991, Musée du Cinema, Brussels, 1991, Kommunales Kino, Hannover, 1991, Kiel, 1991, De Unie, Rotterdam, 1992, 't Hoogt, Utrecht, 1992, Filmmuseum, Frankfurt, 1992, Munich, 1992, Musee Nat. d'Art Moderne, 1992, Calif. Coll. Arts and Crafts, Oakland, 1993, Davis Mus., 1994, U. Iowa, Iowa City, 1996, L.A. Film Forum, 1997, Pacific Film Archive, Berkeley, Calif., 1997, Rocky Mountain Film Ctr., Boulder, Colo., 1998, Boston U., 1998, Harvard Film Archive, Cambridge, 1998, exhibited in group shows at Viper, Lucerne, Switzerland, 1995, Sydney Internat. Film Festival, 1997, Vue Sur Les Docs Festival, Marseilles, 1998, Goethe Inst., Chgo., 1999, numerous others; filmmaker: Matrice, 1975; Design and Debris, 1979; Mexican Sketch, 1980; Displaced Person, 1981; Native Shore, 1983; To A Brother In Asia, 1983; Motion Studies, 1979—90; Cooperation of Parts, 1987; Persistance, 1997; Something More Than Night, 2003. Named Berlin artist-in-residence, Deutscher Akademischer Austauschdienst, 1991, 1997; recipient Outstanding Film award, New Eng. Film Festival, 1981, CEBA awards for excellence, 1988, Hon. Mention, New Eng. Film Festival, 1988, Grand prize, Black Maria Film and Video Festival, 1988—89; fellow in film, Mass. Artists Found., 1982; grantee Mass. Prodns. grantee, Mass. Coun. on Arts, 1986—88, Sch. Art Inst. Faculty Enrichment, 1995, 1997; New Eng. Regional fellow, Nat. Endowment Arts, 1982, Media Arts grantee, 1989—92, artist fellow, The MacDowell Colony, 1990, fellow in film, Mass. Artists Found., 1991, John Simon Guggenheim Meml. Found. fellow, 1999—2000, Ill. Coun. Arts Fellowship, 2001. Home: 1411 W Edgewater Ave Chicago IL 60660-4208 E-mail: deisen@artic.edu.*

EISENBERG, DOROTHY, federal judge; b. 1929; LLB, Bklyn. Law Sch., 1950. Bar: N.Y. 1951, U.S. Dist. Ct. (ea. and so. dists.) N.Y., U.S. Ct. Appeals (2nd cir.), U.S. Supreme Ct. Assoc. Otterbourg, Stiendler, Houston & Rosen, N.Y.C., 1950-51, Goldman, Horowitz & Cherno, Mineola, NY, 1970-80; pvt. practice Garden City, NY, 1981; ptnr. Shaw, Licitra, Eisenberg, Esernio & Schwartz, P.C., Garden City, 1981-89; bankruptcy judge ea. dist. U.S. Bankruptcy Ct., NY, 1989—. Mem. Com. on Character and Fitness, Appellate divsn., 2nd Dept., 1983-89; panel trustee U.S. Bankruptcy Ct. (so. dist.) N.Y., 1979-89, U.S. Bankruptcy Ct. (ea. dist.) N.Y., 1975-89. Fellow: Am. Bar Found.; mem.: ABA, Fed. Bar Coun. (mem. adv. coun. 2nd cir.), Nassau Suffolk Women's Bar Assn. (former pres.), Bar Assn. Nassau County, Am. Bankruptcy Inst., N.Y. State Women's Bar Assn. (Nassau County chpt.), Nat. Assn. Women Judges. Office: LI Fed Courthouse 290 Federal Plz PO Box 9013 Central Islip NY 11722-4437

EISENBERG, HOWARD BRUCE, law educator; b. Chgo., Dec. 9, 1946; s. Herman Levy and Margie M. (Meyers) E.; m. Phyllis Terry Borenstein, Aug. 25, 1968; children: Nathan, Adam, Leah. BA, Northwestern U., 1968; JD, U. Wis., 1971. Bar: Wis. 1971, D.C. 1980, Ill. 1983, U.S. Dist. Ct. (ea. and we. dists.) Wis. 1971, U.S. Ct. Appeals (8th cir.) 1983, U.S. Supreme Ct. 1974, U.S. Ct. Appeals (D.C. cir.) 1978, U.S. Dist. Ct. (ea. and we. dists.) Ark. 1991. Mem. staff Wis. Judicare Legal Svcs. Agy. OEO, Madison, 1968-71; law clk. to justice Wis. Supreme Ct., 1971-72; asst. state pub. defender State of Wis., 1972, state pub. defender, 1972-78; dir. defender divsn. Nat. Legal Aid and Defender Assn., Washington, 1978-79, exec. dir., 1979-83; assoc. prof. law, dir. clin. edn. So. Ill. U., Carbondale, 1983-91, assoc. prof., 1983-87, prof., 1987-91; dean Sch. Law, prof. law U. Ark., Little Rock, 1991-95; dean, prof. law Law Sch. Marquette U., 1995—. Mem. Wis. Bd. Bar Examiners, 1996—, chmn., 2001; bd. dirs. appellate practice sect. Bar of Wis., 1999—, chmn., 2001—; dir. Coalition for Legal Assn., 1981—82, Ill. Guardianship and Protective Svcs. Assn., 1990—91, Ark. CLE Bd., 1991—95, Pulaski County Bar Assn., 1991—95, Ark. Inst. CLE, Assn. Religiously Affiliated Law Schs.; chair Fed. Jud. Nominating Commn., Ea. Dist., Wis., 1995—. Contbr. articles to profl. jours. Bd. dirs. Hospice So. Ill., 1988-91, Milw. Legal Aid Soc., 1997—. Ill. State scholar, 1964-68; NDEA grantee, 1967. Mem. ABA, Am. Acad. Appellate Lawyers, Nat. Acad. Elder Law Attys., State Bar Wis., Wis. Assn. Criminal Attys., Ark. State Bar Assn., 7th Cir. Bar Assn., Ill. State Bar Assn., Milw. Bar Assn., Milw. Bar Assn. Found. (bd. 1997—), Equal Justice Coalition (bd. mem. 1998—), Nat. Assn. Criminal Def. Lawyers, Northwestern U. Alumni Assn., Wis. U. Alumni Assn., Phi Beta Kappa. Democrat. Jewish. Office: Marquette U Sch of Law PO Box 1881 Milwaukee WI 53201-1881

EISENBERG, HOWARD MICHAEL, neurosurgeon; b. NYC, May 4, 1939; s. Monroe L. and Regina (Fish) Eisenberg; children: Nancy M. Hoy, John A. BA, Syracuse U., 1960; MD, SUNY, NYC, 1964. Diplomate Am. Bd. Neurol. Surgery. Intern NY Hosp., 1964-65; resident, fellow Cornell U. Med. Sch., 1964-66; resident neurosurgeon Peter Bent Brigham Hosp., Boston, 1966-70; surgery instr. Harvard U., 1972-75; assoc. prof. U. Tex. Med. Br., Galveston, 1975-80, prof., chief neurosurgery, 1980-92; head divsn. neurosurgery U. Md., Balt., 1992-96, dir. med. svcs. Shock Trauma Ctr., 1992-96, prof. chair dept. neurosurgery, 1996—, R.K. Thompson prof., 2000—. Chmn. neurology A study sect. NIH, Bethesda, Md., 1980—87; numerous vis. professorships and guest lectureships. Mem. editl. bd. Jour. Neurosurgery, 1989—99, chair, 1997—99; editor: (book) The Cerebral Microvasulature, 1980, Neurobehavioral Recovery from Head Injury, 1987, Mild Head Injury, 1989, Neurosurgery Clinics of North America-Mangement of Head Injury, 1991, The Frontal Lobes, 1991; contbr. articles to profl. jours. Mem. devel. bd. Houston Grand Opera, 1989—92. Lt. comdr. USN, 1970—72. Recipient William Cavernes award, Nat. Head Injury Found., 1994, Wakeman award, 1990; numerous grants in field. Mem.: ACGME (mem. residency rev. com. neurosurgery 2001—02, v.p.), ACS (chair neurosurgical adv. coun.), Am. Surg. Assn., Acad. Neurol. Surgeons (v.p.), Soc. Neurol. Surgeons (v.p., pres.-elect, pres.), Am. Bd. Neurol. Surgery (bd. dirs., sec.-treas., bd. dirs. 1990—95, chmn. 1995—96), NY Yacht Club (mem. seamanship com.), Cruising Club Am., Annapolis Yacht. Club, Cosmos Club. Office: U Md Med Systems Dept Neurosurgery 22 S Greene St Ste S12D Baltimore MD 21201-1544 Office Phone: 410-328-3514. Business E-Mail: heisenberg@smail.umaryland.edu.

EISENBERG, LEON, psychiatrist, educator; b. Phila., Aug. 8, 1922; s. Morris and and Elizabeth (Sabreen) E.; m. Ruth Harriet Bleier, June 11, 1948 (div. 1967); children: Mark Philip, Kathy Bleier; m. Carola Blitzman Guttmacher, Aug. 31, 1967; children: Laurence, Alan. AB, U. Pa., 1944, MD, 1946; MA (hon.), Harvard U., 1967; DSc (hon.), U. Manchester, Eng., 1973, U. Mass., 1991. Diplomate: in child psychiatry and psychiatry Am. Bd. Psychiatry and Neurology. Intern Mt. Sinai Hosp., N.Y.C., 1946—47; instr. physiology U. Pa., 1947-48; resident psychiatry Sheppard-Pratt Hosp., Towson, Md., 1950-52; with Johns Hopkins, 1952-67, prof. child psychiatry Med. Sch., 1961-67; psychiatrist-in-charge children's psychiat. service Harriet Lane Home, 1958-67; prof. psychiatry Harvard U. Med. Sch., Boston, 1967—, Maude and Lillian Presley prof. psychiatry, 1975-80, chmn. exec. com. dept. psychiatry, 1973-80, Maude and Lillian Presley prof. social medicine, 1980-93, chmn. dept., 1980-91, prof. of social medicine emeritus, 1993—; psychiatrist-in-chief Mass. Gen. Hosp., 1967-74, mem. bd. consultation, 1974—; sr. assoc. in psychiatry Children's Hosp., Boston, 1974—; prof. emeritus, 1993—. Paley lectr. Cornell U., 1983; Schilder lectr. NYU, 1984; Eli Robins lectr. Washington U., St. Louis, 1985; plenary session lectr. Internat. Pediat. Assn., Amsterdam, 1998; lectr. Italian Psychiat. Soc., Bologna, 1998; Alpha Omega Alpha lectr. U. Rochester, 1999; plenary lectr. World Psychiat. Assn., Athens, 1999; vis. lectr. Yale U., 1987, John Peters lectr., 2002; R.W. Johnson vis. prof. U. Rochester, 1987; Carolyn Voorsanger lectr. Stanford U. Med. Sch., 1989; Willard Sears Simpkins lectr. Johns Hopkins U., 1989; William Potter lectr. Thomas Jefferson U., 1992; vis. prof. McMaster U., Canada, 1991, Charles U., Prague; psychiat. cons. Crownsville (Md.) State Hosp., 1954—58, Rosewood State Tng. Sch., Owings Mills, Md., 1957—60, Balt. City Hosp., 1959—62, Children's Guild, Balt., 1954—61; cons. Sinai Hosp., Balt., 1963—67; Mapother-Lewis ann. lectr. Maudsley Hosp., London, 1977; Baan Meml. lectr. Netherlands Psychiat. Soc., Amsterdam, 1978; Royal Soc. Medicine vis. prof., London, 83; mem. subcom. psychiat. nomenclature com. vital stats. USPHS; chmn. WHO Conf. Devel. Regulation, 1964—67; mem. Joint Commn. Mental Health of Children; cons. divsn. mental health WHO, 1974—, chmn. sci. group on evaluation of psychiat. treatment, 1989; mem. adv. com. to dir. NIH, 1977—80; lectr. Can. Royal Coll. Psychiatry, 1993, Italian Soc. for Biol. Psychiatry, Cagliari, Sardinia, 1994; Richard Goldbloom lectr. Dalhousie U., Halifax, N.S., Canada, 1995; Wolfe Adler lectr. Sheppard-Pratt Hosp. Sys., Balt., 1995; spl. lectr. Health of the Child of the Eve of the Yr. 2000, Bologna, Italy, 1995; plenary lectr. Royal Australian & New Zealand Coll. Psychiatry, 1999, World Congress of Psychiatry, Hamburg, 1999, XII World Congress of Psychiatry, Yokohama, Japan, 2002. Editor Am. Jour. Orthopsychiatry, 1963-73; editorial bd.: Culture, Medicine and Psychiatry, Psychol. Medicine, Jour. Psychiat. Research, 2005. Capt. M.C., U.S. Army, 1948-50. Recipient Theobald Smith award Albany Med. Coll., 1979, Orton award Orton Soc., 1980, Disting. Alumnus award U. Pa., 1992, Presdl. Commendation Am. Psychiat. Assn., 1992, Agnes Purchell McGavin award, 1994, Camille Cosby World of Children award Judge Baker Children's Ctr., 1994, Salmon medal N.Y. Acad. Medicine, 1995, Mumford award and lecture, 1996, Walshe McDermott Medal, Inst. of Medicine, 2003, Ruane prize for child and adolescent psychiatry rsch. Nat. Alliance for Rsch. on Schizophrenic and Affective Disorder, 2003, Child Psychiatry Rsch. award, Nat. Assn. Rsch. in Schizophrenia and Affective Disorder, 2005. Fellow: AAAS, Royal Soc. Medicine, Soc. Rsch. Child Devel. (Pub. Policy award 2003), Royal Coll. Psychiatrists (hon.; Eli Lilly lectr. 1986), Am. Psychiat. Assn. (life; trustee 1973—76, Disting. Svc. award 2003, Human Rights award 2005), Am. Orthopsychiat. Assn. (life Ittleson Meml. award 1996); mem.: I.O.M. (chair com. on planned childbearing 1993—95, chair com. bridging the brain, behavioral and clin. scis. 1999—2000), AAUP (past pres. Johns Hopkins chpt.), Mass. Med. Soc., Soc. Neurosci., Psychiat. Rsch. Soc. (past pres.), Am. Acad. Arts and Scis. (comm. sec. 1995—2002), Md. Psychiat. Soc. (past pres.), Ecuadorean Soc. Neurosci. (hon.), Greek Soc. Neurology and Psychiatry (hon.), Am. Psychopath. Assn., Assn. Rsch. Nervous and Mental Disease, Can. Pediat. Soc. (Queen Elizabeth II lectr. 1986), Am. Pediat. Soc., Am. Acad. Pediat. (Dale Richmond lectr. 1989, Aldrich award 1980), Inst. Medicine NAS (coun. 1975—77, program and membership coms. 1979—82, bd. on health sci. policy 1989—91, Rhoda and Bernard Sarnat prize in mental health 1996),

Johns Hopkins Soc. Scholars, Alpha Omega Alpha (lectr. Jefferson Med. Coll. 1994), Sigma Xi, Phi Beta Kappa (chpt. pres. 1958, vis. scholar 1994—95). Home: 9 Clement Cir Cambridge MA 02138-2205 Office: Harvard U Med Sch Dept Soc Med Boston MA 02115 E-mail: Leon_Eisenberg@HMS.Harvard.edu.

EISENBERG, MARVIN JULIUS, art history educator; b. Phila., Aug. 19, 1922; s. Frank and Rosalie (Julius) E. BA, U. Pa., 1943; M.F.A., Princeton, 1949, PhD, 1954; D.Litt. (hon.), St Andrews, 2003. Mem. faculty U. Mich., Ann Arbor, 1949-89, prof. art history, chmn. dept., 1960-69, Collegiate prof., 1974-75, prof. emeritus, 1989—; mem. Inst. for Advanced Study, Princeton, N.J., 1970. Vis. com. dept. fine arts, Freer Gallery Art, Washington, 1970-96, Harvard U., 1975-81, Commn. on Preservation and Access, Washington, 1991-94, Ga. Mus. Art, 1997—; vis. prof. Stanford U., 1973, Mt. Holyoke Coll., 1995; disting. Berg prof. Colo. Coll., 1990, 93, 95, 97, 2000, 02; Hooker disting. vis. prof. McMaster U., 1993; Robert Lehman lectr. Bowdoin Coll., 1985; Saunders lectr. St Andrews U., 1998; lectr. U. Dayton, 2002; adv. com. Center for Advanced Study in Visual Arts, Nat. Gallery, Washington, 1981-84. Author: Lorenzo Monaco, 1989; co-author: The Confraternity Altarpiece by Mariotto di Nardo, 1998; contbr. articles to profl. jours Served with AUS, 1943-46. Recipient Star of Solidarity II Italy, 1966; Coll. Art Assn. Disting. Teaching of Art History award, 1987; Guggenheim fellow, 1959. Fellow Japan Soc. for Promotion of Sci.; mem. Coll. Art Assn. Am. (dir. 1965-70, v.p. 1966-67, pres. 1968-69), Royal Soc. Arts (Benjamin Franklin fellow 1969), Phi Beta Kappa, Phi Kappa Phi, Pi Gamma Mu. Home: 2200 Fuller Ct Apt 1002 Ann Arbor MI 48105-2307

EISENBERG, MELVIN A., law educator; b. NY, Dec. 3, 1934; s. Max and Laura (Wallance) E.; m. Helen Garlitz, Feb. 5, 1956; children: Bronwyn, David Abram (dec. 1997). AB, SCL, Columbia U., 1956; LLB, SCL, Faye Diploma in Law, Harvard U., 1959; LLD (hon.), U. Milan, 1998; LLD (hon.), U. Cologne, 2004. Bar: N.Y. 1960. Assoc. Kaye Scholer Fierman Hays & Handler, 1959-63, 64-66; corp. counsel City of N.Y., 1966; acting prof. U. Calif.-Berkeley, 1966-69, prof. law, 1969-83, Koret prof. law, 1983—. Vis. prof. Harvard U., 1969-70; vis. prof. law Columbia U., 1998—, Stephen and Barbara Friedman vis. prof. law, 2005; asst. counsel Pres. Commn. on Assassination Pres. Kennedy, Warren Commn., 1964; counsel mayor's task force on reorgn N.Y.C. govt., 1966; mem. mayor's task force on N.Y.C. transp. reorgn., 1966; mem. mayors' task force on mcpl. collective bargaining, 1966; reporter Am. Law Inst., principles of corporate governance: analysis and recommendations, 1980-84, chief reporter, 1984-94, Ammi Cutter chair, 1991-93; adviser, restatement 3d of agy. 1996—; adviser, restatement 3d of restitution, 1998—; prof.-in-residence, Cologne U., 1984, U. Milan, 1992; mem. ABA com. on corp. laws, 1992—; U. Iowa Inaugural lectr., 1987, Roy R. Ray lectr. So. Meth. U., 1993, Robert L. Levine Distg. lectr., Fordham U., 1993; Pillegi lectr. Weidener U., 2004; chmn. AALS contracts sect., 1989, AALS contracts workshop, 1986; chmn. AALS bus. assns. sect., 1998; visitor-in-residence U. Murdoch, U. Western Australia, 1992, McGill U., 1981; Sobeloff lectr. U. Md., 1994; Freehill, Hollingsdale and Page vis. fellow U. New South Wales, Australia, 1994. Author: The Structure of the Corporation, 1977 (Coif Triennial Book award honorable mention 1980), The Nature of the Common Law, 1988, (with L. Fuller) Basic Contract Law, 2001, Cases and Materials on Corporations and Other Business Organization, 2000; also numerous articles. Pres. Queen's Child Guidance Ctr., 1963-66. Guggenheim fellow, 1971-72, Canterbury vis. fellow U. Canterbury, New Zealand, 1988, Kimber fellow York U., Toronto, 1989, Rabin fellow Yale Sch. Law, vis. fellow Doshisha U., Kyoto, Japan, 2003—; Fulbright Sr. scholar, Australia, 1987, Disting. Mellon scholar U. Pitts., 1989, Manuel F. Cohen vis. scholar George Washington U. Sch. Law; Cooley lectr. U. Mich., 1985; Baron de Hirsch Meyer lectr. U. Miami Sch. Law, 1983, Wythe lectr. William and Mary Law Sch., 1999, TePoel lectr. Creighton U. Sch. Law, 1982; recipient Faye Diploma Harvard U. Law Sch., Rudder Outstanding Tchg. award Boalt Hall Law Sch., 2002, Disting. Tchg. award U. Calif., Berkeley, 1990. Fellow AAAS; mem. ABA (com. on corp. law 1992--), Am. Law Inst., Am. Assn. Law Schs. (chair contracts sect. 1989, chair bus. assns. sect. 1999), Phi Beta Kappa. Office: U Calif Sch Law 331 Boalt Hl Berkeley CA 94720-0001 also: 201 E 79th St New York NY 10021-0830 also: Columbia U Law Sch 435 W 116th St New York NY 10027-7201 Office Phone: 510-642-1799. E-mail: eisenberg@law.berkeley.edu.

EISENBERG, MEYER, lawyer; b. Bklyn., Dec. 15, 1931; BA, Bklyn. Coll., 1953; LLB, Columbia U., 1958. Bar: N.Y. 1960, D.C. 1970, U.S. Supreme Ct. 1963. Law clk. to Chief Justice William McAllister Supreme Ct. Oreg., Salem, 1958-59; atty. SEC, Washington, 1959-70, counsel spl. study securities markets, 1962-64, asst. gen. counsel, 1966-68, exec. asst. to chmn., 1968-69, assoc. gen. counsel, 1969-70; with firm Lawler, Kent & Eisenberg, Washington, 1970-79, Rosenman, Colin, Freund, Lewis & Cohen, Washington, 1980-87, Ballard, Spahr, Andrews & Ingersoll, Washington, 1987-93, Kramer, Levin, Naftalis & Frankel, Washington, 1994-98; dep. gen. coun. sec. SEC, Washington, 1998—. Adj. prof. law George Washington U., 1972-75, Georgetown U. Law Sch., 1988-90; vis. prof. law U. Calif., Berkeley; dir. Nat. Ctr. Fin. Svcs., 1985-86; mem. adv. com. Calif. Securities Regulation Inst.; cons. in field. Contbr. articles to profl. publs. Mem. internat. bd. govs. B'nai B'rith, 1978-92; mem. nat. exec. com. Anti-Defamation League, 1980—, nat. vice chmn., 1994—, chmn. Nat. Civil Rights Com., 1992-94, Nat. Legal Affairs Com., 1980-92. Mem. ABA (chmn. com. on devels. in investment svcs. 1981-86, chmn. com. on long-range issues affecting bus. law practice 1986-90, coun. sect. bus. law 1990-94, chmn. com. on internat. tech. assistance 1994—, sec. bus. law), Fed. Bar Assn. (chmn. securities law com. 1984-85). Home: 8216 Lakenheath Way Potomac MD 20854-2740 Office: SEC Office of Gen Counsel 450 5th St NW Washington DC 20549-0001 E-mail: eisenbergm@sec.gov.

EISENBERG, PABLO SAMUEL, non-profit organization executive; b. Paris, July 1, 1932; came to U.S. 1939; s. Maurice and Paula (Halpert) E.; m. Helen Leone Cierniak, June 5, 1960; 1 child, Marina. BA, Princeton U., 1954; BLitt, Oxford (Eng.) U., 1957; LLD (hon.), Princeton U., 2004. Fgn. svc. officer USIA, 1960-63; program dir. Operation Crossroads Africa, N.Y.C., 1963-65; coord. Pa. Office Econ. Opportunity, 1965-67; dep. dir. Rsch. and Demonstration Office, Office of Econ. Opportunity, Washington, 1967-68; asst. dir. Nat. Urban Coalition, Washington, 1968-73; ind. cons. Washington, 1973-75; pres. Ctr. for Cmty. Change, Washington, 1975-98; sr. fellow, cons. Georgetown Pub. Policy Inst., Washington, 1998—. Author: The Courage to Change, 2004; contbr. articles to profl. jours., chpts. to book; columnist Chronicle of Philanthropy. Mem. exec. com. Nat. Com. for Responsive Philanthropy, Washington, 1976—; pres. Friends of VISTA, Washington, 1976-1998, 1980—; bd. dirs. Eureka Cmtys., Coll. Pub. Svc. and Citizenship, Tufts U., 1993-2000, Milton Eisenhower Found., Citizens Funds. Recipient John Gardner Leadership award, 1998; German Marshall Fund of U.S. travelling fellow, 1988. Democrat. Jewish. Avocations: tennis, antique books, movies, sports. Home: 3729 Massachusetts Ave NW Washington DC 20016-5004 Office: Pub Policy Inst Georgetown U 3240 Prospect St NW Washington DC 20007-3214 Office Phone: 202-244-7885. E-mail: pseisenberg@erols.com.

EISENBERG, PAUL RICHARD, cardiologist, consultant, educator; b. Rome, Mar. 9, 1955; came to U.S., 1956; s. David Marvin and Sonia Maria (Benedetti) E.; m. Patricia Lynn Goodman, Apr. 25, 1982; 1 child, Jamie. BS, Tulane U., 1975, MPH, 1980; MD, N.Y. Med. Coll., Valhalla, 1980. Diplomate Am. Bd. Internal Medicine, Am. Bd. Cardiology. Intern in internal medicine Barnes Hosp., St. Louis, 1980-83, fellow in cardiology, pulmonary medicine, 1983-85, asst. dir. CCU, 1986-91, dir. CCU, 1991-98; asst. prof. Washington U., St. Louis, 1985-91, assoc. prof., 1991-97, prof., 1997-98; med. dir. cardiovasc. therapeutics Eli Lilly & Co., Indpls., 1998-2000, exec. dir. cardiovasc. discovery, 2000—01, v.p. med., 2001—02, v.p. global drug safety, 2003—. Asst. editor: Medical Management of Heart Disease; contbr. over 100 articles to profl. jours. Fellow Am. Heart Assn. (clin. cardiology), Am. Coll. Chest Physicians, Am. Coll. Cardiology; mem. Am. Fedn. Clin. Rsch., Internat. Soc. Thrombosis and Haemostasis. Office: Lilly Rsch Labs Lily Corp Ctr Drop Code 0520 Ctr Indianapolis IN 46285-0001

EISENBERG, R. NEAL, restoration company executive; b. Newark, July 15, 1936; s. William C. and Elsie G. (Greenfield) E.; m. Barbara J. Mayer, Dec. 18, 1966; children: Michael S., Elissa P. Student, Stevens Inst. Tech., 1954-55; postgrad. Coll. Engring., NYU, 1955-57, BS in Acctg., 1960. Sr. acct. Puder & Puder (now Deloitte Touche), Newark, 1958-60, J.H. Cohn & Co., Roseland, NJ, 1960-63; ptnr. Universal Engring. Waterpoofing Svc., Newark, 1963-69; pres. Universal Restoration Waterproofing Svc., Inc., West Orange, NJ, 1970—; v.p. Universal Restoration, Inc., Washington, 1967-69, pres., CEO, 1993-96; v.p. Restoration Svcs., Inc., Washington, 1967-69; pres. Vitrifix N.Am., Inc., Washington, 1986-87; chmn. Universal Family Group, West Orange, 1987—; pres. Universal Waterproofing Svc., Inc., West Orange, 1969—. Cons. expert structural restoration. Co-inventor Dekosit/Permo-Bond Restoration Method. Recipient Second Biennial Design award Gen. Svcs. Administrn., 1967. Mem. Constrn. Specifications Inst., Nat. Assn. Waterproofing Contractors, Nat. Trust Hist. Preservation, NJ Bus. Industry Assn., Masons. Office: Universal Waterproofing Svc 623 Eagle Rock Ave Ste 377 West Orange NJ 07052-2948

EISENBERG, REBECCA S., law educator; b. 1955; BA, Stanford U., 1975; JD, U. Calif., Berkeley, 1979. Bar: Calif. 1979. Law clk. to Hon. Robert F. Peckham U.S. Dist. Ct. (no. dist.) Calif., San Francisco, 1979-80; assoc. Heller, Ehrman, White & McAuliffe, San Francisco, 1980-83, Petty, Andrews, Tufts & Jackson, San Francisco, 1983-84; asst. prof. U. Mich., Ann Arbor, 1984-87, assoc. prof., 1987-89, prof., 1989—, Robert and Barbara Luciano prof. law. Mem. adv. com. to dir. NIH; mem. Panel on Sci., Tech. and Health, NAS; bd. dirs. Stem Cell Genomics and Therapeutics Network, Canada. Office: U Mich Law Sch 407 Hutchins Hall 625 S State St Ann Arbor MI 48109-1215 Office Phone: 734-763-1372, 734-763-9375. E-mail: rse@umich.edu.*

EISENBERG, RICHARD S., chemistry professor; b. NYC, Feb. 12, 1943; s. Paul and Norma (Frommer) E.; m. Marcia Landau, Aug. 6, 1966; children: Alan, Robert. AB, Columbia U., 1963, MA, 1964, PhD, 1967. Asst. prof. chemistry Brown U., Providence, 1967-71, assoc. prof., 1971-73; assoc. prof. chemistry U. Rochester (N.Y.), 1973-76, prof., 1976-96, chair, 1991-94, univ. mentor, 1986-87, assoc. dean Coll. Arts and Scis., 1989-91, Tracy H. Harris prof., 1996—. Vis. scientist Calif. Inst. Tech., 1977-78; vis. scholar Cambridge (Eng.) U., 1978; vis. prof. Columbia U., 1985; vice chmn. Gordon Conf. on Organometallic Chemistry, 1987, chmn., 1988; cons. SOHIO, Cleve., 1982-83, Eastman Kodak, Rochester, 1982; mem. adv. bd. Petroleum Rsch. Fund, 1988-91; Closs lectr. U. Chgo., 1994; vis. prof. Chemistry Rsch. Promotion Ctr., Republic of China, 1994; Coates lectr. U. Wyo., 1966; Varon vis. prof. Weizmann Inst., 1997; Miller vis. prof. U. Calif., Berkeley, 2005; Lady Davis fellow Hebrew U., 1997 Editor (jour.) Inorganic Chemistry, 2001—; contbr. numerous articles on chemistry to profl. jours.; mem. editorial adv. bd.: Jour. Am. Chem. Soc., 1982-84, Inorganic Chemistry, 1997-98, Organometallics, 1998-2000. NSF fellow, 1964-66, George B. Pegram Hon. fellow, 1964-65, Alfred P. Sloan fellow, 1972-74, Guggenheim fellow, 1977-78 Mem. Am. Chem. Soc. (chmn. organometallic subdiv. inorganic div. 1982, alt. councilor inorganic div. 1985-87, editorial adv. bd. jour. 1982-84, councilor inorganic div. 1988-90, chmn.-elect 1992, chmn. 1993, sci. com. 2003-05, Rochester Sect. award 2003, Disting. Svc. award 2003), Chem. Soc. Achievements include rsch. interests in homogeneous catalysts, organometallic compounds of platinum group elements, binuclear complexes, inorganic photochemistry; bond activiation and oxidative addition, parahydrogen induced polarization, metal hydrides, structure-function relationships in catalytically active systems. Home: 175 Parkwood Ave Rochester NY 14620-3403 Office: U Rochester River Campus Dept Chemistry Rochester NY 14627 E-mail: eisenberg@chem.rochester.edu.

EISENBERG, SONJA MIRIAM, artist; b. Berlin, June 10, 1926; arrived in U.S., 1938, naturalized, 1947; d. Adolf and Meta Cecilie (Bettauer) Weinberger; m. Jack Eisenberg, Mar. 31, 1946; children: Ralph, Lynn, Lauren. Student, Queens Coll., 1943—46, Middlebury Coll., 1945, NYU, 1952—54, BA, 1954; postgrad., Nat. Acad. Sch. Fine Arts, 1961. Artist-in-residence Cathedral of St. John the Divine, N.Y.C.; apptd. art dir. Hermes Media B.V., Amsterdam, 1992. One-woman shows include Bodley Gallery, N.Y.C., 1970, 1973, 1975, 1980, Galerie Art du Monde, Paris, 1973, Buyways Gallery, Sarasota, Fla., 1973—75, 1978, Galerie de Sfinx, Amsterdam, Netherlands, 1974, Huntsville (Ala.) Mus. Art, 1974, Anglo-Am. Art Mus., Baton Rouge, 1974, Comara Gallery, L.A., 1974, Palm Spring (Calif.) Desert Mus., 1975, Fordham U., N.Y.C., 1976, Omega Inst., New Lebanon, NY, 1979, Am. Mus., Hayden Planetarium, N.Y.C., 1980, Avila Graphics, Ltd., 1981, YWCA, N.Y.C., 1981, Cathedral of St. John the Divine, 1983, 1985, The Millbrook Gallery, NY, 1989, 1994, Christopher Leonard Gallery, N.Y.C., 1993, Park Hotel, Vitznau, Switzerland, 1994, The Burgenstock (Switzerland) Hotels, 1995, Wainscott Gallery, NY, 1997, Galerie Dussmann, Kulturkaufhaus, Berlin, 1998, Horton Gallery, Phila., 2001, exhibited in group shows at Mus. Fine Arts, St. Petersburg, Fla., 1973, Am. Watercolor Soc., 107th, 108th Exhbn., 1974—75, Galerie Frederic Gollong, St. Paul de Vence, France, 1978, Betty Parson's Gallery, N.Y.C., 1981, Foster Harmon Galleries of Am. Art, Sarasota, Fla., 1988, Tokyo Met. Art Mus. 14th Internat. Art Friendship Exhbn., 1989, Galerie Herbert Leidel, Munich, Germany, 1991, Park Ave. Armory, N.Y.C., 1996, Akim-USA, 1996, Represented in permanent collections Archives Am. Art, Smithsonian Inst., Jewish Mus., N.Y.C., Fordham U. Mus., Palm Springs Desert Mus., Omega Inst., Cathedral of St. John the Divine; designer WFUNA cachet for UN Water Power Conf., 1977, UN Internat. Yr. of Disabled Persons, 1981, commd. commemorative painting Crystal Night for Telecom Telefon Karte, Munich, 1993, completed project Seeing the Gospel According to St. John (text and 41 paintings) for Cathedral of St. John, 1987; author: From Here to There and Back Again, 2001, Poems and Paintings, 2002, The Red Painted House, 2002. Regent Cathedral of St. John the Divine, 1990. Recipient Gold medal for artistic merit, Internat. Parliament for Safety and Peace, 1983, Palma D'Oro Europe, 1986. Mem.: Accademia Italia delle Arti e del Lavoro (Gold medal 1981). Home and Office: 1020 Park Ave New York NY 10028-0913 Personal E-mail: sonjaeisenberg@aol.com. *When you focus your mind, you may break through the Known with its borders of words and ideas, and get a glimpse of the "nothing" that is so creative.*

EISENBERG, THEODORE, law educator; b. Bklyn., Oct. 26, 1947; s. Abraham Louis and Esther (Waldman) E.; m. Lisa Wright, Nov. 27, 1971; children: Katherine Wright, Ann Marie, Thomas Peter. BA, Swarthmore Coll., 1969; JD, U. Pa., 1972. Bar: Pa. 1972, N.Y. 1974, U.S. Ct. Appeals (2d cir.) 1974, Calif. 1977. Law clk. U.S. Ct. Appeals, D.C. Cir., 1972-73; law clk. to U.S. Supreme Ct. Justice Earl Warren, 1973; assoc. Debevoise & Plimpton, N.Y.C., 1974-77; prof. law UCLA Law Sch., 1977-81, Cornell U. Law Sch., Ithaca, N.Y., 1981-96, Henry Allen Mark prof. law, 1996—. Vis. prof. law Harvard U. Law Sch., 1984-85, 2004; vis. prof. Law, Stanford U. Law Sch., 1987. Author: Civil Rights Legislation, 1981, 5th edit., 2004, Bankruptcy and Debtor-Creditor Law, 1984, 3d edit., 2004; editor Jour. Empirical Legal Studies; mem. adv. bd. Law and Soc. Rev., Am. Law and Econ. Rev.; contbr. articles to profl. jours. Am. Bar Found grantee, NSF grantee. Fellow Royal Statis. Soc.; mem. ABA, Assn. Bar City N.Y., Law and Soc. Assn., Am. Law and Econ. Assn., Am. Bankruptcy Inst. Office: Cornell U Law Sch Myron Taylor Hall Ithaca NY 14853 E-mail: te13@cornell.edu.

EISENBERG, WARREN, retail executive; Former employee Arlan's; co-founder, co-CEO, co-chmn. Bed, Bath & Beyond, Union, N.J., 1999—. Office: Bed Bath & Beyond 650 Liberty Ave Union NJ 07083

EISENDRATH, CHARLES RICE, journalism educator, farmer, consultant; b. Chgo., Oct. 9, 1940; s. William Nathan and Erna Sarah (Rice) E.; m. Julia Cardozo, Jan. 28, 1967; children: Benjamin Cardozo, Mark William. BA, Yale U., 1962; MA, U. Mich., 1965. Reporter Post-Dispatch, St. Louis, 1962, 64, Evening Sun, Balt., 1966-68; corr. Time Mag., Washington, London, Paris, bur. chief Buenos Aires, 1968-73; prof. U. Mich., Ann Arbor, 1975—. Propr. Overlook Farm, East Jordan, Mich., 1972—; chmn. Grillworks, Inc., Ann Arbor, 1978—; cons. Midland Bank of London, Pfizer, W.K. Kellogg Found.; mem. Pulitzer Prize Jury, 2002—03. Contbr. articles to profl. jours.; inventor in field. Dir. Knight-Wallace Journalism Fellows, 1986—; founding dir. Livingston Awards, Ann Arbor, 1980—; judge nat. barbecue contest, 1994—; pres. task force journalism Columbia U., 2002-03. NEH Mich. Journalism fellow, 1974-75. Mem. Coun. Fgn. Rels., Century Assn. (N.Y.C.), Soc. Profl. Journalists, Com. of Concerned Journalists (founding), Project on the State of the Am. Newspaper (founding bd. dirs. 1998-2000), Landsdowne Club (London), Phi Kappa Phi. Jewish. Office: Wallace House 620 Oxford Rd Ann Arbor MI 48104-2623 E-mail: drath@umich.edu.

EISENHOWER, JOHN SHELDON DOUD, former ambassador, writer; b. Denver, Aug. 3, 1922; s. Dwight David (34th Pres. of U.S.) and Mamie (Doud) E.; m. Barbara Jean Thompson, June 10, 1947 (div. 1986); children: Dwight David II, Barbara Anne, Susan Elaine, Mary Jean; m. Joanne Thompson, Apr. 9, 1990. BS, U.S. Mil. Acad., 1944; MA in English Lit., Columbia, 1950; LHD (hon.), Northwood Inst., 1970. Commd. 2d lt. U.S. Army, 1944, advanced through grades to lt. col., 1963; assigned 1st Army, Europe, 1945, Army of Occupation, Europe, 1945-47, Korean War, 1952-53, Army Gen. Staff, 1957-58, White House Staff, 1958-61; resigned, 1963; brig. gen. USAR, 1974; engaged in writing, 1965-69; U.S. amb. to Belgium, Am. Embassy, Brussels, 1969-71. Cons. to the Pres.; also chmn. Interagency Classification Review Com., 1972-73; chmn. bd. Acad. Life Ins. Co., Atlanta; mem. adv. council Nat. Archives, 1974-77; chmn. President's Adv. Com. on Refugees, 1975; mil. editor Algonguin Books of Chapel Hill. Author: The Bitter Woods, 1969, Strictly Personal, 1974; editor: Letters to Mamie, 1978, Allies, 1982, So Far From God, 1989, Intervention!, 1993, Agent of Destiny, 1997, Yanks, 2001, General Ike, 2003. Mem. diplomatic coun., bd. govs. USO, 1983-85; trustee Alumni Fedn. Columbia U., 1976-80. Decorated Legion of Merit, Bronze Star, Combat Inf. badge, grand cross Order of Crown Belgium, Chungmu Disting. Service medal (Korea); recipient Grad. Faculties Alumni award for excellence Columbia U., 1970. Mem. Diplomatic and Consular Officers Ret., Capitol Hill Club.

EISENHOWER, LAURIE, performing company executive; BA in Dance, MFA in Dance, Arizona State U. Faculty Oakland U., Rochester, 1986—, full professor & head of dance; founder, artistic dir. Eisenhower Dance Ensemble, Rochester Hills, Mich., 1991—. Recipient Oakland U Faculty Recognition Award, 1997. Office: Eisenhower Dance Ensemble 1541 W Hamlin Rd Rochester Hills MI 48309

EISENMAN, PETER DAVID, architect, educator; b. Newark, Aug. 11, 1932; s. Herschel I. and Sylvia H. (Heller) E.; m. Elizabeth Henderson, 1963 (div. 1990); children: Julia, Nicholas; m. Cynthia Davidson, 1990; 1 child, Samuel Chapin. B.Arch. (Charles G. Sands Meml. medal 1955), Cornell U., 1955; MS in Architecture (Alumni tuition scholar 1959, William Kinne fellow 1960-61), Columbia U., 1960; MA, Cambridge (Eng.) U., 1962, PhD, 1963; DFA (hon.), U. Ill., Chgo., 1988, Pratt Inst., 1997; DArch (hon.), U. La Sapienza, Rome, 2003. Prin. firm Eisenman/Robertson Architects, N.Y.C., 1980-88, Eisenman Architects, N.Y.C., 1988—. Founder Inst. Architecture and Urban Studies, N.Y.C., 1967, dir., 1967-82; mem. faculty Cambridge U., 1960-63, Princeton U., 1965-67; faculty Cooper Union, 1970—, adj. prof., 1975-86, Irwin Chanin Disting. prof. 1986—; architect-in-residence Am. Acad. Rome, 1976; Kea prof. U. Md., 1978; Charlotte Davenport prof. Yale U., 1980, Louis I. Kahn prof. arch., 2001—; Arthur Rotch prof. Harvard U., 1982-85, Eliot Noyes vis. critic, 1993; Louis H. Sullivan rsch. prof. architecture U. Ill., Chgo., 1987-93; vis. prof. Ohio State U., 1991-93; John Williams prof. architecture U. Ark., 1997. Author: Diagram Diaries, Choral Works, (with Jacques Derrida) Blurred Zones, Giuseppe Terragni: Transformations, Decompositions, Critiques, 2003, Eisenman: Inside Out, Selected Writings 1963-1988, 2004; editor: Oppositions Books, House X Rizzoli, Houses of Cards; prin. works include pvt. residences Princeton, N.J., Hardwick, Vt., Lakeville and Cornwall, Conn., 1968-76; others Housing Koch-Friedrichstrasse, Berlin, 1980-86, Wexner Ctr. for Visual Arts, Columbus, Ohio, 1983-89, U. Cin. Coll. Design, Art, Architecture and Planning, 1988-96, Columbus (Ohio) Conv. Ctr., 1988-93, Koizumi Sangyo Bldg., Tokyo, 1989-90, Nunotani Office Bldg., 1990-92, Emory U. Art Ctr., 1991-95, Rebstock Pk., Frankfurt, Germany, 1991-95, U.S. Pavilion, Venice Biennale, 1991, Max Reinhardt Haus, Berlin, 1992, Haus Immendorff, Dusseldorf, Germany, 1993-94, Staten Island Inst. Arts and Scis., 1997-2001, Multi-Purpose Stadium, Glendale, Ariz., 1997—, Holocaust Meml., Berlin, Germany, 1998—, City of Culture, Santiago de Compostela, Spain, 1999—, Meml. to the Murdered Jews of Europe, Berlin, Germany, 2005. Served with U.S. Army, 1955-57. Fellow Graham Found., 1966; Guggenheim Found., 1976; grantee Princeton U., 1964, 66; recipient Arnold W. Brunner Meml. prize in architecture Am. Acad. and Inst. Arts and Letters, 1984, medal of honor N.Y.C. AIA, 2001, Cooper-Hewitt Nat. Design award for arch. Smithsonian Instn., 2001, Premio Internacional de Artes Plásticas de la Fundación Cristóbal Gabarrón, Spain, 2003 Fellow AIA; mem. Am. Acad. Arts and Scis., Am. Acad. Arts and Letters, Archtl. League N.Y. (v.p. 1970), Conf. Architects Study Environ. (co-founder 1964) Clubs: Century Assn. (N.Y.C.). Office: Eisenman Architects 41 W 25th St New York NY 10010-2021*

EISENMAN, ROBERT N., research scientist; BA, NYU; PhD in biophysics, U. Chgo., 1971; postdoctoral fellow, Swiss Inst. Exptl. Cancer Rsch., 1975, MIT, 1976. Staff mem. divsn. basic scis. Fred Hutchinson Cancer Rsch. Ctr.; affiliate prof. biochemistry U. Wash. Sch. Medicine. Mem. sci. adv. bd. Swiss Inst. Exptl. Cancer Rsch., Lineberger Cancer Ctr. (UNC), Agensys Inc., Otogene Inc. Recipient The Harvey Lecture, Rockefeller U., 2001, Chiron Lectures, U. Calif., Berkeley, 2004. Mem.: Nat. Acad. Scis. (fellow 1998), Am. Acad. Arts and Scis. (fellow 2003), Am. Assn. Cancer Rsch. (Landon AACR prize 2002), Am. Assn. Advancement Sci., Am. Soc. Microbiology. Office: Fred Hutchinson Cancer Rsch Ctr MS A2-015 PO Box 19024 Seattle WA 98109-1024

EISENMAN, RUSSELL, psychology educator; b. Savannah, Ga., Apr. 17, 1940; s. Abram and Georgia (Russell) E.; m. Frances Bradley, June 12, 1965 (div. Dec. 1972); children: David, Susan. Student, U. N.C., 1958; BA, Oglethorpe U., 1962; MS, U. Ga., 1963, PhD, 1966. Asst. to assoc. prof. Temple U., Phila., 1966-88; sr. clin. psychologist State of Calif., Norwalk, 1988-90; assoc. prof. psychology McNeese State U., Lake Charles, La., 1990-96, Ky. Wesleyan Coll., Owensboro, 1998-99; asst. prof. U. Tex. Pan Am., 2000—. Vis. assoc. prof. U. Calif., Santa Cruz, 1972-73; rsch. assoc. Haverford (Pa.) Coll., 1970-71, Hahnemann Med. Coll. and Hosp., Phila., 1971-72. Author: From Crime to Creativity, 1991, Studies in Personality Social and Clinical Psychology, 1994, Political Issues and Social Problems, 1994, Contemporary Social Issues, 1994, Readings in Psychology, 1995, Readings for Introductory Abnormal and Social Psychology, 1995; co-author: The New Families, 1972. Recipient Cert. of Merit, Kappa Alpha Psi. Mem. Nat. Assn. Creative Children and Adults, Southwestern La. Psychol. Assn. (pres. 1992), Internat. Assn. Correctional Tng. Pers., Soc. Advancement Social Psychology, Policy Studies Orgn., Psi Chi. Avocations: walking, watching sports, talking with people. Office Phone: 956-381-3327, 956-381-3327. E-mail: eisenman@panom.edu.

EISENSTADT, G. MICHAEL, diplomat, writer, educator, researcher; b. Free City of Danzig (now Gdansk, Poland), Nov. 16, 1928; s. Isidor and Edith (Lange) E.; 1 child, Judith Luzann. BA, Queens Coll., 1951; MS, U. Wis., 1952; postgrad., Russian Inst. Columbia U., 1954—56, Fgn. Svc. Inst., 1982—83. Instr. history Queens Coll., Flushing, NY, 1955-60; jr. officer Am. Embassy, Belgrade, Yugoslavia, 1960-61; cultural officer Am. Consulate Gen., Guayaquil, Ecuador, 1962-63; asst. cultural affairs officer Am. Embassy, Belgrade, Yugoslavia, 1963-67, cultural attaché Warsaw, 1968-71, br. pub. affairs officer Bonn, Fed. Republic of Germany, 1973-76, counselor for pub. affairs Budapest, Hungary, 1977-80, dep. counselor for pub. affairs Bonn, 1983-84, counselor for pub. affairs Belgrade, 1984-88; dep. policy officer Voice of Am., Washington, 1971-73; dir. Office Internat. Visitors USIA, Washington, 1980-82; mem. sr. seminar State Dept., Washington, 1982-83; dir. Office European Affairs USIA, Washington, 1988-89; diplomat-in-residence NYU, 1989-90; dir. N.Y. Reception Ctr. USIA, 1990-92; sr. rsch. scholar Inst. East Ctrl. Europe Columbia U., 1992-94. Cons. on the Balkans,

Ea. and Ctrl. Europe, countries of the former Soviet Union; chmn. coordinating com., chmn. drafting com. Conf. on Peace and Tolerance, Istanbul, 1994; chmn. coordinating com. Conflict Resolution Conf., Vienna, 1995; election observer OSCE in Serbia, 1997; coord. Peace and Tolerance Conf. on Kosovo, Vienna, 1999; election observer Appeal of Conscience Found. in Russia, 1999. Sec. Appeal of Conscience Del. to Switzerland, 1997; dir. internat. programs Appeal Conscience Found. With U.S. Army, 1952-54. Mem. Internat. Conf. and Seminar Assn. (pres.). Home: 880 5th Ave Apt Phe New York NY 10021-4951 E-mail: gme1@earthlink.net.

EISENSTADT, THOMAS, protective services official; b. Boston, Mass., May 21, 1939; s. Benjamin and Mary Ellen Eisenstadt; m. Deirdre C. O'Wril, Apr. 8, 1972; children: Timothy, Cassandra, Katarina; 1 child, Kristin V. BA, Boston U., 1958; JD, Boston U. Sch. of Law, 1961. Asst. atty. gen. Cmty. Mass, Boston, 1962—69; sheriff Suffolk County, Boston, 1969—78. Chair Boston Sch. Com., Boston, 1961—69. Named one of Outstanding Young Men of Boston, Boston C. of C., 1961, Outstanding Young Men of Am., 1963. Office: Law Offices Thomas S Eisenstadt 60 Adams St Milton MA 02186 Office Phone: 617-696-6900. Office Fax: 617-696-1013.

EISENSTAT, DAVID H., lawyer; b. Scranton, Pa., May 23, 1951; BA, MA, U. Pa., Phila., 1973; JD, Syracuse U., 1976. Bar: DC 1976, US Dist. Ct. (DC dist.) 1978, US Ct. of Appeals (DC cir.) 1980, US Ct. of Appeals (11th cir.) 1982, US Ct. of Appeals (8th cir.) 1985. Ptnr., head nat. health industry practice group and mem. mgmt. com. Akin, Gump, Strauss, Hauer & Feld, Washington. Rsch. editor Syracuse Law Rev., 1975—76. Mem.: Am. Health Lawyers Assn., DC Bar. Office: Akin Gump Strauss Hauer & Feld Ste 400 1333 New Hampshire Ave NW Washington DC 20036-1564 Office Phone: 202-887-4056. Office Fax: 202-887-4288. Business E-Mail: deisenstat@akingump.com.

EISENSTAT, THEODORE ELLIS, colon and rectal surgeon, educator; b. N.Y.C., Sept. 24, 1942; m. Sharon Diane Leonard, July, 1966; children: Maren Elise, Loren Aline. BA, Vanderbilt U., 1964; MD, N.Y. Med. Coll., 1968. Diplomate Am. Bd. Surgery, Am. Bd. Colon and Rectal Surgery, Nat. Bd. Med. Examiners. Rotating intern St. Vincent's Hosp., Worcester, Mass., 1968-69; resident in surgery Thomas Jefferson U. Hosp., Phila., 1969-71; chief resident in surgery Pa. Hosp., Phila., 1971-73; fellow in colon and rectal surgery Muhlenberg Hosp.-Robert Wood Johnson Sch. Medicine, N.J., 1977-78; dir. surg. endoscopy U. Md., 1975-80, dir. colon & rectal svc., 1976-80; asst. prof. surgery U. Md. Sch. Medicine, 1975-80; sr. attending surgeon Muhlenberg Regional Med. Ctr., Plainfield, NJ, 1979—, John F. Kennedy Med. Ctr., Edison, 1979—; clin. assoc. prof. surgery U. Medicine and Dentistry of N.J., Newark, 1981—, clin. prof. surgery Robert Wood Johnson Med. Sch. New Brunswick, 1979-91, clin. prof. surgery, 1991—, dir. colon and rectal residency program, 1993—; dir. colon and rectal surgery Robert Wood Johnson U. Hosp. Cons. surgeon Lock Raven VA Hosp., Balt., 1975-80, U.S. Army, Kimbrough Army Hosp., Ft. Meade, Md., 1975-80; bd. dirs., ACS rep. Am. Bd. Colon and Rectal Surgery, 1990-96, pres., 1995-96; attending surgeon Robert Wood Johnson U. Hosp., New Brunswick, N.J., 1984—; exhibitor and presenter in field; vis. prof. U. Md. Sch. Medicine, 1983, Abington (Pa.) Meml. Hosp., 1985, York (Pa.) Hosp., 1990, Pa. Hosp., Phila., 1990, others. Contbr. articles to profl. jours. Maj. U.S. Army, 1973-75. Fellow ACS (adv. coun. colon and rectal surgery), Am. Soc. Colon and Rectal Surgeons (Walter A. Fansler award 1977, Purdue Frederick fellow 1977, 1st prize sci. exhibit 1979); mem. AMA, Soc. for Surgery of Alimentary Tract, Assn. for Acad. Surgery, Soc. Am. Gastrointestinal Endoscopic Surgeons (founder 1981, bd. govs. 1986-89), Am. Soc. Gastrointestinal Endoscopy, N.Y. Soc. Colon and Rectal Surgeons (mem. coun. 1983-85, sec.-treas. 1986-87, v.p. 1988-89, pres. 1990-92, 1st prize film 1978), Pa. Soc. Colon. and Rectal Surgeons, N.J. Soc. Colon and Rectal Surgeons (sec.-treas. 1983-85, pres. 1989-90), N.J. Soc. Gastroenterology, N.J. Soc. Gastrointestinal Endoscopy, Assn. Mil. Surgeons U.S., Soc. Surgeons N.J., Crohn's and Colitis Found. Am.

EISENSTEIN, ELIZABETH LEWISOHN, historian, educator; b. N.Y.C., Oct. 11, 1923; d. Sam A. and Margaret V. (Seligman) Lewisohn; m. Julian Calvert Eisenstein, May 30, 1948; children: Margaret, John (dec.), Edward. AB, Vassar Coll., 1944; MA, Radcliffe Coll., 1947, PhD, 1953; LittD (hon.), Mt. Holyoke Coll., 1979; LHD (hon.), U. Mich., 2004. From lectr. to adj. prof history Am. U., Washington, 1959-74; Alice Freeman Palmer prof. history U. Mich., Ann Arbor, 1975-88, prof. emerita, 1988—. Scholar-in-residence Rockefeller Found. Ctr., Bellagio, Italy, June 1977; mem. vis. com. dept. history Harvard U., 1975-81, vice-chmn., 1979-81; dir. Ecole des Hautes Etudes en Sciences Sociales, Paris, 1982; guest spkr., participant confs. and seminars; I. Beam vis. prof. U. Iowa, 1980; Mead-Swing lectr. Oberlin Coll., 1980; Stone lectr. U. Glasgow, 1984; Van Leer lectr. Van Leer Fedn., Jerusalem, 1984; Hanes lectr. U. N.C., Chapel Hill, 1985 first resident cons. Ctr. for the Book, Libr. of Congress, Washington, 1979; mem. Coun. Scholars, 1980-88; pres.'s disting. visitor Vassar Coll., 1988; Pforzheimer lectr. N.Y. Pub. Libr., 1989, Lyell lectr. Bodleian Libr., Oxford, 1990, Merle Curti lectr. U. Wis., Madison, 1992, Jantz lectr. Oberlin Coll., 1995, Clifford lectr. Austin, Tex., 1996; vis. fellow Wolfson Coll., Oxford, 1990; sem. dir. Folger Inst., 1999. Author: The First Professional Revolutionist: F. M. Buonarroti, 1959, The Printing Press as an Agent of Change, 1979, 2 vols. paperback edit., 1980 (Phi Beta Kappa Ralph Waldo Emerson prize 1980), The Printing Revolution in Early Modern Europe, 1983 (reissued as Canto Book, 1993), Grub Street Abroad, 1992; mem. editorial bd. Jour. Modern History, 1973-76, 83-86, Revs. in European History, 1973-86, Jour. Library History, 1979-82, Eighteenth Century Studies, 1981-84; contbr. articles to profl. jours., chpts. to books. Bd. dirs. Folger Shakespeare Libr., 2000—. Belle Skinner fellow Vassar Coll., NEH fellow, 1977, Guggenheim fellow, 1982, fellow Ctr. Advanced Studies in Behavioral Scis., 1982-83, 92-93, Humanities Rsch. Ctr. fellow Australian Nat. U., 1988. Fellow Am. Acad. Arts and Scis., Royal Hist. Soc.; mem. Soc. French Hist. Studies (v.p. 1970, program com. 1974), Am. Soc. 18th Century Studies (nominating com. 1971), Soc. 16th Century Studies, Am. Hist. Assn. (com. on coms. 1970-72, chmn. Modern European sect. 1981, coun. 1982-85, Scholarly Distinction award 2003), Renaissance Soc. Am. (coun. 1973-76, pres. 1986), Am. Antiquarian Soc. (exec. com., adv. bd. 1984-87), Phi Beta Kappa. Office: U Mich Dept History Ann Arbor MI 48109 E-mail: eisenst@mindspring.com.

EISENSTEIN, LAURENCE JAY, lawyer; b. Balt., Oct. 24, 1960; s. Allen Morton and Ruth (Segel) E.; m. Robin Laura Zimelman, Aug. 31, 1986. BA, Harvard U., 1982, JD, 1985. Bar: Md. 1985, D.C. 1986, U.S. Dist. Ct. Md. 1986, U.S. Ct. Appeals (4th cir.) 1986, U.S. Dist. Ct. D.C. 1988, U.S. Ct. Appeals (D.C. cir.) 1988, U.S. Supreme Ct. 1991. Jud. clk. to judge U.S. Dist. Ct. Md., 1985-86; assoc. Covington & Burling, Washington, 1986-94; ptnr. Swidler Berlin Shereff Friedman, LLP, 1994—2002; founding ptnr. Eisenstein Malanchuk LLP, 2002—. Chair pro bono com. Year 2000 Task Force; guest commentator Courtroom TV Network, 1991. Author: (play) Make Believe World, 1980, Refuge Denied, 1989, Forced Back and Forgotten, 1989; exec. dir. Harvard Environ. Law Rev., 1984-85; ofcl. reporter Conf. on Inter-Am. Human Rights System, Washington, 1988; contbr. articles to profl. jours. Mem. Presdl. Transition Team civil rights divsn. Justice Dept., 1992; del. Dem. Nat. Conv., 1980; pres., bd. dirs. New Dem. Coalition 5th Dist., Balt., 1985—; bd. dirs., chair Md. Disability Law Ctr.; bd. dirs. Friends Modern Art, Balt. Mus. Art. Mem. ABA, Internat. Human Rights Law Group (Pro Bono Svc. award 1988), Md. Disability Law Ctr., Mensa (award 1978), Harvard Club of Md. (schs. and scholarships com. 1985—). Office: Eisenstein Malanchuk LLP 1048 Potomac St NW Washington DC 20007 Office Phone: 202-965-4700. Business E-Mail: leisenstein@em-law.com.

EISENSTEIN, TOBY K., microbiology educator; b. Phila., Sept. 15, 1942; d. Edward and Sylvia (Mandel) Karet; m. Bruce A. Eisenstein, Sept. 8, 1963; children: Eric, Andrew, Ilana. BA, Wellesley Coll., 1964; PhD, Bryn Mawr Coll., 1969. Instr. Med. Sch. Temple U., Phila., 1969-71, asst. prof., 1971-79, assoc. prof. microbiology and immunology Med. Sch., 1979-84, prof., 1984—, acting chair, 1990-92, co-dir. Ctr. Substance Abuse Rsch., 1992—. Mem. bacteriology and mycology study sect. NIH, 1976—80, 1988—92, mem. drugs abuse and AIDS study sect., 1994—2004. Contbr. articles to profl. jours. Recipient Rsch. prize, Temple U., 2003; NIH fellow, 1965—69, USPHS grantee, 1971—. Fellow: Am. Acad. Microbiology; mem.: AAAS, Coll. Problems Drug Dependence (bd. dirs. 2005—), Psychoneuroimmunology Rsch. Soc., Soc. Neuroimmune Pharmacology (Joseph Wybran award), Internat. Endotoxin Soc., Soc. Leukocyte Biology (sec. 1998—2000), Am. Assn. Immunologists, Am. Soc. Microbiology (pres. eastern Pa. br. 1983—86, mem. coun. policy com. 1993—96, chair membership bd. 2003—), Sigma Xi (pres. Temple U. chpt. 1981—83). Office: Temple U Sch Medicine Dept Microbiology and Immunology 3400 N Broad St Philadelphia PA 19140-5104 Office Phone: 215-707-3585. Business E-Mail: tke@temple.edu.

EISER, ARNOLD ROBERT, physician executive, bioethicist, nephrologist, internist; b. Newark, NY, Jan. 2, 1949; s. Harold H. and Anne Eiser; m. Barbara Joyce Andrews, June 15, 1975; 1 child, Arielle Veronica. BA magna cum laude, U. Pa., 1970; MD, Northwestern U., 1974. Intern Pa. Hosp., 1974-75; resident Med. Coll. Pa., 1975-77; fellow Hahnemann U., 1977-79; nephrologist Elmhurst (N.Y.) Hosp. Ctr., 1979-95, assoc. chief nephrology, 1993-95, dir. ambulatory care, 1995-97, dir. med. residency program, 1996-97; chief sect. gen. internal medicine U. Ill., Chgo., 1997—2001, prof. medicine, 1997—2003; v.p. Med. Edn. Mercy Health Sys., Darby, Pa., 2003—. Assoc. prof. medicine Mt. Sinai Sch. Medicine, NYC, 1986-97; adj. assoc. Hastings Ctr., Briarcliff Manor, NY, 1994-98; prof. medicine Drexel U., 2003—. Contbg. author: The Kidney in Collagen Vascular Diseases, 1993, Violence Against Women: Philosophical Perspective, 1998; contbr. articles to profl. jours. Fellow: ACP, Coll. Physicians Phila., Inst. Medicine Chgo. (pres. Chgo. clin. ethics program 2001—03); mem.: Am. Coll. Physician Execs. Avocations: travel, fitness, cross-training. Office: 1500 Lansdowne Ave Darby PA 19023 E-mail: aeiser@mercyhealth.org, aeiser@drexel.edu.

EISERER, LEONARD ALBERT CARL, publishing executive; b. Polar, Wis., June 3, 1916; s. Herman Frederick and Anna Elizabeth (Schnieder) E.; m. Lorraine Elizabeth Hickey, June 28, 1941; children: Carol Jean, Elaine Roberta, Leonard Arnold, Beverly Arlene. BA, Roosevelt U., Chgo., 1937; MS in Journalism, Northwestern U., 1939. Editor Am. Aviation Publs., Inc., Washington, 1939—42, v.p., gen. mgr., 1946—57, exec. v.p., sec., 1958-62; pres., pub. Sports Age, Inc., Washington, 1962-63; chmn., CEO Bus. Pubs., Inc., Silver Spring, Md., 1963—. Chmn. Carol Jean Cancer Found., Inc.; bd. dirs. U. N.C. at Greensboro Excellence Found.; pres., dir. Eiserer-Hickey Found., Inc.; dir. Univ. Club of Washington Found. Lt. USN, 1942-46. Named to Hall of Fame Newsletter Pubs. Found., 1994, Man of Yr. Univ. Club of Washington, 1995; inductee Hall of Achievement, Northwestern U. Medill Sch. Journalism, 1997. Mem.: Air and Waste Mgmt. Assn., Water Environ. Fedn., Soc. Profl. Journalists, Newsletter Pubs. Assn., Nat. Press Club, Univ. Club. Home: 9101 Sligo Creek Pky Silver Spring MD 20901-3360 Office: Bus Pubs Inc 8737 Colesville Rd Silver Spring MD 20910-4400 Office Phone: 301-587-6300.

EISERT, EDWARD GAVER, lawyer; b. N.Y.C., May 26, 1948; s. Israel Jay and Bess (Gaver) E.; div.; children: Carolyn B., Stephen J. AB, Cornell U., 1969; JD, NYU, 1973. Bar: N.Y. 1974. Law clk. to Judge Charles L. Brieant U.S. Dist. Ct. (so. dist.) N.Y., N.Y.C., 1973-74; assoc. Simpson Thacher & Bartlett, N.Y.C., 1974-76, Schulte Roth & Zabel, N.Y.C., 1976-80, ptnr., 1981—2002; sr. v.p., gen. corp. counsel Fiduciary Trust Co. Internat., N.Y.C., 2002—. Bd. dirs. N.Y. Small Bus. Venture Fund LLC., 1998—2004. Note and comment editor NYU Law Rev., 1972-73. Mem. ABA (com. on fed. regulation of securities 1983—, subcom. on ann. rev. fed. regulation of securities 1983-89, subcom. on mcpl. and govtl. obligations 1984-92, subcom. on investment cos. and investment advisors 1992—), Internat. Bar Assn., N.Y. Stat Bar Assn., Assn. Bar City N.Y., Univ. Club N.Y.C. Home: 302 Church St White Plains NY 10603-3525 Office: Fiduciary Trust Co International 600 Fifth Avenue New York NY 10020

EISLER, SUSAN KRAWETZ, advertising executive; b. N.Y.C., Aug. 18, 1946; d. Aaron and Bertha (Platt) Krawetz; m. Howard Irwin Eisler, June 8, 1980; 1 stepchild, Robin Joy; 1 adopted child, Joseph. BA, U. Pitts., 1967; MA, New Sch. for Social Rsch., 1971. Analyst Marplan, Inc., N.Y.C., 1968-69; project dir. Market Facts, Inc., N.Y.C., 1969-70; assoc. rsch. mgr. Gen. Foods, Inc., White Plains, N.Y., 1970-75, product mgr., 1975-80; rsch. dir. Elizabeth Arden, N.Y.C., 1980-81; v.p., assoc. rsch. dir. Lintas: N.Y. (formerly SSC&B: Lintas Worldwide), N.Y.C., 1981-87, sr. v.p., assoc. rsch. dir., 1987-92, exec. v.p., dir. strategic planning and rsch., 1992-94, Gotham, Inc., 1995—, mng. ptnr., dir. rsch. and info. svcs. Named Woman of Yr., YWCA Acad. Women Achievers, 1989. Mem.: Advt. Rsch. Found. (copy rsch. coun.), Am. Mktg. Assn. Office: Gotham Inc 100 5th Ave Fl 16 New York NY 10011-6996

EISMANN, DANIEL T., state supreme court justice; b. Eugene, Oreg. m. Sheila Wood, 1982; 1 child, Matthew stepchildren: Catherine Richardson, Christine Putz. Grad. cum laude, U. Idaho, 1976. Former law clerk to justice Donaldson Idaho State Supreme Ct., Boise; magistrate judge Owyheee County, 1986—95; dist. judge Fourth Jud. Dist., 1995—98, adminstrv. dist. judge, 1998—2000; justice Idaho Supreme Ct., Boise, 2001—. Chair Idaho State Supreme Ct. Civil Rules Com., Idaho State Supreme Ct. Criminal Jury Instructions Com., Idaho State Supreme Ct. Drug Court Coordinating Com. Mem. Ada County Domestic Violence Task Force, Region III Coun. for Children and Youth; judge Ada County Drug Ct. With USAR. Decorated 2 Purple Hearts. Mem.: Inns of Ct. (Boise Chpt.), Idaho Bar Assn. (mem. Bar Exam Preparation Com.). Office: Idaho Supreme Ct PO Box 83720 Boise ID 83720*

EISMEIER, JORDAN MATTHEW, music educator; b. Ft. Oglethorpe, Ga., Mar. 20, 1981; s. Frederick Lloyd and Janet Louise Eismeier. B in Music Edn. cum laude, La. State U., 2003. Cert. tchr. La. State Dept. Edn., 2003. Counselor, performer, tchr. Blue Lake Fine Arts Camp, Twin Lake, Mich., 2002—02; mid./high sch. band dir. DeSoto Parish Schs., Mansfield, La., 2003—04; instr. bassoon Lee U., Cleveland, Tenn., 2004—04; substitute tchr. k-12, music specialist Cleveland City Schs., 2004—. Composer: Symphony No. 1 The Cross, Symphony No. 2 Double Cross, (handbell ensemble) Grace Variations, (chamber wind ensemble) Dectet Summer Grove. Prin. bassoon performer/tchr. Shreveport (La.) Met. Concert Band, 2003—04; prin. bassoonist Prevailing Winds Cmty. Band, Bossier City, La., 2003—04; ch. orch. bassoonist Summer Grove Bapt. Ch., Shreveport, 2003—04; handbell ringer/guest condr. U. Bapt. Ch., Baton Rouge, 2000—03, ch. choir mem., 1999—2002. Scholar, La. State U., 1999—2004; $12, 000 Academic/Music scholar, U. Miami, 1999, John Patterson scholar, La. State U., 2000. Mem.: Music Educators Nat. Conf., Golden Key (life), Pi Kappa Lambda (life). Republican. Avocations: freelance bassoon and clarinet teacher, composer. Home: 2109 Eugenia Ave NW Cleveland TN 37311 Office Phone: 423-614-8264. Personal E-mail: bassoonist1@excite.com.

EISNER, DIANA, pediatrician; b. Houston, May 7, 1951; d. Elmer and Edith (Dubow) E. BA in Biology cum laude, Brandeis U., 1973; MD, Southwestern Med. Sch., 1977. Diplomate Am. Bd. Pediatrics. Intern, resident Baylor Coll. Medicine, Houston, 1977-80; pvt. practice Houston, 1981—. Chmn. dept. pediat. Meml. N.W. Hosp., Houston, 1990. Recipient Commendation award Children's Protection Com. Tex. Children's Hosp., 1978, Physician's Recognition award AMA, 1983. Mem. Am. Acad. Pediatrics, Tex. Med. Assn., Tex. Pediatric Soc., Houston Pediatric Soc. (treas. 2001-02, sec. 2002-), Harris County Med. Soc. Avocations: ballet, swimming, walking. Office: 2030 North Loop W Ste 125 Houston TX 77018-8132 Office Phone: 713-688-8393. Personal E-mail: dr.diana@sbcglobal.net.

EISNER, ELLIOT W., education educator; MA in art and edn., Roosevelt U., 1954; MS in art edn., Ill. Inst. Tech., 1955; MA in edn., U. Chgo., 1958, PhD in edn., 1962. Prof. Stanford U., Edn., Art Depts., Stanford, Calif., 1970—; HS art tchr. Chgo., 1956—58; art tchr. U. Chgo., 1958—60; instr., art edn. Ohio State U., 1960—61; instr. edn. U. Chgo., 1961—62, asst. prof. edn., 1962—65; assoc. prof. edn. & art Stanford U., 1965—70, prof. edn. & art, 1970—. Consulting editor Curriculum Perspectives, 1981—; mem. editl. bd. Kappan, 1995—2000; mem. editl. advisory bd. Just & Caring Edn., 1995—2000; mem. editl. bd. Critical Inquiry into Curriculum & Instruction, 1998—. Contbr. articles various profl. jours.; co-author (with David W. Ecker): Readings in Art Education, 1966; co-author: (with Alan Peshkin) Qualitative Inquiry in Education: The Continuing Debate, 1990; co-author: (with Elizabeth Vallance) Conflicting Conceptions of Curriculum series on Contemporary Educational Issues, 1974; author: Confronting Curriculum Reform, 1971, Educating Artistic Vision, 1972, The Arts, Human Development, and Education, 1976, The Education Imagination: On the Design and Evaluation of School Programs, 1979, The Art of Educational Evaluation: A Personal View, 1985, The Role of Discipline-Based Art Education in America's Schools, 1988, The Enlightened Eye: Qualitative Inquiry and the Enhancement of Educational Practice, 1991, Cognition and Curriculum Reconsidered, 1994, Evaluating and Assessing the Visual Arts in Education: International Perspectives, 1996, The Kind of Schools We Need: Personal Essays, 1998, The Arts and the Creation of the Mind, 2002 (The Grawemeyer award for Edn., U. Louisville, 2005). Recipient Harold McGraw Jr. prize in Edn., Nat. Art Edn. Assn., 1998. Mem.: Nat. Acad. of Edn., John Dewey Soc. (pres. 1998—2000), J. Paul Getty Ctr. for Edn. in the Arts. Achievements include research in the rold of artistic thinking in the conduct of social sci. rsch., programs to further arts edn. in Am. schs., the role of artistry in ednl. theory and practice. Office: Stanford U Sch of Edn 485 Lasuen Mall Stanford CA 94305-3096 E-mail: eisner@stanford.edu.

EISNER, HOWARD, engineering educator, engineering executive; b. N.Y.C., Aug. 8, 1935; s. Samuel Eisner and Mary Wegodner; m. Joan Arlene Knopfer, Feb. 9, 1957(div. 1994); children: Seth Eric, Susan Rachel, Oren David; m. June B. Linowitz, Nov. 8, 1995. BEE, CCNY, 1957; MS, Columbia U., 1958; DSc, George Washington U., 1966. Teaching asst. Columbia U., 1957; lectr. dept. physics Bklyn. Coll., 1957-59; lectr., asst. professorial lectr. George Washington U., 1961-67; prof. U. Maryland, 1987-89; various engrng. positions ORI, Inc., Rockville, Md., 1959-68, v.p., 1968-71, exec. v.p., 1971-84, corp. exec. v.p., 1984-85, also dir.; pres. Intercon Systems Corp. subs. ORI, Group, Inc., Rockville, 1985-89, Atlantic Research Services Corp., Alexandria, Va., 1987-89; Disting. rsch. prof. George Washington U., Washington, 1989—. Author: Advanced Algebra, 1960, Computer-Aided Systems Engineering, 1988, Essentials of Project and Systems Engineering Management, 1997, 2d edit., 2002, Reengineering Yourself and Your Company: From Engineer to Manager to Leader, 2000; contbr. articles in field. Fellow IEEE, N.Y. Acad. Scis.; mem. AIAA, INFORMS, Sigma Xi, Tau Beta Pi, Eta Kappa Nu, Omega Rho. Avocations: personal computers, tennis, choral singing, writing. Office: George Washington U Rm 157 SEAS-EMSE 1776 G St NW Washington DC 20052 Office Phone: 202-994-0584. Business E-Mail: heisner@gwu.edu.

EISNER, JONATHAN DAVID, lawyer; b. Silver Spring, Md., Apr. 13, 1967; BSEE, Drexel Univ., 1990; JD with honors, Univ. Md., 1993. Bar: Md. 1993. Law clk. Chief Judge Robert C. Murphy Ct. of Appeals, Md.; ptnr., chmn. Trusts & Estates practice group DLA Piper Rudnick Gray Cary LLP, Balt. Asst. sec., legal counsel South Atlantic divsn. Am. Cancer Soc.; profl. adv. counsel, mem. steering com. Balt. Cmty. Found.; bd. dirs. Hittman Family Found., Md. Sci. Ctr. Mem.: Md. Sci. Ctr. (bd. mem.). Office: DLA Piper Rudnick Gray Cary LLP 6225 Smith Ave Baltimore MD 21209-3600 Office Phone: 410-580-4142. Office Fax: 410-580-3001. Business E-Mail: jonathan.eisner@dlapiper.com.

EISNER, MICHAEL DAMMANN, entertainment company executive; b. Mt. Kisco, N.Y., Mar. 7, 1942; s. Lester and Margaret (Dammann) E.; m. Jane Breckenridge; children: Breck, Eric, Anders. BA, Denison U., 1964. Began career in programming dept. CBS; asst. to nat. programming dir. ABC, 1966-68, mgr. spls. and talent, dir. program devel.-East Coast, 1968-71, dir. program devel. East Coast, 1968-71, dir. feature films and program devel., 1969, v.p. daytime programming, 1971-75, v.p. program planning and devel., 1975-76, sr. v.p. prime time prodn. and devel., 1976; pres., chief operating officer Paramount Pictures, 1976-84; chmn. Walt Disney Co., Burbank, Calif., 1984—2004, CEO, 1984—; founder The Eisner Found. Governor Mighty Ducks of Anaheim, 1993; mem. bus. steering com. Global Business Dialogue on Electronic Commerce. Author: (book) Work in Progress, 1998, (memoir) Camp, 2005. Trustee Denison U., Calif. Inst. Arts; bd. dirs. Am. Hosp. of Paris Found., UCLA Exec. Bd. for Med. Sci. Office: Walt Disney Co 500 S Buena Vista St Burbank CA 91521-0006

EISNER, PETER NORMAN, journalist, writer; b. Jersey City, Aug. 27, 1950; s. Bernard and Lorraine (Gropper) Eisner; m. Musha Salinas, Aug. 27, 1981; children: Isabel, Marina. BA, Rutgers U., 1972. Reporter Hudson (N.Y.) Register-Star, 1974-75, Poughkeepsie (N.Y.) Jour., 1975-76; newsman AP, Columbus, N.Y.C., 1978-1979, Brazil corr. Brasilia, 1979-81, Venezuela bur. chief. Caracas, 1982, news editor, Mex., Cen. Am. Mex. City, 1982-83; dep. fgn. editor Newsday, N.Y.C., 1984-85, sr. editor fgn. news, 1985-89, sr. corr., 1989-94; mng. dir. NewsCom, Coral Gables, Fla., 1994-98, Ctr. for Pub. Integrity, Washington, 1999—2001; dep. fgn. editor Washington Post, 2003. Author editor, translator: Death Beat, 1994, America's Prisoner, 1997; author: The Freedom Line, 2004. Mem bd advisors Ctrl. Am Jounalists Program, 1989—93. Recipient Christopher award, 2005. Mem.: Interamerican Press Asn (freedom of press comt 1988—94, bd dirs 1988—94). Personal E-mail: peisner@bigfoot.com.

EISNER, SIGMUND, retired English language educator; b. Red Bank, N.J., Dec. 9, 1920; s. Victor and Helene Eisner; m. Nancy Fereva Eisner, June 15, 1949; children: Kirpal Singh, Charles, Nicholas, Victoria, Halley, Cassandra. BA in English, U. Calif., Berkeley, 1947, MA in English, 1949; PhD in English, Columbia U., 1955. Instr., asst. prof. Oreg. State Coll., Corvallis, 1954—58; Fulbright fellow Inst. for Advanced Studies, Dublin, 1958—59; asst. prof. English Alameda (Calif.) State Coll., 1960; asst. and assoc. prof. English Dominican Coll. San Rafael, Calif., 1960—66; prof. English U. Ariz., Tucson, 1967—95, prof. emeritus English, 1995—. Vis. assoc. prof. English U. Ariz., Tucson, 1966—67. Author: (book) A Tale of Wonder: A Source Study of "The Wife of Bath's Tale", 1957 (U. Chgo. Folklore prize, 1958), The Tristan Legend: A Study in Sources, 1969, The Kalendarium of Nicholas of Lynn, 1980, The Variorum Edition of Chaucer's Treatise on the Astrolabe, 2002; contbr. articles to profl. jours. With U.S. Army, 1942—45. Recipient faculty rsch. support in humanities grant, Grad. Coll. of U. Ariz., 1972, Sabbatical award for study, London, 1972—73, Oxford, Eng., 1980—81, Spring Sabbatical award, 1989. Democrat.

EISNER, SUSAN PAMELA, communications executive, management consultant, educator; b. N.Y.C., Apr. 19, 1950; d. Nathaniel Julius and Frances Rochelle (Linick) Eisner. Student, Smith Coll., 1968-69; BA, Wellesley Coll., 1971; MPA, Kennedy Sch. Govt., Harvard U., 1974. Mem. staff HEW, Washington, 1971; asst. to dir. comm. Dem. Nat. Com., Washington, 1972; nat. coord. press ops. McGovern Presdl. Campaign, Washington, 1972; dir. comm. Dem. Nat. Com. Telethons II and III, Washington, N.Y.C., L.A., 1973-74; creative dir. Ways and Means, Inc., Louisville, 1974; prodr., writer Sta. WNET-Thirteen TV, N.Y.C., 1975-79, asst. dir. broadcasting, 1979-81, dir. acquisitions, scheduling and spls., 1981, dir. broadcasting, 1981-83, spl. advisor to sr. v.p., 1983; pres., mgmt. and comm. cons., project devel. production Susan Eisner Assocs., N.Y.C., 1983—; staff intern to Senator Javits U.S. Senate, Washington, 1970. Mem. adj. faculty NYU, N.Y.C., 1994—, globalization adv. bd., 1994-95; asst. prof. mgmt. Ramapo Coll., N.J., 1995-99, assoc. prof. mgmt., 1999-,; acad. reviewer Irwin/McGraw Hill, Simon & Schuster, Southwestern, 1997—; profl. connection advisor Harvard U., 1998—; presenter in field. Folk singer, Boston, 1969-71; dir. broadcasting various TV programs and mini series including Cinema Thirteen, Classics Showcase, Star Movie, Viewer's Choice, Gala of Stars, Astaire, Hepburn, Years of Darkness, The American Worker, Black History, Celebrate Dance, Chanukah.Christmas, Disarmament, Remember the Holocaust, A Salute to Britain, First Person Reports, others; exec. producer and producer various TV specials, spots, reports, segments including Listening to You (Nat. Assn. Ednl. Broadcasters Graphics and Design award 1978), Masterpiece Theatre Quotes

Montage (Nat. Assn. Ednl. Broadcasters Graphics and Design award 1978), Haven't Stopped Dancin' Yet (Nat. Assn. Edn. Broadcasters Graphics and Design award 1979), Window on the World (Nat. Assn. Ednl. Broadcasters Graphics and Design award 1979), Everything Beautiful At the Ballet (Nat. Assn. Ednl. Broadcasters Graphics and Design award 1979), Making Poldark--Location (Nat. Assn. Ednl. Graphics and Design award 1979), Work in Progress--Dance in America (Nat. Assn. Ednl. Graphics and Design award 1979), Cavett Conversation with Baryshnikov-Gregory, I Claudius/Poldark/Duchess of Duke Street/Upstairs-Downstairs Farewells, Masterpiece Theatre's Tenth Anniversary Party, On location--Dance Grand Finale, Thirteen: The First Twenty Years, Newsline, Artists at Work, Culture Spots, Eliot Feld audition, Lenoni, Metro Minutes, Preview, You're the Top: Empire State, Be There, Go Public, The Next Twenty Years, People and Programs, Think Again, Think Thirteen, We Are You, Where Every Minute County, others; creator, The Premier Way, 1984; dir. communications various nat. multimedia prodns. for March of Dimes including Witness to Conquesta, A Tribute to Jonas Salk (cabinet and congl. wives' dinner), Mommy Don't (prenatal care campaign), Beautiful Babies: Right from the Start, Journey to Birth; Nat. Communications Adv. Com. Symposiums on Drug Use and Pregnancy and Environ. Risks and Pregnancy, Nat. Vol. Leadership Conf., Nat. Program Tng. Conf., various nat. pub. svc. announcements and campaigns, nat. promotional and instl. campaigns; internatl. cons. various spl. events inclusding Fiftieth Anniversary, Nat. Telethons. Cons. pre-publ. rsch. for book on Bill Cosby, 1987. Creator, Mediasmarts, 1993. Writer contemporary folk songs, 1969-75; author of speeches, presentations, reports, press, ednl., instl. and promotional materials; rsch. on various topics; contbr. articles to profl. jours. Dir. comm. March of Dimes Birth Defects Found., N.Y., 1985-87; spl. cons. to exec. dir. Nat. Urban League, 1969-71; tutor MIT, 1972. Recipient award for Citizenship Am. Legion, 1965, Mayor's award for Young Citizenship Mayor of New Rochelle, N.Y., 1965, Thomases award for faculty excellence, 1999, Outstanding Tchr. award Sch. Adminstrn. and Bus., Ramapo Coll., 1998, 2003, Best Paper award Internat. Bus. and Econ. Rsch. Conf., 2001; named one of Outstanding Young Women Am., U.S. Jayvees, 1981; Durant scholar Wellesley Coll., 1971; Harvard U. Kennedy Sch. adminstrn. fellow, 1971-75; SBR grantee, 1997, Ramapo Coll. Found. grantee, 1997, 2000, FIPSE grantee, 1997, Sanyo grantee, 1995, 98, Pres. award for excellence in tchg., 1999, Expert Tchr., Ramapo Coll, 2003. Mem. AAUW (mem. conv. planning com. 1999, BD minority scholar program mentor 1999, 2000), NAFE, Soc. Advancement Mgmt. (mem. editl. rev. bd. 2000-), Soc. Bus. Ethics, Assn. Bus. Comm., Omicron Delta Kappa, Delta Mu Delta (hon.). Office: Ramapo Coll 505 Ramapo Valley Rd Mahwah NJ 07430-1623

EISNER, THOMAS, biologist, educator; b. Berlin, June 25, 1929; s. Hans Edouard and Margarete (Heil) E.; m. Maria Lobell, June 10, 1952; children: Yvonne, Vivian, Christina. BA, Harvard U., 1951, PhD, 1955; DSc (hon.), U. Wüzburg, Germany, 1982, U. Zürich, Switzerland, 1983, U. Göteborg, Sweden, 1989, Drexel U., 1992. Postdoctoral fellow Harvard U., 1955—57; asst. prof. biology Cornell U., Ithaca, NY, 1957—62, assoc. prof., 1962—66, prof., 1966—76, Jacob Gould Schurman prof. chem. ecology, 1976—, dir. Cornell Inst. for Rsch. in Chem. Ecology, 1992—; sr. fellow Cornell Ctr. for the Environment, 1994—. Vis. scientist dept. entomology Sch. Agr., Wageningen, The Netherlands, 1964—65; vis. scientist Smithsonian Tropical Rsch. Lab., Barro Colorado Island, C.Z., 1968; sr. vis. scientist Max Planck Inst. fur Verhaltensphysiologie, Seewiesen, Germany, 1971, Divsn. Entomology, CSIRO, Canberra, Australia, 1972—73; Rand fellow Marine Biol. Labs., Woods Hole, Mass., 1974; vis. rsch. prof. U. Fla., Gainesville, 1977—78; disting. vis. fellow NY Inst. Humanities, NYU; chief scientist Biodiversity IMAX Film, 1996—2001; mem. internat. adv. bd. INBio, 1997—98, FUNDAQUIM U. de la Republica, Uruguay, 1997—, Butterfly Discovery Pk., 1997—2001; rsch. assoc. Archbold Biol. Sta., 1973—; vis. prof. Stanford U., 1979—80, U. Zürich, 1980—81. Co-author: Animal Adaptation, 1964, Life on Earth, 1973, 7 other books; mem. editl. bd.: Sci., 1970—71, Am. Naturalist, 1970—71, Jour. Comparative Physiology, 1974—80, Jour. Chem. Ecology, 1974—, Behavioral Ecology and Sociobiology, 1976—97, Sci. Yr. World Books, 1979—82, Human Ecology Forum, 1981—85, Living Bird Quar., 1982—88, Experientia, 1982—96, Quar. Rev. Biology, 1983—87, Chemoecology, 1997—, Zoology, 1993—, Chemistry and Biodiversity, 2004—; co-editor: Explorations in Chemical Ecology Series, 1987—; contbr. articles to profl. jours. Recipient Archie F. Carr medal, 1983, Procter prize, Sigma Xi, 1986, Karl Ritter von Frisch medal, 1988, Centennial medal, Harvard U., 1989, Tyler Environ. Achievement prize, U. So. Calif., 1990, Esselen award, 1991, Silver medal, Internat. Soc. Chem. Ecology, 1991, Nat. medal sci., 1994, NWF Nat. Conservation Achievement award, 1997, Green Globe award, 1997, John Wiley Jones award, 1999, Iscol Disting. Environ. Lectr. award, 2000; Guggenheim fellow, 1964—65, 1972—73. Fellow: Entomol. Soc. Am., Animal Behavior Soc., Royal Soc. Arts, Am. Acad. Arts and Scis.; mem.: AAAS (chmn. biology sect. 1980—81, com. on sci. freedom and responsibility 1980—87, chmn. subcom. sci. and human rights 1981—87), NAS (rsch. opportunity in biology com. 1985, film com. 1986—96, com. on human rights 1987—90), Ency. of Biodiversity (internat. adv. bd. 1997—2000), Ctr. of Biodiversity Conservation Am. Mus. Natl. History (adv. com. 1995—2000), Nat. Mus. Natural History (adv. com. 1996—2001), Xerces Soc. (sci. adv. com. 1990—, pres. 1992—), Union Concerned Scientists (bd. dirs. 1993—), Com. Concerned Scientists (nat. sponsor 1988—), World Resources Inst. (adv. coun. 1988—95), Monell Chem. Senses Ctr. (adv. coun. 1988—95), Am. Soc. Naturalists (pres. 1989—90), Mo. Botanical Garden Ctr. Plant Conservation (adv. bd. econ. potential rare and threatened plants 1992), Am. Inst. Biol. Sci. (task force for 90s 1990—), Ctr. on Consequences Nuclear War (steering com. 1983—90), Fedn. Am. Scientists (coun. mem. 1977—81), Nat. Audubon Soc. (bd. dirs. 1970—75), Zero Population Growth (bd. dirs. 1969—70), Acad. Europaea, Am. Philos. Soc., World Wildlife Fund (sci. adv. coun. 1983—91), Nature Conservancy (nat. sci. adv. coun. 1969—74), Deutsche Acad. Naturforscher Leopoldina, Explorers Club. Office: Cornell U W347 Seeley Mudd Hall Dept Neurobiology & Behavior Ithaca NY 14853 *I am a naturalist, interested primarily in field exploration and discovery. My research deals with the behavior and chemical ecology of insects, and with the photographic and cinematographic documentation of little-known aspects of the life of these animals. My chief goal in life is to relate my findings to the cause of wildlife and wilderness preservation.*

EISSMANN, ROBERT FRED, retired manufacturing engineer; b. Bklyn., Jan. 17, 1924; s. Fred Arno and Katherine Elizabeth (Petersohn) E.; m. June I. Vreeland, Dec. 29, 1950; 1 child, Roy Norman. Student, Pratt Inst., 1942-43, 46. Wireman Western Electric Co., Kearney, N.J., 1946-49; assembler Indsl. TV, Clifton, N.J., 1949-51; leadman Bogue Electric, Paterson, N.J., 1951-60, 65-68; wireman, engring. asst. Kearfott, Gen. Precion, West Paterson, N.J., 1960-65; assembler-wireman Henderson Industries, Fairfield, N.J., 1968-72; prodn. mgr. Mipco Inc., West Caldwell, N.J., 1972-80, plant mgr. Fairfield, 1980-84, product support mgr., 1984-85, value engr., 1985-86; advance product design engr., 1986-87; design engr. indsl., elec. products Amerace Corp., 1987-90; ret., 1990. Staff mem. Russellstoll divsn. Midland Ross Corp., Livingston, N.J., 1980-83. Mem. freight contrainer stds. com. Elec. Task Force. With Signal Corps, U.S. Army, 1943-46. Methodist.

EISSMANN, WALTER JAMES, consulting company executive; b. Newark, Apr. 20, 1939; s. Walter Curt Eissmann and Alice Delice (Irving) Clark; m. Dorothea Ann Donaldson, June 1, 1963; children: Patricia Helene Ridenhour, Walter William. BS in Indsl. Engring., Rutgers U., 1962. Account mgr. Gen. Electric, Engelwood Cliffs, N.J., 1962-67; regional sales mgr. Tymshare, Engelwood Cliffs, 1968-71, Buffalo, N.Y., 1971-73, v.p. mktg. svc. divsn. Cupertino, Calif., 1974-79, divsn. v.p., 1980-84; sr. v.p. McDonnell Douglas Corp., Cupertino, 1984-86; gen. ptnr. Archer Assocs., Cupertino, 1985-92; pres., chmn. bd. Walter J. Eissmann Inc., Napa, Calif., 1989—. Bd. dirs. NSF Corp., Nutri/system Franchisee Corp.; chmn. bd. BusinessWise Inc., 1992-93; mng. gen. ptnr. Grand Tyme Partnership, 1992-98. Lead singer: Soc. for Preservation and Encouragement of Barber Shop Quartet Singing in Am., 2001—; lead singer (octet) Men of Note, 2005—. Bd. dirs. Saratoga Little League, Calif., 1976-81, Saratoga Boosters, 1981-84; active Vienna Theatre Players, Va., 1973; mem. Church Men's Choir, Saratoga, 1980-82. Named to President's club Tymshare, Golden Circle, Nutri/system Master of the Keys. Mem. Pi Tau Sigma. Republican. Home and Office: 27 Reno Ct Napa CA 94558

EISWERTH, BARRY NEIL, architect, educator; b. Williamsport, Pa., Sept. 16, 1942; s. Eugene Lewis and Mary Jane (Winters) E.; m. Anne Caroline Essl, Apr. 8, 1967; children: Jason Andreas, Brendan Eugene. BArch., Pa. State U.-University Park, 1965. Registered architect, Pa. Assoc. H2L2 Architects/Planners, Phila., 1967-77, ptnr., 1977-88, sr. ptnr., 1988—; pres. H2L2 Design Co., Phila., 1980—; asst. prof. archtl. design Drexel U., 1975-81; mem. faculty, thesis advisor Phila. Coll. Art. Archtl. works include Children's Hosp., Phila., bldgs. Phila. '76 Bicentennial, Phila. Bourse Bldg., Cypress Sq. Townhouse Complex Phila. (recipient Design award Old Phila. Devel. Corp., Preservation Alliance award for Design Offices and Montgomery McCracken Warker & Rhodes), Constitutional Pavillion for We The People 200, Master Plan and New Classroom Adminstrn. Bldg. Cairo Am. Coll., Engring. and Computer Sci. Campus-Am. U. Cairo, Master Plan Am. Internat. Sch., Tel Aviv, Master Plan and New Classroom Bldgs. Am. Embassy Sch., New Delhi, Master Plan and Design new campus Am. Sch. of Warsaw, Brit. Internat. Sch., Cairo; Master Plan and Expansion Am. Sch. Paris; design of hdqrs. Arab Bank, Cairo. Trustee curator Phila. City Inst.; bd. dirs. Marymount Internat. Sch., Paris; bd. mem. World Affairs Coun., Penverdel Coun. Recipient awards for archtl. designs, Alumni Achievement award Pa. State U., 2000. Mem. AIA, Pa. Soc. Architects, Nat. Acad. Design, Phila. Club. Democrat. Roman Catholic. Office: H2L2 Architects/Planners 714 Market St 6th Fl Philadelphia PA 19106-2372 Office Phone: 215-925-5300. Business E-Mail: eiswerth@hzlz.com.

EISZNER, JAMES RICHARD, lawyer; b. Chicago Heights, Ill., June 6, 1953; s. James R. Sr. and Joyce Carolyn (Holland) E.; m. Barbara Lynn Bonavita, Aug. 15, 1976; children: Nicole, James, Richard. AB, Princeton U., 1975; JD, NYU, 1978. Bar: N.Y. 1979, Mo. 1997, U.S. Dist. Ct. (so., ea., and we. dists.) Mo., U.S. Ct. Appeals 1982, U.S. Supreme Ct. 1982. Assoc. Lord, Day & Lord, N.Y.C., 1978-86; ptnr. Coudert Brothers, N.Y.C., 1986-97, Shook, Hardy & Bacon, LLP, Kansas City, 1997—. Mem. ABA, Hallbrook Country Club. Republican. Presbyterian. Home: 11704 Norwood Dr Leawood KS 66211-3002 Office: Shook Hardy & Bacon LLP 2555 Grand Blvd Kansas City MO 64108-2613 Business E-Mail: jeiszner@shb.com.

EITNER, LORENZ EDWIN ALFRED, art historian, educator; b. Brunn, Czechoslovakia, Aug. 27, 1919; came to U.S., 1935, naturalized, 1943; s. Wilhelm and Katherina (Thonet) E.; m. Trudi von Kathrein, Oct. 26, 1946; children: Christy, Kathy, Claudia. AB, Duke U., 1940; MFA, Princeton U., 1948, PhD, 1952. Research unit head Nuremberg War Crimes Trial, 1946-47; from instr. to prof. art U. Minn., Mpls., 1949-63; chmn. dept. art, dir. mus. Stanford U., Calif., 1963-89. Organizer exhbn. works of Gericault for museums of Los Angeles, Detroit and Phila., 1971-72 Author: The Flabellum of Tournus, 1944, Gericault Sketchbooks in the Chicago Art Institute, 1960, Introduction to Art, 1951, Neo-Classicism and Romanticism, 1969, Gericault's Raft of the Medusa, 1972, Gericault, His Life and Work, 1983 (Mitchell prize 1984, C.R. Morey award 1985), An Outline of 19th Century European Painting from David through Cezanne, 1987, Nat. Gallery, Washington, French Nineteenth Century Paintings, 2000; (with others) The Arts in Higher Education, 1963, Stanford Mus. Art, The Drawing Collection, 1993; contbr. articles to profl. jours. Mem. Regional Area Arts Coun. San Francisco Bay Area. Officer OSS, AUS, 1943-46; sect. head ministries divsn. Nuremberg War Crimes Trial, 1946-47. Fulbright grantee, Belgium, 1952-53; Guggenheim fellow, Munich, Federal Republic Germany, 1956-57; recipient Gold Medal for Meritorious Service to Austrian Republic, 1990. Mem. AAAS, Am. Acad. Arts and Scis., Coll. Art Assn. Am. (bd. dirs., past v.p.), Phi Beta Kappa Home: 684 Mirada Ave Stanford CA 94305-8475*

EITTREIM, RICHARD MACNUTT, lawyer; b. Neptune, N.J., Feb. 10, 1945; s. Wilbur Lawrence and Leta Blanch (MacNutt) E.; m. Margaret Anne Nolan, June 11, 1967; children: Theodore Scott, Elisabeth Marie, Samantha Leta. AB, Yale U., 1967; JD, U. Va., 1973. Bar: N.J. 1973, U.S. Dist. Ct. N.J. 1973, U.S. Ct. Appeals (3d cir.) 1984, (11th cir.) 1996, U.S. Supreme Ct. 1998. Assoc. McCarter & English, Newark, N.J., 1973-80, ptnr., 1980—. Trustee Children's Psychiat. Ctr., Eatontown, N.J., 1977-87, Riverview Hosp. Found., Red Bank, N.J., 1988-93. Mem. ABA, N.J. State Bar Assn., Essex County Bar Assn., Phi Alpha Delta, Sea Bright Lawn Tennis and Cricket Club (pres. 2000—, bd. govs. 1994—), Monmouth Boat Club (treas. 1983-86), Essex Club, Yale Club (pres. 1986-87). Democrat. Presbyterian. Home: 111 Beechwood Dr Shrewsbury NJ 07702 Office: McCarter & English 4 Gateway Ctr 100 Mulberry St Newark NJ 07102-4004 Office Phone: 973-622-4444. Business E-Mail: reittreim@mccarter.com.

EITZEN, DAVID STANLEY, sociologist, educator; b. Glendale, Calif., Aug. 4, 1934; s. David Donald and Amanda Emma (Heidebrecht) E.; m. Florine Kay Voran, May 29, 1956; children: Keith, Michael, Kelly. AB in History, Bethel Coll., 1956; MS, Emporia State U., 1962; MA in Sociology, U. Kans., 1966, PhD in Sociology, 1968. Recreational therapist Menninger Found., Topeka, Kans., 1956-58; tchr. Galva (Kans.) High Sch., 1958-60, Turner (Kans.) High Sch., 1960-65; asst. prof. sociology U. Kans., 1968-72, asso. prof., 1972-74; prof. sociology Colo. State U., Ft. Collins, 1974-95, prof. emeritus, 1995—. Author: Social Structure and Social Problems, 1974, Sociology of American Sport, 1978, In Conflict and Order: Understanding Society, 1978, Sport in Contemporary Society, 1979, Social Problems, 1980, Elite Deviance, 1981, Criminology, Crime and Criminal Justice, 1985, Diversity in American Families, 1987, Society's Problems: Sources and Consequences, 1989, Crime in the Streets and Crime in the Suites: Perspectives on Crime and Criminal Justice, 1989, The Reshaping of America: Social Consequences of the Changing Economy, 1989, Paths to Homelessness, 1994, Solutions to Social Problems: Lessons from Other Societies, 1997, Fair and Foul: Beyond the Myths and Paradoxes of Sport, 1999, Experiencing Poverty: Voices from the Bottom, 2003, Globalization: The Transformation of Social Worlds, 2005; editor Social Sci. Jour., 1978—84; contbr. articles to profl. jours. NDEA fellow, 1965-67 Mem. Internat. Sociol. Assn., Am. Sociol. Assn., Midwest Sociol. Soc., Soc. Study Social Problems, Western Social Sci. Assn., Southwestern Social Sci. Assn., Internat. Com. for Sociology Sport., N.Am. Soc. for Sociology of Sport (pres. 1986-87). Democrat. Mennonite. Home: 303 Lakewood North Newton KS 67117

EIZENSTAT, STUART ELLIOT, lawyer, former ambassador; b. Chgo., Jan. 15, 1943; m. Fran Eizenstat; children: Jay, Brian. AB cum laude, U. N.C., 1964, LLD (hon.), 2000; LLB, Harvard U., 1967; LLD (hon.), Yeshiva U., 1998, Weizmann Inst. Sci., 1999, Jewish Theol. Sem., 2000, Hebrew Coll., 2000, Brandeis U., 2001, Fla. Atlantic U., 2002. Bar: Ga. 1967, D.C. 1981. Mem. White House staff, 1967-68; mem. nat. campaign staff Hubert H. Humphrey, 1968; law clk. U.S. Dist. Ct. No. Dist. Ga., 1968-70; ptnr. Powell, Goldstein, Frazer & Murphy, Washington, 1970-77, vice chmn., 1981-93; asst. to Pres. U.S. for domestic affairs and policy, 1977—81, dir. White House Domestic Policy Staff, 1977—81; amb. to European Union Brussels, 1993-96; spl. envoy Dept. State Property Claims in Ctrl. Europe, 1995-2001; undersec. for internat. trade Dept. Commerce, Washington, 1996-97; envoy Pres. of U.S. for Promotion of Democracy in Cuba, 1996-97; undersec. of state for econ., bus. and agrl. affairs Dept. State, Washington, 1997-99; alt. gov. World Bank, 1998-99, Regional Devel. Banks, 1998-99; dep. sec. Dept. Treasury, 1999-2001; now ptnr., Internat. Trade Practice Group & Trade Regulation Practice Group Covington & Burling, Washington. Spl. rep. of Pres. and Sec. of State on Holocaust Issues, 1999-2001; adj. lectr. J.F. Kennedy Sch. Govt., Harvard U., 1981-92; guest scholar Brookings Inst., Washington, 1981; mem. Energy Coord. Coun., Econ. Policy Group, 1977-81, Pres. Bush task force on U.S. Internat. Broadcasting, 1991; head U.S. del. CSCE Econ. Forum, 1994; lectr. coll., bus. and civic groups; bd. dirs. Mirant Corp., 2001-; trustee Black Rock Funds, 2001-; internat. adv. bd. Coca-Cola, 2001-; chmn. internat. bd. govs. Weizmann Inst. Sci., 2002—. Author: Imperfect Justice: Slave Labor, Looted Assets and the Unfinished Business of World War II, 2003, paperback edit., 2004; co-author: Andrew Young: The Path to History, 1973, Environmental Auditing Handbook, 1984; co-editor: The American Agenda: Report to the 41st President of the United States, 1988, reprint, 1989; contbr. articles to profl. jours. and newspapers. V.p. Jewish Publ. Soc., 1981-85; chmn. Inst. U.S. Jewish-Israeli Rels., 1982-86; bd. dirs. Woodrow Wilson Ctr. for Internat. Scholars, 1978-87, Jerusalem Found., 1992-93, Eurasia Found., 1993; pres. Greater Washington Jewish Cmty. Ctr., 1989-91; mem. exec. com. Ctr. for Dem. Policy, 1982-93; bd. visitors U. N.C., Chapel Hill, 1987-90, bd. trustees Ctr. for Jewish Studies; co-dir. The Am. Agenda (with Pres. Ford and Pres. Carter), 1991; trustee Jerusalem Inst. Mgmt., 1987-93; mem. coun. Harvard Law Sch. Assn., 1988-92, Gov.'s Commn. on Fed. Funding, Commonwealth of Va., 1986, Com. on Federalism and Nat. Purpose, 1984-85; chmn. Econ. and Budget Strategy Com., Montgomery County Coun., 1986; v.p., bd. dirs. Am. Assocs., Ben-Gurion U. of the Negev, N.Y.C., 1981-89; trustee Washington Inst. for Jewish Leadership and Values, 1988—, Brandeis U., 1991—; commr. Commn. on Jewish Edn. in N.Am., 1988-90; v.p. Atlanta Bur. Jewish Edn., 1973-76; mem. exec. com. Atlanta Jewish Cmty. Ctr., 1970-76; mem. B'nai Brith Youth Commn., Washington, 1981-82; bd. dirs. United Synagogues Am., 1981-84.; internat. bd. dirs. Weizmann Inst., 1989-93, chmn. bd. govs., 2002—; active in Dem. party and polit. campaigns. Decorated Legion of Honor (France); pub. policy scholar Woodrow Wilson Ctr. Internat. Scholars, 2001; recipient Man of Yr. award Nat. Capital Assn., State Dept. award for Pub. Svcs., 1996, 99, B'nai B'rith Lodges, 1982, Outstanding Svc. to Summer Youth Program U.S. Dept. Labor, 1980, Outstanding Svc. award Hebrew Aid Immigration Soc., 1980, Outstanding Svc. award Opportunities Industrialization Ctrs., 1979, award Washington Internat. Bus. Coun., 1978, award Nat. Coalition Involved People, 1977, Young Man of Yr. award Am. Assn. Jewish Edn., 1973-74, Leadership award Acad. Jewish Religion, 1989, Tree of Life award Hadassah, Boston, 1989, Myrtle Wreath award Fla. Atlantic Region Hadassah, 1991, Benjamin Cardozo Professionalism award Atlanta Jewish Fedn., 1992, Export Fin. award Coalition for Employment Through Exports, 1993, award for pub. svc. Sec. of State, 1996, Moral Statesman award Anti-Defamation League, 1997, Phillip Klutznick B'nai B'rith award for Outstanding Pub. Svc., 1996, award for transatlantic svc. European Inst., 1997, Myrtle Wreath award Hadassah, 1997, 98, Transatlantic Svc. award European Inst., 1997, award for courage and conscience Israeli Knesset, 1998, Leadership award Sec. of State, 1999, B'nai B'rith Leadership award, 2000, Auschwitz Holocaust Ctr. award, 2000, Washington Inst. Jewish Leadership and Values, 2001, award for leadership Sec. of State, 1999, Alexander Hamilton award Sec. of Treasury, 2001, Humanitarian award Inst. Leadership and Values, 2001, knight comdr.'s cross Fed. Rep. Germany, 2002, Leadership award United Jewish Cmtys., 2002, Great Negotiator award Harvard Negotiation Group, 2003, medal of honor Czech Coun. Victims of Nazism, 2005. Fellow Nat. Acad. Pub. Adminstn., Ctr. for Excellence in Govt.; mem. ABA (spl. com. on lawyers in govt., mem. com. govt. stds. 1992-93), Atlanta Bar Assn., D.C. Bar Assn., Ga. Bar Assn., U.S. C. of C. (internat. policy com. 1982-89), Nat. Fgn. Trade Coun. (internat. trade com.), Washington Policy Coun. (Internat. Mgmt. and Devel. Inst.), Phi Beta Kappa, Phi Eta Sigma. Democrat. Jewish. Office: Covington & Burding 1201 Pennsylvania Ave NW Washington DC 20004-2401 Office Phone: 202-662-5745. Office Fax: 202-662-6291. Business E-Mail: seizenstat@cov.com.

EK, ALAN RYAN, forester, educator; b. Mpls., Sept. 5, 1942; BS in Forestry, U. Minn., St. Paul, 1964, MS, 1965; PhD, Oreg. State U., Corvallis, 1969. Rsch. officer Can. Dept. Forestry and Rural Devel., Sault Ste Marie, Canada, 1966-69; from asst. prof. to assoc. prof. forestry U. Wis., Madison, 1969-77; from assoc. prof. to prof. U. Minn., St. Paul, 1977—, head dept. forest resources, 1984—. Mem. forestry rsch. adv. coun. USDA, 1994—96, 1998—99, chair, 1998—99; cons. in field. Contbr. chapters to books, articles to profl. jours. Fulbright scholar, Finland, 1997. Fellow: Soc. Am. Foresters (various coms., chmn. forest sci. and tech. bd. 1989—90); mem.: AAAS, Am. Soc. Photogrammetry and Remote Sensing, Am. Statis. Assn., Nat. Assn. Profl. Forestry Schs. and Colls. (chmn. rsch. com. 1993—95, 1999—2002), Sigma Xi, Gamma Sigma Delta, Xi Sigma Pi. Avocations: reading, sports. Home: 4744 Kevin Ln Saint Paul MN 55126-5849 Office: U Minn Dept Forest Resources Saint Paul MN 55108 Office Phone: 612-624-3400. Business E-Mail: aek@umn.edu.

EKANGER, LAURIE, retired state official, contractor; b. Salt Lake City, Mar. 4, 1949; d. Bernard and Mary (Dearth) E.; m. William J. Shupe, Nov. 6, 1973; children: Ben, Robert. BA in English, U. Oreg., 1973. Various pos. Mont. State Employment & Tng. Divsn., Helena, 1975-80, dep. adminstr., 1980-82; adminstr. Mont. State Purchasing Divsn., Helena, 1982-85, Mont. State Personnel Divsn., Helena, 1985-93; labor commr. Mont. Dept. Labor & Ind., Helena, 1993-97; dir. Mont. Dept. Pub. Health and Human Svcs., 1997-2000; rsch. & analysis projects, 2000—. Council chair State Employee Group Benefits Coun., 1985-93; bd. dirs. Pub. Employee Retirement Bd., 1988; mem. various state adv. couns. for health and human svcs. Home: 80 Pinecrest Rd Clancy MT 59634-9505

EKDAHL, JON NELS, lawyer; b. Topeka, Nov. 15, 1942; s. Oscar S. and Dorothy O. (Ekdahl) M.; m. Marcia Opp, May 24, 1975; children: Kirsten, Erika, Kristofer. AB magna cum laude, Harvard U., 1964, LLB, 1968; MS in Econs., London Sch. Econs., 1965. Bar: Ill. 1969, U.S. Ct. Appeals (7th cir.) 1981, U.S. Supreme Ct. 1981. Assoc. Sidley & Austin, Chgo., 1968—73, ptnr., 1973—75; mng. ptnr., gen. counsel Andersen Worldwide SC, Chgo., 1975—2000; sr. v.p., gen. counsel AMA, Chgo., 2001—. With USAR, 1968-74. Mem. ABA, Chgo. Bar Assn., Mid-Am. Club, Chgo. Club. Office: Am Med Assn 515 N State St Chicago IL 60610 E-mail: jon_ekdahl@ama-assn.org.

EKELMAN, DANIEL LOUIS, lawyer; b. Cleve., May 1, 1926; s. William Harry and Edna Mae (James) E.; m. Ann Jane Farnacy, Aug. 5, 1950 (dec. June 1993); children: Sally, Karen, Barbara, Beth; m. Phyllis E. Patton, Oct. 18, 1997. BA, Ohio Wesleyan U., 1950; LLB, Case Western Res. U., 1952. Bar: Ohio 1952, U.S. Dist. Ct. (no. dist.) Ohio 1953, U.S. Tax Ct. 1955. Assoc. Calfee, Halter & Griswold, Cleve., 1952-59, ptnr., 1959-77, mng. ptnr., 1977-85, sr. ptnr., 1985-95; ret., 1996. Gen. ptnr. Sawmill Creek Resort, Huron, Ohio, 1968-80. Trustee Brentwood Hosp., Cleve., 1960-94, Greater Cleve. Hosp. Assn., 1975-78 (Outstanding Trustee award 1992), Case Western Res. Law Sch., 1984-87, Meridia South Pointe Hosp., 1995, Brentwood Found., 1995-99. With USN, 1944-46, PTO. Fellow ABA; mem. Ohio Bar Assn., Cleve. Bar Assn., Soc. Benchers, Order of the Coif, The Country Club (Pepper Pike, Ohio, trustee 1988-91), Union Club, Jupiter Hills Club (Jupiter, Fla.). Republican. Home: 22029 Douglas Rd Shaker Heights OH 44122

EKHOLM, COLLYER M., psychiatrist; b. Camp LeJeune, N.C., Sept. 13, 1957; d. Robert Parker and June (Edwards) Marden; m. Steve L. Ekholm, Dec. 1985; 1 child, Sarah. BS in Life Scis., MIT, 1979; MD, U. Iowa, 1983. Diplomate Am. Bd. Psychiatry and Neurology in Psychiatry and Geriatric Psychiatry. Resident U. Kans. Med. Ctr., Kansas City, 1983—87; pvt. practice Ft. Collins, Colo., 1987—89, 1995—99; med. dir. Mohave County Mental Health Clinic, Kingman, Ariz., 1989—92, Larimer County Mental Health, Ft. Collins, 1992—95; staff psychiatrist McFarland Clinic, Ames, Iowa, 1999—2001, Abbe Ctr. for Cmty. Mental Health, Cedar Rapids, Iowa, 2001—. Mem.: Am. Psychiat. Assn. Office: Abbe Ctr for Cmty Mental Health 520 11th St NW Cedar Rapids IA 52405-3811 Office Phone: 319-398-3562.

EKICI, EYLEM, computer engineer, educator; b. Istanbul, Turkey, Aug. 24, 1974; BS, Bogazici U., 1997; MS, Bogazici U., Istanbul, 1998; PhD, Ga. Inst. Tech., 2002. Asst. prof. elec. and computer engring. Ohio State U., Columbus, 2002—. Mem.: ACM, IEEE. Office Phone: 614-292-0495.

EKMAN, DONALD J., lawyer, retail executive; b. 1952; BA, U. Wash.; JD, Willamette U. Bar: Oreg. 1979. Ptnr. Ekman & Bowersox, 1992-93; with Hollywood Entertainment Corp., Wilsonville, Oreg., 1993—, v.p., gen. counsel, sr. v.p., gen. counsel, sec. Office: Hollywood Entertainment Corp Hollywood Video 9275 SW Peyton Ln Wilsonville OR 97070 Office Phone: 503-570-1600. Office Fax: 503-570-1680.

EKMAN, PETER ERIK, urologist, educator; b. Umea, Sweden, Oct. 23, 1943; s. Erik Wilhelm and Margareta Emma Hildegard (Duse) Ekman; m. Amelie Margareta Sundblad, May 4, 1968 (div. Jan. 1991); children: Johan, Kristoffer, Niklas, Jenny; m. Soili Annikki Kupiainen, Sept. 2, 2000; 1 child, Alexandra Anna Margareta. MD, Karolinska Inst., 1969, PhD, 1978. Resident surgery Sabbatsberg, Stockholm, 1972-75; resident urology Karolinska Inst., Stockholm, 1975-79, assoc. prof., 1980-90, prof., dept. chair, 1991—. Co-dir. WHO G.U. Cancers, Stockholm, 1991—. Contbr. chpts. in books, articles to profl. jours. Lt. Swedish Marine Corps, 1969-86. Recipient Fogarty Rsch. award NIH, 1981. Mem. Am. Assn. Genito Urinary Surgeons, Am. Urology Assn., Swedish Urol. Soc. (v.p. 1999-2002, pres. 2002—), Assn. Acad. European Urologists, European Assn. Urology. Avocations: choir singing, skiing, swimming, sports. Home: Odengatan 52 S 11351 Stockholm Sweden Office: Karolinska Hosp Dept Urology S 17176 Stockholm Sweden

EKSIOGLU, MAHMUT, engineering educator; MS in Aerospace Engring., Wichita State U., 1990, MS in Indsl. Engring., 1992, PhD in Indsl. Engring., 1996. Ergonomics cons. Advanced Ergonomics, Inc., Dallas, 1997—98; rsch. scientist Nat. Inst. for Occupl. Safety and Health, Morgantown, W.Va., 1999—2000; asst. prof. Morgan State U., Balt., 2000—01, The U. of Michigan-Dearborn, Dearborn, Mich., 2001—. Mem.: Human Factors and Ergonomics Soc., Inst. of Indsl. Engrs. Achievements include patents pending for Computer-Controlled Universal Hand-Force Analysis System. Office: The Univ Michigan-Dearborn 2231 EC 4901 Evergreen Rd Dearborn MI 48128-1491 Office Phone: 313-593-0326. E-mail: meksiogl@umich.edu.

EKSTRAND, JOHN ROBERT, physician, educator, military officer; b. Lincoln, Nebr., Aug. 5, 1961; s. James Gordon and Elaine Ester Ekstrand; m. Carolyn Joy Olsen, Aug. 19, 1989; children: Charlotte Christine, Christian Joseph, Jonathan James, Jessica Joy. MD, Creighton U., 1988; MPH, Uniformed Svcs. U. of Health Scis., 2000. Diplomate Am. Bd. Internal Medicine, 1991. Commd. 1st lt. U.S. Army, 1991, advanced through grades to col., 2003—, staff physician Bad Cannstatt, Germany, 1991—92, Heidelberg, Germany, 1992—95; chief internal medicine clinic Trippler Army Med. Ctr., Honolulu, 1995—98; tchg. faculty Walter Reed Army Med. Ctr., Washington, 1998—2000; chief internal medicine svc. Brooke Army Med. Ctr., San Antonio, 2000—02, chief family practice svc., 2002—03; dep. comdr. clin. svcs. Gen. Leonard Wood Army Cmty. Hosp., Fort Leonard Wood, Mo., 2003—. Assoc. prof. Sch. Medicine U. Hawaii, Honolulu, 1996—98; assoc. prof. medicine Uniformed Svcs. U. of Health Scis., Bethseda, Md., 1998—2000. Decorated Meritorious Svc. medal U.S. Army, Army Commendiation medal. Fellow: ACP; mem.: Order Mil. Med. Merit. Avocation: music. Office Phone: 573-596-0415.

EL-AASSER, MOHAMED S., engineering educator, academic administrator; b. Egypt, Feb. 10, 1943; naturalized, US; married; 2 children. BS, Alexandria U., Egypt, 1962, MS, 1966; PhD, McGill U., Montreal, Can., 1972. Post-doctoral fellow Ctr. for Surface and Coatings Rsch. Lehigh U., 1972—74, asst. prof. dept. chem. engring., 1974—78, assoc. prof., 1978—82, prof., 1982—, co-dir. Emulsion Polymers Institute, 1978—89, dir., 1989—, dir. Ctr. for Polymer Sci. and Engring., 1988—2001, dir. Polymer Interfaces Ctr., 1991—96, Iacocca Endowed Chair of Engring. and Applied Sci., 1992—2001, chmn. dept. chem. engring., 1996—2001, dean P.C. Rossin Coll. of Engring. and Applied Sci., 2001—04, provost, v.p. acad. affairs, 2004—. With Centre National de Recherche Scientifique Laboratoire Materiaux Organique, Vernaison, France, 1983—84; bd. mem. Pa. Infrastructure Tech. Alliance, 2001—; bd. dirs. Discovery Ctr., 2004—. Author: over 300 papers. Co-recipient NASA Inventor of Yr. Award, 1985; recipient Kuwait Award, 1983, Best Paper Award, Tech. Transfer Workshop, Coun. Chem. Rsch., 1987, Eleanor and Joseph Libsch Rsch. Award, Lehigh U., 1988, O. Hugo Schuck Best Paper Award, Am. Automatic Control Coun., 1998, R.R. and E.C. Hillman Award, Lehigh U., 1999, Roy W. Tess Award in Coatings, Am. Chem. Soc. Divsn. of Polymeric Materials Sci. and Engring., 2002. Mem.: Assn. Engring. Colleges of Pa. (chair 2003—04), Am. Chem. Soc., Am. Soc. Engring. Edn. (Engring. Dean's Coun. 2001—), Am. Inst. Chem. Engineers, AAAS, Coun. Chem. Rsch., Sigma Xi, Phi Beta Delta (Beta Pi Chpt., Faculty Award 1998). Office: Lehigh Univ Provost Office 27 Memorial Dr W Bethlehem PA 18015

ELACHI, CHARLES, aerospace engineer; b. Beirut, Apr. 18, 1947; m. Valerie Gifford; 2 children. BS, U. Grenoble, France, 1968; MS, Calif. Inst. Tech., 1969, PhD in Elec. Sci., 1971; MBA, U. So. Calif., 1978; MS, UCLA, 1983. Rsch. fellow Calif. Inst. Tech., Pasadena, 1971-74, leader Radar Remote Sensing Team, 1974-80, sr. rsch. scientist Jet Propulsion Lab., 1981—87, asst. lab. dir. space and sci. instruments, 1987-95, dir. space and earth sci. programs Jet Proplusion Lab., 1995—2000, prof. elec. engring., 1982—2000, dir. Pasadena, 2000—, v.p. Prin. investigator NASA, 1973-87, mem. Solar Sys. Exploration Com. Coun., 1988—, Astrophysics Coun., 1988—; mem. Electromagnetic Acad., 1990-95; participant in archeological expeditions; spkr. in field. Contbr. over 200 articles to profl. jours.; patentee in field. Chmn. JPL United Way Campaign. Recipient Prof. R.W.P. King award for outstanding contbrn. in field of electromagnetics, 1973, Nevada Medal Outstanding Achievement in Sci. and Engring., Desert Rsch. Inst., 1995, Wernher Von Braun award, 2000, Takeda award, 2002, Mem. AIAA (Dryden Lecturship in Rsch., 2000), NAE, IEEE (Geosensing and Remote Sensing Disting. Achievement award 1987, Engring. Excellence medal 1992), Am. Astronautical Soc., Electromagnetic Soc., Am. Geophys. Union, Planetary Soc., Internat. Acad. Astronautics, Sigma Xi. Achievements include development of a series of imaging radar systems for the Space Shuttle that allowed scientists to study the earth and other planets of the solar system. Avocations: skiing, woodworking, travel, history. Office: Jet Propulsion Lab MS 180-704 4800 Oak Grove Dr Pasadena CA 91109-8001

ELAM, BARBARA SUE, artist, retired art educator; b. Wichita Falls, Tex., Mar. 31, 1940; d. John L. and Della Dora (Bennett) E.; children: Stephen W., Jolie Dimock-Humphrey, Keith Elam Dimock. BFA, U. Tex. at Dallas, Plano, 1978; MFA, East Tex. State U., 1986. Bunting fellow Mary Ingraham Bunting Inst. of Radcliffe, Cambridge, Mass., 1989-90; asst. prof. art DePauw U., Greencastle, Ind., 1990-93, Rockford (Ill.) Coll., 1994—2005, assoc. prof., 2005; ret., 2005. Vis. artist U. Tex., Tyler, 1988, U. Oreg., Eugene, Am. U., Guadalahara, Mex., Hillcountry Art Mus. Tex. One woman show at Irving (Tex.) Art Ctr., 1998, Boston Coll., Tex. A&M U., Bryan, 2001, Ill. State U., Normal, Edith Baker Gallery, Dallas, Sheridan Gallery, Dallas, San Angelo Art Mus., Tex.; exhibited in group shows at Fogg Art Mus. of Harvard U., Mary Ingraham Bunting Inst., Indpls. Mus. Art, Edith Baker Gallery, Dallas, Fogg Art Mus, Harvard U., Ind. Mus. Art, Wilwalkie Mus. Art, Wichita Fall Tex. Mus. of Art, Radcliffe Inst.; over 200 natural and several internat. exhbns.; represented in permanent collections at Fogg Art Mus., Milw. Art Mus., Indpls. Art Mus., numerous univs. and pvt. collections. Mem. Mid Am. Print Coun. (bd. dirs. 1991-94). Office: Rockford Coll Clark Art Ctr 5950 Lindenshire #103 Dallas TX 75230 Home: 716 Medford Dr Rockford IL 61107-3708

ELAM, FRED ELDON, retired military officer; b. Seminole, Okla., July 10, 1937; s. Jack Eldon Elam and Maye (Gaskill) E.; m. Judy Teller, Feb. 21, 1959; children: Jacqueline Marie Elam Kabat, Justin Eldon. BS, U. Ark., 1960; MBA, Mich. State U., 1964; grad. strategy mgmt. and naval ops., Naval War Coll., 1977; grad., Harvard Grad. Sch. Bus. Admin., 1998. Commd. 2d lt. U.S. Army, 1960, advanced through grades to maj. gen., 1986, with Div. G-4, 101st Airborne (Air Assault) Fort Campbell, Ky., 1976-77, comdr. Materiel Support Ctr. Waegwan, Republic of Korea, 1977-79, dir. programs and evaluation Army Materiel Command Alexandria, Va., 1979-82; comdg. gen. 19th Support Command, Taegu, Republic of Korea, 1982-84; dir. mgmt. Hdqrs. Dept. Army, Washington, 1984-85; chief U.S. Army Transp., Hdqrs. Transp. Ctr. Fort Eustis, Va., 1985-88; comdr. Joint U.S. Mil. Mission for Aid to Turkey Ankara, 1988-90; asst. dep. chief of staff for logistics, Dept. Army Washington, 1990—2003; v.p. profl. tech. svcs. Advancia Corp., Arlington, Va., 1993—2002; pres. Elam Consulting, 2003—. Mem. lifetime staff and faculty Army Logistics Mgmt. Ctr., Fort Lee, Va., 1971—, Va. Mil. Commn., 1986-88; disting. mem. Transp. Corps Rgt., U.S. Army; counselor Sr. Corps. Ret. Exec. Decorated D.S.M., Def. Superior Svc. medal, Legion of Merit, Bronze Star with two oak leaf clusters, Meritorious Svc. medal with two oak leaf clusters, Air medal, Army Commendation medal with three oak leaf clusters, Armed Forces expeditionary medal, Vietnam Svc. medal with four oak leaf clusters, Overseas Svc. ribbon with "4" device, Republic of Vietnam campaign medal, Republic of Korea Svc. medal, Medal of Merit of Turkish Armed Forces, Meritorious Svc. medal; named to Hall Fame, Transp. Corps. Mem. Assn. U.S. Army, Air Traffic Control Assn., Soc. of 173d Airborne Brigade, Nat. Def. Transp. Assn., Res. Officers Assn., Am.-Turkish Friendship Assn., Sr. Corps of Ret. Execs., Beta Gamma Sigma. Avocations: running, reading, military history. Office Phone: 703-644-0753. Personal E-mail: elamjf@msn.com.

ELAM, JOHN RICHARD, mortgage company executive; b. Kansas City, Mo., Dec. 4, 1945; s. Jonnie Elam; m. Kathy Elam, Aug. 1996; 1 child, MacKenzie. BS, Auburn U., 1967; MA, U. Ga., 1973; MBA, Harvard U., 1985, Golden Gate U., 1986. With Sallie Mae, Tampa, Fla., 1988-92; divsn. supt. Chase Manhattan Mgmt., Tampa, 1992-96; gen. mgr. CIS, Champaign, Ill., 1996-98; CIO ops. N.Am. Mortgage Co., Santa Rosa, Calif., 1998—. Col. U.S. Army, 1968-88. Avocations: running, weightlifting, golf, reading. Office: N Am Mortgage Co 3883 Airway Dr Santa Rosa CA 95403 Home: 5014 Givendale Ln Tampa FL 33647-2731 E-mail: jaelam@namc.com.

ELAM, LESLIE ALBERT, retired museum director; b. Balt., May 12, 1938; s. Albert and Mary (Walker) E.; m. Judith Anne Clark, Apr. 4, 1964; children— Jennifer Helen, Jeffrey Walker. BA, Lehman Coll., City U. N.Y., 1973. Editor J.J. Augustin, Inc. Pub., Locust Valley, N.Y., 1958-61; editorial asst. Am. Numis. Soc., N.Y.C., 1963-66, editor, 1966-89, adminstrv. officer, 1966-69, sec., 1969-99, dir., 1972-97, exec. dir., 1997-99; cons., 1999-2000. Editor: Am. Numis. Soc. Museum Notes, 1966-89. Served with AUS 1961-63. Mem. Phi Beta Kappa. Home: 8305 Cherokee Trail Crossville TN 38572 Personal E-mail: LAElam@aol.com.

ELAM, MATTHEW, industrial engineer, educator; BS in Math., U. Tex., Tyler, 1991, MS in Math., 1994; PhD, Okla. State U., 2001. Asst. prof. indsl. engring., mem. grad. faculty applied stats. U. Ala., Tuscaloosa, 2001—. Contbr. numerous articles to profl. jours. and conf. proceedings. Recipient Inst. for Ops. Rsch. and Mgmt. Scis. award for outstanding Tchg. Asst., Okla. State U., 1999, 2001; grantee, George C. Marshall Space Flight Ctr., NASA, 2003—04, Am. Cast Iron Pipe Co., 2004—05; Eugene L. and Doris L. Miller Disting. Grad. fellow, Okla. State U., 1998—2001. Mem.: Inst. Indsl. Engrs., Am. Soc. Quality (cert. quality engr.), Am. Soc. Engring. Edn., Am. Statis. Assn., Alpha Chi Nat., Alpha Pi Mu, Tau Beta Pi.

ELAM, RICK, accounting educator; b. Hannibal, Mo., Feb. 11, 1944; s. Albert Gray and Helene (Richards) E.; m. Karen J. Morgan, Nov. 19, 1979; 2 children. BSBA and Econs., Culver-Stockton Coll., 1966; MA in Acctg., U. Mo., 1969, PhD in Acctg., 1973. CPA, Mo. V.p. Al Elam, Inc., Realtor, Lake Ozar, Mo., 1969-70; tchg. asst. U. Mo., Columbia, 1970-73, asst. prof. acctg., 1973-78, assoc. prof., 1978-83, prof., 1983-86, dir. Sch. Accountancy, 1979-86; dean Rutgers U. Sch. Bus., New Brunswick, N.J., 1986-89; v.p. edn. AICPA, 1989-96; dean Mid. Tenn. State U. Coll. Bus., Murfreesboro, 1996—99. Mgmt. cons. Ernst & Whinney, 1978; mem. acctg. accreditation com. Am. Assembly Collegiate Schs. Bus., 1985-88, mem. visitation com. of accreditation coun., 1982-89. Contbr. numerous articles to profl. jours. Scholar Price Waterhouse Found., 1969-73; summer rsch. grantee U. Mo., 1975. Mem. AICPA (chmn. acctg. careers com. 1982, bus., govt. and edn. com. 1981), Am. Acctg. Assn. (consortium rep. 1972, chmn. curriculum and degree subcom. of 5-yr. acctg. edn. program com. 1980-81, treas. mgmt. advt. svcs. sect. 1978-79, winner nat. manuscript contest 1974), Fedn. Schs. Accountancy (v.p. 1984, pres. 1985-86), Beta Alpha Psi, Beta Gamma Sigma. Office: Mid Tenn State U Coll Bus Murfreesboro TN 37132-0001 Home: 3805 Majestic Oaks Dr Oxford MS 38655-8153

ELANAYAR, SUNIL K., research and development engineer; arrived in U.S., 1986; s. Sivadasan Arangott and Komalam Sivadasan; m. Seema S. Nair, Dec. 27, 1996; 1 child, Adira Nair. BS in Tech., ITT, Delhi, India, 1986; MS, Univ. Ala., Tuscaloose, Ala., 1988; PhD, Purdue Univ., W. Lafayette, Ind., 1993. Rsch. fellow Purdue Univ., W. Lafayette, Ind., 1993—94; sr. engr. Computervision, Pune, India, 1994—96; dir. Gentech Corp., Tokyo, 1996—98; sr. rsch. engr. Caice Corp., Tampa, Fla., 1998—2000; sr. engr. Knowledge Tech., Lexington, Mass., 2000—. Fellow David Ross Found., W. Lafayette, Ind., 1991—93. Contbr. scientific papers. Achievements include research in neural networks in mfg. process monitoring knowledge based engring. Avocations: travel, tennis, photography. Home: 561 Ambergate Pl Concord NC 28027 Office: Dassault Systems 10330 David Taylor Dr Charlotte NC 28262

ELANDER, RICHARD PAUL, microbiologist, consultant; b. Worcester, Mass., Sept. 17, 1932; s. Arthur Waldemar and Edith Alma Louise (Engstrand) E.; m. Barbara Ann Sudz, Feb. 8, 1958; children: Tracy, Richard, Ronald. BS with honors, U. Detroit, 1955, MS, 1956; PhD, U. Wis., 1960; postgrad., U. Minn., 1965—66. Rsch. scientist Eli Lilly and Co., Indpls., 1960-67; assoc. dir. Wyeth Labs., West Chester, Pa., 1967-72, Smith Kline and French, Phila., 1972-75; dir. fermentation devel. Bristol-Myers Squibb Co., Syracuse, NY, 1975-80, sr. dir. biotech. and rsch. devel., 1980-83, v.p. biotech., 1983-97; cons. to biotech./pharm. industry, 1997—; sci. adv. Nereus Pharm. Inc., 1999—2005. Lectr. Butler U., Indpls., 1965-66, Rensselaer Poly. Inst., 1983-88; rsch. prof. Syracuse U., 1983-97; biotech. adv. bd., Dartmouth, MIT, Cornell; mem. adv. bd., Engring. and Sci., Detroit Mercy Univ., 1997—, Coll. Agr. and Life Scis., Cornell U., 1998. Mem. editl. bd. Biotech. Letters, 1985-97, Jour. Indsl. Microbiology, 1985-94, Applied and Environ. Microbiology, 1974-83; contbr. articles to profl. jours., also chpts. to books in field; patentee in field. Fellow Am. Acad. Microbiology, Am. Inst. Chemists, Soc. Indsl. Microbiology (sec. 1968, pres. 1974, Charles Thom award 1984); mem. AAAS, Am. Soc. Microbiology (chmn. divsn. 1977), Am. Chem. Soc., Lions (bd. dirs. 1970-73), N.Y. Acad. Sci., Sigma Xi (v.p. Syracuse chpt. 1991, pres. Syracuse chpt. 1992). Avocations: music, skiing, gardening, writing. Home and Office: 318 Gravilla St La Jolla CA 92037-6006 Office Phone: 858-551-4146. E-mail: relander1@san.rr.com.

ELARABY, NABIL A., diplomat, judge; b. Cairo, Mar. 15, 1935; m. Nadia Teymour; children: May, Marwan, Hisham. Licencie en Droit, Cairo U., Egypt; LLM in Internat. Law, JSD, NYU, U.S.A. Legal advisor to Egyptian del. UN Mid. East Peace Conf., Ministry of Fgn. Affairs, Geneva, 1973-75; counsellor to mission from Egypt UN, Geneva, 1974-76, amb., dep. permanent rep. of Egypt N.Y.C., 1978-81, 91-99, amb. extraordinary and plenipotentiary, permanent rep. of Egypt Geneva, 1987-91, permanent rep. N.Y.C., 1991—99; legal advisor, dir. legal and treaties dept. Ministry of Fgn. Affairs, Geneva, 1976-78, 83-87; Egyptian amb. India, 1981-83; arbitrator (Suez Canal dispute) ICC Internat. Ct. of Arbitration, Paris, 1989—92; judge Jud. Tribunal Orgn. Arb Petroleum, 1990; commr. UN Compensation Commn., 1999—2001; mem. Internat. Ct. Justice, The Hague, Netherlands, 2001—. Ptnr. Zaki Hashem & Ptnrs., Attys. at Law; mem. bd. Internat. Coun. Arbitration for Sport, Stockholm Internat. Peace Rsch. Inst.; mem. governing coun. UNIDROIT; rep. Egypt in UN orgns. including The Gen. Assembly, Security Coun., Econ. and Social Coun., Human Rights Commn., 1966—; head Egyptian Del. UN Conf. on Disarmament, 1987—91; leader Egyptian Delegation to Egyptian-Israeli Arbitration Tribunal Taba Talks, 1986—89; former chair numerous UN coms. and working groups; pres. Security Coun., 1996; lectr. The Hague acad. of Internat. Law, Columbia U., NYU, Duke U., Yale U., The Egyptian Soc. Internat. Law, Am. Soc. Internat. Law, many others. Contbr. to profl. jours. and internat. law publs. Adlai Stevenson fellow UN Inst. for Tgn. and Rsch., 1968, Spl. fellow, 1973. Mem. Egyptian Soc. Internat. Law (bd. dirs.). Address: 23 Kasr El Nil St Cairo 11211 Egypt also: Internat Ct Justice Peace Palace 2517 KJ The Hague Netherlands

ELBAUM, CHARLES, physicist, educator, researcher; b. May 15, 1926; married; 3 children. MASc, U. Toronto, 1952, PhD in Applied Sci., 1954; MA (hon.), Brown U., 1961. Rsch. fellow in metal physics U. Toronto, 1954-57, Harvard U., 1957-59; asst. prof. applied physics Brown U., Providence, 1959-61, assoc. prof. physics, 1961-63, prof. physics, 1963—, chmn. dept. physics, 1980-86, also Hazard prof. physics, 1991—. Cons. to industry. Fellow Am. Phys. Soc.; mem. AIME, AAAS, Soc. Neurosci. Office: Brown U Dept Physics PO Box 1843 Providence RI 02912-1843 Business E-Mail: elbaum@physics.brown.edu.

EL-BAZ, FAROUK, science administrator, educator; b. Zagazig, Egypt, Jan. 1, 1938; came to U.S., 1967, naturalized, 1970; s. El-Sayed Mohammed and Zahia Abul-Ata (Hammouda) El-B.; m. Catherine Patricia O'Leary, 1963; children: Monira, Soraya, Karima, Fairouz. BSc, Ain Shams U., 1958; MS, U. Mo., 1961; PhD, U. Mo. and MIT, 1964; DSc (hon.), New England Coll., 1989; PhD (hon.), Mansoura U., 2004, Am. U., Cairo, 2004. Demonstrator geology dept. Assiut U., Egypt, 1958-60; lectr. Mineralogy-Petrography Inst., U. Heidelberg, Germany, 1964-65; geologist exploration dept. Pan Am.-UAR Oil Co., Egypt, 1966; supr. lunar exploration Bellcomm and Bell Tel. Labs., Washington, 1967-72; rsch. dir. Center for Earth and Planetary Studies, Nat. Air and Space Mus., Smithsonian Instn., Washington, 1973-82; v.p. sci. and tech. Itek Optical Sys., Litton Industries, Lexington, Mass., 1982-86; cons. geology, prof. geology and geophysics U. Utah, 1975-77; prof. geology Ain Shams U., Egypt, 1976-81, 95—; sci. adviser Pres. Anwar Sadat of Egypt, 1978-81; sr. advisor Nat. Rsch. Inst. for Astronomy and Geophysics, Helwan, Egypt, 1996—; dir. Ctr. for Remote Sensing Boston U., 1986—. Author: Say It in Arabic, 1968, Astronaut Observations from the Apollo-Soyuz Mission, 1977, Egypt as Seen by Landsat, 1979, The Geology of Egypt: An Annotated Bibliography, 1984; co-author: Coprolites: An Annotated Bibliography, 1968, Glossory of Mining Geology, 1970, The Moon as Viewed by Lunar Orbiter, 1970, Apollo Over the Moon: A View from Orbit, 1978; co-editor: Apollo-Soyuz Test Project Summary Science Report: Earth Observations and Photography, 1979, Desert Landforms of Southwest Egypt: A Basis for Comparison with Mars, 1982, Physics of Desertification, 1986, Remote Sensing and Resource Exploration, 1989, Sand Transport and Desertification in Arid Lands, 1990, The Gulf War and the Environment, 1994, Atlas of State of Kuwait from Satellite Images, 2000, Wadis of Oman, 2002, Sultanate of Oman, Satellite Image Atlas, 2004; editor: Deserts and Arid Lands, 1984; contbr. articles to profl. jours. Decorated Order of Merit 1st class Egypt; recipient certificate merit U.S. Bur. Mines, 1961, Exceptional Sci. Achievement medal NASA, 1971, Alumni Achievement award U. Mo., 1972, Honor citation Assn. Arab-Am. U. Grads., 1973, Outstanding Contbns. to Sci. and Space Tech. award Am.-Arab Anti-Discrimination Com., 1995, Achievement award Egyptian-Am. Profl. Soc., 1995, Human Needs award Am. Assn. Petroleum Geologists, 1996. Fellow: AAAS (Pub. Understanding of Sci. and Tech. award 1992), Geol. Soc. Am. (cert. commendation 1973), Royal Astron.; mem.: Desert Rsch. Inst. (Nev. medal 2003), Nat. Acad. Engring., Internat. Inst. of Boston (Golden Door award 1992), World Aerospace Edn. Orgn. (Cert. of Merit 1973), Explorers Club, Sigma Xi. Office: Boston U Ctr Remote Sensing 725 Commonwealth Ave Boston MA 02215-1401 E-mail: farouk@bu.edu.

ELBER, RON, computer science educator; b. Rehovot, Israel, Mar. 28, 1957; s. Yair and Rachel Neter Elber; m. Victoria Buch, Aug. 1983 (div. Aug. 1996); 1 child, Dassi; m. Virginia Yip, 2000; children: Nurit, Nir. BSc, Hebrew U., 1981, PhD in Chemistry and Physics, 1984. Postdoctoral Harvard U., Boston, 1984-87; asst. prof. chemistry U. Ill., Chgo., 1988-91, assoc. prof. chemistry, 1992-94; assoc. prof. chemistry and biology Hebrew U., Jerusalem, 1994-96, prof. chemistry and biology, 1996-98; prof. computer sci. Cornell U., Ithaca, N.Y., 1999—. Cons. Tera Computers, Israel, 1996-98, Peptor, Israel, 1996—; acting dir. NIH Resource for Parallel Computing, Ithaca, 1999—; organizer numerous scientific meetings. Editor: Recent Development in the Theoretical Studies of Proteins, 1996. Sgt. Israel Def. Forces, 1978-81. Scholar U. Ill., 1990-92; recipient Alon fellow State of Israel, 1992; recipient numerous grants. Mem. AAAS, N.Y. Acad. Sci., ACS, Israel Chem. Soc., Soc. Indsl. and Aplied Maths. Avocations: chess, hiking. Office: Cornell U 4130 Upson Hall Ithaca NY 14853-7501 E-mail: ron@cs.cornell.edu.

ELBERGER, RONALD EDWARD, lawyer; b. Newark, Mar. 13, 1945; s. Morris and Clara (Denes) Elberger; m. Rena Ann Brodey, Feb. 15, 1975; children: Seth, Rebecca. AA, George Washington U., 1964, BA, 1966; JD, Am. U., 1969. Bar: Md. 1969, D.C. 1970, Ind. 1971, U.S. Ct. Appeals (7th cir.) 1971, U.S. Supreme Ct. 1973. Atty. Balt. Legal Aid Bur., 1969-70; chief counsel Legal Services Orgn., Indpls., 1970-72; ptnr. Elberger & Stanton, Indpls., 1974-76; assoc. Bose, McKinney & Evans, LLP, Indpls., 1972—74, 1976—80, ptnr., 1980—; asst. sec. Chip Ganassi Racing Teams, Inc., 1998—. V.p. Worldwide Slacks, Inc., 1984—92, Cardboard Shoe Prodns., Inc., 1989—93; v.p., gen. counsel Emmis Comm. Corp., 1986—98, asst. sec., v.p., litig. counsel, 1998—2002. Mem., v.p. Med. Licensing Bd., Ind., 1982—98; pres., chmn. bd. dirs. Ind. Civil Liberties Union, Indpls., 1972—77, bd. dirs., 1980—82; mem. nat. coun. media and pub. affairs George Washington U., 2000—; bd. dirs. Jewish Cmty. Rels. Coun., 1997—2000, ACLU, N.Y.C., 1972—77; trustee Children's Mus. Indpls., 1994—2003, Disting. advisor, 2003—; bd. dirs. Flanner Ho. Indpls., Inc., 1999—. Fellow Reginald Heber Smith, U. Pa., 1969—71. Fellow: Ind. Bar Found., Indpls. Bar Found.; mem.: ABA, DC Bar, Bar Assn. 7th Cir., Ind. Bar Assn. Democrat. Jewish. Avocations: fishing, music, gardening. Office: Bose McKinney & Evans LLP 2700 First Indiana Pla 135 N Pennsylvania St Indianapolis IN 46204-2400 Office Phone: 317-684-5195. Business E-Mail: relberger@boselaw.com.

ELBERT, CHARLES STEINER, lawyer; b. St. Louis, May 18, 1950; s. Harold I. and Carol B. (Steiner) E.; m. Karen Berry, Dec. 9, 1979; children: Matthew Berry, Lisa Beth. AB, Washington U., 1972; JD cum laude, St. Louis U., 1976. Bar: Mo. 1976, Ill. 1977, U.S. Dist. Ct. (ea. dist.) Mo. 1977, U.S. Ct. Appeals (8th cir.) 1977, U.S. Supreme Ct. 1985. Assoc. Kohn, Shands, Elbert, Gianoulakis & Giljum, LLP, St. Louis, 1976-81, ptnr., 1982—. Spl. rep. 22d Jud. Bar Com., St. Louis, 1978-88; spk. labor and employment law CLEs. Contbr. articles to profl. jours. Trustee Clayton Gardens Neighborhood Assn., Mo., 1983-84, 85-86, pres., 1984-85; bd. dirs. St. Louis chpt. Am. Diabetes Assn., 1998-2004, St. Louis chpt. Am. Jewish Com., 1984-97, mem. nat. legal com., 1997—; sec., 1994-97; v.p. Nursery Found., St. Louis, 1988-89; bd. dirs., Mo. Coalition Against Censorship, 1986-92, sec., 1988-92; bd. dirs. St. Louis Jewish Cmty. Rels. Coun., 2005—; mentor Dunbar Sch., 1995-2001. Mem. ABA (labor law sect. 1984—, corp. banking and bus. law sect. 1987—), Mo. Bar Assn. (labor law com. 1977—), Ill. State Bar Assn., Bar Assn. Met. St. Louis (labor law com. 1977—, grievance com. 1978-87, Clayton Hockey Club (pres. 2001-02). Jewish. Home: 8137 University Dr Saint Louis MO 63105-3726 Office: Kohn Shands Elbert et al Ste 2410 One US Bank Plaza Saint Louis MO 63101 Office Phone: 314-241-3963. E-mail: celbert@ksegg.com.

ELBERT, JAMES PEAK, independent insurance agent, minister; b. Pampa, Tex., Feb. 5, 1937; s. James Monteen and Nannie Pearle (Harwell) E.; m. Jean Coburn, June 25, 1960 (div. Jan., 1983); children: James Michael, Steven Lawrence; m. Ann English Smith, Apr. 23, 1983; 1 child, Jennifer English Aberle. BA, Southwestern U., Georgetown, Tex., 1959; MDiv, So. Meth. U., 1962. Minister First Meth. Ch., Glen Flora, Tex., 1962-65, Falvey Meml. Meth. Ch., Wells, Tex., 1965-67; assoc. minister First United Meth. Ch., Orange, Tex., 1967-69; minister of edn. Trinity United Meth. Ch., Beaumont, Tex., 1969-70; minister First United Meth. Ch., Murchiston, Tex., 1970-71; campus minister Henderson County Jr. Coll., Athens, Tex., 1970-71; v.p., owner Elbert Insur. Agy., Lake Jackson, Tex., 1971-76, Bennett-Elbert Co., Lake Jackson, 1976-83; v.p., gen. mgr. Jahn-Austin Insur., Galveston, Tex., 1983-96; prin., owner Brazoria (Tex.) Ins. Agy., 1998—. Pres. Galveston Ins. Bd., 1986-88; Elbert Ins. Agy., Lake Jackson, Tex., 1995—, pres., Insurco, Inc., 1997—; apptd. to Windstorm Study com. Tex. Dept. Ins., 1992, liaison to Tex. Dept. Ins. bldg. code study com., 1992—; supernumerary Tex. Conf. United Meth. Ch. Bd. dirs. Jr. Achievement of Brazoria County, 1980-81; active Lake Jackson Little League, 1974-77, Lake Jackson Teenage League, 1978-79, Lake Jackson Babe Ruth League, 1980; bd. dirs. Galveston

Windstorm Action Com., 2003—, pres., 2004—; pres. Galveston Housing Fin. Corp., 1993-95, City of Galveston Property Fin. Authority, Inc., 1993-95; v.p. Bay Area coun. Boy Scouts Am., 1988—; pres. Ball H.S. Band Boosters, Galveston, 1991-92; mem. Mayor's Roundtable on Housing, City of Galveston, 1993-95; chmn. com. on ministries Moody Meml. First United Meth. Ch., 1994-95. Recipient Merit award Bay Area Coun. Boy Scouts Am. Quintana Dist., Lake Jackson, 1979, Silver Beaver award Bay Area Coun. Boy Scouts Am., Galveston, 1985. Mem.: Tex. Windstrom Ins. Assn. (bd. dirs. 1998—, Tex. fair plan governing com. 2002—), Ind. Ins. Agts. Tex. (chmn. com. 1991—95, liaison to Tex. Windstrom Pool Assn. 1993—95, bd. dirs. 1995—98, Chmn. of the Yr. 1993—94), Cert. Ins. Counselors (pres. Tex. chpt. 1992, edn. com. 2002, cert.), Brazosport C. of C. (mem. bd. 1980—81), Galveston C. of C. (bd. dirs. 1992—95), Rotary of Galveston Island (pres. 1993—94, Paul Harris fellow 1990, Bd. Mem. of Yr. 1991, Rotarian of Yr.), Phi Delta Theta. Avocations: family camping, gardening. Home: 7754 Beaudelaire Cir Galveston TX 77551-1625 Office: Elbert Ins Agy PO Box 4009 107 W Way Ste 21 Lake Jackson TX 77566-2409 also: Brazoria Ins Agy 100 E Hwy 332 PO Box 1240 Brazoria TX 77422-1240 Office Phone: 979-297-2433. E-mail: eia_james@elbertinsurance.com.

ELBERT, JEROME WILLIAM, physicist, writer; s. Milferd Simon and Irene June Elbert; m. Nancy Ruth Mottet, July 5, 1975. BS, Iowa State U., 1964; MS, U. of Wis., 1966, PhD, 1972. Tchg./rsch. asst. physics dept. U. of Wis., Madison, 1964—71; rsch. assoc., assoc. instr. physics. dept. U. of Utah, Salt Lake City, 1971—73, rsch. asst. prof. physics dept., 1974—80, rsch. assoc. prof. physics dept., 1980—86, rsch. prof. physics dept., 1986—94; self-employed Tacoma, 1994—. Vis. prof. Nat. Inst. Nuclear Physics, Naples, Italy, 1989—90. Author: (non-fiction book) Are Souls Real?, 2000. Mem.: AAAS, Am. Phys. Soc. Avocations: hiking, kayaking, deep-sky astronomy. Personal E-mail: demythologizer@cs.com.

ELBLE, RODGER JACOB, neurologist, researcher; b. Alton, Ill., Aug. 10, 1948; s. Rodger Jacob, Sr. and Blanche Dee (Baughman) E.; m. Suzanne Louise Marshall, Aug. 14, 1971; children: Rodger Jacob III, Joseph Marshall, Ann Elizabeth. BS in Aero. Engring., Purdue U., 1971; PhD in Physiology, Ind. U., 1975; MD, Ind. U., Indpls., 1977. Diplomate Am. Bd. Psychiatry and Neurology. Resident in neurology Washington U., St. Louis, 1978-81; asst. to assoc. prof. neurology So. Ill. U., Springfield, 1981—96, prof., 1996—, chmn. dept. neurology. Dir. regional Alzheimer disease assistance ctr., dir. neurology residency program So. Ill. U., Springfield. Co-author: Tremor, 1990; contbr. articles to profl. jours. Nat. Inst. Neurol. Disorders and Stroke grantee; Nat. Inst. on Aging grantee; The Whitaker Found. grantee, 1987—. Fellow Am. Acad. Neurology; mem. Am. Physiol. Soc., Soc. Neurosci. Avocations: fishing, computers. Office: So Ill U Sch Medicine PO Box 19643 Springfield IL 62794-9643 E-mail: relble@siumed.edu.

ELCANO, MARY S., lawyer; BA cum laude, Lynchburg Coll., 1971; JD, Cath. U., Washington, 1976. Litigation atty. Balt. Legal Aide Bur., 1976; staff atty. Office Solicitor Dept. Labor, 1979; gen. trial and appellate atty. Office Labor Law U.S. Postal Svc., 1982, exec. dir. Office EEO, 1984, regional dir. human resources N.E. region, 1987, sr. v.p., gen. counsel, 1992-99, exec. v.p., gen. counsel, 1999-2000; ptnr. Sidley Austin Brown & Wood LLP, Washington, 2000—03; gen. counsel, corp. sec. ARC, Washington, 2003—. Office: ARC 2025 E St NW Washington DC 20006 Office Phone: 202-303-5422. Business E-Mail: ElcanoM@usa.redcross.org.

ELCHYNSKI, SHERRY A., secondary school educator; b. Indpls., Jan. 7, 1959; d. Charlotte Margaret Nickell; children: Bryan, Justin, Jordan. BS in Health and Phys. Edn., Slippery Rock U., 1981. Cert. CPR instr. ARC, 1988, lifeguard ARC, 2000, aerobic instr. Calif., 1991. Tchr. health, phys. edn. Holy Rosary Sch., Erie, Pa., 1972—87, North East H.S., 1987—. Coach volleyball North East H.S., 1982—85, 2000—. Mem., past pres. North East Recreation Commn., 1986—; pres. Twins Mothers Club Erie, 2004—05. Mem.: NEA, Pa. State Edn. Assn., Am. Coun. Exercise (group fitness instr.). Avocations: aerobics, dance, volleyball, track coach. Office: North East Sch Dist 1901 Freeport Rd North East PA 16428

ELCIK, ELIZABETH MABIE, fashion illustrator; b. Bklyn., Sept. 16, 1933; d. Cornelius Peter and Anna Julia (Cunningham) Mabie; m. John Joseph Elcik, Apr. 20, 1963. Grad., Jamesine Franklin Sch. Profl. Arts, N.Y.C., 1954; student in painting, NYU; student life class, Art Students League, N.Y.C., Alliance of Queens Artists, 2003. Fashion illustrator Vogue patterns Conde Nast Publs., 1954-59; freelance illustrator various clients, N.Y.C., 1960-74; fashion illustrator Butterick Fashion Mktg. Co., N.Y.C., 1974-82, McCall Pattern Co., N.Y.C., 1982—2001. Monitor profl. sketch classes, N.Y.C., 1962—79. Exhibitions include Cedar House Gallery, 2004. Scholar N.Y.C Art, 1951, Jamesine Franklin Sch., 1952. Mem.: Women's Studio Ctr. Inc., Nat. Mus. Women in Arts. Roman Catholic. Avocation: travel.

ELDEN, GARY MICHAEL, lawyer; b. Chgo., Dec. 11, 1944; s. E. Harold and Sylvia Arlene (Diamond) E.; m. Phyllis Deborah Mandler, Apr. 20, 1975; children: Roxanna Mandler, Erica Mandler. BA, U. Ill., 1966; JD, Harvard U., 1969. Bar: Ill. 1969, U.S. Dist. Ct. (no. dist.) Ill. 1969, U.S. Ct. Appeals (7th cir.) 1973, U.S. Supreme Ct. 1973, U.S. Dist. Ct. (ea. dist.) Mich. 1985, U.S. Ct. Appeals (8th cir.) 1988, U.S. Ct. Appeals (6th and 10th cirs.) 1990, U.S. Dist. Ct. (ea. dist.) Wis. 1992. Ptnr. Kirkland & Ellis, Chgo., 1969-78, Reuben & Proctor, Chgo., 1978-86, Isham, Lincoln & Beale, Chgo., 1986-88, Grippo & Elden, Chgo., 1988—. Contbr. articles to profl. jours. Fellow Am. Coll. Trial Lawyers; mem. ABA, Chgo. Bar Assn. (sec. com. appellate procedures 1975-77), Chgo. Coun. Lawyers, Appellate Lawyers Assn. (bd. dirs. 1975-77), Met. Club. Home: 3750 N Lake Shore Dr Chicago IL 60613-4238 Office: Grippo & Elden LLC 111 S Wacker Ste 5100 Chicago IL 60606 Office Phone: 312-704-7700.

ELDER, CHRISTIAN, race car driver; b. Mpls. Race car driver Elko Speedway, Minn., NASCAR Busch Series. Achievements include winner of 1999 Daytona Season Opener. Avocations: skydiving, scuba diving, skiing, hunting, fishing. Office: Akins Motorsports 185 McKenzie Rd Mooresville NC 28115-7976

ELDER, FRED KINGSLEY, JR., physicist, educator, researcher; b. Coronado, Calif., Oct. 19, 1921; s. Fred and Ethel S. (Tait) E.; m. Elinor Jean Goertz, July 5, 1947; children: Nancy Elisabeth Elder Backus, Jessie Custer Elder James, Jacqueline Lesesne Elder Shafer, Elinor Tait Elder Powell, Lydia Jean Elder Archer, Robert Abraham, Mary Grace Elder Graham, John Philip. BS in Physics, U. N.C., 1941; MS in Physics, Yale U., 1943, PhD, 1947. Instr., Yale U., 1943-44; instr. U. Pa., 1947-49; physicist Nat. Bur. Standards, summer 1949; asst. prof. U. Wyo., 1949-50; sr. physicist applied physics lab. Johns Hopkins U., 1950-53; assoc. prof. physics Wabash Coll., Crawfordsville, Ind., 1953-55; prof., chmn. physics dept and div. natural scis. and math. Belhaven Coll., Jackson, Miss., 1955-59; research physicist U.S. Naval Ordnance Lab., White Oak, Md., summers 1957-59; head research br. antisubmarine warfare lab. U.S. Naval Air Devel. Center, Johnsville, Pa., 1959-65; prof. physics Rochester Inst. Tech., N.Y., 1965-91, prof. emeritus, 1991—, head dept., 1965-72. Scientist Physics Research Labs., Eastman Kodak Co., summer 1982; hon. vis. lectr. physics Aston U., Birmingham, Eng., 1985-86; vis. research fellow Lanchester Poly., Coventry, Eng., 1985-86 Scoutmaster, Nat. Capital Area council Boy Scouts Am., 1950-53; Scoutmaster Central Indiana council, 1953-55; trustee Westminster Theol. Sem., Phila., 1960-99, hon. trustee, 1999—, sec. bd. trustees, 1981-83, mem. exec. com., 1965-78; trustee Presbyn. Guardian Pub. Corp., 1958-79; bd. dirs. Presbyn. Jour. Corp., 1979-87, mem. exec. com., 1979-84, mem. editorial com., 1984-87, mem. various denominational bds.; coms. gen. assembly Orthodox Presbyn. Ch., 1952—; trustee Great Commn. Publs., 1975-99, v.p., 1975-76, 77-78, pres. 1978-79, 86-87, 90-91, 92-93. Served to lt. comdr. USNR, 1944-46; physicist U.S. Naval Research Lab. Washington. Mem. Am. Assn. Physics Tchrs. (vice chmn. N.Y. State sect. 1976-78, chmn. 1978-82), Netherlands, Am. phys. socs., Am. Geophys. Union, Am. Soc. for Engring. Edn., Inst. Physics (Gt. Britain), Franklin Inst., U.S. Naval Inst., Phi Beta Kappa, Phi Kappa Phi, Sigma Pi Sigma, Sigma Xi. Orthodox Presbyterian (ruling elder 1952—). Research, publs. on physics of fluids, physics edn. Home: 3026 County Rd 40 Bloomfield NY 14469-9365 Office: Rochester Inst Tech Physics Dept Rochester NY 14623 E-mail: kingsleyelder@aol.com.

ELDER, IRMA, retail automotive executive; b. Xicotencalt, Mex., 1934; m. James Elder, 1963 (dec.); 3 children. Owner, CEO Elder Automotive Group, 1983—. Mem. VIP panel 36th Annual Northwood U. Internat. Auto Show; founder Woman's Automotive Assn. Internat. Bd. dirs. Northwood U., Coll. Creative Studies, Oakland Family Svcs., Econ. Club Detroit. Named Woman Yr., Woman's Automotive Assn. Internat., 2001; named one of 100 Most Influential Women, Crain's Detroit Bus., 100 Leading Women, Automotive News, 2000; recipient Automotive Hall Fame Svc. Citation award, 2000, Pres. award, Ford Motor Co., 2000, 2001, Pride of Jaguar award, 1999, 2000. Achievements include frequently honored for many charitable assn; first woman to own Ford dealership in metropolitan Detroit market; successfully expanded co. from one dealership to eight after death of husband, founder of Elder Automotive; number one Saab dealership in US in volume of automobile sales (Saab of Troy); number one Jaguar dealership in N. Am. in volume of automobile sales (Jaguar of Troy); Elder Automotive consistently ranks top ten of Hispanic Bus. mag. top 500 Hispanic owned co. Office: 777 John R Rd Troy MI 48083 Office Fax: 248-583-0815.*

ELDER, JAMES CARL, lawyer; b. Detroit, Mar. 11, 1947; s. Carl W. and Alta M. (Bradley) E.; m. Margaret Ford, Apr. 6, 1974; children: James B., William J., Michael L., Samuel F. BA, U. Okla, 1969, JD, 1972. Bar: Okla. 1972, U.S. Dist. Ct. (we. dist.) Okla. 1972. Ptnr., dir. Crowe & Dunlevy, Oklahoma City, 1972-82; dir., mem. Mock, Schwabe, Waldo, Elder, Oklahoma City, 1982-96, 98—; ptnr. Gable Gotwals Mock Schwabe Kihle Gaberino, 1996-98. Nat. coun. rep. Last Frontier Coun. Boy Scouts Am., 1989—, pres., 1997-99; trustee Norman (Okla.) Pub. Sch. Found., 1988-97, pres., 1995-97; elder Meml. Presbyn. Ch., Norman, clk. of session, 1992-95; dir. Cmty. Coun. Ctrl. Okla., 1999-2003, v.p., 2002-03; mem. exec. com. United Way Ctrl. Okla., 2004—. Capt. 95th Inf. Div. USAR, 1972—78. Recipient Silver Beaver award Boy Scouts Am., Oklahoma City, 1989, Silver Antelope award, 1999. Fellow Okla. Bar Found. (life), Baden Powell World Fellowship; mem. ABA (mem. title ins. com. real property, probate and trust law sect. 1993—, chmn. closing issues subcom. 1995—2003), Rotary Club, Beta Theta Pi Corp. of Okla. (trustee, v.p., chpt. counselor 1975-86, 95—, pres. 1995-2002). Avocations: scouting, skiing, reading. Office: Mock Schwabe Waldo et al 211 N Robinson 2 Leadership Sq 14th Fl Oklahoma City OK 73102

ELDER, LAMAR ALEXANDER, JR., lawyer; b. Athens, Ga., June 16, 1945; s. Lamar Alexander Sr. and Johnnie Lucile (Aycock) E.; m. Jane Ellen Lindauer, July 25, 1970; children: Jennifer, Jonathan. AB, U. Ga., 1967, JD, 1970. Bar: Ga. 1970, U.S. Supreme Ct. 1974, U.S. Dist. Ct. (so. dist.) Ga. 1985. Assoc. Cook, Pleger & Noell, Athens, 1970-71; asst. gen. counsel USDA, Atlanta, 1975-77; assoc. J. Harold Mimbs, Hazlehurst, Ga., 1977-79; sole practice Hazlehurst, 1979—. Atty. Jeff Davis County, Hazlehurst, 1980—; judge Mcpl. Ct. of Hazlehurst, 1985-86. Mem. Dem. Exec. Com., Jeff Davis County, Ga., 1980—; chmn. adminstrv. bd. 1st United Meth. Ch., Hazlehurst, 1985. Capt. JAGC USAF, 1971-75. Mem. Ga. Bar Assn., Hazlehurst-Jeff Davis County C. of C. (bd. dirs. 1980—, past pres.). Lodges: Rotary (bd. dirs. Hazlehurst chpt. 1982-84, v.p. 1984-85, pres. 1985-86). Avocations: fishing, gardening, refinishing antiques. Home: 11 Woodhaven Dr Hazlehurst GA 31539-6615 Office: # 7 Jeff Davis St PO Box 632 Hazlehurst GA 31539-0632 Office Phone: 912-375-3681.

ELDER, MARY LOUISE, librarian; b. Ann Arbor, Mich., Sept. 7, 1937; d. John Dyer and Elsie (Phelps) Elder. BA, St. Louis U., 1959; MA, U. Chgo., 1962; postgrad., U. Calif., Berkeley, 1965-69. Libr. U. Chgo., 1961-63; rare book cataloger U. Kans., Lawrence, 1963-65; rare books libr. St. Louis Pub. Libr., 1969-74; rare book cataloger Duke U., Durham, N.C., 1979-84, Smithsonian Inst., Washington, 1984-91, Libr. Congress, Washington, 1991—2002; ret. Mem. ALA, Am. Printing History Assn., Bibliog. Soc., Bibliog. Soc. Am., Cath. Libr. Assn., Soc. History Authorship, Reading and Publishing, Alpha Sigma Nu.

ELDER, RICHARD BRUCE, artist, writer; b. Hawkesbury, Ont., Can., June 12, 1947; s. David Murdoch and Edrie Maud (Campbell) E.; m. Kathryn LeRoy, Sept. 4, 1970. Student, McMaster U., 1969; MA, U. Toronto, 1970; B of Applied Arts in Media Studies, Ryerson Poly. Inst., 1976. Curator film programs for Can. Coun., 1982, Can. Images, 1982, 83, Festival of Festivals, 1984, Art Gallery Ont., 1986, 89, Internat. Exptl. Film Congress, 1989; rsch. chair Ryerson U. Prodr. (films) The Book of All the Dead, 1975-94. The Book of Praise, 1997—; works exhibited at Mus. Modern Art, Millennium, N.Y.C., San Francisco Cinematheque, Hood Mus., Atlanta, Kino Arsenal, Berlin, Festival of Festivals, Ctr. Georges Pompidou, George Eastman House, Albright-Knox Gallery, Munich Stadtmuseum, Cineteca, Bologna, Italy, Le Fresnoy, France, Cinema: Nouvelles Ecrisures, Paris; retrospectives of film work Art Gallery Ont., 1985, Cinémathèque Québecoise, 1986, Anthology Film Archives, 1988, 95, Senzatitolo, Treno, Italy, 1996, Images '97, Toronto, The Antechamber, Regina, Can., 2000; author: Image and Identity: Reflections on Canadian Film and Culture, 1989, The Body in Film, 1989, Stan Brakhage: A Retrospective, 1977-95, 1995, A Body of Vision, 1997; author: The Films of Stan Brakhage in the American Tradition of Ezra Pound, Gertrude Stein, and Charles Olson, 1998; contbr. articles to profl. jours. Recipient Can. Film award for best exptl. film, 1976, L.A. Film Critics Circle award for best ind. exptl. film, 1980, Auswortiges Amt. F.G.R. study tour, 1986; grantee Can. Coun., Ont. Arts Coun., Social Scis. and Humanities Rsch. Coun. Can.; Sarwan Sahoto Disting. scholar Ryerson U. Rsch., 2000, Creation in Fine Arts grant, SSHRC Rsch, New Media Initiative Grant CC/NSERC, Ryerson U. Rsch. Chair grant. Address: Unit 5 692 St Clarens Ave Toronto ON Canada M6H 3X1 E-mail: elderb@acm.org.

ELDER, RICHARD C., chemistry educator; b. Ann Arbor, Mich., June 9, 1939; s. John D. and Elsie P. Elder; m. Katherine Tepperman, Sept. 15, 1979; children: Elizabeth Samantha, Sarah Helen. BS (hon.), St. Louis U., 1961; PhD, Mass. Inst. Tech., 1964. Instr. Chemistry U. Chgo., 1965-67, asst. prof. Chemistry, 1967-70; assoc. prof. Chemistry U. Cin., 1970-78; vis. rsch. fellow Australian Nat. U., 1976-77; assoc. dir. Biomedical Chemistry Rsch. Ctr., U. Cin., 1986-88, acting dir., 1988-91; prof. Chemistry U. Cin., 1978—; guest appointment Brookhaven Nat. Lab., Upton, N.Y., 1985—; dir. Biomedical Chemistry Rsch. Ctr., U. Cin., 1991—. Fellow grad. schs. U. Cin., 1996—; named Chemist of Yr. Am. Chem. Soc. Cin. sect., 1996, Scientist of Yr. Scientists and Engrs. Soc. of Cin., 1997. Office: University of Cincinnati PO Box 210172 Cincinnati OH 45221-0172 Office Phone: 513-556-9224.

ELDER, SAMUEL ADAMS, retired physics professor; b. Balt., July 13, 1929; s. Fred Kingsley and Ethel (Tait) E.; m. Sylvia Maynard, Jan. 1, 1955; children: Susan Spottiswoode (Mrs. Lawrence E. Erikson), Sheila Jean (Mrs. Daniel L. Korzep) (dec.), Sarah Maynard, Sandra Louise (Mrs. James A. Chestnut), Sharon Elizabeth (Mrs. Eric H. Thayer). BS, Hampden-Sydney Coll., 1950; Sc.M., Brown U., 1953, PhD, 1956. Sr. staff physicist Johns Hopkins Applied Physics Lab., Silver Spring, Md., 1956-64; asso. prof. physics U.S. Naval Acad., 1964-68, prof., 1968—2000; ret., 2000. Mem. computer policy bd. USN, 1968-2000, chmn., 1973-74. Author (textbook): (with Jerome Williams) Fluid Physics for Oceanographers and Physicists, 1989, 2nd edit., 1996; composer: Random Afternoon, 1969; research and publs. in acoustics, non-linear acoustics, musical acoustics, phys. acoustics, optical pyrometry, computer-aided edn. Pres. bd. dirs. Annapolis Area Christian Sch. Soc., 1974; trustee Covenant Coll., 1966-67; chmn. Mission to N.Am. com. Potomac Presbytery, Presbyn. Ch. in Am., 1990-95. Fellow Acoustical Soc. Am. (chmn. Washington chpt. 1969-70, mem. tech. com. on mus. acoustics 1970-76, tech. com. on phys. acoustics 1984-90); mem. Phi Beta Kappa, Sigma Xi. Republican. Presbyterian (elder). Home: 308 Halsey Rd Annapolis MD 21401-3219 Business E-Mail: elder@usna.edu.

ELDER, STEWART TAYLOR, dentist, retired military officer; b. Darlington, Pa., Aug. 6, 1917; s. William Carl and Olive Gertrude (Taylor) E.; m. Loretta Tersa Vitlo, Apr. 23, 1946; children: Donna Lou, Susan Loretta. BS, Mt. Union Coll., 1940; DDS, Ohio State U., 1945; postgrad., Naval Dental Sch., Nat. Naval Med. Center, Bethesda, Md., 1952-53. With Deming Pump Co., Salem, Ohio, 1935-36, prodn. mgr., 1952-53; commd. lt. (j.g.) U.S. Navy, 1945; advanced through grades to capt. Dental Corps, 1960; prosthetics officer 50th Field Hosp., Paris, 1946-47; asst. dental officer Norfolk Naval Shipyard, Portsmouth, Va., 1948-50, U.S.S. Wisconsin, 1950-52; postgrad. resident in prosthodontics Naval Weapons Plant, Washington, 1953-54; prosthetics officer Norfolk Naval Shipyard, Portsmouth, 1954-55, 57-60; dental officer, prosthetics officer U.S.S. Vulcan, 1955-57; prosthetics officer, exec. officer Naval Dental Clinic, Guantanamo Bay, Cuba, 1960-62; prosthetics officer Naval Dental Clinic Marine Corps Base, Camp Pendleton, Calif., 1962-66; comdg. officer 11th Dental Co., Republic of Vietnam, 1966-67; chief dental service Naval Hosp., Camp Pendleton, 1967-71; exec. officer Naval Dental Clinic, Washington, 1971-73, comdg. officer, 1973-75, Naval Regional Dental Center, Washington, 1975-76, Nat. Naval Dental Center, Bethesda, Md., 1976-79; lectr., instr. Navy Dental Corps Continuing Edn. Program, 1963—, Dental Intern and Postdoctoral Fellowship Programs, 1967—. Practice gen. dentistry, Salem, Ohio, 1947-48, lectr. and condr. clinics in field Mem. ADA (life), Am. Prosthodontic Soc. (life), Fedn. Prosthodontic Orgns. (life). Home: 1436 Patriot Dr Melbourne FL 32940-6818

ELDERFIELD, JOHN, art historian, museum curator; b. Yorkshire, Eng., Apr. 25, 1943; s. Henry and Rhoda May (Risbrough) E.; m. Joyce Davey, Jan. 9, 1965; children: Matthew, Jonathan; m. Jill Elizabeth Moser, Jan. 8, 1989 (div. 1995). Student, U. Manchester, 1961-62; BA with honors, U. Leeds, 1966, M.Phil.; with distinction, 1970; PhD, U. London, 1975. Lectr. art history Winchester Sch. Art, 1966-70; Harkness fellow Yale U., 1970-72; lectr. art history U. Leeds, 1973-75; curator painting and sculpture Mus. Modern Art, N.Y.C., 1975-93, dir. dept. drawings, 1979-93, chief curator at large, 1993—. Author: Hugo Ball: The Flight Out of Time, 1975, Fauvism and Its Affinities, 1976, European Master Paintings, 1976, Matisse, 1978, The Cut-outs of Henri Matisse, 1978, The Masterworks of Edvard Munch, 1979, New Work on Paper, 1981, The Modern Drawing, 1983, The Drawings of Henri Matisse, 1984, Kurt Schwitters, 1985, Morris Louis, 1986, Drawings of Richard Diebenkorn, 1988, Helen Frankenthaler, 1988, (co-author) Matisse in Morocco, 1990, Matisse: A Retrospective, 1992. Recipient Mitchell prize, 1986, chevalier des Arts et Lettres, 1989; Guggenheim fellow, 1972-73; Named one of Time Mag. 100 Most Influential People, 2005. Fellow Royal Soc. Arts; mem. Internat. Assn. Art Critics, Century Assn. Office: Mus Modern Art 11 W 53rd St New York NY 10019-5498*

ELDERGILL, KATHLEEN, lawyer; b. Mt. Kisco, N.Y., Jan. 16, 1953; d. William E. and Isabel E.; m. Bruce S. Beck. BA in Anthropology, U. Conn., 1976, JD, 1981. Cert. civil trial advocacy. Assoc. Beck & Pagano, Manchester, Conn., 1981-83; ptnr., then prin. Beck & Eldergill P.C., Manchester, 1983—. Mem. Fed. Grievance Com., New Haven, 1993-96, chair, 1996-99. Mem. legal adv. bd. Conn. Fund for Environment, 1994—. Fellow Am. Coll. of Trial Lawyers; mem. Am. Trial Lawyers Assn., Conn. Employment Lawyers Assn., Nat. Employment Lawyers Assn., Conn. Trial Lawyers Assn. Office: Beck & Eldergill PC 447 Center St Manchester CT 06040-3998

ELDERKIN, CHARLES EDWIN, retired meteorologist; b. Seattle, Aug. 6, 1930; s. Andrew Charles and Hilda Olena E.; m. Mary DuPriest, May 28, 1959; 1 child, Christopher Charles. BS, U. Wash., 1953, PhD, 1966. Meteorologist Gen. Electric Co., 1959-65; mgr. atmospheric physics sect. Battelle Pacific N.W. Lab., Battelle Meml. Inst., Richland, Wash., 1965-72, assoc. mgr. atmospheric scis. dept., 1972-79, program mgr. wind characteristics program element of fed. wind energy program, 1976-79, mgr. atmospheric scis. dept., 1979-82, assoc. mgr. geoscis. research and engring. dept., 1982-84, mgr. Hanford environ. oversight office, 1984-85, assoc. mgr. earth scis. dept., 1985-86, sr. program mgr. earth and environment scis. ctr., 1986-92. Sci. dir. multi-lab. rsch. program Atmospheric Studies in Complex Terrain, Dept. Energy, 1989-92. Served with USAF, 1954-55. Recipient E.O. Lawrence award U.S. Energy Rsch. and Devel. Adminstrn., 1975. Mem.: Sigma Xi. Home: 531 Holly St Richland WA 99354-1822

ELDERKIN, E(DWIN) JUDGE, retired lawyer; b. Missoula, Mont., Oct. 25, 1932; s. Emerson Winston and Valma Agnes (Judge) E.; m. Marie Jane Fletcher, June 20, 1954; children: Susan Marie, Michael Judge. BS in History, U. Oregon, 1954; LLB, U. Calif., Berkeley, 1959. Bar: Calif. 1960, U.S. Ct. Appeals (9th crct.) Calif. 1960, U.S. Supreme Ct. 1967. Assoc. Brobeck, Phleger & Harrison, San Francisco, 1959-66, ptnr., 1966-92, mng. ptnr., 1984-88, ret., 1992. Pvt. judge Pvt. Adjudication Ctr., Inc.; advisor Ctr. Pub. Resources; lectr. in field; bd. dirs. MPC Ins. Ltd., The Renewal Project; mem. policy com. Aetna dental. Pscyhol. lay counsel for low income families. Named Counselor of the Yr. 1996. Fellow Am. Coll. Trial Lawyers, Am. Bar Found.; mem. Am. Cancer Soc. (driver, Driver of Yr. 1996). Mem. Evangel. Covenant Ch. Avocations: hiking, swimming, golf, tennis.

ELDERS, JOYCELYN (MINNIE JOCELYN ELDERS, MINNIE JOYCELYN LEE), public health service officer, endocrinologist, former Surgeon General; b. Schaal, Ark., Aug. 13, 1933; d. Curtis and Haller Jones; m. Oliver B. Elders, Feb. 14, 1960; children: Eric D., Kevin M. BA in Biol., Philander Smith Coll., 1952; MD, U. Ark. Med. Sch., 1960; MS in Biochemistry, U. Ark., 1967. Pediatric intern U. Minn. Hosp., Mpls., 1960-61; pediatric resident U. Ark. Med. Ctr., Little Rock, 1961-63, chief pediatric resident, 1963-64, pediatric rsch. fellow, 1964-67, asst. prof. of pediatrics, 1967-71, assoc. prof. of pediatrics, 1971-76, prof. of pediatrics, 1976-87; dir. Ark. Dept. of Health, Little Rock, 1987-93; pres. Assn. of State & Territorial Health Officers, 1992; surgeon gen. US Dept. Health & Human Services, 1993-94; prof. pediatrics Univ. Ark. Med. Ctr., Little Rock, 1994—98, prof. emeritus, pediatric endocrinology, 1998—. Bd. dirs. Nat. Bank of Ark., North Little Rock, 1979-89. Editorial bd. Jour. Pediatrics, 1981—; contbr. articles on pediatrics to profl. jours. Bd. dirs. Northside YMCA, Little Rock, 1973—; vol. vols. in pub. schs., Little Rock, 1973—. 1st lt. U.S. Army, 1953-56. Recipient NIH Career Devel. award, Worthen Bank's Ark. Profl. Woman of Distinction award, 1987; named one of 100 Women of Ark., 1980, Ark. Dem. Woman of Yr. statewide newspaper, 1988, Presdl. award, Ark. Sociological and Anthropological Assn., 1993. Mem. So. Soc. Pediatrics (rsch. pres. 1979-80), Lawson Wilkins Endocrine Soc. (com. chair 1976), Ark. Sci. and Tech. Commn. (sec. 1975-89), Little Rock C. of C. (bd. dirs. 1980—), Endocrine Soc., Acad. Pediatrics, Am. Pediatric Soc. First African Am. US surgeon general. Office: U Ark Med Ctr 4301 W Markham # 820 Little Rock AR 72205*

ELDRED, GERALD MARCUS, performing company executive; b. Cambridge, Ont., Can., Oct. 5, 1934; s. Albert Harold and Ethel Emily Hope (Bardwell) E.; m. Marjorie Christine Kidd, Aug. 4, 1956; 1 child, Peter Marcus (dec.). Diploma, Nat. Theatre Sch., Montreal, 1965. Adminstr. Nat. Ballet Can., Toronto, 1972-79; adminstrv. dir., acad. prin. Nat. Ballet Sch., Toronto, 1979-82; exec. dir. Stratford Festival, (Ont.), 1982-86; dir. fin. and ops. Harbourfront Corp., 1987-97. Cons. in field; mem. arts adv. com. The Laidlaw Found., 1980-90. Stage producer, dir., adminstr. Canadian Players, Toronto, 1965-66, Man. Theatre Centre, Winnipeg, 1966-72, Shaw Festival, Niagara-on-the-Lake., Ont., 1967, Expo '67, Montreal, 1967, Rainbow Stage, Winnipeg, 1968, Kawartha Summer Festival, Lindsay, Ont., 1966, producer commd. opera for Nat. Arts Centre, Ottawa, 1969— . Mem. adv. com. program in art York U., 1982-90; mem., officer, bd. dirs. The Theatre Mus. Corp., 1988-2001, The Pleiades Theatre, Toronto, 1996. Named to Stairway of Excellence, Galt Collegiate Inst., 2003. Mem. Can. Actors Equity Assn., Assn. Cultural Execs., Can. Coun. (adv. arts panel 1970-72, adv. bd. touring office 1983-85). mem. bd. dir. Region Waterloo Arts Fund. Home: 5-260 Deer Ridge Dr Kitchener ON Canada N2P 2M3 E-mail: gm.eldred@sympatico.ca.

ELDRED, HEATHER ANN, librarian; b. Racine, Wis., Sept. 4, 1942; d. Sverre S. and Fern (Fulton) Elsmo; m. John Walter Eldred, Feb. 26, 1966. BA, U. Wis., 1964, MLS, 1965. Cert. libr., Wis. Children's libr. Cudahy (Wis.) Pub. Libr., 1966; cataloger/acting dir. Marquette U. Law Sch. Libr., Milw., 1966-70; cataloger Holy Redeemer Coll., Union Grove, Wis., 1970-72; cons. Wis. Valley Libr. Svc. Wausau, Wis., 1972-75, system administrator, 1975-83, dir., 1983—. Mem. ALA, Wis. Libr. Assn. (v.p. to pres.-elect 1987, pres. 1988, past pres. 1989, Muriel Fuller award 1995). Methodist. Avocations: family and neighbors, reading, writing, travel. Office: Wisconsin Valley Libr Svc 300 N 1st St Wausau WI 54403-5405 Office Phone: 715-261-7251.

ELDRED, KENNETH MCKECHNIE, acoustician, consultant; b. Springfield, Mass., Nov. 25, 1929; s. Robert Moseley and Jean McKechnie (Ashton) E.; m. Helene Barbara Koerting Fischer, May 31, 1957; 1 dau., Heidi Jean. BS, MIT, 1950, postgrad., 1951-53, UCLA, 1960-63. Engr. in charge vibration and sound lab. Boston Naval Shipyard, 1951-54; supervisory physicist, chief phys. acoustics sect. U.S. Air Force, Wright Field, Ohio, 1956-57; v.p., cons. acoustics Western Electro-Acoustics Labs., Los Angeles, 1957-63; v.p., tech. dir. sci. services and systems group Wyle Labs., El Segundo, Calif., 1963-73; v.p., dir. div. environ. and noise control tech. Bolt Beranek and Newman Inc., Cambridge, Mass., 1973-77, prin. cons., 1977-81. Dir. Ken Eldred Engring.; mem. exec. stds. coun. Am. Nat. Stds. Inst., 1979-89, vice-chmn., 1981-83, chmn., 1985-87, bd. dirs., 1983-87; bd. dirs., Ince Found.; mem., past chmn. Acoustical Stds. Bd.; mem. com. hearing, bioacoustics and biomechanics NRC, 1963-88; chmn. Internat. Stds. Orgn. Tech. Com. TC108 Mechanical Shock and Vibration, 1994-99; bd. dirs., treas. Earcraft Tech. Inc., 1999-2003. Served with USAF, 1954-56. Fellow Acoustical Soc. Am. (stds. dir. 1987-93, past chmn. coordinating com. environ. acoustics, Silver Medal in Noise 1994); mem. NAE, Inst. Noise Control Engring. (pres. 1976, bd. dirs. 1987-91), Boothbay Harbor Yacht Club, Down East Yacht Club. Home: Meadow Cove East Boothbay ME 04544 Office: PO Box 501 East Boothbay ME 04544-0501 Office Phone: 207-633-5991. Personal E-mail: keldred@alum.mit.edu.

ELDREDGE, CHARLES CHILD, III, art history educator; b. Boston, Apr. 12, 1944; s. Henry and Priscilla Marion (Bateson) Eldredge; m. Jane Allen MacDougal, June 11, 1966; children: Henry Gifford, Janann Bateson. BA in Am. Studies, Amherst Coll., 1966; PhD in Art History, U. Minn., 1971. Curator asst. Minn. Hist. Soc., St. Paul, 1966-68; mem. edn. dept. Mpls. Inst. Arts, 1967-69; tchg. assoc. art history U. Minn., 1968-70; curator collections Spencer Mus. Art U. Kans., Lawrence, 1970—71, dir., 1971-82, asst. prof. art history, 1970-71, assoc. prof., 1974-80, prof., 1980-82, Hall Disting. Prof. Am. Art and Culture, 1988—; dir. Nat. Mus. Am. Art, Washington, 1982-88. C.H. Hynson vis. prof. U. Tex., Austin, 1985; trustee Watkins Cmty. Mus., Lawrence, 1972-76, Assn. Art Mus. Dirs., 1982, 87, Reynolda House Mus. Am. Art, 1986-88, Amherst Coll., 1987-93, trustee Georgia O'Keeffe Found., 1989-95, Amon Carter Mus., 2003—; rsch. assoc. Smithsonian Instn., 1988—; founder Smithsonian Studies in Am. Art, 1987. Author: Marsden Hartley: Lithographs and Related Works, 1972, Ward Lockwood, 1894-1963, 1974, American Imagination and Symbolist Painting, 1979, Charles Walter Stetson, Color and Fantasy, 1982, Pacific Parallels: Artists and the Landscape in New Zealand, 1991, Georgia O'Keeffe, 1991, Georgia O'Keeffe: American and Modern, 1992, The College on the Hill, 1996, Reflections on Nature: Small Paintings by Arthur Dove, 1997, The Floor of the Sky: Artists and the North American Prairie, 2000, Tales from the Easel: American Narrative Paintings, 2004; co-author: The Arcadian Landscape: 19th Century American Painters in Italy, 1972, Art in New Mexico, 1900-1945, 1986, Georgia O'Keeffe and The Calla Lily in American Art, 2002; gen. editor: The Register of Mus. Art, 1971—82; mem. editl. bd. Am. Studies, 1974—77, Am. Art, 1996—. Fulbright scholar N.Z., 1983; Smithsonian Instn. fellow Nat. Collection Fine Arts, 1979, Found. Visitor fellow U. Auckland, 1993, Smithsonian fellow Nat. Mus. Am. Art, 1995, W.T. Kemper fellow for tchg. excellence, 2003; recipient Outstanding Alumnus award U. Minn., 1986. Mem. Coll. Art Assn. Am., Am. Studies Assn., Am. Assn. Mus., Assn. Art Mus. Dirs. (hon.), Phi Beta Kappa (hon.). Office: U Kans Dept Art History 209 Spencer Mus Art 1301 Mississippi St Lawrence KS 66045-0001 Office Phone: 785-864-4713. Business E-Mail: cce@ku.edu.*

ELDREDGE, JONATHAN DEFOREST, medical librarian, educator; s. LeRoy Lincoln Jr. and Elizabeth Belding Eldredge; m. Regina Leslie Wolfe, Nov. 19, 1994; children: Nicolas-Etienne, Gabriela Regina. BA cum laude, Beloit Coll., 1976; MLS, U. Mich., 1978; PhD, U. N.Mex., 1993. Cert. Acad. Health Info. Profls. Med. Libr. Assn., 1989. Libr. dir. Ea. N.Mex U., Clovis, 1981—83; asst. prof., chief Collections and Info. Resources Devel. U. N.Mex, Albuquerque, 1986—2000, assoc. prof., acad. and clin. svcs. coord., 2001—. Oversight com. Nat. Libr. Medicine, Bethesda, Md., 2001—. Assoc. editor: Biomed. Digital Librs., 2003—, jour. rev. editor: Jour. AMA, 1994—2000, mem. adv. bd.: New Eng. Jour. Medicine, 2001—04; contbr. articles to profl. jours. Sec., bd. mem. Friends Librs., N.Mex., Albuquerque, 1995—2003; pres. Serendipity Day Sch. PTA, Albuquerque, 1999—2000. Mem.: ALA (life), Med. Libr. Assn. (Louise Darling medal for disting. achievement in collection devel. in health scis. 1999). Unitarian Universalist/Buddhist. Achievements include one of the main founders of the international Evidence-Based Librarianship movement. Avocations: alpine skiing, surfing, mountain biking, hiking, travel. Office: Univ NMex Health Sci Lib and Informatics Ctr Albuquerque NM 87131-5686 Office Phone: 505-272-0654. E-mail: jeldredge@salud.unm.edu.

ELDREDGE, TODD, figure skater; b. Chatham, Mass., Aug. 28, 1971; U.S. figure skating champion, 1990-91, 95, 97; world bronze medalist, 1991; winner Skate Am., Pitts., 1994; Silver medalist World Figure Skating Championships, Birmingham, U.K., 1995, Gold Medalist, 1996; Silver Medalist World Figure Skating Championship, 1997. Office: Kingswood Sq 1994A S Woodward Ave # 356 Bloomfield Hills MI 48302-0527

ELDRIDGE, AMY HELENE, social worker, dean; b. Chgo., May 10, 1953; d. Stanley Howard and Barbara Mae Lader; m. Howard Earl Eldridge, Aug. 18, 1973 (div. Dec. 1998); children: Brian Howard, Elizabeth Ashley. BA, U. Ill., 1977; MSW, Loyola U., Chgo., 1981; PhD, Inst. for Clin. Social Work, 1992. Diplomate, lic. clin. social work. Clin. staff Juvenile Protective Assn., Chgo., 1981-86, co-dir. infant devel. project, 1986-87; clin. staff Josselyn Ctr. for Mental Health, Northfield, Ill., 1987-90, coord. case assignment, 1990-93, dir. treatment, 1993-94; acad. dean, chief adminstrv. officer Inst. for Clin. Social Work, Chgo., 1997—. Adj. prof., lectr. Loyola U., 1990-97; cons. Lawrence Hall Youth Svcs., Chgo., Ravinia Nursery Sch., Highland Park, Ill., 1993-99. Author: (with others) Progress in Self Psychology, 1997; contbr. articles to profl. jours. Former mem. Child Welfare Coun. of Highland Park, Highwood, Ill., 1990-92, Profl. Connection Group for Learning Disabilities, Highland Park, 1995-99, Adolescent Issues com. PTA Edgewood Sch., Highland Park, 1995-97. Mem. Ill. Soc. for Clin. Social Work (bd. dirs. 1991, 95-98), Alumni Assn. Inst. for Clin. Social Work, Coun. on Social Work Edn., Ill. Assn. of Deans and Dirs. in Social Work. Avocations: biking, hiking, gardening. Office: Ste 1E 565 Vine Ave Highland Park IL 60035 E-mail: Leld@aol.com.

ELDRIDGE, DAVID CARLTON, art and antique appraiser; b. Lansing, Mich., July 15, 1949; s. Carlton Brady and Blythe (Axford) E.; m. Suzanne Hamrick, Dec. 12, 1970; 1 child, Morgan Worth B.F.A., Ill. Wesleyan U., 1971; postgrad., U. Denver, 1972-73; M.F.A., So. Ill. U., 1974. Curator exhibits Nature Sci. Park, Winston Salem, N.C., 1974; curator exhibits Tenn. State Mus., Nashville, 1974-80; exec. dir. Mus. Arts and Scis., Macon, Ga., 1980-82; dir. Eldridge Appraisals, Naples, Fla., 1982—. Mem. Am. Soc. Appraisers (sr.), Appraisers Assn. Am. Office: 1839 Imperial Golf Course Blvd Naples FL 34110-8140 Office Phone: 239-598-2225. Personal E-mail: dceldrid@comcast.net.

ELDRIDGE, DOUGLAS ALAN, lawyer; b. Boulder, Colo., Mar. 15, 1944; s. Douglas Hilton and Clara Effie (Young) E.; m. Benna June Germann, June 24, 1967; children: Heather Dana, Ethan Douglas, Hilary Beca. BA, Yale U., 1966; LLB, U. Pa., 1969; cert., Nat. Inst. Trial Advocacy, Boulder, 1973. Bar: N.Y. 1972, U.S. Dist. Ct. (no. dist.) N.Y. 1973, U.S. Supreme Ct. 1975. Staff atty. Onondaga Neighborhood Legal Svcs., Syracuse, N.Y., 1971-74, exec. dir., 1974-76; counsel N.Y. State Divsn. of Substance Abuse Svcs., Albany, 1976-79; dep. counsel N.Y. State Health Dept., Albany, 1979-80, N.Y. State Energy Office, Albany, 1980-82, asst. counsel, 1982-87; gen. counsel Commn. for Siting Low-Level Radioactive Waste Disposal Facilities, Troy, N.Y., 1987-95; sole practice, 1995—. Govt. affairs counsel N.Y. Rehab. Assn., Inc., 1995-2000. Contbr. articles to legal jours. Bd. dirs. Coun. Cmty. Svcs. United Way of Northeastern N.Y., Albany, 1980-90, pres., 1986-88; bd. dirs. United Way Ea. N.Y., 1986-88, Mohawk-Hudson Found., 1986-89; law guardian Schenectady County, 1996—. Recipient Reginald Heber Smith Cmty. Lawyer fellowship OEO, 1969-71. Mem. N.Y. State Bar Assn., Albany County Bar Assn. (chair legis. com. 1998-2000), Onondaga County Bar Assn., Assn. of Bar of City of N.Y., Yale Alumni Schs. Com., Yale Alumni Assn. Northeastern N.Y., Assn. of Yale Alumni (rep. 1985-88, 94-97), University Club (bd. dirs. 1998-2004). Home: 9 Pinedale Ave Delmar NY 12054-3012 Office Phone: 518-475-0393. E-mail: eldesq@nycap.rr.com.

ELDRIDGE, GLORIA NICOLE, health care policy expert; b. Nashville, Sept. 15, 1972; d. Clyde Owen and Iliana Eldridge. BA in Ethics, Politics, and Econs., Yale U., 1994; MSc in Internat. Health Policy, London Sch. of Econs., 2000; PhD in Pub. Policy, U. Tex., 2001. Health fin. and policy analyst, pharm. econs. analyst The Lewin Group/Quintiles Transnational, Washington and London, 1995—98; health financing evaluator U.S. GAO, Washington, 1998—99; advisor WHO — Europe (UN), Copenhagen, 2000; rsch. assoc. Georgetown U., Health Policy Inst., Washington, 2001; fellow U. Tex., 2001. Author: (report) Policies on pricing and reimbursement of medicines in Europe: networking for information exchange among policy makers, The Impacts on Hospitals of Youth Mentoring Projects: The Commonwealth Fund's Hospital Youth Mentoring Project. Recipient acad. grant, London Sch. Econ. and Polit. Sci., 2000, Asst. Computer Gen. of U.S. Team Excellence award, GAO, 1998, U.S. GAO Merit awards, 1998, 1999. Home: 1458 Church Hill Pl Reston VA 20194

ELDRIDGE, J. CHARLES, endocrinologist, researcher, medical educator; b. Chgo., June 7, 1942; s. John Godfrey Eldridge, Carol Boedeker Eldridge; m. Pat Hudler. BA in Biology, North Cen. Coll., Naperville, Ill., 1965; MS in Physiology, No. Ill. U., 1967; PhD in Endocrinology, Med. Coll. Ga., 1971. Instr. biology Orange County C.C., Middletown, NY, 1967—68; rsch. assoc. I.N.S.E.R.M., Bordeaux, France, 1971-72, Med. Coll. Ga., Augusta, 1973; asst. prof. lab. medicine Med. U. S.C., Charleston, 1974-79; asst. prof. physiology and pharmacology Wake Forest U. Sch. Medicine, Winston-Salem, NC, 1979—87, assoc. prof. physiology and pharmacology, 1987—99, prof. physiology and pharmacology, 1999—. Grant reviewer Nat. Inst. Aging, NIH, Bethesda, Md., 1990—93; rsch. cons. EPA, Washington, 1999—, mem. endocrine disruptors methods validation com., 2001—; cons. Internat. Life Scis. Inst., Washington, 1992—94; med. edn. cons. various schs., 1988—; faculty Harvard Macy Inst. Med. Educators, 2001—. Mng. editor: Basic Sci. Educator, 1999—2002, mem. editl. bd.: Biology of Reproduction, 2000—, Jour. Internat. Assn. Med. Sci. Educators, 2002—; contbr. articles to profl. jours. Coord. United Way, Winston-Salem, 1986—98; elder, deacon, other positions Reynolda Presby. Ch., 1992—. Recipient Disting. Alumni award, Med. Coll. Ga., 2002; grantee, NIH, 1976—97, Nat. Inst. Drug Abuse, 1990—98; Macy fellow in edn., Harvard Med. Sch., 2001. Mem.: Soc. for Study of Reproduction, Internat. Assn. for Med. Sci. Educators, Soc. Neurosci., Endocrine Soc., Shriners (bd. dirs. 1988—91), Masons. Presbyterian. Avocations: music, travel, cuisine. Office: Wake Forest U Sch Medicine Dept Physiology and Pharmacology Winston Salem NC 27157-1083 Office Phone: 336-716-8570.

ELDRIDGE, JAMES FRANCIS, insurance executive, lawyer; b. Appleton, Wis., Nov. 6, 1946; s. C.H. and Florence M. (Dorschel) E.; m. Mary E. Evenson; children: Stacy M., Thomas J., Michael P., Kevin J. BA, Dartmouth Coll., 1968; JD, Marquette U., 1971. Bar: Wis. Assoc. counsel Kivett and Kasdorf, Milw., 1971-74; claim counsel Am. Family Mut. Ins. Co., Milw., 1974-81, regional claim counsel Madison, Wis., 1981-84, regional claim mgr., 1984-85, v.p., claims, 1985-90, exec. v.p. corp. legal, sec., 1990—. Mem. Civil Trial Counsel of Wis., Wis. Acad. Trial Lawyers, Dane County Bar Assn., Am. Arbitration Assn., Nat. Assn. Ind. Insurers (laws com.). Republican. Roman Catholic. Avocations: golf, tennis, racquetball, softball, tropical fish. Home: 1830 Cobblestone Ct Sun Prairie WI 53590-3520 Office: Am Family Ins Group 6000 American Pky Madison WI 53783-0001 Office Phone: 608-249-2111. Business E-Mail: jeldridg@amfam.com.

ELDRIDGE, MAURICE GRAY, academic administrator; b. Washington, Feb. 17, 1940; s. Schuyler Thomas and Thelma (Gray) E.; m. Susannah Stone, Aug. 25, 1962 (div. Dec. 1968); m. Joan Alice Tibbs, June 21, 1969; children: Maria Teresa, Jonathan Kenneth. BA, Swarthmore Coll., 1962; MEd, U. Mass., 1976. Cert. tchr., counselor, Mass.; cert. prin., D.C. Tchr. English and creative writing Pennsbury H.S., Fallsington, Penn., 1962-65; tchr. English and U.S. history Windsor Mountain Sch., Lenox, Mass., 1965-67, asst. headmaster, 1967-75; ednl. specialist Mass. Dept. Edn., Pittsfield, 1976-79; prin./dir. Duke Ellington Sch. Arts, Washington, 1979-89; assoc. dir., then dir. devel. Swarthmore (Pa.) Coll., 1989-93, assoc. v.p., 1993-98, exec. asst. to pres., v.p. Coll. and Cmty. Rels., 1998—. Ind. arts cons., Washington and Swarthmore, 1987—. Editor: Network Bibliography: The Arts High School Library, 1991; contbr. articles to profl. publs. Co-chairperson Chester-Swarthmore Coll. Cmty. Coalition, 1992—; mem. sch. bd. Suburban Music Sch., Media, Pa., 1989-95; co-founder Internat. Network Schs. of Arts, Washington, pres., 1982, 87-89. Ednl. policy fellow Inst. for Ednl. Leadership, Boston and Washington, 1978-79; recipient Whitney M. Young Jr. Meml. award Washington D.C. Urban League, 1982. Mem. Nat. Soc. Fundraising Execs. (bd. dirs. Greater Phila. chpt. 1992-94), Coun. for Advancement and Support of Edn. Avocations: reading, gardening, tropical fish, music, stamp collecting/philately. Office: Swarthmore Coll 500 College Ave Swarthmore PA 19081-1306 Office Phone: 610-328-8312. Business E-Mail: meldrid1@swarthmore.edu.

ELDRIDGE, RICHARD MARK, lawyer; b. Okmulgee, Okla., June 20, 1951; s. H.G. and Marcheta (Barnes) E.; m. Nellene Jane Mark, Aug. 20, 1971; children: Richard Mark Jr. (dec.), Christopher Bryan, Ryan Matthew, Michael Jonathan. BA, Okla. State U., 1973; JD, U. Tulsa, 1975. Bar: Okla. 1976, U.S. Dist. Ct. (no. dist.) Okla. 1976, U.S. Dist. Ct. (ea. dist.) Okla. 1989, U.S. Ct. Appeals (10th cir.) 1977, U.S. Dist. Ct. (we. dist.) Okla. 1991, U.S. Dist. Ct. (ea. dist.) Ark. 2001. Ptnr. Jacobus, Green & Eldridge, Tulsa, 1976-78; spl. judge Dist. Ct., Tulsa, 1979-81; ptnr. Rhodes, Hieronymus, Jones, Tucker & Gable, Tulsa, 1981—2001, Eldridge Cooper Steichen & Leach, PLLC, Tulsa, 2001—. Adj. prof. Oral Roberts U., Tulsa, 1985. Tchr. Couples for Christ, Asbury United Meth. Ch., Tulsa, 1979—; pres., sec. Christian Businessmen's Com., Tulsa, 1981-93; chmn. Asbury Presch. Bd., Tulsa, 1985-95; trustee Metro. Christian Acad., 1998-2004, 1st v.p., 2001-02, chmn., 2002-03. Recipient Cert. of Achievement, Am. Acad. Jud. Edn., 1979. Mem.: ABA, Okla. Assn. Def. Coun., Am. Judicature Soc., Def. Rsch. Inst., Tulsa County Bar Assn., Okla. Bar Assn. Republican. Avocation: coaching baseball and basketball. Home: 2985 E 45th Pl Tulsa OK 74105 Office: Eldridge Cooper Steichen & Leach PLLC 110 W 7th St Ste 200 Tulsa OK 74119 Office Phone: 918-388-5555. Business E-Mail: reldridge@ecslok.com.

ELDRIDGE, TRUMAN KERMIT, JR., lawyer; b. Kansas City, Mo., July 27, 1944; s. Truman Kermit and Nell Marie (Dennis) E.; m. Joan Ellen Jurgeson, Feb. 9, 1965; children: Christina Joanne, Gregory Truman. AB, Rockhurst Coll., 1966; JD, U. Mo., Kansas City, 1969. Bar: Mo. 1969, U.S. Dist. Ct. (we. dist.) Mo. 1969, U.S. Ct. Appeals (8th cir.) 1977, (10th cir.) 1995, U.S. S. Ct., 1992, U.S. Dist. Ct. Kans. 1998. Assoc. Morris, Foust, Moudy & Beckett, Kansas City, 1969-70, Dietrich, Davis, Dicus, Rowlands & Schmitt, Kansas City, 1971-74, ptnr., 1975, Armstrong, Teasdale, LLP, Kansas City, 1989-2000; sr. counsel Schlee, Huber McMullen & Krause, 2001—. Author: (with othrs) Missouri Environmental Law Handbook, 1990, 2d edit., 1993, 3d edit., 1997; contbr. articles to profl. jours. Chmn. bd. dirs. Loretto Sch., Kansas City, 1981-83; mem. Energy and Environ. Commn. City of Kansas City, 1990-91, 1994, bd. dirs. Sheffield Place, 1997-2003, 2005—, vice-chair, 1998-99, chair, 1999-2000. Master Ross T. Roberts Inn of Ct.; mem. ABA, Mo. Bar Assn., Kansas City Met. Bar Assn. (fed. ct. com., vice chair 1989-90, chair 1990-91), Am. Arbitration Assn. (arbitrator), Nat. Arbitration Forum (arbitrator), Kansas City Club (athletic com. 1990-2001, chair 19-2001, house com. 1993-96, 98-99, long range planning com. 1993-97, fin. com. 2004—, bd. dirs. 1997-2001). Roman Catholic. Avocations: sailing, reading, photography, raquetball. Home: 448 W 68th Ter Kansas City MO 64113-1933 Office: PO Box 32430 4050 Pennsylvania Ste 300 Kansas City MO 64171-5430 Office Phone: 816-360-2522. Personal E-mail: truman_eldridge@hotmail.com. Business E-Mail: teldridge@schleehuber.com.

ELEAZER, ALAN GARRETT, church musician, music educator; b. Flint, Mich., July 17, 1957; s. John William and Billie Ruth Eleazer; m. Vicki Sue Tull, May 27, 2000; children: Jason Pitts, Joshua Alan, Melanie Sue Pitts, David William. MusM, U. Tenn., Knoxville, 1995. Min. of music Concord United Meth. Ch., Knoxville, Tenn., 1989—; coll. faculty Pellissippi State Tech. C.C., Knoxville, Tenn., 1997—; mem. coll. faculty Roane State C.C., Harriman, Tenn., 2001—. State repertoire and standards chair Am. Choral Directors Assn., Lawton, Okla., 2003—05. Staff sergent (e-5) USAF, 1975—80. Master: Masons. Democrat. Methodist. Avocations: sailing, golf, hiking, shag dancing, photography. Home: 10705 Sallings Road Knoxville TN 37922 Office: Concord United Methodist Church 11020 Roane Drive Knoxville TN 37922 Office Phone: 865-966-6728. Home Fax: 865-966-3624; Office Fax: 865-966-3624. Personal E-mail: aeleazer@tds.net.

ELEAZER, G. PAUL, geriatrics services professional, educator; b. Columbia, S.C., Dec. 8, 1954; s. George Bennett and Pauline Eleazer; m. Adele Golbinec, Sept. 23, 1983; children: Mary Rebecca, Kevin Paul, Leigh Bennett. Grad. in Medicine, U. S.C., 1982. Cert. Nat. Bd. of Med. Examiners, 1980, diplomate Am. Bd. of Internal Medicine, 1983, cert. spl. competence in geriatric medicine Am. Bd. of Internal Medicine, 1988. Internist, Berea, Ky., 1983—86; clin. asst. prof. of medicine U. S.C. Sch. of Medicine, Columbia, 1987—89; dir. profl. svcs. C.M. Tucker, Jr. Human Resources Ctr., Columbia, SC, 1988—89; sect. chief geriat. sect. U. S.C. Sch. of Medicine, Columbia, 1990—92; med. dir. PRMH, Palmetto Sr. Care, Columbia, SC, 1990—96; dir. James F. Byrnes Ctr. For Geriatric Medicine, Edn. and Rsch., Columbia, SC, 1992—97; county med. dir. Lowman Nursing Home Ctr., White Rock, SC, 1991—2001; from acting dir to dir., divsn. of geriat. U. S.C. Sch. of Medicine, Columbia, 1992—. Leader (academia) Senior Mentor Program (Leader in Geriatric Innovations Award, 2004). Leader Boy Scouts Am., Columbia, SC, 1990—2005; del. White House Conf. on Aging, Columbia, SC, 2005—05. Recipient Physician's Recognition award, AMA, 1998 -2001, Tchg. Advancement award, U. S.C. Sch. of Medicine, 1998, 1999, 2001. Fellow: Am. Geriatrics Soc. (vice chair profl. ednl. exec. com. 2003—, program chair 2004, edn. com. 2000, dep. dir. thoracic surgery, geriatrics for specialists project 2005—, Geriatrics Recognition award 1999—2003); mem.: Assn. Am. Med. Colls. (geriatrics curriculum adv. panel 2001—), Assn. of Dirs. of Geriatric Acad. Programs (chair spl. interest group 1997—2005, John A. Hartford Geriatrics Leadership Scholars Program award 2002—05). Avocations: running, camping, church. Office: Univ SC Sch of Medicine 15 Medical Pk Ste 211 Columbia SC 29208 Office Phone: 803-434-4333. Office Fax: 803-434-4334. Personal E-mail: pauleleazermd@cs.com.

ELECTRA, CARMEN (TARA LEIGH PATRICK), actress; b. Sharonville, Ohio, Apr. 20, 1972; m. Dennis Rodman, 1998 (div. 1999); m. Dave Navarro, Nov. 22, 2003. Actor(co-host): (TV series) Singled Out, 1997, Baywatch, 1997—98, Hyperion Bay, 1999, BattleBots, 2002, Livin Large, 2002—03, 2003—04, Manhunt, 2004; celebrity judge (TV series) Dance Fever, 2003, host Automotive Showcase, 2003, VH1's 100 Greatest Artists of Hard Rock; actor: (TV series) Til' Death Do Us Part: Carmen & Dave, 2004, (TV) Carmen & Dave: An MTV Love Story, 2002; (TV films) Christmas in Malibu, 1999, Baywatch Hawaiian Wedding, 2003; (films) An American Vampire Story, 1997, Starstruck, 1998, The Mating Habits of the Earthbound Human, 1999, Scary Movie, 2000, The Great White Dope, 2000, Sol Goode, 2000, Perfume, 2001, Get Over It, 2001, Whacked!, 2002, Rent Control, 2002, Uptown Girls, 2003, My Boss' Daughter, 2003, Searching for Bobby D, 2004, Starsky & Hutch, 2004, Max Havoc: Curse of the Dragon, 2004, Dirty Love, 2005; voice (TV series) The Simpsons, 2002, King of the Hill, 2003, (video) Lil' Pimp, 2005, American Dad!, 2005; actor: (video) The Chosen One: Legend of the Raven, 1998, Won-G, 2000, Aerobic Striptease, 2003; appears in music video for Moby, "We Are All Made of Stars", guest appearance MADtv, 1997, 2000, Just Shoot Me!, 1997, The Drew Carey Show, 2000, The Osbourne Family Christmas Special, 2003, Punk'd, 2004, Monk, 2004, Hope & Faith, 2005, Summerland, 2005, House, M.D., 2005, and several others.

ELEFANTE, TOM PETER, management consultant; b. Charleroi, Pa., May 30, 1941; ABA, Dade County Coll., Miami, Fla., 1968. Exec. v.p. Loews Theaters, N.Y.C., 1956-90; pres. T.P. Cons., Ringwood, NJ, 1991; sr. v.p. Warner Bros. Internat. Theaters, Burbank, Calif., 1992-96; pres. T.P. Cons., Ringwood, NJ, 1997—2002, Marietta, Ga., 2002—. Home and Office: 3329 Keenland Rd Marietta GA 30062-

ELEQUIN, CLETO, JR., retired physician; b. Antique, Philippines, Oct. 18, 1933; s. Cleto and Enriqueta (Tengonciang) E.; m. Nancy Johnson, May 14, 1958; children: Tracy, Thomas Kyle, Stuart Scott MD, Far Eastern U., Philippines, 1957. Rotating intern Good Samaritan Hosp., Lexington, Ky., 1957-58; gen. practice resident Central Bapt. Hosp., Lexington, 1958-59; psychiat. resident State Hosp., Danville, Pa., 1959-60, 61-62, psychiat. resident with child psychiatry New Castle, Del., 1962-63; staff physician Eastern State Hosp., Lexington, 1960-61, dir. Fayette County Project, dir. intensive treatment service, 1964-67, supt., 1969-71; dep. commr. Dept. Mental Health, State Ky., 1967-69; practice medicine, specializing in family practice Pecos, Tex., 1971-72, Austin, Tex., 1974-89; ret. Cons. psychiatrist Texas Youth Commn., Peyote, Tex., Permian Basin Cmty. Mental Health-Mental Retardation, Odessa, Tex., Prude Ranch for Emotionally Disturbed Children and Adolescents, Ft. Davis, Tex., Dept. Mental Health-Mental Retardation State of Tex.; vis. lectr. in medicine and psychiatry Am. U. of the Caribbean, Plymouth, Montserrat; asst. dep. commr. Tex. Dept. Mental Health and Mental Retardation, Austin, 1973-74, dep. commr. mental health, 1974; pvt. practice family practice and psychiatry, Austin, 1974-85; mem. attending staff Brackenridge Hosp., St. David Med. Ctr., Seton Med. Ctr., Shoal Creek Hosp.; med. dir. Mary Lee Sch. and Found., 1974-80, bd. trustees, 1980-85; attending psychiatrist U. Ky. Med. Ctr., 1964-71, Good Samaritan Hosp., 1969-71, Ctrl. Bapt. Hosp., 1966-71; cons. psychiatrist U. Ky. Student Health Svc., 1965-71, Peace Corps, 1966-68, Bur. Rehab. State Ky., 1965-71, Blue Grass Cmty. Care Ctr., 1967-71, Covington (Ky.) Cmty. Care Ctr., 1969-71, Hazard Cmty. Care Ctr., 1969-71, Danville (Ky.) Cmty. Ctr., 1969-71, Maysville (Ky.) Cmty. Care Ctr., 1969-71; clin. instr., asst. clin. prof. dept. psychiatry U. Ky. Med. Ctr., 1964-69, assoc. clin. prof., 1969-71; cons. psychiatrist Tex. Youth Commn. Tex. Dept. of MH-MR, State of Tex.; pvt. practice in psychiatry, Austin, 1974-85; attending staff Brackenridge Hosp., St. David Med. Ctr., Seton Med. Ctr., Shoal Creek Hosp.; med. dir. Mary Lee Sch. and Found., 1974-80, bd. trustees, 1980-85. Profl. adv. coun. Cmty. Mental Health-Retardation Ctr., Lexington, 1967-71; active Lexington Hosp. Coun., 1969-71. Mem. AMA, Am. Psychiat. Assn., Am. Acad. Family Physicians (life), Assn. Med. Supts. Mental Hosps., Tex. Med. Assn., Travis County Med. Soc., Austin Psychiat. Soc. Home: 10101 Jupiter Hills Dr Austin TX 78747-1322 Office Phone: 512-280-9508. Personal E-mail: c1nelequin@aol.com.

ELETTO, PATRICIA ANN, principal; d. Louis Michael and Minnie Pybus Eletto; m. John Haywood Dowling Maury, July 15, 1995; children: Pauline Karasulu, Margaret Diaz. BA, U. Conn., 1969; MA, U. Minn., 1978. Speech pathologist Farmington Pub. Schs., Conn., 1969—73; tchr. Julius Sprauve Sch., Cruz Bay, 1973—78, Columbus Magnet Sch., Norwalk, 1983—89; adminstr. Norwalk Pub. Schs., 1979—; prin. Kendall Elem. Sch., Norwalk,

1989—99. V.p. Fairfield County Coun. for Exceptional Children, Conn., 1980—81; accreditation team New Eng. Assn. Schs. & Colls., Bedford, Mass., 1986—2000; co-dir. Conn. Odyssey of the Mind, Fairfield, 1988—89; presenter in field. Dir.: children's choral group (Ctr. Character Excellence award, Conn., 1994). Dir. United We Sing Chorus Communitarian Conf., 1996—97. Recipient Tchr. of Yr., VI Govt., 1978, Dedicated Prin. award, Norwalk Mentor Program, 1994, Pride In Norwalk award, Norwalk C. of C., 1997, Outstanding Sch. award, Conn. Down Syndrome Congress, 1998, Communities In Sch. Recognition award, Comms. in Schs., 1998. Mem.: Assn. U. Women, Assn. Curriculum Devel. Achievements include being co-founder of Norwalk Communities in Schools. Avocations: sailing, snorkeling, travel, cooking. Home: 73 Noyes Rd Fairfield CT 06824 Home Fax: 203-255-2713. Personal E-mail: patmaury@yahoo.com.

ELEUTERIUS, NANCY LEA, health facility administrator; b. Biloxi, Miss., Aug. 19, 1943; d. Leo and Mary (Cochran) E.; m. Nick Cefalu, Sept. 9, 1961 (div. Oct. 1975); children: Deborah, Cindy. Student, Thomas Nelson Coll., 1972-73, Ind. U., 1975-76, Va. Wesleyan Coll., 1986-87. Dir. patient adminstrv. svcs. Riverside Hosp., Newport News, Va., 1970-80; dir. adminstrv. svcs. Sentara Norfolk (Va.) Gen. Hosp., 1980-86; COO, Sentara Health Sysm., Norfolk, 1986-89; pres. Sentara Mental Health Mgmt., Virginia Beach, Va., 1989—. Workshop leader Ea. Va. Med. Sch., Norfolk, 1981. Contbr. articles to profl. jours. Bd. dirs. local unit Am. Cancer Soc., 1979-80, Jackson Field Homes, 1991-93, Virginia Beach Health Clinic, 1991-93, Cmty. Alliance Drug Rehab. and Edn., 1991—. Named Hampton Roads Bus. Woman of Yr., 1997. Mem. Nat. Assn. Hosp. Admitting Mgrs. (accredited; regional facilitator 1984, reginal rep. to edn. com. 1983—), Tidewater Assn. Hosp. Admitting Mgrs. (pres., founder 1979, bd. dirs. 1979—, v.p. 1981—), Va. Hosp. Assn. (prin. spkr. 1980), Am. Hosp. Assn., Norfolk Gen. Hosp. Vols. Roman Catholic. Avocations: music, theater, sailing. Home: 1024 Saw Pen Point Trail Virginia Beach VA 23455-5638 Office: Sentara Mental Health Mgmt 4417 Corporation Ln Ste 250 Virginia Beach VA 23462-3162

ELEWSKI, BONI ELIZABETH, dermatologist, educator; b. Cleve., Aug. 7, 1953; d. John Stanley and Alberta (Gulish) E.; married. BA summa cum laude, Miami U., Oxford, Ohio, 1975; MD cum laude, Ohio State U., 1978. Intern U. N.C., Chapel Hill, 1978-79, resident, 1979-82; staff dermatologist Akron (Ohio) Clinic, 1982-88; prof. dermatology Univ. Hosps. of Cleve., Case Western Res. U., 1988-99; prof. U. Alabama, 1999—. Author chpts. to books; editor: Cutaneous Fungal Infections, 1992, 2d edit., 1998; contbr. articles to profl. jours. Fellow Cleve. Dermatology Soc. (sec. bd. dirs., chair skin cancer screening program 1988—, pres. 1994), Am. Acad. Dermatology (bd. dirs. 1996-2000, v.p. elect, 2000, v.p. 2001, pres.-elect 2003-04, pres. 2004); mem. Am. Dermatol. Assn., Women's Dermatology Soc. (sec.-treas., pres.-elect 1999, pres. 2000), Dermatology Found. (trustee 1987-91). Roman Catholic. Home: PO Box 430037 Birmingham AL 35243 Office: U Alabama Birmingham Dept Derm 700 18th St S Birmingham AL 35233-1856 Office Fax: 205-934-5766. E-mail: BEElewski@aol.com.

ELEY, ANDREW D., music educator; b. Madison, Wis., Dec. 14, 1976; s. Dennis William Eley and Gloria Joyce Archer; m. Jennifer Sue Dietiker, July 12, 2003. BA, Luther Coll., 1999. Assoc. vocal music dir. Jefferson High Sch., Cedar Rapids, Iowa, 1999—2004, dir. vocal music, 2004—. Choir dir. Lutheran Ch. Resurrection, Marian, Iowa, 1999—2004. Mem.: Iowa Choral Dirs. Assn., Am. Choral Dirs. Assn. Avocations: golf, hunting, travel. Home: 228 24th St Dr SE Cedar Rapids IA 52403 Office: Jefferson High Sch 1243 20th St SW Cedar Rapids IA 52404 Office Phone: 319-558-1371. Business E-Mail: aeley@c.k12.ia.us.

ELEY, LYNN W., political science professor, retired mayor; b. Zearing, Iowa, Oct. 23, 1925; s. Wilbur Charles and Myrtle (Wolford) E.; m. Elizabeth Sherwood Hill, Aug. 25, 1950 (div. 1970); children— Thomas Wendell, David Matthew, Mary Sherwood; m. Janet Burdy, Aug. 26, 1971; children— Benjamin Charles, Margaret Burdy. BA, Harvard U., 1949; MA, U. Iowa, 1951; PhD, 1952. Orgn. and methods analyst Dept. Agr., Washington, 1952-55; research assoc., supr. Lansing Office, Inst. Pub. Adminstrn., 1955-58; assoc. dir. Extension Service; assoc. prof. polit. sci. U. Mich., 1959-64; dean Sch. Continuing Edn., and Summer Sch.; assoc. prof. polit. sci. Washington U., St. Louis, 1964-68; asst. chancellor U. Wis., Milw., 1968-72, prof. dept. govtl. affairs, 1972-91, prof. emeritus govtl. affairs, 1991—, chmn. dept., 1985-91. Editorial asst. com. on appropriations U.S. Ho. of Reps., 1953; instr. U.S. Dept. Agr. Grad. Sch., 1954-55; mayor City of Mequon, Wis., 1980-86 Author: The Executive Reorganization Plan: A Survey of State Experience, 1967, The Regionalization of Business Services in the Agricultural Research Service, 1967, Local Ombudsmen in America, 1973, An Ombudsman for Milwaukee? 1974; with others Representation of the Poor in Milwaukee's War on Poverty, 1977, A Guide to Citizen Participation in Government: Administrative Rule Making, 1979, 80; Sr. editor: with others The Politics of Fair-Housing Legislation: State and Local Case Studies, 1968, Wisconsin Government and Politics, 4th edit., 1987; mem. editorial bd.: Pub. Adminstrn. Rev, 1969-72. Sec. Gov.'s Adv. Com. Reorgn. State Govt. Mich., 1958-62; city councilman Ann Arbor, Mich., 1961-63; mem. Milw. Model Cities Policy Commn., 1970-75; bd. dirs. Wis. Congress on Aging, 1979-82, N.W. Gen. Hosp., Milw., 1990-94; exec. dir. Mid-Moraine Mcpl. Assn., 1986-95; pres. Riveredge Nature Ctr., Newburg, Wis., 1993-95; mem. planning and zoning comm. City of Bisbee, Ariz., 1998-99; pres. Unitarian-Universalist Ch., Sierra Vista, Ariz., 1999-2000. With USNR, 1944-46. Ellis L. Phillips Found. Postdoctoral intern in acad. adminstrn., 1963—64.

EL FAKHRI, GEORGES, education educator; b. Niha, Lebanon, Apr. 23, 1972; s. Nehme and Sonia El Fakhri. MSEng, Ecole Centrale, France, 1994; MSBME, U. Paris XI, France, 1995; MSECE, U. Tex., Austin, Tex., 1994; PhD, Univ. Paris XI, Paris, France, 1998. Med. Physics, U. Paris, 1998. Instr. radiology Harvard Med. Sch., Brigham & Women's Hosp., Boston, 2001—03, asst. prof. radiology, 2003—. Recipient Dana Found. Award, Dana Found., 2005, Mark-Tetalman, Soc. of Nuc. Medicine, 2005. Mem.: IEEE Nuc. Sci. (assoc.), European Assn. of Nuc. Medicine (assoc.), Soc. of Nuc. Medicine (assoc.). Achievements include research in Quantitative nuc. medicine cardiac and brain imaging. Office Phone: 617-732-6695.

ELFIN, MEL, magazine editor; b. Bklyn., July 18, 1929; s. Joseph and Bess (Margolis) E.; m. Margery Lesser, June 21, 1953; children: David, Dana. AB, Syracuse U., 1951; MA, Harvard U., 1952; postgrad., New Sch. Social Research, 1955-58; LHD, Ill. Wesleyan U., 1997. Copywriter Marvin and Leonard, Boston, advt. staff, 1953-54; successively reporter, travel editor, asst. city editor L.I. Daily Press, Jamaica, N.Y., 1954-58; mem. staff Newsweek mag., 1958—, gen. editor, 1964-65; chief Washington bur., 1965-85, sr. editor, 1985-86; editor spl. projects U.S. News and World Report, 1986-97; editor emeritus U.S. News Coll. Guides, 1997—. TV panelist; cons. Ednl. Facilities Lab., N.Y.C. Author: (with others) Bricks and Mortarboards, 1963; editor America's Best Colleges, 1987-97, Guide to America's Best Graduate Schools, 1987-97, Triumph Without Victory, 1992; contbr. articles to various publs. Served as officer SAC, USAF, 1952-53. Recipient George Polk Meml. award reporting, 1957, N.Y. Newspaper Guild Page One award, 1957; award Edn. Writers Assn., 1966 Mem. Phi Beta Kappa Home: 4515 30th St NW Washington DC 20008-2126 E-mail: melfin@aol.com.

ELFMAN, DANNY, composer; b. Amarillo, Tex., May 29, 1953; m. Bridget Fonda, Nov. 29, 2003; 3 children. Lead singer, songwriter (band) Oingo Boingo, 1979—. Albums (with Oingo Boingo): Oingo Boingo, 1980, Only a Lad, 1981, Nothing to Fear, 1982, Good for Your Soul, 1984, Dead Man's Party, 1986, Boi-ngo, 1987, Boingo Alive, 1988, Skeletons in the Closet, 1988, Dark at the End of the Tunnel, 1990, Best O' Boingo, 1991, Boingo, 1994; composer: (film scores) Forbidden Zone, 1980, Back to School, 1985, Pee-wee's Big Adventure, 1985, Wisdom, 1987, Summer School, 1987, Beetlejuice, 1988, Hot to Trot, 1988, Midnight Run, 1988, Scrooged, 1988, Batman 1989 (Grammy award), Dick Tracy, 1990, Darkman, 1990, Edward Scissorhands, 1990, Nightbreed, 1990, Pure Luck, 1991, Article 99, 1992, Batman Returns, 1992, Somersby, 1993, March of the Dead Theme (Army of Darkness), 1993, The Nightmare Before Christmas, 1993, Black Beauty, 1994, Dolores Claiborne, 1995, Mission Impossible, 1996, The Frighteners, 1996, Bordello of Blood, 1996, Extreme Measures, 1996, Mars Attacks!, 1996, Men in Black, 1997 (Oscar nomination), Flubber, 1997, Good Will Hunting, 1997 (Oscar nomination), A Civil Action, 1998, Instinct, 1999, Sleepy Hollow, 1999, Proof of Life, 2000, The Family Man, 2000, Spy Kids, 2001, Planet of the Apes, 2001, Novocaine, 2001, Spiderman, 2002, Men in Black II, 2002, Red Dragon, 2002, Chicago, 2002, Hulk, 2003, Big Fish, 2003, Spider-Man 2, 2004, Charlie and the Chocolate Factory, 2005, Corpse Bride, 2005; (TV series score, Grammy nomination) The Simpsons (Emmy nomination), (TV) Tales of the Crypt, Pee-wee's Playhouse, 1986, Amazing Stories (2), Alfred Hitchcock Presents (1), Fast Times, 1986, Sledgehammer, 1986, Beetlejuice (animated), 1989, The Flash, 1990, Family Dog, 1992, Batman, 1992, Wierd Science, 1994, Perversions of Science, 1997, Dilbert, 1999, Desperate Housewives, 2004; (albums) So-lo, 1984, Music for a Darkened Theatre, 1990. Office: The Kraft-Engel Management 15233 Ventura Blvd Ste 200 Sherman Oaks CA 91403

ELFMAN, JENNA (JENNIFER MARY BUTALA), actress; b. LA, Sept. 30, 1971; m. Bodhi Rice Elfman, Feb. 18, 1995. Studied with Milton Katselas, LA. Actress in Dharma & Greg Moore Metavoy, L.A., 1997—2002. TV: Townies, 1996, Dharma & Greg 1997-2002; guest appearances include Roseanne, 1995, NYPD Blue, 1995, The Monroes, 1995, Murder One, 1995, Almost Perfect, 1996, The Single Guy, 1997, Two and a Half Men, 2004; TV films include Her Last Chance, Obsessed, 2002; films include Grosse Point Blank, 1997, Krippendorf's Tribe, Can't Hardly Wait, 1998, (voice) Dr. Dolittle, 1998, EdTV, 1999, Keeping the Faith, 2000, Town & Country, 2001, Looney Tunes: Back In Action, 2003; (voice) Clifford's Really Big Movie, 2004, What's Hip, Doc?, 2005; starred in many music videos including Antrax video for Crossroads Films. Recipient TV Guide award, 1999, 2000, Spirit of the Cmty. award, Assn.for Better Living and Edn., 2005. Avocation: performing ballet. Mailing: c/o CAA 9830 Wilshire Blvd Beverly Hills CA 90212-1825

ELFNER, ALBERT HENRY, III, retired portfolio manager; b. Boston, Oct. 6, 1944; s. Albert Henry and Nellie May (Stewart) E.; m. Norma Elfner (div.); 1 child, Nicholas Stewart; m. Jane Colgrove, Oct. 10, 1980; 1 child, Kimberly Ann Stockwell. AB, Middlebury Coll., 1966; postgrad., Harvard U., 1993; D of Comml. Sci. (hon.), Merrimack Coll., 1999. CFA. Investment analyst Bank of Boston, 1966-69; portfolio mgr. Keystone Custodian Funds, Inc., Boston, 1969-81, pres., 1983-91; chmn. Keystone Investment Mgmt. Corp., Boston; pres. Keystone Group, Boston, 1990-95, pres., CEO, 1995—; CEO Keystone Investments, 1995; chmn., CEO Evergreen Investment Mgmt., 1996—99. Bd. dirs. NGM Ins., Jacksonville (Fla.) Unitil Corp., Hampton, N.H. Trustee Anatolia Coll., Middlesex Sch., Optimum Q Funds, Cambridge, Mass.; pres. Trustees of the Donations, Boston, Mass., 2004. Mem. Boston Soc. Security Analysts, Union Boat Club (bd. dirs., pres. 1983-86), Somerset Club, Boston Econs. Club, The Country Club (Brookline, Mass.), Ausable Club. Republican. Episcopalian. Avocations: skiing, squash, golf, gardening. Home: 53 Chestnut St Boston MA 02108-3506 E-mail: chipelfner@aol.com.

ELFVIN, JOHN THOMAS, federal judge; b. Montour Falls, N.Y., June 30, 1917; s. John Arthur and Lillian Ruth (Dorning) E.; m. Peggy Pierce, Oct. 1, 1949. B.E.E., Cornell U., 1942; JD, Georgetown U., 1947. Bar: D.C. 1948, N.Y. 1949. Confidential clk. to U.S. Circuit Ct. Judge E. Barrett Prettyman, 1947-48; asst. U.S. atty., Buffalo, 1955-58; U.S. atty. Western Dist. N.Y., 1972-75; with firm Cravath, Swaine & Moore, N.Y.C., 1948-51, Dudley, Stowe & Sawyer, Buffalo, 1951-55, Lansdowne, Horning & Elfvin, Buffalo, 1958-69, 70-72; justice N.Y. Supreme Ct., 1969; judge U.S. Dist. Ct., Buffalo, 1975—, now sr. judge. Mem. bd. suprs. Erie County, N.Y., 1962-65, mem. bd. ethics, 1971-74, chmn., 1971-72; mem., minority leader Buffalo Common Council Delaware Dist., 1966-69. Mem.: Tech. Socs. Niagara Frontier (pres. 1960—61), Engring. Soc. Buffalo (pres. 1958—59), Erie County Bar Assn., Am. Judicature Soc., Saturn Club, Cornell Club (pres. 1957—58), Phi Kappa Tau. Republican. Office: US Dist Ct 716 US Courthouse 68 Court St Buffalo NY 14202-3405 Office Phone: 716-551-4226. E-mail: rosaliezavarella@nywd.uscourts.gov.

ELFVING, DON C., horticulturist, educator; b. Albany, Calif., June 20, 1941; BS in Botany, U. Calif., Davis, 1964, MS in Horticulture, 1966; PhD in Plant Physiology, U. Calif., Riverside, 1971. From asst. prof. to assoc. prof. pomology Cornell U., Ithaca, N.Y., 1972-79; rsch. scientist Hort. Rsch. Inst. Ontario, Simcoe, Can., 1979-91, mgr. rsch. programs Vineland, Can., 1991-93; supt. tree fruit rsch. and extension ctr. Wash. State U., Wenatchee, 1993-97, horticulturist, prof., 1997—. Cons. U.S. AID, 1977; cons. Internat. Agrl. Devel. Svc., Ark., 1981-82. Author: Training and Pruning of Apple and Pear Trees, 1992. Recipient U.P. Hedrick 1st Pl. award Am. Pomological Soc., 1992. Fellow Am. Soc. Hort. Sci.; mem. Am. Soc. for Hort. Sci. (bd. dirs. 1993-95, chair publs. com. 1993-95), Internat. Dwarf Fruit Tree Assn. (R.F. Carlson Disting. lectr. 1993). Office: Tree Fruit Rsch & Ext Ctr 1100 N Western Ave Wenatchee WA 98801-1230 Business E-Mail: delfving@wsu.edu.

ELG, ANNETTE, food products executive; b. Culdesac, Idaho; d. Ralph and Shirley Steigers; m. Brad Elg, 1977; 2 children. B in Acctg., U. Idaho, 1978. With Arthur Andersen LLP; corp. contr. J.R. Simplot Co., Boise, Idaho, 1990, CFO, 2002—. Office: JR Simplot One Capital Ctr 999 Main St PO Box 27 Boise ID 83707-0027

ELGAFY, AHMED Z, education educator, researcher; b. Cairo, Egypt, June 1, 1960; s. Zaky H. Elgafy and Kawther M. Gadelmawla; m. Amani M. Rizk, July 14, 1994; children: Karim, Mariam. BSc in mech. engring., Zagazeg U., 1984; MSc in mech. engring., Zagazig U., 1990; PhD in mech. engring., Mansoura U., 1996. Asst. prof. Banha Inst. Tech., Egypt, 1996—2001; vis. scholar Cin. U., 2002; assoc. rsch. scientist Dayton U., Ohio, 2002—. Contbr. scientific papers. Soldier Signals, 1984—86, Egypt. Mem.: Egyptian Engring. Mech. Soc., Am. Soc. Mech. Engring., Ahly Nat. Club. (Egypt). Avocations: reading, walking, soccer, swimming. Business E-Mail: azelgafy@yahoo.com.

EL-GAFY, MOHAMED A., engineering educator; b. Ismailia, Egypt, Nov. 10, 1977; s. Anwar El-Gafy and Hoda Ali. BSc, Cairo U., 1999, MSc, 2002; PhD, Fla. State U., 2005. Rsch. asst. Fla. State U., Tallahassee, 2003—05; asst. prof. Ill. State U., Normal, 2005—. Contbr. articles to profl. jours. Named Outstanding Tchg. Asst. of Yr., Fla. State U., 2004—05; recipient Best Overall Performance prize, Faculty of Engring., Cairo U. Egypt, 1999; Dissertation Rsch. grantee, Fla. State U., 2004. Mem.: ASCE, Internat. Computational Intelligence Soc., Tau Beta Pi. Office: Ill State U Turner Hall Rm 210 Campus Box 5100 Normal IL 61790-5100 Office Phone: 309-438-3661. E-mail: mgafy@eng.fsu.edu.

ELGAR, SHARON KAY, science educator; b. Geneseo, Ill., June 27, 1950; BA, Aurora (Ill.) U., 1972. Lic. EMT Waubonsee Coll.; cert. outdoor edn. and survival tng. courses U. Wis., death and dying, outdoor edn. issues, drugs and society, and gifted edn. courses No. Ill. U., tchr. Ill. Tchr. physics, chemistry, biology Aurora Cen. Cath. H.S., 2001—. Beauty cons. Mary Kay, Inc., Mich.; mem. adv. bd. Kane County Pre-Sch., Geneva; mem. homebound tutoring Kaneland Sch. Dist., Maple Park, Ill. Mem. Town & Country Libr. Dist., Elburn; counselor, aide for grief Conley Outreach Ctr., Elburn. Recipient Gold Ivy Leaf Scholar's honors, Aurora U., 1972. Mem.: Boy Scouts Am. Venture Crew, Am. Girl Scouts Assn., Rockford Cath. Diocese Tchrs. Assn., Ill. Tchrs. Assn. (sec. 1972—), Am. Chem. Soc., Nat. Sci. Tchrs. Assn., St. Peters Women Soc., Elburn Lion's Club, Elburn Legion Aux. Republican. Roman Catholic. Avocations: canoeing, hiking, swimming, exercise, reading. Home: 200 Oak Dr Elburn IL 60119 Office: Aurora Cen Cath H S 1255 N Edgelawn Dr Aurora IL 60506

ELGART, LARRY JOSEPH, orchestra leader; b. New London, Conn., Mar. 20, 1922; s. Arthur M. and Bessie (Aisman) E.; m. Lynn Walzer, June 28, 1963; children by previous marriage: Brock, Brad. Altosaxophonist, formed Les and Larry Elgart Orch., 1947, rec. artist for Decca, RCA, Victor, MGM, Columbia labels. Recipient Billboard award, 1959, Downbeat Most Played Band award Disc Jockey poll, 1959, Downbeat, Cashbox and Billboards awards in popularity polls, Gold record album for Hooked on Swing, 1982, Platinum, 1984.

ELGART, MERVYN L., retired dermatologist, educator; b. Bklyn., Aug. 12, 1933; s. Jacob and Sally R. E.; m. Sheila Ruth Cliff, June 13, 1954; children— Brian, George, Paul, Adam, James. AB, Bklyn. Coll., 1953; MD, Cornell U., 1957. Intern Buffalo Gen. Hosp., 1957-58; resident in dermatology Walter Reed Gen. Hosp., Washington, 1960-63; chief dermatology Andrews AFB Hosp., Washington, 1964-66; mem. faculty George Washington U. Med. Sch., 1967-97, prof. dermatology, 1974-97, chmn. dept., 1975-97, prof. pediatrics, 1974-97, prof. medicine, 1974-97; clin. prof. dermatology, medicine and pediatrics Univ. Dermatology Assocs., Washington, 1997—2002, emeritus prof. dermatology, 2002—; ret., 2003. Mem. med. adv. com. Nat. Orgn. Rare Diseases, 2000—. Served as officer M.C. USAF, 1958-66. Fellow Am. Acad. Dermatology; mem. AMA, So. Med. Assn., Internat. Soc. Dermatology, Washington Dermatol. Soc., Am. Dermatol. Assn., Phi Beta Kappa, Alpha Omega Alpha. Roman Catholic. Personal E-mail: elgartm@aol.com.

ELGEE, NEIL JOHNSON, retired internist, endocrinologist, educator; b. Oxford, N.S., Can., Apr. 3, 1926; arrived in U.S., 1946, naturalized, 1955; s. William Harris and Lucile (Nevers) Elgee; m. Leona Victoria Karlsson, Aug. 18, 1951; children: Joan, Susan, Laurie, Steven, Karen. BSc, U. N.B., Can., 1946; MD, U. Rochester, 1950. Intern Peter Bent Brigham Hosp., Boston, 1950—51; resident Strong Meml. Hosp., Rochester, NY, 1951—52; fellow in endocrinology U. Wash., 1952—54, co-chief resident in medicine Seattle, 1954—55, clin. prof. medicine, 1968—93, emeritus clin. prof. medicine, 1993—; practice medicine specializing in endocrinology Seattle, 1957—93; retired, 1993. Founder, pres. Ernest Becker Found., 1993—. Capt. USAF, 1955—57. Master: ACP (gov. for Wash. and Alaska 1965—71, regent 1974—78); mem.: Inst. Medicine, Endocrine Soc. Home: 3621 72nd Ave SE Mercer Island WA 98040-3330 Office Phone: 206-232-2994. Business E-Mail: nelgee@u.washington.edu.

ELGER, WILLIAM ROBERT, JR., accountant; b. Chgo., Mar. 20, 1950; s. William Robert and Grace G. (LaVaque) E.; m. Kathryn Michele Johnson, July 10, 1971; children: Kimberly, William, Kristin, Joseph. AS in Applied Sci., Coll. of DuPage, Glen Ellyn, Ill., 1970; BS magna cum laude, U. Ill.-Chgo., 1972. CPA, Ill. Staff acct. Ernst & Whinney, Chgo., 1973, in-charge acct., 1973-74, sr. acct., 1974-78, mgr., 1978-82, sr. mgr., 1982-88; chief fin. officer U. Ill. Eye and Ear Infirmary, 1988-89; CFO U. Mich. Med. Sch., Ann Arbor, 1989-99, exec. dir. adminstrn., CFO, 2000—. Chair fin. controls frame work task force U. Mich., 1999—2004, chmn. internal controls adv. group, 2005—; presenter various confs. in field. Author, developer: (tng. course) Auditing Third Party Reimbursement, 1986, 87. Active Union League Civic and Arts Found., Chgo., 1982-89, Union League Found. for Boys and Girls Clubs, Chgo., 1982-89; treas. Newport Assn., Carol Stream, Ill., 1982-83; coach Tri-City Soccer Assn., St. Charles, Ill., 1984, 87, Saline Soccer Assn., 1990, 91, 93, 94, 95, Saline H.S. Soccer Club, 1996, 97. Mem. AICPA, Healthcare Fin. Mgmt. Assn. (advanced mem., acctg. and reimbursement com. 1982-87, chpt. task force com. 1986, 87, auditing com. 1986, 87, Spl. Recognition award 1986, Follmer Bronze Merit award 1999), Ill. Soc. CPAs (mem. long term healthcare com. 1983, hosps. com. 1988-89), Nat. Coun. Univ. Rsch. Adminstrs., Assn. of Univ. Technology Mgrs., Med. Group Mgmt. Assn., Assn. Am. Med. Colls. (group on bus. Affairs steering com. 2004, chair Midwest region 2004, profl. devel. com. 2004—). Methodist. Avocation: golf. Office: PO Box 624 1301 Catherine St Ann Arbor MI 48109-0624 Office Phone: 734-763-5202. Business E-Mail: welger@umich.edu.

ELGERT, PAUL A., cytotechnologist; s. Louis G. and Lillian J. Elgert; m. Carol Lee Jaeger, Apr. 28, 1979; children: Caroline A., Susanna G. BA in Biology, Concordia Coll., Bronxville, NY, 1978. Cert. cytotechnologist Am. Soc. Clin. Pathologists, Internat. Acad. Cytology; in bioterrorism preparedness Hunter Coll., NY. Student cytotechnologist Meml. Sloan-Kettering Cancer Ctr., NYC, 1980—81; cytotechnologist Columbia Presbyn. Hosp., NYC, 1981—82, St. Luke Roosevelt Hosp. Ctr., NYC, 1982—84; cytopathology mgr. Montefiore Med. Ctr., Bronx, 1984—95; cytopathology supr. NYU Sch. Medicine, Bellevue Hosp. Ctr., NYC, 1995—. Downstate coord. Profl. Standards Coalition for Clin. Lab. Pers., NYC, 1989—99. Contbr. articles to profl. jours. and papers to confs., chapters to books. Sr. choir St. Luke Luth. Ch., Dix Hills, NY, ch. coun., bd. stewardship chair, 2005—. Mem.: Am. Soc. Clin. Pathology (asst. editor, editl. adv. bd. Lab Medicine 2004—), Am. Soc. Cytotechnology (pres.-elect 1999—2000, region 10 dir., legis. cons. 1999—2003, pres. 2000—01), Greater NY Assn. Cytotechnologists (v.p. 1990—99, pres.-elect 1992—93, pres. 1993—94, Spindle editor 1994—99). Office: Cytopathology 462 First Ave New York NY 10016

ELGIN, RON ALAN, advertising executive; b. Milw., Sept. 15, 1941; s. Carl John and Vivian Elaine (Phillips) E.; m. Bonnie Kay Visintainer, Dec. 3, 1968; 1 child, Alison. BA in Advt., U. Wash., 1965. With Cole & Weber, Seattle, 1965-81; pres. Elgin Syferd, Seattle, 1981-89; chmn. Elgin Syferd/Drake, Boise, Idaho, 1987—; pres., CEO Elgin DDB, 1989-99; pres. DDB Needham Retail, Seattle, 2000—. Chmn. Hornall Anderson Design Works, Seattle, 1982-91; ptnr. Christiansen & Fritsch Direct, Seattle, 1988-96; bd. dirs. Hart Crowser; bd. dirs. Ctrl. Media, Inc., Knowledge Anywhere. Bd. dirs. Ronald McDonald House, Seattle, 1984—, Big Bros., Seattle, 1986—, Spl. Olympics, Seattle, 1987-90, Pacific N.W. Ballet, Seattle, 1988-98, Poncho, Seattle, 1991—, Odyssey, 1993-99, Swedish Hosp., 1995—; mem. adv. bd. U. Wash., Wash. State U. Lt. U.S. Army, 1965-69. Mem. Am. Assn. Advt. Agencies, Am. Mktg. Assn., Mktg. Comm. Execs. Internat. Office: DDB Seattle 1000 2nd Ave Seattle WA 98104-1004

ELGIN, SARAH CARLISLE ROBERTS, biology researcher and educator; b. Washington, July 16, 1945; d. Carlisle Bishop and Lorene (West) Roberts; m. Robert Lawrence Elgin, June 9, 1967; children: Benjamin Carlisle, Thomas James. BA in Chemistry, Pomona Coll., 1967; PhD in Biochemistry, Calif. Inst. Tech., 1971. Research fellow Calif. Inst. Tech., Pasadena, 1971-73; asst. prof. biochemistry and molecular biology Harvard U., Cambridge, Mass., 1973-77, assoc. prof., 1977-81; assoc. prof. biology Washington U., St. Louis, 1981-84, prof., 1984—, prof. edn., 2001, prof. genetics, 2003; mem. Nat. Com. on Sci. Edn. Stds. and Assessment, NAS/NRC, 1992. Mem. editorial bd. Jour. Cell Biology, N.Y.C., 1980-82; exec. editor Nucleic Acids Research, 1983-88; editorial bd. Jour. Biol. Chemistry, 1985-88, Molecular Cellular Biology, 1989—; assoc editor Molecular Cell, 1998-, Bio Med Net; co-editor-in-chief Cell Biology Edn, 2002-05; contbr. papers in field. Mem. molecular biology study sect. NIH, 1986-89. Rsch. grantee NIH, 1987, 88, 91, 93, 98, 99, 2003, 05, NSF, 1986. Fellow AAAS (sect. on biol. scis. 1991—); mem. Am. Soc. Biol. Chemists (program com. 1984), Am. Soc. Cell Biology (coun. 1983-85, 92-94, publs. com. 1989-91, edn. com. 1992—), Genetics Soc. Am. Office: Washington U Biology Dept PO Box 1229 One Brookings Dr Saint Louis MO 63188-1229 Office Phone: 314-935-5348. Office Fax: 314-935-5125. E-mail: selgin@biology.wustl.edu.

ELGISON, MARTIN J., lawyer; b. Miami, Fla., Feb. 22, 1951; s. Hyman and Rose (Lang) E.; m. Juli E. Elgison, June 2, 1984. BA, U. South Fla., 1972; JD, U. Miami (Fla.), 1981. Bar: Ga. 1981. From assoc. to ptnr. Alston & Bird LLP, Altanta, 1981—, founder, intellectual property practice. Contbr. articles to profl. jours. Avocations: golf, tennis. Office: Alston & Bird LLP 1 Atlantic Ctr 1201 W Peachtree St NW Ste 4200 Atlanta GA 30309-3424 Office Phone: 404-881-7167. Office Fax: 404-881-7777. Business E-Mail: melgison@alston.com.

EL-HADIDY, BAHAA, information scientist, consultant; b. Cairo, June 21, 1931; arrived in U.S., 1961; s. Sadek Ayoub El-Hadidy and Tafida Mostafa Fahmy; m. Lily Ayad, Mar. 27, 1965. BSc, Cairo U., 1954; MLS, Rutgers U., New Brunswick, N.J., 1963; PhD, U. Pitts., Pitt., 1974. Advanced cert. U. of Pitts., 1966. Sci. info. officer Nat. Rsch. Ctr., Cairo, 1955—61; info. analyst and chem. info. specialist U. Pitts., 1967—72, libr., 1972—74; asst. prof. Cath. U. Am., Washington, 1974—84; asst. sr. exec. and v.p. Islamic Internat. Bank, Cairo, 1984—87; assoc. prof. U. South Fla., Tampa, 1987—96; internat. cons. Tampa, Fla., 1996—. Cons. NSF, Washington, 1975, The Franklin Inst., Phila., 1977—78, African Regional Ctr. Tech., Dakar, Senegal, 1983—84, UN Indsl. Devel. Orgn., Vienna, 1989—95, Inst. Applied Sci. & Tech., Guyana, 1989, Acad. Sci. Ministry Sci. Rsch., Manila, 1990, Acad. Sci. Rsch. & Tech., Cairo, 1994—98; sr. cons. Ga. Inst. Tech., Atlanta, 1979—84; prin. project investigator and cons. NASA Sci. Info. Facility, Balt., 1984; vis. prof. Cairo U., 1985—87; chmn. tng. Profl. Mgmt. Svcs. Ctr., Kuwait, 1987. Editor: Infrastructure of an Information Society; principal investigator (research project) Training of a Core of Information Specialists from Egypt, chairman of an international conference (international conference) Infrastructure of An Information Society; contbr. chapters to books, scientific papers, articles to profl. jours. Asst. rep. friends group Bibliotheca Alexandrina, Egypt; bd. mem. U.S. Nat. Com. UNESCO Gen. Info. Program, Washington, 1981—84; chmn. U.S. interim com. Internat. Fedn. Documentation, Washington, 1982—84; bd. mem. Sertoma Club at U. South Fla., Tampa, 1997—99; v.p. north Tampa aux. The Children's Home of Tampa, 2000—03; chmn. bd. Am. Soc. Info. Sci./SIG Internat. Info. Issues, Washington, 2001—02; chmn. internat. rels. Am. Soc. Info. Sci., Washington, 1981—83, chmn. bd. (so. Fla. chpt.) Tampa, Fla., 1992—93. Recipient Oustanding Svc. Info. Sci. Profession, Info. Sci. and Tech. Coun., 1984; grantee, NSF, 1979—82, UN Indsl. Devel. Orgn., 1989. Mem.: AAUP, ALA (life), Suncoast Info. Specialists, Assn. Libr. and Info. Sci. Edn., Assn. Egyptian-Am. Scholars, Spl. Libraries Assn., Assn. Computing Machinery, Am. Soc. Info. Sci. and Tech. (certs. appreciation and recognition outstanding svcs. 1984—2004, SIG mem. of yr. award 2000), Tampa Palms Golf & Country Club (bd. mem. 2001—03), Beta Phi Mu (recognition guidance, tchg., and advising 1996). Achievements include development of economical system for searching large database in the 1970s; multifaceted approach for training information specialists from developing countries in the United States; research in bibliographic control among geoscience abstracting and indexing services. Avocations: classical music, travel, tennis. Home: 16104 Stowe Ct Tampa FL 33647-1147 Office: 16104 Stowe Ct Tampa FL 33647-1147 Office Phone: 813-978-1551. Home Fax: 813-978-1551; Office Fax: 813-978-1551. Personal E-mail: elhadidy@cas.usf.edu.

ELHAUGE, EINER RICHARD, law educator; b. NYC, May 28, 1961; s. Einer Eduardo and Maria Ines (Robatto) Elhauge. AB, Harvard U., 1982, JD, 1986. Bar: Pa. 1986, US Ct. Appeals 9th Cir. 1987. Law clk. Office Solicitor Gen., Washington, 1986; law clk. to Judge William Norris US Ct. Appeals 9th Cir., LA, 1986-87; law clk. to Assoc. Justice William J. Brennan US Supreme Ct., Washington, 1987-88; assoc. prof. law U. Calif., Berkeley, 1988-92, prof., 1992-95; prof. law Harvard U., Cambridge, Mass., 1995—. Olin faculty fellow Yale U., 1993; vis. prof. law Harvard U., 1994, U. Chgo., 1995. Co-author: Antitrust Law, 1996. Office: Harvard Law Sch 1563 Massachusetts Ave Cambridge MA 02138 Office Phone: 617-496-0860. Office Fax: 617-496-0861. Business E-Mail: elhauge@law.harvard.edu.*

ELIAS, ANTONIO L., aerospace transportation executive; b. Mar. 3, 1949; married, 1972; 4 children. BS, EAA, PhD Aeronautics, Astronautics, MIT. Rschr., staff mem. Space Guidance & Nav. Divsn., CS Draper Lab., 1972—80; asst. prof. aeronautics and astronautics MIT, 1980—86, sr. v.p. engring., 1986—93, sr. v.p. adv. project group, 1993—96; sr. v.p., chief tech. officer Orbital Sci. Corp., Dulles, Va., 1996—97, exec. v.p., gen mgr. advanced prog., 1997—. Contbr. numerous articles to sci. jours.; patentee in field. Recipient Nat. Medal Tech., 1991, Nat. Air & Space Mus. Trophy. Fellow: AIAA (Engineer of the Year 1991, Aircraft Design award), Am. Astron. Soc. (Brouwer award); mem.: Nat. Acad. Engring. Office: 21839 Atlantic Blvd Dulles VA 20166-6801 E-mail: ae@orbital.com.*

ELIAS, ARTURO, automotive executive; b. Columbia; BEE, Purdue U., 1977, M in Industrl. Engring., 1978; MBA, U. Chgo., 1984. Mfg. engring. GM Corp. Delco Electonics, 1978; sr. analyst GM Treasurer's Office, N.Y.; mgr. GM Corp. European Borrowings Fgn. Exch.; treas. GM de Méx., Mexico; fin. dir. GM Venezuela, Caracas, Venezuela; mng. dir. GM Corp., Santiago, Chile, 1993, asst. vehicle line exec. Pontiac, Mich., 1996—99; vehicle line exec. GM Corp. Adam Opel, Russelsheim, Germany; mng. dir. GM Argentina; pres. mng. dir. GM Méx., Mexico, 2001—. Office: GM Corp 300 Renaissance Ctr PO Box 300 Detroit MI 48265-3000

ELIAS, BARTHOLOMEW, psychologist, researcher; b. S.I., N.Y., Apr. 8, 1967; BA, Franklin and Marshall Coll., 1989; MS, Ga. Tech. Inst., 1991, PhD, 1994. Human factors intern IBM Corp., Charlotte, N.C., 1990; cognitive engring. intern NCR Human Interface Tech. Ctr., Atlanta, 1990-92; rsch. psychologist USAF Armstrong Lab., Dayton, Ohio, 1992—. Mem. Human Factors and Ergonomics Soc. Roman Catholic. Avocations: flying, bicycling. Office: Armstrong Lab Noise Effects Br AL/OEBN 2610 7th St Wright Patterson Afb OH 45433

ELIAS, JUDITH HELEN, music educator; b. Painesville, Ohio, Oct. 5, 1946; d. Harold Edgar Brichford and Mardith Helen CLine; divorced; children: Lori, Kimberly. B of Music Edn., Youngstown State U., 1968; postgrad., Kent State U., 1989—90. Tchr. music Mentor Pub. Schs., Ohio, 1968—69; instr. flute Fine Arts Assn., Willoughby, 1968—, Cuyahoga C.C., Highland Hills, 1991—; substitute tchr. Mentor Pub. Schs., 1991—94; dir. flute choir Lake Erie Coll., Painesville, 2001—. Avocations: sewing, baking. Home: 8272 Eastmoor Rd Mentor OH 44060-7512 Office: Fine Arts Assn 38660 Mentor Ave Willoughby OH 44094 Office Phone: 440-951-7500.

ELIAS, LORI ANNE, music educator, journalist, photojournalist; b. Willoughby, Ohio, Sept. 4, 1969; d. M. J. and Judith Helen Elias. MusB magna cum laude, Bowling Green State U., 1991; MusM, Cleve. State U., 2005. Music educator Rossford Exempted Village Schs., Rossford, Ohio, 1993—94, Tipp City Exempted Village Schs., Ohio, 1994—97, Wickliffe H.S., Wickliffe, Ohio, 1997—2001, Willoughby-Eastlake City Schs., 2001—. Presenter in field. Contbr., website, e-zine, articles to profl. jours. Presser scholar, Bowling Green State U., 1990. Mem.: Soc. Ethnomusicology, Can. Soc. Traditional Music, Lake County Music Educators Assn. (pres. 2001—03, v.p. 2003—05), Ohio Music Educators Assn., Music Educators Nat. Conf., Kappa Delta Pi, Pi Kappa Lambda, Sigma Alpha Iota. Avocations: coaching tennis, travel to major league ballparks.

ELIAS, MAURICE JESSE, psychology educator; b. Bronx, N.Y., Dec. 1, 1952; m. Ellen Sue Rosen, Aug. 7, 1976; children: Sara Elizabeth, Samara Alexandra. BA in Psychology summa cum laude, CUNY, 1974; MA in Clin. Psychology, U. Conn., 1977, PhD in Clin. Psychology, 1980. Psychotherapist mental health svc. U. Conn., Storrs, 1977-78; prevention planning cons. Conn. Dept. Children and Youth Svcs., 1978-79; asst. prof. psychology Rutgers U., New Brunswick, NJ, 1979-85, assoc. prof., 1985—94, prof., coord. internship program in applied-cmty. psychology, 1979—, field supr. psychol. clinic grad. sch., 1979—. Mem. co-adj. faculty dept. psychiatry U. Medicine and Dentistry N.J.-Robert Wood Johnson Med. Sch., 1985, Schwartzman family parenting program Am. Jerusalem Acad. for Contemporary Judaic Studies, 1987—; cons. to numerous pub. sch. dists., pvt. schs., community groups, presenter in field. Author: Social Problem Solving Interventions in the Schools, 1996, Promoting Social & Emotional Learnings: Guidelines for Educators, 1997, Emotionally Intelligent Parenting, 1999; contbr. articles to profl. jours. Treas., trustee Middlesex County Resources for the Menatlly Handicapped, Inc., 1981-83; bd. dirs. Nat. Orgns. Adv. Coun. for Children, 1981-85, Prevention Coalition N.J., 1990-92; mem. Interagy. Youth Devel. Consortium, 1982-86, Nat. Coalition Against TV Violence, 1979—; pres. religious sch. bd. edn. Highland Park Conservative Temple and Ctr., 1992—, trustee, 1992—; trustee Assn. for Children of N.J., 1992—; exec. com. Collaborative for Advancement of Social and Emotional Learning, 1995. Grantee Rutgers U., 1979-83, 84-85, 85-87, William T. Grant Found., 1982-90, 99—, NIMH, 1982-85, 88, 99—, Middlesex County Mental Health Bd. and Bd. Chosen Freeholders, 1984-87, Schumann Found. N.J., 1987-89, 90-93, Fetzer Inst., 1995-99; Lilly Endowment grantee William T. Grant Found., 1991-94, 99—, Surdna Found., 1999—. Mem. ASCD, APA (Nat. Psychology award 1986, 88, Nat. Psychol. Cons. to Mgmt. award 1990, Disting. Contbn. to Practice award 1993, Ethnic Minority Mendoring award, 1998), Nat. Assn. Sch. Psychologists, Phi Beta Kappa. Home: 139 N 5th Ave Highland Park NJ 08904-2924 Office: Tillett Hall Livingston Campus Rutgers U Dept Psychol New Brunswick NJ 08903

ELIAS, PATRIK, professional hockey player; b. Trebic, Czechoslovakia, Apr. 13, 1976; Mem. HC Kladno, 1993—95, Albany River Rats (AHL), 1995—97, New Jersey Devils, 1997—. Mem. Czech Nat. Hockey Team, Olympic Games, Salt Lake City, 2002, Czech Nat. Hockey Team, World Cup of Hockey, 2004. Named to NHL All-Rookie Team, 1998, NHL All-Star game, 2000, 2002, NHL First All-Star Team, 2001. Achievements include mem. Stanley Cup Champion New Jersey Devils, 2000, 2003. Office: c/o New Jersey Devils 50 Rte 120 North East Rutherford NJ 07073

ELIAS, PAUL S., retired marketing executive; b. Chgo., July 5, 1926; s. Maurice I. and Ethel (Tieger) E.; m. Jennie Lee Feldschreiber, June 28, 1953; children— Eric David, Stephen Mark, Daniel Avrum. BS, Northwestern U. Sch. Bus., 1950; hon. degree, N.Y. U. Sch. Continuing Edn., 1972. Buyer Mandel Bros., Chgo., 1950-53; salesman Internat. Latex Corp., Chgo., 1953-56; v.p. Hy Zeiger & Co., Milw., 1957-59; exec. v.p. K-Promotions, Inc., Milw., 1960-78, pres., 1979-80; chief exec. officer, pres. consumer promotions Carlson Mktg. Group, Mpls., 1981-84, chief exec. officer promotions div. Milw., 1985-86; pres. K-Promotions Div. Carlson Promotion Group, 1987-88, Giftmaster Div. Carlson Promotion Group, 1989—2001, Elias Mktg., Inc., 1989—2001. Officer, dir. Milw. Jewish Community Center; pres. regional bd. Anti-Defamation League; pres. Regional Bd. Jewish Nat. Fund, 1993-96. Served with USAAF, 1945-46. Mem. Am. Jewish. Achievements include developing inflight mail order mktg. programs for airlines. Office: Elias Mktg Inc 10134 N Gettysburg Ct Mequon WI 53092 Office Phone: 262-242-5978.

ELIAS, RAYMON TODD, lawyer; b. Corpus Christi, Aug. 3, 1968; s. Raymon K. and Susan Elias; m. Rose Sabrina Elias, Nov. 19, 1998; children: Raymon Andrew, Rose Alyssa. BSBA The Citadel, 1990; JD, Tex. Tech. U. Sch. of Law, 1993. Bar: Tex., (Licensed in all Tex. State Courts, Fed. Cts. Ea. and So. Dist. of Tex.). Of counsel Law Offices of J. Michael Black, Houston, 1993—95, Green, Downey and Black, LLP, Houston, 1995—98; ptnr. Black and Elias, 1998—2000, Gordon and Elias, LLP, Tex., 2000—. Mem.: Houston Trial Lawyers Assn., Am. Trial Lawyers Assn. Office: 5821 SW Frwy Ste 422 Houston TX 77057

ELIAS, SHERMAN, obstetrician, gynecologist, educator, clinical geneticist; b. Rome, Mar. 21, 1947; MD, U. Ky., 1972. Diplomate Am. Bd. Med. Genetics, Am. Bd. Ob-gyn. Resident in ob/gyn U. Louisville, 1976; postdoc. fellow in med. genetics Yale U., New Haven, 1975, Northwestern U., 1978; prof. ob/gyn. genetics U. Tenn., Memphis; prof. ob/gyn., molecular and human genetics Baylor Coll. Medicine, 1994—98; prof., head dept. ob-gyn. U. Ill., Chgo., 1998—2003; chair ob-gyn. Prentice Women's Hosp., Northwestern Meml., Chgo., 2003—; John J. Sciarra prof., chair dept. ob-gyn. Feinberg Sch. Medicine, Northwestern U., Chgo., 2003—. Contbr. articles to profl. jours. Mem. AAAS, Am. Soc. Human Genetics, Soc. Gynecologic Investigation, Am. Gynec./Obstet. Soc. Office: Northwestern U Feinberg Sch Medicine 333 E Superior St # 490 Chicago IL 60611

ELIAS, STEVEN, surgeon; b. Bklyn., Feb. 14, 1953; s. Hyman and Arlene Elias; m. Maria Casella, Nov. 2, 1997; children: Erika, Jeremy, Mia, Sam. BA, The Johns Hopkins U., 1975; MD, SUNY, Buffalo, 1979. Dir. ctr. vein diease Englewood Hosp. and Med. Ctr., NJ, 2000—. Cons. Smith and Nephew Inc., Andover, Mass., 2000—, Diomed Inc., 2003—, U.S. Surg. Inc., Norwalk, Conn., 2002—. Vascular fellowship, England Hosp., 1984. Fellow: ACS, Soc. Clin. Vascular Surgery, Am. Coll. Phlebology, Am. Venous Forum; mem.: Internat. Soc. Vascular Surgery. Achievements include development of Minimally Invasive Vein Surgery. Avocation: trialthlons. Office: Englewood Hospital and Med Ctr 350 Engle St Englewood NJ 07631 Office Phone: 201-816-0666. Personal E-mail: veininnovations@aol.com.

ELIAS, THOMAS SAM, botanist, author; b. Cairo, Ill., Dec. 30, 1942; s. George Sam (dec.) and Anna (Clanton) E.; m. Barbara Ana Boyd (dec.); children: Stephen, Brian; m. Hiromi Nakaoji, 2000. BA in Botany, So. Ill. U., 1964, MA in Botany, 1966; PhD in Biology, St. Louis U., 1969; PhD (hon.), Russian Acad. Scis., Moscow, 2003. Asst. curator Arnold Arboretum of Harvard U., Cambridge, Mass., 1969-71; adminstr., dendrologist Cary Arboretum, N.Y. Botanical Garden, Millbrook, 1971-73, asst. dir., 1973-84; dir., CEO Rancho Santa Ana Bot. Garden, Claremont, Calif., 1984-93; chmn., prof. dept. botany Claremont Grad. Sch., 1984-93; dir. U.S. Nat. Arboretum, Washington, 1993—. Lectr. in extension Harvard U., 1971; adj. prof. Coll. Environ. Science and Forestry, Syracuse, N.Y., 1977-80; coord. U.S.A/U.S.S.R. Botanical Exch., Program for U.S. Dept. of Interior, Washington, 1976—, U.S.A./China Botanical Exch., Program for U.S. Dept. of Interior, 1988-94; sr. exec. svc. USDA, 1993—. Editor: Extinction is Forever, 1977 (one of 100 Best Books in Sci. and Tech. ALA 1977), Conservation and Management of Rare and Endangered Plants, 1987; author: Complete Trees of North America, 1980 (one of 100 Best Books in Sci. and Tech. ALA 1980), Field Guide to Edible Wild Plants of North America (one of 100 Best Books in Sci. and Tech. ALA 1983). Recipient Cooley award, Am. Soc. Plant Taxonomists, 1970, Disting. Alumni award, So. Ill. U., 1989, Presdl. Rank award, 2000, Writer's Artist and Photographer's award, Bonsai Clubs International, 2001. Home: 6276 15th Rd N Arlington VA 22205 Office: US Nat Arboretum 3501 New York Ave NE Washington DC 20002-1958 Office Phone: 202-245-4539. E-mail: tselias@msn.com.

ELIASHBERG, YAKOV, mathematician, educator; arrived in U.S., 1988; Doctorate, Leningrad U., 1972. Assoc. prof. Syktyvkar U., Russia, 1972—75, chair dept. math., 1975—79; head computer software group Russia, 1981—87; with Math. Scis. Rsch. Inst., Berkeley, Calif., 1988—89; prof. Stanford U., Calif., 1989—. Recipient Oswald Veblen prize, Am. Math. Soc., 2001; Guggenheim fellow, 1995. Mem.: NAS. Office: Dept Math Bldg 380 Stanford U Stanford CA 94305-2125

ELIASI, JENNIFER REBECCA, dietician, consultant; b. L.I., N.Y., July 21, 1975; d. Hooshang Henry and Mahin May Eliasi; m. Jonathan Teich, Nov. 23, 2003. BA, Queens Coll., CUNY, 1997; MSc, Tufts U., Sch. of Nutrition Sci. and Policy, 1999; registered dietitian, Frances Stern Nutrition Ctr. at New Eng. Med. Ctr., 1999. Cert. Dietitian Nutritionist NY, 2002. Nutrition intern God's Love We Deliver, N.Y.C, 1996—97; AIDS rsch. vol. New Eng. Med. Ctr., Boston, 1998—99; rsch. asst. Frances Stern Nutrition Ctr., Boston, 1997—99; nutrition counselor Bklyn. AIDS Task Force, 2001—02; dir. nutrition svcs. AIDS Treatment and Health Program Bklyn. (N.Y.) Hosp., 1999—2005; nutrition cons. Millennium Biotechnologies, Bernardsville, NJ, 2001—; key account mgr. Serono, Inc., 2005—. Sec. Bklyn AIDS Task Force Treatment Adherence Com., NY, 1999—; team leader Bklyn Hosp. World AIDS Day Team, NY, 1999—; cons. MTI Biotech, Inc., Ame, Iowa, 2000—, Agouron-Pfizer Pharmaceuticals, N.Y.C, NY, 2000—. Contbr. articles to profl. jours. Recipient Campus Ministries award for Promoting Racial Harmony, Queens Coll., CUNY, 1997, Dietetics Svc. award, 1997, Recognized Young Dietitian of the Yr., Am. Dietetic Assn., 2003, Alumni award, Tufts U., 2005; scholarship, N.Y. State Dietetic Assn., 1998. Mem.: Am. Dietetic Assn. Nutrition Entrepreneurs, Am. Dietetic Assn. HIV/AIDS Dietetic Practice Group (quality mgmt. chair 2002—03, chair elect 2003—04, chair 2004—), Nutritionists In AIDS Care (co-chair 2000—). Independent. Jewish. Achievements include research in relationship of testosterone deficiency and side effects; effect of steroids, nutrition and exercise in HIV/AIDs. Avocations: walking, travel, writing. Office: Bklyn Hosp Ctr Programs for AIDS Treatment and Health 100 Parkside Ave 5th Fl Brooklyn NY 11226 Personal E-mail: jenneliasi@aol.com.

ELIASON, BIRDELL, painter, educator; d. Herman A. Eliason and Stella Berenice Fenney; m. Howard A. Wendt (dec.); 1 child, Mary Birdell Tagge. Diploma, Portland Art Sch., Oreg., 1943; diploma in portrait painting, 1994; cert., Portrait Inst., N.Y.C., 1987. Tchr. parochial sch., Chgo., 1967—69; artist-in-residence Mt. Prospect (Ill.) Hist. Soc., 1980—97; lectr. art, painting Mcpl. Art League, Chgo., 1990—. Art tchr. Zio Luth. Sch., Chgo., 1967—69; contbg. artist Troutdale Hist. Soc., 1996—2004. Mural, YSleta Mission, Anapra, Mex., 2004, Dr. Vanbucek Orthodontics office, Mt. Prospect, 1989; artist, illustrator Story Community - Mt. Prospect, 1992; Represented in permanent collections Rand McNally Co. Tchr. stroke victims Am. Health Care Ctr., Arlington Heights, Ill., 1979—80; tchr. Mexican children Ysleta Mission St. Paul Luth. Ch., El Paso, Tex., 2000—04. Named to Ency. of Living Art, Nat. Women's Libr., Washington, 1997; recipient We the People 1st Pl. award, BiCentennial Com., Mt. Prospect, 1976, Gold medal for art, Nat. PTA, CHgo., 1989—90, Statue of Victory, Cremona, Italy, 1985. Lutheran. Avocations: gardening, sketching, writing, painting, teaching. Home: 12 N Owen St Mount Prospect IL 60056

ELIASON, BONNIE MAE, county treasurer; b. Stanley, N.D., Jan. 10, 1947; d. Melvin Otis and Mabel Isabel (Borst) Howell; m. Murrey Allen Eliason, June 23, 1971; 1 child, Christal Medora. BA, Minot State Coll., 1970. Clk. N.D. Personal Property Tax Collector, Bismarck, 1965, Mountrail County Auditor, Stanley, 1970—74; dep. Mountrail County Treas., Stanley, 1974—77, treas., 1979—. Vice pres., mem. Am. Legion Aux., Stanley, 1980. Mem. Stanley Women's Bowling League (sec., treas. 1973-74, v.p. 1976-77, pres. 1977-78), Stanley Women's Bowling Assn. Presbyterian. Avocations: reading, crossword puzzles, sewing. Home: 7915 70th NW Stanley ND 58784-9013 Office: PO Box 69 Stanley ND 58784-0069

ELIASON, JON TATE, electrical engineer; b. Menominee, Mich., Mar. 23, 1938; s. Edwin Adolph and Irene Albertyn (Longlais) E.; m. Barbara Ann Love, July 2, 1960 (div. Dec. 1980); children: Ellen Artimese, Eric Alan, Eileen Amber; m. Kathleen Ann Vitell, May 25, 1996. BS in Sci. Engring., U. Mich., 1960; MS in Physics, Oreg. State U., 1966. Registered profl. engr., Ala., Ill. Engr. Vallecitos Nuclear Lab. GE, Pleasanton, Calif., 1964—66; sr. staff engr., engring. cons. Sperry Rand Corp., Huntsville, Ala., 1966—76; sr. staff engr. Martin Marietta Corp., Denver, 1976—84; master program engr., group engr. Sundstrand Corp., Rockford, Ill., 1984—92; engr. Insight Industries, Inc., Platteville, Wis., 1993—96, Insight Info. Inc., Platteville, Wis., 1996; project engr. electronic sys. Smiths Aerospace (formerly known as Barber-Colman Co.), Rockford, 1996—2003; founder Eliason Applied Engring., Rockford, 2003—. Recipient New Tech. award NASA, 1973, 75; Regents/Alumni scholar U. Mich., 1956-60. Mem. IEEE, AIAA, Am. Phys. Soc., Sigma Pi Sigma, (chpt. pres. 1963-64). Achievements include patents in field. Avocations: amateur radio, private pilot. Office: PO Box 7231 Rockford IL 61126-7231 Office Phone: 815-394-3983. Personal E-mail: jteliason@worldnet.att.net.

ELIASON, RUSSELL ALLEN, judge; b. Mpls., Jan. 28, 1944; s. Walter Joseph and Hazel Agnes Pearl (Jensen) Eliason; m. Karen L. Stevens; children: Nathaniel, Heidi, Justine, Danielle. At, U. Minn., 1964—65, JD, 1970; BA, Yale U., 1967; at, Wake Forest Law Sch., 1967—68. Bar: Minn. 1970, Iowa 1971, Nebr. 1975, U.S. Dist. Ct. (no. dist.) Iowa 1971, U.S. Dist. Ct. (mid. dist.) N.C. 1974, U.S. Dist. Ct. Nebr. 1975, U.S. Ct. Appeals (8th cir.) 1971, U.S. Ct. Appeals (4th cir.) 1976. Law clk. to judge U.S. Ct. Appeals (8th cir.), 1970—71; asst. U.S. atty. Dept. Justice, Sioux City, Iowa, 1971—72; law clk. to judge U.S. Dist. Ct. (mid. dist.) N.C., 1972—74; assoc. Ryan, Scoville & Uhlir, South Sioux City, Iowa, 1974—75; asst. U.S. atty. Dept. Justice, Greensboro, NC, 1975—76; U.S. magistrate judge U.S. Dist. Ct. (mid. dist.) N.C., Winston-Salem, NC, 1976—. Lectr. in field; active law sch. skills programs. Trumpeter Salem Band, Old Salem Band. Mem.: ABA, Nebr. Bar Assn., Minn. Bar Assn., Forsyth County Bar, N.C. Bar Assn., Sons of Norway, Phi Alpha Delta. Mem. Moravian Ch. Office: 224 Fed Bldg 251 N Main St Winston Salem NC 27101-3914 Office Phone: 336-734-2520.

ELIASSEN, JON ERIC, retired utilities executive, corporate financial executive; b. Omak, Wash., Mar. 10, 1947; s. Marvin George and Helen Grace (Meyer) E.; m. Valerie A. Foyle, Aug. 14, 1971; 1 child, Michael T. BA in Bus., Wash. State U., 1970. Staff acct. Wash. Water Power Co., Spokane, 1970-73, tax acct., 1973-76, fin. analyst, 1976-80, treas., 1980-86, v.p. fin., CFO, 1986-96; sr. v.p., CFO Avista Corp., Spokane, 1996—2003; ret., 2003. Bd. dirs. Itron Corp., West Coast Hospitality Corp.; pres., CEO Spokane Area Econ. Devel. Coun. Trustee Wash. State U. Found., Pullman, 1987-99, N.W. Mus. Art and Culture, 1998-2003; treas. Wash. State U. Found., 1995-97; trustee Spokane Symphony, 1989-95, treas., 1990-95, mem. symphony endowment bd., pres. 2002-04; pres., trustee Spokane Intercollegiate Rsch. and Tech. Inst. Found., 1996-2000; bd. dirs. Western Energy Inst., chair, 2001-02; bd. dirs. Wash. Tech. Ctr., 2002—, Wash. State U. Rsch. Found., 2002—. Mem. Fin. Exec. Inst. (Seattle chpt. 1983—). Episcopalian. Avocations: skiing, travel, bicycling, photography. Office: Spokane Area Econ Devel Coun 801 W Riverside Ave Ste 302 Spokane WA 99201 Office Phone: 509-742-9350.

ELIASSON, JAN K., ambassador; b. Goteberg, Sweden, Sept. 17, 1940; s. John H. and Karin (Nilsson) E.; m. Kerstin E. Englesson; children: Anna, Emilie, Johan. Grad., Swedish Naval Acad., Stockholm, 1962; MA, Sch. of Econs., Goteborg, 1965; Doctorate (hon.), Am. U., 1994, Goteborg U., 2001. Attaché Ministry of Fgn. Affairs, Stockholm, 1965-67, dir., 1977-80, dep. undersec., 1980-82, undersec. for polit. affairs, 1983-87; 2d sec. Embassy of Sweden, Bonn, Fed. Republic of Germany, 1967-70, 1st sec. Washington, 1970-74; advisor Prime Minister's office, Stockholm, 1982-83; amb., permanent rep. to UN, N.Y.C., 1988-92, under-sec.-gen. for humanitarian affairs, 1992-94; amb., chmn. Minsk Conf. on Nagorno-Karabach, 1993—94; state sec. fgn. affairs Govt. of Sweden, 1994—2000; amb. to U.S., 2000—. V.p. UN Econ. and Social Coun., 1991-92; pers. rep. to Sec.-Gen. of UN on Iran-Iraq matters, 1988-92; chmn. UN Trust Fund for South Africa, 1988-92; bd. dirs. Inst. for East-West Security Studies, N.Y., 1988-92, Internat. Peace Acad., N.Y., 1988-2001; vis. prof. dept. peace and conflict rsch. Uppsala (Sweden) U., 1994—; lectr. on fgn. policy and diplomacy. Served to comdr. Swedish Mil. Reserves. Recipient decorations from France, Netherlands, Germany, Egypt, Brazil, Portugal, Luxembourg, Denmark, Estonia, Latvia, Austria, Ukraine, Italy. Lutheran. Fax: 202-467-2699. Office Phone: 202-467-2611. E-mail: jan.eliasson@foreign.ministry.se.

ELIAZ, ROM EZER, chemical engineer, educator; b. Beer-Sheva, Israel, May 16, 1971; s. Joseph Arie and Bruria (Moskovitch) E.; married Yael Rozenberg, Mar. 18, 1997; 1 child, Kinor. BSChemE, BSc in Biotech., Ben-Gurion U. Negev and Weizmann Inst. Scis., Beer-Sheva, Israel, 1993, MSc (hon.), 1995, MBA, 1997, PhD, 1998. Cert. chem. engr. Israeli Engring. Assn., 1993. Rschr. Ben-Gurion U., Beer-Sheva, 1993-94; project coord., process engr. UPS Techs. Ltd., Beer-Sheva, 1994-95; process engr. Baran Group Ltd., Beer-Sheva, 1995-96; rschr. Ben-Gurion U., Beer Sheva, 1993-94. Postdoctoral fellow, asst. prof. U. San Francisco, 1998-2001. Contbr. numerous articles to profl. jours.; patentee pharmacetics, 1996, 2000, 2001. Concert musician. Recipient Sixth Internat. Tumor Necrosis Factor Outstanding Rsch. award, The Nagai Found. Tokyo Grad. Student award Controlled Release Soc., 1996, Post-doctoral award, 2000, Rothschild Post-doctoral Fellowship Honorarium award Rothschild Found., 1998, Cancer Rsch. Coordinating Com. Post-doctoral fellowship U. Calif. San Francisco, 1998-99. Mem. AAAS, Am. Assn. Gene Therapy, Controlled Release Soc., Israel Polymers Assn., Israel Soc. Polymers and Plastics. Avocations: basketball, diving, music. Office: U Calif Dept Biopharm Sci PO Box 0446 San Francisco CA 94143 also: 513 Parnassus Ave San Francisco CA 94143-0446 E-mail: eliaz@itsa.ucsf.edu.

ELIBOL, DAVID HAKAN, lawyer; b. LI, May 31, 1968; s. Tarik Elibol and Karen Elizabeth Andersen; m. Lynn Marie Price, Aug. 8, 1998; children: Cassidy Marie, Hannah Elisabeth. BS, Fla. State U., 1986; JD, Thomas M. Cooley Law Sch., 1995. Bar: NY 1996, U.S. Dist. Ct. (we. dist.) NY 1997, U.S. Supreme Ct. 2001. Assoc. Lipsitz, Green, Fahringer et. al., Buffalo,

1997—98; shareholder Gross, Shuman, Brizdle & Gilfillan, P.C., Buffalo, 1998—. Mem.: ATLA, Sports Lawyer's Assn., Erie County Bar Assn., W. N.Y. Trial Lawyers Assn., N.Y. State Bar Assn. Office: Gross Shuman Brizdle and Gilfillan PC 465 Main St Ste 600 Buffalo NY 14203 Business E-Mail: delibol@gross-shuman.com.

ELIBOL, TARIK, gastroenterologist, educator; b. Sept. 1, 1939; s. Ismail Cemal and Nuriye (Tutkun) E.; m. Eileen Elibol, Aug. 30, 1997; children: Kimberly, Lisa, David, Adam, John. MD, U. Istanbul, 1964. Resident in internal medicine E.J. Meyer Hosp. U. Buffalo, 1964-66; fellow in gastroenterology Cleve. Clinic, 1966-68; clin. asst. prof. medicine U. Buffalo, 1975—; practice medicine specializing in digestive diseases Buffalo, 1969—. Former chief of staff DeGraff Meml. Hosp.; mem. staff Erie County Med. Center. Fellow ACP, Am. Coll. Gastroenterology; mem. Am. Soc. Internal Medicine, Am. Soc. Gastrointestinal Endoscopy, N.Y. State Med. Soc., Erie County Med. Soc., Western N.Y. Soc. Gastrointestinal Endoscopy (past pres.), Western N.Y. Gastrointestinal Liver Soc. (pres. 1980—), Western N.Y. Physician Found. (pres. 1980—). Home: 55 Leicester Rd Buffalo NY 14217-2111 Office: 2949 Elmwood Ave Kenmore NY 14217-1356

ELICKER, GORDON LEONARD, retired lawyer; b. Cleve., May 27, 1940; BA in Math., U. Mich., 1962, JD, 1965; postdoctoral, U. Aix-Marseille, Aix-En Provence, France, 1965-66. Bar: Mich. 1967, N.Y. 1968, U.S. Dist. Ct. (so. dist.) N.Y. 1973. Stagiaire EEC, Brussels, 1966-67; assoc. Shearman & Sterling, N.Y.C., 1967-77, ptnr., 1977-91, Nixon Peabody LLP (formerly Nixon, Hargrave, Devans & Doyle), N.Y.C., 1991—2001; ret., 2001. Dir., sec. The World Affairs Forum, Stamford, Conn., 2001—; spkr. in field. Contbr. articles to profl. jours. Mem. legal com. U.S.-U.S.S.R. Trade and Econ. Coun., N.Y.C., 1978-91; chmn. legis. com. N.Y. Dist. Export Coun., N.Y.C., 1980-86; mem. Dem. Town Com., New Canaan, 1985-87; mem. bd. edn., New Canaan, Conn., 1986-90, chmn., 1989-90. Fulbright scholar, 1965. Democrat. E-mail: elicker@earthlink.net.

ELIE, JEAN ANDRÉ, investment banker; b. Montreal, Que., Can., Oct. 8, 1943; s. Jean-Paul and Violet (Trempe) E.; m. Josée Langevin. BA, Coll. Jean de Brébeuf, 1962; BCL, McGill U., 1965; MBA, U. Western Ont., 1968. Bar: Que. 1966. With Rolland Inc., Montreal, 1968-81, sec., 1974-81, counsel, 1974-81, v.p. administrn., 1978-81; dir. corp. services Burns Fry Ltd., Montreal, 1981-88; v.p., dir. corp. and govt. svcs. Burns Fry Lte., Montreal, 1988-94; fin. cons. Birinco Holdings Internat., Inc., Montreal, 1994—. Mem. adminstrv. coun. Coopers & Lybrand, 1996; mng. dir. Corp. and Investment Banking, Can., Soc. Genérale, 1998; bd. dirs. Mount Copperwind Power Energy Inc., Alimentation Couchetard, Inc., Cambior, Inc.; pres. Jelinco Internat., 2003—. Bd. dirs. Montreal Symphony Orch.; bd. dirs., v.p. Found. Hosp. U. De Montreal Mem. Can. Bar Assn., Que. Bar Assn., Investment Dealers Assn. Can. (exec. com., bd. dirs.), Mt. Royal Club, St. Denis Club. Roman Catholic. Home: 1929 Laird Blvd Mount Royal PQ Canada H3P 2V2 Office: 1929 Laird Blvd Mount Royal PQ Canada H3P2V2 Office Phone: 514-738-4520. Business E-Mail: jeanelie@videotron.ca.

ELIEFF, LEWIS STEVEN, stockbroker; b. Sofia, Bulgaria, Aug. 2, 1929; s. Steven and Vera (Svetcoff) E.; m. Evanka Brown, May 25, 1958; children; Nancy Ann, Robert and Richard (twins). BBA, U. Mich., 1953, MBA, 1954. Statistician, tax acct. Gen. Motors Corp., Flint, Mich., 1954-60; stockbroker Roney & Co., Flint, 1960-73, ltd. ptnr., 1973-79, gen. ptnr., 1979—; stockbroker Raymond James & Assoc., St. Petersburg, Fla., 1999—. Tchr. stock market curriculum Flint Pub. Schs., 1960-68, Genesee County Community Coll., 1968-73, U. Mich. Extension and Grad. Study Ctr. Flint Campus, 1974—. Served with AUS, 1954-56. Mem.: U. Mich. Alumni Club and Assn., Genesee Valley Rotary. Home: 6612 Kings Point Rd Grand Blanc MI 48439-8711 Office: 3499 S Linden Rd Ste 4 Flint MI 48507-3022 Office Phone: 810-733-2810. E-mail: lewis.elieff@raymondjames.com.

ELIEFF, RICHARD GEORGE, energy industry consultant; b. Flint, Mich., July 11, 1960; s. Lewis Steven and Evanka Marie (Brown) E. BSCE summa cum laude, U. Mich., 1982; MBA, U. Pa., 1987. Cost/schedule engr. Bechtel Power Corp., Ann Arbor, 1982-85; constrn. scheduling cons. Hovnanian Enterprises, Inc., Red Bank, N.J., 1986; strategic planning cons. Mendenhall (Pa.) Assocs., Inc., 1987; devel. specialist Wesley Housing Devel. Corp., Alexandria, 1988-91; prin. Vertumnus Enterprises, Alexandria, 1991-97; pres. IntelliPro Software Inc., Alexandria, 1995-98; project mgr. Pace Global Energy Svcs., Fairfax, Va., 1997—. Mem. adv. com. for multifamily loan program Va. Dept. of Housing and Cmty. Devel., Richmond, 1989-91. Author: (software) Secrets to a Happy Car, 1996. William J. Branstrom scholar U. Mich., 1979, scholarship 1980; fellowship Associated Gen. Contractors, 1981. Mem. Tau Beta Pi, Chi Epsilon. Republican. Orthodox. Avocations: stock market, automotive mechanics, piano. Office: Pace Global Energy Svcs 4401 Fair Lakes Ct Ste 400 Fairfax VA 22033-3848 Home: 20870 Lisburn Terrace Apt 304 Ashburn VA 20147-7790

ELIEL, ERNEST LUDWIG, chemist, educator; b. Cologne, Germany, Dec. 28, 1921; came to US, 1946, naturalized, 1951; s. Oskar and Luise (Tietz) E.; m. Eva Schwarz, Dec. 23, 1949; children: Ruth Louise, Carol Susan. Student, U. Edinburgh, Scotland, 1939-40; degree in phys.-chem. sci., U. Havana, Cuba, 1946; PhD, U. Ill., 1948; DSc (hon.), Duke U., 1983, U. Notre Dame, 1990, Babes-Bolyai U., Cluj, Romania, 1993, U. Havana, Cuba, 2004. Mem. faculty U. Notre Dame, South Bend, Ind., 1948-72, prof. chemistry, 1960-72, head dept., 1964-66; W.R. Kenan Jr. prof. chemistry U. N.C., Chapel Hill, 1972-93, prof. emeritus, 1993—. Le Bel Centennial lectr., Paris, 1974, Geoffrey Coates lectr. U. Wyo., 1989, Smith, Kline and French lectr. U. Ill., 1990, Richard and Doris Arnold lectr. U. So. Ill., 1997, Fry lectr. U. Ark., 2005; Sir C.V. Raman vis. prof. U. Madras, India, 1981. Author: Stereochemistry of Carbon Compounds, 1962, Elements of Stereochemistry, 1969, From Cologne to Chapel Hill, 1990; co-author: Conformational Analysis, 1965, Stereochemistry of Organic Compounds, 1994, Basic Organic Stereochemistry, 2001; co-editor: Topics in Stereochemistry, vols. I-XXI, 1967-94. Pres. Internat. Rels. Coun., St. Joseph Valley, Ind., 1961-63; chmn. bd. U.S.-Mex. Found. for Sci., 1994-96. Recipient Coll. Chem. Tchrs. award Mfg. Chemists Assn., 1965, Laurent Lavoisier medal French Chem. Soc., 1968, Amoco Teaching award U. N.C., 1975, Thomas Jefferson award U. N.C., 1991, N.C. award in Sci., 1986, Chirality medal Internat. Symposium on Chiral Discrimination, 1996; NSF sr. rsch. fellow Harvard U., 1958, Calif. Inst. Tech., 1958-59, E.T.H. Zurich, Switzerland, 1967-68, Guggenheim fellow Stanford U., Princeton U., 1975-76, Duke U., 1983-84; named One of Top 75 Disting. Contbrs. to Chem. Enterprise, Chem. and Engring. News, 1998. Fellow AAAS (chmn. chemistry sect. 1991-92), Royal Soc. Chems.; mem. NAS (award for chemistry in svc. to society 1997), AAUP (chpt. pres. 1971-72, 78-79), Am. Acad. Arts and Scis., Am. Chem. Soc. (chmn. St. Joseph Valley sect. 1960, councillor 1965-73, 75—, chmn. com. publs. 1972, 76-78, dir. 1985-93, chmn. bd. dirs. 1987-89, pres. 1992, Morley medal Cleve. sect. 1965, Harry and Carol Mosher award Santa Clara Valley sect. 1982, Herty medal Ga. sect. 1991, So. Chemist award Memphis sect. 1991, Madison Marshall award North Ala. sect., 1993, George C. Pimentel award in Chem. Edn. 1995, Priestley medal 1996), Coun. Sci. Soc. Pres.'s (pres. 1996), Royal Spanish Chem. Soc. (hon.), Argentine Chem. Assn. (hon.), Peruvian Chem. Soc. (corr.), Mex. Chem. Soc. (hon.), Mex. Acad. Scis. (corr.), Chilean Chem. Soc. (hon.), Cuban Chem. Soc. (hon.), Sigma Xi (pres. U. Notre Dame chpt. 1968-69), Phi Lambda Upsilon, Phi Kappa Phi. Home: 345 Carolina Meadows Villa Chapel Hill NC 27517-7519 Office Phone: 919-962-6198. Business E-Mail: eliel@email.unc.edu.

ELIEL, RUTH LOUISE, performing company executive; b. South Bend, Ind., Feb. 6, 1953; d. Ernest Ludwig and Eva Eliel; m. William N. Cooney, Aug. 31, 1990. V.p. Chase Manhattan Bank, N.Y.C., NY, Hong Kong, 1976—84; cons. McKinsey's Co., Inc., N.Y.C., 1984—86; mng. dir. MG Fin. Ltd., Hong Kong, 1986—87; sr. mgr. consulting divsn. Deloitte & Touche, LA, 1987—91; mng. dir. Lewitzky Dance Co., L.A., 1991—97; exec. dir. LA Chamber Orch., 1997—. Mem. adv. bd. Com. Restoration of Freeman House, LA, 1990—93; bd. dirs. ARTS, Inc., LA, 1997—2001; exec. com. mem. Arts for L.A., 1999—. Mem.: Am. Symphony Orchestra League, Assn. Calif. Symphony Orch. (bd. dirs. 2001—04). Democrat. Jewish. Avocations: swimming, tai chi, skiing, hiking. Office: LA Chamber Orch 707 Wilshire Blvd Ste 1850 Los Angeles CA 90017

ELIEZER, DAVID, biochemist, educator; s. Isaac and Naomi Eliezer. PhD, Stanford U. Post-doctoral fellow Scripps Rsch. Inst., San Diego, 1994—99; asst. prof. biochemistry Weill Med. Coll., Cornell, N.Y.C., 1999—2004, assoc. prof. biochemistry, 2004—. Office: Weill Medical College of Cornell 1300 York Ave New York NY 10021 Office Phone: 212-746-6557.

ELIN, RONALD JOHN, pathologist, educator; b. Mpls., Apr. 14, 1939; s. John Matthew and Helen Sophia (Lind) E.; m. Susan May Krogh, June 14, 1969; children: Derek, Justin. BA, U. Minn., 1960, BS, 1962, MD, 1966, PhD, 1969. Diplomate Am. Bd. Pathology, Am. Bd. Clin. Chemistry. Intern U. Hosp. Calif., San Diego, 1969-70; commd. med. officer USPHS, 1970, advanced through grades to med. dir., 1975; staff assoc. Nat. Inst. Allergy and Infectious Diseases NIH, Bethesda, Md., 1970-73, resident clin. pathology dept., 1973-74, chief clin. pathology dept., 1975-97, chief chemistry svc., 1977-97; vice chmn. pathology U. Louisville, Ky., 1997—2001, chmn. dept. pathology and lab. medicine, 2002. Clin. prof. Uniformed Svcs. U. of Health Scis., Bethesda, 1978-97; initiator, first chmn. Gordon Rsch. Conf. on Magnesium in Biomed. Processes and Medicine, 1978. Contbr. more than 220 articles to profl. jours. Decorated Commendation medal USPHS, 1980, Meritorious Svc. medal USPHS, 1984. Fellow Am. Coll. Nutrition, Coll. Am. Pathologists, Am. Soc. Clin. Pathologists; mem. Am. Assn. Pathologists, Am. Assn. Clin. Chemistry (Outstanding Contbns. to Clin. Chemistry in a Selected Area of Rsch. award 1994), Acad. Clin. Lab. Physicians and Scientists (sec.-treas. 1985-87, pres. 1990-91, Gerald T. Evans award 1995). Lutheran. Achievements include research on magnesium metabolism, properties of endotoxin. Office: U Louisville Hosp Dept Pathology and Lab Medicine 512 S Hancock St Rm 203 Louisville KY 40202-1675 Office Phone: 502-852-4464. Business E-Mail: rjelin01@gwise.louisville.edu.

ELINGBURG, WESLEY R., health products executive; Sr. v.p. fin., treas. Roche Biomedical Labs., Inc., 1988-95; sr. v.p. fin. Lab Corp. Am. Holdings, Burlington, N.C., 1995-96, exec. v.p., CFO, treas., 1996—. Office: Lab Corp Am Holdings 358 S Main St Burlington NC 27215

ELINSON, JACK, social sciences educator; b. N.Y.C., June 30, 1917; s. Sam and Rebecca (Block) Elinson; m. May Gomberg, July 5, 1941; children: Richard, Elaine, Mitchell, Robert. BS, CCNY, 1937; MA, George Washington U., 1946, PhD, 1954. Social sci. analyst Dept. Def., Washington, 1942-51; sr. study dir. Nat. Opinion Research Center, 1951-56; asst. prof. sociology U. Chgo., 1954-56; assoc. prof. adminstrv. medicine Columbia U., N.Y.C., 1956-64, prof. adminstrv. medicine, 1964-68, prof. sociomed. scis. and sociology, 1968-86, prof. emeritus, 1986—; Service fellow Nat. Center Health Stats., 1977-81; vis. prof. behavioral scis. U. Toronto, 1969-77; Disting. vis. prof. Inst. Health Care Policy, Rutgers U., 1986-89, Disting. sr. scholar, 1990—; vis. prof. Robert Wood Johnson Med. Sch. (formerly Rutgers Med. Sch.), Univ. Medicine and Dentistry of N.J., 1986—; dir. program evaluation dept. patient care Harlem Hosp. Ctr., 1966-71. Bd. dirs. Med. and Health Rsch. Assn., N.Y.C., 1977—89, Bergen County N.J. Tb and Health Assn., 1960—65; mem. adminstrv. bd. Bur. Applied Social Rsch. Columbia U., 1970—75; co-dir. health care orgn. and adminstrn. track Program for Master's in Pub. Health Rutgers U.-U. Medicine and Dentistry of N.J., 1983—92. Co-author (with R.E. Trussell): Chronic Illness in a Rural Area, 1959; co-author: (with J.J. Williams and R.E. Trussell) Family Medical Care Under Three Types of Health Insurance, 1962; co-author: (with E. Padilla and M. Perkins) Public Image of Mental Health Services, 1967; editor (with A.E. Siegmann): Sociomedical Health Indicators, 1979; editor: (with A. Mooney and A. Siegmann) Health Goals and Health Indicators: Policy, Planning and Evaluation, 1977; editor: (with N.K. Wenger, M.E. Mattson and C.D. Furberg) Assessment of Quality of Life in Clinical Trials of Cardiovascular Therapies, 1984. Named Jack Elinson Sociomed. Scis. Libr., Columbia U. Sch. Pub. Health, 1998; recipient Nat. Merit award, Delta Omega Soc., 1982, Festschrift, spl. issue of Social Sci. and Medicine, 1989. Fellow: APHA (1st award Assn. Social Scis. in Health 1984), Am. Assn. Pub. Opinion Rsch. (pres. 1979—80, Exceptionally Disting. Achievement award 1993), Am. Sociol. Assn. (chmn. med. sociology, Leo G. Reeder award 1985), AAAS; mem.: Med. and Health Rsch. Assn. N.U.C. (bd. dirs.), N.J. Pub. Health Assn. (exec. bd., Dennis J. Sullivan award 1990), N.Y.C. Pub. Health Assn. (bd. dirs.), Inst. Medicine NAS. Office: Columbia U Sch Pub Health Dept Sociomed Scis 600 W 168th St New York NY 10032-3722 Office Phone: 212-305-4027. Business E-Mail: je7@columbia.edu. E-mail: jelinson@juno.com.

ELION, ELAINE ANNE, science educator; MS, PhD, Albert Einstein Coll. of Medicine, 1985. Helen Hay Whitney fellow Whitehead Inst. for Biomed. Rsch., Cambridge, Mass., 1986—90; assoc. prof. Harvard Med. Sch., Cambridge, 1991—. Office: Harvard Med Sch Dept BCMP 240 Longwood Ave Boston MA 02115 Office Phone: 617-432-3815. Personal E-mail: elaine_elion@hms.harvard.edu.

ELIOT, ALEXANDER, writer; b. Cambridge, Mass., Apr. 28, 1919; s. Samuel Atkins, Jr. and Ethel (Cook) E.; m. Jane Winslow Knapp, May 3, 1952; children: May Rose, Jefferson, Winslow. Student, Black Mountain Coll., 1936-38, Boston Mus. Sch., 1938-39. Dir. Pinkney St. Artists Alliance, Boston, 1940-41; asst. to producer March of Time newsreel, 1941-42; asst. dir. films Office of War Info., 1942-43; editor films Office of Coord. Inter-Am. Affairs, 1943-45; art editor Time mag., 1945-60. Prof. emeritus program Hampshire Coll., 1977. Editor Parabola mag., 1995-96; contbg. editor Harvard mag., 1988-95; author: Proud Youth, 1953, Three Hundred Years of American Painting, 1957, Sight and Insight, 1959, Earth, Air, Fire and Water, 1962, Greece, 1963, Love Play, 1966, Creatures of Arcadia, 1967, Socrates, 1967, A Concise History of Greece, 1972, Myths, 1976, Zen Edge, 1979, (with Jane Winslow Eliot) Fisher's Guide to Greece, 1984, Abraham Lincoln, 1985, The Universal Myths, 1990, The Global Myths, 1993, The Timeless Myths, 1996; (film with Jane Winslow Eliot) The Secret of Michelangelo, Every Man's Dream, 1968. Guggenheim fellow, 1960; Japan Found. sr. fellow, 1975 Mem. Century Assn., Dutch Treat Club (N.Y.C.). Home: 105 Paloma Ave Venice CA 90291-2572 *The moon, the planets, pass around my heart. The sun shines into me, and in me as well. Yet what am I? A goose-pimpled crazy on a skewed glass bicycle, continually crashing into scribbled walls. And this moment, this being is the thing.*

ELIOT, CHARLES WILLIAM JOHN, former university president; b. Rawalpindi, Pakistan, Dec. 8, 1928; s. William Edmund and Ann Catherine (McDougall) E.; m. Mary Williamson, Sept. 2, 1954; children: Charles, Sophia (dec.), Nicholas, Johanna, Luke. BA, U. Toronto, Ont., Can., 1949, MA, 1951, PhD, 1961; DCL, King's Coll., 1988; DLitt, St. Mary's, 1999. Lectr., asst. prof., assoc. prof., prof. U. B.C., Vancouver, Can., 1957-71; prof. archaeology Am. Sch. Classical Studies, Athens, Greece, 1971-76; prof. classics Mount Allison U., Sackville, N.B., Can., 1976-85, acad. v.p., 1981-83; pres. U. P.E.I., Charlottetown, Can., 1985-95, pres. emeritus, 1996—. Mem. Acad. Panel of the Social Scis. and Humanities Rsch., 1978-82, chmn., 1980-81. Author: Coastal Demes of Attika, 1962, Campaign of the Falieri and Piraeus in the Year 1827; or a Journal of a Volunteer, 1992. Contbr. revs. and articles to profl. jours. Mem. Sch. Bd. Dist. 14 N.B., 1983-85 Mem. Order of Can., 1994; scholar Am. Sch. Classical Studies, 1952-54, Can. Coun., 1965-66, Dumbarton Oaks, 1980, Social Scis. and Humanities Rsch. Coun. Can., 1984-85. Mem. Classical Assn. Can. (pres. 1992-94). Anglican. Avocation: works of john galt. E-mail: wmeliot@pei.sympatico.ca.

ELIOT, JOHN F., human performance educator, consultant; b. Boston, Apr. 24, 1971; s. Richard Eliot and Marcia Bates Worcester. AB, Dartmouth Coll., 1993; MEd, U. Va., 1995, PhD, 1997. Instr. Dartmouth Coll., Hanover, NH, 1990—93; prof. U. Va., Charlottesville, 1995—2000, Rice U., Houston, 2000—; founder, pres. The Milestone Group, Dallas, 2002—. Adj. faculty So. Meth. U., U. Houston, Tex. Med. Ctr., 2000—; bd. dirs. Ctr. for Performance Arts Medicine, Houston, Nat. Ctr. for Human Performance; cons. numerous elite performers; spkr. in field. Author: (book) Overachievement, 2004, (video and CD programs) The Psychology of Success, 2003; contbr. articles to profl. jours. Vol. coach Little League Baseball, 1988—; vol. Spl. Olympics, 1994—; alumni vol. Dartmouth Coll., 1993—. Mem.: Acad. Mgmt., Am. Coll. and Sports Medicine, Dartmouth Coll. Alumni Assn. Achievements include numerous radio, TV and print media performances; college and professional sport national and international championships. Home: 4128 Childress St Houston TX 77005 Office: Rice Univ MS545 6100 Main St Houston TX 77005 Office Phone: 713-348-5762. Business E-Mail: eliot@rice.edu.

ELIOT, THEODORE LYMAN, JR., former ambassador, consultant; m. Patricia P. Peters. BA, Harvard U., 1948, M.P.A., 1956; LL.D., U. Nebr., Omaha, 1975. With U.S. Fgn. Svc., 1949-78; spl. asst. to under sec. of state; to sec. treasury; country dir. for Iran Dept. State; exec. sec. State Dept.; also spl. asst. to sec. of state Dept. State; ambassador to Afghanistan; insp. gen. Dept. State., Washington; dean Fletcher Sch. Law and Diplomacy, Tufts U., 1979-85; exec. dir. Ctr. for Asian Pacific Affairs Asia Found., San Francisco, 1985-87. Bd. dirs. Neurobiol. Tech. Trustee Asia Found. Mem. Am. Acad. Diplomacy, Univ. Club (San Francisco).

ELISHA, LARISA, musician, performer, educator; b. Baku, Russia, Jan. 12, 1963; d. Vladimir Chumakov and Mariya Chumakova; m. Steven Kenneth Elisha, May 19, 2002; 1 child, Patrick A. BA, A. Lunatcharsky Conservatory of Music, Minsk, Belarus, 1986, MMus, 1987—89; D in Violin performance, K. Lipinski Acad. Music, Wroclaw, Poland, 1996—97; cert. in chamber music, U. Wis., Milw., 1997—99. Prof., violin M. Glinka Coll. Music, Minsk, Belarus, 1985—89, A. Lunatcharsky Conservatory of Music, Minsk, Belarus, 1987—89, K. Szymanowski Coll. of Music, Wroclaw, Poland, 1989—97, K. Lipinski Acad. Music, Wroclaw, Poland, 1989—97, prof., strings methodology, 1996—97, Inst. U. Wis., Milw., 1997—99; prof., violin Wis. Conservatory of Music, Milw., 1998—99; violinist artist in residence Washburn U., Topeka, 1999—. Concertmaster State Witold Lutaslawski Philharm. Symphony Orch., Wroclaw, Poland, 1989—97, Topeka Symphony Orch., 1999—, Wichita Grand Opera, 2002—; prin. violin Chamber Orch. Leopoldinum, Wroclaw, Poland, 1990—93; first violinist, artistic dir. String Quartet Wratislavia of Philharm. Hall, Wroclaw, Poland, 1995—97; violinist, Piano Trio U. Wis. Inst. Chamber Music, Milw., 1997—99; assoc. concertmaster Green Bay Symphony Orch., Waukesha, Wis., 1997—99; co-founder, violinist Elaris Duo, 2000—, Chamber Music Series, Elaris String Academy, 2004—. Author: (books) The Russian Violin School's Traditions, 1986, Methodology of Teaching Violin Players, 1986; violinist (solo recitals and solo with orchestras) Musica Polonica Nova, Poland, 1989, Acad. Music Concert Hall, Krakow, Poland, 1990, Chamber Music Festival, Kolobrzeg, Poland, 1991, State Witold Lutoslawski Philharm. Symphony Orch., Wroclaw, Poland, 1991, Koszalin Philharm. Orch., Poland, 1991, Leopoldinum, Samstag, Germany, 1992, K. Lipinski Acad. Music Concert Hall, Wroclaw, Poland, 1993, Gioventi Musicale d'Italia Festival, Bergamo, Italy, 1993, Wieniawski Festival, Szczawno Zdroj, Poland, 1993, Theater Hall Acad. Music, Wroclaw, Poland, 1997, The Topeka Symphony, 1999, 2000, 2003, 2005, Pittsburg State U., Kans., 2001, 2002, 2003, (recitals) Elaris Duo, Washburn U., Topeka, 2000, 2001, 2002, 2003, 2004, Sunflower Music Festival, 2000—, Miss. Symphony Orch., 2003, Colo. Music Festival, Boulder, 2000, 2001, Bergen Internat. Festival, Norway, 2004 (Musician Yr., Kans. Fedn. Music Clubs (KFMC), 2003), Koncertgebouw Hall, Amsterdam, Warsaw Nat. Philharmony Hall, World Famous Concert Halls, Karajan Hall, Berlin. Named to Kans. Touring Program. Mem.: Chamber Music Am., Am. String Tchrs. Assn., Coll. Music Soc., Northeast Kans. Music Tchrs. Assn., Music Tchrs. Nat. Assn. Office Phone: 785-670-1891. E-mail: elarisduo@cox.net.

ELITZUR, MOSHE, physicist, researcher; b. Borzcow, Poland, Apr. 29, 1944; came to the U.S., 1977; s. Yechiel and Sofia (Brandwein) E.; m. Shlomit Yoskowitz, Apr. 7, 1970; children: Ofer, Haggai, Ben. BS, Hebrew U., Jerusalem, 1964; MSc, Weizman Inst., Rehovot, Israel, 1965; PhD, Weizmann Inst., Rehovot, Israel, 1971. Scientist Weizman Inst., 1973-75, sr. scientist, 1975-80; assoc. prof. U. Ky., Lexington, 1980-86, prof., 1986—. Author: Astronomical Masers, 1992. Lt. Israeli Army, 1965-70. NSF grantee, 1980—. Office: U Ky Dept Physics Astronomy Lexington KY 40506-0001

ELIX, DOUGLAS THORNE, computer company executive; b. Adelaide, Australia, July 27, 1948; s. David Llewellyn and Margaret Thorne (Martin) E.; m. Robin Claire Wallace; children: Claire, Penelope, David, Sarah. Dir. banking region IBM Australia Ltd., 1987-89; dir. fin. industry IBM Asia Pacific, Tokyo, 1990-91; dir. of ops. IBM Australia Ltd., 1991-92, gen. mgr. fin. svcs., 1992-93, asst. mng. dir., CEO, 1993-96; pres., CEO Integrated Sys. Solution Corp., Somers, N.Y., 1996-97; gen. mgr. IBM Global Svcs., N.A., 1997-98, IBM Global Svcs. Ams., 1998-99; sr. v.p., group exec. IBM Global Svcs., 1999—2004, IBM Global Sales & Distbn., 2004—. Bd. dirs. Royal Bank of Can. Fellow Australian Inst. Mgmt.

ELIZABETH, HER MAJESTY, II, (ELIZABETH ALEXANDRA MARY), Queen of United Kingdom of Great Britain, Northern Ireland and of her other Realms and Territories; Head of Commonwealth, Defender of Faith; b. Apr. 21, 1926; d. King George VI (formerly Duke of York) and Queen Elizabeth (formerly Duchess of York); m. Prince Philip, Duke of Edinburgh, Nov. 20, 1947; children: Charles Philip Arthur George (now The Prince of Wales), 1948, Anne Elizabeth Alice Louise (now The Princess Royal), 1950, Andrew Albert Christian Edward (now The Duke of York), 1960, Edward Antony Richard Louis (now The Earl of Wessex), 1964. Succeeded to throne following death of father, Feb. 6, 1952; crowned Queen, June 2, 1953. Address: Buckingham Palace London SW1A 1AA England*

ELIZONDO, HECTOR, actor; b. N.Y.C., Dec. 22, 1936; s. Martin Echevarria and Carmen Medina (Reyes) E.; m. Carolee Campbell, Apr. 13, 1969; 1 son, Rodd. Student, CCNY, 1955-56, Ballet Arts Co. of Carnegie Hall. Appearances include (plays) The Price (Broadway), Drums in the Night, Steambath, 1970 (OBIE award), Prisoner of Second Avenue, 1974, The Great White Hope, 1977, Sly Fox (Dr. Desk-Nun award), Medal of Honor Rag, American Playhouse; (movies) Report to the Commissioner, 1975, The Taking of Pelham-1-2-3, 1975, Cuba, 1978, American Gigolo, 1979, The Fan, 1979, Young Doctors in Love, 1983, The Flamingo Kid, 1984, Nothing in Common, 1985, Leviathan, Pretty Woman, 1990 (Golden Globe nominee best supporting actor), Chains of Gold, Paydirt, Necessary Roughness, Frankie and Johnny, 1991, Being Human, 1992, Exit to Eden, 1993, Getting Even with Dad, 1993, Beverly Hills Cop III, 1993, Safe House, 1996, Turbulence, 1996, Dear God, 1996, Romy & Michelle, 1996, The Other Sister, 1998, Runaway Bride, 1998-99, The Princess Diaries, 2001, sequel, 2004, Celestine Prophecies, 2004, The Princess Diaries 2: The Royal Engagements, 2004; (CBS series) Kate Brasher, 2001, Tortilla Soup, 2001, How High, 2001, Miracles, 2003, Without a Trace, 2003; (TV series) Popi, 1976, Freebie and the Bean, Foley Square, 1985, Great Performances, WCET, 1987, The Impatient Heart, All in the Family, Chicago Hope (Emmy award best supporting actor, 3 nominations), 1994-2000, The West Wing, 2002, Century City, 2003-2004; (TV films) Casablanca, 1983, Medal of Honor Rag, 1982, Mrs. Cage (Emmy nominee for best supporting actor), 1992, The Dain Curse, 1978, Courage, 1986, Honey Boy, 1982, Out of the Darkness, 1985, Natica Jackson, 1987, Addicted to His Love, 1988, Your Mother Wears Combat Boots, 1989, The Amnesty File, 1990, The Burden of Proof, (nomination Emmy best supporting actor), 1992, Borrowed Hearts, 1997, American Playhouse The American Experience Discovery. Recipient Lifetime Achievement Image award, 1997, ALMA award for best actor, 1998, Best Actor in Drama Series, 2000, Latin Legends award, N.Y.C., 2000, Lifetime Achievement IMPACT award, 2002. Mem. Amnesty Internat., The Creative Coalition. Roman Catholic.

ELKES, TERRENCE ALLEN, communications executive; b. N.Y.C., Apr. 28, 1934; s. Sidney and Beatrice (Sachnin) E.; m. Ruth Jerkowsky, June 14, 1959; children: Steven Andrew, David Adam, Daniel Arthur. BA cum laude,

CCNY, 1955; JD, U. Mich., 1958. Bar: N.Y. 1959. Atty. Prentice Hall, Inc., 1958-59; counsel internat. div. Norwich Pharmacal Co., 1959-65; corp. counsel, also v.p., sec. Parsons & Whittemore, Inc., 1965-72; corp. counsel Black Clawson Co., 1965-72; treas. Prince Albert Pulp Co. Ltd., 1966-72; v.p., sec., gen. counsel Viacom Internat., Inc., N.Y.C., 1972-76, exec. v.p., 1976-78, pres., 1978-87, chief exec. officer, 1984-87; prin. Apollo Ptnrs., LLC-NY, N.Y.C., Conn., 1987—. Bd. dirs. IDC Svcs. Corp., Doane Agrl. Svcs., Inc., The Tennis Channel, 2001—; mng. dir. Apollo Radio, Ltd., 1989-96; chmn. Compact Video Corp., 1991-93, Internat. Post Ltd., 1994-97; chmn. Video Svcs. Corp., 1997-2000. Trustee U. Mich. Law Sch., 1992, mem. pres. adv. group U. Mich., 1992, mem. investment adv. group & tech. transfer group, 1992; pres. Jewish Outreach Inst., 1999; chmn. Ctr. Security Policy Bd. Regents, 2003. Home: 12 Trails End Rye NY 10580-2227 Office: Apollo Ptnrs LLC 500 5th Ave New York NY 10110-0002

EL KHADEM, HASSAN SAAD, chemistry professor, researcher; b. Cairo, Mar. 24, 1923; naturalized, 1975; s. Saad S. and Nimet (Zulficar) El K.; m. Nadia M. Said, Sept. 6, 1951 (dec. 2002); children: Samiha, Saad. DSc Tech., ETH Zurich, Switzerland, 1950; PhD, Imperial Coll., London, 1952; DSc, U. London, 1967; BSc with honors, Cairo U., 1946; DSc, U. Alexandria (Arab Republic of Egypt), 1963. Lectr. Alexandria U., 1952-58, asst. prof., 1958-64, prof. organic chemistry, 1964-71; prof. chemistry Mich. Tech. U., Houghton, 1971-74, head dept. chemistry and chem. engring., 1974-80, pres. prof. chemistry, 1980-84; Isbell prof. chemistry The Am. U., Washington, 1984-93, Isbell prof. chemistry emeritus, 1993—. Mem. editorial bd. Carbohydrate Rsch., 1966-92; contbr. over 170 articles on carbohydrates and medicinal chemistry to profl. jours.; author 15 books including Carbohydrate Chemistry: Monosaccharides and their Oligomers, Synthetic Methods for Carbohydrates, Anthracycline Antibiotics; patentee in field. Fulbright scholar U.S. Dept. State, Ohio State U., Columbus, 1963-64; recipient Phys. Sci. award Washington Acad. Sci., 1992. Mem. AAAS, Am. Chem. Soc. (chmn. carbonhydrate div. 1984-85, Melville L. Wolfrom award 1989), Sigma Xi. Achievements include discovery of a lost Greek manuscript by Zosimos (300 A.D.) translated to Arabic in a twelveth century Alchemy book (donated to the Libr. of Congress). Home: 4948 Sentinel Dr Apt 101 Bethesda MD 20816-3586 Office: Am U Dept Chemistry Beeghly Bldg 4400 Massachusetts Ave NW Washington DC 20016-8001 Personal E-mail: helk@erols.com. *One reason why many students stop asking questions in class is that they do not get satisfying answers.*

ELKIES, NOAM D., mathematics professor; b. 1966; BA summa cum laude in Math. and Music, Columbia U., 1985; MA in Math., PhD in Math., Harvard U., 1987. Jr. fellow Harvard U., Cambridge, Mass., 1987-90, assoc. prof. math, John L. Loeb prof. Natural Scis., 1990-93, prof. math, 1993—. Cons. Bell Labs, 1991, Inst. Def. Analysis, 1986— Recipient W.O. Baker award for Initiatives in Rsch., NAS, 1991, Prix Peccot, Coll. de France, 1992; named Presdl. Young Investigator, 1991. Office: Harvard U Sci Bldg/Dept Math 1 Oxford St Cambridge MA 02138-2901

ELKIN, JUDITH, lawyer; b. NYC, Jan. 1, 1956; BA with honors in Am. History, summa cum laude, SUNY at Binghamton, 1978; JD cum laude, U. Wis., 1981. Bar: Wis. 1981, Tex. 1982, NY 2004, admitted to practice: Tex. Supreme Ct., US Supreme Ct., US Ct. Appeals (5th Cir.), US Ct. Appeals (6th Cir.), US Ct. Appeals (10th Cir.), US Ct. Appeals (11th Cir.), US Dist. Ct. (No. Dist.) Tex., US Dist. Ct. (So. Dist.) Tex., US Dist. Ct. (Ea. Dist.) Tex., US Dist. Ct. (We. Dist.) Tex. Ptnr., Bus. Reorganization & Bankruptcy Practice Group Haynes and Boone LLP, Dallas, co-chair, Fin. Sect. Spkr. in field. Bd. dir., exec. bd., sec. Dallas Zoological Soc., 1998—2004. Mem.: Internat. Women's Insolvency and Restructuring Confederation (IWIRC) (sec./trea. 2002—06), COMBAR (Hon. N. Am. Mem., Comml. Bar Assn. United Kingdom), Am. Bankruptcy Inst., Internat. Bar Assn. (com. J, Internat. Insolvency), ABA (cohmn. bankruptcy and insolvency litig. com., Litig. Sect. 1997—2001, bus. bankruptcy com., Bus. Law Sect.), Phi Beta Kappa. Office: Haynes and Boone LLP 399 Park Ave New York NY 10022 Office Phone: 212-659-4968. Office Fax: 212-884-8228. Business E-Mail: judith.elkin@haynesboone.com.

ELKIN, MICHAEL S., lawyer; b. Richmond, Va., May 18, 1957; Attended, L'Université de la Sorbonne, Paris, 1977, L'Université de Tours, 1978; AB, Rutgers U., 1979, MSW, 1981; JD, Bklyn. Law Sch., 1984. Bar: NY 1985, NJ 1985. Ptnr., comml. litig. dept. Thelen Reid & Priest LLP, NYC. Exec. comments editor Bklyn. Jour. of Internat. Law. Mem.: French-Am. C. of C., Assn. Bar City NY (sec. internat. trade com. 1988—90, arbitration & alternative dispute resolution com. 1992—95), Paris-Am. Club. Fluent in French. Office: Thelen Reid & Priest LLP 875 Third Ave New York NY 10022-2001 Office Phone: 212-603-6510. Office Fax: 212-603-2001. Business E-Mail: melkin@thelenreid.com.

ELKIND, ARTHUR H., physician; b. N.Y.C., Oct. 28, 1932; s. Samuel and Marian (Tobias) E.;m. Arlene R. Hirsch, July 3, 1955; children: Stephanie R., Melissa A., Mitchell S. BA, Columbia Coll., 1953; MD, SUNY, 1957. Diplomate Am. Bd. Internal Medicine. Med. intern Maimonides Hosp., Bklyn., 1957-58, med. resident, 1958-59, Montefiore Hosp., Bronx, 1959-61, NIH fellow in renal disease, 1961-62; dir. Montefiore Headache Unit, Bronx, N.Y., 1973-78, Elkind Headache Ctr., Mt. Vernon, N.Y., 1978—. V.p. Nat. Headache Found., Chgo., 1994, pres., 2005—. Author: Handbook of Headache Disorders, 1st edit., 1993, 2nd edit., 1994. Pres. Nat. Headache Found., Chgo. Jewish. Office: Elkind Headache Ctr 12 N 7th Ave Mount Vernon NY 10550-2026 Office Phone: 914-667-2230.

ELKIND, DAVID, psychology professor; b. Detroit, Mar. 11, 1931; s. Peter and Bessie (Nelson) E.; children: Paul Steven, Robert Edward, Eric Allen. BA, UCLA, 1952, PhD, 1955; DSc (hon.), R.I. Coll., 1987; DHL (hon.), Mitchell Coll., 2000. Diplomate: Am. Bd. Profl. Examiners in Psychology. Research asst. to David Rapaport, Austen Riggs Ctr., Stockbridge, Mass., 1956-57; staff psychologist Beth Israel Hosp., Boston, 1957-59; asst. prof. Wheaton Coll., Norton, Mass., 1959-61; asst. prof. med. psychology U. Calif. Med. Sch., Los Angeles, 1961-62; assoc. prof., dir. Child Study Ctr., U. Denver, 1962-66; prof., dir. grad. tng. in developmental psychology, dept. psychology U. Rochester, N.Y., 1966-78; chmn. Eliot Pearson dept. child devel. Tufts U., Medford, Mass., 1978-83; prof. child devel. sr. resident scholar Lincoln Filene Ctr. Eliot Pearson dept. child study Tufts U., Medford, Mass.; research dir. World of Inquiry Evaluation-NSF, 1970; project dir. Tng. of Early Childhood Specialists, U.S. Office Edn., 1970; psychol. cons. VA, 1962-74, Rochester Mental Health Center, 1966-74, Rochester Family Ct., 1967-73; headmaster Mt. Hope Sch., Rochester, 1974-77. Seamus Heany lectr. U. Coll., Dublin, 2000; co-host Lifetime TV series "Kids These Days". Author: (with H.J. Flavell) Studies in Cognitive Development, 1969, Children and Adolescents, 1974, A Sympathetic Understanding of the Child, 1974, (with I. Weiner) Child Development: A Core Approach, 1972, (with others) Psychology: An Introduction, 1973, Child Development and Education, 1976, (with D. Hetzel) Readings in Human Development: Contemporary Perspectives, (with I. Weiner) Development of the Child, 1978, The Child's Reality: Three Developmental Themes, 1978, The Child and Society, 1979, The Hurried Child, 1981, All Grown Up and No Place to Go, 1984, Miseducation: Preschoolers at Risk, 1987, Grandparenting: Understanding Today's Children, 1988; editor: Perspectives in Early Childhood Education, 1991, Parenting Your Teenager in the Nineties, 1993, Images of the Young Child, 1993, Understanding Your Child, 1994, A Sympathetic Understanding of the Child Birth to Sixteen, 1994, Ties that Stress: The New Family Imbalance, 1994, Reinventing Childhood, 1998. Recipient Great Friends to Kids award Assn. Youth Mus., 2001, Dale Richmond award Child and Adolescent Divsn. Am. Acad. Pediat.; NSF Sr. Postdoctoral fellow Geneva, 1964-65. Fellow Am. Psychol. Assn. (recipient Nicholas Hobbs Award div. 26), AAAS, Nat. Assn. Edn. of Young Children (pres. 1986-88). Home: 7 Lloyd Ln East Sandwich MA 02537-1225 Office: Tufts U Dept Child Devel Medford MA 02155 E-mail: delkind@emerald.tufts.edu.

ELKINS, ALFRED DAVID, insurance company executive; b. NYC, Sept. 16, 1946; s. Nathaniel and Emily Elkins; m. Ethel Lehman, Sept. 24, 1978. AB, Herbert H. Lehman Coll., 1969. Corp. proofreader Mut. of Am., N.Y.C., 1985-96, documents file adminstr., 1996—. Recipient Golden Poet Trophy, World of Poetry, 1991, Editor's Choice award, Nat. Libr. Poetry, 1994, Internat. Libr. Poetry, 2004. Mem.: Internat. Soc. Poets, Acad. Am. Poets, Poetry Soc. Am., Am. Hist. Assn. Avocations: reading and writing poetry, music. Home: 2145 Matthews Ave Bronx NY 10462-2028

ELKINS, CYNTHIA JANE, artist, educator; b. Charleston, W.Va., Apr. 30, 1962; d. Denver Boy and Frances Ella Elkins; 1 child, Adain Joseph Christopher. BFA, Colo. State U., 1989. Cert. tchr. Colo. Tchr. art Estes Park (Colo.) Elem. and Intermediate Schs., 1989—2002; specialist art instrn. Eagle Rock Sch. and Profl. Devel. Ctr., Estes Park, 2002—. Actor: (plays) locally. Mem.: Nat. Art Edn. Assn., Colo. Art Edn. Assn. (presenter), Cultural Arts Estes Pk. Avocations: painting, stained glass artist, quilting, acting. Home: PO Box 776 Estes Park CO 80517

ELKINS, DAN, small business owner, educator; b. Bisbee, Ariz., Jan. 19, 1947; AA, Cochise Coll., 1967; BA, Lowell State Coll., 1975; MBA, Lowell U., 1980. Cert. secondary and bilingual edn. tchr. Mass. Seaman USN, 1967, commd. lt. jr. grade, 1979, advanced through grades to lt. comdr., 1986, res. intelligence program officer Naval Air Facility Detroit Mt. Clemens, Mich., 1980-83, staff officer hqrs. U.S. So. Command Quarry Heights, Panama, 1984-87, manpower officer hqrs. Naval Intelligence Command Washington, 1987-90, instr. Joint Mil. Intelligence Tng. Ctr., 1990-94; ret., 1994; grad. asst. Lowell (Mass.) U., 1979-80; fin. analyst Simplex Time Recorder Co., Gardner, Mass., 1980; proprietor DWE Enterprises, Alexandria, Va., 1995—. Dir. DWE Inst., Alexandria, 1998—; cons. Cmty. Mgmt. Staff, Washington, 1996-97, Hdqs. U.S. Naval Security Group Command, Ft. Meade, Md., 2000, Litton TASC, Rosslyn, Va., 1997-98, MITRE Corp., Vienna, Va., 1999. Author: ref. manuals. Vol. tutor Draper Elem. Sch., Washington, 1988—. Recipient Exemplary Svc. award DC Pub. Schs., 1992; named Instr. of Quarter Def. Intelligence Coll., 1991. Mem. Naval Res. Assn. (life), Lowell U. Alumni Assn. (chmn. fin. com. 1980), U. Mass. Lowell Alumni Assn. Avocations: tennis, crossword puzzles, chess, bowling. Office: DWE Enterprises PO Box 4514 Alexandria VA 22303-0514

ELKINS, FRANCIS CLARK, historian, educator, director; b. Scranton, Ark., Feb. 24, 1923; s. Frank and Auby (Moore) E.; m. Norma Trice, Aug. 18, 1946; 1 dau., Annette. BA, U. Cen. Ark., 1943; MA, U. Ark., 1947; PhD, Syracuse U., 1953; postdoctoral, U. Minn., 1956. From instr. to prof., chmn. div. social sci. Henderson State U., Arkadelphia, Ark., 1946-61; pres. Chadron (Nebr.) State Coll., 1961-67, N.E. Mo. State Coll., Kirksville, 1967-69; coordinator Univ. Coll., Ark State U., 1969-70, v.p. instrn., 1970-78, v.p. univ. rels., 1979-80; v.p. univ. rels. and devel. No. Ariz. U., Flagstaff, 1980—88, prof. history, 1980-88, president's coord. univ. rels., 1983-88. Edn. cons., 1988—; mem. exec. com. Rocky Mountain Edn. Lab., 1965-67; examiner North Cen. Assn. Colls. and Schs.; examiner, cons. Nat. Council Accreditation Tchr. Edn., chmn. visitation and appraisal com., 1963-68; mem. Nebr. Ednl. TV Council Higher Edn., 1966-67, Ark. Council Econ. Edn., 1970-81. Mem. adv. coun. Mo. 4-H Found., 1968-69; mem. Ark Adv. Coun. on Career Edn.; bd. dirs. United Way, 1980-88. Served with USAAF, 1943-45. Decorated D.F.C., Air medal with four oak leaf clusters, Unit citation with 1 star; recipient John Vaughn Excellence in Edn. award, North Ctrl. Assn. Colls. and Schs. Commn. on Schs., 1988, Disting. Svc. award, Chadron (Nebr.) State Coll., 1989. Mem. NEA (life), Am. Assn. Colls. for Tchr. Edn. (dir. 1968-71, state liaison rep. 1974-77), Assn. Orgns. Tchr. Edn. (adv. coun.), Ark. Hist. Assn., Ark. Edn. Assn. (life), Ark. Assn. Colls. for Tchr. Edn. (charter pres. 1973-75), Flagstaff C. of C. (dir. 1980-88), Craighead County Hist. Assn. (life), Elks, Rotary Internat. (Paul Harris fellow), Phi Delta Kappa, Kappa Delta Pi, Phi Alpha Theta, Alpha Chi, Phi Kappa Phi, Sigma Tau Gamma, Sigma Nu. Methodist. Home and Office: 3004 Hillridge Cv Jonesboro AR 72401-5937 Office Phone: 870-932-5651.

ELKINS, GLEN RAY, retired diversified financial services company executive; b. Winnsboro, La., May 23, 1933; s. Ceicel Herbert and Edna Mae (Lewallen) E.; m. Irene Kay Hildebrand, Aug. 25, 1951 (div. 1990); children: Steven Breen, Douglas Charles, Karen Anne, Michael Glen; m. Diane Hodgson, Mar. 2, 1992. AA in Indsl. Mgmt., Coll. San Mateo, 1958. Successively mgr. prodn. control, mgr. logistics, plant mgr., asst. v.p. ops. Aircraft Engring. and Maintenance Co., 1957-64; from mgr. field ops. to pres. Internat. Atlas Svc. Co., Princeton, NJ, 1964-85; sr. v.p. Atlas Corp., Princeton, NJ; chmn., CEO, dir. Global Assoc., 1973-85; pres. Global Assoc. Internat. Ltd., 1975-84; pres., CEO Triad Am. Svc. Corp., 1985-2000; pres. Pacific Mgmt. Svc. Corp., TASC Enterprises Inc., dba, Gottschall Engraving Co., 1993-2000; ret., 2000. Area chmn. Easter Seals drive, 1974; bd. dirs. Utah Children's Mus. Served with USN, 1950—54. Mem. Nat. Mgmt. Assn., Electronic Industries Assn., Lakeview Club, Willow Creek Country Club (past pres.). Home: 1445 Harvard Ave Salt Lake City UT 84105-1917 Personal E-mail: grelkinsut@msn.com.

ELKINS, JAMES ANDERSON, JR., banker, director; b. Galveston, Tex., Mar. 24, 1919; s. James Anderson and Isabel (Mitchell) E.; m. Margaret Wiess, Nov. 24, 1945; children— Elise, James Anderson III, Leslie K. BA, Princeton U., 1941. With First City Nat. Bank, Houston, 1941—, v.p., 1946-50, pres. then chmn. bd., 1950-82; dir. First City Bancorp., Houston, 1982-88. Bd. dirs. Central Houston Inc. Bd. dirs. Houston Grand Opera; trustee Tex. Children's Hosp., Tex. Med. Ctr., 1991; chmn. bd. trustees Baylor Coll. Medicine, 1970—; trustee Menil Found.; mem. vestry Christ Ch. Cathedral. Episcopalian. Address: 1001 Fannin St Ste 1166 Houston TX 77002-6708 Office Phone: 713-652-2020.

ELKINS, JAMES ANDERSON, III, financial consultant; b. Houston, May 21, 1952; s. James Anderson Jr. and Margaret K. (Wiess) E.; m. Mary Virginia Arnold, Dec. 8, 1984; children: Margaret Wiess, James Anderson IV, Buck Arnold, John Caldwell, Harry Carothers, Samuel Hill, Lucy Gray. BA, Princeton U., 1974; MBA, U. Tex., 1976. Asst. treas. Morgan Guaranty Trust Co., N.Y.C., 1976-79; exec. v.p. First City Tex., Houston, 1979-93; chmn. Houston Trust Co., 1994—. Bd. govs. Rice U., Houston, 1982—; chmn. Tex. Children's Hosp., Houston, 1997—, trustee, 1989—; trustee Children's Mus., Houston, 1988—, Houston Mus. Natural Sci., 1993—, Houston Zoo Inc., 1993—, Baylor Coll. Medicine, 2001—, The Meth. Hosp., Houston, Tex., 2003—, Houston Police Found., 2005; bd. advisors U. Tex. Health Sci. Ctr., Houston, 1990; vice chmn. Salvation Army, 1990—; pres. Houston Parks Bd. Mem. Am. Bankers Assn. (exec. bd. corp. council), Houston Club, Tex. Bankers Assn., Forum Club. Methodist. Office: Houston Trust Co 1001 Fannin St Ste 700 Houston TX 77002-6707

ELKINS, KATHERINE MARIE, elementary school educator; b. Denver, Mo., Apr. 13, 1942; d. Eugene Forrest and Erma Louise (Wasson) Huber; m. Robert Wayne Ferguson, May 15, 1965 (dec. Apr. 1977); 1 child, Michael Harve. BS in Edn., Mo. Western Coll., 1972; MEd, Kans. State U., 1985. Cert. tchr., Mo., Kans. Proofreader St. Joseph (Mo.) News Press, 1961-68; tchr. spl. edn. North Platte Sch. Dist., Camden Point, Mo., 1972-75; tchr. Troy (Kans.) Elem. Sch., 1981-85, Unified Sch. Dist. 406, Wathena, Kans., 1985—. Mem. Kans. Reading Assn. (v.p., pres. 1984-88), Wathena Edn. Assn. (sec. 1986-88, 90-91), VFW Aux., Delta Kappa Gamma (sec. 1988-90). Mem. Christian Ch. (Disciples Of Christ). Avocations: reading, ceramics, gardening, travel. Home: PO Box 65 Troy KS 66087-0065 Office: Unified Sch Dist 406 705 Jessie Wathena KS 66090

ELKINS, KEN JOE, retired broadcast executive; b. Prenter, W.Va., Oct. 12, 1937; s. Ernest Eugene Elkins and Gay (Avis) Dodrill; married; children: James, Diana. Student, Nebr. U., 1966-69. Engr. Sta. KETV-TV, Omaha, 1960-67, asst. chief engr., 1967-70, ops. mgr., nat. sales, gen. sales mgr., 1972-75, gen. mgr., 1975-80; chief engr. Sta. KOUB-TV, Dubuque, Iowa, 1970-71, gen. mgr., 1971-72, Sta. KSDK-TV, St. Louis, 1980-81; v.p., CEO Pulitzer Broadcasting Co., St. Louis, 1981-84, pres., CEO, 1984-99; ret., 1999. Bd. dirs. Commerce Bank St. Louis, Maximum Svc. Telecasters, Washington; chmn. BMI; pres. Nebr. Broadcasters, Omaha, 1979-80; chmn. NBC Affiliate Bd. Govs. Bd. dirs. BJC Health Sys. With USAF, 1957-61. Inducted into Nebr. Broadcasters Hall of Fame, 1990. Mem. Nat. Assn. Broadcasters (1st amendment com. Washington chpt. 1986-91, 1st amendment com. 1986, bd. dirs.), Found. Broadcasters Hall of Fame (bd. dirs., trustee 1990), TV Operators Caucus, Algonquin Club. Avocations: golf, water sports. Home: 720 Twin Fawns Dr Saint Louis MO 63131-4722 Personal E-mail: k_elkins@sbcglobal.net.

ELKINS, ROBERT N., association executive; b. N.Y.C., June 5, 1943; s. Jacob B. and Lee (Marcus) E.; m. Mary Beth Ackerley (div. 1991). BA, U. Pa., 1965; MD, SUNY, N.Y.C., 1975. Gen. ptnr. Hampstead (N.H.) Hosp. Physician Group, 1976-79; pres. Cen. Md. Health Systems, Inc., 1978-80; gen. ptnr., co-founder Continental Care Group, Md., 1980-86; chmn., chief exec. officer Integrated Health Svcs., Inc., Owings Mills, Md., 1986—2000. Active Associated Jewish Charities, Balt. Recipient Entrepreneur of Yr. award Ernst & Young Inc. Mag., Merrill Lynch, 1991. Mem. Am. Entrepreneurs for Econ. Growth (co-chair), Caves Valley Club.

ELKINS, STANLEY MAURICE, historian, educator; b. Boston, Apr. 27, 1925; s. Frank and Frances (Reiner) E.; m. Dorothy Adele Lamken, June 22, 1947; children: Susan Roselyn, Robert Joel, Barbara Marion, Sara Ann. AB, Harvard, 1949; MA, Columbia, 1951, PhD, 1959. Tchr. Fieldston Sch., N.Y.C., 1951-54; asst. prof. history U. Chgo., 1955-60; faculty Smith Coll., Northampton, Mass., 1960—, prof. history, 1964-69, Sydenham Clark Parsons prof. history, 1969—94; fellow Inst. for Advanced Study, 1970-71, 76-77. Author: Slavery: A Problem in American Institutional and Intellectual Life, 1959, The Age of Federalism, 1993 (Bancroft prize Soc. Cin. Book Prize 1995). Served with AUS, 1943-46. Social Sci. Research Council fellow, 1963-64; Rockefeller fellow, 1954-55; Guggenheim fellow, 1976-77 Mem. Orgn. Am. Historians, Am. Hist. Assn., Soc. of Am. Historians. Home: 126 Vernon St Northampton MA 01060-2905 E-mail: s-elkins@mediaone.net.

ELKINS-ELLIOTT, KAY, law educator; b. Dallas, Nov. 21, 1938; d. William Hardin and Maxidine (Sadler) E.; m. Michael Gail Hodgson, July 7, 1960 (div. Dec. 1974); children: Michael Brett, Ashley Kim, Samantha; m. Frank Wallace Elliott, Aug. 15, 1983. AA with honors, Stephens Coll., 1958; JD, U. Okla., 1964; LLM, So. Meth. U., 1984; MA, U. Tex., Dallas, 1990. Bar: Okla. 1964, Tex. 1982, U.S. Dist. Ct. (no. dist.) Tex. 1982, U.S. Supreme Ct. 1984, U.S. Dist. Ct. (we. dist.) Okla. 1989. Assoc. Ben Hatcher and Assocs., Oklahoma City, 1964-65; dir., gen. counsel Take-A-Tour Swaziland, Mbabane, Swaziland, 1966-74; atty. Dept. Health and Human Svcs., Dallas, 1975-80; hearing officer EEOC, Dallas, 1980-84; atty. pvt. practice, Dallas, 1984-92; vis. assoc. prof. Tex. Wesleyan U. Sch. Law, Dallas, 1992-95; arbitrator State Farm Ins., Dallas, 1991-96; assoc. Dale O'Neal Civil Mediators, Ft. Worth. Adj. prof. Wesleyan U. Sch. Law, 1995—, coach nat. ABA champion negotiation team, 1998; mediator pvt. practice, Dallas, Ft. Worth, Granbury, 1991—; coord. cert. in conflict resolution program Tex. Woman's U., 1996—; coach internat. champion online dispute resolution competition, 2002; cons. in field. Author: (with others) West Texas Practice, 1995; (with Frank Elliott) State Bar of Texas ADR Handbook, 2003. Dir. diversity tng. State Bar Tex. 9/11 project; founder, dir. and pres. Ala. Legal Reform Found., 2005—; registered lobbyist Ala., 2005—. Mem. ABA (negotiation and tng. coms., alternative dispute resolution sect.), Tex. Bar Assn. (ADR sect. coun. mem. 1998-2001, chair publs. com.), Tex. Bar Found., Tex. Initiatives for Mediation in Edn. (founder, planning com. 1993-95), Assn. for Conflict Resolution (pres. Dallas region 1995-97), Tex. Mediator Credentialing Assn. (bd. dir., disting. mediator), Tex. Assn. Mediators, Dallas Bar Assn. (coun. mem. 1993-94), Inst. for Responsible Dispute Resolution (charter), Toastmasters (v.p. 1993-94, pres. 1996-97). Avocations: singing, public speaking. Home: 1609 Sunset Terrace Fort Worth TX 76102 Personal E-mail: k4mede8@swbell.net.

ELKISS, MITCHELL LAWRENCE, neurologist; b. Detroit, Feb. 12, 1950; s. Stanley and Audrey Elkiss; m. Sally Rosenberg, May 3, 1981; children: Elizabeth Rose, Isaac Joseph. BS, U. Mich., 1973; DO, Mich. State U., 1978. Diplomate Am. Bd. Neurology, cert. spl. proficiency osteo. manipulative medicie. Intern Botsford Gen. Hosp., Farmington Hills, Mich., 1978—79, resident in neurology, 1979—82; neurologist Assocs. in Neurology, Farmington Hills, 1982—. Co-author: Foundations of Osteopathic Medicine, 1997. Fellow: Am. Acad. Med. Acupuncture, Am. Coll. Neurology. Office: Assocs in Neurology 27555 Middlebelt Farmington MI 48334

ELKOWITZ, LLOYD KENT, dental anesthesiologist, dentist, pharmacist; b. Bklyn., Jan. 26, 1936; s. Paul and Lillian (Applebaum) E.; m. Deanna A. Weinger; children: Sheryl, Andrew, Marc. BS in Pharmacy, Columbia U., 1956; DDS, Case Western Res. U., 1960, postgrad., 1961. Diplomate Am. Dental Bd. Anesthesiology, Am. Soc. Dentist Anesthesiologists. Resident in anesthesiology U. Ctr. Hosp, Pitts., 1961, fellow in anesthesiology, 1966; anesthesiologist Walson Army Hosp., Fort Dix, N.J., 1962-64; pvt. practice Great Neck, N.Y., 1964—. Dir. divsn. dental anesthesiology dept. dentistry Nassau County Med. Ctr., East Meadow, L.I., 1975—; chmn. dept. dental anesthesiology Flushing (N.Y.) Hosp. Med. Ctr., 1989-95; pres. dental adv. coun. Adelphi U., Tufts U., Garden City, N.y., 1986—; adj. prof. dental biology Adelphi U., 1982—. Trustee Kings Point (N.Y.) Civic Assn., 1978-95. Capt. U.S. Army, 1962-64. Recipient Callahan Meml. award Ohio State Dental Assn., 1960. Fellow Am. Coll. Dentists, Am. Dental Soc. Anesthesiology, Acad. Gen. Dentistry (diplomate), Am. Soc. Dentist Anesthesiologists, Am. Soc. for Advancement of Anesthesia in Dentistry (pres. 1995-2000), Internat. Coll. Dentists; mem. ADA, Am. Pharm. Assn., N.Y. State Dental Assn., Queens Dental Assn., Queens County Dental Soc. (trustee 1995), Internat. Anesthesia Rsch. Soc., Am. Soc. Dentistry for Children, Queens Inst. for Continuing Dental Edn. (charter), Alpha Zeta Omega, Alpha Omega, Alpha Epsilon Delta. Avocations: piano, skiing, sailing, boating, tennis. Office: 107 Northern Blvd Great Neck NY 11021-4309 Office Phone: 516-829-3310.

ELKUS, RICHARD J., JR., electronics company executive; b. San Francisco, Feb. 25, 1935; s. Richard J. and Ruth (Kahn) E.; m. Helen Morrison, Aug. 17, 1956; children: Miriam Lyster, Richard M., Kevin J. BA, Stanford U., 1957; MBA, Dartmouth Coll., 1959. Prodn. control mgr. Ampex Corp., Redwood City, Calif., 1959-64, asst. to pres., 1968-71, mem. ops. bd., 1969-71, gen. mgr. ednl. and indsl. products divsn., 1969-72; pres., CEO, dir. Eyrle Co., Santa Clara, Calif., 1964-67; gen. mgr. Gould Med. systems, Santa Clara, Calif., 1973-74; exec. v.p., gen. mgr. Geometrics, Inc., Sunnyvale, Calif., 1974-80. Bd. dirs., chmn. bd. Integrated Systems, Inc., Santa Clara, 1985-92; bd. dirs. KLA-Tencor, San Jose, Calif., Lam Rsch., Fremont, Calif., SOPRA, Paris, Virage Logic, Fremont, Calif.; CEO Voyan Tech., Santa Clara. Mem. coun. on competitiveness, chmn. panel High Defination products and systems, NSF; mem. adv. bd. Ctr. Strategic and Internat. Studies Inst., 1990-96, Sch. Engring., Ga. Inst. Tech., 1996-98. Capt. USAR, 1957-65; bd. dirs. Nat. Sci. and Tech. Medals Found.; turstee Palo Alto Med. Found., Scripps Rsch. Ints.; pres. bd. sci. and innovation U. Calif. Mem. Am. Mgmt. Assn. (pres.'s coun.), Am. Electronics Assn. (bd. dirs., co-chmn. task force high resolutin systems), Electronics Assn. Calif. (vice chmn. nat. medal tech. nomination evaluation com. 1992-94, chmn. 1994-97), Econ. Strategy Inst. (adv. bd.), Foothills Tennis and Swim Club (Palo Alto, Calif.), Menlo Circus Club (Atherton, Calif.). Office: Voyan Tech 2700 Augustine Dr # 145 Santa Clara CA 95054

ELL, TRAVIS EUGENE, electronics engineer; b. Minot, N.D., Oct. 3, 1951; s. Walter Joseph and Irene Dorthy (Ruby) E.; m. Deborah LouAnn Sorensen, Aug. 23, 1975 (div. June 1985); children: Joshua Michael, Jacob Matthew, John Thadeus; m. Sonia Ovsep Yazgulian. BSEE, N.D. State U., 1974, MSEE, 1978. Tchg. asst. N.D. State U., Fargo, 1974-77; servo engr. IBM Corp., Rochester, Minn., 1977-94; engring. mgr. Micropolis Corp., Chatsworth, Calif., 1994-96; servo engr. Lumonics Corp., Oxnard, Calif., 1996-97, Seagate Tech., Inc., Moorpark, Calif., 1997—. Recipient IBM Market-Driven Quality award, 1993. Mem. IEEE (chmn. N.D. State U. student br. 1993-94),

Sigma Phi Delta (sec. 1993-94). Unitarian-Universalist. Achievements include patent for data disk drive velocity estimator. Home: 2609 Dante Ct Austin TX 78748 Office: Oak Technology 7000 W William Connor Dr Bldg One Ste 120 Austin TX 78735 E-mail: t.e.ell@att.net.

ELLEBY, GAIL, management consultant; b. Seattle, Sept. 15, 1949; d. William Lee and Marie (Davis) E.; 1 child, Courtney Champion. BA, U. Wash., 1973, MPA, 1975; MSA in Sports Adminstrn., Ohio U., 1980. Cert. nat. ofcl. U.S. Am. track and field. Adminstrn. specialist Mayor's Office, City of Seattle, 1986-87; adminstrv. asst. Seattle 1990 Goodwill Games, 1987-88; adminstr. Met. Enrichment Ctr., San Francisco, 1988-90; assoc. v.p. United Way of the Bay Area, San Francisco, 1990-93; cons., pres. Gail Elleby & Assocs., Daly City, Calif., 1993—. Dir. Even Start San Francisco Unified Sch. Dist., 1997-98, mgmt. and tng. specialist Western Ky. U., 1998—. Active San Mateo County Child Care Coun., 1992-97, San Mateo County Commn. on Status of Women, 1994-98; adv. bd. United Way Met. Atlanta Dekalb. Mem. SAMCEDA, Cons. Group (founder). Mem. Ch. of Christ. Avocations: music, sports, reading, cooking, collecting dolls. Home: 111 Timber Springs Way Lawrenceville GA 30043 Office Phone: 770-339-0103. Personal E-mail: gewku@aol.com.

ELLEDGE, GLENNA ELLEN TUELL, journalist; b. Welch, W.Va., Aug. 2, 1931; d. William Jackson and Ellen Annabelle (Jackson) Tuell; div.; children: Carl Gene, Jerry Elwood, Ernest Everett. Certificate in comptometer, Capital City Coll., 1949; student, Wytheville (Va.) C.C., S.W. Va. C.C., Richlands, Va. Intermont Coll. Accounts clk. Household Fin. Corp., Charleston, W.Va., 1951-52; with incest divsn. FBI, Washington, 1953; asst. bookkeeper and acctg. clk. Ft. McNair Officers Open Mess, Washington, 1953-54; stat. analyst Office Strategic Intelligence, Washington, 1954-55; stock control 836th Supply Squadron, Langley AFB, Va., 1957-59; acct., office asst. Comml. Contracting, Troy, Mich., 1970-71; office svcs. asst. Southwestern State Hosp., Marion, Va., 1971-95; staff writer, photographer Saltville (Va.) Progress, 1977-81, Saltville News-Messenger, 1981-93, Family Cmty. Newspapers, Marion, 1993-2000, Saltville Progress, 2000—. Fire brigade Southwestern State Hosp., Marion, 1986-93, instr. CPR, 1986-89, adv. bd., 1986-93. Editor, keyboardist Grandma's Favorite Recipes, 2000, Lucy's Secret, 2001-02. Vol. Air Force Family Svcs., 1956-69, den mother Cub. Scouts Am., 1962-67; bd. dirs. Smyth County Crisis Ctr., Marion, 1971-81; sec., pres. Smyth Coun. Santa's Elves, Marion, 1974-78, Family Oriented Group Home parent Group Home Juveniles 28th Juvenile Domestic Rels. Ct., Abingdon, Va., 1978-81; EMT, instr. Am. Heart Assn., Smyth, Wise, Grayson Counties, 1986-89; mem. and former sunday sch. tchr., supr. Laural Springs United Meth. Ch.; chairperson Mayor's promotional com., Marion, 1994-95; mem. Surry County (N.C.) Hist. Soc., Grayson County (Va.) Hist. Soc. Mem. Nat. Fedn. Press Women (del. 1978, awards), Va. Press Women (del. 1978, awards), Va. Press Assn. (awards), Nat. Press Assn., Nat. Soc. DAR, Nat. Soc. Col. Dames XVII Century. Jamestowne Soc. Republican. Avocations: writing, reading, travel. Office: PO Box 901 Marion VA 24354-0901 Personal E-mail: ellglen@hotmail.com.

ELLEDGE, STEPHEN JOSEPH, medical educator; b. Paris, Ill., Aug. 7, 1956; s. Joseph and Sarah (Greco) E.; m. Mitzi Kuroda. BS in Chemistry, U. Ill., 1978; PhD, MIT, 1983. Asst. prof. Baylor Coll. of Medicine, Houston, 1989-93, assoc. prof., 1993-96, asst. investigator, 1993-96, H. Hughes investigator, 1996—, prof., 1995—. Office: Baylor Coll Medicine One Baylor Plaza T307 Houston TX 77030

ELLEGARD, ROY WHITNEY, appraiser; b. Hartford, Conn., Sept. 16, 1957; s. Roy Taylor and Jeanette (Whitney) E.; m. Bernadette O'Brien, May 22, 1999. BA in Econs., U. Richmond, 1980. Appraiser Stone & Webster, Inc., N.Y.C., 1980-82; cons. Arthur Andersen & Co., N.Y.C., 1983; sr. cons. Arthur D. Little, Inc., Metro Park, N.J., 1984-87; nat. dir. machinery and equipment valuation advisors Ernst & Young LLP, N.Y.C., 1987-98; mng. dir. corp. value consulting Pricewater House Coopers LLP, 1998—2001, Standard & Poor's, 2001—03; ptnr. Ernst & Young, N.Y.C., NY. Mem. Am. Soc. Appraisers (sr., pres. Princeton chpt. 1992-93, 98-99), Kappa Alpha Alumni Assn. (treas. Princeton chpt. 1990-92), Princeton Club N.Y. Republican. Episcopalian. Home: 175 E 96th St Apt 8K New York NY 10128-6204 also: 211 Kent Rd Kent CT 06757 Office: Ernst & Young 5 Times Sq New York NY 10036 Office Phone: 212-773-3363. Business E-Mail: roy.ellegard@ey.com.

ELLEMAN, BARBARA, editor; b. Coloma, Wis., Oct. 20, 1934; d. Donald and Evelyn (Kissinger) Koplein; m. Don W. Elleman, Nov. 14, 1970. BS in Edn., Wis. State U., 1956; MA in Librarianship, U. Denver, 1964. Sch. libr. media specialist Port Washington (Wis.) High Sch., 1956-59, Homestead High Sch., Thiensville-Mequon, Wis., 1959-64; children's libr. Denver Pub. Libr., 1964-65; sch. libr. media specialist Cherry Creek Schs., Denver, 1965-70, Henry Clay Sch., Whitefish Bay, Wis., 1971-75; children's reviewer ALA, Chgo., 1975-82, children's editor, 1982-90, editor Book Links, 1990-96. Vis. lectr. U. Wis., 1974-75, 81-82, U. Ill., Circle Campus, 1983-85; Disting. scholar children's lit., Marquette U., 1996—; cons. H.W. Wilson Co., 1969-75; mem. Libr. Congress Adv. Com. on selection for children's books for blind and physically handicapped, 1980-88, Caldecott Calendar Com., 1986; judge The Am. Book Awards, 1982, Golden Kite, 1987, Boston Globe/Horn Book, 1990; mem. faculty Highlights for Children Writers Conf., 1985-90; mem. orgn. com. MidWest Conf. Soc. Children's Books Writers, 1974-76; chair Hans Christian Andersen Com., 1987-88; advisor Reading Rainbow, 1986-96, Ind. R.E.A.P. project, 1987-93; jury mem. VI Catalonia Premi Children's Book Exbhn., Barcelona, Spain, 1994; adv. bd. Parent's Choice, Cobblestone Publ., Georgia Pub. TV's 2000, The New Advocate mag., 20th Century Children's Writers, Encyclopedia of Children's Literature, Cooperative Children's Book Ctr., U. Wis., Madison, Riverbank Rev., 1998—, Ency. of Children's Lit., 1998—; lang. arts com. NCTE Notable Books, 1997—; spkr. in field. Author: Reading in a Media Age, 1975, 20th Century Children's Writers, 1979, rev. edit., 1984, What Else Can You Do With a Library Degree?, 1980, Popular Reading for Children, 1981, Popular Reading II, 1986, Children's Books of International Interest, 1984, Tomie dePaola, His Art and His Stories, 1999, Virginia Lee Burton: A Life in Art, 2002; contbr. articles to profl. jours. Publicity chair Internat. Bd. Books for Young People Congress, Williamsburg, Va., 1990; bd. trustees Eric Carle Mus. Picture Book Art, 2004-. Recipient Jeremiah Ludington award Ednl. Paperback Assn., 1996, Hope S. Dean award Found. Children's Lit., 1996. Mem. ALA (2000 Caldecott Com. 1999—), Soc. Children's Book Writers (mem. orgn. com. MidWest Conf. 1974-76), Internat. Bd. Books for Young People (U.S. assoc. editor Bookbird 1978-86, chair nominating com., 1985, bd. dirs. 1990-92), Children's Reading Round Table Chgo. (award 1987), Nat. Coun. Tchrs. English (bd. dirs. children's lit. assembly 1986-88, mem. editl. adv. bd. CLA bull. 1989-91, mem. using nonfiction in classroom com. 1990-96, 2000 Caldecott com., Laura I. Wilder com. 2001--). Address: 20 Bayon Dr Apt 5 South Hadley MA 01075

ELLEN, MARTIN M., financial services executive; b. Chgo., Dec. 28, 1953; BS in Acctg., U. Ill., 1975; postgrad in mgmt., Northwestern U., 1987. CPA, Ill. Auditor Price Waterhouse, Chgo., 1975-78, sr. auditor, 1978-81, mgr. auditing, 1981-84, sr. mgr. auditor, 1984; controller D&K Fin., Chgo., 1984-86, v.p. fin., 1986—. Mem. Fin. Exec. Inst., Am. Inst. CPA's, Ill. CPA Soc.

ELLENBERGER, JACK STUART, law librarian; b. Lamar, Colo., Sept. 5, 1930; s. Emmert C. and Ruby F. (Overstreet) E. BS, Georgetown U., 1957; M.L.S., Columbia U., 1959. Law libr. HEW, 1957; libr. Carter, Ledyard & Milburn, N.Y.C., 1957-60, Jones, Day, Reavis & Pogue (and predecessor firm), Cleve., 1960, Bar Assn. of D.C., Washington, 1961-63, Covington & Burling, Washington, 1963-78, Shearman & Sterling, N.Y.C., 1978-93, law libr. emeritus, 1994-95; ret., 1995. Editor: (with Mahar) Legislative History of the Securities Act of 1933 and the Securities Exchange Act of 1934, 1973. Served with USAF, 1951-54. Mem. Am. Assn. Law Libraries (pres. 1976-77, M.G. Gallagher Disting. Svc. award 1994), Spl. Libraries Assn.

ELLENBOGEN, GEORGE, poet, educator; b. Montreal, Que., Can., Nov. 19, 1934; came to U.S., 1966; s. Moses and Jenny (Borenstein) E.; m. Karia Doris Feinzig, Dec. 18, 1960 (div. 1984); children: Sara Rachel, Adam. BA, McGill U., Montreal, 1955; MA, U. Montreal, 1962; PhD, Tufts U., 1969. Mem. faculty Bentley Coll., Waltham, Mass., 1965—, prof. English, 1980—, chmn. dept., 1980-85, dir. Forum for Creative Writing, 1987—2004; poetry editor Boston Today, 1978-81. Vis. prof., writer-in-residence U. Siegen, Germany, 1996. Author: Winds of Unreason, 1957, The Night Unstones, 1971, Along the Road from Eden, 1989, The Rhinogate Poems, 1996, La Porte aux rhinos et autres poemes (bilingual edit.), 1997; Winterfischer, 2002; subject of German documentary film produced by Wolfgang Lippke George Ellenbogen: A Canadian Poet in America; contbr. numerous articles and poems to mags. and anthologies. Recipient award Karolyi Meml. Found., 1986, Va. Ctr. for Creative Arts, 1987, 92, 93, 2000, 02, 03, 04, Montalvo Assn., 1987, Whiting Found., 1994; grantee Can. Internat. Cultural Rels., 1997, Gesellschaft for Kanada Studies, 1998, Can. Dept. Fgn. Affairs, 2003, Ledig-Rowohlt Found., 2004. Mem. AAUP, MLA, Coll. English Assn., Nat. Council Tchrs. of English Home: 21 Wren St West Roxbury MA 02132-2625 Business E-Mail: gellenbogen@bentley.edu.

ELLENBOGEN, LEON, nutritionist, biochemist, retired pharmaceutical executive; b. N.Y.C., May 3, 1927; s. Martin and Bella (Zalesnick) E.; m. Roslyn Barban, June 30, 1951; children: Kenneth Alan, Richard Glen, Cheryl Sue. BS, CCNY, 1949; MS, NYU, 1951; PhD, Ind. U., 1954. Technician and med. corpsman USN, 1945-47; rsch. technician Columbia U., N.Y.C., 1949-51; teaching asst. gen. chemistry and biochemistry Ind. U., Bloomington, 1951-53; rsch. biochemist Lederle Labs., Am. Cyanamid Co., Pearl River, N.Y., 1953-59, sr. rsch. biochemist, group leader, 1959-77, chief nutritional sci., sr. assoc. dir. med. pharm. devel., 1977-95; asst. v.p. nutritional scis. Lederle Consumer Health divsn. Whitehall Robins Health Care, Am. Home Products, Madison, N.J., 1995-97; ret., 1997. Adj. prof. nutrition in medicine Cornell U. Med. Coll., 1978—; adj. prof. nutrition N.Y. Med. Coll., 1981—; adj. prof., adv. com. intrinsic factor Nat. Formulatory Com.; mem. sci. affairs com. Proprietary Assn., 1980-89. Contbr. numerous articles to profl. jours., tech. books; author, presenter abstracts and papers profl. meetings; editor Contemporary Issues in Clin. Nutrition, 1980—, guest editor vols. 2 and 12; editor Drug Nutrient Interactions, 1982-91; cons. editor Biochemistry, Jour. AMA, Am. Jour. Clin. Nutrition, Sci., The Med. Letter, Nutrition Reports Internat., Thrombosis Rsch., Jour. Medicinal Chemistry, Archives Biochem. and Biophys., Annals Internal Medicine, Jour. Biol. Chemistry, Biochem. Pharmacology. Pharmacists mate USN, 1945-47. Recipient Steuben apple for contbns. to sci. rsch. Coun. for Responsible Nutrition. Fellow Am. Soc. Nutritional Scis., N.Y. Acad. Scis. (steering com. biochem. pharmacology discussion group 1973-77); mem. Am. Heart Assn., Am. Soc. Hematology, Am. Inst. Nutrition (nomenclature com.), Am. Soc. Clin. Nutrition, Am. Soc. Biol. Chemists, Am. Soc. Pharmacology and Exptl. Therapeutics, Am. Chem. Soc. (chmn. biochem. discussion group N.Y. sect. 1959, counselor divsn. biol. labs. 1977-79), Soc. Exptl. Biology and Medicine (editor proc. 1961-62), U.S. Pharmacopeia (com. on revision 1990-95, subcom. for nonprescription drugs and nutritional supplements 1995-2000, U.S. Pharmacopia Nutrition and Electrolytes Expert Com., expert com. on rbioavailabilty and nutrient absorption of U.S. pharmacopia 2000-05), Sigma Xi, Phi Lambda Upsilon. Avocation: sports. Home: 16 Morris Dr New City NY 10956-4652 Office: Wyeth Consumer Healthcare Madison NJ 07940-0871 Office Phone: 973-660-5767. E-mail: ellenbl@wyeth.com, ellenblr@aol.com.

ELLENBOGEN-HANDELSMAN, JOAN, lawyer, accountant; b. Pitts., June 30, 1954; d. Alex and Marjory (Blons) Ellenbogen; m. George B. Handelsman, July 30, 1982; 1 child, Michelle Josephine. BBA summa cum laude, Duquesne U., 1976, JD magna cum laude, 1981. Bar: Pa. 1981, U.S. Dist. Ct. (we. dist.) Pa. 1981, U.S. Tax Ct. 1982, U.S. Supreme Ct. 1985; CPA, Pa. Mng. dir. Crawford Ellenbogen, LLC, Pitts., 1972—. Instr. U. Pitts., 1983; adj. prof. Duquesne U. Sch. Law, 1987-88, mem. adv. bds. acctg. program, masters in taxation adv. bd.; past pres. Allegheny County Bar Found.; v.p. Pitts. chpt. 1999-2000, past pres.; mem. estate planning coun. Pitts. Past bd. dirs., fin. com. Riverview Ctr. Jewish Srs., past bd. dirs. Internat. Affiliation CPA firms, Estate Planning Coun.; mem. guardianship adv. com. Jewish Family & Children's Svc.; asst. leader Brownie Troop #657; pres.-elect Exec. Women's Coun. Named one of Outstanding Young Women Am., 1984. Fellow Allegheny County Bar Assn.; mem. ABA, Am. Inst. CPA's, Pa. Bar Assn., Pa. Inst. CPA's (mem. various coms.), Allegheny County Bar Assn. (treas. 1994, mem. various coms.), Internat. Network Accts. and Auditors, Pitts. Tax Club (past pres.). Office: 640 Allenby Ave Pittsburgh PA 15218-1306 Office Phone: 412-731-1500.

ELLENBROOK, CAROLYN KAY, religious organization administrator; b. Denton, Tex., Sept. 2, 1943; d. Herman and Winnie Louise (Garrett) Baker; m. Edward Charles Ellenbrook, Jr., Apr. 13, 1968; 1 child, Margaret. A, Cameron Jr. Coll., 1963; BS in Edn., Okla. State U., 1965. Child welfare caseworker State of Okla., Lawton, 1965—68; religious edn. sec. Comanche-Cotton Bapt. Assn., Lawton, 1981—. Contbr. chapters to books Heart Call-The Call to Prayer, 1998; co-author: (book) Comanche-Cotton Baptist Association A Centennial History, 1902-2002, 2002. Area adv. City PTA, Lawton, 1977—80, mem., 1973—86; treas. Eisenhower H.S. PTA, 1984—86; pres. So. Bapt. Women's Missionary Union, Okla., 1993—98. Named Ch. Women of Yr., DAR, 2000. Mem.: Nat. So. Bapt. Sec. Orgn., Okla. So. Bapt. Sec. Orgn., So. Bapt. Assoc. Religious Educators (pres. 2002). Avocations: hiking, history, writing, travel, working with children. Home: 1603 Keystone Dr Lawton OK 73505 Office: Comanche-Cotton Baptist Assoc 2612 E Ave Lawton OK 73505 Personal E-mail: ecebrook@sirinet.net.

ELLENS, J(AY) HAROLD, philosopher, educator, psychotherapist, minister; b. McBain, Mich., July 16, 1932; s. John S. and Grace (Kortmann) E.; m. Mary Jo Lewis, Sept. 7, 1954; children: Deborah, Jackie, Dan, Beckie, Rocky, Brenda, Brett. AB, Calvin Coll., 1953; BD, Calvin Sem., 1956; ThM, Princeton Sem., 1965; PhD, Wayne State U., 1970; MDiv, Calvin Sem., 1986; MA, U. Mich., 2000, PhD, 2005. Ordained to ministry Christian Reformed Ch., 1956; ordained theologian and pastor Presbyn. Ch., 1978. Pastor Newton Christian Reformed Ch., NJ, 1961-65, North Hills Ch., Troy, Mich., 1965-68; pvt. practice psychotherapy Farmington Hills, Mich., 1967—; pastor Univ. Hills Ch., Farmington Hills, Mich., 1968-78, Westminster Presbyn. Ch., 1980-84, Erin Presbyn. Ch., 1986-88, Cherry Hill Presbyn. Ch., 1994-96, White Lake Presbyn. Ch., 1998-2000, Troy Presbyn. Ch., 2000—01, 2004—, Mt. Clemens 1st Presbyn. Ch., 2001—02, Peoples Presbyn. Ch., Milan, Mich., 2003—04. Religious broadcaster TV, weekly, 1970-74, periodically to date; lectr. humanities and classics Wayne State U., John Wesley Coll., Oakland U., 1970-90, Wayne C.C., Oakland C.C., Calvin Sem.; vis. lectr. Princeton Theol. Seminary, 1977-79; with Inst. for Antiquity and Christianity, Claremont U.; lectr. U.S. and abroad. Author: Program Format in Religious Television, 1970, Models of Religious Broadcasting, 1974, Chaplain (Major General) Gerhart W. Hyatt: An Oral History, 1977, (with others) Internat. Standard Bible Encyclopedia, 1979-89, Eternal Vigilance, 1980, God's Grace and Human Health, 1982, Life and Laughter, 1983, Psychology in Worship, 1984, (with others) Baker's Encyclopedia of Psychology, 1984, 1995, Psychotheology: Key Issues, 1986, (with others) Psychotherapy in Christian Perspective, 1987, (with others) Christian Counseling and Psychotherapy, 1987, Love, Life and Laughter, 1988, (with others) Psychology and Religion, 1988, (with others) The Church and Pastoral Care, 1988, (with others) Moral Obligation and the Military, 1988, (with others) God se genade is genoeg, 1989, (with others) Counseling and the Human Predicament, 1989, (with others) Turning Points in Pastoral Care, (with others) Christian Perspectives on Human Development, 1992, The Ancient Library of Alexandria and Early Christian Theological Development, 1993, 95, Alexander The Great and Hellenistic Culture, 1997, Human Disfunction, 1998, (with others) Humanistic Psychology, 1998, (with others) Dictionary of Pastoral Care and Counseling, 1990, (with others) The Interpretation of the Bible, 1998, Jesus as Son of Man, 2003, (with others) The Destructive Power of Religion (4 vols.), 2004, 05, (with others) God's Word for Our World, 2004, (with others) Psychology and the Bible (4 vols.), 2004, 05, (with others) Jesus as Son of Man, The Literary Character, A Progression of Images, 2004, (with others) Holy Way & Jihad, 2005, three books in Portuguese and one in Spanish; editor: CAPS Internat. Directory vols. II-V, 1976-87, Ethical Reflections, 1977, The Beauty of Holiness, 2d edit., 1985, God's Grace in Free Verse, 1987, (with others) Eerdmans Dictionary of the Bible, 2000, with others; editor in chief Jour. Psychology and Christianity, 1975-88; contbr. more than 165 articles to profl. jours. Served to col. AUS, 1956-61, ret., 1992. Created knight, Queen Juliana, The Netherlands, 1974. Mem. 23 profl. socs. including Christian Assn. Psychol. Studies (now exec. dir. emeritus), Soc. Bibl. Lit., Mil. Chaplain Assn., Ret. Officers Assn., Archeol. Inst. Am., Mil. Order World Wars. Home and Office: 26705 Farmington Rd Farmington MI 48334-4329 Office Phone: 248-231-4433. Personal E-mail: jharoldellens@juno.com. *Secular and religious communities alike tend continually to shift their focus toward some orthodoxy or other, usually in the form of according ultimate authority to an aspect of the community's traditional thought or behavior, thus imposing constraints upon the quest for growth and for truth which are not responsive to reality or authenticity or relevant and wholesome freedom. Orthodoxy is always, therefore, a form of idolatry; it is a psychological phenomenon; it is the posture of arrogance in those who see themselves as "the chosen" or the elect; it is lunge for security vs. growth; it is designed to guard against the destablizing effect of change; it is, therefore inherently imperialistic, arbitrary, propagandist, and abusive.*

ELLENTUCK, ELMER, journal editor; b. N.Y.C. s. Max and Deena (Bregman) E.; m. Beatrice Reiner, Nov. 25, 1946 (dec. Feb. 1982); m. Tara Marcus, June 28, 1985; 1 child, Daniel. BBA, CCNY, 1939; LLB, St. John's U., N.Y.C., 1948. Bar: N.Y. Gen. asst. O.N. Heilbut, N.Y.C., 1948-49; pvt. practice law N.Y.C., 1949-60; editor Prentice Hall, Inc., N.J., 1960-64, Bus. Rsch. Pubs., 1964-96, Employee Rels., 1996—. Co-author: Business Management Handbook, 1968; author: Employee Discipline, 1968. Sgt. USAAF, 1945-46. Mem. N.Y. County Lawyers Assn., Nat. Press Club, Masons. Avocations: reading, fishing, walking. Home and Office: 750 Kappock St Apt 915 Bronx NY 10463-4615

ELLER, MARLIN, security firm executive; BA magna cum laude in Math. & Physics, U. Wash., 1979. Mgr. software devel. Microsoft Corp., 1982—95; founder, CEO, pres. Sunhawk.com, Seattle, 1995—. Vis. instr. in computer sci. Williams Coll., 1980—82; bd. dir. Fire Donations, Gig Harbor, Wash. Co-author: Barbarians Led by Bill Gates, 1998. Office: Sunhawk.com Corp 1463 E Republican St Seattle WA 98112-4517

ELLER, TIMOTHY R. (TIM ELLER), real estate company executive, construction executive; b. 1948; BS in construction mgmt., U. Nebr., 1972. Joined Centex Homes, Ill., 1973, project mgr., 1975, v.p., 1977, divsn. pres., 1981, pres., CEO, 1991, chmn., 1998—2003; exec. v.p. Centex Real Estate Corp./Centex Homes, Dallas, 1985—90; pres., COO Centex Real Estate Corp, Dallas, 1990—98, CEO, 1991—, chmn., 1998—; exec. v.p. Centex Corp., Dallas, 1998—, pres., COO, 2002—, chmn., CEO, 2004—, dir., 2002—. Bd. chmn., High Production Home Builders Coun. Nat. Assn. of Home Builders; life trustee Nat. Housing Endowment. Chmn., policy adv. bd. Harvard U. Joint Ctr. for Housing Studies, 2002; bd. trustees Nature Conservancy Tex. Office: Centex Corp 2728 N Hardwood St Dallas TX 75201-1516 Office Phone: 214-981-5000. Office Fax: 214-981-6859.

ELLERBEE, LINDA (LINDA JANE SMITH), reporter; b. Bryan, Tex., Aug. 15, 1944; m. Mac Smith, 1964 (div. 1966), m. Van Veselka, 1968 (div. 1971), children: Vanessa, Joshua, m. Tom Ellerbee, 1973 (div. 1974). Student, Vanderbilt U., Nashville, 1962—64. Newscaster, disc jockey Sta. WVON, Chgo., 1964-67; program dir. Sta. KSJO, San Francisco, 1967-68; reporter Sta. KJNO and AP, Juneau, Alaska, 1969-72; news writer AP, Dallas, 1972; TV reporter KHOU, Houston, 1972—73; gen. assignment reporter Sta. WCBS-TV, N.Y.C., 1973-76; Washington corr. NBC News, 1976—78; co-anchor Weekend, NBC News, NBC-TV, 1978—79; corr. NBC Nightly News, 1979—82; co-anchor NBC News Overnight, 1982-84, Summer Sunday, 1984; corr., reporter Today Show, NBC-TV, 1984—86; reporter Good Morning America, 1986; writer, anchor Our World, ABC-TV, 1986—87; prodr., writer, host Nick News, Nickelodeon Network, 1993—; founder, pres. Lucky Duck Prodns., N.Y.C., 1987—; commentator Cable News Network, 1989; writer, host On the Record, Microsoft online, 1996—. Author: And So It Goes: Adventures in Television, 1986, Move On: Adventures in the Real World, 1991, Take Big Bites: Adventures Around the World and Across the Table, 2005; exec. prod. (TV spls.) A Conversation with Magic (Cable ACE award 1992), It's Only Television (Peabody award 1992); exec. prod., writer, host (news/mag. program) Nick News (Columbia duPont award 1993, Parents' Choice Found. Gold TV award); writer, anchor, Our World (Emmy for best writing 1986); weekly syndicated columnist King Features, N.Y.; (narrator) Baby Boom, 1987, Addicted, 1997 (also exec. prodr., writer, filmography prodr.); filmography prodr. (miniseries) Oh What a Time It Was, 1999; exec. prodr. (TV) several Intimate Portraits 1998-2003, Feeding the Beast: The 24-Hour News Revolution, 2004; prodr. (TV mini series) Oh What a Time It Was, 1999; exec. prodr. (TV series) When I Was a Girl, 2001; prodr. Inside TV Land: Primetime Politics, 2004 (also writer), Inside TV Land: Tickled Pink, 2005; guest appearances Murphy Brown, 1989, 1993, Ellen, 1998. Office: Lucky Duck Prodns 96 Morton St Fl 4 New York NY 10014-3326*

ELLERBROOK, NIEL COCHRAN, gas company executive; b. Rensselaer, Ind., Dec. 26, 1948; s. James Harry and Margaret (Cochran) E.; children: Jennifer, Jeffrey, Jayma. BS, Ball State U., 1970. CPA, Ind. Staff acct. audit Arthur Andersen & Co., Indpls., 1970-72, audit sr., 1972-75, audit mgr., 1975-80; asst. to sr. v.p. adminstrn. and fin. Ind. Gas Co., Inc., Indpls., 1980-81, v.p. fin., 1981-84, v.p. fin., chief fin. officer, 1984-87, sr. v.p., CFO, 1987—; v.p., treas., CFO Ind. Energy, Inc., 1986, also bd. dirs.; now chmn, pres., CEO Vectren, Evansville, Ind. Bd. dirs. Ind. Gas Co., Ind. Energy, Inc. 5th 3d Bank of Ctrl. Ind Bd. dirs. Crossroads of Am. Coun. Boy Scouta Am., Indpls. Civic Theatre. Mem. AICPA, Ind. CPA Soc. (bd. dirs. Indpls. chpt., past pres. 1977-83, state bd. dirs. 1984-87), Fin. Exec. Inst., Ind. Fiscal Policy Inst. (bd. dirs. 1985—, vice chmn. 1988-91, chmn. 1991-94), Ind. C. of C. (taxation com. 1982-94, chmn. 1987-94), Ind. Gas Assn. (treas., asst. sec. 1988—). Office: Vectren Inc 20 NW Fourth St Evansville IN 47708*

ELLERMAN, LINDA ANN, music educator; b. Decatur, Ill., Aug. 26, 1978; d. George Charles and Chong Suk Carter. BMus, Millikin U., 2001; grad. asst., publ. & mktg., Ill. State U., Normal, 2004. Cert. tchr. Ill. Asst. band dir. Greater Decatur (Ill.) Youth Band, 1998—99; band dir. Meridian Ctrl. Unified Sch. Dist., Decatur, 2000—02; grad. asst., 2002—. Mem.: Am. Coll. Personal Assoc. (ACPA), Phi Kappa Phi. Home: 1102 E Van Buren St Clinton IL 61727

ELLETT, ALAN SIDNEY, real estate developer; b. Seven Kings, Essex, Eng., Jan. 6, 1930; came to U.S., 1974, permanent resident, 1974; s. Sidney Walter and May (Fowler) E.; children: Denise, Michelle, Wayne. BSc in Bldg. Constrn., 1951, MBA. Mng. dir. Gilbert Ash Structures, 1960-68; dir., gen. mgr. Lyon Group (real estate), 1968-70; mng. dir. (pres.) Gilbert Ash Ltd., 1970-72; dir. Bovis Ltd.; chief exec. Bovis Property divsn. Audley Properties Ltd., 1972-74; chmn. bd. Forest City Dillon, Inc., 1974-88; exec. v.p., dir. Forest City Enterprises, Inc., Cleve., 1974-89; chmn. Forest City Rental Properties, 1982-89; chmn., pres. Forest City Comml. Constrn. Co., Inc., 1987-89; exec. v.p., COO Am. Malls Internat., Washington, 1997—2000; prin., owner Intercontinental Devel. and Investment Corp., Plantation, Fla., 1997—. Contbr. articles to profl. jours. Fellow Inst. Builders, Inst. Dirs. Mem. Conservative Party. Mem. Church of England. (London).

ELLETT, JOHN SPEARS, II, retired taxation educator, accountant, lawyer; b. Richmond, Va., Sept. 17, 1923; s. Henry Guerrant and Elizabeth Firmstone (Maxwell) E.; m. Mary Ball Ruffin, Apr. 15, 1950; children: John, Mary Ball, Elizabeth, Martha, Henry. BA, U. Va., 1948, JD, 1957, MA, 1961; PhD, U. N.C., 1969. CPA, Va., La.; bar: Va. 1957. Lab. instr. U. Va., Charlottesville, 1953-58; instr. Washington and Lee U., 1958-60; asst. prof. U. Fla., 1967-71;

assoc. prof. U. New Orleans, 1971-76, prof. taxation, 1976-94, prof. emeritus, 1994—. Trainee Va. Carolina Hardware Co., Richmond, 1948-51; acct. Equitable Life Assurance Soc., Richmond, 1951-52; staff acct. Musselman & Drysdale, Charlottesville, 1952-54; staff acct. R.M. Musselman, Charlottesville, 1957-58; mem. U. New Orleans Oil and Gas Acctg. Conf., 1973-92; bd. dirs., publicity chmn. U. New Orleans Energy Acctg. and Tax Conf., 1993-94, bd. dirs. publicity com.; pres. Maxwelton Farm and Timber Corp., 1994—; treas. U. New Orleans Estate Planning Seminar, 1975-78, lectr. continuing edn.; CPCU instr. New Orleans Ins. Inst., 1975-78. Author books; contbr. articles to profl. jours. Served with AUS, 1943-46. Mem. AICPA (40 yr. hon. mem. 2000—), Am. Acctg. Assn., Am. Assn. Atty.-CPAs (chmn. ptnrship. taxation continuing edn. com. 1989, ptnrship. taxation com. 1990, organized La. chpt., v.p. 1991-93), Va. Soc. CPAs, Soc. La. CPAs, Va. Bar Assn. (40 yr. hon. mem. 2000—). Democrat. Episcopalian. Home: 177 Maxwelton Rd Charlottesville VA 22903-7859

ELLETT, TED (E. TAZEWELL ELLETT), lawyer; b. Richmond, Va., June 9, 1952; s. Tazewell III and Marguerite (Rucker) E.; m. Alice Lee Withers, June 11, 1977; children: Elizabeth Pender, E. Tazewell Jr., Dabney McGuire. BA, Davidson (N.C.) Coll., 1974; JD, U. Va., 1977. Bar: Va. 1977, D.C. 1978, U.S. Dist. Ct. (D.C. dist.) 1979, U.S. Ct. Appeals (D.C. cir.) 1979. Law clk. D.C. Ct. Appeals, 1977-78; assoc. Hogan & Hartson, Washington, 1978-82; spl. asst. to mem. Nat. Transp. Safety Bd., Washington, 1982-84; spl. counsel to adminstr. FAA, Washington, 1984-85, chief counsel, 1985-88; ptnr. Hogan & Hartson, Washington, 1988—. Mem. aviation adv. bd. U. So. Calif., L.A., 1988—. Mem. editorial adv. bd. Aviation Noise Report, 1990—, editl. bd. Va. Law Rev. 1976-77; contbr. articles to profl. jours. Bd. mem. Big Bros. of Nat. Capital Area, Washington, 1980-83; past pres. No. Va. Coun. Big Brothers; vestry mem. Christ Ch. Alexandria, Va., 1985-88. Mem. ABA (mem. forum com. air and space law 1983-, aviation law com. tort and ins. law sect. 1986-), Fed. Bar Assn. (mem. air and space law com. 1983-, adv. bd. transp. law sect. 1987, vice chmn. 1991-92, chmn. 1992-93, chmn. steering com. transp. law sect. 1988-90), Nat. Transp. Safety Bd. Bar Assn., Internat. Bar Assn., Lawyer-Pilots Bar Assn., Va. Bar Assn. (mem. bus. law sect. 1981-, mem. transp. law sect. 1993-, chmn., 1993-95, mem. exec. com. 2000-02, chmn. bd. govs. 2002, pres.-elect 2003, pres. 2004-), Bar Assn. D.C., Aero Club of Washington (trustee 1986—), City Club of Washington, Assawoman Fishing Unltd. Club. Republican. Episcopalian. Avocations: running, fishing, hiking, camping, canoeing. Office: Hogan & Hartson LLP Columbia Square 555 13th St NW Ste 800E Washington DC 20004-1109 Office Fax: 202-637-5910. Business E-Mail: etellett@hhlaw.com.

ELLICKSON, BRYAN CARL, economics professor; b. Bklyn., Feb. 12, 1941; s. Raymond Thorwald and Loene (Gibson) E.; m. Phyllis Lynn Rutter, June 19, 1965; 1 child, Paul Bryan. BA, U. Oreg., 1963; PhD, MIT, 1970. From asst. prof. to assoc. prof. UCLA, 1968-83, prof., 1983—, chair econs. dept., 1996-99. Cons. Rand, Santa Monica, Calif., 1970—. Author: Competitive Equilibrium, 1993; contbr. articles to profl. jours. Rsch. grantee HUD, 1979-81, NSF, 1982-87. Mem. Am. Econ. Assn., Econometric Soc. Avocation: scuba diving. Home: 18409 Wakecrest Dr Malibu CA 90265-5620 Office: UCLA Dept Econs 405 Hilgard Ave Los Angeles CA 90095-1477 Office Phone: 310-825-4556. Business E-Mail: ellickson@econ.ucla.edu.

ELLICKSON, PHYLLIS LYNN, political scientist; b. Springfield, Mass., Apr. 22, 1942; d. Frank Walter Rutter and Winifred Annette Grayston; m. Bryan Carl Ellickson, June 19, 1965; 1 child, Paul Bryan. BA, Mount Holyoke Coll., 1963; PhD, MIT, 1973. Rschr. Arthur D. Little Inc., Cambridge, Mass., 1964—66; asst. prof. UCLA, 1973—74; social scientist Rand, Santa Monica, Calif., 1974—85, sr. behavioral scientist, 1985—. Mem. ednl. adv. bd. The Best Found., L.A., 1994—; mem. nat. adv. bd. Monitoring the Future, Ann Arbor, Mich., 1998—; expert panel mem. Dept. Edn., Washington, 1998—2000. Contbr. articles to profl. jours. Adv. bd. Partnership for a Drug Free Am., N.Y.C., 2002—. Mem.: Soc. for Prevention Rsch., Phi Beta Kappa. Achievements include development of award-winning drug prevention program Project ALERT. Avocations: travel, opera. Home: 18409 Wakecrest Dr Malibu CA 90265 Office: Rand 1776 Main St Santa Monica CA 90407 E-mail: phyllis_ellickson@rand.org.

ELLICKSON, ROBERT CHESTER, law educator; b. Washington, Aug. 4, 1941; s. John Chester and Katherine Heilprin (Pollak) Ellickson; m. Lynn Hammer; children: Jenny, Owen. AB, Oberlin Coll., 1963; LLB, Yale U., 1966. Bar: D.C. 1967, Calif. 1971. Atty. adviser Pres.'s Com. Urban Housing, Washington, 1967-68; mgr. urban affairs Levitt & Sons Inc., Lake Success, NY, 1968-70; prof. law U. So. Calif., LA, 1970-81; prof. Stanford U., Calif., 1981-85, Robert E. Paradise prof. natural resources law, 1985-88; Walter E. Meyer prof. property and urban law Yale U., New Haven, 1988—, dep. dean, 1991-92. Author: (with Tarlock) Land-Use Controls, 1981, Order Without Law, 1991 (Triennial award Order of the Coif), (with Rose & Ackerman) Perspectives on Property Law, 3d edit., 2002, (with Been) Land Use Controls, 3rd edit., 2005. Mem. Am. Acad. Arts and Scis., Am. Law and Econs. Assn. (pres. 2000-01), Am. Law Inst. Office: Yale U Law Sch PO Box 208215 New Haven CT 06520-8215 E-mail: robert.ellickson@yale.edu.

ELLICOTT, JOHN LEMOYNE, lawyer; b. Balt., May 26, 1929; s. Valcoulon LeMoyne and Mary Purnell (Gould) Ellicott; m. Mary Lou Ulery, June 19, 1954 (dec. Jan. 1995); children: Valcoulon, Ann; m. Beatrice Berle Meyerson, Sept. 14, 1996. AB summa cum laude, Princeton U., 1951; LLB cum laude, Harvard U., 1954. Bar: D.C. 1957, U.S. Supreme Ct. 1959. Assoc. Covington & Burling, Washington, 1958-65, ptnr., 1965-98, chmn. mgmt. com., 1986-90, sr. counsel, 1998—. Pres. Fairfax County Fedn. Citizens Assn., Va., 1964; mem. governing bd. Nat. Cathedral Sch., Washington, 1973—80, 1989—90, chmn., 1978—79; trustee Landon Sch., Bethesda, Md., 1972—76; bd. dirs. Protestant Episc. Cathedral Found., Washington, 1980—88. Mem.: ABA (sect. internat. law and practice), Washington Inst. Fgn. Affairs, Am. Bar Found. (life), Phi Beta Kappa. Democrat. Home: 5117 Macomb St NW Washington DC 20016-2611 Office: Covington & Burling 1201 Pennsylvania Ave NW Washington DC 20004

ELLIFF, J(OHN) ERIC, lawyer; b. Sterling, Colo., Dec. 28, 1961; s. John Edgar and Gladys Vera (Cline) E. BS, Washington U., 1984; JD, U. Colo., 1987. Bar: Colo. 1987, U.S. Dist. Ct. Colo. 1987, U.S. Ct. Appeals (10th cir.) 1987. Assoc. Morrison & Foerster LLP, Denver, 1987, mng. ptnr.-Denver office. Instr. legal writing U. Colo., Boulder, 1986. Recipient Am. Jurisprudence award, 1987. Mem. ABA, Colo. Bar Assn., Denver Bar Assn., ASCE, Order of Coif. Democrat. Avocations: skiing, antique automobiles. Office: Morrison & Foerster LLP 5200 Republic Plz 370 Seventeenth St Denver CO 80202-5638 Office Phone: 303-592-2240. Office Fax: 303-592-1510. Business E-Mail: jelliff@mofo.com.

ELLIG, BRUCE ROBERT, personnel director; b. Manitowoc, Wis., Oct. 15, 1936; s. Robert Louis and Lucille Marie (Westphal) Ellig; m. Janice Reals; 1 child from previous marriage, Brett Robert. BBA, U. Wis., 1959, MBA, 1960. With Pfizer, Inc., N.Y.C., 1960-96, mgr. compensation and pers. rsch., 1968-70, corp. dir. compensation and benefits, 1970-78, v.p. compensation and benefits, 1978-83, v.p. employee rels., 1983-85, v.p. pers., 1985-95, v.p. employee resources; ret., 1996. Spkr. in field; mem. standing coms. Pfizer, 1985—96; corp. edn. Employee Compensation and Mgmt. Devel., Retirement Plan, Retirement Plan Assets, Savs. and Investment, Corp. Adv. Coun., 1996—2001; cons. Orgn. Resources Counselors Inc., 1996—2001; mem. adv. panel, wave adv. bd. Career Ctrl., 2001—03. Author: Compensation and Benefits: Analytical Strategies, 1978, Executive Compensation: A Total Pay Perspective, 1982, Compensation and Benefits: Design and Analysis, 1985, Future Focus: Human Resources in the 21st Century, 1998, The Complete Guide to Executive Compensation, 2002, The Evolution of Employee Pay in the United States, 2005; contbg. author: Encyclopedia of Professional Management, 1978, Handbook of Business Administration, 1984, Tomorrow's Human Resources Management, 1997; contbg. author The Future of Human Resource Management, 2005; cons. editor: Compensation and Benefits Rev., 1984—96, mem. adv. bd.: Jour. Compensation and Benefits, 1984—96, adv. bd.: Executive Compensation Reports, 1999—2002; contbr. more than 80 articles to profl. jours. Mem. Mayor's Adv. Pay Commn., N.Y.C., 1977—78, chmn., 1980; mem. Presdl. Quadrennial Pay Commn., 1976; mem. merit pay task force U.S. Civil Svc. Commn., 1979; mem. sector staff Coun. Wage and Price Stability, 1979—80; mem. Ctr. Advanced Human Resource Studies Cornell U., 1985—95; adv. bd. Ky. Ednl. TV, 1987—90, Global Remuneration Orgn.; mem. dean's adv. bd. Sch. Bus. U. Wis., 2004—. Named Person of the Yr., U. Wis. Alumni Club N.Y., 1995, Human Resources Exec. of the Yr., Human Resource Exec. Mag., 1995; recipient Am. Compensation's Keystone award, 1999; fellow Aresty, Wharton Bus. Sch. Fellow: Wharton's Aresty Inst., Employer Benefits Rsch. Inst., Nat. Acad. Human Resources (life); mem.: Sr. Execs. Forum, Human Resources Roundtable Group, Bus. Roundtable Conf. Bd. (adv. coun. human resource mgmt.), Soc. Human Resource Mgmt. (life; chmn. bd. dirs. 1996, faculty staff 1996—, Lifetime Achievement award 1999), Am. Compensation Assn. (life; cert. program developer 1996—2005), Pers. Round Table (life), N.E. Sr. Human Resources Exec. Mtg. Group, N.Y. Pers. Mgmt. Assn. (past pres.), Am. Mgmt. Assn., N.Y. Assn. Compensation Adminstrs. (charter pres.), U. Wis. Bus. Sch. Alumni (bd. dirs. emeritus), Wharton/Spencer Stuart Dir. Inst., N.Y. C. of C., Wall of Fame, Ind. C. of C. (human resource com.), U. Ill. Ctr. Human Resource Mgmt. (past ptnr.), U. So. Calif. Ctr. Effective Orgns. (adv. bd. emeritus), Phi Beta Kappa, Phi Eta Sigma, Beta Gamma Sigma. Republican. Roman Catholic. Personal E-mail: bellig@teminandco.com.

ELLIMAN, DONALD M., JR., magazine company executive; b. Bronxville, NY, Sept. 4, 1944; s. Donald M. Elliman; m. Mary Elliman; children: Kristin, Lindsay, Anderw, Mack. BA, Middlebury Coll., 1967. Mktg. svc. dept. Time Inc., 1967, advt. staff, 1971—76, sales and mktg., 1982—85; circulation dir. People Mag., 1976—78; circulation mgr. Time Internat., 1978—81; various positions Time Inc., 1985—91, People Mag., 1985—91; pres., sales and mktg. divsn. Time Inc., 1991; exec. v.p. Time Warner; pres. Sports Illustrated; pub. People Mag.; mgr., sports assets Ascent, 1999; pres. Kroenke Sports Enterprises, LLC. Bd. dirs. Operation Sail; trustee N.Y. Yacht Club, Jimmie Heuga Ctr; hon. chmn. United Hosp. Fund. N.Y. Avocations: skiing, sailing. Office: Kroenke Sports Enterprises 1000 Chopper Cir Denver CO 80204

ELLIN, MARVIN, lawyer; b. Balt., Mar. 6, 1923; s. Morris and Goldie (Rosen) E.; children: Morris, Raymond, Elisa; m. Marta I. Quintana, Aug. 15, 2001. JD, U. Balt., 1953. Bar: Md. 1953, U.S. Supreme Ct. 1978; diplomate Am. Bd. Forensic Examiners. Practice law, Balt., 1953—; mem. firm Ellin & Baker, 1957—; specialist in med. malpractice law. Cons. on med. and legal trial matters; lectr. ACS, U. Md. Law Sch., U. Balt. City, Yale U. Sch. Medicine, Johns Hopkins Hosp., U. Calif., San Francisco, U. N.J.; former mem. chmn.'s adv. coun. com. on judiciary U.S. Senate. Mem. editl. adv. bd.: Ob/Gyn Malpractice Prevention; contbr. chpts. on med. malpractice to various profl. publs. including Radiation Therapy of Benign Diseases. Fellow Internat. Acad. Trial Lawyers; mem. ABA, Am. Soc. Law and Medicine. Home: 13414 Longnecker Rd Glyndon MD 21136-4839 Office: 1101 Saint Paul St Baltimore MD 21202-2662 E-mail: EllinLaw@aol.com.

ELLINGBURG, C. MICHAEL, lawyer; b. Indianola, Miss., Jan. 27, 1951; m. Linda Jameson Ellingburg; 5 children. BA, Millsaps Coll., 1973; JD, Univ. Miss., 1976. Bar: Miss. 1976. Mem., profl. liability, comml. litigation Daniel Coker Horton & Bell, Jackson, Miss. Mem.: ABA, Fed. Bar Assn., Miss. Bar, Miss. Def. Lawyers Assn., Hinds County Bar Assn., Federalist Soc., Phi Delta Phi. Presbyterian. Office: Daniel Coker Horton & Bell PO Box 1084 4400 Old Canton Rd Jackson MS 39215-1084 Office Phone: 601-914-5230. Office Fax: 601-969-1116. Business E-Mail: mellingburg@danielcoker.com.

ELLINGHAUS, WILLIAM MAURICE, communications executive; b. Balt., Apr. 19, 1922; m. Erlaine Dietrich, May 30, 1942; children: Marcia A. Barone, Eric J., Douglas A., Barbara E. Gurne, Raymond W., Mark D., Christopher C., Jonathan P. LLD, Iona Coll., 1974, Pace U., 1976, St. John's U., 1976, Poly. Inst. N.Y., 1976; LL.D., W.Va. Wesleyan Coll., 1981; L.H.D., Manhattan Coll., 1975, Union Coll., 1982; D.BA, Curry Coll., 1978; D.Sc. (hon.), Washington Coll., 1979; D.Sc., NYU, 1981. With Bell System, 1940-84; comml. mgr. Chesapeake & Potomac Tel. Co. Md., Balt., 1950-51; pub. office mgr. Chesapeake & Potomac Tel. Co. Va., Norfolk, 1951-52, dist. comml. mgr. Culpeper, 1952-55; from gen. comml. supr. to v.p. dir. Chesapeake & Potomac Tel. Co. W.Va., Charleston, 1955-62; from v.p. accts. to v.p. pers. Chesapeake & Potomac Tel. Cos., Washington, 1962-65; from asst. v.p. planning to exec. v.p. AT&T, N.Y.C., 1965-70, exec. v.p., 1970, vice-chmn. bd., 1976-79, pres., also bd. dirs., 1980-84, pres., 1970-76. Pres. N.Y. Telephone Co., 1970-76; exec. vice chmn. bd dirs N.Y. Stock Exchange, 1984-86; 1st chmn. N.Y. Mcpl. Assistance Corp., 1975; mem. N.Y. Emergency Fin.Ctrl. Bd., 1975-76. Trustee Lawrence Hosp.; hon. trustee Mt. Sinai Med. Ctr. With USNR, 1943-45. Mem. Am. Soc. Corp. Execs., Monroe County Telecomm. Authority, Sovereign Order Knights of Malta, Equestrian Order Holy Sepulchre of Jerusalem. Home: Apt 3-H Stoneleigh 2 Bronxville NY 10708 Personal E-mail: wme419@aol.com.

ELLINGSON, JILL EVELYN, psychologist, educator; b. Mpls., Sept. 2, 1972; d. George Warren and Evelyn Wherry Sonnichsen; m. Christopher John Ellingson, Dec. 30, 1994. BA, U. Minn., 1994, PhD, 1999. Undergrad. rsch. asst. U. Minn., Mpls., 1991—93; project mgr. Devel. Resources, Mpls., 1993; NSF trainee U. Minn., Mpls., 1993—94, grad. rsch. asst.; rsch. project mgr. ProStaff Pers. Svcs., Mpls., 1995—97; instr. U. Minn., Mpls., 1995—96; asst. prof. Ohio State U., Columbus, 1999—. Mem. tech. rev. bd. Avert, Inc., Ft. Collins, Colo., 2001—; exec. coach Limited, Inc., Columbus, 2001—; cons. Marathon Ashland Petroleum, Findley, Ohio, 2002—. Contbr. articles to profl. jours. Named Most Published Female Author, Indsl./Orgnl. Psychologist, 2000; fellow dissertation fellow, Human Resource Rsch. Orgn., 1998. Mem.: APA, Acad. Mgmt., Phi Beta Kappa. Methodist. Achievements include research in faking a personality assessment is less detrimental than previously thought; multi-predictor composites are a key way to alleviate ethnic group differences on intelligence tests; temporary employees are a heterogeneous population and yet their performance is homogenous. Avocations: interior design, hiking, classical music, skiing. Office: Ohio State U 734 Fisher Hall 2100 Neil Ave Columbus OH 43210 E-mail: ellingson@cob.osu.edu.

ELLINGSWORTH, LINDA BENOIT, freelance/self-employed writer; b. Troy, NY, May 6, 1953; d. Raymond L. and Marie L. Benoit; m. John D. Ellingsworth, Aug. 14, 1976; 1 child, Craig L. BA in Math., Siena Coll., 1975. Freelance writer, Granville, NY, 1994—; exec. dir. Hometown Blues, Inc., Glens Falls, NY, 1998—2001; event coord. Glens Falls Civic Ctr., Glens Falls, NY, 1999—2000; mktg. & publicity coord. Adirondack Stampede Rodeo, Glens Falls, NY, 2000—04; staff writer The Chronicle, Glens Falls, NY, 1989—94; event coord. Lake George Elvis Festival, 2004. Dir. Glens Falls Blues Festival Hometown Blues, Inc., NY, 1994—2001. Author: (historical book) Alarm From Box 33. Mem. Kiwanis, Glens Falls, NY, 1997—2000; den leader Boy Scouts of Am., Queensbury, NY, 1990—93. Mem.: Glens Falls C. of C. (v.p. 1996—98), Lake George Arts Project, Kiwanis. Achievements include founded Hometown Blues Inc., a non-profit organization to present the annual Glens Falls Blues Festival. Avocation: equestrian sports. Personal E-mail: noble94@localnet.com.

ELLINGTON, CAROL J., artist, printmaker; b. LeMars, Iowa, Nov. 5, 1950; d. Richard Joseph and Mary Jane (Kreber) Meis; m. Richard Wayne Ellington, July 1, 1972; children: Michelle Kay Ellington McNeil, Gina Anne Ellington Arp. BFA in Printmaking magna cum laude, Bellevue U., 1989. One-woman shows include Offutt AFB, Bellevue, Nebr., 1990 (1st Pl. award), Plattsmouth (Nebr.) State Bank, 1992; exhibited in group shows at N.Mex. Internat. Art Exhbn., Clovis, 1986, King Korn Karnival Art Show, Plattsmouth, Nebr., 1982-95, Offutt AFB, 1988 (hon. mention), Nebr. State Office Bldg., 1989, Peter Kiewit Conf. Ctr., Omaha, 1990, 91 (hon. mention) (award of merit), St. Barnabus Episcopal Parish Ch., Omaha, 1990, Assn. Nebr. Art Clubs, Columbus, 1990, Sioux City (Iowa) City Art Ctr., 1990-91, LAEX Gallery, Omaha, 1990, Mus. Nebr. Art, Kearney, 1992 (Merit award), Nebr. Wesleyan U., Lincoln 1993 (Purchase award), Assn. Nebr. Art Clubs, 1993-96 (hon. mention 1995-96), U. S.D. Art Galleries, 1993, Great Plains Chautauqua Art Show, Plattsmouth, 1993, 1200 Landmark Ctr., Omaha, 1994, Mus. Nebr. Art U. Nebr., 1994, Omaha-Douglas County Bldg., 1994-95, Wrightstone Fine Arts Gallery, McCook (Nebr.) C.C., 1995, 97 (Patron award), Artists Coop. Gallery, Omaha, 1995-96, Assn. Nebr. Art Clubs, Fremont, 1996, Nicolet Coll. LRC Gallery, Rhinelander, Wis., 1996, Arts Coun. S.E. Mo., Cape Girardeau, Mo., 1996, Ea. N.Mex. U., Portales, 1996, Trenton (N.J.) State Coll. Art Gallery, 1997, Moss-Thorns Gallery, Ft. Hays, Kans., 1997, 2000, Hilmer Art Gallery, Omaha, 1999, Period Gallery, Omaha, 1999. Recipient 1st place awd. Charleston (S.C. awd.) AFB, Pres. awd. Bellevue U., 1986, 89-90, 94. Mem. Bellevue Artists Assn. (sec., hon. mention,1990, 1991 2 Bronze awds., 1992 2 bronze awds., 2 silver medals, 1993, bronze awd., 1994, bronze awd., hon. mention, 1995, hon. mention, 1996), Assn. Nebr. Artists, Joslyn Art Mus., Artists' Cooperative Gallery, Associated Artists Omaha, Alpha Chi. Roman Catholic. Avocations: reading, travel, sewing. Home: 120 Debra St Plattsmouth NE 68048-2427

ELLINGTON, CHARLES RONALD, lawyer, educator; b. Cuthbert, Ga., Sept. 3, 1941; s. Charles Bartlett and Annie Claire (Moore) E.; m. Jean Alice Spencer, Apr. 29, 1967; children— Gregory Spencer, Alicia Nicole. AB summa cum laude, Emory U., 1963; LL.B., U. Va., 1966; LL.M., Harvard U., 1978. Bar: Ga. 1967, D.C. 1967. Assoc. firm Sutherland, Asbill and Brennan, Atlanta, 1966-69; mem. law faculty U. Ga. Sch. Law, 1969—, prof. law, 1977—, Thomas R.R. Cobb prof. law, 1983-93, dean, 1987-93, J. Alton Hosch prof. law, 1993-99, A. Gus Cleveland prof. legal ethics and professionalism, 1999—. On leave as scholar in residence U.S. Dept. Justice, Washington, 1979-80; reporter Standards of the Profession Com., State Bar of Ga., mem. formal adv. opinion bd. Harvard U. fellow in law and humanities, 1973—74. Mem.: Am. Law Inst. Avocation: hiking. Office: Univ Ga Sch Law Herty Dr Athens GA 30602 Business E-Mail: cre@uga.edu.

ELLINGWOOD, BRUCE RUSSELL, structural engineer, educator; b. Evanston, Ill., Oct. 11, 1944; s. Robert W. and Carolyn L. (Ehmen) E.; m. Lois J. Drager, June 7, 1969; 1 son, Geoffrey D. BSCE, U. Ill., 1968, MSCE, 1969, PhD, 1972. Profl. engr., D.C. Structural engr. Naval Ship Rsch. and Devel. Ctr., Bethesda, Md., 1972—75; rsch. structural engr., leader structural engrng. group Ctr. Bldg. Tech., Nat. Bur. Standards, Washington, 1975—86; prof. civil engrng. Johns Hopkins U., Balt., 1986—2000, chmn. dept., 1990—97; chmn. sch. civil and environ. engrng. Ga. Inst. Tech., Atlanta, 2000—02, prof. civil engrng., 2002—. Lectr., cons. Editor Jour. Structural Safety; mem. editl. bd. Engrng. Structures, Probabilistic Engrng. Mechanics; contbr. articles to profl. jours. Recipient Dural Research prize U. Ill., 1968, Nat. Capital award for Engrng. Achievement D.C. Joint Council Engrng. and Archtl. Socs., 1980, Walter L. Huber prize ASCE, 1980, Silver medal U.S. Dept. Commerce, 1980, Markwardt Rsch. prize Forest Products Rsch. Soc., 1988; named Engr. of Yr. of U.S. Dept. Commerce, Nat. Soc. Profl. Engrs., 1986. Mem. ASCE (pres. Md. sect. 1998-99, State of Art in Civil Engrng. award 1983, 88, Norman medal 1983, 98, Moisseiff award 1988, Walter P. Moore award 1999), Am. Concrete Inst., Am. Nat. Stds. Inst., Am. Inst. Steel Constrn. (T.R. Higgins lectureship 1988), Nat. Acad. Engring., Sigma Xi, Chi Epsilon, Tau Beta Pi. Presbyterian. Achievements include administered the secretariat of American National Standard Committee A58 on minimum design loads from 1977-84 and was responsible for coordinating and directing revisions to the A58 Standard that culminated in the publication of ANSI A58.1-1982 (now ASCE Standard 7), the first load standard in the U.S. to contain probability-based load combinations for limit states. Such load combinations now are used in Canada, the U.S. and in the Eurocodes now being developed in the common market. Was instrumental in the move by the steel industry toward limit states design. Office: Ga Inst Tech Sch Civil and Environ Engring Dept Civil Engring Atlanta GA 30332-0355 Office Phone: 404-894-1635. Business E-Mail: bruce.ellingwood@ce.gatech.edu.

ELLIOT, CAMERON ROBERT, lawyer; b. Portland, Oreg., Jan. 6, 1966; s. James Addison and Dianne Louise (Youngblood) Elliot. BS, Yale U., 1987; JD, Harvard U., 1996. Bar: Calif 1996, DC 1999. Jud. clk. US Dist. Ct., Reno, 1996-98; atty. civil divsn. US Dept. Justice, Washington, 1998—2001; asst. US atty., 2001—. Editor-in-chief: jour Harvard Environ Law Rev, 1995—96. Mem Reno Environ Bd, 1996—97. Lt USN, 1987—92. Office: US Attys Office 147 Pierre Pont St Brooklyn NY 11201 Home: 4 Lexington Ave Apt 12L New York NY 10010 Business E-Mail: cameron@justice.com.

ELLIOT, DAVID HAWKSLEY, geologist, educator; b. Chilwell, Eng., May 22, 1936; came to U.S., 1966; m. Ann Elliot, 1963. BA, Cambridge U., Eng., 1959; PhD, Birmingham U., 1965. Mem. faculty Ohio State U., Columbus, 1969—, prof. dept. geol. scis., 1979—, dir. Byrd Polar Reseach Ctr. (formerly Inst. Polar Studies), 1973-89. Mem. Geol. Soc. Am., Geol. Soc. London, Ohio Acad. Sci., Am. Geophys. Union, Sigma Xi. Office: Ohio State Univ Dept Geol Scis Columbus OH 43210 Business E-Mail: elliot.1@osu.edu.

ELLIOT, JARED, financial management consultant; b. Albany, N.Y., Oct. 15, 1928; s. Henry Melvin and Gladys Dolores (Richter) E.; children: Michael B., Lynn Elliot Sims, Blake R., Jared. B.C.E., Yale U., 1950; MBA, Stanford U., 1955. Mgr. electronic data processing and mfg. scheduling Lenkurt Electric Co. Inc., San Carlos, Calif., 1955-58; sec., treas. Spectracoat Inc., San Carlos, 1958-61; mng. asso. mgmt. services dept. Arthur Young & Co., San Francisco, 1961-69; v.p. Tex. Gas Resources Corp., Owensboro, Ky., 1969—, treas., 1979-84; v.p. fin. Lightnet, New Haven, 1984-86, ret., 1987; pvt. practice fin. mgmt. cons., 1988—. Bd. dirs. United Way, Owensboro, 1969-80, pres., 1972; bd. dirs. Community Concert Assn., Owensboro, 1974-77. Served with USN, 1950-53. Democrat.

ELLIOT, JEFFREY M., political science professor, department chairman; b. L.A., June 14, 1947; s. Gene and Harriet (Sobsey) E. BA, U. So. Calif., 1969, MA, 1970; ArtsD in Govt., Claremont Grad. Sch., 1978; LittD (hon.), Shaw U., 1985; LLD (hon.), City U. L.A., 1986; cert. in grantsmanship, Grantsmanship Tng. Ctr., 1980; cert. in internat. trade and devel., N.C. Ctrl. U., 1995; cert. in conflict resolution, Ctr. for Peace Edn., 1997. Rsch. asst. U. So. Calif., 1969-70; instr. polit. sci. Glendale Coll., 1970-72, Cerritos Coll., 1970-72; asst. prof. history and polit. sci. U. Alaska-Anchorage C.C., 1973-74; asst. prof. history and polit. sci., dean curriculum Miami-Dade C.C., 1974-76; asst. prof. polit. sci. Va. Wesleyan Coll., Norfolk, 1978-79; sr. curriculum specialist Edn. Devel. Ctr., Newton, Mass., 1979-81; prof. polit. sci., dir. grad. studies, dir. internat. progs. N.C. Ctrl. U., 1981—. Disting. advisor fgn. affairs Congressman Mervyn M. Dymally (Dem. Calif.), 1985-94. Author: 150 books, including Keys to Economic Understanding, 1976, Science Fiction Voices, 1979, Literary Voices, 1980, Analytical Congressional Directory, 1981, Deathman Pass Me By: Two Years on Death Row, 1982, Tempest in a Teapot: The Falkland Islands War, 1983, Kindred Spirits, 1984, Black Voices in American Politics, 1985, Urban Society, 1985, The Presidential-Congressional Political Dictionary, 1985, Fidel Castro: Nothing Can Stop the Course of History, 1986, The State and Local Government Political Dictionary, 1986, The Third World, 1987, The Arms Control, Disarmament, and Military Security Dictionary, 1988, Dictionary of American Government, 1988, Fidel, 1988, Conversations with Maya Angelou, 1988, Voices of Zaire: Rhetoric or Reality?, 1990, Brown & Benchmark Reader in American Government, 1991, Brown and Benchmark Reader in International Relations, 1991, The Trilemma of World Oil Politics, 1991, Starclimber: The Autobiography of Raymond Z. Gallon, 1991, Adventures of a Free-Lancer: The Autobiography of Stanton A. Coblentz, 1991, The Work of Jack Dann: An Annotated Bibliography and Guide, 1991, The Work of George Zebrowski: An Annotated Bibliography and Guide, 1991, Brown & Benchmark Reader in American Government, 1992, Brown & Benchmark Reader in International Relations, 1992, The Third World, 1992, Into the Flames: The Life Story of a Righteous Gentile, 1992, After All These Years: Sam Moskowitz On His Science Fiction Career, 1992, The Encyclopedia of African-American Politics, 1994, The Work of Raymond Z. Gallun: An Annotated Bibliography and Guide, 1994, Fidel By Fidel, 1994, The African-American Historical Atlas, 1994, The Historical Dictionary of OPEC, 1995, The Dictionary of State and Local Government, 1995, The Historical Dictionary of the Third World, 1995, The Work of Pamela Sargent: An Annotated Bibliography and Guide, 1996, The Work of George Zebrowski:

An Annotated Bibliography and Guide, 1996, The Work of Jack Dann: An Annotated Bibliography and Guide, 1997; contbr. 550 articles and revs. to profl. and popular jours.; contbg. editor Negro History Bull., 1976-80, West Coast Writers' Conspiracy, 1978-80, Trumphet of Conscience, 2000—. Mem. cmty. svcs. adv. coun. Miami (Fla.) Comty. Svcs., 1974-76; mem. Los Angeles Mayor's Adv. Com., 1971-72; speechwriter, rsch. asst., campaign strategist U.S. Sen. Howard W. Cannon of Nev., 1969—; cons. Calif. Clean Environment Act, 1970-72; commr. Human Rels. Commn., Durham, N.C., 1999—; co-chmn. Sister Cities Program, Durham, 1999—; bd. dirs. Justice Policy Ctr., Durham, 1999—, N.C. Student Rural Health Projec, 1999—. Recipient 100 literary and scholarly awards including Fair Enterprise Medallion award, 1965, Outstanding Polit. Sci. Scholar citation, 1970, Outstanding Tchr. award, 1971, Outstanding Am. Educator citation, 1975, Disting. Svc. Through Community Effort award, 1976, Outstanding Rsch. prize, 1987, 91, Disting. Scholarship award, 1987, Outstanding Rsch. Prize, 1991, Nancy Susan Reynolds award, 1991, Disting Svc. award Acad. Help Ctr., 1992, Gen. News, Election Analysis Associated Press award, 1993, Documentary Profile Cmty. TV award, 1994, Excellence award, Soc. Internat. Develop., 1995, meritorious contributions for Human and Civil Rights award, City of Durham, NC, 2002. Mem. AAUP, ASCD, Cmty. Coll. Social Sci. Assn. (dir. 1970-77, pres. 1975-77), So. Assn. Coll. and Sch. (accreditation team 1974-76), Am. Polit. Sci. Assn., Nat. Coun. for Social Studies, Rocky Mountain Social Sci. Assn., Soc. Internat. Devel. Coun. Fgn. Affairs, Internat. Studies Assn., Assn. Third World Studies, Am. Hist. Assn., Pi Sigma Alpha, Phi Delta Kappa. Home: 511 N Water's Edge Dr Durham NC 27703-6722 Office: NC Cen Univ Dept Polit Sci Durham NC 27707 Office Phone: 919-530-5303. Personal E-mail: jmelliot@aol.com. *I have attempted to live those ideals which inspire me to fight for a more humane world love, honor, courage, integrity, and truth. I have also taken to heart the wisdom of the prophets who implore us to live and love as though life and love were one. Although this is a difficult and frustrating task, it is the only way to live. And finally, I have come to recognize that what matters most, after everything is said, are people-close family and friends who reach out and say in a host of ways, "I care.".*

ELLIOTT, BETTE GREENE, art educator, artist; b. Manfield, Ohio; d. Rupert Adelbert Greene and Addie May Nichols; widowed; children: Brady Allen, Casey Cook. BA, BFA, Otterbein Coll., 1942. Tchr. Alliance (Ohio) Arts Ctr., 1969—80, North Canton (Ohio) Little Art Ctr., 1969—80, Canton (Ohio) Mus. Art, 1972—80; tchr. continuing edn. Kent State U., Canton, 1979—80; tchr. Wayne Gen. Coll., Orville, Ohio, 1979—80; tchr. workshops Ohio, Pa., 1980—90; tchr., self-employed artist North Canton, Ohio, 1980—. Lectr. in field. One-woman shows include, Kent State U., Duke U., prin. works include, Am. Embassy, Nepal. Recipient 1st pl., Headwinds to Miami, 1990. Mem.: Canton Artist League (newletter editor 1999—2000, founder), Ohio Watercolor Soc. (v.p. 1990—95, bd. dirs. 1990—2002). Avocations: walking, sketching, reading, music. Home: 806 Portage St NW North Canton OH 44720 Personal E-mail: bette_elliott@msn.com.

ELLIOTT, BILL, race car driver; b. Dawsonville, Ga., Oct. 8, 1955; m. Cindy Elliott; children: Starr, Brittany, Chase. Race car driver, 1974—. Named winner, Daytona 500, 1985, 1987, Coca-Cola 500, 1985, Winston 500, 1985, Budweiser 500, 1985, 1988, Van Scoy 500, 1985, Miller 400, 1985, 1986, 1989, Pocono 500, 1985, Champion Spark Plug 400, 1985, 1986, 1987, So. 500, 1985, 1988, Atlanta Jour. 500, 1985, 1987, The Winston, 1986, AC Delco 500, 1987, Oakwood Home 500, 1987, Talledaga 500, 1987, Busch Clash, 1987, Del 500, 1988, Summer 500, 1988, Firecracker 400, 1988, 1991, Valleydale 500, 1988, Autoworks 500, 1989, AC Spark Plug 500, 1989, Peak 500, 1990, Pepsi 400, 1991, GM Goodwrench 500, 1992, Pontiac Excitement 400, 1992, Motorcraft Quality PArts, 1992, Tran South 500, 1992, Hooters 500, 1992, So. 500, 1994, Winston Cup Champion, 1988, Most Popular Driver, 1991—2000; recipient Spirit of Ford award, 2000. Achievements include 40 career Winston Cup victories, 49 career pole positions.*

ELLIOTT, CLARK ALBERT, archivist, librarian, historian; b. Ware, Mass., Jan. 22, 1941; s. Leroy and Bertha Lyons Elliott; m. Priscilla Alden Jordan, 1965; children: Andrew, Glenn. AB, Marietta Coll., Marietta, Ohio, 1963; MSLS, Case Western Reserve U., 1965, MA, 1968, PhD, 1970. Asst. prof. Sch. of Libr. Sci., Simmons Coll., Boston, 1969—71; asst. curator Harvard Univ. Arch., 1971—74, assoc. curator, 1974—97; librarian Burndy Libr., Dibner Inst. for History of Sci. and Tech., Cambridge, Mass., 1997—2000; cons. Am. Acad. Arts and Sci., 2000—05. Author: Biographical Dictionary of American Science: The Seventeeth through the Nineteenth Centuries, 1979, History of Sci. in the United States: A Chronology and Research Guide, 1996; co-editor (with Margaret W. Rossiter): Science at Harvard University: Historical Perspectives, 1992; co-editor: (with Pnina Abir-Am) Commemorative Practices in Science: Historical Perspectives on the Politics of Collective Memory, 1999. Mem.: New Eng. Archivists, History Sci. Soc. Personal E-mail: claelliott@earthlink.net.

ELLIOTT, CLIFTON LANGSDALE, lawyer; b. Kansas City, Mo., Oct. 26, 1938; s. John Miller and Kate (Langsdale) E.; m. Bronwyn Ann Reese, Mar. 31, 1963 (div. Mar. 1983); children— Evan R., Kate L.; m. Marjorie A. Critten, Apr. 4, 1987. B.A., Dartmouth Coll., 1960; J.D., Northwestern U., 1963. Bar: Mo. 1963, Wash. 1991, Calif. 1992, U.S. Dist. Ct. (we. and ea. dists.) U.S. Ct. Appeals (8th cir.) 1965, U.S. Ct. Appeals (4th cir.) 1968, U.S. Ct. Appeals (D.C. cir.) 1973, U.S. Ct. Appeals (10 cir.) 1975, U.S. Ct. Appeals (2d, 5th and 9th cirs.) 1980, U.S. Supreme Ct. 1979. Assoc., ptnr. Spencer, Fane, Britt & Browne, Kansas City, Mo., 1963-79; ptnr. Elliott & Kaiser, Kansas City, 1979-87, Smith, Gill, Fisher & Butts, Kansas City, 1987-88, Watson, Ess, Marshall & Enggas, Kansas City, 1988-91; of counsel, ptnr. Davis Wright Tremaine, Seattle, 1991—; instr. labor law U. Mo., 1966; spl. counsel Am. Hosp. Assn., 1973-75; mem. U.S. C. of C. Nat. Labor Relations Act Task Force, 1980— . Mem. ABA, Mo. Bar, Wash. State Bar, Calif. Bar, Am. Soc. Hosp. Attys. (ad hoc com. labor relations 1975—). Contbr. articles to profl. jours. Avocations: boating, fishing. Office: Davis Wright Tremaine 1501 4th Ave Ste 2600 Seattle WA 98101-1688 Office Phone: 206-628-7648. E-mail: clifelliot@dwt.com.

ELLIOTT, DALE STEPHEN, cultural organization administrator; s. Donald S. Elliott; m. Diane L. Otis, 2000; children: Rachel E. Arents, D. Stephen Jr., Andrew G., William A. Landon, George K. Landon, Mary E. Landon. BA, Cornell U., 1971; postgrad., Coll. William and Mary, 1973, Dartmouth's Tuck Bus. Sch., 1990. V.p. planning, info. mgmt., quality performance and corp. sec. Colonial Williamsburg Found., 1982—88, v.p., chief adminstrn. officer, 1988—93, v.p. edn., 1993—2000; exec. dir. Coun. for Am.'s First Freedom, Richmond, 2000—05; pres. Farmer's Museum & NY State Historical Assn., Cooperstown, 2005—. Bd., exec. com. mem. Nat. History Day, College Park, Md.; gov. coun. Am. Assn. State and Local History, Nashville; bd. liaison Nat. Coun. History Edn., Westlake, Ohio; bd. mem. Hampton Rds. Pub. TV and Radio. Vice chair Williamsburg Cmty. Hosp.; chair Williamsburg-James City County Sch. Bd.; pres. United Way Greater Williamsburg; bd. exec. com. Va. Air and Space Ctr., Hampton, Va.; organizer, chair Housing Partnerships; organizer, vice chair Hist. Triangle Cmty. Svcs. Ctr. Office: Farmer's Museum & NYS Historical Assn PO Box 800 Cooperstown NY 13326 Office Phone: 804-643-1786. Office Fax: 804-644-5024. E-mail: selliott@firstfreedom.org.

ELLIOTT, DAVID DUNCAN, III, science company executive; b. L.A., Aug. 4, 1930; s. David Duncan Elliott II and Mildred B. (Young) Mack; m. Arline L. Leckrone, Aug. 18, 1962; children: Lauren, Elliott Croft. BS, Stanford U., 1951; MS, Calif. Inst. Tech., 1953, PhD, 1959. Mem. tech. staff Lockheed Rsch. Lab., Palo Alto, Calif., 1959-61; postdoctoral fellow U. Paris., 1962; dept. head Aerospace Corp., El Segundo, Calif., 1962—70; sci. advisor Nat. Aeronautics and Space Coun., Washington, 1970-72; sr. staff mem. exec. office of pres. NSC, Washington, 1972-77; v.p. SRI Internat., Menlo Park, Calif., 1977-86; sr. v.p. Sci. Applications Internat. Corp., San Diego, 1986-91, Syst Control Tech., Palo Alto, Calif., 1991-94; corp. v.p. Sci. Applications Internat. Corp., Palo Alto, Calif., 1994-95; cons., 1995-99; cons. prof. Ctr. Internat. Security & Coop., Stanford U., Calif., 1999—. Mem. Army Sci. Bd., The Pentagon, Washington, 1982-89; cons. NRC, NAS, 1988—; mem. bd. visitors U. Calif., Davis, 1997-2003. Mem. editorial bd. Jour. Def. Rsch., 1988—. Recipient Outstanding Civilian Svc. award U.S. Army, 1989. Mem. AIAA, AAAS, Am. Phys. Soc., Am. Geophys. Union. Home: 2434 Sharon Oaks Dr Menlo Park CA 94025-6829 Office: CISAC Encina Hall Stanford CA 94305-6165 E-mail: ddelliott3@aol.com.

ELLIOTT, DAVID LEROY, mathematician, educator, engineering educator; b. Cleve., May 29, 1932; m. Kiyoko Akaeda, Mar. 24, 1956 (div. 1980); children: Marguerite, Philip David; m. Pauline Wei-Ying Tang, Oct. 31, 1984. BA, Pomona Coll., 1953; MA, U. So. Calif., 1959; PhD, UCLA, 1969. Mathematician U.S. Naval Ocean Systems Ctr., Pasadena, Calif., 1955-69; lectr. UCLA, 1969-71; mem. faculty Washington U., St. Louis, 1971—, prof. dept. systems sci. and math., 1980-94, prof. emeritus, 1994—; with NSF, Washington, 1987-89. Vis. prof. Brown U., Providence, 1979, UCLA, 1987; vis. rsch. scientist U. Md., 1992—; sr. rsch. scientist NeuroDyne, Inc., 1993-99. Editor: Neural Systems for Control, 1997. Fellow IEEE; mem. Am. Math. Soc., Soc. Indsl. Applied Math., Math. Assn. Am., Sigma Xi. Avocations: music, science fiction. E-mail: delliott@isr.umd.edu.

ELLIOTT, DAVID LINDSEY, literature educator; b. Mpls., Dec. 26, 1944; s. Clarence Smith and Lorraine Lindsey Elliott; m. Carolyn Conrad Sayre, Aug. 8, 1970; children: Matthew Thomas, Gregory Richard. BA, Middlebury Coll., 1966; PhD, Syracuse U., 1978. Prof. English Keystone Coll., La Plume, Pa., 1976—, chair divsn. lang. arts and humanities, 1978—2000, dir. honors program, 2003—, trustee, 2005—. Author: (book of poetry) Wind in the Trees. Mem.: MLA, Haiku Soc. Am., Nat. Coun. Tchrs. English. Avocations: hiking, jazz musician. Office: Keystone College One College Green La Plume PA 18440 Office Phone: 570-945-8453. Business E-Mail: david.elliott@keystone.edu.

ELLIOTT, DOROTHY GAIL, music educator writer; b. Kennard, Ind., Oct. 23, 1918; d. Clyde Harrison and Hazel Uvah (Houk) Copeland; m. Robert E. Elliott, Aug. 22, 1948 (dec. Mar. 1997); children: R. Bruce, Marla Beth, John H. BS in Edn., Ball State Tchrs. Coll., 1940; student Chgo. Theol. Sem., U. Chgo., 1944—47. Tchr. music and math. New Castle (Ind.) Jr. H.S., 1940-43; dir. religious edn. Bethany Union Ch., Chgo., 1945-47; dir. youth activities Hillfields Congl. Ch., Coventry, Eng., 1947-48; music tchr. grades 4, 5, 6 and 7 Silberstein Elem. Sch., Dallas, 1967-70; dir. H.S. choir Singapore Am. Sch., 1970-71; music tchr. grades 4, 5, 6 and 7 Degolyer Elem. Sch., Dallas, 1971-72; music edn. writer J. Weston Walch, Pub., Portland, Maine, 1973—; proprietor Noteman Press, Dallas, 1982—. Author (three books, two tapes) Harmonious Recorder, 1969-2005, (book, worksheets, tapes) ZOUNDS!, 1973-2003; (book, worksheets) Sight-Singing for Young Teens, 1981-97, (reproducible book) Rediscovered Songs, 1991, (historical musical) G.T.T. (Gone to Texas), 1984-2005; author, editor: JUBILEE!, 1987-2004, Dancing with Cancer, 1995-2005; contbg. author: Music and You, 1991. Named Music Alumni of Yr., Ball State U., Muncie, Ind., 1979. Mem. Am. Recorder Soc., Music Educators Nat. Conf., Am. Orff-Schulwerk Assn. Democrat. Avocations: gardening, crafts, theater, concerts. Home and Office: 2603 Andrea Ln Dallas TX 75228-3503 E-mail: dorothyell@aol.com.

ELLIOTT, DOUGLAS S., secondary school educator; b. Harvey, Ill., July 6, 1960; s. Donald A. and Marigenne (Ryburn) E.; m. Jacqueline McIlwaine, Sept. 19, 1987; children: Eric, Logan. BS in Biology, Millikin U., 1982; MS in Biology, U. Houston, Clear Lake, 1993. Biology tchr. Marquette H.S., Alton, Ill., 1984-88, Alton H.S., 1988-89; sci. tchr. I. Weiner Secondary Sch., Houston, 1989-96; sci. coord. St. John's Middle Sch., Houston, 1996—. Biology instr. Houston C.C., 1993-95, U. Houston at Clear Lake, 1993-94; author workbooks Software Mktg., Phoenix, 1992-96/ Avocations: camping, fishing, guitar, softball. Office: St Johns Sch Houston TX 77019 E-mail: delliott@sjs.org.

ELLIOTT, EDWARD, investment executive, financial planner; b. Madison, Wis., Jan. 11, 1915; s. Edward C. and Elizabeth (Nowland) Elliott; m. Letitia Ord, Feb. 20, 1943 (div. Aug. 1955); children: Emily, Ord; m. Melita Uihlein, Jan. 1, 1958 (dec.); 1 child, Deborah; m. Sally Dodds Combs, Jan. 5, 2002. BS in Mech. Engring, Purdue U., 1936. Engr. Gen. Electric Co., Schenectady, 1936—37; with. Pressed Steel Tank Co., Milw., 1937-41, 46-58; v.p. sales Cambridge Co. div. Carrier Corp., Lowell, Mass., 1958-59; mgr. indsl. and med. sales Liquid Carbonic div. Gen. Dynamics Corp., Chgo., 1959-61; v.p. Haywood Pub. Co., Chgo., 1961-63; pres. Omnibus, Inc., Chgo., 1963-67; gen. sales mgr. Resistoflex Corp., Roseland, N.J., 1967-68; investment exec. Shearson, Hammill & Co., Inc., Chgo., 1968-74; v.p. McCormick & Co., Inc., 1974-75, Paine Webber, Inc., Naples, Fla., 1975-91, ret., 1991. Mem. pres.' coun. Purdue U. Lt. col. USAAF, 1941-46. Decorated officer Order Brit. Empire; inducted Indiana Basketball Hall of Fame. Mem.: ASME, Air Force Assn., Rotary, Family Club (San Francisco), Naples Yacht Club, Royal Poinciana Golf Club, Hole-in-Wall Golf Club, Naples Athletic Club, Phi Delta Theta. Episcopalian.

ELLIOTT, EDWIN DONALD, JR., lawyer, educator, federal agency administrator; b. Chgo., Apr. 4, 1948; s. Edwin Donald and Mary Jane (Bope) E.; m. Geraldine Gennet (div. 1980); m. Mary Ellen Savage, Nov. 22, 1980 (div. 1999); children: Eve Christina, Ian Donald; m. Gail Charnley. BA, Yale U., 1970, JD, 1974. Bar: D.C. 1975, U.S. Dist. Ct. D.C. 1975, U.S. Ct. Appeals (2d cir.) 1982. Law clk. to judge U.S. Dist. Ct. D.C., Washington, 1974-75, U.S. Ct. Appeals, Washington, 1975-76; assoc. Leva, Hawes et al, Washington, 1976-80; assoc. prof. law Yale U., New Haven, 1981-84, prof. law, 1984-89, 91-92; asst. adminstr., gen. counsel U.S. EPA, Washington, 1989-91; Julien & Virginia Cornell chair environ. law and litigation Yale U., New Haven, 1992-94, adj. prof. law, 1994—; cons. Fried, Frank, Harris, Shriver & Jacobson, N.Y.C., Washington, 1991-93, ptnr., head of DC Environ. Practice Washington, 1993-96; ptnr., co-chair nat. environ. practice group Paul, Hastings, Janofsky & Walker, Washington, 1996—2003; ptnr., chair environ. dept. worldwide Willkie Farr & Gallagher LLP, Washington, 2003—. Adj. prof. law Georgetown U., Washington, 1997—; advisor Fed. Cts. Study Com., UN Environment Programme, 1993; cons. Asian Devel. Bank, 1994, Carnegie Com. Sci., Tech. and Govt., 1989-93, chair Role of Sci. and Risk Assessment; with Nat. Environ. Policy Inst., 1994—, Overseas Pvt. Investment Corp., Washington, 1983-85, Adminstrv. Conf. U.S., 1987-89, Aetna Ins. Co., 1987-89, G.D. Searle Co., 1988-89; spl. litigation counsel GE Co., Fairfield, Conn., 1985-89; gen. series editor Prentice Hall Environ. Series; bd. toxicology and environ. studies Nat. Acad. Scis., 2003. Co-author: Sustainable Environmental Law, 1993; bd. advisors Environment Law Reporter; mem. editl. bd. Jour. Indsl. Ecology. Resources for the Future fellow, 1989. Mem. ABA (vice chmn. com. on separation of powers 1985-89, jud. rev. 1992—, environ. values 1993—, chair govt. policy liaison), Environ. Law Inst., Gruter Inst. for Law and Behavioral Rsch. (adv. bd. 1986—), Nat. Environ. Policy Inst. (chair sci. and risk assessment), Yale Club N.Y.C., New Haven Lawn Club. Republican. Presbyterian. Address: 56 Beach Ave Milford CT 06460-8156 also: Yale Law Sch PO Box 208215 New Haven CT 06520-8215 Home: 222 11th St NE Washington DC 20002-6218 Office: Willkie Farr and Gallagher LLP 1875 K St NW Washington DC 20006 Office Phone: 202-303-1120. E-mail: delliott@willkie.com.*

ELLIOTT, ELEANOR THOMAS, foundation executive, volunteer; b. N.Y.C., Apr. 26, 1926; d. James A. and Dorothy Q. (Read) Thomas; m. John Elliott, Jr., July 27, 1956. BA, Barnard Coll., 1948; DHL (hon.), Duke U., 2002. Assoc. editor Vogue mag., 1948-52; asst. dir. research and speech writing div. N.Y. State Republican Com., 1952; social sec. to Sec. of State and Mrs. John Foster Dulles, 1952-55; dir. James Weldon Johnson Community Centers, N.Y.C., 1955-60; bd. dirs. Celanese Corp., 1974-87, CIT Fin. Corp., 1978-81, INA Life Ins. Co. of N.Y., 1983-1998. Author: Glamour Magazine Party Book, 1966. Trustee Barnard Coll., 1959—, chmn. bd., 1973-76; bd. dirs. Maternity Center Assn., 1960-70, pres., 1965-69; bd. govs. N.Y. Hosp., 1972—, v.p., 1979—; bd. dirs. Found. for Child Devel., N.Y.C., 1969—, chmn., 1972-79, 1973—; bd. dirs. United Way Greater N.Y., 1977-86, NOW Legal Def. and Edn. Fund, 1983-90, Catalyst Inc., 1978-83, Am. Women's Econ. Devel. Corp., 1980-86, Woodrow Wilson Nat. Fellowship Found, 1983—, chmn. 1993-1999, co-chair, Nat. Adv. Coun., 2000—, Edna McConnell Clark Found., 1984-93, Coun. on Women's Studies, Duke U.; overseer Cornell U. Med. Coll., 1995—. Recipient Alumni medal, Columbia U., 1977, medal of distinction, Barnard Coll., 1979, Red Cross Humanitarian award, 1986, Extraordinary Woman of Achievement award, NCCJ, 1978, Disting. Trustee award, United Hosp. Fund., 1991, Disting. Cmty. Svc. award, 1994, award for disting. svc. to City of New York, St. Nicholas Soc., 2002. Mem.: Colony Club of N.Y.C. Episcopalian. Home: 1035 5th Ave New York NY 10028-0135 Fax: (212)472-6506.

ELLIOTT, EMERSON JOHN, education consultant, policy analyst; b. Ann Arbor, Mich., Nov. 13, 1933; s. Clarence Hyde and Ella Ruth (Kohl) E.; m. Joyce Ann Dodge, Aug. 19, 1956; children— Douglas, Stuart, Susan BA, Albion Coll., Mich., 1955; M.P.A., U. Mich., 1957. Chief edn. br. OMB, Washington, 1967-70, dep. chief human resources programs div., 1970-72; dep. dir. Nat. Inst. Edn., Washington, 1972-77; dir. ednl. staff seminar Inst. for Ednl. Leadership, Washington, 1977-79; dir. sch. fin. study U.S. Dept. Edn., Washington, 1979-81, dir. planning and evaluation, 1981-82, dir. issues analysis, 1982-84; head Nat. Ctr. for Edn. Stats., Washington, 1984-92; com. of edn. stats., 1992-95; dir. spl. projects Nat. Coun. Accreditation Tchr. Edn., Washington, 1995—. Recipient Disting. Alumnus award Albion Coll., 1975; Dirs. Superior Service award Nat. Inst. Edn., 1979; Presdl. Rank awards for Meritorious Service U.S. Govt., 1983, 91. Disting. Service U.S. Govt., 1987. Office: Nat Coun Accred Tchr Edn Ste 500 2010 Massachusetts Ave NW Washington DC 20036-1023 Office Phone: 202-466-7496. Business E-Mail: emerson@ncate.org.

ELLIOTT, EMORY BERNARD, language educator, school system administrator; b. Balt., Oct. 30, 1942; s. Emory Bernard and Virginia L. (Ulbrick) E.; m. Georgia Ann Carroll, May 14, 1966; children: Scott, Mark, Matthew, Laura, Constance. AB, Loyola Coll., Balt., 1964; MA, Bowling Green State U., 1966; PhD, U. Ill., 1972. Instr. Cameron Coll., Lawton, Okla., 1966-67, U.S. Mil Acad., West Point, N.Y., 1967-69; from asst. prof. to prof. English, Princeton U., N.J., 1972-89, chmn. Am. studies program, 1976-82, master Lee D. Butler Coll., 1982-86, chmn. English dept., 1987-89; Pres.'s chair English U. Calif., Riverside, 1989-91, disting. prof., 1992—, univ. prof., 2001—; dir. Ctr. for Ideas and Soc., 1996—. Writing cons. Bell Labs., Holmdel, N.J., 1975-79, RCA, Princeton, 1980-81; edn. cons. Western Electric Corp. Edn. Ctr., Hopewell, N.J., 1974-79 Author: Power and the Pulpit in Puritan New England, 1975, Puritan Influences in American Literature, 1979, Revolutionary Writers: Literature and Authority in the New Republic, 1982, The Literature of Puritan New England in The Cambridge History of American Literature, Vol. 1, 1994, The Cambridge Introduction to Early American Literature, 2002, New Directions in American Literary Scholarship, 1980-2002, 2004; editor: Dictionary of Literary Biography, 3 Vols., 1606-1810, 1983-84; Columbia Literary History of the United States, 1988 (Am. Book award 1988), American Literature: A Prentice Hall Anthology 3 Vols., 1990, Columbia History of The American Novel, 1991, The Jungle, 1991, Wieland, 1994, Huckleberry Finn, 1998, Aesthetics in a Multicultural Age, 2002; series editor Am. Novel Series, 1985—, Critical Studies in Contemporary Am. Fiction, 1987—; mem. editorial bd. Am. Quar., 1976-80, PMLA, 1990-92, Am. Lit., 1995—98, Modern Fiction Studies, 1993—, Ill. Studies Lang. Lit., 1993—, Studies in Am. Puritan Spirituality, 1991—; mem. adv. com. Gale Bibliography of Am. Lit., 1981—; editor-at-large Am. Studies Internat., 1993—. Served to capt. U.S. Army, 1966-69. Recipient Am. Book award, 1988, Disting. Tchr. award U. Calif., Riverside, 1993, Outstanding Advisor/Mentor award, 2004, Rosemary Schaer Humanitarian award, 1997; fellow Woodrow Wilson Found., 1971-72, Am. Coun. Learned Socs., 1973, Guggenheim Found., 1976, Nat. Humanities Ctr. 1979-80, NEH, 1986-87, Inst. for Rsch. in the Humanities, 1991-92, Ford Found., 1998-99, 2000-2003, 2002—, Rockefeller Found., 2000-03, Ford Found., 2002-05; Richard Stockton preceptor Princeton U., 1975-78. Mem. MLA (chmn. Early Am. lit. div., Am. lit. div. 1991, regional del.), Am. Studies Assn. (pres.-elect 2005—) Office: U Calif Dept English Riverside CA 92521-0001 Office Phone: 951-827-4332. Business E-Mail: Emory.Elliott@ucr.edu.

ELLIOTT, ERIC S, insurance company executive; B in mgmt. and fin., MBA, Temple U. Sr. v.p. managed care/pharmacy services Rite Aid Corp., 1989; CEO Eagle Managed Care (Rite Aid); with Mellon Bank; sr. v.p. pharmacy mgmt. CIGNA, 2000—03; sr. v.p. bus. mgmt. PCS Health Systems; v.p. pharmacy mgmt. Aetna Inc., 2003—. Office: Aetna Inc 151 Farmington Ave Hartford CT 06156

ELLIOTT, FRANK NELSON, retired college president; b. Dunkirk, N.Y., Mar. 18, 1926; s. Warren D. and Ima M. (Wilson) E.; m. Mary Elizabeth Neish, July 26, 1952; children: Robert Frank (dec.), Susan Marie, Ann Neish. BA cum laude with dept. honors, Alfred U., 1949, LL.D., 1972; MA, Ohio U., 1950; PhD, U. Wis., 1956; LLD (hon.), Rider U., 1994. Grad. asst. Ohio U., 1949-50; Draper fellow Wis. Hist. Soc., 1951-52, field rep., field supr., 1952-56; curator history, asst. prof. history Mich. State U., 1956-61; asso. dean Sch. Gen. Studies, Columbia U., 1961-64, acting dean, 1964; dir. div. arts and scis. State U. N.Y. Coll. at Cortland, 1964-65, acting dean, 1965-66; v.p. Hofstra U., Hempstead, N.Y., 1966-69; pres. Rider Coll., Lawrenceville, N.J., 1969-90. Contbr. articles to profl. jours. Mem. adv. coun. N.J. State Libr., 1972-87; bd. dirs. N.J. Coun. for Humanities, 1972-76, Deleware Valley United Way, 1986-92, Presbyn. Homes N.J., 1990-96, Granville Acad., Trenton, N.J., 1990-94; bd. dirs. Mercer Med. Ctr., 1980-97, chmn., 1992-95; trustee Alfred U., 1964-69; elder Presbyn. Ch. With AUS, 1944-46, PTO. Mem. Am. Assn. State and Local History (coun. 1960-62), Mich. Hist. Soc. (trustee 1959-61, award for TV lectures 1960), Mercer County C. of C. (dir. 1975-88, Citizen of Yr. 1990). Home: 46 Meadow Lakes Apt LB Hightstown NJ 08520-3332

ELLIOTT, FRANK WALLACE, lawyer, educator; b. Cotulla, Tex., June 25, 1930; s. Frank Wallace and Eunice Marie (Akin) E.; m. Winona Trent, July 3, 1954 (dec. 1981); 1 child, Harriet Lindsey; m. Kay Elkins, Aug. 15, 1983. Student, N.Mex. Mil. Inst., 1947-49; BA, U. Tex., 1951, LLB, 1957. Bar: Tex. 1957, U.S. Supreme Ct. 1962, U.S. Ct. Mil. Appeals 1974, U.S. Dist. Ct. (no. dist.) Tex. 1987, U.S. Dist. Ct. (so. dist.) Tex. 2003, U.S. Ct. Appeals (5th cir.) 1988. Asst. atty. gen. State of Tex., 1957; briefing atty. Supreme Ct. Tex., 1957-58; prof. U. Tex. Law Sch., 1958-77; dean, prof. law Tex. Tech U. Sch. Law, 1977-80; pres. Southwestern Legal Found., 1980-86; ptnr. Baker, Mills & Glast, Dallas, 1987-88; of counsel Ramirez & Assocs., 1988—; dean Dallas/Ft. Worth Sch. Law, 1989-92; dean Sch. Law Tex. Wesleyan U., 1992-94, prof., dean emeritus, 1994—. Parliamentarian Tex. Senate, 1969-73; dir. rsch. Tex. Constl. Revision Commn., 1973 Author: Texas Judicial Process, 2d edit., 1977, Texas Trial and Appellate Practice, 2d edit., 1974, Cases on Evidence, 1980, West's Texas Forms, 20 vols., 1977—, West's Texas Practice, vol. 11, 1990, vol. 14, 1996. Served with U.S. Army, 1951-53, 73-74. Decorated Purple Heart. Mem. ABA, Judge Advs. Assn., Am. Judicature Soc., Am. Bar Found., Tex. Bar Found., Dallas Bar Found., Am. Law Inst., N.Mex. Mil. Inst. Alumni Hall of Fame. Home: 1609 Sunset Terr Fort Worth TX 76102 Office: 1515 Commerce St Fort Worth TX 76102-6572 Office Phone: 817-212-3926. Business E-Mail: felliott@law.txwes.edu.

ELLIOTT, GEORGE ARMSTRONG, III, artist, journalist; b. Wilmington, Del., July 24, 1929; s. George Armstrong Elliott Jr. and Amy Lewis (Rupert) Thomas; m. Shirley Barbara Henin, Oct. 16, 1965. BA, Colgate U., 1951; cert. in journalism, Columbia U., N.Y.C., 1964. Reporter, copy editor, corr. local and nat. newspapers and news agys., 1950-66, Balt. Sun, 1955-62, N.Y. Herald Tribune, 1964, New York Daily News, 1965-66; adminstrv. asst./press sec. Spiro T. Agnew, Baltimore County Exec., Towson, Md., 1962-65, campaign press mgr., 1962; campaign press sec., speechwriter Spiro T. Agnew, Gov. of Md., 1966; pub. affairs dir. Md. State Rds. Commn., Balt., 1967-69; legis. asst. U.S. Congresswoman from Mass. Margaret M. Heckler, Washington, 1969-71; spl. asst. U.S. Sec. of Commerce Peter G. Peterson, Washington, 1972; campaign writer John H. Chafee for U.S. Senator, Providence, 1972; speechwriter Chmn. of FTC Lewis Engman, Washington, 1973; dir. nat. campaign for 55 m.p.h. speed limit U.S. Dept. Transp., Washington, 1976-77; spl. asst., speechwriter U.S. Congressman from Minn. Albert H. Quie, Washington and Mpls.-St. Paul, 1978; press sec. Rep.

Margaret M. Heckler, Washington, 1979-81; prin. writer Nat. Alcohol Fuels Commn., Washington, 1980; writer Nat. Commn. on Air Quality, Washington, 1980-81; internat. pub. rels. counsel A. F. Sabo Assocs., Washington, 1981; Washington and East Coast corr. Jet Cargo News, Washington, 1984-93; profl. Chinese brush painting artist, 1993—. Writer former Md. Gov. Theodore R. McKeldin for Mayor, Balt., 1963; writer for numerous congrl. and local polit. campaigns, 1962-63. Exhibitions include M-Pac Fine Arts Shows, Sugarloaf Mt. Works Shows, Towson, Md., Invitational Art Exhibit, Waterford, Va., Art Mart and Garden tour, Wilmington, Brandywine Arts Festival, Sydney (NSW, Australia) Internat. Art Soc., 1996, Internat. Salon de Haute-Loire, Puy-en-Velay, France, 1997, 99, 7th St. Internat., Washington, 1997, 99, Lalit Kala Nat. Acad. Art, New Delhi, 1998, 99-2000, 2002, Overseas Chinese Culture and Art Festival, Wash., 2000, Internat. Cultural Union, Haifa, 2000-2001, Balt. City Hall Courtyard Galleries, 2000, Marlboro Gallery, Largo, Md., 2000, Mus. Contemporary Art, Wash., 1996, 2001, 03, Russian Cultural Centre, Wash., 2002, 04, Acad. Arts and Design, Tsinghua U., Beijing and Capital Normal U., Beijing, 2002, The Warehouse, Washington, 2003, Gorohavaya 6 EGO Gallery, St. Petersburg, Russia, 2003, All India Fine Arts and Crafts Soc. Galleries, New Delhi, 2004, Vision Gallery, Washington, 2005. With U.S. Army, 1951-54. Ford Found. fellow in advanced internat. reporting Grad. Sch. Journalism, Columbia U., 1963-64. Mem. Nat. Assn. Govt. Communicators, Overseas Press Club Am., Washington Ind. Writers, Montgomery County Art Assn., Internat. Artists Support Group (pres. 1999-2001), Sumi-e Soc. Am., Weekend Art Group. Address: 5826 Bradley Blvd Bethesda MD 20814-1128 Office Phone: 301-263-2788.

ELLIOTT, GRAHAM JOHN, music educator, director; s. Charles and Kathleen Emily Elliott. BMus with honors, U. London, 1968; MA, U. Wales, 1982, PhD, 1985. Sub-organist Llandaff Cathedral, Cardiff, Wales, 1968—70; organist, master of the choristers St. Asaph Cathedral, 1970—81; dir. music Lowther Coll., St. Asaph, Wales, 1972—81; master music Chelmsford Cathedral, England, 1981—99; prof. Guildhall Sch. of Music and Drama, London, 1982—99; founder/dir. Chelmsford Cathedral Festival, England, 1983—99. Diocesan organ adviser Diocese of Chelmsford, England, 1981—99. Author (composer): (academic book) Benjamin Britten: The Spiritual Dimension, composer musical works various publ. for Mayhew. Recipient award, Royal Acad. of Music, 1985, Royal Sch. of Ch. Music, 1998; fellow, Royal Coll. Organists, 1967, Trinity Coll. Music, 1982, London Coll. Music, 1983, Guild of Ch. Musicians, 1999. Mem.: Am. Guild of Organists, Royal Soc. of Musicians, Assn. of Anglican Musicians, Royal Coll. of Organists, Athenaeum, London. Episcopalian. Avocations: swimming, architecture, reading. Office: St Paul's Episcopal Ch Rock Creek Ch Rd & Webster St NW Washington DC 20011 Office Phone: 202-726-2080. Home Fax: 202-726-1084; Office Fax: 202-726-1084. Personal E-mail: graham.elliott@rockcreekparish.org.

ELLIOTT, HERSCHEL, agricultural engineer, educator; BSChemE, U. Tenn., 1972; MS in Civil Environ. Engring., U. Del., 1976, PhD in Civil Environ. Engring., 1979. Registered profl. engr., Pa. Vis. prof. chemistry U. Cape Town, Rondebosch, South Africa, 1991, U. Newcastle (Australia), 1991-92; prof. agrl. engring., coord. environ. resource mgmt. program Pa. State U., University Park, 1990-94, prof. agrl. engring., coord. undergrad. environ. program, 1994-95, prof. agrl. engring., chmn. grad. environ. pollution control, 1995—. Contbr. numerous articles to profl. jours. Recipient Young Engr. of Yr. award North Atlantic Region Am. Soc. Agrl. Engrs. Mem. Am. Water Works Assn., Am. Soc. Agronomy, Soil Sci. Soc. Am., Pa. Assn. Environ. Profls. (bd. dirs. 1988-89), Tau Beta Pi, Alpha Epsilon. Office: Pa State U Environmental Poll Control Prog 249 Ag Eng Bldg University Park PA 16802

ELLIOTT, HOWARD, JR., lawyer, gas industry executive; b. St. Louis, July 4, 1933; s. Howard and Ruth Ann (Thomas) E.; m. Susan Jane Spoehrer, Sept. 2, 1961; children: Kathryn Elliott Love, Elizabeth Elliott Niedringhaus. Student Brown U., 1956; JD, Washington U., St. Louis, 1962. Bar: Mo. 1962. Assoc. Boyle, Priest, Elliott & Weakley, St. Louis, 1962-65, ptnr., 1965-67; mem. Mo. Pub. Svc. Commn., 1967-70, U.S. Postal Rate Commn., 1970—73; assoc. gen. counsel Laclede Gas Co., St. Louis, 1973-77, v.p. adminstrn., 1977-92, sr. v.p. adminstrn., 1992-93, cons., 1993-94, atty., counselor, 1994—. Mem. com. on electricity and nuclear energy Nat. Assn. Regulatory Utility Commrs., 1968-70, mem. exec. com., 1971-73. Charter mem. Com. of 30 for Adoption St. Louis and St. Louis County Jr. Coll. Dist., 1962. With U.S. Army, 1956-58. Mem.: ABA, Bar Assn. Met. St. Louis, Mo. Bar, Loblolly Golf Club (Hobe Sound, Fla.), Chevy Chase (Md.) Club, St. Louis Country Club, St. Louis Club. Republican. Presbyterian. Home: 46 Clermont Ln Saint Louis MO 63124-1351 also: 6820 SE Wood Lark Ln Hobe Sound FL 33455-8048 Personal E-mail: aceelliott@aol.com.

ELLIOTT, J. RAYMOND, medical products executive; Graduate, Univ. We. Ontario. Pres. Far East div. Am. Hosp. Supply Corp.; pres. & CEO J.R. Elliott & Assoc., Cybex Inc., 1995—97; pres. Zimmer Inc., 1997—2001; chmn., dir., pres. & CEO Zimmer Holdings Inc., Warsaw, Ind., 2001—. Dir. Centerpulse Ltd., 2003—. Dir. State of Ind. Workplace Devel. Bd.; dir., chmn. orthopaedic sect. AdvaMed; trustee Orthopaedic Rsch. & Edn. Found. Office: Zimmer Holdings Inc 345 E Main St Warsaw IN 46580*

ELLIOTT, JAMES A., oceanographer, researcher; b. Pierceland, Sask., Can., Feb. 24, 1941; s. James John and Dorothy (Spear) E.; m. Gillian Hope, May 13, 1967; children: Rebecca Jean, Jonathan James Patrick. BSc, U. Sask., 1962; MSc, U. B.C., 1965, PhD, 1970. Rsch. scientist Bedford Inst. Oceanography, Dartmouth, Canada, 1962-78, rsch. mgr., 1979-85, rsch. dir., 1985-97, project dir., 1998, emeritus scientist, 1999—. Contbr. articles to profl. jours. Dir. A.G. Huntsman Found., 1980-98. Office: Bedford Inst Oceanography PO Box 1006 Dartmouth NS Canada B2Y 4A2 Business E-Mail: eljgj@eastlink.ca.

ELLIOTT, JEAN ANN, retired library director; b. Martinsburg, W.Va., Jan. 18, 1933; d. Howard Hoffman and Dorothy Jean (Horn) E. AB in edn., Shepherd U., 1954; MS in libr. sci., Syracuse U., 1957; MS, Shippensburg (Pa.) U., 1974. Asst. libr. Fairmont U., W.Va., 1957-60; reference asst. U. Pitts., 1960-61; acting libr. Shepherd U., 1961-62, coord. libr. sci., 1962-97. Compiler Jefferson County Hist. mag., 1990. Nat. treas. Palatines of Am., Columbus, Ohio, 1986-88. Mem. ALA, AAUW, DAR (W.Va. treas. 1980-83, 86-89, 95-98, state regent 1998-2001, hon. state regent 2001—), W.Va. Libr. Assn. (election chmn. 1988-90), Jefferson County Hist. Soc., Nat. Soc. Daus. Am. Colonies (nat. libr. 1991-94, hon. state regent 1991—), Nat. Soc. Daus. 1812 (nat. libr. 1994-96), W.Va. Soc. Daus. 1812 (state pres. 1991-94, hon. state pres. 1994—), Nat. Soc. Daus. Colonial Wars (state pres. 2001—), Alpha Beta Alpha (nat. exec. sec. 1968-76), Phi Kappa Phi. Presbyterian. Avocations: genealogy, travel, knitting, computers. Home: PO Box 1649 Shepherdstown WV 25443-1649 E-mail: jaelliot@ix.netcom.com.

ELLIOTT, JENNIFER LANDRUM, lawyer; BS, Centre Coll., Danville, Ky., 1996; JD, St. Louis U., 2001. Atty. Stites & Harbison PLLC, Lexington, Ky., 2001—. Mng. editor: St. Louis U. Law Jour., 2000—01; contbr. chapters to books, articles to profl. jours. Mem. Jr. League of Lexington, Lexington, Ky., 2002—05; dir. Centre Coll. Alumni Assn., Danville, 2004—. Mem.: ABA, Fayette County Bar Assn., Ky. Bar Assn. (sec. 2004—), Am. Health Lawyers Assn. Roman Catholic. Office: Stites & Harbison PLLC Ste 2300 250 West Main St Lexington KY 40507 Office Phone: 859-226-2300. Office Fax: 859-425-7890. Business E-Mail: jlelliott@stites.com.

ELLIOTT, JOHN, accountant, educator, dean; b. Sacramento, Calif., Sept. 27, 1945; s. John William and Martha (Arnold) E.; children: Elizabeth Dawn, Jesse John. BS Econs. with high honors, U. Md., 1967, MBA, 1972; PhD Acctg., Cornell U., 1982. CPA, N.Y. Instr. acctg. U. Md., 1970-72; asst. prof. St. Lawrence U., 1972-76, Ctrl. Washington State Coll., 1976-77; vis. prof. U. Chgo., 1983, 88; prof. Johnson Sch. Cornell U., 1982—, assoc. dean, 1997—. Mem. Fin. Policies and Procedures Staff Westinghouse Electric, 1969-70; staff mem. Arthur Andersen & Co., 1967-69. Author (with C. Horngren, G. Sundem) Introduction to Financial Accounting; assoc. editor Contemporary Acctg. Rsch., 1996-97; edit. bd. The Acctg. Review, 1984-87, 89-92, Jour. Acctg. and Pub. Policy, 1983-85, Jour. Fin. Statement Analysis, 1995-98; contbr. articles to profl. jours. Trustee Hangar Theatre, Ithaca, N.Y., 1985-94, Cayuga Med., Ithaca, N.Y., 1992-2001. Mem. AICPA, Am. Acctg. Assn. Home: 220 Prospect Hill Rd Horseheads NY 14845-7979 Office: Johnson Grad Sch Mgmt Cornell U 346 Sage Hall Ithaca NY 14853-6201

ELLIOTT, JOHN, JR., advertising agency executive; b. N.Y.C., Jan. 25, 1921; s. John and Audrey Neilson (Osborn) E.; m. Eleanor Lansing Thomas, July 27, 1956. AB, Harvard U., 1942. Copywriter Batten, Barton, Durstine & Osborn, 1945-49, account exec., 1949-60, v.p., 1956-60, dir., 1958-60; sr. v.p., dir. Ogilvy, Benson & Mather, 1960-65; chmn. Ogilvy & Mather (U.S.), N.Y.C., 1965-75, Ogilvy & Mather Internat., N.Y.C., 1975-82, chmn. emeritus, 1982—. Dir. Fireman's Fund Am. Life Ins. Co. N.Y., 1972-82. Author: Inventing Christmas, 2002. Trustee, pres. Alumni Assn. Browning Sch., 1950-60; trustee St. Paul's Sch., 1978-81, Internat. House, 1967—, Wildlife Conservation Soc., 1979—, Park Assn., N.Y.C., 1956-60, Sta. WNET/Channel 13, 1983—; v.p. Mus. City of N.Y., 1956-65; gen. chmn Red Cross Campaign for Mems. and Funds, N.Y.C., 1970-71; TV advisor Rep. Party, 1950-53; bd. overseers Meml. Sloan-Kettering Cancer Care Center, 1980-84; bd. dirs. Advt. Ednl. Found., 1984-99, Ctr. for Communication, 1982-90; pres. Scottish Nat. Trust Golden Jubilee Found., 1980-93; mem. President's Adv. Council Pvt. Sector Initiatives, 1983-85, Pres.'s Adv. Bd., 1985-89. Served to maj. USMCR, 1942-45. Mem. Am. Assn. Advt. Agys. (chmn. 1974-75), Advt. Council (dir. 1972—, vice chmn. 1979-84, chmn. 1984-85), Advt. Hall Fame (elected 1983). Clubs: Bedford Golf and Tennis, Harvard (N.Y.C.), Century Assn., Hon. Company Edinburgh Golfers, Grolier. Office: Ogilvy & Mather 309 W 49th St Fl 12 New York NY 10019-7316 Office Phone: 212-237-4444.

ELLIOTT, JOHN MICHAEL, lawyer; b. Girardville, Pa., July 8, 1941; s. John T. and Clair C. E.; children: John P., Heather D., Kirwan B., Kyle M. AB in Econs. magna cum laude, St. Vincent Coll., 1963, LLD (hon.), 1985; LLB, Georgetown U., 1966. Bar: Pa. 1966, U.S. Dist. Ct. (ea., we. and mid. dists.) Pa. 1967, U.S. Ct. Appeals (3d cir.) 1967, U.S. Supreme Ct. 1968,. Chmn., CEO Elliott, Greenleaf & Siedzikowski, Phila., 1990—. Pa. counsel Del. River Port Authority, 1987-95; mem. Phila. Coal Rail Task Force, Rockefeller Commn., White House Coal Adv. Commn., 1980; bd. dirs. James A. Finnegan Fellowship Found., 1976-90; bd. dirs. Irish Edn. Devel. Found., Inc., chmn., 1986-2002; mem. Pa. Citizens Adv. Coun. Dept. Environ. Resources, 1970-78, chmn. urban com.; mem. environ. quality bd. Commonwealth of Pa., 1970-78; commr. Del. River Port Authority; rep. auditor Gen. Robert P. Casey; mem. Phila. City Planning Commn., 1970-75, Del. Valley Citizens Coun. for Clean Air; chmn. Disciplinary Bd. Supreme Ct. Pa., 1985-86, vice chmn., 1985, chmn. rules com., 1982, Pa. Bar Inst., 1988-94; mem. Commn. on Security and Coop. in Europe Conf. on the Human Dimension, Paris, 1989, Conf. on Dem. Instns., Oslo, 1991; mem. coun. of advisors Sch. of Humanities and Fine Arts; bd. dirs. St. Vincent Coll., 2002. Contbr. articles to profl. jours. Bd. dirs. Mann Music Ctr., 1988-91, Walnut St. Theatre, 1988-93, Internat. League for Human Rights, 1988-95; mem. adv. coun. Arts and Humanities, 2002—. Recipient St. Patrick's Coll. Maynooth Ireland Salamanaca Archives Dedication, Cahal B. Cardinal Daly, 1995, Gold medal St. Patrick Desmond Cardinal Connell Dublin, 2001; Williston rsch. fellow, 1965. Fellow Pa. Bar Found.; mem. ABA (lectr. on trial practice), Pa. Bar Assn. (ho. of dels. 1983-91, task force on civil ct. rules), Pa. Bar Inst. (bd. dirs. 1987-93, course planner, faculty), Am. Law Inst. (ABA appelate practice program), Nat. Inst. Trial Advocacy (lectr.), Phila. Bar Assn., Nat. Lawyers Com. for Civil Rights Under Law, Braehon Law Soc., Mil. History Soc. Ireland. Home: 1202 Penllyn Blue Bell Pike Blue Bell PA 19422-2108 Office: Elliott Greenleaf & Siedzikowski 925 Harvest Dr Blue Bell PA 19422-1956 Office Phone: 215-977-1004. Business E-Mail: jme@elliottgreenleaf.com.

ELLIOTT, LARRY PAUL, radiologist, educator; b. Manhattan, Kans., Oct. 16, 1931; s. Leonard Paul and Mary Elizabeth (Myers) E.; m. Betty Lou Hawkins, June 23, 1956; children: Laurie Lou, Mary Elizabeth, Larry Paul. BS, U. Fla., 1954; MD, U. Tenn., 1957. Intern John Gaston Hosp., Memphis, 1957-58; resident in pediat. and pediat. cardiology U. Fla. Hosp., 1958-61; resident in cardiac pathology and cardiovasc. radiology U. Minn. Hosp., 1961-65; assoc. prof. cardiac radiology Washington U. Med. Sch., St. Louis, 1966-67; prof. cardiac radiology U. Fla. Med. Sch., 1967-76; prof. radiology, dir. divsn. cardiac radiology U. Ala. Med. Sch., Birmingham, 1976-81; prof., chmn. dept. radiology Georgetown U. Sch. Medicine, 1981—97, clin. prof., chmn. emeritus, 1996—; clin. prof. radiology Emory U. Med. Ctr., Atlanta, 1997—, Med. U. S.C., 1999—. Chmn. Fac. Practice Group, 1989—; clin. prof. Med. U. S.C., 1999—. Author: Pekannens, 1959, The X-Ray Diagnosis Heart Disease, 1968, 79; editor: Radiology, 1967—, Cardiovascular and Interventional Radiology, 1979—, The Fundamentals of Cardiac Imaging in Infants, Children and Adults, 1990; assoc. editor cardiovasc. sect. Taveras Radiology, 1986; contbr. over 200 articles to med. jours. Vol. Charleston Area Therapeutic Riding Group; camp counselor North Charleston Recreation Inner City Group; tutor Gethsesman's Cmty. Ctr., North Charleston, SC. Recipient Disting. Alumnus award U. Fla., 1981, Outstanding Alumnus award U. Tenn. Med. Sch., 1993; grantee cardiac radiology Nat. Heart Inst., 1968-76, Allied Health Profl. Act, 1970. Fellow N.Am. Soc. Cardiac Radiology (pres. 1977-78), Am. Coll. Cardiology; mem. Radiol. Soc. N.Am., Soc. Cardiac Angiography, Am. Heart Assn., Soc. Thoracic Radiology (founding mem., pres. faculty practice group 1989-93). Home: 3 Ocean Point Dr Isle Of Palms SC 29451-3852 *In my own success, I have found 5 key ingredients. (1) A mentor who ignited the switch or literally turned me on. (2) Superb training, especially in sound fundamental principles. (3) An obsessive enthusiasm, a prime feature I look for in all postgraduate students. (4) An element of discipline, which has prevented succumbing to the siren song of private practice. (5) Reward, the only fountain of youth that exists - a close association with each generation of students.*

ELLIOTT, LISA M., psychologist, director; d. Paul A. Elliott and Barbara A. Skidmore, James G. Skidmore (Stepfather); m. Homer L. Dansby, Nov. 5, 1983; children: Hunter L. Dansby, Grace M. Dansby. BBA, Wichita State U., Kans., 1982; MS, U. of North Tex., Denton, 1992, PhD, 1994. Lic. psychologist Tex. State Bd. of Examiners of Psychologists, 1995, cert. Nat. Register Health Providers, 1996. Sr. exec. Macy's, Kansas City, Mo., 1983—84; dir. of human resources LDI, Inc., Minden, La., 1984—88; staff counselor Tex. Acad. of Math and Scis., Denton, Tex., 1992—93; psychology intern VA Med. Ctr., Dallas, 1993—94; adj. prof. U. of North Tex., Denton, Tex., 1994—; lic. psychologist and clinic dir Cook Children's Med. Ctr., Denton, Tex., 1994—. Cons. and adv. Liberty Christian Sch., Denton, Tex., 2001—; truancy cons. Denton County Courts, Tex., 2002—. Contbr. articles to profl. jours. Mem. Denton Drug Task Froce, Denton, Tex., 1997, Denton ISD Safe & Drug Free Bd., Denton, Tex., 2003—03; bd. mem. Family Counseling & Chilrens Services, Shreveport, La., 1988—89. Recipient Outstanding Alumni award, U. of North Tex., 2003. Mem.: APA, Ft. Worth Neuropsychological Assn., Tex. Psychol. Assn., Delta Gamma Frat. (sec. 1979). Achievements include development of truancy prevention program for the court system; learning disability program for a private school. Avocations: travel, water and snow skiing, cooking, entertaining, reading. Office: Cook Childrens Med Ctr 3201 Teasley # 202 Denton TX 76201 Business E-Mail: lelliott@cookchildrens.org.

ELLIOTT, MARIAN KAY, real estate manager; b. Wheatland, Wyo., Aug. 29, 1950; d. James Beal Jr. and Marian L. Angle; m. William Paul Elliott, June 1, 1978; children: Kenneth James Judd, L.R. Dedee Judd, William Paul, Joseph G., Christina Hope, Denise Faith. Cert. Mont. Comml. Credit Mgmt. Assn.; therapeutic foster parenting Dept. Family Svcs.; lic. real estate agt. Wyo. Comml. credit mgr. Pacific Steel, Mills, Wyo., 1978—79; mgr. investment real estate Casper, Wyo., 1981—; real estate assoc. Associated Brokers, Casper, 1982—85. Local reporter National Voter; editor: (newsletter) Wyoming Recycler. Chair fundraising com. Casper Jaycee Jinx, 1974—76; Wyo. scholastic pageant judge Casper Jaycees, 1993; amb. Casper Area C. of C., 1995—96; guardian Youth in Crisis and Mentally Disabled Adults, Casper, 1996—2002; ct. apptd. spl. advocate for abused and neglected children CASA of Natrona County, Casper, 2002—05; vol. Blue Envelope Health/ Elem. Strep Prevention Program, Casper, 1975—78; vol. resource class aide Elem. Sch., Casper, 1975—76, PTA bd. mem., 1979—83; foster parent Dept. Family Svcs., Casper, 1986—96, spkr. new foster parent tng., 1987—98; advocate, lobbyist foster children's rights Foster Parents of Natrona County, Casper, 1989—91; v.p. St. Christopher's Presch. Guild, Casper, 1976; confirmation class tchr. St. Mark's Episcopal Ch., Casper, 1975—78. Mem.: Hat Club/ Resources for Women in Spl. Circumstances (pres. 1997—2001), Big Bros./ Big Sisters Ctrl. Wyo. (adv. coun. 2002—03). Democrat. Achievements include sued for and won the right to sue elected officials in the State of Wyoming; helped change Wyoming laws to allow earlier adoption of foster children. Avocations: gardening, fine arts. Home: 1434 S Beech St Casper WY 82601 Personal E-mail: chadelliott1@msn.com.

ELLIOTT, MARK LEE, lawyer; b. Wertzberg, Germany, July 28, 1956; BA, U. Va., 1977, JD, 1980. Bar: Ga. 1980. Assoc. Troutman Sanders LLP, Atlanta, 1980—87, ptnr., 1988—, practice group leader, comml. leasing dept. Mem. State Bar Ga. Office: Troutman Sanders 600 Peachtree St NE Ste 5200 Atlanta GA 30308-2216 Office Phone: 404-885-3603. Office Fax: 404-962-6551. Business E-Mail: mark.elliott@troutmansanders.com.

ELLIOTT, MISSY, musician; b. Portsmouth, Va., July 1, 1971; d. Ronnie and Pat Elliott. Grad., Manor H.S., Portsmouth, 1990. With Elektra Entertainment, 1996—; owner Gold Mind. Musician: Supa Dupa Fly, 1997 (Platinum), Da Real World, 1999 (Platinum), Miss E...So Addictive, 2001 (Platinum), Under Construction, 2002 (2 times Platinum), This Is Not A Test!, 2003. Nominee 3 Grammy awards, 2002, 2 Grammy awards, 2003; named Best Female Hip-Hop Artist, BET, 2002, 15th of 50 Greatest Hip Hop Artists, VH1, 2003; recipient Best Video of Yr. for The Rain, Rolling Stone, 1997, Soul Train Lady of Soul award for Best R&B/Soul or Rap Music Video for Get Ur Freak On, 2001, Grammy award for Best Rap Solo for Get Ur Freak On, 2002, Soul Train Lady of Soul award for Best R&B/Soul or Rap Music Video for One Minute Man, 2002, Grammy award for Best Female Rap Solo Performance for Scream aka Itchin, 2003, Soul Train Music award for Best R&B/Soul or Rap Music Video for Work It, 2003, Soul Train Lady of Soul awards for Best Song and Best Music Video for Work It, 2003, Video of Yr., Best Hip Hop Video for Work It, 2003, Favirote Rap/Hip-Hop Female Artist, Am. Music Awards, 2003. Office: Elektra Entertainment 75 Rockefeller Plz New York NY 10019

ELLIOTT, OSBORN, journalist, educator, retired dean; b. N.Y.C., Oct. 25, 1924; s. John and Audrey N. (Osborn) E.; m. Deirdre M. Spencer, May 8, 1948 (div. Dec. 1972); children: Diana, Cynthia, Dorinda; m. Inger McCabe, Oct. 20, 1973; stepchildren: Kari, Alexander, Marit. Grad., St. Paul's Sch., 1942; AB, Harvard U., 1946; LHD (hon.), Mich. State U., 1972; LittD (hon.), Marlboro Coll., 1996; LHD (hon.), Marymount Manhattan Coll., 1998. Reporter N.Y. Jour. Commerce, 1946-49; contbg. editor Time mag., 1949-52, assoc. editor, 1952-55; sr. bus. editor Newsweek, 1955-59, mng. editor, 1959-61, editor, 1961-69, 72-75, editor-in-chief, vice chmn., pres., CEO, chmn. bd., 1969-76; former dir. Washington Post Co., A.S. Abell Co. (Balt. Sun); dep. mayor econ. devel. City of NY, 1976—77; dean Grad. Sch. Journalism, Columbia U., N.Y.C., 1979-86, George Delacorte prof., 1986-94, pub. Columbia Journalism Rev., 1979-86. Author: Men At the Top, 1959, The World of Oz, 1980; editor: The Negro Revolution in America, 1964. Bd. overseers Harvard Coll., 1965—71; trustee N.Y. Pub. Libr., 1968—72, 1977—79, St. Paul's Sch., 1969—73, Am. Mus. Natural History, 1958—80, Lincoln Ctr. Theater, 1987—92, Pulitzer Prize Bd., 1979—86; judge Livingston Journalism Awards; chmn. China Seas, Inc., 1973—90, Bernstein Book award N.Y. Pub. Libr.; chmn. bd. dirs. Citizens for N.Y.C., 1975—79, 1990—2003; bd. dirs. New Yorkers for Children, 1999—; organizer 250,000 person Save Our Cities! Save Our Children! March on Washington, 1992. With USNR, 1944—46, Pacific Theatre. Named to Hall of Fame, N.Y.C. Deadline Club, 2000; recipient Carr Van Anda award, Ohio U., 1969, Frederick Douglass award, N.Y. Urban League, 1993, Editor's Hall of Fame award, Am. Soc. Mag. Editors, 1996, Creative Spirit award, Black Alumni Pratt Inst., 1997, Browning Sch. Alumni award, 2001. Fellow Am. Acad. Arts and Scis.; mem. Coun. Fgn. Rels. (trustee), Asia Soc. (1966-93, life trustee 2003—), Harvard Club, Century Assn., Ellis Island Yacht Club (commodore). Home: 84 Water St Stonington CT 06378

ELLIOTT, PETER R., retired athletic organization executive; b. Bloomington, Ill., Sept. 29, 1926; s. Joseph Norman and Alice (Marquis) E.; m. s. Joan Connaught Slater, June 14, 1949; children: Bruce Norman, David Lawrence. BA, U. Mich., 1949. Asst. football coach Oreg. State U., 1949-50, U. Okla., 1951-55; head football coach Nebr. U., 1956, U. Calif., Berkeley, 1957-59, U. Ill., 1960-66, U. Miami, Fla., 1973-74, dir. athletics, 1974-78; asst. football coach St. Louis Cardinals, 1978; exec. dir. Pro Football Hall of Fame, Canton, Ohio, 1979-96, ret., 1996. Served with USNR, 1944-45. Named to Mich. Sports Hall of Fame, 1983, Coll. Football Hall of Fame, 1994. Mem. Am. Football Coaches Assn. (Region 8 Coach of Yr. 1958, Region 5 Coach of Yr. 1963). Presbyterian. Home: 3003 Dunbarton Ave NW Canton OH 44708-1818

ELLIOTT, RALPH H., minister, educator; b. Danville, Va., Mar. 2, 1925; s. Earl A. and Consuela (Arnn) E.; m. Virginia Ellen Case, Oct. 14, 1945; children: Virginia Lee, Beverly A. AB, Carson Newman Coll., 1949; BD, Southern Bapt. Theol. Sem., 1952, ThD, 1956; LHD (hon.), Cen. Philippines U., 1987; DD (hon.), Alderson Broaddus Coll., 1989; LHD (hon.), Hebrew Coll., 1999. Ordained to ministry Bapt. Ch., 1945. Prof. Old Testament Crozer-Midwestern Southern Bapt. Sems., 1956-64; sr. pastor Emmanuel Bapt. Ch., Albany, N.Y., 1964-71, 1st Bapt. Ch., White Plains, N.Y., 1971-77, North Shore Bapt. Ch., Chgo., 1977-89; v.p. acad. life, dean of faculty Colgate Rochester Div. Sch., Rochester, N.Y., 1989-91; interim sr. min. First Bapt. Ch., Rochester, N.Y., 1992-93; interim pres. Andover Newton Theol. Sch., Newton Centre, Mass., 1993-94; interim sr. min. First Bapt. Ch., Worcester, Mass., 1994-96, 1st Bapt. Ch., White Plains, NY, 2000—01. Trustee U. Chgo. Div. Sch., 1978—; vis. prof. U. Melbourne, Australia, 1992. Author: The Message of Genesis, 1961, Reconciliation and the New Age, 1973, Church Growth that Counts, 1982, The Genesis Controversy and Continuity in Southern Baptist Chaos--A Eulogy for a Great Tradition, 1992; contbr. articles to profl. jours. Served with U.S. Infantry, 1943—45. Recipient Courage award, William H. Whitsitt Bapt. Heritage Soc., 1994, Murray I. Rothman award for contbns. toward advancement of Jewish-Christian understanding, 1995. Mem. Internat. Bonhoeffer Soc. Home: 41 Waterford Cir Rochester NY 14618-5422 Personal E-mail: ralphhelliott@msn.com.

ELLIOTT, RICHARD HOWARD, lawyer; b. Astoria, NY, Apr. 30, 1933; m. Judith A. Kessler, Dec. 26, 1956 (dec. 1987); children: Marc Evan, Jonathan Hugh, Eve; m. Diane S. Schaefer, Nov. 18, 1978; children: Alexis, Sara Jane, Benjamin, David. BS, Lehigh U., 1954; JD cum laude, U. Pa., 1962. Bar: US Dist. Ct. (ea. dist.) Pa. 1962, Pa. Supreme Ct. 1962, US Ct. Appeals (3d cir.) 1963, US Dist. Ct. (mid. dist.) Pa. 1976. Assoc. Clark, Ladner, Fortenbaugh & Young, Phila., 1962-69, ptnr., 1970-75, Elliott & Magee, Doylestown, Pa., 1976—. Moderator Permanent Jud. Commn., Presbytery Phila.; v.p., dir. Bucks County Soc. Prevention Cruelty Animals; former pres., dir. Pa. Soc. Prevention Cruelty Animals; gen. counsel, dir. Fedn. Humane Socs. Pa., adj. faculty Bucks County Cmty. Coll.; mem. Pa. Navigation Commn., 1977-80. Lt. USN, 1954-59. Mem. ABA, Pa. Bar Assn., Phila. Bar Assn., Bucks County Bar Assn. Republican. Home: 1205 Victoria Rd Warminster PA 18974-3923 Office: Elliott & Magee 11 Duane Rd PO Box 885 Doylestown PA 18901-0885 Office Phone: 215-230-9900. Personal E-mail: relli59360@aol.com.

ELLIOTT, STANLEY B., chemist, researcher; s. Louis Alexander Elliott and Nellie Cecilia Bennett; m. Elizabeth Marie Seitz, Aug. 2, 1958. Student, Wittenberg Coll., 1935—36; BA, Case We. Res. U. Analytical chemist Harshaw Chem., Cleve., 1936—38, rsch. chemist, 1938—41, Ferro Corp. and U.S. O.S.R.D., Cleve., 1941—45, chem. engr., 1941—45; v.p. Ferro Chem., Cleve., 1945—48, pres., 1948—55; rschr. self-employed, Walton Hills, Ohio,

1955—. Author (A.C.S. Monograph No. 103): Metallic Soaps; contbr. articles Encylopedia of Chemistry 1973. Mem.: Sigma Xi, N.Y. Acad. of Sci., Am. Chem. Soc. Achievements include patents in field of Practical electrical superconductors of high temperature power and performance. Office: Management/Research 7125 Conelly Blvd Walton Hills OH 44146 Office Phone: 440-232-5139.

ELLIOTT, SUSAN SPOEHRER, information technology executive; b. St. Louis, May 4, 1937; d. Charles Henry and Jane Elizabeth (Baur) Spoehrer; m. Howard Elliott Jr., Sept. 2, 1961; children: Kathryn Elliott Love, Elizabeth Elliott Niedringhaus. AB, Smith Coll., 1958. Systems engr. IBM, St. Louis, 1958-66; founder, chmn., CEO, SSE (Sys. Svc. Enterprises, Inc.), St. Louis, 1966—; systems analyst Mo. State Dept. Edn., Jefferson City, Mo., 1967-70; systems coord. Bank of Am. (formerly Boatmen's Nat. Bank), St. Louis, 1979-83. Bd. dirs., exec. com. Mo. Automobile Club; class C dir., dep. chmn. Fed. Res. Bd., St. Louis, 1996-98, chmn., 1999-2000; bd. dirs. Ameren Corp., Angelica Corp., Regional Bus. Coun., St. Louis Regional Commerce and Growth Assn., sec. bd. dirs., 1991-94; bd. dirs. AAA Mo. Trustee, vice-chmn. Mary Inst., St. Louis, 1976-89, Webster U., 1987-96; commr., vice-chmn. St. Louis Civil Svc. Commn., 1985-86, Mo. Lottery Commn., Jefferson City, 1985-87; bd. dirs. St. Louis Zoo, 1990-96, St. Louis Sci. Ctr., 1995-2004; mem. pres.'s adv. coun. area coun., tech. com. Girl Scouts U.S.; chair women bus. owner's com. United Way, 1996-97. Mem. Internat. Women's Forum. Republican. Presbyterian. Avocations: golf, exercise. Office: SSE (Sys Svc Enterprises Inc) 77 West Port Plz Ste 500 Saint Louis MO 63146-3126 Office Phone: 314-439-4701. Business E-Mail: sselliott@SSEinc.com.

ELLIOTT, THOMAS MICHAEL, retired association executive, educator, consultant; b. Evansville, Ind., Aug. 4, 1942; s. Thomas Ira and Pauline (Dawson) E.; m. Susan M. Spiers, July 8, 1967 (div. Aug. 1975); 1 son, Christopher Michael; m. Loretta S. Glaze, Jan. 28, 1976. AB in Zoology, Ind. U., 1965, MS in Higher Edn., 1967, EdD, 1970. Asst. to pres. Purdue U., West Lafayette, Ind., 1972-73, asst. provost, 1973-74; exec. dir. Nat. Commn. United Meth. Higher Edn., Nashville, 1974-77; ptnr. Planning Mgmt. Services Group, Washington, 1976-82; dep. commr. Mo. Dept. Higher Edn., Jefferson City, 1977-79; exec. dir. Ark. Dept. Higher Edn., Little Rock, 1979-82; exec. dir., CEO IEEE Computer Soc., Washington, 1982-2000; ret., 2001—. Cons. numerous colls. and univs. Author: Computer Simulation System, 1975; contbr. articles to profl. jours. Bd. dirs., mem. exec. com. So. Regional Edn. Bd., Atlanta, 1980-82; mem. Cabinet of Gov. Bill Clinton and Gov. Frank White, State of Ark., 1979-82. Mem. IEEE (sr.), IEEE Computer Soc., State Higher Edn. Exec. Officers Assn., Am. Soc. Assn. Execs., Am. Mgmt. Assn., Assn. Computing Machinery. Home: 1735 Q St NW Washington DC 20009-2407 E-mail: melliott@computer.org.

ELLIOTT, TOMMY, secondary school educator; b. Memphis, Tenn., Nov. 22, 1971; s. Martha R. and Betty Jean Wallace; 1 child, Shirlesa Rushawn. BS in Edn., U. Tenn., Martin, 1995; MEd, Cambridge Coll., 2001; EdD in Edn. Leadership, Argosy U., 2005. Educator Youth Villages, Memphis, 1995—96; spl. edn. tchr. Memphis City Schools, 1996—99; tchr. Memphis City Schs., 1999—2001; educator DeKalb County Sch. Sys., Decatur, Ga., 2002—. Mentor, trainer U. Memphis, 1998—2001. Author: (educator's guide) Strategies for Behavior Modification. Rep. Memphis Beautiful Commn., Memphis, Tenn., 1998. Nominee Disney's Am. Tchr. award, 1999—2000; recipient Congl. Recognition for Meritorious Achievement, US Govt., 1998, Contbn. to Cmty. award, Memphis City Coun., 2000, State of Ga. Gov.'s Office Citation Jr. Achievement Vol. Mem.: NEA (Read Across Am. Program award 2004), Assn. Supervision and Curriculum Devel., Nat. Fedn. of State H.S. Assns., Alpha Phi Alpha. Office Phone: 901-340-2999. E-mail: drtommyelliott@aol.com.

ELLIOTT, VIRGINIA F. HARRISON, retired anatomist, publisher, educator, investment advisor, kinesiologist, philanthropist; b. St. Louis, Mar. 15, 1918; d. George Benjamin and Florence Gertrude (McManus) H.; m. William Hector Marsh, Dec. 1, 1963 (dec. Dec. 1986); m. George William Elliott, Oct. 27, 1991; stepchildren: Carolyn Frances Roberts, George William II, Robert Bonner (dec. Apr. 1995), Cathrine Susan Dimino. BS, U. Wis., 1940, PhD, 1959; MA, Columbia U., 1944. Lectr. Columbia U., NYC, 1943-46; asst. prof. Mary Washington U., Fredericksburg, Va., 1946—48, Oreg. State U., Corvallis, 1948-50, assoc. prof., 1950-59; instr. Army Med. Acad./Brooks Army Med. Ctr., San Antonio, 1959-60, assoc. prof., 1960-64; lectr. Hadassah Med. Sch., Hebrew U. of Jerusalem, 1965; pvt. practice Washington, 1969—87; ret., 1987. Fashion model, 1936-47, with John Robert Powers Schs., Phila., Pitts., NYC, 1943-47; cons. U. Tex. Med. Sch., 1962-64, U.S. Pentathlon Team, San Antonio, 1960-64, Dentists for Treatment of Pain from Muscular Tension, San Antonio, 1960-64; vis. prof. grad. sch. U. Wash., Seattle, 1961; lectr. in field Contbr. articles to profl. jours. Bd. visitors Sch. Edn., U. Wis., Madison, 1992-95, now emeritus; mem. Washington com. Nat. Coun. on Women's Giving. Recipient Civilian Meritorious Svc. award U.S. Civil Svc., 1965; Amy Morris Homans fellow, 1958; hon. fellow U. Wis., 1956, 58, 59. Fellow AAHPERD, Tex. Acad. Sci.; mem. Am. Alliance Health, Phys. Edn., Recreation and Dance, Am. Assn. Anatomists divsns. Fedn. Am. Socs. for Exptl. Biology (emeritus), Cosmos Club (emeritus). Presbyterian. Avocations: designing clothing, furniture, landscaping and boats, sculpting, painting. Home: 6333 Cavalier Corridor Falls Church VA 22044-1301

ELLIOTT, WARREN G., lawyer; b. Pueblo, Colo., Jan. 3, 1927; s. Wallace Ford and Hazel (Ellsworth) E.; m. Martha McCabe, June 20, 1953 (div. Sept. 1980); children: Mark, Winthrop, Carolyn, Byron. Student, U. Nebr., 1944-45, U. Colo., 1947-49, AB, 1973; JD, U. Mich., 1952. Bar: Colo. 1952, Conn. 1976, D.C. bar 1978. Asst. city mgr., city atty., Pueblo, 1952-55; adminstrv. asst., legislative counsel U.S. Senator Gordon Allott, 1956-61; asst. gen. counsel Life Ins. Assn. Am., Washington, 1961-68; gen. counsel Aetna Life & Casualty Co., Hartford, Conn., 1968-78; mem. firm Hedrick & Lane, Washington, 1978-79; ptnr. Nossaman, Guthner, Knox & Elliott, Washington, 1979-85, of counsel, 1986—. Epstein, Becker & Green, P.C., Washington, 1986—. Bd. dirs. Friends of the Hopkins Ctr., VISTAS; trustee Opera North. Served with USAAC, 1944-46. Mem. ABA, Fed. Bar Assn., Phi Gamma Delta, Phi Alpha Delta. Office: 3703 Magnolia Ln Santa Barbara CA 93105-2462 Office Phone: 805-687-8302. E-mail: warrengelliott@hotmail.com.

ELLIOTT-NELSON, LINDA J., literature and language professor, director; B, No. Ariz. U., 1978; MBA, Ariz. State U., 1985, MA in Spanish, 1996. Prof. Spanish Ariz. Western Coll., Yuma, 1994—, dicsn. chair modern langs., 1997—. Mem. site coun. Desert Mesa Elem. Sch., Yuma, 1999—. Mem.: Ariz. Assn. Chicanos Higher Edn., Modern Lang. Assn. (com. cmty. colls. 2001—04). Office: Ariz Western Coll Yuma AZ 85365

ELLIOTT-ZAHORIK, BONNIE, nurse, administrator; b. Algona, Iowa; AAS, Coll. Lake County, Grayslake, Ill., 1979; student, U. Iowa; BS, U. St. Francis, Joliet, Ill., 1988; MS, Nat. Louis U., Evanston, Ill., 1989; grad., Northwestern U., 2001. Bd. cert. nurse adminstr.-advanced, critical incident stress debriefing provider, ACLS provider. Chair coordinating coun. Vista Health, Waukegan, Ill., 1998, chair managerial coun., 1998—2002; dir. med./surg. oncology, inpatient pediat., adolescent and outpatient units across the life span Vista Health/Victory Meml. Hosp., 2000—04, nursing adminstrn. mgr., 2004—. Preceptor/mentor Graceland U., Parkside and St. Xavier U.; fellow doctorate program adminstrn. Walden U., 1995—96. Contbr. articles to profl. jours. Mem. combined appeal com., vol. Am. Heart Assn., 1995—2003; co-chair Victory Healthcare Svcs. Combined Appeal Campaign, 1997; mem. Ill. Gov. Blagojevich's Workforce Met. Chgo. Health Care Coun., 2004—, Workforce Coun. Health Care Leadership Critical Skills Shortage Initiative, 2004—; mem. healthcare adv. bd. Ill. Inst. Tech., 2004—. Mem.: AACN, Ill. Orgn. Nurse Leaders (bd. dirs. 1991—, pres. 1998, past pres., state chmn. bylaws com. 1998—99, pres. 2000, strategic planning com. 2000—, pres. IONL region 2-B 2001), Ill. Coalition Nursing Resources (exec. bd. dir. 2000—, legis. funding com. 2001—, pres. 2004), Ill. Coun. Nurse Mgrs. (past pres. Region 2B), Am. Orgn. Nurse Execs.

ELLIS, ALBERT, clinical psychologist, educator, author; b. Pitts., Sept. 27, 1913; s. Henry Oscar and Hettie (Hanigbaum) E. BBA, CCNY, 1934; MA, Columbia U., 1943, PhD, 1947. Diplomate: Am. Bd. Profl. Psychology; in clin. hypnosis Am. Bd. Psychol. Hypnosis; Am. Bd. Med. Psychotherapists, Am. Bd. Sexology. Free-lance writer, 1934-38; personnel mgr. Distinctive Creations, 1938-48; sr. clin. psychologist N.J. State Hosp., Greystone Park, 1948-49; instr. psychology Rutgers U., 1948-49, adj. prof., 1971-83; instr. psychology N.Y. U., 1949; adj. prof. Union Grad. Sch., 1971-77, U.S. Internat. U., 1974-80, Pittsburg State U., 1978—; chief psychologist N.J. State Diagnostic Center, Menlo Park, 1949-50, N.J. Dept. Instns. and Agys., Trenton, 1950-52; pvt. practice psychotherapy and marriage and family therapy N.Y.C., 1943-68; exec. dir. Albert Ellis Inst. for Rational Emotive Behavior Therapy, N.Y.C., 1959-89; pres., 1989—. Cons. clin. psychology VA, 1961-67 Author: An Introduction to the Principles of Scientific Psychoanalysis, 1950, The Folklore of Sex, 1951, (with A.P. Pillay) Sex, Society and the Individual, 1953, The American Sexual Tragedy, 1954, Sex Life of the American Woman and the Kinsey Report, 1954, New Approaches to Psychotherapy Techniques, 1955, (with Ralph Brancale) The Psychology of Sex Offenders, 1956, How to Live With a Neurotic, 1957, Sex Without Guilt, 1958, What Is Psychotherapy, 1959, The Place of Values in the Practice of Psychotherapy, 1959, The Art and Science of Love, 1960, (with Robert A. Harper) A Guide to Successful Marriage, 1961, (with R.A. Harper) A Guide to Rational Living, 1961, (with Albert Abarbanel) The Encyclopedia of Sexual Behavior, 1961, Reason and Emotion in Psychotherapy, 1962, The Intelligent Woman's Guide to Manhunting, 1963, If This Be Sexual Heresy, 1963, Sex and the Single Man, 1963, The Origins and the Development of the Incest Taboo, 1963, Nymphomania, A Study of the Over-Sexed Woman, 1964, Homosexuality, 1965, Suppressed: Seven Key Essays Publishers Dared Not Print, 1965, The Case for Sexual Liberty, 1965, The Search for Sexual Enjoyment, 1966, (with others) How to Raise an Emotionally Healthy, Happy Child, 1966, (with Roger O. Conway) The Art of Erotic Seduction, 1967, Is Objectivism a Religion, 1968, (with John M. Gullo) Murder and Assassination, 1971, (with others) Growth Through Reason, 1971, Executive Leadership: A Rational Approach, 1972, The Civilized Couple's Guide to Extra-marital Adventure, 1972, How to Master Your Fear of Flying, 1972, The Sensuous Person: Critique and Corrections, 1972, (with others) Sex and Sex Education: A Bibliography, 1972, Humanistic Psychotherapy: The Rational-Emotive Approach, 1973, (with Robert A. Harper) A New Guide to Rational Living, 1975, Sex and the Liberated Man, 1976, Anger How to Live With and Without It, 1977, (with Russell Grieger) Handbook of Rational-Emotive Therapy, 1977, (with W. Knaus) Overcoming Procrastination, 1977, (with E. Abrahms) Brief Psychotherapy in Medical and Health Practice, 1978, (with J.M. Whiteley) Theoretical and Empirical Foundations of Rational-Emotive Therapy, 1979, The Intelligent Woman's Guide to Dating and Mating, 1979, (with I. Becker) A Guide to Personal Happiness, 1982, (with M. Bernard) Rational-Emotive Approaches to the Problems of Childhood, 1983, (with M. Bernard) Clinical Applications of Rational-Emotive Therapy, 1985, Overcoming Resistance, 1985, (with Russell Grieger) Handbook of Rational-Emotive Therapy, Vol. 2, 1986, (with Windy Dryden) The Practice of Rational-Emotive Therapy, 1987, (with others) Rational-Emotive Treatment of Alcoholism and Substance Abuse, 1988, How To Stubbornly Refuse to Make Yourself Miserable About Anything-Yes Anything!, 1988, (with others) Rational-Emotive Couples Therapy, 1989, (with R. Yeager) Why Some Therapies Don't Work: The Dangers of Transpersonal Psychology, 1989, (with Windy Dryden) The Essential Albert Ellis, 1990, (with Patricia Hunter) Why Am I Always Broke: How to Be Sane about Money, 1991, (with Windy Dryden) A Dialogue with Albert Ellis: Against Dogma, 1991, (with Emmett Velten) What To Do When AA Doesn't Work For You: Rational Steps to Quitting Alcohol, 1992, (with Lidia Dengelegi and Michael Abrams) The Art and Science of Rational Eating, 1992, (with Arthur Lange) How to Keep People from Pushing Your Buttons, 1994, (with Michael Abrams) How to Cope with a Fatal Illness, 1994, Reason and Emotion in Psychotherapy Revised, 1994, Better, Deeper and More Enduring Brief Therapy, 1996, (with Jack Gordon, Michael Neenan and Stephen Palmer) Stress Counseling: A Rational Creative Behavior Therapy Approach, 1996, (with R.A. Harper) A Guide To Rational Living, 1997, (with R.C. Tafrate) How to Control Your Anger Before It Controls You, 1997, (with Catherine MacLaren) Rational Emotive Behavior Therapy: A Therapist's Guide, 1998, How to Control Your Anxiety Before It Controls You, 1998, (with Shawn Blau) The Albert Ellis Reader, 1998, (with Emmett Velten) Optimal Aging: How to Get Over Growing Older, 1998, How to Make Yourself Happy and Remarkably Less Disturbable, 1999, (with Marcia Grad Powers) The Secret of Coping With Verbal Abuse, 2000, (with S.L. Nielsen and Brad Johnson) Counseling and Psychotherapy With Religious Persons: A Rational Emotive Behavior Therapy Approach, 2001, Feeling Better, Getting Better, Staying Better, 2001, Overcoming Destructive Beliefs, Feelings, and Behaviors, 2001, (with Ted Crawford) Intimate Connections, 2001, (with Robert A. Harper) Dating, Mating, and Relating: How To Build a Healthy Relationship, 2001, (with Jerry Wilde) Case Studies in Rational Emotive Behavior Therapy with Children and Adolescents, 2001, (with Stevan Nielsen and W. Brad Johnson) Counseling and Psychotherapy with Religious Persons: A Rational Emotive Behavior Therapy Approach, 2001, Overcoming Resistance: A Rational Emotive Behavior Therapy Integrative Approach, 2002, (with Ira L. Reiss) From The Dawn of The Sex Revolution, 2002, Anger: How To Live With and Without It, 2003, Ask Albert Ellis, 2003, Sex Without Guilt in the Twenty-First Century, 2003, (with W. Dryden) Albert Ellis, Live!, 2004, Rational Emotive Behavior Therapy: It Works for Me, It Can Work for You, 2004, The Road To Tolerance, 2004, The Myth of Self-Esteem, 2005. Fellow APA (pres. divsn. cons. psychology 1961-62, exec. com. divsn. psychotherapy 1969-73, coun. reps. 1963-64, 72-74), AAAS, Am. Assn. Marriage and Family Therapists (exec. com. 1957-59), Soc. Sci. Study Sex (exec. com. 1957-58, pres. 1958-60), Am. Orthopsychiat. Assn., Am. Sociol. Assn., Am. Assn. Applied Anthropology; mem. ACA, Am. Assn. Sex Educators, Counselors and Therapists (bd. dirs. 1981-82), Nat. Acad. Practice, Soc. Psychotherapy Rsch., N.Y. Assn. Clin. Psychologists in Pvt. Practice (chmn. 1952-54), N.Y. Joint Coun. Psychologists on Legislation (exec. com. 1951-53), Am. Group Psychotherapy Assn., Am. Acad. Psychotherapists (exec. com. 1954-64, v.p. 1962-64), Mensa, Am. Assn. Advancement Psychotherapy, N.Y. State Psychol. Assn., Soc. Exptl. and Clin. Hypnosis. Office: Albert Ellis Inst 45 E 65th St New York NY 10021-6508 Office Phone: 212-535-0822. Personal E-mail: aiellis@aol.com. *I now see that I have given up any addiction to MUSTurbation many years ago—to thinking that I must do well; that others must treat me considerately or fairly; and that the world must provide me with the things I want easily and quickly. I now almost always think that it would be better or nicer if I did well, others treated me fairly, and the world proved easy and pleasant. But it doesn't have to turn out those ways—and that makes quite a difference!.*

ELLIS, ALBERT LUTHER, III, political science professor; b. Raleigh, N.C., Feb. 12, 1946; s. Albert Luther and Marion (Carney) Ellis; m. Helen Neal Scott; children: Emery, Albert IV. BA, U. N.C., Chapel Hill, 1967, MPH, 1975; MA, Rice U., Houston, 1985, PhD, 1991. Cert. real estate broker State of N.C., 1975. Owner Ellis Realty & Constrn., Raleigh, NC, 1973—81; political sci. prof. Texas A&M U., Galveston, 1985—87; pub., bus., health adminstrn. instr. U. Houston, 1987—89; rsch. fellow Rice U., Houston, 1990—91; prof., political sci. & pub. adminstrn. Tex. A&M U., Corpus Christi, 1992—99; Escheats Scholarship fund dir. N.C. State Treasury, Raleigh, 2000—01; prof. polit. sci. Tex. A&M U., Kingsville, 2001—. Chief adminstr. Wake County Health Dept., Raleigh, NC, 1975—77; adj. prof. Coastal Bend C.C., 2004—. Consolidation cons. C. of C., Corpus Christi, Tex., 1994—95, Nueces County Commrs. Ct., Corpus Christi, Tex., 1994—96. E-4 Army Airborne, 1967—73, Ft. Bragg, N.C. Mem.: Law Sch. Admissions Coun. (pre-law advisor 2001—). Home: 418 Sheridan Dr Corpus Christi TX 78412 Office: Tex A&M Univ 300 Rhode Hall MSC165 Kingsville TX 78363 Office Phone: 361-698-1228. E-mail: kfale00@tamuk.edu.

ELLIS, ALFRED WRIGHT (AL ELLIS), lawyer; b. Cleve., Aug. 26, 1943; s. Donald Porter and Louise (Wright) E.; m. Kay Genseke, June 1965 (div. 1976); 1 child, Joshua Kyle; m. Sandra Lee Fahey, Feb. 11, 1989. BA with honors, U. Tex., Arlington, 1965; JD, So. Meth. U., 1971. Bar: Tex., U.S. Dist. Ct. (no., so., ea. and we. dists.) Tex., U.S. Ct. Appeals (5th cir.), U.S. Supreme Ct.; cert. personal injury and civil trial lawyer, Internat. Acad. Trial Lawyers. Capt. U.S. Army, 1965—69; atty. Woodruff, Kendall & Smith, Dallas, 1972; ptnr. Woodruff & Ellis, Dallas; pvt. practice Dallas, 1983-96; of counsel Howie & Sweeney, 1996—2003, Sommerman & Quesada, 2003—. Instr. So. Meth. U. Law Sch. Trial Advocacy; past pres. Law Focused Edn., Inc. Past mem. City of Dallas Urban Rehab. Stds. Bd., Dallas Assembly, Salesmanship Club, Dallas; trustee Hist. Preservation League, 1992—94; dir. Dallas Regional Golden Gloves Tournament, 1976—96; pres., bd. dirs. Dallas Coun. on Alcoholism, 1980; pres. Dallas All Sports Assn., 1980; bd. dirs. Dallas Habitat for Humanity, 1998—2002, 2005—. Named Boss of Yr., Dallas Assn. Legal Secs., 1978; named one of Outstanding Young Men of Am., 1977; recipient Certs. of Recognition (8), Dallas Ind. Sch. Dist., 1971—83, Wall Street Jour. award, So. Meth. U. Law Sch., 1972, Hayward McMurray award, Dallas Jaycees, 1975—76, Spl. Recognition award, All Sports Assn., 1977, Cert. of Appreciation for Exceptional & Disting. Vol. Svc., Gov. Mark White, 1983, Cmty. Spirit award, Dallas Bus. Jour., 1993, Disting. Svc. award, Dallas All Sports Assn., 1993, Nancy Garms Meml. award for Outstanding Contbns. to Law Focus Edn., 1996—, Leon Jaworski award, Dallas Minority Bar Assn., 2002, Excellence award, D.A.Y.L. Found., 2004; fellow, Roscoe Pound Found. Fellow: Dallas Bar Found., Tex. Bar Found. (sustaining life, Dan R. Price Meml. award 2003, "D" Mag. Best Personal Injury Lawyers, Dallas 2003, Tex. Monthly Super Lawyers 2003—05), Dallas Assn. Young Lawyers (life); mem.: ATLA, Best Lawyers Am., William Mac Taylor Inn of Ct., Tex. Legal Svcs. Ctr. (bd. dirs. 1999—2002), Tex. Ctr. for Legal Ethics and Professionalism (bd. dirs. 1999—, chmn. 2002—04), Tex. Commn. Lawyers Discipline, Coll. State Bar of Tex. (bd. dirs. 1997—99), Am. Coll. Barristers, Tex. Equal Access to Justice Found. (bd. dirs. 1994—96), Am. Coll. Legal Medicine (assoc.), Tex. Trial Lawyers Assn., Dallas Trial Lawyers Assn. (pres. 1977, Disting. Cmty. Svc. award 1990), Dallas Bar Assn. (bd. dirs. 1978, v.p. 1987—88, pres. 1990, chmn. bd. dirs. 1998), State Bar Tex. (bd. dirs. 1991—94, lectr. seminars, Outstanding Young Men Am. 1977, Excellence in Diversity award 1994, Outstanding 3d Yr. Dir. award, Judge Sam Williams Local Bar Leadership award), Legal Svcs. of North Tex. (bd. dirs., Outstanding Svc. award 1990), Million Dollar Advocates Forum, Am. Bd. Trial Advocates (sec.-treas. Dallas chpt. 1998, pres. 1999, diplomate, Dayl Found. Excellence award 2004). Avocations: tennis, skiing. Office: 3811 Turtle Creek Blvd #1400 Dallas TX 75219-4461 Office Phone: 214-720-0720. Personal E-mail: al@textrial.com.

ELLIS, ANDREW JACKSON, JR., lawyer; b. Ashland, Va., June 23, 1930; m. Dorothy L. Lichliter, Apr. 24, 1954; children: Elizabeth E. Attkisson, Andrew C., William D. BA, Washington and Lee U., 1951, LLB, 1953. Bar: Va. 1952. Ptnr. Campbell, Ellis & Campbell, Ashland, 1955-70, Mays, Valentine, Davenport & Moore, Richmond, Va., 1970-88, Mays & Valentine, Richmond, 1988-96, sr. counsel, 1998—2002, Troutman & Sanders, Richmond, 2002—. Substitute judge County of Hanover (Va.) Ct., 1955—63, 15th Jud. Dist., 1990—96; commr. chancery cir. ct. Hanover County, 1955—96; commonwealth atty., 1963—70; county atty., 1970—78; judge 15th Dist. Juvenile and Domestic Rels. Ct., 1996—98; capital adv. bd. NationsBank Va., 1960—93. Mem. Ashland Town Coun., 1956—63; mayor Town of Ashland, 1958—63; trustee J. Sargent Reynolds CC, 1972—80. 1st lt. U.S. Army, 1953—55. Fellow: Va. Law Found., Am. Coll. Trial Lawyers; mem.: S.R., Hanover Bar Assn. (past pres.), 15th Jud. Cir. Bar Assn. (past pres.), Richmond Bar Assn., Va. Trial Lawyers Assn., Va. State Bar (coun. 1968—74), Va. Bar Assn., Kiwanis. Episcopalian. Home: 15293 Old Ridge Rd Beaverdam VA 23015-1610 Office: PO Box 1122 Richmond VA 23218-1122

ELLIS, BRENDA ANN, music educator; b. Boiling Springs, N.C., Oct. 27, 1958; d. John Pinkney and Charlie Mae Ellis. BA, Hiram Coll., 1981; diploma, Fontainebleu Conservatory Music, France, 1982; MA, Case Western Res. U., 1983; MEd, Columbia U., 1988, EdD, 1990. Cert. tchr. Ohio, N.Y. Music tchr. grades K-8 St. Henry Cath. Sch., Cleve., 1982—85; coord. music Cleve. Music Sch. Settlement, 1985—86; music tchr. grades K-6 Yonkers (N.Y.) Pub. Schs., 1988—91; prof. Potsdam (N.Y.) Coll., 1991—95, Wright State U., Dayton, Ohio, 1995—. Pvt. music tchr., Cleve., 1981—85; ch. musician St. Henry's Advent Luth., Cleve., 1982—86; music instr. Cleve. Music Sch. Settlement, 1983—86; grad. asst., cmty. music supr. Columbia U., NY, 1986—88; instr., coord. Wright State U. Consortium-Gospel Music Workshop Am., 1996—. Creator: music series Art of Black Music, 1997—. Recipient Meritorious Achievement award, John F. Kennedy Ctr.-Am. Coll. Theater Festival, Washington, 1997. Mem.: Gospel Music Workshop Am. (faculty), Ohio Music Edn. Assn., Am. Choral Dirs. Assn.

ELLIS, BRET EASTON, writer; b. LA, Calif., Mar. 7, 1964; s. Robert Martin and Dale Jeffa (Dennis) E. BA, Bennington Coll., 1986. Author: Less Than Zero, 1985, The Rules of Attraction, 1987, American Psycho, 1991, The Informers, 1994, Zombies, 1996, Glamorama, 2000, Lunar Park, 2005; contbr. to periodicals including Rolling Stone, Wall St. Jour., Vanity Fair, Interview. Mem. Authors Guild. Office: c/o Amanda Urban ICM 40 W 57th St New York NY 10019-4001*

ELLIS, CHARLOTTE POPE, elementary school educator; b. Haralson County, Ga., Dec. 27, 1941; d. Hoyt Hensol and Wilma Ann (Chandler) Pope; m. Thomas Anthony Ellis, Apr. 27, 1963; children: Anthony, Christy. BS in Elem. Edn., West Ga. Coll., 1963, MEd, 1970. Cert. tchr. Classroom tchr. Haralson County Bd. Edn., Buchanan, Ga. Named Tchr. of the Yr. in Haralson County, 1991. Mem. NEA, Ga. Assn. Educators, Haralson County Assn. Educators, Alpha Delta Kappa. Home: 2982 Highway # 100 Tallapoosa GA 30176

ELLIS, CHRISTOPHER L., manufacturing executive; b. Phila., 1945; Degree, U. Va., 1969, U. Pa., 1972. Sr. v.p. fin., treas., CFO USF Corp., Chgo., 1991—. Office: USF Corp 8550 W Bryn Mawr Ave Ste 700 Chicago IL 60631

ELLIS, CLAUD M. BUDDY, diversified financial services company executive; b. Oklahoma City, July 2, 1950; s. Charles and Cloal Marie (Shirley) E.; 1 child, Carla Mohler. BA in Polit. Sci. and Mktg., Columbia U., 1970; MBA in Internat. Banking and Econs., London Sch. Econs., 1972. Dir. govt. rels. and pub. policy Aero Comdr. divsn. Rockwell Internat. Corp., Seal Beach, Calif., 1973-83; White Ho. fellow V.P. George Bush, Washington, 1984-85; pres., CEO Banco Resources Ltd., London, 1985—. Office: Banco Resources Ltd 18 Trafalgar St London England E-mail: bancor@swbell.com.

ELLIS, DAVID ROY, lawyer; b. N.Y.C., Nov. 6, 1947; s. Paul R. and Esther Ellis; m. Susan Beth Gottenberg, July 23, 1972; children: Sharon Rachel, Dana Michelle. S.B., MIT, 1968; JD, Harvard, 1971. Bar: N.Y. 1972, Fla. 1978, U.S. Dist. Ct. (mid. dist.) Fla. 1978, U.S. Ct. Appeals (5th and 11th cirs.) 1981; reg. patent atty. Pvt. practice, N.Y.C., 1971-73; atty. RCA Corp., N.Y.C., 1973-76, Piscataway, N.J., 1976-77; gen. atty. Paradyne Corp., Largo, Fla., 1977-81; pvt. practice, Clearwater and Largo, Fla., 1981—. Adj. prof. U. Fla. Law Sch., Stetson U. Coll. Law, 1989-99. Author: A Computer Law Primer, 1986; lectr. computer law. Contbr. articles to profl. jours. Mem. ABA, Am. Intellectual Property Law Assn., Clearwater Bar Assn., St. Petersburg Bar Assn., Tau Beta Pi. Clubs: MIT Tampa Bay (pres. St. Petersburg 1981-83), Harvard of West Coast Fla. Home: 1904 Oakdale Ln N Clearwater FL 33764-6443 Office: 3233 E Bay Dr Ste 101 Largo FL 33771-1900 Fax: 727-531-5088. Office Phone: 727-531-1111. E-mail: ellislaw@alum.mit.edu.

ELLIS, DAVID WERTZ, retired museum director; b. Huntingdon, Pa., Feb. 8, 1936; s. Calvert Nice and Elizabeth Oller (Wertz) E.; m. Marion Elizabeth Schmitt, June 24, 1961; children: Kathryn Dana, Lorna Beth, Audrey Heather. BA with honors in Chemistry, Haverford Coll., 1958; PhD in Chemistry, MIT, 1962; LLD (hon.), Lehigh U., 1979, Lafayette Coll., 1990; DSc (hon.), Susquehanna U., 1982, Ursinus Coll., 1985; LHD (hon.), Juniata Coll., 1989; DCL (hon.), U. of the South, 2000; DSc (hon.), Northeastern U., 2002. Asst. prof. chemistry U. N.H., 1962-67, assoc. prof., 1967-78, acting asst. dean

Grad. Sch., 1967, asst. dean Coll. of Tech., 1968, assoc. acad. v.p., 1968-71, vice provost, v.p. acad. affairs, 1971-78; pres. Lafayette Coll., Easton, Pa., 1978-90; pres., dir. Mus. of Sci., Boston, 1990—2002, pres. emeritus, 2003—; sr. fellow The Boston Found., 2003—04. Mem. Adv. Com. for The Directorate on Edn. and Human Resources, NSF, 1998-2001, chmn., 2000-01; mem. vis. com. radiation oncology Mass. Gen. Hosp., 1994—. Author: (with others) Calculations of Analytical Chemistry, 7th edit., 1971; contbr. articles to profl. jours. Bd. dirs. Giant Screen Theater Assn., 1992-94, 96-98, chmn. mktg. com., 1992-94, mem. liaison com., 1994-98, chmn. liaison com., 1996-98; bd. dirs. Assn. Sci. Tech. Ctrs., 1992-93, 95—2002, v.p., 1997-99; convener Nat. Health Scis. Consortium, 1994-96; bd. dirs. Sci. Mus. Exhibits Collaborative, 1990—2002, sec.-treas., 1992-93, chmn., 1993-95; bd. dirs. Elderhostel, 1983-87, 89-2000, chmn., 1990-95, 96-2000; bd. dirs. Mus. Film Network, 1990—2002, chmn., 1993-97; bd. dirs. Sta. WGBH, pub. broadcasting, 1990-2000, mem. exec. com., 1992-2000, chmn. audit com., 1993-2000, mem. tech. com., 2000—; mem. bd. overseers Tufts U., Colls. of Arts and Sci., 1995-2001; bd. dirs. U. N.H. Found., 1997—, vice chmn., 1999-2002; mem. Am. Coun. on Edn. commn. on leadership devel., 1988-90; mem. bd. visitors U. Maine, Machias, 2001—; bd. advisors Whitehead Inst., 1996—, Seacoast Sci. Ctr., 1998—, trustee, 2004—, Bermuda Biol. Sta. for Rsch., 1998-2004, Flaschner Inst., 2000-03, MIT Mus., 2000—, Rappaport Inst., 2001—, Lemelson Ctr. of the Smithsonian Instn., 2003—; dir. Conservation Law Found., 2004—. Dupont fellow, 1960-61. Mem. AAAS, Am. Chem. Soc., Am. Assn. Mus., Nat. Assn. Ind. Colls. and Univs. (vice chmn. 1987-88, chmn. 1988-89), The Mus. Group, Harvard Faculty Club. Mem. United Ch. of Christ. Home: 10 Barberry Coast Rd Newmarket NH 03857 Office Phone: 617-494-1123.

ELLIS, DONALD LEE, lawyer; b. Oct. 2, 1950; s. Truett T. and Rosemary (Tarrant) Ellis; children: Angela Nicole, Laura Elizabeth, Natalie Dawn, Donald Lee II. BS, U. Tulsa, 1973; JD, Okla. City U., 1976. Bar: Tex. 1979, Okla. 1977, U.S. Dist. Ct. (ea. dist.) Tex. 1978, U.S. Dist. Ct. (we. dist.) Okla. 1978, U.S. Ct. Appeals (5th cir.) 1984, U.S. Ct. Appeals (11th cir.), U.S. Supreme Ct. 1984. Spl. agt. FBI, Washington, 1976—78; asst. dist. atty. Smith County, Tyler, Tex., 1979—80; mem. firm Barron & Ellis, Tyler, 1980—85; pvt. practice, 1985—. Bd. dir. Mental Health Assn. Mem.: Lawyers-Pilot Bar Assn., FBI Agents Assn., Tex. Trial Lawyers Assn., Soc. Former Spl. Agts. FBI, Smith County Bar Assn., Okla. Bar Assn., Tex. Bar Assn., Assn. Trial Lawyers Am. Home: PO Box 131221 Tyler TX 75713-1221 Office: 3311 Woods Blvd Tyler TX 75707 Office Phone: 903-597-7777.

ELLIS, DORSEY DANIEL, JR., lawyer, educator; b. Cape Girardeau, Mo., May 18, 1938; s. Dorsey D. and Anne (Stanaland) E.; m. Sondra Wagner, Dec. 27, 1962; children: Laura Elizabeth, Geoffrey Earl. BA, Maryville Coll., 1960; JD, U. Chgo., 1963; LLD, Maryville Coll., 1998. Bar: N.Y. 1967, U.S. Ct. Appeals (2d cir.) 1967, Iowa 1976, U.S. Ct. Appeals (8th cir.) 1976. Assoc. Cravath, Swaine & Moore, N.Y.C., 1963-68; assoc. prof. U. Iowa, Iowa City, 1968-71, prof., 1971-87, v.p. fin. and univ. svcs., 1984-87, spl. asst. to pres., 1974-75; dean Washington U. Sch. Law, St. Louis, Mo., 1987-98, prof. law, 1998-99; disting. prof. law, 1999—. Vis. mem. sr. common room Mansfield Coll., Oxford U., Eng., 1972-73, 75; vis. prof. law Emory U., Atlanta, 1981-82, Victoria U., New Zealand, 1999; vis. sr. rsch. fellow Jesus Coll. Oxford U., Eng., 1998; bd. dirs. Maryville Coll., 1989-98, 99—, vis. scholar U. Va., 2003. Contbr. articles to profl. jours. Trustee Mo. Hist. Soc., St. Louis, 1995-2000. Nat. Honor scholar U. Chgo., 1960-63; recipient Joseph Henry Beale prize, 1961, Alumni award Maryville Coll., 1988. Mem. ABA, Am. Law Inst., Bar Assn. Metro St. Louis, Mound City Bar Assn., Iowa Bar Assn., AALS Acad. Resource Corps., Order of Coif. Home: 6901 Kingsbury Blvd Saint Louis MO 63130 Office: Box 1120 1 Brookings Dr Saint Louis MO 63130-4862 E-mail: ellis@wulaw.wustl.edu.

ELLIS, EARLE WESLEY, retired secondary school educator; b. Birmingham, Apr. 30, 1950; s. Earle James and Nina Clarke Ellis; children: Wesley, Adam. BS in Edn., Jacksonville State U., 1971; MS in Edn., Jacksonville State U., 1976. Band dir. Cedar Hill M.S., Cedartown, Ga., 1971—2000. Home: PO Box 677 Cedartown GA

ELLIS, EDWARD R., career officer; BS in Bus. Mgmt., Va. Polytechnic Inst. and State U., 1968; MA in Bus. Stats., U. Ala., 1970; grad., Squadron Officer Sch., 1975, Air Command and Staff Coll., 1984, Air War Coll., 1986, Nat. Security Mgmt. Course, 1988, Nat. War Coll., Fort Lesley J. McNair, Washington, DC, 1991, Harvard Ukranian Nat. Security Program, John F. Kennedy Sch. Govt., Harvard U., 1999. Commd. 2d lt. USAF, 1971, advanced through grades to major gen., 1998; student, undergraduate pilot tng. Craig AFB, Ala., 1971—72; T-37 instr. pilot, 43rd Flying Tng. Squadron, later, flight examiner, 29th Flying Tng. Wing, 1972—77; F-4E pilot, asst. flight comdr. 18th Tactical Fighter Squadron, Elmendorf AFB, Alaska, 1977-80; sect. comdr., ops. officer for dir. student ops. Squadron Officer Sch., Maxwell AFB, Ala., 1980-83, exec. officer to comdt., 1980-83; F-4E pilot, asst. ops. officer then ops. officer 36th Tactical Fighter Squadron, Osan Air Base, Republic of Korea, 1984-86; exec. officer to comdr. 51st Tactical Fighter Wing, Osan Air Base, Republic of Korea, 1984-86; faculty instr., comdr. 3823rd Air Command and Staff Coll. Student Squadron, Maxwell AFB, 1986-88; comdr. 35th Flying Tng. Squadron, Reese AFB, Tex., 1988-90; chief Caribbean Basin br. then chief We. Hemisphere div. Directorate of Strategic Plans and Policy, Joint Staff, Pentagon, Washington, 1991-94; chief flying tng. div. Hdqs. Air Edn. and Tng. Command, Randolph AFB, Tex., 1994-95; comdr. 71st Flying Tng. Wing, Vance AFB, Okla., 1995-97; comdt. Squadron Officer Sch., Maxwell AFB, 1997; comdr. Air Force Accession and Tng. Schs., Maxwell AFB, 1997-99; dep. comdr. 5th Allied Tactical Air Force, Vicenza, Italy, 1999—2000, Combined Air Ops. Ctr. Seven, Larissa, Greece, 2000—01; comdr. Combined Task Force Operation Northern Watch, US European Command, Incirlik AB, Turkey, 2001—02; asst. chief of staff for ops. Hdqs. Allied Air Forces Southern Europe, NATO, Naples, Italy, 2002—04; comdr. 19th Air Force, Air Edn. and Tng. Command, Randolph AFB, Tex., 2004—. Decorated Defense Superior Svc. medal with two oak leaf clusters, Legion of Merit with oak leaf clusters, Meritorious Svc. medal with four oak leaf clusters, Air medal with oak leaf cluster, Aerial Achievement medal with oak leaf cluster, Air Force Commendation medal with oak leaf cluster, NATO medal with Bronze Star (Kosovo). Office: 12FTW/PA Randolph Afb TX 78150

ELLIS, ELDON EUGENE, surgeon; b. Washington, Ind., July 2, 1922; s. Osman Polson and Ina Lucretia (Cochran) E.; m. Irene Eaves Clay, June 26, 1948 (dec. 1968); m. Priscilla Dean Strong, Sept. 20, 1969 (dec. Feb. 1990); children: Paul Addison, Kathe Lynn, Jonathan Clay, Sharon Anne, Eldon Eugene, Rebecca Deborah; m. Virginia Michael Ellis, Aug. 22, 1992. BA, U. Rochester, 1946, MD, 1949. Intern surgery Stanford U. Hosp., San Francisco, 1949—50, resident and fellow surgery, 1950—52, 1955; Schilling fellow pathology San Francisco Gen. Hosp., 1955; ptnr. Redwood Med. Clinic, Redwood City, Calif., 1955—87, med. dir., 1984—87; semi-ret. physician, 1987—; med. dir. Peninsula Occupl. Health Assocs., San Carlos, Calif., 1991—94, physician, 1995—99, Sequoia Med. Clinic, Redwood City, 1999—. Asst. clin. prof. surgery Stanford U., 1970-80; dir. Sequoia Hosp., Redwood City, 1974-82. Pres. Sequoia Hosp. Found., 1983-92, bd. dirs.; pres., chmn. bd. dirs. Bay Chamber Symphony Orch., San Mateo, Calif., 1988-91; mem. Nat. Bd. Benevolence Evang. Covenant Ch., Chgo., 1988-93; mem. mgmt. com. The Samarkand Retirement Cmty., Santa Barbara, Calif., 1991-2000; past pres. Project Hope Nat. Alumni Assn., 1992-94, bd. dirs., 1994—; med. advisor Project Hope, Russia Commonwealth Ind. States, 1992. With USNR, 1942-46, 50-52. Named Outstanding Citizen of Yr., Redwood City, 1987. Mem.: AMA, Calif. Thoracic Soc., Cardiovasc. Coun., San Mateo Individual Practice Assn. (treas. 1984—97), Stanford Surg. Soc., San Mateo Surg. Soc., San Mateo County Comprehensive Health Planning Coun. (v.p. 1969—70), San Mateo Med. Soc. (pres. 1969—70), San Mateo County Heart Assn. (pres. 1961—63), Calif. Heart Assn. (pres. 1965—66), Am. Heart Assn. (v.p. 1974—75), Am. Coll. Chest Physicians, Calif. Med. Assn. Republican. Mem. Peninsula Convenant Ch. Home: 2305 Wooster Ave Belmont CA 94002-1549 Office: Sequoia Med Clinic 633 Veterans Blvd Redwood City CA 94063-1408 also: Sequoia Occupl Health 454 Forest Ave Palo Alto CA 94301 Personal E-mail: eldonellis@hotmail.com.

ELLIS, ELMO ISRAEL, broadcast executive, consultant, columnist; b. Birmingham, Ala., Nov. 11, 1918; s. Samuel B. and Bertha F. (Seletz) Israel; m. Ruth M. Ballinger, Dec. 26, 1944; children: Janet Faye, William Bryan. AB, U. Ala., 1940; MA, Emory U., 1948; postgrad., Am. Mgmt. Assn., 1959, Emory U., 1965; LittD (hon.), Oglethorpe U., 1995. Dir. publicity, prodn. mgr. Sta. WSB-AM-FM, Atlanta, 1940-42; writer, prodr. "We The People," CBS and other network radio programs, 1946—47; prodn. mgr. Sta. WSB-TV, 1948-52; instr., radio-tv Emory U., 1948—52, Ga. State U., 1956—60; mgr. programming Sta. WSB-AM-FM, 1952-63, v.p., gen. mgr., 1963—; v.p. Cox Broadcasting Corp., 1969-82. Former chmn. Radio Advt. Bur.; syndicated radio commentator Jacor Communications, Inc., 1982-87; syndicated columnist Neighbor newspapers, 1982—; former chmn. NAFMB, NBC Radio Affiliates, Radio Code Bd. Nat. Assn. Broadcasters; lectr. Oglethorpe U., bd. trustees, 1975—; bd. visitors Coll. Comm., U. Ala., 1997; mem. journalism adv. bd. Emory U., 1997—; pres. Elmo Ellis Prodns., 1982—. Co-author: Radio Station Management, 1960; author: Sleepy Hollow Poems, 1942, Removing the Rust from Radio, 1954, Happiness is Worth the Effort, 1970, Opportunities in Broadcasting Careers, 1986, 5th edit., 1999, The Youthful Option, 1997, The Phoenix-Civil War Centennial Pageant, 1961, Power of the South and other comml. films, articles, poems, TV and radio commercials; contbg. author: Diagnosis and Prognosis in Journalism, 1962, A Forward Look for Communications, 1967, Business and the Media, 1979. Pres. Ga. Safety Coun., 1981-82; past chmn. S.E. regional adv. bd. Anti-Defamation League, B'nai B'rith, hon. life mem. nat. adv. commn., 1983; chmn. Atlanta Christmas Seals Drive, 1977, 78; asst. to dir. Dem. Nat. Convs., 1952, 56, 60, 64; bd. dirs. Atlanta Landmarks, Inc.; chmn. Friends of the Libraries, Emory U., 1985-90; past mem. exec. com., bd. dirs. Peach Bowl; founder Elmo Ellis Profl.-in-Residence Fund U. Ala., 1987; former trustee, mem. adv. bd. Multiple Sclerosis Soc., Ga., Ga. State . Coll. Bus. Adminstrn.; bd. visitors Emory U., Clark Coll. Comms. Dept., Ctr. for Holocaust Studies, Washington, Girl Scouts Greater Atlanta, Boy Scouts Metro Atlanta, Am. Jewish Com., Ga., Consumer Credit Svcs., Ga. Coun. on Child Abuse, Gerontology Ctr. Ga. State U., Jr. Achievement Greater Atlanta. Capt. USAAF, 1942—46. Recipient Ga. Libr. Assn. award, 1965, Silver Medal award Atlanta Advt. Club, 1965, Peabody awards, 1954, 66, Alfred P. Sloan award, 1966, Sch. Bell award Ga. Edn. Assn., 1967, Citizen of Yr. award Ga. Assn. Broadcasters, 1965, Southeastern Father of Yr. award, 1978, Natl. Media Cancer Awd., 1976, Thomas Alva Edison award, 1966, Red Cross Disting. Svc. award, 1968, 25 yr. Svc. Awd., 1967, Big Drop Awd., 1979, Abraham Lincoln awards So. Bapt. Radio-TV Commn., 1972, 77, Silver Beaver award Boy Scouts Am., 1972, Pioneer Broadcaster Ga. award Phi Gamma Kappa, 1972, Meritorious Svc. award Am. Heart Assn., 1970, Disting. Alumnus award U. Ala., 1971, Gavin Disting. Broadcaster award, 1971, 72, 84, Disting. Svc. award Nat. Safety and Ga. Safety Coun., 1973, 79, Nat. Found. for Hwy. Safety award, 1974, George Washington Honor medals and Disting. Svc. awards Freedom's Found., 1973-99, Abe Goldstein award Anti-Defamation League, 1975, Gold Boot award March of Dimes, 1975, George Erwin award Ga. Assn. Realtors, 1975, 76, 77, 78, Humanitarian award Nat. Jewish Hosp., 1979, Mass Media award Protestant Radio-TV Ctr., 1981, Emory Univ., Disting. Svc. award, 1985, 2001, Nat. Bronze award Jr. Achievement, 1985; 1st appointee to Atlanta chpt. U. Ala. Hall of Fame, 1987; named one of Atlanta's Leaders of Tomorrow Time mag. 1951; Disting. Svc. award Arthritis Found., 1966, news and editl. awards AP, UPI, SDX; U.S. Presdl. Commendation, 1970, Heroes, Saints and Legends award Wesley Woods Found., 1995; Ga. Music Hall of Fame, 1995, U. Ala. Coll. of Comm., Hall of Fame, 1999; Georgian of the Century award, Ga. Trend Mag., 2000; named lt. col. Aide-de-Camp Gov.'s Staff State of Ga., 1990, Hugo Black Award, U. of Alabama, 2000. Mem. NARAS (Hall of Fame elections com. 1987-95), Broadcast Pioneers, Internat. Radio-TV Soc., Ga. Assn. Broadcasters (bd. dirs., past pres., Hall of Fame 1987), Am. Values Inc. (nat. adv. bd. 1987-), Soc. Profl. Journalists (past pres., Ralph McGill award 1993), Acad. Am. Poets, U. Ala. Alumni Assn. (Disting. Alumnus award 1993), Commerce Club, Phi Beta Kappa, Phi Eta Sigma, Tau Kappa Alpha, Omicron Delta Kappa. Home: 6345 Aberdeen Dr NE Atlanta GA 30328-4208 Office: Elmo Ellis Prodns 6345 Aberdeen Dr NE Atlanta GA 30328 *Just look around at the unfinished work of the world, and you can see our reason for being.*

ELLIS, ERLE CHRISTOPHER, ecologist, educator; b. Washington, Mar. 11, 1963; s. Robert Andrews Ellis and Ingrid Ehrlich; m. Ariane Carole de Bremond, Sept. 29, 2001; 1 child, Ryan Andrews. AB, Cornell U., 1986, PhD, 1990. Asst. prof. geography and environ. sys. U. Md., Balt., 2000—. Grantee, NSF, 2000—05. Mem.: Ecol. Soc. Am. Office Phone: 410-455-3078.

ELLIS, EUGENE JOSEPH, cardiologist; b. Rochester, N.Y., Feb. 23, 1919; s. Eugene Joseph and Violet (Anderson) E.; m. Ruth Nugent, July 31, 1943; children: Eugene J., Susan Ellis Renwick, Amy Ellis Miller. AB, U. So. Calif., L.A., 1941; MD, U. So. Calif., 1944; MS in medicine, U. Minn., 1950. Diplomate Am. Bd. Internal Medicine and Cardiovascular Diseases. Intern L.A. County Hosp., 1944, resident, 1946; fellowship Mayo Clinic, Rochester, Minn., 1947-51; dir. dept. cardiology St. Vincent's Hosp., L.A., 1953-55, Good Samaritan Hosp., L.A., 1955-84, ret., 1984; prof. emeritus medicine U. So. Calif., 1984—. Mem. Med. Bd. of Calif., 1984-91; pres., 1988; pres. Div. of Med. Quality, State of Calif., 1985-89; exec. com. trustees U. Redlands, 1976-86. Lt. USN, 1944-46. Contbr. articles to profl. jours. Bd. dirs. Cancer Found. Santa Barbara, Casa Dorinda Retirement Facility, Alcohol Coun. Santa Barbara; trustee Sansum-Santa Barbara Clinic, 2002-, Santa Barbara Mus. Natural History. Lt. USN, 1944-46. Mem. L.A. Country Club, Birnam Wood Golf Club (bd. dirs. 1994-95), Valley Club of Montecito. Republican. Avocations: golf, fly fishing. Home: 450 Eastgate Ln Santa Barbara CA 93108-2248

ELLIS, FRANK HALE, retired English literature educator; b. Chgo., Jan. 18, 1916; s. Frank Hale and Gay (Shepherd) E.; m. Constance Dimock, Dec. 20, 1940; 1 dau., Gay. BS with honors, Northwestern U., 1939; PhD, Yale U., 1948. Mem. faculty U. Buffalo, 1941-42; mem. faculty Yale U., 1945-51, 1955—57; with Dept. State, Washington, 1951-54; mem. faculty Smith Coll., 1958-86, Mary Augusta Jordan prof. English lit., 1974-86; ret., 1986. Author: Swift, A Discourse of the Contests, 1967, Twentieth Century Interpretations of Robinson Crusoe, 1969, Poems on Affairs of State, 1697-1714, 2 vols., 1970, 75, Swift vs. Mainwaring, 1985, Sentimental Comedy: Theory and Practice, 1991, John Wilmot Earl of Rochester: The Complete Works, 1994, The ABC of Lit Crit, 2005, Swift: A Tale of a Tub, 2005; contbr. articles to profl. jours. and Oxford Dictionary of Nat. Biography. Served with AUS, 1942-45, ETO and PTO. Decorated Bronze Star; Morse fellow, 1950-51; Huntington Library fellow, 1975 Mem. Cum Laude Soc., Conn. Acad. Arts and Scis., Phi Beta Kappa. Clubs: Elizabethan, Lawn (New Haven). Home: 64 Gothic St # 201 Northampton MA 01060-3042 Office Phone: 413-585-3308.

ELLIS, FRANKLIN HENRY, JR., surgeon, educator; b. Washington, Sept. 20, 1920; s. Franklin Henry and Katherine (McClintock) E.; m. Mary Jane Walsh, Dec. 2, 1978; children: Katherine de Saulles, Elizabeth Dunston (Mrs. Joseph Browning), Franklin Henry III, Margot McClintock, Laura Lawson (Mrs. David Milliken), Marie-Armide Longer (Mrs. Charles Storey), Hedrick Watson, Michael Garrison. AB, Yale U., 1941; MD, Columbia U., 1944; PhD, U. Minn., 1951. Diplomate: Am. Bd. Surgery, Am. Bd. Thoracic Surgery. Intern Bellevue Hosp., N.Y.C., 1944-45; fellow surgery Mayo Clinic, 1945-46, 48-52, fellow thoracic surgery, 1952-53, asst. to surg. staff, 1952-53, cons. surgery, 1953-70; mem. faculty Mayo Grad. Sch. Medicine, 1952-70, prof. surgery, 1964-70, chmn. thoracic surg. sect., 1966-70; chief cardiovascular surgery Lahey Clinic Found., Boston, 1970-75; chief thoracic and cardiovascular surgery Lahey Clinic Med. Ctr., 1975-86, sr. cons., 1986-90; chmn. dept. thoracic and cardiovascular surgery New Eng. Deaconess Hosp., Boston, 1971-90; lectr. surgery Harvard Med. Sch., 1970-74, asso. clin. prof. surgery, 1974-80, clin. prof. surgery, 1980-91, prof. emeritus, 1991—. Served with USNR, 1946-48. Mem. AMA (Billings Gold medal 1955), ACS, Am. Assn. Thoracic Surgery, Internat. Soc. Surgery, Boston Surg. Soc. (pres. 1985-86), New Eng. Surg. Soc., Soc. Clin. Surgery, Soc. Vascular Surgery (pres. 1971), Soc. Thoracic Surgeons (pres. 1977), Assn. Cardiothoracic Surgeons Gt. Britain and Ireland (hon.), Am. Surg. Assn., European Assn. Cardiothoracic Surgery, European Soc. Thoracic Surgeons (hon.), Internat. Soc. Diseases of Esophagus (hon.). Home: 21 Fairmount St Brookline MA 02445-5905 Office: BI-Deaconess Med Ctr 110 Francis St Ste 2A Boston MA 02215-5501 Office Phone: 617-632-8383. Personal E-mail: mwalshellis@msh.org. Business E-Mail: hellis@caregroup.harvard.edu.

ELLIS, GEORGE EDWIN, JR., chemical engineer; b. Beaumont, Tex., Apr. 14, 1921; s. George Edwin and Julia (Ryan) E. BSChemE, U. Tex., 1948; MS, U. So. Calif., 1958, MBA, 1965, MS in Mech. Engring., 1968, MS in Mgmt. Sci., 1971, Engr. in Indsl. and Systems Engring., 1979. Rsch. chem. engr. Tex. Co., Port Arthur, 1948-51, Houston and Long Beach, Calif., 1952-53, Space and Info. Divsn., N.Am. Aviation Co., Downey, Calif., 1959-61, Magna Corp., Anaheim, Calif., 1961-62; chem. process engr. AiResearch Mfg. Co., L.A., 1953-57, 57-59; chem. engr. Petroleum Combustion & Engring. Co., Santa Monica, Calif., 1957, Jacobs Engring. Co., Pasadena, Calif., 1957, Sesler & Assocs., L.A., 1959; rsch. specialist Marquardt Corp., Van Nuys, Calif., 1962-67; sr. project engr. Conductron Corp., Northridge, Calif., 1967-68; info. systems asst. L.A. Dept. Water and Power, 1969-92. Instr. thermodynamics U. So. Calif., L.A., 1957. With USAAF, 1943-45. Mem. ASTM, ASME, AIChE, Inst. Supply Mgmt., Nat. Contract Mgmt. Assn., Am. Inst. Profl. Bookkeepers, Am. Soc. Safety Engrs., Am. Chem. Soc., Am. Soc. Materials, Am. Electroplaters and Surface Finishers Soc., Nat. Assn. Corrosion Engrs., Inst. Indsl. Engrs., Am. Prodn. and Inventory Control Soc., Am. Soc. Quality, Soc. for Protective Coatings, Soc. Plastics Engrs., Inst. Mgmt. Accts., Soc. Mfg. Engrs., Fedn. Socs. for Coatings Tech., Assn. Finishing Processes, Soc. Tribologists and Lubrication Engrs., Soc. Human Resources Mgmt., Soc. Engring. and Mgmt. Systems, Pi Tau Sigma, Phi Lambda Upsilon, Alpha Pi Mu. Home and Office: 1344 W 20th St San Pedro CA 90732-4408

ELLIS, GEORGIANA KEHR, internist, oncologist; b. Buffalo, Jan. 25, 1947; MD, U. Wash., 1982. Diplomate Am. Bd. Internal Medicine. Intern U. Wash. Affiliate, Seattle, 1982-83, resident in internal medicine, 1983-85, fellow in med. oncology, 1985-88; asst. prof. U. Wash., Seattle, 1988—99, assoc. prof., 1999—. Office: Seattle Cancer Care Alliance 825 Eastlake Ave E Seattle WA 98109 Office Phone: 206-288-6711. Business E-Mail: gellis@u.washington.edu.

ELLIS, GREGORY SCOTT, elementary school educator; b. Riverside, Calif., June 17, 1959; s. Norman Raymond and Janice Elaine Ellis; m. Shawna MArie Ellis, Mar. 26, 1983; children: Ruth, Scott, Christopher. BA in Music, Calif. State U., Fullerton, 1981; MA in Edn., U.S. Internat. U., 1987; Min. Music, Newport Ctr. UMC, 2000. Single subject credential music Calif. Tchr. Huntington Beach (Calif.) H.S., 1982—86, McFadden Intermediate Sch., Santa Ana, Calif., 1986—. Named Tchr. of Yr., 1996; recipient Bravo award, Music Ctr. Edn. Divsn., L.A., 1996, Golden Bell award, Calif. Sch. Bd. Assn., 1994, Ireme Schoepfle Meml. award for outstanding music educator, 1995. Mem.: So. Calif. Vocal Assn. (bd. dirs. 1982—94), Music Educators Nat. Conf., Am. Choral Dirs. Assn., Phi Kappa Lambda, Phi Kappa Phi. Avocations: gardening, woodworking, swimming. Home: 24892 Knollwood Lake Forest CA 92630 Office: McFadden Intermediate Sch 2701 S Raitt Santa Ana CA 92704 Office Phone: 714-435-3700.

ELLIS, HELENE RITA, social worker; b. St. Paul, Sept. 20, 1935; d. Moe and Cele (Sidletsky) Weisman; m. Bernard M. Ellis, Sept. 30, 1956; children: Miriam, Arienne, Elia, Evie. BS, U. Minn., 1956; MSW, Loyola U., 1974; PhD, Inst. Clin. Social Work, Chgo., 1996. Lic. clin. social worker, Ill.; bd. cert. diplomate. Tchr. Roosevelt High Sch., Mpls., 1957-58, Barrington (Ill.) High Sch., 1958-59; social worker Dist. #39 Schs., Wilmette, Ill., 1974—2003; pvt. practice Wilmette, 1996—. Adj. prof. Loyola U. of Chgo., 1996—; chairperson Dist. 39 Health and Safety Curriculum Project, Wilmette, 1987-92. Named Ill. Sch. Social Worker of Yr., Ill. Assn. Sch. Social Workers, 1997-98. Mem. NASW, Sch. Social Work Assn. Am., Am. Group Psychotherapy Assn., Ill. Assn. Sch. Social Workers (Social Worker of Yr. 1997-98), Pi Lambda Theta, Phi Beta Kappa, Alpha Sigma Nu. Office: 3330 Old Glenview Rd Wilmette IL 60091 Office Phone: 847-800-4408. E-mail: ellish18@comcast.net.

ELLIS, JAMES D., communications executive, lawyer; b. Ottumwa, Iowa, 1943; BBA, U. Iowa, 1965; JD, U. Mo., 1968. Bar: Mo. 1968, U.S. Ct. Appeals (D.C. cir.) 1977, Tex. 1980. Atty. AT&T, Kansas City, Mo., 1972-74, AT&T Long Lines, NYC, 1974—79; gen. atty. Southwestern Bell Telephone Co., San Antonio, 1979-83; v.p., gen. counsel AT&T centralized svc., Basking Ridge, NJ, 1983-84, Bellcore, 1984; v.p., gen. counsel, sec., Tex. divsn. Southwestern Bell Telephone Co., Dallas, 1984—86; sr. v.p., gen. counsel Southwestern Bell Corp., St. Louis, 1986—88, SBC Comm., San Antonio, 1988—89, sr. exec. v.p., gen. counsel, 1989—. With U.S. Army, 1968-72. Office: SBC Communications Inc 175 E Houston St San Antonio TX 78205-2255

ELLIS, JAMES HENRY, lawyer, management consultant; b. Hartford, Conn., May 6, 1933; s. Robert Isaac and Eve (Alperin) Ellis; m. Linda Abess, Feb. 22, 1959; children: James Arthur, Nancy Jean, Arthur Ungar. BS, U. Conn., 1955; MBA, Harvard U., 1957; JD, U. Miami, 1968. Bar: Fla. 1968, DC 1969, NY 1975. V.p., sec. Fed. Fire & Casualty Co., Miami, Fla., 1959-68; atty. SEC, Washington, 1968-70; exec. v.p., sec., gen. counsel CNA Mgmt. Corp. and 5 related mut. funds, N.Y.C., 1970-79; pres., gen. counsel Mut. Fund Cons. Group, Scarsdale, N.Y., 1979—. Founder, pres. Sentry Savs. and Loan Assn., Stamford, Conn., 1983—90; chmn. edn. com., assocs. divsn. No. Load Mut. Fund Assn., 1986—89. Prodr.: (plays, Off Broadway); (films, short film) Italian Lessons, 2000 (best narrative short film Westchester N.Y. Film Festival, 2000); contbr. articles to profl. jours. Bd. dirs., v.p. White Plains (NY) Symphony Orch., 1975-87; bd. dirs. Stanford Ctr. for the Arts, 1994—; pres., bd. dirs. Parsons Dance Found., 1998-2004, pres. emeritus, 2004—. Mem. ABA, N.Y. State Bar Assn. (co-chmn. theater and performing arts com. 2001--), Harvard Club (N.Y.C.). Democrat. Jewish. Home: 36 Butler Rd Scarsdale NY 10583-2214 Office Phone: 914-725-5514. E-mail: jhellis@cyburban.com.

ELLIS, J(AMES) NICHOLAS, lawyer; b. Newport News, Va., Apr. 3, 1960; s. James Byrd and Loretta Shirley (Walker) E.; m. Susan Wilson Kuhn, May 16, 1987; 1 child, James Samuel. BS in Mktg., Va. Poly. Inst. & State U., 1982; JD, Wake Forest, 1986. Bar: N.C. 1986, U.S. Dist. Ct. (ea. dist.) N.C. 1987, U.S. Ct. Appeals 1988, US Supreme Ct. Tech. engr. N.N. Shipbuilding, Newport News, Va., 1982-83; law clk. Judge Thomas M. Moore, US Bankruptcy Ct. Ea. Dist. NC, Wilson, 1986-87; assoc. Ward & Smith, New Bern, NC, 1987—91; ptnr., bus. litig. Poyner & Spruill LLP, Rocky Mount, NC, 1991—. Instr. of basic law enforcement Craven Community Coll., New Bern, 1988; co-chmn. NC Gen. Assembly Civil Litig. Study Commn., 2000. Co-chmn. New Bern Bank of the Arts, 1988. Mem. ABA, NC Bar Assn. (chmn. litig. sect. 1999-2000, bd. gov. 2001-04), NC Assn. Def. Attys. (dir. 1998-2001, exec. v.p. 2002, pres. 2004), Craven County Bar Assn., Ea. NC Inn of Ct. (v.p. 2003-04). Avocations: tennis, water sports. Office: Poyner & Spruill LLP 130 S Franklin St Rocky Mount NC 27804 Office Phone: 252-972-7115. Office Fax: 252-972-7045. Business E-Mail: jnellis@poynerspruill.com.

ELLIS, JAMES O., JR., retired military officer; m. Paula Matthews; children: Lauren, Patrick. BS, U.S. Naval. Acad., 1969; MS in Aerospace Engring., Ga. Inst. Tech.; MS in Aero. Sys., U. West Fla.; grad., U.S. Naval Test Pilot Sch., 1975; grad. in U.S. naval nuc. power tng., 1987; grad. sr. officer program in nat. security strategy, Harvard U., 1989. Commd. ensign USN, 1969, advanced through grades to adm., 1999; various assignments; designated naval aviator, 1971; insp. gen. U.S. Atlantic Fleet, 1993; mem. staff CINCLANT Fleet, 1993; comdr. Carrier Group Five/Battle Force

Seventh Fleet USS Independence (CV 62), 1995; dep. chief of naval ops., plans, policy and ops., 1996-98; comdr.-in-chief allied forces So. Europe U.S. Naval Forces, 1998—2001; pilot Fighter Squadron 92 USS Constellation (CV-64); pilot Fighter Squadron 1 USS Ranger (CV-61); exptl., operational test pilot; navy office legis. affairs; F/A 18 program coord., dep. chief naval ops. (airwarfare); dep. comdr., chief staff joint task force Five U.S. Pacific Command Counter Narcotics Force; comdg. officer Strike Fighter Squadron 131, F/A 18 Hornet USS Coral Sea (CV-43), 1985; comdg. officer strike fighter squadron 131, F/A 18 Hornet XO USS Carl Vinson (CVN-70), 1988; comdg. officer USS LaSalle (AGF 3), 1989—90, USS Abraham Lincoln (CVN 72), 1991—93; insp. gen. U.S. Atlantic Fleet, 1991, staff comdr. in chief, 1993; dir. ops. plans and policy (N3N5); comdr.-in-chief U.S. Naval Forces and Allied Forces So. Europe, 1998; comdr. U.S. Strategic Command, Offutt AFB, Nebr., 2001—04; pres., CEO Inst. Nuclear Power Ops., Atlanta, 2005—. Decorated Navy D.S.M., Legion of Merit with 3 oak leaf clusters, Def. Meritorious Svc. medal with oak leaf cluster, Def. Disting. Svc. medal with oak leaf cluster, Meritorious Svc. medal, Navy Commendation medal; grand officer Order of Merit (Italy). Office: Inst Nuclear Power Ops 700 Galleria Pkwy SE Ste 100 Atlanta GA 30339

ELLIS, JAMES REED, retired lawyer; b. Oakland, Calif., Aug. 5, 1921; s. Floyd E. and Hazel (Reed) E.; m. Mary Lou Earling, Nov. 18, 1944 (dec.); children: Robert Lee, Judith Ann (dec.), Lynn Earling, Steven Reed. BS, Yale, 1942; JD, U. Wash., 1948; LLD (hon.), Lewis and Clark U., 1968, Seattle U., 1981; PSD (hon.), Whitman Coll., 1992. Bar: Wash. 1949, D.C. 1971. Ptnr. Preston, Thorgrimson, Horowitz, Starin & Ellis, Seattle, 1952-69, Preston, Thorgrimson, Starin, Ellis & Holman, Seattle, 1969-72, Preston, Thorgrimson, Ellis, Holman & Fletcher, Seattle, 1972-79; sr. ptnr. Preston, Thorgrimson, Ellis & Holman, Seattle, 1979-90, Preston, Thorgrimson, Shidler, Gates & Ellis, Seattle, 1990-92; of counsel Preston, Gates & Ellis, Seattle, 1992—2002; chmn., CEO Wash. State Convention and Trade Ctr., Seattle, 1986—2002. Dep. pros. atty. King County, 1952; gen. counsel Municipality of Met. Seattle, 1958-79; dir., mem. exec. com. Key Bank of Wash., 1969-94, KIRO, Inc., 1965-95; dir. Blue Cross of Wash. and Alaska, 1989-98. Mem. Nat. Water Commn., 1970-73; mem. urban transp. adv. council U.S. Dept. Transp., 1970-71; mem. Wash. Planning Adv. Council, 1965-72; mem. Washington State Growth Strategies Commn., 1989-90; pres. Forward Thrust Inc., 1966-73; chmn. Mayors Com. on Rapid Transit, 1964-65; trustee Ford Found., 1970-82, mem. exec. com., 1978-82; bd. regents U. Wash., 1965-77, pres., 1972-73; trustee Resources for the Future, 1983-92; mem. council Nat. Mcpl. League, 1968-76, v.p., 1972-76; chmn. Save our Local Farmlands Com., 1978-79, King County Farmlands Adv. Commn., 1980-82; pres. Friends of Freeway Park, 1976-99; bd. dirs. Nat. Park and Recreation Assn., 1979-82; trustee Lewis and Clark U., 1988-94; pres. Mountains to Sound Greenway Trust, Inc., 1991-2001; trustee Henry M. Jackson Found., 1992—. 1st lt. USAAF, 1943-46. Recipient Bellevue First Citizen award, 1968, Seattle First Citizen award, 1968, Nat. Conservation award Am. Motors, 1968, Distinguished Service award Wash. State Dept. Parks and Recreation, 1968, Distinguished Citizen award Nat. Municipal League, 1969, King County Distinguished Citizen award, 1970, La Guardia award Center N.Y.C. Affairs, 1975, Environ. Quality award EPA, 1977, Am. Inst. for Public Service Nat. Jefferson award, 1974, State Merit medal State of Wash., 1990, Nat. Founders award Local Initiatives Support Corp., 1992, Henry M. Jackson Disting. Pub. Svc. medal, 1998, U. Wash. Alumnus Summa Laude Dignatus award, 1999, Lifetime Achievement award Am. Lawyer mag., 2005 Fellow: Am. Bar Found.; mem.: ABA (ho. dels. 1978—82, past chmn. urban, state and local govt. law sect.), AIA (hon.), Acad. Pub. Adminstrn., Am. Judicature Soc., D.C. Bar Assn., Seattle Bar Assn. (Pres.'s award 1993), Wash. Bar Assn., Nat. Assn. Bond Lawyers (com. stds. of practice), Mcpl. League Seattle and King County (past pres.), Coun. Fgn. Rels., Rainier Club (Seattle), Order of Coif (hon.), Phi Gamma Delta, Phi Delta Phi. Home: 903 Shoreland Dr SE Bellevue WA 98004-6738 Office: 925 4th Ave Seattle WA 98104-1158 Office Fax: 206-623-7022.

ELLIS, JAMES W., law educator; b. 1946; AB, Occidental Coll., 1968; JD, U. Calif. Berkeley, Boalt Hall, 1974. Bar: D.C. 1975. Law prof. U. N. Mex. Sch. Law, 1975—; with Bazelon Ctr. Mental Health Law, Washington. Conscientious objector Yale Psychiatric Inst. Co-author: Least Restrictive Alternative: Principles & Practices, 1981, Consent Handbook, 1977; author: Some Observations on Juvenile Commitment Cases: Reconceptualizing What Child Has At Stake, 1998, Voluntary Admission & Involuntary Hospitalization of Minors, 1996. Successfully argued before U.S. Supreme Ct. in Atkins v. Virginia, execution of people with mental retardation violate 8th amendment U.S. Constn. Named Lawyer of Yr., Nat. Law Jour., 2002. Mem.: ABA (Paul Hearne Award for Disability Advocacy), ARC of US (Call to Action Award), Am. Assn. Mental Retardation. Office: University of New Mexico School of Law 1117 Stanford NE MSC11 6070 1 University New Mexico Albuquerque NM 87131-0001 Office Phone: 505-277-4830. Office Fax: 505-277-0068. E-mail: ellis@law.unm.edu.

ELLIS, JANICE RIDER, nursing educator, consultant; BSN, U. Iowa, 1960; MN, U. Wash., 1971; Phd, U. Tex., 1990. RN, Wash. Staff nurse various hosps., Wash., Oreg., Iowa; prof., dir. nursing edn. Shoreline C.C., Seattle. Rschr. in field.; nursing edn. cons., Seattle Author textbooks; contbr. to profl. jours.; cons. in field. Mem. ANA, Nat. League Nursing, Wash. State Nurses Assn., Sigma Theta Tau, Phi Kappa Delta. Office: Shoreline C C 16101 Greenwood Ave N Seattle WA 98133-5667

ELLIS, JOHN, small business owner; b. Amherst, Ohio, Sept. 15, 1929; s. Edward Pierson and Jean (Scott) E.; m. Carolyn Elizabeth Collier, Dec. 29, 1951; children: Linda Ellis Wieand, Jeanine Ellis Klausing, Jeanette Ellis Hale, John Edward. BS, Bowling Green State U., 1953; MA, Case Western Res. U., Cleve., 1958; EdD, Harvard U., 1964. Tchr. pub. schs., Lorain, Ohio, 1953-54, prin., 1957-61, from asst. supt. to supt. schs. Massillon, Ohio, 1963-66, supt. schs. Lakewood, Ohio, 1966-71, Columbus, Ohio, 1971-77; exec. dep. commr. edn. U.S. Office Edn., Washington, 1977-80; supt. schs. pub. schs., Austin, Tex., 1980-90; commr. N.J. Dept. Edn., 1990-92; owner Ellis Broadcasting Corp., Wimberley, Tex., 1992-2000; cons. Wimberley, Tex., 2000—. Adj. prof. ednl. adminstrn. Ohio State U., Columbus, 1971-77. Elder local Presbyn. Ch. With USAF, 1947-49, 54-57. Recipient Massillon Young Man of Yr. award, 1965; named to Saturday Rev. Honor Roll, 1977. Mem. Rotary, Phi Delta Kappa, Pi Kappa Alpha, Phi Alpha Theta, Kappa Delta Pi, Gamma Theta Upsilon. Home: 500 Leath Hollow Dr Wimberley TX 78676-5207

ELLIS, JOHN, urban designer; BA, MA, Cambridge (Eng.) U. Designer Anshen & Allen, San Fancisco; sr. designer Kaplan McLaughlin Diaz, San Francisco; ptnr. Solomon, ETC (a WRT Co.), San Francisco, 1996—99, prin., 2000—02, dir. urban design, 2002—. Adj. prof. Calif. Coll. Arts and Crafts, San Francisco, 1984; contbg. writer Arch. Rev., London, 1984; designs include Oakland Fed. Bldg., Plaza Tower, Sacramento, Reno Fed. Courthouse, Flood Bldg. renovation. Mem.: RIBA, AIA. Office: Solomon ETC 1328 Mission St 4th Fl San Francisco CA 94103

ELLIS, JOSEPH JOHN MICHAEL, III, historian, history professor; b. Washington, July 18, 1943; s. Joseph J. and Jeanette H. (Sigafoose) E.; m. Ellen Wilkins; children: Peter, Scott. BA, William and Mary Coll., 1965; MA, Yale U., 1967, PhD, 1969. Asst. prof. U.S. Mil. Acad., West Point, N.Y., 1969-72, Mount Holyoke Coll., South Hadley, Mass., 1972-75, assoc. prof., 1975-79, prof. history, 1979—, dean, 1980—90. Bd. dirs. Progressive Policy Inst. Author: The New England Mind in Transition: Samuel Johnson of Connecticut, 1696-1772, 1972, School for Soldiers: West Point and the Profession of Arms, 1974, After the Revolution: Profiles of Early American Culture, 1979, Passionate Sage: The Character and Legacy of John Adams, 1993, American Sphinx: The Character of Thomas Jefferson (Nat. Book award, 1997), 1997, Founding Brothers: The Revolutionary Generation (Pulitzer prize, 2001), 2000, His Excellency George Washington, 2004. Mem. exec. com. Mass. Found. for Humanities, 1978-81. Served to capt. U.S. Army 1969-72. Nat. Endowment for Humanities fellow, 1976-77, Guggenheim fellow, 1988-89. Mem. Am. Hist. Assn., Inst. Early Am. History and Culture, Nat. Humanities Faculty, William and Mary alumni Assn. (bd. dirs.), Progressive Policy Inst., Phi Beta Kappa.

ELLIS, JOSEPH NEWLIN, retired wholesale distribution executive; b. Tenn., Oct. 19, 1928; s. Richard M. and Pearl A. (Fuqua) E.; m. Barbara Harpster, Sept. 17, 1955; 1 child, Patricia Anne. BS, Northwestern U., 1954. Co-founder LaSalle-Deitch Co., Inc., Elkhart, Ind., 1963, exec. v.p., 1969-72, pres., chief exec. officer, 1972-89, chmn. of the bd., chief exec. officer, 1989-94. With U.S. Army, 1950-52. Home: 1160 Benders Ferry Rd Gallatin TN 37066-5703

ELLIS, LAWRENCE DOBSON, internist, educator; b. Pitts., Oct. 11, 1932; s. Robert S. and Elizabeth (Dobson) E.; m. Jacqueline Coogan, June 8, 1954; children: Christine, Thomas, Holly Anne, Jerome. BS, U. Notre Dame, 1954; MD, U. Pitts., 1958. Diplomate Am. Bd. Internal Medicine. Intern in internal medicine U. Pitts. Health Center Hosps., 1958-59; resident in internal medicine Presbyn.-Univ. Hosp., Pitts., 1959-60, 62-63, fellow in hematology, 1963-64; practice medicine specializing in internal medicine, hematology and oncology Pitts., from 1964; clin. asst. prof. medicine U. Pitts., 1966-71; clin. assoc. prof. U. Pitts, 1971-81; clin. prof. U. Pitts., from 1981; prof. medicine Presbyn.-Univ. Hosp., 1994—, mem. active staff, sec., treas. med. staff, 1972-76, v.p. med. staff, 1976-78, pres., from 1978. Mem. cons. staff Shadyside Hosp., Pitts., from 1964, Allegheny County Bd. Health, from 1976; bd. commrs. Health Edn. Ctr., Pitts., from 1976; mem. Pa. State Bd. Medicine, from 1986, vice chmn. 1987; mem. active staff Montefiore Hosp. Contbr. articles to profl. jours., chpts. to med. books. Trustee Leukemia Soc. Am., from 1972, chmn. profl. edn., from 1973, nat. pres., 1985-87; trustee Presbyn.-Univ. Hosp., from 1981, U. Pitts., from 1986. Served to lt. M.C. USN, 1960-62. Recipient Bicentennial medallion of distinction U. Pitts., 1987, honors convocation, 1989. Fellow ACP, Royal Soc. Medicine London; mem. AMA, Pa. Med. Soc. (del. 1974), Allegheny County Med. Soc. (pres. 1976, chmn. bd. 1977, bd. dirs. from 1970, Frederick M. Jacob Physician of Merit award 1981), Pitts. Acad. Medicine (pres. 1984), Royal Soc. Medicine, N.Y. Acad. Scis., Am. Soc. Hematology, Leukemia Soc. Am. (exec. com. from 1978, John J. Kenny award 1981, Spiral of Life award 1988), Med. Alumni Assn. U. Pitts. (pres. 1979-80), Alpha Omega Alpha. Clubs: Pitts. Field, Univ., Pitts. Athletic Assn. Republican. Roman Catholic. Office Phone: 412-687-1210.

ELLIS, LEE, social sciences educator; b. Iola, Kans., Mar. 1, 1942; s. Lee Ellis, Sr. and Dorothy Ellis; children: Lasha, Holly. BA, Pittsburg (Kans.) State U., 1966, MS, 1970; PhD, Fla. State U., 1981. Prof. sociology Minot (N.D.) State U., 1976—. Author (with Anthony Walsh): Criminology: A Global Perspective, 2000; author: (with foreword by Hans J. Eysenck) Theories of Rape: Inquiries into the Causes of Sexual Aggression, 1989; editor (with L. Ebertz, foreword by Milton Diamond): Males, Females, and Behavior: Toward Biological Understanding, 1998; editor: (with L. Ebertz, foreword by Brian Gladue) Sexual Orientation: Toward Biological Understanding, 1997; editor: (foreword by Robert Retherford) Social Stratification and Socioeconomic Inequality, Volume II: Reproductive and Interpersonal Aspects of Dominance and Status, 1994; editor: Research Methods in the Social Sciences, 1994; editor: (forward by Lionel Tiger) Social Stratification and Socioeconomic Inequality, Volume I: A Comparative Biosocial Analysis, 1993; editor: (with Harry Hoffman, foreword by Larry Siegal) Crime in Biological, Social and Moral Contexts, 1990; contbr. over 100 articles to profl. jours., chapters to books. Office: Minot State U 500 University Ave Minot ND 58707 Office Phone: 701-858-3241. Business E-Mail: lee.ellis@minotstateu.edu.

ELLIS, LESTER NEAL, JR., lawyer; b. Washington, Aug. 1, 1948; s. Lester Neal and Marie (Brooks) E. BS, U.S. Mil. Acad., 1970; JD, U. Va., 1975. Bar: Va. 1975, U.S. Ct. Appeals (5th cir.) 1977, D.C. 1978, U.S. Ct. Appeals (4th and D.C. cirs.) 1979, U.S. Ct. Appeals (11th cir.) 1982, N.C. 1985, U.S. Supreme Ct. 2000, U.S. Dist. Ct. (ea., mid., we. dists.) N.C., U.S. Dist. Ct. (ea., we. dists.) Va., U.S. Ct. Claims. Trial atty. litig. divsn. Office of JAG, U.S. Dept. Army, Washington, 1975-78; assoc. Hunton & Williams, Richmond, Va., 1978-84, ptnr. Raleigh, NC, 1984—. Maj. U.S. Army, 1970-78, col. USAR, 1993-99. Recipient Judge Paul Brosman award U.S. Ct. Mil. Appeals, 1975. Mem.: ABA (chair tort and trial practice steering com., editor-in-chief Tort Source, chair comml. torts commn., chair trial techniques com., tort and ins. practice sect., editor-in-chief Tort and Ins. Law Jour., coun. mem., sect. coun.), D.C. Bar Assn. (Wake County bd. elections 1986—93, chmn. 1987—93, ct. rules com.), Va. Bar Assn. (spl. issues com. 1982), Phi Kappa Phi. Republican. Episcopalian. Home: 1116 Wagon Ridge Rd Raleigh NC 27614 Office: Hunton & Williams One Hanover Sq PO Box 109 Raleigh NC 27602-0109 Office Phone: 919-899-3019. Business E-Mail: nellis@hunton.com.

ELLIS, LLOYD H., JR., emergency physician, art historian; b. Denver, Apr. 7, 1936; s. Lloyd Harris and Lura Lou (Wallace) E.; m. Nancy Kay Greenamyre, June 4, 1962 (div. June 1979); children: Peter, Amanda Hunt Thurber; m. Eva Marie Bevan, Sept. 1, 1984; children: Gwendolyn Ruth, David Bevan. BA, Yale U., New Haven, Conn., 1960, MA, 1961; MD, Case Western Reserve U., Cleve., 1970; MA, Case Western Reserve U., 1990, PhD, 2002. Diplomate Am. Bd. Emergency Medicine. Farm mgr., Hastings, Nebr., 1961-62; vice consul Dept. of State, Lourenco Marques, Mozambique, 1963-64, intelligence analyst Washington, 1965-66; dir. emergency dept. Univ. Hosps., Cleve., 1976-84, emergency physician, 1985-94, Emergency Profl. Svcs., Wooster, Ohio, 1995-96, Chardon, Ohio, 1997, Warren, Ohio, 1998. Instr. in surgery Case Western Reserve U., Cleve., 1976-78, asst. prof. surgery, 1979-94; mng. ptnr. Ellis Family Ltd. Partnership, 1992—. Med. dir. Cleve. Emergency Svc., 1976-94; pres. Jeffrey Wallace Ellis Found., Hastings, 1993—; sr. warden Good Shepard, Lyndhurst, Ohio, 1985-86; jr. warden St. Christopher's, Gates Mills, 1998, sr. warden, 1999, Diocesan Coun., 1999-2002; trustee Luna Lou Wallace Ellis Trust, 1992—. 1st Lt. Army, 1956-59. Recipient Ford scholar Ford Found., New Haven, 1952-55. Mem. Am. Coll. Emergency Physicians, Am. Acad. Emergency Medicine, Rowfant Club. Republican. Episcopalian. Home and Office: 32250 Woodsdale Ln Cleveland OH 44139-1335

ELLIS, LYNN WEBSTER, retired finance educator, retired telecommunications consultant; b. San Mateo, Calif., Feb. 27, 1928; s. Lynn Webster, Sr. and Mary Eleanor (Barstow) Ellis; m. Eileen Mary Gallagher; children: Lynn W. Jr., Margaret, Katherine. BEE, Cornell U., 1948; MS, Stevens Inst. Tech., 1954; D Profl. Studies in Mgmt., Pace U., 1979. Exec. ITT Corp., 1948-79; v.p. engring. Bristol Babcock Co., Waterbury, Conn., 1980-82; cons. Lynn W. Ellis Assocs., Westport, Conn., 1982-85; prof. U. New Haven, West Haven, Conn., 1985-94, scholar-in-residence, 1994-97, prof. emeritus, 1997—. *Named to position of Director of Research with International Telephone & Telegraph Corporation, 1976-1979. Previously was Director of Telecommunications, 1975-1975. Responsible for planning ITT's long range research program, managing the corporate research and advanced technology budget, and directing and coordinating the research program of the ITT laboratories. Also, Alternate Director, Fundación Chile, 1972-1979. Has been associated with ITT for 27 years, undertaking technical work in the operating and manufacturing sectors of telecommunications and research and development in military electronics. Spent 11 years of his ITT service overseas in engineering management positions in subsidiaries in Spain, England, and Australia, where he rose to be Assistant Managing Director, 1963-1966, of ITT's Australian telecommunications manufacturing company, STC (Pty) Ltd.* Author: Evaluating R&D Processes, 1996, Financial Side of Industrial Research Management, 1984; contbr. articles to profl. jours.; patentee in field. Mem. five panels and coms. NRC, Washington, 1970—95; chmn. adv. com. Dept. of Commerce, Washington, 1973—75. Capt. U.S. Army, 1948—52. Fellow: AAAS, IEEE (Internat. Communication award 1983). Home: 1301 Gulf Blvd Apt 115 Clearwater FL 33767-2803 Office: U New Haven 300 Orange Ave West Haven CT 06516-1916

ELLIS, MARTIN F., insurance company executive; AS in Bus., Nebr. Western Coll., Lincoln; BS in Bus. Adminstrn., U. Nebr., Lincoln. Br. claims mgr. Union Ins. Co., Denver, 1984—88; lit. specialist Allied Group Ins., Denver, 1988—91; sr. claims specialist major case unit Royal Ins., Englewood, Colo., 1991—96; acting risk mgr., claims supervisor risk mgmt. and safety divsn. internal svcs. dept. City of Aurora, Colo., 1996—98; dir. risk mgmt. Broe Co., Inc., 1998—2001; comml./farm ranch claims specialist, casualty claims examiner comml. claims unit Am. Family Ins., 2002—. Mem. Colo. Claim Mgr. Coun., 1985—88, 1996—98, treas., 1997, sec., 98. Co-author: What To Do When You Can't Find The Policy, 1995. Bd. dirs. Summit Cove Recreation Assn., Dillion, Colo., 1994—, bd. pres. Mem.: CPCU Soc., Denver and Colo. Claims Assn.

ELLIS, MARY LOUISE HELGESON, retired insurance company executive, business consultant; b. Albert Lea, Minn., May 29, 1943; d. Stanley Orville and Neoma Lois (Guthier) Helgeson; m. David Readinger, Nov. 5, 1994; children from previous marriage: Christopher, Tracy. BS in Pharmacy, U. Iowa, 1966; MA in Pub. Adminstrn., Iowa State U., 1982, postgrad., 1982—83. Faculty Duquesne U., Pitts., 1977; cons. in pharmacy Colville, Wash., 1978—79; dir. pharmacy Mt. Carmel Hosp., Colville, 1978—79; clin. pharmacist Iowa Vets. Home, Marshalltown, Iowa, 1980—81; instr. Iowa Valley C.C., Marshalltown, 1981—83; dir. Iowa Dept. Substance Abuse, Des Moines, 1983—86, State of Iowa Pub. Health; dir. Iowa Dept. Pub. Health, Des Moines, 1986—90; spl. cons. health affairs Blue Cross/Blue Shield of Iowa, 1990—91; v.p. Blue Cross/Blue Shield of Iowa and S.D., 1991—2000; ret., 2000; bus. cons., 2001—. Chair Iowa Health Data Commn., Des Moines, 1986—90; bd. dirs. Health Policy Corp. Iowa, 1986—90; adj. asst. prof. U. Iowa, Iowa City, 1984—; commd. officer U.S. FDA, 1989—90; mem. alumnae bd. dirs. U. Iowa Coll. of Pharmacy, 1989—; chair Nat. Commn. Accreditation of Ambulance Svcs., 1992—97; commencement spkr. U. Iowa, Iowa City, 2003. Mem. Iowa State Bd. Health, 1981—83, v.p., 1982—83; mem. adv. coun. Iowa Valley C.C., 1983—85. Recipient Woman of Achievement award, Des Moines YWCA, 1988, Alumnae of Yr. award, U. Iowa, Coll. Pharmacy, 2005. Mem.: APHA, Iowa Pub. Health Assn. (bd. dirs., Henry Albert award 1990), Iowa Pharmacists Assn., Pi Sigma Alpha, Phi Kappa Phi, Alpha Xi Delta. Republican. Home: 2912 Caulder Ave Des Moines IA 50321-2637

ELLIS, MISSIE LYNNE, music educator; b. Pitts., July 22, 1975; d. Gary Edward and Linda Clymer Ellis. B in Music Edn., Fla. So. Coll., 1998. Dir. of bands Meadowbrook Mid. Sch., Orlando, Fla., 1998—2001, Lakeview Mid. Sch., Winter Garden, Fla., 2001—. Dir. all-county honors band Orange County Pub. Schs., 2005—. Deacon Wekiva Presbyn. Ch., Longwood, Fla., 2005—. Named Tchr. of Yr. at Meadowbrook Mid. Sch., Orange County Pub. Schs., 2002. Mem.: Nat. Assn. for Music Edn., Fla. Music Educators Assn., Fla. Band Masters Assn. Republican. Presbyterian. Avocations: golf, walking, reading, shopping, computers. Home: 500 Golf Tee Ln # 232 Longwood FL 32779 Office: Lakeview Mid Sch 1200 W Bay St Winter Garden FL 34787 Fax: 407-877-5019. Office Phone: 407-877-5010 ext 275. Business E-Mail: ellism4@ocps.net.

ELLIS, NORMANDI, writer; b. Sept. 24, 1953; BA, U. Ky., 1976; MA, U. Colo., 1981. Exec. editor Bookmakers Guild, Longmont, Colo., 1986-88; tchr. fiction U. Ky., Lexington, 1992-98; artist in schs. Ky. Arts Coun., 1993—. Lectr. in field. Author: Awakening Osiris, 1988, Sorrowful Mysteries, 1991, Dreams of Isis, 1994, Voice Forms, 1998, Feasts of Light, 1999. Named Writers Voice fellow, YMCA, 1996, Al Smith fellow, Ky. Arts Coun., 2000; named to FCHS Hall of Fame, 2001; recipient Bumbershoot Weyerhauser award, 1991; grantee, Ky. Found. for Women, 1996. Address: PO Box 51 Frankfort KY 40602-0051

ELLIS, BROTHER PATRICK (H. J. ELLIS), academic administrator; b. Balt., Nov. 17, 1928; s. Harry James and Elizabeth Alida (Evert) E. AB, Cath. U. Am., Washington, 1951; AM, U. Pa., 1954, PhD, 1960; postgrad., Barry Coll., 1963-64, Inst. Catholique, Paris, 1958; LHD (hon.), Assumption Coll., 1982, La Salle U., 1992; HHD (hon.), King's Coll., 1987; LLD (hon.), U. Scranton, 1988, C.C. Phila., 1992, Quincy U., 1993; PdD, Manhattan Coll., 1993; DEd, Anna Maria Coll., 1993, Loyola U., 1997; LHD (hon.), Villa Julie Coll., 2002. Joined Bros. of Christian Schs., Roman Cath. Ch., 1946. Tchr. English dept. West Cath. High Sch. for Boys, Phila., 1951-60, chmn. English dept., 1956-58, guidance dir., 1959-60; dir. practice teaching, sch. prin. St. Gabriel's Hall, Phoenixville, Pa., summers 1960-61, 65-66; asst. prof. English La Salle U., Phila., 1960-62, assoc. prof., 1968-73, prof., 1973—, dir. housing, 1961-62, dir. honors program, 1964-69, dir. devel., v.p., 1969-76, pres., 1977-92; prin. La Salle HS, Miami, Fla., 1962—64; pres. Cath. U. Am., Washington, 1992-98. Author: Called To Teach: Persons Are Forever, 2001; condr.: series for How To Read Gt. Books, U. of the Air, WFIL-TV, Phila., 1961, 65; Contbr. articles to profl. publs. Trustee Manhattan Coll., N.Y.C., Calvert Hall H.S., Balt., to 2001; bd. dirs. Cathedral Fedn. Balt., 2004-, Phila. Cath. Charities, 1986-92, Greater Phila. Urban Coalition, Police Athletic League, Phila., Free Libr. Phila., 1991-92, Del. Valley Citizens Crime Commn., Fed. City Coun., D.C. Econ. Club, D.C. Bd. Trade; former trustee Cmty. Leadership Seminars, BBB; mem. recognition com. Coun. for Higher Edn. Accreditation, 1999-2001. Recipient Lindback award for disting. teaching LaSalle Coll., Phila., 1965 Mem. Sunday Breakfast Club (Phila.), Phila. Club, Univ. Club (Washington), Phi Beta Kappa, Knights of Holy Sepulchre. Home and Office: Calvert Hall HS 8102 La Salle Rd Baltimore MD 21286-8022 Office Phone: 410-296-6031. E-mail: brotherpatrickellis@erols.com.

ELLIS, RANDALL POOR, economist, educator; b. Newton, Mass., 1954; s. George Hathaway and Sylvia (Poor) E.; m. Joyce H. Huber; children: Richard G., Scott R., Karina J. B.A., summa cum laude, Yale U., 1976; M.S., London Sch. Econs., 1977; Ph.D., M.I.T., 1981. Asst. prof. econs. Boston U., 1981-89, assoc. prof., 1989-95, prof., 1995—; sr. scientist DxCG, Inc. Mem. APHA, Am. Econ. Assn., Econometric Soc., Internat. Health Econ. Assn. (dir.), Am. Soc. Health Economists (dir.), Acad.Health, Phi Beta Kappa. Office: Boston U Dept Econs 270 Bay State Rd Boston MA 02215-1403 E-mail: ellisrp@bu.edu.

ELLIS, RANDALL SPENCER, diversified company director; b. Sedalia, Mo., Feb. 25, 1948; s. Isaac Barnett and Margaret Virginia (Hoffman) E.; m. Cecelia Marie Jones, Sept. 18, 1971. BS in Mech. Engring., Kans. State U., 1970; MBA, Northwestern U., 1972. Mfg. analyst/svc. mgr. Bell & Howell, Chgo., 1972-76; auditor FMC Corp., Chgo., 1977, proposals/fin. mgr. ground sys. divsn. San Jose, Calif., 1978-80, contr. ground sys. divsn., 1981-86, gun sys. dir. armament sys. divsn. Mpls., 1987-88, ops. mgr. petroleum equipment divsn. Sens, France, 1989-92, corp. devel. dir. Chgo., 1993—. Treas. Triton Mus. Art, Santa Clara, Calif., 1982-86; vol. Fund for Aging and Disability, Chgo., 1995—; bd. mem. Nonprofit Fin. Ctr., Chgo., 1995—. Mem. SAR. Office: FMC Corp 200 E Randolph St Ste 5200 Chicago IL 60601-6662

ELLIS, RICHARD SALISBURY, astronomer, educator; b. Colwyn Bay, Wales, May 25, 1950; s. Arthur (dec.) and Marion (Davies) E.; m. Barbara Williams, July 28, 1972; children: Hilary Rhona, Thomas Marc. BSc with honors, U. Coll., London, 1971; PhD, Oxford U., 1974; DSc (hon.), Durham U., 2002. From sr. demonstrator to lectr. in astronomy Durham U., 1974-83, prof. astronomy, 1985-93, Calif. Inst. Tech., 1999—2002; Plumian prof. astronomy Cambridge U., England, 1993-99; Steele prof. astronomy Calif. Inst. Tech., 2002—; prin. rsch. assoc. Royal Greenwich Obs., 1983-85; dir. Inst. Astronomy, Cambridge, 1994-99, Palomar Obs., Pasadena, Calif., 2000—02, Caltech. Optical Obs., 2002—. Vis. prof. Princeton U., 1992, Calif. Inst. Tech., 1991, 97, U. Coll. London, 2004. Sr. Rsch. fellow Sci. and Engring. Rsch. Coun., 1989-94, Professorial fellow Magdalene Coll., Cambridge, 1994-99; fellow Univ. Coll., London. Fellow AAAS, Royal Astron. Soc., Inst. of Physics, Royal Soc. London; mem. Am. Astron. Soc., Astron. Soc. Pacific. Avocations: travel, skiing. Office: Calif Inst Asronomy MS 105-24 1200 E California Blvd Pasadena CA 91125 Business E-Mail: rse@astro.caltech.edu.

ELLIS, RICHARD W., lawyer; b. Raleigh, N.C., Apr. 20, 1942; AB, U. N.C., 1964, JD with high honors, 1969. Bar: N.C. 1969. Mem. Ellis & Winters, Raleigh. Assoc. editor N.C. Law Rev., 1968-69. With USNR, 1964-66. Mem. Am. Coll. Trial Lawyers, Interant. Assn. Def. Counsel, Def. Rsch. Inst., N.C. Assn. Def. Attys., Order of Coif. Office: Ellis & Winters LLP PO Box 33550 Raleigh NC 27636 Office Phone: 919-865-7007. Business E-Mail: dick_ellis@elliswinters.com.

ELLIS, ROBERT HARRY, retired broadcast executive, academic administrator; b. Cleve., Mar. 2, 1928; s. John George Ellis and Grace Bernice (Lewis) Ellis Kline; m. Frankie Jo Lanter, Aug. 7, 1954; children: Robert Harry Jr., Kimberley Kay Ellis Murphy, Shana Ellis Antonio. BA, Ariz. State U., 1953; MA, Case Western Res. U., 1962. Newswriter, announcer Sta. KOY, Phoenix, 1953-55, continuity dir., 1955-61; dir., radio ops. Ariz. State U., Tempe, 1959-61; gen. mgr. Sta. KAET-TV, Tempe, 1961-87; assoc. v.p. Ariz. State U., Tempe, 1986-90. Exec. com. bd. dirs. Pub. Broadcasting Svc., Washington, 1972-77, 80-86; founder Pacific Mountain Network, Denver, 1972, pres., 1973-75; mem. ednl. telecomm. com. Nat. Assn. Ednl. Broadcasters, Washington, 1973-77, 80-86. Mem. Sister City, Tempe, Tempe Ctr. For the Handicapped, East Valley Mental Health Alliance, Mesa, Ariz., Ariz. Acad., State Ariz. Behavior Health Bd. of Examiners, 1991-92. Recipient Bd. Govs. award Pacific Mountain Network, 1987, achievement award Ariz. State U., 1997; named to Ariz. Broadcasters Hall of Fame, 1999. Mem. Nat. Assn. TV Arts and Scis. (life, v.p., bd. trustees 1969-70, bd. dirs. Phoenix chpt. 1986, silver circle award 1992), Nat. Assn. Pub. TV Stas. (bd. dirs. 1988-94), Tempe C. of C. (diplomate, bd. dirs. 1987-90), Sundome Performing Arts Assn. (bd. dirs. 1986-90), Ariz. Zool. Soc. (bd. dirs., sec. 1984-90), Ariz. State U. Alumni Assn. (life), Ariz. State U. Retirees Assn. (founder, pres. 1991-92), Tempe Conv. and Visitors Bur. (founder, sec./treas. 1988-93), Tempe Sports Authority (founder 1989-95), ASU Faculty Emeritus Orgn. (pres. 1992-93). Methodist. Avocations: tennis, bridge.

ELLIS, ROSS, non-profit organization executive; Co-owner Visions & Images; pres. Elegant Events; v.p., dir. corp. affairs and events pharm. comm. co.; dir. resource devel. child abuse prevention group; founder, CEO Love Our Children, USA, 1999—. Active with Starlight Children's Found.; mem Phillip Morris Domestic Violence Coun. Mem.: NY Entertainment Publicists Soc. (bd. dirs.), NY Women's Agenda, NY Women in Comm. (bd. dirs.). Achievements include created and ran Dreams Come True program at Mt. Sinai Med. Ctr. Office: Love Our Children USA 220 E 57th St New York NY 10022 Office Phone: 888-347-5437. Business E-Mail: info@loveourchildrenusa.org.

ELLIS, SAMUEL LEE, JR., music educator; b. Rome, Ga., Mar. 5, 1980; s. Samuel Lee Ellis, Sr. and Rebecca A. Ellis. BA in Music Edn., Jacksonville State U., Ala., 2004. Resident asst. Jacksonville State Housing Dept., Ala., 2002—04; band dir. Childersburg H.S., Ala., 2004—. Dir. of music Greater St. Paul CME Ch., Bessemer, Ala., 2004—05. Mem.: Ala. Bandmasters Assn. Home: 1435 Cahaba River Parc Birmingham AL 35243 Office: Childersburg High Sch Band 122 Fay S Perry Dr Childersburg AL 35044 Office Phone: 256-315-5485. Office Fax: 256-315-5495. Personal E-mail: samjsu@aol.com. E-mail: sellis@tcboe.org.

ELLIS, SARAH AMES, clinical psychologist; b. St. Paul, Jan. 10, 1925; d. Charles Lesley and Linda (Baker) Ames; m. Francis Martin Ellis, Sept. 13, 1947 (div. 1982); children: Carolyn Terry, Francis Lyman, Nathan Ames; m. Adam Yarmolinsky, Feb. 3, 1990 (dec. 2000). AB, Barnard Coll.; MSW, Columbia U.; MA in Psychology, New Sch. for Social Rsch., 1973; cert. in Psychoanalytic Psychotherapy and Psychoanalysis, Inst. Contemporary Psychotherapy, 1975; PhD in Clin. Psychology, New Sch. for Social Rsch., 1982. Lic. psychologist, N.Y., D.C. Counselor Women's Intensive Treatment Ward, 1964-66; psychiat. caseworker Mental Hygiene Clinic, 1966-69; psychiat. social worker family therapy unit Bellevue Psychiat. Hosp., N.Y.C., 1964-71; pvt. practice N.Y.C., 1972-90; staff therapist Inst. Contemporary Psychotherapy, N.Y.C., 1975-90; psychology cons. Inst. Reconstructive Plastic Surgery-NYU Med. Ctr., N.Y.C., 1978-86; pvt. practice Washington, 1990—2000; staff psychotherapist D.C. Inst. for Mental Health, Washington, 1990-93. Rsch. psychologist Project H.E.L.P., Gouverneur Hosp., N.Y.C., 1989-90; instr. NYU Med. Sch.; vol. tchr. George Washington Med. Sch., 1997-2000. With WAC, 1945-46. Mem.: APA, Washington Psychologists for Study of Psychoanalysis (bd. dirs. 1993—94). Avocations: travel, animal behavior, hiking. Home and Office: 299 W 12th St New York NY 10014

ELLIS, SCOTT, theatrical director; Grad., Goodman Sch. of Drama, Chgo. Assoc. artistic dir. Roundabout Theatre Co. Dir. plays 1776 (Drama Desk, Outer Critics Circle and Tony nominations), Steel Pier (Drama Desk, Outer Critics Circle and Tony nominations), Company, She Love Me (Tony nomination, Outer Critics Circle award Best Dir., Best Revival, Olivier award), Picnic (Outer Critics Circle nomination), A Month in the Country, Dark Rapture, The World Goes Round: The Music of Kander and Ebb (Drama Desk, Outer Critics Circle awards Best Director, Best Musical Revue), Flora, the Red Menace, 110 in the Shade, A Little Night Music (Drama Desk award Best Director, Best Revival), Sondheim: A Celebration at Carnegie Hall, The Boys from Syracuse, 2002, Tartuffe, 2003, A Day in the Dearth of Joe Egg, 2003, Nine, 2003, The Look of Love, 2003, Master Harold and the Boys, 2003, Big River, 2003, Assassins, 2004, Twentieth Century, 2004, After the Fall, 2004, Twelve Angry Men, 2004 Office: Roundabout Theatre Co Ste 1200 231 W 39th St New York NY 10018

ELLIS, SHARON HENDERSON, arbitrator, mediator; b. Wenatchee, Wash., May 31, 1944; d. Marvin T. and Nola Henderson; m. Alfred D. Ellis, Aug. 1972. BA, U. Wash., 1967; JD, Suffolk U., 1975. Adminstrv. law judge Mass. Labor Rels. Commn., Boston, 1978-81; arbitrator, mediator Brookline, Mass., 1982—. Adj. prof. New Eng. Sch. Law, 2002—. Contbg. author: (book) Labor and Employment Arbitration, 1988. Vol. II, tchr. U.S. Peace Corps, Tunisia, 1967-69. Mem. Am. Arbitration Assn., Nat. Acad. Arbitrators (regional chair 1997-99), Mass. Bar Assn. (sect. co-chair 1999-2000), Assn. for Conflict Resolution. Home: 36 Salisbury Rd Brookline MA 02445-2105 Office Phone: 617-731-3358. Personal E-mail: sharonhendersonellis@rcn.com.

ELLIS, STANLEY WESTON, musician, educator; b. Plymouth, Mass., Dec. 23, 1945; s. Milton Weston and Claudia Bryant Ellis; m. Ann Leslie Semple, June 1, 1968; children: Scott Weston, Stacey Anne. B in Music Edn., Berklee Coll. Music, Boston, 1968. Cert. tchr. Mass. Band dir. Duxbury (Mass.) Pub. Schs., 1976—81, Old Hammondtown Sch., Mattapoisett, 1981—; jazz band dir. Old Rochester Regional Jr. HS, Mattapoisett, Mass., 1989—90; marching percussion dir. Barnstable HS, Hyannis, Mass., 1991—95; jazz combo dir. Old Rochester Regional HS, Mattapoisett, 1999—, jazz band dir., 2001—. Clinician elem. jazz band All State Mass. Music Edn., 1998—2005. Author: Hi-Hat Rhythms for the Modern Drummer, 1982; author, composer: I Never Noticed Until Now When Monday Rolls Around, 1996—98, music dir., composer: albums Old Rochester HS Jazz Combo, 2004. Music dir. Christmas in Pk. Town of Mattapoisett, 2003—04; card artist Animal Advs., New Bedford, Mass., 2000—01. Named Condr. of the Yr., Mass. Instrumental and Choral Assn., 1999, Mattapoisett Man of the Yr., New Bedford Std. Times, 2002. Mem.: ASCAP, Mass. Tchrs. Assn., Mass. Music Educators Assn., Internat. Assn. Jazz Edn. (elem. jazz chairperson Mass. 1998—, state chair combo/choir competition Mass. 2004—05), Mass. Soc. Mayflower Descs. Avocations: drawing, bicycling, musical composition, genealogy. Home: PO Box 327 West Falmouth MA 02574 Office: Old Hammondtown Elem Sch PO Box 477 Mattapoisett MA 02739 Office Phone: 508-758-9226. Personal E-mail: ann1stann@aol.com.

ELLIS, STEPHEN C., lawyer; b. Portland, Oreg., Apr. 17, 1945; s. Donald E. Ellis and Francis E. (Shainholts) Cordiner; m. Helen Stevens, Jan. 1, 1981; children: Donald, Peter. BA cum laude, U. Wash., 1967; JD cum laude, U. Mich., 1970. Bar: Wash., 1970, U.S. Dist. Ct. (We. dist. Wash.). Assoc. Reed McClure Moleri & Thonn, Seattle, 1970-73, ptnr., 1973-86; founder, mng. ptnr., pres. Weiss Jensen Ellis & Botteri (combined with offices Holland & Knight LLP), Seattle, 1986—2001; ptnr. Holland & Knight LLP, Seattle, recruiting and lateral hiring ptnr. Chmn. Com. of Law Examiners, Seattle, 1981-84; mem. WSBA Character and Fitness Com., Seattle, 1985-91. Contbr. articles to profl. jours. Bd. trustee Seattle Chidren's Home, 1987-91; bd. trustee, sec. N.W. Theol. Union, Seattle, 1986-1994; bd. dir., officer Village Theatre Issaquah, Wash., 1994-, current pres. Mem. Seattle-King County Bar Assn., Washington State Bar Assn. (Bar Examiners Com. mem. 1975-86, chmn., com. law examiners, 1983-86, law clerk com. 1983-97, corp., banking law and internat. law, sect. mem., character and fitness com. 1986-91), ABA (mem., sect. on corp., banking and bus. law), Athletic Club, Harbor Club. Avocations: racquetball, book collecting, writing. Home: 12225 188th St SE Snohomish WA 98296-8153 Office: Holland & Knight LLP 520 Pike St 2600 Pike Tower Seattle WA 98101 Office Phone: 206-340-9573. Business E-Mail: stephen.ellis@hklaw.com.

ELLIS, STEVEN GEORGE, public relations/corporate communications executive; b. Mar. 14, 1949; s. George G. and Betty (Chow) E.; m. Sylvia Regina Ellis; children: Steven Andrew, Christopher John, Katharine Marie. BA, U. Ga., 1971. V.p. Burson-Marsteller, Washington, 1976-83; v.p., gen. mgr. Earle Palmer Brown Pub. Rels., Bethesda, Md., 1983-84, pres., 1987-88; v.p. corp. comms. RKO Gen. Co. subs. GenCorp, Inc., N.Y.C., 1984-86; pres. Steve Ellis Comms. Inc., 1988-95; sr. v.p. Jefferson-Waterman Internat., Washington, 1995-98; dir. corp. comms. SAGA Software, Inc., 1998-2000; v.p. global corp. comm. Metiom, Inc., N.Y.C., 2000-01; sr. dir. global corp. comm. Think Tools AG, Zurich, Switzerland, 2001—02; prin. Ellis Internat. Comm., 2003—. Mem. adv. bd. Henry W. Grady Coll. Journalism and Mass Comm. Recipient Gold Key award Pub. Rels. News, 1985, 86.

ELLIS, STUART L., lawyer; b. Milw., Dec. 16, 1952; s. Lester S. and Luverne A. Ellis. BA, U. Wis., 1975; JD, John Marshall Sch. Law, 1981. Bar: Ill. 1981, U.S. Dist. Ct. (no. dist.) Ill. 1981, Wis. 1985. Ptnr. Karp and Ellis, Chgo., 1981—. Mem. Ill. State Bar, State Bar Wis., Chgo. Bar Assn. Office: 77 W Washington St Ste 1020 Chicago IL 60602-2805 Office Phone: 312-726-9382.

ELLIS, TERRY, vocalist; b. Austin, Tex., Sept. 5, 1966; Vocalist En Vogue, Acto/Eastwest Records, N.Y.C., 1988—. Albums include Born to Sing (Platinum 1990), Funky Divas, Remix to Sing, Runaway Love, The Best of En Vogue, 1999. Recipient Soul Train Music award, 1991; nominated Grammy award. Office: care En Vogue Atco/Eastwest Records 75 Rockefeller Plz New York NY 10019-6908

ELLIS, WALTER LEON, minister; b. McKinney, Tex., Oct. 22, 1941; s. Erwin Ballard and Mary Edra (Bray) E.; m. Susan Elizabeth Elder, Nov. 23, 1960; children: Bruce Walter, David Anthony, Patrick Durward. BA, U. North Tex., 1964, MA, 1966; MDiv, Va. Sem., 1977; DMin, Austin Presbyn. Theol. Sem., 1993. Ordained to ministry Episc. Ch., 1977. Vicar St. Michael & All Angels', Longview, Tex., 1977-79, St. Mark's, Gladewater, Tex., 1977-79; rector St. Michael & All Angel's, Longview, Tex., 1979-82, St. Christopher, League City, Tex., 1982-2001, Ch. of the Ascension, Houston, 2001—. Dean Galveston Convocation, League City, 1989-97; mem. Diocesan Standing Com., Houston, 1996-99, pres., 1998; Order of St. Luke Chaplain, 1996-2001, Diocesan E xec. Bd., 1998-2001, Cursillo Secretariat, 1997-99; trustee St. James House, Baytown, Tex., 1983-84, 90-93, Camp Allen, Navasota, Tex., 1987-90, Bishop Quin Found., Houston, 1991-97, St. Vincent's House, Galveston, 1996-99, 2000-01; chmn. dept. environment Diocese of Tex., 1993-95; b.d dirs. Interfaith Caring Ministries, League City, 1993-94; stewardship cons. Episcopal Ch. Ctr., N.Y.C., 1990-95. Contbr. articles to profl. jours. Bd. dirs. pres. Parents Anonymous, Longview, 1980; mem. exec. bd. Bay Area coun. Boy Scouts Am., Tex., 1983-86; pres. Rotary Club, League City, 1989-90; chmn. bd. Ascension Episc. Sch., 2001— Paul Harris fellow Space Ctr. Rotary Club, Houston, 1989. Mem. West Houston Assistance Ministry. Office: 10915 Chevy Chase Houston TX 77042 E-mail: rector@ascensionchurch.org. *You have been blessed by God through others. Find something you admire in each person you meet. Then bless those people by telling them what you admire in them.*

ELLIS, WILLIAM BEN, environmental educator, retired utility executive; b. Vicksburg, Miss., July 4, 1940; s. Conrad Ben and Viola Elizabeth (Stigall) E.; children by previous marriage: Bradford, Katherine, Emily, Ben; m. Elaine Klutsavage, July 10, 1988; children: John, David. BS, Carnegie Mellon U., 1962; PhD, U. Md., 1966. Process engr. Standard Oil N.J., Baton Rouge, 1962-67; assoc. McKinsey & Co., Inc., Washington, 1969-75, prin., 1975-76; exec. v.p., CFO Northeast Utilities and Subs., Hartford, Conn., 1976-78, pres., cfo, 1978-80, pres., coo, 1980-83, chmn., ceo, 1983-93, chmn., 1993-95. Sr. vis. fellow Yale U. Sch. of Forestry and Environ. Studies, 1995—; trustee Northeast Utilities, Hartford, Conn., 1977-95; bd. dirs. Mass. Mutual Life Ins. Co., Catalytica Energy Sys., Inc., numerous others. Bd. dirs. Smithsonian Natural History Mus., 1993-2002, Pew Ctr. Global Climate Change, 1998-. With U.S. Army, 1967-69. Mem. Metro Hartford C. of C. (bd. dirs. 1978—, chmn. 1985).

ELLIS, WILLIAM GRENVILLE, academic administrator, management consultant; b. Teaneck, N.J., Nov. 29, 1940; s. Grenville Brigham and Vivian Lilian (Breeze) E.; m. Nancy Elizabeth Kempton, 1963; children: William Grenville, Bradford Graham. BS in Bus. Adminstrn., Babson Coll., 1962; MBA, Suffolk U., 1963; MEd, Westfield State Coll., 1965; EdD, Pa. State U., 1968; MS, Concordia U., 1991; MLE (Sears Roebuck Found. scholar), Harvard U., 1980; postgrad., U. Chgo., 1983, MIT, 1984, Harvard U., 1988, 96. Asst. prof. bus. Rider U., 1968-69; div. dir., assoc. prof. Castleton (Vt.) State Coll., 1969-72; exec. v.p., prof. St. Joseph Coll. in Vt., Rutland, 1972-73; acad. v.p., dean grad. sch. Thomas Coll., Waterville, Maine, 1973-82; pres. Wayland Acad., Beaver Dam, Wis., 1982-95, New Eng. Coll., Henniker, N.H., 1995-97; dean Sch. Bus. and Legal Studies, Concordia U. Wis., Mequon, 1997—. Mem. adv. bd. CFX Bank, 1996-97; corporator 1st Consumers Savs., 1974-81, Maine Savs., 1981-82, BankOne, 1983-95. Author: The Analysis and Attainment of Economic Stability, 1963, The Relationship of Related Work Experience to the Teaching Success of Beginning Business Teachers, 1968, Marketing for Educational Administrators, 1991, A Gunner's Moon, 1997; contbr. numerous articles and abstracts to profl. jours. Trustee C.C. Vt., 1972-73, Marian Coll., 1988-91, Wayland Acad., 1982-95, New Eng. Coll., 1995-97; auditor Town of Castleton, 1969-71; pres. Kennebee Valley Youth Hockey, Augusta, Maine, 1975-77; pres. Beaver Dam C. of C., 1985, 86, Midwest Classic Athletic Conf., 1989, Wis. Assn. Ind. Schs., 1984-86; chair bd. dirs. Beaver Dam Cmty. Hosp., 1985-95; dir. North Ctrl. Assn. Colls. and Secondary Schs., 1991-94, Ind. Schs. Ctrl. States, 1991-95; dir. N.H. Coll. and Univ. Coun., 1995-97; dir. Ozaukee County Indsl. Devel. Corp., 2003-04, Internat. Assembly Collegiate Bus. Edn., 2004-. Recipient Cmty., Svc. award Rutland C. of C., 1973, Disting. Svc. citation Wayland Acad., 1995, Excellence in Edn. award Pa. State U., 2001; named Cons. of Yr., SBA, 1975, 77, Prof. of Yr. Concordia U. Wis., 1999. Mem. APA, Nat. Assn. Intercollegiate Athletics (cert. of merit 1979), Soc. for Advancement of Mgmt., Cum Laude Soc., Pheasant City Club, Rotary, Alpha Chi, Pi Omega Pi, Alpha Delta Sigma, Delta Pi Epsilon, Phi Delta Kappa. Home: 8655 N Regent Rd Fox Point WI 53217-2362 Office: Concordia U Sch Bus & Legal Studies 12800 N Lake Shore Dr Mequon WI 53097-2418 E-mail: william.ellis@cuw.edu.

ELLISON, BOBBIE DILWORTH, retired music educator, composer; b. San Antonio, Apr. 06; m. Rothchild Ellison, Dec. 24, 1958; 1 child, Arnold. BS, EdM, Prairie View A/M U; additional studies, W TX State U, Canyon, TX. Cert. administration TX A&I U. Tchr.: third grade Brockman Elem. Sch., Monahans, Tex., 1958—61, Hilltop Elem. Sch., Amarillo, Tex., 1963—70; tchr. Alice Landercin Elem. Sch., Amarillo, Tex., 1970—71, Belmar Elem. Sch., Amarillo, Tex., 1971—74, T.G. Allen Elem. Sch., Corpus Christi, Tex., 1975—98. Composer: (songs) Secret Closet, 1999; author: The Healing Heart. Home: 3525 Crestdale Corpus Christi TX 78415-3703

ELLISON, CYRIL LEE, literary agent, retired publishing executive; b. NYC, Dec. 11, 1916; m. Anne N. Nottonson, June 4, 1942 (dec. June 2000). Assoc. pub., v.p. Watson-Guptill Publs., 1939-69, v.p., advt. dir., 1939-69, assoc. pub. Am. Artist mag.; exec. v.p. Communication Channels, Inc., N.Y.C., 1969-88; pub. emeritus Fence Industry, Access Control, Pension World, Trusts & Estates, Nat. Real Estate Investor, Shopping Center World; pres. Lee Comms., 1980—; assoc. Kids Countrywide, Inc., 1987-94; literary agent, 1994—. Pub. cons., book rep., advt. and mktg. cons., 1987-94; assoc. Mark Clements Rsch. N.Y., Inc., 1994—; pub. cons. Mag. Rsch. Co., 1994—; assoc. publisher Plants, Sites & Parks. Served with USAAF, 1942-46, PTO. Named Gray-Russo Advt. Man of Year Ad Men's Post Am. Legion, 1954; recipient Hall of Fame award Internat. Fence Industry Assn., 1985. Mem. Nat. Art Material Trade Assn. (v.p., cons.), Amateur Artists Assn. Am., Am. Legion (life, comdr. advt. men's post 1954, 64). Home: 6839 N 29th Ave Phoenix AZ 85017-1213 Office: Lee Communications 5060 N 19th Ave Phoenix AZ 85015-3210 Business E-Mail: intern@azpra.org.

ELLISON, EARL OTTO, computer scientist; b. Elizabeth, N.J., Apr. 26, 1938; s. Thorleif and Reidun E. (Anderson) Ingeborg; m. Judith Roque Impoc, Feb. 2, 1997; children: Reidun Impoc, Arnfinn Alejandro. BS, Am. U., Washington, 1964, postgrad., 1964-66. Head supplies and equipment at Pentagon C & P Telephone Co. (now Verizon), Arlington, Va., 1956-62; tax acct. Trust Dept. Nat. Bank of Washington, 1964-65; methods analyst Automation Industries, Consol. Am. Svcs. Mgmt. Cons. Subs., Washington, L.A., 1965; mgmt. instr. fed. supply svc. GSA, Washington, 1965-67, contract negotiator info. tech. svc., 1967-77, computer sys. contracting officer, 1977-97; pres. Teledesic Svcs., Inc., Washington, 1997—. Author: Revenue Code of 1962: Effects on the Multi-National Firm, 1965. Judge ballroom dancing U.S. Ballroom Dancing Assn., Eastern seaboard, 1986—; swimming and diving coach Pike Br. Swim and Tennis Club, Alexandria, Va., 1966-2001. With USNR, 1961-62. Mem. The Beethoven Soc. Am. (exec. bd. 1993—), Norwegian Soc., Sons of Norway (prin. bldg. fund 1985—, Washington chpt. pres. 1994, 95, counselor 1993, 96, 97, investment adv. 1979—, internat. del. to conv. 1988, 94, trustee 2002—) Presbyterian. Avocations: swimming, diving, ballroom dancing. Home: 6324 Telegraph Rd Alexandria VA 22310-2969 Office: 710 W Peachtree St NW Atlanta GA 30308-1139 also: Rosfjord 4580 Lyngdal Norway

ELLISON, EDWIN CHRISTOPHER, surgeon, educator; b. Columbus, Ohio, Jan. 10, 1950; s. Edwin Homer and Molly (Scheeler) E.; m. Mary Pat Borgess, Dec. 23, 1978; children: Jonathan Scott, Eric Christopher. BS, U. Wis., 1972; MD, Med. Coll. Wis., 1976. Diplomate Am. Bd. Surgery. Resident surgery Ohio State U., Columbus, 1976—83, asst. prof. surgery, 1983—93, assoc. prof., 1993—99, prof., 1999—; chief divsn. gen. surgery, bd. dirs. Ohio Digestive Disease Inst., Columbus, 1987—93; chief of staff Ohio State U. Med. Ctr., Columbus, 1999—2000, vice chmn. dept. surgery, 1996—99, 1interim chair surgery, 0999—2000, chmn. surgery, 2000—, assoc. v.p. health sci., 2002—, vice dean clin. affairs, 2002—. Fellow ACS. Office: 327 Means Hall 1654 Upham Dr Columbus OH 43210-1240 Office Phone: 614-293-8701.

ELLISON, HERBERT JAY, historian, educator; b. Portland, Oreg., Oct. 3, 1929; s. Benjamin F. and Esther (Anderson) Ellison; m. Alberta M. Moore, June 13, 1952; children: Valery, Pamela. BA, U. Wash., 1951, MA, 1952; PhD (Fulbright fellow), U. London, 1955. Instr. history U. Wash., 1955-56, prof. Russian and Eastern European studies, 1968—, dir. divsn. internat. programs, 1968-72, vice provost for ednl. devel., 1969-72, dir. Inst. Comparative and Fgn. Area Studies, 1973-78, chmn. Russian and East European studies, 1979-83; asst. prof. U. Okla., 1956-62; assoc. prof. history, chmn. Slavic studies program U. Kans., 1962-67, prof., 1965-68, dir. NDEA Lang. and Area Ctr. Slavic Studies, 1965-67, assoc. dean faculties internat. programs, 1967-68; sec. Kennan Inst. Advanced Russian Studies, Washington, 1983-85. Trustee Nat. Coun. Russian and E. European Rsch., 1983—87; dir. Russian rsch. Nat. Bur. Asian Rsch., 1990—, bd. dirs., 1993—; chmn. bd. dirs. Internat. Rsch. and Exchs. Bd., 1992—98; dir. new Russia in Asia rsch. and conf. project, 1993—96; chmn. acad. coun. Kennan Inst. Advanced Russian Studies, 1997—2001; bd. govs. Blakemore Found., 1998—. Author: (book) History of Russia, 1964, Sino-Soviet Conflict, 1982, Soviet Policy Toward Western Europe, 1983, Japan and the Pacific Quadrille, 1987; co-author: Twentieth Century Russia, 1999; contbr. articles to profl. jours.; chief cons., exec. dir. (TV series) Messengers from Moscow, 1995, Yeltsin, 2000. Named Ellison Ctr. Russian, East European and Ctrl. Asian Studies Ctr. and Ellison Disting. Professorship Russian History, U. Wash., 2005. Mem.: AAUP, Am. Assn. Advancement Slavic Studies, Am. Hist. Assn., Univ. Club. Home: 12127 SE 15th St Bellevue WA 98005-3821 Office: Univ Wash Jackson Sch Internat Study PO Box 353650 Seattle WA 98195-3650 Business E-Mail: hellison@u.washington.edu.

ELLISON, JULIAN, JR., economist; b. Albany, Ga., Dec. 16, 1942; s. Julian and Johnnie Ruth (White) E.; m. Patricia E. Bynoe, Jan. 31, 1970 (div. 1974); m. Barbara A. Britton, Sept. 1974 (div. 1976); 1 child, Akissi M.; 1 stepchild, Kiani; m. Shirleeta Diane Bing, Dec. 22, 1980; children: Afoué K., Kofi A.; stepchildren: Teloria L., Latia N., Alvin III. AB, Lincoln University (Pa.), 1967; MA, Columbia U., 1972, PhD (all but dissertation), 1974. Intern U.S. Dept. Def., Washington, 1967; economist N.Y.C. Dept. Personnel, 1968; econ. planner Brownsville Community Coun., Bklyn., 1969-71; instr. econs. and Afro-Am. studies Bklyn. Coll., CUNY, 1970-72; economist, sr. economist Black Econ. Rsch. Ctr., N.Y.C., 1972-76; instr. Coll. New Rochelle, Bronx, N.Y., 1977; asst. prof. Hunter Coll., CUNY, N.Y.C., 1977; dir. econ. devel. programs Nat. Rural Ctr., Washington, 1977-79; vis. asst. prof., rsch. assoc. Susquehanna U., Selinsgrove, Pa., 1983-85; pres., dir. Mid-Atlantic Econ. Rsch. Corp., Washington, 1976-90; economist U.S. Treasury Dept., 1991—. Cons. subcom. on Africa U.S. Ho. of Reps., Washington, 1972-73, com. on small bus., 1972-77; bd. dirs. Emeka Enterprises, N.Y.C., West Africa Timber Imports Inc., Wilmington, Del. Author: Abram L. Harris, Jr., Economist: A Biography, 1990; editor: The Economic Theory of Transfer Pricing, 2002, Celestial Mechanics and the Location of William H. Dean Jr., 1930-1952, American Economic Theory Review, 1991; author of papers in field. Assoc. sec. gen. for N.Am. 6th Pan African Congress, Washington, 1973-74; pres. Com. for Coop. Devel., Washington, 1979-82; candidate U.S. Congress, 1979-80; mem. TransAfrica, Washington, 1979—. Sgt. U.S. Army, 1960-63. Woodrow Wilson Found. fellow, Princeton, N.J., 1967-68, So. Fellowships Fund fellow, Atlanta, 1968-70; grantee Ford Found., N.Y.C., 1972, Opportunity Funding Corp., Washington, 1975-76, Chgo. Econ. Devel. Corp., 1975-76, Presbyn. Econ. Devel. Corp., N.Y.C., 1975-76. Mem. Am. Econ. Assn., Nat. Econ. Assn. (dir. 1969-73), African Heritage Studies Assn., Assn. for Study of African Am. Life and History, Am. Fin. Assn., Assn. for Evolutionary Econs., Assn. for Social Econs. Avocations: chess, bao, Go, jazz. Home: 1193 River Rd Teaneck NJ 07666-2015 E-mail: julianellison@aol.com.

ELLISON, LARRY (LAWRENCE JOSEPH ELLISON), computer software company executive; b. Chgo., Aug. 17, 1944; m. Ada Quinn, 1967 (div. 1974); m. Nancy Wheeler, 1976 (div. 1977); m. Barbara Boothe, 1983 (div. 1986); m. Melanie Craft, Dec. 18, 2003; 2 children. Student, U. Illinois, U. Chgo. With Amdahl, Inc., Santa Clara, Calif., 1967—71, systems architect; pres. systems divsn. Omex Corp., 1972—77; co-founder (with Bob Miner & Ed Oates) Oracle Corp. (formerly Software Devel. Laboratories), Redwood, Calif., 1977; CEO Oracle Corp., Redwood, Calif., 1977—, pres., 1978—96, chmn., 1990—92, 1995—2004, Mem., bd. dir. Oracle Corp., 1977—, Apple Computer, Inc., 1997—2002. Recipient Entrepreneur of the Year, Harvard Sch. of Bus., 1990, Leadership Award for Global Integration, 1994, Disting. Info. Scis. Award, Assn. Info. Tech. Profls., 1996, Industry Achievement Award, 1997, Bio-IT Champion, Bio-ITWorld, 2002. Office: Oracle Corp 500 Oracle Pkwy Redwood City CA 94065-1675

ELLISON, LOIS TAYLOR, internist, educator, medical association administrator; b. Fort Valley, Ga., Oct. 28, 1923; d. Robert James and Annie Maude (Anderson) Taylor; m. Robert Gordon Ellison, Feb. 11, 1945; children—Robert Gordon, Gregory Taylor, Mark Frederick, James Walton, John

Charles. BS, U. Ga., 1943; MD, Med. Coll. Ga., 1950. Fellow, Univ. Hosp., Augusta, Ga., 1950-51; mem. faculty Med. Coll. Ga., Augusta, 1951—, prof. medicine and surgery, 1971—2000, assoc. dean, 1974-75, provost, 1975-84, assoc. v.p. planning (hosps. and clins.), 1984—2000, prof. emeritus medicine and surgery, 2000, med. historian, provost emeritus, 2000—. Attending VA Med. Ctr., Augusta; civilian cons. Eisenhower Army Med. Ctr., Fort Gordon, Ga.; mem. coal mine health research adv. council Nat. Inst. Occupational Safety and Health, 1972-75; bd. dirs. East Central Ga. Health Systems Agy., 1975-79, treas., 1979—; bd. dirs. Oak Ridge Associated Univs., 1978-84; mem. adv. council Univ. Systems Ga., 1975-84; mem. exec. com. Ga. Health Coordinating Council, 1980 Contbr. numerous articles to profl. jours. Bd. dirs. United Way Greater Augusta, 1975-78, chair div. hosp. and health, 1978, chair div. colls. and univs., 1980; mem. adminstrv. bd. Trinity-on-the-Hill United Methodist Ch., Augusta, 1974-77, mem. pastor-parish com., 1978— NIH grantee, 1963-68; included in Changing the Face of Medicine-Celebrating Am.'s Women Physicians exhbn., Nat. Libr. Medicine, NIH, 2003. Fellow Am. Coll. Chest Physicians; mem. Am. Physiol. Soc., Am. Med. Women's Assn., AMA, Assn. Am. Med. Colls., Am. Lung Assn. (dir. 1967—, sec. 1982-85, pres.-elect 1985-86, pres. 1986-87), Am. Heart Assn. (pres. Ga. affiliate chpt. 1982-83, dir. 1979—), So. Soc. Clin. Investigation, Am. Lung Assn. of Ga. (pres. 1984-85), Ga. Heart Assn. Office: Med Coll Ga 1120 15th St AE-3055 Augusta GA 30912 Office Phone: 706-721-4013. Business E-Mail: ellisonl@mcg.edu.

ELLISON, LUTHER FREDERICK, oil industry executive; b. Monroe, La., Jan. 2, 1925; s. Luther and Gertrude (Hudson) E.; m. Frances Williams, July 18, 1948 (dec.); children: Constance Elizabeth, Carolyn Williams; m. Patsy Hunter, Nov. 23, 1996. Student, Emory U., 1943-44; BS in Petroleum Engring., Tex. A&M U., 1949, BS in Geol. Engring., 1950. Registered profl. engr., Tex., La. Jr. petroleum engr. Sun Prodn. Co., Kilgore and McAllen, Tex., 1950-52, area petroleum engr. Garcia Field, Tex., 1952-54, Delhi (La.) unit engr., 1954-60, asst. region supt. Dallas, 1960-62, dist. drilling engr. Corpus Christi, 1962-63, dist. engr. McAllen, 1963-65, supr. engring. Dallas, 1965-66, div. chief petroleum engr., 1966-70, regional mgr. engring., 1970-75, region mgr., 1975-78, dir. devel., 1978-80, v.p. devel., 1980-84; div. v.p., dir. Sun Exploration and Prodn. Co., 1984-86, pres., bd. dirs., 1986—; pres., chief exec. officer Oil & Gas Experts, Inc., Dallas, 1986—, Am. Energy Enterprises Inc., Dallas, 1988—. Pres., dir., mem. exec. com. Nabors-Sun Drilling Co.; dir., mem. exec. com. East Tex. Salt & Water Disposal Co.; CEO, pres. Oil & Gas Experts Inc., 1986; speaker in field. V.p. Northwood Jr. H.S. PTA, Dallas, 1967—68, pres., 1968—69; elder, trustee Preston Hollow Presbyn. Ch. Found.; sr. trustee, 2005—; bd. dirs. Glen Lakes Assn. Mem. Tex.-Mid-Continent Oil and Gas Assn. (Outstanding Achievement award 1964, chmn. area 1964-65, mgr. north region, operating com., Outstanding Performance award 1985—), Am. Petroleum Inst., Soc. Petroleum Engrs., Dallas Engrs. Club, Petroleum Engrs. Club, Dallas Petroleum Club, Park City Club, Northwood Club (Dallas), Lions Club, Premier Club (Dallas), Parents League, Sigma Alpha Epsilon (pres. 1944-45). Home: 526 Preston Trail Loop Kerrville TX 78028-6406 Office: PO Box 822066 North Richland Hills TX 76182 Office Phone: 830-896-6809, 830-896-9480.

ELLISON, NICHOLAS HOWELL, literary agent; b. N.Y.C., Mar. 18, 1948; s. William and Virginia (Howell) Soskin; children: Gustave Nicholas, Catherine Hannah. BA, Boston U., Sorbonne, 1969. Sr. editor Thomas Y. Crowell Pub. Co., N.Y.C., 1972-76; sr. editor Harper & Row Pubs., N.Y.C., 1976-79; editor-in-chief Delacorte Press, N.Y.C., 1979-81; pres. Nicholas Ellison, Inc., 1983—. Prof. writing Fairfield U., 1980—; dir. Verreaux Enterprises. Editor numerous books. Pres. Bell Island Assn., Rowayton, Conn., 1972. Recipient Outstanding Achievement award Folio Mgmt. Tng. Seminars, 1979 Mem.: Shore and Country (Norwalk, Conn.). Congregationalist. Home: 92 Mather Rd Stamford CT 06903-3026 Office: 55 5th Ave New York NY 10003-4301

ELLISON, WILLIAM THEODORE, marine engineer; b. Wilmington, N.C., Nov. 30, 1941; s. Robert Jay and Marie Catherine (Robinson) E.; m. Annelise Manecky, Dec. 18, 1987; children: Britt Kirsten, Hans Salter, Katerina Astri-Marie. BS, U.S. Naval Acad., 1963; MSME, MIT, 1968, PhD, 1970. Scientist, v.p. Cambridge (Mass.) Acoustical Assn., Inc., 1974-83; pres., CEO Marine Acoustics, Inc., Newport, R.I., 1983—. Contbr. articles to profl. jours. Capt. USNR, ret. Named Disting. Alumni of Yr. The Breck Sch., 2001. Fellow Explorers Club; mem. Acoustical Soc. Am., Tau Beta Pi, Sigma Xi. Achievements include designing passive acoustical whale tracking system for population assessment of endangered species in the Arctic; pioneering work in impact of underwater sound on marine resources, breakthrough tech. in handheld voice translation sys. Address: PO Box 340 Litchfield CT 06759

ELLIS-SCRUGGS, JAN, theater arts educator; b. Phila., Apr. 7, 1951; d. Roger C. and Greta M. Ellis; m. William Marquis Scruggs, Aug. 8, 1970; children: William Marcus Jr., Christopher Michael. BA, Cheyney U., 1987; MA, Villanova U., 1991. Lectr., instr. U. Conn., Storrs, 1989-90; theatre arts instr. Delaware County C.C., Media, Pa., 1994-95; asst. prof. theatre arts Cheyney (Pa.) U., 1993-94, 97—; actor, singer, dir., theater educator, adminstr. U.S. and London. Assoc. prodr., Citeaux, Inc., London, 1979-83; dir. Cheyney U., 1997—. Mem. editl. adv. bd., Collegiate Press, San Diego, 1999—. Missionary, Mother Bethel African Meth. Episc. Ch., Phila., 1994—. Mem. AFTRA, SAG (Screen Actors Guild), Actors Equity Assn., Alpha Psi Omega. Home: 7942 Cedarbrook Ave Philadelphia PA 19150 Office: Cheyney U of Pa Marian Anderson Music Ctr Cheyney PA 19319 Business E-Mail: jellis-scruggs@cheyney.edu. E-mail: jebs267@aol.com.

ELLMAN, MICHAEL H., rheumatologist, educator; b. Chicago, Ill., Apr. 4, 1939; married. MD, U. Ill., Chicago, 1964. Diplomate Am. Bd. Internal Medicine, Am. Bd. Rheumatology. Prof. of medicine U. Chgo., 1990—. Capt. U.S. Army, 1965—68, Canal Zone. Fellow: Am. Coll. Rheumatology. Achievements include research in scleroderma. Office: U Chgo 5841 S Maryland Chicago IL 60637 E-mail: mellman@medicine.bsd.uchicago.edu.

ELLMANN, DOUGLAS STANLEY, lawyer; b. Detroit, July 15, 1956; s. William Marshall and Sheila Estelle Ellmann. AB, Occidental Coll., 1978; JD, U. Mich., 1982. Bar: Mich. 1982, U.S. Dist. Ct. (ea. dist.) Mich. 1982, U.S. Ct. Appeals (6th cir.) 1982. Prin. Ellmann & Ellmann, P.C., Ann Arbor, Mich., 1989—. Spl. asst. atty. gen., 1986; trustee U.S. Panel, 1989—; sec. bankruptcy trustee assoc. U.S. Bankruptcy Ct. (ea. dist.) Mich., 1993—. Author: Selected Issues in Asset Protection, 1994, My Advice: Next Time Go Solo, 1994, LWUSA; co-author: Winning Labor Arbitrations, 1987. Mem. U. Mich. Law Sch. Fund, 1986—87. Mem.: ABA (vice chair bankruptcy com. 1995—2001), Washtenaw County Bar Assn. (chmn. banking, bus., bankruptcy com. 1995—2000), State Bar Mich. (mem. manditory CLE com. 1989—96, chmn. 1995—96, mem. jud. qualifications com. 2000—), Mich. Bar Assn. (rep. assembly 1983—89, 1990—92, 1998—, exec. counsel young lawyers sect. 1985—87, mem. client security fund com. 1987—95). Office: 308 W Huron St Ann Arbor MI 48103-4204 Office Phone: 734-668-4800. Business E-Mail: dse@ellmannlaw.com.

ELLMANN, SHEILA FRENKEL, investment company executive; b. Detroit, June 8, 1931; d. Joseph and Rose (Neback) Frenkel; m. William M. Ellmann, Nov. 1, 1953 (dec. Jan. 16, 2002); children: Douglas Stanley, Carol Elizabeth, Robert Lawrence. BA in English, U. Mich., 1953. Dir. Advance Glove Mfg. Co., Detroit, 1954—78; v.p. Frome Investment Co., Detroit, 1980—96, pres., 1996—. Mem.: U. Mich. Alumni Assn., Nat. Trust Hist. Preservation, VFW Aux. Home: 28000 Weymouth Dr Farmington Hills MI 48334 Personal E-mail: sheilaellmann@yahoo.com.

ELLNER, CAROLYN LIPTON, non-profit organization executive, dean, consultant; b. Jan. 17, 1932; d. Robert Mitchell and Rose (Pearlman) Lipton; m. Richard Ellner, June 21, 1953; children: D. Lipton, Alison Lipton. AB cum laude, Mt. Holyoke Coll., 1953; AM, Columbia Tchrs. Coll., 1957; PhD with distinction, UCLA, 1968. Tchr., prof., administr. N.Y. and Md., 1957-62; prof. dir. tchr. edn., assoc. dean Claremont Grad. Sch., Calif., 1967-82; prof., dean sch. edn. Calif. State U., Northridge, 1982-98, dean emerita, 1998—. Pres., CEO On-the-Job Parenting. Co-author: Schoolmaking, 1977, Studies of College Teaching, 1983 (Orange County Authors award 1984). Trustee Ctr. for Early Edn., L.A., 1968-71, Oakwood Sch., L.A., 1972-78, Mt. Holyoke Coll., South Hadley, Mass., 1979-84, Pacific Oaks Coll. and Children's Sch., 2004—; commr. Economy and Efficiency com., L.A., 1974-82, Calif. Commn. Tchr. Credentialing, 1987-90, 93—, vice chair, 1995-96, chair, 1996-98; bd. dirs. Found. for Effective Govt., L.A., 1982, Calif. Coalition for Pub. Edn., 1985-88, Valley Hosp. Found., 1992-94, Mt. Holyoke Alumnae Assn. Bd., 1993-96; founding dir. Decade of Edn., 1990; assoc. dir. New Devel. in Sci. Project NSF, 1985-94; bd. dirs., chair edn. com. Valley Industry and Commerce Assn., 1990-93, v.p. 1993-94; co-prin. dir. Mid South Calif. Arts Project, 1991-98; mem. coun., trustees L.A. Alliance for Restructing Now (LEARN), 1992-2000; bd. dirs. Inner City Arts Found., 1993-96; involved with L.A. Annenberg Met. Project (LAAMP); exec. bd. DELTA, 1995—, Calif. Subject Matter Projects, 1998—. Ford Found. fellow 1964-67, fellow Ednl. Policy Fellowship Program, 1989-90; recipient Office of Edn. award U.S. Office of Edn., 1969-72, Alumnae medal of honor Mt. Holyoke Coll., 1998; W.M. Keck Found. grantee, 1983, 94. Mem. ASCD, Am. Edn. Rsch. Assn., Am. Assn. Colls. for Tchr. Edn., Nat. Soc. for Study of Edn. Home and Office: 1205 S Oak Knoll Ave Pasadena CA 91106-4442 E-mail: ellner@otjp.org.

ELLNER, JERROLD JAY, infectious diseases specialist; b. 1945; MD, Johns Hopkins U., 1970. Diplomate Am. Bd. Internal Medicine, Am. Bd. Infectious Disease. Resident in internal medicine Johns Hopkins Hosp., Balt., 1970—72; formerly with Case Western Res. U. Med. Sch., Cleve.; chair dept. medicine, prof. medicine N.J. Med. Sch., 2000—, head Inst. for Emerging Pathogens; dir. Ctr. for Emerging Infectious Diseases U. Medicine and Dentistry N.J., 2000—. Founding mem. Acad. Alliance for AIDS Care and Prevention in Africa, 2001. Named one of Top Drs. in N.Y. Metro Area, Castle Connolly, Top Drs. 2003, N.J. Monthly Mag. Office: UMDNJ Med Sch Dept Medicine MSB Rm I 506 185 S Orange Ave Newark NJ 07103 E-mail: ellnerjj@umdnj.edu.

ELLNER, MICHAEL WILLIAM, art educator; b. N.Y.C., Apr. 1, 1938; s. Charles and Sylvia May (Golub) E.; m. Josephine Helene Bilello, Aug. 24, 1957; children: Eileen Lorraine, Deborah Lynn, Laurence Steven. AA in Engring., San Jose City Coll., 1963, AA in Art, 1966; BA, Notre Dame De Namur U., 1970; MA, San Jose State U., 1971, postgrad., 1973-74, U. Calif., Santa Cruz, 1980. Cert. secondary art tchr., c.c. art tchr., Calif. Chair art dept. John Muir Jr. High Sch., San Jose, Calif., 1973-80; assoc. prof. art San Jose State U., 1974; chair art dept. Willow Glen Edn. Park, San Jose, 1980-91; visual arts coord. A. Lincoln AVPA Magnet High Sch., San Jose, 1991-96. Cons. Coll. Bd., San Jose, 1989-97, San Jose Unified Sch. Dist., Saturday Acad., San Jose, 1996—; prof. art San Jose City Coll., 1996—; advisor Nat. Art Honor Soc., San Jose, 1991—; intern advisor Casa Program, San Jose, 1991—; co-convenor Lincoln HS Magnet Curriculum Coun., San Jose, 1991-96; mentor tchr. San Jose Unified Sch. Dist., 1985-94. Paintings included in more than 200 collections including San Jose Mus. Art, Calif., De Saisset Mus., Santa Clara, Calif., Foot Mus., Long Beach, Calif., Coll. Notre Dame De Namur U., Belmont, Calif.; guest curator Egyptian Mus. Art Gallery, San Jose, Calif., New World Gallery, San Jose, Calif., San Jose Art League, Calif.; guest curator Macla Gallery, San Jose, Calif., Genesis Gallery, San Jose, Calif., 1970—; exhibited in more than 300 group and one-person shows; created 21 cmty. murals; curator over 100 art exhbns.; represented in several art books on painting, and murals and poetry. Past pres. San Jose Art League; past treas. Cambrian Art League; mem. Anti-Graffiti Program, San Jose. Recipient Program Stds. award Nat. Art Edn. Assn., 1993, 94, 95, 96, Art grant City of San Jose, 1994, Mural grant Rose Garden Assn., San Jose, 1996, grant Nat. League Am. Pen Women, 1996, 97, 98, 99, Program awards Nat. Blue Ribbon Sch., 1998, Magnet Sch. of Am., 1991, 92, 93, Calif. Disting. Sch. award, 1992, 96, Golden Bell award, 1994, Kennedy Ctr. award for the arts, 1995, State Farm Good Nieghbor award Nat. Art Edn. Assn., 1996; inductee Calif. State Senate Youth Mentor's Hall of Fame award, 1999, Excellence in Edn. award City of San Jose, 2000, Youth Focus award, 1999; named Tchr. of Yr., Willow Glen Edn. Park PTA, 1985, San Jose Shrine, 1986. Mem. Calif. Tchrs. Assn., NEA, San Jose Tchrs. Assn., San Jose Inst. Contemporary Art, Artists Alliance Calif., South Bay Artists Assn. (adv. com.), Cmty. Partnership Santa Clara County, San Jose Art League (past pres.), Cambrian Art League (past treas.), Phi Kappa Phi. Avocations: painting, poetry, murals. Home: 1429 Scossa Ave San Jose CA 95118-2456

ELLNER, PAUL DANIEL, microbiologist; b. N.Y.C., May 2, 1925; s. George and Cele (Weis) E.; m. Estelle Ziswasser, 1948 (div. 1960); 1 child, Diane; m. Cornelia Johns, Jan. 15, 1965; children— David, Jonathan BS, L.I. U., 1948; MS, U. So. Calif., 1952; PhD, U. Md., 1956. Diplomate Am. Bd. Med. Microbiology; cert. clin. lab. dir. N.Y.C. Dept. Health. Clin. bacteriologist Los Angeles hosps., 1948-52; rsch. asst. Mt. Sinai Hosp., N.Y.C., 1952-53; instr. microbiology U. Fla. Coll. Medicine, 1956-60; asst. prof. U. Vt. Coll. Medicine, 1960-63, Columbia U. Coll. Physicians and Surgeons, N.Y.C., 1963-66, assoc. prof., 1966-70, prof. microbiology, 1971-78, prof. microbiology and pathology, 1978-89, prof. emeritus, 1989, dir. clin. microbiology service, 1971-89; assoc. microbiologist Presbyn. Hosp., N.Y.C., 1966-70, attending staff, 1971-89. Cons. in field; vis. prof. N.Y. Med. Coll., Valhalla, 1979; ASM Latin Am. vis. prof., Medellín, Colombia, 1982; Am. Bur. Med. Advancement in China vis. prof., Taiwan, 1982; regional coordinator Nat. Disaster Med. System; v.p. Am. BioSci. Cons. Author: Current Procedures in Clinical Bacteriology, 1978, Understanding Infectious Disease, 1992; editor: Infectious Diarrheal Diseases: Current Concepts and Laboratory Procedures, 1984; mem. editorial bd. Sexually Transmitted Diseases, 1982-84, European Jour. Clin. Microbiology, 1985-89; contbr. chpts. to books, numerous articles to profl. jours. With AC, USN, 1943-44; to capt. USPHS Res.; health project officer USCG, 1982-91. Rsch. fellow USN, 1954-56. Fellow Am. Acad. Microbiology, Assn. Clin Scientists, N.Y. Acad. Medicine (assoc.), Infectious Diseases Soc. Am.; mem. AMA (spl. affiliate), Am. Soc. Microbiology (chmn. clin. divsn. 1980-81, Sonnenwirth Meml. award 1992), Acad. Clin. Lab. Physicians and Scientists, Am. Venereal Disease Assn., Sigma Xi. Republican. Jewish. Avocations: fishing, gardening, photography. E-mail: pdel@columbia.edu. *The greatest satisfaction for the scientist is recognition by his peers for honesty and integrity in his studies, fairness and impartiality to his colleagues, and guidance and encouragement to his students.*

ELLNER, RUTH H., realtor; b. Jerusalem, Feb. 27, 1945; arrived in US, 1981; d. Shalom and Yona Avishi Morchi (Mizrahi) Toby; m. Paul Hatchett; m. Larry Ellner (div.); m. Alfred Santo, July 30, 2002; 1 child; 1 child from previous marriage. Diploma, HS, Israel. Realtor Keyes Co., Miami, Fla., 1997—2003, Ocean View, Miami, Fla., 2003—; singer, songwriter, screen playwright self employed. With Israel Airforce. Home: 19001 NE 14 Ave 111 Miami FL 33179 Home Fax: 305-354-4085. Personal E-mail: ruthellner@hotmail.com.

ELLROY, JAMES, writer; b. L.A., Mar. 4, 1948; s. Geneva (Hillaker) E.; m. Mary Doherty, 1988. Author: (novels) Brown's Requiem, 1981, Clandestine, 1982, Blood on the Moon, 1984, Because the Night, 1984, Killer on the Road (formerly Silent Terror) 1986, Suicide Hill, 1986, The Black Dahlia, 1987, The Big Nowhere, 1988 (Prix Mystere award 1990), L.A. Confidential, 1990, White Jazz, 1992, Hollywood Nocturnes, 1994, Dick Contino's Blues, American Tabloid, 1995, My Dark Places, 1996, Crime Wave, 1999, The Cold Six Thousand, 2001, Destination Morque, 2003, (non-fiction) Scene of the Crime: Photographs from the LAPD Archive, 2004; contbr.: Fallen Angels: Six Noir Tales Told for Television, 1993; contbr., editor: Best American Mysteries, 2002. Office: care Warner Books Publicity Dept 1271 Ave of Americas New York NY 10020*

ELLSWEIG, PHYLLIS LEAH, retired psychotherapist; b. Irvington, N.J., Apr. 19, 1927; d. Sumar and Jeanette (Geffner) Schwartz; m. Martin Richard Ellsweig, Dec. 25, 1947; children: Bruce, Steven. BS, East Stroudsburg U. (Pa.), 1947; EdM, Lehigh U., 1966, EdD, 1972. Tchr. Stroud Union High Sch., 1963-66; guidance counselor East Stroudsburg (Pa.) Schs., 1966-68; asst. prof. edn. East Stroudsburg U., 1968; staff psychologist, outpatient supr. Mental Health Center Carbon, Monroe and Pike Counties, Stroudsburg, Pa., 1968-80; pvt. practice in psychotherapy and clin. hypnosis Stroudsburg, 1969-87. Mem. staff Pocono Hosp., 1968—80; pub. spkr. in field; cons. to schs. and pvt. orgns.; tchr. adult edn., Palm Beach County, Fla. Mem. Am. Soc. Clin. Hypnosis, Internat. Soc. Hypnosis, NOW (profl. cons. 1973—). Home: 2584 NW 12th St Delray Beach FL 33445-1353

ELLSWORTH, FRANK L., not-for-profit executive; b. Wooster, Ohio, May 20, 1943; s. Clayton Sumner and Frances (Fuller) E.; 1 child, Kirstin Lynne. BA, Western Res. Coll., 1965; MEd, Pa. State U., 1967; MA, Columbia U., 1969; PhD, U. Chgo., 1976; LLD, Pepperdine U., 1997, Southwestern U., 2004. Asst. dir. devel. Columbia Law Sch., 1968-70; dir. spl. projects, prof. lit. Sarah Lawrence Coll., N.Y., 1971; asst. dean Law Sch., U. Chgo., 1971-79, instr. social sci. collegiate div., 1975-79; pres., prof. polit. sci. Pitzer Coll., Claremont, Calif., 1979-91; pres. Ind. Colls. So. Calif., L.A., 1991-97; v.p. Capital Rsch. & Mgmt. Co., 1997—2003; pres. Japan Soc., 2003—. Pres. endowments The Japan Soc., 1997-2003, Japan Soc., 2003. Author: The Foundation of the 21st Century, 2002, Law on the Midway, 1977, Student Activism in American Higher Education; contbr. articles to profl. jours. Trustee Japanese Am. Nat. Mus., Give2Asia Pitzer Coll., Southwestern U.; chmn. Global Ptnrs. Inst., Ctr. for the Preservation of Democracy; trustee Am. Friends, Portrait Gallery, London. Recipient Disting. Young Alumnus award Case Western Res. U., 1981, True of Life award United Jewish Fund, 1991. Mem. Coun. for Advancement of Secondary Edn., Young Pres.'s Orgn., Ukiyo-e Soc., Asia Soc., Grolier Club Home: 240 East 27th St 10B New York NY 10018 Office Phone: 212-715-1221. Business E-Mail: fellsworth@japansociety.org.

ELLSWORTH, JAMES BYRON, national security educator; s. James B. and Shirley A. Ellsworth; m. Lynne Phillips-Ellsworth, June 7, 2000. BS, Clarkson U., 1986; MBA, Syracuse (N.Y.) U., 1988, PhD, 1998; MA, U.S. Naval War Coll., 2003. Student dir. ednl. computing Clarkson U., Potsdam, NY, 1983—86; grad. asst. Sch. Mgmt. Syracuse (N.Y.) U., 1986—88, grad. asst. Computing and Network Svcs., 1988—89; edn. specialist, dir. tng. and doctrine U.S. Army Armor Ctr. and Sch., Fort Knox, Ky., 1989—91; instrnl. design specialist, dir. evaluation and standardization U.S. Army Intelligence Sch., Fort Devens, Mass., 1991—92, instrnl. sys. adv., intelligence and elec. warfare dept., 1992—94; chief tng. support U.S. Army Intelligence Ctr., Fort Huachuca, Ariz., 1994—95, chief WWW, 1995—97, chief evaluation rsch., office of registrar, 1997—2000, chief automation and performance tech., office of registrar, 1999—2000; prof. Coll. Distance Edn. U.S. Naval War Coll., Newport, RI, 2000—. Sec., distance learning coordinating com. Mil. Edn. Coord. Coun., Washington, 2002—, bd. dirs.; mem. intelligence adv. coun. Am. Mil. U., 2005—. Author: (weblog) Education * Innovation * National Security, SURVIVING CHANGE: A Survey of Educational Change Models; co-author: Sustaining Distance Training, Educational Media and Technology Yearbook; contbr. articles to profl. jours. Planning and zoning commn. observer Mayor's Youth Adv. Coun., Oneida, NY, 1982—83; student senator Clarkson U. Student Govt., Potsdam, NY, 1984—86; comm. dir. Coll. Rep. Syracuse (N.Y.) U., 1986—89; sec. pastoral coun. Holy Family Cath. Parish, Fort Huachuca, 1997—99; mem. choir St. Catherine Cath. Parish, Warwick, RI, 2001—02, St. Anthony Cath. Parish, Portsmouth, 2002—. Decorated Gen. Carl A. Spaatz award USAF Aux., Army Achievement medal Civilian Svc.; grantee, Ednl. Comm. and Tech. Found., 1998. Mem.: U.S. Army Mil. Intelligence Corps Assn. (sr. intelligence officer Patriots chpt. 2003—, Lt. Col. Thomas Knowlton award 1995), Internat. Soc. Performance Improvement (pres. armed forces chpt. 2001—02), Assn. Ednl. Comm. and Tech. (bd. dirs. 2000—02, pres. divsn. sys. change 2001—02, bd. dirs. 2005—), Am. Ednl. Rsch. Assn., Assn. U.S. Army (life). R-Liberal. Roman Catholic. Achievements include one of the first to use the worldwide web as an educational medium; development of unifying framework for the major models of educational change and innovation; design of strategic architecture for the Naval War College's award-winning Web-enabled correspondence Program; research in adaptation of United States military organizations and doctrinal concepts to the post-cold-war security environment. Avocations: running, poetry, computers. Home: Post Office Box 5162 Newport RI 02841-0102 Office: US Naval War College 686 Cushing Road (Code 1G-41) Newport RI 02841-1207 Office Phone: 401-841-2215. Home Fax: 401-683-9569; Office Fax: 401-841-2457. Personal E-mail: jbellsworth@aol.com. E-mail: ellswor@nwc.navy.mil.

ELLSWORTH, LAURA E., lawyer; b. NYC; BA, Princeton Univ., 1980; JD magna cum laude, Univ. Pitts., 1983. Bar: Pa. 1983. Ptnr.-in-charge Pitts. office Jones Day. Adv. com. for study of rules and practices US Dist. Ct., Western Dist. of Pa., 2003; adj. prof. law Univ. Pitts. Sch. of Law. Named a Leader in the Law, Legal Intelligencer, 2004; named one of the top female litigators in Pa., Pa. Law Weekly, 2004; recipient President's award, Pa. Bar Assn., 2002. Fellow: Am. Bar Assn.; mem.: Acad. of Trial Lawyers of Allegheny County, Pa. Bar Assn. (bd. mem.), Order of Coif. Office: Jones Day One Mellon Bank Ctr 31st Fl 500 Grant St Pittsburgh PA 15219 Office Phone: 412-394-7929. Office Fax: 412-394-7959. Business E-Mail: leellsworth@jonesday.com.

ELLSWORTH, PHOEBE CLEMENCIA, psychology professor; b. Hartford, Conn., Jan. 22, 1944; d. John Stoughton and Edith (Noble) E.; m. Samuel Raymond Gross, Nov. 7, 1979; children: Alexandra Ellsworth, Emma Beth Ellsworth. AB, Harvard U., 1966; PhD, Stanford U., 1970. Asst. prof. Yale U., New Haven, 1971-75, assoc. prof., 1975-79, prof., 1979-81, Stanford U., 1981-87; prof. psychology and law U. Mich., Ann Arbor, 1987—, Frank Murphy Disting. U. Prof. law and psychology, 2003—. Assoc. editor JESP, 1977-80; mem. social sci. rev. com. NIMH, 1973-77, com. on law and social sci. SSRC, 1975-84, rev. panel on law and social sci. NSF, 1983-85; mem. rev. bd. Am. Bar Found., 1987-91; bd. trustees Russell Sage Found., 1992—. Author: (with others) Emotions in the Human Face: Guidelines for Research And a Review of the Findings, Methods of Research in Social Psychology, Person Perception; contbr. articles to profl. jours. Fellow APA, Am. Acad. Arts and Scis.; mem. Soc. Exptl. Social Psychology, Am. Psychology Law Assn., Internat. Soc. Research on Emotion (charter)., Law and Soc. Assn. Home: 442 Huntington Pl Ann Arbor MI 48104-1800 Office: U Mich Sch Law 970 Legal Rsch 625 S State St Ann Arbor MI 48109-1215 E-mail: pce@umich.edu.*

ELLSWORTH, RICHARD GERMAN, psychologist; b. Provo, Utah, June 23, 1950; s. Richard Grant and Betty Lola (Midgley) E.; m. Carol Emily Osborne, May 23, 1970; children: Rebecca Ruth, Spencer German, Rachel Priscilla, Melanie Star, Richard Grant, David Jedediah. BS, Brigham Young U., 1974, MA, 1975; PhD, U. Rochester (N.Y.), 1979; postgrad., UCLA, 1980-84; PhD, Internat. Coll., 1983. Cert. Am. Bd. Med. Psychotherapy, (fellow), Am. Bd. Sexology. Instr. U. Rochester, 1976-77; rsch. assoc. Nat. Tech. Inst. for Deaf, Rochester, 1977; instr. West Valley Coll., Saratoga, Calif., 1979-80, San Jose (Calif.) City Coll., 1980; psycholinguist UCLA, 1980-81, rsch. assoc., 1982-85; psychologist Daniel Freeman Meml. Hosp., Inglewood, Calif., 1981-84, Broderick, Langlois & Assocs., San Gabriel, Calif., 1982-86, Beck Psychiat. Med. Group, Lancaster, Calif., 1984-87, Angeles Counseling Ctr., Arcadia, Calif., 1986-89, Assoc. Med. Psychotherapists, Palmdale, Calif., 1988-2001, Taft Correctional Instn., 2003—; prof. Chapman U., 1995—2002; pvt. practice Lancaster, Calif., 2001—; adj. prof. Calif. State U., Bakersfield, Calif., 2000—. Cons. LDS Social Svcs. Calif. Agy., 1981—, Antelope Valley Hosp., 1984—, Palmdale Hosp., 1984-96, Treatment Ctrs. of Am. Psychiat. Hosps., 1985-86, Hollywood Cmty. Hosp., 1994-01, Lancaster Cmty. Hosp., 1996—; commr. Calif. State Bd. Psychology, 1994—2000. Contbr. articles to profl. jours. Scoutmaster, Boy Scouts Am., 1976-79. UCLA Med. Sch. fellow in psychiatry, 1980-81. Mem.: APA, Am. Soc. Clin. Hypnosis, Assn. Mormon Counselors and Psychotherapists (editor AMCAP jour. 2000—), Am. Assn. Sex Educators, Counselors and Therapists, Psi Chi. Office: 1672 W Ave J Ste 207 Lancaster CA 93534 Office Phone: 661-945-9892.

ELLSWORTH, ROBERT FRED, investment executive, former government official; b. Lawrence, Kans., June 11, 1926; s. W. Fred and Lucile (Rarig) E.; children: Robert William, Ann Elizabeth; m. Eleanor L. Biscoe, July 14, 2002 BS, U. Kans., 1945; JD, U. Mich., 1949. Bar: D.C., Mass., Kans., U.S. Supreme Ct. Mem. 87th to 89th Congresses from 2d and 3d Dist., Kans., 1961-67; asst. to Pres. of U.S., Washington, 1969; U.S. ambassador to NATO, 1969-71; gen. ptnr. Lazard Freres & Co., N.Y.C., 1971-74; asst. sec. for internat. security affairs U.S. Dept. Def., Washington, 1974-75, dep. sec. Def., 1975-77. Bd. dirs. Price Comm. Corp.; founder Hamilton Bio Ventures, L.P. Lay reader Episcopal Ch. Knight Honor Johanniterorden. With USNR, 1944-46, 50-53. Recipient Presdl. Nat. Security medal, 1977. Mem. Coun. Fgn. Rels., Internat. Inst. Strategic Studies (v.p.), Atlantic Coun. of the U.S. (dir.), Coun. of Am. Amb. Office: 12555 High Bluff Dr Ste 310 San Diego CA 92130 Home: 2505 Caminito del Barco Del Mar CA 92014 Office Phone: 858-314-2353. Business E-Mail: rellsworth@hamiltonventures.com.

ELLURU, RAVINDHRA G., pediatric otolaryngologist; MD, PhD. (hon.), U. Tex. Southwestern Med. Ctr. at Dallas, 1996. Doctor of Medicine Ohio, 2001, American Board of Otolaryngology Am. Bd. of Otolaryngology, 2002. Pediatric Cin. Children's Hosp. Med. Ctr., 2001—03, asst. prof., 2003—. Dir., voice ctr. Cin. Children's Hosp. Med. Ctr., Cincinnati, Ohio, 2005—. Contbr. articles to profl. jours. Grantee, NIH, 2004—. Fellow: ACS (assoc.); mem.: Soc. for Ear, Nose and Throat Advances in Children, Inc., AMA, Assn. of Indian Physicians, Assn. for Rsch. in Otolaryngology, Am. Acad. Otolaryngology, The Am. Soc. for Cell Biology (assoc.). Achievements include research in Genetic Determinents of the upper respiratory tract developments. Office: Cincinnati Children's Hospital Medical 3333 Burnet Avenue ML 2018 Cincinnati OH 45229 Office Phone: 513-636-7536. Office Fax: 513-636-8133. Personal E-mail: ravi.elluru@cchmc.org.

ELLWANGER, ALBERT THOMPSON, III, secondary school educator; b. Richmond, Va., Aug. 5, 1948; s. Albert Thompson Ellwanger, Jr. and Frances Henrietta Sadler. BFA, Pratt Inst., 1970; MFA, George Washington U., 1981. Tchr. Richmond (Va.) Pub. Schs., 1970; designer Scan Furniture, Greenbelt, Md., 1972—74; educator Montgomery County Pub. Schs., Rockville, Md., 1974—. Dir. Visual and Performing Arts Acad., Kensington, Md., 2001—02. Benefactor Am. Arch. Found., Mariners' Mus., Newport News, Va., Nassau County (N.Y.) Mus. Art; founder Sadler Collection, Va. Mus., Richmond, 1974, Ellwanger-Mescha Collection, Nat. Gallery of Art; vestry mem. St. Bartholomew's Ch., Balt. With U.S. Army, 1970—72. Named Silver Spring (Md.) Tchr. of Yr., Silver Spring C. of C., 1994, Montgomery County Art Tchr. of Yr., Md. Art Edn. Assn., 1998. Mem.: Legacy Cir. Nat. Gallery Art (charter), Nat. Art Edn. Assn. Democrat. Episcopalian. Home: 2517 Pickwick Rd Baltimore MD 21207 Office: Albert Einstein HS 11135 Newport Mill Rd Kensington MD 20895 Office Phone: 301-962-1058. Personal E-mail: toferdinand@msn.com.

ELLWANGER, THOMAS JOHN, lawyer; b. Summit, N.J., Feb. 26, 1949; s. James Warren and Lorean (Nicholson) E.; m. Sabine S. Ellwanger; children: James Hunter, Margaret Lorean. BA, Northwestern U., 1970; JD, U. Fla., 1974. Bar: Fla. 1975, U.S. Dist. Ct. (mid. dist.) Fla. 1976, U.S. Ct. Appeals (11th cir.) 1976, U.S. Dist. Ct. (so. dist.) Fla. 1977, U.S. Tax Ct. Mem. Fowler, White, Gillen, Boggs, Villareal & Banker P.A. (now Fowler, White, Boggs, Banker P.A.), Tampa, Fla., 1975—. Instr. law U. Fla., Gainesville, 1975; adj. prof. Stetson U. Coll. Law, 1997-2000. Editor: Gadsden County Times, 1970-72. Fellow Am. Coll. Trust and Estate Counsel, Fla. Bar (cert. tax lawyer), Hillsborough County Bar Assn. (chmn. com. probate liaison 1985-86, real property probate and trust law sect. 1987-89, 2004-05), Tampa Bay Estate Planning Counsel (pres. 1994-95). Avocations: music, literature, sports. Office: Fowler White Boggs Banker PA 501 E Kennedy Blvd Ste 1700 Tampa FL 33602-5239 Office Phone: 813-222-1161. E-mail: tellwang@fowlerwhite.com.

ELLWOOD, DAVID TABOR, public policy educator, dean; b. Mpls., Sept. 16, 1953; s. Paul and Ann Ellwood; m. Marilyn Rymer. AB in Econs. summa cum laude, Harvard U., 1975, PhD in Econs., 1981. Rsch. asst. to prof. Martin S. Feldstein Harvard U., Cambridge, Mass., 1974-75, 77; rsch. assoc. health policy program U. Calif., San Francisco, 1975-76; tchg. fellow labor econs. Harvard U., Cambridge, 1977-79; rsch. asst. Nat. Bur. Econ. Rsch., Cambridge, 1978-80; asst. prof. pub. policy John F. Kennedy Sch. Govt., Harvard U., Cambridge, 1980-84, assoc. prof. pub. policy, 1984-88, prof. pub. policy, 1988-92, Malcolm Wiener prof. pub. policy, 1992-98, Lucius N. Littauer prof. polit. economy, 1998—2003, Scott M. Black prof. polit. economy, 2003—; co-dir. Malcolm Wiener Ctr. Pub. Policy, Harvard U., Cambridge, 1992-93; acad. dean John F. Kennedy Sch. Govt. Harvard U., Cambridge, 1992-93, 95-97, dean Kennedy Sch. Govt., 2004—; asst. sec. planning and evaluation HHS, Washington, 1993-95. Rsch. assoc. Nat. Bur. Econ. Rsch., 1984-93; faculty mem. retreat U.S. House Ways and Means com.; panel mem. Work and Welfare Demonstration Manpower Demonstration Rsch. Corp., 1985-93, 95—; bd. overseers panel study income dynamics, 1986-88; dir. domestic strategy group The Aspen Inst., 1998—2003; bd. dirs. Abt Assocs.; cons. in field. Author: Poor Support: Poverty and the American Family, 1988 (notable books N.Y. Times Book Review 1988, outstanding book 1988 Policy Studies Orgn.); co-editor Welfare Policies for the 90s; co-author Welfare Realities: From Rhetoric to Reform, 1994; contbr. numerous articles, book reviews to profl. jours. Panel Com. Status Black Ams., NAS, 1986-91; adv. bd. Children's Program Edna McConnell Clark Found., 1989-93; mem. Nat. Forum Future Children and Their Parents, Nat. Rsch. Coun., 1988-91; mem. Task Force Poverty and Welfare Mario Cuomo, gov. State N.Y., 1986-87, Project Welfare Families Bruce Babbitt, gov., State Ariz., 1986-87. Recipient George Kershaw award Assn. Pub. Policy Analysis and Mgmt.; Lehman fellow Harvard U. Fellow Am. Acad. Arts and Scis.; mem. NAS (panel poverty and family assistance), Phi Beta Kappa. Office: Harvard U John F Kennedy Sch Govt 79 John F Kennedy St L-218 Cambridge MA 02138-5801 Office Phone: 617-495-1122.

ELLWOOD, SCOTT, lawyer; b. Boston, July 8, 1936; s. William Prescott and Doris (Cook) E.; m. Suzanne M. Timble; children: Victoria, William Prescott II, Marjorie. Student, Williams Coll., 1954-56; AB, Eastern Mich. U., 1958; LLB, Harvard U., 1961. Bar: Iowa 1961, Ill. 1961, U.S. Dist. Ct. (no. dist.) Ill., 1961. Assoc. McBride & Baker, Chgo., 1961-67, ptnr., 1968-84, McDermott, Will & Emery, Chgo., 1984-99. Pres. Miller Investment Co., 1973-93, bd. dirs.; pres. SMI Investment Corp., 1978—. Pres., bd. dirs. 110 N Wacker Dr Found., 1974-84, Northfield Found., 1978-84, Leadership Found., 1979-84, Woodbine Found., 1980-84, The Cannon River Found., 1982-84, L.M. McBride Found., 1982-84, Bellarmine Found., 1982-84, Mark Morton Meml. Fund, 1982—. Mem. Iowa Bar Assn., Ill. State Bar Assn., Harvard Law Soc. Ill. (bd. dirs. 1983-98, treas. 1987-88, sec. 1988-89, v.p. 1989-93, pres. 1993-95), Harvard Club Chgo. (bd. dirs. 1993-95), Monroe Club (bd. dirs. 1988-98), Skokie Country Club (Glencoe, Ill.). Republican. Episcopalian. Home: 1296 Hackberry Ln Winnetka IL 60093-1606 Office: McDermott Will & Emery 227 W Monroe St 58th Fl Chicago IL 60606-5096

ELM, DAWN RAE, management educator; b. Seattle, Nov. 3, 1957; d. Arthur Lewis and Elizabeth Mower (Stevens) Lomker; m. Chance Raymond Elm, Oct. 17, 1981; children: Courtney Meryl-Lomker, Kendra Daneille-Lomker. BSChemE, U. Mass., 1980; PhD in Strategic Mgmt., U. Minn., 1989. Project mgr. The Procter & Gamble Co., Cin., 1980—84; prof. U. St. Thomas, St. Paul, 1989—; mgmt. concentration dir. grad. programs U. St. Thomas Coll. Bus., St. Paul, 1998—. Mem. editl. bd.: Jour. Bus. Ethics, 1997—; contbr. articles to profl. jours. Mem.: Internat. Assn. Bus. and Soc., Acad. Mgmt. (program chair SIM divsn. 1998—99, chair elect SIM divsn. 1998—99, chair/pres. SIM divsn. 2000—01). Avocation: ballroom dancing. Office: U St Thomas Coll Bus Mail #TMH343 1000 Lasalle Ave Minneapolis MN 55403

ELMAHBOUB, WIDAD BRAHIM, science educator; arrived in US, 1989; d. Ibrahim Ahmed Elmahboub and Naima Abdel Hamid; m. Abdelmagegd Ahmed Elmustafa, June 27, 1986; 1 child, Moe. BS in astronomy physics, Cairo U., 1982; PhD in civil and environ. engring., U. Wis., 2000. Asst. prof. Hampton U. Sch. of Sci. Co-author: Dislocation Simulation, 2004, Bilinear Behavior, 2004; author: Simulated Linear Mixture Model, 2004. Chair 9th World Multi Conf. on Systemics, Cybernetics and Info.; chmn. of bd. Nauotab Inc. MUI grant, NASA, 2004—. Mem.: IEEE, Internat. Geoscience Remote Sensing Soc. Achievements include development of algorithm for atmospheric correction of aerosols for remote sensing data. Home: 200 Eric Nelson Run Yorktown VA Office Phone: 757-727-5909. Office Fax: 757-727-5084. E-mail: widad-elmahboub@hamptonu.edu.

EL MALLAKH, DOROTHEA HENDRY, editor, publishing executive; b. Emmett, Idaho, July 16, 1938; d. David Lovell Parker and Lygia Teressa (Dalton) Hendry; m. Ragaei William El Mallakh, Aug. 26, 1962 (dec. Mar. 19, 1987); children: Helen Alise, Nadia Irene. BA in Modern Langs., Lewis and Clark Coll., 1960; MA in History, U. Colo., 1962, PhD in History, 1972; postgrad., Georgetown U., 1962-63. Exec. adminstr., treas. Internat. Rsch. Ctr. Energy & Econ. Devel., Boulder, Colo., 1973-87, exec. dir., 1987—. Assoc. editor Jour. Energy & Devel., Boulder, 1975-87, mng. editor, 1987—; bd. dirs. Rocky Mountain Eye Found., Boulder. Author: The Slovak Autonomy Movement, 1979; author (with others): The Genius of Arab Civilization, 1983; editor: The Energy Watchers I-IX, 1990-98; author and editor: Saudi Arabia, 1982. Perrine Meml. fellow, U. Colo., 1960-61, Rare Lang. fellow, U.S. Govt., U. Colo., 1961-62, Rotary Internat. fellow, Boise, Idaho, 1962. Mem. Internat. Assn. Energy Econs. (v.p. internat. affairs 1989-91, sec. 1988-89). Office: ICEED 850 Willowbrook Rd Boulder CO 80302-7439 Office Phone: 303-442-4014. Business E-Mail: iceed@colorado.edu.

ELMAN, GERRY JAY, lawyer; b. Chgo., Oct. 7, 1942; s. Earl Samuel and Lucille Paulyne Elman; m. Lois Suzanne Bermet Levine; children: Jason Farrel, Floren Haley. BS, U. Chgo., 1963; MS in Chemistry, Stanford U., 1964; JD, Columbia U., 1967. Bar: N.Y. 1967, Pa. 1969, U.S. Dist. Ct. (so. and ea. dists.) N.Y. 1971, U.S. Dist. Ct. (ea. dist.) Pa. 1973, U.S. Dist. Ct. (mid. dist.) Pa. 1974, U.S. Ct. Appeals (Fed. cir.) 1987, U.S. Ct. Appeals (3d cir.) 1989, U.S. Patent Office, 1967, U.S. Supreme Ct. 1973, U.S. Dist. Ct. Colo. 2002. Assoc. Hubbell, Cohen & Stiefel, N.Y.C., 1967-68; patent atty., enzymes and health products Rohm and Haas Co., Phila., 1968-72; dep. atty. gen. Pa. Dept. Justice, Harrisburg, 1972-76; trial atty. Mid. Atlantic office antitrust divsn. U.S. Dept. Justice, Phila., 1976-82; pvt. practice Phila., 1982-83; mem. Elman Assocs., Phila., 1984-88, Lipton, Famiglio & Elman, Media, Pa., 1988-89, Elman Wilf & Fried, Media, 1990-95, Elman & Fried, Media, 1995-96, Elman & Assocs., Media, 1996—2002, Elman Tech. Law, P.C., Swarthmore, Pa., 2002—. Instr. short course in computer law Temple U., Phila., 1984; faculty in intellectual property mgmt. U. Phoenix Online Campus, 1995-98; webmaster Stanford Club of Phila., 2001-. Contbg. author: Lawyers' Microcomputer Users Group Jour., 1985-88; editor: Columbia Jour. Transnat. Law, 1966-67; mem. editl. bd. Jour. Trademark Reporter, 1968, Jour. Computer Law Reporter, 1983-90, BNA Spl. Reports Biotech., 1989-90, Licensing Jour., 1998—; founder, editor in chief Biotech. Law Report, 1982—; mem. bd. advisors Santa Clara Computer and High Tech. Law Jour., 1994-2003; mem. Global CyberLaw Network, 1997-2002, World Tech. Network, 2001-. Chmn. Three Steps Nursery Sch., Phila., 1977; arbitrator Phila. Ct. Common Pleas, 1971-72, 83-88, U.S. Dist. Ct. (ea. dist.) Pa. 1983—, Am. Arbitration Assn., 1987-96, Delaware County Ct. Common Pleas, Pa., 1993—, Forum Sysop, CompuServe online svc., 1994-99. Mem. ABA, Licensing Execs. Soc., Am. Intellectual Property Law Assn., Phila. Bar Assn. (chmn. jurimetrics com. 1975-77), Phila. Intellectual Property Law Assn. (chmn. biotech. subcom. 1982-86, continuing legal edn. com. 1995-97, PTO coord. com. 2003—), Delaware County Bar Assn., Computer Law Assn., Benjamin Franklin Am. Inn of Ct. (mem. bd. govs. 2004-). Home: 406 Yale Ave Swarthmore PA 19081-2024 Office: Elman Tech Law PC 406 Yale Ave PO Box 209 Swarthmore PA 19081-0209 Office Phone: 610-892-9942. E-mail: elman@elman.com.

EL-MANSY, YOUSSEF A., computer company executive; BSEE, Alexandria (Egypt) U., 1966, MSEE, 1970; PhD in Elec. Engring., Carlton U., Ottawa, Can., 1974. Mgr. tech. evaluation group Portland Tech. Devel. Intel Corp., 1979—80, program mgr. 64K DRAM, 1981—83, program mgr. 1MB CMOS DRAM, 1983—85, engring. mgr. Logic Techs., 1985—90, group v.p., 1993, corp. v.p. tech. and mfg. group, dir. logic tech. devel. Santa Clara, Calif., 2001—. Fellow: IEEE (exec. VLSI com., electron devices exec. com., VLSI symposia).

ELMER, BRIAN CHRISTIAN, lawyer; b. Washington, Apr. 18, 1936; s. Arthur Christian and Kathryn Aleen (O'Brien) E.; m. Sonja Kay Glass, Sept. 3, 1966; children: Mark Christian, Kimberly Kay, Robin Ann. BA in Arts and Sci., Cornell U., 1960; JD, U. Mich., 1962. Bar: D.C. 1963. Law clk. U.S. Ct. Appeals for D.C. Cir., Washington, 1962-64; ptnr. Jones, Day, Reavis and Pogue, Washington, 1964-79, Crowell and Moring, LLP, Washington, 1979—. Author: Fraud in Government Contracting, 1985; contbr. articles to profl. jours. Mem. ABA, D.C. Bar Assn., Met. Club. Office: Crowell & Moring LLP 1001 Pennsylvania Ave NW Washington DC 20004-2595 Office Phone: 202-624-2550. E-mail: belmer@crowell.com.

ELMER, LAWRENCE WILLIAM, neurologist, researcher; b. Gainesville, Fla., Jan. 31, 1958; s. Joseph William and Jean (Maguire) Elmer; m. LeAnn Wolitarsky, Jan. 17, 1953; children: Stephen William, Caroline Grace. BA, Davidson Coll., NC, 1980; MS, Fla. State U., 1983; MD, U. Fla., 1987, PhD, 1988. Diplomate Am. Bd. Psychiatry and Neurology. Asst. prof. U. Mich., Ann Arbor, 1994—98, Med. Coll. Ohio, Toledo, 1998—2004; assoc. prof. Med. U. Ohio, Toledo, 2004—. Dir., Parkinson's Disease and Movement Disorders program Med. U. Ohio, Toledo, 1998—, dir. ctr. for neurol. disorders, 2003—, pres.-elect faculty senate, 2004—05. V.p. Washtenaw Christian Acad., Saline, Mich., 2000—02; bd. dirs. ctrl. Ohio chpt. Huntington's Disease Soc., Columbus, 1999—2001, bd. dirs. Mich. chpt. Lansing, 2001—03; med. dir. NW Ohio Parkinson's Found., Toledo, 1998—2005; APMCO credentials com. mem. Med. Coll. Ohio, Toledo, 2000—04, chair, clin. rsch. ctr. subcom., 2004—04. Recipient Nat. Rsch. Svc. award, NIH, Baylor Coll. Medicine, 1987—88, Humanism in Medicine award, Med. Sch. Class of 2003, 2002, Golden Apple Award for Tchg., 2003, Med. Sch. Class of 2004, 2004, Dean's Tchg. award, Dean's Office, Sch. Medicine, 2003; fellow, U. Fla. Sch. of Medicine, 1983—87; scholar, Pfizer Pharms., 1995—97. Mem.: Soc. for Neuroscience, NY Acad. Sci., Am. Acad. Neurology. Office: Med Univ Ohio 3120 Glendale Ave Toledo OH 43614 Office Phone: 419-383-3544.

ELMER, MICHAEL BENDIK, legal administrator; b. Feb. 26, 1949; life ptnr. Annette Andersen; 1 child. Cand. jur., U. Copenhagen, 1973. Civil servant Min. of Justice, 1973-76, 77-82, head of divsn., 1982-87, 88-91; dep. judge Hillerød, 1976-77; high ct. judge Eastern High Ct., Copenhagen, 1987-88; v.p. a.i. Maritime and Comml. Ct., Copenhagen, 1988; dep. permanent sec. for justice, head of cmty. law and human rights dept., 1991-94; advocate gen. EC Ct. of Justice, Luxembourg, 1994—97; v.p. Maritime & Comml. Ct., Copenhagen, 1998—. Assoc. prof. U. Copenhagen, 1975-85; asst. pub. prosecutor, 1980-81; part time judge Ct. of Ballerup, 1981-82; external examiner Danish law schs., 1985—; internat. comml. arbitrator, 2000—; chmn., mem. numerous govt. and internat. orgns. Author of several books and articles, especially on property law, cmty. law and penal law. Recipient Grand Cross, Order of Merit, Luxembourg, Knight of the Order of Dannebrog, Denmark. Mem.: UNIDROIT (governing coun.), Assn. of European Competition Law Judges (London) (v.p.). Home: Skovalléen 16 DK-2880 Bagsvaerd Denmark Office: Maritime & Comml Ct Bredgade 70 DK-1260 Copenhagen Denmark Office Phone: +45 33 47 92 22. E-mail: michael@elmer.as.

ELMER, RUSSELL S., diversified financial services company executive, lawyer; BA in Polit. Sci. and Internat. Rels., Stanford (Calif.) U.; JD, U. Calif., Berkeley, Calif. Ptnr. Gray, Cary, Ware & Freidenrich; asst. gen. counsel E*TRADE Fin. Corp., Menlo Pk., Calif., 2000—01, gen. counsel, corp. sec., 2002—. Office: 135 E 57th St New York NY 10022 also: E*TRADE Financial Corp 4500 Bohannon Dr Menlo Park CA 94025*

ELMES, DAVID GORDON, psychologist, educator; b. Newton, Mass., Feb. 15, 1942; s. Leslie and Ruth (Adams) E.; m. Anne Louise Lawrence, June 7, 1963; children: Matthew David, Jennifer Anne. BA, U. Va., 1964; MA, U.Va., 1966; PhD, U. Va., 1967. Mgmt. trainee C & P of Va., 1963; asst. prof. psychology Washington and Lee U., Lexington, Va., 1967-71, assoc. prof., 1971-74, prof., 1975—, head dept. psychology, 1990-2000, co-dir. cognitive sci., 1987-2000. Rsch. assoc. Human Performance Ctr., U. Mich., 1973-74; vis. fellow Univ. Coll., Oxford (Eng.) U., 1987. Author: Readings in Experimental Psychology, 1978, Research Methods in Psychology, 2005; contbr. articles to profl. jours. Bd. dirs. Rockbridge Mental Health Clinic, 1968-73. Fellow Am. Psychol. Soc.; mem. Psychonomic Soc., Va. Acad. Sci., Coun. on Undergrad. Rsch. (past pres.), Phi Beta Kappa. Office: Washington and Lee U Dept Psychology Lexington VA 24450-0303 Business E-Mail: elmesd@wlu.edu.

ELMORE, CENIETH CATHERINE, music educator; b. Wilson, NC, July 4, 1930; d. Thomas Onestrus Elmore and Effie Lee Morris. MusB in Theory, U. N.C., Greensboro, 1953; MusM in Composition, U. N.C., 1962, MA in Musicology, 1963, PhD in Musicology, 1972. Piano tchr. pub. sch., Fuquay Springs, NC, 1953—57, Louisburg, NC, 1957—60; grad. asst. piano tchr. U. N.C., Chapel Hill, 1960—63; music prof. Campbell U., Buies Creek, NC, 1963—94, prof. emeritus, 1994—. Lectr. in field; pvt. piano tchr., 1998—. Author. Active Franklin County Arts Coun., Louisburg, NC, 1970—, Franklin County Person Place Preservation Soc., Louisburg, 1980—, Perry's Chapel Bapt. Ch., Franklinton, NC, 1948—. Named Artist of Yr., Franklin County Arts Coun., 1995. Mem.: N.C. Music Tchrs. Assn., Am. Musicological Soc., Raleigh Piano Tchrs. Assn. (first v.p. 1996—98, 2000—02, pres. 2002—04, chair young artist auditions composition competition 2004—). Republican. Avocations: painting, reading, gardening, travel, internet. Home: 981 Perry's Chapel Church Rd Franklinton NC 27525-8263 Personal E-mail: ceniethelmore@aol.com.

ELMORE, EDWARD WHITEHEAD, lawyer; b. Lawrenceville, Va., July 15, 1938; s. Thomas Milton and Mary Norfleet (Whitehead) E.; m. Gail Harmon, Aug. 10, 1968; children: Mary Jennifer, Edward Whitehead Jr. BA, U. Va.-Charlottesville, 1959, JD, 1962. Bar: Va. 1962. Assoc. firm Hunton & Williams, Richmond, Va., 1965-69; staff atty. Ethyl Corp., Richmond, 1969-78, asst. gen. counsel, 1978-79, gen. counsel, 1979-80, gen. counsel., sec., 1980-83, v.p., gen. counsel, sec., 1983-94, spl. counsel to exec. com., corp. sec., 1994-97; sr. v.p., gen. counsel, sec. Albemarle Corp., Richmond, 1994-2001, exec. v.p., sec., 2001—02, exec. v.p., 2002—. Served to capt. AUS, 1962-65. Decorated Army Commendation medal Mem. ABA, Va. Bar Assn., Internat. Bar Assn., Va. State Bar, Am. Corp. Counsel Assn., Bar Assn. Richmond, Am. Soc. Corp. Secs., Raven Soc., Phi Beta Kappa Office: Albemarle Corp 330 S 4th St Richmond VA 23219-4350

ELMORE, JAMES WALTER, architect, educator, retired dean; b. Lincoln, Nebr., Sept. 5, 1917; s. Harry Douglas and Marie Clare (Minor) E.; m. Mary Ann Davidson, Sept. 6, 1947; children: James Davidson, Margaret Kay. AB, U. Nebr., 1938; MS in Architecture, Columbia U., 1948. Mem. faculty Ariz. State U., 1949-86, prof. architecture, 1959-86, founding dean Coll. of Architecture, 1964-74. Cons. architect, 1956— Trustee Heard Museum, Phoenix, 1968-79; bd. dirs. Valley Forward Assn., 1969-89, pres., 1985; bd. dirs. Central Ariz. chpt. Ariz. Hist. Soc., 1973-89; bd. dirs. Ariz. Architects Found., 1978-86, Rio Salado Devel. Dist., 1980-87. Served to col., C.E. U.S. Army, 1940-46. Decorated Bronze Star. Fellow AIA; mem. Ariz. Acad. Home: 7550 N 16t St 6304 Phoenix AZ 85020-4618

ELMORE, JULIE ANN JOHANN, special education educator; d. George Callender Johann, Jr. and Hilda Lucille (Wortman) Johann (Stepmother), H. Marie Ann (Nenne) Johann; m. Leroy Elmore, Jr., June 23, 1972 (div. Dec. 5, 1995); children: Michael Wayne, Patrick Scott, Heather Lynn Elmore Westbrook. BA in Elem. Edn. magna cum laude, N.Mex Highlands U., 1994; MA in Edn., N.Mex State U., 2004; Initial Administrator's Lic., Portland State U., 2005. Teller Bank Va. Beach, Virginia Beach, 1983—84, Ctrl. Carolina Bank, Durham, NC, 1985—88; trust investment asst. Jefferson Nat. Bank, Charlottesville, Va., 1988—90; spl. edn. tchr. Bloomfield Mcpl. Schs., N.Mex., 1994—99, Ctrl. Consol. Sch. Dist., Kirkland, N.Mex., 1999—2002, Klamath County Sch. Dist., Klamath Falls, Oreg., 2002—. Leader Boy Scouts of Am., Norfolk, Va., 1985—86; mem. Springer Cmty. Choir, N.Mex., 1990—94, Klamath Chorale, 2003—05. R-Consevative. Methodist. Avocations: singing, travel, crocheting. Office Phone: 541-783-2321. Personal E-mail: elm276@charter.net.

ELMORE, LEONARD JOSEPH, lawyer; b. Bklyn., Mar. 28, 1952; s. Moses Leonard and Gladys (Henson) E.; m. Gail Segal, Sept. 5, 1987; 1 child, Stephen. BA in English, U. Md., 1978; JD, Harvard Law Sch., 1987. Bar: N.Y. 1988. Asst. dist. atty. Kings County Dist. Atty., Bklyn, 1987-90; pres., CEO Test U., 2001—03; sr. counsel LeBoeuf, Lamb, Green & MacRae. Basketball player NBA, 1974—84; commentator Nat. Pub. Radio, Washington; basketball analyst CBS Sports, N.Y.C., Jefferson Pilot/Raycom Sports, Charlotte, NC, 1985—92; coll. basketball analyst ESPN. Com. mem. Chancellor's Task Force on Academics., U. Md., 1986; bd. mem. Univ. Sys. of Md. Found., 1990—98; mem. Tourism Devel. Bd. U. Md., College Park, 1998—; bd. mem. 1 800 Flowers.com, NBA Retired Players Assn., John and James L. Knight Found.'s Knight Commn. on Intercollegiate Athletics, 2003—. Recipient Citizenship award U. Md., 1974, Alumni Achievement award Black Alumni Assn. U. Md., 1988. Mem. N.Y. Bar Assn. (Sports and Entertainment Com.), Sport Lawyers Assn. (bd. mem.) Avocations: cinema, baseball, literature, history, politics. Office: LeBoeuf, Lamb, Greene & MacRae LLP 125 W 55th St New York NY 10019-8000 Office Phone: 212-424-8000. E-mail: lelmore@llgm.com.

ELMORE, RICHARD F., education educator; B in Polit. Sci., Whitman Coll.; M in Polit. Sci., Claremont U.; EdD in Edn1. Policy, Harvard U. Prof. edn. Harvard U., 1991—. Sr. rsch. fellow Consortium for Policy Rsch. in Edn., co-dir. rsch. project on sch. accountability. Co-author (with B. Fuller and G. Orfield): Who Chooses, Who Loses? Culture, Institutions, and the Unequal Effects of School Choice, 1996; co-author: (with S. Fuhrman) The Governance of Curriculum; co-author: (with P. Peterson and S. McCarthey) Restructuring in the Classroom, 1996; co-author: (with C. Abelmann) Building a New Structure for School Leadership, 2000; contbr. articles to profl. jours. Grantee, OERI/ED. Mem.: NAS, NAE (bd. mem., bd. on testing and assessment), Nat. Rsch. Coun., Am. Ednl. Rsch. Assn. Office: Harvard Grad Sch Edn Gutman 448 Cambridge MA 02138

ELMORE, WALTER A., electrical engineer, consultant; b. Bartlett, Tenn., Oct. 2, 1925; s. Walter Alcorn and Lucile (Tapp) E.; m. Jane Ann Huey, June 3, 1950; children: Robin, Jamie, Laura. BSEE, U. Tenn., 1949. Registered profl. engr., Fla. Mgr. cons. engring. sect. Protective Relay div. Westinghouse Elec. Corp., Newark, 1951-79, Protective Relay div. ABB Power T & D Co., Coral Springs, Fla., 1979-89; mgr. cons. engring. sect. protective relay divsn. ABB Power T&D Co., Coral Springs, Fla., 1989-94, cons. engr. high voltage protection, 1994-96, ret., 1996. Author: (with others) Applied Protective Relaying, 1976, Protective Relaying Theory and Application, 1994, Pilot Protective Relaying, 1999. Fellow IEEE (chmn. IEEE/PES tech. coun. 1988-89, Gold medal for engring. excellence 1989); mem. NAE, Tau Beta Pi, Eta Kappa Nu, Phi Kappa Phi. Republican. Home: 104 Macgregor Dr Blue Ridge VA 24064-1526

EL-MOSLIMANY, ANN PAXTON, paleoecologist, educator, writer; b. Fullerton, Calif., Aug. 2, 1937; d. Donald Dorn and Sarah Frances (Turman) Paxton; m. Mohammed Ahmad El-Moslimany, May 31, 1962 (dec.); children: Samia, Ramsey, Rasheed. BS, N.Mex. State U., 1959; MS, Am. U., Beirut, 1961; PhD, U. Wash., 1983. Tchr. various schs., 1959-83, Kuwait U., 1984—86, Seattle Ctrl. C.C., 1986-90; prin., tchr. Islamic Sch. Seattle, 1989-99, curriculum coord., 1999—. Paleoecological rschr. Palynological Consultants, 1987—; founding dir. Islamic Sch. of Seattle; adv. bd. Islamic Sch. League Am. Author: Zaki's Ramadan Fast, 1994; contbr. articles to sci.

jours.; mem. adv. bd. Aziah mag. Speaker Children of Abraham Organization. Mem. Amnesty Internat., Am. Quaternary Assn., Islamic Sch. League. Moslem. Avocations: travel, literature, history. Home: PO Box 367 Seahurst WA 98062-0367 Office: Islamic Sch Seattle 720 25th Ave Seattle WA 98122-4902 Mailing: PO Box 367 Seahurst WA 98062 E-mail: annelmoslimany@yahoo.com.

ELMOUCHI, JOAN LESLIE, library director; b. Atlantic City, Feb. 18, 1952; d. William Nathaniel Solkin and Ann Herman; m. Gary William Stewart (div. 1984); m. Robert Alan Elmouchi, Sept. 21, 1986. BA, Rutgers U., 1974; MLS, U. Mich., 1975. Librs. permanent profl. cert. Children's libr. Troy (Mich.) Pub. Libr., 1976-78; reference libr. Waterford Twp. (Mich.) Libr., 1979-85; libr. dir. Auburn Hills (Mich.) Libr., 1985-93, Garden City (Mich.) Libr., 1993—. Adv. coun. mem. Wayne (Mich.)-Oakland Libr. Fedn., 1989-90; mem. Libr. Network Steering Com., 2001—; mem. exec. com. SASUG, 2000—; sec. Women's Nat. Book Assn., 2001 Author: Beach Freaks' Guide to Michigan's Best Beaches, 1999. Grantee Dept. Edn. and State Mich., 1997. Mem. ALA, Mich. Libr. Assn. (pub. libr. rep. 1994-95), Metro-Detroit Book and Author Soc. (pres. 1995-99), No Kidding! (Detroit area rep. 1997-99). Avocations: reading, cross country skiing, dance. Office: Garden City Libr 2012 Middlebelt Rd Garden City MI 48135-2895 E-mail: elmouchi@tln.lib.mi.us.

EL-MOURSY, MAGDY, electronics engineer; b. Cairo, Giza, Egypt, Oct. 10, 1974; s. Ali El-Moursy and Naima Ahmed. PhD, U. Rochester, 2004. Software developer Internat. Computer and Communication Consultants (ICCC), Cairo, 1999—2000; rsch. asst. Nat. Inst. Standards, Cairo, 1997—99, Electronics Rsch. Inst., Cairo, 1999—2000; tchg. asst. U. Rochester, Rochester, NY, 2000—01, rsch. asst., 2001—04; integrated circuit designer STMicroelectronics Corp., San Diego, 2003—03; sr. design elec. engr. Intel Corp., Portland, Oreg., 2004, 2004—. Author: (book chapter) Design Methodologies for On-Chip Inductive, Optimizing Inductive Interconnect for Low Power, (journal paper), Resistive Power in CMOS Circuits, Power Characteristics of Inductive Interconnect, Optimum Wire Sizing of RLC Interconnect With Repeaters, Shielding Effect of On-Chip Interconnect Inductance. Tchg. Islamic Ctr. Rochester, Rochester, NY, 2003. Office Phone: 971-214-3547.

ELMS, BEN, actor, theater director; b. Syracuse, N.Y., July 1, 1935; s. Benjamin Charles and Sarah Mildred (Nourse) E. BA, Syracuse U., 1957. Appeared in TV shows including Unsolved Mysteries, 1990; films include Man Who Knew Too Much, 1985, The Judgement, 1990; musicals include The Fantasticks, 1987, Jesus Christ Superstar, 1987, Phantom, 1997, Hello Dolly, 1998, Annie, 2004; plays include Death of a Salesman, 1989, Foxfire, 1991, Noises Off, 1996, Hamlet, 1997, Our Town, 1999, Julius Caesar, 2000, The Diary of Anne Frank, 2001, The Miracle Worker, 2002, Joseph & The Amazing Technicolor Dreamcoat, 2002, The Crucible, 2002, Jekyl & Hyde, 2003, Alice in Wonderland, 2003, Midsummer Night's Dream, 2003, Romeo and Juliet, 2004; dir. plays including Butterflies Are Free, 1978, Extremities, 1987; also commls. Capt. U.S. Army, 1958-60. Mem. SAG, Actors Equity Assn. Republican. Roman Catholic. Home: 60 Presidential Plz Syracuse NY 13202-2292

ELMS, C. LEE, lawyer; b. Marfa, Tex., Sept. 4, 1952; s. Lee W. and Audrey (Elmendorf) E.; children: Robert, William. BBA with honors, N.Mex. State U., 1975; JD, St. Mary's U., 1978. Bar: Tex. 1979, U.S. Dist. Ct. (we. dist.) Tex. 1980, U.S. Ct. Appeals (5th cir.) 1981, U.S. Supreme Ct. 1983, U.S. Dist. Ct. (no. dist.) Tex. 1983, U.S. Dist. Ct. (ea. and so. dists.) Tex. 1990. Assoc. Law Offices of O'Neal Munn, San Antonio, 1978-81; ptnr. Brown, Douglas & Elms, San Antonio, 1981-84; mng. ptnr. Douglas & Elms, San Antonio, 1984-97; mgr. Elms Harmon, LLC, San Antonio, 1997—. Mem. State Bar Tex., San Antonio Bar Assn., Bar Assn. 5th Fed. Cir., Tex. Assn. Bank Counsel, San Antonio Bar Found., ATLA, Assoc. Gen. Contractors, Lions. Office: Elms Harmon LLC 7800 Ih 10 W Ste 600 San Antonio TX 78230-4750 Office Phone: 210-349-8888. Fax: 210-349-8805. Business E-Mail: lelms@elmslaw.com.

EL-NAKIB, HESHAM MOUSSA, diplomat; b. Cairo, Sept. 2, 1961; s. Moussa Morsi El-Nakib and Kariman Radwan. BA in Polit. sci., Am. U., Cairo, Egypt, 1984; diploma in Polit. sci., Inst. of Diplomacy, Berlin, 1986; M in Internat. Rels., The Internat. Inst. of Pub. Adminstrn., Paris, France, 1987; D in Polit. sci., Inst. of Oriental Studies of the Russian Acad. Sci., Moscow, 2000. Diplomatic attache Egyptian Diplomatic Inst., Cairo, 1985—86; third sec. The Cabinet of the Min. of Fgn. Affairs, Cairo, 1987—88, Embassy of Egypt, Vienna, 1988—89; rsch. analyst The UN Devel. Program, N.Y.C., 1989—90; second sec. Office of the Polit. Dir. of the Egyptian President's Bur. (Dr. Osama El Baz), Cairo, 1990—92; first sec. Embassy of Egypt, Washington, 1992—97; dir. (first sec.) North Am. Dept., Ministry of Fgn. Affairs, Cairo, 1997—99; dir. (counselor) Cabinet of the First Undersec. to the Min. of Fgn. Affairs, Ministry of Fgn. Affairs, Cairo, 1999—2001; dir. (press counselor and head of office) Press and Info. Office, Embassy of Egypt, Washington, 2001—. Lectr., guest spkr. Participant youth com. Nat. Dem. Party, Cairo, 1982—85. Recipient Wall of Tolerance, Nat. Campaign for Tolerance, 2002; Honor Scholarship, Am. U., 1986. Mem.: Nat. Press Club, Acad. of Polit. Sci. in NY, Bd. of Diplomatic Club, Cairo (dep. pres. 1999—2000). Office: Egyptian Press and Info Office 1666 Connecticut Ave NW Suite 440 Washington DC 20009 E-mail: egyprsinfo@aol.com.

ELNAQA, ISSAM M., research scientist; b. Beirut, Sept. 14, 1968; arrived in U.S., 1998; s. Uutafei A and Roba O.; married, Nov. 20, 2004. BSc, U. Jordan, 1992, MS, 1995; PhD, Ill. Inst. Tech., 2002. Rsch. assoc. Wash. U., St. Louis, 2002—; software programmer CFB, Jordan, 1995—96. Contbr. scientific papers in field. Mem.: Inst. Elec. Office: Wash U 660 S Eulid Saint Louis MO 63110

ELRIFI, IVOR R., lawyer; b. 1961; BS in Biology, Queen's U. at Kingston, Can., 1982, PhD in Biology, 1986; LLB, Osgood Hall Law Sch., Toronto, Can., 1989. Bar: Can. 1991, NY 1991, ON 1991, Mass. 1998, US Ct. Appeals. (Fed. Cir.), registered: US Patent & Trademark Office. Assoc. Fish & Neave, NY; patent counsel CytoThearapeutics Inc., Providence, gen. counsel & v.p.; patent counsel Modex Therapeutics, Lausanne, Switzerland; ptnr. Mintz Levin Cohn Ferris Glovsky & Popeo PC, Boston, mem. policy com., co-chmn., Intellectual Property Sect. Mem.: Law Soc. Upper Can. Office: Mintz Levin Cohn Ferris Glovsky & Popeo PC One Financial Ctr Boston MA 02111 Office Phone: 617-348-1714. Office Fax: 617-542-2241. Business E-Mail: irelrifi@mintz.com.

ELROD, BEN MOODY, academic administrator; b. Rison, Ark., Oct. 13, 1930; s. Benjamin Searcy and Frances Othello (Sadler) E.; m. Betty Lou Warren, Aug. 7, 1951; children: Cynthia Lou, William Searcy. BA, Ouachita Baptist U., 1952; ThD, Southwestern Bapt. Theol. Sem., 1962; EdD, Ind. U., 1975. Ordained to ministry Baptist Ch., 1950; pastor First Bapt. Ch., Atkins, Ark., 1951-53, Tioga, Tex., 1955-57, Marlow, Okla., 1957-60, South Side Bapt. Ch., Pine Bluff, Ark., 1960-63; pres. Oakland City (Ind.) Coll., 1968-70, Georgetown (Ky.) Coll., 1978-83, Ind. Colls. of Ark., 1983-88; v.p. devel. Ouachita Bapt. U., Arkadelphia, Ark., 1963-68, 70-78, pres., 1988-97, chancellor, 1998—. Commr. Ark. Econ. Devel. Commn., 2002—08; vis. lectr. in field; cons. in higher edn. Contbr. articles to religion jours. Page U.S. Ho. of Reps., 1946-47; trustee Clark County (Ark.) Hosp., 1973-77, chmn., 1975-77; trustee Ark. Bapt. Med. System, 1978, 1989-2001. Mem. Nat. Assn. Ind. Colls. and Univs. (chmn. tax policy commn. 1993), Ark. State C. of C. (bd. dirs. 1990-98), Assn. So. Bapt. Colls. and Schs. (pres. 1996-97), Consortium for Global Edn. (chmn. bd. dirs. 1997-99, mem. exec. com. bd. dirs. 1997-2002). Home: 1008 Village Dr Arkadelphia AR 71923-2922 Office: Ouachita Bapt Univ Elrod Ctr for Family and Cmty Box 3790 Ouachita Sta Arkadelphia AR 71923-3221 Office Phone: 870-245-5320.

ELROD, EUGENE RICHARD, lawyer; b. Roanoke, Ala., May 14, 1949; s. James Woodrow and Selma Fromer (Steinbach) E. AB, Dartmouth Coll., 1971; JD, Emory U., 1974. Bar: Ga. 1974, D.C. 1976, U.S. Ct. Appeals (D.C. cir.) 1985, U.S. Ct. Appeals (5th cir.) 1987, U.S. Dist. Ct. D.C. 1987, U.S. Ct. Appeals (11th cir.) 1987, U.S. Supreme Ct. 1987, U.S. Ct. Appeals (10th cir.) 1997. Trial atty. Fed. Power Com., Washington, 1974-76; atty.-advisor Fed. Energy Adminstrn., Washington, 1977; assoc. Sidley & Austin, Washington, 1977-80, ptnr., 1981—. Adv. bd. Inst. for Energy Law, 2004—, Keplinger Cos., Houston. Mem. selection com. for Woodruff scholars Emory U. Law Sch., Dartmouth '71 Exec. Com. Mem. ABA, D.C. Bar Assn., Ga. Bar Assn., Energy Bar Assn. (chmn. oil pipeline com. 1982-83, tax com. 1980-81, 92-95, liaison with adminstrv. law judges 1986-87, ethics com. 1997-2001, bd. dirs. 2000-03, bd. dirs. Charitable Found.), Dartmouth Club (exec. com. class of 1971), Book Club of Calif. Avocations: running, book collecting, gardening. Home: 4300 Hawthorne St NW Washington DC 20016-3571 Office: Sidley Austin Brown & Wood 1501 K St NW Ste 900 Washington DC 20005 Office Phone: 202-736-8206. Business E-Mail: eelrod@sidley.com.

ELROD, LU, retired music educator, actress; b. Chattanooga, Apr. 23, 1935; d. John C. Elrod and Helen Pauline (Kohn). MusB, Ga. State U., 1960; M in Music Edn., U. Ga., 1970, EdD, 1971; PhD, U. London, 1975. Prof. music, music coach U. Md., Balt., 1972-78, Calif. State U., L.A., 1978—2004, now prof. emerita. Singer with Dallas Opera, 1957. Appeared in movies Charly, 1969, Brewster's Millions, 1986, Major Pettigrew and Me, 1976, Seduction of Joe Tynan, 1977, Atlanta Child Murders, 1985, Children Don't Tell, 1986, For Love or Money, 1986, High School High, 1996, Wag the Dog, 1997, The Big Lebowski, 1998, Primary Colors, 1998, Lloyd the Ugly Kid, 1999, Beautiful, 1999, Glory Days, 2001, Freaky Friday, 2004, Kicking and Screaming, 2005; appeared on TV in Lazarus Syndrome, 1980, Hill Street Blues (Emmy award), 1988, Superior Court, 1988, TV Bloopers, 1989, Beakman's World (Emmy award), Dream On, 1993, Misery Loves Company, 1995, Caroline in the City, 1995, Louie, 1996, George and Alana, 1996, Maggie, 1998, Two Guys and a Girl, 2000, Glory Days, 2001, I Love the 90's, 2004; appeared in TV commls Recipient Leadership Devel. award Ford Found., 1967, Leadership Fellows award Ford Found., 1968; Tift Coll. voice scholar, 1953, Baylor U. voice scholar, 1956; Lu Elrod scholarship named at Calif. State U., L.A., 1989; named to Calif. State U., L.A. Wall of Fame, 1993. Mem. AAUP, AFTRA, SAG, Am. Guild Variety Artists, Calif. Faculty Assn., Coll. Music Soc. Achievements include established 23 music scholarships through fundraising activities for Friends of Music Board of Directors 1978-2005. Office: Calif State Univ 5151 State University Dr Los Angeles CA 90032-4226 Business E-Mail: lelrod@calstatela.edu.

ELROD, STEVEN M., lawyer; b. Chgo., July 12, 1957; BA magna cum laude with spl. honors, Tulane U., 1979; JD, Northwestern U., 1982. Bar: Ill. 1982. Exec. ptnr. Holland & Knight LLP, Chgo., Oakbrook Terrace, Ill., mem. dir. com., chair, fed. polit. action com. Bd. dir. Constitutional Rights Found., Chgo., 1988—, participates in Lawyers in the Classroom; mem., lectr. Nat. Coll. Dist. Attys.; village atty., Northbrook, Ill.; corp. counsel, Highland Park, Ill.; spkr. and lectr. in the field. Contbr. articles to profl. jours. Mem.: Chgo. Bar Assn. (chmn., local govt. com. 1989—90, mem. real property law com.), ABA (mem. state and local govt. law sect.), Lambda Alpha Land Economics Soc. Office: Holland & Knight LLP 131 S Dearborn St 30th Fl Chicago IL 60603 Office Phone: 312-578-6565. Business E-Mail: steven.elrod@hklaw.com.

ELS, ERNIE (THEODORE ERNEST ELS), professional golfer; b. Kempton Park, South Africa, Oct. 17, 1969; s. Cornelius and Hester E. Diploma, Jan de Klerk Tech. Coll. Golf Course Designer Mem. nat. teams Dunhill Cup, 1992, 93, 94, 95, 96, 97, 98, 99, 2000, World Cup, 1992, 93, 96, 97, 2001 Pres.'s Cup, 1996, 98, 2000, 2003, host, Ernie Els Invitational, South Africa. Established the Ernie Els Foundation for Children 1999 Winner, 14 Career PGA Tour Victories,U.S. Open, 1994, 1997, British Open, 2002, 35 Career Internat. Victories; named PGA European Player of Yr., 1994; South African Sportsman of the Yr., 1994, recipient, Lifetime membership, PGA European Tour, 1998. Mem. Ocean Club (Paradise Island, The Bahamas). Avocations: squash, movies, winemaking. Address: c/o PGA European Tour Wentworth Dr Virginia Water Surrey GU25 4LX England

ELSAS, LOUIS JACOB, II, medical educator; b. Atlanta, Feb. 10, 1937; s. Herbert R. and Edith (Levy) E.; m. Nancy Terrell, July 15, 1961; children: Nancy Louise, Margaret Edith, Louis Jacob, III. BA, Harvard U., 1958; MD, U. Va., 1962. Diplomate Am. Bd. Internal Medicine, Am. Bd. Med. Genetics. Intern Yale-New Haven Hosp., 1962-63, resident in internal medicine, 1963-65; NIH postdoctoral fellow in med. genetics Yale U., 1965-68, from instr. to asst. prof. sect. genetics, dept. medicine and pediatrics, 1968-70; faculty Emory U. Med. Sch., Atlanta, 1970—2002, prof. pediatrics and biochemistry, 1977—2002, prof. emeritus, 2002—. Dir. Ga. Comprehensive Genetic System, 1978; vis. prof. Japan Soc. Promotion Sci., 1976; Professore a contratto, Italy, 1985—; U.S. advisor Congress of Inborn Errors of Metabolism, 1980-2000; bd. dirs. The Howard Sch., 1994—; prof., dir. Dr. John T. MacDonald Found. Ctr. Med. Genetics U. Miami, 2002-. Contbr. numerous articles to profl. jours. Mem. alumni coun. Phillips Acad., 2001—. Recipient Rsch. Career Devel. award NIH, 1972-77, John Horsley Meml. prize U. Va. Med. Sch., 1972, A.E. Levy Faculty Rsch. award Emory U., 1989, Big Heart award Civitans, 1992, Claude Fuess award Phillips Acad., 2000; named hon. citizen Interlaken, Switzerland, 1980. Fellow Am. Acad. Pediat., Am. Coll. Med. Genetics (founder, bd. dirs. 1996—); mem. UNICEF, Soc. Inherited Metabolic Disorders (founding pres.), Am. Soc. Clin. Investigation, Soc. Pediat. Rsch., Am. Soc. Biol. Chemistry, Am. Soc. Human Genetics, Assn. Am. Physicians, Assn. Profs. Human and Med. Genetics (pres. 1998-2001), S.E. Genetics Group (chmn. 1983-94), Coun. Regional Networks (pres. 1994-2001), Emory U. Faculty Club, Druid Hills Golf Club, The Temple, Sigma Xi (past chpt. pres.). Clubs: Emory U. Faculty, Druid Hills Golf, Civitan (Humanitarian award 1979, Big Heart award 1992). Office: Dr John T Macdonald Found Ctr Med Genetics U Miami Sch Medicine Rm 6001 MCCD Bldg 1601 NW 12 Ave Miami FL 33136 Home: 3940 Braganza Ave Miami FL 33133-6355 Office Phone: 305-243-7105. Business E-Mail: lelsas@med.miami.edu. *The successful biomedical scientist must develop a personal balance between science and humanism; innovation and application; learning and teaching. This goal can be met if one starts at an early age and continues as a student of fundamental science; is curious and tests central dogma; uses truth and the scientific method as standards of conduct and is sympathetic to the needs of individuals and society.*

ELSASSER, GLEN ROBERT, journalist; b. Marion, Ohio, Oct. 18, 1935; s. Glen Robert and Mary Louise (Hogan) E.; m. Katharine Macy Kersting, Sept. 8, 1973; 1 child, Daniel. BA, Ohio State U., 1957; MS, Columbia U. Sch. Journalism, 1961. Reporter UPI, Louisville, 1957-58; reporter, writer Indpls. Star, 1961-63; reporter, writer, editor Chgo. Tribune, Chgo., N.Y.C., Washington, 1963—. With U.S. Army, 1958-60, Kansas City, Mo. Recipient Gavel award ABA, 1979. Home: 319 C St NE Washington DC 20002-5709 Office: Chgo Tribune 1325 G St NW Ste 200 Washington DC 20005-3129

ELSAYES, KHALED MOHAMED, radiologist; b. Alexandria, Egypt, Oct. 13, 1969; arrived in U.S., 2001; s. Mohamed Nour (Eleyon) and Amal Mahmoud Elsayes; m. Samah Mahmoud Elkhouly; children: Omar, Ahmed, Mariam. B of Surgery and Medicine, Sch. Medicine, Cairo, 1993, M of Radiology. Resident radiology Theodor Bilhart Inst., Cairo, 1996—99, lectr. radiology, staff radiologist, 1999—2001; body MRI fellow Washington U. Sch. Medicine, St. Louis, 2001—. Contbr. articles to profl. jours. Mem.: Am. Ray Roentgen Soc., Radiol. Soc. N.Am. (cert. merit 2003, 2004). Office: Mallinchrodt Inst Radiology Washington U 510 S Kings Hwy Saint Louis MO

ELSBERG, JOHN WILLIAM, editor-in-chief; b. N.Y.C., Aug. 4, 1945; s. John Christian and Paula Hutter E.; m. Constance Waeber, June 17, 1967; 1 child, Stephen John. BA in History magna cum laude, Columbia Coll., 1967; BA in History with honors, Cambridge U., 1969, MA in History, 1973. Editor U.S. Army Ctr. Mil. History, Washington, 1974-80, acting chief editl. br., 1981, chief editl. br., 1982, editor-in-chief, 1983, chief prodn. svcs. divsn., 1988—. Judge numerous writing competitions; lectr. Manassas campus Am. history and We. civilization No Va. C.C., 1974-75, 75-76; freelance rschr. bicentennial project Nat. Pub. Affairs Ctr. T.V., 1974; adj. prof. European div. U. Md., 1970-73; counselor, adminstr. residential Upward Bound program Columbia U., 1965-67. Editor: Gargoyle, 1977—80, Bogg: A Jour. Contemporary Writing, 1980—, author numerous poems, fifteen books and chapbooks of poetry; contbr. articles to profl. jours. MC poetry readings, chair various pub. panel discussions The Writer's Ctr., Bethesda, Md; former mem. poetry com. Folger Shakespeare Libr., Washington. Kellett fellow U. Cambridge. Fellow Va. Ctr. Creative Arts; mem. Coun. Lit. Mags. and Pubs., Poets and Writers, Columbia U. Club Washington, Phi Beta Kappa. Avocations: bicycling, hiking, travel, raising dogs. Home: 422 N Cleveland St Arlington VA 22201 Office: US Army Ctr Mil History 103 Third Ave Washington DC 20319

ELSBREE, LANGDON, English language educator; b. Trenton, N.J., June 23, 1929; s. Wayland Hoyt and Miriam (Jenkins) E.; m. Aimee Desiree Wildman, June 9, 1952; 1 child, Anita. BA, Earlham Coll., 1952; MA, Cornell U., 1954; PhD, Claremont Grad. Sch., 1963. Instr. in English Miami U., Oxford, Ohio, 1954-57, Harvey Mudd Coll., Claremont, Calif., 1958-59; instr. humanities Scripps Coll., Claremont, Calif., 1959-60; instr., prof. Claremont McKenna Coll., 1960-94, prof. emeritus, 1994; mem. grad. faculty Claremont Grad. Sch., 1965—. Part-time lectr. Calif. State U., L.A., 1968-70; vis. prof. Carleton Coll., 1987. Author: The Rituals of Life, 1982, Ritual Passages and Narrative Structures, 1991; co-author: Heath College Handbook, 6th-12th edits., 1967-90; guest editor D.H. Lawrence Rev., 1975, 87. Bd. dirs. Claremont Civic Assn., 1964-66; mem. founding com. Quaker Studies in Human Betterment, Greensboro, N.C., 1987. Fulbright Commn. lectr., 1966-67; grantee NEH, 1975, Claremont McKenna Coll., 1980, 82, 87. Mem.: MLA, Sci. Fiction Rsch. Assn., Virginia Woolf Soc., Friends Assn. Higher Edn., D.H. Lawrence Soc. (exec. bd. 1990), Phi Beta Kappa. Democrat. Soc. Of Friends. Avocations: travel, reading, swimming, films, photography. Office: Claremont McKenna Coll Bauer Ctr 890 Columbia Ave Claremont CA 91711-3901 Personal E-mail: le.ade@verozen.net.

ELSE, CAROLYN JOAN, retired library director; b. Mpls., Jan. 31, 1934; d. Elmer Oscar and Irma Carolyn (Seibert) Wahlberg; m. Floyd Warren Else, 1962 (div. 1968); children: Stephen Alexander, Catherine Elizabeth. BS, Stanford U., 1956; MLS, U. Wash., 1957. Cert. profl. libr. Wash. Libr. Queens Borough Pub. Libr., N.Y.C., 1957—59, U.S. Army Spl. Svcs., France, Germany, 1959—62; info. libr. Bennett Martin Libr., Lincoln, Nebr., 1962—63; br. libr. Pierce County Libr., Tacoma, 1963—65, dir., 1965—94; ret., 1994. Wellness cons. Nikken, Inc., 1994—. Mem. Higher Edn. Coun., South Puget Sound, 1988—92; bd. dirs. Tacoma Philharmonic, 2005—; mem. distbn. com. Greater Tacoma Cmty. Found., 2005—; mem. study commn. Wash. State Local Governance, 1985—88; bd. dirs. Campfire, Tacoma, 1984—92, Cmty. Health Care, 1997—2003. Mem.: Pacific N.W. Libr. Assn. (sec. 1969—71), Wash. Libr. Assn. (v.p. 1969—71), ALA, Tacoma Rotary #8 Club (bd. dirs. 1995—97), City Club (Tacoma). Personal E-mail: carolyn.else@stanfordalumni.org. E-mail: cjelse@harbornet.com.

ELSEN, SHELDON HOWARD, lawyer; b. Pitts., May 12, 1928; m. Gerri Sharfman, 1952; children: Susan Rachel, Jonathan Charles. AB, Princeton U., 1950; AM, Harvard U., 1952, JD, 1958. Bar: N.Y. 1959, U.S. Supreme Ct. 1971. Ptnr. Orans, Elsen & Lupert LLP, N.Y.C., 1965—. Adj. prof. law Columbia U. Law Sch., 1969—; chief counsel N.Y. Moreland Act Commn. on UDC, 1975-76; asst. U.S. atty. So. Dist. N.Y., 1960-64; cons. Pres.'s Commn. Law Enforcement Adminstrn. Justice, 1967; mem. faculty Nat. Inst. Trial Advocacy, 1973; panel chair 1st dept. disciplinary com. N.Y., 1992-96. Contbr. articles to profl. jours. Fellow Am. Coll. Trial Lawyers; mem. Assn. of Bar of City of N.Y. (v.p. 1988-89, chmn. com. on fed. legislation 1969-72, chmn. com. on fed. cts. 1983-86, chmn. nominating com. 1986-87, chmn. com. amenities in land use process for N.Y.C. 1987-88), Am. Law Inst. (adviser Transnat. Rules of Civil Procedure 1999—), Phi Beta Kappa. Office: 875 Third Ave 28th Fl New York NY 10022 Office Phone: 212-586-2211. Business E-Mail: selsen@oellaw.com.

EL-SERAG, HASHEM BESHIR, gastroenterologist, educator; b. Benghazi, Libya, July 30, 1966; came to U.S., 1992; MD, Al-Arab Med. U., 1991. Cert. in internal medicine, gastroenterology, 1997. Intern St. Michael's Med. Ctr.-Seton Hall U., Newark, N.J., 1992-93; resident in internal medicine Greenwich (Conn.) Hosp.-Yale U. Sch. Medicine, 1993-95; fellow in gastroenterology U. N.Mex., 1995-97, asst. prof., 1997—. Office: U New Mexico Hosp ACC-5 2211 Lomas Blvd NE Albuquerque NM 87106-2745

ELSER SMITH, JEANNE ELIZABETH, elementary school educator; b. Danville, Pa., June 25, 1975; d. Michael E. and Donna Jeanne Elser; m. Carter Alexander Smith, Jan. 4, 1972. BSc, MEd, Lesley U., 2004. Tchr. Lilja Elem. Sch., Natick, Mass., 2003—.

ELSEY, GEORGE MCKEE, retired foundation administrator; b. Palo Alto, Calif., Feb. 5, 1918; s. Howard McKee and Ethel May (Daniels) E.; m. Sally Phelps Bradley, Dec. 15, 1951; children: Anne Kranz, Howard McKee. AB, Princeton U., 1939; A.M., Harvard U., 1940; L.H.D., Am. Internat. Coll., 1982. Mem. staff The White House, 1947-53; with ARC, 1953-61, v.p., 1958-61; with various divs. Pullman Inc., 1961-65, asst. to chmn. and pres., 1966-70; pres. Am. Nat. Red Cross, 1970-82, pres. emeritus, 1983—. Bd. dirs. Security Storage Co. Suburban Health Found., chmn., 1996-98; mem. Washington adv. bd. MNC Fin., 1991-93; bd. dirs. The White House Hist. Assn., pres., 1990-95, dir. emeritus 1995— Pres. Meridian House Internat., Washington, 1961-66, vice chmn., 1967-68, counselor, 1971—; trustee Brookings Instn., 1971-83, George C. Marshall Rsch. Found., 1973-83, Harry S. Truman Libr. Inst., 1973-95, PCC Charitable Found., 1997-2005; mem. Nat. Archives Adv. Coun., 1974-79, mem. com. on presdl. librs., 1988-95; trustee emeritus Nat. Trust Hist. Preservation, 1976—; fin. chmn. League Red Cross and Red Crescent Socs., Geneva, 1977-87; mem. adv. bd. Nature's Best Found., 1999—; bd. dirs. U.S. Capitol Hist. Soc., 1993-95. Comdr. USNR, 1941-47. Decorated Legion of Merit, Order Brit. Empire, medals from Red Cross Socs. Finland, Korea, Greece, Netherlands, Fed. Republic Germany, Can. and Magen David Adom (Israel), comdr. Order of St. John; recipient Disting. Pub. Svc. medal Dept. Def. Internat. Humanitarian award Am. Red Mogen David for Israel, Henry Dunant medal Internat. Red Cross and Red Crescent, 1989. Mem. Hist. Soc. Washington, Nat. Geog. Soc. (trustee 1977-93), Met. Club (Washington), City Tavern Club (Washington), White House Mil. Aides Assn. (hon. chmn. 1998—), Phi Beta Kappa. Presbyterian. Home: 5351 Macarthur Blvd NW Washington DC 20016-2539

EL SHAHAWY, MAHFOUZ, internist, educator, cardiologist; b. Cairo, Aug. 1, 1936; came to U.S., 1967, naturalized U.S. citizen; married; 2 children. Diploma Medicine summa cum laude, U. Vienna, Austria, 1962, diploma cardiovasc. dis., 1966; MSc in Medicine and Cardiovasc. Diseases, U. Minn., Rochester, 1971. Diplomate Am. Bd. Internal Medicine, Am. Bd. Cardiovasc. Disease; cert. Can. Bd. Internal Medicine. Resident in medicine and cardiology U. Vienna-Algemeines Krankenhaus, 1962-67; rotating intern Flushing (N.Y.) Hosp. and Med. Ctr., 1967-68; fellow in medicine Mayo Clinic, Rochester, 1968-70, rsch. fellow in medicine and cardiovasc. disease, 1970-71; fellow, tchg. fellow, instr. cardiology Med. Coll. Ga., Augusta, 1971-73; asst. prof. medicine and cardiology U. Fla., Gainesville, 1973-75, mem. clin. professorial faculty, 1976—, clin. prof. medicine; pvt. practice, Sarasota, Fla., 1976—. Dir. adult cardiac catheterization lab., dir. heart sta. Shands Tchg. Hosp.-U. Hosp., 1973-74, dir. CCu, 1974-75; mem. staff Sarasota Meml. Hosp., 1975-83, Columbia-HCA Doctors Hosp., Sarasota, 1975—; chief medicine Doctors Hosp., Sarasota, 1980-81, trustee, 1986-90, vice chmn. bd., 1987-88, chmn. bd. 1988-89, med. dir. cardiac catheterization lab., 1995—; asst. clin. prof. medicine and cardiology U. South Fla., Tampa, 1976-78; chmn. long term investment com. Sarasota County Pub. Hosp., 1991-92, trustee, 1990-92; pres. Cardiovasc. Inst. Sarasota, 1989-95, Cardiovasc. Inst. Sarasota Found. for Edn. and Rsch., 1995—; mem. Rehab. Inst. Sarasota, 1986—; presenter to nat. and internat. meetings, 1971—; organizer, dir. nat. and internat. cardiovasc. symposia, 1988—. Contbr. articles and abstracts to med. jours., including Chest, Circulation, Jour. Fla. Med. Assn., Brit. Heart Jour., Cardiovasc. Rsch. Jour., Am. Heart Jour., Jour. Med. Assn. Ga., Jour. AMA, Lancet, Circulation Rsch. Supplement, Clin. Rsch. Bd. dirs. YMCA, Ringling Mus., Selby Gardens, Sarasota Opera Soc., New Coll. Libr. Assn., Boys Club Sarasota, Sarasota County Pub. Health Clinic, Sun Coast Heart Assn. United Arab Republic scholar, 1962-67. Fellow ACP, Am. Coll. Chest Physicians (coun. on critical care), Am. Coll. Cardiology, Am. Soc. Echocardiology; mem. AMA, Am. Heart Assn. (fellow coun. on clin. cardiology), Internat. Soc. for Holter and Non-Invasive Electrocardiology, Am. Med. Soc. Vienna (life), Fla. Med. Assn., Sarasota County Med. Soc., N.Y. Acad. Scis., Mayo Clinic Cardiovasc. Alumni Assn., Sarasota County C. of C. (bd. dirs.) Century Club Meml. Hosp., Longboat Key Club. Office: Cardiovasc Ctr Sarasota 1851 Arlington St Ste 206 Sarasota FL 34239-3517 Fax: 941-366-2781.

ELSHEIKHA, HANY MOHAMED, research scientist; b. Elmahalla Elkubra, Al Gharbyia, Egypt, Feb. 1, 1971; s. Mohamed Abdel Khalek Elsheikha. B in Vet. Scis., Cairo U., 1992, MS, 1998; PhD, Mich. State U., 2004. Cert. vet. medicine Gen. Adminstn. Vet. Svcs., Egypt, 1993. Rsch. assoc. Mich. State U., East Lansing, 2000—04; post-doctoral fellow U. Conn., Farmington, 2005—. Translator ednl. materials; contbr. scientific papers. Program com. Am. Assn. Vet. Parasitologists, East Lansing, Mich., 2005; grad. student rep. Mich. State U. Coun. Grad. Students, 2002—03, Com. Grad. Studies and Rsch., 2003. Res. officer Foo Security and Vet. Svcs., 1993—94, Egypt. Govtl. scholar, Mansoura U., Egypt, 2000. Mem.: Am. Soc. Microbiologists (assoc.), Am. Soc. Parasitologists (assoc.), Am. Assn. Vet. Parasitologists (assoc.; grad. student rep. 2005, Young Investigator Travel grant 2002, 2003). Achievements include research in molecular evolution of cyst-forming coccidian parasites; development of a vaccine to control EPM disease in horses; discovery of DNA site in SAG1 gene in Sarcocystis neuroba under positive selection pressure; new parasite species known as Sarcocystis inghami. Office: Mich State U B43 Nat'l Food Safety and Toxicolgy Ctr East Lansing MI 48824 Office Phone: 517-432-3100 114. Office Fax: 517-432-2310. E-mail: elsheik2@msu.edu.

EL-SHERIF, MAHMOUD A., electrical engineering educator, engineering executive; b. Cairo, July 7, 1942; came to U.S., 1981; s. Abd-El-Rahman E. and Hakmat Kaleb (El-Saied) E.; m. Jeylan Talaat El-Mansoury, Mar. 15, 1950; children: Dina, Dalia, Mohamed. BSc in Comm. Engring., Cairo U., 1966; Diploma in Electronic Engring., Alexadria (Egypt) U., 1977, MSc in Electro-Physics, 1980; MSEE, U. Pa., 1983; PhD in Elec. Engring., Drexel U., 1987. Engr. The Egyptian Telecom. Orgn., Cairo, 1966-67; radar instr. Air Def. Inst., Alexandria, 1967-77, radar dept. chmn., 1977-81; dean engring. edn. Air Def. Coll., Alexandria, 1987-89; rsch. prof. Drexel U., Phila., 1989-94, dir., founder Fiber Optics and Photonics Lab., 1994—, dir., founder Fiber Optics and Photonics Mfg. Engring. Ctr., 1997—. Prin. investigator NASA Lewis Rsch. Ctr., 1991-95, Dept. Def., 1990—; pres. Photonics, Inc., Wilmington, Del. and Phila., 1990—; cons. David Sarnoff Rsch. Ctr., Princeton, 1996—. Mem. laser tech. delegation U.S. Citizen Ambassador Program, Spokane, Wash., 1996—. Recipient 1st Class Medal of Disting. Performance Pres. of Egypt, Pres. of Egypt, 1971, Medal and cert. of Appreciation, Egyptian Engring. assn., 1987, Am. medal of Honor, 2001. Fellow Optical Soc. Am.; mem. IEEE, Am. Ceramic Soc., Internat. Soc. Optical Engrs., Soc. for Advancement of Material and Processing Engrs. Achievements include research in on optical fibers as active devices; invention of first fiber-optic modulator, coupler, switch and multiplexers; novel structure of Bragg optical fibers; novel process for manufacturing of sapphire optical fibers (core, clad, jacket) for IR transmission and application up to 1700 degress centegrade; design of and devel. of intelligent, smart structures with fiber optic sys. embeddded in composites, ceramic, metallic materials for in-situ real-time characterization/health monitoring structures; development of smart soldier's uniform with embedded fiber optic biological sensors for automatic detection of battle field biological threats; of smart parachutes with embedded fiber optic strain sensors for remote sensing of stresses during air drop. Avocations: chess, history, movies, classical music. Home: 1117 Hillcrest Rd Narberth PA 19072-1223 Office: Drexel Univ Dept Material Engring 32d and Chestnut Sts Philadelphia PA 19104 also: Photonics Labs Inc 3619 Market St Philadelphia PA 19104 Office Phone: 215-387-9970.

ELSHTAIN, JEAN BETHKE, social sciences educator; b. Windsor, Colo., Jan. 6, 1941; d. Paul G. and Helen L. Bethke; m. Errol L. Elshtain, Sept. 3, 1965; children: Sheri, Heidi, Jenny, Eric, (adopted) Bobby Bethke. BA in History, Colo. State U., 1963; MA in History, U. Colo., 1965; PhD in Politics, Brandeis U., 1973; LLD (hon.), Gonzaga U., 1996; DHL (hon.), Valparaiso U., 1996, Grinell Coll., 1997, Maryville U., 1997, Messiah Coll., 1999, Carthage Coll., 2000, Lake Forest Coll., 2001, Siena Coll., 2002, North Park Coll., 2002; DHL (hon.), U. West Timisoara, Romania, 2005. Prof. polit. sci. U. Mass., Amherst, 1973-88, Vanderbilt U., Nashville, 1988-94; vis. prof. Harvard U., Cambridge, Mass., 1994; prof. ethics U. Chgo., 1995—. Author: Public Man, Private Woman: Women in Social and Political Thought, 1982, 2d edit., 1992 (Top Choice acad. book), Czech transl., 1999, Ukrainian transl., 2002, Women and War, 1987, Japanese translation, 1994, Power Trips and Other Journeys, Essays on Feminism as Civic Discourse, 1990, Meditations on Modern Political Thought: Masculine/Feminine Themes Luther to Arendt, 1992, Democracy on Trial, 1995 (NY Times Notable Book 1995), Augustine and the Limits of Politics, 1996; co-author: But Was It Just? Reflections on the Morality of the Gulf War, 1992; editor: The Family in Political Thought, 1982, Just War Theory, 1991, The Jane Addams Reader, 2002, Just War Against Terror: The Burden of American Power, 2003 (one of Best Non-Fiction books of 2003 Pub. Weekly); co-editor: Women, Militarism and War, 1990, Politics and the Human Body, 1995, Promise to Keep, Decline and Renewal of Marriage in America, 1996, Real Politics, Political Theory and Everyday Life, 1997, New Wine in Old Bottles: International Politics and Ethical Discourse, 1998 (Top Choice acad. book), Who are We? Critical Reflection, Hopeful Possibilities, 2000 (Best Acad. Book, Am. Theol. Booksellers Assn. 2000), Jane Addams and the Dream of American Democracy, 2002, Just War Against Terror: The Burden of American Power in a Violent World, 2004 (named one of top non-fiction books of yr. Pubs. Weekly). Trustee Inst. for Advanced Study, 1994-99, Nat. Humanities Ctr., NC, 1996—; chair Coun. on Civil Soc., NYC and Chgo., 1995—, Coun. on Families in Am., NYC, 1995—; bd. dirs. Nat. Endowment for Democracy, 2002-. Recipient Award for Disting. Scholarship, C.S. Lewis Soc., 2005. Fellow AAAS; mem. Am. Polit. Sci. Assn. (v.p. 1998-99, Maguire chmn. ethics at Libr. of Congress 2003—2004, Goodnow award for lifetime svc. 2002), Am. Soc. Polit. and Legal Philosophy (v.p. 1996-97). Avocations: movies, reading. Home: 4010 Wallace Ln Nashville TN 37215-2308 Office: U Chgo Div Sch 1025 E 58th St Chicago IL 60637-1509 Office Phone: 773-702-7252. Business E-Mail: jbelshta@uchicago.edu.

ELSILA, DAVID AUGUST, editor; b. Detroit, Feb. 2, 1939; s. Edward J. and Sylvia (Mikkola) E.; m. Kathlyn Deutch, July 17, 1965; children: Mikael, Jamie and Kari (twins). BA, Eastern Mich. U., 1960, postgrad., 1962. Tchr. pub. schs., Livonia, Mich., 1960-64; editor-in-chief Livonia Observer, 1964-65; dir. publs., editor Am. Tchr., also, Changing Edn., Am. Fedn. Tchrs., Washington, 1965-76; editor UAW Solidarity, 1976—98; asst. dir. pub. rels. and publs. dept. UAW, 1976-98; sr. editor Working USA, 1997—99. Editor ofcl. publs. ACLU, Mich., 1964—67; del. Greater Washington Ctrl. Labor Coun., AFL-CIO; mem. adv. bd. (TV show) We Do The Work, 1992—2001; instr. Labor Studies Ctr., Wayne State U., 1999—2004, Nommos Ednl. Svcs., 1999—2001. Co-author: Union Town: A Labor History Guide to Detroit, 1980; contbg. author: Working Detroit, 1986, The New Labor Press, 1992; exec. prodr. Forgotten: A Jazz Opera, 2004. Nat. sec. Workers Edn. Local 189, 1978—86, Great Lakes bd. mem., 1986—88, Mich. chpt. bd. mem., 1992—99, exec. bd., 1994—99; co-chair Detroit Laborfest, 1997—; coord. Mich. Labor Legacy Project, Inc., 2001—; trustee Cranbrook Peace Found., 2001—; treas. SE Mich. Jobs. with Justice, 2002—; exec. bd. mem. Dem. Socialists of Am. SE Mich. Recipient Page 1 award, Chgo. Newspaper Guild, 1967, 1st awards in journalism, Internat. Labor Comm. Assn., 1968—69, 1972—73, 1975—76, 1983—97, Ednl. Press Assn. Am., 1968—76, Joady award, Film Arts Found., 1991, Pollie award, Am. Assn. Polit. Cons., 1992, Max Steinbock award, Saul Miller award, Internat. Labor Comm. Assn., 1996, Eugene V. Debs award, Dem. Socialists Am., 1998, Solidarity award, UAW, 1998, Communicator of Yr. award, Met. N.Y. Labor Comm. Coun., 2000, Eugene V. Debs award, Midwest Labor Press Assn., 2000, Journalism award, Mich. Labor Press, 2001, Spl. award, Matrix Theatre Co., 2001. Mem. Washington-Balt. Newspaper Guild (mem. exec. bd. 1970-71), Detroit Newspaper Guild, Ednl. Press Assn. Am. (pres. Washington chpt. 1971), Internat. Labor Comms. Assn. (v.p. 1983-89, sec.-treas. 1990-91), ACLU (mem. exec. bd. Detroit chpt. 1993—, sec. 1999-2003, v.p. 2004—), Mich. Labor History Soc. (program com. 2002—, editor publ. 2003—), Phi Delta Kappa. Home: 1411 Three Mile Dr Grosse Pointe Park MI 48230-1125 E-mail: davelsi@aol.com.

ELSMAN, JAMES LEONARD, JR., lawyer; b. Kalamazoo, Sept. 10, 1936; s. James Leonard and Dorothy Isabell (Pierce) E.; m. Janice Marie Wilczewski, Aug. 6, 1960; children— Stephanie, James Leonard III. BA, U. Mich., 1958, JD, 1962; postgrad., Harvard Div. Sch., 1958-59. Bar: Mich. 1963. Clk. Mich. Atty. Gen.'s Office, Lansing, 1961; atty. legal dept. Chrysler Corp., Detroit, 1962-64; founding ptnr. Elsman, Young, O'Rourke, Bruno & Bunn, Birmingham, Mich., 1964-72; pvt. practice Elsman Law Firm, Birmingham, 1972—. Owner Radio Sta. WOLY, Battle Creek, Mich. Author: The Seekers, 1962; screenplay, 1976, 200 Candles to Whom?, 1973; contbr. articles to profl. jours.; Composer, 1974, 76; talk show host Citizen's Court, TV-48, Detroit. Mem. Regional Export Expansion Coun., 1966-73, Mich. Ptnrs. for Alliance for Progress, 1969-80; cand. U.S. Senate, 1966, 76, 94, 96, U.S. Ho. of Reps., 1970. Rockefeller Bros. Found. fellow Harvard Div. Sch., 1959. Mem. ABA, Am. Soc. Internat. Law, Econ. Club Detroit, World Peace Through Law Center, Full Gospel Businessmen, Bloomfield Open Hunt Club, Pres. Club (U. Mich.), Circumnavigators Club, Naples Bath and Tennis, Rotary. Republican. Mem. Christian Ch. Home: 4811 Burnley Dr Bloomfield Hills MI 48304-3781 Office: 635 Elm St Birmingham MI 48009-6768 Office Phone: 248-645-0750. Personal E-mail: elsmanlawlaw@aol.com. *Christianity is not a religion. It is knowing Jesus, i.e. God, personally. It does not hinge on man's works or effort. Christianity is the only way to God, as Christ is the only Mediator between God and man. Choose! You can be sincerely wrong and still go to Hell eternally. Just a country lawyer in a big city, representing the common man in mass tort and class actions and other litigation, whose priority client is Jesus.*

ELSON, ALEX, lawyer, educator, arbitrator; b. nr. Kiev, Russia, Apr. 17, 1905; came to U.S., 1906, naturalized, 1913; s. Jacob and Rebecca (Brodsky) E.; m. Miriam Almond, July 6, 1933; children: Jacova Silverthorne (dec.), Karen O'Neil. PhB, U. Chgo., 1925, JD, 1928. Bar: Ill. 1928. Bill drafter Legislative Reference Bur., Springfield, Ill., 1929; atty. Legal Aid Bur., Chgo., 1929-34; assoc. atty. Tolman, Chandler & Dickinson, 1934-38; regional atty. Wage-Hour Div., Chgo., 1938-41; regional atty., asst. gen. counsel OPA, 1941-45; sr. ptnr. Elson, Lassers & Wolff, 1952—79. Of counsel Rosenthal & Schanfield, 1979-99; lectr. U. Chgo., intermittently 1933-48, 79-99, Yale Law Sch., 1946, seminar-labor rels. Northwestern U. Sch. Law, 1961-65; seminar constl. law Ariz U., 1971 Author: Civil Practice Forms, 1934; co-author: Civil Practice Forms, Illinois-Federal, 1952, rev., 1965; contbr.: articles to profl. jours., also to Ency. Brit. Former pub. mem. Regional War Labor Bd.; former chmn. Chgo. Rent Commn.; pres. Fund for Justice, 1972-76; former chmn. Ill. divsn. ACLU (hon. mem. bd. dirs. Ill. divsn.); former vice chmn. Ill. Commn. on Children; former chmn. Bd. Mental Health Commrs. State Ill., 1960-69; v.p. Law in Am. Soc. Found.; pres. Nat. Acad. Arbitrators Rsch. and Edn. Found., 1987-90; bd. govs. Orthogenic Sch., U. Chgo.; mem. instnl. rev. bd. divsn. social sci. U. Chgo., 1994-97; cons. Ford Found., 1963-68; bd. dirs. Hull House Assn., 1955-65. Fellow Am. Bar Found., Emeritus fellow Coll. of Labor and Employment Lawyers, 1998—; mem. ABA, Ill. Bar Assn., Chgo. Bar Assn. (bd. mgrs.), Am. Law Inst. (life), Nat. Acad. Arbitrators (hon. life mem., v.p. 1983-85); Inst. Psychoanalysis (pres. 1976-79) Home: 5550 South Shore Dr Chicago IL 60637

ELSON, CHARLES MYER, law educator; b. Atlanta, Nov. 12, 1959; s. Edward Elliott and Suzanne (Goodman) E.; m. Aimee F. Kemker, Dec. 18, 1993; children: Caroline Kemker, Charles MacKenzie. AB magna cum laude, Harvard U., 1981, postgrad., 1981—82; JD, U. Va., 1985. Bar: N.Y. 1987, D.C. 1988, U.S. Dist. Ct. (so. and ea. dists.) N.Y. 1987, U.S. Ct. Appeals (11th cir.) 1987. Law clk. to judge U.S. Ct. Appeals (11th cir.), Atlanta, 1985—86; assoc. Sullivan & Cromwell, N.Y.C., 1986—90; asst. prof. Stetson U. Coll. Law, St. Petersburg, Fla., 1990—93, assoc. prof., 1993—96, prof., 1996—2001; Edgar S. Woolard Jr. prof. corp. governance U. Del., 2000—, dir. John L. Weinberg Ctr. for Corp. Governance, 2000—. Vis. prof. law U. Ill., Champaign-Urbana, 1995, Cornell U. Law Sch., Ithaca, N.Y., 1996, U. Md. Law Sch., Balt., 1998; cons. Holland & Knight, 1995—, Towers, Perrin, 1998; bd. dirs. Alderwoods Group, Inc., Auto Zone, Inc., Health South Corp., Nuevo Energy Co., 1998-2004, Investor Responsiblity Rsch. Ctr. Bd. dirs. Big Apple Circus, Ltd., N.Y.C., 1987-93, Circon Corp., 1997-99, Sunbeam Corp., 1996-2002; trustee Talladega Coll., 1994-2001, Tampa Bay Performing Arts Ctr., 2000-2004, Tampa Mus. Art, 1993-99, Del. Mus. Natural History, 2003—. Salvatori fellow Heritage Found., 1993-94. Mem.: ABA (vice chair com. on corp. governance, mem. com. on corp. laws), Nat. Assn. Corp. Dirs. (commn. dir. compensation 1995, commn.dir. professionalism 1996, com. on securities litig. reform and fraud detection 1997, adv. coun. 1997—, com.on succession planning 1998, com. on audit coms. 1999, com on role of bd. in strategic planning 2000, com. on dir. evaluation 2001, com. on exec. compensation 2003, com. on bd. leadership 2004), Assn. of Bar of City of N.Y., Am. Law Inst., Century Assn., Univ. Club N.Y.C., Down Town Assn., Harvard Club N.Y.C., Chevaliers du Tastevin. Home: 906 Cecil Rd Wilmington DE 19807 Office: U Del Coll Bus and Econs Alfred Lerner Hall Newark DE 19716 Office Phone: 302-831-6157. Business E-Mail: elson@lerner.udel.edu.

ELSON, EDWARD ELLIOTT, diplomat; b. N.Y.C., Mar. 8, 1934; s. Harry and Esther (Cohn) E.; m. Suzanne Wolf Goodman, Aug. 24, 1957; children: Charles Myer, Louis Goodman, Harry Elson II. Grad., Phillips Acad., 1952; BA in Polit. Sci. with honors, U. Va., 1956; JD, Emory U., 1959; DHL (honoris causa), Talladega Coll., 1995; JD (hon.), Brenau U., 1997. With Atlanta News Agy., Inc., 1959-86, pres., 1967-82, chmn. bd. dirs., pres., 1982-85, chmn. bd. dirs., 1985-86; pres. Airport News Corp., Atlanta, 1961-82, chmn. bd. dirs., 1982-85; pres. Elson's, Atlanta, 1963-82, chmn. bd. dirs., 1982-86; chmn. Gordon County Bank, 1979-83; chmn. bd. dirs. W.H. Smith & Son Holdings, PLC, 1985-88; amb. to Denmark Dept. State, 1993—. Bd. dirs. NationsBank of Ga., Citizens and So. Ga. Corp., Atlantic Am. Corp., Citizens and So. Trust Co., Inc., Genesco Inc., Specialty Coffee Holdings Inc., Mitre Sports Internat. Ltd., RF & P Corp., New & Lingwood Holdings Ltd., Thorkild Kristensen AG, Köllmann AG, Hamton Investment Funds; chmn. W.H. Smith Group PLC, 1986—, Majestic Wine Corp., 1988; hon. pres. Am. Club, Copenhagen, 1993-98; mem. hon. com. European Assn. for Jewish Studies' 5th Cong., 1993—; vis. prof. Aalborg (Denmark) U. Mem. publs. com. Commentary Mag., 1967—, chmn., 1975-80. Dir., Am. Coun. Ambs.; bd. dirs. So. Regional Coun., 1966—, exec. com., 1986—; bd. govs. Am. Jewish Com., 1966—, trustee, 1977—, chmn. bd. trustees, 1986-89, v.p., 1982-84, treas., 1984-86; v.p. Nat. Found. Jewish Culture, 1990—; mem. Presdl. Commn. on Obscenity and Pornography, 1967-71, Nat. Adv. Commn. Pub. Edn. and Desegregation, 1976-77; mem. funds appeals rev. bd. City of Atlanta, 1971-73, Atlanta-Fulton County Recreation Authority, 1973-80, vice chmn., 1975-80; adv. com. to U.S. Commn. on Civil Rights, State of Ga., 1974—, chmn., 1974-82; chmn. bd. dirs. Nat. Pub. Radio, 1977-80, chmn., 1992—; chmn. Nat. Pub. Radio Found.; chmn. so. regional adv. com. to U.S. Commn. on Civil Rights, 1978, U. Va. Bayley Mus., 1986—; pres.'s coun. Brandeis U., 1967—, dir. Reading is Fundamental program, 1975-86, fellow, 1979; trustee Am.-Skandanavian Found., 1998—; bd. visitors U. Va., 1984-92, rector, 1990-92, exec. com. Health Sci. Coun., 1989—, chmn. Real Estate Found., 1990-92; bd. visitors Clark Coll., 1973—, chmn., 1982; trustee Brown U., 1988—, U. Va. Med. Ctr., 1987—, exec. com., 1987—; trustee Am. Briends Brit. Mus., Talladega Coll., 1973—, U. Mid-Am., 1979-82, Am. Fedn. Arts, 1985—, Brenau Coll., 1986—, Hampton Inst., 1986—. Hebrew Union Coll., 1992—, Spellman Coll., 1992—, Jewish Mus., 1992—, Glyndebourne Assn. Am., 1992—; mem. alumni coun. Phillips Acad., Andover, Mass., 1973-76, charter trustee, 1997; pres. coun. Agnes Scott Coll., 1973-82, chmn., 1975-82; mem. coun. White Burkett Miller Ctr. Pub. Affairs, 1990—; dean's adv. bd. Columbia U. Sch. Internat. Affairs and Pub. Affairs; chmn. adv. bd., bd. dirs. Southeastern Ctr. Contemporary Art, 1976—; chmn. bd. vis. Emory U. Mus. Art and Archaeology, 1985-92; resource planning com. Nat. Gallery, Washington, 1986—, trustee's coun., 1990—, dir. Coun. Am. Ambs.; chmn. U. Va. Real Estate Found., 1990-92; presdl. del. returning Crown of Stephen to Hungary, 1978; exec. com. U. Va. Health Sci. Coun., 1989—; gov. J.C. Brown Libr., R.I., 1989—; bd. dirs. Acad. for Corp. Governance, Fordham U.; chmn. bd. trustees Jeffersonian Restoration, 1992—; trustee Nat. Symphony Orch., 1992—; hon. pres. Copenhagen Theatre Cir., 1993-98; exec. com. Assn. Friends Hans Christian Andersen Mus., 1993-98; active Internat. Inst. Strategic Studies, 1995—; assoc. dir. The Met. Opera, 2000—; dir. Am. Coun. Ambassadors; trustee Game Conservancy; trustee Presbyn. Soc. of Palm Beach, 2004—; trustee Soc. of Four Arts, 2004—; gov. Addison Gallery Am. Art. Recipient Robert B. Downs award Grad. Sch. Library Sci., U. Ill., 1971, Human Relations award Am. Jewish Com., 1975, Disting. Service award Nat. Pub. Radio, 1979, Inst. Human Relations award, 1982, Merkonom award, 1997, Outstanding Alumnus award Emory U. Law Sch., 2002; Guggenheim fellow, 1994. Mem. Ga. Bar Assn., L.Q.C. Lamar Soc. (v.p. 1973-74, chmn. bd. dirs. 1974-80), Jewish Publ. Soc. (trustee 1974-82, 85—, v.p. 1986-87, pres., 1987-90, chmn. 1990—), Asia Soc. (trustee exec. com. 1999—), Am. Jewish Hist. Soc. (exec. com. 1980—, v.p. 1982-85), Am. Scandinavian Found. (vice chmn. 1998—, St. George's Ho. coun.), Muscular Dystrophy Assn. Am. (v.p. 1972-73, corp. 1973-74), U. Va. Alumni Assn. (bd. mgrs. 1982-84), Assn. Governing Bds. Univs. and Colls. (bd. dirs.), Nat. Peace Garden Found. (dir.), Inst. Study Europe (co-chair 1999—), European Assn. Jewish Studies (hon. com. 5th congress 1993-98), Coun. Fgn. Rels., Royal Copenhagen Shooting Soc. and Danish Brotherhood, Farmington Country Club, Univ. Club (N.Y.C.), Century Assn., Game Conservancy, USA (trustee), Palm Beach Country Club, Sailfish Club (Palm Beach, Fla.), Whites Club (London). Home Fax: 561-833-5044.

ELSON, GERALD, automotive executive; BS in Mech. Engring., Mich. State U., 1964, MME, 1965; post grad., Stanford U. Exec. Mgmt. Program, 1986. Design engr. GM Corp. Saginaw Div., Saginaw, Mich., 1965, chief assembly engr., 1970, gen. supr. mfg. devel., 1972, asst. supt. mfg., 1974, supt. mfg., 1978; plant mgr. GM Ltd., 1980; dir. mfg. sys. GM Corp, 1982; exec. dir. adv. mfg. engring. GM Corp., 1984—87; gen. mgr. GM Harrison Div., 1990, GM Inland Fisher Div., 1991, GM Cadillac Luxury Car Div., 1994; v.p., gen. mgr. ops. GM Mid Size, Luxury Car Group, 1996, GM North Am. Car Group, 1999—2002; v.p., gen. mgr. vehicle ops. Gm Corp., 2002—. Mem.: Nat. Coalition Advanced Mfg. (bd. dirs.), Partnership Advancement CAD/CAM/CAE Edn. (co-chair), GM Warren, Mich. Cmty. Rels. Com. (chairperson), Bd. Visitors Oakland U. (bd. mem.). Office: GM Corp 300 Renaissance Ctr PO Box 300 Detroit MI 48265-3000

ELSON, HANNAH FRIEDMAN, biologist, researcher; b. Lublin, Poland, July 10, 1943; came to U.S., 1949; m. Edward C. Elson; 2 children. BA, Vassar Coll., 1964; PhD, MIT, 1970. Arthritis Found. postdoctoral fellow Med. Rsch. Coun. Lab Molecular Biology, Cambridge, Eng., 1970-72; asst. prof., then asst. rsch. biologist U. Calif.-San Diego, La Jolla, 1972-79; rsch. sci. MEDSAT Rsch. Co., Bethesda, Md., 1986-90, 94-00; sr. resident rsch. assoc. Nat. Rsch. Coun. Walter Reed Army Inst. Rsch., Washington, 1988-90; sr. staff fellow Nat. Heart, Lung, Blood Inst. NIH, Bethesda, 1990-92, expert Nat. Cancer Inst., 1992-94; pres. Kenwood Park Citizens Assn., Inc., Bethesda, 1995-99; prin. investigator, sci. mgr. McKesson BioSvcs., Rockville, Md., 2000—. Contbr. articles to sci. jours. Bd. dirs. Kenwood Park Citizens Assn., 1995—, editor newsletter, 1998—. Mem.: AAAS, Am. Chem. Soc., MIT Club Washington (bd. dirs. 2000—), Sigma Xi (treas. D.C. chpt. 1996—). Achievements include research on protein synthesis, membrane changes during development of skeletal muscle, membrane fusion by HIV, and gene therapy.

ELSON, JAMES MARTIN, retired landmark director; b. N.Y.C., Nov. 25, 1932; s. John James and Elizabeth Jane (Slights) E.; m. Joan Mary Scott Elson, Aug. 21, 1965 (dec. Feb. 15, 1991); children: Elizabeth Joan Elson, Christina Marie Elson, James Scott Elson; m. Karen Sue Porter Elson, Aug. 22, 1992. BA, U. Tenn., 1955; MS, The Juilliard Sch., 1961; Mus. AD, W.Va. U., 1970. Chmn. vocal dept. Dana Sch. Music, Youngstown (Ohio) State U., 1962-68; grad. asst. Creative Arts Ctr., W.Va. U., Morgantown, 1968-70; chmn., vocal dept. Sch. Music, Winthrop U., Rock Hill, 1970-72; chmn., dept. visual and performing arts Huntingdon Coll., Montgomery, Ala., 1972-76; chmn., dept. fine arts High Point (N.C.) U., 1976—83; exec. dir. Acad. of Music Theatre, Lynchburg, Va., 1984-88; exec. v.p. Patrick Henry Meml. Fdn., Brookneal, Va., 1988-2000, exec. v.p. emeritus, 2000—. Performing arts critic High Point (N.C.) Enterprise, 1977-83. Author: Academy of Music, Lynchburg, Virginia: The Golden Age of Live Performance, 1993, Lynchburg, Virginia: The First Two Hundred Years, 1786-1986, 2004; author, editor: Patrick Henry Essays, 1994, Patrick Henry and Thomas Jefferson, 1997; editor Lynch's Ferry mag., 2000—; contbr. articles to profl. jours. 1st lt. U.S. Army, 1955-57. Fulbright grant Fulbright Commn., 1961-62. Mem. Coll. Music Soc. (life), Res. Officers Assn. (life), Kappa Sigma. Episcopalian. Home: 34 N Princeton Cir Lynchburg VA 24503-1547 Office Phone: 434-845-0452. Personal E-mail: jelson@inmind.com.

ELSON, JOHN S., legal educator; b. 1943; AB, Harvard U., 1964, JD, 1967; MA, U. Chgo., 1968. Bar: Ill. 1967. Staff lawyer Mandel Legal Aid Clinic, U. Chgo., 1971-75; assoc. prof. Northwestern U. Law Sch., Chgo., 1976-79, prof., 1979—. Contbr. articles to profl. jours. Mem.: Chgo. Coun. Lawyers (chair Chair, Com. Ethics and Profl. Responsibility 1998—). Office: Northwestern U Law Sch 357 E Chicago Ave Chicago IL 60611-3069 Office Phone: 312-503-8573. Office Fax: 312-503-8977. E-mail: j-elson@law.northwestern.edu.*

ELSON, SARAH LEE, art historian, consultant; b. Valley Forge, Pa., Oct. 1, 1962; d. John Everett and Ione (Coker) Lee; m. Louis Goodman Elson, Aug. 26, 1989; children: Isabel Coker Elson, Everett Esther Elson, Edward Lee Elson. BA, Princeton U., 1984; MA, MPhil in Art History, Columbia U., 1992. Prof. English Beijing Normal U., 1984-85; pub. affairs asst. Guggenheim Mus., N.Y.C., 1985-87; lectr. Met. Mus. Art, N.Y.C., 1990-92; freelance lectr. Nat. Gallery, London, 1994-98; founder Galatea Contemporary Art Advisors, London, 1998—. Rschr. Met. Mus., 1990-92, Tate Gallery, London, 1992-93; fellow The Frick Collection, N.Y.C., 1990—. Author catalogs. Nat. Endowment for Arts fellow, 1988, Pres.'s fellow Columbia U., 1988-90, Luce Travel grant, 1992. Mem. Woolnoth Soc. in the City of London. Democrat. Home: 26 Upper Phillimore Gardens London W8 7HA England Office Phone: +442079377000.

ELSON, SUZANNE GOODMAN, social services administrator; b. Memphis, Oct. 17, 1937; d. Charles F. and Isabel (Ehrlich) Goodman; m. Edward Elliott Elson, Aug. 24, 1957; children: Charles Myer, Louis Goodman, Harry II. Student, Randolph-Macon Women's Coll., Lynchburg, Va.; BA, Agnes Scott Coll., 1959. Sec. Nat. Coun. Jewish Women, N.Y.C., 1977-79; pres. Nat. Mental Health Assn., 1980-82; trustee emeritus Randolph Macon Women's Coll., 1988-98, 99. Chmn. Am. Craft Coun., 1989-92, hon. chmn., 1992-94, hon. trustee, 1994-; bd. dirs. Rosalynn Carter Inst., 1990-, Nat. Coun. Medicine Emory U., 1990-95; trustee Va. Mus. of Fine Art., 1992-96, High Mus. Fine Art, 1972-92, Am. Craft Mus., 1999-; bd. regents U. System of Ga., 1993-97; adv. bd. Breast Cancer Rsch. Found., 1998-; bd. dirs. Friends of Art and Preservation in Embassies, 1999- (trustee 1998); bd. govs. Mus. of Art and Design, 1998-; trustee Soc. for the Four Arts, 2003-, Preservation Soc. of Palm Beach, 2004- Home: 180 Cocoanut Row Palm Beach FL 33480-4121

ELSTEAD, JOHN CLIFTON, lawyer; b. San Bernardino, CA, Nov. 11, 1942; s. Lawrence Martin and Eleanor Elizabeth (Clifton) E.; 1 child, Logan Elizabeth. BA, U. Calif., Riverside, 1964; MA, U. West Fla., 1971; JD, U. Calif., Berkeley, 1974. Bar: Calif. 1974, U.S. Dist. Ct. (no. dist.) Calif. 1974,

U.S. Dist. Ct. (cent. dist. Calif. 1975, U.S. Dist. Ct. (so. dist.) Calif. 1979, U.S. Supreme Ct. 1982. Lawyer Wells & Chesney, Oakland, Calif., 1974-77, Sterns, Smith, Elstead & Walker, San Francisco, 1977-86; pvt. practice Pleasanton, Calif., 1986—. Tchg. fellow internat. law U. Pisa, Italy, 1973-74. Naval aviator, USN, 1966-71. Democrat. Roman Catholic. Avocations: reading, handball. Office: 5820 Stoneridge Mall Rd Ste 203 Pleasanton CA 94588-3200

ELSTON, ROBERT C., medical educator; BA with honors, Cambridge (Eng.) U., 1955, diploma in agr., 1956, MA, 1957; PhD, Cornell U., 1959; postgrad., U. N.C., 1960. Asst. prof. U. N.C., Chapel Hill, 1960-62, assoc. prof., 1964-69, prof., dir. genetics lab. Sch. Pub. Health, 1969-79; sr. rsch. fellow biometric medicine U. Aberdeen, 1962-64; prof., head dept. biometry & genetics La. State U. Med. Ctr., New Orleans, 1979-95; prof. dept. epidemiology and biostats. Case Western Res. U., Cleve., 1995—. Vis. prof. Yale U., 1965-66, London U., 1967, Cambridge U., 1970, Fourth Mil. Med. Coll. Xian, China, 1987, U. Calif., Irvine, 1988-89; dir. Ctr. Molecular & Human Genetics La. State U. Med. Ctr., 1991-95; mem. internat. adv. bd. Genetics Selection Evolution, 1992-97; exec. com. mem. teaching of stats. in health scis. sect. Am. Stats. Assn., 1992-94, chair, 1993; pres. Internat. Genetic Epidemiology Soc., 1997. Assoc. editor Biometrics, 1967-71, 1984-88, Am. Jour. Human Genetics, 1974-82, Stats. in Medicine, 1997—; editl. bd. Thrombosis Rsch., 1972-76, Neuropsychobiology, 1974-79, Am. Jour. Med. Genetics, 1977-99, Genetic Epidemiology, 1984-96, T. Human Genetics, 2000; contbr. articles to profl. jours. Recipient Career Devel. award NIH, 1966-76, Rsch. Scientist award, NIMH, 1977-79, Hoch award Am. Psychopath. Assn., 1992, Wick R. Williams Meml. award Fox Chase Cancer Ctr., 1994, Leadership award Internat. Genetic Epidemiology Soc., 1995, William Allan Meml. award Am. Soc. Human Genetics, 1996, Merit award NIH, 1998, Marvin Zelen Leadership award statis. sci. Sch. Pub. Health, Harvard U.; King George VI Meml. fellow, 1956-57, John Simon Guggenheim Meml. fellow, 1973-74; Coulthurst scholar, 1955-56, Cornell scholar, 1956-59. Fellow Am. Stats. Assn. Office: Case Western Res U Wolstein Rsch Bldg 2103 Cornell Rd Rm 1303 Cleveland OH 44106-7281 Office Phone: 216-368-5630. E-mail: rce@darwin.cwru.edu.

ELSTUN, ESTHER NIES, foreign language educator; b. Berkshire Heights, Pa. d. Frank Emory and Florence Mae (Sweigart) Nies; m. James Palmer Elstun, Sept. 1, 1956; 1 child, John Dudley. BA magna cum laude, The Colo. Coll., 1960; MA, Rice U., 1964, PhD, 1969. Asst. prof. to prof., German George Mason U., Fairfax, Va., 1969—. V.p., faculty senate ov Va., 2001-2003; pres. Va. Coun. for Study Abroad, 1981-82, Va. Humanities Conf., 1989-90; mem. exec. bd. Va. Conf. of the AAUP, 1990-92, 2002-04. Author: The Life and work of Richard Beer-Hofmann, 1983; contbr. articles to profl. jours. Vol. Amnesty Internat., 1978—. Recipient Amerika-Kreis Munster scholar, Univ. of Munster, Germany, 1954-55; rsch. grant George Mason Univ. Found., Houghton Libr., Harvard and the Leo Baeck Inst., N.Y., 1974. Mem. AAUP, Am. Assn. Tchrs. of German, Modern Lang. Assn. Am., German Studies Assn., Internat. Arthur Schnitzler Rsch. Assn., Phi Beta Kappa, Delta Phi Alpha. Presbyterian. Avocations: gardening, piano, travel, needlecrafts. Office: George Mason Univ 4400 University Dr Fairfax VA 22030-4444

ELTAHLAWY, HANAN S., entomologist; d. Salah A. Eltahlawy and Aida A. Elafandi; m. Mohamed K. Fakhr, Sept. 22, 1993; children: Ahmed M. Fakhr, Omar M. Fakhr. MS in Entomology, Benha U. Instr. Benha U., Egypt; rsch. asst. N.D. State U., Fargo, 2002—. Scholar, N.D. State U., Grad. Coll. Mem.: Entomol. Soc. Am. Achievements include research in Pheromone Biosynthesis in Eurobian Corn Borer.

ELTAYEB, EMIL, pharmacist, researcher; b. Salzburg, Austria, May 24, 1975; arrived in U.S., 1975; s. Ali and Maia Eltayeb. BS cum laude, St. John's U., 1998, PharmD, 2002. Intern Mary Immaculate Hosp., Jamaica, NY, 1995—97, Rite Aid, Jamaica, NY, 1999—2000. Author: The Mystery of Cancer and Alzheimer's Disease is Revealed. Mem.: N.Y. Acad. Scis., Rho Chi, Golden Key. Achievements include application of Einstein's theory of relativity, law of conservation of energy, and quantum mechanics to the understanding of the pathophysiology of various diseases and their treatment. Avocation: reading. Personal E-mail: meltayeb@msn.com.

ELTERICH, JOACHIM GUSTAV, agricultural economics professor; b. Dresden, Germany, May 22, 1930; came to U.S., 1958, naturalized, 1973; m. Martha Munson Slagel, June 17, 1961; children: Stefan, Karin, Christian. Diploma in sci. agr., Rhein-Friedr Wilhelms U., 1956; MS in Agrl. Econs., U. Ky., 1960; PhD in Agrl. Econs., Mich. State U., 1964; Dr. honoris causa, Agrl. U. Slovakia, 2000. Research asst. dept. agrl. econs. U. Ky., Lexington, 1958-60, Mich. State U., Lansing, 1960-64; research assoc. Inst. for Agrl. Econs. U. Bonn, Fed. Republic of Germany, 1964-67; prof. agrl. econs. U. Del., Newark, 1967—98, chair ops. rsch. com., 1986—96, prof. emeritus, 1998—. Cons. Ford Found., 1976, Minimum Wage Commn., 1980-81, U.S. AID, 1976-83; del. U.S. Dept. Labor, 1980-85; vis. prof. U. Kiel, Fed. Republic Germany, 1974, U. Bonn, Fed. Republic Germany, 1985, 90, 94-2003, U. Nitra, Slovakia, 1990, 95-2003. Contbr. numerous articles to profl. jours.; mem. editorial bd. N.E. Jour. Agrl. Econs., 1977-83. Fulbright rsch. scholar U. Bonn., 1985-86. Mem. Am. Agrl. Econs. Assn., Internat. Assn. Agrl. Economists, Ops. Rsch. Soc. Am., Sigma Xi, Gamma Sigma Delta, Phi Kappa Phi. Home: 145 Timberline Dr Newark DE 19711-7446 E-mail: elterich@udel.edu.

ELTRINGHAM, DANA KRISTIN, writer; b. Santa Monica, Calif., Apr. 28, 1974; d. Lee Gordon and Gail Ann (Minett) Eltringham. B in English, Goucher Coll., 1996; MFA in Creative Writing, George Mason U., 2003. Sr. tech. writer Lockheed Martin, Arlington, Va., 1998-2000; mgr. methods and procedures Nextel Comm., Reston, Va., 2000—01; documentation team lead, sr. tech. writer ATS, Inc., McLean, Va., 2001—. Writer, Alexandria, Va., 1996—, Providence; adj. instr. in English NOVA CC, 2001—02. Contbr. articles to profl. jours. Avocation: fiber art. Home: 68 Fremont St Providence RI 02906 E-mail: danaeltringham@hotmail.com.

ELUHOW, LJILJANA SKORIC, musician, educator; arrived in U.S., 1969; d. Nikola and Terezija (Vukovic) Skoric; m. Raymond Eluhow, July 4, 1970 (dec. Oct. 1991); 1 child, Nicholas Skoric. Diploma, Music Acad., Zagreb, Croatia, 1961; artist diploma, Hochschule fur Musik, Frankfurt, Germany, 1965. Music instr. Wetzlar Music Sch., Germany, 1965—69, Mainz Conservatory, Germany, 1969—71, Shenandoah Conservatory, Winchester, Va., 1971—72, Peabody Prep., Balt., 1972—74; music instr., lectr. No. Va. Cmty. Coll., Alexandria, 1979—. V.p., bd. Arlington Symphony, Va., 1998—2000, pres., womens' com., 2001—; competition co-chair Symphony League of Alexandria, Va., 2002—03. Mem. The Arlington Com. of 100, Va., 2003. Republican. Roman Catholic. Avocations: painting, gardening, writing. Office: No Va Cmty Coll 3001 N Beauregard Alexandria VA 22311 Office Phone: 703-845-6026.

ELVERUM, GERARD WILLIAM, JR., retired electronics executive, diversified financial services company executive; b. Mpls., Sept. 29, 1927; m. Mary Jean Proverbs, Dec. 28, 1948. Student, U. Nebr., 1945, S.D. State U., 1945; B in Physics, U. Minn., 1949. Engr. Jet Propulsion Lab., Pasadena, Calif., 1949-59; sect. head, mgr. dept. Space Tech. Lab., El Segundo, Calif., 1959-62; dir. lab. Systems Group TRW, Redondo Beach, Calif., 1963-66, mgr. ops. Def. and Space Systems Group, 1969-81, v.p., gen. mgr. Applied Tech. Div./Space and Tech. Group, 1981-91, ret., 1991. Mem. adv. panel NASA/Aerospace Safety Bd., Washington, 1982-91; mem. NASA Access to Space Panel, 1995-2001; mem. space studies bd., NRC, 1996-99, com. AF Dept. Def. Aerospace Propulsion, 2005—; mem. space transp. subcom. NASA adv. coun., 1996-2002. Contbr. articles to profl. jours.; patentee in field. Commr. Commn. on Engring. and Tech. Systems, Nat. Rsch. Coun., 1991-94. Served with USAF, 1944-46. Named Outstanding Engr., Inst. Advancement Engring., 1972; recipient Spl. Achievement award, ASME, 1971. Fellow AIAA (James H. Wyld Propulsion award 1973); mem. Am. Def. Preparedness Assn., Nat. Acad. Engring. Personal E-mail: jerryelverum@msn.com. *Preparation, perseverance, patience with others, and absolute integrity will create the career opportunities that many will simply attribute to being at the right place at the right time.*

ELVEY, MALCOLM, venture capitalist; b. Aug. 1941; m. Annette Elvey. Chartered acct., U. Witwatersand; MBA, U. Cape Tow. Dir. ADT Ltd., 1985—87; founder, chmn., CEO Esquire Comm., Ltd., 1988—2000; founder, CEO Qlimo; mng. ptnr. Collaborative Capital, 1999—. Bd. dirs. Children's Place Retail Stores, 2002—, Algol S.p.A.; chmn. US Masters Squash Teams, Maccabiah Games, Israel, 1997. Active with Young Pres. Orgn., 1973—, World Pres. Orgn., 1973—; chmn. fin. com. Friends of Bezalel, Israel's Nat. Acad. Arts & Design. Avocation: squash. Office: Collaborative Capital 535 Park Ave New York NY 10021 Office Phone: 212-421-5007. Office Fax: 206-666-6076. Business E-Mail: malcolm@elvey.com.

ELVIN, GEORGE, architecture educator; b. Washington, Sept. 9, 1958; m. Meg Calkins, May 30, 1998; children: Jackson Calkins, Annabel Calkins. BS, U. Md., 1991; MA in Architecture, U. Calif., Berkeley, 1995, PhD, 1998. Asst. prof. U. Ill., Urbana, 1999—2005; assoc. prof. Bldg. Futures Inst., Ball State U., Muncie, Ind., 2005—. Contbr. The Architect's Guide to Design-Build Services, 2003. Fellow, Inst. for Advanced Study in Humanities, U. Edinburgh, 2005. Achievements include research in nanotechnology, biotechnology, architecture, and design. Office: Ball State Univ Coll Arch and Planning Dept Arch Muncie IN 47306-0305 Office Phone: 765-285-1900.

ELVIR, JOSE M., language educator; s. Jose Elvir and Lucila Maradiaga; m. Rosa M. Elvir; 1 child, Gabriela. Degree, East Stroudsburg U., 1995. Spanish tchr. Palmerton Area Sch. Dist., 1995—. Seventh Day Adventist.

ELWAY, JOHN ALBERT, retired professional football player; b. Port Angeles, Wash., June 28, 1960; s. Jack Elway; m. Janet Elway; children: Jessica Gwen, Jordan Marie. BA in Econs., Stanford U., 1983. Quarterback Denver Broncos, 1983—98; ret., 1998; owner John Elway AutoNation. Mem. Mayor's Coun. on Phys. Fitness City of Denver; chmn. Rocky Mountain regional Nat. Kidney Found. Named first overall pick in NFL draft by Balt. Colts, 1983, NFL MVP/Player of Yr., Associated Press, 1987, Am. Football Conf. Offensive MVP/Player of Yr., 1987, 1993, Super Bowl MVP, 1998; named to Sporting News Coll. All-Am. Team, 1980, 1982, Sporting News NFL All-Pro Team, 1987, Am. Football Conf. Pro Bowl Team, 1987, 1988, 1990, 1992, 1994, 1995, 1997—99, 1990's All-Decade Team. Achievements include winning Super Bowls XXXII and XXXIII (with Denver Broncos), 1997, 1998; inducted in NFL Hall of Fame, 2004.

ELWELL, ROWLAND JOHN, pharmacist, researcher; b. Niskayuna, NY, Mar. 21, 1967; s. Karen A. Pasquariello; m. Heather W. Roy, June 3, 1995; children: Calla R., Andie F. BS in Pharmacy, Albany Coll. Pharmacy, NY, 1994—99; PharmD, Albany Coll. Pharmacy, 1998—2000. Pharmacy practice resident Med. U. SC, Charleston, 2000—01; clin. rsch. fellow Albany Coll. Pharmacy, NY, 2001—03, asst. prof. pharmacy practice, 2003—. Contbr. articles. Deacon First Presbyn. Ch., Schenectady, NY, 2002; med. adv. bd. mem. Nat. Kidney Found. of NE NY, Albany, 2003. Named an Inductee, Rho Chi Nat. Pharm. Honor Soc., 1997; recipient Corp. Scholarship award, NY State Coun. Health-System Pharmacists, 1998, Dr. Rudolph Blythe Rsch. Scholarship, Albany Coll. Pharmacy, 1999, PharmD Student Rsch. award, NY State Chpt. Am. Coll. Clin. Pharmacy, 2000. Mem.: Am. Coll. Clin. Pharmacy, Am. Soc. of Nephrology (assoc.). Conservative. Presbyterian. Achievements include Clinical research studies evaluating the pharmacokinetics of antibiotics administered to peritoneal dialysis patients. Avocation: music. Office: Albany Coll Pharmacy 106 New Scotland Ave Albany NY 12208 Office Phone: 518-445-7347. Business E-Mail: elwellr@acp.edu.

ELWES, CARY, actor; b. London, Oct. 26, 1962; s. Dominic and Tessa (Kennedy) E. Stage debut in Equus, 1981; films include Another Country, 1984, Oxford Blues, 1984, The Bride, 1985, Lady Jane, 1986, Maschenka, 1987, The Princess Bride, 1987, Glory, 1989, Days of Thunder, 1990, Hot Shots!, 1990, Leather Jackets, 1991, Bram Stoker's Dracula, 1992, The Crush, 1993, Robin Hood: Men In Tights, 1993, Rudyard Kipling's Jungle Book, 1994, The Chase, 1994, Twister, 1996, Liar Liar, 1997, Kiss the Girls, 1997, The Informant, 1997, Quest for Camelot (voice), 1998, Cradle Will Rock, 1999, Shadow of the Vampire, 2000, The Cat's Meow, 2001, Wish You Were Dead, 2002, Ella Enchanted, 2004, Saw, 2004. Office: William Morris Agy c/o Michael Gruber 151 S El Camino Dr Beverly Hills CA 90212-2775

ELWORTHY, BRUCE REA, lawyer; b. San Francisco, June 27, 1945; s. John Sherman and Helen Louise E.; m. Anne Bradley Marshall, Aug. 25, 1979. BS, San Jose State U., 1974, MS, 1976; JD, U. Pacific, 1979. Bar: Calif. 1979, Wyo. 1994, Mont. 1994, US Tax Ct. 1980, US Supreme Ct. 1985. Owner Pro Am Racers, Palo Alto, Calif., 1970-76; rsch. atty. Placer County Superior Ct., Auburn, Calif., 1978-79; atty. pvt. practice, San Francisco, 1979-83; ptnr. Elworthy & Marshall, Carmel & Tahoe City, Calif., 1983-97, mng. ptnr. Sheridan, Wyo., 1994-98; pres. Elworthy & Marshall, P.C., Sheridan, 1998—2005; of counsel Gordon & Reed LLP, San Francisco, 2005—. Mng. dir. Elworthy & Marshall, P.C., Tahoe City, 1986-98, Carmel, 1983-86, pres. Author: The San Rafael Project: Format for a Model Reserve Organization, 1975. Mem. Rep. Ctrl. Com., Monterey County, Calif., 1984-85; asst. dir. Davis for U.S. Senate, Monterey County, 1985. With USMC, 1965-66. San Jose State U. Dean's scholar, 1973-74. Mem. State Bar Calif., State Bar Wyo., State Bar Mont. Office: Gordon Reed LLP 275 Battery St Ste 2000 San Francisco CA 94111 Office Phone: 415-986-5900. Business E-Mail: belworthy@gordonreed.com.

ELY, DONALD J(EAN), retired clergyman, secondary school educator; b. Frederick, Md., July 15, 1935; s. George Kline and Jennie Mabel (Boyer) E. m. Lois Jean Kirkpatrick, Aug. 27, 1967; children: Kathleen Rose, Stephen David, Yvonne Elaine. AB, Gettysburg Coll., 1955; BD, Lancaster Sem., 1958; MEd, Bloomsburg U., 1972. Ordained to ministry Evang. and Reformed Ch., 1958. Pastor St. John Evang. and Reformed Ch., Riegelsville, Pa., 1958-61, Zion's Reformed Ch., Ashland, Pa., 1961-64, Augusta Reformed Parish, Sunbury, Pa., 1964-74, Salem United Meth. Ch., Middleburg, Pa., 1974-79, Salem Ind. Brethren Ch., Middleburg, 1979-83; tchr. social studies Shikellamy H.S., Sunbury, 1966-98; ret., 1998. Bd. dirs. Sunbury Area YMCA, 1966—, sec., 1973-80, 88-2000; bd. dirs. Greater Susquehanna Valley YMCA, 1993—, sec. 1999—; bd. dirs. Northumberland County unit Am. Cancer Soc., 1971-74, Snyder County unit, 1974-84; rep. candidate state legis., 1982; vice chmn. Govt. Study Commn. of City of Sunbury, 1989-91; mem. Northumberland County Rep. com., 1987—, state committeeman, 1992—. Mem.: SAR (chaplain 1971—, chpt. pres. 1981—86, 1992), Pennsylvanians for Effective Govt., Greater Susquehanna Valley C. of C., Intercollegiate Studies Inst., Heritage Found., Federalist Soc., Am. Conservative Union, Hist. Soc. Evang. and Ref. Ch., Northumberland County Hist. Soc. (life; trustee 1972—83), Snyder County Hist. Soc. (life; pres. 1980—83), Union County Hist. Soc., Hereditary Register of U.S., Commonwealth Found., Rolls Royce Owners' Club, Susquehana Valley Country Club, Antique Auto Club Am., Masons. Home and Office: PO Box 765 Sunbury PA 17801-0765 Fax: 570-286-4444.

ELY, DUNCAN CAIRNES, social services administrator; b. Phila., Apr. 3, 1951; s. Donald and Barbara Dercum (Mifflin) E.; m. Elizabeth Caroline Wickenberg, June 14, 1984; 1 child, Penn Wickenberg Ely. BA, U. Ariz., 1974; MDiv, Gen. Theol. Sem., N.Y.C., 1988; cert. mentor Edn. for Ministry, U. of South, 1985. Cert. in clin. pastoral edn. Bapt. Med. Ctr., 1985; cert. human svcs. adminstrn. Human Svcs. Inst., 1991. Nat. exec. dir. Assn. for Independence of Disabled, Inc., Tucson, 1974-77; exec. dir. Frat. of Alpha Kappa Lambda, Inc., Indpls., 1977-79; asst. St. Stephen's Episcopal Ch., Phila., 1979-80; exec. dir. The Youth Alternatives Camps, Inc., Tucson, 1980-83, Crisis Assistance Clothing Ministry, Charlotte, N.C., 1989-93, N.C. Harvest, Inc., Charlotte, 1993-96, Spartanburg (S.C.) Cmty. Events, Inc., 1996-98; dir. Camp Gravatt, Aiken, S.C., 1998—. Chmn. bd. advisors Expanded Foods and Nutrition Edn. Program N.C. State U., 1989-96; mem. foster care rev. bd. child protective svcs. Dept. Social Svcs., Charlotte, 1991-96. Author, editor: The Truth and the Word, 1978; also numerous articles in books, jours., mag. and newspapers. Past pres. Ely Assn., Inc., N.Y.C.; trustee Wildlife Guard, Inc., 1973—, past nat. pres., also past chmn. bd. advisors The Relatives, Inc., Charlotte, 1989-96, Ret. Sr. Vol. Program, Charlotte, 1990-96, Vol. Ctr. Charlotte, 1990-96; bd. dirs. Charlotte Emergency Housing, Inc., 1989-96, Met. Music Ministries, Inc., 1993-96, Piedmont Area Girl Scouts, Inc., 1997—, S.C. Inst. Nonprofit Leadership, Share the Vision resource com. City of Spartanburg, 1997—; mem. Vol. Leadership Devel. Program, Charlotte, 1991; grad. class XIII, Leadership Charlotte, 1991; grad. class III Carolinas Leadership Program, 1994; grad. class I Leadership N.C., 1995; chmn. bd. dirs. Spartanburg Caregivers, Inc., 1996—; grad. class 17 Leadership Spartanburg, 1997; grad. class 19 Leadership S.C., 1998; commr. for nat. and cmty. svc. State of N.C.; mem. N.C. Gov.'s Commn. on Nat. and Cmty. Svc.; mem. christian formation steering com. Episcopal Diocese Upper S.C., 1998—, mem. mission and outreach steering com., 1998—, mem. peer ministry conf., 1998. Recipient gold pin Phila. State Hosp., 1973, One of Nine Who Care award Sta. WSOC-TV and United Way, Charlotte, 1991, 94. Mem. S.R., Internat. Festivals and Events Assn., Nat. Soc. Am. Royal Descent, Barorial Order Magna Charta, Colonial Order of the Crown, Soc. Mayflower Descendants, Am. Mgmt. Assn., Am. Soc. Assn. Execs., Nat. Christian Counselors Assn. (lic. pastoral counselor), Metrolina Assn. for Vol. Adminstrn. (past pres.), N.C. Assn. Vol. Adminstrs. (past v.p.), S.C. Festival Assn., Penn Laurel Poets, Soc. Nonprofit Execs., Soc. Cin., Pen and Pencil Club, Alpha Kappa Lambda (past pres.), Alpha Phi Omega (past pres.), Theta Kappa Psi (past pres.), Theta Omega (past pres.), Psi Chi (past pres.), Country Club of Spartanburg, Piedmont Club, Fripp Island Club (S.C.), numerous others. Republican. Episcopalian. Avocations: arts, genealogy, historic preservation horticulture, reading, sports and outdoor activities. Office: Camp Gravatt 1006 Camp Gravatt Rd Aiken SC 29805-8730 Office Phone: 864-415-6338. E-mail: DuncanEly@Hotmail.com.

ELY, GARY G., utilities company executive; Grad., Brigham Young U.; postgrad., U. Idaho, Stanford U., Edison Elec. Inst. Leadership. With Avista Corp., Spokane, 1967—, v.p. mktg., 1986-91, v.p. natural gas, 1991-95, sr. v.p., 1996-97, pres., CEOm chmn. bd., 1997—. Mem. State Bldg. Code Coun. Mem. Pacific Coast Gas Assn. (chmn. gas mgmt. exec. com., chmn. mktg. exec. com., bd. dirs.), N.W. Electric Light and Power Assn. (bd. dirs.), Spokane Valley C. of C. (exec. bd.), N.W. Gas Assn. (bd. dirs.). Office: Avista Corp 1411 E Mission Ave Spokane WA 99220-3727*

ELY, JOE, musician; b. Feb. 9, 1947; With Flatlanders Band, Joe Ely Band; albums include Joe Ely, 1977, Honky Tonk Masquerade, 1978, Down on the Drag, 1979, Live Shots, 1980, Musta Notta Gotta Lotta, 1981, Hi-Res, 1984, Lord of the Highway, 1987, Milkshakes & Malts, 1988, Dig All Night, 1988, Live at Liberty Lunch, 1990, Love and Danger, 1992, From Chippy, 1994, Letter to Laredo, 1995, Twistin' in the Wind, 1998, Los Super Seven, 1999 (Grammy 1999), Live at Antone's, 2000, Best of Joe Ely, 2001, Poet, A Tribute to Townes Van Zandt, 2000 (Grammy nominee), Now Again (The Flatlanders, 2002), Streets of Sin, 2003, Wheels of Fortune (The Flatlanders, 2004), 20th Century Masters Collection, 2004, Heard it on the X Los Super Seven, 2005. Address: LC Media Attn: Lance Cowan PO Box 965 Antioch TN 37011-0965

ELY, PARRY HAINES, dermatologist, educator; b. Washington, Sept. 19, 1945; s. Northcutt and Marica (McCann) E.; m. Elizabeth Magee, June 24, 1969 (div. June 1998); children: Sims, Rebecca, Meredith, Tess; m. Kathleen O'Brien, May 3, 2000. AB, Stanford U., 1967; MD, U. So. Calif., 1971. Diplomate Am. Bd. Dermatology, Am. Bd. Pathology; lic. dermatologist, Calif. Intern in medicine U. So. Calif.-L.A. County Med. Ctr., 1971-72, resident in dermatology, 1972-75; clin. prof. dermatology U. Calif., Davis, 1975—. Bd. dirs. Nevada City Wineries Mem. editl. bd. Calif. Physician, 1994—; manuscript reviewer Archives of Internal Medicine, 1988—, Annals of Internal Medicine, 1980—, Archives of Dermatology, 1977—; contbr. articles to med. jours. Fellow Am. Acad. Dermatology (asst. editor jour. 1988-94, manuscript reviewer 1994—), Am. Soc. Dermatopathology; mem. AMA, Internat. Soc. for Tropical Dermatology, Am. Fedn. for Clin. Rsch., Am. Soc. for Dermatologic Surgery, N.Am. Clin. Dermatologic Soc., Calif. Med. Assn. (alt. del. 1995—, rep. to Calif. Telehealth/Telemedicine coord. project planning com. 1996—), Pacific Dermatologic Soc. (Nelson Paul Anderson Meml. Essay 1st pl. award 1979, Mini Presentation of Yr. award 1984), Noah Worcester Dermatol. Soc., Cutaneous Therapy Soc., Soc. Investigative Dermatology, Sacramento Valley Dermatol. Soc. (pres. 1990-91), Placer Nev. Med. Soc. (bd. dirs. 1978-79, 91-93, v.p. 1994, pres. 1995), Skin Cancer Found. (med. coun. 1987—), Tri-County Am. Cancer Soc. (bd. dirs. 1978-79, 91-92), Royal Soc. Medicine (London), Dermatology Found., Space Dermatology Found. (founding mem.), Shivas Irons Soc. (founding mem.) Office: Brunswick E # 7 10565 Brunswick Rd Grass Valley CA 95945-9053 E-mail: haines@netshel.net.

ELY, ROBERT EUGENE, lawyer, author, educator; b. Ft. Wayne, Ind., Aug. 18, 1949; s. Virgil Eugene and Alberta Irene (Steiner) E.; m. Jackline Sue Meyer, Apr. 14, 1973; l child, Elizabeth Vanessa. BA, Manchester Coll., 1971, MA, 1975; JD, Ind. U., 1983. Bar: Ala. 1985, U.S. Dist. Ct. (mid. dist.) Ala. 1988. Sales promotion cons. Lincoln Nat. Corp., Ft. Wayne, 1971-73; asst. dir. humanities Manchester Coll., North Manchester, Ind., 1973-75; assoc. instr. English Purdue U., West Lafayette, Ind., 1975-77; instr. English Ala. State U., Montgomery, 1977-81, dir. honors, 1984-86, asst. v.p., 1984-85, assoc. prof. English, 1986—; pvt. practice law Montgomery, 1985—. Communications cons. Cummins Internat., Columbus, Ind., 1982; adj. prof. paralegalism Auburn (Ala.) U., 1990-95. Author: The Humanities, 1979, Mose T.'s Slapout Family Album (children's verse), 1996 (Shaw-Montgomery prize for poetry 1985), Encanchata, 2001; contbr. articles to profl. jours. Named to Order of Reyes del Monte do Gozo; fellow Summer Inst., NEH, 1981, Rsch. fellow, Ala. State U., 1978, for Islamic Studies in Turkey, Mobil Found., 1999, for East-West studies U. Hawaii, Henry Luce Found., 2000, for ancient and modern studies in Egypt, Fulbright Found., 2002. Mem. ABA, Ala. Bar Assn., Montgomery County Bar Assn., Am. Acad. Poets, Nat. Coun. Tchrs. English, Lower Audubon Brook Soc., Coventry Motoring and Aviation Soc., The Writs. Democrat. Presbyterian. Avocations: serious and light verse, fishing, folk art, sports cars. Home: 3212 LeBron Rd Montgomery AL 36106-2334 Office: 659 S Hull St Montgomery AL 36104-5807 Office Phone: 334-265-2002. E-mail: relylaw@juno.com.

ELYN, MARK, retired vocalist; b. Seattle, Feb. 4, 1932; s. Isadore and Goldie Elyn; m. Jaclyn Rendall, 1956. Student, U. Wash., 1948-51, Seattle U., 1951-52; student of Robert Weede. Bd. mem. Bel Canto Inst., NY. Debut, N.Y.C. Opera, 1956, leading roles, San Francisco Opera, NBC Opera, Phila. Lyric Opera, leading bass, Cologne, Munich, Hamburg, Stuttgart, Vienna, Monte Carlo, Geneva, Barcelona; roles include: Don Giovanni, Sarastro in The Magic Flute, Philip II in Don Carlo, Figaro in The Marriage of Figaro; prof. music, U. Ill., Urbana, 1977—, chmn. voice dept., 1990-98, prof. emeritus, guest lectr., 1998—. Mem. Am. Guild Mus. Artists, Deutsche Buehnengenossenschaft, Nat. Assn. Tchrs. of Singing. Home: 1238 10th Ave E Seattle WA 98102-4324

ELY-RAPHEL, NANCY, diplomat; b. N.Y.C, Feb. 4, 1937; d. Thomas Clarkson and Margaret (Merritt) Halliday; widowed; children: John Duff Ely, Robert Duff Ely, Stephanie Joyce Raphel. AB, Syracuse U., 1957; JD, U. San Diego, 1968. Bar: Calif. 1968, U.S. Supreme Ct. 1976. Dep. city atty. City of San Diego, 1969—70; asst. U.S. atty. So. Dist. Calif., 1970—71; assoc. Tyler, Cooper, Grant, Bowerman and Keefe, New Haven, 1971—72; from asst. to assoc. dean Sch. Law Boston U., 1972—75; atty.-advisor U.S. Dept. State, Washington, 1975—77; spl. atty. Boston Strike Force U.S. Dept. Justice, 1977—78; asst. legal advisor African Affairs U.S. Dept. State, Washington, 1978—87, asst. legal advisor Nuclear Affairs, 1988—89; dep. asst. Sec. of State Bur. Democracy, Human Rights and Labor Affairs, Washington, 1878—83, prin. dep. asst., 1993—95; Balkan coord. Bur. European and Can. Affairs, Washington, 1995—98; U.S. amb. to Slovenia, Am. Embassy,

Ljubljana, 1998—2001, sr. advisor to sec., 2001—03; counselor on internat. law, 2003; v.p. Save the Children, Washington, 2003—. Mem. Coun. on Fgn. Rels., 1990—. Recipient Outstanding Alumni award U. San Diego Law Sch., 1979, Superior Honor award U.S. Dept. State, Washington, 1983, 84, Presdl. Meritorious Svc. award U.S. Govt., Washington, 1986, 94, 98, Presdl. Disting. Svc. award, 1992, Author Hughes Career Achievement award, 2001, U.S. Dept. State Dir. Gen.'s Cup, 2004. Home: 1304 30th St NW Washington DC 20007-3343 E-mail: nancyelyraphel@earthlink.net.

ELZA, BETTY ANN, retired librarian; b. Wymer, W.Va., Feb. 27, 1944; d. Floyd and Gertrude (Snyder) E. BS, Clarion U., 1966, MSLS, 1971, postgrad., 1971—, U. Dundee, Scotland, Summer 1969. Libr. Brookville (Pa.) Area Sch. Dist., 1966—97, mem. steering com. for self study for evaluation, 1976—77; ret, 1997. Presenter workship on parliamentary procedure Tall Tree Coun. Boardmanship Tng., Clarion Holiday Inn, June 1991; mem. task force Pa. Guidelines for Media Programs, 1975-76; chairperson joint rev. com. Pa. Libr. Master Plan Report, 1975; vis. faculty Clarion U. Pa., 1972-73; inst. adviser U. Pitts., 1976. Contbr. articles to profl. publs. Organizer parish libr. Immaculate Conception Ch., Brookville, 1968-69, First Bapt. Ch., Brookville, 1976-77; mem. steering com. for strategic planning Brookville Sch. Dist., 1994-95; mem. capital stewardship campaign Immaculate Conception, Brookville, 2002; bd. trustees Summerville Pub. Libr., 1997-2003. Mem. NSDAR, Pa. Sch. Librs. Assn. (chairperson profl. stds. com. 1974-76), Embroiderers' Guild Am. (Nydill chpt.), Pa. Assn. Sch. Retirees, Alpha Delta Kappa. Roman Catholic. Avocations: crafts, reading, travel, photography. Home: 618 Simpson Rd Corsica PA 15829-9409

EL-ZAWAHRY, M.A. MONEIM, retired epidemiologist; b. Hehia, Sharkyia, Egypt, Jan. 17, 1926; s. M. A. El-Karim and Sany'ia M. (Aly) El-Zawahry; m. Grace Ellen Ransdell, Dec. 31, 1956 (dec.); 1 child, A. Sabry. MD, Cairo U., 1952; MPH, U. NC, 1957; MPH, PhD, Johns Hopkins U., 1959. Resident in internal medicine Kings Hosp., Cairo, 1952-53; chief med. officer Rural Tng., Demonstration and Rsch. Ctrs., Cairo, 1953—57; pediatrician cardiac clinic Johns Hopkins Hosp., Balt., 1957-59; demonstrator, lectr., assoc. prof., chair prof. epidemiology High Inst. Pub. Health, Alexandria (Egypt) U., 1957-73; sec., med. rsch. coun. Ministry of Rsch., Egypt, 1961—68; WHO prof. Inst. Medicine, Rangoon, Burma, 1968-75; WHO reg. advisor SEARO, New Delhi, 1975-79; WHO rep. Jakarta, Indonesia, 1979—86; WHO sr. health adviser to UNICEF Hdqs., NYC, 1988; sec. WHO/UNICEF Joint Com. Health Policy, Geneva; ret. Cons. primary health care UN Devel. program and WHO, 1986—87; WHO and UN cons. in Yemen, Egypt, Morocco, Ethiopia, Switzerland, U.S., India, Indonesia, Burma, Thailand, Nepal, Saudi Arabia, and Mongolia, 1987—96; cons. to voluntary health projects, Chillicothe, Ohio, 1986—; guest lectr. internat. health Coll. Medicine and Pub. Health & Children Hosp. Ohio State U., Columbus, 1987—; lectr. HIV/AIDS Ohio U., Chillicothe, 2001—; WHO cons. on HIV/AIDS EMRO, 1990—93; spokesperson Child Immunization Coalition, 1997—2002; mem., chair numerous adv. and rsch. coms. WHO & several countries; keynote spkr. on HIV/AIDS in Africa Hospice Orgn., Zimbabwe, 2004. Co-editor: Egyptian Jour. Pub. Health, 1960—68, author 68 publ.; contbr. over 146 articles sci. reports and WHO documents, 25 WHO publ. Panelist Global Health Forum Ohio State U., Columbus, 2001—; chmn. Polio-Plus and World Cmty. Svcs. Com., Rotary, Chillicothe, 1986—2001; cons. AIDS Task Force, Ross County, Ohio, 1995—; mem. bd. dirs. Family Healthcare, Inc., Chillicothe, Ohio, 1999—. Recipient honors and awards, U.S. Internat. Coop. Adminstrn., Johns Hopkins U., Rockefeller Found., Gold Caduceus pin, Burma Med. Assn., Govt. Indonesia, WHO, U. N.C., Rotary, APHA, Govt. Saudi Arabia, Egyptian Med. Syndicate, Family Healthcare, Inc., others. Mem.: APHA (hon. life, awards), Mass. Med. Soc., Burma Med. Assn. (hon., life), Johns Hopkins Med. and Surg. Assn. (Paul Harris fellow 1986—2004, hon. life), Egyptian Family Planning Assn., Egyptian Assn. Tb and Chest Diseases, Egyptian Pub. Health Assn. (governing coun. 1960—68), Tropical Medicine Soc., Egyptian Med. Syndicate (awards), W.H.O. Network for Future Studies, Johns Hopkins U. Alumni Assn. (life), U. N.C. Alumni Assn. (life), Rotary Internat., Chillicothe Rotary. Avocations: classical music, nature photography, fishing. Home: 72 N Courtland Dr Chillicothe OH 45601-2149

ELZAY, RICHARD PAUL, retired dean, dental educator, department chairman; b. Lima, Ohio, Dec. 6, 1931; s. Paul William and Edna Virginia (Moyer) E.; 1 child, Mark S. BS, Ind. U., Indpls., 1957, DDS with honors, 1960, MS in Dental Surgery, 1962. Diplomate Am. Bd. Oral Maxillofacial Pathology. Gen. practice dentistry, Brownsburg, Ind., 1960-62; instr. dept. oral pathology Med. Coll. Va. Sch. Dentistry, Richmond, 1962-64; asst. prof. Sch. Dentistry Med. Coll. Va., Richmond, 1964-66, assoc. prof., 1966-69, prof., chmn. dept. oral pathology, 1969-86, asst. dean acad. affairs, 1970-74; prof., dep. v.p. for health scis., dean Sch. Dentistry U. Minn., Mpls., 1986-96.

ELZINGA, KENNETH GERALD, economics professor; b. Coopersville, Mich., Aug. 11, 1941; s. Clarence Albert and Lettie (Albrecht) E.; m. Barbara Ann Brunson, June 17, 1967 (dec. 1978); m. Terry M. Maguire, Aug. 9, 1981. BA, Kalamazoo Coll., 1963; MA, Mich. State U., 1966, PhD, 1967; LHD, Kalamazoo Coll., 2000. Rsch. economist Senate Antitrust and Monopoly Subcom., 1964; asst. instr. Mich. State U., 1965-66; asst. prof. U. Va., Charlottesville, 1967-71, assoc. prof., 1971-73, prof., 1973—; fellow in law and econs. U. Chgo., 1974; vis. prof. econs. Trinity U., 1984; Thomas Jefferson fellow Cambridge U., 1990, Cavaliers Disting. Tchg. Professorship, 1992-97, Robert C. Taylor prof. econ., 2002—. Spl. econ. advisor to asst. atty. gen., antitrust divsn. Dept. Justice, 1970-71; trustee Hope Coll., 1983-90, Inter-Varsity Christian fellowship, 1992-2000; mem. editl. bd. Antitrust Bull., 1977—; Univ. Disting. vis. prof. Pepperdine U., 2004. Author: (with others) The Antitrust Penalties, 1976, The Fatal Equilibrium, 1985, Murder at the Margin, 1993, A Deadly Indifference, 1995, The Antitrust Casebook, 3rd edit. 1996. Recipient Thomas Jefferson award U. Va., 1992, Commonwealth of Va. Outstanding Faculty award, 1992, Kenan Enterprise award for tchg. econs., William R. Kenan Jr. Charitable Trust, 1996, Templeton Honor Roll award for Edn. in a Free Soc. John Templeton Found., 1997, Disting. Alumni award Mich. State U., 1999; named Tchr. of the Yr. Phi Eta Sigma, 1992. Mem. ABA, Am. Econs. Assn., Mystery Writers of Am., Am. Law and Econs. Assn., So. Econ. Assn. (pres. 1991), Internat. J.A. Shumpeter Soc., Indsl. Orgn. Soc. (pres. 1979). Presbyterian. Avocations: water-skiing, travel. Office: U VA Dept Econs PO Box 400182 Charlottesville VA 22904-4182 Business E-Mail: elzinga@virginia.edu.

EMANO, DENNIS M., psychotherapist, educator; b. Sorsogon, Philippines, Nov. 7, 1967; s. Nestor D and Enemina M Emano; life ptnr. Pedro M Garcia-Alonso. BA, U. Ill., Chgo., 1991; MA, Roosevelt U., 1995. LCPC Dept. of Profl. Regulation, Ill., 1997. Staff therapist Cmty. Counseling Ctrs. of Chgo., 1994—98; cons. Meth. Hosp. of Chgo., 1999—2002; pre-doctoral psychology intern U. of So. Calif., L.A., 2002—03; adj. faculty Oakton C.C., Des Plaines, Ill. Bd. dirs. Ch. of the Resurrection, MCC, Chgo., 1993—97. Recipient Outstanding Svc. to Internat. Students, Roosevelt U., 1993;, Ill. Consortium for Ednl. Opportunity Program fellow, 1999—2003, Anonymous Donor scholar, Roosevelt U., 1992—93, Tuition scholar, Wright Coll., 1987, First Prize scholar, Am. Acad. Art, 1986—87. Mem.: ACA, Ill. Counseling Assn., Am. Mental Health Counselors Assn. Democrat. Avocations: surfing, martial arts, weightlifting, camping, travel.

EMANS, ROBERT LEROY, academic administrator, education educator; b. Madison, Wis., June 12, 1934; s. Lester Meeker and Anita Margaret (Jones) E.; m. Jeanne Elizabeth Faughnan, June 21, 1958; children: Charlotte, Jennifer, Rebecca. BS with honors, U. Wis., 1957; MA, U. Chgo., 1958, PhD, 1963; postdoctoral, Harvard U., 1980. Cert. elem. tchr. Tchr. 6th grade Montreal Pub. Schs., Que., Can., 1959-60; from instr. to asst. prof. edn. U. Wis., Milw., 1963-64; asst. prof. edn. Chgo. Tchrs. Coll., 1964-66; research assoc. U. Chgo., 1965-66; assoc. prof. edn. Temple U., Phila., 1966-68; prof. edn., chmn. Ohio State U., Columbus, 1968-74; dean, prof. edn. U. Md., College Park, 1974-76; assoc. dean, prof. edn. Coll. William and Mary, Williamsburg, Va., 1976-84; prof. edn., dean U. S.D., Vermillion, 1984-90, Tenn. State U., Nashville, 1990—. Vis. asst. prof. U. Chgo., 1966, research assoc., 1965-66; vis. prof. U. Hawaii, Honolulu, 1971; mem. State Task Force on Tchr. Induction, S.D., 1986, State Task Force on Cert. of Tchrs., S.D., 1986, Gov.'s Scholarship com., S.D., 1987, Gov.'s Task Force on Tchr.'s Pay, S.D., 1987; cons. U.S. Office Edn., Washington, State Govts. of Ohio, Md., Va., S.D. Author: A Question of Competence, 1972; contbr. articles to profl. jours. Served to 1st lt. U.S. Army, 1958. Fellow Nat. Council Research in English (pres. 1974-75); mem. Am. Assn. Coll. for Tchr. Edn., Assn. Tchr. Educators, S.D. Assn. of Coll. for Tchr. Edn., Phi Delta Kappa. Avocations: tree farming, travel. Home: 1229 Caldwell Ave Nashville TN 37212-3918 Office: Tenn State U Dept Teaching and Learning Nashville TN 37209 E-mail: reintn@aol.com.

EMANUEL, GLORIA PAGE, retired secondary school educator; b. Dallas, Apr. 5, 1947; d. Daniel and Leola (Green) Page; m. Lawrence Ray Emanuel, Oct. 2, 1971; children: Lawrence Ray Jr., Kevin Lawrence. Student, Paul Quinn Coll., 1966—67; BS, Ea. Tex. State U., 1970; MEd, Prairie View A&M U., 1975. Cert. tchr. Tex., profl. counselor Tex. Tchr. social studies Waco (Tex.) H.S., 1971—82, Univ. Mid. Sch., Waco, 1982—2004, ret., 2004. Chairperson solcial studies, block leader, 1985—93; assn. rep. Univ. Mid. Sch., 1985—93, coord. Adopt-a-Sch., 1992—, coord. Ptnrs. in Edn., 2003—04; mem. Campus Action Com., 1985, Campus Adv. Coun., 1990—91, Supt. Adv. Coun. for Social Studies, 1991—92. Mem. North Tex. Min. Wives, Waco-Temple, 1971—; asst. sec. area II Waco-Temple Missionary Soc.; mem. Joshua Chapel AME Ch., Waxahachie, Tex.; historiographer Gloria Emanuel Unit AME, 1985. Mem.: NAFE, NEA, Heart of Tex. Counselors Assn., Tex. State Tchrs. Assn., Order Ea. Star, Sigma Gamma Rho. Avocations: travel, photography, collecting historical stamps, collecting scenic post cards, collecting scenic slides. Home: 2024 King Cole Dr Waco TX 76705-2749

EMANUEL, JOHN F., lawyer; BBA in acctg. with honors, U. Wis., 1975; JD, Stanford U., 1978. Bar: Wis. 1978. Atty. Whyte Hirschboeck Dudek SC, Milw.; outside gen. counsel Roundy's Inc. Mem.: State Bar Wis.-Bus. Law & Tax Sects., Wiscraft, Inc.-Wis. Enterprises for Blind (bd. dirs.), Associated Industries for Blind (bd. dirs.), Am. Lung Assn. Wis. Inc. (bd. dirs.). Office: Whyte Hirschboeck Dudek SC 555 Wells St Ste 1900 Milwaukee WI 53202-3819 Office Phone: 414-978-5430. Business E-Mail: jemanuel@whdlaw.com.

EMANUEL, MYRON, corporate communications specialist, consultant; b. NYC, Oct. 25, 1920; s. Levy A. and Anna (Ullman) E.; m. Maud Margaret Wenkenbach, Sept. 5, 1947; children: Christina Ann, Robin Duhamel, Anna Lee Chatty, Heather. BA, NYU, 1941. Mem. editl. staff Newsweek mag., 1941-42, Life mag., 1943-47, Sci. Illus., 1947-48, New Republic mag., 1949, Esquire, 1950-51; mgr. pub. affairs dept. E.I. DuPont de Nemours & Co., Inc., Wilmington, Del., 1951-75; dir. bus. comm. programs Towers, Perrin, N.Y.C., 1975-81; pres. Myron Emanuel/Comm., Inc., 1982—. Lectr. Hunter Coll., 1985—; lectr. various colls., univs., 1960—; condr. workshops, seminars, 1965—; vis. prof. Pub. Rels. John Curtin U., Perth, Australia, 1994—. Author: Faces of Freedom, 1972, (with others) Corporate Economic Education Programs-An Evaluation and Appraisal, 1980, Communications Handbook for Human Resources Managers; contbr. chpts. Inside Organizational Communications, 1981, 2d edit., 1985; contbr. numerous articles to profl. jours. Recipient Freedoms Found. medals, 1971, 72, 74; named Vis. Fellow of Pub. Rels. Inst. Australia. Fellow Internat. Assn. Bus. Communicators (named one of 25 most significant contbrs. to the success of Internat. Assn. Bus. Communicators 1995); mem. AAAS, Coun. Comm. Mgmt. (dir. 1972-80), Pub. Rels. Soc. Am., Nat. Assn. Sci. Writers, Delaware Press Club (dir. 1952—). Home: 8 Whitfield Pl Newport RI 02840-2963 Office: 350 E 30th St New York NY 10016-8323 E-mail: memanuel@nyc.rr.com.

EMANUEL, RAHM, congressman; b. Chgo., Nov. 29, 1959; m. Amy Rule; 3 children. BA in Liberal Arts, Sarah Lawrence Coll., 1981; MA in Speech and Comm., Northwestern U., 1985. Nat. campaign dir. Dem. Congl. Campaign Com., 1988; sr. advisor, chief fundraiser Mayoral Campaign Richard M. Daley, 1989; nat. fin. dir. Clinton/Gore Campaign, 1991—92; asst. to Pres., dir. polit. affairs, dep. dir. comm. The White House, Washington, 1993-99, dir. spl. projects, sr. advisor for policy & strategy, 1995—98; mng. dir. Dresdner Kleinwort Wasserstein, Chgo., 1999—2002; U.S. rep. from 5th Dist. Ill., 2003—. Recipient Alumni Achievement Citation, Sarah Lawrence Coll., 2001. Democrat. Jewish. Office: US Ho Reps 1319 Longworth House Office Bldg Washington DC 20515 also: 3742 W Irving Park Rd Chicago IL 60618*

EMANUEL, WILLIAM JOSEPH, lawyer; b. Oct. 31, 1938; s. Lawrence John and Henrietta (Moser) Emanuel; m. Elizabeth Wolfe, Mar. 14, 1964; children: Christina, Michael, Steven. AB, Marquette U., 1960; JD, Georgetown U., 1963. Bar: Nebr. 1963, Calif. 1965, U.S. Supreme Ct. 1976. Assoc. Musick, Peeler & Garrett, L.A., 1963—70, ptnr., 1970—76, Morgan, Lewis & Bockius, L.A., 1976—97, Jones, Day, Reavis & Pogue, L.A., 1998—. Mem. labor rels. com. Am. Hosp. Assn., also mem. spl. subcom. to analyze report of Nat. Commn. on Nursing, Comparable Worth Task Force; mem. adv. com. NLRB, 1994—. Author (with Michael L. Wolfram): California Employment Law, A Guide to California Laws Regulating Employment in the Private Sector, 1989; contbr. articles to profl. jours. Mem.: ABA (com. on devel. of law under Nat. Labor Rels. Act, sect. on labor and employment law), State Bar Nebr., Am. Soc. Hosp. Attys., So. Calif. Labor Law Symposium (founding chmn. 1980, 1981), Los Angeles County Bar Assn. (chmn. labor law sect. 1983—84, exec. com. 1974—86), State Bar Calif. (labor and employment law sect.). Home: 345 17th St Santa Monica CA 90402 Office: Jones Day 555 W 5th St Ste 4600 Los Angeles CA 90013-1025

EMANUELE, R.M., pharmaceutical executive; V.p. rsch. and bus. devel. Cytrx Corp., Norcross, Ga. Office: Cytrx Corporation 11726 San Vicente Blvd Los Angeles CA 90049-5044

EMANUEL-SMITH, ROBIN LESLEY, special education educator; m. Allen Weston Smith, Apr. 14, 1983; children: David, Ariel, Weston. BS in Engring., U.S. Mil. Acad., 1981; BS in Health-Phys. Edn. summa cum laude, Cameron U., Lawton, Okla., 1992; M Spl. Edn., Coll. of St. Rose, Albany, 1995. Cert. spl. edn., health and phys. edn. tchr., N.Y. Enlisted U.S. Army, 1974-76, commd. 2nd lt., 1981, advanced through grades to capt., 1984, resigned, 1990; tchr. spl. edn. Ulster County Bd. Coop. Ednl. Svcs., Port Ewen, N.Y., 1992—. Roman Catholic. Avocations: weightlifting, coaching and officiating youth soccer, softball and baseball. Office: Ulster County Bd Coop Ednl Svs Rt 32 New Paltz NY 12561 Personal E-mail: prteacher@msn.com.

EMANUELSON, JAMES ROBERT, retired insurance company executive; b. Hammond, Ind., Sept. 12, 1931; s. Clarence Harry and Ethel Janet (Anderson) E.; m. Dolores Patricia Fordyce, Aug. 10, 1957; children: James Robert, John Thomas, Karen Lynn. BS, Denison U., 1953. With Midland Mut. Life Ins. Co., Columbus, Ohio, 1953-67, mgr. gen. accounting, 1957-62, dir. cost accounting, 1962-67; with Columbus Mut. Life Ins. Co., 1967—, comptroller, 1969—, apptd. v.p., 1970-76, v.p., elected officer, 1976-91, v.p., comptroller, treas., 1991-93, ret., 1993—. Mem. Ins. Acctg. and Statis. Assn. (chpt. pres. 1954-69, pres. 1966-67, mem. interco. fin. rev. com. 1972-82, chmn. com. 1978-82, mem. fin. planning and control coun. 1978-91, cost acctg. com. 1982-91), Sigma Chi. Republican. Home: 3635 Cedar Circle Powell OH 43065-9148

EMBDEN, DAWN TERRIS, medical/surgical nurse, writer; d. Clarence Washington and Nina Valdaline Embden. ASN, Miami Dade CC, 1989. RN Fla. RN Nursing Agy., Miami, 1989—99, Cedar Med. Ctr., Miami, 1999—2004. Author, editor: book The Dawn of a New Day, 2000, Queen Esther, 2003. Mem. Fountainside Christian Fellowship, Miramar, Fla., 2003—. Home: 9711 SW 16th Ct Pembroke Pines FL 33025 Office: Cedars Med Ctr 1400 NW 12th Ave Miami FL 33136 Office Phone: 305-325-4877. Home Fax: 954-436-6241. Personal E-mail: dembden02@aol.com.

EMBER, CAROL R., anthropology educator, writer; b. Bklyn., July 7, 1943; d. Hy and Elsie (Kardonsky) Ruchlis; m. Lawrence Baldwin, 1963 (div. 1969); m. Melvin Ember, Mar. 21, 1970; children: Katherine Ann, Julie Beth. BA, Antioch Coll., 1965; postgrad., Cornell U., 1965-66; PhD, Harvard, 1971. Lectr. Hunter Coll. CUNY, 1970-71; from asst. prof. to assoc. prof. CUNY, 1971-80; prof. Hunter Coll., 1981-97; exec. dir. Human Rels. Area Files Yale U., New Haven, 1997—. First author: Anthropology, 1973, 2005, Cultural Anthropology, 1973, 2004, Anthropology: A Brief Introduction, 1991, 2000, Cross-Cultural Research for Social Science, 1998; author: Research Frontiers in Anthropology, 1998, Cross-Cultural Research Methods, 2001, New Directions in Anthropology, 2004, Encyclopedia of Medical Anthropology, 2004, Encyclopedia of Sex and Gender, 2004; co-author (with M. Ember): Marriage, Family and Kinship: Comparative Studies of Social Organization, 1983; co-author: (with Burton Pastemak and M. Ember) Sex, Gender and Kinship: A Cross-Cultural Perspective, 1997; co-editor: Portraits of Culture, 1998, Countries and Their Cultures, 2001, Encyclopedia of Diasporas, 2005. Woodrow Wilson Fellow, 1965-66, predoctoral fellow NIMH, 1969-70; rsch. grantee NSF, 1983-84, 86-98, U.S. Inst. Peace, 1990-92. Mem.: Human Behavior and Evolution Soc., Soc. for Psychol. Anthropology, Soc. for Cross-Cultural Rsch. (pres. 1985), Am. Anthrop. Assn. Office: Yale U Human Rels Area Files 755 Prospect St New Haven CT 06511-1225

EMBER, MELVIN LAWRENCE, anthropologist, educator; b. NYC, Jan. 13, 1933; s. Martin William and Ida F. (Trebuchovskaya) E.; m. Irma Stalberg, July 11, 1954 (div. Jan. 1970); children: Matthew, Rachel; m. Carol Lee Ruchlis, Mar. 21, 1970; children: Katherine, Julie. BA, Columbia Coll., 1953; PhD, Yale U., 1958. Postdoctoral fellow Yale U., New Haven, 1958-59; rsch. anthropologist NIH, Bethesda, MD, 1959-63; from asst. to assoc. prof. anthropology Antioch Coll., Yellow Springs, Ohio, 1963-67; assoc. prof. Hunter Coll., CUNY, 1967-70, prof., 1971-87; pres. Human Rels. Area Files, Inc., Yale U., New Haven, 1987—. Chmn. dept. anthropology Hunter Coll., CUNY, 1968-73, exec. officer PhD program in anthropology Grad. Sch., 1973-75. Co-author: Anthropology, 1973, Cultural Anthropology, 1973;: 11th edit., 2004, Marriage, Family and Kinship, 1983, Anthropology: A Brief Introduction, 1992, 5th edit., 2003, Sex, Gender and Kinship: A Cross-Cultural Perspective, 1997, Cross-Cultural Research Methods, 2001; co-editor: Portraits of Culture, 1998, Research Frontiers in Anthropology, 1998, Cross-Cultural Research for Social Science, 1998, Encyclopedia of Cultural Anthropology, 1996, American Immigrant Cultures: Builders of a Nation, 1997, Cultures of the World, 1999, Countries and Their Cultures, 2001, Encyclopedia of Prehistory, 2001—02, Encyclopedia of Urban Cultures, 2002, Archaeology: Original Readings in Method and Practice, 2002, Physical Anthropology: Original Readings in Method and Practice, 2002, Encyclopedia of Sex and Gender, 2003, Encyclopedia of Medical Anthropology, 2004, Encyclopedia of Diasporas, 2004; editor: Cross-Cultural Rsch.: The Jour. of Comparative Social Sci., 1982—. Fellow AAAS, Am. Anthrop. Assn.; mem. Soc. for Cross-Cultural Rsch. (pres. 1981-82). Office: Yale U Human Rels Area Files Inc 755 Prospect St New Haven CT 06511-1225 Office Phone: 203-764-9401.

EMBERGHER, MARY LOUISE, elementary school educator; b. Bklyn., July 22, 1943; d. Joseph and Anna Buonfiglio E. BS in Elem. Edn., St. John's U., 1964; MS in Elem. Edn., Bklyn. Coll. U. of N.Y., 1966. Cert. elem. tchr., Fla. Tchr. N.Y.C. Pub. Schs., Ozone Park, 1964-68, Broward County Pub. Schs., Pembroke Pines, Fla., 1968—. Adminstr. summative for master tchr. program State of Fla., Pembroke Pines, 1984-87; mem. tchr. rep. Broward county Quality Incentive coun. Broward County Pub. Sch. Bd., Ft. Lauderdale, 1983-84, peer tchrs., coach for new tchrs. Broward County Pub. Schs., Pembroke Pines, 1980-98; supr. tchr. for intern tchrs., 1970-98. Publicity chmn. Greater Hollywood Young, Fla., 1969; sec. Reps., 1970. Named Outstanding Young Educator Pembroke Pines Jaycees, 1973, Fla. Master Tchr. State of Fla., 1984-87; recipient Achievement in Edn. award Pembroke Pines Optimist Club. Mem. Women Educators (chpt. pres. 1980-82), Delta Kappa Gamma (yearbook chair 1972-73, chpt. 1st v.p. 1978-80). Republican. Roman Catholic. Avocations: travel, reading, music, politics, working with children. Office: Lakeside Elem Sch 900 NW 136th Ave Pembroke Pines FL 33028 Office Phone: 754-323-6400.

EMBERLAND, GORM PETTER, software developer, computer programmer; b. Bergen, Norway, Aug. 28, 1958; came to the U.S., 1960; s. Rolf Bjarne and Sylvia Ekrheim Emberland; m. Joan Marie Judge, June 18, 1983; children: Ann Elizabeth, Colin Rolf. BS in Zoology, U. Md., 1981, BS in Computer Sci., 1986. Landsat computer ops. mgr. Earth Satellite Corp., Chevy Chase, Md., 1981-84; sys. programmer, mgr. prime ops. Program Resources, Inc., Annapolis, Md., 1984-87; prime applications mgr. AGB TV Rsch., Inc., Columbia, Md., 1987-88; sr. sys. analyst Unisys Corp., Washington, 1988-91; computer specialist, software engr. USDA, Agrl. Rsch. Svc., Nat. Germplasm Resources Lab., Beltsville, Md., 1991—. Contbr. numerous articles to EPA nat. newsletter. Mem. Rep. Nat. Com. (Cert. Appreciation, 1988, Cert. of Recongition, 1990, 92). Recipient Cert. of Merit for Technol. Transfer Activities Aimed at Preservation and Use of Genetic Resources, USDA, 1996, Cert. of Merit Outstanding Support of Nat. Germplasm Resources Lab., 1996, Cert. Merit Using Data Processing Tecnnols.to Produce Databases of Nat. and Internat. Plant Germplasm Systems, 1997, Award of Merit for Excellence in Technol. Transfer Fed. Lab. Consortium, 1997, Cert. of Merit Devel. of Plant Germplasm Info. System Implemented On a Personal Computer, USDA, 1998. Mem. Nat. Trust for Hist. Preservation, Smithsonian Instn., The Civil War Trust (Friends of the Field award 1998), Disabled Am. Veterans (Commdrs. Club 1994). Republican. Lutheran. Achievements include development of Germplasm Resources Information Network for the Personal Computer. This software which has been translated into other languages is now a leading force in standardizing Germplasm management and documentation systems worldwide. E-mail: emberland@olg.com.

EMBLETON, TONY FREDERICK WALLACE, retired Canadian government official; b. Hornchurch, Essex, Eng., Oct. 1, 1929; emigrated to Can., 1952; s. Frederick William Howard and Lucy Violet Muriel (Wallace) E.; m. Eileen Loraine Blackall, Nov. 14, 1953; 1 dau., Sheila. B.Sc. with honours, U. London, 1950, PhD in Physics, 1952, D.Sc., 1964. Postdoctoral fellow NRC, Ottawa, Ont., Can., 1952-53, asst. research officer, 1954-57, asso. research officer, 1957-62, sr. research officer, 1962-74, prin. research officer, 1974-90, ret., 1990. Vis. lectr. U. Ottawa, 1959-69, MIT, 1964, 67, 72; John Wiley Jones award lectr.Rochester Inst. Tech., 1976; adj. prof. Carleton U. 1977-90. Patentee in field; contbr. articles to profl. jours. Mem. Rockcliffe Park Pub. Sch. Bd., 1966-69; bd. dirs. Youth Sci. Found., 1967-72. Recipient Arch T. Coldwell award Soc. Automotive Engrs., 1974 Fellow Acoustical Soc. Am. (assoc. editor jour., exec. coun., v.p. 1977-78, pres. 1980-81, stds. dir. 1993-97, Biennial award 1964, Silver medal in Noise 1986, Gold medal 2002), Royal Soc. Can. (hon. treas. 1982-85); mem. NAE (fgn. assoc.), Can. Acoustical Assn. (founding sec. 1961-64, founding editor jour. 1971-74), Inst. Noise Control Engring. (dir. tech. group 1983-87, editl. bd. jour. 1983-93), Internat. Inst. of Noise Control Engring. (bd. dirs. 1992-2003, v.p. devel. 1998-2002). Home: PO Box 786 80 Sheardown Dr Nobleton ON Canada L0G 1N0

EMBODY, DANIEL ROBERT, biometrician; b. Ithaca, N.Y., July 10, 1914; s. George Charles and Mary Madeline (Riceman) E.; m. Margaret Constance Gran, Mar. 21, 1946 (dec. Mar. 1961); children: James Michael, Daniel Robert, David Richard. BS, Cornell U., 1938, MS, 1939, postgrad., 1939-42, N.C. State Coll., summer 1940. Instr. limnology Cornell U., Ithaca, N.Y., 1940-42; sr. math. analyst Arnold Bernard & Co., N.Y.C., 1947-48; statistician Wash. Water Power Co., Spokane, 1949-53; head statistics sect. E.R. Squibb & Sons-Olin, New Brunswick, N.J., 1953-57, mgr. electronic data processing svc. ctr., 1958-63, coord. sci. computations, 1964-65; math. statistician Bur. Ships, Navy Dept., Washington, 1965-67; biometrician Dept. Agr., Beltsville, Md., 1967-72, staff biometrician animal and plant health inspection svc. Hyattsville, Md., 1972-87; sr. ptnr. EIC Assocs., Hyattsville, 1981—. Cons. Idaho Fish and Game Dept., 1950-60, U.S. Geol. Survey,

1953-58, N.J. Dept. Fish and Game, 1953-60. Contbr. articles to profl. jours. Lt. comdr. USNR, 1942-46, ETO. Mem. IEEE, NRA, Am. Statis. Assn., Biometric Soc., Entomol. Soc. Am. (cert.; emeritus), N.Y. Acad. Scis., Assn. Computing Machinery, Am. Legion, Am. Fisheries Soc., Sigma Xi, Gamma Alpha. Home and Office: 7414 Jefferson St Hyattsville MD 20784-1758

EMBREE, AINSLIE THOMAS, history professor; b. N.S., Can., Jan. 1, 1921; came to U.S., 1958, naturalized, 1965; s. Ira Thomas and Margaret (Langley) E.; m. Suzanne Helene Harpole, May 24, 1947; children: Ralph Thomas, Margaret Louise. BA, Dalhousie U., Halifax, N.S., 1941; BD, Pine Hill Theol. Sem., Halifax, 1946; MA, Union Theol. Sem., 1947, Columbia U., 1955, PhD, 1960; LLD (hon.), Juniata Coll., 1982. Prof. history Indore (India) Christian Coll., 1948-58; asst. prof., assoc. prof. history Columbia U., 1958-69, prof., 1972-91, prof. emeritus, 1991; assoc. dean Sch. Internat. Affairs, 1972-78, chmn., 1982-85, acting dean, 1989-90. Prof. Duke U., 1969-72; counsellor for cultural affairs Am. Embassy, New Delhi, 1978-80, cons., 1994-95; vis. disting. prof. Brown U., 1996-97, vis. prof. Sch. Advanced Internat. Studies, Johns Hopkins U., 2002-04. Author: Charles Grant and British Rule in India, 1962, India, 1967, India's Search for National Identity, 1971; editor: The Hindu Tradition, 1966, Alberuni's India, 1971, Pakistan's Western Borderlands, 1978; editor in chief The Encyclopedia of Asian History, 4 vols., 1988, Imagining India, 1989, Utopias in Conflict, 1990. Served with RCAF, 1942-45. Recipient Van Doren award, 1985, Bancroft award, 1991, T. Das award, 1999, Tannenbaum award, 1999; Can. Council fellow, 1953-54; Am. Council Learned Socs. fellow, 1967; Am. Inst. Indian Studies fellow, 1968-69, 85-86; NEH fellow, 1977. Fellow AAAS; mem. Council Fgn. Relations, Assn. Asian Studies (pres. 1982-83), Am. Hist. Assn., Am. Inst. Indian Studies (pres. 1970-73), Cosmos Club. Home: 10450 Lottsford Rd Apt 1008 Mitchellville MD 20721-2745 E-mail: atembree@aol.com.

EMBREE, MARY EVELYN, retired secondary school educator; b. Columbus, Ohio, May 10, 1940; d. Francis Marion and Mary Edith (Howdyshell) E. BFA, Ohio U., 1962; MS, Nova Southeastern U., 1982; postgrad., Oxford U., Eng., 1987—96. English tchr. Chillicothe (Ohio) Pub. Schs., 1962-67, Columbus (Ohio) Pub. Schs., 1967-74, Palatka (fla.) H.S., 1974—99, chair dept., 1994—99. Coach acad. competition Palatka H.S., 1996-97; adj. faculty mem. St. Johns River C.c., Palatka, 1990-94. Mem. Sch. Improvement Team, Palatka, 1990-92. Tchrs. as Advisors grantee State of Fla., 1989-91. Mem.: Putnam Fedn. Tchrs., Nat. Coun. Tchrs. English, Pi Lambda Theta, Alpha Delta Kappa (internat. dist. officer 1994—96). Democrat. Methodist. Avocations: world study courses, travel, writing. Office: Palatka HS 302 Mellon Rd Palatka FL 32177-4018 E-mail: embree@teacher.com.

EMBRY, MICHAEL DALE, writer, editor; b. Louisville, Oct. 30, 1948; s. G.T. Dale and Dolores Lorraine (Colburn) E.; m. Mary Elizabeth Frederick, Aug. 7, 1971; children: Justin Michael, Sean Russell. AB in journalism, Ea. Ky. U., 1975. Sports editor Messenger, Madisonville, Ky., 1975-77; sports writer Lexington (Ky.) Herald, 1977-80; newsman AP, Louisville, 1980-82, sports writer N.Y.C., 1982-83, state sports editor Milw., 1983-85, corr. Lexington, 1985—98; editor Ky. Mo., 1998—. Mem. adv. bd. Ea. Ky. U. Dept. Comms., 1990-2005, Ea. Ky. Progress, 1990-2005; judge Ky. Lit. Awards, 2005. Author: Basketball in the Bluegrass State, 1983, March Madness, 1985, The Touch, 1999, Baron of the Bluegrass, 2000, A Long Highway, 2001; contbr. articles to profl. publs. With USAF, 1969-73. Recipient Writing award Ky. chpt. Am. Cancer Soc., 1986-87, 89-90, 93, Ea. Ky. U. Comms. Alumni of Yr. 1983, DeDe award Ky. Devel. Planning Coun., 1988. numerous writing awards Ky. Press Assn., Louisville chpt SPJ. Mem. AARP, Nat. Sportscasters and Sportswriters Assn., Blue Grass Soc. Profl. Journalists (pres. 1985-86), Ky. Writers Coalition, Ky. Romance Writers, Romance Writers of Am., Amnesty Internat., U.S. Basketball Writers Assn., Milw. chpt. Basketball Writers Assn. (pres. 1983), Milw. Pen and Mike Club (2nd v.p. 1985), Sierra Club, Friends of Paul Sawyer Libr. (bd. dirs.), Hon. Order of Ky. Cols., Ky. Athletic Hall of Fame (selection com.). Avocations: tennis, music, reading, hiking, travel. Home: 152 Skyview Dr Frankfort KY 40601-9154 Business E-Mail: membry@kentuckymonthly.com.

EMBRY, STEPHEN CRESTON, lawyer; b. Key West, Fla., Feb. 13, 1949; s. Jewell Creston and Julia Martine (Taylor) E.; m. Priscilla Mary Brown, Aug. 21, 1971; children: Nathaniel, Julia, Jessamyn. BA, Am. U., 1971; JD, U. Conn., 1976. Bar: Conn. 1976, U.S. Dist. Ct. Conn. 1976, U.S. Ct. Appeals (2d, 5th and 9th cirs.). Staff aide to Pres. The White House, Washington, 1969-72; assoc. Turner & Hensley, Great Bend, Kans., 1976, O'Brien, Shafner, Bartinik, & Stuart, Groton, Conn., 1976-85, Embry and Neusner, Groton, Conn., 1985—. Editor: Longshore and Harborworkers Textbook; mem. editl. bd. Matthew Bender, BRB Reporter; contbr. articles to profl. publs. Mem. Groton Rep. com., 1976-83, North Stonington Rep. com., 1984-88; chmn. Groton Housing Authority, 1979-80; mem. dean's adv. coun. Am. U. Sch. Internat. Svc., 2002—. Mem. ATLA (chair workers compensation sect. 1984-85, bd. dirs. workplace injury litigation group, sec. 1999-2000, pres.-elect 2001-02, pres. 2002-03), Maritime Claimants Attys. Assn. (bd. dirs.), Conn. Trial Lawyers, Conn. Bar Assn. (exec. bd.), Thames Club, Grange. Democrat.

EMDEN, CRAIG A., lawyer; b. Cin., Apr. 10, 1955; BS magna cum laude, Miami U., 1977; JD with honors, George Washington U., 1980; LLM in Taxation, Georgetown U., 1984. Bar: DC 1980, US Tax Ct. Ptnr., nonprofit org., real estate & taxation Venable LLP, Washington, 1999—. Author: (journal articles) Current Decision, Redding v. Commissioner, 1979; co-author: The Low-Income Housing Credit Provides Shelter from the Cold and Taxes, 1995, IRS Rulings May Significantly Reduce Eligible Basis in Tax Credit Transactions, 2001. Mem.: ABA (mem. taxation section, affordable housing forum), DC Bar Assn. Office: Venable LLP 575 7th St NW Washington DC 20004 Office Phone: 202-344-8521. Office Fax: 202-344-8300. Business E-Mail: caemden@venable.com.

EMEAGWALI, GLORIA THOMAS, humanities educator; b. Trinidad, West Indies, Feb. 6, 1950; came to U.S., 1991; BA, U. W.I., 1973; edn. dipl., London U., 1975; MA, Toronto U., 1976; PhD, Ahmadu Bello U., Zaria, Nigeria, 1986. Asst. prof. Ahmadu Bello U., Zaria, Nigeria, 1979-86; assoc. prof. Nigerian Def. Acad., 1986, Ilorin U., Nigeria, 1986-89; vis. prof. U. W.I., Trinidad, 1989, Oxford U., U.K., 1990-91; assoc. prof. history and African studies Conn. State U., New Britain, 1991-96, tenured prof. history and African studies, 1996—. Vis. prof. Internat. Devel. Ctr., Oxford (Eng.) U., spring 2000; mem. editl. bd. Review of African Political Economy, U.K, chief editor Africa Update, CCSU.; mem. adv. bd. Encyclopedia of the History of Science, Technology and Medicine, Hampshire Coll., Amherst. Keynote speaker, Third World Foundation, Chicago March 2001. Keynote Speaker, Southern cntrl and East African Libr. assn. SCESAL, 2002. Editor: Historical Development of Science and Technology in Nigeria, 1992, Science and Technology in African History, 1992, African Systems of Science Technology and Art, 1993, Women Pay the Price: Structural Adjustment in Africa and the Caribbean, 1995, African Civilization, 1997. Recipient UNESCO award, 1999; Oxford U. fellow, 1990; grantee Old Dominion U., 1986, 88. Mem. AAUP (Conn. state award 1992, 97, 2002), Internat. Soc. for Study of Comp. Civilization (mem. governing body, exec. com. 1992—), World Anthrop. Soc., World Archeaol. Congress, Am. Hist. Assn., African Studies Assn. Avocations: keyboard playing, ping pong/table tennis. Office: Cen Conn State U History/African Studies Dept New Britain CT 06050 Office Phone: 860-832-2815. Business E-Mail: emeagwali@mail.ccsu.edu.

EMEK, SHARON HELENE, risk management consultant; b. Bklyn., Oct. 23, 1945; d. Hyman Sampson and Cynthia Gertrude (Roth) Rabinowitz; children: Aleeza Judith, Joshua Michael, Elana Yael. BA, CCNY, 1967; MA, Bklyn. Coll., 1970; EdD, Rutgers U., 1977. Cert. ins. counselor. Dir. preliminary program for small coll. Bklyn. Coll., 1969-71, 73-74; dir. Am. Ctr. Reading Skills, Tel Aviv, 1972; asst. prof. Brookdale C.C., Lincroft, NJ, 1975-77, Rutgers U., New Brunswick, NJ, 1977-82; pres. The Emek Group, Inc., NYC, 1980-98, CEO Metro Ptnrs., Inc., NYC, 1998—2001; ptnr. CBS Coverage Group, Inc., 2001—. Spkr. profl. meetings. Author: Answers for Managers, 1986, Dealing Successfully with key Management Issues, 1986; contbr. articles to profl. jours. Mem. Mayor's Small Bus. Adv. Bd., N.Y.C., 1998—2001, Small Bus. Rsch. and Tech. Adv. Coun. IBM, 1998—2000; mem. adv. bd. Ctr. Women's Bus. Rsch., 2000—; mem. adv. coun. Women's Fin. Network Siebert, 2000—02; founding bd. dirs. Nat. Mus. Women's History, 1997—2002; bd. dirs. Family Bus. Coun. Greater N.Y., 1997—98, Women's Econ. Devel. Task Force, N.Y.C., 1999—2001; bd. dirs., v.p. N.Y. Women's Agenda, 2000—04; vice chair bd. dirs. Inst. Student Achievement, 1999—; mem. adv. bd. Women's Leadership Exch., 2002—; chair elect Ind. Ins. Agents & Brokers, NY, 2004—. Recipient Promising Rsch. award, Nat. Coun. Tchrs. English, 1978, Woman of Power and Influence award, NOW, 1999. Mem.: Ind. Ins. Agts. and Brokers N.Y., Coun. Ins. Brokers Greater N.Y., Women's Pres. Orgn., Assn. Profl. Ins. Women, Nat. Assn. Ins. Women (Helen Garvin Outstanding Achiever in Ins. Industry award 1999), Coun. Ins. Brokers Greater N.Y., Nat. Assn. Women Bus. Owners (bd. dirs., pres. 1997—98, Mem. of the Yr. 1997), Profl. Ins. Agts. Assn., Ind. Ins. Agts. and Brokers Am. (chair elect bd. dirs.), Emily List (majority coun.). Avocations: writing, reading, jogging, tennis, travel. Office Phone: 212-779-6251. Business E-Mail: semek@cbsinsurance.com.

EMELY, CHARLES HARRY, trade association executive, consultant; b. Phila., Oct. 30, 1943; s. Charles Walter and Jane Beatty (Stott) E.; m. Susan Elizabeth Lawton, June 18, 1966 (dec. Mar. 1977); 1 child, Charles Walter II; m. Mary Ann Horvath, Sept. 1, 1979; 1 stepchild, Wendy A. Vellrath. Student, Drexel Inst. Tech., 1961-62; BA, Temple U., 1967; MA, Fairfield U., 1974; postgrad., NYU, 1974-76; PhD, Calif. Western U., 1978; postgrad., Ohio U., 1981-82. Adminstrv. asst. City of Phila., 1966-68; nat. rep. ARC, Washington, 1968-70; exec. dir., chief exec. officer Bridgeport, Conn., 1970-77; pres., chief exec. officer Comprehensive Bus. Cons., Ft. Washington, Pa., 1977-86; exec. v.p., chief exec. officer Adhesive & Sealant Council, Washington, 1987-88; pres., CEO Comprehensive Bus. Cons., Inc., Fairfax, Va., 1988—; exec. dir., CEO Internat. Assn. Law Firms, 1988—; exec. dir., COO Am. Soc. Hort. Sci., Alexandria, Va., 1994-97; CEO Am. Railway Engring. and MOW Assn., Landover, Md., 1998—. Chmn. Cmty. Cons. Corps, Ft. Washington, 1980—; sr. cons. Philippine Nutrition Ctr., Manila, 1980; adj. faculty Ohio U., Athens, 1982-83, bd. dirs. ICM Internat., Inc.; comunications officer, U.S.A. Nat. Disaster Med. Sys., 1992—. Mem. bd. mgrs. YMCA, Fairfield, Conn., 1971-75; bd. dirs. Hope Ctr., Inc., Bridgeport, 1972-76, Comprehensive Health Planning Agy., Bridgeport, 1973-74, Found. for Internat. Meetings; mem. Mayor's Energy Adv. Com., Bridgeport, 1973-74, Fayetteville (N.Y.) United Meth. Ch., 1985; trustee, v.p. Mental Health Assn. Conn., 1973-77; mem. adminstrv. bd. Nichols United Meth. Ch., Trumbull, Conn., 1975-77; adv. com. campaign coun. Rep. Nat. Com.; mem. Patriots Soc. Germantown Acad., Ft. Washington, 1978-80; pres. Ambler (Pa.) Symphony Orchestra, 1979-80; mem. Pvt. Industry Council, Ambler, 1979-80, Zanesville, Ohio, 1981-83; mem. parents council Hartwick Coll., Oneonta, N.Y., 1987. Mem.: Associated Pub. Safety Comm. Officers, Found. for Internat. Meetings, Am. Railway Engring. and Maint. of Way Assn. (CEO 1998—), Nat. Assn. Corp. Dirs. (sec./treas. Washington chpt.), Am. Soc. Assn. Execs. (cert. assn. exec. 1977), Adminstrv. Mgmt. Soc., Am. Mgmt. Assn., Heritage Found. (exec. com.), Officers Club Nat. Naval Med. Ctr. (Bethesda), U. Conn. Alumni Assn. (life), Mensa, Officers Club Marine Corps Base Quantico, Renewable Natural Resources Found. (bd. dirs.), Armed Forces Comms. and Electronics Assn., Aircraft Owners and Pilots Assn., Am. Radio Relay League, Rep. Nat. Com. Campaign Coun., Rotary, Nat. Assn. Execs. Club, City of Washington Club, Univ. Club, Vesper Club, Phila. Aviation Country Club, Rep. Nat. Com. Pres.'s Club, Elks, Shriners, Masons. Avocations: music, amateur radio, aviation, stamp collecting/philately, travel. Home: 7 Beaver Ridge Rd Stafford VA 22556-6677 Office: Comprehensive Bus Cons Inc PO Box 545 Garrisonville VA 22463-0545 E-mail: chemely@cbc.org.

EMELY, MARY ANN, association executive; b. Bridgeport, Conn., Aug. 10, 1947; d. John and Stefanie Maria (Hutta) Horvath; m. Timothy Vellrath, Sept. 7, 1968 (div. Mar. 1975); 1 child, Wendy Amethyst Vellrath Delbrook; m. Charles H. Emely, Sept. 1, 1979. BA, U. Conn., 1969; postgrad., U. Bridgeport, 1975-76, Ohio U., 1982-83. Adminstrv. asst. ARC, Bridgeport, 1973-78; dir. mem. svcs. Comprehensive Assn. Cons., Ft. Washington, Pa., 1978-81; exec. dir. Muskingum County Respiratory Disease, Zanesville, Ohio, 1981-83; assoc. exec. dir. The Vol. Ctr., Syracuse, N.Y., 1984-86; dir. mem. programs NEA, Washington, D.C., 1986-91; dir. mem., mktg. Am. Geophys. Union, Washington, 1991-93; sr. dir. membership Coun. for Exceptional Children, Reston, Va., 1993-94; dep. exec. dir. Spl. Librs. Assn., Washington, 1994-95; exec. dir. Fedn. Govt. Info. Processing Couns., Fairfax, Va., 1995-99; mng. dir. Nat. Assn. Profl. Employer Orgns., Alexandria, Va., 2000—01; v.p. ops. Am. Coun. Engring. Cos., 2001—. Cons. Comprehensive Assn. Cos., Garrisonville, Va., 1991—. Editor Husky P.A.W. Print, 1995-96, Fedn. Facts, 1995-99; columnist Female Exec., 1994-95. Bd. dirs. Pub. Employees Roundtable, Washington, 1995-99; mem. Nat. Rep. Coalition for Choice, Washington, 1993—. Jr. League of Washington, 1986—. Mem. NAFE, Am. Soc. Assn. Execs. (cert., mentor diversity programs 1994-95), Am. Radio Relay League, Greater Washington Soc. Assn. Execs., Found. for Internat. Meetings, Mercedes Benz Club of Am., U. Conn. Alumni Assn. (Washington chpt., pres. 1996-99, nat. bd. dirs. 2002-, nat. fundraising com. 2001-), Kappa Alpha Theta. Methodist. Avocations: gardening, flower arranging, reading, travel. Home: PO Box 96 Garrisonville VA 22463-0096 Office: 1015 15th St NW Washington DC 20005

EMENHISER, JEDON ALLEN, political science professor, dean; b. Clovis, N.Mex., May 19, 1933; s. Glen Allen and Mary Opal (Sasser); m. Patricia Ellen Burke, Jan. 27, 1954; 1 child, Melissa Mary Emenhiser Westerfield. Student, Am. U., 1954; BA, U. Redlands, 1955; PhD, U. Minn., 1962. Cert. community coll. adminstr. Calif. Instr. to prof. polit. sci. Utah State U., Logan, 1960-77, acting dean, 1973-74; prof. Humboldt State U., Arcata, Calif., 1977—, dean, 1977-86, acting v.p., 1984; chair Social Sci. Rsch. and Instrnl. Coun. Calif. State U., 1994-95; prof. Jr. Statesmen Summer Sch., Stanford U., 1989—2002, 2005. Vis. instr. U. Redlands, Calif., 1959—60; vis. prof. U. Saigon, Vietnam, 1964—65; asst. dean Colgate U., Hamilton, NY, 1972—73; staff dir. Utah Legislature, Salt Lake City, 1967, cons., 1968—77; dir. Bur. Govt. and Opinion Rsch., Logan, 1965—70; cons. USCG, McKinleyville, Calif., 1982; v.p. Exch. Bank, New Franklin, Mo., 1970—76; reader advanced placement exam. U.S. Govt. Coll. Bd., 1990—98; vis. fellow govt. divsn. Congl. Rsch. Svc., Libr. of Congress, 1996; vis. fellow Nat. U. Ireland, Galway, 2002; vis. prof. U. Mons-Hainaut, Belgium, 2002; vis. prof. Am. studies Royal Libr., Belgium, 2003. Author: Utah's Governments, 1964, Freedom and Power in California, 1987; editor, contbr. Dragon on the Hill, 1970, Rocky Mountain Urban Politics, 1971; producer, dir. TV broadcasts The Hawks and the Doves, 1965-66; contbr. articles to profl. jours. Sec. Cache County Dem. Party, Logan, 1962-63; chmn. Mayor's Commn. on Govt. Orgn., Logan, 1973-74; campaign mgr. various candidates and issues, Logan, 1965-75; bd. dirs. Humboldt Connections, Eureka, Calif., 1986-96, pres., 1989-92; elder Presbyn. ch. Sr. Fulbright-Hays lectr. Com. Internat. Exch. of Persons, Vietnam, 1964-65; Adminstrv. fellow Am. Coun. Edn., Colgate U., 1972-73; Paul Harris fellow Rotary Internat.; Fulbright prof., Belgium, 2003. Mem.: Am. Polit. Sci. Assn., Western Polit. Sci. Assn., Am. Studies Assn., Phi Beta Kappa, Omicron Delta Kappa. Presbyterian. Avocations: gardening, photography, travel. Home: 2898 Sand Pointe Dr Mckinleyville CA 95519 Office: Humboldt State U Dept Polit Sci Arcata CA 95521 Office Phone: 707-826-4117. Personal E-mail: jaepat@cox.net. Business E-Mail: jae1@humboldt.edu.

EMERICK, JOHN L., library director; b. Fleetwood, Pa., Apr. 26, 1937; s. Leo J. and Rachael E. Emerick; divorced; 1 child, Michael J. BS in Libr. Sci., Kutztown U., 1959; MLS, Villanova U., 1965; media cert., Temple U., 1969. Librarian, English tchr. Daniel Boone Sch. Dist., Birdsboro, Pa., 1959-62; English tchr. Fleetwood Area Sch. Dist., 1962-65; librarian, head dept. Muhlenberg Sch. Dist., Laureldale, Pa., 1965-72; dir. sch. libs. Boyertown (Pa.) Area Sch. Dist., 1972-93; dir. sch. libr. media svcs. Pa. Dept. Edn., Harrisburg, 1993—. Mem. adv. bd. dept. libr. sci. Kutztown U., 1984—; cons. Phila. Sch. Dist., 1994-95, Ctrl. Bucks Sch. Dist., Doylestown, Pa., 1992-94. Contbr. articles to profl. jours. Pres. Berks County (Pa.) Sch. Librarians, 1982-84, Berks County Libr. Assn., 1990-92; mem. sch. bd. Oley (Pa.) Valley Sch. Dist., 1984-90; supr. Ruscomb Manor Twp., Fleetwood, 1983-87, Mem. ALA (mem. com. 1976-80), Am. Assn. Sch. Librarians (mem. com. 1982-86), Pa. Assn. for Ednl. Comms. and Tech. (chmn. com. 1989-91, award 1997), Pa. Sch. Librarians (chmn. com. 1990-93, award 1999), Pa. Ednl. Tech. (planning com. 1993—, Spl. Svc. award 1997). Democrat. Lutheran. Avocations: travel, swimming, reading, biking, camping. Home: 315 Charleston Ln Wyomissing PA 19610 Office: Pa Dept Edn 333 Market St Harrisburg PA 17126 Office Phone: 717-783-9542. E-mail: jemerick@state.pa.us.

EMERICK, ROBERT EARL, retired sociologist, educator; b. Cleve., Mar. 17, 1942; s. Merl Lowell and Virginia Melissa (Newmyer) E.; m. Carol Ann Carter, Nov.24, 1963; children: Laura Lee, Lynn Lee Emerick Hall. BA, U. Calif., Santa Barbara, 1964; PhD, Northwestern U., 1971. Prof. sociology San Diego State U., 1968—2004, chmn., dept. sociology, 2000—04; ret, 2004. Contbr. numerous articles to profl. jours. Home: 3829 Albatross St San Diego CA 92103-3017 Office: San Diego State U Dept Sociology San Diego CA 92182 E-mail: remerick@mail.sdsu.edu.

EMERLING, CAROL G., management consultant; b. Cleve., Sept. 13, 1930; d. Bernard and Florence A. Greenbaum; m. Norton Harvey Noll, Oct. 1, 1950 (dec. July 1951); m. Stanley Justin Emerling, May 2, 1953 (div. Aug. 1971); children— Keith S., Susan C.; m. Jerrold A. Fadem, Aug. 24, 1974 (div. Oct. 1977). Student, Vassar Coll., 1948-49, Case Western Res. U., 1949-50; LL.B. summa cum laude, Cleve. State U., 1955. Bar: Ohio 1955, Calif. 1975, N.Y. 1982, U.S. Supreme Ct. 1975. Instr. Cleve. Coll., 1956-59; from staff atty. to atty.-in-charge Legal Aid Defenders Office, Cleve., 1962-70; regional dir. FTC, Cleve., 1970-74, L.A., 1974-78; sec. Am. Home Products Corp., N.Y.C., 1978-96; chmn. bd. Global Health Coun., 1998—2002. Adv. com. criminal rules Supreme Ct. Ohio, 1970-73; chmn. Cleve. Fed. Exec. Bd., 1973; internat. health policy cons.; mem. nat. adv. com. Cleve. State U. Law Sch. Co-author: The Allergy Cookbook, 1969; contbr. articles to legal jours. Founder Pepper Pike (Ohio) Civic League, 1959; sec. Pepper Pike Charter Commn., 1966. Recipient Claude E. Clarke award Legal Aid Soc., 1967, Disting. Service award FTC, 1972. Mem. State Bar Calif., State Bar Ohio. Personal E-mail: cgemerling@earthlink.net.

EMERSON, ANNE DEVEREUX, museum administrator; b. Boston, Oct. 6, 1946; d. Kendall and Margaret (Drew) E.; (div. 1980); children: Josephine, Hannah; m. Peter Alexander Altman, 1992. BA magna cum laude, Brown U., 1968; MA, Fletcher Sch. Law and Diplomacy, Tufts U., 1969; MBA, Boston U., 1990. Exec. asst. to v.p. adminstrn. Boston U., 1977—85, dir. adminstrn., program devel., 1985—88; exec. dir. Ctr. for Internat. Affairs Harvard U., Cambridge, 1988—98, acting exec. dir. David Rockefeller Ctr. for L.Am. Studies, 1995—96; pres. Bostonian Soc., Boston, 1998—2002; exec. dir. The Boston History Ctr. and Mus., Inc., 1999—, pres., 2004—. Bd. dirs. Integrated Foster Care, Cambridge, 1985-89; trustee Winsor Sch., 1989-91, Internat. Honors Program, 1995-2003; bd. dirs. World Affairs Coun., Boston, 1991-94, Urban Edge, 2003-; mem. exec. com. Boston Com. Fgn. Affairs, 1997-99. Mem.: Phi Beta Kappa. Office: The Boston Mus Project 55 Court St Boston MA 02108

EMERSON, CARTER WHITNEY, lawyer; b. Oak Park, Ill., Mar. 18, 1947; s. Garner P. and Daisy M. (Carter) E.; m. Susan D. Emerson, June 28, 1969. BS in Fin., Miami U., Oxford, Ohio, 1969; JD magna cum laude, Northwestern U., 1972. Law clk. to judge U.S. Dist. Ct. (no. dist.) Ill., 1972-73; assoc. Kirkland & Ellis, Chgo., 1974-78, ptnr., 1978—. Mem. ABA (business corps. and banking sect.), Order of Coif. Clubs: Mid-Am. (Chgo.). Office: Kirkland & Ellis 200 E Randolph St Fl 54 Chicago IL 60601-6636

EMERSON, CHARLES P., research scientist; PhD. Dir. Boston Med. Rsch. Inst., 2003—, Penn Ctr. Devel. Biology, 1999—2003; prof., dept. chair cell and devel. biology U. Pa. Sch. Medicine, 1994—2003. Author: Methods in Muscle Biology, 1997. Office: Boston Biomedical Rsch Inst 64 Grove St Watertown MA 02472 Business E-Mail: emersonc@bbri.org.

EMERSON, DANIEL EVERETT, retired communications company executive; b. Passaic, N.J., Oct. 22, 1924; s. Daniel T. and Jennie (VanBeveren) E.; m. Patricia Thorston, June 14, 1947; children— Patricia Sue, Nancy Ellen, Pamela Thorston. B.E.E., Cornell U., 1949; postgrad., George Washington U., Boston U., N.Y. U., 1951-56, Dartmouth Coll., 1956, U. Pa., 1959-60. With A.T.&T., 1949—, v.p. fed. relations, 1968-74; v.p. network ops. N.Y. Telephone, N.Y.C., 1974-75, v.p. ops. analysis and methods, 1975-76, exec. v.p. corp. devel., dir., 1976-83; exec. v.p. NYNEX Corp., 1983-86; chmn. bd. NYNEX Mobile Communications Co., 1983-86, NYNEX Info. Resources Co., 1983-86. Bd. dirs. Adams Express Co., Petroleum and Resources Corp., bd. trustees, chmn. YMCA of the USA Fund., Inc. Former mem. bd. dirs., chmn. YMCA U.S.A.; former dir., trustee, chmn. YMCA of Greater N.Y.; former trustee, pres. Kent Pl. Sch., Summit, N.J. 1st lt. USAAF, 1943-45. Decorated Air medal. Mem. U.S. C. of C. (communications com. 1972-74), Canoe Brook Country Club (Summit), Vero Beach (Fla.) Country Club, Cornell Club (N.Y.C.), Vero Beach Yacht Club, Tau Beta Pi, Eta Kappa Nu, Theta Xi.

EMERSON, HARRIETT ANNE, small business owner; b. Corsicana, Tex., Apr. 28, 1925; d. Harold Ralph and Willie Pearl (Richey) E. BME, U. Tex., 1945, MusM, 1947. Concert violinist, N.Y.C., 1949-64; founder Emerson Travel, Inc., N.Y.C., 1964--; mgr. and ptnr. Emerson & Emerson, Cattle, Farms and Real Estate, Powell, Tex., 1990—2000; pvt. practice Powell, 2000—; developer Pearl Valley Estates Gates Cmty., Powell, Tex., 2000—. Bd. dirs. Am. Soc. Travel Agents, Wash. 1981-87; bd. adv. travel and tourism N.Y. State, Albany 1985--. Composer: Violin Solo, Cowboy Dance 1957. Recipient Disting. Achievement award U. Tex., 1975, Austrian Gold Medal award Austria Tourist Office, Vienna 1977, Tourism award Irish Tourist Office, N.Y.C. 1977, Sean Moses award N.Y. A.S.T.A. 1977. Mem. Daughters Am. Revolution, Am. Soc. Composers Authors and Publishers, 41-74 Club N.Y.C., U. Tex. Alumni N.Y.C., Am. Soc. Travel Agents. Home and Office: PO Box 204 Powell TX 75153-0204

EMERSON, JO ANN, congresswoman; b. Bethesda, Md., Sept. 16, 1950; d. Ab and Sylvia Hermann; m. Bill Emerson, 1975 (dec.); children: Victoria, Katharine; m. Ron Gladney, 2000; stepchildren: Elizabeth, Abigail, Alison, Jessica, Stephanie, Sam. BA in Polit. Sci., Ohio Wesleyan U., 1972; DHL (hon.), Westminster Coll., Fulton, Mo. Mem. 105th-109th Congress from 8th Mo. dist., 1997—; appropriations com. 106th Congress, 1998—. Sr. v.p. Am. Ins. Assn.; dir. state rels. and grassroots programs Nat. Restaurant Assn.; dep. dir. comm. Nat. Rep. Congl. Com.; mem. Sub-Com. Agriculture, Transp. Energy & Water Devel. Mem. PEO Womens's Svc. Group (FY chpt.), Cape Girardeau; mem. adv. bd. Arneson Inst. Practical Politics and Pub. Affairs, Ohio Wesleyan U.; co-chair Congl. Hunger Ctr.; bd. dirs. Bread for the World; hon. and life trustee Westminster Coll. Mem.: Copper Dome Soc. Republican. Presbyterian. Office: 2440 Rayburn HOB Washington DC 20515-2508*

EMERSON, KATHY, writer; b. Liberty, N.Y., Oct. 25, 1947; d. William Russell Gorton and Theresa Marie Coburg; m. Sanford M. Emerson, May 10, 1969l AB, Bates Coll., 1969; MA, Old Dominion U., 1972. Freelance writer, Wilton, Maine, 1976—. Author: (reference book) Writer's Guide to Everyday Life in Renaissance Eng., 1996, (mystery novels) Face Down series, 1997—, Diana Spaulding Mysteries, 2003—, also romance novels and children's books. Mem.: Sisters in Crime, Novelists Inc., Am. Crime Writer's League. Home: PO Box 156 Wilton ME 04294-0156 E-mail: emerson@megalink.net.

EMERSON, KIRK, government agency administrator; BA in Psychology, Princeton U.; M in City Planning, Mass. Inst. Tech.; PhD, Indiana U. Dir. U.S. Inst. for Environmental Conflict Resolution, 1998—. Mem.: Am. Political Science Assoc. (William Anderson Award 1998), Am. Inst. of Certified Planners, Am. Planning Assoc., Am. Arbitration Assoc., Arizona's Dispute Resolution Assoc., Am. Bar Assoc. Dispute Resolution Sec., Assoc. for Conflict Resolution. Office: 130 S Scott Ave Tucson AZ 85701-1922

EMERSON, MARION PRESTON, mathematics professor; b. Washburn, Mo., Feb. 24, 1918; s. William Alfred and Alice Maud (Wilson) E.; m. Jane Cornwell Barber, Sept. 20, 1947; children: William David, Anne Ellen, Alice Marie. BS, S.W. Mo. State U., 1938; MS, U. Wis., 1948; PhD, U. Ill., 1952. Cert. pub. sch. tchr. Asst. prof. math. SUNY, Binghamton, 1952-56; assoc. prof. math. S.W. Mo. State U., Springfield, 1956-61; chmn. math. dept. Emporia (Kans.) State U., 1961-79, prof. math., 1979-87, prof. emeritus, 1987—. Co-author: College Albebra, 1955. Capt. USAF, 1942-46. Methodist. Avocation: genealogy. Home and Office: 1425 Luther St Emporia KS 66801-6040

EMERSON, NORENE ROGERS, music educator; b. Ogden, Utah, May 14, 1931; d. Cecil Clay Rogers and Idella Ethel Carter; m. Raymond Maurice Emerson, Sept. 17, 1954. BA with high honors, U. Utah, 1953. Pvt. piano tchr., Salt Lake City, 1946—. Piano soloist Utah Artist, Utah Concerts Coun., Salt Lake City, 1963—64. Mem. Temple Sq. Concert Series Com., Salt Lake City, 1996—; organizer downtown outdoor concert series, Salt Lake City. Recipient Piano Tchr. Recognition award, Keith Jorgensen Music Co., Salt Lake City, 1992. Mem.: Music Circle, Utah Music Tchrs. Assn., Nat. Fedn. Music Clubs, Piano Club, Mu Phi Epsilon Internat., Phi Beta Kappa. Republican. Mem. Lds Ch. Avocation: photography. Home and Studio: 3543 Monte Verde Dr Salt Lake City UT 84109 Personal E-mail: norbird70@aol.com.

EMERSON, RICHARD B., marketing company executive; Past positions in copywriting, pub. rels. and sales promotions; past v.p., past acct. supr. Cabot Advt.; founding ptnr., pres., CEO, acct. supr. Sperry Top Sider, Fidelity Investments, Marriott Corp., Stop & Shop, Thom McAn Emerson Lane Forkino, 1981-91; COO integrated divsns., sr. accts. mgr. Century 21, The Hartford, Stop & Shop (merged with Arnold Advt.), 1991; mng. ptnr., COO Arnold Comm., Inc., Boston, 1991—99; ptnr., COO Toth Brand Imaging, Concord, Mass., 1999—. Past pres. Leukemia Soc. Am., Mass. Mem. 4A's (past chmn. New England bd. govs.), Ad Club (chmn. bd. dirs.). Office: Toth Brand Imaging 30 Monument Sq Concord MA 01742

EMERSON, STERLING JONATHAN, lawyer; b. Pasadena, Calif., July 2, 1929; s. Sterling H. and Mary Foote (Randall) E.; m. Virginia Beabes, July 3, 1954; children: Margaret Ellen, Henry Rollins, Peter Randall. BA in Econs. with honors, U. Calif., Berkeley, 1955; JD, U. Mich., 1957. Bar: Pa. 1958, U.S. Dist. Ct. (ea. dist.) Pa. 1958, U.S. Ct. Appeals (3d cir.) 1958. Assoc. Montgomery, McCracken, Walker & Rhoads, Phila., ptnr., 1966-97; pvt. practice Media, Pa., 1998—. Asst. editor: Law Rev. U. Mich., 1957. With third inf. divsn. U.S. Army, 1950—52, Korea. Fellow Am. Coll. Trust and Estate Counsel; mem. ABA, Fiduciary Law Soc., Pa. Bar Assn., Phila. Bar Assn. (former bd. govs., former chmn. sect. on probate and trust law), Delaware County Bar Assn. Avocations: tennis, gardening, travel. Home: 16 Oberlin Ave Swarthmore PA 19081-1512 Office: Monroe Profl Bldg 117 N Monroe St Media PA 19063-3037

EMERSON, WILLIAM ALLEN, retired investment company executive; b. Columbia, Tenn., July 13, 1921; s. Henry Houston and Mabel N. (Allen) E.; m. Jane Stannard, Oct. 5, 1944; children: Marshal Henry, Shelley, Stacey, Kimberly. AA, St. Petersburg Jr. Coll., 1941; BSBA, U. Fla., 1946. With Merrill Lynch, Pierce, Fenner & Smith, Inc., 1947-87, dir. gen. services div. N.Y.C., 1968-72, Southeast regional dir., corp. dir. Atlanta, 1972-81, sr. v.p., nat. sales dir., 1981-86; dir. Merrill Trust Co. Past vice chmn. bd. trustees St. Joseph-St. Anthony Health Sys. Trustee Oglethorpe U., Atlanta, Mus. Fine Arts, St. Petersburg, Salvadore Dali Mus., St. Petersburg; trustee, past pres. U. Fla. Found. Pilot with USMC, 1942-45. Named Emerson Alumni Hall at U. Fla. in his honor, 2003. Mem.: Feather Sound Country Club (St. Petersburg), St. Petersburg Yacht Club, Capital City Club, Masons. Republican. Baptist. Home: 3050 82nd Way N Saint Petersburg FL 33710-2220 Personal E-mail: ladyjane1@webtv.net. *I believe that what you give away returns to bless you in many ways, and that what you have left is worth more than before the gift.*

EMERSON, WILLIAM HARRY, retired lawyer; b. Rochester, N.Y., Jan. 13, 1928; s. William Canfield and Alice Sarah (Adams) E.; m. Jane Anne Epple, Dec. 27, 1956; children: Elizabeth Anne, Carolyn Jane. BA, Cornell U., 1951, LLB, 1956. Bar: Ill. 1974. Atty. Amoco Corp., 1956-91; sec., dir. Amoco Gas Co., 1979-91. Pres., dir. Undercroft Montessori Sch., Tulsa, 1965-67, Tulsa Figure Skating Club, 1969; bd. dirs. Lake Forest (Ill.) Found. for Hist. Preservation, 1983-2001; mem. vestry Ch. Holy Spirit, Lake Forest, 1988-91. Home: 593 Greenvale Rd Lake Forest IL 60045-1526

EMERSON, WILLIAM KARY, engineering company executive; b. Enid, Okla., July 15, 1941; s. Kary Cadmus and Mary Rebecca (Williams) E.; m. Marcie Louise Stogner, Mar. 13, 1965; children: Rebecca A., Phillip W. BS, Okla. State U., 1965, MS, 1974; diploma, Command and Gen. Staff Coll., 1979, Def. Systems Mgmt. Coll., 1980. Commd. 2d lt. U.S. Army, 1965, advanced through grades to lt. col., 1985; prin. program mgr. Honeywell, Inc., Minnetonka, Minn., 1985-90; sr. program mgr. Alliant Techsystems, Inc., Minnetonka, 1990-92; dep. dir. engring. Teledyne Brown Engring. Co., Huntsville, Ala., 1992-96, dir. advanced engring., 1996-97; sr. program mgr. PEI Electronics, Huntsville, 1997-2001; pres. Emerson Consulting, Inc., 2001—. Disting. guest lectr. Def. Systems Mgmt. Coll., 1997 Author: Chevrons, 1983, Encyclopedia of Insignia, 1995, Marksmanship in the U.S. Army, 2004; contbr. articles to profl. jours. and ency. Adv. com. Dist. 281 Sch. Bd., Minn., 1986-88, summer sch. concept com., 1988-89; mem. Huntsville Land Trust, 1994-2004; chmn. recycling com. N. Ala. Sierra Club, 1994-98; citizen mem. City of Huntsville Ordinance Rewrite Com., 1995-97; lay leader Asbury Meth. Ch., 1997-00, chair adminstrv. bd., 2000-02; bd. mgmt. Anne S.K. Browne Collection, Brown U., Providence, 1998—; pres., bd. dirs. Non Profit Counseling Ctr., 2000-02. Decorated Legion of Merit, Bronze Star with V and one oak leaf cluster, Purple Heart with two oak leaf clusters; inducted into Madison County (Ala.) Hall of Heros, 1996. Fellow Co. Mil. Historians (bd. dirs. 1983-86, 2000—, editor 1986-92, pres. 2003—, Miller award 1977, 2004); mem. VFW (life), Am. Soc. Mil. Insignia Collectors (editor jour. 1993—, Best Nat. Display award 1984), Am. Def. Preparedness Assn., Assn. U.S. Army, Am. Assn. Mil. Uniform Collectors (Writing award 1999, 2000, Achievement medal 2002), Orders and Medals Soc. Am. (bd. dirs. 2003-04, chmn. publs. 2003—, Lit. award 1998, 2005, Silver medal 2000, 02, Commendation medal 2005), Mil. Order Purple Heart, Sierra Club (local chmn. recycling com.). Methodist. Avocations: running, fishing, racquetball. Office: Emerson Cons Inc 124 Kensington Dr Madison AL 35758

EMERT, JOHN WESLEY, mathematician, musician; s. Howard Mitchell and Dorthia Mae Emert; m. Elizabeth Joan Jared. PhD, U. of Tenn., 1989. Prof. math Ball State U., Muncie, Ind., asst. chmn. Dept. Math. Scis. Composer songs; contbr. articles to profl. jours. Office: Ball State University Department of Mathematical Sciences Muncie IN 47306-0490 E-mail: emert@bsu.edu.

EMERY, ALAN ROY, museum administrator, marketing executive; b. Trinidad, West Indies, Feb. 21, 1939; s. Roy W. and Ruth I. (Jackson); m. Frances H. Ruttan, June 23, 1962; children: Katherine, Timothy. BSc with honors, U. Toronto, Ont., Can., 1962; MSc, McGill U., Montreal, Que., Can., 1964; PhD, U. Miami, 1968. Rsch., teaching asst., Toronto and Montreal, 1959-65; rsch. asst. Inst. of Marine Scis., Miami, Fla., 1965-68; rsch. scientist Ont. Ministry of Natural Resources, Maple, 1968-72; from rsch. assoc. to assoc. curator Royal Ont. Mus., Toronto, 1969-80, curator, Ichthyology and Herpetology, 1980-83; assoc. prof. U. Toronto, 1976-83; pres. Can. Mus. Nature, Ottawa, 1983-96, KIVU Nature Inc., 1997—. Bd. dirs. Ctr. Traditional Knowledge, sec.-treas., 1993—2000; pres. Kivu Nature, Inc., 1997—; sr. v.p. mktg. Emery Internat. Devels. Ltd., 2001—04; CEO, chmn. of the bd. Free Impressions, Inc., 2004—; cons. in field. Author: The Coral Reef, 1981; contbr. articles to profl. jours. Recipient Citation Sports Fishing Inst., Washington, Marine Environ. award Found. for Ocean Rsch., Toronto, 1986, Reconocimiento de honor Fundacian Cultural Banesto, Spain, 1992. Mem. World Conservation Union (pres. nat. com. Can. 1995-98), Assn. Systematics Collections (pres. 1987-89), Royal Can. Inst. (pres. 1983), Am. Soc. Ichthyologists and Herpetologists (editor, bd. govs. 1976-86). Avocations: photography, writing, music.

EMERY, CAROLYN VERA, civilian military employee, retired noncommissioned officer; d. Earl Woodrow and Joan Ruth Emery. AA, Ctrl. Tex. Coll., 1988. Commd. 2d. lt. U.S. Army, 1982, master sgt., 2000, noncommissioned officer in charge force protection br. HHC U.S. Army Pacific Fort Shafter, Hawaii, 1999—2003; retired, 2003; force protection program mgr. Dept. Def., U.S. Army, Alaska, 2003—. Decorated Bronze Order of the Marechaussee. Office: HHC US Army Pacific Fort Shafter HI 96858 Home: PO Box 5246 Fort Richardson AK 99505-0246

EMERY, CHARLES CHRISTIAN, JR., health care and information systems executive; b. Pitts., Oct. 11, 1946; s. Charles C. and Gloria V. (Nutridge) E.; m. Marcia A. Balestrino, May 7, 1988; children: Charles C. III, Sandra J. BSME in Aero. Engring., U. Pitts., 1968, MS, 1972, MBA, 1982; PhD in Mgmt., Claremont U., 1990. Engr. AVCO Lycoming, Bridgeport, Conn., 1968-69, Westinghouse Co., Pitts., 1969-71; systems mgr. U. Pitts., 1971-72; v.p. hosp. info. systems Monsour Hosp. and Clinic, Jeannette, Pa., 1972-73; assoc. exec. dir., chief fin. officer St. Elizabeth Hosp. Med. Ctr., Youngstown, Ohio, 1973-85; v.p. info. svcs. Samaritan Health Svc., Phoenix, 1985--; chief info. officer U. Tex. M.D. Anderson Cancer Ctr., Houston, Sisters of the Humility of Mary, Ohio; v.p. & chief info. officer Horizon Blue Cross Blue Shield of N.J., 1996—99, sr. v.p. & chief info. officer, 1999—. Fellow Coll. of Healthcare Info. Mgmt. Executives. Bd. dirs. YW-YMCA, Phoenix, 1987. Recipient Award for Excellence in Healthcare Info. Tech., 1993, John E. Gall Jr. CIO of Yr. award, Healthcare Info. Mgmt. Sys. Soc. and Coll. of Healthcare Info. Mgmt. Executives, 2001. Mem. Am. Coll. Healthcare Execs., Healthcare Fin. Mgmt. Assn. (adv. mem.), Moon Valley Country Club. Methodist. Avocation: golf. Office: SVP & CIO Horizon Blue Cross Blue Shield PO Box 820 Newark NJ 07101

EMERY, HENRY ALFRED, petroleum engineer; b. Northfield, NH, Feb. 9, 1926; s. Henry A. and Ruth (Trask) Emery; children: Trask, Timothy, Ptarmigan. BA, U. Maine, 1950; diploma in, Colo. Sch. Mines, 1956; MBA, U. Denver, 1966. Registered profl. engr., Colo. With Mobil Pipeline Co., 1950-53, Portland Montreal Pipeline Co., 1956-59; maintenance design engr., planning supr., engring. supt., project mgr. Pub. Svc. Co., Colo., 1959-72; pres. Computer Graphics Co., Denver, 1972-78; divsn. mgr. Kellogg Corp., Littleton, Colo., 1978-82; chmn., CEO Emery DataGraphic Inc., Englewood, Colo., 1982-86; pres. Emery DataGraphic divsn. Harris-McBurney Co., 1987-93, Emery & Assoc., Inc., Greenwood Village, Denver, 1993—. Mem.: Am. Water Works Assn., Urgan Regional Info. Sys. Assn., Geospatial Info. Tech. Assn. (past pres.), Tau Beta Pi. Democrat. Home and Office: 11 S Adams St #701 Denver CO 80209 Office Phone: 303-355-2524. Personal E-mail: emery@ecentral.com.

EMERY, HERSCHELL GENE, lawyer; b. Hobart, Okla., Oct. 19, 1923; s. W. Herschell and L. Noreen Emery; m. Charlotte Chrisney, Oct. 29, 1948; children: Kathy Emery Miller, Steve. AB, U. Ill., 1945; LLB, Harvard U., 1948. Bar: Ind. 1949, Tex. 1955, U.S. Tax Ct. 1956, U.S. Ct. Appeals (5th cir.) 1980, U.S. Ct. Claims 1980. Assoc. Ross McCord Ice & Miller, Indpls., 1948—55; assoc. to ptnr. Thompson Knight Wright & Simmons, Dallas, 1955—65; ptnr. Rain, Harrell Emery Young & Doke, Dallas, 1965—87, Locke Purnell Rain Harell, 1987—98, Locke Liddell & Sapp, 1999—2000, of counsel, 2002—. Fellow: Am. Coll. Tax Counsel; mem.: ABA, Dallas Bar Assn., Tex. Bar Assn., Am. Coll. Trust and Estate Counsel, Birnam Wood Club, Dallas Petroleum Club, Dallas Country Club, Phi Beta Kappa. Presbyn. Office: Locke Liddell & Sapp 2200 Ross Ave Ste 2200 Dallas TX 75201-6776 Office Phone: 214-740-8405.

EMERY, NANCY BETH, lawyer; b. Shawnee, Okla., July 9, 1952; d. Paul Dodd Finefrock and Kathryn Jo (Saling) Hutchens; m. Lee Monroe Emery, May 18, 1974. BA with highest honors, U. Okla., 1974; JD, Harvard U., 1977. Bar: D.C. 1981. Atty. advisor Office Gen. counsel, USDA, Washington, 1977-79; legal advisor Fed. Energy Regulatory Commr. Matthew Holden, Jr., Washington, 1979-81; assoc. Pierson, Ball & Dowd and predecessor Sullivan & Beauregard, Washington, 1981-83, Paul Hastings, Janofsky & Walker, Washington, 1983-87, ptnr., 1987-93, Sutherland, Asbill & Brennan, Washington, 1993-97; v.p., gen. counsel, corp. sec. Calif. Ind. Sys. Operator Corp., 1997-99; ptnr. Hopkins & Sutter, Washington, 1999-2001, Ballard, Spahr, Andrews & Ingersoll, LLP, Washington, 2001—03; sr. v.p., gen. counsel, corp. sec. CPS Energy, San Antonio, 2003—. Nat. adv. bd. USAID Tng. Program, 1994—98. Bd. dirs., sec. Park Place Condominium Assn., Inc., Washington, 1982—84; page Continental Congress DAR, 1978—82, chpt. del., 1981, 1984; bd. dirs. New Hope Housing, Inc., Alexandria, Va., 2001—03, chmn. strategic planning com., 2002—03, exec. com., 2003; bd. dirs. Carver Cultural Arts Ctr. Devel. Bd., 2005—. Mem.: ABA (natural resources energy and eviron. law sect. 1990—98, bd. editors Natural Resources & Environment 1990—98, pub. utility law sect., vice chmn. electricity com. 1998—, chmn. program com. 2000—01, chmn. mem. com. 2001—02, chmn. strategic planning com. 2001—02, mem. coun. 2002—, chmn. cmty. involvment 2002—04), Soc. Profl. Journalists, Fed. Energy Bar Assn. (chair tax com. 1986—87, chair FERC ops. and adminstrn. com. 1991—93, chair elec. utility regulation com. 1995—97, chair program com. 1997—98), Mortar Bd., Phi Beta Kappa. Democrat. Office: CPS Energy PO Box 1771 San Antonio TX 78296-1771 Office Phone: 210-353-2406. Business E-Mail: nbemery@cpsenergy.com.

EMERY, PAUL EMILE, psychiatrist; b. Montreal, May 2, 1922; arrived in U.S., 1951; s. Esdras Fernand and Julia (Benoit) E.; m. Virginia Olga B. Kennick, July 27, 1979. BA, U. Montreal, 1942, MD, 1948. Diplomate in gen. psychiatry and forensic psychiatry, Am. Acad. Experts in Traumatic Stress. Staff psychiatrist Austen Riggs Ctr., Stockbridge, Mass., 1958-60; chief mental hygiene VA, Bridgeport, Conn., 1960-62, staff psychiatrist, chief of psychiatry Manchester, NH, 1988-99; pvt. practice Concord, NH, 1962-85, 99—; clin. dir. Ctr. for Stress Recovery, Brecksville, Ohio, 1985-87, dir., 1987-88. Med. dir. forensic unit N.H. Hosp., Concord, 1980-82; cons. VA med. Ctr., Manchester, 1962-64, 82-85, pub. health State of N.H., Concord, 1962-71, St. Paul's Sch., Concord, 1971-78; mem. faculty Dartmouth Coll. Med. Sch., 1971—, Western Res. Sch. Medicine, 1985—. Contbr. articles to profl. jours.; author: Trauma Psychology Model of the Mind, 1993. Sec. adv. commn. health and welfare State of N.H., Concord. Capt. U.S. Army, 1953-55. Recipient Salutation plaque N.H. Program on Alcoholism, 1971, cert. honor for scholarly achievement Internat. Assn. Psychohistory, 1998. Fellow Am. Psychiat. Assn. (life, disting., founder N.H. dist. br. 1972, chair ethics com.), Am. Acad. Experts in Traumatic Stress; mem. N.H. Med. Soc. (cert. commendation 1972), Mass. Psychiat. Soc. (pres. 1965), N.H. Psychiat. Soc. (pres. 1980). Office: 15 Buckingham Dr Bow NH 03304-5207

EMERY, ROBERT ALLAN, minister; b. Rutland, Vt., Aug. 17, 1943; s. Dexter Scott and Frances Elizabeth (Cook) Emery; m. Mary Ann Whiteford, Sept. 1, 1979; children: Allan, Kimberly, Steven, Gregory. BRE, Northeastern Bible Coll., Essex Fells, N.J., 1965; MA with honors, Dallas Theol. Sem., 1976. Ordained to ministry Bapt. Ch., 1971. Assoc. pastor 1st Bapt. Ch., Foxboro, Mass., 1965-67; pastor Grace Bapt. Ch., Attleboro, Mass., 1967-69, Vance Bible Ch., Bristol, Tenn., 1970-71; assoc. pastor 1st Bapt. Ch., Wayne, Mich., 1971-78; chaplain Syracuse (N.Y.) Rescue Mission, 1979-85; assoc. pastor North Syracuse (N.Y.) Bapt. Ch., 1985—. Pres. Search the Scriptures Ministries, Liverpool, NY, 1986—; mem. bd. reference Evang. Counseling Ctr., 1987—88; founder, pres. Greater Syracuse Singles Fellowship, 1990—; lectr. Internat. Leadership, Moscow, Chennai, India, Syracuse U. Author: Divorce Recovery, 1985, How to Study the Bible, 1986. Chief arbitrator Wayne-Westland Sch. Sys., 1976; bd. dirs. Syracuse Rescue Mission, 1986—87. Staley Found. Disting. Christian scholar, lectr., 1988. Republican. Office: North Syracuse Bapt Ch 420 S Main St Syracuse NY 13212-2861 *In life the only constant has been Jesus Christ. He has been Lord and friend, my source of joy and strength.*

EMERY, VICKI MORRIS, school library media administrator; b. Kansas City, Mo., Sept. 7, 1948; d. Arthur Paul and Merna Alva (Powell) Morris; m. Harvey William Emery Jr., July 19, 1974. BS in Edn., Emporia (Kans.) State U., 1970; M in Urban Affairs, Va. Poly. Inst. and State U., 1980; MS in Libr. Sci., Cath. U. Am., 1995; postgrad. student in ednl. leadership, U. Va., 1997—. Tchr. St. Pius X Sch., Mission, Kans., 1970-72, Shawnee Mission (Kans.) Pub. Schs., 1973-74; editing supr. CTB/McGraw-Hill, Monterey, Calif., 1975-76; sch. libr. media specialist Fairfax County (Va.) Pub. Schs., 1995-99, sch. libr. adminstr., 1999—. Mem. adv. bd Fairfax County Sch. Bd., 1996-99. Contbr. revs. and articles to profl. jours. Pres. PTA Sangster Sch., Springfield, Va., 1994-95, 96-98, scholarship chair Fairfax County Coun. PTAs, 1995-99; pres., bd. dirs. Spring-Mar Coop. Presch., Springfield, 1989-90. Recipient Outstanding Svc. award Va. Coop. Presch. Coun., 1991. Mem. ALA, ASCD, Am. Assn. Sch. Librs. (mem. pres.'s program com. 1998, chair ann. conf. com. 2004-05, co-chair 2005—), Va. Ednl. Media Assn., Va. Soc. Tech. Edn., Va. Congress Parents and Tchrs. (hon. life mem.), Beta Phi Mu (local chpt. sec. 2000—04, pres.-elect 2005). Office: Lake Braddock Secondary Sch 9200 Burke Lake Rd Burke VA 22015-1682

EMERY, VIRGINIA OLGA BEATTIE, psychologist, researcher; b. Cleve., Apr. 9, 1938; d. W. Joseph P. and Antoinette Pauline (Misjak) Kennick; m. Paul Hamilton Beattie Sr., 1960 (div. 1975); children: Tamsan Beattie Tharin, Paul Hamilton Beattie Jr.; m. Paul E. Emery, 1979. BA, U. Chgo., 1962, PhD, 1982; MA, Ind. U., 1973. Diplomate Am. Bd. Disability Analysts, Am. Acad. Traumatic Stress; lic. psychologist, NH, Ohio; cert. brief therapist Nat. Acad. Brief Therapists; cert. cognitive therapist Nat. Bd. Behavioral Therapists, cert. domestic violence counselor endorsement; cert. expert traumatic stress, cognitive therapist. Asst. prof. psychology Case Western Res. U., Cleve., 1986—89, asst. clin. prof. psychiatry, 1986—89; sr. faculty assoc. Ctr. on Aging and Health, Concord and Hanover, NH, 1986—89, dir., 1989—; adj. clin. asst. prof. psychiatry Dartmouth Med. Sch., Lebanon, NH, 1983—85, clin. assoc. prof., 1989—. Mem. com. human devel. NIMH, Adult Devel. & Aging Traineeship, U. Chgo., 1974-76; sub-project dir. Case Western Res. U. Sch. Medicine, 1986-90; sec. women's faculty assn. Case Western Res. U., 1987-89; cons. Vets. Affairs Med. Ctr., Manchester, NH, 1989—; sub-project dir. NIMH Mental Health Clin. Rsch. Ctr. Grant, Case Western Res. U. Sch. Medicine, 1986-90; mem. Dartmouth Coll. and Dartmouth Med. Sch. Neurosci. Group, 1990—; Paul Janssen lectr. U. Goteberg, Sweden, 1997; lectr. in field. Author: Language and Aging, 1985, Pseudodementia: A Theoretical and Empirical Discussion, 1988, Language Impairment in Dementia of the Alzheimer Type: A Hierarchical Decline, 2000, Interface between Vascular Dementia and Alzheimer Syndrome: Nosologic Redefinition, 2000, Retrophylogenesis of Memory in Dementia of the Alzheimer Type: A New Evolutionary Memory Framework, 2003, Noninfarct Vascular Dementia and Alzheimer Syndrome Spectrum, 2005; editor: Dementia: Presentations, Differential Diagnosis, and Nosology, 1994, 2d edit., 2003; contbr. chapters to books, articles to profl. jours. Bd. dirs. Frontiers of Knowledge Civic Trust, Concord, 1990—, pres. 1990-95. Recipient Adult Devel. and Aging grant, traineeship NIH/NIMH, 1974-76, Rsch. prize Am. Aging Assn., 1983, Havighurst prize for aging rsch. U. Chgo., 1984, NH Hosp. award for outstanding rsch. in dementia, 2003; named Frontiers of Knowledge Atlee Zellers lectr., 1994, Paul Janssen Med. Inst. lectr., 1997; rsch. grantee Western Res. Coll., 1986-87, NIMH Mental Health Clin. rsch. grantee, 1986-89. Fellow Gerontol. Soc. Am. (Disting Creative Contbn. award 1989; clin. medicine membership com. state liaison 1998—; lectr. Boston 2002), Am. Psychol. Assn., NH Psychol. Assn. (bd. dirs. 1991-93, chair com. acad. rsch. interests 1992-94, sec. 1994—, Riggs Disting. Contbn. award 1991, chmn. Women and Minorities com. 2001—), APA (student rsch. award 1984), Am. Acad. Experts in Traumatic Stress; mem. AAAS, AAUW, Internat. Psychiat. Rsch. Soc., Internat. Psychogeriatric Assn. (Pfizer lectr. 1997, 2d place award for rsch. paper 1995, 2nd Pl. Rsch. award in psychogeriatrics for paper 1995, IPA/Bayer Rsch. award in psychogeriat. 1995), Boston Soc. Gerontol. Psychiatry, Acad. Psychosomatic Medicine, NY Acad. Scis., Am. Acad. Experts in Traumatic Stress, Assn. Alzheimer's Disease Scientists, Am. Mensa Ltd. Home: 15 Buckingham Dr Bow NH 03304-5207 Office: Dartmouth Med Sch Dept Psychiatry Box HB 7750 Lebanon NH 03756 Personal E-mail: vobemeryphd@aol.com. Business E-Mail: v.olga.emery@dartmouth.edu.

EMGE, DEREK JOHN, lawyer; b. Glendale, Calif., Aug. 27, 1967; s. Carl Richard and Heather Anne Emge; m. Suzanne Katleman, Aug. 5, 1989; children: Zachary Brayton, Allison Leigh. BA, Claremont McKenna Coll., Claremont, Calif., 1989; JD, U. San Diego, 1992. Bar: Calif. 1992, U.S. Dist. Ct. (so. dist.) Calif. 1992. Atty. Edwards, White & Sooy, San Diego, 1992-96, Booth, Mitchel & Strange, San Diego, 1996-99; prin. Gilliland & Emge, LLP, San Diego, 1999-2000, Emge & Assocs., San Diego, 2000—. Author: Hidden Trails of San Diego, 1994. Mem. Consumer Lawyers of San Diego. Avocations: bicycling, running, backpacking. Office: Emge & Assocs 550 W C St #1770 San Diego CA 92101

EMIL, ARTHUR D., lawyer; b. N.Y.C., Dec. 29, 1924; s. Allan D'lugasch and Kate Silverman Emil; m. Jane Allen Emil, Sept. 15, 1948 (dec. 1973); children: David A., Jennie, Suzanne Emil Pleskunas; m. Lydia Moffat, July 6, 1976. BE, Yale U., 1945; LLB, Columbia U., 1950. Bar: N.Y. 1950, U.S. Dist. Ct. (so. dist.) N.Y. 1950, U.S. Ct. Appeals (2d cir.) 1950. Trial atty. Cahill, Gordon, Reindel & Ohl, N.Y.C., 1950-52, U.S. Dept. Justice, Washington, 1952-53; assoc. McLaughlin & Fougner, N.Y.C., 1953-55, Arthur D. Emil, N.Y.C., 1955-60, Emil & Kobrin, N.Y.C., 1960-70, 77-79, Emil, Kobrin, Klein & Garbus, N.Y.C., 1970-77, Surrey & Morse, N.Y.C., 1979-86, Jones, Day, Reavis & Pogue, N.Y.C., 1986-93, Kramer, Levin, Naftalis & Frankel LLP, N.Y.C., 1994—2003, Cohen Tauber Spievack and Wagner LLP, N.Y.C., 2003—. Co-chmn. fin. com. Gov. Hugh Carey re-election campaign, N.Y., 1977-78. Lt. (j.g.) USNR, 1943-46, ETO, NATOUSA. Office: Cohen Tauber Spievack and Wagner LLP 420 Lexington Ave New York NY 10170 Office Phone: 212-381-8772.

EMILSON, HENRY BERTIL, artist; b. Sundals-Ryr, Dalsland, Sweden, June 1, 1933; came to U.S., 1951; s. Harry Cristoffer Emilsson and Hanna (Nilsson) Svensson. BFA, Okla. U., 1960; MFA, Inst. Allende San Miguel, Mexico, 1967. Dir. U.S. Army Arts and Crafts Recreation Svcs., U.S. and overseas, 1962-88; artist Bollungsnas, Bralanda, Sweden, 1988—. Exhibited in one-man shows in Erlangen, Germany, 1979, Bad Windsheim, Germany, 1981, Gothenburg, Sweden, 1990, Vanersborg, Sweden, 1994, also others; represented in nat. and internat. pub. and pvt. collections. With USAF, 1952-56. Office: Bollungsnas 460 65 Bralanda Sweden

EMINEM, (MARSHALL MATHERS III), rap artist; b. St. Joseph, Mo., Oct. 17, 1973; s. Debbie; m. Kimberly Scott, 1999 (div. 2001); 1 child, Hailie Jade. Founder Shady Records, N.Y., 1999—; performer D12. Performer: (albums) Infinite, 1997, The Slim Shady LP, 1999, The Marshall Mathers LP, 2000, The Eminem Show, 2002 (Best Selling Album in U.S., 2002), Encore, 2004, with D12: (albums) Devil's Night, 2001, D12 World, 2004; prodr.: albums My Band (D12), 2004; actor: (films) 8 Mile, 2002. Nominee 5 Grammy awards, 2003; recipient 2 Grammy awards, 1999, 3 Grammy awards, 2000, 2 Grammy awards, 2002.

EMISON, EWING RABB, JR., lawyer; b. Vincennes, Ind., Feb. 3, 1925; s. Ewing and Tuley (Sheperd) E.; m. Kathleen M. Crowley, Nov. 28, 1952; children: Susan, Anne Emison Wishard. AB, DePauw U., 1947; JD, Ind. U., 1950. Bar: Ind. 1950. Of counsel Emison Doolittle Kolb & Roellgen, Vincennes; dep. atty. gen. State of Ind., 1968-69. Lectr. CLE seminars, ABA Nat. Conf. for Diversity, 2002. Contbg. columnist Res Gestae, Ind. State Bar mag., 1987—. Mem. Wabash Valley Interstate Commn., 1959-62, Ind. Flood Control and Water Resources Commn., 1961-65; mem. bd. visitors Ind. Univ. Sch. Law, 1984-87. With USN, 1943-46, 52-53. Mem. ABA (Spirit of Excellence award commn. on racial and ethnic diversity in the profession 2003), Nat. Bar Assn., Ind. State Bar Assn. (bd. of mgrs. 1975-77, chmn. ho. of dels. 1979, pres. 1986-87), Phi Delta Phi, Phi Kappa Psi. Republican.

Presbyterian. Avocations: golf, assistance to minority law students, military history. Office: Emison Doolittle Kolb & Roellgen PO Box 215 8th and Busseron Sts Vincennes IN 47591 Office Phone: 812-882-2280. Business E-Mail: emison@emisonlaw.com.

EMISON, JAMES WADE, petroleum company executive; b. Indpls., Sept. 21, 1930; s. John Rabb and Catherine (Stanbrough) E.; divorced; children: Catherine Emison Stoick, Elizabeth Ann, Thomas Weston, William Ash; m. Jane Bale Larson, Feb. 14, 1983. BA, DePauw U., 1952, HHD, 2003. Gen. mgr. C&C Oil Co. Inc., Huntington, Ind., 1954-59; pres. May Petroleum Co. Inc., Lima, Ohio, 1959-61; sales mgr. Oskey Bros. Petroleum Corp., St. Paul, 1961—65; v.p. mktg. Nfld. Refining Co. Ltd., N.Y.C., 1965—69; v.p. Oskey Gasoline & Oil Co., Mpls., 1969-76; chmn., CEO Western Petroleum Co. (successor to Oskey Gasoline & Oil Co.), Mpls., 1977—. Pres. Western Internat. Trading Co., Eden Prairie, Minn., 1981—; bd. dirs. Hydrocarbon Trading & Transport Co., Houston, Community Bank Group, Inc., Eden Prairie, Minn.; ptnr. Bellwood Ptnrs., RBP Realty and RBP Realty II. Trustee DePauw U., Greencastle, Ind., 1981—, former vice chair bd. trustees, co-founder Ctr. for Mgmt. and Entrepreneurship; trustee USMC Marine Corps U. Found. Inc., Quantico, Va., 1984—95; past chair bd. trustees Phi Kappa Psi Endowment Found. Capt. USMC, 1952—54. Recipient Old Gold Goblet, DePauw U., 1987. Mem.: Nat. Assn. Scholars, Nat. Petroleum Coun., Assn. Governing Bds. of Univs. and Colls. (bd. dirs. 1993), Marine Corps Assn. (bd. govs. 1981—84), Minn. Petroleum Assn., Am. Petroleum Inst., Ind. Acad. (hon.), The Continental Soc. Sons of the Indian Wars, Nat. Soc. Sons of Am. Revolution, DePauw U. Alumni Assn. (bd. dirs. 1975—81, pres. 1979—81), Army and Navy Club (Washington), Woodhill Country Club, Spring Hill Country Club, Tralee Golf Club, Ballybunion Golf Club, Monterey Peninsula Country Club, The Minikahda Club, Sagamore of the Wabash, Am. Legion. Republican. Avocations: golf, fly fishing. Home: 3340 Hill Ln Wayzata MN 55391-2602 Office: Western Petroleum Co 9531 W 78th St Ste 102 Eden Prairie MN 55344-3897

EMLER, BRIAN THOMAS, secondary school educator; b. New Brighton, Pa., July 22, 1971; s. Thomas Eugene and Pearl Irene Emler; m. Karen Lea Lawrence, Oct. 21, 1995; children: Rachel Elyse, Lauren Elizabeth. BS in Secondary Edn., Pa. State U.; MS in Edn., Youngstown State U. Cert. earth and space sci. tchr. Pa., 1993, ednl. adminstrn. Pa., 1999. Tchr. Beaver Valley Christian Acad., Rochester, Pa., 1993—95, Mohawk Area Sch. Dist., Bessemer, 1995—97, Ctr. Area Sch. Dist., Monaca, 1997—. Envirothon advisor Ctr. Area Sch. Dist., 1997—2005. Named Environ. Educator of Yr., Beaver County Conservation Dist., 2002. Mem.: Ctr. Area Edn. Assn. (assoc.; bldg. rep. 2003—05). Republican. Office Phone: 724-775-4300. Personal E-mail: btemler@hotmail.com.

EMMANOUILIDES, GEORGE CHRISTOS, physician, educator; b. Drama, Greece, Dec. 17, 1926; came to U.S., 1955; s. Christos Nicholas and Vassiliki (Jordanopoulos) E.; married; children: Nicholas, Elizabeth, Christopher, Martha, Sophia. MD, Aristotelion U., 1951; MS in Physiology, UCLA, 1963. Diplomate in pediatric cardiology and neonatal-perinatal medicine Am. Bd. Pediat. Asst. prof. UCLA, 1963-69, assoc. prof., 1969-73, prof., 1973-95, prof. emeritus, 1995—. Chief divsn. pediatric cardiology Harbor UCLA Med. Ctr., Torrance, Calif., 1963-95. Co-author: Practical Pediatric Electrocardiography, 1973; co-editor: Heart Disease in Infants, Children and Adolescents, 2d edit., 1977, Moss' Heart Disease in Infants, Children and Adolescents, 5th edit., 1995, Neonatal Cardiopulmonary Distress, 1988; contbr. more than 70 articles to profl. jours. and 25 chpts. to books. Served as 2d lt. M.C., Greek Army, 1953-55. Recipient Sherman Mellincoff award UCLA Sch. Medicine, 1982, several rsch. awards Am. Heart Assn., 1965-83. Fellow Am. Acad. Pediat. (cardiology sect., chmn. 1978-80, Founders award 1996), Am. Coll. Cardiology; mem. Am. Pediatric Soc., Soc. for Pediatric Rsch., Hellenic-Am. Med. Soc. (pres.), Acad. of Athens (corr.), Hellenic Univ. Club (LA, bd. dirs.). Democrat. Greek Orthodox. Avocation: gardening. Home: 4619 Browndeer Ln Rolling Hills Estates CA 90275-3911 Office: Harbor-UCLA Med Ctr 1000 W Carson St Torrance CA 90502-2004 Business E-Mail: gemmanou@ucla.edu.

EMMANUEL, JORGE AGUSTIN, chemical engineer, environmental consultant; b. Manila, Philippines, Aug. 28, 1954; came to U.S., 1970; s. Benjamin Elmido and Lourdes (Orozco) E.; 1 child, Andres Layanglawin. BS in Chemistry, N.C. State U., 1976, MSChemE, 1978; PhD in Chem. Engring., U. Mich., 1988. Registered profl. engr., Calif., environ. profl.; cert. hazardous materials mgr. Process engr. Perry Electronics, Raleigh, N.C., 1973-74; rsch. asst. N.C. State U., Raleigh, 1977-78; rsch. chem. engr. GE Corp. R & D Ctr., Schenectady, N.Y., 1978-81; Amoco rsch. fellow U. Mich., Ann Arbor, 1981-84; sr. environ. analyst TEM Assocs., Inc., Emeryville, Calif., 1988-91; pres. Environ. & Engring. Rsch. Group, Hercules, Calif., 1991—. Environ. cons. to the Philippines, UN Devel. Program, 1992, 94; rsch. assoc. U. Calif., Berkeley, 1988-90. Contbr. articles to profl. jours. Mem. Assn. for Asian Studies, Ann Arbor, 1982-88; sec. Alliance for Philippine Concerns, L.A., 1983-91; assoc. Philippine Resource Ctr., Berkeley, 1988-92; bd. dirs. ARC-Ecology, San Francisco, 1990—, Asia Pacific Ctr., Washington, 1995-2000; bd. advisors Urban Habitat, 1995-2002; chmn. bd. Filipino-Am. Coalition for Environ. Solutions, 2001-03; internat. cons. WHO, UN Devel. Program, Healthcare Without Harm, 2005—. Grantee, NC State U., 1976; Phoenix grant, U. Mich., 1982. Mem. NSPE, AAAS, APHA, Air and Waste Mgmt. Assn., Assn. Profl. in Infection Control and Epidemiology, Calif., Scis., N.Y. Acad. Sci., Filipino-Am. Soc. Architects and Engrs. (exec. sec. 1989-90, Svc. award 1990). Avocations: classical guitar, ethnomusicology, asian studies. Office: The Environ & Engring Rsch Group 628 2nd St Rodeo CA 94572-1111 Office Phone: 510-799-2551.

EMMELUTH, BRUCE PALMER, investment company executive, venture capitalist; b. LA, Nov. 30, 1940; s. William J. and Elizabeth L. (Palmer) E.; children: William J. II (dec.), Bruce Palmer Jr., Carrie E.; m. Canda S. Samuels, Mar. 29, 1987. Sr. investment analyst corp. fin. dept. Prudential Ins. Co. Am., LA, 1965—70; with Seidler Amdec Securities, Inc., 1970—90, sr. v.p., mgr. corp. fin. dept., 1974—90; gen. ptnr. VK Ventures, VK Capital, 1990—2000; exec. v.p., sr. mng. dir. Wells Fargo Van Kasper, LA, 2000—01; exec. v.p., sr. mng. dir. investment banking Van Kasper & Co., LA, 1990—99, First Security Van Kasper, 1999—2000, Wells Fargo Securities, 2001—03; pvt. practice, 2004—. Pres., bd. dirs. SAS Capital Corp., venture capital subs. Seidler Amdec Securities, 1977-90; bd. advisors Entreprenurial Studies program Anderson Grad. Sch. Mgmt. UCLA, 1985 With U.S. Army N.G., 1965-71. Presbyterian. Home: 16 Augusta Ln Santa Barbara CA 93108

EMMENS, MATTHEW, research and development company executive; BS in Bus. Adminstrn., Fairleigh Dickenson U., East Rutherford, NJ. Various sales, marketing, and training positions Merck & Co., 1974; helped establish Astra Merck (joint venture with Astra Pharm.); pres., CEO Astra Merck Inc.; joined Merck KGaA; established EMD Pharm.; pres., global prescription pharm. bus. Merck, Darmstadt, Germany; CEO, bd. dir. Shire Pharm. Group, Wayne, Pa., 2003—. Office: Shire Pharm 725 Chesterbrook Blvd Wayne PA 19087-5637 Office Phone: 484-595-8800. Office Fax: 484-595-8900. Business E-Mail: dmilbourne@us.shire.com.

EMMERICH, ADAM OLIVER, lawyer; b. NYC, Dec. 15, 1960; s. André and Constance Ruth (Marantz) E.; m. Pamela Anne Nadler, Dec. 8, 1991; children: Sarah Abigail, Rebecca Elizabeth, Benjamin Ezekiel. BA, Swarthmore Coll., 1981; JD with honors, U. Chgo., 1985. Bar: NY 1987. Law clk. to Abner J. Mikva U.S. Cir. Ct., Washington, 1985-86; assoc. Wachtell, Lipton, Rosen & Katz, N.Y.C., 1986-91, ptnr., 1992—. Mem. ABA, N.Y. State Bar Assn., N.Y. County Lawyers Assn., Assn. Bar City N.Y. Democrat. Jewish. Avocations: running (marathons), squash. Office: Wachtell Lipton Rosen & Katz 51 W 52nd St New York NY 10019-6150 Office Phone: 212-403-1234. Business E-Mail: aoemmerich@wlrk.com.

EMMERICH, ROLAND, director, producer, writer; b. Stuttgart, Germany, Nov. 10, 1955; Prodr. The Thirteenth Floor, 1999, The High Crusade, 1994; dir. Universal Soldier, 1992, Moon 44, 1990; dir., exec. prodr., writer Godzilla, 1998 (Best Dir. Audience award European Film Awards), The Day After Tomorrow, 2004; exec. prodr. Godzilla The Series (TV series), 1998, Independence Day, 1996, Eye of the Storm, 1991; dir., writer Stargate, 1994 (Sci-Fi Universe Mag. Reader's Choice award), Hollywood-Monster, 1987, Joey, 1985, Das Arche Noah Prinzip, 1984; creator, exec. prodr. (TV series) The Visitor; editor, writer, dir. Franzmann, 1979; actor Die 120 Tage von Bottrop, 1997; exec. prodr., dir. The Patriot, 2000. Office: Creative Artists Agy 9830 Wilshire Blvd Beverly Hills CA 90212-1825

EMMERICH, WERNER SIGMUND, physicist, educator; b. Dusseldorf, Germany, June 3, 1921; s. Adolph and Julia (Frank) E.; m. Eva G. Pauson, June 13, 1953; children— Fay Lillian, Ralph Austin, Bertram Frank BS, Ohio State U., 1949, MS, 1950, PhD, 1953. Research physicist Westinghouse Research and Devel. Ctr., Pitts., 1954-57, adv. physicist, 1957-64, mgr. arc and plasma research, 1964-73, dir. applied physics, 1973-75, dir. corp. research, 1975-79, dir. power systems, 1979-83, dir. corp. and comml. research, 1983-86; retired, 1986. Author: Fast Neutron Physics, 1963; patentee in field Served with AUS, 1942-46, ETO Fellow Am. Phys. Soc.; mem. AAAS (life), Sigma XI, Phi Beta Kappa, Zeta Beta Tau Home: 1883 Beulah Rd Pittsburgh PA 15235-5004 E-mail: wemrick@aol.com.

EMMERMAN, MICHAEL N., financial analyst; b. Bklyn., Oct. 7, 1945; s. Leon and Ida E.; m. Janet Louise Goldman, Dec. 20, 1969 (div. Apr. 1978); children: Daniel Blake, Karen Stacey; m. Patricia Anne Stockhausen, Sept. 9, 1995; 1 child, Thomas Justin Stockhausen Emmerman. BBA, Pace U., 1966; MBA, L.I. U., 1967. Bd. cert. forensic examiner; diplomate Am. Bd. Forensic Examiners. Security analyst Standard & Poor's Inc., N.Y.C., 1965-68; sr. security analyst Arnhold & S. Bleichroeder Inc., N.Y.C., 1968-69; dir. managed accounts Lombard, Nelson, McKenna & Paganucci, N.Y.C., 1970-72; pres. Dominick Mgmt. Co., N.Y.C., 1972-74; mng. dir., money mgr. Neuberger Berman L.L.C., N.Y.C., 1974—. Author: Flying and Diving: A New Look, 1987; contbr. articles to jours. in med. and underwater sci. fields. Vice chmn. Fed. Drug Agts. Found., Inc.; hon. dep. chief N.Y.C. Police Dept.; advisor N.Y. Police Dept. Harbor Unit Scuba Team; hon. battalian chief Fire Dept. N.Y.; govt. liaison officer ARC; trustee Long Island U. Fellow Fin. Analysts Fedn., Explorers Club; mem. N.Y. Soc. Security Analysts (accredited sr. security analyst), Undersea and Hyperbaric Med. Soc., Am. Acad. Underwateer Scis., Nat. Assn. Underwater Instrs. (life), Profl. Assn. Diving Instrs. (instr. 1986—), Princeton Club. Avocations: underwater exploration, squash, music. Office: Neuberger Berman LLC 605 3d Ave 38th Fl New York NY 10158-3698

EMMERT, GILBERT ARTHUR, retired engineering educator; b. Merced, Calif., June 2, 1938; s. Allan Valentine and Mildred (Vanderbilt) E.; m. Nancy Sue Johnson, June 12, 1964; children: David Allan, Daniel Andrew. BS, U. Calif., Berkeley, 1961; MS, Rensselaer Poly. Inst., Troy, N.Y., 1964; PhD, Stevens Inst. Tech., Hoboken, N.J., 1968. Analytical engr. United Tech. Corp., East Hartford, Conn., 1961-64; asst. prof. U. Wis., Madison, 1968-72, assoc. prof., 1972-79, prof., 1979—2001, prof. emeritus, 2001—, dept. chair, 1992-01. Contbr. articles to profl. jours. Mem. AIAA, Am. Physical Soc., Am. Nuclear Soc. Office: U Wis Dept Engring Physics 1500 Engineering Dr Madison WI 53706-1609 E-mail: emmert@engr.wisc.edu.

EMMERT, MARK ALLEN, academic administrator, educator; b. Tacoma, Dec. 16, 1952; s. Chester Eugene and Naomi Abigale E.; m. DeLaine Sharon Smith, June 24, 1977; children: Stephen Kenneth, Jennifer Ashley. BA in Polit. Sci., U. Wash., 1975; MPA, Syracuse U., 1976, PhD, 1983. Asst. prof. Northern Ill. U., DeKalb, 1983-85; prof., adminstr. U. Colo., Denver, 1985-91; provost, prof. Mont. State U., Bozeman, 1991-94; chancellor, prof. U. Conn., Storrs, 1994-99, La. State U., Baton Rouge, 1999—2004; pres. U. Wash., 2004—. Contbr. articles to profl. jours. Bd. dirs. Boy Scouts Am., Baton Rouge, 1999—, La. Rsch. Park, 1999—, LUMCON, 1999—; coun. chmn. Nat. Assn. State Univ. and Land Grant Coll., 1998-99. Am. Coun. on Edn. fellow U. Colo., 1988, Fulbright fellow, Germany, 1990-91. Mem. Rotary, Phi Kappa Phi, Golden Key Honor Soc., Alpha Lambda Delta. Avocations: reading, golf, scuba diving, fly fishing. Office: Office of the Pres 301 Gerberding Hall Box 351230 Seattle WA 98195-1230*

EMMERT, RICHARD EUGENE, retired industrial and professional association executive; b. Iowa City, Iowa, Feb. 23, 1929; s. Frank Thomas and Okie Leona (Seydel) E.; m. Marilyn Ruth Marner, June 19, 1949; children: Debra Sue Emmert Warrington, Andrea Gale Emmert Mazzuca, Lisa Alison Emmert Grant. BS, U. Iowa, 1951; MS, U. Del., 1952, PhD, 1954; DSc (hon.), Manhattan Coll., 1992. Supt. mfg. textile fibers dept. E.I. du Pont de Nemours & Co., Martinsville, 1966-67, mgr. engring. tech. and materials rsch. Wilmington, 1969-73, dir. rsch. and devel. pigments dept., 1973-75, dir. instrument products, photo products dept., 1975-77, dir. electronic products, photo products dept., 1977-79, gen. mgr. textile fibers dept., 1979-80, v.p. corp. plans, 1980-83, v.p. electronics dept., 1984-87; exec. dir. AIChE, N.Y.C., 1988-96, ret., 1996. Trustee U. Del. Rsch. Found., Newark, 1987—, pres., 1994-2000; commencement spkr. Coll. Engring., U. Iowa, 1995. Author: Gas Absorption and Solvent Extraction, 1963; contbr. articles to profl. jours. Vice chmn. Stanton Sch. Bd., Del., 1961-64; chmn. adv. bd. Coll. Engring., U. Iowa, Iowa City, 1974-80; chmn. adv. bd. dept. chem. engring. U. Calif., Berkeley, 1978-87, chmn., 1982-83; co-chmn. adv. bd. dept. chem. engring. U. Del., Newark, 1984-88, mem. Coll. Engring. adv. coun., 1995—; trustee Christiana Care Health Sys., Wilmington, 1983—; pres. Del. Found. for Phys. Edn. (now Del. Tennis Found.), Wilmington, 1984-86. With U.S. Army, 1954-56. Recipient 1st Disting. Engring. Alumni award U. Del., 1984, Medal of Distinction, U. Del., 1993, Disting. Alumni award U. Iowa, 1988, Kenneth Andrew Roe award Am. Assn. of Engring. Socs., 1996, Disting. Engring. Alumni Acad. award U. Iowa, 1996. Fellow AIChE (Van Antwerpen award 1998); mem. Nat. Acad. Engring., Del. Tennis Assn. (pres. 1982-83), United Engring. Found. (trustee 1988-2001), Chem. Heritage Found. (dir. 1998—), Tau Beta Pi, Sigma Xi, Phi Eta Sigma. Republican. Presbyterian. Avocation: tennis. Home: 24 Brandywine Falls Rd Wilmington DE 19806-1002 E-mail: emmertr@comcast.net.

EMMET, THOMAS ADDIS, JR., college administrator, consultant; b. Detroit, July 26, 1930; s. Thomas Addis and Leona Marguerete (Schneider) E.; m. Anne Marie Baker, Mar. 3, 1972; children: Lynn, Anthony, William Novitsky. PhB, U. Detroit, 1952, ME, 1954; EdS, EdD, U. Mich., 1963. Asst. dean U. Detroit, 1953-57, dean men, 1957-64, dean evening coll. arts and scis., 1964-66, asst. prof. higher edn., 1964-67; spl. asst. to pres., prof. edn. Regis U., Denver, 1972-91, pres. higher edn. exec. assocs., 1967-72, 84-86, 89—. Adj. prof. higher edn. Wayne State U., Detroit, 1968-70; chmn. bd. Higher Edn. Group, 1986-89; pres. Thomas A. Emmet & Assos., 1972-84; cons. collective negotiations in higher edn. Edn. Commn. of States, 1971-84; cons. higher edn. Opinion Research Corp.; dir. leadership seminars, sr. adviser Am. Council on Edn., 1979-85. Editor: The Acacemic Department and Division Chairman, 1972, Collective Bargaining in Postsecondary Institutions: The Impact on the Campus and the State, 1974; assoc. editor Coll. and Univ. Bus., 1969-71; pub. The Department ADvisor, 1985-92. Staff dir. Mich. State Senate Student Unrest Com., 1968-69; exec. sec. Conf. Jesuit Student Personnel Adminstrs., 1956-64; sec. Coun. Student Personnel Assns. in Higher Edn., 1966-69. Recipient Bernard Webster Reed award, 1963, John P. McNichols award U. Detroit, 1986. Mem. Adult Student Personnel Assn. (v.p. 1961-64), Nat. Assn. Student Personnel Adminstrs. (editor Jour. 1962-63), Phi Kappa Phi, Alpha Sigma Nu, Alpha Sigma Lambda, Phi Delta Kappa, Phi Eta Sigma. Home: PO Box 549 Franktown CO 80116-0549 Office: Regis U New Ventures 50th St and Lowell Blvd 3333 Regis Blvd Denver CO 80221-1154

EMMETT, JAMES ROBERT, retired lawyer; b. Gary, Ind., Jan. 24, 1940; s. Robert Gerald and Jeannette Louise (Pinkerton) E.; m. Marian Carol Yanney, Jan. 28, 1967; children: Jennifer Kathleen, Robert Yanney. BCE, Purdue U., 1963; JD, Ind. U., 1966. Bar: Ind. 1967, U.S. Dist. Ct. (so. dist.) Ind. 1967, U.S. Ct. Internat. Trade 1993, U.S. Supreme Ct. 1993. Engr. design GE Snyder & Assocs., Jackson, Mich., 1968-70; atty. real estate Amoco Oil Co., Chgo., 1970-72; rep. property tax Amoco Corp., Chgo., 1972-74, atty. state tax, 1974-86, sr. tax atty., 1986—2000; ret., 2000. Bd. dirs. St. Charles Singers, Ill., 2002—. Avocations: golf, guitar, horses, reading, drums.

EMMETT, JOHN COLIN, retired inventor, consultant; b. Bradford, Yorkshire, Eng., Apr. 27, 1939; BS, PhD, London U. Former rsch. team leader SmithKline Beecham Corp.; cons. Euromedica Ltd.; freelance cons., 2001—. Co-inventor over 100 patents in field. Named to National Inventors Hall of Fame, 1990. Office: Nat Inventors Hall of Fame 221 S Broadway St Akron OH 44308-1505

EMMETT, RITA, speech professional; b. Chgo., Apr. 12, 1943; d. Thomas Henry Dorney and Helen Fischer; m. Bruce Karder, May 21, 1994; children: Robb Sean, Kerry Shannon. BA in English, Northeastern Ill. U., 1979; MS in Adult and Cont. Edn, Nat. Louis U., Evanston, Ill., 1985. Coord. edn. programs Leyden Family Svc., Franklin Park, Ill., 1977-95; pres. Emmett Enterprises, Inc., Des Plaines, 1994—. Adj. faculty Triton Coll., River Grove, Ill., 1977-99, Wright Coll., Chgo., 1985-99; presenter in field. Author: The Procrastinator's Handbook: Mastering the Art of Doing It Now, 2000; The Procrastinating Child: Helping Your Child Do It Now!, 2002, The Clutter-Busting Handbook, 2005, Great Speakers Anthology; contbr. articles to newspapers and mags. Pres. Parent's Club, River Grove, 1987-88; keynote spkr. Gov.'s Mansion, Springfield, Ill. Mem. Bus. and Profl. Women (Achievement award 1986), Assn. Consultation and Edn. (sec.), Ill. Prevention Network, Century Club, Nat. Spkrs. Assn., Profl. Spkr.'s of Ill. (bd. dirs. 1995-96, 2002-03). Roman Catholic. Avocations: reading, writing, travel, friends. Office Phone: 847-699-9950. E-mail: rita@ritaemmett.com.

EMMONS, ROBERT DUNCAN, diplomat; b. LA, Mar. 1, 1932; s. Richard Norman and Margaret Houston (Kelly) E.; m. Susan Mary Likeman, Aug. 23, 1958; 1 child, Robert Campbell; m. Carolyn Elizabeth Kingsley, Sept. 27, 1995. BA, UCLA, 1954, LL.B., 1957. Contract adminstr. N.Am. Aviation, Inc., Los Angeles, 1958-60, 62-63; contract adminstr. Litton Industries, Los Angeles, 1961; fgn. service officer Dept. State, Washington, 1963-88; vice consul, 3d sec. Am. embassy, Beirut, 1963-65; consul Am. consulate, St. John, N.B., Can., 1966-68; program officer AID, Saigon, Vietnam, 1968-70; sr. watch officer Dept. State, Washington, 1970-71; chief consular sect. Am. embassy, Warsaw, Poland, 1972-74, counselor of embassy Copenhagen, 1974-76, consul gen. Kingston, Jamaica, 1976-78; office dir. Dept. State, Washington, 1978-80; chief immigration br. Am. embassy, London, 1980-84; consul gen. Am. consulate gen., Tijuana, Mex., 1984-87; retired, 1988. Recipient Vietnam award, Dept. State, 1969. Mem.: Calif. State Bar.

EMMONS, ROBERT JOHN, corporate executive, poet; b. Trenton, NJ, Sept. 18, 1934; s. Charles Glunk and Ruth Marie (Heilhecker) E.; m. Christine Young Bebb, July 13, 1980; children: Bradley Thomas, Cathy Lynne, Christopher Robert, Ryan Hunter. AB in Econs, U. Mich., 1956, MBA, 1960, JD, 1964. V.p. Baskin-Robbins Co., Burbank, Calif., 1964-68; pres. United Rent-All, Los Angeles, 1968-69, Master Host Internat., Los Angeles, 1969-71; prof. Grad. Sch. Bus., U. So. Calif., 1971-82; pres. LTI Corp., Monterey, Calif., 1982-84; chmn., CEO, dir. Casino USA/SFI Corp., Santa Barbara, Calif., 1984-98; mng. ptnr. Emmons Capital Investments, Santa Barbara, Calif., 1999—. Author: The American Franchise Revolution, 1970, The American Marketing Revolution, 1980; poetry Other Places, Other Times, 1974, Love and Other Minor Tragedies, 1980, The Road to Paradise, 2003, The Wanderer, A Poet's Journey, 2005. Mem. AAUP, Am. Mktg. Assn., European Mktg. Assn., Am. Econ. Assn., Calif. Yacht Club (L.A.), Hawaii Yacht Club (Honolulu), The Valley Club of Montecito (Calif.), Useppa Island Club (Fla.), St. Petersburg Yacht Club (Fla.), The Calif. Club (LA), Ocean Reef Club (Fla.), Beta Gamma Sigma, Pi Kappa Alpha. Office: Emmons Capital Investments PO Box 50243 Santa Barbara CA 93150-0243

EMMRICH, MARY KAYLENE, librarian; b. Lafayette, Ind., Sept. 18, 1955; d. Harold Clifton and Helen Nora (Dewitt) Martin; m. Roger H. Emmrich, June 18, 1999. BS, Ball State U., 1978, MLS, 1983. Cert. Ind. libr. I Ind. State Library. Tchr., libr. Cannelton (Ind.) City Schs., 1978-81; tchr. North Newton H.S., Morocco, Ind., 1981-82; grad. asst., abstractor Ball State U., Muncie, Ind., 1982-83; historian Ball Meml. Hosp., Muncie, 1983; libr. Jasper County Pub. Libr., Rensselaer, Ind., 1983-94; libr. dir. Newton County Pub. Libr., Lake Village, Ind., 1994—. Cmty. tchg. fellow St. Joseph's Coll., Rensselaer, 1995—; com. chair Incolsa Membership Adv. Coun., Indpls., 1994-96. Cmty. rels. com. mem. Jasper County Hosp., Rensselaer, 1993-96; fed. fin. aid forms asst. Purdue U. Calumet, Hammond, Ind., 1995-1998; active Morocco Sesqui. Commn., 2001, Purdue U. Ext. Svcs. Coun., 2002—, v.p., 2003-05, co-sec., 2005—; active Morocco Planning Commn., 2002—, sec., 2003—, Morocco BZA, 2002—, sec., 2002—; active Newton-Jasper County Lifelong Learning Network, 2002-04, sec., 2002-05; active Friends of Alexander M. Bracken Libr., Crochet Ptnrs Recipient Margaret McNamara Reading award Rensselaer Ctr. Mid. Sch., 1988; named Woman of Yr. Am. Bus. Women's Assn., 1989. Fellow Coun. of Fellows St. Joseph's Coll.; mem. Nat. Hot Rod Assn., Tech. Svc. Librs. (Ohio Valley group), Andy Griffith Show Rerun Watchers Club (pres. Pucka Pucka Pucka chpt. 1995—), Morocco Ladies Literary Club (pres. 1994-95, 96-97, treas. 1997-99), Am. Leg. Aux, Post 146, Ball State U. Alumni Assn., Kappa Kappa Kappa. Democrat. Avocations: walking, reading, auto racing, dogs, handwork. Office: Newton County Pub Libr 9458 N 315 W PO Box 206 Lake Village IN 46349-0206 Office Phone: 219-992-3490. Personal E-mail: auntthrax@hotmail.com.

EMORY, MEADE, lawyer; b. Seattle, Feb. 26, 1931; s. DeWolfe and Marion (Burton) E.; m. Deborah Carley, Apr. 30, 1959; children: Ann, Campbell, Elizabeth. AB, George Washington U., 1954, LL.B., 1957; LL.M. in Taxation, Boston U., 1963. Bar: D.C. 1958, Wash. 1958, Iowa 1966. Trial atty. IRS, Boston, 1961-64; teaching fellow N.Y.U. Sch. Law, 1964-65; mem. faculty U. Iowa Sch. Law, 1965-70; legislation atty. Joint Com. on Taxation, U.S. Congress, 1970-72; mem. faculty U. Calif. Sch. Law, Davis, 1972-75; asst. to commr. IRS, 1975-77; ptnr. firm LeSourd & Patten, Seattle, 1978-90; of counsel Lane Powell Spears Lubersky, Seattle, 1991—; prof. law and dir. grad. program in taxation U. Wash. Sch. Law, Seattle, 1995—2005, prof. emeritus law, 2005—. Vis. prof. law UCLA, 1987, Tulane U. Law Sch., 1990, Duke U., 1991, 92, Northwestern U. Sch. of Law, 1993, Georgetown U. Law, 1993, U. Pa. 1995; Mason Ladd dist. vis. prof. U. Iowa Law, 1994; Earl Dunlap dist. vis. prof. U. Nebr. Law, 1994; Charles S. Lyon vis. prof. taxation from practice NYU, 1989. Co-author: Federal Income Taxation of Corporations and Shareholders-Forms, 1981, rev. edit., 1989; mem. bd. editors Jour. Taxation. Trustee Seattle Symphony Orch., 1978-89; bd. dirs. Cornish Inst. Art, Seattle, 1979— . Recipient Commr.'s award IRS 1976. Mem. Am. Bar Assn., Am. Law Inst. Clubs: Rainier (Seattle), Seattle Tennis (Seattle), Univ. (Seattle); Cosmos (Washington). Office: U Wash William Gates Hall Box 353020 Seattle WA 98195-3020

EMPLIT, RAYMOND HENRY, electrical engineer; b. Darby, Pa., May 2, 1948; s. Henry Raymond and Caroline Winifred (Parker) E.; m. Patricia Jean Jezl, Aug. 7, 1976; children: Eric, Susan. BS summa cum laude in Engring., U. Pa., 1978, MS in Engring., 1979. Engr. Custom Controls Co., Broomall, Pa., 1972-75, tech. dir., 1975-78, v.p., 1979-82; chief engr. Robertshaw Controls, Havertown, Pa., 1982-87; pres. Electronic Devel. Corp., Edgemont, Pa., 1987-89; project engr. Gt. Lake Instruments, Edgemont, Pa., 1989-91; v.p. Interlink Techs., Broomall, Pa., 1991-97, pres., 1997—. Patentee indsl. level instrumentation in U.S. and Can. With U.S. Army, 1968-71. Recipient Hugo Otto Wolf Meml. prize U. Pa., 1978. Mem. IEEE, Eta Kappa Nu, Tau Beta Pi. Republican. Avocations: reading, wine, investing. Home: 71 Sweetwater Rd Glen Mills PA 19342-1710 Office: Interlink Techs 1000 Sussex Blvd Broomall PA 19008-4315

EMR, SCOTT DAVID, biology professor, consultant; b. Jersey City, Feb. 8, 1954; s. John Frank and Evelyn Grace (Metzger) E.; m. Michelle Christine Therrien, July 16, 1977; children: Bryanna Michelle, Kevin Scott. BS, U. R.I.,

1976; PhD, Harvard U., 1981. Vis. scholar NCI Frederick (Md.) Cancer Research Facility, 1979-81; traveling scholar Pasteur Inst., Paris, 1978; rsch. fellow Miller Inst. U. Calif., Berkeley, 1981-83; asst. prof. Calif. Inst. Tech., Pasadena, 1983-89, assoc. prof., 1989—95; prof. cellular & molecular medicine U. Calif., San Diegor, 1995—; investigator Howard Hughes Medical Inst., 2002—. Contbr. articles to profl. jours. Named Presdl. Young Investigator NSF, 1985-90; Searle Scholars Program grantee, 1984-87. Fellow: Am. Acad. Arts & Sci.; mem.: AAAS, Genetics Soc. Am., Am. Soc. Cell Biology, Am. Soc. Microbiology, Phi Kappa Phi. Office: Howard Hughs Med Inst Div Cellular & Molecular Inst U Calif San Diego Sch Med La Jolla CA 92093-0668*

EMRICK, CHARLES ROBERT, JR., lawyer; b. Lakewood, Ohio, Dec. 19, 1929; s. Charles R. and Mildred (Hart) E.; m. Lizabeth Keating; children—Charles R. III, Caroline K. B.S., Ohio U., 1951, M.S., 1952; J.D., Cleve. State U., 1958. Bar: Ohio 1958. Ptnr. Calfee, Halter & Griswold, Cleve., 1965—2000, ret.; v.p. Transaction Group, Cleve., 2000-; lectr. U. Services Bus. Ctr., John Carroll U., 1970—; former Cleve. dir. Best Sand Co., Gt. Lakes Lithograph, Clamco Corp., Hunter Mfg. Co., Ken-Mac Metals, S & H Industries, Somerset Techs., Inc., Wedron-Silica Sand Co. Former trustee, br. bd. chmn. YMCA; former officer, trustee Lake Erie Jr. Nature and Sci. Ctr.; former adj. prof. Baldwin Wallace U.; adv. mem. Hartzell Propeller, Lake Erie Elec. Co., Bil-Jac Dog Food Co.; lectr. Chartered Life Underwriters Assn.; former adj. lectr. Case Western Res. U.; trustee Rocky River Pub. Library; trustee, treas. Cleve. Area Devel. Fin. Corp.; trustee Fairview Gen. Hosp., prin. enterprise bd. Cleve. Zool. Soc., Lake Ridge Acad.; former mem. nat. policy adv. com. New Eng. Mut. Life Ins. Co.; mem. vis. com. Cleve. State Law Sch.; bd. dirs. N.E. chpt. Am. Cancer Soc. Mem. Nat. Assn. Corp. Dirs. (sec., bd. dirs.); dir., adv. bd. Great Lakes Fastener LLC, Willow Hill Corp., Austin Capital, Westney Corp., C.E. White; trustee Ohio U. (bd. chair), ohio U. Found. (medal of merit, founders medal), O.U. Cutler Scholar bd.; dir. Cleve. Clinic Urology Inst., Cleve. Orch. Planned Giving Comm. Methodist. Clubs: Westwood Country (former sec., legal counsel), Union, Cleveland Yachting, The Clifton. Office: Calfee Halter & Griswold 800 Superior Ave E Ste 1800 Cleveland OH 44114-2688

EMSDEN, KATHARINE NICELY, history educator, researcher, writer; b. New York, NY, May 10, 1939; d. James Mount Nicely and Katharine Hendrick Terry; m. Leslie Clare Emsden (div.); children: Maya Asiano, Christopher, Pamela Lyons. BA in history, Swarthmore Coll., 1961; MA in english lit., U. Denver, 1981. Tchr. Douglas County Sch., Castle Rock, Colo., 1971—83, Colo. Acad., Denver, 1983—91, Shady Hill Sch., Cambridge, Mass., 1991—93; math head, reading specialist The Carroll Sch., Lincoln, Mass., 1993—95; dir. Marble Charter Sch., Marble, Colo., 1995—97; instr. in humanities Arapahoe Cmty. Coll., Littleton, Colo., 1998—99; dir. Francisco Ft. Mus., La Veta, Colo., 2002—05. Creator, dir. Denver's Autistic Daycare, 1972—73. Author: Trails West, 1992, The Way West, 1994, Tonty: Italian Lieutenant with La Salle on the Mississippi, 2005; editor: Coming to America: New Life in a New Land, 1995; writer, dir.: (one-act historical plays) Francisco Ft. Mus., 2001—02. Reading and writing instr. Canon City Prison, 1984—86; builder Habitat for Humanity, Alamosa, Colo., 2001—02; bd. mem. Friends of La Veta Pub. Libr., Huerfano County Hist. Assn., 2004—; chmn. PTA, Colo., 1974—75. Summer Reading grant, Nat. Endowment for the Humanities, 1992, Creative Arts grant, Rocky Mountain Women's Inst., 2000. Mem.: Am.-Italian Hist. Assn. Democrat. Home: PO Box 907 La Veta CO 81055 Office: Francisco Ft Mus 3065 Main La Veta CO 81055 Personal E-mail: katharineemsden@hotmail.com.

EMSLIE, WILLIAM ARTHUR, electrical engineer; b. Denver, Oct. 30, 1947; s. William Albert and Hazel Esther (Niles) E.; m. Tracey Jane Palmer, Feb 22, 1975; children: David Barrett, Andrew Niles, Charles William, Alexis Claire. BSEE, US Naval Acad., 1971; MSEE, Mich. State U., 1972. Registered profl. engr., Colo. Commd. ensign USN, 1971, advanced through grades to capt., 1997; commdg. officer 6 naval res. units USNR, 1978—2001; energy conversion engr. Pub. Svc. Co. of N.Mex., Albuquerque, 1978-79; mgr. engr. Horizon Tech., Ft. Collins, Colo., 1979-80; staff engr. Platte River Power Authority, Ft. Collins, 1980-85, planning supr., 1985-89, mgr. quality improvement, 1989-92, exec. engr., 1992-95, supr. engring. svcs., 1995-97, bus. planning mgr., 1997-2001, sr. project engr., constrn. mgr. GE Combustion Turbines, 2001—02, project engr., 2003—. Mem. renewable task force Electric Power Rsch. Inst., Palo Alto, Calif., 1982-85, mgt. com. Western Energy Supply and Transmission Assocs., Albuquerque, 1991-2000, vice chair, 1994-95, chair, 1996—; chmn. Am. Pub. Power Assn. Demonstration of Energy Efficient Devels. Bd., Washington, 1992-94; project engr. installation three Gen. Electric 7 EA combustion turbines Platte River Power Authority's Rawhide Energy Sta.; pres. Shamrock Irrigation Co., 1996—. Chmn. campaign Ft. Collins Area United Way, 1986, pres. bd. dirs., 1988; chmn. Sch. Mill Levy Tax Com., Ft. Collins, 1988. Grantee State of Colo., Am. Public Power Assn./Demonstration of Energy Efficient Devels., Western Energy Supply and Transmission Assocs., US Dept. Energy, City of Colorado Springs, 1986-90. Mem. IEEE, Foothills Rotary of Ft. Collins (pres. 1995-96), After Work Rotary. Achievements include research in photovaltics which provided a solar insolation assessment that is more accurate than the typical meterological year and a comprehensive evaluation of the effectiveness of 4 types of photovaltic systems; development of conceptual design and managing construction of Fair Winds Farm, a 36-acre farm equestrian facility and residence. Home: 825 E Pitkin St Fort Collins CO 80524-3839 Office: Platte River Power Auth 2000 E Horsetooth Rd Fort Collins CO 80525-5721 Personal E-mail: emslieb@frii.com.

ENARSON, HAROLD L., retired academic administrator; b. Villisca, Iowa, May 24, 1919; s. John and Hulda (Thorson) E.; m. Audrey Pitt., June 7, 1942; children: Merlyn Pitt Prentice, Elaine, Lisa. BA, U. N.Mex., 1940, L.H.D., 1981; MA, Stanford U., 1946; PhD, Am. U., 1951; L.H.D., Kent State U., 1972, U. Detroit, 1975, Ohio State U., 1981; D.P.S., Bethany Coll., 1975; LL.D., Miami U., Oxford, Ohio, 1978, U. Akron, 1981, Central State U., 1981; Dr. Pub. Service (hon.), U. W. Fla., 1986; LLD (hon.), SUNY, 1987; LHD (hon.), Cleve. State U., 1990, U. Nebr., CCNY, 1993; HHD, No. Mich. U., 1993. Teaching asst., research asst. Stanford U., 1940-41, asst. prof., 1949-50; examiner Bur. Budget, Washington, 1942-43, 46-49; asst. prof. Whittier Coll., 1949; exec. sec. Steel Industry Bd., summer 1949; cons. Nat. Security Resources Bd., summer 1950; spl. asst. White House, Washington, 1950-52; pub. mem. WSB, 1952-53; asst. dir. commerce City Phila., 1953; exec. sec. mayor Phila., 1954; exec. dir. Western Interstate Commn. Higher Edn., 1954-60, sr. advisor, 1981-99; adminstrv. v.p. U. N.Mex., 1960-61, acad. v.p., 1961-66, past project dir.; Internships in Latin Am.; pres. Cleve. State U., 1966-72, Ohio State U., Columbus, 1972-81, pres. emeritus, 1981—; Carl Hatch chair pub. adminstrn. U. N.Mex., 1982-83; Regents' prof. U. Calif., San Francisco, spring 1984. Carnegie Corp. adminstrs. fellowship, 1958; mem. Nat. Dental Research Council, 1958-62, surgeon gen.'s cons. group on med. manpower, 1960; cons. Ford Found., Egypt, 1960, C.Am., 1961-63, AID, 1965; dir. edn. svcs. Office Human Resources and Social Devel., 1963-64; nat. adv. health coun. USPHS, 1964-68, task force on reorgn., 1967, Nat. Com. on U.S.-China Rels., 1976—, Nat. Commn. for Coop. Edn., 1968-78, adv. com. U.S. Army Command and Gen. Staff Coll., 1975-78; planning com. Coun. for Fin. Aid to Edn., 1977-81; panelist nat. identification program for advancement women in higher edn. Am. Coun. on Edn., 1977-80, commn. on internat. edn., 1965-67, past mem. commn. on acad. affairs, coun. overseas liaison com., 1977-80, bd. dirs., 1970-73, 79-82; chmn. Inter-Univ. Coun. Ohio, 1979-80; sr. cons. Kellogg Nat. Fellows program W.K. Kellogg Found., 1981-85; pub. mem. U.S. Med. Licensing Exams., 1991-94. Trustee Am. Coll. Testing Program, 1979-82; mem. Nat. Coun. on Ednl. Rsch., 1980-81; mem. nat. sponsors com. Coun. for Internat. Exch. of Scholars, 1981-84; co-chmn. Com. on Future of SUNY, 1984; bd. visitors Air U., 1968-70; chmn. bd. dirs. Acad. Ind. Scholars, 1984-88. With AUS, 1943-46. Recipient Disting. Svc. award Pub. Sector, Assn. of Governing Bds. of Univs. and Colls., 1992. Mem. Nat. Assn. State Univs. and Land-Grant Colls. (chmn. internat. affairs com., mem. com. on financing higher edn., commn. on arts and scis. 1978, chmn. assn. and exec. com. 1980-81), Coun. of Presidents (chmn. 1978-79, mem. exec. com. 1978-79), Nat. Acad. Pub. Adminstrn., Assn. Urban Univs. (pres. 1971-72), Assn. Am. Univs. (health policy joint com. 1978-88), Am. Optometric Assn. (coun. on optometric edn. 1984-88), Rotary. Home: 2994 Nogales Ct Boulder CO 80301-1518

ENBERG, DICK, sportscaster; m. Barbara Enberg; 6 children. Grad., Cen. Mich. U., 1957; PhD in Health Sci., Ind. U., 1961. Asst. prof., asst. baseball coach Calif. State U., Northridge, 1961-65; sportscaster, 1965—; with NBC Sports, N.Y.C., 1975—. Spokesperson: GTE Acad. All-Am. Program, 1985—. Sportscaster: Super Bowl (5 times), Rose Bowl (9 times), Orange Bowl (4 times), World Series, Am. and Nat. League Playoffs (3 times), French Open (8 times), Wimbledon (13 times), NCAA Basketball Finals (5 times), Heavyweight Boxing Championships (3 times), NBA Playoffs (2 times), NBA All-Star Game, Olympic Games (3 times), and many others; former host nat. series: Sports Challenge; co-prodr.: The Way It Was, PBS (Emmy award 1978); author, (non-fiction) Oh, My! 50 Years of Rubbing Shoulders with Greatness, 2004. Bd. trustees Suomi Coll., Ind. U., State of Calif. C.C. Recipient Calif. Sportscaster of Yr. award Nat. Sportscasters and Sportswriters Assn., 1967-68, 70, 73, 79-81, Local Emmy award, 1974, Sportscaster Emmy award 1981, 83, 90, Sports Writer Emmy award, 1988, Eclipse award, 1984, Ronald Reagon Media award, Victor award, NFL Press Box award, 1989; named Tennis Play-by-Play Man of Yr., Tennis Mag., 1989, Disting. Alumnus, Ctrl. Mich. U., Disting. Alumnus, Ind. U. Office: care NBC Sports 30 Rockefeller Plz New York NY 10112-0002*

ENCARNACION, JOSE M. IZQUIERDO, Secretary of State Puerto Rico; Sec. transp. and pub. works Puerto Rico, sec. of state, 2004—, acting gov., 2004. Pres. Am. Concrete Inst., Farmington Hills, Mich., 2003. Office: Secretary of State PO Box 9023271 San Juan PR 00902-2121

END, WILLIAM THOMAS, marketing executive; b. Milw., Oct. 31, 1947; s. Jack Arthur and Cecil (O'Brien) E.; m. Nancy Kolb, June 10, 1969 (div. 1974); 1 child, Laura; m. Elyse Soucy, Feb. 23, 1980; children— Alison, David BA, Boston Coll., 1969; student, U. Vienna, Austria, 1967-68; MBA, Harvard U., 1971. Group product mgr. Gillette Toiletries, Boston, 1971-75; exec. v.p. L.L. Bean, Inc., Freeport, Maine, 1975-90, Lands' End, Inc., Dodgeville, Wis., 1991-92, pres., CEO, 1992-95; chmn., CEO Cornerstone Brands Inc., Portland, Maine, 1995—, also bd. dirs. Bd. dirs. Hannaford Bros. Co., Scarborough, Maine, Ariel, Inc., Augusta, Maine, Cinmar, Cin., Travel Smith, San Rafael, Calif., Internat. Cornerstone Group, The Territory Ahead, Santa Barbara, Calif., Garnet Hill, Franconia, N.H., Ballard Designs, Atlanta. Republican. Roman Catholic. Avocations: hunting, fishing, camping, canoeing, skiing. Home: PO Box 339 34 Castle Rd South Freeport ME 04078 Office: Cornerstone Brands Group Inc 5568 W Chester Rd West Chester OH 45069-2914

ENDAHL, ETHELWYN MAE, elementary education educator, consultant; b. Duluth, Minn., May 27, 1922; d. Herman and Florence Jenny (Mattson) Johnson; m. John Charles Endahl Sr., Nov. 27, 1943; children: Merrilee Jean, Marsha Louise, John Charles Jr., Kimberly Ann. BS in Library Science, U. Minn., Mpls., 1943; MA in Edn., Fairfield U., 1978; attended, Elmhurst (Ill.) Coll., 1966-68, U. Bridgeport, Conn., 1981-83, Northeastern U., Martha's Vineyard, Mass., 1982-85, U. Conn., 1971. Cert. Tchr. Conn. Librarian children's hosp. Davenport (Iowa) Pub. Library, 1943-44; librarian Omaha (Nebr.) Pub. Library, 1944; tchr. 4th gr. Center Elem. Sch., New Canaan, Conn., 1968-81, writing coord., 1981-83; staff devel. Dept. Edn. State of Conn., 1986-88; writing coord. East Elem. Sch., New Canaan, 1986-88; instr. Grad. Sch. Edn. Simmons Coll., Boston, 1989. Leader Reminiscence Writing Courtland Gardens Nursing Home, Stamford, Conn., 1985-86; leader adult writing group Charlotte Hobbs Library, Lovell, Maine, 1987-89; leader writing process-children's group Cmty. Ctr., Boca Grande, Fla., 1994; cons. writing process Banyan Elem. Sch., Sunrise, Fla., 1995-96; writing tchr. John Knox Village Retirement Ctr. Mem. AAUW, Nat. League of Pen Women, Older Women's League. Democrat. Quaker. Avocations: women's studies, book groups, writing groups, hiking, writing classes at John Knox Village. Home: 528 Village Dr Pompano Beach FL 33060-7718 Personal E-mail: ettaend@aol.com.

ENDELMAN, SHARON JEAN, librarian; b. Detroit, Apr. 11, 1948; d. Clarence Richard and Elsa Albertina (Beutler) Bice; m. Gary Edward Endelman, June 3, 1973; children: Heather Miriam (dec.), Jonathan Charles, Gabriela Tamar. BA in History, Kalamazoo Coll., 1970; MA in History, Brown U., 1972, PhD in History, 1976; MLS, Emory U., 1980. Teaching fellow in history Brown U., Providence, 1974-75; asst. prof. history Paine Coll., Augusta, Ga., 1976-79; asst. archivist Houston Pub. Library, 1979-80, social scis. librarian, 1980; coord. materials selection Houston Pub. Libr., 1985-88; serial records librarian U. Houston, 1980-82, head current jours. dept., 1982-83, head reference dept., 1983-85. Research advisor Houston Women's History Project, 1985-88; mem. collection devel. com. Houston Area Research Libr. Consortium, 1985-88. Contbr. articles to profl. jours. Pres. Greater Houston chpt. SIDS Alliance; mem. bd. edn. Robert M. Beren Acad., 2000-02; bd. dirs. United Orthodox Synagogues, 2001-02. Recipient fellowship U.S. Dept. Def., 1971-74. Mem. ALA (standards and guidelines com. reference and adult services div. 1983-86), Serial Forum (vice chair, chair 1983-85), Assn. Research Libraries (steering com. collection analysis project at U. Houston 1983-85), Alpha Lambda Delta, Phi Beta Kappa, Beta Phi Mu. Democrat. Jewish. Home and Office: 4418 Osby Dr Houston TX 77096-4423

ENDERS, ALLEN COFFIN, anatomy educator; b. Wooster, Ohio, Aug. 5, 1928; s. Robert Kendal and Abbie Gertrude (Crandell) E.; m. Alice Hay, June 15, 1950 (div. Dec. 1975); children: Robert H., George C., Richard S., Gregory H.; m. Sandra Jean Schlafke, Aug. 5, 1976. AB, Swarthmore Coll., 1950; AM, Harvard U., 1952, PhD, 1955. From asst. prof. to assoc. prof Rice Inst., Houston, 1954-63; from assoc. prof. to prof. Washington U., St. Louis, 1963-75; prof., chmn. dept. human anatomy U. Calif., Davis, 1976-86, prof. cell biology and human anatomy, 1986—. Cons. NIH, Bethesda, Md., 1964-68, 70-73, 76-80, 83-93. Author: (with others) Bailey's Microscopic Anatomy, 1984; editor: Delayed Implantation, 1964; contbr. numerous articles on anatomy and reproduction to profl. jours. Nat. pres. Perinatal Rsch. Soc., 1981. Grantee NIH, 1959-99. Fellow AAAS; mem. Am. Assn. Anatomists (v.p. 1980-82, pres. 1983-84), Pioneer Reprodn. Res. Home: 39707 Barry Rd Davis CA 95616-9415 Office: U Calif Sch Medicine Cell Biology & Anatomy Davis CA 95616

ENDERS, ANTHONY TALCOTT, banker; b. Hartford, Conn., June 22, 1937; s. Ostrom and Alice (Talcott) E.; m. Elizabeth McGuire, June 9, 1962; children: Charles, Alexandra, Camilla, Ostrom. AB, Harvard U., 1959, MBA, 1962. With Brown Bros. Harriman & co., 1962—, asst. mgr., Boston, 1967-69, dep. mgr., 1969-73, mgr., Boston, London, N.Y.C., 1973-81, ptnr., N.Y.C., 1981-95, mng. ptnr., 1995—; exec. dir. Brown Harriman & Internat. Banks, Ltd., London, 1973-77, now mng. ptnr., CEO. Trustee Conn. Coll., New London, 1967-73, Bryn Mawr (Pa.) Coll., 1986—. Office: Brown Bros Harriman & Co 59 Wall St New York NY 10005-2808

ENDERS, ELIZABETH MCGUIRE, artist; b. New London, Conn., Feb. 18, 1939; d. Francis Foran and Helen Cuseck (Connolly) McGuire; m. Anthony Talcott Enders, June 9, 1962; children: Charles Talcott, Alexandra Eustis, Camilla, Ostrom II. BA, Conn. Coll., 1962; MA, NYU, 1987. Trustee Artists Space, N.Y.C., 1986-95, Conn. Coll., New London, 1988-93; assoc. dept. prints and illustrated books Mus. Modern Art, 1993—, Lyman Allyn Art Mus., 1994—. One-woman shows include Paul Schuster Gallery, Cambridge, Mass., 1966, Ulysses Gallery, N.Y.C., 1992, 1994, Lyman Allyn Art Mus., New London, Conn., 1994, Charles Cowles Gallery, N.Y.C., 1995, Norbert Considine Gallery, Princeton, N.J., 1997, Artists Space, N.Y.C., 2001, Charles Shain Libr., Conn. Coll., 2004, Real Art Ways, Hartford, Conn., 2004, exhibited in group shows at Boston Symphony Orch., 1982, NYU, 1983, Conn. Coll., 1988, Bronx Coun. on Arts, 1990—91, Addison Gallery Am. Art, 1993, Angel Art, LA, 1993, Lyman Allyn Art Mus., New London, Conn., 1994—95, 1998, 1999, So. Alleghenies Mus. Art, Loretto, Pa., 1994, Artists Space Multiple, 1995, New Mus. Contemporary Art, N.Y.C., 1995, Denise Bibro Fine Art, 1995, 1998, N.Y. Studio Sch., 1995, 2002, Divine Design '95, LA, Spring Benefit Raffle, Sculpture Ctr., N.Y.C., 1996, 1997, 1998, 2000, 2003, 2004, 2005, Charles Cowles Gallery, 1996, 1998, 2000, 2001, 2002, 2003, Fax Art Week, Copenhagen, Assn. Danish Graphic Artists, 1996, Open Studio, Downtown Arts Festival, N.Y.C., 1997, 1998, Dieu Donne Papermill, 1997, 1999, 2001, Robert Brown Gallery, Wash. D.C., 1999, 2001, 2002, 2003, 2004, NY Acad. of Art Benefit Auction, 1999, Cooley Gallery, Old Lyme, Conn., 1999, 2002, (Benefit for the Nature Conservancy), Nielsen Gallery, Boston, 2001, Artwalk, Coalition for the Homeless, 2001, Pfizer Inc., 2004, 2005, traveling group show Artists Space, 1992, 1994, Southeastern Ctr. Contemporary Art, Winston-Salem, N.C., 1993, Allentown (Pa.) Art Mus., 1994, Cleve. Ctr. Contemporary Art, 1994, Salt Lake Art Ctr., Salt Lake City, 1995, Kemper Ctr. Contemporary Art and Design, Kansas City, Mo., 1996, Bass Mus. of Art, Miami Beach, Fla., 1997, Flint (Mich.) Inst. Arts, 1998, Blaffer Gallery, U. Houston, Tex., 1998, Contemporary Art Ctr., Va. Beach, 1998, Tampa Mus. of Art, 1998—99, Art Mus. of Southeast Tex., 1999, Fresno Metropolitan Mus., Calif., 2000, www.sfnbotanicalart.com, 2003, 2004, 2005, Represented in permanent collections Addison Gallery of Am. Art, Andover, Mass., Graham Gund, Cambridge, Dow Jones, N.Y.C., Agnes Gund, Lyman Allyn Art Mus., Conn. Coll., New London, Pfizer Inc., Wadsworth Atheneum, Hartford, Conn. Recipient Citation of Appreciation, Conn. Coll., 1990, medal, 1993. Mem. The Bklyn. Mus., Contemporary Art Coun. Home: 530 E 86th St New York NY 10028-7535 E-mail: eenders3@earthlink.net.

ENDERS, WALTER, economics professor; m. Linda Enders. BA, U. Toledo, 1969, MA, 1970; MPhil, Columbia U., 1974, PhD in Economics, 1975. Asst. prof. Iowa State U., 1974—79, assoc. prof., 1979—85, prof., 1985—96, U. prof., 1996—2000; prof. U. Ala., Tuscaloosa, 2000—, Lee Bidgood Chair of Economics and Fin. Vis. asst. prof. McGill U., 1980—81; vis. scholar/assoc. prof. U. Calif., San Diego, 1985—86, vis. scholar, 1995—96; vis. prof. U. Glasgow, 1990—91, Queensland U. of Tech., 2000, U. Tech., Sydney, 2001; external assessor U. Pertanian, Malaysia, 1987—96; short-term cons. to World Bank, 2002; mem. editl. bd. Jour. Internat. Econ. Integration, Jour. Internat. Fin.; editl. coun. Rev. Internat. Economics. Co-author (with Harvey E. Lapan): International Economics: Theory and Policy, 1987; author: Applied Econometric Time-Series, 1995, RATS Handbook for Applied Econometrics, 1996. Co-recipient Estes Award for Behavioral Rsch. Relevant to the Prevention of Nuclear War, NAS, 2003—06; grantee NSF. Office: Dept Economics Fin and Legal Studies Culverhouse Coll Commerce U Ala Tuscaloosa AL 35487-0024 Office Phone: 205-348-8972. Office Fax: 205-348-0590. E-mail: wenders@cba.ua.edu.*

ENDICOTT, WILLIAM F., journalist; b. Harrodsburg, Ky., Aug. 26, 1935; s. William O. and Evelyn E.; m. Mary Frances Thomas, Dec. 27, 1956; children: Gene, Fran, Greg. Student, Am. U., 1955; BA in Polit. Sci., Transylvania U., 1957. With Lexington (Ky.) Leader, 1957; sports writer Louisville Courier-Jour., 1958-62; reporter Tulare (Calif.) Advance-Register, 1963; reporter, city editor Modesto (Calif.) Bee, 1963-66; city editor Sacramento Union, 1966-67; with Los Angeles Times, 1968-85; Capitol bur. chief Sacramento Bee, 1985-95, asst. mng. editor, 1995-98, dep. mng. editor, 1998-2000, ret. Hearst vis. prof. U. Tex., 1993. Served with USMCR, 1957-58. Recipient various journalism awards Disting. Alumnus award Transylvania U., 1980 Episcopalian.

ENDRENYI, JANOS, research engineer, educator; b. Budapest, Hungary, Nov. 9, 1927; came to Can., 1957; s. Sandor and Lilly (Szegvari) E.; m. Edith Bernat, Dec. 5, 1956. Diploma in Engring., Tech. U., Budapest, 1951; MASc, U. Waterloo, Ont., Can., 1965; PhD, U. Toronto, Ont., 1972. Registered profl. engr., Ont., Can. Tchg. asst. Tech. U., Budapest, 1949—52; rsch. engr. Rsch. Inst. for Electric Power, Budapest, 1952-56; engr. Toronto Hydro, 1957-59; rsch. engr. rsch. divsn. Ont. Hydro, Toronto, 1959-79, head reliability and stats. sect., 1979-90, prin. rsch. engr., 1990-92, prin. scientist emeritus, 1992—. Lectr. U. Toronto, 1972-80, adj. assoc. prof., 1980-83, adj. prof., 1983—; spkr. at seminars worldwide. Author: Electric Shock Prevention (in Hungarian), 1956, Reliability Modeling in Electric Power Systems, 1978 (translated into Russian and Chinese); contbr. papers to profl. jours. Fellow IEEE; mem. Toronto Mozart Soc. (pres. 2001—). Home: 80 Front St E Apt 201 Toronto ON Canada M5E 1T4 Office: Kinectrics Inc 800 Kipling Ave Toronto ON Canada M8Z 6C4 Business E-Mail: john.endrenyi@utoronto.ca.

ENDRES, ARTHUR P. (SKIP ENDRES), rail transportation executive; BA, Univ. Md.; JD, Cath. Univ. Sch. of Law. Held various positions in house com. including staff dir. of the full com., House Judiciary Com., exec. dir. and gen. counsel Congl. Commn. on Internat. Migration and Coop. Econ. Devel., 1970—94; majority staff dir. sub com. on transp. and hazardous material House Energy and Commerce Com.; spl. coun. to the sub com. on Commerce and Consumer Protection; asst. v.p. govtl. affairs Burlington No. Santa Fe, 1994—96, v.p. govtl. affairs, 1996—. Office: Burlington Northern Santa Fe Corp 2650 Lou Menk Dr 2nd Fl PO Box 961057 Fort Worth TX 76161-0057

ENDRES, LORAINE KATHRYN, gynecologist, obstetrician; b. Dayton, Ohio, June 7, 1969; MD, Ohio State U., Columbus, 1995. Diplomate Am. Bd. Maternal-Fetal Medicine, Am. Bd. Ob-Gyn. Residency U. Pa., Phila., 1995—99; fellowship Northwestern U., Chgo., 1999—2002; asst. prof. U. Ill., Chgo., 2002—. Office: Univ Ill Chgo MC 808 820 S Wood St Chicago IL 60612 Office Phone: 312-996-7300. Office Fax: 312-996-4238. E-mail: lendres@uic.edu.

ENDRISS, MARILYN JEAN, lawyer; b. New Haven, June 27, 1953; BA, Duke U., 1975; JD, Golden Gate U., 1981. Bar: Wash. 1981, U.S. Dist. Ct. (we. dist.) Wash., U.S. Ct. Appeals (9th cir.) 1990. Staff atty. N.W. Women's Law Ctr., Seattle, 1981-82; pvt. practice Seattle, 1982-83; legal advisor Seattle Human Rights Dept., 1984, mgr. enforcement divsn., 1984-87; assoc. Law Office Judith Lonnquist, Seattle, 1987-90; prin. Endriss & Shear, PS, Seattle, 1990-95; pvt. practice Seattle, 1995-99; adminstrv. judge U.S. Equal Employment Opportunity Commn., 1999—. Mem. Wash. State Supreme Ct. Pattern Jury Instrn. Com., 1997-2000. Mem. King County Affirmative Action Adv. Com., Seattle, 1986-88; mem. Edmonds Sch. Dist. Citizens Planning Com., 1993-99, chair 1994-96. Mem. ABA (labor and employment law and ind. rights and responsibilities sects., plaintiff contact Seattle EEOC/ABA joint tng. initiative program 1999—), Nat. Women and the Law Assn. (bd. dirs. 1985-86, mem. steering com. various confs.), Seattle-King County Bar Assn. (labor law sect.), Nat. Employment Lawyers Assn., Wash. Employment Lawyers Assn. (chair 1993-99), Wash. Women Lawyers, Wash. State Bar Assn. (mem. civil rights com. 1987-90, chairperson 1989-90), Wash. State Trial Lawyers (employment law sect.), N.W. Women's Law Ctr. (mem. legal com. 1981-89, bd. dirs. 1983-87, pres. 1985-87). Office: US Equal Employment Opportunity Commn Seattle Dist Office 909 1st Ave Ste 400 Seattle WA 98104-3626

ENDRIZ, JOHN GUIRY, retired electronics executive; b. Oak Park, Ill., Jan. 10, 1942; s. John Daniel and Florence (Guiry) E.; m. Sally Jean Doubleday, July 19, 1975. BSEE, MSEE, MIT, 1965; PhD in EE, Stanford U., 1970. Guest rschr. Linkoping (Sweden) U., 1970-72; project mgr. R.C.A. Rsch. Lab., Princeton, N.J., 1972-77; engring. mgr. Varian Assocs., Palo Alto, Calif., 1977-88; v.p. engring. S.D.L., Inc., San Jose, Calif., 1988-97, v.p. power delivery bus. unit, 1997-99; ret., 2002. Contbr. 53 articles to profl. jours.; patentee more than 30 inventions. Home: 5 Heritage Ct Belmont CA 94002-2944

ENDSLEY, DONAL E., architectural firm executive; Degree, George Washington U. Lic. Calif., Ariz., Nev. Sr. v.p. HMC Group, Ontario, Calif., 1972—, prin., 1972—. Mem.: AIA, Nat. Coun. Archtl. Registration Bds. Office: HMC Group 3270 Inland Empire Blvd Ontario CA 91764-4854

ENDY, DREW, science educator; Studied civil, environ., biochemical engring., Lehigh U., Thayer Sch., Dartmouth Coll. Helped establish Molecular Sciences Inst., Berkeley, Calif., 1998—2001; fellow, dept. biology and biol. engring. divsn MIT, Cambridge, Mass., 2002, joined, 2004—, asst. prof., biological engring. divsn. Co-founded MIT Synthetic Biology Working Group, Registry of Standard Biol. Parts; organized First Internat. Conf. on Synthetic Biology; taught 2003 and 2004 MIT Synthetic Biology Labs; organized Synthetic Biology Competition, 2004; lectr. in field. Contbr. articles to profl. jours. Nominee Rave award in Science, WIRED, 2005. Office: MIT Biological Engring 31 Ames St 68-580a Cambridge MA 02139 Address: MIT Biological Engring 31 Ames St 68-564d Cambridge MA 02139 Office Phone: 617-258-5152. Business E-Mail: endy@mit.edu.

ENENBACH, MARK HENRY, community action agency executive, educator; b. Chgo., July 28, 1949; s. Joseph Henry and Antonette Regina (Kasko) E.; children: Joy Elizabeth, Erin Regina; m. Kai Lindquist Bergin, Sept. 28, 1985; 1 child, Faith Marie. BA in Polit. Sci. with honors, Loyola U., Chgo., 1971, MA in Urban Studies with honors, 1973. Cmty. resource specialist Model Cities, Chgo., 1974—79; grad. prof. Govs. State U., Park Forest South, Ill., 1977—89; dir. energy program City of Chgo., 1980—83; prof. St. Augustine's Coll., Chgo., 1981—82; coord. cmty. svcs. Dept. Human Svcs., Chgo., 1984—91; prof. urban planning and pub. adminstrn. DePaul U., Chgo., 1987—; dir. cmty. svcs. block grant programs Cmty. and Econ. Devel. Assn. Cook County, Inc., Chgo., 1992—96, v.p./COO, 1997—; CEO CEDA Neighborhood Devel. Corp., Chgo., 2000—05. Mem. adv. bd. City Colls. Chgo., 1984-88; spkr. Nat. Headstart Assn., Washington, 1995; mem. task force Ill. Dept. Commerce and Cmty. Affairs, Springfield, 1996—; spkr. Nat. Assn. Cmty. Action Agys., 1996-2000, Nat. Assn. State Cmty. Svcs. Programs, 2000. Pres. Lincoln Park Interagy. Coun., Chgo., 1986-91; mem. adv. bd. Salvation Army, Chgo., 1987-91. Grad. rsch. fellow Loyola U., 1972-73. Mem. Nat. Assn. Cmty. Action Agys., Ill. Assn. Cmty. Action Agys. Avocations: urban research, writing and travel in over 40 countries. Office: Cmty and Econ Devel Assn 208 S Lasalle St Ste 1900 Chicago IL 60604-1119 Business E-Mail: menebach@cedaorg.net.

ENFIELD, DONALD MICHAEL, insurance company executive; b. LA, Jan. 24, 1945; s. Fred Donald Jr. and Suzanne Arden (Hinkle) Enfield; children: Susan Ann, Michael David, Peter Christian. BA in Polit. Sci., U. San Francisco, 1967. Mgmt. trainee Marsh & McLennan, Inc., San Francisco, 1967-70, acct. exec., 1970-77, asst. v.p., 1977-79, v.p., 1979-81, sr. v.p., 1981-82, mng. dir., 1982-89; chmn., CEO Frank B. Hall & Co. of No. Calif., San Francisco, 1989-92; founder, chmn., CEO Metro/Risk, Inc., San Francisco, 1992—. Cons. in field. Contbr. articles to profl. jours. Bd. dirs. Ronald McDonald Ho., San Francisco, 1989—92, Philharmonica Baroque Orch., San Francisco, 2003—; chmn. bd. dirs. Midsummer Mozart Festival, San Francisco, 1985—90; trustee Lamplighters Music Theater, 1996—2003. Mem.: Wine Adv. San Francisco (founder), San Francisco C. of C. (dir. bus./arts coun. 1987—93), Club des Oenophiles Gastronome de Paris (dep. pres. 2000—), Olympic Club San Francisco, City Club of San Francisco, Lotus Club N.Y., Soc. Calif. Pioneers (county v.p. 1974—). Avocation: classical music. Office: Metro/Risk Inc 153 Townsend St San Francisco CA 94107 Office Phone: 415-249-0111. E-mail: enfield@metrorisk.com.

ENG, CATHERINE, health facility administrator, physician; b. Hong Kong, May 20, 1950; came to U.S., 1953; d. Doi Kwong and Alice (Yee) E.; m. Daniel Charles Chan; 1 child, Michael B. BA, Wellesley Coll., 1972; MD, Columbia U., 1976. Diplomate Am. Bd. Internal Medicine, Am. Bd. Gastroenterology; cert. added qualifications geriat. Intern in internal medicine Presbyterian Hosp./Columbia U., Presbyterian Med. Ctr., 1976-77, resident in internal medicine, 1977-79; fellow in gastroenterology/hepatology N.Y. Hosp./Cornell U. Med. Coll., 1979-81; instr. medicine Cornell U. Coll. Medicine, NYC, 1980-81; staff physician On Lok Sr. Health Svcs., San Francisco, 1981-86, supervising physician, 1986-91, med. dir., 1992—. Asst. clin. prof. dept. family and cmty. medicine U. Calif., San Francisco, 1986-95, asst. clin. prof. dept. medicine, 1992-95, assoc. clin. prof. dept. medicine, 1995-2001, clin. prof. medicine, 2001—; primary care specialist Program of All-inclusive Care for the Elderly, San Francisco, 1987-94; asst. chief dept. medicine Chinese Hosp., San Francisco, 1993-98, chmn. com. credentials, 1994—. Instr. BLS Am. Heart Assn., San Francisco, 1988-92; mem. nominating com. YWCA of Marin, San Francisco, San Mateo, 1991-95; mem. mgmt. com. YWCA-Chinatown/North Beach, San Francisco, 1989-95; bd. dirs. Chinatown Cmty. Children's Ctr., San Francisco, 1987-90. Durant scholar Wellesley Coll., 1972. Fellow ACP; mem. Am. Geriat. Soc., Am. Soc. Aging, Am. Gastroent. Assn., Calif. Med. Assn. (assoc.), San Francisco Med. Soc. (assoc.), Sigma Xi, Alpha Omega Alpha. Avocations: reading, hiking. Home: 130 Dorchester Way San Francisco CA 94127-1110 Office: On Lok Sr Health Scvs 1333 Bush St San Francisco CA 94109-5691 Office Phone: 415-292-8886. E-mail: cathy@onlok.org.

ENG, HOLLY S.A., lawyer; b. 1966; BA in English & Econ., St. Cloud State Univ., 1989; JD, Georgetown Univ., 1993. Bar: Minn. 1993. Atty. Dorsey & Whitney LLP, Mpls., 1993—2001, ptnr., labor, employment practice group, 2001—; spl. assignment Mpls. City Atty. Off., 1997. Guardian ad Litem Minn. Guardian ad Litem Program; instr. Univ. St. Thomas Grad. Sch. Bus., 1999—2001. Grantee Nat. Lawyer's Guild Fellowship, Georgetown Univ. Mem.: Minn. Women Lawyers. Office: Dorsey & Whitney LLP Ste 1500 50 S Sixth St Minneapolis MN 55402-1498 Office Phone: 612-343-2164. Office Fax: 612-340-2868. Business E-Mail: eng.holly@dorsey.com.

ENG, MAMIE, librarian; b. Oceanside, NY, May 21, 1954; d. Yen Wah and Hong Lew (Lum) Eng. BA in History and Edn., Vassar Coll., 1976; MS in Libr. Sci., Columbia U., 1977, MA in Ednl. Psychology, 1979. Asst. dir. Henry Waldinger Meml. Libr., Valley Stream, NY, 1979—. Recipient Excellence award, LDA Publishers, 2004. Mem.: ALA, Internat. Reading Assn. (bd. dirs. Manhattan coun. 1985—90), Suffolk County Libr. Assn., N.Y. Libr. Assn., Nassau County Libr. Assn. (hon.; editor assn. newsletter 1985—88, divsn. pres. 1986—87, bd. dirs. 1988—89, editor assn. newsletter 1989—92, pres. elect 1992, pres. 1993, editor assn. newsletter 1994—, divsn. pres. 1999, editor salary schedules and pers. benefits publ. 2001—, media svcs. divsn. pres. 2002, v.p., young adult svcs. divsn. pres. 2004), Reading reform Found., Phi Delta Kappa. Avocations: flower arranging, reading, flowers. Office: Henry Waldinger Meml Libr 60 Verona Pl Valley Stream NY 11580-5468 Office Phone: 516-825-6422. Personal E-mail: hwmlcontact@hotmail.com.

ENG, VINCENT ADRIAN, lawyer; b. Vandenburg AFB, Calif., Dec. 30, 1970; s. Vincent K. and Candy T. (Choung) Eng; m. Claudia Ann Lewis, Apr. 5, 1997. BA, Brandeis U., 1992; MS, JD, Am. U., 1995. Bar: Md., U.S. Supreme Ct. Atty., advisor U.S. Dept. Justice, Washington, 1995-97; mgr. legal divsn. Bernan Assocs., Lanham, Md., 1997-2000; mgr. Almanac and directory pub. Almanac Pub., Washington, 1998-99; mgr. Benan Press, 1999; legal dir. Nat. Asian Pacific Am. Legal Consortium, Washington, 2000—. Mem. U.S. Dept. Justice Atty. Gen.'s com. pro bono, Washington, 1996—97; adj. prof. law Washington Coll. Law Am. U., Washington, 1997—; dir. Bernan Press, Bernan Assocs. Editor: (book) Bernan's Case Summaries: Maryland Criminal Law, 1997, Bernan's Case Summaries: Maryland Jury Instructions, 1998, The Almanac of the Executive Branch, 2000, 2001, Biographical Directory of the Federal Judiciary: 1779-2000, 2001; author: Sanctions, Sentencing and Corrections, 2002. Mem.: John Sherman Myers Soc., Md. State Bar Assn., Md. Trial Lawyers Assn., Brandeis U. Alumni Assn. (mem. coun. 1997—). Avocation: automobiles. Office: Nat Asian Pacific Am Legal Consortium Ste 1200 1140 Connecticut Ave NW Washington DC 20036*

ENGBER, CHERYL ANN, retired language educator, linguist; b. East Chicago, Ind., Oct. 12, 1945; d. James Ward and Beryl Ann (Crowe) Biddle; m. Michael David Engber, Nov. 25, 1967; children: Sara Ann, Kimberly Sue. BA in Spanish with honors, Ind. U., 1967, PhD in Linguistics, 1992, MA in Spanish, 1974; MA in Tchg. ESL, Ball State U., 1979. Instr. Spanish Anderson (Ind.) U., 1979-82; assoc. instr. intensive English program Ind. U., Bloomington, 1983-86, adminstrv. asst. com. for R & D, 1989-91, instr. semi-intensive English program, 1991-93; assoc. prof. linguistics Truman State U., Kirksville, Mo., 1993—2004; ret., 2004; adminstrv. asst. Rotary Club, Bloomington, 2005—. Instr. ESL Ind. U., Kuala Lumpur, Malaysia, 1985—86; grader for Test of Written English Ednl. Testing Svc., Princeton, NJ, 1989—98, reader for AP exams, 2001—03; asst. to editor Studies in Second Lang. Acquisition Ind. U., 1987—89; spkr. in field. Contbr. Understanding English: A Listening Approach to ESL, 1983; contbr. articles to profl. jours. Founder Muncie (Ind.) Internat. Ctr., 1974; vol. tchr., founder internat. summer workshops for children, Muncie, 1977; deacon, elder, mem. com. First Christian Ch., Bloomington, Ind., 1987-92, 2004—. Ind. U. fellow, 1982; Truman State U. grantee, 1994, 2001. Mem. Linguistic Soc. Am., Tchrs. ESL, Am. Assn. for Applied Linguistics, Phi Beta Kappa, Phi Kappa Phi Avocations: travel, gourmet cooking, master gardener. Home: 4672 Compton Blvd Bloomington IN 47401 Personal E-mail: cmengber@att.net.

ENGDAHL, TODD PHILIP, editor; b. Jamestown, N.Y., Feb. 8, 1950; s. George Philip and Janice Marie (Wallin) E.; m. Caroline C.N. Schomp, Dec. 29, 1973; children: Anders Justus Schomp, Mats Philip Schomp. BA, Pomona Coll., 1971; MS, Northwestern U., 1972. Reporter Oregonian, Portland, 1972-75; reporter Denver Post, 1975-80, asst. city editor, 1980-83, night city editor, 1983-85, Sunday editor, 1985-86, city editor, 1986-90, exec. city editor, 1990-95; editor DenverPost.com, 1995—2003; perspective editor Denver Post, 2003—. Lectr. journalism Portland State U., 1974. Democrat. Lutheran. Avocations: reading, gardening, woodworking. Office: Denver Post PO Box 1709 Denver CO 80201-1709 Business E-Mail: tengdahl@denverpost.com.

ENGEBRETSON, DOUGLAS KENNETH, architect, interior designer; b. Dawson, Minn., Nov. 5, 1946; s. Melvin Kenneth and Mary Louise (Jackson) Engebretson; m. Kathleen Stella Jefferies, June 14, 1969; children: Leif Erik, Kristin Ann. BArch, U. Ariz., 1969. Registered arch., Mass., Vt., N.H., Conn., N.Y., R.I., Maine. Draftsman William B. Tabler, FAIA, N.Y.C., summer 1969, Wheeler Petterson Coffeen, Tucson, 1968-69; assoc. Alderman & MacNeish, West Springfield, Mass., 1970-78; pres. Tessier Assocs., Springfield, 1978—. Mem. Mass. Bd. Registration Archs., 1996—, chair, 2002—; dir. Nat. Coun. Archtl. Registration Bds., 2000—03, 2nd v.p., 2002—, nat. sec., 2003—05, 2nd v.p., 2005—, pres., 2005—; corporator Chicopee (Mass.) Savs. Bank, 1996—, trustee, 2000—, mem. bd. investment, 2005—. Prin. works include Putnam Vocat. Tech. Sch., Springfield, Palmer HS and Elem. Schs., Cmty. Savs. Bank, South Hadley, Mass., Ring Nursing Home, Springfield, Mt. Everett Regional Sch., Sheffield, Mass., Heritage Bank Hdqrs., Holyoke, Mass.; co-author: Norway, 1978. Mem. Zoning Bd. Appeals, Southampton, Mass., 1976—84, Pers. Policy and Procedures Bd., 1983—85; trustee Brightside Families and Chidren, West Springfield, 1992—96; trustee, bd. tribunes Sta. WGBY-TV, Springfield, 1992—2001, chmn., 2000; trustee Colony Club, 2001—, bd. govs., 2002—; bd. dirs. Sisters Providence Health Sys. Found., 1999—2005; trustee Bay Path Coll., Longmeadow, Mass., 1991—. Recipient Philanthropist to Distinction award, Nat. Soc. Fundraising Execs., 1996. Fellow: AIA (nat. dir. 1986—89, nat. sec. 1991—92, pres. New Eng. regional coun. 1985—86, pres. western Mass. chpt. 1980—82, Richard Upjohn fellow 1992); mem.: Mass. State Assn. Archs. (pres. 1982—83), Rotary (pres. 1985—86, Group Study Exch. award to Norway 1978). Republican. Lutheran. Home: 6 Madison Ave Southampton MA 01073-9520 Office: Tessier Assoc Inc Tower Sq Ste 250 1500 Main St PO Box 15169 Springfield MA 01115-5169 Office Phone: 413-736-5857. Business E-Mail: douglase@tessierarchitects.com.

ENGEBRETSON, ERIK JOHN, music educator, director; b. Kalispell, Mont., June 20, 1960; s. Rik and Marcia Engebretson; m. Jeanne Arnott, July 21, 1984; children: Kristen, Peter, Elizabeth. BA, Luther Coll., 1982; MS, Univ. of Ill., 1986. Cert. tchr. Office of Pub. Instrn., 2002. Band dir. Wolf Point (Mont.) Sch. Dist., 1982—85, Malta (Mont.) HS/Jr. High, 1986—. Del. ELCA Nat. Conv., Denver, 1999. Mem.: Mont. Bandmaster Assn. (pres. 1996—98). Lutheran. Office: Malta High School 1 High School Lane Malta MT 59538

ENGEL, ANDREW GEORGE, neurologist; b. Budapest, Hungary, July 12, 1930; s. Alexander and Alice Julia (Gluck) E.; m. Nancy Jean Brombacher, Aug. 15, 1958; children: Lloyd William, Andrew George. BSc, McGill U., 1953, MD, 1955. Diplomate: Am. Bd. Internal Medicine, Am. Bd. Psychiatry and Neurology. Intern Phila. Gen. Hosp., 1955—56; sr. asst. surgeon, clin. asso. USPHS, NIH, Bethesda, Md., 1958-59; fellow in neuropathology Columbia U., N.Y.C., 1962-64; with Mayo Clinic, Rochester, Minn., 1956-57, 60-62; cons. Rochester, Minn., 1965—; prof. neurology Mayo Med. Sch., Rochester, 1973—, William L. McKnight-3M prof. neurosci., 1984—; disting. investigator Mayo Clinic, 1995—. Mem. sci. adv. com. Muscular Dystrophy Assn., 1973-99; mem. rev. com. NIH, 1977-81. Mem. editl. bd. Neurology, 1973-77, Annals Neurology, 1978-84, 90-95, Muscle and Nerve, 1978-97, 2000—, Jour. Neuropathology, 1981-83, 1996-2000, European Neurology, 1989—, Jour. Neuroimmunology, 1991-98, Molecular Meurobiology, 1997—; contbr. over 300 articles to med. jours. Served with USPHS, 1957-59. Mem. Am. Acad. Neurology (hon.), Am. Neurol. Assn. (hon.), Am. Soc. Cell Biology, Soc. Neuroscis., AAAS, Inst. of Medicine of Nat. Acad. Sci., 2004. Home: 2027 Lenwood Dr SW Rochester MN 55902-1051 Office: Mayo Clinic 200 1st St SW Rochester MN 55905-0002

ENGEL, BARBARA ALPERN, history professor; BA in Russian Studies, CCNY, 1965; MA in Russian Studies, Harvard U., 1967; PhD in Rusian History, Columbia U., 1974. Part-time instr. Drew U., Madison, NJ, 1972—73; instr. Columbia U., N.Y.C., 1974; asst. prof. Sarah Lawrence Coll., 1974—76, U. Colo., Boulder, 1976—82, assoc. prof., 1982—92, prof., 1992—, dir. Ctrl. and Ea. European studies, 1993—95, chair dept. history, 1995—98. Author, co-editor: Five Sisters: Women Against the Tsar, 1975; author: Spanish transl., 1980, new edit., 1992, Mothers and Daughters: Women of the Intelligentsia in Nineteenth Century Russia, 1983; author, co-editor: Russia's Women: Accomodation, Resistance, Transformation, 1991; author: Between the Fields and the City: Women, Work and Family in Russia, 1861-1914, 1994, paperback edit., 1996; co-editor: A Revolution of their Own. Voices of Women in Soviet History, 1998; cons. editor Feminist Studies, 1979—98, mem. editl. bd. Frontiers, 1980—86, Slavic Rev., 1996—2001; contbr. articles. Recipient Heldt Article award, 1991, cert. tchg. excellence, Mortar Bd. Sr. Honor Soc., 1994, Heldt prize for Outstanding Achievement in Slavic Studies, AWSS, 1996, numerous other awards, grants; Wallenberg fellow, Rutgers Ctr. Hist. Analysis, 1995, fellow, John Simon Guggenheim Meml. Found., 2003, Sr. Exch. grant with the Soviet Union, IREX, 1985, 1987, 1991, Fulbright-Hays tng. grant, Faculty Rsch. Abroad program, 1987, Woodrow Wilson fellow, 1991, John D. and Catherine T. MacArthur Found. grantee, 1993—95, NEH fellow, 2003—. Mem.: Am. Assn. for Advancement of Slavic Studies, We. Assn. Women Historians (book prize com. 1990), Internat. Fedn. Socs. Rsch. Women's History (mem. U.S. com. 1988—91), Am. Hist. Assn. (com. on women historians 1987—89, mem. profl. divsn. 1990—92, mem. program com. 1994—95), Phi Beta Kappa. Office: U Colo Dept History Boulder CO 80309-0234

ENGEL, BERNARD THEODORE, psychologist, educator; b. Chgo., Apr. 18, 1928; s. Marvin I. and Hannah (Hollander) E.; m. Rae Goldberg, Mar. 10, 1951; children: Sandra E., Jeffrey P., Lauren C. BA, UCLA, 1954, PhD, 1956. Jr. rsch. psychologist UCLA, 1956; rsch. psychologist Inst. Psychosomatic and Psychiatric. Research and Tng., Michael Reese Hosp., Chgo., 1957-58; lectr. med. psychology, mem. sr. staff Cardiovasc. rsch. Inst., Sch. Medicine U. Calif., San Francisco, 1959-67; chief behavioral physiology sect., chief Lab. Behavioral Scis. Gerontology Research Center, Nat. Inst. Aging, NIH, Balt., 1967-95; assoc. prof. behavioral biology Johns Hopkins Sch. Medicine, Balt., 1970-82, prof., 1982—. Bd. dirs. Insts. for Behavioral Resources, Inc.; adj. prof. psychiatry and behavioral scis. Duke U. Sch. Medicine, Durham, N.C., 1999—. Contbr. 175 articles to sci. jours.; editorial bds. Applied Psychophysiology and Biofeedback, Jour. of Behavioral Medicine. Served U.S. Army, 1950—52. Recipient award Pavlovian Soc., 1979; cert. of Appreciation, N.C. State Hwy. Patrol, 2003. Fellow AAAS, Gerontol. Sci.; mem. Soc. Psychophysiol. Rsch. (pres. 1970-71), Assn. Applied Psychophysiology and Biofeedback (pres. 1981-82, Disting. Scientist award 2001), Am. Psychosomatic Soc. (sec.-treas. 1981-85, pres. 1985-86, Patricia R. Barchas award in sociophysiology 1999), Gerontol. Soc. Am., Acad. Behavioral Medicine Rsch., Sigma Xi. Personal E-mail: btere@aol.com.

ENGEL, BRADFORD CHARLES, educational association administrator, secondary school educator; b. Washington, Feb. 28, 1959; s. Jane and W. King Engel, Wala Askanas (Stepmother); m. Jackie Engel, Sept. 15, 2001; children: Ryan Bender, Rachel Bender, Bradford. BA, U. of Md. Balt. County, 1982—89. Advanced Profl. Tchg. Cert. Md., 1999. Tchr. Kent Island H.S., Stevensville, Md., 1989—; leadership devel. coord. Md. State Dept. of Edn., Balt., 1999—. Founder Mentor Adv. Program(M.A.P.), Stevensville, Md., 2001—. Author: (textbook) The 4 Challenges of Leadership, (book) Closing the Character Gap, (classroom management system) Quality Classroom Customer Service, Opportunity Dynamics. Coord. Hand in Hand Project, The Achievement Challenge, Leadership Olympics, Stevensville, Md., 1989—. Recipient Md. Tchr. of the Yr., Md. State Dept. of Edn., 2004—, Queen Anne's County Tchr. of the Yr., Queen Anne's County Bd. of Edn., 2004, Kent Island H.S. Tchr. of the Yr., Kent Island H.S. Adminstrn., 1999. Achievements include founder of the leadership honors program for the state of Maryland. Office: Kent Island HS 900 Love Point Rd Stevensville MD 21666 Office Phone: 410-604-2070. E-mail: engel6@gacb.k12.md.us.

ENGEL, CHARLES T., lawyer; BBA, B Journalism, Kans. State U.; JD, U. Kans. Ptnr. Cosgrove, Webb & Oman, Topeka. Mem. bd. regents Washburn U., 1997—. Mem.: Washburn Endowment Assn. (trustee), Washburn Alumni Assn. (former pres.). Office: Cosgrove Webb & Oman 1100 Nations Bank Tower 534 S Kansas Ave Topeka KS 66603 Home: 2824 SW Plass Ave Topeka KS 66611

ENGEL, DAVID, historian; m. Ronit Librozen, Feb. 26, 1975; children: Karen Shapiro, Michelle, Natalie. BA, UCLA, 1972, PhD, 1979. Lectr. history San Francisco State U., 1980—82; sr. lectr. Jewish history Tel Aviv U., 1983—91; Skirball prof. of modern Jewish history NYU, N.Y.C., 1991—2000, Greenberg prof. of holocaust studies, prof. history, prof. Hebrew and Judaic studies, 2000—. Mem. acad. coun. U.S. Holocaust Meml. Mus., Washington, 2001—. Author: In the Shadow of Auschwitz, 1987, Facing a Holocaust, 1993, Between LIberation and Flight (in Hebrew), 1996, The Holocaust: The Third Reich and the Jews, 2000; editor: (diary) Confession: The History of a Jewish Family in Poland under Nazi Occupation, 2004, (journal) Gal-Ed: On the History of Polish Jewry, 1988—. Mem.: Assn. Jewish Studies. Office: NYU 51 Washington Sq South New York NY 10012 Office Phone: 212-998-8980.

ENGEL, DAVID LEWIS, lawyer; b. NYC, Mar. 31, 1947; s. Benjamin and Selma (Fruchtman) Engel; m. Edith Greetham Smith, June 9, 1973; children: Richard William, Jonathan Martin. AB in Gen. Studies in Econ. cum laude, Harvard U., 1967, JD magna cum laude, 1973; Disting. Naval grad., U.S. Naval Officer Candidate Sch., 1969. Bar: Mass. 1975. Law clk. to Judge Henry J. Friendly U.S. Ct. Appeals (2d cir.), N.Y.C., 1973-74; assoc. Goodwin, Procter & Hoar, Boston, 1974-76, 79-80; asst. prof. law Stanford U., Calif., 1976-79; ptnr. Berman, Dittmar & Engel, P.C., Boston, 1980-84, Bingham McCutchen LLP, Boston, 1984—2005, co-chmn. corp. practice area, 2002—05, of counsel, 2005—. Pres. Harvard Law Rev., 1972—73. Mem. bd. visitors Stanford U. Law Sch., 1982—84; bd. dirs. Project Joy, 1995—2001. Lt. j.g. USNR, 1969—71. Recipient Sears prize, 1968, John Bingham Hurlbut award, 1979; John Harvard scholar, Harvard Coll. scholar, Nat. Merit scholar, 1964—67. Mem.: ABA, Boston Bar Assn. (working group of task force on revision of Mass. corp. statute 1987—2001), Phi Beta Kappa. Office: Bingham McCutchen LLP 150 Federal St Boston MA 02110-1713 Business E-Mail: david.engel@bingham.com.

ENGEL, DAVID WAYNE, lawyer, federal official; b. Salisbury, Md., Nov. 29, 1956; s. Robert Peter Engel and Joan (King) Bradshaw; m. Laura Marie Tuck, June 25, 1983; children: Michael Andrew, Jennifer Lynn, Matthew Alan. AB, William & Mary Coll., 1978; JD, Washington & Lee U., 1981; LLM, Judge Advocate Gen.'s Sch., Charlottesville, Va., 1988. Bar: Va. 1981, U.S. Dist. Ct. (ea. and we. dists.) Va. 1981, U.S. Ct. Mil. Appeals 1981, U.S. Ct. Appeals (4th cir.) 1981, U.S. Tax Ct. 1982, U.S. Ct. Appeals (5th cir.) 1985, Tex. 1985, U.S. Dist. Ct. (we. dist.) Tex. 1985, U.S. Supreme Ct. 1988, U.S. Ct. Appeals Vets. Claims 1990, U.S. Ct. Appeals (Fed. cir.) 1991, U.S. Ct. Appeals (10th cir.) 1998, U.S. Dist. Ct. (no. dist.) Okla. 1998. Capt. U.S. Army, 1981-89, active duty, 1989, USAR, 1989-97; appellate litigation atty. U.S. Dept. Vets. Affairs, Washington, 1989-92, spl. asst. to acting asst. gen. counsel, 1992-93; deputy asst. Gen. Coun., 1993-97; U.S. adminstrv. law judge Social Security Adminstrn., Office Hearings & Appeals, Tulsa, Okla, 1997—; col. USAF Res., 1997—; hearing office chief judge, 2002—. Office: Office of Hearings & Appeals Social Security Adminstrv 5110 South Yale Ste 204 Tulsa OK 74135-7481 E-mail: david.engel@ssa.gov.

ENGEL, DREW GARRETT, lawyer; b. Oxford, Ohio, Sept. 11, 1962; s. Alan Stewart and Sondra Frances (Uttanoff) E. BA, Miami U., Oxford, 1984; JD cum laude, U. Dayton, 1987. Bar: Ohio 1987, D.C. 1988, Calif. 1992; qualified/cert. death penalty trial atty., Ohio. Law clk. to Judge Froelich, Trotwood, Ohio, 1985-86; law clk. Louis & Froelich, Dayton, 1986-87; assoc. Crowell & Moring, Washington, 1987-88; asst. county prosecutor Butler County, Hamilton, Ohio, 1988-92; acting pub. defender City of Middletown, Ohio, 1993—; pvt. practice Oxford, 1993—; acting city prosecutor City of Hamilton, 1996—. Guest lectr. Miami U., Oxford, 1990-96; guest commentator Court TV, N.Y.C., 1995—. Articles editor: (law jour.) U. Dayton Sch. of Law Rev., 1987. Mem., vice chair Oxford Civil Svc. Commn., 1995—; hon. ringmaster Am. Heart Assn., Marion County, Ind., 1994; vol. aid ARC, St. Charles, Mo., 1993. Mem. Ohio Assn. Criminal Def. Lawyers, Calif. State Bar (criminal law sect.), Butler County Bar Assn. (pub. rels. com., com. on new lawyers). Avocations: triathlons, marathons, scuba diving, hockey, photography.

ENGEL, ELIOT L., congressman; b. N.Y.C., Feb. 18, 1947; s. Philip and Sylvia (Bleend) E. BA, CUNY, 1969, MS, 1973. Counselor, advisor N.Y. Urban Corps, 1968; tchr., dept. chmn. N.Y. Bd. Edn., 1969-76; guidance counselor N.Y. Pub. Schs., 1973-75; mem. N.Y. State Assembly, 1977-89, U.S. Congress from 17th N.Y. dist., 1989—; mem. econ. and ednl. opportunity com., energy and commerce com.; mem. internat. rels. com. Columnist Co-op City News, 1972. V.p. Park-East Ind. Dem. Club, N.Y., 1970-71; del. Bronx Com. for Dem. Voters, 1971-76, v.p., 1975-76; del., mem. steering com. Youth Caucus, Dem. Nat. Conv., 172; v.p. Ind. Dems. of Co-op City, 1972-73, pres., 1974-75; committeeman Bronx County Dem. Com., N.Y., 1972—; mem. exec. coun. N.Y. State New Dem. Coalition, 1973-75; founder New Dem. Club Co-op City, 1975, pres., 1975-76; jud. del. N.Y. Supreme Ct. Conv., 1st Jud. Dist., 1975-76, dist. leader, 1976—. Recipient Man of Yr. award FDR Ind. Dem. Club, 1976. Mem. United Fund Tchrs., Ams. for Dem. Action (bd. dirs. N.Y. 1974—), Zionist Orgn. Am., K.P. Democrat. Jewish. Office: US Ho of Reps 2264 Rayburn Hob Washington DC 20515-0001*

ENGEL, JOAN MARCIA LEZAR, psychologist, applied animal behaviorist; b. Boston, June 7, 1946; d. Morris and Thelma M. (Goldman) Lezar; m. Robert Lee Engel, Feb. 2, 1969 (div. 1982). BA, U. Mass., Boston, 1970; MA, New Sch. for Social Rsch., 1977; PhD, Fordham U., 1989. Asst. rsch. scientist NYU Med. Ctr., N.Y.C., 1988; adj. asst. prof. Coll. Mt. St. Vincent, Riverdale, N.Y., 1989-90, Lehman Coll., Bronx, N.Y., 1990, John Jay Coll., N.Y.C., 1990, Coll. of New Rochelle, N.Y., 1990; asst. prof. Marist Coll., Poughkeepsie, N.Y., 1990-91; statis. R&D Block Drug Co. Inc., Jersey City, 1991-94. Rschr., cons. in canine behavior, 1994—; cons. ASPCA Animal Behavior Clinic, 1999-2001, Animal Rescue League Behavior Dept., 2002—. Author: Manual for Foster Parent Training, 1980. Mem. APA, Assn. Behavior Analysis, Am. Psychol. Soc., Animal Behavior Soc., Assn. Pet Dog Trainers, AVSAB Personal E-mail: jmengelphd@verizon.net.

ENGEL, JOEL STANLEY, telecommunications executive; b. N.Y.C., Feb. 4, 1936; s. Fred and Pauline (Bienstock) E.; m. Marian Myers, Feb. 1, 1959; children: Stewart Allen, Mark Edward, Amy Ruth. BEE, CCNY, 1957; MSEE, MIT, 1959; PhD in Elec. Engring., Poly. Inst. Bklyn., 1964. Rsch. staff instrumentation lab. MIT, Cambridge, 1957-59; mem. tech. staff Bell Labs., Holmdel, NJ, 1959-64, supr., 1967-73, dept. head, 1975-83; mem. tech. staff BellComm, Washington, 1964-65; R & D mgr. Page Communications, Washington, 1965-67; div. mgr. AT&T, N.Y.C., 1973-75; v.p. Satellite Bus. Systems/MCI, McLean, Va., 1983-87, Ameritech, Chgo., 1987-97; pres. JSE Consulting, 1997—. Exec. adv. coun. Internat. Comms. Forum, Chgo., 1990—; bd. dirs. Syracuse (N.Y.) Rsch. Corp. Contbr. numerous articles to profl. jours.; patentee in field. Recipient Nat. Medal of Tech., 1994. Fellow IEEE (guest editor Transactions on Comm./Vehicular Tech. Jour. 1973, Alexander Graham Bell medal 1987); mem. Nat. Acad. Engring. Office: JSE Consulting 5 Hemlock Hollow Pl Armonk NY 10504-3016 Office Phone: 914-273-0318. Personal E-mail: jsecons@att.net.

ENGEL, JOHN, lawyer; b. N.Y.C., Mar. 8, 1943; s. Ralph and Ann (Unterman) E.; m. Gayle Iselin, May 25, 1980; children: Samuel Albert, Maxwell Robert. BA, Yale U., 1965; JD, Georgetown U., 1971. Bar: D.C. 1971, Va. 1984. Atty. The Rouse Co., Columbia, Md., 1971-75, Shaw Pittman Potts & Trowbridge, Washington, 1976-84, ptnr., 1984—2005; ptnr., Real Estate practice Pillsbury Winthrop Shaw Pittman, Washington, 2005—. Mem. regional adv. bd. Chgo. Title Ins. Co. Chmn. Va. Govt. affairs Internat. Coun. of Shopping, 1987-89; mem. task force City of Alexandria, Va.; bd. dirs. Family Respite Ctr. Mem. ABA, No. Va. Bldg. Industry Assn., DC Bldg. Industry Assn., Internat. Council of Shopping Ctrs. Office: Pillsbury Winthrop Shaw Pittman 2300 N St NW Washington DC 20037-1128 Office Phone: 202-663-8863. Office Fax: 202-663-8864. Business E-Mail: john.engel@pillsburylaw.com.

ENGEL, MARGARET, journalist; b. West Point, N.Y., July 3, 1951; d. Jack and Eleanor Elsie (Frick) E.; m. Bruce Tinsley Adams, Oct. 9, 1983; children: Emily Engel, Hugh Wilson. BJ, U. Mo., 1973. Reporter Lorain (Ohio) Jour., 1973-76; reporter Washington corr. Des Moines Register, 1976-81; reporter, editor Washington Post, 1981-87; pres. Alicia Patterson Found., Washington, 1987—; mng. editor The Newseum, 2001—. Lectr. Smithsonian Instn., Washington, 1998, 99. Author: Food Finds, 1984, 91, 2000, Baseball Vacations, 1997, 99, 2001; columnist Glamour Mag., 1981-86. Bd. dirs. Fund for Investigative Journalism, Washington, 1988—; food mgr. Bethesda Big Train Baseball, 1999. Nieman fellow Harvard U., 1979-80; recipient numerous journalism awards AP, 1980s, Penny-Mo. awards, 1980s. Mem. Soc. for Comml. Archeology, Investigative Reporters and Editors, Chagrin Falls Alumni Assn. Avocations: reading, travel, films. Home: 7211 Exeter Rd Bethesda MD 20814-2347 Office: Alicia Patterson Found Ste 850 1730 Pennsylvania Ave NW Washington DC 20006-4706 Office Phone: 703-284-3550. Business E-Mail: engel@alaciapatterson.org.

ENGEL, PAMELA MARIE, secondary school educator; b. Antigo, Wis., Apr. 22, 1956; d. Donald Otto and Dorothy Ann (Janssen) Wirth; m. Richard Alvin Engel, July 14, 1979; children: Erika Pamela, Richard Alvin, Jr. BS, U. Wis. Stevens Point, 1978; MA in Ednl. Leadership, Marian Coll., 1998. Cert. history, broad field social studies, and econ. tchr.; cert. K-12 sch. adminstrn., Wis. Summer info. booth attendant Langlade County Economic Devel. Com., Antigo, Wis., 1974-78; tchr. St. John's Elem., Antigo, Wis., 1978-79; receptionist Mallard Coach, West Bend, Wis., 1979-80; receptionist, acct. payable Zenith Sintered Products, Menomonee Falls, Wis.; receptionist, typist Lieds Nursery, Sussex, Wis., 1980-81; social studies tchr. Howard Suamico Sch. Dist., Wis., 1981-86, Pulaski Community Schs., Wis., 1986—, dean of students, 1986-87; chmn. dept. social studies Pulaski H.S., 2002—; cert. Tribes trainer Pulaski HS, Wis., 2004—. Jr. varsity volleyball coach Bay Port H.S., Green Bay, Wis., 1981-82, pol. club advisor, 1981-82, acad. excellence com., 1989-93, forensics asst., judge, 1989-93; mem. dist. social studies steering com., 1992, chairperson dist. social studies steering com., 1993-94; co-advisor Nat. Honor Soc., Pulaski, Wis., 1986-97, mem. social studies dist. curriculum com., 1996—; N.E. rep. Wis. Coun. Soc. Studies, 2005—; site based mgmt. core com., site based mgmt. steering com., PHS, 1994-97, chair alt. scheduling com. 1998-99, chair word of the month com. 1997-2003, dist. supr., evaluation steering com. 2001-04, dist. unit planner trainer 2001—. Coord. for nursery schedule Atonement Luth. Ch., Green Bay, 1987-88, Sunday sch. tchr., 1985-92, mem. choir, 1985, 92-94, edn. com., 1988-90, 93-94; confirmation guide Peace Luth. Ch., 1998-2000; mem. Wis. State Hist. Soc., 1999—, World Wildlife Fund. Recipient Brown County Disting. Tchr. award, 1999, 2004, 2005, 2005. Mem. Wis. Coun. for Social Studies (N.E. Wis. rep. 2005—, del. to bd. 2005—), Pulaski Edn. Assn. (sec. 1993-95, rep. convs. 1991–, pub. rels. com. co-chair 1999-2000), Pulaski Lion Club. Democratic. Lutheran. Avocations: golf, reading, travel. Home: 1056 Sunlite Dr Oneida WI 54155-9175

ENGEL, PHILIP L., retired insurance company executive; BA, U. Chgo., 1961, MBA, 1980. With CNA, Chgo., 1961, asst. v.p. corp. planning and control divsn., 1972-76, v.p., 1976-78, v.p. mktg., 1978-90, v.p. sys. and svcs., 1990, exec. v.p. claims, mktg., svcs., sys., underwriting, 1990-92; pres. CNA Ins. Cos., Chgo., 1992-99. Bd. dirs. CNA Fin. Corp., Agy. Mgmt. Svcs., Inc. Vice chmn. bd. trustees Pacific Garden Mission, Chgo.; pres., bd. dirs. Shakespeare Repertory Theater, Chgo. Fellow Soc. Actuaries, Casualty Actuarial Soc.; mem. Am. Acad. Actuaries, Quality Ins. Congress (chmn. bd. dirs.). Office: CNA Cna Plz Chicago IL 60685-0001

ENGEL, RALPH MANUEL, lawyer; b. N.Y.C., May 13, 1944; s. Werner Herman and Ruth Fredericke (Friedlander) E.; m. Diane Linda Weinberg, Aug. 10, 1968; children— Eric M., Daniel C., Julie R. BA in Econs. with highest honors, NYU, 1965, JD, 1968. Bar: N.Y. 1968, U.S. Supreme Ct. 1972. Assoc. Gilbert, Segall and Young, N.Y.C., 1968—71, Trubin Sillcocks Edelman & Knapp, N.Y.C., 1971—76; assoc., then ptnr. Summit Rovins & Feldesman and predecessor firms, N.Y.C., 1976—91; ptnr. Rosen & Reade, LLP, N.Y.C., 1991—2001, Sonnenshein Nath & Rosenthal LLP, N.Y.C., 2001—. Lectr. Sch. Law, Fordham U., 1990—91. Contbr. articles to legal and other publs.; editor-in-chief The Commentator, NYU, 1968. Mem. Planning Bd., Larchmont, NY, 1992—. Fellow Am. Coll. Trust and Estate Counsel; mem. N.Y. State Bar Assn. (trust and estate law sect. com. on practice and ethics 1991—, elder law sect., com. on guardianships and fiduciaries 1991-97, com. on estates and tax planning 1997—), Estate Planning Coun. Westchester County (bd. dirs. 1985-91) Home and Office: 6 Rockwood Dr Larchmont NY 10538-2537 Office: Sonnenschein Nath & Rosenthal LLP 1221 Ave of the Americas New York NY 10020 Office Phone: 212-768-6700. Personal E-mail: engelesq@yahoo.com. Business E-Mail: rengel@sonnenschein.com.

ENGEL, RICHARD L., career officer; b. L.A., July 2, 1946; s. Richard Leroy and Margret Ellen (Wilson) E.; m. Connie Jean Ricks, Sept. 8, 1973; children: Lindsey, Jennifer, Shelly. BS in Mech. Engring., Tex. A&M U., 1968; MS in Indsl. and Sys. Mgmt. Engring., Ariz. State U., Tucson, 1975; student, Air Force Test Pilot Sch., 1976-77, Armed Forces Staff Coll., 1981; M in Nat. Security Strategic Studies, Naval War Coll., 1988. Commd. 2d lt. USAF, 1968, advanced through grades to maj. gen., 1996, pilot spl. ops., 1970-71, instr. pilot Williams AFB, Ariz., 1971-74; air staff officer Hdqs. Air Tng. Command, Randolph AFB, Tex., 1974-76; advanced simulator rsch. flight test officer Air Force Human Resources Lab., Williams AFB, 1978-81; chief of acads. Air Force Test Pilot Sch., Edwards AFB, Calif., 1981-83; dep. dir. F-16 LANTIRN Test Program, Edwards AFB, 1983-85; comdr. F-16 and LANTIRN Combined Test Forces, Edwards AFB, 1985-87; divsn. chief weapons sys. divsn. Office of Legis. Liaison for Sec. of Air Force, Washington, 1988-89; comdr. 3246th Test Wing, Air Force Devel. Test Ctr., Eglin AFB, Fla., 1989-92, 412th Test Wing, Edwards AFB, 1992-93, Air Force Flight Test Ctr., Edwards AFB, 1993-98; commandant Indsl. Coll. of the Armed Forces, Ft. McNair, 1998—2000; ret. Decorated Legion of Merit, D.F.C. with two oak leaf clusters, Air medal with nine oak leaf clusters, Air Force Commendation medal. Mem. AIAA, Soc. Exptl. Test Pilots.

ENGEL, RICHARD LEE, lawyer, educator; b. Syracuse, NY, Sept. 19, 1936; s. S. Sanford and Eleanor M. (Gallop) E.; m. Karen K., Dec. 26, 1965; children: Todd Sanford, Gregg Matthew. BA, Yale U., 1958, JD, 1981. Bar: NY 1961. Law asst. justices Appellate Divsn. NY 4th Jud. Dist., 1961-63; law clk. judge NY Supreme Ct., 1963—65; sr. ptnr. Nottingham, Engel, and Kerr, LLP, Syracuse, 1970—. Adj. prof. law Syracuse U. Coll. of Law; equine law trial practice, law and medicine Am. Arbitration Assn.; AP com. reviewer Prudential Class Action; lectr. in field; mem. various editl. adv. bds. Contbr. articles to profl. jours. Pres. Temple Soc. Concord, 1985-87; bd. dir. Am. Field Svc. Inter-cultural Programs, Inc., 1974-81. Mem. ABA, Am. Bd. Trial Advocates, Am. Coll. Legal Medicine, NY State Bar Assn., Onondaga Bar Assn. (mem. trial lawyers com. 1978-80, chmn. med. legal liaison com. 1976-77, chmn. spl. ins. com. 1988, Bench and Bar com. 1991, found. bd. 1992-98, grievance com. 1998—), NY State Trial Atty. Assn., Upstate Trial Attys. Assn. (pres. 1973-74, chmn. bd. 1974-77), No. Dist. NY Fed. Ct. Bar Assn. Inc. (trustee, program chmn. 2003—), Thoroughbred Owners and Breeders Assn. (owners coun.), Cavalry Country Club, Saratoga Reading Rooms, Inc., Yale Club (pres. Ctrl. NY). Office: Nottingham Engel and Kerr LLP One Lincoln Ctr 6th Fl Syracuse NY 13202 Home: 603 Kimry Moor Fayetteville NY 13066-1832 Office Phone: 315-474-6055. Office Fax: 315-474-6049. Personal E-mail: EquineEsq@aol.com.

ENGEL, ROBERT RALPH, chemist, educator, dean; b. Pitts., Aug. 30, 1942; s. Ralph Emil and Clara Elizabeth (Schmidt) Engel; m. Elizabeth Ella Neidigh, Oct. 1, 1966 (dec. May 22, 2002); children: Cheryl Noel, Erik Michael. BS, Carnegie Inst. Tech., 1963; PhD, Pa. State U., 1966. Prof. chemistry Queens Coll. CUNY, Flushing, NY, 1968—, dean rsch. and grad. study Queens Coll., 1998—2004. Author: 12 Books; contbr. over 120 articles to profl. jours. Capt. U.S. Army, 1966—68. Fellow, NATO, 1975, Rohm & Haas Co., 1986. Mem.: Am. Chem. Soc., Royal Soc. Chemistry, Internat. Coun. Main Group Chemistry (exec. sec. 1997—, treas. 1997—). Achievements include patents in field. Office: Queens College CUNY 65 30 Kissena Blvd Flushing NY 11367 E-mail: robert_engel@qc.edu.

ENGEL, TALA, lawyer; b. N.Y.C. d. Volodia Vladimir Boris and Risia (Modelevska) E.; m. James Colias, Nov. 22, 1981 (dec. Nov. 1989). AA, U. Fla., 1952; BA in Russian and Spanish, U. Miami, 1954; JD, U. Miami, Coral Gables, 1957; postgrad., Middlebury Coll., 1953. Bar: Fla. 1957, Ill. 1962, U.S. Dist. Ct. (so. dist.) Fla. 1957, U.S. Dist. Ct. (no. dist.) Ill. 1962, U.S. Supreme Ct., 1965, D.C. 1982; cert. mediator, arbitrator, Fla., 2005. Pvt. practice, Miami, Fla., 1957—61, Chgo., 1966—86, 1990—93, Washington, 1987—89, 1993—2002, Miami, Fla., 2002—; mediator, arbitrator Broward County, Fla., 2005—. Atty. Immigration and Naturalization Svc., Chgo., 1961-62; parole agt. Ill. Youth Commn., Chgo., 1963-66. Editor The Lawyer, 1956; mem. editl. bd. Miami Law Quar., 1955-57, 10 ML Q 110 Criminal Law, 10 ML Q 608 Ins. Law, 1955-56. Bd. dirs. Cordi-Marian Settlement, Chgo., 1977-93. Mem.: Fla. Bar Assn., Fed. Bar Assn., Chgo. Bar Assn. (entertainment com. 1971—72, devel. of law com. 1985—87), Ill. Bar Assn. (gen. assembly 1984—86), Fla. Bar Found. (life; qualified mediator and arbitrator 2005), Chgo. Bar Found. (life), Nu Beta Epsilon, Alpha Lambda Delta. Avocations: theater, singing, computers, Russian and Spanish languages, travel in 93 countries. Home: 601 Three Islands Blvd #215 Hallandale Beach FL 33009 Office Phone: 954-455-7044. Personal E-mail: talaengel@aol.com.

ENGEL, THOMAS, chemistry professor; b. Yokohama, Japan, Apr. 2, 1942; came to U.S., 1947; s. George Walter and Juliane (Urban) E.; m. Esther Neeser, Aug. 23, 1979; 1 child, Alex. BS, Johns Hopkins U., 1963, MS, 1964; PhD, U. Chgo., 1969; Dr. rer. nat. habil., U. Munich, Fed. Republic Germany, 1979. Instr. Tech. U. Clausthal, Clausthal-Zellerfeld, Fed. Republic Germany, 1969-75, U. Munich, 1975-78; staff mem. IBM Rsch. Lab., Zurich, Switzerland, 1978-80; assoc. prof. chemistry U. Wash., Seattle, 1979-84, prof., 1984—, chmn. dept. chemistry, 1987-90. Contbr. papers and book chpts. to profl. publs. Recipient numerous grants NSF, Air Force Office Sci. Rsch., Office Naval Rsch, Am. Chem Soc. award in Colloid or Surface Chemistry, 1995. Mem. Am. Chem. Soc. (Surface Chemistry award 1995), Am. Vacuum Soc. Office: U Wash Dept Chemistry Box 1700 Seattle WA 98195 E-mail: engel@chem.washington.edu.

ENGEL, TODD SANFORD, lawyer; b. Syracuse, N.Y., Mar. 28, 1967; s. Richard Lee and Karen Kutner E.; m. Dawn Allison Susskind, July 8, 1995; children: Geoffrey Adam, Nicole Kayla. BS, Syracuse U., 1990, JD, 1996. Bar: N.Y. 1998, U.S. Dist. Ct. (no. dist.) N.Y. 1998. Atty. Nottingham, Engel & Kerr LLP, Syracuse, 1998—. Arbitrator, small claims ct. Syracuse City Cts., 1998—. Bd. dirs. Syracuse Jewish Family Svcs., Syracuse, 1998-2003, pres., 2002-2003, Temple Soc., Concord, 1999-2002, exec. com., 2002-; candidate N.Y. State Assembly 121st Dist., Onondaga County, 1998; mem. Manlius Town Dem. Com., Onondaga County Dem. Com., 1998—, exec. com., 1998-2000, lawyer's com., 1998—, rules com., 2001. Mem. ABA, ATLA, N.Y. State Bar Assn., N.Y. State Trial Lawyer's Assn., Onondga County Bar Assn. (CLE com. 1998—, chair newly admitted atty. program 1999, family law). Democrat. Jewish. Office: Nottingham Engel & Kerr LLP One Lincoln Ctr Syracuse NY 13202 Office Phone: 315-474-6055, 315-474-6055. Business E-Mail: tengel@nottinghamlaw.com.

ENGEL, WALBURGA See VON RAFFLER-ENGEL, WALBURGA

ENGELAGE, JAMES ROLAND, management consultant; b. Springfield, Mo., Dec. 5, 1945; s. Roland C. and Dorothy (Dixter) E.; m. Marcia Cooley, July 5, 1968. BS, S.W. Mo. State U., 1965; MS, Troy U., 1968; PhD, St. Louis U., 1977; MA, Ctrl. Mich. U., 1978. Dept. chmn. Montgomery (Ala.) Pub. Schs., 1968-69; asst. prin. Francis Howell Sch. Dist., St. Charles, 1969-74, asst. supt., 1974-75; commd. 2d lt. U.S. Army, 1975—93, advanced through grades to col., 1987; dean Randolph Macon Acad., Front Royal, Va., 1993-94; CEO JAMARC Mgmt. Corp., Winchester, Va., 1994—2003. Evening dir. Temple Schs., Silver Spring, Md., 1982-84; adj. prof. Park Coll., Ft. Myer, Va., 1980-82. Editor: Operation Desert Shield, 1992; contbr. articles to publs. Recipient legion of merit award Dept. Army, Washington, 1993. Mem. Res. Officers Assn. (pres. Chgo. chpt. 1992, Louisville chpt. 1993), Civil Air Patrol (capt. 1973-74), Lions Club (charter 1970-71), Civitans. Republican. Methodist. Avocations: computers, aviation. Home: 411 Windsor Ln Winchester VA 22602-2333 Office: JAMARC Mgmt Corp 29 E Jabel Eraly Rd Winchester VA 22601-7001

ENGELBERG, GAIL MAY, fine arts patron; m. Alfred B. Engelberg, May 5, 1990. Trustee Engelberg Charitable Found.; bd. trustee Solomon R. Guggenheim Mus., NYC; bd. dir. Jazz at Lincoln Ctr., NYC. Office: Engelberg Foundation 30 W 68th St New York NY 10023 also: Guggenheim Mus Trustees 1071 Fifth Ave New York NY 10128-0173 Office Phone: 212-877-4050.*

ENGELBRECHT, RUDOLF, electrical engineering educator; b. Atlanta, Apr. 18, 1928; s. Walter and Dorothea Engelbrecht; m. Christel M. Kluth, Sept. 10, 1050; children: Richard, Rolf, Erika. BS, Ga. Inst. Tech., 1951, MSEE, 1953; PhD in Elec. Engring., Oreg. State U., 1979. Mem. tech. staff Bell Labs., Whippany, N.J., 1953—60, supr. Murray Hill, N.J., 1961—63, dept. head, 1964—69; dir. RCA Tech. Ctr., Somerville, N.J., 1970—72; group leader RCA Labs., Zurich, Switzerland, 1972—77; assoc. prof. Oreg. State U., Corvallis, 1977—93. Co-author: Microwave Devices, 1969; contbr. articles to profl. jours. Named to Oreg. State U. Engring. Hall of Fame, 1998. Fellow: IEEE (life Centennial award 1984, Third Millennium medal 2000); mem.: Sigma Xi. Achievements include patents in field. Office: Oreg State U Dept Elec Computer Eng Corvallis OR 97331

ENGELBREIT, MARY, art licensing entrepreneur; b. St. Louis, 1952; m. Phil Delano, 1977; 2 children. Illustrator greeting card cos., 1983; founder, pres. Mary Engelbreit Studios Retail and Pub. Cos., St. Louis, 1983—; founder, head The Mary Engelbreit Store; founder, creator Mary Engelbreit's Home Companion mag., 1996—. Illustrator The Snow Queen, 1993, The Night Before Christmas, 2001. Office Phone: 314-726-5646.

ENGELHARDT, ALBERT GEORGE, physicist; b. Toronto, Ont., Can., Mar. 17, 1935; came to U.S., 1957, naturalized, 1965; s. Samuel and Rose (Menkes) E.; m. Elzbieta Szajkowska, June 14, 1960; children— Frederick, Leonard, Michael. BASc., U. Toronto, 1958; MS, U. Ill., 1959, PhD (grad. fellow), 1961. Research asst. elec. engring. U. Ill., Urbana, 1958-61; staff research and devel. center engr. Westinghouse Electric Co., Pitts., 1961-70, mgr., 1966-69, fellow scientist, 1969-70; sr. research scientist, group leader Hydro-Que. Research Inst., Varennes, Can., 1970-74; mem. staff Los Alamos Sci. Lab., 1974-86; adj. prof. elec. engring. Tex. Tech. U., Lubbock, 1976—; pres., chief exec. officer, founder Enfitek, Inc., Los Alamos, N.Mex., 1982—. Vis. prof. U. Que., 1970-77 Contbr. articles to profl. jours. Group leader Boy Scouts Can., 1972-74. Mem. IEEE Nuclear and Plasma Scis. Soc., Am. Phys. Soc. Home and Office: 549 Bryce Ave Los Alamos NM 87544-3607 Personal E-mail: a.g.engelhardt@ieee.org. Business E-Mail: agengelhardt@mailaps.org. *Since 1959 my basic research interest has been plasma physics and concomitantly nuclear fusion. The importance of the latter is that it shows great promise for providing us with renewable energy resources with acceptably small environmental and ecological perturbation.*

ENGELHARDT, HUGO TRISTRAM, JR., physician, educator; b. New Orleans, Apr. 27, 1941; s. Hugo Tristram and Beulah Engelhardt; m. Susan Gay Malloy, Nov. 25, 1965; children: Elisabeth, Christina, Dorothea. BA, U. Tex., Austin, 1963, PhD, 1969; MD with honors, Tulane U., 1972. Asst. prof. U. Tex. Med. Br., 1972-75, assoc. prof., 1975-77; mem. Inst. Med. Humanities, 1973-77; Rosemary Kennedy prof. philosophy of medicine Georgetown U., 1977-82; sr. research scholar Kennedy Inst. Center for Bioethics, Washington, 1977-82; prof. depts. internal medicine, community medicine and ob-gyn. Baylor Coll. Medicine, Houston, 1983-2001, prof. emeritus, 2001—; mem. Ctr. for Med. Ethics and Health Policy, Houston, 1983-2001; prof. dept. philosophy Rice U., Houston, 1983—. Chmn. adv. panel on infertility prevention and treatment for office of tech. assessment of the U.S. Congress, 1986-87; vis. scholar Internat. Akad. für Philosophie, Liechtenstein, 1997, Liberty Fund, spring, 1998. Author: Mind Body: A Categorial Relation, 1973, The Foundations of Bioethics, 1986, rev. edit., 1996, Bioethics and Secular Humanism, 1991, The Foundations of Christian Bioethics, 2000; co-author: Bioethics: Readings and Cases, 1987; assoc. editor: Ency. of Bioethics, 1978—83; assoc. editor Jour. Medicine and Philosophy, 1974—84; mem. editl. adv. bd.: Teaching Philosophy, 1975; mem. editl. bd. Poiesis & Praxis, 2001—, Chinese and Internat. Philosophy Medicine, 1998—; editor: Jour. Medicine and Philosophy, 1984—, (series) Philos. Studies in Contemporary Culture, 1992, Philosophy and Medicine series, 1974—, Clin. Med. Ethics, 1987—2002, Evaluation and Explanation in the Biomedical Sciences, 1975, Philosophical Medical Ethics, 1977, Mental Health, 1978, Clinical Judgment, 1979, Concepts of Health and Disease, 1981, New Knowledge in the Biomedical Sciences, 1982, Scientific Controversies, 1987, The Use of Human Beings in Research, 1988, Sicherheit und Freiheit, 1990, Hegel Reconsidered, 1994, The Philosophy of Medicine, 2000, Allocating Scarce Medical Resources, 2002; senior editor: Christian Bioethics, 1995—. Mem. bioethics com. Nat. Found. March of Dimes, 1975—. Recipient McDonald-Merrill-Ketcham Meml. Excellence award in law and medicine, 2003; Fulbright fellow, 1969-70, Woodrow Wilson vis. fellow, 1988; fellow Inst. for Advanced Studies, Berlin, 1988-89. Mem. Am. Philos. Assn., European Acad. Scis. and Arts. Office: Rice U Dept Philosophy PO Box 1892 Houston TX 77251-1892 Office Phone: 713-348-2491. Business E-Mail: htengelh@rice.edu.

ENGELHARDT, IRL F., coal company executive; b. Oct. 19, 1946; m. Suzanne C.; children: Joel, Erin, Evan. BS in Acctg., U. Ill., 1968; MBA, So. Ill. U., 1971. From mem. staff to pres., CEO Peabody Energy, St. Louis, 1979-90, pres., CEO, 1990—, now chmn., CEO. Bd. dirs. U.S. Bank N.A., St. Louis. Mem. Nat. Mining Assn. (bd. dirs., chmn. 1995-96), Nat. Coal Assn. (chmn. 1995-96), Internat. Energy Agy. (coal industry adv. bd., chmn., special com. mem.), Nat. Assn. Mfrs. (bd. dirs.), Coal Utilization Rsch Group (co-chmn.), Coal Based Stockholders Group (co-chmn.), St. Louis Arts and Edn. Council, St. Louis Area Council (exec. bd.), Boy Scouts of Am. Office: Peabody Energy 701 Market St Saint Louis MO 63101 Fax: 314-342-7797. E-mail: lengelhardt@peabodyenergy.com.*

ENGELHARDT, JOHN HUGO, lawyer, bank executive; b. Houston, Feb. 3, 1946; s. Hugo Tristram and Beulah Lillie (Karbach) E.; m. Jasmin Inge Nestler, Nov. 12, 1976; children: Angelique D., Sabrina N. BA, U. Tex., 1968; JD, St. Marys U., San Antonio, 1973. Bar: Tex. 1973. Tchr. history Pearsall HS, Tex., 1968-69; pvt. practice New Braunfels, Tex., 1973-75, 82—; exam. atty. Comml. Title Co., San Antonio, 1975-78, San Antonio Title Co., 1978-82. Adv. dir. M Bank Brenham, Tex., 1983-89. Fellow Coll. State Bar Tex.; mem. ABA, Pi Gamma Mu. Republican. Roman Catholic.

ENGELHARDT, LEROY A., retired paper company executive; b. Saginaw, Mich., Mar. 15, 1924; s. Herman J. and Alma (Engelhard) E.; m. Arlene L. Papineau, July 12, 1947; children— Richard C., Kay C., Douglas R. BBA, U. Mich., 1949, MBA, 1950. Plant, div. or subsidiary controller Chrysler Corp., 1950-60; mgmt. controls cons. Diehl K.G., Nuremberg, Germany, 1960-63; sec. Genesee Brewing Co., Rochester, N.Y., 1963-67; v.p. fin. Consol. Papers, Inc., Wisconsin Rapids, Wis., 1967-89, also ret. dir. Served with AUS, 1943-46. Home: 444 Two Mile Ave Wisconsin Rapids WI 54494-6559 E-mail: arlroy@wctc.net.

ENGELHARDT, THOMAS ALEXANDER, editorial cartoonist; b. St. Louis, Dec. 29, 1930; s. Alexander Frederick and Gertrude Dolores (Derby) E.; m. Katherine Agnes McCue, June 25, 1960; children— Marybeth, Carol Marie, Christine Leigh, Mark Thomas. Student, Denver U., 1950-51, Ruskin Sch. Fine Arts, Oxford (Eng.) U., 1954-56, Sch. Visual Arts, N.Y.C., 1957. Free-lance cartoonist, comml. artist, N.Y.C., 1957-60, Cleve., 1961-62, asst. editl. cartoonist, Newspaper Enterprise Assn., Cleve., 1960-61; editl. cartoonist St. Louis Post-Dispatch, 1962-97; freelance cartoonist, 1998—; one-man exhbns. of cartoons at Fontbonne Coll. Art Gallery, St. Louis, 1972, Old Courthouse (Jefferson Nat. Meml.), St. Louis, 1981, Mark Twain Bank, Frontenac, Mo., 1989; group exhbns. Washington U., St. Louis, 2000, Nat. Press Club, Washington, 2001, St. Louis Artists Guild, 2001. Served with USAF, 1951-53. Recipient Ethical Humanist of Yr. award St. Louis Ethical Soc., 1986, Kay and Leo Drey Environ. Leadership award Mo. Coalition for Environment, 1999. Roman Catholic. Office: 7830 Lafon Pl Saint Louis MO 63130-3805 Office Phone: 314-863-1165. E-mail: kengel7@juno.com.

ENGELL, JAMES THEODORE, language educator, department chairman; b. Danville, Pa., Sept. 6, 1951; s. Frederick Jacob and Ruth Louise Engell; m. Ainslie Sheridan Brennan, June 2, 1984; children: Marleny Brennan, Alexander E. BA, Harvard Coll., 1973; PhD, Harvard U., 1978. From asst. prof. to prof. Harvard U., Cambridge, Mass., 1978—83, prof. English and comparative lit., 1983—2000, chmn. English and Am. lit. and lang., 2004—. Author: The Creative Imagination, 1981 (Thomas Wilson prize 1982), Forming the Critical Mind, 1989, The Committed Word: Literature and Public Values, 1999, Saving Higher Education in the Age of Money, 2005; editor: Coleridge: The Early Family Letters, 1994, Coleridge, Poetry for Young Readers, 2003; co-editor: Coleridge, Biographia Literaria, 1983; editor, contbr.: Johnson and His Age, 1984, Teaching Literature: What Is Needed Now, 1988; editl. advisor Jour. History of Ideas, 1986—, Coll. Lit., 1990-, 1650-1850 Ideas, Aesthetics, and Inquiries in the Early Modern Era, Eighteenth-Century Thought, Literature and Religion. Corporator Emerson Hosp. and Health Sys., Concord, Mass., 1989-94. Recipient Levenson Tchg. prize, 1995, Roslyn Abramson Tchg. award, 1997, Coun. for Advancement and Support Edn. Gold award, 1999, Phi Beta Kappa Tchg. award, 2002, John Marquand Advising prize, 2003; grantee Ford Found., 1978, Baker Found., 2002-04; Cabot fellow, 2001. Mem. AAAS, MLA, Am. Soc. 18th Century

Studies, Johnsonians (chair 1990-91), Assn. Lit. Scholars and Critics (pres. 2001-02, sec. 2002-04), Friends of Coleridge. Avocations: travel, sports, music. Office: Harvard U Barker Ctr Dept English 12 Quincy St Cambridge MA 02138-3804

ENGELMAN, DONALD MAX, molecular biophysics and biochemistry educator; b. LA, Jan. 25, 1941; s. Francis Leopold and Mildred Lillian (Bordsen) E.; m. Pamela Alice Rackliff, Dec. 14, 1963 (div. 1986); children: Ian Kenton, Bevin Page; m. Susan Froshauer, Jan. 1, 1994. BA, Reed Coll., Portland, Oreg., 1962; MS, Yale U., 1964, PhD, 1967. Postdoctoral fellow U. Calif., San Francisco, 1967-68, Kings Coll., London, 1968-70; asst. prof. Yale U., 1970-74, assoc. prof., 1974-78, prof. molecular biophysics and biochemistry, 1978—, Eugene Higgins prof., 1995—, chmn. dept., 1987-92; acting dean Yale Coll., 1992-93; prof. de recherche Blaise Pascal, Ile de France, 1997—. Bd. dirs. Stryker Corp., Kalamazoo, Mich.; vis. prof. Coll. de France, 1993; editor-in-chief Ann. Rev. Biophysics, 1982-92; vis. prof. Cambridge U., Eng., 1978-79, Stanford U., 1984; Swiss Nat. lectr., 1993; guest biophysicist Brookhaven Nat. Lab., Upton, N.Y., 1974—, chair sci. and tech. steering com., 1998—; series cons. U.S. News Books, Washington, 1980-82. Editor: Biophysics Jour., Jour. Membrane Biology, Jour. Cell Biology, Biosci. Report, Proteins: Structure and Function; editor-in-chief: Ann. Rev. Biophysics, 1982-92; contbr. numerous articles to internat. jours., sci. jours. Guggenheim fellow, 1978-79; NSF, NIH research grantee, 1970— Mem. AAAS, NAS, Orgn. Biophys. Soc., Am. Chem. Soc., Conn. Acad. Arts and Scis.; Fellow Am. Acad. Arts & Sci. Office: Yale U PO Box 208114 New Haven CT 06520-8114 E-mail: Donald.engelman@yale.edu.*

ENGELMAN, KARL, physician; b. N.Y.C., June 23, 1933; s. Samuel and Lillian (Wachs) E.; m. Elaine Kaufman, June 10, 1956; children— Harold Kent, Ross Mitchell, Jeffrey Steven. BS, Men's Coll. Arts and Scis., Rutgers U., 1955; MD, Harvard U., 1959; MA (hon.), U. Pa., 1971. Diplomate Am. Bd. Internal Medicine. Intern, asst. resident, resident in medicine Mass. Gen. Hosp., Boston, 1959-64; clin. asso., sr. investigator, attending physician Nat. Heart Inst., NIH, Bethesda, Md., 1961-70; assoc. prof. medicine and pharmacology Sch. Medicine U. Pa., Phila., 1971-95; chief hypertension sect., dir. clin. research center Sch. Medicine U. Pa. Cons. physician Phila. VA Hosp., 1971-95, Children's Hosp., Phila., 1971-95; clin. prof. medicine Med. U. of S.C., 1996—; cons. Beaufort-Jasper Comprehensive Health Svcs., 1996—. Patentee in field. Med. staff Vols. in Medicine, 2002--. Served with USPHS, 1961-63. Mem. ACP, Am. Coll. Clin. Pharmacology, Internat. Soc. of Hypertention (sci. coun. on hypertension), U.S. Pharmacopeia and Nat. Formullary (adv. coun.), Coun. for High Blood Pressure Rsch. (adv. bd.), Am. Heart Assn., Phila. Doctors Golf Assn., Sea Pines Club. Jewish. Home: 20 Turnberry Ln Hilton Head Island SC 29928-4108

ENGELMAN, MELVIN ALKON, retired dentist, dental products executive; b. Waterbury, Conn., July 27, 1921; s. Herman B. and Marion (Halpern) E.; m. Muriel Phillips, Aug. 27, 1949; children: Curtis Land, Suzanne Ruth. AB, Ohio U., 1942; DDS, Western Res. U., 1944. Diplomate: Am. Bd. Oral Electrosurgery. Pvt. practice dentistry, Wappingers Falls, N.Y., 1949-89; chmn. oral diagnosis and oral pathology sect., dir. oral diagnostic ctr. St. Francis Hosp., Poughkeepsie, N.Y., 1963-77, attending dentist, 1963-89, dir. dept. dentistry, 1967, 71-74, 78, hon. staff, 1989—; pres. Di-Equi Dental Products Inc., 1980-99, Dentifax Internat. Inc., 1982-99. Observer Meml. Hosp. Cancer and Allied Diseases, N.Y.C., 1962-66; mem. adv. bd. Dutchess Community Coll., 1963-69, lectr. dental assts. program, 1960-63; dir. 1st regional sci. fair, Dutchess County, N.Y., 1960-61; project dir. USPHS community cancer demonstration project, St. Francis Hosp., 1963-66; asst. chief med. officer Dutchess County N.Y. CD, 1963-68; cons. Nat. Cancer Inst., mem. clin. cancer tng. com., 1968-71, Profl. edn. com. for cancer control, 1972-73; attending dentist Central Dutchess Nursing Home, 1970-85; cons. VA Hosp., Castle Point, N.Y., 1976-77, Lactona Corp., div. Warner Lambert, 1976-80; internat. lectr. on fixed prosthodontics, premedication, oral cancer, metallurgy. Co-author: Oral Cancer Examination Procedure, 16 edits., 1967-83; contbr. articles to profl. jours.; patentee for feeder bar, spruing assembly, sprue pin, and hollow movable reservoir. Chmn. Wappinger Red Cross Fund Drive, 1956; committeeman Troop 6, Boy Scouts Am., Chelsea, N.Y., 1963-67; pres. Dutchess County unit Am. Cancer Soc., 1969-71. From ensign to lt. comdr. Dental Corps, USNR, FMF PAC, 1942-46; lt. comdr. ret., 1986. Fellow AAAS (life), Royal Soc. Health (Eng.), Am. Pub. Health Assn., Acad. Gen. Dentistry; mem. ADA (life), Internat. Assn. Dental Rsch., Mil. Officers Assn., Assn. Mil. Surgeons (life mem.), 9th Dist. Dental Soc. (life mem.), Dutchess County Dental Soc. (pres. 1965), Am. Acad. Dental Electrosurgery (pres. 1983), Wappinger Conservation Assn. (v.p. 1970-71), Wappingers Falls C. of C. (pres. 1952-54), Masons (32 deg.), Shriners, B'nai B'rith (pres. So. Duchess lodge 1963-64), Am. Legion, Jewish War Vets., Marine Corps League, Alpha Omega Alpha. Address: 5720 Cottonwood St Bradenton FL 34203-8806 E-mail: mur4545@aol.com.

ENGELMAN, ROSALYN ACKERMAN, artist, marketing executive; b. Liberty, N.Y., Jan. 2, 1938; d. Nathan and Lillie (Schultz) Ackerman; m. Irwin Engelman, Nov. 24, 1956; children: Madeleine Florence, Marianne Leslie. BA, CCNY, 1958; MS, U. Rochester, 1978. Tchr. art, N.Y.C., 1958, N.J., 1964-66; lectr., fund raiser, docent Meml. Art Gallery, Rochester, N.Y., 1972-74; rschr. Meml. Arts Gallery, Rochester, 1975-78; co-chair arts Westport (Conn.) Bicentennial Com., 1975-76; mem. Met. Arts Resources Com., Rochester, 1977-78; pres. Westport-Weston Arts Coun., 1980-81; devel. officer Conn. Pub. TV, 1982-83; v.p. mktg. Praxis Media, 1984—. Exhibits include regional N.J. galleries, Gronsky Gallery, Kravetz Gallery, Rochester, Temple Israel, N.Y.C., 1997, T-Zart Gallery, N.Y.C., 1994, Baruch Coll., N.Y.C., 1998, Nigerian Embassy, 1998, Nat. Arts Club, N.Y.C., 1999, Adelphi Univ. Gallery, 1999, Masters Mystery Show, Fla. Internat. U., 2004, Norwalk (Conn.) Symphony, 2004; one woman shows: Nat. Arts Club, NY, 1999, Mishkin Gallery Baruch Coll., 2001, Nico Gallery Seattle Wash., 2001, All Commemorative Show NAC NY, 2002, Earthplace Westport, 2003, Thomas Walsh Art Gallery Fairfield U., 2003, Barbara Gillman Gallery, Miami, Fla., 2004, Art Miami Fla., 2004, Caelum Gallery, N.Y.C., 2004, Maters Mystery Show, Miami, 2004, Art Miami Gillman Gallery, 2005, Queensborough CC Art Gallery, Bayside, NY, 2005, Phthalo Gallery, Bay Harbor, Fla., 2005; commissioned to paint: Substantive and Procedural Aspects of Internat. Criminal Law, The Hague Netherlands, 2000 Bd. dirs. Long Wharf Theatre, 1980-83, Performers Conn., 1980-84, Mus. Art Sci. and Industry, Bridgeport, Conn., 1990; chair bd. dirs. Westport-Weston Arts Coun., 1982—; bd. dirs. Nat. Corp. Theatre Fund, 1981-88, treas., 1982, pres., 1984. Recipient citation Town of Westport, 1981, Gold medal Grumbacher award, 1998. Mem. Alumni Assn. U. Rochester, Birchwood Country Club, Nat. Arts Club. Office Phone: 212-213-1569. Personal E-mail: ra936@aol.com.

ENGELMANN, KYLE ANDREW, music educator; s. Kenneth Rex and Mildred Marie Engelmann; m. Kimberly Jane Engelmann, Oct. 29, 1994; children: Jon Kenneth, Carl Jay. BS in Music Performance, Oakland U., Auburn Hills Mich., 1988. Music tchr. Cornerstone Schs., Detroit, 2000—; vocal program dir. First Congl. Ch., Rochester, Mich., 2002—. Musician (composer, arranger and condr.): (composed many choral and symphonic works) Three Poems For Orchestra (SCHOLARSHIP, BAY VIEW CONSERVATORY OF MUSIC, 1984); composer (arranger): (piano works) Devious Boy On A Rocking Horse; composer: (vocal coach) (choral works) Stopping By The Woods On A Snowy Evening; musician (organist): (performance and conducting) Go, Jonah Go. Vol. Clinton River Cleanup, Shelby Twp, Mich. Recipient Recognition From Pres. George Bush Sr. For Composing Song For First Gulf War; scholar Bay View Conservatory Of Music scholar, Bay View Assn., 1986. Mem.: Choristers Guild (corr.), Am. Guild Of Organists (assoc.), Am. Choral Dirs. Assn. (assoc.; mem.). R-Liberal. Christian. Achievements include development of Leading developer of prepared accompaniments for pedegogical training of the young musician.

ENGELMANN, RUDOLPH HERMAN, electronics consultant, writer; b. Hewitt, Minn., Mar. 5, 1929; s. Herman Emil Robert and Minna Louise (Kniep) E.; children: Guy Robert, Heidi Louise, Christopher Eugene, Hallé Marie (dec.). BA, U. Minn., 1953. Electronic designer Lawrence Livermore (Calif.) Lab., 1959-61; cons. Atlantic Rsch. Corp., Manchester, N.H., 1961-64, Gen. Radio Co., West Concord, Mass., 1963-69, Possis Engring., Mpls., 1970—, 3M Co., St. Paul, 1977-78, Pako Photo, Mpls., 1977-78, Litton Microwave, Mpls., 1977-79. Author: The Emperor's Last Man, 2000, Father Fathers Day, 2000; contbr. articles to profl. jours. 1st lt. USAF, 1946-53. Achievements include developments and patents in gigahertz digital frequency scalers and counters and time interval meters, touchtone telephone for U.S. Army, automatic photographic focus control, automatic temperature monitor and control for grain and petroleum storage safety and volume correction, optical character recognition, high efficiency battery charging systems, end-of-charge detector, rudderless flight control, ultra lightweight muscle prostheses, flight controls, power management, stealth penetrating radar, high efficiency shape memory alloy modulation and linear circuitry, high-efficiency electronic orthetic muscle, digitally variable 90db A.C. power source, raster scanning microscope, linear wave blood pump. Office Phone: 904-241-2219. Personal E-mail: rhengelmann@hotmail.com.

ENGELS, BEATRICE ANN, artist, poet, retired real estate company executive; b. N.Y.C., Oct. 1, 1925; d. Sydney and Marguerite Agnes (Carroll) Jonap; m. James J. Engels, May 10, 1944 (dec.); children: James J. Jr.(dec.), Edward R., Marguerite Mary McHale. Brokers degree, Dowling Coll., 1970. Agt. real estate sales Kathleen Hart Real Estate, Bayport, NY, 1969—70; pres., real estate broker Beatrice A. Engels Realty, Patchogue, NY, 1970—76, Blue Point, NY, 1976—95; dir., pres. Beatrice A. Engels Art Gallery, Patchogue, 1970—76, Petite Pallette Art Gallery, Bayport, 1989—91; ret., 1995. Mem. real estate bd. Suffolk County, 1970—80; ecology adv., Blue Point, 1974—94; columnist LI Advance, Patchogue, NY, 1971—75, Suffolk County News, Sayville, NY, 1971—75. Author: Morning Song, 1996 (Editor's Choice award, 1996), Sea Sonnets and Other Poems, 1997, Endless Skies of Blue (Editor's Choice award, 1997), Best Poems of 1997, Celebration of Poets, 1997, Outstanding Poets of 1998 (Editor's Choice award, 1998), Best Poems of 1998; author: (compiled by Famous Poets Press) Our 100 Most Famous Poets, 2004; author, illustrator: Marguerite, The Story of a Dolly, 2003; author: (songs) Best Christmas Present, 1998. Mem. Blue Point Rep. Club, 1970—88. Mem.: Famous Poets Soc., Rosary Soc. (pres.), Internat. Soc. Poets (life), Wet Paints Studio Group (life). Roman Catholic. Achievements include ecological efforts that helped to save the wetlands near Blue Point, N.Y. E-mail: beabysea@bellsouth.net.

ENGELS, LAWRENCE ARTHUR, retired metal products executive; b. Darlington, Wis., Sept. 26, 1933; s. Henry Morris and Nell Ellen (O'Connor) E.; m. Marilyn Rae Stellick, Sept. 6, 1958; children: Laurie, Michael, Thomas, Stephen BBA, U. Wis., 1959; MBA, Northwestern U., 1970. Dist. credit mgr. U.S. Steel Corp., Chgo., 1959-69; asst. treas. Nat. Can Corp., Chgo., 1969-77; corp. treas. Comml. Metals Co., Dallas, 1977—, chief fin. officer and treas., 1979—, v.p., treas., chief fin. officer Dallas, 1981-99, retired, 1999. Served with USN, 1952-55. Fellow Nat. Inst. Credit; mem. Cash Mgmt. Practitioners Assn. (Chgo. sec. 1975), Chgo. Midwest Credit Mgmt. Assn. (dir. 1973-75), Chgo. Midwest Credit Service Corp. (dir. 1975), Fin. Execs. Inst., Nat. Assn. Corp. Treas.

ENGELSON, ROBERT ALLEN, music educator; b. Litchfield, Minn., Nov. 21, 1950; s. Kenneth Robert and Phyllis Marjorie Engelson; m. Thea Ann Sikora, Aug. 31, 1953; 1 child, Matthew. BA in music edn., Augsburg Coll., 1972; DMA in choral music, Ariz. State U., 1974; MFA in choral conducting, U. Minn., 1979. Adj. instr. music Augsburg Coll., Mpls., 1973—81; interim instr. music U. Minn., Mpls., 1978—79; music instr. Coll. St. Catherine, St. Paul, 1979—81; assoc. prof. music St. Andrews Presbyn. Coll., Laurinburg, NC, 1981—91, Teikyo Westmar U., Le Mars, Iowa, 1991—95; music prof. The Franciscan U., Clinton, Iowa, 1995—. Music dir. RiverChor, Clinton, Iowa, 2004—. Contbr. articles various profl. jours.; co-author: In Heavenly Love Abiding, 1979. Pres., bd. dirs. Clinton Symphony Orch., Clinton, Iowa, 2002—. Recipient Outstanding Music Edn. Dissertation award, Coun. for Rsch. in Music Edn., 1994. Mem.: Iowa Music Educators Assn., Music Educators Nat. Conf., Am. Choral Dirs. Assn. Democrat. Luth. Avocations: reading, sports, crossword puzzles. Home: 1113 N 13th St Clinton IA 52732 Office Phone: 563-242-4023. E-mail: rtmengel@clinton.net.

ENGER, EDWARD HENRY, JR., retired editor, writer; b. Mpls., Mar. 16, 1930; s. Edward Henry Sr. and Anastasia (Barber) E.; m. Carolyn Sue Bush, June 1, 1964. BS in Edn., U. Minn., 1952. Cert. tchr., Calif. Tchr. Downers Grove (Ill.) Pub. Sch., 1956-58; editor Harper & Row, Evanston, Ill., 1958-62, author NYC, 1975—78; editor Silver Burdett Co., Morristown, N.J., 1962-68, Dell Pub. Co., N.Y.C., 1968-75; author Nat. Textbook Co., Chgo., 1979-81; editl. dir. Amsco Sch. Publs., N.Y.C., 1982-97; ret., 1997. Author: Writing by Doing, 1981, (textbook series) Language Basics, 1975-78. Served to cpl. U.S. Army, 1954-56, Korea. Mem. Nat. Council Tchrs. English. Democrat. Avocations: gardening, cooking, hiking, jogging.

ENGERMAN, DAVID CHARLES, history educator; s. Stanley Lewis and Judith Rader Engerman; m. Stephanie Lou Wratten, Oct. 13, 2002; 1 child, Nina. BA with honors, Swarthmore Coll., 1988; MA, Rutgers U., 1993; PhD, U. Calif.-Berkeley, 1998. Dir. instl. rsch. Beloit Coll., Wis., 1988—91; history lectr. U. Calif.-Berkeley, 1998—99; asst. prof. history Brandeis U., Waltham, Mass., 1999—. Editor: (book) God That Failed, 2001; co-editor, contbr. (book) Staging Growth, 2003; author: (book) Modernization From the Other Shore, 2003. Office: Brandeis U Dept History Waltham MA 02454

ENGERMAN, STANLEY LEWIS, economist, educator, historian; b. Bklyn., Mar. 14, 1936; s. Irving and Edith (Kaplan) E.; m. Judith Rader, June 21, 1963; children— David, Mark, Jeffrey. BS cum laude, N.Y. U., 1956, MBA, 1958; PhD, Johns Hopkins, 1962. Asst. prof. econs. Yale, 1962-63; asst. prof., then asso. prof. U. Rochester, N.Y., 1963-71, prof. econs. and history, 1971—. Co-author: Time on the Cross: The Economics of American Negro Slavery, 1974; Co-editor: The Reinterpretation of American Economic History, 1971, Race and Slavery in the Western Hemisphere: Quantitative Studies, 1975, Between Slavery and Free Labor: The Spanish Speaking Caribbean in the Nineteenth Century, 1985, Long-Term Factors in American Economic Growth, 1986, British Capitalism and Caribbean Slavery: The Legacy of Eric Williams, 1987, Cambridge Economic History of the U.S., 1996—, A Historical Guide To World Slavery, 1998. Mem. AAAS, Econ. History Assn., Am. Econ. Assn., Am. Hist. Assn., Social Sci. History Assn., Assn. Caribbean Historians, Orgn. Am. Historians, Econ. Hist. Soc., Southern Hist. Assn., Cliometrics Soc. Home: 30 Thornwood Dr Rochester NY 14625-2108 Office: U Rochester Dept Econs Rochester NY 14627

ENGERRAND, DORIS DIESKOW, business educator; b. Chgo., Aug. 7, 1925; d. William Jacob and Alma Willhelmina (Cords) Dieskow; m. Gabriel H. Engerrand,Oct. 26, 1946 (dec. June 1987); children: Steven, Kenneth, Jeannine. BS in Bus. Adminstrn., N. Ga. Coll., 1958, BS in Elementary Edn., 1959; M. Bus. Edn., Ga. State U., 1966, PhD, 1970. Tchr., dept. chmn. Lumpkin County H.S., Dahlonega, Ga., 1960-63, 65-68; tchr. Gainesville, Ga., 1965; asst. prof. Troy (Ala.) State U., 1969-71; asst. prof. bus. Ga. Coll. and State U., Milledgeville, 1971-74, assoc. prof., 1974-78, prof., 1978-90, chmn. dept. info. sys. and comms., 1978-89; retired, 1990. Contbr. articles on bus. edn. to profl. publs. Named Outstanding Tchr. Lumpkin County Pub. Schs., 1963, 66; Outstanding Educator bus. faculty Ga. Coll., 1975, Exec. of Yr. award, 1983. Fellow Assn. for Bus. Communication (v.p. S.E. 1978-80, 81-84, 89-92, bd. dirs.), Nat. Bus. Edn. Assn., Ga. Bus. Edn. Assn. (Postsecondary Tchr. of Yr. award 10th dist. 1983, Postsecondary Tchr. of Yr. award 1984), Am. Vocat. Assn., Ga. Vocat. Assn. (Educator of Yr. award 1984, Parker Liles award 1989), Profl. Secs. Internat. (pres. Milledgeville chpt. 1996-97), Ninety-nines Internat. (chmn. N. Ga. chpt. 1975-76, named Pilot of Yr. N. Ga. chpt. 1973). Methodist. Home: 1674 Pine Valley Rd Milledgeville GA 31061-2465

ENGERRAND, KENNETH G., lawyer, educator; b. Atlanta, June 30, 1952; s. Gabriel H. and Doris A. (Dieskow) E.; m. Anne Walts, Mar. 16, 1985; children: Caroline Elizabeth Turner, Catherine Anne Denton. BA, Fla. State U., 1973; JD, U. Tex., 1976. Bar: Tex. 1976, U.S. Dist. Ct. (so. dist.) Tex. 1977, U.S. Ct. Appeals (5th cir.) 1978, U.S. Supreme Ct. 1980, U.S. Ct. Appeals (11th cir.) 1981, U.S. Dist. Ct. (ea. dist.) Tex. 1987. Assoc. Royston, Rayzor, Vickery & Williams, Houston, 1976-80, Brown, Sims & Ayre, Houston, 1980; v.p., gen. counsel Huthnance Offshore Corp., Houston, 1980-86; ptnr. Brown, Sims, Wise & White, Houston, 1986-2000, Brown Sims PC, Houston, 2000—. Adj. prof. law S. Tex. Coll. Law, 1978-93; columnist The Reporter, 1984-87; contbr. articles to profl. jours.; faculty advisor to spl. maritime edits. S. Tex. Law Jour., 1981-86. Fund drive vol. Houston Grand Opera, 1985-93, trustee, 1986-93; trustee Judge John R. Brown Scholarship Found., 1994—. Recipient outstanding contbn. to cmty. award Houston Jaycees, 1983. Mem. ABA (vce chmn. admiralty and maritime law com., tort and ins. practice sect. 1986-89), Def. Rsch. Inst., Maritime Law Assn., Coll. of State Bar Tex., Order of Coif, Phi Beta Kappa, Phi Delta Phi. Republican. Episcopalian. Avocations: legal writing, cultivating roses. Home: 3511 Durness Way Houston TX 77025 Office: Brown Sims PC 1177 West Loop S STE 1000 Houston TX 77027-9083 Business E-Mail: kengerrand@brownsims.com.

ENGH, N. ROLF, lawyer; b. Scotts Bluff, Nebr., Oct. 26, 1953; s. N.A. and Dolcie (Cuplin) E.; m. Nancy A. Carroll, Jan. 17, 1986. BA, U. Minn., 1976; JD cum laude, William Mitchell Coll., 1982. Bar: Minn. 1982. Grain merchandiser Cook Industries, Memphis, 1976-78; assoc. corp. dept. Lindquist & Vennum, Mpls., 1982-86, ptnr. corp. dept., 1986-93; gen. counsel The Valspar Corp., Mpls., 1993—. Trustee Breck Sch. Mem. ABA, Minn. State Bar Assn., Hennepin County Bar Assn., Mpls. Club, Westminister Church, Phi Beta Kappa. Home: 1928 Humboldt Ave S Minneapolis MN 55403-2815 Office: The Valspar Corp 1101 S 3rd St Minneapolis MN 55415-1259 Business E-Mail: Rengl@valspar.com.

ENGIBOUS, THOMAS (TOM) JAMES, electronics company executive; b. St. Louis, Jan. 31, 1953; s. James C. and Emma E. (Buck) E.; m. Wendy; children: Ryan T., Mandie, Christopher Megan. B of Elec. Engring., Purdue U., 1975, M of Elec. Engring., 1976, D of Engring. (hon.), 1997. Design engr. SCG, Tex. Instruments, Dallas, 1976-80, dept. mgr., 1980-86, v.p., 1986-91, sr. v.p., 1991-93; exec. v.p., pres. semi-condr. group Tex. Instruments, Dallas, 1993-96; pres., CEO Tex. Instruments Inc., Dallas, 1996-98, chmn., pres., CEO, 1998—2004, chmn., 2004—. Mem. vis. com. Purdue U. Engring., 1995—; bd. dirs. J.C. Penny Co., Catalyst, US-Japan Bus. Coun., Nat. Ctr. for Ednl. Accountability. Dir. Dallas Citizens Coun., 1996—; trustee So. Meth. U.; bd. dir. Southwest Med. Found. Mem. IEEE, Bus. Roundtable, Bus. Coun., Nat. Acad. Engring. Roman Catholic. Avocations: boating, water sports, skiing. Office: Tex Instruments Inc 12500 TI Blvd Dallas TX 75266-4136*

ENGLAND, ANTHONY WAYNE, engineering educator, dean, science educator; b. Indpls., May 15, 1942; s. Herman U. and Betty (Steel) E.; m. Kathleen Ann Kreutz, Aug. 31, 1962. SB, MIT, 1965, PhD, 1970, SM, 1965. With Texaco Co., 1962; field geologist Ind. U., 1963; scientist-astronaut NASA, 1967-72, 79-88; with U.S. Geol. Survey, 1972-79; crewmember on Spacelab 2, July, 1985; adj. prof. Rice U., Houston, 1987-88; prof. elec. engring. and computer sci. U. Mich., Ann Arbor, 1988—, prof. atmospheric, oceanic and space sci., 1989—, assoc. dean Rackham Grad. Sch., 1995-98, assoc. dean Coll. Engring., 2004—. Mem. space studies bd. NRC, 1992-98. Assoc. editor Jour. Geophys. Rsch. Recipient Antarctic medal, Spaceflight medal NASA, Spaceflight award Am. Astron. Soc., Outstanding Scientific Achievement medal NASA. Fellow IEEE; mem. Am. Geophys. Union. Home: 7949 Ridgeway Ct Dexter MI 48130-9700 Office: U Mich Dept Elec Engring-Comp Sci Ann Arbor MI 48109-2122

ENGLAND, ARTHUR JAY, JR., lawyer, former state justice; b. Dayton, Ohio, Dec. 23, 1932; s. Arthur Jay and Elsbeth (Weiskopf) E.; m. Morley Tenenbom, June 24, 1959 (div.); children: Andrea, Pamela, Ellen, Karen; m. Deborah J. Miller, Mar. 31, 1984; children: Rachel, Aaron. BS, U. Pa., 1955, LLB, 1961; LLM, U. Miami, 1971; LLD (hon.), John B. Stetson Coll. Law, 1979, Nova U., 1982. Bar: Fla. 1961, N.Y. 1962, Colo. 1997. Assoc. Dewey, Ballantine, Bushby, Palmer & Wood, NYC, 1961-64; ptnr. Culverhouse, Tomlinson, Taylor & DeCarion, Miami, Fla., 1964-69, Scott, McCarthy, Steel, Hector & Davis, Miami, 1969-70; spl. tax counsel Fla. Ho. Reps., 1971-72; consumer adviser, spl. counsel to gov. Fla., 1972-73; ptnr. Paul & Thomson, Miami, 1973-74; justice Supreme Ct. Fla., 1975-81, chief justice, 1978-80; ptnr. Steel, Hector & Davis, Miami, 1981-84, Fine Jacobson Schwartz Nash Block England, Miami, 1984-92, pres., chief exec. officer, 1988-89; shareholder Greenberg Traurig Hoffman Lipoff Rosen & Quentel, Miami, 1992, Greenberg Traurig, P.A. (and predecessor firm), Miami, 1992—, and group head, appellate practice group. Dep. chmn. Conf. of Chief Justices, 1978-80; chmn. Coun. of State Ct. Reps., Nat. Ctr. for State Cts., 1979-80; mem. Commn. on Interest on Lawyers' Trust Accounts, 1986-90, chmn., 1989-90; chmn. adv. bd. Nat. Interest on Lawyers' Trust Accounts Clearinghouse, 1983-86; adj. prof. Coll. Law, Fla. State U. Contbr. articles to legal jours. With AUS, 1955-57. Recipient Medal of Honor, Fla. Bar Found., 1983, Herbert Harley award Am. Judicature Soc., 1986, Jurisprudence award Anti-Defamation League, 1991. Mem. ABA (Pro Bono Pub. award 1988), Am. Acad. Appellate Lawyers (pres. 1990-92), Am. Law Inst., Fla. Bar Assn. (chmn. appellate practice cert. com. 1993-94, cert. appellate lawyers), N.Y. State Bar Assn., Order of Coif, Beta Gamma Sigma. Jewish. Office: Greenberg Traurig LLP 1221 Brickell Ave Miami FL 33131-3224 Office Phone: 305-579-0605. Office Fax: 305-579-0717. Business E-Mail: englanda@gtlaw.com.

ENGLAND, GORDON R., civilian military employee; BS in Elec. Engring., U. Md., 1961; MBA, Tex. Christian U., 1975. Engr. Honeywell Internat., 1961—66; with Gen. Dynamics Corp., 1966—2001, v.p., pres., land systems Falls Church, Va., 1986—91, pres. aircraft sys. Ft. Worth divsn., exec. v.p., 1991, exec. v.p. Falls Church, Va., 1991—93, pres. Lockheed Ft. Worth, 1993-95; owner consulting co., 1995-97; exec. v.p. combat sys. group Gen. Dynamics Corp., Falls Church, Va., 1997—2001; sec. USN, Washington, 2001—03, 2003—; dep. sec. US Dept. Homeland Security, Washington, 2003; acting dep. sec. US Dept. Def., Washington, 2005—. Mem. Def. Sci. Bd. Vice-chmn. Goodwill Internat.; bd. govs. USO; bd. visitors TCU. Recipient award, Boy Scouts Am., Nat. Def. Indsl. Assn., Nat. Mgmt. Assn., Centennial award, IEEE, inductee, Aviation Hall of Fame. Mem.: Beta Gamma Sigma, Omicron Delta Kappa, Eta Kappa Nu. Office: US Dept Def Sec of Navy The Pentagon Rm 4E686 Washington DC 20350

ENGLAND, JULIE SPICER, computer company executive; BS in Chem. Engring., Tex. Tech. U., 1979. First line engr. Tex. Instruments, 1979—89, sr. mem. tech. staff, 1989—94, quality mgr. Semiconductor Group, 1994—98, v.p., 1994—, gen. mgr. radio frequency identification bus., 2004—. Mem. bus. adv. coun. Tex. Tech. Rawl Coll.; founder 3/2 program Tex. Women's U. Recipient Women of Achievement award Richardson Tex. YWCA, inductee Hall of Fame Women in Tech. Internat., 1998, Henry Laurence Gantt Medal, ASME, 2004. Mem. IEEE (sr.), Soc. Women Engrs. (life), Dallas C. of C. (mem. exec. women's roundtable), Dallas Women's Found. (circle of honor award). Achievements include patents for related to infrared focal plane array process technology. Office: Tex Instruments Inc 8505 Forest Ln Dallas TX 75243-4136 Fax: 972-995-4360.

ENGLAND, KATHLEEN JANE, lawyer; b. Boston, July 29, 1953; d. Frank W. and Kathleen E. (Van DenHouten) E. BA cum laude, Mich. State U., 1975; postgrad., U. Exeter, summer 1977; JD, Suffolk U., Boston, 1978. Bar: Mass. 1979, Nev. 1979, U.S. Dist. Ct. Nev. 1980, U.S. Ct. Appeals (9th cir.) 1980. Intern Middlesex Dist. Atty. Bur., Cambridge, Mass., 1978; law clk. Withington, Cross, Park & Groden, Boston, 1976-78, City of Las Vegas, Nev., 1978-79, dep. city atty., 1979-82; assoc. Vargas & Bartlett, Las Vegas, 1982-89; ptnr. Combs & England, Las Vegas, 1989-93; pres. England & Assocs., Las Vegas, 1994-99; ptnr. Kummer Kaempfer Bonner & Renshaw,

Las Vegas, 1999—. Bd. dirs., legal counsel Planned Parenthood So. Nev., Las Vegas; mem. Nev. Supreme Ct. Task Force on Gender Bias, 1987—; bd. dirs. Nat. Conf. Women's Bar Assn., 1992—; vice chair, chair character and fitness com. State Bar of Nev., 1993—. Contbr. articles to profl. jours. Bd. dirs. Nat. Kidney Found. of So. Nev., Las Vegas, 1983, U. Nev., Las Vegas Womens Ctr.; active Amnesty Internat., Campaign for Choice, 1990, Nev. Women's Lobby, chair Ethics Review Bd. City Las Vegas, 1994-97; v.p. Frontier Girl Scouts, 1995—. Recipient Woman of Yr. award Desert Sands Bus. & Profl. Women's Club, 1993; named Disting. Woman of So. Nev., 1992, Woman of Achievement, Legal Women's Coun., C. of C., 1994, Women Helping Women award Soroptimist Internat. of Greater Las Vegas, 1995. Mem. ABA, AAUW, So. Nev. Assn. Women Attys., Nev. Inn of Ct. (chmn. programs 1992-95), State Bar Nev. (founder chair young lawyers sect.). Avocations: travel, reading, horseback riding. Office: Kummer Kaempfer Bonner and Renshaw 7th Fl 3800 Howard Hughes Pkwy Ste 700 Las Vegas NV 89109-0913

ENGLAND, RICHARD JAY, retired chemist; b. Springfield, Ill., Aug. 5, 1926; s. James Clyde and Hazel Vera (Jay) England; m. Elsie Margaret Landes, May 19, 1951; children: Mark, James, Janet. AS, Springfield Jr. Coll., 1948, St. Louis U., 1949; BS in chemistry, Bradley U., Peoria, Ill., 1951. Cert. in chemistry Am. Chem. Soc., 1951. Rsch. and devel. officer U.S. Air Force, Dayton, Ohio, 1951—53; process chemist E.I. DuPont, Gibbstown, NJ, 1953—56, rsch. chemist Martinsburg, W.Va., 1956, Richmond, Va., 1957, Kinston, NC, 1957—59, sr. rsch. chemist Circleville, Ohio, 1959—87, cons., 1987—92; ret., 1987. Contbr. articles to profl. jours. With USNR, 1944—46, 1st lt. USAFR, 1951—53. Roman Catholic. Achievements include patents in field. Avocations: amateur radio, music, electronics, photography, computers. Home: 370 Meadow Ln Circleville OH 43113

ENGLAND, ROBERT STOWE, writer; b. York, S.C., Jan. 14, 1944; s. Hershel Stowe and Myrtle Lorene (Deal) E. BA in English, Duke U., 1967. Reporter Hartford (Conn.) Times, 1967-68; editor, pub. Washington, A Tabloid Rev., 1973-76; editor Del. Valley Bus. Mag., Phila., 1976-77; sr. editor Ingersoll-Rand Co. Corp. Mag., Washington, N.J., 1977-79; editor Metro Newark Mag., 1982-84; writer Insight Mag., Washington, 1985-88; ind. writer bus., fin. and polit. mags., Arlington, Va., 1988—. Adj. fellow, dir. rsch. for global aging initiative, Ctr. for Strategic and Internat. Studies, Washington, 1999-2003. Author: The Fiscal Challenge of an Aging Industrial World, 2002 (One of the 25 Best Books, World Future Soc., 2002), Global Aging and Financial Markets: Hard Landings Ahead?, 2002, The Macroeconomic Impact of Global Aging: A New Era of Economic Frailty?, 2002, Aging China: The Demographic Challenge to China's Economic Prospects, 2005. Pres. Harsimus Cove Neighborhood Assn., Jersey City, 1982-84. Recipient Blue Smoke and Mirrors award Insight mag., Washington, 1986. Mem. Washington Ind. Writers. Episcopalian. Avocations: piano, genealogy. Home: 3116 Military Rd Arlington VA 22207-4136 Office Phone: 703-522-7847. Personal E-mail: rengland@us.net.

ENGLANDER, ISRAEL A., financier; m. Caryl Englander. Ptnr. Aegis Ptnrs.; pres. Englander Capital Corp. Capital Corp., 1984—90; co-founder Jamie Securities, 1985—89; founder Israel A. Englander & Co.; CEO First Millennium Ptnrs., Inc., 1990—; mng. gen. ptnr. Millennium Ptnrs. LLC; sole mgr. Millennium Mgmt. LLC. Mem. bd. govs. AMEX. Bd. mem. Met. NY Coordinating Coun. Jewish Poverty, Mt. Sinai Children's Ctr. Found. Office: First Millennium Ptnrs Inc 666 Fifth Ave 8th Fl New York NY 10103

ENGLANDER, JOHN C., lawyer; BS, Cornell Univ., 1980; JD, Boston Univ., 1983. Bar: Mass. 1984. Law clerk, Hon. Bailey Aldrich US Dist. Ct. Appeals (1st cir.); law clerk, Justice William H. Rehnquist US Supreme Ct.; ptnr., comml. litig. Goodwin Procter, LLP, Boston, co-chair, litig. group, mem. exec. com. Office: Goodwin Procter LLP Exchange Pl 53 State St Boston MA 02109 Office Phone: 617-570-1268. Office Fax: 617-523-1231. Business E-Mail: jenglander@goodwinprocter.com.

ENGLAR, JOHN DAVID, finance educator, textiles executive, lawyer; b. Baldwin, N.Y., Feb. 19, 1947; s. Jack Donald and Edith (Blackwell) E.; m. Linda Meter, May 10, 1986. BA magna cum laude, Duke U., 1969, JD, 1972. Bar: N.Y. 1973. Assoc. Davis Polk and Wardwell, N.Y.C. and Paris, 1972-78; corp. atty. Burlington Industries, Inc., Greensboro, N.C., 1978—, v.p., gen. counsel, sec., 1984-93, CFO, 1994-96, sr. v.p. corp. devel. and law, 1995—2003, also bd. dirs., 1990—2003; exec. in residence Fuqua Sch. Bus., Duke U., 2004—. Chmn. bd. trustees Cen. N.C. chpt. Nat. Multiple Sclerosis Soc., 1984-86, mem. nat. adv. coun., 1988-89; mem. bd. visitors Wake Forest U. Sch. Law, 1984-95, Duke U. Fuqua Sch. Bus., 1995—. Mem. N.C. Bar Assn., Order of Coif, Phi Beta Kappa. Home: 215 Ridgeway Dr Greensboro NC 27403-1526

ENGLAR, NANCY ELLEN, nurse, consultant, nursing educator; b. Excelsior Springs, Mo., Jan. 23, 1955; d. Billy Paul and Mary Helen Slater; m. Jack M. Englar, Jan. 22, 1972; children: Brian, Nathan, Sara. Assoc. Nursing, Frederick (Md.) C.C., 1985; BSN, U. Md., 2001; M Health Law, Nova Southeastern U., 2004. Cert. clin. transplant coordinator, Am. Bd. Transplant Coordinators, oncology nurse, Oncology Nursing Soc., 2005. Transplant coord. NIH, 1990—2000, clin. nurse Bethesda, Md., 2000; transplant coord. U. Md. Med. Ctr., Balt., 1998—2000; clin. nurse Johns Hopkins Hosp., Balt., 1989—90; clin. nurse oncology Frederick (Md.) Meml. Hosp., 1985—89; legal nurse cons. NSE Legal Nurse Cons., Mount Airy, NC; nurse cons., project mgr. Nat. Insts. Allergy and Infectious Diseases, Bethesda, 2004—05, project mgr., transplant coord., 2005—. Mem.: Assn. Clin. Rsch. Profls., Am. Assn. Legal Nurse Cons., N.Am. Transplant Coord. Orgn., Oncology Nursing Soc. Office: U Md Dept Nuclear Medicine 22 S Green St Baltimore MD 21201 Office Phone: 410-328-7803. Business E-Mail: nenglar@umn.edu.

ENGLE, CAROLE RUTH, aquaculture economics professor; b. Harrisburg, Pa., July 7, 1952; d. Morris Mumma Engle and Mildred Evelyn (Orris) Wambold; m. Nathan Mayhew Stone, May 30, 1981; children: Reina, Eric, Cody. BA, Friends World Coll., 1975; MS, Auburn U., 1978, PhD, 1981. Vis. prof. U. Centroamericana, Managua, Nicaragua, 1981-83; fisheries economist Inter-Am. Devel. Bank, Santiago, Panama, 1984-85; asst. prof. econs. Auburn U., Montgomery, Ala., 1985-88; assoc. prof. aquaculture econs. U. Ark., Pine Bluff, 1988-94, prof., 1994—; dir., Aguacultural Fisheries Ctr., U. Ark., Pine Bluff, 1989—. Aquaculture coord. U. Ark., Pine Bluff, 1989—; cons. FAO, Rome, 1986, 88. Contbr. articles to profl. jours.; editor conf. proceedings. Mem. World Aquaculture Soc., Am. Fisheries Soc., Am. Assn. Agriculture Econs., So. Agriculture Econs. Assn., Ark. Acad. Scis. Avocations: gardening, reading, swimming. Office: U Ark PO Box 108 1200 University Dr Pine Bluff AR 71601-2799 Business E-Mail: cengle@uaex.edu.

ENGLE, CHRIS B., social worker, publishing executive; b. Louisville, Sept. 30, 1963; s. George Richard and Jaquelyn Engle; m. Terri S. Klingelhoefer, May 1970. BA in Criminal Justice, Ind. U., 1985; MS in Social Work, U. Louisville, 1987. LCSW Ind., cert. ACSW. Social worker So. Hills Counseling, Jasper, Ind., 1988—89, South Ctrl. Mental Health, Martinsville, Ind., 1989—96; pvt. practice Engle Counseling Solutions, Mooresville, Ind., 1996—99; social worker Hamilton Ctr. Mental Health, Sparcer, Ind., 1999—2003, Counseling and Psychol. Svcs., Bloomington, Ind., 2003—. Pub. Hamster Press, Ellettsville, Ind., 1995—; puppeteer Klinger Engle Puppets, Ellettsville, Ind., 2003—. County chair First Steps, Martinsville, Ind., 1995—98. Mem.: NASW. Democrat. Muslim. Achievements include invention of Matrix games. Avocations: war games, book publishing/production, puppetry. Home: 7251 Str @ 46 W Ellettsville IN 47429

ENGLE, DONALD EDWARD, retired rail transportation executive, lawyer; b. St. Paul, Mar. 5, 1927; s. Merlin Edward and Edna May (Berger) E.; m. Nancy Ruth Frank, Mar. 18, 1950; children: David Edward, Daniel Thomas, Nancy Ann. BA, Macalester Coll., St. Paul, 1948; JD, U. Minn., 1952, BSL., 1950. Bar: Minn. 1952, Mo. 1972. Law clk., spl. atty. Atty. Gen.'s Office Minn., 1951-52; atty., asst. gen. solicitor, asst. gen. counsel G.N. Ry., St. Paul, 1953-70; asso. gen. counsel Burlington No., Inc., 1970-72; v.p., gen. counsel S.L.-S.F. Ry., St. Louis, 1972-80, v.p. law, sec., 1979-80; v.p. law Burlington No., Inc., St. Paul, 1980-81, Burlington No. Ry., St. Paul, 1981-83, sr. v.p. law and govt. affairs, sec., 1983-86, also dir.; ptnr., chmn., chief exec. officer Oppenheimer, Wolff & Donnelly, 1986-93, chmn., chief exec. officer, 1991-93, of counsel, 1993—2004. Continuing edn. lectr. U. Minn.; bd. dirs. Regions Hosp. Found., 2001—05. Bd. dirs. YMCA, St. Paul, 1981-84, ARC, 1981-84; bd. dirs. Boy Scouts Am., 1991-2005. Mem. ABA, Mo. Bar Assn., Minn. Bar Assn., Ramsey County Bar Assn., St. Louis Bar Assn., St. Paul C. of C. (bd. dirs. 1994-97), North Oaks Golf Club, Phi Delta Phi. Republican. Lutheran. Home: 9 W Bay Ln North Oaks MN 55127-2601

ENGLE, HOWARD A., retired pediatrician; b. Wis., Sept. 11, 1919; married; three children. BS, U. Wis., 1939, MS, 1941, MD, 1943. Diplomate Am. Bd. Pediatrics. Intern Michael Reese Hosp., Chgo., 1943, resident in pediatrics, 1943-44; pvt. practice Miami Beach, Fla., 1947—; assoc. clin. prof. U. Miami Sch. of Medicine, assoc. prof. pediatrics emeritus. Sr. cons., past chmn. dept. pediatrics, Mount Sinai Med. Ctr., Miami Beach; com. mem., operation newborn U. Miami Sch. of Medicine; instr. dept. pediatrics U. Fla. Sch. of Nursing; pediatric preceptor Fla. Internat. U. Sch. Nursing; sr. cons. pediatrics Mount Sinai Med. Ctr.; courtesy staff Miami Childrens Hosp.; sr. attending pediatrics Jackson Mem. Hosp.; cons. Fla. Atlantic U. Dept. Spl. Edn., neuropediatrics, Childrens Home Soc. of Fla.; cons., lectr. Dupont de Nemours Found., State Miss.; cons. pediatric neurology Hope Sch.; dir. Symposium Cerebral Palsy, Miami; med. rep. Symposia Cerebral Palsy, State of Tex.; lectr. in field. Contbr. articles to profl. jours. Com. mem. Edn. and Therapy for the Handicapped, Dade County Sch. Bd.; past med. dir. United Cerebral Palsy of Miami; cons. neuropediatrics United Cerebral Palsy of Fla.; past. mem. clin. adv. bd. United Cerebral Palsy; nat. del. World Commn. on Cerebral Palsy, Copenhagen, 1963; med. cons. divsn. exceptional student edn. Miami-Dade County Sch. Bd. Recipient Ralph Hawley award for 50 yrs. svc. to medicine and the cmty. U. Wis., 1993. Mem. Am. Acad. Pediat., Child Neurology Soc., Am. Acad. Cerebral Palsy (exec. com.), Am. Acad. Neurology, Am. Assn. on Mental Retardation, Am. Population and Reproduction Assn. (pres., founder), Fla. Rehab. Assn., Internat. Soc. for Rehab. of Crippled and Disabled, Am. Acad. Phys. Medicine and Rehab., Internat. Soc. for Cerebral Palsy, Internat. Child Neurology Assn. (assoc.), Japanese Soc. Child Neurology, Dade County Med. Assn., Fla. Med. Assn., Fla. Pediatric Soc., Miami Pediatric Soc. (past pres.), Southeastern Med. Assn., European Paediatric Neurology Soc., World Med. Assn., Internat. Population and Reproduction Com. (chmn. edn. programs, bd. dirs., past pres. 1981-82), Alpha Omega Alpha, Sigma Sigma.

ENGLE, JAMES BRUCE, ambassador; b. Billings, Mont., Apr. 16, 1919; s. Bruce Wilmot and Verbeaudah Margaret (Morgan) E.; m. Priscilla Joyce Wright, June 10, 1950; children: Stephen, Judith, Philip, Susan, John, Peter. Diploma, Burlington (Iowa) Jr. Coll., 1938; BA, U. Chgo., 1940, postgrad., 1940-41, 46; diploma, Grad. Sch. Bus. Adminstrn., Harvard, 1945; Honours BA (Rhodes scholar), Exeter Coll., Oxford (Eng.) U., 1950, Honours MA, 1954; diploma, U. per Stranieri, Perugia, Italy, 1949; Fulbright scholar, Istituto Italiano Studi Storici, Naples, 1950-53; postgrad., Am. U., Washington, 1956-58; diploma, Goethe Institut, Germany, 1958; postgrad., King's Coll., Cambridge (Eng.) U., 1958-59. Dept. State liaison officer with Bd. Econ. Warfare, Washington, 1941-42; vice consul Quito, Ecuador, 1942-44, Rio de Janeiro, 1946-47, Naples, 1951-53; 2d sec. Am. embassy, Rome, 1953-54; Italian desk officer Dept. State, Washington, 1955-58; 1st sec. Am. embassy, London, 1958-59; consul Frankfurt, Germany, 1959, Duesseldorf, Germany, 1959-60; labor attache Am. embassy, Bonn, Germany, 1960-61, 1st sec. Accra, Ghana, 1961-62, acting dep. chief mission, 1962-63, charge d'affaires, 1963; dep. chief mission, counselor embassy Managua, Nicaragua, 1963-67; charge d'affaires, 1967; mem. sr. seminar in fgn. policy Dept. State, Washington, 1967-68; dep. chief reports and analysis div. CORDS, Mil. Assistance Command, Saigon, Vietnam, 1968; province sr. advisor Phu Yen mil. region II, Tuy Hoa, Vietnam, 1969-70; dir. Vietnam working group Dept. State, sec. Nat. Security Council com. on Indochina, Washington, 1970-71; spl. advisor to ambassador-at-large on trade and currency negotiations, 1971-72; diplomatic advisor to sec. of treasury, 1972; spl. asst. to U.S. ambassador to North Atlantic Council, Brussels, 1972; exec. sec. spl. interdepartmental task force on Indochina Dept. State, Washington, 1972-73; consul gen. Nha Trang, Vietnam, 1973; dep. chief mission, counselor of embassy Phnom Penh, Cambodia, 1973-74; charge d'affaires, 1974; ambassador to People's Republic of Bénin (Dahomey), Cotonou, 1974-76; polit. advisor with rank of ambassador to U.S. Comdr.-in-Chief Atlantic and Supreme Allied Comdr. Atlantic, 1976-78; sr. fgn. service insp. Dept. State, Washington, 1978-82; cons. on war gaming, 1983-84; dir. U.S. representation U.S.—Saudi Arabian Joint Commn. on Econ. Cooperation Riyadh, Saudi Arabia, 1984-85; Joint Commn. Advisor to Sr. Level Coms. U.S. and Saudi Arabian govts., 1985-87; cons. on fgn. affairs, 1987—; pres. Vermont Coverts: Woodlands for Wildlife, 1991-96, chmn. bd., 1996—, pres. emeritus, 2001. Mem. Vt. Forestry Communications Coun., 1991-95. Mem. Vt. Citizens Adv. Com., No. Forest Lands Coun., 1992-94, U. Vt. Extension Adv. Coun., 1993—. Served to lt. (j.g.) USN, 1944-46; mil. govt. officer Japan, 1945-46. Recipient Rockefeller Pub. Service award, 1958; named Tree Farmer of Yr. Caledonia County, Vt., 1997, Vt. Tree Farmer of Yr., 2001. Mem. The Oxford Union, Phi Beta Kappa. Congregationalist. Achievements include leading 11 U.S. Andean expdns. in Ecuador, 1942-43. Home: PO Box 64 Peacham VT 05862-0064 Mailing: 443 Bayley Hazen Rd Peacham VT 05862-0064

ENGLE, KATHLEEN FAYE, elementary education educator; b. Rapid City, S.D., July 8, 1958; d. Frank Denton and Marie Lucille (Coffield) Packard; m. Steven S. Engle, June 1, 1984; children: Kirstin Marie, Kalin Kathleen. BS in Edn., Black Hill State Coll., 1980. Tchr. physical edn. Campbell County Sch. Dist., Gillette, Wyo., 1980-84, Weston County Sch. Dist., Newcastle, Wyo., 1985—. Mem. evaluatin team Conestiga Rep., Gillette, 1982-83; mem. adv. team Newcastle Mid. Sch., 1981—, evaluation team, 1992—. Middle Sch. Physical Edn. Teacher or the Year, Nat. Assn. for Sport & Phys. Edn., 1995. Mem. Wyo. Edn. Assn., Wyo. Alliance Physical Edn. Health Recreation and Dance, Wyo. Coaching Assn., Newcastle Edn. Assn., Delta Kappa Gamma. Avocations: aerobics, weightlifting. Office: Newcastle Mid Sch 116 Casper Ave Newcastle WY 82701-2705

ENGLE, LARS, language educator; b. NYC, June 4, 1953; s. Alan William and Jessie Ann Engle; m. Holly Laird, May 27, 1989; children: Carl Joseph Engle-Laird, Sage Menglian Engle-Laird. AB (magna cum laude), Harvard Coll., 1974; MA in English, Cambridge U., 1976; PhD in English, Yale U., 1983. Lectr. U. Stellenbosch, South Africa, 1977—79; asst. prof. Yale U., New Haven, 1982—86, U. Tulsa, Okla., 1988—92, assoc. prof., 1993—, chair English, 2003—. Author: Shakespearean Pragmatism: Market of His Time, 1993; editor: (Norton anthology) English Renaissance Drama, 2002. Recipient Excellence in Tchg award, U. Tulsa, 2000, Outstanding Tchr. award, 2001; fellow Mellon fellow, U. Va., 1986—88. Mem.: MLA, U.S. Tennis Assn., Shakespeare Assn. Am., Cole's Black Belt Club, Phi Beta Kappa. Avocations: tennis, singing, martial arts. Office: English University of Tulsa 600 S College Avenue Tulsa OK 74104

ENGLE, LINDA JANE, molecular biologist; b. Summit, N.J., Nov. 5, 1960; d. Thomas Edward and Patricia E.; m. John Edward Landers, Aug. 8, 1998. BS, Rutgers U., 1982; PhD, U. Pa., 1995. Sr. rsch. assoc. Children's Hosp. Phila., 1982-87; postdoctoral rsch. fellow Harvard Med. Sch., Boston, 1995-99; rsch. fellow McLean Hosp./Mass. Gen. Hosp., Boston, 1995-99; v.p., dir. rch. & devel., co-founder PolyGenyx, Inc., Worcester, Mass., 1999—. Cons. neurobiologist Nathan Kline Rsch. Inst. NYU Med. Sch., 1997-2000; cons. CytoMatrix, Cambridge, Mass., 1997-98, U. Pa., Phila., 1993-94. Grantee NIH, 1999-2000. Avocations: classical pianist, tennis, hiking, horticulture, creative writing. Address: Polygenyx Inc care of MBI 25 Winthrop St Worcester MA 01604-4516 E-mail: lengle@polygenyx.com.

ENGLE, MARY ALLEN ENGLISH, retired physician; b. Madill, Okla., Jan. 26, 1922; d. Russell C. and Vera (Apperson) English; m. Ralph Landis Engle, Jr., June 7, 1945 (dec. Oct. 2000); children: Ralph Landis III (dec.), Marilyn Elizabeth. AB cum laude, Baylor U., 1942; MD, Johns Hopkins U., 1945; D.Sc. (hon.), Iona Coll., 1982. Diplomate: in pediatric cardiology Am. Bd. Pediatrics. Intern pediatrics Johns Hopkins Hosp., 1945-46, asst. dir. pediatrics out-patient dept., 1946-47, fellow pediatric cardiology, 1947-48; instr. pediatrics Johns Hopkins U., 1946-48; asst. resident Sydenham Hosp. Contagious Diseases, Balt., 1946, N.Y. Hosp., 1948-49, asst. attending pediatrician, 1952-60, assoc. attending pediatrician, 1960-62, attending pediatrician, 1962-92, hon. staff, 1992—; fellow in pediatrics Cornell U., N.Y.C., 1949-50, mem. faculty, 1950-92, prof., 1969-92, prof. emeritus, 1992—, Stavros S. Niarchos prof. pediatric cardiology, 1979-92, emeritus, 1992—. Med. dir. Insts. in Care Premature Infant, 1952-55, dir. pediatric cardiology, 1963-92. Recipient Spence-Chapin award for contbns. to pediatrics, 1958, award of merit Philoptochos Soc. N. and S. Am., 1978, Woman of Conscience award Nat. Council Women, 1979, citation Nat. Bd. Med. Coll. Pa., 1979, Disting. Achievement award Baylor U., 1981, Disting. Alumna award Baylor U., 1988, Maurice Greenberg Disting. Svc. award N.Y. Hosp.-Cornell Med. Ctr., 1991; hon. fellow Cornell U. Med. Coll. Alumni, 1984; Mary Allen Engle Div. Pediatric Cardiology, N.Y. Hosp.-Cornell U. Med. Coll. dedicated in her honor, 1992, Johns Hopkins U. Soc. Scholars award, 1992, Alumni Assoc. Detlev Bronk award, 1993, Disting. Alumna award, 2002. Mem. Am. Acad. Pediat. (charter mem. sect. cardiology, Founder's award cardiology sect. 1983), Am. Clin. and Climatological Assn. (recorder 1992-2000, pres. 2003-04), Am. Heart Assn. (bd. dirs. 1975-78, award of merit 1975, Helen B. Taussig award 1976), N.Y. Heart Assn. (bd. dirs. 1980-86), N.Y. Acad. Medicine, N.E. Pediatric Cardiology Soc., Harvey Soc., Soc. Pediatric Rsch., Assn. European Pediatric Cardiologists (corr.), Royal Soc. Medicine (bd. dirs. Found. 1983-92, hon. bd. dirs. 1992-2000), Am. Coll. Cardiology (master tchr. 1969, 73, 76, trustee 1974-79, bd. govs. 1990-94, pres. N.Y. State chpt. 1991-92, Theodore and Susan Cummings Humanitarian award 1973, 76), Am. Pediatric Soc., Pediatric Cardiology Soc. Greater N.Y., N.Y. Cardiology Soc. (bd. dirs., pres. 1986-87), Soc. Scholars, Phi Beta Kappa, Alpha Omega Alpha. Presbyterian. Home: 27213 Baileys Neck Rd Easton MD 21601-8503

ENGLE, RICHARD VICTOR, publishing executive; b. Chicago, Oct. 7, 1961; s. Frank J. and Margaret Anne (Fogarty) Wenglewski; m. Denise Marie Denning, July 23, 1985; 1 child, Destiny René. AD, Christ for the Nations Inst., Dallas, 1983. Commr. of archives and records State of Okla., 1998—; pub. Bell West, Am. Bethany, Warr Acres, and Nichols Hills Quail Creek Tel. Directories, Okla., 2000—. Mem. City Coun., Bethany, Okla., 1998—2002; pres. Nat. Fedn. Rep. Assemblies, 2003—, Assembly Edn. Fund, 2004—; v.p. Okla. Conservative PAC, 2000—; chmn. Okla. Fedn. Young Rep., 1997—2001; alt. del. Rep. Nat. Conv., Okla., 1996, del., mem. nat. rules com., 2000. Mem. Okla. Press Assn., (legis. affairs com. 1998-2001). Republican. Avocation: cross country bicycling. Office: 4028 Coronado Plz Warr Acres OK 73122 Office Phone: 405-789-9350. Business E-Mail: president@GOPwing.com.

ENGLE, ROBERT F., finance educator; b. Syracuse, NY, Nov. 1942; m. Marianne Eger, Aug. 10, 1969; children: Jordan, Lindsey. BS in Physics with honors, Williams Coll., 1964; MS in Physics, Cornell U., 1966, PhD in Econs., 1969. Asst. prof. MIT, Cambridge, 1969—74, assoc. prof., 1974—75, U. Calif., San Diego, 1975—77, prof. econs., 1977—2003, chair econs. dept., 1990—94, emeritus prof., 2003—; vis. prof. fin. NYU Stern Sch. Bus., 1999, Michael Armellino prof. Mgmt. of Fin. Svcs., 2000—. Rsch. assoc. Nat. Bur. Econ. Rsch., 1987—. Editor: Cointegration, Casuality, and Forecasting: A Festschrift in Honour of Clive W.J. Granger, 1999; co-editor: Jour. Applied Econometrics, 1985—89; assoc. editor:, 1988—, Jour. Regional Sci., 1978—, Jour. Forecasting, 1985—, mem. editl. bd.: Real Estate Econs., 2004—. Recipient Excellence in Tchg. award, MIT Grad. Econ. Assn., 1974—75, Nobel prize for Econ. Scis., 2003. Fellow: Am. Statis. Assn., Econometric Soc. (coun. mem. 1994), Am. Acad. Arts and Sci. Office: NYU Kaufman Mgmt Ctr-KMC 9-62 44 W Fourth St New York NY 10012-1126

ENGLE, ROBERT IRWIN, music educator, translator; b. New Kensington, Pa., Feb. 11, 1945; s. Dale Clair Engle and Rosalyn Imogene (Timblin) Erickson, 1 child, adopted Emmanuel Glémaud. BS in Music Edn., U. Cin., 1967; postgrad., Stanford U., 1967-68, Ind. U., 1969, U. So. Calif., 1969-71; MA in Music, U. Hawaii, 1973, cert. in Samoan, 1986; PhD in Music, U. Wash., 1994. Cert. tchr. music grades K-12, Calif. Choral instr. Terminal Island Prison, San Pedro, Calif., 1969-71; choral music tchr. Palos Verdes (Calif.) High Sch., 1968-72; dir. music Makiki Christian Ch., Honolulu, 1978-84, 1st United Meth. Ch., Honolulu, 1986-88; tchr. music and French Redemption Acad., Kailua, Hawaii, 1988-91; dir. music Kapiolani Community Coll., Honolulu, 1975-99; dir. choral activities U. Hawaii, Hilo, 1995-96; asst. dir. music Hilo First Samoan Assembly of God, 1995-96; dir. music Good Samaritan Samoan Ch., Honolulu, 1997-98, Tacoma, 1999-2001, San Diego, 2001—02; chair music dept. Northwest Coll., Kirkland, Wash., 1999-2001; choral music tchr. Mt. Carmel H.S., San Diego, 2001—03; artistic dir. San Diego Men's Chorus, 2002—03; music tchr., french tchr. Century HS, Santa Ana, Calif., 2003—; asst. dir. music Long Beach First Samoan Assembly of God, 2005—. Cons. Performing Arts Abroad, Kalamazoo, 1979-99, Pacific Basin Choral Festival in Hawaii, Berkeley, Calif., 1989, Gateway Music Festivals, 1997-99; tchr. music theory, piano S. Seattle C.C., 1993-94; choral music tchr. Inglemoor H.S., Bothell, Wash., 1994; prof. Polynesian music and dance U. Pitts., summer 1996; spkr. Internat. Soc. Music Edn. Convention, Tampa, Fla., 1994, Pretoria, South Africa, 1998; spkr. nat. conf. Soc. Ethnomusicology, L.A., 1995, Music Educators Nat. Conf., Kansas City, 1996; spkr. in field.; accompanist Honolulu Boy Choir, 1996; coord. summer course in Tahitian dance and music, Papeete, Tahiti, 1998; dir. model choir, State Conv. Calif. Music. Edn. Assn., 2003; dir. various choirs, Internat. Festival L.A., 2003-05. Author: Taking Note of Music, 1988, Piano is My Forte, 1989; editor: Pacific Island Choral Series, 1995—99; composer: Tatalo A Le Alii, 1984 (3d pl. state competition); composer, rec. artist Pese Pa'ia, 1988, (rec.) Music at Northwest, 2000, '01 In the Spirit, 2001, profl. rec. Christmas Aloha, dir., composer of new repertoire New Samoan Ch. Choir Repertoire Project, Am. and Western Samoa, 1997; contbr. articles to profl. jours. Founder E Himeni Kakou Colls. Choral Festival, Honolulu, 1976-99; founder, dir. Maile Aloha Singers, Honolulu, 1973-92, Carols at the Centerstage Festival, Honolulu, 1989-99, Lokahi Choral Festival, Honolulu, 1989-99, Aloha, America! Invitational Choral Festival, Honolulu, 1995; dir. Northwest Singers, Kirkland, 1999-2000, Northwest A Cappella, 2000-01; founder Wash. Collegiate Choral Festival, Seattle, 1999-2001, CANTATE! Mid. Schs. Honor Choir, 2002; Gospel piano seminars, Samoa, 2005—. Dir. mus. group representing Hawaii, Cultural Office for Territorial Activity, Papeete, Tahiti, 1982, World U. Games, 1983, Casa De La Cultura, Southeastern Mex., 1984, La. World EXPO, 1984, EXPO '86, Vancouver, Hawaiian Airlines, 1987, Goodwill Tour Am. Samoa, 1989, Artists in the Schs. Auckland, N.Z., 1991, Paris, 1999, Detroit, 2000; dir. mus. group representing U.S.A., U.S. Dept. State, EXPO '85, Tsukuba, Japan, 1985; Dir. award 2d pl. group Collegiate Showcase, Chgo., 1988, Dir. award 1st place Choral Groups All Am. Festival, Orlando, Fla., 1994, 7 NW States H.S. Honor Choir, 2000, Nat. Samoa Pastors Choir, Denver, 2005. Mem. AAUP, Am. Choral Dirs. Assn. (Hawaii chpt. 1978-99, editor newsletter 1987-89, 97-99, state pres. 1989-91, state sec. 1997-99, ethnic music chair NW divsn.), Samoa Fealofani Club, Delta Tau Delta (life). Republican. Mem. Pentecostal Ch. Avocations: languages, weightlifting, polynesian dance, drumming, translating. Home: 4141 Hathaway Ave 23 Long Beach CA 90815 Personal E-mail: drrobertengle@hotmail.com. Business E-Mail: bengle@hawaii.edu.

ENGLE, STEPHEN DOUGLAS, history educator; b. Charlestown, W.Va., Feb. 26, 1962; s. Donald A. Engle; m. Stephanie D. Mickey, July 27, 1985; children: Taylor Benjamin, Caroline Claire. BA, Stepherd Coll., 1984; MA, Western Ill. U., 1985; PhD, Fla. State U., 1989. Prof. Am. history Fla. Atlantic U., Boca Raton, 1990—. Author: Yankee Dutchman, 1993, Most Promising Dutchman of All, 1999, Struggle for the Heartland, 2001. Fulbright scholar,

1995-96. Mem. Am. Hist. Assn., Orgn. Am. Historians, Soc. Civil War Historians, Soc. German-Am. Studies. Office: Fla Atlantic U Dept History 777 Glades Rd Boca Raton FL 33431-6424

ENGLE, STEVE EUGENE, artist; b. Honolulu, Dec. 27, 1950; BFA in Sculpture, Santa Barbara Art Inst., 1973; MFA in Sculpture, Ind. U., 1980; postgrad., Pa. Acad. Fine Art, 1982-84. One person shows include Lisa Harris Gallery, Seattle, 1990, 92, The Contemporary Mus., Honolulu, 1996, Davis/Cline Gallery, Ashland, 2000, Thorndike Gallery, So. Oreg. U., Ashland, 2001, Hypotenuse Gallery, Sinclair C.C., Dayton, Ohio, 2001; exhibited in group shows Santa Barbara (Calif.) Art Inst., 1973, Ind. U., Bloomington, 1980, Contemporary Arts Ctr., Honolulu, 1981, Honolulu Acad. Art, 1982, Shreveport (La.) Art Guild, 1984, Woodmere Art Mus., Phila., 1985, U. Del., Newark, 1986, Roger Lapelle Gallery, Phila., 1987, Phila. City Hall, 1988, Bellevue (Wash.) Art Mus., 1988, 92, U. Wash. Med. Ctr., Seattle, 1990, Port Angeles (Wash.) Fine Arts Ctr., 1990, Seattle Ctr., Modern Art Pavillion, 1990, Alt. Mus., N.Y.C., 1991, Whatcom Mus., Bellingham, Wash., 1991, 92, Honolulu Advt. Gallery, 1991, Microsoft Corp., Redmond, Wash., 1992, WestOne Bancorp, Wash., Oreg., and Idaho, 1992, Seattle Ctr. Pavillion, 1993, Jonson Gallery, U. N.Mex., Albuquerque, 1999; represented in permanent collections WestOne Bancorp, Boise, Microsoft Corp., Redmond, Wash. State Arts Commn. Collection, Sch. Dist. Lacey, Wash., Seattle Arts Commn., Portable Works Collection, 1st Hawaiian Bank, Honolulu, Linda and Robert Kanter, Seattle, Hirschl Adler, N.Y.C., Contemporary Arts Ctr., Honolulu, Laila and Thurston Twigg-Smith, Honolulu, others; works included in publs. Jour. Am., The Herald, Seattle Times, Alt. Mus. Exhbn. Catalog, The Weekly, Artweek, Star-Bull, Impact Weekly, Dayton, Ohio, Sunday Jour., Albuquerque, Contemporary Mus. News, Honolulu. Recipient Betty Bowen Meml. Recognition award Seattle Art Mus., 1989, Juror award Bellevue Art Mus., 1992, Best of Category award Paris Gibson Sq. Mus. Art, 1993, Anita Chadwick award Chautauqua Ctr. Visual Arts, N.Y., 1997; tuition scholar Santa Barbara Art Inst., 1972-73; Ford grantee N.Y. Sch. Painting, Drawing and Sculpture, 1979, Nat. Endowment for Arts visual artists fellowship grantee in sculpture, 1990; Seattle Artists project grantee Seattle Arts Commn., 1990. E-mail: sengleart@yahoo.com.

ENGLE, STEVEN B., biotechnology company executive; BSEE, MSEE, U. Tex. Mgmt. cons. Strategic Decisions Group, 1979—84, SRI Internat., 1979—84; v.p. mktg. and divsnl. gen. mgr. Micro Power Systems, 1984—87; CEO Quantum Mgmt. Co., 1987—91; v.p. mktg. Cygnus Inc., 1991—93; exec. v.p., COO La Jolla Pharm. Co., San Diego, 1993—94, pres., dir., sec., 1994—95, CEO, 1995—, chmn. bd., CEO, 1997—. Chmn. BIOCOM; dir. CareLinc Corp. Office: La Jolla Pharmaceutical Co 6455 Nancy Ridge Dr San Diego CA 92121-2249

ENGLEHART, HUD, communications company executive; Grad., U. Mich., 1969. V.p. corp. comms. Lockheed Corp., 1988-90; various positions Hill and Knowlton, Pitts., 1982-96, former creative dir., global account mgr. Kraft Gen. Foods Chgo., former exec. mng. dir.; pres., COO KemperLesnik Comms., Chgo. Pres. bd. trustees Chgo. Victory Gardens Theater; bd. dirs. Chgo. Internat. Film Festival; mem. devel. bd. U. Mich. Bus. Sch. Mem. PRSA, Arthur Page Soc. Office: KemperLesnik Comms 455 N Cityfront Pl Dr #1500 Chicago IL 60611

ENGLEMAN, EPHRAIM PHILIP, rheumatologist; b. San Jose, Calif., Mar. 24, 1911; s. Maurice and Tillie (Rosenberg) E.; m. Jean Sinton, Mar. 2, 1941; children: Ephraim Philip, Edgar George, Jill. BA, Stanford U., 1933; MD, Columbia U., 1937. Intern Mt. Zion Hosp., San Francisco; resident U. Calif., San Francisco, Jos. Pratt Diagnostic Hosp., Boston; rsch. fellow Mass. Gen. Hosp., Boston, 1937-42; practice medicine specializing in rheumatology San Francisco, 1948—; mem. faculty U. Calif. Med. Ctr., San Francisco, 1949—, clin. prof. medicine, 1965—; dir. Rosalind Russell Arthritis Ctr., 1979—. Staff U. Calif., Mills Meml., Peninsula Hosps.; chmn. Nat. Commn. Arthritis and Related Diseases, 1975-76. Author: The Book on Arthritis: A Guide for Patients and Their Families, 1979; also articles, chpts. in books. Served to maj. M.C. USMCR, 1942-47. Recipient medal of Honor, U. Calif., San Francisco, 1999; Nat. Inst. Arthritis grantee; recipient citation Arthritis Found., 1973; Ephraim P. Engleman Disting. Professorship in Rheumatology named in his honor U. Calif., San Francisco, 1991. Fellow ACP; mem. Internat. League Against Rheumatism (pres. 1981-85), Am. Coll. Rheumatology (founding fellow, master, pres. 1962-63, Presdl. Gold medal 2002), Nat. Soc. Clin. Rheumatologists, AMA, Am. Fedn. Clin. Rsch.; mem. Japanese Rheumatism Soc. (hon.), Spanish Rheumatism Soc., Uruguay Rheumatism Soc., Australian Rheumatism Assn., Chinese Med. Assn., French Soc. Rheumatology, Internat. League against Rheumatism, Gold-Headed Cane Soc. (U. Calif., San Francisco), Family Club (San Francisco). Republican. Jewish. Office: U Calif Rosalind Russell Med Rsch Ctr Arthritis 350 Parnassus Ave Ste 600 San Francisco CA 94117-3608 Office Phone: 415-476-1141. Business E-Mail: ephraim@itsa.ucsf.edu.

ENGLEMAN CONNORS, ELLEN G., federal agency administrator; b. Indpls., Ind., Sept. 21, 1959; BA in Eng. and Comm., Ind. U., 1983, JD, 1987; MPA, Harvard U., 1994. Bar: Ind. 1987, U.S. Dist. Ct. (no. and so. dists.) 1987. Pub. affairs exec. GTE, 1987—92; pres., CEO Electricore, Ind., 1994—2001; adminstr. rsch. and spl. programs adminstrn. U.S. Dept. Transp., Washington, 2001—03; mem. Nat. Transp. Safety Bd. (NTSB), Washington, 2003—, chmn., 2003—05. Dir. Corporate & Govt. Affairs, Direct Relief Internat., 1993—94. Bd. dirs. Direct Relief Internat., dir. corp. & govt. affairs. Lt. USNR, 1999—. Recipient Disting. Pub. Svc. award, USCG, 9/11 medal, U.S. Dept. Transp., 2003 Laurel, Aviation Week. Mem.: Pub. Rels. Soc. Am. (cert. pub. rels.). Office: NTSB Headquarters 490 L'Enfant Plaza SW Washington DC 20594*

ENGLER, BRIAN DAVID, association executive; b. Palmerton, Pa., Oct. 9, 1947; s. David James and Doreen Estelle (Sheldon) E.; m. Margaret Mary Hurlock, Dec. 31, 1969 (div. Apr. 1981); children: Donna, David; m. Maxine Sue Richard, May 24, 1981; children: Rachel, Stacey. BS with merit, U.S. Naval Acad., 1969; MS in Ops. Rsch., Naval Postgrad. Sch., Monterey, Calif., 1978; MBA in Fin., Acctg., Marymount U., 1986. Commd. ensign USN, 1969, advanced through grades to comdr., 1983, naval flight officer, mission comdr., ops. analyst, 1969-89, ret., 1989; ops. analyst, project leader Systems Planning and Analysis., Alexandria, Va., 1989-90, asst. program mgr., 1990-91, program mgr., 1991-2000; exec. v.p. Mil. Ops. Rsch. Soc., 2000—. Assoc. editor (alumni newsletter) O.R. News, 1976-78. Mem. Big Bros./ Big Sisters of Balt., Annapolis, Md., 1968-69; sec.-treas. bd. dirs. Gov.'s Sq. Homeowners Assn., Williamsburg, Va., 1989-97. Decorated Navy Commendation medals (2), Meritorious Svc. medal; recipient Juvenile Decency award Kiwanis Club, 1965, Cert. of Proficiency, Civil Air Patrol, 1963, Best Cadet award Temple U., 1965. Mem. Am. Soc. Assn. Execs., Greater Washington Soc. Assn. Execs., Mil. Ops. Rsch. Soc. (bd. dirs. 1991—, sec.-treas. 1993-94, v.p. for adminstrn. 1994-95. v.p. fin. and mgmt. 1999-2000), VFW (post comdr. 2002-05), Am. Legion, Mil. Applications Soc., Inst. for Ops. Rsch. and Mgmt. Sci., Washington Inst. for Ops. Rsch. and Mgmt. Sci., Delta Epsilon Sigma. Avocations: running, sailing, reading, music, fencing, bowling. Home: 5918 Clermont Landing Ct Burke VA 22015-2565 Office: Mil Ops Rsch Soc Ste 450 1703 N Beauregard St Alexandria VA 22311-1717 E-mail: brian@mors.org.

ENGLER, EVA KAY, dental and veterinary products company executive; b. Czechoslovakia, May 7, 1927; m. Alfred Engler (dec. 1979); children: Raya, Michael David. Pres., founder med. and dental mfg. co. Engler Engring. Corp., Hialeah, Fla., 1964—. Avocations: languages, painting. Office: Engler Engring Corp 1099 E 47th St Hialeah FL 33013-2139 Fax: 305-685-7671. Office Phone: 305-688-8581. Personal E-mail: eengler@bellsouth.net.

ENGLER, JOHN M., trade association administrator, former governor; b. Mt. Pleasant, Mich., Oct. 12, 1948; s. Mathias John and Agnes Marie (Neyer) E.; m. Michelle; children: Margaret Rose, Hannah Michelle, Madeleine Jenny; B.S. in Agrl. Econs., Mich. State U., 1971; J.D., Thomas M. Cooley Law Sch., 1981. Mem. Mich. Ho. of Reps., 1971-78; mem. Mich. Senate, 1979-90, Republican leader, 1983, senate majority leader, 1984-90; gov., 1991-2003; pres. state and local govt. EDS, 2003-04; pres., CEO, Nat. Assn. Mfrs., 2004—; bd. dirs. Dow Jones & Co., 2005-, Northwest Airlines, Universal Forest Products, Munder Capital; trustee Annie E. Casey Found. Del. White House Conf. on Youth, 1972; U.S. Trade Reps.' Intergovernmental Policy Adv. com., 1988, Intergovernmental Adv. Coun. on Edn., 1988; chmn. Presdl. Scholars, 1991-92; One of 5 Outstanding Young Men of Mich., Mich. Jaycees, 1983, Governing Magazine Public Official of the Yr. pres. Gerald R. Ford Found.; mem. Nat. Gov.'s Assn. (welfare reform task force 1993-96, edn. goals panel 1993-2002, chair 2001-02). Republican. Roman Catholic. Office Phone: 202-637-3106.

ENGLER, RENATA JOHANNA MARTHA, allergist, immunologist, internist, educator; b. Frankfurt, Germany, 1949; MD, Georgetown U., 1975. Diplomate Am. Bd. Internal Medicine, Am. Bd. Allergy and Immunology (bd. dirs.). Intern Nat. Naval Med. Ctr., Bethesda, Md., 1975-76, resident in internal medicine, 1978-80; fellow in allergy and immunology Walter Reed Army Med. Ctr., Washington, 1980-82, mem. staff, 1982—, chief allergy & immunization svcs. Assoc. prof. Uniformed Svcs. U. Health Sci., Bethesda. Mem. ACP, Am. Acad. Allergy and Immunology, Am. Coll. Allergy, Am. Fedn. Clin. Rsch. Home: 1900 Wallace Ave Silver Spring MD 20902-1302 Office: Sair Hosp and Clinic Allergy-Immunology Dept Walter Reed Army Med Ctr Washington DC 20307-0001

ENGLER, ROBERT, political science professor; b. N.Y.C., July 12, 1922; s. Isidore and Esther (Haber) E.; m. Rosalind Elowitz, May 16, 1946 (div. June 1960); children: Richard J., Elise P.; m. Inea Bushnaq, Sept. 5, 1968; 1 dau., Nadya Kate. BSS., CCNY, 1942; MA, U. Wis., 1946, PhD, 1947. Mem. faculty U. Wis., 1946-47, Syracuse U., 1947-50, Columbia U., 1959-63; prof. polit. sci. Queens Coll., CUNY, 1964-69, Grad. Sch. and Bklyn. Coll., CUNY, 1969-91, prof. emeritus, 1991—; prof. polit. sci. Sarah Lawrence Coll., 1951-71; mem. faculty New Sch. Social Research, 1961-64; chair, vis. prof. world politics of peace and war Princeton U., 1988-89. Vis. prof. U. P.R., 1961, U. Sask., 1973, Ctr. for Rsch. in Rural and Indsl. Devel., India, 1992, 2001, U. Havana, 1987, 92, 93; disting. vis. scholar Indian Coun. Social Sci. Rsch., 2001-02; disting. vis. prof. Am. U., Cairo, 1978; assoc. fellow Inst. for Policy Studies, Washington, 1979-80. Author: The Politics of Oil: Private Power and Democratic Directions, 1961, The Brotherhood of Oil: Energy Policy and the Public Interest, 1977; also articles, reviews; contbg. author: The Dissenting Academy, 1968, Winning America, 1988; editor: America's Energy: Reports From the Nation on 100 Years of Struggle for the Democratic Control of Our Resources, 1980. Asst. to pres. Nat. Farmers Union, Washington, 1950-51; dir. Encampment for Citizenship, N.Y.C., 1961, 63. Served with AUS, 1943-46, ETO. Recipient Sidney Hillman Found. prize award polit. writing, 1955. Home: 444 Central Park W Apt 12F New York NY 10025-4358 Office: CUNY Grad Ctr 365 5th Ave New York NY 10016-4309

ENGLERT, DAVID JOHN, music educator; b. Lancaster, Pa., June 18, 1951; s. Ethel Englert; m. Suzy Sullivan, July 7, 1990. BMus, Oberlin Conservatory, 1973; MMus, Cleve. Inst. Music, 1976. Prof. music Montgomery Coll., Conroe, Tex., 1995—2004; instr. music Sam Houston State U., Huntsville, Tex., 2004—. Permanent organist Resurrection Luith. Ch., Spring, Tex., 2003—. Mem. Woodlands Symphony Bd., The Woodlands, Tex., 1997—2000. Home: 25727 Oakridge Forest Ln Spring TX 77386 Personal E-mail: docdave87d@netscape.net.

ENGLERT, HELEN WIGGS, writer; b. Nashville, June 1, 1927; d. Lawrence Raymond and Frances Eloise (Smith) Wiggs; m. Roy Theodore Englert Sr., Sept. 25, 1948; children: Lee Ann Englert Regan, Roy Theodore Jr. AA, Ward Belmont., Nashville, 1948; AB, George Washington U., Washington, 1954, postgrad., 1969-71. Lectr. Weight Watchers, Washington & Va., 1972-84. Author: Hey, Wait a Minute! Dealing with Feelings and Weight Control, 1992, We Hold These Values...What is Uniquely American about Being an American, 2002. Elder Old Presbyn. Meeting House, Alexandria, Va., 1982—; bd. mem. Sr. Citizens Employment & Svcs. Inc., Alexandria, 1994-97. Mem. George Washington U. Club, Campagna Ctr. (Alexandria), Nat. Mus. Women in Arts, Phi Theta Kappa. Avocations: walking, travel, tennis, grandchild, geneology.

ENGLERT, PETER, academic administrator, director; Grad., U. Cologne, Germany. Faculty mem., adminstr. San Jose State U., Calif.; pro vice chancellor, dean sci., architecture and design Victoria U., Wellington, New Zealand, 1995—2002, U. Hawaii, Manoa, 2005—, CEO, chancellor, 2002—05. Founder support group Maori and Pacific nation students U. Victoria; elected adminstrv. bd. Internat. Assn. Univs. (IAU), 2004—. Office: U Hawaii Hawaii Inst Geophysics and Plan 1680 E-W Rd, Post 602 Honolulu HI 96822 Office Phone: 808-956-5033. Office Fax: 808-965-6322. Business E-Mail: penglert@hawaii.edu.

ENGLERT, ROY THEODORE, lawyer; b. Nashville, Sept. 11, 1922; s. Roy T. and Ruth Rowe (Tindall) E.; m. Helen Frances Wiggs, Sept. 25, 1948; children: Lee Ann, Roy Jr. BA, Vanderbilt U., 1943; JD, Columbia, 1951; LLM, George Washington U., 1953. Bar: Tenn. 1951, U.S. Dist. Ct. D.C. 1951, U.S. Supreme Ct. 1955, Internat. Trade 1975. Asst. counsel Office Comptroller of Currency, U.S. Treasury Dept., 1951-58, chief counsel, 1958-62, asst. gen. counsel of dept., 1962-66, dep. gen. counsel, 1966-73; sole practice Washington, 1973-96. Bd. dirs., sec. Walker/Potter Assocs., Inc., Washington, 1973-96; mem. Sr. Seminar in Fgn. Policy, Dept. State, 1963-64, U.S. Assay Commn., 1975; lectr., writer on banking law. Contbr. articles to profl. jours. Judo tech. ofcl. Atlanta Olympics; bd. dirs. Westminster Ingleside Found. Lt. USNR, 1943—46. Recipient Exceptional Service award U.S. Treasury, 1972, Gen. Counsel's award, 1973; named US Track Nat. Masters Champion 10,000 meter run, 1998. Mem. ABA, Tenn. Bar Assn. Presbyterian. Home: 12183 Cathedral Dr Woodbridge VA 22192-2227 Office: 6720 Bellamy Ave Springfield VA 22152-3023

ENGLERT, WALTER GEORGE, classics and humanities educator; b. Oakland, Calif., June 30, 1952; s. Walter George and Isobel Ann (O'Hearne) E.; m. Mary Ellen Mecchi; children: Francesca, Molly. BA summa cum laude, St. Mary's Coll. Calif., 1974; MA, U. Calif. Santa Barbara, 1976; postgrad., Am. Sch. Classical Studies, Athens, 1979; PhD, Stanford U., 1981. Teaching asst. U. Calif., Santa Barbara, 1974-76, Stanford U., 1977-78; vis. lectr. U. Mich., Ann Arbor, 1980-81; vis. assoc. prof. U. Calif., Berkeley, 1986, Intercollegiate Ctr. Classical Studies, Rome, 1992-93; Omar and Althea Hoskins prof. Reed Coll., Portland, Oreg., 1981—. Organizer and lectr. Reed Latin Symposium for H.S. Students, 1988-2005; participant TAG Spring Interdisciplinary confs., 1988; tchr. Paideia Class, 1989, 91, 96, 97, Reed MALS Seminar, 1988, 93, 97, 2001, 05, Reed Elderhostel Program, 1989; mem. faculty Reed Alumni Coll., 1989, 95; lectr. Seattle Reed Alumni Group, 1991; guest Town Hall TV show, 1991. Contbr. articles to profl. jours. Grantee NEH, 1983, 95, Mellon Faculty Seminar, 1986-87, Sloan Found., 1987-88. Office: Reed Coll 3203 SE Woodstock Blvd Portland OR 97202-8138 Office Phone: 503-517-7310. Business E-Mail: walter.englert@reed.edu.

ENGLES, GREGG L., food company executive; Chmn. bd., CEO various predecessors Suiza Foods, Dallas; chmn. bd., CEO Dean Foods (name changed from Suiza Foods), Dallas, 2001—. Bd. dirs. Evercom, Inc., Tex. Capital Bankshares. Office: Dean Foods 2515 Mckinney Ave Ste 1200 Dallas TX 75201-1945

ENGLESE, DAMON JOSEPH, director; b. Secaucus, N.J, Aug. 8, 1979; s. Dennis L. and Theresa Englese. BS, Seton Hall U., 2001; MA in Edn., St. Peter's Coll., 2003. Tchr. Union City Bd. Edn., NJ, 2001—03, whole sch. reform facilitator, 2003—. Chair Sch. Leadership Coun., Union City, 2003—05. Democrat. Roman Catholic. Avocations: golf, travel. Office: Union City Bd Edn 1401 Central Ave Union City NJ 07087 Office Phone: 201-348-5602.

ENGLESMITH, TEJAS, actor, television producer, curator; b. London, Nov. 28, 1941; came to U.S. 1957; s. George and Lydia Julia (Johnson-Briet) E. Student in art history, U. St. Thomas, Houston, 1959-63. Asst. dir. Whitechapel Gallery, London, 1963-69; curator Contemporary Art Jewish Mus., N.Y.C., 1969-70; dir. Leo Castelli Gallery, N.Y.C., 1970-76, Max Hutchinson Gallery, Houston, 1976-78; pvt. art cons. Houston, 1978-80; auction mgr. Sta. KUHT-TV, Houston, 1980-84, exec. prodr., 1980-86, assoc. dir., devel. managing editor Public Times, 1984-86; prodr., announcer Sta. KUHF-FM, Houston, 1987-90; ind. broadcast cons. and prodr. Houston, 1990—; subscriber svcs./pub. rels. rep. Theatre Under the Stars, Houston, 1992-99. Judge Roanoke (Va.) Art Festival, 1972; judge, lectr. S.W. Tex. State U., San Marcos, 1978. Narrator: (film) Pas de Deux: A Dance of Two Countries: China and America, 1980, Just a Closer Walk With Thee, 1989, The English Countryside, 1992 (Silver Telly award narration 1994), Hall of the Americas, 1998, Voyages of Discovery, 2000, Houston Mus. of Natural Sci., numerous travel and indsl. videos; actor (TV series) Gamera 2: Region shurai, 1996, Kino no tabi, 2003; interviewee: Inflatable Sculpture, CBS-TV, 1969, Views on Art, Sta. WNYC-FM, 1975, Curtain!, Sta. KUHT-TV, 1980-81; prodr./host: Conversations with People in Arts, Sta. KPFT-FM, 1977; exec. prodr. 30th Anniversary Sta. KUHT Sock Hop, 1983; writer mus. catalogues; organizer various exhbns. Mem. selection com. N.Y. Drawing Soc., 1970; reader Taping For the Blind, 1987—; adv. bd. Cultural Arts Council Houston, 1978. Recipient Silver award Assn. for Community TV, 1981, Gold award Assn. for Community TV, 1982. Fellow Royal Soc. Arts. Clubs: TLC Four Seasons. Home: 7839 Fondren Rd Houston TX 77074-4601 Office: Pastorini/Bosby Talent Agy 3013 Fountain View Dr Houston TX 77057-6124 Personal E-mail: tejase@sbcglobal.net. *The learning and practice of good manners would alleviate most of the problems we face today ... and tomorrow.*

ENGLING, EZRA SAMUEL, Spanish language and literature educator, researcher; b. Kingston, Jamaica, June 3, 1957; 1 child, El Hassane Aghazzaf. BA in Spanish and English with honors, U. W.I. Mona, St. Andrew, Jamaica, 1980, MA in Spanish, 1983, PhD in Spanish, 1986. English tchr. Calabar H.S., St. Andrew, 1980-81; asst. lectr. Spanish U. W.I., Mona, 1981-82, grad. asst. Spanish, 1984-86; Spanish tchr. Campion Coll., St. Andrew, 1982-84; lectr. in English Coll. Arts, Scis. and Tech. (now U. Jamaica), St. Andrew, 1983-84; prof. Spanish and world lit. Lincoln (Pa.) U., 1987-2001, chair dept. langs., 1993-98; prof. Spanish, Tex. A&M Internat. U., Laredo, 2001—. Founding mem., adv. bd. Moroccan Cultural Studies Ctr., Fes, 1996—. Author: A Critical Edition of Calderon's "La Aurora en Copacabana," 1994; contbr. articles to profl. jours. Translator Oxford (Pa.) Dist. Ct., 1990—; contbr. Oxford Neighborhood Svcs. Scholar NEH, 1989, Spanish Ministry of Culture, Almagro, Spain, 1991; Summer Lang. Inst. grantee United Negro Coll. Fund, 1996; sr. rsch. fellow Fulbright Found., Morocco, 1996-97. Mem. MLA, AAUP (sec. local chpt. 1992-94), Coll. Lang. Assn. (mem. study abroad scholarship com.), Assn. Hispanic Classical Theater. Avocations: reading, travel, music, computers. Office: Tex A&M Internat U Dept Lang & Lit Laredo TX 78045 E-mail: engling@tamiu.edu.

ENGLISH, BETTY JO BOONE, business educator; b. Suffolk, Va., Sept. 22, 1952; d. Robert Simon and Katherine Irene (Stringfield) B.; m. William Edwin English, Sept. 10, 1977; children: Robin, Melissia, William, Stephen, Katherine. BS, James Madison U., Harrisonburg, Va., 1974. Teaching cert. in Bus. edn. Va., nat. bd. cert. tchr. career and tech. edn., cert. master Microsoft Office user. Jr. programmer Smith Transfer Corp., Staunton, Va., 1974-75; programmer, analyst S & K Sales Inc., Norfolk, Va., 1976; programming instr. ECPI of Norfolk, 1976-77; bus. edn. tchr. The Pruden Ctr. for Industry and Tech., Suffolk, Va., 1977—2003; tchr. career and tech. edn. Suffolk Pub. Schs., 2003—. Ednl. presenter Classroom Connect, El Segundo, Calif., 1997-98. Contbr. articles to profl. jours. Bd. dirs., v.p. The Suffolk Va. Employees Fed. Credit Union, 1991—; co-chmn. Goober Gang, The Peanut Fest, Inc., Suffolk, Va., 1996-98. Named Walter Shell Va. Bus. Educator of Yr., Va. Bus. Edn. Assn., Fairfax, 1997, Suffolk Pub. Sch. H.S. Tchr. of Yr., 1999, Excellence in Tech. award Consortium for Interactive Instrn., 1999, Career and Tech. Edn. Tchr. of Yr. Suffolk Pub. Schs., 2004, Bus. Tchr. of Yr. Va. Mid. Sch., 2004 Mem.: Va. Soc. Tech. in Edn., Va. Bus. Edn. Assn. (bd. dirs. 2001—, pres. 2005—), Va. Assn. Career and Tech. Educators, Nat. Bus. Edn. Assn. Home: 5403 Pruden Blvd Suffolk VA 23434-6848 Office: Kings Fork Mid Sch 350 Kings Fork Rd Suffolk VA 23434 Office Phone: 757-925-5750. Office Fax: 757-925-6754. Business E-Mail: betenglish@spsk12.net.

ENGLISH, BRUCE VAUGHAN, environmentalist, consultant; b. Richmond, Va., Aug. 6, 1921; s. Pollard and Lucy Kelly (Rice) E.; m. Virginia Tejas McCall Shaw, Feb. 6, 1949. BS in Physics and Math., Randolph-Macon Coll., 1942; MS in Physics and Math., Ind. U., 1943; PhD in Physics, U. Va., 1958. Grad. asst. instr. army specialized tng. program/rsch. asst. Manhattan Dist. Engrs. Project; physics instr. Ind. U., Bloomington; asst. prof. physics army specialized tng. program Randolph-Macon Coll., Ashland, Va., 1943-44, assoc. prof., acting chmn. dept. physics, 1948-58, prof., chmn. dept., 1958-64; physicist, head hip pressure lab. U.S. Navy Underwater Sound Reference Lab., Orlando, Fla., 1946-48; physicist, cons. historic preservation, pollution control and environment Ashland, 1964—; dir. Poe Found., Inc., Richmond, 1968-97, pres., 1973-92, life hon. pres., 1998—; pres., dir. Edgar Allan Poe Mus., Richmond, 1973-92. Pres. Pollution Control Assocs., Richmond, 1967-70. Pub.: Conway Thompson, A Retrospective, 2000; co-pub.: Poe's Richmond, 1978; columnist Herald-Progress, 1971—; contbr. articles to Poe Messenger mag. Founding mem. Richmond Symphony, 1956; mem. Patrick Henry Scotchtown Com., Hanover County, Va., 1958—; pres. Hist. Richmond Found., 1967-70; bd. dirs. Church Hill Model Neighborhood Bd., Richmond, 1968-73; chmn. Bicentennial Com. for Hanover County, 1974-92, Drainage Com., Ashland, 1980s, Courthouse Com. for Hanover County, 1985—; lay reader, mem. vestry St. John's Ch., Church Hill, Richmond, Va., 1969-70; hon. pres. Poe Found., Inc., 1998. With USN, 1944-45. Named Hon. Citizen State of Md., 1990; Ford Faculty fellow, 1951-52, Danforth fellow, 1956-57, du Pont fellow, 1957-58; recipient Smithey Math Gold medal, 1942. Mem. AAAS, Am. Phys. Soc., Va. Acad. Sci., Va. Hist. Soc., Nat. Trust for Hist. Preservation, Irish Georgian Soc., Cousteau Soc. (founding), Air and Waste Mgmt. Assn., Nat. Soc. for Clean Air Gt. Britain, Soc. Descs. of Peter Francisco (founder, advisor), Nat. D-Day Mus. WWII (charter), City Tavern Club, Commonwealth Club, Farmington Country Club, Downtown Club, Phi Beta Kappa, Sigma Xi, Omicron Delta Kappa, Chi Beta Phi, Pi Delta Epsilon. Episcopalian. Achievements include research in project developing atomic bomb, increasing awareness of hazards of pollution since 1955, of Edgar Allan Poe's cosmology, cryptography, and other scientific writings.

ENGLISH, BURTON CLYDE, agricultural economics educator; b. Darien, Conn., Nov. 29, 1951; s. Gerald Raymond and Vivian (Moehling) E.; m. Beth Ellen Nansel, June 1, 1974; children: Iva, Marla, Evan, Eldon. BS, Iowa State U., 1974, PhD, 1981; MS, N.Mex. State U., 1976. Grad. rsch. asst. N.Mex. State U., Las Cruces, 1974-76, rsch. specialist, 1976; rsch. asst. Ctr. for Agrl. and Rural Devel., Iowa State U., Ames, 1976-77, rsch. assoc., 1977-81, staff economist, 1981-86, asst. prof., 1984-86; assoc. prof. agrl. econs. U. Tenn., Knoxville, 1986—, prof. agrl. econs., 2002—. Mem. biomass roundtable Electric Power Rsch. Inst. and Audubon Soc., 1989—. Editor: Future Agriculture Technology and Resource Conservation, 1984, Crop and Livestock Technologies, 1997, Evaluating Natural Resource Use in Agriculture, 1998. Recipient Cert. of Appreciation, USDA, 1989. Mem. Am. Agrl. Econs. Assn., Western Agrl. Econs. Assn., North Ctrl. Agrl. Econs. Assn., So. Agrl. Econs. Assn. Lutheran. Avocations: coaching soccer, constructing models, stamp collecting/philately. Home: 9404 Ravenwood Cir Knoxville TN 37922-3549 Office: U Tenn Dept Agrl Econs 2621 Morgan Cir Knoxville TN 37996-4518 Office Phone: 865-974-3716. E-mail: benglish@utk.edu.

ENGLISH, DAVID FLOYD, lawyer; b. Corning, N.Y., Feb. 21, 1948; s. Floyd W. English Jr. and Carolyn C. E.; m. Marcia Lynn Allen, Sept. 5, 1970; children: Eric Allen, Lynne Marie. BS, U. Rochester, 1970; JD, U. Miami, 1977. Bar: Fla. 1977, N.Y. 1978, U.S. Dist. Ct. (mid. dist.) Fla. 1978, U.S.

Dist. Ct. (we. dist.) N.Y. 1978. Ptnr. English and English, Corning, 1978-80, Yorio, Tunney and English, Painted Post, N.Y., 1980-87, Yorio and English, Painted Post, 1988-90, Yorio, English and Roche, Painted Post, 1990-94; sr. counsel, dir. contracts, asst. sec. Dresser-Rand Co., Corning, N.Y., 1994-99; corp. and comml. legal cons., 1999-2000; asst. gen. counsel, asst. sec. World Kitchen, Inc., 2000—. Atty. Erwin-Painted Post Consol. Bd. Health, 1988—; atty. Town or Erwin, N.Y., 1988—; gen. counsel, Three Rivers Devel. Found., Inc., Corning, 1982-94, vice chmn., 1994—, Erwin Indsl. Devel. Agy., 1988—; trustee Painted Post Church Facilities Corp., 1992-95. Troop com. Boy Scouts Am. Steuben Area Coun., Bath, N.Y., 1986-89; committeeman Steuben County Rep. Com., Bath, 1980-85; dir. Stueben & Chemung Counties United Way. With USN, 1970-74; Capt. USNR, 1974-99. Named to Corning Sports Hall of Fame, 1987. Mem. ABA, Am. Corp. Counsel Assn., Def. Rsch. Inst. (product liability sect.), N.Y. Bar Assn., Fla. Bar Assn., Steuben County Bar Assn., Corning Bar Assn. (treas. 1980-87). Presbyterian. Avocations: sports, sailing, cross country skiing, model railroads, coin collecting/numismatics. Home and Office: 215 Watauga Ave Corning NY 14830-3233

ENGLISH, EDMOND, retail company executive; Grad., Northeastern U. With Filene's Basement; buyer T.J. Maxx, 1983, various sr. level merchandising positions, 1983-95; sr. v.p., group exec. TJX Cos., Inc., Framingham, Mass., 1998-99, COO, 1999—2000, pres., bd. dirs., 1999—, CEO, 2000—. Office: TJX Cos Inc 770 Cochituate Rd Framingham MA 01701-4672*

ENGLISH, FLOYD LEROY, telecommunications industry executive; b. Nicholas, Calif., June 10, 1934; s. Elvan L. and Louise (Corliss) E.; children from previous marriage: children: Roxane, Darryl; m. Elaine Ewell, July 3, 1981; 1 child, Christine. AB in Physics, Calif. State U., Chico, 1959; MS in Physics, Ariz. State U., 1962, PhD in Physics, 1965. Divsn. supr. Sandia Labs., Albuquerque, 1965-73; gen. mgr. Rockwell Internat.-Collins, Newport Beach, Calif., 1973-75; pres. Darcom, Albuquerque, 1975-79; cons in energy mgmt. and acquisitions Albuquerque, 1980-81; v.p. U.S. ops. Andrew Corp., Orland Park, Ill., 1981-82, pres., 1981-82, COO, 1981-82, CEO, 1983-92, also bd. dirs., 1982—, chmn. bd. dirs., pres., CEO, 1992—2000, 2000—01, chmn., bd. dirs., CEO, 2001—02, chmn. bd. dirs., 2002—04, chmn. emeritus, 2004. Contbr. articles to profl. jours. 1st lt. U.S. Army, 1954-57; capt. Res., 1957-69 Mem.: IEEE. Republican. Presbyterian. Office Phone: 708-846-2280. Personal E-mail: eee81@comcast.net.

ENGLISH, JAMES FAIRFIELD, JR., former college president; b. Putnam, Conn., Feb. 15, 1927; s. James Fairfield and Alice Bradford (Welles) English; m. Isabelle Spotswood Cox, July 9, 1955; children: Alice, James Fairfield, Margaret, William. Grad., Loomis Sch., 1944; BA, Yale U., 1949; MA, Cambridge (Eng.) U., 1951; JD, U. Conn., 1956; HLD, Northeastern U., 1982, Trinity Coll., 1989; LLD, U. Hartford, 1971, St. Joseph Coll., West Hartford, Conn., 1982. With Conn. Bank & Trust Co., Hartford, 1951—, sr. v.p., 1961-63, exec. v.p., 1963-66, pres., 1966-70, chmn. bd., 1970-80; v.p. fin. and planning Trinity Coll., Hartford, 1977-81, pres., 1981-89. Trustee emeritus Loomis Chaffee Sch., Mystic Seaport Mus.; bd. dirs. Cmty. Found. S.E. Conn. With AUS, 1944—46. Episcopalian. Home: 31 Potter St Groton CT 06340-5734 also: 777 Prospect Ave West Hartford CT 06105-4204

ENGLISH, JERRY FITZGERALD, lawyer, educator; b. Houston, Dec. 18, 1934; d. William Edward Michael and Viola Catherine (Christopherson) Fitzgerald; m. Alan Taylour English, July 23, 1955; children: Holly, Christopher, Anderson, Eric. BA, Stanford U., 1956; JD, Boston Coll., Harvard Law Sch., 1963. Bar: N.J. 1965, U.S. Dist. Ct. N.J. 1965. Clk., assoc., ptnr. Moser, Griffin, Kerby & Cooper, Summit, N.J., 1964-74; mem. N.J. Senate, 1971-72, asst. counsel to, 1972-74; legis. counsel Gov. N.J., Trenton, 1974-79; commr. N.J. Dept. Environ. Protection, 1979-82; of counsel Kerby, Cooper, English, Schaul & Garvin, Summit, 1982—85, ptnr., 1985, Cooper Rose & English, Summit, NJ. Adj. prof. N.J. Inst. Tech., 1983—; lectr. nationally for many orgns. Assoc. editor, editl. bd. N.J. Law Jour. Commr. Port Authority of N.Y. and N.J., 1979-88; trustee N.J. Ctr. for Visual Arts, N.J. Harvard Law Sch. Assn., 1973-; bd. dirs. Regional Plan Assn.; mem. Gateway Nat. Recreation Area Adv. Commn., 1981; mem. exec. coun. Dem. Nat. Com., 1978-84; mem. chem. events com. Nat. Acads. Sci., 2001-03, mem. mustard gap processing com., 2004-05; chair N.J. Election Law Enforcement Commn., 2004—. Master Environ. Inn of Ct.; mem. ABA (co-chair subcom. hazardous waste & CERCLA), Internat. Bar Assn., N.J. Bar Assn., Summit Bar Assn.; fellow ABA, Harvard Club. Unitarian Universalist. Office: Cooper Rose & English 480 Summit Ave Summit NJ 07901 Office Phone: 908-273-1212. Business E-Mail: jenglish@crelaw.com.

ENGLISH, JOHN DWIGHT, lawyer; b. Evanston, Ill., Mar. 28, 1949; s. John Francis English and Mary Faye (Taylor) Butler; m. Claranne Kay Lundeen, Apr. 22, 1972; children: Jennifer A., Katharine V., Margaret E. BA, Drake U., 1971; JD, Loyola U., 1976. Bar: Ill. 1976, U.S. Dist. Ct. (no. dist.) Ill. 1976, U.S. Tax Ct. 1977. Assoc. Bentley DuCanto Silvestri & Forkins, Chgo., 1976-79; ptnr. Silvestri Mahoney English & Zdeb, Chgo., 1979-81; assoc. Coffield Ungaretti Harris & Slavin, Chgo., 1981-83; ptnr. Ungaretti & Harris, Chgo., 1983—. Instr. estate planning Loyola U., Chgo., 1982-87; instr. Ill. Inst. Continuing Edn. Estate Planning Short Course, 1998, 2001. Bd. dirs. Prince of Peace Luth. Sch., Chgo., 1977-83, Bethesda Home for the Aged, Chgo., 1981-89, 2000-03, Luth. Family Mission, Chgo., 1985-91; alderman Park Ridge (Ill.) City Coun., 1991-95; pres. congregation coun. St. Luke's Luth. Ch., Park Ridge, 2000-03, 05-. Mem.: Chgo. Bar Assn. (former chmn. divsn. II probate practice com.), Ill. State Bar Assn., Phi Beta Kappa. Lutheran. Home: 631 Wisner St Park Ridge IL 60068-3428 Office: Ungaretti & Harris 3500 Three 1st Nat Bank Plz Chicago IL 60602 Office Phone: 312-977-4401. Business E-Mail: jdenglish@uhlaw.com.

ENGLISH, MARLENE CABRAL, management consultant; b. Lawrence, Mass., Apr. 28, 1954; d. Amick John and Mary Rose (Vasconcelos) Cabral; m. Richard Gayle English, June 24, 1978. BBA, U. Mass., 1976. Acct. mgr. Revlon, Inc., N.Y.C., 1977-79; tech. rep. Rapidata, Inc., N.Y.C., 1979-80; mgr.acctg. systems group Pannell, Kerr, Forster, Dallas, 1980-83; mgmt. cons. Blythe/Nelson, Dallas, 1983-84, Prism Cons., Arlington, Tex., 1984—. Sec., treas. Highland-Avery Industries, Inc., Dallas, 1988-95. Author: And God Created Woman, 1995. Tech. systems procurement & installation Rep. Nat. Conv., Dallas, 1984; dir. Faith Harvest Ministries, Inc., Dallas, 1990-95; sys. cons. Van Cliburn Internat. Piano Competition, Ft. Worth, 1985. Roman Catholic. Avocations: Victorian studies, antique linen restoration, gardening, Christian writing, classical piano. Home and Office: Prism Cons 4320 Rambling Creek Dr Arlington TX 76016-3418 Personal E-mail: jicky@sbcglobal.net.

ENGLISH, MICHELA, entertainment company executive; married; 2 children. BA in Internat. Affairs, Sweet Briar Coll.; M Pub. and Pvt. Mgmt., Yale U. Policy analyst Fed. Energy Adminstrn.; sr. mgr. McKinsey & Co.; v.p. corp. planning and bus. devel. Marriott Corp.; sr. v.p. Nat. Geog. Soc.; pres. Discovery.com, Bethesda, Md. Bd. dirs. Riggs Nat. Corp., Washington; cons. in field. Bd. dirs. Sweet Briar (Va.) Coll. Mem. Nat. Found. for Improvement of Edn. (bd. dirs.). Office: Discovery.com 7700 Wisconsin Ave Fl 5 Bethesda MD 20814-3557 Fax: 301-986-4826.

ENGLISH, NICHOLAS CONOVER, lawyer; b. Elizabeth, N.J., Apr. 12, 1912; s. Conover and Sara Elizabeth (Jones) E.; m. Agnes N. Perry, Mar. 18, 1939 (div. 1947); children— Henry H. P., Ann Whitall (Mrs. Edward J. Wardwell); m. Eleanor Morss, May 1, 1948; children— Priscilla English Vincent, Sara (dec.), Sherman, Eleanor English Folta. Grad., Pingry Sch., 1929; AB magna cum laude, Princeton, 1934; LL.B., Harvard, 1937. Bar: N.J. 1937. Since practiced in, Newark; partner firm McCarter & English, 1947-77, of counsel, 1978—. Bd. dirs. Summit (N.J.) YMCA, 1950-57, pres., 1953-55; bd. dirs. Newark YMWCA, also pres.; chmn. exec. com. Ctrl. Atlantic Area YMCA, 1957-63; mem. nat. coun. YMCA, 1954, 58-81, v.p., 1959-60, mem. nat. bd., 1960-71, 73-81, vice chmn., 1969-71, treas., 1977-81; trustee N.J. Nat. Land Trust, 1983-93, Kent Place Sch., 1959—, pres., 1961-72, Pingry Sch., 1954-73; bd. dirs. Nat. Legal Aid Assn., 1953-56. Lt. USNR, 1943—45. Mem. ABA (ho. of dels. 1957-58), N.J. Bar Assn., Essex County Bar Assn., Am. Bible Soc. (bd. trustees 1964-93, sr. trustee 1993—), Am. Law Inst. Congregationalist. Home: 46 Meadow Lks Apt 04L Hightstown NJ 08520-3332 Office: McCarter & English 4 Gateway Ctr 100 Mulberry St Newark NJ 07102-0652

ENGLISH, PATRICIA DORZELL, women's health nurse practitioner; d. Robert William and Irma Mary English. BSN, St. Xavier U., 2000. RN State Ill. Dept. Regulation and Edn., 2002, lic. practical nurse, State Ill. Dept. Regulation and Edn., 1983, cert. childbirth educator, ARC, 1983. Nurse Daniel Hale Williams Med. Ctr., Chgo., 1984, St. Francis Xavier Cabrini Hosp., Chgo., 1985—86, Michael Resse Health Plan, Chgo., 1986—89, Rush Presbyn. St. Luke's Med. Ctr., Chgo., 1989; educator, couselor South Side Pregnancy Ctr., Oak Lawn, Ill., 2004—; pvt. tchr., 1989—2004. Editor Block Club, Chgo., 1994—97. Recipient Outstanding Vol. Svc. award, Oak Forest Hosp., 1980—90, Vol. award, ARC, 1983—89. Mem.: Sigma Theta Tau. Avocations: ceramics, sewing, crafts, singing, writing poetry.

ENGLISH, PHILIP SHERIDAN, congressman; b. Erie, Pa., June 20, 1956; s. John Sr. and Otilie English; m. Christiane Weschler. BA in Polit. Sci., U. Pa., 1978. Contr. City of Erie, Pa., 1986-90; chief of staff Senator Melissa Hart, Harrisburg, Pa., 1990-92; ex-dir. Pa. Senate Fin. Com., Harrisburg, 1992-94; mem. U.S. Congress from 3rd Pa. dist. (formerly 21st), 1995—; mem. ways and means com., joint econ. com. Republican. Roman Catholic. Avocations: hiking, history, archaeology. Office: US Ho of Reps 1410 Longworth Ho Office Bldg Washington DC 20515-0001*

ENGLISH, RAY, library administrator; b. Brevard, N.C., Dec. 11, 1946; s. Daniel Leon and Lois (Dorsett) E.; m. Allison Scott Ricker, Oct. 19, 1985; children: John, Michael. AB with honors in German, Davidson Coll., 1969; MA in German Lit., U. N.C., 1971, MSLS, 1977, PhD, 1978. Teaching asst. German dept. U. N.C., Chapel Hill, 1970-73, 74-75, rsch. asst., 1976; reference libr. Alderman Libr. U.Va., Charlottesville, Va., 1977-79; head reference libr. Oberlin (Ohio) Coll. Libr., 1979-89, assoc. dir., 1986-90; dir. librs. Oberlin (Ohio) Coll., 1990—, acad. advisor, 1980—. Lectr. in German, 1986—2000; vis. lectr. Sch. Libr. Sci., U. N.C., Chapel Hill, 1981; spkr. in field; mem. steering com. Scholarly Pub. and Acad. Resources Coalition, 1999—. Mem. editl. bd. Portal: Libraries and the Academy; contbr. articles to profl. jours. German Acad. Exchange Svc. fellow, 1973-74. Mem.: ALA, Acad. Libr. Assn. Ohio, Libr. Adminstrn. and Mgmt. Assn., Assn. Coll. and Rsch. Librs. (bd. dirs., exec. com. 1996—98, chair scholarly comm. com. 2002—). Home: 83 S Cedar St Oberlin OH 44074-1559 Office: Oberlin Coll Library 148 W College St Oberlin OH 44074-1575 Office Phone: 440-775-5666. E-mail: ray.english@oberlin.edu.

ENGLISH, RICHARD ALLYN, sociologist, educator; b. Winter Park, Fla., Aug. 29, 1936; s. Wentworth and Mary English; m. Ireita Geraldine Williams, June 29, 1978 AB, Talladega Coll., 1958; MA (Woodrow Wilson fellow), U. Mich., 1959, MSW., 1964, PhD, 1970. Cert. Oxford U., Internat. Summer Sch. Forced Migration Refugee Ctr., Queen Elizabeth Hse, Oxford, England, 2001. Dir. vocat. and youth services Flint Urban League, Mich., 1959-61, acting exec. dir., 1961-62; social group worker Neighborhood Service Orgn., Detroit, 1963-65; mem. faculty Sch. Social Work, Wayne State U., 1965-67; lectr. U. Mich., Ann Arbor, 1967-70, asst. prof. social work, 1970-72, assoc. prof., 1972-83, prof., 1983—85, assoc. v.p. acad. affairs, 1974-81; dean Howard U. Sch. Social Work, 1985—2000, prof., 1985—; interim provost and chief acad. officer Howard U., 2003—04, provost and chief acad. officer, 2004—. Vis. scholar Paul Baerwald Sch. Social Work, Hebrew U., Jerusalem, 1975; vis. prof. Howard U., fall 1981; Am. Psychol. Assn.-Nat. Inst. Edn. fellow, 1981; Robert L. Sutherland chair in mental health and social policy U. Tex.-Austin Sch. Social Work, 1983-84, 84-85; cons. to various schs., social work, public sch. dists. and pvt. founds., 1969—; pres. Council on Social Work Edn., 1981-84; bd. dirs. Nat. Resource Ctr. for Spl. Needs Adoption, Spaulding Sch. for Children, Chelsea, Mich., 1986—, Nat. Coun. Aging. Author: (with others) Inheriting the Earth: Child Welfare Policies and Practices for Minority Children, 1990; co-editor: Human Service Organizations: A Book of Readings, 1974; The Challenge for Mental Health: Minorities and Their World Views, 1984, (with W. Allen and J. Hall) Black Families, 1960-84: A Classified, Selectively Annotated Bibliography, 1986; co-editor: (with C. Guzzetta and A.J.Katz) Education for Social Work Practice: Selected International Models; The Professional School Dean: The Roles of Leadership (co-editor with M.J. Austin and F.L. Ahearn), 1997; mem. editorial bd. Black Caucus: Jour. Nat. Assn. Black Social Workers; contbr. articles to profl. jours. Mem. adv. panel Refugee Policy Group, mem. adv. bd. Nat. Assembly; bd. visitors Sch. Social Work U. Pitts.; bd. dirs. Youth for Understanding Internat. Exch., 1991—, Coalition for the Homeless; bd. advisors Ill. Inst. Mil. and Occupational Studies; adv. bd. Enterprise Found.; mem. vestry St. Mary's Episcopal Ch. Recipient Outstanding Service award Nat. Assn. Black Social Workers, 1983; Nat. Assn. for Equal Opportunity in Higher Edn. Disting. Alumni award, 1985, Presdl. award for Excellence in Social Work Edn., 1997; Whitney Young, Jr. scholar, Western Mich. U., 1988. Mem. Nat. Assn. Social Workers, Nat. Coun. Family Rels., Am. Sociol. Assn., Internat. Council Social Welfare, Internat. Assn. Schs. Social Work (bd. dirs.), ACLU (bd. dirs. nat. capitol area 1986—), The Emeritus Found. (bd. dirs.), Dept. Human Svcs. Commn., D.C. Govt., Nat. Network for Social Work Mgrs. (adv. bd.), Internat. Coun. Social Welfare (U.S. com., internat. bd.), Coun. on Social Work Edn., Nat. Assn. Black Social Workers. Home: 2724 Abilene Dr Chevy Chase MD 20815-3051 Office: Howard U Office of Provost 2400 6th St Ste 405 Washington DC 20059-0001 Business E-Mail: renglish@howard.edu.

ENGLISH, ROBERT JOSEPH, electronics executive; b. Jersey City, Dec. 5, 1932; s. John Joseph and Mary (Budrawiz) E.; m. Robyn Adele Allan, Dec. 27, 1958; children: Robert Joseph, Mark Allan, John Frederick. BS, St. Peters Coll., 1954; LL.B., Georgetown U., 1958; MBA, NYU, 1963. Bar: DC 1958, NJ 1959, NY 1984. Subcontract adminstr. ITT Fed. Labs. div., Nutley, N.J., 1959-60; with Fed. Electric Corp., Paramus, N.J., 1960—, sec., gen. counsel, 1964-66, dir. legal contracts, 1967-70; gen. counsel ITT Govt. and Comml. Services Group, 1970-72; v.p., sec., gen. counsel ITT Def. Communications and ITT Avionics divs., Nutley, 1972—; sec., gen. counsel Internat. Electric Corp., 1972—. Dir. ITT Fed. Support Services Inc., ITT Tech. Services Inc., Intelex Systems Inc., Providence, Base Services Inc., Paramus, Internat. Standard Engrng. Inc., Paramus. Author: Business Contract Forms, Federal Government Subcontract Forms; contbr. articles to profl. jours. Trustee Mahwah Hist. Soc., N.J., 1978—. Served to 1st lt., Chem. Corps, U.S. Army, 1954-56. Mem. Am., Bergen, NJ, DC, NY Bar Assns., Phi Delta Phi. Home: 36 Sunnyside Rd Mahwah NJ 07430-1418 Office: 492 River Rd Nutley NJ 07110-3609 Personal E-mail: esquire@aol.com.

ENGLISH, STEPHEN FRANCIS, lawyer; b. Portland, Oreg., Jan. 17, 1948; BA, Hons. Coll., U. Oreg., 1970; JD, U. Calif., San Francisco, 1973. Bar: Oreg. 1973; U.S. Dist. Ct. Oreg. 1973; U.S. Ct. Appeals (9th cir.) Oreg. 1980; U.S. Supreme Ct. 1982. Ptnr. Bullivant Houser Bailey, Portland, Oreg., 1983—. Mem. faculty Hastings Coll. Trial Advocacy, 1998—; mem. Bus. Litigation Inst., 2000; bd. dirs. Dr. Martens AirWair USA, 2002—, Fellow Am. Coll. Trial Lawyers; Mem. ABA (vice-chair products liability com., 1996—, chair self insurers and risk mgrs. com. 1994-95, editor Self Insurers Newsletter 1987-89, chair non-profit, charitable and religious orgns. com. 1990-92, mem. Tort and Insurance Practice Sect.), Multnomah County Bar Assn., Oreg. State Bar Assn. (chair litigation sect. 1990-91, exec. com. 1987-91), Am. Bd. Trial Adv. (treas. Oreg. chpt. 1996-98, bd. dirs. 1997—, sec. 1998—, pres. 2002-, pres. Oreg. chpt., 2003-04), Oreg. Assn. Def. Counsel (chair products liability practice group 1997-98), Def. Rsch. Inst., Oreg. State Bar Masters of Trial Advocacy. Office: Bullivant Houser Bailey 300 Pioneer Tower 888 SW 5th Ave Portland OR 97204-2089 E-mail: steve.english@bullivant.com.

ENGLISH, STEPHEN RAYMOND, lawyer; b. Key West, Fla., Nov. 25, 1946; s. Jack Raymond and Jean Clyde (Peightal) E.; m. Molly Munger, Oct. 7, 1978; children: Nicholas, Alfred. BA, UCLA, 1975; JD, Harvard U., 1975. Bar: Calif. 1975, U.S. Dist. Ct. (ctrl. dist.) Calif. 1976, U.S. Dist. Ct. (so. dist.) Calif. 1978, U.S. Dist. Ct. (ea. dist.) Calif. 1988, U.S. Ct. Appeals (9th cir.) 1992. Assoc. Agnew, Miller & Carlson, L.A., 1975-78, Morgan, Lewis & Bockius, L.A., 1978-85, ptnr., 1985-98, English, Munger & Rice, L.A., 1998—, co-dir. Advancement Project, 2000—. Lawyer rep. Ninth Cir. Jud. Conf., 1996-97. Pres. bd. dirs. Pub. Counsel, L.A., 1988-89, Inner City Law Ctr., L.A., 1992-93; bd. dirs. L.A. Legal Aid Found., 1999—. Mem. L.A. County Bar Assn. (mem. barristers exec. com. 1980-82, trustee 1990-92, chair pro bono coun. 1990-92, chair legal svcs. for poor 1993-95, mem. exec. com. litig. sect. 1994—, chair litig. sect. 2003-04), L.A. County Bar Found. (pres. 1998-99). Office: English Munger & Rice 1545 Wilshire Blvd Ste 800 Los Angeles CA 90017-4694

ENGLISH, THOMAS FRANCIS, lawyer; b. Washington, Mar. 8, 1958; s. Joseph Martin and Dorothea Mary (Jackal) E.; m. Margaret Catherine Hitselberger, May 29, 1982; children: Carolyn Sara, Pamela Marie. AB, Georgetown U., 1980, JD, 1983. Bar: Mass. 1983, DC 1988, NY 2000, U.S. Dist. Ct. Mass. 1985. Atty. Mass. Mut. Life Ins., Springfield, Mass., 1983-85, asst. counsel, 1985-88; sr. v.p. & gen. counsel New York Life, NYC. Mem. ABA, Nat. Assn. Life Underwriters, Assn. Life Ins. Counsel, DC Bar, Knights of Columbus. Republican. Roman Catholic. Office: New York Life Ste 10 SB 51 Madison Ave New York NY 10010

ENGLISH, WILLIAM DESHAY, lawyer, director; b. Piedmont, Calif., Dec. 25, 1924; s. Munro and Mabel (Michener) E.; m. Nancy Ames, Apr. 7, 1956; children: Catherine, Barbara, Susan, Stephen. AB in Econs., U. Calif., Berkeley, 1948, JD, 1951. Bar: Calif. 1952, D.C. 1972. Trial atty., spl. asst. to atty. gen. U.S. Dept. Justice, Washington, 1953-55; sr. atty. AEC, Washington, 1955-62; legal advisor U.S. Mission to European Communities, Brussels, 1962-64; asst. gen. counsel internat. matters COMSAT, Washington, 1965-73; counsel Internat. Telecomm. Satellite Orgn., 1965-73; v.p., gen. counsel, dir. COMSAT Gen. Corp., 1973-76; sr. v.p. legal and govtl. affairs Satellite Bus. Sys., McLean, Va., 1976-86; v.p., gen. counsel Satellite Transponder Leasing Corp. (IBM), McLean, Va., 1986-87; pvt. practice Washington, 1987—; counsel Am. Space Transp. Assn., 1987-93, Washington Space Bus. Roundtable; gen. counsel Iridium, LLC, 1992-96, spl. counsel, 1996-2000. With USAAF, 1943-45. Decorated Air medal. Fellow Coun. on Econ. Regulation, 1985-91; mem. ABA, AIAA (chmn. com. legal aspects aeronautics and astronautics,1993-2000, chmn. allocation space launch risks subcom. 1987, chmn. orbital debris legal subcom.), Am. Competitive Telecomm. Assn. (bd. dirs. 1976-84, pres. 1983), D.C. Bar Assn., Fed. Comm. Bar Assn., State Bar Calif., Fgn. Policy Discussion Group, Met. Club, Chevy Chase Club. Home: 7420 Exeter Rd Bethesda MD 20814-2352 Personal E-mail: w.english2@verizon.net.

ENGLISH, WOODROW DOUGLAS, lawyer; b. San Antonio, Dec. 1, 1941; s. Woodie Douglas Jr. and June Louise (Wasik) E.; m. Marcia Anne Mathwig, Dec. 19, 1969 (div. Aug. 1981); children: Kristina Renee, David Douglas; m. Carol Jordan, July 11, 1987; children: Leanne Alexander Cassidy, Lisa Alexander Cook. BS in Physics, Trinity U., 1967; JD, Western State U., 1981. Bar: Calif. 1989, U.S. Patent Office 1982, U.S. Supreme Ct. 1992. Sales engr. Mfrs. Rep., Seattle, 1972-75; real estate salesperson, broker Sherwood & Roberts Realtors & Coldwell Banker, Seattle, 1975-78; safety engr. Boeing Aerospace, Seattle, 1978-79; ins. agt., broker Farmers Ins. Group, San Diego, 1979-81; U.S. patent agt. Dept. Def., China Lake, Calif., 1981-87; corp. counsel Del Mar Avionics, Irvine, Calif., 1987-97; pvt. practice Ventura, Calif., 1991—. Real estate broker, Ventura, ins. broker, Ventura. Capt. USAF, 1961-65. Mem. Masons, Shriners, Elks, Kiwanis, Am. Legion, Sigma Pi Sigma, Phi Alpha Delta, Nu Beta Epsilon. Republican. Avocation: flying. Home: 1215 Lost Point Ln Oxnard CA 93030-6770 Office: County Sq Profl Offices 674 County Square Dr Ventura CA 93003-5454

ENGLISH-ANDERSON, SAN DEI, minister; b. Jacksboro, Tex., Aug. 27, 1945; d. Robert March English and Ressie English; m. Donald Loren Anderson, Dec. 19, 2001; children: Traci Dixon, Tiara Cunningham, Joshua English. AA, Jarvis Christian Coll., Hawkins, Texas, 1965. Minister, assoc. pastor New Creation Outreach, Anaheim, Calif., 2001—02; producer/host Sonic Cable TV, San Luis Obispo, Calif., 1982—86; CEO Tiara Prodns., Mission Viejo, Calif., 1987—2002. V.p. ways & means Laguna Niguel Rep. Women Federated, 2000—01. Served USAF, 1964—65. Named Model of Yr., Foxes and Hares Model Assn., 1967, Ms. Royal Ambassador 2002, Mrs. Orange County Am., 2003, Mrs. Irvine Am., 2004. Mem.: Ctr. Stage/ Performing Arts Guild, Phenomenal Women Orgn. (treas.). Avocation: writing, sewing, reading, dancing, meditating. Office Phone: 949-347-9822. Personal E-mail: sandeienglishanderson@yahoo.com.

ENGLISH-BARRETT, KATHLEEN THERESE, artist; b. Windsor, Ont., Can., Sept. 10, 1958; came to U.S., 1980; d. Michael and Dorothy Anne (Carruthers) English; m. Robert Edward Barrett, Sept. 1, 1984.l BFA, U. Windsor, 1980; MA, Wayne State U., Detroit, 1983. Sole proprietor English Rebel Designs, Ltd., Rochester, Mich., 1984-88, v.p., owner Auburn Hills, Mich., 1988—. Oil paintings include Uncle Tom, 1983 (Best of Show award 1983). Mem. Detroit Inst. Arts. Republican. Roman Catholic. Avocations: travel, art history. Home: 2441 Dexter Rd Auburn Hills MI 48326-2311 Office: English Rebel Designs Ltd 2441 Dexter Rd Auburn Hills MI 48326-2311

ENGLUND, GAGE BUSH, dancer, educator; b. Sept. 7, 1931; d. Morris Williams and Margaret Wallace (Gage) Bush; m. Richard Bernard Englund, Dec. 1, 1959; children: Alixandra Gage, Rachel Rutherford. Student, Sch. Am. Ballet, 1960. Founder Birmingham Civic Ballet, 1952; mem. Robert Joffrey Ballet, N.Y.C., 1957-60, soloist, 1959-60; mem. Am. Ballet Theatre, N.Y.C., 1960-63, Huntington Dance Ensemble, L.I., N.Y., 1968-69; soloist Dance Repertory Co., 1969-72; tchr. ballet, assoc. chmn. Friends of Am. Ballet Theatre, N.Y.C., 1972—. Dir. Ala. By-Products Corp., 1971—77; rehearsal coach Am. Ballet Theatre II, 1973—85; mem. scholarship com. Am. Ballet Theatre Sch., N.Y.C., 1974—; rehearsal coach Joffrey Ballet II, 1985—95, Am. Ballet Theatre Studio Co., 1995—. Trustee Ballet Theatre Found., 1974—87, v.p., 1980—81; trustee Chapin Sch., 1982—2003, Animal Med. Ctr., N.Y.C., 1982—, Cancer Rsch. Inst., 1984—, Episcpoal Sch. N.Y., 1979—83; bd. dirs. Children's Hosp. Clinic, Birmingham, 1955—57, Spoleto Festival, U.S.A., 1980—83, Ala. State Ballet, 1967—, Birmingham Civic Ballet, 1952—67. Named Queen, Birmingham Festival Arts, 1957; recipient Silver Bowl award, 1957, Lucia Chase award for svcs. to Am. Ballet Theatre, Soc. Fine Arts U. Ala., 2001, Patron of the Arts award, 2002; scholar Ford Found., 1960. Mem.: Am. Guild Mus. Artists, Jr. League N.Y.C., Colonial Dames Ala., Colony Club, Lakewood Country Club. Episcopalian. Home: PO Box 469 17367 Scenic Hwy 98 Point Clear AL 36564

ENGLUND, ROBERT, actor, director, producer; b. Glendale, Calif., June 6, 1949; s. C. Kent and Janice (McDonald) E.; m. Nancy Ellen Booth, Oct. 1, 1988. Student, Oakland U., U. Calif., Northridge, UCLA, Royal Acad. Dramatic Arts, Rochester, Mich. Actor, dir., producer; resident artist Meadow Brook Theatre, Rochester, 1969-72, guest artist, 1973; resident actor Gt. Lakes Shakespeare Festival, Cleve., 1970—71; resident actor Judas in Godspell, Cleve., 1971. Appeared as Freddy Krueger in A Nightmare on Elm Street, 1984, A Nightmare on Elm Street, Part 2: Freddy's Revenge, 1985, A Nightmare on Elm Street 3: Dream Warriors, 1987, A Nightmare on Elm Street 4: The Dream Master 1988, A Nightmare on Elm Street 5: The Dream Child, 1989, Freddy's Dead: The Final Nightmare, 1991, Wes Craven's New Nightmare, 1994; also appeared in films Buster and Billie, 1973, Hustle, 1974, Last of the Cowboys, 1976, Stay Hungry, 1975, A Star Is Born, 1976, Bloodbrothers, 1977, Big Wednesday, 1978, Galaxy of Terror, 1980, Dead and Buried, 1981, Don't Cry, It's Only Thunder, 1982, Never Too Young to Die, 1986, Phantom of the Opera, 1989, Dance Macabre, 1992, Steven King's The Mangler, 1995, Tobe Hoopers Night Dreams, 1992, Ford Fairlane, 1990, Killer Tongue, 1996, Wishmaster, 1997, Disney's Meet the Deedles, 1997,

Dee Snyder's Strangeland, 1997, Urban Legend, 1998, Nobody Knows Anything, 1999, The Prince and the Surfer, 1999, Wish You Were Dead, 2000, The Return of Caligostro, 2000, Python, 2000, Cold Sweat, 2000, Windfall, 2001, Like A Bad Dream, 2002, 2002 Maniacs, 2002, Homecoming, 2002, others; dir. 976-EVIL, 1988; appeared on TV in series Downtown, 1986-87, Freddy's Nighymares, 1987-89, Nightmare Cafe, 1992-93, Young Joe, the Forgotten Kennedy, 1977, The Ordeal of Patty Hearst, 1979, V, 1983, Hobson's Choice, 1983, I Want to Live, 1983, Hunter, 1985, Knight Rider, 1986, MacGyver, 1986, also on Police Woman, Soap, Charlie's Angels, Police Story, Married With Children, also others; TV films Mortal Fear, 1995, Unspoken Truth, 1996; also stage actor and producer. Mem. SAG, AFTRA, Actors Equity Assn., Dirs. Guild Am. Office: 1616 Santa Cruz St Laguna Beach CA 92651-3350

ENGSTRAND, BEATRICE C., neurologist, educator; b. Oceanside, NY, July 16, 1960; d. Donald Daniel and Claudia Helen Engstrand. BA, Lehigh U., 1982, doctorate (hon.); MD, Med. Coll. Pa., 1984. Diplomate Am. Bd. Psychiatry and Neurology, bd. cert. in neurology; lic. physician, NY. Resident in medicine North Shore U. Hosp., Manhasset, NY, 1984-85; resident in neurology NY Hosp., NYC, 1985-86, SUNY Health Sci. Ctr., Bklyn., 1986-88; attending physician Met. Hosp., NYC, 1988-92; asst. prof. neurology NY Med. Coll., Valhalla, 1988—; pvt. practice Huntington, NY, 1992—. Founder, pres. Neuro-Degenerative Disease Found., 1993—; radio host Sta. WOR; presenter and lectr. in field. Author: (book) A Gift of Healing—A Legacy of Hope, 1990; host, prodr. WOR Radio Mem. adv. bd. arts and sci. Lehigh U., Bethlehem, Pa., 1992—, women's adv. study bd., 1993—; mem. legis. com. Suffolk County Med. Soc., 1994-97; com. fundraiser Gov. George Pataki Election, 1995; mem. People for Ethical Treatment of Animals, Physicians for Responsible Medicine, other animal rights groups. Recipient Woman of Distinction award Soroptomist Internat.; named one of Outstanding Young Woman of Am., 1997. Fellow Am. Acad. Neurology (diplomate); mem. AMA, ACP, Am. Med. Student Assn., Am. Acad. Neurology, Nat. Bd. Med. Examiners (diplomate), Med. Soc. NY State, NY County Med. Soc. (pub. rels. com.), Westchester County Med. Ctr. (bioethics com.), Bklyn. Neurol. Soc., Med. Coll. Pa. Alumni Assn., Cornell U. Alumni Assn., Rotary Club Upper Manhattan (v.p. 1990-91, pres. 1991-92, Paul Harris award 1991). Republican. Avocations: travel, animals, languages, opera, writing. Office: 76 E Main St Ste 1 Huntington NY 11743-2837 Office Phone: 631-423-2100. Personal E-mail: neurologydoctor@aol.com.

ENGSTROM, ERIK, publishing executive; b. Taby, Stockholm, Sweden; s. Kjell and Alice (Klarstrom) E. BS in Econs. & Bus. Adminstrn., Stockholm Sch. Econs., 1986; MS in Engring., Royal Inst. Technology, 1986; diploma Internat. Mgmt. Program, Ecole des Hautes Etudes Comml., Paris, 1986; MBA, Harvard U., 1988. Cons. and engagement mgr. McKinsey & Co., N.Y., 1988-91; v.p. corp. devel. Bantam Doubleday Dell Pub. Group, Inc., N.Y., 1991-92, sr. v.p., CFO, 1992-93, exec. v.p., chief adminstrv. officer, 1993-94, exec. v.p., COO, 1994-96, pres., COO, 1996-98; pres., CEO BDD N.Am., 1998; pres., COO Random House Inc., N.Y.C., 1998-2001; ptnr. Gen. Atlantic Ptnrs., Greenwich, Conn., 2001—04; CEO Elsevier, 2004—. Bd. dirs. Bonnier Books, Eniro AB, Reed Elsevier PLC. Bd. dirs. Graham-Windham Svcs. to Families and Children, 1999—; mem. bus. com. Met. Mus. of Art, 1998—. Sgt. Swedish Army, 1983-84. Scholar Fulbright Commn., 1986. Office: Elsevier 360 Park Ave S New York NY 10010

ENHORNING, GORAN, obstetrician, gynecologist; b. Birkdale, Eng., Mar. 18, 1924; came to US 1986; s. Emil Augustin and Maria Rosina (von Haartman) E.; m. Louise Christina Carlberg, Apr. 16, 1955; children: Ulf, Dag and Peder (twins), Marianne. MD, Karolinska Inst., Stockholm, 1952, PhD in Physiology, 1961. Asst. prof. ob-gyn. Karolinska Inst., Stockholm, 1952—61; Fulbright scholar U. Utah, Salt Lake City, 1961—63, UCLA, 1963—64; assoc. prof. ob-gyn. Karolinska Inst., 1964—71, U. Toronto, Canada, 1971—75, prof. ob-gyn., 1975—86; prof. ob-gyn. and physiology SUNY, Buffalo, 1986—2002. Contbr. articles to profl. jour. initiation of concept that symptoms of asthma and infectious bronchiolitis may be due to a surfactant dysfunction, caused by airway inflammation, an allergic reaction, an inhalation of cold air, or a hydrolysis of surfactant phospholipids, catalyzed by phospholipase A2 (PLA2) and by lysophospholipase (LPL) from eosinophils. The way the surfactant dysfunction causes airway blockage, and thus breathing difficulties is demonstrated with the Capillary Surfactometer, a new instrument developed to simulate surfactant function in terminal airways. Home: 1112 Old Galleon Ln Vero Beach FL 32693 Business E-Mail: gee1@buffalo.edu.

ENIS, CHARLES RICHARD, accountant, educator; b. Balt., Sept. 15, 1946; s. Bernard Anthony and Ellen Norma Enis; m. Gloria Louise Enis, Dec. 15, 1974; children: Megan May, Mark Richard. BS in Fin., U. Md., 1968, BS in Acctg., 1972, MBA, 1974, PhD, 1981. CPA Md., 1973. Lectr. acctg. U. Md., College Park, 1974—81; assoc. prof. acctg. Pa. State U., University Park, 1981—. Contbr. over 80 articles to profl. jours. With USAR, 1969—90. Mem.: Am. Tax Assn., Md. Assn. of CPAs. Roman Catholic. Office: Pa State Univ Smeal Coll of Bus University Park PA 16802

ENKE, CHRISTIE GEORGE, chemistry professor, consultant; b. Mpls., July 8, 1933; s. Alvin Christie Enke and Mae Eileen (Ferris) Nichols; m. Mary Crane, June 23, 1956; children: Paul F. (dec.), David M., Anne; m. Bea Reed, Dec. 25, 1988; 1 child, Gillian. BA, Principia Coll., 1955; PhD, U. Ill, 1959. Instr. to asst. prof. Princeton U., 1959-66; assoc. to prof. chemistry Mich. State U., East Lansing, 1966-94; prof. chemistry U. N.Mex., Albuquerque, 1994—. Author: Electronics and Instrumentation, 1982; patentee in field. Sloane Found. fellow, 1969. Fellow AAAS, Am. Chem. Soc. (chmn. divsn. computers, chair elect analytical divsn, 2004-05, Chem. Instrumentation award 1974, Computers in Chemistry award 1989, J.C. Gidding award for Excellence in Edn., 2003); mem. Am. Soc. Mass Spectrometry (pres. 1994-96, Disting. Contbn. award 1994). Avocation: stained glass. Office: U NMex Clark Hall Albuquerque NM 87131 Office Phone: 505-277-3159. E-mail: enke@unm.edu.

ENLOW, DONALD HUGH, retired anatomist, dean; b. Mosquero, N.Mex., Jan. 22, 1927; s. Donald Carter and Martie Blairene (Albertson) E.; m. Martha Ruth McKnight, Sept. 3, 1945; 1 child, Sharon Lynn. BS, U. Houston, 1949, MS, 1951; PhD, Tex. A&M U., 1955. Instr. biology U. Houston, 1949-51; asst. prof. biology West Tex. State U., 1955-56; instr. anatomy Med. Coll. S.C., 1956-57; asst. prof. U. Mich. Med. Sch., Ann Arbor, 1957-62, assoc. prof., 1962-67, prof. anatomy, 1969-72; dir. phys. growth program Center for Human Growth and Devel., 1966-72; prof., chmn. dept. anatomy W.Va. U. Sch. Medicine, Morgantown, 1972-77; Thomas Hill disting. prof., chmn. dept. orthodontics Case Western Res. Sch. Dentistry, Cleve., 1977-89, prof. emeritus, 1989—, asst. dean for rsch. and grad. studies, 1977-85, acting dean, 1983-86. Adj. prof. U. N.C., 1992—; guest lectr. 29 fgn. countries, 1963—. Author: Principles of Bone Remodeling, 1963, The Human Face, 1968, Handbook of Facial Growth, 1975, 3d edit., 1990, Essentials of Facial Growth, 1996; contbr. chpts. to 30 books, numerous articles to profl. jours. Served with USCGR, 1945-46. Recipient Outstanding Research award Tex. Acad. Sci., 1952 Fellow Royal Soc. Medicine, Am. Assn. Anatomists, Internat. Assn. Dental Research; hon. mem. Am. Assn. Orthodontists (Mershon Meml. lectr. 1968, Spl. Merit award 1969, award for outstanding contbns. to orthodontia, 1984), Gt. Lakes Orthodontic Soc., Cleve. Dental Soc., Cleve. Orthodontic Soc., Omicron Kappa Upsilon. Republican. Methodist. Home: 5 Arbutus Ln Whispering Pines NC 28327-9465 Personal E-mail: donnlo@pinehurst.net.

ENMAN, JOHN AUBREY, science educator; b. Newton, Mass., Sept. 11, 1921; s. John Aubrey and Grace Elizabeth (Johnston) Enman; m. Betty Ann Buckels. BA, U. Maine, 1943; MA, Harvard U., 1948; PhD, U. Pitts.U., 1963. Instr., asst. prof. Wash. Jefferson Coll., Wash., Pa., 1948—59; assoc. prof., prof. Bloomsburg U., Bloomsburg, Pa., 1959—85; ret., 1985. Rschr. Coal, Coke Heritage Ctr., Uniontown, Pa., 1990. Sgt. U.S. Army, 1943—46, India. Mem.: Assn. Am. Geographers. Democrat. Avocations: photography, reading, travel. Home: 249 Frosty Valley Rd Danville PA 17821

ENNEKING, WILLIAM F., orthopedist, educator; b. Madison, Wis., May 9, 1926; s. William Frank and Francesca Kayser Enneking; m. Margaret Olivia Little, Sept. 11, 1947; children: William, Bonnie, Margaret, Olivia, Florence, Francesca, Christjohn. BS, U. Wis., Madison, 1946, MD, 1949; PhD (hon.), U. Coimbra Causa, Portugal, 1997. Diplomate bd. cert. Am. Bd. Orthop. Surgery, 1958. Prof. orthopedic surgery U. Miss., Jackson, 1956—60; disting. svc. prof. orthopedic surgery U. Fla. Coll. of Medicine, Gainesville, Fla., 1960—. Chmn. bd. dirs. Musculoskeletal Transplant Found., Edison, NJ, 1987—. Author: Musculoskeletal Tumor Surgery, 1983; editor: Musculoskeletal Limb Salvage, 1985. Lt. (j.g.) USN, 1950—52, Korea. Recipient Heath award Outstanding Clin. Control Cancer Treatment, MD Anderson, Dallas, 1988, Sheen award Outstanding Contbn. to Medicine, Am. Coll. of Surgeons, 1988. Mem.: Am. Acad. Orthop. Surgery (exec. com. 1966, Kappa Delta award 1967, 1972, 1980), Am. Bd. Orthop. Surgery (chmn. 1973—80), Am. Orthop. Assn. (pres. 1984—85, Lifetime Achievement in Rsch. 1994, Disting. Clinician Educator 2002). Independent. Roman Catholic. Avocation: fishing. Office: U Fla Orthopeadic Inst 3450 Null Rd Rm 3341 PO Box 112 727 Gainesville FL 32611-2727 Home: 5246 SW 24th Dr Gainesville FL 32607 Personal E-mail: BillKingFisher@aol.com.

ENNIS, BRUCE CLIFFORD, retired lawyer; b. Dover, Del., Mar. 22, 1941; s. Clifford Morgan and Mary Elizabeth (Jones) E.; m. Diane Wallace, July 19, 1969; 1 child, Heather Diane. BA, W.Va. Wesleyan Coll., 1963; JD, Dickinson Law Sch., 1966. Bar: Del. 1969, U.S. Dist. Ct. Del. 1971. Ptnr. Schmittinger & Rodriguez, P.A., Dover, 1969—2001; ret. Instr. Wesley Coll., Dover, 1970-78, Del. Tech. and C.C., Dover, 1978-98. Active United Meth. Ch., Dover. With U.S. Army, 1966-68. Mem. Del. State Bar Assn., Kent County Bar Assn. Home: 444 Troon Rd Dover DE 19904-2343

ENNIS, EDGAR WILLIAM, JR., lawyer; b. Macon, Ga., May 20, 1945; s. Edgar W. and Nelle (Branan) E.; m. Judith Anne Godfrey, June 29, 1974; children: William, Branan. BS in Engring. Sci., USAF Acad., Colorado Springs, Colo., 1967; JD, U. Ga., 1971. Bar: Ga. 1971. Commd. 2d lt. USAF, 1967, advanced through ranks to capt., 1970, resigned, 1975; asst. U.S. atty. U.S. Atty.'s Office-Mid. Dist. of Ga., Macon, 1975-88; U.S. atty. U.S. Dept. Justice, Macon, 1988-93; of counsel Haynsworth, Baldwin, Johnson & Harper, Macon, 1993-97; ptnr. Haynsworth, Baldwin, Johnson & Greaves LLC, Macon, 1998-99, Constangy, Brooks & Smith LLC, Macon, 1999—. Office: Constangy Brooks & Smith LLC 577 Mulberry St Ste 710 Macon GA 31201-8588 Office Phone: 478-750-8600. E-mail: eennis@constangy.com.

ENNIS, LOIS, municipal official; b. Greenville, N.C., Nov. 21, 1945; children: Jose, April, Uta, Djuan, Ameera. B in Sociology, Rutgers U., 1980, M in Pub. Policy, 1983. Asst. adminstr. Forum for Policy Rsch., Rutgers U., Camden, N.J., 1979-84; community devel. officer N.J. Housing and Mortgage Fin., Trenton, 1985-87; data cons. Chase Manhattan Bank, Wilmington, Del., 1987; neighborhood coordinator Berlin (N.J.) Twp., 1987—. Real estate sales assoc. various real estate agys., Magnolia, N.J., 1980-85; coordinator workshops in field; devel. officer N.H.M.F. Agy., Trenton, 1985-86; instr. Rutgers U., Camden County Sch., Pittsgrive Sch. Contbr. articles to profl. publs.; author manual, booklets. Block capt. Thurman St. Assn., Camden, 1976-80; chmn. Liberty Park Civic Assn., Camden, 1979-80; vol. housing counselor nonprofit agys., Camden County, 1987-88; dir. svcs. Girl Scout County Assn., Camden County, 1984-85; pres. Black People Unity Movement Day Care, 1975-80. Recipient Cert. of Honor, Lung Assn., 1978, Good Neighborhood Citizen award Mayor of Camden, 1979. Mem. Rutgers Alumni Assn., Neighborhood Pres. Coordinators Assn. Democrat. Baptist. Avocations: reading, travel.

ENNIS, THOMAS MICHAEL, management consultant; b. Morgantown, W.Va., Mar. 7, 1931; s. Thomas Edson and Violet Ruth (Nugent) E.; m. Julia Marie Dorety, June 30, 1956; children: Thomas John, Robert Griswold (dec.). Student, W.Va. U., 1949-52; AB, George Washington U., 1954; JD, Georgetown U., 1960. With Gov. Employees Ins. Co., Washington, 1956, 59, Air Transport Assn. Am., Washington, 1959-60; dir. ann. support program George Washington U., 1960-63; nat. dir. devel. Project HOPE, People to People Health Found., Inc., Washington, 1963-66; nat. exec. dir. Epilepsy Found. Am., Washington, 1966-74; exec. dir. Clinton, Eaton, Ingham Community Mental Health Bd., Lansing, Mich., 1974-83; nat. exec. dir. Alzheimer's Disease and Related Disorders Assn., Inc., Chgo., 1983-86; exec. dir., pres. The John Douglas French Alzheimers Found., L.A., 1986-96, pres. emeritus, 1996—. Clin. instr. dept. cmty. medicine and internat. health Georgetown U., 1967-74; adj. assoc. prof. dept. psychiatry Mich. State U., 1975-84; lectr. Univ. Ctr. for Internat. Rehab., 1977; cons. health and med. founds., related orgns.; cons. Am. Health Found., 1967-69, Reston, Va.-Georgetown U. Health Planning Project, 1967-70. Editl. bd. Am. Jour. Alzheimer's Disease, 1997—. Mem. adv. bd. Nat. Center for the Law and the Handicapped, 1971-74; advisor Nat. Reye's Syndrome Found.; mem. Nat. Com. for Research in Neurol. Disorders, 1967-72; mem. nat. adv. bd. Developmental Disabilities/Tech. Assistance System, U. N.C., 1971-78; nat. trustee Nat. Kidney Found., 1970-74, mem. exec. com. and bd. Nat. Capitol Area chpt., pres., 1972-74; bd. dirs. Nat. Assn. Pvt. Residential Facilities for Mentally Retarded, 1970-74; bd. dirs., mem. exec. com. Epilepsy Found. Am., 1977-84, Epilepsy Center Mich., 1974-83; nat. bd. dirs. Western Inst. on Epilepsy, 1969-72; bd. dirs., pres. Mich. Mid-South Health Systems Agy., 1975-78; sec. gen. Internat. Fedn. Alzheimer's Disease and Related Disorders, 1984-86; mem. panel Alzheimer's Disease Edn. and Referral Ctr., 1990-93; mem. Calif. State Coun. on Developmental Disabilities, 1997—2003; med. adv. bd. EdenCare Sr. Living Svcs., advisor Ctr. Aging, Washington, 1998—. World Rehab. Fund fellow Norway, 1980. Mem. Nat. Epilepsy League (bd. dirs. 1977-78), Mich. Assn. Cmty. Mental Health (pres. 1977-79), Nat. Coalition Rsch. Neurol. Disorders (dir. at-large 1991—), Scan Health Plan (bd. govs.), Phi Alpha Theta, Phi Kappa Psi. Home and Office: 23740 Killion St Woodland Hills CA 91367-5822 Office Phone: 818-999-2273.

ENO, AMOS STEWART, natural resource foundation administrator; b. Princeton, N.J., Jan. 26, 1950; s. Amos and Alice Pardee (Stewart) E.; m. Marjorie Theresa Belli, Sept. 18, 1982; children: Amos Pinchot L., Angus Connelly. BA, Princeton U., 1972; MA, Cornell U., 1977. Staff asst. to asst. sec. U.S. Dept. Interior, Washington, 1974-76, spl. asst. to chief, office of endangered species, 1978-81; asst. dir. wildlife affairs Nat. Audubon Soc., Washington, 1981-82, dir. wildlife programs, 1982-86; dir. conservation programs Nat. Fish and Wildlife Found., Washington, 1986-91, exec. dir., 1991-99; pres. Resources First Group, South Freeport, Maine, 2000—. Pres. Resources First Found.; exec. dir. New Eng. Forestry Found., 2002—; bd. dirs. Strategic Environ. Rsch. and Devel. Program, U.S. Dept. Def., Light-Stream Corp., Hydrophilix Corp.; mem. coun. N.Am. Wetlands Conservation Coun., U.S. Dept. Interior. Editor FY 1987-93 Federal Agency Needs Assessment; editor reports. Recipient Frederick Douglas award, Princeton, 1972, Profl. Conservationist award Chevron, 1992, Pres. Conservation Achievement Awd., 1993, Nature Conservancy. Mem. Ivy Club. Avocations: tennis, running, photography. E-mail: amoseno@aol.com.

ENO, PAUL FREDERICK, editor, writer; b. Hartford, Conn., Mar. 30, 1953; s. Earl Bryan and Bernice Sarah (Landers) E.; m. Jaclyn Ann Blackmon, June 7, 1981; children: Jonathan David, Benjamin Thomas. AA, St. Thomas Sem., Bloomfield, Conn., 1973; BA in Philosophy, Wadhams Hall Coll., Ogdensburg, N.Y., 1975; postgrad., Trinity Coll., Hartford, Conn., 1976-78. Book series editor Warbrooke Pub. Ltd., Montreal, Que., Can., 1974-76; staff writer Pawtuxet Valley Daily Times, West Warwick, R.I., 1979-80; mng. editor Observer Publs., Smithfield, R.I., 1980-83; copy editor Providence Jour., 1985-91; freelance editor, writer and publisher, 1976—. Owner New River Press, Woonsocket, R.I., 1990—; exec. dir. Pickering Inst. for New Eng. Studies, 1999—. Author: Best of Times, 1992, Rhode Island: A Genial History, 2005, Underhill Days, 1998, Faces at the Window, 1995, Footsteps in the Attic, 2002; editor: John Brown's Adirondack Empire, 1988, Flexography: Principles and Practices, 1990; contbr. articles to mags. Vice chmn. Cumberland Hist. Dist. Commn., 1987-92; bd. dirs. New Eng. Confedn., 1997—. With USCGR, 1983—89. Recipient medal R.I. Hist. Soc., 1987. Mem. R.I. Press. Assn. (bd. dirs., treas. 1982-89, Best Editorial of Yr. 1981, 82), Cumberland Beagle Club. Avocations: riding, boating, model railroading, shooting. Home: 645 Fairmount St Woonsocket RI 02895-4012 Office Phone: 800-244-1257. E-mail: pauleno@cox.net.

ENO, WOODROW E., lawyer, retired insurance company executive; b. Lincoln, Nebr. m. Ann Eno; 3 children. BA in History/Econs., Pittsburg (Kans.) State U., 1968; JD, U. Nebr., 1971; LLM, Judge Advocate Gen. Sch., Charlottesville, Va. Trial atty., regional counsel criminal investigation command U.S. Army; dir. law dept. market support div. CNA Ins. Co.; with legal/state affairs dept. Health Ins. Assn. Am., Appleton, Wis., 1975, v.p., gen. counsel, dir. state affairs, 1975—96; sr. v.p., gen. counsel, sec. Thrivent Financial for Lutherans, Mpls., 1996—2001, sr. v.p., gen. counsel, 2002—05. Developer model laws and regulators on timely issues Nat. Assn. Ins. Commrs. Contbr. articles to profl. jours. Fundraiser several Washington area charities. Lt. col. JAGC U.S. Army. Mem. Nat. Health Lawyers Assn. (bd. dirs. 1992). Methodist.

ENOCH, CRAIG TRIVELY, retired judge; b. Wichita, Kans., Apr. 3, 1950; BA, So. Meth. U., 1972, JD, 1975; LLM, U. Va., 1992. Bar: Tex. 1975, U.S. Dist. Ct. (no. dist.) Tex. 1976, U.S. Ct. Appeals (5th cir.) 1979; cert. Civil Trial Law. Assoc. Burford, Ryburn & Ford, Dallas, 1975-77; ptnr. Moseley, Jones, Enoch & Martin, Dallas, 1977-81; judge 101st Dist. Ct., Dallas, 1981-87; chief justice Tex. Ct. Appeals (5th dist.), 1987-92; justice Tex. Supreme Ct., Austin, 1993—2003; chair appellate practice, mem. litigation and govt. rels. practice Winstead Sechrest & Minick P.C., Austin, 2003—. Pres. Appellate Judges Edn. Inst., 2002—. Mem. exec. bd. Dedman Sch. Law So. Meth. U., 1990—. Capt. USAFR, 1973-81. Recipient Outstanding Young Lawyer in Dallas, 1985, Disting. Alumni award for judicial svc. So. Meth. U. Dedman Sch. Law, 1999, J. Edward Finch Law Day Speech award, 2001. Fellow: Dallas Bar Found., Tex. State Bar Found., Am. Bar Found.; mem.: ABA (past chair exec. bd. appellate judges conf. jud. divsn.), Tex. Supreme Ct. (liaison to State Bar of Tex. 1999—2003), Am. Law Inst. Episcopalian. Office Phone: 512-370-2883. Business E-Mail: cenoch@winstead.com.

ENOCH, JAY MARTIN, optometrist, research scientist; b. NYC, Apr. 20, 1929; s. Jerome Dee and Stella Sarah (Nathan) E.; m. Rebekah Ann Feiss, June 24, 1951; children: Harold Owen, Barbara Diane, Ann Allison. *Grandchildren, Jordan Michael and Ryan Samuel Enoch, David Jacob Dryfoos, and Julia Rose and Maxwell Jay Perry. Enoch's career stems from inspiration received at the Bronx High School of Science. Stimuli were provided by mentors at Columbia U. by Isidore Finkelstein and George Smelser, at OSU by Glenn Fry, at NPL in Teddington, England, by Walter Stanley Stiles, at Washington U. in St. Louis by Bernard Becker, in Berne by Hans Goldmann, and at U. Florida by Herbert Kaufman. Throughout, he was encouraged by his parents, grandfather Harry Nathan, and his wife.* BS in Optics and Optometry, Columbia U., 1950; post grad., Inst. Optics U. Rochester, 1953; PhD in Physiol. Optics, Ohio State U., 1956; DSc (hon.), SUNY, 1993, Poly. U., Barcelona, Spain, 2002. Asst. prof. physiol. optics Ohio State U., Columbus, 1956-58; assoc. supr. Ohio State U. (Mapping and Charting Rsch. Lab.), 1957-58; fellow Nat. Phys. Lab., Teddington, England, 1959-60; rsch. instr. dept. ophthalmology Washington U. Sch. Medicine, St. Louis, 1958-59, rsch. asst. prof., 1959-64, rsch. assoc. prof., 1965-70, rsch. prof., 1970-74; fellow Barnes Hosp., St. Louis, 1960-64, cons. ophthalmology, 1964-74; rsch. prof. dept. psychology Washington U., St. Louis, 1970-74; grad. rsch. prof. ophthalmology and psychology Coll. Medicine U. Fla., Gainesville, 1974-80, grad. rsch. prof. physics, 1979-80; dir. Ctr. for Sensory Studies, 1976-80; dean Sch. Optometry, chmn. Grad. Group in Vision Sci. U. Calif., Berkeley, Calif., 1980-92, prof. optometry and vision sci., 1980-94, prof. of Grad. Sch., 1994—; prof. physiol. optics in ophthalmology U. Calif., San Francisco, 1980—. Exec. sec. subcom. on vision and its disorders of nat. adv. Neurol. Diseases and Blindness Coun., NIH, 1963-66; chmn. subcom. contact lens stds. Am. Nat. Std. Inst., 1970-77; mem. nat. adv. eye coun. Nat. Eye Inst., NIH, 1975-77, 80-84; exec. com., com. on vision NAS-NRC, 1973-76; mem. US Nat. Com. Internat. Commn. Optics, 1976-79; health sci. com. Systemwide Adminstrn. U. Calif., 1989-93, co-chmn. subcom. on immigrant health in Calif., 1993-94; mem. sci. adv. bd. Fight-for-Sight, 1988-92, Allergan Corp., 1991-93; mem. Lighthouse Internat., NY, 1989-05, chair, 1995, Pisart award com., bd. dir. 2001-07; mem. com. on Refractive Errors WHO, 2002-2005; founder Elite Sch. Optometry, Chennai, Tamil Nadu, India, dedication lectr., 1985, plenary spkr. 20th Ann., 2005 *As Executive Secretary of the Subcommittee on Vision and its Disorders, Enoch had opportunity to draft the plan for the future National Eye Institute, NIH. With modifications, this proved to be a seminal document. Enoch served for decades as liaison between ophthalmology and optometry, helped develop the infrastructure of modern visual and ophthalmic science, and aided in organizing modern optometry in India. He derived satisfaction during years in neonatal vision-care practice, as well as from his research on retinal receptor optics, etc., during his service as Dean at Berkeley, and in development of low vision services in the U.S.A. and India.* Mem. editl. bd.: Investigative Ophthalmology and Vision Sci., 1965—75, 1983—88, Vision Rsch., 1974—80, Sight-Saving Rev., 1974—84, Sensory Processes, 1974—80, Internat. Ophthalmology, 1977—93, mem. editl. bd. optical scis.: Springer-Verlag, 1978—87, mem. editl. bd.: Binocular Vision, 1984—, Clin. Vision Sci., 1986—93, Biomed. Optics, 1988—90, mem. editl. bd. biomed. scis.: Springer-Verlag, 1988—95, mem. editl. bd.: Annals of Ophthalmology, 1997—2005, assoc. editor for vision: Handbook of Optics, Optical Soc. Am., 1997—, mem. internat. editl. bd.: Ophthalmic and Physiol. Optics, 2002—; contbr. chpts. and articles on visual sci., photoreceptor optics, perimetry, contact lenses, infant and aged vision, myopia, history of earliest lenses and mirrors to profl. jours. Nat. sci. adv. bd. Retinitis Pigmentosa Found., 1977-95; US rep. Internat. Perimetric Soc., 1974-90, also exec. com., chmn. Rsch. Group Standards; bd. dirs. Friends of Eye Rsch., 1977-88, Lighting Rsch. Bd., 1988-95; trustee Illuminating Engring. Rsch. Inst., 1977-81; mem. bd. counselors U. Calif. San Francisco Sch. Dentistry, 1995-2003. 2d lt. US Army, 1951-52. Named one of 250 Alumni Ahead of Their Time, Columbia Univ., 2004; recipient Career Devel. award, NIH, 1963—73, Everett Kinsey award, Contact Lens Soc. Ophthalmologists, 1991, Berkeley citation, Festschrift U. Calif. Berkeley, 1996, Pisart award, Lighthouse Internat., 2001, Gaspar de Portola award, U. Calif. and Govt. of Catalunya, 2001, 2004. Fellow AAAS, Am. Acad. Optometry (co-founder eye disease sect., Glenn A. Fry award 1972, Charles F. Prentice medal award 1974, 50 Yr. award 2004), Optical Soc. Am. (chmn. vision tech. sect. 1974-76, mem. book pub. com. 1996-2000), Am. Acad. Ophthalmology (low-vision com., honor award 1985); mem. Assn. for Rsch. in Vision and Ophthalmology (trustee 1967-73, pres. 1972-73, Francis I. Proctor medal 1977), Assn. for Rsch. in Vision and Ophthalmology Found., Concilium Ophthalmologicum Universale (chmn. visual functions com. 1982-86), Am. Optometric Assn. (low vision sect., Vision Care award 1987), Internat. Perimetric Soc. (hon. mem., chair com. stds.), Ocular Heritage Soc. (medal 1997), Cogan Ophthalmic History Soc. (trustee 2000-02, pres. 2002-04, pres. 2005-), Cosmos Club (Washington), Sigma Xi. Home: 54 Shuey Dr Moraga CA 94556-2621 Office: U Calif Sch Optometry Berkeley CA 94720-2020 Office Phone: 510-642-9694. Business E-Mail: jmenoch@berkeley.edu.

ENOS, PAUL, geologist, educator; b. Topeka, July 25, 1934; s. Allen Mason and Marjorie V. (Newell) E.; m. Carol Rae Curt, July 5, 1958; children: Curt Alan, Mischa Enos Martin, Kevin Christopher, Heather Enos Wohlert. BS, U. Kans., 1956; postgrad., U. Tübingen, W.Ger., 1956-57; MS, Stanford U., 1961; PhD, Yale U., 1965. Geologist Shell Devel. Co., Coral Gables, Fla., 1964-68, research geologist Houston, 1968-70; from assoc. prof. to prof. geology SUNY, Binghamton, 1970-82; Haas Disting. prof. geology U. Kans., Lawrence, 1982-2000, prof., 2001—03, Disting. prof. emeritus, 2003—. Cons. to industry; sedimentologist Ocean Drilling, 1975, 92; rsch. vis. Oxford U., 1989, U. Erlangen, Germany, 1995-96; fgn. scientist Ministry Geology, People's Republic China, 1988; with Global Sedimentary Geology Project, 1988—, co-convener Working Group 4, 1992-2000. Co-author: Quaternary Sedimentation of South Florida, 1977, Mid-Cretaceous, Mexico, 1983; editor: Field Trips: South-Central New York, 1981, Deep-Water Carbonates, 1977; contbr. articles to sci. jours. Served to 1st lt. C.E., U.S. Army, 1957-59.

Recipient Pettijohn medal Sedimentology, 2001, Excellence in Tchg. award, Geology Dept., 2003; fellow U. Liverpool, 1976-77, NSF, 1959-62, Fulbright, 1956-57; Summerfield scholar, 1954-56. Mem. Soc. Sedimentary Geology (assoc. editor 1976-80, 83-87, Best Paper award 1969), Internat. Assn. Sedimentologists (assoc. editor 1983-87), Am. Assn. Petroleum Geologists, Geol. Soc. Am., Omicron Delta Kappa. Avocations: photography, diving, bicycling, history. Office: U Kans Dept Geology Lawrence KS 66045-2124 Home: 1825 Castle Pine Court Lawrence KS 66047-2017 Office Phone: 785-864-2744.

ENOS, RANDALL, cartoonist, illustrator; b. New Bedford, Mass., Jan. 30, 1936; s. Eugene and Isabel (Da Costa) E.; m. Leann Walker, June 23, 1956. Student, Boston Mus. Sch. Fine Arts, 1954-55. Art tchr. Famous Artists Schs., Inc., Westport, Conn., 1956-64; film designer Pablo Ferro Films, Inc., N.Y.C., 1964-66; free-lance illustrator and film designer Westport, 1966—; part-time tchr. Parsons Sch. Design, N.Y.C., 1975-84; lectr., tchr. Syracuse U. Designed films for maj. Am. corps.; illustrator for maj. publs. including N.Y. Times, Time Mag., also children's books, posters; represented in numerous illustrators and art dirs. anns., other anthologies and mus. collections; created comic strips. Recipient Cannes TV award, 1964. Mem. Soc. of Illustrators. Democrat. Avocations: collecting antique harpoons and other whale craft, studying history of American whaling, creating limited edition prints of whaling subjects. Home: 402 N Park Ave Easton CT 06612-1248 Office Phone: 203-445-8376. E-mail: renos@optonline.net.

ENRICO, EUGENE JOSEPH, music educator; b. Red Lodge, Mont., July 25, 1944; s. Joseph Eugene Enrico and Margaret Elizabeth Souders; m. Sherry Lee Enrico, Aug. 12, 1970. MusB, BA, MA in Musicology, U. Mont., 1966; PhD of Musicology, U. Mich., 1970. Asst. prof. Saginaw Valley State Coll., University Center, Mich., 1970—73; postdoctoral rsch. fellow Smithsonian Instn., Washington, 1973; asst. prof. U. Louisville, 1973—76; assoc. prof. U. Okla., Norman, 1976—83, prof., 1983—95, Ruth Vern Davis Reaugh prof. music, 1995—. Dir. Early Baroque Performance Workshop, Lake Tahoe, NY, 1980—84; artistic dir. Accademia Filarmonica, Norman, Okla., 1983—; dir. Ctr. for Music TV, Norman, 1990—; lectr. nat. lecture tours Waverly Consort, 1989, 91, 92. Author: (book) The Orchestra at San Petronio, 1976; pro-dr.(dir.): (PBS TV program) 1492: A Portrait in Music, 1992, Isabella d'Este: First Lady of the Renaissance, 2002, (early music TV series) www.ou.edu.earlymusic. Recipient Gov.'s Art award, State of Okla., 1993, Outstanding Fine Arts Faculty award, Coll. Fine Arts, U. Okla., 1996. Mem.: Am. Musical Instrument Soc., Early Music Am., Am. Musicol. Soc. Office: Univ of Oklahoma Sch of Music Norman OK 73019 Business E-Mail: ejenrico@ou.edu.

ENRIGHT, CYNTHIA LEE, illustrator; b. Denver, July 6, 1950; d. Darrel Lee and Iris Arlene (Flodquist) E. BA in Elem. Edn., U. No. Colo., 1972; student, Minn. Sch. Art and Design, Mpls., 1975-76. Tchr. 3d grade Littleton (Colo.) Sch. Dist., 1972-75; graphics artist Sta. KCNC TV, Denver, 1978-79; illustrator No Coast Graphics, Denver, 1979-87; editorial artist The Denver Post, 1987—. Illustrator, editor "Tiny Tales" The Denver Post, 1991-94. Recipient Print mag. Regional Design Ann. awards, 1984, 85, 87, Phoenix Art Mus. Biannual award, 1979, third pl. Best of the West award for illustration, 2004. Mem. Mensa. Democrat. Home: 1210 Ivanhoe St Denver CO 80220-2640 Office: The Denver Post 1560 Broadway Denver CO 80202-5177

ENRIGHT, ROBERT D., social sciences educator; s. William F. and Margaret R. Enright; children: Shawn M., Kevin D. BA, Westfield Coll., 1973; PhD, U. Minn., 1976. Prof. U. Wis., Madison, 1978—. Editor: Exploring Forgiveness, 1998; author: Helping Clients Forgive, 2000, Forgiveness Is a Choice, 2001, (children's book) Rising Above the Storm Clouds, 2004; contbr. articles to profl. jours. Founder, bd. dirs. Internat. Forgiveness Inst., Madison, 1994—. Recipient Tchg. award, U. of Wis. Student Assn., 1991, Aaron T. Beck Inst.'s Nat. award, Assumption Coll., 1997—98, Outstanding Rsch. award, Nat. Alliance for the Mentally Ill, 2003. Mem.: APA. Achievements include organization of first national conference on interpersonal forgiveness at a university; publication of first social scientific article on person-to-person forgiving; publication of first social scientific article on a forgiveness intervention; publication of first comprehensive literature review of interpersonal forgiveness; research in publication of first cross-cultural studies of interpersonal forgiveness; establishment of first community-based and school-based intervention on forgiveness in Belfast, Northern Ireland; development of Enright Forgiveness Inventory. Office: U Wis-Madison 1025 W Johnson St Madison WI 53706 Office Phone: 608-262-0835. Personal E-mail: forgive@sbcglobal.net.

ENRIQUEZ, CAROLA RUPERT, museum director; b. Washington, Jan. 2, 1954; d. Jack Burns and Shirley Ann (Orcutt) Rupert; m. John Enriquez, Jr., Dec. 30, 1989. BA in History cum laude, Bryn Mawr Coll., 1976; MA, cert. in mus. studies, U. Del., 1978. Pers. mgmt. trainee Naval Material Command, Arlington, Va., 1972-76; tchg. asst. dept. history U. Del., Newark, 1976-77; asst. curator/exhibit specialist Hist. Soc. Del., Wilmington, 1977-78; dir. Macon County Mus. Complex, Decatur, Ill., 1978-81, Kern County Mus., Bakersfield, Calif., 1981—. Pres. Kern County Mus Found., 1991—2002; advisor Kern County Heritage Commn., 1981-88; chmn. Hist. Records Commn., 1981-88; sec.-treas. Arts Coun. of Kern, 1984-86, pres., 1986-88; county co-chmn. United Way, 1981, 82; chmn. steering com. Calif. State Bakersfield Co-op Program, 1982-83; mem. cmty. adv. bd. Calif. State U.-Bakersfield Anthrop. Soc., 1986-88; bd. dirs. Mgmt. Coun., 1983-86, v.p., 1987, pres., 1988; bd. dirs. Calif. Coun. for Promotion of History, 1984-86, v.p., 1987-88, pres., 1988-90; mem. cmty. adv. bd. Calif. State U.-Bakersfied Sociology Dept., 1986-88; mem. women's adv. com. Girls Scouts U.S., 1989-91; bd. dirs. Greater Bakersfield Conv. and Visitors Bur., 1993-95; co-chair 34th St. Neighborhood Partnership, 1994—. Hagley fellow Eleutherian Mills-Hagley found., 1977-78; Bryn Mawr alumnae reg. scholar, 1972-76. Mem. Calif. Assn. Mus. (regional rep. 1991—2002, v.p. legis. affairs 1992—2002), Am. Assn. State and Local History (chair awards com. Calif. chpt. 1990, regional vice chair 1999—2002). Presbyterian. Office: Kern County Museum 3801 Chester Ave Bakersfield CA 93301-1345

ENRIQUEZ, MANUEL HIPOLITO, physician; b. Angeles City, Philippines, Aug. 19, 1953; came to U.S., 1982; s. Antonio S. and Milagros D. (Hipolito) E.; m. Mary Diane Maloney, June 22, 1985; children: Steven. Katie. BS, U. of the East, 1974, MD, 1979; MPH, Med. Coll. Wis., 2004. Diplomate internal medicine, pulmonary disease, critical care medicine, and occupational medicine. Intern Philippine Gen. Hosp., Manila, 1980; resident Mercy Hosp., Buffalo, 1982-85; fellow Wayne State U. Sch. Medicine, Detroit, 1985-87; dir. respiratory therapy Humana Hosp. Clinch Valley, Richlands, Va., 1987-88; staff pulmonologist VA Med. Ctr., Asheville, NC, 1989—99, also dir. med. ICU, 1990—99, med. dir. respiratory therapy, 1997—99; staff physician VA Outpatient Clinic, Chattanooga, 1999—2001; flight surgeon USAF Clinic, Charleston AFB, SC, 1991—99; cons. assoc. Duke U. Med. ctr., Durham, NC, 1989-99; sr. physician TVA Nuclear, Chattanooga, 2001—; sr. flight surgeon 134th Med. Squadron McGhee Tyson Air NG Base, Tenn. Cons. in field. Med. officer CAP, Asheville, 1990-99, sr. programs officer, 1993-99. Fellow: ACP, Am. Coll. Chest Physicians; mem.: Soc. USAF Flight Surgeons, Res. Officers Assn., Aerospace Med. Assn., Am. Coll. Occupl. and Environ. Medicine. Roman Catholic. Avocations: flying, jogging, reading, computers. Office: TVA EB 10B-C 1101 Market St Chattanooga TN 37402

ENROTH-CUGELL, CHRISTINA ALMA ELISABETH, neurophysiologist, educator; b. Helsingfors, Finland, Aug. 27, 1919; came to US, 1956, naturalized, 1962; d. Emil and Maja (Syren) E.; m. David W. Cugell, Sept. 5, 1955. MD, Karolinska Inst., 1948, PhD, 1952; Hon. Doctors Degree, U. Helsinki, Finland, 1994. Resident in ophthalmology Karolinska Sjukhuset, 1949-52; intern Passavant Meml. Hosp., 1956-57; with Northwestern U., Evanston, Ill., 1959-91, prof. emeritus, 1991—, prof. dept. neurobiology and physiology and dept. biomedical engring., 1974—; mem. vision rsch. program com. Nat. Eye Inst., 1974-78, mem. nat. adv. eye coun., 1980-84. Contbr. articles to profl. jours. Recipient Ludwig von Sallman award Internat. Assn. Rsch. in Vision and Ophthalmology, 1982. Fellow Am. Inst. Med. and Biol. Engring., Am. Acad. Arts and Sci.; mem. Am. Assn. Rsch. in Vision and Ophthalmology (co-recipient Friedenwald award 1983, recipient W.H. Helmerich III award 1992), Soc. Neurosis., Am. Physiol. Soc., Physiol. Soc. (U.K.) Office: Northwestern U McCormick Sch Engring Technl Inst 2145 Sheridan Rd Evanston IL 60208-0834 Office Phone: 847-491-7673. Business E-Mail: enroth@northwestern.edu.

ENSARI, SEMSI, biochemical engineer, researcher; MS, U. Calif., Irvine, 1998; BS, Bogazici U., 1994; PhD, U. Calif., 2001. Postdoctoral rschr. U. Calif., Irvine, 2001—02; engr. Schering-Plough Rsch. Inst., Union, NJ, 2003—. Contbr. articles to profl. jours. Fellow, Bogazici U., 1994; Regents' fellowship, U. Calif., 1997—2000. Mem.: AIChE, Am. Chem. Soc. Office: Schering-Plough Research Institute 1011 Morris Avenue Union NJ 07083 Office Phone: 908-820-6354. Business E-Mail: semsi.ensari@spcorp.com.

ENSEKI, CAROL, museum director; Deputy dir. N.Y. Brooklyn Children's Mus., dir. programs, dir. exhbn. & collections, exhibit devel., 1989—96, pres., 1997—. Mem.: Assn. Children's Mus., Arts & Bus. Coun., Am. Assn. Mus. Office: Bklyn Children's Mus 145 Bklyn Ave Brooklyn NY 11213

ENSENAT, DONALD BURNHAM, ambassador, lawyer; b. New Orleans, Feb. 4, 1946; s. A.G. and Genevieve (Burnham) E.; m. Taylor Harding, June 5, 1976; children: Farish, Will. BA, Yale U., 1968; JD, Tulane U., 1973. Bar: La. 1973, U.S. Ct. Appeals (5th cir.) 1974, U.S. Supreme Ct. 1975, U.S. Ct. Appeals (11th cir.) 1982, Tex. 1991. Legis. asst. Congressman Hale Boggs, U.S. Ho. of Reps., Washington, 1969-70, legis asst. Congresswoman Lindy Boggs, 1973-74; personal aide Hon. George Bush, Houston, 1970; asst. atty gen. State of La., New Orleans, 1975-80; assoc., dir., mng. dir. Carmouche, Gray, & Hoffman, A.P.L.C., New Orleans, 1981-89; mng. dir. Hoffman Sutterfield Ensenat, A.P.L.C., New Orleans, 1989-92, sr. dir., 1994-97; of counsel Locke Liddell & Sapp, PC, New Orleans, 1997-2001; U.S. Chief of Protocol Washington, 2001—. U.S. amb. to Brunei, 1992-93. Bd. dirs. World Trade Ctr., New Orleans, chmn. fin. com., 1990-92, exec. com., 1993-2001, pres.-elect, 1995, pres., 1996, chmn. bd. dirs., 1997. With USAR, 1968-74. Mem. State Bar Tex., La. State Bar Assn., Maritime Law Assn. U.S., Yale Alumni Assn. La. (bd. dirs. 1976-92, 94—, pres. 1980-82), Assn. Yale Alumni (rep. 1976-79). Republican. Roman Catholic. Avocation: sports. Home: 5527 Hurst St New Orleans LA 70115 Office: US State Dept S/CPR 2201 C St NW Washington DC 20520

ENSIGN, JOEL FRANCIS, musician; s. William James and Joan Marie (Kennedy) Ensign. BA in Music, Ohio Dominican Coll., Columbus, 1974; post graduate study, Capital U., Bexley, Ohio, 1980. Recreation leader City of Columbus, Recreation and Parks Dept., 1986—95; liturgist, music dir., organist St. Matthias Ch., Columbus, 1993—. Recitialist Cotos and Am. Guild Organist, Columbus, 1995—. Election precinct judge Franklin County Bd. Elections, Columbus, 2000—. Mem.: Ctrl. Ohio Theatre Organ Soc. (pres. 2001—04, sec.), World Black Belt Bureau (life). Achievements include Grand Master Black Belt Tae Kwon Do, World Black Belt, Nashville, Tenn., 1994. Home: 4538 Maize Rd C-33 Columbus OH 43224-1168

ENSIGN, JOHN E., senator, former congressman; b. Roseville, Calif., Mar. 25, 1958; s. Mike and Sharon E.; m. Darlene Sciarretta Ensign; 3 children. Student, UNLV; B in Gen. Sci., Oreg. State U., 1981; D of Veterinary Medicine, Colo. State U., 1985. Owner animal hosp., Las Vegas; gen. mgr. Gold Strike Hotel & Casino, 1991, Nev. Landing Hotel & Casino, 1992; mem. U.S. Congress from 1st Nev. dist., Washington, 1995—99; mem. ways and means com., subcom. health, subcom. human resources; mem. com. on resources, 1995-98; U.S. senator from Nev., 2001—. Candidate for U.S. Sen., 1998-99. Republican. Office: 356 Russell Senate Office Building Washington DC 20510 Office Phone: 202-224-6244.*

ENSIGN, MICHAEL S., resort company executive; Gen. mgr. Circus Circus-Las Vegas; COO, exec. v.p. Circus-Circus Enterprises; also bd. dirs.; rejoined as COO, vice-chmn., 1995-98; CEO, chmn., 1998; CEO, COO, chmn. Mandalay Resort Group, Las Vegas, 1998—. Office: Mandalay Resort Group 3950 Las Vegas Blvd S Las Vegas NV 89119

ENSIGN, RICHARD PAPWORTH, transportation executive; b. Salt Lake City, Jan. 20, 1919; s. Louis Osborne and Florence May (Papworth) E.; m. Margaret Anne Hinckley, Sept. 5, 1942; children: Judith Ensign Lantz, Mary Jane Ensign Hofmeister, Richard L., James R., Margaret. BS, U. Utah, 1941. With Western Air Lines, 1941-70, v.p. in-flight service, 1963-70, v.p. passenger service, 1970, Pan Am. World Airways, 1971, sr. v.p. field mgmt., 1972-74, sr. v.p. mktg., 1974-75; exec. v.p. Western Airlines, 1975-82; pres. R.P. Ensign & Assocs., 1982—; spl. asst. to pres. Marriott-Host, Marriott Corp., 1990-91; spl. asst. to chmn. Caterair Internat. Corp., 1991-96. Chmn. Utah Nat. Adv. Coun., 1984-86; bd. dirs. Western Airlines, 1980-81, Pacific Area Travel Assocs., 1976-81, Marriott Airport Svc. Co., Osaka, Japan, 1986-92; resident dir. Marriott Internat. Corp., Seoul, People's Republic of Korea. Patentee in field. Nat. fund raising chmn. U. Utah, 1982-83, 83-84. Recipient Disting. Service award Fla. Internat. U., 1973; named Disting. Alumnus U. Utah, 1976, 86, recipient merit award of honor, 1985. Mem. Nat. Aeros. Assn. Clubs: Lochinvar. Republican. Mem. Lds Ch. Home: 3848 Malibu Country Dr Malibu CA 90265-4717

ENSLEN, PAMELA CHAPMAN, lawyer; b. Detroit, Dec. 29, 1953; d. Ralph Nicholas Chapman and Roberta Margaret Clarke McLaughlin; m. Richard Alan Enslen, Nov. 20, 1985; 1 child, Alan Gennady Robert. BMus, U. Mich., 1976, MMus, 1977; JD, Wayne State U., 1981. Bar: Mich. 1981, Calif. 1996, U.S. Dist. Ct. (ea. and we. dists.) Mich. 1981, U.S. Ct. Appeals (6th cir.) 1983, U.S. Supreme Ct. 1983. Pre-hearing atty. Mich. Ct. Appeals, Detroit, 1981-83; fed. law clk. U.S. Dist. Ct., We. Dist. Mich., Kalamazoo, 1983-85; sr. ptnr. Miller, Canfield, Paddock & Stone, Kalamazoo, 1985-2001; fed. pub. defender We. Dist. Mich., 2001—03; sr. counsel Miller, Canfield, Paddock & Stone, Kalamazoo, 2003—. Lectr., cons., arbitrator and mediator in field; standing com. on US cts. State Bar Mich., Mich., 2004—. Co-founder, bd. dirs. Cmty. Dispute Resolution Ctr. Kalamazoo County, 1988—; bd. dirs. Am. Cancer Soc., Kalamazoo, 1991—. Named Mich. Lawyer of the Yr., Mich. Lawyers Weekly, 1998. Master: Am. Inns of Ct.; fellow: Am. Bar Found.; mem.: ATLA, ABA (standing com. on dispute resolution 1990—93, governing coun. dispute resolution sect. 1994—97, chair dispute resolution sect. 1997—98, sect. del. Ho. of Dels. 1999—, standing com. on fed. jud. improvements 2001—04, standing com on jud. independence 2004—), Fed. Bar Assn. We. Mich. (governing bd. 2003—, bd. dirs.), Nat. Order of Barristers (John Marshall award com. 2003), Women Lawyers of Mich. (regional rep. 1989—90), Kalamazoo Trial Lawyers Assn., Kalamazoo County Bar Assn. (chair law day com. 1989, bd. dirs. 1996—99), Mich. Bar Assn. (counsel sect. on arbitration and alternative dispute resolution 1985—98), Am. Mensa, Pi Kappa Lambda. Democrat. Avocations: reading, music. Office: Miller Canfield 444 W Michigan Kalamazoo MI 49007

ENSLEN, RICHARD ALAN, federal judge; b. Kalamazoo, May 28, 1931; s. Ehrman Thrasher and Pauline Mabel (Dragoo) E.; m. Pamela Gayle Chapman, Nov. 2, 1985; children— David, Susan, Sandra, Thomas, Janet, Joseph, Gennady. Student, Kalamazoo Coll., 1949-51, Western Mich. U., 1955; LL.B., Wayne State U., 1958; LL.M., U. Va., 1986. Bar: Mich. 1958, U.S. Dist. Ct. (we. dist.) Mich. 1960, U.S. Ct. Appeals (6th cir.) 1971, U.S. Ct. Appeals (4th cir.) 1975, U.S. Supreme Ct 1975. Mem. firm Stratton, Wise, Early & Starbuck, Kalamazoo, 1958-60, Bauckham & Enslen, Kalamazoo, 1960-64, Howard & Howard, Kalamazoo, 1970-76, Enslen & Schma, Kalamazoo, 1977-79; dir. Peace Corps, Costa Rica, 1965-67; judge Mich. Dist. Ct., 1968-70; U.S. dist. judge Kalamazoo, 1979—; chief judge, 1995-2001. Mem. faculty Western Mich. U., 1961-62, Nazareth Coll., 1974-75; adj. prof. polit. sci. Western Mich. U., 1982— Co-author: The Constitutional Law Dictionary: Volume One, Individual Rights, 1985; Volume Two, Governmental Powers, 1987, Constitutional Deskbook: Individual Rights, 1987, (with Mary Bedikian and Pamela Enslen) Michigan Practice, Alternative Dispute Resolution, 1998. Served with USAF, 1951-54. Named Person of the Century-Law and Courts, The Kalamazoo Gazette, 1999; named to Great Am. Judges, ABC-Clio, 2003; recipient Disting. Alumni award, Wayne State Law Sch., 1980, Western Mich. U., 1982, Outstanding Practical Achievement award, Ctr. Pub. Resources, 1984, award for Excellence and Innovation in Alternative Dispute Resolution and Dispute Mgmt., Legal Program; scholar, Jewel Corp., 1956—57, Lampson McElhorne, 1957. Mem. ABA (standing com. on dispute resolution 1983-90), Mich. Bar Assn., Am. Judicature Soc. (bd. dirs. 1983-85), Sixth Cir. Jud. Coun. Office: US Dist Ct 410 W Michigan Ave Kalamazoo MI 49007-3757 Office Phone: 616-343-7542.

ENSLER, EVE, playwright, actress; b. NYC, May 25, 1953; m. Richard McDermott, 1978 (div. 1988); adopted stepson Dylan McDermott; life ptnr. Ariel Orr Jordan. BA, Middlebury Coll., Vt., 1975; LittD (hon.), Middlebury Coll., 2003. Founder V-Day, 1998; leader writing group Beford Hills Correctional Facility for Women, 1998—; faculty mem. Omega Inst. Playwright Coming From Nothing, The Vagina Monologues, 1997 (Obie Award, 1997), Necessary Targets, 2002, Conviction, Lemonade, The Depot, Floating Rhoda and the Glue Man, Extraordinary Measures, The Good Body, 2004; exec. prodr.: (documentaries) What I Want My Words to Do to You: Voices From Inside a Women's Maximum Security Prison, 2003; author: Vagina Warriors, 2005. Trustee PEN Am. Ctr., chair, Women's Com. Recipient Berrilla-Kerr Award playwriting, Elliot Norton Award outstanding solo performance, Jury Award theater, US Comedy Arts Festival, Media Spotlight Award for leadership, Amnesty Internat., 2002, Matrix Award, 2002; Guggenheim Fellowship in playwriting. Vagina Monologues has been translated into over 35 languages & enlists many celebrities as performers/activists. Mailing: PEN American Ctr 588 Broadway Ste 303 New York NY 10012 also: Omega Institute 150 Lake Dr Rhinebeck NY 12572*

ENSLEY, JOHN FREDERICK, oncologist, researcher; b. Detroit, Mich., Mar. 22, 1944; m. Margaret Elizabeth Crowe, June 21, 1943; children: Elizabeth Ann Sedano, Laura Marie Laura. BS, Wayne State U., Detroit, 1970, MS, 1973, MD, 1977. Bd. Internal Medicine Am. Bd. of Internal Medicine, 1983, Bd. Med. Oncology Am. Bd. of Internal Medicine, 1984. Co-chmn., head and neck cancer com. SW Oncology Group, San Antonio, 1987—2002; prof. of medicine, oncology and otolaryngology head and neck surgery Wayne State U. Karmanos Cancer Inst., Detroit, 1983—. Author: (testbook) Head and Neck Cancer-Current Perspectives (Woodward and Whites Best Doctors in Am., 2005). Grantee, NIH, 1986—99. Achievements include research in Developed treatment regimens for patients with head and neck cancer that increased cure rates and reduced un-necessary functional and cometic defects due to surgery; Developed laboratory tools for identifying prognostically important subgroups of patients with head and neck cancer. Office: Wayne State Univ 4100 John R Detroit MI 48201 Office Phone: 313-745-9168. Office Fax: 313-993-0559. E-mail: ensleyj@karmanos.org.

ENSLIN, THEODORE VERNON, poet; b. Chester, Pa., Mar. 25, 1925; s. Morton Scott and Ruth May (Tuttle); m. Mildred Marie Stout, Aug. 1, 1945 (div.); children— Deirdre, Jonathan Morton; m. Alison Jane Jose, Sept. 14. 1969; 1 son, Jacob Hezekiah. Studied mus. composition with Nadia Boulanger, Cambridge, Mass., 1943-44. Author: New Sharon's Prospect, 1965, To Come To Have Become, 1966, Forms (5 vols.), 1970-74, The Country of Our Consciousness, 1971, The Median Flow, 1975, Synthesis, 1975, Carmina, 1976, Ranger, 2 vols., 1978-80, Music for Several Occasions, 1985, Small Suite for Solo Flute, 1985, The Weather Within, 1986, Case Book, 1987, From Near the Great Pine, 1988, Love and Science, 1990, Little Wandering Flake of Snow, 1991, Gamma-UT, 1992, The House of the Golden Windows, 1993, Music in the Key of C, 1995, Communitas, 1996, Propositions for John Taggart, 1996, Thumbprint on Landscape, 1997, Skeins, 1998, Then and Now Selected Poems, 1999, Sequentiae, 1999 (in tandem 2003), A Folder for LN, 2003, Nine, 2004; readings and seminars various colls. and univs. Recipient Niemann award for weekly newspaper column The Cape Codder, 1955, Hart Crane Meml. award, 1969; Disting. Vis. Prof. Bowling Green State U., 1989. Mem. Am. Found. for Homeopathy. Address: 379 Kansas Rd Milbridge ME 04658

ENSMINGER, DALE, retired mechanical engineer, retired electrical engineer; b. Mt. Perry, Ohio, Sept. 26, 1923; s. Charles Henry and Mary Elpha (Koehler) Ensminger; m. Lois Elizabeth Hamilton, Mar. 25, 1948; children: Martha Jean, Laura Lee, Charles Robert, Jonathan Dale, Mary Ann, Daniel Joseph; m. Patricia Ann Evans, June 7, 2002. BSME, BSEE, Ohio State U., 1950, postgrad., 1950-53. Registered profl. engr., Ohio. Rschr. Battelle Meml. Inst., Columbus, Ohio, 1950, prin. rschr.; sr. rschr. Battelle Columbus Labs., mgr. ultrasonics, sr. rsch. scientist, 1984—98, ret., 1998. Cons. in field. Author: Ultrasonics, 1973, 2d edit., 1988; contbr. articles to profl. jours., chapters to books; reviewer Am. Society Non-Destructive Testing Handbook, 1989—. Sec. Columbus Prison Assn., 1950—; dean, dir. Columbus Bible Inst., 1952—97; mem. bd. Fundamental Bapt. Mission Trinidad and Tobago; mem. session governing body Calvary Bible Ch., 1953—89, clk.session, 1953—84. With U.S. Army, 1943—46. Recipient cert. of Recognition, NASA, 1975. Mem.: ASM, Ultrasonic Industry Assn., Soc. for Non-Destructive Testing, Acoustical Soc. Am., Am. Registry Outstanding Profls. (life). Achievements include patents in field. Office Phone: 408-732-5165. Personal E-mail: patdens@earthlink.net.

ENSMINGER, JOHN JAY, writer, poet, minister, counselor; b. June 25, 1945; m. Cynthia Re Fugate, Feb. 18, 1983. BTh, Southwest Bible Sem., Springfield, Mo., 1967; PhD, Univ. Metaphysics, Studio City, Calif., 1997. Caseworker State of Mo., 1974—2002, ret., 2002; jewelry designer and gem collector Ageless Wonders, Trenton, Mo., 1984—2003; metaphysical min. Univ. Metaphysics, Studio City, Calif., 1996—. Pub. On Earth Newsletter. Author: On Earth as it is in Heaven, 2003, Joy on Joy, 2005. Recipient Citizenship award, 1959, Editors Choice award, Nat. Poetry Libr., 1991. Mem.: Midwest Artist Assn. (1st prize in photography 2005, Artist of the Month for May 2005), Acad. Am. Poets. Avocations: antiques, gardening, rock and gem collector, rare books.

ENSMINGER, LUTHER GLENN, retired chemist; b. Mt. Perry, Ohio, Oct. 17, 1919; s. Charles Henry and Mary Elfa (Koehler) E.; m. Emma Jean Couch, May 12, 1951 (div. Apr. 1973); children: Luther, Douglas, Phillip, Deborah; m. How Leng Cheng, Nov. 11, 1983 (div. Dec. 1988); m. Lee Rose Olson, Oct. 19, 1992. BSc, Ohio State U., 1942, BSc, 1948. Chemist FDA, Cin., 1948-56, chemist, lab. supr. Los Angeles, 1956-59, sci. adminstr. Washington, 1959-79, ret., 1979; sci. cons. Arlington, Va., 1979—. Vol., tutor for immigrant high sch. and coll. students (YMCA awards for outstanding tutoring work 1992, 93). Contbr. articles to profl. jours. Sec. Lee-Ballston Citizens Assn., 1965-75. Served with U.S. Army, 1942-45. Recipient Seven Who Care award, 1990, Outstanding Svc. to Cmty. award YMCA Met. Washington, 1996. Fellow Assn. Ofcl. Analytical Chemists (exec. sec. 1967-79, mem. exec. com. 1960-79), Beta Gamma Sigma; mem. Am. Shoppers Panel, Nat. Family Opinion World Group. Republican. Presbyterian. Address: 631 N Edison St Arlington VA 22203-1430

ENSOR, LINDA LINEBERGER, literature and language educator; d. David Howard Lineberger and Dorothy Zona Thomas; m. James Robert Ensor, Jan. 7, 1984; children: David James, Katherine Elizabeth. BA in English, Furman U., Greenville, S.C., 1975; MAT in English, U. of S.C., 1976. Cert. secondary edn., English N.J., 1986, elem. edn. N.J., 1986. H.s. English tchr. Columbia H.S., Columbia, SC, 1976—80; coord. of fin. aid Coker Coll., Hartsville, SC, 1980—81; aquatic instr. Cmty. YMCA, Red Bank, 1987—90; assoc. dir. of fin. aid Princeton U., Princeton, NJ, 1984—86, Furman U., Greenville, SC, 1981—84; sat instr. Ednl. Svc. Corp., NJ, 1990—91; tutor-math and english Tutors Unltd., Atlantic Highlands, NJ, 1991—96; h.s. English tchr. Middletown H.S. North, Middletown, NJ, 1995—2002, Shore Regional H.S., West Long Branch, NJ, 2002—. Cons. Catherine E. Gahler Scholarship Fund, Red Bank, NJ, 1993—. Mem. Parent Info. Coun., Middletown, NJ, 1995—2000; pres. Fairview Sch. PTO, Middletown, NJ, 1996—98; recruiter/mem. LWV, Middletown, NJ, 1996—99; trustee Middletown United Meth. Ch., Middletown, NJ, 2003—05, Middletown Twp. Ednl. Found., Middletown, NJ, 1995—2002. Mem.: Shore Regional Edn. Assn., Monmouth County Edn. Assn., N.J. Edn. Assn., Nat. Coun. of Tchrs. of English, NEA, Women's Internat. Bowling Congress. Democrat-Npl. Methodist. Avocations: reading, bowling, archery, calligraphy, jogging. Home: 812 Center St Red Bank NJ 07701-6269 Office: Shore Regional High School 132 Monmouth Park Hwy West Long Branch NJ 07764 Office Phone: 732-222-9300.

ENSTAD, VIRGINIA (GINNY) G., English teacher; b. Portland, Oreg., Dec. 17, 1943; d. Ermel Virginia Anderson and Robert Sizer. Master of Edn./Tech., City U., Bellevue, WA, 1992—93; BA in English, Wash. State U., Pullman, Washington, 1962. H.s. english tchr. Edmonds-Woodway H.S., Edmonds, Wash., 1999—, Meadowdale H.S., Lynnwood, Wash., 1982—99. Co-chair profl. excellence com. Edmonds Sch. Dist./Edmonds Edn. Assn., Edmonds, 1996—; edmonds edn. assn. negotiator Edmonds Edn. Assn., Edmonds, 1987—; profl. edn. adv. bd. mem. (co-chair) U. of Wash., Seattle, 1991—, coll. of edn. adv. bd., 2000—. Campaign worker/patty murray Dem. Party, Lynnwood, Wash. Mem.: Wash. Edn. Assn., NEA, Nat. Coun. of Teachers of English. Democrat-Npl. Avocation: gardening, travel, reading, walking. Office: Edmonds-Woodway High School 7600 212th St SW Edmonds WA 98026

ENSTROM, JAMES EUGENE, epidemiologist; b. Alhambra, Calif., June 20, 1943; s. Elmer Melvin, Jr. and Klea Elizabeth (Bissell) E.; m. Marta Eugenia Villanea, Sept. 3, 1978. BS, Harvey Mudd Coll., Claremont, Calif., 1965; MS, Stanford U., 1967; PhD in Physics, 1970; M.P.H., UCLA, 1976. Research assoc. Stanford Linear Accelerator Center, 1970-71; research physicist, cons. Lawrence Berkeley Lab. U. Calif., 1971-75; Celeste Durand Rogers cancer research fellow Sch. Pub. Health, UCLA, 1973-75; Nat. Cancer Inst. postdoctoral trainee, 1975-76; cancer epidemiology researcher, 1976-81; assoc. research prof., 1981—. Program dir. for cancer control epidemiology Jonsson Comprehensive Cancer Center, 1978-88, research epidemiologist, 1988—, sci. dir. tumor registry, 1984-87, mem. dean's council, 1976—; cons. epidemiologist Linus Pauling Inst. Sci. and Medicine, 1976-94; cons. physicist Rand Corp., 1969-73, R&D Assos., 1971-75; mem. sci. bd. Am. Council on Sci. and Health, 1984—. Author papers in field. NSF predoctoral trainee, 1965-66; grantee Am. Cancer Soc., 1973—, Nat. Cancer Inst., 1979—; Preventive Oncology Acad. award, 1981-87. Fellow Am. Coll. Epidemiology; mem. Soc. Epidemiologic Research, Am. Heart Assn., Am. Pub. Health Assn., Am. Phys. Soc., AAAS, N.Y. Acad. Scis., Galileo Soc. Office: U Calif Sch Pub Health Los Angeles CA 90024

ENTEMAN, WILLARD FINLEY, philosophy educator; b. Glen Ridge, NJ, Oct. 21, 1936; s. Verling Clair and Elizabeth Vance Rutherford (Dailey) E.; m. Kathleen Ffolliott, June 18, 1960; children: Sally Holyoke, David Finley. BA, Williams Coll., 1959, LL.D. (hon.), 1978; MBA, Harvard U., 1961; MA, Boston U., 1962, PhD, 1965; LL.D. (hon.), Colby Coll., 1980. Instr. in philosophy Wheaton Coll., 1963-65, asst. prof., 1965-69, assoc. prof., 1969-70; assoc. prof., chmn. dept. philosophy Union Coll., Schenectady, 1970-72, provost and assoc. prof., 1972-78; pres., prof. Bowdoin Coll., 1978-81; provost, v.p. acad. affairs R.I. Coll., Providence, 1982-90, prof. philosophy, 1982—; exec. v.p., dir. Bibliotech, Inc., 1984-96. Mem. New Eng. Bd. Higher Edn., 1978-81; 2d v.p., trustee Colby-Bates-Bowdoin Ednl. Telecasting Corp., 1978-81. Author: Managerialsim: The Emergence of a New Ideology, Retirement 101: How TIAA-CREF Members Should Deal with the Dramatic Changes in Their Pensions; editor: The Problem of Free Will, 1967; contbr. articles to profl. publs. Trustee Regional Meml. Hosp., Brunswick, Maine, 1978-81, Hotchkiss Sch., 1980-90, Eckerd Coll., 1987—; mem. long-range planning com. Portland (Maine) Sch. Art, 1979-81; vice chmn. bd. trustees R.I. Coun. on Econ. Edn. Named One of 100 Top Young Leaders in Higher Edn., Change mag., 1978. Mem. Nat. Assn. Ind. Colls. and Univs. (dir.), Brunswick C. of C. (trustee 1978-81) Office: RI Coll 600 Mt Pleasant Ave Providence RI 02908-1924 Office Phone: 401-456-9766. Business E-Mail: wenteman@ric.edu.

ENTESSAR, TAHMINEH, political scientist, educator; b. Tehran, June 22, 1953; arrived in U.S., 1972; d. Fatollah and Azar Entessar; m. Robert Beller Weisenfeld, Aug. 18, 1984; 1 child, Aryan Entessar Weisenfeld. BA cum laude, Webster U., 1975; MA, So. Ill. U., Edwardsville, 1977; PhD, St. Louis U., 1983. Tchr. secondary sch. Springboard to Learning, St. Louis, 1978—83; adj. prof. Webster U., St. Louis, 1983—2001, lectr., grad. adviser, 2001—. Guest commentator Sta. KTVI-TV, St. Louis, 1991, World News Report, St. Louis, 1984—97; guest analyst St. Louis Post Dispatch, 1990. Mem.: AAUP, Pi Sigma Alpha. Avocations: classical music, jogging, piano. Office: Webster U 470 E Lockwood Ave Saint Louis MO 63119 E-mail: entessar@webster.edu.

ENTHOVEN, ALAIN CHARLES, economist, educator; b. Seattlle, Sept. 10, 1930; s. Richard Frederick and Jacqueline E.; m. Rosemary Fenech, July 28, 1956; children: Eleanor, Richard, Andrew, Martha, Nicholas, Daniel. BA in Econs., Stanford U., 1952; M.Phil. (Rhodes scholar), Oxford (Eng.) U., 1954; PhD in Econs. MIT, 1956. Instr. econs. MIT, Cambridge, 1955-56; economist The RAND Corp., Santa Monica, Calif., 1956-60; ops. research analyst Office of Dir. Def. Research and Engring., Dept. Def., Washington, 1960; dep. comptroller, dep. asst. sec. U.S. Dept. Def., Washington, 1961-65, asst. sec. for systems analysis, 1965-69; v.p. for econ. planning Litton Industries, Beverly Hills, Calif., 1969-71; pres. Litton Med. Products, Beverly Hills, 1971-73; Marriner S. Eccles prof. pub. and pvt. mgmt. Grad. Sch. Bus. Stanford (Calif.) U., 1973-2000, prof. health care econs. Sch. Medicine, 1973-2000; sr. fellow Ctr. for Health Policy, Stanford U., 2000—. Cons. The Brookings Instn., 1956-60; vis. assoc. prof. econs. U. Wash., 1958; mem. Stanford Computer Sci. Adv. Com., 1968-73; cons. The RAND Corp., 1969—; mem. vis. com. in econs. MIT, 1971-78; mem. vis. com. on environ. quality lab. Calif. Inst. Tech., 1972-77; mem. Inst. Medicine, Nat. Acad. Scis., 1972—; mem. vis. com. Harvard U. Sch. Pub. Health, 1974-80; cons. Kaiser Found. Health Plan, Inc., 1973—; vis. prof. U. Paris, 1985, London Sch. Hygiene and Tropical Medicine, 1998-99; vis. fellow St. Catherine's Coll., Oxford U., Eng., 1985, New Coll., 1998-99; dir. Hotel Investors Trust, 1986-87, PCS Inc., 1987-90, Caresoft, 1996-2002, Rx Intelligence, 2000-03, eBenX Inc, 2001-03. Author: (with K. Wayne Smith) How Much is Enough? Shaping the Defense Program 1961-69, 1971, Health Plan: The Only Practical Solution to the Soaring Cost of Medical Care, 1980; editor: (with A. Myrick Freeman III) Pollution, Resources and the Environment, 1973, Theory and Practice of Managed Competition in Health Care Finance, 1988, In Pursuit of an Improving National Health Service, 1999, (with Laura A. Tollen) Toward a 21st Century Health System: The Contributions and Promise of Prepaid Group Practice, 2004; contbr. articles to profl. jours. Bd. dirs. Georgetown U., Washington, 1968-73, Jackson Hole Group, 1993-96; bd. regents St. John's Hosp., Santa Monica, 1971-73; chmn. Gov's Taskforce Managed Health Care Improvement, 1997-98, vis. com. Harvard U. Kennedy Sch. Govt., 1998-2003. Recipient President's award for disting. fed. civilian svc., 1963, Disting. Pub. Svc. medal Dept. Def., 1968, Baxter prize for health svcs. rsch., 1994, Bd. Dirs.' award Healthcare Fin. Mgmt. Assn., 1995, Ellwood award Found. for Accountability, 1998, Rock Carling fellow, Nuffield Trust, 1999. Mem. Am. Assn. Rhodes Scholars, Am. Acad. Arts and Scis., Integrated Healthcare Assn. (bd. dirs. 1999—), Phi Beta Kappa. Home: 1 McCormick Ln Atherton CA 94027-3033 Office: Stanford Univ Grad Sch Business 518 Memorial Way Stanford CA 94305-5015 Office Phone: 650-723-0641. Business E-Mail: enthoven@stanford.edu.

ENTMAN, ROBERT MATHEW, communications educator, consultant; b. Bklyn., Nov. 7, 1949; s. Bernard and Rose (Jacobson) E.; m. Francie Seymour, June 1, 1979; children: Max, Emily. AB, Duke U., 1971; PhD, Yale U., 1977; M in Pub. Policy, U. Calif., Berkeley, 1980. Asst. prof. Dickinson Coll., Carlisle, Pa., 1975-77, Duke U., Durham, N.C., 1980-89; postdoctoral fellow U. Calif., 1978-80; assoc. prof. comm. Northwestern U., Evanston, Ill., 1989-94; prof. comm. N.C. State U., Raleigh, 1994—2005, dir. Ctr. for Info. Tech. and Policy, 1999—2003; Shapiro prof. media and pub. affairs George Washington U., Washington, 2005—. Adj. prof. U. N.C., Chapel Hill, 1995-98; Lombard vis. prof. Harvard U., 1997; cons. subcom. on telecom. U.S. Ho. of Reps., Washington, 1982, Nat. Telecom. and Info. Adminstrn., Washington, 1984-85, Aspen Inst., Washington and Aspen, Colo., 1986—; mem. working group Commn. on TV Policy, 1990-96; guest scholar Woodrow Wilson Ctr., Washington, 1989. Author: Democracy without Citizens, 1989, (monograph) Blacks in the News, 1991, Diversifying Broadcast Media, 1998, The Black Image in the White Mind, 2000 Projections of Power, 2004; co-author: Media Power Politics, 1981; co-editor Mediated Politics: Communication in the Future of Democracy, 2000, (book series) Communication, Society and Politics, 1998—; also articles. Recipient McGannon award for comm. policy rsch., 1993, Mott award, 2000, Lane award, 2000, Goldsmith Book prize, 2002; rsch. grantee Markle Found., 1984, 86, 88, 95, Chgo. Cmty. Trust, 1989-92, 95-97; rsch. fellow Ameritech., 1989-90. Mem. Am. Polit. Sci. Assn. (coun. polit. comm. sec. 1990-91, mem. editl. bd. Polit. Comm. 1992—, Jour. Comm. 1994-98, Comm. Law and Policy 1994-2002, Critical Studies in Media Comm., 2002-, Comm. Review, 2001-, sec.-treas. polit. comm. sec. 1996-99, vice chair 1999-2000, chair 2000-01), Social Sci. Rsch. Coun. (mem. working group on media and fgn. policy 1990-93). Avocations: wine collecting and tasting, tennis. Office: NC State U Dept Comm PO Box 8104 Raleigh NC 27695-8104

ENTNER, PAUL DWIGHT, psychologist; b. Connersville, Ind., Apr. 9, 1947; s. Charles Leroy and Lenora Frances (Hirschy) E.; m. Ruth Elizabeth Kauffold, Aug. 23, 1968; 1 child, James. BS, Cedarville Coll., 1969; MEd, Wright State U., 1972; MA, Rosemead Grad. Sch. Profl. Psychology, 1974, PhD, 1976. Lic. psychologist, Ohio. Dir. children services Voorman Psychiat. Med. Clinic, Upland, Calif., 1976; psychologist, founder Agape Counseling Ctr., Dayton, Ohio, 1976—. Ednl. cons. Kettering (Ohio) City Schs., 1978-80; supervision cons. Kettering Med. Ctr., 1985-86; indsl. cons. Manville Corp., Richmond, Ind., 1986; speaker in field. Speaker seminars, Centerville, Ohio, 1981-90; pres.' assoc. Cedarville Coll., 1983-90; mem. pres.' circle Biola U., La Mirada, Calif., 1990; advisor five support groups, 1986; past bd. mem., Clergy Care Ctr.; past 3-yr. bd. mem., Middletown Area Crisis Pregnancy Ctr.; bd. mem., Healing Touch Ministries. Mem. Am. Psychol. Assn., Am. Assn. Christian Counselors, Ohio Psychol. Assn., Miami Valley Psychol. Assn., Christian Assn. Psychologists. Evangelical. Avocations: tennis, skiing, photography. Home: 705 W Stroop Rd Dayton OH 45429-1333 Office: Agape Counseling Ctr 175 S Main St Dayton OH 45458-2372

ENTORF, RICHARD CARL, retired management consultant; b. Gettysburg, SD, Feb. 11, 1929; s. Carl Luke and Violet (Carr) E.; m. Dorothy Ann Alexander, Nov. 23, 1951; children: Mark, Kimberly. BS, U. Calif. at Berkeley, 1952. Methods engr. Boeing Aircraft Corp., 1957; successively prodn. mgr., dir. mfg., v.p. ops., v.p., gen. mgr., pres. Riverside Cement Co. div. Amcord, Inc., Los Angeles, 1957-75; successively v.p., gen. mgr. Fla. div., sr. v.p. Gen. Portland Inc., Dallas, 1975-81; sr. v.p. Fla. Crushed Stone Co., Leesburg, Fla., 1982-84, pres., 1984-89; pvt. practice mgmt. cons. Leesburg, 1989-99; retired, 1999. Served with USAF, 1953-57. Home: 248 Island Pointe Dr Medford OR 97504-9453

ENTREKIN, DAVID W, insurance company executive; BSc in indsl. mgmt., Ga. Inst. Tech.; MBA, U. Tex. With Capital Markets Group of Met. Life Ins. Co.; v.p. investor rels. Aetna Inc., 2003; exec. v.p., CFO retirement services, past exec. v.p. strategic develop, sr. investment mgr. Am. Gen. Corp., 1992—2003. Office: Aetna Inc 151 Farmington Ave Hartford CT 06156

ENTREMONT, PHILIPPE, conductor, musician; b. Rheims, France, June 7, 1934; came to U.S., 1953; s. Jean and Renée (Monchamps) E.; m. Andree Ragot, Dec. 21, 1955; children: Félicia, Alexandre. Student, Conservatoire National Superieur de Musique, Paris, Jean Doyen. Founder, artistic dir. Santo Domingo Music Festival, 1997—. Profl. debut at 17, Barcelona, Am. debut at 19, Nat. Gallery, Washington, 1953, pianist-condr. debut Mostly Mozart Festival, N.Y.C, 1971; rec. artist CBS, Teldec, EMI, Schwann and ProArte records; guest condr. Pitts. Symphony, Royal Philharm. Orch. Nat. de France, Montreal Symphony, San Francisco Symphony, Phila. Orch., Detroit Symphony, numerous others; prin. condr. Netherlands Chamber Orch., 1993—; prin.-guest condr. Israel Chamber Orch., 1994-96, condr. laureate, 1996—; lifetime mus. dir. Vienna Chamber Orch., 1975-91, chief laureate, 1991—; mus. dir. New Orleans Symphony Orch., 1981-85, Denver Symphony, 1986-89, others; prin. guest condr. Shanghai Broadcasting Symphony Orch., 2002—. Decorated Officer of the Legion of Honor, Legion of Honor, Officer de l'Ordre National du Merite: Austrian First Class Cross of Honor for the Arts and Scis., Comdr. in Order of Arts and Letters, 1998; A finalist Queen Elizabeth of Belgium Internat. Concours, 1952; Grand Prix Marguerite Long-Jacques Thibaud Competition, 1953; Harriet Cohen Piano medal, 1953; 1st prize Jeunesses Musicales; Grand Prix du Disque, 1967, 68, 69, 70; Edison award, 1968; Nominee Grammy award, 1972. Former mem. Academie Internationale de Musique Maurice Ravel (pres. 1975-80) Office: care Audrey Michaels 122 E 76th St New York NY 10021-2833 E-mail: ampubrel@aol.com.

ENTRIKEN, ROBERT KERSEY, JR., editor, writer; b. Houston, Feb. 13, 1941; s. Robert and Jean (Finch) Entriken (Stepmother); divorced; 1 child, Jean Louise; m. Sandra Jo Miller, Mar. 4, 1989; 1 adopted child, Stephanie Lynn children: Caitlyn Miller, Matthew Kersey 1 stepchild, Jared Ray Adamson. Student, Sch. Journalism, U. Kans., 1961-69. Gen. assignment reporter Salina Jour., Kans., 1969-71, motorsport columnist, 1970-83, courts reporter, 1971-82, Sunday editor, 1972-75, spl. sects. editor, 1975-94, Neighbors editor, 1982-95, TV editor, 1994-95. Contbg. editor Sports Car Mag., Tustin, Calif., 1972—; motorsport columnist Motorsports Monthly, Tulsa, 1983—85, Nat. Speed Sport News, 1996—, Racer mag., 2003—; operator Ikke sa Hurtig Racing. Editor: Kans. Motor Sports Ann., 1996; contbr. articles to mags. With USN, 1969—71. Mem.: Soc. Profl. Journalists, Eastern Motorsports Press Assn., Am. Auto Racing Writers and Broadcasters Assn. (Midwest v.p. 1980—82, gen. v.p. 1982—86, chmn. All-Am. Team selections 1983—, chmn. Legends in Racing selections hall of fame 1989—), Sports Car Club Am. (regional exec. Kans. region 1974, Mid-Am pointskeeper 1974—, founding mem. Salina region 1990, regional exec. Salina region 1994, Midwest Divsn. nat. pointskeeper 1995—2000, Best Story award 1972, 1973, Solo Driver of Yr. Wichita Region 1976, Best Story award 1976—78, Solo II Champion Kans. 1978, Solo Cup nat. award 1981, Solo Driver of Yr. Wichita Region 1982, Best Story award 1983—87, Solo II Champion Kans. 1984, Nat. Solo I champion 1986, Best Story award 1989, England-Stipe award 1989, Best Story award 1992, Road Racing Driver of the Yr. Salina Region 1995, inaugural recipient Vern Jaques Sports Car Contbr. of Yr. nat. award 1999), Sigma Delta Chi. Avocations: sports car racing, autocrossing, skiing. Home and Office: 2731 Scott Ave Salina KS 67401-7858 Office Phone: 785-827-5143. E-mail: rocky@tri.net.

ENTWISLE, DORIS ROBERTS, social studies educator; b. Wilbraham, Mass., Sept. 28, 1924; d. Charles Edwin and Helen (McMenigall) Roberts; m. George Entwisle, Aug. 31, 1946; children: Barbara, Beverly, George H.; m. 2d Donald Roberts, Nov. 12, 1993. BS, U. Mass., 1945; MS, Brown U., 1946; PhD, Johns Hopkins U., 1960. Postdoctoral fellow Social Sci. Research Council Johns Hopkins U., Balt., 1960-61, research assoc. edn. and elec. engring., 1961-64, part-time asst. prof., 1964-67, assoc. prof., 1967-71, prof. sociology and engring. sci., 1971-98, prof. emerita, 1998—2003, rsch. prof., 2003—. Mem. com. on child devel. and pub. policy NRC, 1982—87; Harvard vis. com. for sociology dept., 1986—91. Author: (with S.G. Doering) The First Birth, 1981, (with L.A. Hayduk) Early Schooling, 1982, (with K.L. Alexander and Susan Dauber) The Success of Failure, 1984, 2d edit., 2002, (with K.L. Alexander, L.S. Olson) Children, Schools and Inequality, 1997; editor: Sociology of Education, 1975-78; assoc. editor Am. Sociol. Rev., 1972-75, 95-98; co-editor Jour. Rsch. in Adolescence, 1990-94. Guggenheim fellow, 1976—77. Fellow APA, Am. Sociol. Assn. (chair sect. children); mem. Am. Ednl. Rsch. Assn., Soc. Rsch. in Child Devel. (pub. com. 1987-93, chair 1989-91, governing coun. 1993-99). Office: Johns Hopkins U 530 Mergenthaler Baltimore MD 21218

ENTWISTLE, ANDREW JOHN, lawyer, consultant; b. Rockville Centre, N.Y., Apr. 13, 1959; s. Michael Joseph and Frances (Deluca) E. BA in Govt. and Internat. Relations, U. Notre Dame, 1981; JD, Syracuse U., 1984. Bar: N.Y. 1985, N.J. 1986, U.S. Dist. Ct. (ea. and so. dists.) N.Y. 1986, U.S. Ct. Appeals (2d cir.) 1986, U.S. Dist. Ct. N.J. 1987, U.S. Ct. Appeals (3d cir.) 1989, U.S. Dist. Ct. (no. dist.) N.Y. 1993, U.S. Supreme Ct. 1993, Ill. 2001, D.C. 2001, Tex. 2002, Colo. 2004. Assoc. D'Amato & Lynch, N.Y.C., 1984—86, Wilson, Elser, Moskowitz, Edelman & Dicker, N.Y.C., 1986—89, Mudge Rose Guthrie Alexander & Ferdon, N.Y.C., 1989—91; ptnr., chmn. litigation dept. Wohl & Entwistle, LLP, N.Y.C., 1992—98. Mng. ptnr. Entwistle & Cappucci LLP, N.Y.C., 1998—; chmn. Nattech Security Svcs., 2003-; spl. mediator U.S. Bankruptcy Ct. for So. Dist. N.Y.; N.E. regional editor The Bus. Suit, Def. Rsch. Inst., 1997-. Mem. exec. com. Bd. Cath. Big Bros. of N.Y., 1995-98, bd. dirs., 1998-, co-chair adv. bd., 2005—; mem. Housing Bd. Town of North Salem, N.Y., 1996-2000; chmn. Sports Buddies, Inc., 1998—2005; dir. Linden Hill Sch., 2001-02. Mem. ABA, N.Y. Bar Assn., N.J. Bar Assn., Ill. State Bar Assn., D.C. Bar Assn., Assn. Trial Lawyers Am., Nat. Assn. Pension Plan Attys., Coun. Instnl. Investors (edn. sustainer), Nassau County Bar Assn., N.Y. Trial Lawyers Assn., Westchester County Bar Assn., Assn. Bar City N.Y., Fed. Bar Coun., Def. Rsch. Inst. Avocations: golf, skiing, fly fishing, hunting. Office: 299 Park Ave New York NY 10171 Home: 35 Mianus River Rd Bedford NY 10506-2805 Office Phone: 212-894-7200. Business E-Mail: aentwistle@entwistle-law.com.

ENTZ, GARY R., historian, educator; b. Newton, Kans., Sept. 22, 1959; s. Merle W. and Marilyn Entz. BA, Bethel Coll., 1990; MA, James Madison U., 1993; PhD, U. Utah, 1999. Asst. prof. history McPherson Coll., Kans., 1999—2004, assoc. prof. history, 2005—. Contbr. articles to profl. jours. Sponsor McPherson Coll. Svc. Learning, N.Mex., 2003. With USN, 1981—87. Steffenson Cannon fellow, U. Utah, 1996, 1997, Tanner Grad. Rsch. fellow, 1998. Mem.: Soc. Automobile Historians, We. History Assn. (Arrington-Prucha prize 2002), Kans. State Hist. Soc., Kans. History Tchrs. Assn. Independent. Avocations: travel, hiking. Office: McPherson Coll Box 1402 1600 E Euclid Mcpherson KS 67460 Office Phone: 620-241-0242. Office Fax: 620-241-8443. Business E-Mail: entzg@mcpherson.edu.

ENTZMINGER, JOHN NELSON, JR., federal agency administrator, electrical engineer; b. Memphis, Dec. 17, 1936; s. John Nelson and Josephine Chambers (Marshall) Entzminger; m. Nancy May Burg, Sept. 9, 1961; children: David Marshall, Rebecca Louise. BSEE magna cum laude, U. S.C., 1959; MSEE, Syracuse U., 1968. Elec. engr. Bell Telephone Labs., Winston-Salem, N.C., 1959; project engr. Rome Air Devel. Ctr., Griffiss AFB, N.Y., 1960-66, sect. chief, communications, 1966-73, br. chief, communications and control, 1973-81, tech. dir. intelligence and reconnaissance, 1981-83; dir. tactical tech. Def. Advance Rsch. Project Agy., Washington, 1983-91, chief advanced tech., 1991—93, dir. joint uav program off, 1993—96; sr. staff mem. Inst. for Def. Analyses, Alexandria, Va., 1996-98; dep. for technology Def. Airborne Reconnaissance Office, Washington, 1996-98; pres. Entzminger Assocs. Consulting Firm, 1998—. Contbr. articles to profl jours. Elder Christian Assembly, Vienna, Va., 1985—. Fellow: IEEE, AIAA (assoc.); mem.: Phi Beta Kappa, Tau Beta Pi. Republican. Achievements include patents in field. Avocations: flying, carpentry, mechanics, skiing. Home: 3203 Dominy Ct Oakton VA 22124-2008 E-mail: jentzminger@ieee.org.

ENYEART, JAMES L., museum director; b. Auburn, Wash., Jan. 13, 1943; s. Lyle F. and Emma A. (Ham) E.; m. Roxanne Enyeart Malone, Sept. 7, 1964; children: Mara, Sascha, Megan. BFA, Kansas City Art Inst., 1965; MFA, U. Kans., 1972. Dir. Albrecht Gallery Art, St. Joseph, Mo., 1967-68; curator photography, assoc. prof. Spencer Mus. Art, U. Kans., 1968-76; exec. dir. Friends of Photography, Carmel, Calif., 1976-77; dir., adj. prof. art Ctr. for Creative Photography, U. Ariz., 1977-89; dir. Internat. Mus. Photography at George Eastman House, Rochester, N.Y., 1989-95; emeritus Marion Ctr. Photo. Art Coll. Santa Fe, 1995—2003, Anne and John Marion prof., 1995—. Mem. numerous panels, adv. bds. and commns. in field, including peer panel Nat. Endowment for Arts, Mus. Challenge Grants, 1993; adv. bd. Am. Photography Inst., NYU, 1991—; others; cons. in field. Author: Creative Camera, 1976, Francis Bruguiere, 1977, Jerry Uelsmann: Twenty-Five Years, A Retrospective, 1982, Edward Weston's California Landscapes, 1984 (Am. Inst. Graphic Arts award), Land, Sky, and All That Is Within: Visionary Photographers of the Southwest, 1998, The Nature of Photographs, 1998, Harmony of Reflected Light: The Photographs of Arthur Wesley Dow, 2001, Photographers, Writers, and the American Scene, 2002, others; (with R.D. Monroe, Philip Stokes) Three Classic American Photographs: Texts and Contexts, 1982; contbr. Edward Weston Omnibus, 1984, Contemporary Photographers, 1983, 2d rev. edit., 1986-87; editor: Decade by Decade: A Survey of Twentieth Century American Photography, 1989; co-editor: Henry Holmes Smith: Collected Writings 1935-1985, 1986; contbr. introductions to Andreas Feininger: A Retrospective, 1986, Aaron Siskind: Terrors and Pleasures, 1931-1980, 1982, W. Eugene Smith: Master of the Photographic Essay, 1981, Landscapes 1975-1979, 1981, Photography of the Fifties: An American Perspective, 1980, George Fiske, Yosemite Photographer, 1980, Peekamoose, 1973; editor Kans. Album, 1977, Heinecken, 1980, The Archive, 1988, Image, 1989—; designer print study rm. Spencer Mus. Art, U. Kans., 1976, Ctr. Creative Photography, U. Ariz., 1989; author, curator exhbn. Judy Dater: Twenty Years; represented in collections Albrecht Gallery, St. Joseph, Mo., Mus. Art, U. Kans., Bibliotheque Nationale, Paris, Internat. Mus. Photography at George Eastman House, Rochester, Sheldon Meml. Gallery, Lincoln, Nebr., Nat. Mus. Am. Art; numerous other publs. Commr. Kans. Arts Commn., 1973-74; selection com. Ariz. Gov's. Arts Awards, 1984; creative arts award com. Brandeis U., Waltham, Mass., 1990—; adv. bd. Aaron Siskind Found., 1981—, W. Eugene Smith Meml. Fund, Inc., 1983—; nom. com. MacArthur Found., 1982; rev. panel Bush Found. Fellowships, St. Paul, 1980. Recipient Josef Sudek medal Ministry Culture, Union Visual Arts, Czechoslovakia, 1989, Photokina Obelisk award, Fed. Republic Germany, 1982, Internat. Achievement award Photographic Soc. Japan, 1994, others; grantee NEA, 1973, 74, 75; Hon. Rsch. fellow U. Exeter, 1974, OAS fellow, 1966-67, John Simon Guggenheim Meml. fellow, 1987; fellow John S. and James L. Knight Found. Nat. Millennium Survey, 1998; named 100 Most Important People in Photography Am. Photo, 1998; grantee Nat. Endowment for the Arts, 1973—; other awards in field. Mem. Am. Assn. Art Mus. Dirs., Am. Assn. Art Mus., Am. Photography Inst. (adv. bd. 1991—), Am. Photog. Hist. Soc. (hon. life), Oracle (co-founder), Deutschen Gesellschaft fur Photographie (hon. mem.), others. Office: Coll Santa Fe Marion Ctr Photographic Art 1600 Saint Michaels Dr Santa Fe NM 87505-7615

ENYEDY, GUSTAV, JR., chemical engineer; b. Cleve., Aug. 23, 1924; s. Gustav and Mary (Silay) E.; m. Zoe Agnes Zachlin, Aug. 25, 1956 (div.); children: Louise Elaine, Roseann Marie, Arthur Gustav, Lillian Alice, Edward Anthony; m. Barbara Martha Ludwig Holley, May 9, 1987. BS in Chem. Engring., Case Inst. Tech., 1950, MS, 1955. Registered profl. engr., Ohio. Engr., Rayon Tech. div. E.I. duPont, Richmond, Va., 1950-51; project engr. Grasselli Chem. Div., Cleve., 1951-54; devel. engr. Diamond Alkali (Soda Products), Painesville, Ohio, 1954-60; process engr. Central Engring., Cleve., 1960-61, staff engr. research dept. Painesville, 1961-65, supr. computer services, 1965-68; mgr. Diamond Shamrock Corp., Painesville, 1968-73; engring. cons., 1973-85; pres. PDQS, Inc., 1975—. Lectr. chem. engring. Fenn Coll., Cleve., 1957-61, Cleve. State U., 1975-76 Contbr. articles to tech. jours., textbooks. Treas., cubmaster, chmn. Gates Mills Cub Scout Pack, 1970-71, 75-78. Served with AUS, 1943-46. Decorated Bronze Star medal, Combat Inf. badge. Fellow Am. Inst. Chem. Engrs., Am. Assn. Cost Engrs. (tech. v.p. 1966-68, pres. 1969-70, speakers' bur. program 1971-89, O.T. Zimmerman Founder's award and hon. life mem., 1992); mem. Hungarian Geneal. Soc. of Greater Cleve. (founder 1996), Tau Beta Pi, Pi Delta Epsilon. Home and Office: 7830 Sugarbush Ln Gates Mills OH 44040-9317 Office Phone: 440-423-3520. *Do each job with complete integrity. Do not gain favor by giving in to outside pressure to slant results.*

ENZI, MICHAEL BRADLEY, senator, accountant; b. Bremerton, Wash., Feb. 1, 1944; s. Elmer Jacob and Dorothy (Bradley) E.; m. Diana Buckley, June 7, 1969; children: Amy, Bradley, Emily. BBA, George Wash. U., 1966;

MBA, Denver U., 1968. Cert. profl. human resources, 1994. Mayor City of Gillette, Wyo., 1975—82; pres. NZ Shoes, Inc., Gillette, Wyo., 1969-95, NZ Shoes of Sheridan, Inc., Wyo., 1983-96; acctg. mgr. Dunbar Well Svc., Inc., Gillette, 1985-97; mem. Wyo. Ho. of Reps., Cheynne, 1986—91, Wyo. State Senate, Cheynne, 1991-96; commr. Western Interstate Commn. for Higher Edn., 1995—96; US senator from Wyo., 1997—; mem. fgn. rels. com.; chmn. health, edn., labor and pensions com., 2005—. Chmn. bd. dirs. 1st Wyo. Bank, Gillette, 1978-88; chmn. Senate Revenue Com., 1992-96. Mayor City of Gillette, 1975-82; pres. Wyo. Assn. Mcpls., Cheyenne, 1980-82. Sgt. Wyo. Air NG, 1967-73. Mem. Wyo. Order of DeMolay (state master councilor 1963-64), Wyo. Jaycees (state pres. 1973-74), Masons (Sheridan and Gillette lodges), Scottish Rite, Shriners, Lions, Sigma Chi. Republican. Presbyn. Avocations: fishing, bicycling, soccer, hunting. Office: US Senate 379A Senate Russell Bldg Washington DC 20510-0001 E-mail: senator@enzi.senate.gov.*

ENZOR, GARY R., trucking executive; BS in Computer sci., MBA, Fla. Atlantic U. Formerly with Allied Signal; formerly with fin. dept., gen. mgr. higher edn. bus. Dell Computer; former v.p., CFO aerospace electronic systems bus. Honeywell; CFO Swift Transp. Co., Phoenix, 2002—. Office: Swift Transp Co Inc 2200 S 75th Ave Phoenix AZ 85043

EO, SURAK, plastic surgeon, educator; b. Gwangju, Republic of Korea, Feb. 14, 1968; s. JaeHong Eo and Ju OkSoon; m. InA Jeong; children: DoYang, Douglas Ford. MD, PhD, Chonnam Nat. Med. Sch., Gwangju, 1987—93. Diplomate Korea, 1993. Internat. fellow UCLA Med. Ctr., 2003—; asst. prof. Hallym U. Med. Ctr., Seoul, Republic of Korea, 2005. Contbr. articles to profl. jours. Lt. U.S. Army, 1994—97, Korea. Mem.: Korean Soc. Plastic and Reconstructive Surgery. Home: 827 Levering Ave #508 Los Angeles CA 90024 Office: UCLA Med Ctr 10945 Le Conte Ave #3355 Los Angeles CA 90095 Office Phone: 310-794-7784. Office Fax: 310-206-0063. E-mail: surakeo@yahoo.com.

EOVALDI, THOMAS L., law educator; b. May 9, 1940; married; 2 children. BS, U. Ill., 1962, LLB, 1969. Bar: Ill. 1965. Assoc. Jenner & Block, Chgo., 1965—67; asst. prof. Northwestern U. Law Sch., Chgo., 1967—70, assoc. prof., 1970—73, prof., 1973—. Asst. dean for Clin. Edn. Northwestern U. Law Sch., 1974—76, assoc. dean, 1976—77. Author (with Louis W. Stern): Legal Aspects of Marketing Strategy: Anti-Trust and Consumer Protection Issues, 1984. Mem.: Chgo. Coun. Lawyers (bd. govs.), Ill. Law Rev., Order of Coif. Office: Northwestern U Sch Law 357 E Chicago Ave Chicago IL 60611-3059 Office Phone: 312-503-8541. E-mail: teovaldi@law.northwestern.edu.*

EPCAR, RICHARD MICHAEL, actor, writer, director; b. Denver, Apr. 29, 1955; s. George Buck and Shirley (Learner) E.; m. Ellyn Jane Stern, Aug. 15, 1982; children: Jonathan Alexander, Jacqueline Elizabeth. BFA in Performing Arts, U. Ariz., 1978; postgrad., U. So. Calif., L.A., 1980, U. Calif., 1981, Am. Film Inst., 1982. Pres. Epcar Entertainment, LA, 1986—. Actor (films) including Memoirs of an Invisible Man, DC Collins, Incident of War, Street Hawk, Escape to Love, Not of This World, (TV series) Diagnosis Murder, Columbo, Beverly Hills 90210, Cheers, General Hospital, Guns of Paradise, Matlock, Who's the Boss?, Sonny Spoons, Moonlighting, Highway to Heaven, Amazing Stories, Fast Times, Crazy Like a Fox, Hell Town, Stir Crazy, Santa Barbara, Days of our Lives, (animated series) Teknoman 2 Lead Voices; author 7 episodes, co-dir. Ghost in the Shell (film & lead voice-series), Transformers (co-author and lead voice), Digimon (dir. first season), Lupin the Third (dir. and lead voice), Fighting Spirit (dir. and lead voice), Storm Force (dir. and lead voice), Cyborg 009 (author and lead voice), Daigunder (author and lead voice), Robotech, (lead voice) Shadow Cronicles, Shark Bait, (dir., lead voice) Toy Warrior, (dir.) Pat Labor III, (dir.) Tae Guk Gi, (dir.) Old Boy, (voice) Curious George, (lead voice) Avenging Apes, Bo-Bo-B0-B0, Prince of Egypt, Honey Bee Hutch, X-Men; dir., voice Crimes of Father Amaro (acad. award nomination); dir and author, Betty Blue, Warriors of Heaven and Earth, The Code, The Returner, Widow of St. Pierre (acad. award nomination) Mostly Martha, Emperor and Assassin, Iron Monkey, Mission Kashmir, Shiri, Double Vision, and Omhyosi; dir. The Pearl, Toy Warrior, Shadow Hearts II, Robotech The Game; Onmyoji dir., author, lead voice Eagle Riders, 2 lead voices Digimon, lead voice Flint; co-dir., co-author, lead voices Samurai X; TV and film voice Gladiator, Gods and Generals, Riddick, Independence Day, Seven, Hell Raiser III & IV, Hard Target, Crime Story, Power Rangers, Jack, E.R., Nash Bridges, Xena, Hercules; (on stage) Why a Hero, Dracula, An Evening with Lincoln, Real Inspector Hound, Richard II; actor, writer (play) (on stage) The Vow, Take My Wife...Please!, 1980; wrote and directed English adaptation of Acad. award winning Cinema Paradisco, Belle Epoque (Acad. Award winner), Women on the Verge of a Nervous Breakdown (Acad. Award nomination), Eat Drink Man Woman (Acad. Award nominated), Fencing Master (Acad. Award nominated); dir. (for TV) A Cowboy Christmas; internat. supr. Gladiator, Galaxy Quest, Chicken Run, El Dorado, E.T.; CD-ROM lead voice Medal of Honor, Blackhawk Down, Samurai Warriors, Dynasty Tactics II, Waterworld, Xena-Saga I & II, Aero Wings, Wetlands, Jade Cacoon, Dynasty Warriors IV, dir. Fighting Spirit, dir., lead voice Lupin III, Covenant, others. Mem. L.A. Zoo Assn., 1983-90, 91, 94, Natural History Mus., L.A., 1989-91, Earth Save, L.A., 1990, L.A. Mus. Art, 1991; host fall festival Sta. KCET-Pub. TV, L.A., 1980; active Am. Cancer Soc. Recipient Haldeman Found. scholarship, U. Ariz., 1973-78; named Nat. Best Actor of Yr., Nat. Players, 1977, CPC Repertory Group, 1980; recipient Irene Ryan Soloist award, 1978. Avocations: weightlifting, tennis, music, art. Office Phone: 818-426-3415. E-mail: tallactor@richardepcar.com.

EPEL, DAVID, biologist, educator; b. Detroit, Mar. 26, 1937; s. Jacob A. and Anna K. E.; m. Lois S. Ambush, Dec. 18, 1960; children: Andrea, Sharon, Elissa. AB, Wayne State U., 1958; PhD, U. Calif.-Berkeley, 1963. Postdoctoral fellow Johnson Research Found., U. Pa., 1963-65; asst. prof. Hopkins Marine Sta., 1965-70; assoc. prof., then prof. Scripps Instn. Oceanography, 1970-77; Jane and Marshall Steel Jr. prof. marine scis. Hopkins Marine Sta., Stanford U., Pacific Grove, Calif., 1977—; acting dir. Hopkins Marine Sta., Pacific Grove, 1984—88. Co-dir. embryology course Marine Biol. Lab, Woods Hole, 1974—77. Mem. editl. bd. Acta Histochemica, Zygote. Bd. dirs. Monterey Bay Aquarium Rsch. Inst., 1983-87, 1989, trustee, 1985-88. Guggenheim fellow, 1976-77, Overseas fellow Churchill Coll., Cambridge, Eng., 1976-77, Dist. Fellow Calif. State U., 2004; recipient Allen Cox medal for fostering excellence in undergrad. rsch. Stanford U., 1995. Fellow AAAS (mem.-at-large, sect. G 1979-84, chmn. sect. on biol. scis. 1998—), Calif. Acad. Scis.; mem. Am. Soc. Cell Biology (mem. council 1978-80), Soc. Devel. Biology, Internat. Soc. Devel. Biology, Soc. Integrative and Comparative Biology (chairperson devel. and cell biology sect. 1990-92). Home: 25847 Carmel Knolls Dr Carmel CA 93923-8845 Office Phone: 831-655-6226. Business E-Mail: depel@stanford.edu.

EPHRON, NORA, writer; b. NYC, May 19, 1941; d. Henry and Phoebe (Wolkind) E.; m. Dan Greenburg (div.); m. Carl Bernstein (div.); children: Jacob, Max; m. Nicholas Pileggi. BA, Wellesley Coll., 1962. Reporter N.Y. Post, 1963-68; free-lance writer, 1968—; contbg. editor, columnist Esquire mag., 1972-73, sr. editor, columnist, 1974-78; contbg. editor N.Y. mag., 1973-74. Author: Wallflower at the Orgy, 1970, Crazy Salad, 1975, Scribble Scribble, 1978, Heartburn, 1983, Nora Ephron Collected, 1991; screenwriter: (with Alice Arlen) Silkwood (nominated Acad. award for best original screenplay), 1983, Heartburn, 1986, Cookie, 1989, When Harry Met Sally (nominated Acad. award, BAFTA award for best screenplay), 1989, My Blue Heaven, 1990; dir., screenwriter (with Delia Ephron) This Is My Life, 1992, Mixed Nuts, 1994, Michael, 1996, You've Got Mail, 1998; co-screenwriter, dir. Sleepless in Seattle (nominated Acad. award for best original screenplay), 1993; prodr., dir. Lucky Numbers, 2000; screenwriter, prodr. Hanging Up, 2000; playwright Imaginary Friends, 2002; screenwriter, dir., Bewitched, 2005. Mem. Writers Guild Am., Authors Guild, Dirs. Guild of Am., Acad. Motion Picture Arts and Scis.

EPLER, GARY ROBERT, physician, author, educator; b. Chico, Calif., Apr. 5, 1944; s. Deane Chandler and Kathryn Louise (McNeil) E.; m. Joan Susan Weidman, Sept. 10, 1983; children: Gregory C., Brett H. MD, Tulane U., 1971; MPH, Harvard U., 1978. Diplomate in internal medicine and pulmonary medicine Am. Bd. Internal Medicine. Intern Harlem Hosp., Columbia U., 1971-72; resident U. Hosp., Boston, 1974-76, pulmonary medicine fellowship, 1975-78; asst. prof. medicine Sch. Medicine Boston U., 1978-85, assoc. clin. prof. medicine, 1985-96, Harvard U., Boston, 1995—; med. dir. respiratory therapy, chmn. dept. medicine New England Bapt. Hosp., Boston, 1983-98, med. dir. rehab. unit, 1983-98. Parasitology rsch. fellow Tulane U., Cali, Colombia, 1969-70, USPHS, Ctrs. Disease Control, 1972-74; tuberculosis cons. CDC Vietnamese Refugee Camps, Eglin AFB, Fla. and Indiantown Gap, Pa., 1975, Cuban Refugee Camp, Indiantown Gap, 1980; med. cons. CDC, Vietnamese Refugee Programs in Hong Kong, Thailand, Philippines, Malaysia, Indonesia; vis. attending physician U. Hosp., Boston City Hops. and Boston VA Hosp., 1978-98, Brigham and Women's Hosp., Boston, 1999—; med. dir. Occupational Health Ctr., Wilmington, Mass; vis. prof. Kyoto (Japan) U., 1990; many others. Author book on diseases of bronchioles, 1994; editor book on occupational lung diseases; editl. reviewer New England Jour. Medicine, Annals of Internal Medicine, Jour. AMA, Am. Rev. Respiratory Diseases, Chest, Jour. Respiratory Medicine, Jour. Western Medicine, Jour. Rheumatology, European Respiratory Jour.; contbr. chpts. to books, more than 85 articles to sci. jours. Lt. comdr. USPHS, 1972-74. Recipient cert. of appreciation Am. Lung Assn. Mass.; named one of Outstanding Med. Specialists in U.S., Town and Country Mag., 1989. Fellow ACP, Am. Coll. Chest Physicians (chmn. com. on occupational and environ. health 1987-88, v.p. New England States chpt. 1989-91, pres. chpt. 1991-93); mem. AMA (alt. del. 1987-93), Am. Soc. Law and Medicine (treas. 1983-85, Disting. Svc. award 1985), Am. Coll. Physician Execs., Mass. Thoracic Soc. (mem. coun. 1980-84, sec.-treas. 1984-85, pres. 1986-88), Mass. Med. Soc. Office: Brigham and Women's Hosp Pulmonary/Critical Care Med 75 Francis St Boston MA 02115-6106

EPLEY, LEWIS EVERETT, JR., lawyer; b. Ft. Smith, Ark., Apr. 28, 1936; s. Lewis Everett and Evelyn (Wood) E.; m. Donna Louise Swopes, Feb. 24, 1962. BS, JD, U. Ark., 1961. Bar: Ark. 1961. Formerly practiced in Eureka Springs, Ark.; city atty., 1969-71; chmn. bd. Bank of Eureka Springs, Ark., 1990-93, vice-chmn., 1993—, also bd. dirs. Del. Ark. Constl. Conv., 1969-70; apptd. spl. assoc. justice Ark. Supreme Ct., 1984. Ark. Bldg. Svcs. Coun., 1975-80, chmn., 1976-78; Carroll County Cen. Dem. Com., 1964-68, Beaver Lake Adv. Com., 1982-89; bd. dirs. Eureka Springs Ozark Folk Festival, 1964-69, Ark. Cancer Rsch. Ctr., N.W. Ark. Radiation Therapy Inst., 1984-91, pres. bd. dirs., 1989; chmn. adv. bd. Eureka Springs Mcpl. Hosp., 1963-71; trustee U. Ark., 1989-99, chmn. bd. trustees, 1996-98; bd. dirs. U. Ark. Found., 1994—, chmn., 2004—; bd. dirs. Mashburn Scholarship Found., 1993-2002; past dir., past mem. Washington Regional Med. Found.; mem. Carroll County Com. for Study of Long-Term Health Care Needs, 1990-93; devel. coun. Eureka Springs Hosp., 1997-2001. Fellow Ark. Bar Assn. (del. 1975-78), Am. Inns of Ct. (mem. emeritus W. B. Putnam chpt. 1990-97), Carroll County Bar Assn. (past pres.), Eureka Springs C. of C. (dir., past pres.), Fayetteville Rotary Club, Phi Alpha Delta, Kappa Kappa Psi. Baptist. Home: 2805 Brandon Cir Fayetteville AR 72703 E-mail: epleyoff@sbcglobal.net.

EPLING, RICHARD LOUIS, lawyer; b. Waukegan, Ill., Aug. 16, 1951; s. Carrol Franklin and Mary Teresa Epling; m. Suzanne Braley, Aug. 4, 1973. BA in English and History magna cum laude, Duke U., 1973; JD, U. Mich., 1976. Bar: Ill. 1977, US Dist. Ct. (no. dist.) Ill. 1977, US Ct. Appeals (7th cir.) 1979, Ariz. 1981, US Dist. Ct. Ariz. 1981, US Ct. Appeals (9th cir.) 1982, NY 1988, US Ct. Appeals (2d cir.) 1988, US Dist. Ct. (ea. and so. dists.) NY 1989. Law clk. to presiding justice Mich. Supreme Ct., Southfield, 1976-77; assoc. Katten, Muchin & Zavis, Chgo., 1977-81; ptnr. Brown & Bain, P.A., Phoenix, 1981-88, Sidley & Austin, NYC, 1988-92, Pillsbury Winthrop Shaw Pittman LLP and predecessor firm, NYC, 1992—2005; ptnr., leader Insolvency & Restructuring practice Pillsbury Winthrop Shaw Pittman, NYC, 2005—. Assoc. conferee Nat. Bankruptcy Conf., Washington, 1985-93. Contbr. articles to profl. jours. Mem. Am. Bankruptcy Inst., Phi Beta Kappa. Office: Pillsbury Winthrop Shaw Pittman 1540 Broadway New York NY 10036 Office Phone: 212-858-1649. Office Fax: 212-858-1500. Business E-Mail: richard.epling@pillsburylaw.com.

EPLING-BURNETTE, PEARLIE K., pharmacologist, educator; b. Matewan, W.Va., Feb. 12, 1961; d. Pearley and Marie Epling; m. Michael C. Burnette, June 4, 1983; children: Alexis Burnette, Sean Burnette. BS in Microbiology, U. Ky., 1983; PharmD, U. Fla., 1989; PhD in Med. Sci., U. So. Fla., 1994. Rsch. asst. Med. U. S.C., Charleston, 1984—85; pharmacy resident H. Lee Moffitt Cancer Ctr., Tampa, Fla., 1989—90, clin. pharmacist, 1990—91; rsch. asst. H. Lee. Moffitt Cancer Ctr., Tampa, Fla., 1998—99; fellow U. So. Fla., Tampa, 1995—98, asst. prof., 1999—. R&d com. James A. Haley VA Hosp., Tampa, 2001—05, mem. safety com., 2002—05. Contbr. articles to profl. jours. Mem.: Am. Soc. Hematology. Avocations: horseback riding, reading, skiing, cooking. Office: James A Haley VA Hosp/USF 13000 Bruce B Bowns Tampa FL 33612

EPNER, STEVEN ARTHUR, computer consultant; b. Buffalo; s. Robert and Rosann (Krohn) E.; m. Louise Berke, June 20, 1970; children: Aaron J., Brian D. BS, Purdue U., 1970. Computer operator/programmer Union Carbide, Chgo. and London, 1966-68; system analyst process design III, Chgo., 1969; analyst, sr. systems analyst Monsanto Co., St. Louis, 1970-74; lead analyst Citicorp., St. Louis, 1974-76; cons., pres. The User Group, Inc. (name changed to BSW Consulting, Inc. 1995), St. Louis, 1976—. Lectr. U. Mo., St. Louis Bus. Program, AICPA, Mo., 1983-93; SBA Task Force on Small Bus.; dir. Programming and Systems Cons., Inc. Editor: The Independent, 1977-84; contbg. editor St. Louis Bus. Jour., St. Louis Computing; contbr. articles to profl. jours. Trustee Steven A. Epner/ICAA Scholarship fund; mem. tech. com., founding rep. EDI Coalition of Assns. Mem. Ind. Computer Cons. Assn. (dir., pres. chpt., nat. pres.), Nat. Cons. Council, Nat. Spkrs. Assn. (Cert. Spkg. Profl. award 2000), Internat. Brotherhood Magicians. Office: BSW Cons Inc 1050 N Lindbergh Blvd Saint Louis MO 63132-2912 *I am often asked about starting businesses. My normal reply is, "If it were easy and guaranteed, then it would already be done." Therefore, building a successful organization takes time, effort, and risk.*

EPP, DIANNE NAOMI, secondary school educator; b. Yankton, S.D., Oct. 1, 1939; d. Willard H. and Florence A. (Leigh) Waltner; m. Anthony R. Epp, Aug. 18, 1964; children: Alain-René Epp Weaver, Rachel Epp Buller. BA in Chemistry, Bethel Coll., 1961; MA, U. Mo., 1963; cert. etudes, L'Ecole d'Administration, Brussels, 1965. Chemistry instr. Bethel Coll., North Newton, Kans., 1963-64; sci. tchr. Ecole Secondaire, Sundi-Lutete, Zaire, 1965-67; rsch. chemist FMC Glass Lab., Golden, Colo., 1967-70; vis. instr. Nebr. Wesleyan U., Lincoln, 1973-74, 77-79, 1980-81; chemistry tchr. East High Sch., Lincoln, 1982—93, 1994—2005; vis. scholar Miami U., Oxford, Ohio, 1993-94. Cons. NSF Doing Chemistry Videodisc, 1988; cons. small scale CD ROM Synapse Corp., Lincoln, 1993. Author: Chemical Manfacturing: The Process of Mixing, 2000, Experimental Design: The Chemistry of Adhesives, 1998, Product Testing: The Chemistry of Ice Cream, 1998; cons. editor: Starting at Ground Zero, 1989; author: (monograph series) A Palette of Color, 1995; contbr. articles to profl. jours. Recipient Excellence in Teaching award Cooper Found., 1990, Excellence in High Sch. Chemistry Teaching award Am. Chem. Soc., 1990, 91, Presdl. award for Excellence in Sci. and Math. Teaching NSF, 1994, Kiewit Found. Tchg. award, 1997, 01, Christa McAuliffe award, 2005. E-mail: depp@lps.org.

EPP, ELDON JAY, religion educator; b. Mountain Lake, Minn., Nov. 1, 1930; s. Jacob Jay and Louise (Kintzi) E.; m. ElDoris Balzer, June 13, 1951; children: Gregory Thomas, Jennifer Elizabeth. AB magna cum laude, Wheaton Coll., 1952; BD magna cum laude, Fuller Theol Sem., 1955; STM, Harvard U., 1956, PhD, 1961. Spl. rsch. asst. Princeton Theol. Sem., 1961-62; vis. instr. Drew U. Theol. Sch., 1962; asst. prof. religion U. So. Calif. Grad. Sch. Religion, 1962-65, assoc. prof., 1965-67, assoc. prof. classics, 1966-68; assoc. prof. religion Case Western Res. U., Cleve., 1968-71, prof. religion, Harkness prof. bibl. lit., 1971-98, prof. emeritus, 1998—, dean humanities and social scis., 1977-85, dean emeritus, 1998—; acting dean Western Res. Coll., Cleve., 1984; chmn. dept. religion Case Western Res. U., Cleve., 1982-98. Lectr. Harvard Divinity Sch., 2001-02, vis. prof., 2002-03, 2004-05; Am. exec. com. Internat. Greek New Testament Project, 1968-88; mem. N.Am. Com., 1989—; mem. accreditation rev. coun. North Ctrl. Assn. Commn. on Insts. Higher Edn., 1986-90, mem. appeals panel, 1992-95, cons. evaluator corps, 1983-98; panelist NEH, 1978, 80, 90, 2000; reader John Simon Guggenheim Meml. Found., 1991-94; Kenneth W. Clark lectr. Duke U., 1986; Ratner lectr. Case Western Res. U., 1998; bd. dirs. New Testament Lang. Project, 1999—. Author: The Theological Tendency of Codex Bezae Cantabrigiensis in Acts, 1966, Perspectives on New Testament Textual Criticism, 2005, Junia, First Woman Apostle, 2005; co-author: Studies in the Theory and Method of New Testament Textual Criticism, 1993; co-editor: New Testament Textual Criticism: Its Significance for Exegesis, 1981, The New Testament and Its Modern Interpreters, 1989; assoc. editor Jour. Bibl. Lit., 1971-90; editor Critical Rev. of Books in Religion, 1991-94, Studies and Documents, 1991-05; mem. editl. bd. Soc. Bibl. Lit. Monograph Series, 1969-72, Soc. Bibl. Lit. Centennial Publs., 1975-86, Studies and Documents, 1971-05, Critical Rev. of Books in Religion, 1987-94; exec. sec. Hermeneia: A Critical and Historical Commentary on the Bible, 1962—, mem. editl. bd., 1966—; contbr. about 50 scholarly articles to profl. jours. Active Boy Scouts Am., 1975-78; Bd. mgrs. St. Paul's Episcopal Cathedral, L.A., 1964-68, clk., 1967-68. Harvard Faculty Arts and Scis. fellow, 1958-59, Rockefeller doctoral fellow in religion, 1959-60; postdoctoral fellow Claremont Grad. Sch., 1966-68; Guggenheim fellow, 1974-75; NEH grant, 1988. Mem. AAUP 1963-98 (mem. chpt. exec. com. 1970-72), Am. Acad. Religion 1961-98(sect. pres. 1965-66), Soc. Bibl. Lit. (chmn. textual criticism seminar 1966, 71-84, mem. permanent Centennial com. 1975-80, mem. coun. 1980-82, 85-87, 2002-03, del. Coun. on Study of Religion 1980-82, chair nominating com. 1985-87, mem. fin. com. 1997—, v.p. 2002, pres. 2003, chmn. com. on programs and initiatives 2003—), Studiorum Novi Testamenti Societas, Cath. Bibl. Assn., Am. Soc. Papyrologists, New Testament Colloquium (chmn. 1974), Soc. Mithraic Studies, Egypt Exploration Soc., Phi Beta Kappa. *Personal philosophy: Two essentials for life and livelihood are integrity and maturity. Integrity, in the abstract, is soundness, but in practical terms means incorruptibility, while maturity is basically the capacity to tolerate ambiguity. As individuals and as a society, we cannot afford to abandon integrity or to stifle maturity.*

EPPELE, DAVID LOUIS, columnist, author; b. Jersey City, Apr. 4, 1939; s. Joseph Anton and Lena Marie (Tadlock) E.; m. Gladys Emily Padilla (div. 1975); children: David D., Joseph E.; m. Geneva Mae Kirsch, July 7, 1977. Student, N.Mex. State U., 1958, U. N.Mex., 1966, U. Portland, 1972. Field botanist, SW Deserts and Mex., 1947—2004, N.Mex. Cactus Rsch., Belen, 1953-62; dir. Ariz. Cactus and Succulent Rsch., Bisbee, 1984—; editor Ariz. Cactus News, 1984—; columnist Western Newspapers, 1987—. Columnist: On the Desert, 1986—; author: On the Desert, 1991, On The Desert, vol. 2, 2000; editor: Index of Cactus Illustrations, 1990, Desert in Bloom, 1989. Mem. Mule Mountain Dem. Party, Bisbee, 1978—. With USN, 1958-59. Mem. AAAS, Cactus and Succulent Soc. Am., N.Mex. Acad. Sci., Bisbee C. of C. Avocations: photography, music. Home and Office: Ariz Cactus 8 S Cactus Ln Bisbee AZ 85603-6356 Office Phone: 520-432-7001. E-mail: azcactus@starband.net.

EPPEN, GARY DEAN, business educator; b. Austin, Minn., Apr. 28, 1936; s. Marldene Fredrick and Elsie Alma (Wendorf) E.; m. Ann Marie Sathre, June 14, 1958; children: Gregory, Peter, Paul, Amy. AA, Austin Jr. Coll., 1956; BS, U. Minn., 1958, MSIE, 1960; PhD, Cornell U., 1964; Hon. Doctorate, Stockholm Sch. Econs., 1998. Prof. mgmt. European Inst. Advanced Studies, Brussels, 1972-73; assoc. dean Grad. Sch. Bus., U. Chgo., 1969-75, prof. indsl. adminstrn., 1970—, assoc. dean Ph.D. studies, 1978-85, dir. internat. bus. exchange program, 1977-92, dir. Life Officers Investment Seminar, 1975-88, dir. Fin. Analysts Seminar, 1982-88, Robert Law prof., 1989-97, dir. exec. program, 1989-94, Keller Disting. Svc. prof., 1997-2001, dep. dean part-time programs, 1998-2001, Keller Disting. Svc. prof. emeritus, 2001—. Francqui prof. Cath. U. Leuven, Belgium, 1979; Urwitz vis. prof. Stockholm Sch. Econs., 1994; external examiner U. W.I., 1979-82; dir. Landauer, Inc., Hub Group, Inc., Hornet Capital, LLC. Author: (with F.J. Gould) Quantitative Concepts for Management, 1979, (with Metcalfe and Walters) The MBA Degree, 1979, (with F.J. Gould and C.P. Schmidt) Introductory Management Science, 1984; editor: Energy the Policy Issues, 1975; contbr. articles to profl. jours. FMC Faculty Rsch. scholar, 1986—89. Home: 3107 N Snead Dr Goodyear AZ 85338 E-mail: gary.eppen@chicagogsb.edu.

EPPERSON, ERIC ROBERT, finance executive, film producer; b. Oregon City, Oreg., Dec. 10, 1949; s. Robert Max and Margaret Joan (Crawford) E.; m. Lyla Gene Harris, Aug. 21, 1969; 1 child, Marcie. BS, Brigham Young U., 1973, M of Acctg., 1974; MBA, Golden Gate U., 1977, JD, 1981. Instr. acctg. Brigham Young U., Provo, Utah, 1973-74; supr. domestic taxation Bechtel Corp., San Francisco, 1974-78; supr. internat. taxation Bechtel Power Corp., San Francisco, 1978-80; mgr. internat. tax planning Del Monte Corp., San Francisco, 1980-82, mgr. internat. taxes, 1982-85; internat. tax specialist Touche Ross & Co., San Francisco, 1985-87; dir. internat. tax Coopers & Lybrand, Portland, Oreg., 1987-89; exec. v.p., CFO Epperson Dayton Sorenson Prodns., Inc., Salt Lake City, 1989-90, Epperson Prodns., 1990-92; exec. dir. The Oreg. Trail Found., Inc., Oregon City, 1992-93; pres., chmn. bd. MFD Ltd., Portland, 1993—; pres. Oreg. Trail Films, Ltd., 1998—, Morgan's Ferry Prodns., LLC, 1998—, Lakeboat Prodns., L.L.C., 1999—, Oregon Trail TV, Ltd., 1999, Oregon Trail Promotions, Ltd., 1999. Author: (with T. Gilbert) Interfacing of the Securities and Exchange Commission with the Accounting Profession: 1968 to 1973, 1974; prodr. (film) Without Evidence, 1995, Morgan's Ferry, 1999, Lakeboat, 2000; exec. prodr. (film) Dream Machine, 1989, Live & Learn, 2001, (TV series) Live & Learn, 2000, Dixie Chick Fly Tour, 2000. Scoutmaster Boy Scouts Am., Provo, 1971-73, troop committeeman, 1973-74, 83—, vice-chmn. ranch devel. com., Butte Creek; mem. IRS Vol. Income Tax Assistance Program, 1972-75; pres. Youth First Found. Inc., 2000-, Mut. Improvement Assn., Ch. Jesus Christ of Latter-day Saints, 1972-74, pres. Sunday sch., 1977-79, tchr., 1974-80, ward clk., 1980-83, bishopric, 1983-87; bd. dirs. Oreg. Art Inst. Film Ctr., Oreg. Trail Coordinating Coun., Hist. Preservation League of Oreg. Mem. World Affairs Coun., Japan/Am. Soc., Internat. Tax Planning Assn., Internat. Fiscal Assn., Oreg. Trail Coordinating Coun. (exec. bd.), Oreg. Hist. Soc., U.S. Rowing Assn., Oreg. Calif. Trail Assn., Royal Photog. Soc., Commonwealth Club, Multnomah Athletic Club, Exec. Officers Club. Republican. Office: PMB 180 25 NW 23d Pl Ste 6 Portland OR 97210-5599

EPPERSON, KRAETTLI QUYNTON, lawyer, educator; b. Ft. Eustis, Va., May 2, 1949; s. Dimpster Eugene Sr. and Helen Walter (Davidson) E.; m. Kay Lawrence, Aug. 22, 1970; children: Kraettli L., Kristin J., Kevin Q., Keith W. BA in Polit. Sci., U. Okla., 1971; MS in Urban and Policy Scis., SUNY, Stony Brook, 1974; JD, Oklahoma City U., 1978. Bar: Okla. 1979, U.S. Dist. Ct. (we. dist.) Okla. 1984, Fed. Claims Ct. 1997. Urban planner Gov.'s Office of Community Affairs and Planning, Oklahoma City, 1974-75; adminstr. of pub. transp. planning Okla. Dept. of Transp., Oklahoma City, 1975-79; title examiner Lawyers Title of Oklahoma City, Inc., 1979-80; gen. counsel, v.p. Am. First Land Title Ins. Co., Oklahoma City, 1980-82; assoc. Ferguson & Litchfield, Oklahoma City, 1982-85; of counsel Ames & Ashabranner, Oklahoma City, 1986-88, ptnr., 1989-93, Cook & Epperson, Oklahoma City, 1994-97, Oklahoma City, 1997—2002, Rolston, Hamill, Epperson, Myles & Nelson, 2002—. Adj. prof. law Okla. land titles Oklahoma City U., 1982—; instr. real property Okla. Bar Rev., 1998—; instr. real property titles Grad. Realtors Inst., 1998-99. Author: Basye Clearing Land Titles, 1998-2000, contbr., 2001-; contbg. author, editor: Vernon's Oklahoma Forms 2d-Real Estate, 2000—; contbr. articles to profl. jours. Asst. scoutmaster Boy Scouts Am., Oklahoma City, 1984-88, 1993-2000, asst. cubmaster, 1989-90, cubmaster, 1990-91, webelos leader, 1991-95, dist. vice-chair, 2000-01, dist. chair, 2001—. 2d lt. USAR, 1971. Recipient Dist. Svc. award, Boy Scouts

Am., 2001. Mem. ABA (vice-chmn. conveyancing com. 1987-88, 93-94, chmn. 1991-93, chmn. state customs and practice subcom. 1987-88, project chmn. title exam. standards nat. survey 1988—), Am. Land Title Assn. (legis. com. 1981-82, jud. com. 1981-82), Okla. Bar Assn. (real property sect. 1979—, dir. 1982-88, 94-95, chmn. 1985-86, project chmn. Okla. Title Exam. Standards Handbook project 1982-85, mem. title exam. standards com. 1980—, chmn. 1992—, legis. liaison com. 1986-92, co-chmn. abstracting standards com. 1982-84), Oklahoma City Real Property Lawyers Assn. (dir. 1985-91, pres. 1990-91), Oklahoma City Commml. Law Attys. Assn. Republican. Episcopalian. Avocations: skeet, storytelling, camping. Home: 3029 Rock Ridge Ct Oklahoma City OK 73120-5731 Office: 4334 NW Expressway St Ste 174 Oklahoma City OK 73116-1574 E-mail: kqelaw@aol.com.

EPPERSON, ROBERT DALE, farmer; b. Santa Maria, Calif., Jan. 12, 1947; s. Joseph Cary and Lina Marcille Epperson; m. Loretta Jolan Lambrecht, July 20, 1968; children: Andrea, David, Sara, Mary. BS, Calif. State U., Fresno, 1968, MS, 1970. Farmer, Kerman, Calif., 1974—; v.p. Epperson's Market, Inc., Kerman, 1974-79; dir. grants and contracts Calif. State U., Fresno, 1984-89; sr. environ. planner Calif. Dept. Transp., Fresno, 1989-2000; resource mgr. U.S. Bur. Reclamation, Fresno, 2000—. Mem. Nat. Agrl. Stats. Adv. Com., Washington, 1999-2004, mem. mktg. and strategic planning com. Sun-Maid Growers Bd. Dirs., Kingsburg, Calif., 1987—, mem. fin. com., 1987—, mem. pers. com., 1990—, chair fin. com., 1996—, chair ethics com., 1997—, chair mktg. and strategic planning com., 1990-96; dir. Sun-Diamond Growers, Pleasanton, Calif., 1988-97, mem. audit com., 1995-97, mem. ethics com., 1996-97: mem. Raisin Adminstrv. Com., Fresno, 1985—; mem. audit com. Raisin Adminstrv. Com., Fresno, 1995, vice-chair grades and stds. com., 1992-96. Chair safety and environ. protection subcom. Joint Army, Navy, NASA and Air Force Com. on Rocket Propulsion, L.A., 1979-83; admissions liaison officer USAF Acad., Colorado Springs, 1993-99; youth group leader St. Olaf Luth. Ch., Garden Grove, Calif., 1980-83, Hope Luth. Ch., Fresno, 1984-88; youth group leader Bethel Luth. Congregation, Fresno, 1974-79, pres., 1977-79; v.p. Hope Luth. Ch., Fresno, Calif., 2004—. Explorer Scout liasion Air Force Armament Lab., Eglin AFB, Fla., 1972-74. Capt. USAF, 1979-83. Mem. Am. Chem. Soc. Republican. Avocations: genealogy, history, plant physiology, travel, reading. Home: 6175 No Figarden Dr Apt 121 Fresno CA 93722 Office: US Bur Reclamation 1243 N St Fresno CA 93721-1813 Personal E-mail: r-epperson@comcast.net.

EPPERSON, STELLA MARIE, artist; b. Oakland, Calif., Nov. 6, 1920; d. Walter Peter and Martha Josephine (Schmitt) Ross; m. John Cray Epperson, May 10, 1941; children: Therese, John, Peter. Student, Calif. Coll. Arts & Crafts, 1939, 40-41, 56; postgrad., Art Inst., San Miguel d'Allende, Mex., 1972. Portrait artist Oakland Art Assn., 1956—, San Francisco Women Artists, 1962—, Marin Soc. Artists, Ross, Calif., 1971—. Art docent Oakland Mus., 1969-71, mem. women's bd., 1971—, art chmn. fund raiser, 1971-89, art guild chmn., 1965-69, chmn. exhbt. Japanese artists in Brazil, Kaiser Ctr., Oakland, for honoring artist Xavier Martinez, event honoring Neil Armstrong, Calif. Coll. Arts and Crafts. One-woman shows include Oakland Mus. Auction, 1993, Univ. Club, San Francisco, 1994; exhbns. include Women's Art Gallery, San Francisco, Kaiser Ctr., St. Mary's Coll. Hearst Gallery, numerous others; commd. portrait Mrs. Evangelina Macapagal, Malacalang Palace. Recipient San Francisco Women Artists, 1989, Oakland Art Assn., 1991, 1997, 2000, Marin Soc. Artists, 1992, Figurative Subject First award, Oakland Art Assn. Mem. Oakland Art Assn. (1st award in small format show 1998, 1999 Artistic award in Kaiser Ctr. Gallery Exhibit, Merit award 2000, Artistic award 2001), San Francisco Women Artists, Marin Art Assn., U. Calif. Berkeley Faculty Club, Orinda Country Club. Republican. Roman Catholic. Avocations: dress design, gourmet cooking, tennis. Home: 31 Valley View Rd Orinda CA 94563-1432

EPPERT, LUANA KYLE, retired secondary school educator, sculptor, writer; b. Shreveport, La., June 24, 1918; d. Lewis Francis and Silver Enola (Hatten) Kyle; m. Leo Clinton Eppert. BA, L.A. U., 1960; MA, U. So. Calif., 1962, U. Utah, 1965, U. Nev. Las Vegas, 1972. Cert. secondary tchr. Calif., Nev. Housewife, sculptress, 1948—59; tchr. L.A., 1961—71, Las Vegas, Nev., 1972—84. Author: The Greek Women, 1989; one-woman shows include, Maui, Hawaii, 1963, Las Vegas, 1973, Island of Paros, Greece, 1973. Hostess U.S. State Dept., L.A., 1958—60. Recipient Best of Show award, Las Vegas Art Coun., 1974. Mem. Soc. Of Friends. Avocation: needlecrafts. Home: # C 41633 Maroon Town Dr Bermuda Dunes CA 92203 Personal E-mail: quantumsearch@webtv.net.

EPPES, ELIZABETH MCCALL, art educator; b. Greenville, SC, Dec. 10, 1961; d. Frank and Frankie Eppes; m. Steve A Thackston, Aug. 10, 1991; children: Hadley McCall Thackston, Armistead Jefferson Thackston. BFA in Graphic Design, U. Ga., 1987; MAT in Art Edn., U. SC, 1989. Nat. bd. cert. tchr. 2004. Art tchr. Anderson County Sch., Pendelton, SC, 1990—91, Aiken County Sch. Sys., North Augusta, SC, 1991—97, DeKalb County Sch., Atlanta, 1997—. Chair fine art dept. Druid Hills H.S., Atlanta, 2000—; members exhibit co-chair Ga. Art Edn. Assn., Atlanta, 2002—; lead tchr. for dekalb county visual art DeKalb County Schools, Atlanta, 2004—. Painting, No More Dishes (Works accepted into juried exhibits, 2003). Dist. co- pres. Ga. Art Edn. Assn., Atlanta, 2003—05. Named 2003 Tchr. of Yr., Druid Hills H.S, Tchr. of the Yr., Ga. Project Wet, 2002; recipient Perimerter Coll. Rising Star Educator award, Ga. Perimeter Coll., 2003, Emory Tchr. of Excellence award, Emory U., 2003; grantee Serve And Learn Grant, Dept. of Edn.-, 2000-2003. Mem.: Ga. Art Edn. Assn. (assoc.; dist. co- pres. 2003—05). Democrat. Presbyterian. Office: Druid Hills H.S. 1798 Haygood Dr NE Atlanta GA 30307 Office Phone: 678-874-6356.

EPPES, THOMAS EVANS, advertising executive, public relations executive; b. NYC, Aug. 10, 1952; s. Benjamin F. and Eileen (Evans) E.; m. Jennie Spradling, Aug. 2, 1980; children: Benjamin, Jared, Michael. BS, U. So. Miss., 1974. Reporter Jackson (Miss.) Daily News, 1974-75, 76-77, Clearwater (Fla.) Sun, 1975-76; pub. info. coord. Miss. Rsch. and Devel. Ctr., Jackson, 1976-78; press sec. Gov. Bill Waller for U.S. Senate, Jackson, 1978, Maurice Dantin for U.S. Senate, Jackson, 1978; dir. pub. rels. Days Inns Am., Atlanta, 1978-82, Mgmt. Sci. Am., Atlanta, 1982-85; pres., pub. rels. Eric Mower & Assocs. (formerly Price-McNabb), Asheville, NC, 1985-91, pres., 1992—, sr. ptnr., bd. dirs., 2005—. Spkr. nat. confs. on comms. and mktg. Bd. dirs., communications chmn. United Way of Asheville and Buncombe, 1986-87; campaign dir. Jacksonians for Mayor, Jackson, 1976; bd. advisors U. of Colo., Boulder Inc. Sch. Fellow Pub. Rels. Soc. Am. (counselor's acad., exec. bd. counselor's acad. 1998-2000, Coll. of Fellows 2000, Silver Anvil award 1993), Internat. Assn. Bus. Communicators (Gold Quill award 1980, 81), Internat. Comms. Agy. Network (v.p.2002), Charlotte C. of C. (bd. dirs. 1997). Avocation: golf. Office: Eric Mower & Assocs 1001 Morehad Square Dr #5th Flr Charlotte NC 28203-4253

EPPES, WILLIAM DAVID, arts/humanities supporter; s. Talmadge DeWitt and Annie Lou (McCord) E. AB, Coll. of William and Mary, 1939; BS in LS, Vanderbilt U., 1940; student, U. Miami, U. Manchester (Eng.), 1950, Columbia U., 1950; MA, NYU, 1959; student, U. Durham, Eng., 1987. Reference asst. George Washington U., 1944—48, Calif. State U., San Francisco, 1948—49; head, stack personnel Butler Libr. Columbia U., N.Y.C., 1954-58; assoc. prof. Kean State Coll., N.J., 1958-61; asst. libr. Cooper Union, N.Y.C., 1961-70. Founder Film Classics League, St. Petersburg, Fla., 1950; co-founder Backstage Gallery, St. Petersburg Jr. Coll., 1950, Littlebury Eppes Meml. Libr., Westover Ch., Va.; adv. bd. Coral Gables (Fla.) Hist. Preservation Bd. Rev., 1979-81; trustee Greenwich Village Trust for Hist. Preservation, Inc., 1980, pres., 1980-84, 1984-90; cons. Hist. Buckingham (Va.) Inc., 1987—; hon. commr. Eleanor Roosevelt Monument Fund, Inc., N.Y.C. Author: The Empire Theatre (1893-1953), 1978, Gertrude Michael-A Star of the Golden Age of Hollywood, 1985, Montgomery (Ala.) Theatre 1822-1985, 1986; contbr. articles to mags. and hist. jours. Bd. dirs. St. Petersburg Symphony Orch., 1950-54; exec. bd. Assn. Village Homeowners, N.Y.C., 1969-82, Assocs. of Earl Gregg Swem Libr., Coll. of William and Mary, 1973-86; benefactor Jonathon Daniels Sch., Keene, N.H., 1998, Apple Hill Chamber Orch., Sullivan, N.H., 1998, Kean State Coll., 1999—; benefactor, hist. cons. Redfern Performing Arts Ctr. Keene (N.H.) State Coll., 2000—; pres. coun. Va. Hist. Soc., 1982; profl. advisor McLeod Plantation, Sea Island Hist. Soc., S.C. Mem. Theater Hist. Soc. (rsch. and reference com. 1977-81), Author's Guild, Inc., W&M Choir, Va. Hist. Soc. (pres.'s coun. 1993—, exec. coun. 1995), Sea Island Hist. Soc. (profl. adv. bd. 2000). Episcopalian. Home: 14 Rivermead Rd Peterborough NH 03458-1701

EPPINGER, FREDERICK H., JR., finance company executive; Grad., Coll. Holy Cross, 1981; MBA, Dartmouth Coll., 1985. CPA. Acct. Coopers & Lybrand; ptnr. fin. instn. group McKinsey & Co., 1985—2000; exec. v.p. mktg. and svc. ops. ChannelPoint, Inc., 2000—01; from sr. v.p. strategic mktg. to exec. v.p. The Hartford, 2001—02; pres., CEO Allmerica Fin. Corp., Worcester, Mass., 2003—. Edward Tuck scholar. Office: Allmerica Fin 440 Lincoln St Worcester MA 01653

EPPLE, STEVEN, architectural firm executive; BS in Environ. Design and Arch., Ball State U.; MBA, UCLA. Prin. Callison Arch. Inc., Seattle, 1996—, dir. ops. Retail Ctrs. practice, COO, 2001—, also bd. dirs. Mem.: AIA, Internat. Coun. Shopping Ctrs. Office: Callison Arch Inc Ste 2400 1420 Fifth Ave Seattle WA 98101-2343

EPPLER, JEROME CANNON, investment advisor; b. Englewood, N.J., Mar. 16, 1924; s. William E. and Aileen (Vaughan) E.; m. Debora Nye Eppler; children: Stephen Vaughan, William Durand, Margaret Nye, Elizabeth Scott, Edward Curtis. BSME, Tex. A&M U., 1946; MBA, U. Pa., 1949. With Gen. Electric Supply Corp., Newark, 1949-50; investment banker Equitable Securities Corp., Nashville, mgr. Houston, 1950-53; gen. ptnr. Cyrus J. Lawrence & Sons, N.Y.C., 1953-61; mem. N.Y. Stock Exch.; owner Eppler & Co., Denver, 1961; bd. dirs. Esmark, Inc., 1965—84; ltd. ptnr. Alex Brown & Sons, Balt., 1982-84; bd. dirs. Chgo. Milw. St. Paul & Pacific Ry., 1958-63, Chemex Pharms., 1984-88; prin. Olympic Capital Ptnrs., Seattle, 1995-2000. Dir. Advanced Rsch. Sys., Inc., Seattle, 1997-99, Pvt. Asset Mgmt., Inc., Bellevue, Wash.; chmn. bd. United Screen Arts, Inc., L.A., 1966-73; bd. dirs. VisionTek, Inc., Boulder, Colo., 1998-2001; chmn., bd. dirs. Life Ins. Co. Calif., 1967-77, I.S.I. Corp., 1967-77, Tessco Techs. Inc., Hunt Valley, Md., World Wide Life Assurance Co., London, 1972-77, Windsor Life Ins. Co., London, 1972-77; mem. indsl. adv. com. U. Calif., San Diego, 1978-93; dir. Telecredit, Inc., L.A., 1976-90, Brooktree Corp., San Diego, 1983-86, QTron, Inc., San Diego, 1995-97; chmn. Global Leadership Coun., Coll. Bus., Colo. State U., Ft. Collins, Colo. Trustee emeritus Scripps Clinic and Research Found., La Jolla; former trustee Drew U. (N.J.). 1966-67, Morris Mus. Arts & Scis. (N.J.), 1954-76, Met. Opera Assn., 1980-82, Wharton Grad. Sch. Bus. N.Y., 1972-86. Lt. (j.g.) USNR, 1942-46. Mem. Wharton Grad. Bus. Sch. Club, Castle Pines Golf Club, River Bend Country Club (Tequesta, Fla.). Presbyterian. Home: 2800 S University Blvd #22 Denver CO 80210

EPPLEY, FRANCES FIELDEN, secondary school educator, writer; b. Knoxville, Tenn., July 18, 1921; d. Chester Earl and Beulah Magnolia (Wells) Fielden; m. Gordon Talmage Cougle, July 25, 1942; children: Russell Gordon Eppley, Carolyn Eppley Horseman; m. Fred Coan Eppley, Mar. 8, 1953; 1 child, Charlene Eppley Sellers. BA in English, Carson Newman Coll., 1942; MA, Winthrop U., 1963. Tchr. East Corinth (Maine) Acad., 1942-43, pub. schs., Charlotte, N.C., 1950-53, 59-83, Greenville, S.C., 1954-56, Spartanburg, S.C., 1957-58; Head Start tchr., summers 1964-68. Author: First Baptist Church: Its Heritage, 1982, Flint Hill Church, 1984, Religion and Astrology, 1991, Astrology and Prophecy, 1992, Sammy's Song, Jericho, Aunt Lillian's Sea Foam Candy, The First Astrologer, 1993, The Story of William Fielden, 1998, Search for an Ancestor, 1999, Christmas Magnus, Stella and the Sitting Stone, Messiah, An Immediate Family, 1999, The Signs of Your Life, 2000, Another Mary, 2000, The Winter Solstice, 2001, Of Course Your Child Can Read!, 2002, Columbus: The Race Home, 2003, Canada Trilogy, 2003;: To A Japanese Friend, 2002, Wacky Kings and Mystic Things, 2003, The Yellow River, 2003, To A Japanese Friend, 2004. Mem. hist. com. N.C. Bapt. Conv., 1985-88. Alpha Delta Kappa Grantee, 1970. Mem. NEA, N.C. Social Studies Conf., Writers Assn., Alpha Delta Kappa, Pi Kappa Delta, Alpha Psi Omega. Baptist. Mailing: 251 N Highway 16 Apt 1 Denver NC 28037

EPPS, ANNA CHERRIE, immunologist, educator, dean; b. New Orleans, July 8, 1930; d. Ernest and Anna L. (Johnson) Cherrie; m. Joseph M. Epps, Sr., Nov. 23, 1968. BS, Howard U., 1951, PhD, 1966; MS, Loyola U., New Orleans, 1959. Technologist clin. lab. dept. Our Lady of Mercy Hosp., Cin., 1953-54; asst. prof., acting chmn. dept. med. tech. Xavier U., New Orleans, 1954-60; technologist dept. medicine La. State U. Sch. Medicine, New Orleans, 1954-60; asst. prof. microbiology Coll. Medicine Howard U., Washington, 1961-69; fellow dept. medicine Sch. Medicine Johns Hopkins U., Balt., 1969; asst. prof., USPHS faculty fellow dept. medicine Tulane U. Sch. Medicine, New Orleans, 1969-71, assoc. prof., 1971-75, prof., 1975—97, assoc. dean student svcs., 1970—97; dir. med. edn. reinforcement and enrichment program Tulane U. Med. Ctr., New Orleans, 1969—97; prof. internal medicine Meharry Med. Coll., Nashville, 1994—, dean emeritus Sch. Medicine, 1997—2002, sr. advisor to pres., acting dean, 1994—96, 1997—2002, sr. v.p. acad. affairs, 2002—. Co-editor: Medical Education: Responses to a Challenge; mem. editorial bd. Jour. Med. Edn., 1980—; contbr. articles to med. jours. Trustee Children's Hosp., New Orleans, 1977-79; regent Georgetown U., Washington, 1975—; bd. dirs. Diabetes Assn. Greater New Orleans, 1978; mem. La. Bd. Health and Rehab. Svcs., 1972; adv. mem. Kellogg Nat. Fellowship Program, 1981. Recipient award for meritorious rsch. Interstate Postgrad. Med. Assn. N.Am., 1966, Scroll of Merit, Nat. Med. Assn., 1980, Herbert W. Nickens award, AAMC, 2003. Mem. Am. Soc. Clin. Pathologists (cert. in med. tech. and blood banking), Am. Soc. Med. Technologists, Am. Assn. Blood Banks (cert. in blood banking), Am. Soc. Tropical Medicine and Hygiene, AAUP, Musser-Burch Soc., Albertus Magnus Guild, Washington Helminthol. Soc., Am. Soc. Bacteriologists, Sigma Xi. Home: 769 Sinclair Cir Brentwood TN 37027-2921 Office: Meharry Med Coll 1005 D B Todd Blvd Nashville TN 37208 Office Phone: 615-327-5935. Business E-Mail: acepps@mmc.edu.

EPPS, CHARLES HARRY, JR., retired orthopaedic surgery educator, dean; b. Balt., July 24, 1930; BS magna cum laude, Howard U., 1951, MD, 1955. Intern Freedmen's Hosp., 1955-56, resident, 1956-57, mem. staff, 1961—2001; resident D.C. Gen. Hosp., Washington, 1958-60, vis. staff, 1961-98, orthopaedic med. officer for handicapped and crippled children's svc., 1961-98; instr. orthopaedic surgery Howard U., Washington, 1961-64, asst. prof., 1964-68, assoc. prof., 1968-73, prof., 1973-96, prof. emeritus, 1996—2001, chief divsn. orthopaedic surgery, 1968-88, dean Coll. Medicine, 1988-94, exec. dean Coll. Medicine, 1994-95; v.p. health affairs, acting exec. dir., CEO Howard U. Hosp., Washington, 1994-96; spl. asst. to pres. for health affairs Howard U., 1996-2001; ret., 2001. Assoc. prof. Johns Hopkins U., 1971; mem. staff VA Hosp., Washington, Cafritz Meml. Hosp., Providence Hosp.; cons. USN Med. Ctr., Bethesda, Md., Walter Reed Army Med. Ctr. Capt. M.C., U.S. Army, 1961-62. Fellow ACS; mem. AMA, Nat. Med. Assn., Ea. Orthop. Assn., Am. Orthop. Assn., Am. Acad. Orthop. Surgery.

EPPS, HARLAND WARREN, astronomy educator, optical design consultant; b. Hawthorne, Calif., July 29, 1936; s. Harland Garner and Nydia Dolly (Gall) E.; m. Louise Rodney Daniels, June 5, 1962 (div. Jan. 1970); m. Susan Lou Markowitz, Oct. 10, 1976 (div. Feb. 1983); children: Melody Amanda, Brenden Putty; m. Johanna Helen Archer, Nov. 23, 1991; children: Helena Dolly, Naomi Lauren. Student, U. Vienna, Austria, 1956—57; BA, Pomona Coll., 1959; MS, U. Wis., 1961, PhD, 1964. Asst. prof. astronomy San Diego State U., 1964-65, UCLA, 1965-70, assoc. prof., 1970-76, prof., 1976—89; astronomer, prof. astronomy Lick Obs., Santa Cruz, Calif., 1989—, U. Calif., Santa Cruz, 1989—. Cons. Steward Obs., Tucson, 1972—, Lick Obs., 1970—, Smithsonian Astrophys. Obs., Cambridge, Mass., 1984—, Los Alamos (N.Mex.) Nat. Lab., 1984—, Mount Wilson and Las Campanas Observatories, 1987—, Calif. Inst. Tech., 1988—. Assoc. editor for instrumentation: Publs. of Astron. Soc. of the Pacific, 2003—; contbr. articles to profl. jours. Mem. USAF Sci. Adv. Bd., 1989-93. Grantee NSF, Air Force Cambridge Rsch., U. Calif. Regents Opportunity Fund, NASA. Mem. Am. Astron. Soc., Internat. Astron. Union, Soc. Photooptical Instrumentation Engrs., Sigma Xi. Avocation: classical and flamenco guitar. Office: U Calif UCO/Lick Obs Natural Scis 2 Rm 191 Santa Cruz CA 95064 Office Phone: 831-459-3454. Business E-Mail: epps@ucolick.org.

EPPS, JAMES HAWS, III, lawyer; b. Johnson City, Tenn., Sept. 15, 1936; s. James Haws and Anne Lafayette (Sessoms) E.; m. Jane Mahoney, Oct. 9, 1976; children from previous marriage--James Haws IV, Sara Stuart. BA, U.N.C., 1955-59; JD, Vanderbilt U., 1962. Bar: Tenn. 1962, U.S. Dist. Ct. Tenn. 1962, U.S. Ct. Appeals (6th cir.) 1971, Interstate Commerce Commn. Bar 1962, U.S. Supreme Ct. 1967. Prin. Epps & Epps, Johnson City, Tenn. City atty. Johnson City, 1967—, Johnson City Bd. Edn., 1967-86; spl. counsel State of Tenn., 1966-70; former gen. counsel Appalachian Flying Svc. Inc., ET&WNC Transp. Co., Inc. First bd. govs. Transp. Law Jour. Past bd. dirs. Washington County Mental Health Assn., East Tenn. and Western N.C. Transp. Co., East Tenn. and Western N.C. R.R., Tennolina Corp., Appalachian Air Lines, Inc., Appalachian Flying Svc., Inc., Farmers and Mchts. Bank, Limestone, Tenn., budget com. United Fund of Johnson City, 1964-68, Assault Crime Counsel Early Support Svcs. Inc., Safe Passage Inc., Johnson City Homeless Coalition, Home Base Adv. Coun., Johnson City/Washington County Health Coun. adv. com.; former legal adviser Appalachian coun. Girl Scouts U.S.A.; mem. Tenn. Law Revision Commn., 1970-71; legal counsel Salvation Army, mem. adv. bd. 1974—, exec. com. 1977—, 1st v.p. adv. bd. 1991, pres. adv. bd. 1993, 94, mem. property com.; chmn. Family Violence Coun.; legal counsel Washington County Humane Soc., Inc.; mem. Civil Def., 1967—; chmn. Washington County for Tenn. Leukemia Soc., 1991; mem. exec. com. Washington County Dem. Party, Tenn. Bicentennial Commn., exec. and fin. coms.; past mem. bd. dirs. Tenn. Mental Health ASsn. Fellow Tenn. Bar Found.; mem. ABA, Fed. Bar Assn., Nat. Orgn. Legal Problems Edn., Am. Counsel Assn., Nat. Assn. R.R. Trial Counsel, Internat. Mcpl. Lawyers Assn. (bd. dirs. 1982-2004, state chmn. Tenn. 1988-89, ethics and environ. coms. 1989—, regional v.p. 1989-92, chmn. resolutions com. 1989-90, lectr., trustee, 1992—, chmn. dues and alternatives revenue 1996-97, budget and fin., federalism com. 1996—, state league counsel rev. com. 1997, awards com., 1999—, bd. mem. policy adv. com. 2000, 1st v.p. 2001, pres. 2002-03), Nat. Legal Aid Defender Assn., Tenn. Bar Assn., Am. Judicature Soc., Washington County Bar Assn. (past pres.), Tenn. Mcpl. Attys. Assn., Assn. ICC Practitioners (past com. profl. ethics and grievences), Transp. Lawyers Assn., Motor Carrier Lawyers Assn., Johnson City C. of C. (Disting. Service award 1968), Internat. Platform Assn., Lawyers Com. for Civil Rights Under Law, World Peace Through Law Ctr., Tenn. Lung Assn., Tenn. Correctional Assn., Tenn. Taxpayers Assn. (past bd. dirs.), Tennesseans for Better Transp., U.S. Supreme Ct. Hist. Soc., Def. Rsch. Inst., Tipton Haynes Hist. Assn. (past dir.), Hurstleigh Club, Unaka Rd. and Gun Club, Highland Stable Club, North Johnson City Bus. Club (dir., past pres. 1966-67), Nat. Lawyers Club, East Tenn. State U. Century Club, Boys'Club (charter, Johnson City/Washington County), Masons, Elks (legal counsel 1963-67), Phi Delta Phi, Phi Delta Theta. Episcopalian. Office: 115 E Unaka Ave Johnson City TN 37601-4623 also: PO Box 2288 Johnson City TN 37605-2288

EPPS, OMAR, actor; b. Bklyn., July 23, 1973; m. Keisha Spivey; 1 child, K'mari Mae. Actor: (films) Juice, 1992, The Program, 1993, Major League II, 1994, Higher Learning, 1995, Don't Be a Menace to South Central While Drinking Your Juice in the Hood, 1996, Blossoms and Veils, 1997, Scream 2, 1997, Breakfast of Champions, 1999, The Mod Squad, 1999, The Wood, 1999, In Too Deep, 1999, Love & Basketball, 2000, Brother, 2000, Dracula 2000, 2000, Perfume, 2001, Big Trouble, 2002, Against the Ropes, 2004, Alfie, 2004, (TV films) Daybreak, 1993, Deadly Voyage, 1996, First Time Felon, 1997, Conviction, 2004 (TV series) House M.D., 2004-; TV appearances include Here and Now, 1992, Street Justice, 1993, ER, 1996, 97. Office: The Gersh Agy 232 N Canon Dr Beverly Hills CA 90210-5302*

EPPS, ROSELYN ELIZABETH PAYNE, pediatrician, educator; b. Little Rock, Dec. 11, 1930; d. William Kenneth and Mattie Elizabeth (Beverly) Payne; m. Charles Harry Epps, Jr., June 25, 1955; children: Charles Harry III (dec.), Kenneth Carter, Roselyn Elizabeth, Howard Robert. BS, Howard U., 1951, MD, 1955; MPH, Johns Hopkins U., 1973; MA, Am. U., 1981. Intern Freedmen's Hosp., Howard U., Washington, 1955-56, pediatric resident, 1956-59, chief resident, 1958-59; practice medicine specializing in pediatrics Washington, 1960; med. officer, pediatrics D.C. Dept. Pub. Health, Washington, 1961-64, dir. Clinic for Retarded Children, 1964-67, chief Infant and Pre-Sch. div., 1967-71, dir. children and youth project, 1970-71, dir. maternal and crippled children services, 1971-75; chief Bur. Clin. Services D.C. Dept. Human Services, Washington, 1975-80, acting commr. pub. health, 1980; instr., asst. research investigator Howard U. Coll. Medicine, Washington, 1960-61, prof. Dept. Pediatrics and Child Health, 1980-98, chief divsn. child devel., dir., 1985-89, dir. Child Devel. Ctr., 1985-89; rsch. assoc., vis. scientist smoking tobacco and cancer program, div. cancer prevention and control Nat. Cancer Inst. NIH, Washington, 1989-91; expert Nat. Cancer Inst. NIH, Pub. Health Applications Br., Bethesda, Md., 1991-97; scientific program adminstr. Nat. Cancer Inst. Pub. Health Applications Branch, Bethesda, Md., 1997-98; med. pub. hlth cons., 1998—; sr. program advisor for women's health programs Women's Health Inst., Howard U., Wash., 1999—. Chmn. task force to prepare comprehensive child care plan for D.C. Dept. Human Services, 1973-74; mem. nat. task force on pediatric hypertension Heart, Lung and Blood Inst., NIH, 1975; chmn. rsch. grants rev. com. maternal and child health and crippled children's svcs. HEW, Rockville, Md., 1978-80; sec. Commn. Licensure to Practice Healing Arts, Washington, 1980; trustee med. svc. D.C. Blue Shield Plan Nat. Capital Area, 1980; chmn. sec.'s adv. com. on rights and responsibilities of women HEW, Washington, 1981; dir. high-risk young people's project Howard U. Hosp., 1981-85; Washington coord. Know Your Body Program Am. Health Found., N.Y.C., 1982-91; mem. bd. advs. Coll. Home Econs. Ohio State U., Columbus, Ohio, 1983-87; adv. com. Nat. Ctr. for Edn. in Maternal and Child Health Georgetown U., Washington, 1983-89; nat. steering com., subcom. chmn. Healthy Mothers, Healthy Babies Coalition, Washington, 1983-90, mem. nominating com., 1991; cons. sickle cell disease NIH, 1984-88, Govt. Liberia and World Bank, 1984, UN Fund for Population Activities, N.Y. and Caribbean, 1984, filmstrip Miriam Berg Varian/Parents Mag. Films, 1978; bd. dirs. Vis. Nurse Assn., Inc., Washington, 1983-89; pres. bd. dirs. Hosp. for Sick Children, Washington, 1986-90, bd. dirs., 1984-94; frequent guest lectr. Weekly columnist Your Child's Health, Afro-Am. Newspaper, Washington, 1960-63; contbr. articles syndicated column Nat. Newspaper Pubs. Assn., 1982, Nat. Newspaper Assn., 1986-87; co-author audiocassettes; exhibitor sci. program; exhibit: Women Chage the Faces of Medicine; contbr. more than 90 articles to profl. jours. US trustee Children's Internat. Summer Villages, Casstown, Ohio, 1969—76, pres., 1974—75; trustee nat. bd. Palmer Meml. Inst., Sedalia, NC, 1969—71, Ford's Theater, Washington, 1973—79; bd. mgrs. YWCA of DC, 1970—83, vice chmn., 1975—76; v.p. Jack and Jill of Am., Inc., Washington, 1970—71; nat. bd. dir. Ctr. Population Options, Washington, 1980—86, Alexander Graham Bell Assn. for Deaf, Washington, 1974—78; bd. dir. Washington Performing Arts Soc., DC, 1971—81, v.p., 1979—81, hon. dir., 1981—. Recipient Leadership and Meritorious Service in Medicine award Palmer Meml. Inst., 1968, 14th Ann. Fed. Women's award CSC, Washington, 1974, Superior Performance award D.C. Govt., 1975, Meritorious Community Service award Howard U. Sch. Social Work Alumni Assns. and vis. com., 1980, Cert. Commendation Mayor of DC, 1981, Roselyn Payne Epps M.D. Recognition Resolution of 1983 Council DC, 1983, Disting. Vol. Leadership award March of Dimes Birth Defects Found., 1984, Community Svc. award DC Hosp. Assn., 1990, Physician of Yr. award Women's Med. Assn. N.Y.C., 1990, 91; named Outstanding Vol. in Leadership category YWCA Nat. Capital Area, 1983; inducted into DC Women's Hall of Fame DC Commn. for Women, 1990, Hall of Fame, DC, 2005; grantee Robert Wood Johnson Found., Princeton, N.J., 1982, div. maternal and child health HHS, Rockville, Md., 1986; honored Tribute Resolution of 1981 declaring Feb. 14 Dr. Roselyn Payne Epps Day, Council of D.C., 1981; recipient Ophelia Settle Egypt award Planned Parenthood of Met. Washington, 1991, Advocacy award Soc. Advancement Women's Health, 1996, Horizon award Nat. Assn. Negro Bus. and Profl. Women's Clubs, 1999, Dorothy I Height award, Nat. Coun. of Negro Women, 2001, Lifetime Achievement award, Girls Inc., 2003. Fellow

Am. Acad. Pediatrics (alt. state chmn. D.C. 1973-75, exec. com. D.C. chpt. 1983-94, pres. D.C. chpt. 1988-91, sec. cmty. pediatrics sect. 1973-75, cert. appreciation 1979, mem. coun. of child and adolescent health, cmty. and internat. health sect., charter mem., exec. com. 1992-94); mem. Acad. Medicine, AMA (alt. del. Nat. Med. Assn. 1983-85), Am. Med. Women's Assn. (chmn. pub. health com. 1973-75, pres. br. 1 1974-76, sec. 1988, v.p. 1989, pres-elect nat. 1990, pres. 1991, found. founding pres. 1992, bd. dirs. 1992-97, chmn. nominating com. 1993, Physician of Yr. award 1991, Cmty. Svc. award 1990, Elizabeth Blackwell award 1992), Women's Forum Washington, Med. Soc. D.C. (exec. bd. 1990, sec. 1990, pres.-elect 1991, pres. 1992, chair exec. bd. 1993, ann. Cmty. Svc. award 1982), Am. Pediatric Soc., D.C. Hosp. Assn. (Cmty. Svc. award 1990), Am. Pub. Health Assn. (action bd. 1977-79, joint policy com. 1978-79, gov. council 1978-81), Met. Washington Pub. Health Assn. (gov. council 1975-78, 81-83, ann. award 1981), Nat. Med. Assn. (chmn. pediatric sect. 1977-79, Ross Labs. award 1979, Outstanding Svcs. to Children during Internat. Yr. of Child award 1979, Meritorious Service Appreciation award 1979, W.M. Cobb co-lectr. 1985, mem. Coun. on Maternal and Child Health, 1974-92, chmn. 1979-89, ann. Roselyn Payne Epps Symposium 1994—, Grace Marilyn James award for Disting svc. Pediatric sect. 1991, Achievement award 1993, ann. Roselyn Payne Epps symposium 1994—), Am. Hosp. Assn. (maternal and child health sect. governing coun. 1989, 1992-94, maternal and child health nominating com. 1991), Soc. for the Advancement of Women's Health Rsch. (award for advocacy 1996), The Women's Forum of Washington, Alpha Omega Alpha, Delta Omega, Alpha Kappa Alpha. Mem. United Ch. of Christ. Clubs: Pearls (pres. 1984-86), Carrousels (corr. sec. 1978-80), Links (pres. Met. chpt. 1986-89) (Washington), Cosmos. Lodge: Zonta, Internat. Women's Forum. Home and Office: 1775 N Portal Dr NW Washington DC 20012-1014

EPPS, SUSIE REBECCA SMITH, secondary school educator; b. Concord, N.C., June 12, 1951; d. Wade Francis and Polly Ann (Simpson) Smith; m. Harold Jackson Epps Jr., July 12, 1974; 1 child, David Matthew. BA, Lander Coll., 1972; M in Teaching, U. S.C., 1978. Cert. tchr. theater, speech and social studies S.C., nat. bd. cert. adolescent and young adult Social Studies 2001. Cashier svc. dept. Sky City Stores, Inc., Greenwood, S.C., 1970-74; tchr. Emerald Jr. High, Greenwood, 1973-94, chair dept. social studies, 1994-95; tchr., dir. Performing Arts of Greenwood # 50, 1989-95; tchr., drama dir. Emerald H.S., 1995—. Sponsor Acad. Challenge, Greenwood, 1987-95; coor. Greenwood History Day, 1989-94; drama dir. Emerald Jr. High, Greenwood, 1975-95; chairperson Emerald SACs Com., Greenwood, 1982-83. Actress Greenwood Community Theatre, 1988; tchr. First Presbyn. Ch. Sunday Sch., Greenwood, 1984-92; youth advisor First Presbyn. Ch., Greenwood, 1974-80. Bicentannial Commn. grantee 1987-88, Edn. Enrichment Found. grantee, 1988, S.C. Arts Commn. grantee, 1989, S.C. in Edn. grantee, 1990, S.C. Dept. Edn., 1989, 90, S.C. Arts in Edn. Target 2000 grantee, 1991, S.C. EIA grantee 1991; Coun. for Basic Edn., NEH fellow, 1990. Mem. Internat. Thespian Soc. (sponsor), S.C. Edn. Assn., S.C. Theatre Assn., NEA, Smithsonian Assocs., Delta Kappa Gamma. Avocations: performing, reading, hand crafts. Home: 322 Sagewood Rd Greenwood SC 29646-9249 Office: Emerald High Sch 150 Bypass 225 Greenwood SC 29646-1154

EPSEN, ROBERT A., lawyer; b. Omaha, May 25, 1939; AB, Princeton U., 1961; JD, Stanford U., 1971. Bar: Calif. 1971. Atty. Heller, Ehrman, White & McAuliffe, San Francisco, 1971—, gen. coun. Mem. ABA. Office: Heller Ehrman White & McAuliffe 333 Bush St San Francisco CA 94104-2806 Office Phone: 415-772-6042. Office Fax: 415-772-6268. E-mail: repsen@hewm.com.

EPSTEIN, ALVIN, actor, performance artist, theater director, make-up artist; b. Bronx, N.Y., May 14, 1925; s. Harry and Goldie (Rudnick) E. Student, Queens Coll., 1941-43, Ecole de Mime Etienne Decroux, Paris, 1947-51, Sanford Meisner Profl. Class, N.Y.C., 1951-52. Tchr. Chamber Theatre, Israel, Neighborhood Playhouse, N.Y.C., Circle in Sq. Theatre Sch., N.Y.C., Yale Drama Sch., 1968-77, Am. Repertory Theatre Inst.; acting artistic dir. Yale Repertory Theatre, 1972-73, assoc. artistic dir., 1973-77; artistic dir. Guthrie Theatre, Mpls., 1978-79. Mem. faculty Salzburg Am. Seminar, 1972, Aspen Music Festival, 1980-82. Actor Theatre de Mime Etienne Decroux, Paris, 1947-51, Habima Theatre, Israel, 1952-55; made Am. profl. debut with Marcel Marceau, Phoenix Theatre, N.Y.C., 1955; has appeared in many Broadway, off-Broadway touring and regional prodns., including The Fool in Orson Welles' King Lear, N.Y.C., 1956, Lucky in original Broadway prodn. Waiting for Godot, 1956, Puck in A Midsummer Night's Dream, Empire State Music Festival, N.Y., 1956, O'Killigain in Purple Dust, N.Y.C., Clov in Endgame, N.Y.C., Luc Delbert in No Strings, N.Y.C., title role in Enrico IV, Milw., Chgo., Beranger in The Pedestrian in the Air, Chgo., Theseus and Oberon in A Midsummer's Night Dream, N.Y.C., Octave in Clerambard, N.Y.C., various roles in Postmark Zero, N.Y.C., Landau in The Latent Heterosexual, Los Angeles, Sgt. in Dynamite Tonite, N.Y.C.; appeared in Whores, Wars and Tin Pan Alley, Chgo., New Haven, N.Y.C., Easthampton, A Place Without Doors, Long Wharf Theatre, New Haven, Staircase Theatre, N.Y.C., Goodman Theatre, Chgo., on U.S. tour, Los Angeles, Washington, 3 Plays by Samuel Beckett, Harold Clurman Theater N.Y.C., 1983-84, Mark Taper Forum Los Angeles, Library of Congress, Washington, 1984, Jerusalem Festival, 1985; directed and acted Hamm in Endgame, Samuel Beckett Theatre, Cherry Ln. Theater, N.Y.C., New Mayfair Theater, Los Angeles, Jerusalem Festival, 1985; mem. Yale Repertory Theatre, New Haven, 1968-77; playing leading parts Dynamite Tonite, God Bless, Story Theatre, The Bacchae, Greatshot, Crimes and Crimes, Olympian Games, Gimpel the Fool, Woyzeck, Don Juan, Macbett (Ionesco), The Tempest, Happy End, The Possessed, Bingo, Ivanov. Crossing Niagara, N.Y.C. Manhattan Theatre Club, Ghosts, Three Sisters, School for Scandal, Good Woman of Setzuan, 6 Characters in Search of an Author, Right You Are (If You Think You Are), Uncle Vanya, King Stag (Gozzi), Platanov, Mastergate, In Twilight (Chekhov Short Stories), The Miser (Moliere), Once In A Lifetime (Kaufman and Hart), When We Dead Awaken (Ibsen), Gloucester in King Lear, Polonius in Hamlet, Lord Summerhays in Misalliance (Shaw), Media Amok (C. Durang), Judge Brack in Hedda Gabler, Dr. Lombardi in The Servant of Two Masters (Goldoni), Dream of the Red Spider (Ribman), Iva Vasilyevich in Black Snow (Bulgakov-Dewhurst), Silence, Cunning, Exile (S. Greenman), directed and played Duncan and Scottish Doctor in Macbeth, King Henry in Henry IV Parts 1 & 2 (Shakespeare), Dr. Rance in What the Butler Saw (Orton), Firs in the Cherry Orchard (Chekhov), Patty O'Dowd in "A Touch of the Poet (O'Neill), Krapp's Last Tape, Ohio Impromptu, Agamemnon, Waiting for Godot, Henry V, Threepenny Opera, Beckett Trio: Eh Joe, Ghost Sonata, Nacht Und Träume, The Tempest, Tartuffe, Slaughter City, Am. Repertory Theatre, Cambridge, Mass., Value of Names, Androcles and the Lion, Hartford Stage Co., Waltz of the Toreadors, Roundabout Theatre, N.Y.C., Peachum in Three Penny Opera, Lunt-Fontanne Theatre, 1989; dir. The Rivals, Caligula, Seven Deadly Sins, Bourgeois Gentleman, Rise and Fall of the City of Mahagonny, The Tempest, A Midsummer Night's Dream, Troilus and Cressida, Julius Caesar, Old Times, Marriage of Figaro, Boys From Syracuse, Endgame, Importance of Being Earnest, Heartbreak House, others at Yale Repertory Theatre, Am. Repertory Theatre, Williamstown Theatre Festival, Richard III, Becket Trio; narrator Oedipus Rex, Cantata Singers; appeared in many TV shows on all networks, including The Doctors on NBC-TV, 1981-82, Doing Life NBC-TV film, 1986; dir. The Pretenders, Beggars Opera; appeared in Marriage, A Kurt Weill Cabaret for Guthrie Theatre, with Martha Schlamme in A Kurt Weill Cabaret for Bijou Theater, N.Y.C., on tour throughout U.S., Argentina, Brazil, Israel, 1979-85; co-founder, actor Berkshire Theatre Festival, Stockbridge, Mass., 1966, playing Antrobus in Skin of Our Teeth, Shylock in Merchant of Venice; dir. Colette, Berkshire Theatre Festival, Stockbridge, Mass., 1974; appeared in Schlamme and Epstein Sing Bernstein and Blitzstein, Aspen Music Festival, HB Studio N.Y.C., Am. Repertory Theatre, Cambridge, Mass., 1981, When the World Was Green, Olympic Arts Festival, The Cabinet of Dr. Caligari, Man and Superman; (film) Never Met Picasso, Thomas Edison in The Wizard of Menlo Park with Boston Pops, The Devil in Stravinsky's Soldier's Tale, Jordan Hall, Boston, Alice Tully Hall, N.Y.C., GBS in Dear Liar, on U.S. tour, Cadmus in The Bacchae, Shlink in In The Jungle of Cities, Lee Strasberg in Nobody Dies on Friday, Old Man in When The World was Green, Internat. Festival, Moscow Art Theatre, Russia, 1997-98, voice overs for documentary Africans in America, Old Gobbo and Tubal in Merchant of Venice, Am. Repertory Theatre, Cambridge Mass., narrator Philosopher's Stone by Mozart et al, Boston Baroque, Jordan Hall, Boston, Old Man in Charlie in The House of Rue, American Repertory Theatre, Cambridge, Leonard in film The Living Room Waltz, 1998-99; various roles in series of Samuel Beckett Radio Plays for Nat. Pub. Radio, 1987-88, Voice of the Bookseller in Walt Disney's Beauty and the Beast, 1991, The Gentleman from Boston (film), Passionada (film), Count Shabelsky in Ivanov (Indep. Reviewers New England award: Best Supporting Actor 1999), McLeavy in Loot, Honecker in Full Circle, Camillo in The Winters Tale, Tiresias in Sophocles' Antigone, The General in Chekhov's The Wedding, Dr. Blenkinsop in Shaw's The Doctor's Dilemma, John of Gaunt in Richard II, American Repertory Theatre, 1999-2001, Kurt Weill Songs Dengenerate and Otherwise Market Theatre, Cambridge, Mass, 2001, Ragpicker in The Madwoman of Chaillot, Neighborhood Playhouse, N.Y.C.; Dr. Gianonni in Enrico IV; Herald in Marat/Sade; Old Man in Lysistrata, Am. Repertory Theatre; Mr. Zurmer in Psychoanalysis Changed My Life (film); Morrie in Tuesdays with Morrie, N.Y. Stage and Film Co., Vassar Coll., 2001-02, Minetta Lane Theatre, N.Y.C., 2002-03, Twenty Four Evenings of Wit and Wisdom, Arc Light Theatre, N.Y.C., Law and Order Colleague's Theatre, N.Y.C.; (concert appearances) 92nd St. Y, Bryn Mawr Coll., Maverick Concerts, Woodstock, N.Y., Theatre Works, 2004, Atlantic Theater Co., NYC, 2005. Bd. dirs. Theatre Communications Group, N.Y.C., 1975-77. Served with AUS, 1943-46, ETO. Recipient Brandeis Creative Arts award, 1966, Obie award for Dynamite Tonite, 1968, Torch of Hope award, 1994, Elliot Norton prize Boston Theatre Critics, 1996, Jason Robards award for dedication to the theater, 2001, Best Cabaret award Ind. Reviewers of New Eng., 2002, Spencer Cherashore Lifetime Dedication to Not-for-profit Theatre award, 2003; Ford Found. grantee, 1959-60; Trumbull Coll. fellow, Yale U.; named Most promising Actor, Variety poll, 1956. Address: 57 Montague St Brooklyn NY 11201

EPSTEIN, ANDREW ERNEST, cardiologist, educator; b. N.Y.C., Nov. 30, 1950; s. Frederick Hermon Epstein and Ingeborg Luise (Gunther) Davenport; m. Judith Ann Mullen, Oct. 6, 1979 (div. 1980); m. Eileen Marie Dawson, Dec. 9, 1984 (div. 2005); 1 child, Anne Elizabeth. BA in English, Amherst Coll., 1973; MD, U. Rochester, 1977. Diplomate Am. Bd. Internal Medicine, Am. Bd. Cardiology, Nat. Bd. Med. Examiners, Am. Bd. Clin. Electrophysiology. Intern Barnes Hosp., St. Louis, 1977-78, resident, 1978-80; fellow U. Ala. at Birmingham, 1980-82; chief fellow Divsn. Cardiovascular Disease, 1982-83; instr. U. Ala. at Birmingham, 1982-83, asst. prof. medicine, 1983-87, assoc. prof. medicine, 1988-91, prof. medicine, 1991—. Advisor to many mfrs. cardiac rhythm mgmt. devices and pharm. cos. Contbr over 200 articles, more than 200 abstracts to profl. jours., chpts. to 30 books in field. Vol. Am. Heart Assn., Birmingham and Dallas, 1983—, mem. Ala. emergency cardiac care com., 1993-2000; expert advisory panel cardiovasc. and renal drugs US Pharmacopoeia, 1995-2000; com. mem. Dept. Transp. on Guildlines on Fitness to Drive, 2001. Fellow Am. Coll. Cardiology (chmn. com. on guidelines for implantation of cardiac pacemakers and arrhythmia devices, 2004—), Am. Heart Assn. (clin. coun. 1983—, exec. com. 1992-95, 96-97, chmn. com. on sudden death 1992-95, com. on electrocardiography and arrhythmias 1995-2002, chmn. com. guidelines implantation pacemakers and arrhythmia devices 2004—, chair, 2004—,comm. com. 2004—); mem. Heart Rhythm Soc., Cardiac Electrophysiology Soc. Home: 91 Windsor Dr Birmingham AL 35209 Office: U Ala at Birmingham Divsn Cardiovascular Disease Univ Sta THT 321 1530 3d Ave S Birmingham AL 35294-0001 Office Phone: 205-934-7114. Business E-Mail: aepstein@uab.edu.

EPSTEIN, ARNOLD M., medical educator; MD, Duke U., 1976. John H. Foster prof. health policy and mgmt. Harvard Sch. Pub. Health, Boston, chair dept. health policy and mgmt., prof. medicine; chief sect. on health svcs. and policy rsch. Brigham & Women's Hosp. Contbr. articles to profl. jours. Mem.: Inst. Medicine. Achievements include research on access and quality of care especially for disadvantaged populations. Office: 677 Huntington Ave Boston MA 02115-6028 Fax: 617-432-3417. E-mail: aepstein@hsph.harvard.edu.

EPSTEIN, ARTHUR WILLIAM, physician, educator; b. N.Y.C., May 15, 1923; s. Jacob E. and Anne (Bass) E.; m. Leona Cruce, Mar. 2, 1955; children: David Byron, Nona Kathryn, Emily Vera, James Jacob. AB, Columbia U., 1944, MD, 1947. Intern Mt. Sinai Hosp., N.Y.C., 1947-48, resident, 1949-50; clin. asst. Norristown (Pa.) State Hosp., 1948-49; faculty Tulane U., New Orleans, 1954—, asso. prof. psychiatry and neurology, 1959-64, prof., 1964—; pvt. practice medicine, specializing in neuropsychiatry New Orleans, 1964—; prof. emeritus Tulane U., 1993—. Vis. physician Charity Hosp., New Orleans, 1951-99; cons. U.S. Army Hosp., New Orleans, 1958-64; mem. med. staff Tulane Med. Center Hosp., 1976— Author: An Anatomist's Dream of Love, 1966, The Dissecting Room, 1978, The Lady and the Serpent, 1981, A Contemporary Religious Svc., 1987, Bridge Cross, 1989, Dreaming and Other Involuntary Mentation: An Essay in Neuropsychiatry, 1996, Poems of Later Life, 1999; contbr. articles to profl. jours. Med. adviser Social Security Adminstrn., 1968-93; bd. dirs. Ednl. Rsch. and Treatment Ctr., New Orleans. Served with M.C. USNR, 1956-58. Named Psychiatrist of Yr. La. Psychiatric Assn., 1992. Fellow AAAS, Am. Psychiat. Assn. (life, leisure time and its uses com.), Am. Acad. Psychoanalysis (pres. 1987-88, Silverberg award 1985), Am. Acad. Neurology; mem. Soc. Biol. Psychiatry (v.p. 1979-80, pres.-elect 1980-81, pres. 1981-82), Am. Epilepsy Soc., Alpha Omega Alpha. Office: DePaul-Tulane 1040 Calhoun St New Orleans LA 70118-5914 Office Phone: 504-894-7200. *Amid the hurly-burly, keep awe and wonder. Pursue the ideal.*

EPSTEIN, BARBARA, editor; b. Boston, Aug. 30, 1929; d. Harry W. and Helen (Diamond) Zimmerman; children: Jacob, Helen. BA, Radcliffe Coll., 1949. Editor N.Y. Rev. Books, N.Y.C., 1963—. Office: NY Rev of Books 1755 Broadway Fl 5 New York NY 10019-3743 E-mail: bepstein@nybooks.com.

EPSTEIN, BARBARA MYRNA ROBBIN, language educator; b. Chgo., Oct. 15, 1939; d. Jack M. and Angeline Delores (Benzuly) Robbin; m. Erwin Howard Epstein, Sept. 3, 1961; children: Jack R., Eric M., M. Avi. BS, U. Wis., 1961; MA, U. Chgo., 1964. Bilingual assessment, transitional bilingual, secondary English, elem. tchr. Ill. Tchr. Sch. Dist. 65, Evanston, Ill., 1963—64, Waynesville R-IV Schs., Ft. Leonard Wood, Mo., 1980—82, Am. Sch. Found., Monterrey, Mexico, 1982—83; instr. U. P.R., Rio Piedras, 1964; cons., tchr. Colegio Ingles, Monterrey, 1979—80; English tchr. Rolla Pub. Schs., Mo., 1983—92, Pickerington Local Schs., Ohio, 1992—98; bilingual tchr. Schaumburg Sch. Dist., Ill., 1998—, bilingual assessment liaison, 2003—. Pres. Rolla Cmty. Tchrs. Assn., 1991—92; pres. Ozarks chpt. Phi Delta Kappa, Rolla, 1986; state pres. Ptnrs. of the Americas (Brazil-U.S.), Mo., 1987—88; bd. dirs. South Ctrl. Mo. Arts Coun., 1991—92. Recipient Kemper Knapp scholarship, U. Wis., 1957—61, humanities fellowship, U. Chgo., 1962—64, tchr. recognition, U. Kans., 1991. Mem.: NEA, AAUW (sec. Glenview chpt. 2001—04, pres. 2004—, pres. Glenview Br. 2004—), Ill. Assn. Multilingual-Multicultural Educators, Nat. Coun. Tchrs. of English, Nat. Assn. Bilingual Educators, Hadassah of Chgo. Jewish. Avocations: movies, theater, reading, travel, cooking. Home: 135 Rutgers Ct Glenview IL 60026 Office: Sch Dist 54 524 E Schaumburg Rd Schaumburg IL 60194 Office Phone: 847-357-5073. E-mail: bmepstein@ameritech.net.

EPSTEIN, CHARLES JOSEPH, pediatrician, geneticist, biochemist, educator; b. Phila., Sept. 3, 1933; s. Jacob C. and Frieda (Savransky) E.; m. Lois Barth, June 10, 1956; children: David Alexander, Jonathan Akiba, Paul Michael, Joanna Marguerite. AB, Harvard U., 1955, MD, 1959; DS, Northeastern Ohio U., 1997. Diplomate Am. Bd. Med. Genetics. Intern in medicine Peter Bent Brigham Hosp., Boston, 1959-60, asst. resident in medicine, 1960-61; research assoc., med. officer and sect. chief Nat. Heart Inst. and Nat. Inst. Arthritis and Metabolic Diseases, NIH, Bethesda, Md., 1961-67; rsch. fellow in med. genetics U. Wash., 1963-64; assoc. prof. pediat. and biochemistry U. Calif., San Francisco, 1967-72, prof., 1972—2005, prof. emeritus, 2005—, chief divsn. med. genetics. dept. pediat. San Francisco, 1967—, co-dir. program in human genetics, 1997—2004. Investigator Howard Hughes Med. Inst., 1976-81; mem. human embryology and devel. study sect. NIH, 1971-75; mem. mental retardation rsch. com. Nat. Inst. Child Health and Devel., 1979-83, chmn., 1981-83; mem. com. for study inborn errors of metabolism NRC, 1972-75; mem. sci. adv. bd. Nat. Down Syndrome Soc., 1981-99, chmn., 1984-99, mem. nat. adv. bd., 1999—, also bd. dirs.; mem. recombinant DNA adv. com. NIH, 1985-90, mem. human gene therapy subcom., 1987-91, chmn. residency rev. com. med. genetics, 1993-99; mem. sci. adv. bd. Buck Inst., 2002-, chmn., 2004-, trustee, 2004-; Stanley Wright Meml. lectr. Western Soc. Pediatric Rsch., 1986; William Potter lectr. Thomas Jefferson U., 1987; George H. Fetterman lectr. U. Pitts., 1989; faculty rsch. lectr. U. Calif., San Francisco, 1994; Mary Hulings Edens lectr. U. Tex. Med. Br., Galveston, 1996; Ida Cordelia Beam lectr. U. Iowa, 1998; Donald L. Thurston meml. lectr. Washington U., St. Louis, 1999, others. Author: The Consequences of Chromosome Imbalance: Principles, Mechanisms and Models, 1986; editor: Human Genetics, 1984-95, The Neurobiology of Down Syndrome, 1986, Oncology and Immunology of Down Syndrome, 1987, Am. Jour. Human Genetics, 1987-93, Molecular and Cytogenetic Studies of Non-disjunction, 1989, Molecular Genetics of Chromosome 21 and Down Syndrome, 1990, Morphogenesis of Down Syndrome, 1991, Down Syndrome and Alzheimer Disease, 1992, Phenotypic Mapping of Down Syndrome and other Aneuploid Conditions, 1993, Etiology and Pathogenesis of Down Syndrome, 1995, Inborn Errors of Development. The Molecular Basis of Clinical Disorders of Morphogenesis, 2004; assoc. editor Rudolph's Textbook of Pediatrics, 18th edit., 1986, 20th edit., 1996; mem. editl. bd. Biology Reproduction, 1974-78, Cytogenetics and Cell Genetics, 1975-80; mem. editl. bd. Am. Jour. Med. Genetics, 1977—, sr. editor, 1995-99, adv. editor, 2000—; mem. editl. bd. Devel. Genetics, 1983-85, Jour. Embryology and Exptl. Morphology, 1983-85, Human Gene Therapy, 1990-98, Human Mutation, 1992-99, Human Genetics, 1995-99, Down Syndrome Quar., 1996—, Trends in Genetics, 1997—, Cmty. Genetics, 1998—, Ann. Rev. of Human Genetics and Genomics, 1999—, Mechanisms of Aging and Devel., 2000—; contbr. numerous rsch. articles on human and med. genetics, devel. genetics and biochemistry to profl. publs. Served with USPHS, 1961-63. Named to Hall of Fame, Central High Sch. of Phila., 2001; recipient Henry A. Christian award, Harvard Med. Sch., 1959, Rsch. Career Devel. award, NIH, 1967—72, Nancy and Daniel Weisman Charitable Found. award, 1990, Lifetime Achievement award in genetic scis., March of Dimes Birth Defects Found., Col. Harland Sanders, 1995, 6th World Congress on Down Syndrome award, 1997, Disting. Rsch. award, The Arc of the U.S., 1998, Premio Internat. Phoenix-Anni Verdi Perle Rsch. Genetiche, Italian Soc. Human Genetics, 1999, Allan award, Am. Soc. Human Genetics, 2001. Fellow AAAS, Am. Acad. Arts and Scis.; mem. AMA, Am. Bd. Med. Genetics (bd. dirs. 1988-93, v.p. 1989, pres. 1990-91), Genetics Soc. Am., Am. Fedn. Clin. Rsch., Am. Soc. Human Genetics (bd. dirs. 1972-75, 87-93, 97-98, pres.-elect 1995, pres. 1996), Am. Soc. Biochemistry and Molecular Biology, Soc. Pediatric Rsch. (coun. 1972-75), Am. Coll. Med. Genetics (pres.-elect 2001-02, pres. 2003-2005, past pres. 2005-), Western Soc. Clin. Investigation, Western Soc. Pediatric Rsch., Am. Soc. Clin. Investigation, Am. Soc. Cell Biology, Soc. Devel. Biology, Am. Pediatric Soc., Western Assn. Physicians (coun. 1993-95), Assn. Am. Physicians, Soc. Inherited Metabolic Disorders, Inst. Medicine of NAS, Calif. Acad. Medicine exec. comm. 2002-, v.p. 2004-), Phi Beta Kappa, Alpha Omega Alpha. Jewish. Office: U Calif Dept Pediat Rock Hall GD584B 1550 4th St San Francisco CA 94143-0748 Office Phone: 415-476-2981.

EPSTEIN, CYNTHIA FUCHS, sociology educator, writer; BA in Polit. Sci., Antioch Coll., 1955; postgrad., U. Chgo. Law Sch., 1955-56; MA in Sociology, New Sch. Social Rsch., 1960; PhD, Columbia U., 1968. Instr. anthropology Finch Coll., 1961-62; assoc. in sociology Columbia U., 1964-65, instr. Barnard Coll., 1965; instr. sociology Queens Coll., N.Y.C., 1966-67, asst. prof., 1968-70, assoc. prof., 1971-74, prof., 1974-84; prof. grad. ctr. CUNY, 1974, Disting. prof. Grad. Ctr., 1990; resident scholar Russell Sage Found., 1982-88; co-dir. Program in Sex Roles and Social Change Ctr. Social Scis., Columbia U., 1977-82, co-dir. NIMH tng. grant on sociology and econs. of women and work Grad. Ctr., disting. prof. Grad. Ctr., 1990—. Vis. prof. Health Sci. Ctr. SUNY, Stony Brook, 1975, Stanford Law Sch., 1997, vis. fellow, 2002; vis. scholar Stanford U., 1991, Columbia Law Sch., 2004; Phi Beta Kappa vis. scholar, 1991-92; com. on women's employment and related social issues NRC-Nat. Acad. Scis., 1981-88; adv. com. on econ. role of women Pres.' Council Econ. Advisers, 1973-74; cons., lectr. and speaker in field. Author: Woman's Place: Options and Limits in Professional Careers, 1970, Women in Law, 1981, 2d edit., 1993, Deceptive Distinctions: Sex, Gender and the Social Order, 1988, The Part-time Paradox: Time Norms, Professional Life, Family and Gender, 1999; editor: (with William J. Goode) The Other Half: Roads to Women's Equality, 1971; (with Rose Laub Coser) Access to Power: Cross-National Studies of Women and Elites, 1981, (with A. Kalleberg) Time Limits, 2004, (with Arne L. Kalleberg) Shifting Boundaries of Work and Social Life, 2004; mem. editl. bds. Signs, Women's Studies, Internat. Jour. Work and Occupations, Sociol. Focus, Women 1974, Dissent, Am. Jour. Sociology, CUNY Mag., Gender and Soc.; contbr. chpts. to books, articles to profl. jours. Trustee Antioch U., 1984—97. Recipient Award for Disting. Contbn. to Study of Sex and Gender, ASAN, 1994, Rebecca Rice award Antioch Coll., 1997; grantee Inst. Life Ins., 1974, Ford Found., 1975-77, Rsch. Found. City of N.Y., 1974-76, 90-93, Guggenheim Meml. Found., 1976-77, Ctr. Advanced Study in Behavioral Scis., 1977-78, 2005, Russell Sage Found., 1982-90, Sloan Found., 1995—; fellow NIH, 1963-66, MacDowell Colony, 1973, 74, 77, 80, Guggenheim Found., 1976-77, Ctr. Advanced Study in Behavioral Sci., 1977-78, Va. Ctr. Creative Arts, 1984. Mem. AAAS, Eastern Sociol. Soc. (v.p. 1977-79, exec. coun. 1973-74, pres. 1983-84, I Peter Gellman award, Merit award 2004), Am. Sociol. Assn. (coun. 1974-77, com. exec. office and budget 1978-81, chmn. sect. on orgns. and occupations, chmn. sect. on sociology of sex roles 1973-74, chair culture sect. 2000-01, pres.-elect, 2004-, Jessie Bernard award 2003), Social Rsch. Assn., Internat. Sci. Commn. on Family. Office: CUNY Grad Ctr 365 5th Ave New York NY 10016-4309 Business E-Mail: cepstein@gc.cuny.edu.

EPSTEIN, DANIEL MARK, poet, dramatist, biographer; b. Washington, Oct. 25, 1948; s. Donald David and Louise Marietta (Tillman) E.; m. Wendy Roberts, May 29, 1976 (div. 1994); children: Johanna Ruth, Benjamin Robert; m. Jennifer Bishop, 1994; children: Theodore John, Nathaniel David. AB magna cum laude with highest honors in English, Kenyon Coll., 1970; postgrad., U. Va., 1970-71; M.F.A. h.c., Norwich U. Asst. mgr. Automatic Enterprises, Washington, 1967-70; disting. scholar-in-residence Randolph-Macon Woman's Coll., 1982; writer-in-residence Towson State U., 1983-90. Cons. lit. div. Nat. Endowment for Arts, Washington, 1973; lectr. USIS tour German univs., 1977, tour, Africa, 1978; asst. prof. Johns Hopkins U.; bd. dirs. Balt. Theatre Project; co-founder Balt. Poet's Theatre. Poet-in-residence, NDEA grantee, Garrett County, Md., 1972; master poet Md. Arts Coun. Artists-in-the Schs. program, 1974-77; appeared in numerous poetry readings; books of poetry include Appearances, 1969, No Vacancies in Hell, 1973, The Follies, 1977, Young Men's Gold, 1978, The Book of Fortune, 1982, Spirits, 1987, The Boy In The Well, 1995, The Traveler's Calendar, 2002, stories and essays include Star of Wonder, 1986, Love's Compass, 1990; biographies include Sister Aimee, 1993, Nat King Cole, 1999, Edna St. Vincent Millay, 2001, Lincoln and Whitman, 2004; plays include Jenny and the Phoenix, 1977, The Midnight Visitor, 1981, The Leading Lady 1999, others; translator Euripides' The Bacchae, 1998. Recipient Robert Frost prize, 1969; Prix de Rome AAAL, 1977; Danforth Found. grantee, 1971; Nat. Endowment for Arts fellow, 1974; Guggenheim fellow, 1983 Fellow Am. Acad. in Rome; mem. Phi Beta Kappa. Address: 843 W University Pkwy Baltimore MD 21210-2911

EPSTEIN, DAVID M., publishing executive; b. Chgo., Feb. 20, 1946; s. Bernard G. and Marjorie P. (McCormack) E.; m. Ryba L. Tregilgas, Apr. 11, 1968; children: Daniel, Miriam. AB, UCLA, 1968; MA, U. Ill., 1971. Assoc. editor Scott, Foresman and Co., Glenview, Ill., 1971-80, courseware splst., 1980-81; editor Richard D. Irwin Inc., Homewood, Ill., 1981-83, mgr. composition, 1983-89; assoc. pub. Am. Libr. Assn., Chgo., 1989-98; mgr. Creative Svcs. PricewaterhouseCoopers LLP, Chgo., 1998—2001, Mellon HR Svcs., 2002—05; proposal mgr. Affiliated Computer Svcs., Inc., Chgo.,

2005—. Author: Electronic Text Management, 1984; editor: U.S. in Literature, 1978, Books of the Fairs, 1991, Feeling Overworked: When Work Becomes Too Much, 2001; mng. editor: World Encyclopedia Libr. and Info. Sci., 1996, Frontiers of World Class Learning, 1998. Bd. dirs. Chgo. Concerned Jamaicans. Jewish. Avocations: aviation history, writing, jazz history. Office: Affiliated Computer Svcs Inc 1 North Dearborn Chicago IL 60602

EPSTEIN, EDWARD LOUIS, lawyer; b. Walla Walla, Wash., Jan. 10, 1936; s. Louis and Marie (Barger) E.; m. Marilyn K. Young, Dec. 29, 1962; children: Lisa Marie, Rachel Ann. BA with great distinction, Stanford U., 1958; LLB magna cum laude, Harvard U., 1961. Bar: Oreg. 1962, U.S. Dist. Ct. Oreg. 1962, U.S. Ct. Appeals (9th cir.) 1963. Assoc. Stoel Rives LLP, Portland, Oreg., 1962-67, ptnr., 1967—. Past sec., bd. dirs. Portland Hosp. Facilities Authority; trustee Good Samaritan Hosp. and Med. Ctr., Portland, 1972-78, pres., 1978; past trustee Morrison Ctr. for Youth and Family Svcs., Oreg. Assn. Hosps. Found.; bd. dirs. Banner Corp., Banner Bank. Mem. ABA, Am. Bar Found., Am. Health Lawyers Assn., Oreg. Bar Assn., Multnomah County Bar Assn., Multnomah Athletic Club, Univ. Club, Harvard Law Rev., Phi Beta Kappa. Office: Stoel Rives LLP 900 SW 5th Ave Ste 2600 Portland OR 97204-1268 Office Phone: 503-294-9245. Business E-Mail: elepstein@stoel.com.

EPSTEIN, EMANUEL, plant physiologist; b. Duisburg, Germany, Nov. 5, 1916; came to U.S., 1938, naturalized, 1946; s. Harry and Bertha (Lowe) E.; m. Hazel L. Leask, Nov. 26, 1943; children: Jared H. (dec.), Jonathan H. BS, U. Calif., Davis, 1940, MS, 1941; PhD, U. Calif., Berkeley, 1950. Plant physiologist Dept. Agr., Beltsville, Md., 1950-58; lectr., assoc. plant physiologist U. Calif.-Davis, 1958-65, prof. plant nutrition, plant physiologist, 1965-87, faculty rsch. lectr., 1980, prof. botany, 1974-87, prof. and plant physiologist emeritus (active), 1987—. Cons. in field. Author: Mineral Nutrition of Plants: Principles and Perspectives, 1972, 2d edit. (with A.J. Bloom), 2005; mem. editl. bd. Plant Physiology, 1962-71, 76-92, CRC Handbook Series in Nutrition and Food, 1975-84, The Biosaline Concept: An Approach to the Utilization of Underexploited Resources, 1978, Saline Agriculture: Salt-Tolerant Plants for Developing Countries, 1990, Plant Sci., 1981-89, Advances in Plant Nutrition, 1981-88, Soil Science and Plant Nutrition, 1998—; contbr. articles to profl. jours. With U.S. Army, 1943—46. Recipient Gold medal Pisa (Italy) U., 1962; Guggenheim fellow, 1958; Fulbright sr. research scholar, 1965-66, 74-75, award of honor, Am. Soc. Agronomy Calif. Chapter, 2002. Fellow AAAS (pres. Pacific divsn. 1990, Fifty-Yr. Life mem. award 1999); mem. Nat. Acad. Scis., Am. Soc. Plant Biologists (Charles Reid Barnes Hon. Life Membership award 1986), Japanese Soc. Plant Physiologists, Am. Inst. Biol. Scis., Am. Soc. Agronomy Calif. (award of honor, 2002), Common Cause, Save-the-Redwoods League, U. Calif. Davis Club, Calif. Aggie Alumni Assn. (Alumni citation for Excellence, 1999), Nature Conservancy, Sigma Xi. Achievements include rsch. in ion transport in plants, mineral nutrition and salt rels. of plants, salt tolerant crops, and silicon in plant biology. Office: UC Soils & Biogeochemistry-Land Air & Water Resources One Shields Ave Davis CA 95616-8627 Office Phone: 530-752-0197. Business E-Mail: eqepstein@ucdavis.edu.

EPSTEIN, FRANKLIN HAROLD, internist, educator; b. Bklyn., May 5, 1924; s. Max and Fannie (Geduld) E.; m. Sherrie Spivack, Aug. 12, 1951; children: Mark, Ann, Sara, Jonathan. BA, Bklyn. Coll., 1944; MD, Yale U., 1947; Doctor Honoris Causa, Med. Acad., Gdansk, 1992. Diplomate: Am. Bd. Internal Medicine (chmn. subsplty. bd. in nephrology 1969-72). Asst. prof. medicine Yale U., 1954-59, assoc. prof., 1959-66, prof. medicine, 1966-72, chief, divsn. metabolism, 1965-72; prof. medicine Harvard U., 1972—, H.L. Blumgart prof. medicine, W. Applebaum prof. medicine; dir. Thorndike Meml. Lab., Boston City Hosp., 1972; physician-in-chief Beth Israel Hosp., 1973-80, dir. renal divsn., 1980-93; Macy Found. fellow and vis. scientist Oxford (Eng.) U., 1980-81. Cons. to surgeon gen. U.S. Army, 1964-80; mem. metabolism study sect. USPHS, 1962-66; pres. Mt. Desert Island Biol.Lab., 1986-95. Editor: Yearbook of Medicine, 1967-96; assoc. editor: Jour. Clin. Investigation, 1957-62, New Eng. Jour. Medicine, 1982-2001, Quar. Jour. Medicine, 1984-93; contbr. papers, book chpts. on renal physiology, disease of kidneys. Capt. M.C., U.S. Army, 1950-53. Recipient Rsch. Career award, USPHS, 1964, John P. Peters award, Am. Soc. Nephrology, 1985, Bywaters award, Internat. Soc. Nephrology, 1999, David Hume award, Nat. Kidney Found., 2003. Fellow AAAS, Assn. Physicians Gt. Britain and Ireland, Royal Coll. Physicians; mem. Am. Soc. Clin. Investigation (v.p. 1970), Assn. Am. Physicians, Interurban Clin. Club, Sigma Xi, Alpha Omega Alpha. Jewish. Home: 294 Buckminster Rd Brookline MA 02445-5801 Office: 330 Brookline Ave Boston MA 02215-5400 Office Phone: 617-667-4104. Business E-Mail: fepstein@bidmc.harvard.edu.

EPSTEIN, GARY M., lawyer; b. Newark, Feb. 19, 1948; BA summa cum laude, Yeshiva Coll., 1969; MA in English and Am. Lit., NYU, 1970; JD, Harvard Univ., 1980. Bar: Fla. 1980, US Ct. Appeals (11th cir.) 1980, US Dist. Ct. (so. dist.) Fla. 1981. Shareholder, chair nat. corp. and securities practice, co-chair Israel Initiative Greenberg Traurig LLP, Miami, Fla. Mem.: ABA, Fla. Bar Assn., Am. Israel C. of C., Fla. (chmn. bd.), Miami Beach Jewish Cmty. Ctr. (pres.). Office: Greenberg Traurig LLP 1221 Brickell Ave Miami FL 33131 Office Phone: 305-579-0500. Office Fax: 305-579-0717. Business E-Mail: epsteing@gtlaw.com.

EPSTEIN, GARY MARVIN, lawyer; b. Bklyn., Nov. 28, 1946; s. Arthur and Juliett (Winick) E.; m. Jeralyn Needel, June 29, 1969; children: Daniel, Deborah. BSEE, Lehigh U., 1968; JD, Harvard U., 1971. Bar: D.C. 1971, U.S. Ct. Appeals (3d cir.) 1973, U.S. Supreme Ct. 1975, U.S. Ct. Appeals (9th cir.) 1988. Engr. Gordon Engring. Co., Wakefield, Mass., 1967-70; assoc. Arent, Fox, Kinter, Plotkin & Kahn, Washington, 1971-79, ptnr., 1979-81; chief Common Carrier Bur. FCC, Washington, 1981-83; ptnr., head telecom. group Latham & Watkins, Washington, 1983—. Pub. mem. Adminstrv. Conf. U.S., 1983-86; chmn. adv. com. reduced orbital spacing FCC, 1983-86; chmn. adv. Com. World Radiocomms. Conf., FCC, 1994-96; dir. D.C. Appleseed Ctr., 2001—, vice chmn., 2002—, vice chair, 2003-, Appleseed Found., 2002-, v.p., 2002-. Bd. dirs. Appleseed Found., 2002—. Mem. ABA, D.C. Bar Assn., Eta Kappa Nu, Tau Beta Pi. Home: 1111 23d St NW Apt PH1F Washington DC 20037-2809 Office: Latham & Watkins 555 11th St NW Washington DC 20004-2585 Office Phone: 202-637-2249. Business E-Mail: Gary.Epstein@lw.com.

EPSTEIN, GERALD LEWIS, technology and security policy analyst; b. Washington, Dec. 13, 1956; s. Joseph Bernard and Rosalie E.; m. Ellen Mika, June 30, 1985; children: Alanna, Nathan. SB, MIT, 1978; MA, U. Calif., Berkeley, 1980, PhD in Physics, 1984. Analyst Office Tech. Assessment, Washington, 1983-87, sr. analyst, 1987-89, 91-95, sr. assoc., 1995; project dir. Kennedy Sch. Govt., Harvard U., Cambridge, Mass., 1989-91; sr. policy analyst White House Office Sci. and Tech. Policy, 1996-2000, asst. dir. for nat. security, 2000—01; sr. dir. for sci. and tech. Nat. Security Coun. Staff, 2000—01; rschr. Inst. Def. Analyses, 2001—03; sr. fellow sci. and security Ctr. Strategic & Internat. Studies, 2003—. Vis. lectr. pub. and internat. affairs Princeton U., 1992; mem. adv. bd. Chem. and Engring. News, 1994-97; mem. editl. bd. Biosecurity and Bioterrorism, 2003—; adj. prof. security studies program Georgetown U., 2004—. Co-author: Beyond Spinoff: Military and Commercial Technologies in a Changing World, 1992; project dir.: Starpower: The U.S. and the International Quest for Fusion Energy, 1987, Proliferation of Weapons of Mass Destruction: Assessing the Risks, 1993. Fannie and John Hertz Found. fellow, 1978-83; Congl. fellow Office Tech. Assessment, 1983. Fellow Am. Phys. Soc. (exec. com. forum on physics and soc. 1994-97, mem. com. on internat. sci. affairs, 2005—); mem. Internat. Inst. Strategic Studies, AAAS, Phi Beta Kappa, Sigma Xi, Tau Beta Pi. Home: 6008 Anniston Rd Bethesda MD 20817-3404 Office: Ctr for Strategic and Internat Studies 1800 K St NW Washington DC 20006 Office Phone: 202-775-3125. Business E-Mail: gepstein@csis.org.

EPSTEIN, HARRIET PIKE, public relations executive; b. N.Y.C. d. Samuel and Sonia (Kuchinok) Pike; m. Stanley H. Epstein; children: Lois N., Susan A. BA cum laude, NYU. Pub. rels. exec. Townsend Comm. Inc., Syosset, N.Y., 1970-75; mng. editor L.I. Bus. Rev., Plainview, N.Y., 1975-80; v.p. Howard Rubenstein Assocs., N.Y.C., 1980-81; dir. comm. ways and means com. N.Y. State Assembly, Albany, 1981-87; v.p. GreyCom, Inc., N.Y.C., 1987-88; v.p. media rels. Fin. Svcs. Corp., N.Y.C., 1988-91; dir. comm. Cmty. Svc. Soc. N.Y., N.Y.C., 1991—. Mem. Pub. Rels. Soc. An., N.Y. Women in Comm., L.I. Women's Network (chmn. membeships 1980-82), N.Y. Press Club, Phi Beta Kappa.

EPSTEIN, IRVING ROBERT, chemistry professor; b. Bklyn., Aug. 9, 1945; s. Milton and Marion (Hillsberg) E.; m. Ellen Bea Fisher, Oct. 31, 1971; children: David, Peter. AB, Harvard U., 1966, MA, 1968, PhD, 1971; diploma, Oxford U., 1967. NATO postdoctoral fellow Cambridge U., 1971; asst. prof. chemistry Brandeis U., Waltham, Mass., 1971-75, assoc. prof., 1975-81, prof., 1981—, Helena Rubinstein prof., 1989—94, chmn., 1983-87, dean arts & scis., 1992-94, provost, sr. v.p. for acad. affairs, 1994-2001. NSF faculty profl. devel. fellow Max Planck Inst., Göttingen, Germany, 1977-78. Editl. adv. bd. Jour. Phys. Chemistry, 1982-89; assoc. editor Chaos, 1990—; editl. bd. Interjour. Complex Sys., 1995—; contbr. articles to profl. jours. Recipient tchr.-scholar award Dreyfus Found., 1973; Nat. Merit scholar, 1962-66, Marshall scholar, 1966-67, Woodrow Wilson fellow, 1968, Guggenheim fellow, 1977, 87, Humboldt fellow, 1977, NSF fellow, 1977-78. Mem. Am. Chem. Soc. (Liebmann award), Phi Beta Kappa. Home: 28 Otis St Newton MA 02460-1803 Office: Brandeis U MS 015 Waltham MA 02454-9110 Business E-Mail: epstein@brandeis.edu.

EPSTEIN, JASON, publishing company executive; b. Cambridge, Mass., Aug. 25, 1928; s. Robert and Gladys (Shapiro) E.; children: Jacob, Helen. BA, Columbia U., 1949, MA, 1950. Editor Doubleday & Co., 1951-58; v.p., editorial dir. Random House, Inc., N.Y.C., 1958-97. Co-founder N.Y. Rev. Books; founder Libr. of Am.; founder Reader's Catalog. Author: The Great Conspiracy Trial, 1970; co-author: Easthampton, a history and guide, 1975, Book Business, 2001; contbr. articles to various publs. Recipient John Jay award Columbia Coll., 1988, Lifetime Achievement award Nat. Book Award, 1988, Curtis Benjamin award Assn. Am. Pubs., 1993, Lifetime Achievement award Guld Hall, 2001, Lifetime Achievement award Nat. Book Critics Cir., 2002. Mem. Coun. on Fgn. Rels., Phi Beta Kappa. Home: PO Box 1143 Sag Harbor NY 11963-0039

EPSTEIN, JAY STUART, federal agency administrator; married; 2 children. BA cum laude, Harvard U., 1969; MD, Downstate Med. Coll., 1976. Resident internal medicine George Washington U. Hosp., Washington, 1976-79, clin. fellow infectious diseases, 1979-81; sr. staff fellow rsch. divsn. virology office biologics rsch. & review FDA, Rockville, Md., 1981-85, chief immunochemistry lab., 1984-86, chief retrovirology lab. divsn. transfusion sci., 1986-92, acting dept. dir., 1990-92, dir. divsn. transfusion transmitted diseases, 1993-95, acting. dir. Office Blood Rsch. and Rev., 1993-95, dir., 1995—. Rsch. asst. Moffit Hosp., San Francisco, 1971-73; part time physician Potomac (Md.) Village Med. Ctr., 1981-83; part time house physician Capitol Hill Hosp., Washington, 1981-83. With USPHS, 1985-88. Nat. Merit scholar, 1965, Harvard Coll. scholar, 1965, N.Y. State Regents Medicine scholar, 1969. Mem. AAAS, Infectious Diseases Soc. Am., Greater Washington Area Infectious Diseaes Soc., Alpha Omega Alpha. Home: 1922 Foxhall Rd Mc Lean VA 22101-5535 Office: Office Blood Rsch & Review FDA CBER HFM-300 1401 Rockville Pike Rockville MD 20852-1448 Office Phone: 301-827-3518. E-mail: epsteinj@cber.fda.gov.

EPSTEIN, JEREMIAH FAIN, anthropologist, educator; b. N.Y.C., Feb. 14, 1924; s. Joseph and Carol (Fain) E.; divorced; children: Anne, Louise, Suzanne. BS in Agr., U. Ill., 1949, MA in Anthropology, 1951; PhD, U. Pa., 1957. Lectr. Hunter Coll., N.Y.C., 1954-58; rsch. scientist anthropology U. Tex., Austin, 1958-60, mem. faculty, 1958—, prof. anthropology, 1970—97, prof. emeritus, 1973—. Fieldwork in Mex., Belize, Honduras, France, U.S. Contbr. articles to profl. jours. Served with AUS, 1942-45. Decorated Purple Heart; grantee NSF, 1963, 64; grantee Wenner Gren Found., 1961; grantee U. Tex. Inst. Latin Am. Studies, 1963, 75; grantee U. Tex., 1988; Fulbright-Hays fellow, 1964; Mellon Found. fellow in Latin Am. studies, 1988; U. Tex. faculty rsch. assignment, 1988. Mem. AAAS, Am. Anthrop. Assn., Soc. Am. Archaeology, Soc. Mexicana Anthropologia. Office: U Tex Dept Anthropology Austin TX 78712 Office Phone: 512-471-7529. Business E-Mail: jepstein@mail.utexas.com.

EPSTEIN, JEREMY G., lawyer; b. Chgo., Sept. 28, 1946; s. Joseph and Gayola (Goldman) E.; m. Amy Kallman, Sept. 15, 1968; children: Joshua, Abigail. BA summa cum laude, Columbia U., 1967; BA, Cambridge U., Eng., 1969, MA, 1973; JD, Yale U., 1972. Bar: N.Y. 1973. Law clk. to judge Arnold Bauman U.S. Dist. Ct. (so. dist.) N.Y., 1972-74; asst. U.S. atty. So. Dist. N.Y., 1974-78; ptnr. Shearman & Sterling, N.Y.C., 1982—. Vol. Lawyers for the Arts; bd. dirs. Fund for Modern Cts, City Bar Fund, Inc. Fellow Am. Coll. Trial Lawyers, Phi Beta Kappa. Office: 599 Lexington Ave Fl C2 New York NY 10022-6030 Office Phone: 212-848-4169. Business E-Mail: jepstein@shearman.com.

EPSTEIN, JOHN HOWARD, dermatologist; b. San Francisco, Dec. 29, 1926; s. Norman Neman and Gertrude (Hirsch) E.; m. Alice Thompson, Nov. 1953; children: Norman H., Janice A., Beverly A. BA, U. Calif., Berkeley, 1949, MD, 1952; MS, U. Minn., 1956. Diplomate Am. Bd. Dermatology (dir. 1974-84, pres. 1981-82). Intern Stanford U. Med. Ctr., 1952-53; resident in dermatology Mayo Clinic, Rochester, Minn., 1953-56; practice medicine specializing in dermatology San Francisco, 1956—; chief dermatology Mt. Zion Hosp., 1970-80. Clin. prof. U. Calif. Med. Sch., San Francisco, 1972—; cons. Letterman Army Med. Center, U.S. Naval Hosp., San Diego. Chief editor Archives of Dermatology, 1973-78; asst. editor Jour. Am. Acad. Dermatology, 1978-88; contbr. over 275 articles to profl. jours. With USNR, 1944-46. Recipient Finsen medal, Internat. Soc. Photobiology, 2004. Fellow ACP; mem. Am. Acad. Dermatology (pres. 1981-82, Silver award for exhibit 1962, Gold award 1969), Soc. Investigative Dermatology (v.p. 1979-80), Am. Dermatol. Assn. (bd. dirs. 1983-88, pres. 1990-91), N.Am. Dermatology Soc., Pacific Dermatol. Assn. (pres. 1985-86), Brit. Dermatol. Soc., Danish Dermatol. Soc., Polish Dermatol. Soc., San Francisco Dermatol. Soc. (pres. 1963-64), Am. Soc. Photobiology (councilor 1983-86), Academia Mexicana and Dermatologia (hon.), European Acad. Dermatology and Venerology (hon.), La Societe Francaise de Dermatologie & de Syphiligraphie, Spanish Dermatol. Soc. Office: 450 Sutter St Rm 1306 San Francisco CA 94108-4002

EPSTEIN, JUDITH ANN, judge; b. L.A., Dec. 23, 1942; d. Gerald Elliot and Harriet (Hirsh) Rubens; m. Joseph I. Epstein, Oct. 4, 1964; children: Mark Douglas, Laura Ann. AB, U. Calif., Berkeley, 1964; MA, U. San Francisco, 1974, JD, 1977. Bar: Calif. 1978, U.S. Dist. Ct. (no. dist.) Calif 1978, U.S. Supreme Ct. 1983, U.S. Ct. Appeals (9th cir.) 1984. With social svcs. dept. Sutter County, Yuba City, Calif., 1964-66; bus. devel. assoc. Yuba County C. of C., Marysville, Calif., 1968-70; rsch. clk. Calif. Supreme Ct., San Fransisco, 1977; ptnr. Crosby, Heafey, Roach & May, Oakland, Calif., 1978-91; gen. counsel and sec. Valent USA Corp., 1991-98; fellow The Commonwealth Club of Calif., 1999—2001; appellate judge Calif. State Bar Ct., 2002—. Lectr. U. Calif. Grad. Sch. Journalism in Media Law, Berkeley, 1987-91; bd. dirs. Sierra Pacific Steel, Hayward, Calif.; adj. prof. U. San Francisco, 1999—, exec. dir., East Bay. Bd. dirs., v.p. Oakland Ballet, 1980-92; mem. bd. counselors U. San Francisco Sch. Law, 1994; trustee U. San Francisco, 1996—; bd. dirs. San Francisco Bay area Girl Scouts U.S., 1998—, East Bay Cmty. Found. Recipient Pres.'s award Oakland Ballet, James Madison Freedom of Info. award Soc. Profl. Journalists, 1992; award for Disting. Achievement, Girl Scouts U.S., 1995. Fellow Am. Bar Found.; mem. Calif. Women Lawyers Assn., Alameda Bar Assn., Berkeley Tennis Club.

EPSTEIN, KITTY KELLY, writer, educator; b. L.A., Mar. 24, 1946; d. Andrew Robert and Edna Mary (Manuel) Kelly; m. Kenneth Allen Epstein; 1 child, Jaron Kelly. BA, San Francisco State U., 1968, MA, 1979; PhD, U. Calif., Berkeley, 1989. Dept. chair Emiliano Zapata St. Acad., Oakland, Calif., 1976—89; vis. prof. edn. U. Calif., Berkeley, 1989—; prof. edn. Holy Name Coll., Oakland, 1989—. Cons. Multicultural Project, Children's Hosp., Oakland. (booklet) Back to the Bad Old Days, 2000; contbr. articles to profl. jours. and newspapers. Founding mem. Coun. for Transformation of Urban Schs., Oakland, 1999—; adv. com. Congresswman Barbara Lee, Oakland, 1999—; bd. dirs. Vanguard Pub. Found., San Francisco, 1992—. Recipient Educator of Yr. award, Marcus Foster Found., Oakland, 1983. Mem.: Am. Ednl. Rsch. Assn., Ronald V. Dellums Dem. Club. Avocations: travel, volunteering.

EPSTEIN, LEE JOAN, political science professor; b. N.Y.C., Mar. 17, 1958; d. Kenneth Maurice and Ann (Buxbaum) Spole BA with high honors, Emory U., 1980, MA, 1982, PhD, 1983. Mallinckrodt Disting. Univ. prof. polit. sci. Washington U., St. Louis, 1998—, prof. law, 2000—. Author: Conservatives in Court, 1985; co-author: Supreme Court and Legal Change, 1992, The Choices Justices Make, 1998, The Supreme Court Compendium, 2003, Constitutional Law for a Changing America, 2004; contbr. articles to profl. jours., chpts. in books. Fellow Am. Acad. Polit. and Social Sci.; mem. Am. Polit. Sci. Assn., Midwest Polit. Sci. Assn., Law and Soc. Assn., Pi Sigma Alpha, Alpha Epsilon Phi. Jewish. Avocations: skiing, tennis. Office: Washington U Dept Polit Sci PO Box 1063 Saint Louis MO 63183-4899 Office Phone: 314-935-8580. Business E-Mail: epstein@wustl.edu.

EPSTEIN, LIONEL CHARLES, lawyer; b. N.Y.C., Apr. 7, 1924; s. David and Carrie (Roth) E.; m. Sarah Louise Gamble, June 10, 1951 (div. Apr. 12, 1983); children: David Bradley, James Roth, Richard Aldis, Miles Owen, Sarah Carianne; m. Elizabeth Pendelton Streicher, Nov. 10, 1990. BA, NYU, 1947; LL.B., Harvard U., 1950. Bar: N.Y. 1950, D.C. 1953, U.S. Supreme Ct. 1955. With office gen. counsel U.S. Navy Dept., 1950-52; tax div. U.S. Justice Dept., 1952-57; mem. firms Ginsburg & Leventhal, 1957-67, Epstein, Friedman, Duncan & Medalie, Washington, 1967-74; mem. firm Jones, Day, Reavis & Pogue, Washington, 1975-84, of counsel, 1984-86; chmn. EFO Capital Mgmt. Inc., Washington, 1984—. Spl. asst. to R. Sargent Shriver Peace Corps, 1962; Bd. dirs. Expt. in Internat. Living, Mus. Modern Art, N.Y.C., Com. on Illustrated Books and Prints, Washington Print Club. Author art exhbn. catalogs. Served with inf. AUS, 1942-45. Decorated Purple Heart, Knight's Cross 1st class Order St. Olav (Norway). Mem. ABA, Harvard Club (N.Y.). Clubs: Lawyers (founding mem.), Harvard. Home: 700 New Hampshire Ave NW Washington DC 20037-2406 Office: 21 Dupont Cir NW Ste 330 Washington DC 20036-1549 E-mail: lepstein@efocapitalmgmt.com.

EPSTEIN, MARK ROBERT, electronics executive; b. NYC, Feb. 7, 1943; s. Albert David and Edith (Prager) Epstein; children: Paul, Jeff. BS, MIT, 1963, MS, 1964; PhD, Stanford U., 1968. Rsch. assoc. Stanford Electronic Labs., 1967—68; mgr. R&D Northrop Page Engrs. Inc., Vienna, Va., 1968—74; program dir. Computer Sci. Corp., Falls Church, Va., 1974—76; staff asst. Theater C3 Office of Sec. of Def., Washington, 1976—80; dep. for C3 and intelligence Office of Sec. of Army, Washington, 1980—86; sr. v.p. Qualcomm Inc., San Diego, 1986—. Chmn. Circles bd. Kennedy Ctr. for the Performing Arts, 2003—04; chmn. Washington Com. for the Arts, 2004—; mem. Wilson coun. Woodrow Wilson Internat. Ctr. for Scholars, 2002—; mem. MIT Corp., 2002—. Mem. IEEE (sr.), MIT Club Washington (bd. dirs. 1998—, pres. 2002-03), Sigma Xi. Avocations: swimming, piano, dance, golf. Home: 9209 Fox Meadow Ln Potomac MD 20854 Office: Qualcomm Inc 9209 Fox Meadow Ln Potomac MD 20854 Office Phone: 301-365-6963. Business E-Mail: mepstein@qualcomm.com.

EPSTEIN, MARSHA ANN, public health administrator, physician; b. Chgo., Feb. 4, 1945; 1 child, Lee Rashad Mahmood. BA, Reed Coll., 1965; MD, U. Calif., San Francisco, 1969; MPH, U. Calif., Berkeley, 1971. Diplomate Am. Bd. Preventive Medicine. Intern French Hosp., San Francisco, 1969-70; resident in preventive medicine Sch. Pub. Health, U. Calif., Berkeley, 1971-73; fellow in family planning dept. ob-gyn. UCLA, 1973-74; med. dir. Herself Health Clinic, LA, 1974-79; pvt. adult gen. practitioner LA, 1978-82; dist. health officer LA County Pub. Health, LA, 1982—2001, area med. dir., 2001—. Part-time physician U. Calif. Student Health, Berkeley, 1970-73; co-med. dir. Monsenior Oscar Romero Free Clinic, LA, 1992-93. Mem.: APHA, Calif. Acad. Preventive Medicine, So. Calif. Pub. Health Assn., LA-Am. Med. Women's Assn., Am. Med. Women's Assn., Am. Coll. Physician Execs. Democrat. Jewish. Avocations: dance, native plants, meditating. Office: Tucker Health Ctr 123 W Manchester Blvd Inglewood CA 90301 Office Phone: 310-419-5301. E-mail: mepstein@ladhs.org.

EPSTEIN, MARVIN MORRIS, retired construction company executive; b. Cleve., June 2, 1928; s. Isadore Elchanan and Rose (Gevelber) E.; m. Lois M. DeSure, June 10, 1957; children: Deborah L. Epstein Merkin, David A. BA with highest honors, U. Mich., 1951; attended, Western Res. U., 1947-49, Ohio State U., 1953, Cleve. State U., 1995-98. Reporter Cleve. Plain Dealer, 1951-52; editor AP, Columbus, Ohio, 1953-55; asst. mng. editor Times-Star, Cin., 1956-57; editor internat. news Milw. Jour., 1958—59; cons. Eden & Assocs., Cleve., 1959-60; sr. exec. The Austin Co., Cleve., 1961-93, sr. v.p., 1990—93, ret., 1993. Contbr. articles to profl. jours. Active Greater Cleve. Growth Assn., 1975-90; mem. bd. overseers, visiting com. Case Western Res. U., Case Inst. Tech., Cleve., 1981-85; bd. dirs. The Stearns Collection, Ann Arbor, Mich., 1990-93; bd. dirs. World Affairs Coun. of Desert, 2000-04; trustee Cleve. Music Sch. Settlement, 1989-90; mem. Presdl. Societies, Univ. Mich., 1980—, Vis. Com. Coll. Lit., Sci. and the Arts, U. Mich., 1989-92; trustee Cleveland Heights-University Heights Pub. Libr., 1997-99. With U.S. Army, 1946-47. Recipient McNaught Gold medal U. Mich., 1951, Disting. Svc. award, 1998. Mem. Soc. Profl. Journalists (life), U. Mich. Alumni Assn. (pres. Cleve. chpt. 1975-76), Heights Regional C. of C. (pres. 1992), Democrat. Home: 36598 Fan Palm Way Palm Desert CA 92211-2383 Fax: 760-360-2942. Office Phone: 760-360-9481. E-mail: mmebrain@aol.com.

EPSTEIN, MATTHEW, opera company director; b. N.Y. Grad., U. Pa., 1969. Artistic dir. opera programme Bklyn. Acad. Music, 1987-91; gen. dir. Welsh Nat. Opera, Cardiff, Wales, 1991-94; v.p. Columbia Artists Mgmt., NYC, 1973—99, dir., vocal divsn., 2005—; artistic dir. Lyric Opera Chgo., 1999—2005. V.p., spl. cons. Columbia Artists Mgmt.; artistic cons. San Francisco Opera, Santa Fe Opera, Lyric Opera Chgo., BMG Classics/RCA Records, Sony Classical, Carnegie Hall, 1982-86 Mem. jury panel Cardiff Singer World Competition, 1989, 91, 93. Office: Columbia Artists Mgmt 165 W 57th St New York NY 10019-2201*

EPSTEIN, MELVIN, lawyer; b. Passaic, N.J., Jan. 4, 1938; s. Hyman and Lillian (Rozenblum) E.; m. Rachel Judith Stein, Dec. 20, 1964; children: Jonathan Andrew, Emily E. Landau. AB, Harvard U., 1959, LLB, 1962. Bar: N.Y. 1963. Assoc. Stroock & Stroock & Lavan LLP, N.Y.C., 1962-71, ptnr. securities & corp. fin., 1972—. Mem. schs. com. Harvard U., 1984—; bd. dirs. Manhattan Class Co. Theater, 2005—. Mem. N.Y. State Bar Assn., Assn. of Bar of City of N.Y. Democrat. Jewish. Office: Stroock & Stroock & Lavan LLP 180 Maiden Ln New York NY 10038-4925 Office Phone: 212-806-5864. Office Fax: 212-806-6006. Business E-Mail: mepstein@stroock.com.

EPSTEIN, MICHAEL ALAN, lawyer; b. NYC, June 26, 1954; s. Herman and Lillian (King) E. BA, Lehigh U., 1975; JD, NYU, 1979. Bar: NY, 1980, US Dist. Ct. (So. & Ea. Dists.) NY, 1980. Ptnr. Weil, Gotshal & Manges LLP, NYC, 1979—, co-chair trade practices and regulatory law dept., chair tech. and proprietary rights group, mem. mgmt. com. Lectr. in field. Author: Modern Intellectual Property, 1984, 3rd edit., 1994, International Intellectual Property, 1992, Epstein on Intellectual Property, 4th edit., 2001; editor: Corporate Counsellors Deskbook, 1982, 3rd edit., 1990, Biotechnology Law, 1988, The Trademark Law Revision Act, 1989, Trade Secrets, Restrictive Covenants and Other Safeguards, 1986, Online-Internet Law, 1997 and several others; Co-author several books and articles; bd. editor The Computer

Lawyer 1984-, The Intellectual Property Strategist 1994-, The Cyberspace Lawyer 1996-;co-editor-in-chief, bd. editor Jour. of Proprietary Rights 1988-; contbr. articles to profl. jours. Trustee Jonas Salk Found., North Shore-LIJ Health Sys. Donald L. Brown fellow in trade regulation NYU Sch. Law, 1978-79. Mem. ABA, NY State Bar Assn. Home: 1020 Park Ave New York NY 10028-0913 Office: Weil Gotshal & Manges LLP 767 5th Ave New York NY 10153 Office Phone: 212-310-8432. Office Fax: 212-310-8007. Business E-Mail: michael.epstein@weil.com.

EPSTEIN, NORMAN B., psychologist, educator, marriage and family therapist, educator; b. Worcester, Mass., July 15, 1947; s. Paul (Stepfather) and Irene R. Sherman, Max L. Epstein; m. Carolyn R. Smith, May 24, 1985; children: Meredith B., Christine E. BA, UCLA, 1969, PhD, 1974. Lic. psychologist Md. State Bd. Examiners of Psychologists, 1984, marriage and family therapist Md. State Bd. Profl. Counselors and Therapists, 2002, diplomate Am. Bd. Assessment Psychology. Asst. prof. psychology SUNY, Buffalo, 1974—78; asst. prof. psychology in psychiatry U. Pa. Sch. Medicine, Phila., 1978—83; asst. prof. family studies U. Md., College Park, 1983—86, assoc. prof. family studies, 1986—92, prof. family studies, 1992—. Pvt. practice clin. psychology, Rockville, Md., 1976—. Author: Cognitive-Behavioral Marital Therapy, 1990, Enhanced Cognitive-Behavioral Therapy for Couples: A Contextual Approach, 2002; editor: Depression in the Family, 1986, Cognitive-Behavioral Therapy with Families, 1988; contbr. chapters to books, articles to profl. jours. Grantee, Substance Abuse and Mental Health Services Adminstrn., 2002—03, Substance Abuse and Mental Health Svc. Adminstrn., 2003—04. Fellow: APA; mem.: Groves Conf. on the Family, Assn. for Advancement Behavior Therapy, Am. Assn. for Marriage and Family Therapy. Achievements include development of questionnaires for assessing individuals' cognitions regarding their marital relationships; research in assessment and treatment of marital problems; cross-cultural comparison of marital standards and marital satisfaction of couples in mainland China and in the United States; evaluating couple therapy for domestic abuse; family psychoeducation for families with a member diagnosed with Schizophrenia. Avocations: travel, reading, cooking, running. Office: Dept Family Studies University of Maryland College Park MD 20472 Office Phone: 301-405-4013. Business E-Mail: nbe@umd.edu.

EPSTEIN, RANDY J., physician, ophthalmologist; b. Chicago, Ill., Jan. 8, 1955; s. Benita M. LoGiudice; m. Kayla G. Schieber, June 17, 1979; children: Rachel H., Sarah A, Joshua N. MD, Rush Med. Coll., Chgo., 1976—80; BS, U of Ill., Urbana, IL, 1972—76. Diplomate Am. Bd. of Ophthalmology, 1986. CEO Chgo. Cornea Consultants, Ltd., Highland Pk., Ill., 1986—; prof. Dept. of Ophthalmology, Rush Med. Coll., Chgo., 1986—. Mem. Lions Club, Highland Pk., Ill. Recipient One of Chicago's Top Doctors, Chgo. Mag., 2001, Honor award, Am. Acad. Ophthalmology, Sr. Achievement award, 2004. Office: Chicago Cornea Cons 806 Central Highland Park IL 60035 Office Phone: 847-432-6010. E-mail: corneas@aol.com.

EPSTEIN, RAYMOND, engineering and architectural executive; b. Chgo., Jan. 12, 1918; s. Abraham and Janet (Rabinowitz) E.; m. Betty Jadwin, Apr. 7, 1940; children: Gail, David, Norman, Harriet. Student, MIT, 1934-36; BS, U. Ill., 1938. Registered architect registered profl. engr. With A. Epstein & Sons Internat., Inc., Chgo., 1938—, chmn. bd., 1961-83, chmn. exec. com., 1983—. Bd. dirs., life trustee United Israel Appeal; past sec., hon. dir. Am. Jewish Joint Distbn. Com.; mem. exec. com. Nat. Jewish Cmty. Rels. Adv. Coun.; v.p. nat. bd. Jewish Telegraphic Agy.; mem. citizens bd. Loyola U.; past pres. Coun. Jewish Fedns., Welfare Funds, Inc., Jewish Welfare Fund Met. Chgo., Jewish United Fund, Young Men's Jewish Coun.; past sec. Jewish Fed. Met. Chgo.; past chmn. budget com., bd. govs. Jewish Agy.; past trustee Chgo. Med. Sch; past bd. dirs. United Jewish Appeal; past exec. com. Meml. Found. Jewish Culture; past chmn. pub. affairs com., past chmn. campaign Jewish United Fund Met. Chgo.; past. sec. Welfare Coun. Met. Chgo.; past bd. dirs. Chgo. Bldg. Congress; life dir. Mt. Sinai Med. Rsch. Found.; trustee, past dir. Ampal-Am. Israel Corp. Decorated comdr. Legion of Honor Ivory Coast, 1982; recipient Disting. Alumnus award U. Ill., 1974, Julius Rosenwald Meml. award Jewish Fedn. Chgo., 1974, Citation Brandeis U., 1992; named to City of Chgo. Sr. Citizens Hall of Fame, 1991. Fellow Soc. Civil Engr. France, Soc. Am. Registered Architects; mem. NSPE, ASCE, Am. Concrete Inst., Western Soc. Engrs., Assn. Engrs. and Architects in Israel, French Engrs. in the U.S., Inc., Pi Lambda Phi. Clubs: Standard (past trustee), Illini, MIT, Caxton (Chgo.). Home: 4950 S Chicago Beach Dr Chicago IL 60615-3207 Office: 600 W Fulton St Chicago IL 60661-1100 E-mail: ray@rayepstein.com.

EPSTEIN, RICHARD A., law educator; b. 1943; AB summa cum laude, Columbia U., 1964; BA Juris., Oxford U., 1966; LLB cum laude, Yale U., 1968; LLD (hon.), Univ. Ghent, 2003. Bar: Calif. 1969. Asst. prof. Sch. Law U. So. Calif., L.A., 1968—70, assoc. prof., 1970—73; vis. prof. Law. Sch. U. Chgo., 1972—73, prof. Law Sch., 1973-82, James Parker Hall prof. law, 1982-88, James Parker Hall Disting. Svc. prof., 1988—, interim dean, 2001. Peter & Kirsten Bedford sr. fellow Hoover Inst., 2000—; sr. fellow Ctr. Clinical Medical Ethics, U. Chgo. Medical Sch., 1983—. Author: Skepticism and Freedom: A Modern Case for Classical Liberalism, 2003, Torts, 1999, Cases and Materials in Torts, 7th edit., 2000, Takings: Private Property and the Power of Eminent Domain, 1985, Simple Rules for a Complex World, 1995, Mortal Peril: Our Inalienable Right to Health Care, 1997, Principles for a Free Society: Reconciling Individual Liberty with the Common Good, 1998, Forbidden Grounds: The Case Against Employment Discrimination Laws, 1992, Bargaining With the State, 1993, Modern Products Liability Law, 1980; editor: Jour. Legal Studies, 1981-91, Jour. Law and Econs., 1991—2001; mem. editl. bd. Yale Law Jour. Mem. Am. Acad. Arts and Scis., Order of Coif. Office: U Chgo Law Sch 1111 E 60th St Chicago IL 60637-2776 Business E-Mail: repstein@midway.uchicago.edu.*

EPSTEIN, ROBERT HARRY, lawyer; b. St. Louis, June 22, 1958; s. I. Robert and Marcia Ruth (Marglous) Epstein; m. Donna Jean Brafman, June 21, 1983; children: Jeffrey Evan, Leslie Ellen. BA in History and Polit. Sci. cum laude, Boston U., 1980; JD, Washington U., St. Louis, 1983. Bar: Mo. 1986, U.S. Dist. Ct. (ea. and we. dists.) Mo. 1983, U.S. Ct. Appeals (8th cir.), U.S. Supreme Ct. 1991; cert. Ill., 1984. Assoc. Susman, Schermer, Rimmel & Shifrin, predecessor firms, St. Louis, 1983-89, ptnr., 1989-2000; mem. Gallop, Johnson & Neuman, L.C., 2001—, chmn. real estate dept. Mem.: ABA, Ill. Bar Assn., Bar Assn. Met. St. Louis, Mo. Bar Assn. (mem. real estate com. 1985—). Avocations: coin collecting/numismatics, softball, sailing, reading. Office: Gallop Johnson & Neuman LC 101 South Hanley Fl 17 Saint Louis MO 63105 Office Phone: 314-615-6000.

EPSTEIN, ROBERT MARVIN, anesthesiologist, educator; b. NYC, Mar. 10, 1928; s. Nathan B. and Rebecca Epstein; m. Lillian Ray Cohen, Dec. 31, 1950; children: Judith Susan, Neal Myron, Charles Benjamin. BS with distinction, U. Mich., 1947, MD cum laude, 1951. Diplomate Am. Bd. Anesthesiology (dir. 1972-84, pres. 1979-80). Intern U. Mich. Hosp., 1951—52; resident in anesthesiology Presbyn. Hosp., NYC, 1952—53, 1955—56; instr. in anesthesiology and fellow in medicine Columbia U., 1956—57, assoc., 1957—59, asst. prof., anesthesiology, 1959—65, assoc. prof., 1965—70, prof., 1970—72, U. Va., Charlottesville, 1972—74, Alumni prof., 1974—87, Disting. prof., 1987—92, Harold Carron prof., 1992—2002, dept. chmn., 1972—96, Harold Carron prof. emeritus, 2002—. Mem. anesthesiology tng. com. Nat. Inst. Gen. Med. Scis., NIH, 1966—69; mem. com. on anesthesia NRC, 1970—71; mem. Nat. Bd. Med. Examiners, 1982—90, Am. Bd. Med. Specialities, 1974—95. Editor: Anesthesiology, 1974—79; contbr. numerous articles to profl. jours. Bd. dirs., sec. U. Va. Health Svcs. Found., 1980—90, pres., 1990—93; trustee Ednl. Commn. for Fgn. Med. Grads., 1991—95, vice chmn., 1993—95; bd. dirs. QualChoice of Va., 1997—2000. With U.S. Army, 1953—55. Fellow Guggenheim fellow, Oxford U., England, 1966—67, N.Y. Heart Assn., 1956—57; scholar in-residence, Inst. Medicine NAS, 1997, sr. scholar, Va. Health Policy Ctr., 1997—. Fellow: Royal Coll. Anaesthetists (Eng.); mem.: W.T.G. Morton Soc., Assn. Univ. Anesthesiologists (pres. 1973—74), Anaesthetic Rsch. Soc. (U.K.), Am. Soc. Pharmacology and Exptl. Therapeutics, Soc. Acad. Anesthesia Chmn. (rep. to Coun. Acad. Soc. Assn. Am. Med. Coll. 1984—91, mem. coun.), Am. Soc. Anesthesiologists, Am. Physiol. Soc., Inst. Medicine NAS, AAAS, Alpha Omega Alpha, Sigma Xi, Phi Beta Kappa. Office: Dept Anesthesiology PO Box 800710 Charlottesville VA 22908-0710 Business E-Mail: rme@virginia.edu.

EPSTEIN, SAMUEL ABRAHAM, sales executive; b. NYC, Sept. 14, 1956; s. Isidore and Mamie (Kosofsky) E.; m. Peggy Ann Eisenberg, July 4, 1979; children: David, Daniel, Rebecca. BS in Geology, Bklyn. Coll., 1977; MS in Geology, Rensselear Poly. Inst., 1979. Rsch. asst. Steinetz Marine Lab., Elat, Israel, 1978-79; petroleum geologist Cities Svc. Co., Houston, 1979-82; sr. petroleum geologist Getty Oil Co./Texaco, Houston, 1982-85; with Morgan Stanley, Houston, N.Y.C., 1985—, first v.p. investments, retirement planning specialist N.Y.C., 1998-99, World Trade Ctr. br. taxable fixed income coord., 1996-98, CPA continuing edn. instr. N.Y. State Investment Adv. Svcs., 1996-97, br. equity and taxable fixed income coord., 1999, sales mgr. World Trade Ctr. Office, 1999—2001, sales mgr. Penn Plz., 2001—02, 1st v.p./retiring planning specialist, 2002—. Author articles on interest rates; contbr. articles to petroleum industries profl. publs. Mem. Prime Mins. Club State of Israel Bonds, 1987-92; bd. overseers Lander Coll. for Touro Coll.; bd. dirs. Ohav Zedet, Queens, N.Y. Recipient Bklyn. Coll. Disting. Geol. Alumni award, CUNY, 1990. Mem. Am. Assn. Petroleum Geologists (cert.), NY Acad. Scis. (co-chmn. geol. scis. sect. 1998-2002). Jewish. Avocations: weight training, walking, geology, oceanography. Home: 173 Beach 134 St Far Rockaway NY 11694-1965 Office Phone: 212-613-6701. E-mail: sam_epstein@morganstanley.com.

EPSTEIN, SIDNEY, architect, civil engineer; b. Chgo., 1923; m. Sondra Berman, Sept. 4, 1987; children from previous marriage: Donna Epstein Barrows, Laurie Epstein Lawton. BS in Civil Engring. with high honors, U. Ill., 1943. Various positions A. Epstein & Sons Internat.; chmn. A. Epstein & Sons Internat., Inc., Chgo. Bd. dirs. Polk Bros. Found., Michael Reese Health Trust; trustee emeritus Northwestern Mut. Life Ins. Co. Founder, bd. dirs., past chmn. Chgo. Youth Ctrs.; past chmn. bd. trustees Michael Reese Hosp. and Med. Ctr.; bd. govs., life mem. U. Chgo. Hosps. and Clinics; life trustee Orchestral Assn. Chgo. Mem.: Standard Club (life; past pres.), Chi Epsilon, Phi Eta Sigma, Phi Kappa Phi, Sigma Tau, Tau Beta Pi, Sigma Xi. Home: 1430 N Lake Shore Dr Chicago IL 60610-6682 Office: A Epstein & Sons Internat Inc 600 W Fulton St Chicago IL 60661-1100 Office Phone: 312-429-8000. Business E-Mail: sidneyepstein@epstein-isi.com.

EPSTEIN, SUSAN BAERG, librarian, consultant; b. Chgo., Feb. 28, 1938; d. Philip William and Alice (Mackenzie) Ruppert; m. William Baerg, 1960 (div. 1971); children: Elisabeth Baerg, William Philip Baerg, Sara Margaret Baerg; m. A. H. Epstein, 1977 (div. 1981). BA in Econs., Wellesley Coll., 1960; MLS, Immaculate Heart Coll., 1972. Sys. analyst IBM, San Jose, Calif., 1960-63, Control Data Corp., Palo Alto, Calif., 1963-64; dir. tech. and automation svcs. Huntington Beach (Calif.) Pub. Libr., 1972-74, asst. city libr., 1974-78; spl. asst. to county libr. Los Angeles County Pub. Libr., L.A., 1978-81, chief tech. svcs., 1979-81; pres. Susan Baerg Epstein, Ltd., Costa Mesa, Calif., 1981—. Columnist: Libr. Jour., 1984—. Mem.: ALA (chair com.), Calif. Libr. Assn. (councilor 1973—80). Office: 1992 Lemnos Dr Costa Mesa CA 92626-3534 Office Phone: 714-754-1559. Personal E-mail: sbepstein@aol.com.

EPSTEIN, THEO N., professional sports team executive; b. Dec. 29, 1973; BA in Am. Studies, Yale U.; JD, U. San Diego. From with pub. rels. dept. to dir. baseball ops. San Diego (Calif.) Padres, dir. baseball ops.; gen. mgr. Boston (Mass.) Red Sox, 2002—. Office: 4 Yawkey Way Boston MA 02215

EPSTEIN, WILLIAM, experimental psychologist; b. N.Y.C., Nov. 23, 1931; s. Jacob and Sarah (Kaplan) E.; m. Sheena J. Rogers, Apr. 22, 1989; 1 child: Maggie Eliana Rogers; children from previous marriage: Sara Ann, Edith Lynn. BA, NYU, 1955; MA, New Sch. Social Research, 1957, PhD, 1959; PhD (hon.), U. Uppsala, Sweden, 1992. Asst. prof. psychology U. Kans., 1959—62, assoc. prof., 1962-65, prof., 1965-68; prof. psychology U. Wis.-Madison, 1968-96, prof. emeritus, 1996—, chmn. dept., 1975-79. Vis. prof. Cambridge (Eng.) U., 1972-73, U. Va., 1997—; Fulbright rsch. fellow, vis. prof. Delhi (India) U., 1981-82; vis. fellow Wolfson Coll., Oxford U., Eng. Author: Varieties of Perceptual Learning, 1967, (with F.C. Shontz) Psychology in Progress, 1971, Stability and Constancy in Visual Perception, 1977, (with G. Jansson and S.S. Bergstrom) Perceiving Events and Objects, 1994; (with S. Rogers) Handbook of Perception and Cognition, Vol. 5 Perception of Space and Motion, 1995; cons. editor Perception and Psychophysics, 1971-82; editor Jour. Exptl. Psychology: Human Perception and Performance, 1982-88. NSF sr. postdoctoral fellow U. Uppsala, Sweden, 1966-67; grantee NIMH, 1959—93, NSF, 1987—93. Fellow Am. Psychol. Assn., Soc. Exptl. Psychologists; mem. AAAS, Psychonomic Soc., Sigma Xi. Office: Univ Va Gilmer Hall Charlottesville VA 22840 Home: 1820 Dairy Rd Charlottesville VA 22903-1308 Business E-Mail: we7v@virginia.edu.

EPSTEIN, WILLIAM LOUIS, dermatologist, educator; b. Cleve., Sept. 6, 1925; s. Norman N. and Gertrude (Hirsch) E.; m. Joan Goldman, Jan. 29, 1954; children: Wendy, Steven. AB, U. Calif., Berkeley, 1949, MD, 1952. Mem. faculty U. Calif., San Francisco, 1957—, assoc. prof. div. dermatology, 1963-69, prof. div. dermatology, 1969—, dir. dermatol. rsch., 1957-70, acting chmn. div. dermatology, 1966-69, chmn. dept. dermatology, 1970-85. Cons. dermatology Outpatient Dept.; cons. various hosps. Calif. Dept. Public Health; cons. Food and Drug Adminstrn., Washington, 1972—, Dept. Agriculture, 1979; dir. div. research Nat. Program Dermatology, 1970-73; Dohi lectr., Tokyo, 1982; Beecham lectr., 1988-89; Nippon Boehringer Ingelheim lectr. 18th Hakone Symposium on Respiration, Japan, 1990. Decorated medal of honor Order of the Rising Sun, gold rays with neck ribbon (Japan). Mem. AAAS, AMA, Am. Soc. Cell Biology, Am. Acad. Dermatology and Syphlology (nominating com. 1984), Am. Contact Dermatology Soc. (hon.), Pacific Dermatologic Assn., Am. Fedn. Clin. Rsch., Am. Contact Dermatitis Soc. (hon.), Soc. Investigative Dermatology (bd. dirs., pres. 1985), Am. Dermatol. Assn., Assn. Profs. Dermatology (sr. mem.), Dermatology Found. (pres. 1986-87), Phi Beta Kappa, Sigma Xi. Home: 267 Golden Hinde Psge Corte Madera CA 94925-1953 Office Fax: 415-681-9165. Personal E-mail: wle@itsa.ucsf.edu. E-mail: jngepstn@aol.com.

EPSTIEN, JAY ALAN, lawyer; b. Newark, May 23, 1951; s. Leonard and Lorraine (Pedd) E.; children: Jessica, Shira; m. Nancy Elizabeth Kirsch, June 1, 1996. BS, Case Western Res. U., 1973; JD, Cornell U., 1976. Bar: D.C. 1976, N.J. 1976, U.S. Supreme Ct. 1977. Indsl. engr. Ortho Pharm., Somerset, N.J., 1973, Shaw, Pittman, Potts & Trowbridge, Washington, 1976—2000, ptnr., 1984—96, chmn. bus. dept., 1994-95; mng. ptnr. Rudnick, Wolfe, Epstien & Zeidman, Washington, 1996-99; co-mng. ptnr. Piper Rudnick LLP, Washington, 1999—2003, co-chmn. real estate dept., 2003—04; chmn. real estate dept. DLA Piper Rudnick Gray Cary US LLP, Washington, 2005—. Mem. adv. bd. Advanced Comml. Leasing Inst., Georgetown Univ. Law Ctr., 1998—2001. Editor: Cornell Law Rev., 1975—76. Bd. dirs. greater Washington region Am. Heart Assn., 1998—2001. Named Top Real Estate Lawyer in Washington, Washington Bus. Jour.; named one of Top Lawyers in Washington, Washingtonian Mag., 2004. Mem.: Anglo-Am. Real Property Inst., Am. Coll. Real Estate Lawyers (bd. govs. 2001—), Internat. Coun. Shopping Ctrs. (chmn. D.C. govt. affairs 1989—96), Fed. City Council. Avocation: golf. Office: DLA Piper Rudnick Gray Cary 1200 19th St NW Fl 7 Washington DC 20036-2412 Office Phone: 202-861-3850. Office Fax: 202-223-2085. Business E-Mail: jay.epstien@dlapiper.com.*

ERASLAN, HULYA K., finance educator; b. Kayseri, Turkey, July 8, 1969; d. Kadir and Nesrin Kuzucu; m. Emin Suat Eraslan, June 27, 1993; 1 child, Tobrak Can. BS, Bilkent U., 1991; MA, SUNY Buffalo, 1994; PhD, U. Minn., 2000. Asst. prof. U. Pa., Phila., 2000—. Vis. scholar Fed. Res. Bank Phila., 2005—. Achievements include research in Political economy, bankruptcy reorganizations. Office: Univ Pennsylvania 2300 Steinberg Hall 3620 Locust Walk Philadelphia PA 19104-6367 Office Phone: 215-898-9424.

ERASMUS, CHARLES JOHN, anthropologist, educator; b. Pitts., Sept. 23, 1921; s. Percy Thomas and Alice E.; m. Helen Marjorie O'Brien, Feb. 18, 1943; children: Thomas Glen, Gwendolyn. BA, UCLA, 1942; MA, U. Calif., Berkeley, 1950, PhD, 1955. Field ethnologist Smithsonian Instn., Colombia, 1950-52; applied anthropologist AID, Western S.Am., 1952-54; research assoc. culture exchange project U. Ill., Champaign-Urbana, 1955-59; vis. prof. anthropology Yale U., New Haven, 1959-60; assoc. prof. U. N.C., Chapel Hill, 1960-62, U. Calif., Santa Barbara, 1962-64, prof., 1964-87, prof. emeritus, 1987—, chmn. dept. anthropology, 1964-68. Author: Man Takes Control: Cultural Development and American Aid, 1961, In Search of the Common Good: Utopian Experiments Past and Future, 1977, Contemporary Change in Traditional Communities of Mexico and Peru, 1978. Served with USN, 1942-45. Home: 6190 Barrington Dr Santa Barbara CA 93117-1758 Office: U Calif Dept Anthropology Santa Barbara CA 93106

ERB, BETTY JANE, retired real estate agent; b. Balt., July 10, 1930; d. Edgar Smith Shanks and Delora Hickman Cockrum; m. William Cornelius Smith, Oct. 14, 1950 (div. Aug. 11, 1966); children: Stephen Cole Smith, Scott Douglas Smith, Cindy Lynn Smith; m. George Lewis Erb, Apr. 30, 1982. Grad., Manchester (Md.) HS, 1948. Mainframe computer operator Svc. Bur. Corp., Balt., 1974—86; real estate agt. Carroll County Assn. Realtors, Westminster, Md., 1988—2002. Mem.: Carroll County Coin Club (pres., v.p., sec., bd. dirs.). Baptist. Home: 402 Barnes Ave Westminster MD 21157

ERB, DONALD, composer; b. Youngstown, Ohio, Jan. 17, 1927; s. Tod and Janet (Griffith) E.; m. Lucille Hyman, June 10, 1950; children: Christine, Matthew, Stephanie, Janet. BS, Kent State U., 1950; MusM, Cleve. Inst. Music, 1953, MusD (hon.), 1984; MusD, Ind. U., 1964. Tchr. Cleve. Inst. Music, 1953-61, composer-in-residence, 1966-81, disting. prof. of composition, 1987-96; Meadows prof. composition So. Meth. U., 1981-84; composer-in-residence St. Louis Symphony, 1988-91; resident composer Am. Acad., Rome, 1991. Vis. asst. prof. rsch. electronic music Case Inst. Tech., 1965-67; composer-in-residence Dallas Symphony, 1968-69, Aspen Music Festival, 1993, Schweitzer Inst., 1994, 95; vis. prof. Ind. U., 1975-76, Calif. State U., L.A., 1977; prof. composition Ind. U., 1984-87; staff composer Bennington Composers Conf., 1969-73; resident composer June in Buffalo, 1984-96, composer-librettist panelist Nat. Endowment for Arts, 1973-79, chmn., 1977-79; performed at Warsaw Autumn Festival, 1971, 73, 94—; artist-in-residence Atlantic Ctr. for Arts, 1995. Composer: Dialogue for Violin and Piano, 1958, Correlations for Piano, 1959, Music for Violin and Piano, 1959, String Quartet No. 1, 1960, Sonata for Harpsichord and String Quartet, 1962, Chamber Concerto, 1961, Sonneries for Brass Choir, 1961, Four for Percussion, 1962, Bakersfield Pieces, 1962, Cumming's Cycle, 1963, Concertant for Harpsichord and Strings, 1963, Symphony of Overtures, 1964, VII Misc, 1964, Fallout?, 1964, Reticulation, 1965, Phantasma, 1965, Concert Piece 1, 1966, Diversion for Two, 1966, Stargazing, 1966, Concerto for Solo Percussion and Orchestra, 1966, Andante for Piccolo, Flute and Alto Flute, 1966, String Trio, 1966, Summermusic, 1966, Kyrie, 1967, Reconnaissance, 1967, In No Strange Land, 1968, the Seventh Trumpet, 1969, Basspiece, 1969, Klangfarbenfunk I, 1970, God Love You Now, 1971, Fanfare, 1971, The Purple-Roofed Ethical Suicide Parlor, 1972, Harold's Trip to the Sky, 1972, Concerto for Trombone and Orchestra, 1976, Quintet, 1976, Music for a Festive Occasion, 1976, Concerto for Violoncello and Orchestra, 1976, The Hawk, 1979, Cenotaph, 1979, Sonata for clarinet and percussino, 1980, Concerto for trumpet and orch., 1980, The Devil's Quickstep, 1982, Prismatic Variations, 1983, Concerto for clarinet and orch., 1984, The Rainbow Snake, 1985, The Dreamtime, 1985, Concerto for orch., 1985, Concerto for brass and orch., 1986, Three Poems for violin and piano, 1987, Solstice, 1988, Woody, 1988, Symphony for winds, 1989, String Quartet # 2, 1989, Five Red Hot Duets, 1989, Ritual Observances, 1991, Drawing down the Moon, 1991, Concerto for violin and orch., 1992, Evensong, 1993, Sonata for solo violin, 1994, Remembrances, 1994, Changes, 1994, Sonata for harp, 1995, Sunlit Peaks and Dark Valleys, 1995, String Quartet # 3, 1995, Suddenly It's Evening, 1997, others. Served with USNR, 1945-46. Recipient Disting. Alumni award Ind. U. Sch. Music, Naumberg Rec. award, 1974, Disting. Alumnus award Kent Sate U., 1982, Ohioana citation, 1978, award Am. Acad. Inst. Arts and Letters, 1985, Libr. of Congress Commn., 1987, Grammy nominee, 1994, Koussevitzky Commn., 1994, Fromm Found. Commn., 1994, Meet the Composer Commn., 1994, Ohioana Libr. Career award 1998, letter of distinction Am. Music Ctr., 2001; Ford Found. composer-in-residence Bakersfield, Calif., 1962-63; Rockefeller Found. grantee for performance Symphony of Overtures, 1965, grantee Nat. Coun. on Art, 1967-68, Nat. Endowment for Arts, 1980, 84, 91; Guggenheim fellow, 1965-66, fellow Bellagio Study and Conf. Ctr., 1979, 89, USA-Can. fellow NEA, 1995. Mem. Am. Music Center (pres. 1982-85), Broadcast Music, Cleve. Composers Guild, League ISCM (nat. adv. bd.). Home: 4073 Bluestone Rd Cleveland OH 44121-2465 E-mail: donalderb@aol.com.

ERB, JAMES BRYAN, music educator, conductor, musicologist; b. La Junta, Colo., Jan. 25, 1926; s. Tillman Harvey and Phebe Ann (King) E.; m. Ruth Hildegard Esther Urbancic, Mar. 1, 1952; children: Martin Georg, Paul David, Christina Elizabeth, Jonathan Tillman. BA, Colo. Coll., 1950; Staatszeugnis (Gesang), Staatsakademie Musik, Vienna, Austria, 1952; MM in Singing, Ind. U., 1954; MA, Harvard U., 1964, PhD, 1978. Tchr. City Schs., Cheyenne, Wyo., 1952-53; from instr. to assoc. prof. music U. Richmond, Va., 1954-78, prof., 1978-94, prof. emeritus, 1994—. Music dir. Cafur, Richmond, 1966-94; chorus master Richmond Symphony Chorus, 1971—. Arranger (choral adaptation) Shenandoah, 1975; editor: O. diLasso Sämtl-Werke, Neue Reihe, vols. 13-17, 1981-88; author: O. diLasso, A Guide to Research, 1990. With U.S. Army, 1944-46. Named Outstanding Educator, Va. Coun. Higher Edn., 1993; Tchr. study grantee Danforth Found., 1962-65, Study grantee Martha Baird Rockefeller Fund Music, 1968-69. Mem. Am. Musicological Soc., Am. Brahms Soc., Am. Renaissance Soc., Gesellschaft Für Bayerische Musikgeschichte. Home: 4703 Patterson Ave Richmond VA 23226-1343

ERB, KARL ALBERT, physicist, government official; b. Chgo., June 30, 1942; s. Edgar Gillette and Dorothy (Carsten) E.; children: Janet, Margaret. BA, NYU, 1965; MS, U. Mich., 1966, PhD, 1970. Instr. U. Pitts., 1970-72; instr., asst. prof., assoc. prof. Yale U., New Haven, 1972-80; staff scientist Oak Ridge (Tenn.) Nat. Lab., 1980-86; program dir. NSF, Washington, 1986-89, dep. dir. physics divsn., 1991; asst. dir. White House Office Sci. and Tech. Policy, Washington, 1989-91; acting assoc. dir. for phys. scis. and engring. White House Office of Sci. and Tech. Policy, Washington, 1991-92, assoc. dir. for phys. scis. engring., 1992-93; sr. sci. advisor NSF, 1993-98; dir. office of polar programs NSF and U.S. Antarctic Program, 1998—. Exec. sec. Pres.'s Com. for the Nat. Medal of Sci., 1993-99; exec. com. Fed. Demonstration Partnership, 1996-99; chmn. Com. Mgrs. Nat. Antarctic Program, 2000-04; U.S. rep. Arctic Sci. Coun. Regional Bd.; vice chair APS Com. on Internat. Sci., 1999-2002, mem. U.S. Nuc. Sci. Adv. Com., Washington, 1983-86; vis. prof. J.W. Goethe U., Frankfurt, 1978; bd. govs. U.S.-Indo. S&T forum, 2001-02. Contbr. articles to physics jours. and encys., chpts. to books. Recipient Pres. Sr. Exec. Svc. Meritorious award, 1998, 2003. Fellow AAAS, Am. Phys. Soc. Office: NSF 4201 Wilson Blvd Arlington VA 22230-0001 E-mail: kerb@nsf.gov.

ERB, RICHARD LOUIS LUNDIN, resort and hotel executive; b. Chgo., Dec. 23, 1929; s. Louis Henry and Miriam (Lundin) E.; m. Jean Elizabeth Easton, Mar. 14, 1959; children: John Richard, Elizabeth Anne, James Easton, Richard Louis II. BA, U. Calif., Berkeley, 1951, postgrad., 1952; student, San Francisco Art Inst., 1956. Cert. hotel adminstr. Asst. gen. mgr. Grand Teton Lodge Co., Jackson Hole, Wyo., 1954-62; mgr. Mauna Kea Beach Hotel, Hawaii, 1964-66; v.p., gen. mgr. Caneel Bay Plantation, Inc., St. John, V.I., 1966-75; gen. mgr. Williamsburg (Va.) Inn, 1975-78; exec. v.p., gen. mgr. Seabrook Island Co., Johns Island, S.C., 1978-80; v.p., dir. hotels Sands Hotel and Casino, Inc., Atlantic City, 1980-81; v.p., gen. mgr. Disneyland Hotel, Anaheim, Calif., 1981—82; COO Grand Traverse Resort, Grand Traverse Village, Mich., 1982—93; gen. mgr. Stein Eriksen Lodge, Deer Valley, Utah, 1993-96; pres. The Erb Group, 1996—. Pres. Spruce-Park Mgmt. Co., 1989; mem. adv. bd. travel and tourism Mich. State U., 1992-96; vice-chmn.

Charleston (S.C.) Tourism Coun., 1979-81; bd. dirs. Anaheim Visitors and Conv. Bur., 1981-82, Grand Traverse Conv. and Visitors Bur., 1985-90, U.S. 131 Area Devel. Assn., 1983-93; sr. cons. Cayuga Hosp. Advisors, 1996—. Contbr. articles to trade jours. Vice-pres. V.I. Montessori Sch., 1969-71, bd. dirs., 1968-76; bd. dirs. Coll. of V.I., 1976-79; adv. bd. U. S.C., 1978-82, Calif. State Poly. Inst., 1981-82, Orange Coast C.C., 1981-82, Northwestern Mich. Coll., 1983-93; adv. bd. hospitality mgmt. program Ea. Mich. U., 1989-93; trustee Munson Med. Ctr., Traverse City, 1985-93; bd. dirs. Traverse Symphony Orch., 1984-88, N.A. Vasa, 1987-89; adv. panel Mich. Communities of Econ. Excellence Program, 1984-88; mem. hospitality adv. bd. Utah Valley State Coll., 1994-98. Lt. arty. U.S. Army, 1952-54. Named hon. prof. Mich. State U. Hotel Sch., 1992—. Fellow Edn. Inst.; mem. Am. Hotel and Motel Assn. (dir. 1975-77, 90-94, exec. bd. 1991-94, Service Merit award 1976, Lawson Odde award 1993, Gold Medalist Membership award 1993, trustee Ednl. Inst. 1977-83, mktg. com., exec. com. 1978-83, chmn. projects and programs com. 1982-98, AH&MA resort com. 1986-96, AH&MA condominium com. 1985-96, chmn. ratings com. 1988-96, Ambassador award 1986, Blue Ribbon task force 1988-89, Resort Exec. of Yr. 1988), Caribbean Hotel Assn. (1st v.p. 1972-74, dir. 1970-76, hon. life mem., Extraordinary Service Merit award 1974), V.I. Hotel Assn. (pres. chmn. bd. 1971-76, Merit award 1973), Calif. Hotel Assn. (dir. 1981-82), Caribbean Travel Assn. (dir. 1972-74), Internat. Hotel Assn. (dir. 1971-73), S.C. Hotel Assn. (dir. 1978-82), Am. Hotel Assn. Edn. Inst., (Lamp of Knowledge award 1988), Va. Hotel Assn., Williamsburg Hotel Assn. (bd. dirs. 1975-78), Atlantic City Hotel Assn. (v.p. 1981-82), Atlantic City Casino Assn. (dir. 1981-82), Cornell Soc. Hotelmen, Mich. Travel and Tourist Assn. (bd. dirs. 1983-94, treas. 1986, sec. 1987, v.p. 1988, mktg. com. 1986-93, govtl. affairs com. 1986-93, chmn. edn. com. 1983-84, chmn. bd. 1989-90, Mich. Hotelier of Yr. 1991), Mich. Restaurant Assn. (bd. dirs. 1989-91, chmn. adminstrv. com. 1989-90), Mich. Gov.'s Task Force on Tourism, 1986-87, Grand Island Adv. Commn., Traverse City C. of C. (bd. dirs. 1984-89), Nat. Restaurant Assn., Utah Hotel and Motel Assn. (bd. dirs. 1994-96, treas. 1996), Leadership Grand Traverse (exec. com. 1984-92, fellow 1992), Park City Lodging Assn. (bd. dirs. 1993-96), Park City C. of C. (bd. dirs. 1994-97), Tavern Club, Rotary (Paul Harris fellow 1990), Beta Theta Pi. Congregationalist. Office Phone: 435-649-5605. Personal E-mail: RichardErb@aol.com.

ERB, ROBERT ALLAN, physical scientist; b. Ridley Park, Pa., Jan. 30, 1932; s. John Walter and Roma (Chapman) E.; m. Doretta Louise Barker, June 27, 1953; children: Sylvia Ann, Susan Doretta, Carolyn Joy. BS in Chemistry, U. Pa., 1953; MS, Drexel Inst. Tech., 1959; PhD, Temple U., 1965. Chemist Gates Engrng. Co., Wilmington, Del., 1953-54; with Franklin Rsch. Ctr., divsn. Franklin Inst. (later divsn. Arvin/Calspan), Phila., 1954-93, sr. staff chemist, 1965-68, prin. scientist, 1968-81, Inst. fellow, 1981-84, staff scientist, 1985-93; tech. dir. SiliClone Studio, Valley Forge, Pa., 1993—. Mem. AAAS, Am. Anaplastology Assn. (pres. 1996-97), Am. Chem. Soc., Soc. Plastics Engrs., The Franklin Inst., Sigma Xi. Presbyterian. Inventor human simulators, medical and prosthetic devices, solar collectors, permanent systems for dropwise condensation, contraceptive systems, composites using waste plastics. Home and Office: PO Box 86 Valley Forge PA 19481-0086 *Success is to know God's will for your life and to do it.*

ERBAS, SEYITALI NURI, economist, researcher; b. Izmir, Turkey, Jan. 1, 1953; s. Mahmut and Firuzan Ayse Erbas; m. Chera Lee Sayers, May 19, 1990; children: Serra April, Ayse Juliet. BA, Bogazici U., Istanbul, Turkey, 1975, MA, 1976; PhD, M Phil., Columbia U., N.Y., 1982. Asst. prof. U. Hawaii, Honolulu, 1982—84, U. Houston, 1984—89; sr. economist IMF, Washington, 1989—. Free lectr. IMF, Washington, 1989. Recipient Rectorate Award, Bogazici Univ., 1975. Mem.: Internat. Inst. of Pub. Fin. (assoc.). Achievements include research in Economics. Office: Internat Monetary Fund 700 19th St NW Washington DC 00431 Office Phone: 202-623-8348. Personal E-mail: sebas@imf.org. Business E-Mail: serbas@imf.org.

ERBE, GARY THOMAS, artist; b. Union City, NJ, Sept. 2, 1944; s. Herman Charles and Florance (Bertone) Erbe; m. Zeny Erbe; children: Kim, Chantell. Student pub. schs., Union City. One man shows Pace Gallery, Houston, 1970, Veldman Gallery, Milw., 1971, New Britain Mus. Am. Art, 1976, 95, Summit (NJ) Art Ctr., 1976, Bergen Cmty. Mus., Paramus, NJ, 1979, Alexander Gallery, NYC, 1982, 85, NJ State Mus., Trenton, 1983, Butler Inst. Am. Art, Youngstown, Ohio, 1985, 94-95, Sordon: Art Gallery, Wilkes Barre, Pa., 1985, Montclair Art Mus., NJ, 1988, Westmoreland (Pa.) Mus. Art, 1988, Canton (Ohio) Art Inst., 1988, Woodmere Art Mus., Phila., 1988, James A. Michener Art Mus., Doylestown, Pa., 1995, Boca Raton (Fla.) Mus. Art, 1995, ACA Gallery, NYC, 1998, Springfield (Mo.) Art Mus., 1999, Nat. Arts Club, NYC, 2000; exhibited in group shows at Newark Mus., 1971, Rutgers U., 1971, Heritage Gallery, NYC, 1972, NJ State Mus., 1972, 75, Baseball Hall of Fame, Cooperstown, NY, 1991, Morris Mus., NJ, 1994, ACA Gallery, NYC, 1998, 2000, Springfield Art Mus., Mo., 1999, Albuquerque Mus., 1999, Meridian Internat. Ctr., Washington, 1999, Mus. Fine Arts, Hanoi, Vietnam, 1999, Mus. Fine Arts, Ho Chi Minh, Vietnam, 1999, Painting Inst., Shanghai, China, 1999, Singapore Mus. Art, 1999, CIPTA Gallery, Jakarta (Indonesia) Arts Ctr., 1999—, Met. Mus. of Manila, Iran, Albuquerque Mus., 1999, Met. Mus. Manila, 2000, Bradford Brinton Meml. Mus. Wyo., 2002, Meridian Internat. Ctr., Washington, 2002, Topkapi Mus., Turkey, 2002, Ankara Mus. Turkey, 2002, Hanager Arts Ctr., Cairo, 2003, Alexandria, Egypt, 2003, Rabat, Morocco, 2003, Casablanca, Morocco, 2003, Allied Mus., Berlin, Germany, 2003, Trompe L'Oeil Internat., Eleanor Ettinger Gallery, NYC, 2003, Harmon-Meek Gallery, Naples, Fla., 2003; represented in permanent collections Butler Inst. Am. Art, NJ State Mus., New Britain Mus. Am. Art, Montclair Art Mus., Woodmere Art Mus., Archives Am. Art, Nat. Arts Club, NYC, Springfield (Mo.) Art Mus., Phoenix Art Mus., Bradford Brinton Meml. Mus., Wyo., Nat. Arts Club, NYC Recipient Julius Hallgarten award NAD, 1975, 1st award Salmagundi Club, 1975, Noyes Mus., N.J., 1992, The Gilmore Romans Meml. award Allied Artists Am., 1993; nat. mid-yr. 1st pl. award Butler Inst. Am. Art, 2002, Silver medal Audubon Artists, N.Y.C., 2002. Mem. Allied Artists Am. (Gold medal of honor 1975, 84, 91, John Young-Hunter Meml. award 1982, 85, Emily Lowe award 1989), Conn. Acad. Fine Arts, Assoc. Artists N.J., Audubon Artists (Emily Lowe award 1991, Beatrice Jackson Humphreys Meml. award 1992, Stephan Hirsch Meml. award 1994, gold medal of honor 1998, silver medal 2002), Allied Artists Am. (pres. 1994—), Nat. Arts Club (N.Y.C., 1st award 99th Ann. Members Exhbn., Salzman award 100th Ann. Members Exhbn. 1998, Nat. Midyear 1st pl. award Butler Inst. Am. Art 2002, Art Medal for Life Achievement in the Arts, 2003), Artists Fellowship, Inc. (N.Y.C., trustee 1997—), Trompe L'Oeil Soc. Artists. Achievements include development of contemporary approach to Am. Trompe l'oeil called Levitational Realism, extention of school to 3 dimensional compositions, oil on bronze. Office: 539 42nd St Union City NJ 07087-2606

ERBE, JOAN, artist; b. Balt., Nov. 1, 1926; children from previous marriage: Joan Randolph Edwards, Constance Carver Edwards; m. George Udel, May 22, 1956 (dec. Nov. 1999); 1 child, Jacob. Student, Md. Inst. Coll. Art, 1937-55. Painting tchr., 1956—. Numerous one-woman shows including Balt. Mus. Art, 1966, Nat. Acad. Arts & Letters, NYC, 1980, Gomez Gallery, Balt., 1991; represented in permanent collections Balt. Mus. Art, Corcoran Gallery of Art, U. D., Mcpl. Ct. DC, Morgan State U., Main St. Gallery, Annapolis, Md., Renaissance Gallery, Bethesda, Md., Kent Galleries, Key West, Fla.; represented in pvt. collections. Recipient over 25 best of show and purchase awards. Home: 2909 Fallstaff Rd Apt 18 Baltimore MD 21209

ERBER, THOMAS, mathematics professor, physics professor; b. Vienna, Dec. 6, 1930; m. Audrey Burns. BSc, MIT, 1951; MS, U. Chgo., 1953, PhD in Physics, 1957. Asst. prof. physics Ill. Inst. Tech., Chgo., 1957-62, assoc. prof., 1962-69, prof., 1969—, prof. math., 1986—, disting. prof., 1999—. Vis. scientist Stanford Linear Accelerator Ctr., 1970; prof. physics U. Graz, 1971, 82, hon prof., 1971—; prof. physics UCLA, 1978-79, 84-85, 87-92, 2006, U. Grenoble, 1982; prof. physics U. Chgo., 1998-99; adv. bd. rsch. corp. Mem. editl. bd. Acta Physica Austriaca. Rsch. fellow, Brussels, Belgium, 1963-64. Fellow: Inst. Physics (U.K.), Am. Math. Soc., Am. Phys. Soc.; mem.: IEEE (life sr.), Nuclear, Plasma & Magnetics Soc., Am. Acad. Mechanics, Am. Radio Relay League, Magnetics Soc., Oesterreichische Physikalische Gesellschaft, European Phys. Soc. Office: Ill Inst Tech Dept Physics Chicago IL 60616

ERBER, WILLIAM FRANKLIN, gastroenterologist; b. N.Y.C., June 1, 1941; s. Sigmund and Marcia (Picard) E.; m. Ingrid Amelia Friedler, Dec. 25, 1967; children: Gregory, Karina, Jonathan, Joanna, Jeremy. BS, Muhlenberg Coll., 1963; MD, U. Health Sci., Chgo., 1967. Diplomate Am. Bd. Internal Medicine and Gastroenterology. Intern Maimonides Hosp., 1967-68, resident, 1968-69, 71-72; fellowship in gastroenterology Albert Einstein Coll. of Medicine, 1973-75; rsch. fellow Hadassah Hosp., Jerusalem, 1971-72; clin. asst. prof. Health Sci. Ctr., Bklyn., 1975—. Cons. Crohn's Colitis Found., N.Y.C., 1975—, H.I.P., N.Y.C., 1975—; attending gastroenterologist Maimonides Med. Ctr., Bklyn., 1975—. Author: Internal Medicine Review, 1979; contbr. articles to profl. jours. Maj. USAF, 1969-71. Fellow: ACP, Am. Coll. Gastroenterology; mem.: Am. Soc. Gastroenterol. Endoscopy, Am. Gastroenterol. Assn. Avocations: music, piano, skiing. Office: 591 Ocean Pkwy Brooklyn NY 11218-5913 Home: 159 Beach 147th St Neponsit NY 11694 Office Phone: 718-972-8500. Personal E-mail: ef591@aol.com.

ERBSEN, CLAUDE ERNEST, retired journalist; b. Trieste, Italy, Mar. 10, 1938; came to U.S., 1951, naturalized, 1956; s. Henry M. and Laura Elena (Treves) E.; m. Jill J. Prosky, July 16, 1959; 1 dau., Diana Lisa; m. Hedy Miriam Cohn, Apr. 7, 1970; children: Allan Henry, Michael David. BA cum laude, Amherst Coll., 1959; Inter-Am. Press Assn. scholar, U. Andes, Bogota, Colombia, 1960. Reporter-printer Amherst Jour.-Record, 1955-57; staff reporter El Tiempo, Bogota, 1960; with AP, 1960-1965, newsman in N.Y.C., Miami, Fla., Washington; to chief of bur. Brazil, 1965—69; exec. rep. for Latin Am., 1969—70; bus. mgr., adminstrv. dir. AP-Dow Jones Econ. Report, N.Y.C., 1970-75; dep. dir. world services AP, N.Y.C., 1975-80; v.p., dir. AP-Dow Jones News Svcs., London, 1980—87; v.p., dir. world services AP, N.Y.C., 1987—2003, ret., 2003; sr. cons., dir. Innovation Internat. Media Cons. Group, 2003—. Bd. dirs. World Press Inst., St. Paul. Served to lt. USNR, 1961-65. Recipient San Giusto D'Oro award City of Trieste, 1995. Mem. Internat. Press Inst., Coun. Fgn. Rels., World Assn. of Newspapers. Home: 27 Stratton Rd Scarsdale NY 10583-7556

ERBSTEIN, KEITH SANDY, lawyer; b. N.Y.C., Mar. 6, 1946; s. Leo and Irma (Goldstein) E.; m. Theresa Erbstein; children: David, Sara, Jessica. BA, SUNY, Buffalo, 1967; JD, Temple U., 1970. Bar: Pa. 1970, U.S. Dist. Ct. (mid. and ea. dists.) Pa. 1972, U.S. Ct. Appeals (1st cir.) 1972, U.S. Ct. Appeals (3d cir.) 1976, U.S. Supreme Ct. 1978. Ptnr. The Beasley Firm LLC, Phila., 1970—; judge pro tem Ct. Common Pleas, Philadelphia County. Mem. hearing com. Disciplinary Bd. of Supreme Ct. of Pa., 1988-94. Mem. editorial bd. Temple U. Law Rev., 1969-70. Recipient Disting. Pa. Super Lawyer, 2005. Mem. ATLA (lectr.), Phila. Bar Assn. (med.-legal com. 1981-82, select com. for disposition civil cases 1983), Pa. Bar Assn., Pa.Trial Lawyers Assn. (lectr.), Phila. Trial Lawyers Assn. (bd. dirs. 1982-86, chmn. products liability com. 1983-85, musmanno com., lectr.), Am. Bd. Trial Advocates (advocate). Office: The Beasley Firm 1125 Walnut St Philadelphia PA 19107-4918 Business E-Mail: kse@beasleyfirm.com.

ERBURU, ROBERT F., publishing executive; b. Ventura, Calif., Sept. 27, 1930; BA, U. So. Calif., 1952; JD, Harvard U. Law Sch., 1955. Chmn. bd., CEO, pres. Times Mirror Co., LA, bd. dirs. Chmn. Reserve Bank of San Francisco, 1989—91; bd. dirs. Marsh & McLennan Co., Inc., NYC, 1996—, lead dir., 2004—, non-exec. chmn., 2005—. Mem. trustees coun. Nat. Gallery Art, Washington, DC, 1985—93, mem. bd. trustees, 1993—, chmn., 2000—; chmn. bd. Huntington Libr., Art Collections, and Botanical Gardens; chmn. emeritus J. Paul Getty Trust; trustee William and Flora Hewlett Found., Ahmanson Found. Mem. Newspaper Assn. Am. (bd. govs., exec. bd., exec. com., bd. dirs. 1980-92, officer 1988-92, chmn. 1991-92), Coun. Fgn. Rels. (bd. dirs.), Calif. Bus. Roundtable, Bus. Coun., past dir. C of C of U.S., L.A. Area C of C. Home: 1518 Blue Jay Way Los Angeles CA 90069-1215 Office: Marsh & McLennan Co, Inc 1166 Ave of Americas New York NY 10036*

ERCKLENTZ, ALEXANDER TONIO, investment company executive; b. NYC, July 13, 1936; s. Enno Wilhelm and Hildegard (Schlubach) E.; children: Alexander Tonio Jr., Christina Titaua, Nicholas Ley. BA, Yale U.; postgrad, NYU. Various positions Brown Brothers Harriman & Co., N.Y.C., 1959-77, ptnr., 1978—. Bd. dirs. AXA Art Ins. Corp., Stinnes Corp. Pres. Am. Berlin Opera Found.; trustee Am. U. Beirut. Mem.: Field Club, Stanwich Club, The Links. Roman Catholic. Office: Brown Brothers Harriman & Co 140 Broadway New York NY 10005-1101

ERCKLENTZ, ENNO WILHELM, JR., lawyer; b. N.Y.C., Jan. 27, 1931; s. Enno Wilhelm and Hildegard (Schlubach) E.; m. Mai A. Vilms, Sept. 20, 1969; children: Cornelia, Stephanie. AB, Columbia U., 1954; JD, Harvard U., 1957. Bar: N.Y. 1958. Assoc. Curtis, Mallet-Prevost, Colt & Mosle, N.Y.C., 1957-60; sec., gen. counsel Channing Fin. Corp., N.Y.C., 1960-69; v.p., sec., gen. counsel Inverness Mgmt. Corp., N.Y.C., 1969-75; pvt. practice N.Y.C., 1975-78; ptnr. Whitman & Ransom, N.Y.C., 1978-87, Greeven & Ercklentz, N.Y.C., 1987-98; pvt. practice N.Y.C., 1998—. Author: Modern German Corporation Law, 1979. Mem. ABA, N.Y. State Bar Assn., Assn. of Bar City of N.Y., Am. Fgn. Law Assn. Republican. Roman Catholic. Office: Enno W Ercklentz Jr PC 620 Fifth Ave 5th flr New York NY 10020-2457 Office Phone: 212-632-3560. Business E-Mail: ennoerck@aol.com.

ERDELJAC, DANIEL JOSEPH, retired manufacturing company executive; b. Farmington, W.Va., Aug. 27, 1932; s. Phillip John, Mary M. (Hudak) E.; m. Constance June Sabatino, June 25, 1955; children— Daniel J. II, James M., Mary L., Laurie A. Grad. high sch., Farmington, W.Va. Materials mgr. South Union Coal Co., Edna, W.Va., 1952-60; plant mgr. Interpace Corp., various locations, 1960-70; pres., exec. v.p. Hydro Conduit Corp., Houston, 1970-92, pres., 1980-82, ret., 1992; divsn. mgr. Brooks Products, Houston, 1995-96, ret., 1996. Past chmn. Am. Concrete Pipe Assn. Roman Catholic. Avocations: grandchildren, investments.

ERDELY, STEPHEN LAJOS, music educator; b. Szeged, Hungary, May 6, 1921; came to U.S., 1949, naturalized, 1954; s. Jeno and Vilma (Lengyel) Erdelyi; m. Beatrice Eppinelle, Sept. 28, 1952. Absolutorium, Nat. Franz Liszt Music Acad., 1939-44, Franz Josef U., 1944; PhD, Case Western Res. U., 1962. Faculty Ohio State U., Toledo, 1966-73; prof. music M.I.T., Cambridge, Mass., 1973—, dir. music, 1976—; mem. faculty Divsn. Continuing Edn. Harvard U. Rsch. assoc. Milman Perry Collection, Harvard U., faculty mem. divsn. continuing edn. Soloist, Munich (Ger.) Chamber Music Dept., 1946-49, Cleve. Orch., 1951-66, concert artist with, The Erdely Duo, 1951—; Author: Methods and Principles of Hungarian Ethnomusicology, 1965, Music of South Slavic Epics From The Bihac Region of Bosnia, 1995; contbr. articles to profl. jours. Am. Philos. Soc. grantee, 1962; Am. Council Learned Socs. grantee, 1964; Nat. Endowment for Arts grantee, 1974-77, 83-85 Mem. Am. Musicol. Soc. Soc. for Ethnomusicology (councilor 1970-73), Internat. Folk Music Council, Ohio Folklore Soc. (pres. 1967-69), Internat. Musicology Soc., Coll. Music Soc. Office: MIT Dept Humanities Cambridge MA 02139 Fax: 978-371-7046.

ERDELY-SAYO, SANDRINE, musician, educator; b. Perpignan, France, Oct. 11, 1968; d. Daniele Sayo and Gerald Erdely. MusM, U. Arts, Phila., 1990—92. Accompanist U. Arts, 1990—92; prof. piano and music theory Conservatoire, Phila., 1993—. Musician (concert pianist): Chgo. debut at Preston Bradley Hall, (concerts) Louvre Mus., Festival of Hispanidad, Festival Bach, Internat. Jewish Film Festival. Mem. World Jewish Congress, 1998, B'nai B'rith, 1998. Recipient prize winner, Ibla Internat. Piano Competition, First Prize, Bellan Competition, 1980, D. Reinhardt Medal award, French Min. Culture, France, 1983, Gold Medalist, Scene Française Piano Competition, Paris, 1987, Company Steinway award, 1992; scholar Prize, Mediterranean Festival, France, 1991. Mem.: ULTRANET, Internat. Soc. Philosophical Inquiry, High IQ for Humanity (hon.). Achievements include recordings of integral work of Primitivo Lazaro in two CDs; composed 3 pieces for chamber orchestra played at Châtelet Theater in Paris. Office Phone: 215-546-9659. Home Fax: 215-546-9659. Personal E-mail: erdelysayo@verizon.net. E-mail: sandrine@erdelysayo.com.

ERDEN, SYBIL ISOLDE, artist; b. N.Y.C., Nov. 30, 1950; d. Mark and Annelise (Stautner) E.; m. Philip M. Freund, July 7, 1970 (div. 1978); m. Jerry Buley, June 15, 1991 (div. 1998). Student, Acad. of Art, San Francisco, 1970-71, San Francisco Art Inst., 1971-73, Ariz. State U., 1992-93. Lectr. Calif. Coll. Arts and Crafts, 1978, Tempe Fine Art Ctr., 1985, Collins Gallery, San Francisco, 1986, Collage Art Appreciation Group, Colorado Springs, Colo., 1987, South Park Sch. Dist., Fairplay, Colo., 1987, Al Collins Sch. Graphic Design, 1989-90, Cerro Coso C.C., Calif., 1991, Chico State U., 1991; tchr. workshops City of Phoenix, 1991, Cerro Coso C.C., Calif., 1991, Chico State U., 1991, Phoenix Coll., 1992-94, Cochise Coll., 1993; guest spkr. Tempe Art Ctr. Seminar for Artists, 1993, Mesa C.C., 1994-96; invited spkr. Animal Rights 2003, L.A., 2003, Ann Arbor Bird Club, 2005, Salt Lake Bird Club, 2005, Las Vegas Agr. Soc., 2005, Pittsburgh Bird Club, 2003, Pet Bird Report Conf., 1998, 2001, Long Island Parrot Soc. Conf., 2000, 03, West LA Bird Club, 2000, Las Vegas Avicultural Soc., 1999, TARA (Tucson Avian Rescue and Adoption, 2002, Manhattan Bird Club, 2004. Exhibited in group shows including San Francisco Art Inst., 1973, The Bush Street Gallery, San Francisco, 1977, The Top Floor Gallery, San Francisco, 1979, I-Beam, San Francisco, 1980, Diablo Valley Coll., Walnut Creek, Calif., 1980, The Stable, San Francisco, 1982, Tempe Fine Arts Ctr., 1985, Collins Gallery, San Francisco, 1986, 89—, Berkeley (Calif.) Art Ctr., 1986, The Cave, San Francisco, 1981, Alwun House, Phoenix, 1985, 87-93 (award 1989), Grand Canyon Coll., Phoenix, 1988, N.Mex. Jr. Coll., 1988, 90 (award 1990), San Francisco State U., 1988, Pa. State U., 1989, Ohio State U., 1989, Mendocino Art Ctr., 1990, Jewish Cmty. Ctr., Denver, 1990, Cerro Coso C.C., Kern County, Calif., 1990-91, Chico State U., 1991, Sierra Arts Found., 1991, Ea. N.Mex. U., 1992, Shemer Art Ctr., Phoenix, 1991, Chico (Calif.) State U., 1992, Sierra Arts Found., Reno, 1992, IOA Artspace, Oklahoma City, 1995, Ariz. State U., 1996, Tempe Pub. Libr., 1996, La Bandera Vieja nat. traveling exhibit Ariz. Commn. on Arts; executed mural office of Dr. Peter Eckman, San Francisco, 1977, HandBall Express, San Francisco, 1981; archived by Smithsonian Mus. Archive Am. Art, Washington; columnist Cages Bird Hobbyist, 1996—, Companion Bird Quarterly (formerly Pet Bird Report) 1998-; contbr. articles to popular mags. Founder, dir., pres. Oasis Sanctuary Found., 1996—; co-founder/ bd. mem. Avian Welfare Coalition (AWC), 1999—2003; nat. rescue coord. Avian Welfare Coalition (AWC) Rescue Network, 2003; co-founder Avian Rescue Network (ARN), 2003—. Mem. Am. Surrealist Initiative, Ariz. Visionary Alternative (founder, dir. 1984-85, 87-95), Movemiento Artistico del Rio Salado Artspace (artist mem. 1995-98), LIC Rehabber For the Birds, Am. Fedn. Aviculturists, Assn. Avian Veterinarians, Am. Sanctuary Assn.(ASA), (bd. dirs., sec. 2003-), The Assn. of Sanctuaries (TAOS). Democrat. Jewish. Avocations: motorcycles, wildlife rescue and rehabilitation, animal welfare activist. Mailing: 5411 N Teran Rd Benson AZ 85602 Office Phone: 520-212-4737.

ERDMAN, DAVID WILLIAMS, lawyer; b. Camp Lejeune, NC, July 4, 1949; s. Lawrence Huntington and Marian (Williams) E.; m. Lynn Kendrick, Feb. 4, 1984; children: Natalie, Emily. BSE, Duke U., 1971; JD, Georgetown U., 1975. Bar: NC 1975. Rsch. staff asst. Watergate com. U.S. Senate, Washington, 1973; atty. N.C. State Bd. Edn., Raleigh, 1975-76; mem. campaign staff Jim Hunt for Gov. of N.C., Raleigh, 1976; assoc. Wardlow, Knox & Knox, Charlotte, N.C., 1977-81; ptnr. Erdman and Hockfield LLP, Charlotte, 1981—. Composer, performer 45 RPM recording On My Knees, 1967; developer Juriscan computer program, 1974. Mem.-at-large Charlotte City Coun., 1999; mem. N.C. Employment Security Commn., Raleigh, 1978-82. Angier B. Duke scholar, 1967. Mem. Met. Bus. Coun., Charlotte C. of C. (bd. advisors 2001), Myers Park Country Club. Democrat. Baptist. Avocation: guitar. Home: 251 Huntley Pl Charlotte NC 28207 Office: Erdman and Hockfield LLP 2300 E 7th St Charlotte NC 28204-4366 Office Phone: 704-333-7800. Business E-Mail: erdman@charlotte-nc-law.com.

ERDMAN, JOHN W., nutritionist, educator; m. Edie Erdman; children: Carolyn, Jackie. PhD, Rutgers U., 1975. Asst. prof. Dept. Food Sci. U. Ill., Urbana, prof. Food Sci. and Human Nutrition. Dir. Nutritional Scis. divsn. U. Ill., Urbana, 1989—99, asst. dean Coll. Office Rsch., 1995—99. Contbr. more tha 130 articles to profl. jours. Recipient award, Am. Soc. Nutritional Scis. Fellow: Inst. Food Technologists (Babcock-Hart award 1999); mem.: NAS, Inst. Medicine, 2004, Am. Assn. Nutritional Scis. (pres.-elect 2000—01). Office: Univ Illinois Divsn Nutritional Scis 451 Bevier Hall MC-186 905 S Goodwin Ave Urbana IL 61801

ERDMAN, PAUL EMIL, author; b. Stratford, Ont., Can., May 19, 1932; (parents Am. citizens); s. Horace Herman and Helen E.; m. Helly Elizabeth Boeglin, Sept. 11, 1954; children: Constance Anne Catherine, Jennifer Michele. Student, Concordia Coll., Ft. Wayne, Ind., 1950-51, Concordia Sem., St. Louis, 1952-53; BA, Concordia Coll., St. Louis, 1954; BS, Georgetown U., 1956; MA, PhD, U. Basel, Switzerland, 1958. Econ. cons. European Coal and Steel Community, Luxembourg, Luxembourg, 1958; internat. economist Stanford Research Inst., Menlo Park, Calif., 1958-61; exec. v.p. Electronics Internat. Capital Ltd., Hamilton, Bermuda, 1962-64; vice chmn. United California Bank in Basel A.G., 1965-70. Cons. RAI Corp., TV corp., Italy.; host Moneytalk Sta. KGO, ABC, San Francisco, 1983-86, commentator, 1987—; adv. bd. Sch. Bus. and Econs. Sonoma State U., Ronerd Pk., Calif., 2001—. Author: Swiss-American Economic Relations, 1959, Die Europaeische Wirtschaftsgemeinschaft und die Drittlaender, 1960, The Billion Dollar Sure Thing, 1973, The Silver Bears, 1974, The Crash of '79, 1976, The Last Days of America, 1981, Paul Erdman's Money Book: An Investor's Guide to Economics and Finance, 1984, The Panic of '89, 1987, The Palace, 1988, What Next? 1988, The Swiss Account, 1991, Warning to the Yen, 1992, Zero Coupon, 1993, Tug of War, 1996, The Set-Up, 1997; contbg. editor, columnist M Inc. mag., 1987-92; columnist The Nikon Keizai Shimbun, 1987-88, The Japan Post, 1989—, CBS Market Watch, 1998—; contbr. articles, revs. to popular mags. Mem. bd. advisors program in internat. bus. diplomacy Sch. fgn. Service, Georgetown U., Washington, 1980—, faculty mem. Georgetown leadership seminar, 1982—. Recipient Champion Media award for econ. understanding Amos Tuck Sch. Bus. Administrn., Dartmouth Coll., 1984 Mem. Authors Guild, Mysters Writers Am. (Edgar award 1974), PEN Am. Ctr., Commonwealth Club Calif. (adv. bd. 2005). Lutheran. Address: 1817 Lytton Springs Rd Healdsburg CA 95448-9145 Office Phone: 707-433-4982. Personal E-mail: erdman@sonic.net.

ERDMANN, CHARLES EDGAR, federal judge, former state supreme court justice; b. June 26, 1946; married; 4 children. Student, Mont. State U., 1964-66; BS in Bus./Econs., Eastern Mont. Coll., 1972; JD, U. Mont., 1975. Bar: Mont., U.S. Dist. Ct. Mont., U.S. Ct. Appeals (9th cir.), U.S. Mil. Ct. Appeals. Legal intern Cascade County (Mont.) Atty.'s Office, 1974; asst. atty. gen. Mont. Atty. Gen.'s Office, 1975-76, chief state atty., 1978-79; chief counsel Mont. State Auditor's Office, 1976-78; bur. chief/atty. Medicaid Fraud Control Bur., State of Mont., 1979-82; staff atty. Mont. Sch. Bds. Assn., 1982-86; pvt. practice Helena, Mont., 1986-95; justice Mont. Supreme Ct., Helena, 1995—97; head Human Rights & Law Dept. Office of the High Rep. in Bosnia, 1999—2000; chmn., chief judge Bosnia Election Ct., 2000—02; judge US Ct. Appeals for the Armed Forces, Washington, 2002—. Sgt. USMC, 1967-69, lt. col. Mont. Air NG, 1980—. Pre-Law scholar Yellowstone County Bar Assn., Cascade County Bar Assn. scholar, 1973-74, Albyn F. McCulloch scholar, 1974-75. Mem. Mont. State Bar Assn., Alpha Psi Kappa, Phi Delta Phi. Office: US Ct Appeals Armed Forces 405 E St NW Washington DC 20442

ERDMANN, JAMES BERNARD, educational psychologist; b. Oct. 27, 1937; s. George C. and Emma (Hiltebrand) E.; m. Rebecca Susan Lindsay; children: Theodore Michael, Carolyn Louise, Christopher Joseph, Timothy James. Grad. cum laude, Pontifical Coll., Josephinum, 1959; MA, Loyola U., Chgo., 1964, PhD, 1966. Rsch. asst. Psychometric Lab. Loyola U., 1960-63, rsch. assoc., project dir., 1963-65, acting dir., 1965-66, assoc. dir., 1967-69, instr. dept. psychology, 1964-66, asst. prof. measurement program, 1967-69; assoc. prof. Sch. Edn. and Sch. Human Medicine, eval. coord. Office Med. Edn., R & D, Mich. State U., 1969-70; dir. divsn. ednl. measurement and rsch. Assn. Am. Med. Colls., Washington, 1970-87; clin. assoc. prof. psychiatry and behavioral scis. George Washington U. Sch. Medicine and Health Scis., 1973-87; assoc. dean adminstrn. and spl. projects Jefferson Med. Coll., Thomas Jefferson U., Phila., 1987-89, assoc. dean adminstrn. and univ. registrar, 1990-2001, prof. medicine (edn.) dept. medicine, 1993—, sr. assoc. dean faculty affairs, 2001—; dean Jefferson Coll. Health Professions Thomas Jefferson U., Phila., 2002—. Contbr. articles to profl. jours. Mem. Am. Ednl. Rsch. Assn., Assn. Schs. of Allied Health, Assn. Am. Med. Coll. Roman Catholic. Home: 408 Bickmore Dr Media PA 19086-6909 Office: 130 S 9th St Philadelphia PA 19107-5233 Office Phone: 215-503-6595. Business E-Mail: james.erdmann@jefferson.edu.

ERDMANN, JOACHIM CHRISTIAN, physicist; b. Danzig, June 5, 1928; s. Franz Werner and Maria Magdalena (Schreiber) E.; m. Ursula Maria Wedemeyer, Aug. 24, 1957; children: Michael Andreas, Thomas Christian, Maria Martha Dorothea. Doctorate, Tech. U. Braunschweig, Germany, 1958. Physicist Osram Labs., Augsburg, Germany, 1954-60; sr. rsch. scientist Boeing Sci. Rsch. Labs., Seattle, 1960-72, Boeing Aerospace Co., Seattle, 1972-73; prin. engr. Boeing Comml. Airplane Co., Seattle, 1973-81, sr. prin. engr., 1981-84, Boeing Aerospace (Boeing Def. and Space Group), Seattle, 1984—90; tech. cons., 1990—. Vis. prof. Max Planck Inst. for Metals Rsch., Stuttgart, Germany, 1968-69; lectr. Tech. U. Stuttgart, 1968-69; pres. Optologics Inc., Seattle, 1973-94. Author: Heat Conduction in Crystals, 1969; contbr. articles to profl. jours. Mem. Am. Phys. Soc., Optical Soc. Am., Soc. Photo Optical Instrumentation Engrs. Achievements include research in cryogenics, statistical physics and opto electronics. Home: 14300 Trillium Blvd SE Apt 8 Bothell WA 98012-1300 Office: Boeing Def & Space Group PO Box 3999 Seattle WA 98124-2499 Business E-Mail: jo@juerdmann.com.

ERDMANN, JOHN BAIRD, environmental engineer; b. Mpls., Feb. 24, 1950; s. Robert Keith and Mary Ann (Baird) E.; m. Ann Marie Freed, June 12, 1969 (div. 1976); 1 child, Rachel; m. Diane Lee Johnson, Apr. 24, 1982; children: Saleha, Daniel. AB in Engring. and Applied Physics, Harvard U., 1972; MSCE, U. Minn., 1990, PhD in Civil Engring., 1997. Registered profl. engr., Minn. Rsch. assoc. New Eng. Aquarium Rsch. Dept., Boston, 1972-73; asst. engr. Mass. Div. Water Pollution Control, Westborough, 1973-77; environ. engr. Eugene A. Hickok & Assocs., Inc., Wayzata, Minn., 1977-85; prin. environ. engr. Wenck Assocs., Inc., Maple Plain, Minn., 1985—. Contbr. articles to profl. jours. Dir., water quality chair Charles River Watershed Assn., Newton, Mass., 1974-76. Mem. ASCE, Assn. Ground Water Scientists and Engrs., Minn. Lake Mgmt. Fedn. (sec. 1989-90), North Am. Lake Mgmt. Soc. Democrat. Episcopalian. Achievements include new methods of river water quality data analysis including visualization of dissolved oxygen concentrations in space and time, and calculation of photosynthesis and respiration rates; new understanding of groundwater pumpout capture zone dimensions, important in groundwater contamination cleanup. Office: Wenck Assocs Inc PO Box 249 Maple Plain MN 55359-0249 Office Phone: 612-479-4203. Business E-Mail: jerdmann@wenck.com.

ERDOES, MARY CALLAHAN, investment banker; m. Philip Erdoes. BS in Math., Georgetown Univ.; MBA, Harvard Univ., 1993. With Bankers Trust; portfolio mgr. Meredith, Martin & Kaye; head, fixed income group, JPMorgan Flemming Investment Mgmt Divsn. JPMorgan Private Bank, 1996—2002, mng. dir., global head, investments, 2002, now CEO. Bd. dir. UNICEF, 2005—. Named one of 100 Most Powerful Women in World, Forbes mag., 2005. Office: JP Morgan Pvt Banking 522 Fifth Ave New York NY 10036*

ERDRICH, LOUISE (KAREN ERDRICH), writer, poet; b. Little Falls, Minn., June 7, 1954; d. Ralph Louis and Rita Joanne (Gourneau) E.; m. Michael Anthony Dorris, Oct. 10, 1981 (dec. Apr. 1997); children: Abel (dec.), Sava, Madeline, Persia, Pallas, Aza. BA, Dartmouth Coll., 1976; MA, Johns Hopkins U., 1979. Vis. poet, tchr. N.D. State Arts Council, 1977-78; tchr. writing Johns Hopkins U., Balt., 1978-79; communications dir., editor Circle-Boston Indian Council, 1979-80; textbook writer Charles Merrill Co., 1980. Author: (textbook) Imagination, 1981; (poetry) Jacklight, 1984, Baptism of Desire, 1989; (novels) Love Medicine, 1984 (Nat. Book Critics Circle award for fiction 1984, Virgina McCormick Scully prize 1984, L.A. Times award for best novel 1985, Sue Kaufman prize for first fiction Am Acad. and Inst. of Arts and Letters 1985), The Beet Queen, 1986, Tracks, 1988, (with Michael Dorris) The Crown of Columbus, 1991, (with Dorris) Route 2, 1991, The Bingo Palace, 1994, The Blue Jay's Dance: A Writer's Year with Baby, 1995, Tales of Burning Love, 1996, The Antelope Wife, 1998, Last Report on the Miracles at Little No Horse, 2001, The Master Butchers Singing Club, 2003, Four Souls, 2004; (children's) Grandmother's Pigeon, 1997, The Birchbark House, 1999, Game of Silence, 2005; contbr. short stories, essays and poems to popular mags., other publs. Johns Hopkins U. teaching fellow, 1979; Macdowell Colony fellow, 1980; Yaddo Colony fellow, 1981; vis. fellow Dartmouth Coll., 1981; Guggenheim fellow, 1985-86; recipient numerous awards for profl. excellence including Nelson Algren award, 1982, Pushcart prize, 1983, Nat. Mag. Fiction award, 1983, 87, First prize O. Henry awards, 1987. Mem. PEN (exec. bd. 1985-90), Am. Acad. Arts and Letters, Authors Guild, Western Lit. Assn. Address: c/o Wylie Aitken & Stone Inc 250 W 57th St Ste 2114 New York NY 10107-2199*

ERDTMANN, FREDERICK J., retired military officer, physician; b. Mineola, N.Y., July 28, 1944; m. Jean Erdtmann. BS, Bucknell U.; MD, Temple U. Sch. Medicine, 1970; MPH, U. Calif., Berkeley; grad., Armed Forces Staff Coll., Indsl. Coll. Armed Forces. Intern Allentown Gen. Hosp., Pa., 1970—71; advanced through grades to col. U.S. Army; resident, preventive medicine Walter Reed Army Inst. Rsch., 1974—75; chief, preventive medicine svc. Fitzsimmons Army Med. Ctr., Frankfurt Army Med. Ctr., Germany, Madigan Army Med. Ctr.; divsn. surgeon 2d Infantry Divsn., Tongduchon, Republic of Korea; several tours Office of the Surgeon Gen.; hosp. cmdr. Walter Reed Army Med. Ctr., 1998—99; dir. Med. Follow-up Agy. Inst. Medicine Nat. Acads. Decorated 5 Legions of Merit, Order of Military Med. Merit, George Sternberg Medal for Excellence in Preventive Medicine. Office: Inst Medicine 500 Fifth St NW Washington DC 20001 Office Phone: 202-334-1925. Business E-Mail: rerdfmann@nas.edu.

EREKSEN, CHRISTA ANN, social worker, marriage and family therapist; b. Manville, N.J., Oct. 19, 1973; d. Paul Erek Ereksen and Chris Antoinette Bladzinski; m. Marshall Chandler McCoy, July 2, 1996 (div. Jan. 2001). Cosmetology lic., Richards Beauty Coll., San Bernardino, Calif., 1994; A in Liberal Arts, Victor Valley Coll., 1999; B in Psychology, Calif. State U., San Bernardino, 2002; postgrad., Calif. Bapt. U., 2004; postgrad, Walden U. Cosmetologist Fantastic Sams, Apple Valley, Calif., 1995—99; eligibility worker San Bernardino County, 1999—2000, social worker II, 2000—04. Intern marriage and family therapy Foothills AIDS Project, San Bernardino, 2003—04, MFI Recovery, Riverside, Calif., 2003—04; dist. social worker Calif. Dept. Corrections, Parole and Cmty. Services Divsn., 2004—. Mem.: APA, Calif. Assn. Marriage and Family Therapists, Calif. State Alumni Assn., Phi Kappa Phi. Democrat. Roman Catholic. Avocations: reading, writing, poetry. Office: 303 W 5th St San Bernardino CA 92401 Office Phone: 909-383-4694 2045.

ERENGIL, MEHMET ERDAL, aeronautical engineer, researcher; b. Yalova, Cyprus, Sept. 10, 1964; arrived in U.S.A., 1982; s. Kadir and Sevim Erengil; m. Miriam Jacqueline Balduff, Dec. 28, 1990; children: Haven Kennedy, Justice Remington. BS with hons. in Engring., Case We. Res. U., 1986; MS in Engring., U. Tex., 1989, PhD, 1993. From post-doctoral fellow to rsch. assoc. Inst. Advanced Tech. U. Tex., Austin, 1994—2000, rsch. assoc. Inst. Advanced Tech., 2000—03; rsch. scientist Inst. Advanced Tech., Austin, 2004—. Cons. in field. Contbr. articles to profl. jours. Scholar, Cyprus-Am. Scholarship Program, 1982—86. Mem.: AIAA (sr.), Nat. Def. Indsl. Assn. Achievements include development of guidance, navigation and control concept for precision strike. Avocations: camping, photography, soccer, scuba diving, swimming. Home: 8420 Asmara Drive Austin TX 78750 Office: Inst for Advanced Technology 3925 W Braker Lane Ste 400 Austin TX 78759 Office Phone: 512-232-4456. E-mail: erengil@iat.utexas.edu.

ERENS, JAY ALLAN, lawyer; b. Chgo., Oct. 18, 1935; s. Miller S. and Annette (Goodman) R.; m. Patricia F. Brett, Aug. 21, 1960 (div. May 1985); children: Pamela B., Bradley B.; m. Patrice K. Franklin, June 15, 1985; 1 child, Cameron Jay. BA, Yale U., 1956; LLB, Harvard U., 1959. Bar: Ill. 1960. Law clk. to Justice John M. Harlan U.S. Supreme Ct., Washington, 1959-60; pvt. practice Chgo., 1960-64; founding and sr. ptnr. Levy and Erens (name changed to Erens and Miller 1985), Chgo., 1964-86; sr. ptnr. Hopkins & Sutter, Chgo., 1986-2001; with Foley & Lardner, Chgo., 2001—. Lectr. law Northwestern U., Chgo., 1961-63; spl. asst. atty. gen. State Ill., Chgo., 1964-70. Trustee Latin Sch. Chgo., 1975—80. Mem.: ABA, Chgo. Bar Assn. Office: Foley & Lardner 321 N Clark St Chicago IL 60610 Office Phone: 312-832-4536. Business E-Mail: jerens@foley.com.

ERENSTEIN, ALAN, emergency nurse practitioner; Grad., Aliquippa Hosp Sch. Radiology, Pa., 1974; student, Aliquippa Hosp. Sch. Radiology, New Wilmington, Pa., 1974; AA in Gen. Studies, LPN, Beaver County C.C., Monaca, Pa., 1977, AS in Nursing, RN, 1979. RN, Fla.; registered radiologic technologist. LPN Hamot Med. Ctr., Erie, Pa., 1977-78; team leader Trauma-Neuro ICU and Stepdown Unit Allegheny Gen. Hosp., Pitts., 1979-81, staff nurse Emergency Room, 1981; flight nurse LifeWATCH HCA Wesley Med. Ctr., Wichita, Kans., 1981-91, contigency and float pool, 1991-92, hyperbaric nurse, 1991-92; ER nurse, relief charge nurse, clin. coord., team leader JFK Med. Ctr., Atlantis, Fla., 1992-95; aeromed. specialist Bizjet Air Ambulance, West Palm Beach, Fla., 1994-95; med. edn. cons. Med. Edn. Cons. Am., Tampa, 1994-97; with disaster team Cutler Ridge (Fla.) Field Hosp., 1992; response team Kans. Tornado Wesley Med. Ctr., Wichita, 1991; emergency rm./trauma nurse DelRay Med. Ctr., 1996—. Paramedic clin. coord. Hutchinson (Kans.) C.C., 1989; skills lab coord. Advanced Trauma Life Support Course, HCA Wesley Med. Ctr., Wichita, 1989-92; lectr. various med. ctrs., univs. and confs. Author: Trauma in Pregnancy, 1990; co-author: LifeWATCH Transport Manual, 1988; contbr. Society Trauma Nurses: Instructor's Resource Manual for Trauma Nursing, The Pregnant Trauma Patient Module, 1998.

ERESHEFSKY, LARRY, scientific officer, executive, psychopharmacology educator, consultant; b. Bklyn., Mar. 10, 1952; s. Sam and Claire (Geller) E.; m. Elke S. Weisburd, Sept. 1, 1974; children: Benjamin Jacob, Sabrina Hope. Pharm.D., U. So. Calif., 1976. bd. cert. in psychiat. pharmacy. Resident in psychiat. pharm. practice, Calif.; rsch. asst. UCLA, 1970-73; clin. instr. U. So. Calif., 1976-77; asst. prof. U. Tex., Austin, 1977-82; assoc. prof., 1982-88; Regents chair in psychopharmacology, 1985—2003; prof. pharmacology and psychiatry Health Sci. Ctr., U. Tex., San Antonio, 1982—2003; program dir., 1983—2003; prof. clin. pharmacy, 1988-96; chmn. postdoct. tng., 1990—2003; chief sci. officer, exec. v.p. Calif. Clin. Trials, 2003—. Cons. in field; adv. com. Novartis, Inc., 1988—, Johnson & Johnson, 1995—, Wyeth, Inc., 1995—, Eli Lily & Co., 2000—, Neurogenetics, 2003-, Lundbeck, 2003-, Pfizer, 2000-; mem. adv. com. on psychopharmacologic drugs FDA, 1992-95; co-dir. clin. rsch. unit San Antonio State Hosp., 1995—2003, chief sci. officer, exec v.p. Calif. clin. trials, 2003-; mem. neurology and psychiatry panel U.S. Pharmacopeial Conv., 1985—; co-founder, past chmn., Coll. Psychiat. and Neurologic Pharmacists, pres. 2004—; adj. prof. psychiatry and pharmacology U. Tex. Health Sci. Ctr. at San Antonio, 2003—; mem. rsch. rev. panel pharmacogenetics and depression, NIMH, NIH, 2003-; participant warfighters counter-fatigue measures workgroup, Defense Advanced Rsch. Projects Agency, 2003. Editor: Psychopharmacy Newsletter, 1990-94, Coll. Psychiat. and Neurologic Pharmacists Newsletter, 1994-98; mem. editl. bd. Am. Jour. Hosp. Pharmacy, 1988-98, Drug Therapy Perspectives, 1990—, Primary Psychiatry, 1974-; contbr. articles to over 120 peer reviewed publs. Recipient award Wilford Hall USAF Med. Ctr., Judy J. Saklad Meml. award Coll. Psychiat. and Neurol. Pharmacists, 2002, Robert Leonard Meml. Lectr. award Tex. Soc. Health-System Pharmacists, 2000. Fellow Am. Coll. Clin. Pharmacy (chmn. clin. practice affairs 1987-88, bd. regents 1989-94); mem. Am. Soc. Hosp. Pharmacists (SIG officer 1980-82, mem. coun. edn. affairs 1982-83, chmn. psychopharmacology 1982), AAAS, Am. Assn. Colls. Pharmacy, Am. Soc. Health Sys. Pharmacists (chair-elect clin. pharmacy splsts. coun. 1997-98, chair sect. clin. splsts. 1999—), Coll. Psychiat. and Neurol. Pharmacists (founding mem., pres. 2003-04), N.Y. Acad. Sci., Phi Kappa Phi, Rho Chi. Achievements include development of proof of concept trials accelerating drug development; Phase I dosage formulation and bridging studies; prin. investigator pivotal trials developing psychotropic medications, evaluating drug-drug interactions and pharmacogenetics. Avocations: sailing, snorkeling, hiking, reading, astronomy. Office: Calif Clin Trials 1509 Wilson Ter Glendale CA 91206 Office Phone: 818-254-1650. E-mail: larry.ereshefsky@cctrials.com.

ERGANIAN, LESLIE JEANNE, artist, writer; b. Oak Park, Ill., Sept. 14; d. Alex Mark Erganian and Alice Lovella Forbes. BA in Art History and Painting, U. Calif., Riverside, 1979; MFA in Photography, U. Ill., 1982; MFA in Performing Arts, UCLA, 1993. Tchg. asst. in art U. Ill., Champaign-Urbana, 1980-82; tchg. assoc. in film UCLA, 1984-86; art dir. propaganda films MGM/Warner Bros., L.A., 1992-98; set decorator Dreamworks/Showtime, PBS, L.A., 1992-98; performer Showtime, NBC, Discovery and Hallmark channels, L.A. Founder Lost Continents Fine Gifts & Stationery, L.A., 1996—; TV guest artist Rosie O'Donnell Show, N.Y.C., Christopher Lowell, L.A.; actress, art dir. Radio Inside; vis. lectr. film design UCLA Sch. Theater, Film and TV, 1998—; docent Meet the Masters Palo Alto Unified Sch. Dist., 2004—05. Author: Bye Dad, 1999; editor, contbg. writer: Raphael Soriano, 2002, composer, performer revue: Shakespeare Live!, 2000; Exhibited in group shows at Krannert Art Mus., Champaign-Urbana, Ill., 1982, Phyllis Needleman Gallery, Chgo., 1982, 2002 Cultural Olympiad, Salt Lake City, Represented in permanent collections Calif. Mus. Photography, Riverside, Xerox Corp., Rochester, N.Y.; TV host The Soul of a House, 2003—05. Vol. reader SAG Book Pals, L.A. and San Francisco, 1998—. Grad. fellow UCLA, 1984. Mem.: SAG, Soc. Archtl. Historians (So. Calif. chpt.), Phi Kappa Phi.

ERGEN, CHARLES W., communications professional; married; 5 children. BS in Bus. and Acctg., U. Tenn.; MBA, Wake Forest U. Founder, chmn., CEO Echostar Comms., Littleton, Colo., 1980—. Co-founder Satellite Broadcasting Comm. Assoc. Named Master Entrepreneur of the Year for the Rocky Mountain region, INC. Mag., 1991, Business Person of the Year, Rocky Mountain News, 1996, 2001, Space Industry Business Man of the Year, Aviation Week Mag., 2000; recipient Star award, Home Satellite TV Assn., 1998, CEO of the Year, Frost & Sullivan, 2001. Achievements include leading figure in the movement for the Satellite Home Viewer Improvement Act in 1999 which gave American consumers the right to watch local TV channels via satellite; testified before Congress regarding other video competition issues on several occasions. Office: Echostar Comms 5701 S Santa Fe Littleton CO 80120*

ERIBO, FESTUS, mass communication educator, journalist; b. Benin City, Edo, Nigeria, June 16, 1950; arrived in U.S., 1985; s. Wilfred Omovbe and Grace Iroguehi Eribo; m. Luba N. Eribo, Aug. 24, 1978; children: Brenda, Hilda. MA, Leningrad (Russia) State U., 1979; PhD, U. Wis., 1989. Tchr. Edo Coll., Benin City, 1971; pub. rels. mgr. Ribway Group Cos., Benin City, 1971-73; prin. info. officer Dept. Info., Benin City, 1980-89; asst. prof. East Carolina U., Greenville, 1990—95, assoc. prof., 1995—2002, prof., 2002—. Co-author: Window on Africa: Democratization and Media Exposure, 1993, Press Freedom and Communication in Africa, 1997, Journalism and Mass Communication in Africa: Cameroon, 2002, Development and Communication in Africa, 2003; author: In Search of Greatness: Russia's Communications with Africa and the World, 2001. Mem. Assn. for Edn. in Journalism and Mass Comm. Home: 402 Lancelot Dr Greenville NC 27858-8647 Office: East Carolina U Sch Com Greenville NC 27858

ERICHSEN, PETER CHRISTIAN, foundation administrator; b. Kentfield, Calif., Aug. 4, 1956; s. Hans Skabo and Ruth Elsie (Henderson) E. AB magna cum laude, Harvard U., 1978, JD cum laude, 1981. Bar: Mass. 1981, Pa. 2000. Assoc. Ropes & Gray, Boston, 1981-90, ptnr., 1990-93; dep. asst. atty. gen. U.S. Dept. Justice, Washington, 1993-96; assoc. counsel to Pres. The White House, 1996-97; v.p., gen. counsel U. Pa., U. Pa. Health Sys., 1997—2001; v.p., gen. counsel, sec. J. Paul Getty Trust, 2001—. Bd. govs. Phila. Stock Exch., 1999—; bd. dirs. Music Ctr Performing Arts Ctr, L.A., Reading for the Blind and Dyslexic, Inc., Appleseed Found., Washington, L.A. Appleseed, Appleseed Found., Washington, D.C., Reading for Blind and Dyslexic, Inc., N.J.; trustee Samuel Courtland Trust, London, 2003—; Claymore we. asset treas. Inflation Protected Securities Funds, 2004—. Vestryman Trinity Ch., Boston, 1987-91, 92-93; founding dir. Trinity Hospice, Boston, 1988-93. Office: 1200 Getty Ctr Dr Los Angeles CA 90049-1681 E-mail: perichsen@getty.edu.

ERICKSEN, JERALD LAVERNE, retired science engineering educator; b. Portland, Oreg., Dec. 20, 1924; s. Adolph and Ethel Rebecca (Correy) E.; m. Marion Ella Pook, Feb. 24, 1946; children: Lynn Christine, Randolph Peder. BS, U. Wash., 1947; MA, Oreg. State Coll., 1949; PhD, Ind. U., 1951; DSc (hon.), Nat. U. Ireland, 1984, Heriot-Watt U., 1988. Mathematician, solid state physicist U.S. Naval Rsch. Lab., 1951-57; faculty Johns Hopkins U., 1957-83, prof. theoretical mechanics, 1960-83; prof. mechanics and math. U. Minn., Mpls., 1983-90; cons. Florence, Oreg., 1990—. Served with USNR, 1943-46. Recipient Bingham medal, 1968, Timoshenko medal, 1979, Engring. Sci. medal, 1987. Mem. Internat. Liquid Crystal Soc. (hon.), NAE, Soc. Rheology (Panetti-Ferrari prize and Gold medal 2003), Soc. Natural Philosophy, Soc. Interaction Mechanics and Math., Soc. Engring. Sci., Royal Irish Acad. (hon.). Home and Office: 5378 Buckskin Bob Dr Florence OR 97439-8320

ERICKSON, ALAN ERIC, librarian; b. Boston, Feb. 6, 1928; s. Elmer Eric and Ethel M (Winch) Erickson; m. June Andersen, July 14, 1951; children: Kim, John, Martha, William. AB, Middlebury Coll., 1949; MA, Boston U., 1955, PhD, 1960; MS in L.S., Simmons Coll., 1969. Cert. tchr. Mass. Instr. Boston U., 1954-60; staff scientist Worcester Found. for Exptl. Biology, Shrewsbury, Mass., 1960-66; sci. specialist library Harvard U., Cambridge, Mass., 1966-91; librarian Cabot Sci. Library, 1973-91; assoc. librarian for adminstrn. Harvard Coll., Cambridge, Mass., 1970-72; assoc. librarian Harvard Coll. Sci., 1984-91; ret., 1991. Consult Marine Biol Labs, Wood Hole, Mass., 1981—82; trustee BIOSIS Info Serv, 1988—93, chmn bd dirs, 1993. Contbr. articles to profl jours. Trustee David Turner Scholarship Fund, Needham, Mass., 1970—; bd. govs. Greater Boston 32 degree Masonic Learning Ctr. for Children, Inc., 2001—04; trustee Carter Mem Meth Ch, Needham, Mass., 1964—66. Lt col USAFR, 1951—73, ret USAFR. Recipient Woolsey Bible Prize, Middlebury Col, Vt, 1949. Mem.: Harvard U. Retirees Assn. (pres. 1995—97), Needham Ret. Men's Club (pres. 1999, 2000). Avocations: gardening, woodworking, bicycling.

ERICKSON, ARTHUR CHARLES, architect; b. Vancouver, B.C., Can., June 14, 1924; s. Oscar and Myrtle (Chatterson) E. Student, U. B.C., Vancouver, 1942-44; BArch., McGill U., Montreal, Que., Can., 1950; LLD (hon.), Simon Fraser U., Vancouver, 1973, U. Man., Winnipeg, Can., 1978, Lethbridge U., 1981; D.Eng. (hon.), Novia Scotia Tech. Coll., McGill U., 1971; LittD (hon.), U. B.C., 1985, Frank Lloyd Wright Sch. Arch., 2001, MArch (hon.), 2001. Asst. prof. U. Oreg., Eugene, 1955-56; assoc. prof. U. B.C., 1956-63; ptnr. Erickson-Massey Architects, Vancouver, 1963-72; prin. Arthur Erickson Architects, Vancouver, 1972-91, Toronto, Ont., Can., 1981-91, Los Angeles, 1981-91, Arthur Erickson Archtl. Corp., Vancouver, 1991—. Prin. works include Simon Fraser U., Lethbridge U. Alta., McMillan Bloedel Bldg., Can. Pavilion at Expo '70, Osaka (recipient first prize in nat. competition, Archtl. Inst. of Japan award for best pavilion), Robson Square/The Law Courts (honor award), Mus. of Anthropology (honor award), Eppich Residence (honor award), Habitat Pavilion (honor award), Sikh Temple (award of merit), Champlain Heights Cmty. Sch. (award of merit), San Diego Conv. Ctr., Calif. Plz., L.A., Fresno City Hall, Can. Embassy, Washington, Roy Thompson Hall, Toronto, Bank of Can., Ottawa Hdqs., Koerner Libr., U.B. C. Liu Internat. Conf. Ctr., U. B.C. Scotibank Dance Ctr., Internat. Glass Mus., Tacoma, Wash., 2003. Mem. com. on urban devel. Coun. of Can., 1971; bd. dirs. Can. Conf. of Arts, 1972; mem. design adv. coun. Portland Devel. Commn., Can. Coun. Urban Rsch.; trustee Inst. Rsch. on Pub. Policy. Capt. Can. Intelligence Corps., 1945-46; mem. internat. coun. Mus. Modern Art, N.Y.C., 1982-86. Decorated officer Order of Can., companion Order of Can.; recipient Molson prize Can. Coun. Arts, 1967, Triangle award Nat. Soc. Interior Design, Royal Bank Can. award, 1971, Gold medal Tau Sigma Delta, 1973, residential design award Can. Housing Coun., 1975, August Perret award Internat. Union Architects Congress, 1975, Chgo. Architecture award, 1984, Gold medals Royal Archtl. Inst. Can., 1984, French Acad. Architecture, 1984, AIA, 1986, Pres. award excellence Am. Soc. Landscape Architects, 1979. Fellow AIA (hon., Pan Pacific citation Hawaiian chpt. 1963, Gold medal 1986), Royal Archtl. Inst. Can. (award 1980), Royal Inst. Brit. Archs. (hon.), Royal Inst. Scottish Archs. (hon.), Frank Lloyd Wright Found. (hon., 2000); mem. Archtl. Inst. B.C., ARCAB Wash. State Archtl. Assn., Coll. d'arquitectos de España (hon.), Coll. d'architectos de Mex. (hon.), Royal Can. Acad. Arts (academician), S.F.U. Faculty Club. Office: Arthur Erickson Archtl Corp 1672 W 1st Ave Vancouver BC Canada V6J 1G1 Office Phone: 604-737-9801. E-mail: arthurerickson@lynx.bc.ca.

ERICKSON, BARBARA MARTHA, historian, writer; b. Knoxville, Tenn., July 17, 1932; d. William Vivian and Elza Cleo (Nichols) Slatery; m. Eugene William Erickson, Aug. 21, 1954; children: Randall William, Jacqueline Barbara. BA, U. Tenn., 1954. Asst. bridal cons. LeGrands Jewelers, Chattanooga, Tenn., 1952-54; organizer patient file room Erlanger Hosp., Chattanooga, 1954; floral arranger Stevens Florists, Spring Valley, N.Y., 1956-58; sec. treas. Erickson Olds, Inc., Monsey, N.Y., 1968-92, Toyota of Rockland, Monsey, 1992. Floral arranger Schweizers Florist, Pearl River, N.Y., Dykstras Florists, Spring Valley, N.Y. Author: (children's hist. drama) Lure of the Kakiat, 1956, 200 Years of Brick Church History, 1974, What in the World is a Rotary Ann?, 1983, Diary of the West New Hempstead Dutch Reformed Church, 2000, Sergent. Richard M. Masterson, Life of a Tennessee Farmer and Soldier in the Union Army, 2004; editor Rockland Rep. Reporter Rockland County Young Rep. Club, 1950's, 60's, The Tempo of Brick Church West New Hempstead Reformed Ch., Spring Valley, N.Y., 1958-98; contbr. articles to mags., jours., chpt. to book. Historian West New Hempstead Reformed Ch., 1961-2002; co-chmn. bi-centennial Town of Ramapo, N.Y., 1976; sponsor, participant Canine Companions for Independence, 1990—, Ramapo Children of Chernobyl project, 1998-2000. Recipient Gov.'s Newsletter award Dist. Gov. Rotary Internat., 1984, Town Svc., Humanitarian awards Town of Ramapo, 1991; named First Families of Tenn. East Tenn. Hist. Soc., 1995; Paul Harris fellow, 1981, Fred. Ellen Am. Legion Aux. Mem. Valley Garden Club (hon., pres. 1962-65), Valley Star Order of the Ea. Star (matron, pres. 1960), Suffern Woman's Club (mem. exec. bd. 1996-2002), Sons of Norway (Tubfrim chmn. Norrona chpt. 2001—, exec. bd., 1996-2002), Atlantic Coast Old Timers Racing Assn., Rockland County German-Am. Club (sec. 2002-03), DAR (chpt. scrapbook chmn. 2003, Shatemuc, N.Y., pub. rels. chmn. 2003, assoc. Mary Blount Chpt., regent 2004), Pearl River Rotary Club, German-Am. Club, Phi Mu. Mem. Reformed Ch. in Am. Avocations: writing, golf, scuba diving, camping, travel. Home: 179 W Maple Ave Monsey NY 10952-1733

ERICKSON, CAROL JEAN, literature and language professor; b. St. Cloud, Minn., Dec. 25, 1943; d. Clarence Joseph and Lucille Frances Reiter; m. Eric Bruce Erickson, Aug. 13, 1966 (dec. July 2004); children: Holly Lynn, Kirk Adam. BS in English, St. Cloud State U., Minn., 1962—66; MA in Tchg. and Learning, St. Mary's U. Minn., Winona, 1996—98. Lang. arts educator Sch. Dist. 728, Elk River, Minn., 1966—. Speech coach Vandenberge Jr. High, Elk River, Minn., 1966—2000, lang. arts chair, 1968—85, site coun. chair, 2000—03; past sec., faculty rep., and parliamentarian Elk River Edn. Assn., Minn., 1968—78; lang. arts dist. 728 curriculum com. Dist. 728, Elk River, Minn., 2001—03. State v.p. Jaycee Women, Minn., 1975—76;

founder, past chair, bd. mem. Rivers of Hope, Monticello, Minn., 1989—2005. Nominee Tchr. of Yr., Elk River Edn. Assn., 1980; recipient Key Woman, Minn. Jaycee Women, 1977, Minn. Tchr. Excellence, Minn. Edn. Assn., 1983. Mem.: NEA, Edn. Minn., Elk River Edn. Assn., Delta Kappa Gamma (past chair, past parliamentarian, current mem.). Roman Catholic. Avocations: gardening, reading, travel. Office Phone: 763-241-3400.

ERICKSON, DENNIS, professional football coach; b. Everett, Wash., Mar. 24, 1947; m. Marilyn, children: Bryce, Ryan. BS Phys. Educ., Montana State U. Grad. asst. coach Montana State U., 1969, Washington State U., 1970; head football coach Billings Central H.S., Billings, Mont., 1970; backfield coach Montana State U., 1971-73; offensive coordinator, head coach U. Idaho, 1974-75, 1982-85; offensive coordinator Fresno State U., 1976-78, San Jose State U., 1979-81; head coach U. Wyoming, 1986, Washington State U., 1987-88, U. Miami Hurricanes, 1989-95, Seattle Seahawks, 1995-98, Oregon State U., 1999—2003, S.F. 49ers, 2003—04. All-Big Sky quarterback, 1966-68, honorable All-American; head coach NCAA Divsn. 1A football champions, 1989, co-champions (with U. Wash.), 1991; fishing, golf.

ERICKSON, EDWARD GRANT, electrical engineer; b. Riverside, Calif., Mar. 12, 1933; s. Edward Grant Sr. and Evalyn Lloyd (Henry) Erickson; m. Marilyn Eileen Cox (div.); children: Joyce, Lissa, Linda Jones. Student, USN Aviation Electronics Sch., 1952—53, Chaffey Coll., 1956—61. R&D technician Advanced Techniques Group, Pomona, Calif., 1956—62; rsch. engr. Northrup Space Labs., Palos Verdes and Hawthorne, Calif., 1962—65; project leader Korad divsn. Union Carbide Corp., Santa Monica, Calif., 1966—68; devel. engr. Holobeam, Inc., Paramus, NJ, 1968—71; sr. mem. tech. staff electro-optics orgn. GTE Govt. Sys., Mountain View, Calif., 1973—89; head laser sub-sys. Kestrel program Lawrence Livermore (Calif.) Nat. Lab., 1992; prin. investigator Deltron Laser Corp., Sunnyvale, Calif., 1990—91; sr. mgm. tech. staff advanced laser applications Lawrence Livermore (Calif.) Nat. Labs., 1991—92; pres., CEO, founder Deltron Laser Corp., Sunnyvale, Calif., 1990—91. Presenter in field. Author: Two Hundred and Eleven Days to Eternity, 2004. Mgr. emergency response team Sheriff's Aux. Vols., Pima County, Ariz., 1995—98; capt. High Country Co. Ariz. Rangers, Williams, 2000—02. Comdr./capt. (ret.) USN, 1952—56. Achievements include patents in field. Avocation: cutting and polishing sapphires and other crystals. Home: 10915 N Falcon Ridge Rd Williams AZ 86046

ERICKSON, EDWARD LEONARD, biotechnologist, consultant; b. Chgo., Dec. 7, 1946; s. Leonard Gerald and Eleanore Antoinette (Picek) E.; m. Helen Leonora Masten, Dec. 29, 1979. BS in Math., Ill. Inst. Tech., 1968, MS in Math., 1970; MBA in Gen. Mgmt., Harvard U., 1980. Mktg. rep. IBM, Miami, Fla., 1975-76; sr. systems engr. Advanced Tech., Inc., McLean, Va., 1976-78; cons. Bain & Co., Boston, 1979-80; sr. assoc. Resource Planning Assocs., Washington, 1980-82; dir. RPA Mgmt. Cons., London, 1982-83; dir. corp. devel. Amersham Internat. plc., Little Chalfont, Eng., 1983-86, gen. mgr. internat. ops., 1986-88; v.p. fin. ops. The Ares-Serono Group, Boston, 1988-90; pres. Serono-Baker Diagnostics (The Ares-Serono Group), Allentown, Pa., 1990-91; pres., CEO, dir. Cholestech Corp., Hayward, Calif., 1991-93, DepoTech Corp., La Jolla, Calif., 1993-98; pres., CEO, chmn. Immunicon Corp., 1998—. Bd. dirs. Valeo Med. Contbr. articles to profl. jours. Lt. USN, 1970—75. John L. Loeb fellow Harvard U., 1980, George F. Baker scholar, 1980, NASA fellow, 1968-70. Mem. Am. Soc. Clin. Oncology (affiliate), Am. Assn. Pharm. Scientists, Am. Assn. Advancement of Sci. Republican. Avocations: tennis, skiing. Home: 6887 Tohickon Hill Rd Pipersville PA 18947-1415 E-mail: elerickson@comcast.net.

ERICKSON, ELAINE MAE, composer, educator, poet; b. Des Moines, Iowa, Apr. 22, 1941; d. Iver Carl and Ruth Eloise (Johnson) Erickson. MusB, Wheaton Coll., 1964; MusM, Drake U., 1967. Pvt. piano tchr., Des Moines, 1964—; music libr. Main Pub. Library, Des Moines, 1965-67; composer-in-residence Ford Found. Fellowship, Ft. Lauderdale, Fla., 1967-68; tchr. piano music theory Drake U., Des Moines, 1969-72; pianist Ctr. for New Music State U. Iowa, Iowa City, 1974-76; piano tchr. Waxter Ctr., Balt., 1988-89, Church Lane Elem. Sch., Balt., 1989-90; tchr. music composition Ctrl. Coll., Pella, Iowa, 1993-96; composer-in-residence Charles Ives Ctr. Am. Music, New Milford, Conn., 1981—83, 1993. Guest composer Meet the Composer, Saranac Lake, NY, 1987; touring artist Very Spl. Arts Iowa, 1994—. Author (poetry) Separate Trains, 1988, A Visit Home, 1990, Solo Drive, 1992, Portraits and Selected Poems, 1994, The Cottage, 2001, Summer Evening, 2004; writer 5 operas, 3 performed at Peabody Conservatory, Balt., 1986-91; contbr. poetry to numerous jours. Pianist various retirement homes, Balt., Des Moines, 1978—, music appreciation tchr., Balt., 1991-93, Des Moines, 1993—; organist Divinity Luth. Ch., Towson, Md., 1987-88. Recipient Pyle Commn. award Iowa Composers Forum, Des Moines, 1997, composition award Nat. League Am. Pen Women, 1992; touring grantee Iowa Arts Coun., 1974-75, 81-82. Democrat. Avocation: photography. Home and Office: 3700 Hillsdale Dr Des Moines IA 50322-3947 Office Phone: 515-252-7662.

ERICKSON, ELIZABETH GRAY, marketing professional; b. Princeton, N.J., Aug. 12, 1967; d. Charles Augustus and Rachel Davis Gray; m. Jonathan Loyal Erickson, July 8, 1995. BA, Williams Coll., 1989; M of Mgmt., Northwestern U., 1995. Fin. analyst Credit Suisse First, Boston, 1989-91; client rep. Bloomberg Asia Inc., Tokyo, 1991-93; mktg. mgr. Am. Express, N.Y.C., 1995-97; v.p., co-founder Youth Noise Save the Children, Westport, Conn., 1997—2003. Mem. adv. bd. Youth Noise & Parents' Action for Children. Bd. dirs. Family and Children's Svcs. of Ctrl. N.J., Parents Action. Avocations: reading, time with family, dance. Home: 100 Hunt Dr Princeton NJ 08540-2426

ERICKSON, GERALD MEYER, classical studies educator; b. Amery, Wis., Sept. 23, 1927; s. Oscar Meyer and Ellen Claire (Hanson) E.; m. Loretta Irene Eder, Feb. 11, 1951; children: Rachel, Viki, Kari BS, U. Minn., 1954, MA, 1956, PhD, 1968. Cert. secondary sch. tchr., Minn. Tchr. Edina-Morningside Pub. Sch., Minn., 1956-65, 66-67; vis. lectr. U. Minn., Mpls., 1965-66, asst. prof., 1968-71, assoc. prof., 1971-83, prof. classical studies, 1983-95, prof. emeritus, 1995—. Exchange prof. Moscow State U., 1980, 86; vis. prof. U. Ill., 1967, 68, Coll. of William and Mary, 1984; bd. regents La. Univ. System, 1981, chmn. evaluation team for classics programs; reader Coll. Bds. Advanced Placement Program, 1975-77, chief reader, 1978-81; cons., lectr. in field Assoc. editor, mem. editorial staff Nature, Society and Thought, 1987—; author, lectr. various TV and radio courses Served with U.S. Mcht. Marine, 1945-46, U.S. Army, 1946-47, PTO; served to capt. USAF, 1951-53 NEH grantee, 1977-79; recipient award Horace T. Morse Amoco Found., 1984 Mem. Minn. Classical Conf. (pres. 1971-74), Minn. Humanities Conf. (pres. 1974-75), Classical Assn. Midwest/South (Ovatio award 1971). Avocations: bicycling, short-wave radio. Home: 121 E 51st St Minneapolis MN 55419-2605 Office: U Minn 831 Heller Hall Minneapolis MN 55455 E-mail: erick002@umn.edu.

ERICKSON, HOWARD HUGH, veterinarian, educator, physiology educator; b. Wahoo, Nebr., Mar. 16, 1936; s. Conrad and Laurene (Swanson) E.; m. Ann E. Nicolay, June 6, 1959; children: James, David. BS, DVM, Kans. State U., 1959; PhD, Iowa State U., 1966. Commd. 1st lt. U.S. Air Force, 1959, advanced through grades to col., 1979; veterinarian U.K., 1960-63; vet. scientist Sch. Aerospace Medicine, Brooks AFB, Tex., 1966-75; dir. rsch. and devel. aerospace med. divsn. Brooks AFB, 1975-81; prof. physiology Kans. State U., Manhattan, 1981—, acting head dept. anatomy and physiology, 1989—90, Roy W. Upham prof. vet. medicine, 2001—04. Sci. adv. bd. Morris Animal Found., Englewood, Colo., 1990-93; cons. Tex. Higher Edn. Coordination Bd., Austin, 1990-91; clin. asst. prof. U. Tex. Health Sci. Ctr., San Antonio, 1972-81; vis. mem. grad. faculty Tex. A&M U., College Station, 1967-81; affiliate prof. Colo. State U., Fort Collins, 1970-75. Editor: Animal Pain, 1983; contbr. articles to profl. jours. Founding mem. Kans. State U. Golf Course Rsch. and Mgmt. Found.; trustee Meadowlark Hills Cmty. Found. Recipient Alumni Achievement award Midland Luth. Coll., Fremont, Nebr., 1977, Merck award for Creativity, 1993, Bayer Excellence in Equine Rsch. award Am. Vet. Med. Assn. Coun. on Rsch., 2000. Fellow AAAS, Royal Soc. Health, Aerospace Med. Assn. (assoc.); mem. Am. Vet. Med. Assn. (chmn. coun. on rsch. 1984), Am. Physiol. Soc., Optimists Club. Republican. Lutheran. Home: 1700 Kings Rd Manhattan KS 66503-7550 Office: Kans State U Coll Vet Medicine Dept Anatomy and Physiology Manhattan KS 66506 Business E-Mail: erickson@vet.ksu.edu.

ERICKSON, JAMES CLIFFORD, III, anesthesiologist, educator; b. Phila., Oct. 7, 1927; MD, Temple U., 1953, MS in Anesthesiology, 1958. Diplomate Am. Bd. Anesthesiology, Pain Mgmt. Intern, resident anesthesiology Temple U. Hosp., Phila., 1953-57; from instr. to asst. prof. Temple U., Phila., 1957-67; prof., chief anesthesist Woman's Med. Coll. Pa., 1967-69; prof. anesthesiology Jefferson Med. Coll., 1969-80, Northwestern U. Med. Sch., Chgo., 1980-98, prof. emeritus, 1998—. Anesthesiologist Northwestern Meml. Hosp., Chgo., 1980—98. Vol. cons. Wood Libr.-Mus. Anesthesiology, 1998—; Elderhostel amb., 2002—. Fellow: Soc. Clin. and Exptl. Hypnosis, Am. Coll. Pain Medicine, Am. Coll. Anesthesiology; mem.: AMA, Assn. Late Deafened Adults, Anesthesia History Assn., Soc. Clin. and Exptl. Hypnosis, Am. Soc. Regional Anesthesia, Am. Soc. Clin. Hypnosis, Internat. Assn. Study Pain, Internat. Soc. Hypnosis, Am. Acad. Pain Medicine, Am. Soc. Anesthesiologists, Northwestern Emeriti Orgn. (pres. 2002—03). Office: 2425 Cardinal Ln Wilmette IL 60091-2334 Office Phone: 847-256-4765. Business E-Mail: jceric@northwestern.edu.

ERICKSON, JOHN S., research scientist; s. Merle R. and Geraldine E. Erickson; m. Jill Marie Carey, May 26, 1984; children: Stephanie Jeanne, Heidi Marie. BSEE, Rensselaer Poly. Inst, 1984; MSEE, Cornell U., 1989; PhD in Engring., Dartmouth Coll., 1997. Prin. engr. Digital Equipment Corp., Marlboro, Mass., 1984—92; co-founder and v.p., product & tech. strategy NetRights LLC, Lebanon, NH, 1995—97; v.p. tech. strategy YRM, Divsn. of YBP, Inc, Contoocook, NH, 1997—2000; prin. scientist Hewlett-Packard Labs., Norwich, Vt., 2000—. Mem.: IEEE (assoc.). Achievements include patents for (US 6807534, US 5765152) System and Method for Managing Copyrighted Electronic Media. Home: 707 Rt 132 Norwich VT 05055 Office: Hewlett-Packard Labs PO Box 1158 Norwich VT 05055 Office Phone: 802-649-1683.

ERICKSON, KRISS A., author; b. Paterson, N.J., May 23, 1958; d. Philip Thomas and Elizabeth Ann (Cafera) Hendrick; m. Michael Noel Erickson, Sept. 21, 1986; 1 child, Jason Michael. B.Theology, Ambassador Coll., Pasadena, 1981; postgrad., Mars Hill Coll., Bothell, Wash., 2000—. Exec. sec. Worldwide Ch. of God, Pasadena, 1982-85; apt. preparer Tenari II Apts., Lakewood, Wash., 1985-86; petsitter Pets "R" Inn, Tacoma, Wash., 1988-90; tchrs. aide Pierce County Sch. Dist., Tacoma, 1990-91; free lance writer Bonney Lake, Wash., 2000—. Author: (novel) The Land Behind the Veil, 2000, (cookbook) Healthy Gourmet Cheesecake, 1997. Worship leader Worldwide Ch. of God, Federal Way, Wash., 1997-99, Elm Evang. Free Ch., Puyallup, Wash., 2000; writing mentor Am. Online, 1993—. Avocations: gardening, soapmaking, singing, songwriting. Home and Office: 109 W Intercity Ave Everett WA 98204-2741 E-mail: slverkriss@aol.com.

ERICKSON, LAWRENCE A. (LARRY ERICKSON), electronics executive; b. Duluth, Minn. BS in Acctg., Mt. Mercy Coll., Cedar Rapids, Iowa. With Rockwell Collins, Inc., Cedar Rapids, 1975—, former v.p., contr. Collins Comml. Avionics subs., v.p., fin. and strategic devel., 1996—2001, sr. v.p., CFO, corp. officer, 2001—. Vice chmn. bd. dirs. Collins Cmty. Credit Union. Founding bd. dirs., pres. Friends of Linn County Conservation. Office: Rockwell Collins Inc 400 Collins Rd NE Cedar Rapids IA 52498

ERICKSON, LINDA E., retired academic administrator; b. Longview, Wash., Sept. 20, 1940; d. John Emil and Hazel Rydberg Erickson. BA in Music and Psychology with honors, Lewis and Clark Coll., 1962; MA in Student Pers. Adminstrn., Syracuse U., 1964; MusM in Piano Pedagogy, U. South Fla., 1970. Resident instr. U. South Fla., Tampa, 1964-65, instr., asst. prof., 1964-72, asst. dean of women, 1965-71, asst. to v.p. for student affairs, 1971-73, dir. new student rels., 1973-81, dir. admissions, 1981-86, asst. v.p., univ. registrar, 1986-96; ret., 1996. 1st pres. Fla. Assn. Women Educators, 1966-73; founding mem., 2d pres. Fla. Coll. Pers. Assn., 1975-78; bd. dirs., nat. cons. Nat. Orientation Dirs. Assn., 1977-81; exec. com., pres. Fla. ACT Coun., 1981-96; guardian ad litem Guardian Ad Litem Program, 13th Jud. Cir. Ct., Fla., 1996-2001; vol. neonatal ICU St. Joseph's Women's Hosp., Tampa, 1997-2001. Mem. Mortar Bd., Mu Phi Epsilon, Phi Kappa Phi, Delta Delta Delta. Avocations: music, travel, genealogy, physical fitness, reading. Home: 10217 Devonshire Lake Dr Tampa FL 33647

ERICKSON, MIRIAM MAY, retired school librarian; b. Markesan, Wis., May 21, 1932; d. Erwin Edwin and Eva Sophie Eckert; m. Howard Richard Erickson, Sept. 10, 1955; children: Joanne Barnard, Lizabeth Dickson, Michele Packett, My Chi, Soledad. BS, U. Wis. at Stout, 1954; MA, U. Wis.-Milwaukee, 1974. Home econ. ext. agt. U. Ext., Sturgeon Bay, Wis., 1954—56; home econ. tchr. Gibraltar Area Sch. Dist., Fish Creek, 1960—68, sch. libr. media specialist, 1968—98; owner Shallas Resort, Egg Harbor, 1968—2003; ret. Bd. mem. Coun. on Libr. and Network Develop., Madison, Wis., 1995—2003; bd mem. Corp. Edn. Svc. Agy., Green Bay, 2004—; mem. sch. dist. bd. Gibraltar, 1999—; pres. Nicolet Libr. Sys. Bd., Green Bay, 1995, Green Bay, 1997—99. Moderator Hope United Ch. of Christ, 2002—03; mem. Door County Cmty. Found. Bd., Sturgeon Bay, Wis., 2002, Door County Hosp. Aux., 1998—, Door County Libr. Found., 1997—. Recipient Sch. Libr. Media Specialist of the Yr., Wis. Libr. Assn., 1984, Award of Excellence, Wis. Career Info. Sys., 1986, Spl. Svc. Recognition award, Wis. Edn. Media Assn., 1986, Award of Excellence, 1991, Presdl. award, 1999, Wis. Media Specialist of the Yr., Assn. for Ednl. Communications and Tech., 1992, Award of Outstanding Svc., DoorNet Internet Group, Inc., 1998. Democrat. United Ch. Of Christ. Avocations: reading, travel, needlecrafts, stamp collecting/philately. Home: 8519 Hwy 42 Fish Creek WI 54212

ERICKSON, MITCHELL DRAKE, chemist, environmental scientist; b. Chgo., Aug. 31, 1950; s. Charles O. and Jane (Drake) E.; m. Colleen M. Erickson, June 12, 1976; children: Adam M., Carl J., Brendan C. AB in Chemistry, Grinnell Coll., 1972; PhD in Analytical Chemistry, U. Iowa, 1976. Chemist Research Triangle Inst., Research Triangle Park, N.C., 1976-81; prin. chemist Midwest Rsch. Inst., Kansas City, Mo., 1981-87; group leader Argonne (Ill.) Nat. Lab., 1987-89, 93-97, assoc. dir. R & D program office, 1989-93; lab. dir. Environ. Measurements Lab. U.S. Dept. Energy, N.Y.C., 1997—. Sci. adv. com., Hazardous Substance Rsch. Ctr. for Fed. Regions 7 and 8, Kans. State U., Manhattan, 1991—, chmn., 1994-98. Author: Analytical Chemistry of PCBs, 1986, 2d edit., 1997, Remediation of PCB Spills, 1993; contbr. articles to profl. jours. Recipient R&D Mag. 100 award, 1996, Fed. Lab. Consortium award for excellence in tech. transfer, 1997. Mem. Am. Chem. Soc., Soc. Applied Spectroscopy, Sigma Xi. Office: US DOE Environ Meas Lab 201 Varick St Fl 5 New York NY 10014-4811 Fax: 212-620-3651. E-mail: erickson@eml.doe.gov.

ERICKSON, NANCY LOU, history educator, academic administrator; b. Berea, Ohio, July 14, 1941; d. Douglass Allan and Lucy (Scrivens) Dawson; m. Dennis Harold Erickson, Aug. 22, 1964 (div. Jan. 2001); children: Jeffrey Arthur, Jane Marie. BS in Edn., Kent State U., 1961; AM, U. Ill., 1964; PhD, U. N.C., 1970. Teaching asst. U. Ill., Champaign, 1962-63; tchr. Champaign Sr. High Sch., 1963-64, Maine Twp. High Sch. West, Des Plaines, Ill., 1964-66; part-time instr. U. N.C., Chapel Hill, 1966-70, Elon Coll., N.C., 1969, U. Tenn., summer 1971, 72; prof. history Erskine Coll., Due West, SC, 1974—99; v.p. for acad. affairs Iowa Wesleyan Coll., 1999—. Contbr. articles and revs. to publs. in field. Tutor, mem. Literacy Coun., Greenwood; Sunday sch. tchr. Westminster Presbyn. Ch., Greenwood, SC; elder 1st Presbyn, Ch., Mt. Pleasant, Iowa. Recipient Pres.'s Scholarship, Kent State U., 1958-61; Univ. fellow U. Ill., Champaign, 1961-62, Lily scholar Duke U., Durham, N.C., 1976; Excellence in Teaching award Erskine Coll., 1978. Mem.: AAUW, Phi Alpha Theta (councillor 1986—88), So. Hist. Assn., Conf. on Faith and History, Orgn. Am. Historians, Am. Hist. Assn., Rotary Club. Home: 5007 Oak Ln Mount Pleasant IA 52641-8303 E-mail: nerickson@iwc.edu.

ERICKSON, PETER BROWN, librarian, scholar, writer; b. Worcester, Mass., Aug. 11, 1945; s. Irving Peter and Elinor (Brown) E.; m. Tay Gavin, June 30, 1968 (dec. Oct. 1998); children: Andrew Sven, Ingrid Adriana, Benjamin Peter. BA, Amherst Coll., 1967; postgrad., U. Birmingham, Birmingham, Eng., 1967-68; PhD, U. Calif., 1975; MSLS, Simmons Coll., 1984. Asst. prof. Williams Coll., Williamstown, Mass., 1976—81; fellow Wesleyan U., Middletown, Conn., 1981—82, vis. asst. prof., 1982—83; rsch. lib. Clark Art Inst., Williamstown, Mass., 1985—2003; ret., 2003. Author: Patriarchal Structures in Shakespeare's Drama, 1985, Rewriting Shakespeare Rewriting Ourselves, 1991 (paperback edit. 1994); contbr. articles to profl. jours; editor: Festschrift: Shakespeare's Rough Magic, Renaissance Essays in Honor of C.L. Barber, 1985, Making Trifles of Terrors: Redistributing Complicities in Shakespeare, 1997, Early Modern Visual Culture: Representation, Race, and Empire in Renaissance England, 2000, Approaches to Teaching Shakespeare's Othello, 2005 Amherst Meml. fellow Amherst Coll., 1967-68, Kent fellow Soc. for Values in Higher Edn., 1981-82; Worldwide Books Pub. award, 2001, 03 Mem. Shakespeare Assn. of Am., Renaissance Soc. of Am., Modern Language Assn., Appalachian Mt. Club, Phi Beta Kappa. Avocations: running, hiking, canoeing. Home: 81 Buxton Hill Rd Williamstown MA 01267-2773 E-mail: pberickson@verizon.net.

ERICKSON, PHYLLIS TRAVER, marketing executive; b. N.Y.C., Mar. 31, 1952; d. Harold August and Barbara Lucille (Seifert) T.; m. C. Carl Muscari, June 30, 1979 (div. Nov. 1982); m. Roger C. Erickson, July 8, 1995. BA, Northwestern U., 1974; MBA, Harvard U., 1978. Dir. rsch. Staub, Warmbold and Assocs., N.Y.C., 1974-75; dir. rsch., assoc. cons. Coopers and Lybrand, N.Y.C., 1975-76; asst. product mgr. Nestle Food Corp., White Plains, N.Y., 1978-79, product mgr., mktg. mgr., 1979-83, bus. dir. Purchase, N.Y., 1983-90; pres. PT Ventures, 1990—, Barrier Systems, Inc., Greenwich, Conn., 1991-92; v.p. mktg. Homeview, Inc., Needham, Mass., 1992-94, Media One, Boston, 1995-99. Pres. Erickson Cons., 1999—. Contbr. articles to mktg. jours. Named to Acad. Women Achievers YWCA. Mem. Harvard U. Bus. Sch. Club. Republican. Episcopalian. Home and Office: 133 Washington St Duxbury MA 02332-4520 E-mail: perickson@adelphia.net.

ERICKSON, RALPH D., retired physical education educator, small business owner, consultant; b. Beresford, S.D., June 25, 1922; s. John Henning and Ester Christina (Lofgren) E.; m. Nancy Erickson, Sept. 1949 (div. 1961); m. Patricia Erickson, Apr. 1973 (div. 1975); m. Karen Ann Erickson, June 1, 1989; 1 child, Karina Ann. BS in Phys. Edn., Northwestern U., 1949, MA in Edn., 1953. Swim instr., coach Chgo. Park Dist., 1946-54; social studies tchr., swim coach Elmwood Park (Ill.) High Sch., 1954-65; swimming, water polo coach Loyola Univ., Chgo., 1965-87, assoc. prof. phys. edn., 1971-87; salesman Alexander Hamilton Inst., Chgo., 1966-69; tchr. Chgo. Bd. Edn., 1969-70. Bd. dirs. Capital Investments & Ventures Corp., Santa Ana, Calif., 1983-93, Cosmopolitan Comm., Santa Ana, 1991-93; vice chmn. Internat. Profl. Assn. Diving Inst., Santa Ana, 1966-93. Author: Under Pressure, 1961, Discover the Under Water World, 1971, V/W Navigation, 1972, Search and Recovery, 1973. Sgt US Army, 1942-45 Recipient Reach Out award Diving Equipment Mfg. Assn.; named to Ill. H.S. Swimming Coaches Hall of Fame, 1982, Athletic Hall of Fame Loyola U. Chgo., 1986. Mem. Profl. Assn. Diving Instrs. (co-founder). Home and Office: 17307 Whippoorwill Trl Leander TX 78645-9734 Office Phone: 512-267-7393. Personal E-mail: rerick@msn.com.

ERICKSON, RALPH O., botany educator; b. Duluth, Minn., Oct. 27, 1914; s. Charles W. and Stella (Sjostrom) E.; m. Elinor M. Borgstedt, June 17, 1945; children: Diane Erickson Field, Elizabeth Erickson. BA, Gustavus Adolphus Coll., 1935; MS, Washington U., St. Louis, 1941, PhD, 1944. Instr. Gustavus Adolphus Coll., 1935-39; asst. chemist Western Cartridge Co., East Alton, Ill., 1942-44; instr., then asst. prof. botany U. Rochester, NY, 1944-47; mem. faculty U. Pa., Phila., 1947—, prof. botany, 1954-85, prof. emeritus, 1985—, chmn. grad. group botany, 1957-68, acting dir. divsn. biology, 1961-63, chmn. grad. group biology, 1968-76, acting chmn. dept. biology, 1977-78. Contbr. articles to profl. jours. Guggenheim fellow Calif. Inst. Tech., 1954-55. Mem. AAAS, Bot. Soc. Am., Soc. Devel. Biology (pres. 1959), Am. Inst. Biol. Scis., Sigma Xi. Home: 3300 Darby Rd Apt 3319 Haverford PA 19041-1071 E-mail: erickson@snip.net.

ERICKSON, RAY CHARLES, retired wildlife biologist; b. St. Peter, Minn., Jan. 30, 1918; s. Isaac and Martha Ernestina (Ziebarth) Erickson; m. Patricia Katherine Miles, Jan. 8, 1950 (div. Nov. 8, 1951); 1 child, Susan Eileen; m. Helen Josephine Haworth, Sept. 10, 1953 (dec. Nov. 16, 1996); children: Joanne Louise, David Wayne, Thomas Alan; m. Grace Marjorie Hayes, May 2, 2001. Student, George Washington U., 1939—40; AB, Gustavus Adolphus Coll., 1941; MS, Iowa State U., 1942, PhD, 1948. Wildlife biologist U.S. Fish and Wildlife Svc., Burns, Oreg., 1948—57, rsch. staff specialist divsn. wildlife rsch. Washington, 1957—65, supr. endangered wildlife rsch. program Laurel, Md., 1965—80; ret., 1980. Mem., scientist Oreg. Natural Heritage Adv. Coun., Salem, 1990—2002. Contbr. articles to profl. publs. Lt. (j.g.) USNR, 1943—46, PTO. Named Disting. Alumnus, Gustavus Adolphus Coll., 1991; recipient Disting. Svc. award, U.S. Dept. of Interior, 1968, Spl. Conservation award, Nat. Wildlife Fedn., 1975, Wildlife Conservation award, Zool. Soc. San Diego, 1979. Mem.: Whooping Crane Conservation Assn. (life), Washington Biologists' Field Club (pres. 1967—70). Lutheran. Achievements include federal refuge management studies of the role of grazing and other agricultural practices in wetland wildlife production; conceiving and implementing endangered species research involving coordinated laboratory and ecological investigations; captive propagation to preserve and restore viable wild populations. Avocations: nature watching, fishing, photography, travel. Home: 3010 Twin Oak Pl NW Salem OR 97304

ERICKSON, RICHARD AMES, physicist, emeritus educator; b. Bryant, S.D., Sept. 12, 1923; s. Ray and Mabel Gabriella (Arneson) E.; m. Frances Irene Boyd, June 13, 1943; children: Donna Mae, Jeanne Marie (Mrs. Paul Mahoney), David Ray, Kristine Ann (Mrs. Scott Stewart). B.Sc., S.D. Sch. Mines and Tech., 1944; PhD, Tex. A. and M. U., 1952. Predoctoral fellow Oak Ridge Inst. Nuclear Studies, 1949-51; asst. prof. physics U. Tenn., 1951-54; asst. prof. Ohio State U., 1954-61, assoc. prof., 1961-74, prof., 1974-79, prof. emeritus, 1979—; prof. of physics Ind. U. (ITM/MUCIA), Shah Alam, Malaysia, 1987-89; sec. faculty Ohio State U., 1975-77. Cons. Lockheed Research Lab., Palo Alto, Calif., 1964, AID, India, 1965; Mem. Univ. Area Commn., Columbus, Ohio, 1973-74 Contbg. author: Methods of Experimental Physics, vol. 3, 1961; Contbr. articles to profl. jours. Served with USNR, 1944-46. Home: 325 W Grant St Spearfish SD 57783-2334 E-mail: fizit43@spe.midco.net.

ERICKSON, RICHARD BEAU, insurance and financial company executive; b. Chgo., May 14, 1952; s. Charles Arthur and Carole Annette (Beaumont) E.; m. Dayna Natasha Erickson BS, U. Ky., 1974, MBA, 1975. CLU. Sales rep. Met. Life and affiliated cos., Chgo. Hgts., Ill., 1975-78, sales mgr. Flossmoor, Ill., 1978-80, mktg. specialist Aurora, Ill., 1980-81, branch mgr. Orland Park, Ill., 1981-84; corp. dir. Met. Life Gen. Ins. Agy. Inc., N.Y.C., 1984-86, regional sales mgr. L.A., 1986-89, agy. v.p., sr. mktg. and sales exec., 1989-98, agy. v.p., 1989-95, regional v.p., 1996-98; CEO, pres. Greater L.A. Fin. Group, Inc., L.A., 1999—2003; retirement strategy cons. Erickson and Assoc., 2003—. Rep. (Midwest) Sales Mgr. Adv., N.Y.C., 1979; dir. South Cook County Assn. Life Underwriters, Chgo., 1983. Author: Met. Manpower Development, 1981, Met. Manpower Development: A Guideline for Success, 1986. Mem. Nat. Assn. Securities Dealers, Life Underwriters Tng. Counsel, Chartered Life Underwriters, Nat. Assn. Life Underwriters, Gen. Agts. & Mgrs. Assn., Million Dollar Round Table, Sigma Nu Avocations: coaching soccer, hiking, norwegian elkhound dog shows, mountain climbing. Fax: 310-789-7999. Office Phone: 310-456-8520. E-mail: rickerickson@earthlink.net.

ERICKSON, ROBERT ALLEN, English literature educator; b. Fargo, N.D., Apr. 1, 1940; s. Allen Gerald and Ruth Dorothy (Dahl) E.; m. Liisa Raatikainen, Nov. 21, 1966; children: Martin, Stephen, Annaliisa. AB, Boston U., 1962; MA, Yale U., 1964, PhD, 1966. Asst. instr. in English Yale U., New

Haven, 1965; asst. prof. of English U. Calif., Santa Barbara, 1966-73, lectr. in English with security, 1973-77, assoc. prof. of English, 1977-85, prof. English, 1985—. Author: Mother Midnight, 1986, The History of John Bull, 1976, The Language of the Heart, 1600-1750, 1997; contbr. articles to profl. jours. Vis. scholar Fulbright Sr. fellow, Finland, 1999—2000; Augustus Howe Buck scholarship, Boston U., 1958—60, Woodrow Wilson fellow, 1962—63, Fulbright fellow, U.S. Govt., 1965—69. Mem. Am. Soc. for Eighteenth Century Studies. Home: 2517 Medcliff Rd Santa Barbara CA 93109-1819 Office: Dept English U Calif Dept English Santa Barbara CA 93106 Business E-Mail: erickson@english.ucsb.edu.

ERICKSON, ROBERT W., military officer, educator, consultant; s. Duane and Janice Erickson; m. Theresa Erickson, Apr. 20, 1991; 4 children. BS in Aero. Engring., Embry-Riddle Aero. U., 1990; MBA, Baker Coll., 1998; PhD in Orgnl. Leadership - Bus., Regent U., 2005. Cert. acquisition profl. devel., Program Mgmt. Level III Dept. Def., acquisition profl. devel., Sys. Plan., R & D Level III Dept. Def., acquisition profl. devel., Test & Evaluation Level III Dept. Def. Mgmt. engr. 355th Wing USAF, Davis-Monthan AFB, Ariz., 1991—94; flight test engr. USAF Flight Test Ctr., Edwards AFB, Calif., 1994—97; fellow Lockheed Martin Electronics & Missiles, Orlando, Fla., 1997—98; dep. program mgr. Delta IV (evolved expendable launch vehicle) USAF Space & Missile Ctr., El Segundo, Calif., 1998—2002; chief space planning, programming and budgeting sys. USAF, Washington, 2002—03, space program element monitor operationally responsive space, 2003—; adj. faculty Regent U., Virginia Beach, 2005—, LeTourneau U., Longview, 2005—. Cons. BTC Enterprises, Woodbridge, Va., 2002—. Maj. USAF, 1991. Decorated Commendation medal USAF, Sec. of the Air Force Welch Mgmt. award, Meritorious Svc. medals, David Packard Excellence in Acquisition award Dept. Def.; scholar USAF, 1988—90, Daedalian Found., 1989; Edn. with Industry fellow, USAF, 1997—98. Mem.: Internat. Leadership Assn. (assoc.), So. Mgmt. Assn. (assoc.), Soc. Indsl. and Orgnl. Psychology (assoc.), World Future Soc. (assoc.), Acad. Mgmt. (assoc.). Achievements include research in the antecedents to motivation to lead and the affects of collective efficacy. Home: 4074 Westwind Dr Woodbridge VA 22193

ERICKSON, RODNEY ALLEN, university executive, provost; b. Frederic, Wis., Oct. 3, 1946; s. Reuben Alexander and Elva Imogene (Bergman) E.; m. Sharon Lea Young, May 3, 1969; children: Craig, Jeffrey. BA, U. Minn., 1968, MA, 1970; PhD, U. Wash., 1973. Asst. prof. U. Wis., Madison, 1973-77, Pa. State U., University Park, 1977-79, assoc. prof., 1979-84, prof., 1984—, dean grad. sch., 1995-99, v.p. for rsch., 1997-99, exec. v.p., provost, 1999—. Staff sgt. USAR, 1966-72. Simon Sr. rsch. fellow U. Manchester (England), 1982, Census rsch. fellow NSF, Washington, 1989; sr. rsch. scholar Fulbright Commn., Washington, 1982. Mem. Am. Geographical Soc. (councilor 1984-96). Avocations: grain farming, windsurfing, skiing. Office: Pa State U 201 Old Main University Park PA 16802-1503 Fax: (814) 863-8583. E-mail: rae@psu.edu.

ERICKSON, SUSAN PHILLIANS, secondary school educator; b. Uniontown, Pa., July 31, 1947; d. John William and Louise (Grannell) P.; m. Philip Milton Erickson, July 1, 1972; 1 child, Spencer Philip. BA, Thiel Coll., 1969; student, W.Va. U., 1970-71, SUNY, Fredonia, 1974-92. Cert. tchr., NY. Tchr. Jamestown (NY) Bd. Edn., 1969—2002, ret., 2002. Coord. German-Am. Partnership program Jamestown and Maximilian-Kolbe-Gymnasium, 1978-92, Lessing Gymnasium, 1993-1998; cons. Jamestown Pub. Schs., 2003-04. Mem. NEA ret., 2003; Am. Assn. Tchrs. German, Am. Assn. Tchrs. French, NY Assn. Fgn. Lang. Tchrs., Nat. Edn. Assn. NY, NY State Ret. Tchrs. Assn., Jamestown Tchrs. Assn. (dist. liasion com. 1976-79), DAR, Norden Women's Club, PTA, Delta Epsilon Phi. Republican. Meth. Home: 4471 Bayview Rd Bemus Point NY 14712-9754 Personal E-mail: genny@madbbs.com.

ERICKSON, W(ALTER) BRUCE, business and economics educator, entrepreneur; b. Chgo., Mar. 4, 1938; s. Clifford Eric and Mildred B. (Brinkmeier) E. BA, Mich. State U., 1959, MA, 1960, PhD in Econs., 1965. Rsch. assoc. subcom. on antitrust and monopoly U.S. Senate, 1960-61; asst. prof. econs. Bowling Green (Ohio) U., 1964-66; asst. prof. bus. and govt. Coll. Bus. Adminstrn., U. Minn., Mpls., 1966-70, assoc. prof., 1971-75, prof. dept. mgmt., 1975—, prof., chmn. dept. mgmt., 1977-80, co-chmn., then chmn., 1988-92. Bd. dirs. various bus., non-profit and venture capital orgns.; cons. rock salt antitrust cases for atty. gens. Mich., cons. rock salt antitrust cases for atty. gens. Calif., Ill., Wis., Minn.; cons. U.S. Justice Dept. Author: An Introduction to Contemporary Business, 4th edit., 1985, Government and Business, 1980, 2d edit., 1984, International Business, 1998; co-author: International Business, 1998; bd. editors Antitrust Law and Econs. Rev., Jour. Indsl. Orgn.; contbr. articles to profl. jours. Bd. dirs. Found. for Constl. Edn. and the Citizens League, 1991-92; mem. ethics com. Ebenezer System, Minn. Mem. Am. Econ. Assn., Royal Econ. Soc. Office: Carlson Sch Mgmt 321 19th Ave S Minneapolis MN 55455-0438

ERICKSON, WILLIAM HURT, retired state supreme court justice; b. Denver, May 11, 1924; s. Arthur Xavier and Virginia (Hurt) E.; m. Doris Rogers, Dec. 24, 1953; children: Barbara Ann, Virginia Lee, Stephen Arthur, William Taylor. Degree in petroleum engring., Colo. Sch. Mines, 1947; student, U. Mich., 1949; LLB, U. Va., 1950; PhD in Engring. (hon.), Colo. Sch. of Mines, 2002. Bar: Colo. 1951. Pvt. practice, Denver; state supreme ct. justice Colo. Supreme Ct., 1971-96, state supreme ct. chief justice, 1983-86; faculty NYU Appellate Judges Sch., 1972-85. Mem. exec. Commn. on Accreditation of Law Enforcement Agys., 1980-83; chmn. Pres.'s Nat. Commn. for Rev. of Fed. and State Laws Relating to Wiretapping and Electronic Surveillance, 1976. Chmn. Erickson Commn., 1997, Limitations on use Deadly Force by Police; chmn. gov.'s Columbine Rev. Commn., 1999-2001. With USAAF, 1943. Recipient Disting. Achievement medal Colo. Sch. Mines, 1990. Fellow Internat. Acad. Trial Lawyers (former sec.), Am. Coll. Trial Lawyers, Am. Bar Found. (chmn. 1985), Internat. Soc. Barristers (pres. 1971); mem. ABA, (bd. govs. 1975-79, former chmn. com. on standards criminal justice, former chmn. coun. criminal law sect., former chmn. com. to implement standards criminal justice, mem. long-range planning com., action com. to reduce ct. cost and delay), Colo. Bar Assn. (award of merit 1989), Denver Bar Assn. (past pres., trustee), Am. Law Inst. (coun. 1973—), Practising Law Inst. (nat. adv. coun., bd. govs. Colo.), Freedoms Found. at Valley Forge (nat. coun. trustees, 1986—), Order of Coif, Scribes (pres. 1978). Home: 10 Martin Ln Englewood CO 80113-4821 E-mail: bnderickson@yahoo.com.

ERICSON, BRUCE ALAN, lawyer; b. Buffalo, Feb. 28, 1952; s. Carl H. and Jean (Herman) E.; m. Elizabeth Whitney Burton, Feb. 6, 1988; children: John Cotton, Whitney Burton. AB, U. Pa., 1974; JD, Harvard U., 1977. Bar: Calif. 1977, U.S. Dist. Ct. (no. dist.) Calif. 1977, U.S. Dist. Ct. (ea. dist. and so. dist.) Calif. 1988, U.S. Dist. Ct. Ariz. 1992, U.S. Ct. Appeals (9th cir.) 1981, U.S. Ct. Appeals (11th cir.), 1991, U.S. Ct. Appeals (D.C. cir.) 1994, U.S. Supreme Ct. 1982. Assoc. Pillsbury, Madison & Sutro, San Francisco, 1977-84, ptnr., 1985—2001, Pillsbury Winthrop LLP, San Francisco, 2001—05; ptnr., chmn. Securities Litigation practice Pillsbury Winthrop Shaw Pittman, San Francisco, 2005—. Judge pro tem. San Francisco Mcpl. Ct., 1984—. Contbr. articles to profl. jours. Named No. Calif. Super Lawyer, San Francisco Mag., 2004. Mem. ABA, San Francisco Bar Assn., Phi Beta Kappa. Clubs: Olympic (San Francisco). Republican. Avocations: skiing, squash. Office: Pillsbury Winthrop Shaw Pittman 50 Fremont St San Francisco CA 94105 Office Phone: 415-983-1560. Office Fax: 415-983-1200. Business E-Mail: bruce.ericson@pillsburylaw.com.

ERICSON, DAVID FRANK, political scientist, educator; b. Chgo., June 18, 1950; s. Arthur Edward Ericson and Ruth Irene Kessel. BA in Polit. Sci., Wayne State U., 1972; MA in Polit. Sci., U. Mich., 1973, MA in Journalism, 1976; PhD in Polit. Sci., U. Chgo., 1987. Journalist Jackson (Mich.) Citizen-Patriot, 1977, Detroit News, 1978-80; instr. Oberlin (Ohio) Coll., 1986-87; prof. Wichita (Kans.) State U., 1992—. Vis. prof. Washington U., St. Louis, 1987—89, U. Chgo., 1990—91. Author: (book) The Shaping of American Liberalism: The Debates Over Ratification, Nullification, and Slavery, 1993, The Debate Over Slavery: Antislavery and Proslavery Liberalism in Antebellum America, 2001; editor: The Liberal Tradition in American Politics: Reassessing the Legacy of Amercian Liberalism, 1999; contbr. articles to profl. jours. Postdoctoral fellow, John M. Olin Ctr. Study History Polit. Culture, U. Chgo., 1989—90, Summer Rsch. grantee, NEH, 1994. Mem.: Social Sci. History Assn., Midwest Polit. Sci. Assn., Am. Polit. Sci. Assn., Phi Beta Kappa, Pi Sigma Alpha. Avocations: tennis, basketball. Home: 402 N Bluff St Wichita KS 67208-3729 Office Phone: 316-978-7128. Business E-Mail: david.ericson@wichita.edu.

ERICSON, JON MEYER, academic administrator, language educator; b. Three Forks, Mont., Aug. 1, 1928; s. George Edward and Olga Young (Meyer) E.; m. Amy Knutson, Aug. 19, 1951; children: Jon, Beth, Joel, Ingrid. BA, Pacific Luth. Coll., 1952; MA, Stanford U., 1953, PhD, 1961. Instr. argumentation, pub. speaking, rhetorical theory and criticism Tex. Luth. Coll., Seguin, 1953-54; asst. prof. Pacific Luth. Coll., Tacoma, 1954-57; instr., dir. forensics Stanford (Calif.) U., 1959-61, asst. prof., 1961-64; from assoc. prof. to prof., dept. head Cen. Wash. State U., Ellensburg, 1964-70, prof. dept. speech communication, 1970—98; dean sch. liberal arts Calif. Poly. State U., San Luis Obispo, 1988—95, dept. dir. London Study Program, 1984-96. Co-author: The Debater's Guide, 1961; contbg. author: Demosthenes on the Crown, 1967, Public Speaking as Dialogue, 1970; contbr. articles to profl. jours. and books Pres. Pacific Forensic League, 1961-62, No. Calif. Forensic Assn., 1962-63; mem., trustee Pacific Luth. Theol. Sem., Berkeley, 1961-64. Served with USN, 1946-48. Danforth tchr., 1957; Univ. Honors scholarship Stanford U., 1957-61. Lutheran. Avocations: tennis, gardening. Home: 741 Pasatiempo Dr San Luis Obispo CA 93405-1033

ERICSON, ROBERT WALTER, lawyer; b. Highland Park, Ill., June 24, 1948; BA, Johns Hopkins U., 1970, MA, 1971; JD, U. Va., 1976. Bar: Ill. 1976, N.Y. 1992. Ptnr. Winston & Strawn, N.Y.C. Mem.: N.Y. State Bar Assn. Office: Winston & Strawn 200 Park Ave Fl 41 New York NY 10166-4401 Office Phone: 212-294-6741. Business E-Mail: rericson@winston.com.

ERICSON, ROGER DELWIN, lawyer, forest resource company executive; b. Moline, Ill, Dec. 21, 1934; s. Carl D. and Linnea E. (Challman) E.; m. Norma F. Brown, Aug. 1, 1957; children: Catherine Lynn, David. AB, JD, Stetson U., DeLand, Fla., 1958; MBA, U. Chgo., 1971. Bar: Fla. 1958, Ill. 1959, Ind. 1974. Atty. Brunswick Corp., Skokie, Ill., 1959-62; asst. sec., asst. gen. counsel Chemetron Corp., Chgo., 1962-73; asst. v.p. Inland Container Corp., Indpls., 1973-75, v.p., gen. counsel, sec., 1975-83, Temple-Inland, Inc., 1983-94, of counsel, 1994—. V.p., sec. bd. dirs. Inland Container Corp.; dir., pres., co-CEO Kraft Land Svcs., Inc., Atlanta, 1978-88; bd. dirs., v.p. Guaranty Holdings Inc., Dallas; v.p. Temple-Inland Fin. Svcs., Inc., Austin, 1990-94; bd. dirs. Temple-Inland Forest Products, Temple-Inland Real Estate Investment, Inc., Temple-Inland Realty Inc. Trustee Chgo. Homes for Children, 1971-74; mem. alumni coun. U. Chgo., 1972-76; mem. Palatine Twp. Youth Commn., 1969-72; sect. chmn. Chgo. Heart Assn., 1972, 73; alumni bd. dirs. Stetson U.; bd. dirs. Temple-Inland Found; past mem. Safe and Drug-Free Comm. Collier County Sch. Bd. Mem. ABA, Am. Arbitration Assn. (past nat. panel comml. arbitrators), Am. Soc. Corp. Secs., Am. Forest Products Assn. (past mem. govt. affairs com. and legal com.), Am. Corp. Counsel Assn., Ind. Bar Assn., Fla. Bar Assn., Chgo. Bar Assn., Indpls. Bar Assn. (chmn. corp. counsel sect., mem. profl. responsibility com. 1982), Collier County Bar Assn., Indpls. C. of C. (govt. affairs com.), Plum Grove Club (pres. 1967), The Floridian Club, Omicron Delta Kappa, Phi Delta Phi. Office: PO Box 110218 Naples FL 34108-0104 *Concentrate on the desired final result of any activity. Never forget your family, co-workers, friends.*

ERICSON, WILLIAM B., orthopedic hand surgeon; MD, Harvard U., 1983; BS, MIT, 1979. Diplomate Am. Bd. Orthopedics and Hand Surgery. Orthop. hand surgeon Winchester (Mass.) Hand Surgery, 1990—. Fellow: ACS, Am. Acad. Orthop. Surgeons; mem.: MOA (pres. 1997—98), ASSH. Achievements include discovery of anatomic basis of repetitive strain injuries. Office: Winchester Hand Surgery 19930 Bullinger Way NE Seattle WA 98155 Office Phone: 206-363-6947.

ERICSSON, SALLY CLAIRE, not-for-profit official; b. Madison, Wis., Jan. 16, 1953; d. William H. and JoAnn (Finnell) Ericsson; m. Thomas A. Garwin, Oct. 7, 1979; children: Rachel Garwin, Benjamin Garwin. B in Urban and Regional Planning, U. Ill., 1976; M in Pub. Policy, Harvard U., 1981. Legis. analyst Dem. Steering and Policy Com, Washington, 1982-87; adminstr. asst. Rep. Sam Geidenson U.S. Ho. Reps., Washington, 1987-89; legis. asst. to Sen. John F. Kerry U.S. Senate, Washington, 1989-90; asst. to pres. for policy and rsch. Svc. Employees Internat. Union, Washington, 1990-93; assoc. under sec. for econ. affairs U.S. Dept. Commerce, Washington, 1993-96, dep. chief of staff, 1996-97; assoc. dir. natural resources Coun. Environ. Quality, Exec. Office of the Pres., 1997-99; dir. outreach Pew Ctr. Global Climate Change, Arlington, Va., 1999—2005. Home: 1805 Monroe St NW Washington DC 20010-1014

ERIE, STEVEN PHILIP, political science professor; b. Bakersfield, Calif., Jan. 28, 1946; s. Harlan Eugene Erie (dec.) and Carmen Joyce (O'Brien) Barr. BA, UCLA, 1967, MA, 1969, PhD, 1975. Asst. prof. pub. adminstrn. U. So. Calif., L.A., 1975-78; asst. prof. polit. sci. SUNY, Albany, 1978-80; policy analyst U.S. Dept. Health and Human Svcs., Washington, 1980-81; asst. prof. U. Calif. San Diego, La Jolla, 1981-89, assoc. prof. polit. sci., adj. prof. history, 1989—. Cons. L.A. Pub. Commn. on County Govt., 1975-76, Ednl. Testing Svc., Princeton, N.J., 1989-91; cons. RAND, Santa Monica, 1997—, Metropolitan Forum Project, L.A., 1997—, L.A. Econ. Devel. Corp., 1999—, Orange County Bus. Coun., 1998—; sr. fellow So. Calif. Studies Ctr., L.A., 1997—. Author: Rainbow's End, 1988 (Best Book on Urban Politics, Am. Polit. Sci. Assn. 1989, Robert Park award Am. Sociology Assn. 1989); contbg. editor Metro Investment Report, 1994—; mem. editl. adv. bd. U. Press of Va., Charlottesville, 1993—. Active Citizens Charter Reform Com., San Diego, 1993, 98-00, Pacific Coun. on Internat. Politics, 1998—, San Diego Dialogue, 1995—, Citizens Coordinate for Century Three, San Diego, 1996; bd. dirs. Water and Power Assocs., L.A., 1994—, Gov.'s Commn. on Bldg. for 21st Century, 1998—; mem. Pacific Coun. on Internat. Policy, 1998—. Charles F. Scott Meml. fellow UCLA, 1972-78: Faculty fellow Nat. Assn. Schs. of Pub. Affairs and Adminstrn., Washington, 1980-81; Faculty Rsch. grantee Calif. Policy Seminar, Berkeley, 1990, 94. Mem. Am. Polit. Sci. Assn. (exec. coun. urban politics sect. 1989-91, chair book prize com. 1991), Western Polit. Sci. Assn., Orgn. Am. Historians, Calif. Hist. Soc. Avocations: reading, tennis, swimming. Office: Univ Calif San Diego Dept Polit Sci La Jolla CA 92093

ERIKSEN, CHARLES WALTER, psychologist, educator; b. Omaha, Feb. 4, 1923; s. Charles Hans and Luella (Carlson) E.; m. Garnita Tharp, July 22, 1945 (div. Jan. 1971); children: Michael John, Kathy Ann; m. Barbara Becker, Apr. 1971. BA summa cum laude, U. Omaha, 1943; PhD, Stanford, 1950. Asst. prof. Johns Hopkins U., Balt., 1949-53, research scientist, 1954-55; lectr. Harvard U., Cambridge, Mass., 1953-54; mem. faculty U. Ill., Urbana, 1956—, prof., 1959-93, prof. emeritus, 1993—. Rsch. cons. VA, 1960-80; mem. psycho-biology panel NSF, 1963; mem. exptl. psychology study sect. NIH, 1958-62, 66-70; Pillsbury Meml. lectr. Cornell U., 1966; keynote address 1st Internat. Congress on Visual Search, U. Durham, U.K., 1988, European Congress for Cognitive Psychology, Elsinore, Denmark, 1993; invited lectr. Max Plank Inst., Munich, 1993, Universidad Autonoma de Madrid, 1993, U. of Salamanca, Spain, 1993. Author: Behavior and Awareness, 1962; editor Am. Jour. Psychology, 1968; prin. editor Perception and Psychophysics, 1971-93; cons. editor Jour. Exptl. Psychology, 1965-71, Jour. Gerontology, 1980—; contbr. articles to profl. jours. Recipient Stratton award Am. Psychopath. Assn., 1964, NIMH Research Career award, 1964 Fellow AAAS; mem. Am. Psychol. Soc., Psychonomic Soc., Soc. Exptl. Psychologists, Midwestern Psychol. Assn., Sigma Xi. Home: 22485 State Highway 133 Oakland IL 61943-6822 Office: U Ill Psychol Bldg 603 E Daniel St Champaign IL 61820-6232 Personal E-mail: erikbarb@consolidated.net.

ERIKSON, G(EORGE) E(MIL) (ERIK ERIKSON), anatomist, archivist, historian; b. Palmer, Mass., May 3, 1920; s. Emil and Sofia (Gustafson) Erikson; m. Suzanne J. Henderson, Apr. 23, 1950; children: Ann, David, John, Thomas. BS, Mass. State Coll. (now U. Mass.), 1941; MA in Biology, Harvard U., 1946, PhD in Biology, 1948. Reader in history of sci. and learning Harvard U., 1943—45, asst. prof. gen. edn. in biology, 1949—52, lectr. anthropology, 1965; instr. anatomy Harvard Med. Sch., 1947—49, rsch. fellow anatomy, 1949—52, assoc. in anatomy, 1952—55, asst. prof. anatomy, 1955—65, assoc. curator Warren Anat. Mus., 1961—65; prof. med. sci. Brown U., Providence, 1965—90, chmn. sect. morphology, 1968—85, co-chmn. sect. population biology, morphology & genetics and chmn. for anatomy, 1985—90, prof. emeritus, 1990—; vis. prof., Dept. Anatomy and Cellular Biology Harvard U. Med. Sch., 1990—91; vis. lectr. in surgery Med. Sch. Harvard U., 1990—99; anatomist dept. surgery Mass. Gen. Hosp., Boston, 1990—2004; pres. Erikson Biog. Inst., Inc., Providence, 1990—. Adv. bd. Reed Elsevier, 1990; anatomist various Boston Hosps., 1952—82, Mass. Gen. Hosp. Sch. Med. Illus., 1947—60, Mass. Gen. Hosp., 1990—, Lahey Clinic, Boston, 1947—60; anatomist depts. surgery, orthopedics, rehab. and neurosurgery R.I. Hosp., 1967—; cons. anatomist Surg. Techniques Illus., 1976—80; cons. Dorlands Illus. Med. Dictionary, Rockefeller Found. med. and pub. health, S. Am., 1949; specialist State Dept., Brazil, 1962; adj. mem. faculty R.I. Sch. Design, 1970—; Kate Hurd Mead lectr. Coll. Physicians Phila., 1977; Raymond C. Truex lectr. Hahnemann U. Sch. Med., 1985. Fellow Sheldon Traveling, Harvard Ctrl. Am., 1946, Guggenheim, S. Am., 1949, Fulbright, Brazil, 1962. Mem.: Assn. of Anatomy Chairmen (emeritus), Oral History Medicine, Am. Assn. History Medicine (coun. 1972—74), Am. Assn. Anatomists (historian and archivist 1972—86, archivist 1986—90, historian and archivist 1990—), Am. Assn. Phys. Anthropologists (archivist and co-historian 1981—), History Sci. Soc. (life), Alpha Omega Alpha Honor Med. Soc. (faculty election 1957). Achievements include research in new world primates and gen. intellectual history, especially biology and medicine; development of of database foundation of Erikson Biographical Institute, 1990, with database of 450,000 individuals. also: Erikson Biog Inst 242B Meeting St Providence RI 02906-2221 Office Phone: 401-861-8848. Business E-Mail: gee@biographical.org.

ERIKSON, KAI, sociologist, educator; b. Vienna, Feb. 12, 1931; came to U.S., 1933, naturalized, 1937; s. Erik H. and Joan (Serson) E.; m. Joanna M. Slivka, Jan. 27, 1961; children: Keith S., Christopher J. BA, Reed Coll., 1953; MA, U. Chgo., 1955, PhD, 1963. Instr. psychiatry U. Pitts., 1959-63; assoc. prof. Emory U., Atlanta, 1963-66; prof. sociology and Am. studies Yale U., New Haven, 1966, master Trumbull Coll., 1969-73; editor Yale Rev., 1979-89. Author: Wayward Puritans, 1966, Everything in Its Path, 1976, A New Species of Trouble, 1994. With AUS, 1955-57. Fellow Am. Sociol. Assn. (MacIver award 1967, Sorokin award 1977, pres. 1984-85); mem. Soc. Study Social Problems (pres. 1970-71), Eastern Sociol. Soc. (pres. 1980-81) Home: 53 Quarry Dock Rd Branford CT 06405-4655 Office: Yale U Dept Sociology PO Box 208265 New Haven CT 06520-8265 Business E-Mail: kai.erikson@yale.edu.

ERIKSON, KAROLE JANE, music educator; d. Glen M and Betty J. Erikson; m. Jay D. Miller, Feb. 17, 1957; 1 child, Colin E. Immenschuh Miller. MLS, Ft. Hays U., 2003. Nat. cert. music tchr. Music Tchrs. Nat. Assn., 1990. Piano, organ instr. Barton County C.C., Great Bend, 1984—. Mem.: Music Tchrs. Nat. Assn. Office: Barton County CC 245 NE 30th Rd Great Bend KS 67530 Office Phone: 620-792-9384.

ERIKSON, RAYMOND LEO, biology professor; b. Eagle, Wis., Jan. 24, 1936; m. 1958. BS, U. Wis., 1958, MS, 1961, PhD in Molecular Biology, 1963. Asst. prof. to assoc. prof. U. Colo., Denver, 1965-72, prof. pathology, 1972-82; John F. Drum Am. Cancer Soc. Prof. Cellular and Devel. Biology Harvard U., Cambridge, Mass., 1982—. Mem. adv. coun. GM Cancer Rsch. Found. USPHS fellow, 1963-65; recipient Papaicolau award, 1980, Albert Lasker Basic Med Rsch. award, Lasker Found., 1982, Robert Koch prize, 1982, Alfred P. Sloan Jr. prize GM Cancer Rsch. Found., 1983, Hammer Cancer Rsch. prize, 1984. Mem. NAS, Am. Academia of Arts and Scis., Am. Soc. Biol. Chemists, Am. Soc. Microbiology. Office: Harvard U Biol Labs Rm 2048 16 Divinity Ave Cambridge MA 02138-2020

ERIKSON, SHELDON R., oil field services company executive; b. Chgo., Sept. 23, 1941; s. Roy A. and Florence Mary (Sheldon) E.; children: Steven, Michael. MBA, Harvard U., 1970. Assoc. Booz, Allen & Hamilton, Cleve., 1970-75; gen. mgr. Gen. Electric Co., Houston, 1975-80; group v.p. plastics and chems. Hoover Universal, Ann Arbor, Mich., 1980-82; pres. oilfield services group NL Industries, Houston, 1982-86; pres. Joy Petroleum Equipment Co., Houston, 1986-87; pres., chief exec. officer The Western Co. of N.Am., Ft. Worth, 1987-88, also bd. dirs., 1987-95, chmn., pres., chief exec. officer, 1988-95; pres., chief exec. ofcr. Cooper Cameron Corp., Houston, 1995—, chmn., 1996—. Bd. dirs. Harvard Bus. Sch. Club, Houston. Office: Cooper Cameron Corp 515 Post Oak Blvd Houston TX 77027-9482*

ERION, CAROL ELIZABETH, music educator; b. Quincy, Ill., Jan. 16, 1943; d. Alva Eugene and Margaret Althea (Kaempfer) McKenney; m. David F. Erion, June 19, 1965; children: Elizabeth Celia Erion Matthews, Paul Frederick. MusB, Oberlin Coll., 1965; MusM, New England Conservatory Music, 1982; cert., U. Toronto, Ont., Can., 1978, Mozarteum Acad. Music, Salzburg, Austria, 1979. Music tchr. Montessori Sch. No. Va., Annandale, 1972-84, St. Agnes Episcopal Sch., Alexandria, Va., 1984-85, The Sidwell Friends Sch., Washington, 1985-87; music and fine arts tchr. Arlington (Va.) Pub. Schs., 1988-00; supr. arts edn. Arlington Pub. Schs., 2000—. Music dir. All Saints Episcopal Ch., Alexandria, 1983-90; workshop clinician various music edn. orgns. in U.S., 1980—; adj. instr. George Mason U., Fairfax, Va., 1983-2001; cons. WETA-TV, Washington, 1987. Author: Tales to Tell, Tales to Play, 1982; contbr. articles to profl. jours. Humanities fellow Coun. Basic Edn., 1989. Mem. NEA, AAUW, ASCD, Am. Recorder Soc., Am. Orff Schulwerk Assn. (pres. 1993-95), Arlington Edn. Assn. (pres. 1998-2000). Democrat. Episcopalian. Home: 19 W Linden St Alexandria VA 22301-2621 Office Phone: 703-228-6171. E-mail: cerion@arlington.va.us.

ERIQAT, VICTORIA ALDERMAN, small business owner, lawyer; b. LA, Mar. 20, 1940; d. James William and Ann Alderman; m. Albert Kareem Eriqat, Apr. 18, 1959; children: David Alan, Cheryl Anne, Joseph Michael, Suzanne Michelle. AA, Mesa Coll., 1977; BS, San Diego State U., 1979, MS, 1983; JD, U. San Diego, 1988. Corp. sec./treas. AKE Profl. Engrs., San Diego, 1971, also bd. dirs.; owner, operator Eriqat Enterprises, San Diego, 1971—; pvt. practice law, 1989. Bd. dirs., area chmn. San Diego council Girl Scouts U.S., 1970—; vol. cons. Small Bus. Adminstrn. San Diego, 1978-79. Merit scholar U. San Diego Sch. Law, 1984. Mem. Calif. Bar Assn., San Diego County Bar Assn., Inst. Cert. Fin. Planners, San Diego Bd. Realtors, Phi Kappa Phi, Beta Gamma Sigma. Avocations: piano, accordion, windsurfing, skating, bodybuilding. Home: 8264 Caminito Maritimo La Jolla CA 92037-2204 Office: Law Offices Victoria Enjat 4060 30th St San Diego CA 92104 Office Phone: 619-563-5586.

ERISTOFF, ANDREW S., state agency administrator; b. N.Y.C., Feb. 20, 1963; m. Catherine E. Baxter; 3 children. BA cum laude, Princeton U., 1985; JD cum laude, Georgetown U., 1989. Legis. analyst N.Y. State Senate, 1987; assoc. Webster & Sheffield Law Firm, 1989-91; counsel to Senator Roy M. Goodman, 1991-93; councilman dist. 4 City of N.Y., 1993—99; commr. NYC Dept. Fin., 1999—2002, New York State Dept. Tax and Fin., 2003—. Mem.: Assn. Bar City N.Y. Office: W A Harriman Campus Albany NY 12227 Office Phone: 518-457-2244. Fax: 518-485-8593. Business E-Mail: andrew_eristoff@tax.state.ny.us.

ERKAMP, RAMON QUIDO, medical researcher, consultant; s. Henri Victor and Ursula Erkamp. BS in electrical engring., Hogeschool Enschede, The Netherlands, 1992; Ms in bio engring., U. Mich., 1995, MSE in electrical engring., 1997; PhD in Biomedical Engring., U. Mich., Ann Arbor, 2003. Rsch. asst. U. Mich., Ann Arbor, 1993—2003, postdoctoral rsch. fellow,

2003—05; rsch. scientist Philips Rsch., Briar Cliff Manor, NY, 2005—. Home: 13080 Rawsonville Rd Belleville MI 48111 Office: Philips Rsch 345 Scarborough Rd Briarcliff Manor NY 10510 Office Phone: 734-647-0846. E-mail: erkamp@umich.edu.

ERKINE, ALEXANDRE M., science educator; b. Russia, June 11, 1957; arrived in US, 1993; BSc, MSc, St. Petersburg State U., Russia, 1979; PhD, St. Petersburg STate U., Russia, 1987. Post doctoral position La. State U., Shreveport, 1993—98, rsch. asst. prof., 1998—2003, asst. prof. sch. medicine Vermillion, SD, 2003—. Grantee NSF Rsch. grant, NSF, 2002—. Office: Univ SD Sch of Medicine 414 E Clark St Vermillion SD 57069

ERKKILA-RICKER, BARBARA HOWELL, writer, photographer; b. Boston, July 11, 1918; d. John William and Adelia Parsons (Jones) Howell; m. Onni R. Erkkila, Apr. 27, 1941 (dec. 1981); children: John W., Kathleen L., Marjorie A.; m. G. Ashton Ricker, FEb. 5, 2000. Student, Boston U. Evening Coll., 1959—62. Corr. Gloucester (Mas.) Daily Times, 1936-53, feature writer, 1953—, women's editor, 1967-72, cmty. news editor, 1972-74. Editor weekly mag. Essex County Newspapers, Gloucester, 1973, editl. asst., 1974-85, writer, photographer, 1970—; tchr. Russian, Ipswich (Mass.) Pub. Schs., evenings, 1962-63; jewelry designer; quarry historian. Author: Hammers on Stone, 1981, Village at Lane's Cove, 1989; editor Lane's Cove Cook Book, 1954; contbr. articles to popular mags. Mem. price panel OPA, 1944-46; mem. ARC nurse's aide class Addison Gilbert Hosp., 1942-43; mem. Gloucester Hist. Commn., 1967-69, 93-2000; formerly active Girl Scouts U.S.A.; sec. Lanesville C.C., 1957-94; apptd. granite industry cons. Cape Ann (Mass.) Hist. Assn. Mus., 1997. Recipient 2d prize for feature writing UPI, 1970, historian award Town of Rockport, 1978, First Walker Hancock award City of Gloucester, 1999. Mem. Sandy Bay Hist. Soc., Ohio Geneal. Soc., Westford Hist. Soc., Cape Ann Hist. Assn., North Shore Rock and Mineral (charter), North Shore Button Club. Congregationalist. Home and Office: 7 School St North Chelmsford MA 01863-2109 Personal E-mail: barickgran@aol.com.

ERKONEN, WILLIAM E., radiologist, medical educator; BS, U. Iowa, 1955, MD, 1958. Diplomate Am. Bd. Radiology. Intern U. Oreg., Portland, 1959; pvt. practice; resident in radiology U. Iowa Coll. Medicine, Iowa City, 1968-71; pvt. practice, 1971-87; faculty U. Iowa Coll. Medicine, 1988-94, asst. prof. radiology, 1994-98, assoc. prof., 1995-98, co-dir. Electric Differential Multimedia Lab., 1993—, assoc. prof. emeritus, 1998—. Rschr. in med. informatics and med. student instrn. and edn.; mem. anatomy and interdisciplinary com. Nat. Bd. Med. Licensure Exam., 1999—2001; lectr. history Bates Coll., 2003—. Editor: (textbook) Radiology 101 1st edit., 1998, 2d edit., 2005; contbr. articles to profl. jours.; developer electronic med. textbooks. Recipient numerous certs. of merit Radiology Soc. N.Am.; named Tchr. of Yr., U. Iowa Coll. Med., 1990, 93, 96; recipient Disting. Tchr. award for jr. faculty in clin. scis. Alpha Omega Alpha. Fellow Am. Coll. Radiology.

ERLA, KAREN, artist, painter, collagist, printmaker; b. Pitts., Nov. 17, 1942; d. Jack and Lenore (Kamons) Franklin; children: Stephanie, Joan. BFA, George Washington U., 1965; postgrad., Parsons Sch. Design, 1979-81, Carnegie Inst., 1958-59, Boston U., 1960-62, Pratt Inst., 1980-82, NYU, 1982. Solo exhbns. include Phoenix Gallery, N.Y.C., 1985, E.L. Stark Gallery, N.Y.C., 1988, Bertha Urdang Gallery, N.Y.C., 1986, Bennett and Siegel Gallery, 1989, 90, U. of South, Sewanee, Tenn., Manhattanville Coll., Purchase, N.Y., 1982, Printmaking Council of N.J., 1982, Bennet Siegel Gallery, N.Y.C., 1990, Bryant Gallery, N.Y.C., 1990, Queens Coll., N.Y.C., 1991; group shows include Herbert Johnson Mus. Art, Atlanta Coll. Art, Van Straaten Gallery, Chgo., Greene Gallery, Guilford, Conn., Nat. Mus. of Am. Art, Washington, D.C., Fine Arts Museum of L.I., N.Y., Zimmerli Mus., New Brunswick, N.J., Printmaking Council of N.J., Somerstown Studios and Gallery, Somers, N.Y., Cork Exhbn. in Lincoln Ctr., Fay Gold Gallery, Atlanta, 1984, Boston Printmakers 37th Nat. Exhbn., 1985, The Print Club's 61st Internat. Juried Exhbn., Phila., Schering-Plough Corp. Gallery, Madison, N.J., New Brunswick, N.J., Australian Nat. Gallery, 1989, E.L. Stark Exhbn., 1990, Am. Embassy, 1990, others; represented in permanent collections at Balt. Mus. of Art, Herbert F. Johnson Mus., Cornell U., Bklyn. Mus. Art, Huntsville Mus. Art, Ala., L.A. County Mus. Art, Met. Mus. Art, N.Y., Nat. Museum Am. Art, Australian Nat. Gallery, Smithsonian Inst., New Orleans Mus. Art, Phila. Mus. Art, Tampa Mus., Fla.; featured in Monograph of Karen Erla (text by Ronnie Cohen) 1988, Monoprints Karen Erla (text by Dr. Mary Lee Thompson), Paintings: Karen Erla (text by Bertha Urdang and E.L. Stark); featured in Newsday as New Yorker mag.; solo exhibitions E.L. Stark Gallery, Bertha Urdang Gallery, N.Y.C. Harrison Library, Harrison, N.Y. Manhattanville Coll., Purchase, N.Y., Sound Shore Gallery, N.Y.C., The Print Club 62d Internat., Phila. Recipient Nat. Art award, Pa., 1959, award Herbert F. Johnson Mus., Cornell U., award Mamroneck Artists Guild, 1983, Outstanding Svc. award N.Y. State Assembly, 2004, Outstanding Svc. award Westchester County Bd. Legislators, 2004, Outstanding Svc. award White Plains Bd. Legislators, 2004, Outstanding Svc. award N.Y. Bd. Legislators, 2004. Mem. World Print Council, Printmaking Council N.J., Artists Equity, Pratt Graphic Ctr., L.A. Printmaking Soc. Avocations: music, reading, travel. Address: PO Box 202 North White Plains NY 10603-0202

ERLANDSON, DAVID ALAN, education administration educator; b. Chgo., Jan. 10, 1936; s. Gerald Kenneth and Anna Marie Schlichting E.; m. Gwyneth Ellen Jones, Sept. 21, 1957; children: Paul William, Linda Ann, Daniel Lindsay, Charles David. AB, Wheaton (Ill.) Coll., 1956; MS, No. Ill. U., 1962; EdD, U. Ill., 1969. Cert. supr. all grades, Ill. Tchr. jr. high sch. Geneva (Ill.) Pub. Schs., 1959-62, Unit 4 Schs., Champaign, Ill., 1962-63, dir. gifted program, 1965-68, asst. prin., 1969-71; tchr. Univ. High Sch., Urbana, Ill., 1963-64; asst. prof. SUNY, Buffalo, 1964-65; dir. Ctr. for Upgrading Ednl. Services, Champaign, 1968-69; asst. prof. Queens Coll. CUNY, Flushing, 1971—77; prof. ednl. adminstrn. Tex. A&M U., College Station, 1977—, head dept. ednl. adminstrn., 1984-92. Dir. Prins.' Ctr., Tex. A&M U., 1983-85, 93-01. Author: Strengthening School Leadership, 1976, Doing Naturalistic Inquiry, 1993, Organizational Oversight, 1996; co-author: School Special Services, 1979, Measurement and Evaluation, 1999, The Emerging Principalship; co-editor School Leadership Library; contbr. 130 articles to books and profl. jours. Served to 1st lt. USMC, 1956-59. Mem. Nat. Assn. Secondary Sch. Prins. (commn. on standards for principalship 1985-88), Am. Ednl. Rsch. Assn., Phi Delta Kappa, Phi Kappa Phi. Democrat. Home: 1107 Glade St College Station TX 77840-4434 Office: Tex A&M U Dept Ednl Adminstrn College Station TX 77843-4226

ERLANGER, BERNARD FERDINAND, biochemist, educator; b. N.Y.C., July 13, 1923; s. Leo and Frieda (David) E.; m. Rachel Fenichel, June 23, 1946; children: Laura, Louis, Leon. BS with highest honors, CCNY, 1943; MA, NYU, 1949; PhD, Columbia U., 1951. Chemist U.S. Indsl. Chems. Co., Inc., Newark, 1943-44; tech. adviser Manhattan Project, U.S. Army, Los Alamos, 1944-46; prodn. mgr. Hexagon Labs., Inc., N.Y.C., 1946-48; faculty Columbia, 1951—, prof. microbiology, 1966—; vis. scientist Instituto Superiore di Sanita, Rome, 1961-62, Inst. Cell Biology, Shanghai, People's Republic of China, 1978. Mem. Fulbright-Hays Award Com., 1966-72; invited expert analyst biochem. and molecular biology edit. Chemtracts; mem. study sect. neurol. C, NIH, 1985-88. Recipient 600th Anniversary medal Copernican Med. Acad., Cracow, Poland, 1979,Sigma Alpha/Mu Gamma award N.Y. Heart Assn., Townsend Harris medal CUNY, 1995; Fulbright scholar U. Republic of Uruguay, 1967, Guggenheim fellow Inst. Phys.-Chem. Biology, Paris, 1969, Am. Cancer Soc. scholar Pasteur Inst., Paris, 1979. Recipient Physicians and Surgeons Disting. Svc. award Columbia U., 1996. Mem. Am. Chem. Soc., Am. Soc. Biol. Chemists, Biochem. Soc., N.Y. Acad. Scis. (mem. conf. com. 1978), Soc. Exptl. Biol. Medicine (assoc. editor proceedings 1981-88), Harvey Soc., Am. Soc. Immunologists, N.Y. Heart Assn., Am. Soc. Photobiology, Phi Beta Kappa, Sigma Alpha Mu (Gamma award). Achievements include research in mode of action of antibiotics and on cancer; investigation of mechanisms of enzyme catalysis; investigation of macromolecules concerned with genetics immunology of fullerenes, photoregulation, biological receptors; investigation of immunochemistry of buckminsterfullerenes, nanobiotechnology. Office: Columbia U 701 W 168th St New York NY 10032-2704 Home: 333 E 30 St New York NY 10016 Business E-Mail: bfe1@columbia.edu. *The scientist, like the artist, contributes most when he allows his work to be an extension of his individuality. The risks to his ego and security are great, but success brings with it the satisfaction of making a personal imprint on the future of society.*

ERLEBACHER, ARLENE CERNIK, retired lawyer; b. Chgo., Oct. 3, 1946; d. Laddie J. and Gertrude V. (Kurdys) Cernik; m. Albert Erlebacher, June 14, 1968; children: Annette Doherty, Jacqueline McCarthy. BA, Northwestern U., 1967, JD, 1973. Bar: Ill. 1974, U.S. Dist. Ct. (no. dist.) Ill. 1974, U.S. Ct. Appeals (7th cir.) 1974, Fed. Trial Bar 1983, U.S. Supreme Ct. 1985. Assoc. Sidley & Austin, Chgo., 1974-80, ptnr., 1980-95, ret., 1996. Fellow Am. Bar Found.; mem. Order of Coif. E-mail: Erlebacher@comcast.net.

ERLEBACHER, MARTHA MAYER, artist, educator; b. Jersey City, Nov. 21, 1937; d. Desiderius and Mary Mayer; m. Walter Erlebacher, June 26, 1961 (dec. Aug. 1991); children: Adrian Immanuel, Jonah Daedalus. Student, Gettysburg (Pa.) Coll., 1955-56; B of Indsl. Design, Pratt Inst., 1960, MFA, 1963. Indsl. designer, illustrator Arthur Wagner Assocs., N.Y.C., 1956-61; tchr. anatomy and figure drawing U. of Arts, Phila., 1978-94. Tchr. Phila. Coll. Art, 1966-68, 78-94; tchr. anatomical drawing and painting Grad. Sch. Figurative Art, N.Y. Acad. Art, N.Y.C., 1992—, others; guest lectr. Grad. Sch. Art Yale U., 1974, Vassar Coll., Poughkeepsie, N.Y., 1975, Phila. Coll. Art, 1976, U. Conn., Storrs, 1977, Tyler Sch. Art Temple U., 1978, Med. Coll. Pa., Phila., 1987, N.Y. Acad. Art, 1990, others; vis. artist colls. and univs. including U. Wis., Oshkosh, 1979, Syracuse U., 1986-87, U. Mich., 1988, Calif. State U., 1989, 91, Tulane U., New Orleans, 1992, Kalamazoo Inst. Arts, 1989; panelist arts shows, 1978—; juror U. Del., 1979, N.Y. Statewide Bi-Annual, Trenton, 1984, Moss Rehab. Hosp., Phila., 1985, Tex. Nat. '98, Nacogdoches. Exhibited in one-person shows at Robert Schoelkopf Gallery, N.Y.C., 1973, 75, 78, 80, 82, 85, Dart Gallery, Chgo., 1976, 78, 83, Koplin Gallery, L.A., 1989, 91, Kalamazoo Inst. Arts, 1989, Fischbach Gallery, N.Y.C., 1993, 95, The More Gallery, Phila., 1993, 97, 2000, Hackett-Freedman Gallery, San Francisco, 1999, 2002, Arnot Mus., Elmira, NY, 2001, Forum Gallery, N.Y.C., 2003, Seraphin Gallery, Phila., 2005, others; exhibited in group shows Bklyn. Mus., 1960, Phila. Art Alliance, 1967, Suffolk Mus., Stony Brook, N.Y., 1971, Pratt Manhattan Ctr., 1971, Am. Acad. Arts and Letters, N.Y.C., 1973, 76, 87, Yale U. Art Gallery, 1973, Phila. Civic Ctr., 1974, Mus. Art, Penn. State U., 1974, 76, N.Y. Cultural Ctr., 1975, Libr. Congress, 1975, U. Notre Dame, 1976, Ringling Mus. Art, Sarasota, Fla., 1976, Fogg Art Mus. Harvard U., Cambridge, Mass., 1976, Art Gallery Boston U., 1977, Penn. Acad. Fine Arts, 1978, 81, 82, Phila. Mus. Art, 1979, Centro Colombo Americano, Bogota, Colombia, 1979, Fendrick Gallery, Washington, 1980, Print Club, Phila., 1980, 88, Albright-Knox Gallery, Buffalo, 1981, Woodmere Art Gallery, Phila., 1982, Univ. Art Mus., Santa Barbara, Calif., 1983, N.J. State Mus., Trenton, 1984, Hudson River Mus., Yonkers, N.Y., 1986, Sch. Fine Arts Gallery Ind. U., 1987, Sherry French Gallery, N.Y.C., 1988, 91, 92, Jack Wright Gallery, Palm Beach, Fla., 1992, Contemporary Realist Gallery, San Francisco, 1993, 94, Gerald Peters Gallery, Sante Fe, 1993, Fletcher Gallery, Sante Fe, 1994, Arnot Mus., Elmira, 2000, many others; represented in pvt. and pub. collections including Cleve. Mus. Art, Ball State U., Muncie, Ind., AT&T Co., Inc., Chgo., U. Notre Dame, Art Inst. Chgo., Fogg Mus. of Art, Fed. Reserve Bank, N.Y.C., Penn. Acad. Fine Arts, Phila., Valparaiso U., Phila. Mus. Art, Libr. Congress, Flint Inst. Arts, N.J. State Mus., others. Recipient Bertha Shay award Cheltenham Art Ctr., 1967, Netsky-Sernaker Meml. prize, 1973, Vivian and Meyer P. Potamkin prize, 1974; Yaddo fellow, 1966, 73, sr. fellow Nat. Endowment for Arts, 1982, fellow Pa. Coun. on Arts, 1988; grantee Ingram Merrill Found., 1978, Mellon Venture Fund, 1987; also other grants and awards. Home: 7733 Mill Rd Elkins Park PA 19027-2708 Personal E-mail: mmayererlebacher@aol.com.

ERLENMEYER-KIMLING, L., psychiatrist, researcher; b. Princeton, NJ; d. Floyd M. and Dorothy F. (Dirst) Erlenmeyer; m. Carl F. E. Kimling. BS magna cum laude, Columbia U., 1957, PhD, 1961; DSc (hon.), SUNY, Purchase, 1997. Sr. rsch. scientist N.Y. State Psychiat. Inst., N.Y.C., 1960-69, assoc. rsch. scientist, 1969-75, prin. rsch. scientist, 1975-78, dir. div. devel. behavioral studies, 1978—, chief med. genetics, 1991—; asst. in psychiatry Columbia U., 1962-66, rsch. assoc., 1966-70, from asst. prof. to assoc. prof. psychiatry and genetics, 1970—78, prof., 1978—. Vis. prof. psychology New Sch. Social Rsch., 1971—97; mem. peer rev. group NIH, 1976—80; mem. work group guidance and counseling Congl. Commn. Hungtinton's Disease, 1976—77; mem. task force intervention Pres.'s Commn. Mental Health, 1977—78; mem. initial rev. group NIMH, 1981—85; mem. adv. bd. Croatian Inst. Brain Rsch., 1991—93. Editor: Life-Span Research in Psychopathology, 1986; issue editor: Differential Reproduction, Social Biology, 1971, Genetics and Mental Disorders, Internat. Jour. Mental Health, 1972, Genetics and Gene Expression in Mental Illness, Jour. Psychiat. Rsch., 1992, Measuring Liability to Schizophrenia: Progress Report, 1994; mem. editl. bd. Social Biology, 1970—79, Schizophrenia Bull., 1978—2004; issue editor: Schizophrenia Bull., 1994; mem. editl. bd. Jour. Preventive Psychiatry, 1980—84, Croatian Med. Jour., 1991—. Neurology/Psychiatry/Brain Rsch., 1991—97, Am. Jour. Med. Genetics: Neuropsychiat. Genetics, 1992—. Recipient Disting. Investigator award, Merit award, NIMH, 1989—96, William K. Warren Schizophrenia Rsch. award, Internat. Congress Schizophrenia Rsch., 1995, Lifetime Achievement award, Internat. Soc. of Psychiatric Genetics, 2002; grantee, NIMH, 1966—69, 1971—, Scottish Rite Com. Schizophrenia, 1970—74, 1984—87, 1989—94, W. T. Grant Found., 1978—86, MacArthur Found., 1981, Stnaley Found., 1995—, Nat. Alliance Rsch. on Schizophrenia and Depression, 1996—2000. Fellow: APA, Am. Psychol. Soc., Am. Psychopath. Assn. (Joseph Zubin award 2005); mem.: AAAS, Soc. Study Social Biology (bd. dirs. 1969—84, 1992—96, sec. 1972—75, pres. 1975—78), N.Y. Acad. Scis., Internat. Soc. Psychiat. Genetics (Lifetime Achievement award 2002), Behavior Genetics Assn. (mem.-at-large 1972—74, Theodosius Dobzhansky award 1985), Am. Soc. Human Genetics, Sigma Xi, Phi Beta Kappa. Office: NY State Psychiat Inst Dept Med Genetics 1051 Riverside Dr Mail Unit 6 New York NY 10032-2603 Office Phone: 212-543-5475. Business E-Mail: le4@columbia.edu.

ERLICH, REESE WILLIAM, journalist; b. L.A., July 5, 1947; s. I.J. Erlich; m. Elizabeth Erlich, Jan. 20, 1972; 1 child, Jason. BA, U. Calif., Berkeley, 1970. Staff writer Ramparts mag., San Francisco, 1968-69; freelance journalist Calif., 1969—, Christian Sci. Monitor, Boston, 1983—, Monitor Radio, 1986-97, Nat. Pub. Radio, 1987—. Prodr. The Russia Project, 2002. Recipient Silver Hugo, Chgo. Internat. Film Festival, 1996, Bronze medal for the Russia Project Radio Documentary, 2002, Most Censored Story In America award, Project Censored, 2003. Mem. Soc. Profl. Journalists, Assn. Ind. in Radio. Office: PO Box 19261 Oakland CA 94619-0261 E-mail: rerlich@pacbell.net.

ERLICH, VICTOR, Slavic languages educator; b. Petrograd, Russia, Nov. 22, 1914; came to U.S., 1942, naturalized, 1943; s. Henryk and Sophie (Dubnov) E.; m. Iza Sznejerson, Feb. 27, 1940; children: Henry Anthony, Mark Leo. MA, Free Polish U., Warsaw, 1937; PhD, Columbia U., 1951; MA (hon.), Yale U., 1963. Asst. lit. editor New Life mag., Warsaw, 1937-39; research writer Yiddish Ency., 1942-43; from asst. prof. to prof. Slavic lit. and langs. U. Wash., 1949-63; Bensinger prof. Russian lit. Yale U., 1963-85, chmn. dept. Slavic langs., 1963-68, 78-81, prof. emeritus, 1985—; Del. congress Fedn. Modern Lang. and Lit., 1957, Internat. Congress Slavists, Sofia, 1963, Congress Internat. Comparative Lit. Assn., Belgrade, 1967. Author: Russian Formalism: History, Doctrine, 1955, The Double Image: Concepts of The Poet in Slavic Literatures, 1964, Gogol, 1969, Modernism and Revolution: Russian Literature in Transition, 1994; editor: Twentieth Century Russian Criticism, 1975, Pasternak: Twentieth-Century Views, 1977. Served with AUS, 1943-45, ETO. Decorated Purple Heart.; Ford Fellow, 1953-54; Fulbright lectr. U. Leyden, 1957-58; Guggenheim fellow, 1958, 64, 76-77; Nat. Endowment for Humanities fellow, 1968-69 Mem. Am. Assn. Advancement Slavic Studies (v.p.), MLA (exec. council), Internat. Assn. Slavic Langs. and Lits. (exec. council 1957-62), AAUP, Am. Comparative Lit. Assn., Am. Soc. Aesthetics. Home: 25 Glen Pkwy Hamden CT 06517-1402 Office: Yale Univ Dept of Slavic Languages New Haven CT 06520

ERLICHSON, HERMAN, physics professor; b. Bklyn., Mar. 22, 1931; m. Barbara H. Erlichson, Apr. 3, 1966; children: J. Peter, Andrew, Mark, Ellen. PhD in Philosophy, Columbia U., 1968; PhD in Physics, Rutgers U., 1980. Asst. prof. to prof. Coll. of S.I., 1960—. Contbr. articles to profl. jours. Mem. History of Sci. Soc., Am. Assn. Physics Tchrs. E-mail: erlichson@postbox.csi.cuny.edu.

ERLICHT, LEWIS HOWARD, broadcasting company executive; b. N.Y.C., Aug. 6, 1939; s. Harry and Estelle (Silk) E.; m. Wilma Binder, June 10, 1961; children: Paul Jon, Jamie Blake. BA in Psychology, L.I. U., 1962. With ABC-TV, 1962—, account exec., 1965-70; sales mgr. Sta. WABC-TV, 1970-73, gen. sales mgr., 1973-74; gen. mgr. Sta. WLS-TV, Chgo., 1974-77, v.p. programming N.Y.C., 1977-79; v.p., asst. to pres. ABC Entertainment, Los Angeles, 1979-80, sr. v.p., asst. to pres., 1980-81, sr. v.p. prime time programming, 1981-83, pres., 1983-85, ABC Circle Films, 1985-86; pres., chief operating officer New World Broadcasting, Los Angeles, 1986-87; pres. LHE, Inc., 1986—. Cons. Scandinavian Broadcasting Systems, 1989-91. Served with USAF, 1956-60.

ERMAN, AILA, small business owner; b. State Island, N.Y., Mar. 8, 1941; d. Theodor Diatlo and Selma Eva (Anderson) Erman; m. Marvin Ross Cutson, Nov. 2, 1962 (div. Oct. 31, 1981); children: Craig Bernard, Jaana Erman; m. Jospeh McEwen, Nov. 19, 1983 (div. Jan. 6, 2004). BS in Mktg., Fla. State U., 1962; MLA, U. Pa., 1992. Asst. dept mgr. Sears Roebuck, Tampa, Fla., 1962; social worker State of Fla., Tampa, 1962-64; owner Aila's Decorative Hardware & Bath Gallery, St. Petersburg, Fla., 1965—79; v.p., sec. So. Lock & Supply Co., Inc., St. Petersburg, 1968-81; pres. Mills Travel Svc., Inc., St. Petersburg, 1983—2004; jewelry designer Saint Petersburg, Fla., 2004—. Mem., benefactor Am. State Theater, St. Petersburg, Fla., 1988—, Dali Mus., St. Petersburg, Ctr. Against Spouse Abuse (CASA); bd. dirs. PAVA, Guatemala Highland Maya assistance group; docent Mus. Fine Arts, St. Petersburg, 1982. Mem.: N.C. Friendship Force, Fla. Goldsmith, Assn. Sr. Profls. Eckerd Coll., Arts Ctr., Am. Stage Theater, Suncoast Friendship Force, Am. Soc. Goldsmiths, Dali Mus., Fla. Suncoast Club, St. Petersburgh Yacht Club, Tiger Bay Club (founding mem.), Fla. State U. Pres.'s Club, Century Club, Alpha Chi Omega (past pres. Delta Sigma chpt.). Democrat. Jewish. Avocations: exotic travel, creative decorative arts, gardening. Home: 1910 Kansas Ave NE Saint Petersburg FL 33703-3430 Home (Summer): 309 Old Forbes Rd Bakersville NC 28705

ERMOLAEV, HERMAN SERGEI, Slavic languages educator; b. Tomsk, Russia, Nov. 14, 1924; came to U.S., 1949, naturalized, 1956; s. Sergei and Vera (Kozminykh) E.; m. Tatiana Kuzubova, June 8, 1975; children: Michael, Natalia, Katherine. Student, U. Graz, Austria, 1949; BA, Stanford U., 1951; MA, U. Calif.-Berkeley, 1954, PhD, 1959. Mem. faculty Princeton U., 1959—, prof. Slavic langs. and lits., 1970—. Author: Soviet Literary Theories, 1917-1934, The Genesis of Socialist Realism, 1963, 77, Mikhail Sholokhov and His Art, 1982, Censorship in Soviet Literature, 1917-1991, 1997, Mikhail Sholokhov and His Art (in Russian), 2000; co-author: Sholokhov's Tikhii Don, A Commentary, 1997; also articles; translator: Untimely Thoughts (Gorky), 1968, 95. McCosh fellow, 1967-68 Mem. Am. Assn. Advancement Slavic Studies, Am. Assn. Tchrs. Slavic and East European Langs. (pres. 1971-72) Home: 206 Moore St Princeton NJ 08540-3404 Office Phone: 609-258-4726. Business E-Mail: ermolaev@princeton.edu.

ERMOLAEVA, MARIA D., biophysicist, researcher; Diploma in biophysics with honors, Moscow State U., 1995, PhD in Physics and Math., 1997. Postdoctoral rschr. Pa. State U., University Park, 1997—99; staff scientist Inst. Genomic Rsch., Rockville, Md., 1999—; lectr. Johns Hopkins U., Rockville, Md., 2002—. Contbr. articles to profl. jours. Office: Inst Genomic Rsch 9712 Medical Ctr Dr Rockville MD 20850 Business E-Mail: mariae@tigr.org.

ERNEST, DOUGLAS JEROME, librarian; b. Billings, Mont., Mar. 31, 1947; s. Clarence Henry and Ruth (Imhof) E. BA in History, U. Colo., 1969, MA in History, 1975; MA in Libr. Sci., U. Denver, 1970. Reference libr. Florence (S.C.) County Libr., 1970-73, Mo. Western State Coll., St. Joseph, 1975-81; social scis., humanities libr. Colo. State U., Ft. Collins, 1981—. Author: Agricultural Frontier to Electronic Frontier, 1996; co-editor (with Stephen W. Green): Information Sources of Political Science, 2005; contbr. articles to profl. jours. Chair High Plains Regional Libr. Svc. Sys. Bd., 2000-01. Recipient Lit. award Colo. Libr. Assn., 1996. Mem. Nature Conservancy, Phi Beta Kappa, Beta Phi Mu. Unitarian Universalist. Avocations: hiking, nature study. Home: 1625 W Elizabeth St Apt J-1 Fort Collins CO 80521-4465 Office: Colo State Univ Morgan Libr Fort Collins CO 80523-1019 Office Phone: 970-491-1861. Business E-Mail: Doug.Ernest@colostate.edu.

ERNEST, J. TERRY, ocular physiologist, educator; b. Sycamore, Ill., June 26, 1935; married (div.); 1 child. BA, Northwestern U., 1957; MD, U. Chgo., 1961, PhD in Visual Sci., 1967. Prof. ophthalmology U. Wis., 1977-79; prof., chmn. ophthalmology Ind. U., 1980-81; prof. ophthalmology U. Ill., 1981-85; prof., chmn. ophthalmology U. Chgo., 1985—2004, Cynthia Chow prof., 2002—. Mem visual sci. A study sect., NIH, 1975-78, chmn. 1978-79, chmn. visual disorders study sect., 1979-80; rsch. prof. Rsch. to Prevent Blindness, Ind., 1981-84; mem. Vision Rsch. Program Com., 1982-84. Founding editor, Key, 1986-88; editor, Year Book of Ophthamology, 1982-88, Investigative Ophthalmology and Visual Sci., 1988-92. Recipient Rsch. Career Devel. award NIH, 1972. Mem. AAAS, Am. Ophthalmol. Soc., Am. Acad. Ophthalmology (Honor award 1982), Assn. Rsch. Vision and Ophthalmology. Achievements include research in ocular circulation with special emphasis on glaucoma and diabetic retinopathy using various methods of in vivo blood flow measurements. Office: U Chgo Visual Sciences Ctr 5841 S Maryland Ave MC2114 Chicago IL 60637-1454

ERNEST, TABI ELISE, art educator, photographer; b. New Orleans, Mar. 4, 1978; d. Gary John and Dawn Elizabeth Ann (Marshall) Ernest. BFA in Art Edn. with honors, Ga. State U., 2003. Cert. tchr. Ga. Art tchr. North Gwinnett H.S., Suwanee, Ga., 2003—. Soccer coach North Gwinnett H.S., 2003—04. Fellow: Nat. Art Educators Assn. Avocations: music, travel, soccer. Home: 1791 Piedmont Ave Atlanta GA 30324 Office Phone: 678-482-1053.

ERNEWEIN, PHILIPPE, educational consultant, educator; b. Turnhout, Flanders, Belgium, May 4, 1972; s. James and Renny Kesler; m. Jennifer-Rebecca Richards Ernewein, Jan. 1, 2004. BA, Longwood Coll., 1994; MA, U. Colo., 2003. Tchr. East St. John H.S., Reserve, La., 1994—96; park ranger Chaco Culture NHP, Chaco Canyon, N.Mex., 1996; tchr. Denver Acad., 1997—, coord., 2002—. Mem.: Colo. Lang. Arts Soc. (presenter), Tch. for Am. (corps mem. 1994—96), Learning Disabilities Assn. (mem. bd. 1997—2004), Student Conservation Assn. (recruiter 1997). Home: 2820 S Lincoln St Englewood CO 80113-1541

ERNSBERGER, DONALD CRAIG, secondary school educator, director; b. Fremont, Ohio, Sept. 26, 1947; s. Donald LaMar and Mary Elizabeth (Ward) Ernsberger; m. E. Louise Mould, Aug. 2, 1969; children: Michelle Louise, Michael. BS, Pa. State U., 1969; MA, Temple U., 1975. Cert. secondary edn. tchr. Pa. Founder, dir. Soc. Individual Liberty, Warminster, Pa., 1969—; tchr. Coun. Rock H.S., Newtown, Pa., 1969—99, dept. chmn., 1977—80, 1984—96. Adj. prof. Gwynedd Mercy Coll., 1998—; Civil War lectr. Pub. (CDRom) The Great Charge, Civil War battlefield guide; author: Paddy Owen's Regulars, 2004. Candidate U.S. Congress, 1988, U.S. Senate, 1994; mem. Libertarian Nat. Com., 1987—95; dep. chief staff U.S. House

Rep., 2001—. Avocations: guitar, travel, Civil War history and reenacting. Home: 105 Williamsburg Way Lansdale PA 19446-4373 Office Phone: 202-225-2415. Personal E-mail: ernscave@aol.com.

ERNST, CALVIN BRADLEY, retired vascular surgery educator; b. Detroit, May 12, 1934; s. Edward William and Irene Marie (Doelker) E.; m. Elizabeth Abbott, Dec. 21, 1957; children: Lisa Anne, Matthew Abbott, David William, Susan Elizabeth. MD, U. Mich., 1959. Diplomate Am. Bd. Surgery (bd. dirs. 1991-97). Intern Ohio State U. Med. Ctr., Columbus, 1959-60; resident U. Mich. Med. Ctr., Ann Arbor, 1960-65; instr. surgery U. Mich., 1968-69, asst. prof., 1969-72, assoc. prof., 1972, U. Ky., Lexington, 1972-74, prof., 1974-79; prof. surgery Johns Hopkins U., 1979-85, surgeon hosp., 1979-85; chmn. surg. scis. Balt. City Hosps., 1979-85; clin. prof. surgery U. Mich., Ann Arbor, 1985-97; prof. surgery Case Western Res. U., Cleve., 1994-97; head vascular surgery Henry Ford Hosp., Detroit, 1985-97; prof. surgery, chief vascular surgery Med. Coll. Pa., Hahnemann Univ., Phila., 1997-99. Cons. surgeon Loch Raven VA Hosp., Balt., 1979-85. Assoc. editor Jour. Vascular Surgery, 1986-91, editor, 1991-97, emeritus editor, 1997—; mem. editl. bd. Archives of Surgery, 1983-93, Surgery, 1983-93; editor 7 vascular surgery textbooks; contbr. chpts. to books. Dir. Am. Bd. Surgery, 1991-97. Served to capt. U.S. Army, 1966-68. Fellow ACS; mem. Soc. Vascular Surgery (sec. 1984-88, pres.-elect 1989-90, pres. 1990-91, Am. Surg. Assn., Internat. Cardiovascular Soc. (recorder 1977-82), So. Assn. Vascular Surgery (sec. treas. 1976-81, pres. 1982-83), Alpha Omega Alpha. Home: 3904 N Farway Dr Jupiter FL 33477 E-mail: cbernst@earthlink.net.

ERNST, DANIEL PEARSON, lawyer; b. Des Moines, Sept. 30, 1931; s. Daniel Ward and Thea Elaine (Pearson) E.; m. Ann Robinson, April 14, 1956; children: Ellen, Daniel R., Ruth Ann. BA, Dartmouth Coll., 1953; JD, U. Mich., 1956. Bar: Iowa 1956, Ill. 1964, Mich. 1980. Assoc. Clewell Cooney & Fuerste, 1960-64; ptnr. Nelson Stapleton & Ernst, Stapleton & Ernst, Stapleton Ernst & Sprengelmeyer, East Dubuque, Ill., Nelson Stapleton & Ernst & Sprengelmeyer, Dubuque, Iowa, 1964-79; pvt. practice Dubuque, 1979-80; ptnr. Ernst & Cody, Dubuque, 1981-84, Daniel P. Ernst, P.C., Dubuque, 1984-90, Vincent Roth & Ernst, P.C., Galena, Ill., 1991; pub. defender State of Iowa, Dubuque, 1991-96; pvt. practice Dubuque, 1997—. U.S. trustee, 1979—91. Capt. USAF, 1957-60, U.S. Coast Guard Aux. Mem. ABA, Iowa State Bar Assn. (bd. govs. 1985-89), Dubuque County Bar Assn. (2d v.p. 1979-80, 1st v.p. 1980-81, pres. 1981-82), Ill. State Bar Assn., Jo Daviess County Bar Assn., State Bar Assn. Mich., Grand Traverse-Leelanau-Antrim Bar Assn. Democrat. Avocations: swimming, boating. Fax: 563-582-0324. Office Phone: 563-582-0324. E-mail: ernstdan@mchsi.com.

ERNST, EDWARD WILLIS, retired electrical engineering educator; b. Great Falls, Mont., Aug. 28, 1924; s. Paul Wilson and Grace Vio (Woodmore) E.; m. Helen Kitty Todd, Jan. 29, 1950 (dec. Mar. 1975); children: Deborah Kitty, Thomas Edward (dec.); m. Margaret Frances Patton, Sept. 13, 1975 (dec. Feb. 2002); children: Alan Harmon, Ruth Margaret, Betty Carol; m. Barbara Allen Moye, Apr. 26, 2003. BSEE, U. Ill., 1949, MSEE, 1950, PhD in Elec. Engring., 1955. Rsch. engr. GE, Syracuse, N.Y., 1955, Stewart-Warner, Chgo., 1955-58; assoc. prof. U. Ill., Urbana, 1958-68, prof., 1968-89, assoc. head elec. engring., 1970-85, assoc. dean engring., 1985-89; Allied-Signal prof. engring. U. S.C., Columbia, 1990-2000, disting. emeritus engring. prof., 2000; ret., 2000. Program dir. NSF, Washington, 1987-90; chmn. Engring. Accreditation Commn., Accreditation Bd. for Engring. Tech., N.Y.C., 1985-86, pres., 1989-90. Pres. Mckinley Found., Champaign, Ill. 1968-72. Recipient Linton Grinter award Accreditation Bd. Engring. and Tech., 1992. Fellow IEEE (v.p. 1981-82, Centennial medal 1984, EAB Meritorious Achievement award in accreditation activities 1985), AAAS, Accreditation Bd. for Engring. Tech., Internat. Engring. Consortium (bd. dirs.), Am. Soc. for Engring. Edn. (editor Jour. Engring. Edn. 1992-96). Presbyterian. Avocations: photography, reading. Business E-Mail: ernst@engr.sc.edu.

ERNST, JAMES ALLAN, safety engineer, consultant; b. Pittsburgh, Pa., Feb. 15, 1943; s. Charles Joseph and Ellen Black McKenzie Ernst; m. Tamara Sue Kugel, July 28, 1947; children: Tina Rae Evans, Tela Fae Cooper. BS Mgmt., Cardinal Stritch U., Edina, Minn. Campus, 1997—99; AAS Electronic Engring. Tech., CC Of The Air Force, Maxwell Air Force Base, AL, 1978—81. Cert. paramedic NY, 1985. Electronics technician USAF, 1961—81; sys. safety/human factors engr. GE/Martin Marietta/Lockheed Martin, Syracuse, NY, 1981—95; paramedic Syracuse U. (Carrier Dome), 1987—95; EMT instr. NY State Dept. of Health, Syracuse, 1990—95; EMT/paramedic Greater Baldwinsville Ambulance Corps, Baldwinsville, NY, 1983—95; project safety engr. United Def. LP, Mpls., 1995—2004; system safety engring. cons., 2005—. Dir. of ops. Greater Baldwinsville Ambulance Corps, Baldwinsville, 1992—92. Firefighter Jefferson Twp Vol Fire Dept., Bowersville, Ohio, 1967—70, Ocean Springs Fire Dept., Ocean Springs, Miss., 1970—71; aux. police officer Chelmsford Aux. Police Force, Chelmsford, Mass., 1979—81; deacon Bklyn Ctr. Ch. Of Christ, Brooklyn Center, Minn., 1998—2001; boy scout leader BSA, Chelmsford, Mass., 1976—81. Msgt (e7) USAF, 1961—81, Various. Decorated AFCM w/ 1 oak cluster, Humanitarian Svc. Medal w/ 1 oak cluster, AFLSM w/ 4 oak clusters, NDSM, AF Orgnl. Excellence Award USAF, NCO Acad. Grad. Ribbon, AFGCM w/ 5 oak clusters. Mem.: Human Factors and Ergonomics Soc., Internat. Sys. Safety Soc. Christian. Avocations: travel, camping, woodworking. Home: 1730 Van Ct Alamogordo NM 88310 E-mail: je43@prodigy.net.

ERNST, MARCIA MCCRORY, lawyer; b. Orlando, Fla., Aug. 10, 1961; d. Oscar William and Nancy Diane (Parrish) McCrory; m. Michael Joseph Ernst, May 24, 1986. BBA, U. Ga., 1984, JD, 1987. Bar: Ga. 1987, U.S. Dist. Ct. (no. dist.) Ga. 1987, U.S. Ct. Appeals (11th cir.) 1988. Lobbyist Bus. Council Ga., Atlanta, 1983; legal intern Athens (Ga.) Planning Commn., 1984; law clk. Northeast Ga. Planning Commn., Athens, 1986-87; assoc. Webb & Daniel, Atlanta, 1987-92; ptnr. Smith, Gambrell & Russell LLP, Atlanta, 1992—. Editorial bd. Ga. Journal of Internat. and Comparative Law 1985-86. Mem. Ga. Vol. Lawyers for Arts, Atlanta, 1988, Atlanta Vol. Lawyers Found., 1988, Dekalb Vol. Lawyers Found., Decatur, Ga., 1988. Named Outstanding Young Women of Am., 1988. Mem. ABA, Ga. Bar Assn., Atlanta Bar assn., Phi Mu Alumni Assn. Democrat. Episcopalian. Avocation: photography. Office: Smith Gambrell & Russell Ste 3100 Promenade II 1230 Peachtree St NE Atlanta GA 30309-3592 E-mail: mernst@sgrlaw.com.

ERNST, MARK A., diversified financial services company executive; m. Annette Ernst; two children. Degree in Acctg. & Fin. summa cum laude, Drake U.; MBA, U. Chgo. With tax, investment and corp. adv. svcs. dept. Coopers & Lybrand; v.p., gen. mgr. tax and bus. svcs. divsn. Am. Express Co., Mpls., sr. v.p. workplace fin. svcs., sr. v.p.; exec. v.p., COO H&R Block, Inc., 1998-99, pres., COO, 1999—2001, pres., CEO, 2001—, chmn., 2002—. Adv. Initiative Fin. Security Aspen Inst.; bd. trustees U. Mo. Kans. City; bd. dirs. Great Plains Energy, Knight-Ridder Inc., 2004—. Bd. dir. Civic Coun. Greater Kans. City, Greater Kans. City Area C. of C., Kansas City Area Devel. Coun., H&R Block Found., Am. Royal. Office: H&R Block 4400 Main St Kansas City MO 64111-1812*

ERNST, RANDY, radiologist; b. Atlanta, July 18, 1951; BA in Psychology, U. Tex., 1981, MD, 1990. Diplomate Am. Bd. Radiology, Am. Bd. Diagnostic Radiology. Intern U. Tex., Galveston, 1990—91, resident in internal medicine, 1991—95; fellow Beth Israel Hosp./Harvard Med. Sch., Boston, 1995—96; faculty dept. radiology U. Tex. Med. Sch., Houston, 1996, U. Tex. Med. Br., Galveston, 2001—, Emory U., Atlanta, 1999—2001. Office: UTMB Dept Radiology Galveston TX 77555-0709 Business E-Mail: rdernst@utmb.edu.

ERNST, RICHARD ROBERT, chemist, educator; b. Winterthur, Zurich, Switzerland, Aug. 14, 1933; s. Robert and Irma (Brunner) E.; m. Magdalena Kielholz, Oct. 9, 1963; children: Anna Magdalena, Katharina Elisabeth, Hans-Martin Walter. Diploma Chemistry, ETH-Zurich, 1956, DSc in Tech., 1962; PhD (hon.), ETH-Lausanne, Switzerland, 1986, Technische Hochschule, Munich, 1989, U. Zurich, 1994, U. Antwerp, 1997, U. Cluj-Napoca, 1998, U. Montpellier, 1999, Charles U., Prague, 2002, Babes-Bolyai U. Scientist ETH-Zurich, 1962-63, privatdozent, 1968-70, asst. prof., 1970-72, assoc. prof., 1973-76, prof., 1976—, dir. Phys. Chemistry Lab., pres. Rsch. Coun.; scientist Varian Assocs., Palo Alto, Calif., 1963-68. Cons. Spectrospin AG, Fällanden, Switzerland, 1978—, v.p. bd. dirs. Editl. bd. mem. of 10 sci. jours; numerous inventions, patents in field. 1st lt. ACS-Dienst, 1953-88, Swiss mil. Recipient Silver medal ETH-Zurich, 1962, Ruzicka prize, 1968, Gold medal Soc. Magnetic Resonance in Medicine, San Francisco, 1983, Benoist prize Swiss Fedn. Confedn., Berne, 1986, Kirkwood award Yale U., 1989, Ampere prize, 1990, Wolf prize in chemistry, 1991, Louisa Gross Horwitz prize Columbia U., 1991, Nobel prize in chemistry, 1991, award for Achievements in Magnetic Resonance EAS, 1992. Mem. NAS (India), Deutsche Akademie Leopoldina, Acad. Europaea, Schweizerische Chemische Gesellschaft, Royal Soc. London, Österreichische Gesellschaft für Analytische Chemie, Am. Phys. Soc., U.S. Nat. Acad. Sci., Am. Acad. Arts and Scis., Schweizerische Akademie d. Tech. Wiss., Russian Acad. Scis, IOM (elected 2004), Swiss Sci. Coun., COST Com., Found. Marcel Benoist (prize, 1986). Avocations: tibetan art, music. Office: Lab F Phys Chem ETH-Honggerberg 8093 Zurich Switzerland Office Phone: 41 1 632 4368. E-mail: ernst@nmr.phys.chem.ethz.ch.

ERNST, WALLACE GARY, geology educator; b. St. Louis, Mo., Dec. 14, 1931; BA, Carleton Coll., 1953; MS, U. Minn., 1955; PhD, Johns Hopkins U., 1959. Geologist U.S. Geol. Survey, Washington, 1955-56; fellow (Geophys. Lab.), Washington, 1956-59; mem. faculty UCLA, 1960-89, prof. geology and geophysics, 1968-89, chmn. geology dept. (now earth and space scis. dept.), 1970-74, 78-82, dir. Inst. Geophysics and Planetary Physics, 1987-89; dean Stanford Sch. of Earth Scis., 1989-94; prof. geol. and environ. scis. Stanford (Calif.) U., 1989—, Benjamin M. Page prof., 1999—, dean Sch. of Earth Scis., 1989-94. Author: Amphiboles, 1968, Earth Materials, 1969, Metamorphism and Plate Tectonic Regimes, 1975, Subduction Zone Metamorphism, 1975, Petrologic Phase Equilibria, 1976, The Geotectonic Development of California, 1981, The Environment of the Deep Sea, 1982, Energy for Ourselves and Our Posterity, 1985, Cenozoic Basin Development of Coastal California, 1987, Metamorphic and Crustal Evolution of the Western Cordillera, 1988, The Dynamic Planet, 1990, Integrated Earth and Environmental Evolution of the Southwestern United States, 1998, Planetary Petrology and Geochemistry, 1999; editor: Earth Systems: Processes and Issues, 2000, (with R.G. Coleman) Tectonic Studies of Asia and the Pacific Rim--A Tribute to Benjamin M. Page, 2000, (with J.G. Liou) Ultrahigh-Pressure Metamorphism and Geodynamics in Collision-Type Orogenic Belts, 2000, Frontiers in Geochemistry, 2002, (with S.L. Klemperer) The Lithosphere of Western North America, 2004, Serpenite and Serpentinites, 2004. Trustee Carnegie Instn. of Washington, 1990—. Recipient Miyashiro medal Geol. Soc. Japan, 1998. Mem. NAS (chmn. geology sect. 1979-82, chair class I 2000—), AAAS, Am. Philos. Soc., Am. Geophys. Union, Am. Geol. Inst., Geol. Soc. Am. (pres. 1985-86), Am. Acad. Arts and Sci., Geochem. Soc., Mineral Soc. Am. (recipient award 1969, pres. 1979-80). Office: Stanford U Dept Earth & Environ Scis Green Earth Sci #209 Palo Alto CA 94303-1823

ERNST-FONBERG, MARY LOU, biomedical researcher, educator; b. Harrisburg, Pa., Jan. 18, 1937; d. Donald Hafer Ernst and Margaret Florence Snyder; m. Ignacy B. Fonberg; children: Margaret Sandra Fonberg, Chasity Ann Stoots-Fonberg. BA, Susquehanna U., Selinsgrove, Pa., 1958; MD, Temple U., Phila., 1962; PhD, Yale U., New Haven, Conn., 1967. Vis. scientist Weizmann Inst. Sci., Rehovoth, Israel, 1966—67; chemistry fellow Harvard U., Cambridge, Mass., 1967—69; assoc. prof. biology Yale U., New Haven, 1969—78; prof. biochemistry, molecular biology East Tenn. State U., Johnson City, Tenn., 1978—, adj. prof. biology, 1978—. Contbr. articles to profl. jours. Grantee rsch., NSF, NIH, AHA. Mem.: Am. Soc. Biochemistry and Molecular Biology, AAAS. Office Phone: 423-439-2025. E-mail: ernstfon@mail.etsu.edu.

ERON, LEONARD DAVID, psychology professor; b. Newark, Apr. 22, 1920; s. Joseph I. and Sarah (Hilfman) E.; m. Madeline Marcus, May 21, 1950; children: Joan Hobson, Don, Barbara Christensen. BS, CCNY, 1941; MA, Columbia U., 1946; PhD, U. Wis., 1949. Diplomate Am. Bd. Profl. Psychology. Asst. prof. psychology and psychiatry Yale U., New Haven, 1948-55; dir. rsch. Rip Van Winkle Found., 1955-62; prof. psychology U. Iowa, Iowa City, 1962-69; rsch. prof. U. Ill.-Chgo., 1969-89; emeritus rsch. prof. of the social sci. in psychology, 1989—; rsch. scientist, prof. psychology Inst. for Social Rsch., U. Mich., Ann Arbor, 1992—2003. Author 8 books; editor Jour. Abnormal Psychology, 1973-80; assoc. editor Am. Psychologist, 1986-90; contbr. numerous articles to profl. jours. Served to 1st lt. AUS, 1942-45 Fulbright lectr., Free U. Amsterdam, 1967-68; recipient Fulbright Sr. Scholar award, Queensland U., Australia, 1976-77, James McKeen Cattell Sabbatical award, U. Rome, 1984-85. Fellow AAAS, Am. Psychol. Assn. (chair comm. violence and youth 1991-93, Disting. Contbns. to Knowledge award 1980, Gold medal award for Life Contbn. to Psychology in the Pub. Interest 1995, Lifetime Contbn. to Media Psychology award 2003), Am. Orthopsychiat. Assn.; mem. Midwestern Psychol. Assn. (pres. 1985-86), Internat. Soc. for Rsch. in Aggression (pres. 1989-90).

EROZAN, YENER SAHIR, pathologist, educator; arrived in U.S., 1959; s. Celal Sahir and Sevim Erozan; m. Brenda Martin, July 7, 1966. MD, Istanbul (Turkey) U., 1954. Cert. practice medicine and surgery Bd. Med. Examiners State Md., 1971, anatomic pathology Am. Bd. Pathology, 1974, added qualification in cytopathology Am. Bd. Pathology, 1989. Resident in pathology Haydarpasa Numune Hosp., Istanbul, 1956—59, Suburban Hosp., Bethesda, Md., 1959—62; fellow in pathology Johns Hopkins U., Balt., 1962—64; instr. pathology Johns Hopkins U. Sch. Medicine, Balt., 1964—65, asst. prof. pathology, 1969—75, assoc. prof. pathology, 1975—95, prof. pathology, 1995—; asst. prof. pathology Hacettepe U. Sch. Medicine, Ankara, Turkey, 1965—68. Dir. The John K. Frost cytopathology lab. The Johns Hopkins Hosp., Balt., 1989—95. Editor: (book) Fine Needle Aspiration of Subcutaneous Organs and Masses, 1996. Named Otago Trust Vis. Prof., Dunedin Sch. Medicine, New Zealand, 1998; recipient Disting. Svc. award, Am. Soc. for Clin. Pathology, 2002; Yener S. Erozan, M.D. fellowship established in his name, Johns Hopkins U. Sch. Medicine Dept. Pathology, 2003. Fellow: Am. Coll. Chest Physicians, Internat. Acad. Cytology, Coll. Am. Pathologists; mem.: AMA, Md. Soc. Pathologists, The Johns Hopkins Alumni and Faculty Assn., Am. Soc. Cytopathology (pres. 1985—86, Papanicolaou award 1997), Johns Hopkins Club. Avocations: photography, travel, swimming. Office: The Johns Hopkins Hosp 600 North Wolfe St Baltimore MD 21287 Office Phone: 410-955-1180. Business E-Mail: yerozan@jhmi.edu.

ERPELDING, DONNA M, elementary school educator; b. Herington, Kans., Jan. 4, 1946; d. John Anton Spackek and Beatrice Eleanor Spachek; m. Lawrence H Erpelding; children: Angela, Brad, Craig. AS, Ctrl. Rural State U., 1964; BS, Kans. State U., 1980, MS, 1988. Library Media Specialist Kans. State U., 1988. Tchr. USD 383, Manhattan, Kans., 1980—. Finalist Kans. Tchr. of the Yr., 1993; recipient Nancy Landon Kassenbaum Excellence in Tchg., State of Kans., 1993, Bob Srack Excellence in Tchg., Manhattan, Kans., 1993, Presdl. award, Kans., 1990. Home: 1732 Westbank Way Manhattan KS 66503

ERRANTE, VALERIE, music educator, soprano; d. Ernest Alfred and Hilda Joyce Haskins; BM, Ithaca Coll., 1977; MME, No. Mich. U., Marquette, 1980; DMA, Eastman Sch. Music, Rochester, N.Y., 1995. Leading coloratura soprano Opera House, Kiel, Germany, 1984—90; assoc. prof. U. Wis., Milw., 1997—. Adj. instr. Folkwang Hochschule Musik, Essen, Germany, 1991—92; assoc. in voice Eastman Sch. Music, Rochester, NY, 1993—96; vis. prof. U. Iowa, Iowa City, 1996—97; bd. dirs. Wis. Dist. Met. Auditions, Milw. Performer (solo singer): (CD) Puccini: Gianni Schicchi/ Angelica, 1988, Songs of Alec Wilder, 2000. Named Artist to Watch, Milw. Jour. Sentinel, 2000; fellow Internat. fellow, AAUW, 1997. Office: Univ Wis PO Box 413 Milwaukee WI 53201 Fax: 414-962-8829. Business E-Mail: verrante@uwm.edu.

ERRECART, JOYCE, lawyer; b. Vergennes, Vt., July 1, 1950; d. Lloyd Maurice and Lillian Adela (Jay) Hier; m. Michael Terry Errecart, Mar. 30, 1971; children: Michael Jay, Jacqueline Marie. BA, Wellesley Coll., 1972; JD, Am. U., 1976; LLM in Taxation, Georgetown U., 1981. Bar: Md. 1976, U.S. Tax Ct. 1977, Vt. 1984, U.S. Dist. Ct. Vt. 1984. Law clk. to spl. trial judge U.S. Tax Ct., Washington, 1975-76; trial atty. dist. counsel IRS, Washington, 1976-83; assoc. Dinse, Erdmann & Clapp, Burlington, Vt., 1983-86; sole practice Burlington, 1986-91; commr. Vt. Dept. of Taxes, Montpelier, Vt., 1991—. Mem. ABA (tax sect.), Vt. Bar Assn. (tax sect.). Republican. Avocation: quilting. Office: Vt Dept Taxes Pavilion Office Bldg Montpelier VT 05602

ERRINGTON, NORMAN, television producer, photographer; b. Middlesbrough, Yorkshire, England, Nov. 13, 1936; s. Nathan Errington and Ruth Havercroft; 1 child, Mark. Leading aircraftsman RAF/ Fighter Command, Leeming, England, 1951—54; mng. dir. Mark Printing Co., Middlesbrough, England, 1954—60; pres. Vistavision TV Prodn., Tampa Bay, Fla., 1961—78; photo journalist New Port Richey Press, New Port Richey, Fla., 1978—84; tv prodr. Telemart Programming & Prodn., Bayonet Point, Fla., 1993—. Publisher: TV Today, 1986; prodr.: (TV series) What's New, 1989; (TV films) In Search of.The Fountain of Youth, 1984; author: One Life Less Ordinary, A Memoir, 2002. Founder, pres. Brit. Am. Assn., Tampa Bay, Fla., 1986—90. With Fighter Command Royal Air Force, 1954—57, England. Master: Freemasons (25 yr. pin 1998). Avocations: world war 2 historian, travel. Office: Norman Errington TV Productions Box 34669 Bayonet Point FL 34669 Personal E-mail: NormanErrington@aol.com.

ERSEK, GREGORY JOSEPH MARK, lawyer; b. Cleve., Aug. 30, 1956; s. Joseph Francis and Mary H. (Hurchanik) E. AB, Columbia U., 1977; MBA, U. Pa., 1979; JD, U. Fla., 1984; cert. cir. civil mediator, Fla. Internat. U., 1998. Bar: Fla. 1986, U.S. Dist. Ct. (so. dist.) Fla. 1987. Cons. fin. valuation Am. Appraisal Co., Princeton, N.J., 1979-80; mgr. import-export Marie L. Veslie Co., Coral Gables, Fla., 1980-85; dir. corp. fin. dept. and capital markets group Dunhill Diversified, Ltd., L.A., 1980—2001; assoc. Lunny, Tucker, Karns & Brescher, Ft. Lauderdale, Fla., 1986; dir. legal dept. Horizons Rsch. Labs. Inc., Ft. Lauderdale, 1986-89, sr. corp. planner, 1988-89; gen. counsel Unisco Corp., Ft. Lauderdale, 1989-93, TRICORD Corp., Ft. Lauderdale, 1990-93, Irish Times, Inc., Ft. Lauderdale, 1993-97; dir. corp. fin. dept. & sr. corp. counsel Canton Fin. Svcs. Corp., subs. Cyber Am. Corp., Salt Lake City, 1995-96; gen. counsel Greenstreet Capital Corp., Investment Bankers, Las Vegas, 1996-99, Gaelic Pub. Devel., Inc., Ft. Lauderdale, 1998—2002, Premier Fin. Corp., Jacksonville, 1998—2002. Rsch. asst. jurisprudence U. Fla., 1982-84; tchg. fellow U. Fla. Law Sch., 1983; sec.-treas. Sorkar Group, Inc., Ft. Lauderdale, 1987-89; CEO Am. CompuShopper, Inc., 1989-98; with legal dept. Pfizer Inc., NYC, 1983; co-founder, mgr. Poland/US Trade and Mktg. Consortium, 1989—; mem. Philip C. Jessup Internat. Moot Ct. team, 1983; gen. counsel Biltmore Vacation Resorts, Inc., f/k/a Cyber Info., Inc., Las Vegas, 1997-99, Avalon Group, Inc., Cedar Rapids, Iowa, 1997-99; rsch. asst. in jurisprudence to Prof. Robert Moffat, U. Fla., 1982-84; gen. counsel HLO Custom Internat. Tours, Orlando, 1992—, Custom Archtl. Builders, Inc., Boca Raton, 2002—; rschr. Ctr. of Excellence in Functional Recovery in Spinal Cord Injury, Miami VA Med. Ctr., 2004—; mem. Miami Project to Cure Paralysis, 2004—. Editor Medscanner, med. industry newsletter, 1987-89. Mem. venture coun. forum; alumnus Internat. House, N.Y.C., 1984; mem. The Miami Project to Cure Paralysis, 2004—, South Fla. Regional Spinal Cord Injury Model Sys., 2004—. Tchg. fellow, U. Fla. Law Sch., 1983. Mem.: Nat. Register Practicing Lawyers with Spinal Injury (exec. sec. 2005—), Nat. Assn. Disabled Attys., Execs. and Dirs. (pres. 2005—), Fla. Bar Assn., Nat. Assn. Securities Dealers (nat. arbitration com. 1991—98), Assn. Disabled Attys. (exec. dir. 2002—), Coun. on Fgn. Rels. (local com.), United Spinal Assn., Corp. Execs. and Dirs. Pub. Cos. with Spinal Cord Injury (sec. 2002—, pres. 2002—, sec. 2004—), Wharton Club South Fla., Phi Delta Phi. Avocations: travel, books. Home and Office: 17820 NW 18th Ave Miami Gardens FL 33056-4949

ERSEK, ROBERT ALLEN, plastic surgeon; b. Ridley Twp., Pa., June 19, 1938; s. Joseph Martin and Theda Louise (Kromes) E.; m. Gerry Avenelle Mullins, Mar. 28, 1958; children: Stephanie Louise, Cynthia Leigh. BS, Morris Harvey Coll., 1961; MD, Hahnemann Med. Coll., 1966. Diplomate Nat. Bd. Med. Examiners; cert. Am. Bd. Plastic Surgery. Intern surgery U. Minn. Hosps., Mpls., 1966-67; research fellow U. Pa., 1962, Hahnemann Med. Coll., Phila., 1963-65; med. fellow dept. surgery U. Minn., 1967-73; resident dept. plastic and reconstructive surgery Tulane U., New Orleans, 1975-77; fellow in plastic surgery U. Miss., Jackson, 1978; clin. instr. plastic surgery U. Tex. Health Sci. Center, San Antonio, 1979. Chmn. bd., dir. Med. Gen. Inc., 1969—; dir., med. dir. Genetic Labs., 1970—, Emerald Airlines, Inc.; chmn. bd. Remedco, 1980—; bd. dirs., med. dir. Genetic Labs Wound Care; chmn. Personique Inc., 1996; bd. dirs. Plastic Surgery Co.; dean Lipoplasy Univ. Author: Pain Control, 1981; Co-editor: Organ Perfusion and Preservation, 1969; contbr. articles to med. jours.; patentee numerous surg. devices. Bd. dirs. Austin Civic Ballet. Served to maj. USAF, 1973-75. Recipient Alan Edelsohn prize Hahnemann Med. Coll., 1966; Grand award for exhibit Student Am. Med. Assn. Squibb Nat. Contest, 1967; award of excellence in med. writing Minn. Medicine, 1970 Fellow ACS; mem. AMA, AAUP, NAS, Am. Coll. Emergency Physicians, La. Med. Soc., Soc. for Cryosurgery, Am. Soc. Plastic and Reconstructive Surgeons, Am. Soc. Artificial Internal Organs, Am. Med. Writers Assn., Smithsonian Inst., Nat. Assn., Flying Physicians, Am. Trauma Soc., Tex. Med. Assn., Travis County Med. Soc., Am. Burn Assn., Lipoplasty Soc. N.Am. (bd. dirs.), Serpent Soc., Aesculpulation Soc., Austin Knights of Symphony (chmn. Personique Inc. 1996), Phi Kappa Delta. Office: 630 W 34th St Austin TX 78705-1229 Office Phone: 512-459-6800. Personal E-mail: ersek@ensek.com.

ERSHLER, WILLIAM BALDWIN, biogerontologist, educator; b. Syracuse, N.Y., Jan. 13, 1949; s. Irving Leonard and Eunice (Baldwin) E.; m. Joan Lipstein, Nov. 6, 1971; children: Rachel Eve, Leah Rose. BA, Case Western Res. U., 1970; MD, SUNY Upstate Ctr., Syracuse, 1974. Diplomate Am. Bd. Internal Medicine, Am. Bd. Med. Oncology, Am. Bd. Hematology. Asst. prof. U. Vt., Burlington, 1980-85; assoc. prof. U. Wis., Madison, 1985-89, prof. medicine, 1989-96, dir. U. Wis. Inst. on Aging, 1989-96, head geriatrics, 1989-96; dir. geriatric rsch. Edn. and Clin. Ctr. William Middleton VA Hosp., Madison, 1991-96; prof. medicine, dir. Glennan Ctr. Geriatrics & gerontolog Eastern Va. Medical Sch., Norfolk, 1996-97; dir. Inst. Advanced Studies in Aging and Geriatric Medicine, Washington, 1998—, Nat. Geriatrics Rsch. Consortium, 1998—; rsch. edn. dir. Extended Care Info. Network, 1999—. Dir. Geriatric Oncology Consortium, 2001—; sr. investigator Nat. Inst. Aging, NIH. Editor Jour. Gerontology, 1996-2000; contbr. articles to profl. jours. Recipient Geriatric Leadership award NIH, 1990-96; NIH grantee, 1989—. Fellow Gerontologic Soc. Am.; mem. Am. Geriatrics Soc., Am. Assn. Cancer Rsch., Am. Soc. Clin. Oncology, Am. Soc. Hematology, Assn. Dirs. Acad. Geriatrics (councilor). Jewish. Avocations: running, photography, travel. Office: 1700 Wisconsin Ave NW Washington DC 20007 E-mail: wershler@iasia.org.

ERSKINE, JAMES LORENZO, physics professor; b. Seattle, Oct. 25, 1942; s. Lawrence A. and Elizabeth (Woodbury) E.; m. Julie Ann Grant; children: Michael Grant, John Lawrence. BSEE, U. Wash., 1964, MSEE, 1966, PhD in Physics, 1973. Sr. engr. and cons. Boeing Co., Seattle, 1967-74; rsch. asst. prof. dept. physics U. Ill., Urbana, 1974-77; asst. prof. dept. physics U. Tex., Austin, 1977-82, assoc. prof., 1982-86, prof., 1986—. Trull Centennial prof. Trull Found. U. Tex., 1986. Contbr. numerous articles in fields of solid state physics, magnetism and magnetic materials, surface physics, surface chemistry, and instrumentation. Grantee NSF, R.A. Welch Found., other fed. and pvt. agys. Fellow Am. Phys. Soc.; mem. Am. Vacuum Soc. Office: U Tex Grad Sch Dept Of Physics Austin TX 78712 Office Phone: 512-471-1464. Business E-Mail: erskine@physics.utexas.edu.

ERSKINE, JANIS JAN, educational association administrator; d. Warren Edward and Dorothy Annabelle Hoglund; 1 child, Marcella Lynn. BS in Edn., Chgo. State U.; MA in Edn. Adminstrn., U. Colo., 1977. Uniserve dir. Tchrs.

Assn. Anne Arundel County, Annapolis, 1989—95; examiner U.S. Senate Productivity and Md. Quality Awards, Md., 1996—97; tchr. Denver Pub. Sch., 1975—89; orgnl. specialist, edn. reform Md. State Tchrs. Assn., Annapolis, 1998—. Bd. dirs. Annapolis Adv. Bd. for Parks and Recreation, 1995—2000; vendor com. chairperson Md. Seafood Fesitval, C. of C., Annapolis, Md., 1990—92; chairperson First Night Annapolis, 1999—2001. Recipient Hazel F. Petrocco Women's Leadership award, Colo. Edn. Assn.-NEA Women's Caucus, 1989. Mem.: NEA (com. apptd., women's caucus, release time local pres. 1982—89), Assn. Supervision and Curriculum Devel. Democrat-Npl. Avocations: sailing, travel, scuba diving, ballroom dancing. Office: Md State Tchrs Assn 140 Main St Annapolis MD 21401 Office Phone: 410-263-6600.

ERSKINE, JOHN MORSE, surgeon; b. San Francisco, Sept. 10, 1920; s. Morse and Dorothy (Ward) E. BS, Harvard U., 1942, MD, 1945. Diplomate Am. Bd. Surgery. Surg. intern U. Calif. Hosp., San Francisco, 1945-46; surg. researcher Mass. Gen. Hosp., Boston, 1948; resident in surgery Peter Bent Brigham Hosp., Boston, 1948-53; George Gorham Peters fellow St. Mary's Hosp., London, 1952; pvt. practice in medicine specializing in surgery San Francisco, 1954-98; asst. clin. prof. Stanford Med. Sch., San Francisco, 1956-59; asst., assoc. clin. prof. U. Calif. Med. Sch., San Francisco, 1959—. Surg. cons. San Francisco Vets. Hosp., 1959-73. Contbr. articles to profl. jours., chpts. to books. Founder No. Calif. Artery Bank, 1954-58, Irwin Meml. Blood Bank, San Francisco, commr., pres., 1969-74; bd. dirs. People for Open Space-Greenbelt Alliance, 1984-98, adv. coun., 1998—; chmn. adv. coun. Dorothy Enskine Open Space Fund. Capt. with U.S. Army, 1946-48. Fellow ACS; mem. San Francisco Med. Soc. (bd. dirs. 1968-72), San Francisco Surg. Soc. (v.p. 1984), Pacific Coast Surg. Assn., Am. Cancer Soc. (bd. dirs. San Francisco br. 1965-75), Calif. Med. Assn., Olympic Club, Sierra Club. Democrat. Unitarian Universalist. Avocations: mountains, tree farming, gardening, walking, reading, music. Office: 233 Chestnut St San Francisco CA 94133-2452

ERSKINE, RODNEY D., oil industry executive; m. Jackie Erskine. BS in petroleum engring., Tex. A&M U., 1966. With Union Tex. Petroleum, 1975—91; pres. and CEO Nerco Oil & Gas, Inc.; with Coastal Oil & Gas (merged with El Paso Corp. 2001), 1994—97, sr. v.p., 1997—2001, pres., 2001; pres. prodn. El Paso Corp., Houston, 2001—.

ERSKINE, WILLIAM CRAWFORD, retired academic administrator, accountant, health facility administrator; b. Seattle, Feb. 29, 1924; s. Alwin Crawford and Emilie Hildred (Davies) E.; m. Mary Jean Hopkins, Feb. 28, 1946; children: Scott Crawford, Nancy Page. BA in Bus. Adminstrn., U. Wash., 1950. CPA, Wash. Auditor Arthur Andersen & Co., 1950-54; sr. auditor Ansell Johnson & Co., CPAs, Seattle, 1956-59; contr. Food Giant Stores, Seattle, 1959-64; comptr. U. Wash., Seattle, 1964-70; v.p. bus. U. Colo., Boulder, 1970-74; exec. v.p. U. Nebr. Sys., Lincoln, 1974-80; v.p. bus. affairs U. Tex., El Paso, 1980-88; ret., 1988. Dir. West Tex. Higher Edn. Authority, El Paso, 1982-88, Sunwest Bank El Paso, 1986-96, Providence Hosp. P.H.A., Inc., 1994-96; cons. Educator Cons. Panel GAO, 1978-86. Treas. St. Francis on the Hill Episcopal Ch., 1996-99; mem. exec. com. Nat. Assn. State Univs. and Land Grant Colls., 1977-80. With U.S. Air Corps, WWII. Mem.: Coronado Country Club (treas. 1990—93). Home: 6136 Los Robles Dr El Paso TX 79912-1933 E-mail: werskine@elp.rr.com.

ERSTAD, LEON ROBERT, lawyer; b. Tyler, Minn., Aug. 3, 1947; s. Clifford and Josie (Dellberg) E.; m. Nancy Youel, July 19, 1969; children: Eric, Andrew, Jonathan. BSBA, U. Minn., 1969; JD cum laude, Temple U., 1976. Bar: Minn. 1976, U.S. Dist. Ct. Minn. 1976, U.S. Ct. Appeals (8th cir.) 1992, U.S. Supreme Ct. 1994; cert. ct. mediator. Ptnr. Chadwick, Johnson & Condon, P.A., Mpls., 1976-90, Erstad & Riemer P.A., 1990—. Adj. instr. law William Mitchell Coll., St. Paul, 1985-94; bd. dirs. Minn. Fulbright Assn.; lectr. in field; spkr. in field Contbr. articles to profl. jours. Bd. dirs. Loring Nicollet Cmty. Ctr., Mpls., 1981-91, Minn. Returned Peace Corps Vols., Mpls., 1980-86, pres., 1980-81; trustee Lynnhurst Congrl. Ch., 1997—, deacon, 1994-97. Named alumni of notable achievement U. Minn. Mem. ABA, Minn. State Bar Assn., Minn. Def. Lawyers Assn. (bd. dirs. 1999-2000, sec. 2000-01, treas. 2001-02, v.p. 2002-03, pres. 2003-04, pres. emeritus 2004—05), Def. Rsch. Inst., Def. Lawyers Assn. Home: 4700 Dupont Ave S Minneapolis MN 55409-2324 Office: Erstad & Riemer PA 200 Riverview Office Tower 8006 34th Ave S Minneapolis MN 55425 Office Phone: 952-896-3700. Business E-Mail: lerstad@erstad.com.

ERTAN, ATILLA, medical educator, physician, researcher, health facility administrator; b. Eskisehir, Turkey, June 21, 1940; arrived in US, 1969; s. Rasim and Veliye E.; m. Inci E. Ertan, June 2, 1973; children: Basak, Baris R. MD, Ankara (Turkey) U. Med. Sch., 1963, Internal Medicine, 1967. Intern Ankara U. Med. Sch., 1963—64, resident in internal medicine, 1964—67; instr. medicine U. Pa., Phila., 1969—71, fellow in gastroenterology, 1971; assoc. prof. Ankara U. Med. Sch., 1972—76, prof., 1976-—82, Tulane U. Med. Sch., New Orleans, 1982—90, chief gastrointestinal sect., 1985—90, interim chair, 1989—90; prof., chief GI BCM/TMH, Houston, 1990—2000; prof., med. dir. dept. digestive diseases Meth. Hosp., Houston, 1990—. Founder Turkish GI Rsch. Fund, Ankara, 1996. Editor: Best Practice of Med. Gastroent., 1998; mem. editl. bd.: Digestive Disease Sci., 1994—, Ann. Med. Sci., 1999—, Med. Sci., 2002—; contbr. over 140 articles to profl. jours., chapters to books. Named Hon. Citizen, City of New Orleans, 1989, Best Physician, Crohn's and Colitis Found. Am., 1996, Man of Yr., Assembly of Turkish Am. Assn., 2004; named one of Top Drs. in Am., Nat. Registry, 1997—2005; recipient Med. Sci. award, Turkish Sci. and Tech. Rsch. Assembly, 1992. Master: Am. Coll. Gastroenterology; mem.: ASGE, AAAS, Am. Gastroenterol. Assn. (Disting. Clinician award 2003), Turkish GI Soc. (hon. pres. 1996), L'Union Med. Balkanique (hon. Best Rschr. award 1973), So. Soc. Clin. Investigation, Am. Fedn. Med. Rsch. Achievements include research in biliary and pancreatic disorders, Barrett's esophagus and inflammatory bowel diseases. Avocations: travel, reading, exercise. Home: 6337 Mercer St Houston TX 77005 Office: 6560 Fannin St Ste 2208 Houston TX 77030

ERTL, WOLFGANG, German language and literature educator; b. Sangerhausen, Germany, May 27, 1946; came to U.S., 1969; m. Mary R. Clough, Aug. 30, 1969. BA equivalent in German and English, Philipps U., Marburg, Germany, 1969; MA in German, U. N.H., 1970; PhD in Germanic Langs. and Lits., U. Pa., 1975. Lectr. German U. Pa., Phila., 1974-76; asst. prof. German Swarthmore (Pa.) Coll., 1976-77, U. Iowa, 1977-82, assoc. prof., 1982-88, prof., 1988—, chmn. dept. German, 1988-96. Author: Stephan Hermlin and Tradition, 1977, Nature and Landscape in the Poetry of the GDR: Walter Werner, Wulf Kirsten, and Uwe Gressmann, 1982, (with Christine Cosentino) On Volker Braun's Lyric Poetry, 1984; co-editor: GDR Poetry in Context, 1988; co-editor Glossen: An Internat. Bi-Lingual Scholarly Jour. on Lit., Film, and Art in the German Speaking Countries After 1945; co-editor (with C. Cosentino and W. Muller) Taking Stock--German Literature after Unification: Contributions to the 1st Carlisle Symposium on Modern German Literature, Glossen 10, 2000-, Crosscurrents--German Literature(s) and the Search for Identity: Selected Papers from the 2nd Carisle Symposium on Modern German Literature, Glossen 15, 2002; co-editor At the Milennium: Focus on German Literature, 2003; co-editor, America in German Literature and Film: Selected Papers from the 3rd Carlisle Sympsium on Modern German Literature, Glossen 19, 2004; contbr. chpts. to books, revs. and articles to profl. jours. Resident dir., Academic Year In Freiburg, Germany, 2000-01, 2004-05. May Brodbeck Humanities fellow, 1987. Mem. MLA, N.E. MLA, Am. Assn. Tchrs. German, German Studies Assn. Office: U Iowa Dept German 526 Phillips Hall Iowa City IA 52242-1323

ERTMER, PEGGY ANN, education educator, consultant; b. Detroit, Oct. 31, 1951; m. David J. Ertmer. BA, U. Denver, 1973; MA, Cardinal Stritch Coll., Milw., 1976; PhD, Purdue U., 1995. Tchr. Holy Rosary Elem. Sch., Milw., 1973-74; tchr. learning disabilities Milw. Pub. Schs., 1975-78; ednl. diagnostician Arapahoe Pub. Schs., Littleton, Colo., 1978-79; tchr. learning disabilities Fremont RE-1 Schs., Canon City, Colo., 1979-83; grad. tchg. asst. Purdue U., W. Lafayette, Ind., 1991-95, asst. prof., 1997—2002, assoc. prof., 2002—. Adj. prof. Boise State U., 1997—; cons., Lafayette, Ind., 1994—. Author: The ID CaseBook: Case Studies in Instructional Design, 1999, 2d edit., 2003, Education on the Internet: The Worldwide Classroom, 2000; contbr. Articles to profl. jurs. Recipient Best Rsch. Study award Soc. Info. Tech. and Tchr. Edn., 2000, Book of Yr. award, Assn. Ednl. Commns. and Tech. Mem. Am. Ednl. Rsch. Assn., Assn. Ednl. Comms. and Tech.

ERTSGAARD, EDWIN PAUL, physicist; b. Mpls., Minn., Jan. 24, 1922; s. Edwin and Anna Christine (Hafstrom) Ertsgaard; m. Marian Eschmeyer, Mar. 6, 1954; children: Jon Edwin, Thomas Steven, Katherine Ann, Susan Karen. BS, U. Rochester, 1951. With Nat. Bur. Standards, 1940; with Dept. Terrestrial Magnetism Carnegie Instn., Washington, 1940—42; with Applied Physics Lab. Johns Hopkins U., 1942—46; sr. project engr. Eastman Kodak, Rochester, NY, 1946—70, sr. rsch. assoc., 1970—83. Cons. U.S. Army, 1944—83. Contbr. articles to profl. jours. Maj. U.S. Army, 1944—45, ETO. Recipient Army/Navy Cert. of Appreciation, 1947, Naval Ordnance Devel. Award, 1945. Achievements include patents in field; research in radio proximity fuze project during WWII, infrared proximity fuze, space satellite program, microwave and ultrasound research. Avocations: photography, computers, amateur radio. Home: 1674 Highland Ave Rochester NY 14618 Personal E-mail: ke2p@arrl.net.

ERVIN, BILLY MAXWELL, management consultant; b. Dante, Va., July 29, 1933; s. Willie Beldon and Ollie Lowel (Biggs) Ervin; m. Barbara Frances Walsh, June 27, 1971; 1 child, Honore McDonough 1 stepchild, Kerry Thompson; 1 child from previous marriage, Michael. BS, U.S. Naval Acad., 1955; grad., Navy Nuclear Power Training, 1961; M in Marine Affairs, U. R.I., 1971; postgrad., U. Mass., 1989. Commd. ensign USN, 1955, advanced through grades to capt., 1975, chief engr. aircraft carrier, 1969-70, destroyer capt., 1971-73, project mgr. Washington, 1973-78, head logistics br., 1978-80, head rsch. and devel. br., 1980-82, insp. gen. Europe London, 1982-85, ret., 1985; adminstr. Baystate Eye Care, P.C., Springfield, Mass., 1986-88; mgr. engring. adminstrn. and planning Kaman Aerospace Corp., Bloomfield, Conn., 1990-92; chief oper. officer Conn. Orthopaedic and Sports Medicine Ctr., Vernon, CT, 1992-97; bus. mgr. engring. Kaman Aerospace Corp., Bloomfield, 1997-2000; mgmt. cons. Bloomfield, 2000—. Decorated Bronze Star; recipient Meritorious Svc. Medal award Pres. of the U.S., 1985. Mem. Naval War Coll. Found., Navy League, St. Andrew's Soc., Clan Irwin Assn. Avocations: antique cars, genealogy. Home: 20 Magnolia Ter Springfield MA 01108-2512 Personal E-mail: max.ervin@1955.usna.com.

ERVIN, CHARLES PHIFER, JR., education educator, retired military officer; b. Morganton, NC, Nov. 30, 1942; s. Charles P. Ervin Jr. and Eunice (Cuthbertson) Ervin; m. Margie Berry Ervin, Sept. 10, 1962 (div. Aug. 1989); children: Eunice Anita, Charles III, Todd. BS in Sociology, N.C. A&T State U., 1965; MA in Mgmt., Ctrl. Mich. U., 1978; PhD in Social Found. of Edn., Ga. State U., 2001. Commd. 2d lt. U.S. Army, 1965, advanced through grades to lt. col., chief pers. svcs. officer Ft. Bragg, NC, 1980—81, insp. gen., auditor Camp Casey, Republic of Korea, 1983—84, manpower staffing officer, Pentagon, 1984—87, dep. cmty. comdr., resource mgr. Camp Red Cloud, Republic of Korea, 1987—89; prof. mil. sci. SROTC Ft. Valley State Coll., Ft. Valley, 1989—93; ret. U.S. Army, 1993; sr. army ROTC instr. Northeast H.S., Macon, Ga., 1993—96; state coord. edn. homeless children and youth program Fla. Dept. Edn., Fla. A&M U., Tallahassee, 1996—2003; asst. prof. Fla. A&M U., Tallahassee, 2001—. Bd. dirs. Tallahassee Coalition for Homeless, 1997—, Fla. Coalition for Homeless, Orlando, 1998—2004. Named one of 100 Black Men of Mid. Ga., CME Ch., Warner Robins, Ga., 1991; Fulbright scholar, Turkey, 2004. Mem.: NAACP, Ret. Officers Assn., Nat. Assn. for Edn. Homeless Children & Youths, Urban League, Mason, Phi Delta Kappa, Phi Lambda Theta, Kappa Delta Pi, Alpha Phi Alpha. Democrat. Methodist. Avocation: running. Home: 8691 Alexandrite Ct Tallahassee FL 32309 Office: Fla A&M Univ Dept Secondary Edn Coll Edn Tallahassee FL 32301 Office Phone: 850-412-7190. Personal E-mail: cervin42@aol.com.

ERVIN, CLARK KENT, former federal agency administrator; b. Apr. 1, 1959; m. Carolyn A. Harris. BA in Govt., Harvard Coll., 1980, LLD, 1985; MA, Oxford U., 1982. Atty Vinson & Elkins, 1985—89; assoc. dir. policy Office of Nat. Svc., 1989—91; atty. Locke, Liddell & Sapp, 1993—95; asst. sec. of state State of Tex., 1995—99; dep. atty. gen., gen. counsel, dir. adminstrn. Tex. Atty. Gen.'s Office, 1999—2001; insp. gen. U.S. Dept. State, Washington, 2001—03; acting insp. gen. US Dept. Homeland Security, Washington, 2003, insp. gen., 2003—04. Scholar Rhodes scholar.

ERVIN, ROBERT MARVIN, lawyer; b. near Ocala, Fla., Jan. 19, 1917; s. Richard William and Carrie (Phillips) E.; m. Frances Anne Cushing, Dec. 25, 1941; children: Anne Cushing (Mrs. Henry Lamar Rowe), Robert Marvin. BSBA, U. Fla., 1941, LLB, 1947. Bar: Fla. 1947. Of counsel Ervin, Chapman & Ervin, Tallahassee, 1947—; U.S. referee in bankruptcy No. Dist. Fla., part time, 1952-72. Mem. Fla. Constn. Revision Commn., 1966-68; Trustee U. Fla. Law Center Assn.; mem. founders com., mem. bd. visitors Fla. State U. Coll. Law. Served with USMC, 1941-45, PAO; col. ret. Recipient Disting. Svc. award for legal edn. John B. Stetson U., 1966, Disting. Svc. award Armed Forces League, 1966, Medal of Hon. award Fla. Bar Found., 2003; named to Fla. Housing Hall of Fame, 1993. Fellow Am. Bar Found. (chmn. 1989-90); mem. ABA (ho. of dels. 1966-91, bd. govs., 1979-82, chmn. sect. criminal justice 1975-76, mem. resource devel. coun., audit com., vice chmn. sr. lawyers div., chmn. special com. on fiscal policy 1984-85), Am. Coll. Trial Lawyers (bd. regents 1983-84), Am. Law Inst., Am. Judicature Soc., Fla. Bar (pres. 1965-66, Disting. Svc. award 1966), Fla. Supreme Ct. Hist. Soc. (pres. 1986-87, chmn. trustees 1987-98), Am. Bar Retirement Assn. (pres. 1980-82), Nat. Conf. Referees in Bankruptcy (pres. 1963-64), Ret. Officers Assn., Elks, Fla. Blue Key, Phi Alpha Delta, Alpha Kappa Psi. Baptist. Home: 530 North Ride Tallahassee FL 32303-5127 Office: PO Box 1170 Tallahassee FL 32301-1811 Office Phone: 850-224-9135. Personal E-mail: ervin090@comcast.net.

ERVIN-CARR, CHARLESETTA YVONNE, secondary school educator; b. Seattle, June 10, 1946; d. Charles Woodrow and Christene Rosetta (Griffin) Ervin; 1 child, David Anthony Carr. BA in Speech and English, U. Wash., 1969, MEd, 1971. Tchr. Seattle Pub. Schs. Dist. 1, 1971—2002; instr. Seattle Central C.C., part-time, 1977-87; tng. and employee devel. cons. City of Seattle, 1981—; owner, cons. Effective Communication Skills, Seattle, 1980—. Bd. dirs. Shades of Beauty, Seattle, 1979—, Nat. Black Child Devel. Inst.; pres. Mt. Zion Bd. Christian Edn., 1989-2001; faculty field supr. Pacific Oaks Coll. N.W., 2003. Recipient Excellence in Edn. award Top Ten Tchrs. Seattle Pub. Schs., 1987, Outstanding Educator award Seattle U., 1985, Paula Marcus award for Outstanding Cmty. Svc., Child Devel. Inst., Seattle, 1993, Svc. to Edn. award Black Coll. Fair, 1996, Mary McLeod Bethune Outstanding Tchr. award Hall of Fame, 2002. Mem. AAUW, Black Profl. Educators of Greater Puget Sound, Nat. Coun. Negro Women (Seattle sect.), Coun. on Black Am. Affairs, Women's Ednl. Network, Women's Profl. and Managerial Network, Seattle Alliance of Black Sch. Educators (scholarship chair), Delta Kappa Gamma. Personal E-mail: cyegcc@aol.com.

ERVINE, TIMOTHY DUWAYNE, utilities executive; b. Covington, Va., Feb. 15, 1963; s. Randolph DuWayne and Mary Evelyn (McCutcheon) E.; m. Teresa Lee Gadd, Feb. 25, 1984; children: Alison Lee, Casey Beth. Student, Jackson River Vocat., 1981, Tri-County Tech. Coll., 1988-90; BS in Safety Engring, Kennedy-Western U., 1996. Cert. utility safety adminstr. Nat. Safety Coun.; cert. provl. environ. auditor; cert. hazard control mgr. From attendant to asst. mgr. Stonewall Svc. Sta., Covington, 1976-81; safety and loss prevention insp. Va. Power, Warm Springs, Va., 1981-86; with BE & K Constrn. Co., 1985-86, project safety dir. Jacksonville, Fla., 1986, Georgetown, S.C., 1986; safety specialist Duke Power Co., Salem, S.C., 1986-90, safety and security supr., 1990-91, Great Falls, S.C., 1991-94, safety and indsl. hygiene cons. Charlotte, NC, 1994-98, health and safety mgr., 1998—2001, mgr. environ. health and safety, 2001—. Mem., del. Va. Assn. Vol. Rescue Squads, 1978-83; del. Va. Firemen's Assn., 1978-83. Named Fireman of the Yr. Dunlap Fire and Rescue Squad, 1979, 81. Mem. Am. Soc. Safety Engrs., Am. Indsl. Hygiene Assn. Methodist. Avocations: auto racing, hunting, fishing, carpentry. Home: 419 Woodland Rd Covington VA 24426-6321 Office: Duke Power Co 526 S Church St Charlotte NC 28202-1802 E-mail: tdervine@duke-energy.com.

ERVING, JULIUS (JULIUS WINFIELD ERVING II), retired professional basketball player, business executive; b. East Meadow, N.Y., Feb. 22, 1950; s. Callie Erving Lindsey; m. Turquoise Erving; 4 children. Grad., U. Mass., 1986; hon. doctorate, U.Mass., 1983, Temple U., 1983. With Va. Squires, Am. Basketball Assn., 1971-73, N.Y. Nets, Am. Basketball Assn., 1973-76, Phila. 76ers, NBA, 1976-87; mem. NBA Championship team, 1983; broadcaster NBC, 1993; exec. v.p. Orlando Magic, 1997—; v.p. RDV Sports, Orlando, 1997—. Bd. dirs. Meridian Bancorp, Phila. Coca-Cola Bottling Co., DJ Group, Inc.; pres. mgmt. and mktg. firm JDREGI; spokesman Coca-Cola Co., Converse Shoe Co., Advanced Golf Techs., Hardee's. Appeared in film The Fish That Saved Pittsburgh, 1979. Trustee NBA Internat., Basketball Hall of Fame; bd. dirs. N.Y. State Sports Commn. Named Rookie of Yr. Am. Basketball Assn., 1972, Most Valuable Player Am. Basketball Assn., 1974, 76 and mem. championship team, 1974, 76; named to NBA 35th Anniversary All-Star Team, 1980; named Most Valuable Player NBA, 1981, Most Valuable Player All-Star Game NBA, 1971, 83; recipient Cert. Appreciation Easter Seals, 1982, Best Friend award Police Athletic League Phila, 1982, Walter Kennedy Citizenship award, 1983, Jackie Robinson award for Am. Black Achievement Ebony mag., 1983, Whitney M. Young award Urban League, 1984, Father Flanagan award Boys Town Nebr., 1984, Biddy Basketball award, 1984, Sports award Big Bros. Inc., N.Y.C., 1985, Man of Yr. award Am. Express, 1985, Appreciation award Lupus Found. Am., 1985, Sportsman of Yr. award David Zinkoff Meml. Found., 1986; presented Liberty Bell award Mayor Frank Rizzo, Phila., 1978; named to Hall of Fame, U. Mass., 1980, Basketball Hall of Fame. One of 3 players to score 30,000 points in his profl. basketball career; holds NBA All-Star game record for most free-throws attempted in one half, 11, in 1978; shares NBA All-Star game record for most free-throws made in one half, 9, in 1978; one of 7 players to average over 20 points and 20 rebounds per game during NCAA career. Office: care Erving Group Inc PO Box 8269 Cherry Hill NJ 08002-0269 also: Orlando Magic Orlando Arena 8701 Maitland Summit Blvd Orlando FL 32810-5915

ERWIN, BARBARA F., school system administrator; b. Chgo. married; 2 children. BS in Spl. Edn., Ind. U., Bloomington; MS in Sch. Adminstrn., Purdue U., West Lafayette, Ind.; PhD in Sch. Adminstrn., Ind. U., Bloomington. Mid. sch. spl. needs tchr.; Title IV-C cons. Ind. Dept. Pub. Instrn.; spl. edn. diagnostician; tchr.; elem. sch. prin.; supt., Allen (Tex.) Ind. Sch. Dist., 1994—2000, Scottsdale (Ariz.) Pub. Sch., 2000—. Nominee Nat. Supt. of Yr., 1999; named Supt. of Yr., Tex. Assn. of Sch. Bds., 1997, Tex. Assn. Sch. Adminstrs., 1998; recipient Top Suburban Supt. Leadership Learning award, Am. Assn. of Sch. Adminstrs., 1996. Office: Scottsdale Pub Sch Edn Ctr 3811 N 44th St Phoenix AZ 85018-5420

ERWIN, DONALD CARROLL, plant pathology educator; b. Concord, Nebr., Nov. 24, 1920; s. Robert James and Carol Erwin; m. Veora Marie Endres, Aug. 15, 1948; children: Daniel Erwin, Myriam Erwin Casey. Student, Wayne State (Nebr.) Tchrs.Coll, 1938-39; BSc, U. Nebr., 1949, MA, 1950; PhD, U. Calif.-Davis, 1953. Jr. plant pathologist U. Calif., Riverside, 1953-54, asst. plant pathologist, 1954-60, assoc. plant pathologist, 1960-66, prof. plant pathology, 1966—, emeritus prof., 1991. Sr. author: Phytophthora Diseases Worldwide, 1996; editor: Phytophthora: Its Biology, Taxonomy, Ecology and Pathology, 1983; contbr. articles to profl. jours. With U.S. Army, 1942-46; ETO. Nathan Gold fellow, 1949, Guggenheim fellow, 1959 Mem.: Am. Phytopathol. Soc. (fellow), Sigma Xi. Democrat. Roman Catholic. Office: U Calif Dept Plant Pathology Riverside CA 92521-0001

ERWIN, ELMER LOUIS, vintager, consultant; b. Visalia, Calif., Oct. 6, 1926; s. Louis Nelson and Myra Erla (Hector) E.; m. Jeanne Prothero, Feb. 27, 1954; children: Catherine Lynn, Christopher Lawrence. BS, U. Calif.-Berkeley, 1950. Registered profl. engr., Calif. With Kaiser Cement Corp., Oakland, Calif., 1957-80, v.p. mfg. and distbn., 1980-87; freelance vintager. Cons. internat. cement plant projects.

ERWIN, FRANCES SUZANNE, artist; b. Stockton, Calif. d. Frederick Bedford and Clara Jackquiline (Seale) Davis; widow; 9 children. Student, Thomas Leighton Sch. Fine Arts, San Francisco, 1964-70, Sergie Bongart Sch., Rexburg, Idaho, 1972-73, various master artists, various cities, 1972—. Represented by The Main Street Gallery, Pleasanton, Calif., The Phantom Gallery, Hayward, Calif. Portrait painting instr. Roy Johnson Sch., Castro Valley, Calif., 1993—, San Lorenzo (Calif.) Sch., 1995—; lectr. on visual arts, various San Francisco Bay area locations, 1987—. One-woman shows include Hayward Art Coun. Gallery, Hayward, Calif., 2002; group exhbns. include The Triton Mus., San Jose, Calif., 2002; portrait painter numerous pvt. commns include Alameda County Ct. House, 1990, recreation facilities in Castro Valley and Hayward, 1991-92, Moreau H.S., Hayward, 1993, San Francisco World Trade Club, 1994, Eden Hosp., Castro Valley, 1994, Sakura Corp. Mus., Osaka, Japan, 1996; designed image for Sakura Corp. Judge various county fairs and open art shows, Alameda County, Contra Costa County, and Santa Clara County (all in Calif.), 1988—. Recipient Best of Show award Alameda County Fair, Pleasanton, Calif., 1989, Best of Class, 1990; recipient Purchase and Founders awards Pastel Soc. Fla., 1996, Silver Medal awards (3) Alameda County Fair, 1999, 2 Silvar Medal awards, 2002. Mem. Pastel Soc. of Am. (signature mem.), Am. Soc. Portrait Artists, Pastel Soc. of the West Coast (signature mem., co-founder, bd. dirs., events chair 1985-87, v.p. 1987-88, pres. 1988-89, adv. bd. mem. 1989—, Plaques 1988, 89, Art of the West award 1994), Knickerbocker Artists USA (signature mem.), Nat. League Am. Pen Women. Republican. Roman Catholic. Avocations: photography, sculpting, gardening. Home: The Painted Portrait 22125 Orange Ave Castro Valley CA 94546-6937 E-mail: franportraits@aol.com.

ERWIN, FRANK WILLIAM, personnel practices advisor; b. Elizabeth, N.J., Nov. 22, 1931; s. Frank J. and Jessie (Rugero) E.; m. Bridget E. Taddeo, June 26, 1965. BA cum laude, NYU, 1957. With MBS, 1957-62, asst. to pres., asst. sec. to bd. dirs., 1960-62; dep. dir. div. selection, dir. recruiting ops. Peace Corps, 1962-65; exec. asst. to sec. labor, 1965-68; pres., chmn. Richardson, Bellows, Henry & Co., Inc., 1968-99; advisor FBI, 1995—, ePredix, Inc., 1999—, Nat. Skills Stds. Bd., 2001—03. Chmn. fin. com. Our Lady of Lourdes Ch.; pres. Ridge House Condominium, 2002—; v.p. Ridge House Condominium, 2001-2002. Served with AUS, 1949-52. Mem. Am. Psychol. Assn., Internat. Assn. for Advancement Pschology, Soc. for Indsl. and Organizational Psychology (Disting. Profl. Contbn. award, 2005), Personnel Testing Coun. of Metro. Washington. Home and Office: 2310 S Rolfe St Arlington VA 22202-1545 E-mail: niwre@ix.netcom.com.

ERWIN, LINDA MCINTOSH, librarian, consultant; b. Austin, Tex., June 22, 1939; d. William Erwin and Martha (Ferguson) McIntosh; m. Kenneth James Erwin, June 7, 1962 (div. Feb. 1986); 1 child, Jason Emerson. BA magna cum laude, U. Tex., 1961, MLS, 1968. Tchr. Spanish, Victoria (Tex.) H.S., 1961-62, El Campo (Tex.) H.S., 1962-63, Del Valle (Tex.) H.S., 1963-66; libr. U. Tex., Austin, 1968-69, Corpus Christi Pub. Librs., 1981-89; cons. South Tex. Libr. Sys., Corpus Christi, 1989-99, asst. coord., 1999—. Ford Found. scholar, 1966-67. Mem. ALA, Tex. Libr. Assn., Pub. Libr. Assn., Phi Beta Kappa, Alpha Phi, Sigma Delta Pi. Office: South Tex Libr Sys 805 Comanche St Corpus Christi TX 78401-2715

ERWIN-COOK, NANCY ELIZABETH, commercial artist; b. Erwin, Tenn., June 12, 1949; d. Jack Lilly and Shirley (Britton) Sifferd; m. Larry Joe Erwin, Dec. 23, 1966 (div. June 1977); 1 child, Kimberly Beth; m. Jerry Eugene Cook, Mar. 17, 1990. Owner embroidery bus., Erwin, Tenn., 1964-65; salesperson Unaka Stores, Erwin, 1966-68, Matthews-Belk Dept. Store, Gastonia, N.C., 1966; floral designer Mountain View Florist, Erwin, 1968-69; teller, student loan officer Valley Fed. Savs. & Loan, Erwin, 1969-77; br. mgr. Great So. Savs. & Loan, Springfield, Mo., 1977-81; sales agt. Bus. Benefits

Ins. Agy., Tulsa and Springfield, 1981; savs. account mgr. First Tenn. Bank, Johnson City, 1981-82; mktg./pub. rels. Valley Fed., Johnson City, Tenn., 1982-83; self-employed comml. artist Erwin, 1983—; owner import bus., 1984—; asst. to sales rep. for ski-wear bus., 1986—. Bd. mem. March of Dimes, Johnson City, 1982-91, sec., 1990-91, Walkamerica chmn., 1984; treas. Tri Cities Head Injury Assn., 1991; program dir. North Johnson City Bus. Club, 1985. Recipient Vol. Plaque, Sr. Citizens Ctr., Johnson City, 1984. Mem. Watauga Valley Art League (treas. 1983-84, Plaque). Baptist.

ERXLEBEN, WILLIAM CHARLES, lawyer, data processing executive; b. Chgo., Dec. 18, 1942; s. Walter Oscar and Sarah Louise (Githens) E.; m. Gayle Amelia Reichmuth, Aug. 28, 1965; children: David William, Jennifer Renée. BS in Bus., Miami U., Oxford, Ohio, 1963; JD, Stanford U., 1966. Bar: Wash. 1969. Asst. state atty. gen. Wash. State Atty. Gen.'s Office, Olympia, 1968-70; exec. asst. U.S. atty. Dept. Justice, Seattle, 1970-72; regional dir. FTC, Seattle, 1972-79; lectr. Grad. Sch. Bus., U. Wash., Seattle, 1979-85; ptnr. Foster, Pepper & Shefelman, Bellevue, Wash., 1985-91, Lane Powell Spears Lubersky, Olympia, 1991-93; pres., CEO, Data I/O Corp., Redmond, Wash., 1993-98, bd. dirs., 1979-98. Chmn., dir. Advanced Digital Tech., Bellevue, 1983-85. Contbr. articles to law revs. Counsel Wash. Assn. for Children and Adults with Learning Disabilities, Seattle, 1985-93; chmn. Portwatch, Seattle, 1985; mem. advt. rev. com. BBB, Seattle, 1982; bd. dirs. Wash. Citizens for Recycling, Seattle, 1980-84; Dem. nominee for Wash. State Atty. Gen., 1988, Wash.Ho. of Reps., 1982; mem., chmn. Newcastle City Planning Commn., 2002—; mem. Newcastle City Coun., 2002—. Recipient Excellence in Supervision award FTC, 1975, Disting. Svc. award, 1979; Sloan exec. fellow Stanford U. Grad. Sch. Bus., 1975-76. Mem. ABA, Wash. State Bar Assn. (sec.-treas. antitrust subcom 1981-83). Home: 7625 120th Pl SE Newcastle WA 98056-1791 E-mail: billerx3@yahoo.com.

ERZINGER, KATHY MCCLAM, nursing educator; b. Lake City, S.C., July 14, 1951; d. Curtis Brown and Parneace Ora (Timmons) McClam; m. Dennis Eugene Erzinger, Sr., June 22, 1974; children: Amberlyn Marie, Dennis Eugene Jr. AA, Brevard C.C., 1971; BS in Vocat. Edn., Carson-Newman Coll., 1974; degree in Vocat. Nursing, Simi Career Inst., 1994. Lic. vocat. nurse, Calif., 1994, cert. intravenous therapy and blood withdrawal, Calif., 1997; staff devel. Calif., 2001, tchr. Calif., 2001. Tchr. First Bapt. Acad., Thousand Oaks, Calif., 1988—90, Hillcrest Christian Sch., Thousand Oaks, 1990—93; charge nurse Victoria Care Ctr., Ventura, Calif., 1994—95; per diem charge nurse Thousand Oaks (Calif.) Health Care, 1995—; dir. staff devel. Westlake Healthcare Ctr., Westlake Village, Calif., 2001—02; instr. Simi Career Inst., Simi Valley, Calif., 2000—. Vol. Am. Cancer Assn., Simi Valley, 2003. Mem.: Calif. Vocat. Educators, Calif. Coun. for Adult Edn., Simi Educators Assn., Calif. Tchrs. Assn., Health Occupations Student Assn. Republican. Avocations: painting, baking, walking, music, gardening. Office: Simi Valley Adult School 3192 Los Angeles Ave Simi Valley CA 93065 E-mail: erzingerk@msn.com.

ESAKI, LEO, physicist, foundation executive, university president; b. Osaka, Japan, Mar. 12, 1925; arrived in U.S., 1960, permanent resident; s. Soichiro and Niyoko (Ito) Esaki; m. Masako Kondo, May 31, 1986; children from previous marriage: Nina Yvonne, Anna Eileen, Eugene Leo. BS, U. Tokyo, 1947, PhD, 1959. With Sony Corp., Japan, 1956—60; with Thomas J. Watson Research Center, IBM, Yorktown Heights, NY, 1960—92, IBM fellow, 1967—92, mgr. device research, 1965—92; dir. IBM-Japan, 1975—92; pres. U. Tsukuba, Ibaraki, Japan, 1992—98; chmn. Sci. and Tech. Found. of Ibaraki, 1998—; pres. Shibaura Inst. of Tech., Tokyo, 2000—05. Dir. Yamada Sci. Found. Decorated Order of Culture Govt. of Japan, Grand Cordon Order of Rising Sun; recipient Nishina Mem. Prize, 1959, Stuart Ballantine medal, Franklin Inst., 1961, Japan Acad. award, 1965, Nobel prize in Physics, 1973, Internat. Prize for New Materials, Am. Physical Soc., 1985. Fellow: IEEE (Morris N. Liebman Meml. prize 1961, medal of Honor 1991), Am. Vacuum Soc. (bd. dirs. 1973—74), Japan Phys. Soc., Am. Phys. Soc. (councillor-at-large 1971—74); mem.: NAE (fgn. assoc.), NAS (fgn. assoc.), Japan Acad., Russian Acad. Scis. (fgn.), Academia Nacional de Ingenieria Mex. (corr.), Max-Planck Gesellschaft, Am. Philos. Soc., Am. Philos. Soc., Am. Acad. Arts and Scis. Achievements include discovery of Esaki tunnel diode, 1957; pioneering research in semiconductor superlattices and quantum wells. Home: PO Box 851 Katonah NY 10536-0851 Office: Esaki Tokyo Office 25-17 Sakuragaokacho Shibuya Tokyo 150 0031 Japan also: Tsukuba Internat Congress 2-20-3 Takezono Tsukuba 305 0032 Japan E-mail: leoesaki@epochal.or.jp.

ESAMANN, DOUGLAS F., utilities executive; m. Kimberly Esamann; children: Regan, Kalee, Conley. BS, Ind. U., 1979. Various positions to tax mgr. Pub. Svc. Indiana (now subs. of Cinergy), Ind., 1979—94; project mgr., corp. devel. Cinergy Corp., Cin., 1994—96, fin. team, comml. bus. unit, 1996—98, gen. mgr., bus. devel. Cin., 1998—99, v.p., CFO, comml. bus. unit, 1999—2001, pres. Pub. Svc. Ind. Inc., 2001—04, sr. v.p., Energy Portfolio Strategy and Mgmt., Comml. Bus. Unit. Cin., 2004—. Bd. dir. Ctrl. Ind. Corp. Partnership, Ind. Fiscal Policy Inst. Mem.: Ind. Mfrs. Assn. (bd. dir.), Ind. C. of C. (bd. dir.), Indpls. (Ind.) C. of C. (bd. dir.). Office: Cinergy Corp 139 E 4th St Cincinnati OH 45202*

ESCALANTE, DELIA, Spanish educator, translator; b. Tucson, Ariz., Dec. 20, 1950; d. José Francisco Escalante and María Luisa Paredes de Escalante; 1 child, Abraham Antonio Sánchez. BA, U. Ariz., Tucson, 1973, MA, 1975. Adminstrv. asst. Grad. Sch. Libr. U. Ariz., Tucson, 1975—76; mem. Spanish faculty Phoenix Coll., 1976—. Translator Canyon Surgery Ctr., Phoenix, 2000—01. Catechetical facilitator Our Lady of Perpetual Help, Scottsdale, Ariz., 1999—2002, liturgical min., 2000—. Named Fulbright Hayes fellow to Italy, U.S. Dept. Edn., 1980, Fulbright Hayes fellow to Brazil, 1982; recipient Nat. Inst. for Staff and Orgnl. Devel. award, U. Tex., Austin, 1992, 2002. Mem.: AAUP, Ariz. Lang. Assn., Am. Assn. Tchrs. of Spanish and Portuguese, Sigma Delta Mu (life), Sigma Delta Pi (life). Roman Catholic. Avocation: travel, reading, cooking. Office: Phoenix College 1202 West Thomas Road Phoenix AZ 85013 Business E-Mail: delia.escalante@pcmail.maricopa.edu.

ESCALANTE, JUAN, performing company executive; children: Juan, Eduardo. Devel. mgr., human resources dir. Miami City Ballet; asst. dir. fin. N.Y.C. Ballet; mng. dir. Ballet of Fla., Fla., 2002—. Mem. bd. trustees Chaminade-Madonna Coll. Prep., Hollywood, Fla.

ESCALANTE, JUDSON ROBERT, business consultant; b. Schenectady, N.Y., Jan. 31, 1930; s. James S. and Katherine H. (Judson) E.; m. Charlotte D. Carpenter, June 7, 1958; children: David J., Katherine Anne. BA, Union Coll., 1953. Asst. estate planning officer Nat. Comml. Bank, Albany, N.Y., 1955-65; founder, v.p., sec., dir. Fidelity Bank of Colonie, Latham, N.Y, 1966-69; area dir. Gen. Bus. Svcs., Latham, 1969-81, Micro Bus. Svcs., 1981—2003. V.p. fin. Gad Cruise Lines, Inc., 1987-88; instr. in field. Bd. dirs., treas. Capital Artists Opera Co., 1970-74, 79; mem. fund dr. com. Union Coll., 1979-80; vestryman, treas. Episcopal Ch.; treas., chief fin. officer Chatham Vis. Nurse Assn., 1983-89; trustee Chatham Vis. Nurse Assn. Profit Trust, 1985-96; auditor Chatham Conservation Found., 1985-95. With U.S. Army, 1953-55. Mem. Colonie C. of C. (treas., bd. dirs. 1972-76), Union Coll. Alumni Soc. (pres. 1971-73, Alumni Gold medal 1978), Dutch Settlers Soc. Albany. Home: 400 Old Comers Rd Chatham MA 02633-1315 E-mail: judcape@capecod.net.

ESCALET, FRANK DIAZ, small business owner; b. Ponce, P.R., Mar. 16, 1930; s. Frank Thillet and Concepcion Rodriquez (Diaz) E.; m.Shirley Leslie Fanner, Sept. 29, 1953 (div. Aug., 1955); children: Judith Alicia, Sudan Edith Escalet Barry; m. Marjorie Janet Gaydash-Huebner, July 19, 1964; 1 child, Frank Daniel (dec.). Owner, operator Talent Shop, N.Y.C., 1955-58, House of Escalet, N.Y.C., 1958-71, Pandora's Box, Eastport, Maine, 1971-73, Cobbler's Bench Art Gallery, Pembroke, Maine, 1973-82, House of Escalet Gallery, Kennebunkport, Maine, 1982-84, House of Escalet Studios, Kennebunkport, 1984—. Tchr. leathercraft Pasamaquoddy Reservation, Perry, Maine, 1971-72, Vocat. Sch. for Retarded Children, Calais, Maine, 1972-73. One-man traveling show Czechoslovakia, Russia, Poland, Yugoslavia, Hungary, Ukraine, 1991—; represented in permanent collections at Naprstkovo Mus., Prague, Union of Artists, Moscow, Bratslavia Primitive Mus., Slovakia, Frydek-Mistek Mus. No. Moravia, Museo Chicano, Phoenix, S.E. Tex. Art Mus., Beaumont, Arch. M. Huntington Gallery, Austin, Tex., Housatonic Mus., Bridgeport, Conn., Orgn. of Am. States Art Mus., Washington, Maryknoll (N.Y.) Sisters Ctr., Mus. City N.Y., 1998; featured on pub. TV, 1978, 82, 89; works in permanent collections Mus. City of N.Y., Ellen Noel Mus. Art of Permian Basin, Odessa, Tex., Dowd Fine Arts Mus., Cortland, N.Y., New Britain Mus. Am. Art; artist: Song and Dance Man acrylic, 1996. With US Air Force, 1947-54. Recipient numerous internat. and U.S. awards. Avocations: photography, antiques, gardening, travel, reading. Home and Office: House of Escalet Studios 24 Fletcher St Kennebunk ME 04043-6707 Office Phone: 207-985-7782. E-mail: escalet@gwi.net.

ESCALLON, ANA MARIA, museum director, writer, curator; b. Columbia; Dir. Art Mus. of the Ams., Washington, 1996—2004. Author: Gerchman, 1994, Mejia-Guinand, 2002; 18 sculptures by Colombian artist Fernando Botero positioned along Constitution Ave in Washington, DC, 1996, An Architect of Surrealism, works by Roberto Matta, Mus. of the Americas, 2004, Sculpture in Four Dimensions, 2004. Office: Art Mus of the Americas 1889 F St NW Washington DC 20006

ESCARRA, VICKI B., retired airline company executive; b. Atlanta; married; 2 children. Grad., Ga. State U.; exec. mgmt. program, Columbia U.; exec. leadership program, Harvard U. Joined, in-flight svc. div. Delta Airlines Inc., Atlanta, 1973—92, dir. in-flight svc. ops., 1992—94, v.p. reservation sales, 1994-96, v.p. reservation sales and distribution planning, 1996, v.p. airport customer svc. to sr. v.p. airport customer svc., 1996—98, exec. v.p., chief customer svc. officer, 1998—2001, exec. v.p., chief mktg. officer, 2001—04. Serves on Women Build Steering Coun. of Habitat for Humanity, Internat.; bd. dirs. AG Edwards, Atlanta C. of C., Woodward Acad., Atlanta Convention and Visitors Bur., chair elect, 2003—05; bd. visitors Emory Univ. Named Women of Year, Women Looking Ahead mag.; named one of 200 Most Powerful Women in Travel, Travel Agent mag., 1997, 1999, 2000, 2001; recipient Nat. Aviation and Space Exploration Wall of Honor certificate, Nat. Air & Space Mus. of Smithsonian Institution, 2000, YWCA Women of Achievement award, 2002. Mem.: Com. of 200, Internat. Women's Forum, Wings Club, Women in Aviation Internat., Atlanta Rotary Club.

ESCARRAZ, ENRIQUE, III, lawyer; b. Evergreen Park, Ill., Aug. 30, 1944; s. Enrique Jr. and Mary Ellen (Bandy) E.; children from previous marriage; Erin Christine, Martina Mary; m. Patricia Jane Escarraz; children: Sarah Ellen, James Lee, Jason F. BA, U. Fla., 1966, JD, 1968. Bar: Fla. 1969, U.S. Dist. Ct. (so. and mid. dists.) Fla. 1969, U.S. Ct. Appeals (5th cir.) 1971, U.S. Ct. Appeals (11th cir.) 1981. VISTA atty. Community Legal Counsel, Chgo., 1968-69; mng. atty. Fla. Rural Legal Services, Ft. Myers, 1969-71; pvt. practice law St. Petersburg, Fla., 1971-82, 85-87, 88—; ptnr. Anderson & Escarraz, St. Petersburg, 1982-85; asst. gen. counsel U. South Fla., 1987-88; assoc. James L. Eskald Law Office, Largo, Fla., 1988. Part-time atty. Pub. Defender's Office Fla. 6th Cir., St. Petersburg, 1973-74; bd. dirs. Gulf Coast Legal Svcs., Inc., 1989—, pres., 1994-96. Vol. Cmty. Law Prog., Inc.; coord. James B. Sanderlin for Judge, Pinellas County, Fla., 1972-76; mem. ACLU Legal Panel, St. Petersburg, 1972—; cooperating atty. NAACP Legal Def. Edn. Funds, Inc., N.Y.C., 1973—; pres. Creative Care, Inc., Clearwater, Fla., 1974-80; mem. allocations com. United Way, Pinellas County, 1976, 1978-81; pres., treas. Cmty. Youth Svcs., Inc., St. Petersburg, 1977-82; co-chmn. Blue Ribbon Com. Pinellas County Dem. Exec. Com., 1977-82; mem. Fla. HRS Dist. V Adv. Coun., Pinellas County, 1982, St. Petersburg Human Rels. Rev. Bd., 1984, 90—, St. Petersburg Adult Cmty. Band, 1989-2003, Greater St. Petersburg Second Time Around Marching Band, 1990-92; mem. adv. bd. Jacquelyn Elvera Hodges Johnson Fund, 1990—. Mem.: FBA, ATLA, ABA, Five Guys From Fla. Investment Club, St. Petersburg Bar Assn. (pro bono com. 1988, 1995—2001, diversity com. 2000—), Nat. Assn. Social Security Claimant Reps., Show Me the Money Investment Club Pinellas (founding mem., 1st pres. 2002), Greater Pinellas County Dem. Club (sec.-treas. 1989—97, bd. dirs. 1997—2001). Office: 2121 5th Ave N Saint Petersburg FL 33713-8013 also: PO Box 847 Saint Petersburg FL 33731-0847 Office Phone: 727-327-6600. E-mail: rattorne@tampabay.rr.com.

ESCHBACH, JOSEPH WETHERILL, nephrology educator; b. Detroit, Jan. 21, 1933; s. Joseph William and Marguerite (Wetherill) E.; m. Mary Ann Charles, June 16, 1956; children: Cheryl Louise, Ann Elizabeth, Joseph Charles. BA, BS, Otterbein Coll., 1955; MD, Jefferson Med. Coll., 1959. Practitioner nephrology and internal medicine Minor and James Med., Seattle, 1965—; dir. home dialysis U. Wash., Seattle, 1965-72, clin. asst. prof. div. nephrology, 1967-70, clin. assoc. prof. div. nephrology, 1970-75, clin. prof. div. nephrology, 1975-85, clin. prof. divs. nephrology and hematology, 1985—. Cons. Ortho Pharm., Raritan, N.J., 1987-88, Amgen, Thousasnd Oaks, Calif., 1985-91. Co-editor: Erythropoietin: Molecular, Cellular and Clinical Biology, 1991; contbr. articles to jours. in field, chpts. to textbooks. Trustee First Ave. Svc. Ctr., 1976-86; pres. bd. trustees Northwest Kidney Ctr., Seattle, 1985-87 (Haviland award 1991). Recipient Disting. Svc. award Seattle Jaycees, 1979, Alumni Achievement award Otterbein Coll., 1991. Fellow: ACP; mem.: AMA, Washington Assn. Biomed. Rsch. (pres. 1999—2001), King County Med. Soc. (pres. 1987), Internat. Soc. Nephrology, Am. Soc. Nephrology, Inst. Medicine of NAS. Presbyterian. Avocations: squash, woodworking, singing. Home: 101-101st Ave SE 301A Bellevue WA 98004-6502 Office: U Wash NW Kidney Ct 700 Broadway Seattle WA 98122

ESCHELS, PHILIP C., lawyer; b. Grand Rapids, Mich., Dec. 26, 1950; s. Carl W. and Lois L. Eschels; m. Mary Elizabeth Weber, June 23, 1973; 1 child, Mary Katherine. BA, Concordia Coll., 1974; MA, Ball State U., 1977; JD with honors, Ind. U., 1983. Law clk. Ind. Ct. of Appeals, Indpls., 1984; assoc. Greenebaum Doll & McDonald, PLLC, Louisville, 1985—92, shareholder, 1992—. Author: How to Avoid Legal Pitfalls in Hiring and Firing in Kentucky, 2002. Pres. Concordia Luth. Ch., Louisville, 1993—; pres., bd. dirs. Actors Theatre Louisville, 2005—07. Mem.: ABA (mem. labor and employment sect. 1988—), Jr. League (mem. cmty. adv. bd. Louisville 2002—). Office: Greenebaum Doll & McDonald PLLC 3500 National City Twr Louisville KY 40202 Office Phone: 502-587-3665. Business E-Mail: pce@gdm.com.

ESCHENAUER, ROBERT K., assistant to clinical administrator; b. N.Y.C., Dec. 23, 1946; s. George and Adeline Eschenauer; m. Jean Eschenauer, Sept. 8, 1968; children: Jennifer, Christine, Rebecca, Eric, Nancy. BA, St. Francis Coll., 1968; MS, St. John's U., 1976, PhD, 1986. Cert. counselor, nat. Psychotherapist, Bklyn. Mem. faculty dept. pastoral and family counseling Iona Coll. Contbr. article to profl. jours. Mem. Am. Psychol. Assn., AACD.

ESCHENBACH, CHRISTOPH, conductor, pianist; b. Breslau, Silesia, Germany, Feb. 20, 1940; Attended, Hamburg (Germany) Conservatory, State Conservatory Music, Cologne, Germany; D, U. Houston. Performed with leading orchs. including Concertgebouw, Amsterdam, The Netherlands, Paris Orch., London Symphony, Berlin Philharm., Carnegie Hall debut with Cleve. Orch., 1969, toured Europe, N.Am. and S.Am., Israel, Japan, appeared at festivals including, Salzburg, Austria, Lucerne, Switzerland, Bonn, Germany, Aix-en-Provence, France, Pacific Music Festival, 1990—94, chief condr. Staatsphilharmonie Rheinland-Pfalz, Germany, 1979, first prin. guest condr. Tonhalle Orch., Switzerland, 1981, chief condr., 1982, rec. artist Deutsche Gammophon, Polydor, EMI, Virgin Classics, London, 1989, artistic dir. Schleswig-Holstein Music Festival, Germany, music dir. Hamburg NDR Symphony Orch., Orch. de Paris, 2000, Houston Symphony, 1988—99, Phila. Orch., 2003—. Decorated officers cross German Order Merit, comdrs. cross; named artistic dir., Ravinia Music Festival, 1995, award, Munich Internat.; recipient Leonard Bernstein award, Pacific Music Festival, 1993. Office: care Columbia Artists Mgmt Inc 165 W 57th St New York NY 10019-2201 Mailing: Houston Symphony Orch 615 Louisiana St Ste 102 Houston TX 77002*

ESCHENMOSER, ALBERT, chemist; b. Erstfeld, Aug. 5, 1925; s. Alfons and Johanna (Oesch) E.; m. Elizabeth Baschnonga, 1954; 3 children. Dr. Nat. Sci., Swiss Fed. Inst. Tech., 1951; student Collegium Altdorf, Kantonsschule St. Gallen, ETH Zurich; Dr.rer.nat. (hon.), U. Fribourg, 1966; DSc (hon.), U. Chgo., 1970, U. Edinburgh, 1979, U. Bologna, 1989, U. Frankfurt, 1990, U. Strasbourg, 1991, Harvard U., 1993, Scripps Rsch. Inst., La Jolla, Calif., 2000. Privatdozent organic chemistry Swiss Fed. Inst. Tech., 1956, assoc. prof., 1960, prof. organic chemistry, 1965; prof. Skaggs Inst. Chem. Biology Scripps Rsch. Inst., La Jolla, Calif., 1996. Contbr. articles to profl. jour. Recipient Kern award, Swiss Fed. Inst. Tech., 1949, Werner award, Swiss Chem. Soc., 1956, Ruzicka award, Swiss Fed. Inst. Tech., 1958, Fritzsche award, Am. Chem. Soc., 1966, Marcel Benoist prize, Swiss Govt., 1973, R.A. Welch award in Chemistry, Houston, 1974, Kirkwood medal, Yale, 1976, A.W.V. Hofmann-Denkmünze, GDCh., 1976, Dannie Heinemann prize, Akademie der Wissenschaften Göttingen, 1977, Davy medal, Royal Soc. London, 1978, Tetrahedron prize, Pergamon Press, 1981, G. Kenner award, U. Liverpool, 1982, Arthur C. Cope award, Am. Chem. Soc., 1984, Wolf prize for chemistry, Wolf Found., Israel, 1986, Cothenius medal, Leopoldina Halle, 1991, Orden Pour le mérite für Wissenschaften und Künste, Berlin, 1992, Oesterreichisches Ehrenzeichen für Wissenschaft und Kunst, 1993, Nakanishi prize, Chem. Soc. Japan, 1998, Paracelsus prize, Swiss Chem. Soc., 1999, Grande Medaille d'Or, Acad. de Sci., Paris, 2001, A.I. Oparin medal, Internat. Soc. Study Origin of Life, 2002, Roger Adams award, Am. Chem. Soc., 2003, F. H. Westheimer medal, Harvard U., 2004, F. A. Cotton medal, Tex. A&M U., 2004, Sir Derek Barton medal, Royal Soc. Chemistry, London, 2004. Mem. Am. Acad. Arts and Sci. (fgn.), Nat. Acad. Sci. US (fgn. assoc.), Akademie der Wissenschaften (corr. mem. Göttingen), Deutsche Akademie der Naturforscher Leopoldina (Halle), Royal Soc. (fgn. London), Pontificial Acad. (Vatican), Acad. Europe (London), Croatian Acad. Sci. Arts (corr. mem. Zagreb), European Acad. Scis. (Brussels). Home: Bergstrasse 9 8700 Kusnacht Switzerland Office: ETH Hönggerberg HCI H309 CH-8093 Zurich Switzerland Business E-Mail: eschenmoser@org.chem.ethz.ch.

ESCHWEILER, PETER QUINTUS, planning consultant; b. Milw., Nov. 2, 1932; s. Alexander Chadbourne Jr. and Dorothy Quincy (Adams) E. m. Mickie Pauline Symonds, Aug. 13, 1955; children Susan Marie, Steven Adams. BA, Cornell U., 1955, M of Regional Planning, 1957. Assoc. planner Frederick P. Clark & Assocs., Rye, NY, 1960—66; chief planner Westchester County, White Plains, NY, 1967, dep. commr. of planning, 1968—69, commr. of planning, 1969—91; advisor Greenway Cmty. Coun. Hudson River Valley, NY, 1991—2000; advisor Nassau County Planning Commn., NY, 1997—98. Pres. Pleasantville (N.Y.) Housing Devel. Fund Co., Inc., 1997—2002, sec., 2003—; mem. Mt. Pleasant Pub. Libr. Men's Group, 1991—, chmn., 2002—; dir. Westchester County Hist. Soc., 2001—; pres. Pleasantville Cmty. Housing Devel. Orgn., Inc., 2002—03; mem. Pleasantville Bus. Support Coun., 2004—; chmn. Westchester County Drought Mgmt. Task Force, 1991—2002, Westchester County Geographic Info. Sys. Task Force, 1998—; mem. mission planning task force Presbytery of Hudson River, 1994, 1997, 2002, chmn. mission planning task force, 1997. Lt. USAF, 1957—60. Recipient Lifetime Achievement award, Westchester Mcpl. Planning Fedn., 2004, Outstanding Cmty. Svc. award, Pleasantville C. of C., 2004. Mem. Am. Inst. Cert. Planners, Nat. Assn. County Planning Dirs. (pres. 1984-85), N.Y. State Assn. Counties (pres. 1980-81, Recognition award 1991), N.Y. Assn. County Planning Dirs. (pres. 1970, bd. dirs. 1969-91), Nat. Assn. Counties (bd. dirs. 1987-89), Nat. Assn. Regional Couns. (bd. dirs. 1988-89), Am. Soc. for Photogrammetry and Remote Sensing (bd. dirs. North Atlantic region 1987-97, 99—, sec.-treas. 1988-97, Bausch and Lomb Photogrammetric award 1957, Meritorious Svc. award 1997), Cornell Club (N.Y.C.), Rotary (pres. White Plains 1985-86), Sigma Chi. Presbyterian. Avocations: skiing, photography, computers. Home and Office: 36 Wilton Rd Pleasantville NY 10570-2022 Office Phone: 914-747-1445. E-mail: PQuintus@aol.com.

ESCOBAR, ANTHONY, marketing professional, consultant; b. Liverpool, England, Aug. 29, 1948; s. Antonio and Joyce Escobar; m. Randi Medlock, Jan. 3, 1970; children: Danielle Lisa Coletti, Anthony Brandon, Andrea Marie Clawson, Sean Anthony. Concept product designer Total Health Solutions, Salt Lake City, 1991—; rep. Isagenix Internat., Tempe, Ariz., 2002—. Cons. and seminar spkr. Anthony Escobar & Assoc., Salt Lake City, 1992—; herbalist, nutritionist; cons. to network mktg. industry. Author network mktg. ednl. materials; editor: Cleansing Times Newsletter. Mem.: Women's Health Rsch. Soc., N.Y. Acad. Scis., Christopher Reeve's Paralysis Found., Nat. Health Mus. Achievements include having broken every record in network mktg., income and recruiting. Office Phone: 801-381-1925. E-mail: tony@tonyescobar.com.

ESCOBAR, DEBORAH ANN, gifted and talented educator; b. Schenectady, NY, Aug. 21, 1952; d. Richard H. and Rose Marie (Denny) Quay; m. Jorge Escobar, Oct. 25, 1975; children: Rosana, Michael, Jorge R. AA, Schenectady County C.C., NY, 1988; BA, Russell Sage Coll., Troy, NY, 1990; MA, State Univ. Albany, NY, 1995. Lic. tchr. social studies, secondary, gifted and talented edn. NY. Asst. editor, legis. liaison Internat. Assn. Fire Chiefs, Washington, 1972-76; tchr. gifted and talented Guilderland Sch. Dist., NY, 1991—. Author: Answering the Call, 1993, Teaching the History of the Albany Internat. Airport, 2000, Creating Hist. Documentaries, 2001, From Africa to NY: Slavery in NY State, 2001, (website) NYS Archives Legacies, 2003. Named Outstanding New Tchr. Sally Mae and Am. Assn. Sch. Adminstrs., Washington, 1992, NYS Hist. Day Tchr. of the Yr., 2001; Nat. Hist. Day Richard T. Ferrell Tchr. of Merit, 2001, Bruce W. Dearstyne Ann. Archives award, 2004. Mem. NY State Coun. Social Studies, Capital Dist. Coun. Social Studies, Phi Alpha Theta, Phi Kappa Phi, Phi Theta Kappa. Democrat. Avocations: writing, dance, genealogy. Office: Farnsworth Mid Sch State Farm Rd Guilderland NY 12084

ESCOBAR, JAVIER IGNACIO, psychiatrist; b. Medellin, Colombia, July 26, 1943; came to U.S., 1969; s. Ignacio and Ines (Soto) E.; m. Luz M. Zapata, July 7, 1967; children: Javier I. Jr., Linda. BS, San Ignacio de Loyola, Medellin, 1960; MD, U. Antioquia, Medellin, 1967; M Psychiatry, U. Minn., 1973. Diplomate, Am. Bd. Psychiatry and Neurology. Resident in psychiatry U. Minn., Mpls., 1969-73, asst. prof. dept. psychiatry, 1973-76; prof., vice-chmn. dept. psychiatry U. Conn. Health Ctr., Farmington, 1986—; prof., acting chmn. dept. psychiatry U. Conn. Sch. Medicine, Farmington, 1992-94; prof., chmn. dept. psychiatry UMDNJ-Robert Wood Johnson Med. Sch., Piscataway, N.J., 1994—. Adj. prof. Rutgers U., Piscataway, N.J., 1995—; assoc. prof. depts. pharmacology, psychiatry, U. Tenn., Memphis, 1976-79; assoc. prof. dept. psychiatry, UCLA, 1979-85, prof., 1985-86; chief, VA Neighborhood Clinic, L.A., 1979-82, Clin. Rsch. Ctr. at Brentwood VA Hosp., L.A., 1984-86; mem. adv. com. on psychiat. drugs, FDA, Washington, 1989-95; mem. NIMH Rsch. Com., Washington, 1989-93; mem. tech. adv. group, VA, Washington, 1987-89; sr. advisor to the dir. NIMH, 2003—. Co-author: Mental Health and Hispanic Americans, 1982; contbr. to over 200 med. publs. Fellow Am. Psychiat. Assn., Am. Assn. Social Psychiatry, Am. Coll. Psychiatry, Am. Coll. Clin. Psychopharmacology. Democrat. Roman Catholic. Avocations: running, bicycling. Office: UMDNJ-RWJMS Dept Psychiatry 675 Hoes Ln Piscataway NJ 08854-5627 Home: Apt 2025 1 Richmond St New Brunswick NJ 08901 Office Phone: 732-235-4440.

ESCOBAR, MARISOL See MARISOL

ESCOBEDO CABRAL, ANNA, federal official; m. Victor Cabral; children: Raquel, Viana, Catalina, Victor Christopher. BA, UCLA, 1987; MPA, Harvard U., 1990; JD, George Mason U. Exec. staff dir. U.S. Rep. Task Force on Hispanic Affairs, Washington, 1991—99; dep. staff dir. U.S. Senate Com. on Judiciary, Washington, 1993—99; pres., CEO Hispanic Assn. on Corp. Responsibility, Washington, 1999—2003; U.S. treasurer US Dept. Treasury, Washington, 2004—. Dir. Smithsonian Ctr. for Latin Initiatives Smithsonian Inst., 2003—; gov., bd. mem. Am. Red Cross. Office: Dept of Treasury 1500 Pennsylvania Ave NW Rm 2134 Washington DC 20220 Office Phone: 202-622-0100. Office Fax: 202-622-2258.*

ESCOTO, LUZ, language educator; arrived in U.S., 1984; d. Victor Manuel Becerra and Luz Maria Escoto; m. James Cameron, Jan. 4, 1984 (div. 1984); 1 child, Ivan Becerra. BA in Edn., St. Mary's U., San Antonio, 1993; MA in Spanish and Portuguese, Rice U., 1997; student, U. Tex., 1997—. Spanish instr. U. Tex., Austin, 1997—. Spkr. in field. Vol. San Antonio Mus. Art, 1994; vol., ESL organizer Pilgrim Luth. Ch., Houston, 1995. Hon. scholar, St. Mary's U., San Antonio, 1990—93, Presdl. scholar, Rice U., Houston, 1994—96. Mem.: Alfa Sigma Lambda. Avocations: writing, travel, cooking, movies. Office: Univ Tex Austin Spanish and Portuguese Dept University Station B3700 Austin TX 78712-1155

ESCOVER, MATTHEW MANUEL, political science professor; b. San Jose, Calif., Aug. 1, 1957; s. Manuel and Joyce Escover. BA in Polit. sci., MA in Polit. sci., San Jose State U., 1982. Cert. C.C. tchr. Loan officer Union Bank, Hollister, Calif., 1986—90; asst. v.p. San Bonito Bank, Hollister, 1990—94; pvt. practice cons. Hollister, 1994—97; prof. Cabrillo Coll., Aptos, Calif., 1997—. Councilman City of Hollister, 1985—92, mem. planning commn., 1987—88, vice mayor, 1992; vice chmn. Hollister Redevel. Agy., 1992. Recipient Disting. Svc. award, 27th Dist. Calif. State Assembly, 1997, 2000. Mem.: Acad. Polit. Sci., Pi Sigma Alpha, Phi Delta Kappa. Republican. Roman Catholic. Avocations: hiking, photography, reading. Office: Cabrillo Coll 6500 Soquel Dr Aptos CA 95003 E-mail: escover@mindspring.com.

ESENALIEV, RINAT O., science educator, lab administrator; PhD, Russian Acad. Scis., Inst. Spectroscopy, 1992. Contbr. articles to profl. jours. Mem.: SPIE. Achievements include patents for drug delivery, optics, ultrasound, glucose monitoring, oxygenation and hemoglobin monitoring. Office: U Tex Med Branch 301 University Blvd Galveston TX 77555-0456 Office Phone: 409-772-8144. Office Fax: 409-772-8144.

ESFANDIARY, H. AUSTIN, communications executive; b. Wash., D.C. s. Mohsen Sadigh and Mary S. Esfandiary. BA, Columbia U., 1978. News dir. WKCR-FM, N.Y.C., 1976—78; Capitol Hill prodr. INN TV, Wash., 1982—85; v.p. PEGS, Cheverly, Md., 1985—88; CEO ExhibitsInc.com, Md., 1988—. Artist, dance Va. State Open Dance Championship (champion-Hustle, 1997). Negotiator Ft. Gaines Citizens Assn., Wash., 1982—85; commr. Mayor's Citizen's Advisory Com., Wash., 1984—85. Recipient commendation, Wash. D.C. City Coun., 1985. Master: KCCH Club (pres. 2002—04), Potomac Lodge (Lodge #5, F.A.A.M. 1997—98), Robert de Bruce Coun. Kadosh (commdr. 2003—04); mem.: Mensa. Achievements include contbr., crew member yacht racing (award Chesapeake Bay High Point, 1998). Office: ExhibitsInc.com 9602 Rhode Island Ave College Park MD

ESH, LAURA RAE, music educator; b. Hagerstown, Md., Sept. 4, 1976; d. Clyde Irving and Sandra Rae Gaylor; m. Christian Russell Esh, June 19, 1999. BA in Music, Houghton (NY) Coll., 1998. Piano program coord. Lopez Studios, Inc., Reston, Va., 1999—. Pianist College Park (Md.) Wesleyan Ch., 1999—2005. Mem.: Nat. Guild Piano Tchrs. Office: Lopez Studios Inc 11425 Isaac Newton Sq Ste 100 Reston VA 20190 E-mail: lesh@lopezstudios.org.

ES-HAQ, FEREIDOUN, minister, marriage and family therapist; b. Hamadan, Iran, June 7, 1956; arrived in U.S., 1979; s. Samuel Es-Haq and Alice Yeganeh. BA, Azusa Pacific U., 1980, MA, 1987; DMin, Carolina U. Theology, 1997; M in Pastoral Counseling, Andersonville Bapt. Sem., 1999, ThD, 2003. Cert. Internat. Assn. Christian Counselors. Pastor Assyrian Evang. Ch., Turlock, Calif., 1980—85, organizing pastor San Jose, Calif., 1981—92; asst. pastor Santa Teresa Hills Presbyn. Ch., San Jose, 1985—86; organizing pastor Iranian Christian Ch., San Jose, 1987—94, Bet-Eil Assyrian Ch., San Jose, 1992—, S. Bay Iranian Ch., San Jose, 1994—2000. Bd. dirs. Conservative Bapt. Assn. No. Calif. and Nev., Saratoga, Calif.; adj. prof. San Jose Christian Coll., 1987—94. Translator: Disciple, 1982, 1997, Be Mature, 1998, How to Handle Adversity, 1999, other books from English to Farsi. Cmty. adv. Assyrian cmty., San Jose, 1987—; welfare adv. Bet-Eil Assyrian Ch., San Jose, 1992—. Avocations: choir directing, composing music. Office: Bet-Eil Assyrian Ch PO Box 24278 San Jose CA 95154

ESHBAUGH, W(ILLIAM) HARDY, botanist, educator; b. Glen Ridge, N.J., May 1, 1936; s. William Hardy Eshbaugh Jr. and Elizabeth (Wakeman) Henderson; m. Barbara Keller, Sept. 6, 1958; children: David Charles, Stephen Hardy, Elizabeth Wendy Brown, Jeffrey Raymond. BA, Cornell U., 1959; MA, Ind. U., 1961, PhD, 1964. Lectr. in botany Ind. U., Bloomington, 1962; spl. asst. to chief ecology and epidemiology br. Dugway (Utah) Proving Ground, 1964-65; asst. prof., curator herbarium So. Ill. U., Carbondale, 1965—67; from asst. prof. to prof. botany Miami U., Oxford, Ohio, 1967—98, chmn. dept. botany, 1983-88, prof. emeritus, 1998. Cur., Willard Sherman Turrell Herbarium, Miami U., 1967-82; assoc. program dir. NSF, Washington, 1982-83; co-chmn. steering com. Systematics Agenda 2000-Charting the Biosphere; adv. bd. Am. Bot. Coun., 1996—; instr. Internat. Rainforest Workshops, 1991-99. Co-author: (Book) The Vascular Flora of Andros Island, Bahamas, 1988; contbr. articles to profl. jours. Bd. dirs. Childrens Environ. Trust Found., 1992-94; pres. Elizabeth Wakeman Henderson Charitable Found., 1997—. Capt. U.S. Army, 1964-65. Named Citizen of Yr., Oxford, Ohio, 2002. Fellow: AAAS, Inst. Environ. Scis., Ohio Acad. Sci.; mem.: Internat. Field Studies (trustee 1989—95), Internat. Orgn. Plant Biosytematists (coun. 1987—89, ad hoc com. 1989—92, N. Am. treas. 1992—95), Assn. Systemic Collections (bd. dirs. 1981—84, rep.-at-large), Nature Conservancy (vice chmn. Ohio chpt. 1970—75, trustee 1970—77), Atlantic Salmon Fedn. (bd. dirs. 2002—05), Bot. Soc. Am. (pres. 1988—89, Merit award 1992), Soc. Econ. Botany (v.p. 1982—83, pres. 1983—84), Am. Soc. Plant Taxonomists (pres. 1991—92), Am. Inst. Biol. Scis. (pres. 1995), Nat. Audubon Soc. (bd. dirs. 1993—, vice-chmn., Great Egret award 2005), Explorer's Club. Methodist. Avocations: camping, fly fishing, photography, sailing, swimming. Home: 209 Mckee Ave Oxford OH 45056-9059 Office: Miami U Dept Botany Oxford OH 45056 Office Phone: 513-529-4200. Business E-Mail: eshbauwh@muohio.edu.

ESHELMAN, RALPH ELLSWORTH, historian, consultant, paleontologist; b. Mt. Holly, N.J., Mar. 20, 1947; s. Ralph Mengel and Grace Elizha (Bozarth) E.; m. Evelyne Margaret Herman, June 3, 1974; 1 child, Erich Ellsworth. AA, Prince George's C.C., 1967; BS, SUNY, Stony Brook, 1969; MS, U. Iowa, 1971; PhD, U. Mich., 1974. Phys. sci. aide U.S. Geol. Survey, Washington, 1965-69; dir. Calvert Marine Mus., Solomons, Md., 1974-90; rsch. assoc. Smithsonian Inst., Washington, 1976—2005. Owner Eshelman & Assocs., 1994—; cons. Nat. Maritime Initiative, Nat. Park Svc., 1993-2000, USCG, 1995-98; project dir. Md. War of 1812 Initiative, 1998—; cons. Am. Battlefield Protection program Nat. Park Svc., 1999-2002, cons. Star-Spangled Nat. Historic Trail study, 2002—; lectr. on expedition cruise ships, 1991—; study leader for nat. and internat. trips Smithsonian Instn., 1998-2003; dir. palenotological field camp Mus. of Middle Appalachians, 2000-2003. Contbr. articles to profl. jours. Grantee Sigma Xi, 1972, Nat. Geog. Soc., 1981, 86. Mem. Nat. Maritime Preservation Task Force (vice chmn. 1983-84), Md. Soc. Underwater Archeology (trustee 1984-86), Historical Trust, Md. Humanities Coun. (trustee 1984-89, 2d v.p. 1987-89), Coun. Am. Maritime Mus. (exec. com. 1983-89, v.p. 1988-89, pres. 1990), Solomons Environ. and Archeol. Rsch. Consortium (founding chmn. 1987), Nat. Maritime Alliance (co-chair 1994-95), Nat. Lighthouse Mus. (pres. steering com., trustee 1998-2003, 2nd v.p.), The Nature Conservancy (Md. chpt. v.p. sci. and stewardship 1996-2001). Avocations: spelunking, snorkeling, hiking, swimming, kayaking. Home and Office: 12178 Preston Dr Lusby MD 20657-2905 Office Phone: 410-326-4877. E-mail: ree47@comcast.com.

ESHER, BRIAN RICHARD, manufacturing executive; b. NYC, Sept. 1, 1948; s. John Conrad and Elizabeth (Carley) E.; children: Justin John, Christopher Ryan. BS in Bus. Mgmt. magna cum laude, Fairleigh Dickinson U., Madison, N.J., 1971, MBA summa cum laude, 1975. Mgr. Litton Industries, Morristown, 1972-75; industry mgr. AT&T Long Lines, Somerset, N.J., 1975-77; v.p. Transaction Mgmt., Inc., Montgomeryville, Pa., 1977-79; dir. mktg. Burroughs Corp., Detroit, 1980-82, exec. office Detoit, 1982-84, v.p. Rochester, N.Y., 1984-85; sr. v.p., gen. mgr. ITEK Graphic Systems Divsn., 1985-88; exec. v.p. A.B. Dick Co., Chgo., 1988-89; chmn., pres., CEO Environ. Control Group, Inc., Maple Shade, NJ, 1989, pres., CEO, chmn., 1990-96; dir., chmn, CEO MLX Corp., 1990-96, also bd. dirs.; chmn, pres., CEO Pameco Corp., Norcross, Ga., 1992-96; prin. S.E. Tech. Opportunities Fund LLC., 1998—2000; chmn., CEO Storm Consulting LLC, 2000—; chmn., pres & CEO, Coe Mfg. Co., 2002—03, pres., chmn., 2003—04; chmn. Coe Newnes/McGehee, 2002—04, Ace Products Inc., 2003—04, CEO, 2003—04. With U.S. Army, 1967-69, Vietnam. Decorated D.S.C., Silver Star, Bronze Star, Purple Heart (3). Mem. Assn. of MBA Execs., Phi Omega Epsilon (Membership award 1971). Republican. Avocation: tennis. Home: 9185 Old Southwick Pass Alpharetta GA 30022-6253 Office Phone: 678-291-9191. Office Fax: 678-291-9138. E-mail: brian@stormconsultingllc.com.

ESHLEMAN, DIANE VARRIN, bank executive; b. Jan. 1956; d. Robert D. Varrin; m. Gregory V. Eshleman, Sept. 6, 1980. Grad., Princeton U., 1978. With Chemical Banking Corp.; exec. v.p. Chase Manhattan bank; mng. dir., chief procurement officer info. tech. JP Morgan Chase, N.Y.C. Named one of 25 Women to Watch, US Banker Mag., 2003. Office: JP Morgan Chase 270 Park Ave New York NY 10017-2070

ESHLEMAN, VON RUSSEL, electrical engineering educator, aerospace scientist; b. Darke County, Ohio, Sept. 17, 1924; married; 4 children. BEE, George Washington U., 1949; MS, Stanford U., 1950, PhD in Elec. Engring., 1952. Rsch. assoc. Radio Propagation Lab. Stanford (Calif.) U., 1952-56, from instr. to prof. elec. engring., 1956-61, prof. elec. engring., co-dir. Ctr. Radar Astronomy, 1961-82, dir. Radioscience Lab., 1974-83. Cons. NAS, Nat. Bur. Stds., SRI Internat., Jet Propulsion Lab.; mem. Internat. Astronaut Congress, Internat. Astron. Union, Internat. Sci. Radio Union; dir. emeritus Watkins-Johnson Co.; mem. radio sci. teams for Viking, Pioneer, Mariner, Voyager, Galileo spacecraft studies of the planets. Fellow AAAS, IEEE, Am. Geophys. Union, Royal Astronomy Soc.; mem. NAE. Achievements include rsch. in radar astronomy, planetary exploration, ionospheric and plasma physics, radio wave propagation, astronautics. Office: Stanford U Radar Astronomy Ctr Packard EE Bldg 309 Stanford CA 94305-9515 E-mail: eshleman@stanford.edu.

ESHOM-SMITH, CORINA MAY, air transportation executive; b. Moab, Utah, Aug. 25, 1967; d. Marvin Edward Eshom and Sandra Irene Peterson; m. Tyler Smith. BS in Anthropology, U. Utah, 1990. Cert. EMT Utah. Dir. environ. safety and health AgriDyne Techs., Salt Lake City, 1988-94; environ. engr. Dugway (Utah) Proving Ground Lockheed Martin, 1995-99, supr. agt. test support sect. Dugway, 1999—. Vol. firefighter/EMT Terra (Utah) Fire Dept., 1999—2001; instr., instrn. trainer ARC, Salt Lake City, 1984—2003, dir. 1st aid sta. team, mem. health and safety com., 1992—94; leader Utah Girl Scouts, Dugway, 2000—01. Mem. Am. Chem. Soc., Am. Legion Aux. (Secondary Edn. scholar 1985), Am. Philatelic Soc., Utah Firefighters Assn., Tooele County Backcountry Horsemans Club Mem. Lds Ch. Avocations: stamp collecting/philately, hiking, climbing, quilting, carpentry. Home: 261 W Utah Ave Tooele UT 84074 Office: Lockheed Martin Bldg 4239 Dugway Proving Ground Dugway UT 84022 Personal E-mail: neenamay@yahoo.com. E-mail: oviatt@dpg.army.mil.

ESHOO, ANNA GEORGES, congresswoman; b. New Britain, Conn., Dec. 13, 1942; d. Fred and Alice Alexandre Georges; children: Karen Elizabeth, Paul Frederick. AA with honors, Canada Coll., 1975. Chmn. San Mateo County Dem. Ctrl. Com., Calif., 1978-82; chair Human Rels. Com., 1979-82; mem. U.S. Congress from 14th Calif. dist., 1993—; at-large minority whip; mem. energy and commerce com., intelligence com. Chief of staff Calif. Assembly Spkr. Leo McCarthy, 1981; regional majority whip No. Calif., 1993-94. Co-founder Women's Hall of Fame; chair San Mateo County (Calif.) Dem. Party, 1980; active San Mateo County Bd. Suprs., 1982-92, pres., 1986; pres. Bay Area Air Quality Mgmt. Dist., 1982-92; mem. San Francisco Bay Conservation Devel. Commn., 1982-92; chair San Mateo County Gen. Hosp. Bd. Dirs. Democrat. Roman Catholic. Office: US Ho Reps 205 Cannon Ho Office Bldg Washington DC 20515-0001*

ESHRAGHI, ADRIEN A., neurosurgeon, medical educator; b. Nov. 21, 1964; s. Khalil and Pari Eshraghi; m. Rebecca Eshraghi; 1 child, Nicolas. MS, U. Paris, 1993; MD, U. Paris, France, 1994; fellowship in otolaryngology (hon.), UCLA, 1995; DEA, U. Paris, 1997. Cert. otology, neurotology, otolaryngology U. Miami, 2002. Chef de clinique U. Paris, 1996—99; asst. prof. U. Miami Sch. Medicine, 2002—04; chief otolaryngology Miami VA Med. Ctr., 2004; assoc. prof. U. Miami Sch. Medicine, 2005—. Ethic adv. bd. West Palm Beach VA med. Ctr., Fla., 2003, laser safety com., 03; dir. Cochlear Implant Program and Rsch., Miami, 2003—05. Contbr. articles various profl. jours., chapters to books. Recipient First Prize Rsch. award, Shandler Soc., 2000, A.M.B. award, Le HumanityMission, 1990. Mem.: Assoc. for Rsch. in Otolarynology, Am. Acad. Otolarynology Head and Neck Surgery, Am. Neurotology Soc. Office: U Miami Miller Sch of Medicine Otolarynotology Dept 1666 NW 10th Ave Ste 306 Miami FL 33136 Office Phone: 305-585-7126. Business E-Mail: aeshraghi@miami.edu.

ESKANDARIAN, EDWARD, advertising agency executive; b. Telford, Pa., Nov. 20, 1936; s. Michael and Katherine (Arslanian) E.; m. Nancy Rose Boujicanian, June 26, 1965; children: Wendy, Christopher, Jill. BS, Villanova U., 1958; MBA, Harvard, 1965. Engr. Pitman Dunn Labs., Phila., 1958-60; project engr. GE, Phila., 1961-63; v.p., account supr. Compton Advt., Inc., N.Y.C., 1965-71; chmn., chief exec. officer HBM/Creamer Inc., Boston, 1971-88; chmn. Della Femina McNamee, Boston, 1988-89; chmn., CEO Arnold Comm., Boston, 1989-2000, Arnold Worldwide Ptnrs., Boston, 2000—. Overseer Boston Symphony, 1987—; trustee U. Richmond, Dana Farber Cancer Inst.; bd. dirs. HAVAS, Getwell Network. With USAF, 1959-60. Mem. Am. Assn. Advt. Agys. (sec.-treas. 1988-89, ea. region gov.-at-large 1989-91), New Eng. Broadcasters Assn. (pres. 1982-83), Advt. Club Boston (pres. 1977-78, trustee 1980—), Harvard Bus. Sch. Assn. Boston (pres. 1984-85), Harvard Club, Algonquin Club, Weston Golf Club, Jupiter Hills Club, Oyster Harbors Club, Willowbend Club, Caves Valley Club. Home: 300 Boylston St Boston MA 02116-3923 Office: Arnold Worldwide Ptnrs 101 Huntington Ave Boston MA 02199-7606 Office Phone: 617-587-8000. Business E-Mail: ee@arn.com.

ESKEW, HENRY LAWRENCE, JR., economist, consultant; b. Atlanta, July 31, 1937; s. Henry L. and Marian Gresham Eskew; m. Gloria Harrell Eskew (div.); children: Marian Kathryn Eskew Brown, Lauren Claire Eskew Kaniecki. BS in Indsl. Mgmt., Ga. Inst. Tech., 1959, MS in Indsl. Mgmt., 1963; MA in Econs., Am. U., Washington, 1966; PhD in Econs., Am. U., 1988. Ops. analyst Tech. Ops. Inc., Ft. Belvoir, Va., 1963—66; sr. assoc. Planning Rsch. Corp., Washington, 1967—68; founder, pres., CEO Adminstrv. Sci. Corp., Alexandria, Va., 1968—83; prin. Booz Allen & Hamilton, Inc., Washington, 1984—85; rsch. staff, dep. dept. dir. Ctr. for Naval Analyses, Alexandria, 1985—2000; cons. economist, 2000—. Vis. prof. Naval Postgrad. Sch., Monterey, Calif., 1998; profl. lectr. George Washington U., Washington, 1985—95, Am. U., Washington, 1985—95. Contbr. articles to profl. jours. Mem. regional devel. coun. Ga. Inst. Tech., Washington, 1996—99. Commd. officer USAF, 1960—68. Mem.: Mil. Ops. Rsch. Soc., INFORMS, Am. Econ. Assn. Avocations: golf, bridge. Home: 5537 Reading Ave Alexandria VA 22311-2374 Office Phone: 703-820-1025. E-mail: henryesker05@comcast.net.

ESKEW, MICHAEL L., package distribution company executive; BS in Indsl. Engring., Purdue U., 1972; postgrad., Butler U., U. Pa. Various positions UPS, Inc., Germany, 1972-82, indsl. engring. mgr. northwest region, 1982-91, dist. mgr. Cen. Jersey dist., 1991-93, corp. indsl. engring. mgr., 1993, corp. v.p. indsl. engring, 1994—96, group v.p. engring., 1996—99, exec. v.p., 1999—2002, vice chmn., 2000—02, chmn., CEO, 2002—. Bd. dirs. 3M; Mem. Bus. Roundtable. Office: UPS Inc 55 Glenlake Pkwy NE Atlanta GA 30328-3474

ESKEY, LEO JOSEPH, lawyer; b. Lincoln, Nebr., July 4, 1946; s. Joseph George and Hanora Cecilia (Malone) E.; m. Garland Louise Kiner, June 27, 1969; 1 child, Joseph Charles. BA, U. Nebr., 1969, JD, 1971. Bar: Nebr. 1971, U.S. Supreme Ct. 1978. Assoc. atty. Harry Stephens Law Office, Fremont, Nebr., 1971-75; ptnr. Eskey & Gless Law Office, Fremont, Nebr., 1975-81; pvt. practice Fremont, Nebr., 1981—. Police judge, Fremont, Nebr., 1972; spl. prosecutor Washington County, Fremont, 1985, Dodge County, 1975-99. Mem. St. Patrick's Ch. (finance com. mem 1993-95, ch. coun. mem. 1992-95), Fremont, Nebr.; chmn. alternate Dodge County Bd. Mental Health, 1985—. Mem. Nebr. State Bar Assn., Dodge County Bar Assn., Nebr. Trial Attys. Assn., Nebr. Criminal Def. Attys. Assn., Fremont Area Svc. Club, Fremont Golf Club. Roman Catholic. Office: Leo J Eskey Law Office 16 Bell Ctr Fremont NE 68025-3100

ESKINAZI, CHRISTOPHER B., physician assistant; s. Benny and Gwendolyn Lora Eskinazi. BS, Wagner Coll., Staten Island, N.Y., 1995; MS, Wagner Coll., 1996; M in Med. Sci., cert. physician asst., Cornell U., N.Y.C., 2002. Cert. BCLS, PALS, ACLS, ATLS, lic. physician asst. N.Y. Microbiologist Clin. Diagnostic Svcs., Englewood, NJ, 1996—2001, Diagnostic Splty., New City, NY, 1997—2002; physician asst. Nyack (N.Y.) Hosp., 2003—, Haverstraw (N.Y.) Pediat., 2004—. Fellow: Soc. Emergency Medicine Physician Assts. (bd. dirs., Northea. regional dir. 2004—), Assn. Neurol. Physician Assts., Physician Assts. in Orthop. Surgery, Am. Assn. Surg. Physician Assts. (bd. dirs., chmn. membership com. 2003—05, sec. 2004—), Am. Acad. Physician Assts., Am. Coll. Clinicians, N.Y. State Soc. Physician Assts.; mem.: Am. Soc. Microbiology, Am. Soc. Law, Medicine and Ethics, Am. Coll. Legal Medicine, Soc. Critical Care Medicine, Assn. Physician Assts. in Cardiovasc. Surgery, Orthop. Rsch. Soc. Home: 1 Doctor Marquise Dr Thiells NY 10984 Office: Nyack Hosp 161 Midland Ave Nyack NY 10960 Office Phone: 845-248-2345. E-mail: ceskinazi@aol.com.

ESKRIDGE, CAROLE FAY, artist; b. Port of Spain, Trinidad, July 3, 1947; came to U.S., 1948; d. Woodrow Wilson and Lyda Mae (Blanchard) E.; m. Harold Sherman Frye, Aug. 6, 1966 (div. Aug. 1976); children: Sarah Mae Frye, Rebecca Jane Frye. Grad. magna cum laude, Ala. A&M; photography cert., U. Ala., Huntsville, 1981. Founder Visionary Artists Guild for Mentally Ill Artists, Huntsville, 1991—. Mural painter History of Mental Health, 1992; represented in permanent collections Birmingham Mus. Art, Montgomery Mus. Fine Art. Recipient Disting. Svc. award Huntsville-Madison County Mental Health Bd., 1992, Consumer of Yr. award Ala. Alliance Mentally Ill, 1993, Creativity award Mental Health Consumers Ala., 1995, cert. Spl. Congrl. Recognition, 1996. Mem. Docents of Hunsville Mus. Art. Roman Catholic. Avocations: sailing, writing, pub. speaking. Studio: 115 Clinton Ave 1205 Huntsville AL 35801 Office: Visionary Guild Mentally Ill Artists Huntsville AL 35801 Office Phone: 256-539-4161. Office Fax: 256-539-4161.

ESKRIDGE, WILLIAM NICHOL, JR., law educator; b. Princeton, W.Va., Oct. 27, 1951; s. William Nichol Sr. and Elizabeth Beckwith (DeJarnette) E. BA, Davidson (N.C.) Coll., 1973; MA, Harvard U., 1975; JD, Yale U., 1978. Bar: DC 1979. Law clk. to hon. judge Edward Weinfeld US Dist. Ct. (so. dist.) NY, NYC, 1978-79; assoc. Shea & Gardner, Washington, 1979-82; asst. prof. Law Sch. U. Va., Charlottesville, 1982-86; assoc. prof. Georgetown U. Law Ctr., Washington, 1987-90, prof., 1990—98; Garver Prof. of Jurisprudence Yale U., New Haven, 1998—. Vis. prof. NYU Law Sch., 1993, 2004, Harvard Law Sch., 1994, Stanford Law Sch., 1995, Yale Law Sch., 1995-98, Columbia U., 2003. Author: (with Philip Frickey) Statutes and the Creation of Public Policy, 1987, 2d edit., 1994, (with Daniel Farber and Philip Frickey) Constitutional Law: Themes for its third Century; editor, contbr.: A Dance Along the Precipice: Economic and Political Implications of the International Debt Problem, 1985, Cynamic Statutory Interpretation, 1994, (with Philip Frickey) Hart and Sacks, The Legal Process, 1994. Fellow Guggenheim, 1995; mem. ABA. Presbyterian. Office: Yale Law Sch PO Box 208215 New Haven CT 06520 E-mail: william.eskridge@yale.edu.

ESLAMBOLCHI, HOSSEIN, communications executive; BSEE with highest honors, MSEE, PhD in Elec. Engring., U. Calif., San Diego. Joined AT&T Bell Labs., 1986—; v.p. network ops. and chief compliance officer AT&T Corp., v.p., AT&T Data and Network Svcs., 2000, sr. v.p., Packet and Optical Network Svcs., 2000—01, interim pres. Excite@Home Broadband Networks, 2001, pres., AT&T labs, 2001—, pres., AT&T Global Networking Tech. Svcs., chief tech. officer, 2001—, chief information officer. Bd. dirs. Mindspeed Techs., Inc., 2003—, Nat. Action Coun. for Minorities in Engring., Wytec; mem. adv. bd., bd. dir. Nat. Alliance Bus.; serves as AT&T's Accessibility Champion President's Com. on Employment of People with Disabilities; bd. advisor The Catalyst Group, Inc., Pacific Broadband Comm., Conexant; bd. tech. advisors Compaq Computer Corp. Mem. editl. bd.: IEEE Jour. Network and Sys. Mgmt.; contbr. articles to profl. jours. Mem. adv. coun. John Hopkins U. Whiting Sch. Engring. Named Inventor of Yr., NJ Inventors Hall of Fame, 2001, Alumnus of Yr., U. Calif. San Diego, 2002; named one of Top Ten Innovators "Ten award", Exec. Coun. NY, 2003, 10 Internet Bus. Leaders, Cisco IQ Mag., 2003, Premiere 100 IT Leaders, Computerworld, 2004; recipient Thomas Alva Edison award, NJ R&D Coun., 1997. Achievements include patents in field; invention of FASTAR (Fast Automated Restoration System), which instantly reroutes service on AT&T's SONET rings, eliminating or minimizing service outages for customers. Office: AT&T Corp One AT&T Way Bedminster NJ 07921

ESLICK, HEATHER BASS, psychologist; b. Winchester, Tenn., Apr. 1, 1976; s. Gary Evans Bass and Linda Moore Jones; m. Craig Jamison Eslick, July 15, 2000; 1 child, Camden Jefferson. BSc, Tenn. Tech. U., 1998, M in edn. psychology, 2000, EdS in sch. psychology, 2002. Sch. psychologist Franklin County Bd. of Edn., Winchester, Tenn., 2001—. Monitoring chmn. Franklin Co. Spl. Services, Winchester, Tenn., 2002—. Mem.: Nat. Assn. Sch. Psychology, Tenn. Assn. Sch. Psychology. Avocations: boating, scrapbooks, reading. Office: Franklin Co Spl Services 1025 Dinah Shore Blvd Winchester TN 37398

ESLINGER, ELLEN THERESE, historian; d. Norman F. and Dolores E. Eslinger. BS, No. Ill. U., 1977; MA, U. Chgo., 1982, PhD, 1988. Asst. prof. James Madison U., Harrisonburg, Va., 1988—92, DePaul U., Chgo., 1992—97, assoc. prof., 1997—2002, prof., 2002—. Author: (book) Citizens of Zion: The Social Origins of Camp Meeting Revivalism, 1999; editor: Running Mad for Kentucky: Frontier Travel Accounts, 2004. Pres. Rogers Pk. West Ridge Hist. Soc., Chgo., 1999. Recipient Richard H. Collins award, Ky. Hist. Soc., 1995. Mem.: Soc. Hist. Early Am. Republic, Southern Hist. Soc., Orgn. Am. Historians. Office: DePaul Univ 2320 N Kenmore Ave Chicago IL 60614 Business E-Mail: eeslinge@depaul.edu.

ESLINGER, KENNETH NELSON, social sciences educator; s. Kenneth N. and Pearl May E.; m. Denise Marie Juba, July 22, 1979. BA, Ind. State U., Terre Haute, Ind., 1963; MA, The Ohio State U., Columbus, 1968, PhD, 1971. Asst. prof. sociology Ohio State U., Columbus, 1972—73, The Cleve. State U., 1973—80; asst. prof. sociology John Carroll U., University Heights, Ohio, 1980—85, assoc. prof. sociology, 1985—, acting chair dept. sociology, 1995—96, chair dept. sociology, 1997—. Contbr. articles to profl. jours. Mem. Dem. Nat. Com., 1993—2003; adv. com., congressman Cleve., 1983—84; organizer higher edn. field gubernatorial campaign, Cleve., 1982. Mem.: Am. Sociol. Assn., North Ctrl. Sociol. Assn. (v.p. 1997—99), Soc. Study Social Problems, Nat. Coun. Family Rels. Democrat. Avocations: bass fishing, fly fishing. Office: John Carroll U 20700 North Park Blvd University Heights OH 44118 Office Phone: 216-397-4381.

ESLINGER-BROWN, VANESSA PAULINE, humanities educator; b. Murfreesboro, Tenn., Dec. 28, 1951; d. Walter Clarence and Clare Marie Eslinger; m. Wilbur Edwin Brown Jr., Nov. 28, 1987; children: Celeste Gabrielle Brown, Cameron Yates Brown, Savannah Clare Brown. B Speech and Comm., U. Mont., 1973; MEd, U. Va., 1983, EdD, 1986. Cert. secondary tchr. Va. Substitute tchr. Eugene (Oreg.) Pub. Schs., 1976—78; coach, drama dir., English tchr. MatoacaH.S., Ettrick, Va., 1978—82; rsch. asst. U. Va.,

Charlotteville, 1986—87; adj. lectr. Germanna C.C., Locust Grove, Va., 1987—89; adj./asst. prof. No. Va. C.C., Woodbridge, 1987—89; adj./sr. lectr. Mary Washington Coll., Fredericksburg, Va., 1990—94, sr. lectr., 1994—95; prof. gen. studies Stayer U., Fredericksburg, 1996—, chmn. dept. gen. studies, 1999—2005, prof., assoc. dean, 2005—. Piano tchr., Fredericksburg, 1995—98; mem. minority achievement com. Walker Grant Mid. Sch., 2003—; mem. Walker Grant Mid. Sch. Com., 2003—. Vol. magic cir. Women's Shelter for Help and Emergency, Charlottesville, 1982—87; Bible sch. tchr. Shiloh New Site Bapt. Ch., Fredericksburg, 1989—99. Named honoree, Wall of Tolerance; recipient Outstanding Vol. award, Women's Shelter for Help and Emergency, 1985. Mem.: ASCD, So. Poverty Law Ctr., Fredericksburg Sister City Assn., Nat. Coun. Tchrs. English, Va. Assn. Tchrs. English, Nat. Forensics League, Thespians Soc. Democrat. Methodist. Avocations: swimming, piano, reading, cooking. Home: 10415 Edinburgh Dr Spotsylvania VA 22553 Office: Strayer U 4500 Plank Rd Fredericksburg VA 22407 Business E-Mail: veb@strayer.edu.

ESMOND, DONALD V., transportation executive; m. Cheryl Esmond; children: Mike, Dan, Chris. BSc in Bus. and Econs., Ill. Inst. Tech. With Ford Motor Co., 1970—82; from copr. fleet and truck mgr. to sr. v.p. and gen. mgr. Toyota Motor Sales, USA, Inc., Torrance, Calif., 1982—2003, sr. v.p., 2003—, gen. mgr., 2003—. Capt. USMC, Vietnam. Decorated Silver Star USMC, Disting. Flying Cross, Purple Heart; recipient Semper Fidelis award, 1999. Office: Toyota Motor Sales USA Inc 19001 South Western Ave Torrance CA 90509

ESPALDON, ERNESTO MERCADER, plastic surgeon, former senator; b. Sulu, Philippines, Nov. 11, 1926; arrived in Guam, 1963; s. Cipriano Acuna Espaldon and Claudia (Cadag) Mercader); m. Leticia Legaspi Virata, May 31, 1952; children: Arlene Espaldon Ramos, Vivian Espaldon Wolff, James, Diane, Karl, Ernesto Jr. AA, U. Philippines, Manila, 1949; MD, U. Santo tomas, Manila, 1954; postgrad., U. Okla., 1959, Washington U., St. Louis, 1961. Diplomate Am. Bd. Plastic Surgery. Plastic surgeon Guam Meml. Hosp., Agana, 1963—, chief surgery, 1965-69; pres., plastic surgeon Espaldon Clinic, Agana, 1969—; senator Guam Legislature, Agana, 1974-80, 86-92, chmn. Com. on Health, Welfare and Ecology and Com. on Ethics and Standards, 1974-80. Vis. prof. Bicol Med. and Edn. Ctr., Legaspi City, The Philippines, 1980—; cons. plastic surgery U.S. Naval Hosp., Guam, 1972-76; chmn. com. on advance health care Assn. Pacific Islands Legislators, 1988-92, Coll. Assurance Plan Pre-Need Ednl. Plan, Guam, 1979—; bd. dirs. Coll. Assurance Plan Pension, Philippines, Coll. Assurance Plan, Philippines. Author: With The Bravest, 1996. Pres., founder Guam Balikbayan Med. Mission, Agana, 1974—; organizer, co-founder Aloha Med., Mission, Honolulu, 1982—. Guerrilla comdr. Sulu (Philippines) Area Command, 1943-46, 2d lt. Philippine Army, 1946-47. Recipient Thomas Jefferson award for pub. svc. Am. Inst. Pub. Svc., Washington, and Honolulu Advertiser, 1983, Raja Baguinda award for humanitarian svc. 6th Centennial Celebration of Islam in The Philippines, 1980; named Most Outstanding Filipino Overseas Philippine Govt. and Philippine Jaycees for Pub. Svc., 1982, Most Outstanding Cmty. Filipino Leader of Guam Philippine-Am. Cmty., 1979, Man of Yr. and Disting. Svc. award Inst. Philippine Am. Affairs, Hawaii, 1983; named Most Outstanding Alumni Achiever for Humanitarian Svc., U. Santo Tomas, 1981, Ernesto M. Espaldon profl. chairship in plastic and reconstructive surgery U. Santo Tomas, 1995. Fellow ACS, Philippine Coll. Surgeons; mem. AMA, Pan Pacific Surg. Assn., Guam Med. Soc. (pres. 1970-72, chief del. to AMA 1973-76), KC. Republican. Roman Catholic. Home: PO Box CE Hagatna GU 96932-8982

ESPARZA, KACIE LYNNE, military officer; b. Atlantic, Iowa, June 27, 1980; d. Stanton Farrell Campbell and Lisa Luanne Flowers; m. Andrew Arthur Esparza, II, Nov. 3, 2001; 1 child, Andrew Arthur III. Student, CC Air Force, Davis-Monthan AFB, Ariz., 2000—. Asst. mgr. Hy-Vee Food Stores, Souix Falls, SD, 1999—2000; enlisted USAF, 2000; maintenance prodn. mgr. 358 Amu 355 Amxs 355 Wing, Davis-Monthan AFB, 2001—. Dormitory coun. pres. 355 Wing, Davis-Monthan Air Force Base, Ariz., 2001. Republican. Lutheran. Avocations: writing, vocal music, art, softball, dance. Personal E-mail: kacie.esparza@americanamicable.com. Business E-Mail: kacie.esparza@dm.af.mil.

ESPE, MATTHEW J., manufacturing executive; With GE, 1980—2002; pres. GE Plastics Netherlands, 1994—99, GE Plastics Europe, 1999—2000; pres., CEO GE Lighting, 2000—02, IKON Office Solutions, Inc., 2002—, chmn., 2003—. Office: 70 Valley Stream Pkwy Malvern PA 19355

ESPENLAUB, MARGO LINN, women's studies educator, writer, artist; b. Decorah, Iowa, May 1, 1944; d. Lloyd Wilson and Margaret Mary (Seegmiller) Ruid; children: Arn R. Johnson, Cara C. Hubbell. BA in Philosophy, U. Colo., 1983, M in Humanities, 1985; PhD in Women's Studies, The Union Inst. Grad. Sch., 1995. Assoc. dir. student devel., mem. faculty U. Denver, The Women's Coll. Mem. faculty senate; coord. working group in ethical theory Inst. Ethics Ctr. Tchg. and Learning; faculty coord. TWC Student Writer's Club U. Denver. Co-author: Women's Studies: Thinking Women, 1993; gen. editor Voices of the Women's Coll. Mem. biomed. ethics com. Kaiser Permanente, Denver, 1986-96. Mem.: NOW, Nat. Women's Studies Assn., Nat. Mus. Women in the Arts.

ESPENSCHIED, BARBARA KRIEGSMAN, librarian; b. Bklyn., Oct. 29, 1944; d. Leo and Iris (Kovner) Kriegsman; m. Robert Steven Sager, June 19, 1966 (div. Apr. 1971); m. Clyde C. Espenschied, July 28, 1973; 1 child, Mark Daniel. BA, SUNY, Binghamton, 1966; MS, Hofstra U., 1970; MLS, Rutgers U., 1980. Cert. reading specialist, N.J., N.Y.; cert. libr., N.J. Adult svcs. supr. Edison (N.J.) Pub. Libr., 1993—. Bibliographic com. LMxAC, Middlesex County, N.J., 1990—, tng. com., 1992—, tng. coord., 1993; liaison Edison Libr. LMxAC, 1992—; membership com. Pub. rels. officer I.L. Peretz Community Jewish Sch., New Brunswick, 1986-87, sec., 1984-85, mem.-at-large, 1983-84. Mem. N.J. Libr. Assn. Jewish. Avocations: reading, gardening. furniture refinishing. Home: 265 Main St Spotswood NJ 08884-2312 Office: Edison Pub Libr 340 Plainfield Ave Edison NJ 08817-3147

ESPINOSA, LEANDRO, composer, conductor, educator; b. Monterrey, Nuevo Leon, Mexico, Jan. 2, 1955; arrived in US, 1992; s. Leandro Espinosa and Enrriqueta Garay. Undergraduate studies, Formative Sch. Through Arts, Monterrey, Nat. Conservatory Music, Mexico City, Perfecting Sch. Life and Movement; MusM, Peabody Conservatory, Balt., 1999; D in Musical Arts (hon.), U. Mo., Kansas City, 2002. Asst. prof. Formative Sch. Through Arts, Monterrey, 1976—78; assoc. prof. music Superior Sch. Music and Dance Carmen Romano de Lopez Portillo, Monterrey, 1987—90; asst. prof. music Ea. Oreg. U., La Grande, 2002—. Music dir. chamber orch. Technol. Inst. Superior Studies of Monterrey, 1977—78, Superior Sch. Music and Dance Carmen romano de Lopez Portillo, Monterrey, 1987—89, U. Coahuila, Saltillo, 1987—89; asst. condr. Peabody camerata Peabody Conservatory, Balt., 1997—99; music dir., condr. musica nova ensemble U. Mo., Kansas City, 2001—02, vis. adj. prof. music., 2001—02; music dir., condr. Grande Ronde Symphony Orch., La Grande, Oreg., 2002—. Composer: (musical composition) Homage, 1974—76 (Participation in the Internat. Festival Mex. a Work of Art, 1991), rev., 1979, Canto, 1977 (Participation in the Internat. Cervantine Festival, 1991), rev., 1987—88, Senso (ballet), 1984 (Participation in the Berchem Internat. Fesival of Choreography, and Brussels Gestes 85, 1985), Opera Ifigenia Cruel, 1989—91 (Grant to the Creators and Intellectuals of Mex., 1989), La Noche, 1995 (Commisioned by the Nat. Inst. of Fine Arts of Mex., 1995). Recipient Chamber Music 2000, U. of Missouri-Kansas City, 2000, Grad. Asst. Excellence in Tchg. Award, U. of Mo., Kansas City, 2002, Faculty Scholars Award, Ea. Oreg. U., 2003—05; scholar To the Creators and Intellectuals of Mex., Nat. Fonds for Culture and the Arts of Mex., 1989. Mem.: ASCAP (assoc. Raymond Hubbell scholar 2001). Achievements include research in An alternative system of music serialism. Office: Eastern Oregon Univ One University Blvd La Grande OR 97850 Personal E-mail: espinosaleandro@hotmail.com. E-mail: lespinos@eou.edu.

ESPINOSA, NANCY SWEET, artist, anthropologist; b. Jackson, Mich., Feb. 21, 1956; d. Harland Guy and Genevieve Kathryn Sweet; m. John P. Espinosa, 1978 (div. 1998). BFA in Two-Dimensional Art, BS in Anthropology, Ea. N.Mex. U., 1998, MA in Anthropology, 2002. Comm. operator III N.Mex. State Police, Roswell, N.Mex., 1980—88; emergency comm. operator Roswell Police Dept., 1989—96; fellow Ea. N.Mex. U., 1999—2002, archaeol. collections mgr., 2000—02; curator Salmon Ruins Mus. and Rsch. Libr., Bloomfield, N.Mex., 2003—. Exhibited in group shows at Clovis C.C./Ea. N.Mex. U., 1996, BFA Gallery, 1998. Home: PO Box 733 Bloomfield NM 87413-0733 Office Phone: 505-632-2013. E-mail: espnart@hotmail.com.

ESPINOSA, RESURRECCION, playwright, theater director, writer; b. Tijola, Almeria, Spain, Dec. 19, 1956; arrived in U.S., 1978; d. Juan Espinosa Mesas and Carolina Rodriguez Jimenez; m. Charles William Frink, Sept. 12, 1988. Licentiate in philosophy and letters, U. Granada, Spain, 1982. Bilingual tchr. New London (Conn.) Pub. Schs., 1983—84; instr. hispanic studies Conn. Coll., New London, 1985—93; part-time instr. U. R.I., Kingston, 1993—98, dir., founder Teatro Latino Estudiantil, 1998—; dir., founder Teatro Latino de New London, 2000—; master tchg. artist Conn. Commn. on Arts, Hartford, 2001—; theater dir. New London Pub. Schs., 2002—. Pub. spkr. R.I. Com. for Humanities, Providence, 2000—; lectr., evaluator Conn. Humanities Coun., Middletown, 1991, Middletown, 92. Author: (book of plays) El Gaucho Vegeteriano and Other Plays, 1995, Don Quijote in America, Plays in English and Spanish, 2002, (book of poems) Waking Dream, 1998, (comic strip) Amanda y Rocinante, 1995—. Active New London Main St., 2000—, Trinity Encore, Providence, 2000—. Recipient Cmty. Svc. award, Centro de la Comunidad, New London, 1991, Pioneers Project award, 1999, Lambda Upsilon Lambda, 2002; grantee, United Way, New London, 2001—02, Palmer and Bodenwein Funds, Hartford, 2001—02, RISCA, 1998, RICH, 2000, Conn. Com. Arts, 2002. Mem.: Am. Assn. Tchrs. Spanish and Portuguese. Avocations: photography, walking, playing with cat, plants, music. Home: 265 Gardner Ave New London CT 06320-3026 E-mail: teatrol@etal.uri.edu.

ESPINOZA, LUIS ROLAN, rheumatologist, researcher; b. Pisco, Peru, July 3, 1943; arrived in US, 1969, naturalized, 1992; s. Luis R. and Luz Lelia (Bernales) E.; m. Carmen G. Gonzalez, Dec. 20, 1969; children: Luis M., Gabriela M. MD, Cayetano Heredia, Lima, Peru, 1969. CPA; cert. Am. Bd. Internal Medicine, 1973, in rheumatology 1974, in allergy & immunology 1975, diagnostic & clin. immunology 1986. Intern Jersey City (N.J.) Med. Ctr., 1969-70; resident Washington U., St. Louis, 1970-72, rheumatlogy fellow, 1972-73, McGill U., Montreal, Can., 1973-74, asst. prof., 1976-78; immunology fellow The Rockefeller U., N.Y.C., 1974-76; assoc. prof. U. South Fla., Tampa, 1978-83, prof. medicine, 1983-90, La. State U. Sch. Medicine, New Orleans, 1991—, also chief rheumatology sect. Editor: Infection in the Rheumatic Diseases, 1988, Psoriatic Arthritis, 1985, Immun Complexes, 1983; guest editor Infectious Arthritis Rheumatic Disease Clin. N. Am., 1993, 98. Chmn. Lupus Found. Am., Tampa, 1979-90; pres.-elect Pan Am. League Against Rheumatism. Recipient Rsch. award NIH, Tampa, 1981, Arthritis Found., Tampa, 1990. Fellow ACP, Am. Coll. Rheumatology; mem. Am. Assn. Immunologists, So. Soc. for Clin. Investigation, Soc. for Clin. Rsch., Can. Soc. Rheumatologists, Can. Soc. for Clin. Investigation. Avocations: music, swimming, chess. Home: 1212 Conery St New Orleans LA 70115-3340 Office: La State U Med Ctr 1542 Tulane Ave New Orleans LA 70112-2825 Office Phone: 504-568-4630. Business E-Mail: lespin1@lsuhsc.edu. E-mail: luisrolan@msn.com.

ESPIRICUETA, SYLVIA, counseling administrator; b. Chgo., June 17, 1960; d. Zeferino Sáenz and Maria Delua; m. Valentine Espiricueta, July 26, 1986; 1 child, Valentine IV. BS in Edn. magna cum laude, Pan Am. U., Edinburg, Tex., 1983; MS in Edn., Counseling, Guidance, U. North Tex., 1990. Cert. counselor Tex., tchr. Tex. Bilingual tchr. Mission Sch. Dist., Tex., Austin Ind. Sch. Dist., Tex., Irving Ind. Sch. Dist., Tex.; tchr. Spanish Mesquite Ind. Sch. Dist., Tex.; binlingual psychotherapist MHMR, Dallas, Galaxy Ctr., Garland, Tex.; elem. sch. counselor Grand Prairie Ind. Sch. Dist., Tex., Arlington Ind. Sch. Dist., Tex. Whole brain tutor, Dallas, Ft. Worth, 1998—; lectr. in field; bilingual storyteller Arlington Pub. Libr., 2002. Singer (songwriter): (CD) After the Rain Comes the Sun, 2003; author: Positive Choices, 1996, Teach to Reach, 2002, Choosing to Learn to Climb, 2002. Internat. singer, songwriter. Finalist, Festival Cancion Latin Am., Calif., 2003; recipient Honorable Mention, Billboard World Song Contest, 2003, Song of Yr., 2005. Mem.: ASCAP, L.A. Music Network, Ft. Worth Songwriters Assn. Office Phone: 682-365-2894. Personal E-mail: espiricuetasylvia@hotmail.com.

ESPOSITO, JOHN VINCENT, lawyer; b. Logan, W.Va., Dec. 25, 1946; s. Vito T. and Mary Frances (Lamp) E. BA magna cum laude, W.Va. U., 1968, JD, 1971. Bar: W.Va. 1971, S.C. 1980, D.C. 1994, Legis. aide to Congressman Ken Hechler, 4th Dist. W.Va., 1971; counsel to Hans McCourt, Pres. W.Va. State Senate, 1972; instr. So. W.Va. Community Coll., 1972-; founder, sr. ptnr. Esposito & Esposito, Logan, W.Va. and Hilton Head Island, S.C., formerly in Washington, D.C. and N.Y.C., 1972—; arbitrator United Mine Workers Am.-Coal Operators Assn.; spl. judge Cir. Ct. Logan County (W.Va.); commr. in chancery Cir. Ct. Logan County; judge Mcpl. Ct. City of Chapmanville (W.Va.); spl. pros. atty., W. Va.; Citizen Ambassador to People's Republic of China and Soviet Union for U.S. Legal Del.; Founder, Citizens Environ. Quality, 1983.; of coun. to several Nat. & Internat. law firms; coun. to various Internat., Nat., State, and Local leaders; Citizen's Amb. relative to U.S. Legal Sys.; spkr. for Nat. & Internat. Forums; fashion model for Elite Knot; 2d lt. U.S. Army. U. Calif.; Hastings Coll. Law Coll. Advocacy scholar; Mem. ABA, Assn. Trial Lawyers Am., Am. Judicature Soc., W.Va. State Bar, S.C. Bar, D.C. State Bar, U.S. Supreme Ct. Bar, Internat. Platform Assn., Acad. Am. Poets; assisted in formation of Internat. War Crimes Amb., in Democracies establishing their gov., including Solvenia, Bosnia, Romania; Co-author: Laws for Young Mountaineers, 1973-74; Author: Law & Sex Come Together in the 90's; featured in a coll. textbook, Public Speaking/Theory Into Practice by Dr. John Makay; Creator, Dir. & Host of TV program, Law USA. Office: Ste 303 WatersEdge at Shelter Cove Harbour PO Drawer 5705 Hilton Head Island SC 29938 Office Phone: 843-785-6959.

ESPOSITO, LARRY WAYNE, planetary astronomer; b. Schenectady, N.Y., Apr. 15, 1951; s. Albert and Beverly Jane (DeLaMater) E.; m. Diane Marie McKnight, July 26, 1975; children: Rhea, Ariel. SB in Math., MIT, 1973; PhD in Astronomy, U. Mass., 1977. Research assoc. Lab. Atmospheric and Space Physics U. Colo., Boulder, 1977—, lectr., 1979-84, assoc. prof. dept. astrophys., planetary and atmospheric scis., 1984-95, prof., 1995—; prin. investigator NASA, Cassini Space Mission, 1990—. Investigator Pioneer Venus, Pioneer Saturn, Voyager, Galileo, Mars Observer, USSR Phobos and Mars 1994 spacecraft missions, 1977—; mem. NASA Planetary Atmospheres Mgmt. Ops. Working Group, 1981-84, Nat. Acad. Scis. Space Sci. Bd. com. on planetary and lunar exploration, 1982-86, chmn. 1989-92; dep. chmn. Nat. Acad. Scis. Space Sci. Bd. task group on planetary exploration, 1984-86; chair Europa Planetary Protection Task Group, 1999-2000, Task Group Forward Contamination Europa, 1999-2000. Contbr. articles to sci. publs. Recipient Exceptional Sci. Achievement medal NASA, 1986, Richtmyer Lecture award Am. Assn. Physics Tchrs. and Am. Phys. Soc., 1991. Mem. Am. Astron. Soc. (div. planetary scis. com. 1983-86, H.C. Urey prize 1985), Internat. Astron. Union, Am. Geophys. Union, Internat. Council Sci. Unions (exec. mem. com. space research) Clubs: Boulder Go. Methodist. Achievements include discovery of Saturn's 4th ring, 1979 (as part of the Pioneer Saturn Team), first Hubble Space Telescope observations of Venus, 1995. Office: U Colo CB392 Lab Atmosphere Spc P Boulder CO 80309-0001

ESPOSITO, RICHARD JOSEPH, journalist, executive; b. N.Y.C., Dec. 28, 1954; s. Richard and Marie (Croci) E.; m. Diana Claire von Mueffling, Aug. 29, 1992; 1 child, Tatiana Maria von Mueffling. BA with honors, NYU, 1975; postgrad., U. Calif., Berkeley, 1976-77. Clk. N.Y. Daily News, 1977-80, reporter, 1980-81; police bur. chief Phila. Bull., 1981; asst. editor Crains Bus. Mktg., N.Y.C., 1981-82; assoc. editor CBS Venture One, Fairlawn, N.Y., 1982-83; investigative reporter N.Y. Post, 1983-86; police bur. chief N.Y. Newsday, 1986-90, city editor, 1990-93; metro editor N.Y. Daily News, 1993, Sunday editor, 1993-95; sr. v.p. Warner Music Group, N.Y.C., 1995; exec. v.p., CEO Constant Mgmt. (formerly Maroley Media Group), 1995—. Lectr. in field. Author: Dead on Delivery, 1992—. Recipient Silurian award, 1992, AP award, 1990-94; co-recipient Pulitzer Prize city editor Newsday, 1992. Mem. N.Y. Press Club, Internat. Crime Writers, Soc. Profl. Journalists. Avocations: skiing, tennis, sport fishing, shooting. Home: 245 E 72ND St Apt 5A New York NY 10021-4516

ESPREE, MILDRED MICHELLE, language educator, writer; b. Houston, Dec. 13, 1954; d. Mitchell Cornelius and Eunice Vitalee (Delahoussaye) Barlow; m. Réne Jerome Espree; children: Jaréd Hilary, Genevieve Rachel. BJ, U. Tex., Austin, 1977; MEd, U. Houston, 1984. Newspaper reporter, feature writer Brazosport Facts, Clute, Tex., 1979—80; reporter Baytown Sun, Tex., 1980—81; English tchr. Houston Ind. Sch. Dist., 1985—. Adj. coll. English tchr. various cmty. colls., Houston, 1989, 96, 2000; adj. prof. St. Xavier U. Master's Program, Chgo.; cons., reader Coll. Bd. ETS, Princeton, NJ, 1998—2003; tchr. rep., coord. Houston Tchrs. Inst., 2000—; mem. supt. adv. bd. Houston Sch. Dist., 2002—03. Contbr. articles to profl. jours. Adult catechist St. Andrew Cath., 1991—98, lector, 1990—. Named Houston ISD Tchr. of Yr., 2002—03; recipient Joseph B. Whitehead Nat. Educator of Distinction award, Coca Cola, 2003; Walt Disney Tchr's. grant, Walt Disney Corp., 2001, At Challenge grant, DeBakey HS. Mem.: Assn. Supervision and Curriculum Devel., Nat. Coun. Tchrs. English, Kappa Delta Pi. Democrat. Roman Catholic. Avocations: reading, writing, cooking, travel, movies. Home: 303 Haymarket Ln Houston TX 77015 Office: DeBakey HS for Health Professions 3100 Shenandoah St Houston TX 77021 E-mail: mespree@houstonisd.org.

ESQUIBEL, EDWARD V., psychiatrist, health facility administrator; b. Denver, May 28, 1928; s. Delfino C. and Beatrice (Solis) E.; m. Elaine F. Telk (div. 1961); children: Roxanne, Cyndi, Allen, James; m. Lillian D. Robb, 1961; children: Amanda, Ramona. MD, U. Colo., 1958. Diplomate Am. Bd. Psychiatry and Neurology. Assoc. chief svc. Ill. State Psychiat. Inst., Chgo., 1964-66; dir. undergrad. program psychiatry, asst. prof. psychiatry Chgo Med. Sch., 1966-68; cons. and supr. group therapy Lake County Mental Health Clinic, Gary, Ind., 1968-72; pvt. practice Daytona Beach, Jacksonville, Fla., 1972-82; chief forensic svcs., dir. div. maximum security and inst. rsch. Colo. State Hosp., Pueblo, 1981; assoc. clin. prof. psychiatry Quillen-Dishner Coll. Medicine, Johnson City, Tenn., 1982-84; clin. psychiatrist VA Outpatient Clinic, Riviera Beach, Fla., 1984-86; mental health coord., supr. VA, Pensacola, Fla., 1986-88; assoc. chief staff, ambulatory care VA Med. Ctr., Ft. Lyon, Colo., 1988-90, Carl Vinson VA Med. Ctr., Dublin, Ga., 1990-91; staff physician VA Med. Ctr., Sheridan, Wyo., 1993—, chief psychiat. svcs. Lake City, Fla., 1993-94; contract physician, 1995—. Contbr. articles to profl. jours. Sgt. U.S. Army, 1948-52. Recipient Plaque Recognition award Southeastern Psychiat. Inst., 1964, Internat. Pers. Creative award, 1972, Key to City Daytona Beach, 1975, Hosp. Dirs. commendation VA, 1991. Avocations: gardening, arts and crafts, reading. Home and Office: 801 Gospel Island Rd Inverness FL 34450-3592 Office Phone: 352-637-4749.

ESQUIVEL, AGERICO LIWAG, retired research physicist; b. Manila, June 5, 1932; came to U.S., 1957, naturalized, 1971; s. Enrique Frias and P. R. (Liwag) E. AB, Berchmans Coll., Manila, 1955; MA, Berchmans Coll., 1956; PhD, St. Louis U., 1963. Rsch. assoc. St. Louis U., 1961-63; rsch. scientist Research Inst. Advanced Studies, Balt., 1963, Materials Research Lab., Martin Co., Orlando, Fla., 1964-65; sr. rsch. engr. Materials Tech. Labs. Boeing Co., Seattle, 1965-71; postdoctoral fellow Advanced Research Projects Agy., U. So. Calif., L.A., 1971-73; mem. tech. staff Hughes Aircraft Co., Culver City, Calif., 1973-76; mem. tech. staff Semicondr. Process and Device Ctr., Tex. Instuments Inc., Dallas, 1976-98. Presenter internat. symposia, U.S., Japan, Europe. Contbr. articles to sci. jours. NSF postdoctoral fellow, 1963. Mem. IEEE Elec. Devices Soc. (sr. mem.), Am. Phys. Soc., Electrochem. Soc., Sigma Xi, Pi Mu Epsilon. Achievements include 16 U.S. patents issued on submicron CMOS process integration, development, device characterization, process/device computer simulation, trench isolation, buried multilevel interconnect systems, nonvolatile memory devices; contbr. papers to jours. and procs. on X-ray, electron diffaction, radiation hardening, cathodoluminescence in GaAs, deep level transient spectroscopy, x-ray lithography, high density nonvolatile memories, trench isolated electronically programmable read-only memories (EPROMs), sub-0.25 micron Complementary Metal Oxide Semiconductor (CMOS) transistors and fabrication process, 0.18 micron CMOS logic transistor technology, Ultra Large Scale Integrated (ULSI) CMOS device process integration and characterization.

ESREY, WILLIAM TODD, telecommunications company executive; b. Phila., Pa., Jan. 17, 1940; s. Alexander J. and Dorothy (B.) E.; m. Julie L. Campbell, June 13, 1964; children: William Todd, John Campbell. BA, Denison U., Granville, Ohio, 1961; MBA, Harvard U., 1964. With Am. Tel & Tel. Co., also N.Y. Tel. Co., 1964-69; pres. Empire City Subway Ltd., N.Y.C., 1969-70; mng. dir. Dillon, Read & Co. Inc., N.Y.C., 1970-80; exec. v.p. corp. planning United Telecommunications, Inc. (now Sprint), Westwood, Kans., 1980-81, exec. v.p., CFO, 1981-82, 84-85, CEO, 1985—90; chmn., CEO Sprint Corp., Westwood, Kans., 1990—2003. Bd. dirs. Duke Energy Corp., Gen. Mills, Inc.; chmn. bd. dirs. Japan Telecom Co., Ltd., 2003—04. Mem. Birnum Wood, Eagle Springs, Valley Club of Montecito, Phi Beta Kappa.

ESRICK, JERALD PAUL, lawyer; b. Moline, Ill., Oct. 1, 1941; s. Reuben and Nancy (Parson) E.; m. Ellen Feinstein, June 18, 1966; children: Sara Elizabeth, Daniel Michael. BA, Northwestern U., 1963; JD, Harvard U., 1966. Bar: Ill. 1966, U.S. Dist. Ct. (no. dist.) Ill. 1967, U.S. Supreme Ct. 1974, U.S. Ct. Appeals (9th cir.) 1985, U.S. Ct. Appeals (7th cir.) 1967. Law clk. U.S. Dist. Ct. (no. dist.) Ill., 1966-68; assoc. Wildman, Harrold, Allen & Dixon, Chgo., 1968-73, ptnr., 1973—, also chmn. firm mgmt. com., 1987-90. Lectr. Northwestern U., 1984-93, Coll. Arts and Scis. bd. visitors, 1993—, Nat. Panel Comml. Arbitrators, Am. Arbitration Assn. Pres. bd. trustees Nat. Lekotek Ctr., Evanston, Ill., 1989-93, U.S. Toy Libr. Assn., 1987-88; bd. dirs. Evanston Mental Health Assn., 1984-86, Fund for Justice, 1969-95, Lawyers' Com. for Civil Rights, 1974-84. Fellow Am. Coll. Trial Lawyers; mem. ABA, Ill. State Bar Assn., Chgo. Coun. Lawyers (bd. dirs., sec., founding mem.), Chgo. Bar Assn., Lawyers Club Chgo. Avocations: running, skiing, sailing, classical music, bicycling. Home: 1326 Judson Ave Evanston IL 60201-4720 Office: Wildman Harrold Allen & Dixon 225 W Wacker Dr Ste 3000 Chicago IL 60606-1229 Office Phone: 312-201-2508. E-mail: esrick@wildmanharrold.com.

ESSANDOH, HILDA BRATHWAITE, primary school educator; b. N.Y.C., Feb. 19, 1925; d. Charles Christopher and Millicent Marian (Boxill) Brathwaite; m. Samuel O. Essandoh, June 11, 1959; children: Millicent Efua, Yvonne Araba, Dorothy Esi. BA, Hunter Coll., 1959; MS, Bank Street Coll. Edn., 1976, profl. diploma in supervision-adminstrn., 1980. Cert. nursery, kindergarten, 1st-6th grades, sch. adminstrn. and supervision. Tchr. kindergarten N.Y.C. Bd. Edn., 1962-91. Recipient Ely Trachtenberg award. Home: 548 W 165th St New York NY 10032-4942

ESSARY, ANDREW CHARLES, philosopher, educator, financial analyst; b. Dallas, Oct. 6, 1950; s. Charles Eugene and Dorothy (Miller) E.; m. Carol Anne Kuhn, Aug. 15, 1969; 1 child, Kerry Alise Berry. Student, Richland Coll., Dallas, 1974-80; BBA, So. Meth. U., 1984; MA, U. Tex. at Dallas, Richardson, 1994. Fin. analyst Tex. Instruments, Dallas, 1972-93; auditor Trinity Industries, Dallas, 1993-95; dir. Lovers Lane Animal Hosp., Dallas, 1995-98; assoc. prof. philosophy Collin County C.C., Plano, Tex., 1995—; sr. fin. analyst U. Tex. Southwestern Med. Sch., Dallas, 1998—2005, Parkland Health and Hosp. Sys., Richardson, Tex., 2005—. Freelance writer, newspaper columnist on ethics, 1998.d Named Outstanding Alumni, U. Tex. at Dallas, 1997; scholar Endowed Essary Family's Single Parent scholarship,

Collin County C.C. Found., 1998—. Mem. Mensa, Profl. Assn. Dive Instructors (cert. dive master). Avocations: scuba diving, photography, gardening, motorcycling, tai chi. Office Phone: 214-590-0346. Business E-Mail: aessary@ccccd.edu.

ESSELMANN, JESSE J, education educator; s. Norbert P and Veronica S Esselmann; m. Angela E Kura, Apr. 15, 1972; children: Laura E Esselmann-Grisar, Matthew K. M, U. of Wis., 1988—93. Law Enforcement Officer: Standards and Tng. Bd. 1974. Asst. prof. of legal studies Concordia U. Wis., Mequon, Wis., 1993—; pres. Visionary Consulting Inc., Saukville, Wis., 2001—. Ssgt (e-5) Air Force, 1969—73, RAF Chicksands. Avocations: photography, travel. Office: Concordia Univ Wis 12800 N Lake Shore Dr Mequon WI 53097-2402 Office Phone: 262-243-4365.

ESSER, ARISTIDE HENRI, psychiatrist; b. Padalarang, Java, Indonesia, May 11, 1930; came to U.S., 1961; s. Samuel Jonathan and Anganita (Tawalujan) E.; m. Ada Reif; children: Jonathan Hendrik, Jessica. MD, U. Amsterdam, The Netherlands, 1955. Diplomate Am. Bd. Psychiatry and Neurology. Med. dir. N.S. Kline Rsch. Inst., Orangeburg, N.Y., 1962-69; dir. rsch. Letchworth Village, Thiells, N.Y., 1969-71; dir. Ctrl. Bergen Cmty. Mental Health Ctr., Paramus, N.J., 1971-77; med. dir. Mission for Immaculate Virgin, S.I., N.Y., 1977-80; dir. quality assurance Bronx (N.Y.) Psychiat. Ctr., 1980-85; unit chief for supportive rehab. Rockland Psychiat. Ctr., Orangeburg, 1985-88, chief geriat. divsn., 1988-90; pvt. practice, 1989; cons. psychiatrist St. Dominic's Home, Blauvelt, 1990—2001; attending psychiatrist Good Samaritan Hosp., Suffern, NY, 1990—2002, Rye (N.Y.) Hosp. Ctr., 1990—. Rsch. prof. NYU Med. Ctr., NYC, 1985-94; pres. Psychiatry PC, 1989—, Psychiatry Evaluation Treatment and Rehab. Assocs., PLLC, 1999—. Co-author: Mental Illness: A Homecare Guide, 1989, Chi Gong: The Ancient Chinese Way to Health, 1990; co-editor: Behavior and Environment, 1971, Design for Communality and Privacy; editor Jour. Man-Environment Sys., 1969— (Internat. Design award 1973). Travel grant City of Leyden, The Netherlands, 1960; Lederle Labs. fellow Yale U., 1961. Fellow AAAS (life), Am. Psychiat. Assn. (life); mem. Soc. for Biol. Psychiatry, Soc. for Gen. Systems Rsch., Am. Acad. Acupuncture (founding), Assn. for Study Man-Environment Rels. (founding). Home: 435 S Mountain Rd New City NY 10956-5731 Office: 337 N Main St Ste 2 New City NY 10956-4310 Office Phone: 845-639-6723. Office Fax: 845-639-3031. Personal E-mail: pbhppmc@att.net.

ESSER, CARL ERIC, lawyer; b. Montclair, NJ, Feb. 12, 1942; s. Josef and Elly (Graber) E.; m. Barbara A. B. Stelzer, Oct. 12, 1968; children: Jennifer, Eric, Brian. AB, Princeton U., 1964; JD, U. Mich., 1967. Bar: Pa. 1967. Assoc. Reed Smith LLP, Phila., 1967-72, ptnr., 1973—2002; pvt. practice Phila., 2003—. With USMCR, 1960-66. Mem. ABA, Pa. Bar Assn., Pa. Lawyers Fund for Client Security (bd. dirs., chmn.), Octavia Hill Assn. (chmn. bd. dirs.), German Am. C. of C. (bd. dirs.); Racquet Club, Penllyn Club, Mfrs. Golf and Country Club. Republican. Office: 2500 One Liberty Pl Philadelphia PA 19103 Office Phone: 215-851-8181. Business E-Mail: cesser@reedsmith.com.

ESSER, JAMES MARK, cardiovascular and interventional radiologist; b. Madison, Wis., Aug. 1, 1960; s. John Michael Esser and Helen Josephine (Brown) Butterworth. MD, SUNY, Buffalo, 1985. Diplomate Am. Bd. Radiology, Nat. Bd. Med. Examiners. Transitional resident John Burns Sch. Medicine-U. Hawaii, Honolulu, 1985-86, asst. clin. instr. surgery, 1985-86; resident in diagnostic radiology Beth Israel Med. Ctr.-Mt. Sinai Sch. Medicine, N.Y.C., 1986-90; fellow in vascular and interventional radiology St. Luke's-Roosevelt Hosp., N.Y.C., 1990-91; clinical fell. Cardiovasc. and Interv. Rad., Columbia Coll. of Physicians and Surgs., 1990-91; attending staff emergency dept. Bellevue Hosp., N.Y.C., 1988-91; attending radiologist Elmhurst Hosp., N.Y.C., 1990-91, St. Mary's Hosp., West Palm Beach, Fla., 1991-92, Med. Ctr. Hosp., Punta Gorda, Fla., 1992-93, Welborn Hosps. & Clins., Evansville, Ind., 1993-94, St. Mary's Med. Ctr., Evansville, 1993—, Cmty. Meth. Hosp., Henderson, Ky., 1994—98, Perry County Meml. Hosp., Tell City, Ind., 1994—99, St. Mary's Ctr. for Her, Evansville, 1995—, Vencor Hosp., Louisville, 1998—2001, Jasper Meml. Hosp., Jasper, Ind., 1998—2000, Wellington Regional Med. Ctr., West Palm Beach, Fla., 2000—, Regional Med. Ctr., Madisonville, Ky., 2000—; asst. clinical prof. of radiology U. Louisville Sch. Med., 2003—; chairman dept. radiology Granite City, Ill., 2004—. Pres., v.p. N.Y.C. Soc. Physicians for Social Responsibility, 1987-90. Clin. fellow Columbia Coll. Physicians and Surgeons, 1990-91. Mem. AAAS, N.Y. Acad. Sci., Am. Coll. Radiology, Radiol. Soc. N.Am., Soc. Cardiovasc. and Interventional Radiology, Am. Roentgen Ray Soc., N.Y. Roentgen Soc. Roman Catholic. Avocations: jogging, surfing, rock climbing.

ESSER, PATRICK J., communications executive; BA in Comm. Media, MA in Comm. Media, U. No. Iowa. Dir. programming, Hampton Roads Sys. Cox Communications, Inc., 1976; mem. mgmt. team for CableRep (now Cox Media, Inc.), 1981—90, dir. advertising sales, 1990—91, v.p. advertising sales, 1991—99; v.p. ops. Cox Communications, Inc., 1999—2000, sr. v.p. ops., western divsn., 2000—01, exec. v.p. ops. Atlanta, 2001—, COO, 2005—. Co-founder, former bd. dir. Product Information Network; bd. dir. Cable & Telecommunications Assn. for Mktg. Ednl. Found., Nat. Cable Comm.; mem. telecommunications adv. bd. Compaq. Recipient Heritage Honors Alumni Achievement award, U. No. Iowa, 2003, Cable TV Advertising Bur. President's award. Office: Cox Communications Inc 1400 Lake Hearn Dr Atlanta GA 30319 Office Phone: 404-843-5000. Office Fax: 404-843-5975.*

ESSEX, FRANCIS XAVIER, physician, educator; b. N.Y.C., July 17, 1931; s. John A. and Caroline H. (Weber) E.; m. Judith Ann McBride, July 11, 1959; children: Paul F., Anne C., Caroline E., Julia M. BS, Holy Cross Coll., 1953; MD, Creighton U., 1960. Diplomate Am. Bd. Internal Medicine. Commd. ensign USN, 1959, advanced through grades to comdr., 1969; regtl. surgeon 2d Marine div. FMF, FMF, Lant, 1960-61; staff med. officer U.S. Naval Hosp., Phila., 1963-65, from asst. to chief med. svc. Charleston, S.C., 1967-69, chief med. svc., 1969-70; ret. capt. USNR, 1991; asst. prof. Med. Coll. of S.C., Charleston, 1969-70; from instr. to assoc. prof. U. Tex. Med. Br., Galveston, 1970—; pvt. practice, Galveston, 1970—. Clin. assoc. prof. U. Tex. Med. Br., 1983—; chmn. internal medicine dept. St. Mary's Hosp., Galveston, 1984-85. Hon. adm. Tex. Navy, Galveston, 1985—; bd. dirs. Moody House Ret. Cmty., Galveston, 1970-71. Fellow Am. Coll. Physicians; mem. AMA, Am. Soc. Internal Medicine, Tex. Med. Assn., Galveston County Med. Soc. Avocations: sailing, tennis, reading, woodworking. Home: 1203 Harbor View Dr Galveston TX 77550-3113 Office: Internal Medicine Assocs 1203 Harbor View Dr Galveston TX 77550-3113

ESSEX, JOSEPH MICHAEL, visual communication planner; b. Santa Barbara, Calif., May 27, 1947; Student, Montgomery Coll., Rockville, Md., Va. Commonwealth U., Richmond. Art dir. Met. Pitts. Pub. Broadcasting, 1970-73; sr. designer Ctr. for Comm. Planning, 1973-76; assoc. creative dir. Jim Johnston Advt., 1976; design dir. Burson-Marsteller Design Group, Chgo., 1976-86, v.p., dir. visual comm. planning Americas, 1980-88; prin. Design By Objectives, Chgo., 1986-88; ptnr. Essex Partnership, Chgo., 1988-89, Essex Two Inc., Chgo., 1989—. One man poster exhbn. Chgo., 1979; exhibited in group shows: Japan, 1976, Ireland, 1977, Cooper-Hewitt Mus., N.Y.C., 1981. Recipient Silver medals, Merit award Art Directors Club, N.Y.C., 1979, 80, over 300 other awards from design and advt. orgns. Office: Essex Two Inc 2210 W North Ave Chicago IL 60647-5430 Office Phone: 773-489-1400. E-mail: joseph@5x2.com.

ESSEX, MARILYN J., sociologist, educator; b. Phila., May 24, 1950; d. Phillip Hartley Essex and Effie May Amy. BS, U. Wis., Whitewater, 1971; MS, U. Md., 1973, PhD, 1978. Asst. prof. Lawrence U., Appleton, Wis., 1980—84; asst. scientist U. Wis., Madison, 1984—87, assoc. scientist, 1987—90, sr. scientist, 1990—2004, asst. prof., 2004—. Cons. U. Calif., Berkeley, 2002—, Washington U., St. Louis, 2002—. Contbr. articles to profl. jours., chapters to books. Mem. sci. core on non-psychopathology and devel. MacArthur Rsch. Network; mem. John D. and Catherine T. MacArthur Found., 1996—2004. Grantee, NIMH, 1982—85, 1983—88, 1989—93, 1993—2003, 1998—2003, 1999—, 1999—2003, 1999—2004, 2004—, Nat. Inst. Aging, 1985—86, 1992—96, AARP Andrus Found., 1989, U. Wis., 1989—90, John D. And Catherine T. MacArthur Found., 1990, 1991, 1991—93, 1992—93, 1992—94, 1993, 1997—99, 2000—04, U. Wis., Madison, 2003—04, NSF, 2002—05. Mem.: Nat. Coun. Family Rels., Am. Anxiety Disorders Assn., Soc. Rsch. Child Devel. Avocations: gardening, photography. Office: Wis Psychiatric Inst and Clinics 6001 Research Pk Blvd Madison WI 53719

ESSEX, MYRON ELMER, microbiology and virology educator; b. Coventry, R.I., Aug. 17, 1939; s. Myron Elmer Essex and Ruth Hazel (Knight) Esses; m. Elizabeth Katherine Jordan, June 19, 1966; children: Holly Anne, Carrie Lisa. BS, U. R.I., Kingston, 1962; DVM, Mich. State U., East Lansing, 1967; MS, Mich. State U., 1967, DSc (hon.), 1988; PhD, U. Calif., Davis, 1970; MA (hon.), Harvard U., 1979; DSc (hon.), U. R.I., 1987; DSc (hon.), U. Madrid, 1989, U. Md., 1992; DSc (hon.), U. Kinshasa, Zaire, 1995. Research fellow Karolinska Inst., Stockholm, 1970—72; asst. prof. Harvard U., Cambridge, Mass., 1972—76, assoc. prof., 1976—78, prof., chmn. dept. microbiology, 1978—81, chmn. dept. cancer biology, 1981—97, chmn. dept. immunology and infectious diseases, 1997—, Mary Woodard Lasker prof. health scis., 1989—, chmn. AIDS Inst., 1988—. Mem. sci. adv. bd. Cambridge Biosci. Corp., 1982—93, Virus Rsch. Inst., 1993—; cons. Diacrin, Cin. Co-editor: Viruses in Cancer, 1980, AIDS:Etiology, Diagnosis, Treatment and Prevention, 1992, 1997, Human T-cell Leukemia Viruses, 1984, AIDS in Africa, 1994; contbr. articles to profl. jours.; patentee test for human T leukemia virus infection and AIDS blood tests and vaccines. Bd. sci. counselors Nat. Cancer Inst., 1982—93; sci. adv. bd. ARC, 1985—89; v.p. sci. affairs Internat. Retrovirol. Assn. HTLV and Related Viruses, 1995—; sec. gen. Internat. Assn. Rsch. on Leukemia, 1995—97, pres., 1997; mem-.Lasker award jury Albert & Mary Lasker Found., 1982—84, 1987—92; bd. dirs. Pierre Dick/Virbac Found.; mem. adv. bd. AIDS Assn., 1990—; mem. sci. adv. bd. Until There's A Cure, 1995—, Internat. AIDS Vaccine Initiative, Rockefeller Found., 1996—, Sabin Found., 1996—, Inst. for Internat. Vaccine Devel., 1997—, Virus Rsch. Inst., 1992—; bd. dirs. Hong Kong Cancer Ctr., 1994—. Recipient Bronze medal, Am. Cancer Soc., 1978, Ralston-Purina Rsch. award, 1985, Outstanding Investigator award, Nat Cancer Inst., 1985, Lifetime Rsch. award, 1995, Disting. Alumnus award, Mich. State U., Lasker award, 1986, Carnation Rsch. award, 1987, Disting. Alumnus award, U. Calif., Davis, 1987, Presdl. medal of honor, Govt. of Senegal, 1991, Ann. award, Am. Assn. Vet. Epidemiologists, 1992, Gold-Headed Cane award, 1995, Alumni Excellence award, U. R.I., 1994; scholar Leukemia Soc. Am., 1972, Am. Cancer Soc. Nat Cancer Inst., 1973—. Fellow: Infectious Disease Soc. Am., Am. Assn. Microbiology, AAAS; mem.: Internat. Retrovirology Assn. (v.p.), Leukemia Soc. Am. (adv. bd. 1978—83, 1985—), Am. Cancer Soc. (mem. rsch. com. Mass. br. 1975—86), Soc. Gen. Microbiology, Reticuloendothelial Soc., Nat. Acad. Practitioners, Am. Soc. Virology, Internat. Assn. Rsch. in Leukemia (pres.), Am. Assn. Immunologists, Am. Assn. Cancer Rsch., AVMA, Inst. Medicine of NAS. Office: Harvard Sch Pub Health Immunology & Infectious Dis 651 Huntington Ave Boston MA 02115-6009

ESSICK, CAROL EASTERLING, elementary school educator; d. Woodrow Wilson and Laura Byrd Easterling; m. Irving Louis Essick, Mar. 26, 1994. MusB, Berry Coll., 1980. Cert. performance based tchr. Ga. Profl. Stds. Commn. Elem. music specialist McDuffie County Schs., Thomson, Ga., 1980—81, Waycross (Ga.) City Schs., 1981—93, Ware County Schs., Waycross, 1993—98, Glynn County Schs., Brunswick, 1998—. Vice-chairperson Goodyear Elem. Sch. Coun., Brunswick, 2001—02, sec., 2002—. Mem.: NEA, Music Educators Nat. Conf., Sigma Alpha Iota (life Sword of Honor 1979). Methodist. Avocations: golf, photography, coin collecting/numismatics. Office: Goodyear Elem Sch 3000 Roxboro Rd Brunswick GA 31520 Personal E-mail: cessick@adelphia.net. Business E-Mail: cessick@glynn.k12.ga.us.

ESSIEN, FRANCINE B., biologist, educator; BA in Biology, Temple U.; PhD in Genetics, Yeshiva U.; postgrad., U. Conn. Prof. dept. biol. scis. Rutgers U., New Brunswick, N.J., 1997—. Dir. Minority Undergrad. Sci. Programs, Rutgers U., 1988—, founder, co-founder Success in the Scis., Biomed. Careers Program, Rsch. Apprentice Program, ACCESS-MED, mem. adv. bd. Douglass Project for Rutgers Women in Math, Sci. and Engring.; mem. rev. panel NSF/NIH; cons. CUNY, Atlanta U.; lectr. in field. Contbr. articles to profl. jours. Fulbright scholar; recipient Spina Bifida Assn. Am. award, N.J. Women of Achievement award Woodrow Wilson Found. Instns.; named Black Achiever in Sci., Chgo. Mus. Sci. and Industry, U.S. Prof. of Yr. for Rsch. and Doctoral Univs., Carnegie Found. Advancement of Teaching.; Disting. Black Scholar-in-Residence, U. Cin., 1988; CASE Professor of the Yr. 1994-95; recipient W.E.B. DuBois award for edn. NAACP of Cen. N.J., 1997. Office: Rutgers U Nelson Lab/Busch Campus 604 Allison Rd Piscataway NJ 08854-8000

ESSIG, MARK G., steel products company executive; b. Dec. 17, 1957; BS, Loyola U., Chgo.; MBA, U. Ill. Mgmt. and exec. level positions with Washington (Pa.) Steel Corp.; then joined AK Steel Corp., Middletown, Ohio, 1992, v.p. employee rels. and asst. to CEO, exec. v.p.; pres., CEO GS Industries, Charlotte, N.C., 1998—.

ESSIGMANN, JOHN M., chemistry professor; b. Medford, Mass. m. Ellen Essigmann; children: Amy, Nolan. BS, Northeastern U., 1970; MS, MIT, 1972, PhD, 1976. William R. and Betsy P. Leitch prof. chemistry, dept. chemistry MIT, prof. toxicology, biomedical engring. divsn. Contbr. contbn. to prof. jour. Recipient Outstanding Investigator award, Nat. Cancer Inst., 1989, Arthur C. Smith award, 1998, Susan B. Komen Breast Cancer Found. award, 2000, Princess Chulabhorn Gold Medal, Thailand, 2004; Margaret Mac Vicar fellowship, 1997—2007. Mem.: Nat. Assn. Collegiate Scholars, Environ. Mutagen Soc., Am. Soc. Microbiology, Soc. Toxicology, Am. Assn. Cancer Rsch., Am. Chem. Soc. (Mutation Rsch. award for Sci. Excellence 2002). Office: MIT Rm 56-669 77 Mass Ave Cambridge MA 02139

ESSINGER, SUSAN JANE, special education educator; b. Paris, Ill., Oct. 7, 1952; d. Rex Milburn and Virginia Ellen (White) E. BS in Edn., Ea. Ill. U., Charleston, 1973; MS in Edn., Ind. State U., 1981, postgrad. Cert. learning disabilities, elem., educationally mentally handicapped with early childhood endorsement. Elem. tchr. Havana (Ill.) Sch. Dist., 1973-74; tchr. early childhood spl. edn. Paris Sch. Dist. 95, 1974—. Mem. APA, NEA, IDEC, CEC, Assn. for Edn. Young Children, Ill. Edn. Assn., Paris Tchrs. Assn. Avocations: dollmaking, gardening, collecting coins and stamps. Home: 1104 S Main St Paris IL 61944-2823 Office: Paris Sch Dist 95 S Main St Paris IL 61944 E-mail: sessinger@comwares.net.

ESSMAN, ROBERT NORVEL, artist, graphics designer; b. St. Louis, Feb. 6, 1937; s. Paul M. and Rose (Solinsky) E. BFA, State U. of Iowa, 1959. Artist Simplicity Pattern Co., N.Y.C., 1961-62, Life Mag., N.Y.C., 1962-68, art dir., 1969, Show Mag., N.Y.C., 1969-70, Bus. Week Mag., N.Y.C., 1970-74; logo designer, creative dir. N.Y.C. Bicentennial Commn., N.Y.C., 1974-76; art dir. People Weekly Mag., N.Y.C., 1974-82; art dir., pres. Bob Essman: Design, The Cricket Press, N.Y.C., 1982—. Pubr./design dir.: Revival: Theatrical History Revisited, 1992-94. Bd. dirs. League for the Hard of Hearing, 1977-99, recording sec. 1987-95, hon. bd., 1999—; bd. dirs. Hampton-Booth Theatre Libr., 1993-94, sec., 1994. Recipient Vol. of Yr. award League for the Hard of Hearing, 1990, Excellence of Design award Advt. Club NY, 1977, Art Dirs. Club of NY, 1978, Gen. Excellence Nat. Mag. award Am. Soc. Mag. Editors, 1973, Real Masson Founders award, VGSA, 2004. Mem.: Overseas Press Club (Designer Dateline 1991—92, New Club Logo 1994), Soc. Pub. Designers (bd. dirs. 1972—79, pres. 1976—79, Excellence of Design award 1972, 1973, 1975, 1976, 1978), Am. Inst. Graphic Arts (Excellence of Design award 1980), Dutch Treat Club (book designer 1989—, compiled membership history The Whole Who 1995, Gold medal 2003), The Players Club (bd. dirs. 1979—85). Home and Office: Bob Essman Design 33 Follett St Winooski VT 05404-2132 E-mail: bobessman@adelphia.net.

ESSMAN, SUSIE, actress; Actor: (TV series) Baby Boom, 1988—89, (voice) Crank Yankers, 2002—, Curb Your Enthusiasm, 1999—; guest appearances (TV series) Kate & Allie, 1989, Law & Order, 1997, 2004, 2002, The King of Queens, 2002; actor: (films) Crocodile Dundee II, 1988, Punchline, 1988, Teenage Mutant Ninja Turtles II, 1991, Volcano, 1997, The Siege, 1998, Keeping the Faith, 2000, The Secret Lives of Dentists, 2002, The Man, 2005.

ESSMYER, MICHAEL MARTIN, lawyer; b. Abilene, Tex., Dec. 6, 1949; s. Lytle Martin Essmyer and Roberta N. Essmyer Nicholson; m. Cynthia Rose Piccolo, Dec. 27, 1970; children: Deanna, Mike, Brent Austin. BS in Geology, Tex. A&M U., 1972; postgrad., Tex. Christian U., 1976; JD summa cum laude, South Tex. Coll. Law, 1980. Bar: Tex. 1980, U.S. Dist. Ct. (no., so., ea. we. dists) Tex. 1982, U.S. Ct. Appeals (5th cir.) 1981, U.S. Ct. Appeals (9th cir.) 1990, U.S. Ct. Appeals (1st cir.) 1993, U.S. Ct. Appeals (7th cir.) 1995, U.S. Ct. Appeals (fed. cir.) 1985, U.S. Ct. Claims, 1981, U.S. Supreme Ct. 1991. Briefing atty. Supreme Ct. Tex., Austin, 1980-81, Haynes & Fullenweider, Houston, 1981-89, Essmyer & Hanby, Houston, 1989-92; atty. Essmyer & Assocs., Houston, 1992-94; pres. Essmyer & Tritco, LLP, Houston, 1994-95, Essmyer, Tritco & Clary, LLP, Houston, 1995-99, Essmyer & Tritco, LLP, Houston, 1999—. Lead article editor South Tex. Law Jour., 1979. Dem. candidate for state rep., Bryan, Tex., 1972; del. Dem. Party, Houston, 1982, 84; precinct chmn. Harris County Dem. Exec. Com., Houston, 1983-86. Capt. USAF, 1972-78. Nat. Merit Scholar, 1968-72. Mem. ATLA, ABA, Houston Bar Assn., Tex. Trial Lawyers Assn. (dir. 1996—), Harris County Trial Lawyers Assn. (dir. 1997—), Tex. Criminal Def. Lawyers Assn., Tex. Bar Found., Harris County Criminal Lawyers Assn. (dir. 1986-87), Fed. Bar Assn., Houstonian Club, The Petroleum Club of Houston, The Company Onstage (dir. 2001—). Roman Catholic. Home: 1122 Glourie Dr Houston TX 77055-7506 Office: Essmyer & Tritico LLP 4300 Scotland St Houston TX 77007-7328 Office Phone: 713-869-1155. Business E-Mail: messmyer@essmyertritico.com.

ESSNER, ROBERT ALAN, pharmaceutical executive; b. N.Y.C., Oct. 26, 1947; s. Arthur and Charlotte (Levy) E.; m. Rosalind Esser, July 24, 1969 (div. June 1986); children: Elizabeth, Emily; m. Anne Essner, May 23, 1987; children: Elizabeth, Emily, Benjamin. Grad., Miami U., Oxford, OH; MA, U. Chicago. Various positions Sandoz Pharms. Corp., East Hanover, NJ, 1978-86, v.p., 1986-87, corp. v.p., COO bus. mgmt., 1987; pres. Sandoz Consumer HealthCare Group, Parsippany, NJ, 1987, Wyeth-Ayerst Labs., 1993—97, Wyeth-Ayerst Global Pharm., 1997; exec. v.p. Wyeth, Madison, NJ, 1997-2000, COO, 2000, pres., 2000—, CEO, 2001—, chmn., 2003—. Bd. dirs. Mass. Mutual Life Ins. Comp., Pharm. Rsch. & Mfr. Am.; mem. Bus. Roundtable, Bus. Coun. Chmn. Children's Health Fund Corp. Coun.; trustee Penn Medicine. Mem.: Pharm. Mfr. Assn. Avocation: antique photography. Office: Wyeth 5 Giralda Farms Madison NJ 07940-0874*

ESSWEIN, ERIC JOHN, industrial hygienist; b. Denver, Jan. 27, 1957; s. John E. Esswein and Malvina Sutherland, Patricia E. Esswein (Stepmother). AA in Sci., North Seattle (Wash.) Coll., 1983; BS, We. Wash. U., 1986; MS in Pub. Health, U. Utah, 1991. Cert. indoor air quality profl., Assn. Energy Engrs., 1995; indsl. hygienist Am. Bd. Indsl. Hygiene, 1995, registered sanitarian Ohio, 1996. Indsl. hygienist Nat. Inst. Occupl. Safety and Health, Cin., 1991—98, sr. indsl. hygienist Denver, 1998—. Contbr. articles to profl. jours. Comdr. U.S. Pub. Health Svc., 1991—2004. Recipient Cumming award, Soc. Am. Mil. Engrs., 2002, Nat. Excellence in Tech. Transfer award, Fed. Lab. Consortium S.W. Region, 2003, Fed. Lab. Consortium, 2004. Mem.: Am. Conf. Govtl. Indsl. Hygienists, Am. Indsl. Hygiene Assn. (assoc.; mem. indoor environ. com. 2001—03, Outstanding Com. award 2004). Achievements include patents for handwipe disclosing method for the presence of lead. Home: 11523 Hannah Drive Conifer CO 80433 Office: Cdc/Niosh Denver Federal Center PO Box 25226 Denver CO 80225 Office Phone: 303-236-5946. Home Fax: 303-236-6072; Office Fax: 303-236-6072. Personal E-mail: eje1@cdc.gov.

ESTABROOK, ALISON, breast surgeon; b. N.Y.C., Oct. 29, 1951; d. Edwin Burke and Shirley (Butler) E.; m. William Harrington, June 12, 1982. BA, Barnard Coll., 1974; MD, NYU, 1978. Resident in surgery Columbia-Presbyn. Med. Ctr., N.Y.C., 1978-81, 82-84, fellow in surgery, onocology, 1981-82, asst. prof. surgery, 1984—, dir. Breast Clinic, 1985—97, Florence Irving asst. prof., 1989-92, chief breast surgery, 1991-97, assoc. prof. surgery, 1992-95, prof. clin. surgery, 1995—; chief breast surgery St. Luke's Roosevelt Hosp., N.Y.C., 1998—. Mem.: Am. Soc. Breast Disease (bd. dirs. 1996—2001), Soc. Surg. Oncology, N.Y. Surg. Soc., N.Y. Met. Breast Group, Assn. Women Surgeons, Am. Soc. Clin. Oncology, Sigma Xi (Kappa chpt.). Office: St Lukes Roosevelt Hosp 425 W 59th St New York NY 10019-1104 Office Phone: 212-523-7500. Business E-Mail: ae9@columbia.edu.

ESTABROOK, REED, artist, educator; b. Boston, May 31, 1944; s. F. Reed and Nancy (Vogel) E.; 1 son, August. BFA, R.I. Sch. Design, Providence, 1969; MFA, Art Inst. Chgo., 1971. Instr. U. Ill., 1971-74; asst. prof. U. No. Iowa, Cedar Falls, 1974-78, assoc. prof., 1978-83, head dept. photog. program, 1974-83; advisor visual arts Iowa Arts Coun., Des Moines, 1977-78, mem. art purchase com., 1977-78; chmn. photog. dept. Kansas City (Mo.) Art Inst., 1983—94, prof., coord. photography, 2005; prof., coord. photo dept. San Jose (Calif.) State U., 1984—89. Bd. dirs. San Francisco Camera Work, 1987-90; Fulbright exch. tchr. Sheffield Poly., Eng., 1990-91. Exhibited one-man shows, Sioux City Art Ctr., Iowa, 1981, Klein Gallery, Chgo., 1982, James Madison U., Harrisonburg, Va., 1983, Orange Coast Coll., Costa Mesa, Calif., 1983, Portland State U., Oreg., 1983, others, group shows, Isetan Mus. of Art, Tokyo, 1993, U. Colo., Boulder, 1977, 82, Mus. Modern Art, N.Y.C., 1978, 82, 84, Santa Barbara Mus. Art, Calif., 1979, San Francisco Mus. Modern Art, 1982, 90, Hokkaido Obihito Mus. of Art, Tokyo, 1993, Royal Coll. Art, London, 1994, Mus. Fine Art, Santa Fe, N.Mex., 1994, 96, San Jose Inst. Contemporary Art, 1996, San Francisco Mus. Modern Art, 1996, Sheppard Gallery U. Nev., Reno, others; represented permanent collections, Mus. Modern Art, N.Y.C., Mpls. Inst. Arts, Hallmark Collection, Kansas City, Mo., Boise Gallery Art, Idaho, Walker Art Ctr., Mpls., R.I. Sch. Design, U. Colo., Fogg Mus. Art, Harvard U., Spencer Mus. Art, U. Kans., Lawrence, Internat. Mus. Photography, Rochester, N.Y., Art Inst. Chgo., Humbolt State U., Arcata, Calif., Smithsonian Instn., Washington, San Francisco Mus. Modern Art, J. Paul Getty Mus., Santa Monica, Calif., Honolulu Acad. Arts. W.R. French fellow Art Inst. Chgo., 1971; Nat. Endowment for Arts fellow, 1976. Fellow Soc. Contemporary Photo; mem. Soc. for Photog. Edn. Home: 482 Chetwood St Oakland CA 94610-2649 Office: San Jose State U Sch Art & Design San Jose CA 95192-0089 Office Phone: 408-924-4693. Personal E-mail: reed@reedestabrook.net.

ESTABROOK, ROBERT HARLEY, journalist; b. Dayton, Ohio, Oct. 16, 1918; s. Charles and Christianne M. (Harley) E.; m. Mary Lou Stewart, Dec. 22, 1942; children: John Stewart, James Ross, David Morse, Margaret Harley. AB, Northwestern U., 1939; postgrad., Am. Press Inst., Columbia, 1947; LHD (hon.), Colby Coll., 1972. City editor Emmet County Graphic, Harbor Springs, Mich., 1936; editor Daily Northwestern, Northwestern U., 1938-39; reporter Cedar Rapids (Iowa) Gazette, 1939-40, editorial writer, 1940-42, Washington Post, 1946-53, editor editorial page, 1953-61, corr. London, 1961-62, chief fgn. corr., 1962-65, UN and Can. corr., 1966-71; editor, pub. Lakeville (Conn.) Jour., 1971-86, pub. emeritus, cons., 1987—. Lectr. journalism U. Md., 1948-49; India Editor Exchange Program, 1987. Author: Never Dull: From Washington Editor and Foreign Correspondent To Country Publisher, 2005 Served from pvt. to capt. AUS, 1942-46; in charge Army newspaper and radio sta. 1945, Brazil. Recipient John Peter Zenger award U. Ariz., 1979, Eugene Cervi award, 1980, Horace Greeley award, 1980, Yankee Quill award Acad. New Eng. Journalists, 1983; named to New Eng. Cmty. Newspaper Hall of Fame, 2000. Mem. Nat. Conf. Editorial Writers (founder, life mem. pres. 1951), Council Fgn. Relations, Conn. Council on Freedom of

Info. (chmn. 1981-82, Stephen Collins award, 1989), New Eng. Press Assn. (pres. 1983), Rotary Club, Phi Beta Kappa, Sigma Delta Chi (award for best editorial 1954), Deadline Club (Pulitzer Prize juror 1988, 89, award for UN corr. 1969, Golden Quill award for best editorial 1973, 78, Herbert Brucker award 1977), Delta Tau Delta. Unitarian Universalist. Office: Lakeville Jour 33 Bissell St PO Box 1688 Lakeville CT 06039-9989 Office Phone: 860-435-9873.

ESTABROOK, RONALD WINFIELD, chemistry professor; b. Albany, NY, Jan. 3, 1926; s. George Arthur and Lillian Florence (Childs) E.; m. June Elizabeth Templeton, Aug. 23, 1947; children: Linda Estabrook Gilbert, Laura Estabrook Verinder, Jill Estabrook Wisehart, David. BS, Rensselaer Poly. Inst., 1950; PhD, U. Rochester, 1954, D.Sc. (hon.), 1980; MD (hon.), Karolinska Inst., Stockholm, 1981. Johnson Research Found. fellow U. Pa. Sch. Medicine, 1955-58; research assoc., 1958-59; asst. prof. phys. biochemistry, 1959-62; assoc. prof., 1961-65; prof., 1965-68; Virginia Lazenby O'Hara prof. biochemistry, 1968—; chmn. biochemistry U. Tex. Southwestern Med. Ctr., Dallas, 1968-82; dean U. Tex. Health Sci. Center (Grad. Sch. Biomed. Scis.), 1973-76; Cecil and Ida Green Chair of Biomedical Scis., 1990—; acting dir. Green Ctr. for Reproductive Biology Scis. U. Tex. Southwestern Med. Ctr., Dallas, 1997-99; chmn. basic sci. rev. com. VA, 1972-74. Cons. in field; bd. sci. advisors St. Judes Hosp., Memphis, 1978-81; chmn. bd. toxicology and environ. health NAS, 1980-85; governing bd. NRC, NAS, 1986-89; mem. Atlantic Richfield Sci. Adv. Coun., 1981-87; mem. coun. Inst. Medicine, NAS, 1984-89, report rev. com.; chmn. bd. sci. overseers Med. Rsch. Inst. San Francisco; mem. Robert Wood Johnson Found. Commn. on Med. Edn., bd. sci. advisors ILSI Found.; treas. Fedn. Am. Socs. Exptl. Biology, 1992-94; treas. 17th Internat. Congress of Biochemistry and Molecular Biology; chmn. Philip Morris USA SAB, 2002—; mem. SAB Kansas City Life Sci. Inst., 2002—. Exec. editor Archives of Biochemistry and Biophysics, 1966-73, 77-92, chmn. editorial bd., 1984-90; exec. editor Cancer Research, 1980-84; editor Jour. Pharmacology and Exptl. Therapeutics, 1969-74, Xenobiotica, 1970—, Life Scis., 1973-84; contbr. articles to profl. jours. Served with USNR, 1943-46. Recipient Patton Prize British Toxicology Soc., 2002, Disting. Scientist award Fedn. Am. Socs. Exptl. Biology, 1977, Claude Bernard medal U. Montreal, 1969. Mem. NAS, Inst. Medicine, Pan Am. Assn., Biochem. Socs. (sec.-gen. 1972-75), Am. Assn. Med. Schs. (adminstrv. bd. council acad. socs.; task force cost med. edn. 1971-72, liaison com. med. edn. 1975-80), Am. Soc. Biol. Chemists (treas. 1985-91), Internat. Soc. for Study Xenobiotics (pres. 1988-90), Am. Soc. Pharmacology and Exptl. Therapeutics, Acad. Medicine, Engring., and Sci. Tex. (treas., mem. gov. bd.), OXYgene (founder 1989), Sigma Xi. Home: 5208 Preston Haven Dr Dallas TX 75229-3040 Office: U Tex Southwestern Med Ctr 5323 Harry Hines Blvd Dallas TX 75390-9038 Office Phone: 214-648-3456. Personal E-mail: restab6741@aol.com. Business E-Mail: ronald.estabrook@utsouthwestern.edu.

ESTEBAN, MANUEL ANTONIO, academic administrator, language educator; b. Barcelona, June 20, 1940; arrived in U.S., 1970; s. Manuel and Julia Esteban; m. Gloria Ribas, July 7, 1962; 1 child, Jacqueline. BA in French with 1st class honors, U. Calgary, Can., 1969, MA in Romance Studies, 1970; PhD in French, U. Calif., Santa Barbara, 1976. From asst. prof. to prof. French and Spanish langs. and lit. U. Mich., Dearborn, 1973-87, assoc. dean, 1984-86, acting dean Coll. Arts, Scis., and Letters, 1986-87; dean arts and scis. Calif. State U., Bakersfield, 1987-90; provost, v.p. acad. affairs Humboldt State U., Arcata, Calif., 1990-93; pres., prof. French and Spanish Calif. State U., Chico, 1993—2003, pres. emeritus, prof. emeritus, 2003—. Author: (book) Georges Feydeau, 1983; contbr. to book revs. and articles to profl. publs. Trustee Enloe Hosp. Fellow, U. Mich., 1982—83; Woodrow Wilson fellow, 1969, Doctoral fellow, U. Calif., Santa Barbara, 1970—73, Can. Coun. Doctoral fellow, Govt. of Can., 1970—73, Rackham grantee, U. Mich., 1979. Mem.: Am. Assn. State Colls. and Univs., Am. Coun. Edn., Sierra Health Found. (bd. dirs. 1998—). Avocations: golf, woodworking, glass blowing. Office: Calif State Univ O'Connell 407 Chico CA 95929-0003 E-mail: mesteban@csuchico.edu.

ESTEFAN, GLORIA MARIA (GLORIA FAJARDO), singer, lyricist; b. Havana, Cuba, Sept. 1, 1957; came to U.S., 1959; d. Jose Manuel and Gloria G. (Garcia) Fajardo; m. Emilio Estefan, Jr., Sept. 1, 1979; children: Nayib Emil, Emily Maria. BA in Psychology, U. Miami, Fla., 1978, MusD (hon.), 1993. Composer: (popular songs) Anything for You, 1987, Live for Loving You, 1991, Can't Forget You, 1991, Coming Out of the Dark, 1991, Always Tomorrow, 1992, Go Away, 1993; performer songs for Olympics in Korea, 1987, World Series Baseball, St. Louis, 1987, Pan Am. Games, 1988, Superbowl Halftime, Mpls., 1992; albums: Primitive Love, 1986, Let It Loose, 1987, Cuts Both Ways, 1990, Coming Out Of The Dark, 1991, Greatest Hits, 1992, Mi Tierra, 1993 (Best Latin Tropical Album Grammy award, 1994), Christmas Through Your Eyes, 1993, Hold Me, Thrill Me, Kiss Me, 1994, Abriendo Puertas, 1995 (Best Latin Tropical Grammy award 1996), Destiny, 1996, Gloria!, 1998, Santo Santo, 1999, Alma Caribena: Carribean Soul, 2000; contbr. vocals to albums Danzon (Arturo Sandoval), 1993, Duets (Frank Sinatra), 1993, Q's Jook Joint (Quincy Jones), 1994; contbr. to soundtrack of movie The Birdcage, 1996. Benefactress Children's Home Soc., Miami, 1991, Leukemia Soc., 1991, United Way, 1991, United Negro Coll. Fund, 1992, Community Alliance Against AIDS, Miami, 1992, Hurrican Relief Fund, So. Fla., 1992-93; pub. mem. U.S. Del. to 47th Gen. Assembly UN. Recipient Am. Music award, 1987, Victory award, 1991, Songwriter of Yr. award BMI, 1991, Humanitarian of Yr. award B'nai Brith, 1992, Casita Maria Gold Medal award, 1993, Hispanic Heritage award, 1993, Hearst Found. Gold Medal award, 1992, Ellis Island Congl. Medal of Honor, 1993.; named Billboard's Best New Pop Artist and Top Pop Singles Artist, 1986; also numerous Grammy award nominations, 1988-91, Musicares Person of Yr., 1994, Billboard Music Video of Yr. award Everlasting Love, 1995, also over 50 platinum albums worldwide. Achievements include The Miami Sound Machine's single, Conga, being the first to crack the pop, dance, Black and Latin charts simultaneously. Office: care Epic Records 550 Madison Ave New York NY 10022-3211

ESTEP, MYRNA LYNNE, systems analyst, philosophy educator; b. Whitesville, W.Va., Jan. 7, 1944; d. Modest Schaeffer and Mary Magdalene E.; m. Richard Keith Schoenig, June 5, 1971; 1 child, Debora Lynne. BA, Ind. U., 1970, MS, 1971, PhD, 1975; postgrad., U. Tex., 1993. Assoc. instr. Ind. U., Bloomington, 1972-75; asst. prof. U. Tex., San Antonio, 1975-78; rsch. edn. specialist Acad. Health Scis., San Antonio, Tex., 1979-84; program systems analyst, field researcher USMC, U.S. Navy, Quantico, Va., 1984-87; grad. faculty, advisor U. Zimbabwe, 1987-89; rsch. systems analyst San Antonio, 1990—; adj. faculty in philosophy U. of Incarnate Word, San Antonio, 1996-99, Our Lady of the Lake U., San Antonio, 1996-98. Grad. faculty U. Zimbabwe, Harare; advisor to ministries of higher edn. and labour, manpower planning and social welfare, Zimbabwe, 1987-89. Author: The Relation Between Theoretical and Procedural Knowing, 1975, A Theory of Immediate Awareness: Self-Organization and Adaptation in Natural Intelligence, 2003; co-editor (with E.S. Maccia and others): Women and Education, 1975; reviewer (for jours.); contbr. articles to profl. jours. including Applied Sys. and Cybernetics, Pergamon, Ferminista: The On-Line Jour. of Feminist Reconstrn. Recipient Best Paper award U. Vienna, Austria, 1992. Mem. AAAS, Internat. Soc. Gen. Systems Rsch., Austrian Soc. Cybernetics, Math. Assn. Am., N.Y. Acad. Sci., Phi Kappa Phi. Home: 16022 Oak Grove Dr San Antonio TX 78255-1128 Personal E-mail: emathematica@aol.com.

ESTEP, ROBERT LLOYD, lawyer; b. Marion, Va., Dec. 20, 1939; s. Lanson Eugene and Clara Nell (White) E.; m. Elizabeth Grayson Werth, July 10, 1971; 1 child, Laura White. BA with Honors, U. Va., 1962, JD, 1973. Bar: Ill. 1973, U.S. Dist. Ct. (no. dist.) Ill. 1973, Tex. 1984. From assoc. to ptnr. Isham, Lincoln & Beale, Chgo., 1973-83; ptnr. Jones, Day, Reavis & Pogue, Dallas, 1983—. Served to capt. U.S. Army, 1966-70, Vietnam. Woodrow Wilson fellow, U. Va., 1962. Mem. Tex. Bar Assn., Law Club Chgo., Spl. Forces Assn., Phi Beta Kappa. Republican. Lutheran. Home: 6331 Park Ln Dallas TX 75225-2108 Office: Jones Day Reavis & Pogue 2727 N Harwood St Dallas TX 75201-1515

ESTERGARD, JANA KJERSTEN, academic administrator; b. Cambridge, Nebr., June 25, 1971; d. Gary Lloyd and Barbara Jean Estergard; m. Anthony Lee Roberts, Oct. 16, 1962; 1 child, Evan Lee Roberts. BA, Doane Coll., 1992; MRC, Bowling Green State U., 1995. Cert. Rehab. Counselor Commn. on Rehab. Counselor Certification, Ill., 1995. Vocat. rehab. counselor State of Mo., Springfield, 1996—97; dir. disability svcs. SW Mo. State U., 1997—2000, equal opportunity officer, 2000—. Consulting DO-IT prof., U. Wash., Seattle, 2000—02. Bd. mem. Therapeutic Riding of Ozarks, Springfield, 2000—01. Avocations: tennis, travel. Office: SW Missouri State Univ 901 S National Ave Springfield MO 65804 Office Phone: 417-836-4252. Office Fax: 417-836-3055. Business E-Mail: janaestergard@smsu.edu.

ESTERHAI, JOHN LOUIS, JR., surgeon, medical educator; b. Phila., Oct. 23, 1946; s. John Louis and Louise K. (Moyer) E.; m. Carol Jean Keely, Apr. 12, 1969; children: Staci June, Gregory Wayne. BA, Gettysburg Coll., 1968; MD, Temple U., 1972. Intern in surgery Temple U. Health Sci. Ctr., Phila., 1973; flight surgeon USAF, Kadena AFB, Okinawa, Japan, 1973-76; resident in orthop. surgery U. Pa. Sch. Medicine, 1977-80; asst. prof. orthopedic surgery Hosp. U. Pa., Phila., 1980-87, assoc. prof. orthopedic surgery, 1987-2000, prof. orthopedic surgery, 2000—; chief orthopedic surgery Phila. VA Med. Ctr., 2001—. Editor: Musculoskeletal Infection, 1992. Maj. USAF, 1973-76. Recipient award Am. Orthopedic Assn., 1989, Assn. Bone and Joint Surgeons, 1994. Fellow Am. Acad. Orthopedic Surgeons, ACS; mem. Internat. Soc. Fracture Repair, Orthopaedic Rsch. Soc., Musculoskeletal Infection Soc. (pres. 1997-98). Office: Hosp U Pa Dept Orthopaedic Surgery 3400 Spruce St Philadelphia PA 19104-4206

ESTERLY, NANCY BURTON, physician; b. N.Y.C., Apr. 14, 1935; d. Paul R. and Tanya (Pasahow) Burton; m. John R. Esterly, June 16, 1957; children: Sarah Burton, Anne Beidler, John Snyder, II, Henry Clark, II. AB, Smith Coll., 1956; MD, Johns Hopkins U., 1960. Intern, then resident in pediatrics Johns Hopkins Hosp., 1960-63, resident in dermatology, 1964-67; instr. pediatrics Johns Hopkins U. Med. Sch., 1967-68; instr., trainee La Rabida U. Chgo. Inst.; also dept. pediatrics U. Chgo. Med. Sch., 1968-69; asst. prof. Pritzker Sch. Medicine, U. Chgo., 1969-70, assoc. prof., 1973-78; asst. prof. dermatology Abraham Lincoln Sch. Medicine, U. Ill., 1970-72, assoc. prof. dermatology and pediatrics, 1972-73; dir. div. dermatology, dept. pediatrics Michael Reese Hosp. and Med. Ctr., Chgo., 1973-78; prof. pediatrics and dermatology Northwestern U. Med. Sch., 1978; head div. dermatology, dept. pediatrics Children's Meml. Hosp., Chgo., 1978-87; prof. pediatrics and dermatology Med. Coll. Wis., Milw., 1987—2004, prof. emeritus dermatology, 2005—; head div. dermatology, dept. pediatrics Children's Hosp. Wis., Milw., 1987—2004. Editor-in-chief Pediatric Dermatology, 1983—; contbr. numberous articles to profl. jours. Recipient David Martin Carter award, Am. Skin Assn., 2002, Lifetime Career Educator award, Dermatology Found., 2002, Disting. Svc. award, Med. Coll. Wis., 2004. Mem.: Wis. Pediat. Soc., Women's Dermatol. Soc. (Rose Hirschler award), Soc. Pediat. Dermatology (1st Lifetime Achievement award 1998), Soc. Pediat. Rsch., Am. Acad. Pediatrics, Soc. Investigative Dermatology, Wis. Dermatol. Soc., Am. Dermatol. Assn., Am. Acad. Dermatology, Internat. Soc. Pediat. Dermatology, Sigma Xi. Personal E-mail: nesterly@comcast.net.

ESTERN, NEIL CARL, sculptor; b. N.Y.C., Apr. 18, 1926; s. Marc J. and Molly (Sylbert) E.; m. Anne Graham, May 27, 1947; children: Peter, Evan, Victoria. BFA, BS in Edn., Tyler Sch. Fine Arts, 1947; postgrad., Barnes Found., Merion, Pa., 1945-47. One-man shows include Scoville Meml. Libr., Salisbury, Conn., 1985; exhibited in group shows at Nat. Acad., N.Y.C., 1985-2004, Nat. Sculpture Soc., 1985-2004, Sharon Creative Arts Found., 1985, Bklyn. Mus., 1980, Kent, Conn., 1992, Fairfield, Conn., 1994, 96; prin. works include J.F.K. Meml., Bklyn., 1966, Statue of Fiorello H. LaGuardia, LaGuardia C.C., 1983, LaGuardia Meml. Statue of Fiorello La Guardia, N.Y.C., 1994, FDR Meml. Statues of Eleanor, FDR and Fala, Washington, 1997, Nat. Cathedral Statue of Eleanor Roosevelt, D.C., 1998, Claude Pepper Meml., Tallahassee, 2003; portrait busts of Danny Kaye, Gov. Raymond Baldwin, Thomas Buechner, Jack Nicholson, Pres. Carter, Prince Charles, Lady Diana, David Levine, J. Edgar Hoover, Senator Robert Taft, Covington Hardee, Miguel de la Madrid. Recipient 1st prize sculpture Kent Art Assn., 1982, . Fellow Nat. Sculpture Soc. (pres. 1994-97, Lindsey Morris prize 1984, Mildred Victor Meml. prize 1988); mem. NAD (John Gregory award 1964, Samuel F.B. Morse Gold medal 1970, Cert. of Merit 1979, 90, Dessie Green prize 1990, Daniel Chester French award), Century Assn. Avocation: tennis. Home: 82 Remsen St Brooklyn NY 11201-3420 also: Cream Hill Rd West Cornwall CT 06796 Personal E-mail: anneilestern@yahoo.com.

ESTEROW, MILTON, publishing executive; b. Bklyn., July 28, 1928; s. Bernard and Yetta (Barash) E.; m. Jacqueline Levine, Jan. 6, 1951; children: Judith, Deborah. Student, Bklyn. Coll., 1946-49. Reporter N.Y. Times, N.Y.C., 1948-63, asst. to cultural news dir., 1963-68; assoc. dir. Kennedy Galleries, N.Y.C., 1968-72; editor, pub. ARTnews, N.Y.C., 1972—; pub. ARTnewsletter, 1975—; chmn. Esterow Communications Corp., 1981, Annellen Publs., 1982. Lectr. in field. Author: The Art Stealers, 1966. Office: ARTnews LLC 48 W 38th St Fl 9 New York NY 10018-6238

ESTES, ANDREW HARPER, lawyer; b. Pecos, Tex., Dec. 16, 1956; s. Bobby Frank and Gayle (Harper) E.; m. Deidre Dement, Mar. 19, 1976; children: Andrew Kimble, Jada Catherine. BA, Tex. Tech U., 1977; JD, Baylor Sch. Law, 1979. Bar: Tex. 1980, U.S. Dist. Ct. (no. dist.) Tex. 1980, U.S. Dist. Ct. (we. dist.) Tex. 1981, U.S. Ct. Appeals (5th cir.) 1982, U.S. Supreme Ct. 1983, U.S. Tax Ct., U.S. Ct. Appeals (10th cir.) 1987. Ptnr. Lynch, Chappell & Alsup P.C., Midland, Tex., 1980—. Mem. admissions com. Dist. 16, State Bar Tex., 1982-85, bd. dirs., 1999-2002. Mem. Tex. Tech. U. Coll. Edn. Devel. Coun., Lubbock, 1986-87; vol. Big Bros., Midland, 1983—, bd. dirs., 1985-89; bd. dirs. Hearthstone Temporary Children's Shelter, 1988-92; mem. bd. dirs. Tex. Book Festival, 2001-. Named Big Brother of Yr., Big Bros./Big Sisters of Midland, 1985; recipient Trimble Vol. Svc. award, Leadership Midland Alumni, 1986, Pro Bono Atty. award West Tex. Legal Svcs., 1991. Mem. ABA, Midland County Young Lawyers Assn. (sec., treas. 1987-88, Outstanding Young Lawyer of Midland County 1992), Midland County Bar Assn. (sec., treas. 1987-88, v.p. 1992-93, pres. elect. 1993-94, pres. 1995-96), State Bar Tex. (Dist. 16B grievance com. 1990-93, chmn. 1992-93, bd. dirs. 1999-2002), Tex. Young Lawyers Assn. (bd. dirs. 1987-89), Tex. Bd. Legal Specialization (cert.), Phi Delta Phi. Presbyterian. Home: 1505 Princeton Ave Midland TX 79701-5760 Office: Lynch Chappell & Alsup PC The Summit Bldg 300 N Marienfeld St Fl 7 Midland TX 79701-4345 Office Phone: 432-683-3351. Business E-Mail: hestes@lynchchappell.com.

ESTES, CARL LEWIS, II, lawyer; b. Ft. Worth, Feb. 9, 1936; s. Joe E. and Carroll E.; m. Gay Gooch, Aug. 29, 1959; children: Adrienne Virginia, Margaret Ellen. BS, U. Tex., 1957, LL.B., 1960. Bar: Tex. 1960. Law clk. U.S. Supreme Ct., 1960-61; assoc. firm Vinson & Elkins, Houston, 1961-69, ptnr., 1970—2002. Bd. dirs. Houston Grand Opera Assn., Houston Arboretum. Fellow Am. Bar Found., Tex. Bar Found.; mem. ABA, Internat. Bar Assn., Am. Law Inst., Am. Coll. Probate Counsel, Tex. Bar Assn., Internat. Fiscal Assn., Internat. Acad. Estate and Trust Law. Fellow Am. Bar Found., Tex. Bar Found.; mem. ABA, Internat. Bar Assn., Am. Law Inst., Am. Coll. Probate Counsel, Tex. Bar Assn., Internat. Fiscal Assn., Internat. Acad. Estate and Trust Law, Asia Soc. (bd. dirs.).

ESTES, CARROLL LYNN, sociologist, educator; b. Fort Worth, May 30, 1938; d. Joe Ewing and Carroll (Cox) E.; 1 child, Duskie Lynn Gelfand Estes. AB, STanford U., 1959; MA, So. Meth. U., 1961; PhD, U. Calif., San Diego, 1972; DHL (hon.), Russell Sage Coll., 1986. Rsch. asst., asst. study dir. Brandeis U. Social Welfare Rsch. Ctr., 1962-63, rsch. assoc., 1964-65, project dir., 1965-67; vis. lectr. Florence Heller Grad. Sch., 1964-65; rsch. dir. Simmons Coll., 1963-64; asst. prof. social work San Diego State Coll., 1967-72; asst. prof. in residence dept. psychiatry U. Calif., San Francisco, 1972-75, assoc. prof. dept. social and behavioral scis., 1975-79, prof., 1979-92, chair dept. social and behavioral scis., 1981-93, coord. human devel. tng. program, 1974-75; dir. Aging Health Policy Rsch. Ctr., 1979-85, Inst. for Health and Aging, 1985-99; LaSor lectr. Faculty rsch. lectr. U. Calif., 1993; LaSor lectr. Oreg. Health Scis. U, 2005; co-founder Concerned Scientists in Aging, 2005. Author: The Decision-Makers: The Power Structure of Dallas, 1963; co-author: Protective Services for Older People, 1972, U.S. Senate Special Committee on Aging Report, Paperwork and the Older Americans Act, 1978, The Aging Enterprise, 1979 Fiscal Austerity and Aging, 1983, Long Term Care of the Elderly, 1985, Political Economy, Health and Aging, 1984, The Long Term Care Crisis, 1993, The Nation's Health, 2001, 7th edit., 2003, Critical Gerontology, 1999, Social Policy and Aging, 2001, Social Theory, Social Policy and Aging, 2003, Health Policy, 4th edit., 2004; contbr. articles to profl. jours. Mem. Calif. Commn. on Aging, 1974-77; cons. U.S. Senate Spl. Com. on Aging from 1976, Notch Commn. U.S. Commn. Social Security, 1993-94; bd. dirs. Nat. Com. to Preserve Social Security and Medicare, 2002—. Recipient Matrix award Theta Sigma Phi, 1964, award for contbns. to lives of older Californians, Calif. Commn. on Aging, 1977, Helen Nahm Rsch. award U. Calif., San Francisco, 1986, Woman Who Would Be Pres. League of Women Voters, 1998. Mem. Inst. Medicine of NAS, ACLU, Am. Sociol. Assn. (Disting. Scholar award Aging and Life Course 2000), Assn. Gerontology in Higher Edn. (pres. 1980-81, recipient Beverly award 1993, Tibbitts award 2000), Am. Soc. on Aging (pres. 1982-84, Leadership award 1986), Geronotol. Soc. Am. (Kent award 1992, pres. 1995-96), Older Women's League (v.p. 1994-97), Soc. Study Social Problems, Alpha Kappa Delta, Pi Beta Phi. Office: U Calif San Francisco Inst Health & Aging 3333 California St Ste 340 San Francisco CA 94118-1944 Office Phone: 415-476-3236. E-mail: cestes@itsa.ucsf.edu.

ESTES, ELAINE ROSE GRAHAM, retired librarian; b. Springfield, Mo., Nov. 24, 1931; d. James McKinley and Zelma Mae (Smith) Graham; m. John Melvin Estes, Dec. 29, 1953. BSBA, Drake U., 1953, tchg. cert., 1956; MSLS, U. Ill., 1960. With Pub. Libr. Des Moines, 1956-95, coord. ext. svcs., 1977-78, dir., 1978-95, ret., 1995. Lectr. antiques, hist. architecture, librs.; mem. conservation planning com. for disaster preparedness for librs. Author bibliographies of books on antiques; contbr. articles to profl. jours. Mem. State of Iowa Cultural Affairs Adv. Coun., 1986—94, Nat. Commn. on Future of Drake U., 1987—88; chmn. Des Moines Mayor's Hist. Dist. Commn.; mem. nominations review com. Iowa State Nat. Hist. Register, 1983—89; chmn. hist. subcom. Des Moines Sesquecentennial Com., 1993, Iowa Sister State Commn., 1993—95; mem. com. 40th Anniversary Drake U. Alumni Weekend, 50 Yr. Drake Alumni Weekend, 2003; mem. July 4 com. Iowa Sesquecentennial; nat. exch. dir. Friendship Force, 1997; mem. nat. adv. bd. Cowles Libr., 1998—; mem. Gov.'s Iowa Centennial Meml. Found., 2003—; mem. acquisition com. Salisbury House, 2003; mem. cultural ctr. task force African Am. Hist. Mus., 1999—2003; mem. Iowa author com. Pub. Libr. Des Moines Found., 2001—; mem. Terrace Hill Commn., 2001—; bd. dirs. Des Moines Art Ctr., 1972—83, hon. mem., 1983—; bd. dirs. Friends of Libr. USA, 1986—92, Henry Wallace House Found., Iowa Libr. Centennial Com., 1990—91, Wagner Hall Preservation Project, 2004—. Recipient Recognition award Greater Des Moines, YWCA, 1975, Disting. Alumni award Drake U., 1979, Woman of Achievement award YWCA, 1989, Excellence in Hist. Preservation award City of Des Moings, 1994, Contbn. to Cmty. award Connect Found., 1995, Friend of Literacy award Pub. Libr. of Des Moines Found., 2003; named Textbook Project in her honor, Forest Libr., 2002; named to Wall of Fame, YWCA, 2003. Mem.: ALA (30th Anniversary Honor Roll for Intellectual Freedom 1999), Iowa Soc. Preservation Hist. Landmarks (bd. dirs. 1969—97), Libr. Assn. Greater Des Moines Metro Area (chmn. 1992, pres.), Iowa Urban Pub. Libr. Assn., Iowa Libr. Assn. (life; pres. 1978—79), Iowa Antique Assn., Terrace Hill (Gov.'s Mansion) Soc. (bd. dirs. 1972—, v.p. 1991—93, pres. 1993—96), Links Inc. (40th ann. com. 1997), Drake U. 50 Yr. Club, Questers Inc. Club (pres. 1982, state 2d v.p. 1984—86, 1st v.p. 1990—2000, pres. 1997, state pres. 2000—03, pres. 2001—03), Rotary (history com. 2001—), Proteus Club (pres. 2003—04).

ESTES, JACK CHARLES, oil service company executive, scientist; b. Rogers, Ark., Apr. 7, 1935; s. Jack Russell and Merle Clara (White) E.; m. Sandra Jean Reeves, Nov. 10, 1961; children: Michael Lynn, David Russell, Cristi Yvonne. BS in Engring., U. Tulsa, 1965. Computer engr. Remington Rand Univac, Illion, N.Y., 1960; rsch. tech. Pan Am. Petroleum Corp., Tulsa, 1960-65, rsch. engr., 1965-76; rsch. supr. Amoco Prodn. Co., Tulsa, 1976-89; pres. Environ. Drilling Tech., Inc., Tulsa, 1990—; prin. Estes Consulting Group, Tulsa, 1999—. Contbr. articles to profl. jours.; patentee in field. With USAF, 1955-59. Mem. ASME, N.E. Okla. Sq. Dance Assn. (bd. dirs. 1989-92), Am. Petroleum Inst. (chmn. internat. subcom. 13 1982-85, vice chmn. com. 13 1986-89, task group chmn. 1989—, Svc. award 1991), Internat. Drilling Contractors (chmn. drill bit standardization task group 1973-80), Am. Mgmt. Assn., Soc. Petroleum Engrs. (tech. editor Jour. Petroleum Tech. 1977-78, Svc. award 1985, program com. 1989-92), Am. Chem. Soc. (Svc. award 1984), Sci. Rsch. Soc. (internat. sci. fair judge), Sigma Xi. Office Phone: 918-294-0394. E-mail: jestes@olp.net.

ESTES, JAMES W., foundation administrator; b. Denton, Tex., Feb. 3, 1946; s. Frank Moore and Elizabeth Louise Estes; m. Jenifer Lynn Farrell, June 20, 1970; children: W. Todd, J. Brooke Estes Arellano. BS, U. N. Tex., Denton, 1968, MS, 1970; EdS, Vanderbilt U., Nashville, 1977, EdD, 1978. Asst. prof., coach Belmont U., Nashville, 1972—77; athletic dir. Grand Canyon U., Phoenix, 1978—82; psychologist pvt. practice, Phoenix, 1982—84; assoc. athletic dir. U. S. Fla., Tampa, 1984; dir., advancement U. N. Tex., Denton, 1984—86; pvt. cons. pvt. practice, Denton, Tex., 1986—90; regional dir., major gifts Tex. A&M Found., Dallas, 1990—. Cons., vocational guidance So. Baptist Convention, Nashville, 1970—72. Author: A Fast Ride on a Slow Merry-Go-Round, 1971; contbr. articles to profl. jours. Bd. mem. Grand Canyon Broadcasting, Phoenix, 1979—80, Retired Sr. Vol. Program, Denton, Tex., 2001—; deacon First Baptist Ch., Denton, Tex., 2001. Named Nat. Merit Scholar, Sears, 1964. Mem.: Coun. for ADvancement & Support of Edn. Republican. Baptist. Office: Tex A&M Found 1601 Bryan St Rm 02008 Dallas TX 75201 Office Phone: 214-812-7306.

ESTES, KENNETH WILLIAM, history professor, military officer; b. Seattle, Aug. 25, 1947; s. Victor Guy Estes and Lois Bernice Horth; m. Genevieve Perrin, Sept. 24, 2002; children: Caroline Estes Hougen, Gwendolyn Estes Haley. BSc, US Naval Acad., 1969; MA, Duke U., 1974; PhD, U. Md., 1984. Lt. col. USMC, DC, 1969—93; prof. history various edn!. insts., 1995—2004. Cons. Computing Technologies, Inc., Falls Church, Va., 1996—2001. Editor: (guide book) Marine Officer's Guide, (hand book) Handbook for Marine NCOs, (non-fiction) History in Dispute 18: The Spanish Civil War; author: Marines under Armor, Tanks on the Beaches, US Marine Corps Tank Crewman World War II, A European Anabais. Decorated Meritorious Svc. medal USMC, Def. Meritorious Svc. medal, Cruz de Merito (Naval) con Distinctivo Blanco Kingdom of Spain; recipient 3d Pl. Codd award as Outstanding Navy ROTC Instr., Am. Def. Preparedness Assn., 1984; fellow European Acad., Fed. Republic of Germany, 1982. Mem.: US Naval Inst., Soc. for Mil. History, Am. Hist. Assn (Gutenberg-e prize 2001). Home: 19202 39th Ave S Seattle WA 98188-5316 Personal E-mail: ken_estes@compuserve.com.

ESTES, MARY GWYN, art educator; b. Jackson, Miss., Oct. 6, 1953; d. Aubrey Homer and Evelyn Virginia (Fancher) Rone; m. Ray Clinton Estes; 1 child from previous marriage, Faith Victoria Toney. BFA, Delta State U. Cert. Art K-12 U. West Ga. Art tchr., 7-9 Memphis City Schools, 1977—79; art tchr. 7-12 Cross (SC) HS, 1979—94; art tchr. Cobb County Compton Elem., Powder Springs, Ga., 1994—. Head learning com. Compton Elem., Powder Springs, Ga., 1999—2000, head beautification com., 2001—04, mem. leadership team, 2005—. Editor: Collegiate Guidepost Mag., 1973—74, Miss. Delta Newspaper, 1973—75. Recipient 1st Degree Blackbelt award, 1996; grant, to paint mural Chattahoochie River Watershed, 2005. Master: Nat. Art Edn. Assn.; mem.: Ga. Art Edn. Assn., Delta Delta Delta (v.p. sorority 1974), Kappa Pi, Hon. Art Fraternity. Avocations: martial arts, oil painting, stained glass art. Personal E-mail: poohbr@comcast.net.

ESTES, MICHELE DAWN, multimedia designer; b. East Liverpool, Ohio, Jan. 17, 1970; d. Cathy and Charles Oyster; m. Geoffray A Estes, Aug. 17, 1996; children: Christopher, Jacob. BFA, Valdosta State U., 1988—93, MED in instrnl. tech., 1993—94; PhD in instrnl. tech., U. of Ga., 2002. Co-op: video asst. and tech. writing editor IBM, Atlanta, 1991—92; hall dir. Valdosta State U., 1993, instrnl. technolgy grad. asst., 1993—94; edn. program specialist U. Sys. of Ga. Bd. of Regents, 1994—99; instrnl. design and tech. specialist UGA Office of Instrnl. Support and Devel., Athens, Ga., 1999—2000; coord., instrnl. multimedia design and devel. U. of Ga. Office of Instrnl. Support and Devel., 2000—. Co-chmn. streaming com. U. of Ga., 2002—03; chmn., como conf. site selection subcom. Ga. Assn. for Instrnl. Tech., 2001—01, chmn., como conf. registration subcom., 2000; sect. leader, webct conf. planning com. U. of Ga., 2000; chmn., tech. adv. com. U. Sys. of Ga. Bd. of Regents, 1997—98; it student rep. U. of Ga., 2004—05, it doctoral student rep., 2003—04; mem., emma devel. team U. of Ga. Dept. of English, 2004—05; co-instr. U. of Ga., 2003—05. Dir.: (dvd) Universal Design: What Faculty Should Know, Thoughts for Discussion; contbr. chapters to books. Vol. St. Joseph Cath. Sch., Athens, Ga., 2003—05, Champions for Children Daycare, Athens, Ga., 2003—05; eucharistic min. Cath. Ctr. at UGA, Athens, Ga., 2002—05, baptismal class instr., 2002—05. Mem.: AERA (corr.), AECT (corr.; strategic planning taskforce, nat'l. nominating com., reviewer 2005—), Ga. Assn. for Instrnl. Tech. (life; past pres., pres., pres.-elect, bd. mem. at large 2002—). Achievements include research in emma universal design pilot study. Avocations: family, travel, writing, jazz, music. Office: OISD S Instrnl Plaza Univ of Georgia Athens GA 30602 Office Phone: 706-542-1582. Office Fax: 706-542-0518. E-mail: mestes@uga.edu.

ESTES, RICHARD, artist; b. Kewanee, Ill., 1932; Student, Chgo. Art Inst., 1951-55. Exhbns. include Whitney Mus. Am. Art, Mus. Modern Art, Guggenheim Mus., all N.Y.C., Rockhill Nelson Mus., Kansas City, Mo., Toledo Mus., Chgo. Art Inst., Des Moines Art Ctr., Mus. Contemporary Art, Chgo., High Mus. Art, Atlanta, Hirshorne Mus., Washinton, Richmond, Va. Mus. Art, Mus. Contemporary Art, Vienna, Austria, Ludwig Collection, Cologne, Fed. Republic Germany; numerous exhbns. including Documenta V, Kassel, Fed. Republic Germany, 1972, Venice Biennale, 1972, Whitney Mus. Ann., 1972, Va. Mus. Fine Arts, 1974, Boston Mus. Fine Arts, 1975, 78, Allan Stone Gallery, 1983, Adams-Middleton Gallery, Dallas, 1984, Greenville (S.C.) County Mus. Art, 1984, Whitney Mus. Am. Art, N.Y., 1982, Martha White Gallery, Louisville, 1984, Heckscher Mus., Huntington, N.Y., 1984, Walter Moos Gallery, Toronto, Ont., Can., 1984, Byer Mus. Arts, Evanston, 1984, Daimaru Mus., Osaka, Japan, 1985, Mus. Art, Ft. Lauderdale, 1986. Contemporary Art Ctr., New Orleans, 1986, San Francisco Mus. Modern Art, 1986-87, 90, Carpenter Ctr., Harvard U., 1990, Portland (Maine) Mus. Art, 1991, Whitney Mus., Stamford, Conn., 1991-92; traveling retrospective exhibit in Japan, Tokyo, Osaka and Hiroshima, Am. Fedn. of Arts; traveling print show various mus., 1993-95; one-man show at Marlborough Gallery, 1995, 97, 98, Centro Cultural Recoleta, Buenos Aires, 1999, Fine Art (London) Ltd., 2000. Address: 300 Central Park W New York NY 10024-1513*

ESTES, RICHARD MARTIN, lawyer; b. N.Y.C., June 27, 1933; s. Jack Estes and Irene Eva (Dessauer) Schwarz; m. Pamela Jane Graine, Mar. 18, 1965; children: Kenneth Murray, William Jonathan, Jessica Jane. BA, Yale Coll., 1955; LLB, Columbia U., 1959; LLM in Taxation, NYU, 1962. Bar: N.Y. 1959, Fla. 1976; U.S. Supreme Ct. 1962. Assoc. White & Case, N.Y.C., 1959-62, Root, Barrett, Cohen Knapp & Smith, N.Y.C., 1962-65; asst. tax counsel Rockefeller Family & Assocs., N.Y.C., 1965-68; tax counsel Bear, Stearns & Co., N.Y.C., 1968-70; assoc. to ptnr. Spear & Hill, N.Y.C., 1970-75; founding ptnr. Christy & Viener, N.Y.C., 1976-98, Salans, Hertzfeld, Heilbronn, Christy & Viener, N.Y.C., 1999—2004; of counsel Warshaw & Burstein, Cohn Schleimga, Kuh, LLP, 2005—. Lectr. in field. Contbr. articles to profl. jours. Trustee, sec., nomination com. N.Y.C. Police Found., 1971—; bd. mem., v.p., sec. Yale Project 55, Inc., N.Y.C., 1993—; trustee, treas. 1010 Tenants Corp., N.Y.C., 1988—. Maj. USAR, 1955-65. Honored as co-founder N.Y.C. Police Found., 1991. Mem. ABA, Assn. of the Bar of the City of N.Y. (libr. com.), N.Y. State Bar Assn. (tax sect.), Fla. Bar Assn., Univ. Club (coun., libr. and art com. 1976—), Grolier Club, Harmonie Club, Beach Point Club. Avocations: antiquarian book collector, exercise, reading, travel.

ESTES, SIMON LAMONT, opera singer, bass-baritone; b. Centerville, Iowa, Feb. 2, 1938; Studied with Charles Kellis, U. Iowa, 1956-63; student, Juilliard Sch., 1964-65. Appeared with major European and Am. operas including Deutche Opera, Boston Opera, Chgo. Lyric Opera, Met. Opera, Zurich Opera, Vienna Staatsoper, Paris Opera, numerous others; roles include Ramphis in Aida, Figaro in The Barber of Seville, Banquo in Macbeth, Oroveso in Norma, Dutchman in The Flying Dutchman, Amonasro in Aida, Wotan in Ring of the Nibelungen, Amonsaro in Aida, Gremin in Eugene Onegin, Porgy in Porgy and Bess, Amfortas in Parisfal, Orest in Elektra, King Philip in Don Carlos, Fiesco in Simon Boccanegra, Macbeth in Macbeth, London Promenade Concerts, 1989—; recs. include Spirituals, 1986' author (autobiography) In His Own Voice, 1999. Recipient Munich competition prize, 1965; Silver medal Tchaikowsky Competition, Moscow, 1966 Address: IMG Artists Europe 3 Burlington Ln Chiswick W4 2TH England Office: Janice Muyer & Asso LLC Ste 2214 250 W 57th St New York NY 10107-2206

ESTES, WILLIAM KAYE, psychologist, educator; b. Mpls., June 17, 1919; s. George D. and Mona Estes; m. Katherine Walker, Sept. 26, 1942; children: George E., Gregory W. Mem. faculty Ind. U., 1946—62, prof. psychology, 1955—60, research prof. psychology, 1960—62; faculty research fellow Social Sci. Research Council, 1952—55; lectr. psychology U. Wis., 1949; vis. prof. Northwestern U., 1959; fellow Center Advanced Study Behavioral Scis., 1955—56; spl. univ. lectr. U. London, 1961; prof. psychology, mem. Inst. Math. Studies Social Scis., Stanford, 1962—68; prof. Rockefeller U., 1968—79, Harvard U., 1978—89, prof. emeritus, 1989—; prof. Ind. U., 1999—. Chmn. Office Sci. and Engring. Personnel NRC, 1982—85, chmn. com. on prevention of nuclear war, 1984—89. Author: An Experimental Study of Punishment, 1944, Learning Theory and Mental Development, 1970, Models of Learning, Memory and Choice, 1982, Statistical Models in Behavioral Research, 1991, Classification and Cognition, 1994; co-author: Modern Learning Theory, 1954; contbr. articles to profl. jours.; editor: Handbook of Learning and Cognitive Processes, 1962—68, Psychol. Rev., 1977—82, Psychol. Sci., 1990—94; Jour. Exptl. Psychology, 1958—62. With AUS, 1944—46. Recipient U.S. Nat. medal of Sci., 1997. Fellow: AAAS, APA (pres. divsn. exptl. psychology 1958—59, Disting. Sci. Contbn. award 1962, gold medal for lifetime achievement in psychol. sci. 1992), Am. Acad. Arts and Scis.; mem.: NAS, Fedn. Behavioral Psychol. and Cognitive Scis. (v.p. 1988—91), Midwestern Psychol. Assn., N.Y. Acad. Scis. (life), N.Y. Acad. Scis. (hon.), Soc. Exptl. Psychologists (Warren medal 1963). Home: 2714 E Pine Ln Bloomington IN 47401-4423 Office: Ind U Psychology Bldg Bloomington IN 47405 E-mail: wkestes@indiana.edu.

ESTEVE, EDWARD V., lawyer; b. N.Y.C., May 29, 1937; m. Mildred Briand, June 10, 1961; children: Greg, Christopher, Kimberly. Grad., NYU, 1959; LLB, JD, N.Y. Law Sch., 1962. Ptnr. Taitz, Bernard & Esteve, Patchogue, N.Y., to 1997, Pelletreau & Pelletreau, Patchogue, 1997—98, Roe Wallace Esteve Taroff & Taitz, 1999—. Adj. prof. Touro Coll. Law, Huntington, N.Y., 1995—; mem. com. on character and fitness, 2d dept. N.Y. Appellate Divsn., 1991—. Bd. dirs. Red Cross (Suffolk chpt.), Adelante of Suffolk, La Union Hispanica, Three Village Youth Coun., 1972-90, Brookhaven Meml. Hosp., Patchogue, 1995—; v.p., officer Suffolk Acad. Law, 1977-89. Mem. N.Y. State Bar Assn. (gen. practice sect. 10th and 11th jud. dist. v.p. 1981-82, pres. com. access justice 1990-96), Suffolk County Bar Assn. (pres. 1989-90, bd. dirs. and exzc. com. 1977-93). Avocation: aviation. Office: Roe Wallace Esteve Taroff & Taitz LLP 31 Oak St PO Box 352 Patchogue NY 11772

ESTEVEZ, CARLOS IRWIN See SHEEN, CHARLIE

ESTEVEZ, ELIA, secondary education mathematics educator; b. Rio de Janeiro, July 2, 1961; came to the U.S., 1981; d. Benito and Maria Tereza (Vidal) Fernandez; m. Jose Estevez, June 3, 1984; children: Adriana, Gabriel, Alexis. BS, Hofstra U., 1988, MA, 1991; BS, Columbia U., 2002, PhD in Math. Edn., 2005. Cert. secondary math tchr. Math tchr. grades 7-12 Long Beach (N.Y.) Sch. Dist., 1989-91, Hempstead (N.Y.) H.S., 1992—. Rschr. Hofstra U., Hempstead, 1991, summer math. tchr., 1991-93. Avocations: travel, writing, reading, dance. Home: 72 Parma Rd Island Park NY 11558-1043 Office Phone: 516-292-7111.

ESTÉVEZ, L. ANTONIO, chemical engineer, educator; s. Germán Luis Estévez and Elena Victoria De Vidts; m. Mireya Montero Montero, May 18, 1974; children: Claudio Ignacio, Marcel André, Nicolás Sebastián. BS in Chem. Engring., U. Santiago, 1974; MS in Petrochemical Processes, Ctrl. U. Venezuela, 1977; PhD in Engring., U. Calif., Davis, 1983. Registered profl. engr., P.R., 1989. Instr. U. Santiago, Chile, 1973—75; part-time instr. U. Chile, 1975—75; asst. prof. Simón Bolívar U., Caracas, Venezuela, 1975—84, assoc. prof., 1984—86; assoc. prof. Sch. Pharmacy U. PR, San Juan, 1990—90, assoc. prof. Mayagüez, 1990—95, assoc. dir. dept., 1991—95, prof., 1995—, assoc. dean acad. affairs, dir. of grad. studies, 2001—03. Mem. minorities in grad. edn. com. Coun. Grad. Schs., Washington, 2002—03; vis. prof. U. PR, Mayagüez, 1987—90, Cornell U., Ithaca, NY, 1996—97. Contbr. articles to profl. jours. Recipient cert. Acknowledgment Acad. Excellence, Atlantic Richfield Co., 1981; fellow, Nat. Rsch. Fund, Venezuelan Govt., 1980—83. Mem.: Inter-Am. Confeden. Chem. Engring. (v.p. 1995—96, pres. 1996—98, past pres. 1998—2000, sec.-gen. 2000—, Víctor Márquez award 2000), AIChE (mem. societal impact oper. coun. 2001—04, mem. career and edn. oper. coun. 2005—). Office: I PR Dept Chem Engring Mayaguez PR 00681-9046 Office Phone: 787-832-4040 2573. Home Fax: 305-723-0904; Office Fax: 787-265-3818. Personal E-mail: antonio_estevez@netzero.net. E-mail: estevez@uprm.edu.

ESTEVEZ, RAMON See SHEEN, MARTIN

ESTEY, ELIHU HARRIS, medical educator; b. N.Y.C., July 15, 1946; s. Richard and Anne Estey; m. Cynthia Lee David; children: Emily, Anne. AB, Yale U., 1968; MD, Johns Hopkins U., 1972. Diplomate Am. Bd. Internal Medicine, subspecialty med. oncology Am. Bd. Internal Medicine. Asst. prof. medicine U. Tex. M.D. Anderson Cancer Ctr., Houston, 1980—88, assoc. prof. medicine, 1988—96, prof. medicine, 1996—. Mem.: Am. Soc. Clin. Oncology, Am. Soc. Hematology. Office: Univ Tex MD Anderson Cancer 1515 Holcombe Houston TX 77025 Office Phone: 713-792-7544. Business E-Mail: ehestey@mdanderson.org.

ESTILETTE, KATHLEEN C., music educator; b. Ft. Worth, Oct. 6, 1955; d. Thomas William and Norma Dean Crenshaw; m. Randall Bryan Harper, Oct. 1973 (div. 1980); children: Thomas Randall Harper, Stephen Bryan Harper; m. Michael Estilette, Mar. 31, 1989 (div. Apr. 2001). Grad., Jasper (Tex.) H.S., 1973; student in Piano Studies, 1996—. Sec. Jasper Meml. Hosp., 1980—83, Jasper Title and Abstract, 1983—86, Lawyers Title, Carrollton, Tex., 1986—89, Richard Jackson and Assoc., Dallas, 1989—92; sec., office mgr. Law Firm of Bill Reppeto, Dallas, 1992—96; owner, tchr. Piano Studio, Carrollton, 1995—. Asst. tchr. Piano Studio of Dr. Mary Humm, McKinney, Tex., 1997—98; singer and composer Step By Step, Dallas. Editor (scale book): Scale Technique, 1998. Mem., sponsor James Group-A Christ Centered 12-Step Program, Dallas, 1988—. Mem.: Carrollton Music Tchrs. Assn. (pres. 1999—2000, Tchr. of Yr. 1999—2000). Ch. Of Christ. Avocations: piano playing, singing, reading, cross stitching. Home: 3139 Barton Rd Carrollton TX 75007

ESTIN, HANS HOWARD, retired brokerage house executive; b. Prague, Czechoslovakia, Sept. 8, 1928; came to U.S., 1941, naturalized, 1946; m. Martha McCormick, Oct. 1990; children from previous marriage: Hilary Parker, Alexandra Howard; stepchildren: Sargent L. Goodchild, Jr., Abigail Goodchild, McKay Goodchild. AB, Harvard U., 1949; LL.D., Merrimac Coll., 1972, Boston U., 1977. Vice chmn., pres., chmn. bd. Harbor Nat. Bank, Boston, 1964-67; vice chmn. N.Am. Mgmt. Corp., Boston, 1974—2004, vice chmn. emeritus, 2004—. Trustee Putnam Group Mut. Funds, 1972-2001. Former trustee New Eng. Aquarium; chmn. bd. trustees Boston U., 1969-76; mem. Schepens Eye Rsch. Inst.; former bd. overseers Boys and Girls Clubs Boston, Inc. 1st lt. USAF, 1951-55. Decorated Knight, Order of Crown, Belgium, 1983, Order of Leopold, Belgium, 1990; named Hon. Consul of Belgium at Boston, 1970-90. Mem. Essex County Club (Manchester, Mass.). Home: 600 Summer St Manchester MA 01944-1626 Office: NAm Mgmt Corp Ten Post Office Sq Boston MA 02109 Business E-Mail: hestin@namco.nu.

ESTIN-KLEIN, LIBBYADA, advertising executive, medical writer; b. Newark, July 13, 1937; d. Barney and Florence B. (Tenkin) Straver; m. Harvey M. Klein, Sept. 9, 1984. Student, Syracuse U., 1955-57; BS, Columbia, 1960; RN, Columbia-Presbyn. Med. Ctr., 1960; cert., N.Y. Sch. Interior Design, 1962. Med. rsch. tech. writer, N.Y.C., 1960-62; pres. Libbyada Estin Interiors, N.Y.C., 1962-65; v.p. advt. and pub. relations Behrman/Estin Inc., N.Y.C., 1965-67; account exec., dir. pub. rels. J.S. Fullerton, Inc., N.Y.C., 1968-69, Kallir Philips Ross Inc., N.Y.C., 1969-71; copy supr. William Douglas McAdams Inc., N.Y.C., 1971-75, Sudler & Hennessey Inc., N.Y.C., 1975-80; v.p., exec. adminstr., creative dir. Grey Med. Advt. Inc., N.Y.C., 1980-84; founder, ptnr. Estin Sandler Comm. Inc., N.Y.C., 1984; v.p. Barnum Comm. Inc., N.Y.C., 1984-86; sr. v.p. ICE Comm., Inc., Rochester, N.Y., 1986-87; pres. Estin-Klein Comm. Inc., Rochester and Pittsford, N.Y., 1987—. Dir. health group Robert Comm., Inc., East Rochester, N.Y., 1993-95; bd. dirs., Perinatal Network of Monroe County, Pathways to Health. mem. PRSA Health Acad. Mem. Pub. Rels. Soc. Am., Advt. Women N.Y., Am. Advt. Fedn., Advt. Coun. of Rochester, Rochester Sales and Mktg. Execs. Club, Mktg. Communicators of Rochester, Am. Med. Writers Assn., Women in Comm., Healthcare Mktg. and Comms. Coun., Healthcare Bus. Women's Assn., Am. Nurses Assn., Allied Bd. Trade, Columbia-Presbyn. Hosp. Alumnae Assn., Columbia U. Alumnae Assn., Syracuse U. Alumnae Assn., Sigma Theta Tau, Delta Phi Epsilon. Home and Office: 289 Garnsey Rd Pittsford NY 14534-4540 Personal E-mail: libbyada@aol.com.

ESTLER, SUZANNE E., education educator; b. Paterson, NJ, Sept. 16, 1944; d. Louis Calder and Beatrice VanderVoort Estler; life ptnr. Paula D. Johnson. BA, Rutgers U., New Brunswick, N.J., 1966; MA, Ohio U., Athens, OH, 1969; PhD, Stanford U., Calif., 1978. Grad. asst. Stanford U., 1973—76; resident dir. Ohio U., Athens, 1967—69; asst. dir. of residences SUNY Binghamton, Vestal, NY, 1969—70, dir. of residences, 1970—71, coord. of student svcs. coll. in the woods, 1971—73; vis. instr. of higher edn. Claremont Grad. Sch., Claremont, Calif., 1976—77; asst. prof. of higher edn. U. of Wash., Seattle, 1979—84; assoc. prof. of higher ednl. leadership U. of Maine, Orono, 1984—, dir. of equal opportunity, 1986—97. Cons. Nat. Ctr. for Higher Edn. Mgmt. Systems, Boulder, Colo., 1978—80. Author: Who Calls the Shots? Sports and University Leadership Culture and Decision-Making, 2005; contbr. articles to profl. jours., chapters to books. Pres. Audubon Expdn. Inst., Belfast, Maine, 1988—2003. Recipient Janet Badger Vol. award, Rape Response Svcs., 1998, M Club, U. of Maine, 1999; Thomas James Jr. fellowship, Stanford U., 1975—76. Mem.: Assn. for the Study of Higher Edn., Am. Ednl. Rsch. Assn. Avocations: lobstering, boating, travel, reading, gardening. Office: University of Maine Merrill Hall Orono ME 04469-5749 Business E-Mail: estler@umit.maine.edu.

ESTLUND, CYNTHIA, law educator; BA summa cum laude, Lawrence U., 1978; JD, Yale U., 1983. Law clk. to Juege Patricia Wald US Ct. Appeals (DC Cir.), 1983—84; assoc. Bredhoff & Kaiser, Washington, DC, 1985—89; prof. U. Tex. Sch. Law, 1989—99, Columbia Law Sch., NYC, 1999—, Isidor and Seville Sulzbacher prof. law. Contbr. articles to law jours. Office: Columbia U 435 W 116th St New York NY 10027 Office Phone: 212-854-5084. E-mail: ce76@columbia.edu.

ESTREICHER, SAMUEL, lawyer, educator; b. Bergen, Democratic Republic Germany, Sept. 29, 1948; came to U.S., 1951; s. David and Rose (Abramowicz) E.; m. Aleta Glaseroff, Aug. 10, 1969; children: Michael, Hannah. BA, Columbia U., 1970, JD, 1975; MS in Labor Rels., Cornell U., 1974. Bar: N.Y. 1976, D.C. 1978, U.S. Dist. Ct. (so. and ea. dists.) N.Y., U.S. Ct. Appeals (2d and 11th cirs.), U.S. Supreme Ct. Law clk. to assoc. judge Harold Leventhal, U.S. Ct. Appeals (D.C. cir.), 1975-76; assoc. Cohn, Glickstein, Lurie, Ostrin & Lubell, N.Y.C., 1976-77; law clk. to assoc. justice Lewis F. Powell Jr. U.S. Supreme Ct., Washington, 1977-78; prof. law NYU, 1978—; of counsel Cahill, Gordon & Reindel, N.Y.C., 1984-98; labor and employment counsel O'Melveny & Myers LLP, N.Y.C., 1998—2002; spl. counsel Morgan Lewis & Bockius LLP, N.Y.C., 2002—03; of counsel Jones Day, N.Y.C., 2003—. Vis. prof. law Columbia U., 1984-85; dir. NYU-Inst. Jud. Adminstrn., 1991—, Ctr. for Labor and Employment Law at NYU Sch. Law, 1996—; prof. law NYU Sch. Law, 1978—, Charles L. Denison chair, 2002-04, Dwight D. Opperman chair, 2004—. Author: Redefining the Supreme Court, 1986, Labor Law and Business Change, 1988, The Law Governing the Employment Relationship,1990, 2d edit., 1992, Labor Law: Text and Materials, 5th edit., 2003, Procs. of 49th NYU Annual Conference on Labor, 1997, Employee Representation in the Emerging Workplace: Alternatives/Supplements to Collective Bargaining, 1999, Sexual Harassment in the Workplace, 1999, Foundations of Labor and Employment Law, 2000, Employment Discrimination and Employment Law, 2000, 2d edit., 2004, Global Competition and The American Employment Landscape, 2000, Employment Law, 2004, Employment Law Discrimination, 2004, others; editor-in-chief Columbia U. Law Rev., 1974-75; contbr. articles to profl. jours. Pulitzer Fund scholar, 1966-70; Herbert H. Lehman fellow, 1970-72. Mem. ABA (labor and employment law sect. 1978—, sec. sect. on labor and employment law 2004—), N.Y. State Bar Assn. (labor and employment law sect. 1980—), Assn. Bar City N.Y. (chmn. labor and employment law com. 1984-87), Am. Law Inst. (reporter Restatement of Employment Law 2000—). Office: NYU Sch Law 40 Washington Sq S New York NY 10012 Office Phone: 212-998-6226. E-mail: samuel.estreicher@nyu.edu.

ESTREN, MARK JAMES, communications executive, television producer, writer; b. N.Y.C., July 12, 1948; s. Solomon and Elaine Estren; m. S. Amber Gordon, July 4, 1986; children: Meredith, Nicholas. BA in Classics and English cum laude, Wesleyan U., 1968; MS in Journalism, Columbia U., 1970; MA in English and Psychology, U. Buffalo, 1973, PhD in English and Psychology, 1978. Producer, reporter, anchor Stas. WBEN & WBEN-TV, Buffalo, 1971-75; exec. producer Stas. WCBS-Radio and TV, N.Y.C., 1975-76, Sta. WCAU-TV, Phila., 1976-79; sr. producer ABC News, N.Y.C. and Washington, 1979-80; editor Phila. Inquirer, 1980-81, Miami (Fla.) Herald, 1980-81; exec. producer The Nightly Bus. Report, Miami, Fla., 1981-84; sr. v.p., gen. mgr. Fin. News Network, N.Y.C. and L.A., 1984-87; editor-in-chief High Tech. Bus. mag., Boston and N.Y.C., 1987-89; exec. v.p. Infotechnology, Inc., N.Y.C. and Washington, 1987-90, UPI, Washington, 1988-90; founder, pres. UPI TV, Fairfax, Va., 1989-90; pres., chief exec. officer TransCentury Comm., Inc., Easton, Conn. and McLean, Va., 1984—. Adj. prof. Columbia U., 1987-89; webmaster www.infodad.com, 1999—. Author: A History of Underground Comics, 1974, rev. edit., 1987, 89, 93; co-author: In a Word, 1992; contbg. editor Miami Herald, Bottom Line/Personal, Bottom Line/Tomorrow, Boardroom Reports, Bottom Line/Business, Bottom Line/Health, Washington Office Mag., Moneysworth, Parent Weekly, Va. Parent News. Trustee Boston Cath. TV Ctr., 1987-89; vice chmn. Arthritis Found., Washington, 1992-94, chmn. commn. com., 1990-92. Pulitzer Found. fellow, 1970. Avocations: classical music, herpetology. Office: 1163 Old Gate Ct Mc Lean VA 22102-2532 Personal E-mail: infodad@juno.com.

ESTRIDGE, LARRY D., lawyer; b. Rock Hill, SC, Jan. 31, 1944; BA in Hist., cum laude, Furman U., 1966; JD, Harvard U., 1969. Bar: Ga. 1969, SC 1973, admitted to practice: US Dist. Ct., Dist. SC, Dist. Ga., US Ct. of Appeals (4th Cir.). Assoc. Alston, Miller & Gaines (now Alston & Bird), Atlanta, 1971—72, Wyche, Burgess & Parham, P.A., Greenville, SC, 1972—75, mem., 1975—98; mng. mem., econ. develop. dept. and real estate dept. Womble Carlyle Sandridge & Rice, PLLC, Greenville, SC, mem. mgmt. com. Pro bono legal svcs. Habitat for Humanity; bd. dir. Evergreen Resources, Inc., 1988—; lectr. in field. Co-author (chpt.) Oral Advocacy, Apellete Practice Manuel. Former pres. Furman U. Alumni Assn.; SC chair Harvard Law Sch. Fund, 1973—76; legal divsn. chair Greenville United Way, 1974; pres. Citizens for Greenville (local polit. initiatives, 1975—77, Greenville Ctrl. Area Partnership (downtown revitalization), 1982—83; bd. trustee Carolina Piedmont Found. (U. SC-Spartanburg), 1989—96, Lees-McRae Coll., 1990—93; mem. Reedy River Basin Task Force (City of Greenville), 1990—91; bd. gov. Thornblade Club, 1990—2001, pres., 1990—2001; bd. trustee Furman U., 1996—2001, 2001—; bd. dir. Greater Greenville C.ofC., 1997—2000, general counsel, 1997; bd. dir., pres. Children's Mus. of the Upstate, 1998—2001. Capt. U.S. Army, 1969—71, Ft. Jackson, SC, battalion def. counsel for courts martial U.S. Army, S. Vietnam. Decorated Bronze Star, Vietnam Svc. medal. Mem.: ABA, Greenville County Bar Assn., Ga. Bar Assn., SC Bar Assn. (mem., pro bono program and real estate sect., House of Delegates), Southern Club (pres.), Blue Key Honor Soc. Office: Womble Carlyle Sandridge & Rice PLLC 700 Poinett Plz 104 S Main St PO Box 10208 Greenville SC 29603 Office Phone: 864-255-5401. Office Fax: 864-255-5481. Business E-Mail: lestridge@wcsr.com.

ESTRIN, DEBORAH PERRY, human resources executive; b. Waynesboro, Va., Dec. 28, 1948; d. James William and Annie Lee (Miller) Perry; m. Abbott Simon Estrin, Feb. 6, 1982. BS in Humanities, U. Tenn., 1982; MBA, Fairleigh Dickerson U., 1988. Dir. human resources Ciba Geigy Pharms., Summit, N.J., 1983-89; v.p. human resources Geneva Pharms. divsn. Ciba Geigy Pharms., Broomfield, Colo., 1989-91, USPCI subs. Union Pacific, Houston, 1994-96, N.Y. Power Authority, White Plains, 1994-96; sr. v.p. human resources Phila. Gas Works, 1996-98; v.p. human resources Maersk-Sealand, Inc., Madison, N.J., 1999-2000; dir. human resources Thames Water, London and N.J., 2001—04. Adj. prof. Audrey Cohen Coll., 1994-96; dir. S.C. Ctr. for Dispute Resolution; bd. dir. Beaufort County Transportation Authority. Mem. Beaufort County Transp. Authority. E-mail: fitzaddison@aol.com.

ESTRIN, HERBERT ALVIN, financial consultant, consultant, film company executive; b. Jamaica, N.Y., May 4, 1925; s. Joseph and Minnie (Haskell) E.; m. Phyllis Glassman, Jan. 28, 1951; children— Myrna Hope, Richard Lawrence. BS in Acctg, N.Y. U., 1949. With Columbia Pictures Industries, Inc., N.Y.C., 1953-73, v.p., 1971-73; v.p., treas., chief fin. officer Prudential Bldg. Maintenance Corp., N.Y.C., 1973-79; v.p., treas. Bolt Corp., South Laguna, Calif., 1979; sr. v.p. fin. and adminstrn. Warner Home Video Inc. subs. Warner Communications, 1981-83; dir. ops. adminstrn. United Satellite Communications Inc., 1983-85; v.p. fin. and adminstrn. Rainbow Home Video div. Rainbow Program Enterprises Co., 1986-88; fin. cons., 1986—. Served with U.S. Army, 1943-46.

ESTRIN, JUDITH, computer company executive; m. Bill Carrico. BS in Maths. and Computer Sci., UCLA; MSEE, Stanford U. Co-founder Bridge Comms.; pres., CEO Network Computing Devices; chief tech. officer, sr. v.p. Cisco Sys., Inc., San Jose; chmn. Packet Design, Palo Alto, 2002—. Bd. dirs. Fed. Express, Sun Microsystems, Walt Disney Co. Named to, Women in Tech. Internat. Hall Fame. Office: Packet Design Inc 3400 Hillview Ave Bldg 3 Palo Alto CA 94304 Fax: 408-526-4100.

ESTRIN, KARI (KAREN RUTH ESTRIN), theater producer, agent, consultant; b. Plainfield, NJ, Nov. 5, 1954; d. Herman Albert and Pearl (Simon) E. BA with honors, Ramapo Coll. of NJ, 1976. Founder, exec. dir. Black Sheep Concerts and Publs., Inc., Cambridge, Mass., 1980-86; editor The Black Sheep Rev., 1982-85; co-producer (album) Great Acoustics, 1985; artist mgr., agt. Tony Rice/Rounder Records, 1981-85; tour mgr. Suzanne Vega/A&M Records, 1985, Peter Murphy Tour/Island Records, 1987, Kevin Brown Ryko Disc/Chrysalis, 1991; founder, cons. Palomine Mgmt., 1984—92; asst. producer Newport Folk Festival Festival Prodns., Inc., NYC,

1987; artist and tour mgr. 3 Mustaphas 3/Ryko Disc, 1988-91; artist asst. Suzy Bogguss/Capitol Records, 1989; mgr. Kanda Bongo Man, 1991, 93; tour mgr. Irma Thomas/Rounder Records, 1993, Papa Wemba/Real World Records, 1995; booking & spl. events dir. Caffe Milano, 1998; owner. prin. Kari Estrin, Mgr., Cons., Nashville, 1995—. Nat. promoter Rounder Records, Cambridge, Mass., 1979; asst. to dir. Berkshire Mt. Bluegrass Festival, Hillsdale, NY, 1980—81; assoc. prodr. Gt. N.E. Prodns., Townsend, Mass., 1986, Pickin' for Merle series N,C, Pub. TV, Rsch. Triangle Park, 1992; chairperson events ECO, Nashville, 1990; bd. dirs., vol. Sta. WPLN, 1991—92, pres. vol bd. dirs., 1993—94; cons. Marie Watson Meml. Festival, Wilkesboro, NC, 1992—93, asst. festival dir., 1993; co-founder Chris Austin Songwriting Contest, Nashville/Wilkesboro, 1992—93; artist mgr. Wayland Patton, 1993—94, David Llewellyn & Rob Lures, 2003—; talent coord. Pro Events Summer Lights, 1997; nat. advt. mgr. Sing Out ! mag., 1995—96; co-prodr. Americana Music Assn. Conv., Nashville, 2000; club booking agt. Radio Cafe, Nashville, 2000—01, 3rd and Lindsley, Nashville, 2002; prodr. Woody Guthrie Month, Nashville, 2003, Authentic Voice Compilation CD, 2004; local co-chair Folk Alliance Conf. Nat. Conf., Nashville, 2003. Editor: How to be Your Own Booking Agent and Save Thousands of Dollars, 1997. Bd. dirs. Hey, Rube Folk Music Orgn., 1983-86, Folk Arts Network, Cambridge, 1983-85, Folk Arts Ctr. of New Eng., Cambridge, 1982-84; sec., newsletter editor Eastwood Neighbors Bd., 1995-97. Avocations: catering and cooking, travel, performing arts. Home and Office: 1415 Sumner Ave Nashville TN 37206-2533

ESTRIN, MELVYN J., computer products company executive; b. 1942; Co-chmn., co-CEO Nat. Intergroup, Inc., Carrollton, Tex., 1997—; co-chmn, co-CEO McKesson Health Corp., Carrollton, Tex., 1996; also bd. dirs.; chmn. U. Rsch. Corp., Bethesda, Md.; co-CEO Phar-Mor. Inc., Youngstown, Ohio. Mng. ptnr. Centaur Ptnrs., L.P.; chmn., pres., CEO Am. Health Svcs.; v.p., dir. Spectro Industries; founder First Women's Bank of Md.; pres. FWB Bancorporation, Rockville, Md.; chmn. FWB Bancorporation.; chmn. Estrin International, Inc.; with Estrin Realty and Devel. Corp.; bd. dirs. Washington Gas Light Co. Trustee U. Pa.; active Endowment Bd. of the Kennedy Ctr., The Econ. Club of Washington, The Washington Opera; nat. vice chmn. State of Israel Bonds; apptd. by Pres. Bush commr.Nat. Capital Planning Commn.; apptd. Nat. Coun. for the Performing Arts, John F. Kennedy Ctr. Recipient Eleanor Roosevelt Humanities award for Community Svc., 1986. Office: Phar-Mor Inc 20 Federal Plz W Ste 3 Youngstown OH 44503

ESTRIN, RICHARD WILLIAM, real estate broker; b. NYC, Apr. 16, 1932; s. Max and Ruth (Lillienthal) E.; m. Alison Kiendl Stewart, Mar. 13, 1971. BA, CCNY, 1953; grad., Realtor Inst., 2000. Reporter Pk. Row News Svc., NYC, 1953-55; with Newsday, Inc., Long Island, NY, 1955-85, sucessl. Sunday news editor, Part II editor, sr. editor news, until 1983, exec. news editor N.Y.C. Newsday, 1983-85; weekend editor Herald-Tribune, Sarasota, Fla., 1985-86, news editor, 1986-90, asst. mng. editor, 1990-97; v.p. Longview Realty, Longboat Key, Fla., 1999-2001, pres., 2001—. Recipient First Place Lifestyle Journalism awards J.C. Penney-U. M., 1974, 75 Mem. Kiwanis, Phi Beta Kappa. Office Phone: 941-383-6112. Business E-Mail: longviewrealty@att.net.

ESTRUP, FAIZA FAWAZ, physician, educator; came to the U.S., 1951; m. Peder Jan Estrup, Sept. 15, 1960 AB in Physics, Boston U., 1953; MSc in Molecular Biophysics & Biochem., Yale U., 1960, PhD in Molecular Biophysics & Biochem., 1961; MD in Medicine, Brown U., 1975. Diplomate Nat. Bd. Med. Examiners, Am. Bd. Internal Medicine, Am. Bd. Rheumatology; med. lic., R.I., Calif. Postdoctoral fellow Inst. Molecular Biology & Biophysics, U. Geneva, 1960-61; rsch. biophysicist The Bell Tel. Labs., Murray Hills, N.J., 1962-63; vis. asst. prof. Haverford (Pa.) Coll., 1964-65, sr. rsch. assoc. biology, 1965-67; sr. rsch. assoc. divsn. of biology Brown U., 1968-69; asst. prof. C.C. R.I., Providence, 1969-71; dir. Arthritis Ctr. R.I., Providence, 1980—. Chief divsn. rheumatology Meml. Hosp. R.I., Pawtucket, 1983—; clin. asst. prof. medicine Brown U., Providence, 1984-91, assoc. prof. medicine, 1991-99, assoc. dean medicine, 1999—, prof. medicine, 2000—. Mem. editl. bd. Brown U. Medicine mag., 1999; contbr. articles to profl. jours. Mem. med. and sci. com. Arthritis Found., Providence, 1982—, bd. govs. R.I. chpt., 1982-91, 94-95. Named R.I. Woman Physician of Yr., 2002; named one of Am. Top Physicians, rheumatology, Consumers Rsch. Coun. Am., 2003; recipient Education award, Arthritis Found., 1993, Tchg. Excellence award, Brown Med. Sch., 2002; fellow, Wayland Coll., 1999. Fellow ACP (exec. coun. R.I. chpt. 1983-91), Am. Coll. Rheumatology (founder), Am. Rheumatism Assn.; mem. AMA, R.I. Med. Soc., Providence Med. Soc., Sigma Xi. Avocations: travel, lecturing to community on rheumatic diseases. Home: 2221 St James Dr Santa Barbara CA 93105 Office: Brown U Sch Medicine Box G Providence RI 02912

ESTRUP, PEDER JAN, physics and chemistry educator; b. Copenhagen, July 15, 1931; came to U.S., 1956; s. Lauritz A. and Alice (Horneman) E.; m. Faiza Fawaz, Sept. 15, 1960. M.Sc., Poly. Inst. Denmark, Copenhagen, 1954; PhD (Fulbright fellow, Sheffield Sci. fellow), Yale, 1959; Postdoctoral fellow, European Center Nuclear Research, Geneva, 1959-61. Mem. tech. staff Bell Telephone Labs., Murray Hill, N.J., 1961-64; rsch. scientist Bartol Rsch. Found., Swarthmore, Pa., 1964-67; prof. physics, chemistry Brown U., Providence, 1967—, chmn. dept. chemistry, 1989-96, Newport Rogers prof. chemistry and physics, 1992—, dean Grad. Sch. and Rsch., 1996—. Assoc. editor Jour. Vacuum Sci. and Tech., 1988-94; sr. editor Jour. Phys. Chemistry, 1990-95; mem. editorial bd. Progress in Surface Sci., 1982-97, Jour. Phys. and Chem. Reference Data, 1993—. Served to lt. Danish Army, 1954-56. Fellow Am. Phys. Soc., Am. Vacuum Soc. (exec. com. surface sci. divsn.); mem. Am. Chem. Soc. Research in physics and chemistry of surfaces. Home: 15 Adelphi Ave Providence RI 02906-4119

ESTY, DANIEL CUSHING, law educator, lawyer; b. Boston, June 6, 1959; s. John Cushing and Katharine (Cole) E.; m. Elizabeth Henderson, Oct. 20, 1984. AB, Harvard U., 1981; BA, Oxford U., 1983; JD, Yale U., 1986. Bar: Calif. 1986, US Ct. Internat. Trade 1987, DC 1988, US Dist Ct. DC 1988. US Ct. Appeals (Fed. Cir.) 1988. With Arnold & Porter, Washington, 1986-89; spl. asst. to adminstr. EPA, Washington, 1989-90, dep. chief of staff, 1990-91, dep. asst. adminstr. for policy, 1991-93; sr. fellow Inst. for Internat. Econs., Washington, 1993-94; assoc. prof. Environ. Law and Policy Yale U., New Haven, 1994—2004, prof., 2001—, dir. Ctr. for Environ. Law and Policy, 1994—, assoc. dean Sch. Forestry and Environ. Studies, 1998—2002, dir. World Fellows Prog., 2001—. Vis. prof. INSEAD, Fontainebleau, France, 2000—01. Author: Greening the GATT: Trade, Environment, and the Future, 1994, Asian Dragons and Green Trade, 1996, Sustaining the Asia Pacific Miracle: Environmental Protection and Economic Integration, 1997, Thinking Ecologically: The Next Generation of Environmental Policy, 1997, Regulatory Competition and Economic Integration, 2001, Environmental Performance Measurement: The Global Report 2001-2002, 2002, Greening the Americas: NAFTA's Lessons for Hemispheric Trade, 2002, Global Environmental Governance: Options and Opportunities, 2002. Office: Yale Ctr for Environ Law and Policy 205 Prospect St New Haven CT 06511-2106 also: PO Box 208215 New Haven CT 06520 Office Phone: 203-432-1602. Office Fax: 203-432-8095. E-mail: daniel.esty@yale.edu.*

ESTY, DAVID CAMERON, marketing and communications executive; b. Mt. Kisco, N.Y., May 26, 1932; s. John Cushing and Virginia (Place) E.; m. Elizabeth Gunn; children: John Philip, Mary Virginia, David Cameron, Cynthia Elizabeth. BA, Amherst Coll., 1954. Sr. v.p. J. Walter Thompson, N.Y.C., 1960-68; pres., CEO T.D.I., N.Y.C., 1968-75; CEO Douglas Leigh, Inc., N.Y.C., 1975-76; founder Catalyst Corp., 1976-78; CEO BIS Communications Corp., N.Y.C., 1979-82; owner, CEO Esty Assocs., Inc., Darien, Conn.; COO The Alden Group, N.Y.C., 1990-92; owner. CEO MarkeTeam, Inc., 1992—; prin. Adventure Assets, Inc., Cambridge, Mass., 1997—. Bd. dirs. World Sports Humanitarian Hall of Fame, Boise, Idaho, Inst. Internat. Sport., Kingston, R.I.; CEO, Pacific Beacon Co., Seattle. Author: Somebody Close to You is on Drugs, 1971. Mem. Nat. Ski Patrol (dist. svc. award 1995); EMT; pres. Class of '54, Amherst Coll., dist. svc. awd., 1999; pres. Friends Tuckerman Ravine, North Conway, N.H. Capt. USAF Res., 1950-67. Mem. Ad Coun. (dir., mem. exec. com. emeritus), Young Pres. Orgn. (49er) Home: PO Box 756 Waitsfield VT 05673 Office Phone: 802-279-8818. Personal E-mail: daveesty@gmart.net.

ESTY, JOHN CUSHING, JR., writer, educator, not-for-profit developer; b. White Plains, N.Y., Aug. 9, 1928; s. John Cushing and Virginia (Place) E.; m. Katharine Woolsey Cole, Dec. 21, 1955; children: Daniel Cushing, Paul Cameron, Benjamin Cole, Joshua Dwight. BA, Amherst Coll., 1950, LHD (hon.), 1970; MA, Yale U., 1951; postgrad., U. Calif., Berkeley, 1959-60. Asst. dean, asst. dir. admissions Amherst Coll., 1953-58, asso. dean, 1958-63, lectr. math., 1958-63; headmaster Taft Sch., Watertown, Conn., 1963-72; research asso. in edn. Harvard U., 1972-73; scholar-in-residence U. Mass. Sch. Edn., 1972-73; sr. staff asso. Edn. Devel. Center, Newton, Mass., 1973-74; staff asso. Rockefeller Bros. Fund, N.Y.C., 1973-78; pres. Nat. Assn. Ind. Schs., 1978-91; adj. lectr. U. Mass., 1978—2002. Pres. bd. Coun. for Am. Pvt. Edn., 1987-89. Author: Choosing Private School, 1974. Trustee Amherst Coll., 1970-76; trustee, bd. chmn. Greeley Found., Mass., 1991-2000; dir., founder Recruiting New Tchrs., Inc., 1988—2003; assoc. for bd. devel. Nat. Ctr. Nonprofit Bds., 1993—2003. 1st lt. USAF, 1951-53. Mem. Phi Beta Kappa, Sigma Xi. Clubs: Univ. (N.Y.C.), Century Assn. (N.Y.C.).

ESWEIN, BRUCE JAMES, II, human resources specialist; b. San Mateo, Calif., Oct. 26, 1951; s. Bruce James and Janet Gordon (Copeland) Eswein; m. Sarah Anne Shames, Feb. 7, 1981 (div.); children: Thomas Jonathan, Elizabeth Anne. Student, U. Wash., 1969-71; AB, U. Calif.-Berkeley, 1973, MBA, 1977. Brand asst. Clorox Co., Oakland, Calif., 1977-79, coll. rels. mgr., 1979-83; mgr. exec. recruitment and devel. BBDO Worldwide, N.Y.C., 1983-84, v.p., 1984-87, v.p. personnel adminstrn., 1987-88, v.p. human resources, mgr. worldwide tng. and devel., 1988-89, v.p. human resources internat., 1989-90, v.p., dir. human resources internat., 1990-95, sr. v.p., dir. human resources internat., 1995-97; cons. Newman Group, N.Y.C., 1997—. Mem.: Soc. Human Resources Mgmt., U. Calif. Berkeley Bus. Sch. Alumni Assn. (bd. dirs. 1980—83), Phi Beta Kappa, Chi Psi (v.p. 1972—73, bd. dirs. 1979—82, trustee endl. trust 1983—84, trustee emeritus 1984—). Episcopalian. Home: 27 Scenic Dr Apt H Croton On Hudson NY 10520-1822

ETCHEMENDY, JOHN, academic administrator, educator; b. Reno; m. Nancy Etchemendy; 1 child, Max. Bachelors Degree, Masters Degree, U. Nev.; PhD, Stanford U., 1982. Lectr. Princeton U., 1981—82, asst. prof., 1982—83; faculty philosophy dept. Stanford U., 1983—, sr. assoc. dean Sch. Humanities and Scis., 1993—97, provost, 2000—, mem. Symbolic Systems Program, sr. rschr. Ctr. for Study of Language and Info. Faculty mem. Symbolic Sys. Program Stanford U., sr. rschr. Ctr. for the Study of Lang. and Info. Author: Hyperproof, 1994, Language, Proof and Logic, 1999; editor: Jour. Symbolic Logic; mem. editl. bd. Synthese, Philosophia Mathematica. Mem.: Assn. for Symbolic Logic (mem. governing coun.), Am. Philos. Assn. Office: Office of the Provost Bldg 10 Stanford Univ Stanford CA 94305-2061 E-mail: etch@csli.stanford.edu.

ETCHESON, WARREN WADE, business administration educator; b. Bainbridge, Ind., May 15, 1920; s. Raymond W. and Rosetta (Evans) E.; m. Marianne Newgent, May 30, 1947; children: Denise Elene, Crayton Wade. BS, Ind. U., 1943; MA, U. Iowa, 1951, PhD, 1956. Adminstrv. sec., exec. sec., nat. sec. Delta Chi Nat. Fraternity, 1946-56; lectr. Santo Tomas U., Manila, 1946, U. Iowa, 1951-54; asst. prof. U. Wash., 1954-56, assoc. prof., 1956-60, prof. Sch. Bus. Adminstrn., 1960-90, assoc. dean Bus. Adminstrn., 1974-87, prof. emeritus, 1990—. Fulbright prof. Istanbul, Turkey, 1963-64. Author: Pazarlama, 1964, Consumerism, 1972. Served to lt. U.S. Army, 1942-46. Mem. Alpha Kappa Psi, Phi Eta Sigma, Beta Gamma Sigma, Delta Chi. Home: 6625 NE 132nd St Kirkland WA 98034-1614

ETEFIA, FLORENCE VICTORIA, school psychologist; b. Alton, Ill., Feb. 13, 1946; d. Esau and Pearl (Taylor) Anthony. BA, Mich. State U., 1968; MAT, Oakland U., Rochester, Mich., 1972; EdS, Wayne State U., 1977, MA, 1987, postgrad. Cert. tchr. mentally impaired, Mich.; spl. edn. supr., Mich.; cert. tchr. mentally impaired, learning disabled, K-8 gen. edn., psychology, Mich. Special edn. tchr. Sch. Dist. of Pontiac, Mich. Mem. NEA, Mich. Edn. Assn., Pontiac Edn. Assn., Delta Sigma Theta. Home: 3035 Debra Ct Auburn Hills MI 48326-2044

ETGEN, ANN, ballet educator, artistic director, choreographer; b. Dallas; d. Eddy R. Etgen and Myrtle (Applegate) Etgen; life ptnr. Bill Atkinson, Aug. 16, 1961. Dance, active Arts Magnet Sch., 1980, 81, 82, 83. Dancer Met. Opera Ballet, N.Y.C., 1958—60. Artistic dir. Etgen-Atkinson Sch. of Ballet, Dallas, 1962—, Dallas Met. Ballet, 1964—; dance panel Tex. Fine Arts Com., 1978—79. Dancer (Broadway musicals) Brigadoon, Carousel; guest dancer Omnibus History of Dance for Agnes De Mille, 1957, host S.W. Regional Ballet Festival, 1973, Creator (ballets) Dallas Met. Ballet. Recipient choreography plan award, Nat. Assn. Regional Ballet, 1983; grantee NEA choreography grantee, 1976, Tex. Fine Arts Commn., 1973, 1976—77, Mobile Oil, 1979, 500 Inc., 1978—79. Mem.: S.W. Regional Ballet Assn. (membership chmn. 1986—87), Nat. Assn. Regional Ballet. Presbyterian. Office: Etgen Atkinson Ballet School 6815 Hillcrest Ave Dallas TX 75205-1308

ETGES, FRANK JOSEPH, parasitology educator; b. Chgo., June 18, 1924; s. Joseph Peter and Anna Marie (Foss) E.; m. Ruth Camille Storkan, Sept. 20, 1948 (div. June 1984); children: Robert J., William J., Anne C., David J., Thomas J.; m. Lesta Judith Cooper-Freytag, July 6, 1985. AB, U. Ill., 1948, MS, 1949; PhD, NYU, 1953. Asst. prof. U. Ark., Fayetteville, 1953-54, U. Cin., 1954-59, assoc. prof., 1959-66, prof. parasitology, 1966-95; prof. emeritus, 1995—. Rsch. assoc. U.S. Army Tropical Rsch. Med. Lab., San Juan, P.R., 1961-62; guest investigator London Sch. Tropical Medicine and Hygiene, 1971-72. Sgt. U.S. Army, 1943-46, ETO, PTO. NSF rsch. grantee, 1959-65; La. State U. Med. Sch. rsch. fellow, Santo Domingo, P.R., 1961-62, 64, 65, 67, 69; postdoctoral fellow NIH, London, 1971-72, WHO, Egypt, Sudan, Rhodesia, 1975. Mem. Am. Soc. Parasitologists (editorial com.), Am. Soc. Tropical Medicine and Hygiene, Am. Microscopical Soc. (v.p. 1970), Royal Soc. Tropical Medicine and Hygiene, Australian Soc. Parasitology, Soc. Protozoologists, Midwestern Parastiologists (pres. 1969), Helminthol. Soc. Washington, Sigma Xi. Avocations: travel, golf. Home: 8284 Sunfish Ln Maineville OH 45039-8978 Office: U Cin Dept Biol Scis Cincinnati OH 45221-0006 E-mail: cooperlj@ucfwcu.rwc.uc.edu.

ETHAN, CAROL BAEHR, psychotherapist, psychoanalyst; b. N.Y.C., May 30, 1920; d. Irving and Sadie (Goldman) Baehr; m. Sy Ethan, Mar. 18, 1955; children: Willa Capraro, Barbara. Trained, Greenwich Inst. Psychoanalytic Studies, 1965-70; BA in Psychology with honors, NYU, 1978; MA in Psychology, New Sch. Social Rsch., 1981. Tchr. Queens Coll., 1956-57; consumer psychology rschr., cons., 1950-70; staff psychotherapist Fifth Ave. Ctr. Counseling & Psychotherapy, 1965-70; psychotherapist-psychoanalyst pvt. practice, N.Y.C., 1967—. Vol. social rehab. program Queens County Mental Health Soc., 1965—66; Dem. committeewoman Queens County, 1960. Recipient Founders Day award, NYU, 1978; fellow Internat. Coun. Sex Edn. and Parenthood, Am. U. Fellow: Am. Orthopsychiat. Assn.; mem.: APA, Am. Counselors Assn., Nat. Assn. Advancement of Psychoanalysis (cert. psychoanalyst), Am. Psychotherapy Assn. (cert. diplomate), N.Am. Assn. Masters in Psychology (cert.), Internat. Acad. Behavioral Medicine, Counseling and Psychotherapy (clin. mem.), Family and Divorce Mediation Coun. N.Y., Am. Mental Health Counselors Assn., N.Y. State Assn. Practising Psychotherapists (cert.). Address: 235 W 76th St New York NY 10023-8210 Office Phone: 212-595-4657. E-mail: cethan@nyc.rr.com.

ETHEREDGE, EDWARD EZEKIEL, retired surgeon; b. Jacksonville, Fla., May 22, 1939; s. Ezekiel Yonce and Raymer Frances (Johnson) E.; m. Beverly Elizabeth Hooten, Aug. 26, 1961; children: Edward Ezekiel Jr., William Glenn. BA magna cum laude, Yale U., 1961, MD, 1965; PhD, U. Minn., 1974. Diplomate Am. Bd. Surgery. Intern U. Minn. Hosp., 1965-66, asst. resident, 1966-72, chief resident surgery, 1972-73; asst. prof. surgery Wash. U. Sch. Medicine, St. Louis, 1975-79, assoc. prof. surgery, 1979-84; prof. surgery Tulane U. Sch. Medicine, New Orleans, 1984-97, prof. emeritus, 1998—, dir. div. transp., 1984-97. Specialist site visitor residence rev. com. on surgery Accreditation Coun. Grad. Med. Edn., Chgo., 1989-94; assoc. councillor United Network for Organ Sharing, Richmond, Va., 1991-93, councillor, 1993-95; pres. bd. dirs. La. Organ Procurement Agy., 1994-96, End Stage Renal Disease Network # 13, 1995-96. Editor, author (major, with others): Management Techniques in Surgery, 1986; contbr. articles to numerous sci. jours. Pres. Meml. Hall Found., New Orleans, 1990-97, Polk County Hist. Assn., 1999—; bd. dirs. Opera Theatre of St. Louis, 1979-83. Lt. col. U.S. Army, 1973-75. Decorated Commendation medal; recipient Spl. Recognition award Nat. Kidney Found., 1996. Fellow ACS; mem. Am. Surg. Assn., So. Surg. Assn., Soc. Univ. Surgeons, Am. Soc. Transplant Surgeons, Am. Assn. Immunologists. Republican. Methodist. Home: 1850 S Mariposa Ave Bartow FL 33830-7351

ETHEREDGE, ROGER GRAY, band director; b. Demopolis, Ala., Jan. 31, 1960; s. Willie Gray Jr. and Dorothy Jean (Duncan) E. AA, East. Miss. Jr. Coll., 1981; B in Music Edn., Troy State U., 1984. Cert. tchr., Ala. Band dir. Florala (Ala.) High Sch., 1988—. Mem. Music Educators Nat. Conf., Ala. Bandmaster Assn., Nat. Bandmaster Assn., Nat. Educators Assn., Ala. Educators Assn. Baptist. Avocations: car restoration, rescue squad. Office: Florala High Sch PO Box 218 Florala AL 36442-0218

ETHERIDGE, BOB, congressman; b. Lilington, N.C., Aug. 7, 1941; m. Faye Cameron; 3 children. BSBA, Campbell U., 1965; student, N.C. State U.; degree (hon.), Fayetteville State U., Pfieffer Coll., Shaw U. Owner hardware store; tobacco farmer; commr. Harnett County, 1972—76; mem. NC Ho. Reps., 1978—88; supt. Pub. Inst. Dept., Raleigh, NC, 1989—96; mem. U.S. Congress from 2d N.C. dist., Washington, 1997—; mem. agr. com., sci. com.; mem. Select Com. on Homeland Security. Bd. trustees N.C. Symphony; mem. adv. bd. Math./Sci. Edn. Network; past mem. Nat. Coun. Chief State Sch. Officers; bd. dirs. N.C. Coun. Econ. Edn. With U.S. Army, 1965—67. Democrat. Presbyterian. Office: US House of Reps 1533 Longworth Ho Office Bldg Washington DC 20515-3302 Address: 609 North First St PO Box 1059 Lillington NC 27546 also: 225 Hillsborough St Ste 490 Raleigh NC 27603*

ETHERIDGE, DIANA CAROL, internet business executive; b. Alliance, Nebr., Mar. 18, 1940; d. Elvon Lynn and Enola Nadene Howe; m. Brian Newman Etheridge, May 30, 1940; children: Melissa Ann, Juliana Lynn Student, U. Geneva, Switzerland, 1960-61; BA, U. Denver., 1962; MA, Simmons Coll., 1981. Cert. tchr., Colo., Fla.; real estate lic., Fla., 1995, Va., 1982; cert. internatl property specialist Nat. Assn. Realtors. Tchr. French, science, English Denver Pub. Schs., 1962-63, 64-68; tchr. 7th grade, French tchr. preK-7th grade St. Anne's Episcopal Sch., Denver, 1974—76; tchr. 6th grade, French tchr. k-8th grade, co-founder Collegiate Sch., Denver, 1976—80; real estate broker Merrill Lynch, Prudential, Long & Foster, Treder Realty, Potomac, Md. and Titusville, Fla., 1982—, Vincent Keenan Realtors, Cape Canaveral, Fla. Mem. No. Va. Coun. Comml. Realtors, Fairfax, Va., 1993—95, Govtl. Internat. and Info. Svcs. Coms., Fairfax, Internat. Real Estate Inst., Alexandria, Minn., 1996—2005, World Trade Ctr. Inst., Balt., 1995; cert. internat. property specialist Nat. Assn. Realtors, 1994—2000, judge Who is Today's Realtor, 1995; pres., founder e-dea, Inc., Merritt Island, Fla., 1997—, Cybernastics, Inc., Merritt Island, 1999—, Flexystema/Flexhome, Merritt Island, 2000—. Editor: My Hawaii (by Jane Thomas). House bill proofreader Colo. State Legislature, Denver, 1970; campaign staff mem. U.S. Congressman Dave Weldon, Melbourne, Fla., 1996, 1998, 2000; hon. chmn. Fla. bus. adv. coun. Nat. Rep. Congl. Com., 2003. Recipient Lifetime award Prudential Preferred Properties, 1990 Mem.: Md. Assn. Realtors, Fla. Bus. Adv. Coun., Montgomery Assn. Realtors (Lifetime award), Nat. Assn. Realtors, Nat. Assn. Home Builders, Nat. Assn. Women in Constrn., Hospitality and Info. Svcs. Internat. Club, Long and Foster Pres.'s Club (life), Optimists Club (past pres. Capital City), Brevard County Newcomer's Club, Welcome to Washington Internat. Club, Phi Beta Kappa, Pi Beta Phi. Achievements include patents for building construction; tensioned building system. Avocations: skiing, swimming, scuba diving, hiking, aerobics. Office Phone: 321-453-7665. E-mail: diana_etheridge@yahoo.com, info@edea.com.

ETHERIDGE, JACK PAUL, arbitrator, mediator, retired judge; b. Atlanta, Mar. 16, 1927; s. Anton Lee and Jessie Shephard (Brown) E.; m. Ursula Schlatter, Feb. 2, 1952; children: Jack Paul, Margaret Ann, Mary Elizabeth. Grad., Darlington Sch., Rome, Ga., 1945; BS, Davidson Coll., 1949; JD, Emory U., 1955. Bar: Ga. 1955. Since practiced in, Atlanta; mem. firm Huie, Etheridge & Harland, 1959-66; mem. Ga. Gen. Assembly from Fulton County, 1963-66; judge Fulton Superior Ct., 1966-76, sr. judge, 1977—, litigation mgr., 1991; faculty Nat. Jud. Coll., Coll. Criminal Justice, Law Sch., U. S.C., 1977-80; assoc. dean Emory U. Law Sch., Atlanta, 1981-88; chief jud. officer Jud. Arbitration and Mediation Svcs., Inc., Atlanta, 1992-98, spl. master nat. class actions, 1999—. Mem. Ga. Crime Commn., 1971-73; bd. dirs. Atlanta Legal Aid Soc., 1960-70. Trustee Davidson Coll., 1966-75; trustee Arts Festival of Atlanta, 1971-74, Atlanta U., 1977-87; chmn. bd. dirs. Atlanta Neighborhood Justice, Inc., Wolfcreek Wilderness Schs., Inc.; Fellow Harvard Law Sch., 1980. Served with USNR, 1945-46; Served with with AUS, 1949-52. Named Young Man of Year in Professions Atlanta Jr. C. of C., 1962 Fellow ABA, Am. Bar Found., Ga. Bar Assn., Internat. Acad. Trial Judges, Ctr. for Pub. Resources; mem. Atlanta Bar Assn. (pres. 1962-63), Nat. Conf. State Trial Judges (chmn. 1978-79), Atlanta Hist. Soc. (trustee 1969-75), Nat. Acad. Pub. Adminstrn., Beta Theta Pi, Omicron Delta Kappa, Phi Alpha Theta. Presbyterian. Home: 4715 Harris Trl NW Atlanta GA 30327-4409 Office Phone: 770-240-1426. E-mail: jetheridge@mindspring.com.

ETHERIDGE, MELISSA LOU, singer, lyricist; b. Leavenworth, Kans., May 29, 1961; d. John and Elizabeth Etheridge; m. Tammy Lynn Michaels, Sept. 22, 2003; children: Bailey, Beckett. Student, Berklee Coll. of Music, Boston, 1970. Wrote songs for the film, Weeds; albums include Melissa Etheridge, 1988, Brave and Crazy, 1989, Never Enough, 1992, Yes I Am, 1993, Your Little Secret, 1995, Breakdown, 1999, Skin, 2001, Lucky, 2004. Named Entertainer of Year Can. Acad. Recording Arts and Scis., 1990; Grammy award, Best Female Rock Vocal for "Aint It Heavy," 1993, Female Rock Vocal Performance for "Come to My Window," 1994; named one of 100 Most Influential People, Time Mag., 2005. Address: MEIN PO Box 884563 San Francisco CA 94188-4563*

ETHERIDGE, WHITSON BEAZLEY, lawyer; b. Conroe, Tex., Nov. 1, 1917; s. Obie and Florence Hilda (Beazley) E.; m. June 27, 1939; children: Ann Marie, Mary Faye, Whitson B. II, Jo Carol. B in Journalism, U. Tex., 1939; LLB, South Tex. Sch. Law, 1952. Bar: Tex. 1952. Reporter, photographer San Antonio (Tex.) Light, 1939-40; deputy tax collector Montgomery County, Conroe, Tex., 1941-43; trouble shooter Columbian Carbon Co., Conroe, 1943-58; pvt. practice lawyer Conroe, 1958—. Pres. Montgomery County Girl Scouts, Conroe, 1948, 52; deacon First Bapt. Ch., 1946—; mem. Pres. Coun. Houston Bapt. Univ., 1973—, trustee, 1984-91; mem. exec. bd. Tex. Bapt. Conv., 1962-66. Mem. Montgomery Masonic Lodge (past master, grand chaplain Royal Arch chpt. Tex. 1996, dist. Masonic rels. officer 1990-2002), Lions Club (zone chmn. 1988). Avocations: stained glass work, gardening, fishing, painting. Office: 207 Simonton St # 297 Conroe TX 77301-2863

ETHERINGTON, CAROL A., medical association administrator; b. Tenn. married. MSN in Psychology and Mental Health. RN Tenn. With Internat. Med. Corps, Bosnia-Herzegovina, 1994; pres., bd. dirs. U.S. sect. Doctors Without Borders, 1999—; asst. prof. nursing Vanderbilt U. Med. Ctr., Nashville. Founder Victims Intervention Program, Nashville Police Dept., 1975—95; mem. internat. com. ARC, 1980, vol. for disaster relief. Recipient

Internat. Achievement award, Florence Nightingale Internat. Found., Geneva, 2003, Florence Nightingale medal, Internat. Red Cross, 1997—98. Office: Vanderbilt Univ 336 First Hall 461 21st Ave S Nashville TN 37240

ETHINGTON, MARIROSE T., biology professor; MA in Biology, SUNY, Geneseo, 1986. Assoc. prof. Genesee C.C., Batavia, NY, 1991—. Dir. Soil and Water Conservation, Batavia, Youth Soccer Bd. Recipient Chancellors award For Excellence in Tchg., N.Y. State Chancellor Com., 2001, Paragon award, Phi Theta Kappa, 2000. Mem.: Delta Kappa Gamma (assoc.). Office: Genesee Community College College Rd Batavia NY 14020 Office Phone: 585-343-0055. Business E-Mail: mtethington@genesee.edu.

ETHRIDGE, JOSEPH ALFRED, manufacturing executive; BBA in Acctg., U. N. Tex., 1963, MBA in Fin., 1967. Comptr. currency Asst. Nat. Bank Examiner, Dallas, 1968-69; staff acct. to mng. ptnr. Coopers & Lybrand, 1970-90; sr. v.p. fin., treas. Sammons Enterprises Inc., Dallas, 1990—. Office: Sammons Enterprises Inc 5949 Sherry Ln Ste 1900 Dallas TX 75225

ETHRIDGE, LARRY CLAYTON, lawyer; b. Houston, Feb. 27, 1946; s. Robert Pike and Gladys Jeannette (Grant) E.; m. Edith Kirkbride Gilbert, May 21, 1977; children: Elizabeth Kirkbride, Grant Harbin. BA, Duke U., 1968; JD cum laude, U. Louisville, 1975. Bar: Ky. 1975, U.S. Dist. Ct. (we. dist.) Ky. 1980, U.S. Ct. Appeals (6th cir.) 1981, U.S. Dist. Ct. (ea. dist.) Ky. 2003. Intern Adv. Commn. on Intergovtl. Rels., Washington, 1975-76; asst. dir. model procurement code project ABA, Washington, 1976-80; ptnr. Mosley, Clare & Townes, Louisville, 1980-97, Ackerson Mosley & Yann, 1998—2003, Ackerson & Yann, Louisville, 2003—. Cons. ABA model procurement code project, Washington, 1980-82; panel mem. N.Y. State Procurement Rev., 1984—. Co-author: Supplement to Annotations on the Model Procurement Code, 1991, Annotations, 3d edit., 1996. Elder Highland Presbyn. Ch., Louisville, clk. of session, 1989-90, 96-2001; vol. ARC; gen. counsel Mobile Riverine Force Assn., 1995—; mem. bd. overseers U. Louisville, 2003—. Lt. USNR, 1969, Vietnam, Cambodia, and Japan. Recipient Disting. Svc. award Nat. Inst. Govtl. Purchasing, 1987. Fellow Am. Bar Found. (life); mem. ABA (chmn. coord. com. on a model procurement code 1985-96, co-chmn. model procurement code revision project steering com. 1997—, coun. mem., state and local govt. law sect. 1988—, sect. publs. dir. 1990-93, comms. dir. 1993-95, sec. 1995-96, vice-chmn. 1996-97, chmn. elect 1997-98, chmn. 1998-99, Donald M. Davidson award), AAA Ky. (bd. dirs. 1990-96, sec., gen. counsel 1996—), Ky. Bar Assn., Louisville Bar Assn., Jefferson Fordham Soc., U. Louisville Law Alumni Assn. (pres. 1990-92), U. Louisville Alumni Assn. (exec. com., pres.-elect, pres. 2003-2004, Alumni Svc. award), Duke Club Ky. (pres. 1992-94), Waggener H.S. Alumni Assn. (pres. 1996-97, Hall of Fame), Univ. of Louisville Club (bd. dirs. 1997—, treas. 2000—, v.p. 2002-04, pres. 2004—). Republican. Presbyterian. Avocations: gardening, travel, golf, bicycling, reading. Home: 2402 Longest Ave Louisville KY 40204-2125 Office: Ackerson & Yann 401 W Main St Ste 1200 Louisville KY 40202-2806 Office Phone: 502-583-7400. E-mail: lethridge@ackersonlegal.com.

ETHRIDGE, MARK FOSTER, III, newswriter, publishing executive, consultant; b. Winston-Salem, N.C., May 28, 1949; s. Mark F. Jr. and Margaret Burns (Furbee) E.; m. Kay Stover, Aug. 12, 1972; children: Emily Vigland, Mark Furbee. Grad., Phillips Exeter Acad., 1967; AB cum laude, Princeton U., 1971. Reporter AP, Boston, 1971-72, The Charlotte (N.C.) Observer, 1972-88, dep. metro editor, 1978-79, mng. editor, 1979-88; pub. The Bus. Jour. of Charlotte, 1989-98; pres. Carolina Parenting, Inc., 1991—, Cotter Group, Harrisburg, N.C., 1998-2001. Bd. dirs. Bioethics Resource Group Ltd. Mem. exec. com. Princeton Alumni Coun., 2001—03; trustee Charlotte Country Day Sch., 2002—. Nieman fellow Harvard U., 1986. Presbyterian. Home: 5516 Gorham Dr Charlotte NC 28226-6414 Office: Carolina Parenting Inc 2125 South End Dr Charlotte NC 28203 Office Phone: 704-344-1980. Business E-Mail: methridge@charlotteparent.com.

ETIENNE, MICHELE, financial consultant; b. Cap Haitien, Haiti, Oct. 16, 1946; d. Raymond and Claudia (Prophete) Kersaint; m. Ernst Etienne, Mar. 2, 1967; children: Patrick, Bernard. BBA, Baruch Coll., 1976. Dir. fin. Martha Graham Ctr., N.Y., 1973-98; fin. adv. Lee Strasberg Theatrical Inst., N.Y., 1999—. Pres. Primevere Club; mem. Casegha. Home: 84-15 168th St Jamaica NY 11432 Office: Lee Strasberg Theatrical Inst 115 E 15th St New York NY 10003-2188 E-mail: metienne16@aol.com.

ETIENNE, MYRON E., JR., lawyer; b. Pasadena, Calif., May 19, 1924; s. Myron E. Etienne and Lucile B. McClung; m. Charlene A. Pinder; children: Victor, Dirk. BS, U.S. Merchant Marine Acad./U. Calif., Berkeley, 1945; JD, Hastings Coll., 1952. Bar: Calif., D.C. Legal rsch. aide, dist. ct. appeal 1st Appellate Dist., Divsn. I, 1953—54; dep. dist. atty. Monterey County, Calif., 1954—55; mem. Noland, Hamerly, Etienne & Hoss, Salinas, Calif., 1955—. Mem. alumni coun. exec. com. U. Calif., Berkeley, 1969—75; v.p. exec. coun., mem. Coun. Barristers, 1960—61; past mem. Center City Authority, Salinas; pro bono counsel Salinas River Channel Coalition; mem. pro bono referral panel Legal Svcs. for Srs.; vice chmn., bd. dirs. Hastings Coll. Law, 1981—88; past bd. dirs. Hastings Law Ctr. Found.; past pres., bd. dirs. 1066 Found. Hastings Coll. Law; bd. trustees Med. Ctr. Found. Monterey County; bd. dirs. Friends of Historic San Antonio Mission; past bd. dirs. Joe Gheen Found., Salinas, Salvation Army, Salinas, Salinas Valley Fair, King City, Calif., 1968—91; past pres., bd. dirs. Salinas Jr. C. of C.; past pres., bd. dirs., gen. counsel Monterey Jazz Festival, Calif. Rodeo, Salinas; past. pres., bd. trustees Rodeo Info. Found., 1966—70; chmn. humane adv. com. Profl. Rodeo Cowboys Assn.; chmn. bd. harbor commrs. Moss Landing Harbor Dist., Calif., 1957—64. Lt. (j.g.) U.S. Maritime Svc. USNR. Named Outstanding Young Man of Yr., Salinas Jr. C. of C., Citizen of Yr., Salinas C. of C., 2002; named to, Profl. Rodeo Cowboys Hall of Fame, 2001; recipient Alumnus of Yr. award, Hastings Coll. Law, 1982, Chief Justice Phil Gibson award, Monterey County, 1989, Std. of the West award, Outstanding Rodeo Committeeman, 1991. Mem.: ABA, Calif. Trial Lawyers Assn., Monterey County Bar Assn., Profl. Rodeo Cowboys Assn. (hon.). Office: Noland Hamerly Etienne & Hoss 333 Salinas St Salinas CA 93901

ETO, HAJIME, information scientist, educator; b. Tokyo, June 16, 1935; s. Yoshio and Kikuko (Tamari) E. BA, U. Tokyo, 1959, MA, 1962; MS, U. Calif., Berkely, 1967; PhD, Tokyo Inst. Tech., 1979. Rschr. Hitachi Ltd., Tokyo, 1962-76; prof. U. Tsukuba, Japan, 1976-99, Chiba Keizai U., Japan, 1999—; prof. emeritus U. Tsukuba, 1999—. *Having the background of philosophy of natural and social science methodologies and oriental ideas, he uses various methods across disciplines. His recent works on innovation policies consider the cultural, historical, philosophical aspects and combine technology innovations with organizational ones in business and political circles including reforms of obsolete taxation organizations that obstruct innovations.* Author, editor: R & D Management Systems in Japanese Industry, 1984, R & D Strategies in Japan, 1993; mem. editl. bd. Scientometrics Jour., 1979—, Human Sys. Mgmt., 1980-84, Internat. Jour. of the Sci. of Scis., 1994—, Internat. Jour. Svc. Tech. & Mgmt., 1998—, Internat. Jour. Foresight and Innovation Policy, 2003—, Information and Management, 2004—; contbr. sci. articles to profl. jours. Recipient Fulbright scholarship U.S.-Japan Edn. Com., 1966. Mem. AAAS, Internat. Soc. Scientometrics and Informetrics (mem. coun. 1993—, mem. editl. bd. 1995—), Japan Assn. for Philosophy Sci. (mem. coun. 1970-92), Japan Soc. for Sci. Policy (bd. dirs. 1994-96, coun. 1997—), Assn. of France on Cybernetics, Econs. and Tech. (mem. editl. bd. 1985—), N.Y. Acad. Sci. Buddhist. Home: Nakano 3-43-17-305 Nakano-ku Tokyo 164-0001 Japan Personal E-mail: etohajime@peach.ocn.ne.jp. Business E-Mail: eto@cku.ac.jp.

ETRA, LIONEL, lawyer; b. N.Y.C., July 22, 1942; s. Max Jacob and Reba (Zuckerbraun) E. AB, Columbia Coll., 1964; JD, Harvard U., 1967; LLM in Taxation, NYU, 1978. Atty. Karelsen Karelsen Lawrence & Nathan, N.Y.C., 1969-77, Roberts & Holland, N.Y.C., 1977—. Avocations: photography, flute playing, running. Office Phone: 212-903-8721. Business E-Mail: letra@rhtax.com.

ETRIS, SAMUEL FRANKLIN, trade association research consultant; b. Port Huron, Mich., Dec. 3, 1922; s. Samuel and Mildred Susan (Davis) E.; m. Mary Jane Lytle, June 29, 1957; children— Andrew Brooke, Edward Lytle. AB, Temple U., 1947; MS, Rutgers U., 1951. With Foote Mineral Rsch. Labs., Phila., 1947-49, spl. asst. to mng. dir. for nat. affairs, editor, 1967-80; editor ASTM, Phila., 1967-76. Sr. cons. Klein of Saks, Inc., Washington; mgrs. Silver Inst., Gold Inst.; mem. numerical data adv. bd. NRC. Contbr. articles and editorials to profl. publs. Tchr. measurement course Phila. Pkwy. Sch.; Scoutmaster Boy Scouts Am., 1954-57, troop com. chmn., 1957-61; convenor 1st Internat. Conf. on Gold and Silver in Medicine, Bethesda, Md., 1987. Served to 1st lt. USAAF, 1944-46, CBI; Served to 1st lt. USAF, 1951-52. Recipient Scoutmaster's Key award, 1957 Mem. Am. Ceramic Soc. (emeritus). Home and Office: 115 Runnymede Ave Wayne PA 19087-4014 Personal E-mail: sfetris@erols.com.

ETSON, JANET A., librarian; b. River Falls, Wis. 1 child, Maria M. BA, Wis. State U., Oshkosh. determined medically disabled, 2001. Asst. to circulation libr. U. Wis., River Falls, 1971—74; tchr., librarian Pub. Schs., Hannah, ND, 1975—76, libr. Warwick, ND, 1976—78, Minot Daily News, ND, 1983—86, U. N.D. Grad. Ctr., Minot AFB, 1987—89; textbook clk. Cobber Bookstore, Concordia Coll., Moorhead, 1990—93. Vol. Cameron Med. Libr. Trinity Med. Ctr., Minot, 1979-89, Urban Youth 4-H, 1980-86. Mem. ITC (treas. Minot chpt. 1987-89). Personal E-mail: sqhaven@hotmail.com.

ETTE, ENE IKPONG, clinical pharmacologist; b. Nwaniba, Akwa Ibom, Nigeria, Jan. 28, 1954; s. Ikpong Ikpong and Nkaepe Ebrewong Ette; m. Esther Awala Awala, Feb. 11, 1961; 6 children. BSc in Pharmacology, U. Ibadan, Nigeria, 1977; MS in Pharmacology, U. Ife (now Obafemi Awolowo U.), Nigeria, 1980; BS in Pharmacy, Northeastern U., 1983; PhD in Clin. Pharmacology, U. Glasgow, 1992. Cert. pharmacist Nigeria. Grad. asst. Obafemi Awolowo U., Ile-Ife, Nigeria, 1977—78, juinor rsch. fellow, 1978—80. Asst. to assoc. prof. U. Lagos, Nigeria, 1983—92; reviewer to sr. reviewer, rschr. FDA, Rockville, Md., 1992—96, expert scientist (pharmacometrics), 1997; staff scientist Vertex Pharms., Inc., Cambridge, Mass., 1997, head of clin. pharmacology, 1999—2000, dir. to sr. dir. clin. pharmacology, 2002—. Author: Guidance on Population Pharmacokinetics for Industry (CDER(FDA) Excellence in Rev. Sci. Award, 1996). Ministering to the sick and the needy MetroWest Worship Ctr., Ashland, Mass., 1997—2004. Recipient Team Excellence award, Ctr. for Drug Evaluation, 1998; Glaxo Ltd. Travel fellow, Glaxo Nigeria Ltd., 1988, Overseas Rsch. Students awardee, U.K. Overseas Rsch. Students Scholarship, 1989—91. Fellow: Am. Coll. Clin. Pharmacy (Russel Miller award 1999), Am. Coll. Clin. Pharmacology; mem.: Am. Assn. Pharm. Scis. Achievements include patents in field; development of the process of discovering knowledge from population pharmacokinetics data sets; the methodology for estabilishing population model stability and performance; the importance of informative graphics in population pharmacokinetic modeling. Avocations: reading, Christian ministry. Office: Vertex Pharmaceuticals Inc 130 Waverly St Cambridge MA 02139 Office Phone: 617-444-6318. E-mail: ene_ette@vrtx.com.

ETTEL, ZITA MOAK, nursing administrator, food service executive; b. Blythewood, S.C., Feb. 11, 1922; d. George Washington and Johhnie Louise (Halstead) Moak; m. James Hughlon Lylos, Oct. 24, 1949 (dec. June 1960); 6 children; m. James Phillip Ettel, Dec. 25, 1995. RN, Elizabeth Buxton Sch. Nursing, 1941. Carpenter Blythewood Shop, S.C., 1938; RN Elizabeth Buxton, Va., 1942; armament electrician, welder Columbia, SC, 1943; aircraft mechanic Army Air Base, Columbia, 1944; charge nurse Providence Hosp., Columbia, 1945; decorator Macy Dept. Store, N.Y.C., 1947; auto mechanic, 1948; food svc. supr. Columbia Hosp., 1959; psychoanalyst Hall Inst., Columbia, 1964; RN Valley Meml. Hosp., Grand Forks, N.D., 1965; beautician Columbia, 1970—76; orthop. nurse Vet. Hosp., Columbia, 1973, 1980-85. Author: My Abused Childhood, Tommy Turtle, 1955, (poems) Farewell, The Christmas Promise, Too Many; inventor. Nurse Am. Red. Cross, Ft. Monroe, Va., 1942, Ft. Jackson, 1943; driver Blind Assn., Columbia, S.C., 1970; former ch. organist, Sunday Sch. tchr., sec. Luther League. With U.S. Air Force, 1943. Recipient Editor's Choice award Nat. Libr. Poetry, 1996, Golden Poet award World of Poetry, 1989, 91 Mem. N.Y. Acad. Scis. Home: 1001 Confederate Ave Columbia SC 29201

ETTENGER, ROBERT BRUCE, physician, nephrologist; b. Phila., Sept. 17, 1942; s. Ervin Earl and Sylvia (Goodstein) W.; m. Angela Joan Castellano; children: Allison, Jessica. BA, U. Pa., 1964; MD, 1968. Asst. prof. pediat. Children's Hosp. of L.A., 1976-80, Sch. Medicine UCLA, 1980-84, asst. prof., 1984-89, prof., 1989—, head divsn. pediat. nephrology dept. pediat., 1990—, vice chmn. clin. affairs, 1990—; med. dir. pediat. renal transplant program UCLA Med. Ctr., 1983—, dir. historcompatibility lab., 1987—2001, vice chief staff, 2002—. Mem., chair sub-bd. nephrology Am. Bd. Pediat., Chapel Hill, N.C., 1986-91; cons. Immunosuppressive Adv. Com. Food and Drug Adminstrn., Bethesda, Md., 1994—, Biologics and Immune Response Modifiers, Food and Drug Adminstrn., Bethesda, 1994—; mem. biol. sci. adv. com. U.S. Renal Data Sys., Ann Arbor, Mich., 1993-2000. Assoc. editor Am. Jour. Transplantation; mem. editl. bd. Transplantation, Pediat. Nephrology, Pediat. Transplantation; contbr. articles to profl. jours. Coach, mem. exec. bd. AYSO Soccer, Santa Monica, Calif., 1994-2001, Bobby Sox Softball, 1995-97, YWCA Basketball, 1995-2000; mem. med. adv. bd. Nat. Kidney Found., L.A., 1993—; mem. sports and phys. edn. adv. com. Santa Monica Sch. Dist. Maj. U.S. Army, 1971—73. Recipient Ortho Biotech Lectureship Urologic Soc. for Transplantation, 1990, Continuing Svc. award Nat. Kidney Found., L.A., 1991, 92, 94. Fellow Internat. Soc. of Nephrology, Internat. Pediat. Nephrology Assn., Am. Acad. Pediat., Am. Soc. Transplant Physicians (pres. 1984-85), Am. Pediat. Soc., Am. Soc. of Nephrology, Am. Soc. of Pediat. Nephrology, Soc. for Pediat. Rsch., Transplantation Soc (Best Drs. in Am. 1992-2004), United Network For Organ Sharing (regional councillor at region 5, bd. dirs. 2000-02). Jewish. Avocations: distance running, youth sports. Office: UCLA Med Ctr A2-383 Dept Pediatrics 10833 Le Conte Ave Los Angeles CA 90095-3075

ETTENSOHN, FRANK ROBERT, geologist, educator; b. Cin., Feb. 6, 1947; s. Robert Frank and Aileen Frances (Keman) E.; m. Beth Mosher, June 3, 1978; children: Clare Marie, Marc Francis. BS, U. Cin., 1969, MS, 1970; PhD, U. Ill., 1975. Lic. profl. geologist Ky. Tchr. math. Greenhills (Ohio)-Forest Park City Sch. Dist., 1971; from asst. prof. to prof. geology U. Ky., Lexington, 1975—87, prof., 1987—, chmn. dept. geol. sci., 1997—2005. Geology adv. com. Coun. for Internat. Exch. Scholars, 1993-96, chmn., 1994-96; bd. dir., v.p. Ky. Mus. Natural History, 1991-; tech. adv. com. Ea. Oil Shale Symposium, 1992-94; dir. U.K. Geology Field Camp, 1977-81, 84-85, 92-93, 95, 97-98, 2001; adv. com. Ky. Water Resources Rsch. Inst., 1998-2001; faculty math. and sci. edn. program U. Ky. Coll. Edn., 1999-; adv. bd. Appalachian Math. Sci. Partnership, 2003-; cons. in field; expert witness; vis. prof. U. Geosciences, China, 2005. Editor (tech.): Jour. Paleontology, 1994—97; contbr. articles to profl. jours. Capt. C.E., AUS, 1970. Fenneman fellow, 1969-70; U. Ill. fellow, 1971-74; grantee U.S. Dept. Energy, 1976-81, NSF, 1987-90, US Bur. Mines, 1990-91, Ky. Coun. on Higher Edn., 1998-2002, NSF/EPSCOR, 2002-05, Geol. Soc. Am.; Fulbright lectr. US Govt., Soviet Union, 1989. Fellow Geol. Soc. Am. (jt. chmn., field trip chmn. ann. mtg. southeastern sect. 2001-02); mem. AAAS, Paleontol. Soc., Paleontol. Assn., Paleontol. Rsch. Inst., Internat. Paleontol. Assn., Ky. Acad. Sci., Am. Geophys. Union, Nat. Assn. Geosci. Tchr., Nat. Earth Sci. Tchr. Assn., Fulbright Assn., Phi Beta Kappa, Sigma Xi, Phi Kappa Phi, Sigma Gamma Epsilon. Roman Catholic. Avocations: phlately, coin collecting/numismatics, scouting, soccer. Home: 1631 Duntreath Dr Lexington KY 40504-2352 Office: U Ky Dept Geol Scis Lexington KY 40506-0053 Office Phone: 859-257-6232. Business E-Mail: fettens@uky.edu.

ETTER, DELORES M., federal agency administrator; Student, Okla. State U., U. Tex., Arlington; BS in Math., Wright State U., Dayton, Ohio, 1970, MS in Math., 1972; PhD in Elec. Engring., U. New Mex., 1979. Mem. faculty dept. elec. and computer engring. U. N.Mex., 1979-89, assoc. chair dept., 1987-89, assoc. v.p. acad. affairs, 1989; prof. elec. and computer engring. U. Colo., Boulder, 1990-98; dep. under sec. defense sci. and tech. Dept. Defense, Washington, 1998—2001; disting. chair sci. and tech. office naval rsch. U.S. Naval Acad., 2001—. Mem. Naval Rsch. Adv. Com., 1991-97, chmn. 1995-97; vis. prof. info. sys. lab.Stanford U., 1983-84; bd. dirs. Def. Sci. Bd., 1995-98, Nat. Sci. Bd.; prin. U.S. rep. NATO rsch. and tech. bd., tech. cooperation program; mem. bd. vis. Nat. Def. U.; panel mem. numerous studies. Recipient Pub. Svc. award Dept. Navy, 1998, Fed. Women in Sci. and Engring. Lifetime Achievement award. Fellow IEEE (pres., acoustics, speech and signal processing soc. 1988-89, editor in chief Transactions on Signal Processing jour. 1993-95, Disting. lectr. 1996-97, Harriet Rigas award 1998), AAAS, Am. Soc. Engring. Edn.; mem. NAE. Office: US Naval Acad 121 Blake Rd Annapolis MD 21402-5000 Office Phone: 410-293-3174. E-mail: detter@nerc.com.

ETTER, GREGG WAYNE, SR., police officer, educator; b. Hutchison, Kans., Oct. 17, 1952; s. Lendell Wayne and Imojean (Swearingen) E.; m. Pamela Lynn Scoggins, June 30, 1979 (div. Oct. 1989); children: Gregg Jr., Alexander P., Nicholas V., Benjamin J.; m. Bonnie Lou Arnold, Dec. 10, 1991. B of Gen. Studies in Polit. Sci., Wichita State U., 1976, M in Adminstrn. Justice, 1981; diploma, USAF Air Command & Staff Coll., 1978; EdD, Okla. State U., 2000. Lt. Sedgwick County Sheriff's Dept., Wichita, Kans., 1977—; instr. Butler County C.C., El Dorado, Kans., 1991—97, Newman U., Wichita, 1997—. Contbr. articles to profl. jours. Unit comdr. Civil Air Patrol, Wichita, 1974-94. Recipient Frederick Milton Thrasher award, Nat. Gang Crime Rsch. Ctr., 1995, 1998. Mem. Am. Soc. Law Enforcement Tnrs., Kans. Peace Officers Assn., Kans. Sheriff's Assn., North Okla./South Kans. Peace Officers Assn., Am. Correctional Assn., Am. Soc. Criminology, Brit. Soc. Criminology, Acad. Criminal Justice Scis., Am. Jail Assn. Republican. Episcopalian. Office: Sedgwick County Sheriff'sDept 525 N Main St Wichita KS 67203-3702

ETTER, HOWARD LEE, artist; b. Moberly, Mo., Jan. 22, 1931; s. John Harmon and Mildred Lee (Elsea) E.; m. Martha Lou Klepfer, Jan. 20, 1952; 1 child, Cynthia Lou. Student, Art League of Calif., San Francisco, 1954-55, Acad. of Art, 1955-57. Illustrator various studios, San Francisco, 1957-60, New Ctr. Studios, Detroit, 1960-61, Kolyer Studios, Detroit, 1961-62; illustrator, art dir. Wagner Advt. Agy., Detroit, 1962-67; artist, cons. self-employed, Oak Park, Mich., 1967-77; art instr. Lawrence Inst. Tech., Southfield, Mich., 1967-77; artist self-employed, Albuquerque, 1977-80, Camden, Maine, 1980—. Author: Perspective for Painters, 1990. With USNR, 1948-52. Recipient Purchase award Friends of Am. Art, 1975. Avocations: musical instrument making, classical guitar. Home and Office: PO Box 740 Camden ME 04843-0740

ETTER, PAUL COURTNEY, oceanographer; b. Phila., Oct. 27, 1947; s. Richard T. and Ellen M. (Cunliffe) E.; m. Alice D. Eblighatian, June 21, 1969; children: Gregory M., Andrew D. BS in Physics, Tex. A&M U., 1969, MS in Oceanography, 1975. Quality control technician Technitrol, Inc., Phila., 1969; rsch. asst. Tex. A&M U., College Station, 1973-76; sr. engr. MAR, Inc., Rockville, Md., 1976-82; sr. tech. dir. ODSI Def. Systems, Inc., Rockville, Md., 1982-89; sr. scientist Radix Systems, Inc., Rockville, Md., 1989-97; adv. engr. oceanic systems Northrop Grumman Corp., Annapolis, Md., 1998—. Instr. Tech. Svc. Corp., Silver Spring, Md., 1982-92, Applied Tech. Inst., Clarksville, Md., 1993—. Author: Underwater Acoustic Modeling, 1991, 3d edit., 2003; contbr. articles to profl. jours. including Jour. Physical Oceanography, Shock and Vibration Digest, Continental Shelf Rsch., Sea Tech., Jour. Sound and Vibration, Jour. Geophys. Rsch Lt. USN, 1969—73. Fellow Wash. Acad. Scis.; mem. IEEE (sr.), Am. Geophys. Union, Am. Meteorol. Soc., Acoustical Soc. Am. Home: 16609 Bethayres Rd Rockville MD 20855-2043

ETTERS, RONALD MILTON, retired lawyer, former government official; b. San Antonio, Nov. 6, 1948; s. Milton William and Ilse Charlotte (Ostler) E.; m. Anna Colleen Wesson, Feb. 12, 1977; children: William Lawrence, Elizabeth Charlotte, Margaret Lawreen. BA magna cum laude, Am. U., 1971, JD, 1976. Bar: Va. 1976, U.S. Ct. Appeals (D.C. cir.) 1977, U.S. Dist. Ct. (ea. dist.) Va. 1978, U.S. Ct. Appeals (4th and 9th cirs.) 1978, U.S. Supreme Ct. 1979, D.C. 1980, U.S. Dist. Ct. D.C. 1980, U.S. Ct. Appeals (1st and 2d cirs.) 1980, U.S. Ct. Appeals (7th cir.) 1981, U.S. Ct. Appeals (3rd, 11th and fed. cirs.) 1982, U.S. Ct. Appeals (5th cir.) 1983. Intern to gen. counsel Adminstrv. Office of U.S. Cts., Washington, 1970-71; fed. mgmt. intern IRS, Washington, 1971-72, labor rels. officer, 1972-75; ptnr. Nusbaum & Etters, Burke, Va., 1976-80; gen. counsel Nat. Mediation Bd., Washington, 1980—2002; ret., 2002. With Sigma Alpha, 1971; justice Phi Alpha Delta, 1975; professorial lectr. Am. U., Washington, 1978-83; adj. prof. law Georgetown U., Washington, 1985-88; vis. prof. George Mason U. Sch. Law, Arlington, Va., 1999, dir. Ctr. Advanced Study of Law and Dispute Resolution Processes, Arlington, 2000-2002. Sr. bd. editors The Railway Labor Act, 1991-2002. Mem. ABA (co-chmn. com. on railway and airline labor law 1987-93, 1999-2002), Christian Legal Soc., Nat. Lawyers Assn., Fed. Bar Assn. Home: PO Box 2374 Centreville VA 20122-2374 E-mail: etters5@etters.net.

ETTINGER, ALAN B., neurologist; b. Newark, N.J., Feb. 25, 1959; s. Samuel and Lillian Ettinger; m. Deborah M. Weisbrot, June 5, 1988. BA/MD magna cum laude, Boston U., 1983. Lic. physician N.Y., cert. neurology Am. Bd. Psychiatry and Neurology, added qualifications in clin. neurophysiology Am. Bd. Psychiatry and Neurology, Am. Bd. Clin. Neurophysiology. Intern in internal medicine Hartford Hosp., 1983—84; resident in internal medicine Hartford Hosp., U. Conn. Med. Sch., 1984—85; resident in neurology Albert Einstein Coll. Medicine, Bronx, 1985—87, instr. neurology, fellow in EEG, epilepsy and evoked potentials, 1989; dir. inpatient epilepsy monitoring Montefiore Med. Ctr., 1989—92; assoc. prof. neurology Albert Einstein Coll. Medicine, 1989—92; dir. adult epilepsy program, asst. prof. neurology Univ. Med. Ctr., Stony Brook, 1992—99; chief divsn. EEG and epilepsy, dir. Comprehensive Epilepsy Ctr. L.I. Jewish Med. Ctr., New Hyde Park, NY, 1999—. Spkr. and lectr. in field; dir. profl. surgery bd. Epilispy Founstum of LI; assoc. prof. neurology Albert Einstein Coll. of Medicine. Co-author (with A. Kanner): Psychiatric Issues in Epilepsy, 2001; co-author: (with O. Devinsky) Managing Epilepsy and Co-Existing Disorders, 2002; co-author: (with D.M. Weisbrot) The Essential Patient Handbook, 2004. Recipient grants in field. Mem.: AMA, Am. Epilepsy Soc., Am. Acad. Neurology. Office: LI Jewish Med Ctr 270-05 76th Ave New Hyde Park NY 11040

ETTINGER, HARRY JOSEPH, retired industrial hygiene engineer, retired consultant; b. NYC, July 20, 1934; s. Morris and Pauline (Waxman) E.; m. June Kopf, June 14, 1958; children: Linda E., Steven E., Robert A. BCE, CCNY, 1956; MCE, NYU, 1958. Registered profl. engr., N.Mex.; cert. indsl. hygienist. San. engr. USPHS, Bethesda, Md., 1958-61; staff mem. Los Alamos (N.Mex.) Nat. Lab., 1961-71, alt. group leader, 1971-74, group leader, 1974-80, program mgr., 1981-87, tech. rsch. coord., 1989-91, program mgr., 1991-93, chief scientist environ., safety and health divsn., 1993-97, acting dep. divsn. dir., 1995-96, lab. assoc., 1997-99, cons., 1999—2004; project dir. Occupl. Safety and Health Adminstrn., Washington, 1987-89; ret., 2004. Cons. divsn. reactor licensing USAEC, 1970-71, cons. EPA, 1972-74, various industries, 1970—; cons. to adv. com. on nuc. facility safety DOE, 1990-91; mem. adj. faculty U. Ark., Little Rock, 1969-90, San Diego State U., 1981-86; vis. faculty Tex. A&M U., College Station, 1981-99; faculty affiliate Colo. State U., Ft. Collins, 1983—; mem. exec. com. toxic substances rsch. and tchg. program U. Calif., 1984-90; mem. stds. steering group DOE Lab. Dirs. Environ. and Occupl. Health, 1990-96; mem. liaison com. NIOSH Nat. Occupl. Rsch. Agenda, 2000-03. Mem. editl. bd. Jour. Occupl. and Environ. Hygiene, 2004-; contbr. jour. articles and tech. reports on indsl. hygiene, aerosol physics, respiratory protection. Active Los Alamos County Utility Bd., 1968-70, 78-82, chmn., 1970; vice chmn. Los Alamos County Planning and Zoning Commn., 1974-76, mem., 1972-76, 97-2001, 04—. Fellow: Am. Indsl. Hygiene Assn. (chmn. aerosol tech. com. 1968—70, mem. aerosol tech. com. 1968—78, editl. rev. bd. 1979—87, aerosol tech. com. 1980—84, bd. dirs. 1987—90, editl. rev. bd. 1990—91, v.p. 1991—92, pres.-elect 1992—93, pres. 1993—94, editl. rev. bd. 1995—2003, respirator com. 1995—, Edward Baier award 1990, Donald Cummings Lectr. award 2003, Henry Smyth Lectr. and award 2004); mem.: Internat. Occupl. Hygiene Assn.

(bd. dirs. 1994—97), Internat. Soc. Respiratory Protection (bd. dirs. 1985—88, 1995—97, mem. editl. bd. NSC Jour. safety rsch. 2001—), Am. Conf. Govtl. Indsl. Hygiene (Meritorious Achievement award 1985), Am. Bd. Indsl. Hygiene (bd. dirs. 1979—85, chmn. 1983—85), Am. Acad. Indsl. Hygiene (editor newsletter 1997—2001). Democrat. Jewish. Office Phone: 505-662-7132. Personal E-mail: Junee@rt66.com.

ETTINGER, JOHN RICHE, lawyer; b. N.Y.C., June 12, 1951; s. Austen A. and Shirley (Riche) E.; m. Linda A. Simpson, Apr. 19, 1986; children: Katharine Simpson, John Tyler, William Riche. BA summa cum laude, Yale U., 1973; JD, Harvard U., 1978. Bar: N.Y. 1979. Atty. Davis Polk & Wardwell, 1979—86, ptnr. N.Y.C., 1986—, chmn. mgmt. com. Rhodes scholar Oxford (Eng.) U., 1975. Office: Davis Polk & Wardwell 450 Lexington Ave Fl 31 New York NY 10017-3982 Office Phone: 212-450-4232. Office Fax: 212-450-3232. Business E-Mail: john.ettinger@dpw.com.*

ETTINGER, JOSEPH ALAN, lawyer; b. N.Y.C., July 21, 1931; s. Max and Frances E.; children: Amy Beth, Ellen Jane. BA, Tulane U., 1954, JD with honors, 1956. Bar: La. 1956, Ill. 1959. Asst. corp. counsel City of Chgo., 1959-62; pvt. practice, Chgo., 1962-73, 76-80; sr. ptnr. Ettinger & Schoenfield, Chgo., 1980-92; pvt. practice, Chgo., 1993—. Assoc. prof. law Chgo.-Kent Coll., 1973-76; chmn. Village of Olympia Fields (Ill.) Zoning Bd. Appeals, 1969-76; chmn. panel on corrections Welfare Coun. Met. Chgo., 1969-76; spl. state appellate defender State of Ill., 1997-98; delegate inauguration Michael M. Crow to Pres. Ariz. State U., Tulane U., 2002. Contbr. articles to profl. jours. Capt. JAGC U.S. Army, 1956—59. Recipient svc. award, Village of Olympia Fields, 1976. Mem. Chgo. Bar Assn., Assn. Criminal Def. Lawyers (gov. 1970-72). Achievements include del. (Tulane U.) to inauguration of Michael Crow, pres. Ariz. State U., 2002. Office Phone: 312-326-1543. E-mail: joeett@aol.com.

ETTINGER, LAWRENCE JAY, pediatric hematologist, oncologist, educator; b. Bklyn., Dec. 17, 1947; s. Joseph and Blanche (Mittman) E.; m. Alice G. Renick. BA, Case Western Res. U., 1969, MD, 1973. Intern in pediatrics U. Md. Hosp., Balt., 1973-74, resident in pediatrics, 1974-75, Children's Hosp. Buffalo, 1975-76; fellow in pediatric hematology-oncology Roswell Park Meml. Inst. and Children's Hosp. Buffalo, 1976-78; asst. prof. pediatrics U. Rochester (N.Y.) Sch. Med. and Dentistry, 1978-81, U. So. Calif., L.A., 1981-84; assoc. prof. U. Medicine and Dentistry N.J., Robert Wood Johnson Med. Sch., New Brunswick, chief div. pediatric hematology-oncology, 1984-98; lectr. in pediats. Coll. Physicians and Surgeons Columbia U., 1998-2000; chief divsn. pediat. hematology/oncology St. Peter's Univ. Hosp., 1998—; assoc. clin. prof. pediatrics Coll. Physicians and Surgeons Columbia U., 2000—04; clin. prof. pediat. Drexel U. Coll. Medicine, Phila., 2005—. Sickle cell adv. com. N.J. State Dept. Health, 1998—. Contbr. articles to profl. jours.; manuscript reviewer Cancer, Mayo Clinic Proceedings, Jour. Pediat. Hematology-Oncology, Brit. Jour. Cancer, Med. Pediat. Oncology, Am. Jour. Perinatology. Mem. adv. com. Pediatric Oncology Adv. Group, N.J. Commn. Cancer Rsch., 1986—; mem. med. adv. bd. Inst. for Children with Cancer and Blood Disorders, 1991-98; field reader Office of Orphan Products Devel. FDA, 1988—; mem. spl. rev. com. NIH, 1992, 95; mem. cancer ad hoc com. Ocean County (N.J.) Health Dept., 1996-98. Recipient Univ. Excellence award for patient care U. Medicine and Dentistry, N.J., 1991, Pride of N.J. award and Clara Barton Med. Svc. award Gov. of N.J., 1992, N.J. Pride award in health, 1993; grantee N.J. Commn. on Cancer Rsch., Trenton, 1987-89, Valerie Fund, Maplewood, N.J., 1985-90, The Upjohn Co., Kalamazoo, 1984-86, Wyeth-Ayerst Rsch., Phila., 1992-94, Enzon Inc., Piscataway, N.J., 1992-94, Amgen, Inc., Thousand Oaks, Calif., 1992-94, Inst. for Children with Cancer and Blood Disorders, 1991-98, Sanofi Winthrop, 1996; Jr. Faculty Clin. . Fellow Am. Cancer Soc., 1980-83. Fellow: Am. Acad. Pediat. (exec. com. sect. on hematology-oncology 1997—2000); mem.: Children's Oncology Group (prin. investigator 2004—), Internat. Soc. Pediat. Oncology, Children's Cancer Group (prin. investigator 1997—98), Oncology Soc. N.J., Am. Cancer Soc. (svc. and rehab. com. N.J. divsn. 1986—96, vice chmn. 1988—89, 1992—94, chmn. 1994—96, trustee, exec. com. 1994—96), Am. Soc. Pediat. Hematology-Oncology, Am. Soc. Hematology, Am. Soc. Clin. Oncology, Am. Assn. Cancer Rsch., Phi Beta Kappa. Avocations: photography, travel. Office: St Peter's U Hosp 254 Easton Ave PO Box 591 New Brunswick NJ 08903-0591 Office Phone: 732-745-6674. Business E-Mail: lettinger@saintpetersuh.com.

ETTINGER, MICHAEL SAUL, lawyer; b. 1961; s. Leon and Victoria S. Ettinger; m. Joyce Francine Katz, Aug. 18, 1984. BA, SUNY, Binghamton; JD, SUNY, Buffalo. Bar: 1986. V.p., gen. counsel, sec. Henry Schein Inc., Melville, NY. Office: Henry Schein Inc 135 Duryea Rd Melville NY 11747

ETTINGER, STEVE JOEL, music educator; b. King City, Calif., Nov. 16, 1969; s. Arnold and Sheila June Ettinger; m. Aya Nishida Ettinger, July 5, 1998; 1 child, Kayla Anne. B, UCLA, 1991; M, U. Oreg., 1994. Tchr. English Aeon Conversation Sch., Mihawa, Japan, 1995—97; tchr. music Hayward United Sch. Dist., Calif., 1997—98; instr. strings King City Union Sch. Dist., 1998—. Composer: Vision, 1994, Adventures, 2002, 3 songs using texts, 2002. Vol. King City Town Watch, 2000—, various hosps., 1995—. Fellow, U. Oreg., Eugene, 1993—94; grantee, Mr. Holland Opus Found., King City, 2001. Mem.: Calif. Tchrs. Assn., Nat. Assn. Composers USA, Calif. Music Educators Assn. Jewish. Avocations: chess, reading, baseball. Home: 98 River Dr King City CA 93930 E-mail: dallapiccolo@msn.com.

ETTINGER, SUSI STEINITZ, artist; b. Berlin, July 29, 1922; came to U.S., 1939, naturalized, 1944; d. Otto and Grethe Steinitz; B.F.A. cum laude, U. Louisville, 1943; m. Manford F. Ettinger, June 2, 1944; children— Linda, Daniel. Staff lectr. Met. Mus. Art, N.Y.C., 1944-45; staff instr., dir. children's classes Springfield (Mo.) Art Mus., 1960-66; instr. and lectr. art S.W. Mo. State U., Springfield, 1964-84, ret., 1984, also former area head found. art program; one-woman shows include: Ft. Smith (Ark.) Art Mus., 1968, Sch. of Ozarks, 1972, 86, Springfield Art Mus., 1976, S.W. Mo. State U., 1980; two-artist shows, Springfield, 1974, 84; exhibited group shows in Ark., Kans., Mo., Nebr., Tenn., 1966—; represented in permanent collections: Mo. Hist. Soc., Springfield Art Mus., Harwell Art Mus., Poplar Bluff, Mo. Recipient Appreciation cert. Mo. Women in Arts, 1974. Home: 1080 Patterson St Apt 801 Eugene OR 97401-3322

ETTLING, JOHN, history educator; b. Poplar Bluff, Mo., Oct. 30, 1944; s. Albert John and Emily (Tucker) E.; m. Jennifer Beth Tarlin, Sept. 30, 1974; children— Sarah Isabel, Rachel Anne. B.A., U. Va., 1966; A.M., Harvard U., 1972, Ph.D., 1978. Assoc. prof., chmn. dept. history U. Houston. Author: The Germ of Laziness: Rockefeller Philanthropy and Public Health in the New South, 1981. Served to capt. USAF, 1966-71. Recipient Allan Nevins prize Soc. Am. Historians, 1979; Friends of the Dallas Pub. Library prize Tex. Inst. Letters, 1982. Mem. Am. Hist. Assn., Orgn. Am. Historians, So. Hist. Assn., Am. Assn. for History of Medicine, Phi Beta Kappa. Home: 410 Reeves Dr Grand Forks ND 58201-4914 Office: Dept of History Univ of Houston Houston TX 77004

ETTNER, SUSAN L., healthcare educator, economist; PhD in econs., MIT, Cambridge, 1991. Margaret T. Morris asst. prof. Harvard Med. Sch. Dept. of Health Care Policy, Boston, 1991—98, assoc. prof., 1998—99, Sch. of Pub. Health U. Calif., Los Angeles, 2000—03, prof., 2003—; assoc. prof. Divsn. Gen. Internal Medicine and Health Svcs. Rsch. U. Calif., Los Angeles, 1999—2003, prof., 2003—. Recipient Alice S. Hersch New Investigator award, Acad. Health Svcs. Rsch. and Health Policy, 2001. Office: U CA LA Mail Code 173617 911 Broxton Plaza Los Angeles CA 90095

ETTORE, JOSEPH R., retired discount department store chain executive; B, St. Peter's Coll., Jersey City, NJ, 1961. Pres., COO, dir. Stuart's Dept. Store, Inc., 1989—92, chmn., CEO, 1992—93; pres., CEO, Jamesway Corp., 1993—94; pres., CEO Ames Dept. Stores Inc., Rocky Hill, Conn., 1994—99, chmn., 1999—2002; sr. exec. Management Capital LLC, Providence, 2004—. Recipient numerous industry awards and honors, including Humanitarian of Yr. award Housewares Charity Found., Retail Exec. ot Yr. award Discount Merchandiser mag., Discounters in Svc. to Cmty. award Discount Store News, Bus. Leadership award U. Hartford, Corp. Leadership award Nat. Coun. on Aging, 1st award for edn. excellence Sch. and Home Office Products Assn. Found., 1999. Mem. Internat. Mass Retail Assn. (chmn.).

ETTRE, LESLIE STEPHEN, chemist; b. Szombathely, Hungary, Sept. 16, 1922; came to U.S., 1958, naturalized, 1965; s. Stephen and Mary Therese (Dunay) E.; m. Kitty Polonyi, May 16, 1953; 1 child, Julie Suzanne. Diploma Chem. Engring, U. Tech. Scis., Hungary, 1945, D.Tech. Scis. Chemist G. Richter Pharm. Works, Budapest, Hungary, 1946-49; rsch. chemist Rsch. Inst. for Heavy Chem. Industries, Veszprem, Hungary, 1949-51, head tech. office, 1951-53; sr. lectr. chemistry U. Veszprem, 1951-53; head indsl. dept. Research Inst. for Plastics Industry, Budapest, 1953-56; chemist Lurgi Cos., Frankfurt, Fed. Republic Germany, 1957-58; applications chemist Perkin-Elmer Corp., Norwalk, Conn., 1958-60, product specialist, 1960-62, chief applications chemist, 1962-68, sr. staff scientist, 1972-87, sr. scientist, 1987-90. Exec. editor Ency. Indsl. Chem. Analysis John Wiley & Sons, N.Y.C., 1968-72; rsch. assoc. dept. engring. and applied scis. Yale U., New Haven, 1977-78, adj. prof., 1989-95, rsch. affiliate, 1995—; adj. prof. U. Houston, 1978-88; chmn. various symposia on chromatography, intermittantly, 1972-93; co-chmn. Summer Symposium on Analytical Chemistry Miami U., Oxford, Ohio, 1973; lectr. in U.S., Can., Europe, Asia, Africa, Australia; participant lecture tours of Chromatography Coun. of Acad. Scis., USSR, 1976, 78, 79, 80, 81, 86, 88, Estonian Acad. Scis., 1979-81, Chinese Acad. Scis., 1980, 85, 87, Georgian Acad. Sci., 1981. Recipient Commemorative Chromatography medal Acad. Scis., USSR, 1978, M.S. Tswett award, 1978, L.S. Palmer award Minn. Chromatography Forum, 1980, A.J.P. Martin award Brit. Chromatography Discussion Group, 1982, Outstanding Svc. award Western Carolinas Chromatography Discussion Group, 1987, M.J.E. Golay award Internat. Symposium on Capillary Chromatography, 1992, Jubilee award, 1998, Golden Diploma U. Tech. Scis., Budapest, 1995, Dimick award Pitts. Conf. on Analytical Chemistry and Applied Spectroscopy, 1998, Cs Horvath award Conn. Separations Sci. Coun., 2001. Fellow Am. Inst. Chemists; mem. ASTM (chmn. subcom. rsch. com. E-19, 1966-70, subcom. on nomenclature of com. E-19, 1970-73), Am. Chem. Soc. (award in chromatography 1985), Chromatography Soc. (exec. com. 1982-89), N.Y. Acad. Scis., Internat. Union Pure and Applied Chemistry (nomenclature com. 1981-91), Hungarian Chem. Soc. (hon.; Heureka award 2001). Office: 38 Boston Ave Middletown CT 06457-3562

ETZEL, JAMES EDWARD, environmental engineering educator; b. Reading, Pa., Nov. 9, 1929; s. Edward John and Ruth Anna (Getrost) E.; m. Barbara Dawn Shoup, Sept. 3, 1950; children: Pamela Dawn, Gregory John, Mark Raymond, Scott Edward, Christopher James. BS in Sanitation Engring., Pa. State U., 1951; MSCE, Purdue U., 1955, PhD, 1957. Registered profl. engr., Ind. Engr. Capitol Engring. Co., Dillsburg, Pa., 1951, du Pont Co., Wilmington, Del., 1957-58; engr., dir. research Roy F. Weston, engrs., Newtown Sq., Pa., 1958-59; mem. faculty Purdue U., 1959-90, prof. environ. engring., 1964-90, Water Refining Co. prof., 1978-83, head environ. engring. area Sch. Civil Engring., 1971-90, prof. emeritus environ. engring., 1990—; v.p. Heritage Environ. Svcs., Inc., 1990—. Chmn. Tippecanoe County (Ind.) Solid Wastes Com., 1971-86; mem. W. Lafayette Environ. Commn., 1968-76; cons. to industry, 1960—. Patentee in field. Served with C.E., 1951-53, AUS. Named Outstanding Prof. in Civil Engring. Purdue U., 1979 Mem. Water Pollution Control Fedn. Ind. Water Pollution Control Assn. (past pres.) Lutheran. Home and Office: 710 Cardinal Dr Lafayette IN 47909-9036

ETZEL, RUTH ANN, pediatrician, epidemiologist, educator; b. Milw., Apr. 6, 1954; d. Raymond Arthur and Marion Dorothy Etzel. Student, St. Olaf Coll., 1972-73; BA in Biology summa cum laude, U. Minn., 1976; MD, U. Wis., 1980; PhD, U. N.C., 1985. Bd. cert. Am. Bd. Pediat., Am. Bd. Preventive Medicine. Resident in pediat. N.C. Meml. Hosp., Chapel Hill, 1980-83; adj. asst. prof. pediat. Emory U. Sch. Medicine, Atlanta, 1985-87; epidemic intelligence svc. officer Ctr. Environ. Health Ctrs. Disease Control, Atlanta, 1985-87, med. epidemiologist Ctr. Environ. Health and Injury Control, 1987-90, chief air pollution and respiratory health br., 1991-96, asst. dir. preventive medicine residency program, 1992-97; dir. divsn. epidemiology and risk assessment Office Pub. Health and Sci., Food Safety and Inspection Svc., USDA, Washington, 1998—2001; adj. prof. environ. and occupl. health George Washington U., Washington, 2000—. Mem. preventive medicine and pub. health test com. Nat. Bd. Med. Examiners, 1992—94; mem. US Med. Licensing Exam. Step 2 Preventive Medicine and Pub. Health Test Material Devel. Com., 1992—94; mem., trustee Am. Bd. Preventive Medicine, 1992—2001, vice chair pub. health and preventive medicine, 1997—2001; commissioned officer US Pub. Health Svc, 1985—2005. Editor: Am. Acad. Pediat., Pediat. Environ. Health, 1999—; assoc. editor: Current Problems in Pediatrics and Adolscent Medicine, —; contbr. articles to profl. publs. Recipient Arthur S. Flemming award, DC Jaycees, 1991; Robert Wood Johnson Clin. scholar, U. N.C., 1983—85, MacPherson scholar, 1972. Fellow: Am. Coll. Preventive Medicine, Am. Acad. Pediats. (Ctrs. Disease Control and Prevention liaison 1986—94, chmn. sect. epidemiology 1988—92, ex-officio 1993—94, chmn. com. environ. health 1995—99, mem. com. on native Am. child health 2003—); mem.: Internat. Soc. Environ. Epidemiology, Ambulatory Pediatric Assn. (mem. rsch. com. 1987—, comms. dir. 2002—05), Delta Omega, Phi Beta Kappa. Personal E-mail: retzel@earthlink.net.

ETZIONI, AMITAI, sociologist, educator; b. Cologne, Germany, Jan. 4, 1929; s. Willi Falk and Gertrude Hannauer (Falk) E.; m. Minerva Morales, Sept. 14, 1965 (dec. Dec. 20, 1985); children: Ethan, Oren, Michael, David, Benjamin; m. Patricia Kellogg, Nov. 6, 1992. BA, Hebrew U., Jerusalem, 1954, MA, 1956; PhD in Sociology, U. Calif., Berkeley, 1958; LittD (hon.), Rider Coll., 1980, Gov.'s State U., 1987; LLD (hon.), U. Utah, 1991; LHD (hon.), Colo. Coll., 1994, Conn. Coll., 1994. Mem. faculty Columbia U., 1958-80; rsch. assoc. Inst. War and Peace Studies, 1961, prof. sociology, 1967, chmn. dept., 1969-78; dir. Ctr. for Policy Rsch., 1968—; guest scholar Brookings Instn., 1978-79; sr. advisor White House, 1979-80; univ. prof. George Washington U., Washington, 1980—, dir. Inst. for Communitarian Policy Studies, 1995—; Thomas Henry Carroll Ford Found. vis. prof., grad. sch. bus. Harvard U., Cambridge, Mass., 1987-89. Bd. dirs. Ctr. for Policy Rsch., Washington; mem. Econ. Forum The Conf. Bd., 1983-85; founder Ctr. for Comm. Policy Studies, George Washington U., 1995—; dir., founder Inst. Communitarian Policy Studies, 1995; developed organizational analysis, a typology based on means used to control participants in orgns., how orgns. change, survive and are integrated into larger social units. Author: A Comparative Analysis of Complex Organizations, 1961, Modern Organizations, 1964, Political Unification, A Comparative Study of Leaders and Forces, 1965, Studies in Social Change, 1966, the Active Society, 1968, Genetic Fix, 1973, Social Problems, 1975, An Immodest Agenda, 1982, Capital Corruption, 1984, The Moral Dimension, 1988, The Spirit of Community, 1993, The New Golden Rule, 1996, The Limits of Privacy, 1999, The Road to the Good Society, 2001, The Monochrome Society, 2001, My Brother's Keeper, 2003, From Empire to Community, 2004, How Patriotic is the Patriot Act, 2004; editor: The Responsive Community, 1990-2004; mem. editl. bd. Sci. Mag., 1969-71; contbr. numerous articles to profl. jours. With Israeli Army. Social Sci. Rsch. Coun. faculty fellow, 1960-61, 67-68; fellow Ctr. for Advanced Study in Behavioral Scis., 1965-66; Guggenheim fellow, 1968. Fellow AAAS; mem. Am. Sociol. Assn. (pres. 1995), Soc. for the Advancement Socio-Econs. (founder 1989), The Communitarian Network (founder 1993), Inst. Medicine. Office: George Washington U Rm 703 2130 H St NW Washington DC 20052-0001

EUBANK, DAVID LYNN, lawyer, consultant; b. Lexington, Ky., May 3, 1950; s. Elbert H. and Thelma C. Eubank; m. Lenora A. Eubank, Apr. 12, 1980; 1 child, Mitchell. B of Cmty. Planning, U. Cin., 1974; MPA, JD, U. Dayton, 1989. Bar: Ohio 1989, U.S. Supreme Ct. 1996, U.S. Ct. Appeals (6th cir.) 1991, U.S. Dist. Ct. (so. dist.) Ohio 1990. Exec. dir. Longmont (Colo.) Downtown Devel. Authority, 1980-85; city atty. City of Beavercreek, Ohio, 1991-97; law dir. City of Kettering, Ohio, 1997—. Prin. SFDG Cons., Cin., 1975-80. Mem. Montgomery County, Ohio Cmty. Human Svcs. Levy Rev. Bd., Dayton, 1990-96, mem. Montgomery County Criminal Justice Council, Dayton, 2004—. Mem. Am. Inst. Cert. Planners. Office: City of Kettering Law Dept 3600 Shroyer Rd Kettering OH 45429

EUBANK, EDWARD J., music educator; b. Des Moines, Iowa, Feb. 12, 1961; s. Harold F. and Jeannine T. Eubank; m. Christina R. Kowalczyk, May 12, 1984; children: Brandon J., Amanda L. MusB, Am. Conservatory Music, Chgo., 1983; MA in Ednl. Adminstrn., Govs. State U., 1996. Type 75 Administrative Certificate, General Administrative E Ill., 1996, Special K 12, Type 10 Teaching Certificate Music Ill., 1991. Orch./choral dir. Mother Guerin H.s., River Grove, Ill., 1991—93; dir. orch. Cmty. Unit Dist. #300, Algonquin, Ill., 1993—94, Maine Twp. H.S. East, Park Ridge, Ill., 1994—2000, chmn. dept. fine arts, 2000—. Mem. Park Ridge Cultural Arts Coun., 2001—; founder Maine East String Acad. Violinist, cantor music ministry St. Elizabeth Seton Cath. Ch., Orland Hills, Ill., 1990—2002. Mem.: ASCD, Nat. Assn. Music Edn., Tri-M Music Honor Soc. (hon.). Avocations: travel, reading, hiking, golf. Office: Maine Township High School East 2601 W Dempster St Park Ridge IL 60068

EUBANK, J. THOMAS, lawyer; b. Port Arthur, Tex., Mar. 17, 1930; s. J.T. and Ada (White) E.; m. Nancy Moore, Feb.10, 1956; children: John, Marshall, Stephen, Laura. BA, Rice U., 1951; JD, U. Tex., 1954. Bar: Tex. 1954, U.S. Supreme Ct. 1960. With Baker Botts L.L.P., Houston, 1954-90, sr. ptnr., 1979-90, sr. counsel, 1999—; dir. Sentinel Trust Co., L.B.A., 1997—. Mem. joint editl. bd. Uniform Probate code, 1972-86. Bd. govs. Rice U., 1985-91. Mem. ABA (chmn. sect. real property, probate and trust law 1978-79), Am. Coll. Trust and Estate Counsel (pres. 1984-85, pres. Found. 1986-89, Trachtman lectr. 1986), State Bar Tex. (chmn. sect. real estate, probate and trust law 1972-73, Lifetime Achievement award 2003), Am. Bar Found., Tex. Bar Found., Houston Philos. Soc., Rice U. Alumni Assn. (pres. 1979-80, Rice Gold medal 1992), Am. Law Inst., Internat. Acad. Estate and Trust Law, Houston Country, Coronado, Allegro, Thalia, Chevaliers du Tastevin. Home: 26 Liberty Bell Cir Houston TX 77024-6303 Office: 910 Louisiana St Houston TX 77002-4995 Office Phone: 713-229-1688. Business E-Mail: tom.eubank@bakerbotts.com.

EUBANK, WEAVER KEITH, history professor, writer; b. Princeton, N.J., Dec. 8, 1920; s. Weaver Keith and Nancy Grace (Holden) Eubank; m. Marilyn Jean Climenson, Sept. 8, 1951; children: David Keith, Ellen Jane Patrick. BA, Hampden-Sydney Coll., Va., 1942; MA, Harvard U., Cambridge, Mass., 1947; PhD, U. Pa., Phila., 1951. Instr. Bloomfield Coll., NJ, 1950—53; asst. prof., history U. N. Tex., Denton, 1954—56, assoc. prof., history, 1956—59, prof., history, 1959—64, Queens Coll., CUNY, 1964—90, chmn., dept. history, 1967—85. Author: Munich, 1963, The Summit Conferences, 1919-1963, 1966, Summit at Teheran, 1985; co-author: Survey of Historic Costume, 3d edit., 1998, Origins of World War II, 4th edit., 2004. 1st lt. U.S. Army, 1942—46, ETO. Mem.: Am. Hist. Assn., Phi Beta Kappa. Democrat. Presbyterian. Home: 500 Crestwood Dr #1409 Charlottesville VA 22903

EUBANKS, EUGENE EMERSON, education educator, consultant; b. Meadville, Pa., June 6, 1939; s. Nelson Eubanks and Emily (Princes) Jackson; m. Audrey Hunter, Aug. 4, 1962; children: Brian, Regina. BS, Edinboro (Pa.) State U., 1963; PhD, Mich. State U., 1972. Tchr. Cleve. Pub. Schs., 1963-68, unit prin., 1968-70; asst. prof. U. Del., Newark, 1972-74; asst. dean U. Mo., Kansas City, 1974-79, dean, 1979-88, prof. edn. and urban affairs, 1988—; dept. supt. Kansas City Pub. Schs., 1984-85. Contbr. articles to profl. jours. Cons. Urban League, 1978—, legal def. fund NAACP, 1978, Cleve. Found., 1978, U. Wis., 1988; bd. dirs. Operation PUSH, 1982-87, Mid-Continent Girl Scouts, Kansas City, 1983—, Genesis Sch., 1984—; chair Desegration Monitoring Com., 1985—. Mem. Am. Assn. Coll. Tchr. Edn. (pres. 1988-89), Nat. Alliance Found. (chmn. 1984-85), Black Sch. Educators (edn. commn.). Home: 12737 Oakmont Dr Kansas City MO 64145-1140 Office: U Mo Sch Edn 5100 Rockhill Rd Kansas City MO 64110-2481 Office Phone: 816-235-2448. Business E-Mail: EubanksE@umkc.edu.

EUBANKS, KEVIN, jazz guitarist; b. Philadelphia, PA, Nov. 15, 1957; Mem. Art Blakey's big band, 1980—81; joined The Tonight Show band, 1992; music dir. The Tonight Show with Jay Leno, L.A., 1995—. Musician: (albums) Guitarist, 1982, Sundance, 1984, Opening Night, 1985, Face to Face, 1986, The Heat of Heat, 1987, Shadow Prophets, 1988, The Searcher, 1988, Promise of Tomorrow, 1989, Turning Point, 1991, Spiritalk, 1993, Live at Bradley's, 1994, Spiritalk 2, 1994, The Best of Kevin Eubanks Collection, 1996; composer musical score: HBO Pictures Rebound - The Legend of Earl "The Goat" Manigault, 1996, PBS documentary series Black Westerners.

EUBANKS, RONALD W., lawyer, commentator; b. Montgomery, Ala., Sept. 17, 1946; s. William Shell and Violet Lavern (Walker) E.; 1 child, Edward Todd. Student, Auburn U., 1964-65; BA, U. Ala., 1968; JD, U. Utah, 1974. Bar: Utah 1974, Nebr. 1979, Minn. 1983, Wash. 1985, U.S. Ct. Appeals (10th cir.) 1977, U.S. Ct. Appeals (8th cir.) 1979, U.S. Supreme Ct. 1977, U.S. Ct. Appeals (9th cir.) 1985. Gen. mgr. Sta. WVMI and Sta. WQID, Biloxi Gulfport, Miss., 1968-71; with FCC, Washington, 1974-75; assoc. Hansen & Hansen, Salt Lake City, 1975-77; with law dept. Union Pacific R.R., Omaha, 1977-83; asst. gen. counsel Burlington No. R.R. Co., St. Paul, 1983-84, gen. counsel western region, 1984-87; v.p. law and corp. affairs Glacier Park Co., 1987-88; exec. v.p. Ecos Corp., 1988; CEO Capital Comms., Montgomery, 1991-97; pres. ET Comms., Montgomery, 1988-97; regional v.p. Clear Channel Comm., 1997—2002; mng. ptnr. WDJR-WESP-WZND Radio Sta., Dathan, Ala., 2002—. Dir. Camas Prairie R.R., Longview Switching Co.; adj. prof. comms. dept. Ala. State U. Co-author: Practical Law in Utah, 1978, Defense of Mary Carter, 1984; contbr. articles to profl. publs. Bd. dirs., mem. exec. com., legal counsel Utah Boys Ranch, Salt Lake City, 1977-79; bd. dirs. Children and Youth Svcs., Salt Lake City, 1977-84, Nebr. affiliate Am. Diabetes Assn., 1982-83, Greater Montgomery Sickle Cell Found., 1990—, Ala. Broadcasters Assn., 1998—, Oreg.-Wash. R.R., 1984-87, Camas Prairie R.R., 1984-87, Longview Switching Co., 1984-87; chmn. Wash. R.R. Assn., 1984-87; co-chmn. Montgomery Father and Son Banquet Com., 1993—; bd. dirs., mem. exec. com. Montgomery Mental Health Assn., 1995—, treas., 1996—; bd. dirs., mem. exec. com. Montgomery Area Coun. on Aging, 1998-99; bd. advisors, dept. comm. Ala. State U., 1995—. Recipient Friend of Youth award YMCA, 1993; named Role Model of Yr. Southlawn Sch., 1996-97. Mem. ABA (sect. on litigation, coms. on publs. and trial techniques, sect. on tort and ins. practice, com. on r.r. law), Washington State Bar Assn., Seattle-King County Bar Assn., Wash. R.R. Assn. (chmn. 1984-87), Def. Rsch. Inst. (chmn. com on r.r. law 1984-86, mem. com. on practice and procedure), Jason's Soc., Phi Alpha Delta, Alpha Tau Omega. Presbyterian. Office: Capital Comm 648 Perry St Montgomery AL 36104

EUBANKS-POPE, SHARON G., real estate company executive, entrepreneur; b. Chgo., Aug. 26, 1943; d. Walter Franklyn and Thelma Octavia (Watkins) Gibson; m. Larry Hudson Eubanks, Dec. 20, 1970 (dec. Jan. 1976); children: Rebekah, Aimée; m. Otis Eliot Pope, June 7, 1977; children: O. Eliot Jr., Adrienne. BS in Edn., Chgo. Tchrs. Coll., 1965; postgrad., Ill. Inst. Tech., 1967, John Marshall Law Sch., 1970, Governor's State U., 1975-76. Educator, parent coord. Chgo. Bd. Edn., 1965-77; owner, ptnr. Redel Rentals, Chgo., 1977—. Realtor, 1990—. N.W. regional dir. Jack and Jill Am. Found., 1993-95, nat. treas., 1998-2000; adminstrv. bd. St. Mark United Meth. Ch., Chgo., 1967, bd. trustees, 1988; com. chair Englewood Urban Progress Ctr., Chgo., 1973; coord., educator LWV, 1975-76; chair comms. Marian Cath. H.S., 1999—, adv. bd. Named Outstanding Sch. Parent Vol., Chgo. Bd. Edn., 1977; recipient Outstanding Cmty. Law Class award LWV, 1975-76, Christian Leadership award United Meth. Women, Chgo., 1985. Mem.: NAACP, NAFE, Nat. Assn. Realtors, Am. Soc. Profl. and Exec. Women, St. Mark Cmty. Devel. Corp. (v.p. 2003—), Links, Inc., Jack and Jill Am., Inc. (Chgo. chpt. journalist 1989—91, parliamentarian 1991, founder Parents for Parity in Edn. 1992, pres. Eubanks-Pope Devel. Co., Inc. 1993, Midwestern region sec.-treas. 1993—95, nat. treas. 1998—2000), Alpha Beta Gamma (female exec. del. to China People to People Amb. program 1998). Office: Redel Rentals 4338 S Drexel Blvd Chicago IL 60653-3536

EUCLIDE, WILLIAM L., art educator, department chairman; m. Sandra Euclide; children: Brian, Gregory. EdB, U. Wis., Oshkosh, 1970; M in Edn. Art, Concordia U., 1987. Tchr., dept. chair Grafton (Wis.) HS, 1970—. Bd. dirs. WEA Trust Ins. Co. Bd. dirs. Town of Cedarburg, Wis., 1974—80, mem. planning com., 1974—98. Named North Shore Educator of the Yr. Mem.: Wis. Edn. Assn. (bd. dirs.). Home: 5722 Oakdale Ct Grafton WI 53024 Office: Grafton HS 1950 Washington St Grafton WI 53024-2199

EUDALY, OLIVIA COGGIN, not-for-profit executive, educator; b. Dec. 23, 1945; BA, Tex. Christian U., 1967; MA, Southwestern Bapt. Theol. Sem., Ft. Worth, 1972. Spl. events mgr. Rafter Seven Ranch, Ft. Worth, 1970-99; tchr. Western Hills H.S., Ft. Worth, 1992-94; adj. prof. Tex. Christian U., Dallas Bapt. U., Tarrant City Coll., 1989—; dep. dir. Tarrant Area Food Bank, Ft. Worth, 1996—2003; v.p., fund devel. Big Brothers Big Sisters of North Tex., 2003—. Bd. dirs. Happy Hill Farm. Committeewoman State Rep. Exec. Com., Tex., 1994-98; candidate U.S. Ho. of Reps., 1995-96; trustee Hardin Simmons U.; mem. Leadership Ft. Worth. Recipient Gt. Women of Tex. award, 2001, Outstanding Woman in the Workplace, City of Ft. Worth Mayor's Com. Mem.: Petroleum Club, Assn. Fundraising Profls. (v.p.), Leadership Ft. Worth (v.p.), Rotary Club of Ft. Worth. Office: Big Brothers Big Sisters of North Texas 205 W Main St Arlington TX 76016 Office Phone: 817-277-1148.

EUGENIDES, JEFFREY, writer; b. Detroit, Mar. 8, 1960; married; 1 child. BA in English, Brown U., 1983; MA in English and Creative Writing, Stanford U., 1986. Fellow Berliner Kunstlerprogramm of DAAD, Am. Acad. Berlin. Author: (book) The Virgin Suicides, 1993, Middlesex, 2002 (Pulitzer prize for fiction, 2003); contbr. fiction to popular mags. and anthologies. Recipient Whiting Writer's award, Henry D. Vursell Meml. award, Am. Acad. Arts and Letters, Pulitzer prize for fiction, 2003; fellow, Guggenheim Found., NEA. Office: Farrar Straus & Giroux 19 Union Sq W New York NY 10003*

EUGSTER, ALBRECHT KONRAD, veterinarian, laboratory director; b. Langenegg, Austria, Dec. 10, 1938; came to US, 1964; s. Anton Ferdinand and Joseffina (Laesser) E.; m. Kathe Ella Dittrich, Feb. 12, 1965; children: Cristopher, Susan. D.V.M., Vet. Coll., Vienna, Austria, 1963; PhD, Colo. State U., 1970. Diplomate Am. Coll. Vet. Microbiologists. Practice vet. medicine, Austria, 1963-64; rsch. assoc. S.W. Found. Rsch. and Edn., San Antonio, 1964-67; head diagnostic microbiology Tex. Vet. Med. Diagnostic Lab., Coll. Sta., 1970-80, exec. dir., 1980—2002, vet. med. cons., 2002—. Columnist jour. The Cattleman Mem. Am. Assn. Vet. Lab. Diagnosticians (pres. 1987), AVMA, Tex. Veterinary Med. Assn. (Disting. Achievement award 1984), World Assn. Vet Lab Diognosticians (pres. 1999-2001), Am. Veterinarian Epidemiology Soc. (hon. diploma) Lodges: Kiwanis (pres. 1984-85). Roman Catholic. Avocation: skiing. E-mail: keugster@tamu.edu.

EUGSTER, JACK WILSON, retail executive; b. Mound, Minn., Oct. 7, 1945; s. George and Helen M. (Kerr) E.; m. Camie M. Rust; children: Nicholas J., Wilson M. BA in Chemistry, Carleton Coll., 1967; MBA in Fin., Stanford U., 1969. Mgr. ops. and merchandising Target Stores Inc., Mpls., 1970-72; exec. v.p. The Gap Stores, San Bruno, Calif., 1972-80; chmn., pres., CEO The Musicland Group, Inc., Mpls., 1980—2001. Bd. dirs. Donaldson Corp., Midwest Resources Inc., Des Moines, Damark Inc., Mpls., Carleton Coll., Northfield, Minn., Best Buy Co., ShopKo Stores, Inc., Green Bay, Wis., chmn. bd. dirs., 2001— Divsn. chmn. campaign United Way, Mpls., 1980—; bd. dirs. Children's Home Soc. Minn. Recipient Human Relations Music and Video Div. award Anti-Defamation League, N.Y.C., 1986. Mem. Nat. Assn. Recording Merchandisers (bd. dirs. 1981-88, pres. 1985-86), Country Music Assn. (bd. dirs. 1985-88, chmn. 1987-88), Wayzata Country Club, Mpls. Club. Home: 2655 Kelly Ave Excelsior MN 55331-9532 Office: Chairman Shopko Stores inc 700 Pilgrim Way Green Bay WI 54304

EULE, NORMAN LOUIS, lawyer; b. Bklyn., Jan. 5, 1947; m. Ellen D. Luks, June 21, 1971; 1 child, Alex. BA in Polit. Sci. cum laude, Bklyn. Coll., 1968; JD with highest honors, George Washington U., 1974; postgrad., Columbia U., 1968—71. Bar: D.C. 1974, Md., 1986. Assoc. Pierson, Ball & Dowd, Washington, 1974-81, ptnr., 1981-89, Reed, Smith, Shaw & McClay, 1989-94, Ridberg, Sherbill & Aronson, LLP, Bethesda, Md., 1995—. Adj. prof. Am. U./Washington Coll. of Law, George Washington U. Law Sch., Washington; spkr. and author tax, bus. and employee benefits matters. Mem. editl. bd. Tax Strategies; contbr. articles to profl. jours. Past pres. Congregation Beth El, Montgomery County, Md. Mem. ABA, Fed. Comm. Bar Assn., Bar Assn. of D.C., Bar Assn. of Md., Order of Coif. Office: Ste 650 Three Bethesda Metro Ctr Bethesda MD 20814 E-mail: neule@rpslaw.com.

EURICH, JUDITH, art appraiser, printmaker; Tchr. Acad. Art Coll., Hearst Art Gallery, St. Mary's Coll., Moranga, Calif., Univ. Calif. Ext., San Francisco; curatorial asst., asst. curator, curator, prints, drawings, 19th century photogs. San Francisco Arts Mus. Achenbach Found. for Graphic Arts, 1981—92; specialist to dir., print dept. Butterfield & Butterfield (now Bonhams & Butterfields), San Francisco, 1995—. Lectr. in field. Office: Bonhams & Butterfields 220 San Bruno Ave San Francisco CA 94103 Office Phone: 415-503-3259. Office Fax: 415-861-8951. Business E-Mail: judith.eurich@bonhams.com.

EURICH, NELL P., education educator; b. Norwood, Ohio, July 28, 1919; d. Clayton W. and Adah (Palmer) Plopper; m. Alvin C. Eurich, Mar. 15, 1953 (dec. 1987); children: Juliet Ann, Donald Alan; m. Maurice Lazarus, 1988. AA, Stephens Coll., 1939; BA, Stanford U., 1941, MA, 1943; PhD, Columbia U., 1959. Dir. student union U. Tex., 1942-43; resident counselor Barnard Coll., 1944-46; asst. to pres. Woman's Found., 1947-49; officer charge pub. relations State U. N.Y., 1949- 52; acting pres. Stephens Coll., 1953-54; asst. prof. English NYU, 1959-64; academic dean New Coll., Sarasota, Fla., 1965; dir. project to reorganize curriculum Aspen (Colo.) Pub. High Sch., 1966; dean faculty, prof. English Vassar Coll., 1967-70; provost, dean faculty, prof. English, v.p. acad. affairs Manhattanville Coll., N.Y., 1971-75; sr. cons. Internat. Council for Ednl. Devel., 1975-82, Acad. for Ednl. Devel., 1982-88. Mem. nat. selection com., chmn. Rocky Mountain regional com. Nat. Endowment Humanities, 1966-67, cons., 1970-71; mem. Middle States commn. Marshall Scholarships, 1967-68; chmn. Northeastern region, 1969-71; mem. U.S. Commn. on Ednl. Tech., HEW, 1968-69; mem. overseer's vis. com. on summer sch. and univ. extension Harvard, 1969-75; mem. panel of judge's Fed. Woman's award, 1969; cons. Acad. for Ednl. Devel., 1970-71; mem. career minister rev. bd. U.S. Dept. State, 1972; participant Ditchley Conf. V, 1973; mem. Rhodes Scholarship Selection Com., 1976; moderator exec. seminar Aspen Inst. for Humanistic Studies, 1977, 79, 80; dir. Adult Learning Project Carnegie Found. for Advancement Teaching, 1985-90; advisor Nat. Acad. of Engring., 1987-88; vis. com. Neuro Scis., Mass. Gen. Hosp. Author: Science in Utopia, 1967, Higher Education in Twelve Countries: A Comparative View, 1981, (with B. Schwenkmeyer) Great Britain's Open University, 1971, Corporate Classrooms, 1985, The Learning Industry, 1991; contbg. author: (Alvin Toffler) Learning for Tomorrow, 1974, From Parnassus: Essays for Jacques Barzun, 1976; contbr. articles to profl. jours. Past trustee Bank Street Coll., Salisbury Sch., Hudson Guild Neighborhood House, Colo. Rocky Mountain Sch., Bennington Coll.; trustee Carnegie Coun. on Policy Studies in Higher Edn., 1977—80, Carnegie Found. for Advancement of Teaching, 1978—84; trustee emeritus New Coll. Found., 1964—2001. Mem. MLA, Am. Assn. Colls. (spl. com. on liberal studies 1966-70), World Soc. Ekistics, Nat. Coun. Women (hon.), Century Assn. N.Y.C. Home: 144 Brattle St Cambridge MA 02138-2202

EURICH, RICHARD REX, lawyer; b. Lancaster, Pa., Apr. 12, 1947; s. Richard Roy and Mary Elizabeth (Kiehl) E.; m. JoAnn Samsa, June 27, 1970; 1 child, Richard. BA cum laude, Am. U., 1969; JD cum laude, Harvard U., 1972. Bar: Mass. 1972, U.S. Dist. Ct. Mass. 1973, U.S. Ct. Appeals (1st cir.) 1975. Assoc. Morrison Mahoney, LLP, Boston, 1972-76, ptnr., 1976—. Elected Town Meeting Mem., Town of Lexington, 1996-99; mem. exec. bd. Lexington Town Meeting Mems. Assn., 1998-99, Lexington Appropriation Com., 2000— Fellow Mass. Bar Found.; mem. ABA, Mass. Bar Assn. (mem. budget and fin. com., chmn. ins. com.), Def. Rsch. Inst., Mass. Def. Lawyers Assn., Internat. Assn. Def. Counsel. Roman Catholic. Home: 7 Pitcairn Pl Lexington MA 02421-7108 Office: Morrison Mahoney LLP 250 Summer St Fl 1 Boston MA 02210-1181 Office Phone: 617-439-7508. E-mail: reurich@morrisonmahoney.com.

EUSDEN, JOHN DYKSTRA, theology studies educator, minister; b. Holland, Mich., July 20, 1922; s. Ray Anderson and Marie (Dykstra) E.; m. Joanne Reiman, June 14, 1950; children: Andrea Bonner, Alan Tolles, John Dykstra Jr., Sarah Jewell. AB, Harvard U., 1943; postgrad., Harvard Law Sch., 1946; BD cum laude, Yale U., 1949, PhD in Religion, 1954. Ordained to ministry United Ch. of Christ, 1949. Instr. in religion Yale U., 1953-55, asst. prof., 1955-60; assoc. prof. religion, chaplain Williams Coll., Williamstown, Mass., 1960-70, Nathan Jackson prof. Christian theology, 1970-90, vis. prof. environ. studies, 1990-92; vis. prof. religion and Asian studies Mt. Holyoke Coll., Mass., 1992—93; min. 1st Congl. Ch., Bennington, Vt., 1991—; cons. Asian programs and environ. studies Williams Coll., Williamstown, Mass., 1992—. Lectr., research fellow Kyoto U., 1963-64, 76, 81-82; theologian-in-residence Am. Ch. in Paris, 1972; lectr. Doshisha U., Kyoto, Japan, 1976, 82; bd. dir. Associated Kyoto Program, Japan. Author: Puritans, Lawyers and Politics in Early 17th Century England, 1958, 68, Zen and Christian: The Journey Between, 1981, (with John H. Westerhoff III) The Spiritual Life: Learning East and West, 1982, (with Westerhoff) Sensing Beauty: Aesthetics, the Human Spirit, and the Church, 1998, (with Westerhoff) Thirsting for Healing and Wholeness, 2005; contbr. articles to profl. jours.; translator, editor, author introduction: The Marrow of Theology (William Ames), 1975, 86; author introduction: Zen Buddhism and Christianity in Y. Takeuchi Festschrift (Japanese edition), 1993, Christology: The Dialogue of East and West in Christology in Dialogue, 1993, Chinese Healing: A Practical Mysticism in John Sahadat Festschrift, 2002. Mem. adv. coun., campus ministry program Danforth Found., 1966-70; bd. dirs. Wellesley Coll. Parents Assn., 1972-75, pres., 1974-75; rsch. fellow Ctr. for Study of Japanese Religion, Kyoto, 1976-94; trustee Lingnan Found., N.Y.C., 1964—, Buxton Sch., Williamstown, Mass., 1970-83, Chewonki Found., Wiscasset, Maine, 2002—; leader trips, People's Republic of China, 1978, 81, 86, 88, 90, 94. 1st lt. USMCR, 1943-45. Scholar Harvard U.; faculty fellow Am. Assn. Theol. Schs., 1958-59, Sterling fellow Yale U., 1950-53, fellow Folger Shakespeare Libr., 1958-59, 71-72; Lilly postdoctoral grantee, 1963-64, Danforth campus ministry grantee, 1963-64; fellow Am. Council Learned Socs., 1967-68; Fulbright rsch. travel grantee, 1967-68; research fellow U. Utrecht, Netherlands, 1968; rsch. grantee Williams Coll., 1976. Mem. AAUP, Am. Acad. Religion, Am. Soc. Ch. History, Am. Soc. Christian Ethics, Nat. Assn. Coll. and Univ. Chaplains, Soc. Values in Higher Edn., Appalachian Mountain Club, Randolph Mountain Club (pres. 1973-75). Home: 75 Forest Rd Williamstown MA 01267-2028 Office: Williams Coll Stetson Hall Williamstown MA 01267 Personal E-mail: jeusden@sover.net.

EUSTACE, DUDLEY GRAHAM, diversified financial services company executive; b. July 3, 1936; m. Carol Diane Zakrajsek; 2 children. BA in Econs., U. Bristol. Chartered acct. With John Barrit & Son, Hamilton, Bermuda, 1962, Internat. Resort Facilities, Ont., 1963, Alcan Aluminium, Ltd., Montreal, Vancouver, Buenos Aires, Rio de Janeiro, Madrid & U.K., 1964-87, Brit. Aerospace plc, 1987, fin. dir., 1988-92; mem. group mgmt. com. Philips, 1992—2001, exec. v.p. fin., 1993-97, vice chmn. Amsterdam, 1997—; now chmn. Smith & Nephew plc, London. Mem. coun. dept. exports, credits guarantee Resigweb, 1992; chmn. supervisory bd. Aegon N.V., chmn. Sendo Plc; mem. supervisory bd., 1999-2004, KPN N.V., Hagemeyer N.V.; interim CFO, Royal Ahold N.V., 2003. Avocations: stamp collecting/philately, gardening, reading. Office: Smith & Nephew plc 15 Adam St London WC2N 6LA England Business E-Mail: dudley.eustace@smith-nephew.com.

EUSTACE, NATALIE BENCOWITZ, elementary school educator; b. Offenbach, Germany, Apr. 16, 1946; arrived in U.S., 1947; d. Isaac and Galina (Kapustjan) Bencowitz; m. Tom Lee Eustace, July 6, 1968; children: Natasha Leigh, Tanya Marie. BA, Austin Coll., 1968; MA, So. Meth. U., 1973. Tchr. 2d-6th grade Ft. Bend (Tex.) Ind. Sch. Dist., 1968-71, Plano (Tex.) Ind. Sch. Dist., 1971-74; tchr. 3d grade Ft. Bend Ind. Sch. Dist., 1974-75; tchr. 7th-12th grade Midland (Tex.) Ind. Sch. Dist., 1981-84, tchr. 4th grade, 1984—. Trainer N.J. Writing Project and TTT (TAKS Help). Judge Nat. Guild Piano. Chmn. parent-family coun. Austin Coll., Sherman, Tex., 1999—2001, mem. alumni bd., 1981—93; active 1st United Meth. Ch., Midland, 1981—, Cmty. Bible Study, 1999—, treas., 2005—. Mem.: Midland Music Tchrs. Assn., Tex. Reading Coun., Tex. Music Educators Assn., Tex. State Tchrs. Assn., Music Tchrs. Nat. Assn., Delta Kappa Gamma (chpt. treas. 1994—2000, state ceremonials com. 1999—2001, pres. 2000—02, state music com. 2001—03, area coord. 2003—). Republican. Methodist. Avocations: reading, music, travel, singing. Home: 4007 Crestgate Ave Midland TX 79707-2716 Office: Parker Elem Sch 3800 Norwood St Midland TX 79707-4499 Office Phone: 432-689-1840.

EUSTER, JOANNE REED, retired librarian; b. Grants Pass, Oreg., Apr. 7, 1936; d. Robert Lewis and Mabel Louise (Jones) Reed; m. Stephen L. Gerhardt, May 14, 1977; children: Sharon L., Carol L., Lisa J. Student, Lewis and Clark Coll., 1953-56; BA, Portland State Coll., 1965; MLibrarianship, U. Wash., 1968, MBA, 1977; PhD, U. Calif., Berkeley, 1986. Asst. libr. Edmonds C.C., Lynnwood, Wash., 1968-73, dir. libr.-media ctr., 1973-77; libr. Loyola U., New Orleans, 1977-80; libr. dir. J. Paul Leonard Libr., San Francisco State U., 1980-86, Rutgers State U. N.J., New Brunswick, 1986-89, v.p. info. svcs., 1989-91, v.p. univ. librs., 1991-92; libr. dir. U. Calif., Irvine, 1992-97; ret., 1997. Mem. adv. coun. Hong Kong U. Sci. and Tech. Librs., 1988—, Princeton U. Libr., 1988-92, U. B.C., Can., 1991—; cons. in field Author: Changing Patterns of Internal Communication in Large Academic Libraries, 1981, The Academic Library Director, Management Activities and Effectiveness, 1987; columnist Wilson Libr. Bull., 1993-95; contbr. articles to profl. jours. Pres. Seattle Repertory Orgn.; trustee Seattle Repertory Theatre. Mem. ALA, Calif. Libr. Assn., Assn. Coll. and Rsch. Librs. (pres. 1987-88), Rsch. Librs. Group (chair bd. dirs. 1991-92).

EUSTIS, ALBERT ANTHONY, lawyer, diversified financial services company executive; b. Mahanoy City, Pa., Nov. 8, 1921; m. Mary Hampton Stewart, Apr. 25, 1959; children: Thomas Stewart, David Anthony. BS, Columbia U., 1948; LL.B., Harvard U., 1951. Bar: N.Y. 1952, U.S. Dist. Ct. (So. dist.) N.Y 1955. Atty. firm Kelley, Drye & Warren, N.Y.C., 1951-61; atty. W.R. Grace & Co., N.Y.C., 1961-66, asst. gen. counsel, 1966-76, v.p., gen. counsel, sec., 1976-78, sr. v.p., gen. counsel, sec., 1978-82, exec. v.p., gen. counsel, sec., 1982-87; of counsel Holland & Knight, Washington, 1987—. Chmn. bd. trustees, spl. counsel Found. for President's Pvt. Sector Survey on Cost Control; adj. prof. law Fordham Law Sch. Served with AUS, 1942-46. Mem. ABA, Am. Arbitration Assn. (bd. dirs., comml. arbitration panel)

EUSTIS, ROBERT HENRY, design company executive, mechanical engineer; b. Mpls., Apr. 18, 1920; s. Ralph Warren and Florence Louise E.; m. Katherine Vik Johnson, Mar. 20, 1943; children: Jeffrey Nelson, Karen V. B in Mech. Engring., U. Minn., 1942, MS, 1944; ScD, MIT, 1953. Instr. U. Minn., 1942-44; rsch. scientist NASA, 1944-47; asst. prof. MIT, 1947-51; chief engr. Thermal Rsch. and Engring. Corp., 1951-53; mgr. heat and mech. sect. S.R.I. Internat., 1953-55; mem. faculty dept. mech. engring. Stanford (Calif.) U., 1955-90, prof., 1962, dir. high temperature gasdynamics lab., 1961-80, assoc. dean engring., 1984-88; pres. Menlo Furniture Designs, 2004—. Chmn. tech. adv. coun. Emerson Electric Corp.; prin. Eustis Designs, 1990-00. Contbr. articles to profl. jours. Recipient medal Soviet Sci. Acad., 1973. Fellow: AAAS, ASME, AIAA. Home: 862 Lathrop Dr Palo Alto CA 94305-1053 Office: Stanford Univ Dept Mech Engring Stanford CA 94305 Business E-Mail: rheustis@stanford.edu.

EUTSLER, MARK LESLIE, business services executive, real estate broker; b. Crawfordsville, Ind., May 17, 1958; s. David Lee and Lilian Agnus May (Grant) E., m. Therese Anne Wagner, Oct. 3, 1987. BS, Ind. State U., 1980; MS in Edn., Purdue U., 1984; postgrad., Butler U., 1985. Cert. life tchr., Ind. Broker, assoc. Eutsler Real Estate, Linden, Ind., 1977-86; sec., treas. DEW Advt. Corp., Linden, 1978—; music dir. Frontier Sch. Corp., Chalmers, Ind., 1980-83; band and music dir. McCutcheon High Sch., Lafayette, Ind., 1983-84; acting pub. health sanitarian Montgomery County Dept. Health, Safety and Environ. Mgmt., Crawfordsville, Ind., 1985; asst. editor Lafayette Bus. Digest, 1985-86; field rep. Cen. Ind. Regional Blood Ctr., Lafayette, 1986-87; cons. DEW Advt. Corp., Linden, Ind., 1987—; v.p. mktg. and devel. Wesley Manor Retirement Cmty., 1999—, dir. mktg. & devel., 1999—. Bd. dirs. Hist. Linden, Inc. dba Railway Heritage Network, pres., 1986—; rep. Pub. Assistance Ind., Inc., Crawfordsville, 1984—; program mgr. Arts Ind. Mag. in the Classroom, 1995-99. Contbr. articles to profl. jours. Sec., bd. dirs. John T. Conner Ctr. for U.S.-USSR Reconciliation, Inc., 1985—; mem. Ind. State Police Coun. Emergency Response Team; bd. dirs. U.S. Selective Svc., 1993—; mem. proficiency overview com. Ind. Dept. Edn., 1998—; co-chair bands com. 500 Festival Parade, 1996—; Fanfest/Mus. chair 500 Festival Cmty. Day, 1998—; chair family concerts bands com. 500 Festival, 1998—. Named to Hon. Order of Ky. Cols., Gov. of Ky., Frankfort, 1985; named Disting. Hoosier by Gov. Evan Bayh, 1989; recipient Meritorious Hoosier award Ind. Sec. of State, Indpls., 1985, Cmty. Svc. award Gov.'s Voluntary Action Program, 1996; named Hoosier Hero, U.S. Senator Dan Coats, 1997. Mem. New Richmond Coal Creek Twp. Hist. Soc. Inc. (pub. rels. dir. 1984-87), Crawfordsville-Montgomery County C. of C. (tourism brochure com.), Greater Lafayette C. of C. (ambassador 1985-87), Clinton County C. of C. (bd. dirs. 2000—), Young Audiences Ind. Arts Ptnrs. (steering com. 1995—), Railway Heritage Network (founding prse. 1986—), Arts Coun. Indpls. Task Force, Ind. Arts Commn. (adv. panelist 1997—), Masons. Methodist. Home: PO Box 61 Linden IN 47955-0061 Office: DEW Advt Corp 207 N Main St Linden IN 47955 Office Phone: 765-426-0195. Personal E-mail: eutsler@tctc.com.

EUTSLER, THERESE ANNE, physical therapist; b. Jasper, Ind., Sept. 11, 1959; d. Joseph Martin and Viola Agnes (Rasche) Wagner; m. Mark Leslie Eutsler, Oct. 3, 1987; children: Andrew, Abigail BS, Ind. U., 1982. Physical therapist Reid Meml. Hosp., Richmond, Ind., 1982-84; physical therapist Cen. Convalescent Services, Crawfordsville, Ind., 1984-85, St. Elizabeth Hosp., Lafayette, Ind., 1985-86, 95—, clinical coord., 1986-92; with Indsl. Rehab. of Crawfordville, 1992-94. Panelist to rev. grants Ind. Arts Commn., 1998. Bd. dirs. Arthritis Found. Tippecanoe unit, Lafayette, 1986-89, John T. Conner Ctr. for U.S.-USSR Reconciliation, 1989—; del. Ind. State Dem. Conv., Indpls., 1988. Recipient Sagamore of the Wabash award, 2004. Roman Catholic. Avocations: volleyball, raquetball, railroad walking. Home: 215 N Main St Linden IN 47955 E-mail: eutsler@tctc.com.

EVAN, WILLIAM MARTIN, sociologist, educator; b. Ostrow, Poland, Dec. 17, 1922; BA, U. Pa., 1946; PhD, Cornell U., 1954. Instr. sociology Princeton U., 1954-56; asst. prof. Columbia U., 1956-59; research sociologist Bell Telephone Labs., Murray Hill, N.J., 1959-62; assoc. prof. sociology and mgmt. MIT, 1962-66; prof. U. Pa., Phila., 1966—. Cons. to govt. agys. and pvt. industry, 1960—; Ford vis. prof. sociology Grad. Sch. Bus., U. Chgo., 1971-72; vis. fellow Wolfson Coll., U. Oxford, 1978-79. Author: (with others) Preventing World War III, 1962, Law and Sociology, 1962, Organizational Experiments, 1971, Interorganizational Relations, 1976, Organization Theory, 1976, Frontiers in Organization and Management, 1980, The Sociology of Law, 1980, Knowledge and Power in a Global Society, 1981, The Arms Race and Nuclear War, 1987, Social Structure and Law, 1990, Organization Theory: Research and Design, 1993, (with Ved P. Nanda) Nuclear Proliferation and the Legality of Nuclear Weapons, 1995, (with Mark Manion) Minding the Machines: Preventing Technological Disasters, 2002, War and Peace In An Age of Terrorism, 2005. Social Sci. Rsch. Coun. tng. fellow, 1951-52, Fulbright fellow, 1952-53; Russell Sage Found. resident, 1956-58. Fellow AAAS; mem. Am. Sociol. Assn., Internat. Sociol. Assn., Internat. Inst. Mgmt. Scis., Law and Soc. Assn., Internat. Studies Assn., U. Pa. Faculty Club, Phila. Art Alliance. Home: 200 Harvard Ave Swarthmore PA 19081 Office: Dept Sociology and Dept Mgmt Univ Pa Philadelphia PA 19104 Office Phone: 215-898-7668. Business E-Mail: evanw@wharton.upenn.edu.

EVANGELISTA, ALLAN, podiatrist, medical researcher; b. Quezon City, Manila, The Philippines, June 23, 1970; came to U.S., 1990, naturalized, 2003. s. Go Guan and Ana Evangelista; m. Julia Ann Adams, Nov. 9, 2002; children, Christian Allan, Ryan Connor. BA in Biology, U. La Verne, Calif., 1991; MDiv in Family, Pastoral Care and Counseling, Fuller Theol. Sem., Calif., 1996; MPH in Epidemiology, Loma Linda U., Calif., 1998; D of Podiatric Medicine, Temple U., Phila., 2002. Tchg. asst. U. La Verne, Calif., 1991; project supr., computer graphic designer Interior Corner, Monterey Park, Calif., 1992-93; assoc. pastor New Life Christian Ctr., El Monte, Calif., 1992—98; rsch. assoc. U. So. Calif. Cardiovasc. Lab., L.A., 1993—98; inter libr. loan processor Fuller Sem. Libr., Pasadena, Calif., 1995-96; intern VA, West Los Angeles, Calif., 2002—03; resident VA-Tampa, Fla., 2003—05; fellow in reconstructive surgery of foot, ankle and leg Sarasota (Fla.) Orthop. Assocs., 2005—. Fin. trustee New Life Christian Ctr., El Monte, 1994—98; pastoral care/marriage counselor First Assembly of God Ch., El Monte, 1994—98. Contbr. articles to med. jours. Vol. San Gabriel Valley Med. Ctr., 1992; med. outreach coord. First Assembly of God Ch., El Monte, 1994—98; youth pastoring/Bible tchr. Christian Reform Ch., West Covina, Calif., 1995—97; chaplain UCLA Med. Ctr., Westwood, 1996. Recipient Ednl. Excellence award Alpha Kappa Alpha, Chgo., 1995; Harding Found. scholar, 1995-96, Fuller Theol. Sem. scholar, 1995-96. Mem.: APHA, ACA, AAAS, Am. Coll. Foot and Ankle Surgeons, Am. Diabetes Assn., Am. Heart Assn. (rsch. coun. 1999), Am. Podiatric Med. Assn., Internat. Assn. Marriage and Family Counselors, Am. Fedn. Med. Rsch. (trainee investigator award 1994). Avocations: basketball, swimming, drawing, travel, cooking. Home: 3878 Royal Hanonock Blvd Sarasota FL 34240-8245 Office Phone: 941-951-2663. E-mail: allevan@hotmail.com.

EVANGELISTA, ANITA LORETTA, freelance/self-employed writer, publishing executive, psychologist; b. L.A., Nov. 9, 1952; d. Carl A. and Etta L. (Erickson) Anderson; m. Nick F. Evangelista, 1979; children: Jamie, Justin. Student, Pepperdine U., 1970-71, U. So. Calif., 1972; BSN, S.W. Mo. State U., Springfield, 2001; MSN, S.W. Mo. State U., 2004; MS in Psychology, Mo. State U., 2005; postgrad. in Nursing, Duquesne U., 2004—. RN; cert. family nurse practitioner; cert. clin. hypnotherapist; bd. cert. advanced practice registered nurse; bd. cert. advanced holistic nurse. Asst. to dir. internat. fin. Max Factor, L.A., 1972-73; asst. to 2d mgr. steel dept. Sumitomo Shoji, L.A., 1973-75; freelance writer, 1975—; columnist Mo. Farm Mag., Clark, 1984-87; adminstr. West Plains (Mo.) Coun. on Arts, 1986-91; editor Ranch Dog Trainer mag., West Plains, 1990-92; mng. editor Fencers Quar., 1999—; family nurse practitioner Cox Health, Mo., 2004—. Spkr., lectr. Mid West Hypnosis Conv., Chgo., 1983; cons. film dir. R. Wise, Hollywood, Calif., 1977; reader Llewellyn Pub., 1997—. Author: Hypnosis-A Journey into the Mind, 1980, Dictionary of Hypnotism, 1991, How to Develop a Low-Cost Family Food Storage System, 1995, How To Live Without Electricity and Like It, 1997, Backyard Meat Production, 1997, (with N. Evangelista) Blood Lust Chickens and Renegade Sheep: A First Timer's Guide to Country Living, 1999, (with N. Evangelista) Country Living is Risky Business, 2000, (with N. Evangelista) The Women Fencer, 2001; indexer: Tikkum Olam, 1996; contbr. articles to mags., periodicals including Mother Earth News, Sci. Digest, Reason, Chronicles, Backwoods Home, Small Farmers Jour., Practical Farmer of Iowa, Fate, Maine Organic Gardner, Dairy Goat Jour., numerous others. Vol. Ozark Med. Ctr., West Plains, 1995-98, ARC, 1999. Recipient TZ 1st prize Twilight Zone Mag., 1989, 1st place Fine Arts Heart of the Ozarks Fair, 1989. Mem.: Soc. Scientific Exploration, Advanced Practice Nurses of the Ozarks (treas. 2005—), Parapsychology Assn., Mo. Psychol. Assn., Cath. Med. Assn., Ozark Area Psychol. Assn., Am. Psychol. Soc., Internat. Assn. Clin. Hypnotherapists, Calif. Prof. Hypnotist Assn. (chpt. pres. L.A. 1976—82), Am. Holistic Nurses Assn., Am. Soc. Psychical Rsch., Sigma Theta Tau, Psi Chi, Alpha Sigma Lambda, Phi Theta Kappa. Roman Catholic. Achievements include research in apolipoprotein E4 in Alzheimer's linguistic expression; Parkinson's disease and visual scanning; Alzheimer's disease and divorce; assessing single-question screening tool for problem drinking; learning hypnotizability; nurse license disciplinary actions. E-mail: evangel@atlascomm.net.

EVANGELISTA, NICK FORREST, fencing master, writer, illustrator; b. Glendale, Calif., Jan. 25, 1949; s. Joseph Norman and Marianne (Williamson) E.; m. Anita Loretta Evangelista, Aug. 5, 1979; children: Jamie Alexandre, Justin Alyn. Student, S.W. Mo. State U., 2001—. Fencing master Faulkner Sch. Fencing, L.A., 1973-81, Evangelista Sch. Fencing, L.A., 1981-85, Peace Valley, Mo., 1985—2000, Springfield, Mo., 2001—, St. Louis Classical Fencing Soc., 1998—2003; fencing master, fight arranger S.W. Mo. State U. Fencing Soc., 2001—; farmer Peace Valley, 1985—; historian, 1989—. Author: The Encyclopedia of the Sword, 1995, The Art and Science of Fencing, 1996, Fighting with Sticks, 1998, Blood-Lust Chickens and Renegade Sheep, 1999, The Inner Game of Fencing, 2000, Country Living Is Risky Business, 2000, The Woman Fencer, 2001; pub., editor-in-chief Vet. Fencers Quar. aka Fencers Quarterly Mag., 1999—; fencing editor Ency. Brit., 2000—; contbr. articles to profl. jours. Fundraiser West Plains (Mo.) Coun. on Art, 1987-91. Recipient 1st Ann. Fiction awards Crosscurrents Mag., 1981. Mem. U.S. Fencing Assn., Nat. Soc. Collegiate Scholars, Phi Alpha Theta, Alpha Sigma Lambda. Roman Catholic. Avocations: paleontology, book collecting, cartooning, Latin. E-mail: evangel@atlascomm.net.

EVANICH, KEVIN R., lawyer; b. 1955; BA, U. Wis., Milw., 1976; JD, Northwestern U., 1980. Bar: Ill. 1980. Ptnr., mem. firm com. Kirkland & Ellis, Chgo., 1986—. Named one of World's Leading Lawyers in Corp. M&A, Chambers Global, 2002—05, 2004—05. Mem.: Phi Beta Kappa. Office: Kirkland & Ellis LLP 200 E Randolph Dr Chicago IL 60601 Office Phone: 312-861-2076. Office Fax: 312-861-2200. Business E-Mail: kevanich@kirkland.com.

EVANITSKY, STEPHAN E., film company executive; b. Rochester, N.Y., Jan. 10, 1970; s. Eugene and Tatiana Evanitsky; m. Karen Kreiger, Dec. 16, 1999. BS in Cinema and Photography, Ithaca coll., 2002. N.Y. State fire fighter State of N.Y., 1994. Owner SEE Painters, Pittsford, NY, 1992—2002; firefighter Bushnell's Basin Fire Dept., Perinton, NY, 1993—2002; v.p. Bushnell's Basin Fire Assn., Perinton, 1997—98; owner S.E.E. Productions L.L.C., Burbank, Calif., 2002—; with distbn. dept. New Line Cinema, L.A., 2003—. Prodn. intern DreamWorks SKG's Old Sch., L.A., 2002; intern New Line Cinema, L.A., 2002—03. Dir.(writer): (short film) Tribulation, (writer, cinematographer) Whetting the Scythe (Ithaca College's Best of Show, 2001), Mind Prey; cinematographer (short film) Mercenaries, Triangle, special effects supr. Fine Line, cinematographer (cartoons don't die) Short Film. Home and Office: SEE Prodns LLC 4132 Warner Blvd Ste E Burbank CA 91505-4150 Personal E-mail: see119ff@hotmail.com.

EVANOFF, GEORGE C., retired publishing executive; b. W. Deer, Pa., June 5, 1931; s. Christ and Luba Evanoff; m. Mary E. Yelavich, Nov. 21, 1964; 1 son, Michael. BS cum laude, U. Detroit, 1952, MBA, 1956. Engr. Gen. Motors Corp., Detroit, 1953-57; supervisory, mgmt. and exec. positions in sales, marketing, and product devel. Ford Motor Co., Dearborn, Mich., 1957-68; staff v.p. mktg., v.p. corporate planning, v.p. corporate devel. RCA Corp., N.Y.C., 1968-76; with Norton Simon, Inc., Los Angeles and New York, 1977-82; v.p. corp. planning, interim pres. Max Factor & Co., 1977-78; pres. Max Factor Internat., 1979-82; pres., chief exec. officer Cordura Publs., Inc., San Diego, 1984-86; mgmt. cons., 1987-88; pres., chief exec. officer Tago, Inc., Burlingame, Calif., 1989-92; ret. Ind. cons., pvt. investor, 1993—96. Comms. officer USAF, 1952—53, capt. Res. USAF. Roman Catholic. Home: 10 Ronsard Newport Coast CA 92657-0113

EVANOVICH, JANET, writer; Attended, Douglass Coll. Author: (Stephanie Plum series) One For the Money, 1994, Two For the Dough, 1996, Three to Get Deadly, 1997, Four to Score, 1998, High Five, 1999, Hot Six, 2000, Seven Up, 2001, Hard Eight, 2002, Visions of Sugar Plums, 2002, To the Nines, 2003, Ten Big Ones, 2004 (Publishers Weekly Bestseller list, 2004), Eleven on Top, 2005 (No. 1 NY Times Bestseller hardcover fiction list, 2005, No. 1 Publishers Weekly Bestseller hardcover fiction list, 2005), (Romance novels written under pseudonym Steffie Hall) Hero at Large, 1987, Foul Play, 1989, (Romance novels) The Grand Finale, 1988, Thanksgiving, 1988, Manhunt, 1988, Ivan Takes a Wife, 1989, Back to the Bedroom, 1989, Wife for Hire, 1990, Smitten, 1990, The Rocky Road to Romance, 1991, Naughty Neighbor, 1992, Metro Girl, 2004; co-author (with Charlotte Hughes): (Full series) Full House, 2002, Full Speed, 2003, Full Tilt, 2003, Full Blast, 2004, Full Bloom, 2005. Address: c/o Robert Gottleib Trident Media Group 36th Fl 41 Madison Ave New York NY 10010*

EVANS, ALFRED LEE, JR., advertising executive; b. Kansas City, Mo., Sept. 16, 1940; s. Alfred Lee and Laura Edith (Redman) E.; m. Jean Perpetua Corcoran, Aug. 29, 1970 (div. Mar. 1994); children: Amanda Corcoran, Cynthia Redman, Cassandra Lee, Nicholas Carpenter; m. Georgiana Coyle Mundy, July 9, 1994. BA, Princeton U., 1962. Account exec. Ted Bates & Co., N.Y.C., 1963-66, Papert Koenig Lois Inc., N.Y.C., 1967-68; v.p. account supr. Lois Holland Callaway, Inc., N.Y.C., 1969-74, v.p. mgmt. supr., 1975, sr. v.p. mgmt. supr., 1976, Norman Craig & Kummel, N.Y.C., 1977-80, Laurence, Charles, Free & Lawson, N.Y.C., 1981-84, 85—, exec. v.p., mem. ops., 1988-95, mem. bd. dirs.; sr. v.p. Wolf Group, N.Y.C., 1995-2000, Bates USA, N.Y.C., 2000—03; sr. ptnr., dir. in charge J. Walter Thompson, N.Y.C., 2004—. Recipient summer travel award Carnegie Found., 1960; scholar Princeton U., 1958-62. Episcopalian. Home: 1530 Palisade Ave Fort Lee NJ 07024-5470 Office: J Walter Thompson 466 Lexington Ave New York NY 10017 Office Phone: 212-210-7186. E-mail: al.evans@jwt.com.

EVANS, AUDREY ELIZABETH, physician, educator; b. York, Eng., Mar. 6, 1925; came to U.S., 1957, naturalized, 1962; d. Leonard Llewellyn and Phyllis Mary (Miller) E. Licentiate Sch. Medicine, Royal Coll. Surgeons, Edinburgh, 1950. Intern Royal Infirmary, Edinburgh, 1950-52; physician tumor therapy Children's Hosp., Boston, 1957-65; instr. pediatrics Harvard U. Med. Sch., 1961-65; asst. prof. pediatric hematologist U. Chgo., 1965-69; prof. pediatrics U. Pa., 1969—. Dir. oncology Children's Hosp., Phila., 1969-89. Home: 2010 Spruce St Philadelphia PA 19103-6569 Office: Children's Hosp ARB 902 324 S 34th St Philadelphia PA 19104-4399

EVANS, BARTON, JR., analytical instrument company executive; b. Washington, Dec. 11, 1947; s. Barton and Viola (Gompf) E.; m. Harriet Andrea Neves, Nov. 20, 1983. BA in Econs., Claremont McKenna Coll., 1970; BS in Engring., MS in Engring., Stanford U., 1972. Sr. engr. Lockheed Missiles and Space Co., Sunnyvale, Calif., 1976-77, Dionex Corp., Sunnyvale, 1977-79, engring. mgr., 1979-81, dir. engring., 1981-83, v.p. engring., 1983-84, v.p. ops., 1984-93, sr. v.p. ops., 1993-2001, exec. v.p., COO, 2001—03; pvt. practice, 2003—05. Trustee Claremont McKenna Coll., 2005—. 1st lt. U.S. Army, 1972—75, col. USAR, 1976—2002, ret. Mem.: ASME, Res. Officers Assn., Assn. U.S. Army, Psychol. Ops. Assn., Civil Affairs Assn. (dir.). Achievements include co-inventor conductivity detector. E-mail: baron.evans@comcast.net.

EVANS, BERNARD WILLIAM, geologist, educator; b. London, July 16, 1934; came to U.S., 1961, naturalized, 1977; s. Albert Edward and Marjorie (Jordan) E.; m. Sheila Campbell Nolan, Nov. 19, 1962. BSc, U. London, 1955; PhD, Oxford U., Eng., 1959. Asst. U. Glasgow, Scotland, 1958-59; departmental demonstrator U. Oxford, 1959-61; asst. research prof. U. Calif., Berkeley, 1961-65, asst. prof., 1965-66, assoc. prof., 1966-69; prof. geology U. Wash., Seattle, 1969—2001, chmn. dept. geol. scis., 1974-79; emeritus prof. U. Washington, 2001—. Contbr. articles to profl. jours. Recipient U.S. Sr. Scientist award Humboldt Found., Fed. Republic Germany, 1988-89; Fulbright travel award, France, 1995-96. Fellow Geol. Soc. Am., Mineral Soc. Am. (pres. 1993-94, award 1970), Geochem. Soc., Geol. Soc. London, Mineral. Soc. Gt. Britain, Swiss Mineral. Soc. Home: 8001 Sand Point Way NE Apt C55 Seattle WA 98115-6399 Office: U Wash Dept Earth and Space Scis PO Box 351310 Seattle WA 98195-1310 Office Phone: 206-543-1750. Business E-Mail: bwevans@u.washington.edu.

EVANS, BETH OTTEN, music educator; b. Tallahassee, Fla., Oct. 23, 1958; d. William John Otten and Diana Agnes Wilcox; m. David Robert Evans, June 12, 1982; children: Gwyneth, Heather, Mckenzie Rose. B in Music Edn., Nyack (N.Y.) Coll., 1982; M in Music Edn., Cath. U. of Am., 1990. Cert. tchr. vocal and instrumental music K-12 Va., Kodaly cert. Found. Aesthetic in Music Edn. Gen. music tchr. North Rockland (N.Y.) Sch. Dist., 1982—86; gen. music tchr., piano tchr. Jewels of Ann Pvt. Day Sch., Washington, 1986—88; gen. music tchr. Bethesda (Md.) Country Day Sch., 1988—89; vocal music tchr. Alexandria (Va.) City Pub. Schs., 1989—. Asst. pipe organ resoration, 1999. Brownie co-leader Girl Scouts of Am., Alexandria, 2000—02; sponsor, dir. 4-H Recorder Club, Alexandria, 1999—2001; organist, dir. children's choir Ch. of the Ascension, Silver Spring, Md., 1986—89; organist Messiah Luth. Ch., Alexandria, 1989—97; organist, dir. children's choir and summer music Olivet Episcopal Ch., Franconia, Va., 1997—. Mem.: NEA, Va. Music Educators Assn. (elem. rep. Dist. 10), Music Educators Nat. Conf., Am. Guild Organists. Episcopalian. Avocations: hiking, sewing, flute, piano, organ. Home: 6106 Paulonia Rd Alexandria VA 22310 E-mail: bevans@acps.k12.va.us.

EVANS, BETTY VAUGHN, minister; b. Campbell, Ala., Sept. 3, 1954; children: Robert, Rochelle, James. D in Ministry, Victory Bible Coll., 2003. Ordained evanglist Ch. God in Christ, 1985, ordained minister Ch. God in Christ, 1986, ordained pastor Whole Lifw Christian Ch./TX, 1995, cert. restorative therapist Faith Based Counselor Tng. Inst. Tex., 2000. Pastor Storehouse Ministry Fellowship, Inc., San Antonio, 1995—. Chmn. bus. adv. coun. Tex. chpt. Nat. Rep. Congl. Com., 2005—. Nominee Black Achievement award, San Antonio, Tex., 2003; named Pioneer Woman Pastor, San Antonio Express News, 2003. Office: Storehouse Ministry Fellowship Inc 14100 Nacogdoches Rd San Antonio TX 78247 Office Phone: 210-599-8136. E-mail: storehousemf.org.

EVANS, BOB (ROBERT EVANS), publishing executive; Founding editor Computer Reseller News; with CMP Media Inc., Manhasset, NY, 1983—, v.p., 1989—, v.p. product devel., 1993—, editor-in-chief Info. Week, 1996—2005, mng. dir. Info. Week; editl. dir. CMP Media Inc, 1999—, sr. v.p., web tech., 1999—. Office: CMP Media Inc 600 Community Dr Ste 1 Manhasset NY 11030-3875 E-mail: bevans@cmp.com.*

EVANS, BONITA DIANNE, education educator; b. NYC, Jan. 14, 1940; d. Roy Simon and Verna (Ashton) Evans; m. Robert John Watts, Aug. 1981 (div. 1996); 1 child, Helena Watts. BA, U. Canberra, Australia, 1990; MDS, Monash U., Melbourne, Australia, 1992; PhD, Walden U., Minn., 1996. With Dept. of Prime Minister and Cabinet, Australian Dept. Fgn. Affairs, Canberra, 1986—88; devel. rsch. officer Aboriginal Hostels, Canberra, 1986—88; cultural affairs asst. U.S. Embassy, Canberra, 1988—90; mem. Diplomatic Corps UN Mission to Nambia, S.W. Africa, 1978; field officer Israeli/Egyptian border UN Peacekeeping Forces, 1979—80; adj. prof. English Montclair State U., NJ, 1996—2000; vis. prof. Rutgers U., Newark, 1999—2000; adj. history, women's studies, and African Am. studies depts. William Paterson U., 1997—. Author: Youth in Foster Care, 1997, Kijani, 2002, New Hope Rising, 2002. Recipient Cert. Spl. Congressional Recognition for Outstanding and Invaluable Svc. to Cmty., 2005. Personal E-mail: DrBonitaEvans@peoplepc.com.

EVANS, BRUCE DWIGHT, lawyer; b. Mt. Hope, W.Va., May 27, 1934; s. M. Albert and Eleanor E. (Fowler) E.; m. Sallie Lee Hazen, Aug. 24, 1957 (div. Jan. 1974); children: Scott C., Leigh F., Randolph D.; m. Doris M. Stritzinger Webster, Sept. 2, 1978. AB, Princeton U., 1956; LL.B., Harvard U., 1959. Bar: N.Y. 1960, Pa. 1970. Assoc. Debevoise, Plimpton, Lyons & Gates, N.Y.C., 1959-68; ptnr. Reed Smith Shaw & McClay, Pitts., 1969-96. Trustee Ellis Sch., Pitts., 1972-78. Mem. ABA, Pa. Bar Assn., Allegheny County Bar Assn., Rivers Club, Phi Beta Kappa Republican. Episcopalian. Office: One Oxford Centre Ste 4300 301 Grant St Pittsburgh PA 15219 E-mail: bruce.evans@pobox.com.

EVANS, CAROL ROCKWELL, nursing administrator; b. New Orleans, Jan. 8, 1953; d. Daniel Raymond Sr. and Helen (Fischer) Rockwell; divorced; children: Nikki Elizabeth, Mimi Michelle. ADN, La. State Med. Ctr., 1990. RN, La.; cert. ACLS, BLS, cert. case mgr.; lic. life and health ins. agent. Life and health ins. agt. La. Ins. Agts. Assn., New Orleans, 1975-95; dir. case mgmt. and utilization rev. Associated Med. Rev. Svcs., Metairie, La., 1986-95; charge nurse med-surg. telemetry unit Elmwood Med. Ctr., Jefferson, La., 1990—; RN specialist III ICU dept. St. Charles Gen. Hosp., New Orleans, 1993—; dir. med. mgmt. Nat. Health Resources, Inc., Metairie, La., 1995-99, Med. Care Solutions, Inc., 1999—2002; owner Case Mgmt. Svcs., Metairie, 2002—. Lobby La. Health Care, Baton Rouge, 1991. Mem. ANA, NAFE, Case Mgmt. Soc. Am., Individual Case Mgmt. Assn., Assn. Respiratory Care, New Orleans Continuity Care, La. Managed Healthcare Assn. (Great Nurses award 1997). Republican. Roman Catholic. Avocations: sports, dance, swimming, travel, theater. Home: 6316 York St Metairie LA 70003-3557 Office: Case Mgmt Svcs PO Box 74137 Metairie LA 70033-4132 Office Phone: 504-813-3261. Personal E-mail: crocky108@aol.com.

EVANS, C(AROLINE) SUE, education educator; b. Bethel, Ohio, July 14, 1948; d. Raymond George Brown and Relva Olive Spears-Brown; m. Gary W. Evans, June 18, 1966; children: Rhonda Fannin, Gary Lee, Daniel Ray, Rebekah, David Jonathan Assoc. of Applied Bus., So. State C.C., Hillsboro, Ohio, 1989; BS, Wilberforce U., 1999. Leader, lectr. Weight Watchers, Inc., West Union, Ohio, 1974—80; lab. asst. So. State C.C., Sardinia, Ohio, 1989—92, 1993—99, dir., instr., 1999—; project sec. Ford Motor Co./Morrison Knuedson, Contractor, Batavia, Ohio, 1992—93; adminstrv. asst. So. Ohio Ctr. of Excellence, Ohio Coll. Access Network, 2005—. Mem. adv. bd. Your Place, Sardinia, Family/Cons. Sci., Seaman, Ohio. Author: Broken Wings Fly, 2003. Bd. dirs. United Ch. of God, Portsmouth, Ohio, Adam Brown Counties Econ. Opportunities Inc.; leader Take Off Pounds Sensibly. Home: 1525 Moores Rd Seaman OH 45679 Office: So State CC 12681 US 62 Sardinia OH 45171 Office Phone: 937-695-0307 3540. Business E-Mail: sevans@sscc.edu.

EVANS, CHARLES H., federal judge; b. 1922; BA, U. Ill., 1947, JD, 1948. Asst. atty. gen. State of Ill., 1949—56, 1962—76; pvt. law practice, 1957—62; magistrate judge Ill. Ctrl., Springfield, 1977—. Served with USAAF, 1942—45. Office: 110 US Courthouse 600 E Monroe St Springfield IL 62701-1626

EVANS, CHARLES WAYNE, II, biologist, researcher; b. Athens, Ohio, Aug. 9, 1929; s. Charles Wayne Evans and Florence Louise (Sheets) Evans Claypool; m. Jo F. Burt, 1948 (div. 1959); children: Charles Wayne III, James Friedrich(dec.), John Burns, Elizabeth Burt; m. Patricia Anne Baker, 1971; children: Debbie Jo(dec.), Caralyn Michele. Student, Tex. A&M U., 1947-51, BA, 1957, postgrad., 1963-65, U. Houston, 1969-70. Seismologist Universal Seismic Expt., Beaumont, Tex., 1958-65; marine biologist CRI/VIERS, St. Thomas, U.S. Virgin Islands, 1965-71; geologist Dr. C. B. Claypool, Beaumont, Tex., 1971-76; research biologist Panthera-Marine-Internat., Ltd., Belize, C.A., Beaumont; pres., CEO Panthera-Marine-Internat., Ltd., Belize, 1976—; rsch. biologist Synetics Inc., Las Vegas, 1979-82; bd. dirs., treas. Las Vegas, 1979; rsch. biologist SAC Research Ctr., 1982-88; pres. Jordhammer, Inc., Las Vegas, 1980—; bd. dirs. Ant Fire, Inc., Beaumont, 1985-89, Caribbean World enterprises, Ltd., New Orleans & Belize, 1987—; pres., dir. rsch. Invicta Corp., 1988. Cons. I.Q. Tech., Houston, 1994—96, Eradicator Corp., Houston, 1994—98, Aire-Mate Inc., Westfield, Ind., Terminator Techs., Inc., San Jose, Calif., 1999. Co-inventor Jordhammer, 1982, Earthfire Injection System, 1988. Sus. mem. Rep. Nat. Com., Washington, 1982; charter mem. Ellis Island Found., N.Y.C., 1983—; founder, pres. Caribbean Inst. Natural Sci., St. Thomas, 1967-70; with N.G., 1945-47. SAC Research Ctr. grantee, 1983, Dr. C.B. Clayppol grantee, 1963, 78. Mem. AAAS, Smithsonian Asocs., Am. Mus. Natural History (assoc.)., N.Y. Acad. Sci., Internat. Oceanographic Found., Entomol. Soc. Am., World Wildlife Fund, Aggie Club, Century Club, Lions. Avocations: music, chess, big game fishing. Office: 5380 Grain Mill Rd Pahrump NV 89061 E-mail: Solenopsis@aol.com.

EVANS, CLYDE MERRILL, academic administrator, state representative; b. Gallipolis, Ohio, June 26, 1938; s. Owen Wade and Reva Belle (Hutchinson) E.; m. Rosemary Salser, Aug. 26, 1961; children: Mary Margaret, Sarah Leigh, Nancy Jane, Dylan Owen Wade. BA, Union Coll., 1960; MA, Eastern Ky. State U., 1962; PhD, U. So. Miss., 1972; cert. in adminstrn., Ohio U., Athens, 1967. Cert. secondary tchr., Ohio; cert. counselor, Ohio; cert. supt., Ohio. V.p. student devel. Rio Grande (Ohio) Coll., 1972-77, provost, 1977-84; project dir., assoc. prof. sports mgmt. U.S. Sports Acad., Mobile, Ala., 1984-86; prin. Vinton County Schs., McArthur, Ohio, 1986-89; v.p. adminstrn. U. Rio Grande, Ohio, 1989—. Pres. Rio Grande Village Council, 1968-70, O.O. McIntyre Park Dist., Gallipolis, 1973-84; bd. dirs., treas. Southeastern Ohio Emergency Med. Service, Gallipolis, 1977-80; state rep. 87th H.O. (Ohio). Named one of Outstanding Young Men of Am., Outstanding Ams. Found., 1970. Mem. Ohio Assn. Elem. Sch. Adminstrs., Gallipolis Area C. of C. (bd. dirs. 1990), Gallia County Hist. Soc. (bd. dirs. 1991). Republican. Baptist. Avocations: reading, sports. Home: PO Box 36 Rio Grande OH 45674-0036

EVANS, CRAIG STEVEN, academic administrator; b. Syracuse, NY, Oct. 21, 1962; s. John Evans and Nadeen Cheevers; m. Dwight Stefan Myers. MusB in Edn., Ithaca Coll., 1984; MusM in Performance, MusM in Edn., Fla. State U., 1986; EdD, Univerity of Ctrl. Fla., 1997. Condr. Fla. Symphony Youth Orch., Orlando, Fla., 1986—94; tchr. Polk County Schs., Winter Haven, Fla., 1986—87, Orange County Schs., Orlando, Fla., 1987—90, sch. adminstr., 1990—93, asst. prin., 1993—97, prin., 1998—99; condr. Fla. Young Artist's Orch., Orlando, Fla., 1998—99; prin. Ithaca City Sch. Dist., NY, 1999—2002, asst. to the supt., 2002—04; dir. of individual giving Ithaca Coll., 2004—. V.p. Cayuga Chamber Orch., Ithaca, 2002, Tompkins Learning Ptnrs., 2001. Home: 2002 Ellis Hollow Rd Ithaca NY 14850 Office: Ithaca Coll 238 Alumni Hall Ithaca NY 14850 Office Phone: 607-274-3388. Personal E-mail: cevans@ithaca.edu.

EVANS, DANIEL E., manufacturing and restaurant chain company executive; b. Gallipolis, Ohio, Aug. 24, 1936; With Bob Evans Farms Inc., Columbus, Ohio, 1957—; chmn. bd., sec., CEO, dir., 1971—. Office: Bob Evans Farms Inc 3776 S High St Columbus OH 43207-4000

EVANS, DAVID See THE EDGE

EVANS, DAVID ALLAN, language educator; b. Sioux City, Iowa, Apr. 11, 1940; s. Arthur Clarence and Ruth (Lyle) Evans; m. Janice Kay Johnson, July 4, 1958; children: Shelly Evans Moreau, David Allan Jr., Karlin Evans Bauer. BA, Morningside Coll., 1962; MA, U. Iowa, 1964; MFA, U. Ark., 1973. Asst. U. Iowa, Iowa City, 1965, U. Ark., Fayetteville, 1971-72; asst. prof. English, Adams State Coll., Alamosa, Colo., 1966-68, S.D. State U., Brookings, 1968-78, prof., 1978—, writer-in-residence, 1997—; poet laureate SD, 2002. Faculty exch. prof. Yunnan Normal U., Kunming, China, 1988—89; faculty leader Seminar Abroad S.D. State U., Yunnan Province, China, 2001, Phi Kappa Phi lectr., 03; poet laureate, SD, 2002—. Author: (poetry chapbook) Among Athletes, 1970, (poetry) Train Windows, 1976, Real and False Alarms, 1980, Hanging Out with the Crows, 1990, Decent Dangers, 2001, Bull Riders Advice: New and Selected Poems, 2004, (essays) Remembering the Soos, 1982; (with Jan Evans) Double Happinesss: Two Lives in China, 1995; co-editor: From Language to Idea, 1970, Statement and Craft, 1972, The Sport of Poetry/The Poetry of Sport, 1979; editor: New Voices in American Poetry, 1973; gen. editor, writer What the Tall Grass Says, 1982. Writing mentor S.D. State Prison, Sioux Falls, 2001—; mem. steering com. Brookings Arts Coun., 2001—; active participant artist in schs. SD Arts Coun. Named S.D. Centennial Poet, 1989, Alumni Educator of Yr., Morningside Coll., Sioux City, Iowa, 2003, S.D. Author of Yr., S.D. Coun. Tchrs. English, 2005; recipient Exemplary Tchr. award Guangdong U. Fgn. Studies, 1999, Spl. Recognition, Sports Hall of Fame Banquet, Augustana Coll., 2004; athletic scholarship Augustana Coll., 1958-60, Breadloaf scholar, Vt., 1973, Fulbright scholar, China, 1992-93, 98-99; writing grantee Nat. Endowment for Arts, 1975, 80, grantee S.D. Arts Coun., 1981, artist grantee Bush Found., 1990. Mem. Soc. Midland Authors, Acad. Am. Poets, Sports Lit. Soc., Poetry Soc. Am. (S.D. Poet of Yr. 2004), S.D. Coun. Tchrs. English (S.D. Author of Yr. 2005), Fulbright Assn., Sigma Tau Delta (hon. mem. Alpha Chi chpt.). Democrat. Avocations: racquetball and other exercise, reading, travel. Home: 1432 2nd St Brookings SD 57006 Office: SD State U Scobey Hall 008 Box 504 Brookings SD 57007 Business E-Mail: evanspl@brookings.net.

EVANS, DAVID C., lawyer; b. Nov. 10, 1945; BS in bus. mktg., Ind. U., 1968, JD, 1971. Bar: Ind. 1971, DC 1972, Supreme Ct. Ind. 1971, US Dist. Ct. DC 1972, US Ct. Appeals DC Cir. 1972. Mem. Reed Smith Shaw & McClay (now Reed Smith LLP), Washington, 1971—, dir. practice devel., 1991-95, former mng. ptnr., Washington office, former practice group leader Govt. Services Group, now ptnr., practice group leader, Real Estate Group, 2005—, also treas. polit. action com. Sec. bd. trustees Nat. Bldg. Mus., Washington. Recipient Outstanding Young Alumnus Award, Ind. U. Mem.: Am. Soc. Assn. Executives (mem. legal sect. coun.), ABA, Fed. City Coun., Nat. Eagle Scout Assn., Econ. Club Wash., Chevy Chase Club, Annapolis Yacht Club, Ocean Reef Club. Office: Reed Smith LLP 1301 K St NW Ste 1100 - East Tower Washington DC 20005 Office Phone: 202-414-9221. Office Fax: 202-414-9299. Business E-Mail: devans@reedsmith.com.

EVANS, DENIS ALLEN, medical researcher; b. Detroit, Dec. 31, 1944; s. Edgar and Eleanor Agnes Evans; m. Carla Ann Koziol, June 21, 1969; children: Paul G., Laura E. BS, Cath. U. Am., 1966; MD, U. Mich., 1970. Diplomate Am. Bd. Internal Medicine, 1973, lic. physician Mass., 1976. Intern, resident, fellow Boston (Mass.) City Hosp. Harvard Med. Svc., 1970—76; from instr. to asst. prof. Brigham & Women's Hosp. Harvard U., 1976—90; Jesmer prof. medicine Rush Med. Coll., Chgo., 1990—; dir. Rush Inst. Healthy Aging, Chgo., 1992—. Mem. exec. com. Alzheimer's Disease Ctrs, Nat. Inst. Aging, Chgo., 1993—96; steering com. Nat. Alzheimer's Coordinating Ctr., Chgo., 1999—2002, steering com. Health and Retirement Study, 2000—. Contbr. over 200 articles to profl. jours. Maj. U.S. Army, 1973—75. Recipient Rita Hayworth Gala award, Alzheimer's Assn., 2004; grantee, NIH, 1991, 1993—. Mem.: Alpha Omega Alpha. Office: Rush Institute for Healthy Aging 1645 W Jackson Blvd Suite 675 Chicago IL 60612 Office Phone: 312-942-3350. Office Fax: 312-942-2861. E-mail: denis_evans@rsh.net.

EVANS, DENNIS HYDE, chemist, educator; b. Grinnell, Iowa, Mar. 28, 1939; s. Leonard Hyde and Clara Ethel (Parmley) E.; m. Ruth Elizabeth Turnbull, June 28, 1958 (div. July 1986); children: Susan Katherine, John Hyde, Andrew Turnbull; m. Mary Jean Wirth, Aug.2, 1986. BS, Ottawa U., 1960; AM, Harvard U., 1961, PhD, 1964. Instr. chemistry Harvard U., Cambridge, 1964-66; asst. prof. chemistry U. Wis., Madison, 1966-70, asso. prof., 1970-75, prof., 1975-84, Meloche-Bascom prof. chemistry, 1984-86, chmn. dept., 1977-80, assoc. dean Coll. of Letters and Sci., 1983-86; prof. chemistry U. Del., Newark, 1986—2004, U. Ariz., Tucson, 2004—. Contbr. articles to profl. jours. Danforth fellow, 1960-64, NIH fellow, 1961-64; recipient C.N. Reilley award Soc. for Electroanalytical Chemistry, 1993. Fellow Electrochem. Soc. (M.M. Baizer award Organic and Biol. Electrochemistry Divsn. 2004); mem. Am. Chem. Soc., Internat. Soc. Electrochemistry, Soc. for Electroanalytical Chemistry (pres. 1993-95). Baptist. E-mail: dhevans@email.arizona.edu.

EVANS, DONALD LOUIS, former secretary of commerce, financial services organization executive; b. Houston, July 27, 1946; m. Susan Marinis; three children: Lisa Moon, Jennifer, Donald L. BS in Mech. Engring., U. Tex. Austin, 1969, MBA, 1973; LHD (hon.), U. S.C., 2001. Mgmt. to chmn. bd. dirs. and CEO Tom Brown, Inc., Denver, 1975-2001; sec. U.S. Dept.

Commerce, Washington, 2001—05; CEO Fin. Services Forum, 2005—. Bd. dirs. TMBR/Sharp Drilling, Inc., bd. regents U. Tex., 1995-2001, chmn. bd., 1997-2001. Bd. Trustees Meml. Hosp. & Med. Ctr., 1990-94; bd. dirs. The Gladney Fund, 1992-96, Scleroderma Rsch. Found., 1992-2000; campaign chair United Way of Midland, 1981, pres., 1989; bd. regents U. Tex., 1995-96, chmn., 1997-98; bd. dirs. Scleroderma Rsch. Found; active United Way, campaign chair, 1981, pres., 1989; mem. Gov. Bush gubernatorial campaign, 1994, 98; chmn. Bush/Cheney Presdl. campaign, 2000. Named to U. Tex. Red McCombs Sch. Bus. Hall of Fame, 2002; recipient Disting. Alumnus award, U Tex., 2002. Mem. Independent Petroleum Assn. Am., Young Presidents Orgn., Rocky Mtn. Oil & Gas Assn., Permian Basin Petroleum Assn., All-Am. Wildcatters, Nat. Petroleum Council. Republican. Methodist.*

EVANS, DOUGLAS MCCULLOUGH, surgeon, educator; b. Vandergrift, Pa., July 31, 1925; s. Archibald Davis and Helen Irene (McCullough) E.; m. Thelmajean Volkers, Aug. 1, 1959; children: Matthew Kirk, Daniel Scott. MD, Western Res. U., 1952; postgrad., U. Mich., 1956-58. Diplomate Am. Bd. Surgery. Resident in surgery Henry Ford Hosp., 1952-57, chief resident in surgery, 1957-58, mem. surgery staff, 1959-60, Akron (Ohio) Gen. Hosp., 1960-70; chmn. dept. surgery Akron Gen. Med. Ctr., 1971-90, rsch. cons.; prof. and chmn. surgery emeritus Northeastern Ohio U. Coll. Medicine. Served with AUS, 1943-46. Fellow: ACS; mem.: AAAS, AMA, N.Y. Acad. Scis., Ohio Med. Assn., Midwest Surg. Soc., Soc. Critical Care Medicine, Metastasis Rsch. Soc., Am. Assn. Cancer Rsch. Republican. Presbyterian. Office: 400 Wabash Ave Akron OH 44307-2433

EVANS, ELI NACHAMSON, foundation administrator; b. Durham, N.C., July 28, 1936; s. Emanuel Joshua and Sara (Nachamson) E.; m. Judith London, Nov. 15, 1981; 1 child, Joshua London. BA, U. N.C., 1958; LLB, Yale U., 1963; LHD (hon.), Jewish Theological Seminary, 2003, Hebrew Union Coll., 2005. Bar: N.C. 1963. Asst. to Dr. Eric Goldman, Spl. Cons. Pres. L.B. Johnson White House, Washington, 1964-65; staff dir. to Gov. Terry Sanford Study Am. States, Duke U., Durham, N.C., 1965-67; sr. program exec. Carnegie Corp. N.Y., N.Y.C., 1967-77; pres. Charles H. Revson Found., N.Y.C., 1977—2003; bd. chair Covenant Found., Chgo., 1995—. Bd. dir. Nat. Video Resources, N.Y.C., Next Book, N.Y.C.; mem. Carnegie Commn. on Future of Pub. Broadcasting, N.Y.C., 1977-79, N.C. Task Force on Pub. Telecomm., 1977-79, Commn. on Jewish Edn. in N.Am., N.Y.C., 1989-90, Internat. Commn. of Diaspora Israeli-Rels., N.Y.C., 1995-97; mem. 20th Century Fund Task Force on Pub. Broadcasting, N.Y.C., 1992-93. Author: The Provincials: A Personal History of Jews in the South, 1973, reissued, 1997, 2005, Judah P. Benjamin: The Jewish Confederate, 1988 (La. Book of Yr. 1989), The Lonely Days Were Sundays: Reflections of a Jewish Southerner, 1992. Bd. dir. N.C. State Pub. TV Network, Chapel Hill, 1979-87. Lt. (j.g.) USN, 1958-60, Japan. Mem. State Bar Assn. N.C., Am. Acad. Arts and Sciences, Yale Club. Home: One Lexington Ave 3-C New York NY 10010

EVANS, ELIZABETH ANN WEST, retired real estate agent; b. Xenia, Ohio, Mar. 28, 1933; d. Millard Stanley and Elizabeth Denver (Johns) West. BA, Ohio U., 1966, MA, 1968. Cert. GRI, 1993. Sec. various orgns., Ohio, 1952-61; tchr. Ohio U., Athens, 1966-67, Zanesville, 1968-72, Collier County Pub. Schs., Naples, Fla., 1972-77; sales Helen's Hang Ups, Naples, 1978-79; mgr. pvt. practice Wilmington, Ohio, 1979-87; adminstrv. asst. Powell Assocs., Cambridge, Mass., 1987-90; real estate agt. Bill Evans Realty, Inc., Naples, 1989-90, Howard Hanna Real Estate Svcs., Naples, 1991—93, Downing-Frye Realty, Inc., Naples, 1993—97, Downing-Frye Referral Network Realty Inc., Naples, 1997—2002; ret., 2002. Cape May resident rep. to Ohio Presbyn. Retirement Svcs., 2004—. Fellow: Phi Beta Kappa; mem.: DAR (chaplain 1988—90, chmn. Motion, Picture, Radio and TV 1992—94, asst. chaplain 1994—96, chaplain 2000—01, chmn. pub. rels. 2003—05), Kappa Alpha Theta (50-yr. mem.), Phi Kappa Phi, Phi Sigma Iota. Republican. Presbyterian. Avocation: leading group discussions. Home: 182 Cape May Dr Wilmington OH 45177 Personal E-mail: eevans5@cinci.rr.com.

EVANS, ELOISE SWICK, retired educator, writer; b. Capitol Heights, Md., Sept. 27, 1920; d. Clarence Herbert and Hattie May Swick; m. Latimer Richard Evans, Aug. 24. 1942 (dec. Aug. 1991); children: Carol, Beth, Marget, Scott. BA, Am. U., 1941; MS in Organic Chemistry, Purdue U., 1945. Tchr. chemistry and physics Las Cruces (N.Mex.) Pub. Schs., 1961-73, co-founder, coord. San Andres (Alternative) H.S., 1973-86; ret., 1986. Mem. adv. bd. Adolescent Family Life Ctr., Las Cruces, 1986-90, Los Niños, Las Cruces, 1991-95. Contbr. short stories and articles to profl. and lit. publs. Bd. dirs. United Way S.W. N.Mex., Las Cruces, 1997. Mem.: LWV (pres. Greater Las Cruces 1989, 1992—94, bd. dirs. N.Mex. 1992—97, sec. 1995—96), Las Cruces Assn. Ednl. Retirees (pres. 2001), Desert Writers. Avocations: oral historian on Las Cruces retired teachers, writing. Home: 5120 Oriole Rd Las Cruces NM 88011-7598 E-mail: pevans@zianet.com.

EVANS, ERIC ALAN, lawyer; b. Bend, Oreg., Mar. 17, 1949; s. Byron Fletcher and Margaret Jeanette Evans; m. Anne Van Vechten Myers Evans, July 26, 1975; children: Ryan, Katharine, Andrew. BA, U. of Pa., 1971; JD, Albany Law Sch. of Union U., N.Y., 1976. Bar: N.Y. 1977, Fed. 1977. Banking & comml. lawyer Harter, Secrest & Emery LLP, Rochester, NY, 1976—78, mgmt. labor lawyer, 1978—, chair, labor dept., 1992—95, unit mgr., bus., 1998—2000, mng. ptnr., 2000—. Bd. mem. Kirkhaven, Rochester, NY, 1994—2000; nominating com. United Way of Greater Rochester, NY, 2002; bd. mem. Rochester Bus. Alliance, NY, 2003. Mem.: Mgmt. Attorneys Conf., Genesee Valley Club. Office: Harter Secrest & Emery LLP 1600 Bausch & Lomb Pl Rochester NY 14604-2711 E-mail: eevans@hselaw.com.

EVANS, ERIC CHARLES, management executive; b. Montpelier, Idaho, Oct. 22, 1952; s. Joseph Eschler and Zelda (Cook) E.; m. Elisabeth Anne Lee, May 24, 1980; children: Juliet, Emily, Elisabeth, Erica. Student, Harvard U., 1977, MBA, JD, Harvard U., 1981. Cons. Bain & Co., Menlo Park, Calif., 1981-82; pres. Evans Co., L.A., 1983-87; v.p. Internat. Copeland Corp. divsn. Emerson Electric, St. Louis, 1987-93; pres. internat. Emerson Internat., St. Louis, 1993-96, CFO, group exec., 1996-97, group v.p., 2000—. Office: Copeland Corp Campbell Rd Sidney OH 45365 E-mail: ECEvans@copeland-corp.com.

EVANS, ERSEL ARTHUR, engineering executive, consultant; b. Trenton, Nebr., July 17, 1922; s. Arthur E. and Mattie Agnes (Perkins) E.; m. Patricia A. Powers, Oct. 11, 1945 (div.); children: Debra Lynn (dec.), Paul Arthur. BA, Reed Coll., Portland, Oreg., 1947; PhD, Oreg. State U., 1950. Registered profl. engr., Calif. With Gen. Electric Co., 1951-67, supr. ceramics research and devel. Hanford, Wash., 1961-64; mgr. plutonium devel. Vallecitos Lab., Pleasanton, Calif., 1964-67; mgr. fuels and materials dept. Battelle Meml. Inst., Richland, Wash., 1967-70; with Westinghouse Electric Corp., 1970-87; v.p. Westinghouse Hanford Co., Richland, 1972-87, v.p., lab. tech. dir., 1985-87, ret., 1987, cons., 1987—. Mem. Tech. Assistance Adv. Group for Three Mile Island Recovery, 1981-86; mem. rev. Com. EBR-II, U. Chgo., 1989-91, 94—; mem. Japan Tech. Panel for Nuclear Power, NSF, 1989-90; mem. alt. applications of laser isotope separations tech. com. NRC, 1991-92, separations and tech. study, 1991-95, 96; del. Atlantic Coun. U.S.-Japan Conf. on Global Energy Issues, Maui, 1994, 96. Mem. vis. com. U. Wash. Served with USNR, 1943-45. Recipient Westinghouse Order of Merit; DuPont fellow, 1950-51; recipient Mishima award Am. Nuclear Soc., 1995. Fellow Am. Nuclear Soc. (Spl. Merit award 1964, Spl. Performance award 1980 Fed. Design Achievement award 1991, Walker Cisler medal 2001), Am. Inst. Chemists, Am. Soc. Metals, Am. Ceramic Soc.; mem. NAE, Phi Kappa Phi, Sigma Xi. Achievements include patents in field. Home and Office: Park Row # 82 701 Kettner Blvd San Diego CA 92101-5908 E-mail: ersel3@cox.net. *Inspiration and guidance for my career have often been provided by Justice Oliver Wendell Holmes, "certainty generally is illusion, and repose is not the destiny of man." (Harvard Law Review 1897).*

EVANS, ESSI H., research scientist; b. Bad-Schwalbach, Germany, Jan. 12, 1950; came to U.S., 1951, naturalized, 1957; d. John H. (b. Horst H. Jahn) and Jean E. (von Schwerin); m. Everett M. Turner Jr., Aug. 16, 1974. BS in Agr., U. Md., 1972; MS in Animal Sci., U. Guelph, 1974, PhD in Animal Sci., 1976. Polymer chemist Monarch Rubber Co., Balt., 1972; rsch. asst., tchg. asst. U. Guelph, Ont., 1972-76; project dir. animal nutrition Can. Packers Inc., Toronto, Ont., 1976-85, tech. mgr. animal nutrition and animal health, 1986-89, rsch. mgr., 1989-90, gen. rsch. and nutrition mgr. shur-gain divsn., 1990-93, mgmt. dir., 1993-2000, v.p. Shur Gain, 2000—02; CEO Tech. Adv. Svcs. Inc., 2002—. Farm cons.; guest lectr. Hubbard Farms fellow, 1975-76; NRC Indsl. postdoctoral fellow, 1976-79. Contbr. articles to sci. jours. and profl. and sci. confs. James Harris scholar, U. Md., 1972; recipient Hamilton Milk Prodrs. award, 1973, 74; Ont. Ministry of Agr. and Foods Provincial Lottery grantee, 1980-83. Mem. AAAS, Am. Soc. Animal Sci., Am. Dairy Sci. Assn., Am. Assn. Vet. Nutritionists, Coun. for Agrl. Sci. and Tech., Nat. Feed Industry Assn., Can. Feed Industry Assn. Republican. Home and Office: 64 Scugog St Bowmanville ON Canada L1C 3J1 Office Phone: 905-623-7599. Personal E-mail: essievans@sympatico.ca.

EVANS, EVAN, petroleum executive; b. N.Y.C., May 19, 1925; s. John William Jr. and Therese Rosemary (Guilfoyle) E.; m. Natalie Coe Holbrook, Feb. 20, 1968; children: Megan, Meredith, Rhys, Valerie, Cynthia, David. Student, St. Lawrence U., 1942-43, 46, BS, 1949, MIT, 1951. Engr. Calif. Tex. Oil Corp., N.Y.C., 1951-55, Bahrain, 1955-57, refinery ops. asst. N.Y.C., 1957-60, Rotterdam, 1960-62, refinery plant mgr. Lebanon, 1963, refinery specialist N.Y.C., 1963-65; refinery project mgr. King Wilkinson, Antwerp, Belgium, 1966-68; v.p. United Refining Co., Warren, Pa., 1972-81, dir., 1974-81, 96—. Pres. Kiantone Pipeline, 1970-81; v.p. Western Crude Oil Inc., 1981-83; pres. Wesco Internat. Inc., 1981-83, Holvan Properties Inc., Madison, Conn., 1985—; dir. U.S. Energy Sys., Belgian Refining Corp., 1993-96, Alexander-Allen Inc., 1994-2002. Chmn. Am. Sch. Rotterdam, 1961-62. With USN, 1943-46. Mem. N.Y. Athletic Club. Address: 331 Old Toll Rd Madison CT 06443-1710

EVANS, FAITH, singer; b. Fla., June 10, 1973; m. Christopher Wallace (The Notorious B.I.G.), 1995 (dec.); 1 child, Christopher Wallace Jr., 1996. Student, Fordham U. Singer: (albums) Faith, 1995, Keep The Faith, 1998 (Grammy award for best rap performance, 1998), Faithfully, 2001, The First Lady, 2005; singer: (background vocals) (Mary J. Blige) My Life, 1994, Ballads, 2001, (Hi-Five) Keep it Goin On, 1992, (Frankie) My Heart Belongs to You, 1997, (The Notorious B.I.G.) Life After Death, 1997, (Eric Benet) Day in the Life, 1999, (Jon B.) Pleasures U Like, 2001, (Kelly Price) Priceless, 2003, and others; singer: (background vocals, assoc. prodr.) (LSG) Levert, Sweat, Gill, 1997. Office: c/o Bad Boy Records 1440 Broadway, 16th Fl New York NY 10018*

EVANS, FRANKLIN BACHELDER, finance educator, consultant; b. Chgo., Feb. 9, 1922; s. Franklin B. and Arline (Brown) E.; m. Barbara V. Both, Sept. 16, 1943; children: Mary A., Amy B., Geoffrey B., Christopher G. AA, U. Chgo., 1941, AB, 1943, MBA, 1954, PhD, 1959. Asst. prof. mktg. U. Chgo., 1957-64; prof. mktg. U. Hawaii, 1964-69; prof. advt. Northwestern U., 1969-80, prof. emeritus, 1981—. Cons. to bus. and industry; researcher on consumer motivation. Contbr. articles to profl. jours. Served with U.S. Army, 1943-45. Decorated Bronze Star. Home: 4215 Harding Pike Apt 708 Nashville TN 37205 *Education should develop intellectual power. The ideal education is not specialized or pre-professional; it is not utilitarian. The intellectual tools for developing the mind start with the three R's and the liberal arts. Specialization can follow later.*

EVANS, FREDERICK JOHN, psychologist; b. Wollongong, Australia, Nov. 17, 1937; came to U.S., 1963; s. Frederick John and Phyllis Lurline (Wiffen) E.; m. Barbara Joan Marcelo, June 8, 1968 (div. 1990); children: Christopher Arthur, David Troy, Mark Fredrick (dec.), Diana Joy; m. Patricia E. Burns, Nov. 26, 1993; children: Mariefred Joy, Ellen Blessing. BA Honors Class I, U. Sydney, Australia, 1959, PhD, 1966. Tchg. fellow U. Sydney, 1959-63; rsch. psychologist Mass. Mental Health Center, 1963-64; from instr. psychology in psychiatry U. Pa. Sch. Medicine, Phila., 1965-66, to assoc. prof. psychiatry, 1972-81, assoc. prof. psychology, 1974-79; sr. rsch. psychologist Unit for Exptl. Psychiatry Inst. of Pa. Hosp., Phila., 1964-79; cons. psychologist pain mgmt. ctr. Med. Ctr. Princeton, NJ, 1998—; mem. cons. staff dept. psychiatry Princeton House, 1998—; cons. psychologist Pain Care Inst., Phila., 1999—, Arthritis Osteoporosis Ctr., West Reading, Pa. Vis. fellow psychology Yale U., 1970-71; trustee Inst. Exptl. Psychiatry, Boston, 1970-79; adj. prof. U. Medicine and Dentistry N.J.-Robert Wood Johnson Med. Sch., 1979-88; dir. rsch. divsn. Carrier Found., Belle Mead, N.J., 1979-88; v.p. Tex. Inst. Behavioral Medicine and Neurosci., 1989-96; pres. Pathfinders, Cons. in Human Behavior; dir. Pain Mgmt. Behavioral Medicine Svcs., Reading, Pa.; consulting psychologist The Elms Nursing Home, 1995—, The Back Rehab. Inst., Cranbury, N.J., Hamilton, N.J., 1997—; dir. psychol. svcs. Pain Mgmt. Ctr. The Med. Ctr. at Princeton, 1998—. Adv. editor: Internat. Jour. Clin. and Exptl. Hypnosis, 1968-69, assoc. editor, 1969—; assoc. editor: Am. Jour. Clin. Hypnosis, 1986-91, 95—; cons. editor: Jour. Abnormal Psychology, 1979-87, assoc. editor, 1989-91; co-editor: Functional Disorders of Memory, 1979, Springer Series in Behavior Modification and Behavioral Medicine, 1980-86; contbr. chpts. to textbooks, articles to profl. jours. Served to capt. Australian Army, 1961-63. Fulbright grantee, 1963-66 Fellow AAAS, APA (divsn. 30 program chmn. 1972, sec-treas. 1973-75, pres. 1978-79), Am. Soc. Clin. Hypnosis (chmn. liaison com. 1975-77, 88-89, cert. cons. 1993—), N.J. Psychol. Soc., Pa. Psychol. Soc., Soc. Clin. and Exptl. Hypnosis (co-chmn. sci. program 1970, 99, chmn. rsch. workshop, 1971, 76, 79, 80, 87-90, 97-2000, sec. 1973-86, co-chmn. publs. com. 1975-77, v.p. 1979-81, pres. 1981-83, chmn. budget com. 1987-89); mem. Am. Pain Soc. (founding dir. 1977-80), Internat. Soc. Hypnosis (sec.-treas. 1973-79, co-chmn. 7th Internat. Congress Hypnosis 1976, vice chmn. bd. dirs. organizing com. 10th Internat. Congress 1985, pres.-elect 1986-88, pres. 1987-91, immediate past pres. 1991-94, chair nominations and election com. 1991-94), Nat. Pain Found. (pres. 1989-92), Royal Soc. Medicine, Internat. Soc. Inner Mental Tng. (v.p. 1993-96). E-mail: aussiedr@aol.com.

EVANS, GARY LEE, communications educator, consultant; b. Davison, Mich., June 26, 1938; s. Joe Howard and Annie Annette (Colden) E.; m. Katherine Strand; children: Gary James, Aimee Lynn; stepchildren: John E. Holkeboer, Maja K. Holkeboer. BA, Wayne State U., 1962; MA, U. Mich., 1965, PhD, 1977. Prof. organizational and intercultural communication Eastern Mich. U., Ypsilanti, 1964—. Pres. Comm. Rsch. and Tng. Assocs.; cons. Volvo Corp., GM Corp., Ford Motor Car Co., Mich. Pub. Schs. and other ednl. instns.; speaker in field; instr., Davos, Switzerland, 1989; internat. program instr., Australia, New Zealand, Switzerland. Mem. Peace Corps Tng. and Teaching. Recipient Outstanding Continuing Educator of Yr. award Ea. Mich. U., 1994, Disting. Sr. Tchg. award 1998, Disting. Faculty Mem. award 1998, Disting. Tchg. award Ea. Mich. U. Alumni, 2001, Martin Luther King Humanitarian award 2005, Gold Medallion award 2005 Mem. Internat. Communication Assn., Speech Communication assn., Mich. Acad. Sci., Arts and Letters (communication chmn. 1982), Mich. Speech Communication Assn. (communication chmn. 1978—), Golden Key Nat. Honorary Soc., Phi Kappa Phi (pres. 1998—), Delta Sigma Rho, Pi Kappa Delta. Home: 11353 Pleasant Shore Dr Manchester MI 48158-9739 Office: Ea Mich U 121 Quirk Hall Ypsilanti MI 48197-2220

EVANS, GERALDINE ANN, academic administrator; b. Zumbrota, Minn., Feb. 24, 1939; d. Wallace William and Elda Ida (Tiedemann) Whipple; m. John Lyle Evans, June 21, 1963; children: John David, Paul William. AA, Rochester Community Coll., 1958; BS, U. Minn., 1960, MA, 1963, PhD, 1968. Cert. tchr., counselor, prin. and supt., Minn. Tchr. Hopkins (Minn.) Pub. Schs., 1960-63; counselor Anoka (Minn.) Pub. Schs., 1963-66; cons. in edn. Mpls., 1966-78; policy analyst Minn. Dept. Edn., St. Paul, 1978-79; dir. personnel Minn. Community Coll. System, St. Paul, 1979-82; pres. Rochester (Minn.) Community Coll., 1982-92; chancellor Minn. C.C. System, St. Paul, 1992-94; exec. dir. Ill. C.C. Bd., Springfield, 1994-96; chancellor San Jose (Calif.) Evergreen C.C. Dist., 1996—. Mem. San Jose Workforce Investment Bd., 2000—; mem. legis. and adv. com. Calif. C.C. League, 1998-2002. Mem. Gov.'s Job Tng. Coun., St. Paul, 1983—94, chair, 1992—94; mem. Silicon Valley Pvt. Industry Coun., 1997—2000, Workforce Silicon Valley, 1998—2002; trustee Golden Gate U., 1997—; chair Rochester (Minn.) United Way, 1985—86; mem. campaign cabinet United Way of Silicon Valley, 2003—; moderator Mizpah United Ch. Christ, Hopkins, 1982; mem. complete count com. U.S. Census, Santa Clara County, 2000; vice chair, bd. dirs. Wayzata (Minn.) Sch. Bd., 1980—83; bd. dirs. Minn. Tech. Ctr., Rochester, 1991—92; bd. mem. Boy Scouts San Clara Coun., 2004—; sec.-treas. Coun. North Ctrl. Cmty. and Jr. Colls., 1990—92; mem. ACE Commn. on Edn. Credit and Credentials, 1992—96. Winner Rochester C. of C. Athena award, 1990, San Jose YWCA Exec. award, 1998; Inst. Ednl. Leadership fellow, Washington, 1978-79. Mem. Nat. League Nursing (bd. assoc. degree accreditation rev. 1990-93, exec. com. 1993-96), Am. Assn. Cmty. Colls. (workforce commn. 2000-03), Am. Assn. Cmty. Jr. Colls. (bd. dirs. 1984-87), North Ctrl. Assn. Cmty. and Jr. Colls. (evaluator 1985-96), Silicon Valley C. of C. (bd. dirs. 2001-04), La Raza Roundtable, Rotary. Congregationalist. Avocations: travel, gardening. E-mail: geraldine.evans@sjeccd.org.

EVANS, HAROLD EDWARD, banker; b. Detroit, Apr. 23, 1927; s. Harold J. and Mary Esther (Keenoy) E.; m. Patricia Mae Persons Willy, Mar. 28, 1982; children by previous marriage: D'lorah Ann, M'liss Lorraine, David Keenoy, Craig Edward. BBA, U. Mich., 1950; cert., Bank Adminstrn. Inst., U. Wis., 1968, Stonier Grad. Sch. Banking, Rutgers U., 1975. Auditor Second Nat. Bank Saginaw, Mich., 1952-61, controller, 1961-73, sr. v.p., cashier, sec., chief fin. officer, 1973-92; founder, chmn. art collection, 1976-92; mem. selection com., 1992-2001; v.p. loan rev. officer Citizens Banking Corp., Flint, Mich., 1986-92. Sec.-treas. 2d Nat. Corp., 1973-88, Century Life Ins. Co., Mich., 1973-93; lectr. Robert Perry Sch. Banking, Ctrl. Mich. U. Mem. Saginaw Citizens Coun. for Ctrl. Bus. Dist., 1970-89; mem. adv. bd. Urban Renewal, chmn. econ. base study com., 1954-55; chmn. Downtown Saginaw Beautification Commn., 1968-83, Greater Saginaw Beautification Residential Com., 1965-68, 1988-97; chmn. Saginaw Valley State U. Humanities Series Com., 1990—; sec., trustee Saginaw Osteo. Hosp., 1960-84; treas., trustee Saginaw Symphony Orch., 1965-72; past trustee Saginaw His. Mus.; treas., dir. United Rehab. Svcs., 1954-65, Temple Theater Arts Assn., 1980-87; fin. officer Saginaw CAP, 1978-84; trustee, treas. Saginaw Valley Dancers, 1977-93; trustee Hartley Nature Ctr. Found., 1987—, Saginaw Hall of Fame, 1989—; mem. adv. bd. Health Source Saginaw, Inc., 1991—, sec. adv. bd., 1993, 96, vice chmn., 1997, chmn., 1998; mem. steering com. Cathedral Dist. Renewal, 1990—; mem. com. for advancement Saginaw Valley State U., 1992—, mem. com. Stuart and Vernice Gross History Lit. award, 1996-2000; mem. com. for advancement Saginaw Area Enrichment Commn., 1992-2002, Saginaw Twp. Art in Pub. Place Commn., 1991—, Delta Coll. Pub. Radio Fund Raiser Com., 1990-97, Temple Theater Film Selection com., 1998-2003; mem. awards panel Theatre Guild Midland Ctr. for the Arts; bd. trustees Mideastern Libr. Coop., 2003. With USNR, 1945—46. Recipient Saginaw Arts award Community Enrichment Commn., 1992; nominee Gov.'s Art award, 1996. Mem. Saginaw C. of C., Bank Adminstrn. Inst. (life; pres. Ea. Mich. conf. 1955-56, v.p. Mich. chpt. 1958-59), Valley Film Soc. (bd. dirs. 1991—), Tri-County Econ. Club, Econ. Club Detroit, Internat. Torch Club (Saginaw Valley chpt. 1993—), U. Mich. Alumni Club (Saginaw chpt.), Optimists (bd. dirs. Breakfast Club 1960-80, treas. 1961-63, pres. 1970-72), Mich. Women's Hall of Fame (elector 1992-93), Friends Theodore Roethke, U.S. Navy League. Home: 17 Riverside Blvd Saginaw MI 48602-1077 also: 1710 N Charles St Saginaw MI 48602-4848

EVANS, SIR HAROLD MATTHEW, editor, publisher, writer; b. Manchester, Eng., June 28, 1928; arrived in US, 1984, naturalized, 1999; s. Frederick Albert and Mary Hannah (Haselum) Evans; m. Enid Parker, Apr. 15, 1953 (div. 1978); children: Ruth, Katherine, Michael; m. Tina Brown, Aug. 20, 1981; children: George, Isabel. BA in politics and economics with honors, Durham U., London, 1952; MA, Durham U., 1966; PhD(hon.), Sterling U., 1982; DCL (hon.), Durham U., 1998; DLitt (hon.), U. Teesside, 2000, London Inst., 2001. Reporter, Ashton-under-Lyne; reporter, editl. writer Manchester Evening News, England, 1952—56, asst. editor, 1958—61; editor Northern Echo, Darlington, England, 1961—67, The Sunday Times, London, 1967-81, The Times, London, 1981-82; dir., exec. bd. Goldcrest Films & TV, London, 1982—84; editor-in-chief Atlantic Monthly Press, NYC, 1984; editorial dir. US News & World Report, Washington, 1984-86, contbg. editor, 1984—; founding editor-in-chief Conde Nast Traveler, NYC, 1986-90; pres., pub. Random House Trade Pub. Group, NYC, 1990-97; vice chmn., edit. dir. US News and World Report, NY Daily News, Atlantic Monthly, Fast Company, 1997-99; author Little, Brown and Co., NYC, 2000—; cons. editor The Week Mag., NYC. Vis. prof. City U., London, 1978-82, Poynter Inst., St. Petersburg, Fla., 1982, Duke U., NC, 1984. Author: Eye Witness, 1981, Good Times Bad Times, 1983, Editing and Design (5 vols.), 1977-78, (with others) We Learned to Ski, 1976, Suffer the Children, 1979, The American Century, 1998, They Made America: From the Steam Engine to the Seach Engine: Two Centuries of Innovators, 2004; exec. producer: (TV prog.) We Learned to Ski, 1983. Served to cpl. RAF, 1946-49. Named one of 50 World Press Heroes, Internat. Press Inst., 2000; recipient Internat. Editor of Yr. Award, World Press Rev., 1974, Editor of Yr. Award, Granada Press Awards, 1982, Lifetime Achievement Award, Internat. Ctr. Photography, 1999, Gold Award for Lifetime Achievement, British Press Awards, 2000; Harkness Commonwealth Fund Fellow in Journalism, U. Chgo. and Stanford U., 1956—57, Knighted for services to journalism, Queen Elizabeth II, 2004. Fellow Soc. Indsl. Designers, Inst. Journalists (European Gold Medal 1978); mem. Royal Photographic Soc. (Hood Medal 1980), Nat. Press Photographers of Great Britain (honoree 1986), Garrick Club (London), Century Club (NY), Yale Club (NY). Avocations: music, swimming, ping pong/table tennis. Office: Little Brown and Co 1271 Ave of the Americas New York NY 10020*

EVANS, HARRY LAUNIUS, pathology educator; b. Mobile, Ala., June 11, 1948; s. Aurelius A. and Anne (Hathaway) E.; m. Cheryl J. Winfrey, June 6, 1970 (div. Dec. 1990); children: Thomas H., Sarah S. BS, Stetson U., 1970; MD, U. Fla., 1974. Diplomate Am. Bd. Pathology. Resident in pathology Vanderbilt U. Med. Ctr., Nashville, 1974-75; fellow in dermatopathology Mayo Clinic, Rochester, Minn., 1977-78; fellow in pathology U.Tex.-M.D. Anderson Cancer Ctr., Houston, 1975-77, asst. prof. pathology, 1978-82, assoc. prof., 1982-90, prof., 1990—. Contbr. articles to med. jours. Mem. U.S.-Can. Acad. Pathology, Arthur Purdy Stout Soc. Surg. Pathologists. Avocations: mountain climbing, music, crossword puzzles. Office: U Tex-MD Anderson Cancer Ctr Dept Pathology 1515 Holcombe Blvd Houston TX 77030-4009 Office Phone: 713-792-3152. E-mail: hevans@mdanderson.org.

EVANS, HELEN RUTH, music educator, pianist; b. Grant City, Mo., May 26, 1913; d. John Larkin and Inez (Florea) Hall; m. Donald Maurice Mathias, Oct. 7, 1934 (div.); m. Thomas Claude Evans, Sept. 1. Grad., No. Colo. U. Piano tchr., Colo., 1940-50, 1950-96; ret., 1996. Mem. AAUW, N.Mex. Music Tchrs. Assn., Delta Kappa Gamma. Republican. Presbyterian. Avocations: pianist, reading, cooking.

EVANS, HIRAM KRAIG, forensic chemist; b. Chula Vista, Calif., July 8, 1953; BA in Chemistry, Ctrl. Coll., Pella, Iowa, 1975; AS in Criminal Justice, Southwestern Coll., Chula Vista, 1976; MS in Criminalistics, Calif. State U., Los Angeles, 1982. Cert. criminalist, controlled substance analyst, ASCLD Lab. inspector. Tech. asst. Harris & Harris, Los Angeles, 1977; criminalist I Ventura County (Calif.) Sheriff's Dept., 1978-79; criminalist San Diego County Sheriff's Dept., 1979-81; supervising criminalist, dep. sheriff San Bernardino County (Calif.) Sheriff's Dept. Forensic Sci. Lab., 1982—. Adj. prof. forensic sci. Nat. U., San Diego, 1980-83; instr. Regional Criminal Justice Tng. Ctr., San Bernardino, 1983—; prof. criminalistics Calif. State U., L.A., 1992—. Contbr. articles to profl. jours, chpt. to book. Fellow Am. Bd. Criminalistics, Am. Acad. Forensic Scis. (criminalistics sect.); mem. Am. Chem. Soc., Calif. Assn. Criminalists (sec. 1986-92, pres. 1999-2000), Calif. Assn. Crime Lab. Dirs. (treas. 2004-05), Ctrl. Coll. Alumni Assn., Internat. Assn. Forensic Scis., Midwestern Assn. Forensic Scientists (ASTM com.

E-30 on forensic sci.), Assn. Ofcl. Analytical Chemists, Pacific S.W. Ry. Mus. Assn., Masons Republican. Avocations: horticulture, railway history. Home: PO Box 782 Highland CA 92346-0782 Office: San Bernardino County Sheriff's Dept PO Box 569 San Bernardino CA 92402-0569 E-mail: HEvans@sanbernardinosheriff.org.

EVANS, HUGH E., pediatrician, educator; b. N.Y.C., July 6, 1934; s. David and Geraldine (Krebs) E.; m. Ruth L. Orloff, June 5, 1960 (dec. Mar. 1999); children: Margo Lynn Evans Manspeizer, Marc Douglas. AB cum laude, Columbia U., 1954; MD, SUNY Downstate Med. Center, 1958. Intern Johns Hopkins Hosp., Balt., 1958-59, asst. resident, 1959-60; sr. asst. resident NIH, Bethesda, Md., 1960-62, chief resident outpatient dept., 1962-63; pvt. practice Bellaire, Ohio, 1963-66; assoc. dir. pediatrics Harlem Hosp. Center, N.Y.C., 1966-73; dir. dept. pediatrics Jewish Hosp. and Med. Center, Bklyn., 1973-85; prof. pediatrics U. Medicine and Dentistry of N.J., Newark, 1985—, prof. preventive medicine and community health, 1991—, chmn. dept. pediatrics, 1985-90; dir. dept. pediatrics U. Hosp., Newark, 1985-90, mem. attending staff, 1985—. Assoc. clin. prof. pediatrics Columbia U., 1968-73; prof. pediatrics SUNY Downstate Med. Center, Bklyn., 1973-85; cons. Englewood (N.J.) Hosp., Hackensack (N.J.) Hosp.; trustee Bergen-Passiac County Lung Assn., 1973-85. Author: (with Leonard Glass) Perinatal Medicine, 1976, Lung Diseases of Children, 1979, 2d edit., 1985, The Hidden Campaign: The Medical History of President Franklin D. Roosevelt and the 1944 Election, 2002; editor: Hospital Care of Children and Youth, 1986, Jour. Perinatology, 1985-2000; contbr. articles to profl. jours., chpts. to textbooks; TV appearances include C-Span, History Channel, Discovery Channel. Served to sr. asst. surgeon USPHS, 1960-62. Recipient Richard L. Day award in pediats., 2003; fellow, Sabin Vaccine Inst., 2004—. Mem. AAUP (bd. govs. 2001—, v.p. 2003—), Soc. Pediat. Rsch., Harvey Soc., Am. Soc. Microbiology, Am. Acad. Pediat. (com. on hosp. care 1982-85, chmn. 1985-88, task force on pediat. AIDS 1987-92), Am. Thoracic Soc., Am. Pediat. Soc., Soc. Exptl. Biology and Medicine, N.Y. Pediat. Soc. (pres. 1982-83), Am. Polit. Sci. Assn., Bklyn. Acad. Pediat. (v.p. 1976, pres. 1977), Infectious Diseases Soc., Med. Soc. N.J. (mem. spl. com. AIDS 1993-95), Rotary Internat., Sigma Xi, Alpha Omega Alpha. Home: 49 Nelson Pl Tenafly NJ 07670 Office: U Medicine and Dentistry NJ MSB-F586 185 S Orange Ave Newark NJ 07103-2757 Office Phone: 973-972-6530. Business E-Mail: evanshe@umdnj.edu.

EVANS, JACK R. (J. GLENN EVANS), writer, poet; b. Wewoka, Okla., Dec. 21, 1930; s. John and Jimmie Devonia (Gordon) Glenn; m. Lucille Wallace, May 28, 1957 (div. 1967); m. Barbara Ann (Lubic) Conroy, Oct. 26, 1968; 1 stepchild, Barbara Ann Conroy. BS, East Ctrl. U., Ada, Okla., 1956. Stockbroker Hinton Jones Co., Seattle, 1966-68; stockbroker, v.p. Fox Roff Co., Seattle, 1968-70, John R. Lewis Co., Seattle, 1970-73; stockbroker, pres. Securities Exch., Seattle, 1973-76; pres., stockbroker, investment banker Securities Corp. of Wash., Seattle, 1976-84; pub. SCW Publs., Seattle, 1984—; poetry editor, pub. PoetsWest Online, Seattle, 1998—; freelance poet, writer, historian Seattle, 1986—; poetry curator Seattle City Coun. "Words' Worth", 2001. Bd. dir. Seattle Freelances, 1995-2002 (pres. 2004-2005); mem. adv. bd. U. Wash. Writers Program; founder SCW Shirt Pocket Book series, 2005 Author: Buffalo Tracks, 2003, Broker Jim, 2002, Chasing His Dreams: Life of Entrepreneur, 2002, Window in the Sky, 1996, Seattle Poems, 1996, Swedes From Whence They Came, 1993, Levant F. Thompson: Hop King, Banker, Senator, 1992, Little History of Pike Place Market, 1991, Little History of North Bend-Snoqualmie, 1990, Little History of Bothell Washington, 1988, Little History of Gig Harbor Washington, 1988, Little History of Renton Washington, 1987, (CD) Window in the Sky, 1999; editor: Klondike Gold Rush Centennial Anthology, 1997. Contest dir., bd. dir. Klondike Gold Rush Centennial Celebration, Wash. State, 1997. Cpl. USAF, 1954. Recipient Faith Beamer Cooke award Wash. Poets Assn., 1999, Seattle FreeLances Outstanding Writer award, 2003, Nat. winner Rock River Poetry Contest, 2003, 2d pl. winner William Stafford award, 2002. Mem. Assn. King County Hist. Orgn. (past pres.), Pacific N.W. Hist. Guild (past v.p.), Wash. Poets Assn. (bd. dirs. 1997-2004), PoetsTable (founding mem.). Avocations: history, reading, poetry reading. Office: SCW Publs 1011 Boren Ave # 155 Seattle WA 98104-1325 Office Phone: 206-682-1268.

EVANS, JAMES D., JR., retail executive; Former prin. L.P. Evans Cos., Miami, Fla.; former v.p. automotive retail group AutoNation, Inc., Ft. Lauderdale, Fla., sr. v.p. industry rels., 2000—. Mem. South Fla. Internat. Auto Show Com.; pres. South Fla. Mercedes-Benz Dealers, Inc. Advt. Coop. Mem.: Am. Internat. Automobile Dealer Assn. (bd. dirs.), Fla. Automobile Dealer Assn. (bd. dirs.), South Fla. Auto Dealer Assn. (past bd. dirs.). Office: AutoNation Inc 110 SE 6th St Fort Lauderdale FL 33301

EVANS, JAMES E., lawyer; b. 1946; BA, Mich. State U., 1968; JD, Ohio State U., 1970. Bar: Ohio 1971. Assoc. Keating, Muething & Klekamp, 1970—76; named v.p., gen. counsel Am. Fin. Corp. (former subsid. Am. Fin. Group Inc.), Cin., 1976; sr. v.p., gen. counsel, dir. Am. Fin. Group Inc., Cin., 1995—. Mem.: Cin. Bar Assn., Ohio Bar Assn., ABA. Office: Am Fin Group Inc 1 E 4th St Cincinnati OH 45202*

EVANS, JAMES HANDEL, academic administrator, architect; b. Bolton, Eng., June 14, 1938; came to U.S., 1965. s. Arthur Handel and Ellen Bowen (Ramsden) E.; m. Carol L. Mulligan, Sept. 10, 1966; children: Jonathan, Sarah. Diploma of Architecture, U. Manchester, Eng., 1965; MArch., U. Oreg., 1967; postgrad., Cambridge (Eng.) U., 1969-70. Registered architect, Calif., U.K.; cert. NCARB. Assoc. dean. prof. architecture Calif. Poly. State U., San Luis Obispo, 1967-78; prof. art and design San Jose (Calif.) State U., 1979—, assoc. exec. v.p., 1978-81, interim exec. v.p., 1981-82, exec. v.p., 1982-91. interim pres., 1991-92, pres., 1992-95; sr. adminstr. Calif. State U., Monterey Bay, 1991—94; vice chancellor Calif. State U System, Long Beach, CA, 1995-96; planning pres. Calif. State U. Channel Islands, Ventura, 1996-2001; pres. HE Cons. Inc., 2001—. Cons. Ibiza Nueva, Ibiza, Spain, 1977-80; vis. prof. Ciudad Universitaria, Madrid, 1977; vis. lectr. Herriott Watt U., Edinburgh, 1970; mem. adv. com. Army Command Staff Coll., Ft. Leavenworth, Kans., 1988. Trustee Good Samaritan Hosp., San Jose, 1987-90; bd. dirs. San Jose Shelter, 1988-90; dir. San Jose C. of C., 1991-94, Ventura County Mus. History and Art. Sci. Rsch. Coun. fellow Cambridge U., 1969-70. Fellow AIA; mem. Royal Inst. Brit. Architects, Assn. Univ. Architects. Avocation: golf. E-mail: hevans@vcccd.net, jhevans@adelphia.net.

EVANS, JAMES HURLBURT, retired transportation and natural resources executive; b. Lansing, Mich., June 26, 1920; s. James L. and Marie (Hurlburt) E.; m. Mary Johnston Head, 1984; children by previous marriage: Eric B. (dec. 1996), Carol E. Jepperson, Joan E. Madsen. AB, Centre Coll., 1943, DHL (hon.), 1987; JD, U. Chgo., 1948; LLD (hon.), Millikin U., 1978. Bar: Ill. 1949. Atty., loan officer Harris Trust & Savs. Bank, Chgo., 1948-56; sec.-treas. Reuben H. Donnelley Corp., Chgo., 1956-57; v.p., dir. Reuben H. Donnelley Corp. (merged with Dun & Bradstreet 1961), N.Y.C., 1957-62; v.p. fin. Dun & Bradstreet, 1962-65, also bd. dirs.; pres. Seamen's Bank for Savs., N.Y.C., 1965-68, chmn. bd., 1968, trustee, 1965-78; pres. Union Pacific Corp., N.Y.C., 1969-77, chmn., CEO, 1977-85. Ret. dir. AT&T, GM Corp., Citicorp/Citibank, Met. Life Ins. Co., Bristol-Myers, Dun & Bradstreet, Anaconda Corp. Bd. govs. ARC, 1970-76, nat. fund chmn. 1974-76; hon. trustee, former vice chmn. John F. Kennedy Ctr. for Performing Arts; life trustee Nat. Recreation Found., pres. 1971-75, U. Chgo., Ctr. Coll. Ky., Ctrl. Park Conservancy; founding mem. Citizens Adv. Com. on Environ. Quality, 1966-70. Served to lt. USNR, 1943-46; life gov. N.Y. Presbyn. Hosp. Mem. ABA, Phi Beta Kappa, Omicron Delta Kappa, Delta Kappa Epsilon. Clubs: Racquet and Tennis, Links, Knickerbocker (N.Y.C.); Metropolitan, Alfalfa (Washington); Maidstone (East Hampton); Bohemian (San Francisco). Presbyterian. Office: 375 Park Ave Ste 2005 New York NY 10152-2099

EVANS, JAMES MIGNON, architect; b. Memphis, May 9, 1938; s. Mignon Kemper and Elizabeth Louise (Fulcher) E.; m. Gayle Jean Dupont, Aug. 21, 1965; children: Matthew Moseby, Benjamin Dupont, Bolin Briscoe. BA, Rice U., 1960; MFA in Architecture, Princeton U., 1962. Registered architect, Tenn., Va., Calif., Ariz., N.Y. Intern architect Perkins & Will Ptnrship., Washington, 1965-66; architect Doxiadis Assocs., Washington, 1966-68, Gassner Nathan & Browne, Memphis, 1969-70, prin., 1970-87, Nathan/Evans/Taylor, Memphis, 1987-95, Nathan/Evans/Taylor/Coleman/Foster, Memphis, 1995—2003, Evans Taylor Foster Childress Archs., Memphis, 2003—. Mem. bldg. code rev. and adv. bd. Memphis and Shelby Counties, 1980-83; mem. Memphis Heritage Adv. Com., 1980-84. Bd. dirs. Dismas Ho., Memphis, 1989—94, pres., 1992, 1993; bd. dirs. Theatre Memphis, 2003—; trustee Grace-St. Luke's Episcopal Sch., Memphis, 1980—86, pres., 1984—85; mem. vestry Grace-St. Luke's Episcopal Ch., 1983—86, 1990—93, 2001—, jr. warden, 1992, 1993, 2004. Served with U.S. Army, 1963—65. Lowell M. Palmer fellow, 1961-62; recipient Sylvan award Lumberman's Club of Memphis, 1983, 85, Excellence award Masonry Inst. Tenn., 1980, 89, 91, Energy Design Honor award TVA, 1988. Mem. AIA (treas. 1978, peer reviewer 1987—, Honor award 1978, 94, mem. exec. com. Memphis chpt., mem. past pres. coun. 2001-03, chmn. 2004, chmn. awards com. 2001-03), Tenn. Soc. Architects (bd. dirs. 1977-80, Excellence award 1978, 81, 96, 97, Honor award 1981, 89, 91), Memphis Inst. Architects (v.p. 1980, pres. 1981), Memphis Rotary (chmn. ambassadorial scholarship com. 2003—). Clubs: Univ. of Memphis. Avocations: jogging, gardening, reading. Office: Evans Taylor Foster Childress-Archs 343 N Main St Memphis TN 38103 Office Phone: 901-525-5344.

EVANS, JANET, publishing executive; b. Raleigh, N.C., Sept. 16, 1956; d. Leonard Odell and Sue J Mills. Mktg. advisor Evans & Wade Advt. Ltd., Raleigh, 1977—79; pres. Ivy Ho. Pub. Group, Raleigh, 1993—. Bd. dirs. Found. Internat. Meetings. Editor various organizational newsletters. Mem. Raleigh C. of C., NC, 1980—2002. Mem.: Pubs. Assn. of the South. Republican. Baptist. Avocations: reading, travel, walking. Home: 5527 Golden Arrow Ln Raleigh NC 27613 Home Fax: 919-781-9042. Business E-Mail: janetevans@ivyhousebooks.com.

EVANS, JO BURT, communications executive, rancher; b. Kimble County, Tex., Dec. 18, 1928; d. John Fred and Sadie (Oliver) Burt; m. Charles Wayne Evans II, Apr. 17, 1949; children: Charles Wayne III, John Burt, Elizabeth Wisart. BA, Mary Hardin-Baylor Coll., 1948; MA, Trinity U., 1967. Owner, mgr. Sta. KMBL, Junction, Tex., 1959-61; real estate broker Junction, 1965-74; staff economist, adv. on 21st Congl. Dist., polit. campaign Nelson Wolff, 1974-75; asst. mgr., bookkeeper family owned ranches/rental property Junction, 1948—; gen. mgr. TV Translator Corp., Junction, 1968—, sec.-treas., 1980—. Treas., asst. to coord. Citizens for Tex., 1972; historian Kimble Hist. Soc.; mem. Com. of Conservation Soc. to Save the Edwards Aquifer, San Antonio, 1973; homecoming chmn. Sesquicentennial Yr., Junction; treas., asst. coord. New Consitution, San Antonio, 1974; legis. chair Hill Country Women, Kimble County, 1990—; cashier Texan Theatre; campaign chmn. for Challenge U. Mary Hardin, Baylor, 2000. Named an outstanding Texan, Tex. Senate, 1973. Mem. AAUW (scholarship named in honor 1973), Nat. Translator Assn., Daus. Republic Tex., Tex. Sheriffs Assn., Nat. Cattlewomens Assn., Internat. Platform Assn., Bus. and Profl. Women (pres. 1981-82). Republican. Mem. Unity Ch. Home: PO Box 283 Junction TX 76849-0283 Office: 618 Main St Junction TX 76849-4635 Office Phone: 325-446-3407.

EVANS, JOHN DAVID DANIEL, judge; b. Feb. 5, 1944; children: Reagan, Quentin Cory, Jonathan. BA, U. Western Ont., 1967; LLB, Windsor Law Sch., 1972. Bar: Ont. 1974. Assoc. W.L.S. trivett, Q.C., Orillia, Ont., 1974, Robert J. Carter, Q.C., Toronto, Ont., 1975-76; ptnr. Evans, Kukurin, Timmins, Ont., 1976-77, Perras, Evans, Kukurin & Huot, Timmins, Ont., 1977-80, Riopelle, Evans, Chornyj and Carr, Timmins, 1980-84; apptd. judge Criminal divsn. Provincial Ct., Ont., 1984-90, apptd. regional sr. judge ctrl. east region, 1990-98, sr. judge. Faculty law St. Clair C.C., No. C.C., Laurentian U. Mem. Criminal Lawyers Assn., Can. Bar Assn., Am. Judges Assn. (bd. govs.). Roman Catholic. Avocations: sports, hockey playing. Office: Ont Ct Justice 3 Dominion St Bracebridge ON Canada P1L 2E6

EVANS, JOHN DERBY, telecommunications company executive; b. Detroit, June 3, 1944; s. Edward Steptoe and Florence (Allington) E.; m. Susan Blair Allan, Apr. 7, 1973 (div. Nov. 1986); children: John Derby, Courtenay Boyd. AB, U. Mich., 1966. Pres. Evans Comm. Sys. Inc., Charlottesville, Va., 1970-72; v.p., gen. mgr. Capitol Cablevision Corp., Charleston, W.Va., 1972-76; regional mgr. Am. TV and Comm. Corp., Denver, 1974-76; exec. v.p., COO Arlington (Va.) TeleCom. Corp., 1976-83; pres. Arlington Cable Ptnrs. Ltd., 1983-94, Suburban Cable Ptnrs., Brooklyn Pk., Minn., 1985-89, Hauser Comm., N.Y.C., 1985-94, Evans Telecomm. Co., 1983—; chmn., CEO Waterford Marine Inc., Middleburg, Va., 1996—2001. Staff asst. sec. planning and devel. Dept. HEW, Washington, 1976; co-founder, bd. dirs. Cable Satellite Pub. Affairs Network (C-SPAN), 1979—, exec. com., 1982—93, 1998—, chmn., 1991—93, chmn. fin. com., 1997—; pres. Montgomery Cablevision (LP), Rockville, Md., 1986—94, Washington Metro Cable Club, 1981—; bd. dirs. Falcon Comm. Co., L.A., Falcon Cable TV, 1998—2000, GBR Sci., Balt., 1999—2000; v.p. North Ctrl. Cable Comm. Co., Roseville, Minn., 1986—92; mng. gen. ptnr. Waterford Farm Partnership, Middleburg, Va., 1993—; Siciliano forum lectr. U. Utah, 1998; future makers lectr. Emory U., 1999, futurist forum panelist, 2004; bd. dirs. Nelson Cable Co., Lovingston, Va.; lectr. Inst. of the Humanities, U. Mich., 2000; keynote spkr. Exec. Summit on Internat. Health Philanthropy Royal Coll. Physicians, London, 2001; inaugural lectr. Mich. State U. Quello Ctr. for Telecom. Law and Regulation, 2001; spkr. in field; bd. dirs. Alescentor Tech. Holdings, Amman, Israel, 2005—. Trustee C-Span Ednl. Found., 1994—; trustee, vice chmn. bd. trustees Signature Theater, Arlington, 1992—2004; chmn. bd. trustees Evans Found., 1994—; chmn. Cancer/AIDS Rsch. Network, Balt.; mem. steering com. Inst. Human Virology U. Md., Balt., 1996—; bd. dir. Internat. Cancer and AIDS Rsch. Found., 1996—2000, Internat. AIDS Vaccine Initiative, N.Y.C., 2002—, treas., 2003—, chmn. fin. and audit com., 2003—; bd. dir. Hollings Cancer Ctr., Charleston, SC, 1998—2004; adv. com. AIDS Rsch. Inst. U. Calif., San Francisco; mem. vis. com. Coll. LS and A, U. Mich., 1994—, mem. pres.'s adv. bd., 1998—, mem. commn. on info. tech., 2000—; chmn. Waterford Project Inc., 2000—03; bd. dir. Eisenhower World Affairs Inst., 1990—2003, chmn. strategic planning com., 1997—2003, vice chmn., 1999—2003; bd. dir. Accerator Tech. Holdings, Amman, Jordan. Named to Va. Comm. Hall of Fame, Richmond, Va., 2004; recipient AIDS Achievement award, League African Am. Women, 2000. Mem.: Cable TV Adminstrn., Mktg. Soc. (bd. dir. 1985), Va. Communication Hall of Fame, Va. Commonwealth U., Asia-Pacific Conf. Sci. and Tech. Leaders (U.S. del. 1996), Va. Cable Assn. (bd. dir. 1979—, v.p. 1982, pres. 1983—84, Hall of Fame 2001), Nat. Cable TV Assn. (nat. chmn. awards com. 1981, bd. dir. 1982—, chmn. govt. rels. com. 1985—86, mem. regulatory policy com. 1991—95, chmn. elections, bylaws com. 1991—97, convention com. 1998—, mem. conv. com. 1999—2000, Pres. award 1979, Vanguard award 1984), Key West Yacht Club, Washington Golf and Country Club (Arlington), Boars Head Sports Club (Charlottesville), Farmington Country Club (Inducted Va. Comms. Hall of Fame 2004). Republican. Episcopalian. Avocations: scuba diving, motorcycling, boating. Home and Office: Evans Telecoms 1617 White St Key West FL 33040 E-mail: jdevans@msn.com, jdevans2000@aol.com.

EVANS, JOHN JOSEPH, management consultant, educator, writer; b. St. Louis, Mar. 1, 1940; s. Roy Joseph and Henrietta Frances (Schweizer) E.; children: Todd, Karlyn, Jane, Mark. BA, Centenary Coll., 1962; postgrad., Syracuse U., 1969, U. Wis., 1971, Harvard Bus. Sch., 1970—73; MBA, Pepperdine U., 1972, DSc (hon.), 1974. Pres., CEO Evans Distbg. Cos., La., 1962—72, Evans & Co., La., 1966—, KOA, L.A., 1968—69; v.p., corp. sec. Lee Nat. Life Ins. Co., La., 1973; pres., CEO La. REIT; v.p. mktg. UMB, 1974; divsn. gen. mgr. AgMet, La., 1974—76; pres., CEO Universal Mfg. Corp., L.A., 1982; gen. mgr. Exxon Ofc Products, L.A., 1976—78; corp. dir. tng. & devel. Mitchell Internat., San Diego, 1983—87, Sun Electric Corp., Crystal Lake, Ill., 1988—90; corp. dir. tng. Chilton Publs., Radnor, Pa., 1990—92. Adj. prof. Centenary Coll., Golf Acad. San Diego. Bd. dirs. ARC; trustee Grad. Sch. Sales Mgmt. and Mktg.; pres. KOA of La., 1964; chmn. bd. dirs. N. La. Mental Health Hosp.; co-chair United Way, 1965-69. Recipient awards United Way, 1965-69, ITVA awards, 1987-88. Mem. Nat. Beer Wholesalers Assn. (adv. dir.), Sales and Mktg. Execs. of Shreveport (pres.), S.W. Sales and Mktg. Execs. Coun. (pres.), Young Pres. Orgn., Pres.'s Assn., Conf. Bd., Aspen Inst., Sales and Mktg. Execs. Internat., Am. Soc. Tng. and Devel., Am. Soc. Pers. Adminstrn., Syracuse U. Grad. Sch. Sales Mgmt. and Mktg. Alumni Assn. (past pres., past trustee), Westlake Village C. of C. (past v.p., bd. dirs.), Air Force Assn., Am. Legion, Shreveport C. of C. Pers. and Indsl. Rels. Assn. (vice chmn., bd. dirs.), Harvard Club San Diego. Home and Office: 11305 Affinity Ct 131 San Diego CA 92131-2758

EVANS, JOHN ROBERT, academic administrator, cardiologist; b. Toronto, Can., Oct. 1, 1929; s. William Watson and Mary Evelyn Lucille (Thompson) E.; m. Jean Gay Glassco, 1954; children: Derek, Mark and Michael (twins), Gillian, Timothy, Willa. MD, U. Toronto, 1952; DPhil (Rhodes scholar), Oxford U., 1955; LLD (hon.), Dalhousie U., McMaster U., McGill U., 1972, Queen's U., 1974, Wilfred Laurier U., 1975, York U., 1977, U. Toronto, 1980, U. Western Ont., 1982, Yale U., 1978; DSc (hon.), Meml. U., 1973, U. Montreal, 1977, Royal Mil. Coll., 1989; DHL (hon.), Johns Hopkins U., 1978; D Univ. (hon.), U. Ottawa, 1978, U. Limbourg, The Netherlands, 1980. Intern Toronto Gen. Hosp., 1952—53, chief resident physician, 1958—59; practice medicine specializing in cardiology Toronto, 1961—72; assoc. dept. medicine U. Toronto Med. Sch., 1961—65, prof., 1972—, pres. univ., 1972—78, pres. emeritus, 1995—; dir. population, health and nutrition dept. World Bank, Washington, 1979—83; chmn. Allelix Inc., Mississauga, 1983—99; physician Toronto Gen. Hosp., 1961—65; dean Faculty Medicine McMaster U., Hamilton, 1965—72, v.p. health scis., 1967—72; chmn. Torstar Corp., Toronto, 1993—, Alcan Aluminium Ltd., Montreal, 1995—2002; vice chmn. NPS-Allelix Inc., 1999—. Bd. dirs. Torstar Ltd., Toronto, MDS Health Group, Toronto, Retirement Residences Income Trust; hon. fellow London Sch. Hygiene and Tropical Medicine, Univ. Coll., Oxford, Eng.; chmn. Can. Found. Innovation, 1997—. Trustee Rockefeller Found., N.Y.C., 1982—95, chmn., 1988—95, African Med. Rsch. Found., Canada, 1986—90; trustee Walter and Duncan Gordon Charitable Found., Toronto, 1991—2000, chair, 1998—2000. Decorated Companion Order of Can., Order of Ont.; named, Can. Med. Hall of Fame, 2000, Can. Bus. Hall of Fame, 2005; recipient Gairdner Found. Wightman award, Gairdner Found., 1992, FNG Starr medal, Can. Med. Assn., 2002, Disting. Leadership medal, Can. Inst. Health Rsch., 2004; Markle scholar, 1960—65. Master: ACP; fellow: Inst. Corp. Dirs., Royal Coll. Physicians (London), Royal Coll. Physicians and Surgeons Can., Royal Soc. Can. Home: 58 Highland Ave Toronto ON Canada M4W 2A3 Office: Torstar Ltd 1 Yonge St Toronto ON Canada M5E 1P9

EVANS, JOHN T., finance educator, consultant, social sciences educator, researcher; b. Albany, NY, Mar. 31, 1941; s. Horace S. and Maurine F. (Sassé) Evans; m. Barbara E. Ferman, Nov. 28, 1982 (dec. June 1993). BA, Columbia U., 1965; MA, New Sch. U., 1969, PhD, 1989. V.p. Syntony Sound, Inc., NYC, 1979—81; pres. Econ. Sys. Corp., NYC, 1981—; instr. Baruch Coll., NYC, 1986—88; prof. Manhattan Inst. Mgmt., NYC, 1988—91; asst. prof. LI U., Bklyn., 1991—98, assoc. prof., 1998—, chmn. bus. dept., 2001—. Author: From Trade Surplus to Deficit, 1995; co-author: Childrens TV Commercials, 1974, Globalization in the 21st Century, 1999, Globalization and Labor Force Composition, 2001. Campaign mgr. Congl. race, Albany, NY, 1968. Mem.: Am. Econ. Assn., Internat. Trade & Fin. Assn., Columbia Club. Avocations: travel, history, reading. Office: LI Univ 1 University Plz Brooklyn NY 11201 Office Phone: 718-488-1158.

EVANS, JOHN THOMAS, lawyer; b. N.Y.C., Feb. 28, 1948; s. John Arthur and Dorothy (Reilly) E.; m. Marie Tolnay, June 2, 1979; children— Claire, Grace. B.A., U. Wis., 1970; J.D., Fordham U., 1973. Bar: N.Y. 1974, U.S. Dist. Ct. (so. and ea. dists.) N.Y., U.S. Tax Ct. Asst. dist. atty. N.Y. County, N.Y.C., 1973-79; assoc. Blumenthal & Lynne, N.Y.C., 1979-81; ptnr. Morris & Duffy, N.Y.C., 1982-85, Belair, Klein, Groman & Evans, N.Y.C., 1985—; cons. Vol. Lawyers for Arts, N.Y.C., 1979-84, Hofstra U. Law Sch. Moot Ct. Program, Uniondale, N.Y., 1982; cons., lectr. N.Y.C. Police Dept. Detectives Endowment Assn., 1981—. Author: Arguing Cases Before A Medical Malpractice Law & Strategy; contbr. articles to profl. jours. Recipient Highest award Manhattan Detective Area, N.Y.C., 1979. Mem. N.Y. State Bar Assn., Assn. Bar City of N.Y., N.Y. Criminal Bar Assn. Club: N.Y. Athletic (N.Y.C.). Home: 362 W Broadway New York NY 10013-5303 Office: Belair & Evans 61 Broadway New York NY 10006-2701

EVANS, JOY, foundation administrator; b. Waterbury, Conn., Feb. 15, 1940; 4 children. Student, Hartford Coll. for Women, 1959. Weekly radio personality Young Stars on Parade Sta. WBRY, Waterbury, 1951-58; exec. sec. dir.'s office Discover Am. Travel Orgns., Washington, 1962-71; exec. sec. adminstr.'s office Nat. Ctr. for Housing Mgmt., Washington, 1971-72; exec. sec. mgr.'s office Nat. Visitor's Ctr. Nat. Park Svc. Dept. Interior, 1972-73; staff asst. divsn. pub. programs NEH, Washington, 1973-81, pub. info. officer, office of the chair, 1981—. Founding chair fed. woman's com. NEH, 1980-82, liaison White House task force on the humanities and arts 1981-82; spkr. commencement address Nat. Coll. Bus. and Tech., Charlottesville, Va., 2002, 04. Staff newsletter editor Not Hardcopy Newsletter, 1996-98. Mem. Annandale Homeowner's Assn. (pres. Terrace Townhouses 1989-92, TTA newsletter editor 1988-92), Soc. Govt. Meeting Planners (D.C. chpt. 1991-92). Roman Catholic. Avocations: music, art, dance, photography, theater, feng shui. Office: Nat Endowment for Humanities Rm 402 1100 Pennsylvania Ave NW Washington DC 20506-0001 Office Phone: 202-606-8446. Business E-Mail: jevans@neh.gov.

EVANS, KARL WESLEY, psychologist; b. Canton, Ohio, Nov. 21, 1974; s. Edwin ElliotCalumry and Betty Valkema Evans; m. Jamie Marie Winters, June 28, 2003; 1 child, Addison Marie. BA, Hanover Coll., 1997; PsyD, Fla. Inst. Tech., 2001. Lic. psychologist Ind. Intern Lexington VA Med. Ctr., Va., 2000—01; trainee Chillicothe VA Med. Ctr., Ohio, 2001—03; rehab. psychologist Columbus Regional Hosp., Ind., 2003—. Youth leader Asbiry United Meth. Ch., Columbus, 2003—. Recipient Disting. Psychology award, Hanover Coll., 1997; Richter grantee, Malawig, Africa, 1996. Mem.: APA. Avocations: golf, travel, basketball, fishing, Bible study. Office: Columbus Regional Hosp 2400 E 17th St Columbus IN 47201

EVANS, KATHRYN MILLER, art educator, department chairman; d. Hampton K and Mary R Miller; m. Robert H. Evans; children: Erin M Schultz, Michael M Schultz. MFA, U.New Mex., 1970—81. Dir. of fine arts Oakridge Sch., Arlington, Tex., 1998—; art tchr. Albuquerque Acad., 1988. Office: Oakridge Sch 5900 West Pioneer Parkway Arlington TX 76013 Office Phone: 817-451-4994. Personal E-mail: kevans@theoakridgeschool.org.

EVANS, LANE, congressman; b. Rock Island, Ill., Aug. 4, 1951; s. Lee Herbert and Joycelene (Saylor) E. BA, Augustana Coll., 1974; JD, Georgetown U., 1978. Bar: Ill. 1978. Mng. atty. Western Ill. Legal Assistance Found., Rock Island, 1978-79; mem. nat. staff Kennedy for Pres., Washington, 1978-80; atty., ptnr. Community Legal Clinic, Rock Island, Ill., 1981-82; mem. U.S. Congress from 17th Ill. Dist., 1983—; mem. nat. security com., ranking mem. vets. affairs com., armed svcs. com. Served with USMC, 1969-71. Mem. AmVets, Am. Legion, Marine Corps League, Vietnam Vets Ill. Democrat. Roman Catholic. Office: US Ho of Reps 2211 Rayburn HOB Washington DC 20515-1317

EVANS, LAWRENCE E., lawyer, educator; b. Houston, Mar. 30, 1950; s. Lawrence Edgar and Edith (Kinzy) E.; m. Nancy Campbell, Aug. 20, 1977; children: Christopher, Laura. BA, Washington & Lee U., 1973; JD, South Tex. Coll., 1977. Bar: Tex. 1977, Mo. 1989; registered patent atty. Lawyer Gunn, Lee & Miller, Houston, 1977-88, Herzog, Crebs & McGhee, St. Louis, 1988-2000, Blackwell, Sanders, Peper, Martin LLP, St. Louis, 2000—. Adj. prof. Washington U. Sch. Law, St. Louis, 2000-04 Mem. Metro. Bar Assn. St. Louis (chmn. Patent, Trademark and Copyright sect. 1994), Internat. Trademark Assn., Am. Intellectual Property Law Assn. Office: Blackwell Sanders Peper Martin LLP 720 Olive St Ste 2400 Saint Louis MO 63101 Office Phone: 314-345-6431. Business E-Mail: levans@blackwellsanders.com.

EVANS, LINDA KAY, publishing company executive; b. Tipton, Ind., June 16, 1945; d. Walter K. and Helen S. (Fakes) E. BA in English, Purdue U., 1968. Asst. to mng. editor Random House Pubs., N.Y.C., 1969-71; asst. to dir. editorial svcs. Sch. div. McGraw-Hill Book Co., N.Y.C., 1971-75, mgr. state contracts and inventory dept., 1975-88; bookstore owner, pres. The Literary Bookshop, N.Y.C., 1988-93; prodn. mgr. trade div. Simon & Schuster, N.Y.C., 1994—2004, sr. prodn. mgr. trade div., 2004—. Pub. cons. for sch. textbooks Prentice-Hall Book Co., Englewood Cliffs, N.J., 1992-93. Recipient Holiday Window Display award to Lit. Bookshop, Greenwich Village C. of C., 1990. Avocations: reading, antique collecting, furniture making, travel. Office: Simon & Schuster Trade Div 1230 Ave of the Americas New York NY 10020-1586 Office Phone: 212-698-7237.

EVANS, LOUISE, investor, retired psychologist; b. San Antonio; d. Henry Daniel and Adela (Pariser) E.; m. Thomas Ross Gambrell, Feb. 23, 1960. BS, Northwestern U., 1949; MS in Clin. Psychology, Purdue U., 1952, PhD in Clin. Psychology, 1955. Lic. marriage, family and child counselor Calif.; Nat. Register of Health Svc. Providers in Psychology; lic. psychologist, Calif., N.Y. (inactive); diplomate Clin. Psychology, Am. Bd. Profl. Psychology. Intern clin. psychology Menninger Found. Topeka (Kans.) State Hosp., 1952-53; postdoctoral fellow clin. child psychology Menninger Clinic, Topeka, 1955-56; staff psychologist Kankakee (Ill.) State Hosp., 1954-55; head staff psychologist child guidance clinic Kings County Hosp., Bklyn., 1957-58; dir. psychology clinic Barnes-Renard Hosp.; instr. med. psychology Sch. Medicine Washington U., 1959-60; clin. rsch. cons. Episc. City Diocese, St. Louis, 1959-60; pvt. practice Fullerton, Calif., 1960—93; fellow Internat. Coun. Sex Edn. and Parenthood, 1984, Am. U., Washington. Psychol. cons. Fullerton Cmty. Hosp., 1961-81; staff cons. clin. psychology Martin Luther Hosp., Anaheim, Calif., 1963-70; chair, participant psychol. symposiums, 1956—; spkr., lectr. in field. Contbr. articles on clin. psychology to profl. publs. Elected to Hall of Fame Ctrl. H.S., Evansville, Ind., 1966; recipient Svc. award Yuma County (Ariz.) Head Start Program, 1972, Statue of Victory Personality of Yr. award Centro Studi E. Ricerche Delle Nazioni, Italy, 1985, Alumni Merit award Northwestern U. Coll. Arts and Scis., 1997; named Miss Heritage, Heritage Publs., 1965. Fellow AAAS (emeritus), APA (clin. divsn. psychology of women divsn., psychotherapy divsn., cons. divsn., dir. exec. bd. 1976-79, Internat. Div., Lifelong Contributions Advancement of Psychology Internat. Recognition award 2002), Acad. Clin. Psychology, Am. Assn. Applied and Preventive Psychology (charter), Royal Soc. Health Eng. (emeritus), Internat. Coun. Psychologists (dir. 1977-79, sec. 1962-64, 73-76, 2 awards 2003, recognition for pioneering leadership in internat. psychology, named amb. for life award 2003), Am. Orthopsychiat. Assn. (life), World Wide Acad. Scholars of N.Z. (life), Am. Psychol. Soc. (charter), L.A. Soc. Clin. Psychologists (exec. bd. 1966-67), Internat. Coun. Psychologists; mem. AAUP (emeritus), Calif. Psychol. Assn. (life, ins. com. 1961-65), L.A. County Psychol. Assn. (emeritus), Orange County Psychol. Assn. (charter founder, exec. bd. 1961-62), Am. Pub. Health Assn. (emeritus), Internat. Platform Assn., N.Y. Acad. Scis. (emeritus), Purdue U. Alumni Assn. (life, past pres. coun., mem. dean's club, Citizenship award 1975, Disting. Alumni award 1993, Old Master 1993), Northwestern U. 1851 Soc. (Coll. Arts and Scis. Merit award 1997), Ctr. Study Presidency, Soc. Jewelry Historians USA (charter), Alumni Assn. Menninger Sch. Psychiatry, Sigma Xi (emeritus). Achievements include development of innovative theories and techniques of clinical practice; acknowledged pioneer in development of psychology as science and profession both nationally and internationally, and in marital and family therapy, and in consulting to hospitals and clinics. Office: PO Box 6067 Beverly Hills CA 90212-1067 Office Phone: 310-474-1361. Office Fax: 310-474-1361.

EVANS, MARGARET ANN, human resources administrator, business owner; b. Great Bend, Kans., Dec. 26, 1947; d. Freddy Florence and Peggy (Hawkins) Green; m. Carl Evans, Aug. 13, 1972 (dir.); children: Carl André, Christopher Dion. B in Psychology, U. Mo., 1971, MPA, 1972. Pers. specialist Met. Jr. Coll., Kansas City, Mo., 1972-73; employee rels. specialist Amoco Oil Co., Kansas City, 1973-74; classification specialist Richards-Gebaur AFB, Mo., 1974-75; employee rels. officer Govt. Employee Hosp. Assn., Kansas City, 1977-84, mgr. pers., 1984-87, dir. human resources, 1987—. Mem. pers. com. Sta. KKFI, Kansas City, 1989—; mem. cert. bd. Human Resource Inst., exam devel. dir., 1994-95, sec.-treas., 1995-96. Sec. and v.p. Booster Club, Hickman Mills High Sch., Kansas City, 1989—; bd. dirs. Saturday Scholars, 2000-02. Ford Found. fellow U. Mo., 1971; recipient Contbr. of Yr. award Human Resource Mgmt. Assn., 1992, Pres. award 1993, 1995; named One of Kansas City's 100 Most Influential Kansas Citians KC Globe Most Influential African Ams. of Kansas City, 1993, 95, 96, 97. Mem. NAFE, Soc. Human Resources Mgmt. (pers. rsch. com. Kansas City chpt. 1989—, nat. com. 1990—, sec.-treas. Mo. state coun. 1992-93, bd. dirs., v.p. at large 1999-2000, v.p. Area IV 2000, 02, 03), Pers. Mgmt. Assn. (co-chmn. coll. rels. 1981), Urban League, NAACP, Links, Inc., ASTD, Alpha Kappa Alpha (chair midwestern regional conf., 1996, Outstanding Grad. Soror). Home: 10216 E 96th St Kansas City MO 64134-2309 Office: Govt Employee Hosp Assn 17306 E Us Highway 24 Independence MO 64056-1808

EVANS, MARGARET GRIFFIN, music educator; MusB, U. NC; MusM, U. Ill.; MusD, Northwestern U. Piano faculty U. Mont., Missoula, Mont., 1982—85; doctoral tchg. fellow Northwestern U., Evanston, 1985—90; piano faculty Meredith Coll., Raleigh, NC, 1994—. Adjudicator numerous competitions and auditions for organizations, 1982—; judge Bartok-Kabalevsky-Prokofiev Internat. Piano Competition, Music Tchrs. Nat. Assn., 1982—, 57th Hong Kong Schs. of Music Competition, Hong Kong, 2005. Musician: (piano recitalist, concerto soloist) Solo recitals, collaborative performances with orchestra, vocalists and instrumentalists in North Carolina, Illinois, Pennsylvania, Washington, Oregon, Montana, and Switzerland. Recipient Phi Kappa Phi, U. Ill. chpt., Pi Kappa Lambda Cert. of Merit, Meredith Coll., Pi Kappa Lambda, U. Mont., Phi Beta Kappa, U. of NC; Faculty Devel. grants, Meredith Coll., 2000, 2001, 2002, 2003, 2004. Mem.: Raleigh Music Club, Nat. Guild of Piano Tchrs., Raleigh Piano Tchrs. Assn., Music Tchrs. Nat. Assn., Raleigh Chamber Music Guild (bd. of directors 2000—03). Avocations: sailing, horseback riding, travel, cooking, painting. Office: Music Dept Meredith Coll 3800 Hillsborough St Raleigh NC 27607 Office Phone: 919-760-8349.

EVANS, MARGARET UTZ, secondary school educator; b. Gladwyne, Pa. d. Joseph H. and Marion Irwin (Laughead) Utz; m. James Irvin Evans. BA, King's Coll., Briarcliff Manor, N.Y.; MA, Ea. Bapt. Theol. Sem., Wynneword, Pa. Tchr. Menaul High Sch., Albuquerque, Haverford Sch. Dist., Havertown, Pa., Penn-Delco Sch. Dist., Aston, Pa. Recipient Wilbor T. Elmore prize in history, James A. Barkley award in history. Mem. NEA.

EVANS, MARK IRA, obstetrician, geneticist; b. Bklyn., May 14, 1952; s. Robert Bernard and Sonia Beatrice Evans. BS in Psychology, Tufts U., 1973; MD, SUNY, Bklyn., 1978. Diplomate Am. Bd. Ob-Gyn, Am. Bd. Med. Genetics. Resident in ob-gyn. U. Chgo., 1979—82; med. genetics fellow NIH, Bethesda, Md., 1982—84; dir. reproductive genetics Hutzel Hosp. Wayne State U., Detroit, 1984—2001, Charlotte B. Failing prof. ob-gyn. and human genetics Ctr. Molecular Med./Path., 1991—2001, disting. prof., 2000, dir. Ctr. for Fetal Diagnosis and Therapy, 1985—2001, dir. human genetics program, 1996—2001, chmn., chief, 1998—2001; prof., chmn. ob-gyn, prof. human genetics, dir. fetal therap Hahnemann Hosp., Phila., 2000—02; dir. fetal therapy program MCP Hahnemann U., 2000—02; dir. Inst. Genetics and Fetal Medicine Columbia U. Coll. of Physicians and Surgeons, N.Y.C., 2002—; prof. ob-gyn St. Lukes Roosevelt Hosp. Ctr./Columbia U., 2002—. Mem. adv. bd. Ehlrs Danlos Found., L.A., 1986—, Corning Metpath, Quest Diagnostics, 1988-2000, Lab. Corp., 2003—, Nat. Adv. Bd. on Ethics in Reproduction, Washington; mem. ethics com. Am. Coll. Ob-Gyn., 1987-90, Molecular Medicine and Genetics, Wayne State U. Author: (textbooks) Pretest: Obsterics and Gynecology, 6th rev. edit., 1991, 9th edit., 2000, (with C.C. Lin) Intrauterine Growth Retardation, 1984, (with others) Fetal Diagnosis Therapy: Science, Ethics and the Law, 1989, Reproductive Risks and Prenatal Diagnosis, 1992, The New Reproductive Genetics, 1993, Maternal Genetic Disease, 1996, Invasive Outpatient Procedures in Reproductive Medicine, 1997, Principles and Practice of Medical Therapy in Pregnancy, 1998, Study Guide, 1998, The Unborn Patient, 2001, Contemporary Therapy for Obstetrics & Gynecology, 2002; (with Evans and Rodeck) Ultrasound and Fetal Therapy, 2000; (with Evans, Platt and De La Cruz) Fetal Therapy, 2000; editor: (with others) The Genetic Revolution and Obstetrics and Gynecology, 2002, New Genetics for the Clinician, 2002; contbr. articles to profl. jours. Fellow Am. Coll. Ob-Gyn. (course coordination com. 1996-99), Am. Coll. Med. Genetics (founder); mem. AMA (nat. ultrasound task force 1990-91), Internat. Fetal Medicine Surgery Soc. (pres. 1986-87, 96-97), Am. Soc. Human Genetics, Soc. Gynecol. Investigation, Ctrl. Assn. Ob-Gyn. (bd. dirs. 1998-2000, pres. 2004), Soc. Perinatal Obstetricians, Am. Gynecol. and Obstetrics Soc., Ctrl. Assn. Obstetrics and Gynecologists (v.p. 2004—). Jewish. Office: Inst for Genetics and Fetal Medicine St Lukes Roosevelt Hosp Ctr 1000 10th Ave Ste 11A-11 New York NY 10019 Office Phone: 212-523-5895. Business E-Mail: IGFM@chpnet.org.

EVANS, MARSHA JOHNSON, non-profit association administrator, former career officer; b. Springfield, Ill., Aug. 12, 1947; d. Walter Edward Johnson and Alice Anne Field; m. Gerard Riendeau Evans, June 30, 1979. AB, Occidental Coll., 1968; MA, MA in Law & Diplomacy, Fletcher Sch., 1977; postgrad., Nat. War Coll., 1988-89. Commd. ensign USN, 1968, advanced through grades to rear admiral, 1993; mideast policy officer Commander-in-Chief, U.S. Naval Forces, Europe, London, 1977-79; spl. asst. to sec. treasury U.S. Treasury Dept., Washington, 1979-80; staff analyst Office of Chief Naval Ops., Washington, 1980-81; dep. dir. Pres. Commn. on White House Fellowships, Washington, 1981-82; exec. officer Recruit Tng. Command, San Diego, 1982-84; commanding officer Naval Tech. Tng. Ctr., San Francisco, 1984-86; battalion officer, sr. lectr. polit. sci. U.S. Naval Acad., Annapolis, Md., 1986-88; chief of staff San Francisco Naval Base, 1989-91, Naval Acad., Annapolis, Md., 1991-92; exec. dir. of the standing com. on mil. and civilian women Dept. of the Navy, 1992-93; comdr. Navy Recruiting Command, Washington, 1993-95; supt. Naval Postgrad. Sch., Monterey, Calif., 1995-97; CEO, nat. exec. dir. Girl Scouts U.S.A., N.Y.C., 1998—2002; president American Red Cross, 2002—. Presidential appointee bd. visitors, U.S. Military Academy at West Point; interim dir. George C. Marshall European Ctr. Security Studies, Garmisch Partenkirchen, Germany, 1996-97; bd. dirs. Lehman Brothers Holdings, Inc., May Dept. Stores Co., AutoZone, Inc. and Weight Watchers Internat., Inc. Advisory bd. Pew Partnership for Civic Change Pew Charitable Trusts; dir. Naval Academy Found. White House fellow, 1979; Chief Naval Ops. scholar, 1976. Mem. Mortar Bd., Phi Beta Kappa. Office: Am Red Cross 430 17th St NW Washington DC 20006-5307

EVANS, MARTIN FREDERIC, lawyer; b. Nashville, June 12, 1947; s. Robert Clements and Adelaide Hawkins (Roberts) E.; m. Margaret Carroll Kidder, Apr. 17, 1982. BA, U. Va., 1969; JD, Yale U., 1972. Bar: N.Y. 1973, U.S. Dist. Ct. (so. dist.) N.Y. 1973, U.S. Ct. Appeals (2d cir.) 1974, U.S. Ct. Appeals (D.C. cir.) 1981, U.S. Supreme Ct. 1981, D.C. 1982. Assoc. Debevoise & Plimpton, N.Y.C., 1972-80, ptnr. litig. dept., 1981—. Mem. ABA (sect. for antitrust law), Assn. of Bar of City of N.Y., Phi Beta Kappa. Office: Debevoise & Plimpton 919 Third Ave New York NY 10022-6225 E-mail: mfevans@debevoise.com.

EVANS, MARY JOHNSTON, corporate director; b. Shawnee, Okla., Feb. 28, 1930; d. Paul Xenophon and Helen Elizabeth (Alford) Johnston; children by previous marriage: Marcy Head Benson, Paul Johnston Head, Eric Talbott Head; m. James H. Evans, 1984. Student, Wellesley Coll., 1947-48, U. Okla., 1949. Dir. Amtrak, 1974-80, vice-chmn., 1975-79. Bd. dirs. Household Internat., Inc., Saint-Gobain Corp., Sunoco, Inc., Delta Air Lines, Inc., Moody's Corp. Pres. Jr. League Oklahoma City, 1968-69; trustee Nat. Coun. Crime and Delinquency, 1971-75, Presbyn. Med. Ctr., Oklahoma City, 1969-75; trustee Brick Presbyn. Ch., 1985-89; bd. dirs. St. Anthony Hosp., 1973-75; bd. visitors U. Pitts. Grad. Sch. Bus., 1978-85; trustee Mary Baldwin Coll., Staunton, Va., 1976-83, Carnegie Hall, 1985-92. Recipient Law Day award-Liberty Bell award Okla. Bar Assn., 1971, Disting. Svc. award U. Okla., 1981; named one of Top 100 Corp. Women Bus. Week mag., 1976; named to Okla. Hall of Fame, 1978 Mem. Conf. Bd. (Sr.), Colony Club, River Club, Maidstone Club (East Hampton, N.Y.), Pi Beta Phi. Presbyterian (elder). Address: 920 5th Ave New York NY 10021-4160 also: 32 Windmill Ln East Hampton NY 11937-3605

EVANS, MICHAEL D., lawyer; b. Columbia, Mo., Oct. 23, 1946; BA, Okla. State U., 1969; JD, U. Okla., 1973. Bar: Okla. 1973. Asst. dist. atty. Third Jud. Dist. Okla., Tillman County, 1975—82, 1998; city atty. Frederick, Okla., 1982—; with Massad, Evans, & Kent, Frederick, Okla. Fellow: Okla. Bar Found., Am. Bar Found. (life); mem.: ABA, Okla. Bar Assn. (chmn. profl. responsibility commn. 1992, 1995, bd. govs. 1996—98, v.p. 2001, pres.-elect 2004—), Tillman County Bar Assn. (past pres.). Office: Massad Evans & Kent 120 N Ninth St Drawer 606 Frederick OK 73542 Office Phone: 580-335-5531. Office Fax: 508-335-5532. E-mail: meklaw@pldi.net.

EVANS, MYRON WYN, physicist, researcher; b. Craigcefnparc, Wales, May 26, 1950; arrived in U.S., 1986, naturalized, 2000; s. Edward Ivor and Mary (Jones) Evans; m. Laura Jean Joseph, Feb. 18, 1988. BSc, Aberystwyth U., Wales, 1971, PhD, 1974, DSc, 1977. Jr. rsch. fellow Wolfson Coll., Oxford, England, 1975; advanced fellow Sci. and Engring. Rsch. Coun., Aberystwyth, Wales, 1978-83; vis. scientist Cornell U., 1989-92, U. Zurich, 1989-90; prof. Alpha Found., Budapest, Hungary, 1995—, dir., chmn. bd. dirs. Inst. Advanced Study, 1998—. Mem. nat. com. Brit. Sci. and Engring. Rsch. Coun.; 1st sci. coord. European Molecular Liquids Group, 1980; rsch. assoc. Pa. State U., 1992, sr. assoc., 90; sci.-tech. advisor Plaid Cymru, 1991; vis. scientist U. Pisa and Schola Normale Superiore, 1980, Cornell U., 1989, 91, U. Zurich, 1990; vis. prof. Trinity Coll., Dublin, 1985, IBM, Kingston, NY, 1986, York U., Toronto, 1995, Indian Statis. Inst., Calcutta, 1995. Author: Molecular Dynamics, 1982, Molecular Diffusion, 1984, Memory Function Approaches to Stochastic Problems in Condensed Matter, 1985, Dynamical Processes in Condensed Matter, 1985, Simulation and Symmetry in Molecular Diffusion and Spectroscopy, 1992, The Photon's Magnetic Field, 1992, The Photomagneton in Quantum Field Theory, 1994, Water in Biology, Chemistry and Physics, 1996, Classical and Quantum Electrodynamics and the B(3) Field, 1999, Generally Covariant Unified Field Theory: The Geometrization of Physics, 2005; editor, author: Enigmatic Photon, 5 vols., 1994—99; editor: Modern Nonlinear Optics, 1997, 2001; contbr. articles to profl. jours. Mem. Civil List Pension, 2005. Recipient Harrison Meml. prize, Royal Soc. Chemistry, London, 1978, Meldola medal, 1979, Disting. Am. Scientist award, Assn. Disting. Am. Scientists, 2000; Leverhulme fellow, Humboldt fellow, Brit. Imperial Chem. Industries fellow, 1974, NRC Can. fellow, 1974, Jr. Rsch. fellow, Wolfson Coll., Oxford, 1975, Brit. Ramsay Meml. fellow, 1976, IBM fellow. Mem.: N.Y. Acad. Scis., Am. Inst. Physics, Optical Soc. Am., Brit. Civil List, Sigma Pi Sigma. Republican Nationalist. Avocations: poetry, landscape photography, athletics. Home: 50 Rhyddwen Rd Craigcefnparc Swansea SA6 5RA Wales Office: Alpha Found Inst Physics 11 Rutafa St Budapest Hungary Home: PO Box 6828 Ithaca NY 14851-6828 Personal E-mail: emyrone@aol.com.

EVANS, NOLLY SEYMOUR, lawyer; b. Augusta, Ga., Sept. 16, 1927; s. Nolly Seymour and Laura (Taylor) E.; m. Judith Anne Leach, Feb. 18, 1965; children: Samantha, Meredydd, Clelia, Nolly. BFA in Music, U. Ga., 1948, MA in English Lit., 1950; LLB, Yale U., 1956; LLD, Yale Law Sch., 1971. Bar: N.Y. 1956. Assoc. firm Milbank, Tweed, Hadley & McCloy, N.Y.C., 1956-64; fin. counsel Amax, Inc., N.Y.C., 1964-70; gen. counsel, sec. Gilman Paper Co., N.Y.C., 1970-74, Crouse-Hinds Co., Syracuse, N.Y., 1976-82; counsel Hancock & Estabrook, Syracuse, N.Y., 1982-83; prin. Nolly S. Evans Law Offices, Syracuse, 1983-93. Docent Homewood House Mus., Balt. With U.S. Army, 1947—48. Mem. Confrerie des Chevaliers du Tastevin (grand officer), Sous Commanderie de Etats-Unis (grand officer), Sous Commanderie de Ctrl. N.Y. (grand senechal, grand officer), N.Y., Bordeaux (comdr.), Le Grand Conseil de Bordeaux, Jurade de St. Emilion, Connetable de Guyenne, Royal Over-Seas Club (London), and others. Home: 647 W University Pkwy Baltimore MD 21210-2907 also: Shadowlands Park Clarks Hill SC 29821

EVANS, OLIVER H., college administrator; b. Burlington, Vt., June 15, 1944; s. Samuel H. and Louise (Lifsey) E.; m. Eileen Beary, Sept. 10, 1973; children: Rachel, Ethan. BA, Albion Coll., 1966; MA, Purdue U., 1969, PhD, 1972. Asst. prof. Dakota State Coll., Madison, S.D., 1972-74, S.D. State U., Brookings, 1974-78, Creighton U., Omaha, 1978-80, Western Mich. U., Kalamazoo, 1980-84; dir. grad. studies Nazareth Coll., Kalamazoo, 1984-87, v.p. acad. affairs, 1987-90, pres., 1990, Kendall Coll. of Art and Design, Grand Rapids. Cons., evaluator North Cen. Assn., Chgo., 1988—. Author: George Henry Boker, 1984; contbr. articles to profl. jours. Office: Nazareth Coll 3333 Gull Rd Kalamazoo MI 49048-1281 also: Kendall College of Art and Design Ferris State U 17 Fountain St Grand Rapids MI 49503-1312*

EVANS, ORINDA D., federal judge; b. Savannah, Ga., Apr. 23, 1943; d. Thomas and Virginia Elizabeth (Grieco) E.; m. Roberts O. Bennett, Apr. 12, 1975; children: Wells Cooper, Elizabeth Thomas. BA, Duke U., 1965; JD with distinction, Emory U., 1968. Bar: Ga. 1968. Assoc. Fisher & Phillips, Altanta, 1968-69, Alston, Miller & Gaines, Atlanta, 1969-74, ptnr., 1974-79; judge US Dist Ct. (No. Dist.) Ga., Atlanta, 1979—, chief judge. Adj. prof. Emory U. Law Sch., 1974-77; counsel Atlanta Crime Commn., 1970-71 Recipient Disting. award BBB, 1972. Mem. Atlanta Bar Assn. (dir. 1979) Democrat. Episcopalian. Office: US Dist Courthouse 1988 US Courthouse 75 Spring St SW Atlanta GA 30303-3309*

EVANS, PAT, mayor; b. Abilene, Tex., Feb. 12, 1943; m. Chuck Evans, 1964; 3 children. BA, U. Tex., Austin, 1964; JD, So. Meth. U., 1991. Atty. Gay & McCall, Inc., 1991—95; family law instr. Southeastern Paralegal Inst., 1996—97; atty., 1991—; dep. mayor pro-tem Plano, Tex., 2000; mayor, 2002—. Tchr. Richardson Ind. Sch. Dist., 1964—70; owner landscape design co. Exec. bd. North Tex. Coun. Govts.; exec. com. Dallas REgional Mobility Coun.; mem. Plano Econ. Devel. Exec. Bd.; past. pres. Jr. League, Plano; mem. Metroplex Mayor's Coun., Collin County Mayor's Coun. Office: City of Plano 1520 Avenue K Plano TX 75074

EVANS, PATRICIA MCCORMICK, psychotherapist; b. Cheraw, S.C. d. Foris Linsley and Mary Lucille Jackson; children: Robert, Antonio, Ronnie Jr. BA in Sociology, Coker Coll., 1996; MA in Counseling, Webster U., 1999; postgrad., Walden U., 2000—. Cashier Wal-Mart, Cheraw, SC, 1996—97; instr. South Piedmont C.C., Polkton, SC, 1997—2001; social worker Richmond County Dept. Social Svcs., Rockingham, SC, 2000—01; facilitator grief counseling group Richmond County Hospice. Founder, dir. Edn. Mentoring/Tutoring Program, Chesterfield, S.C., 2000—; founde,r pres. Maknadifrens, Inc. Author of poems. Vol. Richmond County Hospice. Mem.: Am. Correctional Assn., Am. Counseling Assn. Democrat. Baptist. Home: PO Box 882 Cheraw SC 29520 Office: Carolina Behavioral Svcs LLC Divsn Mentor Network 1219 Rockingham Rd Ste 12 Rockingham NC 28379 E-mail: cateyes@peedeeworld.net.

EVANS, PAUL, osteopath; b. Nutley, NJ, May 23, 1950; m. Roxanne Romack. BS cum laude in Biology, U. Miami, 1972; DO, Phila. Coll. Osteopathic Med., 1979. Diplomate Am. Bd. Family Practice, Nat. Bd. Osteo. Examiners; cert. Am. Osteo. Bd. Family Practice. Commd. 2d lt. U.S. Army, 1972, advanced through grades to col., 1995; ret., 1998; asst. chief mil. pers. U.S. Army Med. Svc. Corps, Frankfurt, Fed. Republic Germany, 1972-75; intern Letterman Army Med. Ctr., San Francisco, 1979-80; resident in family practice Womack Army Community Hosp., Ft. Bragg, N.C., 1980-82; dir. family practice quality assurance Tripler Army Med. Ctr., Hawaii, 1982-84, dir. residency tng. dept. family practice, 1984-86; asst. prof. family practice, physician Uniformed Svcs. U. Health Scis., F. Edward Hebert Sch. Med., Bethesda, Md., 1986-92, clerkship dir., 1986-88, dir. continuing med. edn., 1987-91, asst. prof. mil. and emergency medicine, 1991-92; chief dept. family practice Reynolds Army Community Hosp., Ft. Sill, Okla., 1992-94, chief primary care, 1994-95, chmn. rsch. com., dir. hosp. continuing med. edn., 1992-95, dir. physicians asst. tng. program, dir. quality improvement, 1992-94; tchg. chief dept. family practice Madigan Army Med. Ctr., Tacoma, 1995-97, dir. primary care projects Tricare N.W., 1997-98, dir. primary care, mem. exec. bd. dirs., exec. adv. coun.; clin. assoc. prof. of family medicine U. Wash., 1996-98; assoc. dean curricular affairs, dir. ednl. resources/devel. Okla. State U. Coll. Osteopathic Med., Tulsa, 1998—2003, assoc. prof. family med., exec. coun. curriculum com., learning resources com., 1998—2003, dir. dept. edn. resources and devel., 1998—2003, prof. family medicine, 2003—04; chief acad. officer, vice dean Ga. campus Phila. Coll. Osteo. Medicine, Suwanee, Ga., 2004—. Presenter, lectr., cons. in field; clin. faculty, family practice residency DeWitt Army Hosp., Ft. Belvoir, Va., 1986-89, 91-92, Malcolm Grow USAF Med. Ctr., Andrews AFB, Md., 1989-91. Reviewer Am. Family Physician, Patient Care, Military Medicine, Family Medicine, Farmily Practice Mgmt.; mem. editl. bd. Jour. Am. Osteo. Assn., 2003—; contbr. articles to profl. jours. Asst. med. dir. Old Dominion 100 Mile Run, Front Royal, Va., 1990, med. dir., 1991; asst. med. dir. Am. Diabetes Assn. Youth, Honolulu, 1984, med. dir., 1985. USUHS grantee. Fellow Am. Acad. Family Physicians; mem. Am. Osteo. Assn., Am. Coll. Osteo. Family Physicians, Uniformed Svcs. Acad. Family Physicians (chmn. edn. com. 1993-97, sec.-treas. 1997-98), Soc. Tchrs. Family Medicine (genogram rsch. com. 1989-94, managed care com. 1997-2000, faculty devel. com. 1999-2003), Amer. Osteo. Assn., Amer. Coll. Osteo. Family Phys., Ga. Osteo. Assn., Phila. Coll. Osteo. Medicine Alumni Assn. (life), Omicron Delta Kappa, Alpha Epsilon Delta. Avocations: bicycling, scuba diving, collecting salt water fish, finch breeding, golf. Home: 3201 St Ives Country Club Pkwy Duluth GA 30097 Office Phone: 770-962-4888. Business E-Mail: paulev@pcom.edu.

EVANS, PAUL LAURENCE, horticulturist, educator; b. Bklyn., Apr. 20, 1960; s. Eugene and Julia Gertrude (Ford) E. BS in Horticulture, Cornell U., 1981. Instr. Bklyn. Botanic Garden, 1982-83; curator-conservatory garden Ctrl. Park Conservancy, NYC, 1983-85; dir. horticulture Magnolia Tree Earth Ctr., NYC, 1985—86; asst. shop mgr. Horticulture House, NYC, 1986—87; dir. cmty. svcs. Mass. Hort. Soc., Boston, 1987-90; sr. sci. developer The Children's Mus., Boston, 1990-94; regional coord., commr. office Mass. Dept. of Edn., Malden, 1994-96; dir. Bronx Green-Up, The NY Bot. Garden, 1996—99; NY tchg. fellow NYC Bd. Edn., 2000—01; assoc. edn. officer NYC Dept. Edn., 2001—. Cons., lectr. Mus. of Sci., Boston, 1991; lectr. Lesley Coll., Cambridge, Mass., 1993; guest lectr. NYU, 1997; panelist sci. literacy Mass. Cultural Coun., Boston, 1992. Series host, writer (ednl. TV program) PALMS Electronic Institue: Teaching Beyond Tomorrow, 1995, Kitchen Physics: Windmills, 1994, Kitchen Physics: Ice Cream Making, 1993, Kitchen Physics: Tops/Salad Dressing, 1992, Extra Help: Biology, 1991-92 (Cert. 1992). Sci. mentor, fair judge Woodrow Wilson Middle Sch., Boston, 1992-94, McCormack Middle Sch., Boston, 1993-94; Arbor Day coord. Boston GreenSpace Alliance, Boston, 1990 Recipient Mollie Parnis award Citizens Com. for N.Y., 1985; grantee Chase Manhattan, 1985, Black United Fund N.Y., 1985, NSF, 1992. Mem. AAAS (instr. pub. sci. day 1993), NSTA, Nat. Assn. Television Prodn. Execs., Am. Soc. Hort. Sci., Assn. Sci.-Tech. Ctrs. (panel chmn. 1992—). Avocations: gardening, racquetball/squash. Home: PO Box 1374 Brooklyn NY 11202-1374 Office: NYC Dept Edn Region 9 333 Seventh Ave Rm 722 New York NY 10001 Office Phone: 646-249-6959.

EVANS, PETER JOHN, surgeon, researcher; s. John and Helen Annette Evans; m. Heather Anne Richmond, May 5, 2000; children: Kaitlin Anastasia, Justin John, Lachlan Richmond. AB, Harvard U., Cambridge, Mass., 1979—83; MD, U. Calgary, Can., 1984—87; PhD, U. Toronto, Can., 1989—93. Dir., orthop. rsch. Johns Hopkins Bayview Med. Ctr., Balt., 1999—2001, chief, hand & upper extremity surgery, 1999—2001; dir., peripheral nerve ctr. Cleve. Clinic Found., 2001—, chief, hand surgery, 2001—. Hockey coach Shaker Heights Hockey Assn., Ohio, 2002, Cleve. Skating Club, 2002. Recipient Basic Sci. Award, Plastic Surgery Ednl. Found., 1992, 1993, 1995, Outstanding Orthop. Surgery Rsch. Award, Can. Orthop. Rsch. & Edn., 1995, First Pl., Orthop. Resident Rsch. Award, Smith & Nephew Richards Inc., 1995. Fellow: Royal Coll. Surgeons Can., Royal Coll. Physicians & Surgeons, Ont.; mem.: Soc. for Peripheral Nerve. Achievements include design of all electronic feedback mechanisms of harvesting tools for osteochondral bone grafts; minimally invasive carpal tunnel guide for carpal tunnel surgery. Office: Cleve Clinic Found Crile Bldg/A40 9500 Euclid Ave Cleveland OH 44195 Office Phone: 216-491-9920. Home Fax: 216-445-3694. E-mail: evansp2@ccf.org.

EVANS, PETER KENNETH, advertising executive; b. Brighton, Eng., Apr. 18, 1935; s. Percy Edward and Doris (McCoy) E.; m. Juana Santana Ramirez, Mar. 31, 1956; children: Luis Miguel, Linda Rosa Del Rocio, Pilar De Los Angeles. Student, Varndean Sch., Brighton, 1946-50. Asst. art dir. Grant Advt., Toronto, Ont., Can., 1958-61; creative group head Goodis, Goldberg, Soren, Toronto, 1961-63; v.p., creative dir. Baker/BBDO, Toronto, 1963-65; creative dir. Kenyon & Eckhardt, Toronto, 1965-67, Mexico City, 1967-68; exec. v.p., creative dir. Vladimir & Evans Inc., Miami, Fla., 1968-71; pres., creative dir. Evans & Ciccarone Inc., Miami, 1971-91; mktg. cons., 1991—; proprietor Peter Evans Pipes, 1994—2001, Peter Evans Woodcrafting Solutions, 1998—; cartoonist The Islander News, Key Biscayne, Fla., 1996—; pres. Peter Evans Response Mktg. & Advt., 1996—, Peter Evans Creative Svcs., 1997—. Instr. advt. Fla. Internat. U., Miami, 1974. Author: Jumpstart Marketing for the New Business Owner, 1993, Treasure Your Teeth, 1998; broadcaster radio reading svc. Sta. WLRN-FM (NPR affiliate), Miami, 1990—; playwright: Ruiz, 1982, Unconscious, 1996, Lost, 1997, Bang, 1998; actor: Scrooge, Social Security, 2000; inventor bed elevator, blind dog head protector, perfect wood carvers bench, sander-expander. Leader Jr. Achievement, Miami, 1968; asst. leader Boy Scouts Am., Miami, 1970; bd. dirs. Key Biscayne Music & Drama Club, Miami Bach Soc. Armament technician RAF, Fassberg, Germany, 1953-55, ETO. Recipient awards Can. TV Commercials Festival, N.Y. Art Directors Show, Clio awards, Andy awards, 100 Best U.S. TV Commercials, Printing Industry Am. awards, 24 Top U.S. New Product Introductions, Miami Big Mike awards, Miami Addy awards, Fla. State Addy awards, Fla. Press Assn. awards, Best Editl. Cartoons of Yr., 2005 edit.; named 100 Top U.S. Creative Men Ad Day/USA, Art Dir. of Yr. Greater Miami Ad Fedn., Best Editl. Cartoons of Yr., 2005. Mem. Nat. Assn. Underwater Instrs., Profl. Assn. Diving Instrs., Dramatists Guild, Nat. Wood Carvers Assn., Am. Birding Assn., Miami Bach Soc., Nat. Audubon Soc., Key Biscayne Beach Club, South Fla. Woodcarvers Club. Anglican. Home and Office: 285 W Mashta Dr Key Biscayne FL 33149-2419 E-mail: evanspeter@bellsouth.net.

EVANS, PETER YOSHIO, ophthalmologist, educator; b. Tokyo, Dec. 19, 1925; came to the U.S., 1957; s. Paul Yuzuru Kawai and Vicki Wichgraf Evans; m. Helga Kemp, Sept. 19, 1953; children: Johannes, Marina, Michael, André, Thomas, Ursula, Christiane. MD, Innsbruck U., 1951. Resident Innsbruck (Austria) and Frankfurt (Germany) Univs., 1951-55; intern Sisters Charity Hosp., Buffalo, N.Y., 1957-58; chief dept. ophthalmology D.C. Gen. Hosp., 1958-63; fellow Georgetown U., Washington, 1958-59, program dir. div. ophthalmology, 1963-69, chmn., 1969-83, prof., 1973-92, prof. emeritus, 1992—. Cons. D.C. Columbia Lighthouse for the Blind, 1959-63; sr. cons. D.C. Child and Maternal Welfare Dept., 1961-74; exec. v.p. Joint Commn. Allied Health Pers. in Ophthalmology, St. Paul, 1981-96; bd. dirs. Internat. Eye Found., 1999—. Author, producer scientific films; contbr. articles to profl. jours.; editor numerous jours. Recipient Man of Decade award, Joint Commn. on Allied Health Pers. in Ophthalmology, 1997, Promotion of Peace and Vision award, Internat. Eye Found., 2002. Fellow Am. Acad. Ophthalmology (Disting. Svc. award 1982), Austrian Ophthalm. Soc. (First Fuchs Meml. Lectr. 1975), German Ophthalm. Soc., Am.-Austrian Soc. (pres. 1989-91), Cosmos Club D.C. Lutheran. Avocations: skiing, violin, stamp collecting/philately, photography, bridge. Home and Office: 3113 Lewis Pl Falls Church VA 22042-2511 Office Phone: 703-573-6452. Personal E-mail: pye19@cs.com.

EVANS, ROB, artist; b. Boston; s. Warren H. and June (Loucks) Evans; m. Renee Patton, June 1, 1991; children: Lucas, Elizabeth. BFA summa cum laude, Syracuse U., 1981. Artist (solo exhbns.) Natural Forces, Del. Ctr. Contemporary Arts, Mystery and Allegory: Fifteen Years of Work, National Sci. Found., Arlington, Va., Lancaster Mus. Art, Pa., Seven Rooms, Arlington Arts Ctr., Nat. Arts Club, N.Y., (permanent collections) Corcoran Gallery Art, Wash., James A. Michener Art Mus., Doylestown, Pa., State Mus. Pa., Harrisburg, Allentown Art Mus., So. Alleghenies Mus. Art, Loretto, Pa., Noyes Mus. Art, Oceanville, N.J., Lancaster Mus. Art, (feature article) Am. Artist mag.; traveled to Susquehanna Art Mus., Harrisburg, Peninsula Arts Ctr., Newport News, Va. Exhbn. com. chmn. YorkArts, York, Pa., 1997—2002. Grantee Residency grant, MidAtlantic Arts Found., 1988, Individual Artist grant, Pa. Coun. Arts, 1994, Pollock-Krasner Found., 1997, Visual Arts Fellowship grant, E.D. Found., 1998. Home: 7152 Roundtop Ln Wrightsville PA 17368

EVANS, ROBERT, JR., economics professor; b. Sterling, Colo., Mar. 20, 1932; s. Robert and Mary Louise (Paradise) E.; m. Lois Ellen Herr, Nov. 6, 1955 (dec. 1994); children: Karen E., Robert, Janet K., Thomas W., L. Midori, Laura E., Katherine Joan; m. Marian Elizabeth Grotheer, Dec. 26, 1996. SB, MIT, 1954; PhD (Hillman fellow), U. Chgo., 1959. Asst. prof. indsl. relations MIT, 1959-65; assoc. prof. Brandeis U., Waltham, Mass., 1965-71, prof., 1971—, Atran prof. labor econs., 1975-98, chmn. dept. econs., 1970-72, 73-75, 84-87, dean Coll. Arts and Scis., 1975-81; retired, 1998. Vis. prof. Keio U., Tokyo, 1966-67, 72-73, 82-83, 88-89, 94-95; rsch. dir. study on prison industries Can. Corrections Assn., 1968-69. Author: Public Policy Toward Labor, 1965, The Labor Economics of Japan and the United States, 1971, Developing Policies for Public Security and Criminal Justice, 1973. Mem. Acton (Mass.) and Acton Boxborough Regional Sch. Com., 1971-72, 74-82, 84-88, regional chmn., 1972, 79-80, 85-86, town chmn., 1975-77; mem. Acton Fin. Com., 1997—, chair, 2000-2003. With U.S. Army, 1955-57. Fulbright Rsch. scholar, Japan, 1982-83, 88-89; Abe fellow, Japan, 1994-95. Mem. Am. Econ. Assn. Home: 4 Old Meadow Ln Acton MA 01720 E-mail: revans5557@verizon.net.

EVANS, ROBERT E., bank executive; b. 1940; BS, Ohio No. U., 1962; JD, Capital U., 1967. Bar: Ohio 1967. Chmn. People's Bancorp Inc., Marietta, Ohio, 1980—, CEO, 1980—. Bd. dirs. McDonough Corp.; trustee Marietta Coll. Mem. ABA. Office: Peoples Bancorp Inc 138 Putnam St PO Box 738 Marietta OH 45750-0738

EVANS, ROBERT GEORGE, JR., retail and mail order executive; b. Wabash, Ind., May 6, 1953; s. Robert George and Helen (Kalb) E.; m. Leisa Marie Napier, June 13, 1987. Student, Ind. U., 1970-74; BSBA, Wesleyan U., 1993. Dir. computer services Ind. U. Northwest Campus, Gary, 1972-75; mgr. configuration planning CNA Ins., Chgo., 1975-79; mgr. tech. support Brylane/Ltd. Inc., Indpls., 1979-85, sr. mgr. tech. svcs., 1985-89; dir. MIS Lane Bryant/Ltd., Inc., Indpls., 1989-91; dir. Brylane/Ltd., Inc., Indpls., 1991-93; v.p. MIS Brylane, LP, Indpls., 1993-97, MIS Brylane, Inc., Indpls., 1997-99; sr. v.p., chief info. officer web svcs. Brylane Group, 1999—. Pres. Tri-Star Consulting, Merrillville, Ind., 1983-86; cons., instr. Ind.-Purdue U. Indpls. Continuing Studies Program, 1980-83. Mem. Major of Indpls. Liaison for County Agys. and Twps., 1991. Republican. Methodist. Avocations: tennis, running, weight training, travel.

EVANS, ROBERT JAMES, architect; b. Alameda, Calif., Apr. 15, 1914; s. Edwin Florence and Idella Mary (Cranna) E.; m. Carol Ann Benton, Sept. 11, 1937 (dec. 2004); children: Joan Carlson, Ann Blakeman, Marcia Mothorn. AB, U. Calif., Berkeley, 1935. Registered architect, Calif. Draftsman Wm. C. Hays Architect, San Francisco, 1935-37, U. Calif., 1937-41, architect, 1941-45, univ. architect, 1945-72, asst. v.p., 1971-72; cons. architect Marshall, Calif., 1973—; asst. to chancellor U. Mich.-Flint, 1972-73; supervising architect U. Calif., Davis, 1942-45, Berkeley, 1948-55; cons. architect campus plan U. Ryukus, Okinawa, 1969; cons. architect campus paln U. N.C., Greensboro, 1979-82. Cons. architect campus plan Kabul U., Afghanistan, 1955, U. Hawaii, 1960-62, Salk Inst., San Diego, 1983-84. Founder Tomales Bay Assn., Marshall Calif., 1964. Fellow AIA (emeritus), Assn. Univ. Architects (founder, pres. 1955-57, emeritus 1972), Richmond Yacht Club (treas. 1961) Address: PO Box 788 Marshall CA 94940

EVANS, ROBERT SHELDON, manufacturing executive, director; b. Pitts., 1944; BA in History, U. Pa., 1966; MBA in Fin., Columbia U., 1968. V.p. Evans & Co. Inc., 1971-74; v.p. internat. ops. Crane Co., N.Y.C., 1974-78, sr. v.p., 1978-79, exec. v.p., dir., 1979-84, CEO, 1984—2001, pres., chief ops. officer, 1986-91, chmn., 2001—. Chmn., CEO, bd. dirs. Medusa Corp.; bd. dirs. HBD Industries Inc., Fanstel, Inc. Mem. dean's adv. coun. Columbia Grad. Sch. Bus.; trustee Eaglebrook Sch. Office: Crane Co 100 1st Stamford Pl Stamford CT 06902-6740*

EVANS, ROBERT VINCENT, sales and marketing executive; b. Mobile, Ala., Sept. 21, 1958; s. William Alexander Evans and Katherine Barbara (Doerr) Davidson; children: James Vernon, Chelsea Marie, Layla Annelise; m. Elise Ann Brackmann Evans. BS in Computer Info. Systems, BS in Tech. Mgmt., Regis U., Denver, 1987; postgrad. in Mgmt., U. Wash., 1995. Electrician Climax (Colo.) Molybdenum Co., 1978—82; applications engr. Honeywell, Inc., Englewood, Colo., 1982—83, sales engr., 1983—87; sys. engr. Apple Computer, Inc., Seattle, 1987—88, mgr. regional sys. engring. Portland, Oreg., 1988—96, dist. sales mgr. Seattle, 1997—2002; v.p. Bulldog Beach Interactive, Seattle, 2002—; practice mgr. BEA Systems, Kirkland, Wash. Author: Anthology of American Poets, 1981. Dir. Operation Lookout, Seattle, 1989; mem. Rep. Nat. Com.; commr. dist. chmn. Boy Scouts Am. Recipient USMC Blues award, Marine Corps Assn. Leatherneck award, 1977, Denver Post Outstanding Svc. award, 1983, N.Y. Zool. Soc. Hon. medal, James West fellowship award, Paul Harris fellowship award, Silver Beaver award Boy Scouts Am., 1998. Mem. Am. Mgmt. Assn., Am. Platform Assn., Mensa, Rotary, Kiwanis. Republican. Avocations: reading, church ministry, family activities. Office: BEA Systems Ste 300 10230 NE Points Dr Kirkland WA 98033

EVANS, RONALD M., microbiologist, educator; BA in Bacteriology, UCLA, 1970, PhD in Microbiology and Immunology, 1974. Asst. rsch. prof. dept. molecular cell biology Rockefeller U., N.Y.C., 1975—78; from asst. to assoc. prof. tumor virology lab. Salk Inst. Biol. Studies Howard Hughes Med. Inst., La Jolla, Calif., 1978—84, sr. mem. molecular biology and virology lab. Salk Inst. Biol. Studies, 1984—86, prof. gene expression lab Salk Inst. Biol. Studies, 1986—, investigator, 1985—; prof. Salk Institute for Biol. Studies, San Diego. Adj. prof. dept. biology U. Calif., San Francisco, 1985—, adj. prof. dept. biomedical scis. Sch. Medicine, San Diego, 1989—, adj. prof. dept. neurosciences, 1995—; chmn. faculty Salk Inst. Biol. Studies Howard Hughes Med. Inst., La Jolla, 1993—94, La Jolla, 1997—98; mem. sci. adv. bd. SIBIA, 1983—; mem. external sci. adv. com. City of Hope, 1987; mem. molecular biology study sect. NIH, 1983—86, mem. molecular neurobiology study sect., 1984—85; mem. nat. adv. com. Pew Scholars Program in Biomedical Scis., 1987—2000; founder and chair sci. adv. bd. Ligand Pharm., 1988—; mem. program com. Searle Scholars, 1989—91; mem. Alfred P. Sloan Jr. selection com. GM Cancer Rsch. Found., 1991; organizer numerous confs. in field; mem. external sci. adv. bd. Mass. Gen. Hosp., 1996—; mem. sci. adv. bd. Dana Farber Cancer Inst., 1996—, Osaka Bioscience Inst., 1999—; S. Richard Hill, Jr. vis. prof. U. Ala., 1995; Woodward vis. prof. Meml. Sloan-Kettering, 1996; Burroughs Wellcome vis. prof. U. Mass., 1998; spkr. in field, lectr.; March of Dimes chair in Molecular and Developmental Neurobiology Salk Inst., La Jolla, Calif. Editor: Molecular Endocrinology, 1993—97; editor: (assoc. editor) Molecular Brain Rsch., 1985—93, Jour. Neuroscience, 1985—90, Neuron, 1987—93; mem. editl. bd. Receptors and Channels, 1992—93, Genes and Development, 1992—, Hormones and Signalling, 1996—; co-editor: Current Opinion in Cell Biology, 1993. Mem. fellowship screening com. Am. Cancer Soc., 1987—90. Named Calif. Scientist of Yr., Calif. Mus. Sci., 1994; recipient Gregory Pincus medal, Laurentian Soc., 1988, Louis S. Goodman and Alfred Gilman award, Am. Soc. Pharmacology and Exptl. Therapeutics, 1988, Van Meter/Rorer Pharm. prize, Am. Thyroid Assn., 1989, Gregory Pincus Meml. award, Worcester Found. Exptl. Biology, 1991, Rita Levi Montalcini award, Fidia Rsch. Found. Neuroscience, 1991, Osborne and Mendel award, Am. Inst. Nutrition, 1992, award for cancer rsch., Robert J. and Claire Pasarow Found., 1993, Transatlantic medal, Soc. Endocrinology, 1994, Dickson prize in medicine, U. Pitts., 1994—95, Morton award, U. Liverpool, Biochemical Soc., 1996, Gerald Aurbach Meml. award, Assn. Bone and Mineral Rsch., 1997, Fred Conrad Koch award, Endocrine Soc., 1999, award for disting. achievement in metabolic rsch., Bristol-Myers Squibb, 2000, Alfred P. Sloan Jr. prize, GM Cancer Rsch. Found., 2003, Albert Lasker award for Basic Medical Rsch., 2004; fellow, NIH, 1975—78; Rsch. Assoc. fellow, Cancer Rsch. Com. Calif., 1975. Mem.: NAS, Inst. Medicine, 2004, Am. Assn. Cancer Rsch. (chair cancer rsch. com. 2001, Pezcoller Internat. award 2001, Eleventh C.P. Rhoads Meml. award 1990), Am. Acad. Arts and Scis. (fellow), Harvey Soc., Am. Acad. Microbiology, Am. Soc. Microbiology (fellow), Soc. Neuroscience, Soc. Devel. Biology, Endocrine Soc. (Edwin B. Astwood Lectureship award 1993). Office: Salk Inst Biol Studies Howard Hughes Med Inst 10010 N Torrey Pines Rd La Jolla CA 92037

EVANS, SANDRA HERNANDEZ, secondary school educator; b. Sept. 5, 1950; d. Teme P. and Lauris Tate Hernandez; m. Michael Leo Evans, Oct. 30, 1971; children: Michael T. Hernandez Evans, Andrew W. Hernandez Evans. BS, La. State U., 1985, MS, 2001. Cert. art and social studies tchr. Pvt. practice typist, 1977-83; art tchr. Highland Enrichment Ctr., Highland Elem. Sch., 1986; tchr. EBR Parish Sch. Bd.-Tara High Sch., 1985-86, EBR Parish Sch. Bd.-Southeast Middle Sch., 1986—99, Woodlawn High Sch., 1999—. Instr., developer fine arts survey curriculum for online learning La. Virtual Classroom, 2000—. Exhibited Tchr.'s Art Show, Art and Artists Guild, 1985, 86, Tchr.'s Art Show, B.R. Little Theater, 1987, 89, 90, 91, 92. PTA officer, coord. homeroom mothers, Jefferson Terrace, 1982-83, PTA pres. Buchanan, 1985-86; bd. dirs. Camelot Civic Assn., 1994. Recipient grants La. Bd. Elem. and Secondary Edn., Southeast Middle Sch., 1992—. Mem. Nat. and State Art Educators' Assn., Art and Artists Guild, Arts and Humanities Coun. Avocations: reading, gardening, camping, swimming, computers.

EVANS, SARA, country singer, songwriter; b. Mo., Feb. 5, 1971; m. Craig Schelske; children: Avery, Olivia. Signed contract with RCA, Nashville, 1996; performer with group Sara Evans & North Santiam. Singer: (albums) Three Clouds and the Truth, 1997, No Place That Far, 1998, Girls' Night Out, 1999, Born to Fly, 2000, Restless, 2003, (singles) True Lies, 1997, Three Clouds and the Truth, 1997, Shame About That, 1997, Cryin' Game, 1998, No Place That Far, 1998, Born to Fly, 2000 (Video Yr., Country Music Assn., 2001); background singer: songs "I Never Really Knew You", Key, 1994; singer "Almost New", Clay Pigeon (Original Soundtrack), 1998, "That's the Beat of a Heart", Where the Heart Is (Original Soundtrack), 2000, "Mary of the Wild Moor", Songcatcher (Original Soundtrack), 2001. Office: RCA Record Group 1400 18th Ave S Nashville TN 37212 Office Phone: 615-301-4300.

EVANS, SUSAN A., chemist; Postdoctoral and rsch. fellow Edsel B. Ford Inst. for Med. Rsch. and dept. pathology Henry Ford Hosp., Detroit; v.p. rsch., devel. and engring. LifeScane, Inc., a Johnson and Johnson Co., Milpitas, Calif. Fellow: Nat. Acad. Clin. Biochemistry; mem.: NCCLS (fin. com., nominating com., strategic planning com., area com. on clin. chemistry and toxicology), Internat. Fedn. Clin. Chemistry (sec. and corp. rep. edn. and mgmt. divsn.), Am. Assn. Clin. Chemistry (sec. 2002—, exec. com. bd. dirs., fin. com., ex-officio mem. ho. of dels. steering com., chair program coord. commn., sec., chair, councilor Fla. sect., vice chair San Diego sect. 1993, recording sec. Chgo. sect. 1997, founding mem., treas. industry divsn., mem. long range planning com. 1985—89, mem. coun. steering com. 1987—88, co-chair ann. meeting 1988). Achievements include research in has focused on immunodiagnostic methods.

EVANS, TERENCE THOMAS, federal judge; b. Milwaukee, Wisc., Mar. 25, 1940; s. Robert Hansen and Jeanette (Walters) Evans; m. Joan Marie Witte, July 24, 1965; children: Kelly Elizabeth, Christine Marie, David Rourke. BA, Marquette U., 1962, JD, 1967. Bar: Wis. 1967. Law clk. to justice Wis. Supreme Ct., 1967—68; asst. dist. atty. Milw. County, 1968—70; assoc. Cook & Franke, Wis., 1970—72, ptnr., 1972—74; county judge Milw. County Ct., 1974—78; cir. judge State of Wis., 1978—80; judge, then chief judge US Dist. Ct. (ea. dist) Wis., Milw., 1979—95; judge US Ct. Appeals (7th cir.), 1995—. Mem.: ABA, Judicial Coun. of Seventh Circuit, Seventh Circuit Bar Assn., Milw. Bar Assn., State Bar Wis. Roman Catholic. Office: US Courthouse & Federal Bldg 517 E Wisconsin Ave Rm 721 Milwaukee WI 53202-4504*

EVANS, THELMA JEAN MATHIS, internist; b. East St. Louis, Ill., Jan. 29, 1944; d. Clemmie and Catherine (Rose) Mathis; m. Timothy Charles Evans, June 29, 1968; children: Cynthia Marie, Catherine Elizabeth (twins). BS in Zoology with honors, U. Ill., 1967; MD, U. Ill., Chgo., 1969. Intern, then resident U. Ill. Hosp., Chgo., 1969-71, fellow in pulmonary medicine, 1971-73; med. dir., acute care unit Presbyn.-St. Luke's Hosp., Chgo., 1973-75, asst. to dir. emergency svcs., 1975-77; staff physician Health Specialists, S.C., Chgo., 1977-80, AT&T (Western Electric), Cicero, Ill., 1980-85, Health First, Inc., Chgo., 1985-89, Michael Reese Health Plan, Chgo., 1989-98; mem. adv. bd. Advocate Profl. Group, Chgo., 1998—; bd. dirs. Advocate Health Care Network, Chgo., 2000—. Instr., Rush Med. Coll., Chgo., 1973-84; tuberculosis control officer, infectious disease sect. Chgo. Dept. Health, 1976-77. V.p., Com. to Elect Timothy C. Evans, Chgo., 1989. Grantee, Chgo. Lung Assn., 1972-73. Fellow: ACP; mem.: AMA, AMWA, NAACP. Democrat. African Methodist Episcopal. Avocations: photography, gardening, collecting thimbles, bells and music boxes. Office: Advocate Health Ctrs 9831 S Western Ave Chicago IL 60643-1791 Office Phone: 773-445-3500. Office Fax: 773-445-3500.

EVANS, THOMAS PASSMORE, management consultant; b. West Grove, Pa., Aug. 19, 1921; s. John and Linda (Zeuner) Evans; m. Lenore Jane Knuth, June 21, 1947; children: Paula S., Christina L., Bruce A., Carol L. BSEE, Swarthmore Coll., 1942; M in Engring., Yale U., 1948. Registered profl. engr., Pa. Engr. atomic power divsn. Westinghouse Electric Corp., Pitts., 1948-51; dir. R&D AMF, Inc., N.Y.C., 1951-60; dir. rsch. O.M. Scott & Sons Co., Marysville, Ohio, 1960-62; v.p. R&D W. A. Sheaffer Pen Co., Fort Madison, Iowa, 1962-67; dir. rsch. Mich. Tech. U., Houghton, 1967-80; prof. bus. adminstrn. Berry Coll., Mt. Berry, Ga., 1980-86, dir. rsch., mem. faculty, 1980-88. Lt. USN, 1943—46. Mem.: VFW, AAAS, IEEE, Yale Sci. and Engring. Assn., Soc. Plastics Engrs., Am. Phys. Soc., Nat. Def. Indsl. Assn., Am. Forestry Assn., Nat. Trust Hist. Preservation, Air Force Assn., Am. Legion, Tau Beta Pi, Sigma Xi. Achievements include patents in field. Home: 8333 Seminole Blvd Apt 660F Seminole FL 33772-4391

EVANS, TIMOTHY GRANT, international organization administrator; b. Jan. 10, 1961; BSS, U. Ottawa, Can., 1984; PhD in Agrl. Econ., U. Oxford, Eng., 1989; MD, McMaster U., Can., 1992. Intern Brigham and Women's Hosp., Boston, 1992—93, rsch. resident, 1992—96, jr. asst. resident, internal medicine, 1993—94, sr. asst. resident, internal medicine, 1994—96, attending physician, dept. gen. internal medicine and primary care, 1996—97; MacArthur fellow Harvard Ctr. for Population and Devel. Studies, 1992—94; asst. prof., internat. health econ. Harvard U. Sch. Pub. Health, 1995—97; team dir., health equity program The Rockefeller Found., 1997—2003; asst. dir. gen., evidence and info. for policy WHO, Geneva, 2003—. Fellow, Internat. Exchange of Experts in Rehab., 1994; scholar, Can. Internat. Devel. Agy., 1986—87; Rhodes Scholar, U. Oxford, 1984—88. Office: World Health Orgn Avenue Appia 20 1211 Geneva Switzerland E-mail: evanst@who.int.

EVANS, TOMMY NICHOLAS, obstetrician, gynecologist, educator; b. Batesville, Ark., Apr. 12, 1922; s. James Rufus and Carrye Mae (Goatcher) E.; m. Jessica Ray Osment, June 12, 1945; 1 child, Laura Kathreen AA, Mars Hill Jr. Coll., 1940; student, Duke U., 1940-41; AB, Baylor U., 1942; MD, Vanderbilt U., 1945. Intern U. Mich. Hosp., Ann Arbor, 1945-46, asst. resident ob-gyn, 1948, resident, 1948-49, jr. clin. instr., 1949-50, sr. clin. instr., 1950-51, instr., 1951-54, asst. prof., 1954-56, assoc. prof., 1956-60, prof., 1960-65; prof. ob-gyn Wayne State U., Detroit, 1965-83, dean Sch. Medicine, 1970-72, dir. C.S. Mott Ctr. Human Growth and Devel., 1973-83; sr. attending physician Hutzel Hosp., 1966-83, chief ob-gyn, 1966-82, vice chief of staff, 1967-70, chief of staff, 1970-74, trustee, 1975-78; mem. teaching, surgeon Harper-Grace Hosps., 1965-83, chief gynecology Harper div., 1970-83, chief ob-gyn, 1975-83; chief gynecology, sr. attending physician Detroit Receiving Hosp., 1965-83; chief gynecology U. Colo., Denver, 1983-89, vice chmn. ob-gyn., 1983-89, prof. emeritus ob-gyn., 1989—. Cons. pediatric surgery Children's Hosp.; cons. Sinai Hosp. William Beaumont Hosp., Wayne County Gen. Hosp.; past mem. med. adv. com. Detroit Med. Ctr. Corp. Bd. dirs. Alan Guttmacher Inst. Fellow Am. Assn. Ob-Gyn.; mem. Am. Coll. Obstetricians and Gynecologists (past exec. bd., past pres.), ACS (adv. council ob-gyn credentials com. 1983-85, bd. govs. 1982-86), Am. Fedn. Clin. Research, Am. Fertility Soc., Am. Gynecol. Club (past pres.), Am. Gynecol. Soc. (past pres.), Am. Gynecol. and Obstetrical Soc. (council), AMA, Am. Med. Soc. Vienna, Am. Pub. Health Assn., Am. Soc. Andrology (exec. council), Am. Soc. Study Sterility, Anthony Wayne Soc., Assn. Profs. Ob-Gyn (past chmn. nominating com.), Central Assn. Ob-Gyn (past pres.), Charlie Flowers Ob-Gyn Soc., Chgo. Gynecol. Soc., Continental Gynecol. Soc., Detroit Acad. Medicine, Detroit Cancer Club (past mem. program com.), Engring. Soc. Detroit, Greater Detroit Area Hosp. Council Inc., Internat. Fedn. Ob-Gyn (exec. bd.), Internat. Soc. Advancement Humanistic Studies in Gynecology, Miami Obstet. and Gynecol. Soc., Mich. Assn. Retarded Children, Mich. Cancer Found. (trustee), Mich. Council Study of Abortion, Mich. Soc. Ob-Gyn (past pres.), Mich. State Med. Soc. (past exec. council), Mich. United Cerebral Palsy Assn., Norman Miller Gynecol. Soc. (past pres.), Ob-Gyn Soc. N.Y., Planned Parenthood League, Pan Am. Med. Assn., Royal Soc. Medicine, Soc. Study of Reprodn., Soc. Ob-Gyn of Can., S. Atlantic Assn. Ob-Gyn, numerous others. Republican. Presbyterian. Office: 7501 E Thompson Peak Pkwy Apt 233 Scottsdale AZ 85255-4533 Business E-Mail: tommyevans2000@msn.com.

EVANS, WALTER REED, retired engineering executive, consultant; b. El Paso, Tex., Oct. 25, 1921; s. Charles Reed and Ruby Estelle (Simpson-Rountree) E.; m. Frances Adelaide Lounsbury, Jan. 15, 1942 (dec. 1975); children: Sandra Frances, Roger Reed, Sharon Adelaide; m. Dorothy May Cuthbertson, 1975; stepchildren: Jack W., William D., Charles T. Rogers. BS in Mech. Engring., U. Tex. Registered profl. engr. La., Tex. Engring. and mech. supr. Celanese and Exxon Corps., Tex. and Venezuela, 1948-57; plant mgr., pres. Falcon Chem. Corp., Lake Charles, La., 1957-59; cons. SIP, Inc., Houston, 1960-62; instrument engr. Exxon, Aruba, 1963, mech.supt. Malaga, Spain, 1964—65, chief engr. Pakistan, 1966—71, divsn. head Sriracha, Thailand, 1972; project mgr. S & B, Inc., Houston, 1973-79; mech. mgr. Arabian Am. Oil Co., Ras Tanura, Saudi Arabia, 1979-81; pvt. practice mech. engring. cons., 1982-88; Tex. state coord., lobbyist ASME, Austin, 1988-94; prof., competency monitor Tex. State Bd. Engring. Registration, 1995-99. Founder, v.p. Structural Metals, Inc. divsn. Comml. Metals, Inc., Seguin, Tex., 1947-48; trustee Teal Petroleum Co. divsn. W.R. Grace Co., 1975-79; apprentice mechanic, aircraft engine, Kelly Field, Tex., 1939; owner's rep. Himont, Inc. divsn. Dupont, 1984-85. Author: Aircraft Engine Overhaul, 1942. Enlisted Tex. N.G., 1938; lt. USAAF, 1942-44, ETO. Fellow ASME (life); mem. NSPE (life), NRA, Squires Bus. Men's Orgn., Austin Amateur Radio, Men's Garden Club, Austin Rifle Club. Republican. Episcopalian. Avocations: hunting, fishing, stamp/coin collecting, gardening, reading. Home and Office: 11279 Taylor Draper Ln Apt 329 Austin TX 78759-3965

EVANS, WAYNE, obstetrician, perinatologist; b. Cincinnati, Ohio, Apr. 13, 1954; s. Johnnie Kate and Wilbur Evans; m. Jacqueline Evette Brown, Apr. 1, 2001; children: Karoline Odessa, David Wayne;. BS in Biology, Marietta Coll., 1976; AAS Physician Asst., Cin. Tech. Coll., 1978; MD, Med. Coll. of Ohio, Toledo, 1981. Diplomate Am. Bd. Ob-Gyn., Am. Bd. Maternal-Fetal Medicine. Resident, ob-gyn. Good Samaritan Hosp., Cin., 1981—85; gen. obstetrician-gynecologist Milw. Comprehensive Cmty. Health, Milw., 1985—86, MetroHealth of Ind., Indpls., 1986—89, USPHS, Carl Albert Indian Health Facility, Ada, Okla., 1989—91; fellow, critical care medicine U. of Md./RA Crowley Shock Trauma Ctr., Balt., 1991—92; fellow, maternal fetal medicine U. of Pitts./ Magee Womens Hosp., Pitts., 1992—94; dir. of perinatology/clin. asst. prof. U. of Wis. Med. Sch.- Milw. Clin. Campus, 1994—. Dir. of perinatology Aurora Sinai Med. Ctr., Milw., 1995—. Author:

(novel) I Seek You, 2001. 0-6 comdr. USPHS, 1989—91, Ada, Okla. Mem.: AMA, State Med. Soc. of Wis., Nat. Perinatal Assn., Soc. of Obstetric Medicine, Milw. Gynecologic Soc. (assoc.). Office: Aurora Sinai Med Ctr Bldg A 5th Fl 950 N 12th St Milwaukee WI 53202 Personal E-mail: docdub@excite.com. E-mail: docdub@hotmail.com.

EVANS, WILLIAM JOSEPH, medical educator; b. Beaufort, S.C., Oct. 26, 1950; s. William Theadore and Christine Marie Evans; m. Elizabeth Fisher, Aug. 20, 1984; children: Katherine, Robert, Julia. BA, U. N.C., 1972; MS, PhD, Ball State U., 1980. Chief Human Physiology lab. Tufts U., Boston, 1982—93; dir. Noll Lab. Pa. State U., University Park, 1993—97; prof. U. Ark. Med. Sci., Little Rock, 1997—. Author: Biomarkers and Astrofit, 1991. With U.S. Army, 1972-74. Fellow Am. Coll. Sports Medicine; mem. Am. Dietetic Assn. (hon.), Am. Physiol. Soc., Am. Soc. Nutrition Scis. Democrat. Avocations: golf, skiing, biking. Home: 46 Fontenay Cir Little Rock AR 72223 Office: U Ark Med Scis 4301 Markham Slot 806 Little Rock AR 72205 Office Fax: 501-526-5710. E-mail: evanswilliamj@uams.edu.

EVANSON, BARBARA JEAN, middle school education educator; b. Grand Forks, N.D., Aug. 15, 1944; d. Robert John and Jean Elizabeth (Lommen) Gibbons; m. Bruce Carlyle Evanson, Dec. 27, 1965; children: Tracey, John, Kelly. AA, Bismarck State Coll., 1964; BS in Spl. and Elem. Edn., U. N.D., 1966. Tchr. spl. edn. Winship Sch., Grand Forks, 1966-67, Simle Jr. High, Bismarck, 1967-70; tchr. Northridge Elem. Sch., Bismarck, 1980-86, Wachter Middle Sch., Bismarck, 1986—. Cons. Dept. Pub. Instrn., Bismark, 1988—, Chpt. I, Bismark, 1989—, McRel for Drug Free Schs., Denver, 1990-95. Co-founder The Big People, Bismarck, 1978-95; mem. task force Children's Trust Fund, N.D., 1984; senator N.D. Legislature, Bismarck, 1989-94; mem. N.D. Bridges Adv. Bd., 1991-97, DPI English Adv. Com., 1993—; co-facilitator Lead Mid. Sch. for Carnegie, 1994-97, N.D. Health Adv. Coun., 1993-94, N.D. Tchr.'s Fund for Retirement, State Investment Bd. 1996—; co-founder, bd. dirs. Neighbors Network, 1983—. Recipient Gold Award Bismark Norwest Bank, 1985; named Tchr. of Yr., N.D. Dept. Pub. Instrn., 1989, Legislator of Yr., Children's Caucus, 1991, Outstanding Alumnae, Bismarck State Coll., 1991, Milken Nat. Tchr. of Yr., 1995-96, KX Golden Apple award, 1999. Mem. N.D. Reading Assn., N.D. Coun. of Tchrs. of English., NEA, N.D. Edn. Assn., Bismarck Edn. Assn. Avocations: clown, walking, reading, travel, remodeling. Office: Wachter Middle Sch 1107 S 7th St Bismarck ND 58504-6533

EVANSON, PAUL JOHN, utilities executive; b. NYC, June 16, 1941; s. Edwin F. and Barbara (Marconi) E.; m. Carol Louise Cordaro, Aug. 21, 1965; 1 child, Lisa J. BBA, St. John's U., N.Y., 1963; JD, Columbia U., 1966; LLM, NYU, 1970. CPA, N.Y.; Bar: N.Y. 1966. Mgr. Arthur Andersen & Co., N.Y.C., 1966-73; exec. v.p. Moore McCormack Resources, Inc., Stamford, Conn., 1973-88; pres., chief oper. officer Lynch Corp., Greenwich, Conn., 1988-92; sr. v.p., CFO FPL Group, Inc., Juno Beach, Fla., 1992-95; pres. FPL Co., Juno Beach, 1995—2003; pres., CEO, chmn. Allegheny Energy, Inc., Greensburg, Pa., 2003—. Bd. dirs. Lynch Corp. (AMEX), So. Edison Electric Inst., Southeastern Electric Exch.; bd. govs. St. John's U. Chmn., pres. YMCA, Stamford, 1982-88. Mem. Country Club of Darien. Avocations: tennis, reading. Office: Allegheny Energy Inc 800 Cabin Hill Dr Greensburg PA 15601

EVARTS, HELEN COLEMAN, secondary school educator; b. N.Y.C., Apr. 7, 1928; d. Leighton Hammond and Jane (Fraser) Coleman; m. William M. Evarts Jr., Aug. 28, 1948; children: Holly Bartow, Kate, Alice. Student, Bryn Mawr Coll., 1946-48; BA, Columbia U., 1970; MA, NYU, 1973. Tchr. history Nightingale-Bamford Sch., N.Y.C., 1975-91. Bd. dirs. Aztec Land & Cattle Co., N.Y.C. Docent Met. Mus. Art, N.Y.C., 1992—; bd. dirs. Columbia U. Sch. Gen. Studies, Lower Hudson chpt. The Nature Conservancy, 1984—94, Vidda Found., Civitella Ranieri Found. Mem. Assn. Tchrs. in Ind. Schs. (sec. 1980-87), Nat. Assn. Ind. Schs., Phi Beta Kappa, Cosmopolitan Club, River Club. Democrat. Episcopalian. Avocations: reading, hiking, swimming, sailing, birding. Home: 7 Gracie Sq New York NY 10028-8001 E-mail: evarts@highlands.com.

EVARTS, WILLIAM MAXWELL, JR., lawyer; b. N.Y.C., June 3, 1925; m. Helen Rulison Coleman, Aug. 28, 1948. AB, Harvard U., 1949, LL.B., 1952. Bar: N.Y. 1953, U.S. Ct. Appeals (2d cir.) 1961, U.S. Dist. Ct. (so. and ea. dists.) N.Y. 1974. Assoc. Winthrop, Stimson, Putnam & Roberts, N.Y.C., 1952-62, ptnr., 1962-97, sr. counsel, 1997—. Bd. dirs. United Hosp. Fund, N.Y.C., Scenic Hudson, Poughkeepsie, The Clark Found., N.Y.C.; chmn., 1996-2000, cons. mem., 2001—; chmn. distbn. com. N.Y. Cmty. Trust. Sgt. U.S. Army, 1943-46, ETO. Mem. ABA, Assn. of Bar of City of N.Y. Office: Pillsbury Winthrop Shaw Pittman LLP 1540 Broadway New York NY 10036

EVDOKIMOVA, EVA, prima ballerina assoluta, director, producer, consultant, actress; b. Geneva, Dec. 1, 1948; parents Am. citizens; m. Michael Gregori, 1982. Student, Munich State Opera Ballet Sch., Royal Ballet Sch., London; studied privately with Maria Fay (London), Vera Volkova (Copenhagen), Natalia Dudinskaya (Leningrad), 1964-66; student in Music Studies, Guild Hall Sch. Music, London, 1964—66; student in Drama Studies, H.B. Studio, N.Y.C., 1997—2000. Pres. of jury Rudolf Nureyev Internat. Ballet Competition, Budapest, 1994, 96, 98; chm. Jury Varna Internat. Ballet Competition, Bulgaria, 1996; ballet mistress Boston Ballet, 2002-03; ballet coach; drama performances 5 off offBroadway drama prodns., 1997-2002; contemporary dance performances created for her by Igal Perry, Henning Rübsam, Angela Jones; simultaneous translation and interpretation between English, French, German, Russian, Italian, Danish. Latin Studies. Debut Royal Danish Ballet, Copenhagen, 1966; Prima Ballerina Assoluta, Deutsche Oper Berlin, 1969-90; frequent guest artist with numerous major ballet cos. worldwide including London Festival Ballet, English Nat. Ballet, Am. Ballet Theatre, Paris Opera Ballet, La Scala, Kirov Ballet, Tokyo Ballet, Teatro Colon, Nat. Ballet of Can., Stuttgart Ballet, Royal Danish Ballet, and all other major nat. ballet cos.; premiered roles in Rudolf Nureyev's classical ballet prodns., ptnr., 1971-86; appeared in over 16 classical and modern ballets with Rudolf Nureyev across the world; repertoire of more than 130 roles includes Swan Lake, Giselle, La Sylphide, Sleeping Beauty, Romeo and Juliet, Don Quixote, La Bayadere, Onegin, Raymonda; created roles in many contemporary ballets for stage, film and TV; film appearances include The Nutcracker, La Sylphide, Cinderella, A Family Portrait, The Romantic Era, Invitation to the Dance, Portrait of Eva Evdokimova, and others. Recipient Diploma, Internat. Ballet Competition, Moscow, 1969; winner Gold medal Varna Internat. Ballet competition, 1970; awarded title Prima Ballerina Assoluta, Berlin Senate, 1973, Berlin Critic's Prize, 1974; first fgn. mem. Royal Danish Ballet, first Am. and Westerner to win any internat. ballet competition, first Am. to perform with Kirov Ballet, 1976, first Am. to perform in Peking after the Cultural Revolution, 1978, first and only Am. dancer with portrait in permanent collection, Mus. Drama and Dance, Leningrad, St. Petersburg, Russia, only Am. performer ever to be honored in a German opera house, Grand Défilé ceremony, 1990 Deutsche Oper Berlin; recipient letter for meritorious svc. from Pres. Bush, 1990, numerous other awards; holder world record for 67 curtain calls with 40 minute standing ovation, Berlin, 1990. Achievements include world record performing in two different Giselles, two full length Prokofiev Ballets and eight other works with three companies; at Lincoln Center, New York, in three debuts with three different companies within a three month period.

EVE, (EVE JIHAN JEFFERS), rap artist, actress; b. Phila., Nov. 10, 1978; Formed female rap duo EDGP; former mem. DMX's Ruff Ryders posse; signed one-yr. deal with DMX's new label Aftermath. Performer: (albums) Let There Be Eve...Ruff Rider's First Lady, 1999, Scorpion, 2001, Eve-Olution, 2002; musician: (songs) "Eve of Destruction", 1998; musician: (with Gwen Stefani) "Let Me Blow Ya Mind", 2001 (Grammy award best rap/sung collaboration, 2001); musician: (with The Roots) "You Got Me"; musician: (with Blackstreet & Janet Jackson) "Girlfriend/Boyfriend"; musician: (with Missy Elliott) "Hot Boyz"; actor: (films) XXX, 2002, Barbershop, 2002, The Woodsman, 2003, Barbershop 2: Back in Business, 2004; (TV series) Eve, 2003; co-exec. prodr. (TV series) Eve, 2003; actor(guest appearances): (TV series) Third Watch, 2003, One on One, 2004, (voice): (video game) XIII, 2003. Office: Interscope Records 2220 Colorado Ave Santa Monica CA 90404

EVELETH, JANET STIDMAN, law association administrator; b. Balt., Sept. 6, 1950; d. John Charles and Edith Janet (Scales) Stidman; m. Donald P. Eveleth, May 11, 1974. BA, Washington Coll., 1972; MS, Johns Hopkins U., 1973. Counselor Office of Mayor, Balt., 1973-75; asst. dir. Gov. Commn. on Children, Balt., 1975-78; lobbyist Balt., 1978-80; comm. specialist Med. Soc., Balt., 1980-81; dir. pub. affairs Mid-Atlantic Food Dealers, Balt., 1981-84; dir. comm. Home Builders Assn., Balt., 1984-87, Md. Bar Assn., Balt., 1987—. Contbr. articles to profl. jours. Recipient Gov. citation State of Md., 1993, Citizen citation City of Balt., 1993. Mem.: NAFE, Nat. Assn. Bar Execs. (chmn. pub. rels. sect. 1994—95, Achievement award 1995, E.A. Wally Richter award 1997, Luminary award 1999, 2001, 2003), Md. Soc. Assn. Execs. (pres. 1992—93), Am. Soc. Profl. Women, Pi Lambda Theta, Alpha Chi Omega. Office: Md Bar Assn 520 W Fayette St Baltimore MD 21201-1781 Office Phone: 410-685-7878. E-mail: jeveleth@msba.org.

EVEN, FRANCIS ALPHONSE, lawyer; b. Chgo., Sept. 8, 1920; s. George Martin and Cecilia (Neuman) E.; m. Margaret Hope Herrick, Oct. 16, 1945; children: Janet Beth, Dorothy Elizabeth. BS in Mech. Engring, U. Ill., 1942; JD, George Washington U., 1949. Bar: D.C. 1949, Ill. 1950. Engr. GE, 1945-49; ptnr. Fitch, Even, Tabin & Flannery (patent and trademark law), Chgo., 1952—. Mem. bd. edn., River Forest, Ill., 1963-69; trustee West Suburban Hosp., Oak Park, Ill., 1974-77; mem. bd. Ill. State Hist. Soc., 2000-03. Combat engr., U.S. 3d inf. divsn., 1942-45. Decorated knight French Legion Honors. Fellow Am. Coll. Trial Lawyers (emeritus); mem. ABA, Am. Intellectual Property Law Assn. (bd. mgrs. 1963-66), Ill. Bar Assn., Chgo. Bar Assn., Intellectual Property Law Assn. Chgo. (bd. mgrs. 1972-73, pres. 1984), No. Ill. Ct. Hist. Assn. (pres.), Union League Club (Chgo.), Oak Park (Ill.) Country Club, Chgo. Literary Club. Republican. Home: 1018 Park Ave River Forest IL 60305-1308 Office: 120 S La Salle St Chicago IL 60603-3403 Office Phone: 312-577-7000.

EVEN, RANDOLPH M., lawyer; b. 1943; BS, U. Calif.; JD, Calif. Western Sch. Law. Bar: Calif. 1969. Atty. Even, Crandall, Wade, & Lowe and predecessor firm Genson, Even, Crandall & Wade, P.C., Woodland Hills, Calif., Randolph M. Even & Assocs., PLC, 2002—. With Calif. Med. Legal Com., 2005—. Mem. Am. Bd. Trial Advocates, Assn. So. Calif. Def. Counsel (bd. dirs. 1978-80, 93-98, Calif. med. legal com.). Office: 5550 Topanga Canyon Blvd STE 280 Woodland Hills CA 91367-7471 Office Phone: 818-226-5444.

EVENS, RONALD GENE, radiologist, educator, health facility administrator; b. St. Louis, Sept. 24, 1939; s. Robert and Dorothy (Lupkey) E.; m. Hanna Blunk, Sept. 3, 1960; children: Ronald Jr., Christine, Amanda. BA, Washington U., 1960, MD, 1964, postgrad. in bus. and edn., 1970-71. Intern Barnes Hosp., St. Louis, 1964-65; resident Mallinckrodt Inst. Radiology, St. Louis, 1965-66, 68-70; rsch. assoc. Nat. Heart Inst., 1966-68; asst. prof. radiology, v.p. Washington U. Med. Sch., 1970-71, prof., head dept. radiology, dir., 1971-72, Elizabeth Mallinckrodt prof., head radiology dept. St. Louis, 1972-99, prof. med. econs., 1988—; pres., sr. exec. ofcr. Barnes-Jewish Hosp., St. Louis, 1999—. Radiologist-in-chief Barnes Hosp., St. Louis, 1971-99; radiologist-in-chief Children's Hosp., 1971-99, pres., chief exec. officer, 1985-88; vice chancellor fin. Washington U., St. Louis, 1988-91; mem. adv. com. on splty. and geog. distbn. of physicians Inst. Medicine, Nat. Acad. Scis., 1974-76, Hickey lectr., 1976, Carmen lectr. Calif. U., 1985, Kiewit lectr. Eisenhower Med. Ctr., 1986; Hornick lectr. U. Pitts., 1986; ann. orator Can. Radiol. Soc., 1984; Hodes lectr. Jefferson U., 1991—; Smith lectr. Royal Coll. Physicians, Edinburgh, 1992; Seaman lectr. Columbia Presbyn., 1992; dir. Boatmens Bank Inc., Mallinckrodt Group Inc., Right Choice Inc., Blue Choice, Inc.; chmn. bd. Med. Care Group St. Louis, 1980-86. Contbr. over 210 articles to profl. jours. Active Boy Scouts Am., 1975—; elder Glendale Presbyn. Ch., 1971-74, Kirkwood Presbyn. Ch., 1983-86. Served with USPHS, 1966-68. Advance Acad. fellow James Picker Found, 1970; recipient Disting. Svc. award. St. Louis C. of C., 1972; named Disting. Eagle Scout Nat. Coun., 1983. Fellow Am. Coll. Radiology (chair elect 1995, chair bd. chancellors 1996—); mem. AMA (editl. bd. JAMA), Mo. Radiol. Soc. (pres. 1977-78), Soc. Nuclear Medicine (trustee 1971-75), St. Louis Med. Soc., Mo. State Med. Assn., Soc. Chmn. Acad. Radiology Depts. (pres. 1979), Radiol. Soc. N.Am., Assn. Univ. Radiologists (pres. 1988), Am. Roentgen Ray Soc. (pres. 1989), Phi Beta Kappa, Alpha Omega Alpha (Sheard-Sanford award). Office: Barnes Jewish Hosp Mallinckrodt Inst Radiology Barnes Jewish Plz Saint Louis MO 63110-1016 Address: Barnes-Jewish Hosp One Barnes-Jewish Hospital Plz Saint Louis MO 63110

EVENSON, MERLE ARMIN, chemist, educator; b. LaCrosse, Wis., July 27, 1934; s. Ansel Bernard and Gladys Mabel (Nelson) E.; m. Peggy L. Kovats, Oct. 5, 1957; children— David A., Donna L. BS in Chem. Physics and Math., U. Wis., LaCrosse, 1956; MS in Guidance, MS in Sci. Edn., Madison, 1960, PhD in Analytical Chemistry, 1966. Diplomate Am. Bd. Clin. Chemists, v.p., 1978-81. Tchr. math. and physics St. Croix Falls (Wis.) High Sch., 1956-57; tchr. chemistry Central High Sch., LaCrosse, 1957-59; instr. dept. medicine U. Wis., Madison, 1965-66, asst. prof., 1966-69, asso. prof., 1971-75, prof., 1975—, prof. dept. pathology, 1979—; asst. dir. clin. lab. Univ. Hosps., 1965-66, dir. clin. chemistry lab., 1966-69, dir. toxicology lab., 1971-87. Chmn. Gordon Rsch. Conf. on Analytical Chemistry, 1978; vis. lectr. Harvard Med. Sch., 1969-71; mem. staff Peter Bent Brigham Hosp., Boston, 1969-71; cons. on analytical and clin. chemistry to AEC, 1968-93, Am. Chem. Soc., Nat. Bur. Standards, FDA, NIH, study sect. mem. 1968-72, ad hoc memberships, 1973-87. Bd. editors: Chemical Instrumentation, 1973-87, Analytical Chemistry, 1974-77, Jour. Analytical Toxicology, 1976-79, Selected Methods in Clin. Chemistry, 1977-81; editor: Contemporary Topics in Analytical and Clincal Chemistry, 1974-83; contbr. numerous chpts. to books, articles to profl. jours.; patentee continuous oil hemoperfusion unit. NIH fellow, 1970-71, NSF, 1959-62; recipient Maurice O. Graff Disting. Alumni award U. Wis., LaCrosse, 1981 Mem. AAAS, Acad. Clin. Lab. Physicians and Scientists, Am. Assn. Clin. Chemists (bd. editors Clin. Chemistry 1970-80, nat. chair pub. rels. com. 1973-78, diplomat 1974, v.p. 1978-81), Am. Chem. Soc. (com. on clin. chemistry 1973-93), Sigma Xi, Kappa Delta Pi. Office: U Wis 1300 University Ave Madison WI 53706-1510 *As a teacher, the fostering of the development of creativity in people who then make contributions to our society is an exciting process. The most significant professional reward I receive is the observation of the successes of others with whom I have interacted and taught.*

EVENSON, ROBERT EUGENE, economist, educator; b. Elmore, Minn., July 25, 1934; s. Edven Herbert and Annie Cecelia (O'Toole) Evenson; m. Judith Joan Ungrodt, June 11, 1967; children: Nancy Lynn, Patsy Ann, Joseph Robert, Sarah Judtih. BA in Bus. Adminstrn., U. Minn., 1961, MS, 1964; PhD, U. Chgo., 1968. Farmer E.H. Evenson & Son, Minnesota Lake, Minn., 1952—60; asst. prof. U. Minn., Mpls. and St. Paul, 1966—68; vis. asst. prof. So. Meth. U., Dallas, 1968—69; assoc. prof. econs. Yale U., New Haven, 1969—74; assoc. vis. prof. Agrl. Devel. Coun., N.Y.C., 1974—77; prof. Yale U., New Haven, 1977—. Cons. World Bank, Washington, 1970—, U.S. AID, 1970—. Author: Agricultural Research and Productivity, 1975, Technology and Income, 1990; editor: Science for Agriculture, 1993. Fellow: AAAS (chair Sect. K), Am. Agrl. Econs. Assn.; mem.: Econometric Soc., Am. Econ. Assn. Home: 322 Audubon Ct New Haven CT 06510*

EVERAGE, KAREN BURGESS, mathematics educator; b. Birmingham, Ala., Aug. 27, 1946; d. George Thomas and Angie Manning Monroe; m. Joseph Brannon Burgess, Nov. 22, 1968 (div.); children: Angie Elizabeth Burgess, Michael Brannon Burgess; m. Archie Edward Everage, Dec. 29, 2001. BS, Samford U., 1968; MS, Fla. State U., 1989. Computer programmer, data processor Samford U., Birmingham, Ala., 1966—69; computer programming instr. Birmingham City Sch. Sys., 1969—70; German and math. tchr. Escambia County Sch. Sys., Pensacola, Fla., 1970—72; math. tchr. Dade County Sch. Sys., Miami, Fla., 1973—77; dir. of choirs Northside Bapt. Ch., Brunswick, Ga., 1980—81; adj. instr. in math. Tallahassee C.C., 1984—89; assoc. in math. Fla. State U., Tallahassee, 1989—. Recipient U. Tchg. award, Fla. State U., 1992, 1997, Excellence in Tchg. award, Phi Eta Sigma, 1994, 1998, 2002, 2004, Seminole award, Seminole Leadership Experience and Orgn. and Leadership Svcs., 2001, Disting. Tchr. award, Fla. State U., 2003—04. Mem.: Math. Assn. Am. Baptist. Avocations: needlecrafts, piano, racquetball. Office: Florida State U 208 Lov Tallahassee FL 32306-4510 Office Phone: 850-644-2202. Business E-Mail: everage@math.fsu.edu.

EVERARD, KENNETH EUGENE, business educator; b. Croghan, N.Y., July 4, 1931; s. Gregory Lawrence and Lavina (Sherman) E.; m. Lois Beverly Nudo, June 23, 1956. BS with honors, SUNY, Albany, 1954, MS, 1955; DEd with honors, Ind. U., 1962. Asst. prof. U. Md., College Park, 1962-64; lectr. bus. European divsn. U. Md., Heidelberg, Germany, 1964-66, Far East divsn. U. Md., Japan, 1966-68; prof. bus. and grad. program supr. bus. edn. programs Trenton (N.J.) State Coll., 1968-92, supr. MS in Mgmt. program, 1979-93; prof. emeritus The Coll. of N.J., 1999—. Author: Business Principles and Management, 1973, 79, 84, 90, 96, 2001; (with Robert J. McCullough) Bank Reconciliation Projects, 1959, 80, 87. Recipient Cmty. Svc. award Trenton State Coll., 1972, rsch. grantee, 1977, 81, 83, 87, 90, career devel. grantee, 1988, 90, 92, sabbatical leave grantee, 1978, 85-86, 93, merit award, 1980, 85. Mem. ASTD, Assn. for Bus. Comm. (group II chmn.), Soc. Human Resource Mgmt., Nat. Bus. Edn. Assn., Acad. Adminstrv. Mgmt. (regent, chair acad. coun.). Eastern Acad. Mgmt., Mid-N.J. Soc. Tng. and Devel. (assoc. editor newsletter, author Bookshelf Column), Phi Delta Kappa, Delta Pi Epsilon, Kappa Delta Pi. E-mail: everardl@voicenet.com.

EVERBACH, OTTO GEORGE, lawyer; b. New Albany, Ind., Aug. 27, 1938; s. Otto G. and Zelda Marie (Hilt) E.; m. Nancy Lee Stern, June 3, 1961; children: Tracy Ellen, Stephen George. BS, U.S. Mil. Acad., 1960; LLB, U. Va., 1966. Bar: Va. 1967, Ind. 1967, Calif. 1975, Mass. 1978. Counsel CIA, Langley, Va., 1966-67; corp. counsel Bristol-Meyers Co., Evansville, Ind., 1967-74, Alza Corp., Palo Alto, Calif., 1974-75; sec., gen. counsel Am. Optical Corp., Southbridge, Mass., 1976-81; assoc. gen. counsel Warner-Lambert Co., Morris Plains, N.J., 1981-83; v.p. Kimberly-Clark Corp., Neenah, Wis., 1984-86, sr. v.p., gen. counsel, 1986—, sr. v.p. law & govt. affairs, 1988—2003. Served with U.S. Army, 1960-63. Mem. Am. Bar Assn., Mass. Bar Assn., Ind. Bar Assn., Calif. Bar Assn. Office: Kimberly-Clark Corp DFW Airport Sta PO Box 619100 Dallas TX 75261-9100

EVERDELL, WILLIAM, retired lawyer; b. N.Y.C., May 29, 1915; s. William and Rosalind (Romeyn) E.; m. Eleanore Darling, July 2, 1940; children: William Romeyn, Coburn Darling, Preston. BA, Williams Coll., 1937; LLB, Yale U., 1940. Bar: N.Y. 1941. Assoc. Debevoise & Plimpton, N.Y.C., 1940-49, ptnr., 1949-85, of counsel, 1986-88. Contbr. articles to profl. jours. Trustee Woods Hole Oceanographic Instn., Mass., 1978-86; mem. exec. com., 1981-86, hon. trustee, 1987—; trustee, mem. exec. com. Cold Spring Harbor Lab., N.Y., 1987-93. Served to lt. comdr. USNR, 1942-45, PTO, ATO. Decorated with seven battle stars. Fellow Am. Bar Found.; mem. ABA, Assn. of Bar of City of N.Y. (mem. exec. com. 1960-64), N.Y. State Bar Assn. (chmn. com. corp. law 1971-73). Clubs: The Links (gov. 1959-62) (N.Y.C.). Episcopalian. Avocations: sailing, golf.

EVERETT, C(HARLES) CURTIS, retired lawyer; b. Omaha, Aug. 9, 1930; s. Charles Edgar and Rosalie (Cook) E.; m. Joan Rose Bader, Sept. 7, 1951; children: Jeffrey, Ellen, Amy, Jennifer. BA cum laude, Beloit Coll., 1952; JD, U. Chgo., 1957. Bar: Ill. 1957. Pvt. practice, Chgo., 1957-91; ptnr. Bell, Boyd, Lloyd, Haddad & Burns, 1965-81, successor firm Bell, Boyd & Lloyd, 1981-91; v.p. law, sec., gen. counsel AMRE, Inc., Dallas, 1991-96; v.p. law, sec., gen. counsel, bd. dirs. Am. Remodeling, Inc., Dallas, 1992-96; v.p. Canre Remodelling, Inc., Dallas, 1992-94. V.p., sec. Hans Bader, Cons., Inc., Clearwater, Fla., 1954-99, also bd. dirs.; vis. com. U. Chgo. Law Sch., 1986-89; lectr. Ill. Inst. CLE. Mem. editl. bd. U. Chgo. Law Rev., 1956-57; contbr. articles to profl. jours. Chmn. So. Suburban area Beloit Coll. Ford Found. challange program, 1964-65; pres. The Players, Flossmoor, 1970-71; bd. govs. Lake Shore Dr. Condominium Assn., 1986-91. With AUS, 1952-54. Mem. ABA, Ill. Bar Assn., Chgo. Bar Assn. (mem. securities law com. 1960-91), U. Chgo. Law Sch. Alumni Assn. (dir. 1973-76, pres. Chgo. chpt. 1979-80), Legal Club, Law Club, Monroe Club (bd. govs. 1976-97), Univ. Club Chgo., Order of DeMolay (past master counselor Rock River chpt.), Order of Coif, Sigma Chi, Phi Alpha Delta. Mem. Cmty. Ch. (deacon). Home: 532 Long Reach Dr Salem SC 29676-4214 Personal E-mail: curtandje@aol.com.

EVERETT, CLAUDIA KELLAM, retired special education educator; b. Mobile, Ala., Dec. 28, 1933; d. Claude M. and Minnie L. Kellam; m. Thomas Sherwood Everett Sr., June 18, 1953; children: Thomas Sherwood Jr., Sherilisa Ann. BA magna cum laude, Roberts Wesleyan Coll., 1958; MS summa cum laude, Barry U., 1988. Cert. English, spl. edn. tchr. Fla., N.Y. Tchr. Dade County Pub. Schs., Miami, Fla., 1959-67, Carol City Elem. Sch., Miami, 1967-77; pers. mgr., payroll supr. Harrington Cos., Miami, 1977-81; honors English tchr. Citrus Grove Jr. HS, Miami, 1981-87; spl. edn. tchr. Citrus Grove Mid. Sch., Miami, 1987-90; tchr. severely emotionally disturbed children Hilton (N.Y.) HS, 1990-91; tchr. emotionally disturbed and mentally retarded, learning disabled Hill Elem. Sch., Brockport, NY, 1991-92; tchr. emotionally/learning disabled, mentally retarded Oliver Mid. Sch., Brockport, 1991—2001; ret., 2001. Cons. cmty. benevolent agys., Miami, 1969—83; pvt. tutor, 2001—. Author: numerous poems. Youth dir. Ctrl. Alliance Youth, Miami, 1960—80; cmty. advisor youth affairs Carol City, Miami, 1970—87; founder, pres. Tchr.-Parent Study Group, Miami, 1970—80; 1st v.p., sec., treas. PTA Carol City, 1967—77; pres. Teens to S.Am. Christian Missionary Alliance, Miami, 1978—80, cons. tech. action, 1980—90. Recipient Svc. award, Christian Missionary Alliance Cmty., 1980, Youth in Action award, S.Am. Missions, 1978. Mem.: S.E. Edn. Opportunities Handicapped, Coun. Exceptional Children (mem. divsn. learning disabilities 1989—, mem. divsn. mentally retarded 1989—, mem. divsn. emotionally handicapped 1989—). Republican. Avocations: reading, photography, tutoring, writing for children, visiting elderly in nursing homes. Home: 2355 Westside Dr Rochester NY 14624-1933

EVERETT, GRAHAM, English language educator, poet, publisher; b. Oceanside, N.Y., Dec. 23, 1947; s. James H. and Jacqueline (Vaughn) E.; m. Elyse Arnow, Dec. 27, 1981; 1 child, Logan James. BA in English, Canisius Coll., 1970; MA in English, SUNY, Stony Brook, 1987, PhD in English, 1994. Pub., editor Street Press, Port Jefferson, N.Y., 1972-92; dir. Backstreet Editions, Inc., Port Jefferson, 1980-86; asst. dir. Poetry Ctr. SUNY, Stony Brook, 1988-91. Prof., acad. tutor Adelphi U.; writer in residence N.Y. State Poets in Sch. Program, L.I., 1973-86. Author: (poetry) Strange Coast, 1979, Sunlit Sidewalk, 1985, Minus Green, 1992, Minus Green Plus, 1995, Corps Calleux, 2000; editor: The Doc Fayth Poems, 1998; co-editor: Paumanok Rising, 1980. Office: Street Press PO Box 772 Sound Beach NY 11789-0772 Office Phone: 516-877-3447. Personal E-mail: tgle47@yahoo.com. Business E-Mail: everett@adelphi.edu.

EVERETT, HOBART RAY, JR., engineer, naval officer, consultant, researcher; b. Charleston, S.C., Nov. 29, 1949; s. Hobart Ray and Ruth (Humphreys) E.; m. Rachael Patricia Lewis, Dec. 30, 1971 (div. Dec. 1995); children: Todd Ashley, Rebecca Nicole. BEE, Ga. Inst. Tech., 1973; MSME, Naval Postgrad. Sch., 1982. Commd. ensign USN, 1973, advanced through grades to comdr., 1988, asst. engr. USS Nitro, 1975-77, engrng. recruiter for officer programs Montgomery, Ala., 1977-80, robotics coord. Naval Sea Sys. Washington, 1983-84, dir. Office of Robotics and Autonomous Sys., 1984-86, autonomous sys. project office Naval Ocean Sys. Ctr. San Diego, 1986-88, chief engr. USMC teleoperated vehicle program, 1988-89, assoc. head advanced sys. divsn., 1988-93. Cons. to Computer Scis. Corp., Falls Church, Va., 1993-94; assoc. divsn. head robotics Space and Naval Warfare Sys. Ctr., San Diego, 1994—; founder DoD Robotics and Artificial Intelligence Database, 1983; Navy rep. to tri-svc. Joint Tech. Panel for Robotics, 1984-86; guest lectr. in robotics U. Md., U. PA., 1983-86, U. Calif., San Diego, 1988; robotics rschr. Naval Ocean Sys. Ctr.; prin. tech. cons. U.S. Army Mobile

Detection Assessment and Response Sys. interior program, 1990-93; tech. dir. Joint Army-Navy Mobile Detection Assessment and Response Sys. interior and exterior program, 1993—. Author: Sensors for Mobile Robots, 1995, (with Borenstein and Feng) Sensors and Techniques for Mobile Robot Positioning, 1996; contbg. author Robotics Age mag., 1982-86, Sensors mag., 1987—; mem. editl. bd., contbg. author Robotics and Autonomous Sys. mag.; contbr. 90 tech. publs.; inventor 1st autonomous sentry robot; patentee in field. Decorated Navy Commendation, 1981, 86; recipient Naval Sea Sys. Command award for Acad. Excellence, 1982, Woelful award for Acad. Excellence, Naval Sea Sys. Command, 1983, Gen. Dynamics award for Acad. and Mil. Accomplishment, 1973, Spl. Act award Dept. Def., 1999, Navy Meritorious Civilian Svc. award, 2000, SSC San Diego Lauritsen-Bennet award for excellence in engring., 2001. Mem. IEEE, Soc. Mfg. Engrs. (sr.), Robotics Inst. Am., Nat. Svc. Robot Assn. (bd. dirs. 1991-93), Assn. Unmanned Vehicle Sys. Internat., Sigma Xi. Office: Space & Naval Warfare Sys Ctr Code D3701 53406 Woodward Rd San Diego CA 92152-7383 E-mail: everett@spawar.navy.mil.

EVERETT, JAMES JOSEPH, lawyer; b. San Antonio, May 7, 1955; BA, St. Mary's U., San Antonio, 1976; JD, Tex. So. U., 1980. Bar: U.S. Dist. Ct. Ariz. 1987, U.S. Tax Ct. 1980, U.S. Ct. Appeals (9th cir.) 1988. Sr. trial atty. IRS, Phoenix, 1980-87; ptnr. Brnilovich & Everett, Phoenix, 1987-89; owner Law Offices of James J. Everett, Phoenix, 1989—; of counsel Broadbent, Walker & Wales, 1991-95; prin., owner James J. Everett & Assocs., P.C., Phoenix, 2005—. Pres. No Nonsense Networking Group, 2004—; chair Univ. Club Tax Study Group, 2005; owner James J. Everett & Assocs. P.C., Phoenix, 2005—. Mem. ATLA, ABA (bus. and tax sects.), Fed. Bar Assn., Tex. Bar Assn., Ariz. Bar Assn., State Bar Ariz. (cert. tax specialist), Maricopa County Bar Assn., Ariz. Tax Controversy Group, Valley Estate Planners (Phoenix), Ctrl. Ariz. Estate Planners, Ariz. Soc. Boutiques, St. Thomas Moore Soc., No Nonsense Networking Group (pres. 2004-05), Univ. Club Tax Study Group (chair 2005). Office: Ste 225 2999 N 44th St Phoenix AZ 85018 Office Phone: 602-230-2212. Business E-Mail: James.Everett@azbar.org.

EVERETT, JAMES W., JR., lawyer; b. Buffalo, Oct. 26, 1957; s. James William and Esther (Kratzer) Everett. BA in Polit. Sci., Coll. Wooster (Ohio), 1979; JD, SUNY, Buffalo, 1984; LLM in Banking Law with honors, Boston U., 1985. Bar: N.Y. 1985, U.S. Dist. Ct. (we. dist.) N.Y. 1989, U.S. Dist. Ct. (no. dist.) N.Y. 1990, U.S. Supreme Ct. 1991. Officer Emil A. Kratzer Co., Inc., Buffalo, 1980—2001; assoc. John C. Peters, P.C., Hartford, Conn., 1986-87; assoc. counsel for banks, corps., ins. and sml. bus. N.Y. State Assembly, Albany, N.Y., 1987-88; asst. counsel for banks, commerce, securities, real property, state and local fin. N.Y. State Senate Majority, 1988-94; v.p., counsel for state procs. and taxation Securities Industry Assn., 1995-98; gen. ptnr. Everett Law, 1998—; capital markets counsel NY State Ins. Dept., 2001—. Speechwriter for chair policy com. for nat. adv. counsel on women's edn. programs. Observer, Nat. Conf. Commr. on Uniform State Laws Trust Code Drafting Com.; spkr. fin. svcs. Nat. Conf. State Legislators, Exec. Enterprise Inst. Author N.Y. Law Revision Commn. Review on Leasing (Art. 2A (Remedies), Forward to Bowne Securities Regulation Compilations; contbg. editor Barnert Reports; contbr. to Buffalo News, Bus. Ins., Corp. Fin. Week, The Bank Letter, The Bond Buyer, Compliance Reporter. Mem. judicial nominating com. Erie County (N.Y.) Rep. Com., 1979-2001; deacon N. Presbyn. Ch., Amherst, N.Y. Recipient Cummings-Rumbaugh prize Coll. of Wooster, Ohio, Harmony Heights Sch. Pub. Svc. award. Mem. Assn. Corp. Counsel, N.Y. State Bar Assn., Assn. Bar City N.Y., Nat. Assn. Life Cos. Avocations: hiking, bicycling, travel. Home: 602 Baxter Ct Delmar NY 12054 Office Phone: 518-408-1593.

EVERETT, KAREN JOAN, retired librarian, genealogist, educator; b. Cin., Dec. 12, 1926; d. Leonard Kelly and Kletis V. (Wade) Wheatley; m. Wilbur Mason Everett, Sept. 25, 1950; children: Karen, Jan, Jeffrey, Jon, Kathleen, Kerry, Kelly, Shannon. BS in Edn. magna cum laude, U. Cin., 1976, postgrad., 1982-85, Coll. Mt. St. Joseph, 1981-86, Xavier U., Cin., 1985-87, U. Cin., 1982-85, Miami U., 1987. Libr. S.W. Local Schs., Harrison, Ohio, 1967-97, dist. media coord., 1980-97, dist. vol. dir., 1980-97, ret., 1997; instr. genealogy U. Cin., 1998—. Tchr. genealogy U. Cin., 1997—; cons. in field; bd. dirs. U. Cin. ILR; lectr. in field. Contbr. articles to profl. jours. Pres. Citizens Adv. Coun., Harrison, Ohio, 1981-84, 88—, Citizens Adv. Coun., 1989; state chmn. supervisory div. Ohio Ednl. Libr./Media Assn.; mem. Ohio Ambulance Licensing Bd., 1991—. Named Woman of the Yr., Cin. Enquirer, 1978, Xi Eta Iota, 1979; named PTA Educator of the Yr., 1981, others. Mem. NEA, Ohio Ednl. Libr./Media Assn. (chair supervisory div. 1990—, bd. dirs. 1993-94), Ohio Edn. Assn., S.W. Local Classroom Tchrs. Assn., Hamilton County Geneal. Soc. (bd. dirs. 1992—). Avocations: flying, travel, genealogy. Personal E-mail: karywib@aol.com.

EVERETT, MARK ALLEN, dermatologist, educator; b. Oklahoma City, May 30, 1928; s. Mark Ruben and Alice (Allen) E.; 1 son, Howard Dean. BA in Polit. Sci., U. Okla., 1947, MD, 1951; USAF intern in pub. health. Intern in pediatrics U. Mich. Med. Sch., 1951, resident in dermatology, 1954-57, instr. dermatology, 1956-57; intern in pub. health Tulane Med. Sch., 1951; mem. faculty U. Okla. Med. Sch., 1959-98, chmn. dept. dermatology, 1964-96, prof. dermatology, head dept., 1967-96, adj. prof. pathology and anatomy, 1975-98, prof., interim head dept. pathology, 1979-84, Regents prof., 1982-98, Regents prof. emeritus, 1998—, chmn. faculty bd., 1974-90; chief staff Okla. Meml. Hosp., 1980-85. Vice chmn. bd. Bone and Joint Hosp., Oklahoma City, 1976-85; chmn. Internat. Com. for Dermatopathology, 1980-86; bd. dirs. Am. Bd. Dermatology, 1985-96, pres. elect, 1994, pres., 1995. Author 200 articles in field, chpts. in books. Pres. Okla. Ballet Soc., 1973, 77-80, Oklahoma City Chamber Orch., 1979-81, Chamber Music Okla., 1989-2001; pres. bd. trustees Everett Found., 1961-; adv. bd. World Lit. Today, 1970-85, Bizzell Libr. Soc., 1982—; bd. visitors Coll. of Fine Arts, U. Okla., 1990-2002, Coll. of Arts and Scis., 1996-99; bd. dirs. Red Earth Inc., 1997-, trustee, 2000, v.p., 2001-04; chair Mus. Com., 1997-2001, Art Com., 2001-03; bd. dirs. Jacobson House, 2002-. With USAF, 1952-54. Recipient Bronze medal U. Okla. Fedn., Mayor's award for Lifetime Contbn. to Arts, Oklahoma City, 1989, Gov.'s Arts award, 1993; grantee Am. Cancer Soc., NIH. Mem. AMA, Am. Acad. Dermatology (chmn. long-range planning coun. 1975-80, dir. 1978-82, chmn. coun. on sci. assembly 1985), Assn. Profs. Dermatology (pres. 1976-78), Am. Soc. Dermatopathology (pres. 1980), Am. Assn. Cancer Rsch., Internat. Acad. Pathology, Am. Dermatol. Assn. (bd. dirs. 1990-95, pres. 1995-96), Am. Soc. Clin. Investigation, Soc. Investigative Dermatology, Radiation Rsch. Soc., Okla. Med. Soc., Coll. Physicians Phila., N.Y. Acad. Scis., N.Mex. Dermatol. Soc., Pacific Dermatol. Assn., South Ctrl. Dermatol. Soc., Austrian Dermatology Soc. (hon.), Polish Dermatology Soc. (hon.), Brit. Assn. Dermatology (hon.), RRC Dermatology RRC Dermapathology, Gourgerot Soc., Société Française de Dermatologie (hon.), Lotos Club (N.Y.C.), Equestrian Order of the Holy Sepulchre, Phi Beta Kappa. Democrat. Roman Catholic. Home and Office: 1211 N Shartel Ave Ste 202 Oklahoma City OK 73103-2425 Fax: 405-235-8000.

EVERETT, PAUL MARVIN, physicist; b. Toledo, Mar. 15, 1940; s. Arthur Marvin and Elizabeth Bernice Everett; m. Sandra Lee McClelland; children: David, Christopher. BS Physics, Case Inst. Tech., Cleve., 1962; PhD, Case Western Res. U., 1968. Rsch. assoc. La. State U., Baton Rouge, 1968—71, adminstrv. asst., 1971—72; asst. prof. physics U. Ky., Lexington, 1972—79; tech. staff Tex. Instruments Ctrl. Rsch. Labs., Dallas, 1979—83; unit mgr., sect. mgr., br. mgr. McDonnell Douglas Microelectronics Ctr., St. Louis, 1983—89; br. mgr. McDonnell Douglas Electronic Sys. Co., St. Louis, 1989—90; chief scientist, product mgr. Magnavox New Eng. Rsch. Ctr., Sudbury, Mass., 1990—91; bus. devel. mgr., program mgr. Litton Electron Devices, Tempe, Ariz., 1992—96; pres., owner Everett Cos. LLC, Phoenix, 1996—. Apptd. Ahwatukee Foothills Village Planning Com. - City of Phoenix, 1998—. Fellow, NASA, 1965—67; grantee, The Rsch. Corp., 1974—76. Mem.: IEEE, IEEE Phoenix Sect. (mem. exec. com. 2002—04), IEEE Phoenix Area Cons. Network (mem. exec. bd. 2000—, pres. 2002—05), Sigma Xi. Office: Everett Companies LLC 3825 E Mtn Vista Dr Phoenix AZ 85048-7374 Office Phone: 480-706-4753. Personal E-mail: peverett@everettinfrared.com.

EVERETT, RALPH BERNARD, lawyer; b. Orangeburg, S.C., June 23, 1951; s. Francis G.S. and Alethia (Hilton) E.; m. Gwendolyn Harris, June 22, 1974. BA, Morehouse Coll., 1973; JD, Duke U., 1976. Bar: N.C. 1977, D.C. 1979. Adminstrv. asst. N.C. Dept. Labor, 1976-77; legis. asst. Office of Sen. Ernest F. Hollings, Washington, 1977-82; minority chief counsel, staff dir. U.S. Senate Com. on Commerce, Sci., Transp., Washington, 1983-87, chief counsel, staff dir., 1987-89; ptnr. Paul, Hastings, Janofsky and Walker, LLP, Washington, 1989—. Bd. dirs. Shenandoah Life Ins. Co., Cumulus Media Inc.; mem. adv. bd. Norfolk So. Corp., Washington, 1991—; life mem. bd. visitors Duke U. Sch. Law; former mem. Pres.'s Bd. Advisors on Historically Black Colls. and Univs.; head U.S. Del. to World Telecomm. Conf., 1998; U.S. amb. to 1998 Internat. Telecomm. Union Plenipotentiary Conf.; bd. trustees Sci. Mus. Va. Former trustee Nat. Urban League, N.Y.C., 1990, 92; senate liaison Clinton/Gore Presdl. Campaign, Washington, 1992; former mem. Congl. Award Found., McLean, Va., 1993—; former mem. Fed. City Coun. Mem.: Econ. Club Washington, Phi Beta Kappa, Alpha Phi Alpha. Office: Paul Hastings Janofsky & Walker LLP 875 15th St NW Washington DC 20005 Office Phone: 202-551-1700. E-mail: ralpheverett@paulhastings.com.

EVERETT, REYNOLDS MELVILLE, JR., lawyer; b. Davenport, Iowa, Jan. 29, 1946; s. Reynolds Melville and Annette (Young) E. BS in Agr., U. Ill., 1968; postgrad., U. Tulsa, 1970-71; JD, Loyola U., Chgo., 1972. Bar: Ill. 1972, U.S. Dist. Ct. (no. dist.) Ill. 1972, U.S. Dist. Ct. (cen. dist.) Ill. 1974. Staff atty. State Nat. Bank, Evanston, Ill., 1972-74; pres. Barash & Everett, LLC, Galva, Ill., 1974—. Panel trustee U.S. Bankruptcy Ct. (cen. dist.) Ill., 1987—; bd. dirs. Peoples Nat. Bank of Kewanee. Bd. dirs. Bishop Hill Heritage Assn., Bishop Hill, Ill., 1976-84, Jet Oil Co., Tulsa, 1978-84; sec. Galva Econ. Devel. Assn., 1983—. With U.S. Army, 1968-70, Vietnam. Mem. ABA (assembly mem. 1976-82, chmn. real estate sec. 1976-82), Am. Coll. Trust and Estate Counsel, Ill. State Bar Assn., Estate Planning, Probate & Trust Coun., Henry County Bar Assn., Midland Country Club (Kewanee, Ill., bd. govs. 1983—), Rotary (local pres. 1978), Shriners, Elks. Office: Everett & Luymes PC Yocum Bank Bldg Galva IL 61434

EVERETT, RUPERT, actor; b. Norfolk, Eng., May 29, 1959; Actor (films) Another Country, 1984, Dance With A Stranger, 1985, Duet For One, 1986, The Right Hand Man, 1987, Hearts of Fire, 1987, Chronicle of a Death Foretold, 1988, The Comfort of Strangers, 1990, The Madness of King George, 1994, Ready to Wear, 1994, Dunston Checks In, 1996, My Best Friend's Wedding, 1997, A Midsummer Night's Dream, 1998, B. Monkey, 1998, Shakespeare in Love, 1998, The Next Best Thing, 1999, An Ideal Husband, 1999, Inspector Gadget, 1999, The Next Best Thing, 2000, South Kensington, 2001, The Importance of Being Earnest, 2002, Unconditional Love, 2002, The Wild Thornberrys Movie (voice), 2002, To Kill a King, 2002, Stage Beauty, 2004, Shrek 2 (voice), 2004; (tv movies) The Manhood of Edward Robinson, 1981, Soft Targets, 1982, Princess Daisy, 1983, Arthur the King, 1985, Mr. Ambassador, 2003; (tv series) The Far Pavilions, 1984, Les Liaisons dangereuses, 2003. Office: William Stein 8942 Wilshire Blvd Beverly Hills CA 90211-1934

EVERETT, TERRY, congressman; b. Dothan, Ala., Feb. 15, 1937; m. Barbara Pitts. Owner, pres. The Union Springs Herald; mem. U.S. Congress from 2nd Ala. Dist., Washington, 1993—; nat. security com., agriculture com., veterans' affairs com., and select com. on intelligence. Served in USAF, 1955—59. Republican. Baptist. Office: US Ho of Reps 2312 Rayburn Bldg Washington DC 20515-0102

EVERETT, TOM, actor; b. Oreg. BA cum laude, Adelphi U.; MFA, NYU Sch of Arts, London Acad. Music/Drama Arts. Actor: (films) The Alamo, The Island, Beautiful Dreamer, XXX, Intellectual Property, Pearl Harbor, Air Force One, My Fellow Americans, Dances With Wolves, Thirteen Days, Crazy as Hell, Mi Amigo, Vaya Con Dios (aka Hard Time Romance), Best of the Best, The Goodbye Girl, Beverly Hills Cops, Prison, Messenger of Death, Die Hard 2, Earth and the American Dream, Leatherface, Hollywood Vice Squad, others; (Broadway plays) Elizabeth I, Habeas Corpus, Emminent Domain, A Midsummer Night's Dream; numerous Off-Broadway and regional theatre plays; (TV movies) The Elizabeth Smart Story, Last Rites, Crash Landing: The Rescue of Flight 232, To Heal A Nation, Gore Vidal's Billy the Kid, Lady Mobster, Double Jeopardy, The Return of Mike Hammer, Thirteen Days to Glory, others; (TV shows) C.S.I. Miami, Alias, The Beast, The District, C-16, Pretender, JAG, E.R., Profiler, Picket Fences, Space Above and Beyond, Murder She Wrote, Cheers, LA Law, Hill Street Blues, Cagney and Lacy, Birdland, Newhart, Secret Agent Man, others; songwriter/singer (RCA album): Porchlight On In Oregon; (ind. album) Still Waters (A Collection of Years). Scholar Jacobs Pillow Dance Festival, Perry Mansfield Dance and Drama Sch.; fellow NYU Sch. of Arts, ITT Internat. Fellowship/Fulbright Competition, London Acad. of Music and Dramatic Arts. Mem. The Actors Studio. Roman Catholic. Avocations: cello, guitar, country-western music.

EVERETT, WOODROW WILSON, electrical engineer, educator; b. Newton, Miss., Oct. 11, 1937; s. Woodrow Wilson and Katherine (Thrash) E.; m. Cherry Donna Sarff, Aug. 23, 1958; children: Woodrow W., Leanne Everett Traver. B.E.E., George Washington U., 1959; MS, Cornell U., 1965, PhD, 1968. Project engr. Scott Paper Co., 1959, Ithaca (N.Y.) Rsch. Labs., Atlantic Rsch. Corp., 1962-64; postdoctoral program dir. Rome (N.Y.) Air Devel. Ctr., 1964-75; chmn. bd. N.E. Consortium for Engring. Edn., St. Cloud, Fla., 1975—. Bd. dirs. Device Assos. Corp. N.Y., Masonwood, Inc., Sunoric Corp., ITG, Inc., Thrash Homestead Corp., The Cherwood Corp., SCEEE Svc. Corp. Contbr. articles to profl. jours. Democratic committeeman, Madison County, N.Y., 1976-79; pres. Village of Groton (N.Y.) Appeals Bd., 1966-69; chmn. Groton Planning Bd., 1968-69. Served with USAF, 1959-62. Fellow IEEE (life); mem. Air Force Assn. (life), Res. Officers Assn. (life), Am. Soc. Engring. Edn. Clubs: Rotary. Home: Cherwood Pond King George PO Box 68 Port Royal Sq Port Royal VA 22535-0068 Office: 1101 Massachusetts Ave Saint Cloud FL 34769-3733

EVERETT NOLLKAMPER, PAMELA IRENE, legal association administrator, educator; b. L.A., Dec. 31, 1947; d. Richard Weldon and Alta Irene (Tuttle) Bunnell; m. James E. Everett, Sept. 2, 1967 (div. 1973); 1 child, Richard Earl; m. Milton Nollkamper, Dec. 20, 2000. Cert. Paralegal, Rancho Santago Coll., Santa Ana, Calif., 1977; BA, Calif. State U.-Long Beach, 1985; MA, U. Redlands, 1988. Owner, mgr. Orange County Paralegal Svc., Santa Ana, 1979—; pres. Gem Legal Mgmt. Inc., Fullerton, Calif., 1986—; co-owner Bunnell Publs., Fullerton, Calif., 1992-96. Instr. Rancho Santiago Coll., 1979-96, chmn. adv. bd., 1980-85; instr. Fullerton Coll., 1989-2002, Rio Hondo Coll., Whittier, Calif., 1992-94; advisor Saddleback Coll., 1985—, North Orange County Regional Occupational Program, Fullerton, 1986-99, Fullerton Coll. So. Calif. Coll. Bus. and Law; bd. dirs. Nat. Profl. Legal Assts. Inc., editor PLA News. Author: Legal Secretary Federal Litigation, 1986, Bankruptcy Courts and Procedure, 1987, Going Independent--Business Planning Guide, Fundamentals of Law Office Management, 1994; co-author: The Limited Liability Company, 2005. Republican. Avocation: reading. Office: 940 Manor Way Corona CA 92882 E-mail: 2Pan@attbi.com.

EVERHARD, MARTIN E., surgeon; b. Pitts., Jan. 28, 1933; s. Martin and Anna (Golaki) E. BS, William & Mary Coll., 1953; PhD, U. Va., 1959; MD, NYU, 1967. Mem. med. bd. Phelps Meml. Hosp., Tarrytown, 1989-94, dir., 1991. Contbr. articles to profl. jours. Bd. dirs., trustee Phelps Meml. Hosp. Lt. USN, 1953-59. Merit scholar NYU, 1963-67, Rubin scholar, 1963-67. Fellow ACS, Internat. Coll. Surgeons; mem. Westchester Surg. Soc. Office: Surg Group 8 Tarrow Ridge Rd Savannah GA 31411-3048

EVERHART, JAMES GRAY, retired manufacturing executive; b. Pitts., Aug. 29, 1915; s. Samuel Dunlap Everhart, Frances Pillow Gray; m. Levada Marie Hamilton, Mar. 9, 1940; children: Rodney Lee, Gary Eugene, Barbara Eileen Phillips. BSEE, Pa. State U., 1938; grad. mgmt. course, Am. Mgmt. Assn., 1960. Registered profl. engr., Ohio, 1938. From engring. inspector to mgr. engring. Transformer divsn. Line Material Industries, Zanesville, Ohio, 1938—55; mgr. plant Tex. Fibre Products McGraw-Edison Co., Sherman, Tex., 1955—57, v.p., gen. mgr., pres. Ill. Edison Porcelain divsn. Line Material Industries Macomb, Ill., 1957—66, gen. mgr. Line Material Industries Zanesville, 1966—70; v.p. mfg., gen. mgr. Utility Sys. divsn. A.B. Chance Co., Centralia, Mo., 1970—80; exec. v.p., 1970—80; pres. Pitman divsn. Emerson Electric Co., Kansas City, Mo., 1976—80; ret., 1980. Author: Strategic Business Planning, 1974, 1991, Business Insights for the Advancing Supervisor, 1975, Comprehensive Plan for the City of Centralia, Mo., 1987. Chmn. planning and zoning commn. City of Centralia, 1985—. Fellow: IEEE (life); mem.: Am. Mgmt. Assn. (lectr., seminar leader 1969—75, v.p. mfg. coun. 1973—75, pres.'s coun. 1977—80, Disting. Svc. award 1975), Nat. Elec. Mfrs. Assn. (distbn. transformer sect. 1948—55, chmn. high voltage insulator sect. 1964—65, bd. dirs. power equipment divsn. 1973—77, chmn. high voltage insulator sect. 1974—76), Boone County Hist. Soc. (bd. dirs. 1999—2002, exec. com. 1990—2001, Long Range Planning Program author 2001), Centralia Hist. Soc. (bd. dirs. 1995—2001), Rotary Internat., Toastmasters Internat., Eta Kappa Nu, Sigma Tau, Tau Beta Pi. Republican. Methodist. Achievements include patents for electric transformers. Avocation: music. Home: 902 Eastmont Dr Centralia MO 65240

EVERHART, LEON EUGENE, retired career officer; b. Abilene, Kans., Jan. 14, 1928; s. Charles Francis and Florence Etta (Amess) E. BS with distinction, Ariz. State U., 1957; postgrad., U. Tenn., 1965. Commd. 2d lt. USAF, 1952, advanced through grades to col., 1970, ops. officer Berlin Air Safety Ctr., 1961-63, project officer Missile Devel. Ctr. Holloman AFB, N.Mex., 1963-65, chief spl. projects div. Missile Devel. Ctr., 1965-66, tactical fighter pilot, flight commander South Vietnam, 1967-68, system program dir. Aero. Systems Div. Wright Patterson AFB, Ohio, 1968-72, dir. test engring. Devel. and Test Ctr. Eglin AFB, Fla., 1973-78, comdr. Air Force Western Test Range Vandenberg AFB, Calif., 1978-82, ret., 1982. Cons. in field. Speaker on big-game hunting in Africa and wildlife conservation for various civic and ednl. orgns. Mem. Amateur Trapshooting Assn. Ohio, NRA. Avocations: golf, trapshooting, big-game hunting, deep-sea fishing. Home: 1285 Oak Knolls Rd Santa Maria CA 93455-4302

EVERHART, ROBERT PHILLIP (BOBBY WILLIAMS), entertainer, songwriter, recording artist; b. St. Edward, Nebr., June 16, 1936; s. Phillip McClelland and Martha Matilda (Meyer) E.; m. Sheila Dawn Armstrong, Feb. 14, 1992; 1 child, Bobbie Lhea. Student, U. Nebr., 1959-62; Assoc. in Radio-TV, Iowa Western Coll., 1971, Assoc. in Graphic Arts, 1974; diploma in Journalism, London Sch. Journalism, 1983; spl. studies Mex. Indian culture, U. Okla., 1990—. Disc jockey various stas., Omaha and Juneau, Alaska, 1959-63; songwriter Royal Flair Music, BMI Pub., Walnut, Iowa, 1964—. Prodr. Bus Stop radio program, 2000—. Host prodr. (TV series) Old Time Country Music, (radio show) Old-Time Music Hour; prodr. The Great Plains and Prairie music Tour, World Music Events, American Traditional Music and Dance Festival, 1998, 2000--; rec. artist Folkway Records, N.Y.C., 1970—, Smithsonian Inst., Westwood Records, Wales, 1981, Folk Variety Records, Europe, 1980—, Allied Records, The Philippines, OGA Records, Austria, Otro Records, Poland, Prairie Music Records, Unltd. Prodns., internat. concert artist performing traditional Am. country and folk music; curator, owner Pioneer Music Instrument Mus., Am. Country Music Hall of Fame, Am. Old Time Fiddlers Hall of Fame, Capt.'s Quarters Bed & Breakfast, all located in Walnut, Iowa, and Vera Cruz, Mex., Oaktree Opry, Anita, Iowa; festival promoter Nat. Old-Time Country Music Contest and Pioneer Exposition, 1976—, Am. Traditional Music and Dance Festival, Nat. Traditional Music Performer Awards, 1991—; pres. Nat. Traditional Country Music Assn., Inc., 1982—; regular performer La. Hayride, 1985—; editor: Tradition Country Music Mag., 1980—; author: Clara Bell, 1976, Hart's Bluff, 1977, Listen to the Mockingbird, 1995; (poetry) Silver Bullets, 1979, Savage Trumpet, 1980, Prairie Sunrise, 1982, Snoopy Goes to Mexico, 1983; prodr. (TV shows) Bus Stop, Tradition, Country Life, Country Style; (TV scripts) The Life of Jimmie Rodgers, 1984, Matecombe Treasure, 1984, The Ghost of Carl Herrmann, 1993, Listen to the Mockingbird, 1998; recs. include: Let's Go, Dream Angel, She Sings Sad Songs, Love to Make Love, Bad Woman Blues, Fishpole John, Time After Time, Street Sleepers, No One Comes Near, Berlin Folksinger My Sweet Love Aint Around Compact Disc release on Otro Records, Dear Grand Ole Opry, 2001; host (TV) Old Time Country Music, 1990-97. With USN, 1954—59. Named to Profl. Musicians and Entertainers Club Iowa Hall Fame, 1994, Country Music Showcase Internat. Hall Fame, 1995, Am.'s Old Time Country Music Hall Fame; Ky. col., 1995, South Tex. Music Hall Fame, 2003; recipient Lifetime Achievement award World Music Events, Vienna, 1998, Kitty Wells/Johnny Wright Country Music Leadership award, 2000, Inspiration award Calif. Group Gordon, 2004; honored as Tenn. Amb. Goodwill by Gov. Don Sundquist, 2000; honored by Iowa State Legis., 2001, 03, Am. Profile Mag., 2004, Midwest County News, 2004. Mem. Internat. Coun. Festivals Fedn., Great Plains Old Time Music Assn., Acad. Country Music, Nat. Bluegrass Assn., Ill. Traditional Country Music Assn., Tri-State Bluegrass Assn., Ky. Cols., Internat. Bluegrass Music Assn., Soc. for Preservation of Bluegrass Music of Am., Profl. Musicians Club of Iowa, Midwest Prodrs. Assn. (chmn.), Internat. Assn. Fairs and Expositions, Carribean Club. Lutheran. Avocations: scuba diving, travel. Office: Country Opera House PO Box 492 Anita IA 50020-0492 also: Nat Traditional Country Music Assn PO Box 492 Anita IA 50020-0492 E-mail: bobeverhart@yahoo.com.

EVERHART, THOMAS EUGENE, retired academic administrator, engineering educator; b. Kansas City, Mo., Feb. 15, 1932; s. William Elliott and Elizabeth Ann (West) E.; m. Doris Arleen Wentz, June 21, 1953; children: Janet Sue, Nancy Jean, David William, John Thomas. AB in Physics magna cum laude, Harvard, 1953; MSc, UCLA, 1955; PhD in Engring., Cambridge U., Eng., 1958. Mem. tech. staff Hughes Research Labs., Culver City, Calif., 1953—55; mem. faculty U. Calif., Berkeley, 1958—78, prof. elec. engring. and computer scis., 1967—78, Miller research prof., 1969—70, chmn. dept., 1972—77; prof. elec. engring., Joseph Silbert dean engring. Cornell U., Ithaca, 1979—84; prof. elec. and computer engring., chancellor U. Ill., Urbana-Champaign, 1984—87; prof. elec. engring. and applied physics, pres. Calif. Inst. Tech., Pasadena, 1987—97, pres. emeritus, 1997—. Fellow scientist Westinghouse Rsch. Labs., Pitts., 1962-63; guest prof. Inst. Applied Physics, U. Tuebingen, Germany, 1966-67, Waseda U., Tokyo, Osaka U., 1974; vis. fellow Clare Hall, Cambridge, U., 1975; chmn. Electron, Ion and Photon Beam Symposium, 1977; cons. in field; mem. sci. and ednl. adv. com. Lawrence Berkeley Lab., 1978-85, chmn., 1980-85; mem. sci. adv. com. GM, 1980-89, chmn., 1984-89; bd. dirs. Saint-Gobain Corp., Raytheon Co.; tech. adv. com. R.R. Donnelly & Sons, 1981-89; sr. sci. advisor W.M. Keck Found., 1997—; pro-vice chancellor Cambridge U., 1998. Chmn. Sec. of Energy Adv. Bd., 1990-93; bd. dirs. KCET, 1989-97, Corp. for Nat. Rsch. Initiatives; trustee Calif. Inst. Tech., 1998—; mem. bd. overseers Harvard U., 1999-05, pres., 2004-05. Marshall scholar Cambridge U., 1955-58, NSF sr. fellow, 1966-67, Guggenheim fellow, 1974-75. Fellow IEEE, AAAS, ASEE, Royal Acad. Engring.; mem. NAE (ednl. adv. bd. 1984-88, mem. com. 1984-89, chmn. 1988, coun. 1988-94, 96-2002), Microbeam Analysis Soc. Am., Electron Microscopy Soc. Am. (coun. 1970-72, pres. 1977), Coun. on Competitiveness (vice-chmn. 1990-96), Assn. Marshall Scholars and Alumni (pres. 1965-68), Athenaeum Club, California Club, Sigma Xi, Eta Kappa Nu. Home: PO Box 1639 Goleta CA 93116 Business E-Mail: everhart@caltech.edu.

EVERITT, ALICE LUBIN, labor arbitrator; b. Dec. 13, 1936; d. Isador and Alice (Berliner) Lubin. BA, Columbia U., 1968, JD, 1971. Assoc. Amen, Weisman & Butler, N.Y.C., 1971-78; spl. asst. to dir. Fed. Mediation and Conciliation Svc., Washington, 1978-81; pvt. practice labor arbitration Washington, N.Y.C., 1981-87, Petersburg, Va., 1987—. Mem. various nat. mediation and arbitration panels including Fed. Mediation and Conciliation

Svc., U.S. Steel and United Steelworkers, Am. Arbitration Assn. Editor: Dept. Labor publ., 1979. Mem. Petersburg Libr. Found., Inc. Mem. Am. Arbitration Assn., Soc. Profls. Dispute Resolution, Indsl. Rels. Rsch. Assn., Civil War Roundtable of Richmond, Petersburg Planning Comm. Office: 541 High St Petersburg VA 23803-3859 Office Phone: 804-733-3200.

EVERITT, ELIZABETH M., school system administrator; d. William Stith; m. Tom Everitt; 1 stepchild, Brian. BS, MA, East Carolina U.; PhD in Spl. Edn., U. N.Mex., 1983. Asst. prin. Mark Twain Elem. Sch., Northeast Heights, prin.; dir. spl. svcs. Albuquerque Pub. Schs., 1995—97, asst. supt. for curriculum and instrn., 1997—98, assoc. supt., 1998—2002, one of 4-person superintendency team, 2002—03, supt., 2003—. Office: Albuquerque Pub Schs 725 University Blvd SE Albuquerque NM 87106

EVERITT-NEWTON, KATHERINE EVELYN, international management consultant; b. Cleve., Sept. 2, 1957; BS, Bowling Green State U., 1979, MBA, 1981. Sci. systems analyst Eli Lilly & Co., Indpls., 1981-83, systems tng. cons., 1983-84; customer liaison mgr. Ind. U., Bloomington, 1985, prodn. ops. mgr. Indpls., 1985-86; prin. systems cons. Wang Labs., Inc., Carmel, Ind., 1986-93; mgmt. cons. AMT-Sybex (I) Ltd., Dublin, 1994-99; sr. cons. mgr. AMT-Sybex, Ltd., U.K., Letchworth, 1999—2004; ptnr. Cogantus Ltd., Berkshire, England, 2004—. Cons. Ind. Univ., Bloomington, 1984-85, Allied Irish Bank, Dublin, Ireland, 1990-91. Contbr. (book) Introduction to Business, 1980, Introduction to Accounting, 1981, Computers and Data Processing, 1981. Republican. Presbyterian. Avocations: scuba diving, photography, biking, crafts, horseback riding. Home and Office: 2 Beaulieu Close Berkshire RG12 9QL England Office Phone: 44-07968017403. E-mail: kevoss@compuserve.com.

EVERLY, JACK, conductor; b. Richmond, VA; Grad., Ind. U. Prin. condr. Am. Ballet Theatre, N.Y.C., 1984—98; mus. dir. & condr. Ameritech's Yuletide Celebration, Indianapolis Symphony Orchestra, 1994—; music advisor Symphonic Pops Consortium, 1998—; principle pops condr. Indianapolis Symphony Orchestra, 2002—. Conducted shows including Hello, Dolly!, 1978, A Chorus Line, They're Playing Our Song, Showboat, Kismet, Carousel, The Mikado, Hazel Kirk, others; conductor Vancouver Symphony, San Diego Symphony, Lake George Opera Festival, Pacific Symphony, Ravinia Festival; music dir., orchestrator In Performance at the White House; conductor world premiers at Am. Ballet Theatre include Sir Kenneth MacMillan's Requiem, Agnes de Mille's The Informer, Mikhail Baryshnikov's Giselle and Swan Lake. Office: Indianapolis Symphony Orchestra 32 E Washington St Ste 600 Indianapolis IN 46204*

EVERROAD, JOHN DAVID, lawyer; b. Columbus, Ind., Jan. 6, 1940; s. Henry and Margaret L. (Eckleman) E.; m. Patricia Diane Hayworth, June 10, 1967; children: Andrew Quinn, Matthew Oldham. BA, Vanderbilt U., 1962, JD, 1969. Bar: Ariz. 1970, Calif. 1997. Atty. Fennemore Craig PC, Phoenix, 1969—. Mem. panels Nat. Inst. Trial Advocacy programs; lawyer Com. Uniform Jury Standards State of Ariz.; mem. faculty Continuing Edn. Legal Programs. Pres. Parochial Sch. Bd., Phoenix, 1972-78; mem. Christ Luth. Ch., Phoenix, 1969—, sec., 1986, 88-89, pres., 1979-80; bd. dirs. Combined Metro. Phoenix Arts and Scis., 1996-98. With USMC, 1962-66. Fellow ABA, Ariz. Bar Found. (founder), Maricopa County Bar Found. (founder), Am. Coll. Trial Lawyers; mem. Am. Bd. Trial Advocates, Maricopa County Bar Assn. (pres. 1992-93), Ariz. State Bar Assn. (chmn. edit. bd. Law Jour., com. revisions uniform jury instructions 1984-89, Disciplinary com. 1984-90), Phi Delta Phi. Republican. Lutheran. Avocations: scuba, skiing, sport fishing, bow hunting. Home: 6625 N 3rd Dr Phoenix AZ 85013-1103 Office: Fennemore Craig PC 3003 N Central Ste 2600 Phoenix AZ 85012-2913 Office Phone: 602-916-5302. Business E-Mail: jeverroa@fclaw.com.

EVERS, DIANE ROBERTS MACIVER, elementary school educator; b. Brookline, Mass., Mar. 13, 1944; d. Malcoln Neil and Helen Louise (McIntosh) MacIver; m. Richard Paul Evers, June 30, 1967; children: Laurel Beth, Kurt William. BSEd, Northeastern U., 1967; MEd, U. N.C., Wilmington, 1981; student, Boston U. Cert. tchr. 1st-8th grades, Mass., tchr. kindergarten-3rd grades, N.C. Tchr. 1st-2nd grades Newton (Mass.) Pub. Schs., 1967-69; tchr. kindergarten, 1st and 3rd grades New Hanover County Schs., Wilmington, N.C., 1969-70, 79-83; tchr. 1st grade Cape Fear Acad., Wilmington, 1985-86, St. Mary Sch., Wilmington, 1987—. Mem. N.C. Assn. for Edn. Young Children (past local pres.), Nat. Cath. Edn. Assn., U. N.C. Alumni Assn. (Wilmington Watson Sch. Edn. chpt. v.p. 1999-2000, chpt. pres. 2001, 02). Home: 301 Gregory Rd Wilmington NC 28405-3957 Office: St Mary Sch 217 S 4th St Wilmington NC 28401-4597

EVERS, GENE, writer; b. N.Y.C., Mar. 26, 1951; s. Lee Evers and Pauline (Leviton) Stein. AA in Liberal Arts, Nassau C.C., Garden City, N.Y., 1973; BA in Humanities, SUNY, Old Westbury, 1982. Writer L.I. Bus. Rev., Plainview, N.Y., 1978-82; staff Quaker Homecraft, Plainview, 1983-84; ind. writer Bethpage, NY, 1992—. Staff Nassau Ctr. for the Developmentally Disabled, Woodbury, N.Y., 1978-84. Author: (movie script) The Ancient Star of Christmas, 1997, (poem) I Long for the Love of Thee, (poem) My Beloved; songwriter Where My Heart Lies, The Summer Rain A Christmas Song, 1997, Candles of Love, The Northern Wind, We're Flying, Ohio, The Very Last Time; author of poetry, short stories. Named Disting. Poet of the Yr., Internat. Soc. Poets, Owings Mills, Md., 1997; inductee Hall of Fame, Internat. Soc. Poets, 1996. Avocations: model trains, weightlifting, studying history, philosophy and literature. Home: 15 Kensington Circle Apt E Garnerville NY 10923

EVERS, WILLIAM C., III, lawyer; b. Alton, Ill., June 13, 1945; s. William C. Evers Jr. and Doroty M. Gehrecke; m. Lynda Sue Vandewater, Dec. 22, 1973; children: Caren E. and W. Clark. BA, Blackburn Coll., 1967; JD, U. Kans., 1972. Bar: Kans. 1972, Ill. 1972, U.S. Dist. Ct. (so. and cen. dists.) Ill. 1972, U.S. Ct. Appeals (7th cir.) 1973, U.S. Tax Ct. 1993. Asst. atty. U.S. Dept. Justice, East St. Louis, 1972-76; pvt. practice Collinsville, Ill., 1976—; asst. atty. gen. State of Ill., Springfield, 1979-82, atty. for sec. of state, 1988-90; asst. state's atty. Madison County, Edwardsville, Ill., 1980-85. Precinct committeeman Republican Com., Collinsville, Ill., 1976—. Presbyterian. Avocations: history, politics, economics. Office: 2014 Ravenwood Dr Collinsville IL 62234-4935

EVERS, WILLIAM DOHRMANN, lawyer; b. San Francisco, May 6, 1927; s. Albert John and Sepha (Pischel) E.; m. Edwina Bigelow Benington, Aug. 26, 1950 (div. May 1978); children: Elliot B., Anne B., Albert John II, William Dohrmann Jr.; m. Britte-Marie Emblad, May 27, 1978. BA, Yale U., 1949; LLB, JD, U. Calif., Berkeley, 1952. Bar: Calif. 1952. Assoc. Chickering & Gregory, San Francisco, 1953-56; legal asst. to commr. SEC, 1956-57; assoc. atty. Allen, Miller, Groezinger, Keesling & Martin, San Francisco, 1957-60; ptnr. Pettit, Evers & Martin, San Francisco, 1960-78; chmn. On-Line Bus. Sys., Inc., 1980-82; chmn., CEO Precision Techs., 1982-87; ptnr. Chickering & Gregory, San Francisco, 1986-89, Sullivan, Roche & Johnson, San Francisco, 1989-95, Miller, Mailliad & Culver LLP, San Francisco, 1995-96, Evers & Andelin LLP, San Francisco, 1996-97, Evers & Hendrickson LLP, 1997-2000, Foley & Lardner, 2000—04; CEO QOL Health Programs, 2004—. Pres. Econ. Devel. Council City and County of San Francisco, 1978-80; chmn. San Francisco Bay Conservation and Devel. Commn., 1972-75; pres. Calif. Roadside Council, 1959-60; chmn. SPUR, San Francisco, 1975-78; chmn. assistance and adv. council Calif. Gov.'s Office Planning and Research, 1977-78; founder, pres. Planning and Conservation League, 1965-68; mem. air quality adv. bd. EPA, 1970-73; vice chmn. San Francisco Republican County Central Com., 1959-63; trustee Marin County Day Sch., 1967-70, 79-82, Katherine Branson Sch., 1976-78; bd. dirs. Yosemite Nat. Inst., 1981—, chmn. 1988-90; mem. governing council Wilderness Soc., Washington, 1984-96; chmn. Calif. Capital Access Forum, 1996. With USN, 1944-45. Mem. ABA, San Francisco Bar Assn., State Bar Calif., Bohemian Club (San Francisco). Home: 2019 Lyon St San Francisco CA 94115-1609 Office Phone: 415-202-0906. Business E-Mail: be@qolhp.com. *Intelligence, industry, integrity and humor are the essential elements for business or professional success and, of these, integrity is the most important.*

EVERS, WILLIAMSON MOORE, education policy analyst, political scientist; b. San Francisco, Oct. 18, 1948; s. Henry Kaspar and Emily Stout Evers; m. Leslie Carver Johnson, Apr. 30, 1994; m. Mary Therese Gingell (div.); children: Daniel Kenneth, Pamela Ruth. BA in Polit. Sci., Stanford U., 1972, MA in Polit. Sci., 1978, PhD in Polit. Sci., 1987. Editor-in-chief Inquiry Mag., San Francisco, 1976—80; vis. asst. prof. Emory U., Atlanta, 1987—88; nat. and vis. fellow Hoover Instn., Stanford (Calif.) U., 1988—94, rsch. fellow, 1995—; sr. advisor edn. to Amb. Paul Bremer Coalition Provisional Authority, Iraq, 2003. Adj. assoc. prof. Santa Clara (Calif.) U., 1995—98; commr. State Calif. Commn. for the Establishment Academic Content and Performance Stds., Sacramento, 1996—98; mem. math. content rev. panel State Calif. Standardized Testing and Reporting Program, Sacramento, 1998—, mem. history-social sci. content rev. panel, 1999—; mem. adv. bd. Calif. History-Social Sci. Project, Davis, 1999—; mem. Koret Task Force on K-12 Edn., Hoover Instn., Stanford, 1999—, Nat. Ednl. Rsch. Policy and Priorities Bd., Washington, 2001—02; commr. White Ho. Commn. on Presdl. Scholars, Washington, 2001—; mem. content rev. panel, history textbook adoption State of Calif., 2005. Author: (public policy research) Victims' Rights, 1996; editor, contbr.: public policy research National Service: Pro & Con, 1990, What's Gone Wrong in America's Classrooms, 1998; co-editor: School Reform: The Critical Issues, 2001, School Accountability, 2002, Teacher Quality, 2002, Testing Student Learning, Evaluating Teaching Effectiveness, 2004. Mem. edn. adv. com. Bush-Cheney Transition, 2000—01; co-chmn. Gov. Schwarzenegger's Coalition for Edn. Reform, 2005; edn. policy advisor Richard Riordan Gubernatorial Campaign, 2001—02, William Simon Gubernatorial Campaign, 2002; bd. dirs. East Palo Alto (Calif.) Charter Sch., 1997—, 1997—2004; trustee Santa Clara County Bd. Edn., 2004—. Episcopalian. Office: Hoover Instn Stanford Univ Stanford CA 94305-6010

EVERSE, JOHANNES, biochemist, researcher; b. Yerseke, The Netherlands, Dec. 2, 1931; came to U.S., 1960; s. Marinus Everse and Cornelia Geertruida Mulder; m. Kathleen Eleanor Dervin (dec. Mar. 1988); children: Magdalena Cornelia, Stephen Jay, Linda Ann; m. Melissa Lea Gunn, July 30, 1993. MA, Brandeis U., 1971; PhD, U. Calif., San Diego, 1973. Lab. asst. Philips-Duphar, N.V., Weesp, The Netherlands, 1952-60; rsch. assoc. Brandeis U., Waltham, Mass., 1960-69; assoc. specialist U. Calif., San Diego, 1969-73, asst. rsch. chemist, 1973-76; assoc. prof. Tex. Tech U. Health Sci. Ctr., Lubbock, 1976-80, prof., 1980—. NATO sr. vis. prof. U. Milan, Italy, 1980-81; vis. prof. U. Utrecht, The Netherlands, 1989; vis. rsch. scientist Letterman Army Inst. of Rsch., San Francisco, 1989-91. Contbr. over 60 articles to profl. jours.; co-editor 5 books; patents immobilization of streptokinase. Grantee NIH, 1975—, Am. Cancer Soc., 1980-81, Robert A. Welch Found., 1977-83, US Dept. Edn., 1996-2000. Mem. Am. Cancer Soc., Am. Soc. Biol. Chemists, Am. Assn. Cancer Rsch., Tex. Faculty Assn. (exec. com. 1999—). Avocation: restoration of 1953-1955 Kaiser automobiles. Home: 2613 Newcomb St Lubbock TX 79415-1707 Office: Tex Tech U Health Scis Ctr 3601 4th St Lubbock TX 79430-0001 Office Phone: 806-743-2506. E-mail: johannes.everse@ttuhsc.edu.

EVERSLEY, FREDERICK JOHN, sculptor, engineer; b. Bklyn., Aug. 28, 1941; s. Frederick William and Beatrice Agnes (Syphax) E. BSE.E., Carnegie-Mellon U., 1963. One-man shows include Whitney Mus. Am. Art, N.Y.C., 1970, Nat. Acad. Sci., Washington, 1976, 81, L.A. Inst. Contemporary Art, 1976, Santa Barbara Mus., 1976, Newport Harbor Art Mus., 1976, Oakland Mus. Art, 1977, Palm Springs (Calif.) Desert Mus., 1978, AIA, 1981, Va. Mus., 1981, Bacardi Art Gallery, Miami, 1984, Laband Art Gallery, 1985, Loyola Marymount U., L.A., Hokin Gallery, Palm Beach, Fla., 1988, Juda Gallery, London, 1988, Eva Cohen Gallery, Chgo., 1991, Lorenzelli Arte, Milan, 1992, Pavilion of Saudi Arabia, Expo 92, Seville, Spain, 1992, Capa Gallerie, Brussels, 2003-04, European Space Agy., The Hague, 2004, Osuna Art, Bethesda, 2004; represented in permanent collections Smithsonian Instn., Washington, IRS Nat. Hdqtrs., New Carrollton, Md., Calif. State Coll., L.A., Oakland (Calif.) Art Mus., Milw. Art Center, Whitney Mus. Am. Art, N.Y.C., John Marin Meml. Collection, N.Y.C., U. Kans. Art Gallery, Lawrence, Long Beach (Calif.) Mus. Art, Currier Gallery Art, Manchester, N.H., Taft Mus. Art, Cin., Cranbrook Art Gallery, Bloomfield Hills, Mich., Nat. Acad. Sci., Washington, Nat. Collection Fine Arts, Washington, MIT, Cambridge, Neuberger Mus. Art, Purchase, N.Y., Newport Harbor Art Mus., Newport Beach, Calif., Guggenheim Mus., N.Y.C., Smith Coll. Mus. Art, Northhampton, Mass., Nat. Air and Space Mus., Mus. Contemporary Art, L.A., Palm Springs Desert Mus., Rose Mus. of Art, Brandis U., Boston, Sammlung Goetz, Munich Germany, IRS hdqs., New Carrollton, Md., 1996, Rossini Sculpture Park, Briosco, Italy, 1999, Katzen Art Ctr. Am. U., Washington; artist in residence Nat. Air and Space Mus., Washington, 1977-80. Nat. Endowment Arts grantee, 1972 Mem. L.A. Inst. Contemporary Art, Artworkers Coalition. Address: 1110 Abbot Kinney Blvd Venice CA 90291-3314 E-mail: fredever@bigfoot.com.

EVERSON, CHARLES WEBSTER, musician, director; s. Charles Scott Everson and Lori Lynn Moore, Mark Richard Moore (Stepfather). BA in Bibl. Studies, Ouachita Bapt. U., 2002. Assoc. pastor Christpoint Ch., Arkadelphia, Ark., 2001—02; missionary Internat. Mission Bd., Paris, 2002—04; dir. liturgical music St. Lawrence Cath. Campus Ctr., Lawrence, Kans., 2004—. Roman Catholic. Office: St Lawrence Catholic Center 1621 Crescent Road Lawrence KS 66044 Personal E-mail: charleseverson@pobox.com.

EVERSON, JEAN WATKINS DOLORES, librarian, media consultant, educator; b. Forest City, N.C., Feb. 14, 1938; d. J.D. Watkins and Hermie Roberta (Dizard) Watkins; children: Curtis Bryon, Vincent Keith. BS Elem. Edn., U. Cin., 1971, M Secondary Edn., 1973. Cert. X-ray technician. Educator Cin. Pub. Schs., Cin., 1965—2002, classroom tchr., parent/school coord., 1965—2002; work study coord. Butler County Edn. Ctr., Fairfield, Ohio, 1997—98; long term sub. Brown County -Georgetown Sch. Sys., Gerogetown, Ohio, 1993; sr. staff asst., cpc/alcohol substance abuse, inc. Cin. Pub. Schs., Cin., 1992—93; libr. tech. media; libr. media tech. asst. langsam libr. University of Cin.cinnati-Langsam Library, Cincinnati. Dir. and coord. tutoring program So. Baptist Ch., Cincinnati, 1990—91. Author: (booklet) Gospel Music: Copywrite Laws, 1987 (1987). Prodr./dir./coord. city music festival in music hall Cin. Pub. Schs., 1972—77. Mem.: Ohio Assn. Suprs. and Work Study Coords., Music Educator Nat. Conf. Baptist. Avocations: travel, walking. Home: PO Box 8337 West Chester OH 45069 Office: Cin City Pub Schs-Woodward 7001 Reading Rd Cincinnati OH 45237 Home Fax: 513-858-6880; Office Fax: 513-758-1279. Personal E-mail: jeanwatkinseverson@msn.com. Business E-Mail: eversoj@cpsboe.k12.oh.us.

EVERSON, MARK WHITTY, federal agency administrator; b. NYC, Sept. 10, 1954; s. Leonard Charles and Marjory (Whitty) Everson; m. Nanette Rutka; 2 children. BA, Yale U., 1976; MS in acctg., NYU Sch. Bus., 1977. Staff acct., audit mgr. Arthur Andersen & Co., N.Y.C., 1976—82; with Reagan Adminstrn., 1982—88, spl. asst. to the dir., asst. dir., U.S. Information Agency, USIA, 1982—85, spl. asst. to Atty. Gen. Edwin Meese, Dept. Justice, 1985—86, exec. assoc. commr., Immigration and Naturalization Svc., 1986—87, dep. commr., Immigration and Naturalization Svc., 1987—88; various fin. and oper. positions in the United States, France and Turkey Pechiney Group, 1988—98; group v.p. fin. SC Internat. Svcs., Inc., 1998—2001; contr. fed. fin. mgmt. Off. of Mgt. and Budget, Washington, 2001—02, dep. dir. for mgmt., 2002—03; commr. IRS, Washington, 2003—. Office: IRS 1111 Constitution Ave NW Washington DC 20224-0002

EVERS-WILLIAMS, MYRLIE BEASLEY, advocate, cultural organization administrator; b. Vicksburg, Miss., Mar. 17, 1933; m. Medgar Evers (dec. June 11, 1963); 3 children; m. Walter Edward Williams 1975 (dec. 1995). Student, Alcorn State U.; BA in Sociology, Pomona Coll., 1968, Doctorate (hon.); cert., Simmons Coll.; Doctorate (hon.), Medgar Evers Coll., Spelman Coll., Columbia Coll., Chgo., Bennett Coll., Tougaloo Coll., Willamette U. Mem. staff, sec. NAACP; asst. dir. planning Clarmont (Calif.) Colls., 1968—70; v.p. advt. & publicity Seligman & Latz, N.Y.C., 1973-75; dir. consumer affairs Atlantic Richfield Co.; commr. Pub. Works Bd., L.A., 1987-95; chairwoman NAACP, 1995-98. Civil rights leader, lectr. Author: For Us the Living, 1967, Watch Me Fly, 1999; co-author (with Steven Kasher) The Civil Rights Movement, 1996, (with Harriet Jacobs) Incidents in the Life of a Slave Girl, 2000, (with Russell J. Rickford) Betty Shabazz, 2003, editor: (with Manning Marable)The Autobiography of Medgar Evers, 2005; contbg. editor Ladies Home Jour. Candidate for Congress in Calif., 1970; candidate for L.A. City Coun., 1987; head So. Calif. Dem. Women's Divsn.; convener Nat. Women's Polit. Caucus; founder, chmn. Medgar Evers Inst.; mem. adv. bd. Boys & Girls Clubs Ams. Youth for Unity and Allstate Found., 2004. Named Woman of Yr., Glamour Mag., 1995, Ms. Mag., 1995, one of Women of Yr., Ladies Home Jour., 1996, one of 200 most influential women, Vanity Fair mag., Jan. 1999; recipient Mary Church Terrell award Delta Sigma Theta, 1996, Althea T.L. Simmons Social Action award, 1998, Spingarn award, NAACP, Atlanta, 1998, Trumpeter's award, Nat. Consumers League, New Orleans, 1998, U.S. Congl. Black Caucus Achievement award, Woman of Honor award LWV, Image award for civil rights NAACP, Woman of the Yr. award State of Calif. Mem.: NAACP (chmn. emeritus, nat. bd. dirs.). Office: MEW Assocs Inc 15 SW Colorado Ave Bend OR 97702-1150*

EVERT, CHRIS (CHRISTINE MARIE EVERT), retired professional tennis player; b. Ft. Lauderdale, Fla., Dec. 21, 1954; d. James and Colette Evert; m. John Lloyd, Apr. 17, 1979 (div.); m. Andy Mill, July 30, 1988; children: Alexander James, Nicholas Joseph, Colton Jack. Amateur tennis player, until Dec. 1972; profl. tennis player, 1972-89; ret. from tennis, 1989; owner Evert Enterprises/IMG, Boca Raton, Fla., 1989—; Olympics commentator CBS Sports, 1992. Commentator NBC Sports tennis events; winner numerous tournaments including U.S. Jr. Championship, 1970, 71, U.S. Open, 1975, 76, 77, 78, 80, 82, Wimbledon Singles, 1974, 76, 81, doubles, 1976, Australian Open, 1982, 84, French Open Singles, 1974, 75, 79, 80, 83, 85, 86, Virginia Slims, 1972, 73, 75, 77, 87, European Women's Open, Geneva, 1987, Eckerd Open, 1987; spl. advisor to U.S. Nat. Tennis Team by U.S. Tennis Assn.; bd. dirs. Internat. Tennis Hall of Fame; trustee Womens Sports Found. Corp. spokesperson and rep., appearing in TV commls. and print advertisements; host and organizer Chris Evert Pro-Celebrity Tennis Classic, 1989, 90, 92, 93, 94, 95, 96, 97, 98, 99. Founder Chris Evert Charities, Inc., Healthy Start. Recipient Lebair Sportsmanship trophy, 1971; named Female Athlete of Yr. AP, 1974, 75, 77, 80, Athlete of Yr. Sports Illustrated, 1976, Greatest Woman Athlete of Last 25 Years Women's Sports Found., 1985, Flo Hyman award Women's Sports Found., 1990, Providencia award Palm Beach County Conv. and Visitors Bur., 1991; named one of Top 10 Romantic People of 1989, Korbel; inducted Madison Sq. Garden Walk of Fame, 1993, inductee, Internat. Tennis Hall of Fame, 1995. Mem. U.S. Lawn Tennis Assn. (Top Women's Singles Player award 1974), Nat. Honor Soc., Fla. Sports Found. (bd. dirs.), Women's Tennis Assn. (pres. 1982-91, exec. com., Sportsmanship award 1979, Player Svc. awards 1981, 86, 87).

EVERT, RAY FRANKLIN, botany educator; b. Mt. Carmel, Pa., Feb. 20, 1931; s. Milner Ray and Elsie (Hoffa) E.; m. Mary Margaret Maloney, Jan. 2, 1960; children: Patricia Ann, Paul Franklin. BS, Pa. State U., 1952, MS, 1954; PhD, U. Calif. at Davis, 1958. Mem. faculty Mont. State U., 1958-60; mem. faculty U. Wis.-Madison, 1960—, prof. botany, 1966-77, prof. botany and plant pathology, 1977-88, Katherine Esau prof. botany and plant pathology, 1988-2001, emeritus prof. botany and plant pathology, 2001—, chmn. dept. botany, 73-74, 77-79, 1994-98. Vis. prof. U. Natal, Pietermaritzburg, S. Africa, winter, spring 1971, U. Göttingen, W.Ger., summer 1971, 74-75, summer 1988; mem. gen. biology and genetics fellowship rev. panel NIH, 1964-68, NSF Adv. Com. for Biol. Research Ctrs. Program, 1987-88; forensic plant anatomy cons. Co-author: Biology of Plants; sci. editor Physiol. Plantarum, 1983-98; mem. editl. bd. Trees, 1991-2000, Internat. Jour. Plant Scis., 1991-98; contbr. articles on food conducting tissue in higher plants and leaf structure-function relationships. Recipient Alexander von Humboldt award, 1974-75, Emil H. Steiger award for excellence in tchg. U. Wis., 1981, Bessey Lectr. award Iowa State U., Ames, 1984, Benjamin Minge Duggar lectureship award Auburn U., 1985, Disting. Svc. citation Wis. Acad. Scis., Arts and Letters, 1985, Hilldale award in biol. sci., 1998; Guggenheim fellow, 1965-66 Fellow Am. Acad. Arts and Scis., AAAS; mem. Bot. Soc. Am. (pres. 1986-87, Merit award 1982), Am. Inst. Biol. Scis., Wis. Acad. Scis., Arts and Letters, Am. Soc. Plant Physiol., Internat. Assn. Wood Anatomists, Deutschen Botanischen Gesellschaft, Golden Key Nat. Honor Soc., Sigma Xi, Phi Kappa Phi, Phi Sigma, Phi Epsilon Phi., Pi Alpha Xi. Home: 810 Woodward Dr Madison WI 53704-2238 Office Phone: 608-262-2678. Business E-Mail: rfevert@wisc.edu.

EVERT, SANDRA FLORENCE (SANDRA WHEELER), medical/surgical nurse; b. Saginaw, Mich., Sept. 18, 1949; d. Charles William and Florence Arlene (Babcock) Wheeler; m. Raymond Clyde Evert, Jan. 20, 1968; children: Christine Michelle, Raymond Clyde II. AD cum laude, Lansing C.C., 1986. Med./surg. staff nurse E.W. Sparrow Hosp., Lansing, Mich., 1986—. Mem. First United Pentecostal, The Liberty Ch. of Grand Ledge, Mich. Mem. Apostolic Ch. Avocations: camping, bible reading, christian music, family, church functions. Home: 10 Willard Ct Grand Ledge MI 48837-1356

EVERT, THOMAS L., III, music educator; b. Phila. AA, Bucks County C.C., 1988; BA, Trenton State Coll., 1990; MA in Edn., Beaver Coll., 1991, MEd, 2001. Cert. music tchr. K-12, supr. curriculum and instrn., elem. prin., secondary prin. Pa., music tchr. K-12, supr., prin./supr., sch. bus. adminstr., sch. adminstr. N.J. Tchr. Music Trenton Sch. Dist., NJ, 1992—99, disciplinarian, 1999—. Coord., supr. summer sch. Trenton Sch. Dist., 2000—; adj. prof. Music Beaver Coll./Arcadia U., Glenside, Pa., 1993—, acting chairperson Music Dept., 2002—. Mem.: Musician Union Phila. #77, Trenton Educators Assn., N.J. Educators Assn. Office: Arcadia Univ Music Dept 450 S Easton Rd Glenside PA 19038-3215

EVERTS, CONNOR, artist; b. Bellingham, Wash., Jan. 24, 1926; s. William Edward and Sophia (Mehan) E.; children: Anon Connor, Meigan Mariko, Geoffrey, Tamura; m. Judith Asa Colman, Dec. 12, 1994. AA, El Camino Coll., 1950; BA, U. Wash., 1952. Mem. faculty dept. art Calif. State U., Northridge, 1960-62; mem. faculty dept. art Calif. Inst. Arts, 1962-65, Calif. State U., Long Beach, 1965, San Francisco Art Inst., 1966, U. So. Calif., 1967-69, U. Calif., Riverside, 1972-76; graphics chmn. Cranbrook Acad. Art, Bloomfield Hills, Mich., 1976-81. Exchange prof. Prahran Coll. Advanced Studies, Melbourne, Australia; artist in residence Calif. Inst. Tech., 1970-71 One man shows include Pasadena Art Mus., 1960, Michael Walls Gallery, San Francisco, 1967-69, Los Angeles Mcpl. Gallery, 1971, Meckler Gallery, Los Angeles, 1979, World Print Council, 1982, retrospective exhibit, Los Angeles Mus., 1983, Orange County Ctr. for Contemporary Art, 1986, Whatcom Mus. Art, 1987, Print Works Gallery, Chgo., 1988, 90, Ruth Bachofner, L.A., 1986, 89, Dominguez Hills State U., 1989, Joy Emery Gallery, Detroit, 1990, Claremont Gallery, L.A., 1995, Flowers Gallery, London, 1999, Oceanside Mus., 2001; Retrospective 1948-2002 at Union Ctr. for the Arts, L.A., 2004; review indiffernet media, El Camino Gallery, 1948-2004; exhibited in group shows at Tokyo Biann. Painting Exhbn, 1967, Homage to Lithography, Mus. Modern Art, N.Y.C., 1969, Printmaking, Oskokunst Forening, Oslo, Norway, 1974, Mint Mus., 1987, Kunstsamm-Luggen Der Veste Coburg, 1988, Norton Simon Mus., 2004; represented in permanent collections, Chgo. Art Inst., Long Beach Mus. Art, Los Angeles County Mus. Art, Milw. Art Mus., Mus. Modern Art, N.Y.C., Pasadena Art Mus., Norton Simon Mus., San Francisco Mus. Modern Art, Washington Gallery Modern Art, others. Pres. adv. bd. Los Angeles Mcpl. Gallery, 1968. With USCG, 1946. Mem. AAUP, L.A. Printmakers Soc., Mich. Assn. Printmakers, Artists Equity. Studio: 2351 Sonoma St Torrance CA 90501-3130 Office Phone: 310-328-1624. Personal E-mail: connoreverts@socal.rr.com. *Circumstances, time and place of birth, sex, race, religion, economic status, and the resultant formulative years,* *determine the rough shape of our lives. But we, above all, are the largest factors in determining the kinds of persons we become. Let it be by conscious choice. If we will be shaped, let it be by ideas and challenge.*

EVIATAR, LYDIA, pediatrician, neurologist; b. Bucharest, Romania, Apr. 7, 1936; came to U.S., 1966; d. Joseph and Ghitea (Scheinberg) Tamir; m. Abraham Eviatar, Oct. 9, 1956; children: Joseph, Daphne. BSc, Faculte des Scis., Strasbourg, 1954; MD, Hadassah Hebrew U., Jerusalem, 1961. Diplomate Am. Bd. Pediatrics, Am. Bd. Neurology with spl. competence in child neurology. Intern and resident Tel Hashoner Hosp., Tel Aviv, 1961-65; U.C.P. fellow UCLA, 1966-67, fellow in pediatric neurology, 1967-69; pediatric neurologist Bronx (N.Y.) Lebanon Hosp., 1970-79; resident in neurology Montefiore Hosp. Med. Ctr., Bronx, 1973-75; pediatric neurologist L.I. Jewish Med. Ctr., 1979-86; chief pediatric neurology Schneider Children's Hosp., New Hyde Park, N.Y., 1986-99; from assoc. prof. to prof. pediatrics and neurology Albert Einstein Coll. Medicine, Bronx, N.Y., 1989-99, chief emeritus prof. Pediat. Neurology Sch., 1999—. Co-author: (with others) Pediatric Neurology, 1988, 2004. Grantee Nat. Inst. Neurol. Disease and Blindness, 1970-77, Acad. Cerebral Palsy, 1980-81, Richmond award, 1981; recipient teaching award Am. Acad. Otolaryngology, 1983. Fellow Am. Acad. Pediatrics, Am. Acad. Neurology (cert. neurologist, child neurologist); mem. Epilepsy Soc., Child Neurological Soc. Office Phone: 718-470-3450. Business E-Mail: eviatar@lij.edu.

EVINS, DAN W., food products executive; Co-founder Cracker Barrel Old Country Stores, Lebanon, Tenn., 1969, pres., CEO, bd. chmn., 1974—2004, CBRL Group (holding company of Cracker Barrel), 1998—2004, chmn. emeritus Lebanon, Tenn., 2004—. Office: CBRL Group 305 Hartmann Dr Lebanon TN 37087

EVNIN, ANTHONY BASIL, venture capital investor; b. N.Y.C., Mar. 10, 1941; s. Oscar B. Evnin and Nina (Fradkin) Schick; m. Judith P. Ward, June 9, 1962; children: Luke B., Timothy W. BA, Princeton U., 1962; PhD, MIT, 1966. With Union Carbide Corp., 1966-71, Story Chem., 1971-74; gen. ptnr. Venrock Assocs., N.Y.C., 1974—. Bd. dirs. Icagen, Inc., Durham, NC, Memory Pharms. Corp., Montvale, NJ, Renovis, Inc., South San Francisco, Calif. Trustee Princeton U., 1997—, Rockefeller U., 1999—. Office: Venrock Assocs 30 Rockefeller Plz Fl 56 New York NY 10112-0256

EVSLIN, TOM, internet telephone service executive; b. Warner-Robins, Ga., Aug. 28, 1943; AB cum laude, Harvard U., 1965. Owner Solutions, Inc., 1972-91; dir. Microsoft, 1991-94; v.p. AT&T, Bridgewater, N.J., 1994-97; chmn., CEO ITXC Corp., 1997—. Chmn. Policy Com. of The Voice on the Net Coalition. Office: ITXC Corp 750 College Rd E 200 Princeton NJ 08540-6617

EWALD, ROBERTA GRANT, artist, writer; b. Mpls., Aug. 25, 1915; d. Oscar and Hanna Theolinda (Johannson) Grant; m. Henry C. Ewald, Sept. 7, 1946; 1 child, Grant Christian. Student, U. Minn., Calif. Sch. Fine Arts, Coll. San Mateo, Golden Gate Coll. Asst. various firms, San Francisco, 1946—64; owner, artist Travers Art Gallery, South San Francisco, 1973—86; owner, adminstr. Ewald Travel Svc., South San Francisco and San Bruno, Calif., 1967—86; founder, pres. Keyboard Prodns., 1990—. Cons. Capuchino Cmty. Theater, 1984; creator, curator WestWing Art Gallery at Sanchez Art Ctr., Pacifica, 1996—2000. Lead role, author: (musical) The Wanderers, 1978; co-producer revision, 1982, 1992; poetry, I'm All I Know, 1983; co-producer: (TV show) Pacifica, 1982; dir.: children's choirs, music events; songwriter, singer, actress, musician (piano and guitar):; writer, illustrator: poetry My View; writer, prodr., lead: (musicals) Madam Bella's Saloon, 1983; Coastside Bowl, 1988; We Meant Well, 1989; prodr.: Moving Matters, 1991, Annual Producer's Showcase, 1993—. Founder Seaside Music Acad., San Francisco State U., 1999. Recipient Merit award, Capuchino Cmty. Theater, 1983, 1984, Lifetime Achievement in Arts, City of Pacifica, 1998, numerous awards for paintings, San Francisco and Calif. art exhibits, Lifetime Achievement award, City of Pacifica. Mem.: Crystal Springs Creative Writers, Citizens Against Waste, Pacific Art Connections, Pacifica Spindrift Players (named Outstanding Mem. 1980), Art Guild, Kiwanis.

EWALD, WILLIAM BRAGG, JR., writer, consultant; b. Chgo., Dec. 8, 1925; s. William Bragg and Mary Ann (Niccolls) E.; m. Mary Cecilia Thedieck, Dec. 6, 1947 (dec. Feb. 1997); children: William Bragg, Charles Ross, Thomas Hart Benton. AB, Washington U., 1946; MA, Harvard U., 1947, PhD, 1951. Instr. English, humanities Harvard U., Cambridge, 1951-54; spl. asst. on White House staff, asst. to Sec. Interior Washington, 1954-61; with IBM, Armonk, 1961-88. Author: The Masks of Jonathan Swift, 1954, The Newsmen of Queen Anne, 1956, Eisenhower the President, 1981, Who Killed Joe McCarthy?, 1984, McCarthyism and Consensus, 1987, Tramneule Crow: A Legacy of Real Estate Bus. Innovation, 2005; asst. to former Pres. Eisenhower in preparation of 2-vol. memoirs, White House Years, 1961-64. Pres. Bruce Mus. Assocs., Greenwich, 1972-73; vestry mem. Christ Ch., Greenwich, 1986-89; bd. dirs. Eisenhower World Affairs Inst., 1984-91. Grantee Am. Philos. Soc., 1952, Harvard Found. Advanced Study and Research, 1952-53; Eisenhower Exchange fellow, 1960. Mem. Judson Welliver Soc., Phi Beta Kappa. Clubs: Cosmos (Washington); Round Hill (Greenwich). Republican. Episcopalian. Home and Office: 3 Dewart Rd Greenwich CT 06830-3418

EWALD, WILLIAM BRAGG, III, law educator, philosopher; b. Washington, Sept. 30, 1954; s. William Bragg Ewald Jr. and Mary Thedieck. BA, AM, Harvard U., 1976, JD, 1981; PhD, Oxford (England) U., 1978. Jr. rsch. fellow Queen's Coll., Oxford, 1982—88; mem. Inst. for Advanced Study, Princeton, NJ, 1988—89; Jean Monnet fellow European U. Inst., Florence, Italy, 1989—91; asst. prof. law and philosphy U. Pa., Phila., 1991—96, prof. law and philosophy, 1996—, William Ewald prof. law. Editor: From Kant to Hilbert, 1996; contbr. articles to law jours. Trustee St. Mark's Sch., Southborough, Mass., 1999—. Grantee, Alexander von Humboldt Stiftung, Göttingen, Germany, 1984—86. Home: 1520 Flat Rock Rd Narberth PA 19072 Office: U Pa Law Sch 3400 Chestnut St Philadelphia PA 19104-6204 Fax: 215-573-2025. E-mail: wewald@law.upenn.edu.*

EWALT, HENRY WARD, lawyer; b. Pitts., July 3, 1940; s. H. Ward and Jane Ewalt; m. Mary Alice Jabsen, June 1, 1968; children: Andrew, Sarah. BA in Polit. Sci. cum laude, Allegheny Coll., 1962; MA in Polit. Sci., U. Mich., 1963, JD, 1966. Bar: U.S. Dist. Ct. Pa. 1966, Pa. 1967, U.S. Ct. Appeals (3d cir.) 1975, U.S. Supreme Ct. 1984. Field atty. NLRB, Pitts., 1966-71; ptnr. Reding, Blackstone, Rea & Stewart, Pitts., 1971-75; chief labor counsel Allegheny County, Pitts., 1971-87; founder, pres. Brooks & Ewalt, Pitts., 1975-84; ptnr. Tucker Arensberg, P.C., Pitts., 1984-87; assoc., gen. counsel labor and employment law Westinghouse Electric Corp., Pitts., 1987-92, assoc., gen. counsel litigation and employment law, 1993-95; v.p., assoc. gen. counsel litigation CBS Corp., 1995-98; ptnr. Pepper Hamilton, LLP, 1998—2000. Vice-chmn. Allegheny Regional Asset Dist., 1993-96; cons., lectr. in field. Author: Practical Planning - A How to Guide for Solos and Small Law Firms, 1985, Through the Clients Eyes, 1994, 2d edit., 2002. Mem. Pitts. City Planning Commn., 1978-82; trustee Children's Home of Pitts., 1976-85; bd. dirs. Zoar Home, Pitts., 1984-88; pres. Perry Hilltop Citizens Coun., Pitts., 1970-76, pres., Depreciation Lands Mus., 1991-93; mem. Hampton Parks and Recreation Bd., 1991-93, chmn., 2000—; mem. Allegheny Land Trust, 1997—, pres., 1998-2000; bd. dirs. City Theater, 1997—, treas., 2000; bd. dirs. Pitts. Garden Place, 1999-2000; bd. dirs. Phipps Conservatory and Botanical Gardens, 2000—. Decorated Bronze Star, Purple Heart. Fellow Coll. Law Practice Mgmt. (trustee 2000—); mem. ABA (chmn. practice mgmt. divsn. econs. of law practice sect. 1986), Fed. Bar Assn. (past pres. Pitts. chpt.). Avocations: outdoor sports, gardening. Home: 4436 Mt Royal Blvd Allison Park PA 15101-2669 Office: Pepper Hamilton LLP 500 Grant St 50th Fl Pittsburgh PA 15219-2502 Office Phone: 412-874-5009.

EWAN, DAVID E., lawyer; b. Camden, N.J., June 23, 1959; s. Eugene H. and Catherine T. (Stannard) E.; m. Lisa J. Draves, Sept. 12, 1998. BA, Dickinson Coll., 1981; JD, Rutgers U., 1991. Bar: N.J. 1991, Pa. 1991, Fla. 1992, Colo. 1994, U.S. Dist. Ct. N.J. 1991, U.S. Ct. Appeals (3d cir.) 1992. Legal intern Camden County Prosecutor, 1989; law clk. U.S. Ct. Appeals (3d cir.), Phila., 1990-91; assoc. Begley, McCloskey & Gaskill, Moorestown, NJ, 1991—2001; pres. Computer Network SOS, Inc., 2002—. Cons. N.J. Land Title Assn., 2000—; sr. adj. prof. paralegal program Burlington County Coll., Pemberton, N.J., 1996—. Mem.: Assn. for Info. and Image Mgmt. Internat., Property Records Industry Assn. (bd. dirs. 2003—, co-chair real property law com. 2003—), Am. Ednl. Rsch. Assn. Home: 1009 Woodhill Ct Williamstown NJ 08094 Office: PO Box 102 Haddonfield NJ 08033

EWAN, GEORGE THOMSON, physicist, researcher; b. Edinburgh, Scotland, May 6, 1927; arrived in Can., 1952; s. Alexander Farmer and Jeannie Young (Taylor) E.; m. Maureen Louise Howard, Aug. 7, 1952; children: Elizabeth Louise, Robert Alexander. BS with 1st class honors, Edinburgh U., 1948, PhD, 1952; DSc (hon.), Guelph U., 2001, Laurentian U., 2002, Queen's U., 2005. Asst. lectr. Edinburgh U., 1950-52; rsch. assoc. McGill U., Montreal, Que., Can., 1952-55; asst. to sr. rsch. officer Atomic Energy of Can., Ltd., Chalk River, 1955-70; prof. physics Queen's U., Kingston, Ont., Can., 1970-94; prof. emeritus, 1994—; head dept. Queen's U., Kingston, Ont., Can., 1974-77. Vis. scientist Lawrence Berkeley (Calif.) Lab., 1966. Ford Found. fellow Niels Bohr Inst., Copenhagen, Denmark, 1961-62; Japan Soc. Promotion of Sci. fellow, Tokyo, 1986; recipient Radiation Industry award Am. Nuclear Soc., 1967. Fellow Royal Soc. Can., Royal Soc. Edinburgh, Am. Phys. Soc.; mem. Can. Assn. Physicists (Gold medal Achievement in Physics 1987). Mem. United Ch. Can. Avocations: golf, walking, reading. Office: Queen's U Physics Dept Kingston ON Canada K7L 3N6

EWBANK, THOMAS PETERS, lawyer, retired banker; b. Indpls., Dec. 29, 1943; s. William Curtis and Maxine Stuart (Peters) E.; m. Alice Ann Shelton, June 8, 1968; children: William Curtis, Ann Shelton. Student, Stanford U., 1961-62; AB, Ind. U., 1965, JD, 1969. Bar: Ind. 1969, U.S. Tax Ct. 1969, U.S. Dist. Ct. (so. dist.) Ind. 1969, U.S. Supreme Ct. 1974; cert. trust & fin. advisor. Legis. asst. Ind. Legis. Coun., 1966-67; estate and inheritance tax adminstr. Mchts. Nat. Bank, Indpls., 1967-69; assoc. Hilgedag, Johnson, Secrest and Murphy, Indpls., 1969-71; asst. gen. counsel Everett I. Brown Co., Indpls., 1971-72; with Mchts. Nat. Bank & Trust Co. (now Nat. City Bank), Indpls., 1972-95; from probate adminstr. to sr. v.p. & sr. trust officer, pres. Mechants Capital Mgmt., Inc., Ind., 1990-93; ptnr. Krieg DeVault LLP, Indpls., 1995—. Contbr. articles to profl. jours. Asst. treas. Ruckelshaus for US Senator Com., 1968; candidate for Ind. Legislature, 1970, 74; bd. dir. Noble Found. Ind., 1997-99, Indpls. Art Ctr., 1997-2002, Ruth Lilly Found., 1997-2002, Ctr. Philanthropy, Ind. U., Indpls., 1998-2002, Benjamin Harrison Home Found., 1994—, v.p., 1996-98, pres., 1998-2000, sec., 2003—; bd. dirs. Arthur Jordan Found., 2002—, sec., 2003-2004, vice chmn., 2004—; chmn. adv. com. ARC, 1987—. Fellow: Ind. Bar Found. (life); mem.: ABA, Indpls. Bar Found. (treas. 1976-81), Ind. Bar. Assn., Indpls. Bar Assn., Estate Planning Coun. Indpls. (pres. 1982—83), Soc. Ind. Pioneers, English Speaking Union Indpls., Kiwanis (Circle K Internat. trustee 1963-64, pres. 1964-65, chmn. internat. com. 1988-90, George Hixson Diamond fellow, past treas. Indpls. club) (Career Achievement award 2001, Tablet of Hon., Sapphire Cir. Hon.), Meridian Hills Country Club, Blue Key. Republican. Baptist. Office: One Indiana Sq Ste 2800 Indianapolis IN 46204-2017 Office Phone: 317-238-6252. Business E-Mail: tewbank@kdlegal.com.

EWELL, A. BEN, JR., lawyer, small business owner; b. Elyria, Ohio, Sept. 10, 1941; s. Austin Bert and Mary Rebecca (Thompson) Ewell; m. Suzanne E. Ewell; children: Austin Bert III, Brice Ballantyne, Harrison Dale, Jonathan Eli, Tucker Benjamin. BA, Miami U., Oxford, Ohio, 1963; JD, Hasting Coll. Law, U. Calif., San Francisco, 1966. Bar: Calif. 1966, U.S. Dist. Ct. (ea. dist.) Calif. 1967, U.S. Ct. Appeals (9th cir.) 1967, U.S. Supreme Ct. 1982. Pres. A.B. Ewell, Jr., A. Profl. Corp., Fresno, Calif., 1984-98, The Clarksfield Co., Inc., Fresno, 1989—; formerly gen. counsel to various water dists. and assn.; gen. counsel, chmn. San Joaquin River Flood Control Assn., 1984-88; CEO Millerton New Town Devel. Co., 1988-94, chmn., 1994-96; pres. Millerton Open Space and Natural Resource Plan, 1999—; regional v.p. Western Water Co., Fresno, 2001—03; pres. Lake Millerton Marinas, LLC. Mem. task force prosecution, cts. and law reform Calif. Coun. Criminal Justice, 1971—74; bd. dirs. Fresno (Calif.) Bulldog Found. Calif. State U.; bd. dirs. Fresno (Calif.) Sports Coun., 2005—. Columnist: The Wellington Enterprise. Mem. adv. com. St. Agnes Med. Ctr. Found., 1983—89; mem. San Joaquin Valley Agrl. Water Commn., Fresno County Water Adv. Com., 1989; trustee U. Calif. Med. Edn. Found., 1989—90, Fresno Met. Mus. Art, History and Sci., 1989—, mem. adv. coun., 1993—94; bd. dirs. Citizens for Cmty. Enrichment, Fresno, 1990—93; mem. Police Activities League; bd. dirs. Fresno Conv. and Visitors Bur., 1997—, pres., 2003—; chmn. various area polit. campaigns and orgns. including Reagan/Bush, 1984, Deukmejian for Gov., 1986; co-chmn. min. resources 1st Congrl. Ch., 2003—; bd. dirs. Fresno E. Cmty. Ctr., 1971—73; mem. Fresno Sports Coun., 2004—. Mem.: SBA, Millerton Lake C. of C., Brighton Crest Golf and Country Club (pres. 1989—96), Copper River Country Club, Sigma Nu, Phi Alpha Delta. Office: 410 W Fallbrook Ave Ste 102 Fresno CA 93711-5830 Office Phone: 559-437-1990.

EWELL, DENA LYNETTE, administrative management executive; b. Washington, May 27, 1966; d. Deo and Connie (Hoskinson) Clure; m. Charles Raymond Ewell, Jr., Feb. 2, 1993. Computer Sci., George Mason U., 1987. Security officer CIA, Washington, 1984-88; customer svc. rep. Sprint, Reston, Va., 1988-89; exec. asst. Summer Cons., Inc., McLean, Va., 1989-91; adminstr. Waterfall Trucking, Centreville, Va., 1991-95; bookkeeper Greg Sound & Comm., Chantilly, Va., 1994-96; fin. cons. Genesis Tech. Group, Sterling, Va., 1996; sr. fin. analyst, fin. adminstr. Gestalt Sys., Inc., Vienna, Va., 1996-99; exec. asst., strategic alliances specialist Motient Corp., Reston, Va., 1999-2000; mgr., bus. devel. eStara, Inc., 2000—03; adminstrv. mgr. Lansdowne (Va.) Cmty. Devel., LLC, Va., 2001—03; adminstr. Convergys Corp., Reston, 2003—. Recipient Presdl. Acad. Achievement award Dept. Edn., 1984. Mem.: NAFE, Nat. Assn. for Search and Rescue, The Wolf Edn. and Rsch. Ctr. Avocations: reading, hiking, auto racing, contemporary dancing. Office: Convergys Corp 11800 Sunrise Valley Dr #800 Reston VA 20191 E-mail: dena.ewell@convergys.com.

EWELL, GARY L., lawyer; b. Dallas, Nov. 13, 1952; s. Harry L. E. and Nancy (Usher) McKelvy; m. Teresa A. Oppedal, Nov. 14, 1987; children: Madeline, Anna. BA, Brown U., 1975; JD, U. Tex., 1978. Bar: Tex., 1978, D.C., 1980, Calif., 1981. Assoc. Vinson & Elkins LLP, Houston, 1978-81, Morrison & Poerster, San Francisco, 1982-83; pvt. practice San Francisco, 1983-86; ptnr. Seltzer, Ewell & Cravet, San Francisco, 1986-87, Ewell & Levy, San Francisco, 1987-97, Kuenzel & Ewell, San Francisco, 1997; ptnr., co-head Litig. Sect. Vinson & Elkins LLP, Austin, Tex. Bd. trustees Nat. Urban League, N.Y.C., 1980-86. Mem. San Francisco Bar Assn. (bd. dirs. 1983), Barristers Club (bd. dirs. 1983). Office: Vinson & Elkins LLP Ste 100 2801 Via Fortuna Austin TX 78746 Office Phone: 512-542-8526. E-mail: gewell@velaw.com.

EWELL, JOHN ALBERT, III, mathematician, educator; b. Newellton, La., Feb. 28, 1928; s. John Albert Ewell II and Carolyn E. (Fay) Ewell; m. Perdy Viola Lavik, Oct. 15, 1960; children: Ginger Astri, Lars Albert, Philip Adrian. BS, Morehouse Coll., 1948; postgrad., U. Colo., 1949—51; MA, UCLA, 1955, PhD, 1966. Tchr. Sci. Lincoln H.S., Camden, Ark., 1948—49; asst. prof. Math. So. U., Baton Rouge, 1955—57, Calif. State U. Long Beach, 1961—66; postdoctoral fellow U. Manitoba, Winnipeg, Canada, 1966—67; asst. prof. Math. York U., Toronto, Canada, 1967—70; assoc. prof. Math. Calif. State U., Rohnert Park, 1970—73, No. Ill. U., DeKalb, 1973—98, prof. emeritus, 1998—. Contbr. articles to profl. jours. Avocations: opera, music, walking. Office: Northern Ill Univ Dekalb IL 60115 Office Phone: 815-753-6746.

EWEN, H.I., physicist; b. Chicopee, Mass., Mar. 5, 1922; s. Arthur and Ruth Frances (Fay) E.; m. Mary Ann Whitney, Feb. 11, 1956; children: Donald, Jim, Bruce, Mark, David, Deborah, Daniel, Rebecca. BA, Amherst Coll., 1943; MA, Harvard U., 1948, PhD, 1951. Mem. faculty Amherst Coll., 1943; co-dir. Harvard Radio Astronomy Program, 1952-58, rsch. assoc. astronomy dept., 1958—80; v.p. Millitech Corp., South Deerfield, Mass., 1989-2000; rsch. prof. Sch. Engring. U. Mass., 2000—. Pres. Ewen Knight Corp., Weston, Mass., 1952-88, Ewen Dae Corp., 1958-88, E.K. Assocs., 1993—; sci. advisor to Cin. Electronics Corp. for USAF Air Weather Svc.; mem. Global Solar Radio Telescope Network, 1977-86. Contbg. author: Advances in Microwaves, vol. 5, 1970, Electromagnetic Sensing of the Earth from Satellites, 1967, Geoscience Instrumentation, 1974, also articles; co-discoverer 21 cm interstellar hydrogen line, 1951; remote sensing of atmospheric ozone distribution (resonant line at 102 GHz), 1966. Served to lt. USNR, 1943-46. NRC fellow, 1946-49; recipient svc. award Harvard Coll., 1977. Fellow AAAS (life), IEEE (Morris E. Leeds award 1970), Am. Acad. Arts and Scis.; mem. Am. Astron. Soc. (Tinsley prize 1988), Phi Beta Kappa, Sigma Xi. Office Phone: 413-665-7435. Personal E-mail: docewen@comcast.net. Business E-Mail: ewen@mirsl.ecs.umass.edu. E-mail: docewen@msn.com.

EWEN, JOHN A., chemist; b. 1945; m. Pamela Binnings Ewen. BS in chemistry, U. West Indies, 1972; D in organic chemistry, Tulane U., 1979. Founder ExxonMobil Chemical Co., Baytown, Tex., 1980; pres. Catalyst Rsch. Corp., Houston; sr. rsch. cons. Baseel Corp., Netherlands. Recipient Nat. Medal Tech., USA, 2002. Achievements include his innovations are documented in 49 patents and in over 24 articles in refereed jour. Office: Catalyst Consulting Inc Houston TX 77008

EWEN, PAMELA BINNINGS, retired lawyer; b. Mar. 22, 1944; d. Walter James and Barbara (Perkins) Binnings; m. Jerome Francis Ayers, Aug. 22, 1965 (div. July 1974); 1 child, Scott Dylan Ayers; m. John Alexander Ewen, Dec. 13, 1974 (div. Feb. 2003); m. James Craft Lott, Dec. 27, 2003. BA, Tulane U., 1977; JD cum laude, U. Houston, 1979. Bar: Tex. 79, U.S. Dist. Ct. (so. dist.) Tex. 81, U.S. Ct. Appeals (5th cir.) 81. Law clk. Harris, Cook, Browning & Barker, Corpus Christi, Tex., 1977—79; assoc. Kleberg, Dyer, Redford & Weil, Corpus Christi, 1979—80; atty. law dept. Gulf Oil Corp., Houston, 1980—84; assoc. Baker & Botts, L.L.P., Houston, 1980—84, ptnr., 1988—2004; ret. Author: Faith On Trial, 1999. La. Legis. scholar, New Orleans, 1976—77. Mem.: ABA (forum com. on franchising 1983—85, law practice mgmt. sect., subcom. Women Rainmakers Assn.), Tex. Assn. Bank Coun., Tex. State Bar (bd. dirs. 1994—97), Am. Petroleum Inst. (com. on product liability 1982—85, spl. subcom. to gen. com. on law), Order of Barons, Jr. Achievement S.E. Tex. (bd. dirs. 1997—2001, bd. dirs. Inprint, Inc. 2002—04). Home: 715 Kiskatom Ln Mandeville LA 70471 E-mail: pamela.ewen@charter.net.

EWER, SUZETTE ALLYNNE, music educator; b. Evansville, Ind., Aug. 20, 1962; d. Robert Wayne and Lucille Imogene (Parlier) Ewer. Student, Ind. U., 1983—84; MusB, U. Evansville, 1985; studied with, Robert H. McIver, 1991—97, David E. Brunell, 1992—, Dennis E. Northway, 2002—05. Pvt. piano/voice tchr., Evansville, Ind., 1985—, Schuttler Music Store, Evansville, 1993—2004; piano/voice tchr. Grand Prodns., Evansville, 2004—05. Musician: Evansville Philharm. Chorus, 1985—92, Owensboro (Ky.) Symphony Chorus, 1999—2002. Mem.: Am. Coll. Musicians, Keyboard Edn. Youth Soc. (adv. bd. 2003—04), Ind. Music Tchrs. Assn. (adv. bd. 2004—), Ind. Fedn. Music Clubs (judge 2000—04). Republican. Avocations: gardening, travel, ballroom dancing.

EWERS, ANNE, opera company director; BA in Theatre, MusB, Frontbonne Coll.; MusM in Opera Prodn., U. Tex. Gen. dir. Boston Lyric Opera, 1984—89, Utah Opera, Salt Lake City, 1990—2005; CEO Utah Symphony & Opera, Salt Lake City, 2002—. Bd. trustees OPERA Am.; panelist NEA. Dir.: (60 productions for more than 25 opera cos.); (Operas) Dreamkeepers, The Seven Deadly Sins of the Petite Bourgeoisie, 2003, Pierrot humare, 2005. Founder Utah Opera Young Artist Program, 1992; hon. trustee Big Bros./Big Sisters, 1999—; bd. advisors Opera Boston, 1998—, Salt Lake City Downtown Alliance, 1999—2002; mem. auditions adv. bd. Met. Opera, Utah, 1999—2004; cons., panelist NEA, 1987—; bd. trustees Salt Lake Conv. & Visitors Bur., 1995—2002; hon. chair Muscular Ddystrophy Found., Salt Lake City, 1994. Mem.: Utah Women's Forum (mem.-at-large 1997—2002), Internat. Women's Forum (mem.-at-large 1995—). Office: Utah Symphony & Opera 123 W South Temple Salt Lake City UT 84101-1403 Office Phone: 801-533-5626. Business E-Mail: aewers@utahsymphonyopera.org.

EWERS, ROBERT THOMAS, military officer; b. Lincoln, Nebr., Apr. 23, 1967; s. Robert Thomas Ewers and Donna M. Hodder; m. Elizabeth A. Robbins, Mar. 9, 1995; 1 child, Lauren M. BS in Aerospace Engring. Scis., U. Colo., 1994; M in Aero. sci., Embry-Riddle Aero. U., 2004. Flight comdr., munitions accountable systems officer 898 Munitions Sq., Kirtland AFB, 1995—98; flight comdr., sortie generation 14 Fighter Sq., Misawa AFB, Japan, 1998—2000; ops. flight comdr. 13 Space Warning Squadron, Clear AFS, Alaska, 2000—01; chief, emergency war order plans 341st Ops. Group, Malmstrom AFB, Mont., 2001—. Capt. USAF, 1999—. Office: 341st Ops Group Malmstrom A F B MT 59402 Office Phone: 406-731-6226. Business E-Mail: robert.ewers@malmstrom.af.mil.

EWERSEN, MARY VIRGINIA, retired school system administrator, poet; b. Van Wert County, Ohio, June 7, 1922; m. Herbert Ewersen (dec.); 2 children. BS in Elem. Edn., Bowling Green, 1966, Toledo and Ohio State U. Cert. tchr. K-12, reading, Ohio. Remedial reading tchr. Port Clinton (Ohio) City Schs., 1966-70, reading tchr. chpt. I/coord., 1970-94; ret. Lyrics writer Hilltop Records. Author: Keepsakes and Celebrations!, 1997, (activity card set) From Hyperactive to Happy-Active in Limited Spaces, 1979, The Lures of Pan, 2001, of poems. Mem. Internat. Reading Assn., Sandusky Choral Soc., Acad. Am. Poets, Internat. Soc. Poets, Kappa Delta Pi. Home: 1786 S Hickory Grove Rd Port Clinton OH 43452-9637 Office: 431 Portage Dr Port Clinton OH 43452-1724

EWERT, QUENTIN ALBERT, lawyer, consultant; b. Griggsville, Ill., Aug. 19, 1915; s. Albert Merritt and Anna Mabel (Beard) E.; m. Frances Norfleet, Dec. 25, 1941; children: David Norfleet, Gregory Albert, Catherine Ann, Mary Frances, Jane Cranston; m. Arlayne Joy Brown, May 1973 (div. June 1981). BA, Mich. State U., 1938; JD, U. Mich., 1946. Bar: Mich. 1946. Atty. Auto Owners Ins. Co., Lansing, Mich., 1946-47; ptnr. Ewert and Fagan, Lansing, Mich., 1947-48; sole practice Lansing, Mich., 1948-53; pres., bd. chmn. Guardsman Ins. Co., Pasadena, Calif., 1953-55; ptnr. Loomis, Ewert, Ederer, Parsley, Davis & Gotting, P.C., Lansing, 1955-87, of counsel, 1988—. Owner, bd. chmn. Communications, Inc., Grand Rapids, Mich., 1972-87; cons. TIE/communications, Inc., Shelton, Conn., 1988-91. Met. area chmn. Rep. party, Lansing, 1952. Served to lt. cmdr. USNR, 1941-45. Mem.: The Springs Country Club. Home: 16747 Thorngate Rd East Lansing MI 48823-9772 Home (Winter): 11 Mount Holyoke Dr Rancho Mirage CA 92270-3667 Office: Loomis Ewert Parsley Davis & Gotting 232 S Capitol Ave Ste 1000 Lansing MI 48933-1526 Office Phone: 517-482-2400.

EWIN, DABNEY MINOR, surgeon; b. New Orleans, Dec. 7, 1925; s. James Perkins and Lucille Havard (Scott) E.; m. Ethelyn Alexander Sherrouse, June 6, 1951 (div. 1968); children: Dabney Jr., Constance, Walton, Christopher, Leila; m. Marilyn Allison Abernathy, June 29, 1968. MD, Tulane U., 1951. Intern Jefferson-Hillman Hosp. U. Ala., Birmingham, 1951, resident, 1951-54, Ochsner Found. Hosp., New Orleans, 1954-56; chief resident Huey P. Long Charity Hosp., Pineville, La., 1956-57; pvt. practice, 1957—99; staff physician Concentra Med. Ctrs., 1999—. Staff surgeon Touro Infirmary, New Orleans, East Jefferson Gen. Hosp., Metairie, La., Charity Hosp. La.; clin. prof. surgery and psychiatry Tulane Med. Sch.; clin. prof. psychiatry La. State U. Contbr. articles to profl. jours. Bd. dirs. Christ Sch., 1979-85; sr. class Sunday sch. tchr. Trinity Episc. Ch., 1960-66. Fellow ACS; mem. AMA (life), Am. Trauma Soc. (dir. 1975-79), Am. Burn Assn., Am. Coll. Occup. and

Environ. Medicine (spkr. Ho. of Dels., 1973-75), Am. Bd. Med. Hypnosis (past pres.), Am. Soc. Clin. Hypnosis (past pres.), La. State Med. Soc., Orleans Parish Med. Soc., Surg. Assn. La., New Orleans Surg. Soc., Alton Ochsner Surg. Soc. (past sec.), So. Med. Assn. (chmn. sect. on indsl. medicine and surgery 1966-67), Soc. for Clin. and Exptl. Hypnosis, La. Psychiat. Med. Assn. Republican. Avocations: fishing, tennis. Office: 318 Baronne St New Orleans LA 70112-1606 Personal E-mail: dabneyewin@aol.com.

EWING, ALEXANDER COCHRAN, retired chancellor; b. N.Y.C., Feb. 25, 1931; s. Thomas and Lucia (Chase) E.; m. Carol Sonne, Feb. 15, 1958 (dec.); children: Alexander, Eric, Caroline; m. Sheila Cobb, Oct. 31, 1970. BA, Yale U., 1953. Bus. mgr., gen. dir. Joffrey Ballet, N.Y.C., 1963-70, assoc. dir., 1990-91; pres. Hillbright Enterprises Inc., Millbrook, N.Y., 1973-90; chancellor N.C. Sch. of the Arts, Winston Salem, 1990—2000; ret., 2000. Home: 500 S Main St Winston Salem NC 27101-5328

EWING, ANN TWAY, psychology educator; b. Tucson, Jan. 27, 1952; d. Irwin D. and Helen W. Tway; m. Robert William Ewing, Aug. 11, 1973; children: James, Michael, Steven. BA Psychology/Sociology, Occidental Coll., 1974, MA Psychology, 1975; PhD Psychology, Ariz. State U., 1995. Prof. Mesa Comm. Coll., Mesa, AZ, 1977—. Recipient Excellence in Teaching award Mesa Comm. Coll., AZ, 1997; named Advisor of Yr., Mesa Comm. Coll., AZ, 1998. Fellow recipient, WPA Outstanding Tchr. award Mem. APA (chair, comm. coll. working grp. 1997—), Western Psychol. Assn., Soc. for Teaching of Psychology (chair, long range planning 1999-2000), Coun. Tchrs. of Undergraduate Psychology; liaison Bd. Ednl. Affairs, Psi Beta Nat. Honor Soc. (pres. 1995-96, coun. mem. 1991-97). Office: Mesa Comm Coll 1833 W Southern Ave Mesa AZ 85202-4822 Business E-Mail: ewing@mail.mc.maricopa.edu.

EWING, BENJAMIN BAUGH, environmental engineer, educator, consultant; b. Donna, Tex., Apr. 4, 1924; s. Joshua Fulkerson and Bula Betty (Baugh) E.; m. Elizabeth Malone, Apr. 3, 1947; children: Melissa, Douglas Malone, Frederick Joshua. BS, U. Tex., Austin, 1944, MS, 1949; PhD, U. Calif. at Berkeley, 1959. Diplomate: Am. Acad. Environ. Engrs. Instr., asst. prof. U. Tex., Austin, 1947-55; assoc. in civil engring., asst. research engr. U. Calif. at Berkeley, 1955-58; assoc. prof., prof. U. Ill., Urbana, 1958-85, prof. emeritus, 1985—, dir. Water Resource Center, 1966-73, dir. Inst. for Environ. Studies, 1972-85, dir. emeritus, 1985—. Cons. engr., 1959— Research and publs. in water quality mgmt. and pollution control, water treatment, wastewater treatment, water resources mgmt. Trustee Urbana and Champaign San. Dist., 1974-80; public mem. Ill. Water Resources Commn., 1975-84. Served to lt. (j.g.) CEC. USNR, 1943-46. Recipient Epstein award dept. civil engring. U. Ill., 1961, Harrison Prescott Eddy award for noteworthy research, 1968 Fellow ASCE; mem. Am. Water Works Assn. (life), Water Environment Fedn. (life), Assn. Environ. Engring. Profs. Emeritus. Home: 4374 Cedar Pl Lummi Island WA 98262-8672

EWING, BLAIR GORDON, federal official; b. Kansas City, Mo., Dec. 3, 1933; s. Lynn Moore and Margaret (Blair) E.; m. Barbara F. Thompson, Jan. 3, 1959 (div. Nov. 1991); children: Blair Gordon, Chatham Boyd; m. Martha L. Brockway, Apr. 30, 1994. AB, U. Mo., 1954; postgrad., U. Bonn, Germany, 1957—58; AM, U. Chgo., 1960. Reporter Chgo. City News Bur., 1958-59, UPI, 1959-60, Traffic World Mag., 1960-61; instr. polit. sci. Chgo. City Jr. Coll., 1961-62, SUNY, Binghamton, 1962-67; planning and mgmt. cons. Harold Wise and Assocs., Washington, 1967-69; program analyst Office of Asst. Sec. HEW, Washington, 1969-70; dir. criminal justice planning DC Govt., 1970-72; dir. dept. pub. safety Met. Washington Coun. Govts., 1972-74; dir. planning and evaluation divsn. U.S. Dept. Justice, Washington, 1974-78; dep. dir. Nat. Inst. Law Enforcement and Criminal Justice Dept. Justice, 1976—. Acting dir.U.S. Office Pers. Mgmt., Washington, 1977-79, asst. dir., 1979-81, dep. dir., 1981-83; sr. exec. U.S. Office Mgmt. and Budget, 1983-86; dir. Mgmt. Improvement, Dept. Def., 1986-98; adj. prof. Law Ctr., Georgetown U., 1971-74. Author: Peace Through Negotiation: The Austrian State Treaty, 1966; contbr. articles to profl. jours. Mem. Montgomery County (Md.) Human Rels. Commn., 1975-76; mem. Montgomery County Bd. Edn., 1976-98, pres., 1982-83, 90-91; elected mem. coun. Montgomery County, 1998-2002 pres., 2000-01. With U.S. Army, 1954-56. Recipient Disting. Svc. award Office Pers. Mgmt., 1981, U.S. Dept. Def. Disting. Civil Svc. award, 1990, Presdl. Rank award Meritorious Sr. Exec., 1990; Rotary Found. fellow U. Bonn, 1957-58; Woodrow Wilson fellow, 1956-57. Mem. Phi Beta Kappa. Democrat. Home: 3 Park Valley Rd Silver Spring MD 20910-5424 E-mail: priorities@erols.com.

EWING, BRIAN KIM, engineering executive, writer; b. Viroqua, Wis., July 23, 1957; s. Myron Edward and Betty Lavonne (Crook) Ewing; divorced; children: Rebecca, Bradley, Deanna, Amy. AA in Mktg., Blackhawk Tech. Coll., Janesville, Wis., 1997; DDiv (hon.), Progressive Universal Life Ch., 2002. Various tech. and cons. positions, 1979—91, 1994—98; maintenance mgr. Panoramic, Inc., Janesville, Wis., 1991—94; lead tech. Tailormade Products, Elroy, Wis., 1998—2001; maintenance coord. U.S. Army Corp. Engrs., Eastman, Wis., 2001—. Combat sys. planner Royal Saudi Navy, Jubail, Saudi Arabia, 1986—87. Author: Surviving the Beast, 1996, numerous poems. Govs. commn. USS Wis., Madison, 1988. With USN, 1975—79. Recipient award, Wis. Sesquicentennial Commn. Mem.: Disabled Am. Vets. (life), WIs. Am. Legion, Sons of Union Vets. of Civil War (jr. vice-comdr. 2002—). Republican. Methodist. Avocations: gardening, hunting, photography, writing, poetry. Home: 43666 Hounsell Dr Soldiers Grove WI 54655 Office: US Army Corp Engrs 24545 St Hwy 35 Eastman WI 54626

EWING, DAVID CHARLES, automobile dealership executive; b. Canton, Ohio, Sept. 27, 1942; s. Stanley Clement; m. Penni Lynn West, Sept. 10, 1966; 1 child, Amy Lynn. BSBA, Bowling Green State U., 1964; MBA, Western Res. U., 1966. 1st lt. USAR, 1966-72; mgr. truck sales Ewing Chevrolet, Canton, 1966-72, mgr. lease sales, 1972-75, mgr. new car sales, 1975-81, gen. mgr., 1981-88; owner, pres. Ewing Chevrolet, Inc., Canton, Ohio, 1988—. Chmn. adminstrv. bd. Ch. of Savior United Meth. Ch., 1989—92; trustee Malone Coll., Canton, Ohio, State Coll. Found., Ohio & Erie Canalway Coalition. Mem. Greater Canton C. of C., Nat. Automobile Dealers Assn., Ohio Automobile Dealers Assn. (trustee), Stark County Automobile Dealers Assn. (past pres.), Antique Automobile Club Am. (life), Brookside Country Club, Rotary (pres. Canton 1989-90, dist. 6650 gov. 1996-97), Elks, Vintage Chevrolet Club of Am. (life), Alpha Tau Omega. Republican. Home: 2545 Glenmont Rd NW Canton OH 44708-1341 Office: Ewing Chevrolet Inc 929 Cleveland Ave NW Canton OH 44702-1895 E-mail: dce1914@aol.com.

EWING, ELISABETH ANNE ROONEY, priest; b. San Bernardino, Calif. m. James E. Ewing. Student, Mt. San Antonio Coll., 1978. Ordained priest Communion Evang. Episcopal Ch., 1998, ordained to ministry Meth. Ch. Pastor, gen. overseers, CEO St. Matthew's Nationwide Chs., N.Y.C. Mem. Rand Rsch. Corp.; mem. diplomat cir. L.A. World Affairs Coun. Co-editor: (book) Church History, 1996—98, The Church Visible, 1996—98, Life After Death, 1996—98, Bible Lessons, 1996—98; head pub. rels., assoc. editor Pinnacle Today Internat. Mag.; assoc. editor: St. Matthew Tribune. Recipient St. Augustine cross, Archbishop of Canterbury. Mem.: Knights of Malta (dame).

EWING, FRANK MARION, paper company executive, real estate developer; b. Albany, Ga., Apr. 24, 1915; s. Frank Marion and Alpharetta (Tucker) E.; m. Hanna Anderson, June 15, 1935; children: Grace Marit (Mrs. Paul Atherton), Linda Tucker (Mrs. Richard R. Mace), Frances Marion (Mrs. Brian Tennery); m. Jo Anne Bacon Hilley, Mar. 12, 1964; children: (adopted) Kathleen Melinda, Wayne Edgar, Andrew L.; m. Marilyn Hassett Petrie, Mar. 2, 1973; m. Judith H. Viets, July 24, 1999. BA (Sereno Gaylord scholar), Yale U., 1936. Pres., chmn. bd. Frank M. Ewing Co., Inc., Washington, 1937—, Lumber Distbn. Co., Petersburg, Va., 1942-57; Pres., chmn. bd. Ewing Lumber & Millwork Corp., Beltsville, Md., 1958-71; chmn. bd. Kettler Bros. Inc., Gaithersburg, Md., 1965-88; developer Beltsville Indsl. Center, 1950-89. Bd. dirs. Washington Mut. Investors Fund.; mem. industry adv. com. WPB, 1942-46; industry adv. com. to sec. commerce, 1947-50, dep. and later acting asst. sec. def., 1955-56; mem. bd. Met. Washington Bd. Trade, 1957-61 Gen. campaign chmn. Prince Georges Community Chest, 1955; bd. dirs. Childrens Hosp., Washington. Mem. Prince Georges C. of C. (pres. 1956-57) Clubs: Kiwanian (bd. dirs. Prince Georges 1948-52), Mason., Chevy Chase, Metropolitan, Burning Tree (Washington); St. Andrew's Royal and Ancient Golf (Scotland), Tryall Club (Jamaica). Home and Office: 5610 Wisconsin Ave PH20C Chevy Chase MD 20815-4415 Home: 4951 Gulf Shore Blvd N Naples FL 34103 Office Phone: 301-656-7337.

EWING, JACK ROBERT, accountant; b. San Francisco, Feb. 14, 1947; s. Robert Maxwell and Blanche Julia (Diak) E.; m. Joan Marie Coughlin Ewing, Nov. 25, 1967; children: Theresa Marie Ewing, Christina Ann Ewing. BS, U. Mo., 1969. CPA. Staff acct. Fox & Co., St. Louis, 1969-70; radio station opr. USAF, Mountain Home, Idaho, 1970-72; internal auditor Air Force Audit Agy., Warren, Wyo., 1972-74; supr. auditor Fox & Co., St. Louis, 1974-79; audit mgr. Erickson, Hunt & Spillman, P.C., Ft. Collins, Colo., 1979-82; stockholder, owner Hunt, Spillman & Ewing, P.C., Ft. Collins, Colo., 1982-93; owner Jack R. Ewing, CPA, 1993—. Mem., pres. Parent Adv. Bd., Beattie Elem. Sch., 1982-83, 86-87; mem. Entrepreneur of Yr. Selection Com., Ft. Collins, Colo., 1989-92, Suicide Resource Ctr. of Larimer County, Ft. Collins, Colo., 1992—, pres., 1998—, bd. dirs.; mem. Leadership Ft. Collins-Class of 1992, State of Colo. Mental Health Planning Coun., 1993—; dir. treas. One West Contemporary Art Ctr., 1989-97—, Ctr. for Diversity in Work Place, 1991—; pres., adv. bd. Larimer County Bd. Mental Health, 1992-99; v.p. Colo. Behavioral Healthcare Coun., 1995-97; mem. mental health pro bono project, 1996-97; mem. gov.'s citizen panel on suicide prevention, 1998—; indicators and outcomes com. Mental Health Performance; planning steering com. Mental Health and Substance Abuse. Mem. Am. Inst. CPAs, Colo. Soc. CPAs. Avocations: writing, hiking. Office: 3112 Meadowlark Ave Fort Collins CO 80526-2843

EWING, JAMES E., priest; m. Elisabeth Anne Rooney. DD, ThD. Ordained priest Communion Evang. Episcopal Chs., 1951. Sr. pastor, gen. overseer, pres. bd. govs. and counselors St. Matthew's Nationwide Chs., N.Y.C., 1951—. Mem. Rand Rsch. Corp.; mem. diplomat cir. L.A. World Affairs Coun. Co-author, editor: book Church History, The Church Visible, Life After Death, Bible Lessons, pub., editor, author: Pinnacle Today. With USAF, 1953—57. Recipient St. Augustine cross, Archbishop of Canterbury. Mem.: Sovereign Order St. John of Jerusalem, Knights of Malta.

EWING, JOHN HARWOOD, mathematics professor, department chairman, professional society administrator; b. Bronxville, NY, Nov. 25, 1944; s. Robert Edward and Virginia (Harwood) E.; m. Janice Rusche, May 22, 1965; children: Scott Andrew, Jennifer Beth, Amy Sarah. BS, St. Lawrence U., Canton, N.Y., 1966; MS, PhD, Brown U., 1971; DS (hon.), St. Lawrence U., 1996. Instr. Dartmouth Coll., Hanover, N.H., 1971-73; asst. prof., assoc. prof. math. Ind. U., Bloomington, 1973, prof., chmn. dept., 1986-89, 92-95; exec. dir. Am. Math. Soc., Providence, 1995—. Sci. and Engring. rsch. Coun. fellow U. Newcastle, Eng., 1980-81; Sonderforschungsbereicht fellow U. Goettingen, Germany, 1985-86; series editor Springer-Verlag, N.Y.C., 1987-95. Author: Puzzle It Out, 1981; editor: Numbers, 1990, Celebrating 50 Years of Mathematics, 1991, A Century of Mathematics, 1994, Towards Excellence, 1999; editor-in-chief Math. Intelligencer, 1980-86, Am. Math. Monthly, 1992-96; also over 40 articles. Recipient Lester R. Ford award, 1976, George Polya Lectr. award, 1991—92, Polya award, 1996. Fellow, mem. AAAS; mem. Am. Math. Soc., Math. Assn. Am., Soc. Indstl. & Applied Math., Assn. Women in Math. Episcopalian. Office: Am Math Soc 201 Charles St Providence RI 02904 Office Phone: 401-455-4100. Business E-Mail: jhe@ams.org.

EWING, JOSEPH NEFF, JR., retired lawyer; b. Bryn Mawr, Pa., Nov. 10, 1925; s. Joseph Neff and Anne (Ashton) Ewing; m. Margaret Converse Howe, Dec. 22, 1951; children: Margaret E. Lloyd, Anne A., Elizabeth M. Peifer. AB, Princeton U., 1947; JD, U. Pa., 1953. Bar: Pa. 1954, U.S. Supreme Ct. 1978, U.S. Tax Ct. 1992. Assoc. Saul, Ewing, Remick & Saul, Phila., 1953-63, ptnr., 1963-95, of counsel, 1996—. Bd. govs. Main Line Health, Inc., 1988—95; trustee Bryn Mawr Hosp., 1969—96, Bryn Mawr Hosp. Found., 1981—98, Hist. Sugartown, Inc., Malvern, Pa., 1990—98, Dunwoody Village, Inc., 1997—, 1st vice chmn., 1999—2004, chmn., 2004—; chancellor Clan Ewing in Am., 1998—2004. Chmn. Willistown Twp. Planning Commn., Malvern, 1960—69, chmn. bd. suprs., 1970—82, chmn. zoning hearing bd., 1985—95, East Goshen Twp., 1996—; chmn. spl. contacts divsn. Phila. United Fund, 1965—66; mem. hosp. coun. southeastern Pa. Mental Health Assn., Phila., 1967—68; elder Paoli (Pa.) Presbyn. Ch., 1970—72; pres. bd. trustees Embreeville (Pa.) State Hosp., 1965—72. Sgt. USMC, 1944—46, sgt. USMC, 1950—51. Mem.: ABA, Pa. Soc. Healthcare Attys. (pres. 1975—77), Nat. Assn. R.R. Trial Counsel, Phila. Assn. Def. Counsel (pres. 1973), Phila. Bar Assn. (med.-legal com. 1962—76, chmn. 1971), Waynesborough Country Club (v.p. 1965—69). Avocations: sailing, photography, gardening, genealogy. Home: 1109 Lincoln Dr West Chester PA 19380-5721 Personal E-mail: joenewing@aol.com.

EWING, KY PEPPER, JR., lawyer; b. Victoria, Tex., Jan. 7, 1935; s. Ky Pepper and Sallie (Dixon) E.; m. Almuth Rott, Apr. 6, 1963; children: Kenneth Patrick, Kevin Andrew, Kathryn Diana. BA cum laude, Baylor U., 1956; LLB cum laude, Harvard U., 1959. Bar: D.C. 1959, U.S. Supreme Ct 1963. Assoc. firm Covington & Burling, Washington, 1959-64; partner firm Prather, Seeger, Doolittle, Farmer & Ewing, Washington, 1964-77; dep. asst. atty. gen. antitrust div. Dept. Justice, Washington, 1978-80; ptnr. Vinson & Elkins, Washington, 1980—2001, of counsel, 2002—03. Mem. Washington Inst. Fgn. Affairs. Author: Competition Rules for the 21st Century: Principles from America's Experience, 2003; co-editor-in-chief: State Antitrust Practice and Statutes, 3 Vols., 1990; mem. antitrust adv. bd. Antitrust and Trade Regulation Report Bur. Nat. Affairs, 1990—; mem. edit. bd. Antitrust Report Matthew Bender & Co., 1993—. Pres. Potomac Valley League, 1977, Carderock Springs Citizens Assn., 1975-78. Fellow: Am. Bar Found. (life); mem.: ABA (chmn. legis. com. antitrust sect. 1987—91, coun. antitrust sect. 1991—94, fin. officer antitrust sect. 1994—96, chmn. FTC/Dept. Justice working group 1994—97, mem. Ho. of Dels. 1996—98, vice chair antitrust sect. 1998—99, chair-elect antitrust sect. 1999—2000, chair antitrust sect. 2000—01, chmn. nominating com. antitrust sect. 2002—03), D.C. Bar Assn., Internat. Bar Assn. (editl. bd. Bus. Law Internat.), Met. Club. Republican. Episcopalian. Home: 8317 Comanche Ct Bethesda MD 20817-4561 Office: The Willard Office Bldg Rm 719 1455 Pennsylvania Ave NW Washington DC 20004-1013 Office Phone: 202-639-6580. Business E-Mail: kewing@velaw.com.

EWING, PATRICK ALOYSIUS, professional basketball coach; b. Kingston, Jamaica, Aug. 5, 1962; m. Rita Ewing; children: Patrick Aloysius, Randi. BFA, Georgetown U., 1985. Basketball player N.Y. Knickerbockers, NYC, 1985—2000, Seattle SuperSonics, 2000—01, Orlando Magic, Fla., 2001—02; asst. coach Washington Wizards, 2002—03, Houston Rockets, 2003—. Mem. U.S. Olympic Basketball Teams, 1984, 92. Named Divsn. I Most Outstanding Player, NCAA, 1984, Coll. Player of Yr., Sporting News, 1985, 1985, Rookie of Yr., NBA, 1986; named to All-Am. 1st team, Sporting News, 1985, All-Star team, 1986, 1988—93, All-Am. 2d team, 1983—84, NBA All-Star team, 1986—95, All-NBA 2d team, 1988, All-Defensive 2d team, 1988, 1989, All-NBA 2d team, 1989, All-NBA 1st team, 1990, All-NBA 2d team, 1991, All-Defensive 2d team, 1992, All-NBA 2d team, 1992; recipient Naismith award, 1985, Gold medal, U.S. Olympic Basketball Team. Achievements include being a player in NCAA divsn. I championship team, 1984; being a holder of NBA Finals series record for most blocked shots (30), 1994; being co-holder of NBA finals single-game record most block shots (8), 1994. Office: Houston Rockets 1510 Polk St Houston TX 77002-1099*

EWING, R. STEWART, telecommunications company executive; BA in Bus., Northwestern State U., Natchitoches, La. CPA. V.p. fin. Century Tel Inc., Monroe, La., 1983-84, v.p., contr., 1984-89, sr. v.p., CFO, 1989-99, exec. v.p., CFO, 1999—. Bd. dirs. Progressive Bank. Sr. warden St. Alban's Episcopal Ch.; bd. dirs. N.E. La. Children's Mus.; treas. St. Frederick's H.S. Athletic Assn., Monroe, La.; bd. dirs., treas. Grace Episcopal Sch., Monroe. Mem. AICPA, Am. Mgmt. Assn., Nat. Assn. Accts., La. Soc. CPAs. Office: Century Tel Inc 100 Century Park Dr Monroe LA 71203

EWING, RAYMOND CHARLES, retired ambassador; b. Cleve., Sept. 7, 1936; s. Thomas Davis and Marion (Andrews) E.; m. Jerelyn Patten, Jan. 19, 1962; children: Gregory, Thomas, Joyce, Lillian Patten. BA, Occidental Coll., 1957; MPA, Harvard U., 1970. Joined Fgn. Svc., Dept. State, 1957; various assignments in Washington, Bern, Switzerland, Rome, Lahore, Pakistan, Vienna, Tokyo, 1957-1977; dir. Office So. European Affairs, Dept. State, Washington, 1977-79; mem. Sr. Seminar, Washington, 1979-80; dep. asst. sec. of state for European affairs, 1980-81; amb. to Cyprus Nicosia, 1981-84; dean Sch. Lang. Studies Fgn. Svc. Inst., Washington, 1985-87; dir. Office Career Devel. and Assignments, Dept. State, 1987-89; amb. to Ghana, 1989-92; chargé d'affaires, a.i. to Tanzania Dar es Salaam, 1992; ret., 1993; mng. editor Mediterranean Quarterly, Washington, 1994—. Mem. Am. Fgn. Svc. Assn., Diplomatic and Consular Officers (ret., bd. govs., 2005-), Cyprus Am. Archaeol. Rsch. Inst. (bd. dirs. 2000), Sr. Seminar Alumni Assn. (pres. 2004—). Presbyterian. Avocations: tennis, golf, travel, reading.

EWING, RICHARD EDWARD, mathematics, chemical and petroleum engineering educator; b. Kingsville, Tex., Nov. 24, 1946; s. Floyd Ford and Olivia Clara (Henrichson) E.; m. Rita Louise Williams, Aug. 8, 1970; children: John Edward, Lawrence Alan, Bradley William. BA, U. Tex., 1969, MA, 1972, PhD, 1974; doctorate (hon.), U. Bergen, Norway, 1996, Shadong U., China, 1987. Asst. prof. Oakland U., Rochester, Mich., 1974-77, Ohio State U., Columbus, 1977-80, assoc. prof., 1980-81; sr. rsch. mathematician Mobil R & D Corp., Dallas, 1980-82, assoc. mathematician, 1982-83; prof. math., petroleum and chem. engring. U. Wyo., Laramie, 1983-92, J.E. Warren dist. prof. energy and environ., 1984-92, dir. Enhanced Oil Recovery Inst., 1984-92, dir. Inst. for Sci. Computation, 1986-92, dir. Ctr. for Math. Modeling, 1986-92, Wold Centennial chair in energy, 1991-92; dean Coll. Sci. Tex. A&M U., College Station, 1992-2000, prof. math. and engring., 1992—, dir. Inst. for Sci. Computation, 1992—, disting. rsch. chair TEES, 1992, dir. Acad. Advanced Telecom. and Learning Techs., 1996-2000, Dist. prof. math. and engring., 1998—, v.p. for rsch., 2000—; chair in sci. computing Mobil Tech. Co., 1999—, Harrison Endowed chair in Sci., 1999—. Adj. prof. Rice U., Houston, 1980—84, U. Tex., 1998—; adv. res. Inst. Petroleum, Beijing, 1987—; adv. Rsch. Inst. Petroleum, 1987—; steering com. Ctr. for Fluid Dynamics and Geoscis., Columbia, SC, 1987—; hon. prof. Shandong U., China, 1987; adv. bd. Ctr. Sci. Computing, Jyväskylä, Finland, 1990—, Improved Oil Recovery Ctr., Bergen, Norway, 1990—, Interdisciplinary Ctr. Computational Sci., Heidelberg, Germany, 1992—, Inst. Biosci. Tech., Houston, 1992—; acad. adv. bd. Dow Chem., 1994—; exec. com. Patrnership Computational Scis., Oak Ridge Nat. Lab., 1991—98; pres. Environ. Modelling and Analysis Corp., 1991—; sci. adv. bd. Inst. for Math. Scis., Alta, Canada, 1996—; bd. dirs. Nat. space Biomed. Rsch. Inst., Houston Tech. Ctr., Associated Western U., Southeastern U. Rsch. Assocs., Oak Ridge Assocs. U., Tex. Healthcare and Biosci. Inst., Tex. Soc. Biomed. Rsch., Tex. Inst. for Genomic Medicine; adv. coun. NASA, 2001—03, Tex. Coun. on Environ. Tech., 2001—; hon. guest rschr. Wuhan U., China, 1997—; adj. prof. U. Tex., Houston, 1998—; sci. bd. Indsl. Math. Inst., U.S.C., 1999—; cons. in field; coun. mem. Harte Rsch. Inst., 2001—; pres. Tex. Giga POP, 2002—04; fgn. mem. Acad. Europaea, 2005. Author: The Mathematics of Reservoir Simulation, 1983, Mathematical Modeling in Energy and Environmental Sciences, 1988; contbr. articles to sci. jours., chpts. to books. Cubmaster Boy Scouts Am., Dallas, 1981, Webelos leader, 1982, asst. scoutleader, Laramie, 1984, asst. scoutmaster, College Station, 1995—. Recipient NASA Pub. Svc. medal, 2003, Innovative Rsch. award Chinese Assn. for Sci. and Tech., 2004, Humboldt Rsch. award Sr. U.S. Scientists, 2005; numerous rsch. grants NSF, Dept. Energy, NRC, DOD, oil cos., others, 1978—. Fellow AAAS; mem. Soc. Petroleum Engrs., Soc. Indsl. and Applied Math. (trustee 1986-93), Am. Math. Soc., Math. Assn. Am., Internat. Assn. for Math. and Computers in Simulation, Internat. Assn. Computer Mech. (trustee 1991—), Inst. for Advancement Sci. Computing (trustee 1987-93), Geoscis. Inst. (bd. dirs. 1988-92), N.Y. Acad. Scis., Internat. Computer Club (sci. coun. 1989—). Democrat. Avocations: skiing, tennis, stamp and coin collecting. Home: 2004 Indian Trl College Station TX 77845-5600 E-mail: richard-ewing@tamu.edu.

EWING, ROBERT CLARK, lawyer; b. Lower Merion, Pa., Nov. 26, 1957; m. Cheralynn Kennedy, Mar. 22, 1986; children: Edward, Jaesun; stepchildren: Kristin, Shannon. BS in Fin., Pa. State U., 1980; JD, Villanova U., 1983. Bar: Pa. 1983, U.S. Dist. Ct. (ea. dist.) Pa. 1985, U.S. Ct. Appeals (3rd cir.) 1987, U.S. Supreme Ct. 1987. Ranger Pa. State Park Svc., 1976-78, Valley Forge Nat. Park, 1979; police officer Ocean City (Md.) Police Dept., 1980-81, Springfield Twp. Delaware County, 1992-99; assoc. Lagoy & Lyons, West Chester, Pa., 1983-86, Ronald H. Silverman, P.C., King of Prussia, Pa., 1986-88, Anthony J. McNulty & Assocs., Media, Pa., 1988-91; pvt. practice Media, Pa., 1991—. Contbr. articles to profl. jours. Mem. Lima (Pa.) Fire Co., 1973—, bd. dirs., 1981-88; mem. Media (Pa.) Fire Co., 1988—; bd. dirs. Hank Nacrelli Scholarship Fund, 1988-97, Delaware County Emergency Health Svcs. Coun., 1986-93; active Delaware County Critical Incident Stress Mgmt. Program, Media, 1987—. Mem. ATLA, Delaware County Bar Assn., Pa. Trial Lawyers Assn. Office: 115 N Monroe St PO Box 728 Media PA 19063

EWING, RUSSELL CHARLES, II, physician; b. Tucson, Aug. 16, 1941; s. Russell Charles and Sue M. (Sawyer) E.; children: John Charles, Susan Lenore. BS, U. Arizona, 1963; MD, George Washington U., 1967. Diplomate Am. Bd. Family Practice. Intern L.A. County-U. So. Calif. Med. Ctr., L.A., 1967-68; gen. practice in medicine and surgery Yorba Linda and Placentia, Calif., 1970—96; correctional psychiatrist, 1998—; gen. practice in medicine and surgery Brea, Calif., 1996-97; mem. staff St. Jude's Hosp., Fullerton, Calif., 1970-98, Placentia Linda Cmty. Hosp., 1972-98; vice chief staff, 1977-78; chief staff, 1978-80; bd. dirs., 1974-81; sec., dir. Yorba Linda Med. Group, Inc., 1974-90. Bd. dirs. We. Empire Savs. & Loan Assn., Calif., Ewing Enterprises. Prin. Yorba Linda YMCA, 1973-88, pres., 1973-74, 81. With USN, 1968-70. Fellow Am. Acad. Family Practice; mem. AMA, Am. Coll. Physician Execs., Calif. Med. Assn. (ho. of dels. 1978-90, 92-99, trustee 1990-92), Orange County Med. Assn. (bd. dirs. 1983-90, pres. 1988-89). Republican. Episcopalian. Home and Office: 2300 Iron Pt Rd #1113 Folsom CA 95630-8489

EWING, SCOTT EDWIN, physiatrist, educator; b. Seattle, July 2, 1956; s. Edwin Stanley Jr. and Mary Alice (Castleman) E.; m. Eileen Smith, June 9, 1990; 1 child, Edwin Stanley III. BS, U. Mich., 1980; DO, Midwestern U., 1989. Diplomate Am. Osteo. Bd. Neurology and Psychiatry; MD, Mass. Resident in psychiatry Mass. Gen. Hosp., Boston, 1991-94; clin. fellow in psychiatry Harvard Med. Sch., Boston, 1991-94; chief resident in psychiatry Mass. Gen. Hosp., Boston, 1993-94; fellow in psychopharmacology Harvard Med. Sch., Boston, 1994-95; psychiatrist in charge short term unit McLean Hosp., Belmont, Mass., 1995-96; instr. in psychiatry Harvard Med. Sch., Boston, 1995—; dir. depression and anxiety disorders outpatient clinic McLean Hosp., Belmont, 1996—. Cons. Harvard Pilgrim Health Plan, Boston, 1995-2003. Contbg. author: (book) Challenges in Psychiatric Treatment: Pharmacologic and Psychosocial Strategies, 1996; patentee in field. Mem. Nat. Trust for Hist. Preservation, Washington, 1995—. Recipient Outstanding Resident award NIMH, 1992, Laughlin fellowship Am. Coll. Psychiatrists, 1993, Dupont-Warren fellowship Harvard Med. Sch. Dept. of Psychiatry, 1994-95, Livingston award, 1995. Mem. AMA, Am. Psychiat. Assn., Am. Osteo. Assn., N.Y. Acad. Scis., Am. Coll. Neuropsychiatrists, Harvard Club of Boston, Harvard Faculty Club, Sigma Sigma Phi. Avocations: creative writing, photography, athletics. Office: Harvard U Place Ste 200N 124 Mt Auburn St Cambridge MA 02138

EWING, SIDNEY ALTON, veterinary medical educator, parasitologist; b. Emory University, Ga, Dec. 1, 1934; s. Aubrey Coleman and Grace Eliza (Prickett) E.; m. Margaret Jane Steffens, Aug. 16, 1963; children— Holly Annette, Ann Krull, Leah Grace. BSA, DVM, U. Ga., 1958; MS, U. Wis., 1960; PhD, Okla. State U., 1964. Instr. U. Wis., 1960; mem. faculty Okla. State U., Stillwater, 1960—65, 1968—72, prof., head dept. vet. parasitology, microbiology and public health, 1968—72, 1979—84, prof., 1984—91, interim assoc. dean for acad. affairs, 1991—92, 2001—03, Wendell H./Nellie G. Krull endowed prof. vet. parasitology, 1992—2003, Wendell H./Nellie G. Krull prof. emeritus, 2004—; assoc. prof. Kans. State U., 1965—67; prof., head dept. Miss. State U., 1967—68; prof., dean Coll. Vet. Medicine, U. Minn., St. Paul, 1972—78. Mem. adv. bd. Morris Animal Found., Denver, 1967-69, cons., 1969-78; mem. animal health com. NRC, 1971-75; mem. adv. panel U.S. Pharmacopeial Conv., 1980-95. Recipient Outstanding Tchr. of Yr. award Okla. State U. Coll. Vet. Medicine, 1970, SmithKline Beecham award for rsch. excellence Okla. State U., 1991, A.M. Mills award for outstanding contbns. to vet. medicine, 1993, Good Neighbor award Radio Sta. WCCO, Mpls.-St. Paul, 1978; commendation Gov. Minn., 1978; named Veterinarian of Yr., State of Okla., 1997; named to Okla. Higher Edn. Hall of Fame, 2000, Disting. Vet. Parasitologist Am. Assn. Vet. Parasitologists, 2002. Mem. AAUP, AVMA, Am. Assn. Vet. Parasitologists, Am. Soc. Parasitologists, Am. Vet. Med. History Soc., Am. Soc. Rickettsiology, World Assn. Advancement Vet. Parasitology, Conf. Rsch. Workers in Animal Diseases (coun. 1980-85, v.p. 1983-84, pres. 1984-85), Soc. Vector Ecology, Soc. Tropical Vet. Medicine, Minn. Vet. Med. Assn., Okla. Vet. Med. Assn., NY Acad. Sci., Southwestern Assn. of Parasitologists (program officer, pres. elect 2001-02, pres. 2002-2003), Sigma Xi, Phi Kappa Phi, Phi Zeta, Alpha Zeta, Alpha Psi (past nat. pres.), Gamma Sigma Delta, Aghon, Omicron Delta Kappa. Office: Okla State U Dept Vet Pathobiology Stillwater OK 74078-2005 Office Phone: 405-744-8177. Business E-Mail: saewing@cvm.okstate.edu.

EWING, SUSAN R., art educator, artist; b. Lawrenceville, Ill., 1955; AA in Music, Stephens Coll., 1974; BA in Jewelry, Metalsmithing, Ind. U., 1976, MFA in Jewelry, Metalsmithing, 1980. Head metals program Miami (Ohio) U., 1981—. One-person shows include Hans Hansen Sølv, Copenhagen, Denmark, Nat. Tech. Mus., Prague, Czech Republic, Phoenix Mus. Art, Ohio Craft Mus., Columbus, Ork. Art Ctr., Little Rock; group shows include Aspects Gallery, London, Park Ryu Sook Gallery, Seoul, Korea, Schweizerisches Landesmuseum, Zurich, Switzerland, Cercle Mcpl. Galerie Oféo, Luxembourg, Mus. Kunsthandwerk, Frankfurt, Germany, Deutsches Klingenmuseum, Solingen, Germany, Schmuckmuseum, Pforzheim, Germany, Galerie Matter, Cologne, Germany, Galerie Ende, Cologne, Mathildenhohe Mus., Darmstadt, Germany, Galerie Spectrum, Munich, Germany, Galerie Ventil, Munich, Fortunoff's N.Y.C., Urban BobKat Gallery, N.Y.C., Lever House, N.Y.C., Seventh Regiment Armory, N.Y.C., Am. Craft Mus., N.Y.C.; represented in permanent collections White House. Recipient Dolibois Faculty Devel. award, disting. Lifetime Achievement award Ohio Designer Craftsmen; Summer Rsch. fellow Miami U., Ohio Arts Coun. Individual Artist fellow, 1987, 89, 91, Fulbright grantee, 1997, 98; Rsch. Challenge grantee Ohio State Bd. Regents. Office: Sch Art Fine Arts Dept Miami U Oxford OH 45056

EWING, THOMAS WILLIAM, congressman, lawyer; b. Atlanta, Ill., Sept. 19, 1935; m. Connie Lupo, 1981; children: Jane, Kathryn, Sam, Christine Lupo, John Lupo, Stephanie Lupo. BS, Millikin U., 1957; JD, John Marshall Law Sch., Chgo., 1968. Asst. state atty. Livingston County, 1968-73; ptnr. Satter Ewing Beyer & Spires, Pontiac, Ill., 1969-91; mem. Ill. Ho. of Reps., 1974-91, U.S. Congress from 15th Ill. Dist., 1991-2001; mem. sci. com., agr. subcom., transp. and infrastructure coms., house adminstrn. com.; of counsel Davis and Harman L.L.P., Washington. Mem. agr. com. Ill. Ho. Reps., chmn. subcom. on risk mgmt. and specialty crops, subcom. on dept. ops., nutrition and fgn. agr., transp. and infrastructure com., aviation subcom., water resources and environment subcom., joint econ. com., former dep. minority leader, chmn. policy com., house revenue com., 1980, co-chmn. Ill. Econ. and Fiscal Commn., co-chmn. Legis. Space Needs Commn.; mem. biotech adv. coun. Monsanto, chmn. grower adv. coun.; chmn. biomass R&D tech. adv. com. Dept. Agr., Dept. Energy; bd. dirs. Pontiac Nat. Bank Holding Co., Inst. Representative Govt., Washington, D.C. Rep. precinct committeeman; del. Rep. Nat. Conv., 1980, 84, 88, 96, 2000; committeeman 15th Congl. Dist., 1986-93; mem. nat. advocacy com. Am. Diabetes Assn.; bd. dirs. Nat. Futures Assn. With U.S. Army, 1958, USAR, 1957-63. Recipient Best Legislator award Nat. Rep. Legislator of the Yr. award, 1982, Ill. Small Businessmen Assn., 1983, 85, 87, Friend of Agr. award Ill. Agrl. Assn., 1985, 87, 89, 91, Legislator of Yr. award Ill. Assn. Homes for the Aging, 1986. Mem. Livingston County Bar Assn., Pontiac C. of C. (past exec. dir., past pres.), Livingston County Farm Bur., Elks, Moose, Masons. Republican. Methodist. Home: 1647 Mockingbird Ln Pontiac IL 61764-9249 E-mail: TWewing@yahoo.com.

EWING, WAYNE TURNER, coal company executive; b. Beech Creek, Ky., Dec. 1, 1933; s. O.E. and Elizabeth E.; m. Jane Gray, June 3, 1960; children—Allyson, Sally. BA, Georgetown Coll.; MA, Western Ky. U. With Peabody Coal Co., 1963-85, pres. St. Louis, 1983-85, Peabody Devel. Co., St. Louis, 1985-90; cons. Peabody Holding Co., St. Louis, 1992-93; sr. v.p. Kerr McGee Corp., Oklahoma City, 1993-96; owner The Ewing Co., Bonita Springs, Fla., 1996—. With U.S. Army, 1955-57. Mem. Pelican Nest Country Club. Office Phone: 239-948-0718. Personal E-mail: wewing@mindspring.com.

EWY, GORDON ALLEN, cardiologist, researcher, educator; b. Brenham, Kans., Aug. 5, 1933; s. Marvin John and Hazel Miller (Allen) E.; m. Priscilla Ruth Weldon; children: Kim Elizabeth (dec.), Gordon Stuart, Mark Allen. BA, U. Kans., 1955, MD, 1961. Resident, house officer Georgetown U. Hosp., Washington, 1961-64, cardiology fellow, 1964-65; instr. medicine Georgetown U., Washington, 1965-68, asst. prof., 1968-69, U. Ariz., Tucson, 1969-70, assoc. prof., 1970-75, prof. medicine, 1975—, chief cardiology, dir. cardiology fellowship program, 1982—, assoc. head dept. medicine, 1986-94, dir. Sarver Heart Ctr., 1991—, The Gordon A. Ewy MD Disting. Endowed Chair Cardiovasc. Medicine, 2002—. Editor: Cardiovascular Drugs and Management of Heart Disease, 1982, 93, Current Cardiovascular Drug Therapy, 1984, Manual of Cardiovascular Diagnosis and Therapy, 5th edit., 2002; author numerous sci. publs.; contbr. numerous revs. to profl. jours., chpts. to books. Lt. (j.g.) USNR, 1955-57. Fellow ACP, Am. Heart Assn. (mem. clin. coun., nat. faculty advanced cardiac life support 1982-84, chmn. nat. programs subcom. 1982, bd. dirs. Ariz. chpt. 1975-82, 84-89, tchg. fellow 1970-75), Am. Coll. Cardiology (chmn. learning ctr. com. 1988-91, trustee 1992-97), Alpha Omega Alpha. Republican. Avocation: travel. Office: Ariz Health Scis Ctr 1501 N Campbell Ave Tucson AZ 85724-0001 Office Phone: 520-626-2000. Personal E-mail: gaewy@aol.com.

EXNICIOS, VAL PATRICK, lawyer; b. New Orleans, Aug. 29, 1959; s. Samuel Richard and Glendora Marie (de Bouchel) E.; m. Carol Ann Carlton (div.); m. Victoria Cotton, Jan. 1997; 1 child, Valerie Marie. BA in Polit. Sci., U. New Orleans, 1986; JD, Loyola U., New Orleans, 1989. Bar: La. 1989, U.S. Dist. Ct. (ea. and mid. dists.) La. 1990. Assoc. Liska, Exnicios & Nungesser, New Orleans, 1989-93, ptnr., 1993-95, mng. dir., 1995—. Author case note Loyola Law Rev., 1989. Pres. Lawyers Against Crime Inc., New Orleans, 1996—; bd. dirs. St. Thomas More Soc., New Orleans, 1996—. Mem. ATLA, La. State Bar Assn. (environ. law sect., sect. on ins., negligence, compensation and admiralty law), New Orleans Bar Assn., La. Trial Lawyers Assn., Cosmopolitan Club of New Orleans (pres. 1994-96). Republican. Roman Catholic. Avocations: skiing, water-skiing. Office: Liska Exnicios & Nungesser 9701 Lake Forest Blvd New Orleans LA 70127-5402 E-mail: vexnicios@aol.com.

EYER, JULIA ARLENE, speech pathology/audiology services professional, educator; b. Shawnee, Okla., Dec. 2, 1955; d. Kenneth Verle and Nell Arlene (Smith) Eyer; m. Michael Leo Parchman, Mar. 13, 1982. BA, Okla. Bapt. U., 1977; MA, U. Kans., 1979; PhD, U. Tex., 1988. Cert. deaf educator Coun. Edn. Deaf. Fellow Gallaudet U., Washington, 1979—80; speech-lang. pathologist various sch. dist., Tex., 1980—87; asst. prof. U. Okla., Oklahoma City, 1988—91; vis. prof. Okla. State U., Stillwater, 1991—92; rsch. assoc. Purdue U., West Lafayette, Ind., 1993—95; assoc. prof. U. Tex., El Paso, 1995—98; prof., Woolfolk chair Our Lady of the Lake U., San Antonio, 1998—. Cons. in field. Contbr. articles to profl. jours. Mem.: Internat. Assn. Study of Child Lang., Am. Speech-Lang.-Hearing Assn. (cert.), Friends Meeting San Antonio. Office: Our Lady of the Lake Univ 411 SW 24th St San Antonio TX 78207

EYERMAN, JAMES DAVID, psychiatrist, educator, writer; b. St. Louis, Mo., Jan. 3, 1948; s. Edward Louis and Mary Cecilia (Robinson) Eyerman; m. Janice Kay Teece, Apr. 14, 1993. AB in Classics, Coll. of the Holy Cross, Worcester, Mass., 1965—69; MD, St. Louis U. Med. Sch., 1969—74. Psychiat. resident Washington U., St. Louis, 1974—75, 1976—78; instr., dept. psychiatry U. So. Calif., L.A., 1978—80, clin. asst. prof., 1980—82, St. Louis U., 1982—86; unit dir. Boulder Cmty. Hosp., Colo., 1986—88; med. dir. Epworth Children's Hosp., St. Louis, 1982—86, 1989—2001, Masters & Johnson Inst., St. Louis, 1993—97, La Montaigne Eating Disorder Program, St. Louis, 1998—2001; dir. Transpersonal Inst., St. Louis, 2001—. Psychopharmacologist Napa State Hosp., Calif., 2003—. Mem.: Assn. for Holotropic Basatawork Internat., Acad. Clin. Psychiatry, Am. Psychiat. Assn. Democrat. Roman Catholic. Avocations: sailing, running, yoga, dance. Office: Neuropsychiat & Transpersonal Inst PO Box 7243 Napa CA 94558 Office Phone: 707-815-1625.

EYLER, DAVID PAUL, music educator; s. Thomas Eyler and Ruth Bergeron; m. Barbara Johnson, Aug. 12, 1978. BS, Frostburg (Md.) State U., 1977; MusM, The Ohio State U., 1979; DMA, La. State U., 1985. Music dir.: Frostburg State U. percussion ensemble Frostburg State U., Frostburg, Md., 1973—77; grad. tchg. assoc. Sch. Music Ohio State U., Columbus, Ohio, 1977—79; grad. tchg. asst. Sch. Music La. State U., Baton Rouge, 1979—84; dir. of bands/dept. chairperson Redemptorist Jr. and Sr. HS, Baton Rouge, 1984—85; asst. prof. of music Ind. U. of PA, Ind., Pa., 1986—86; dir. of bands St. Jude Sch., Baton Rouge, 1986—87; assoc. prof. of music Concordia Coll., Moorhead, Minn., 1987—. Prin. Percussionist Susquehanna Festival Theater Orch., Harford, Md., 1971—73; prin. timpanist Potomac Symphony Orch., Potomac, Md., 1976—77; percussionist Columbus (Ohio) Symphony Orch., 1977—79; prin. percussionist Baton Rouge (La.) Symphony New Hyperion Ragtime Orch., 1979—84, Baton Rouge (La.) Symphony Orch., 1979—87; trap set drummer La. Soundstage Orch., Baton Rouge, 1981—85; prin. percussionist Baton Rouge (La.) Opera Orch., 1982—87; percussionist Rapides (La.) Symphony Orch., Alexandria, 1986—86, Lake Charles (La.) Symphony Orch., 1986—86; prin. timpanist Fargo-Moorhead Symphony Orch., Fargo, ND, 1987—. Author: Twenty-Two Progressive Studies, Etudes and Duets for Snare Drum, Music For Percussion, Inc.; composer: (music compositions) Triple Threat, Perpetual Motion, Fanfare and Dance for Solo Timpani, 7/8 Stomp, Watching The Time Go By, Latino: Trio for Latin Instruments, Tricastourine: A Multiple Percussion Solo, March Time for Percussion Trio, Changing Times for Solo Snare Drum, Bajo Los Pinos, Arrangements of Silent Night, Somewhere Over the Rainbow; contbr. articles to profl. jours. Chmn. orch. com. Baton Rouge (La.) Symphony Orch., 1986—87; chair, orch. com. Fargo-Moorhead (N.Dak.) Symphony Orch., 2000—; v.p. Minn. Percussive Arts Soc. Chpt., 1995—; bd. of trustees Fargo-Morhead (N.Dak.) Symphony Assn., 1995—2001; bd. trustees Percussive Arts Soc., 1998—. Fellow Danforth Grad. fellowship, 1977; grantee NEXUS grant, Lake Region Arts Coun., 1998, N.Dak. State U., 1999, Lake Region Arts Coun., 2001, Hendrickson Study grant, Concordia Coll., 2002, Lake Region Arts Coun., 2002; scholar Charles E. Lutton Meml. Merit-scholarship, 1976. Mem.: Music Educators Nat. Conf. (corr.), Coll. Music Soc. (corr.), Percussive Arts Soc. (assoc.; bd. of dir. 1998—2002, grants 1990—99), Pi Kappa Lambda Nat. Music Honor Soc. (hon.), Phi Mu Alpha Sinfonia Frat. (corr.; pres. 1976—77). Conservative. Pentecostal. Home: 2545 S 14th Street Fargo ND 58103 Office: Concordia College 901 S 8th Street Moorhead MN 56562 Office Phone: 218-299-4414.

EYLER, JOHN H., JR., retail toy and game company executive; b. 1948; m. Dolores Eyler; 3 children. Grad., U. Wash.; MBA, Harvard U. With May Dep. Stores Co.; pres., CEO, May D&F, Denver, from 1980; chmn., CEO MainStreet divsn. Fed. Dept. Stores, Inc.; CEO retail subs. Hartmarx, Chgo.; chmn., CEO FAO Schwarz, 1992-2000; pres., CEO Toys 'R' Us, Inc., Paramus, NJ, 2000—, chmn., 2001—. Bd. dirs. Donna Karan Internat. Inc.

EYMAN, SUSANNE KOHN, clinical psychologist; b. L.A., Oct. 3, 1956; d. Abraham Joseph and Wila (Rottstein) Kohn; m. James Randall Eyman, June 5, 1982 (div. 1999); children: Adrianne Sarah, Ethan James. BA, U. So. Calif., 1977; PhD, U. Nev., 1984. Lic. psychologist, Kans. Asst. prof. Washburn U., Topeka, 1983-85; staff psychologist Topeka State Hosp., 1985-86; postdoctoral fellow Menninger Clinic, 1986-88; pvt. practice Southwind Counseling Svcs., Manhattan, Kans., 1989—. Contbr. articles to profl. jours., chpts. to books. Pres. Mother to Mother of Shawnee County, 1998—2003, Temple Bethsholom, Topeka, 2005—; bi-state advisory bd. Jewish Cmty. Rels., Bur./Am. Jewish Com., 2005—. Mem. APA, NOW, Kans. Psychol. Assn. Democrat. Jewish. Avocation: women's issues. Office: Southwind Counseling Svcs 225 Southwind Pl Manhattan KS 66503-3123 Office Phone: 785-776-5858.

EYMANN, RICHARD CHARLES, lawyer; b. Hanover, N.H., June 6, 1945; BS, U. Oreg., 1968; JD, Gonzaga U., 1976. Bar: Wash. 1976, U.S. Dist. Ct. (ea. dist.) Wash. 1978, U.S. Ct. Appeals (9th cir.) 1987, U.S. Dist. Ct. (we. dist.) Wash. 1989, U.S. Supreme Ct. 1995. Ptnr. Eymann, Allison, Fennessy, Hunter Jones, P.S., Spokane, Wash. Mem. ABA (founder, chmn. nat. appellate advocacy competition 1975-84, bd. advs. 1985-93), ATLA, Wash. State Bar Assn. (bd. govs. 1997-98, pres. elect 1998-99, pres. 1999-2000), Wash. State Trial Lawyers Assn. (bd. govs. 1984-86, 88-95, legis. steering com. 1990-96, membership chair 1984-85, v.p. East 1991-92, fin. com. 1994-95, Trial Lawyer of Yr. 1995, pres. 1996-97), Wash. Trial Lawyers for Pub. Justice (bd. dirs. 1994-98), Am. Bd. Trial Advocates, Spokane County Bar Assn., Am. Inns of Ct. (barrister 1986, master of the bench 1990, Charles L. Powell & Inn pres. 1991-93), Damage Attys. Round Table. Office: Eymann Allison Fennessy Hunter & Jones PS 601 W Main Ave Ste 801 Spokane WA 99201 E-mail: eymann@eahjlaw.com.

EYRE, IVAN, artist; b. Tullymet, Sask., Can., Apr. 15, 1935; s. Thomas and Kay E.; m. Brenda Fenske, June 14, 1957; children: Keven, Tyrone. Mem. faculty U. N.D., 1958-59; mem. faculty U. Man., Winnipeg, Can., 1959-92, prof. drawing and painting, 1975-92, head drawing dept., 1974-78, prof. emeritus, 1994—; founding mem. Winnipeg Art Gallery, 1996. One-man shows include: Montreal Mus. Fine Arts, 1964, Winnipeg Art Gallery, 1964, 66, 74, 82, 88, 92, 2005, Fleet Galleries, Winnipeg, 1965, 69, 71, Albert White Galleries, Toronto, 1965, Atelier Vincitore Gallery, Brighton, Eng., 1967, Yellow Door Gallery, Winnipeg, 1966, Mount Allison U., 1968, Mendel Art Gallery, Saskatoon, 1968, Jerrold Morris Gallery, Toronto, 1969, 71, 73, Frankfurter Kunst Kabinett, Frankfurt, Ger., 1973, Burnaby Art Gallery, 1973, McIntosh Gallery, U. W. Ont., 1973, Siemens Werk, Erlangen, Germany, 1974, N.B. Mus., St. John, 1976, Gallery I.I.I., U. Man., 1977, 94, Nat. Gallery Can., Ottawa, 1978, Equinox Gallery, Vancouver, 1978, 81, 82, Robert McLaughlin Gallery, Oshawa, 1980, Mira Godard Gallery, Toronto, 1978-80, 90, 92, 94, 96, 99, 2002, Rodman Hall Arts Centre, St. Catherines, Ont., 1980, Art Gallery Windsor, Ont., 1981, Beaverbrook Art Gallery, Fredericton, N.B., 1981, London (Ont.) Regional Art Gallery, 1981, Sir George Williams Galleries, Montreal, 1981, MacDonald Stewart Art Centre, Guelph, Ont., 1981, Brian Melnychenko Gallery, Winnipeg, 1981, 87, The Ctr. for Inter-Am. Rels. NY, 1982, Burlington (Ont.) Art Ctr., 1982, Can. Cultural Centre, Paris, 1982, Can. House Gallery, London, Eng., 1982, Talbot Rice Gallery, Edinburgh, Scotland, 1982, The Art Gallery of Greater Victoria, Can., 1973, 82, 99, Evelyn Aimis Fine Art Gallery, Toronto, 1985, 87, Nat. Gallery of Can., Ottawa, 1988, Ivan Eyre: Personal Mythologies: Images of the Milieu: Figurative Paintings 1957 to 1988 touring Can., Winnipeg Art Gallery, 1989, Nickle Arts Mus., Calgary, 1989, Edmonton Art Gallery, 1989, London (Can.) Regional Art Gallery, 1989; 49th Parallel Gallery, NYC, 1988, Edmonton Art Gallery, 1995, Mackenzie Art Gallery, 1996, Assiniboine Park Pavilion Gallery, Winnipeg, 1998-2004, Art Gallery of Hamilton, 1999, Loch & Mayberry Fine Art, Winnipeg, 2000, Winnipeg Art Gallery, 2005; group shows include: London Regional Art Gallery, 1964, Agnes Lefort Gallery, Montreal, 1964, Nat. Gallery, Ottawa, 1965, 67, 74, Yellow Door Gallery, Winnipeg, 1965, Art Gallery of Ont., Toronto, 1968, Montreal Mus. Fine Arts, 1964, 70, 76, Primera Biennial Americana De Artes Graficas, Cali, Columbia, 1971, Art Gallery Ont., 1970, 76, Winnipeg Art Gallery, 1967, 76, 90, 92, 95, 2002, Glenbow-Alta. Inst., Calgary, 1976, Vancouver Art Gallery, 1977, Mendel Art Gallery, Saskatoon, 1977, 82, 2002, Harbourfront Art Gallery, Toronto, 1977, Edmonton (Alta., Can.) Art Gallery, 1981, 99, 2000, Printworld, US, 1982, Barcelona, Spain, 1982, Seattle Art Fair, 1987, LA Art Fair, 1986-87, Chgo. Art Fair, 1989, Maison de la Culture Cotes-des-Neiges, Montreal, 1992, Galerie de la Ville Dollard-des-Ormeaux, Que., Can. Coun. Art Bank, 1993, Drabinsky Gallery, Toronto, 1993, Hong Kong Art Fair, 1993, Expo '93, Taejon, South Korea, 1993, Loch and Mayberry Fine Art, Winnipeg, 1997, Mira Godard Gallery, Toronto, 1998, 2001, Royal Can. Acad. Arts Prairie Region Exhbn., Winnipeg, 1997, travelling to Regina, 1998, Calgary, 1998, Victoria, 1999, Markham, Ont., 1999, Provinciaal Centrum Voor Kunst En Culture (Patershol) Gent, 2001, Mackenzie Art Gallery, Regina, 2001-02, 04, Gallery I.I.I., U. Manitoba, 2003-04, McMichael Can. Art Collection, Kleinburg, Ont., Can., 2004; represented in permanent collections, Assiniboine Pk. Pavilion Gallery Art Collection, Winnipeg, Winnipeg Art Gallery, Nat. Gallery, Ottawa, Vancouver Art Gallery, Edmonton Art Gallery, Montreal Mus. Fine Arts, Art Gallery Ont., Toronto. Decorated Queen's Silver Jubilee medal, Queen's Golden Jubilee medal; nominee Molson prize, 1996; named sr. grantee, Can. Coun., 1966, 1977; recipient Gold medal, Acad. of Italy, 1980, Jubilee award, U. Man. Alumni, 1982, Outstanding Achievement medal, Internat. Biograph.Ctr., 1998. Mem. Royal Can. Acad. Arts Achievements include being subject of books Ivan Eyre (Woodcock), 1981, Ivan Eyre Drawings by Tom Lovatt, 2003, Ivan on Eyre-The Paintings, 2004; subject of various documentary films. Home: 1098 Des Trappistes St Winnipeg MB Canada R3V 1B8

EYRE, PAMELA CATHERINE, retired career officer; b. Chgo., Nov. 3, 1948; d. Francis Thomas and Jane (Burd) E. BA, Ctrl. State U. Okla., 1972; MPA, U. Okla., 1976; postgrad., U. Tex., 1998—. Commd. 2d lt. U.S. Army, 1973, advanced through grades to lt. col., 1991, test and evaluation officer Ft. Gordon, Ga., 1982-85, R&D coord. Ft. Monmouth, N.J., 1985-88, with army gen. staff Pentagon Washington, 1988-91, acquisition policy staff officer Army Secretariat Pentagon, 1991-94, asst. project mgr. Def. Telecom. Svc., 1994-95, test and evaluation officer Army Secretariat Pentagon, 1995-96; ret., 1996; program mgr. unmanned aerial vehicles Mission Techs., Inc., San Antonio, 2000—. Home: 200 PR 4660 Castroville TX 78009 E-mail: eyre@texas.net.

EYRE, PAUL P., lawyer; b. Dublin, Mar. 13, 1947; BA with honors, U. Wis., 1971, JD with honors, 1975. Bar: Wis. 1975, Ohio Supreme Ct. 1982, US Dist. Ct., No. Dist., Ohio, 1982, US Ct. of Appeals, Sixth Circuit, 1991, Second Circuit, 1994. Asst. regional dir. FTC, Washington, 1977-79, regional dir., 1979-82; assoc. then ptnr. Baker & Hostetler, Cleve., 1982—2001, chmn. litigation dept., mng. ptnr. NYC, 2001—, mem. policy com. With USN, 1967-69. Mem. Ohio Bar Assn. Office: Baker & Hostetler 666 Fifth Ave New York NY 10103 Office Phone: 212-589-4210. Office Fax: 212-589-4201. Business E-Mail: peyre@bakerlaw.com.*

EYRING, HENRY BENNION, bishop; b. Princeton, N.J., May 31, 1933; s. Henry and Mildred (Bennion) E.; m. Kathleen Johnson, July 27, 1962; children: Henry J., Stuart J., Matthew J., John B., Elizabeth, Mary Kathleen. BS, U. Utah, 1955; MBA, Harvard U., 1959, DBA, 1963; DHum (hon.), Brigham Young U., 1985. Asst., then assoc. prof. Stanford U., Palo Alto, Calif., 1962—71; pres. Ricks Coll., Rexburg, Idaho, 1972—77; dep. commr. edn., then commr. LDS Ch., Salt Lake City, 1977—85, presiding bishopric, 1985—92, mem. 1st Quorum of the Seventy, 1992—95, mem. Quorum of the Twelve, 1995—. Author: To Draw Closer to God, 1997, Because He First Loved Us, 2002; co-author: The Organizational World, 1973. With USAF, 1955—57. Recipient Sloan faculty fellowship, MIT, 1963—64. Avocations: painting, woodcarving. Office: LDS Ch Quorum of the Twelve 47 E South Temple Salt Lake City UT 84150-9701

EYSTER, MARY ELAINE, hematologist, educator; m. Robert E. Dye, Jan. 2, 1965; children: Robert E. Dye, Charles Dye. AB, Duke U., 1956, MD, 1960. Intern. N.Y. Hosp.-Cornell Med. Coll., N.Y.C., 1960-61, resident in medicine, 1961-63, fellow in hematology, 1963-66, instr. medicine, 1966-67, asst. prof. medicine, 1967-70; asst. prof. medicine Milton S. Hershey Med. Ctr. Pa. State U., Hershey, 1970-73, assoc. prof. Milton S. Hershey Med. Ctr., 1973-82, prof. Milton S. Hershey Med. Ctr., 1982—, chief hematology divsn., dept. medicine Coll. Medicine, 1973-96. Bd. dirs. Hemophilia Ctr. Cen. Pa., 1973—, AIDS Clin. Trials Unit Pa. State U., 1987—; faculty rsch. assoc. Am. Cancer Soc., 1966-71; mem. State Hemophilia Adv. Com, 1973—, chmn., 1977-79, 1988-90; mem. policy bd. Coop. F VII inhibitor study Nat. Heart, Lung and Blood Inst., 1975-79; mem. med. and sci. adv. counc. Nat. Hemophilia Found., 1976-77, 83-89, chmn. med. adv. com. Del. Valley chpt., 1979-82; co-investigator, mem. multi-agy. task force on AIDS HHS, 1982-83; mem. blood products adv. com. FDA, 1985-89; exec. com. NIH-NIAID Clin. Trials, 1988-90; mem. forum on blood safety and availability Inst. of Med., 1993-95. USPHS grantee, 1976-95. Fellow ACP; mem. Am. Fedn. Clin. Rsch., World Fedn. Hemophilia, Am. Soc. Hematology, Internat. Soc. Thrombosis and Haemostasis, Internat. Soc. Hematology, Pa. Soc. Hematology and Oncology (bd. dirs. 1982-85), Am. Assn. for Study of Liver Diseases, Phi Beta Kappa, Alpha Omega Alpha. Office: Milton S Hershey Med Ctr PO Box 850 Hershey PA 17033-0850 Office Phone: 717-531-8399.

EZELL, MARGARET M., language educator; John Paul Abbott prof. of liberal arts Tex. A&M U., College Sta., 1997—. Author: The Patriarch's Wife: Literary Evidence and the History of the Family, Writing Women's Literary History, Social Authorship and the Advent of Print; editor: (series) Women Writers in English, 1350-1830. Fellow, John Simon Guggenheim Meml. Found., 2003. Office: Tex A&M U Dept English 243D Blocker Bldg (MS 4227) College Station TX 77843

EZELLE, ROBERT EUGENE, diplomat; b. Mattoon, Ill., Dec. 5, 1927; s. Zonner Robert and Nina Leora (Smith) E.; m. Lesly Marion Hopkins, Apr. 30, 1955; children: Robert, Lesley, John, Paul. Student, U. So. Calif., 1947-49, U. Bonn, 1954-56, U. Munich, 1956-57; PhD, U. Vienna, 1960; MS (Sloan fellow), Stanford Grad. Sch. Bus., 1977; Dr.h.c., Nat. U., 1981. Instr. Bonn, Munich and Vienna, 1954-60; dir. lang. sch., San Mateo, Calif., 1960-61; joined U.S. Fgn. Svc., 1961; internat. rels. officer State Dept., Washington, 1961-62, staff asst. Nat. Interdeptl. Seminar, 1962-63; assigned Hong Kong, 1963-65, Bern, Switzerland, 1965-69, Naples, Italy, 1969-72; chief consular affairs sect. Am. Embassy, Bonn, 1972-75; internat. rels. officer State Dept., Washington, 1975-76; dep. consul gen. Am. Embassy, London, 1977-80; consul gen. Am. Consulate Gen., Tijuana, Mex., 1980-84, Am. Embassy, Paris, 1984-88, Haiti, 1988—90; cons., internat. trade, 1990—. Served with USAF, 1949-53. Recipient Gold medal City of Paris, 1988, Superior Honor award Dept. State, 1988. Address: 1608 NE 17th St Battle Ground WA 98604

EZELL-GRIM, ANNETTE SCHRAM, business management educator, academic administrator; b. West Frankfort, Ill., June 19, 1940; d. Woodrwo C. and Rosa (Franich) Schram; m. John R. Grim III; children: Michael L., Rona Maria. BS, U. Nev., 1962, MS in Physiology, 1967, postgrad., 1969; EdD in Pub. Adminstrn., Brigham Young U., 1977. Mem. staff Washoe Med. Ctr., Reno, Nev., 1962; tchg. asst. U. Nev., Reno, 1962-63, instr., 1963-64, 65-67, asst. prof., 1967-71; curriculum specialist U. Nev. Med. Sch., 1971-72; project mgr. Fed. Grant Intercampus Edn. Project, 1969-71; assoc. prof., curriculum specialist rural practitioner program, 1971-73; staff assoc. Mountain States Regional Med. Program, 1974-75; cons. Nev. Dept. Edn., 1975-77; asst. dean acad. affairs U. Utah, Salt Lake City, 1977-80, acting dean, 1981, dir., prof. doctoral program Edn. Adminstrn.; prof., dept. head Coll. Human Devel. Pa. State U., 1982-85; dean Coll. Profl. Studies, prof. bus. adminstrn. U. So. Colo., Pueblo, 1985-87; sr. asst. to pres. Towson State U., Balt.,

1987-94, assoc. prof. mgmt. sch. bus., 1994-95; assoc. dean prof. bus. mgmt. Wor Wic C.C., Salisbury, Md., 1995—. Cons. higher edn., TV edn., research methology; adviser to various research, polit. and ednl. bds. Mem. Am. Ednl. Rsch. Assn., AAAS, Am. Acad. Arts and Scis., AAUP, Am. Coun. on Edn., Am. Assn. Higher Edn., Soc. for Coll. & Univ. Planning, Decision Scis. Inst., Sigma Xi, Phi Kappa Phi, Delta Kappa Gamma. Office: Wor Wic CC 32000 Campus Dr Salisbury MD 21804-1485

EZENWA, JOSEPHINE NWABUOKU, social worker; b. Oct. 20, 1959; d. H.M. Eze-Igwe Silas O. and H.R.H. Veronica Ezenwa; children: Bryan, Brenda, Sean. BA in Psychology and Human Svc. (hon.), Fontbonne Coll., St. Louis, 1980; MSW, Washington Univ., St. Louis, 1981; postgrad., St. Louis U., 1991—93. Diplomate Am. Coll. Profl. Mental Health Practitioners, 2002. Rsch. dir. Nat. Benevolent Assn., St. Louis, 1981-89; tchr. U. City Sch. Dist., St. Louis, 1989-94; therapist Presbyn. Children's Home, St. Louis, 1994-95; social worker St. Louis Regional Med. Ctr., 1995-97; founder, chair St. Louis Regional Med. Ctr. Dialysis Support Group, 1995-97; social worker St. Louis U. Hosp., 1997; CEO, pres. BBS Care U.S.A., Inc., St. Louis, 1997—; pres. BBS Charities, Inc., St. Louis, 2000—; chair Bus. Adv. Coun. Nat Rep. Congl. Com., St. Louis, 2002—. Founder and chair St. Louis Regional Med. Ctr. Dialysis Support Group, 1995-97; chair long range planning com. Washington U.; co-chair Bus. Adv. Coun., 2002; presenter in field. Chair bus. adv. coun. Nat. Rep. Congl. Com., 2002—. Named Businesswoman of Yr., Nat. Rep. Congl. Com., 2003; recipient Nat. Leadership award, St. Louis Regional Med. Ctr. Dialysis Support Group, 2002, Gold Medal award, Nat. Rep. Congl. Com., 2003. Mem. NASW, NAFE, Coun. Nephrology Social Workers; Nat. Assn. Forensic Counselors; Nat. Assn. Cognitive Behavioral Therapists, Washington U. Sch. Social Work Alumni Assn. (bd. dir.); Creve Coeur-Olive C. of C.; Lions Club. Avocations: choreography, fashion cons., event coord., design, travel. Office: St Louis U Hosp 3536 Vista Grand Saint Louis MO 63110 also: BBS Care USA Inc 7151-7155 Olive Blvd Saint Louis MO 63130 Office Phone: 314-725-7733.

EZOLD, NANCY O'MARA, lawyer; d. Francis L. and Edna Mae (Jackson) O'Mara; m. William L. Keenan; children: Christopher E. Ezold, Matthew F. Ezold. BA, U. Maine, 1964; JD, Villanova U., 1980. Bar: Pa. 1980, U.S. Dist. Ct. (ea. dist.) Pa. 1980, U.S. Ct. Appeals (3rd and fed. cirs.) 1982, U.S. Claims Ct. 1989, U.S. Dist. Ct. (mid. dist.) Pa. 1989, U.S. Supreme Ct. 1989, U.S. Dist. Ct. Ariz. 1991. Adminstrv. positions fed., state and local govt. agys., 1964-77; assoc. Kirschner, Walters & Willig, Phila., 1980-81, Phillips & Phelan, Phila., 1981-83, Wolf Block Schorr & Solis-Cohen, Phila., 1983-89, Rosenthal & Ganister, West Chester, Pa., 1990-94; pres., chief counsel BES Environ. Specialists, Larksville, Pa., 1989-90; pvt. practice Bala Cynwyd, Pa., 1994—. Spkr. in field. Chmn. Women's Law Project, Phila., 1999-00. Mem. ATLA, Nat. Employment Lawyers Assn., Phila. Bar Assn., Nat. Assn. Women Lawyers (pres.' award 1991). Office: 401 City Ave Ste 904 Bala Cynwyd PA 19004-1131 Fax: 610-660-5595. Office Phone: 610-660-5585. E-mail: nezold@ezoldlaw.com.

EZRATI, MILTON JOSEPH, investment manager, economist, writer; b. N.Y.C., May 22, 1947; s. Al and Edythe Ezrati; m. Lynda Lamare, July 1970 (div.); m. Susan Arlene Graham, June 19, 1976; 1 child, Isabel Diana. BA in Econs., SUNY, Buffalo, 1969; M Social Sci. in Math. Econs., Birmingham (Eng.) U., 1973. Econ. specialist Citibank, N.Y.C., 1971-73; economist Chase Manhattan Bank, N.Y.C., 1973-77, Lionel Edie & Co., N.Y.C., 1977-78, chief economist, 1978-81, Mfrs. Hanover Investment Corp., N.Y.C., 1981-83, chief economist and strategist, 1983-85, sr. v.p., dir. rsch., 1985-87; chief investment officer Nomura Asset Mgmt., N.Y.C., 1987-99; sr. economist and strategist Lord, Abbett & Co., Jersey City, N.J., 2000—. Author: Kawari: How Japan's Economic and Cultural Transformation Will Alter the Balance of Power Among Nations, 1999; contbr. articles to profl. and popular jours. Mem. Am. Econs. Assn., Nat. Assn. Scholars, Old Westbury Horseman's Assn. Methodist. Avocations: riding and training horses, skiing. Office: Lord Abbett & Co 90 Hudson St Jersey City NJ 07302

EZRIN, MYER, director, consultant; b. Boston, June 23, 1926; s. Joseph and Ida Ezrin; m. Madeline Frager, Aug. 22, 1946; children: Jane Barbara Yourish, Andrea Louise Silverstein, Jonathan Charles. BS in Chemistry summa cum laude, Tufts Coll., 1948; PhD in Chemistry, Yale U., 1954. Chemist Dupont Coated Fabrics, Fairfield, Conn., 1948—50, Monsanto Chem. Co., Springfield, Mass., 1953—65; project mgr. Springborn Labs., Enfield, Conn., 1965—80; dir. IMS Assocs. Program U. Conn., Inst. Materials Sci., Storrs, 1980—. Expert witness in patent infringement and product liability litig. Springborn Labs., Enfield, 1969—80; expert witness in field, Longmeadow, Mass., 1980—; vis. prof. polymer analysis and characterization U. Conn., Storrs, 1978—79. *He has testified and consulted in patent infringement and product liability litigation in plastics in the United States, Canada, England, Australia, and New Zealand. He is the keynote speaker in Society of Plastics Engineers Technical Conference in plastics failure and also is the winner (with coauthor Gary Lavigne) of Best Paper award in Society of Plastics Engineers Polymer Analysis Division Annual Conference in 2002.* Co-author: Plastics Analysis Guide - Chemical and Instrumental Methods, 1983; author: Plastics Failure Guide - Cause and Prevention, 1996. Jewish religious sch. tchr., 1955—69; lay rabbi for religious svcs. at coll., 1955—60. Electronic tech mate 2nd class NAVY, 1944—46, England. Phi Beta Kappa Undergrad. scholar, Tufts Coll., 1947. Fellow: Soc. Plastics Engrs. (chmn. failure group 1989—91, pres. Western New Eng. sect. 1991—92, new tech. com.); mem.: Am. Chem. Soc. (emeritus), Sigma Xi. Jewish. Achievements include research in electron exchange polymers was the first for synthetic polymers capable of controlled reversible oxidation and reduction; discovery of acid rain contributed to the failure of fiberglass support rod on electrical transmission line; Patent infringement litigation on chemically embossed vinyl flooring, invented an analytical method of analysis that proved infringement resulting in damages of many millions of dollars; aromatic hydrocarbons, including benzene, in air from gasoline vapors are absorbed by plastics; patents for combined electron- and ion-exchange copolymers; biazially oriented crystalline polystyrene; process for the manufacture of biaxially oriented crystalline polystyrene; uniaxially oriented crystalline polymers. Avocation: bible study. Office: Univ Conn 97 North Eagleville Rd Storrs CT 06269-3136 Home: 173 Academy Dr Longmeadow MA 01106 Office Phone: 413-567-3803. Office Fax: 860-486-4745. Business E-Mail: myer.ezrin@uconn.edu.

FAATZ, JEANNE RYAN, councilperson; b. Cumberland, Md., July 30, 1941; d. Charles Keith and Elizabeth (McIntyre) Ryan; children: Kristin, Susan. BS, U. Ill., 1962; postgrad.; MA, U. Colo., Denver, 1985. Instr. speech dept. Met. State Coll., Denver, 1985-98; sec. to majority leader Colo. Senate, 1976-78; mem. Colo. Ho. Reps. from Dist. 1, 1979-98; dir. Colo. Sch.-to-Career, 1999—2001; councilwoman City of Denver, 2003—. Former ho. asst. majority leader. Past pres. S.W. Denver YWCA Adult Edn. Club; former mem. bd. mgrs. S.W. Denver YMCA; past pres. Harvey Park (Colo.) Homeowners Assn. Gates fellow, Harvard U., 1984. Home: 2903 S Quitman St Denver CO 80236-2208 Office Phone: 303-763-8562. E-mail: jeanne.faatz@ci.denver.co.us.

FABBRI, ANNE R., critic, curator; b. Norristown, Pa. d. Remo and Anna Wild (Butterworth) F.; m. Joseph Henry Butera (div.); children: Virginia, Remo, Joseph F. (Jay). AB cum laude, Radcliffe Coll.; MA in Art History, Bryn Mawr Coll., 1971. Art lectr. Villanova U., Pa., 1971-73, Drexel U., Phila., 1974-76; art critic, art editor The Drummer, Phila., 1976-79; art critic The Bulletin, Phila., 1978-80; dir. Alfred O. Deshong Mus., Widener U., Chester, Pa., 1980-82, The Noyes Mus., Oceanville, N.J., 1982-91; dir. Paley Design Ctr. Phila. U., 1991-2001; art critic Phila. Daily News, Art in Am., Art Matters, The Art Newspaper, Am. Artist, 1998—, Phila. Style mag., 2002—; lectr. arts adminstrn. Rosemont Coll., 2000—03, lectr. humanities, 2001—03. Bd. dirs. Phila. Vol. Lawyers for the arts, 2001-03; mem. adv. com. Main Line Art Ctr.; chair adv. com. Art in City Hall, Phila., 1999-2003; chair New Visions, Phila. Furniture Exhbn., 1998-2004. Chair, mem. adv. com. Art in City Hall, 1999—. Vis. NEH fellow U. Calif.-Berkeley, 1980, Princeton U., 1981; recipient John Cotton Dana award Mus. N.J. Assn. Mus., 1991. Mem. Am. Assn. Museums, Coll. Art Assn., Internat. Assn. Art Critics. Home and Office: 642 Valley View Ln Wayne PA 19087-2024 Office Phone: 610-989-0588. E-mail: arfabbri@aol.com.

FABE, DANA ANDERSON, state supreme court justice; b. Cin., Mar. 29, 1951; d. George and Mary Lawrence (Van Antwerp) F.; m. Randall Gene Simpson, Jan. 1, 1983; 1 child, Amelia Fabe Simpson. BA, Cornell U., 1973; JD, Northeastern U., 1976. Bar: Alaska 1977, U.S. Supreme Ct. 1981. Law clk. to justice Alaska Supreme Ct., 1976-77; staff atty. pub. defenders State of Alaska, 1977-81; dir. Alaska Pub. Defender Agy., Anchorage, 1981—88; judge Superior Ct., Anchorage, 1988—92; deputy presiding judge Third Judicial Dist., 1992—95; justice Alaska Supreme Ct., Anchorage, 1996—, chief justice, 2000—03. Chair Alaska Supreme Ct. Civil Rules Com., Alaska Supreme Ct. Judicial Outreach Commn., Alaska Ct. System Law Day Steering Comm., Alaska Teaching Justice Network. Named alumna of yr. Northeastern Sch. Law, 1983; recipient Northeastern Sch. Law Alumni Pub. Svc. award, 1991. Mem.: Am. Judicature Soc. (bd. dirs.), Alaska Bar Assoc. (bd. govs. 1987—88, co-chair Gender Equality Sect.). Office: Alaska Supreme Ct 303 K St Fl 5 Anchorage AK 99501-2013 Office Phone: 907-264-0622.

FABENS, ANDREW LAWRIE, III, lawyer; b. Washington, Apr. 8, 1942; s. Andrew Lawrie Jr. and Alicia Gordon (Hail) F.; m. Martha Leigh Leingang, June 24, 1966; children: Andrew Lawrie IV, Jennie Leigh. AB, Yale U., 1964; JD, U. Chgo., 1967. Bar: Ohio 1967. Assoc. Thompson, Hine and Flory, Cleve., 1967-74; ptnr. Thompson Hine LLP (formerly Thompson, Hine and Flory), Cleve., 1974—, chmn. estate planning and probate area, 1988-94. Contbr. articles on estate planning and related topics to profl. pubis. Pres. Family Health Assn., Cleve., 1978-80, 83-84; trustee A.M. McGregor Home, East Cleveland, Ohio, 1991—, chmn., 2001—; trustee Bascom Little Fund, Cleve., 1985—, Great Lakes Basin Conservancy, 1999—; vestryman Christ Episcopal Ch., Shaker Heights, Ohio, 1972-77. Fellow Am. Coll. Trust and Estate Counsel; mem. Ohio State Bar Assn. (coun. estate planning, trust and probate law sect. 1983—, treas. 1997-99, sec. 1999-2001, vice-chmn. 2001-03, chmn. 2003-05), Probate Law Jour. Ohio (adv. bd.), Cleve. Bar Assn. (speaker, com. mem. 1976—), Cleve. Skating Club, Rowfant Club (fellow 2000-03), The Novel Club (sec. 1986-88, pres. 1995-97), The Union Club. Home: 2280 Woodmere Dr Cleveland OH 44106-3604 Office: Thompson Hine LLP 3900 Key Ctr 127 Public Square Cleveland OH 44114-1216 Office Phone: 216-566-5736. Business E-Mail: andy.fabens@thompsonhine.com.

FABER, DAVID ALAN, federal judge; b. Charleston, W.Va., Oct. 21, 1942; s. John Smith and Wilda Elaine (Melton) F.; m. Deborah Ellayne Anderson, Aug. 24, 1968; 1 dau., Katherine Peyton. BA, W.Va. U., 1964; JD, Yale U., 1967; LLM, U. Va., 1998. Bar: W.Va. 1967, U.S. Ct. Mil. Appeals 1970, U.S. Supreme Ct. 1974. Assoc. Dayton, Campbell & Love, Charleston, W.Va., 1967-68, Campbell, Love, Woodroe, 1972-74; ptnr. Campbell, Love, Woodroe & Kizer, Charleston, 1974-77, Love, Wise, Robinson & Woodroe, Charleston, 1977-81; US atty. US Dept. Justice, Charleston, 1982-86; ptnr. Spilman, Thomas, Battle & Klostermeyer, Charleston, 1987-91; judge US Dist. Ct. (So. Dist.) W.Va., Bluefield, 1991—, chief judge. Counsel to ethics commn. W.Va. State Bar, Charleston, 1974-76 Served to capt. USAF, 1968-72, to col. W.Va. Air N.G., 1978-92. Nat. law scholar Yale Law Sch. New Haven, 1964-65 Mem.: W.Va. Bar Assn., W.Va. State Bar, Phi Beta Kappa. Republican. Episcopalian. Office: US Dist Ct PO Box 5009 110 N Heber St Beckley WV 25801 Fax: (304) 253-6811.

FABER, GEORGE DONALD, communications executive; b. Mpls., June 17, 1921; s. Morris William and Lowella (Whitman) F.; m. Marjorie Alice Knodel; children: Kathie Diane Goodman, Michael William, Patricia Netzley. Student, Wis. Coll. Music, 1940; BA, Northwestern U., 1941. Writer, announcer, actor Sta. WHBL, Sheboygan, Wis., 1937-39; prodn. mgr. Sta. WMFD, Wilmington, N.C., 1939-41; columnist and author Behind the Mike series, Cape Fear Pub. Co., Wilmington, N.C., 1940-41; news editor NBC, Chgo., 1943-46; news dir., writer CBS, 1946-56; internat. mgr. CBS films, L.A., 1956-71; internat. dir. client rels. Viacom Prodsn. divsn. Paramount TV, 1971—2000. Dir. communications, bd. dir. Callahan and Assocs. L.A. Emmy nomination. Vol. fundraising Childrens Hosp. Mem. Internat. Photo Journalists (hon. life), TV Programs Execs. Com. (publicity), Sigma Delta Chi. Avocations: photography, fundraising for charities. Home: 10760 Cushdon Ave Los Angeles CA 90064-3219 E-mail: georgedfaber@aol.com.

FABER, MICHAEL WARREN, lawyer; b. NYC, June 7, 1943; s. Carl Faber and Harriet Ruth Cohen; m. Adele Zolot, Apr. 16, 1975; children: Evan, Jenna. AB, Hunter Coll., 1964; JD, Fordham U., 1967. Bar: N.Y. 1967, D.C. 1972, U.S. Ct. Claims, 1972, U.S. Supreme Ct. 1972, Colo. 1993. Gen. atty. FCC, Washington, 1967-69, trial atty., 1969-71, atty. advisor to Commr. T.J. Houser, 1971; assoc. Peabody, Rivlin, Lambert & Meyers, Washington, 1971-73; ptnr. Peabody, Lambert & Meyers, Washington, 1973-84, Reid and Priest, Washington, 1984-93, mem. exec. com., 1986-92; prin. The Faber Group, Cascade, Colo., 1993-94; pres. USA Volleyball Ctrs. LLC, Colorado Springs, Colo., 1995-96; owner The Pantry Restaurant, Green Mountain Falls, Colo., 1996—2001; prin. Crossroads Cons., LLC, Cascade, 2001—. Dir. Workforce Partnership study Pikes Peak Workforce Investment Bd., Colorado Springs, 2003; cons. White House Office Telecom. Policy, 1971; chmn. organizing com. Nat. Volleyball League. Bd. dirs. Washington Very Spl. Arts, 1986-93; chair Telecom. Policy Adv. Com., Colo. Springs, 2002—, SAFE Com., Colo. Springs, 2002—; v.p. devel. Pikes Peak United Way, 2003-04, chair campaign, 2003. Mem. NY Bar Assn., DC Bar Assn., Fed. Comm. Bar Assn., Colo. Bar Assn., Manitou Springs Edn. Assn. (pres. 2002-04).

FABER, PETER LEWIS, lawyer; b. N.Y.C., Apr. 29, 1938; s. Alexander W. and Anne L. Faber; m. Joan Schuster, June 14, 1959; children: Michael, Julia, Thomas. AB, Swarthmore Coll., 1960; LLB, Harvard U., 1963. Bar: N.Y. 1964. Assoc. Wiser, Shaw, Freeman, Ickes & Williams, Rochester, N.Y., 1963-65, Parker, Chapin & Flattau, N.Y.C., 1965-66; ptnr. Harter, Secrest & Emery, Rochester, N.Y., 1966-82, Winthrop, Stimson, Putnam & Roberts, N.Y.C., 1982-84, Kaye, Scholer, Fierman, Hays & Handler, N.Y.C., 1984-95, McDermott, Will & Emery, N.Y.C., 1995—. Mem. adv. com. NYU Ann. Inst. on State & Local Taxation; mem. N.Y. State Coun. on Fiscal and Econ. Priorities, 1991-95. Contbr. articles to profl. jours. Chmn. Rochester Econ. Devel. Com., 1979-82; pres. Rochester Philharm. Orch., Inc., 1980-82; bd. dirs. Met. Rochester Devel. Coun., Harley Sch., 1978-81, Partnership for N.Y.C., 1985-; mem. fin. com. Monroe County Dem. Party, 1979-82. Fellow Am. Bar Found., Am. Coll. Tax Counsel; mem. ABA (chmn. tax sect. 1991-92, vice chmn. 1986-88, chmn.-elect 1990-91, chmn. com. corp. stockholder relationships tax sect. 1980-82, liaison to IRS for North Atlantic region, vice chmn. spl. com. on integration 1979-81, sec. tax sect. 1984-86), N.Y. State Bar Assn. (chmn. sect. taxation 1976-77, exec. com. sect. taxation 1969—), N.Y. C. of C. (chmn. tax com. 1988—, trustee 1989—, exec. com. 1990—), Monroe County Bar Assn., Am. Law Inst. (tax project adv. group), Rochester Area C. of C. (trustee 1980-82). Home: 300 Central Park W New York NY 10024-1513 Office: McDermott Will & Emery 50 Rockefeller Plz Fl 12 New York NY 10020-1605 Office Phone: 212-547-5585. Business E-Mail: pfaber@mwe.com.

FABER, SANDRA MOORE, astronomer, educator; b. Boston, Dec. 28, 1944; d. Donald Edwin and Elizabeth Mackenzie (Borwick) Moore; m. Andrew L. Faber, June 9, 1967; children: Robin, Holly. BA, Swarthmore Coll., 1966, DSc (hon.), 1986; PhD, Harvard U., 1972; DSc (hon.), Williams Coll., 1996. Asst. prof., astronomer Lick Obs., U. Calif., Santa Cruz, 1972-77, assoc. prof., astronomer, 1977-79, prof., astronomer, 1979—; Univ. Prof. U. Calif., Santa Cruz, 1996—. Mem. astronomy adv. panel NSF, 1975-77; vis. prof. Princeton U., 1978, U. Hawaii, 1983, Ariz. State U., 1985; Phillips visitor Haverford Coll., 1982; Feshbach lectr. MIT, Cambridge, Mass., 1990; Darwin lectr. Royal Astron. Soc., 1991; Marker lectr. Pa. State U., 1992; Bunyan lectr. Stanford U., 1992; Tomkins lectr. U. Calif., San Francisco, 1992; Mohler lectr. U. Mich., 1994; mem. Nat. Acad. Astronomy Survey Panel, 1979-81Nfat. Acad. Com. on Astronomy and Astrophysics 1993-1995; chmn. vis. com. Space Telescope Sci. Inst., 1983-84; co-chmn. sci. steering com. Keck Obs., 1987-92, leader DEIMOS spectrograph team, 1993—; mem. Wide Field Camera team Hubble Space Telescope, 1985-97, user's com., 1990-92, mem. advanced radial camera selection team, 1995,co-chmn. TAC review comm., 2002; mem. treas. pgm. advis. comm. 2002-; mem. Calif. Coun. on Sci. and Tech., 1989-94,; Com. on Future Smithsonian Instn., 1994-95; mem. White House Space Sci. Workshop, 1996, Waterman Awards Com., NSF, 1997-99, Nat. Medal of Sci. selection com., 1999-2001; mem. Plumian Prof. selection com. Cambridge U., 1998—. Assoc. editor: Astrophys. Jour. Letters, 1982-87; editorial bd.: Ann. Revs. Astronomy and Astrophysics, 1982-87; contbr. articles to profl. jours. Trustee Carnegie Instn., Washington, 1985—; bd. dirs. Ann. Revs., 1989—, SETI Inst., 1997—; editl. affairs com. Ann. Revs., 1996—; exec. com. Ann. Revs., 1998—; Scripps Instn. Oceanography Coun., 2000--; bd. overseers Fermilab, 2002--. Recipient Bart J. Bok prize Harvard U., 1978, Director's Distinguished Lectr. award Livermore Nat. Lab., 1986; NASA Group Achievement award, 1993, DeVaucouleurs medal U. Tex., 1997; Carnegie Lectr. Carnegie Inst. Washington, 1988, 99; NSF fellow, 1966-71; Woodrow Wilson fellow, 1966-71; Alfred P. Sloan fellow, 1977-81; listed among 100 best Am. scientists under 40, Sci. Digest, 1984, listed among 50 best Am. Women scientists, Discover Mag., 2002; Tetelman fellow, Yale U., 1987. Fellow Calif. Coun. on Sci. and Tech.; mem. NAS (vice chair adv. panel on cosmology 1993, rsch. in astronomy commn. on orgn. and mgmt. astrophysics 2001, co-chmn. TAC rev. commn. 2002, mem. treas. program adv. commn. 2002--), Am. Philos. Soc. Am. Acad. Arts and Scis., Calif. Acad. Scis., 1998—, Am. Astron. Soc. (councilor 1982-84, Dannie Heineman prize 1986), Internat. Astron. Union, Am. Philos. Soc., Phi Beta Kappa, Sigma Xi. Office: U Calif Lick Obs Santa Cruz CA 95064 E-mail: faber@ucolick.org.

FABER, SEBASTIAAN, humanities educator; b. Amsterdam, Netherlands, Oct. 17, 1969; arrived in U.S.A., 1995; s. Aart Faber and Adelheid Zwollo; m. Kim Tungseth, Aug. 8, 1997; children: Jakob Tristan, Maya Jasmijn. Degree, U. Amsterdam, 1995; PhD, U. Calif., Davis, Calif., 1999. Tchg. asst. Spanish U. Calif., Davis, 1995—98, assoc. instr. Spanish, 1998—99; asst. prof. hispanic studies Oberlin (Ohio) Coll., 1999—2004, assoc. prof. Hispanic studies, 2004—. Contbr. articles to profl. jours.; author: (book) Exile and Cultural Hegemony: Spanish Intellectuals in Mex., 2002. Recipient J.H. Scheps prize, Inden=Reiss-fonds, Netherlands, 1995, George Watt Meml. prize, Abraham Lincoln Brigade Archives, 2000; fellow, Ministry Fgn. Affairs, Spain, 1999, Social Sci. Rsch. Coun., Am. Coun. Learned Socs., 2000; grantee, Ministry Culture Spain, 1997. Mem.: MLA, Inst. Internat. Lit. Iberoamericana, Am. Assn. Tchrs. Spanish and Portuguese, Latin Am. Studies Assn. Office: Oberlin College 50 N Professor St Oberlin OH 44074 Home: 331 Eastern Ave Oberlin OH 44074 Office Phone: 440-775-8189.

FABER, TRUDY, music educator; b. Clifton, N.J., Dec. 10, 1938; d. Jacob Gerard and Olive Kievit; m. J. Arthur Faber, Aug. 5, 1960; children: James Stephan, Jonathan Leigh. BA in Music, Calvin Coll., 1960; postgrad., Amsterdam Conservatory, 1960—61, U. Toronto, Can., 1962—63; MA in Music, Smith Coll., 1966. Cert. ch. musician Presbyn. Ch. Am. Asst. instr. organ Calvin Coll., Grand Rapids, Mich., 1961—62; elem. music tchr. Sylvan Christian Schs., Grand Rapids, Mich., 1961—62; H.S. English tchr. Northampton (Mass.) H.S., 1963—64; prof. music Wittenberg U., Springfield, Ohio, 1966—, chair dept. music, 1995—2004. Organ, harpsichord recitalist Covenant Presbyn. Ch., Springfield, 1972—, organist, 1973—; clinician Am. Guild Organists, 1986—; organ and harpichord recitalit, 1971—; pre-concert lectr. Springfield Symphony Orch., 1988—; lectr. in field. Fulbright scholar, 1960. Avocations: reading, bicycling, boating, hiking, travel. Home: 2910 Nauset St Springfield OH 45503 Office: Wittenberg Univ Box 720 Springfield OH 45501 Office Phone: 937-327-7352. E-mail: tfaber@wittenberg.edu.

FABERMAN, AUSTIN S., lawyer; b. NYC, Feb. 6, 1970; BSBA, Bucknell U., Pa., 1992; JD, St. John's U. Sch. Law, NY, 1995. Assoc. Thacher Proffitt & Wood, NYC, 1995—97, Ballard Spahr Andrews & Ingersoll, LLP, Phila., 1997—2000, Drinker Biddle & Reath LLP. Bd. mem. Anti Defamation League, Phila. Office: Drinker Biddle & Reath LLP One Logan Sq 18th & Cherry Sts Philadelphia PA 19103-6996 Office Phone: 215-988-2700. Office Fax: 215-557-9162.

FABIAN, HANS J., education educator; b. Elbing, Germany, Aug. 1, 1926; arrived in U.S., 1941; s. Morris F. and Johanna E. Fabian; m. Myra Lou Williamson, Aug. 19, 1951. BA, Syracuse U., 1950, MA, 1952, MS, 1954; PhD, Ohio State U., 1963. Dir. libr., asst. prof Wilmington Coll., Ohio, 1954—61; asst. prof. German Ohio U., Athens, 1962—63; libr. Ohio State U., Columbus, 1963—64; asst. prof. German U. Mich., Ann Arbor, 1964. Resident dir. Study Abroad U. Mich., Ann Arbor, Mich., 1968—69, Ann Arbor, 1975—76, asst. dean, 1970—73, dir. German House, 1975. Contbr. articles to profl. jours. Cpl. intelligence U.S. Army, 1944—46, Germany. Rsch. Grant, NEH, Washington, 1979, U. Mich., 1980. Mem.: Modern Lang. Assn. (life). Avocations: sailing, skiing, swimming, travel. Home: 2320 Walter Dr Ann Arbor MI 48103-3453 Personal E-mail: hjf@umich.edu.

FABIAN, JOHN MATTHEW, psychologist; s. Dee Kennedy and Wayne Fabian. D Psycology, Chgo. Sch. of Profl. Psychology, Chgo., 1999; JD, Cleve. Marshall Coll. of Law, Cleve., 2003. Licensed Psychologist Ohio, 2001. Forensic psychologist Lake County Ct. of Common Pleas, Painesville, Ohio, 1999—, Minn. State Operated Forensic Svcs., St. Peter, Minn., 2004—05. Consulting forensic psychologist Cuyahoga County Juvenile Ct., Cleve., 2001—04. Contbr. articles pub. to profl. jour. Office Phone: 507-931-7117.

FABIAN, LARRY LOUIS, academic administrator; b. Aurora, Ill., May 25, 1940; s. Louis and Emma F.; m. Terese Sulikowski, Dec. 1, 1978; children: Christopher, Laura. BA, Cath. U. Am., 1961, MA, 1963; PhD, Columbia U., 1971. Staff mem. Bur. Intelligence and Research, Dept. State, Washington, 1962; staff mem. Carnegie Endowment for Internat. Peace, N.Y.C., 1964; research staff fgn. policy studies program Brookings Instn., Washington, 1965-71, research asso., co-dir. program on tech. and Am. fgn. policy, 1971-73; sr. assoc., dir. Middle East program Carnegie Endowment for Internat. Peace, Washington, 1974-77, sec., 1977-94; sr. v.p., COO, Coun. on Fgn. Rels., N.Y.C., 1994-95; v.p. Shorebank Corp., Chgo., 1996-98; deputy commr. Chgo. Dept. Housing, 1998; v.p., exec. sec. bd. trustees, exec. dir. N.Y. office Am. U. in Cairo, 1998—. Cons. Hudson Inst., N.Y.C., Rockefeller Found. Author: Soldiers without Enemies, 1971, (with others) Regimes for the Ocean, Outer Space and Weather, 1973, Andrew Carnegie's Peace Endowment, 1985; co-editor: Israelis Speak: About Themselves and the Palestinians, 1976. Mem. Coun. on Fgn. Rels., Century Assn. Roman Catholic. Office: Am U in Cairo NY Office 420 5th Ave Fl 3D New York NY 10018-2729

FABING, SUZANNAH, museum director; b. Cin., Oct. 1, 1942; d. Howard Douglas John and Esther Clare (Marting) F.; m. Peter B. Doeringer, June 19, 1965 (div. June 1981); 1 child, Eric Atchley; m. James Alexander Muspratt, Aug. 21, 1993. AB in Art History with hons., Wellesley Coll., 1964; AM, Harvard U., 1965. Asst. to curator of Ancient art to dep. dir. mus. Fogg Art Mus./Harvard U., 1965-83; curator of records Nat. Gallery of Art, Washington, 1983-84, mng. curator of records and loans, 1984-91, head Divsn. of Rsch. on Collections, 1991-92; dir., chief curator Smith Coll. Mus. of Art, Northampton, Mass., 1992—2005. Overview panel NEA, 1993-94; reviewer NEH, 1992-94; surveyor AAM Mus. Assessment Program, 1991—; mem. Art Info. Task Force, Getty Art Info. Program, 1990-94; vis. com. Wellesley Coll. Mus., 1988—, Fitchburg Art Mus., chmn. 1983-88, others; trustee Fitchburg Art Mus., 1975-82, Revels, Inc., 1981-82, 88-92), others. Contbr. articles to profl. jours. Mem. New Eng. Mus. Assn. (panelist), Mus. Computer Network (bd. dirs. 1984-90, sec. 1988, v.p. 1988-89, pres. 1989-90), Phi Beta Kappa. Avocation: languages. Office: Hillyer Hall Smith Coll Northampton MA 01063-0001 E-mail: sfabing@smith.edu.

FABIO, THEA MARIE, lawyer; b. Boston, Mar. 8, 1955; d. Faust F. and Mary R. (Bonafede) F.; m. Richard L. Merrill, Aug. 4, 1979; children: Alessandra, Maria, Livia. BA, Smith Coll., 1976; JD, U. Tex., 1979. Bar: Tex. 1979, Mass. 1987, U.S. Dist. Ct. (so. dist.) Tex. 1980, U.S. Ct. Appeals (5th cir.) 1980. Atty. Groom, Miglicco & Gibson, Houston, 1979-85; shareholder/ptnr. Botschen & Fabio, Houston, 1986-87; pvt. practice Thea M. Fabio, Houston, 1987-90; ptnr. Fabio & Merrill, Houston, 1990—. Vol. Houston Vol. Lawyers Program, 1988—; trainer Alternative Dispute Resolution, Houston, 1987-90; pres. Univ. Pl. Assn., 1999-2000. Pres. Southgate Civic Club, Houston, 1992-97; troop leader San Jacinto Girl Scouts, Houston, 1991-2002; chair various coms. Roberts Elem. Sch., Houston, 1989-2002. Mem. Houston Bar Assn., Smith Coll. Club Houston, Greater S.W. Houston C. of C. Office: Fabio and Merrill Twelve Greenway Plz Ste 101 Houston TX 77046 Business E-Mail: tfabio@fabiomerrill.com.

FABRE, NIZA ELSIE, literature educator; b. Guayaquil, Guayas, Ecuador; BA, CUNY, 1980, MA, 1982, MPhil, 1989, PhD, 1991. Assoc. prof. Ramapo Coll. N.J., Mahwah, 1992—. Author: Americanismos, Indigenismos, Neologismos y Creación Léxica en la Obra de Jorge Icaza, 1993; contbr. articles to profl. jours. Mem. MLA, N.E. MLA, Circulo de Cultura Panamericano, Circulo de Escritores y Poetas Iberoamericanos, Assn. Ecuadorianists in N.Am., Popular Culture Assn

FABRE, RAUL, management consultant; arrived in U.S., 1982; s. Raul Fabre-Pimienta and Morales de Fabre Maria Concepcion; m. Liese Sherwood-Fabre, May 17, 1987; children: Raul, Roberto, Fernanada. MBA, Ind. U., 1984. Cert. project mgmt. profl. Project Mgmt. Inst., SAP, change mgmt. Price Waterhouse. Sr. mgr. PriceWaterhouse, Washington, 1985—93, ptnr. mgmt. consulting Moscow, 1993—98; ptnr. telecom. practice PwC Consulting, Dallas, 1998—2002, ptnr. oil and gas industry Milan, 1998—99; bus. solutions leader IBM Global Svcs., Dallas, 2002—. Named to IBM Hundred Percent Club, IBM, 2004; recipient 1st SAP Award of Excellence in Russia, SAP, AG, 1987, IBM Award of Excellence, IBM, 2004, IBM High Performance award, 2003, PriceWaterhouse Chmn. award, Price Waterhouse, 1987. Mem.: Fraud Examiners Assn. (assoc.), Project Mgmt. Inst. (assoc.). Home: 673 West Pennsula Coppell TX 75019 Office: IBM Global Svcs 1000 Belleview St Dallas TX 75215 Office Phone: 972-304-8651. Personal E-mail: raul.fabre@comcast.net.

FABREGAS, J. ROBERT, retail appearel executive; M Bus. Adminstrn., Rutgers U. Exec. v.p. Credit Suisse, Los Angeles; exec. v.p., head corp. fin. Am. Savings Bank; pres., founder Stonepine Holdings, Ltd.; CFO, exec. v.p. Easyriders, Inc., 1999—. Office: Easyriders Inc 28210 Dorothy Dr Agoura Hills CA 91301

FABRICAND, BURTON PAUL, physicist, researcher; b. N.Y.C., Nov. 22, 1923; s. Irving Kermit and Frances (Sobler) F.; m. Heather C. North, Dec. 15, 1972; children by previous marriage: Nicole Diane, Lorraine Stewart. AB, Columbia U., 1947, A.M., 1949, PhD, 1953. Project engr. Philco Corp., Phila., 1952-54; lectr., research asso. U. Pa., 1954-56; sr. research scientist Columbia Hudson Labs., Dobbs Ferry, N.Y., 1957-69; prof. physics Pratt Inst., Bklyn., 1969-92, prof. emeritus, 1992—; mng. ptnr. Fabricand Assocs., 1970—. Cons. Moore Sch. Elec. Engring., U. Pa., 1954-60, Indsl. Electronic Hardware Corp., N.Y.C., 1960-64; investment mgr. Beating the Street Fund, 1996—; bd. dirs. Murphey, Marseilles, Smith & Nammack, N.Y.C. Author: Horse Sense: A New and Rigorous Application of Mathematical Methods to Successful Betting at the Track, 1965, Beating the Street, 1969, Horse Sense: Updated and Expanded Edition, 1976, The Science of Winning: A Random Walk on the Road to Riches, 1979, Abolish the Income Tax: A New and Rigorous Inquiry into the Wealth of Nations, 1986, Symmetry in Free Markets in Symmetry—Unifying Human Understanding, 1989, The Science of Winning: A Random Walk Along the Road to Investment Riches, 1996, 2002; contbr. numerous articles on atomic and nuclear physics and oceanography. Served U.S. Army, 1942-46. Mem. Am. Phys. Soc., Sigma Xi. Home: PO Box 1107 New Milford CT 06776 Office: PO Box 1107 New Milford CT 06776-1107

FABRICANT, ARTHUR E., lawyer, corporate financial executive; b. N.Y.C., Aug. 8, 1935; s. Henry and Rita (Wilson) F.; children: Jill, Mary, John, James, Ann. AB, U. St. Andrews, Scotland, 1954, Union Coll., 1956; JD, Harvard U., 1959. Bar: N.Y. 1960. Atty. spl. group organized crime Office U.S. Atty. Gen., 1959-60; mem. firm Abeles & Clark, N.Y.C., 1960-61; v.p. Seligman & Latz Inc., N.Y.C., 1962-67, pres. internat. divsn. London, 1967-84, COO, pres., 1984-85; chmn. Essanelle Holdings, Ltd., Bermuda, 1985-96, Elizabeth Arden, Inc., 1992-2000. Bd. dirs. Elizabeth Arden Holdings Inc. Fellow Inst. Dirs.; mem. Royal Wimbledon Golf Club; Lyford Cay Club. Home: Old Warren Farm Wimbledon Common England Office: AE Fabricant & Co 39 Camp Rd London SW19 4UR England E-mail: arthurfab@aol.com.

FABRICANT, JILL DIANE, technology company executive; b. L.A. d. I. Robert and Lillian (Solid) F. BA, Mills Coll., 1971; MA, Occidental Coll., 1971; PhD, McGill U., 1976. Postdoctoral fellow Pasteur Inst., Paris, 1976-78; scientist NASA-Johnson Space Ctr., Houston, 1978-79; asst. prof. U. Tex. Med. Br., Galveston, 1979—82; pres. Biosyne Corp., Houston, 1982-88; v.p. bioscis. KVM Techs., Inc., 1989—90; pres. OvTex Corp., 1991—96; dir. The Enterprise NASA, Johnson Space Ctr., Houston, 1993—96; pres., CEO FlowGenix Corp., Webster, 1996—99; CEO Medicine for Humanity, San Juan Capistrano, Calif., 2000—01; dir. emerging technologies O'Melveny Consulting, LLC, L.A., 2002; pres. JFabricant and Assocs., Dana Point, 2002—03; pres. and CEO Neuros Corp., 2003—04, Vasix Corp., 2004—. Adv. bd. Houston Tech. Ctr., 1999—2003; trustee Mills Coll., 2000—, ATSC, Newport Beach, 2002—04; bd. dirs. San Gabriel Childrens Ctr. Contbr. articles to sci. jours. Mem.: Sigma Xi. Achievements include patents in field of sperm sexing and early-embry sexing, ovulation detection and FlowRad cell surface modification. Home: 34363 Dana Strand Dana Point CA 92629-2706 Personal E-mail: jf@jfabricant.com.

FABRICANT, MONA, mathematics and computer science educator; b. N.Y.C., Apr. 22, 1946; BA, Queens Coll., N.Y.C., 1966; MA, Queens Coll., 1967; EdD, Rutgers U., 1974. Editor Harcourt Brace Jovanovich, N.Y.C., 1970-72; asst. prof. math. LaGuardia C.C., Long Island City, N.Y., 1972-74; freelance author and editor, 1974-82; asst. prof. dept. math. and computer sci. Queensborough C.C., Bayside, N.Y., 1982-87, assoc. prof., 1987-90, prof., 1990—, chair dept. math. and computer sci., 1993—2002. Tchr. edn. program Co-Pi Timegcc, 2002—. Author: Algebra 2 with Trigonometry, 1990, Advanced Mathematics: A Precalculus Approach, 1993 (TAA Excellence award 1994); author articles. Recipient Queensborough C.C. award for Excellence in Faculty Scholarship, 2002. Mem. Nat. Coun. Tchrs. Math., N.Y. State Math. Assn. Two-Yr. Colls. (award for outstanding contbns. to math. edn. 1992), Math. Assn. Am. (vice chair for two-yr. colls. N.Y. Met. Region 1987-89, Disting. Coll. or Univ. Teaching Math. award 1997), Phi Beta Kappa, Kappa Delta Pi. Office: Queensborough CC 56th Ave & Springfield Blvd Bayside NY 11364 Office Phone: 718-631-6361. Business E-Mail: mfabricant@qcc.cuny.edu.

FABRICANT, ROBERT EDMUND, lawyer; b. N.Y., 1963; BA, Drew U., 1985; JD, Cath. U., 1990. Law clk. to Hon. Melvin P. Antell NJ Superior Ct., appellate div., 1990—91; dep. atty. gen NJ Dept. Law & Pub. Safety, 1992—94; asst. counsel for environmental issues Office of the Gov., NJ, 1994—97; pvt. practice, 1997—98; dep. chief counsel Gov. Christine Todd Whitman, 1998—2000, chief counsel, 2000—01; gen. counsel EPA, Washington, 2001—03; spl. counsel, environmental law dept. Willkie Farr & Gallagher LLP, NYC, 2004—. Adj. prof. Rutgers U. Office: Wilkie Farr & Gallagher LLP 787 Seventh Ave New York NY 10019-6099 E-mail: rfabricant@wilkie.com.

FABRIKANT, CRAIG STEVEN, psychologist; b. Buffalo, Jan. 8, 1952; s. Benjamin and Laurine Miriam (Zucker) F.; m. Carol Diane Golub, Nov. 6, 1977; children: Chad Adam, Carly. BA, Fairleigh Dickinson U., 1974, MA, 1977; PhD, Fla. Inst. Tech., 1983. Intern in psychology N.J. Dept. Human Svcs., Trenton, 1977-78; clin. psychologist North Jersey Devel. Ctr., Totowa, 1978-85, Cedar Grove Residential Ctr.; chief psychologist Hackensack (N.J.) Med. Ctr., 1985-96; pvt. practice, 1984—. Adj. instr. Montclair State Coll., 1980-82; part-time instr. Fairleigh Dickinson U.; lectr. Bergen C.C., 2004—; cons. psychology N.J. Dept. Labor and Industry, Newark, 1980—. Author profl. papers. Mem. APA, Assn. Advancement Behavior Therapy, N.J. Psychol. Assn. Home: 750 Martin Ave Oradell NJ 07649-2300 Office: 106 Old Hook Rd Westwood NJ 07675-2421 Office Phone: 201-664-7418. Personal E-mail: shrink106@aol.com.

FABUGAIS, TRISHA, law librarian; d. Berzelius and Violanda (Bradbury) Fabugais. BA, Houston Bapt. U., 1985—89; MLS, U. of Wis. - Milw., 1991—93. Law libr. dir. Sewell & Riggs, PC, Houston, Tex., 1993—95; law libr. Gardere Wynne Sewell, L.L.P., Houston, 1995—. Spkr. in field. Author: (workshop reference guide) Attorneys' Guide to Understanding and Using the Internet. Type III fellowship, Am. Assn. of Law Libraries, 1991, Advanced Opportunity Program fellowship, U. Wis.-Milw., 1992. Mem.: Am. Assn. of Law Librs. (chair local arrangements-assn. luncheon 2005 conf.), Spl. Librs. Assn., Houston Area Law Librs. (v.p. 2003—04, pres. 2004—). Office: Gardere Wynne Sewell LLP 1000 Louisiana St Ste 3200 Houston TX 77002

FACCINI, ERNEST CARLO, mechanical engineer; b. Livo, Trento, Italy, May 28, 1949; parents Am. citizens; s. Carlo and Elena Agnes (Pancheri) F.; m. Sharon L. Finisecy; 1 child, Carlo Ernesto. AA, Western Wyo. Community Coll., 1969; BS, U. Wyo., 1972, MS, 1976. Registered profl. engr. Wyo., Md., N.Mex. Engring. technician Laramie (Wyo.) Energy Rsch. Ctr., 1968-71; field engr. Mountain Fuel Supply Co., Rock Springs, Wyo., 1972; research engr. Aberdeen (Md.) Proving Grounds, 1972-73; rsch. asst. mech. engring. U. Wyo., Laramie, 1973-76; engring. asst. Bridger Coal Co., Rock Springs, Wyo., 1973; mech. engr. Naval Explosive Ordnance Disposal Facility, Indian Head, Md., 1976-85; sr. scientist TERA/NMIMT, Socorro, N.Mex., 1986-89; prin. scientist Textron Systems Corp., Wilmington, Mass., 1989—99; rsch. engr. Raytheon Co., Tewksbury, Mass., 1999—. Contbr. articles to profl. jours.; patentee in field. Mem. ASME (chmn. student sect. 1971-72), TMS, Am. Phys. Soc., Internat. Assn. of Bomb Technichians and Investigators. Roman Catholic. Achievements include rsch. in ballistics, shaped charge design, explosively formed projectile and explosive effects; also rschr. in fabrication of Ta metal for warhead liners, application of orbital forging to warhead liners, use of powdered metall. techniques to obtain starting material for forging liners, use of end-game analysis, vulnerability lethality analysis codes in the design of warheads, use of reactive/energetic materials and insensitive explosives applications to warheads; patentee in field. Home: 9 Spring Rd Londonderry NH 03053-2912 Office: Raytheon Co 50 Apple Hill dr Tewksbury MA 01876-0901 Business E-Mail: Ernest_Faccini@Raytheon.com.

FACCINTO, VICTOR PAUL, artist, gallery administrator; b. Albany, Calif., Oct. 30, 1945; s. Victor A. and Betty Jean (Smith) Pearson; 1 dau., Denise Michelle. BA in Psychology, Calif. State U.-Sacramento, 1969, MA in Art, 1972. Instr. art Calif. State U., 1972-74; asst. to dir. Nancy Hoffman Gallery, N.Y.C., 1974-78; dir. art gallery Wake Forest U., Winston-Salem, NC, 1978—, art faculty, 1983—. Founding mem. multi-media performance group Three People, 1990. One-person shows include Millennium, 1996, 2003, Mus. Modern Art, N.Y.C., 1975, Collective for Living Cinema, N.Y.C., 1976, Phyllis Kind Gallery, N.Y.C., 1980, 82, 87, 2004, N.C. Mus. Art, 1986, Helander Gallery, N.Y.C., 1991, Millennium Film Workshop, N.Y.C., 1996, 2003, Cleve. Performance Art Festival, 1998, Southeastern Ctr. for Contemporary Art, N.C., 1999, Madison (Wis.) Art Ctr., 2000; group shows include Am. Visionary Art Mus., Md., 2002, Whitney Mus. Am. Art, 1972, 73, 74, Mus. Modern Art, N.Y.C., 1978, Barbara Gladstone Gallery, N.Y.C., 1983, Monique Knowlton Gallery, N.Y.C., 1983, Helander Gallery, Palm Beach, Fla., 1988, 90; represented in film study collection Mus. Modern Art, N.Y.C., Philip Morris, Inc.; animated film maker: Shameless, 1974. N.Y. CAPS fellow, 1977; N.C. Arts Coun. fellow, 1982, 86, 2000; recipient 1st prize NYU Small Works Competition, 1983. Home: 1950 Cliffside Dr Pfafftown NC 27040-9507 Office: Wake Forest U PO Box 7232 Winston Salem NC 27109-7232 Office Phone: 336-758-5795. Business E-Mail: faccinto@wfu.edu.

FACE, E. JOSEPH, JR., state agency administrator; Grad., U. Ala., Ctrl. Mich. U. With Va. State Corp. Commn. Bur. Fin. Instns., Richmond, 1979—, dep. commr. fin. instns., 1993-99, commr., 1999—. Rep. state regulators Operation Jump-Start Coalition, Am. Fin. Svcs. Assn. and NACCA; mem. com. computerized loan origination working group U.S. Dept. Housing and Urban Devel.; spkr. in field. Contbr. articles to profl. jours. Office: Fin Instns Bur 1300 E Main St Ste 800 Richmond VA 23219-3630

FACHNIE, H(UGH) DOUGLAS, film manufacturing company official; b. Windsor, Ont., Can., Sept. 8, 1952; arrived in U.S., 1958; s. Harold Lennox Fachnie and Mary Jane (Schultz) MacKenzie. B Gen. Studies, U. Mich., 1973. Salesman Quarry, Inc., Ann Arbor, Mich., 1974, store mgr. Ann Arbor and Saginaw, Mich., 1974-77; dist. mgr. Fotomat Corp., San Diego, 1977-80, dir. ops. Wilton, Conn., 1980-81, dir. merchandising, 1981-83; mgr. optical products Fuji Photo Film U.S.A., Inc., N.Y.C., 1983-84, product mgr. consumer film Elmsford, N.Y., 1984-89, sr. product/packaging mgr. film and one-time use cameras, 1989-94, mktg. mgr. consumer photo, 1995-97, 98-00; comml. planning and logistics mgr. profl. and photofinishing Fuji Phot Film USA, Inc., Elmsford, N.Y., 1998-2000, dir. mktg., color paper and chems., comml. imaging divsn., 2000—. Mem. AAAS, Photog. Mktg. Assn., Digital Imaging Mktg. Assn., Am. Prodn. and Inventory Control Soc., Profl. Photographers Assn. Republican. Avocations: home maintenance, flying, photography, audiophile, curling. Home: 30 Fleetwood Dr Danbury CT 06810-7010 Office: Fuji Photo Film USA Inc 555 Taxter Rd Elmsford NY 10523-2394 E-mail: d.fachnie@att.net.

FACINI, MICHELLE, conservator; b. Jersey City, July 27, 1973; d. Sime and Maria Facini; m. Walter J. Ploskon, June 27, 1998; 1 child, Alexander Ploskon. BS in Art History, Towson State U., 1996; MS in Art Conservation, U. Del., 2002. Paper conservation tech. Balt. Mus. Art, Baltimore, 1996—99; Samuel H. Kress conservation fellow Fine Arts Mus. San Francisco, 2002—03; Andrew W. Mellon fellow in paper conservation Nat. Gallery Art, Washington, 2003—04; paper conservator Nat. Archives & Records Adminstrn., College Park, Md., 2004—. Presenter in field. Fellow, Nielson & Bainbridge, 2002—03. Mem.: Inst. Paper Conservation, Am. Inst. Conservation Hist. & Artistic Works, Golden Key.

FACKLER, ELIZABETH, writer; b. Lansing, Mich., May 23, 1947; d. Edward John and Mabel Marion (Jackson) Fackler; m. Michael Stoner Sinkovitz, Mar. 2, 1985. BA in Sociology cum laude, U. Calif., San Diego, 1977. Author: (novels) Arson, 1984, Barbed Wire, 1986, Blood Kin, 1992, Backtrail, 1993, Road From Betrayal, 1994, Legend of El Chivato, 1995, Billy the Kid, 1995, Badlands, 1996, Texas Lily, 1997, Breaking Even, 1998, Patricide, 2000, When Kindness Fails, 2003, Endless River, 2005, short stories, poetry. Mem.: Capitan Women's Club (pres.). Avocation: southwest history. E-mail: elizasin@trailnet.com.

FACKLER, JOHN PAUL, JR., chemistry educator; b. Toledo, July 31, 1934; s. John P. and Ruth (Moehring) F.; m. Naomi Paula Steege, Sept. 2, 1956; children: Katherine G., Cheryl R., Karla S., John M., Dorothy L. Student, MIT, 1952; BA, Valpraiso U., 1956, D.Sc. (hon.), 1987; PhD, MIT, 1960. Jr. chemist Sun Oil Co., 1953-56; teaching asst. MIT, 1956-59, research assoc., 1960; asst. prof. U. Calif., 1960-62, Case Inst. Tech., 1962-64; assoc. prof. chemistry Case Western Res. U., 1964-69, prof., 1970-82, chmn. dept., 1972-77; dean Coll. Sci., Tex. A&M U., 1983-91, Disting. prof. chemistry, 1987—; Wilhelm Manchot Forschung prof. Tech. U., Munich, 1992. Vis. prof. U. Calif. at Santa Barbara, 1969; Fulbright lectr. Colombia, 1969; cons. in chemistry Central State U., 1967-69; chmn. Inorganic Synthesis Corp., 1987-90. Author: Symmetry in Coordination Chemistry, 1971; editor: Symmetry in Chemical Theory, 1973, Inorganic Syntheses, Vol. 21, 1982, Modern Inorganic Chemistry Series, Plenum; contbr. articles to profl. jours. Bd. dirs. Luth. Met. Ministry, 1969-72; bd. dirs. Luth. High Sch. Assn., 1974-80, chmn., 1979. NSF summer fellow, 1959; J.S. Guggenheim fellow, 1976; Bye fellow Robinson Coll., U. Cambridge, 1992; recipient Tech. Achievement award Cleve. Tech. Soc., 1971 Fellow AAAS, Am. Inst. Chemists; mem. Am. Chem. Soc. (councilor 1972-73, chmn. elect 1974, chmn. Cleve. sect. 1975, chmn. elect 1978, chmn. inorganic divsn. 1979, Morley medal Cleve. sect. 1987, Southwest regional award 1990, Disting. Achievement award 2001, chair, Chemistry Sect.), Gordon Rsch. Conf. (council 1979-82, trustee 1982-89, chmn. 1989), Tex. Acad. Sci. (bd. dirs. 1987-90), Chem. Soc. London, Am. Crystal. Assn., N.Y. Acad. Scis., Sigma Xi, Phi Lambda Upsilon, Phi Delta Theta. Lutheran. Home: 4770 Enchanted Oaks Dr College Station TX 77845-7649 Office: Tex A&M U Chem Dept College Station TX 77842-3012

FACKLER, NAOMI PAULA, retired librarian; b. NYC, Sept. 30, 1935; d. Martin Theodore and Lucie Clara Louise (Cloeter) Steege; m. John Paul Fackler, Sept. 2, 1956; children: Katherine G., Cheryl R., Karla S., John M., Dorothy L. AA, Concordia Collegiate Inst., 1954; BA, Valparaiso U., 1956; MILS, U. Tex. Austin, 1986. Med. technician New Eng. Deaconess Hosp., Boston, 1956—60; libr. tech. svcs. Med. Scis. Libr. Tex. A&M U., College Station, 1986—94, mgr. collection devel. Med. Sci. Libr., 1995—2000; ret., 2000. Editor: Collection Development Policy, 1993; mem. editl. bd. Biomed. Libr. Acquisitions Bulletin, 1993-2000, The Serials Libr., 1995-2000. Co-pres. LWV Brazos County, Tex., 1995-96, pres. 1993-94, South Euclid, Ohio chpt., 1975-77; sec., bd. dirs. Dispute Resolution Ctr. Ctrl. Brazos Valley. Democrat. Lutheran. Avocations: reading, crocheting, gardening, golf, swimming.

FACTOR, MAX, III, mediator, arbitrator; b. L.A., Sept. 25, 1945; s. Sidney B. and Dorothy (Levinson) F.; BA in Econs. magna cum laude, Harvard U., 1966; JD, Yale U., 1969. Bar: Calif. 1970, U.S. Ct. Appeals (6th cir.) 1971, U.S. Dist. Ct. (cen. dist.) Calif. 1971. Law clk. U.S. Ct. Appeals (6th cir.), 1969-71; exec. dir. Calif. Law Ctr., Los Angeles, 1973-74; dir. Consumer Protection Sect., Los Angeles City Atty., 1974-77; pvt. practice Factor & Agay, Beverly Hills, Calif, 1978—. expert witness numerous state and fed. bds., 1974-78; guest lectr. UCLA, U. So. Calif., Los Angeles County Bar Assn., Calif. Dept. Consumer Affairs, 1974-76; hearing examiner City of Los Angeles, 1975. Contbr. articles to profl. jours. Bd. dirs. Western Law Ctr. for the Handicapped, Los Angeles, 1977-79, Beverly Hills Unified Sch. Dist., 1979-83; pres. Beverly Hills Bd. Edn., 1983; bd. councilors U. So. Calif. Law Ctr., Los Angeles, 1983—; chmn. Beverly Hills Visitors Bur., 1989-90. Recipient scholarship award Harvard Coll., 1965; Max Factor III Day proclaimed in his honor Beverly Hills City Council, 1979; recipient Disting. Service to Pub. Edn. award Beverly Hills Bd. Edn., 1979. Mem. Los Angeles County Bar Assn. (chmn. various coms. 1976-78), Beverly Hills C. of C. (pres. 1987-88), Beverly Hills Edn. Found. (pres. 1977-79). Office: 345 N Maple Dr Ste 294 Beverly Hills CA 90210-3878

FADAMIRO, HENRY Y., science educator, researcher; arrived in U.S., 1996; s. Joseph A. and Esther O. Fadamiro; m. Helen F. Fadamiro, July 3, 1990; children: Seyi, Fara, Moni. PhD, U. Oxford, 1995; MSc, BS, Fed. U. Tech., Akure, Nigeria, 1989, Fed. U. Tech., 1992. Lectr. Fed. U. Tech., Akure, Nigeria, 1990—92; tchg. asst. U. Oxford, 1993—95; postdoctoral rschr. Iowa State U., Ames, 1996—98, U. Minn., St. Paul, 1998—99; rsch. scientist Minn. Dept. Agr., St. Paul, 1992—2002; asst. prof. Auburn U., Ala., 2003—. Contbr. over 25 rsch. papers in peer rev. jours. and over 50 ext. related articles. Rhodes scholar, Oxford-Rhodes Trust, 1992—95. Mem.: Entomol. Soc. Am. Avocations: soccer, basketball, fishing. Office: Auburn U Dept Entomology 301 Funchess Hall Auburn University AL 36849 Office Phone: 334-844-5098.

FADAOL, ROBERT FREDERICK, lawyer; b. Opelousas, La., Oct. 3, 1939; s. Joseph Charles and Marie (Nassar) F.; m. Carolyn Ann Chapman, Jan. 1, 1970; children: Charles, Tracy, Robert. BS in Pharmacy, Auburn U., 1962; JD, Loyola U., New Orleans, 1970. Bar: La. 1971, U.S. Dist. Ct. (ea. and mid. dists.) La. 1971, U.S. Ct. Appeals (5th cir.) 1971, U.S. Dist. Ct. (we. dist.) La. 1975, U.S. Ct. Appeals (11th cir.) 1980, U.S. Tax Ct. 1984, U.S. Ct. Appeals (fed. cir.) 1994, U.S. Supreme Ct. 1976. Sole practice, New Orleans, 1971—. Judge ad hoc Parish Ct., 1986. Served to 2nd lt. U.S. Army, 1962-67. Mem. ABA, La. Bar Assn., Assn. Trial Lawyers Am., La. Trial Lawyers Assn. Republican. Roman Catholic. Home: 348 Terry Pky Gretna LA 70056-2637 Office: 1108 Stumpf Blvd Gretna LA 70053-3612

FADDEN, SISTER R. PATRICIA, academic administrator, nun; b. Canonsburg, Pa. d. Gerald and Ruth Fadden. AB in Math., Immaculata Coll.; MA in Edn., Ohio State U.; EdD in Edn., Immaculata Coll. Tchr. elem. sch., 1960—68; tchr. West Cath. H.S. Girls, 1968—77; dir. of studies Cardinal O'Hara H.S., 1977—85; prin. Archbishop Prendergast H.S., Upper Darby, Pa., 1985—90; dir. secondary curriculum and instr. Office of Edn. Archdiocese of Phila., 1991—99; prin. Villa Maria Acad., Malvern, Pa., 1999—2002; pres. Immaculata U., Immaculata, Pa., 2002—. Mem. bd. trustees Immaculata Coll., 1991—2000, adj. faculty, 1991—2000; vice chair exec. com. Commn. on Secondary Schs. Mid. States Assn., mem. strategic planning com., mem. com. on instn.-wide accreditation, mem. com. to restructure; chair IHM Profl. Devel. Com., 1995—2000. Office: Immaculata Coll 1145 King Rd Immaculata PA 19345

FADDEN ZETTS, MARY JO, music educator, director; d. Joseph H. and Mary E. Fadden; m. Eric J. Zetts, June 29, 1991. BS in Music Edn., Ind. U. Pa., 1987, MA in Music Performance, 1988, MA in Music Edn., 1989. Cert. tchr. Ind. U. Pa., 1987. Dir. bands and chorus Blairsville-Saltsburg Sch. Dist., Saltsburg, Pa., 1990—; prof. tuba and euphonium Seton Hill U., Greensburg, Pa., 2001—. Performing mem. (tuba) Slippery Rock Musicians Concert Band, Pa., 1994—, Keystone Brass Quintet, Greensburg, 2001—; prin. tuba Westmoreland Symphonic Winds, Greensburg, 1997—. Named Tchr. of the Yr., Blairsville-Saltsburg Sch. Dist., 2000. Mem.: Music Educators Nat. Conf., Ind. Music Educators Assn. (treas. 1999—2005), Pa. Music Educators Assn. (curriculum coord. HS 2001—05). Avocations: boating, attending concerts and plays. Home: 1090 East Pike Indiana PA 15701 Personal E-mail: tuba@adelphia.net.

FADEL, MITCHELL E., rental company executive; Regional mgr. Thorn Americas, 1983—91; pres., CEO ColorTyme Inc.; pres. Rent A Ctr., Plano, Tex., 2000—, COO, 2002—. Office: Rent A Center 5700 Tennyson Pkwy Plano TX 75024

FADELY, JAMES PHILIP, writer, educator; b. New Castle, Ind., Jan. 10, 1953; s. Harry Ellison and Viola (Clapp) F.; m. Sally Jane Fehsenfeld, Aug. 16, 1975; children: James Philip Jr., Adele Langsdale. BA, Hanover Coll., 1975; MA, Ind. U., 1977, PhD, 1990. Tchr. Brookstone Sch., Columbus, Ga., 1975-76, Savannah (Ga.) Country Day Sch., 1979-83; lectr. Ind. U., Indpls., 1984—2000; tchr., asst. headmaster St. Richard's Sch., Indpls., 1988-90, tchr., 1990-91, dir. admission and fin. aid, tchr., 1991-2000; dir. mktg. and pub. rels. Univ. H.S., 2000—05, tchr. history, dir. coll. counseling, 2000—. V.p. Ind. Libr. and Hist. Bd., 1997—, Ind. State Libr. and Hist. Bur. Found., 2004—; lectr. Butler U., 1985, U. Indpls., 1995. Author: A Brief History of St. Richard's School, 1960-1995, 1995, Thomas Taggart: Public Servant, Political Boss, 1856-1929, 1997, The Origins of Woodstock Club, 1997; contbr. articles to profl. jours. Dem. nominee 6th Dist. of Ind. for Congress, 1990; friend Woodrow Wilson House. Mem.: Indpls. Mus. Art, Hist. Madison, Nat. Assn. Coll. Admission Counseling, Ind. Hist. Soc. (mem. com. jrs. 1992—2002, mem. com. bd. resources 2002—, grant 1991—94), Ind. Assn. Historians, Hist. Landmarks Found., Ind., Nat. Coun. for History Edn., Am. Hist. Assn., Eng. Speaking Union (chmn. membership Indpls. (Ind.) br.

1994—98, chmn. membership region VI 1996—99, chmn. nat. membership com. 1997—2000, nat. bd. dirs. 1997—2003, exec. com. 1998—2001, pres. Indpls. br. 2002—), Soc. Ind. Pioneers (bd. govs. 2001—02), Hanover Coll. Alumni Assn. (bd. dirs. 1985—88), Marion County Hist. Soc. (treas. 1985—86, bd. dirs. 1985—98), Nat. Trust for Hist. Preservation, Leelanau Hist. Soc., Woodstock Club, Hanover Club Indpls. (bd. dirs. 1988—96), Indpls. Lit. Club, Leland (Mich.) Yacht Club, Phi Delta Theta. Democrat. Roman Catholic. Avocation: travel. Home: 9146 N Kenwood Dr Indianapolis IN 46260-1400 Office: Univ HS 2825 W 116th St Carmel IN 46032-8730 Personal E-mail: fadely@att.net.

FADEN, ALAN IRA, neurology educator; b. Phila., Jan. 11, 1945; BA in Physics, U. Pa., 1966; postgrad., Ind. U., 1966-67; MD, U. Chgo., 1971. Resident in neurology U. Calif., San Francisco, 1972-75; research neurologist Walter Reed Army Inst. Research, Washington, 1975-80; assoc. prof. neurology and medicine Uniformed Services U. of Health Scis., Bethesda, Md., 1978-81, prof. neurology and physiology, 1981-84, vice chmn. neurology, 1980-82; chief neurobiol. research unit Uniformed Serviced U. of Health Scis., Bethesda, Md., 1982-84, prof. neurology, 1984-91; vice chmn. dept. U. Calif., San Francisco, 1984-90; chief neurology VA Med. Ctr., San Francisco, 1984-90; dir. Ctr. for Neural Injury, San Francisco, 1984-91; dean rsch. Sch. of Medicine Georgetown U., 1991—. Sci. dir. Nat. Research Inst. for Neural Injury, Washington, 1983—; vis. prof. Dept. Chem. and Biochem. James Cook U., Townsville, Australia, 1990-91. Assoc. editor J. Neurotrauma; mem. editorial bd. Arch Neurol and CNS Trauma; contbr. articles to profl. jours.; patentee in field. Named one of 100 Top Leaders of Washington, Washington mag., 1982. Fellow ACP, Am. Acad. Neurology, Soc. for the Advancetment of Socio-econs., Internat. Asss. for the Study of Common Property, Japan Studies Assn. of Can.; mem. Am. Soc. Pharmacolgy and Exptl. Therapeutics, Am. Soc. Clin. Investigation, Am. Physiol. Soc., Am. Neurol. Assn., Neurotrauma Soc. (pres.), Soc. Neural Spectroscopy (coun.), San Francisco Neurol. Soc. (sec., v.p., treas., pres.). Avocations: jogging, history, art collecting. Office: Georgetown U Med Ctr 3950 Reservoir Rd NW Washington DC 20007-2126 Home: 5430 Chevy Chase Pkwy NW Washington DC 20015-1706

FADEN, RUTH R., medical educator, ethicist, researcher; BA, U. Pa., 1970; MA, U. Chgo., 1971; MPH, U. Calif., Berkeley, 1973, PhD, 1976. Sr. rsch. scholar Kennedy Inst. Ethics, Georgetown U., 1978—; prof. health policy and mgmt. Johns Hopkins U., Balt., 1986—, joint appointment in medicine, Sch. of Medicine, 1992—, prof., Philip Franklin Wagley chair in biomed. ethics, 1995—, exec. dir. Phoebe R. Berman Bioethics Inst., 1995. Chair pres.'s adv. com. on human radiation expts., 1994—95; chmn. adv. panel on reproductive hazards in workplace Office Tech. Assessment, 1984—85; mem. com. on risk perception and comm. NAS, 1987—88; mem. panel on confidentiality and data access om. on Nat. Stats. and Social Sci. Rsch. Coun., 1989—91; mem. Alcohol, Drug Abuse, and Mental Health Adminstrn., AIDS Adv. Com., 1990—92; mem. Workshop on Biomed. Ethics in U.S. Pub. Policy Office Tech. Assessment, 1992; mem. adv. bd. Finding Common Ground Project: The Reproductive Rights and Needs of Women and the Emerging Conflict in Maternal and Child Health, 1992—93; mem. Adv. Panel on Prospects for Health Tech. Assessment Office Tech. Assessment, 1992—93; co-chair com. on legal and ethical issues relating to inclusion of women in clin. studies Inst. Medicine, 1992—93, mem. com. on clin. rsch. in pub. interest, 1996—97, mem. bd. on health scis. policy, 1995—, mem. com. on battlefield radiation exposure criteria, Med. Follow-Up Agy., 1996—98, mem. adv. com. on strategies to protect health of deployed U.S. forces, 1998—99; chmn. acv. com. on human radiation expts. Human Radiation Expts., 1996; mem. nat. adv. coun. for human genome rsch. NIH, 1996—97; mem. adv. bd. to nat. info. resource on ethics and human genetics Kennedy Inst. Ethics, 1996—99; mem. privacy law adv. com. Ctrs. for Disease Control and Prevention, Coun. State and Territorial Epidemiologists, Assn. State and Territorial Epidemiologists, and Nat. Coun. State Legislators, 1998—; mem. genetics adv. com. Genetics Legis. Project, 1999—2001. Author (with T.L. Beauchamp, J. Wallace and L. Walters): Ethical Issues in Social Science Research, 1982; author: (with T.L. Beauchamp) A History and Theory of Informed Consent, 1986; author: (with G. Geller, M. Powers) AIDS, Women and the Next Generation, 1991; author: (with A.C. Mastroianni, D. Federman) Women and Health Research: Ethical and Legal Issues of Including Women in Clinical Studies, vol. I, 1994, vol. II, 1994; author: (with N. Kass) HIV, AIDS and Childbearing: Public Policy, Private Lives; mem. editl. bd.: The Millbank Quarterly, 2000—. Fellow: APA, Hastings Ctr. (fellow's coun.); mem.: APHA, Am. Soc. for Bioethics and Humanities, Forum on Bioethics (co-founder, former chmn.), Am. Assn. Bioethics (organizing com.), Inst. Medicine. Office: Phoebe R Berman Bioethics Inst Hampton House 352 624 N Broadway Baltimore MD 21205-1996 E-mail: rfaden@jhsph.edu.

FADER, BRUCE E., lawyer; b. Bklyn., Nov. 6, 1948; BS in Acctg. cum laude, CUNY, 1970; JD cum laude, Bklyn. Law Sch., 1974. Bar: NY 1975, US Dist Ct, NY Eastern Dist, Southern Dist 1975, US Dist Ct., Calif., Northern Dist. 1982, US Ct Appeals, Second Circuit 1984, US Ct Appeals, Seventh Circuit 1993, US Ct Appeals, Federal Circuit 1993, US Supreme Ct. 2000, US Ct. Appeals, Third Circuit 2002. Law clk. to Hon. Edward R. Neaher U.S. Dist. Ct. (ea. dist.) N.Y., 1974-76; mem. exec. com., atty. litigation & dispute resolution dept. Proskauer Rose LLP, NYC, 1976—. Notes editor Bklyn. Law Rev., 1973-74. Mem.: Am. Judicature Soc., NY Bar Assn. Office: Proskauer Rose LLP 1585 Broadway Fl 27 New York NY 10036-8299

FADER, HENRY CONRAD, lawyer; b. Bronx, NY, Dec. 2, 1946; s. Michael and Ruth (Filler) F.; m. Linda L. Koch, Nov. 23, 1969; children: Melanie, Danielle. AB, U. Rochester, N.Y., 1968; MEd, Temple U., 1970; JD, Syracuse (N.Y.) U., 1973. Bar: Pa. 1973, U.S. Dist. Ct. (ea. dist.) Pa. 1973, N.J. 1988. Ptnr. Fox, Rothschild, O'Brien & Frankel, Phila., 1973-92, chmn., 1985—92; ptnr. Schnader, Harrison, Segal & Lewis, Phila., 1992—2003, chmn. health law dept., 1993—2003; ptnr. Pepper Hamilton LLP, Phila., 2003—. Chmn. bd. dirs. Phila. Chamber Bus. & Industry, 2004—. Mem. Pa. Health Care Cost Containment Coun., 2004—; bd. dirs., solicitor Eagleville (Pa.) Hosp., 1987—; bd. dirs. Beth Am Synagogue, Abington, Pa., 1988—, Pa. Chamber Bus. and Industry, 1994—; chmn. bd. dirs. Intercultural Family Svcs., Inc., 1998—. Mem. ABA, Pa. Bar Assn., Phila. Bar Assn., Nat. Assn. Bond Lawyers, Am. Health Lawyers Assn. Avocations: tennis, reading, gardening. Office: Pepper Hamilton LLP 3000 Two Logan Sq 18th and Arch Sts Philadelphia PA 19103 Office Phone: 215-981-4640. Business E-Mail: faderh@pepperlaw.com.

FADER, SHIRLEY SLOAN, writer; b. Paterson, N.J. d. Samuel Louis and Miriam (Marcus) Sloan; m. Seymour J. Fader; children: Susan Deborah, Steven Micah Kimchi. BS, MS, U. Pa. Writer, journalist, author, Paramus, N.J. Chmn., coord. ann. writers seminar Bergen C.C., 1973-76. Author: (books) The Princess Who Grew Down, 1968, From Kitchen to Career, 1977, Jobmanship, 1978, Successfully Ever After, 1982 (Brit. edit. 1985), Wait a Minute: You Can Have It All, 1993, paperback edit., 1994; (columns) Jobmanship, People and You, Family Weekly mag., 1971-82, How to Get More From Your Job, Glamour mag., 1978-81, Start Here, Working Woman mag., 1980-88, Work Strategies, Working Mother mag., 1987-88, Women Getting Ahead, Ladies Home Jour., 1980-90, How Would You Handle It, New Idea mag., 1984—, Moving Up, Woman mag., 1989-90, Career Expert "Ask the Experts", Woman's World mag., 1992-95; contbg. editor Family Weekly, 1971-82, Glamour mag., 1978-81, Working Woman mag., 1980-88, Working Mother mag., 1987-88, Ladies Home Jour., 1980-90, Woman mag., 1989-90; contbr.: (book) Foundations of English, 2002; contbr. articles on career, relationships and travel to mags. worldwide. Mem. Authors Guild, Am. Soc. Journalists and Authors (moderator ann. writer's conf. 1971-2000, nat. v.p. 1976-77, mem.-at-large nat. exec. coun. 1976-78, 83-86, nat. sec., mem. exec. coun. 1995-96), Nat. Press Club, Newswomen of N.Y. Address: 377 Mckinley Blvd Paramus NJ 07652-4725

FADIEL, AHMED, research scientist; Post doctoral fellow in bioinformatics/proteomics Hosp. for Sick Children, Toronto, Canada, 2002; assoc. rsch. scientist Sch. Medicine Yale U., New Haven, 2002—. Mem.: Yale Club (NYC).

FADIMAN, ANNE, writer, educator; b. NYC, Aug. 7, 1953; d. Clifton and Annalee Whitmore (Jacoby) F.; m. George Howe Colt, Mar. 4, 1989; children: Susannah, Henry. BA, Harvard U., 1975. Contbr. editor Harvard Magazine, Cambridge, Mass., 1973-75; instr. Nat. Outdoor Leadership Sch., Lander, Wyo., 1975-76; columnist Country Journal, Manchester, N.H., 1978-79; asst. sci. editor Life, N.Y.C., 1979-81, columnist, 1986-87, staff writer, 1981-88; columnist, editor-at-large Civilization, Washington, 1994—97; editor The Am. Scholar, Washington, 1997—2004; Francis writer-in-residence Yale U., New Haven, 2005—. Bd. incorporators Harvard Magazine, Cambridge, Mass., 1985— (bd. dirs., 1985-91), vis. lectr. Smith Coll., 2000-02. Author: The Spirit Catches You and You Fall Down, 1997 (Nat. Book Critics Circle award for nonfiction, 1997, LA Times Book Prize for Current Interest, 1997, Ann Rea Jewell Non-Fiction Prize, Boston Book Rev., 1997), Ex Libris: Confessions of a Common Reader, 1998; editor: Best American Essays, 2003, Rereadings, 2005. Recipient Nat. Magazine award for Reporting, Am. Soc. Magazine Editors, 1987, Nat. Mag. award for essays, 2003; named John S. Knight fellow in Journalism Stanford (Calif.) U., 1991-92. Mem. Phi Beta Kappa (hon.).

FADIMBA, KOFFI BAANA, mathematics professor; s. Banena and Ahouda Fadimba; m. Foga Boma Atta, Aug. 25, 1986; children: Bogmsa, Jennifer Wenmi, Marie-Salveria Pehessi. BS (Licence) in Math., U. Bordeaux I, Talence, France, 1980; MS (DEA) in Math. and Applications, U. of Bordeaux I, Talence, France, 1982; PhD in Math., U. SC, Columbia, 1993. Jr. lectr. U. Lome, Togo, 1983—88, tenured asst. prof., 1994—2000; post doctoral fellow Inst. Sci. Computations Tex. A&M, College Station, 1994; vis. scholar, lectr. U. RI, Kingston, 2000—02; asst. prof. math. U. SC, Aiken, 2002—. Contbr. profl. papers to math. jours. Pres. Assn. Sons. and Daus. from Kongah Residing in Lome, Togo, 1995—96. Grantee, U. SC, Aiken, 2004; Fond d'Aide et de Cooperation fellow, Ministry of Cooperation, France, 1986—88, African Grad. fellow, Africa Am. Inst., NYC, 1988—93, post doctoral fellow, U. SC, Columbia, 1993. Mem.: Reseau African de Mathematiques Appliquees pour le Developpement, Math. Assn. Am., Soc. Indsl. and Applied Math., Am. Math. Soc. Home: 30 Early Ct Aiken SC 29803 Office: Univ SC - Aiken 471 University Pky Aiken SC 29801 Office Phone: 803-641-3537. Home Fax: 803-641-3726; Office Fax: 803-641-3726. Personal E-mail: koffif@usca.edu.

FADIRAN, OLADIPO O., electrical engineer, researcher; b. Ile-Ife, Osun State, Nigeria; B of Elec. Engring., U. Ilorin, 1996; MSEE, U. Cape Town, 2001. Registered engr., Coun. Registered Engrs. Nigeria, 1997. Rsch. fellow Elec. Engring. Dept., U. Cape Town, South Africa, 2001—02, Ctr. Theoretical Study Phys. Systems and Elec. Engring. Dept., Clark Atlanta U., 2002—. Contbr. articles to profl. jours. Mem., engring. student coun. U. Ilorin Engring. Student Coun., Nigeria, 1995—96. Recipient Acad. Excellence award, Clark Atlanta U., 2003. Mem.: IEEE. Avocation: soccer. Office: Ctr Theor Stud Phy Sys 223 James P Brawler Dr SW Hiram GA 30141 Office Phone: +1-404-880-6432.

FADOOL, MARGOT CUSHING-BROWN, education educator; b. Cleveland, Ohio, Nov. 22, 1962; d. James Maxwell and Gretchen Halbin Brown; m. John Gerard Fadool, June 17, 1989; children: John Maxwell, Jacob James. BS, Pa. State U., 1981—85; MEd, Cabrini Coll., 1989—91; EdD, U. of Cin., 1991—95. Asst. prof. Bowling Green State U., Ohio, 1994—96; tchr. Nido de Aguilas, Santiago, Chile, 1997—99; vis. asst. prof. Agnes Scott Coll., Atlanta, 2004—05. Tchr. trainer Escuela Campo Alegre, Caracas, Venezuela, 1999—2002.

FAENZA, MICHAEL M., mental health association administrator; b. Dec. 5, 1950; BA, Ind. U., Gary, 1975; MSSW, U. Tex., Arlington, 1982. Counseling Lansing (Ill.) Assn. for Retarded Citizens, 1974-76; dir. work adjustment and placement svcs. Tradewinds Rehab. Ctr., Inc., 1976-78; sr. mental health cons. Tri-City Cmty. Mental Health Ctr., Inc., East Chicago, Ind., 1978-79; vocat. program coord. Independence House, Dallas County MHMR Ctr., 1979; child placement worker Dallas County Child Protective Svcs. Tex. Dept. Human Resources, Dallas, 1981; program Dallas County Juvenile Detention Ctr., Dallas, 1982-83; adminstr., clin. dir. Letot Ctr.-Dallas County, Dallas, 1983-88; exec. dir. Mental Health Assn. Greater Dallas, 1988-94; pres., CEO Nat. Mental Health Assn., Alexandria, 1994—. Contbr. chpt. to book. Recipient Advocacy award Alliance for Mentally Ill., 1989, Disting. Mental Health Profl. award Dallas Child Guidance Ctr., 1991, Excellence in Nat. Exec. Leadership award Nat. Assembly of Health and Human Svc. Orgns., 1999. Mem. Alpha Delta Mu.

FAERBER, GARY J., surgeon, educator; s. John and JoAnn Faerber; m. Kathleen A. Cooney; children: Meg, Tim. BS in Biology, Washington U., 1980; MD, Temple U., 1984. Resident urol. surgery U. Mich., Ann Arbor, 1989—92; asst. prof. U. Mich. Med. Sch., Ann Arbor, 1992—98, assoc. prof., 1998—. Cons. Olympus Inc. Mem.: Endonigl. Soc., Am. Urology Assn., Mich. Urologic Soc. (pres. 2003). Office: Univ Mich Med Ctr 1500 E Medical Center Dr Ann Arbor MI 48109

FAFIAN, JOSEPH, JR., management consultant; b. N.Y.C., Apr., 1939; s. Joseph M. and Mary (Alonso) F.; m. Nathalie Coluccio, Oct. 5, 1963; children: John Joseph, Michael Francis. BA, Bklyn. Coll., 1959. Assoc. actuary U.S. Life Ins. Co., N.Y.C., 1967; 2d v.p. USLIFE Corp., 1967-69, v.p., 1969-72, sr. v.p. ops., 1972-76, exec. v.p. life ins., 1976-77, sr. exec. v.p. life ins., 1977-78; pres., chief exec. officer, dir. U.S. Life, 1978-80; pres., dir. Beneficial Nat. Life Ins. Co., N.Y.C., 1980-82, chmn. bd., CEO, 1982-84; founder, pres., CEO, Fafian and Assocs., Inc., S.I., N.Y., 1984—. Dir. Assoc. Madison, pres., COO, 1982-84; acting pres. Maine & Fidelity Life Ins. Co., 1985-86; bd. dirs. Columbian Mut., Columbian Family, Columbia Life. Served with N.G., 1962-67. Fellow Soc. Actuaries; mem. Acad. Actuaries. Home: 74 Mason St Staten Island NY 10304-3106 Office: 74 Mason St Staten Island NY 10304-3106 Office Phone: 718-727-0880. E-mail: josephfafian@cs.com. *Guide my actions by three principles: Always be proud of what I am doing; Always seek to improve what I am doing; Always learn more about what I am doing.*

FAGALY, WILLIAM ARTHUR, curator; b. Lawrenceburg, Ind., Mar. 1, 1938; s. William James and Dorothy Rae (Wheeler) F. BA, Ind. U., 1962, MA, 1967. Asst. registrar Art Mus., Ind. U., Bloomington, 1965-66; registrar New Orleans Mus. Art, 1966—67, curator collections, 1967-73, chief curator, 1973-80, asst. dir for art, 1980-2001, Francoise Billion Richardson curator African art, 1997—; curator art U. Art Mus. U. La. Lafayette, 2002—03. Guest curator La. Folk Painting exhibit, Mus. Am. Folk Art, 1973, Exhbn. of Contemporary Painting, Corcoran Gallery of Art, Washington, 1989, Preacher Art, Arthur Roger Gallery, New Orleans, 1990, Geography of the Body: The Art of Mignon Faget, Contemporary Arts Ctr., 1995, Preacher Art, Phyllis Kind Gallery, N.Y.C., 1997, Watercolor U.S.A. 1999, Springfield (Mo.) Art Mus., 1999, Nat. Works on Paper, McNeese State U., Lake Charles, La., It's a Wonderful World, Contemporary Arts Ctr., New Orleans, 2003, Aristides Logothetis, Cue Art Found., N.Y.C., 2003, Tools of Her Ministry: The Art of Sister Gertrude Morgan, Am. Folk Art Mus., 2004, Resonance from the Past: African Sculpture from the New Orleans Mus. of Art, Mus. for African Art, N.Y.C., 2005; adv. panel visual arts and crafts divsn. arts La. Arts Coun., 1978—81, 1992; guest lectr. S.S. Rotterdam, 1983, H.M.S. Queen Elizabeth II, 1986, Sotheby's, NY, 1996; cons. Liberian Pavilion La. World Expn., 1984, Shapes of Power, Belief and Celebration: African Art from New Orleans Collections, 1989, Fritz Bultman: A Retrospective, 1993, Wyo. Art Mus., Laramie, 1995, Oreg. Biennial, Portland Art Mus., 1995, Roots of Am. Jazz: African Mus. Instruments from New Orleans Collections, 1995, He's the Prettiest: A Tribute to Big Chief Allison "Tootie," Montana's 50 Yrs. of Mardi Gras Indian Suiting; selection panelist McKnight Found. Fellowship Program, Minn. Coll. Arts and Design, Mpls., 1986, So. Arts Fedn., NEA Arts Regional Artists Fellowships, 1990; selecton panelist 1984 Visual Arts Fellowships, Wyo. Arts Coun., 1993; selection panelist Adolph and Esther Gottlieb Found. Artist Fellowships, N.Y.C., 1995, Western States Art Fedn./NEA, 1996; bd. dirs. Ctr. for African and African-Am. Studies, So. U., New Orleans, Sac-O-Lait-The Keith Sonnier Found., 2002—; bd. advisors Wilkinson County Mus., Woodville, Miss.; adj. curator Univ. Art Mus., U. La., Lafayette, 2002—; founder art activities bus. FUN (Fagaly Unltd.), 2001—. Contbr. articles to profl. jours. NEA fellow, 1985, Visual Arts and Media fellow Miss. Arts Commn., 1994, Visual Arts fellow Wyo. Art Coun., 1994; recipient Mayor's Arts award City of New Orleans, 1997, Gov.'s Arts award La. State Arts Coun., 1997, Charles E. Dunbar Jr. Career Svc. award La. Civil Svc. League, 1999, Isaac Delgado Meml. award Fellows of New Orleans Mus. of Art, 2001. Mem. Am. Assn. Mus. (mem. vis. com. for Tampa Mus. Art accreditation program 1999). Episcopalian. Home: 915 Saint Philip St New Orleans LA 70116-2407 Office: PO Box 19123 New Orleans LA 70179-0123 Office Phone: 504-483-2630. Business E-Mail: bfagaly@noma.org.

FAGAN, ALANNA, artist, printmaker; b. New Bedford, Mass., Sept. 20, 1939; d. Arthur William and Dorothy Virginia (Crawshaw) Raybold; m. Leo James Fagan, Apr. 25, 1965; children from previous marriage: Charles Downing Lay II, Daniel Mackintosh Lay II. Student, U. Bridgeport, 1963—65, Silvermine Guild Sch. Art, 1965. Painting instr. Silvermine Guild Sch. Art, New Canaan, Conn., 1977—84. Author: (filmstrip) Drawing Animals, 1981, Drawing People, 1981; one-woman shows include Salmagundi Club, NY, 1975, Northeast Harbor Gallery, Maine, 1980, Silvermine Guild Arts Ctr., Conn., 1981, 1986, Fairfild U., Conn., 1983, Greene Art Gallery, 1986, Darien Pub. Libr., 1986, Les Castelets, St. Barthelemy, 1991—92, La Galerie, 1992, exhibited in group shows at Pastel Soc. Am., NY, 1974—92, Springfield (Mass.) Art Mus., 1975, Salmagundi Club, NY, 1976—2004, Art of the Northeast, Conn., 1977, 1984—85, 1995, 1999—2000, Circle Gallery, NY, 1978, Copley Mus., Mass., 1979, Central Falls Gallery, NY, 1984, Galerie du Mus., Paris, 1985, Nat. Acad. Design, NY, 1986, Greene Art Gallery, Conn., 1986, Westport Arts Ctr., 1988—2005, Allied Artist Am., NY, 1989—91, Craven Gallery, Mass., 1997, Ctr. for Contemporary Printmaking, Conn., 1997—2004, Am. Watercolor Soc., 1997, Stamford Art Assn., Conn., 1998, Brush and Palette Club, 2002, New Haven Paint and Clay Club, 2004, 2005, Represented in permanent collections Harvard Club, NY, New Eng. Sch. Law, Mass., Cohen and Wolf PC, Conn., Ctr. for Creative Leadership, NC, Inst. Geografico de Agostini, Italy. Mem.: Ctr. for Contemporary Printmaking, Westport Arts Ctr., Silvermine Guild Artists, Allied Artists Am., New Haven (Conn.) Paint and Clay Club. Home: 73 Housatonic Dr Milford CT 06460

FAGAN, CHRISTOPHER BRENDAN, lawyer; b. South Bend, Ind., Sept. 1, 1937; s. Christopher J. and Clara A. (Poirier) F.;m. Mary K. O'Neill, Feb. 11, 1961 (div. July 1977); children: Kathleen, Patricia, Colleen, Matthew, Timothy, Daniel; m. Janyce R. Brock, Sept. 1, 1978 (div. May 1997); m. Barbara A. Vargo, Apr. 10, 1999. BSME, U. Notre Dame, 1959; JD, Georgetown U., 1965. Bar: Ohio 1965, U.S. Dist. Ct. (no. dist.) Ohio 1967. Patent examiner U.S. Patent Office, Washington, 1963-65; patent atty. Eaton Corp., Cleve., 1965-67; assoc. Fay, Sharpe, Fagan, Minnich & McKee, Cleve., 1967-70, ptnr., 1970—. Lt. USN, 1959-63. Mem. Ohio State Bar Assn., Cleve. Bar Assn., Am. Patent Law Assn., Cleve. Patent Law Assn. Republican. Roman Catholic. Home: 3040 N Windsor Ct Westlake OH 44145-6717 Office: Fay Sharpe Fagan Minnich & McKee 1100 Superior Ave E Ste 700 Cleveland OH 44114-2518

FAGAN, FREDERIC, neurosurgeon; b. Bklyn., Oct. 18, 1935; s. Jack and Sophie (Altschuler) F.;m. Donna Fagan, Mar. 1, 1969; children: Gabrielle, Samantha. BA, Ohio State U., 1958. Intern Santa Monica (Calif.) Hosp., 1959; resident N.Y. Hosp., N.Y.C., 1960. Cons. AMA, L.A., 1980—. Dir. Smithsonian Assocs., Washington, 1995, U.S. Holocaust Meml. Mus., Washington, 1995. Named Surgeon of Yr. MacMillan Industries, Santa Clara, Calif., 1989. Mem. N.Y. Acad. Scis., NRA (dir. 1995). Home: 11102 Excelsior Dr Apt 9E Norwalk CA 90650-5646 Office: Woodruff Hosp 3800 Woodruff Ave Long Beach CA 90808-2125 Office Phone: 562-420-2847.

FAGAN, JEFFREY A., law educator; b. Dec. 17, 1946; BE, NYU, 1968; MS in Human Factors Engring., SUNY, Buffalo, 1971, PhD in Policy Sci., 1975. Dir. Coll. Urban Studies SUNY, Buffalo, 1970—74; assoc. rsch. analyst Office of Criminal Justice Planning, Oakland, Calif., 1974—75; rsch. dir. No. Calif. Svcs. League, San Francisco, 1975—76; dir. Ctr. Law and Soc. Policy URSA Inst., San Francisco, 1977—86; sr. rsch. fellow NYC Criminal Justice Agency, 1986—88; assoc. prof. Dept. Law and Politics John Jay Coll. of Criminal Justice, CUNY, assoc. dir. rsch.; assoc. prof. criminal justice CUNY Grad. Ctr., 1988—89; assoc. prof. to prof. Sch. Criminal Justice, Rutgers U., 1989—95; dir. Ctr. for Violence Rsch. and Prevention Mailman Sch. of Pub. Health, Columbia U., NYC, prof. Depts. of Epidemiology and Sociomedical Scis., 1995—; vis. prof. Columbia Law Sch., NYC, 1998—2001, prof., co-dir. Ctr. for Crime, Cmty. and Law, 2001—. Co-author: Workin' Hard for the Money: The Social and Economic Lives of Women Drug Dealers, 2000, The Changing Borders of Juvenile Justice: Waiver of Adolescents to the Criminal Court, 2002; contbr. articles to law jours. Office: Coilubia Law Sch Rm 634, Box D-18 435 W 116th St New York NY 10027 Home: 28 Old Fulton St Apt 7D Brooklyn NY 11201 Office Phone: 212-854-2624. Office Fax: 212-854-7946. E-mail: jfagan@law.columbia.edu.

FAGAN, JOHN ERNEST, lawyer; b. Phila., June 30, 1949; s. George Vincent and Ernestine (Hudak) F. BA with highest honors, U. Notre Dame, 1971; JD, Northwestern U., 1974; LLM, NYU, 1986. Bar: Ill. 1974, Wis. 1977, N.Y. 1979, Va. 1991. Assoc. McDermott Will & Emery, Chgo., 1974-76; internat. tax analyst Allis-Chalmers Corp., Milw., 1976-78; tax counsel Mobil Corp., N.Y.C. and Fairfax, Va., 1978-99, Exxon Mobil Corp., Fairfax, 2000—. Mem. Am. Petroleum Inst. (com. mem.). Office: Exxon Mobil Corp 3225 Gallows Rd Rm 3C2129 Fairfax VA 22037-0002 E-mail: john.e.fagan@exxonmobil.com.

FAGAN, TARA J., counseling administrator, educator; b. East Northport, N.Y., July 22, 1970; d. Lawrence Fagan and Susan McLaughlin. BS, SUNY, Oneonta, 1992; MS, LI U., 1997. Admissions counselor C. W. Post Campus LI U., Brookville, 1997, N.Y. Coll. Health Professions, Syossett, 1998—99; adj. instr., asst. dir. student svc. St. Joseph's Coll., Patchogue, NY, 1999—2002; adj. asst. prof., counselor campus activities Suffolk CC, Brentwood, NY, 2002—, acting dir. campus activities, 2003—04. Advisor Dance Club, Brentwood, 2002—04; coach dance team Suffolk County CC, Brentwood, 2004—. Recipient cert. of Appreciation, Student Govt. St. Joseph's Coll., 1999—2000, award of honor, Campus Activities Bd., 2003—04. Mem.: Am. Coll. Pers. Assn., Western Suffolk Counselors Assn., LI Coll. Pers. Assn. (sec. 2002—03). Avocations: dance, camping, bicycling, photography, windsurfing. Office: Suffolk CC Captree Commons 110 1001 Crooked Hill Rd Northport NY 11768

FAGEL, BRUCE G., lawyer, former emergency physician; b. Chgo., Ill., Oct. 11, 1946; BA with high honors, U. Ill., 1968; MD, U. Ill. Coll. Medicine, 1972; JD with high honors, Whittier Coll. Sch. Law, LA, 1982. Bar: Calif. 1982; lic. to practice medicine Ill., 1973, Calif., 1975. Practiced emergency medicine, 1972—82; atty. Bruce G. Fagel & Associates., Beverly Hills, Calif., 1982—. Seminar spkr. Consumer Attys. Calif., Consumer Attys. Assocs. LA. Author: Liberty on Hold, Families of Victims Need Help Not Lawsuits; guest appearances on CBS, NBC & ABC, featured in LA Times, Sacramento Bee, Oakland Tribune. Mem. Birth Trauma Litigation Group, Inner Circle of Advocates. Capt., medical corps. USAF, 1974—76. Nominee Trial Lawyer of Yr. (6 Times); named one of Top 10 Litigators, Nat. Law Jour., 2003. Fellow: Am. Coll. of Law and Medicine; mem.: LA County Med. Assn., Calif. Med. Assn., Assn. of Trial Lawyers Am., ABA, President's Club of Consumer

Attorneys Assn. of LA, Calif., Phi Beta Kappa. Office: Bruce G Fagel & Associates 445 S Beverly Dr Ste 200 Beverly Hills CA 90212 Office Phone: 310-277-1288. Office Fax: 310-277-0835. Business E-Mail: bgfagel@aol.com.

FAGEN, LESLIE GORDON, lawyer; b. N.Y.C., Apr. 12, 1950; s. Herman and Estelle F. BA, Yale U., 1971; JD, Columbia U., 1974. Bar: N.Y. 1975, D.C. 1985, U.S. Dist. Ct. (so. and ea. dists.) N.Y. 1975, U.S. Ct. Appeals (2d cir.) 1975, U.S. Ct. Appeals (3d cir.) 1991, U.S. Ct. Appeals (7th and fed. cirs.) 1993; U.S. Supreme Ct. 1978. Law clk to judge U.S. Dist. Ct. (ea. dist.) N.Y., Bklyn., 1975; assoc. Milbank, Tweed, Hadley & McCloy, N.Y.C., 1975-76; from assoc. to ptnr. Paul, Weiss, Rifkind, Wharton & Garrison, N.Y.C., 1976—, co-chair litigation dept. Former adj. faculty Cardozo Law Sch., CCNY. Vice-chmn., pres. and trustee The Ednl. Alliance, Inc., 1993-2000; bd. dirs. Maimonides Med. Ctr., 2001—. Fellow Am. Coll. Trial Lawyers; mem. N.Y. State Bar Assn., Assn. Bar City N.Y. Office: Paul Weiss Rifkind Wharton & Garrison 1285 Avenue Of The Americas New York NY 10019-6028

FAGER, EVERETT DEAN, minister; b. Redkey, Ind., Apr. 6, 1947; s. Luther Von and Nola Marceil (Elliott) F.; m. Kathy Jo McKean, Mar. 17, 1973 (div. Aug. 1989); children: Holly Renee (dec.), Ryan Christopher; m. Janet A. Caskey, June 12, 1993; children: Benjamin Dean, Sarah Ashley; stepchildren: Eric, Mike, Nick Caskey. BA, U. Evansville, 1969; ThM, Boston U., 1972; D of Ministry, Drew U., 1981. Ordained to ministry Meth. Ch. as elder, 1973. Youth and edn. min. First United Meth. Ch., Decatur, Ind., 1972-76, St. Mark's United Meth. Ch., Decatur, 1972-76; min. Albany (Ind.) United Meth. Ch., 1976-82, Osceola (Ind.) United Meth. Ch., 1982-86; sr. pastor Taylor Chapel United Meth. Ch., Ft. Wayne, Ind., 1986-91; assoc. dir. for local ch. ministries North Ind. Conf., 1991-94; ptnr. GROW Ministries, Ft. Wayne, 1983-93; pastor Main St. United Meth. Ch., Peru, Ind., 1994—2001, 1st United Meth. Ch., Plymouth, Ind., 2001—. Chaplain Jaycees, Decatur, 1975-76; mem. area comm. com. United Meth. Ch., 1980-86, conf. comm. chair., 1980-86, 94—; mem. conf. program com. United Meth. Ch., 1984-90; assoc. faculty Bethel Coll., Mishawaka, Ind., 1985-86; chmn. Membership Recruitment Task Force Ch. Builders of Ft. Wayne Dist., 1987-91; mem. com. on Investigation N. Ind. Conf. United Meth. Ch., 1988-91, chair Kokomo dist. com. on superintendency, 1998—; bd. dirs. Assoc. Chs. Allen County, Ft. Wayne, 1988-91. Chmn. Walkathon, Adams County March Dimes, Decatur, 1973-75; mem. Publicity Com. Osceola Days, 1984-86; vice chmn. Osceola Bd. Zoning Appeals, 1985-86; mem. new ch. devel. task force North Ind. U. Meth. Ch., 1989-93; mem. local coord. coun. Gov.'s Task Force for a Drug-Free Ind., 1994-2001; mem. C.O.M.P.A.S.S., 1995-97. Named Outstanding Young Man Am., Jaycees, Decatur, 1975; recipient Ch. Growth awards N. Ind. Conf. United Meth. Ch., 1988. Mem. Peru Min. Assn. (pres. 1995-96), Peru Rotary Club (sgt.-at-arms 1998-99, chaplain, 1999-2001), Plymouth Rotary Club, Plymouth Optimist Club. Democrat. *The worst of life is tolerable if one believes that the best is yet to come. The best of life is put in perspective if one believes that the best is yet to come. This is my one overeaching and unconquerable hope: the best is yet to come.*

FAGER, JEFFREY, broadcast executive; b. Wellesley, Mass., Dec. 10, 1954; m. Melinda Fager; 3 children. B in Eng. and polit. sci., Colgate U., 1977. Prodn. asst. Sta. WBZ-TV, Boston, 1977—78; news writer Sta. WEEI Radio, Boston, 1978—79; assignment editor Sta. WGBH-TV, Boston, 1978—79; broadcast prodr. Sta. KPIX-TV, San Francisco, 1979—82; prodr. various broadcasts including weekend edit. CBS Evening News and Nightwatch CBS News, 1982—84; prodr. CBS Evening News, NYC, 1984—85, London, 1985—88, 48 Hours, NYC, 1988—89, 60 Minutes, 1989—94; sr. broadcast prodr. CBS Evening News, 1994—96; exec. prodr. CBS Evening News with Dan Rather, 1996—98, 60 Minutes II, 1998—2004, 60 Minutes, 2004—. Office: 60 Minutes 524 W 57th St New York NY 10019 Office Phone: 212-975-3247.*

FAGER, WESLEY M., writer, editor; b. Norfolk, Va., Mar. 1, 1946; s. William Bartlett Fager and Dorothy Louise Mooney; m. Catherine Pierce, Oct. 20, 1968; children: William, Penelope Williams, Wesley (dec.). BS, Va. Polytech. Inst., 1970. Author: A Clockwork Straight, 2000. Lt. U.S. Army, 1970-72. VPI scholar, 1964. Mem. Masons (3e deg.), Am. Legion. Avocation: exposing destructive-mind cults. Home: 3126 Valentino Ct Oakton VA 22124 Office: Oakton Inst Cultic Studies 3126 Valentino Ct Oakton VA 22124 Fax: 703-281-2647. E-mail: wesfager@thestraights.com.

FAGERBERG, ROGER RICHARD, lawyer; b. Chgo., Dec. 11, 1935; s. Richard Emil and Evelyn (Thor) F.; m. Virginia Fuller Vaughan, June 20, 1959; children: Steven Roger, Susan Vaughan, James Thor, Laura Craft. BS in Bus. Adminstrn., Washington U., St. Louis, 1958, JD, 1961, postgrad., 1961-62. Bar: Mo. 1961. Grad. teaching asst. Washington U., St. Louis, 1961-62; assoc. firm Rassieur, Long & Yawitz, St. Louis, 1962-64; ptnr. Rassieur, Long, Yawitz & Schneider and predecessor firms, St. Louis, 1965-91; pvt. practice St. Louis, 1991—. Mem. exec. com. Citizens' Adv. Council Pkwy. Sch. Dist., 1974—, pres.-elect, 1976-77, pres., 1977-78; bd. dirs. Parkway Residents Orgn., 1969—, v.p., 1970-73, pres., 1973—; scoutmaster Boy Scouts Am., 1979-83; Presbyn. elder, 1976—, pres. three local congs. 1968-70, 77-78, 83-84. Mem. ABA, Mo. Bar Assn., St. Louis Bar Assn., Christian Bus. Men's Com. (bd. dirs. 1975-78, 87-91), Full Gospel Bus. Men's Fellowship, Order of Coif, Omicron Delta Kappa, Beta Gamma Sigma, Pi Sigma Alpha, Phi Eta Sigma, Phi Delta Phi, Kappa Sigma. Lodges: Kiwanis (bd. dirs. 1988-91), Masons, Shriners. Republican. Home and Office: 13812 Clayton Rd Chesterfield MO 63017-8407

FAGG, GEORGE GARDNER, federal judge; b. Eldora, Iowa, Apr. 30, 1934; s. Ned and Arleene (Gardner) Fagg; m. Jane E. Wood, Aug. 19, 1956; children: Martha, Thomas, Ned, Susan, George, Sarah. BSBA, Drake U., 1965, JD, 1958. Bar: Iowa 1958. Ptnr. Cartwright, Druker, Ryden & Fagg, Marshalltown, Iowa, 1958—72; judge Iowa Dist. Ct., 1972—82, U.S. Ct. Appeals (8th cir.), 1982—99, sr. judge, 1999—. Faculty Nat. Jud. Coll., 1979. Mem.: Iowa Bar Assn., Order of Coif. Office: US Ct Appeals US Courthouse Annex 110 E Court Ave Ste 455 Des Moines IA 50309-2044

FAGG, KERI BETH (MYERS), speech pathology/audiology services professional; b. Terre Haute, Ind., Mar. 26, 1955; d. James Chester and Geraldine Beth Myers; children: Derik Alan, Tashawna Nicole. BS, Ind. State U., 1997, MS, 1998. Cert. speech pathologist Am. Speech Lang. Assn. and Ind. Speech Hearing Asn., 1998, lic. Ind. Professions Bur. Standards. Sec. Whiteco Outdoor Advt., Terre Haute, Ind., 1978—84; customer svcs. Cinergy PSI, Brazil, 1985—91; speech therapist Putnam County Schools, 2000—05, Intrepid Home Healthcare, Brazil, 2001—05, Healthcare Therapy Svcs., Terre Haute, 2001—05. Singer (cast/actor/singer): (community therater) numerous. Fundraising sec. Spl. Olympics, Greencastle, Ind., 2000—05; bd. dird. Putnam County Spl. Olympics, Putnam County, 2000—05. Mem.: Ind. Speech Hearing Assn. (licentiate), Am. Speech Lang. Assn. (licentiate). Office: Old Nat Trail Spl Edn 522 Anderson Greencastle IN 46135 Office Phone: 765-653-2781. Personal E-mail: kbfslp@yahoo.com.

FAGG, LAWRENCE WELLBURN, nuclear physicist, researcher, educator; b. East Orange, N.J., Oct. 10, 1923; s. Lawrence Wellburn Fagg and Doris Virginia Shea Fagg Gedney; m. Simone Fastres, May 5, 1950 (div. 1956); m. Patricia Menendez, Dec. 14, 1958 (div. 1962); m. Mary Skipp, Apr. 18, 1993. MS in Physics, U. Md., 1947; MA in Physics, U. Ill., 1948; PhD in Physics, Johns Hopkins U., 1953; MA in Religion, George Washington U., 1981. Physicist Naval Rsch. Lab., Washington, 1953-58; sr. physicist Atlantic Rsch. Corp., Alexandria, Va., 1958-63; physicist Naval Rsch. Lab., Washington, 1963-76; rsch. prof. physics Cath. U. Am., Washington, 1977—. Author: Two Faces of Time, 1985, The Becoming of Time, 1995, Electromagnetism and the Sacred, 1999; contbr. chpts. to Ionization in High Temperature Gases, Electric and Magnetic Giant Resonances in Nuclei, Themes in Nuclear Physics, New Perspectives on Problems in Classical and Quantum Physics; contbr. more than 80 articles to sci. and profl. jours. With AUS, 1942-45. Recipient Meritorious Civilian Svc. award Naval Rsch. Lab., 1975. Fellow Am. Phys. Soc.; acad., fellow Inst. on Religion in Age of Sci. (v.p. 1981-85); mem. Internat. Soc. for Study Time. Avocations: farming, skiing, writing. Office: Cath U Am Dept Physics 4th St and Michigan Ave NE Washington DC 20064-0001 E-mail: lfagg@shentel.net.

FAGG, RUSSELL, judge, lawyer; b. Billings, Mont., June 26, 1960; s. Harrison Grover and Darlene (Bohling) F.; m. Karen Barclay, Feb. 15, 1992. BA, Whitman Coll., 1983; JD, U. Mont., 1986; MJS, U. Nev., 1999. Law clk. Mont. Supreme Ct., Helena, 1986-87; atty. Sandall Law Firm, Billings, 1987-89; city prosecutor City of Billings, 1989-91; dep. atty. Yellowstone County, Billings, 1991-94; mem. Mont. State Legislature, Helena, 1991-94; judge State Dist. Ct. (13th dist.) Mont., Billings, 1995—. Dir. Midland Empire Pachyderm Club, 1988-94, pres. 1990-91; chmn. judiciary com. House of Reps., 1993-94. Named Outstanding Young Montanan, Mont. Jaycees, 1994; recipient Young Life Spirit award Billings Young Life, 2002. Avocations: hiking, fishing, skiing, reading. Home: 3031 Rimview Dr Billings MT 59102-0955 Office: PO Box 35027 Billings MT 59107-5027 Office Phone: 406-256-2906.

FAGGIN, FEDERICO, electronics executive; b. Vicenza, Italy, Dec. 1, 1941; arrived in U.S., 1968, naturalized, 1978; s. Giuseppe and Emma (Munari) Faggin; m. Elvia Sardei, Sept. 2, 1967; children: Marzia, Marc, Eric. Grad., Perito Industriale Instituto A. Rossi, Vicenza, 1960; D.Physics, U. Padua, Italy, 1965. Sect. head Fairchild Camera & Instrument Co., Palo Alto, Calif., 1968-70; dept. mgr. Intel Corp., Santa Clara, Calif., 1970-74; founder, pres. Zilog Inc., Cupertino, Calif., 1974-80; v.p. computer systems group Exxon Enterprises, N.Y.C., 1981; co-founder, pres. Cygnet Techs., Inc., Sunnyvale, Calif., 1982-86; co-founder, CEO Synaptics, Inc., San Jose, Calif., 1986-99, chmn., 1999—; pres., CEO Foveon, Inc., 2003—. Named to Nat. Inventor's Hall of Fame, 1996; recipient W. Wallace McDowell award, IEEE Computer Soc., 1994, Kyoto prize, 1997; Marconi Fellowship award, 1988. Achievements include development of silicon gate technology for MOS fabrication, first microprocessor. Office: Foveon Inc 2820 San Tomas Expwy Santa Clara CA 95051 Business E-Mail: federico.faggin@foveon.com.

FAGIEN, STEVEN, ophthalmologist, consultant; b. Neptune, NJ, Mar. 7, 1957; s. Melvin Blumenthal and Sondra Parker; m. Debra L Rattner, Dec. 26, 1981; children: Samantha Michelle, Alyssa Nicole, Kayla Danielle. BS, U. of Fla., 1975—79, MD, 1979—83. Bd. cert. Ophthalmology, 1988, Am. Soc. of Ophthalmic Plastic and Reconstructive Surgery, 1989. Internal medicine U. Fla., resident-ophthalmology, 1979—83; fellow- ophthalmic plastic surgery U. Ill., 1987—88; dir. self-employed, Boca Raton, Fla., 1988—2004. Founder Collagenesis, Inc., Beverly, Mass., 1975—2002; educator, instr. Am. Soc. Aesthetic Plastic Surgery, Los Alamitos, Calif.; founder and co-director SEE Internat., Santa Barbara, Calif., 1991—96; cons., med. advisor Allergan, Inc., Irvine, Calif., 1997—, Medicis, Inc, Scottsdale, Ariz., 2002—; founder, pres. Collagen Matrix Technologies, Boca Raton, Fla., 2002—; cons., med. advisor Dermik Aesthetics, Inc, Berwyn, Pa.; chief; dept. surgery Boca Raton Cmty. Hosp., Boca Raton, Fla. Contbr. articles to profl. jours. Bd. mem. Boca Raton Cmty. Hosp. Recipient Man of the Yr., Cystic Fibrosis Found., 2001, Dr. of the Yr., Boca Raton Women's Club, 2002. Fellow: Am. Soc. of Ophthalmic Plastic and Reconstructive Surgery, Am. Acad. of Ophthalmolgy; mem.: Am. Soc. of Aesthetic Plastic Surgery (assoc.). Achievements include research in new techiques in blepharoplasty; advanced techniques for the use of botulinum toxin type A in facial enhancement; advanced techniques in injectable soft tissue augmentation agents; development of inectable human collagen matrix; research in soft tissue augmentation. Office: Steven Fagien MD PA 660 Glades Road Ste 210 Boca Raton FL 33431 Office Phone: 561-393-9898. Office Fax: 561-347-0772.

FAGIN, ALLEN IAN, lawyer; b. Bronx, N.Y., Oct. 22, 1949; s. Carl and Frieda (Ehrlich) F.; m. Judith H. Rosenberg, June 29, 1970; children: Robert, Charles. BA summa cum laude, Columbia Coll., NYC, 1971; MPP, JD cum laude, Harvard U., 1975. Bar: NY 1976, US Dist. Ct., NY Eastern & Southern Dist. 1977, US Ct Appeals, Second Circuit 1984, US Ct Appeals, Eleventh Circuit 1989, US Dist. Ct., NY Northern Dist. 1992, US Ct. Appeals, Sixth Circuit 1997, US Supreme Ct. 1998. Law clk. to Hon. Robert L. Carter U.S. Dist. Ct. (so. dist.) N.Y., 1975-76; assoc. Proskauer Rose LLP, NYC, 1976-83, ptnr., 1983—, former co-chair, labor & employment law dept, 1997—2004, now chmn., 2005—. Fellow: Coll. Labor & Employment Lawyers. Office: Proskauer Rose LLP 1585 Broadway Fl 20 New York NY 10036-8299

FAGIN, BARRY STEVEN, computer science educator, writer; b. Boston, Sept. 2, 1960; s. Arnold D. Fagin and Lois R. Roisman; m. Michele Berdinis Fagin, Aug. 11, 1985; children: Max, Erica. AB magna cum laude, Brown U., 1982; PhD, U. Calif., Berkeley, 1987. Asst. prof. engring. sci. Thayer Sch. of Engring., Dartmouth Coll., Hanover, N.H., 1987-94; prof. computer sci. USAF Acad., Colorado Springs, Colo., 1994—. Program annotator Colo. Springs Symphony, contbr. articles to profl. jours. Co-founder Families Against Internet Censorship, Colorado Springs, 1996—; former info. dir. ACM SIGCAS, N.Y.; mem. Rocky Mountain Skeptics, Colorado Springs. Recipient Civil Liberties award ACLU, 1996; sr. fellow Independence Inst.; Fulbright scholar St. Petersburg (Russia) Tech. State U., 2001. Jewish. Avocations: snowboarding, mountain climbing, scuba, freestyle frisbee, speaking Russian. Office: USAF Acad Dept Computer Sci 2354 Fairchild Dr Colorado Springs CO 80840 Fax: 719-333-3338. Office Phone: 719-333-7377. E-mail: barry.fagin@usafa.af.mil.

FAGIN, CLAIRE MINTZER, nursing educator, nursing administrator; b. NYC; d. Harry and Mae (Slatin) Mintzer; m. Samuel Fagin, Feb. 17, 1952; children: Joshua, Charles. BS, Wagner Coll., 1948; MA, Tchrs. Coll. Columbia, 1951; PhD, NYU, 1964; DSc (hon.), Lycoming Coll., 1983, Cedar Crest Coll., 1987, U. Rochester, 1987, Med. Coll. Pa., 1989, U. Md., 1993, Wagner Coll., 1993, Loyola U., 1996, Case Western Res. U., 2002; LLD (hon.), U. Pa., 1994, U. Toronto, 2004; DHL (hon.), Hunter Coll., 1993, Rush U., 1996, Johns Hopkins U., 2003. Staff nurse, clin. instr. Sea View Hosp., S.I., NY; clin. instr. Bellevue Hosp., N.Y.C.; psychiat. nurse cons. Nat. League for Nursing, N.Y.C.; asst. chief psychiat. nursing svc. clin. ctr. NIH; rsch. project coord. dept. psychiatry Children's Hosp., Washington; instr., assoc. prof. psychiat.-mental health nursing NYU, N.Y.C., dir. grad. programs in psychiat. mental health nursing, 1965—69; chmn. nursing dept., prof. Herbert H. Lehman Coll., CUNY, N.Y.C., 1969—77; dir. Health Professions Inst., Montefiore Hosp. and Med. Ctr., 1975—77; Margaret Bond Simon dean sch. of nursing U. Pa., Phila., 1977—92, Leadership chair prof., 1992—96, interim pres., 1993—94, dean emeritus, prof. emeritus, 1996—. Bd. dirs. Provident Mut. Ins. Co., 1988—96, chmn. audit com., 1985—96, exec. com., 1986—96, adv. com., 1996—2003; bd. dirs., mem. audit com. Salomon, Inc., 1994—97; bd. dirs. Vis. Nurse Soc., NY, Radian Inc., 1994—2002, Van Ameringen Found., 1996—2004; dir. program bldg. acad. geriatric nursing John A. Hartford Found., 2000—05; spkr., cons. in field. Contbr. articles to profl. jours. Named Disting. Dau. Pa., 1994; recipient Achievement award, Wagner Coll., 1956, Tchrs. Coll., 1975, Disting. Alumna award, NYU, 1979, Founders award, Sigma Theta Tau, 1981, Hon. Recognition award, ANA, 1988, Woman of Courage award, Women's Way, 1990, Alumni Merit award, U. Pa., 1991, First Leadership award, Trustee Coun. Pa. Women First, 1991, Caring award, Phila. Vis. Nurses Assn., 1994, Lillian Wald award, N.Y. Vis. Nurses Assn., 1994, Hildegard Peplau award outstanding contbn. psych-nursing, 1994, Pres. medal, NYU, 1998, Nightingale Lamp award, Am. Nurses Found., 2002; disting. scholar, 1984, hon. fellow, Royal Coll. Nursing, 2002. Mem.: Nat. League for Nursing (pres. 1991—93), Am. Orthopsychiat. Assn. (bd. dirs. 1972—75, exec. com. bd. dirs. 1973—75, pres. 1985—86), Am. Acad. Nursing (governing coun. 1976—78, Living Legend award 1998), Inst. Medicine of NAS (governing coun. 1981—83, chmn. bd. health promotion and disease prevention 1991—94, mem./chair Lienhard Com. 1999—2004). Address: 200 Central Park S Apt 12E New York NY 10019-1415 Office: U Pa Sch Nursing 354 Neb Bldg Philadelphia PA 19104-6096 Office Phone: 202-651-7047. Personal E-mail: cfagin@att.net.

FAGIN, DAN, writer, reporter; b. Oklahoma City; m. Alison Frankel; 2 children. B, Dartmouth Coll., 1985. Polit. and govt. reporter Sarasota Herald-Tribune, Newsday, environ. writer, 1991—. Co-author (with Marianne Lavelle): (books) Toxic Deception (finalist Investigative Reporters & Editors award), 1997. Recipient AAAS Journalism award, 2003. Mem.: Soc. of Environ. Journalists (pres. 2003). Office: Environment Writer Newsday 235 Pinelawn Rd Melville NY 11747

FAGIN, DAVID KYLE, gas industry executive; b. Dallas, Apr. 9, 1938; s. Kyle Marshall and Frances Margaret (Gaston) F.; m. Margaret Anne Hazlett, Jan. 24, 1959 (dec. July 1999); children: David Kyle, Scott Edward; m. Terry Lee Craig, Dec. 6, 2002. BS in Petroleum Engring., U. Okla., 1960; postgrad., Am. Inst. Banking, So. Meth. U. Grad. Sch. Bus. Adminstrn. Registered profl. engr., La., Okla., Tex. Trainee Exxon-Mobil (formerly Magnolia Petroleum Co.), 1955—56; jr. engr., engr., then ptnr. W.C. Bednar Petroleum Cons., Dallas, 1958—65; petroleum engr. Bank of Am. N.A. (formerly First Nat. Bank Dallas), Dallas, 1965—68; v.p. Rosario Resources Corp. (merged 1980 with AMAX Inc.), N.Y.C., 1968—75; pres. Alamo Petroleum Corp., 1968—82; exec. v.p. Rosario Resources Corp. (now Alcoa/Phelps Dodge), N.Y.C., 1975—77, dir., 1975—80, pres., COO, 1977—82; chmn., dir., pres., CEO Fagin Exploration Co., Denver, 1982—86; pres., COO, bd. dirs. Barrick Gold Ltd. (formerly Homestake Mining Co.), Toronto, Canada, 1986—91; CEO & chmn. Golden Star Resources Ltd., Denver, 1992—96, dir., 1992—; chmn., CEO Western Exploration and Devel. Ltd., Denver, 1997—2000, dir., 1997—2001. Bd. dirs. all T. Rowe Price Pub. Mut. Funds, Balt., Pacific Rim Mining Corp. (formerly Dayton Mining Co.), Vancouver, B.C., Canyon Resources Corp. Bd. dirs. Denver Area coun. Boy Scouts Am., 1993—, Mineral Info. Inst.; bd. visitors U. Okla. Sch. Engring., 1995-98, 99—, chmn., 2002—04; Nat. Mining Hall of Fame and Mus., 1997—. Mem. AIME (chmn. Dallas sect. of Soc. Petroleum Engrs. 1975, chmn. investment fund 1979-82), Soc. Mining, Metallurgy and Exploration (dir. 1996-97), Soc. Petroleum Engrs., Mining and Metall. Soc. Am., Internat. Mining Profls. Soc. (dir., exec. com., v.p. 1999, pres. 2001-2002). E-mail: dkfagin@aol.com.

FAGUNDO, ANA MARIA, language educator; b. Santa Cruz de Tenerife, Spain, Mar. 13, 1938; came to U.S., 1958; d. Ramón Fagundo and Candelaria Guerra de Fagundo. BA in English and Spanish, U. Redlands, 1962; MA in Spanish, U. Wash., 1964, PhD in Comparative Lit., 1967. Prof. contemporary lit. of Spain and creative writing U. Calif., Riverside, 1967—. Vis. lectr. Occidental Coll., Calif., 1967; vis. prof. Stanford U., 1984. Author 11 books of poetry including Invention de la Luz, 1977 (Carbala de Oro Poetry prize Barcelona 1977), Obra Poetica: 1965-90, 1990, Isla En Si., 1992, Antologia, 1994, El Sol, La Sombra En El Instante, 1994, La Miriada de Los Sonambulos, 1994, Trasterrado Marzo, 1999, Pacabras Sobre Las Dias, 2004, The Poetry of Ana Maria Fagundo: A Bilingual Anthology, 2005; founder, editor Alaluz, 1969—. Grantee Creative Arts Inst., 1970-71, Humanities Inst., 1973-74; Summer faculty fellow U. Calif., 1968, 77; Humanities fellow, 1969. Mem. Am. Assn. Tchrs. Spanish and Portuguese, Sociedad Gen. de Autores de Espana. Roman Catholic. Avocations: tennis, jogging, walking. Office: U Calif Spanish Dept Riverside CA 92521-0001 Home: Valdevarnes 13 5o D 28039 Madrid Spain

FAHERTY, DAVID MILES, musical instrument repairman; b. Ft. Worth, Tex., July 8, 1954; s. Frank Patrick and Laura Gene Faherty. Grad., Tarrant County Jr. Coll., 1977. Owner, pres. D.M. Faherty Music Co., Ft. Worth, 1978—. Active US Jaycees, Ft. Worth, 1985-94; pres. Tarrant County Jaycees, 1988-89. Mem. Ft. Worth City Band (v.p. 1984-85), Nat. Assn. of Profl. Band Instrument Repair Technicians (clinician tchr.). Roman Catholic. Avocations: hunting, fishing, musical performance. Office: D M Faherty Music Co PO Box 11102 Fort Worth TX 76110-0102 Office Phone: 817-923-9904. E-mail: milessax@napbirt.org.

FAHERTY, ROBERT LOUIS, publishing executive; b. St. Louis, Sept. 26, 1939; s. Justin Louis and Elizabeth Veronica (Quigley) F.; m. Claudia C. Hutchison, Jan. 10, 1969; children: Kathleen Marie, Timothy Robert, Mark Robert, Megan Elizabeth, Bridget Justine. BA magna cum laude, Cath. U. Am., 1961, MA, 1962; STL cum laude, Pontifical Gregorian U., Rome, 1966. Editor St. Louis Rev., 1967-69, Ency. Britannica, Chgo., 1969-72; mng. editor sci./Benefic Press Harcourt Brace Jovanovich, Chgo., 1972-73; mng. editor Scholarly Press, Detroit, 1973-75; co-founder, editor-in-chief Reference Publs., Algonac, Mich., 1975-77; editor-in-chief Congl. Budget Office, Washington, 1977-84; dir. Brookings Instn. Press, Washington, 1984—; v.p. Brookings Instn., 2002—. Lectr. Howard U. Book Pub. Inst., 1985-89; mem. adv. com. on pub. and comm. programs U. Va., 1994—, instr., 1995—. Contbr. articles to profl. jours. Trustee, treas. Ela Area Pub. Libr. Dist., Lake County, Ill., 1973-74; bd. dirs. United Cmty. Ministries, Fairfax County, Va., 1992-99, pres., 1995-99; chmn. Algonac Recreation Commn., 1976-77; mem. bioethics com. for Mid-Atlantic region Kaiser Permanente HMO, 1989-99; mem. Fairfax County, Va., Human Svcs. Coun., 1999—. Curators' scholar U. Mo., 1957, Basselin Found. scholar Cath. U. Am., 1959. Mem. Assn. Am. Univ. Presses (bd. dirs. 1991-94, 97-2000, pres. 1998-99), Assn. Am. Pubs. (bd. dirs. 2001—). Home: 4303 Mission Ct Alexandria VA 22310-3353 Office: Brookings Instn 1775 Massachusetts Ave NW Washington DC 20036-2103 E-mail: rfaherty@brookings.edu.

FAHEY, HENRY MARTIN, information technology executive; b. Cin., Jan. 27, 1963; s. Richard H. and Gloria A. (Benson) F.; m. Pamela S. Gille, May 23, 1991; children: Jeffrey W. Winton (dec.), Suzy M. Winton. BS in Computer Sci., U. Colo., 1986; MBA, So. Meth. U., 1990. Software engr. Digital Equipment Corp., Colorado Springs, Colo., 1986-89, tech. cons. Ft. Worth, 1990-92; network specialist Galderma Labs, Inc., Ft. Worth, 1993-95, mgr. tech. svcs. N.Am., 1995-98; mgr. tech. svcs. ChannelPoint, Inc., Colorado Springs, Colo., 1998-99, dir. worldwide support svcs., 1999—. Tech. adv. bd. student work consortium U. Tex., Arlington, 1995-98. Mem. Oracle Applications Users Group, Digital Equipment Computers Users Soc. Republican. Mem. Ch. LDS. Avocations: black belt taekwondo, downhill skiing, laser tag gaming, scuba diving, martial arts. Office: ChannelPoint Inc 5825 Mark Dabling Blvd Colorado Springs CO 80919-2266 Home: 6512 N Missouri Ave Oklahoma City OK 73111-7928

FAHEY, JAMES EDWARD, brokerage house executive; b. N.Y.C. s. John Michael and Kathleen Rose Fahey; 2 children. BBA, MBA, Iona Coll. Registered investment advisor. Territory asst. European Am. Bank, N.Y.C., 1978—80; internat. analyst Texaco, Inc., White Plains, 1981—83; mgr. internat. treasury Am. Standard Inc., N.Y.C., 1984—88; asst. treas. Perkin Elmer Internat., Inc., 1988-91; sr. mgr. internat. treasury Perkin Elmer Corp., Norwalk, Conn., 1988-91; sr. v.p. investments, corp. client group dir. Smith Barney, N.Y.C., 1991—2005; v,p. Merrill Lynch, N.Y.C., 2005—. Active Friends of Am. Cancer Soc., N.Y.C., 1986—; mem. leadership com. Tristate Cure Autism Now, 2002—. Mem.: Friendly Sons of St. Patrick (N.Y.C.). Office: Smith Barney 450 Lexington Ave New York NY 10017

FAHEY, JOHN M., JR., book publishing executive; b. NYC; m. Heidi Fahey; children: Christopher, Kenneth, Allison. BS in Engring., Manhattan Coll.; MBA, U. Mich. Exec. v.p., COO Time Life Books, 1986—89; pres., CEO, chmn. Time Life Inc., Alexandria, Va., 1989—96; exec. v.p., chair ops. office Nat. Geog. Ventures, Washington, 1996—; pres., CEO Nat. Geog. Soc., Washington, 1998—, Explorers Hall, Washington. Adv. com. mem. Newseum; bd. dir. Jason Found. for Edn., Johnson Outdoors Inc., Exclusive Resorts. Named one of top 100 Irish Americans, Irish Am. mag. Office: Nat Geographic Soc 1145 17th St NW Washington DC 20036-4701*

FAHEY, MIKE, mayor; b. Kansas City, Kansas; 4 children. BA, Creighton Univ., 1973. Former owner Am. Land Title Co., 1978—90, ret. CEO, 1978—97; mayor City of Omaha, 2001—. Bd. Holy Name Housing, Am. Red Cross Heartland Chpt., Creighton Prep H.S.; chmn. Omaha Planning Bd., 1981. Office: 1819 Farnam St Ste 300 Omaha NE 68183 Business E-Mail: mfahey@ci.omaha.ne.us.*

FAHEY, RICHARD PAUL, lawyer; b. Oakland, Calif., Nov. 2, 1944; s. John Joseph and Helene Goldie (Whetstone) F.; m. Suzanne Dawson, June 8, 1968; children: Eamon, Aaron Chad. AA, Meritt Coll., 1964; BA, San Francisco State U., 1966; JD, Northwestern U., 1971. Bar: N.Mex., 1971, U.S. Dist. Ct. N.Mex., 1972, U.S. Ct. Appeals (10th cir.) 1972, Ohio 1973, U.S. Dist. Ct. (no. and so. dists.), U.S. Supreme Ct. 1975. Atty. in charge Dinebeiina Nahiilna Be Agaditahe, Shiprock, N.Mex., 1971-73; asst. atty. gen. State of Ohio, Columbus, 1973-76; ptnr. Fahey & Schraff, 1976-80; atty. Sanford, Fisher, Fahey, Boyland & Schwarzwalder, 1980-84; of counsel Knepper, White, Arter & Hadden, 1984-85; ptnr. Arter & Hadden, 1985-99; of counsel Vorys Sater Seymour and Pease LLP, 2000—02, ptnr., 2003—; adj. prof. law Capital U., 1976-86, Ohio State U., 1986-87; chmn. Ohio Oil and Gas Regulatory Rev. Commn., 1986-87. Author: Underground Storage Tanks A Primer of the Federal Regulatory Program, 2nd edit., 1995; contbr. articles to profl. jours. Vol. Peace Corps., Liberia, 1966—68; active Columbus Pub. Schs. Bd. Edn., 1986—93, pres., 1989; trustee Godman Guild Settlement House, 1976—82, Ohio Environ. Coun., 1981—83; adv. bd. WCBE Pub. Radio; Charter rev. com. Columbus City, 1998—99; pres. Audobon Ohio, 1999—2002; mem. sewer and water adv. bd. City of Columbus, 2004—; exec. com. Dem. Party, Ohio, 1996—2002; trustee Downtown Columbus, Inc., 1989, Pilot Dogs, Inc., 1993—2004, pres., 2001, Cmty. in Sch., 2000—. Grantee, Russell Sage Found., 1969. Mem. ABA (vice chair Sonreel water quality com. 1993-97), Ohio Bar Assn., N.Mex. Bar Assn., Columbus Bar Assn., Columbus Bar Found. Democrat. Unitarian Universalist. Avocations: travel, fishing, reading, jogging, skiing. Home: 449 E Dominion Blvd Columbus OH 43214-2216 Address: 58 Camino Nevoso Sante Fe NM 87505 Office: Vorys Sater Seymour and Pease LLP 52 E Gay St Columbus OH 43215 Office Phone: 614-464-5601. Business E-Mail: rpfahey@vssp.com.

FAHIEN, LEONARD AUGUST, physician, educator; b. St. Louis, July 26, 1934; s. John Henry and Alice Katherine (Schubkegel) F.; m. Rose Marian Burmeister, June 21, 1958; children: Catherine Fahien Reuter, Lisa Fahien Uldrich, James. AB, Washington U., St Louis, 1956; MD, Washington U., 1960. Intern U. Wis., Madison, 1960-61; surgeon NIH, Bethesda, Md., 1964-66; asst. prof. dept. pharmacology U. Wis. Med. Sch., Madison, 1966-69, asso. prof., 1969-74, prof., 1974—, asso. dean, 1979-83; vis. prof. Inst. Protein Rsch. Osaka U., Japan, 1991; prof. El Julios U. Barcelona (Spain), 1997. Contbr. chapters to books, articles to profl. jours. Served with USPHS, 1964—66. Numerous NIH grants, 1966—. Mem.: Phi Beta Kappa, Sigma Xi. Lutheran. Home: 3212 Topping Rd Madison WI 53705-1435 Office: 426 S Charter St Madison WI 53715-1626 Business E-Mail: lafahien@facstaff.wisc.edu.

FAHIEN, ROSE MARIAN, small business owner; b. Union, Mo., June 28, 1933; d. William Henry and Ella Caroline (Kissling) Burmeister; m. Leonard August Fahien, June 21, 1958; children: Catherine Fahien Reuter, Lisa Fahien Uldrich, James Robert. BA, Washington U., 1955; student, U. Wis., 1956-57, Madison (Wis.) Tech. Coll., 1972. Cert. secondary tchr. Mo., Wis. Tchr. English Mehlville Jr. HS, Lemay, Mo., 1955-57, Kirkwood (Mo.) HS, 1957-60, 61-62, Ctrl. HS, Madison, Wis., 1960-61; tchr., buyer Ch. Day Nurseries, Madison, 1971-75; Panhellenic advisor U. Wis., Madison, 1984-91; founder, owner Bog Lake Outfitters, La Pointe, Wis., 1989—. Co-owner Trippers Too, Ltd., Madison, 1985—; customer sales rep. Lands' End, Cross Plains, Wis., 1990—2005. Author: Research Paper Manual for High School Students, 1959, 101 Things to do in Apostle Island Country, 1999, A History of the University League: 1901-2001, 2001; editor: (newsletter) U. League, 1978; contbr. articles to profl. jours. Pres. Shorewood Hills PTA, Madison, Shorehawk Square Dancers, 1983; chairperson Van Hise-Shorewood Neighborhood Girl Scouts, 1977; bus. mgr. Midwest Assn. Edn. Young Children; pres., sec. Bethel Luth. Ch. Women. Mem.: PEO Sisterhood (pres. 1985), Attic Angel Assn. (expansion chair 1989—90, mem. fin. com. 1993—95), Shorewood Garden Club (pres.), Univ. League (pres. 1981), Civics Club (pub. affairs spkr.). Lutheran. Avocations: photography, literature, writing, gardening. Home: 3212 Topping Rd Madison WI 53705-1435 Office Phone: 715-747-2685. Personal E-mail: boglakeotftr@yahoo.com.

FAHLE, MANFRED, ophthalmology researcher; b. Duesseldorf, Germany, Dec. 10, 1950; s. Fritz and Helma (Westerfeld) F.; m. Sigrid Henke, Aug. 3, 1979; children: Nora Katharina, Till Patrick Jakob; m. Karoline Spang, Aug. 4, 2001. Degree in Biology, U. Goettingen, Fed. Republic Germany, 1972; degree in medicine, U. Giessen, Fed. Republic Germany, 1973; MA in biology, U. Mainz, Fed. Republic Germany, 1975; MD, U. Tuebingen, Fed. Republic Germany, 1977. Fellow Max-Planck Inst. for Biol. Cybernetics, Tuebingen, 1977-81; head electrophysiol. lab. Univ. Eye Clinic, Tuebingen, 1981-88; vis. scientist U. Calif., Berkeley, 1984, MIT, Cambridge, Mass., 1989-90; fellow German Rsch. Coun., Tuebingen, 1990-93; prof. ophthalmology, head sect. visual sci. Univ. Eye Hosp., Tuebingen, 1994-98; head Inst. Brain Rsch. IV, human-neurobiology U. Bremen, Germany, 2000—, dir. Ctr. Cognitive Sci., 2005—. Wiersma vis. prof. Calif. Inst. Tech., Pasadena, 1996; prof., head dept. optometry and visual sci. City U., London, 1998-99; prof. human neurobiology U. Bremen, Germany, 1999—; dir. Inst. for Brain Rsch., 2003-; vis. prof. Univ. Coll., London, 1999-2002, vis. prof. Applied Vision Rsch. Ctr., City Univ., 2000—; mem. acad. senate, U. Bremen, 2003—. Mem. editl. bd. German Jour. Ophthalmology, 1991-97, Neuroophthalmology, 1993-2003, Vision Rsch., 1994-2004; author: (with T. Poggio) Perceptual Learning, 2002, (with M. Greenlee) Visual Neuropsychology, 2003. Bd. dirs. Grad. Program Neurobiology, Tuebingen, 1986-91, Drug Rsch. Program, Tuebingen, 1996-99. Recipient Heisenberg award German Rsch. Coun., 1989, prize von Humboldt/Max-Planck Soc., 1992. Avocations: music, literature, sailing, windsurfing. Home: Graf-Moltkestr 56 D28211 Bremen Germany Office: Inst Human Neurobiology Argonnenstr 3 D28211 Bremen Germany Office Phone: 49-421-218-9522. E-mail: mfahle@uni-bremen.de.

FAHMY, IBRAHIM MOUNIR, hotel executive; b. Alexandria, Egypt, July 4, 1943; came to U.S., 1986; s. Ambassador Mounir Ibrahim and Aziza (Kelada) F.; m. Brenda Lee Chenier, Sept. 18, 1970 (div. Jan. 1991); children: Susan Lee, Christine Lynn; m. Ann Marie Jones, Oct. 15, 1995; 1 child, Laila Ann. Certs., St. Mark's Coll., Alexandria, 1949-63; student, U. Alexandria, 1962-63. V.p., gen. mgr. King Edward Hotel, Toronto, Canada, 1982—86; sr. v.p. Can. Forte Hotels Inc., N.Y.C., 1986—95; exec. v.p. Forte Hotels Inc., San Diego, 1986—95; mng. dir. The Carlton, Washington, 1995—99, The Essex House, NY, NY, 1999—2002, Egypt-Starwood Hotels and Resorts Worldwide, Cairo, 2002—. Former dir. Hotel Assn. Met. Toronto, Ont. Hostelry Inst.; mem. adv. com. Humber Coll. Vol. Kidney Found., Muscular Dystrophy, The Can. Children's Found. Mem. Internat. Wine and Food Soc. Avocations: skiing, english riding, squash, theater, skeet and sporting clay shooting. Home and Office: Sheraton Cairo Hotel Towers and Casino PO Box 11 Cairo 11511 Egypt Office Phone: +202 3369700/800.

FAHMY, NABIL, ambassador; b. NY, Jan. 5, 1951; married; 3 children. BS in Physics and Math., Am. U. Cairo, 1974, MA in Mgmt., 1976. Advisor Cabinet of V.P. of Egypt, 1974—76; mem. Cabinet of the Sec. of the Pres. for External Comms., 1974—76; 2nd sec. Egyptian Mission to UN, Geneva, N.Y.C., 1978—82; mem. Cainet of the Dep. Prime Minister of Fgn. Affairs, Egypt, 1982—84; 1st sec. UN, 1986—; sr. disarmament ofcl. Dept. Internat. Orgns., Min. of Fgn. Affairs, 1991—; polit. advisor to fgn. minister Govt. of Egypt, 1993—97, amb. to Japan, 1997—99, amb. to U.S. Washington, 1999—. Mem. UN Sec. Gen.'s Adv. Bd. of Disarmament Matters, 1999, chmn., 2001; head Egyptian delegation to Middle East Peace Process Steering Com., 1993, Egyptian delegation to Multilateral Working Group on Regional Security and Arms Control, Madrid Peace Conf., 1991; vice-chmn. 1st com. on disarmament and internat. security affairs 44th session UN Gen. Assembly, 1986. Office: Embassy of the Arab Republic of Egypt 3521 International Ct NW Washington DC 20008

FAHMY HUDOME, RANDA, lawyer; b. Syracuse, N.Y., Feb. 4, 1964; d. Mahmoud Hussein and Irandukht (Vahidi) F.; m. Michael Hudome; 1 child, Alexandria. BA summa cum laude, Wilkes U., 1986; JD, Georgetown U., 1990. Fin. dir. Holtzman for Congress, Wilkes-Barre, Pa., 1986; lobbyist Citizens for Am., Washington, 1987; legal asst. Hamlin Blaszkow, Washington, 1987; with Koonz, McKenney & Johnson, Washington, 1988, Willkie, Farr & Gallagher, Washington, 1989-90, assoc., 1990—94; fgn. policy counsel to Sen. Spencer Abraham U.S. Senate, 1994—2001; assoc. dep. sec. energy Pres. George W. Bush, 2002—03; pres. Fahmy Hudome Internat., 2004—. Apptd. Md. Comm. for Women; dir. Muslim Women Lawyers for Human Rights. Adminstrv. editor Law and Policy in Internat. Bus., 1989-90. Mem. Rep. Nat. Lawyers Assn., Washington, 1990—. Mem. Internat. Law Soc. Georgetown U. Law Sch. (bd. dirs. Washington chpt. 1988-89), Md. Bar Assn., DC Bar Assn., U.S. Ct. Internat. Trade. Office: Fahmy Hudome Internat LLC 815 Connecticut Ave NW #200 Washington DC 20006 Office Phone: 202-429-5566. Office Fax: 202-429-5577. E-mail: randa@fahmyhudome.com.

FAHN, LARRY, former environmental organization administrator; JD, Univ. Calif., 1976. Atty. private practice, San Francisco; exec. dir. As You Sow, San Francisco, 1998—; bd. dirs. Sierra Club, San Francisco, 1999—2005, nat. v.p. conservation, 2002—03, pres., 2003—05.*

FAHN, STANLEY, neurologist, educator; b. Sacramento, Nov. 6, 1933; s. Ernest and Sylvia F.; m. Charlotte, June 21, 1958; children: Paul N., James D. BA, U. Calif.-Berkeley, 1955, MD, 1958. Diplomate Am. Bd. Neurology. Resident in neurology Neurol. Inst., N.Y., 1959-62; rsch. assoc. NIH, 1962-65; mem. faculty Columbia U., N.Y.C., 1965-68, prof. neurology, 1973-78, H. Houston Merritt prof., 1978—, dir. Morris K. Udall Parkinson Disease Rsch. Ctr., 1999—2003; mem. faculty U. Pa., Phila., 1968-73. Dir. Dystonia Rsch. Ctr., 1981-97; sci. dir. Parkinson's Disease Found., 1979—; chmn. adv. com. peripheral and ctrl. nervous sys. drugs FDA, 1987-89, 91-96. Editor Movement Disorders, 1985-95; assoc. editor Neurology, 1977-87. With USPHS, 1962-65 Grantee NIH, 1974—77, 1980—82, 1984—91, 1994—. Mem.: Inst. of Medicine, Dystonia Med. Rsch. Found. (hon. life, bd. dirs. 1998—), Movement Disorder Soc. (pres. 1988—91), Am. Neurol. Assn. (v.p. 1987—88, chair jour. oversight com. 1994—96), Am. Acad. Neurology (chair edn. com. 1986—93, v.p. 1993—97, pres.-elect 1999—2001, pres. 2001—03). Home: 155 Edgars Ln Hastings On Hudson NY 10706-1107 Office: 710 W 168th St New York NY 10032-2603

FAHNER, JAMES BYRON, physician; b. East Grand Rapids, Mich., May 14, 1957; s. Byron Carl and A. Vivian (Skeoch) F.; m. Gail Marie DeSmet, Oct. 13, 1984; children: Therese Anne, Jill Marie. BS, U. Mich., 1979, MD, 1983. Diplomate in pediatrics and pediatric hematology/oncology Am. Bd. Pediatrics. Intern, resident in pediatrics U. Mich., Ann Arbor, 1983-86; fellow in pediat. hematology and oncology C.S. Mott Children's Hosp., Ann Arbor, Mich., 1986-89; divsn. chief pediat. hematology and oncology DeVos Children's Hosp., Grand Rapids, Mich., 1989—. Contbr. articles to profl. jours. Bd. dirs. Hospice of Mich., Southfield, 1993-2001, vice chair, 1996-99, chair, 1999-2000; bd. dirs. Make-a-Wish Found., Lansing, 1995-01, 2003—, vice chair, 1997-2000, chmn., 2000-01; bd. dirs. Ronald McDonald House, Grand Rapids, 1994-2000. Grantee Richard and Helen DeVos Found., 1990; recipient Miracle Maker award Children's Miracle Network, 1994. Fellow Am. Acad. Pediats.; mem. Am. Soc. Pediat. Hematology and Oncology. Avocations: reading, travel, writing. Office: DeVos Childrens Hosp MC 85 100 Michigan St NE Grand Rapids MI 49503-2560

FAHNER, TYRONE C., lawyer, former state attorney general; b. Detroit, Nov. 18, 1942; s. Warren George and Alma Fahner; BA, U. Mich., 1965; JD, Wayne State U., 1968; LLM, Northwestern U., 1971; m. Anne Beauchamp, July 2, 1966; children— Margaret, Daniel, Molly. Bar: Mich. 1968, Ill. 1969, Tex. 1984, U.S. Dist. Ct. (ea. dist.) Mich. 1968, US Dist. Ct. (no. dist.) Ill. 1969, US Ct. Appeals (7th cir.) 1969, US Ct. Appeals (5th cir.) 1981, US Ct. Appeals (D.C. cir.) 2002, US Supreme Ct. 2002. asst. US atty. for No. Dist. Ill., Chgo., 1971-75, dep. chief consumer fraud and civil rights, 1973-74, chief ofcl. corruption, 1974-75; ptnr. Freeman, Rothe, Freeman & Salzman, Chgo., 1975-77; dir. Ill. Dept. Law Enforcement, Springfield, 1977-79; ptnr. Mayer, Brown, Rowe & Maw, Chgo., 1979-80, 83—, co-chmn. mgmt. com. 1998-2001, chmn. mgmt. com., 2001-; atty. gen. State of Ill., Springfield, 1980-83; instr. John Marshall Law Sch., 1973-76, 78-84; former chmn. Coun. Great Lakes Govs.; chmn. Govs. Adv. Bd. Law Enforcement, 1980-83, Ill. Jud. Inquiry Bd, 1988-92, Chgo., Com. Honest Elections, 1984-92, Com. Internat. Trade and Tourism, Chgo. com. Chgo. Coun. Fgn. Rels. Mem. Toronto sister city com. Chgo. Sister Cities Internat. Program; former bd. dirs. Mex.-Am. Legal Defense and Ednl. Fund; mem. corp. adv. com. U. Mich. Coll. Lit., Sci. & The Arts, mem. major gifts com.; Mex.-Am. Legal Def. and Ednl. Fund; mem. William J. Fulbright bd. fgn. scholarships USIA, 1988-93; active Law Sch.'s Com. Visitors Wayne State U., US Info. Agy., Ill. Racing Bd., 1979-80, United Cerbral Palsy, Chgo., 1981-84, Epilepsy Found. Greater Chgo., Evanston Hist. Soc., Bureau Ednl. and Cultural Affairs, 1988-93. Mem. ABA, Am. Coll. Trial Lawyers, Internat. Assn. Gaming Attys., Mich. Bar Assn., Tex. Bar Assn., Chgo. Bar Assn., Law Club Chgo., Am. Inns of Ct. (Chgo. chpt.), Ill. Ambs. (bd. dirs., past pres.), Northwestern U. Sch. Law Alumni Assn. (bd. dirs. 1990-95, chmn. Class 1967 James B. Haddad professorship fundraising com.), Econ. Club of Chgo., Chgo. Club, Chgo. Commonwealth Club, Legal Club Chgo., Am. Effective Law Enforcement (com. cts. and justice), Commercial Club Chgo., U. Mich. Major Gifts com., Just The Beginning Found. Named, Person of Yr. Chgo. mag., 2002. Republican. Lutheran. Office: Mayer Brown Rowe & Maw LLP 71 S Wacker Dr Chicago IL 60606-4637

FAHOUR, AHMED, investment company executive; b. Almoun, Lebanon; B in econ., La Trobe U.; MBA, Grad. Sch. Mgmt. U. Melbourne, 1988. Ptnr. Boston Consulting Group; mng. dir. iFormation Group; sr. v.p. corp. devel. Citigroup, 2000—02; mem. Citigroup Mgmt. com., 2000—; CEO Citigroup Alternative Investments Group, NY, 2002—, Citigroup Australasia, 2004—. Dep. chmn. Australian Bankers' Assn., 2004—. Office: Citigroup 399 Park Ave New York NY 10043 also: Citigroup Centre 2 Park St Sydney NSW 2000 Australia Office Phone: 800-285-3000, 61-2-8225 1000.

FAHRBACH, RUTH C., state legislator; b. N.Y.C. Grad. high sch., East Meadow, N.Y. Mem. Dist. 61 Conn. Ho. of Reps., 1981—, minority whip, mem. select com. on inquiry. Appropriations com., pub. health com., legis. mgmt. com., select com. of inquiry. Active Windsor Rep. Town Com.; mem. Windsor Bd. Edn., 1977-81, v.p., 1979-80; bd. dirs. Celebrate Windsor, Inc., 2001-04. Mem. First Dist. Rep. Womens Club, Fedn. Rep. Women, Civitan Club Windsor (past pres), Nat. Order of Women Legislators, Conn. Order of Women Legislators (sec.), Conn. Fedn. of Rep. Women, Nat. Fedn. of Republican Women, St. Casimir's Lithuanian Club Women's Aux. Home: 592 Poquonock Ave Windsor CT 06095-2204 Office: Legis Office Bldg Rm 4200 Hartford CT 06106-1591 Business E-Mail: ruth.fahrbach@housegop.po.state.ct.us.

FAHRENKROG, EUGENE HENRY, JR., lawyer; b. St. Louis, Jan. 20, 1946; s. Eugene Henry and Jeffie (Hanpeter) F.; m. Linda L. Stoutenburgh, Aug. 8, 1970; children— Jeffrey, Stacy, Dana. B.A., Ohio U., 1968; J.D., Washington U., St. Louis, 1971. Bar: Mo. 1971. Asst. pros. atty. Pros. Atty.'s Office, St. Louis, 1971-74; assoc. James F. Koester, Inc., St. Louis, 1975-77; ptnr. Eugene H. Fahrenkrog Jr. P.C., St. Louis, 1977—1990, founding ptnr., Walther/Glenn Law Assoc., 1990-; pub. St. Louis Met. Jury Verdict Reporting Service. Mem. Mo. Assn. Trial Attys. (pres. 1983-84), Christian Legal Soc. (pres. 2004-2005). Mem. United Ch. Christ. Office: Walther Glenn Law Assoc 1034 S Brentwood Blvd Saint Louis MO 63117 Office Phone: 314-725-9595.

FAHRINGER, CATHERINE HEWSON, retired savings and loan association executive; b. Phila., Aug. 1, 1922; d. George Francis and Catherine Gertrude (Magee) Hewson; m. Edward F. Fahringer, July 8, 1961 (dec.); 1 child, Francis George Beckett. Grad. diploma, Inst. Fin. Edn., 1965. Notary pub. Fla. With Centrust Bank (formerly Dade Savs. and Loan Assn.), Miami, 1958-85, v.p., 1967-74, sr. v.p., 1974-82, sec., 1975-79, head savs. personnel and mktg. divsn., 1979-83, exec. v.p. office of chmn., 1984, dir., 1984-90, co-chmn. audit com. of bd. dirs., 1990; referral assoc. Referral Network Inc. subs. Coldwell Banker, 1990—. Pub. arbitrator NASD, 1999—. Contbr. articles to profl. jours. Trustee United Way of Dade County (Fla.), 1980-87, chmn. audit com. 1982-84, trustee, Pub. Health Trust, Dade County, 1974-84, sec. 1976, vice chmn., 1977-78, chmn. bd., 1978-81; mem. adv. coun. Women's Bus. Devel. Ctr., Fla. Internat. U., 1993-95; mem. spl. steering com. Breast Cancer Task Force, Jackson Meml. Hosp., 1991; hon. bd. govs. U. Miami, Soc. for Rsch. in Med. Edn.; trustee South Fla. Blood Svc., Miami, 1979-84, vice chmn., 1980, chmn., 1981-84; trustee Dade County Vocat. Found., 1977-81; trustee Fla. Internat. U. Found., 1976-90; trustee emeritus, 1990, v.p. bd., 1978-81, pres. 1982-84; bd. dirs. Sta. WPBT-TV, 1984-2002, founding lifetime dir., 1995, chmn. budget and fin. com., 1986, mem. exec. com. 1985-92, sec. 1987, investment com., 1988-90, vice chmn. 1988-92, mem. fin. com., 1992, chmn. audit and control com., 1994, 2000, 2001, mem., 1997-98; bd. dirs., mem. nominating com. Girl Scout Coun., Tropical Fla., 1985-89, chmn. 1988-89, mem. long range planning com., 1986-88; citizens oversight com. Dade County Pub. Sch. System, 1986-90, chmn. 1988-90; bd. dirs. New World Sch. of Arts, 1987-90, chmn. devel. com., 1987-90, chair New World Sch. of Arts Gala, 1990; mem. Disaster Relief Com., chair Hurricane Disaster Relief Distbn. Ctr., 1992; mem. fin. commn., chmn. capital improvement fund com. Coral Gables Congrl. Ch., summer concert series com., chmn. refreshement sub-com.; commd. Stephen min., 1995—; mem. grievance com. 11th Jud. Cir. Fla. Bar, 1988-92; bd. trustees United Protestant Appeal, 1994-96; mem. parking adv. bd. City of Coral Gables, 1997-98, bd. of adjustments, 1998—, vice chmn., 2001—2003, chmn.2003—; mem., 3rd v.p. Bush chpt. Women's Cancer Assn. U. Miami, 1997-99, 2nd v.p., treas. and parliamentarian, 1999-2001, chmn. meml. fund, 1998-2003, 3rd v.p., 2002-03. Named Women of Yr. in fin., Zonta Internat., 1975, amb., Air Def. Arty., 1970, U.S. Army Air Def. Command, 1970, Woman of Yr. in Sports, Links Club, 1986, First Lady of Athletics, Fla. Internat. U., 2003; recipient Trail Blazer award, Women's Coun. of 100, 1977, Cmty. Headliner award, Women in Comm., 1983, Outstanding Citizen of Dade County award, 1984, Honors and Recognition award, Golden Panthers Club of Fla. Internat. U., 1989, Disting. Svc. and Leadership award, Fla. Internat. U., 1991, apprecation, New World Sch. of the Arts, 1990, Meritorious Pub. Svc. award, Fla. Bar, 1991, Outstanding Svc. award, Country Club Coral Gables, 2001, hon. BA, U. Hard Knocks Alderson-Broaddus Coll., 1987, Key to City of Coral Gables for Cmty. Svc., 2000, Dedicated Svc. award, Women's Cancer Assn. of U. Miami, 2001, Outstanding Svc. Award, 2001. Mem.: LWV, Women's Union Russia, Fla. Women's Alliance (bd. dirs. 1983—91, pres. 1987—89), Internat. Women's Alliance, Savs. and Loan Pers. Soc. South Fla., Savs. and Loan Mktg. Soc. South Fla. (past pres.), Inst. Fin. Edn. (life; nat. dir., past pres. Local Greater Miami chpt.), Greater Miami Women's Golf Assn. (social dir. 1999—2001), Greenway Women's Golf Assn. (treas. 1988—89), Balt. Women's Golf Assn., Fla. Internat. U. Athletics Club, Golden Panther Club (bd. dirs. 1988—, v.p. 1991, pres. 1992—94), Links Fla. Internat. U. Club (v.p. 1992, bd. dirs., sec.), Country Club Coral Gables (treas. women's golf assn 1988—89, sec., bd. dirs., found. trustee 1993, v.p. bd. dirs. 1994, pres. 1995, chmn. bldg. restoration, capital improvement and maintenance com. 1995—99, bd. advisor 1996—99, liaison City of Coral Gables 1997—99, rear commodore, vice commodore, historian, adv., chair The Fleet 1998, commodore 1999, publicity chmn. woman's bd. 2000—01, pres. women's golf assn. 2001—02, golf adv., directory chair 2003—04, mem. adv. bd. govs. 2003—, mem. adv. bd. dirs. 2002—), Dade Bus. and Profl. Women's Club (past pres.). Democrat. *Success is putting forth your full effort and loving what you do. Dreams take time, but you can make them happen if you believe in yourself and in your dreams.*

FAHS, PAMELA STEWART, nursing educator, researcher; b. Lexington, Ky., Mar. 30, 1952; d. James Robert and JoAnn Howard Stewart; m. James Edward Fahs, May 12, 1990; children: Alexander James, Laura Ashley. ADN, 1978, BSN, 1982; MS in Nursing, SUNY, Binghamton; DSN, U. Ala., Birmingham, 1991. Staff nurse U. Ky. Med. Ctr., Lexington, 1978—80, team leader A-dialysis, 1980—82; nurse care mgr. St. Joseph Hosp., Lexington, 1982—83; lectr. Binghamton (N.Y.) U. Decker Sch. Nursing, 1985—91, asst. prof., 1991—2001; assoc. prof. Binghamton U., 2001—. Dir. O'Connor office of rural health studies Decker Sch. Nursing Binghamton U. Recipient Cmtys. Working Together for a Healthier N.Y. award, N.Y. State Dept. Health, 1998; grantee AREA grantee, NINR, 1988—90, Binghamton U. Decker Sch. Nursing, 1999, N.Y. State Dept. Health, 1999, Kennth Axtell Found., 2003, SUNY, 2003—. Mem.: Nat. Rural Health Assn., Rural Nurse Orgn., Am. Acad. Nursing (mem. coun. for the advancement nursing sci. 2000), Assn. Womens Health, Obstet. and Neonatal Nursing (mem. cardiovasc. health for women team), N.Y. State Nursing Assn. Achievements include research in PI Studies of Cardiovascular Risk of Rural Women. Office: Bingamton Univ Decker Sch Nursing Vestal Parkway East Binghamton NY 13902-6000 Office Phone: 607-777-6805. Business E-Mail: psfahs@binghamton.edu.

FAHY, JOHN J., lawyer; b. Carlstadt, N.J., Aug. 26, 1954; s. John and Mary (Roche) F.; m. Anne Dixon, Oct. 4, 1985. BS in Acctg., Fairleigh Dickinson U., Rutherford, N.J., 1976, MBA, 1978; JD, Seton Hall U., 1981. Bar: N.J. 1981, U.S. Dist. Ct. N.J. 1981, N.Y. 1982, U.S. Ct. Appeals (3d cir.) 1983; CPA, N.Y.; cert. criminal trial atty. Asst. prosecutor Hudson County, Jersey City, 1982-84; asst. U.S. atty. Office U.S. Atty., Newark, 1984-90; county prosecutor Bergen County, Hackensack, NJ, 1990-95; ptnr. Cole, Schutz, Meisel, Forman & Leonnard, Hackensack, 1995-96, Waters McPherson McNeill, Secaucus, NJ, 1996-99, Reed Smith, Newark, 1999—2002, Fahy Choi, Rutherford, NJ, 2002—. Instr. writing Seton Hall U. sch. law, Newark, 1989-90; commr. N.J. Commn. on Hate Crimes, Trenton, 1992—. Fellow ABA; mem. Fed. Bar Assn. (v.p. N.J. sect. 1993—), N.J. Bar Assn., Bergen County Bar Assn., Leadership N.J., Seton Hall Law Sch. Alumni Assn. (trustee 1991—), Inns Ct. (barrister 1992—). Democrat. Roman Catholic. Avocations: basketball, golf, reading. Office: Fahy Choi 201 Rte 17 N Rutherford NJ 07070 Office Phone: 201-438-0200. E-mail: jfahy@fahychoi.com.

FAIG, HAROLD, information technology executive; Grad., U. Cin., Coll. Mt. St. Joseph; MBA in Multinational Bus., Xavier U. Joined Milacron Inc., Cincinnati, 1967, Co. officer, v.p. plastics tech., 1990—93, group v.p. plastic tech., 1993—2002, pres., COO, 2002—03; pres., CEO The Tech Group, Inc., 2003—. Adv. bd. Tech Group, Inc. Trustee Coll. Mt. St. Joseph; adv. coun. Bus. Sch., Xavier U., Sch. Engring., U. Cin. Recipient Hero of U.S. Mfg., Fortune. Fellow: Soc. Mfg. Engrs. (Donald C. Burnham Mfg. Mgmt. Award); mem.: Machinery and Allied Products Inst. (mem. pres. coun.), Soc. Plastics Industry (bd. dirs. exec. com.), Soc. Plastic Engrs. Achievements include patents in field of of plastics and control systems for plastic processing and metalworking. Office: The Tech Group, Inc 14677 N 74th St Scottsdale AZ 85260

FAIGEN, ANNE GUSSIN, writer, educator; d. Carl and Yetta Smilovitz Gussin; m. Mark R. Faigen, June 15, 1952; children: Susan L., Lynne E. Faigen (Deceased), Janet Faigen Schultz, David S. BA, U. of Pitts., 1948—52, MA, 1958—62. Cert. tchr. Pa. Bd. Edn., 1970. Tchr. Penn Hills Sch. Dist., Pitts., Pa., 1971—84. Author: (young adult novel) Finding Her Way, New World Waiting, Brave Salamander. Vol. reader of novels for blind and print-impaired Radio Info. Svc., Pitts., 1977—2005; spkr. H.S. classes, mother/daughter book groups; Allegheny County com. woman Dem. Party, Pitts., 1996—99; bd. of trustees Temple Sinai, Pitts., 1999—2005; bd. dirs. Friends of Carnegie Libr., Pa.; spkr. to educators/parents of gifted adolescents Pa. Assn. for Gifted Edn., Pitts., 1998. Avocations: travel, hiking, reading, theater, reviewing books. Home: 5561 Woodmont St Pittsburgh PA 15217 Personal E-mail: marknann@pghmail.com.

FAIGLEY, JOSEPH RAYMOND, social studies educator; b. Canton, Ohio, July 4, 1948; s. Raymond Charles and Mary Ellen (Gockstetter) Faigley; m. Mary Evelyn Simpson, Nov. 3, 1979. BA, Walsh U., 1972, MA, 1990. Cert. superintendent Ashland, Ohio, 1992, permanent tchr. Ohio DOE. Tchr. St. Thomas Aquinas HS, Louisville, Ohio, 1974—; lectr. Walsh U., North Canton, Ohio, 1990—98. Dept. chair, humanities St. Thomas Aquinas HS, 1997—99, dept. chair, social studies, 1999—, parents adv. bd., 2000—; social studies curriculum com. Diocese of Youngstown, Youngstown, Ohio,

1997—98; negotiator Youngstown Diocese Confederation of Tchrs., 2002. Workshop participant Nat. First Ladies Mus., Canton, Ohio, 2003. Named Tchr. of Week, WHBC Radio, 1992. Mem.: Nat. Coun. of Hist. Edn., Organ. of Am. Hist., Phi Delta Kappa. Office: St Thomas Aquinas HS 2121 Reno Dr NE Louisville OH 44641 Office Phone: 330-875-1631. E-mail: jfaigley@neo.rr.com.

FAILING, GEORGE EDGAR, editor, clergyman, educator; b. Kingston, Ont., Can., Nov. 25, 1912; s. Roy Augustus and Nellie (Richardson) F.; m. Phyllis Ogden, Apr. 12, 1939; children: Bunnie Jean, Alice Joy, Lynn Odgen. BA magna cum laude, Houghton Coll., 1940, Litt.D., 1960; MA, Duke U., 1947; D.D., So. Wesleyan U., 1996. Ordained to ministry Wesleyan Meth. Ch., 1938. Pastor in, Fillmore, N.Y., 1935-41, Louisville, 1941-44, Marion, Ind., 1953-56; prof. Cen. S.C. Wesleyan Coll., 1944-47; prof. theology Houghton (N.Y.) Coll., 1947-53, dir. pub. rels., 1947-53; editor Sunday sch. lit., pastor Wesleyan Meth. Ch., Marion, Ind., 1956—59; editor Wesleyan Meth., 1959-68; chancellor Satellite Christian Inst., San Diego, 1968-73; prof. Greek and N.T. United Wesleyan Coll., Allentown, Pa., 1973; gen. editor Wesleyan Advocate, Marion, 1973-84. Author: I Corinthians, 1963, The Way of Holiness, 1970, Presence, 1977, Secure and Rejoicing, 1980, Did Christ Die for All?, 1980; contbg. author: Ency. World Methodism, 1974; contbg. author, editor: And They Shall Prophesy, 1978, With Open Face, 1983, Way of Wonder, 1983, History of the Wesleyan Ch., 1991, Death Has No Dominion, 1991. Mem. gen. bd. trustees Wesleyan Meth. Ch. Am., 1959-68, 74-84; pres. Presence, Inc., 1979—. Recipient Spl. Alumnus award United Wesleyan Coll., 1969, Houghton Coll., 1983. Mem. Soc. Bibl. Lit. and Exegesis, Evang. Press Assn. (pres. 1965-67), Am. Schs. Oriental Rsch. Avocations: photography, travel. Home: PO Box 1867 Easley SC 29641-1867 Office: 102 Fernwood Dr Easley SC 29640-8831

FAILS, THOMAS GLENN, geologist; b. Unity Twp., Ohio, Feb. 28, 1928; s. T. Glenn and Mary C. (Adams) Fails; m. Mary Ivy Schmid, Mar. 1, 1959; children: Glenn Michael, Nora Anne. Degree in geol. engring., Colo. Sch. Mines, 1954; MA in Geology, Columbia U., 1955. Cert. petroleum geologist, profl. geologist. Geologist Shell Oil Co., New Orleans, 1956—66; dist. geologist Trend Exploration Ltd., New Orleans, 1967—69, v.p., London, 1970—75; ind. geologist, petroleum prodr. Denver, 1975; pres., owner Raven Exploration Corp., Denver, 1977—; v.p., dir. Pannonian Energy, Inc., Denver, 1998—2000; pres., dir. Pannonian Internat., Ltd., Denver, 2000—. Trustee Bridge Trust, Denver, 1990—93; mem. adv. com. Colo. Geol. Survey, 1991—94. Author: Gulf Coast, U.S.; contbr. articles to profl. jours. Bd. dirs. Belcaro Park Homeowners Assn., Denver, 2004—. With USMC, 1946—48, with USMC, 1950—51. Fellow: Geol. Soc. London; mem.: Rocky Mountain Assn. Geologists (Disting. Pub. Svc. to Earch Sci. award 1993), Petroleum Exploration Soc. Gt. Britain (bd. dirs. 1974—75), Am. Inst. Profl. Geologists (pres. 1999, v.p. 1995, Martin van Couvering Meml. award 2001, Parker medal 2004), Am. Assn. Petroleum Geologists. Republican. Lutheran. Home: 965 S Monroe St Denver CO 80209-4939 Office: 4101 E Louisiana Ave Ste 412 Denver CO 80246-3431 Office Phone: 303-759-9733. Personal E-mail: thomgeol@aol.com.

FAIN, JOHN NICHOLAS, biochemistry educator; b. Jefferson City, Tenn., Aug. 18, 1934; s. Samuel Clark and Virginia Manson (Hunt) F.; m. Ann Duff, June 7, 1958; children: Margaret Ann, John Nicholas Jr., James Clark. BS magna cum laude, Carson-Newman Coll., 1956; PhD in Biochemistry, Emory U., 1960. Rsch. assoc. Emory U., Atlanta, 1960-61; NSF fellow NIH, Bethesda, Md., 1961-62, postdoctoral fellow USPHS, 1962-63; biochemist NIH and Nat. Inst. Arthritis and Metabolic Diseases, Bethesda, 1963-65; asst. prof. Brown U., Providence, 1965-68, assoc. prof., 1968-71, prof., 1971-85, chmn. biochemistry, 1975-85; Van Vleet prof., dept. chmn. U. Tenn., Memphis, 1985-2000, Van Vleet prof. of molecular scis., 2000—. Contbr. numerous articles to sci. jours. Del. gen. assembly United Presbyn. Ch., Providence, 1972. Recipient Disting. Alumnus award Carson-Newman Coll., 1986; fellow Cambridge U., 1977-78; NIH Fogarty fellow, 1984-85; Macy Faculty scholar, 1977-78. Mem. Am. Soc. Biol. Chemists. Democrat. Office: U Tenn Health Scis Ctr Coll Medicine Dept Mol Scis 858 Madison Ste GO1 Memphis TN 38163 Fax: 901-448-7360. Office Phone: 901-448-4343. E-mail: jfain@utmem.edu.

FAIN, RICHARD DAVID, cruise line executive; b. Boston, Oct. 9, 1947; s. Morton Edgar and Libby Miriam (Winer) F.; m. Colleen Jo Ferris, July 27, 1969; children: Julie Meredith, Sara Elizabeth, Benjamin Alfred, Jessica Lynn. BS, U. Calif., Berkeley, 1969; MBA, U. Pa., 1972. Mgr. internat. fin. IU Internat. Corp., Phila., 1972-75; joint mng. dir., dir. Gotaas Larsen Shipping Corp., London, Eng., 1975-88; chmn., chief exec. officer Royal Caribbean Cruise Line, Miami, Fla., 1988—. Chmn. Internat. Coun. Cruise Lines, Washington, 1993-95; bd. dirs. Assurance Foreningen Gard, SunTrust Bank, Miami, Semi-conductor Packaging Materials, Inc. Chmn. Greater Miami Conf. and Visitors Bur., 1995-97; trustee U. Miami, United Way Miami. Decorated Legion of Honor (France); named ARC Humanitarian of Yr., Dade County, Fla. Mem. Chaine de Rotisseurs. Home: 700 Arvida Pkwy Miami FL 33156-2325

FAIN, THOMAS ALTON, JR., music educator; b. Baytown, Tex., July 10, 1958; s. Thomas Alton and Velala Arnold Fain; m. Anita Muncy Fain, Oct. 17, 1998; children: Austin Thomas, Katherine Christina, Jacqueline Cecille. BS, Lamar U. - Beaumont, 1976—80; MusM, Tex. A&M U. - Commerce, 1983—85. Dir. of bands Cleve. Jr. High, Tex., 1980—81; asst. dir. of bands Bowman Mid. Sch., Plano, Tex., 1981—91, dir. of bands, 1991—98; assoc. dir. bands Highland Park Mid. Sch., Dallas, 2002—05; dir. bands Meml. Prep. Sch., Garland, Tex., 2005—. Recipient Outstanding Performance, Am. Classics Bluebonnet Festival - San Antonio, TX, 2004. Mem.: Tex. State Tchrs. Assn., Tex. Music Educators Assn. (region iii mid. sch. band chmn. 1991—92), Nat. Band Assn., Internat. Percy Grainger Soc., Tex. Bandmasters Assn., Phi Mu Alpha Sinfonia, Kappa Kappa Psi (life; pres. 1978—80). Home: 3625 Longbow Lane Plano TX 75023-3757 Office: Meml Prep Sch 2825 S First St Garland TX 75041 Office Phone: 972-926-2650. Office Fax: 972-926-2651. Personal E-mail: tfain@wt.net.

FAINBERG, ANTHONY, physicist; b. London, Jan. 14, 1944; came to U.S., 1947; s. Benjamin and Elizabeth (Martelli) F.; m. Louise Vasvari (div. 1986); m. Diane August, Sept. 7, 1986. AB, NYU, 1964; PhD, U. Calif., Berkeley, 1969. Physicist INFN U. of Turin, Italy, 1970-72; rsch. prof. Syracuse (N.Y.) U., 1973-78; physicist Brookhaven Nat. Lab., Upton, N.Y., 1978-83; legis. aide Office of Senator Bingaman, Washington, 1983-84; sr. assoc. Office of Tech. Assessment, Washington, 1985-95; dir. Office Policy and Planning for Civil Aviation Security Fed. Aviation Adminstrn., 1996-99; fellow Ctr. for Internat. Security & Arms Control, Stanford, 1991-92; chief advanced concepts divsn. Advanced Sys./Concepts Office Def. Threat Reduction Agy., Dept. of Def., 1999—2002; spl. asst. tech. Transp. Security Adminstn., Washington, 2002—; dir. office transformational R&D, Domestic Nuc. Detection Office Dept. Homeland Security, Washington, 2002—. Editor: (book) The Energy Source Book, 1991. Fellow Am. Phys. Soc. (mem. panel on pub. affairs 1990-92, 95-96, congl. fellow 1983-84); mem. AAAS. Office: Dept Homeland Security Murray Ln Washington DC 20528 Office Phone: 202-254-6019. Business E-Mail: tonyfainberg@dhs.gov.

FAINGOLD, EDUARDO DANIEL, language and linguistics educator, researcher; b. La Plata, Argentina, Sept. 6, 1958; arrived in US, 1990; s. Enrique and Annie (Turkenich) Faingold; m. Sonia D Hocherman; 1 child, Noam. BA in English and French, Hebrew U., Jerusalem, Israel, 1984, MA in English, 1987; PhD in Linguistics, Tel-Aviv U., 1992. Vis. scholar Tech. U. Berlin, 1988-89, UCLA, 1990-92, SUNY, Stony Brook, 1992-95; asst. prof. U. Tulsa, 1995—2002, assoc. prof., 2003—. Advisor UNESCO, 1998; guest prof. Hebrew U., Jerusalem, 1984; vis. prof. U. Calif., Santa Barbara, 2001; vis. scientist Max Planck Inst., Leipzig, 2002. Author: The Case for Fusion: Ladino in Balkans and the Eastern Turkish Empire, 1989, Child Language, Creolization and Historical Change, 1996, Composition Codex, 2002, The Development of Grammar in Spanish and the Romance Languages, 2003, Multilingualism from Infancy to Adolescence, 2003, mem. editl. bd.: S.W. Jour. Linguistics, 1997, book rev. editor:, 1999—2005; contbr. articles to profl. jours. Recipient Fozis Research Prize, 1989, Tel-Aviv Univ Cult Doctoral Prize, 1991, Teaching Award, Univ Tulsa, 1997; grantee, NEH, 2002—; Book Publ. grantee, German Sci. Found., 1996, Faculty rsch. grantee, U. Tulsa, 1996—2004, DAAD fellow, 2002. Mem.: MLA, Internat. Phonetic Assn., Internat. Acad. Linguistic Law, Salzburg Seminal Alumni Assn., Internat. Linguistic Assn., Linguistic Soc. Am., Linguistic Assn. S.W., Internat. Clin. and Linguistics Assn. Office: U Tulsa 600 S College Ave Tulsa OK 74104-3126

FAINSTEIN, NORMAN, academic administrator; m. Susan Fainstein; 2 children. BS with highest honors, MIT, 1966, PhD with highest distinction, 1971. Prof., dep. chair undergrad. programs in gen. studies, dir. summer session dept. sociology Columbia U., N.Y.C., 1971—76; prof., assoc. dean acad. affairs Grad. Sch. Mgmt. and Urban Professions New Sch. for Social Rsch., N.Y.C., 1983—87; prof., dean Sch. Liberal Arts and Scis. Baruch Coll. CUNY, 1987—95; prof., dean of faculty Vassar Coll., Poughkeepsie, NY, 1996—2001; pres. Conn. Coll., New London, 2001—. Author: 4 books; contbr. numerous articles to profl. jours. Active Poughkeepsie Inst., Andrew W. Mellon Found. Fellow Woodrow Wilson, NSF, Stouffer, Harvard-MIT Joint Ctr. for Urban Studies. Office: Conn Coll 270 Mohegan Ave New London CT 06320

FAINTUCH, SALOMAO, radiologist, physician; b. São Paulo, Brazil, Dec. 21, 1976; s. Joel and Bluma Linkowski Faintuch. MD, Fed. U. São Paulo, 1999. Resident in radiology Fed. U. São Paulo, 2000—; clin. fellow cascular and interventional radiology Beth Israel Deaconess Med. Ctr., Harvard Med. Sch., Boston, 2004—. Mem. med. ethics com. Fed. U. São Paulo, 2001—02; lectr. and presenter in field. Contbr. articles to profl. jours., chpts. to books. Named Student Rsch. fellow, CNPq - Brazilian NRC, 1995—99; recipient Best Poster awards (4), Jour. Paulista de Radiologia and Brazilian Congress Radiology, 2001, Walter Leser prize, Fed. U. Sao Paulo, 2002, Disting. Reviewer award, Jour. Vascular and Interventional Radiology, 2005; Rsch. fellow vascular and interventional radiology, Beth Israel Deaconess Med. Ctr., Harvard Med. Sch., 2003—04. Mem.: Soc. Clin. and Exptl. Hypnosis, New Eng. Soc. Interventional Radiology, Soc. Interventional Radiology, Am. Roentgen Ray Soc., Radiol. Soc. N.Am. (scholar Internat. Young Academics Seminar 2000). Office: Beth Israel Deacones Med Ctr Harvard Med Sch Radiology Dept 1 Deaconess Rd WCC 308 Boston MA 02215

FAIR, HARRY DAVID, academic administrator, physicist; b. Indiana, Pa., Dec. 2, 1936; s. Harry Dale and Ruth Roxanne (Crawford) F.; m. Isabelle Cadwallader (div. 1985); children: David Eric, Martin Crawford, Courtney Tyler; m. Nancy Jo Shiro, Dec. 19, 1986; 1 child, Katie Anne. BS, Indiana U. Pa., 1958; MS, U. Del., 1960, PhD, 1966. Rsch. physicist Picatinny Arsenal, Dover, N.J., 1960-67, chief energy conversion sect., 1967-70, chief solid state physics br., 1970-73, chief solid state physics and chemistry br., 1973-75, chief Energetic Materials Lab., 1976-76, chief Propulsion Tech. Lab., 1977-81; dir. land warfare div. Def. Advanced Rsch. Projects Agy., Washington, 1981-85; dir. Joint Program Office Def. Advanced Rsch. Projects Agy., U.S. Army, USMC, Washington, 1985-87; dir. Inst. for Advanced Tech., U. Tex., Austin, 1988—. Vis. prof. U. Paris, 1974, Royal Instn. Gt. Britain, 1975. Editor: Physics and Chemistry of Azides, Vols. I and II, 1977; also over 200 articles on solid state physics and electromagnetic propulsion; patentee in field. 1st lt. U.S. Army, 1960-62. Recipient R and D awards U.S. Army, 1972-75, 1st citation for achievement Indiana U. Pa., 1977, Edison medal IEEE, 1982, Founder's award IEEE Electromagnetic Launch Symposium, 1988, Lavrentyev medal Russian Acad. Scis.; fellow Sec. Army, 1974. Mem. AIAA, AASA, Am. Phys. Soc., Sigma Xi, Sigma Pi Sigma. Home: PO Box 645 Dripping Springs TX 78620-0645 Office: U Tex Austin Inst Advanced Tech Ste 400 3925 W Braker Ln Austin TX 78759-5316

FAIR, JAMES RUTHERFORD, JR., engineering educator, consultant; b. Charleston, Mo., Oct. 14, 1920; s. James Rutherford and Georgia Irene (Case) Fair; m. Merle Innis, Jan. 14, 1950; children: James Rutherford III, Elizabeth, Richard Innis. Student, The Citadel, 1938-40; BS, Ga. Inst. Tech., 1942; MS, U. Mich., 1949; PhD, U. Tex., 1955; DSc (hon.), Wash. U., 1977; HHD (hon.), Clemson U., 1987. Rsch. engr. Shell Devel. Co., Emeryville, Calif., 1954-56; with Monsanto Co., 1942-52, 56-79, engring. dir. corp. engring. dept. St. Louis, 1969-79; McKetta chair chem. engring. U. Tex., Austin, 1979—. Dir., v.p. Fractionation Rsch., Inc., Bartlesville, Okla., 1969—79; pres. James R. Fair, Inc., 1981—2004. Author: North Arkansas Line, 1969, Distillation, 1971, 1998, Louisiana and Arkansas, 1997; contbr. articles to profl. jours. Recipient Profl. Achievement award, Chem. Engring. mag., 1968, King award, U. Tex., 1987. Fellow: AIChE (bd. dirs. 1965—67, inst. lectr. 1979, Walker award 1973, Practice award 1975, Founders award 1977, Separation Tech. award 1994); mem.: NAE, NSPE, Am. Soc. Engring. Edn., Am. Chem. Soc. (Separation Sci. and Tech. award 1993, Acad. Achievement award 2005), Headliners Club (Austin), Faculty Club U. Tex., Sigma Nu. Republican. Presbyterian. Home: 2804 Northwood Rd Austin TX 78703-1603 Office: U Tex Dept Chem Engring Separations Rsch Progr Austin TX 78712 Office Phone: 512-471-0939. Personal E-mail: j.fair@sbcglobal.net. Business E-Mail: fair@che.utexas.edu.

FAIR, JEAN EVERHARD, retired education educator; b. Evanston, Ill., July 21, 1917; d. Drury Hampton and Bess Marion (Everhard) F. BA, U. Ill., 1938; MA, U. Chgo., 1939, PhD, 1953. Tchr. Evanston (Ill.) Twp. High Sch., 1940-48, 1954-58; tchr. U. Minn. High Sch., 1948-49, U. Ill. High Sch., 1951-53; prof. edn. Wayne State U., Detroit, 1958-82, now prof. emeritus. Cons. in edn.; cons. Mich. Ednl. Goals, Objectives and Assessment in Social Studies; reviewer of position statements for teaching and learning, standards, assessment and other manuscripts for Nat. Coun. Social Studies. Contbr. articles to profl. jours. Mem. AAUW, Nat. Council for Social Studies (pres. 1972, dir. 1958-61, 73-75), Assn. for Supervision and Curriculum Devel., Social Sci. Edn. Consortium, LWV, Phi Beta Kappa. Mem. United Ch. Christ. Home: Apt 281 16351 Rotunda Dr Dearborn MI 48120-1158

FAIR, RAY CLARENCE, economics educator; b. Fresno, Calif., Oct. 4, 1942; s. Clarence and Goldie Marie (Smith) F.; m. Sharon Monica Oster, May 14, 1977; children— Emily, Stephen, John BA in Econs., Fresno State Coll., 1964; PhD in Econs., MIT, 1968. Asst. prof. econs. Princeton U., N.J., 1968-74; assoc. prof. econs. Yale U., New Haven, 1974-79, prof., 1979—. Vis. assoc. prof. MIT, Cambridge, 1977; mem. Cowles Found., Yale U., 1974—; research assoc. Nat. Bur. Econ. Research, Cambridge, 1979—. Author: Specification, Estimation and Analysis of Macroeconometric Models, 1984; contbr. arteicles to profl. jours. Fellow Econometric Soc. Democrat. Home: 233 Everit St New Haven CT 06511-1335 Office: Yale U Dept Econs New Haven CT 06520

FAIRBAIRN, JOYCE, Canadian government official; b. Lethbridge, Alta., Can., Nov. 6, 1939; m. Michael Gillan (dec.). BA in English, U. Alta., 1960; B Journalism, Carleton U., 1961. Mem. news staff Ottawa (Ont., Can.) Jour., 1961; mem. staff parliamentary press gallery UPI, Ottawa, 1962-64; mem. staff parliamentary bur. F.P. Publs., 1964-70; legis. asst., sr. legis. advisor Prime Minister of Can. Pierre Elliott Trudeau, 1970-84, comms. coord., 1981-83; mem. Senate for Province of Alta., 1984—, appt. to privy coun., leader govt., 1993-97, minister with spl. responsibility for literacy, 1993-97, spl. advisor for literacy, 1997. Mem. Spl. Senate Com. on Youth, Senate Standing Coms. on Transp. and Comm., Legal and Constl. Affairs, Fgn. Affairs, Agr. and Forestry, mem. senate social affairs com.; founding mem. standing com. on Aboriginal peoples; chair spl. com. on Anti-Terrorism, 2001, 05; vice chair Nat. Liberal Caucus and Western and No. Liberal Caucus, 1984-91; co-chair nat. campaign com. Liberal Party of Can., 1991. Past mem. senate U. Lethbridge; inducted into Kainai Chieftanship, Blood Nation, pres., 2004—; chmn. Friends of Can. Paralympics, 1998-2003; chmn. bd. dirs. Can. Paralympic Found., 2003—. Named hon. col. 18th Air Def. Regt., Royal Can. Army. Office: Can Senate 571-S Centre Block Ottawa ON Canada K1A 0A4 Office Phone: 613-996-4382. E-mail: fairbj@sen.parl.gc.ca.

FAIRBAIRN, URSULA FARRELL, human resources executive; b. Newark, Feb. 5, 1943; d. Henry C. and Clara J. (Ziefle) Otte; m. William Todd Fairbairn III, May 14, 1978; children: W. Todd, Mary. BA, Upsala Coll., 1965; MAT in Math., Harvard U., 1966. Instr., numerous mktg. positions IBM, N.Y.C., 1966-78; exec. asst. to sec., White House fellow U.S. Treasury Dept., Washington, 1973-74; exec. asst. to chmn. bd., group dir. IBM, Armonk, N.Y., 1978-79, v.p. mgmt. svcs., then v.p. mktg. ops. west, 1980-84, dir. pers. resources, 1984-87, dir. bus. and mgmt. edn., 1987, dir. edn., 1987-89, dir. edn. and mgmt. devel., 1989-90; sr. v.p. human resources Union Pacific Corp., Bethlehem, Pa., 1990-96; exec. v.p. human resources and quality Am. Express Co., N.Y.C., 1996—2005; pres, CEO Fairbairn Group, LLC, 2005—. Bd. dirs. VF Corp., Greensboro, N.C., Air Products Corp., Allentown, Pa., Sunoco Corp., Phila., Circuit City Stores, Inc., Centex Corp. Contbg. author: Managing Human Resources in the Information Age, 1991. Mem. Com. of 200, Catalyst, N.Y.C.; vice-chair Nat. Acad.-HR; chair Pers. Round Table. Mem. Bus. Roundtable, Employee Rels. Com., Labor Policy Assn. (bd. dirs., mem. exec. com.), Nat. Acad. Human Resources (vice-chair). Avocations: gardening, art, reading, walking, travel. Office: Centex Corp 2728 N Harwood St Dallas TX 75201-1516 Office Phone: 214-981-5000. Office Fax: 214-981-6859.*

FAIRBANK, JANE DAVENPORT, editor, civic worker; b. Seattle, Aug. 21, 1918; d. Harold Edwin and Mildred (Foster) Davenport; m. William Martin Fairbank, Aug. 16, 1941; children: William Martin, Robert Harold, Richard Dana. AB magna cum laude, Whitman Coll., 1939; postgrad., U. Wash., 1940—42. Sci. staff mem. Radiation Lab. Mass. Inst. Tech., Cambridge, 1942—45; chmn. Second Careers for Women, Stanford, Calif., 1970—75; chmn. annual continuing edn. program Whitman Coll. Sr. Alumni Coll., 1986—96. Tchg. asst. U. Wash., 1940—42; mem. Canada Coll. Citizens Adv. Com. for Cmty. Edn., 1968; founding mem. Bay Area Consortium on Ednl. Needs of Women, 1971; mem. organizing com. for conf. on frontiers of physics Stanford U., 1982. Editor: Radar Maintenance Manual, 1945; co-editor: Near Zero: New Frontiers of Physics, 1988, Second Careers for Women: A View from the San Francisco Peninsula, 1971, Second Careers for Women, 1975. Mem.: Calif. Congress Parents and Tchrs. (hon. life), Mortar Bd., Whitman Coll. Alumni Assn. (bd. dirs. 1986—96), Stanford Univ. Women's Club (pres. 1975—76), Alpha Chi Omega, Phi Beta Kappa. Mem. United Ch. Of Christ. Deceased.

FAIRBANK, RICHARD D., diversified financial services company executive; BA, Stanford Univ., 1972, MBA, 1981. Chmn., CEO Capital One Fin. Corp., McLean, Va., 1994—. Mem. MasterCard U.S. Region Bd. Dir., 1995—2004, chmn., 2002—04; dir. MasterCard Internat. Global Bd., 2004—. Named Best CEO, Institutional Investor mag., Bus. Leader of the Year, Washingtonian Mag. Office: Capital One Financial Corp 1680 Capital One Dr Mc Lean VA 22102-3491

FAIRBANK, ROBERT HAROLD, lawyer; b. Northampton, Mass., Mar. 4, 1948; s. William Martin and Jane (Davenport) F.; m. Valerie Baker; children: Sarah Julia, David Kivy. AB in Polit. Sci., Stanford U., 1972; MLS, U. Calif.-Berkeley, 1973; JD, NYU, 1977. Bar: Calif. 1977, U.S. Dist. Ct. (cen. and no. dists.) Calif. 1978, U.S. Dist. Ct. (so. dist.) Calif. 1993. Assoc. Gibson, Dunn & Crutcher, L.A., 1977-84, ptnr., 1985-96; co-founding ptnr. Fairbank & Vincent, 1996—. Lawyer rep., co-chair 9th cir. Jud. Conf. Ctrl. Dist., 2000—02; bd. dirs. 9th Jud. Cir. Hist. Soc.; adj. prof. U. So. Calif. Law and Bus. Schs., 2004—. Author: Effective Pretrial and Trial Motions, 1983, California Practice Guide: Civil Trials and Evidence (The Rutter Group 1993, with yearly updates); mem. editl. bd. NYU Law Rev., 1975-76. Named One of Top 100 Bus. Lawyers in L.A., L.A. Bus. Jour., 1995. Mem. Assn. Bus. Trial Lawyers (co-founder San Francisco and Orange County chpts., bd. govs. 1984-85, treas. 1986-87, sec. 1987-88, v.p. 1988-89, pres. 1989-90), L.A. County Bar Assn. (fed. cts. com. 1983-85), Jud. Coun. Calif. Adv. Com. on Local Rules (subcom. chair on civil trial rules). Office: Fairbank & Vincent 11755 Wilshire Blvd Ste 2320 Los Angeles CA 90025-1501 Office Phone: 310-996-5520. E-mail: rfairbank@fairbankvincent.com.

FAIRBANKS, CHARLES F., law educator; Student, Johnson Wales Jr. Coll., Providence, 1968; AA in Bus., Nebr. We. Jr. Coll., Scottsbluff, 1972; BS in Criminal Justice, U. Nebr., Omaha, 1974; MA in Edn., U. Nebr., Kearney, 1994; postgrad., Walden U.; PhD Criminal Justice mgmt., Columbus U., 2004. Dep. sheriff Hall County, Grand Island, Nebr., 1974-79, sheriff, dir. adult correctional facility, 1979-87; dir. adult correctional facility Scotts Bluff County, Gering, 1987-94, sheriff, 1987-95; instr. criminal justice We. Nebr. C.C., Scottsbluff, 1995-2000, Metro. C.C., Omaha, 2001—. Presenter in field. Active Boy Scouts Am., Gering New Horizons. Recipient Outstanding Svc. award United Vets. Grand Island, 1987, Outstanding Loss Prevention award Nebr. Inter-Gov. Risk Mgmt. Assn., 1990, Law Enforcement Cmty. Leadership award US Atty. Dist. Nebr., 1990, Recognition Svc. award Boy Scouts Am., 1990. Phi Theta Kappa Excellence in Edn. award, 1996-97. Mem.: Internat. Soc. Crime Prevention Practitioners, Am. Jail Assn., Nat. Assn. Police Planners, Law Enforcement Intelligence Network, We. Intelligence Narcotics Group (grant dir.), Nebr. Assn. County Officials (Pres. award 1987), Nebr. Sheriff's Assn. (Pres. award 1986), Nebr. Crime Prevention Assn. (Outstanding Support, Guidance and Leadership award 1992). Office: 5730 N 30th St Bldg N Omaha NE 68111 Office Phone: 402-451-6425. Personal E-mail: eju101@cox.net. Business E-Mail: cfairbanks@metropo.meeneb.edu.

FAIRBANKS, DAVID NATHANIEL FOX, otolaryngologist, surgeon, educator; b. Ann Arbor, Mich., Mar. 31, 1936; s. Avard Tennyson and Beatrice Maude (Fox) F.; m. Sylvia West, June 17, 1959; children: David W., Lisa Marie, E. Jefferson, Galen J. BS, U. Utah, 1959, MD, 1963. Diplomate Am. Bd. Otolaryngology. Resident in otolaryngology surgery Johns Hopkins Hosp., Balt., 1963-69; grands adminstr. NIH, Bethesda, Md., 1969-71; mem. rotating staff Project HOPE, Kingston, Jamaica, 1971; clin. prof. otolaryngology George Washington U., Washington, 1970—, dir. divsn. otolaryngology, 1976-84. Med. bd. Project HOPE, Millwood, Va., 1971—; cons. NIH, Bethesda, Md., 1971—; co-dir. Sleep Disorders Ctr., Sibley Meml. Hosp., Washington D.C., 1994—. Author: Antimicrobial Therapy in Otolaryngology, 1981, 12th edit., 2005, Snoring and Obstructive Sleep Apnea, 1987, 3d edit., 2002; contbr. articles to profl. jours., chpts. to books. Missionary Ch. of Jesus Christ of Latter-day Saints, Calif., 1956-58. With USPHS, 1969-71. Johns Hopkins U. fellow, 1968-69. Fellow ACS, Am. Acad. Otolaryngology (dir. 1983-85, Disting. Svc. award 1999), Am. Rhinological Soc., Triol. Soc.; mem AMA, Med. Soc. D.C. (bd. dirs. 1984-86), Met. Ear, Nose and Throat Soc. (pres. 1976), Phi Beta Kappa, SAR, Sons of the Utah Pioneers. Republican. Mem. Lds Ch. Avocations: banjo, folk music, farming, family band. Office: Ear Nose and Throat Med Group 2021 K St NW Ste 210 Washington DC 20006-1003

FAIRBANKS, JONATHAN LEO, art company executive, museum curator, artist; b. Ann Arbor, Mich., Feb. 19, 1933; s. Avard T. and Beatrice Maude (Fox) F.; m. Louise Ann Eckenbrecht, Feb. 12, 1954; children: Theresa Louise Fairbanks Harris, Hilary-Ann. BFA, U. Utah, 1953; student, Pa. Acad. Fine Arts, 1956-57; MFA, U. Pa., 1957; MA, U. Del., 1961. From curatorial asst. to assoc. curator Winterthur Museum, Del., 1961-71; co-founder Am. Prints Confs., 1970—; founder dept. Am. decorative arts and sculpture Mus. of Fine Arts Boston, 1971—99, Katharine Lane Weems curator Am. decorative arts/sculpture; v.p. Antiques Am., Inc., Boston, 1991—; v.p. rsch. Artfact, 2005—. Adj. lectr. U. Del.; instr. U. Utah Ext., Brigham Young U. Ext., W.Va. U. Ext.; adj. prof. Am. New Eng. studies program Boston U.; trustee Tex. Pioneer Arts Found.; trustee, incorporator Dublin Seminar for Early New Eng. Folklife; rsch. assoc. Dept. Art History, Boston U. Curator exhbns. and catalogues Paul Revere's Boston--1735-1818, New England Begins, The Seventeenth Century, Glass Today, U.S. Dept. State, 2003; one-man shows Washington County Mus. Fine Arts, Hagerstown, Md., 2004; exhibited paintings at Haley & Steele, Boston, 2001, 02; author: American Furniture 1620 to the Present, 1981; mural executed Hall of Earth History, Acad. Natural Scis., Phila., 1957. Bd. dirs. Revere House, Boston, Fairbanks House, Dedham, The Connick Found.; former mem. Com. for Preservation White

House; pres. Decorative Arts trust; former trustee Forest Hills Cemetery, Longfellow's Wayside Inn, Shirley-Eustis House. Winterthur fellow, 1959-61; recipient Disting. Service award Antiques Monthly, 1983, Robert H. Lord award for excellence in hist. studies. Emmanuel Coll., 1983, medal Excellence Craft, Soc. Arts & Crafts, Boston, 1997, Ellen Banning Ayer award for Contbns. to the Cultural Life of Boston, 1999, award of distinction The Furniture Soc., 2003. Fellow Pilgrim Soc., Am. Inst. Conservation, Am. crafts Coun. (hon.); mem. Victorian Soc. Am. (past v.p., Lifetime Achievement award Am., New Eng. chpt. 2000), Internat. Inst. Conservation, Am. Assn. Mus., Soc. Archtl. Historians, Nat. Trust for Hist. Preservation, Colonial Soc. Mass., Decorative Arts Soc. (v.p. 1978-79, C.F. Montgomery award 1983), Westwood Hist. Soc. (pres. 1978-81), Am. Soc. Interior Designers (hon.), Mass. Hist. Soc., Am. Antiquarian Soc., Colonial Soc., Walpole Soc., St. Botolph Club. Office: VP Rsch Artfact 2 Canal Pk Cambridge MA 02141 Office Phone: 617-252-5001. Office Fax: 617-252-5001. Personal E-mail: jleofairbanks@yahoo.com. Business E-Mail: jfairbanks@artfact.com.

FAIRBANKS, RICHARD MONROE, III, lawyer, retired ambassador; b. Indpls., Feb. 10, 1941; s. Richard Monroe, Jr. and Mary Evans (Caperton) F.; m. Ann Shannon O'Connor, June 13, 1962; children: Woods Alexander, Jonathan Barcroft. AB, Yale U., 1962; JD magna cum laude, Columbia U., 1969. Bar: D.C. Assoc. Arnold & Porter, 1969-71; spl. asst. to adminstr. EPA, 1971; staff asst. Domestic Council, Exec. Office of Pres., White House, 1971-72, assoc. dir. energy, environ. and natural resources, 1972-74; founding ptnr. firm Ruckelshaus, Beveridge & Fairbanks, Washington, 1974-81; asst. sec. congressional relations Dept. State, 1981-82, ambassador, spl. negotiator for Middle East peace process, 1982-83, ambassador-at-large, 1984-85; ptnr. Paul, Hastings, Janofsky & Walker, 1986-89, mng. ptnr., 1990-92, sr. counsel, 1992-94, Ctr. for Strategic and Internat. Studies, Washington, 1992-94, mng. dir. for domestic and internat. issues, 1994-99, pres., CEO, 1999-2000, counselor, 2000—. Adj. prof. law Georgetown U., Washington, 1971-72; dir. Fairbanks Broadcasting Co., 1974-81; bd. dirs. SEACOR Holdings Inc., GATX Corp., SPACEHAB, Inc.; sr. counselor Am. Enterprise Inst., 1985-90; pres. U.S. nat. com. for Pacific Econ. Coop., 1986-92; internat. chair Pacific Econ. Coop. Coun., 1991-92, U.S. vice chair 1992—; mem. Pres.'s Task Force on U.S. Internat. Broadcasting, 1991. Founder, 1st pres. Washington chpt. Am. Refugee Com., 1978, mem. nat. bd. dirs., 1977-93; trustee Meridian House Internat., 1978-81; mem. com. natural resources Rep. Nat. Com., 1977-80; mem. Pres.'s Citizens Adv. Com. Environ. Quality, 1974-77; bd. visitors Columbia U. Sch. Law, 1999—. Officer USN, 1962-66. Mem.: ABA, Ctr. for Strategic and Internat. Studies (adv. bd. 1989, bd. trustees 2000), Coun. Am. Ambassadors, Coun. Fgn. Rels., D.C. Bar Assn., Indian Creek Club, Roaring Fork Club, Chevy Chase Club, Yale Club (N.Y.C.), Met. Club Washington, Burning Tree Club, Anglers Club. Office: Ctr Strategic & Internat Studies 1800 K St NW Washington DC 20006-2202 Office Phone: 202-775-3130. Business E-Mail: rfairban@csis.org.

FAIRBANKS, ROBERT ALVIN, lawyer; b. Oklahoma City, July 9, 1944; s. Albert Edward and Lucille Imogene (Scherer) F.; m. Linda Gayle Geer, Aug. 26, 1967; children: Chele Lyn, Kimberly Jo, Robert Alvin II, Michael Albert, Richard Alan, Joseph Alexander. BS in Math., U. Okla., 1967, JD, 1973; MBA, Oklahoma City U., 1970, MCJA, 1975; LLM, Columbia U., 1976; MA, Stanford U., 1984; MEd, Harvard U., 1993. Bar: Okla. 1974, U.S. Dist. Ct. (we. dist.) Okla. 1974, U.S. Ct. Customs and Patent Appeals 1974, U.S. Ct. Mil. Appeals, 1974, U.S. Tax Ct. 1974, U.S. Claims Ct. 1975, U.S. Customs Ct. 1975, U.S. Ct. Appeals (10th cir.) 1975, U.S. Supreme Ct. 1977, U.S. Dist. Ct. (ea. dist.) Okla. 1984, Minn. 1993. Commd. 2d lt. USAF, 1967, advanced through grades to capt., 1970, col., 1986; asst. staff judge adv., chief of claims div. Office of Staff Judge Adv., Tinker AFB, Okla., 1974-75; legal asst. to Justice William A. Berry, Okla. Supreme Ct., 1977; pvt. practice Norman, Okla., 1974—; v.p. St. Gregory's U., Shawnee, Okla., 1997—; prof. math. Univ. Ctrl. Okla., 2004—. Instr. bus. adminstrn. U. Md. Far East div., Nha Trang, Viet Nam, 1970-71, Rose State Coll., Midwest City, Okla., 1974; rsch. assoc. in law U. Okla., Norman, 1974, spl. lectr., 1974-75, vis. asst. prof., 1976-77, adj. prof. law, 1984—; vis. asst. prof. law Oklahoma City U., 1977; asst. prof. law U. Ark., Fayetteville, Arks., 1977-81; assoc. prof. law La. State U., Baton Rouge, 1981; rsch. asst. dept. family, community and preventative medicine Stanford (Calif.) Med. Sch., 1981-82; adj. asst. prof. govt. contract law Air Force Inst. Tech., Wright-Patterson AFB, Ohio, 1985—; v.p. St. Gregory's U., Shawnee, Okla.; prof. bus. adminstrn. U. Phoenix; adj. prof. law and mgmt. Okla. Christian U. Coll. Bus.; cons. Cheyenne Tribe, Clinton, Okla., 1977-81, 90, Citizens Band of Pottawatomie Tribe, Shawnee, Okla., 1977-79, Inst. for Devel. of Indian Law, Washington, 1976-81; dir. Native Am. Coll. Prep. Ctr. Bemidji State U., Minn., 1993—; prof. math. U. Cen. Okla., 2004—. Editor-in-chief Am. Indian Law Rev., 1973; editor Okla. Law Rev., 1971-73; producer, dir.: (with Barbara P. Ettinger) "Aa-Niin" film, 1994; author book revs.; contbr. articles to profl. jours. Mem. bd. control Fayetteville (Ark.) City Hosp., 1977-81; cubmaster Boy Scouts Am., Norman, 1982-83, asst. scoutmaster, Stanford, 1981, scoutmaster, Norman, 1990-91, com. mem., den leader, 1988; softball coach Jr. High Girls League, Fayetteville, 1977-81; mem. adv. bd. Native Am. Prep. Sch., Santa Fe; pres., chmn. bd. Native Am. Coll. Prep. Ctr., Bemidji, Minn.; mem. exec. adv. bd. Aerospace Sci. and Tech. Edn. Ctr. of Okla., Okla. City Univ.; mem. legal edn. com., Okla. Bar Assn. U.S. Dept. Edn. fellow Stanford U. Med. Sch.; Charles Evans Hughes fellow Columbia U. Law Sch., 1976; Sequoyah fellow Assn. Am. Indian Affairs, 1975-76; Mellon fellow Harvard U. Sch. Edn., 1993; nominee Pulitzer prize for Disting. Commentary, 1997. Mem. ABA, Okla. Bar Assn., Fed. Bar Assn., Am. Trial Lawyers Assn., Okla. Trial Lawyers Assn., Okla. Indian Bar Assn., Oklahoma County Bar Assn., Assn. Am. Law Schs., N.G. Assn. U.S., Air Force Assn. (life), Res. Officers Assn. (life), Nat. Contract Mgmt. Assn., Soc. Logistics Engrs., Phi Alpha Delta, Phi Delta Epsilon, Phi Delta Kappa. Republican. Roman Catholic. Office: 2212 Westpark Dr Norman OK 73069-4012 Personal E-mail: rafairbanks@sbcglobal.net. Business E-Mail: rfairbanks@ucok.edu.

FAIRBANKS, WILLIAM LOUIS, II, anthropologist, educator; b. San Francisco, Mar. 26, 1937; s. William Louis and Drusilla Talbot Fairbanks; m. Carole Anne Fairbanks, Jan. 24, 1959; children: William Louis Fairbanks III, Christine Genevieve Holdstock, Judy Diane Irons. AA, Santa Rosa Jr. Coll., Santa Rosa, CA, 1957; BA, San Jose State Coll., San Jose, CA, 1961, MA, 1962; PhD, U. Calif. Santa Barbara, Santa Barbara, CA, 1975. Social sci. educator Yuba City Union H.S., Yuba City, Calif., 1962—66; anthropology educator Cuesta Coll., San Luis Obispo, Calif., 1966—. Mem.: Am. Anthrop. Assn., Calif. Mission Studies Assn. (exec. bd. mem. 2001—02), Southwestern Anthrop. Assn. (pres. 2000—00). United Methodist. Achievements include Organized program for community college students to travel across the U.S. and interview people in their fields. Avocations: basketball, bridge, wine, walking, rose gardening. Office: Cuesta College PO Box 8106 San Luis Obispo CA 93403 Office Phone: 805-546-3100 2675.

FAIRBANKS, WILLIAM Z., III, music educator; b. Biloxi, Miss., Dec. 28, 1961; s. William Z. Fairbanks, Jr. and Patricia J. Fairbanks; children: William Zerfing IV, Rebekah Anne, Sarah Ashlee. B in Music Edn., West Tex. State U., 1983; MDiv., Boston U., 1988; MusM, Stephen F. Austin State U., 2004. Cert. instr. Am. Tae Kwon Do Assn./Calif., 1992, peer mediator/mediation instr. Peer Assistance Network Tex., 1995, soccer coach North Tex. Soccer Assn., 1995, profl. rescuer/instr. Am. Red Cross/Tex., 2003, lifeguarding/CPR/first aid instr. Am. Red Cross/Tex., 2003. Intern First United Meth. Ch., Honolulu, 1984—85, Milton, 1987—88; assoc. min. Foothills United Meth. Ch., La Mesa, Calif., 1988—91, Newport Ctr. United Meth. Ch., Newport Beach, Calif., 1991—93; dir. bands Kaufman (Tex.) H.S., 1993—97, Trinity Valley C.C., Athens, Tex., 1997—. Adjudicator area music/arts contests, Tex., 1983—; clinician area music contests, Tex., 1983—; dir./instr. Leadership Camp, Tex., 1993—; co-coord. Young People's Conv., L.A., 1993—93; dir. drum maj. camp Trinity Valley C.C., Athens, 1997—, coord. area honor band, 1997—; dir. Athens Cmty. Band, 1998—; dir. aquatics/head lifeguard Cain Ctr., Athens, 2002—; poolside/lakeside lifeguard Christian Youth Found./Disciples Crossing Camp, Athens, 2002—; band booster pres. Athens H.S. Bands, 2002—03. Actor: (plays) Forever Plaid, Greater Tuna, Clue, the Musical, Smoke on the Mountain, Little Shop of Horrors, Some Enchanted Evening, The Butler Did It (ALTY, Best Supporting Male Actor, 2004), Lend Me a Tenor, Singing in the Rain, You're a Good Man, Charlie Brown, Children of Eden; arranger: band/instrumental music arrangements. Entertainer Tony Orlando's Veteran's Day Telecast, Branson, Mo., 2004—04; fundraiser Am. Heart Assn., Athens, 1997—2005, Am. Cancer Soc., Athens, 1998—2005, Juvenile Diabetes Found., Athens, 2002—02; mem. TVCC WildCard Jazz Band, Athens, 1997—2005; fundraiser/performer Henderson County Performing Arts Ctr., Athens, 1998—2005. Mem.: Tex. C.C. Tchrs. Assn., Coll. Band Dirs. Nat. Assn., Tex. Music Educators Assn., Tex. Bandmasters Assn. Methodist. Avocations: soccer, Tae Kwon Do, swimming, art, crafts. Home: 704 W College St Athens TX 75751 Office: Trinity Valley Community College 100 Cardinal Dr Athens TX 75751 Office Phone: 903-675-6222. Office Fax: 903-675-6316. Business E-Mail: wfairbanks@tvcc.edu.

FAIRCHILD, PHYLLIS ELAINE, school counselor; b. Franklin, La., Feb. 23, 1927; d. Joseph Virgil and Georgiana (Bourgeois) F. BS in Chemistry and Biology, U. Southwestern La., 1946; postgrad., La. State U., 1949-50, MEd in Guidance, 1966. Cert. chemistry, biology, gen. sci., Spanish and social studies tchr., counselor, La. Tchr. sci. St. Mary Parish Sch. Bd., Franklin, 1952—58, counselor, 1977—82; tchr. sci. Am. Dependent Schs., Yokohama, Japan, 1958—60, London, Lakenheath, England, 1960—61, Ramey AFB, PR, 1961—62, Norfolk City Schs., Va., 1962—63, Iberville Parish Sch. Bd., Plaquemine, La., 1963—66; tchr. sci., counselor East Baton Rouge Parish Sch. Bd., Baton Rouge, 1966—77; counselor Hanson Sch. Bd., Franklin, 1982—94, 1996—98; ret., 1998. Mem. adv. com. La. Dept. Edn., Baton Rouge, 1976, 78. Mem. DAR (regent Attakapas chpt. 2003—, dir. 6th Dist. 2004—), Coun. on Aging Bd., La. Landmarks Soc., Cath. Daus. Am. (co-chmn. religious litergy 1992-94), Fortnightly Lit. Club (pres. 1982-83), Sigma Delta Pi, Pi Gamma Mu, Kappa Kappa Gamma, Delta Kappa Gamma (chmn. membership, scholarship, profl. affairs 1971-77, parliamentarian 1996-98). Avocations: reading, walking, piano, writing. Home: 214 Morris St Franklin LA 70538-6127 Personal E-mail: Phyllis@teche.net.

FAIRCHILD, ROBERT CHARLES, pediatrician; b. Kansas City, Mo., Dec. 22, 1921; s. Charles Clement and Ada Mae (Baker) F.; m. Patricia Louise Russell, May 28, 1964; children— Robert, Nancy, Rex Hartman, Dan Hartman Student, Kansas City Jr. Coll., 1938-40; BA, U. Kans., 1942, MD, 1950. Diplomate Am. Bd. Pediatrics. Intern Kansas City Gen. Hosp., 1950-51; resident in pediatrics U. Kans. Med. Ctr., 1951-53; practice medicine specializing in pediatrics Mission, Kans., 1953-70; dir. area clinics Children's Mercy Hosp., Kansas City, Mo., 1970-74, dir. outpatient services, 1974-88, ret., 1991. Prof. pediatrics emeritus U. Mo.-Kansas City Sch. Medicine; mem. adv. com. Assoc. Degree nursing program Johnson County Community Coll. Contbr. articles to med. jours. Served to maj. U.S. Army, 1942-46 Decorated Bronze Star; recipient Physician's Recognition award AMA, 1990; Porter scholar U. Kans. Sch. Medicine, 1950. Mem. AMA, Am. Acad. Pediatrics, Mo. State Med. Assn., Met. Med. Soc. of Kansas City, Greater Kansas City Pediatric Soc., Kansas City S.W. Clin. Soc., Alpha Omega Alpha, Nu Sigma Nu, Sigma Nu. Home: Claridge Ct 8101 Mission Rd Apt 233 Prairie Village KS 66208-5247

FAIRCHILD, SAMUEL WILSON, professional services company executive, retired federal agency administrator; b. Ft. Eustis, Va., July 16, 1954; s. Henry Howell and Ruby Mae (Love) F.; m. Linda Elizabeth Doremus, May 17, 1986; children: Elizabeth Christine, Samuel Bruce. BS, BA, Coll. of William and Mary, 1977. Cons. ITT, Inc., Smithfield, Va., 1977; v.p., gen. mgr. P.A., Inc., Hampton, Va., 1977-83; sr. policy advisor Exec. Office of the Pres., Washington, 1983-89; dep. asst. sec. U.S. Dept. Transp., Washington, 1989-91; v.p., sr. fellow Ctr. for Tech. and Pub. Policy Rsch. BDM Internat., Inc., McLean, Va., 1991-94; ptnr. Galland, Kharasch, Morse & Garfinkle, p.c., Washington, 1993-99; v.p. PA Cons. Group, Washington, 1999—2004; pres. Tadpole Group, Morris Plains, NJ, 2004—; mng. dir. Thesus Cap. Ptnrs., Morris Plains, NJ, 2004—. Chmn. bd. dirs. Schiphol N.Am. Holdings; bd. dirs., founder, pres. GKMG Cons. Svcs., Washington; cons. Innova Aviation Consulting, Chevy Chase, Md., 2005—; bd. dirs. BodyBlue, Inc., Toronto, Inline Technologies, LLC, Skillman, N.J., PropertyBank, LLC, Hagerstown, Md. Author, editor: Moving America, 1989. Active Boy Scouts Am., Irving, Tex., 1972—, mem. World Scout Bur., Geneva, 1972-80, Coun. for Excellence in Govt.; mem. exec. bd. Nat. Capital Area Coun. Boy Scouts Am., 1990—, Patriots Path coun., 1999—, Scouting Century Found., 1999—; co-chmn. ARC, Alexandria, Va., 1988-90. Recipient Disting. Alumni award Christopher Newport Coll., 1990; Usry Garland scholar Coll. William and Mary/Christopher Newport Coll., 1975. Mem. Nat. Aviation Assn., Coun. for Excellence in Govt., Aero Club. Presbyterian. Avocations: photography, music. Home: PO Box 341 Brookside NJ 07926-0341 Office Phone: 973-267-9083. Personal E-mail: samchild7@aol.com. Business E-Mail: sam@tadpolegroup.com.

FAIRCHILD, THOMAS EDWARD, federal judge; b. Milw., Dec. 25, 1912; s. Edward Thomas and Helen (Edwards) Fairchild; m. Eleanor E. Dahl, July 24, 1937; children: Edward, Susan, Jennifer, Andrew. Student, Princeton, 1931—33; AB, Cornell U., 1934; LLB, U. Wis., 1938. Bar: Wis. 1938. Practiced, Portage, Wis., 1938—41, Milw., 1945—48, 1953—56; atty. OPA, Chgo., Milw., 1941—45; hearing commr. Chgo. Region, 1945; atty. gen. Wis., 1948—51; consultant Office of Price Stabilization, 1951; U.S. atty. for Western Dist. Wis., 1951—52; justice Supreme Ct. Wis., 1957—66, U.S. Ct. Appeals for 7th Circuit, 1966—; chief judge, 1975—81; sr. judge, 1981—. Dem. candidate Senator from Wis., 1950, 1952. Mem.: KP, FBA, ABA, Am. Law Inst., Am. Judicature Soc., Dane County Bar Assn., 7th Cir. Bar Assn., Milw. Bar Assn., Wis. Bar Assn., Phi Delta Phi. Democrat. Mem. United Church Of Christ. Office: US Courthouse Rm 2764 219 S Dearborn St Chicago IL 60604-1702 Office Phone: 312-435-5800.

FAIRCLOTH, MARY WILLIAMS, minister, educator; d. Willie Sylvester and Katie Ruth Williams; m. Alonzo Vernon Faircloth, Nov. 23, 1978. BS in Mgmt., Rutgers U., 1978; MDiv, New Brunswick Theol. Sem., 1995. Mgmt. staff Port Authority N.Y. and N.J., N.Y.C., 1967—95, adminstrv. asst., 1978—84; clin. chaplain Ctr. for Hope, Linden, NJ, 1995—96, Dobbs Youth Devel. Ctr., Kinston, NC, 1997—2000; pastor Anderson Chapel AME Ch. AME Ch., Greenville, NC, 1998—; prof. ethics/religion/philosophy Shaw U., Raleigh/Greenville, NC. Ch. growth and devel. AME Ch., Greenville, 1999—. Tchr., organizer, youth leader Dobbs Youth Devel. Ctr., Kinston, 1998—2002. Recipient Cert. of Achievement, Pitt County Meml. Hosp., 1997, 1998, 1999. Mem.: Assn. Seminarians (life; pres./v.p. 1992—94, Cert. of Achievement 1995). Methodist. Avocations: travel, reading, writing, antiques, cooking. Home: 208 Buckingham Dr Winterville NC 28590-9418 Office: Anderson Chapel AME Church PO Box 30791 3788 Ivan Harris Rd Greenville NC 27833 Office Phone: 252-746-8427. Personal E-mail: andersonchapame@aol.com.

FAIRES, IAN MATTHEW, music educator; b. Charlotte, N.C., Sept. 26, 1977; s. Steven Rossell Faires and Rebecca Lynn Schneider. MusB, Appalachian State U., 1999. Lic. edn. for music grades K-12. Band dir. Charlotte-Mecklenburg Schs., Charlotte, NC, 2000; music dir. Mooresville (N.C.) Intermediate Sch., 2000—; pianist Southside Bapt. Ch., Mooresville, 2001; assoc. music min. Mt. Zion United Meth. Ch., Cornelius, NC, 2002—; pvt. piano tchr. Music & Arts Ctr., Huntersville, NC, 2003—04. Mem., tenor Joyful Hearts, Mooresville, 2003—04, Blessing, Cornelius, 2001—02; asst. dir. Davidson (N.C.) Coll. Pep Band, 2000—. Composer: (recorder method book) Mooresville Intermediate School Recorder Method, 2002. Mem.: N.C. Music Educators Assn., Music Educators Nat. Conf., N.C. Assn. for Educators. Independent. Methodist. Home: 20917 Academy St Cornelius NC 28031 Office: Mooresville Intermediate Sch 233 Kistler Farm Rd Mooresville NC 28115

FAIRES, ROSS NORBERT, manufacturing executive; b. Indpls., July 20, 1934; s. Herbert C. and Thelma (Wood) F.; m. Glady Ann Caley, Dec. 20, 1954; children: Kurt J., Eric S., Jay A. BA, Wabash Coll., 1958; MBA, Ind. U., 1959. Advt. mgr. Cummins Engine Co., Columbus, Ind., 1959-62; pres. Arvin Industries div. Housewares, Columbus, 1962-75, Tibbals Flooring Co., Oneida, Tenn., 1976-91; chmn. Faires Group, Chattanooga, 1991—. Bd. dirs. AmSouth Bank, Knoxville, Tenn. Bd. dirs. Knoxville Zoo, Knoxville Mus. Art, Nat. Symphony Orch., Washington, Webb Sch., Knoxville, St. Mary's Hosp. Found., Am. Symphony Orch. League, East Tenn. Comm. Found., Helen Ross McNabb Found.; bd. regents State of Tenn., 1984-91; mem. bd. advisors McCallie Sch. for Boys, Chattanooga; trustee Wabash (Ind.) Coll., Maryville Coll. Mem. Tenn. Bus. Assn. (bd. dirs.), Tenn. BAnd Assn., Leadership Knoxville, Cherokee Country Club, Sea Pines Country Club. Presbyterian. Home and Office: 6512 Sherwood Dr Knoxville TN 37919

FAIRFIELD, BILL L., finance company executive; BS in Engring., Bradley U.; MBA in Bus. Admistrn., Harvard U. Sr. exec. Eastman Kodak, 1969-73; sr. v.p. Lindsay Mfg. Co., 1975-79; pres. mktg. domestic irrigation divsn. Valmont Industries Inc., 1979-81, pres., gen. mgr. irrigation divsn., 1981-82; pres., CEO, Inacom Corp., Omaha, 1982-99, also bd. dirs.; chmn. Dreamfield Ptnrs. Inc., Dreamfield Capital Ventures, 2000—. Bd. dirs. Fed. Res. Bank Kansas City., Omaha, Sitel Corp., others. Trustee U. Nebr., Lincoln; bd. trustees Boy Scouts Am.; mem. Chancellor's Adv. Coun., U. Nebr., Omaha. Office: The Fairacres Project 206 Fairacres Rd Omaha NE 68132-2706

FAIRFIELD, PAULA KATHLEEN, sound recording engineer; b. Halifax, N.S., Can., Sept. 17, 1961; d. Henry Alfred and Sylvia Kathleen Fairfield; life ptnr. Carla Mary Murray. BFA, N.S. Coll. of Art and Design, Halifax, 1984. Freelance sound editor, Toronto, Canada, 1987—97; freelance picture editor, 1987—96; gen. mgr. Charles St. Video, Toronto, Canada, 1987—94; sec. treas. Pandora Pictures Inc, Toronto, Canada, 1987—98; pres. MHz Sound Design Inc, Toronto, Canada, 1997—2000, L.A., 1998—. Cons., design arts Ont. Arts Coun., Toronto, 1992; sr. tech. wirer CTV Networks, Network Relocation and Olympic installation, Toronto, 1994—95; instr., post prodn. sound Ont. Coll. of Art and Design, Toronto, 1997. Dir.: (electronic media installation) MIRAGE, (short film) Screamers, Livewires, Fragments;, sound effects editor and sound designer (feature film) Sin City, sound supervisor and sound designer (television series) La femme Nikita, sound effects editor and sound designer Due South, artist (exhibition group) Retrospective of Canadian Film and Video, George Pompidou Centre, Paris, Anteneo Femista De Madrid, Madrid, sound supr. and sound designer (feature film) Assault on Precinct 13, artist (exhibition group) Olympic Musem, Sarajevo, Museum of Modern Art, Zagreb, Croatia, Bienal De La Imagen En Movimento, Madrid, Infermental 10: There-Between-Here, Osnabruck, sound effects editor (feature film) A Love Song for Bobby Long, sound effects editor and sound designer Terminator 3: Rise of the Machines, Spy Kids 3D: Game Over. Jury mem. and adjudicator Can. Coun. for the Arts, Ottawa, 1989—97, Toronto Arts Coun., Toronto, 1989—97, Ont. Arts Coun., Toronto, 1990—97. Recipient B award, Can. Coun. for the Arts, 1992, Gemini Award for Achievement in Sound Editing: Due South, Acad. of Can. Cinema and TV, 1996, Can. Musicvideo VideoFACT Award, 1994; grantee audio prodn. grantee, Can. Coun. for the Arts, 1990, Explorations grantee, Can. Coun. for the Art, 1990, Video Prodn. grantee, 1989, 1987, Photography grantee, 1986, Film Prodn. grantee, Ont. Arts Coun., 1993, Video Prodn. grantee, 1992, Audio Prodn. grantee, Can. Coun. for the Arts, 1999, 1992, Film Prodn. grantee, 1994. Mem.: Am. Film Inst., Women in Film, L.A., Am. Working Malinois Assn., United Schutzhund Clubs of Am., Audio Engring. Soc., Soc. of Motion Picture and TV Engrs., Motion Picture Editors Guild, Internat. Alliance of Theatrical Stage Emplyees, Moving Picture Technicians, Artists and Allied Crafts, Profl. Orgn. of Women in Entertainment Reaching Up (founding mem. 2000—03), S.W. Working Dog Assn. Office Phone: 818-980-0306.

FAIRFIELD-SONN, JAMES WILLED, management educator, management consultant; b. Nashua, N.H., Aug. 21, 1948; s. David Alexander and Christine Mary (Fairfield) Sonn; m. Lynn Groark, July 3, 1982; children: Anne Madeline, James Willed, Jr., John Thomas. MS, Cornell U., 1979; MA, Yale U., 1980, MPhil, 1982, PhD, 1985. Mgr. office adminstrn. Hartford Ins. Group, Indpls., 1972-76; asst. prof. mgmt. U. Hartford, West Hartford, Conn., 1982-88, assoc. prof., 1988—2002, prof., 2002—, chmn. mgmt. dept., 1987-90, dir. exec. MBA, 1993-95, interim dean, 2004—05, dean, 2005—. Pres. Fairfield-Sonn Assocs., Centerbrook, Conn., 1981—; v.p. bd. dirs. ENCOMPASS Software. Author: Corporate Culture and the Quality Organization, 2001; contbr. articles and revs. to profl. jours. Named Outstanding Tchr. of Yr., Barney Sch., 1999; Cornell U. indsl. and labor rels. fellow, 1977-78, Yale U. fellow, 1978-82, Olin fellow, 1981. Mem.: Assn. Yale Alumni (chmn. grad. and profl. schs. com. 1982—83), Ea. Acad. Mgmt., Acad. Mgmt. Republican. Congregationalist. Avocations: tennis, travel, gardening. Home and Office: PO Box 1047 Old Lyme CT 06371-0998 E-mail: jimfs@fairfield-sonn.net.

FAIRHURST, MARY E., state supreme court justice; b. 1957; BA in Polit. Sci. cum laude, Gonzaga U., 1979, JD magna cum laude, 1984. Bar: Wash. 1984. Jud. clk. to Hon. William H. Williams Wash. Supreme Ct., 1984, jud. clk. to Hon. William C. Goodloe, 1986; chief revenue, bankruptcy and collections divsn. Wash. Atty. Gen.'s Office, 1986—2002; justice Wash. Supreme Ct., Olympia, 2003—. Mem. Wash. Supreme Ct. Gender and Justice Commn., Access to Justice Bd. Com. Established Lawyers and Students Engaged in Resolution Program; mem. Girl Scouts Bd. of Pacific Peak Council; mem. bd. advisors Gonzaga Law Sch. Recipient Steward of Justice award, 1998, Allies for Justice award, LEGALS, P.S., 1999. Mem.: Wash. Women Lawyers (past pres., Passing the Torch award 1999), Wash. State Bar Assn. (past. pres., mem. bd. govs.). Office: Wash Supreme Ct PO Box 40929 415 12th Ave SW Olympia WA 98504-0929 Business E-Mail: J_M_Fairhurst@courts.wa.gov.

FAIRMAN, JOEL MARTIN, broadcasting consultant; b. N.Y.C., Mar. 12, 1929; s. Philip A. and Isabelle (Glackman) Feinberg; m. Claire Martin, Oct. 1, 1959; children: Elizabeth, David, Helen. BA, Amherst Coll., 1952; JD, Yale U., 1955. Assoc. Patterson Belknap & Webb, N.Y.C., 1956-61; asst. to pres., v.p. Gianis & Co., Inc., N.Y.C., 1961-65; sr. v.p. and mng. dir. corp. fin. communications group Prudential-Bache Securities and predecessor firms, N.Y.C., 1965-83; chmn. Faircom Inc., 1984-98; vice chmn. Regent Comm., Inc., 1998—2001; chmn. North Shore Strategies Inc., 2001—. Home: Bayville Rd Locust Valley NY 11560-2003 Office: North Shore Strategies PO Box 46 Glen Head NY 11545-1947

FAIRMAN, MARC P., lawyer; b. May 25, 1945; BA, U. Calif., Berkeley, 1967; JD cum laude, Harvard U., 1970. Bar: Calif. 1971. Ptnr. McDermott, Will & Emery, Menlo Park. Northern Calif. adv. bd. Entrepreneurship Inst.; bd. trustees Mills Coll. Mem. Am. Inns of Ct., Assn. of Bus. Trial Lawyers. Office: 3150 Porter DR Palo Alto CA 94304-1212

FAIROBENT, DOUGLAS KEVIN, computer programmer; b. Detroit, Jan. 10, 1951; s. Jack Edward and Doris Kathleen (Kennedy) F.; m. Paulette Marie Gillig, June 13, 1981. BS in Physics, U. Mich., 1972, MS in Physics, 1975, PhD in Theoretical Condensed Matter Physics, 1978. Engr. Ford Motor Co., Allen Park, Mich., 1978-80; lectr. physics Ohio State U., Columbus, 1980-82; sr. systems programmer Rockwell Internat., Columbus, 1982-85, Cin. Milacron, 1985-90, Quantum Chem. Co., Cin., 1990-96; sys. adminstr. Cath. Healthcare Ptnrs., Cin., 1996—. Contbr. articles to Phys. Rev., other publs. Mem. Am. Phys. Soc. (life). Avocations: ice hockey, classical piano. Office: Catholic Healthcare Partners 615 Elsinore Pl Cincinnati OH 45202-1459 E-mail: dkfairobent@health-partners.org.

FAIRSTEIN, LINDA A., prosecutor, writer; b. Westchester County, NY, May 5, 1947; m. Justin N. Feldman BA in English Lit., Vassar Coll.; JD, Univ. Va. Joined Manhattan District Atty.'s Office, 1972, chief sex crimes unit, 1976—. Author: (non-fiction) Sexual Violence, 1994 (NY Times notable book, 1994), (novels) (Alexandra Cooper series) Final Jeopardy, 1996, Likely to Die, 1997, Cold Hit, 1999, The Dead House, 2001, The Bone Vault, 2003, The Kills, 2004, Entombed, 2005. Active in human-rights and legal organizations. Fellow: Am. Coll. Trial Lawyers. Office: Office Dist Atty Sex Crimes/Spl Victims Bur 210 Joralemon St Brooklyn NY 11201-3745 Mailing: PO Box 226 New York NY 10021-0014*

FAIRWEATHER, DANIEL EDWARD, music educator; b. Elizabeth, N.J., Oct. 19, 1978; s. Dorothy and Gilbert Fairweather. BMus, Ga. So. U., Statesboro, 1996—2001. Cert. tchr. Ga. Dept. Edn., 2002. Band dir. Atlanta Pub. Schs., 2002—. Pvt. lesson instr. Century Music Ctr., Decatur, Ga., 2003—. Young musicians mentor Salvation Army, Decatur, Ga., 2002—05. Mem.: Ga. Music Educators Assn. (assoc.). Conservative. Achievements include invention of the Fairweather Method - The process of playing rhythm guitar using a small maraca in your hand and foot, in order to simulate the sound of a full rhythm section. Avocations: basketball, art, poetry, travel. Home: 5533 Mountain View Pass Stone Mountain GA 30087 Personal E-mail: defairweather@gmail.com.

FAIRWEATHER, ROBERT GORDON LEE, retired lawyer; b. Rothesay, N.B., Can., Mar. 27, 1923; s. Jack H.A.L. and Agnes Charlotte (Mackeen) F.; m. Nancy E. Broughall, June 1, 1946 (dec. Aug. 2003); children— Michael, Wendy, Hugh. B.C.L., U. N.B., 1949, LL.D. (hon.), 1973, St. Thomas U., 1977, Queens U., 1978, St. Francis Xavier U., 1980, York U., 1993. Called to bar N.B 1949, created Queen's Counsel 1958. Partner firm McKelvey, MacAulay, Machum & Fairweather, St. John, 1957-77; atty. gen. N.B., 1958-60; chief Can. Human Rights Commn., Ottawa, Ont., 1977-87; chmn. Immigration and Refugee Bd., Ottawa, 1987-92. Mem. Legis. Assembly N.B., 1952-62, M.P., 1962-77. Served with Royal Can. Navy, 1941-45. Decorated officer Order of Can.; recipient Outstanding Achievement award of pub. svc. Govt. Can., 1990, Humanitarian of the Yr. award Can. Red Cross, 1999, New Brunswick Pioneer of Human Rights award, 2002, Order of New Brunswick award, 2005; Ryerson Poly. U. fellow, 1993. Home: 2865 Rothesay Rd Apt 43 Rothesay NB Canada E2E 5V1

FAIRWEATHER, SCOTT JAMES, music educator; b. Robbinsdales, Minn., Jan. 20, 1974; s. James Burness and Diane Louise Fairweather. BS in Instrumental Music, Minn. State U., Mankato, 1997. Band dir., music tchr. Richfield (Minn.) Jr. HS, 1997—98; band dir. Wayzata (Minn.) West Mid. Sch., 1998—99, Cretin-Derham Hall, St. Paul, 1999—. Drum line coach Blaine HS, 1998—2001, Minn. HS, 2001—02, Rosemont HS, 2002, Red Wing HS, 2000—04, Pk. Ctr. HS, 2002. Mem.: Internat. Assn. for Jazz Music Edn., Music Educators Nat. Conf. Avocation: playing rock music. Office: Cretin-Derham Hall 550 S Albert St Saint Paul MN 55126 Personal E-mail: sjf74@yahoo.com.

FAISON, BEVERLY ANN, librarian; b. Wilmington, N.C., Feb. 3, 1960; d. Samuel Ellerby and Edith Reaves Faison; children: Derico, Eukia, Jasmine. AA, Cape Fear Tech. Sch., Wilmington, 1981; grad., Tidewater C.C., Norfolk, Va, 1998. Cert. microcomputer software. Pers. asst. Earl Industries, Portsmouth, Va., 1995—96, quality assurance tech. libr., 1996—99; personal care asst., 2004—. Author: The Healing Process, 2001, poetry. Mem.: United Order of Tents (rec. sec. 1992—).

FAISON, LUGENIA MARION, special education educator; b. Bklyn., Apr. 17, 1954; d. Jerry Faison and Marion Braxton-Faison. BA in Elem. Edn., U. V.I., St. Croix, 1982; MA in Learning Disabilities and Reading, U. Fla., Coral Gables, 1989; MA in Counseling and Guidance, Point Loma Nazarene U., 2002. Profl. clear multiple tchg. credential, profl. clear spl. edn. credential, profl. clear pupil pers. svcs. credential. Elem. tchr., St. Croix, 1976—93; spl. edn. tchr. Pasadena, Calif., 1994—. Mem.: ASCD, NAACP. Democrat.

FAISON, RALPH E., communications equipment manufacturing executive; BS in Mktg., Ga. State Univ., Atlanta; MS in Mgmt., Stanford Univ. Various exec. positions AT&T wireless bus. unit; v.p. advt., brand mgmt. Lucent Tech., v.p., new ventures group, 1997—2001; pres., CEO Celiant Corp.(acquired by Andrew), 2001—02; COO Andrew, Orland Park, Ill., 2002, pres., 2002—, and CEO. Bd. dir. WatchMark Corp., NETGEAR, Inc.; bd. adv. New Venture Ptnrs. LLC. Bd. dir. Exec. Club, Chgo. Office: Andrew 10500 W 153rd St Orland Park IL 60462 Office Phone: 708-349-3300.*

FAISON, SETH SHEPARD, retired insurance broker; b. N.Y.C., Jan. 18, 1924; s. John Williams and Caroline Goree (Shepard) F.; m. Susan Tyler, Apr. 14, 1956 (dec. 1978); children: Katharine Faison Spencer, Seth Shepard, Sarah, Ann Badger; m. Sara Williams Rose Chew, Mar. 29, 1980; stepchildren: Sara Holten Chew, Katherine Rose Chew, Arthur Duncan Chew (dec.). BA with honors and distinction, Wesleyan U., 1947. Personnel mgr. NBC, N.Y.C., 1948-53; divsn. mgr. Am. Mgmt. Assn., N.Y.C., 1953-58; asst. v.p. Johnson & Higgins, N.Y.C., 1958-68, v.p., 1968-89; ret., 1989. Chmn. Bklyn. Acad. Music, 1966-72, hon. chmn., 1979—; trustee Bklyn. Inst. Arts and Scis., 1963-81, v.p., 1965-71, exec. v.p., 1971-74, vice-chmn., 1974-79, chmn., 1979-81; trustee/gov. The Bklyn. Mus., 1972-91, vice-chmn. 1976-91, trustee 1993—; trustee Bklyn. Hosp., 1963—, v.p. 1968-82, vice-chmn., 1982-93, chmn., 1993-02, chmn. emeritus, 2003—; bd. govs. Hosp. Trustees of N.Y. State, 1992-97, chmn., 1995-97; trustee Poly Prep., 1962-77, N.Y. Presbyn. Healthcare Sys., 1998-03; bd. dirs. Police Athletic League N.Y., 1957-73, Chelsea Theater Center, 1969-77; regent St. Francis Coll., Bklyn., 1961-70; mem. N.Y.C. Commn. for Cultural Affairs, 1981-91. Lt. (j.g.) USNR, 1943-46. Recipient N.Y. State award for Bklyn. Acad. Music, 1969, BAM award for disting. svc., Bklyn. Acad. Music, 1975, Poly. Prep. Disting. Alumnus award, 1997, Forsythia award, Bklyn. Bot. Garden, 2003, Disting. Trustee award, United Hosp. Fund, 2003, Founders medal, Bklyn. Hosp. Ctr., 2003. Mem. Citizens Union, Huguenot Soc. Am., The Heights Casino Club, Rembrandt Club, Ihpetonga Club (Bklyn.), Bellport Bay Yacht Club (N.Y.). Unitarian (sr. deacon). Home: 1 Pierrepont St Apt 10B Brooklyn NY 11201-3302 E-mail: maisonfaison@earthlink.net.

FAISS, ROBERT DEAN, lawyer; b. Centralia, Ill., Sept. 19, 1934; s. Wilbur and Theresa Ella (Watts) F.; m. Linda Louise Chambers, Mar. 30, 1991; children: Michael Dean Faiss, Marcy Faiss Ayres, Robert Mitchell Faiss, Philip Grant Faiss, Justin Cooper. BA in Journalism, Am. U., 1969, JD, 1972. Bar: Nev. 1972, D.C. 1972, U.S. Dist. Ct. Nev. 1973, U.S. Supreme Ct. 1977, U.S. Ct. Appeals (9th cir.) 1978. City editor Las Vegas (Nev.) Sun, 1957-59; pub. info. officer Nev. Dept. Employment Security, 1959-61; asst. exec. sec. Nev. Gaming Commn., Carson City, 1961-63; exec. asst. to gov. State of Nev., Carson City, 1963-67; staff asst. U.S. Pres. Lyndon B. Johnson, White House, Washington, 1968-69; asst. to exec. dir. U.S. Travel Adminstrn., Washington, 1969-72; ptnr., chmn. adminstrv. law dept. Lionel, Sawyer & Collins, Las Vegas, 1973—. Mem. bank secrecy Act Adv. Group U.S. Treasury. Co-author: Legalized Gaming in Nevada, 1961, Nevada Gaming License Guide, 1988, Nevada Gaming Law, 1991, 95, 98. Recipient Bronze medal Dept. Commerce, 1972, Chris Schaller award We Can, Las Vegas, 1995, Lifetime Achievement award Nev. Gaming Attys. Assn., 1997; named One of 100 Most Influential Lawyers in Am. and premier U.S. gaming atty., Nat. Law Jour., 1997. Mem. ABA (chmn. gaming law com. 1985-86), Internat. Assn. Gaming Attys. (founding, pres. 1980), Nev. Gaming Attys. Office: Lionel Sawyer & Collins 300 S 4th St Ste 1700 Las Vegas NV 89101-6053

FAIT, CINDA RUTH MCGILL, elementary school educator; b. Meadville, Pa., July 14, 1950; d. Gaylord A. and Margaret A. (Kebert) McGill; m. William Lance, Nov. 21, 1978; children: Jacob Ian, Sarah Min. BS, Edinboro (Pa.) U., 1972, MS, 1975. Tchr. 4th grade Cochranton (Pa.) Elem. Sch., Crawford Ctrl. Schs., 1972-75, tchr. 3rd grade, 1975—. Mentor Crawford Ctrl. Schs., Meadville, coop. tchr., Allegheny Coll., Edinboro U., Clarion U., Grove City Coll. Mem. commn. edn. Grace United Meth. Ch., Meadville, 1986—. Mem. NEA, Pa. State Edn. Assn., Crawford Ctrl. Edn. Assn. (treas.). Avocations: swimming, travel, children. Home: 166 Reynolds Ave Meadville PA 16335-1717

FAIT, GLENN A., lawyer, law educator; BA, Calif. State Univ., Sacramento; JD, Univ. Pacific. Assoc. dean McGeorge Sch. Law, Univ. Pacific, spl. counsel; dir. Inst. for Adminstrv. Justice, Univ. Pacific. Former mayor City of Folsom, Calif. Office: University of the Pacific McGeorge School of Law 3200 Fifth Ave Sacramento CA 95817

FAIT, GRACE WALD, writer, retired language educator; d. Samuel and Evelyn Ragosin Wald; m. Jerome Myles Portman (div.); m. Irwin Fait, Sept. 10, 1966 (dec.). AA, Miami-Dade C.C., 1982. Self-employed home developer, Delray Beach, Fla., 1958—68; officer mgr., legal sec. Milton Grusmark, Miami Beach, 1968—70; exec. legal sec. Courshon & Courshon, Miami Beach, Fla., 1972—77; exec. sec. to pres. Funding, Inc., North Miami Beach, Fla., 1970—72; ESL tchr. Broward C.C., Coconut Creek, Fla., 1983—99; ret., 1999. Liaison Broward C.C./Voice of Wynmoor, Coconut Creek, 2001—04. Asst. editor, staff reporter: Voice of Wynmoor, 1983—2004; contbr. articles, revs., poems to profl. publs. Pub. rels. vol., advisor Friends of North Regional Libr., Coconut Creek, 2003—. Avocations: piano, reading, writing. Home: 3403 Bimini Ln A2 Coconut Creek FL 33066 Office: Voice of Wynmoor 3403 Bimini Ln A2 Coconut Creek FL 33066

FAITH, MARSHALL E., grain company executive; Chmn., dir. The Scoular Co., Omaha. Sect. Bishop Clarkson Mem. Found., Episcopal Diocese Nebr. Office: The Scoular Co Scoular Bldg 2027 Dodge St Ste 300 Omaha NE 68102-1229

FAITH, THOMAS IAIN, historian, educator; b. Phila., May 31, 1979; s. Donald and Eileen Faith. BA, Temple U., Phila., 1997—2001; MPh, George Wash. U., 2004; postgrad., George Wash.U., 2004—. Rsch. asst. George Wash. U., Washington, 2002—04; tchr. U.S. Ho. of Reps. Page Sch., Washington, 2004; editl. asst. Eleanor Roosevelt Papers, Washington, 2004; grad. tchr. George Wash. U., Washington, 2004—. Bd. mem. Abraham Lincoln Commn., Washington, 2004—; mem., history com. N.Y. Ave. Ch., Washington, 2004—. Deacon Presbyn. Ch. Mem.: Soc. for Mil. History, Am. Hist. Assn., Phi Alpha Theta. Liberal. Presbyterian. Office: George Washington Univ Phillips Hall 801 22nd St History Dept Washington DC 20052 Personal E-mail: tomfaith@gwu.edu.

FAITZ, ANN PAULA, lawyer; b. St. Louis; d. Victor Joseph and Pauline (Crimi) Manganello; m. Dean Faitz; 1 child, Nicholas. BA, Fontbonne, St. Louis, 1973; JD, U. Ark., Little Rock, 1986. Bar: Ark. 1986, Mo. 1988. Assoc. Hale Law Firm, North Little Rock, 1986-88; atty. specialist Ark. Dept. Environ. Quality, Little Rock, 1988-92; assoc. Chisenhall, Nestrud & Julian, Little Rock, 1993—. Cons. Ark. Dept. Environ. Quality; assoc. coun. Ark. Environ. Fedn., State C. of C., Little Rock; arbitrator BBB; facilitator N.W. Ark. Watershed Summit; lectr. in field. Contbr. articles to profl. jours. Bd. dirs. Main St. Argenta, Our Way, Inc. Mem. ABA, Ark. Bar Assn., Pulaski County Bar Assn., Ark. Wildlife Fedn., Ark. Environ. Fedn., Ark. C. of C. Office: Chisenhall Nestrud & Julian 400 W Capitol Ave Ste 2840 Little Rock AR 72201-3467 Office Phone: 501-372-5800. Business E-Mail: afaitz@cjlaw.com.

FAIZ, ALEXANDRIA, researcher, writer; d. Robert Lee and Eileen Helen (Wagner) F. BA in English and Biology with honors, Fairfield U., 1993; postgrad., Columbia U., 1993-94. Nat. outreach coord. Thirteen/Sta. WNET, NYC, 1996—98; rsch. cons. SCIENS Pub. Rels., 1999—2000; sr. rsch. mgr. Studley, Inc., 1999—. Mem. editl. bd. Columbia: A Magazine of Poetry and Prose, 1993; author, editor: In Honor of the Earth, 1997. Founding mem. Alumnae Forum, Fairfield, 1995; co-founder Student Adv. Coun., Lit. Vols. Southeastern Fairfield County, 2002-2004; trustee Alfred Adler Inst. N.Y., 1997—. Recipient Outstanding Women of Conn., 2003. Mem.: PEN (mem. freedom to write com.), Nat. Writers Union (asst. nat. grievance officer 2002—04), History of Sci. Soc., Philosophy of Sci. Assn., U.N. Assn. U.S. (interim chair UNA YPIC), Gt. Books Found., Nature Conservancy, Toastmasters, Am. Mus. Natural History. Roman Catholic. Avocations: issues concerning intellectual property and freedom of expression, professional ethics. Office Phone: 203-947-2497. E-mail: afprofessional@hotmail.com.

FAJANS, STEFAN STANISLAUS, retired internist; b. Munich, Mar. 15, 1918; arrived in U.S., 1936, naturalized, 1942; s. Kasimir M. and Salomea (Kaplan) Fajans; m. Ruth Stine, Sept. 6, 1947; children: Peter S., John S. BS, U. Mich., Ann Arbor, 1938, MD, 1942. Intern Mount Sinai Hosp., N.Y.C., 1942—43; research fellow U. Mich., 1946—47, rsch. fellow, 1949—51, resident, 1947—49; mem. faculty U. Mich. Med. Sch., 1950—, prof., 1961—88, active prof. emeritus, 1988—. Mem. endocrinology study sect. NIH, 1958—62, mem. diabetes and metabolism tng. grants com., 1966—70, mem. nat. diabetes adv. bd., 1987—91; chief divsn. endocrinology and metabolism Mich. Diabetes Rsch. and Tng. Ctr., 1973—87, dir., 1977—86; chmn. Am. zone internat. sci. adv. com. Congresses Internat. Diabetes Fedn., 1977—79; Banting meml. lectr., 1978. Contbr. articles med. publs. Mem. career devel. com. VA Med. Rsch. Svcs., 1987—91. Officer M.C. U.S. Army, 1943—46. Fellow rsch. fellow in medicine, ACP, 1949—50, Life Ins. Med. Inst., 1950—51. Master: ACP; mem.: NAS (sr. mem. inst. med.), Ctrl. Soc. Clin. Rsch., Assn. Am. Physicians, Am. Soc. Clin. Investigation, Am. Fedn. Clin. Rsch., Endocrine Soc. (v.p. 1970—71, coun. 1967—71, 1978—81), Am. Diabetes Assn. (pres. 1971—72, Banting medal 1972, Banting Meml. award 1978), Alpha Omega Alpha, Sigma Xi. Home: 827 Asa Gray Dr # 360 Ann Arbor MI 48105-2566 Office: PO Box 0354 Ann Arbor MI 48109-0354 Office Phone: 734-936-5039. Business E-Mail: sfajans@umich.edu.

FAJARDO, LUIS FELIPE, pathologist, educator, director; b. Bogotá, Colombia, Jan. 23, 1927; arrived in US, 1952; s. Luis Antonio and Maria Teresa (Lobo Guerrero) Fajardo; m. Lorela M. Enterline, July 6, 1958; children: Anna Luisa, Marta, Andrés. MD, Nat. U. Colombia, Bogotá, 1952. Diplomate Am. Bd. Pathology. Pathologist New Britain Gen. Hosp., Conn., 1959—60; chief pathology Hosp. Mil. Ctrl., Bogotá, 1962—65, Vets. Hosp., Palo Alto, Calif., 1977—; assoc. prof. pathology Stanford U., Calif., 1972—84, prof. pathology, 1984—. Vis. prof. Yale U., U. Mich., Oxford U., U. Utah, U. Calif., San Francisco, U. Geneva, U. Alberta. Author: Radiation Pathology, 2001, 152 rsch. articles; contbr. 20 chpts. sci. books. Mem.: South Bay Pathology Soc., Radiation Rsch. Soc., Internat. Acad. Pathology. Avocations: photography, hiking, backpacking. Office: Pathology Vets Med Ctr 3801 Miranda Ave Palo Alto CA 94304

FAJORS, NIQUE, marketing executive; b. Boston, Nov. 2, 1967; s. Herb and Blanche Christine Fajors; m. Faiza Abdallah Zarroug. BSBA, Suffolk U., 1989; MBA, Harvard U., 1993. Brand mgmt. Procter & Gamble, Cin., 1993-95; exec. v.p. Digital Telemedia, Inc., N.Y.C., 1995-97; pres. Valuecreation.com LLC, N.Y.C., 1997—99; pres. consumer mktg. svcs. Bounty SCA Worldwide, Chgo., 1999—2001; sr. policy advisor Office of the Sec. Dept. Commerce, 2002—04; v.p. ptnr. mgmt. CMI Mktg. Inc., N.Y.C., NY, 2004—05; v.p. Global Brand Mgt., Atari, Inc., N.Y.C., 2005—. Bd. dirs. ProMonde, Inc., bd. mem. Nat. Childhood Obesity Found. Prodr. (ednl. video) The Invisible Men, 1995; author: Cultural & Economic Revitalization, 1999. Avocations: travel, photography. Home: 440 Riverside Dr Apt 28 New York NY 10027 Office: 417 5th Ave New York NY 10016 Office Phone: 212-726-6553. E-mail: nfajors@earthlink.net.

FAJT, KAREN ELAINE, art educator; d. E. Albert and Angeline Louise DeLuca; m. Henry Gervase Fajt, Jr., June 22, 1974; children: Merritt Lynn, Holly Elizabeth. BA, Seton Hill U., 1970; MEd, U. Pitts., 1973. Art educator Hempfield Area Sch. Dist., Greensburg, 1970—. Bd. trustees Laurel Ballet Theatre, Greensburg, 1989—93; mem. St. Lucy's Aux. to the Blind., Pitts., 1994—, Frick Art and Hist. Ctr., 2001—, Westmoreland Mus. Am. Art, 1985—; bd. dirs. Lawyers' Aux., Greensburg, 1978—. Recipient Sullivan award, Seton Hill U., 1970. Mem.: NEA, Hempfield Area Edn. Assn., Pa. State Edn. Assn., Nat. Art Edn. Assn., Greensburg Coll. Club (bd. trustees 1970—, parliamentarian 1970—, chmn. scholarship com.), Univ. Club. Avocations: painting, travel, reading, gardening, shopping. Office: Hempfield Area School Dist RD # 6 Greensburg PA 15601

FAKAHANY, AHMASS L., finance company executive; BS summa cum laude, Boston U.; MBA, Columbia U. Fin. staff Exxon Corp.; with Merrill Lynch & Co., Inc., NYC, 1987—, COO global mkts. & investment banking, 2001—02, exec. v.p., CFO, 2002—. Office: Merrill Lynch & Co Inc Four World Financial Ctr New York NY 10080

FAKE, INGRID CHRISTINE, middle school educator; b. Ashland, Pa., May 28, 1968; d. Klaus Bernd and Diane Adrian (Robbins) Runge; m. Michael William Fake, Aug. 24, 1991. Grad., Kutztown U., 1990. Asst. mgr. Frugal Frank's Shoes, Media, Pa., 1985-86; cashier Burger King, Brookhaven, Pa., 1987-89; recreator Elwyn (Pa.), Inc., 1988-91; art tchr. elem. Kutztown (Pa.) Area Sch. Dist., 1990-91; art tchr. middle sch. Owen J. Roberts Middle Sch., Pottstown, Pa., 1991—; arts and crafts coord. Muhlenberg Twp., Hyde Park, Pa., 1992. Mem. AAUW, Nat. Art Edn. Assn., Pa. Art Edn. Assn. Lutheran. Avocations: physical fitness, camping, travel, gardening. Home: 629 Elm Ave Reading PA 19605 Office: Owen J Roberts Sch Dist 881 Ridge Rd Pottstown PA 19465-9801

FAKIRANANDA, MIRA B., academic administrator; b. St. Johnsbury, Vt., Oct. 15, 1946; children: Joe Mendle Williams, Kate Beloved McIntyre. BA, U. Vt., 1969; MA, U. Wash., 1971. Tchg. asst., adminstrv. asst. U. Wash., Seattle, 1969-78; adminstrv. asst. U. Vt., Burlington, 1995—. Mem. Burlington Human Rights Coun., 1993-95, The Women's Union, Burlington, 1994—, Race Edn. Action Project, Burlington, 1995—, Burlington Cmty. Justice Initiative, 1998; active First United Meth. Ch., Burlington. Recipient Making a Difference for Women in Vt. award, Gov.'s Commn. award, 1999. Mem. Sanatana Dharma. Avocations: cross country skiing, cooking, singing, advocating the creation of more low-income housing. Home: 19 Woods St Burlington VT 05401-1858 E-mail: mfakiran@zoo.uvm.edu.

FALA, HERMAN C., lawyer; b. Phila., Oct. 15, 1949; s. Herman Anthony and Rose Maria (Iannetti) F.; m. Helen E. Perry, June 26, 1971; 1 child, Danielle. BS summa cum laude, U. Notre Dame, 1971; JD cum laude, Harvard U., 1974. Bar: Pa. 1974, U.S. Dist. Ct. (ea. dist.) Pa. 1974. Assoc. Wolf, Block, Schorr & Solis-Cohen, Phila., 1974-82, ptnr., 1982—. Chair real estate dept. Wolf, Block, Schorr & Solis-Cohen. Editor: The Philadelphia Lawyer, 1977—. Bd. dirs. The Wilma Theatre, Phila., 1986—, chmn., 1995-97, Charter H.S. Arch. Design, 2005—. Mem. ABA, Pa. Bar Assn., Phila. Bar Assn. (v.p. 1997, chair exec. com. real property sect. 1998), Am. Coll. Real Estate Lawyers, Phi Beta Kappa. Avocations: photography, amateur astronomy, travel, cooking, writing. Office: Wolf Block Schorr & Solis-Cohen 22d Fl 1650 Arch St Fl 22D Philadelphia PA 19103-2029

FALB, PETER LAWRENCE, mathematician, educator, investment company executive; b. N.Y.C., July 26, 1936; s. Harry and Bertha (Kirschner) F.; m. Karen Forslund, Oct. 9, 1971; children: Hilary, Alison. AB, Harvard U., 1956, MA, 1957, PhD, 1961. Mem. staff MIT Lincoln Lab., Cambridge, 1960-66; assoc. prof. applied math. U. Mich., Ann Arbor, 1966; prof. Brown U., Providence, 1967—; prin., treas. Dane, Falb, Stone & Co., Inc., Boston, 1977—. Chmn. Barberry Corp., 1968-85; also bd. dirs.; bd. dirs. FES Computing Co., LTCQ, Inc., Toreador Royalty, Infolenz, LTC Media; mng. dir. F-Co. Holdings Co.; vis. prof. Lund (Sweden) Inst. Tech., summers 1971, 72, 74, 76, 78; cons. NASA, Bolt, Beranek & Newman Co. Author: (with M. Athans) Optimal Control: An Introduction to the Theory and its Applications, 1966, (with R. Kalman and M. Arbib) Topics in Mathematical System Theory, 1969, (with J. deJong) Some Successive Approximation Methods in Control and Oscillation Theory, 1969; Methods of Algebraic Geometry in Control Theory, Part I: Scalar Linear Systems and Affine Algebraic Geometry, 1989, Methods of Algebraic Geometry in Control Theory, Part II: Multivariable Linear Systems and Projective Algebraic Geometry, 1999. Home: 245 Brattle St Cambridge MA 02138-4614 Office: Dane Falb Stone & Co Inc 15 Broad St Ste 406 Boston MA 02109-3803 also: Brown U Box F Providence RI 02912 Office Phone: 617-742-0666. Personal E-mail: plf245@aol.com.

FALCAM, LEO A., former Micronesian government official; b. Nov. 20, 1935; V.p. Federated States of Micronesia, 1997-99, pres., 1999—2003. Office: Office of the Pres POB PS-53 Palikir Pohnpei FM 96941

FALCO, CHARLES MAURICE, physicist, researcher; b. Fort Dodge, Iowa, Aug. 17, 1948; s. Joe and Mavis Margaret (Mickelson) F.; m. Dale Wendy Miller, May 5, 1973; children: Lia Denise, Amelia Claire. BA, U. Calif., Irvine, 1970, MA, 1971, PhD, 1974. Trainee NSF, 1970-74; asst. physicist Argonne (Ill.) Nat. Lab., 1974-77, physicist, 1977-82, group leader superconductivity and novel materials, 1978-82; prof. physics and optical scis., research prof. U. Ariz., Tucson, 1982-97, prof. optical scis., chair condensed matter physics, 1998—, dir. lab. x-ray optics, 1986—. Vis. prof. U. Paris Sud, 1979, 86, U. Aachen, 1989; lectr., 1974—; mem. panel on artificially structured materials NRC, 1984-85; co-organizer numerous internat. confs. in field, 1978—; mem. spl. rev. panel on high temperature superconductivity Applied Physics Letters, 1987—; mem. panel on superconductivity Inst. Def. Analysis, 1988—; researcher on artificial metallic superlattices, X-ray optics, auperconductivity, condensed matter physics, electronic materials; curatorial advisor Solomon R. Guggenheim Mus., 1997—, cocurator The Art of the Motorcycle exhbn. Editor: Future Trends in Superconductive Electronics, 1978, Materials for Magneto-Optic Data Storage, 1989; contbr. articles to profl. jours.; patentee in field. Mem. divsn. condensed matter physics Exec. Com. Arts, 1992-94. Alexander von Humboldt Found. sr. disting. grantee, 1989; recipient Art Motorcycle Exbhn. award Internat. Assn. Art Critics, 1999. Fellow Am. Phys. Soc. (counselor 1992-94, exec. com. div. condensed matter physics 1992-94, exec. com. div. internat. physics 1994-98), Optical Soc. Am.; mem. IEEE (sr.), Materials Rsch. Soc., Sigma Xi. Achievements include rsch. on artificial metallic superlattices, X-ray optics, superconductivity, condensed matter physics, electronic materials. Home: 13005 E Cape Horn Dr Tucson AZ 85749-9734 Office: U Ariz Optical Scis Ctr Box 210077 Tucson AZ 85721-0077 Office Phone: 520-621-6771. E-mail: falco@u.arizona.edu.

FALCO, EDIE, actress; b. Northport, NY, July 5, 1963; 1 adopted child, Anderson. BFA, SUNY, Purchase, NY, 1986. Appeared in films Sweet Lorraine, 1987, The Unbelievable Truth, 1990, Trust, 1990, Time Expired, 1992, Laws of Gravity, 1992, I Was on Mars, 1992, Bullets Over Broadway, 1994, Backfire!, 1995, The Addiction, 1995, Layin' Low, 1996, The Funeral, 1996, Breathing Room, 1996, Firehouse, 1997, Cost of Living, 1997, Cop Land, 1997, Trouble on the Corner, 1997, A Price Above Rubies, 1998, Hurrican Streets, 1998, Judy Berlin, 1999, Random Hearts, 1999, Overnight Sensation, 2000, Death of a Dog, 2000, Sunshine State, 2002 (Best Supporting Acress award LA Film Critics Assn. 2002, Golden Satellite award best supporting actress 2003); appeared in TV movies The Sunshine Boys, 1995, Jenifer, 2001; appeared in TV series Oz, 1997-99, The Sopranos, 1999- (Golden Globe award best actress in a drama 2000, 03, Emmy for best actress 1999, 2001, 2003, Actor of Yr., Am. Film Inst. 2001, Golden Satellite award 2002, SAG award 2003); TV guest appearances include Homicide: Life on the Street, 1993-94, 97, Law & Order, 1993-94, 97, New York Undercover, 1995; film dir. Rift, 1993; TV prodr. Stringer, 1999; theater appearances include Side Man, 2000, The Vagina Monologues, 2001, Frankie and Johnny in the Clair de Lune, 2002. Office: c/o Sandra Marsh Mgmt 9150 Wilshire Blvd Ste 220 Beverly Hills CA 90212-3429

FALCO, MARIA JOSEPHINE, political scientist; b. Wildwood, N.J., July 7, 1932; d. John J. and Mafalda M. (Barbieri) F. AB, Immaculata (Pa.) Coll., 1954; student, U. Florence, Italy, 1954-55; MA, Fordham U., 1958; PhD, Bryn Mawr (Pa.) Coll., 1963; postdoctoral rsch. fellow, Yale, 1965-66; quantitative data analysis, U. Mich., 1968; mgmt. program, Carnegie-Mellon U., 1983. Instr., then asst. prof. history and polit. sci. Immaculata Coll., Pa., 1957-63; asst. prof. polit. sci. Washington Coll., Chestertown, Md., 1963-64; rsch. asst. Genevieve Blatt; candidate for U.S. Senator from Pa., 1964-65; asst. prof., then assoc. prof. polit. sci. Le Moyne Coll., Syracuse, N.Y., 1966-73, chmn. polit. sci. dept., 1967-73; prof. polit. sci. Stockton State Coll., Pomona, N.J., 1973-76; chmn. social and behavioral scis. faculty U. Tulsa,

1976-79; dean Coll. Arts and Scis., Loyola U., New Orleans, 1979-85; prof. polit. sci. Loyola U., New Orleans, 1985-86; v.p. acad. affairs DePauw U., Greencastle, Ind., 1986-88, prof. polit. sci., 1988-93, prof. emerita, 1993—. Speaker in field; adj. prof. polit. sci. Tulane U., New Orleans, 1996-97. Author: Truth and Meaning in Political Science: An Introduction to Political Inquiry, 1973, Bigotry: Ethnic, Machine and Sexual Politics in a Senatorial Election, 1980; editor: Through the Looking Glass: Epistemology and the Conduct of Political Inquiry: An Anthology, 1979, Feminism and Epistemology: Approaches to Research in Women and Politics, 1987, Feminist Interpretations of Mary Wollstonecraft, 1996, Feminist Interpretations of NiccolÓ Machiavelli, 2004; cons. editor Political Parties and the Civic Action Groups:; contbr. articles and book revs. to profl. jours Mem. Mayor's Task Force on Future of New Orleans, 1983-85, Women's Equity Action League, 1979-81, LWV, 1960-63, 82-84; bd. dirs. Inst. for Human Rels., Loyola U., Inst. Human Understanding, New Orleans, 1985-86; pres. Syracuse chpt. New Dem. Coalition, 1970-71; mem. pres.'s coun. Loyola U., New Orleans, 1997-2000. Fulbright scholar U. Florence, Italy, 1954-55; faculty fellow in state and local politics Nat. Ctr. for Edn. in Politics, 1964. Mem. AAUP (v.p. LeMoyne chpt. 1971-72), Womens Caucus Polit. Sci. (pres. 1976, named Mentor of Distinction 1989), Am. Polit. Sci. Assn. (Benjamin Evans Lippincott award com. 1976, chmn. sect. program com. 1975, com. acad. freedom and profl. ethics, chair com. for outstanding conv. paper award women and politics rsch. sect. 1990-91), Midwestern Polit. Sci. Assn. (com. status of women), Northeastern Polit. Sci. Assn., S.W. Polit. Sci. Assn. (outstanding conv. paper com.), Founds. Polit. Theory Group, Common Cause, Great Lakes Coll. Assn. (dean's coun. 1986-88), Assn. Jesuit Colls. and Univs. (dean's coun. 1979-85), Assn. Am. Colls. (coun. for liberal learning 1985-87), Western Polit. Sci. Assn., Ind. Polit. Sci. Assn. (pres., chair 1992-93), Ind. Social Sci. Assn., So. Polit. Sci. Assn., Jefferson Parish LWV (bd. dirs. 1999—, pres. 2001-02), Jefferson Parish Bus. and Profl. Women (1st v.p. 2002-04, pres. 2004-05) Roman Catholic. Home: 4817 Belle Dr Metairie LA 70006-2274 E-mail: falco@loyno.edu. *Despite the fact that it's difficult being a woman in a man's world, I'm glad I'm a woman.*

FALCO, RICHARD GERARD, music educator; b. Worcester, Mass., Apr. 19, 1951; s. Santo Michele and Nancy Rita Falco; m. Lucia Marie Clemente, May 5, 1977; 1 child, Mattina Clemente. Studied, Berklee Coll. Music, Boston, 1971—75; BA, U. Mass., Amherst, 1989; MA, Clark U., Worcester, Mass., 1992. Dir. jazz studies Worcester Polytech. Inst., Mass., 1979—; dir., jazz ensembles Clark U., Worcester, Mass., 1990—93, jazz guitar instr., 1990—93. Dir.(narator): (edn. program for children) Conversations in Jazz. Mem.: R.I. Music Educators (festival judge 1990—), Mass. Music Educators (adjudicator 1985—), Internat. Assn. Jazz Educators (adjudicator 1988—), New England Jazz Alliance (web site coord. 1991—). Home: 88 Longfellow Rd Worcester MA 01602 Office: Worcester Polytech Inst 100 Institute Rd Worcester MA 01609 Office Phone: 508-831-5794. Business E-Mail: rfalco@wpi.edu.

FALCON, ARMANDO, JR., financial consultant, lawyer; b. San Antonio, June 4, 1960; married; 2 children. BA, St. Mary's U., 1983; M in Pub. Policy, Harvard U., 1983; JD, U. Tex., 1988. With San Antonio Econ. Devel. Found.; legis. asst. com. on edn. State Senate, Tex., 1983; law clk. to atty. gen. Tex., 1986—88; atty. pvt.practice; of counsel com. on banking and fin. svcs. U.S. Ho. of Reps., 1989—91, dep. gen. counsel, 1991—95, gen. counsel, 1995—97; dir. Office Fed. Housing Oversight, 1999—2005; ptnr. The Canonbury Group, London, 2005—. Office: Canonbury Group Buckingham Ct 78 Buckingham Gate London SW1E 6PE England Office Phone: 44-20-7222-7730.*

FALCON, RAYMOND JESUS, JR., lawyer; b. N.Y.C., Nov. 17, 1953; s. Raymond J. and Lolin (Lopez) F.; m. Debra Mary Bomeisl, June 4, 1977; children: Victoria Marie, Mark Daniel. BA, Columbia U., 1975; JD, Yale U., 1978. Bar: N.Y. 1979, U.S. Dist. Ct. (so. and ea. dist.) N.Y. 1979, U.S. Ct. Appeals (D.C. and 2d cirs.) 1983, Fla. 1987, N.J. 1988, U.S. Dist. Ct. N.J. 1988. Assoc. Webster and Sheffield, N.Y.C., 1978-82; ptnr. Falcon and Hom, N.Y.C., 1982-85; sr. atty. Degussa Corp., Ridgefield Park, N.J., 1985-88, v.p., sec., gen. counsel, 1989-94; pvt. practice Woodcliff Lake, N.J., 1994-95; prin. Falcon & Singer PC, Woodcliff Lake, 1995—. Contbr. articles to profl. jours. Dem. candidate Town Justice, Town of Rye, N.Y., 1983; Dem. jud. del., Westchester, N.Y., 1984-89; mem. planned giving adv. coun. Eastern N.Y. region Am. Cancer Soc., 2001--. Mem. ABA, N.J. State Bar Assn., Fla. Bar Assn., Bergen County Bar Assn., Nat. Acad. Elder Law Attys., Park Ridge Rotary (bd. dirs. 1997-2001, officer 2001-03), Columbia Alumni of Westchester County (v.p., bd. dirs. 1983-90, 97—). Home: 582 Colonial Rd River Vale NJ 07675-6107 also: 14 Harwood Ct Scarsdale NY 10583-4121 Office Phone: 201-307-0074. E-mail: rfalcon@falconsinger.com.

FALCONE, ANTHONY M., music educator; b. Arlington, Va., Mar. 20, 1963; s. Ralph Gilbert and Barbara Simpkins Falcone; m. Lori Elizabeth Payne, Aug. 3, 1991. B in Music Edn., James Madison U., 1986, MusM, 1988. Adj. instr. music Culver Stockton Coll., Canton, Mo., 1988—90; instr. music Truman State U., Kirksville, Mo., 1988—90, James Madison U., Harrisonburg, Va., 1990—93; adj. instr. music Bridgewater (Va.) Coll., 1990—93; adj. instr. of music Ea. Mennonite U., Harrisonburg, Va., 1990—93; vis. asst. prof. U. Ark., Fayetteville, 1993—98; assoc. dir. bands U. Nebr., Lincoln, 1998—. Camp dir. 1000 Hills Youth Camp, Kirksville, Mo., 1989—90; prin. percussionist North Ark. Symphony Orch., Fayetteville, 1993—98; percussionist Ark. Symphony Orch., Little Rock, 1995—98; dir. Ark. Winds Cmty. Band, Fayetteville, 1996—98; camp dir. U. Nebr. Summer Marching Band Camp, Lincoln, 2002—; clinician in field; guest condr. in field; profl. percussionist. Arranger (marching percussion); contbr. articles and revs. to jours. Mem. James Madison U. Alumni Bd. Dirs., Harrisonburg, Va., 1991—93. Named Outsanding Young Am., Outstanding Young Americans, 1998, winner concedrto competition, Va. Music Tchrs. Assn., 1985; recipient Cert. of Recognition for Contributions to Students, Parents Assn. and Tchg. Coun. of the U. of Nebraska—Lincoln, 2002, 2003, 2005. Mem.: Nebr. State Bandmasters Assn. (marching band com. mem. 2004), Nebr. Music Educators Assn., Nat. Band Assn., Coll. Band Dirs. Nat. Assn., Music Educators Nat. Conf., JMU Faculty Senate, Percussive Arts Soc. (Nebr. state chpt. pres. 2003), Pi Kappa Lambda, Phi Beta Mu, Kappa Kappa Psi (hon.; faculty sponsor 2002), Phi Mu Alpha - Sinfonia (hon.; faculty advisor 1995—98). Achievements include Member, All-American College Marching Band, Walt Disney World, 1983; member, Crossmen Drum and Bugle Corps, 1984; Member, All-American College Marching Band, 50th Presidential Inaugural, 1985; Member, All-American College Marching Band, Statue of Liberty 100th Anniversary, 1986. Avocation: cooking. Home: 2310 Jenna Ln Lincoln NE 68512 Office: Univ Nebr—Lincoln 220 Westbrook Music Bldg Lincoln NE 68588 Office Phone: 402-472-2505. Office Fax: 402-472-2326. Personal E-mail: afalcone@neb.rr.com. Business E-Mail: afalcone2@unl.edu.

FALCONE, FRANK S., academic administrator; b. Kenosha, Wis., Sept. 26, 1940; s. Frank R. and Theresa (Barca) F.; m. Judith Herbert, Aug. 17, 1963; children: Jennifer, F. Jeffrey. BS, U. WIs., 1963; MA, U. Denver, 1965; PhD, U. Mass., 1973. Prof., provost Ithaca (N.Y.) Coll., 1969-80; v.p., dean Pace U., White Plains, N.Y., 1980-82, exec. v.p. Pleasantville, N.Y., 1982-85; pres. Springfield (Mass.) Coll., 1985-93, Carroll Coll., Waukesha, Wis., 1993—. Bd. dirs. Springfield YMCA, 1990-92, Basketball Hall of Fame; bd. visitors Air U., Maxwell AFB, Ala., 1989-90; exec. com. Boy Scouts, 1994—, United Way Exec. Comm., 1994. Mem. Assn. Ind. Colls. and Univs. in Mass. (exec. com. 1987-89, chmn. 1990-91), Assn. Ind. Colls. Mass. (pres. 1990-91), Greater Springfield C. of C. (bd. dirs. 1987-92), Waukesha C. of C. (bd. dirs. 1994-98, exec. com. 1995—, v.p. 1995), Wis. Found. for Ind. Colls. (treas. 1995-99). Home: 115 S East Ave Waukesha WI 53186-6207 Office: Carroll Coll Office of Pres 100 N East Ave Waukesha WI 53186-3103 E-mail: ffalcone@carroll1.cc.edu.

FALCONE, THOMAS WILLIAM, finance educator; b. Ind., Pa., Oct. 22, 1947; s. Dominick Thomas and Ann Helen Falcone; m. Catherine Lynn McAnulty, Aug. 29, 1971; children: Ryan, Shannon. BS, Penn State Univ., State Coll., Pa., 1967; MBA, Mankato State Univ., Mankato, Minn., 1972; DBA, Kent State Univ., Kent, Ohio, 1985. Mktg. specialist B.F. Goodrich Corp., Independce, Ohio, 1973—77; instr. mktg. Kent State Univ., Kent, Ohio, 1977—79; prof. mgmt. Ind. Univ. of Pa., Ind., Pa., 1979—. Co-dir. mgmt./svcs. Ind. Univ. of Pa., Ind., Pa., 1990—, chmn. mgmt./mktg. dept., 1984—92. Author: Imagining the Entrepreneurial Sys., 2005. Chmn. Ind. County Solid Waste Authority, Ind., Pa., 1989—; bd. mem. Ind. County Redevelopement Authority, Ind., Pa., 1996—, Pa. Resources Coun., Media, Pa., 1982—. SP4 U.S. Army, 1969—71, Panama. Recipient SBA 2003 Rsch. Adv., Small Bus. Adminstrv., 2003, Faculty of the Yr., Eberly Coll. of Bus., 1996, 4 Nat. Runner -ups Case of the Yr., Small Bus. Inst. Dirs. Assn., 1992, 1996, 1999, 2005. Mem.: Acad. Mgmt. Independent. Christian. Achievements include cons. Pa. Dept. of transp. Ind., Regional Med. Ctr., Westmoreland County Girl Scouts, Keystone Carbon Co., Tri-county Workforce Investment Bd. Avocations: golf, landscaping. Home: 2560 Warren Rd Indiana PA 15701 Office: Ind Univ of Pa 308K Ecobit Indiana PA 15705

FALCONE, TOMMASO, reproductive endocrinologist; b. Montreal, Que., Can., Nov. 28, 1953; came to U.S., 1995; s. Michele and Domenica Falcone. Med. degree, McGill U., Montreal, 1981. Bd. cert. in reproductive endocrinology and laparoscopic surgery. Reproductive endocrinologist McGill U., Montreal, 1984-94, Cleve. Clinic Found., 1995—. Editor: Congenital Malformations of Female Genital Tract, 1999; co-author: Atlas of Endoscopic Techniques in Gynecology, 2000. Mem. Am. Soc. Reproductive Medicine. Office: Cleve Clinic Found Dept Gyn-A-81 9500 Euclid Ave Dept Gyn-a81 Cleveland OH 44195-0001 Office Phone: 216-444-1758. E-mail: falcont@ccf.org.

FALCONES, ETTA Z., mathematician, math and computer science education and administration; b. Tupelo, Miss. AB in Math., Fisk U., 1953; MS, U. Wis., 1954; PhD, Emory U., 1969. Instr. Okolona Coll., 1954—63; tchr. Chattanooga Sch. Sys., 1963—64; asst. prof. Spelman Coll., Atlanta, 1964—71, assoc. prof. math., 1972—90, Calloway Prof. Math., 1990—. Asst. prof. math. Norfolk State U., 1971—72; founder NASA Women in Sci. Program, 1987, NASA Undergrad. Sci. Rsch. Program, 1987; assoc. provost for sci. programs and policy Spelman Coll., Atlanta, 1990—. Recipient AWM Louise Hay award, 1995. Mem.: AAAS, Atlanta Minority Women in Sci. Network, Am. Math. Soc., Nat. Assn. Mathematicians (founder). Office: Spelman Coll Math Dept Box 953 350 Spelman Ln SW Atlanta GA 30314-4399

FALEOMAVAEGA, ENI FA'AUAA HUNKIN, congressman; b. Vailoatai Village, Am. Samoa, Aug. 15, 1943; m. Hinanui Bambridge Cave; children: Temanuata Tuilua'ai, Taualai, Nifae, Vaimoana, Leonne. BA in Polit. Sci. and History, Brigham Young U., 1966; JD, U. Houston, 1972; LLM, U. Calif., Berkeley, 1973. Bar: Am. Samoa, U.S. Supreme Ct. Adminstrv. asst. Am. Samoa del. to Washington, 1973-75; staff counsel to house com. on interior and insular affairs U.S. House of Reps., Washington, 1975-81; dep. atty. gen. Am. Samoa, 1981-84, lt. gov., 1984-89; territorial del. from Am. Samoa U.S. Ho. Reps., 1988; rep. U.S. Congress from Samoa, 1989—; mem. internat. rels. com., resources com. Chmn. Gov.'s Task Force for Reorgn. of the Adminstrn., Am. Samoa Adv. Fisheries Council, 1985—, Gov.'s Adv. Com. on Grants Programs, 1985—; mem. nat. lt. gov.'s mission to Egypt, Jordan and Saudi Arabia, South Pacific Leaders Orientation Mission to Paris, 1987; leader Am. Samoa's del. to South Pacific Conf., Noumea New Caledonia, 1987; keynote speaker and leader Am. Samoa's del. to Pacific Trade/Investment Conf., 1986. With U.S. Army, 1966-69, including Vietnam, USAR, 1985—. Recipient Alumni Svc. award Brigham Young U., 1979; named Chieftain Faleomavaega, leone Village. Mem. Nat. Conf. of Lt. Govs., Nat. Assn. Secs. of State, Navy League of U.S., VFW, Nat. Am. Indian Prayer Breakfast Group, Lions (charter mem. Pago Pago chpt.), Go for Broke Assn. (life; pres. Samoa chpt.). Democrat. Office: US Ho Reps 2422 Rayburn HOB Washington DC 20515*

FALES, HALIBURTON, II, lawyer; b. N.Y.C., Aug. 7, 1919; s. DeCoursey and Dorothy Mildred (Mitchell) F.; m. Katharine Ladd, Dec. 27, 1941; children: Nancy, Haliburton, Priscilla, Lucy, William E. Ladd. Student, Harvard U., 1938—41; LLB, Columbia U., 1947. Bar: NY 1948, U.S. Supreme Ct. 1957. Assoc. White & Case, NYC, 1947-58, ptnr., 1959-88, of counsel, 1988-90, ret., 1991. Spl. master Appellate divsn. 1st dept. NY State Supreme Ct., 1983—, chmn. departmental discipline com., 1991—96, spl. counsel, 1997—; nat. ctr. for state cts Warren Burger Assoc., 2002. Author: Trying Cases A Life in the Law, 1997; contbr. articles to profl. jours. Trustee Pierpont Morgan Libr., 1966-2000, pres., 1979-89, trustee emeritus, 2000—; trustee St. Barnabas Hosp., 1949-96, trustee emeritus, 1996—; sr. warden St. Luke's Ch., 1967-93; bd. dirs. Union Theol. Sem., 1986-94; bd. visitors Columbia Law Sch., 1993-98, emeritus, 1998—. Lt. comdr. USNR, 1941-45. Recipient Columbia U. medal, 1994. Fellow Am. Bar Found., NY Bar Found., Inst. Jud. Adminstrn., Am. Coll. Trial Lawyers; mem. ABA, Albert Gallatin Assocs., Am. Judicature Soc., Am. Law Inst. (life), Assn. Bar City of NY, NY County Lawyers Assn. (William Nelson Cromwell award 1998), NY State Bar Assn. (pres. 1983-84, chair task force on the prof., 1994-96), Columbia Law Sch. Assn., Inc. (pres. 1991-92), St. Paul's Sch. Alumni Assn. (v.p. 1988-92), Alumni Fedn. Columbia U. Home: 560 Pottersville Rd Gladstone NJ 07934-2046 Office: c/o White & Case 1155 Ave of Americas New York NY 10036-2711

FALES, HENRY MARSHALL, chemist; b. N.Y.C., Feb. 12, 1927; s. Henry Marshall and Cecile Marie (Vatet) F.; m. Caroline Eleanor McCullagh, Dec. 20, 1947; children: Marsha Kent Fales Mazz, Suzanne Kent Fales Palmer, Henry Richard. BSc in Chemistry, Rutgers U., 1948, PhD in Organic Chemistry, 1953. Instr. Rutgers U., New Brunswick, N.J., 1953; rsch. chemist, lab. chief Nat. Heart, Lung and Blood Inst., NIH, Bethesda, Md., 1953—2003, mem. sr. biomed. rsch. svc., 2005; adj. prof. anatomy, physiology and genetics Uniformed Svcs. U. Health Scis., 2001—. With USN, 1944-46. Recipient Superior Svc. award U.S. Govt., 1973, 86, Profl. Svc. award Wash. Chpt. of Alpha Chi Sigma, 50 Yr. Svc. award, NIH, Nat. Heart, Lung, and Blood Inst. Mem. Am. Chem. Soc., Am. Soc. Mass Spectrometry (mem.-at-large, sec., v.p. programs, pres., past pres.). Avocations: fishing, stained glass. Home: 3114 Gracefield Rd Apt # 315 Silver Spring MD 20904-7854 Office: NIH NHLBI Bldg 50 Rm 3305 50 South Dr MSC 8014 Bethesda MD 20892-8014 Office Phone: 301-496-2135. E-mail: hmfales@helix.nih.gov.

FALES, LISA JOSE, lawyer; b. Indianapolis, Indiana, Apr. 3, 1962; BA, U. Md., 1984; JD, U. Balt., 1990. Bar: Md. 1990, DC 1992, US Dist. Ct., Md. 1992. Legislative specialist, consumer protection div. Md. Atty. Gen. Office, 1983—89; summer assoc. Venable LLP, Balt., 1989; ptnr., govt. antitrust practice group Howrey Simon Arnold & White LLP, Washington; ptnr., regulatory practice group Venable LLP, Washington, 2004—. Co-chair, moderator & presenter Nat. Inst. for Women Corp. Counsel conference, 2003. Bd. dirs. Women's Law Ctr. for Md.; mem. benefits com. NOW Legal Defense and Education Fund. Mem.: ABA (mem. antitrust section), DC Bar Assn. (chair consumer affairs com. 1994—96, mem. steering com. 1996—97, mem. antitrust section), Md. Bar Assn. (mem. antitrust section). Office: Venable LLP 575 7th St NW Washington DC 20004 Office Phone: 202-344-4349. Office Fax: 202-344-8300. Business E-Mail: ljfales@venable.com.

FALGOUST, DEAN THOMAS, lawyer, accountant; b. Vacherie, La., Oct. 21, 1958; s. Joseph Bienvenue and Rose Mary (Landry) F.; m. Janet Marie Dolese, Aug. 7, 1982; children: Luke Bienvenue, Laura Katherine. BS in Acctg., Nicholls State U., 1978; JD, Loyola U., New Orleans, 1982; LLM in Taxation, NYU, 1983. Bar: La. 1982; CPA, La. Auditor A.A. Harmon & Co., New Orleans, 1978-79; pvt. practice acctg. New Orleans, 1980-81; assoc. Chaffe, McCall, Phillips, Toler & Sarpy, New Orleans, 1982-85; dir. tax, v.p. Freeport-McMoRan Inc., New Orleans, 1985-97; v.p., tax and legal Freeport McMoran Copper & Gold, Inc., New Orleans, 1997—, v.p., gen. counsel, 2003—, McMoran Exploration Co., 1997—. Bd. dirs., chmn. First Am. Bank & Trust, One Am. Corp., Vacherie, legal cons., 1984—. Mem. Loyola Law Rev., 1980-82. Mem. ABA, La. Bar Assn. Republican. Roman Catholic. Home: 9631 Garden Oak Ln River Ridge LA 70123-2005 Office: Freeport McMoRan Copper & Gold Inc 1615 Poydras St PO Box 61119 New Orleans LA 70161-1119 E-mail: dean_falgoust@fmi.com.

FALGUIERE, SHARON ELLEN, costume designer; b. White Plains, N.Y., Jan. 31, 1968; d. Joel Albert Falguiere and Barbara Jean (Bruns) Meeker. Student, Western Carolina U., 1985-88; cert. in filmmaking and costume, Valencia C.C., 1989. Stylist numerous comms., 1989—2002, costume designer, 1991—2002. Costume designer: Unsolved Mysteries, 1989, 93, What Would You Do?, 1991, 92, Clarissa Explains It All, 1992, HBO-One Night Stands, 1992, Fortune Hunter, 1994, Bermuda Triangle, 1995, Shootfighter II, 1995, The Good Life, 1996, Good Guys, Bad Guys, 2000, In the Shadows, 2000; designer feature film Emmett's Mark, 2001; asst. designer, buyer: The Adventures of Superboy, 1990-91, Automatic Avenue, 1997, Wild Things, 1997, Holyman, 1997, Gone in 60 Seconds, 2001, Assassination Tango, 2001 (filmed in Argentina); set costumer: The Grand Pardon, 1992, Extralarge II, 1992-93, Drop Zone, 1994, Two Much, 1995, Rosewood, 1996, The Pest, 1996, Armaggedan, 1997, Something About Mary, 1998, Any Given Sunday, 2000, Gone in Sixty Seconds, 2000; stylist: Disney World Co., Pepsi, Sears, Maxwell House Coffee, Labott's Beer, Publix, Craven Cigarettes, Timotei Shampoo, Disney Cruise Lines, Italian Vogue, T.J. Maxx, Bacardi Rum, Delta Airlines, Am. Express, and numerous others. Fundraiser Dem. Party, Orlando, Fla. 1996—. Mem. Women of the Motion Picture Industry, Mus. Art and Scis. (Miami), IATSE, Costume Designers Guild. Roman Catholic. Avocations: politics, boating, traveling, photography, paintings. E-mail: ellefab@aol.com.

FALK, ARMAND ELROY, retired English educator, writer; b. Yankton, S.D., May 16, 1933; s. Robert Leo and Palma Rocelia (Hugelen) F.; m. Ardis Laurene Johnson, July 14, 1956; children: Sean L., Eric B. BA, Concordia Coll., 1955; MA, U. Mont., 1965; PhD, Mich. State U., 1968. Prof. English St. Cloud (Minn.) State U., 1968-96; ret., 1996. Sr. lectr. Fulbright Commn., La Cote d'Ivoire, 1985-86, Burkina Faso, 1994-95. Contbr. short stories to profl. publs. Cpl. U.S. Army, 1956-58. Bush Foud. grantee, 1993. Home: 210 3rd St S Apt 102 Saint Cloud MN 56301-4443

FALK, BERNARD HENRY, trade association executive; b. N.Y.C., Sept. 10, 1926; s. Max and Sadie (Orwin) F.; m. Iris G. Tannenbaum, June 13, 1954; children: Cindy, Amy, David. BEE, CCNY, 1950; postgrad., Columbia Sch. Bus., 1954. Field engr. RCA, 1950-52; sales engr. Gen. Precision Corp., 1953-56; exec. sec. Nat. Elec. Mfrs. Assn., 1956-65, v.p. govt. rels., 1966-71, pres., 1972-91, vice chmn., 1991-92; chmn. adv. com. elec. goods Dept. Commerce; pres. elect Internat. Electrotech. Commn., 1994-95, pres., 1995—2000. Mem. exec. adv. com. nat. power survey FPC; mem. Bus. Adv. Coun. on Fed. Reports; chmn. liaison com. White House Trade Assn.; bd. dirs. Underwriters Labs., trustee, 1992-2001; co-chmn. EC 92 com. Dept. Commerce, 1991—. Served with USNR, 1944-46. Mem. Am. Nat. Standards Inst. (dir.), Am. Soc. Assn. Execs. (v.p. 1978, dir., chmn. Key industries assn. Council 1985-86), N.Y. State Soc. Assn. Execs. (pres. 1975), U.S. C. of C. (bd. dirs.). Home: 14 Bermuda Lake Dr Palm Beach Gardens FL 33418-4583

FALK, CHARLES H. (HARRY FALK), stock exchange executive; With Czarnikow-Rionda, 1958—82, Richco Sugar, 1982—84; chmn. Coffee, Sugar & Cocoa Clearing Assn., 1983—91; with Louis Dreyfus Corp., 1984—; bd. mgrs. Coffee, Sugar & Cocoa Exch., Inc., 1989—90, vice chmn., 1990, chmn., 1991—95; vice chmn. N.Y. Bd. Trade, LI, 2000, chmn., 2000—, acting pres. & CEO, 2002—03, pres., CEO, 2003—. Office: NY Bd Trade 1 North End Ave New York NY 10282-1101 Office Phone: 212-748-4000.*

FALK, EDGAR ALAN, public relations consulting executive, writer; b. Bklyn., Nov. 4, 1932; s. Ralph P. and Lillian (Freud) F. AB, NYU, 1954, postgrad., 1957-59. Pub. rels. asst. Western Electric Co., N.Y.C., 1957-59; dir. pub. rels. Ritter, Sanford, Price & Chalek, N.Y.C., 1959-60; account supr. pub. rels. Batten, Barton, Durstine & Osborn, N.Y.C., 1960-67; group dir. pub. rels. N.W. Ayer & Son, N.Y.C., 1967-73; v.p., dir. pub. rels. div. Cunningham & Walsh, Inc., N.Y.C., 1973-79; dir. communications NBA, 1979-81; pres. Ed Falk Communications, N.Y.C., 1981—. Spkr. nat. convs. retailing orgns. Author: 1,001 Ideas To Create Retail Excitement, 1994; rev.edit. 2003, contbg. editor, writer for several retail publs. Mem. Kings County Rep. County Com., 1958-61. 1st lt. U.S. Army, 1954-56; lt. col. Res. ret. Recipient Freedoms Found. award, 1971 Mem. Pub. Rels. Soc. Am. (recipient Silver Anvil award 1970, 71, 73), The Author's Guild, Res. Officers Assn., Retired Officers Assn. Home and Office: 301 E 78th St New York NY 10021-1322

FALK, ELLEN STEIN, media specialist, educator; b. Mobile, Ala., Aug. 19, 1942; d. Louis James and Elizabeth Jeffers Stein; m. Michael Marc Falk, July 3, 1968; 1 child, Rachel Mara. BS in Fine Arts, Spring Hill Coll., 1964; student, St. Thomas Aquinas, 1981—85; MEd, William Paterson U., 2005. Cert. tchr. N.J., 1986. Flight attendant United Airlines, N.Y.C., 1965—68, flight ops. office Newark, 1968—73; tchr. Meml. Sch., Montvale, NJ, 1986—2001, media specialist, 2001—. Del. People To People Amb. Program, China, 1994, New Zealand, Australia, 2001. Named Tchr. of Yr., Govs. Tchr. Recognition Program, 1994. Mem.: Montvale Tchrs. Assn. (negotiation com.), Ednl. Media Assn. N.J., Nat. Coun. Tchrs. English, Internat. Reading Assn., Friends of Libr., Parent Tchr. Orgn., Kappa Delta Pi, Pi Lambda Theta. Home: 77 Akers Ave Montvale NJ 07645 Office: Memorial School 53 West Grand Avenue Montvale NJ 07645 Office Phone: 201-391-2900 503. E-mail: efalk@mail.montvale.k12.nj.us.

FALK, EUGENE HENRY, artist; b. Turlock, Calif. s. Henry Gustav and Inez Mattie Falk. BPA, Brooks Inst. Photography, Montecito, Calif., 1958—61. Pres., CEO Gem Graphics, Inc., Madison, Tenn., 1986—, CEO Sedona, Ariz., 2005—. Co-author: Summer Jobs in National Parks, 1965. Mem. Citi Rd. Methodist Ch. Sgt. Army Air Corps., 1943—46, Burma. Named Videographer of Distinction, Video Mag., 2000. Mem.: Madison Art Ctr. Avocations: skiing, hiking. Office: Gem Graphics 405 Churchill Crossing Madison TN 37115 also: Gem Graphics 90 Wild Turkey Rd Sedona AZ 86351 Home: 200 E Webster #917 Madison TN 37115

FALK, HENRY, pediatrician, epidemiologist, researcher; b. N.Y.C., N. Y., Feb. 7, 1943; m. 1971; 3 children. BA, Yeshiva Coll., 1964; MD, Albert Einstein Coll. Medicine, 1968; MPH, Harvard U., 1976. Intern Children's Hosp., Phila., 1968-69; resident Bronx Mcpl. Hosp. Ctr., N.Y.C., 1969-72; med. epidemiologist Ctr. Disease Control, Atlanta, 1972-75, 1976—; dir. div. of environ. hazards and health effects Nat. Ctr. for Environ. Health (NCEH), 1985—99, dir., 2003—; asst. adminstr. Agency for Toxic Substance and Disease Registry (ATSDR), 1999—2003. Mem. Am. Acad. Pediat. (liaison mem. com. environmental health 1978), Am. Coll. Epidemiology Rsch., Am. Pub. Health Assn., Soc. Pediatric Rsch. Epimediologi rsch. on etiology of cancer; environmental and occupational exposures; evaln. vinyl chloride exposed individuals and devel. hepatic tumors. Office: NCEH 1600 Clifton Rd NE Atlanta GA 30333

FALK, JAMES HARVEY, SR., lawyer; b. Tucson, Aug. 17, 1938; s. George W. and Elsie L. (Higgins) F.; m. Bobbie Jo Vest, July 8, 1960; children: James H. Jr., John Mansfield, Kathryn Colleen. BS, BA, U. Ariz., 1960, LLB, JD, U. Ariz., 1965. Bar: Ariz. 1965, U.S. Dist. Ct. Ariz. 1968, U.S. Dist. Ct. D.C. 1971, U.S. Dist. Ct. Md., 1990, U.S. Ct. Appeals (fed., 4th, 6th and 9th cirs.) 1981, U.S. Ct. Claims 1985, U.S. Supreme Ct. 1972. Counsel El Paso (Tex.) Natural Gas Co., 1965-66, The Anaconda Co., Tucson, 1967-68; ptnr. Waterfall Economidis, Falk & Caldwell, Tucson, 1968-71; staff asst. to pres. Office of the Pres., Washington, 1971-73; assoc. dir. Domestic Coun., The White House, Washington, 1973-76; assoc. Touche Ross & Co., Washington, 1976-78; ptnr. Coffey, McGovern, Noel & Novogroski, Washington, 1978-81, Larkin, Noel & Falk, Washington, 1981-86, Thompson & Mitchell, Washington, 1986-87, McGovern, Noel & Falk, Ltd., Washington, 1987-90, Falk & Causey, Washington, 1991-92, Falk Law Firm, Washington, 1993—2003, Epstein Becker & Green, PC, 2003—. Rep. of U.S. Pres. to state and local govts., D.C., U.S. ters., 1974-75, U.S. Govs. Conf., 1974-75, U.S. Conf. Mayors, 1974-75, U.S. Del. Peoples Republic of China, 1974; asst. city prosecutor, city atty., Tucson, 1966-67; chmn. Tucson Transit Authority, 1971-72; apptd. D.C. Bar Jud. Evaluation Com., 1992-95, 95-98. Mem. ABA. Republican. Congregationalist. Home: 9430 Cornwell Farm Rd Great Falls VA 22066-2702 Office: Epstein Becker & Green PC 1227 25th St NW Ste 700 Washington DC 20037 Office Phone: 202-861-1895. Business E-Mail: jfalksr@ebglaw.com.

FALK, JEROME B., JR., lawyer; b. May 25, 1940; AB with honors, Univ. Calif., Berkeley, 1962, JD, 1965. Bar: Calif. 1966, US Supreme Ct. Law clk. Justice William O. Douglas, U.S. Supreme Ct.; sr. dir., civil & appellate litigation Howard Rice Nemerovski Canady Falk & Rabkin, San Francisco. Adj. prof. Univ. Calif. Berkeley, 1968—78; mem. Ninth Cir. Com. Judicial Evaluation, 1980; lawyer rep. Ninth Cir. Judicial Conf., 1983—85; lectr. CLE programs. Bd. chmn. KQED Inc., 1999—2001. Named one of Top 100 No. Calif. Super Lawyers, San Francisco Mag., 2004. Mem.: Calif. Acad. Appellate Lawyers (pres. 1994—95), Assn. Bus. Trial Lawyers No. Calif. (pres. 1993—94), Bar Assn. San Francisco (pres. 1985), Order of the Coif. Office: Howard Rice Nemerovski Canady Falk & Rabkin 7th Fl 3 Embarcadero Ctr San Francisco CA 94111-4024 Office Phone: 415-434-1600. Office Fax: 415-217-5910. Business E-Mail: jfalk@howardrice.com.

FALK, JOHN H., educational administrator; b. L.A., Dec. 6, 1948; s. Ivan and Edith Teresa (Marx) F.; m. Amanda Sue Archerd, Dec. 21, 1969 (div. 1984); children: Joshua, Daniel, Lara; m. Lynn Diane Dierking, July 20, 1990. BA in Zoology, U. Calif., Berkeley, 1970, MA in Zoology, 1972, PhD in Biology and Edn., 1974. Lic. Calif. State tchr. biology. Assoc. dir. Chesapeake Bay Ctr. for Environ. Studies, Edgewater, Md., 1974-83; dir. Smith Office of Ednl. Rsch., Washington, 1983-85; spl. asst., asst. sec. rsch. Smith Instn., Washington, 1986-87; dir. Inst. for Learning Innovation, Annapolis, Md., 1987—. Cons. in field; advisor Nat. Mus. Natural History, Washington, Calif. Sci. Ctr., others. Author: Museum Experience, 1992, Learning from Musemus, 2000; creator learning assessment: Personal Meaning Mapping, 1997; editl. bd. Sci. Edn., Curator. NSF grantee, 1991-92, 93-95, 93-98, 98—. Mem. AAAS, Visitor Studies Assn., Nat. Assn. for Rsch. in Sci. Tchg., Am. Assn. Mus. Avocations: painting, japanese gardening, volleyball, tennis. Office: Inst for Learning Innovation 166 West St Annapolis MD 21401-2824 E-mail: falk@ilinet.org.

FALK, ROBERT BARCLAY, JR., anesthesiologist, educator; b. Lancaster, Pa., July 1, 1945; s. Robert Barclay and Miriam (Neff) F.; m. Carol Anne Gundel, May 30, 1970; 1 child, Juliana Gundel. BA, Franklin and Marshall Coll., 1967; MD, Jefferson Med. Coll., 1971. Diplomate Am. Bd. Anesthesiology. Intern Conemaugh Valley Meml. Hosp., Johnstown, Pa., 1971-72; resident in anesthesiology M.H. Hershey Med. Sch. Hosp., 1974-77; ptnr. Anesthesia Assocs., Lancaster, 1977—, sr. v.p., 1993-94, pres., 1994-2000, exec. v.p., 2000—. Staff anesthesiologist Lancaster Gen. Hosp., 1977—, vice chmn. dept. anesthesiology, 1984-85, chmn., 1985-92; clin. asst. prof. dept. anesthesiology Hershey (Pa.) Med. Sch., 1977-2002. Contbr. articles to profl. jours. Participant alumni phonathon Franklin and Marshall Coll., 1978-81, vice chmn., 1981, chmn., 1983, mem. alumni admissions com., 1977-79, chmn., 1980-87, chmn. 20th reunion gift com.; mem. Lancaster Regional Alumni Coun., 19987-91, trustee athletic com., 1988-96, 98; mem. Lancaster Area Arts Coun., 1989-91; Sunday sch. tchr. Trinity Luth. Ch., Lancaster, 1977-80; bd. dirs. Lancaster Summer Arts Festival, 1981—, v.p., 1982-84, pres., 1985-90; bd. dirs. Pa. Acad. Music, 1991—, vice-chmn., 1991-92, chmn., 1993—; bd. mgrs. Lancaster Assembly, 2000—, chmn., 2003—. Lt. M.C., USNR, 1972-74. Mem. Am. Soc. Anesthesiologists, Pa. Soc. Anesthesiologists, Intenat. Anesthesia Rsch. Soc., Pa. Med. Soc., Lancaster Country Club, Hamilton Club (v.p. 1995-97, pres. 1997-99), Masons, Shriners, Chaine des Rotisseurs. Republican. Home: 1025 Marietta Ave Lancaster PA 17603-3106 Office: Anesthesia Assocs 133 E Frederick St Lancaster PA 17602-2222 Office Phone: 717-394-9821. Personal E-mail: rbfalkjr@aol.com.

FALK, STEVEN B., newspaper publishing executive; Various positions Gannett Newspapers, 1983—87; various positions, including circ. dir. San Francisco (Calif.) Newspaper Agy., 1987—98, pres., CEO, 1998—2000; pres., assoc. pub. & COO San Francisco (Calif.) Chronicle, 2000—03, pres. & pub., 2003—. Office: San Francisco Chronicle 901 Mission St San Francisco CA 94103-2905

FALK, THOMAS J., paper company executive; b. Waterloo, Iowa, 1958; m. Karen Falk; 1 child. B in Accounting, U. Wis., 1980; MS in Management, Stanford U., 1988. With Alexander Grant & Co.; joined internal audit staff Kimberly-Clark Corp., Neenah, Wis., 1983, sr. auditor, 1984, sr. fin. analyst, 1986, dir. corp. strategic analysis, 1987, operations mgr. infant care, diaper plant Beech Island, SC, 1989, v.p. operations analysis and control, 1990, sr. v.p., analysis and admin., 1991, group pres. infant and child care, 1993, group pres. No. Am. consumer products, 1995, group pres., global tissue and paper, 1998, pres., COO, 1999, also bd. dirs. Irving, Tex., 1999—, CEO, 2002—, chmn., 2003—. Bd. dirs. Centex Corp.; Dallas regional advisory bd. JP Morgan Chase. Nat. trustee Boys and Girls Clubs of Am. Sloan Fellow, Stanford U. Grad. Sch. Bus., 1988. Office: Kimberly-Clark Corp 351 Phelps Dr Irving TX 75038-6507*

FALK, WILLIAM JAMES, lawyer; b. Kew Gardens, NY, 1952; s. Sam and Bertha Falk; m. Laurie Falk; children: Douglas, Andrew, Edward. BS, Ill. Inst. Tech., 1973; JD cum laude, Suffolk U., 1977; LLM in Taxation, Washington U., St. Louis, 1982. Bar: Mass. 1977, Mo. 1981. Trial atty. IRS Office of Dist. Counsel, St. Louis, 1977—81; assoc. Thompson & Mitchell, St. Louis, 1982—83, ptnr., 1984—96, Thompson Coburn LLP, St. Louis, 1996—99; mem. Lewis, Rice & Fingersh, L.C., St. Louis, 1999—. Contbg. author: Missouri Taxation Law and Practice, 1987, 96; contbr. articles to legal jours. Mem. ABA, Mo. Bar Assn., Bar Assn. Met. St. Louis (chmn. taxation sect. 1992-93, mem. exec. com. 1992-93). Avocation: music. Office: Lewis Rice & Fingersh LC 500 N Broadway Ste 2000 Saint Louis MO 63102-2147

FALKENBERG, MARY ANN THERESA, realtor; b. Dec. 8, 1931; d. Joseph and Catherine (Bausch) Haselsteiner; m. Charles V. Falkenberg Jr., Apr. 9, 1955; children: Catherine, Grace Ann, Susan Marie, Charles V., Robert, Thomas, Martin, Mary, Elizabeth, Joseph. Student, Barat Coll., 1953. Cert. home protection cons. Piano tchr., 1946—73; organist St. Thomas of Villanova Ch., 1960—, choir dir., 1960—; sales staff Quinlan & Tyson, Realtors, Inc., Palatine, Ill., 1970—77; pres., co-owner, broker, mgr. Assoc. Realty Corp., Palatine, 1978—91; mgr. Prudential Preferred Properties, 1991—, Coldwell Banker, 1998—. Named Palatine Woman of Yr., Suburban Press Found., 1962. Mem.: NAFE, Women in Sales, Women in Sales, N.W. Suburban Bd. Realtors (edn. com. 1977—78, non-resident com. 1982, broker-lawyer com. 1986—91, grievance com. 1988—2004), Nat. Assn. Realtors (accredited profl. residential appraiser, cert. real property appraiser), Ill. Assn. Realtors (life mem. five million dollar club, mem. seven million dollar club, Gold award 1980, leading edge award), Am. Mgmt. Assn., Women in Mgmt., Barat Coll. Alumni Assn., Multiple Listing Orgn. (bd. dirs. 1986—2004, sec. 1988—90, treas. 1990—91, v.p. 1991—92, pres. 1993—96), Women's Club. Republican. Roman Catholic. Home: 517 Warwick Ave Palatine IL 60074-3875 Office: 792 E Rand Rd Arlington Heights IL 60004-4006 Office Phone: 847-222-8633. E-mail: haselfalk@sbcglobal.net.

FALKENBERG, MARY ELAINE, small business owner; b. Romeo, Mich., Jan. 10, 1940; d. Paul Emerson and Florence Irene (Joughin) Teal; m. Theodore Henry Falkenberg, June 19, 1965; children: Wendy Elaine, Amy Elizabeth, Theodore Paul. AB in Speech, Geography, Ctrl. Mich. U., 1962. Tchr. West Bloomfield (Mich.) H.S., 1962-63, Coopersville (Mich.) H.S., 1963-65; tchr. forensics Harbor Beach (Mich.) H.S., 1966-69; owner Falkenberg's Screenprinting & Honey, Harbor Beach. Trustee Harbor Beach Sch. Bd., 1991-95. Mem. Thumb Area Reading Coun.; active ch. choir, bible study; chair Zion Luth. Pray Chain, 2005 Mem. Mich. Edn. Assn., Mich. Beekeepers Assn. (sec., treas.), Huron County Homemaker Club, Women's Club (program dir.), Luth. Women's Missionary League (pres., sec., treas.), Luth. Brotherhood, Port Hope Sr. Citizens, Altar Guild, Ladies of Zion (pres.), Evangelism (sec. 1994-95, pres. 1995-2000), Bloomer's Garden Club, Jaycettes (pres., v.p., sec., treas., Spark Plug), Ski Club, Thumb Rose Soc. (corr. sec., 2003, 04, 05), Luth. Bible Study, Mom's-in-Touch Prayer Group, Presbyn. Bible Study, Thrivent Fin. for Luth. Huron County (pres. 2005), Women's Nat. Farm and Garden Assn. (v.p. 2005), Harbor Beach Cmty. Choir, Cath. Bible Study, Mich. Edn. Assn., Luth. Laymen's League, Aid Assn. for Luth., Harbor Beach Hosp. Aux., Harbor Beach Garden Club, Nat. Farm and Garden Assn. (v.p. 1993, 2005) Republican. Avocations: reading, advanced master gardener, crafts, clarinet playing, skiing. Home and Office: 1205 S Klug Rd Harbor Beach MI 48441-9723 Office Phone: 989-479-9075. E-mail: mfalkenbergm@yahoo.com.

FALKENBERG, WILLIAM STEVENS, architect, contractor; b. Kansas City, Mo., July 21, 1927; s. John Joseph and Maraba Elizabeth (Stevens) F.; m. Janis Patton Hubner, Apr. 13, 1951; children: Ruth Elizabeth, Christopher Joseph, Charles Stevens. BS in Archtl. Engring., U. Colo., 1949. Pres. Falkenberg Constrn. Co., Denver, 1951-71, 74-84, devel. cons., 1984-94; broker Hogan & Stevenson Realty, Denver, 1971-74. Chmn. constrn. Archdiocesan Housing Com., Inc., pres. 1997-98; chmn. restoration 9th Street Hist. Park; chmn. bldg. comm. Four Mile House Hist. Park; chmn. Housing Trust Coun., Denver, 1986-90; chmn. Rocky Mountain Better Bus. Bur., 1965-67; pres. Denver Friends Folk Music, 1966. Lt. (j.g.) USNR, 1945-51. Mem. AIA (bd. dirs. Denver chpt. 1978-81, treas. 1981), Home Builder Assn. Met. Denver, Colo. Hist. Soc. Found. (trustee, sec. 1987-97), Serra Internat. (pres. 1971, dist. gov. 1973), Nat. Assn. Atomic Vets., Colo. Archeol. Soc., Denver Athletic Club, Equestrian Order of Holy Sepulchre, Cactus Club (pres. 1995-98). Home and Office: Apt 4B 1501 Wazee St Denver CO 80202-1476

FALKIE, THOMAS VICTOR, mining engineer, mining executive; b. Mount Carmel, Pa., Sept. 5, 1934; s. Victor J. and Aldona H. Falkie; m. Jean C. Broscius, Nov. 27, 1957 (dec. Apr. 2001); children: Ann, Thomas, Lawrence, Michael, Christine. BS in Mining Engring., Pa. State U., 1956, MS in Mining Engring., 1958, PhD in Mining Engring., 1961. Fellow, rsch. asst. Pa. State U., University Park, 1956-61, prof., head mineral engring. dept., 1969-73; various staff and managerial positions Internat. Minerals and Chem. Corp., Skokie, Ill., 1961-69, Bartow, Fla., 1961-69; dir. U.S. Bur. Mines Dept. of Interior, Washington, 1974-77; pres., CEO Berwind Natural Resources Corp., Phila., 1977—98, chmn. bd., 1999—2003, bd. dirs., 2004—. Adj. prof. indsl. engring. U. Fla., U. So. Fla., 1966; cons. UN, 1971—73; nat. arbitrator joint industry health and safety com. United Mine Workers and Bituminous Coal Operators Assn., 1973; chmn. coal task force project ind. study U.S. Govt., 1974; chmn. interagy. task force Fed. Coun. Sci. and Tech., 1975—76; mem. bd. mineral and energy resources NRC, 1982—88; mem. adv. com. mining and mineral resources rsch. Dept. of Interior, 1988—94. Contbr. articles to profl. jours. Recipient Disting. Alumnus award, Pa. State U., 1995, 2004. Mem.: NAE (councillor 1994—2000), AIME (hon.), Am. Coal Found. (chmn. 1993—), Mining and Metall. Soc. Am., Nat. Mining Assn. (bd. dirs. 1979—2002, hon. dir. 2002—), Pa. Coal Assn. (bd. dirs. 1980—90), Soc. Mining Engrs. of AIME (bd. dirs. 1971—75, v.p. 1977—79, chmn. Phila. sect. 1980—81, bd. dirs. 1984—87, pres. 1988, disting. mem., Erskine Ramsay medal 1991, Disting. Svc. award 2001), Union League Club (Phila.), Tau Beta Pi, Sigma Gamma Epsilon. Republican. Roman Catholic. Home: 347 Echo Valley Ln Newtown Square PA 19073-1619 Office: Berwind Natural Resources Corp 3000 Centre Sq W 1500 Market St Philadelphia PA 19102-2100 Personal E-mail: tfalkie@comcast.net. Business E-Mail: tfalkie@berwind.com.

FALKOWSKI, BRENDA LISLE, retail buyer, director; b. Lexington, Ky., July 2, 1943; d. Edward Spencer and Evelyn (Wright) Lisle; m. Edward John Falkowski, Oct. 19, 1963; children: Brenda June Falkowski-Ashway, Richard Spencer, Lance Edward. AA in Liberal Studies, Neumann Coll., Aston, Pa., 1994, BS in Liberal Studies, 1998. Pres., v.p. Tokyo Am. Club Women's Group, Tokyo, 1981-85; assoc. Webb Jewelers and Silversmiths, West Chester, Pa., 1986-89; realtor Fox and Lazo Realtors/Prudential Preferred Properties, West Chester, 1990-92; internat. cons. corp. svcs. Fox and Lazo Relocation Mgmt., Paoli, Pa., 1993-95; pres. Touch of Glass Inc., Mt. Pleasant, SC, 1993—2000; v.p. Brenlan Assocs. Inc., Mt. Pleasant, 1995—; exclusive buyers agt. The Real Buyers Agt., Mt. Pleasant, SC, 2001—. Bd. govs. Tokyo Am. Club, 1981—85; cons. cross-cultural relocation, West Chester, Pa., 1996—98; internat. cons. Chamness Relocation, Mt. Pleasant, SC, 2002—. Monthly contbr. newspaper column The Tokyo Am., 1983-95. Membership chair Reps. Abroad, Tokyo, 1984; neighborhood vol. Am. Cancer Soc., Am. Heart Assn., Am. Kidney Found. Mem.: NAFE, AAUW, Nat. Assn. of Exclusive Buyers Agts., Nat. Assn. Realtors, Nat. Assn. Bus. Coaches (E. Cooper Prof. Women), Adult Women's Network, Internat. Women's Club. Methodist. Avocations: breeding of rare dogs, personal fitness training, retirement home pet therapy. Home: 3527 Stockton Dr Mount Pleasant SC 29466-6990

FALKOWSKI, EDWARD J., executive consultant, business coach; b. Manchester, Conn. s. John E. and Carmella M. Falkowski; m. Brenda L. Falkowski, July 2, 1943; children: B. June Ashway, Richard S., Lance E. BS in Chem. Engring., Worcester Poly. Inst., 1965; MBA, We. New Eng. U., 1968. Various positions E.I. duPont, Wilmington, Del., 1966—79; regional dir. DuPont Japan Ltd., Tokyo, 1979—85; bus. dir. E.I. duPont, Wilmington, 1985—95; v.p., gen. mgr. Ceco Environ., Conshohocken, Pa., 1996—99; pres. Brenlan Assoc. Inc., Mt. Pleasant, SC, 1999; bd. dir. Touch of Glass, 2000—01; ad. bd. Media Services, Mr. Pleasant, SC, 2000—01. Com. mem., Nat. Recycling Coalition, Washington, 1993-95; mem. Environ. Export Coun., Washington, 1996-99; com. chmn., Am. Polyester Film Mfrs., 1994-95. Mem. Nat. Assn. Bus. Coaches (dir. adv. bd. 2000-01), Charleston Metro C. of C. Avocation: golf. Office: Brenlan Assocs Inc Suite C-171 1150 Hungry Neck Blvd Mount Pleasant SC 29466 E-mail: brenlan@onebox.com.

FALKOWSKI, PAUL GORDON, biological oceanographer; b. N.Y.C., Jan. 4, 1951; s. Edward J. and Helen H. Falkowski; m. Sari G. Ruskin; children: Sasha, Mirit. BS in Biology, CCNY, 1972, MA in Biology, 1973; PhD in Biology, U. B.C., Vancouver, 1975. Head oceanographic and atmospheric scis. divsn. Brookhaven Nat. Lab., Upton, N.Y., 1988-92, sr. scientist, 1976—. Cons. Alt. Fluorocarbon Adv. Study Bd., 1990-93; mem. adv. bd. NRC, 1993-94. Co-editor: Global Biogeochemical Cycles, 1992, Limnology and Oceanography, 1994—; contbr. articles to profl. jours. John Simon Guggenheim fellow, N.Y.C., 1992; Greene Disting. prof., 1995. Mem. Am. Assn. Plant Physiologists, Am. Soc. Limnology and Oceanography. Achievements include 2 patents on fluorometer instrumentation.

FALKOWSKI, THERESA GAE, chemistry educator; b. El Paso, Tex., Mar. 19, 1958; d. Chester Doan and Patricia Ann Harman; m. Henry Steven Falkowski, May 16, 1981. AA, Potomac State Coll., 1978; BA, W.Va. U., 1980. Lab. asst. Potomac State Coll., Keyser, W.Va., 1977-78, gen. chem. prep rm. mgr., 1986—, chem. lab. instr., 1995-99; chem. lab. tchg. asst. W.Va. U., Morgantown, 1981-83, chem. lab. tech., 1981-85, adj. instr. chemistry, 1999—. Cons. USS N.C. Battleship Meml., Wilmington, 1981—; mem. haz-mat response team Potomac State Coll., 1993—. Author: Clark Hall of Chemistry: A Pictorial History, 1996, Laboratory Manual for Chemistry 112, 1996; illustrator: Laboratory Manual for Chemistry 115/116, 1991. Mem. Am. Chem. Soc., W.Va. Acad. Sci., Carnegie Mus. Natural History and Sci. Ctr., The Nat. Maritime Ctr., The N.C. Aquarium Soc., The Mote Marine Lab. Avocations: model building, world war ii history, aircraft identification, science fiction. Office: Potomac State Coll Fort Ave Keyser WV 26726

FALL, DOROTHY, artist, art director, art association administrator; b. Rochester, N.Y., Apr. 7, 1930; d. Isadore and Esther Paula (Rudman) Winer; m. Bernard B. Fall, dec. Feb. 1967; children: Nicole Francoise, Elisabeth Anne, Patricia Madeleine Marcelle. BFA, Syracuse U., 1952; postgrad., Am. U., 1956-58, 66; student, Acad. de la Grande Chaumiere, Paris, 1961, Acad. Julian, 1965. Dep. art dir. AMERIKA Mag. U.S. Info. Agy., Washington, 1956-80; owner, art dir. Fall Design Comms., Washington, 1980-88; dir. Gallery 10, Washington, 1994—. Bd. dirs. Pyramid Atlantic, Riverdale, Md. Editor: Last Reflections on a War, 1967, 2d edit., 2000; art dir., designer Space Science Comes of Age, 1981; one-woman shows include Mickelson Gallery, Washington, 1969, 73,79, 84, Plum Gallery, Kensington, Md., 1989, O St. Studio, Washington, 1989, 92, AVA Gallery, Lebanon, N.H., 1990, Covington & Burling, Washington, 1990, Am. Hort. Soc., Alexandria, Va., 1993, Gallery 10, Washington, 1996, 2000, Cosmos Club, 2000, Galerie Internationale, N.Y.C., 1968, Maison de France, Phnom Penh, Cambodia, 1962; group shows include Hanoi (Vietnam) Fine Arts Coll., 2000, Assioma Gallery, Prato, Italy, 2000, 01, Marino Marini Mus., 2001, Pistoia, Italy, Venezia Viva, Venice, 2001, UN, N.Y.C., 2001; represented in permanent collections and by Verve Art Gallery, Leuven, Belgium, Gallery 10, Washington, AVA Gallery, Lebanon, N.H., Aries East, Brewster, Mass. Recipient gold medal award Art Dirs. Club of Met. Washington Exhibits, 1965, 66, 69, 79, distinctive merit Art Dirs. Club of N.Y. Exhibits, 1969, 74, 77, 78, 79, 81, 82, 83, silver medal N.Y. Soc. Illustrators, 1969. Mem. Women's Caucus on Arts, Washington Sculptors Group, Artists Equity, Cosmos Club. Home: 4535 31st St NW Washington DC 20008-2130

FALL, DOROTHY ELEANOR, librarian; b. Havre de Grace, Md., Feb. 4, 1945; d, James Huey Jr. and Blanche Cecelia (JOhnson) Fall. BA, Lake Erie Coll., 1967; MEd, Westfield State Coll., 1976; EdD, Nova U., 1995. Cert. tchr. Mass, Va. Tchr. Big Spring (Tex.) Sch. System, 1968; substitute tchr. Dept. Defense Schs., Clark AFB, Philippines, 1969-70; tchr. Fayetteville (N.C.) Sch. System, 1971-72, Granby (Mass.) Pub. Schs., 1973-78; eligibility tech. State of Conn., Danbury, 1980-85; libr. Loudoun Country Day Sch., Leesburg, Va., 1990—. Ednl. liaison Granby Pub. Schs., Granby Pub. Libr., 1973-78; libr. trustee Loudoun County Libr. System, 1990-94; lectr. Shenandoah U., Winchester, Va., 1994—; adj. prof. edn. Mary Baldwin Coll. Contbr. articles to newspapers and jours. Vol. ARC, Ala, Ohio, Philippines, 1960-69, United Way, Conn., Va., 1984-86, Am. Cancer Soc., Va., 1988; pres. P.E.O. sisterhood, 1988-90; bd. dirs. Vol. Svcs., Loudoun County, 2002—; mem. Cmty. of Caring. Named Hidden Heroine Girl Scouts Am., 1976. Mem. ALA, ASCD, Va. Libr. Assn., Va. Edn. Media Assn., P.E.O. Presbyterian. Avocations: herb gardening, catering, decorating, calligraphy, sewing. Office: Loudoun Country Day Sch 237 Fairview St NW Leesburg VA 20176-2009

FALL, NICOLE FRANÇOISE, artist, educator; b. Washington, Sept. 18, 1957; d. Bernard B. and Dorothy Fall; m. Blake Martin Conroy, Nov. 19, 1982; children: Blake Bernard Fall-Conroy, Lisette Elizabeth Mary Fall-Conroy. Student, Pratt Inst., Bklyn., 1980; BFA, Md. Inst. Coll. Art, 1981; MFA, Towson U., 1991. Cert. advanced profl. tchr., Md. Instr. Anne Arundel (Md.) C.C., 1984, 86; instr. arts and the aging program Md. Inst. Coll. Art., Balt., 1982-85; instr. art Friends Sch. Balt., 1985-93; founding instr. sculpture and printmaking Carver Ctr. Arts and Tech., Towson, 1993-2000; dir. cmty. art programs Balt. Clayworks, 2000—; asst. prof. Balt. City C.C., 2004—. Art com. for congrl. art exhibit Office Congressman Ben Cardin, Balt., 1990-94; guest lectr. Balt. Sch. Arts, 1992, Coll. Notre Dame, Balt., 1994, U. Md., College Park, 1997 One-woman shows include Gallery K, Washington, 1989, 91, 95, Sch. 33 Art Ctr., Balt., 1990, Arnold and Porter Internat. Sculpture Ctr., Washington, 1993, Hanoi (Vietman) Coll. Fine Art, 2000. Condr. workshops Balt. Book Festival, 1997, 98, 99, 2000; participant in protests, Women's Right to Choose, Washington. Recipient Visual Artist award Alpha Delta Kappa Found., Kansas City, 1991; fellow Md. State Arts Coun., 1992, Vt. Studio Ctr., Johnson, Vt., 1999; named Outstanding Tchr. of Sculpture Internat. Sculpture Ctr., 2000. Mem. NEA, Balt. Clayworks, Balt. Co. Pub. Schs. (svc. learning award 1998, recognition 2000) Democrat. Office: Baltimore Clayworks 5707 Smith Ave Baltimore MD 21209 E-mail: mindartpower@verizon.net.

FALLAT, DALE WILLIAM, lawyer; b. Cleve., Dec. 16, 1944; s. Walter and Susan (Hoshko) F.; m. Sandra Jean Sondgerath, Jan. 31, 1967; children—Amie, Bridget, Colleen, Kathryn. B.A., St. Joseph's Coll., 1966; J.D., U. Toledo, 1970. Bar: Ohio, 1970, U.S. Dist. Ct. (no. dist.) Ohio 1971. Asst. gen. counsel The Andersons, Maumee, Ohio, 1974-79, counsel for govt. affairs, 1979-83, gen. ptnr., mgr. govtl. affairs, 1983-88, mem. mng. com., 1986—, v.p. corp. svcs., 1988—, also bd. dirs. Trustee St. Joseph's Coll., Rensselaer, Ind., 1978-86, McAuley High Sch., Toledo, Ohio, 1982-85; bd. dirs., pres. Toledo Soc. for the Handicapped, 1985-95; bd. dirs. Jr. Achievement Northwest Ohio; trustee Anderson Found., Anderson Fund, 1996—. Named Outstanding alumnus St. Joseph's Coll., 1982; recipient Disting. Alumnus award U. Toledo Law Sch. Mem. ABA, Ohio Bar Assn. (chmn. agrl. law com. 1984), Toledo Bar Assn., Ohio C. of C. (bd. dirs. 1987—), Toledo C. of C. (chmn. legis. affairs. com.). Lodge: Rotary (pres. 1983—, chmn. bd. dirs. Rotary Service Found., 1986—). Home: 6675 Embassy Ct Maumee OH 43537-9648

FALLCREEK, STEPHANIE JEAN, non-profit organization executive; b. Springfield, Mo., May 6, 1950; d. Martha Jean (Barton) Wertz; m. Jerry R. Tillman, 1987; children: Ernest, Daniel, Christopher, Joseph; stepchildren: Shannon, Tiffanie. AB in History, U. Okla., 1972; MSW in Social Welfare, U. Calif., Berkeley, 1974, DSW in Social Welfare, 1984. Dir. Inst. for Geron. Research and Edn., N.Mex. State U., Las Cruces, 1983-87, N.Mex. State Agy. on Aging, Santa Fe, 1987-91; dir. Office of Planning N.Mex. Dept. of Health, 1991-92; dir. div. long term care N.Mex. Dept. Health, Albuquerque, 1992; exec. dir. Fairhill Ctr. for Aging, Cleve., 1992—. Pres. Fallcreek & Assocs., Cleve., 1982—; sr. assoc. Age Wave Inc., Emeryville, Calif., 1985-87; cons. various hosps. and health care orgns.; speaker confs. and trade shows; guest radio and TV programs on aging. Author: (with others) A Healthy Old Age: A Sourcebook for Health Promotion with Older Adults, Health Promotion and Aging: Strategies for Action, Health Promotion and Aging: A National Resource of Selected Programs; also articles and book chpts.; mem. editl. bd. Generations, 1999-2002. Bd. dirs. Am. Soc. on Aging, 1992-1995, Nat. Assn. State Units of Aging, 1987-91, S.W. Soc. on Aging, 1992-97, Goodwill Industries Cleve., 1999-2004; moderator First Bapt. Ch. of Greater Cleve., 1997-98; treas., fin. chair Laurel Lake Retirement Cmty., 1999-2004; bd. dirs. RSVP Greater Cleve., 2002—, chmn. governance com., 2004—. Danforth fellow, 1972-78; named to Women of Note, Crains Cleve. Bus., 2004. Mem. AAUW, Nat. Coun. on the Aging (policy com. 2004-05), Soc. for Values in Higher Edn., Nat. Assn. Social Workers, Am. Soc. on Aging. Office: Fairhill Ctr 12200 Fairhill Rd Cleveland OH 44120-1013 Office Phone: 216-421-1350. E-mail: sfallcreek@aol.com, sfc@fairhillcenter.org.

FALLDING, HAROLD JOSEPH, sociology educator; b. Cessnock, New South Wales, Australia, May 3, 1923; s. Frederick and Alice Bessie (Chopping) F.; m. Margaret Hurlstone Hardy, Dec. 18, 1954; children: Marion, Ruth, Helen. Cert. Libr. Sch., Pub. Libr. New South Wales, 1941; BSc, U. Sydney, Australia, 1950, BA, 1951, diploma of edn., 1952, MA with honors, 1955; PhD, Australian Nat. U., 1957. Tchr. h.s. English and history New South Wales Dept. Edn., 1952-53; sr. rsch. fellow in sociology, dept. agrl. econs. U. Sydney, 1956-58; sr. lectr. sociology U. New South Wales, 1959-62; vis. assoc. prof. Grad. Sch., Rutgers U., N.J., 1963-65; prof. U. Waterloo, Ont., Can., 1965-88, disting. prof. emeritus, 1989—. Author: The Sociological Task, 1968, The Sociology of Religion: An Explanation of the Unity and Diversity in Religion, 1974, Drinking, Community and Civilization. The Account of a New Jersey Interview Study, 1974, The Social Process Revisited, 1990; poems Word of the Tangling Fire, 1969, Collected Poetry, 1997, The Complete Poems to 2005, 2005. Mem. Clare Hall, U. Cambridge. Fellow Royal Soc. Can.; mem. Am. Sociol. Assn., Can. Inst. Internat. Affairs, Can. Soc. Sociology and Anthropology, Internat. Sociol. Assn., Soc. Sci. Study of Religion, Assn. Sociology of Religion, Social Sci. Fedn. Can. (dir.) Mem. United Ch. Can. Home: 40 Arbordale Walk Guelph ON Canada N1G 4X7 Office: Sociology Dept U Waterloo Waterloo ON Canada N2L 3G1 *My life has seemed like a series of arrivals at the same crossroads, compelling me to confirm a decision on priorities made very early, that loyalty to truth comes before achievement. Any achievements have consequently seemed surprises—like spin-offs from giving effect to that loyalty.*

FALLER, DONALD E., marketing and operations executive; b. Jersey City, Mar. 1, 1927; s. Louis John and Gertrude Louise (Hupfield) F.; m. Dolores Adeline Smith, Aug. 28, 1948; children: Mark William, Kyle Lindsay Fernandez, Kimberly Willard, Donald Mark, Krystn Judith, Kelly Bridget Christina Weir. BS, Mich. State U., 1948. Prodn. mgr. Sealtest Foods Kraft, Detroit, 1958-60, dist. mgr., 1960-67, div. mktg. mgr. Cleve., 1967-70; v.p. mktg. Citrus Cen. Inc., Orlando, Fla., 1970-78, exec. v.p. mktg. and adminstrn., mktg. divsn., 1978-83, chief exec. officer, 1980-83; gen. sales mgr. Sunkist Growers Inc., Ontario, Calif., 1984-88, dir. sales, fin. and ops., 1988-90; pres., CEO Trinity Mktg. Cons., Longwood, Fla., 1990—. Bd. dirs. Combank Apopka Freedom Savs. & Loan Assn., Winter Park, Fla., Calif.-Ariz. Citrus League. Bd. dirs. Pace Sch., Alamonte Springs, Fla., 1976-82. Mem. Nat. Juice Products Assn. (pres.), Blue Key, Sweetwater Country Club (Longwood, Fla.), Orlando Country Club, Errol Estate Country Club, Alpha Zeta (pres. 1947-48). Republican. Office: Trinity Mktg Cons 732 Riverbend Blvd Longwood FL 32779-2349

FALLER, DOROTHY ANDERSON, international training consultant; b. Chgo., July 6, 1939; d. Albert T. and Lillian G. (Chalbeck) Anderson; m. Adolph Faller, Sept. 5, 1959; children: Carl, Kurt. Student, Ill. Wesleyan U., 1956—59; AB, U. Ill., 1960; MS in Social Adminstrn., CASE Western Res. U., 1975. Lic. ind. social worker. Child welfare worker Klamath County Pub. Welfare Commn., Klamath Falls, Oreg., 1960-67; social svc. cons. Ind. State Dept. Pub. Welfare, 1968-72; adminstrv. asst. Berea (Ohio) Children's Home, 1974; rsch. asst. Case Western Res. U., Sch. Applied Social Scis., 1975, Mandel Sch. Applied Social Scis.; social svcs. supr. Ohio Dept. Pub. Welfare, Cleve., 1975-81; exec. dir. Cleve. Internat. Program, 1981-99; exec. gen., CEO Coun. Internat. Programs USA, 1999—2002; pres. Faller Internat. Tng., 2002—. Cons. Cleve. Found., Am. Sickle Cell Anemia Found., John A. Yankey & Assocs.; field instr. Case Western Reserve U., 1976—77; dir. African Internship Project Substance Abuse Prevention, 1992—95, Ghana Conf., 1995; assisted founding Sch. of Social Work, Addis Abba U., Ethiopia, 2002—; instr. conflict resolution and fundraising Addis Ababa, NGO Fiscal Mgmt., Ukrainian Women's Group, NGO Issues for Japanese Mcpl. Workers for Cleve. Coun. World Affairs, 2004; mem. adv. coun. Mandel Ctr. Non-Profit Orgns., 1995—96, CASE Western Res. U.; strategic planning Coun. Internat. Fellowship, Goa, India, 2003, Riga, Latvia, 04, Bonn, Germany, 05; cons. Ethiopian programs U. Ill., Chgo., 2002—; tchr. 1st master social work class Addis Ababa U., 2004; faculty assoc. U. Ill., Chgo., 2004; lectr. in field. Editor, contbr.: Ohio Children's Budget Project: A Public Policy Study, 1975. Bd. dirs. West Shore Unitarian Ch., 1978-81, 2000-03, Volgograd Free Speech Forum, 1995-2001. Grantee Cmty. Criminal Justice Adminstrn., Romania, 1999-2001; hon. by Fulbright Assn., 1999, Cleve. Rotary, 2003. Mem. Acad. Cert. Social Workers (cert.), Nat. Assn. Social Workers (unit chair state bd., exec. com. nat. bd. dirs. 1985-88, chmn. Internat. Activities Com. of Nat. Bd. 1986-89, program com. 1989-91, del. Internat. Fedn. Social Workers, Sweden, 1988, Cleve. unit Social Worker of Yr. 1986, del. from Ohio to del. assembly 1990, conf. chair ann. meeting profession 1993), Nat. Fulbright Assn. (life), CASE Western Res. U. Sch. Applied Social Scis. Alumni Assn., Sigma Kappa (pres. 1959), Alpha Lambda Delta (pres. 1956). Home and Office: 6889 Columbia Rd Olmsted Falls OH 44138-1523 E-mail: dorothyfaller@sbcglobal.net.

FALLER, JAMES ELLIOT, physicist, researcher; b. Mishawaka, Ind., Jan. 17, 1934; s. Elmer Edward and Leona Maxine (Forstbauer) F.; m. Jocelyne T. Bellenger, March 7, 1996; children: William Edward, Peter James. AB summa cum laude, Ind. U., 1955; MA, Princeton U., 1957, PhD, 1963; MA (hon.), Wesleyan U., Middletown, Conn., 1972. Instr. Princeton U., 1959-62; mem. Joint Inst. Lab. Astrophysics, Boulder, Colo., 1963-66, fellow, 1972—; asst. prof. physics Wesleyan U., 1966-68, assoc. prof. physics, 1968-71, prof., 1971-72. Nat. Acad. Sci./NRC postdoctoral fellow, 1963-64; Sloan fellow, 1972-73; recipient Precision Measurement award Nat. Bur. Standards, 1970, Arnold O. Beckman award Instrument Soc. Am., 1970, Exceptional Sci. Achievement medal NASA, 1973, Gold medal Dept. Commerce, 1990, Fed. Lab. Consortium Tech. Transfer award, 1992, Joseph F. Keithley award, 2001. Mem. Am. Phys. Soc., AAAS, Am. Geophysical Union, Phi Beta Kappa, Sigma Xi. Home: 303 Hollyberry Ln Boulder CO 80305-5230 Office: JILA Univ Colorado Boulder CO 80309-0001

FALLER, JOHN W., chemistry professor, researcher; b. Louisville, Jan. 7, 1942; PhD, MIT, Cambridge, Mass., 1966. Prof. Yale U., New Haven, Conn., 1966—. Fellow, A. P. Sloan Found., 1970—72, John Simon Guggenheim Found., 1972. Mem.: Am. Crystallographic Soc., Am. Chem. Soc. Office: Yale Univ 225 Prospect St New Haven CT 06520-8107 Office Phone: 203-432-3954. Office Fax: 203-432-6144. Personal E-mail: jack.faller@yale.edu.

FALLER, RHODA, lawyer; b. NYC, Dec. 21, 1946; d. Benjamin and Marion (Mediasky) Sragg; m. Stanley Grossberg, Apr. 12, 1973 (div. Oct. 1983); children: Joseph Seth, Daniel Benjamin; m. Bernard Martin Faller, May 31, 1987. BS, SUNY, Stony Brook, 1967; MS, Pace U., 1973; JD, NY Law Sch., 1978. Bar: N.Y. 1979, N.J. 1979, U.S. Dist. Ct. N.J. 1979, Fla. 1980, U.S. Dist. Ct. (ea. and so. dists.) N.Y. 1982, Ky. 1996, U.S. Dist. Ct. (ea. dist.) Ky. 1997. Assoc. Fuchsberg & Fuchsberg, N.Y.C., 1982-91, DeBlasio & Alton, P.C., N.Y.C., 1991-95, Rhoda Grossberg Faller, Esq., Teaneck, 1995-96, Becker Law Office, Louisville, Ky., 1997-2000; pvt. practice Louisville, 2000—. Mem.: Women Lawyers Assn., Louisville Bar Assn., Fla. Bar Assn., N.Y. State Bar Assn., Ky. Bar Assn., Ky. Acad. Trial Attys., Nat. Assn. Women Bus. Owners, Assn. Trial Lawyers Am., Million Dollar Advocates Forum. Democrat. Jewish. Home: 213 Mockingbird Gardens Dr Louisville KY 40207-5718 Office: Law Office of Rhoda Faller PLLC 455 S 4th St Ste 310 Louisville KY 40202 Office Phone: 502-582-2212. Business E-Mail: rfaller@fallerlaw.com.

FALLER, SUSAN GROGAN, lawyer; b. Cin., Mar. 1, 1950; d. William M. and Jane (Eagen) Grogan; m. Kenneth R. Faller, June 8, 1973; children: Susan Elisabeth, Maura Christine, Julie Kathleen. BA, U. Cin., 1972; JD, U. Mich., 1975. Bar: Ohio 1975, Ky. 1989, U.S. Dist. Ct. (so. dist.) Ohio 1975, U.S. Ct. Claims 1982, U.S. Ct. Appeals (6th cir.) 1982, U.S. Supreme Ct. 1982, U.S. Tax Ct. 1984, U.S. Dist. Ct. (ea. dist.) Ky., 1991. Assoc. Frost & Jacobs, Cin., 1975-82; ptnr. Frost & Jacobs LLP, Cin., 1982-2000; mem. Frost Brown Todd LLC, Cin., 2000—. Assoc. editor Mich. Law Rev., 1974-75; contbg. author: MLRC 50-State Survey of Media Libel and Privacy Law, 1982-93, MLRC 50-State Survey of Media Libel Law, 1999-, MLRC State Survey of Employment Libel and Privacy Law, 1999-. Bd. dirs. Summit Alumni Coun., Cin., 1983-85; trustee Newman Found., Cin., 1980-86, Cath. Social Svc., Cin., 1984-93, nominating com., 1985-88, sec., 1990; mem. Class XVII Leadership Cin., 1993-94; mem. exec. com., def. counsel sect. Media Law Resource Ctr., 1998-2002, chmn. membership com., 2003—; pres., def. counsel sect. Libel Def. Resource Ctr., 2001; mem. parish coun. St. Monica-St. George Ch., 1996-2000. Recipient Career Women of Achievement award YWCA, 1990. Mem. ABA (co-editor newsletter media litig. 1993-97), FBA, Ky. Bar Assn., No. Ky. Bar Assn., No. Ky. Women's Bar Assn., Ohio Bar Assn. (chair media law com. 2001-02), Cin. Bar Assn. (com. mem.), Potter Stewart Inn of Ct., U. Cin. Alumni Assn., Arts & Scis. Alumni Assn. (bd. govs. U. Cin. Coll. 1988-2000), U. Mich. Alumni Assn., Mortar Bd., Leland Yacht Club, Coll. Club, Clifton Meadows Club, Phi Beta Kappa, Theta Phi Alpha. Roman Catholic. Home: 5 Belsaw Pl Cincinnati OH 45220-1104 Office: Frost Brown Todd LLC 2200 PNC Ctr 201 E 5th St Cincinnati OH 45202-4182 Office Phone: 513-651-6941. E-mail: sfaller@fbtlaw.com.

FALLESEN, GARY DAVID, journalist; b. Rochester, N.Y., July 24, 1959; s. Karl David and Mary Lou (Putnam) F.; m. Elaine Gertrude Busse, July 3, 1982; children: Jesse Dane, Hayley Hope. BA, St. John Fisher Coll., Rochester, 1981. Sports clk. Democrat & Chronicle, Rochester, 1979-82, sports writer, 1982-88, sports columnist, 1988-92, sports writer, 1992-96; outdoor writer, 1996—. Contbr. articles to Sporting News, Golf World, Golf Journal, CBS Sportsline, Adirondack Explorer, Escape Mag., Altrec.com, other sports publs; author: (book) Peak Experiences and Mount Everest Confessions of an Amature Peakbugs, 2000. Worship side leader Luth. Ch., NY. Named Sports Writer of the Yr., N.Y. State Wrestling Coaches Assn., 1984, Rochester Press-Radio Club, 1986, Hon. Mention, N.Y. State AP Writers Contest, 1989, 2nd place column, Profl. Football Writers, 1990, 1st place column Profl. Football Writers, 1991, honorable mention column Profl. Football Writers, 1992, 2nd place enterprise Football Writers Assn., 1995, hon. mention column Football Writers Assn., 1996, N.Y. Newspaper Pub. Assn. award of excellence, 1996-97, 98, hon. mention N.Y. State AP Writers Contest, 1998. Mem.: Newspaper Guild (exec. com. 1992—, v.p. 1995—2001, officer Local 17), N.Y. State Outdoor Writers Assn., Outdoor Writers Assn. Am. (2nd outdoors page 2001, 3d pl. big game hunting, outdoors page 1999, 1st boating, 3d outdoors page 2000), Rochester Christian Writers Guild (co-dir.), Am. Alpine Club. Lutheran. Avocations: mountain climbing, photography, drama . Office: Dem & Chronicle 55 Exchange Blvd Rochester NY 14614-2001 Business E-Mail: gfallesn@democratandchronicle.com.

FALLETTA, JO ANN, conductor; b. N.Y.C., Feb. 27, 1954; d. John Edward and Mary Lucy (Racioppo) F.; m. Robert Alemany, Aug. 24, 1986. BA in Music, Mannes Coll. Music, N.Y.C., 1976; MA in Music, Juilliard Sch., N.Y.C., 1983, PhD in Musical Arts, 1989; doctorate (hon.), Marian Coll., Wis., 1988, Old Dominion U., 1996, Canisius Coll., 2000. Music dir. Queens Philharmonic, N.Y.C., 1978-91, Den. Chamber Orch., Colo., 1983-92; assoc. condr. Milw. Symphony, Wis., 1985-88; music dir. Women's Philharmonic, San Francisco, 1986-96; music dir., condr. Long Beach Symphony, Calif., 1989-00; music dir. Va. Symphony, Norfolk, 1991—, Buffalo Philharm., 1999—. Over 30 recordings with the London Symphony, the Buffalo Philharmonic, the Virginia Symphony, the English Chamber Orchestra, the New Zealand Symphony, the Long Beach Symphony, the Czech National Symphony and the Women's Philharmonic. Stokowski Conducting Competition, Toscanini Conducting award, John S. Edwards Award, Am. Symphony Orchestra League, Seaver/Nat. Endowment for the Arts Conductors Award, 2002. Office: ICM Artists LTD 40 W 57th St Fl 16 New York NY 10019-4098

FALLETTA, JOHN MATTHEW, pediatrician, educator; b. Arma, Kans., Sept. 3, 1940; s. Matthew John and Norma (Luke) F.; m. Carolyn Ontjes, June 22, 1963; children: Elizabeth, Matthew. AB, U. Kans., 1962, MD, 1966. Diplomate Am. Bd. Pediat., Am. Bd. Hematology-Oncology. Intern in mixed medicine Kans. U. Med. Ctr., Kansas City, 1966-67; surgeon Epidemic Intelligence Svc., Tex. Children's Hosp. USPHS, Houston, 1967-69; asst. instr. pediat. Baylor Coll. Medicine, Houston, 1967-69, resident, 1969-71, chief resident Tex. Children's Hosp., 1971, postdoctoral fellow hematology-oncology, 1971-73, asst. prof. pediat., 1973-76; assoc. prof. Duke U., Durham, NC, 1976-83, prof., 1984—, chief divsn. hematology-oncology, 1976-94, dir. Clin. Pediat. Lab., 1976-95. Chmn. transfusion com. Duke U. Med. Ctr., 1978—, mem. exec. com. med. staff, 1978—, instl. rev. bd. human rsch., 1979—, chmn., 1994—; mem. instl. rev. bd. human rsch. Baylor Coll. Medicine, 1974-76; mem. acad. coun. Duke U., 1982-86, 87-96, 98-2000, exec. com., 1988, faculty compensation com., 1988—, faculty com. on univ. governance, 1988, trustee-faculty com. to rev. pres., 1989, search com. for pres., 1992; cons. pediat. hematologist-oncologist Charlotte (N.C.) Meml. Hosp., 1978-94, mem. Copernicus Independent Rev. Bd., 2002—, vice-chair, 2004—; mem. med. adv. bd. Children's Cancer Rsch. Fund, 2001—; mem. coun. on accreditation Assn. for the Accreditation Human Rsch. Protection Programs, Inc., 2005— Contbr. more than 120 articles to Nature, Am. Jour. Ophthalmology, Pediat., New Eng. Jour. Medicine, Clin. Pediat. Oncology, others. Cons. pediat. hematologist-oncologist Project Hope, Pediatric Inst., Krakow, Poland, 1979—; prin. investigator Pediat. Oncology Group, 1981-95, chmn. epidemiology com., mem. prin. investigator's exec. com., new agts. and pharmacology com.; chmn. prophylactic penicillin study I Nat. Heart, Lung and Blood Inst., NIH, 1982-86, chmn. study II, 1987-95; active Cancer Ctr. Support Rev. Com. Nat. Cancer Inst. NIH, 1986-90, NIH Reviewers Res., 1990—, Cancer Clin. Investigation Rev. Com., 1991-96, chmn., 1995-96; trustee Ronald McDonald House Charities, 1986—. Mem. Am. Acad. Pediat., Am. Pediat. Soc., Am. Soc. Clin. Oncology, So. Soc. Pediat. Rsch. (pres. 1981-82), Soc. Pediat. Rsch., N.C. Pediat. Soc., N.C. Med. Soc., Phi Beta Kappa, Alpha Omega Alpha. Office: Duke U Med Ctr PO Box 2991 Durham NC 27710-2991

FALLIN, DICKY GRAYSON, music educator, musician; b. Martinsville, Va., 1955; s. Charles Grayson and La Honda Fallin; m. Wanda Faye Eanes, 1979; children: Sherry, William, Benjamin. B in Music Edn., Appalachian State U., 1980; MMus, Norfolk (Va.) State U., 1991. Trumpet instr. Armed Forces Sch. Music, Norfolk, 1985—91, brass br. supr., 1994—96; 1st sgt. 434 Army Band, Ft. Gordon, Ga., 1996—98; band dir. Glenn Hills Mid. Sch., Augusta, Ga., 1999—2001, Cross Creek H.S., Augusta, 2001—03, Taft Mid. Sch., 2003—05; humanities prof. Augusta State U., 1998—. 1st trumpet Fairbanks (Alaska) Symphony Orch., 1992—94; 3d trumpet Augusta Symphony, 1998—99; 2d trumpet Augusta Opera, 1999—2002. Avocation: record collecting. Home: 4715 Oakley Pirkle Rd Augusta GA 30907 Office: Taft Mid Sch 495 Boy Scout Rd Augusta GA 30906

FALLIN, MARY COPELAND, lieutenant governor; b. Warrensburg, Mo., Dec. 9, 1954; d. Joseph Newton and Mary (Duggan) Copeland; children: Christina, Price. BS, Okla. State U., 1977. Bus. mgr. Okla. Dept. Securities, Oklahoma City, 1979-81; state travel coord. Okla. Dept. of Tourism, Oklahoma City, 1981-82; sales rep. Associated Petroleum, Oklahoma City, 1982-83; mktg. dir. Brian Head (Utah) Hotel & Ski Resort, 1983-84; dir. sales Residence Inn Hotel, Oklahoma City, 1984-87; dist. mgr. Lexington Hotel Suites, Oklahoma City, 1988-90; real estate assoc. Pippin Properties, Inc., Oklahoma City, 1990-94; state rep. Okla. Ho. of Reps., Oklahoma City, 1990-94; lt. gov. State of Okla., Oklahoma City, 1995—. Chmn. Nat. Conf. Lt. Govs. Mem., del. Okla. Fedn. Rep. Women; mem. Am. Legis. Exch. Coun., Nat. Conf. State Legislatures; former bd. mem. United Way Oklahoma City, YWCA; mem. adv. bd. Trail of Tears; former hon. chair Organ Donor Network; former hon. co-chair Indian Territory Arts and Humanities Coun.; former co-chair Festival of Hope; active Crossings Cmty. Ch. Named Woman of Yr., Ladies in Comm., 1998, Girl Scouts Am., 1998, Nat. Legislator of Yr., Okla. Ladies in the News, Disting. Former Student, U. Ctrl. Okla.; recipient Bi-liner award, 1997, Guardian of Small Bus. award, Small Bus. Adv. award, Nat. Fedn. Ind. Small Bus., Women in the News award, Women in Comm. Mem.: Aerospace States Assn. (chmn. 2003—05). Republican. Office: State Capitol Rm 211 Office of Lt Governor Oklahoma City OK 73105 Office Phone: 405-521-2161. Business E-Mail: mary.fallin@ltgov.state.ok.us.

FALLINGS, GLORIA VONDELL, special education educator; b. Barnesville, Ga., Oct. 2, 1956; d. Grady and Minnie Akins Fallings. BA in Psychology, Albany State U., Albany, 1978. Related vocat. instrn. program coord. Newton County Schools, Covington, Ga., 1994—; mentor tchr. Newton County Sch., 2002—. Rec. steward, sec. Mt. Sinai Christain Meth. Ch., Milner, Ga. Mem.: GAE, NEA, Zeta Phi Beta Sorority, Inc. Democrat. Npl. Methodist. Home: 75 Saratoga Ct Covington GA 30016 Office: Newton High Sch 140 Ram Dr Covington GA 30014 Office Phone: 770-787-2250. Personal E-mail: fallingsg@aol.com. E-mail: www.newton.k12.ga.us.

FALLIS, STEPHEN JAMES, lawyer; b. Oceanside, N.Y., Nov. 7, 1942; 1 child, Scott. BA, Columbia Coll., 1964; LLB, Harvard U., 1967. Bar: N.Y. 1967, U.S. Ct. Appeals (2d cir.) 1974, U.S. Dist. Ct. (so. and ea. dists.) N.Y. 1975. Asst. dist. atty. N.Y. County Dist. Attys. Office, N.Y.C., 1967-72; bur. chief N.Y. State Spl. Prosecutor's Office, N.Y.C., 1972-76; dep. chief counsel U.S. House Reps., Select Com. on Assassinations, Washington, 1976-77; ptnr., head litigation dept. Carb, Luria, Cook & Kufeld LLP, N.Y.C., 1977—. Mem. mediation panel U.S. Dist. Ct. (so. dist.) N.Y., 1994—. Mem. N.Y. City Bar Assn., Harvard Club of N.Y. Avocations: tennis, golf, bridge. Office: Carb Luria Cook & Kufeld 521 5th Ave New York NY 10175-0003 E-mail: sfallis@carbluria.com.

FALLON, JIMMY, actor; b. Bklyn., Sept. 19, 1974; s. Jim and Gloria Fallon. Attended, Coll. St. Rose. Actor: (TV series) Saturday Night Live, 1998—2004; (TV films) Sex and the Matrix, 2000; (TV miniseries) Band of Brothers, 2001, (guest appearance): (TV series) Spin City, 1998,; (films) Almost Famous, 2000, Anything Else, 2003, The Entrepreneurs, 2003, Taxi, 2004, Fever Pitch, 2005; co-author (with Gloria Fallon): (book) I Hate This Place: The Pessimist's Guide to Life, 1999; performer: (comedy album) The Bathroom Wall, 2003. Named one of 50 Most Beautiful People in the World, People mag., 2002. Office: Creative Artist Agency 9830 Wilshire Blvd Beverly Hills CA 90212*

FALLON, PAT, artist, educator; b. Cartagena, Colombia, Nov. 2, 1939; d. Carlos Fallon and Maureen (Bryne) Fallon Laird; m. Ronald Patrick Conner, Dec. 26, 1960 (div. June 1976); children: Haldey Kathryn Conner, Kenneth Fallon Conner. BA, Antioch Coll., 1962; BFA, Cleve. Inst. Art, 1980; MFA, Kent State U., 1982. Prof. Ursuline Coll., Cleve., 2001—. Exhibitions include nat. and internat., U.S., Ireland, Germany. Vol. N.E. Ohio Coalition Homeless, Cleve. Fellow, Ohio Humanities Coun., 1986—94. Mem.: Mus. Contemporary Art Cleve., So. Poverty Ctr. Democrat. Roman Catholic. Home: 3300 Kenmore Rd Shaker Heights OH 44122-3462 Office: Ursuline Coll 2550 Lander Rd Cleveland OH 44124-4318

FALLON, PATRICK R., advertising executive; b. 1946; With Leo Burnett, Chgo., 1967-69, Stevson & Assocs., Mpls., 1969-76, v.p.; with Martin/Williams Advt., Mpls., 1976-81, v.p.; chmn. bd. dirs. Fallon McElligott, Inc., Mpls., 1981—; CEO Fallon. Office: Fallon-McElligott Inc Ste 2800 50 S 6th St Minneapolis MN 55402-1550*

FALLON, RICHARD H., JR., law educator; b. Augusta, Maine, Jan. 4, 1952; AB in History, Yale U., 1975, JD, 1980; BA in Philosophy, Politics, and Economics, Oxford U., 1977. Bar: Mass. 1988. Law clk. to Hon. J. Skelly Wright US Ct. Appeals DC Cir., 1980-81; law clk. to Hon. Lewis F. Powell Jr. US Supreme Ct., Washington, 1981-82; asst. prof. law Harvard Law Sch., Cambridge, Mass., 1982-87, prof., 1987—, Ralph S. Tyler, Jr. prof. constl. law, 2004—. Vis. prof. Wash. U., Seattle, spring 1991. Author: Implementing the Constitution, 2001, The Dynamic Constitution - An Introduction to American Constitutional Law, 2004; co-author: Constitutional Law: Cases, Comments, Questions, 2001, Hart & Wechsler's The Federal Courts and The Federal System, 1973, 1988, 1996, 2003. Office: Harvard Law Sch 1563 Massachusetts Ave Cambridge MA 02138 Office Phone: 617-495-3215. Office Fax: 617-496-5156. Business E-Mail: rfallon@law.harvard.edu.*

FALLON, WILLIAM J., career military officer; b. East Orange, NJ, Dec. 30, 1944; m. Mary Elizabeth Trapp; children: Susan, Barbara, William, Christina. BA, Villanova U., 1967; MA in Internat. Studies, Old Dominion. Advanced through grade to adm. USN; pilot USS Ranger, 1969; comdr. attack squadron 65 USS Dwight D. Eisenhower, 1984-85; dep. comdr. carrier air wing 8 USS Nimitz; comdr. attack wing 1 Naval Air Sta. Occana, Va., 1989-90, USS Theodore Roosevelt, 1991, comdr. carrier group 8, 1995; comdr. Theodore Roosevelt battle group, comdr. Battle Force 6th Fleet; dep. comdr. in chief, chief staff US Atlantic Fleet, Norfolk, Va., 1996-98, commdr. 2d Fleet, Striking Fleet Atlantic, 1997—2000; vice chief naval ops. US Navy, Washington, 2000—03; comdr. US Fleet Forces Command and US Atlantic Fleet, Norfolk, Va., 2003—, US Pacific Command, Honolulu, 2005—. Office: US Pacific Command PO Box 64031 Camp H M Smith HI 96861*

FALLS, KATHLEENE JOYCE, photographer; b. Detroit, July 3, 1949; d. Edgar John and Acelia Olive (Young) Haley; m. Donald David Falls, June 15, 1974; children: Daniel John, David James. Student, Oakland Community Coll., 1969-73, Winona Sch. Profl. Photography, 1973-80, postgrad., 1988, 90. Lic. amateur radio-technician class, cert. photographic specialist Profl. Photographers Am., 1988, photog. craftsman Profl. Photographers Am., 1990, cert. electronic imaging Profl. Photographers Am., 1990, master artist Profl. Photographers Am., 1990, profl. photographer Profl. Photographers Am., 2004, master electronic imaging Profl. Photographers Am., 2004. Printer Guardian Photo, Novi, Mich., 1967-69; printer, supr. quality control N.Am. Photo, Livonia, 1969—76; free lance photographer, 1969—76; owner, pres. Kathy Falls, Inc., Camden, 1976—2001. Instr. continuing edn. Monroe County (Mich.) C.C., 1981—83, instr. digital imaging, 1994—95; instr. Internat. Photography and Art Sch., Indpls., 2004; nat. artisan judge Congl. H.S. Art Competition, 1985—2000; owner Picture Perfect, Carlton, Mich., 1987; co-owner Haleys Gift Shoppe, Dundee, 1989; pub. info. officer Am. Radio Relay League, 1998—2000. Author: (booklet) Emergency Photo-Retouching for Photographers, 1988; photographer (represented in spl. categories) Profl. Photographers Am. Nat. Loan Collection, 1980, 1981, 1983, 1987, 2002, 2004, (permanent collections) Monroe County Hist. Mus., Archives Notre Dame; editor: The Hertzian Herald, 1998; contbr. articles to profl. jours. Active Big Bros. and Big Sisters, Monroe, 1986—87; corr. sec. Monroe Women's Ctr., 1986—88; mem. Amateur Radio Emergency Svc.; pres. Our Lady of Knock divsn. Laoh Adrian, Laoh State Bd., 2001—03; Catechist St. Parick's Ch., Carleton, 1984—87, mem. parish coun., 1998—2000; bd. dirs. Ladies Ancient Order of Hibernians. Mem.: NAFE, Nat. Orgn. Women Bus. Owners, Monroe C. of C. (chmn. council women bus. owners), Monroe County Fine Arts Coun., Am. Photog. Artisans Guild (bd. dir. 1987—, Photog. Artisan degree 1989, Artisan Laurel degree 1991, pres. 1992, editor Palette Page 2001—04, exec. sec. 2001—, exec. dir. 2002, coun. mem., Fuji Masterpiece award 2005), Profl. Photographers Am., Profl. Photographers Mich. (artisan chair 1982—83, bd. dir. 2000—, dir. 2001—02, Best of Show award 1976, Artist of Yr. 1980, Best of Show award 1981, Artist of Yr. 1991, Best of Show award 2001), Detroit Profl. Photographers Assn. (artisan chmn. 1981—82, bd. dir. 1987—, Best of Show award 1981, 1983), Am. Soc. Photographers, Hillsdale Art Guild, Toastmasters, Monroe County Radio Comms. Assn., Ladies Ancient Order of Hibernians (bd. dir. 1998—99), Monroe Camera, Hillsdale County Amateur Radio Club, Scarab Club Detroit, Internat. Club. Republican. Roman Catholic. Avocations: guitar, piano, drawing, travel, camping. Home and Office: 14940 Carpenter Rd Camden MI 49232 Office Phone: 517-368-4995. E-mail: katfalls@tdi.net.

FALOON, WILLIAM WASSELL, physician, educator; b. Pitts., July 6, 1920; s. Joseph Coulter and Martha Louise (Wassell) F.; m. Roberta Jane Emery, Sept. 11, 1948; children: Karen F. Durham, Nancy F. Dodd, William W. BA, Allegheny Coll., 1941; MD, Harvard U., 1944. Diplomate Am. Bd. Internal Medicine; cert. registered arbitrator; ordained as deacon Presbyterian, 1958, elder, 1963. Intern Pa. Hosp., Phila., 1944-45; asst. resident in medicine Albany (N.Y.) Hosp., 1945-46, resident in medicine, 1946-47; rsch. fellow in medicine Harvard Med. Sch., Thorndike Meml. Lab., Boston City Hosp., 1947-48; asst. prof. oncology, instr. medicine Albany Med. Coll., 1948-50; instr. medicine SUNY Coll. Medicine, Syracuse, 1950-51, asst. prof., 1951-56, assoc. prof., 1956-64, prof. medicine, 1964-68; program dir. Adult Clin. Rsch. Ctr., Syracuse, 1965-68; physician-in-chief, dir. clin. rsch. and edn. Santa Barbara (Calif.) Gen.-Cottage Hosps., 1968-69; prof. medicine U. Rochester (N.Y.) Sch. Medicine, 1969-92, emeritus prof. medicine, 1992—; mem. Univ. Senate, 1971-74; mem. staff Strong Meml. Hosp., Rochester, Highland Hosp., 1969-90, chief medicine, 1970-80, dir. gastroenterology and nutrition, 1970-86; sr. attending physician The Genesee Hosp., 1990-91. Mem. editl. bd. Am. Jour. Clin. Nutrition, 1970-76; contbr. articles to profl. jours. Bd. mgrs. Camp Dudley YMCA, 1962-67, 69-74, chmn. bd., 1966-67, 71-73; bd. dirs. Onondaga County Met. Health Coun., Syracuse, 1959-61; mem. adv. com. Onondaga County Health Dept., 1966-68; bd. dirs. Am. Liver Found., 1982-92, pres. we. N.Y. chpt., 1982-83. Fellow ACP, Rochester Acad. Medicine (dir. 1979-82); mem. Am. Fedn. Clin. Rsch. (councillor 1956-59), AAAS, Onondaga County Med. Soc. (exec. com. 1964-66), Am. Assn. for Study Liver Disease, Am. Inst. Nutrition, Am. Soc. Clin. Nutrition, Endocrine Soc., Am. Gastroent. Assn., Western Soc. for Clin. Rsch., Med. Soc. Monroe County, Internat. Assn. for Study Liver, Assn. Program Dirs. Internal Medicine (councillor 1978-80), N.Y. State Dept. Health (bd. profl. med. conduct N.Y. State 1986-97), Island Profl. Rev. Orgn. (cons. 1991-94), Nat. Health Lawyers Assn. (dispute resolver), Gt. Lakes Interurban (sec. 1977-84), Ea. Gut, Oak Hill Country Club (Rochester). Presbyterian. Home: 4 Whitecliff Dr Pittsford NY 14534-2926 Office Phone: 585-381-6239. E-mail: remfaloon@aol.com.

FALSGRAF, WILLIAM WENDELL, retired lawyer; b. Cleve., Nov. 10, 1933; s. Wendell A. and Catherine J. F.; children: Carl Douglas, Jeffrey Price, Catherine Louise. AB cum laude, Amherst Coll., 1955, LLD (hon.), 1986; JD, Case Western Res. U., 1958. Bar: Ohio 1958, U.S. Supreme Ct. 1972. Ptnr. Baker & Hostetler, Cleve., 1971—2002; ret., 2002. Chmn. vis. com. Case Western Res. U. Law Sch., 1973-76; trustee Case Western Reserve U., 1978-90, chmn. bd. overseers, 1977-78; trustee Cleve. Health Mus., 1975-90, Hiram Coll., 1989—; chmn. bd. trustees Hiram Coll., 1990-99. Recipient Disting. Service award; named Outstanding Young Man of Year Cleve. Jr. C. of C., 1962. Fellow Am. Bar Found., Ohio Bar Found.; mem. ABA (chmn. young lawyers sect. 1966-67, mem. ho. of dels. 1967-68, 70—, bd. govs. 1971-75, pres. 1985-86, bd. dirs. Am. Bar Endowment 1974-84, 87-97), Am. Bar Ins. Plans Cons. (pres. 1991—), Ohio Bar Assn. (mem. coun. of dels. 1968-70), Cleve. Bar Assn. (trustee 1979-82), Amherst Alumni Assn. (pres. N.E. Ohio 1964), The Country Club, LaPaloma Country Club. Home: 616 North St Chagrin Falls OH 44022-2514 Office: Baker & Hostetler LLP 3200 National City Ctr Cleveland OH 44114-3485 Office Phone: 216-861-7376. Business E-Mail: wfalsgraf@bakerlaw.com.

FALSONE, JACK JOSEPH, physician; b. Queens, N.Y., Nov. 6, 1923; s. Joseph and Margaret (Cutelli) F.; m. Anna Mandracchia, Dec. 23, 1945; children: Margaret, Catherine. AB, Columbia Coll., 1944; MD, L.I. Coll. Medicine, 1947. Diplomate Am. Bd. Internal Medicine. Intern Bklyn. Hosp., 1947-48, resident in internal medicine, 1948-51; attending physician Norwalk (Conn.) Hosp., 1954—91, assoc. chief chest diseases, 1970-87; instr. coll. medicine Yale U., 1955-61, asst. clin. prof. medicine, 1961-69; sr. rsch. assoc. Beulah Hinds Ctr., Norwalk Hosp., 1991—; vol. physician AmeriCare Free Clinic, Norwalk, 1994—, vol. med. dir., 1999—. Served with AUS, 1943-46, USAF, 1951-53. Fellow ACP; mem. Norwalk Heart Assn. (pres. 1955), Norwalk Med. Soc. (pres. 1975), Am. Coll. Chest Physicians. Roman Catholic. Office: Beulah Hinds Ctr Norwalk Hosp Norwalk CT 06856 Office Phone: 203-855-3615. E-mail: jack.falsone@norwalkhealth.org.

FALTER, ROBERT GARY, realtor, educator; b. NYC, Sept. 14, 1945; s. Lawrence Zane and Helen (Smith) F.; m. Kathleen Ann Burrill, July 9, 1982; children: John William Wright III, Jason Michael Wright. AA, St. John's U., 1965, BA, 1967; MA, Kean U., 1973; MBA, Cornell U., 1976; PhD, Walden U., 1993. Lic. real estate salesperson, notary pub. Adminstrv. resident N.Y. Hosp./Cornell Med. Ctr., N.Y.C., summer 1975; mgr. ophthalmology Hahnemann Med. Coll. & Hosp., Phila., 1976-77; dir. out-patient clinic USPHS Ctr. for Disease Control, Atlanta, 1977—78; project officer ambulatory care data systems USPHS Divsn. Hosps. and Clinics, West Hyattsville, Md., 1978-80; assoc. dir. ambulatory care USPHS Hosp., Boston, 1980-81; adminstr. family medicine Sch. of Medicine U. Tenn., Memphis, 1981-82; asst. v.p. customer svc./instnl. benefits Blue Cross/Blue Shield of N.Y., N.Y.C., 1982-86; assoc. v.p. ops. S.I. Hosp., 1986-87; assoc. dir. adminstrv. svcs. divsn. fed. employee occupl. health USPHS Region II, N.Y.C., 1988-89; health/resources and svcs. adminstr. Rockville, Md., 1989; materiel mgmt. officer, dep. br. chief, 1989; health care adminstr. individual ready rsch. USPHS, Rockville, 1989-90, chief program liaison unit, 1990-91, chief budget officer BOP/HSD, 1991-93, chief br. budget and mgmt. support, 1993-99; chief health svcs. officer Office of the Surgeon Gen./Pub. Health Svc., 1995-99; adminstrv. officer Fed. Med. Ctr., Fed. Bur. Prisons, Devens, Ayer, Mass., 1999-2000, quality risk mgr., 2000; health care adminstr. correctional med. svcs. MCI-Shirley-Medium, Mass., 2000—02; adminstr.-in-tng. Clark Manor Healthcare Ctr., 2002; asst. adminstr. Tower Hill Ctr. for Health and Rehab., Canton, Mass., 2002—03, Harborlights Nursing and Rehab. Ctr., 2002; interim adminstr. Avery Manor Rehab. and Nursing Ctr., Needham, Mass., 2003; adminstr. Linda Manor Extended Care Facility, Leeds, Mass., 2003—04; realtor Coldwell Banker Residential Brokerage Park Ave., Worcester, Mass., 2004—. Chmn. hosp. and med. care adminstrs. Health Care Profls. Adv. Com., 1989—91; co-chmn. centennial symposium planning com. Health Svcs. Officers, 1989; lectr. fiscal mgmt. Christian Bros. U., Memphis, 1982; lectr. health econs. grad. program in health svcs. adminstrn. Salve Regina Coll., Newport, RI, 1984; mem. assoc. grad. faculty, acad. advisor Ctrl. Mich. U. Coll. Extended Learning Health Svcs. Adminstrn., 1995—2004; adj. asst. prof. divsn. nursing rsch. Uniformed Svcs. U. Health Scis. Grad. Sch. Nursing, Bethesda, 1996—2001; adj. instr. Vanderbilt U. Sch. Nursing, Nashville, 1999—2005; sr. lectr. Western New Eng. Coll., Springfield, Mass., 2000—; bd. dirs. Nat. Commn. on Correctional Health Care, 1991—94, mem. program com., 1991—92, mem. publs. com., 1991—94, mem. exec. com., 1992—94, mng. editor Jour. Correctional Health Care, 1994—97; adj. asst. prof. preventive medicine and biometrics, Health Svcs. Adminstrn., Uniformed Svcs. U. of Health Scis., Bethesda, 1999—2001. Bd. dirs. Vis. Nurse Assn. Memphis, Inc., 1982; mem. cmty. adv. bd. Primary Health Care for Srs., Allston-Brighton Med. Care Coalition, Boston, 1981; usher coord. St. Michael's Cath. Ch., Poplar Springs, 1989-91; mem. ARC. Served with U.S. Army, 1968-71; capt. USPHS, 1977-81, 88-2001. Recipient Capt. Stanley J. Kissel, Jr. award USPHS/Health Svcs. Officer, 1994, Surgeon Gen.'s Exemplary Svc. medal USPHS, 1996, 99. Fellow: Am. Coll. Healthcare Execs. (editl. bd. Healthcare Execs. 1986—88, book reviewer Hosp. and Health Svcs. Adminstrn.), Am. Acad. Med. Adminstrs. (hon.); mem.: Worcester Regional Assn. Realtors (mem. edn. com. 2005—), Mass. Assn. Realtors, Nat. Assn. Realtors, Mil. Officers Assn. Am. (pres. Worcester (Mass.) county chpt. 2002—04), D.C.-Md.-Va. Hosp. Assn. (chmn. liaison com. 51st ann. conv. 1991), Commd. Officers Assn. USPHS (sec. Atlanta chpt. 1978), Assn. Mil. Surgeons U.S. (reviewer Mil. Medicine 1989—, cons.), Healthcare Mgmt. Assn. Mass., Assn. Health Care Adminstrs. Nat. Capital Area, Anchor and Caduceus Soc. (charter), Reserve Officers Assn. U.S. (newsletter editor Montgomery County chpt. 1989), KC (warden St. Michael's of Poplar Springs coun. 1990—91, chancellor 1991—92). Independent. Roman Catholic. Avocations: teaching, travel, writing, consulting. Home: 50 Deerfield Rd Shrewsbury MA 01545-1571 Office Phone: 508-635-6712. Personal E-mail: rgf4@cornell.edu. Business E-Mail: bob.falter@nemoves.com.

FALVEY, PATRICK JOSEPH, lawyer; b. Yonkers, N.Y., June 29, 1927; s. Patrick J. Falvey and Nora Rowley Falvey; m. Eileen Ryan, June 29, 1963; 1 child, Patrick James. Student, Iona Coll., 1944-47; JD cum laude, St. John's U., Jamaica, N.Y., 1950. Bar: N.Y. 1951, U.S. Supreme Ct. 1972. Law asst. Port Authority of N.Y. and N.J., 1951, atty., 1951-65, chief condemnation and litigation, 1965-67, asst. gen. counsel, 1967-72, gen. counsel, 1972-91, gen. counsel, asst. exec. dir., 1979-87, dep. exec. dir., 1987-91, spl. counsel, 1991—. Advisor U.S. del. to UN Com. on Internat. Trade Law, U.S. State Dept. Pvt. Trade Law; advisor to U.S. del. UN diplomatic confs. on treaty on liability of ops. of transport terminals, N.Y. County Lawyers Assn., 1992—. With USN, 1945-46. Recipient Howard S. Cullman Disting. Svc. medal Port Authority of N.Y. and N.J., 1982, 91; Loftus award and Trustee's Honoree Iona Coll., 1982. Fellow Am. Bar Found.; mem. ABA (chmn. urban state and local govt. law sect. 1983-84, vice-chmn. model procurement code project 1979—, sect. del. 1987-90, Award for Lifetime Achievement in Local Law 2000), Assn. Bar City N.Y., N.Y. County Lawyers Assn., Internat. Assn. Ports and Harbors (hon., legal counsellors, arbitrator, mediator trade and comml. matters, cons. transp. and trade studies). Address: PMB 81 Pondfield Rd Ste 338 Bronxville NY 10708-3818 Office Phone: 718-324-6244. Personal E-mail: woodlawnfalvey@aol.com.

FALWELL, JERRY L., minister; b. Lynchburg, Va., Aug. 11, 1933; s. Carey H. and Helen V. (Beasley) Falwell; m. Macel Pate, Apr. 12, 1958; children: Jerry L., Jeannie, Jonathan. BA, Bapt. Bible Coll., Springfield, Mo., 1956; DD (hon.), Tenn. Temple U.; LLD (hon.), Calif. Grad. Sch. Theology, Cen. U., Seoul, Korea. Founder, pastor Thomas Rd. Bapt. Ch., Lynchburg, Va., 1956—; founder Liberty U. (formerly Lynchburg Baptist Coll.), 1971, chancellor, 1971—; founder Moral Majority Inc., 1979—89; founder, nat. chmn. Moral Majority Coalition, 2004—. Host TV show Old Time Gospel Hour; lectr in field. Author: Listen, America!, 1980, The Fundamentalist Phenomenon, 1981, Finding Inner Peace and Strength, 1982, When It Hurts Too Much to Cry, 1984, Wisdom for Living, 1984, Stepping Out on Faith, 1984, Champions for God, 1985, IF I Should Die Before I Wake, 1986, Strength For the Journey, 1987, New American Family, 1992, Falwell: A Autobiography, 1997, Fasting Can Change Your Life, 1998, The How To Book: God's Principles for Mending Broken Lives, 1999, Disarming the Powers of Darkness: Personal Victory in the Spiritual World, 2002; co-author: Church Afflame, 1971, Capturing a Town for Christ, 1973. Named Christian Humanitarian of Yr., Food for the Hungry Internat., Number One Most Admired Conservative Man Not in Congress, Conservative Digest, 1983, Most Influential Ctrl. Virginian of 20th Century, News and Advance, Lynchburg, Va., 1999; named one of Most Influential People in Am., U.S. News & World Report, 1983, 10 Most Admired Men, Good Housekeeping, 1982, 1984, 1986; named to Hall of Fame, Nat. Religious Broadcasters, 1985; recipient Clergyman of Yr. award, Religious Heritage Am., 1979, Jabotinsky Centennial medal, 1980, Two Hungers award, Food for the Hungry Internat., 1981. Mem.: Nat. Assn. Religious Broadcasters (bd. dirs.). Baptist. Address: Liberty U 1971 University Blvd Lynchburg VA 24502-2269

FALZONE, KEITH EDWARD, emergency medical technician; b. Columbus, Ohio, Sept. 6, 1961; s. Edward William and Virgiania Lee (Verhoff) Kumler; m. Denise Marie Scheem, July 4, 2000. AA in interpreting, Columbus State Cmty. Coll., 1985. Cert. paramedic Grant Med. Ctr., 1991. Paramedic Delaware County EMS, Delaware, Ohio, 1993—96; newborn transport tech, paramedic Children's Hosp., Albuquerque, 1998—2000; flight paramedic U. N. Mes. Hosp., Albuquerque, 1996—2000; sign lang. interpretor, ednl. Fairbanks No. Star Sch. Dist., Fairbanks, Alaska, 2000—01; sign lang. interpretor, dir. The Bridge Interpreters Referral Svc. Inc., Fairbanks, 2000—; phlebotomist Fairbanks Meml. Hosp., Fairbanks, 2003—04, home med. equipment tech., 2004—. Interpreter for the deaf Columbus State Cmty. Coll., Columbus, 1983—93, Cmty. Ctr. for the Deaf, Columbus, 1985—88; paramedic Physicians Medic Transport, Columbus, Ohio, 1991—93. Author: Northern Lights Above, Distant Wispers Below, 2004. Mem.: Fire Dept. Honor Guard. Green Party. Avocations: walks with wife and dogs, jazz music appreciation, martial arts, contra dancing. Office Phone: 907-479-2205. Office Fax: 907-374-0351. E-mail: keithfalzone@hotmail.com.

FAMBROUGH, REINHARD EUGENE, director, music educator; b. Atlanta, Apr. 10, 1969; d. John Warren and Martha Heerman Fambrough; m. Anna Sheree Graves, Dec. 9, 2000; 1 child. B of Music Edn., U. Ga., 1993; MusM, East Carolina U., 1995; D of Musical Arts, U. Ala., 2002. Asst. dir. bands Oak Grove High Sch., Bessemer, Ala., 1998—2000, dir. bands, 2000—01; instr. percussion Mars Music, Birmingham, 1999—2001; asst. dir. band U. Ala., Birmingham, 2001—. Composer: Three Cycles, 1994, Digital Reflections, 2002, Distant Light, 2003. Mem. Prince Peace Sch. Bd., Hoover, Ala., 2003—04. Grantee, U. Ala. Birmingham, 2001—05. Mem.: Kappa Kappa Phi, Percussive Arts Soc. (tech. com.), Ala. Pervussive Arts Soc. (v.p. 2001—04), Pi Kappa Lambda. Roman Catholic. Avocations: reading, golf. Office: U Ala 950 13th St S Birmingham AL 35294

FAN, CHIEN, aerospace engineer, researcher; b. Haimen, China, Apr. 1, 1930; s. Chin Meng Fan and Shi Mei Shih; m. Ning Sun Chang, May 3, 1958; children: Albert W., May S., Marie S. BSME, Nat. Taiwan U., 1954; MSME, U. Ill., 1958, PhD, 1964. Asst. prof. Fla. State U., Tallahassee, 1961—65; rsch. specialist Lockheed Missiles and Space Co., Huntsville, Ala., 1965—74, staff engr. Sunnyvale, Calif., 1974—79, project engr., 1980—84, supr., 1985—91, sr. staff engr., 1989—94; ret., 1994. Vis. scientist to Republic of China NSF, Washington, 1970; lecturing scientist China Sci. and Tech. U., Hei-Fe, 1995. Contbr. articles to profl. publs. Chmn. bd. dirs. Fan Chin-Meng/Fan Heng Father/Son Scholarship Fund Found., Haimen, China, 1994—2004. Recipient Hdqrs. award, NASA, 1986, Hdqrs. award (2), 1994, The LMSC Pres. award, 1984. Mem.: AIAA, ASME, N.Y. Acad. Scis., Am. Soc. Engring. Edn., Sigma Xi, Pi Mu Epsilon. Achievements include development of Monte Carlo computer simulation techniques for molecular flow problems. Avocations: bridge, travel.

FAN, CHONGLUN, materials scientist, researcher; b. Beijing; B Engring., Beijing U. Sci. and Tech., 1982; PhD, Cath. U. Leuven, Belgium, 1990. Invited rschr. Polytechnic Inst., U. Montreal, Canada, 1990—95; mem. tech. staff Lucent Technologies, Bell Labs, Electroplating Chemicals and Svcs., Murray Hill, NJ, 1995—99; R&D prin. investigator Lucent Technologies, Electroplating Chemicals and Svcs., S.I., NY, 1999—2002; sr. scientist Cookson Electronics, Enthone Inc., Jersey City, 2002—. Contbr. articles to profl. jours. Recipient Johnson Matthey medal award, Trans. Inst. Metal Finishing, 1999, Best U.S. Tech. Paper award, APEX, 2002, 2004. Mem.: Surface Mt. Tech. Assn., Am. Electroplaters and Surface Finishers Soc. Achievements include 9 U.S. patents granted; 5 U.S. patents pending. Office: Cookson Electronics 600 Route 440 Jersey City NJ 07304 Business E-Mail: clfan@cooksonelectronics.com.

FAN, CONG, music educator; d. Shi-Huang Fan and Feng-Li Guo. Mus D Arts, Temple U., Phila., 2000—03, MusM Arts, 1998—2000; MusB Arts, Ctrl. Conservatory of Music, Beijing, China, 1993—97. Opera coach Nat. Opera Ho. of China, Beijing, 1997—98; piano tchr. Ctrl. Conservatory of Music, Beijing, 1997—98; opera coach Temple U., Phila., 1998—2000, piano tchr., 2000—, recital accompanist, 2000—, part-time faculty, 2003—. Ch. organist United Meth. Ch., Phila., 1998—; concert pianist Rotary Clubs, Phila., 2000—, Music Teachers Nat. Assn., Phila., 2000—, Piano Teachers Congress of NY, New York, NY, 2002—. Recipient William A. Singer Meml. Award, Temple U., 1999; fellow Martha Ellen Fisher Tye Fellowship, Am. Inst. of Musical Studies, 2002; scholar Kennedy Music Scholarship, Am. Embassy, 2001, Ann. Full-tuition Scholarship, Temple U., 1998-2003, Ann. Tchg. Assistantship, 1998-2003. Mem.: Music Teachers Nat. Assn. (licentiate; cin. 2000—03), Pi Kappa Lambda Music Soc. (hon.; phila. 1999—2003, first prize 1999), Nat. Music Honor Soc. (hon.; phila. 1999—2003, first prize 1999). Achievements include Winning of Frinna Awerbuch International Piano Competition; Winning of Pennsylvania Piano Competition; Winning of Pi Kappa Lambda Competition; Winning of Young Artist's Competition; Winning of Competition's of Chinese Piano Compositions. Avocations: travel, aerobics, walking.

FAN, GUANGWEI, seismologist; b. Tianjin, China; arrived in U.S., 1986; s. Jingtao and Jingli (Wang) F.; m. Lin Guo; 1 child, Diana Ying. PhD, U. Ariz., 1992. Tchg./rsch. asst. N.Mex. State U., Las Cruces, 1986-89; rsch. assoc. U. Ariz., Tucson, 1990-92, rsch. scientist, 1992-96; postgrad. rschr. U. Calif., Santa Cruz, 1996—. Editl. bd. Seismol. Abstract, Beijing, 1979-86; contbr. articles to profl. jours. Recipient Amoco prize Amoco Corp., 1992. Mem. Am. Geophys. Union, Seismol. Soc. Am., Sigma Pi Sigma. Avocations: music, reading. Office: IGPP Dept of Earth Sci U Calif Santa Cruz 1156 High St Santa Cruz CA 95064

FAN, LIANG-SHIH, chemical engineering educator; BS, Nat. Taiwan U., 1970; MS, West Va. Univ., 1973, PhD, 1975; MS in Statistics (with honors), Kansas State Univ., 1978. Disting. Univ. prof. dept. chem. engring., C. John Easton prof. in engring. Ohio State U., Columbus. Recipient Alexander von Humboldt Rsch. award for U.S. Sr. Scientists, 1993, Institution Eminent Spkr. award, Institution Engrs., Australia, 1994, Thomas Baron award in fluid-particle sys. AIChE, 1994, Alpha Chi Sigma award AIChE for Chem. Engring., 1996, Union Carbide Lectureship award Chem. Engring. Divsn. ASEE, 1999, Malcolm E. Pruitt award, Coun. for Chem. Rsch., 2000. Mem. NAE. Office: Ohio State U Dept Chem Engring 140 W 19th Ave Columbus OH 43210-1110 E-mail: fan@chbmeng.ohio-state.edu.

FAN, LIANG-SHING, economics educator; b. Taoynan, Taiwan, June 18, 1932; s. Chung-Chang and Chien-Moi Fan; m. Chuen-mei Lee, Dec. 22, 1965; children: Elliot T., Frieda T. BA, Nat. Taiwan U., 1956; MA, U. Minn., 1960, PhD, 1965. Instr. U. Minn., Mpls., 1962-64; asst. prof. Kans. State U., Manhattan, 1964-68; assoc. prof. Colo. State U., Ft. Collins, 1968-72, prof. econs., 1972—. Vis. asst. prof. U. Minn., Mpls., summer 1965, 66, vis. assoc. prof., summer 1969; vis. prof. People's U., Beijing, 1987, Fudan U., Shanghai, 1992; Fulbright prof. Nat. Cheng-Chi, U., Taipei, 1977-78. Mem. Am. Econ. Assn., So. Econ. Assn., Western Econ. Assn., Taiwan Econ. Assn. Avocation: fishing. Home: 1504 Teakwood Ct Fort Collins CO 80525-1954 Office: Colo State U Dept Econs C312 Clark Fort Collins CO 80523-0001

FAN, PENG, mathematician; s. Chuang-Tu and Sun-Fen Fan; m. Li-Chih Wang, June 8, 1974; 1 child, DerZen. BS, Nat. Taiwan Normal U., 1970; MS, Nat. Tsing Hua U., 1972; PhD, Ind. U., 1980. Assoc. prof. Tex. Christian U., Fort Worth, 1983—. Vis. assoc. prof. Nat. Chiao Tung U., Hsing Chu, Taiwan, 1989—90. Contbr. articles to profl. jours. Grantee, NRC, Taipei, Taiwan, 1989—90. Mem.: Am. Math. Soc. (reviewer 1983—, translator 1983—). Avocations: ping pong/table tennis, tennis, racquetball. Office: Tex Christian U Dept Math Box 298900 Fort Worth TX 76129 Office Phone: 817-257-6195. E-mail: p.fan@tcu.edu.

FAN, SHIRLEY TSUI-YU, music educator; b. Taipei, Taiwan, July 12, 1964; arrived in U.S., 1984; d. David Fan and Mary Tseng Fan; m. Robert Kao, Oct. 29, 1988; children: Amy Kao, Wilson Kao, Kenneth Kao. MusB, Juilliard Sch. Music, 1989; MusM, Rider U., 1996. Cert. music tchr. N.J. Cashier Tangy Fast Food Restaurant, N.Y.C., 1985—88; receptionist, clk. comm. office Juilliard Sch. Music, N.Y.C., 1985—88; tchr. Chinese Zi-Sen Chinese Sch., Queens, NY, 1985—88; piano tchr. Golden Rhythmic Music Sch., Queens, 1989—95; piano artist faculty mem. Westminster Conservatory, Princeton, NJ, 1995—2001; piano chmn. Piano Tchr. Forum of Ctrl. Jersey, 2003—; pvt. piano tchr. Edison, NJ. Tchr. New Sch. Music, Kingston, NJ, 1994—97. Mem.: N.J. Chinese Music Tchrs. (publicity events com. 2004—), Piano Tchrs. Soc. Am., N.J. Music Tchrs. Assn. (piano chmn. 2000—), Edison Music Club. Home: 12 Rolling Brook Dr Edison NJ 08820 Fax: 908-668-8628. Office Phone: 908-294-3266. E-mail: shirleyfanty@yahoo.com.

FAN, WEIGUO, technology professor, researcher; PhD, U. Mich., 2002. Asst. prof. Va. Tech, Blacksburg, Va., 2002—. Office: Virginia Tech 3007 Pamplin Hall Blacksburg VA 24061 Office Phone: 540-231-6588. E-mail: wfan@vt.edu.

FANAROFF, AVROY A., pediatrician, educator; b. 1937; MD, South Africa, 1960; MD (hon.), U. Witwatersrand, Johannesburg, South Africa, 2004. Bd. cert. med. oncology. Eliza Henry Barnes prof. pediat. Case Western Res. U. Sch. Medicine, Cleve., prof. neonatology and reproductive biology; chair dept. pediat. U. Hosps. Cleve., 2003—. Author: The Year Book of Neonatal and Perinatal Medicine, 1990, 1991, 1992, 1994, 1998, 2002, Neonatal-Perinatal Medicine: Diseases of the Fetus and Infant, 2001, Care of the High-Risk Neonate, 2001. Recipient Nat. Neonatology Edn. award, Am. Assn. Pediat., 1999, Virginia Apgar award, 2002. Fellow: Royal Coll. Pediat. and Child Health (hon.). Avocations: golf, tennis. Office: Case Western Res Univ Sch Medicine Pediat 11100 Euclid Ave 784 Cleveland OH 44106-6003 Office Phone: 216-884-3884. Business E-Mail: aaf2@curu.edu.

FANCHER, EVELYN PITTS, librarian; b. Marion, Ala.; d. D.C. and Nell Lenora Pitts; B.S., Ala. State U., 1946; M.S.L.S., Atlanta U., 1961; Ed.S., George Peabody Coll., 1969, Ph.D., 1975; m. Charles B. Fancher, Dec. 20, 1947; children— Charles B., Mark Pitts, Adrienne Lenore. Tchr. biology, chemistry public schs., Marion, Ala., 1946-56; library tech. asst. A&M U., Huntsville, 1956; dir. media center Council High Sch., Huntsville, Ala., 1959-62; circulation, reference librarian, instr. Tenn. State U., Nashville, 1962-74, dir. univ. library, 1976—; cons. Tenn. State Library Adv. Bd. on Libraries, 1983-85. Bd. dirs. Tenn. Girl Scouts U.S.A., 1982-85. Mem. ALA, Southeastern Library Assn., Tenn. Library Assn., (pres. 1984-85), Mid State Library Assn., Nashville Library Club, AAUW, Phi Delta Kappa. Baptist. Home: 3948 Drakes Branch Rd Nashville TN 37218-1846

FANCHER, MICHAEL REILLY, editor, publishing executive; b. Long Beach, Calif., July 13, 1946; s. Eugene Arthur and Ruth Leone (Dickson) F.; m. Nancy Helen Edens, Nov. 3, 1967 (div. 1982); children: Jason Michael, Patrick Reilly; m. 2d Carolyn Elaine Bowers, Mar. 25, 1983; Katherine Claire, Elizabeth Lynn. BA, U. Oreg., 1968; MS, Kans. State U., 1971; MBA, U. Wash., 1986. Reporter, asst. city editor Kansas City Star, Mo., 1970-76, city editor, 1976-78; reporter Seattle Times, 1978-79, night city editor, 1979-80, asst. mng. editor, 1980-81, mng. editor, 1981-86, exec. editor, 1986—, v.p., exec. editor, 1989-95; sr. v.p., 1995—. Bd. dirs. Blethen Maine Newspapers, Walla Walla Union-Bulletin, Yakima Herald Rep. Ruhl fellow Hall of Achievement, U. Oreg., 1983 Mem. Am. Soc. Newspaper Editors, Soc. Profl. Journalists, Nat. Press Photographers Assn. (Editor of Yr. 1986). Office: Seattle Times PO Box 70 1120 John St Seattle WA 98111-0070 Business E-Mail: mfancher@seattletimes.com.

FANELLI, MICHAEL PAUL, musician, educator, writer; b. Evanston, Ill., Feb. 12, 1943; s. George and Gloria (Del Carlo) F.; m. Carla Jean Saiger, May 28, 1978. BMus, U. Ill., 1968, EdD in Music Edn., 2001; MA in Music History, U. Mo., 1981. Cert. tchr. K-12, Webster U. Instr. music U. Ill., 1963—67, U. Mo., Columbia, 1968-74; instr. music, artist-in-residence Stephens Coll., Columbia, 1968-75; profl. double bassist Chgo. Sinfonetta, 1963—65, Mo. Symphony Soc., 1973—78, Gateway Festival Orchestra, 1978—84, St. Louis String Enselble, 1978—87, St. Louis Philharmonic, 1983—87, Champaign-Urbana Symphony Orchestra, 1992—94; instr. instrumental music Sch. Dist. of the City of Ladue, Mo., 1983-87; instr. music U. No. Iowa, Cedar Falls, 1987—2002, asst. prof. distance learning Iown Comms. Network, 1995—, asst. prof. dept. ednl. psychology & foundations, 2002—; instr. of double bass Grinnell (Iowa) Coll., 1996—, U. No. Iowa Skuki Sch., 2001—. Founder, music dir. No. Iowa Jr. Orchestra, Cedar Falls, 1990-92; music dir. No. Iowa Youth Orchestra, 1994—2001; adv. bd. Iowa Alliance for Arts Edn., Des Moines, 1994—2001; presenter in field. Contbr. articles to profl. jours.; contbg. author: American String Teacher, 1997. Double bassist U. Ill., U.S. State Dept. tour of S.Am., 1964. Microcomputer grantee U. No. Iowa, Cedar Falls, 1989, 92, 95-98, 2005. Mem. Iowa String Tchrs. Assn. (editor 1988-92, pres. 1996-98, historian 2004-, Disting. Svc. award 1992, Cert. for Outstanding Contbn. 1996), Iowa Sch. Orchestra Assn. (pres. 1992-96), Am. String Tchrs. Assn. (editl. com. 1997—2005, columns editor, reviewer 2005-, Outstanding Contbr. 1995-97, 99, 2003), Suzuki Assn. of the Americas (column editor 1992-, double base com. 1992-), Mo. String Tchrs. Assn. (sec.-treas. 1983-87), Kappa Delta Pi, Phi Kappa Delta, Phi Kappa Lambda, Phi Mu Alpha. Avocations: American art history, photography, fly fishing, painting. Home: 203 Parkgate Rd Cedar Falls IA 50613-1953 Office: Univ No Iowa Schindler Edn Ctr Cedar Falls IA 50613 Business E-Mail: michael.fanelli@uni.edu.

FANETTI, MARY-JUNE, writer, editor; b. Oklahoma City, June 22, 1921; d. Robert and Catherine Quinn; m. Donald Louis Fanetti, Nov. 23, 1940; children: Donald Louis Jr., Donna Louise, Robert Adam, Dennis Lee, Mary-June II, Dale Louise, JoAnn Marie, Daniel Louis, David Lee, Dina Marie. Attended, St. Elizabeth Acad., St. Louis. Owner Quinn Linoleum and Wallpaper, St. Louis, 1945; co-founder, owner Bugle Newspaper & Printing, St. Louis, 1945-77, owner, editor, 1977-86; columnist Bugle Newspaper, St. Louis, 1986-96; columnist, roving editor Network News, St. Louis, 1996—. Columnist Matter of Opinion, Lotta Baloney Sezs. Roman Catholic. Avocations: reading, writing. Home: PO Box 6595 Saint Louis MO 63125-0595 Office: Network News 7832 Ivory at Primm Saint Louis MO 63111-3532

FANG, CHENG-SHEN, chemical engineering professor; b. Taipei, Taiwan, Mar. 29, 1936; came to U.S., 1962; s. Hou-Chin and Roumouy Fang; m. Fei-Ying Fang, Oct. 5, 1972. BSChemE, Nat. Taiwan U., Taipei, 1958; MSChemE, U. Houston, 1965, PhD in Chem. Engring., 1968. Registered profl. engr., La. Postdoctoral fellow U. Houston, 1968-69; prof. chem. engring. U. La., Lafayette, 1969—. Presenter in field. Co-author: Oceanography-Contemporary Reading, 1996; creater (computer software) ChemCalc 2, ChemCalc 3, 1985; contbr. articles to profl. jours. Mem. AIChE, Soc. Petroleum Engrs. Office: U La Dept Chem Engring Madison Hall Rex St Lafayette LA 70504-4130 Office Phone: 337-482-5350. Personal E-mail: csfang@att.net. Business E-Mail: fangcs@louisiana.edu.

FANG, JOONG, philosopher, mathematician, educator; b. Piongyang, Korea, Mar. 30, 1923; arrived in U.S., 1948, naturalized, 1962; s. Gabiong and Igab (Kim) Fang; children: Eva Maria, Guido Andreas. Student, Chuo U.,

Tokyo, 1939-41; BS, Coll. Tech. Seoul, Korea, 1944; MA, Yale U., 1950; PhD, U. Mainz, Germany, 1957. Asst. prof. math. Jinhae Coll., also U. Pusan, Republic of Korea, 1945-48, Valparaiso (Ind.) U., 1958-59, St. John's U., 1959-61, U. Alaska, 1961-62; assoc. prof. No. Ill. U., 1963-67; prof. math. and philosophy Memphis State U., 1967-73; prof. philosophy Old Dominion U., Norfolk, Va., 1974-90, prof. emeritus, 1990—. Vis. prof. U. Münster, Germany, 1971. Author: (book) Das Antinomienproblem, 1957, Abstract Algebra, 1963, Kant-Interpretation, I, 1967, Numbers Racket: The Aftermath of the "New Math", 1968, Towards a Philosophy of Modern Mathematics, I, Bourbaki, 1970, II, Hilbert, 1970, Mathematicians from Antiquity to Today, I, 1972, Sociology of Mathematics and Mathematicians, 1975, The Illusory Infinite: A Theology of Mathematics, 1976, Logic Today, Basics and Beyond, 1979, Linguistic Sense of the Japanese (in Japanese), 1984, Kant and Mathematics Today, 1997, Learning, East and West, 2002, Docta Ignorantia, 2003, Ecrasez l'Infame!, 2004; editor: Philosophia Mathematica, 1964—92. Mem.: Am. Philos. Assn., Am. Math. Soc. Address: 9745 Oakview Dr North VA 23128-9041

FANG, XIANGYU, materials scientist; m. Yi Zhou, July 22, 1993; 1 child, Ziheng. BS in Materials sci. and Engring., East China U. Chem. Tech., 1984; MS in Materials sci. and Engring., Shanghai Inst. Ceramics, Chinese Acad. Scis., 1990; PhD of Ceramic Engring., U. Mo.-Rolla, 2000. Asst. lectr. East China U. Chem. Tech., Shanghai, 1984—87; sr. rsch. assoc. Shanghai Inst. Ceramics, Chinese Acad. Scis., 1987—96; sr. vis. scholar Grad. Ctr. Materials Rsch. and Ceramic Engring. Dept. U. Mo.-Rolla, 1996—98, rsch. asst. Grad. Ctr. Materials and Ceramic Engring. Dept., 1998—2000; sr. r&d engr. Mo-Sci Corp., Rolla, 2000; sr. engr. Axt Inc., Fremont, Calif., 2000—. Vis. scholar U. Newcastle Upon Tyne, England, 1994. Mem.: Am. Chem. Soc. (licentiate), Am. Ceramic Soc. (licentiate). Achievements include development of new wafer process techniques for semi-conducting materials, such as GaAs, InP and Sapphire wafers; research in providing novel information about the processing and properties of the chemical duable and mechanically strong iron phosphate glasses to be used in nuclear waster dispose and new fiber generation; a novel composition and processing of the oxynitride glass and glass-ceramics to be used as the grain boundary in the high temperature structural materials; composition and processing of the transparent glass-ceramics with the nano-sized mullite crystals used in tunable lasers and in solar concentrator applications; novel technique to determine the nucleation rate and crystal growth rate in glass by using the tool of Differential Thermal Analysis (DTA); coordinated project for designing and adjusting of the first glass-ceramic production line in China. Office: AXT Inc 4487 Technology Dr Fremont CA 94538 Office Phone: 510-438-4737. E-mail: xiangyu_fang@yahoo.com.

FANGER, DONALD LEE, Slavic language and literature educator; b. Cleve., Dec. 6, 1929; s. Max Leon and Rae (Bercu) F.; m. Margot Taylor, June 18, 1955; children: Steffen, Ross, Katharine. BA, U. Calif., Berkeley, 1951, MA, 1954; PhD, Harvard U., 1962. Mem. faculty Brown U., 1960-66, assoc. prof. Slavic langs. and lit., 1964-66; assoc. prof. Slavic langs., dir. div. Stanford U., 1966-68; prof. Slavic and comparative lit. Harvard U., 1968-98, chmn. dept. Slavic langs and lits., 1973-82, Harry Levin rsch. prof. lit., 1998—2003. Mem. bd. syndics Harvard U. Press, 1968-73. Author: Dostoevsky and Romantic Realism, 1965, The Creation of Nikolai Gogol, 1979; editor: Brown U. Slavic Reprint Series, 1962-66. Mem. program com. Internat. Rsch. and Exchanges Bd., 1968-69, 70-73. With AUS, 1953-55. Guggenheim Found. fellow, 1975-76. Mem. Am. Acad. Arts and Scis., Acad. Lit. Studies, Internat. Comparative Lit. Assn. Office: Harvard U Widener Study L Cambridge MA 02138 Home: 75 Richdale Ave Ste 3 Cambridge MA 02140-2608 Office Phone: 617-495-4092. E-mail: fanger@fas.harvard.edu.

FANGER, MICHAEL W., medical educator; b. Ft. Wayne, Ind., July 3, 1940; BA in Chemistry and Zoology, Wabash Coll., 1962; PhD in Biochemistry, Yale U., 1967. NIH postdoctoral fellow Nat. Inst. Med. Rsch., London, 1967-68, U. Ill. Med. Sch., Chgo., 1968-70; from asst. prof. to assoc. prof. microbiology Case Western Res. U., Cleve., 1970-81; faculty dept. immunology Middlesex Hosp., London, 1977-78; prof. microbiology and medicine Dartmouth Med. Sch., Lebanon, N.H., 1981—, chmn. dept. microbiology, 1992—2002, dir. immunology program, 1981-92. Dir. immunology program Norris Cotton Cancer Ctr., 1984-92, dir. monoclonal antibody libr., 1984-2000; cons. Verax Corp., Lebanon, 1982-87, mem. sci. adv. bd., 1984-87; founder Medarex Inc., Annandale, N.J., 1987, dir., 1987-2004, chmn. sci. adv. bd., cons., 1987-2004. Contbr. numerous articles to profl. jours.; patentee in field. Mem. Am. Assn. Immunologists. Office: Dartmouth Med Sch Dept Microbiology 1 Medical Center Dr Lebanon NH 03756-0001

FANGEROW, KAY ELIZABETH, nurse; b. Thomas, Okla., June 27, 1952; d. Byron Frederick and Wilma Jean (Bickford) Mayfield; children: David Andrew, Sarah Elizabeth. Student, Oral Roberts U., 1970-71; BS in Nursing magna cum laude, Calif. State U., Long Beach, 1975; MS in Health Care Adminstrn., U. LaVerne, 1991. RN, Calif.; cert. pub. health nurse. Staff nurse pediatrics service Long Beach Meml. Hosp., 1974-75, Riverside (Calif.) Community Hosp., 1975-76, Parkview Community Hosp., Riverside, 1982-84; supervising pub. health nurse County Health Dept., San Bernardino, Calif., 1976—, coord. sch. based and sch. linked health care svcs., 1994—; dir. Westside Park Sch. Based Health Ctr. FQHC Clinic, 2002; grant writer County Health Dept., San Bernardino, Calif., 1994—. Cons. Am. Home Health, Santa Ana, Calif., 1986—2000. Instr. Inland Counties chpt. Am. Cancer Soc., Riverside, 1977—; mem. cmty. action coun. San Bernardino County Youth Justice Ctr., 1999—; chair child death rev. team San Bernardino County, 2005—. Mem. Am. Pub. Health Assn. (co-author abstract 1986, 87, 89, coordinator hypertension worksite project, diabetes control project, pub. health nursing homeless project, presenter ann. meeting 1986, 87, 89), Pub. Health Nurse Group (chmn. 1977-78, vice chmn. profl. performance com. 1978, sec. peer rev. com. 1978), San Bernardino County Asthma Coalition, Sigma Theta Tau (Gamma Alpha chpt., honoree for child abuse prevention supervising pub. health nurse of yr. 2002) San Bernardino County Child Death Review Team (chair, 2005). Democrat. Home: 555 Oak Hill St Ontario CA 91761 Office Phone: 909-388-0479. Business E-Mail: kfangerow@dph.sbcounty.gov.

FANIZZA, JOANNE, lawyer; b. Bklyn., Jan. 22, 1957; d. John Carmelo and Mary Carmela (Spadafora) F. BA, U. Fla., 1981, JD, 1987. Bar: Fla., U.S. Dist. Ct. (so. dist.) Fla. 1988, U.S. Ct. Appeals (5th and 11th cirs.) 1988, U.S. Dist. Ct. (mid. dist.) Fla. 1989, U.S. Supreme Ct. 1997. Newspaper editor and reporter Ft. Lauderdale (Fla.) News/Sun-Sentinel, 1977-79, 1981-85; newspaper reporter, editor Gainesville (Fla.) Sun, 1979-81, 1985-86; assoc. Ferrero & Middlebrooks, P.A., Ft. Lauderdale, 1988-94, Law Offices of Joanne Fanizza, P.A., Ft. Lauderdale, 1995—. Adj. prof Broward C.C., Coconut Creek, Fla., 1988-91; Broward County Commn. on Status of Women, 2000-02. Rsch. editor U. Fla. Jour. of Law and Pub. Policy, 1986-87. Mem. city coun. City of Wilton Manors, 1998—2002, mem. bd. adjustment, 1992—98, chair bd. adjustment, 1993—98; mem. Wilton Manors Bus. Assn., Tropical Pines Civic Assn.; bd. dirs., sec. Abandoned Pet Rescue, Inc., 1996—. Recipient Am. Jurisprudence award constitutional law AmJur, 1986, spl. citation John Marshall Bar Assn., 1987; named one of Outstanding Young Women of Am., 1982, Atty. of Yr., 1998, 2003, Broward Lawyers Care, Best of the Bar, 2004, Pres.' Pro Bono Svc. award South Fla. Bus. Jour., 17th Jud. Cir., 2005. Mem. ABA, Broward County Trial Lawyers Assn. (bd. govs. 1995-2004), Broward County Bar Assn., Broward Lawyers Care (pro bono). Democrat. Avocations: sports, cooking, travel. Office: Law Offices Joanne Fanizza PA 1995 E Oakland Park Blvd Ste 210 Fort Lauderdale FL 33306-1623 Office Phone: 954-565-5445. Fax: 954-565-1941. E-mail: jfanizza@bellsouth.net.

FANN, MARGARET ANN, counselor; b. Pasco, Wash., July 16, 1942; d. Joseph Albert David and Clarice Mable (Deaver) Rivard; m. Jerry Lee Fann, June 13, 1986; children: Brenda Heupel, Scott Sherman, Kristin Johnson, Robert Lack III. AA, Big Bend C.C., Moses Lake, Wash., 1976; BA in Applied Psychology magna cum laude, Ea. Wash. U., 1977, MS in Psychology, 1978. Cert. mental health counselor, Wash.; cert. chem. dependency counselor II, nat. cert. addictions counselor II, cert. in chronic psychiat. disability. Intern counselor Linker House Drug Rehab., Spokane, Wash., 1976-78; drug counselor The House drug program, Tacoma, Wash., 1978-80; exec. dir. Walla Walla (Wash.) Commn. Alcohol, 1980-82; dir. Cmty. Alcohol Svcs. Assn., Kennewick, Wash., 1982-86; primary care coord. Carondelet Psychiat. Care Ctr., Richland, Wash., 1986-90; part-time instr. Ea. Wash. U., Cheney, 1981-88; instr. Columbia Basin Coll., Pasco, 1990-93; adminstr. Action Chem. Dependency Ctr., Kennewick, 1993—. Bd. dirs. Benton-Franklin County Substance Abuse Coalition, Pasco, Kennewick, Richland, 1990—. Vol. Pat Hale for Senator, Kennewick, 1994. Mem. Am. Counselors Assn., Nat. Mental Health Counselors Assn., Wash. State Mental Health Counselors Assn., Tri-Cities Counselors Assn., Phi Theta Kappa. Avocations: swimming, bicycling, running. Office: Action Chem Dependency Ctr 552 N Colorado St Ste 5525 Kennewick WA 99336-7779 also: Benton-Franklin County MICA Detoxification Ctr 1020 E 7th Ave Kennewick WA 99336-5936

FANN, TERRY ANDREW, lawyer; b. Franklin, Tenn., July 22, 1961; s. Hayes A. and Margaret E. (Smithson) F.; m. Vicki Raikes, June 25, 1983; children: Lee Andrew, Steven Chase. BS, U. Tenn., 1983; JD, Memphis State U., 1987. Bar: Tenn. 1988, U.S. Dist. Ct. (mid. dist.) Tenn. 1988, U.S. Ct. Appeals (6th cir.) 1988, cert. Civil Trial Splist. 1995. Asst. to treas. Murfreesboro (Tenn.) Prodn. Credit Union, 1983-85; law clerk Wampler, Pierce, Hagemeyer, Memphis, 1986-87; extern U.S. Attys. Office, Memphis, 1987; law clerk Shelby County Cir. Ct., Memphis, 1987; atty. Waldron & Fann, Murfreesboro, Tenn., 1988—. Mem. Tenn. Supreme Ct Bd. Profl. Responsibility Hearing Com., 2005. Mem. ABA, ATLA, Rutherford County Bar Assn., Tenn. Bar Assn., Tenn. Trial Lawyers Assn., Tenn. Assn. Criminal Def. Attys., Nat. Assn. Criminal Def. Lawyers, Outstanding Lawyers Am. Baptist. Office: Waldron & Fann 202 W Main St Murfreesboro TN 37130-3581 Office Phone: 615-890-7365. E-mail: tfann@bellsouth.net.

FANNIN, DAVID CECIL, lawyer; b. Catlettsburg, Ky., Feb. 5, 1946; s. Cecil and Marie (Conley) F.; m. Lucille Ann Stewart, Jan. 1, 1985; children: Christopher, Brian, Catherine. BA, U. Ky., 1968, JD, 1973; MA, U. Ill., 1971. Bar: Ky. 1974. Assoc. Wyatt, Tarrant & Combs, Louisville, 1974-79, ptnr., 1979—93; authorized house counsel Fla., 1994; exec. v.p., gen. counsel Sunbeam Corp., 1994—98; sr. v.p., gen. counsel Office Depot, Inc., Delray Beach, Fla., 1998—2000, exec. v.p., gen. counsel, 2000—. Bd. advisors VenuLex Corp. Woodrow Wilson fellow, 1968. Mem. ABA, Ky. Bar Assn., Lousville Bar Assn, Am. Corp. Counsel Assn., Am. Soc. Corp. Secretaries, Phi Beta Kappa, Order of the Coif. Democrat. Baptist. Avocations: music, running. Office: Office Depot Inc Legal Dept 2200 Old Germantown Rd Delray Beach FL 33445-8299

FANNIN, JOSEPHINE JEWELL, social services administrator; b. W.Va., Feb. 12, 1944; Student, Davis Coll., Am. Inst. Banking, L.A., 1962-65, Nat. Floral Inst., 1966-68; lic., Bucks Coll., Newtown, Pa., 1984; AAS in Human Svcs., Ariz. Western Coll., 1994; MA in human svc., U. of Wexford, 2000, PhD in Human Svc. Leadership Mgmt., 2004. Women's program dir. for Europe, USN, Rota, Spain, 1976-77; with mktg. svcs. dept. Bank of Am., Fairfield, Calif., 1962-65; comml. accounts specialist Commerce Bank, St. Charles, Mo., 1970-73, 75-76, comml. accounts rep., 80-82, Pa. Nat. Bank, Phila., 1978-81; info. and referral field nurse Upjohn Health Care, Newtown, 1982-85, info. and referral specialist Jacksonville, Fla., 1985-89; dir. vol. and ret. sr. vol. program Western Ariz. Coun. Govts., Yuma, 1992-94; sr. program adminstr. Mid East Area Agy. on Aging, Brentwood, Mo., 1994-99; exec. dir. Hosp. Hospitality Ho., Huntington, W.Va., 1999—. Spkr. Internat. Platform Assn., 1985-95. Bd. dirs. Ch. Women United, Bucks County, Pa., 1980-85, Yuma Regional Med. Ctr., 1992-94; bd. dirs., mem. fin. com. Jacksonville and Yuma hospices, 1985-94; ombudsman adv. Western Ariz. Coun. Govts., 1989-94; mem. adv. bd. vol. clearing house and human svcs. program St. Charles C.C., 1995, bd. dirs., 1997; exec. dir. Hosp. Hospitality House, 1999—; bd. dirs. St. Charles Cmty. Coun., 1997, City of Huntington Found., 2000. Recipient Outstanding Employee award Western Coun. Govts., 1994. Mem. AAUW, Assn. Fundraising Profls., Nat. Soc. Fund Raising Execs., Zonta (past bd. dirs. and program dir. Yuma), Rotary Internat. (bd. dirs.), Phi Theta Kappa (Alumni award 1994). Avocations: travel, writing, speaking on current events and senior advocacy and volunteer programs. Office: Hosp Hospitality House 2801 S Staunton Rd Huntington WV 25702 Home: 1661 Washington Blvd Huntington WV 25701 E-mail: huntingtonhhh@aol.com.

FANNING, BARRY HEDGES, lawyer; b. Olney, Tex., Dec. 5, 1950; s. Robert Allen and Carolyn (Parker) F.; m. Rebecca Sue Cobbs, May 24, 1975 (dec. Mar. 1997); m. Sherri Winn Perry, Mar. 6, 1999. BBA, Baylor U., 1972, LL.B., 1973. Bar: Tex. 1973, Fla. 1974, U.S. Dist. Ct. (no., ea. we. and so. dists.) Tex. 1974, U.S. Ct. Appeals (5th and 11th cirs.) 1974. Mem. firm Fanning, Harper & Martinson, Dallas, 1974—. Social v.p. Dallas Symphony Orch. Guild, 1975-77; mem. Dallas Regional Young Life Bd., 1977—, fund raising chmn., 1982-84, 86-88, 97—; bd. dirs., membership/mktg. com., Downtown YMCA, 1997—, chmn. cmty. svcs. fund dr., 2003; mem. Russell Perry Free Enterprise Banquet Com., chmn., 2004; mem. Dallas Bapt. U.; mem. Miss Tex. Pageant Bd., 2003—. Recipient Sam Winstead award, YMCA, 2005. Mem. ABA (vice chmn. young lawyers com. 1980, pub. rels. com. torts sect.), Baylor U. Student Found. (steering com. 1971-72), Baylor Alumni Assn. (bd. dirs. 1978-82, 95), Tryon Coterie (pres. 1971), Highland Park Forensics Found. (pres. 1993-95), Preston Ctr. Legal Assn. (sec. 1993-94, bd. dirs. 1994-95), Dervish Club, Calyx Club, Dallas Baylor Club (bd. dirs. 1976-84, pres. 1981-82), Christian Men's Club, Phi Eta Sigma, Omicron Kappa Delta, Phi Delta Theta. Baptist. Home: 4400 Lorraine Dallas TX 75205 Office: Fanning Harper & Martinson 4849 Greenville Ave Ste 1300 Dallas TX 75206 Office Phone: 972-860-0327. E-mail: bfanning@fhmlaw.com.

FANNING, DAKOTA, actress; b. Conyers, Ga., Feb. 23, 1994; d. Steve and Joy Fanning. Actor: (films) Tomcats, 2001, I Am Sam, 2001 (Best Young Actor/Actress award Broadcast Film Critics Assn.), Father Xmas, 2001, Trapped, 2002, Sweet Home Alabama, 2002, Hansel & Gretel, 2002, Uptown Girls, 2003, The Cat in the Hat, 2003, Man on Fire, 2004, Hide and Seek, 2005, Nine Lives, 2005, War of the Worlds, 2005, (voice): (TV films) Kim Possible: A Stitch in Time, 2003,: (TV miniseries) Taken, 2002, (guest appearances): (TV series) ER, 2000, Ally McBeal, 2000, Strong Medicine, 2000, CSI: Crime Scene Investigation, 2000, The Practice, 2000, Spin City, 2000, Malcolm in the Middle, 2001, The Fighting Fitzgeralds, 2001, The Ellen Show, 2001, Friends, 2004, (guest appearances, voice) Family Guy, 2001. Office: Osbrink Talent Agy 4343 Lankershim Blvd Ste #100 North Hollywood CA 91602 Office Phone: 818-760-2488.*

FANNING, DELVIN SEYMOUR, soil science educator; b. Copenhagen, N.Y., July 13, 1931; s. Clarence Roscoe and Faye Theodora (Hays) F.; m. Mary Christine Balluff, Nov. 22, 1958 (dec. Aug. 1994); children: Michael Christopher, Maurine Faye, Christine Kay; m. Emily Louise Wenzel Manning, Nov. 15, 1997. BS, Cornell U., 1954, MS, 1959; PhD, U. Wis., 1964. Cert. profl. soil scientist. Soil scientist Soil Conservation Svc., USDA, 1954, 59-62; grad. rsch. asst. dept. of soils U. Wis., Madison, 1960-64; from asst. prof. to prof. dept. natural resource scis. and landscape arch. U. Md., College Park, 1964-99, emeritus prof., 1999—. Vis. prof. Tech. U. of Munich, Germany, 1971-72, USDA Soil Conservation Svc., Washington, 1986; rsch. assoc. Tex. A&M U., College Station, 1979. Co-author: (with M.C.B. Fanning) Soil: Morphology, Genesis, and Classification, 1989; co-editor Acid Sulfate Weathering, 1982; contbr. entries in Encys., chpts. in books, articles to profl. jours. Bass singer Holy Redeemer Ch. Choir, College Park, Md., 1968—. With U.S. Army, 1954-56. Fellow Am Soc. Agronomy, Soil Sci. Soc. Am. Democrat. Roman Catholic. Achievements include definition, description and naming of processes for sulfide mineral accumulation in soils sulfidization and sulfide mineral oxidation to form sulfuric acid, and reaction of sulfuric acid with soils to form new minerals sulfuricization. Home: 4809 Ravenswood Rd Riverdale MD 20737-1115 Office: U Md Dept Nat Resource Scis and Landscape Arch College Park MD 20742-4452 Office Phone: 301-405-1308. Personal E-mail: delvindel@aol.com. Business E-Mail: dsf@umd.edu. *Know the earth and live in harmony.*

FANNING, ELLEN, biology professor, research scientist; BS in chemistry, U. Wis.-Madison; PhD in virology, Univ. Cologne, Germany, 1977. Asst. prof. Univ. Konstanz, Germany; prof. and acting chair Inst. for Biochemistry Univ. Munich; now Stevenson Prof. Molecular Biology, Dept. Biological Sciences Vanderbilt Univ., Nashville. Vis. prof. Dept. Genetics Harvard Med. Sch.; mem. editl. bd. Jour. of Virology; assoc. dir. Nat. Inst. Health Tng. Grant of Viruses, Nucleic Acids and Cancer; prof. Howard Hughes Med. Inst. Mem.: German Science Found. Peer Review Bd., Milwaukee Found. Corp. (Shaw Scholar Sci. Adv. Bd.), European Molecular Biology Orgn. Office: Vanderbilt U 2325 Stevenson Ctr 1161 21st Ave S Nashville TN 37235 Office Phone: 615-343-5677. Office Fax: 615-343-6707. E-mail: ellen.h.fanning@Vanderbilt.Edu.

FANNING, FRANCIS GERARD, lawyer; b. Chgo., Nov. 20, 1947; s. Francis Joseph and Catherine Beatta (Heatherly) F.; m. Muriel Anne Knoblauch, Aug. 22, 1970; children: Michael G., Christopher J., Patrick D. BA, U. Ill., 1970; MEd, U. Ariz., 1974; JD, Ariz. State U., 1978. Bar: Ariz. 1978, U.S. Dist. Ct. Ariz. 1978, U.S. Ct. Appeals (9th cir.) 1992, U.S. Supreme Ct. 1995, U.S. Ct. Appeals (10th cir.) 1996. Prosecutor intern City Atty., Tempe, Ariz., summer 1977; law clk. Justice William Holohan Ariz. Supreme Ct., Phoenix, 1978-79; assoc. atty. Law Office of Carl Divelbiss, Phoenix, 1979-81; pvt. practice Tempe and Mesa, Ariz., 1981-88, 90—; assoc. Bill Stephens & Assocs., Phoenix, 1988-90. Judge pro tempore Maricopa County Superior Ct., Phoenix, 1991-96, commr. pro tempore, 1982-83; mem. local bd. Supreme Ct. Foster Care Rev. Bd., Phoenix, 1981-85. Vol. Maricopa County Bar Assn. Vol. Lawyers Assn., Phoenix, 1981—; mem. troop com. Troop 7 Boy Scouts Am., Tempe, 1993-98; vol. coach YMCA, Tempe, 1989-93. Named Atty. of Yr., Maricopa County Bar Assn. Vol. Lawyers Program, Phoenix, 1987. Mem. Ariz. Employment Lawyers Assn. (bd. dirs. 1996-97), Nat. Employment Lawyers Assn. Democrat. Avocations: choral music, music composition. Home: 1941 E Los Arboles Dr Tempe AZ 85284-2586 Office: 500 E Southern Ave Ste B Tempe AZ 85282-5210 Office Phone: 480-731-9142. Business E-Mail: fanning@azbar.org.

FANNING, RONALD HEATH, architect, engineer; b. Evanston, Ill., Oct. 5, 1935; s. Ralph Richard and Leone Agatha (Heath) F.; m. Jenine Vivian Schnelle, Jan. 9, 1960; children: Anthony Lee, Traycee Anne. BArch, Miami U., Oxford, Ohio, 1959. Registered architect in 24 states; registered profl. engr. in 13 states Nat. Coun. of Archtl. Registration Bds., Nat. Coun. of Engring. Examiners. Pres., CEO, Fanning/Howey Assocs., Inc., Celina, Ohio, 1959—2000, chmn. bd., 2000—. Mng. ptnr. Manning Partnership, Celina 1978-2003, F/H Bldg. Partnership, 1986—; trustee Fanning Family Charitable Remainder Trust, 2003—. Chmn. Mercer County Young Reps., Celina, 1962-65. Recipient Fred B. Joyner Profl. Achievement award Delta Gamma chpt. Pi Kappa Alpha, 1997. Mem. NSPE, AIA, Coun. Ednl. Facility Planners Internat. (Great Lakes Midwest regional membership chmn. 1992-97, pres. Great Lakes Midwest region coun. ednl. facility planners internat. 1997-98), Ohio Soc. Profl. Engrs., Ohio Soc. Architects, Soc. Mktg. Profl. Svcs., Fla. Ednl. Facilities Planners Assn., Buckeye Assn. Sch. Adminstrs., Coun. Ednl. Faculty Planners Internat. (membership chmn. 1994-96, dir. 1997-2005, pres.-elect 2002-03, pres. 2003-04, past. pres. 2004-05, cert.), CEFPI Found. & Charitable Trust (dir. 2001-). Methodist. Avocations: tennis, bowling, golf. Home: 422 Magnolia St Celina OH 45822-1254 Office: Fanning Howey Assoc Inc PO Box 71 Celina OH 45822-0071 Office Phone: 419-586-7771. Business E-Mail: rfanning@fhai.com.

FANNING, WILLIAM HENRY, JR., computer specialist; b. N.Y.C., Feb. 12, 1917; s. William Henry and Terese Genevieve (Moloney) F.; m. Mary Major Winter, Sept. 5, 1940; children: Hugh M. (dec.), Helen A. Smith, Mary M., Gerard, William Henry III. BA, Fordham U., 1940; postgrad., Cath. U., 1940-41, Jersey City State Coll., 1977, Pace U., 1989-91. Exch. clerk N.Y. Times, 1938-40; Greek and German instr. Gonzaga High Sch., Washington, 1940-41; reporter, copy editor Nat. Cath. News Svc., Washington, 1941-48, news editor, 1948-55; dir. Rome News Bur., Radio Free Europe, 1955-57, dir. news and info. svcs. Munich, 1957-59, dir. Paris News Bur., 1959-60; editor The Cath. News, N.Y.C., 1960-66; freelance writer CBS-TV, N.Y.C., 1966-68, Harcourt Brace Jovanovich, NYC, 1967—72; v.p. promotion and advt., pop music producer/agt. Diamond Prodns., Ltd., NYC, 1967—69; analyst CGA Computer Assocs., Holmdel, N.J., 1969-73; programmer/analyst to sr. systems specialist Equitable Life Assurance Soc. U.S., N.Y.C., 1973-87; computer and network mgr. Mayor's Office of Midtown Enforcement, N.Y.C., 1988-94. Cons. Bill Fanning Productivity Systems, Westport Point, Mass., 1966—; lectr. journalism Good Counsel Coll., White Plains, N.Y., 1967-69; head U.S. Cath. Bishops Press Rels. Office, Rome-2d Vatican, 1962; mem. pres.'s com. Employment of the Handicapped, 1947-66. Bd. dirs. Westchester Cath. Edn. Coun., N.Y.C., 1963-69; mem. Archdiocese Edn. Coun., N.Y.C., 1961-66. Lt. USNR, 1942-45. Mem. N.Y. Acad. Scis., Writers Guild Am., Phi Kappa Theta (hon.). Roman Catholic. Home and Office: Box 234 Westport Point MA 02791-0234 Personal E-mail: fanningjrw@aol.com.

FANNING, WILLIAM JAMES, professional sports team executive, commentator; b. Chgo., Sept. 14, 1927; s. Frank and Gladys Leona (Lighter) F. BA in phys. edn., Buena Vista Coll, 1951; M in Phys. Edn., U. Ill., 1961. Profl. baseball player Chgo. Cubs, 1954, 56, 57; player, mgr. Tulsa Oilers, Tex. League, 1958, Dallas Rangers, Am. Assn., 1959-60, Venezuela, Eau Claire Braves, Wis., 1961-62; spl. assignment scout Milw. Braves, 1963-64, asst. gen. mgr., 1964-66; asst. gen. mgr., farm and scouting dir. Atlanta Braves, 1966-67; 1st dir. Major League Scouting Bur., 1968; gen. mgr. Montreal Expos., 1968-73, v.p., gen. mgr., 1973-77, v.p. player devel., 1977-81, field mgr., 1981-84, v.p. player devel. and scouting, 1982-86, spl. cons. baseball ops., 1989—; radio and TV broadcaster, 1987-88. Spl. cons. baseball ops., 1989-92; major league scout Colo. Rockies, 1993-99; radio baseball show CJAD, Montreal, 1993-2000; spl. asst. to gen. mgr. Toronto Blue Jays, 2001; amb. to amateur baseball Toronto Blue Jays 2002, 03, 04, 05. Served with U.S. Army, 1945-47. Inducted into Can. Baseball Hall of Fame, 2000, Montreal Expos Hall of Fame, 2000. Pentecostal. Home and Office: 154 Tiner Ave Dorchester ON Canada N0L 1G2 Address: One Blue Jays Way Ste 3200 Toronto ON Canada M5V 1J1 Office Phone: 519-268-1634. E-mail: wordsarepoetry@rogers.com.

FANNJIANG, ALBERT, mathematician, educator; arrived in U.S., 1987; s. W.-C. and W.-Y. Fannjiang; m. Jean Fannjiang, Mar. 19, 1988; children: Clara, Dominic. PhD, NYU, 1992. Asst. prof. computational and applied math. UCLA, 1992—95; asst. prof. U. Calif., Davis, 1995—99, assoc. prof., 1999—2003, prof. math., 2003—. Contbr. rsch. articles to profl. jours. Recipient U. Calif.-Davis Chancellor fellowship, U. of Calif., 2001—06; grantee, NSF, 1996—2003. Mem.: Am. Math. Soc. (Centennial fellow 2002). Achievements include research in mathematical theory of random media. Office: U Calif Dept Math One Shields Ave Davis CA 95616-8633

FANOS, KATHLEEN HILAIRE, osteopathic physician, podiatrist; b. Bremerhaven, Germany, Aug. 18, 1956; came to U.S., 1957; d. Homer Dantangelo and Ilse Helmar (Ochs) F. AAS in Music, Nassau C.C., Garden City, N.Y., 1976; BS in Music Edn., Hofstra U., 1978, postgrad., 1978-79; D Podiatric Medicine, Coll. Podiatric Med. and Surgery, Des Moines, 1987, DO, 1994. Diplomate Am. Bd. Internal Medicine. Tchr. music McKenna Jr. H.S. and Eastlake Elem. Sch., Massapequa, NY, 1978—79; musician numerous profl. orgns., N.Y., Iowa, 1979—; preceptorship in podiatry Bayshore, N.Y., 1987-88; pvt. practice podiatry Hyde Park, West Roxbury and Brookline, Mass., 1988-91; resident in internal medicine Winthrop U. Hosp., Mineola, NY, 1994-97; internist Cmty. Med. Assocs., Jackson, NJ, 1997-2000, Ocean County Family Care, Jackson, 2000—03, Hinds Internal Medicine, Jackson, 2003. Ins. med. examiner Portamedic, Burlington, Mass., 1988-91. Mem. AMA, ACP, Am. Bd. Internal Medicine, Am. Soc. Internal. Medicine, Am. Osteo. Assn., Am. Coll. Osteo. Family Physicians, N.Y. State Internal Medicine Soc., Phi Theta Kappa, Pi Kappa Lambda, Sigma Sigma Phi, Phi Delta Epsilon. Avocations: music, tennis, bowling, skiing, travel. Office Phone: 601-372-2616. Personal E-mail: kfanos@jam.rr.com.

FANSELOW, MICHAEL SCOTT, psychology professor; b. Bklyn, May 2, 1954; BS magna cum laude with honors, CUNY, Bklyn., 1976; PhD in Behavioral Psychology, U. Wash., 1980. Asst. prof. Rensselaer Poly. Inst., Troy, N.Y., 1980-81, Dartmouth Coll., Hanover, N.H., 1981-86, assoc. prof., 1986-88, UCLA, 1988-89, prof., 1989—. Recipient Troland Rsch. award NAS, 1995. Fellow AAAS, APA (Edwin B. Newman award 1979, D.O. Heb Young Scientist award 1983, Disting. Sci. award 1985). Office: UCLA Dept Psychology PO Box 951563 Los Angeles CA 90095-1563

FANSLER, BRIAN CALDWELL, budget analyst; b. Charlottesville, Va., June 4, 1971; s. Stephen Douglas and Donnetta Fern F. BA, No. Ariz. U., 1993, MPA, 1995. Zoning asst. Beus, Gilbert and Morrill, Phoenix, 1995-96; staff svcs. analyst Calif. Pub. Employee Retirement Sys., Sacramento, 1996-97; budget analyst Calif. Dept. Transp., Sacramento, 1997—. Founder Lincoln Meml. Mus., Washington, 1994. Mem. Am. Soc. Pub. Adminstrs., Calif. State Employees Assn., No. Ariz. U. Alumni Assn. (founder), 20/30 Club. E-mail: bfansler@msn.com.

FANTA, GEORGE FREDERICK, chemist, researcher; b. Chgo., Aug. 30, 1934; s. George and Hermina Fanta; m. Carmen Viola Amado, Sept. 7, 1957; children: Steven George, Linda Carmen Troemel, Julie Anita Carson. BSc, Purdue U., 1956; PhD, U. Ill., 1960. Rsch. chemist Ethyl Corp., Ferndale, Mich., 1960—63, USDA, Peoria, Ill., 1963—. Contbr. articles to profl. jours. Mem.: Am. Chem. Soc. Achievements include patents in field. Home: 33 Diamond Point Morton IL 61550-1186 Office: USDA 1815 N University St Peoria IL 61604 Business E-Mail: fantagf@ncaur.usda.gov.

FANTA, PAUL EDWARD, chemist, educator; b. Chgo., July 24, 1921; s. Joseph and Marie (Zitnik) F.; m. LaVergne Danek, Sept. 3, 1949; children—David, John. BS, U. Ill., 1942; PhD, U. Rochester, 1946. Postdoctoral research fellow U. Rochester, 1946-47; instr. Harvard, 1947-48; mem. faculty Ill. Inst. Tech., 1948—, prof. chemistry, 1961-84, prof. emeritus, 1984—. Exchange scholar Czechoslovak Acad. Sci., Prague, 1963-64, Soviet Acad. Sci., Moscow, 1970-71 Contbr. articles to profl. jours. NSF fellow Imperial Coll., London, Eng., 1956-57 Mem. Am. Chem. Soc., Sigma Xi, Phi Lambda Upsilon. Home: 947 Clinton Ave Oak Park IL 60304-1821

FANTACI, JAMES MICHAEL, lawyer; b. Rochester, N.Y., Dec. 23, 1946; s. Anthony and Shirley F.; m. Ellen Louise Steman, Apr. 26, 1969; children: Michael, Matthew. BA, U. Rochester, 1968; JD, U. Va., 1971. Bar: Va. 1971, La. 1972, U.S. Dist. Ct. (ea. dist.) La. Law clk. to Hon. E. Gordon West U.S. Dist. Ct. (ea. and mid. dist.) La., 1971-72; atty. Monroe & Lemann, New Orleans, 1972-84, McGlinchey Stafford, New Orleans, 1984—. Mem. The Chamber/New Orleans and the River Region East Jefferson Coun., 1988-93; chmn. East Jefferson Coun., 1992; chmn. Area Couns. Coord. Com., 1993; chmn. bd. commrs. Jefferson Parish Econ. Devel. Commn., 1999. Contbr. articles to jours. and legal revs. Mem. ABA (bus. law sect., small bus. com., franchising subcom.), La. Bar Assn., Va. Bar Assn., Jefferson C. of C. Home: 114 Sycamore Dr Metairie LA 70005-4025 Office: McGlinchey Stafford 643 Magazine St New Orleans LA 70130-3477 E-mail: jfantaci@mcglinchey.com.

FANTAZOS, HENRYK MICHAEL, painter, graphic artist; b. Kamionka, Lvov, Poland, Jan. 18, 1944; came to U.S., 1975; s. Antoni and Katarzyna Danuta Ziembicka; 1 child, Jessica. MA, Acad. Fine Arts, Cracow, Poland, 1969. One-man shows include Desa Gallery, Cracow, Poland, 1970, 75, Pegasus Gallery, Zakopane, Poland, 1971, Mus. Teatraine, Cracow, 1972, Karstadt Gallery, Cologne, Germany, 1973, Gallery of the Sparkasse der Stadt Hagen, Germany, 1974, Koszykowa Gallery, Warsaw, 1975, The Nippon Club, N.Y.C., 1976, Old Warsaw Gallery, Alexandria, Va., 1977, 81, Westlake Gallery, White Plains, N.Y., 1978, French Art Gallery, Gallipolis, Ohio, 1983, Birke Gallery, Marshall U., Huntington, W.Va., 1983, Judge Gallery, Durham, N.C., 1986, 90, McIntosh Gallery, Atlanta, 1987, Lee Scarfone Gallery, U. Tampa, Fla., 1988, Carrboro Art Ctr., N.C., 1988, Hanes Art Ctr., U. N.C., Chapel Hill, 1989, Phila. Art Alliance, 1989, Rockland Art Ctr., Balt., 1989, Dorothy McRae Gallery, Atlanta, 1993, Horace Williams House, Chapel Hill, 1994, Tyndall Gallery, Durham, N.C., 1995, Durham (N.C.) Art Guild, 1996, Nat. Bldg. Mus., Washington, 2000. Recipient numerous art awards including First prize Mannassas (Va.) Art Competition, 1984, Winner Internat. Print Competition San Diego Art Inst., 1994, Best in Show award New Works Exhibition, Raleigh, N.C., 1996; fellow Art Coun. N.C., 1996; grantee Aldegrewer Gesselschaft, West Germany, 1973, Sparkasse der Stadt Hagen, West Germany, 1974, Kosciuszko Found., N.Y., 1976, Artist in Residence, W. Va., 1982-83. Avocations: rose gardening, crystal collecting. Home: 227 West Hill Ave Hillsborough NC 27278

FANTE, RONALD LOUIS, engineer; b. Phila., Oct. 27, 1936; s. Frank Louis and Jeanne Gloria (Bossone) F.; m. Clara Connie Patalano, Apr. 23, 1961; children: Robert, Richard, Karen. BS, U. Pa., 1958; MS, MIT, 1960; PhD, Princeton U., 1964. Sr. scientist AVCO Corp., Wilmington, Mass., 1964-71, Air Force Cambridge Rsch. Labs., Bedford, Mass., 1971-80; asst. v.p. Textron Def. Systems, Wilmington, 1980-87; corp. fellow The MITRE Corp., Bedford, 1988—. Author: Signal Analysis and Estimation, 1988; contbr. numerous articles to jours. in field; mem. editl. bd. Waves in Random Media. Recipient Atwater Kent prize U. Pa., 1958, Dept. Labs. Achievement award USAF, 1974, Marcus O'Day prize USAF, 1975, I Migliori award Pirandello Lyceum, 1989, MITRE Corp. Best Paper prize, 1992, 2002, IEEE Disting. Lectr., 1995, 96. Fellow IEEE (editor in chief Transactions 1983-86, Third Millennium medal 2000, Schekluneff prize 2002), Optical Soc. Am., Inst. Physics; mem. Electromagnetics Acad., Internat. Union Radio Sci. Roman Catholic. Home: 26 Sherwood Rd Reading MA 01867-3743 Office: MITRE Corp Burlington Rd Bedford MA 01730-1306 E-mail: rfante@mitre.org.

FANTINI-KING, JULIE ANN, language educator; b. Mich. d. Gerald and Dorothy Fantini; m. Mark King; children: Griffin King, Duncan King. BA, U. Mich., 1994. Cert. tchr. Tex., 1994, Mich., 1994. Tchr. Galena Pk. H.S., Tex., 1994—, chair dept. lang. arts, 1996—, Nat. Honor Soc. advisor, 1997—. Office: Galena Park HS 1000 Keene St Galena Park TX 77547 Office Phone: 832-386-2950.

FANTON, JONATHAN FOSTER, foundation administrator; b. Mobile, Ala., Apr. 29, 1943; s. Dwight F. F. and Marion (Foster) Fanton Bemer; m. Cynthia Greenleaf, Aug. 2, 1986. BA, Yale U., 1965, M.Phil., 1977, PhD, 1978. Carnegie teaching fellow in history Yale U., 1965-66, lectr. history, 1966-78, spl. asst. to pres., 1970-73, exec. dir. Summer Plans, 1973-76, assoc. provost, 1976-78; v.p. planning U. Chgo., 1978-82; pres., prof. history New Sch. Social Rsch., N.Y.C., 1982—99; pres. John D. and Catherine T. MacArthur Found., Chgo., 1999—. Author: The University and Civil Society, Vol. 1, 1995, Vol. 2, 2002; co-editor: John Brown, The Manhattan Project, 1991. Advisor, trustee Rockefeller Bros. Fund; bd. dirs. Human Rights Watch Mem. Am. Hist. Assn., Coun. on Fgn. Rels., Econ. Club. Home: 4375 Congress St Fairfield CT 06430-1722 Office: 140 S Dearborn St Chicago IL 60601

FANTOZZI, PEGGY RYONE, geologist, environmental planner; b. Providence, Feb. 2, 1948; d. Eugene Baker and Cynthia (Bragg) Ryone; m. Thomas Allen Collins, Jan. 4, 1969 (div. 1985); children: Christin, Cindi; m. Thomas Edward Fantozzi, Mar. 22, 1985 (div. 1989); 1 child, Amy. BA in Earth Scis., Bridgewater State Coll., 1969; MS in Geology, Franklin and Marshall Coll., 1971. Registered sanitarian, Mass.; cert. wastewater treatment operator grade 4-M; cert. soil evaluator. Project mgr. Coastal Zone Mgmt. Grant, Eastham, Mass., 1980—81; geologist, project mgr. BSC Group/Cape Cod, Barnstable Village, Mass., 1982—88; sr. environ. scientist A.M. Wilson Assocs., Osterville, 1988—94, Daylor Consulting Group, Braintree, Mass., 1994—97. Instr. earth scis. and geology Bridgewater (Mass.) State Coll., 1972-74, Cape Cod C.C., West Barnstable, Mass., 1979-82; cons. conservation and health bds. Town of Bourne, Mass., 1984-85; mem., chair State Comm. for the Conservation of Soil, Water and Related Resources, 1996—; mem. Nat. Resources Conservation and Devel. Coun., 1998. Bd. dirs., v.p. Assn. for Preservation of Cape Cod, Orleans, Mass., 1979-85; bd. trustees Cape Cod Mus. Natural History, Brewster, 1982-85; advisor Barnstable County Marine Resources program, 1980-82; chmn. Eastham Conservation Commn., 1978-82, Selectmen's Task Force on Local Pollution, Bourne, 1985-87; del. Barnstable County Water Resources Adv. Coun., 1979-89, Bourne Shore and Harbor Com., 1989-92; rep. Tri-Town Septage treatment Facilities Planning Commn., Eastham, Orleans, citizen's adv. com. groundwater discharge program Mass. Dept. EPA, 1987-88, Surface Water Quality, 1990, 93, Mass. Bays Program Citizen Adv. Steering Com., 1992—; pres. Mass. Assn. Conservation Dists., 1995-98; chair Mass. State Commn. for the Conservation of Soil, Water and Related Resources, 1998—. Grantee USDA-Natural Resources Conservation Svc., 1997-98. Mem. Nat. Assn. Conservation Dists. (dir.), Mass. Health Officers Assn., Mass. Water Works Assn., Monument Beach Civic Assn. Home: 25 Shore Rd Buzzards Bay MA 02532-5425 Office: Land Use Permitting 25 Shore Rd Bourne MA 02532-5425

FANUELE, FRANK JOHN, engineering executive, mechanical engineer; b. N.Y.C., June 19, 1938; BSEE, Rensselaer Poly. Inst., 1960. Elec. engr. GE, 1960-64; project engr. Fairchild Electrometrics Corp., 1964-69; sys. engring. mgr. Mech. Tech. Inc., 1969-84; tech. sales mgr. Brown & Sharpe Mfg. Co., 1984-86; tech. mktg. mgr. Robotic Vision Sys., 1989; pres. Fanuele Enterprises, Albany, NY, 1986—. Achievements include research in field of automation. Office: Fanuele Enterprises 256 Partridge St Albany NY 12208-2624 Office Phone: 518-438-0603. Personal E-mail: afanuele@nycap.rr.com.

FANUELE, MICHAEL ANTHONY, retired electronics engineer, research engineer; b. Bronx, NY, Feb. 24, 1938; s. Joseph A. and R. Fanny (Rubino) F.; m. Joyce L. Cassidy, May 23, 1964; children: Gina M., Peter A. BEE, NYU, 1959; MSEE, Rutgers U., 1968. Electronics engr. U.S. Army Combat Surveillance & Target Acquisition Lab., Fort Monmouth, N.J., 1960-72, sr. electronics engr., 1972-80, project officer, 1980-81, dir. ISTA systems div., 1981-85; chief systems and signals analysis div. U.S. Army Electronic Warfare, Reconnaissance Surveillance and Target Acquisition Ctr., Fort Monmouth, N.J., 1985-88; sr. rsch. engr. Ga. Tech. Rsch. Inst., Ga. Inst. Tech., 1988-2001; ret., 2001. Cons. in field; chmn. dept. electomagnetic engring. U.S. Army Internal Tng. Program, Ft. Monmouth, 1968-78, advisor, 1978-88; Army chmn. Tri-Svc. Radar Symposium Steering Group, Ft. Monmouth, 1973-88; Army mem. Internat. Tech. group, 1977-81, Internat. Radar Panel, 1984-88; coord., instr. radar short course Ga. Tech. Patentee in field; contbr. articles to profl. jours. 2d lt. U.S. Army, 1959-60. Mem. IEEE (sr.), Assn. Old Crows, KC (treas. Brickton, NJ 1968-70), Elks Club, Vintage Auto Club Ocean County, Classic Thunderbird Club Internat. Roman Catholic. Avocations: photography, woodworking, collecting records, model railroading, auto restoration. Home: 440 Colleen Ct Toms River NJ 08755-7376 Personal E-mail: mfanuele@verizon.net.

FANWICK, ERNEST, lawyer; b. N.Y.C., Feb. 28, 1926; s. Jacob and Jeanette (Lossof) F.; m. Lee Nathan, Sept. 1, 1951; children: Lewis, Leslie, Eric. BS in Elec. Engring., Pa. State U., 1948; JD, Columbia U., 1951. Bar: N.Y. 1952, Conn. 1988, U.S. Patent Office 1952, U.S. Ct. Appeals (2d cir.) 1952, U.S. Supreme Ct. 1958, U.S. Ct. Appeals (fed. cir.) 1982. Sr. patent atty. ITT Fed. Telecom. Labs., Nutley, 1951-55; div. counsel Avion div. ACF, Paramus, N.J., 1955-57; patent counsel Burndy Corp., Norwalk, Conn., 1957-65, dir. legal dept., 1965-75, gen. counsel, 1975-82, v.p., gen. counsel, sec., 1982-89. Mem. faculty Practising Law Inst., N.Y.C., 1964-97; lectr. Conf. Legal Execs., Pa., 1970, 72. Bd. dirs. Aid to Retarded, Stamford, Conn., 1982-87, mem. exec. com., 1997—; bd.dirs. Assn. Jewish Family and Children's Agys., 1992-2000, Jewish Family Svcs., Stamford, 1989-2000; alternate mem. Zoning Bd. Appeals, Stamford, 1990-96; active Am. ARbitration Assn.; mem. Arbitration panel N.Y. Stock Exch., Am. Stock Exch., Nat. Assn. Security Dealers. Lt. U.S. Army, 1943-47. Mem. ABA, Conn. Bar Assn., Conn. Patent Law Assn. (pres. 1966), N.Y. Intellectual Property Law Assn., The Corp. Bar Assn., Am. Intellectual Property Assn., Am. Arbitration Assn., Masons. Fax: 203-322-4764. Office Phone: 203-322-5752. E-mail: ernest@fanwick.com.

FARABI-NANCE, KHADIJAH, writer; b. Junction City, Kans., Apr. 30, 1938; d. Signey Charles Rucker and Maxine Lillian Barnes; m. Lawrence Lorenzo Hammond, May 10, 1952 (div. Oct. 1, 1966); children: Lawrence Hammond, Jeffrey Hammond, Charisse Hammond, Crystal Hammond, Roger Hammond, Leann Hammond, Syadia Hammond. BA in English, African-Am. studies, Met. State Coll., Denver, 1977. Founder, pres. Syadia Creations; founder Nudijah Prodns. Mem. adv. bd. Operation Push, Denver, 1975, Cleo Parker Dance Co., Denver, 1976—82; cons. Compton Welfare Rights, Calif., 1991—97. Author: Wish Words Story Poet, Chocolate Thief. Mem.: Internat. Black Writer and Artist (Poetry prize 1999). Avocations: refinishing furniture, renewing throw away items, reading. Home: 1051 Pioneer Ave Wilmington CA 90744

FARABOW, FORD FRANKLIN, JR., lawyer; b. Charlotte, N.C., Jan. 6, 1938; s. Ford Franklin and Louise (Botts) F.; children— Ford Franklin, III, Amy Kathryn, Andrew Leighton. BS in Chem. Engring., Clemson U., 1959; JD with honors, George Washington U., 1963. Bar: D.C. bar 1965, S.C. bar 1963. With law dept. Swift & Co., Washington, 1959-62; assoc. Nexsen & Pruet, Columbia, S.C., 1962-64; with patent dept. Hercules, Inc., Wilmington, Del., 1964-65; ptnr. Finnegan, Henderson, Farabow, Garrett & Dunner, Washington, 1965—. Lectr. to ABA, Am. Patent Law Assn., also others. Contbr. articles to profl. publs. Named one of best lawyers in intellectual property law, Best Lawyers in Am., 2005—06. Mem. ABA, S.C. Bar Assn., Am. Judicature Soc., Bar Assn. D.C., Am. Patent Law Assn., U.S. Trademark Assn. (chmn. internat. adv. group), Am. Chem. Soc., Clemson U. Alumni Assn., Giles S. Rich Am. Inns of Ct., Tiger Brotherhood, Order of Coif, Phi Eta Sigma, Delta Theta Phi, Bethesda (Md.) Club (bd. dirs. 1987), TPC Club at Avenel, Franklin Sq. Club, Clemson IPTAY. Office: Finnegan Henderson Farabow Garrett & Dunner LLP 901 New York Ave NW Washington DC 20001-4413 Office Phone: 202-408-4000. Office Fax: 202-408-4400. Business E-Mail: ford.farabow@finnegan.com.

FARACI, JOHN VINCENT, JR., paper company executive; b. Summit, N.J., Feb. 16, 1950; s. John V. and Joan (Abbot) F.; m. Heath Holland. BA, Denison U., 1972; MBA, U. Mich., 1974. With Internat. Paper Co., 1974-88; fin. analyst N.Y.C., 1974-75; bus. analyst Statesville, N.C., 1975-76; plant contr. Kalamazoo, 1976-77; staff analyst N.Y.C., 1977-78; mgr. mktg. Mobile, Ala., 1978-80; dir. planning N.Y.C., 1980-83; gen. mgr. western ops. Gardiner, Oreg., 1983-85; gen. mgr. wood products group Dallas, 1985-88; v.p., gen. mgr. Masonite div., Chgo., 1988-91; CEO, mng. dir., Carter Holt Harvey Ltd., 1995—99; sr. v.p. finance, CFO International Paper, Purchase, NY, 1999—2000, exec. v.p., CFO, 2000—03, pres., 2003, chmn., CEO, 2003—. Republican. Avocations: mountain climbing, flying, collecting American Antique funiture, tennis, water sports. Office: Internat Paper 400 Atlantic St Stamford CT 06921 Office Phone: 203-541-8000.

FARAG, BRENDA KAY, music educator; b. Kans. City, Kans. d. Richard Irwin Chandler and Willa Sean Christy; m. Hany Nabil Farag, Dec. 20, 2003; children: Jackie L. Sutton, Noel S. Sutton, Christine N. Sutton. BS in Music Edn., Otterbein Coll., Westerville, Ohio, 1998. Cert. tchr. Ohio. Vocal music tchr. Columbus Pub. Schs., Ohio, 1998—. Cons. Columbus Symphony Orch., Ohio, 2004. Mem.: NEA, Nat. Music Edn. Conf.

FARAG, NOHA HASSAN, medical researcher; arrived in U.S., 1998; d. Hassan Hassan Farag and Rawia Niazy Ali; m. Tarek Mohamed Gamal El-Din Rashed, Aug. 27, 1994; children: Ali Tarek Rashed, Fatma Tarek Rashed. MD, Assiut U. Sch. Medicine, Egypt, 1993; B Medicine and Surgery, Assiut U., 1993. Lectr. Assiut U. Sch. Medicine, Egypt, 1994—98; clin. rsch. assoc. Reproductive Endocrine Assoc., San Diego, 1999—2000; post grad. rschr. U. Calif., San Diego, 2000—03; rsch. fellow U. Okla., Oklahoma City, 2003—. Contbr. articles to ency., abstracts, articles to profl. jours. Recipient Gen. Clin. Rsch. Ctr. award, Am. Psychosomatic Soc., 2001; grantee, HIV Neurobehavioral Rsch. Ctr., 2004—. Mem.: Soc. Egyptian Physicians, Am. Psychosomatic Soc., Sigma Xi. Muslim. Achievements include research in internat. collaborative study examining effects on neurocognitive function of immune pathways involved in HCV infection. Avocations: travel, gardening. Office: U Okla HSC 151A 921 NE 13th St Oklahoma City OK 73104 Office Phone: 405-270-0501 3123. Office Fax: 405-290-1839. Business E-Mail: noha-farag@ouhsc.edu.

FARAG, WALEED E, science educator; b. Zagazig, Sharkiya, Egypt, Aug. 26, 1971; s. Ezzat M Farag and Mahaseen Y Shawer; m. Nervana Mahmoud, June 4, 1998; 1 child, Jannah W. BSc, Zagazig U., Egypt, 1993; MSc, Zagazig U., 1997; PhD, Old Dominion U., 2002. EIT Egypt, 1993. Grad. tchg. asst. Zagazig U., Egypt, 1993—98; grad. rsch. asst. Old Dominion U., Norfolk, Va., 1998—2002; assoc. prof. Ind. U. Pa., Ind., 2002—. Peer reviewer Internat. Conf. On Parallel Processing, Vancouver, British Colombia, Canada, 2001—02, IEEE Infocom Conf., Washington, 2001—02; tech. reviewer Info. Resources Mgmt. Assn., Hershey, Pa., 2003—; peer reviewer Hawaii Internat. Conf., Computer Scis., Honolulu, 2003—. Contbr. chapters to books various info. text, articles various profl. jours and tech. conf. papers. Social activity coord. Ind. U. Pa., Ind., Pa., 2002; curriculum com. mem. Ind. U. Pa., 2002, recruitment com. mem., 2002, senate grant proposal com. mem., 2002. Scholar Studying doctorate degree, Egyptian Govt., 1998-2022. Mem.: IEEE, Hawaii Intern. Conf., IRMA, Engring. Syndicate. Moslem. Achievements include research in digital video steganography; network security; content-based access to video databases; distance learning application; neural network and optimization techniques. Office: Ind U Pa 210 S 10th St - Stright Hall Rm 319 Indiana PA 15705

FARAGE, MIRANDA A., research scientist; BSc in Pub. Health, U. Ill., 1982, MSc in Biology, 1984, PhD, 1987. Prin. scientist clin. sect. Feminine Care and Family Care, Cin. Office: Procter and Gamble Co 6110 Ctr Hill Ave Cincinnati OH 45224 Office Phone: 513-634-5594. Office Fax: 513-634-7364. E-mail: farage.m@pg.com.

FARAGO, JOHN MICHAEL, law educator, consultant; b. N.Y.C., Mar. 8, 1951; s. Ladislas and Liesel (Mroz) F.; m. Sharon Cramer, Nov. 11, 1972 (div.); m. Jeanne Elaine Martin, Dec. 5, 1985; 1 child, Max Farago; stepchildren: Belle Iskowitz, Sarah Iskowitz. BA, MAT, Harvard U., 1972; JD, NYU, 1978, postgrad., 1975-78. Assoc. dean, prof. Valparaiso (Ind.) U. Sch. Law, 1978-82; assoc. prof., assoc. dean for acad. planning CUNY Law Sch., N.Y.C., 1982—86, assoc. prof., dir. systems, 1986—90, assoc. dean for acad. affairs N.Y. Law Sch., N.Y.C., 1990—92; assoc. prof. CUNY Law Sch., N.Y.C., 1992—2004, prof., 2004—. Spl. edn. hearing officer Ind. Edn. Dept., 1979-82, N.Y.C. Bd. Edn., 1982—; hearing officer N.Y. State vocat. Edn., N.Y.C., 1993-98; adj. prof. Tchrs. Coll., 1998; cons. in field Co-author: Junk Food, 1978, Current & Emerging Issues in Special Education, 2002, Special Education Primer; editor: The Family, 1975; editl. bd. Ctr. for Computer-Assisted Legal Instrn., 1997—; contbr. articles to profl. jours. Search coord., chancellor search N.Y.C. Bd. Edn., 1995; v.p. NY State Assn. of Adminstrv. Law Judges, 2005—. Home: 1225 Park Ave New York NY 10128-1758 Office: CUNY Law Sch 65-21 Main St Flushing NY 11367 Office Phone: 212-348-0815. E-mail: Farago@mail.law.cuny.edu.

FARAH, BADIE NAIEM, computer information systems educator, consultant; b. Nazareth, Palestine, Jan. 15, 1946; came to U.S., 1970; naturalized, 1983. s. Naim R. and Afifi F. BS, Damascus U., 1967, MA, 1968; MS, Wayne State U., 1973; MSIE, Ohio State U., 1976, PhD, 1977. Teaching asst. Wayne State U., Detroit, 1971-73; research assoc. Ohio State U., Columbus, 1973-77; sr. systems analyst Gen. Motors Co., Detroit, 1977-78; asst. prof. Oakland U., Rochester, Mich., 1978-82; asst. prof. computer systems Eastern Mich. U., Ypsilanti, 1982-86, assoc. prof., 1986-90, prof., 1990—. Advisor to bd. dirs. S & G Grocer Co., Detroit, 1979-81, vis. gen. mgr., 1980-81. Author: Business Information Systems: Development and Implementation, 1990, 2nd edition, 1995; co-author: Integrated Case Studies in Accounting Information Systems, 1987; contbr. articles to profl. jours. Mem. Am. Inst. Indsl. Engrs., Assn. for Computing Machinery (exec. council Met. Detroit chpt.), Ops. Research Soc. Am., Inst. Mgmt. Scis. (sec. SE Mich. chpt.), Mich. Acad. Sci., Arts and Letters, AAUP, Alpha Pi Mu, Beta Gamma Sigma, Phi Kappa Phi. Syrian Orthodox (pres. local ch. bd.). Research on data communications and networks of computers, e-commerce, management information. Home: 37 Foxboro Dr Rochester Hills MI 48309 Office: Ea Mich U Computer Info Sys Ypsilanti MI 48197 Office Phone: 734-487-1098. Business E-Mail: badie.farah@emich.edu.

FARAH, CAESAR ELIE, language educator; b. Portland, Oreg., Mar. 13, 1929; s. Sam Khalil and Lawrice Farah; m. Irmgard Tenkamp, Dec. 13, 1987; 1 child, Elizabeth;children from previous marriage: Ronald, Christopher, Ramsey, Laurence, Raymond, Alexandra. Student, Internat. Coll. Am. U. Beirut, 1941—46; BA, Stanford U., 1952; MA, Princeton U., 1955, PhD, 1957. Pub. affairs asst., cultural affairs officer ednl. exchanges USIS, New Delhi, 1957-58, Karachi, Pakistan, 1958; asst. to chief Bur. Cultural Affairs, Washington, 1959; asst. prof. history and Semitic langs. Portland State U., 1959-63; asst. prof. history Calif. State U., LA, 1963-64; assoc. prof. Near Eastern studies Ind. U., Bloomington, 1964-69; prof. Mid. Eastern and Islamic history U. Minn., Mpls., 1969—, chmn. South Asian and Mid. Eastern studies, 1988-91. Guest lectr. Fgn. Ministry, Spain, Iraq, Iran, Ministry Higher Edn., Saudi Arabia, Yemen, Turkey, Kuwait, Qatar, Tunisia, Morocco, Syrian Acad. Scis., Acad. Scis., Beijing; vis. scholar Cambridge U., 1974; resource person on Middle East media and svc. group, Minn., 1977—; bd. dirs., chmn. Upper Midwest Consortium for Middle East Outreach, 1980—; vis. prof. Harvard U., 1964, 65, Sanaa U., Yemen, 1984, Karl-Franzens U. Austria, 1990, 91, 1997—98, Ludwig-Maximilian U., Munich, 1992—93; vis. Fulbright-Hays scholar U. Damascus, 1994; vis. lectr. Am. U. Beirut, 2001; exec. sec., editor Am. inst. Yemeni Studies, 1982—86; sec.-gen., exec. bd. dirs. Internat. Com. for Pre-Ottoman & Ottoman Studies, 1988—2000, v.p., 2000—; fellow Rsch. Ctr. Islamic History, Istanbul, 1993, Ctr. Lebanese Studies & St. Anthony Coll., Oxford, England, 1994; vis. cons. Sultan Qaboos U., Oman, 2000; mem. exec. bd. Arab Am. Cultural Inst., 2001—. Author: The Addendum in Medieval Arabic Historiography, 1968, Islam: Beliefs and Observances, 7th edit., 2003, Eternal Message of Muhammad, 1964, 3d edit., 1981, Tarikh Baghdad li-Ibn-al-Najjar, 3 vols., 1980—83, 2d edit., 1986, al-Ghazali on Abstinence in Islam, 1992, Decision Making in the Ottoman Empire, 1992, The Road to Intervention: Fiscal Policies in Ottoman Mount Lebanon, 1992, The Politics of Interventionism in Ottoman Lebanon, 2000, The Sultan's Yemen, 2002, Ottomans & Arabs, 2002, First Arab Traveler to Latin America, 2003; contbr. articles to profl. jours.; mem. editl. bd.: Digest of Middle East Studies. Mem. Oreg. Rep. Committeeman, 1960—64. Named Fulbright-Hayes lectr., 1993—94; recipient cert. of merit, Syrian Ministry Higher Edn.; fellow, Am. Coun. Learned Socs., 1953, Am. Rsch. Ctr. Egypt, 1966—67, Fulbright Tgn. and Rsch., Germany, 1992—93, Ford Found., 1966, Am. Philos. Soc., 1970—71; grantee Participants Program, Dept. State Am., 1981, 1984, 1993, Minn. Humanities Commn., 1981, 1985, 1989, 1995, 1998, 2001, Am. Inst. Yemeni Studies, 1999, Coun. Am. Overseas Rsch. Ctrs., 2000, Travel to Collection, NEH, 1989, others; scholar Fulbright Rsch., 1966—67, 1985—86, 1992—93. Mem.: Turkish Studies Assn., Am. Assn. Tchrs. Arabic (exec. bd.), Mid. East Studies Assn. N.Am., Am. Hist. Assn., Royal Asiatic Soc. Gt. Britain, Am. Oriental Soc., Stanford U. Alumni Assn. (pres. upper Midwest Assn. 1978—79, Leadership Recognition award), Princeton Club, Stanford Club Minn. (dir., pres. 1979), Phi Alpha Theta, Pi Sigma Alpha. Greek Orthodox. Home: 5125 Blake Rd S Edina MN 55436-1125 Office: Univ Minn 839 Soc Sci Towers Minneapolis MN 55455 Office Phone: 612-624-0580. Business E-Mail: farah001@umn.edu.

FARAIDY, ABDULAZIZ ABDULLAH, retired national public security officer; b. Saudi Arabia, May 15, 1945; m. Nora; children: Faris, Waleed, Yasir, Najah, Nayef, Bander, Nouf. BS, Calif. State U. L.A., 1970; MPA, U. So. Calif. L.A., 1978, PhD of Pub. Adminstrn., 1982. Comdr. of shooting range Pub. Security, Riyadh, 1970—72, chief armament dept., 1972—73, chief instr. officers inst., 1973—75, chief instr. non-commd. officers inst., 1975; dir. gen. hosp. Security Forces Hosp., Riyadh, 1975—76, 1982—84;

dir. officers dept. Civil Def., Riyadh, 1986—87, dir. warning and monitoring dept., 1987—90; dir. region Civil Def. for Baha, 1990—92; vice comdr. Civil Def. for Riyadh Region, 1992—97, gen. dir., 1997—2004; ret., 2004. Mem. Am. Soc. for Pub. Adminstrn., Am. Soc. Safety Engrs., Fire Engring. Soc. Avocations: swimming, tennis. Home: PO Box 46918 Riyadh 11542 Saudi Arabia Office Phone: 966500415415.

FARAJ, ALI, information technology executive; arrived in U.S., 1979; BA in Polit. sci., U. Ill., Chgo., 1997. Cert. info. security mgr. Info. Sysy. Audit and Cntl. Assn.; project mgmt. profl. Project Mgmt. Inst., project mgr. Project Mgmt. Leadership Group. Mgr. ops. and IT APC Rsch., Chgo., 1995—99, Northwestern Med. Faculty Found., Chgo., 1999—2000; global program mgr. Exodus Comm./Cable and Wireless, Oak Brook, Ill., 2000—03; IT dir., chief project owner, IBS-FT contractor Kraft Foods N.Am., Oak Brook, 2003; sr. dir. tech. Thomson NETg, Naperville, Ill., 2003—. Lead project mgr. BestBuy.com. Bd. dirs. Kenneth Young Ctr., Carbini Connections. With USAF, 2000—01. Recipient Unsung Hero award, Exodus Comm., 2001. Master: Investment Decisions Everyone Agrees upon (life; pres. 2002—04). Office: Thomson NETg 1751 W Diehl Rd Naperville IL 60563 Office Phone: 630-695-8905. Personal E-mail: alifaraj2002@hotmail.com.

FARARA, JOSEPH MONTGOMERY, library director; b. Boston, Mar. 19, 1958; s. Joseph Clinging and Elizabeth Mary (Mulcahy) F.; m. Nancy Ruth Blood, Nov. 24, 1984; 1 child, Keegan James. BA in English, Bates Coll., 1980; MS in Info. Sci., Simmons Coll., 1984. Cataloging asst. Mus. Fine Arts, Boston, 1984; reference libr. RISD, Providence, R.I., 1984-85; rsch. libr. F.W. Faxon Co., Westwood, Mass., 1985-87; reserves and circulation libr. Hilles Libr., Harvard U., Cambridge, 1987-90; libr. dir. Johnson (Vt.) State Coll., 1990—, assoc. dean tech., 1995—2002, chief tech. officer, 2002—; dir. libr. planning Vt. State Colls., 2003—. Host: (radio show) Fancy Eatin' Table, 1990—. Recipient Faculty Rsch. grant Johnson (Vt.) State Coll., 1992, Learning Communities grant Vt. State Colls., Waterbury, 1993, 2005. Mem. Lamoille County Librs. Assn. (pres. 1993—), Vt. State Colls. Libr. Coun. (chmn. 2002—), Sandinista Track Club, B.A.B. Office Club at West Main. Republican. Episcopalian. Office: John Dewey Libr Johnson State Coll Johnson VT 05656

FARARO, THOMAS JOHN, sociologist, educator; b. NYC, Feb. 11, 1933; s. Joseph and Anna (Marcello) F.; m. Irene Johanna Fannasch, Dec. 30, 1955; children: Ramona, Raymond. BA, CCNY, 1959; PhD, Syracuse U., 1963. Asst. prof. sociology Syracuse (N.Y.) U., 1963-64; vis. scholar Stanford (Calif.) U., 1964-67; prof. U. Pitts., 1967-99, chmn. dept. sociology, 1980-85, Disting. Svc. prof., 1999—. Author: Mathematical Sociology, 1973, Mathematical Sociology, Japanese translation, 1980, The Meaning of General Theoretical Sociology, 1989 (transl. into Japanese 1996), Social Action Systems, 2001; co-author: A Study of a Biased Friendship Net, 1964, Generating Images of Stratification, 2003; editor: Mathematical Ideas and Sociological Theory, 1984; co-editor Rational Choice Theory, 1992, The Problem of Solidarity, 1998; assoc. editor Jour. Math. Sociology, 1978—; mem. editl. bd. Am. Jour. Sociology, 1977-79, Am. Sociol. Rev., 1980-82, Social Networks, 1978-82, Sociol. Theory, 1988-90, Sociol. Forum, 1989-92. With USAF, 1952-56. Grantee Social Sci. Rsch. Coun., 1968, NSF, 1969-72. Mem. Am. Sociol. Assn. (chair math. sociol. sect. 1998-99), Internat. Network for Social Network Analysis, Sociol. Rsch. Assn. Office: U Pitts Dept Sociology 230 S Bouquet St Pittsburgh PA 15213-4015 E-mail: tjf2@pitt.edu. *I have devoted my intellectual life to the advancement of theoretical sociology by the use of mathematical methods in presenting theories, clarifying and formalizing concepts, representing social processes and social structures, and explaining social phenomena.*

FARB, THOMAS FOREST, financial executive; b. N.Y.C., Oct. 28, 1956; s. Peter and Oriole (Horch) F.; m. Stacy Siana Valhouli, Apr. 29, 1961; children: Peter Forest Valhouli-Farb, Siana Louisa Valhouli-Farb, Andreas John Valhouli-Farb. AB, Harvard U., 1980. Rsch. assoc. Mass. House Ways and Means Com., Boston, 1976-78; asst v.p. Bank of Boston, 1980-83; v.p., CFO and gen. mgr. ea. ops. Symbolics, Inc., Burlington, Mass., 1983-89; sr. v.p., CFO, contr. Airfund Corp., Lexington, Mass., 1989-92; v.p. corp. devel., CFO, treas. Cytyc Corp., Marborough, Mass., 1992-94; exec. v.p., CFO, treas. Indevus Pharms., Inc., Lexington, Mass., 1994-98; gen. ptnr., CFO Summit Ptnrs., Boston, 1998—2003; mng. dir. New Am. Ptnrs., LLC, Waltham, Mass., 2003—, Cappello Capital Corp., 2003—. Bd. dir. Fair, Issac and Co., San Rafael, Calif., Redwood Trust, Inc., Mill Valley, Calif., Saf-T-Med. Inc., Barrington, Ill., Symon Comm., Dallas, Norton Motorsports, Gladstone, Oreg., Zencheng Power Corp., Guangzhou, China, Chameleon Network, Concord, Mass. Mem. Fin. Execs. Inst., Bus. Assocs. Club, Treas. Club Boston, Newcomen Soc. Home: 1228 Lowell Rd Concord MA 01742-5527 Office: New Am Ptnrs 1050 Winter St Waltham MA 02451 Office Phone: 978-201-9081. E-mail: tfarb@newamericapartners.com.

FARBANISH, THOMAS, sculptor; b. Endicott, N.Y., Mar. 21, 1963; BFA, Rochester Inst. Tech., 1986. Asst. Artpark, Lewiston, N.Y., 1986, Wheaton Village, Millville, N.J., 1989; instr. Golden Glass Sch., Cin., 1990, Corning Bus. Devel. Ctr., 1991; faculty Tyler Sch. Art, Pa., 1991, Urban Glass, N.Y., 1992, Pilchuck Glass Sch., Stanwood, Wash., 1993-94, 97, gaffer, 1996-97; faculty Haystack Sch. Crafts, Maine, 1993, Penland Sch., N.C., 1993, Rochester (N.Y.) Inst. Tech., 1994, 97. Tchg. asst. Pilchuck Glass Sch., Stanwood, 1986, 87, 90, 2004, Saxe emerging artist in residence, 1988; lectr. in field. One-man and two-man shows include Snyderman Gallery, Phila., 1987, Sarah Squeri Gallery, Cin., 1990, AVA Gallery, Lebanon, N.H., 1992, Artspace, Kohler Art Ctr., Sheboygan, Wis., 1993, Robert L. Kidd Gallery, Birmingham, Mich., 1994, William Traver Gallery, Seattle, 1991, 94, 95, Heller Gallery, N.Y.C., 1995; group shows include Glass Gallery, Bethesda, Md., 1984, 85, Germanow Gallery, Rochester, 1984, Morris Mus., Morristown, N.J., 1985, Upton Hall Galleries, Buffalo, 1985, Courtyard Galleries, Balt., 1986, Huntington (W.Va.) Mus. Art, 1986, Heller Gallery, N.Y.C., 1986, 87, 91, 92, 94, 95, 97, Ward Gallery, 1987, Somerstown Gallery, Somers, N.Y., 1987, Snyderman Gallery, Pa., 1987, Am. Craft Mus., N.Y.C., 1988, So. Alleghenies Mus. Art, Loretto, Pa., 1988, Grohe Gallery, Boston, 1989, Robert L. Kidd Gallery, Birmingham, 1989, 96, William Traver Gallery, Seattle, 1990, 92, 93, Sotheby's, N.Y.C., 1990, Gallery Nakama, Tokyo, 1991, Lehman Gallery, N.Y.C., 1993, Christies, N.Y.C., 1993, Bellevue (Wash.) Art Mus., 1994, Habitat Galleries, Birmingham, 1994, Leedy Voulkos Gallery, Kansas City, Mo., 1995, Philabaum Gallery, Tucson, 1995, Huntsville (Ala.) Mus. Art, 1996, William Traver Gallery, Seattle, 2004; represented in permanent collections Huntsville Mus. Art, Am. Craft Mus., Prescott Collection, Wash., Huntington Mus. Art, Davis Wright and Jones, Wash., Wheaton (N.J.) Mus. Am. Glass, Pilchuck Glass Sch., Wash., Rochester Inst. Tech. Creative Glass Ctr. Am. fellow Wheaton Village, 1985, 90, Visual Artist fellow Nat. Endowment Arts, 1988, 94; Pilchuck Glass Sch. scholar, 1987; Mid Atlantic Arts Found. grantee, 1990. Office: c/o William Traver Gallery 110 Union St Ste 200 Seattle WA 98101-2028

FARBER, BERNARD JOHN, lawyer; b. London, Feb. 27, 1948; arrived in US, 1949; s. Solomon and Regina (Wachter) F.; m. Mary Lee Mueller, Feb. 14, 1987; children: Zachary, Anne. BS, U. of State of N.Y., Albany, 1978; JD, Ill. Inst. Tech., 1983. Bar: Ill. 1983, U.S. Dist. Ct. (no. dist.) Ill. 1983, U.S. Ct. Appeals (7th cir.) 1985, U.S. Tax Ct. 1986, U.S. Ct. Mil. Appeals 1986, U.S. Supreme Ct. 1987, U.S. Ct. Appeals (6th cir.) 1988, U.S. Ct. Appeals (4th cir.) 1989, U.S. Ct. Appeals (11th cir.) 1990. Instr. legal writing Chgo.-Kent Law Sch. Ill. Inst. Tech., 1983-85, computer rsch. atty., 1985-86, adj. prof. law, 1987—; legal editor Longman Fin. Svcs., Chgo., 1986-87; rsch. counsel publs. Ams. for Effective Law Enforcement, Chgo., 1987—. Instr. Law Scholastic Aptitude Test; preparation course BAR/BRI, Chgo., 1984-88; v.p. Brickton Montessori Sch., Chgo., 1992-93; sec. bd. dirs., 1993-95. Mng. editor: Chgo.-Kent Law Rev., 1981-82, editor-in-chief, 1982-83; co-author: Protective Security Law, 1996; editor: (with others) Dow Jones-Irwin Handbook of Micro Computer Applications in Law, 1987, Illinois Law of Criminal Investigation, 1986; contbr. articles to profl. jours. Elected mem. Local Sch. Coun., Agassiz Elem. Sch., Chgo., 1996-2004, chmn., 1999-2004, vice-chmn. 2002-2003. Mem. ABA, Ill. State Bar Assn., Chgo. Bar Assn., Sci. Fiction Rsch. Assn., Mensa. Avocations: history, computers, science fiction. Home and Office: 1126 W Wolfram St Rear Chicago IL 60657-4330 Personal E-mail: bernfarber@aol.com. Business E-Mail: bernardjfarber@voyager.net.

FARBER, DONALD CLIFFORD, lawyer, educator; b. Columbus, Nebr., Oct. 19, 1923; s. Charles and Sarah (Epstein) F.; m. Ann Eis, Dec. 28, 1947; children: Seth, Patricia. BS in Law, U. Nebr., 1948, JD, 1950. Bar: NY 1950. Assoc. Newman, Hauser & Teitler, N.Y.C., 1950-58; pvt. practice, N.Y.C., 1958-80; of counsel Conboy, Hewitt, O'Brien & Boardman, N.Y.C., 1980-84; ptnr. Tanner Propp Fersko & Sterner, N.Y.C., 1984-95, Farber & Rich LLP, N.Y.C., 1995-98; of counsel Hartman & Craven LLP, N.Y.C., 1998—2000, Jacob Medinger & Finnegan LLP, N.Y.C., 2000—. Prof. law York U., Toronto, Ont., Canada, 1970, Toronto, 1972—73; prof. theatre law Hofstra Law Sch., Hempstead, NY, 1974—75; prof. New Sch. for Social Rsch., N.Y.C., 1972—, Hunter Coll., 1978. Author: From Option to Opening, 1968, 5th edit., 2005, 1st Limelight edit., 1988, Producing on Broadway, 1969, Actor's Guide: What You Should Know About the Contracts You Sign, 1971, Producing, Financing and Distributing Film, 1973, 2d edit., 1991, The Amazing Story of the Fantasticks: America's Longest Running Play, 1991, 2d edit., 2005, Producing Theatre: A Comprehensive Legal and Business Guide, 1981, 3d Limelight edit., 1997, Common Sense Negotiation-The Art of Winning Gracefully, 1996; gen. editor (10 vol. series, author theatre vol.) Entertainment Industry Contracts-Negotiating and Drafting Guide. With AUS, 1941—44, ETO. Mem.: Order of Coif. Home: 14 E 75th St New York NY 10021-2657 Office: Jacob Medinger & Finnegan LLP Attn Donald C Farber 1270 Ave of Americas New York NY 10020 Office Phone: 212-524-5035. Personal E-mail: donaldc14@aol.com. Business E-Mail: dcfarber@jmfnylaw.com.

FARBER, EMMANUEL, pathology educator, biochemistry educator; b. Toronto, Ont., Can., Oct. 19, 1918; s. Morris and Mary (Madorsky) Farber; m. Ruth Diamond, Apr. 21, 1942 (dec. Apr. 22, 1993); 1 child, Noami Beth; m. Henrietta K., Apr. 28, 2000. MD, U. Toronto, 1942; PhD in Biochemistry, U. Calif., 1949; D Medicine and Surgery (hon.), U. Turin, Italy, 1985. Diplomate Am. Bd. Pathology. Intern, then resident in pathology Hamilton (Ont.) Gen. Hosp., 1942-43; fellow in cancer rsch. Am. Cancer Soc. U. Calif., 1947-49, Hektoen Inst. Med. Rsch., Cook County Hosp., Chgo., 1949-50; from instr. to assoc. prof. pathology and biochemistry Tulane U., New Orleans, 1950-59, Am. Cancer Soc. Rsch. prof., 1959-61; prof., chmn. pathology dept. U. Pitts., 1961-70; Am. Cancer Soc. Rsch. prof., sr. investigator Fels Rsch. Inst., Temple U. Sch. Medicine, Phila., 1970-74, prof., dir., 1974-75; prof., chmn. pathology dept. U. Toronto, 1975-85, prof. dept. pathology, dept. biochemistry, 1985, prof. emeritus, 1985—; mem. staff, pathologist-in-chief Toronto Gen. Hosp., 1975-85; chmn. dept. pathology Toronto Western Hosp., 1975-85; prof. dept. pathology and cell biology Jefferson Med. Coll., Phila., 1994—; prof. dept. pathology S.C. Cancer Ctr.-U. S.C. Sch. Medicine, Columbia, 1999—, rsch. prof./cons., 1999—; cons., 2001—. Vis. scientist Toxicology Rsch. Unit Med. Rsch. Coun. Lab., Carshalton, Eng., 1959; vis. prof. Courtauld Inst. Biochemistry. Middlesex Hosp. Med. Sch., London, Eng.,1968-69; vis. prof., lectr. Krakower U. Ill., Chgo., 1989; mem. Surgeon Gen.'s adv. com. on smoking and health, 1962-64; mem. pathology B study sect. NIH, 1962-66, chmn. 1963-66, chem. pathology study sect, 1980-82, metabolic pathology study sect., 1987-89; mem. pathology com. NAS Nat. Rsch. Coun., 1965-66; mem. adv. panel 5 on med. scis. U.S.-Japan coop. sci. program, 1965, panel D Nat. Cancer Inst. Can., 1977-79, panel I com. on food safely and food safety policy NAS, 1978-79; mem. rev. bd. Alachlor Can., 1985-87; mem. sci. adv. bd. Armed Forces Inst. Pathology, 1966-70, Nat. Ctr. Toxicology Rsch., 1973-74; mem. nat. adv. cancer coun. USPHS, 1966-70; mem. com. Cancer Rsch. Tng. Grants Nat. Cancer Inst., 1971-72; mem. bd. sci. overseers Jackson Lab., 1972-81, trustee 1972-74; cons. HEW, 1964-67, St. Michael's Hosp., Toronto, 1976-85, Sunnybrook Med. Centre, Toronto, 1976-85, Wellesley Hosp., 1976-85, Mt. Sinai Hosp., 1976-85, N.Y. Gen. Hosp., 1977-85. Editor: Biochemical Pathology, 1966, The Biochemistry of Disease Series Vols. 1-12, 1971-87, Toxic Liver Injury, 1979, Toxic Injury of the Liver, 1980, Pathogenesis of Liver Diseases, 1987; mem. editorial bd., assoc. editor Cancer Rsch., Teratogenisis Carcinogenesis and Mutagenesis; mem. editorial bd. Oncology News, Internat. Jour. Cancer, Chem. Biological Interactions, Carcinogenesis, Liver, Hepatology, Lab. Investigation; assoc. editor Toxicologic Pathology; contbr. numerous articles to profl. jours. Capt. Med. Corp. Royal Can. Army, 1942-46. Recipient Parke-Davis award Am. Soc. Exptl. Pathology, 1958, Bertha Goldblatt Teplitz Meml. award, 1961, Samuel R. Noble Found. award, 1976, fellow Royal Soc. Can., Eastman Kodak award Nat. Acad. Clin. Biochem., 1986, Founders' award Chem. Industry Inst. Toxicology, 1987, Disting. Pathologist award U.S. and Can. Acad. Pathologists, 1992; named Schofield Meml. lectr. U. Guelph, 1984, Alexander Breslow Meml. lectr. George Washington U., 1986, Robert E. Greenfield lectr. U. Nebr., 1987, Disting. lectr. Roswell Pk. Meml. Inst., 1988; NIH fellow Nat. Cancer Inst., 1969-70. Mem. AAAS, Am. Assn. Cancer Rsch. (GHA Clowes Meml. award 1984, hon. mem. 1995), Am. Assn. Pathologists (Rous-Whipple award 1982), Am. Chem. Soc., Am. Soc. Biochemistry Molecular Biology, Am. Soc. Investigative Pathology (Gold Headed Cane award 1995), Am. Gastroenterol. Assn., Am. Assn. Study Liver Disease, Biochem. Soc., Can. Assn. Pathologists (William Boyd lectr. 1986), Can. Biochem. Soc., Histochem. Soc., U.S.-Can. Acad. Pathology (Maude E. Abbott lectr. 1987, Disting. Pathologist award 1992), Jap. Cancer Assn. (hon.), N.Y. Acad. Scis., Ont. Assn. Pathologists, Ont. Med. Assn., Pathol. Soc. Gt. Britain Ireland (hon.), Soc. Exptl. Biology and Medicine, Soc. Toxicology (U.S. chpt.), Soc. Toxicology Can., Soc. Toxicologic Pathologists (hon.). Office: U SC Sch Medicine Dept Pathology & Cancer Ctr Columbia SC 29209 Personal E-mail: twoakinlov@aol.com.

FARBER, EVAN IRA, librarian; b. N.Y.C., June 30, 1922; s. Meyer M. and Estelle H. (Shapiro) F.; m. Hope Wells Nagle, June 13, 1966; children: Cynthia, Amy, Jo Anna, May Beth; stepchildren: David Nagle, Jeffrey Nagle, Lisa Nagle. AB, U. N.C., 1944, MA, BLS, U. N.C., 1953; DHL (hon.), St. Lawrence U., 1980, Susquehanna U., 1989, Ind. U., 1996. Instr. polit. sci. U. Mass., Amherst, 1948-49; librarian State Tchrs. Coll., Livingston, Ala., 1953-55; chief serials and binding div. Emory U. Library, Ga., 1955-62; head librarian Earlham Coll., Richmond, Ind., 1962-94, coll. libr. emeritus, 1994—. Cons. Bates Coll., Eckerd Coll., Colo. Coll., Hartwick Coll., Macalester Coll., Maryville Coll., Knox Coll., Ill. Coll., Messiah Coll., Hiram Coll., Centenary Coll., Colby Coll., Ga. State U., Ripon Coll., Hampshire Coll., Reed Coll., Williams Coll., NEH, Lilly Endowment, North Ctrl. Assn., Assn. Am. Colls., Pew Meml. Trust. Author: (with Andreano and Reynolds) Student Economists Handbook, 1967, Classified List of Periodicals for the College Library, 5th edit., 1972; assoc. editor: Southeastern Librarian, 1959-62; asst. editor: Explorations in Entrepreneurial History, 1964-66; co-editor: Earlham Rev., 1965-72; editor: Combined Retrospective Index to Book Revs. in Scholarly Jours., 1886-1974, 1979-83, Combined Retrospective Index to Revs. in Humanities Jours., 1802-1974, 1983-85, (with Ruth Walling) Essays in Honor of Guy R. Lyle; columnist: Choice Mag., 1974-80, Library Issues, 1982-88; mem. editl. bd. Coll. and Undergrad Librs., Internet and Higher Edn. Recipient Acad./Rsch. Libr. of the Yr., 1980, B.I. Libr. of Yr. award, 1987. Mem. Assn. Coll. and Rsch. Librs. (pres. 1978-79, bd. dirs. 1989-93), ALA (council 1969-71, 79-83). Home: 304 SW H St Richmond IN 47374-5243 Office: Earlham Coll Lilly Libr Richmond IN 47374 E-mail: evanf@earlham.edu.

FARBER, GEORGE ALLAN, dermatologist, educator; b. Miami, Fla., Jan. 4, 1934; s. Charles R. and Clara M. (Milman) F.; m. Nancy Graves, Dec. 26, 1955; children: George Allan, Michael G., Jeffrey N., Guy C., Scott Q. BS, La. State U., 1955, MD, 1959. Diplomate Am. Bd. Cosmetic Surgery., Am. Bd. Dermatology. Intern So. Bapt. Hosp., New Orleans, 1959-60; resident Charity Hosp. of New Orleans, 1963-66; commd. 2d lt. M.C. USAF, 1955, advanced through grades to lt. col., 1965; chief aviation medicine and mil. pub. health Luke AFB, Phoenix, 1960-63; flight surgeon, chief dermatology and syphilology 12th USAF Hosp., Cam Ranh Bay, Vietnam, 1966-67; chief dermatology svc., cons. to Surgeon Gen. S.E. region USAF Med. Referral Ctr., Keesler AFB, Miss., 1967-70; ret. USAF, 1970; asst. prof. medicine Tulane U. Sch. Medicine, New Orleans, 1970-75, assoc. prof., 1976-84; pvt. practice dermatology, 1970—; clin. assoc. prof. dermatology Tulane U. Sch. Medicine, New Orleans, 1975-84; mem. staff Kenner Regional Ctr. Hosp., 1994-2000. Past mem. staff Charity Hosp. New Orleans, East Jefferson Hosp., So. Bapt. Hosp., Kenner (La.) Regional Med. Ctr.; mem. courtesy staff LifeCare Hosp., Kenner; prof., med. dir. resident and postgrad. accredited tng. program Gulf South Med. and Surgery Inst., Kermer, La.; mem. profl. staff Kenner Dermatology Clinic; ret. dir. Fairground Corp., New Orleans; mem. courtesy staff Northshore Regional Med. Ctr., Slidell, La.; bd. dirs. La. Divsn. Am. Lukemia Soc. Mem. Kenner Med. Soc. (founder, sec./treas. 1998), N.Am. Acad. Cosmetic and Reconstructive Surgery (founder, bd. dirs., pres. 1998-99), Am. Soc. Dermatologic Surgery (co-founder, past officer and dir.), Am. Acad. Cosmetic Surgery (co-founder, past officer and dir.), Am. Bd. Cosmetic Surgery (examiner, rev. course lectr., past officer and dir.). Home: 3705 Florida Ave Kenner LA 70065-2473 Office: Gulf South Med Surg Inst 3705 Florida Ave Kenner LA 70065-2473 Office Phone: 504-471-3100.

FARBER, ISADORE E., psychologist, educator; b. St. Joseph, Mo., May 21, 1917; s. Jacob and Rose (Malkin) F.; m. Billie Frances Gulko, May 5, 1942, (dec.); children: Ronna Ellen (dec.), Deborah. Student, St. Joseph Jr. Coll., 1934-36; BA, U. Mo., 1939, MA, 1940; PhD, U. Iowa, 1946. Instr. psychology U. Rochester, 1946-47; asst. prof. to prof. psychology U. Iowa, 1947-64; vis. prof. U. Wis., 1955, Stanford, 1960; research cons. Med. Sch., U. of Okla., 1956-57; prof. psychology U. Ill., Chgo., 1964-84, prof. emeritus, 1984—, head dept. psychology, 1964-68, 76-81. Vis. prof., sr. Fulbright fellow Hebrew U., Jerusalem, 1971-72. Founding editor Jour. Exptl. Research in Personality, 1965-71; editor Psychology series, Dodd, Mead & Co., 1965-73; cons. editor Jour. Abnormal and Social Psychology, 1955-61, Jour. of Personality, 1955-61, Jour. Abnormal Psychology, 1973-79; contbr. articles to profl. jours. Served with Q.M.C. AUS, 1941-42; to 2d lt. USAAF, 1942-45. Fellow APA, Am. Psychol. Soc.; mem. Midwestern Psychol. Assn. (past pres.), Psychonomic Soc., Midwest Com. for Rational Inquiry, Phi Beta Kappa, Sigma Xi. Jewish. Home: 2601 Chestnut Ave #1303 Glenview IL 60026

FARBER, JOHN J., chemical company executive; b. Timisoara, Rumania, Aug. 23, 1925; s. Eugene and Magda (Reiter) F.; m. Maya Kleyman, June 28, 1953; children: Sandra, Deborah, Michael, Claudia. MS, U. Cluj, Timisoara, 1948; PhD, Poly. Inst. Bklyn., 1956. Rsch. chemist Sun Chem. Co., N.Y.C., 1951-52; cons. Soc. des Peintures et Vernis Bouvet, Tournus, France, Verneba A.G. Neuallschwill, Basel, Switzerland, Foster Grant Co., Inc., Leominster, Mass., Chemische Fabrik Kalk GmbH, Koln, Kalk, Germany, Asahi Chem. Industry Co., Ltd., Tokyo, 1953-56; chmn. bd., chief exec. officer ICC Industries, Ind., N.Y.C.; chmn. Primex Plastics Corp., Oakland, N.J.; pres. Dover Chem. Corp., Ohio. Dir., chmn. Electrochem. Industries (Frutarom) Ltd., Haifa, Israel. Mem. Am. Chem. Soc., Soc. Plastics Industry, Soc. Plastics Engrs., Nat. Petroleum Refiners Assn., Chem. Mfrs. Assn. Office: ICC Industries Inc 460 Park Ave New York NY 10022-1906

FARBER, PATRICIA ANN, secondary school educator; b. Balt., June 15, 1945; d. George Earle and Joy Lucille (Hankins) Reynolds; m. Stuart L. Farber. BA in English and Music, Calif. State U., Long Beach, 1967, MA in Edn. Adminstrn. summa cum laude, 1983, postgrad., 1987. Cert. tchr. math., English and music, cert. in adminstr. svcs., Calif. Instr. kindergarten-6th grade Garden Grove (Calif.) Unified Sch. Dist., 1968-72, math. and English curriculum specialist, 1976-78; field curriculum cons. Allied Edn. Coun., Chgo., 1973-75; tchr. math./computers Palm Desert (Calif.) Mid. Sch., 1983-85; mentor math. tchr. Bellflower (Calif.) H.S., 1985-98, chair dept. math., 1993-98; math. tchr. La Quinta H.S., 1998—. Author curricula, math. placement and proficiency exams. Chair jr. aux. Children's Meml. Hosp., Long Beach, 1978-83; v.p. Long Beach Civic Light Opera Guild, 1978-83. Recipient Jaime Escalante award L.A. Ednl. Partnership/ARCO, 1992, Outstanding Educator award Johns Hopkins U., 1994, Congl. Dist. citation 1996, NBC TV Crystal Apple award, 1997, Golden Apple award KESQ (ABC) TV, 2001; Mark Taper fellow, 1994; Tandy Tech. scholar, 1994, 95. Mem. ASCD, NEA, Calif. Tchrs. Assn., Assn. for Elem. Edn., Calif. State U. Alumni Assn., Phi Delta Kappa. Avocations: boating, travel, tennis. Home: 350 Monrovia Ave Long Beach CA 90803-1933 Office: La Quinta HS 79-225 Westward Ho Dr La Quinta CA 92253 E-mail: patriciaf@surf.dsusd.k12.ca.us.

FARBER, SAUL JOSEPH, physician, educator; b. N.Y.C. s. Isodor and Mary (Bunim) Farber; m. Doris Marcia Balmuth; children: Joshua M., Beth Mina Farber Loewentheil. AB, NYU, 1938, MD, 1942; PhD (hon.), Tel Aviv U., 1983. Diplomate Am. Bd. Internal Medicine. Intern Sinai Hosp., Balt., 1942—43; rsch. resident Goldwater Meml. Hosp., N.Y.C, 1946—47; resident Bellevue Hosp., N.Y.C, 1947—48; fellow NYU, 1948—49, instr., asst. prof. medicine N.Y.C., 1953—62, assoc. prof., 1962—66, prof., chmn. dept. medicine, 1966—, Frederick H. King prof. medicine, 1978—, dean for acad. affairs Sch. Medicine, 1978—98, acting dean Sch. of Medicine, 1963—66, 1979—81, 1982—, provost, dean sch. medicine, 1987—98, chmn., 1998—99. Co-chmn. N.Y. State Health Adv. Coun., 1975—80; chmn. Com. on Resource Requirements of VA Health Care Systems NRC, 1974—77; mem. adv. com. on long term care chronic illness Robert Wood Johnson Found., 1979—, co-chmn. clin. nurse scholars adv. com., 1982—; mem. med. adv. bd. Hadassah; mem. adv. com. Harold C. Simmons Arthritis Rsch. Ctr., U. Tex. Health Sci. Ctr., Dallas, 1983—86; organizing chmn. Fedn. Coun. Internal Medicine, 1975; splty. advisor Naval Med. Command, Washington, 1985—86. Contbr. articles to profl. jours. Recipient Career Scientist award, Health Rsch. Coun., N.Y.C., 1960—65, Med. Alumni Achievement award, NYU Sch. Medicine Alumni Assn., 1966, Gt. Tchr. award, NYU Alumni Fedn., 1973, Alumni Assn. Achievement award, Washington Sq. Coll. Arts and Sci., NYU, 1978, Alumni Meritorious Svc. award, NYU Alumni Fedn., 1984, Wise medal, Tel Aviv U., 1990, The Albert Gallatin medal, NYU, 1993, The Abraham Flexner award for Disting. Svc. to Med. Edn., 1995. Master: ACP (pres. 1984—85, regent 1978—86, Disting. Tchr. award 1986, Alfred Stengal Meml. award 1992); mem.: Acad. Health Ctrs. (adv. com. 1981—), Am. Physiol. Assn., Am. Clin. and Climatol. Assn., Inst. Medicine NAS, Interurban Clin. Club, Assn. Am. Physicians, Am. Soc. Clin. Investigation (sec.-treas. 1951—60, councillor 1960—63), Am. Soc. Internal Medicine (Disting. Internist of Yr. award 1976), Sigma Theta Tau (hon.). Office: NYU Sch Medicine 550 1st Ave New York NY 10016-6402

FARBER, SETH C., lawyer; b. San Francisco, Jan. 2, 1964; AB summa cum laude, Harvard Univ., 1986, JD cum laude, 1989. Bar: Mass. 1989, N.Y. 1990, US Dist. Ct. (ea., so. dist. N.Y., ea. dist. Mich., Mass.), US Ct. Appeals (2d, 4th cir.). Law clk. Judge Joseph L. Tauro, US Dist. Ct. Mass.; asst. U.S. atty. so. dist. N.Y.; ptnr. litigation dept. & chmn. Pro Bono com. Dewey Ballantine LLP, N.Y.C. Mem. Criminal Justice Act Panel, So. Dist. N.Y. Editor: Harvard Law Rev.; contbr. articles to profl. jour. Mem.: ABA (chmn. Programming subcom., Criminal Litigation com.). Office: Dewey Ballantine LLP 1301 Ave of the Americas New York NY 10019-6092 Office Phone: 212-259-7227. Office Fax: 212-259-6333. Business E-Mail: sfarber@dbllp.com.

FARBER, STEPHEN D., health facility administrator; BS in Econs., U. Pa.; grad. advanced mgmt. program, Harvard U. Investment banker Donaldson, Lufkin & Jenrette, L.A., 1993—97; v.p. corp. fin. Tenet Healthcare Corp., Santa Barbara, Calif., 1997—98; v.p. health care investment banking J.P. Morgan & Co., NY, 1998—99; sr. v.p. corp. fin., treas. Tenet Healthcare Corp., Santa Barbara, Calif., 1999, CFO, 2002—. Bd. dirs. Tenet Healthcare Found. Office: Tenet Healthcare Corp 3820 State St Santa Barbara CA 93105

FARBER, STEVEN ARTHUR, electrical engineer, educator; s. Jerome and Phyllis Sandra Farber; m. Christine Michelle Weston, July 8, 1990; children: Elias Max Weston-Farber, Zachary David Weston-Farber. BSEE, Rutgers U., 1986; SM, MIT, 1991, PhD, 1994. Post doctoral fellow MIT, Cambridge, Mass., 1993—94; vis. scientist Boston U., 1994; post doctoral fellow Carnegie Instn., Balt., 1995—2000; asst. prof. Thomas Jefferson U., Phila., 2000—04; adj asst. prof. Johns Hopkins U., Balt., 2004—; staff mem. Carnegie Instn., Balt., 2004—. Recipient Alumni Leadership award in tech.

and policy, MIT, 1987; Barbara McClintock post doctoral fellow, Carnegie Instn. Wash., 1997—98, Pew scholar, Pew Trust, 2002—. Mem.: AAAS. Office: Carnegie Instn 115 West University Pky Baltimore MD 21210 Office Phone: 410-554-1200.

FARBERMAN, HAROLD, conductor, composer; b. N.Y.C., Nov. 2, 1930; s. Louis and Lena (Kramer) F.; m. Corinne Curry, June 22, 1958; children: Thea, Lewis. Diploma, Juilliard Sch. Music, 1951; BS, New England Conservatory Music, 1956, MS, 1957. Prin. guest condr. Bournemouth Sinfonietta; founder, dir. Conductors Inst., 1980—. Dir. Stokowski Conducting Competition, 1994; prof. conducting Hartt Sch. Author: The Art of Conducting Technique; percussionist, Boston Symphony Orch., 1951-63, condr., New Arts Orch., Boston, 1955-63, guest condr., Royal Philharm. Orch., London, Denver Symphony Orch., BBC Symphony, Victoria (Can.) Philharm., Miami (Fla.) Philharm., N.Y. Philharm., New Philharmonia Orch., London, Orchestre de Lille, France, Stockholm Philharm., Swedish Radio Orch., Danish Radio Orch., Malmö (Sweden) Symphony Orch., Sydney (Australia) Symphony, Melbourne (Australia) Symphony, Perth (Australia) Symphony, Brisbane (Australia) Symphony, London Smyphony Orch., English Chamber Orch., condr., Colorado Springs (Colo.) Philharm., 1967-68, music dir., condr., Oakland Symphony Orch., 1971-79, rec. artist (condr. or composer) for, Columbia, Capitol, Mercury, Vanguard, Cambridge, Serenus, Boston records, rep. U.S. in, Paris Internat. Composition Competition, 1959; Composer symphonies, string quartet, chamber music, operas, jazz.; pioneered recorded works of Charles E. Ives., Michael Haydn. Scholar Juilliard Sch. Music, 1947-51. Mem. Condrs. Guild (founder, bd. dirs. summer inst.), Nat. Assn. Composers and Condrs. Address: PO Box 543 Germantown NY 12526 Office Phone: 518-537-5955. E-mail: corkycf@aol.com.

FARBISH, ALFRED B., waterproofing materials executive; b. Phila., Sept. 18, 1923; s. Sidney Almeyer and Rachel Bucks Farbish; m. Rita Fayer, Oct. 11, 1951 (dec. July 1995); children: Michael Bucks, Peter Bertram. Student, Oxford (Eng.) U., 1945; BA, U. Pa., 1948. Civil engr. Corps of Engrs., Phila., 1956-59; quality control Barrett divsn. Allied Chem., N.Y.C., 1959-65; sales mgr. Am. Cyanamid, Wakefield, Mass., 1965-71; v.p. Rubber & Plastics Corp., Long Island City, NY, 1972-89; pres., owner Nervastral, Inc., Greenwich, Conn., 1989—. Patentee in field. 1st lt. arty. U.S. Army, 1948-53; lt. col. USAR ret., 1983. Republican. Avocations: rowing, fencing. Home: 351 Pemberwick Rd Apt 916 Greenwich CT 06831 Office: Nervastral Inc 100 Melrose Ave Ste 206 Greenwich CT 06830

FARELL, DAN, utilities executive; B in Acctg. and Fin., East Tex. State U.; grad. advanced mgmt. program, Harvard U. CPA Tex. Treas., sec. TU Electric and TU Svcs. subsidiaries Tex. Utilities Co., v.p. TU Electric and TU Svcs. subsidiaries, 1991, chief acctg. officer, 1994, CFO TU Electric subsidiary, 1994, chmn. Ea. Energy, 1995; mng. dir. TXU Australia, 1995, pres. distbn. divsn. Oncor, 2000; pres. TXU Gas, 2002; CFO, exec. v.p. TXU Corp., Dallas, 2003; sr. v.p., CFO TXU Electric Delivery, Dallas, 2004—. Bd. dirs. Victorian Power Exch., Australia, So. Gas Assn., Assn. Tex. Intrastate Natural Gas Pipelines, Energy Reliability Coun. Tex., Leadership Coun. Am. Gas Assn., North Tex. Commn. Dir. North Tex. Commn. United Way; bd. dirs. United Way Met. Dallas; trustee First Bapt. Acad. Mem.: AICPA, Fin. Execs. Inst., Tex. Soc. CPA. Office: TXU Electric Delivery 500 N Akard St Dallas TX 75201-3411 Office Phone: 214-812-4600.

FARENTHOLD, FRANCES TARLTON, lawyer; b. Corpus Christi, Tex., Oct. 2, 1926; d. Benjamin Dudley and Catherine (Bluntzer) Tarlton; children: Dudley Tarlton, George Edward, Emilie, James Doughterty, Vincent Bluntzer (dec.). AB, Vassar Coll., 1946; JD, U. Tex., 1949; LLD, Hood Coll., 1973, Boston U., 1973, Regis Coll., 1976, Lake Erie Coll., 1979, Elmira Coll., 1981, Coll. Santa Fe, 1985. Bar: Tex. 1949. Pvt. practice, 1949-65, 67-76, 80—; mem. Tex. Ho. of Reps., 1968-72; dir. legal aid Nueces County, 1965-67; pres. Wells Coll., Aurora, N.Y., 1976-80; asst. prof. law Tex. So. U., Houston, Thurgood Marshall disting. vis. prof., 1994-95. Lawyer; b. Corpus Christi, Tex., Oct. 2, 1926; d. Benjamin Dudley and Catherine (Bluntzer) Tarlton; children: Dudley Tarlton, George Edward, Emilie, James Doughterty, Vincent Bluntzer (dec.). AB, Vassar Coll., 1946; JD, U. Tex., 1949; LLD, Hood Coll., 1973, Boston U., 1973, Regis Coll., 1976, Lake Erie Coll., 1979, Elmira Coll., 1981, Coll. of Santa Fe, 1985. Bar: Tex. 1949. Pvt. practice, 1949-65, 67-76, 80—. mem. Tex. Ho. of Reps., 1968-72; dir. legal aide Nueces County, 1965-67; asst. prof. law Tex. So. U., Houston; pres. Wells Coll., Aurora, N.Y., 1976-80; disting. vis. prof. Thurgood Marshall Tex. So. U., Houston, 1994-95. Mem. Human Relations Com., Corpus Christi, 1963-68, Corpus Christi Citizen's Com. Community Improvement, 1966-68; mem. Tex. adv. com. to U.S. Commn. on Civil Rights, 1968-76; mem. nat. adv. council ACLU; mem. Orgn. for Preservation Unblemished Shoreline, 1964—; Dem. candidate for Gov. of Tex., 1972; del. Dem. Nat. Conv., 1972, 1st woman nominated to be candidate v.p. U.S., 1972; nat. co-chmn. Citizens to Elect McGovern-Shriver, 1972; chmn. Nat. Women's Polit. Caucus, 1973-75; mem. Dem. platform com., 1988; trustee Vassar Coll., 1975-83; bd. dirs. Fund for Constl. Govt., Ctr. for Devel. Policy, 1983—, Mexican Am. Legal Def. and Ednl. Fund, 1980-83; chmn. Inst. for Policy Studies, 1986-91; mem. bd. dirs. Rothko Chapel, 1997—. Recipient Lyndon B. Johnson Woman of Year award, 1973. Mem. State Bar Tex. Mem. Human Rels. Com., Corpus Christi, 1963-68, Corpus Christi Citizens Com. Cmty. Improvement, 1966-68; mem. Tex. adv. com. to U.S. Commn. on Civil Rights, 1968-76; mem. nat. adv. coun. ACLU; mem. Orgn. for Preservation Unblemished Shoreline, 1964—; Dem. candidate for Gov. of Tex., 1972; del. Dem. Nat. Conv., 1972, 1st woman nominated to be candidate v.p. U.S., 1972; nat. co-chair Citizens to elect McGovern-Shriver, 1972; chmn. Nat. Women's Polit. Caucus, 1973-75; mem. Dem. Platform Com., 1988; trustee Vassar Coll., 1975-83; bd. dirs. Fund for Constl. Govt., Ctr. for Devel. Policy, 1983—, Mexican Am. Legal Def. and Ednl. Fund, 198--83; chmn. Inst. for Policy Studies, 1986-91; bd. dirs. Rothko Chapel, 1997—, chmn., 2001—. Recipient Lyndon B. Johnson Woman of Yr. award, 1973, Lifetime Svc. award, Dem. Party of Tex., 1998. Mem. State Bar Tex. Home: 2929 Buffalo Speedway Apt 1813 Houston TX 77098-1710 Personal E-mail: emailsissy@aol.com.

FARGIS, ALISON K., book developer, literary agent, consultant; d. Paul McKenna Fargis and Elizabeth Fargis-Lancaster; m. Michael W. Buckley, Sept. 17, 2005. BA, Vassar Coll., 1991. English tchr. Gymnasium Pod Svata Horu, Pribram, Czech Republic, 1992—93, Prague Castle, 1995; ednl. coord. Estee Lauder Companies, NYC, 1993—95; book developer, lit. agt. The Stonesong Press, NYC, 1995—. Editor: Words That Built a Nation: A Young Person's Collection of Historic American Documents, The American Film Institute Desk Reference, The New York Public Library Desk Reference, Balancing Pregnancy and Work: How to Make the Most of the Next 9 Months on the Job, The 20/30 Fat & Fiber Diet Plan, The Discover Science Almanac, Chocolate Bar: Recipes and Entertaining Ideas for Living the Sweet Life (Gourmand World Cookbook award, 2004), I'll Be Home for Christmas: The Library of Congress Revisits the Spirit of Christmas During World War II. Fellow, Found. Civil Soc., 1995; grantee, Dana Found., 1990. Mem.: Am. Book Producers Assn. Office: The Stonesong Press 27 West 24th St Ste 510 New York NY 10010 Office Phone: 212-929-4600.

FARGIS, PAUL MCKENNA, publisher, publishing executive, consultant, book designer; b. N.Y.C., NY, Mar. 19, 1939; s. George Bertrand and Elizabeth Harlin (McKenna) F.; m. Elizabeth Hackett, Aug. 22, 1964; children: John Hackett, Alison Katherine; m. Dawn Sangrey, Apr. 23, 1977; 1 child, Christopher Sangrey. Student, Cath. U. Am., 1958; B in Social Sci., Fairfield U., 1961; MA (Publ. Tuition scholar), NYU, 1962. Editorial asst. Prentice-Hall, Inc., Englewood Cliffs, NJ, 1961-62; editor Hawthorn Books, Inc., NYC, 1963-67, v.p., editorial dir., 1967-71; v.p., editor-in-chief Thomas Y. Crowell Co. and Funk & Wagnalls divs. Dun-Donnelley Pub. Corp., NYC, 1971-77; editor-in-chief Apollo Books, NYC, 1972-77; mng. dir. Thomas Y. Crowell div. Harper and Row, NYC, 1977-78; founder, pres. and pub. The Stonesong Press, Inc., 1978—2003. Dir., sec. Round Stone Press, Inc., 1990-2001; pub. Grand Ctrl. Press, 2001-2003; mem. adv. bd. Grad. Sch. Corp. and Polit. Comm., Fairfield U., 1969-81; pub. arbitrator Am. Arbitration Assn., 1982-2002; pub. seminar lectr. Author: The Consumer's Handbook, 1966, rev. edit., 1974, Company's Coming, 1965; Am. editor: Twentieth Century Ency. Catholicism, 1963-67; editor-in-chief: The New York Public Library Desk Reference, 1989; co-author: Perks and Parachutes, 1997; co-editor: The Big Book of Life's Instructions, 1995; contbr. articles to profl. jour.; patentee in field. Exec. dir. Harrison (NY) Town Recreation Commn., 1970-72; dir. Harrison Town Forum, 1969-73; former bd. dir. US Cath. Hist. Soc.; trustee Unitarian Universalist Fellowship of No. Westchester. Mem. Am. Book Coun. (bd. dir. 1987-88), Am. Book Producers Assn. (pres. 1986-87, bd. dir. Charitable Book program 1987-89), Book Industry Study Group. Unitarian Universalist. Avocations: carpentry, stonework, travel, hiking, sculpture. Office: 27 W 24th St New York NY 10010

FARGO, HEATHER, mayor; b. Oakland, Ca, Dec. 12, 1952; m. Alan Moll. BS in environmental planning and mgmt., U. Cal-Davis, 1975. Mem. Sacramento City Coun., 1989—98; mayor City of Sacramento, Calif., 2001—. Office: City Hall 730 I St Ste 321 Sacramento CA 95814 E-mail: hfargo@cityofsacramento.org.*

FARGO, THOMAS BOULTON, retired career military officer; b. San Diego, Calif., 1948; Grad., U.S. Naval Acad., 1970. Commd. ensign USN, 1970, advanced through ranks to adm.; various assignments to comd. U.S. Naval Forces, Cen. Command/Comdr., U.S. Fifth Fleet; dep. chief of naval opers., comdr. U.S. Pacific Fleet; comdr. U.S. Pacific Command, Honolulu, 2002—05. Decorated Disting. Svc. medal (4 times), Def. Superior Svc. medal, Legion of Merit (3 times), others; recipient James Bond Stockdale award for Inspirational Leadership, 1989. Office: US Pacific Command PO Box 64031 Camp H M Smith HI 96861-4031

FARHA, TODD, health products executive; BA magna cum laude econ., Trinity Univ.; MBA with distinction, Harvard Univ. Bus. Sch. CEO Best Doctors, Oxford Specialty Mgmt.; with Physician Corp. Am.; pres., CEO Wellcare Health Plan. Office: WellCare Health Plans Inc Renaissance 1 8725 Henderson Rd Tampa FL 33634 Office Phone: 813-290-6200. Office Fax: 813-262-2802.*

FARHADI, ASHKAN, physician, researcher; b. Shiraz, Iran, Mar. 5, 1965; arrived in U.S., 2000; s. Gholam Ali Farhadi and Sadat Eyni; m. Ziba Ranjbaran, June 20, 1990; children: Arghavan, Nilgoun. Med. Diploma, Shiraz U., Iran, 1989; Internal Medicine Splty., Shiraz U., 1992; Gastroenterology subspeciality, Beheshti (Nat.) U., Tehran, Iran, 1994; M in clin. rsch., Rush U., 2001—03; Internal Medicine Splty., Rush U., Ill., 2003—04, Gastroenterology, 2004. Lic. MD Ill. Regulation dept., 2002, Iran Med. Assn., 1989. Rsch. fellow Rush U., Chgo., 2000—; chmn., dept. of medicine Mazandaran U., Sari, Iran, 1998—99, asst. prof. of medicine, 1994—99, Beheshti (Nat.) U., Tehran, 1992—94. Author: (book) Irritable Bowel Syndrome, Peptic Ulcer. Recipient Presdl. award, Am. Coll. of Gastroenterology, 2002, Sr. Fellow award, 2002, Third Pl. in the Bd. of Gastroenterology, Mister of Health and Sciences, Iran, 1994, First Pl. in the Bd. of Internal Medicine, 1992, Best Young Investigator, The Iranian Med. Assn., 1990; Award for Rsch., Am. Coll. of Gastroenterology, 2001. Achievements include invention of creeping colonoscope; automated hot biopsy needle and device; sanitizing container and display; Farhadi's cell culture plate; Farhadi's cell container. Office: Rush Medical Coll 1725 W Harrison St Ste 206 Chicago IL 60612 Office Phone: 312-942-8924. Business E-Mail: ashkan_farhadi@rush.edu.

FARIAN, BABETTE SOMMERICH, artist; b. N.Y.C., June 6, 1916; d. Hugo Joseph and Clara Julia (Hart) Somerich; m. Robert Alan Farian, Sept. 27, 1944 (dec.); 1 child, Robert Alan. Student, N.Y. Sch. Fine and Applied Art, 1933-35, Cooper Union Sch. Art, 1939-42, Modern Mus. Art Sch., 1965-68; pvt. student, Morris Kantor, 1941, Joseph Margulies, 1947-49, Donald Stacy, 1969-89. Instr. color and design Cooper Union, N.Y.C., 1941-42; designer Hanscom Fabrics, Kransom Co., N.Y.C., 1955-57; free lance textile and greeting card designer, 1958-59; asst. head of studio Manhattan Shirt Co., 1960-64. One women shows include Serial Fed. Savs. Bank, N.Y.C., 1976, Walter Reade Theatres, N.Y.C., 1977, 81; exhibited in group shows at Atelier Gallery of Contemporary Art, N.Y.C., 1967, 68, Am. Artist Profl. League, N.Y.C., 1958-59, Impulse Gallery, Martha's Vineyard, 1968, U.S. Fine Arts Registry, 1968, Fine Artists Ctr., Taos, N.Mex., Nat. Arts Club, 1987-97, Audubon Artists Assn., 1988-89, 90, Nat. Soc. Painters in Casein & Acrylic, 1989, 90, Morin-Miller Galleries, 1989, Met. Mus., St. John's U., 1990, Villanova U., 1991, Queens Coll., 1991, 97, Corner Gallery, 1991, Fed. Pla., 1991, and numerous others; represented in permanent collections Bklyn. Botanic Garden Collection, Women's Inter.-Art Mus., N.Y.C., Sloan-Kettering Hosp., Tammassee D.A.R. Sch. Gallery, Unitarian-Universalist Ch. Gallery, also pvt. collections. Recipient Internat. Women's Yr. award, 1976, Grumbacher award Nat. Art League, 1984-87, 1st prize Jackson Hts. Art Club, 1989, Spl. award Jackson Hts. Art Club, 1991, Honorable Mention, Queens Coll., 1991, 97. Mem. Burr Artists (meml. chair), Composers, Authors and Artists Am. (watercolor prize 1980, 83, 1st prize short story 1981), Nat. Arts Club, Artist's Equity Assn., N.Y. Nat. League Am. Pen Women (bd. dirs., Merit award 1979, achievement award 1997), Eleanor Gay Lee Found., Internat. Soc. Artists Internat., Cath. Artists of the 1990's, Orgn. Internat. Artists, Orgn. Ind. Artists, Queens Coun. on Culture of Arts, Eleanor Gay Gallery Found. (bd. dirs.).

FARIAS, BRIAN K., music educator; b. Somerville, N.J., Aug. 19, 1962; s. Arthur E. and Shirley M. Farias. MusB in Edn. cum laude, Boston Conservatory Music, 1984; M in Clarinet Performance, New Eng. Conservatory, 1989; postgrad., Rutgers U., 2002—. Cert. music tchr. N.J., 1984, Pa., 1992, Md., 1998, music tchr.comprehensive grades K-12 Mass., 1984. Music tchr. Sayreville Pub. Schs., Parlin, NJ, 1985—86; band dir. Harvard (Mass.) Pub. Schs., 1989—89, Middlesex (N.J.) H.S., 1990—91, Emmaus (Pa.) H.S., 1991—93, Thomas Pullen Arts Magnet Sch., Landover, Md., 1998—2001; music tchr. Lyndhurst (N.J.) Pub. Schs., 2001—02; band/jazz band dir. Rosa Parks Performing Arts HS, Paterson, NJ, 2002—05. Guest soloist Nutley (N.J.) Symphony Orch., 1983; dir. Best Feet Forward-Holistic Practice, Newton, NJ, 1998—; holistic health practitioner and educator Best Feet Forward, 1999—; healer with music, reflexology, hypnosis and past-life regression, aromatherapy; pvt. lesson instr. Cmty. Conservatory, 1994—97, DeVoe's Music, 1997—98, Calderone Sch. Music, 2000—02, Newton, NJ. Named Competition Winner, Garden State Arts Ctr., 1980, Compeition Winner, Livingston Symphony Orch., 1984, Competiton Winner, Rutgers U., 1990; Performance scholar, Rutgers U. Orch., 2002. Mem.: N.J.-Internat. Assn. for Jazz Edn. (assoc.; pres. N.J. region 1 2002), Nat. Band Assn. (assoc.), Internat. Clarinet Soc. (assoc.), Music Educators Nat. Conf. (assoc.). Achievements include development of Rosa Parks Percussion Ensemble; Louis Armstrong Jazz Award-Rosa Parks HS; John Philip Sousa Band Award-Rosa Parks HS; 1st Place Awards-Music in the Parks for Band-Rosa Parks HS; 1st Place -Music in the Parks for Jazz Band-Rosa Parks HS; Silver Award for Band-NBA festival, Rosa Parks HS; Best Rhythm, Trombone, soloist-NJ-IAJE Jazz Festival-Rosa Parks HS; NJ State Teen Arts Festival Participant-Rosa Parks HS; 1st Place-Music in the Parks for ELEM Chorus-Lyndhurst Public Schools. Home: 52 Plainfield Ave Newton NJ 07860 Office Phone: 973-383-9438. Personal E-mail: healingmusicman@aol.com.

FARICY, JOHN HARTNETT, JR., lawyer; b. Augsburg, Germany, Nov. 5, 1955; came to U.S., 1956; s. John Hartnett and Mary Helen Sarah (Bowe) F. BA, Tulane U., 1977; JD, William Mitchell Coll. Law, St. Paul, 1982. Bar: Minn. 1982, U.S. Dist. Ct. Minn. 1983, U.S. Ct. Appeals (2d cir.) 1987, U.S. Supreme Ct. 1988. Ptnr. Faricy & Roen, P.A., Mpls., 1996—. Mem. Univ. Club of St. Paul. Office: Faricy & Roen PA 333 S 7th St Minneapolis MN 55402-4200 Office Phone: 612-371-4400. Business E-Mail: jfaricy@faricyroen.com.

FARID, FARID O., mathematics professor; MS, U. of London, U.K., 1982; PhD in Math., U. of Calgary, Can., 1988. Vis. math prof. U. of Cin., 1999—2000, Pacific Luth. U., Tacoma, 2000—01; math prof., rschr., supr. U. of Minn., Morris, 2002—; math prof. U. Toledo, 2003—. Author: (author of a research paper in math) Linear and Multilinear Algebra, (math. rsch. papers) Linear Algebra and Its Applications, Procs. of the Am. Math. Soc., Procs. Indian Acad. Sci; co-author: Can. Jour. of Math. Fellow Post Doctoral Fellowship, U. of Toronto, 1989, U. of Guelph, 1992; scholar Rsch. and Tchg. Scholarships, U. of Calgary, 1984—88. Office Phone: 419-530-2804. E-mail: farid.farid@utoledo.edu.

FARINA, DENNIS, actor; b. Chgo., Feb. 29, 1944; Actor: (films) Thief, 1981, Jo Jo Dancer, Your Life is Calling, 1986, Manhunter Deg, 1986, Midnight Run, 1988, Open Admissions, 1988, The Case of the Hillside Strangler, 1989, Blind Faith, 1990, People Like Us, 1990, Men of Respect, 1991, Serious Money, 1991, Another Blowout, 1993, Striking Distance, 1993, Little Big League, 1994, Get Shorty, 1995, Eddie, 1996, That Old Feeling, 1996, Out of Sight, 1998, Saving Private Ryan, 1998, Buddy Faro, 1998, The Mod Squad, 1999, Reindeer Games, 2000, Snatch, 2000, Sidewalks of NY, 2001, Big Trouble, 2002, Stealing Harvard, 2002, Paparazzi, 2004; (TV mini-series) Bella Maffia, 1997; (TV series) In-Laws, 2002-03, Law and Order, 2004-. Office: Geddes Agy 1633 N Halsted St Ste 400 Chicago IL 60614-5517

FARINELLI, JEAN L., management consultant; b. Phila., July 26, 1946; d. Albert J. and Edith M. (Falini) F. BA, Am. U., Washington, 1968; MA, Ohio State U., Columbus, 1969. Asst. pub. relations dir. Dow Jones & Co., Inc., N.Y.C., 1969-71; account exec. Carl Byoir & Assocs., Inc., N.Y.C., 1972-74, v.p., 1974-80, sr. v.p., 1980-82; pres. Tracy-Locke/BBDO Pub. Relations, Dallas, 1982-87, Creamer Dickson Basford, Inc., N.Y.C., 1987-88, chmn., chief exec. officer, 1988-98; pres., chief exec. officer Eurocom Corp. & PR (U.S.), 1991, Corp. Graphics, Inc., 1992; pres. Farinelli Cons. Group, LLC, 1999—, 20 Sutton Pl. South, Inc., 2003—. Dir. The Cologne Life Reinsurance Co., 1997-99. Recipient PR CaseBook, PR Reporter, N.H., 1984, Silver Spur, Tex. Pub. Rels. Assn., Dallas, 1985, Matrix award Women in Comms., 1993. Mem.: Nat. Found. for Infectious Diseases (former trustee), Arthur W. Page Soc. (treas., v.p. adminstrn. and fin.), Internat. Pub. Rels. Assn. (pub. rels. seminar), Nat. Investor Rels. Inst., The Women's Forum (bd. dirs.), Women in Comms. (chmn. 1995, dir. 1999—, Matrix award 1993), Pub. Rels. Soc. Am. (Silver Anvil awards chmn. 1987, acad. exec. bd. 1990—91, trustee found., Silver Anvil award 1980—81, 1985, Excalibur award Houston chpt. 1985, Best of Show Silver Anvil award 1998). Office: 20 Sutton Pl S New York NY 10022-4165

FARIS, GEORGE N., management consultant; b. Juddaya, Lebanon, Mar. 1, 1941; arrived in U.S., 1958; s. Naim George Faris and Emilie Saadi; m. Claude Moujes, Dec. 12, 1969; children: Ron, Danielle. BSc, Miss. State U., 1961, MSME, 1963; PhD in Mech. Engring., Purdue U., West Lafayette, Ind., 1968. Sr. engr. IBM, 1968—69; chmn., CEO Donbar Devel. Corp., 1969—73, ICAT, Inc., 1973—81; chmn. Am. Internat. Refinery, 1988—2000; mng. dir. Medshipping Estruet Petroleum, Ltd., 1997—2001; chmn., CEO Am. Internat. Petroleum Corp., 1981—2002; chmn. Faris Group, Inc., 2002—. Contbr. articles to profl. jours. Adv. coun. chmn. Georgetown U. Sch. Bus.; adv. coun. Harvard U. Kennedy Sch. Govt.; corp. mem. Coun. on Fgn. Rels.; chmn. internat. adv. bd. Lebanese Am. U., 2004—; chmn. fin. com. Rep. Abroad, 1990—92; pres. Gillian Assn., Greenwich, Conn.; bd. trustees Lebanese Am. U.; pres. bd. 570 Park Ave. Apts., N.Y.C. Recipient Ellis Island Medal of Honor, 2002. Mem.: AAAS, N.Y. Acad. Sci., Palm Beach Yacht Club, Beach Club, Doubles Club, Met. Club, Univ. Club. Republican. Roman Catholic. Achievements include patents for rotary head exchange. Avocations: reading, tennis, swimming, exercise. Home: 570 Park Ave New York NY 10021 Office Phone: 212-753-1409.

FARIS, JAMES VANNOY, interventional cardiologist, educator, hospital executive; b. Indpls., July 18, 1943; s. Vannoy and Maudeline (Freeman) F.; m. Jacqueline Claire Bexell, July 1, 1978; children: Nathan James, Jamie Lynn, Jenna Claire, Brittany Jean, James Vannoy III, Janessa Marie. AB, Ind. U., 1965, MD, 1968. Diplomate Am. Bd. Internal Medicine, Am. Bd. Cardiology, Am. Bd. Interventional Cardiology. Intern, resident Ind. U. Med. Ctr., Indpls., 1968-71, asst. prof. medicine, 1976-80, assoc. prof. medicine, radiology, 1980-99; chief of staff Richard L. Roudebush VA Med. Ctr., Indpls., 1983-95, chief sect. cardiology, 1995-99; clin. assoc. prof. medicine, med. scis. program Ind. U., Bloomington, 1999—. Asst. dean sch. medicine Ind. U., 1983-95. Maj. U.S. Army, 1971-73, Vietnam. Grantee Ind. Heart Assn., VA Cooperative Study, 1999-2000. Fellow Am. Coll. Cardiology; mem. AMA, Ind. State Med. Assn. (parliamentarian), Indpls. Med. Soc. (pres. 1998-99), Monroe Owen County Med. Soc. (pres. 2003), Alpha Omega Alpha, Alpha Epsilon Delta. Republican. Methodist. Avocations: skiing, tennis, water-skiing. Office Phone: 877-679-3758. Business E-Mail: jfaris@ima-md.com.

FARIS, LYNNE, minister; b. Galveston, Tex., May 2, 1966; d. Arthur Monroe and Gail Carver Faris. BA English Lit., Colo. Coll., 1988; MDiv, Fuller Theol. Sem., 1994. To ministry Presbyn. Ch. Young adult intern 1st Presbyn. Ch., Colorado Springs, Colo., 1988—89; comm./devel. asst. The Mendenhall Ministries, Miss., 1989—90; substitute tchr. Alhambra, Calif., 1990—94; assoc. pastor outreach Nat. Presbyn. Ch., Washington, 1994—. Bd. dirs. The Reconciliation Inst., Inc., Washington, sec., 1995—; mem. Evangs. for Mid. East Understanding, Chgo., mem. adv. bd., 1998—; mem. Unique Learning Ctr., Washington, mem. adv. bd., 1997—. Mem.: Holy Land Ecumenical Found. (v.p. 1998—, bd. dirs.). Avocations: hiking, travel. Home: 2020 Derby Ridge Ln Silver Spring MD 20910 Office: 516 N 62nd St Lower Apt Seattle WA 98103

FARIS, MARC R, composer, education educator; b. Waynesboro, Va., Aug. 13, 1972; s. Melvin R and Charlotte Duncan Faris; m. Leslie M Vincent, July 1, 2000. MusB, Eastman Sch. of Music, 1990—94; PhD, Duke U., 1998—2003. Vis. asst. prof. Duke U., Dept. of Music, Durham, NC; pub. rels. and performance dir. Pulsoptional Composers' Collective, Durham, NC. Composer: (soprano and sring quartet) Facing (Finalist, ALEA III Internat. Composition Competition, 2000), (ensemble) Alternative Communities, (brass quartet, rock band and amplified string quartet) Cultural Studies, (solo violincello) VLC (William Klenz Composition prize, 2001). James B. Duke Grad. fellowship, Duke U., Grad. Sch., 1998—2003, Composition fellow, Chamber Music Conf. and Composers Forum of the East, 2001. Office: Duke Univ Dept of Music Box 90665 Durham NC 27708-0665 Office Phone: 919-660-3370. Office Fax: 919-660-3370. E-mail: mrf@duke.edu.

FARISH, CHARLES MORRISON, physician; b. Columbia, S.C., Aug. 20, 1946; s. Charles Adams and Louise (Morrison) F.; m. Luanne Grigg, June 13, 1970; children: Cameron Morrison, Geofferey Grigg, Amanda Jane. BS in Bacteriology, U. N.C., 1968, MS in Pub. Health, 1970; MD, Med. U. S.C., 1974. Diplomate Am. Bd. Pediatrics. Research microbiologist S.C. Dept. Health and Environ., Columbia, 1970-71; resident Med. U. S.C., Charleston, 1974-75, Okla. Children's Meml. Hosp., Oklahoma City, 1975-77; with Pee Dee Health Care, Darlington, S.C., 1977-80, pres., 1980-85, Eastern Carolina Pediat. Assocs., Darlington, 1985—. Team physician St. John's High Sch. Darlington, 1977-98; asst. prof. Med. U. S.C. Charleston, 1980—; mem. med. adv. bd. Dept. HHS. Active Darlington County Child Protection Adv. Bd., Darlington, 1978-83; chmn. Darlington County Youth Home, 1978—; past chmn. Pee Dee Mental Health Bd., Florence, S.C., 1979-85. Fellow Am. Acad. Pediatrics (pres. S.C. chpt. 1998-2000), Am. Acad. Sports Medicine. Lutheran. Home: 103 Min Lou Cir Darlington SC 29532-2307 Office: Eastern Carolina Pediatrics 201 Industrial Way Darlington SC 29532-3816 also: 1594 Freedom Blvd Ste 301 Florence SC 29505-6040 Office Phone: 843-667-6710. E-mail: cmfarish@aol.com.

FARISH, WILLIAM S., former ambassador, horse breeder; m. Sarah Farish. Student, U. Va. Stockbroker Underwood, Neuhaus and Co., Houston; pres. Navarro Exploration Co.; founding dir. Eurus, Inc., Capital Nat. Bank, Houston; pres. W.S. Farish and Co., Houston; owner Lane's End Farm, Versailles, Ky., 1980—; U.S. amb. to U.K. U.S. Dept. State, London,

2001—04. Chmn. Churchill Downs Inc., 1992—2001. Past organizing mem. Houston chpt. Nat. Urban League; chmn. Houston Parks Bd. Office: Lane's End Farm PO Box 626 Versailles KY 40383

FARISON, JAMES BLAIR, electrical biomedical engineer, educator; b. McClure, OH, May 26, 1938; s. Blair Albert and Marie Lucille (Ballard) F.; m. Gail Donahue, Mar. 30, 1961; children: Jeffrey James, Mark Donahue. BS summa cum laude in Elec. Engring, U. Toledo, 1960; MS, Stanford U., 1961, PhD, 1964. Registered profl. engr., Tex., Oh. Asst. prof. elec. engring. U. Toledo, 1964-67, assoc. prof., 1967-74, prof., 1974-95, asst. dean engring., 1969-71, dean engring., 1971-80, prof. elec. engring. and computer sci., 1995-98; prof. bioengring., 1996-98; prof. dean Emeritus U. Toledo; prof., chmn. dept. engring. Baylor U., Waco, Tex., 1998—. Adj. prof. Med. Coll. Ohio, 1987-98; mem Accreditation Bd. for Engring. and Tech. Contbr. articles to various profl. jours. Recipient Outstanding Young Man of 1971 award Toledo Jr. C. of C., 1972, Boss of Year award Limestone chpt. Am. Bus. Women's Assn., 1973, Toledo's Engr. Yr. award, 1984, Outstanding Tchr. award U. Toledo, 1986; named Disting. Alumnus, U. Toledo, 1983. Fellow Ohio Acad. Sci. (Centennial honoree 1991); mem. IEEE (sr. mem., Toledo Elec. Engr. of Yr. 1972, 74, 76), NSPE, ASME, Ohio Soc. Profl. Engrs. (Young Engr. of Yr. 1973, Citation 1983, Outstanding Engring. Educator 1984), Toledo Soc. Profl. Engrs. (Young Engr. of Yr. 1973), Accreditation Bd. for Engring. and Tech. (program evaluator 1996-2001), Biomed. Engring. Soc., Am. Soc. Engring. Edn. (Outstanding Campus Rep. 2003, vice chair, program chair, 2002-05, chair 2005—, multidisciplinary engring. divsn. 2002—), Soc. Mfg. Engrs. (sr.), Internat. Soc. Optical Engring., Tex. Soc. Profl. Engrs., Soc. Woman Engrs. (sr.), Blue Key, Sigma Xi, Tau Beta Pi, Pi Mu Epsilon, Phi Kappa Phi, Eta Kappa Nu (Outstanding Young Elec. Engr. 1971). Home: 9613 Old Farm Rd Waco TX 76712-6402 Office: Baylor U One Bear Pl # 97356 Waco TX 76798-7356 E-mail: Jim_Farison@baylor.edu.

FARISS, BRUCE LINDSAY, endocrinologist, consultant; b. Allisonia, Va., July 22, 1934; s. Alven Pierce and Hetty Jo (Lindsay) F.; m. Cheryl Louise Tomasie, Jan. 18, 1975; children: Bruce LIndsay, Melissa, Margaret, Susan, Henry, Sarah Jane, Caroline, Adam. BS, Roanoke Coll., 1957; MD, U. Va., 1961. Diplomate in internal medicine and endocrinology Am. Bd. Internal Medicine. Med. intern U. Va. Hosp., Charlottesville, 1961-62; commd. capt. M.C. U.S. Army, 1962, advanced through grades to col., 1976; gen. med. officer Ft. Monroe, Va., 1962-63; resident in internal medicine Brooke Gen. Hosp., Ft. Sam Houston, Tex., 1963-66; fellow in endocrinology U. Calif., San Francisco, 1966-68; chief endocrine service Madigan Gen. Hosp., Tacoma, 1968-71, chief clin. rsch. svc., 1968-76, asst. chief dept. medicine, 1972-73, dir. endocrine fellowship program, 1971-76, chief dept. clin. investigation, 1979-85, dir. endocrine-metabolism fellowship tng. program, 1979-85; cons. internal medicine MEDCOM Europe, 1976-79; cons. endocrinology to surgeon gen. U.S. Army, 1979-85; with dept. biology Va. Poly. Inst., Blacksburg, 1987-99; sec., treas. Radford Cmty. Hosp., 1998—2000, vice chmn., 2000—02, chmn., 2002—04, chmn. dept. M & D, 2005—. Contbr. articles to profl. jours. Mem. Bd. Suprs., Pulaski County, Va., 1988-2004, vice chmn., 2000-04; mem. Pulaski County Planning Commn., 1992-2004; mem. Pulaski County Recreation Com., 1989-93. Decorated Legion of Merit with oak leaf cluster; recipient Meritorious Svc. aard Office of Surgeon Gen. of Army, 1977, Roanoke Coll. medal, 1982. Fellow: ACP; mem.: AACE, Am. Assn. Clin. Endocrinologists, N.Y. Acad. Sci., So. Med. Assn., Am. Diabetes Assn. (trustee 1986—89), Endocrine Soc. (ednl. com. 1980—83), Am. Fedn. Clin. Rsch., S.W. Va. Med. Soc., Alpha Omega Alpha. Office Phone: 540-674-5900.

FARKAS, CAROL GARNER, nurse, administrator; b. NYC, Apr. 26, 1936; d. Charles Harry and Phyllis (Levine) Schotland; m. Theodore Arthur Garner, 1956 (dec. 1971); children: Charles Hugh Farkas Garner, Judi Beth Garner Farkas, Andrea Lee Garner Farkas Krupen; m. Robin Lewis Farkas, Oct. 17, 1972; adopted children: Bradford Lewis Farkas, Andrew Lawrence Farkas. BSN with distinction, Cornell U., 1976; MPH, Columbia U., 1980. Nursing dir. Am. Inst. Life Threatening Illness and Loss Columbia Presbyn. Med. Ctr., NYC, 1980—. Del. white House Conf. Aging, NY State Gov.'s Conf. Aging; mem. NY State Hospice Adv. Group, 1979-81; mem. adv. com. office health mgmt. NY State Dept. Health, 1979-81; mem. select com. financing and licensure, com. legis. edn. Nat. Hospice Orgn., 1980—; vol. adminstr., practitioner in symptom control psychiatry dept. Meml. Sloan-Kettering Cancer Ctr., NYC, 1981-96; mem. Choice in Dying, 1991-92, Nat. Coun. Death and Dying, 1990-91, Soc. Right to Die, 1982-90; co-chair med. student conf. nursing com. Columbia Presbyn., NYC, 1992. Co-editor: Nursing and Thanatology, 1982; contbr. articles to profl. publs., chpts. to books. Bd. mem. NY State Task Force on Life and the Law, 1994-97. Mem. Sigma Theta Tau. Home: PO Box 9223 485 Indian Springs Dr Jackson Hole WY 83002 Fax: 307-734-8006. Office Phone: 307-734-8005.

FARKAS, DANIEL FREDERICK, food science and technology educator; b. Boston, June 20, 1933; m. Alice Bridgetta Brady, Jan. 25, 1959; children: Brian Emerson, Douglas Frederick. BS, MIT, 1954, MS, 1955, PhD, 1960. Lic. chem. engr., Calif. Commd. U.S. Army, 1954, advanced through grades to major, 1968, ret., 1974; staff scientist Arthur D. Little, Cambridge, Mass., 1960-62; asst. prof. Cornell U. Agrl Expt. Sta., Geneva, N.Y., 1962-66; rsch. leader We. regional rsch. ctr. USDA, Albany, Calif., 1967-80; prin. Daniel F. Farkas Assocs., 1976—; prof., chair dept. food sci. U. Del., Newark, 1980-87; v.p. process R & D Campbell Soup Co., Camden, N.J., 1987-90; Jacobs-Root prof., head dept. food sci. and tech. Oreg. State U., Corvalis, 1990-2000, prof. emeritus, 2000—. Contbr. more than 50 articles to peer-reviewed sci. and tech. jours. Fellow Inst. Food Technologists (Nicholas Appert medal 2002); mem. AICE, Am. Chem. Soc. (profl.), Sigma Xi. Achievements include 5 U.S. patents for centrifugal fluidized bed food drying system, application of ultra-high hydrostatic pressure to food preservation.

FARKAS, JULIUS, chemist; b. Brownsville, Pa., Apr. 9, 1958; s. Julius and Marcella (Stanko) F. BA, Washington and Jefferson Coll., Washington, Pa., 1980; PhD, Pa. State U., University Park, 1985. Tchg./rsch. asst. Washington and Jefferson Coll., 1979-80; lab. technician Stauffer Chem. Co., Washington, 1979-80; tchg./grad. rsch. asst. Pa. State U., University Park, 1980-85; R&D assoc. Noveon, Inc. (formerly known as B.F. Goodrich Co.), Brecksville, Ohio, 1985—. Mem. Am. Chem. Soc., Am. Inst. Chemists, Soc. Plastics Engrs. Presbyterian. Office: Noveon Inc 9911 Brecksville Rd Brecksville OH 44141-3289 Office Phone: 216-447-7323. Business E-Mail: Julius.Farkas@noveon.com.

FARKAS, PAUL STEPHEN, gastroenterologist; b. N.Y.C., 1952; s. Benjamin J. and Ellen (Tanner) F.; m. Esta Miriam Cantor, June 24, 1973; children: Melanie Sharon, Joshua David. AB magna cum laude with distinction in psychology, Brandeis U., 1972; MD, Tufts U., 1976. Diplomate Am. Bd. Internal Medicine, Am. Bd. Gastroenterology. Intern Baystate Med. Ctr., Sprinfield, Mass., 1976-77, resident in internal medicine, 1977-79; fellow in gastroenterology Albert Einstein Coll. Medicine, Bronx, N.Y., 1979-81; asst. clin. prof. medicine Tufts U., Boston, 1985—; med. advisor Med. Assist Program Springfield Tech. C.C., 1989—. Co-dir. med. edn. Mercy Hosp., Springfield, 1990-95, chmn. dept. gastroenterology, 1995—, dir. libr., 1988-97, mem. exec. com., 1995—, treas. med. staff, 1999—; mem. adv. bd. VNA, Springfield, 1984-88; adj. asst. prof. clin. pharmacology Mass. Coll. Pharmacy, Boston, 1982—. Author: Diagnostic Diagrams Gastroenterology, 1985; contbr. book chpts., articles and revs. in field. Bd. dirs. B'nai Jacob Synagogue, Springfield, 1987-88, Com. for Longmeadow, Mass., 1989, Yeshiva, Longmeadow, 1994-99; trustee Mercy Hosp., 1997-98. Fellow ACP (cmty. based excellence in tchg. award 2000); mem. AMA, Am. Coll. Gastroenterology, Am. Gastroent. Assn., Am. Soc. Gastrointestinal Endoscopy, New Eng. Soc. Gastrointestinal Endoscopy. Office: 299 Carew St Springfield MA 01104-2301 Office Phone: 413-737-7951. Personal E-mail: docpsf@aol.com.

FARLESS, FLOYD HUGH, lawyer; b. Rome, Ga., Apr. 28, 1950; s. Floyd and Ruby Lee (Hilburn) F.; m. Lila Dolora Lloyd, Feb. 12, 1977; children: Evan, Anna, Emma. BA, Auburn U., 1972; LLB, Cumberland Sch. of Law, Birmingham, Ala., 1976. Bar: Ga. Assoc. Clary, Kent, Rome, 1976-80; ptnr. Farless, Newton, Wyatt, Rome, 1980-82, Farless & Newton, Rome, 1982—99; pvt. practice Rome, Ga., 1999—2001. Precinct pres. Rep. Party of Ga.'s Floyd County, Rome, 1997—; pres. treas. bd. dirs. Floyd County Wildlife Assn., Rome, 1966-94. Capt. USAR. Mem. F&AM, Am. Legion. Mem. Lds Ch. Avocations: fishing, camping, history. Home: 5878 Alabama Hwy NW Rome GA 30165-8812 Office: 401 Broad St Ste 103 Rome GA 30161

FARLEY, ANDREW NEWELL, lawyer, consultant; b. Brownsville, Pa., Oct. 31, 1934; s. Andrew Polycarp and Sarah Theresa (Landymore) F.; m. Marta Olha Pisetska, May 5, 1963; children— Andrew Daniel, Mark Landymore. AB, Washington and Jefferson Coll., 1956; MPA, U. Pitts., 1962, JD, 1961; diploma, U.S. Army Command and Gen. Staff Coll., 1972, Indsl. Coll. Armed Forces, 1967; grad., U.S. Army War Coll., 1976. Bar: Pa. 1962, U.S. Supreme Ct. 1965. Assoc. Reed Smith Shaw & McClay, Pitts., 1961-65, ptnr., 1966-91; cons. Pitts., 1992—. Bd. dirs. Corp. Devel. USAM Mid-Atlantic and Ohio; mng. dir. USAM-Nat., 1992—; Am. Arbitration Assn. Nat. Panel Comml. Disputes, 1995—; mediator JAMS-Endispute, 1996—; sec.-treas. Internat. Acad. Mediators, 1996-2000; lectr. in fed. jurisprudence and adminstrv. law U. Pitts.; adminstrv. asst. Pa. Atty. Gen., 1959; counsel to Pa. Constl. Conv., 1968; mem. Pa. Atty. Gen.'s Task Force on Adminstrn., 1970; mem. faculty Pa. Bar Inst. Bus. Lawyer Inst., 1999—. Assoc. editor Pitts Legal Jour., 1963— (mem. exec. com.); contbr. articles to profl. jours. Bd. dirs. Ind. Sch. Chmn. Assn., World Affairs Coun., Pitts., Pitts. Opera, 1986-95; sec., bd. dirs. Found. for Calif. U. Pa.,; mem. adv. bd. Western Pa. Advanced Tech. Ctr., Internat. Resuscitation Rsch. Ctr., U. Pitts. Med. Sch., Mon Valley Renaissance; mem. bd. visitors U. Pitts. Grad. Sch. Pub. and Internat. Affairs; trustee Thiel Coll., 1989-95. Brig. gen. U.S. Army. Decorated Meritorious Svc. medals, Dept. Def. and U.S. Army, Army Commendation medals; recipient Gubernatorial citation Commonwealth of Pa., 1978, Omicron Delta Kappa award, 1960; Nat. Def. Transp. Assn. fellow, 1956; named Mon Valley Renaissance MVP, 1987. Mem. Internat. Acad. Mediators, Pa. Bar Assn. (chmn. sect. internat. law, bd. editors, jud. adminstrn. com., statewide computer com. for the cts., alternative dispute resolution com.), In-house Coun. Com., Allegheny County Bar Assn. (fee determination com.), Am. Law Inst., Nat. Health Lawyers Assn., Am. Arbitration Assn., Soc. for Profls. in Dispute Resolution, Assn. U.S. Army (pres. Ft. Pitt chpt., pres. Pa.), Sr. Army Res. Comdrs. Assn. (exec. com.), Pitts. Athletic Assn., Duquesne Club, Pa. State Grange, Masons. Home: 54 N Manorcliff Pl The Woodlands Spring TX 77382 Office Phone: 281-419-9561.

FARLEY, BENJAMIN WIRT, religious studies educator, writer; b. Manila, Aug. 6, 1935; s. Wirt Pamplin and Bessie (Campbell) White F.; m. Alice Anne Gamble; children: John David, Bryan Kirk. AB, Davidson Coll., 1958; BD, Union Theol. Sem., Richmond, Va., 1963, ThM, 1964, PhD, 1976. Ordained to ministry Presbyn. Ch., 1963. Instr. Lees-MacRae Coll., Banner-Elk, NC, 1973-74; asst. prof. bible, religion, philosophy Erskine Coll., Due West, SC, 1974-78, assoc. prof., 1978-84, Younts prof., 1985—2000, chair bible, relgion, philosophy dept., 1978-91, prof. emeritus, 2004—. Author: The Hero of St. Lo, 1986, Mercy Road, 1986, The Providence of God, 1988, Corbin's Rubi-Yacht, 1992, In Praise of Virtue, 1994, Son of the Morning Sky, 1999; translator, editor: Calvins Sermons on the Ten Commandments, 1980, Calvin's Treatises Against the Anabaptists and Against the Libertines, 1982, Calvin's Sermons on the Book of Micah, 2003, Of Time & Eternity, 2004; co-translator: Calvin's Ecclesiastical Advice, 1991; contbr. articles to profl. jours. Chair Bi-Racial Com., Franklin, Va., 1967-68, pres. of the Calvin Studies Soc. in America, 1997—. Named Writer of the Season, Nostalgia mag., 1990; Fund for Theol. Edn. fellow, 1970; Thomas Carey Johnson scholar Union Theol. Sem., 1963. Mem. Am. Philos. Assn., Calvin Studies Soc. (pres. 1997-99), Coloquium on Calvin Studies, Internat. Calvin Congress, Omicron Delta Kappa. Republican. Avocations: golf, sailing, hunting, fishing, hiking. Personal E-mail: aag@infoave.net.

FARLEY, CAROLE, soprano; b. Le Mars, Iowa, Nov. 29, 1946; d. Melvin and Irene (Reid) Farley; m. Jose Serebrier, Mar. 29, 1969; 1 child, Lara Adriana Francesca. MusB, Ind. U., 1968. Fulbright scholar Hochschule für Musik, Munich, 1968-69. (Musician of Month, Musical Am./Hi Fidelity 1977), Am. debut at Town Hall, N.Y.C., 1969, Paris debut, Nat. Orch., 1975, London debut, Royal Philharmonic Soc., 1975, S.Am. debut, Teatro Colon, Philharmonic Orch., Buenos Aires, 1975; soloist with, major Am. and European symphony orchs., 1970—, soloist, Welsh Nat. Opera, 1971, 72, Cologne Opera, 1972-75, Phila. Lyric Opera, 1974, Brussels Opera, 1972, Lyon Opera, 1976, 77, Strasbourg Opera, 1975, Linz Opera, 1969, N.Y.C. Opera, 1976, New Orleans Opera, 1977, Cin. Opera, 1977, Met. Opera Co., N.Y.C., 1977—, Zurich Opera, 1979, Chgo. Lyric Opera, 1981, Can. Opera Co., 1980, Düsseldorf Opera, 1980, 81, 84, Palm Beach Opera, 1982, Theatre Mcpl. Paris, 1983, Theatre Royale dela Monnaie Brussels, 1983, Teatro Regio, Turin, Italy, 1983, Nice Opera (France), 1984, 86, 87, 88, Cologne Opera, 1985, Teatro Comunale, Florence, Italy, 1985, BBC Opera, 1987, TeatroColon, Buenos Aires, 1987, 88, 89, Opera de Montpellier (France), 1988, 94, Theatre des Champs Elysees, Paris, 1988, Helsinki Festival, 1989, Tchaikovsky Opera Arias Pickwick/IMP Records, 1993, Met. Opera Premiere Shostakovich Opera Lady Macbeth of Mtzensk, 1994, Theatre Capitole de Toulouse Wozzeck, 1994, internat. tour with Nat. Chamber Orchestra of Toolouse, 2003; on New Zealand Broadcasting Commn. Orchestral Tour, 1986; TV film for ABC Australia La Voix Humaine, also co-producer compact disc and video for BBC, London, 1990; co-producer compact disc and video The Telephone, 1990; recorded compact disc Weill, 1992, Metro. Opera Shostakovich: "Lady Macbeth", 1994, Strausslieder with Czech Philharmonic, 1995, Les Soldats Morts, 1995 (Grand Prix du Disque); recorded for Deutsche Gramophone (Diapason d'or prize 1997), Chandos, CBS, BBC, ASV, RCA, Ricercar and Varese-Sarabande records, London/Decca Records, IMP Masters, Pickwick; new CD Naxos: Selected Songs Ned Rorem, 2001, The Songs of Ernesto Lecuona For Bis Records, 2003; Argentine premier Bomarzo by Alberto Ginastera, Teatro Colón Buenos Aires, 2003. Recipient Abiati prize for her role as Lulu, Italy, 1984, Deutsche Schallplatten award for recording Carole Farley Sings French Songs, 1988; named Alumni of Year, U. Ind., 1976; two-time Grammy nominee, 2004. Mem.: Am. Guild Mus. Artists. Home: 270 Riverside Dr New York NY 10025-5209 E-mail: caspi123@aol.com. *A young opera singer today has a much greater responsibility than his predecessors 50 years ago. The age of the 200-pound soprano expiring of consumption at the end of La Traviata is a thing of the past. Now we must "look" the part, and be able to act as well as sing.*

FARLEY, EDWARD RAYMOND, JR., mining and manufacturing company executive; b. S.I., N.Y., Sept. 30, 1918; s. Edward Raymond and Ruth Veronica (Joyce) F.; m. Irene Daly, Feb. 19, 1948; children— Thomas Joyce, Nancy Seaver, Jane Campbell, Edward Raymond III. AB, Princeton, 1940; JD, Harvard, 1943. Bar: N.Y. bar 1944. With firm Simpson, Thacher & Bartlett, N.Y.C., 1944-55; v.p. Atlas Corp., N.Y.C., 1956-64, chmn. bd. dirs., 1964-87, pres., 1966-87, also chmn. exec. com. Trustee, chmn. exec. com. Lincoln Savs. Bank, Bklyn., 1973-84; dir. Am. Nuclear Energy Council, 1979-89. Active local United Fund; trustee, pres. bd. Lawrenceville Sch., 1970-85; trustee, chmn. bd. Princeton Med. Center, 1976—; assoc. trustee U. Pa., 1988—. Decorated Knight of Malta Mem. Nat. Football Hall of Fame (pres. Delaware Valley chpt.), Atomic Indsl. Forum, U. Pa. Grad. Sch. Edn. (bd. gov.'s 1988—), Dial Lodge (trustee) Beden's Brook Club (Princeton), Pretty Brook Tennis Club (Princeton), Nassau Club (Princeton), Springdale Golf Club (Princeton). Home: 188 Parkside Dr Princeton NJ 08540-4815 Office: 353 Nassau St Princeton NJ 08540-4623

FARLEY, JAMES NEWTON, retired manufacturing executive, electrical engineer; b. Hutchinson, Kans., Nov. 8, 1928; s. James N. Farley and Elizabeth (Martin) Sanders; m. Nancy J. Hollabaugh, Apr. 30, 1956; children: Sarah Huskey, Timothy, Barbara Carré, James, Stuart. BSEE, Northwestern U., 1950. Registered pro^ engr., Ill. Test engr. GE, Schenectady, N.Y., 1950-51; sales engr. Allen Bradley Co., Milw., 1953-54, Chgo., 1954-60; sales mgr. SpeedFam Corp., Skokie, Ill., 1960-64, pres. Des Plaines, Ill., 1964-87, chmn. bd. dirs., 1987-97; pres., CEO Speedfam-IPEC, Inc., Chandler, Ariz., 1987-92, CEO, chmn. bd. dirs., 1992-97, chmn. bd. dirs., 1997-2001, chmn. emeritus, 2001—02, ret., 2002—. Bd. dirs. Lovejoy, Inc., Downers Grove, Ill., imortgage.com, Scottsdale, Ariz., Ex One, Irwin, Pa. With U.S. Army, 1951-53. Recipient Alumni Merit award Northwestern U., 1996. Mem. Assn. for Mfg. Tech., Oriental Order of Groundhogs. Democrat. Episcopalian. Office: Novellus Sys Inc 300 N 56th St Chandler AZ 85226-2405 Home: 2402 Esplanade Ave PH2 Phoenix AZ 85016

FARLEY, JAMES PARKER, retired advertising agency executive; b. Newark, Sept. 16, 1924; s. James Joseph and Margaret (Parker) F.; m. Irene Florence Reinert, July 1, 1950; children: James Bernard, Catherine Elizabeth, Robert Craig, Margaret Patricia. BA in Bus. Adminstrn, Rutgers U., 1949. Asst. to advt. mgr. Gen. Electric Co., Syracuse, N.Y., 1949-51, merchandising mgr. Bridgeport, Conn., 1951-56; account dir. McCann-Erickson, Inc., N.Y.C., 1956-62; pres., chief exec. officer McCann Erickson-Hakuhodo, Tokyo, 1963-78, chmn., chief exec. officer, 1978-79, chmn., 1979-82; exec. v.p., regional mgr. Pacific, McCann-Erickson Internat., N.Y.C., 1972-82. Dir. McCann-Erickson Internat., N.Y.C., 1974-82, Hakuhodo, Inc., Tokyo, 1963-82. Served with USNR, 1943-46. Mem. Internat. Advt. Assn., Am. C. of C. Japan, Am.-Japan Soc., Fgn. Corr. Club Japan, Fgn. Corr. Club Hong Kong, Japan Soc. N.Y.C., Young Pres. Orgn., Zeta Psi. Clubs: Tokyo Am. (past pres.); Patterson (Fairfield, Conn.), Royal Hong Kong Yacht; Met. (N.Y.C.); N.Y. Athletic. Home: 62 Rivergate Dr Wilton CT 06897-4137

FARLEY, JERRY B., academic administrator; m. Susan Farley. BS in Fin. and Acctg., U. Okla., 1968; MBA, Okla. U., 1972. V.p. bus. and fin. Okla. State U., 1986; CFO Okla. U., Oklahoma City, v.p. adminstrn. and fin., 1994; pres. Washburn U., Topeka, 1997—. Named No. 4 most powerful Topekan, Topeka Capital-Jour., 2000. Office: Washburn U Office of Pres 1700 SW College Ave MO 202 Topeka KS 66621

FARLEY, JOSEPH MCCONNELL, lawyer; b. Birmingham, Ala., Oct. 6, 1927; s. John G. and Lynne (McConnell) F.; m. Sheila Shirley, Oct. 1, 1958 (dec. July 1978); children: Joseph McConnell, Thomas Gager, Mary Lynne. Student, Birmingham-So. Coll., 1944—45; BSME, Princeton U., 1948; postgrad., U. Ala., 1948—49; LLB, Harvard U., 1952; LHD (hon.), Judson Coll., 1974; LLD (hon.), U. Ala. at Birmingham, 1983. Bar: Ala. 1952. Assoc. Martin, Turner, Blakey & Bouldin, Birmingham, 1952-57; ptnr. successor firm Martin, Balch, Bingham & Hawthorne, 1957-65; exec. v.p., dir. Ala. Power Co., 1965-69, pres., dir., 1969-89; v.p. So. Electric Generating Co., 1970-74, pres., dir., 1974-89; exec. v.p. nuclear, bd. dirs. The So. Co., Birmingham, 1989-90; pres., CEO So. Nuclear Oper. Co., Birmingham, 1990-91, chmn., CEO, 1991-92, also bd. dirs.; exec. v.p., corp. counsel So. Co., 1991-92; of counsel Balch & Bingham, LLP, Birmingham, 1993—. Bd. dirs. N.A., Torchmark Corp., SVI Corp.; mem. exec. bd. Southeastern Electric Reliability Coun., chmn., 1974-76; bd. dirs. Edison Electric Inst.; bd. dirs. Southeastern Electric Exch., pres., 1984; adv. dir. So. Co., 1992-97; bd. dir. Am. South Bancorp, 1970-96. Mem. Jefferson County Republican Exec. Com., 1953-65; counsel, mem. Ala. Rep. Com., 1962-65; permanent chmn. Ala. Rep. Conv., 1962; alternate del. Rep. Nat. Conv., 1956; bd. dirs. Ala. Bus. Hall of Fame, Birmingham Area YMCA (hon. dir.); chmn. bd. trustees So. Rsch. Inst., 1970-99; trustee Tuskegee U., 1981-2002; trustee Children's Hosp. Birmingham, pres. bd. trustees 1983-85; mem. Pres.'s Cabinet U. Ala.-Tuscaloosa; bd. visitors U. Ala. Sch. Commerce, chmn., 1991-93. Served with USNR, 1948; now lt. ret. Mem. ABA, NAM (bd. dirs. 1987-92), Ala. Bar Assn., Birmingham Bar Assn., Inst. Nuclear Power Ops. (bd. dirs. 1982-89, chmn. 1987-89), U.S. Coun. for Energy Awareness (bd. dirs. 1985-92), Am. Nuclear Energy Coun. (chmn. bd. dirs. 1987-92), Newcomen Soc. N.Am., Birmingham Country Club, Shoal Creek Club, The Club, Mountain Brook Club, Summit Club, Rotary, Phi Beta Kappa, Kappa Alpha, Tau Beta Pi, Beta Gamma Sigma (hon.). Episcopalian. Home: 3333 Dell Rd Birmingham AL 35223-1319 Office: Balch & Bingham LLP PO Box 306 Birmingham AL 35201-0306 Office Phone: 205-226-3464.

FARLEY, KATHERINE G., real estate company executive; b. 1950; m. Jerry I. Speyer, 1991; 1 child. Grad., Brown U., 1971; MA in Architecture, Harvard Grad. Sch. of Design, 1976. Mgr. bus. devel. for E. Asia Turner Construction; sr. mng. dir. Latin Am. and Global Corp. Mktg. Tishman Speyer Properties, N.Y.C., 1984—. Exec. com. mem. Internat. Rescue Com.; chmn. emeritus Women In Need; exec. com. mem. NY Philharmonic, Brearley Sch.; bd. mem. Lincoln Center for the Performing Arts, Lincoln Center Theater, Alvin Ailey Dance Co. Named one of Top 200 Collectors, ARTnews Mag., 2004. Avocation: Collector of Contemporary Art. Office: Tishman Speyer Properties 520 Madison Ave New York NY 10022 Office Phone: 212-715-0300.*

FARLEY, PEGGY ANN, finance company executive; b. Phila., Mar. 12, 1947; d. Harry E. and Ruth (Lloyd) F.; m. Reid McIntyre, Dec. 31, 1985 (div.); 1 child, Margaret Ruth Farley. AB, Barnard Coll., 1970; MA with high honors, Columbia U., 1972. Admissions officer Barnard Coll., N.Y.C., 1973-76; adminstr. Citibank NA, Athens, Greece, 1976-77; cons. Orgn. Resources Counselors, N.Y.C., 1977-78; sr. assoc. Morgan Stanley and Co. Inc., N.Y.C., 1978-84; mng. dir., CEO AMAS Securities Inc., N.Y.C., 1984-98; also bd. dirs. AMAS Securities, Inc., N.Y.C.; pres., CEO Ascent Asset Mgmt. Adv. Svc., Inc., N.Y.C., 1998-99. Pres., CEO, bd. dirs. Ascent/Meredith Asset Mgmt. Inc., N.Y.C., 1999—, Ascent/Meredith Portfolio Mgmt. Inc., N.Y.C., 1999-2004, Robert R. Meredith & Co. Inc., N.Y.C., 1999-2004, Ascent Capital Mgmt., Inc., 2004—, Ascent Securities, Inc., 2004—; partner Ascent Med. Tech. Fund, 1999—; mng. dir. Ascent Pvt. Equity, 1999—, Ascent Capital Adv., 2001—. Author: The Place Of The Yankee And Euro Bond Markets In A Financing Program For The People's Republic of China, 1982, Ascent Quar. Rev. Mem. Columbia U. Seminar on China-U.S. Bus. Mem. China Inst., Fgn. Policy Assn., Met. Club, Econ. Club of N.Y. Republican. Presbyterian. Avocations: gardening, film, swimming. Home: 908 Owassa Rd Newton NJ 07860-4015 Office: Ascent/Capital Mgmt Inc 152 W 57th St New York NY 10019-4108 Personal E-mail: peggyfarley@hotmail.com.

FARLEY, ROY CARL, counselor educator; b. Dierks, Ark., Feb. 21, 1942; s. Embra and Mildred (Efird) F.; m. Omagene Cowan, May 29, 1969; children: Susanne, Justin. BA, Henderson State U., 1964; MS, Ctrl. Ark. U., 1972; EdD, U. Ark., 1978. Rehab. counselor, adminstr. Ark. Rehab. Svcs., Little Rock, 1967-74; dir., prof. rehab. edn. Ark. Rsch. and Tng. Ctr., Hot Springs, 1974-99; prof., counselor edn. U. Ark., Fayetteville, 1999—2003, chair dept. ednl. leadership, counseling and founds., 2004—. Presenter in field. Author, co-author 15 comprehensive tng. packages for rehab. and mental health profls. including The Advanced Facilitative Case Management Series, Relationship Skills for Career Enhancement, Rational Behavior Problem-Solving, Employability Assessment and Planning, Know Thyself: A Strategy for Empowering and Involving Consumers in the Vocational Assessment Process; contbr. over 50 articles to profl. jours., chpts. to books Home: 2670 E Tulip Ct Fayetteville AR 72701-2889 Office: U Ark 134 Grad Edn Bldg Fayetteville AR 72701 also: U Ark GRAD 234 Fayetteville AR 72701 Office Phone: 479-575-7725. Business E-Mail: rfarley@uark.edu.

FARLEY, TERRENCE MICHAEL, banker; b. N.Y.C., Mar. 6, 1930; s. Terrence M. and Mary A. (Dundon) F.; m. Audrey E. Churchill, June 8, 1952; children: Elizabeth C., Peter, Matthew. BBA, CCNY, 1955. With Brown Bros. Harriman & Co., N.Y.C., 1951—, ptnr., 1972—2004, mng. ptnr., 1983—95, ltd. ptnr., 2005—. Trustee Children's Specialized Hosp., Mountainside, NJ. Mem. Univ. Club, Echo Lake Country Club (Westfield, N.J.), Wianno Club (Osterville, Mass.). Home: 309 Hillside Ave Westfield NJ 07090-2902 Office: Brown Bros Harriman & Co 140 Broadway New York NY 10005-1101

FARLEY, THOMAS T., lawyer; b. Pueblo, Colo., Nov. 10, 1934; s. John Baron and Mary (Tancred) F.; m. Kathleen Maybelle Murphy, May 14, 1960; children: John, Michael, Kelly, Anne. BS, U. Santa Clara, 1956; LLB, U. Colo., 1959. Bar: Colo. 1959, U.S. Dist. Ct. Colo. 1959, U.S. Ct. Appeals (10th cir.) 1988. Dep. dist. atty. County of Pueblo, 1960-62; pvt. practice

Pueblo, 1963-69; ptnr. Phelps, Fonda & Hays, Pueblo, 1970-75, Petersen & Fonda, P.C., Pueblo, 1975—. Bd. dirs. Pub. Svc. Co. Colo., Wells Fargo Pueblo, Wells Fargo Sunset, Health Net, Inc., Colo. Pub. Radio. Minority leader Colo. Ho. of Reps., 1967-75; chmn. Colo. Wildlife Commn., 1975-79, Colo. Bd. Govs., 1979-87; bd. regents Santa Clara U., 1987—; commr. Colo. State Fair; trustee Cath. Found. Diocese of Pueblo, Great Outdoors Colo. Trust Fund. Recipient Disting. Svc. award U. So. Colo., 1987, 93, Bd. of Regents, U. Colo., 1993, Colo. State U.-Pueblo, Presdl. Seal, 2004; named to Pueblo Hall of Fame, 2005. Mem. ABA, Colo. Bar Assn., Pueblo C. of C. (bd. dirs. 1991-93), Rotary. Democrat. Roman Catholic. Office: Petersen & Fonda PC 215 W 2d St Pueblo CO 81003-3251 Office Phone: 719-545-9330.

FARLEY, TOM, real estate company executive; BA, U. Victoria. CRF designation Real Estate Inst. Can. With Morguard Investments, Calgary, Toronto, Canada; various sr. mgmt. positions Brookfield Properties Corp., Toronto, Canada, 1993—99, sr. v.p. Western Can., 1999—2003, exec. v.p., COO Can. comml. ops., 2003, pres., COO Can. comml. ops., 2003—. Office: Brookfield Properties Corp PO Box 770 Ste 330 BCE Pl 181 Bay St Toronto ON Canada M5J 2T3

FARMAKIDES, JOHN BASIL, lawyer; b. Symi Island (Dodecanese), Italy; s. Basil John and Anna Maria (Zouroudis) F.; m. Maria T. Kambanis, July 12, 1964; children: Basil J., George S. BS, Case Western Res. U., 1950; JD with honors, George Washington U., 1956; LL.M., Georgetown U., 1958. Bar: D.C. 1957, U.S. Supreme Ct. 1958, Va. 1986. Patent examiner U.S. Patent Office, 1955-59; atty. U.S. Air Force, 1960-61, NASA, 1961-70, mem. bd. contract appeals, 1968-70; asst. gen. counsel NSF, 1970-72; mem. NRC appeals bd. AEC (NRC), 1972-75; chmn. bd. appeals Dept. Energy, Washington, 1975-84; ptnr. Whitney & Dempsey, Washington, 1985-88; arbitrator, 1988—. Adj. prof. in law Am. U. Law Sch., 1964-72; U.S. del. Internat. Conf. on Govt. Computer Experts, Geneva, 1972; chmn. Fed. Coun. Sci. and Tech. Subcom. on Legal Aspects of Info Sys., 1969-72; cons. HEW, NSF; chmn. Nat. Conf. on Legal Aspects of Computerized Info. Sys.-FCST, 1969-72; comdg. officer, dir. Joint Army, Navy, Air Force Spl. Analyn Divsn., USAR, 1971-74; mem. U.S. Chinese Workshop on Computerized Info. Sys., NAS, 1972. Contbr. articles to profl. jours. Pres. Cosmos Hist. Preservation Found. Recipient letters of appreciation U.S. Army, HEW, NASA, NSF; Exceptional Svc. medal Dept. Energy. Mem. ABA, Fed. Bar Assn., IEEE, Am. Arbitration Assn., Am. Soc. Pub. Adminstrn., NASA Space League, Phi Delta Phi. Clubs: Cosmos, Washington Golf, Nat. Lawyers.

FARMAKIS, GEORGE LEONARD, retired education educator; b. Clarksburg, W.Va., June 30, 1925; s. Michael and Pipitsa (Roussopoulos) F. BA, Wayne State U., 1949, MEd, 1950, MA, 1966, PhD, 1971; MA, U. Mich., 1978; postgrad., Columbia U., Yale U., Queens Coll. Tchr. audio-visual aids dir. Roseville (Mich.) Pub. Schs., 1951-57; tchr. Birmingham (Mich.) Pub. Schs., 1957-61, Highland Park (Mich.) Pub. Schs., 1961-90; substitute tchr. Grosse Pointe Pub. Schs., 1990—2003; ret., 2003. Lectr. Oakland County C.C., 1990-92, Lawrence U., 1990-98, Oakland U., 2000—; instr. Highland Park C.C., 1966-68, Wayne County C.C., 1969-70; assoc. mem. grad. faculty Coll. Edn. Wayne State U., 1988-89; founder Ford Sch. Math. High Intensity Tutoring Program, 1971; chairperson Highland Park Sch. Dist. Curriculum Coun. and Profl. Staff Devel. Governing Bd., 1979-82; pres. Mich. Coun. Social Studies, 1985-86; founder, dir. Mich. Social Studies Olympiad, 1987; founder, editor Mich. Social Studies Jour., 1986; participant ESEA Title I/Nat. Diffusion Network. Author, translator: Letters of Nicholas Gysis, 1842-1901; co-author: Michigan School Finance Curriculum Guide; contbr. poems to books of poetry, articles to Focus jour. Cpl. USNG, 1948-51. Recipient spl. commendation Office of Edn., 1978, Outstanding Svc. award Nat. Coun. Social Studies, 1987, Presdl. award Mich. Coun. Social Studies, 1988, 96. Mem. ASCD (bd. dirs. Mich. chpt. 1983-86), Internat. Reading Assn., Am. History Assn., Nat. Coun. Social Studies (pres. SIG-CASE 1987-88, pres. JESIG 1988-89), Am. Philol. Assn., U. Mich. Alumni Assn., Wayne State U. Coll. Edn. Alumni Assn. (bd. dirs. 1985-86), Mich. Reading Assn., Masons (32 degree), Shriners, Ancient Accepted Scottish Rite, Phi Delta Kappa (Outstanding Educators award 1988). Greek Orthodox. Home: 15215 Windmill Dr Macomb MI 48044-4929

FARMAN, ALLAN GEORGE, radiologist, pathologist, educator; b. Birmingham, Eng., July 26, 1949; came to the U.S., 1980; s. George and Lily (Hewitt) F.; m. Taeko Takemori, May 21, 1996. B Dental Surgery, U. Birmingham, 1971; PhD, U. Stellenbosch, Cape Town, South Africa, 1977, DSc (hon.), 1996; EdS, U. Louisville, 1983, MBA with distinction, 1987. Diplomate Am. Bd. Oral and Maxillofacial Radiology, Japanese Bd. Oral and Maxillofacial Radiology; specialist registration in oral pathology South African Med. and Dental Coun.; lic. Ky. Bd. Dentistry. Sr. lectr. oral pathology U. Stellenbosch, Cape Town, 1974-77; head dept. oral biology U. Riyadh, Saudi Arabia, 1978-79; prof., head divsn. radiology and imaging scis. Dental Sch., U. Louisville, 1980—; clin. prof. dept. diagnostic radiology Med. Sch., U. Louisville, 1990—. Cons. Joint Commn. for Dental Bd. Examination, Chgo., 1984—92, NIH, Bethesda, Md., 1990—; rep. to internat. DICOM com. Am. Dental Assn., 2001—; co-chmn. DICOM Working Group 22, 2003—. Author: Oral and Maxillofacial Diagnostic Imaging, 1993; editor: Advances in Maxillofacial Imaging, 1997, (oral and maxillofacial radiology sect.) Oral Surgery, Oral Medicine, Oral Pathology, Oral Radiology and Endodontics, 1988-95, 2005—; co-editor CARS Procs., Computer-Assisted Radiology and Surgery, 1998-; mem. editl. bd. Cranio, Oral Radiology, Acta Stomatologica Croatia, Safundi; contbr. 250 articles to profl. jours. Mem. Am. Dental Assn., Internat. Assn. Dental Rsch., Japanese Soc. Oral and Maxillofacial Radiology, Internat. Assn. Dento Maxillofacial Radiology (pres. 1994-97, trust fund chmn. 1997-), Internat. Congress and Exposition on Computed Maxillofacial Imaging (initiator, founder, organizer 1995—), Am. Acad. Oral and Maxillofacial Radiology (editor 1988-95), Am. Assn. Dental Schs. (chmn. oral radiology sect. 1988-89). Office: U Louisville Sch Dentistry 501 S Preston St Louisville KY 40292-1701 Office Phone: 502-852-1241. Business E-Mail: agfarm01@louisville.edu.

FARMAN-FARMAIAN, GHAFFAR, investment company executive; b. Tehran, Iran, Jan. 14, 1930; s. Abdol Hossein Mirza and Massoumeh (Tafreshi) F-F.;m. Jahan Aalam, Aug. 5, 1956; children: Massoumeh, Amir Hossein, Ali Reza, Afsar. D.L.C. with honors, Loughborough (Eng.) Coll., 1951; MS, U. Ill., 1953; PhD, U. Calif., Berkeley, 1958. Head power div. Karadj Water & Power Orgn., Tehran, 1961-64; mem. Iranian Nat. Com. on Electro-Tech. Standards, Tehran, 1966-79; pres. Armed Forces Communication & Electronic, Tehran, 1970-71; chmn. IEEE, Tehran, 1972-73; mem. Iranian Nat. Com. on Energy Ministry of Water and Power, Tehran, 1972-79; co-founder, chmn. ASEA Iran Co., Tehran, 1973-79; vice chmn. Bank of Tehran, 1973-79; co-founder, bd. dirs. Tehran Ins. Co., 1975-79; pres. Univest Corp., N.Y.C., 1982—, Astle Properties Inc., Houston, 1989—2005. Author tech. papers. Chmn. bd. trustees Cmty. Sch., Tehran, 1975—79. Recipient 1st prize Inst. Elec. Engrs., 1956, 57, Alfred Noble prize Am. Inst. Civil Engrs., 1958. Mem. IEEE (life), Armed Forces Communication & Electronic Assn. (life). Avocations: financial planning, tennis, hiking. Office: PO Box 3221 CH-1211 Geneva 3 - Rive Switzerland E-mail: gff@ieee.org.

FARMER, CHRISTOPHER J., political scientist, writer; b. Norwich, Conn., Apr. 19, 1965; s. Clifford E. Farmer. Polit. sci., U. New Haven, 1999—2001, MS in Nat. Security, 2004. Author: (novels) Parr Taken, The Oath of the Necromancer, The Fallen Elves, Stale Donuts, 2005. Sapper staff sgt. e-6 US Army, 1986—95, Panama (Just Cause), Somalia (Restore Hope), Sinai Egypt. Decorated Army Commendation Medal, 4th Oakleaf Cluster US Army, Armed Forces Expeditionary Medal with Bronze Star, UN Multinational Force and Observers Mission UN, Valorous Unit award US Army, Joint Meritorious Unit award, Nat. Def. Svc. medal (2nd Award), Army Achievement Medal 4th Oakleaf Cluster; recipient Rollin G. Osterweis award for Excellence in Polit. Sci., U. of New Haven, 2000. Conservative-R. Catholic. Avocations: writing, game theory, travel, skiing, mountain climbing.

FARMER, CORNELIA GRIFFIN, lawyer, consultant, county official; b. NYC, Mar. 3, 1945; d. John Bastin and Elizabeth McCue (Sussman) Griffin; m. William Paul Farmer, Jan. 8, 1972; children: Suzanne Elizabeth, John Paul. BA, Mt. Holyoke Coll., 1967; M in Regional Planning, Cornell U., 1970; JD, Marquette U., 1978. Bar: Wis. 1978, Pa. 1981, Minn. 1996, Oreg. 1999, Ill. 2002. Planner Frederick P. Clark Assoc., Rye, N.Y., 1970-71, Tri State Regional Planning Com., N.Y.C., 1971-72, State of Wis. and City of Milw., 1973-75; assoc. Friebert & Finerty, Milw., 1978-80, Baskin & Sears, Pitts., 1981-82; cons. County of Allegheny, Pitts., 1983; adj. faculty U. Pitts., 1986-94; jud. law clk. Commonwealth Ct. of Pa., Pitts., 1992-95; pvt. practice Mpls., 1996—99; staff atty., hearings ofcl. Lane Coun. Govts., Eugene, Oreg., 1999—2001. Vic-chmn. loan monitoring com. Pitts. Countywide Corp., 1981—87; child adv. Allegheny County Pro Bono Program, Pitts., 1986—92; mediator Dispute Resolution Ctr., St. Paul, 1998—99; adj. faculty U. Wis., Milw., 1978—79. Book reviewer, referee books and articles. Vol. polit. campaigns Milw., Pitts., Mpls., Chgo., and Eugene, 1972-2004; trustee Falk Sch. Fund; v.p. PTA Falk Lab. Sch. U. Pitts., 1985-89; ct. monitor abuse cases WATCH, Mpls., 1996-99; vol. WITS tutoring and mentoring program, 2002-, Start Making A Reader Today, Eugene, Oreg.; mem. Ill. Advisory Council of Midwest Eye-Banks, 2004—; head class agent Mt. Holyoke Coll., 2002—. Mem. ABA, APA, Chgo. Bar Assn., Silver Bay Assn. Coun., Mt. Holyoke Coll. Alumnae Assn. (alumnae vol.). Mt. Holyoke Club Pitts. (past pres., treas.).

FARMER, CROFTON BERNARD, atmospheric physicist; b. Cardiff, Wales, May 30, 1931; came to U.S., 1967; s. Francis Herbert and Cicely (Arnott) F.; m. Roberta Josephine Stewart, June 20, 1956; (div); children: Louise Josephine, Joanna Cicely, Philippa Bernice, Christopher Llewellyn; m. Christine Louise Conaway, Feb. 29, 1992. BS, U. London, 1952, PhD, 1968. Research physicist EMI Electronics, Ltd., Eng., 1952-60, head infrared research dept., 1960-62; led sci. expdns. to Bolivian Andes, 1962, 64; sr. research scientist Jet Propulsion Lab., Calif. Inst. Tech., Pasadena, 1967-72, mgr. planetary atmospheres, 1972-75; prin. investigator NASA Viking Mars, 1975-77, Shuttle Spacelab, from 1977. Vis. prof. divsn. geology and planetary sci. Calif. Inst. Tech., 1978-81; disting. vis. scientist Jet Propulsion Lab., 1989—; mem. subcoms. on planetary atmospheres and stratospheric rsch. NASA; cons., lectr. remote sensing of atmospheres. Contbr. articles on solar-terrestrial spectroscopy and composition of planets' atmospheres to sci. jours. Recipient Exceptional Sci. Achievement medal NASA, 1975, 77, 87, Antarctica Svc. medal, 1987, William T. Pecora award NASA and Dept. Interior, 1996. E-mail: farmer@jpl.nasa.gov.

FARMER, DEWAYNE MARK, director, photographer; b. Morristown, Tenn., Mar. 16, 1960; s. Ernest Jr. and Doris Ann Farmer; m. Daphney Cheri Pilkey, Nov. 16, 1956; children: April Pilkey Akins, Heather Pilkey Barnes, Clinton Pilkey. BS in Music Edn., Tenn. Tech. U., 1983; M in Music Edn., U. So. Miss., 1989, postgrad., 1997—. Profl. tchg. cert. Tenn., tchg. cert. Miss., cert. tchr. evaluator Miss., profl. tchr. Ga. Dir. bands Sweetwater (Tenn.) H.S., 1983—84, Bledsoe County H.S., Pikeville, Tenn., 1985—89, Dougherty Comprehensive H.S., Albany, Ga., 1989—92, Brantly County Mid. Sch., Nahunta, Ga., 1992—93, Jefferson Mid. Sch., Jefferson City, Tenn., 1996—2002, Metter H.S., Ga., 2002—; pvt. practice photographer Jefferson City, 1983—. Supr. music student tchrs. U. So. Miss., Hattiesburg, 2001—02. Recipient Grad. Tchg. assistantship, U. So. Miss., 2001-2002. Mem.: NEA, Ga. Music Educators Assn., Tenn. Edn. Assn., Tenn. Secondary Sch. Band Dirs. Assn., E. Tenn. Sch. Band and Orch. Assn., Music Educators Nat. Conf. Avocation: photography. Office: Metter High School RR3 Box 1500 Metter GA 30439 Personal E-mail: mfarmer@pineland.net.

FARMER, DONALD A(RTHUR), JR., lawyer; b. Wichita, Kans., Apr. 3, 1944; s. Donald Arthur and Ethel Lois (Figge) F.; m. Jane Moran, June 17, 1967; children: Emma Christina, Matthew Todd. AB, Stanford U., 1966, JD, 1969. Bar: Calif. 1970, D.C. 1970. Trial atty. antitrust div. U.S. Dept. Justice, Washington, 1969-74, spl. asst. to head of antitrust div., 1974-77; dir. bur. internat. aviation U.S. CAB, Washington, 1977-79; ptnr. Galland, Kharasch, Calkins & Short, Washington, 1979-81, Beckman & Farmer, Washington, 1981-84, Popham, Haik, Schnobrich & Kaufman, Ltd., Washington, 1984-97, Reed Smith LLP, Washington, 1997—. Mem. ABA, Internat. Bar Assn. Office: Reed Smith LLP Ste 1100-East 1301 K St NW Washington DC 20005-3317

FARMER, EVAN R., academic administrator, dermatologist, researcher; b. Richmond, Va. BS in Biology, Va. Mil. Inst.; MD, M in History Ideas, John Hopkins U. Diplomate Am. Bd. Dermatology, cert. in dermatopathology. Past Kampen-Norins prof., past chmn. dept dermatology Sch. Medicine Ind. U.; formerly with Armed Forces Inst. Pathology, Washington; past resident in dermatology John Hopkins U., past dep. dir. dept. dermatology, dir. depts. dermatopathology, oral pathology, 1977, past rschr. in graft-versus-host disease; dean, provost Ea. Va. Med. Sch., Norfolk. Past vol. All Africa Leprosy Rehab. and Tng. Ctr., Addis Ababa, Ethiopia. Address: 580 Mowbery Arch Norfolk VA 23507

FARMER, GUY OTTO, II, lawyer; b. Washington, Jan. 7, 1941; s. Guy Otto and Rose Marie (Smith) F.; m. Drema Houchins, Jan. 27, 1963; children: Caroline E., Guy Otto III. BA in Polit. Sci., W.Va. U., 1963; JD, U. Va., 1966. Bar: Fla. 1966, U.S. Dist. Ct. (mid. dist.) Fla. 1966, U.S. Ct. Appeals (5th cir.) 1967, U.S. Ct. Appeals (11th cir.) 1970, U.S. Supreme Ct. 1970, U.S. Ct. Appeals (6th cir.) 1991, U.S. Ct. Appeals (2d cir.) 1997, cert.: Fla. Bar (specialist in labor and employment law). Assoc. to ptnr. Mahoney, Hadlow & Adams, Jacksonville, Fla., 1966-82; ptnr. Smith & Hulsey, Jacksonville, 1982-88, Foley & Lardner, Jacksonville, 1988—2003, Holland & Knight, Jacksonville, 2003—. Contbr. articles to profl. jours. Bd. dirs. N.E. Fla. Hospice, Jacksonville, 1987-93, Children's Home Soc., Jacksonville, 1988-91, N.E. Fla. Safety Coun., Jacksonville, 1988—. Fellow: Am. Bar Found.; mem.: ABA (com. on EEO law and Nat. Labor Rels. Act), Acad. Fla. Mgmt. Attys. (bd. dirs. 2000—02), Jacksonville Bar Assn., Fla. Bar Assn., Epping Forest Yacht Club, Ponte Verda Club, The River Club. Democrat. Methodist. Avocations: reading, gardening, boating, sports. Home: 4244 San Jose Blvd Jacksonville FL 32207-6343 Office: Holland & Knight 50 N laura St Ste 3900 Jacksonville FL 32202 Office Phone: 904-353-2000. E-mail: guyfarmer@hklaw.com.

FARMER, HARRY CLAYTON, JR., music educator; s. Harry Clayton Farmer, Sr. and Wanda Gay Farmer; m. Lesley Anne Bowne, July 29, 2004. MusB, W. Va. U., 1996. Band. dir. Forest Mid. Sch., Va., 1996—. Office: Forest Mid Sch 100 Ashwood Dr Forest VA 24551

FARMER, HELEN SWEENEY, psychology professor; b. Ottawa, Can., Dec. 23, 1929; d. Henry Bertrum and Mabel Sarah (Switzer) Sweeney; m. James A. Farmer Jr., Jan. 25, 1955; children: James Sweeney, David Sargent, Paul Alexander. BA, Queens U., Can., 1952; BD, Union Theol. Sem., 1955; MA, Columbia U., 1969; PhD, UCLA, 1972. Lic. psychologist, Ill. Dir. evaluation svcs. INSGROUP, Long Beach, Calif., 1971-74; asst. prof. counseling psychology U. Ill., Urbana, 1974-81, assoc. prof., 1981-87, prof., 1987—98, sr. scholar, 1995—, prof. emerita, 1998—. Author: (with Tom Backer) New Career Options for Women: Counselor's Sourcebook, 1977, New Career Options for Women: A Woman's Guide, 1977, Diversity and Women's Career Development: Adolescence to Adulthood, 1997; contbr. articles to profl. jours. Queens U. scholar, 1949, Can. govt., 1949-52; grantee Nat. Inst. Edn., 1974, 76, 78, NSF, 1991; recipient Mentoring Grad. Students award U. Ill., 1997. Fellow APA (divsn. sec., Disting. Sr. Contbr. to counseling psychology 1995, Divsn. Counseling, Woman of Yr. 1999), Am. Psychol. Soc.; mem. ACA, Am. Ednl. and Rsch. Assn. (divsn. v.p. 1984-86). Avocation: snorkeling. Home: 2204 S Staley Rd Champaign IL 61822-9763 Office: U Ill Sch Edn Dept Ednl Psychology Champaign IL 61820 Fax: 217-244-0726. E-mail: hfarmer@uiuc.edu.

FARMER, JOHN JOSEPH, lawyer, former state attorney general; b. June 24, 1957; m. Beth Gates. BA, Georgetown U., 1979, JD, 1986. Law clk. Hon. Alan B. Handler N.J. Supreme Ct. Justice, Trenton, NJ, 1986—88; assoc. Riker, Danzig, Scherer, Hyland and Perretti, Morristown, 1988—90; asst. U.S. atty. Dist. NJ US Dept. Justice, 1990—94; dep. chief counsel, sr. assoc. counsel to Gov. State of N.J., Trenton, 1994—97, chief counsel to the Gov., chief law enforcement officer, 1997—99, atty. gen., 1999—2002; commr., sr. counsel State of N.J. Commn. on Terrorist Attacks upon the US, Trenton, 2002—05; ptnr. Kirkpatrick & Lockhart Nicholson Graham LLP, Newark, 2005—. Adj. prof. law Seton Hall U. Law Sch., 1993—97; chmn. Juvenile Justice Commn. Mem.: Nat. Assn. Attys. Gen. (co-chair health care fraud, abuse and adv. com.). Republican. Office: Kirkpatrick & Lockhart Nicolson Graham LLP One Newark Ctr 10th Fl Newark NJ 07102 E-mail: jfarmer@king.com.*

FARMER, KENNETH L., JR., military officer; b. Leeds, Ala. married; 4 children. BS, Auburn U.; MD, U. Ala.; grad., Army Command Gen. Staff Coll., Army War Coll. Diplomate Am. Bd. Family Practice. Commd. 2d lt. U.S. Army, advanced through grades to maj. gen.; early assignments include Madigan Army Med. Ctr., Ft. Lewis, Wash., 9th Med. Detachment and Health Clinic, Heilbronn, Germany, 1976-79; dept. chief of family practice residency program Eisenhower Army Med. Ctr., Ft. Gordon, Ga.; chief of family practice dept. Keller Army Hosp., West Pt., NY; divsn. surgeon 101st Airborne divsn., Ft. Campbell, Ky.; dep. comdr. clin. svcs. Ft. Campbell Hosp.; comdr. 85th Evacuation Hosp., Dhahran, Saudi Arabia, 1990-91, Bayne-Jones Army Cmty. Hosp., Ft. Polk, Darnall Army Cmty. Hosp. and U.S. Army Med. Dept. Activity, Ft. Hood, Tex., 22nd Support Group (provisional); command surgeon U.S. European Command, Stuttgart, Germany, 1994-97; dir. Healthcare Svcs. Ft. Bragg, NC; comdg. gen. 44th Med. Brigade, Ft. Bragg, NC, 1999-2000, Western Regional Med. Command, Tacoma, 2000—02, TRICARE NW Region, Ft. Lewis, 2000—02; surgeon 18th Airborne Corps; dep. surg. gen., chief of staff U.S. Army Commd., 2002—04; commdg. gen. N. Atlantic Reg. Med. Command and Walter Reed Army Med. Ctr., Washington, 2004—. Decorated Legion of Merit with 3 oak leaf clusters, Disting. Svc. medal, Defense Superior Svc. medal, Bronze Star, Meritorious Svc. medal with 4 oak leaf clusters, Def. Superior Svc. medal with oak leaf cluster, Army Commendation medal, Army Achievement medal (two awards), Order of Mil. Med. Merit, and others. Fellow Am. Acad. Family Physicians (Robert Graham Physician Exec. award 2001). Office Phone: 202-782-1104. Business E-Mail: kenneth.farmer@na.amedd.army.mil.

FARMER, LILLIAN JEAN, counseling executive; d. Lula Bell Noland. BS, U. Ala., Birmingham, 1985; MA in Counseling, Birmingham Theology Sem., 1996. EMG technologist U. Hosp., Birmingham, 2004—; CEO, exec. dir. 3 Dimensional Mentoring, Birmingham, 1995—; freelance polysomnagraphic technologist Birmingham, 1995—. Author: Recovering All, 2004. Adv. mem. World of Opportunity, Birmingham, 2002—05. Master: Delta Sigma Theta Sorority Inc. (life); fellow: Eta Sigma Gamma (life; charter). Home: 1012 Griswold Rd Birmingham AL 35064

FARMER, NANCY, state official; b. Jacksonville, Ill., 1956; m. Darrell Hartke. Grad., Ill. Coll., 1979. Exec. dir. Skinker-DeBaliviere Cmty. Coun.; state rep. dist. 64 Mo. Ho. of Reps., 1993—2001; asst. treas. State of Mo., 1997—2001, treas., 2001—. Mem. Woman's Polit. Caucus Mo. Ho. of Reps.; dir. intergovernmental affairs City of St. Louis, 1997. Active Woman's Com. Forest Park, Rosedale Neighborhood Assn., mem. exec. com.; active West End Arts Coun.; cand. for Mo. U.S. Senator, 2004. Mem. Ctrl. West End Assn., Women Legislators Mo. Office: PO Box 210 Jefferson City MO 65102

FARMER, PAUL EDWARD, medical anthropologist; MD, PhD, Harvard U., 1990. Founding dir. Ptnrs. in Health; Presley prof. med. anthropology dept. social medicine Harvard Med. Sch., Boston, 1995—; attending physician divsn. infectious disease Brigham and Women's Hosp., Boston; med. co-dir. Clinique Bon Sauveur, Haiti. Mem. internat. sci. com. ids; coord. berculosis; mem. DOTS-Plus working group for the global tuberculosis programme WHO; chief advisor tuberculosis programs Open Soc. Inst.; chief med. cons. tuberculosis treatment project in prisons of Tomsk (Siberia) Pub. Health Rsch. Inst.; mem. sci. com. WHO Working Group on DOTS-Plus for MDR-TB; mem. Commonwealth of Mass. Bur. Communicable Disease Control; mem. sci. rev. bd. 10 internat. confs. on AIDS. Author: (book) AIDS and Accusation: Haiti and the Geography of Blame, 1992, The Uses of Haiti, 1994, Infections and Inequalities, 1998, Pathologies of Power, 2003; co-editor: Women, Poverty and AIDS, 1996, The Global Impact of Drug-Resistant Tuberculosis, 1999; contbr. articles to profl. jours. Recipient, 9th Ann. Heinz Humanitarian award, 2003, Margaret Mead award, Am. Anthrop. Assn., 1999, Humanitarian award, Duke U., Outstanding Internat. Physician award, AMA, Genius award, John D. and Catherine T. MacArthur Found., 1993. Mem.: Inst. of Medicine, 2004 (life). Office: Harvard Med Sch Dept Social Medicine 25 Shattuck St Boston MA 02115

FARMER, PHILLIP W., communications executive; b. 1939; BA, Duke U. Various mgmt. and tech. positions GE, 1962-82; v.p., gen. mgr. govt. support sys. divsn. Harris Corp., Melbourne, Fla., 1982-86, v.p. Palm Bay ops., govt. sys. sector, 1986-88, sr. v.p. sector exec., govt. sys. sector, 1988-89, pres. electronics sys. sector, 1989-91, exec. v.p., 1991, pres., CEO, 1995—, chmn., pres., CEO. Bd. dirs. Mfrs. Alliance, Aerospace Industries Assn. Bd. trustees Fla. Inst. Tech. Mem. Bus. Roundtable, Electronic Industries Assn. Office: Harris Corp 1025 W Nasa Blvd Melbourne FL 32919-0002

FARMER, RICHARD GILBERT, physician, foundation administrator, nursing consultant; b. Kokomo, Ind., Sept. 29, 1931; s. Oscar Irvin and Elizabeth Jane (Gilbert) Farmer; m. Janice Mae Schrank, Nov. 29, 1958; children: Amy Lynn, David Richard. Student, Ind. U., 1949—52; MD, U. Md., 1956; MS in Medicine, U. Minn., 1960. Diplomate Am. Bd. Internal Medicine, Gastroenterology. Fellow in internal medicine Mayo Clinic, Rochester, Minn., 1957—60; mem. staff Cleve. Clinic Found., 1962—91, chmn. dept. gastroenterology, 1972—82, bd. govs., 1974—79, chmn. divsn. medicine, 1975—91, mem. med. exec. com., 1975—91, mem. exec. com. bd. trustees, 1975—77; sr. med. advisor Bur. for Europe Agy. for Internat. Devel. U.S. Dept. State, Washington, 1992—94; cons. health care Ea. Europe and former Soviet Union, 1994—96; med. dir. Quality Health Internat., Boston, 1997—98; cons. Scandinavian Care, 1998—2003; prof. medicine, chief digestive and liver disease unit U. Rochester Med. Ctr., 2004—; clin. prof. medicine (gastroenterology) Georgetown U. Med. Ctr., Washington, 1992—2004; prof., chief digestive diseases unit U. Rochester (NY) Med. Ctr., 2004—. Mem. nat. sci. adv. bd. Nat. Found. Ileitis and Colitis, 1973—91; mem. nat. adv. bd. Nat. Commn. Digestive Diseases, 1977—79; mem. Coun. Subsplty. Socs. in Internal Medicine, 1978—85; chmn. grants rev. com. Nat. Found. Ileitis and Colitis, 1981—85; mem. com. to assess quality care in Medicare program, GAO and ways and means com. U.S. Ho. of Reps., 1986—89; cons. Am. Medico-Legal Found., Phila., 1996—2003, Inst. for Health Policy Analysis, Washington, 1996—2004; med. dir. Eurasian Med. Edn. Program (Russian Fedn.), 1998—2004. Editor 6 books; contbr. over 275 articles to sci. jours., books. Lt. comdr. USNR, 1960—62. Recipient Jubilee medal, Charles U. Prague, 1998. Master: ACP (gov. Ohio 1980—84, health and pub. policy com. 1982—91, chmn. med. tech. assessment com. 1985—86, regent 1985—91, chmn. 1986—88, chmn. clin. practice subcom. 1988—91, del. to AMA 1989—94, Spl. Presdl. citation 1984), Am. Coll. Gastroenterology (trustee, exec. com. 1975—80, pres. 1978—79); mem.: Internat. Orgn. for Study Inflammatory Bowel Disease (dep. chmn. 1982—86), Interstate Postgrad. Med. Assn. (pres. 1983—84), Inst. Medicine of NAS (life), Am. Gastroent. Assn. (commn. on future 1973—74, tng. and edn. com. 1975—78, chmn. subcom. grad. edn. 1975—78), Assn. Program Dirs. in Internal Medicine (founding pres. 1977—79, Founder's award 1993). Democrat. Mem. Soc. Of Friends. Home: 9126 Town Gate Ln Bethesda MD 20817-4111 Office: U Rochester Med Ctr Box 646 Rochester NY 14642 Fax: 585-276-1911. Office Phone: 585-275-7432. Business E-Mail: Richard_Farmer@urmc.rochester.edu.

FARMER, RICHARD T., uniform rental and sales executive; b. Dayton, Ky., Nov. 22, 1934; BBA, Miami U., Ohio, 1956. Chmn. bd. Cintas Corp., Cin. Office: Cintas Corp 6800 Cintas Blvd PO Box 625737 Cincinnati OH 45262-5737

FARMER, ROBERT LINDSAY, lawyer; b. Portland, Oreg., Sept. 29, 1922; s. Paul C. and Irma (Lindsay) F.; m. Carmen E. Engebretson, Sept. 8, 1943; children: Cort W., Scott L., Eric C. BS, UCLA, 1946; LLB, U. So. Calif., 1949. Bar: Calif. 1949. Since practiced in, L.A.; mem. Farmer & Ridley, L.A., 1949—. Trustee Edward James Found., West Dean Estate, Chichester, Eng. Served with AUS, 1943-46. Mem. ABA, Los Angeles County Bar Assn., Order of Coif, Beta Gamma Sigma, Kappa Sigma, Phi Delta Phi, Annandale Golf Club (Pasadena, Calif.). Home: 251 S Orange Grove Blvd Apt 1 Pasadena CA 91105-1766 Office: 444 S Flower St Los Angeles CA 90071-2901

FARMER, SCOTT D., apparel executive; BA, Miami U., 1981. V.p. mktg. & merchandising Cintas Sales Corp., Cin., v.p. nat. account divsn., pres., 1992-94, CEO, 1994—, also chmn. bd. dirs. Office: Cintas Sales Corp 6800 Cintas Blvd Cincinnati OH 45262

FARMER, SUSAN LAWSON, retired broadcast executive, retired executive secretary; b. Boston, May 29, 1942; d. Ralph and Margaret (Tyng) Lawson; m. Malcolm Farmer, III, Apr. 6, 1968; children: Heidi Benson, Stephanie Lawson. Student, Garland Jr. Coll., 1960-61, Brown U., 1961-62; LHD, Bryant Coll., 2004. Mem. Providence Home Rule Charter Commn., 1979-80; sec. of state State of R.I., Providence, 1983-87; pres., CEO Sta. WSBE-TV R.I. PBS, Providence, 1987—. Spl. adv. R.I. Family Ct., 1978-83; mem. nat. voting stds. panel Fed. Election Commn. co-chmn. Nat. Voter Edn. Project; mem. electoral coll., 1984; chmn. Gov.'s Com. on Ethics in Govt., 1985-86; mem. tchg. facility and adv. panel Internat. Ctr. on Election Law and Adminstrn.; mem. nat. edn. adv. com. Pub. Broadcasting System, 1987-89; trustee Eastern Ednl. TV Network, 1987-95; mem. R.I. Task Force on Tech., 1995-04, R.I. Info. Mgmt. Commn., 1997; bd. dirs., mem. exec. com. Program Resources Group, 1993-01; mem. Gov.'s Telecom. Task Force, 2000-04; mem. nat. media adv. com. WomenFuture, 2002-04. Bd. dirs. Justice Resources Corp., Marathon House, Inc., R.I. Council Alcoholism, R.I. Hist. Soc., Planned Parenthood (R.I. chpt.), R.I. Rape Crisis Ctr., The Newport Inst.; mem. Mayor's Task Force on Child Abuse, R.I. Film Commn.; v.p. Miriam Hosp. Found.; mem. adv. com. Women in Polit. and Govtl. Careers Program, U. R.I., 1985-95; mem. adv. bd. Com. for Study of Am. Electorate-Ford Found. Project-Efficacy in State Voting Laws, 1986; mem. Commn. to Study Length of Election Process, 1985-87; steering com. Nat. Fund for America's Future, Project Vote R.I.; bd. dirs. Dawn for Children Tng. Thru Placement; pres. R.I. PBS Found.; bd. dirs. R.I. Anti-Drug Coalition Exec. Com., Nat. Forum for Pub. TV Execs., 1998-2004, chmn., 1999. Named Woman of Yr., Nat. Women's Polit. Caucus, 1980; recipient Nat. Advocacy award Assn. Pub. TV Stas., 2004. Mem. LWV, NATAS (bd. govs. New Eng. chpt. 1995—), N.E. Assn. Schs. and Colls. (com. on tech. and course instns.), So. Ednl. Comms. Assn. (bd. dirs. 1993-96), R.I. Women's Polit. Caucus (Woman of Yr. 1980), Bus. and Profl. Women (Woman of Yr. 1984), Common Cause, Save the Bay, Providence Preservation Soc., Orgn. State Broadcasting Execs, Agawam Hunt Club, Mill Reef Club (Antigua, West Indies), Nat. Assn. of Ams. Pub. TV Stas. (trustee 1996-2002, Nat. Advocacy award, 2004), Nat. Acad. TV Arts and Scis. (bd. govs. N.E. chpt. 1995-2001), Nat. Ednl. Telecomms. Assn. (bd. dirs. 1997-2004, Nat. Forum Pub. TV Execs. (bd. dirs. 1998-2004, chmn. 1999). Home: 190 Upton Ave Providence RI 02906-1552 Personal E-mail: sfarmer10@cox.net.

FARMER, T. BRENT, music educator; b. Louisville, Ky., Feb. 18, 1970; s. Thomas Franklin and Emma LaVerne Farmer; B in music edn., U. Ky., 1993; M in music edn., Valdosia State U., 1996. Cert. tchg. cert. State of Ga. Percussion arranger, tchr. various HS in Ky. NC, and Ga., 1989—96; dir. bands Thomasville HS, Thomasville, Ga., 1996—2003, East Tex. Bapt. U., Marshall, Tex., 2003—. 1st v.p. Marshall Symphony Bd., Marshall, Tex., 2005—; percussionist South Ark. Symphony, El Dorado, Ark., 2004—, Marshal Symphony, Marshall, Tex., 2004—. Named Drum Corps Assoc. World Champion, Corp. Drum and Bugle Corp., 2001. Mem.: Collegiate Band Dirs. Nat. Assn., Tex. Bandmasters Assn., Tex. Music Educators Assn. Home: 705 Slone Dr Marshall TX 75672 Office: E Tex Bapt U 1209 N Grove St Marshall TX 75670 Office Phone: 903-923-2168. Office Fax: 903-934-8114. E-mail: bfarmer@albu.edu.

FARMER, TERRY D(WAYNE), lawyer; b. Oklahoma City, May 1, 1949; s. Gayle V. and Allene (Edsall) F.; m. Nicole M. Charlebois; children: Grant L., Tyler M. BA, U. Okla., 1971, JD, 1974. Bar: Okla. 1974, N.Mex. 1975, U.S. Dist. Ct. N.Mex. 1976, U.S. Ct. Claims 1975, U.S. Ct. Appeals (10th cir.) 1977, U.S. Supreme Ct. 1980. Asst. trust officer First Nat. Bank of Albuquerque, 1974-75; assoc. Nordhaus, Moses & Dunn, Albuquerque, 1975-78, ptnr., 1978-80; dir. Moses, Dunn, Farmer & Tuthill, P.C., Albuquerque, 1980—. Pres. Albuquerque Lawyers Club, N. Mex., 1982-83. Named one of Outstanding Lawyers Am. Fellow N.Mex. Bar Found.; mem. N.Mex. Bar Assn. (pres. Young Lawyers div., 1978-79), Okla. Bar Assn., N.Mex. Trial Lawyers, Am. Trial Lawyers Assn. Office: Moses Dunn Farmer & Tuthill PC PO Box 27047 Albuquerque NM 87125-7047 Office Phone: 505-843-9440.

FARMER, THOMAS WOHLSEN, neurologist, department chairman, science educator; b. Lancaster, Pa., Sept. 18, 1914; s. Clarence R. and Laura (Wohlsen) F.; m. Phyllis McCormick, July 19, 1941; children: Pamela Farmer Henderson, Thomas Wohlsen. AB, Harvard U., 1935, MD, 1941; MA, Duke U., 1937; postgrad., U. Copenhagen, 1957-58, U. Calif., San Diego, 1971-72. Diplomate: Am. Bd. Psychiatry and Neurology (dir. 1969—, pres. 1977). Intern Pa. Hosp., Phila., 1941-42; resident Boston City Hosp., 1942-43, Johns Hopkins Hosp., 1943-44, 46-47; mem. staff N.C. Meml. Hosp., Chapel Hill, 1952—; instr. medicine Johns Hopkins U., 1947-48; asst. prof. neurology Southwestern Med. Sch., U. Tex., Dallas, 1948-49, assoc. prof., 1949-50, prof., 1950-52, prof. medicine, acting chmn. dept. medicine, 1951-52; prof. neurol. medicine, head div. neurology U. N.C., Chapel Hill, 1952—, Sarah Graham Kenan prof. medicine, 1975—. Author: Pediatric Neurology, 1964, 3d edit., 1983, Neurologia Pediatrica, 1972. Served with USNR, 1944-46. Mem. Am. Acad. Neurology (nat. sec. 1955-57), Am. Neurol. Assn., Am. Acad. Neurology, ACP, AMA, Assn. Research Nervous and Mental Diseases, Child Neurology Soc. Home: 1304 Mason Farm Rd Chapel Hill NC 27514-4604 Office: U NC Sch Medicine Clin Scis Bldg Chapel Hill NC 27514

FARNAM, JAFAR, allergist, immunologist, pediatrician; b. Tabriz, Iran, Dec. 18, 1945; MD, Faculty Medicine Tabriz, 1972. Diplomate Am. Bd. Pediat., Am. Bd. Allergy and Immunology. Intern U. Ill. Hosp., Chgo., 1977-78; resident in pediat. Christ Hosp.- Rush U., Oaklawn, 1978-80; fellow in allergy & immunology U. Tex. Med. Br., Galveston, 1980-82, clin. assoc. prof. internal medicine; with Clear Lake Regional Hosp. Mem. Am. Acad. Pediat., Am. Acad. Allergy, Asthma, and Immunology, Am. Coll. Allergy, Asthma, and Immunology, Tex. Med. Assn., Tex. Allergy Soc. Office: Allergy Asthma Ctr 450 Medical Center Blvd Ste 204 Webster TX 77598-4229 Office Phone: 281-338-2246. Business E-Mail: farnammd@bluegate.com.

FARNATH, DOROTHY WHITMYER, recruitment company executive; b. Hammonton, N.J., Mar. 3, 1942; d. Theodore George and Dorothy Priest Whitmyer; children: Melissa Scott Ciliberti, Theodore George. BS in Med. Tech., U. Pa., 1964. Med. tech. Thomas Jefferson U. Medicine, Phila., 1966-69; supr. South Jersey Urology Assocs., Cherry Hill, N.J., 1977-84; supr., mgr. 227 Labs., Phila., 1984-88; pres. Dorothy Whitmyer Farnath & Assocs., Inc., Marlton, N.J., 1988—. Pres. Championship Family Restaurant, Trenton, N.J., 1995—; gen. mgr. GDV Enterprises, Trenton, 1995—; owner Hair Sta., Haddon Heights, N.J., 1994—; co-owner Hardshell Cafe, Marlton, N.J., 2000—. Mem. Rep. Nat. Com., Washington, 1994—. Mem. U.S. C. of C. Avocations: reading, genealogy. Office: 104 Centre Blvd Ste B Marlton NJ 08053-4130

FARNESE, ROSANNA, language educator; b. Caracas, Venezuela, Sept. 22, 1960; d. Salvatore Della Vecchia and Rosina Vinci; m. Sergio Farnese, Apr. 22, 1958; 1 child, Michele. BA Spanish, St. Peter's Coll., 1985. Tchr. Spanish Acad. Sacred Heart, Hoboken, NJ, 1985—98, Palisades Park Jr./Sr. H.S., NJ, 1998—.

FARNGALO, ROSEMARIE MERRITT, school psychologist; d. Ormond StClair and Elaine Louis Merritt; children: Aisha Ferngalo, Zuri Ferngalo. BS in Criminal Justice, CUNY, 1980, MEd in Sch. Psychology, 1993; PhD in Guidance and Counseling, Union Inst. & U., 2004. Cert. sch. psychologist Ga. Instr. Interborn Inst., NYC, 1980—81; health rschr. WHO, Trinidad and Tobago, 1981—84; educator NYC Bd. Edn., Bklyn., 1984—93; sch. psychologist Dekalb County Schs., Decatur, Ga., 1995—. Behavior cons. DPCH, Decatur, 2004—; cons. United Way, Atlanta, 2005—. Named Outstanding Presenter, Peer Helpers Dekalb County, 2004, Unity Cmty. Coalition, Ga., 2004. Mem.: Nat. Assn. Sch. Psychologists, Order Ea. Star (chaplain 2002—04), Zeta Phi Beta (Outstanding Presenter 2003). Democrat. Avocations: travel, music, reading. Office: Deklab County Schs 5839 Meml Dr Stone Mountain GA 30083 Office Phone: 678-676-1930. E-mail: rfarngalo@comcast.net.

FARNHAM, ANTHONY EDWARD, language educator, department chairman; b. Oakland, Calif., July 2, 1930; s. Willard Edward and Frances Fern (Hicks) F.; m. Frances Anne Larkey, Dec. 28, 1957; children: Allen Nicholas, Timothy John. AB, U. Calif.-Berkeley, 1951; MA, Harvard U., 1957, PhD, 1964. Instr. English Mt. Holyoke Coll., South Hadley, Mass., 1961-64, asst. prof., 1964-69, assoc. prof., 1969-72, prof., 1972-99, dept. chmn., 1979-85, prof. emeritus, 1999—. Editor: A Sourcebook in the History of English, 1969; author: Statement and Search in the Confessio Amantis, Mediaevalia 16, 1993. Served with M.I. U.S. Army, 1953—56. Mem. MLA, Am. Cath. Hist. Assn., Medieval Acad. Am., Assn. Literary Scholars and Critics, Dante Soc., New Chaucer Soc., Phi Beta Kappa. Roman Catholic. Home: 23 Atwood Rd South Hadley MA 01075-1601 Office: Mt Holyoke Coll Dept English 50 Coll St South Hadley MA 01075-6421

FARNHAM, CLAYTON HENSON, lawyer; b. New Brunswick, N.J., Aug. 18, 1938; s. Richard Bayles and Naomi Shropshire (Henson) F.; m. Katharine Gross, Sept. 16, 1967; children: Julia Kernan, Richard Bayles II. BA, U. of the South, 1961; LLB, U. Ga., 1967. Bar: Ga. 1968, U.S. Dist. Ct. (no., so. and mid. dists.) Ga. 1968, U.S. Supreme Ct. 1978, U.S. Dist. Ct. (no. dist.) Miss. 1978, U.S. Dist. Ct. (ea. dist.), Tenn. 1997, U.S. Ct. Appeals (5th cir., 11th cir.) 1968, (4th cir.) 1981, U.S. Ct. Appeals (8th cir.) 1992. Law clk. to judge U.S. Dist. Ct., Atlanta, 1967-69; from assoc., to ptnr. Swift, Currie, McGhee & Hiers, Atlanta, 1969-82; ptnr. Drew, Eckl & Farnham, Atlanta, 1983—. Contbr. articles to profl. jours. Lt. (j.g.) USNR, 1961-64. Mem. ABA (coun. TIPS sect. 1989-92), Internat. Assn. Def. Counsel (com. chmn. 1987-89), Ansley Golf Club, Lawyer's Club Atlanta, Old War Horse Lawyer's Club. Home: 30 Inman Cir NE Atlanta GA 30309 Office: Drew Eckl & Farnham 800 W Peachtree St NW PO Box 7600 Atlanta GA 30357 Office Phone: 404-885-1400. Business E-Mail: cfarnham@deflaw.com.

FARNHAM, ROBERT E., health facility administrator; CPA. Acct. PricewaterhouseCoopers LLP; from mem. staff to sr. v.p., CFO Health Mgmt. Assocs., Inc., Naples, Fla., 1985—2001, sr. v.p., 2001—, CFO, 2001—. Office: Health Management Associates Inc 5811 Pelican Bay Blvd Ste 500 Naples FL 34108-2710

FARNHAM, TIMOTHY, information technology executive; b. Arlington, Calif., Mar. 1, 1947; s. Jack Pershing and Joyce Maureen (Evans) F.; m. Sue Ann Newton Frantz, Oct. 25, 1969 (div. Jan. 1975); children: Kevin, Kara; m. Paula Eleen Kerner, Nov. 25, 1978; children: Melinda, Elyse. BBA summa cum laude, Nat. U., 1990. Equipment engr. Pacific Bell, San Diego, 1980-86, design engr., 1986-87; mgr. instrn. and devel. Bellcore, Lisle, Ill., 1987-89, mgr. tng. and edn., 1991-95; tech. engr. Pacific Bell, San Ramon, Calif., 1989-91, 95-96; regional mgr. new tech. and applied R & D Teleport Comm. Group, Walnut Creek, Calif., 1996-99; dir. tng. and edn. Telecordia Techs. Inc., Benicia, Calif., 1999—2005; product and tech. trainer Redback Networks, San Jose, Calif., 2005—. Lead presenter wireless comm. curriculum Bellcore; presenter UN APEC Agy., Bangkok, USTA Showcases, Western Comm. Forum, Network '90s Conf., San Francisco, Expo Comm, Mex., Mexico City, Inst. for Internat. Rsch., Beverly Hills, Calif. Contbr. articles to profl. conf. procs. Sgt. USAF, 1965-68. Mem. IEEE, N.Y. Acad. Scis. Avocations: reading, playing guitar, genealogy research. Office: 863 Dover Cir Benicia CA 94510-3651 Personal E-mail: farnham4@pacbell.net.

FARNHOLTZ, SHARYN ANN, minister; b. Utica, N.Y., May 18, 1945; d. James Arthur and Evelyn Florence McCurdy; m. David Frederick Farnholtz, July 31, 1965; children: Jodee Lynn Farnholtz Cook, Nathaniel David. Student, Oneonta State U., 1963-65. Lic. to ministry Agape New Testament Fellowship, 1985. Nursery supt. Macungie (Pa.) Bapt. Ch., 1970-77; v.p. Women's Missionary Soc., Macungie, 1975-76; ch. sec. Agape New Testament Fellowship, Schnecksville, Pa., 1977-81, 91, supt. Sunday sch., 1977-84, 88, dir. youth, 1978-85, 89, elder, team pastor, 1985—. V.p. Christian Action Coun. of Lehigh Valley, Allentown, Bethlehem, Pa., 1990-91. Republican. Office: Agape New Testament Fellowship 2259 Rt 873 Schnecksville PA 18078-9469 *When trials and hardships come to us, it is the time to turn obstacles into opportunities to learn a better way, to live a better life, and to become a better person; it is God's way.*

FARNSWORTH, ELIZABETH, broadcast journalist; b. Mpls., Dec. 23, 1943; d. H. Bernerd and Jane (Mills) Fink; m. Charles E. Farnsworth, June 20, 1966; children: Jennifer Farnsworth Fellows, Samuel. BA, Middlebury Coll., 1965; MA in History, Stanford U., 1966; LLD (hon.), Colby Coll., 2002. Reporter, panelist PBS World Press, KQED, San Francisco, 1975-77; reporter InterNews, Berkeley, Calif., 1977-80; freelance TV and print reporter, San Francisco, 1980-91; fgn. corr. MacNeil/Lehrer News Hour, San Francisco, 1991-95; chief corr., prin. substitute anchor News Hour with Jim Lehrer, Arlington, Va., 1995-97, San Francisco, 1997-99, sr. corr., 1999—. Co-author: El Bloqueo Invisible, 1974; prodr., dir. documentary Thanh's War, 1991 (Cine Golden Eagle award); contbr. articles to various publs. Mem. adv. bd. Berkeley Edn. Found., 1990-95, U. Calif. Sch. Journalism, Berkeley; mem. nat. adv. bd. Ctr. Investigative Reporting, 2001-; bd. dirs. Data Ctr., Oakland, Calif., 1993-95. Recipient Golden Gate award San Francisco Film Festival, 1984, Best Investigative Reporting award No. Calif. Radio, TV News Dirs.' Assn., 1986, Blue Ribbon, Am. Film and Video Festival, 1991, Silver World medal N.Y. Film Festivals, 2001; nominee Emmy award, 2002. Mem. AFTRA, NATAS, World Affairs Coun. No. Calif. (bd. dirs. 1998—), Nat. Adv. Writers Corps, Phi Beta Kappa. Presbyterian. Avocations: gardening, hiking, poetry.

FARNSWORTH, FRANK ALBERT, retired economics professor; s. Frank Adelbert and Lancing Claudine (Miller) F.; m. Ruth Coburn, June 26 1943 (dec. Dec. 1970); children: Frank A., Ruth Farnsworth Eldridge, John C.; m. Elizabeth Hoyt Martire, Dec. 26, 1971 (dec. June 1988); children: Elizabeth M. Cutter-Hickman, Amy Martire, John Martire. AB in Econs. with honors, Colgate U., 1939; AM, Harvard U., 1946, PhD, 1952. With dept. econ. Colgate U., 1941-87, prof., 1957-87, ret., 1987. Dept. chmn., vis. rsch. assoc. Grad. Bus. Sch., Harvard U., 1947-48; Fulbright prof. Norwegian Sch. Econ., Bergen, 1954-55; vis. prof. small bus. Wake Forest U., 1975; vis. fellow Massey Coll.-U. Toronto, Ont., Can., 1968; ex-officio mem. Madison County Indsl. Devel. Agy.; bd. dir. Otter Valley Press, Inc., Am. Tree Farmer, Svc. Corp. of Ret. Execs.; cons. in field. Mem. AAUP, Am. Mgmt. Assn., N.Y. State Econ. Devel. Coun., Masons, Alpha Chi Epsilon, Alpha Delta Phi. Republican. Baptist. Home: 17 E Kendrick Ave Hamilton NY 13346-1311 Office: 1119 Wheeler Rd Brandon VT 05733-8922 Personal E-mail: farnsworth@Mail.Colgate.Edu. Business E-Mail: vtotter@together.net.

FARNSWORTH, NED STEPHEN, Spanish language and literature educator; b. Reading, Pa., Apr. 4, 1965; s. Glennis Kay and Marilyn Ruth Farnsworth. BA, Houghton Coll., 1987; postgrad., U. Md., 1988, Bibl. Theol. Sem., Hatfield, Pa., 1992—. Tchr. Camp Springs (Md.) Christian Sch., 1988-89; program coord. Spearhead, Mexico City, 1989-91; bilingual customer svc. rep. Meridian Bank, Reading, 1992-96; tchr. Berks Christian Sch., Birdboro, Pa., 1996-01; children's min. coord. Liebenzell Missions, Ecuador, 2001—. Big brother Allegeny County Outreach, Houghton, N.Y., 1983-87; vol. Olivet Boys & Girls Club, Reading, 1992-94. Avocations: music, writing, photography, theater, cooking. Office: Liebenzell Mission USA PO Box 66 Schooleys Mountain NJ 07870

FARNSWORTH, STEVEN ROBERT, safety engineer; s. Robert Wayne and Ruth Marie Farnsworth; m. Lynette Rae Dass, Sept. 23, 1973; children: Stephanie Lynn Hudson, Shane Robert. AA, Iowa Lakes C.C., 1982. Cert. welding inspector, Am. Welding Soc., 1992, welder, Profl. Svc. Industries, 1998. Shipfitter U.S.S. Basilone U.S. Navy, San Diego, 1973—77, technician hull maintenance U.S.S. White Plaines U.S. Naval Base, 1984—86, inspector quality assurance USS Hunley Norfolk, Va., 1987—88; welder, heavy equipment operator Spencer (Iowa) Constrn. Co., 1977—79; instr. welding Iowa Lakes C.C., Emmetsburg, Iowa, 1979—84, welding instr., 1988—. With USN, 1973—77. Mem.: Am. Welding Soc. (assoc.), Kiwanis. Democrat. Methodist. Avocations: hunting, golf. Home: 3506 1st Street Emmetsburg IA 50536 Office: Iowa Lakes Community College 3200 College Drive Emmetsburg IA 50536 Office Phone: 712-852-3554. Home Fax: 712-852-2152; Office Fax: 712-852-2152. Personal E-mail: sfarnsworth1@iowalakes.edu.

FARNSWORTH, T. BROOKE, lawyer; b. Grand Rapids, Mich., Mar. 16, 1945; s. George Llelwyn and Gladys Fern (Kennedy) Farnsworth; m. Connie D. Hedblom, June 15, 1996; children: Leslie Erin, T. Brooke. BS in Bus., Ind. U., 1967; JD, Ind. U., Indpls., 1971. Bar: Tex. 1971, U.S. Dist. Ct. (so. dist.) Tex. 1972, U.S. Tax Ct. 1972, U.S. Ct. Appeals (5th cir.) 1977, U.S. Ct. Appeals (D.C. Cir.) 1977, U.S. Supreme Ct. 1978, U.S. Ct. Appeals (11th cir.) 1982, U.S. Dist. Ct. (we. dist.) Tex. 1988, U.S. Dist. Ct. (no. dist.) Tex. 1994, U.S. Ct. Appeals (10th cir.) 2003. Adminstrv. asst. to treas. of State of Ind., Indpls., 1968-71; assoc. Butler, Binion, Rice, Cook & Knapp, Houston, 1971-74; counsel Damson Oil Corp., Houston, 1974-78; prin. Farnsworth & Assocs., Houston, 1978-90, Farnsworth & von Berg, Houston, 1990—. Contbr. articles on law to profl. jours. Fellow: Tex. Bar Found., Coll. State Bar Tex.; mem.: ATLA, ABA, Houston Bar Assn., State Bar Tex., Champions Golf Club, Olympic Club. Republican. Home: 6038 Pebble Beach Dr Houston TX 77069 Office: Farnsworth and von Berg 333 N Sam Houston Pkwy E Ste 300 Houston TX 77060-2414 E-mail: tbfarnsworth@farnsworthvonberg.com.

FARNY, NATASHA HOLT, musician, educator; b. Concord, Mass., Apr. 27, 1971; d. Michael Holt and Ethel Hooper Farny. Cert., The Curtis Inst. Music, 1990; BA in Humanities, Yale U., 1995; MusM in Performance, SUNY, Rochester, N.Y., 1998; MusD, The Juilliard Sch., 1998—2003. Tchr. cello Third St. Music Sch. Settlement, N.Y., 1998—2000; asst. prin. cellist R.I. Philharm., Providence, 2001; sect. cellist Colo. Music Festival, Boulder, Colo., 2003—; asst. prof. cello SUNY, Fredonia, NY, 2005—. Musician: (radio) Sonata Recital, Beethoven Triple Concerto, The Cottonwood Festival. Recipient Performer's cert., The Eastman Sch. Music, 1998; grantee, Citibank and the Juilliard Sch., 2000—01. Mem.: Am. Fedn. Musicians (assoc.). Avocations: hiking, travel, crossword puzzles, music, dance.

FARON, FAY CHERYL, private investigator, writer; b. Kansas City, Mo. d. Albert David and Geraldine Fay (Morgan) F. Student, Glendale (Ariz.) C.C., 1967-68, Ariz. State U., 1968-71, U. Ariz., 1971-72. Lic. pvt. investigator, Calif. Owner Monogramation, San Francisco, 1976-80; assoc. prodr. Sta. KGO-TV, San Francisco, 1980-81, Power/Rector, San Francisco, 1982-83; owner Office in the City, San Francisco, 1982-83, The Rat Dog Dick Detective Agy., San Francisco, 1983—. Lectr., spkr. San Francisco U., 1984—, San Francisco Assn. Legal Assts., 1984—, Commonwealth Club San Francisco, 1987, Calif. Collectors Coun., San Francisco, 1992—, Book Passage Mystery Writers Conf., 1997-99. Author: A Private Eye's Guide to Collecting a Bad Debt, 1991, Missing Persons, 1997; author/editor: The Instant National Locator Guide, 1991, 2nd edit., 1993, 3rd edit, 1996, Rip-Off, 1998; columnist Ask Rat Dog, 1993—; host, writer: (Court TV Crime Story Spl.) Rip-Offs and Scams, 2000. Co-founder, pres. bd. ElderAngels, San Francisco. Subject of Jack Olsen's book, Hastened to the Grave, 1998. Mem. Nat. Assn. Investigative Specialists, Nat. Assn. Bunco Investigators (asst.), Profls. Against Confidence Crimes (asst.), Sisters in Crime. Avocations: biking, camping, horseback riding, river rafting, travel.

FARQUHAR, JAMES, geochemist, researcher; b. Chgo., Jan. 6, 1965; s. James Douglas and Sue (Wakeman) F.; m. Lisa Joan Tuit, Dec. 31, 1994; children: James Henry, Anna Ruth. BS, Washington and Lee U., 1987; MSc, U. Chgo., 1990; PhD, U. Alta., Edmonton, Can., 1995. Fellow Carnegie Instn. Washington, 1995-97; NSF fellow U. Calif., San Diego, 1997-99, rsch. chemist, 1999-2001; asst. prof. geochemistry U. Md., College Park, 2000—05, assoc. prof. geochemistry, 2005—. Assoc. prof. Earth Sci. Interdisciplinary Ctr., dept. geology U. Md., 2000-05. Assoc. editor Geochimica et Cosmachanica Acta, 2003—; mem. editl. bd. Geobiology, 2000—. Killam grad. fellow Killam Found., Can., 1993-95; recipient F. W. Clarke medal Geochem. Soc., 2000. Mem. AAAS, Am. Chem. Soc., Am. Geophys. Union. Office: UMCP Dept Geology and ESSIC College Park MD 20742 E-mail: jfarquha@essic.umd.edu.

FARQUHAR, JOHN WILLIAM, physician, educator; b. Winnipeg, Man., Can., June 13, 1927; arrived in U.S., 1934; s. John Giles and Marjorie Victoria (Roberts) Farquhar; m. Christine Louise Johnson, July 14, 1968; children: Margaret F., John C.M.;children from previous marriage: Bruce E., Douglas G. AB, U. Calif., Berkeley, 1949; MD, U. Calif., San Francisco, 1952. Intern U. Calif. Hosp., San Francisco, 1952—53, resident, 1953—54, 1957—58, postdoctoral fellow, 1955—57; resident U. Minn., Mpls., 1954—55; rsch. assoc. Rockefeller U., N.Y.C., 1958—62; asst. prof. medicine Stanford (Calif.) U., 1962—66, assoc. prof., 1966—73, prof., 1978—, C.F. Rehnborg prof. in disease prevention, 1989—2000; dir. Stanford Ctr. Rsch. in Disease Prevention, 1973—98; dir. collaborating ctr. for chronic disease prevention WHO, 1985—99; prof. health rsch. and policy, 1988—. Mem. staff Stanford U. Hosp.; chair Victoria Declaration Implementation com. Author: The American Way of Life Need Not Be Hazardous to Your Health, 1978, 1987; author: (with Gene Spiller) The Last Puff, 1990; author: The Victoria Declaration for Heart Health, 1992, How to Reduce Your Risk of Heart Disease, 1994, The Catalonia Declaration: Investing in Heart Health, 1996, Worldwide Efforts to Improve Heart Disease, 1997; author: (with Spiller) Diagnosis Heart Disease: Answers to Your Questions about Recovery and Lasting Health, 2001; contbr. articles to profl. jours. Served with U.S. Army, 1944—46. Recipient James D. Bruce award, ACP, 1983, Myrdal prize, 1986, Dana award for Pioneering Achievement in Health, Dana Found., 1990, Nat. Cholesterol award for Pub. Edn., Nat. Cholesterol Edn. Program of NIH, 1991, Rsch. Achievement award, Am. Heart Assn., 1992, Order of St. George for Svc. to Autonomous Govt. of Catalonia, 1996, Joseph Stokes Preventive Cardiology award, Am. Soc. Preventive Cardiology, 1999, Ancel Keys Meml. lectureship, Am. Heart Assn., 2000. Mem.: Internat. Heart Health Soc., Soc. Behavioral Medicine (pres. 1991—92), Am. Heart Assn. (coun. epidemiology and prevention), Am. Soc. Clin. Investigation, Inst. Medicine NAS, Gold Headed Cane Soc., Alpha Omega Alpha, Sigma Xi. Episcopalian. Office: Stanford U Sch of Medicine Stanford Prevention Rsch Ctr 211 Quarry Rd Stanford CA 94305-5705 E-mail: JFarquhar@stanford.edu.

FARQUHAR, MARILYN GIST, cell biologist, pathologist, educator; b. Tulare, Calif., July 11, 1928; d. Brooks DeWitt and Alta (Green) Gist; m. John W. Farquhar, June 4, 1952; children: Bruce, Douglas (div. 1968); m. George Palade, June 7, 1970. AB, U. Calif., Berkeley, 1949, MA, 1952, PhD, 1955. Asst. rsch. pathologist Sch. Medicine U. Calif., San Francisco, 1956-58, assoc. rsch. pathologist, 1962-64, assoc. prof., 1964-68, prof. pathology, 1968-70; rsch. assoc. Rockefeller U., N.Y.C., 1958-62, prof. cell biology,

1970-73, Sch. Medicine Yale U., New Haven, 1973-87, Sterling prof. cell biology and pathology, 1987-90; prof. pathology cell molecular medicine U. Calif., San Diego, 1990—, chair divsn. cellular and molecular medicine, 1991-99, prof. cellular & molecular medicine, chair dept. cellular & molecular medicine, 1999—. Mem. editorial bd. numerous sci. jours.; contbr. articles to profl. jours. Recipient Career Devel. award NIH, 1968-73, Disting. Sci. medal Electron Microscope Soc., 1987, Gomori medal Histochem. Soc., 1999, A.N. Richards award Internat. Soc. Nephrology, 2003. Mem.: NAS, Internat. Soc. Nephrology (A.N. Richards award 2003), Am. Soc. Nephrology (Homer Smith award 1988, Gottschalk award 2002), Am. Assn. Investigative Pathology (Rous Whipple award 2001), Am. Soc. Cell Biology (pres. 1981—82, E.B. Wilson medal 1987), Am. Acad. Arts and Scis. Home and Office: U Calif San Diego Sch Med 12894 Via Latina Del Mar CA 92014-3730

FARQUHAR, ROBERT MICHAEL, lawyer; b. Chelsea, Mass., Apr. 28, 1954; s. Robert Vociel and Helen Margaret (Stevens) F.; m. Carol Elizabeth Auch, Dec. 16, 1978; children: Stephanie Elizabeth, Andrew Michael. BS, So. Meth. U., 1977, JD, 1980. Bar: Tex. 1980, U.S. Dist. Ct. (no. and ea. dists.) Tex. 1980, U.S. Ct. Appeals (5th and 11th cirs.) 1980, U.S. Supreme Ct. 1990; cert. bus. bankruptcy law Tex. Bd. Legal Specialization. Assoc. Carter Jones MaGee Rudberg Moss & Mayes, Dallas, 1980-82; ptnr. Johnson & Cravens, Dallas, 1982-88; shareholder Winstead Sechrest & Minick, P.C., Dallas, 1988—. Mem. ABA, Dallas Bar Assn. Republican. Episcopalian. Avocations: bicycling, computers. Office: Winstead Sechrest Minick PC 1201 Elm St Ste 5400 Dallas TX 75270-2199

FARQUHAR, ROBERT NICHOLS, lawyer; b. Dayton, Ohio, Apr. 23, 1936; s. Robert Lawrence and Mary Frances (Nichols) F.; m. Elizabeth Lynn Bryan, Aug. 29, 1959 (div. 1971); children: Robert Nichols, Jensen; m. Carol A. Smith, Dec. 27, 1975. AB, Kenyon Coll., 1958; JD, Cornell U., 1961. Bar: Ohio 1961, Mich. 1993, U.S. Dist. Ct. (so. dist.) Ohio 1962, U.S. Ct. Appeals (6th cir.) 1966, U.S. Supreme Ct. 1978. Assoc. Altick & McDaniel, Dayton, 1961-69; ptnr. Gould, Bailey & Farquhar and predecessor firms, Dayton, 1969-78, Brumbaugh, Corwin & Gould, Dayton, 1978-80, Altick & Corwin, Dayton, 1981—, pres., 1996—2005. Bd. dirs. Ohio Law Abstract Pub., Columbus; city atty., Centerville, Ohio, 1969-2004, Oakwood, Ohio, 1997—2003; sec., gen. counsel Miami Conservancy Dist., 1990-2004; bd. commrs. character and fitness Ohio Supreme Ct., 1987-94, 97-2003, chair, 2000-02. Mem. Montgomery County Rep. Ctrl. Com, 1965-69, exec. com., 1968-69; bd. dirs. Centerville Hist. Soc., 1971-75, pres. 1973-74; trustee Montgomery County Legal Aid Soc., 1972-76; trustee Dayton Law Libr. Assn., 1972—, pres., 1980-86; mem. governing bd. Carillon Hist. Park, Dayton, chair, 1999-2001; mem. congressional screening com. U.S. Naval Acad., 1979-83. Mem. ABA (ho. of dels. 2001-2004), Ohio State Bar Assn. (chmn. legal ethics and profl. conduct com. 1982-86, exec. com. 1988-91, coun. of dels. 1988—), Dayton Bar Assn. Found. (pres. 1984-90), New England Hist. Genealogical Soc. (coun. mem.), Dayton Bicycle Club, Dayton Lawyers Club, Delta Phi, Phi Delta Phi. Episcopalian. Home: 1731 Ladera Trl Dayton OH 45459-1403 Office: Altick & Corwin 1700 One Dayton Ctr 1 S Main St Dayton OH 45402-2024 Office Phone: 937-223-1201. Personal E-mail: nikfar@aol.com. Business E-Mail: farquhar@altickcorwin.com.

FARQUHAR, ROBIN HUGH, educational consultant, former university president; b. Victoria, B.C., Can., Dec. 1, 1938; s. Hugh Ernest and Jean (MacIntosh) F.; m. Frances Harriet Caswell, July 6, 1963; children: Francine Jean, Katherine Lynn, Susan Ann. BA with honors, U. B.C., 1960, MA, 1964; PhD, U. Chgo., 1967; Hon. Diploma in Adult Edn., Red River C.C., 1989. Tchr., counsellor, coach Edward Milne Secondary Sch., Sooke, B.C., 1962-64; assoc. dir., then dep. dir. Univ. Council Ednl. Adminstrn., Columbus, Ohio, 1966-71; chmn. ednl. adminstrn. dept., asst. dir. Ont. Inst. Studies in Edn., Toronto, 1971-76; prof. U. Toronto, 1974-76; prof., dean Coll. Edn., U. Sask., Saskatoon, 1976-81; prof., pres. U. Winnipeg, 1981-89, Carleton U., Ottawa, Canada, 1989—96, prof. policy pub. and adminstrn., 1996—2004, prof. emeritus, 2004—; spl. advisor to pres. of Salzburg Seminar, 2002. Author: The Humanities in Preparing Educational Administrators, 1970, Preparing Educational Leaders: A Review of Recent Literature, 1972; editor: Social Science Content for Preparing Educational Leaders, 1973, Educational Administration in Australia and Abroad: Analyses and Challenges, 1975, Canadian and Comparative Educational Administration, 1980, The Canadian School Superintendent, 1989, Advancing Education: School Leadership in Action, 1991, Advancing the Canadian Agenda for International Education, 2001; mem. editl. bd. Jour. Edn. Adminstrn., 1973-86. Served with Can. Navy Res., 1956-64. Recipient Edward L. Bernays Found. prize, 1968, Commemorative medal for 125th Anniversary of Confedn. of Can., 1993, Ottawa-Carleton Partnership award of excellence for leadership, 1996, Can. Bur. Internat. Edn. award of Merit, 1998; named Hon. Citizen, City of Winnipeg, 1989; hon. mem. Scouts Can., 1992. Fellow Commonwealth Coun. Ednl. Adminstrn. (former pres.); mem. Can. Bur. Internat. Edn. (former chmn.), Can. Soc. Study Edn. (former pres.), Can. Edn. Assn. (former dir.), InterAm. Soc. for Ednl. Adminstrn. (former dir.), Ottawa-Carleton Econ. Devel. Corp. (former dir.), Ottawa-Carleton Rsch. Inst. (former dir.), Corp. Higher Edn. Forum (former dir.), Nat. Acad. of Sch. Execs. (former dir.). Office Phone: 613-230-4735. E-mail: rfarquha@connect.carleton.ca.

FARQUHARSON, GORDON MACKAY, lawyer, director; b. Charlottetown, P.E.I., Can., July 12, 1928; s. Percy Alfred and Rachel Lillian (MacKay) F.; m. Judy Lynne Bridges, Oct. 10, 1980; children: Trevor, Jordan; children by previous marriage: Douglas, Tanyss, Rob, Caryn. BA, U. Toronto, 1950; LL.B., Osgoode Hall Law Sch., 1954. Bar: Called to Ont. bar 1954; Queen's Counsel 1965. Pvt. practice, Toronto, 1954—; ptnr. Lang Michener, 1964—. Dir. Doverhold Investments Ltd. Recipient The Queen's Golden Jubilee medal, 2003. Mem. University Club (Toronto), Craigleigh Ski Club, Phi Gamma Delta (pres. 1950). Home: 419 Brunswick Ave Toronto ON Canada Office: BCE Pl 181 Bay St Ste 2500 Toronto ON Canada M5J 2T7 Office Phone: 416-307-4067. Business E-Mail: gfarquharson@langmichener.ca.

FARQUHARSON, PATRICE ELLEN, primary school educator; b. West Haven, Conn., Feb. 10, 1956; d. Robert Douglas and Margaret Ellen (Dietle) Farquharson; children: Julia, Elena. BS in Edn., U. Conn., 1978; MS in Edn., So. Conn. State U., 1984; EdD, Nova Southeastern U., 1995. Cert. tchr., adminstr., Conn. Asst. dir. West Haven (Conn.) Child Devel. Ctr., 1978-82, exec. dir., 1982-96, 97—; edn. cons. dept. pediatrics div. child and family studies U. Conn., 1993-95; mgmt. cons. West Haven Child Devel. Ctr., Inc., 1996—; asst. prof. early childhood edn. Teikyo-Post U. (now Post U.), Waterbury, Conn., 1996—, dir. early childhood, 1996—2004. Adj. prof. U. Conn. Inst. Pub. Policy, 1996; profl. cheerleader The New Eng. Patriots football team, 1980; dir., ptnr. New Eng. Cheerleading Camp, West Haven, 1982-84; cheerleading coach U. New Haven, 1982-90; textbook webguide developer Thomson Pub., 2001; online course developer Teikyo Post U., Charter Oak State Coll., faculty, 2000—; cons., presenter in field Conn. Early Childhood Edn. Coun. scholar, 1993-96, 2004. Mem. AAUW, Nat. Assn. Edn. Young Children, Conn. Assn. Edn. Young Children, Dirs. Forum, South Ctrl. Conn. Agy. on Aging (adv. coun.), Rotary Avocations: ballet, jazz dancing, horseback riding, reading, travel. Home: 5 Sunflower Cir West Haven CT 06516-6229 Office: West Haven Child Devel Ctr 201 Noble St West Haven CT 06516-6047

FARR, BARRY MILLER, physician, epidemiologist; b. Ft. Leonard Wood, Mo., Nov. 15, 1951; s. Alonza Lewis and Alice Louise (Miller) F.; m. Ann Katherine Henry, Oct. 22, 1977; children: Eric Christopher, Ryan Anthony, Jason Alexander. BA in Chemistry, U. Miss., Oxford, 1975; MD, Washington U., St. Louis, 1978; MSc in Epidemiology, London Sch. Hygiene, 1984. Diplomate Am. Bd. Internal Medicine, Am. Bd. Infectious Diseases. Intern U. Va. Hosp., Charlottesville, 1978-79, resident in internal medicine, 1979-81, fellow in infectious diseases, 1981-83; asst. prof. U. Va., 1983-89, assoc. prof., 1989—, William S. Jordan Jr. prof., 1989, prof. medicine, 1995—. Contbr. articles to profl. jours. Carrier scholar, 1970-74, Culley scholar, 1974-78, Milbank Meml. scholar, 1983-88. Fellow ACP, Infectious Diseases Soc. Am.; mem. Soc. Hosp. Epidemiology of Am., Soc. for Epidemiologic Rsch. Avocations: hunting, fishing, photography, writing. Office: U Va Hosp Dept Epidemiology & Virology PO Box 473 Charlottesville VA 22902-0473

FARR, CHARLES SIMS, lawyer; b. Hewlett, N.Y., June 29, 1920; s. John Farr and Hazel (Zealy) Sims; m. Mary Randolph Rue, Dec. 21, 1946 (dec. Dec. 1980); children: Charles Sims, Virginia Farr Ramsey, Randolph Rue, John II; m. Muriel Tobin Byrnes, Oct. 13, 1990. Student, Princeton U., 1938-40; LLB, Columbia U., 1948. Bar: N.Y. 1949, Fla. 1984. Assoc. White & Case, N.Y.C., 1948-58, ptnr., 1959-88, of counsel, 1989-92, ret. Contbr. articles to profl. publs. Chmn. Commonwealth Fund, N.Y.C., 1976-93; trustee St. Luke's-Roosevelt Hosp. Ctr., 1968-92, Gen. Theol. Sem., 1968-77, N.Y. Zool. Soc., Kent Sch.; mem. bd. fgn. parishes Protestant Episcopal Ch., 1954-78, pres. 1977; chancellor to pres. bishop Protestant Episcopal Ch. in U.S.A., 1977-85; vestryman St. James Ch., N.Y.C., 1966-76; sr. warden, 1973-76, jr. warden, 1984-86; mem. coun. Rockefeller U., 1980-92; former mem. bd. visitors Columbia U. Sch. Law. Lt. comdr. USN, 1941—45, ETO, MTO, PTO. Recipient medal Columbia U. Alumni Assn., 1977. Fellow Am. Coll. Probate Counsel (regent 1960-75), Am. Bar Found.; mem. ABA (chmn. tax aspects decedent's estates 1974-76, bd. dirs. real property, probate and trust law sect. 1976-78, chmn. com. application securities laws to fiduciaries 1974-76), N.Y. State Bar Assn. (chmn. trusts and estates com. 1966-68), Assn. of Bar of City of N.Y. (com. profl. responsibility 1972-74), Century Club (trustee 1992-95), Links Club, River Club, Pilgrims Club, Yeamans Hall (S.C.). Independent. Home: PO Box 9455 900 Yeamans Hall Rd Charleston SC 29410 also: 200 E 66th St Apt E802 New York NY 10021-9192 also: PO Box 835 Flat Rock NC 28731

FARR, DAVID N., electronics executive; married; 2 children. BS in Chemistry, Wake Forest U.; MBA, Vanderbilt U. From mem. staff to CEO Emerson, 1981—2000, CEO, 2000—, chmn., 2004—. Mem. The Bus. Coun., Washington; bd. dirs. Delphi Corp. Bd. trustees Webster U.; bd. dirs. Municipal Theatre Assoc., St. Louis; bd. dirs., Greater St. Louis Area Coun. Boy Scouts of Am.; mem. Civic Progress. Office: Emerson 8000 W Florissant Ave PO Box 4100 Saint Louis MO 63136

FARR, DONALD EUGENE, engineering scientist; b. Clinton, Iowa, July 1, 1933; s. Kenneth Elroy and Nellie Irene (Bailey) F.; m. Sally Joyce Brauer, Mar. 8, 1954; children: Erika Lyn Farr Leventis, Jolene Karyn Farr Walters. BA in Engring. Psychology, San Diego State U., 1961; MT with honors, Nat. U., 1974; postgrad., Calif. Pacific U., 1976-80. Human factors specialist Bunker Ramo Corp., Canoga Park, Calif., Germany, 1964-69; sr. design specialist Gen. Dynamics, San Diego, 1955-63, 69-76; tech. staff Sandia Nat. Labs., Albuquerque, 1977-80; group supr., sr. tech. advisor The Babcock and Wilcox Co., Lynchburg, Va., 1980-82; dir. human factors sys. Sci. Applications, Inc., Lynchburg, 1982-83; human engring. scientist Lockheed Calif. Co., Burbank, 1983-91; MANPRINT mgr. Teledyne Electronic Sys., Northridge, Calif., 1991-94; human engring. scientist, program mgr. Symvionics, Inc., Pasadena, Calif., 1994—. Ergonomics safety cons. govt., industry and academia, 1977—; instr. human factors/design psychology Art Ctr. Coll. of Design, Pasadena, Calif., 2000—. Contbr. articles to profl. jours. and tech. books. Precinct capt., voter registration vol. Rep. Party, 1963—; lectr., support group Am. Diabetes Assn., L.A., 1993—. With USN, 1952-53. With USN, 1952—53. Scholarship USN, 1953; recipient Admiral's award NSIA, 1963. Mem. Human Factors and Ergonomics Soc. (pres. San Diego, L.A. chpt.), Internat. Numismatic Soc. (pres. 1973-75), Am. Nuclear Soc. (human factors chair 1980-82), Am. Legion, NRA Golden Eagles (honor role). Conservative. Lutheran. Achievement include 50 years human interface design, test, & management aerospace programs including, space shuttle, advanced stealth technology, nuclear weapons, tactical operating systems, commercial nuclear power, computer systems, security systems, human modeling and simulation. Home: 20054 Avenue Of The Oaks Newhall CA 91321-1361 Office: Symvionics Inc 190 Sierra Ct Ste A3 Palmdale CA 93550-7609 Personal E-mail: dfarr@earthlink.net.

FARR, IVANNE ESTELLE, small business owner, consultant, artist, sculptor; b. Texarkana, Ark., Feb. 7, 1940; d. Franklin Lynnwood and Leone Faye (Seedig) F.; m. William D. Alsup, Aug. 27, 1960 (div. Aug. 1975); children: Joe Farr, Mark De Witt, Lara LeAnne. Attended, Tex. State U.; cert. diamond, Gemological Inst. Am., 1980. Founder, owner Ivanne et Cie, Inc., Corpus Christi, Tex., 1976—; v.p. Internat. Agri-Ventures, Inc., Corpus Christi, 1985—89; owner Bosque River Valley Breeders, Ltd., Emu prodn. facilities, Meridian, Tex., 1990—97. Cons. C.I.C.C., Inc., Montreal, Can., 1985, Mexican Jewelers Assn., Mexico City, 1988, Jireh Resources, Inc., Paris, 1988, CEI, St. Thomas, 2003-04; co-founder, charter pres. Bosque County Tourism Coun., Inc., 1992; co-founder Farr Rsch. Internat., 1997; cons. Bibl. Archaeology Mus., Springfield, Mo., 1997; co-founder, chmn., chair Odyssey of Flight, 1991-94; chmn. John A. Lomax Gathering Trading Post Silent Auction, 1991-94 Active Mus. Oriental Culture, Jr. League, Corpus Christi, 1974-96, Charity League, Inc., 1974-92; bd. dirs. Chem. Dependency Unit South Tex., Coastal Bend Youth City, Palmer Drug Abuse Program; bd. of govs., chmn. membership com. Art Mus. South Tex.; chmn. bd. govs., co-founder Alliance for Justice Found., Inc., 1988—; docent Fossil Rim Wildlife Ctr., Glenrose, Tex.; pres. Bosque County Tourism Coun., 1992-96, 99-2003; co-founder Bosque County Chisholm Trail Cowboy Gathering Trail Ride and Rendezvous, 2000-01, Tex. Chisholm Trail Heritage Celebration, 2002-03, co-chmn., 2003; founding pres. Tex. Chisholm Trail Assn., Inc., 2003; founding pres. bd. officers GIA Caribbean Islands Alumni Chpt., 2004; internat. com. Corpus Christi Area Econ. Devel. Corp. Mem. Gemological Inst. Am. (pres., bd. dir. Caribbean Islands alumni chpt.), Coast Conservation Assn., Inst. Tex. Cultures (amb.), Jewelers Assn. Am., Marine Mil. Acad. Parents Assn., Navy League (bd. dirs.), Norwegian Soc. Tex., PTA, Scandinavian Soc. South Tex. (co-founder), Tex. Jewelers Assn., Internat. Group (co-founder), Corpus Christi C. of C. (bd. dirs.), Am. Emu Assn., Tex. Emu Assn., Emu Coop., Am. Assn. Museums, Ducks Unltd., Mid-Morning Group (co-founder), Daus. of the King Internat., Tex. State U. Alumni Assn. Republican. Episcopalian. Avocations: water-skiing, skiing, travel, sailing, opera. Personal E-mail: farrlands@hotmail.com.

FARR, JESSE F., federal agency administrator; b. Scranton, Pennsylvania, Feb. 5, 1915; s. Edward Farr Jr. and Leah Frisby Farr; m. Mary Elizabeth Davison; children: Lee Anne Geiger, Jesse Edward. Student, Powell Bus. Coll., Scranton, 1934—35; BS, Lafayette Coll., 1938. Chief indsl. rate analysis Phila. Electric Co., 1941—42; asst. legal attaché Am. Embassy, Paris, 1965—68; spl. agent unit chief FBI, Washington, staff supr. Balt. Author: (short stories) Nuke Sub Sold. Former pres. Beach Lake Vol. Fire Dept.; 1st reader Christian Sci. Ch., Towson, Md. Mem.: Beach Lake Hunting Club (former pres.). Home: 2501 North Nelson St Arlington VA 22207

FARR, JUDITH BANZER, literature educator, writer; b. N.Y.C., Mar. 13, 1936; d. Russell John and Frances Anna (Wissell) Banzer; m. George F. Farr, Jr., June 30, 1962; 1 child, Alec Winfield. BA, Marymount Manhattan Coll., 1957, LHD, 1992; MA, Yale U., 1959, PhD, 1965. Instr. in English Vassar Coll., Poughkeepsie, N.Y., 1961-63; asst. prof. St. Mary's Coll., Moraga, Calif., 1964-68; assoc. prof. SUNY, New Paltz, 1968-77, Georgetown U., Washington, 1978-90, prof. of English and Am. Lit., 1990-99, prof. emerita, 1999—. Vis. assoc. prof. Georgetown U., 1977—78. Author: The Life and Art of Elinor Wylie, 1983, The Passion of Emily Dickinson, 1992, I Never Came to You in White: A Novel, 1996, The Gardens of Emily Dickinson, 2004 (Crayshaw award of the Byron, Keats and Shelley Meml. Trust Brit. Acad., 2005); editor: Twentieth Century Interpretations of Sons and Lovers, 1970, New Century Views: Emily Dickinson, 1995; contbr. articles, poems, short stories to profl. and comml. publs. Recipient Alumnae award for Distinction in Arts and Letters, Marymount Manhattan Coll., NYC, 1976, Alpha Sigma Nu Best Book award, 1993, Alumnae award for scholarly distinction, Mary Louis Acad., 2001, Rose Mary Crawshay prize, Byron, Keats and Shelley Meml. Trust, The Brit. Acad., 2005; grantee, N.Y. State Rsch. Found., 1974, Am. Coun. Learned Socs., 1984, 1986, Georgetown U. Ctr. German Studies, 1992; Morgan-Porter fellow, Yale U., 1960—61, Am. Philos. Soc. fellow, 1983. Mem. AAUP, Authors' Guild, Emily Dickinson Internat. Soc., Cosmos Club. Avocations: antiques, gardening, art. Home: 5064 Lowell St NW Washington DC 20016-2616

FARR, MARCIA ELIZABETH, English and linguistics educator; b. Berkeley, Calif., Mar. 25, 1944; d. Richard Arthur and Margaret Mary (Bollinger) F.; m. David Lee Whiteman, July 30, 1966 (div. July 1981); 1 child, Julianna Downing; m. Michael David Maltz, Dec. 2, 1984; stepchildren: David Selby, Robert Reeves. BA in English, Ohio Wesleyan U., 1965; MA in Linguistics, Am. U., 1970; PhD in Linguistics, Georgetown U., 1976. Sr. rsch. assoc. Nat. Inst. Edn., Washington, 1976—82; assoc. prof. to prof. English and linguistics U. Ill., Chgo., 1982—2002; prof. of edn. and English Ohio State U., Columbus, 2002—. Adv. bd. Ctr. for the Study of Writing, U. Calif., Berkeley, 1986-96. Co-author: Language Diversity and Writing Instruction, 1986; editor: Variation in Writing, 1981, Ethnolinguistic Chicago: Language and Literacy in the City's Neighborhoods, 2004, Latino Language and Literacy in Ethnolinguistic Chicago, 2005; author: (with others) Cultural Performances, 1994, Literacy Across Communities, 1994, Mexico en Fiesta, 1998; editl. bds. jours.; gen. editor rsch. series Hampton Press, Cresskill, N.J., 1992-2000, Ablex Publs., Norwood, N.J., 1982-92. Rsch. fellow in Mex., Fulbright Found., 1995-96; rsch. grant Spencer Found., 1990-93, 95-98, 99-00, NSF, 1988-90; recipient Mentor Network award Spencer Found., 1995-97. Fellow Am. Anthropol. Assn.; mem. Am. Assn. for Applied Linguistics (exec. com., program chair 1981), Internat. Assessment of Literacy (U.S. nat. com.), Nat. Coun. of Tchrs. of English (commn. on English lang.). Avocations: Flamenco dance, mystery novels and films. Office: Ohio State U Coll Edn 29 W Woodruff Ave Columbus OH 43210 Office Phone: 614-292-0095. E-mail: farr.18@osu.edu.

FARR, MICHAEL KEOGH, investment company executive; b. Washington, Apr. 24, 1961; s. Harry Hull and Joyce Keogh Farr; m. Laurie Fishburn, Apr. 1, 1989; children: Robert, Margaret. BA, U. of the South, 1984. Sch. master Pomfret (Conn.) Sch., 1984-87; stock broker, v.p. Wheat First Securities, Washington, 1987-90; stock broker, prin. Alex Brown & Sons, Washington, 1990-96; pres. Farr, Miller & Washington, LLC, 1996—; chmn. FMW Trust Co., Sioux Falls, SD, 1999—2001. Expert commentator CNN TV, 1998—, WJLA Channel 7 TV. Chmn. Paul Berry Acad. Scholarship Found., Washington, 1995-2000, Nation's Capital Progress Found., Washington, 1997-2002; bd. dirs. The Salvation Army, Washington, 1999—; trustee The Heights Sch., Potomac, Md., 1995-2001; trustee Sibley Meml. Hosp., 2002—, Fords Theater, 2005—. Recipient Outstanding Young Alumnus Achievement award U. of the South, 1999; named Top 10 Outstanding Brokers of Yr. Registered Rep. mag., 1994. Mem. Washington Assn. of Money Mgrs., Nat. Econs. Club, Met. Club of Washington, Chevy Chase Club, Rehoboth Beach County Club. Republican. Roman Catholic. Avocations: hunting, fishing, golf, sailing. Office: Farr Miller & Washington LLC 1020 19th St NW Ste 200 Washington DC 20036-6101

FARR, REETA RAE, special education administrator; b. Edhube, Tex., Jan. 15, 1926; d. Paul Ray and Verna (Biggerstaff) Wright; m. Gerald Edward Self, June 1, 1946 (dec. Dec. 1977); children: Eddie, Lee; m. Barnie B. Farr Jr., Dec. 28, 1978 (wid. Mar. 1997). BS, Southeastern Okla. State U., 1959, MS, 1963. 1st grade tchr. Sherman (Tex.) Pub. Schs., 1959-61, Denison (Tex.) Pub. Schs., 1961-64, spl. edn. tchr., 1964-72, spl. edn. counselor, 1972-76, spl. edn. diagnostician, 1976-85, dir. spl. edn., 1985-94. Named Educator of Yr. Denison Edn. Assn., 1991. Mem. NEA, AAUW (pres. 1981-83), Tex. State Tchrs. Assn. (local pres. 1971), Tex. Ednl. Diagnostician Assn., Tex. Assn. Counseling and Devel., Phi Delta Kappa (sec.-treas. 1983, del. 1978-99), Delta Kappa Gamma. Mem. Ch. Of Christ. Avocation: reading. Home: 23000 2nd Fork Rd Ola ID 83657-5015 E-mail: rfarr@bigskytel.com.

FARR, SAM, congressman; b. Calif., July 4, 1941; m. Shary Baldwin; 1 child, Jessica. BSc Biology, Willamette U., 1963; student, Monterey Inst. Internat. Studies, U. Santa Clara Law Sch. Vol. Peace Corps, 1963-65; budget analyst, cons. Assembly com. Constl. Amendments; bd. suprs. Monterey (Calif.) County; rep. Calif. State Assembly, 1980-93; mem. U.S. Congress from 17th Calif. dist., 1993—; mem. appropriations com., agr. and military constrn. subcoms. Named Legislator of Yr. Calif. 9 times. Democrat. Avocations: photography, skiing, fly fishing, spanish. Office: Ho of Reps 1221 Longworth Bldg Washington DC 20515-0517

FARR, WILLIAM JOSEPH, secondary school educator; b. Manchester, Conn., June 12, 1947; s. Joseph N. and Ann Rose (Kominski) F.; m. Ann Elizabeth Farr, July 1, 1977; children: Joseph William, Christopher Michael, Jonathan Thomas. BS, Cen. Conn. State U., 1969, MA, 1974; PhD in Curriculum and Instrn., U. Conn., 2004. Tchr. Bolton (Conn.) High Sch., 1969-72, Bolton (Conn.) Ctr. Sch., 1972—; tchr. communications course Bolton Ctr. Sch., 1974-80, tchr. study skills course, 1980—, chmn. lang. arts dept., coach debate team, 1987-89; assoc. edn. cons. Conn. State Dept. Edn., 1996-97, dir. Celebration of Excellence, Blue Ribbons Schs., Tchr. of Yr. Program, 1997-99; reading/lang. arts cons. Wethersfield (Conn.) Pub. Schs., 1999-2000; lectr.-in-residence Reading/Lang. Arts Ctr Neag Sch. Edn., U. Conn., Storrs, 2000—04; asst. prof.-in-residence U. Conn., Storrs, 2004—. Leader Gt. Books Discussion Programs, 1987-89; presenter Celebration of Excellence Program, 1986, 87, 91, asst. facilitator summer inst., 1992. Recipient Celebration of Excellence Teaching award Conn. State Dept. Edn., 1986, 91, Connl. Coun. Tchrs. English Tchr. Yr. award, 2003. Mem. NEA, Conn. Edn. Assn., Bolton Edn. Assn. (sec.), Nat. Assn. Tchrs of English, New England Assn. Tchrs of English, Conn. Educator Talent Pool (award Conn. State Dept. Edn. 1990), Pi Lambda Theta. Avocations: antiques, early american architecture, collecting first editions of American and European literature, travel. Home: 21 Westminister Rd Manchester CT 06040-5433 Office: U Conn Neag Sch Edn 249 Glenbrook Rd Unit 2033 Storrs CT 06269 Office Phone: 860-486-0285. E-mail: wfarr01@snet.net.

FARRAKHAN, LOUIS, religious leader; b. N.Y.C., May 11, 1933; changed name from Louis Eugene Wolcott to Louis X, then to Louis Farrakhan; m. Betsy Wolcott; 9 children. Student, Winston-Salem (N.C.) Tchrs. Coll. Vocalist, calypso singer, dancer and violinist, Boston; joined Nation of Islam, 1955—, formerly leader of Harlem mosque N.Y.C., nat. spokesman, founder reorganized Nation of Islam, 1977—. Founder newspaper The Final Call, 1979—. Author: A Torchlight for America, 1993. Founder Louis Farrakhan Prostate Cancer Found., 2003—. Achievements include organized the Million Man March on the Mall in Wash., D.C., 1995. Office: Nation of Islam 7351 S Stony Island Ave Chicago IL 60649-3106*

FARRAN, DALE CLARK, education educator; Student, Wesleyan Coll., Macon, Ga., 1961—63; BA in Psychology, U. N.C., 1965; PhD in Edn. and Child Devel., Bryn Mawr Coll., 1975. Rsch. assoc., curriculum specialist N.C. Advancement Sch., Winston-Salem, 1965—67; rsch. assoc. Pa. Advancement Sch., Phila., 1967—71; with psychology dept. Children's Aid Soc., Phila., 1971—74; NICHHD postdoctoral fellow Frank Porter Graham Child Devel. Ctr. U. N.C., Chapel Hill, 1974—75, instr. Sch. Edn., 1975—76, clin. asst. prof. divsn. spl. edn., Sch. Edn., 1976—80, rsch. assoc. Health Svcs. Rsch. Ctr., 1980—86, faculty Bush Inst. for Child and Family Policy, Faculty, Rsch. Tng. Program for Rsch. in Mental Retardation, 1979—84, clin. assoc. prof. divsn. spl. edn Sch. Edn., 1980—84; assoc. prof. psychology dept. U. Hawaii, 1984—87; head child devel. rsch. dept. Ctr. for Devel. Early Edn. Kamehameha Schs./Bishop Estate, 1984—87; prof. dept. human devel. and family studies U. N.C., Greensboro, 1987—96; prof. depts. tchg. and learning, psychology and human devel. dir. Susan Gray Sch. for Children, assoc. dir. John F. Kennedy Ctr. for Rsch. Human Devel Peabody Coll., Vanderbilt U., Nashville, 1996—. Co-author (with D. Cooper): (book) Cooper-Farran Behavioral Rating Scale, 1991; co-editor (with J. D. McKinney): Risk in Intellectual and Psychosocial Development, 1986; co-editor: (with L. Feagans) The Language of Children Reared in Poverty: Implications for Evaluation and Intervention, 1982; contbr. articles to profl. jours. and chpts. to books. Named Profl. of Yr., Mayor's Adv. Coun. on Disabilities, 1999, hon. coach, Vanderbilt U. Women's Basketball Team, 1998, 2000;

recipient Peabody Award for Excellence in Rsch., 1984, Outstanding Young Scholar award, Spencer Found., 1978, 1980. Fellow: Am. Psychol. Soc.; mem.: CEC (divsn. early childhood), Nat. Assn. for Edn. of Young Children, Am. Ednl. Rsch. Assn. (early childhood spl. interest group), Internat. Soc. for Study of Behavioral Devel., Soc. for Rsch. in Child Devel., Phi Beta Kappa. Office: Vanderbilt U Peabody Coll Dept Tchg and Learning PO Box 330 Nashville TN 37203

FARRAND, JAMES CLINTON, minister, consultant; b. Oklahoma City, Nov. 3, 1947; s. Robert Lee and Gladys Marie Farrand; m. Linda Kay Wilkins, Dec. 24, 1967; children: Carri Danielle, Clinton Robert Vernon. MusB in EDn., Okla. Bapt. U., Shawnee, 1971; MusM, Southwestern Sem., Fort Worth, Tex., 1978; post grad. in Leadership Theory and Devel., post grad. in Exec. and Life Skills Coaching, post grad. in Orgnl. Health and Team Building. Assoc. pastor First Bapt. Ch., McAlester, Okla., 1979—89, Shawnee, 1989—. Adj. prof. Okla. Bapt. U., Shawnee, 1990—93, guest lectr.; condr. Shawnee Choral Soc. Contbg. editor: The Church Musician; contbr. articles to profl. jours. Mem. Shawnee Youth Coalition, Okla., 2002—, Okla. Alliance Liturgy and the Arts, Oklahoma City, 2003—, Shawnee Youth Baseball Assn., 1992—96; pres. The CenturyMen, N.Y.C., 2004—, Faculty Coun. Camerata for Okla. Bapt. U., Shawnee, Okla., 2003—, Gateway to Prevention and Recovery, 2000—, Arts and Humanities Coun., McAlester, 1985—89, Cmty. Concert Series, 1983—88. With U.S. Army, 1969—73. Mem.: Am. Choral Directors Assn. (assoc.), Am. Guild English Handbell Ringers (assoc.). Home: 1 Seneca Shawnee OK 74801 Office: First Baptist Ch 227 N Union Shawnee OK 74801 Office Phone: 405-275-6111.

FARRAND, WILLIAM RICHARD, geology educator; b. Columbus, Ohio, Apr. 27, 1931; s. Harvey Ashley and Esther Evelyn (Bowman) F.; m. Claudine Brickmann, Aug. 17, 1962 (div. 1983); children: Frederic Hervé, Anne Marie; m. Carola Hill Stearns, Dec. 6, 1988; 1 child, Michelle Diane. BS in Geology, Ohio State U., 1955, MS in Geology, 1956; PhD, U. Mich., 1960. Rsch. assoc. Lamont Geol. Obs. Columbia U., N.Y., 1960-61, asst. prof., 1961-64; rsch. assoc. in geology U. Mich., Ann Arbor, 1962; postdoctoral rsch. fellow NAS/NRC, Strasbourg, France, 1963-64; asst. prof. geol. scis. U. Mich., Ann Arbor, 1965-67, assoc. prof. geol scis., 1967-74, prof., 1974-2000, prof. emeritus, 2000—, curator analytical collections Mus. Anthropology, 1975-2000, dir. Exhibit Mus., 1993-2000. Vis. prof. U. Strasbourg, France, 1964-65, Hebrew U., Jerusalem, 1971-72, U. Colo., Boulder, 1983, U. Tex., Austin, 1986; fellow Inst. for Advanced Study, Ind. U., 1985; mem. archaeometry panel NSF, 1989-91; apptd. mem. U.S. Nat. com. Internat. Quaternary Assn., 1989-99, chair, 1995-99; sr. fellow Inst. for Study Earth and Man, So. Meth. U., Dallas, 1991—. Mem. editorial bd. Quaternary Sci. Review, Paleorient, Jour. Archaeological Sci., Review Archaeology, Stratigraphica Archaeologica; contbr. articles and maps to profl jours. With U.S. Army, 1951-53. Fellow AAAS, Geol. Soc. Am. (mem. panel quaternary geology and geomorphology divsn. 1978, vice chmn. archaeological geology divsn, 1979, chmn, 1980, Archaeological Geology award 1986), Ohio Acad. Sci., 1994-96; mem. Am. Quaternary Assn. (sec. 1978-90, program chmn. biennial meeting 1980, pres. 1994-96), Mich. Acad. Sci., Arts and Letters, Internat. Union for Quaternary Rsch. (chmn. working group on Southwest Asia commn. paleoecology early man 1975-83), L'Assn. Francaise pour l'Etude de Quaternaire, Sigma Xi, Phi Beta Kappa. Office: U Mich Mus Anthropology 4009 Ruthven Mus Ann Arbor MI 48109-1079 Office Phone: 734-764-6589. Business E-Mail: wfarrand@umich.edu.

FARRAR, DONALD KEITH, retired finance company executive; b. Indio, Calif., May 18, 1938; s. Keith and Sarah S. Farrar; m. Jo Ann Puttler, Dec. 16, 1961; children: Daniel K., Donald S., Douglas S., Kimberly. BSBA, U. So. Calif., 1960; MBA, Harvard U., 1965. With planning div. Paul Revere Life Ins. Co., Worcester, Mass., 1965, budget supr., 1966, asst. to pres., 1967, asst. sec., 1968-73, v.p. investment, 1969-73; v.p. planning Avco Corp., Greenwich, Conn., 1973-74, sr. v.p., chief acct. officer, 1975-77, exec. v.p., 1978-81, pres., 1981-85, also bd. dirs.; sr. exec. v.p., pres. Avco Ops. Textron Inc., Providence, R.I., 1985-89, sr. exec. v.p. ops., 1985-89, also bd. dirs.; pres., CEO IMO Industries, Lawrenceville, N.J., 1993-94, chmn., CEO, 1994-97. Pvt. investor 1990-93, 98—, retired. With USNR, 1960-63. Home: 5 Prairie Grass Irvine CA 92603

FARRAR, DONNA BEATRICE, health facility administrator; b. Ayer, Mass., Feb. 4, 1950; d. Raymond H. and Shirley E. (Perham) F. B Music Edn., U. Mass., Lowell, 1971; MDiv, Bangor Theol. Sem., 1979; D Ministry, Christian Theol. Sem., 1987; M Family Studies, U. Ky., 1997. Tchr. music Billerica (Mass.) Pub. Schs., 1971-76; chaplain intern various hosps., Bangor, Maine, 1979; assoc. pastor Emanuel United Ch., Hales Corners, Wis., 1980-82; chaplain resident Ind. U & Meth. Hosp., Indpls., 1982-85; assoc. chaplain Ohio State U. Hosp., Columbus, 1985-87; assoc. dir., dir. Ind. U. Med. Ctr., Indpls., 1987-92; dept. dir. U. Ky. Hosps., Lexington, 1992—. Mem.: Am. Assn. Marriage and Family Therapists (lic. marriage family therapist). Democrat. Mem. Christian Ch. Avocations: reading, felines, dance, travel, art. Office: U Ky 800 Rose St # H-118 Lexington KY 40536-0293

FARRAR, ELAINE WILLARDSON, artist; b. L.A. d. Eldon and Gladys Elsie (Larsen) Willardson; children: Steve, Mark, Gregory, JanLeslie, Monty, Susan. BA, Ariz. State U., 1967, MA, 1969, PhD, 1990. Tchr. Camelback Desert Sch., Paradise Valley, Ariz., 1966-69; mem. faculty Yavapai Coll., Prescott, Ariz., 1970-92, chmn. dept. art, 1973-78, instr. art in watercolor, oil, acrylic painting, intaglio, 1971-92, instr. art relief intaglio and monoprints, 1971-92; grad. advisor Prescott Coll. Master of Arts Program, 1993-97, 2004—. One-woman shows include R.P. Moffat's, Scottsdale, Ariz., 1969, Art Ctr., Battlecreek, Mich., 1969, The Woodpeddler, Costa Mesa, Calif., 1979, numerous group shows including most recently, exhibited in group shows at Prescott Fine Arts Assn., 1999, 2001, 2002, The Elements, 2001, Collage & Works on Paper, 2002, Faces & Forms To The Edge, 2004. Mem., curator Prescott Fine Arts Visual Arts com., 1992-97, Works on Paper, 2002; mem. exec. com., 1996-98; bd. dirs. Prescott Fine Arts Assn., 1995-98, Friends Y.C. Art Gallery Bd., 1992-97; active PTA Gawery, Prescot, Ariz. Mem. Northern Ariz. Watercolor Assn., Mountain Artists Guild (past pres.), Women's Nat. Mus. (charter Washington chpt.), mus. of North Ariz. and Phoenix Art Mus., Kappa Delta Pi. *Through the visual arts many ideas and feelings are expressed that would otherwise be lost to the communication of these thoughts to others—a vital link to understanding...and vital to helping release ideas through art therapy when one has been unable to verbalize thoughts and ideas, whether analyzed or not the path is cleared away...universal as is music and dance!.*

FARRAR, FRANK LEROY, lawyer, former governor; b. Britton, S.D., Apr. 2, 1929; s. Virgil William and Venetia Soule (Taylor) F.; m. Patricia Jean Henley, June 5, 1953; children— Jeanne Marie, Sally Ann, Robert John, Mary Susan, Ann M. BS, U. S.D., 1951, LL.B., 1953; LL.D., Huron Coll. Bar: S.D. 1953. Practiced law, Britton, 1957-63; agt. IRS, 1955-57; judge Marshall County, S.D., 1958, state's atty., 1959-62; atty. gen. State of S.D., 1963-69, gov., 1969-70; ptnr. Farrar & Spiry, Britton, S.D., 1970—. Chmn. Cardinal and Gold Ins. Co., Frank L. Farrar & Assocs., Performance Bankers, Inc., Capital, Fulda, Beresford, Wanbay, Sidney, Uptown, Versailles, Glenrock, Wolf Point Bancorps., Inc., NW Investment Inc., Carlton Agy., Inc., 1st Agy. Hasting, Cairo, First, Inc., Peoples Holding Co.; adv. bd. dirs. Citicorp, Correspondent Resources Inc. Past pres. Pheasant council Boy Scouts Am.; past chmn. S.D. March of Dimes; past fund raising chmn. S.D. Mental Health Assn.; bd. dirs. Rural Coalition Am.; chmn. Marshall County Republican Party, 1959; asst. sgt.-at-arms Rep. Nat. Conv., 1960. Served to capt. U.S. Army Recipient Alumnus Achievement award U. S.D., 1981, named Alumnus of Yr. Sch. Bus., 1979; named Sr. Olympics Athlete of the Yr. for S.D., 4th All Am. for Triathlon, 1999; named to Hall of Fame Sr. Olympics, S.D. Mem. S.D. Bar Assn., Ind. Bar Assn., Wash. Bar Assn., S.D. States Attys. Assn. (asst. pres.), Nat. Dist. Attys. Assn., Alpha Tau Omega, Phi Delta Phi. Lodges: Masons, Shriners, Jesters, Lions, Elks, Odd Fellows, Sportsmen. Address: PO Box 936 Britton SD 57430-0936 Office Phone: 605-448-2643. Business E-Mail: ffarrar@wiltonsd.com.

FARRAR, JOHN EDSON, II, finance company executive, consultant, investment advisor; b. Williamsport, Pa., Oct. 9, 1938; s. John Edson and Ruth (Price) F.; 1 child, John Edson III. BA in Psychology, Pasadena Coll., 1963; postgrad., U. Calgary (Alta.), 1967, pub. relations cert.; postgrad., Claremont Grad. Sch., 1963-64, U. Calif. at Riverside, 1968-71. Evaluating social services dir. Head Start dental rsch. project Loma Linda (Calif.) Sch. Dentistry, 1966-67; coordinator Head Start Riverside County Econ. Opportunity Bd., Riverside, Calif., 1967; dir. community relations San Bernardino County Welfare and Probation Depts., San Bernardino, Calif., 1968-73; publicity and promotions coordinator in charge tourism and indsl. devel. Econ. Devel. Dept. San Bernardino County, 1973; dir. pub. relations Middle East Boeing Comml. Airplane Co., Seattle, 1973-76, Northwest Hosp., Seattle, 1976-77; owner Craig & Farrar Pub. Relations and Advt., 1977-80; exec. v.p. Environ. Research and Devel. Corp., Seattle, 1980-82; owner Aamco Transmissions Ctr. of Bremerton, Wash., 1982-86; stockbroker Prudential-Bache Securities, Seattle, 1984-86; note broker Afamya, Ltd., London, 1986-87; ind. fin. and bus. cons. and broker Kent, Wash., 1987-93; pres. Professionally Managed Portfolios, Acton, Calif., 1993—. Lectr. mktg. pub. relations, investment techniques and options strategies Antelope Valley College and College of the Canyons, Valencia, Calif.; former chmn. dept. pub. relations and advt. City Coll., Seattle; instr. pub. relations U. Wash.; pub. relations cons. to pvt. bus., govt. Pres. bd. dirs. Frazee Community Center, 1970-71; bd. dirs., pub. relations chmn. Chief Seattle council Boy Scouts Am., promotions chmn. for camping in Southwestern U.S.; exec. bd. Seattle-King County Visitors and Conv. Bur.; mem. Republican Presdl. Task Force, 1982-84. Mem. Pub. Relations Soc. Am. (chpt. pres. 1971, 72, dist. chmn. govt. sect.), Calif. Social Workers Orgn. (v.p. 1970-71), Soc. for Internat. Devel., Nat. Pub. Relations Council Health and Welfare Services, Internat. Pub. Relations Assn., U.S.-Arab C. of C. Lodges: Rotary. Business E-Mail: john@pmpmanagement.com.

FARRAR, JOHN THRUSTON, health facility administrator; b. St. Louis, June 26, 1920; s. Benedict and Ruth Elizabeth (Gregg) F.; m. Joan Hayward Niedringhaus, May 20, 1947 (div. Feb. 1964); children: John Hayward, Leslie Tweedy; m. Pamela Sedgwick Gibson, May 15, 1966 (div. Mar. 1994); children: Elizabeth Gregg, Anne Dandridge; m. Rowena Kay Bryan, Oct. 28, 1995. AB, Princeton U., 1942; MD, Washington U., St. Louis, 1945. Diplomate Am. Bd. Internal Medicine, Am. Bd. Gastroenterology. Intern St. Louis County Hosp., Clayton, Mo., 1945-46; asst. resident in pathology Boston City Hosp., 1948-49; intern in medicine Mass. Meml. Hosps., Boston, 1949-50, asst. resident in medicine, 1950-51, rsch. assoc. divsn. gastroenterology, 1951-54; instr. medicine Boston U. Sch. Medicine, 1954-55; asst. prof. clin. medicine Cornell U. Coll. Medicine, N.Y.C., 1956-63; assoc. prof. medicine Med. Coll. Va., Richmond, 1963-65, chmn. divsn. gastroenterology, 1963-78, prof. medicine, 1965-92, assoc. dean vets. affairs, 1979-90, prof. emeritus, 1992—. Chief gastroenterology sect. med. svc. Vets. Hosp., N.Y.C., 1955-63; assoc. chief of staff rsch. devel. Vets. Affairs Med. Ctr., N.Y.C., 1956-63; cons. gastroenterology McGuire Vets. Affairs Med. Ctr., Richmond, 1963-78, chief of staff, 1979-90; nat. adv. panel nat. program rev. com. VA, 1965-69; adv. com. gastrointestinal drugs FDA, Washington, 1971-74, 77-82, cons., 1976-77; grants rev. com. Nat. Found. Ileitis Colitis, Inc., 1975-79, nat. scientific adv. com. 1975-79; chmn. long range planning com. Nat. digestive Diseases Edn. Info. Clearinghouse, 1983-85, chmn. scientific Evaluation subcom. 1983-85, chmn. exec. com. advisors, 1983-90; mem. steering com. Internat. Conf. Gastrointestinal Motility, 1975-81, chmn. steering com., 1977-79; chmn. Am. Bd. Gastroenterology, 1979-83; mem. bd. govs. Am. Bd. Internal Medicine, 1979-85; first vice-chmn. Coalition Digestive Desease Orgns., 1983-85; pres. Digestive Disease Nat. Coalition (formerly Coalition Digestive Disease Orgns.), 1986-91; rsch. com. Am. Fedn. Aging Rsch., 1983-89; assoc. dep. chief med. dir. Dept. Vets. Affairs, Vets. Affairs Ctrl. Office, Washington, 1990-91, dep. chief med. dir., 1991-93, acting under sec. health, 1993-94, dep. under sec. health, 1994-95; assoc. chief of staff extended care Vets. Affairs med. Ctr., Martinsburg, W.Va., 1995—. Author: (chpts.) Miniaturization, 1961, Modern Trends in Gastroenterology, 1961, Medicine, Essentials of Clinical Practice, 1970, Medical Engineering, 1974, Gastrointestinal Motility, 1971, Scientific Foundations of Gastroenterology, 1980, Tratado De Gastroenterologia Y Hepatologia, 1982, Clinics in Gastroenterology, 1982, Clinical Medicine, 1983, Social Security Practice Guide, 1986, Surgical Management of the Elderly Patient, 1992; editor: Practice of Medicine, Vol. Gastroenterology, 1973-78; mem. editl. bd. Am. Jour. Digestive Diseases, 1959-64, 88—, editor, 1968-76, Gastroenterology, 1964-68, Am. Jour. Med. Electronics, 1962-82; mem. editl. coun. Rendiconti Romani di Gastro-enterologia, 1969-89; contbr. over 55 articles to profl. jours. Bd. trustees Elk Hill Farm for Boys, 1974-80; pres. Goochland Family Svc. Soc., 1975-76, 79-81. Capt. U.S. Army Med. Corps., 1946-48. Mem.: ACP (coun.subspecialty socs. 1985—88, chmn. gastroenterology com. 1985—88, chair Washington 1986, chair San Francisco 1987), Am. Liver Found. (bd. dirs. 1986—, chmn. 1990—94), Am. Clin. Climatol. Assn., Am. Gastroent. Assn. (rssch. com. 1968—71, nat. liaison com. 1971—73, 1977—80, treas. 1972—77, chmn. publs. com. 1977—80, gov. bd. 1972—77, 1980—89, v.p 1980—81, pres.-elect 1981—82, pres. 1982—83, chmn. com. pub. policy and govt. rels. 1986—89, historian, archivist 1989—98), Am. Fedn. Clin. Rsch. Home: 431 Dogleg DR Williamsburg VA 23188-7411 E-mail: jtfarrar@widomaker.com.

FARRAR, STANLEY F., lawyer; b. Santa Ana, Calif., Mar. 24, 1943; BS, U. Calif., Berkeley, 1964, JD, 1967. Bar: Calif. 1968, NY 1969. Of counsel Sullivan & Cromwell LLP, LA. Mem. ABA (chmn. subcom. on bank holding cos. and nonbank activities banking law com. 1980-85, chmn. letters credit subcom. uniform comml. code com. 1982-88, sect. bus. law), State Bar Calif. (chmn. fin. instns. com. 1981-82). Office: Sullivan & Cromwell LLP 1888 Century Park E Los Angeles CA 90067-1725 Business E-Mail: farrars@sullcrom.com.

FARRAR, STEPHEN PRESCOTT, glass products manufacturing executive; b. Concord, N.H., Jan. 27, 1944; s. Prescott Samuel and Katherine (Hitchcock) F.; m. Kathleen D. Clark, Dec. 28, 1968 (dec.); children: Sheila E. Bermudez, Stephen Prescott Jr.; m. Rose Marie Bucar, July 4, 1998. BA, Bowdoin Coll., 1965; MSFS, Georgetown U., 1967. Internat. economist U.S. Dept. Commerce, Washington, 1966-72, Office of Mngt. and Budget, Washington, 1972-80, chief econ. affairs br. IAD, 1980-86; dir. internat. econ. affairs NSC, Washington, 1986-88, spl. asst. to Pres. and sr. dir. internat. econ. affairs, 1988-89; dep. exec. sec. Econ. Policy Coun., The White House, Washington, 1989-92; spl. asst. to Pres. for Policy Devel. Office of Policy Devel., the White House, Washington, 1989-92; chief of staff Office of the U.S. Trade Rep., Washington, 1992-93; dir. internat. bus. Guardian Industries Corp., Auburn Hills, Mich., 1993—. Mem. Coun. on Fgn. Rels. Republican. Avocations: tennis, running. Office: Guardian Industries Corp 2300 Harmon Rd Auburn Hills MI 48326-1714 Office Phone: 248-340-2104. Business E-Mail: sfarrar@guardian.com.

FARRAR, THOMAS C., chemist, educator; b. Independence, Kans., Jan. 14, 1933; s. Otis C. and Agnes K. F.; m. Friedemarie L. Farrar, June 22, 1963; children: Michael, Christian, Gisela. BS in Math., Chemistry, Wichita State U., 1954; PhD in Chemistry, U. Ill., 1959. NSF fellow Cambridge U., Eng., 1959-61; prof. chemistry U. Oregon, Eugene, 1961-63; chief, magnetism sect. Nat. Bur. Standards, Washington, 1963-71; dir. R & D Japan Electron Optics Lab., Cranford, N.J., 1971-75; dir. instr. NSF, Washington, 1975-79; prof. chemistry U. Wis., Madison, 1979—. Chmn. adv. com. MIT Nat. Magnetics Lab., Cambridge, Mass., 1979-84. Author: Introduction to Pulse NMR Spectros, 1989, Density Matrix Theory, 1995; contbr. over 120 articles to profl. jours. Recipient Silver medal Dept. Commerce, Washington, 1971, Silver medal Nat. Science Found., Washington, 1979. Fellow Wash. Acad. Science; mem. Am. Chem. Soc. (sec.-treas. Wis. sect. 1986-89), Am. Physical Soc. Office: Univ Wis Dept Chemistry 1101 University Ave Madison WI 53706-1322 Office Phone: 608-262-6158. E-mail: tfarrar@chem.wisc.edu.

FARRELL, COLIN JAMES, actor; b. Castleknock, Dublin, Ireland, May 31, 1976; s. Eamonn and Rita Farrel; m. Amelia Warner, 2001 (div. 2001); 1 child, James. Actor: (films) Drinking Crude, 1997, The War Zone, 1999, Ordinary Decent Criminal, 2000, Tigerland, 2000, Am. Outlaws, 2001, Hart's War, 2002, Minority Report, 2002, Phone Booth, 2002, The Recruit, 2003, Daredevil, 2003, Veronica Guerin, 2003, S.W.A.T., 2003, Intermission, 2003, A Home at the End of the World, 2004, Alexander, 2004; (TV films) Falling for a Dancer, 1998, David Copperfield, 1999; (TV series) Ballykissangel, 1998—99, Love in the 21st Century, 1999. Office: The Lisa Richards Agy 15 Lower Pembroke St Dublin Ireland

FARRELL, DONNA MARIE, photographer, graphic artist; b. Hackensack, N.J., Jan. 24, 1968; d. Raymond Patrick and Rosemarie Farrell. BFA, Va. Commonwealth U., 1991. Freelance artist Murals in Motion, 1991—; photographer/graphic artist McFarlane Design Group, Bloomingdale, NJ, 1999—. Capt. The Rave, Montclair, NJ, 1998—2002; photographer Goodwill Games, New York, 1998—98, Paraylmic Games, Atlanta, 1996—96; adj. prof. William Paterson U., Wayne, NJ, 1991—92. Prin. works include mural Olympic Athlete Commemorative Mural Project. Vol., photographer Revlon Run/Walk, New York, 2002—02, Goals for Life, Montclair, 2000—02. Named Women of Distinction World of Art, Lenni Lenape Girl Scout Coun., 1993; recipient Gold medal, Ga. Games, 1994, 1995, 1997; grantee Art & Photography grant, Summer Olympics, 1992, 1996, Winter Olympics, 1994, 1998. Mem.: N.J. Club Printing Ho. Craftsmen, Nat. Mus. Women in Arts, U.S. Soccer Found., Women's Sport Found., Sportfriends Soccer Club. Roman Catholic. Office: McFarlane Design Group 15 Hamburg Turnpike Bloomingdale NJ 07403 Office Phone: 973-709-0943. Personal E-mail: donnamarie.farrell@att.net. E-mail: dfarrell@mcfarlane.com.

FARRELL, EDGAR HENRY, building components manufacturing executive, lawyer; b. Aug. 31, 1924; s. Edgar Henry and Lillian Sarah (Lancaster) Farrell; m. Mary Louise Whelan, May 3, 1952; children: Brooke Larkin Cragan, Elizabeth Lancaster, Kimberley Hopkins. Student, Tex. A&M U., 1943, Stanford U., 1943—45, George Washington U., 1948—49; JD, U. Md., 1950; postgrad., Harvard U., 1965. Exec. sales asst. A.C. Gilbert Co., N.Y.C., 1950; asst. legal counsel U.S. Senate Crime Com., 1951; zone mgr. Life Mag., N.Y.C., 1951—52; account exec. Time Mag., N.Y.C., 1952—55, Phila., 1955—59, Detroit, 1959—62; nat. automotive sales mgr. Worldwide Automotive Products, Detroit, 1962—64, divsn. sales mgr., 1964—68, sales mgr., 1968; regional mgr. Comms./Rsch. Machines, Inc., Mich., Ohio, 1968; ctrl. advt. dir. Petersen Pub. Co., Detroit, 1969; CEO Internat. Concrete Bldg. Group, London, 1972—79; asst. to pres. Dillon Co., Akron, Ohio, 1979—80; pres., CEO Component Bldgs. Group, Woodbury, Conn., 1980—96; v.p. Mktg. Contrs. Mkt. Pl., Cornwall Bridge, Conn., 1993—96; assoc. pub. Bus. Digest Housatonic Valley Pub. Co., New Milford, Conn., 1996—97; mem. constrn. panel Am. Arbitration Assn., 1992; pres. Motorhome Holidays Internat., Camp Can. Inc., BEK Press, Camp Am., Inc. Housing cons. Saudi Arabia, Nigeria, Sri Lanka. Author: Computer Center Construction, 1984, Walls on Wheels, 1993. Trustee Baldwin Libr., Birmingham, Mich., 1962—65; publicity chmn. Youth for Eisenhower Com., N.Y.C., 1952. Lt. U.S. Army, 1945—46, PTO. Recipient Low Cost Housing award, Ministry of Housing, Sri Lanka, 1979. Mem.: Nat. Assn. Home Bldrs., Am. Mktg. Assn., Gen. Soc. Mayflower Descendants, Phi Alpha Sigma, Gamma Eta Gamma, Phi Delta Theta. Republican. Episcopalian. Home: 44D Heritage Village Southbury CT 06488 Office: Bee Publ Co 5 Church Hill Rd Newtown CT 06470-1605 Office Phone: 203-426-3141.

FARRELL, EDMUND JAMES, retired English language educator, writer; b. Butte, Mont., May 17, 1927; s. Bartholomew J. and Lavinia H. (Collins) F.; m. Jo Ann Hayes, Dec. 19, 1964; children: David (dec.), Kevin, Sean. AB, Stanford U., 1950, MA, 1951; PhD, U. Calif., Berkeley, 1969. Chmn. English dept. James Lick H.S., San Jose, Calif., 1954-59; supr. secondary English U. Calif., Berkeley, 1959-70; adj. prof. English U. Ill., Urbana, 1973-78; prof. English edn. U. Tex., Austin, 1978—92, prof. emeritus, 1992—; pres. Farrell Ednl. Svcs., Inc., Austin, 1981-97; ret., 1997; sr. editl. cons. EMC Paradigm Pub. Co., 1993—. Participant revision lit. objectives Nat. Assessment of Ednl. Progress, Denver, 1972-73, 78; adv. com. Ctr. for the Book, Libr. of Congress, 1980-86; chmn. adv. com. on English, Coll. Bd., NYC, 1974-79, council acad. affairs, 1978-79; guest lectr. local, state and nat. confs. of English tchrs., 1954—; reader compositions for advanced placement program Rider Coll., Princeton, NJ, 1969, 72-77; pres. Calif. Assn. Tchrs. English, 1962-63; sr. cons. EMC Masterpiece Series, 1999—. Author: (with others) Exploring Life Through Literature, 1964, Counterpoint in Literature, 1967, Projection in Literature, 1973, Outlooks Through Literature, 1973, Fantasy: Forms of Things Unknown, 1974, Science Fact/Fiction, 1974, Comment, 1976, Myth, Mind and Moment, 1976, I/You, We/They, 1976, Traits and Topics, 1976, Reality in Conflict, 1976, To Be, 1976, Arrangement in Literature, 1979, Purpose in Literature, 1979, Album U.S.A., 1983, Discoveries in Literature, 1985, classic edit., 1989, Patterns in Literature, 1985, classic edit., 1989, Transactions with Literature, 1990, The Perceptive I, 1997. With USN, 1945-46. Fellow Nat. Conf. Rsch. on Lang. and Literacy; mem. Nat. Coun. Tchrs. English (field rep. 1970-71, asst. exec. sec. 1971-73, assoc. exec. dir. 1973-78, chmn. commn. lit. 1979-83; trustees rsch. found. 1983-85; fund for tchg. of English 1993-96, Disting. Svc. award 1982, James R. Squire award 1999), Tex. Joint Coun. Tchrs. of English (pres. 1986-87, Disting. English Educator award 1989-90, Disting. Lifetime Svc. award 1999). Unitarian Universalist. Home: 6500 Sumac Dr Austin TX 78731-4117 Office: U Tex Dept Curriculum and Instrn Austin TX 78712 Business E-Mail: farrell@mail.utexas.edu.

FARRELL, EDWARD WAGNER, retired dentist, educator; b. Jan. 12, 1921; Dentist VA Ohio, 1948—50; pvt. practice dentistry Youngstown, Ohio, 1952—62; dental dir. Ariz. Dept. Health, Phoenix, 1965—69, Fla. Dept. Health, Jacksonville, 1969—75; dir. dental aux. edn. Ind. U. Shc. Dentistry, N.W. Campus, Gary, 1975—86, ret. Served with U.S. Army, 1943—45, served with USN, 1946—48. Republican.

FARRELL, GREGORY ALAN, biomedical engineer; b. Bklyn., May 12, 1942; s. Edmond William and Edna Florence (Williams) F.; m. Mary Louise Lupiani, Sept. 3, 1966; children: Juliana Eden, Cristina Elizabeth. BSME, Cooper Union, 1964; MS in Biomed. Engring., Columbia U., 1972, postgrad., 1972—. Mech. engr. Gen. Dynamics, San Diego, 1964-65, Rochester, N.Y., 1965-67; rsch. asst. Columbia U. Med. Sch., N.Y.C., 1968-69; instr. pathology N.Y. Med. Coll., 1969-72; rsch. engr. Technicon Instruments Corp., Tarrytown, N.Y., 1972-82; mgr. mech. engring. Baker Instruments Corp., Allentown, Pa., 1982-84, prin. mech. engr., 1984-86; prin. engr. Nat. Patent Devel. Corp., N.Y.C., 1986-87; project engr. Bayer Diagnostics (divsn. Bayer Healthcare), Tarrytown, 1987—90, new product devel. mgr., 1990—99; prin. staff engr. Tarrytown, 2000—; mgr. mech. engring., 2001—05. Patentee in field; contbr. articles to profl. jours. Winner med. design excellence award, Indsl. Designers Soc. Am., 1998. Democrat. Roman Catholic. Achievements include development of several automated clinical hematology, chemistry and immunology instruments. Home: 447 Hillcrest Rd Ridgewood NJ 07450-1520 Office: Bayer Diagnostics 511 Benedict Ave Tarrytown NY 10591-5005 Office Phone: 914-524-3466. E-mail: gregory.farrell.b@bayer.com.

FARRELL, JOHN L., JR., lawyer, consultant, corporate financial executive; b. N.Y.C., Jan. 24, 1929; s. John Lawrence and Edna (Ziegler) F.; m. Beverly H. Farrell; children: John Lawrence III, Maureen, Jayne, Dianne, Michael. BA, St. Peters Coll., N.J., 1950; LL.B., St. John's U., 1955; MBA, NYU, 1960. Bar: N.Y. 1956. Asst. counsel ACF Industries, Inc., N.Y.C., 1955-61; counsel, sec., asst. to chmn. Knox Glass, Inc., N.Y.C., 1961-68; adminstrv. liaison Williams Cos., Tulsa, 1968-69; cons. on mergers and acquisitions, 1969-71; sr. v.p. law and adminstrn., sec. U.S. Filter Corp., N.Y.C., 1971-82; pres., chief operating officer FRACORP, Tulsa, 1983-84; cons. on mergers, acquisitions and fin. Frates Enterprises, Tulsa, 1984-87; prin. The Morgan Investment Group, Tulsa, 1988—; chmn. exec. com. Diagnetics, Inc., Tulsa, 1989-96. Mem. Ardsley (N.Y.) Sch. Bd., 1965-68. Served to 1st lt. U.S. Army, 1951-53. Republican. Roman Catholic. Home: 2128 E 60th Pl Tulsa OK 74105-7021

FARRELL, JOHN MARSHALL, architect; b. Poplar Bluff, Mo., Nov. 2, 1942; s. Marshall Dee and Frieda Mae (Burk) F.; m. Susan Martha Garbett, Dec. 7, 1968; children— Kevin, Elizabeth. B.Arch., Tex. Tech U., 1965. Registered architect Tex., N.Mex., Calif., Fla. Designer Skidmore Owings & Merrill, Chgo., 1968-70; project architect Bernard Johnson Inc., Houston, 1970-72; project architect NSHD Inc., Houston, 1972-73; prin., corp. dir., project mgr. Golemon & Rolfe Assocs. Inc., Houston, 1973-83; former pres. Farrell-Robson Architects Inc.; prin. FKP Architects, Tex., 1998- .Mem. zoning and planning commn. City of West University Place (Tex.), 1980-82; v.p. West University Little League, 1981-83; mem. adminstrv. bd. St. Luke's United Methodist Ch., Houston, 1982-84. Served as officer USNR, 1965-68; Vietnam. Mem. AIA (past dir. Houston chpt.), Tex. Soc. Architects, NCARB (cert.), Council Ednl. Facility Planners. Club: Briar. Archtl. works: U. Houston at Clear Lake City, 1975; Riverwalk Marriott Hotel, San Antonio, 1978; Oak Ridge High Sch., Conroe, Tex., 1981; Saida Hilton Condominium, South Padre Island, 1982; Crowne Plaza West Loop Hotel, Houston, 1983. Office: FKP Architects 8 Greenway Plaza, Ste 300 Houston TX 77046-6501

FARRELL, JOSEPH, film producer, financial analyst, film company executive, sculptor, writer; b. N.Y.C., Sept. 11, 1935; s. John Joseph and Mildred Veronica (Dwyer) F. AB summa cum laude, St. John's Coll., 1958; A.M., U. Notre Dame, 1959; JD, Harvard U., 1965. Bar: N.Y. 1965. With firm Milbank, Tweed, Hadley & McCloy, N.Y.C., 1964-65; exec. assoc. Carnegie Corp. N.Y., 1965-66; exec. v.p., chief oper. officer Am. Council of Arts, 1966-71; cons. Rockefeller Bros. Fund, Spl. Projects, 1966-74, exec. v.p., 1974-77; vice chmn. Louis Harris & Assocs. (Harris Poll), N.Y.C., 1978; chmn., CEO, Nat. Rsch. Group, Inc., subs. VNU, L.A., London and Tokyo, 1978—. Movie market analyst and cons., 1978—; movie exec. producer, 1986—; sculptor, 1958—; designer Farbino Furniture, 1982—. Author, editor: Americans and the Arts, 1973, 75, Museums: USA, 1973, The Cultural Consumer, 1973, The U.S. Arts and Cultural Trend Data System, 1977; author: (novel) Birds of Prey, 1998; screenwriter The Foundation, Second Son, 1990—. Mem. Gov. N.Y. Task Force on Arts, 1975; founder, bd. dirs. Vol. Lawyers for Arts, 1968-76; bd. dirs. Arts and Bus. Coun. N.Y., 1973-76; bd. advisors Actors Studio, 1983-90. Woodrow Wilson fellow, 1958; named among Top 100 Influential People in Hollywood, Premiere mag., 1998, 99. Office: 6255 W Sunset BLVD #19TH-FLR Los Angeles CA 90028-7403

FARRELL, JOSEPH MICHAEL, water transportation executive; b. Yonkers, N.Y., June 7, 1922; s. Joseph Michael and Mary Elizabeth (Powers) F.; m. Cloatta Grace Pennington, Dec. 6, 1946; children: Cloatta M., Anthony J., Christopher J., Janice E. BS in Marine Transp., U.S. Mcht. Marine Acad., 1943; postgrad., Columbia U., 1948-50, Fordham U., 1947-48. Commd. ensign USNR, 1943, advanced through grades to capt., 1960; ret., 1968; mgr. Great Lakes Svc., States Marine LInes, 1960-62; European mgr. States Marine Lines, Bremerhaven, Germany, 1962-65; exec. v.p Waterman S.S. Corp., Washington, 1965-95. V.p. Hammond Leasing Corp., Mobile, Ala., 1967-89, Waterman S.S. Co. of Del., 1967-89; pres. Waterman Oceanic Corp., 1974-89; sr. v.p. Ctrl. Gulf Lines, 1993-95; v.p. Internat. Shipholding Corp., 1993-95. Recipient Outstanding Profl. Achievement U.S. Merchant Marine ACad., 1968-88; invested Knight of Malta, 1988. Mem. Propeller Club U.S. (v.p., bd. govs. 1967-68, U.S. Exec. com. 1984-95), Nat. Def. Transp. Ass.n, Navy League, Congressional Country Club, Univ. Club, George Town Club (Washington), Siwanoy Country Club (Bronxville, N.Y.). Home: 4701 Willard Ave Apt 1214 Chevy Chase MD 20815-4625

FARRELL, KENNETH ROYDEN, economist; b. Ont., Can., Jan. 17, 1927; naturalized, 1958; s. William R. and Velma V. (Wood) F.; m. Mary Souter, Sept. 7, 1951; children: Janet, Betty, Deborah, Robert, Patricia, Lisa. BS, U. Toronto, Ont., 1950; MS, Iowa State U., 1955, PhD, 1958. Economist U. Calif., Berkeley, 1957-71; dep. adminstr. USDA, Washington, 1971-77, adminstr., 1977-81; dir. Nat. Ctr., Resources for the Future, Washington, 1981-87; v.p. U. Calif., Oakland, 1987-95, v.p. emeritus, 1995—. Economist Nat. Food Commn., Washington, 1965-66, Nat. Productivity Commn., Washington, 1972-73; mem. Presdl. Task Force, Washington, 1982; cons. Robert Nathan Assocs., 1983-84. Contbr. articles to profl. jours.; author (with others) books. Lt. Royal Can. Navy Res., 1946-48. Fulbright scholar U. Naples, Italy, 1963-64. Fellow AAAS, Am. Agrl. Econs. Assn. (bd. dirs. 1973-76, pres. 1976-77, named for Disting. Pub. Policy Contbn. 1980, 92); mem. Internat. Assn. Agrl. Econs., Commonwealth Club Calif., Phi Kappa Phi, Gamma Sigma Delta. Avocations: golf, gardening, literature. Office: Univ Calif 300 Lakeside Dr Ste 701 Oakland CA 94612-3534 Office Phone: 510-987-0035. Personal E-mail: fkenmar2001@aol.com. Business E-Mail: Kenneth.farrell@ucop.edu.

FARRELL, KEVIN WALTER, history professor; b. Port Chester, N.Y., Aug. 5, 1964; s. William Edward Farrell and Carol Heithaus; m. Sheila Jeannette Newman, Dec. 8, 1990; children: Elizabeth Clare, William Patrick, Caroline Newman. BS, U.S. Mil. Acad., 1986; MA in Modern European History, Columbia U., 1995, MPhil in Modern European History, 1997, PhD in Modern Brit. History, 1999. Commd. 2d. lt. U.S. Army, lt. col.; chief rsch. and pub. team Combat Studies Inst., 2002—04; adv., tng. officer Afghan Nat. Army, Kabul, Afghanistan, 2003; assoc. prof. Command and Gen. Staff Coll., Ft. Leavenworth, Kans., 2004; battalion comdr. U.S. Army, Ft. Stewart, Ga., 2004—. Contbr. articles to profl. jours., chapters to books. Lt. col. U.S. Army. Mem.: Assn. U.S. Army, KC (3d degree knight), Phi Alpha Theta. Home: 17 Wynn Pl Fort Stewart GA 31315 Office: 1st Battalion 64th Armor 3d Infantry Divsn Mechanized Fort Stewart GA 31314

FARRELL, MARGARET DAWSON, lawyer; b. Bellingham, Wash., July 23, 1949; d. Sterling Jacob and Irene Hegg; m. David S. Farrell, June 10, 1972; children: Lindsay S., Charles D. BA cum laude, Smith Coll., 1971; postgrad., Georgetown U., 1971-72; JD, U. Cin., 1974. Bar: Ohio 1974, U.S. Dist. Ct. (so. dist.) Ohio 1974, R.I. 1976, U.S. Dist. Ct. R.I. 1976. Assoc. Frost & Jacobs, Cin., 1974-76; from assoc. to ptnr. Tillinghast, Collins & Graham, Providence, 1976—81; ptnr. Hinckley, Allen & Snyder LLP, Providence, 1981—. Lectr. Bryant Coll., 1979-80; dir., sec. Bank R.I., 1996—, Bancorp R.I., Inc., 2000—. Trustee Women and Infants Hosp., Providence, 1981—, sec., 1982-96, vice chair, 1996—2003, chair 2004—; bd. dirs. Women and Infants Corp., Providence, 1989—2003, chair 2004—, sec., 1989-96, vice chair, 1996-2003, chair, 2004—; trustee, sec. Providence Preservation Soc. Revolving Fund, 1982-88; trustee Butler Hosp., 1995—, Care New England Health Sys., 1996—, R.I. Hist. Soc., 1980-85, Gordon Sch., East Providence, R.I., 1990-95; trustee Hosp. Assn. R.I., 1989-2003, mem. exec. coun., 1998-2003; trustee, sec., pres. Found. for Repertory Theatre, R.I., 1978-84; R.I. del. Am. Hosp. Assn. Congress Hosp. Trustees, 1993-98; mem. R.I. Bd. Regents for Elem. and Secondary Edn., 1987-90. Mem. ABA, R.I. Bar Assn. Avocations: golf, sailing, skiing, horseback riding. Office: Hinckley Allen & Snyder LLP 1500 Fleet Ctr Providence RI 02903-2319 Office Phone: 401-274-2000.

FARRELL, MICHAEL W., judge; b. 1938; Grad., U. Notre Dame; MA, Columbia U.; JD, Am. U. Law clerk to Assoc. Judge John P. Moore Md. Ct. Spl. Appeals, 1973; atty. criminal divsn. U.S. Dept. Justice; chief appellate divsn. Office U.S. Atty. D.C., 1982-89; assoc. judge D.C. Ct. Appeals, 1989—. Chmn. Eng. dept. Georgetown Prep. Sch. Office: Ct Appeals 500 Indiana Ave NW Rm 6000 Washington DC 20001-2131*

FARRELL, MIKE, actor; b. St. Paul, Feb. 6, 1939; s. Michael and Agnes Farrell; m. Judy Hayden, 1963 (div.); children: Michael, Erin; m. Shelley Fabares, 1984. Ed., UCLA, Jeff Corey Workshop, Hollywood. Profl. debut in little theatre prodn. Rain, 1961; motion pictures include: Captain Newman, M.D, 1964, The Americanization of Emily, 1964, The Graduate, 1967, Targets, 1968; numerous TV appearances; regular on TV series Days of Our Lives, NBC-TV, The Interns, CBS-TV, 1970-71, The Man and the City, ABC-TV, 1971-72, M*A*S*H, CBS-TV, 1975-83, The Killers Within, 1995, Superman, 1996, Providence, 1999—; TV spls. include Ladies of the Corridor, PBS, 1975, Child Sexual Abuse, PBS, 1984, JFK, A One-Man Show; TV movies include: The Questor Tapes, The Longest Night, Battered, Sex and the Single Parent, Damien, The Leper Priest, Prime Suspect, 1982, Choices of the Heart, 1983, Memorial Day, 1984, Private Sessions, 1985, Vanishing Act, 1986, A Deadly Silence, 1989, (also co-author) Incident at Dark River, 1990, The Whereabouts of Jenny, 1991, Silent Motive, 1991, Hart to Hart: Old Friends Never Die, 1994, Vows of Deception, 1996, Tangled Web, 1996, Behind the Laughs, 1997, Sins of the Mind, 1997, The Crooked E: The Unshredded Truth About Enron, 2003, Miracle Dogs, 2003, The Clinic, 2004; co-producer motion picture Dominick and Eugene, 1988; dir. M*A*S*H episodes, (TV movie) Run Till You Fall, CBS-TV, 1988; prodr. (films) Memorial Day, 1983, Dominick and Eugene, 1988, Incident at Dark River, 1989, Silent Motive, 1991, Patch Adams, others; dir. M*A*S*H, 1972, Run Till You Fall, 1988; TV guest appearances include Bonanza, 1959, I Dream of Jeannie, 1965, The Monkees, 1966, Ghost Story, 1972, The Six Million Dollar Man, 1974, Murder, She Wrote, 1984, Matlock, 1986, others. Involved in polit. and social causes; active Human Rights Watch, CONCERN/Am., Calif. State Commn. on Jud. Performance; pres. Death Penalty Focus. Served USMC. Recipient Valentine Davies award, Writers Guild Am., 1996. Mem. AFTRA, Screen Actors Guild.

FARRELL, PATRICIA ANN, psychologist, educator, writer; b. NYC; d. Joseph and Pauline Farrell. BA, Queens Coll.; MA, PhD, NYU. Lic. psychologist, NJ, Fla.; cert. online computer instr. Assoc. editor Pubs. Weekly Mag., NYC; editor Bestsellers Mag., NYC; assoc. editor King Features Syndicate, NYC; staff psychologist, intake coord. Mid-Bergen Cmty. Mental Health Ctr., Paramus, NJ; instr. Bergen C.C., Paramus, 1978-94; prof. clin. psychology Walden U., 1995—2001. Resident clin. psychology Am. Inst. for Counseling, NJ, 1990-91; cons. Family Counseling Svc. of Ridgewood, NJ, 1984; clin. psychology intern Marlboro (NJ) Psychiat. Hosp., 1984-85, staff psychologist, 1985-87; rsch. analyst Mt. Sinai Sch. Medicine, 1987-88; account exec., sr. med. writer Manning, Selvage and Lee, NYC, 1988-90; sr. clin. psychologist, mem. med. staff Greystone Pk. (NJ) Psychiat. Hosp., 1990-96; pvt. practice psychology, Englewood, NJ; health sci. editor Time Warner Cable, Channel 10 News, 1995-2000; med. specialist NJ Divsn. Disability Determination, 1997—; police surgeon Boro Ft. Lee, NJ, 1998—; psychiatry preceptor U. Medicine and Dentistry NJ Med. Sch.; cons. pharm. clin. protocols; psychologist, expert moderator on anxiety and panic WebMD, 2000—. Guest radio and TV shows including The Today Show, Crier Live, Nat. Geog. TV, MSNBC, The Abrams Report, The Big Idea, Ron Reagan's Connections, Hollywood at Large, The View, The O'Reilly Factor, ABC Sports Spl., VH1, E!, ABC World News Tonight, Court TV, Rapid Fire, CNN Radio, Geraldo Rivera Show, Newsweek-on-Air, Voice of Am., Family Talk, Up Front Tonight, Buchanon & Press, Pros and Cons, Local Live, USA Radio Network, Ken Hamblin Show, KNU Radio, Fox Beyond the News, Real Talk, Jay Thomas Radio Show, Sally Jessy Raphael, Montel Williams, Gordon Elliott Show, Inside Edit., Am. Jour., Joan Rivers Show, Fox Cable News, Good Day NY, Mark Walberg, Am. After Hours, Dini, The Shirley Show, Camilla Scott, USA Live, Alive and Wellness with Carol Martin, News Talk, Maury Povich, Caucus NJ, It's Your Call, One-on-One, The Carnie Wilson Show, AP Newswire, Judge for Yourself TV Show, NYC 10 O'Clock News, Cosmo, Redbook, Self, Shape, Fitness, Latina, Maxim, Good Housekeeping, AARP, Cooking Light, Smart Money, Ct. TV Investigative Reports, In Touch, Woman's World, Achieve Solutions, All You, First for Women, Washington Post, Fox & Friends, Eyewitness News, Reuters TV, Timeout NY, Detroit News, Knight-Ridder News, Chgo. Tribune, Home Office Computing, Working Woman, NY Post, Boston Globe, NY Daily News, NY Times, Chateleine, New Woman, Phila. Enquirer, WPIX-TV, NY, UPN 9 News, WWOR-TV News, WNRR-TV, In Your Interest, LTV, Channel 10 News, On Campus, Sta WTTM, WSNJ, WHSI-TV, Bloomberg News, UPI News, KGAB, WSAR, Don Weeks Show, Common Concerns, WHSE-TV, Alan Nathan's Battle Lines, Dirk Van NBC radio, Ruth Koscielak Show, Voice of Am., WTOP, Redbook, Ramp, Eyewitness News, Cork Talks Back, TalkSport, The Week, Pink, Life & Style, Ladies Home Jour., Reuters TV, Bev Smith Show, Fitness, Shape, Prevention, In Touch, Life & Style, More, The Oregonian, Arnie Arneson Show, Talk Am., Real Simple, Marie Claire, Seventeen, Parents, Shape, Prevention, AARP Bull., Women's Health, Inside TV, Baby Talk, Family Circle, Women's Day, Metro NY, Physical, Christian Single, Mental Health Law Report; author: (manual) Alzheimer's Disease Assessment Scale test, How To Be Your Own Therapist, 2004; contbr. book chpt. to Innovations in Clin. Practice: A Source Book, 15th edit., 2000, Counseling and Psychotherapy; contbr. articles to Writer's Digest, Real World, Postgrad. Medicine, newspapers. Bd. dirs., chmn. med. liaison com. liaison to dept. psychiatry Bergen Pines County Hosp., Paramus, 1994-95. McDonald's rsch. grantee, 1994-95; recipient Sci. award Rotary Club. Avocations: exercise, racquetball, kite-flying. Office: PO Box 1525 Englewood Cliffs NJ 07632-0283 Personal E-mail: pfarrell@ix.netcom.com.

FARRELL, PEG (MARGARET FARRELL), magazine publisher; BA, Fordham U. Mgmt. positions Gillette Co., Boston, Vitt Media, NY, BBDO, NY; with Time Magazine, Sports Illustrated, Time Inc., 1975—90; assoc. pub. Reader's Digest, 1990—92; founding pub. Marie Claire, 1994-97; v.p., pub. Country Living Gardens, NYC, 1997—2000; sr. v.p. Family Cir. G+J USA, 2000—, pub. Family Cir., 2000—. Office: G+J USA Publishing 375 Lexington Ave New York NY 10017-5514 Office Phone: 212-499-1888. Office Fax: 212-499-8153. E-mail: pfarrell@familycircle.com.*

FARRELL, PHILIP M., dean, physician, educator, researcher; b. St. Louis, Nov. 26, 1943; m. Alice Yeakle; children: Michael Henry, David Sean, Bridget Mary. AB, St. Louis U., 1964, MD, PhD, St. Louis U., 1970. Diplomate Am. Bd. Pediatrics. Intern U. Wis. Hosps., 1970—71, resident in pediatrics, 1971—72; fellow pediatric metabolism br. Nat. Inst. Arthritis, Metabolism and Digestive Diseases, NIH, Bethesda, Md., 1972—74, sr. investigator pediatric metabolism br., 1974—75; chief Neonatal and Pediatric Medicine Br., Nat. Inst. Child Health and Human Devel., NIH, Bethesda, Md., 1975—77, Chief, Sect. Devel. Biology and Clin. Nutrition, 1975—77; Asst. prof. dept. child health George Washington U., Washington, 1975; asst. prof. pediatrics U. Wis., Madison, 1977-78, dir. Cystic Fibrosis Ctr., 1977—83, co-dir., 1983—88, affiliate scientist Wis. Regional Primate Research Ctr., 1978, affiliate faculty dept. nutrition scis., 1978, assoc. prof. pediatrics, 1978-82, dir. Pediatric Pulmonary Specialized Ctr. of Research, 1981-85, prof. pediatrics, 1982—, chmn. dept. pediatrics, 1985-95, med. dir. Children's Hosp., 1988—95, Alfred Dorrance Daniels Prof. on Diseases of Children, 1990—, interim dean Med. Sch., 1994—95, dean Med. Sch., 1995—, vice-chancellor med. affairs, 2001—. Editor: Lung Development: Biological and Clinical Perspectives, 1982. Avalon Found. scholar, 1965-67, Thurston Meml. scholar, 1966-70; Fogarty Internat. fellow, 1985. Mem. Am. Chem. Soc., Am. Acad. Pediatrics, Soc. Pediatric Rsch., Am. Thoracic Soc., Soc. Exptl. Biology and Medicine, Am. Inst. Nutrition, Am. Soc. Clin. Nutrition, Wis. Assn. Perinatal Care, Sigma Xi, Phi Beta Kappa, Alpha Omega Alpha. Office: Univ Wis Office of Dean 1300 University Ave Rm 1217 Madison WI 53706-1510

FARRELL, RICHARD T., human resources administrator; m. Jennifer Farrell; children: Elizabeth, Connor. B in Polit. Sci. magna cum laude, Fla. State U., 1969, M in Govt., 1970. Chief of staff, legis. dir. to U.S. Senator Lawton Chiles, Washington; v.p. govt. affairs Syntex Corp.; sec. Fla. Dept. of Bus. and Profl. Regulation; dir. Human Resources and Adminstrn., Dept. of Energy, Washington, 1998-99; assoc. adminstr. for reinvention EPA, Washington, 1999—. With U.S. Army. Nat. Def. Edn. Act fellow, 1970.

FARRELL, STEPHEN PETER, lawyer; b. N.Y.C., Aug. 21, 1947; s. Peter T. and Agnes M. Farrell. AB, Coll. Holy Cross, 1968; JD, Fordham U., 1971; LLM, NYU, 1979. Bar: N.Y. 1972, (U.S. Supreme Ct.) 1975. Law clk. Hon. William H. Mulligan U.S. Ct. Appeals 2d cir., N.Y.C., 1971—73; assoc. Kelley, Drye & Warren, N.Y.C., 1973—80; assoc., ptnr. Morgan, Lewis & Bockius LLP, N.Y.C., 1980—. Mem.: ABA, N.Y. State Bar Assn., Assn. Bar City of N.Y. Office: Morgan Lewis Bockius LLP 101 Park Ave New York NY 10178-0060

FARRELL, SUZANNE, ballerina; b. Cin., Aug. 16, 1945; d. Robert Ficker and Donna (Von Holle) Holly; m. Paul Mejia, Feb. 21, 1969 (div. 1997). Studies with Marian LaCour, Cin. Conservatory Music; student, Sch. Am. Ballet, 1960—61; LHD (hon.), Georgetown U., 1984, Fordham U., 1987; DFA (hon.), Yale U., 1988; LLD (hon.), U. Notre Dame, 1990; D of Performing Arts (hon.), U. Cin., 1990; ArtsD (hon.), Middlebury Coll., 1992; LHD (hon.), Coll. Mt. St. Vincent, 1995; Doctorate (hon.), Harvard U., 2004. With N.Y.C. Ballet, 1961—69, 1975—89, became featured dancer, 1962, prin. dancer, 1965—69, 1975—89; artistic dir. The Suzanne Farrell Ballet, 2000—. Hon. lectr. dance U. Cin.; guest tchr. Sch. Am. Ballet, Kennedy Ctr. for Performing Arts. Appeared in film version Midsummer Night's Dream, Bejart Ballet of 20th Century, Brussels, 1971—75, appeared as Juliet in Romeo and Juliet, appeared with N.Y.C. Ballet in New Ravel Festival, Tzigane, in G Major, 1976, (documentary) Elusive Muse, 1996, created roles in other ballets Ah, Vous Dirais Je, Maman?, the young girl in Rose in Nijinsky, Clown of God, 1971, Laura in I Trionfi, (N.Y.C. Ballet) Chaconne, Mozartiana, Diamonds, featured in TV show Balanchine Dance in Am., Parts I-IV, featured in Exploring Ballet with Suzanne Farrell at the Kennedy Ctr., 1993—; author: (autobiography) Holding on to the Air, 1990; repetiteur for George Balanchine Trust. Mem. sr. adv. bd. N.Y. chpt. Arthritis Found.; mem. arts adv. bd. Princess Grace Found.-USA. Recipient Merit award Mademoiselle mag., 1965, Dance mag. award, 1976, award of honor for arts and culture N.Y.C., 1979, Spirit Achievement award Albert Einstein Coll. Medicine, 1980, Merit award Brandeis U., Emmy award, 1985, Golden Plate award Am. Acad. of Achievement, 1987, N.Y. State Gov.'s Arts award, 1988, Nat. Medal of Arts, 2003.

FARRELL, THOMAS FRANCIS, energy executive; b. Ft. Buckner, Okinawa, Japan, 1954; BA in Econs., U. Va., 1976, JD, 1979. Ptnr. McGuire Woods Beatle & Booth, 1981-95; sr. v.p., gen. counsel Dominion Resources Inc., Richmond, Va., 1995-97; CEO Va. Power, Richmond, 1995—; sr. v.p. corp. affairs Dominion Resources, Richmond, 1997-99; CEO Dominion Generation, Inc., Richmond, 1999—; exec. v.p. Dominion Resources, Richmond, 1999—2003, pres., COO, 2003—. Chmn. nominations to the appellate ct. com. State of Va. Mem. Va. Bar Assn. (exec. com., chmn. young lawyers sect.), Va. Law Found. (mem. continuing legal edn. com.). Office: Dominion Resources PO Box 26532 120 Tredegar St Richmond VA 23219-4306*

FARRELL, W. JAMES, metal products manufacturing company executive; b. N.Y.C., 1942; married; 5 children. BA in Electrical Engring., U. Detroit, 1965. Joined Ill. Tool Works., Inc., Glenview, Ill., 1965, sales corr., Shakeproof div., 1965—68, sales engr., 1968—70, automotive acct. mgr., 1972—77, v.p., group pres. Fastener Group, 1977—83, exec. v.p. Glenview, Ill., 1983—94, pres., 1995—96, CEO, 1995—2005, chmn. bd., 1996—. Bd. dirs. Allstate Ins. Co., Sears, Roebuck and Co., 1999—, Kraft Foods, 2001—, United Airlines, Fed. Reserve Bank Chgo., chmn., 2001—03, 2004—. Dir. Big Shoulders Fund, Chgo. Public Library Found.; chmn. Jr. Achievement Chgo.; trustee Northwestern U.; advisory bd. mem. J.L. Kellogg Grad. Sch. Mgmt.; trustee Rush Presbyterian-St. Luke's Medical Ctr.; chmn. bd. trustees Mus. Sci. and Industry; dir. Lyric Opera Chgo.; vice chmn. United Way Crusade of Mercy. Served criminal investigation div. U.S. Army, 1965—67, Alaska. Mem.: Econ. Club Chgo. (chmn.), Chgo. Club (pres.), Comml. Club Chgo. (civic com.), Executives Club Chgo., Mid-Am. Com., Ill. Bus. Roundtable, Bus. Coun. Office: Illinois Tool Works Inc 3600 W Lake Ave Glenview IL 60025-5811*

FARRELL, WILLIAM JOSEPH, university chancellor; b. Milw., Aug. 17, 1936; s. William John and Rita (Taggart) F.; m. Carol Mary Leeming, Aug. 1, 1959; children: William Jr., Charles, Elizabeth. BS summa cum laude, Marquette U., 1958, MBA, 1976; MA, U. Wis., 1959, PhD, 1961; DHL (hon.), St. Anselm's Coll., 1998. Instr. U. Chgo., 1961-63, asst. prof., 1963-68; assoc. prof. Marquette U., Milw., 1968-75, dir. of Found. Support, 1970-75; assoc. v.p. of research U. Iowa, Iowa City, 1975-84; pres. Plymouth (N.H.) State Coll., 1984-92; chancellor Univ. System of N.H., 1992—2000. Vis. prof. U. Calif., Berkeley, 1967-68; trustee Univ. Sys. N.H., 1984—, St. Anselm's Coll., 1992—, chair ednl. policy com., 1995—, mem. exec. com., 1995—, state del. New Eng. Bd. Higher Edn., 1984—, chair N.H. del., 1995—. Co-editor English Literature 1600-1800: A Bibliography of Modern Studies, 1972; editor: (jour.) Renascence: Essays on Values in Literature, 1969-72; contbr. numerous articles to profl. jours. Bd. dirs. N.H. Music Festival, Center Harbor, 1984-93, Bus. and Industry Assn. of N.H., 1998—; mem. N.H. Postsecondary Edn. Commn., 1984—, mem. exec. com., 1988-93, chmn., 1990-92. Woodrow Wilson fellow, 1958, Danforth fellow, 1958. Mem. N.H. Coll. and Univ. Coun. (chmn. 1989-91), Am. Assn. State Colls. and Univs., Am. Coun. on Edn., Nat. Assn. Sys. Heads, Nat. Assn. State Univs. & Land Grant Colls., State Higher Edn. Exec. Officers, N.H. Bus. and Industry Assn. (bd. dirs. 1998—). Roman Catholic. Home: PO Box 873 17 Denbow Rd Durham NH 03824-3104 Office: Univ System NH Dunlap Ctr 25 Concord Rd Durham NH 03824-6624

FARRELLY, BOBBY (ROBERT LEO RARRELLY JR.), scriptwriter, film director, film producer; b. Cumberland, R.I., 1958; m. Nancy Farrelly; 2 children. Student, Rensselaer Poly. Inst. Writer, prodr. Outside Providence, 1999; writer, co-prodr., dir. Dumb and Dumber, 1994; exec. prodr., writer, dir. There's Something About Mary, 1998; writer, prodr., dir. Me, Myself and Irene, 2000, Shallow Hall, 2001. Stuck on You, 2003; writer Bushwacked, 1995; dir. Kingpin, 1996; dir., prodr. Osmosis Jones, 2001; prodr. Say It Isn't So, 2001; exec. prodr. The Ringer, 2005, (TV series) Ozzy & Drix, 2002; dir. Fever Pitch, 2005. Recipient Screenwriter of Yr. ShoWest Conv., 1999. Office: Creative Artists Agy c/o Adam Kantor 9830 Wilshire Blvd Beverly Hills CA 90212-1825*

FARRELLY, JOHN WILLIAM, music educator; b. Sheffield, England; s. Derick and Clarice Farrelly; m. Meg Farrelly. Degree in Music Ed. Choral, C.S.U, 1998; degree in Elem. Edn., Citadel U., 2004. Airman Royal Air Force, England, 1980—90. Coach tennis Snee Farm Athletic Club, Charleston, 2001—04. Office: Lambs Elem School 6800 Dorchester Rd Charleston SC 29418 Office Phone: 843-767-5900. Personal E-mail: soninit@aol.comjkm.

FARRELLY, PETER JOHN, screenwriter; b. Phoenixville, Pa., Dec. 17, 1956; s. Robert Leo and Mariann (Neary) F. BA, Providence Coll., 1979; MFA, Columbia U., 1987. Salesman U.S. Lines, Inc., Boston, 1979-81; bartender various libationary locales, Boston, 1981-85; screenwriter Paramount Columbia and Disney Studios, Los Angeles, 1985—. Author Outside Providence, 1988; co-writer (TV spls.) Our Planet Tonight, 1987, Paul Reiser: Out on a Whim, 1987; writer (film) Dumb & Dumber, 1994, Bushwhacked, 1995, There's Something About Mary, 1998; dir. (film) Dumb & Dumber, 1994, Kingpin, 1996, There's Something About Mary, 1998, Fever Pitch, 2005; prodr. There's Something About Mary, 1998, Outside Providence, 1999; writer, co-dir, prodr.: Me, Myself & Irene, 2000, Shallow Hal, 2002; exec. prodr. (TV series) Oxxy & Drix, 2002; writer, dir., prodr. Stuck on You, 2003. Mem. Writers Guild Am. West. Roman Catholic.*

FARREN, J. MICHAEL, former government official, lawyer; b. Waterbury, Conn., Nov. 21, 1952; s. Joseph W. and Elizabeth (Sayers) Farren; m. Mary Margaret Scharf, May 3, 1997. BA in polit. sci., Fairfield U., 1977; MA in pub. policy analysis, Trinity Coll., 1982; JD, U. Conn., 1982. Bar: Conn., DC. Dist. rep., campaign dir. US Rep. Ronald A. Sarasin, Conn., 1973-78; v.p. Greater Waterbury C. of C., Conn., 1978-81; dir. White House liaison Rep. Nat. Com., 1981-83, exec. asst. to the dep. chmn., 1981—83; dir. Office Bus. Liaison US Dept. Commerce, Washington, 1983-85, counsellor to the sec., 1985, dep. under sec. internat. trade, 1985-88, under sec. internat. trade, 1989-92; dep. dir. transition team Office Pres.-Elect George Bush, 1988-89; of counsel Wiggin & Dana, New Haven, 1988—89; dep. campaign mgr. Bush-Quayle Re-election Campaign Com., 1992; v.p. external affairs Xerox Corp., Washington, 1992—94, corp. v.p. external affairs, 1994—2003, corp. v.p. external and legal affairs, gen. counsel Stamford, Conn., 2003—. Office: Xerox Corp 800 Long Ridge Rd Stamford CT 06904

FARRER, CLAIRE ANNE RAFFERTY, anthropologist, educator; b. NYC, Dec. 26, 1936; d. Francis Michael and Clara Anna (Guerra) Rafferty; 1 child, Suzanne Claire. BA in Anthropology, U. Calif., Berkeley, 1970; MA in Anthropology and Folklore, U. Tex., 1974, PhD in Anthropology and Folklore, 1977. Various positions, 1953-73; fellow Whitney M. Young Jr. Meml. Found., NYC, 1974-75; arts specialist, grant adminstr. Nat. Endowment for Arts, Washington, 1976-77; Weatherhead resident fellow Sch. Am. Rsch., Santa Fe, 1977-78; asst. prof. anthropology U. Ill., Urbana, 1978-85; assoc. prof., coord. applied anthropology Calif. State U., Chico, 1985-89, prof., 1989—2001, prof. emerita, 2002—, dir. Multicultural and Gender Studies, 1994. Cons. in field, 1974—; mem. film and video adv. panel Ill. Arts Coun., 1980-82; mem. Ill. Humanities Coun., 1980-82; vis. prof. U. Ghent, Belgium, 1990; vis. prof. Southwestern studies Colo. Coll., Colorado Springs, 2002—, Hulbert chair in Southwestern studies, 1997; bus. mgr. Calif. Folklore Soc., 1994-99; NEH and Harry J. Gray disting. vis. prof. in humanities U. Hartford, Conn., 2002-03. Author: Play and Inter-Ethnic Communication, 1990, Living Life's Circle: Mescalero Apache Cosmovision, 1991, Thunder Rides a Black Horse: Mescalero Apaches and the Mythic Present, 1994, 96, others; co-founder, co-editor Folklore Women's Commn., 1972; editor spl. issue Jour. Am. Folklore, 1975, 1st rev. edit., 1986; co-editor: Forms of Play of Native North Americans, 1979, Earth and Sky: Visions of the Cosmos in Native North American Folklore, 1992; contbr. numerous articles to profl. jours., mags. and newspapers, chpts. to books. Recipient J. Gordon prize in S.W. Studies, Colo.Coll.; numerous fellowships and grants. Fellow Am. Anthrop. Assn.; mem. Authors Guild, Am. Ethnol. Soc., Am. Folklore Soc., Am. Soc. Ethnohistory, Astronomy in Culture. Home: PO Box 50293 Colorado Springs CO 80949-0293 E-mail: clairerfarrer@aol.com.

FARRINGTON, BERTHA LOUISE, retired nursing administrator; b. Poteet, Tex., Jan. 20, 1937; d. Leonard Gilbert and Janie (Hernandez) Lozano; m. James Charles Farrington, Jan. 30, 1965; children: Mark Hiram, Robert Lee. BSN, Tex. Women's U., 1960; NP, U. Tex., 1984. RN, Tex. Charge nurse emergency rm. Parkland Meml. Hosp., Dallas; head nurse emergency rm./day surgery Bapt. Meml. Hosp., Pensacola, Fla.; asst. dir. health svcs. U. Tex. Southwestern Med. Ctr., Dallas, dir. student health svcs., ret., 2002. Cons. Student Health Com. E-mail: j.bfarrington@sbcglobal.net.

FARRINGTON, GREGORY C., academic administrator; b. Bronxville, N.Y. B in Chemistry, Clarkson U., 1968; AM in Chemistry, Harvard U., 1970, PhD in Chemistry, 1972; degree (hon.), U. Uppsala, Sweden, 1984. Staff sci. GE, Schenectady, N.Y., 1972-79; assoc. prof. materials sci. and engring. U. Pa., 1979-84, prof., 1984, chair dept. materials sci. and engring., 1984-87, dir. Lab. for Rsch. on Structure of Matter, 1987-90, dean Sch. Engring. and Applied Sci., 1990-98; pres. Lehigh U., 1998—. Bd. trustees St. Luke Hosp. & Health Network, Nat. Mus. of Indsl. History, Lehigh Valley Partnership, Lehigh Valley Econ. Devel. Corp. Contbr. chapters to books, articles 100 articles to tech. jours. Achievements include holding or sharing more than two dozen patents. Office: Lehigh U Office of the Pres 27 Memorial Dr West, Alumni Memorial Bld Bethlehem PA 18015*

FARRINGTON, JOHN WILLIAM, academic administrator, dean, research scientist; b. New Bedford, Mass., Sept. 25, 1944; s. John James Grace and Hazel Evelyn F.; m. Shirley Gale Hutchinson, May 28, 1966; children: Karen Lee Sabetta, Jeffrey William. BS in Chemistry, U. Mass. Dartmouth, 1966, MS in Chemistry, 1968; PhD in Oceanography, U. R.I., 1972. Grad. tchg. asst. U. Mass. Dartmouth, New Bedford, 1966—68; summer rsch. fellow Biochem. Rsch. Labs. Dow Chem. Co., Midland, Mich., 1968; grad. rsch. asst. Grad. Sch. Oceanography U. R.I., Kingston, 1968—69, fed. water quality adminstrn. fellow Grad. Sch. Oceanography, 1968—71; postdoctoral investigator, asst., assoc., sr. scientist Chemistry dept. Woods Hole Oceanographic Inst., Mass., 1971—88, dir. coastal rsch. ctr., 1982—87; Michael P. Walsh prof., dir. Environ. Scis. Program U. Mass., Boston, 1988—90; assoc. dir. edn., dean, sr. scientist Woods Hole Oceanographic Inst., 1990—2002, v.p. for acad. programs, dean, 2002—. Cons. several cos., adv. nat., internat. orgns. with respect to oceanography. Contbr. over 120 sci. jour. articles and book chpts. Trustee Bermuda Biological Station for Rsch, Bermuda, N.Y., 1990—, New Bedford Aquarium, 1998—, Big Brother/Big Sisters, Cape Cod and the Islands, Mass., 1998-2002; asst. cub master, Weblos leader Falmouth Pack, St. Barnabas Ch., Falmouth, Mass., 1978-79; overseer Sea Edn. Assn.,2005—. Recipient Best Paper award Organic Geochemistry Divsn./Geochemical Soc., Marine Educator award Mass. Marine Educators Assn., 1996, Excellence in Rsch. award U. R.I. Alumni/ae Assn., Kingston, 1998, USGS Amb. of Sci. award, 2001, David B. Stone award N.E. Aquarium, 2001, Bostwick H. Ketchum award WHOI, 2003, named nat. assoc. U.S. Nat. Academies, 2003 Mem. AAAS, Am. Chem. Soc., Am. Geophysical Union, Oceanography Soc., Estuarine Rsch. Fedn., N.Y. Acad. Sci., Sigma Xi (pres. Woods Hole chpt. 1995-96), Nat. Assoc. of the Nat. Academies. Protestant. Office: Woods Hole Oceanographic Inst MS #31 360 Woods Hole Rd Woods Hole MA 02543-1536

FARRIOR, EVAN BELL, special education educator, writer; b. Jersey City, June 2, 1952; BA, N.J. City U., 1977. Cert. tchr. of the handicapped. Supr. Hudson County Enterprise, Jersey City, 1978—83; tchr. spl. edn. Jersey City Pub. Sch., 1983—. Advocate for spl. needs Farrior Advocacy Svc., Jersey City, 1983—. Author: (book) Enoch: A Faith Tale, 1995, Love Is a Strange Thing, 2003. Notary pub., signing agt. Farrior Notary & Fax Svcs., Jersey City, 1995—; pres., owner Farrior Enterprise, Jersey City, 2002—; bus. adv. coun. Nat. Rep. Congl. Com.; pres. Evan B. Farrior Ministries Internat., Jersey City, 1995—. Named Golden Poet, World of Poetry, 1986, 1987, 1988, 1989, 1990, 1991, 1992; recipient citation, County of Hudson, 1991, Svc. award, Afro Am. Indsl. Women's Club, 1988, citation, County of Hudson, 1999, Businessman Yr., Nat. Rep. Congl. Com., 2003, 2004, Leadership award, 2003, Ronald Reagan Gold medal. Mem.: CEC, Nat. Rep. Congressional Com., Internat. Soc. Poet (Poet Yr. 1999, 2000, 2001, 2002, 2003, 2004), Flagship Interval Assn. Inc., Interval Internat., Spl. Olympics, N.J. State Coun. on Arts, Hudson County Coun. on Arts, Nat. Notary Assn., Famous Poet Soc. (Famous poet 1998, 1999, 2000, Famous Poet 2001, 2002, 2003), Internat. Soc. Poets (Editor's Choice 2000, 2001, 2002), Authors League of Am., Inc., Author's Guild, Am. Christian Writers, Feed the Children, N.J. Performing Arts Ctr., Learning Resource Ctr.-N/NS, N.J. Edn. Assn., Hudson County Edn. Assn., Jersey City Edn. Assn. Avocations: travel, writing, cooking, singing, listening to music. Home: 79 Charles St Jersey City NJ 07307 Office Phone: 201-656-0177. Personal E-mail: Enoch348@aol.com.

FARRIOR, JAMES L., III, lawyer; b. Vallejo, Calif., Jan. 21, 1962; s. James L. Jr. and Lee A. (Williams) F. BA, U. So. Miss., 1984; JD, U. Miss., 1987. Bar: Miss. 1987. Assoc. Fielding L. Wright Jr., Pascagoula, Miss., 1987-90; pvt. practice Pascagoula, Miss., 1990-94; asst. pub. defender Jackson County, Pascagoula, Miss., 1994-96; asst. dist. atty. Harrison County, Gulfport, Miss., 1996-97; pvt. practice Biloxi, Miss., 1997—. Office: 2555 Marshall Rd Biloxi MS 39531-4705

FARRIS, G. STEVEN, oil and gas production company executive; Graduate history, accounting, Okla. State Univ. Exec. v.p. Robert W. Berry Inc., 1978—83; v.p. & treas. Terra Resources, 1983—88; v.p. exploration and prodn. Apache Corp., Houston, 1988-91, sr. v.p., 1991-94, pres., COO, 1994—, CEO, 2002—, mem. exec. com. Mem. Nat. Petroleum Council. Mem. steering com. Energy for Teachers. Office: Apache Corp 2000 Post Oak Blvd Ste 100 Houston TX 77056-4400

FARRIS, JEFFERSON DAVIS, university administrator; b. Springdale, Ark., Sept. 30, 1927; s. Jeff D. and Loretta J. (Grunder) F.; m. Patricia Ann Camp, July 31, 1948; children— Rebecca, Elizabeth, Jefferson Davis III. BS in Engring, U. Central Ark., 1949; MA, Peabody Coll., 1950; M.P.H. (USPHS fellow), U. Mich., 1957; Ed.D., U. Ark., 1963; DHL, Sch. of Ozarks, 1981. Tchr. public high sch., Pine Bluff, Ark., 1950-57; dir. public health edn. Ark. Dept. Health, Little Rock, 1957-61; prof. health edn. U. Central Ark., Conway, 1961-86, chmn. dept. health and phys. edn., 1961-68, dean, 1968-75, univ. pres., 1975-86; nat. exec. dir. Nat. Assn. Intercollegiate Athletics, Kansas City, Mo., 1986-91. Mem. adv. com. Nat. Endowment Humanities; chair U.S. Collegiate Sports Coun., 1988-91. Editor: A Guide for School Health Education, 1956, Handbook for Elementary Physical Education, 1964. Mem. Ark. Gov.'s Council on Youth Fitness; bd. dirs. Conway (Ark.) Meml. Hosp., 1971-86, civilian aide for Ark. to sec. of army, 1979-81. Served with USN, 1946-48. Named Layman of Yr. Ark. Assn. Dentistry for Children, 1970 Mem. Ark. Assn. Deans (pres. 1968-75), Nat. Assn. Intercollegiate Athletics. Clubs: Rotary (pres. local, Paul Harris fellow 1986). Methodist. Home: 2 Delavaga Cir Hot Springs National Park AR 71909-6009 E-mail: jeffpat@cox.net.

FARRIS, JEROME, federal judge; b. Birmingham, Ala., Mar. 4, 1930; s. William J. and Elizabeth Farris; 2 children. BS, Morehouse Coll., 1951, LLD, 1978; MSW, Atlanta U., 1955; JD, U. Wash., 1958. Bar: Wash. 1958. Mem. Weyer, Roderick, Schroeter and Sterne, Seattle, 1958—59; ptnr. Weyer, Schroeter, Sterne & Farris and successor firms, Seattle, 1959—61, Schroeter & Farris, Seattle, 1961—63, Schroeter, Farris, Bangs & Horowitz, Seattle, 1963—65, Farris, Bangs & Horowitz, Seattle, 1965—69; judge Wash. State Ct. of Appeals, Seattle, 1969—79, U.S. Ct. of Appeals (9th cir.), Seattle, 1979—95, sr. judge, 1995—. Lectr. U. Wash. Law Sch. and Sch. Social Work, 1976—; mem. faculty Nat. Coll. State Judiciary, U. Nev., 1973; adv. bd. Nat. Ctr. for State Cts. Appellate Justice Project, 1978—81; founder First Union Nat. Bank, Seattle, 1965, dir., 1965—69; mem. US Supreme Ct. Jud. Fellows Commn., 1996—2002, Jud. Conf. Com. on Internat. Jud. Rels., 1997—2000; chmn. Ninth Circuit Judicial Conf. Com., Ninth Circuit Standing Com. on Fed. Pub. Defenders. Del. The White House Conf. on Children and Youth, 1970; mem. King County (Wash.) Youth Commn., 1969—70; vis. com. U. Wash. Sch. Social Work, 1977—90; mem. King County Mental Health-Mental Retardation Bd., 1967—69; past bd. dirs. Seattle United Way; mem. Tyee Bd. Advisers, U. Wash., 1984—88, bd. regents, 1985—97, pres., 1990—91; trustee U. Law Sch. Found., 1978—84, Morehouse Coll., 1999—; mem. vis. com. Harvard Law Sch., 1996—2005. With Signal Corps U.S. Army, 1952—53. Recipient Disting. Svc. award, Seattle Jaycees, 1965, Clayton Frost award, 1966. Fellow: Am. Bar Found. (chair of fellows 2000, bd. dirs. 1987, exec. com. 1989—97); mem.: ABA (exec. com. appellate judges conf. 1978—84, chmn. conf. 1982—83, exec. com. appellate judges conf. 1987—88, del. jud. adminstrn. coun. 1987—88, sr. lawyers divsn. coun. 1998—), State-Fed. Jud. Coun. State Wash. (vice-chmn. 1977—78, chmn. 1983—87), Wash. Coun. on Crime and Delinquency (chmn. 1970—72), U. Wash. Law Sch., Order of Coif (mem. law rev.). Office: US Ct Appeals 9th Cir 1200 6th Ave Ste 313 Seattle WA 98101

FARRIS, PAUL LEONARD, agricultural economist; b. Vincennes, Ind., Nov. 10, 1919; s. James David and Fairy Julia (Kahre) F.; m. Rachel Joyce Rutherford, Aug. 16, 1953; children: Nancy, Paul, John, Carl. BS, Purdue U., 1949; MS, U. Ill., 1950; PhD, Harvard U., 1954. Asst. prof. agrl. econs. Purdue U., West Lafayette, Ind., 1952-56, assoc. prof., 1956-59, prof., 1959-90, prof. emeritus, 1990—, head dept. agrl. econs., 1973-82; agrl. economist Dept. Agr., Washington, 1962; project leader for meat and poultry Nat. Commn. Food Mktg., Washington, 1965-66. Editor: Market Structure Research, 1964, Future Frontiers in Agricultural Marketing Research, 1983; contbr. articles to profl. jours. Served with AUS and USAAF, 1941-46. Fellow Am. Agrl. Econs. Assn.; mem. Am. Econ. Assn. Home: 1510 Woodland Ave West Lafayette IN 47906-2376 Office: Purdue U Dept Agrl Econs West Lafayette IN 47907

FARRIS, ROBERT HAROLD, JR., artist, educator; b. Lynn, Mass., Mar. 22, 1954; s. Robert Harold Sr. and Helen Louise (Castle) F. Student, Mass. Coll. Art, 1972-73. Assembler Western Electric Co., North Andover, Mass., 1973-74; designer's asst. Star Divsn./London Fog, Lynn, Mass., 1974-77; operator New Eng. Tel., Boston and Salem, Mass., 1977-87; customer svc. rep. Nynex Yellow Pages, Lynn, 1987-91; portrait artist East Boston Courthouse, 1991; artist Am. Embassy, Lima, Peru, 1992; owner Wood End Studio, Lynn, 1991—, tchr., 1995—; ptnr. Saltbox Gallery, Topsfield, Mass., 1994—, v.p., 1999. Contbg. artist WGBH 2 Collection, Boston, 1995—, Christopher Gallery, Cohasset, Mass., 1996—. Inductee Annual Grumbacher Calendar, 1997. Lectr. Greater Lynn Sr. Citizens, 1993; artistic supr. Sterling Cmty. Svcs., Lynn, 1994; fine art donor New Eng. Home for the Deaf, Danvers, Mass., 1996, North Shore Assn. Retarded Citizens, Salem, 1996-97. Recipient 4 Grumbacher Silver medalions Koh-I-Nor Corp., N.J., 1991-98, 3 Grumbacher Gold medallions Koh-I-Nor Corp., N.J., 1997; named to Grumbacher Hall of Fame, Koh-I-Nor Corp., N.J., 1996. Mem. Am. Soc. Classical Realism, Oil Painters Am. (assoc.), Soc. Egg Tempera Painters (artist), North Shore Art Assn. (artist), Lynnfield Art Guild (artist, bd. dirs. 1993, 6 awards 1992-95), Greater Lynn Arts and Crafts Soc. (artist, pres. 1993-94, 16 awards 1991-97). Avocations: antique collecting, gardening, woodworking, travel. Home and Office: Wood End Studio 188 Chatham St Lynn MA 01902-2221

FARRIS, ROBERT LINSY, ophthalmologist, director; s. Joseph Dean and Virginia Kelly Farris; m. Vivian Welk Welk, Apr. 2, 1960; children: Karen Farris Neus, Alan Linsy, Andrew Lawrence. MD, Duke U., 1961; MPH in Pub. Health, Columbia U., 1992. Diplomate Am. Bd. Ophthalmology, 1968. Dir. ophthalmology Harlem Hosp. Columbia U., N.Y., 1973—, prof. clin. ophthalmology, 1990—2005; intern Phila. Gen. Hosp., 1961—62; resident Columbia-Presbyn. Hosp., 1964—67. Contbr. articles to profl. jours. Pres. John Harms Performing Art Ctr., Englewood, NJ, 1985—87. Capt. USPHS, 1962—64. Recipient 1st prize for exhibit at ann. sci. meeting, Am. Acad. Ophthalmology, 1978; grantee, NIH, 1980—85. Mem.: Am. Ophthal. Soc. Presbyn. Achievements include development of tear osmolarity measurement. Avocations: music, jazz, performing bass player. Office: Columbia Ophthlmology Consultants 635 West 165th St New York NY 10037 Office Phone: 212-939-8305. E-mail: rlf1@columbia.edu.

FARRIS, TRUEMAN EARL, JR., retired newspaper editor; b. Sedalia, Mo., June 2, 1926; PhB in Journalism, Marquette U., Milw., 1948; MA in Polit. Sci., U. Wis.-Milw., 1989. Reporter Milw. Sentinel, 1945-62, asst. city editor, 1962-75, city editor, 1975-77, mng. editor, 1977-89. Juror Pulitzer Prizes, 1985-86; mem. dean's coun. Student Publs. Bd., Coll. of Comm., Journalism and Performing Arts, Marquette U., 1987-92; mem. bd. visitors U. Wis., Milw., 1991-2000; mem. commitment adv. panel, U. Wis., Milw., 2000; bd. dirs. Wis. Masonic Jour., Newspaper of State Grand Lodge, 1993—, pres. 2004—. Author series of stories: Japan, 1980. Served with U.S. Army, 1955 Recipient By-Line award Marquette U., 1987; named to Milw. Press Club Media Hall of Fame, 1989. Mem. AP Mng. Editors Assn. (dir. 1980-87, editor ann. reports 1979-85), Milw. Soc. Profl. Journalists (pres. 1982-83), Milw. Press Club (pres. 1968, several reporting awards, editorial writing award 1957, included Media Hall of Fame 1989), Civil War Round Table (sec.), Mil. Order Loyal Legion of U.S. (recorder). Methodist. Avocations: reading, genealogy, civil war history. Home: 3192 S 80th St Milwaukee WI 53219-3501 Office: Milwaukee Sentinel PO Box 371 Milwaukee WI 53201-0371

FARRIS, VERA KING, former college president; b. Atlantic City, July 18, 1940; BA in Biology magna cum laude, Tuskegee Inst., 1959; MS in Zoology, U. Mass., 1962, PhD in Zoology/Parasitology, 1965; LHD (hon.), Marymount Manhattan Coll., 1985; LLD (hon.), Monmouth Coll., West Long Branch, N.J., 1987; DSc honoris causa, Johnson and Wales Coll., 1988. Dean spl. programs, assoc. prof. pathology and biology SUNY, Stony Brook, 1968-72, vice provost acad. affairs, prof. biological sci. Brockport, 1973-80; v.p. acad affairs, prof. biological sci. Kean Coll. N.J., Union, 1980-83; pres. Stockton State Coll., Pomona, NJ, 1983—2003. Contbr. articles to profl. jours. Founding mem. Gov.'s Pride award acad., 1986—, Gov.'s adv. coun. Holocaust Edn. in N.J., 1982—. Recipient Golden Trefoil award, Delaware Valley Coun. Girl Scouts Am., 1987,Chancellors Medal for Exemplary and Extraordinary Svc., U. Mass., 1986, Honor Roll Ednl award Wash. Ctr. for Internships and Acad. Seminars, Commendation for Outstanding Achievement in Edn., N.J. Assembly, 1993, others; named Lifetime Honorary citizen of Atlanta, 1984, N.J. Woman or Yr. N.J. Woman's Mag. Mem. Am. Coun. Edn. (bd. dirs. 1988-91), Coun. Post-Secondary Accreditation (bd. dirs. 1988—), Middle States Assn. Colls. and Secondary Schs. (pres. bd. trustees), Am. Assn. State Colls. and Univs. (nominating com.), N.J. State Bd. Examiners, N.J. State Coll. Pres. (chair 1987-89), B'naiB'rith (life hon.), Cosmos Club (Washington). Home: 689 St Andrews Dr Egg Harbor City NJ 08215-5119

FARROW, MARGARET ANN, former lieutenant governor; b. Kenosha, Wis., Nov. 28, 1934; d. William Charles and Margaret Ann (Horan) Nemitz; m. John Harvey Farrow, Dec. 29, 1956; children: John, William, Peter, Paul, Mark. Student, Rosary Coll., 1952-53; BS in Polit. Sci. and Edn., Marquette U., 1956, postgrad., 1975-77. Tchr. Archdiocese of Milw., 1956-57; trustee Elm Grove Village, Wis., 1976-81, pres., 1981-86; mem. Wis. Assembly, Madison, 1986-89, Wis. Senate from 33rd dist., Madison, 1989—2001; lt. gov. State of Wis., 2001—03; dir. local govt. affairs Whyte Hirshboeck Dudek Govt. Affairs, 2003—. Chair govt. effectiveness, 1998-2001, asst. majority leader, 1998; mem. joint com. on audit, 1993-97, mem. joint survey com. on tax exemptions, 1993-97, chair Wis. women's coun., 1991—, Rep. caucus chair, 1996, 99, mem. coun. on workforce excellence, 1995—, mem. Wis. glass ceiling commn., 1993—; mem. Senate Com. on edn., 1999, Senate com. on labor, 1999. Republican. Home: W 262 # 2402 Deer Haven Dr Pewaukee WI 53072-4572*

FARRUG, EUGENE JOSEPH, SR., retired lawyer; b. Detroit, May 22, 1928; s. Michael and Bridget Mary (Foley) F.; m. Dolores Marie Augustine, Apr. 14, 1951; children: Elizabeth Marie Streit, Eugene Joseph Jr., Matthew Augustine, Pamela Ann, Bridget Louise, Donna Michele. BBA, U. Mich., 1950, JD, 1958. Bar: Ill. 1958, U.S. Dist. Ct. (no. dist.) Ill. 1958; U.S. Supreme Ct. 1980. With Lincoln-Mercury divsn. Ford Motor Co., Dearborn, Mich., 1950, with Aircraft Engine divsn., 1951; assoc. McKenna, Storer, Rowe White & Farrug, Dearborn, 1958-62, ptnr., 1962-92, of counsel, 1992—. Mem. Citizens of Greater Chgo., 1970-80, pres., 1976-79. Served with USN, 1951-55. McGreggor Fund scholar, 1946; Mich. Bd. Realtors scholar, 1949. Mem. Ill. Bar Assn., Chgo. Bar Assn., DuPage County Bar Assn., Am. Judicature Soc., Cath. Lawyers Guild, Phi Alpha Delta. Lodges: Kiwanis (pres. 1964). Home: 708 W Hinsdale Hinsdale IL 60521 Fax: 630-323-1162.

FARSHEE, MARLENA W., title company executive; b. Prattville, Ala., Sept. 30, 1964; d. Albert G. Wallace Jr. and Mary Margaret Gray; m. Charles Morgan King, Feb. 6, 1981 (dec. Jan. 1985); 1 child, Candice King; m. William B. Farshee, Jr., Aug. 8, 1999; children: Carly, Anna, William. Legal sec. Sasser & Littleton, PC, Mont., Ala., 1992—94; mgr. Closing Assocs., Prattville, 1994—98; pres. Flagship Closing Svcs., Mont., 1998—2004; owner Advantage Closing, LLC, Mont., 2004—. Mem.: Greater Montgomery Homebuilders Assn. (assoc. com. chair 2001—02, Assoc. of Yr. 2002), Women's Coun. Realtors, Real Estate Assn. Ala. (affiliate com. 2000—03). Republican. Methodist. Avocations: gardening, reading, boating. Home: 120 Huckleberry Dr Deatsville AL 36022 Office: Advantage Closing LLC 6767 Taylor Cir Montgomery AL 36117 Office Phone: 334-558-0166. Office Fax: 334-558-0213.

FARSON, DAVE FOREST, engineering educator; b. Marietta, Ohio, Sept. 10, 1958; s. Robert F. and Martha Clark F.; m. Paula M. Mourant, Aug. 31, 1991; children: Forrest, Ellis. PhD, Ohio State U., 1987. Rsch. assoc. Pa. State U., State College, 1988-95; assoc. prof. Ohio State U., Columbus, 1995—. Fellow Laser Inst. Am. (pres. 1997, dir. 1993—); mem. Am. Welding Soc. (Adams Meml. membership award 1998). Office: Ohio State U 1971 Neil Ave Columbus OH 43210

FARSON, RICHARD EVANS, psychologist; b. Chgo., Nov. 16, 1926; s. Duke Mendenhall and Mary Gladys (Clark) F.; m. Elizabeth Lee Grimes, May 21, 1954 (div. 1962); children: Lisa Page, Clark Douglas; m. 2d Dawn Jackson Cooper, Jan. 4, 1964 (div. 1990); children: Joel Andrew, Ashley Dawn, Jeremy Richard. BA, Occidental Coll., 1947, MA, 1951; postgrad., UCLA, 1948-50; PhD, U. Chgo., 1955. Dean Sch. Design Calif. Inst. Arts, Valencia, 1969-73; pres. Esalen Inst., Big Sur and San Francisco, 1973-75; faculty Saybrook Inst., San Francisco, 1975-79; pres. Western Behavioral Scis. Inst., La Jolla, Calif., 1958-68; chmn. bd. Western Behavior Scis. Inst., La Jolla, Calif., 1968-79, pres., 1979—. Dir. Internat. Design Conf. in Aspen, Colo., 1971-2001, pres. 1976-80, 94-97; pub. dir. AIA, 1999-2001. Editor: Science and Human Affairs, 1967; author: Birthrights, 1974, Management of the Absurd: Paradoxes in Leadership, 1996, (with others) The Future of the Family, 1969, (with Ralph Keyes) Whoever Makes the Most Mistakes Wins: The Paradox of Innovation, 2002. Served to lt. j.g. USNR, 1955-57. Fellow, World Acad. Arts. and Scis.; Ford Found. fellow, Harvard U. Bus. Sch., 1953—54, Sr. fellow, Design Future Coun. Fellow World Acad. Art Sci., Design Futures Council; mem. Am. Psychol. Assn., Sigma Xi, Psi Chi Home: 252 Prospect St La Jolla CA 92037-4225 Office Phone: 858-454-2048. E-mail: rfarson@wbsi.org.

FARTHING, CHARLES FRANK, medical educator, AIDS researcher; b. Christchurch, New Zealand, Apr. 22, 1953; came to U.S., 1989; s. Jack Raymond and Ngaire Emily (Green) F. MB, ChB, Otago Med. Sch., Dunedin, New Zealand, 1976; MD in Infestious Disease, SUNY, 1993. Diplomate Am. Bd. Internal Medicine. Intern, resident Christchurch Hosp., 1977-81; fellow in renal medicine Riyadh (Saudi Arabia) Mil. Hosp., 1981-82; registrar in genitourinary medicine St. Thomas' Hosp., London, 1982-83; resident in dermatology, AIDS rsch. fellow St. Stephen's Hosp., Westminster Hosp., London, 1983-89; acting investigator div. infectious disease NYU Med. Ctr., N.Y.C., 1989—; dir. Bellevue Hosp. AIDS program, 1992—; clin. asst. prof. medicine, 1993—. Bd. dirs. Found. for AIDS Counseling and Treatment, London, 1988—, Elton John AIDS Found., 1992—. Author: Colour Atlas of AIDS, 1986, AIDS Treatment, 1988; also articles. Mem. All Party Parliamentary Com. on AIDS, London, 1986-89; patron London Lighthouse, 1988—. Recipient award for svcs. to AIDS, Terence Higgins Trust, London, 1986; fellow Winston Churchill Meml. Trust, 1988. Fellow Royal Australasian Coll. Physicians, Royal Soc. Medicine; mem. ACP, AMA, Royal Coll. Physicians, Brit. Med. Assn. Episcopalian. Avocations: theater, skiing, travel, ballet, opera. Office: NYU Med Ctr 550 1st Ave New York NY 10016-6402 Address: 6415 W Olympic Blvd Los Angeles CA 90048-5329

FARUQI, ABDUL RAB, physician, consultant, researcher; arrived in U.S., 1997; s. Abdul Jabbar and Rehmat (Nisa) Faruqi; m. Noshaba Anjum, Apr. 22, 1974; children: Abdul Ali, Sana Rab. MBBS, Dow Med. Coll., Karachi, Pakistan, 1972, DCH, 1980. Cert. pulmonary medicine and infectious disease. Intern Dow Med. Coll., Civil Hosp., Karachi, 1972; med. dir. S. Asia Merrel Dow Pharm., Hong Kong, 1986—88, Marion Merrel Dow, Australia, 1992—95; assoc. global med. dir. Merrl Dow, Pakistan, 1989—92; med. dir. S. Asia Hoechst Marion Roussel, Singapore, 1996—97, sr. dir. clin. rsch. Bridgewater, NJ, 1997—98; head arthritis bone/clin. ops. Aventis Pharm., Bridgewater, 1998—2002; cons. med. dir. gen. medicine Aventis U.S. Med. Rsch., Bridgewater, 2003—. Hon. editor-in-chief: Asian Med. News, 1985. Fellow: Chinese Anti Tuberculosis Assn., Am. Coll. Chest Physicians; mem.: Am. Thorasic Soc., Societa Italiana di Chemitoterapia, Japan Anti Tuberculosis Assn. (hon.), Internat. Union Against Tuberculosis and Lung Disease, N.Y. Acad. Scis. Avocations: travel, squash, cricket. Home: 1020 Sunset Ridge Bridgewater NJ 08807 Office Phone: 908-243-6857. Office Fax: 908-243-7871. Personal E-mail: rabfaruqi@yahoo.com.

FARVARDIN, NARIMAN, engineering educator; b. Tehran, Iran, July 15, 1956; m. Hoveida Farvardin. BS in elec. engring., Rensselaer Poly. Inst., Troy, NY, 1979, MS in elec. engring., 1980, PhD in elec. engring., 1983. Asst. prof. elec. and computer engring. U. Md., 1984—88, assoc. prof., 1988—93, prof., 1993—, joint appt. Inst. for Systems Rsch., chair dept. elec. and computer engring., 1995—2000, dean A. James Clark Sch. Engring., 2001—; vis. prof. Ecole Nationale Superieure des Telecommunications, Paris, 1990—91. Co-recipient Award of Excellence, Md. Indsl. Partnerships Program, 1992, Invention of Yr. Award, U. Md., 1999; recipient George Corcoran Award, Dept. Elec. Engring., U. Md., 1987, Presdl. Young Investigator Award, NSF, 1987, Outstanding Systems Engring. Faculty Award, Inst. for

Systems Rsch., U. Md., 1993. Fellow: IEEE; mem.: Am. Soc. Engring. Edn. Avocations: racquetball, reading, music. Office: Clark Sch Engring U Md 3110 Kim Enring Bldg College Park MD 20742 Business E-Mail: farvar@umd.edu.

FARVER, JANE, museum director; Dir. Lehman Coll. Art Gallery, CUNY, 1989—92; dir. exhbns. Queens Mus. Art, 1992—97; dir. List Visual Arts Ctr., MIT, 1999—. Curator Global Conceptualism: Points of Origin, 1950s-1980s. Office: List Visual Arts Ctr 20 Ames St Bldg E15 Cambridge MA 02139 E-mail: jfarver@mit.edu.*

FARWELL, ELWIN D., minister, consultant; b. Branch County, Mich., May 1, 1919; s. Don J. and Dessa (Clingan) F.; m. Helen Irene Hill, Aug. 23, 1942; children: Don Lucian, Helen Kay, James Lyman, Judith Anne. BS, Mich. State U, 1943, MS, 1947; EdD, U. Calif. at Berkeley, 1959; BD, Pacific Lutheran Theol. Sem., Berkeley, 1959; LLD (hon.), Loras Coll., 1969, Valparaiso U., 1980, Luther Coll., 1986, Dana Coll., 1992, Calif. Luth. U., 1994; LHD (hon.), St. John's U., 1981, St. Olaf Coll., 1982. Instr. animal husbandry Mich. State U., 1947-49, asst. prof., 1949-55; cons. point 4 program State Dept. U. Nacional, Colombia, 1952; adminstrv. asst. to chmn. Center Study Higher Edn., U. Calif. at Berkeley, 1956-59; ordained to ministry Luth. Ch., 1958; pastor in Andrew, Iowa, 1959-61; academic dean Calif. Luth. Coll., Thousand Oaks, Calif., 1961-63; pres. Luther Coll., Decorah, Iowa, 1963-82; vis. scholar U. Calif.-Berkeley, 1982; profl. cons., 1983—; pres. Dana Coll., Blair, Nebr., 1985-86; dir. study theol. edn. Luth. Ch. U.S.A., 1984-86; adminstrv. cons. Pacific Luth. Theol. Sem., 1987-88; interim bishop Nebr. Synod Evan. Luth. Ch. in Am., 1990; interim pastor St. Paul Luth. Ch., Monona, Iowa, 1990-91, 97; interim bishop Rocky Mountain Synod Evangel. Luth. Ch. in Am., 1993-94. Author: Livestock Development and Selection, 1951, (with others) Stability of Change, 1964; contbr. articles to profl. jours., encys. Mem. Iowa Gov.'s Com. Conservation Natural Resources, 1964-68, Iowa Gov.'s Commn. Coop. State and Local Govt., 1964-66; mem. Iowa Coordinating Coun. Higher Edn., 1967-70, pres., 1968-69; chmn. Com. Intergovtl. Coop. and Comm., 1964-65, Gov.'s Com. on Govt. Reorgn., 1966, State Adv. Com. on Cmty. and Jr. Coll., 1965-69; mem. exec. com. Iowa Assn. Pvt. Colls. and Univs., 1964-73, 76-78, chmn., 1971-72; chmn. Coun. Coll. Pres.'s Am. Luth. Ch., 1976-77; mem. exec. com. Norwegian-Am. Mus. Assn., 1965-71; chmn. World Brotherhood Found., 1962-77; chmn. Iowa Coll. Found., 1968-69; mem. Iowa Campaign Fin. Disclosure Commn., 1977-91, chmn., 1980-81, 87-89; mem. Iowa Mental Health Adv. Coun., 1978-81, Am. Scandinavian Found.; bd. govs. Calif. Luth. Ednl. Found., 1957-59; bd. dirs. Inst. European Studies, 1977-81; bd. Nat. Luth. Campus Ministry, 1966-69; pres. Luth. Ednl. Conf. N.Am., 1973-74, mem. legis. policy com., 1978-81; counselor Luth. Coun. U.S.A., 1975-79; bd. dirs. Gundersen Med. Found., La Crosse, Wis., 1976-81; bd. regents Dana Coll., 1986-95; trustee Iowa Natural Heritage Found., 1983-92, Iowa Humanities Found., 1992-2002; bd. dirs. Luth. Social Svc. of Iowa, 1992-95, Winneshiek County Hosp. Found., 1992-97. Capt. U.S. Army, 1943-46, PTO. Decorated Knight's Cross 1st class Order St. Olav, 1975, Knight's Cross 1st class Order No. Star, 1977 (Sweden); recipient Disting. Patriarchs award Mich. State U., 1993. Mem. Ctrl. State Coll. Assn. (dir. 1964-76, chmn. 1967), Nat. Assn. Ind. Colls. and Univs. (bd. dirs. 1977-78), Oneota Golf and Country Club (pres. 1987-89), Rotary, Phi Beta Kappa, Phi Delta Kappa, Alpha Gamma Rho, Alpha Zeta. Lutheran. Home: 504 Locust Rd # 3 Decorah IA 52101-1002 Personal E-mail: farwelle@luther.edu.

FARWELL, NANCY LARRAINE, public relations executive; b. Sellersville, Pa., May 2, 1944; d. Warren Gregory and Mary Rita (Zaniboni) F. BA, Pa. State U., 1966. Asst. TV rep. H.R. TV Reps., Phila., 1966-68; various positions Hawthorne Advt. Inc., Phila., 1968-73; dir. employee rels. Colonial Penn Group, Inc., Phila., 1973-75, mgr. press rels., 1976-78, mgr. pub. rels., 1978-82; dir. comm. Provident Mut. Life Ins. Co., Phila., 1982-83, asst. v.p., comm., 1983-87; pres. Nancy Farwell Assocs., Phila., 1987-90; v.p. Anne Klein & Assocs., Inc., Mt. Laurel, NJ, 1990-92, sr. v.p., 1992-97, sr. v.p., COO, 1998-2001, sr. v.p. strategic planning, 2001—03, sr. councilor, 2003—. Adv. bd. City of Phila. Century IV Tall Ships, 1982. Author: (photo essay) Philadelphia, 1976; contbr. chpt. to home health care mktg. book. Founder, co-chair Portico Row Neighborhood Assn., Phila., 1989-92; bd. dirs. Washington Sq. West Project Area Com., Phila., 1990-92, Boys and Girls Clubs of Metro Phila. Adv. Coun., 1991—; adv. com. Phila. 6th Police Dist., 1990-92. Mem. Pub. Rels. Soc. Am. (9 Pepperpot awards, Award of Excellence, Silver Anvil award of Excellence), Phila. Pub. Rels. Assn. Office: Anne Klein and Assoc Inc 401 Route 73 N Ste 108 Marlton NJ 08053-3429 Office Phone: 856-988-6564.

FARWELL, WALTER MAURICE, vocalist, educator; b. Sidney, Iowa, Mar. 29, 1928; s. Clyde Ross and Erma Leona (Liggett) F. B.Mus.Edn., U. Mo., Kansas City, 1950; MA, U. Iowa, 1953. Vocal music tchr. pub. schs., Fayette, Iowa, 1953-59; head voice tchr. Wartburg Coll., Waverly, Iowa, 1960-61; vocal music tchr. pub. schs., Tipton, Iowa, 1961-67, music educator Davenport, Iowa, 1967-90. Choir dir. Meth. Ch., Fayette, Tipton, 1953—; vocal soloist, 1953—; organist Replacement Tng. Ctr., Ft. Bragg, N.C., 1951-52. Author: (4 vols.) History of Fremont County, Iowa, 1968-91; contbr.: Bells of Stony Creek, 1994; editor: Court Records Atchison County, Mo. (pamphlet), 1985; cons. (county history) Thumbprints in time, 1996; contbr. historical articles to profl. pubs. Cpl. U.S. Army, 1950-52. Recipient Am. Legion award, 1941. Mem. NEA, Davenport Area Ret. Tchrs. Assn., Fremont County Hist. Soc. (charter). Methodist. Avocation: historical and genealogical research. Home: 549 E 4th St Tipton IA 52772-1933 E-mail: farwellwalter@hotmail.com.

FASANO, ANTHONY JOHN, marketing consultant; b. San Antonio, Sept. 22, 1947; s. Patrick Joseph and Frances (Greco) F.; m. Leatine Winders, June 21, 1984. AA, Iowa State U., 1968, BS, 1969. Program dir. KDMI-FM, Des Moines, 1966-68; asst. dir. Sta. WHO-TV, Des Moines, 1968-71; advt. assoc. San Antonio Light Newspaper, 1971-75; advt. dir. San Antonio Mag., 1976-77; pres. Anthony J. Fasano & Assocs., San Antonio, 1977—; dir. mktg. cons. Southwestern Bell Yellow Pages, San Antonio, 1997-98; v.p. account supr. Dialogue Works, 1999; prodr. DM programs Leukemia and Lymphoma Soc., 1999—2003. Mktg. dir. Environ. Delivery Systems, San Antonio, 1988-90; v.p. prodn. devel. Parent Banc, 1990-95, co-developer children's product, 1990-95. Direct mail campaign mgr. Exec. Tel., 1985, Security Link, 1987-92; account mgr. DM program Tie Communication Dealer Co-op., 1987-89; creative dir. campaign The Gun Cleaning Sys., 1988-90. Active Tex. Rep. Party, 1979—. Mem. Direct Mktg. Assn. Roman Catholic. Avocations: stamp collecting/philately, bicycling, exercise. Home and Office: 555 Crooked Oak Dr Spring Branch TX 78070-4927 Office Phone: 830-228-4648. E-mail: afasano@ajfdirect.com.

FASEL, IDA, literature and language professor, writer; b. Portland, Maine, May 9, 1909; d. I.E. Drapkin and Lilian Rose Harwich; m. Oscar A. Fasel, Dec. 24, 1946 (dec. Apr. 1973). BA summa cum laude, Boston U., 1931, MA, 1945; PhD, U. Denver, 1963. Mem. faculty English U. Conn., New London, Midwestern U., Wichita Falls, Tex., Colo. Woman's Coll., Denver; prof. English U. Colo., Denver, 1962-77, prof. emerita of English, 1977. Presenter in field; contest judge. Transl. from French and Italian, editl. cons.: Renaissance and Baroque Lyrics, 1962; author (poetry): On the Meanings of Cleave, 1979 (Nortex Publ. award), Where Is the Center of the World?: Selections From Seven Chapbooks, 1981-1991, 1999 (U. Fla. and Before the Rapture Press prize chapbooks), All Real Living Is Meeting, 2000, The Difficult Inch, 2000, Journey of a Hundred Years, 2002 (Colo. Book award, 2003), Air, Angels and Us, 2002, Waking to Light, 2002 (Best Chapbook Angels Without Wings Found., 2003), Aureoles, 2002, The True Purpose of Planes, 2004; contbr., editl. cons.: The Study and Writing of Poetry, 1983; contbr. articles to profl. jours., chpts. to books, poetry to anthologies and jours.; author: (poetry) Leafy as a Locust Tree, 2005. Faculty Rsch. fellow U. Colo., 1979; recipient Disting. Alumni honor Boston U., 1979, Alumni Poetry prize, 1983, 85, Before the Rapture Chapbook prize, 1985, Colo. Poet Honor, Friends of Denver Pub. Libr., 1991, Panhandler Chapbook prize, U. West Fla., 1991, Prize Poems award Colo. Authors League, 1993-94. Mem. Milton Soc. Am. (life), Friends of Milton's Cottage (charter), Assn. Literary Scholars and Critics, Conf. on Christianity and Lit., Poetry Soc. Tex., Colo. Endowment for the Humanities, Denver Woman's Press Club, Phi Beta Kappa. Avocations: ballet, Star Trek, collecting angels, piano, translating French poetry. Home: 165 Ivy St Denver CO 80220-5846

FASH, VICTORIA R., business executive; Sr. v.p. bus. strategy Dun & Bradstreet Corp., 1995-96; exec. v.p., CFO Cognizant, 1996—; exec. v.p., chmn., CEO IMS Internat., Westport, Conn., 1999—. Bd. dirs. Orion Capital Corp. Office: IMS Health Inc 1499 Post Rd Fairfield CT 06430-5940

FASHING, EDWARD MICHAEL, ranch owner, physical science educator; b. Chgo., Jan. 27, 1936; s. Michael George and Leontine (LeClercq) F.; m. Annette Louise Lubker, Jan. 29, 1959; children: Anita Fashing Kiska, Mary Fashing Schillig, Edward Jr., James, John. BS in Chemistry, Loyola U., Chgo., 1960; MS in Chemistry, DePaul U., 1968; postgrad., U. Mo., 1982-84. Cert. jr. coll. chemistry tchr., Ill. Instr. geology, phys. sci., chemistry of hazardous materials Triton Coll., River Grove, Ill., 1969-81; Simmental cattle rancher and vinologist Cedar Ln. Farm, Sturgeon, Mo., 1973—; asst. prof. N.E. Mo. State U. (Truman State), Kirksville, Mo., 1981-82; chemistry asst. U. Mo., Columbia, 1982-84; instr. physics Columbia (Mo.) Coll., 1986; summerreading tchr. Centralia Elem. Sch., 1998—. Writer, news commentator, show moderator, producer Farm Forum Sta. KOPN-Radio, 1985-89; freelance reporter, columnist, proofreader Am. Agr. Reporter; editor Mo. Am. Agr. Newsletter, 1990—; mem. editl bd., writer religious and cultural cyber jour. Just Good Company, 2002—. Nat. v.p. coms. Am. Agr. Movement, 2003—; leader 4H, Sturgeon, 1974—84, 1988; creator posters Mo. Rural Crisis Ctr., Columbia, 1986—93, bd. dirs., 1989—92; publicity dir. Am. Agrl. Movement Grassroots, 1985, demonstrator, 1985, spokesman Chgo. demonstrations, 1984, 1985, 1986; mem. Nat. Farm Org.; v.p. coms. Am. Agr. Movement Inc. of Mo., 1991—; bd. dirs. Farm Alliance of Rural Mo., 1986—89, 1995—, pres., 1997—99, v.p., 1999—2001; mem. N.Am. Farm Alliance, Orgn. for Competitive Markets; lobbyist Nat. Farmers Union, 1990; Dem. rep. Mo. State Conv., 1988; Roman Cath. ch. cantor, lector, extraordinary min. NSF grantee, 1966, 76; 2d place winner steer carcass judging contest Mo. State Fair, 1995; breeder of 10 winning steer carcasses, 1973-99, Boone County, Mo. and Mo. State Fair, 1995, 2000. Mem.: AAAS, Am. Chem. Soc., Am. Corn Growers Assocs., Mo. Stockmans Assn., Am. Chem. Soc. Democrat. Avocations: rockhounding, gardening, writing, entomology. Address: Cedar Ln Farm 2898 Audrain Road 114 Sturgeon MO 65284-2023 E-mail: emfashing@socket.net.

FASICK, ADELE MONGAN, library and information scientist, educator; b. N.Y.C., Mar. 18, 1930; d. Stephen Leo and Florence (Geary) Mongan; m. Frank Fasick, Aug. 14, 1955 (div. 1986); children: Pamela, Laura, Julia. BA, Cornell U., 1951; MA, Columbia U., 1954, MSLS, 1956; PhD, Case Western Reserve U., 1970. Libr. N.Y. Pub. Libr., 1955-56, L.I.U., Bklyn., 1956-58; asst. prof. Rosary Coll., River Forest, Ill., 1970-71; prof. U. Toronto, 1971-96, dean Faculty of Libr. and Info. Sci., 1990-95. Adj. prof. San Jose State U., 1999—, U. .C., 2002—. Author: Managing Children Services in Public Libraries, 1991, 2d edit., 1998, Beauty Who Would Not Spin, 1987; co-author: ChildView, 1987; editor: Lands of Pleasure, 1990; editor International Research Abstracts: Youth Library Services, 1993—. Mem.: ALA (com. on accreditation 1990—92), Assn. Librs. and Info. Sci. Edn. (pres. 1992), Internat. Fedn. Libr. Assn. (sec./treas. sect. on reading 1997—2003), Assn. Libr. Svc. to Children (exec. bd. 1980—84). E-mail: amfasick@earthlink.net.

FASKE, DONNA See KARAN, DONNA

FASMAN, ZACHARY DEAN, lawyer; b. Chgo., Oct. 27, 1948; s. Irving D. and Lillian V. (Vilatzer) F.;m. Andrea L. Udoff; children: Jonathan, Benjamin, Rebecca. BA, Northwestern U., 1969; JD, U. Mich., 1972. Bar: Ill. 1972, D.C. 1977, N.Y. 2001, U.S. Supreme Ct. 1977. Assoc., then ptnr. Seyfarth, Shaw et al, Chgo. and Washington, 1972-81; ptnr. Wald, Harkrader et al, Washington, 1981-83, Crowell & Moring, Washington, 1983-88, Paul, Hastings, Janofsky & Walker, Washington, 1988—2000, NYC, 2000—. Author: Equal Employment Audit Handbook, 1983, Employment Law Compliance Manual, 1988, What Business Must Know About The ADA, 1992. Mem. ABA (labor law sect., litig. sect.), Coll. Labor and Employment Lawyers, Order of Coif. Office: Paul Hastings Janofsky & Walker 75 E 55th St New York NY 10022 Home: 52 Game Farm Rd Pawling NY 12564 Office Phone: 212-318-6315. Office Fax: 212-318-6837. E-mail: zacharyfasman@paulhastings.com.

FASNACHT, HEIDE ANN, artist, educator; b. Cleve., Jan. 12, 1951; BFA, R.I. Sch. Design, 1973; MA in Studio Art, NYU, 1981. Vis. artist Bennington Coll., Vt., 1980, 1983, Cranbrook Acad., Bloomfield Hills, Mich., 1984, Cleve. Art Inst., 1981; asst. prof. art SUNY-Purchase, 1981—87; art instr. Parson's Sch. Design; vis. artist R.I. Sch. Design, 1985, Md. Inst. Coll. Art, 1985; asst. prof. dept. visual and environ. studies Harvard U., Cambridge, Mass., 1993—94, Pilchuck artist-in-residence, 2004. One-woman shows include New Gallery of Contemporary Art, Cleve., 1981, Vanderwoudel/Tananbaum Gallery, N.Y.C., 1983, 1985, Hill Gallery, Birmingham, Mich., 1984, 1986, Germans van Eck Gallery, N.Y.C., 1988, Yale U. Art Gallery, 2002, Kent Gallery, N.Y.C., 2003, 2005, Galeria Trama, Barcelona, 2003, Galerie les Filles du Calvaire, Paris and Brussels, 2005. Fellow, MacDowell Colony, 1981, 1983, 2005, Yaddo, 1980, 1985, Hand Hollow Found., 1983, Rockefeller Found., 2003, Lucas Vusiual Arts Program, Montalvo; grantee, NEA, 1979, 1994, Athena Found., 1983, Louis Comfort Tiffany Found., 1986, Guggenheim Mus., 1991, Adolph and Esther Gottlieb Found. Home: 4 White St Apt 4A New York NY 10013-2469 Personal E-mail: heidestudio@earthlink.net.

FASS, PAULA SHIRLEY, history educator; b. Hannover, Fed. Republic Germany, May 22, 1947; d. Chaim Harry and Bluma Rose F.; m. John Emmett Lesch, July 13, 1980; children: Bluma Jessica Fass Lesch, Charles Harry Taylor Lesch. AB, Barnard Coll., 1967; MA, Columbia U., 1968, PhD, 1974. Lectr. Rutgers U., New Brunswick, N.J., 1972-73, asst. prof., 1973-74; from asst. prof. to prof. U. Calif., Berkeley, 1974—98, Chancellors prof., 1998—2001, Margaret Byrne prof., 2002—. Cons. Aspen Inst. for Humanistic Studies, 1975-76, Poynter Inst. for Media Studies. Author: The Damned and the Beautiful: American Youth in the 1920's, 1977, Outside In: Minorities and the Transformation of American Education, 1989; editor: The American Social Experience, Kidnapped: Child Abduction in America, 1997, Childhood in America, 2000, Teh Encyclopedia of Children in History and Society (3 vols.), 2004; contbr. articles to profl. jours. Fellow NEH, 1979, 85-86, 91, 94-95, Rockefeller Found., 1976-77, U. Calif. Regents, 1980-81, 91, Ctr. for Advanced Study in Behavioral Scis., 1991-92. Mem. Am. Hist. Assn., Orgn. Am. Historians, History Edn. Soc., Phi Beta Kappa. Jewish. Avocations: poetry, cooking, gardening, travel. Office: U Calif Dept History Berkeley CA 94720-0001

FASS, PETER MICHAEL, lawyer, educator; b. Bklyn., Apr. 11, 1937; s. Irving and Bess (Fordin) F.; m. Deborah K. Orshan, May 6, 1989; 1 child, Olivia Jae; children from previous marriage: Brian Samuel, Lyle Williams. BS in Econs. with honors, U. Pa., 1958; JD cum laude, Harvard U., 1961; LLM, NYU, 1964. Bar: N.Y. 1965; CPA. From assoc. to ptnr. Carro, Spanbock, Fass, Geller, Kaster & Cuiffo, N.Y.C., 1968-86; ptnr. Kaye, Scholer, Fierman, Hayes & Handler, N.Y.C., 1988-95, Battle Fowler LLP, N.Y.C., 1995-2000, Proskauer Rose LLP, N.Y.C., 2000—. Adj. asst. prof. real estate NYU; lectr. Practicing Law Inst., N.Y. Law Jour., Instl. mag., Ill. Inst. Continuing Legal Edn.; spl. cons. Calif. Commr. of Corps Real Estate Adv. Com.; mem. ad hoc com. Real Estate Securities and Syndication Inst., chmn. regulatory legis. and taxation com., 1975-76; mem., dir. participant/real estate com. NASD, 1991-94. Co-author: Tax Advantaged Securities, 1977—, Real Estate Syndication Handbook, 1985-87, Tax Aspects of Real Estate Investments, 1988—, Blue Sky Practice Handbook, 1987—, Real Estate Investment Trusts Handbook, 1987—, S Corporation Handbook, 1985—, Tax Advantaged Securities Handbook, 1979—; contbr. articles to profl. jours. Recipient Haskins award for outstanding achievement in N.Y. State CPA's exam., 1964. Mem. ABA (chmn. real estate investment com., real property, probate and trust sect.), N.Y. State Bar Assn., Am. Inst. CPA's, N.Y. State Soc. CPA's, Pi Lambda Phi, Beta Gamma Sigma, Beta Alpha Psi. Home: 115 Central Park W New York NY 10023-4153 Office: Proskauer Rose LLP 1585 Broadway New York NY 10036-8299 Office Phone: 212-969-3445. Personal E-mail: reitman411@aol.com. Business E-Mail: pfass@proskauer.com.

FASSEL, DIANE MARY, organizational consultant; b. San Antonio, Sept. 12, 1945; d. Robert Alois and Mary Jane (Stokman) F. BA, Webster U., 1968; MA, Harvard U., 1974; PhD, Union Inst., 1987. Chair English dept. Loretto H.S., Kansas City, Mo., 1968-72; cmty. life coord. Loretto Cmty., Denver, 1974-78; pvt. practice Denver, 1978—92, Boulder, Colo., 1994—; v.p. Wilson Schaef Assoc., Boulder, 1992-94; pres. Newmeasures, Inc., Boulder, 1997—. Advisor Am. Arbitration Assn., Denver, 1978-84. Author: The Addictive Organization, 1988, Working Ourselves to Death, 1990, Growing Up Divorced, 1991, Organizational Capabilities, 1996. Bd. dirs. St. Mary's Acad., Denver, 1978-86; exec. com. Loretto Cmty., Denver, 1978-82; mediator CDR Assoc., Boulder, 1984, bd. dirs., 2001—. Democrat. Roman Catholic. Avocations: horseback riding, snorkeling, bicycling, movies.

FASSEL, JIM (JAMES E. FASSEL), professional football coach; b. Anaheim, Calif., Aug. 31, 1949; m. Kitty Fassel; children: John, Brian, Jana, Mike. Coach Fullerton Coll., 1973; player, coach Hawaii Hawaiians, WLF, 1974; coach U. Utah, 1976, head coach, 1985—89; coach Weber St., 1977—78, Stanford U., 1979—83; asst. coach New Orleans Breakers, USFL, 1984; asst. head coach/offensive coord. Denver Broncos, 1993—94; quarterback coach Oakland Raiders, 1995; offensive coord., quarterback coach Ariz. Cardinals, 1996; asst. coach N.Y. Giants, 1991-92, head coach, 1997—2003; sr. cons. Baltimore Ravens, 2004—05, offensive cord., 2005—. Named NFL Coach of the Yr., 1997. Office: c/o Baltimore Ravens 1101 Russel St Baltimore MD 21230

FASSOULIS, SATIRIS GALAHAD, communications company executive; b. Syracuse, N.Y., Aug. 19, 1922; s. Peter George and Anastasia P. (Limpert) F. BA, Syracuse U., 1945. V.p. Commerce Internat. Corp., 1949—75; chmn. Global Comm. Co., N.Y.C., 1976—, Global Def. Products Inc., N.Y.C., 1976—; pres. CIC Internat. Ltd., 2000—, Columbia Def. Corp., 2000—; chmn. CIC Aerospace Corp. Dir Comml. Exports (Overseas) Ltd., U.K., CIC Internat. Ltd., NYC, Colombia Tech. Corp., Colombia Energy Corp., Africa One Ltd. Mem. U.S. Congl. Adv. Bd.; bd. dirs. Better Life Enterprises for the Blind, Inc.; chmn. Internat. Cultural Exch. 1st lt. USAAF, 1941-45. Decorated Purple Heart, Air medal with 3 oak leaf clusters, Prisoner of War medal. Mem. N.Y. C. of C., Am. Def. Preparedness Assn., Navy League U.S., Armed Forces Comm. and Electronics Assn., U.S. Naval Inst., Air Force Assn., Assn. U.S. Army, Internat. Platform Assn., N.Y. Athletic Club, Order Ahepa. Republican. Episcopalian. Home: 20 Waterside Plz New York NY 10010-2612 Office: 5 Marine View Plz Apt 310 Hoboken NJ 07030 Office Phone: 201-792-1800. Personal E-mail: sgfcic@compuserve.com.

FAST, ERIC CARSON, diversified financial services company executive; b. Boston, July 10, 1949; s. Robert Eberle and Carol (Waters) F.; m. Patricia Nelson, May 30, 1980; children: Allison, Christina, Lillian. BA, U. N.C., 1971; MBA, NYU, 1978. Asst. treas. U.S. Industries Inc., N.Y.C., 1975-80; treas. Macmillan Inc., N.Y.C., 1980-84; v.p. Salomon Bros. Inc., N.Y.C., 1984-88, dir., 1988-89, mng. dir., 1989-91, co. head domestic corp. fin., co-head of global investment banking; bd. dir. Crane Co., 1999—, pres., COO, 1999—2001, pres. CEO, 2001—. Office: c/o Crane Co. 100 First Stamford Place Stamford CT 06902*

FAST, HENRYK, mathematician, educator; s. Leon and Regina (Stiel) Fast; m. Nora Elisabeth Vazquez, Apr. 1990 (div. Aug. 2003); children: Monica, Tamara, Maximiuk, Simon, Sheila, Jessica. MS, U. Wroclaw, Poland, 1951; PhD in Math., Polish Acad. Sci., Warsaw, 1958. Adj. instr. U. Wroclaw, Poland, 1956—60; asst. prof., math. U. Notre Dame, Ind., 1962—66; prof., math. Wayne State U., Detroit, 1966—94. Contbr. articles to profl. jours. Avocation: painting. Home: 13751 Rustic Dr Royalton OH 44133 E-mail: hfast@earthlink.net.

FAST, JULIUS, writer, editor; b. NYC, Apr. 17, 1919; s. Barnett Arthur and Ida (Miller) F.; m. Barbara Hewitt Sher, June 8, 1946; children: Jennifer, Melissa, Timothy Hewitt. BA, NYU, 1941. Sr. writer Smith, Kline & French Pharms., Phila., 1955-57; chief dept. med. communications Purdue Fredericks, N.Y.C., 1957-62; feature editor Med. News, 1962-63; sr. editor Med. World News, 1963-64; editor Ob-Gyn Observer, N.Y.C., 1965-75. Author: (mystery novels) Watchful at Night, 1945, Bright Face of Danger, 1946, Walk in Shadow, 1948, Model for Murder, 1956, Street of Fear, 1959, A Trunkfull of Trouble, 2002, (fiction) What Should We Do About Davey?, 1987, (sci. fiction) League of Grey-Eyed Women, 1970, (nonfiction) Blueprint for Life, 1963, Beatles, 1968, What You Should Know About Sexual Response, 1966, Body Language, 1970, Incompatibility of Men and Women, 1971, You and Your Feet, 1971, The New Sexual Fulfillment, 1972, Bisexual Living, 1974, The Pleasure Book, 1975, Creative Coping, 1976, The Body Language of Sex Power and Aggression, 1977, Psyching Up, 1978, Weather Language, 1979, Talking Between the Lines, 1979, Body Politics, 1980, The Body Book, 1981, Sexual Chemistry, 1983, Ladies Man, 1983, The Omega-3 Breakthrough, 1987, Subtext, 1990, Legal Atlas of the United States, 1996, Courtroom Communication Skills, 1994. Served with AUS, 1942-46. Recipient Mystery Writers Am. award, 1944 Home: 720 West End Ave Apt 1608 New York NY 10025-6299

FAST, KENNETH H., lawyer; b. Newark, Apr. 1929; s. Moe M. and Eva H. Fast; m. Judith Nicholson, Nov. 23, 1969; children: Jonathan Nicholson, Madelaine M. BA, Lafayette Coll., 1951; LLB, Yale U., 1954. Bar: N.J. 1954, D.C. 1954, U.S. Ct. Appeals (3d cir.) 1958, U.S. Supreme Ct. 1960. Ptnr. Fast & Fast, East Orange, N.J., 1957-86, Fox & Fox, Livingston, N.J., 1987—. Trustee Weisberger Fund for Age, Poor and Needy, Livingston, N.J., 1969—. 1st lt. USAF, 1955-57. Mem. N.J. State Bar Assn., Essex County Bar Assn. Home: 91 Fairfield Dr Short Hills NJ 07078-1718 Office Phone: 973-597-0777.

FAST, LARRY GLEASON, psychologist; b. Bartlesville, Okla., June 14, 1946; s. Edwin and Evelyn Marie Fast; m. Brenda Sue Dossey, Oct. 11, 1969; children: Tamarah Lea, Ryan Scott. BA, Baylor U., 1968; MS, Kans. State U., 1973. Cert. sch. psychologist Nat. Assn. Sch. Psychologists, 1979. Grad. asst. Dept. Psychology Kans. State U., Manhattan, Kans., 1971—73; dir. McPherson (Kans.) Youth Ctr., 1973—75, Grace Children's Home, Henderson, Nebr., 1976—78; house parent Youth Outreach, Vancouver, Wash., 1978—79; psychologist Evergreen Sch. Dist., Vancouver, 1979—. Tchr. various chs., 1968—. 1st lt. U.S. Army, 1968—71, Vietnam. Mem.: Nat. Assn. Sch. Psychologists, Wash. State Sch. Psychol. Assn. Republican. Bapt. Avocations: reading, hiking, camping, travel. Home: 9105 NE 68 St Vancouver WA 98662 Office: Evergreen Sch Dist Spl Svc 49th St Vancouver WA 98668 Office Phone: 360-604-6400 x7508. Personal E-mail: lbfast@pacifier.com.

FASTENAU, PHILIP S., neuropsychologist, educator; s. Emmett H. and Doris P. Fastenau; m. Dana R. Atkinson. BA in Sociology, Concordia Coll., 1984; MS in Exptl. Psychology, Appalachian State U., 1988; PhD in Clin. Psychology, Mich. State U., 1994. Lic. health svc. provider in psychology Ind. Lectr. Appalachian State U., Boone, NC, 1989; instr. Mich. State U., East Lansing, 1991—93; postdoctoral fellow U. of Mich. Med. Ctr., Ann Arbor, 1994—96; asst. prof. Ind. U. Purdue U. Indpls., 1996—2002, assoc. prof., 2002—; mem. exec. bd. Ctr. for Therapeutic Behavioral Neurosci., Indpls., 2002—. Instr. Appalachian State U., Boone, NC, 1989; assessment coord., supr. Mich. State U. Psychol. Clinic, East Lansing, 1991—93; instr. Mich. State U., East Lansing, 1991—93; mem. grad. faculty Purdue U., West Lafayette, Ind., 1996—, assoc. mem. grad. faculty, 1997—; affiliated scientist Ind. U. Ctr. for Aging Rsch., Indpls., 1999; cons. neuropsychologist Riley

Hosp. for Children, Indpls., 1999—; team neuropsychologist Indpls. Colts, 1999—; adj. asst. prof. clin. psychology Ind. U. Sch. Medicine, Indpls., 2001—; presenter in field. Contbr. articles to profl. jours. Recipient Jr. Investigator Travel award, Nat. Inst. of Neurol. Disorders and Stroke and The Epilepsy Found., 2000, Jr. Investigator Rsch. award, Epilepsy Found. of Am., 1996; grantee, NIH/Nat. Inst. of Neurol. Disorders and Stroke, 2000—07, NIH/Nat. Inst. of Nursing Rsch., 2002—04, Cyberonics, Inc., 1998—99, Epilepsy Found., 1999—2000, Eli Lilly & Co., 2000, U.S. Dept of Edn. and Rehab. Svcs. Adminstrn., 1997—2000, NIH/Nat. Inst. of Nursing Rsch., 1997—2002, Clarian Health Ptnrs., 1999—2001. Mem.: AAUP, APA (Dissertation award 1992), Ind. Psychol. Assn., Midwestern Neuropsychological Group, Epilepsy Found. Am. (grantee 1997—98), Am. Epilepsy Soc., Nat. Acad. of Neuropsychology, Internat. Neuropsychol. Soc., Alpha Kappa Delta (life), Psi Chi (life). Achievements include invention of Extended Complex Figure Test, a psychometric test of visual-spatial memory used in diagnosing neurological disorders. Office: Ind U Purdue U Indpls Psych (LD 124) 402 N Blackford St Indianapolis IN 46202-3275

FASUSI, JIMMY ADEBAYO, small business owner; s. John Olawole Fasusi and Harold Harford; m. Patricia Elizabeth Harford, Feb. 15, 2002. BSc, U. Ibadan, Nigeria, 1995. Cert. engr., Nat. Inst. Sci. and Tech., Nigeria. Mgr. Circuit City, Frederick, Md., 1998—2002; pres., CEO X-Class Corp., Kensington, Md. Mem.: IEEE. Home: 5630 Duchaine Dr Lanham MD 20706 Office: X-Class Corp 3827 Plyers Mill Rd Kensington MD 20895 Office Phone: 301-946-0800. Office Fax: 301-946-0801. Personal E-mail: jfa820@aol.com. E-mail: jimmy@kensingtonofficemachines.com.

FATEMI, FARAMARZ SAIFPOUR, history and political science educator, consultant; b. Isfahan, Iran, Aug. 6, 1935; came to US, 1949; s. Nasrollah Saifpour Fatemi and Shayesteh (Ostovar) F.; m. Afsar Nouri-Esfandiary, Dec. 15, 1962; children: Faranak, Roshanak. BA, Earlham Coll., Richmond, Ind., 1955; MA, Columbia U., 1958; PhD, New Sch. for Social Rsch., 1976. Prof. Fairleigh Dickinson U., Teaneck, NJ, 1961—, chair dept. history, polit. sci. and internat. studies, 1984-95, dir. Sch. Polit. and Internat. Studies, 1996-99, dir. Sch. History, Polit. and Internat. Studies, 2000—; CEO Nouri Enterprises, Ho-Ho-Kus, NJ, 1991—; pres. acad. senate Fairleigh Dickinson U., Teaneck, NJ, 1994-96, participant bd. trustees. Vis. prof. Shippensburg (Pa.) State Coll., 1964-65, 69; dir., CFO Fairleigh Dickinson Credit Union, Madison, NJ, 1987—; pres. Lakeland chpt. NJ Credit Union League, 1998-99; mem. Ctr. for Internat. Studies, Bergen C.C., Paramus, NJ, 1980-95, chmn., 1992-93; vis. scholar Wolfson Coll., Cambridge (Eng.) U., 1984, Consortium on Global Interdependence, Princeton, 1985; fellow Peace Inst., Kyung Hee U., Seoul, 1985—. Author: USSR in Iran, 1980; co-author: Sufism: Message of Brotherhood, Harmony and Hope, 1976 (Internat. Book award UNESCO 1977), Love, Beauty and Harmony in Sufism, 1978; editor: Reflections on the Time of Illusion, Vol. II, 1991, Editor, Reflection on the Time of Illusion, Vo. III, 2002. Mem. adv. bd. Internat. Awareness Network, NYC, 1991—; mem. NJ World Trade Coun., Trenton, 1992—, bd. dir., 1996—, vice chmn., 2001-; advisor Persian Humanitarian and Cultural Soc., Passaic, NJ, 1988—. Recipient Kurt Riezler Meml. award New Sch. for Social Rsch., 1976, Disting. Faculty Svc. award Fairleigh Dickinson U., 1993, Meritorious Svc. award Credit Union Affiliatees NJ, 1999. Mem. Phi Alpha Theta, Pi Sigma Alpha. Office Phone: 201-692-2272. Business E-Mail: fatemi@fdu.edu.

FATEMI, KHUSROW, academic administrator, economics educator; BA, Abadan Inst. Tech., Iran; MBA, PhD in internat. rels., Univ. So. Calif. Sr. economist Nat. Iranian Oil Co., 1972—79; asst. prof. Middle Tenn. State Univ., 1979—82; prof. internat. bus. Tex. A&M Univ., 1982—90, dean coll. bus., grad. sch. internat. trade & bus. adminstrn., 1990—98; dean, prof. internat. bus. San Diego State Univ., Imperial Valley, 1998—2004; pres. Ea. Oreg. Univ., La Grande, 2004—. Editor (founding): Global Economy Quarterly, The Internat. Trade Jour.; contbr. articles to profl. jours. Bd. dir. U.S.-Mex. C. of C. Mem.: Internat. Mgmt. Develop. Assn. (past pres., Internat. Dean of the Year 1999). Office: Eastern Oregon Univ Office of the President 1 University Blvd La Grande OR 97850-2899*

FATHAUER, THEODORE FREDERICK, meteorologist; b. Oak Park, Ill., June 5, 1946; s. Arthur Theodore and Helen Ann (Mashek) Fathauer; m. Mary Ann Neesan, Aug. 8, 1981. BA, U. Chgo., 1968. Cert. cons. meteorologist. Rsch. aide USDA No. Devel. Labs., Peoria, Ill., 1966, Cloud Physics Lab., Chgo., 1967; meteorologist Sta. WLW Radio/TV, Cin., 1967-68, Nat. Meteorol. Ctr., Washington, 1968-70, Nat. Weather Svc., Anchorage, 1970-80, meteorologist-in-charge Fairbanks, Alaska, 1980-98, lead forecaster, 1998—. Instr. USCG Aux., Fairbanks, Anchorage, 1974—, U. Alaska, Fairbanks, 1975—76; specialist in Alaska meteorology. Co-author: Denali's West Buttress, 1997, Living with the Coast of Alaska, 1997; contbr. articles to mags. and jours. Bd. dirs. Fairbanks Concert Assn., 1988—, Friends U. Alaska Mus., 1993—, pres., 1993—95, sec., 1997—98; bd. dirs. Fairbanks Symphony Assn., 1994—, sec., 1994—2001, treas., 2001—; trustee U. Alaska Found., 1997—, mem. coll. fellows, 1993—, mem. exec. com., 1997—, vice chair, 1998—99, chair, 2000—01; mem. adv. bd. Salvation Army, Fairbanks, 1997—; bd. dirs. No. Alaska Combined Fed. Campaign, 1996—, campaign chmn., 1996—97; bd. visitors U. Alaska, Fairbanks, 1995—. Recipient Fed. Employee of the Yr. award, Fed. Exec. Assn., Anchorage, 1978. Fellow: Royal Meteorol. Soc., Am. Meteorol. Soc. (mem. sci. and tech. adv. com. coastal environments 1998—2004, TV and radio seals approval, co-chmn. Conf. Coastal Environment 2003); mem.: AAAS, Am. Sailing Assn., Can. Meteorol. and Oceanog. Soc., Oceanography Soc., Arctic Inst. N.Am. (exec. sec. U.S. Corp. 1998—2003, bd. govs. U.S. Corp. 2003—), Western Snow Conf., Am. Geophys. Union, Greater Fairbanks C. of C. Republican. Lutheran. Avocations: reading, music, skiing, canoeing. Home: 1738 Chena Ridge Rd PO Box 80210 Fairbanks AK 99708-0210 Office: Nat Weather Svc Forecast Office Internat Arctic Rsch Ctr U Alaska PO Box 757345 Fairbanks AK 99775-7345 Office Phone: 907-474-5606. Business E-Mail: ted.fathauer@gi.alaska.edu.

FATOVIC, ROBERT DEAN, lawyer, transportation executive; b. Englewood, NJ, Mar. 1965; m. Leeanna D. Black. BS in fin., magna cum laude, Boston Coll., 1987, JD, 1990. Bar: NJ 1991, NY 1991, Fla. 1997. Assoc. Hannoch Weisman, PC, NJ, 1990—94; asst. div. counsel Ryder System Inc., Miami, 1994—96, assoc. div. counsel, 1996, chief counsel, 1996, sr. v.p. US Supply Chain Operation, High-Tech and Consumer Industries, now exec. v.p., gen. counsel, corp. sec. Mem.: ABA. Office: Ryder System Inc 11690 NW 105 St Miami FL 33178 Office Phone: 305-500-3726.*

FATT, WILLIAM R., hotel executive; b. Toronto, Ont., Can., Mar. 11, 1951; BA in Econs., York U., Toronto. Auditor Thorne Riddell, Toronto, 1973-75; asst. contr. Revenue Properties Co. Ltd., Toronto, 1975-77; acctg. analyst The Consumers Gas Co., Toronto, 1977-78; asst. treas. Hiram Walker Resources, Toronto, 1978-82, treas., 1982-84, v.p., treas., 1984-86; v.p. Morgan Bank of Can., Toronto, 1986-88; treas. Can. Pacific Ltd., Toronto, 1988, v.p., treas., 1988-90, v.p. fin. and acctg., CFO, 1990-94, exec. v.p. and CFO Toronto and Calgary, 1994; CEO Fairmont Hotels & Resorts (formerly Can. Pacific Hotels Corp.), Toronto, 1998—; also bd. dirs. Vice chmn., trustee Legacy Hotels Real Estate Investment Trust; bd. dirs. Embridge Inc., Sun Life Fin. Inc., EnCana Corp. Office: Fairmont Hotels & Resorts 100 Wellington St W # 1600 Toronto ON Canada M5K 1B7

FATTAH, ABBAS, research scientist; b. Isfahan, Iran, July 5, 1955; m. Sabih Mir; children: Hadi, Shadi, Sara. BS, Shiraz U., Iran, 1978; MS, Isfahan U. of Tech., Iran, 1989; PhD, McGill U., Can., 1995. Lectr. Isfahan U. Tech., 1981—90, asst. prof., 1996—2001; teachnig and resaerch asst. in robotics and mech. sys. McGill U., Montreal, 1990—95; rsch. scholar U. Del., Newark, 2001—. Contbr. articles to profl. jours. Recipient Paper award, Ministry of Sci. Rsch. and Tech., 2000; scholar, McGill U., 1990—95. Mem.: ASME. Office: Univ Del Dept Mech Engring 126 Spencer Lab Newark DE 19716 Office Phone: 302-831-6541. Business E-Mail: fattah@me.udel.edu.

FATTAH, CHAKA, congressman, former state legislator; b. Phila., Nov. 21, 1956; m. Renée Chenault; 3 children. Student, Phila. C.C., 1976; M. in Govt., U. Pa., 1986; student, Harvard U. Mem. Pa. Ho. of Reps., 1982-88, Pa. State Senate, 1988-94; congressman, Pa. 2nd Dist. U.S. House Reps., Washington, D.C., 1995—. Mem. house adminstr. com., com. on appropriations, VA-HUD subcom. Founder Am. Cities Conf. and Found.; leader task force Child Devel. Initiative, Phila.; founder, convenor Grad. Opportunities Conf., Pa.; chmn. exec. com. Pa. Higher Edn. Assistance Agy.; creator Jobs Project. Recognized nationally for outstanding leadership Time Mag.'s roster of Amer.'s most promising leaders, 1994, Ebony Mag.'s one of 50 Future Leaders, 1984; recipient Pa. Pub. Interest Coalition's State Legislator of Yr. award. Democrat. Baptist. Office: US Ho Reps 2301 Rayburn Hob Washington DC 20515-0001: 4104 Walnut St Philadelphia PA 19104*

FATTAL, LAURA RACHEL, arts supervisor; b. N.Y.C., June 25, 1952; d. Carroll and Muriel Gertrude (Schwartz) Felleman; m. Jacob Fattal; children: Alexander Leor, Felix. BA, SUNY, 1974; MA, Hunter Coll., 1976; PhD, U. Tex., 1984. Cert. art K-12 Pa., NJ, NY. Art hist. tchr. U. of Arts, Phila., 1984—88; tchr. of gifted Cheltonham Pub. Sch., Pa., 1988—90; curator of edn. Aimmerli Art Mus., New Brunswick, NJ, 1990—94; dir. of NJ sch. of arts State Dept of Edn., Trenton, NJ, 1995—2002; arts supr. Plainfield Pub. Sch., Plainfield, NJ, 2002—. Indep. art reviewer, 1988—. Contbr. articles various profl. jours. Concert series organizer Cheltenham Music in the Parks. Mem.: NAEA, Coll. Art Assn., Nat. Art Educators, Art Table, AAM, CAA. Jewish. Avocations: bicycling, walking, hiking, reading, travel. Home: 405 Shoemaker Rd Elkins Park PA 19027 Office: Plainfield Pub Sch 925 Arlington Ave Plainfield NJ 07060 Office Phone: 908-731-4200 x 5353. E-mail: jfattal@comcast.net.

FATTORI, RUTH A., human resources specialist, electronics executive; BS, Cornell U. Advanced mfg. engr., various human resources positions Xerox Corp.; mng. dir. European ops., v.p., chief quality officer GE Capital, London; sr. v.p. human resources Siemans Corp., Siemans AG, Asea Brown Boveri; exec. v.p. process and productivity Conseco, Inc.; sr. v.p. human resources, comm. productivity and quality global tech. infrastructure group JPMorgan Chase & Co.; exec. v.p. human resources Motorla, Inc., Schaumburg, Ill., 2004—. Bd. trustees Polytechnic U., Trinity Pawling Sch. Office: Motorola Inc 1303 E Algonquin Rd Schaumburg IL 60196 Office Phone: 847-576-5000. Office Fax: 847-576-5372.*

FAUCETTE, GLORIA MARIE, accountant, educator; b. Burlington, N.C., Aug. 29, 1948; d. Jesse Graham and Mildred Kathryn Faucette. BA in Social Scis., Elon Coll., 1982; BS in Acctg., N.C. A&T State U., 1991; MBA, Elon Coll., 1993. Social worker Alamance County Dept. Social Svcs., Burlington, NC, 1974-89; instr. acctg. and bus. N.C. A&T State U., Greensboro, NC, 1991-99, N.C. AT&T State, Greensboro, NC, 2000—01; acct. Cobb Ezekiel Brown and Co., Graham, NC, 1999—2000; bus. tchr. Hawfields Mid. Sch., 2001—. Mem. acad. rels. com. Inst. Internal Auditors, Greensboro, 1996-97; cons. bus. ednl. career decisions mid/secondary sch. students; small bus. cons. Contbr. articles to profl. jours. Mem. AICPA, N.C. Assn. CPA (mem. acctg. edn. com. 1995-97; chair careers in acctg. com. 1999), Beta Alpha Psi, Beta Gamma Sigma Democrat. Methodist.

FAUCHIER, DAN RAY, arbitrator, mediator, law educator, construction executive; b. Blackwell, Okla., Sept. 27, 1946; s. Wallace Monroe and Betty Lou F.; m. Sylvia Stephanie Chan Fauchier, Mar. 15, 1969; 1 child, Angele Calista Fauchier; m. Jonah Keri, 1997. BA cum laude, Southwestern Coll., 1964-68; student, Sch. Theology, Claremont, Calif., 1968-69, Claremont Grad. Sch., 1969-70. Lic. bldg. contractor, Calif.; cert. arbitrator and mediator. Min. of youth First United Meth. Ch., Winfield, Kans., 1964-68, First Congl. Ch., Riverside, Calif., 1968-69; adminstr. Calif. Youth Authority, Chino and Paso Robles, Calif., 1969-76; tchr. Chaffey Coll., Rancho Cucamonga, Calif., 1971-74; dir. Pacific Fin. Svcs., Beverly Hills, Calif., 1977-81; pres. Littlefields Corp., Santa Maria and Corona del Mar, Calif., 1978-81; cons. Hughes Helicopters, Oasis Oil, Jakarta, Indonesia, 1981; systems designer Teltrans Corp., L.A., 1982-85; project mgr. Pacific Sunset Builders, L.A., 1985-87, DW Devel., Fontana, Calif., 1987-90; owner Fauchier Group Builders, San Diego, 1988—; pres. Empire Bay Devel. Corp., San Bernardino, Calif., 1991-92; project mgr. White Sys. L.A. Ctrl. Libr., 1993; dir. project mgmt. White Sys. divsn. Pinnacle Automation, Inc., San Diego, 1993-95; dir. project mgmt.; dir. design logistics White Systems divsn. Pinnacle Automation, Inc., San Diego, 1995-97; v.p. SDC & Assocs., San Diego and Washington, 1997-2000; tchr. Power Summit, 2000—, dir., bd. advisors, 2001—; dir. constrn. svcs. LaJolla Ctr. Dispute Resolution, 2003—. Founding dir. Neighborhood Restoration Project, San Bernardino, Calif., 1991-92; cons. project mgr. White Sys., Inc., Cin. Pub. Libr., 1997, FCC Document Mechanization Project, 1998; instr. U. Calif. San Diego, 1998-2001; Inst. Constrn. Mgmt., arbitrator and mediator Arbitration Works, 1999—2003 Saddle Island Inst., 1999—; instr. San Diego State U., 2001-02, mediator panelist La Jolla Ctr. Dipsute Resolution, 2003—, dir. constrn. svcs., 2004—; v.p. Realignment Group, Ltd., 2005—. Contbr. cons.: President's Commission on Criminal Justice, 1972; co-author: Consumer Credit, 1984. Deputy Registrar Voters San Bernardino, Calif., 1975; mem. Skid Row Mental Health Adv. Bd., L.A., 1986, Chaffey Coll. Adv. Bd. Rancho Cucamonga, Calif., 1991-95, chmn. Bus. Security Alliance, San Bernardino, Calif., 1992; founding exec. dir. EGCA Found., 2004—. Named Nat. fellow Woodrow Wilson Fellowship, Princeton, N.J., 1968-69; Grad. scholar State of Calif., Claremont, 1969. Mem. Associated Gen. Contractors (chmn. edn. com. 1999-2001), Am. Subcontractor Assn. (chmn. mktg. com. 1999-2000), Associated Builders and Contractors, Nat. Elec. Contractors Assn., Forensics Cons. Assn., Nat. Found. for Dispute Rev. Bds., Engring. Gen. Contractors Assn. (pub. works advocate), ABA Constrn. Industry Forum, Self-Realization Fellowship, Christmas in April (bd. dirs., v.p. 1999-2000), Habitat for Humanity, Internat. Platform Assn., Inst. for Cmty. Econ., Homeless Coalition, People for Ethical Treatment of Animals, Rainforest Alliance. Avocations: painting, photography, writing. Home: PMB249 9921 Carmel Mountain Rd San Diego CA 92129-2813 E-mail: dan@danzpage.com.

FAUCI, ANTHONY STEPHEN, federal agency administrator, allergist, immunologist; b. Bklyn., Dec. 24, 1940; s. Stephen A. and Eugenia A. Fauci. AB, Coll. of Holy Cross, 1962; MD, Cornell U., 1966; DSc (hon.), Coll. Holy Cross, 1987, Georgetown U., 1990, Hahnemann U., 1990, Mt. Sinai Sch. Medicine, 1990, Universita di Roma, 1990, St. John's U., 1991, Long Island U., 1992, Med. Coll. Wis., 1993, Bard Coll., 1993, Bates Coll., 1993, SUNY, Farmingdale, 1994, U. Conn. Health Ctr, 1994, Duke U., 1995. Diplomate Am. Bd. Internal Medicine, Am. Bd. Allergy and Immunology (bd. dirs. 1984 to date), Am. Bd. Infectious Diseases. Intern N.Y. Hosp.-Cornell Med. Ctr., 1966—67, asst. resident in medicine, 1967—68, chief resident dept. medicine, 1971—72; clin. assoc. Nat. Inst. Allergy and Infectious Diseases-NIH, Bethesda, Md., 1968—70, sr. staff fellow, 1970—71, sr. investigator, 1972—74, head, clin. physiology sect., 1974—80, dep. clin. dir., 1977—80, chief Lab. Immunoregulation, 1980—, dir., 1984—; dir. Office of AIDS Rsch., NIH, assoc. dir. NIH for AIDS Rsch., 1988—94. Cons. Naval Med. Ctr., Bethesda, 1972—. Contbr. numerous articles to profl. jours. With USPHS, 1968—96. Named One of the Top 50 Scientific Leaders, Scientific Am., 2003; recipient meritorious svcs. award, USPHS, 1979, Arthur S. Fleming award, 1983, Squibb award, Infectious Diseases Soc., 1983, Commrs. Spl. Citation, FDA, 1984, Clemons von Pirquet award, Georgetown U. Med. Ctr., 1986, Disting Clin. Educator award, NIH Clin. Ctr., 1988, Leadership award, Columbus Citizens Found., Inc., 1988, spl. award for rsch. in AIDS, Nat. Hemophilia Fedn., 1989, Lee P. Brown Nat. Pub. Svc. award, Nat. Acad. Pub. Adminstrn. and Nat. Soc. for Pub. Adminstrn., 1989, numerous awards, Duke U., AMA, Children's Hosp., Nat. Med. Ctr., Surgeon Gen., Am. Assn. Physicians for Human Rights, Nat. Health Coun., Nat. Found. Infectious Disease, Helen Hayes award for med. rsch., 1989, Excellence in Pub. Svc. award, Com. for Support of Pub. Svcs., 1990, Lifetime Sci. award, Inst. Advanced Studies in Immunology and Aging, 1990, Internat. Chiron prize, 1990, Pres. award, N.Y. Acad. Sci., 1990, Thomas H. Ham-Louis R. Wasserman award, Am. Soc. Hematology, 1992, Dr. Nathan Davis award, AMA, 1992, Outstanding Achievement award, Howard U., 1992, Humanitarian award, Tiro a Segno Fedn., 1993, Cartwright prize, Columbia U. Coll. Physicians and Surgeons, 1993, Commr. of Honor award, SUNY-Farmingdale, 1994, Theobald Smith award, Albany Med. Coll., 1995, Coord. Com. award, ABA, 1996, David Rumbough Sci. award, Juvenile Diabetes Fedn. Internat., 1996, award, Nat. Coun. Internat. Health, 1996, March of Dimes Fedn., 1996, Ellen Browning Scripps medal, Scripps Fedn. Medicine and Rsch., 1996, Md. Gov.'s Citation, 1997, Thomas J. D'Alesandro Jr. award, Assoc. Italian Am. Charities, 1997, San Marino prize for medicine, 1997, John P. McGovern award, Am. Med. Writers Assn., 1997, many others, Berry prize in fed. med., 1999, Frank Annunzio award, Christopher Columbus Fellowship Found., 2001, Albany Med. Center prize, 2002, Ellis Island Family Heritage award, Statue of Liberty-Ellis Island Found., 2003. Master: AAAS (Westinghouse award 1988); fellow: Am. Acad. Microbiology, Am. Acad. Arts and Scis., ACP (Richard and Hinda Rosenthal award 1995, John Phillips Meml. award 1997), Am. Acad. Allergy, Am. Acad. Allergy and Immunology (hon.), Am. Med. Writers Assn. (hon.), N.Y. Acad. Medicine (hon.); mem.: Royal Acad. Medicine (Spain), Royal Danish Acad. Sci. and Letters (fgn.), Inst. Medicine of NAS, Assn. of Am. Physicians (recorder 1988—93, councillor 1993—), Am. Soc. for Clin. Investigation, Infectious Diseases Soc. Am., Commd. Officers Assn. USPHS (Pub. Health Leader of Yr. award), Internat. AIDS Soc., Am. Fedn. Clin. Rsch. (pres. 1980—81), Am. Soc. Cell Biology, Am. Soc. Virology, Am. Assn. Immunologists (program chmn. 1982—85, Kober lectr. 1988). Roman Catholic. Avocations: running, tennis. Office: Nat Inst Allergy & Infectious Diseases MSC 6612 6610 Rockledge Dr Bethesda MD 20892-6612

FAUCI, PETER ANTHONY, JR., surgeon; b. N.Y.C., Jan. 13, 1933; s. Peter Anthony and Mary (Mayo) F.; m. Linda Kelly; children: George, Peter III. AB, Columbia U., 1953; MD, Boston U., 1957. Diplomate Am. Bd. Surgery. Intern Jersey City Med. Ctr., 1957-58; resident in surgery Bellevue Hosp./Cornell Univ. Divsn., N.Y.C., 1958-60, Met. Hosp./N.Y. Med. Coll., 1960-62; pvt. practice New Rochelle, N.Y., 1964—. Attending surgeon New Rochelle Hosp. Med. Ctr., 1964; cons. surgeon Calvary Hosp., N.Y.C., 1970—; clin. asst. prof. surgery N.Y. Med. Coll., Valhalla, 1964—. Contbr. articles to med. jours. Capt. U.S. Army, 1962-64. Fellow ACS; mem. Am. Soc. Breast Surgeons, N.Y. State Med. Soc., Westchester Med. Soc., Westchester Surg. Soc., Larchmont Shore Club, Rotary. Democrat. Roman Catholic. Office: 175 Memorial Hwy New Rochelle NY 10801-5635 Office Phone: 914-235-6540. E-mail: pafjrmd@aol.com.

FAUDE, WILSON HINSDALE, museum director, consultant; b. Hartford, Conn., Feb. 20, 1946; s. John Paul and Helen (Hinsdale) Faude; m. Janet Bailey, 1985; children: Sarah Hinsdale, Paul Bailey. BA, Hobart Coll., 1969; MA, Trinity Coll., 1975. Curator Mark Twain Meml., Hartford, 1971—78; exec. assoc. to v.p. for devel. U. Hartford, West Hartford, Conn., 1981—85; exec. dir. Old State House, Hartford, 1978—81, 1985—2001, exec. dir. emeritus, 2002—; guest curator Wadsworth Atheneum, 2004. Commr. Conn. Arts Commn., 1975—83, hon. mem. 350th commn., 1984—86; commr. Conn. Hist. Commn., 1980, chmn., 1984—96. Author: (book) Renaissance of Mark Twain's House, 1977, The Great Hartford Picture Book, 1985, The Old Photograph Series: Hartford, 1994, The Old Photograph Series: Hartford, vol. II, 1995, The Old Photograph Series: Hartford, vol. III, 1997, Lost Hartford, 2000, The Old Photograph Series: West Hartford, 2004; author: (with others) Connecticut Firsts, 1978, 1985, 1996, 2000, Birthplace of Democracy, 1979; contbr. articles to profl. jours.; Cow Parade, 2004. Reader Talking Books for the Blind and Handicapped Conn. Vols. Svcs., 1986—; mem. faculty Cooperstown (NY) Seminars, 1979—80, 1984—88; corporator Hartford Art Sch., West Hartford, 1980—98; mem. Conn. Heritage Task Force, 1980—82; corporator Hartford Hosp., 1992—; bd. dirs. Conn. Equestrian Ctr., 1996, Stowe Ctr., 1996—97, Conn. Women's Hall of Fame, 1996—2004; trustee Renbrook Sch., West Hartford, 1984—85; hon. trustee Mark Twain Ho., 1997—. With U.S. Army, 1969—71. Named Capt., 1st Co. Gov. Foot Guard, 1979—, Civitan Man of the Yr., 1997; recipient 1st prize needlepoint, Ea. State Expn., 1997, Disting. Adv. for the Arts award, State of Conn., 1998, Thomas Hooker award for disting. cmty. svc., Ancient Burying Ground Assn., 1999. Mem.: Pub. Rels. Soc. Am. (Pub. Svc. Merit award 2001), Mark Twain Meml., Century Assn., Nat. Arts Club, Druid Soc. Episcopalian. Home and Office: 42 Fulton Pl West Hartford CT 06107-1128 Office Phone: 860-523-8226. Personal E-mail: wilsonfaude@comcast.net.

FAUGHT, BRENDA DORMAN, health sciences educator; m. Jesse Albert Faught. AA, Phoenix Coll., 1970—73. Master Tchr. Tex. State PTA, 1998. Testing clk. Midland Coll., Tex., 1998—2000, health sciences continuing edn. specialist, 2002—. Tchr., kids coll. Midland Coll., Tex., 1992—97; store mgr. Connie's Fashion, Midland, Tex., 1993—94; owner Party Pizazz, Midland, Tex., 1993—95; substitute tchr. Midland Ind. Sch. Dist., 1994—95; part-time testing clk. Midland Coll., Tex., 1995—98. Pres. Volunteers In Pub. Schools, Midland, Tex., 1988—89, Midland City Coun. of PTA, Tex., 1989—90, Goddard Jr. H.S., Midland, Tex., 1990—91, Midland Freshman H.S., Tex., 1991—92, Midland H.S. PTA, Tex., 1993—94; mem. Midland Symphony Guild, Tex., 1992—99; parade of homes chmn./treas. Jr. Woman's Club, Midland, Tex., 1985—90; pres. Opportunity Ctr. Aux., Midland, Tex., 1983—84, Santa Rita Elem. Sch. Parent, Tchr. Assn., Midland, Tex., 1986—87; by-laws com. mem. Alamo Heights Bapt. Ch., Midland, Tex., 1990—93, spl. events com. chmn., 1989—92, vacation bible sch. chmn., 1989—90, parliamentarian, 1998—99; pres. & mem. Youth Centers, Midland, Tex., 1992—93; pres., treas. Greater Midland Football Cheerleader Bd., Tex., 1989—92; mem. Midland Coll. 25th Anniversary, Tex., 1998—99; pres. Cert. Pub. Accountants Wives Club, Midland, Tex., 1975—81. Recipient Nat. Dean's List, Ednl. Comm., Inc., 1997—98, 1998—99. Mem.: Tex. Administrators of Continuing Edn. for Cmty./Jr. Colleges (assoc.), Tex. PTA (hon.; life mem.), Phi Theta Kappa Hono Soc. (life), Sigma Kappa Nat. Social Sorority (life; pres. of Midland alumnae 1975—80, Ernistine Duncan Collins Pearl Ct. Award 1989). R-Consevative. Southern Bapt. Avocations: ceramics, party decorating, needlecrafts, crewel, tennis. Office: Midland Coll 3600 N Garfield - DHS #228 Midland TX 79705 Personal E-mail: bdfmidtx@aol.com. E-mail: bfaught@midland.edu.

FAUL, JUNE PATRICIA, education specialist; b. Detroit; d. John William and Shirley Olive (Block) Lynch; m. George Johnson Faul, EdD, Dec. 22, 1949; children: Robert M., Alison. BA, U. Calif., Berkeley, 1952. Cert. elem. tchr., Calif. Tchr. Tulare County (Calif.) Schs., 1945-46, Tulare City Schs., 1946-48, Visalia (Calif.) City Schs., 1948-49, Richmond (Calif.) City Schs., 1951-52, Pacific Grove (Calif.) Sch. Dist., 1965-85; designated English tchg. specialist State of Calif., 1969—; edn. cons. Leo A. Meyer Assocs., Inc., Hayward, Calif., 1993—. Prin. Group Four Assocs.; lectr. Calif. State U., Fresno, 1969, U. Calif., Santa Cruz, 1970. Co-author: The New Older Woman, 1996. Apprd. mem. first human rels. commn. City of Richmond, 1962-64; adv. bd. Family Resource Ctr.; founding mem., 1st pres. Monterey (Calif.) Peninsula Child Abuse Prevention Coun., 1974; hon. life mem. Calif. PTA; bd. dirs. Carmel Cultural Commn., 1964-67, Harrison Meml. Libr. Bd., Carmel, Calif., 1978-84; bd. dirs. Monterey Peninsula Airport Dist., 1980-2004; co-founder 100 Women Supporting Women, Monterey Peninsula Coll., 1997; vol. chair Women Mentoring Women, 2004. Mem. Am. Assn. Airport Execs., Friends of Hopkins Marine Sta. (founer, bd. dirs.), Carmel Heritage (founder, bd. dirs.), Monterey NAACP (life), Monterey Mus. Art (life), Monterey Symphony Guild (life). Democrat. Avocation: writing. Home: PO Box 4365 Carmel CA 93921-4365 E-mail: patfaul@aol.com.

FAUL, MAUREEN PATRICIA, healthcare administrator; d. Michael M and Margaret A Faul; life ptnr. Stacey Citrin. BSN, Wheeling Jesuit U., W.Va., 1983. RN Pa., 1983. V.p. Heart Ctr. of Excellence North Broward Hosp. Dist., Ft. Lauderdale, Fla., 1998—2003; pres. The Resh Group, Inc, Coral Springs, Fla., 2003—05; CEO, Pulmonary Physicians of South Fla., LLC, Miami, 2005—. Bd. dirs. Am. Heart Assn., Ft. Lauderdale, Fla., 1998—2003. Office: Pulmonary Physicians of South Fla LLC 3625 NW 82d Ave # 408 Miami FL 33166 Personal E-mail: mpfaul@bellsouth.net.

FAULCONER, ROBERT JAMIESON, pathologist, educator; b. Sedlescombe, Sussex, Eng., July 11, 1923; came to U.S., 1925, naturalized, 1932; s. Robert Hoffman and Gladys Alice (Jamieson) F.; m. Virginia Myrl Davis, Aug. 11, 1945; children: Anne Faulconer Hurley, Elizabeth Myrl, Mary Waite, John Edmund. BS, Coll. William and Mary, 1943; MD, Johns Hopkins U., 1947; DSc (hon.), Ea. Va. Med. Sch., 1998. Diplomate Am. Bd. Pathology. Intern Johns Hopkins Hosp., 1948, fellow, 1948-49; resident Presbyn.-U. Pa. Med. Ctr., Phila., 1949-52; pathologist DePaul Hosp., Norfolk, Va., 1954-78, pathologist, dir. labs., 1965-78; clin. prof. pathology Med. Coll. Va., 1972-79; prof. pathology Ea. Va. Med. Sch., 1974-94, chmn., 1978-93, prof. emeritus, 1994—. Cons. pathologist U.S. Naval Hosp., Portsmouth, Va., VA Hosp., Hampton, Va., Children;s Hosp., Norfolk, Va. Beach Gen. Hosp.; chmn. Health Svcs. Adv. Bd., Norfolk; mem. adv. com. Va. Cancer Registry. Med. editorial bd. Histology and Histopathology Jour.; contbr. articles on pathology to profl. publs. Pres. Va. div. Am. Cancer Soc., 1963-66, mem. nat. bd. dirs., exec. and sci. rev. coms.; bd. visitors Coll. William and Mary, 1972-76, 79-87, chmn. William and Mary Olde Guarde, 1997-98. With USNR, 1943-46, M.C., U.S. Army, 1952-54. Recipient J. Shelton Horsley award merit, Va. div. Am. Cancer Soc., 1966, Alumni medallion, Coll. William and Mary, 1985. Fellow AAAS; mem. AMA, Internat. Acad. Pathology, Am. Soc. Clin. Pathologists, Coll. Am. Pathologists, Am. Assn. Anatomists, Am. Soc. Clin. Oncology, Am. Assn. Phys. Anthropologists, Va. Soc. Pathology (pres. 1958-59), Norfolk Acad. Medicine (pres. 1964-65), Am. Assn. History of Medicine, Am. Assn. Pathologists, Assn. Pathology Chmn., Cypher Soc. (Coll. William and Mary), Norfolk Yacht and Country Club, Town Point Club (bd. govs.), Commonwealth Club (Richmond), Sigma Xi. Episcopalian. Home: 1507 Buckingham Ave Norfolk VA 23508-1354 Office: Ea Va Med Sch Med Coll of Hampton Roads PO Box 1980 Norfolk VA 23501-1980 Business E-Mail: crd@borg.evms.edu.

FAULES, BARBARA RUTH, retired elementary school educator; b. Austin, Tex., Mar. 10, 1940; d. Milton Friedrich Hausmann and Ruth Elizabeth Hornbuckle; m. John Wilson Faules, May 30, 1967. BA cum laude, Harding U., 1962; MA in Curriculum and Instrn., U. Mo., Kansas City, 1995. Cert. elem. tchr., Mo. Tchr. 4th grade Searcy Grammar Sch., Ark., 1962—64, Pulaski County Spl. Sch., Little Rock AFB Elem., Jacksonville, Ark., 1964—67; tchr. grades 3, 4, and 6 Butcher Greene Elem. Consol. Sch. Dist. #4, Grandview, Mo., 1967—98, ret., 1998. Contbr. (poetry) Sunrise and Soft Mist, 1999 (Editor's Choice 1999). Mem. Nat. Congress Parents and Tchr. (hon. life mem.). Mem. Ch. of Christ. Avocations: freelance photography, writing, gardening, reading, travel. Home: 9131 Big Bethel Dr San Antonio TX 78240-2852 Personal E-mail: tchow1101@sbcglobal.net.

FAULK, MARSHALL WILLIAM, professional football player; b. New Orleans, Feb. 26, 1973; Student, San Diego State U. Running back Indpls. Colts., 1994-99, St. Louis Rams, 1999—. Named NFL MVP, 2000, 2001, NFL Offensive Player of the Yr., 1999—2001; named to NFL Pro-Bowl, 1994—95, 1998—2002; recipient Espy Award for Best Football Player, ESPN, 2001, 2002. Achievements include Three-time consensus NCAA All-America; mem. Super Bowl XXXIV Champion St. Louis Rams, 2000; first player in NFL history to gain 2,000 yards from scrimmage in four consecutive seasons. Office: c/o St Louis Rams One Rams Way Bridgeton MO 63045

FAULKNER, ELAINE CHEN, music educator; b. Albuquerque, N.Mex., Oct. 29, 1980; d. Andrew Olanda Faulkner and Hsiu Chen Chang. BMus, Valdosta State U., Ga., 1999—2003. Cert. music tchr. Ga. Profl. Standards Commn., 2003. Orch. tchr. Richards Mid. Sch. Orch., Lawrenceville, Ga., 2003—. Dir., orchs. Richards Mid. Sch. Orch., Lawrenceville, Ga., 2003—. Contbr. violin performance. Scholar, Valdosta Symphony Orch., 1999—2003. Mem.: Music Educator's Nat. Conf. Conservative. Office Phone: 770-338-4808. Personal E-mail: elainetangerine@gmail.com.

FAULKNER, JAMES VINCENT, JR., lawyer; b. N.Y.C., Mar. 25, 1944; s. James Vincent and Josephine Rita (Fitzsimmons) F.; m. Bettina Van Der Plas, Aug. 10, 1968; children: Aylsia, Martina, James III. BA, Georgetown U., 1966, MS, 1968, JD, 1970. Assoc. Appleton, Rich & Perrin, N.Y.C., 1970-72, Lord, Day & Lord, N.Y.C., 1972-75; sr. corp. atty. Union Pacific Corp., N.Y.C., 1975-77, asst. gen. counsel, 1977-80, assoc. gen. counsel, 1980-83, dep. gen. counsel, 1983-88; sr. v.p., gen. counsel USPCI Inc. subs. Union Pacific Corp., Houston, 1988-93; v.p., law atty. Tenneco Inc., Houston, 1993—95; v.p., gen. counsel Tenneco Packaging, 1995—99; v.p., gen. counsel, sec. Pactiv Corp., 2000—. Mem. Sch. bd. St. Patrick's Ch., Bedford, N.Y., 1979-81, parish council, 1981-84. Mem. ABA, Am. Corp. Counsel Assn. (dir. 1985-88), Assn. Bar City N.Y. (com. on uniform state laws 1971-72). Clubs: Bedford Golf and Tennis. Republican. Roman Catholic. Avocations: squash, riding. Office: Pactiv Corp 1900 W Field Court Lake Forest IL 60045

FAULKNER, JULIA ELLEN, opera singer; b. St. Louis, Nov. 1, 1957; d. Seldon and Dona Leah (Clark) F. MusB cum laude, Ind. U., 1980, MusM, 1983. Instr. voice No. Ariz. U., Flagstaff, 1984, Iowa State U., 1984-85; solo artist San Francisco Opera Ctr., 1985-86, Wolftrap Opera Co., Vienna, Va., 1986, Bavarian State Opera, Munich, 1987-91, Vienna (Austria) State Opera, 1991-97, Metropolitan Opera, N.Y.C., 1997—; studio voice tchr., 1998—2002; asst. prof. U. Wis. Sch. Music, 2003—. Solo performances with opera cos. and theaters at La Scala, Carnegie Hall, N.Y.C., Met. Opera, N.Y.C., L.A. Philharm., San Francisco Philharm., also in Miami Fla., Berlin, Hamburg, Germany, Lyon, Jerusalem, Bordeau, Stockholm, Amsterdam and Genoa; dir. Oklahoma and Old Maid and the Thief, Flagstaff, 1984; rec. artist Elektra, 1990, Der Rosenkavalier, 1991, Rossini, Semiramide, Schumann, Genoveva; recorded Pergolese Stabat Mater Deutsche Grammophone Das Paradis und die Peri, Verdi's Falstaff. Recipient award Met. Opera, N.Y.C., 1985, 3d prize Whitaker Internat. Voice Competition, 1985, Festspiel prize Bavarian State Opera, 1988. Democrat. Office: Sch of Music Univ Wis Madison WI 53703 Office Phone: 608-263-1922. E-mail: juliafaulkner@charter.net.

FAULKNER, LARRY RAY, academic administrator; b. Shreveport, La., Nov. 26, 1944; s. James Clifford and Doris Louise (Koch) Faulkner; m. Mary Ann Jordan, Aug. 14, 1965; children: Brian Jordan, Susan Louise. BS, So. Meth. U., 1966; PhD, U. Tex., Austin, 1969; DSc (hon.), So. Meth. U., 2000. Asst. prof. chemistry Harvard U., Cambridge, Mass., 1969—73; prof. chemistry U. Tex., Austin, 1983—84, pres., 1998—; asst. prof. U. Ill., Urbana-Champaign, 1973—75, assoc. prof., 1975—79, prof., 1979—83, prof. chemistry, dept. head, 1984—89, dean Coll. Liberal Arts and Sci., 1989—94, provost and vice chancellor acad. affairs, 1994—98. Mem. Materials Rsch. Lab, 1978—90. Author (with A.J. Bard): Electrochemical Methods, 1980, 2d edit., 2001; editor: Jour. Electroanalytical Chemistry, 1980—85; mem. edit. bd.: Jour. Electrochem. Soc., 1975—80. Recipient U.S. Dept. Energy award, 1986. Fellow: Electrochem. Soc. (v.p. 1988—91, pres. 1991—92, Edward Weston fellow 1969, Young Author's prize 1976, Edward Goodrich Acheson medal 2000), Am. Acad. Arts and Scis.; mem.: Soc. Electroanalytical Chemistry (Charles N. Reilly award 1998), Am. Chem. Soc. (award in analytical chemistry 1992), Phi Kappa Phi, Phi Beta Kappa (Grad. Rsch. award Tex. Gamma chpt. 1969—70). Home: 5310 Western Hills Dr Austin TX 78731-4822 Office: Office of Pres U Tex at Austin PO Box T Austin TX 78713-8920 E-mail: president@po.utexas.edu.*

FAULKNER, ROBERT LLOYD, advertising executive, graphics designer; b. Chgo., Nov. 8, 1934; s. L. Lester and Agnes Elizabeth (Irons) F.; m. Elizabeth Alice Thomas, June 14, 1958; children: Anne Elizabeth, Lynn Marie, Thomas Robert. BFA in Advt. Design, U. Ill., 1958. Account exec. Brad Sebstad Advt., Chgo., 1966—67; sr. account exec. D'Arcy Advt. Co., Chgo., 1967—70; v.p. Wm. A. Robinson Inc., Northbrook, Ill., 1970—71; nat. mdse. and promotion mgr. James B. Beam Distilling Co., Chgo., 1971—73; v.p. Coord. Advt., Chgo., 1973—77, Grant/Jacoby Inc., Chgo., 1977—79, Kennedy Advt., Chgo., 1979—86; exec. v.p. Kamen/Faulkner Inc., Chgo., 1986—89; pres., owner Bob Faulkner Corporation, Westchester, Ill., 1989—. Course coord., advt. lectr. grad. level advt. courses Northwestern U. and Roosevelt U., Chgo., 1980-85; computer instr. Senior Net. Author: Learn to Cross Country Ski, 1976; co-author: Cross-Country Skiing for Everybody, 1975. Dir. Western Springs Hist. Soc., 1992-95; mem. Illegitimate Theatre of Western Springs. Recipient numerous advt. awards. Mem. Bus. Mktg. Assn. (Cert. Bus. Communicator), Nat. Ski Patrol (life), Model T Ford Owners Assn., Sports Car Club Am., Portage Lake Yacht Club. Episcopalian. Avocation: fine art painting. Home and Office: 11523 Burton Court Westchester IL 60154 Office Phone: 708-492-1330. E-mail: bofaulk@netzero.net.

FAULKNER, SCOT, management consultant; b. Northampton, Mass., July 3, 1953; s. Clarence and Irene Faulkner; m. Vicki Clements Hunter, Feb. 12, 1997; 1 child, Amanda Marie Hunter. BA, Lawrence U., 1975; MPA, Am. U., Washington, 1978. Dir. pers. Presidents Ronald Reagan and George H. W. Bush, Washington, 1980; White Ho. staff Pres. George H. W. Bush, 1981; exec. asst. GSA, 1981—82, 1983—84; acting dep. adminstr. U.S. Dept. Edn., 1982; country dir. U.S. Peace Corps, Malawi, 1984—86; expert USDA, Washington, 1987; dep. assoc. adminstr. FAA, 1988—89; v.p. Philip Crosby Assoc., 1990—93; CAO U.S. Ho. Reps., 1994—97; global practice leader AMA, 1998—2000; dir. European Inst., 2001; sr. ptnr. global ops. Phoenix Cons. Assoc., 2002—. Adj. faculty U. Md., 1993—2000; lectr. Kennedy Sch. Govt., 1995—96; bd. dir. Kinexum. Co-author: Continuous Quality Improvement; Making the Transition to Education, 1993, Quality in Education Outcomes Report National Governors Association, 1992—94; contbr. articles to profl. jours. Pres. Friends of Harper's Ferry Nat. Hist. Park, 1988—; pres. bd. trustees U.S. Capitol Hist. Soc., 1995—97; bd. trustees Md. Mus. African Art, 0990—1998. Mem.: Civil War Preservation Trust, Reagan Alumni Assn., Capitol Hill Club. Office: 253 Prospect Ave Harpers Ferry WV 25425 Office Phone: 304-535-2757.

FAULKNER, WALTER THOMAS, lawyer, director; b. New Haven, Sept. 17, 1928; s. Walter Thomas and Alice Marion (McGushin) F.; m. Joan Lee Hills, Mar. 17, 1956; children: John, Andrew, George, Susan. AB, Providence Coll., 1952; LL.B., Columbia U., 1955. Bar: N.Y. State 1956. Since practiced in, N.Y.C.; assoc. firm Rogers, Hoge & Hills, 1959-65, ptnr., 1965-86, Kelley Drye & Warren, 1987—. Sec. Sterling Drug Inc., 1973-78, Bacardi Corp., 1975-96. Bd. govs. Sound Shore Med. Ctr. Westchester. Served with AUS, 1946-48. Mem. Assn. of Bar of City of N.Y., ABA, N.Y. State Bar Assn., Am. Soc. Corp. Secs. Home: 64 Woodbine Ave Larchmont NY 10538-3525 Office: Kelley Drye & Warren 101 Park Ave New York NY 10178-0062

FAULMANN, ROGER RAY, retired music educator; b. Mt. Clemens, Mich., Jan. 27, 1938; m. Jo E. Dunbar, Dec. 27, 1964; 1 child, Bryan A. BME, Baldwin-Wallace Coll., 1960; MusM, U. of Mich., 1967. Cert. tchr. Fla., 1985. Instrumental gen. music dir. Fraser (Mich.) Pub. Schs., 1960—63; instrument/gen. music tchr. Port Huron (Mich.) Pub. Schs., 1963—64; dir. of bands Lake Orion (Mich.) Cmty. Schs., 1963—67; percussion prof. and band dir. Ill. State U., Normal, Ill., 1967—80; dir. of bands and percussion S.Dak. State U., Brookings, SD, 1980—83; dir. of bands Miami-Dade (Fla.) County Schs., 1985—2000; ret., 2000. Faculty Interlochen (Mich.) Arts Ctr., 1963—76; prof. and band dir. Ill. State U., 1967—80; cons. Fleisher-Hinton Music, Denver, 1983—85; guest condr. in field; rep. So. Fla. and No. Mich. Collegiate Apparell, Herff Jones, Inc. Contbr. articles to profl. jours.; percussionist: numerous internat. venues. Mem.: Music Educators Nat. Coll., Am. Sch. Bandmasters Assn., Fla. Bandmaster Assn. Liberal. Episcopalian. Avocations: model trains, holocaust research, political activist. Home: 10386 West Marion Dr Traverse City MI 49686 Office Phone: 231-357-5965. Personal E-mail: rfaulmann@aol.com.

FAULS, TED (THOMAS E. DUB. FAULS), lawyer; b. Fredericksburg, Va., 1961; AB, Coll. William & Mary, 1983, JD, 1986. Bar: Va. 1986. Ptnr., practice group leader, lending and structured fin. Troutman Sanders LLP, Richmond, Va. Mem.: ABA, Va. Bar Assn. Office: Troutman Sanders LLP Bank Am Ctr 1111 E Main St Richmond VA 23219 Office Phone: 804-697-1397. Office Fax: 804-697-1339. Business E-Mail: ted.fauls@troutmansanders.com.

FAUNCE, SARAH CUSHING, retired curator; b. Tulsa, Aug. 19, 1929; d. George Jr. and Helen Pauline (Colwell) F. BA, Wellesley Coll., 1951; MA, Washington U., St. Louis, 1959; postgrad., Columbia U., 1960-63. Tchr. history Hartridge Sch., Plainfield, N.J., 1954-56; tchr. art Mary C. Wheeler Sch., Providence, 1958-59; instr. art history Barnard Coll., N.Y.C., 1962-64; sec. adv. council art history Columbia U., 1963-70, registrar, curator, 1965-70; exhbn. cons. Jewish Mus., N.Y.C., 1968-70; curator paintings and sculpture Bklyn. Mus. Art, 1970-98, curator emeritus, project dir. Courbet Catalogue Raisonné project, 1998—. Author: Courbet, 1993; exhbn. catalog author: Anne Ryan Collages, 1974, Carl Larsson, 1982; author, editor: Belgian Art 1880-1914, 1980, Courbet Reconsidered, 1988, In the Light of Italy: Corot and Early Plein Air Painting, 1996; editor: Northern Light: Realism and Symbolism in Scandinavian Painting 1880-1910, 1982. Travel grantee Columbia U., 1963 Mem. AAM-ICOM, Coll. Art Assn., Phi Beta Kappa. Democrat. Home: 28 E 92nd St New York NY 10128-0616 Office: Courbet Catalogue Raisonne Project 22 E 71st St New York NY 10021 Office Phone: 646-878-2707. Personal E-mail: faunce.courbet@mindspring.com.

FAUNTLEROY, ANGELA COLLEEN, music educator; b. Phila., Dec. 16, 1956; d. Rudolph Simmons and Marlyn Fauntleroy. MusB in Applied Piano, Boston Conservatory Music, 1978; MusB in Music Edn., U. of the Arts, 1989; MusM in Edn. Adminstrn., Cheyney U., 1994. Cert. secondary educator Pa., 1996. Music tchr. Sch. Dist. of Phila., 1980—. Mem.: Nat. Assoc. Female Execs., The Schoolmen's Club of Phila., Sigma Alpha Iota, Kappa Delta Pi, Nu Theta Chpt., Internat. Honor Soc. in Edn. Avocations: travel, dance. Home: 4533 Sansom St Philadelphia PA 19139-3624 Office Phone: 215-299-7000. E-mail: afauntleroy@phila.k12.pa.us.

FAURE, GUNTER, geology educator; b. Tallinn, Estonia, May 11, 1934; s. Arnulf and Stella (von Harpe) F.; m. Barbara L.L. Goodell, Sept. 5, 1959 (div. Feb. 1985); children: Mary Jennifer, John Eric, Pamela Anne, David Christopher; m. Teresa M. Mensing, June 4, 1988. B.Sc., U. Western Ont., 1957; PhD, MIT, 1961; fellow, Sch. Advanced Studies, 1961-62. Asst. prof. geology Ohio State U., 1962-65, assoc. prof., 1965-68, prof., 1968—2002, prof. emeritus, 2002—; field work Antarctica. Author: (with J.L. Powell) Strontium Isotope Geology, 1972, Principles of Isotope Geology, 1977, 2d edit., 1986, Principles and Applications of Geochemistry, 1991, 2d edit., 1998, Origin of Igneous Rocks, 2001, Isotopes: Principles and Applications, 2005; editor-in-chief Jour. Isotope Geoscience, 1983-88; exec. editor Geochimica et Cosmochimica Acta, 1989-97; assoc. editor Geochimica et Cosmochimica Acta, 1989-97; contbr. articles to profl. jours. Named an Honoree, Applied Geochemistry, 2004; recipient univ. gold medal in honours geology, U. Western Ont., 1957, Disting. Tchg. award, Ohio State U., 1970, 1983, 1999, Antarctic Svc. medal, 1976. Fellow Geol. Soc. Am., Geochem. Soc. (Disting. Svc. award 2005), European Assn. Geochemistry; mem. Planetary Soc., Meteoritical Soc., Internat. Assn. Geochemistry and Cosmochemistry (v.p. 1992-96, pres. 1996-2000, treas. 2005—, newsletter editor 1999-2002), Ohio Acad. Scis. Office: 125 S Oval Mall Columbus OH 43210-1308 Office Phone: 614-292-3454. Business E-Mail: faure.1@osu.edu.

FAUSEL, ALAN, art appraiser; BA in Art Hist., UCLA; MA in Art Hist., Stanford Univ. Asst. curator, European sculpture, decorative arts Fine Arts Mus., San Francisco, 1986—89; curator Frick Art Mus., Pittsburgh, 1989—91; dir., European painting dept. and mus. svcs. dept. Butterfield & Butterfield, San Francisco, 1991—94; sr. v.p., dir., painting, drawing dept. Doyle New York, 1994. Adj. lectr. NYU Grad. Sch. Edn.; lectr. Appraisal Assn. Am.; appraiser Antiques Roadshow, WGBH-PBS. Office: Doyle New York 175 E 87th St New York NY 10128 Office Phone: 212-427-4141 ext. 238. Office Fax: 212-369-0892. Business E-Mail: alan@doylenewyork.com.*

FAUSOLD, MARTIN LUTHER, history educator; b. Irwin, Pa., Nov. 11, 1921; s. Samuel and and Edna (Breegle) F.; m. Daryl Ethel Clement, June 18, 1949 (dec. May 1995); children: Sharon Ann, Cynthia Lynn, Marti Clement, Martin Samuel; m. Marjorie F. Dimpfl, June 22, 1996. BA, Gettysburg Coll., 1944; PhD, Syracuse U., 1953. Ptnr. Fausold Dairy Co., Blairsville, Pa., 1946-49; from asst. prof. to prof. history and govt. State U. N.Y., Cortland, 1952-58; prof. history and govt., chmn. social sci. divsn. SUNY, Geneseo, 1959-69, prof. Am. history, 1969-85, disting. svc. prof. Am. history, 1985-92, prof. emeritus, 1992—. Mem. univ. awards com. SUNY, chmn., 1970-78, joint awards coun., 1970-82; co-dir. permanent exhibit Valley Village Collage SUNY Geneseo; dir. SUNY Oral History Project, 1983—. Author: Gifford Pinchot: Bull Moose Progressive, 1961, James W. Wadsworth Jr.: The Gentleman from New York, 1975, The Presidency of Herbert Hoover, 1985, also articles, book reviews to profl. jours.; editor: The Hoover Presidency: A Reappraisal, 1974; co-editor: The Constitution and the American Presidency: A Reappraisal, 1991. Chmn. Cortland Bd. Pub. Works, 1956; trustee Wadsworth Library, 1976-87. Served to lt. (j.g.) USNR, 1942-46. SUNY Faculty Exchange Scholar, 1978-92. Mem. Faculty Assn. State U. N.Y. (pres. 1964- 67). Democrat. Presbyterian (elder 1968-70, 84-86). Home: Valley Manor 1570 East Ave Apt 315 Rochester NY 14692 Personal E-mail: mlfausold@aol.com.

FAUSS, DAVID H., management consultant; b. Jacksonville, Fla., Mar. 17, 1961; s. G. Herman Fauss Jr and Carole Cook Fauss; m. Melissa A. Pigott. BS, Jacksonville U., 1983; MS in Mgmt., Ga. Inst. Tech., 1991. Photographer, pres. PhotoWorks, Jacksonville, Fla., 1984—91; v.p. bus. devel. Trial Cons., Inc., Miami, 1991—93; CEO, dir. cons. svcs. Magnus Rsch. Cons., Inc., Pompano Beach, 1993—. Mem. personnel appeals bd. City of Lighthouse Point, Fla., 2000—. Mem. Leadership Broward, Ft. Lauderdale, Acad. Mgmt. Scholar, Rotary Found. Office: Magnus Rsch Cons Inc 1305 NE 23d Ave Ste 1 Pompano Beach FL 33062-3748

FAUST, ANNE SENECHAL, artist; b. New Britain, Conn., Mar. 11, 1936; d. George Augustus and Louise Mary (Schmalz) Senechal; m. Jacob Faust, Oct. 20, 1979. BFA cum laude, Boston U., 1958; M in Art Edn., U. Hartford, 1977. Cert. tchr. Conn. Draftsman Conn. Light & Power, Berlin, 1959—67, Fafnir Bearing Co., New Britain, 1967—69; art instr. New Britain Bd. Edn., 1969—79. Illustrator: The Audubon Society Handbook for Birders, 1981, The Audubon Soc. Guide to Attracting Birds, 1985. Named Master Wildlife Artist, Leigh Yawkey Woodson Art Mus., Wausau, Wis., 1999; recipient 1st pl., Lafayette (La.) Art Assn., 1996, Hilton Head (S.C.) Art League, 1999. Mem.: La. Art and Artists Guild, Soc. Animal Artists (award of excellence 1992). Republican. Avocations: birdwatching, cooking, travel. Home: 2345 Dogwood Ave Baton Rouge LA 70808

FAUST, DAVID E., lawyer; b. Allentown, Pa., Apr. 10, 1942; s. Henry J. and Helene J. F.; m. Dianne L. Faust, Dec. 26, 1964; children: Michelle M., Allison J. BS, Northwestern U., 1964, JD, 1967. Bar: Pa. 1968. Atty. Penn Cen. Transp. Co., Phila., 1971-76; assoc. Post and Schell, P.C., Phila., 1976-78, ptnr., 1978—. With U.S. Army, 1968-71, Vietnam. Mem. Nat. Assn. R.R. Trial Counsel, Phila. Bar Assn., Def. Rsch. Inst. Avocation: travel. Office: Post and Schell PC 1600 John F Kennedy Blvd Fl 14 Philadelphia PA 19103-2808 E-mail: dfaust@postschell.com.

FAUST, DONNY D., music educator; b. Durango, Colo., May 24, 1953; s. Melvin E. and Eloise L. Faust; 1 child, Jennifer Jo. BA, Ft. Lewis Coll., Durango, Colo., 1976; MPA, U. Colo., Colorado Springs, 1979; grad. in MAED Adminstrn., U. Phoenix, 2002. Cert. K-12 prin., K-12 music tchr. Ariz., 1992, Community College; Music, History, ESL, Ed Admin. State of Ariz. Coll. Bd., 1992. Tchr. band/music Willcox Pub. Sch., Ariz., 1994—95; asst. prin. Marana Sch. Dist., Ariz., 1995—96; tchr. music/band and history Superior Sch. Dist., Ariz., 1996—97; tchr. band 5-12 San Carlos Sch. Dist.; tchr. K-8 music and 5-8 band Roosevelt Sch. Dist., Phoenix, 1997—. Adj. instr. Cochise C.C., Willcox, Ariz., 1996; ballet folklorico Roosevelt Sch. Dist., Phoenix, 1997—; adj. instr. music Chandler-Gilbert C.C., Ariz., 1998—; adj. instr. ESL Mesa C.C., Ariz., 2000—; trombone musican Fiesta Bowl parade, Phoenix, 2001—. Contbr. H.S. NCAA accreditation team. Water cmty. of bond issues City of Chandler, Ariz. Recipient Outstanding Band award, Rodeo Parade Com., 1994, Best Band in Class, Colo. State Fair, 1988, Outstanding Student Dance performance, Nat. Assn. for Bilingual Edn., 2001. Mem.: NEA (assoc.), Music Educators Nat. Conf. (corr.), Nat. Assication for Bilingual Edn. (assoc.), Phi Delta Kappa (corr.). Achievements include research in Color-coding of Musical Notes to Music Instruction; San Carlos Apache Study, National Endowment Fellowship Study 1994. Home: PO Box 7648 2119 West Tulsa St Chandler AZ 85246 Personal E-mail: dondfaust@earthlink.net.

FAUST, DREW GILPIN, historian, educator; b. N.Y.C., Sept. 18, 1947; d. McGhee Tyson and Catharine (Mellick) G.; m. Stephen Faust, Dec. 28, 1968 (div. 1976); m. Charles E. Rosenberg, June 7, 1980; 1 child, Jessica Rosenberg. BA magna cum laude, Bryn Mawr Coll., 1968; MA, U. Pa., Phila., 1971, PhD, 1975. Asst. prof. Am. civilization U. Pa., Phila., 1976-80, assoc. prof., 1980-84, prof., 1984-89, Stanley I. Sheerr prof. history, 1988-89, Annenberg prof. history, 1989—2000; dean Radcliffe Inst. for Advanced Study at Harvard U., 2000—; Lincoln prof. history Harvard U., 2001—. Walter Lynwood Fleming lectr. La. State U., 1987; mem. edtl. adv. bd. Guggenheim Found., 1988—; cons. Before Freedom Came: African American Life in the Antebellum South, exhbn. at Mus. Confederacy, 1988-91; NEH panel Interpretive Rsch. Program, 1987; mem. Pulitzer Prize History Jury, 1986, 90; lectr. various colls. and univs. Author: A Sacred Circle: The Dilemma of the Intellectual inthe Old South, 1977, paperback edit., 1986, James Henry Hammond and the Old South: A Design for Mastery, 1982, The Creation of Confederate Nationalism: Ideology and Identity in the Civil War South, 1988, Southern Stories: Slaveholders in Peace and War, 1992, Mothers of Invention: Women of the Slaveholding South in the American Civil War, 1996 (Parkman prize, Avery Craven prize 1996, Honoarble metion annual awards, Asn. Am. Pub., 1997, Francis Parkman prize, 1997, mem. editl. bd. Jour. Am. History, 1991—, Pa. Mag. History and Biography, 1986-89, Jour. So. History, 1981-86; contbr. articles to profl. jours. Recipient Jules F. Landry award James Henry Hammond and the Old South, 1982, Charles Sydnor award, Prize Soc. Historians of Early Am. Republic, 1983, article prize Berkshire Conf. Women's Historians, 1991; U. Pa. Rsch. Found. grantee, 1982; assoc. fellow Stanford Humanities Ctr., Stanford U., 1983-84, Am. Coun. Learned Socs. fellow, 1986, Guggenheim fellow, 1987, Mass. Hist. Soc. fellow, 2002, Elizabeth Hall fellow Concord Acad., 2003. Mem. So. Hist. Assn. (chair nominating com. 1993, exec. coun. 1987-90, Frank L. Owsley prize com. 1987, pres. 1999-2000), Am. Hist. Assn. (v.p. profl. divsn. 1992-95, coun. mem. 1992—), Orgn. Am. Historians (chair Avery Craven Prize Com. 1991, 97, chair program com. 1987, mem. coun. 1999-2002), Am. Studies Assn. (mem. coun. 1988-90, Honoable metion Hope Franklin award, 1997), Hist. Soc. Pa. (mem. bd. 1988-91), So. Assn. Women Historians (membership com. 1988—, pres. 1998-99). Office: Radcliffe Inst Adv Study Harvard Univ Cambridge MA 02139

FAUST, ELIZABETH ANNE, medical affairs executive; b. Gainesville, Fla., Mar. 25, 1965; d. Phil and Barbara Brady; m. William Perry Faust, July 29, 1989; children: Gregory Evan, Alan Brady, Carl Roberson. BS, Auburn U., 1987; MA, U. Calif., Riverside, 1989; PhD, UCLA, 1995. Tchg. asst. U. Calif., Riverside, 1987—89, UCLA, 1989—90; post-doctoral fellow Amgen, Inc, Thousand Oaks, Calif., 1995—98, sr. med. writer, 1998—2001, mgr. profl. svcs., 2001—02, assoc. dir. med. affairs, 2002—05, dir. med. affairs, 2005—. Contbr. chapters to books, articles to profl. jours. Mem. West L.A. Parents of Multiples, 1993—95. Scholar, Allison Eberlin Found., 1990; Immunology Tng. grantee, NIH, 1990, 1991, Biotechnology Tng. grantee, 1993, 1994, UCLA Warsaw fellow, Warsaw Family Found., 1990. Mem.: AAAS, Internat. Soc. Med. Publ. Profls. (mem. steering com.), Coun. Sci. Editors, Am. Soc. Hematology, Am. Soc. Clin. Oncology, Am. Med. Writers Assn. (core curriculum cert. 2002, pres. elect Pacific S.W. chpt.). Office: Amgen Inc One Amgen Center Dr MS 24-2-A Thousand Oaks CA 91360 E-mail: efaust@amgen.com.

FAUST, EMANUEL, JR., lawyer; b. Columbia, SC, May 1, 1958; BA, U. SC, 1980; JD, Duke U., 1983. Bar: DC 1983, US Dist. Ct. DC 1984. Assoc. Davis Polk & Wardwell, 1983—87, Dickstein Hapiro Morin & Oshinsky LLP, Washington, 1987—92, ptnr., 1992—, co-chmn. diversity com./ quality of life com. Mem.: DC Bar. Office: Dickstein Shapiro Morin & Oshinsky LLP 2101 L St NW Washington DC 20037-1526 Office Phone: 202-861-9127. Office Fax: 202-887-0689. E-mail: fauste@dsmo.com.

FAUST, JOHN JOSEPH, JR., performing arts educator, theater director; b. St. Louis, Feb. 16, 1939; s. John J. and Elinor (Cafferata) F.; m. Deborah Doyle, Aug. 18, 1969; children: John Charles, Mark Doyle. AB in Speech, St. Louis U., 1961; MA in Speech and Dramatic Arts, State U. Iowa, 1964. Tchr. speech/theatre Columbus High Sch., Waterloo, Iowa, 1963-64; chair English dept., dir. theatre Augustinian Acad., St. Louis, 1964-70; chair fine arts dept., dir. activities De Smet Jesuit High Sch., St. Louis, 1970-79; dir. theatre John Burroughs Sch., St. Louis, 1979-88, Barrington (Ill.) High Sch., 1988-94. Dir. nat. high sch. inst. theatre Northwestern U., Evanston, Ill., 1963-72, 89, Webster U. High Sch. Inst., St. Louis, 1978-80, creative drama workshop Barrington Area Arts Coun., 1990-93; adjudicator, panel mem. arts recognition and talent search Nat. Found. Advancement Arts, Miami, Fla., 1978-88; tchr. Mark Twain Summer Inst., St. Louis, 1985-88; founder, exec. dir. Theatre Whatever A Prodn. Co. For, By and With Young Adults, 1996. Assoc. editor: Theatre Technology & Design, 1984; contbg. editor: Model/Theatre Curriculum. Americorps vol. in HIV/AIDS awareness in teenagers ARC, 1994-95. Mem. Am. Alliance Theatre and Edn. (John Barner award 1992, Secondary Theatre Tchr. of Yr.), Ednl. Theatre Assn. Home and Office: Apt 207 564 Sarah Ln Creve Coeur MO 63141-6992

FAUST, NAOMI FLOWE, education educator; b. Salisbury, N.C. d. Christopher Leroy and Ada Luella (Graham) Flowe; m. Roy Malcolm Faust, Aug. 16, 1948. AB, Bennett Coll.; MA, U. Mich., 1945; PhD, NYU, 1963. Tchr. elem. Pub. Schs. Gaffney, SC; tchr. English, French, phys. edn. Atkins H.S., Winston-Salem; instr. English Bennett Coll. and So. U., Scotlandville, La., 1944—46; prof. English Morgan State Coll., Balt., 1946—48; tchr. English Greensboro Pub. Schs., NC, 1948—51, N.Y.C. Pub. Schs., 1954—63; prof. edn. Queens Coll. of CUNY, Flushing, 1964—82; writer, lectr., poetry readings, 1982—. Lectr. in field. Author: Discipline and the Classroom Teacher, 1977; (poetry) Speaking in Verse, 1974, All Beautiful Things, 1983, And I Travel by Rhythms and Words, 1990; contbr. poetry to jours. Named Tchr.-Author of 1979, Tchr.-Writer; recipient Cert. of Merit for Poem Cooper Hill Writers Conf., 1970, Achievement award L.I. br. AAUW, 1985, Poet of the Millennium award Internat. Poets Acad., Excellence in World Poetry award Internat. Poets Acad., 2002; named Internat. Eminent Poet, Internat. Poets Acad. Mem. AAUP, AAUW, Acad. Am. Poets, Nat. Coun. Tchrs. English, Nat. Women's Book Assn., Nat. Assn. Univ. Women (L.I. br.), World Poetry Soc. Intercontinental, N.Y. Poetry Forum, Poetry Soc. Am., NAACP, United Negro Coll. Fund, Alpha Kappa Alpha, Alpha Kappa Mu., Alpha Epsilon. Home: 11201 175th St Jamaica NY 11433-4135

FAUSTMAN, DENISE L., immunologist; b. Royal Oak, Mich., 1958; BS in Zoology and Chemistry, U. Mich., Ann Arbor, 1978; PhD in Transplantation Immunology, Washington U., St. Louis, 1982, MD, 1985. Intern and resident in medicine Mass. Gen. Hosp., Boston; rsch. assoc. Harvard Med. Sch., 1996—; dir. Immunology Lab., Mass. Gen. Hosp., Boston. Sr. editor: Jour. Women's Health. Recipient Arnold B. Zetcher award for excellence in rsch., Bay State chpt. Juvenile Diabetes Found., 1997, Lily Found. award, award, Am. Soc. for Reproductive Medicine, 2000; selected as part of, NIH's "Changing the Face of Medicine" exhbn., 2003. Mem.: AAAS, Diabetes Rsch. Internat. Network (co-founding mem.), Cell Transplant Soc. (founding mem.), Soc. for Women's Health Rsch. (chair bd. dirs. 1998—). Achievements include head of study that cured type I diabetes in mice, 2003. Office: Mass Gen Hosp E Bldg 149 13th St Charlestown MA 02129

FAUTH, JOHN J., venture capitalist; BS, Georgetown Univ. Vp, sr. credit off. Citicorp U.S.A.; pres., CEO Churchill Industries, Mpls., 1982—; chmn., dir., pres., CEO Churchill Capital, Inc., Mpls., 1987—. Chmn., bd adv, Georgetown Univ. Grad. Sch. Bus. Adminstrn.; bd. dir. Georgetown Univ. Office: Churchill Capital Inc 333 S 7th St Ste 2400 Minneapolis MN 55402-2435

FAVALORA, JOHN CLEMENT, archbishop; b. New Orleans, Dec. 5, 1935; s. Felix J. and Leona M. (Stevens) F. BA in Philosophy and History, Notre Dame Sem., New Orleans, 1958; STL, Pontifical Gregorian U., Rome, 1962; MEd, Tulane U., 1969. Ordained priest Roman Cath. Ch., 1962. Asst. pastor St. Theresa of the Child Jesus Ch., New Orleans, 1962—70; sec. to archbishop Archdiocese of New Orleans, 1963—65, vice chancellor, 1963—65; vice rector St. John Prep., New Orleans, 1964—67, 1968—71; dir. Office of Permanent Diaconate, New Orleans, 1971—74; adminstrv. asst. Notre Dame Sem., New Orleans, 1971—73, rector-pres., 1981—86; pastor St. Angela Merici Ch., Metairie, La., 1973—79; dir. Office of Vocations, New Orleans, 1979—81; bishop Diocese of Alexandria, La., 1986—89, Diocese of St. Petersburg, Fla., 1989—94; archbishop Diocese of Miami, 1994—. Ecclesiastical notary Archdiocese of New Orleans, 1962—64, pro-synodal judge, 1973—79; dean East Jefferson Deanery, New Orleans, 1974—77; vicar Pastoral Planning, New Orleans, 1976—81; chmn. Permanent Diaconate Adv. Com., New Orleans, 1984; consultor Archdiocese of New Orleans, 1984—86. Office: Archdiocese of Miami Pastoral Ctr 9401 Biscayne Blvd Miami Shores FL 33138*

FAVARO, MARY KAYE ASPERHEIM, pediatrician, writer; b. Edgerton, Wis., Sept. 30, 1934; d. Harold Wilbur and Genevieve Catherine (Hyland) Asperheim; m. Biagino Philip Favaro, May 31, 1969; children: Justin Peter, Gina Sue. BS, U. Wis., 1956; MS, St. Louis Coll. Pharmacy, 1965; MD, U. Wis., 1969. Instr. pharmacology St. Louis U. and St. Mary's Hosp. Sch. Practical Nurses, 1959-64; staff pharmacist U. Hosps., Madison, Wis., 1964-65; intern Albany (N.Y.) Med. Center, 1969-70; resident, 1970-71; resident in pediatrics U. S.C., Charleston, 1971-72, asst. prof. pediatrics, 1973-75; pvt. practice pediatrics, 1974-99; ret. Author: Pharmacology, an Introductory Text, 2005; The Pharmacologic Basis of Patient Care, 1985. Mem. AMA. Roman Catholic. Home: 1407 Southwood Dr Surfside Beach SC 29575 Personal E-mail: maryfav@aol.com.

FAVERO, MICHELE MAREE, music educator, musician; b. Omaha, June 6, 1970; d. Valentino Reno and Caryl June (O'Brien) F.; m. Thomas Rex Kluge, June 13, 1998. B in Music, So. Meth. U., 1993; M in Music, U. Nebr., 1997; diploma, Royal Acad. Music, London, Eng., 1994, Liszt Acad. Music, Budapest, Hungary, 1995. Freelance pianist, Budapest, Hungary, 1994-95; pvt. piano instr., 1994-95; accompanist Omaha Pub. Schs., 1997-98; freelance pianist, 1995—; pvt. piano instr., 1995—2000, 2004—; chmn. piano dept., exec. dir. Omaha Conservatory Music, 2000—04. Mem. Mu Phi Epsilon. Republican. Roman Catholic. Avocations: reading, studying languages, drawing, exercising, cooking.

FAVISH, JACQUELINE RAPPAPORT, elementary school educator; b. Chgo., Aug. 17, 1929; d. Bernard J. and Bella (Gan) Rappaport; m. Richard Jay Favish, Oct. 18, 1953; children: Lisa Renee Dembo, Pamela Elayne Levin, Sharon Rose Meserve. BS in Math., Roosevelt U., 1951; MEd, Nat.-Lewis U., Wilmette, Ill., 1976. Cert. tchr. K-12, spl. edn., learning disabled, emotionally disabled, culturally disadvantaged, Ill. Title I educator Evanston (Ill.) Sch. Dist. 65, 1964-69; ednl. therapist Lincolnwood (Ill.) Dist. 74, 1969-89. Coun. mem. Ill. Coun. on Developmental Disabilities, Springfield, Ill., 1989—. Mem. Nat. Tourette Syndrome Assn. (bd. dirs., exec. bd. 1986—), Tourette Syndrome Assn. Ill. (founder, bd. trustees). Jewish. Avocations: travel, gardening, creative crafts, civic involvement. Home: 18616 N 44th Pl Phoenix AZ 85050-3300

FAVORULE, DENISE, publishing executive; Advt. dir. Stagebill Mag., 1993—96; advt. mgr. Prevention Mag., 1996—98, nat. advt. dir., 1998—99, assoc. pub., 1999—2000, v.p., pub., 2000—. Office: Rondale Press Inc 33 E Minor St Emmaus PA 18098-0099 Office Phone: 212-573-0379. Office Fax: 610-967-7726. E-mail: denise.favorule@rodale.com.*

FAVRE, BRETT LORENZO, professional football player; b. Pass Christian (Gulfport), Miss., Oct. 10, 1969; s. Irvin and Bonita Favre; m. Deanna Tynes, July 14, 1996; children: Brittany, Breleigh. Grad. in Spl. Edn., So. Miss. U., 1991. Quarterback Atlanta Falcons, 1991—92, Green Bay Packers, 1992—; owner Brett Favre's Steakhouse, Brett Favre's Two Minute Grill. Co-author (with Chris Havel): Favre: For the Record, 1997; co-author: (with Bonita Favre and Chris Havel) Favre, 2004; actor: (films) There's Something About Mary, 1998. Founder Brett Favre Found., 1996. Named NFL MVP (only player in history to win 3 times), 1995—97; named to Nat. Football Conf. Pro Bowl Team, 1992, 1993, 1995—97, 2001—03; recipient Espy Award for Best Football Player, Espn, 1996, 1997, Espy Award for Best Moment, 2004. Achievements include mem. Super Bowl XXXI Champion Green Bay Packers, 1997. Office: Green Bay Packers PO Box 10628 Green Bay WI 54307-0628*

FAWBUSH, ANDREW JACKSON, lawyer; b. Miami, Fla., Oct. 7, 1946; s. Andrew T. Fawbush; m. Melinda Wheeley, Dec. 18, 1982; children: Andrew J. Jr., Tyler S., Karin J., Michelle L. BSBA in Acctg., with high honors, U. Fla., 1972, JD, 1974. Bar: Fla. 1975, DC 1994, NY 1995. Assoc. Smith & Hulsey, Jacksonville, Fla., 1975-80, ptnr., 1980-88, LeBoeuf, Lamb, Greene & MacRae LLP, Jacksonville, 1988—, chmn. employee benefits dept., 1993-95, hiring ptnr. Fla. office. Contbg. author The Tax Lawyer. Bd. dirs. YMCA, Jacksonville, 1981-83; bd. dirs., past pres. Employee Benefits Coun. N.E. Fla.; bd. dirs., exec. com. Gator Boosters, Inc.; trustee, tchr. Cert. Employee Benefits Specialists, U. North Fla., 1982-88, Southside United Methodist Church; bd. dirs. U. Fla. Found., 1993. With U.S. Army, 1968-70. Mem. ABA - Tax Sect. (employee benefits com.), Fla. Bar Assn. (spkr. employee benefit sect. 1983-88), D.C. Bar Assn., N.Y. Bar Assn., U. Fla. Alumni Assn. (bd. dirs. 1987-98, pres. 1994), Jacksonville C. of C. (gen. counsel, sports coun., mem. exec. com.), U. Fla. Athletic Assn. (v.p., bd. dirs.). Office: LeBoeuf Lamb Greene MacRae 50 N Laura St Ste 2800 Jacksonville FL 32202-3634 Office Phone: 904-354-5340. Office Fax: 904-353-1673. Business E-Mail: afawbush@llgm.com.

FAWCETT, CHRISTOPHER BABCOCK, civil engineer, construction and water resources company executive; b. NYC, Dec. 17, 1951; s. George Gifford Fawcett Jr. and Andi Adams Emerson; m. Nina Beth Williamson, June 20, 1986 (div. Aug. 1993); 1 child, Kyle Christopher Adams. Student, U. Okla., 1969—72, Concordia U., Montreal, Que., Can., 1979—81; BS, Clarkson U., 1984. Lic. civil engr.; registered civil engr., NY. Owner C.B.F. Handyman Co., NYC, 1974-77; v.p., gen. mgr. Fawcett & Fawcett, Inc., NYC, 1977-84; project mgr. U.S. Army Corps Engrs., NYC, 1985-86; asst. project mgr. N. Kruger Constrn., Inc., Locust Valley, NY, 1986-87; project mgr., engr. Finch, Pruyn & Co., Inc., Glens Falls, NY, 1987-98; propr. Caton Hill Enterprises, 1992—; project mgr., engr. Clough Harbour & Assocs., LLP, Albany, NY, 2000; project mgr. MLB Industries, Inc., Latham, NY, 2001; sr. project mgr. and project exec. Santa Fe Constrn., Inc., NYC, 2002—04; sr. project mgr. J.H. Mack, LLC, Teaneck, NJ, 2004—. Judge, NY Acad. Scis., H.S. Sci. and Engring. Event, NYC, 2003-05; founder, past chmn. Tri-County Nat. Engrs. Week and Nat. Jr. H.S. Mathcounts Competition programs, Glens Falls, 1987-98; founding sponsor Challenger Ctr. for Space Sci. Edn.; bd. dirs. treas. 16 E 96th St. Corp. Mem. NSPE, ASCE, NY Acad. Scis., Nat. Space Soc. (charter), Engrs. for Edn., Order of Engr., Cousteau Soc., Masons. Avocation: scuba diving. Office: Caton Hill Enterprises 16 E 96th St Ste 2A New York NY 10128-

FAWCETT, DAVID B., III, lawyer; b. Pitts., Pa., Aug. 5, 1958; BA, Carnegie Mellon Univ., 1980; JD, Univ. Pitts., 1985. Bar: Pa. 1985. Shareholder, litig. sect. Buchanan Ingersoll PC, Pitts. Trustee Carnegie Mus., Pitts., Carnegie Libr., Pitts.; mem. Allegheny County Council, Allegheny County Bd. Elections. Mem.: ABA, Pa. Bar Assn., Allegheny County Bar Assn. Office: Buchanan Ingersoll PC 20th Fl One Oxford Ctr 301 Grant St Pittsburgh PA 15219-1410 Office Phone: 412-562-3931. Office Fax: 412-562-1041. Business E-Mail: fawcettdb@bipc.com.

FAWCETT, DON WAYNE, retired anatomist; b. Springdale, Iowa, Mar. 14, 1917; s. Carlos J. and Mabel (Kennedy) F.; m. Dorothy Marie Secrest, 1941; children: Robert S., Mary Elaine, Donna, Joseph. AB cum laude, Harvard, 1938, MD, 1942; DSc (hon.), U. Siena, Italy, 1974, N.Y. Med. Coll., 1975, U. Chgo., 1977, U. Cordoba, Argentina, 1978; MD (hon.), U. Heidelberg, Germany, 1977; DVM (hon.), Justus Liebig U., Giessen-Lahn, Germany, 1977; DSc (hon.), Georgetown U., 1987, U. Rome, 1997. Intern surgery Mass. Gen Hosp., Boston, 1942-43; instr. anatomy Harvard Med. Sch., 1946-48, asso. anatomy, 1948-51, asst. prof. anatomy, 1951-55, Hersey prof. anatomy, 1958-80, James Stillman prof. comparative anatomy, 1962-80, sr. asso. dean preclin. affairs, 1975-77; prof. anatomy Cornell Med. Coll., 1955-58; scientist Internat. Lab. Research on Animal Diseases, Nairobi, Kenya, 1980-85. Author: The Cell, 1966, 2d edit., 1981, Textbook of Histology, 1968, 10th edit., 1975, 11th edit., 1986, 12th edit., 1993. Served as capt. M.C. AUS, 1943-46; bn. surgeon A.A.A. John and Mary Markle scholar med. sci., 1949-54; recipient Lederle Med. Faculty award, 1954 Fellow Am. Acad. Arts and Sci., Nat. Acad. Sci. U.S., Royal Microscopical Soc. (hon.); mem. AAAS, N.Y. Acad. Sci., Am. Assn. Anatomists (pres. 1964- 65, Henry Gray award 1983, Centennial medal 1987), N.Y. Soc. Electron Microscopists (pres. 1957-58), Histochem. Soc., Tissue Culture Assn. (v.p. 1954-55), Soc. Exptl. Biology and Medicine, Assn. Anatomy Chairmen (pres. 1973-74), Am. Soc. Zoologists, Am. Soc. Mammalogists, Electron Microscope Soc. Am. (Disting. Scientist award in Life Scis. 1989), Soc. Study Devel. and Growth, Harvey Soc., Am. Soc. Cell Biology (pres. 1961-62), Argentine Nat. Acad. Sci., Anat. Soc. So. Africa (hon.), Japanese Anat. Soc. (hon.), Anat. Soc. Australia and N.Z. (hon.), Japanese Electron Microscope Soc., Internat. Fedn. Soc. Electron Microscopy (pres. 1976-78), Am. Soc. Andrology (pres. 1977-78), Soc. Study Reprodn. (Carl Hartman award 1985), Mexican (hon.), Canadian (hon.) Assn. Anatomists. Address: 1224 Lincoln Rd Missoula MT 59802-3041 Personal E-mail: dfawc20586@aol.com.

FAWCETT, FARRAH LENI, actress, model; b. Corpus Christi, Tex., Feb. 2, 1947; d. James William and Pauline Alice (Evans) F.; m. Lee Majors, July 28, 1973 (div. 1982); 1 son, Redmond James. Student, U. Tex. at Austin. Works as model. Movie debut in Myra Breckenridge, 1970; other film appearances include Love is a Funny Thing, 1970, Logan's Run, 1976, Somebody Killed Her Husband, 1978, Sunburn, 1979, Saturn 3, 1980, Cannonball Run, 1981, Extremities, 1986, See You in the Morning, 1989, Man ofthe House, 1995, The Apostle, 1997, The Love Master, 2000, Dr. T and the Women, 2000; TV movie appearances include Charlie's Angels, 1976, Murder in Texas, 1981, The Red Light Sting, 1984, The Burning Bed, 1984, Between Two Women, 1986, Nazi Hunter: The Beate Klarsfeld Story, 1986, Margaret Bourke-White, 1989, The Substitute Wife, 1994, Dalva, 1996, Silk Hope, 1999, Baby, 2000, Jewel, 2001, Hollywood Wives, 2003; regular on TV series Charlie's Angels, 1976-77, Good Sports, 1991, Spin City, 2001, The Guardian, 2001-02; other TV appearances include Harry O, McCloud, The Six Million Dollar Man, Marcus Welby, M.D., Apple's Way; N.Y.C. Stage debut (off-Broadway) Extremities, 1983; TV miniseries appearances include Poor Little Rich Girl: The Barbara Hutton Story, 1987, Small Sacrifices, 1989, Children of the Dust, 1995; Posed for Playboy, 1995. Mem. Delta Delta Delta.

FAWCETT, GAYLE P., bank executive; m. Ken Fawcett; 2 children. Degree, Mass. Sch. Fin. Studies; student in Fin. Studies, Fairfield U. Cert. para-planner. Joined Berkshire Bank, Pittsfield, Mass., 1977; sr. v.p. Retail Banking and Ops. Bd. dirs. EastPoint Tech. Users Group. Bd. dirs. St.Mark's Ch. Fin. Com. Named One of 25 Women to Watch, U.S. Bankers Mag., 2003. Office: Berkshire Bank 24 North St PPO Box 1308 Pittsfield MA 01202-1308

FAWCETT, H. DANIEL, nuclear medicine physician, radiologist; s. Stanley and Margaret Fawcett; m. Maria Aquino, May 5, 1979; 1 child, Joseph. BSc with honors, Dalhousie U., Halifax, N.S., Can., 1971; MD, Dalhousie U., Halifax, N.S., Can., 1975. Asst. prof. radiology U. Tex. Med. Br., Galveston, 1982—87, assoc. prof. radiology, 1987—90; nuc. physican/radiologist RATC(PA), Ft. Worth, 1990—.

FAWCETT, JOHN SCOTT, real estate developer; b. Pitts., Nov. 5, 1937; s. William Hagen and Mary Jane (Wise) F.; m. Anne Elizabeth Mitchell, Dec. 30, 161; children: Holly Anne, John Scott II (dec.). BS, Ohio State U., 1959. Dist. dealer rep. Shell Oil Co., San Diego, 1962-66; dist. real estate rep. Shell Oil, Phoenix, 1967-69, region real estate rep. San Francisco, 1970-71, head office land investments rep. Houston, 1972-75; pres., CEO Marinita Devel. Co., Newport Beach, Calif., 1976—. Lectr. in land devel. related fields. With U.S. Army, 1960-61. Named Ky. Col., Gov. Ky., 1996. Mem. Internat. Platform Assn., Internat. Coun. Shopping Ctrs., Internat. Right of Way Assn., Internat. Inst. Valuers, Inst. Bus. Appraisers, Nat. Assn. Rev. Appraisers and Mortgage Underwriters, Am. Assn. Cert. Appraisers, Urban Land Inst., Nat. Assn. Real Estate Execs. (pres. L.A. chpt. 1975), Calif. Lic. Contractors Assn., Bldg. Industry Assn., U.S. C. of C., Town Hall of Calif., Ohio State U. Alumni Assn., Toastmasters (pres. Scottsdale Ariz. club 1968, pres. Hospitality T club 1964), U. Athletic Club, Phi Kappa Tau. Republican. Roman Catholic. Avocations: antiques, tennis, skiing. Home: 8739 Hudson River Cir Fountain Valley CA 92708-5503 Office: Marinita Devel Co 3835 Birch St Newport Beach CA 92660-2600 Business E-Mail: scott@marinita.com.

FAWCETT, JOHN THOMAS, archivist; b. West Branch, Iowa, Nov. 27, 1943; s. Floyd Thomas and Mary Helen (Miller) F.; m. Sharon Atchison, July 25, 1971 (div. 1993); children: Allen, Katherine. BA, U. Iowa, 1966; MA, U. Tex., 1978. Archivist, mus. tech. Herbert Hoover Libr., West Branch, Iowa, 1962-67; asst. acting dir., exec. dir. Herbert Hoover Libr. and Assn., West Branch, Iowa, 1983-87; archivist Office Presdl. Librs., Washington, 1967-68, supervisory and acting dir., 1978-83, asst. archivist, 1987-95; mil. aide to President of U.S. Exec. Office, Austin, Tex., 1968-70; supervisory archivist Lyndon B. Johnson Libr., Austin, 1970-78; pres. John T. Fawcett and Assocs., Inc., Washington, 1995—. Trustee Woodrow Wilson Presdl. Libr., 2002—. Mem. exec. bd. Boy Scouts Am., 1984-87. Mem. Masons, Kiwanis (pres. 1985). Business E-Mail: jtfawcett@aol.com.

FAWCETT, JOY LYNN, retired professional soccer player; b. Inglewood, Calif., Feb. 8, 1968; m. Walter Fawcett; children: Katelyn Rose, Carli, Madilyn Rae. Degree in phys. edn., U. Calif., Berkeley, 1990. Women's soccer coach UCLA, 1993-97, 1993—97; mem. U.S. Nat. Women's Soccer Team, 1987—2004; profl. soccer player San Diego Spirit, 2001—03. Named 3-time All-Am., 1987—89, Most Valuable Player, So. Calif., L.A. Times, 1987, World Cup Champion, 1991, 1999, MVP, WUSA, 2002, Defender of Yr., 2002; named to, U. Calif. Berkeley Hall of Fame, 1997; recipient Silver medal, Sydney Olympics, 2000. Achievements include 1995 FIFA World Cup, Sweden; 1994 CONCACAF Qualifying Championship, Montreal; U.S. Olympic Festival, Denver, 1995; FIFA Women's World Cup, Sweden, 1995; gold medal U.S. Women's Soccer Team, Atlanta Olympic Games, 1996, Athens Olympic Games, 2004; mem. Ajax of Manhattan Beach Club Soccer Team (champions U.S. Women's Amateur Nat. Cup, 1992, 93). Office: US Soccer Fedn 1801-1811 S Prairie Ave Chicago IL 60616

FAWCETT, MARIE ANN FORMANEK (MRS. ROSCOE KENT FAWCETT), civic leader; b. Mpls., Mar. 6, 1914; d. Peter Paul and Mary (Stepanek) Formanek; m. Roscoe Kent Fawcett, Mar. 16, 1935; children: Roscoe Kent, Peter Formanek, Roger Knowlton II, Stephen Hart. Cert., Harvard U., 1976-83. Chmn. of vols. Merry Go Round Club House and Mews, Greenwich, Conn., 1949-92, trustee, 1948-90, v.p., bd. dirs., 1949—, corr. sec., 1992—, chmn. entertainment, 1970-90; bd. dirs., vol. chmn., corr. sec. Nathaniel Witherell Hosp., Greenwich, 1952—, chmn. vols., 1956-89, corr. sec. aux. bd., 1956-94; bd. dirs., corr. sec. Nathaniel Witherell Auxiliary Hosp., 1952—. Chmn. vols. Greenwich Hosp., 1953-54; dist. chmn. ARC, Community Chest, Mental Health, 1946-50; vol. mentally retarded children Milbank Sch., Greenwich, 1958-92. Bd. dirs. Cerebral Palsy, Greenwich Symphony, 1956—, Greenwich Symphony Guild, 1956—, Putnam Indian-field Sch.; bd. dirs., corr. sec. Merry Go Round Mews, 1949—; bd. dirs. Multiple Sclerosis Soc., 1948—, v.p., 1970, corr. sec., 1958—; active drives for ARC, Community Chest, Leukemia, Muscular Dystrophy, Mental Health, Mentally Retarded Children Milbank Sch.; bd. dirs. Merry-Go-Round News for the Elderly, 1948—, Nathaniel Whitherell Hosp. for Elderly, 1952—, Greenwich Symphony Guild, 1956—, Travel Club Greenwich, 1982—; participating mem. Huxley Inst. Biosocial Rsch.; mem. polo com. Susan Cancer Fund, Pegasus Therapeutic Riding and Rusk Inst. Rehab. Medicine; trustee Menninger Found., Topeka. Named Woman of Year, Soroptimist Club, 1967; recipient Community Svc. award United Cerebral Palsy Assn. Fairfield County, 1972, Fund Drive award Cerebral Palsy, 1970, citations for 36 yrs. outstanding vol. svcs. Nathaniel Witherell Hosp. Aux., Conn. Dept. Health, 1977. Mem. Internat. Platform Assn., Smithsonian Inst., The Woman's Club of Greenwich, Travel Club of Greenwich (corr. sec., bd. dirs. 1982—), Charles F. Menninger Soc. (mem. Roll of Nonor 1998, Sustaining Excellence award). Home: 8141 12th Ave S Minneapolis MN 55425-1055

FAWCETT, SHERWOOD LUTHER, lab administrator; b. Youngstown, Ohio, Dec. 25, 1919; s. Luther T. and Clara (Sherwood) F.; m. Martha L. Simcox, Feb. 28, 1953; children: Paul, Judith, Tom. BS, Ohio State U., 1941, PhD (hon.); MS, Case Inst. Tech., 1948, PhD, 1950; PhD (hon.), Gonzaga U., Whitman Coll., Otterbein Coll., Detroit Inst. Tech., Ohio Dominican Coll. Registered profl. engr., Ohio. Mem. staff Columbus (Ohio) Labs. Battelle Meml. Inst., 1950-64, mgr. physics dept., 1959-64; dir. Pacific Northwest Labs., Richland, Wash., 1964-67; trustee Battelle Meml. Inst., Columbus, 1968-92, exec. v.p., 1967-68, CEO, 1968-84, pres., 1968-80, chmn., 1981-84, chmn. bd. trustees, 1985-87, assoc. trustee, 1987-94. Chmn. bd. dirs. Transmet Corp. With USNR, 1941-46. Decorated Bronze Star; recipient Washington award Western Soc. Engrs., 1989. Mem. AIME, NSPE, Am. Phys. Soc., Am. Nuc. Soc., Am. Phys. Soc., Sigma Xi, Tau Beta Pi, Delta Chi, Sigma Pi Sigma. Home: 1852A Riverside Dr Columbus OH 43212-1875 Office: Transmet Corp 4290 Perimeter Dr Columbus OH 43228-1036

FAWLEY, JOHN JONES, retired banker; b. Phila., Oct. 1, 1921; s. James L. and Edna (Jones) F.; m. Ann Kemp, Jan. 8, 1944; children: Jo Ann (Mrs. Richard High), Christine, James K. BS in Econs, U. Pa., 1948; grad., Rutgers U., 1957. With First Pa. Bank, Phila., 1948-69, sr. v.p., 1968-69; pres., dir. United Va. Bank/First & Citizens Nat. Bank, Alexandria, Va., 1969-72; exec. v.p. Indsl. Valley Bank, Phila., 1973-83, Dauphin Deposit Bank, Harrisburg, Pa., 1983-87. Lectr. Comml. Lending Sch., U. Okla., 1969 Former trustee Hahnemann U. With AUS, 1942-45. Mem. Robert Morris Assocs. (nat. pres. 1972-73), Masons. Home: Brittany Pointe Estates #2214 1001 Valley Ford Rd Lansdale PA 19446 also: Pinecrest Lake Pocono Pines PA 18350

FAWSETT, PATRICIA COMBS, federal judge; b. 1943; BA, U. Fla., 1965, MAT, 1966, JD, 1973. Pvt. practice law Akerman, Senterfitt & Edison, Orlando, Fla., 1973-86; commr. 9th Cir. Jud. Nominating Commn, 1973-75, Greater Orlando Crime Prevention Assn., 1983-86; judge US Dist. Ct. (Mid. Dist.) Fla., Orlando, 1986—, chief judge. Trustee Legal Aid Soc., 1977-81, Loch Haven Art Ctr., Inc., Orlando, 1980-84, U. Fla. Law Sch., 2001—; hon. trustee Reago Spiritual Scholarship Found., 1999—; commr. Orlando Housing Authority, 1976-80, Winter Park (Fla.) Sidewalk Festival, 1973-75; bd. dirs. Greater Orlando Area C. of C., 1982-85. Mem. ABA (trial lawyers sect., real estate probate sect.), Am. Judicaturs Soc., Assn. Trial Lawyers Am., Fla. Bar Found. (bd. dirs. grants com.), Commn. on Access to Cts., Fla. Coun. Bar Assn. Pres.'s (pres., bd. dirs. 9th cir. grievance com.) Osceola County Bar Assn., Fla. Bar (bd. govs. 1983-86, budget com., disciplinary rev. com., integration rule and bylaws com., com. on access to legal system, bd. of cert., designation and advt., jud. adminstrn., selection and tenure com., jud. nominating procedures com., pub. rels. com., ann. meeting com., appellate rules com., spl. com. on judiciary-trial lawyer rels., chairperson midyr. conv.

com., bd. dirs. trial lawyers sect.), Orange County Bar Assn. (exec. coun. 1977-83, pres. 1981-82), Order of Coif, Phi Beta Kappa. Office: US Dist Ct Federal Bldg 80 N Hughey Ave Ste 611 Orlando FL 32801-2231*

FAX, CHARLES SAMUEL, lawyer; b. Balt., Sept. 12, 1948; s. David Hirsch and Eleanor Shirley (Lobe) F.; m. Nancy Lee Gruenberg, 1980 (div. 1995); children: Joanna May, Benjamin Zachary; m. Michele Weil, 1996. BA, Johns Hopkins U., 1970; JD with honors, George Washington U., 1973. Bar: D.C. 1974, N.Y. 1974, Md. 1990. Office of dist. atty. N.Y.C. (Bronx county), 1973-74; assoc. Truitt & Fabrikant, Washington, 1974-75, Chapman, Duff & Paul, Washington, 1975-79, ptnr., 1979-84, Porter, Wright, Morris & Arthur, Washington, 1985-89; sr. ptnr., co-chmn. lit. dept. Shapiro Sher Guinot & Sandler (formerly Shapiro and Olander), Balt., 1989—; mem. exec. com. Shapiro Sher Guinot & Sandler, Balt., 1999—; gen. counsel Parents and Children Together, Inc., 1992-98; apptd. mediator Cir. Ct. for Balt. City, 1994-98; spl. outside litigation counsel Commonwealth P.R. Dept. Justice, 1998-2001, Balt. City Mayor, 1994—95. Mem. faculty Exec. Enterprises, Inc., N.Y.C., Chgo., 1985-86; lectr. fed. personnel litigation Adminstrv. Law Inst., Washington, Chgo., San Francisco, 1982-83; lectr. Md. Mcpl. League, 1990-98; book rev. Cleve. Plain Dealer. Co-author: Discovery Problems and Their Solutions, 2005; contbr. articles to newspapers and mags. Mem. Washington com. Sch. Arts and Scis., Johns Hopkins U., 1987—89; class of '70 agt. Johns Hopkins U., 1995—; chmn. Jewish Nat. Fund Nat. Makor Leadership Group, 2004—; nat. bd. trustees Jewish Nat. Fund, 2004—, bd. dirs. Md. region, 2002—, chmn. exec. com., 2002—03, chmn. Md. region ann. campaign, 2002, pres., 2003—05, pres. Mid-Atlantic zone, 2005—; bd. dirs. Am. Friends of Haifa Music Festival, 2002—03. Mem. Johns Hopkins U. Soc. for 2d Decade, Tudor and Stuart Club, Johns Hopkins Club, Alpha Delta Phi. Democrat. Jewish. Home: 10720 Gloxinia Dr North Bethesda MD 20852-3404 Office: Shapiro Sher Guinot & Sandler 36 S Charles St Ste 2000 Baltimore MD 21201-3147 E-mail: csf@shapirosher.com.

FAXON, ALICIA CRAIG, art educator, department chairman; b. NYC, July 27, 1931; d. William Donald and Clara Alicia (Harnecker) Craig; m. Richard Bremer Faxon, Feb. 21, 1953; children: Richard Paul, Thomas Hardwick. AB, Vassar Coll., 1952; MA, Radcliffe Coll., 1953, Boston U., 1971, PhD, 1979; DHL (hon.), Simmons Coll., 1998. Lectr. New Eng. Sch. Art and Design, Boston, 1974-77; acting dir. Danforth Mus., Framingham, Mass., 1977; teaching assoc. Boston U. Sch. for Art, 1978-79; vis. lectr. Simmons Coll., Boston, 1979-80, asst. prof. art, 1980-86, assoc. prof., 1986-91, chmn. dept. art and music, 1987-93, prof. art, 1991-93, alumnae endowed chair, 1992-93. Lectr. Sch. for Lifelong Learning, Harvard U., Cambridge, Mass., 1978-80; program chmnn. Women's Studies Adv. Bd., 1982-84; R.I. editor Art New Eng., 1994-99. Author: Catalog Raisonnè of Prints of J.-L. Forain, 1982, Pilgrims and Pioneers, 1987, Dante Gabriel Rossetti, 1989; co-author: (with Liana Cheney and Kathleen Russo) Self-Portraits of Woman Painters, 2000; co-editor (with Susan Casteras) Pre-Raphaelite Art in its European Context, 1995; mem. editl. bd. Woman's Art Jour., 1989—. Mem. acquisitions com. Danforth Mus., 1974—89, trustee, 1975—77. Recipient Nan award for art criticism Art New Eng., 1987; grantee Nat. Endowment for Arts, 1982, Simmons Coll., 1984, NEH, 1989, 92. Mem. Coll. Art Assn. (chmn. preRaphaelite session 1990), Pre-Raphaelites and the Myth Image (chmn. 2005), Women's Caucus for Art (program co-chmn. 1986-88), Victorian Soc., 19th Century Art Historians Group, Vassar Coll. Alumnae Assn. Democrat. Episcopalian. Avocations: travel, writing.

FAXON, DAVID PARKER, cardiologist; b. Manchester, NH, 1944; BA, Hamilton Coll., 1967; MD, Boston U. Med. Sch., 1971. Cert. internal medicine, cardiology. Intern Mary Hitchcock Meml. Hosp., 1971—72; resident, internal medicine Darmouth-Hitchcock Med. Ctr.; resident Mary Hitchcock Meml. Hosp., 1972—74; fellowship, cardiology Boston U. Hosp.; fellowship, cardiol. Mary Hitchcock Meml. Hosp., 1974—76; assoc. prof., medicine Boston U. Sch. Medicine; prof. medicine, dir. interventional cardiol., acting chief of cardiol. Boston U., 1976—93; prof., medicine, chief of divsn. of cardiol. USC, Los Angeles, 1993—2000, USC Med. Ctr., 1993—2000, U. Chgo. Med. Ctr., 2000—. Contbr. articles various profl. jours., chapters to books. Chmn. Am. Heart Assn. Sci. Adv. and Coord. Com.; edit. bd. mem. Circulation, The Am. Jour. of Cardiology, Jour. of the Am. Coll. of Cardiology Group. Mem.: Am. Heart Assn. (former pres., bd. of dirs.), Assn. U. Cardiologists, Soc. Cardiac Angiography and Interventions, Am. Coll. Cardiol. Achievements include first to angioplasty, a non-surgical technique for restoring blood flow through clogged arteries; research in methods to prevent renarrowing of vessels after angioplasty. Office: U Chgo Hosp Cardiol MC 6080 5841 S Md Ave Chicago IL 60637 Address: Ctr for Advanced Medicine 5758 S Md Ave Chicago IL 60637 Office Phone: 773-702-1919.

FAXON, JACK, headmaster; b. Detroit, June 9, 1936; s. Morris Faxon and Pauline Krimsky. BS in Edn., Wayne State U., 1956, MEd, 1958; MA in History, U. Mich., 1963. Tchr. Detroit Pub. Schs., 1956-64; founder, headmaster Internat. Sch., Farmington Hill, Mich., 1968—. Corp. dir. Cellex Bioscis. Corp. Inc., Mpls., 1988-2000; dir. Quest Biotech. Inc., Detroit, 1986—. Paintings exhibited in group shows at Wayne State U. (Arts award 1978), U. Mich., 1981; dancer The Nutcracker Ballet, Detroit Symphony Orch./Dance Detroit, 1979, 88-96, Sleeping Beauty, Mich. Opera Theater, 1994, Romeo and Juliet, 1996; singer Die Fledermaus, Naughty Marietta, Mich. Opera Theater, 1976, 77, 78, 79, 94. Elected del. to Mich. Constnl. Conv., State of Mich., Lansing, 1961-62, elected rep. to State Ho. of Reps., Lansing, 1964-70, elected senator, Lansing, 1970-94; pres. pro tem Mich. Senate, Lansing, 1977-83; bd. dirs. Anti Defamation League, Friends of African Art, Detroit, 1987-91, Friends of Asian Art, Detroit Inst. Arts, 1984-91, Russian Am. Studio Theater, 1991—; trustee Mich. Libr., Lansing, 1976-87; chmn. bd. trustees Harlem Sch. of the Arts, Inc., N.Y.C.; mem. Edn. Commn. of State, Denver, 1975-85, Mich. Hist. Soc., 1981-89, Mus. African Art, N.Y.C., 1993—; mem. com. on Jewish elderly svcs. Detroit Jewish Cmty. Coun.; bd. dirs. Harlem Sch. of the Arts, 1997--, chmn. bd., 2001-03, mem. exec. bd., 2003--. Recipient 1st pl. award Mich. Watercolor Soc., 1978, Citation of Merit, Wayne County Coun. on Smoking Health, 1981, Order of Arts and Letters award Republic France, 1984; Eagleton fellow Rutgers U., 1966. Mem. Founder Soc. Detroit Inst. Arts (life), Mus. African Art (N.Y.C.), Pres.'s Club (U. Mich.). Democrat. Avocations: ballet, performance art in opera, theater, painting, art. Office: The Internat Sch 28555 Middlebelt Rd Farmington Hills MI 48334-4129 E-mail: jackfaxon@msn.com.

FAXON, THOMAS BAKER, retired lawyer; b. Des Moines, Oct. 15, 1924; s. Ralph Henry and Prue (Baker) Faxon; m. Virginia Webb Johnson, Sept. 8, 1949; 1 child, Thomas Baker; 1 child, Rebecca Webb Osgood. BA, Princeton U., 1949; LLB, Harvard U., 1952. Bar: Colo. 1953. Asst. prof., asst. dir. Inst. Govt. U. N.C., Chapel Hill, 1952-53; assoc. Pershing, Bosworth, Dick & Dawson, Denver, 1953-57; ptnr. Dawson, Nagel, Sherman & Howard, Denver, 1957-84; of counsel Sherman & Howard, Denver, 1984-92. Bd. trustees Colo. Legal Aid Found., Denver, 1984-91. Bd. dirs. Urban League Colo., Denver, 1964-67, Colo. chpt. UN Assn. of U.S.A., 1980-81, Recording for the Blind Colo., 1988-94; pres. bd. trustees 1st Unitarian Ch., Denver, 1960; mem. Denver Equality of Edn. Com., 1969. USAAF, 1943-46. Mem.: Cactus Club. Democrat. Address: 431 College Ave Palo Alto CA 94306

FAY, ABBOTT EASTMAN, history professor; b. Scottsbluff, Nebr., July 19, 1926; s. Abbott Eastman and Ethel (Lambert) F.; m. Joan D. Richardson, Nov. 26, 1953; children: Rand, Diana, Collin. Grad., Scottsbluff (Nebr.) Jr. Coll.; BA, Colo. State Coll. Edn., 1949, MA, 1953; postgrad., U. Denver, 1961-63; cert. advanced study, Western State U., 1963. Tchr. Leadville (Colo.) Pub. Schs., 1950-52, elem. prin., 1952-54; prin. Leadville Jr. H.S., 1954-55; pub. info. dir., instr. history Mesa Coll., Grand Junction, Colo., 1955-64; asst. prof. history Western State Coll., Gunnison, Colo., 1964-76, assoc. prof. history, 1976-82, assoc. prof. emeritus, 1982—. Adj. faculty Adams State Coll., Alamosa, Colo., Mesa State Coll., Grand Junction, Colo., 1989—; propr. Mountaintop Books, Paonia, Colo.; bd. dirs. Colo. Assoc. Univ. Press; dir. hist. tours; columnist Valley Chronicle, Paonia, Best Years Beacon, Grand Junction, Free Press, Grand Junction, The Historian, Fruita, Colo., Grand Mesa Byway News, Delta, Colo.; profl. speaker in field; cons. Colo. Welcome Ctr., 1997—. Author: Mountain Academia, 1968, Writing Good History Research Papers, 1980, Ski Tracks in the Rockies, 1984, Famous Coloradans, 1990, I Never Knew That About Colorado, 1993, Beyond The Great Divide, 1999, To Think That This Happened in Grand County!, 1999, A History of Skiing in Colorado, 2000, More That I Never Knew About Colorado, 2000, The Story of Colorado Wines, 2002, Grand Mesa Country, 2005; playwright: Thunder Mountain Lives Tonight!; contbr. articles to profl. jours.; freelance writer popular mags. Founder, coord. Nat. Energy Conservation Challenge; travel cons. Colo. State Welcome Ctr., 1997-99; project reviewer NEH, Colo. Hist. Soc.; steering com. West Elk Scenic & Historic Byway, Colo., 1994—; founder Leadville (Colo.) Assembly, pres., 1953-54; mem. Advs. of Lifelong Learning, 1994—. Named Top Prof. Western State Coll., 1969, 70, 71; fellow Hamline U. Inst. Asian Studies, 1975, 79; recipient Colo. Ind. Pubs. award, 1998. Mem. Western Writers Am., Rocky Mountain Social Sci. Assn. (sec. 1961-63), Am. Hist. Assn., Assn. Asian Studies, Western History Assn., Western State Coll. Alumni Assn. (pres. 1971-73), Internat. Platform Assn. Profl. Guides Assn. Am. (cert.), Rocky Mountain Guides Assn., Colo. Antiquarian Booksellers Assn., Am. Legion (Outstanding Historian award 1981), Phi Alpha Theta, Phi Kappa Delta, Delta Kappa Pi. Home: 679 Brentwood Dr 11A Palisade CO 81526

FAY, CONNER MARTINDALE, retired church administrator; b. Chillicothe, Mo., May 9, 1929; s. Vernon Martindale and Corinne (Conner) F.; m. Evelyn Caffey Buford, Dec. 2, 1961; children: Leslie Conner Francesca, Buford Martindale Edoardo, David Curtis Anselmo. BA, Yale U., 1951; MBA cum laude, Harvard U., 1953. Brand mgr. Procter & Gamble Co., Cin., 1956-62; mktg. mgr. Procter & Gamble Co. Italia, Rome, 1962-69; sr. v.p. Clairol Inc., N.Y.C., 1970-89; mgmt. cons., 1989-93; ret., 1993. Mem. bd. fgn. parishes Am. Episcopal Ch., N.Y., 1977-2005, pres., 1989-2005; bd. dirs. St. Paul's Ch., Rome, 1977-2005, pres., 1989-2001; bd. dirs. St. James Ch., Florence, Italy, 1977-2005, pres., 1989-2000; vice chmn. St. Stephen's Sch., Rome, 1980-94; trustee Samuel and Lois Silberman Fund of N.Y. Cmty. Trust, 1993—; sr. warden St. Mary the Virgin Episcopal Ch., Chappaqua, N.Y., 1982-83, 91-93; chmn. coun. of advisors Hunter Sch. Social Work, CUNY, 1985-97; various offices Yale Alumni Fund, including chmn., 1996-98, agt., 1996-, 50th reunion co-chair Class of 1951, 2001; bd. dirs. Yale Alumni Chorus Found., 2003—, v.p., 2004-; bd. dirs. Katonah Mus. Art, 1995-, treas., 2001-03. Recipient Yale medal, 2000. Mem. Am. Indsl. Health Coun. (bd. dirs. 1979-91, chmn. 1988-89), Yale Glee Club Assocs. (pres. 1979-81, treas. 1996-2001), Yale Club. Republican. Avocation: music. Office Phone: 914-763-4680. Business E-Mail: conner.fay@aya.yale.edu.

FAY, DONALD P., lawyer; m. Patricia W. Fay; children: Carolyn J., Catherine A. BSME, MME, JD, So. Meth. U. Atty. comml. law dept. Johnson & Wortley PC; sr. counsel HCA Inc., 1993—94, v.p. legal, 1994—97, sr. v.p. Pacific Group, 1998—99; exec. v.p., gen. counsel, corp. sec. Triad Hospitals Inc., Plano, Tex., 1999—. Office: Triad Hospitals Inc 5800 Tennyson Pkwy Plano TX 75024

FAY, GLENN MILLS, JR., science educator; b. Middlebury, Vt., July 3, 1954; s. Glenn Mills Sr. and Virginia Field (Powers) F.; m. Donna Sutton, Jul. 11, 1987; children: Addison, Lillian. BS, U. Vt., 1976, EdD, 1995; MEd, Colo. State U., 1981. Sci. tchr. Lake Region Union H.S., Orleans, Vt., 1976—79, Shelburne (Vt.) Mid. Sch., 1982—83, Champlain Valley H.S., Hinesbury, Vt., 1983—. Adj. prof. U. Vt. Burlington, Trinity Coll. Vt. Author: Science in the Service of Reform, 1992; contbr. articles to profl. jours. Recipient Gustav Ohaus award NSTA Ohaus, 1990, Scimat fellowship NSF, 1993, Presdl. award in Excellence in Teaching NSF, 1993. Mem. Vt. Sci. Tchrs. Assn. (bd. dirs. 1991—), Vt. Profl. Standards Bd (bd. dirs. 1995-2001), Nat. Sci. Tchrs. Assn. Avocations: running, hiking. Home: PO Box 177 South Hero VT 05486-0177 Office: Champlain Valley Union HS 369 CVU Rd Hinesburg VT 05461-9403

FAY, JAMES ALAN, mechanical engineering educator; b. Southold, N.Y., Nov. 1, 1923; s. William Joseph, Jr. and Margaret (Keenan) F.; m. Agatha Marie Kelly, Jan. 12, 1946; children: David Anthony, Mark Bernard, Colin Michael, Jamie Martin, Peter Robert, Michele Marie. BS, Webb Inst. Naval Architecture, 1944; MS, MIT, 1947; PhD, Cornell U., 1951. Research engr. Lima-Hamilton Corp., 1947-49; asst. prof. engring. mechanics Cornell U., 1951-55; mem. faculty MIT, 1955-89, prof. mech. engring., 1960-89, prof. emeritus, 1989—. Cons. to govt. and industry; mem. NRC Environ. Studies Bd., 1973-78, 80-83 Author: (Text books) Molecular Thermodynamics, 1965, Introduction to Fluid Mechanics, 1994, Energy and the Environment, 2002; contbr. articles to profl. jours. Chmn. Boston Air Pollution Commn., 1969-72, Mass. Port Authority, 1972-77; bd. dirs. Union Concerned Scientists, 1978—, Conservation Law Found., 1984-94. Served with USNR, 1942-46. Overseas fellow Churchill Coll., Cambridge U., 1980; Fulbright lectr., India, 1990. Fellow Am. Acad. Arts and Scis., Am. Phys. Soc. (exec. com. div. fluid dynamics 1964-67), AAAS, AIAA (chmn. plasmadynamics com. 1966-68); mem. NAE, ASME, Air and Waste Mgmt. Assn., Sigma Xi. Home: 36 Spruce Hill Rd Weston MA 02493-2134 Office: MIT Rm 3-258 Cambridge MA 02139-4307 Office Phone: 617-253-2236. Business E-Mail: jfay@mit.edu.

FAY, KEVIN J., public relations executive; Grad., U. Va.; JD, Am. U. Bar: Va. With Alcalde & Fay, Arlington, Va., 1982—; pres. Exec. dir. Internat. Climate Change Partnership; counsel Alliance for Responsible Atmosphere Policy; appeared on numerous TV and radio shows. Bd. dirs. World Children's Choir; mem. exec. com. Leukemia Soc. Ball. Named Citizen of Yr., McLean Times and Providence Jour.; recipient Lord Fairfax award, Fairfax County Bd. Supervisors, 2000, Cath. Schools Bus. Partnership award, Cath. Bus. Network No. Va., 1999, 2000. Office: Alcalde & Fay 2111 Wilson Blvd 8th Fl Arlington VA 22201 also: 400 N Capitol St NW Ste 475 Washington DC 20001 Office Phone: 202-783-6669, 703-841-0626.*

FAY, SISTER MAUREEN A., university president; BA in English magna cum laude, Siena Heights Coll., 1960; MA in English, U. Detroit, 1966; PhD, U. Chgo., 1976. Tchr. English, speech, moderator student newspaper, student council St. Paul High Sch., Grosse Pointe, Mich., 1960-64; chairperson English dept., dir. student dramatics, moderator student publs. Dominican High Sch., Detroit, 1964-69; co-dir. Cath. student ctr. Adrian (Mich.) Coll., 1969-71; instr. English Siena Heights Coll., Adrian, 1969-71; evaluators inst. criminal justice execs. U. Chgo., 1971-73; instr. English U. Ill., Chgo., 1971-74; dir. evaluation sch. new learning DePaul U., Chgo., 1974-75; fellow in acad. adminstrn. Saint Xavier Coll., Chgo., 1975-76, dean. grad. studies, 1979-83, dean continuing edn., 1976-83; asst. prof. No. Ill. U., Dekalb, 1980-83; pres. Mercy Coll. Detroit, 1983-90, U. Detroit Mercy, 1990—. V.p. VAUT Corp, bd. dirs. four inner city high schs., Archdiocese Chgo.; mem. exec. com. Assn. Mercy Colls.; adv. com. Adult Learning Svcs., The Coll. Bd., Met. Affairs Corp. of Detroit and S.E. Mich., cons. Nat. Assn. for Religious Women, 1974-75, North Cen. Assn. Colls. and Schs., evaluator commn. on higher edn.; trustee Rosary Coll., River Forest, Ill., New Detroit, Inc., 1993; emeritus mem. div. bd. Mercy Hosps. and Health Svcs. of Detroit; bd. dirs. Nat. Bank of Detroit., Detroit Econ. Growth Corp., 1992; mem. Nat. Commn. Ind. Higher Edn.; commr. North Central Assocs., Commn. on Instns. of Higher Edn., 1993. Asst. editor: (book rev.): Adult Education, A Journal of Research and Theory, 1971-74. Bd. dirs. United Way SE Mich., 1991, Assn. Catholic Colls. and Univs., 1992; Steering com. Metro Detroit GIVES; exec. com., edn. task force Detroit Strategic Planning com., 1987; trustee Mich. Opera Theatre; bd. dirs. Greater Detroit Interfaith Round Table Nat. Conf. Christians and Jews, Inc., The Detroit Symphony; mem. Nat. Bipartisan Commn. on Ind. Higher Edn. in U.S., 1993. Mem. Am. Assn. Higher Edn., North Cen. Assn. (cons., evaluator commn. on higher edn.), Nat. Assn. Ind. Colls. and Univs. (bd. dirs.), Assn. Ind. Colls. and Univs. of Mich. (exec. com., chairperson), Am. Assn. Cath. Colls. and Univs., AAUW, Pi Lambda Theta. Office: U Detroit Mercy Office Pres PO Box 19900 4001 W McNichols Rd Detroit MI 48219-0900

FAY, MICHAEL LEO, lawyer; b. Springfield, Mass., Oct. 3, 1949; s. Joseph L. and Marie A. (Wilson) Fay; children: Matthew, Kathryn, Christopher. BA summa cum laude, Dartmouth Coll., 1971; postgrad., Oxford (Eng.) U., 1972; JD, Harvard U., 1975. Bar: Mass. 1975, U.S. Tax Ct. 1992. Assoc. Hale & Dorr, Boston, 1975-80, jr. ptnr., 1980-85, sr. ptnr., 1985—, former chmn. pvt. client dept. Bd. dirs. Family Firm Inst., 1993—99; lectr. Mass. Continuing Legal Edn., Boston, 1984—. Mem. corp. Tenacre Country Day Sch., Wellesley Hills, Mass., 1992—, Ptnrs. Healthcare, 1994—; overseer Aquinas House/Cath. Students Ctr. Dartmouth Coll., Hanover, NH, 1984—; sec. Dartmouth Ednl. Assn., Boston, 1984—. Fellow: Am. Coll. Trust and Estate Counsel; mem.: ABA, Boston Bar Assn., Mass. Bar Assn., Dartmouth Club Greater Boston (sec. 1984—2000), Dartmouth Alumni Coun. Republican. Roman Catholic. Office: Wilmer Cutler Pickering Hale and Dorr 60 State St Boston MA 02109-1816 Office Phone: 617-526-6320. Business E-Mail: michael.fay@wilmerhale.com.

FAY, MIRIAM SOLER, guidance counselor, educator; d. Jose Hugo and Maria Carmen Soler; m. Jack Revelle Fay, Jan. 12, 1984; children: Jessica, Eric. Degree in Law, St. Thomas U., 1969; MEd in Guidance & Counseling, Stetson U., 1992; EdD in Ednl. Leadership, U. Mo., 2004. Labor Law Specialist: Xaverian U., Colombia 1973; State Cert. K-12 Sch. Guidance Counselor Fla., 1995, State Lic. K-12 Sch. Guidance Counselor Kans., 1997, State Cert. K-12 Sch. Guidance Counselor Okla., 1999, Mo., 2000. Creator, labor counselor for women and minors Ministry of Labor and Social Security, 1983—93, govt. mediator for labor unions, 1970—83; guidance counselor Volusia County Schs., 1993—96, co-sponsor of tchrs. as mentors, 1994—95; guidance counselor Tulsa Pub. Schs., 1997—98, Lewis & Clark Mid. Sch., Tulsa, Okla., 1997—98, Neosho R-5 Sch. Dist., Mo., 2001—; rsch. assoc. Mo. So. State U., Joplin, 1998—2001. Career fairs sponsor Osteen, 1994—95, DeLeon Springs, 1994—95; chair students reach-out program; coord. career fairs, testing and parenting groups Neosho R-5 Sch. Dist.; co-sponsor secondary migrant summer inst. for minorities at risk. Creator labor counsel Women and Minors Task Force; career and employability edn. sponsor HS Summer Migrant Inst., 1996. Mem.: Am. Ednl. Rsch. Assn., Am. Sch. Counselors Assn., Phi Delta Kappa Internat. Avocations: home improvement projects, volunteering. Office Phone: 417-437-1670. Personal E-mail: m_fay@sbcglobal.net.

FAY, PETER THORP, federal judge; b. Rochester, NY, Jan. 18, 1929; s. Lester Thorp and Jane (Baumler) Fay; m. Claudia Pat Zimmerman, Oct. 1, 1958; children: Michael Thorp, William, Darcy. BA, Rollins Coll., 1951, LLD, 1971; JD, U. Fla., 1956; LLD, Biscayne Coll., 1975. Bar: Fla. 1956, U.S. Supreme Ct. 1961. Ptnr. firm Nichols, Gaither Green, Frates & Beckham, Miami, Fla., 1956—61, Frates, Fay, Floyd & Pearson (and predecessors), Miami, 1961—70; prof. Fla. Jr. Bar Practical Legal Inst., 1959—65; judge U.S. Dist. Ct. for So. Fla., Miami, 1970—76, U.S. Ct. Appeals (5th cir.), 1976—81, U.S. Ct. Appeals (11th cir.), 1981—94, sr. judge, 1994—; lectr. Fla. Bar Legal Inst., 1959—; faculty Fed. Jud. Center, Washington, 1974—94. Mem. Jud. Conf. Com. for Implementation Criminal Justice Act, 1974—82, Adv. Com. on Codes of Conduct, 1980—87, Ad Hoc Com. on Cameras in the Courtroom, 1983—84, Adv. Com. on Appellate Rules, 1987—90, Eleventh Circuit Standing Edn. Com.; mem. exec. com. Eleventh Circuit Judicial Coun.; co-chmn. Nat. Jud. Coun. for State and Fed. Cts., 1990—. Mem. Orange Bowl Com., 1974—; dist. collector United Fund, 1957—70; mem. adminstrv. bd. St. Thomas U., 1970—; trustee U. Miami, Fla., 1989—; mem., supr. Ind. Counsel, 1994—. Lieutenant USAF, 1951—53. Mem.: ABA, Medico Legal Inst., John Marshall Bar Assn. (past pres.), Dade County Bar Assn., Fla. Bar Assn., Fla. Acad. Trial Attys., Law Sci. Acad., Miami C. of C., U. Fla. Alumni Assn. (dir.), Fla. Coun. of 100, Miami Club, Coral Oaks Club (Miami), Wildcat Cliffs Club (N.C.), Snapper Creek Lakes Club (Miami), Phi Delta Theta (past sec.), Phi Kappa Phi, Pi Gamma Mu (past pres.), Omicron Delta Kappa (past pres.), Phi Delta Phi (past pres.), Order of Coif. Republican. Roman Catholic.*

FAY, REGAN JOSEPH, lawyer; b. Cleve., Sept. 19, 1948; s. Robert J. and Loretta Ann (Regan) F.; m. Michelle P. Fay; children: John, Mary, Matthew, Jessica, Samantha. BS in Chem. Engring., MIT, 1970; JD with honors, George Washington U., 1974. Bar: Ohio 1974, U.S. Dist. Ct. (no. dist.) Ohio 1974, U.S. Patent Office 1973, U.S. Ct. Appeals (fed. cir.) 1974, U.S. Ct. Appeals (9th cir.) 1975, U.S. Dist. Ct. (ea. dist.) Wis. 1976, U.S. Dist. Ct. (no. dist.) Tex. 1986, U.S. Supreme Ct. 1988. Patent examiner U.S. Patent and Trademark Office, Washington, 1970-72; law clk. to presiding justice U.S. Ct. Customs and Patent Appeals, Washington, 1973-75; assoc. Yount & Tarolli, Cleve., 1975-79; assoc., then ptnr. Jones, Day, Reavis & Pogue, Cleve., 1979—. Lectr. patent and trademark law Case Western Res. U., Cleve., 1976-86. Mem. Cleve. Intellectual Property Law Assn (pres. 1996-97). Republican. Roman Catholic. Avocation: skiing. Office: Jones Day Reavis & Pogue 901 Lakeside Ave E Cleveland OH 44114-1190 Office Phone: 216-586-7327. E-mail: rjfay@jonesday.com.

FAY, SARAH L., secondary school educator; b. Anchorage, Alaska, Oct. 7, 1976; d. Grover C. and Jacklyn L. Bowen; m. Ron C. Fay, Mar. 30, 1996. BSc, Calvin Coll., 1998. Cert. tchr. Ill., 2000. Tchr. math, physics Chgo. Christian H.S., Palos Heights, Ill., 1998—2001; tchr. physics Zion (Ill.) Benton Twp. H.S., 2001—. Co-sponsor Healthy Youth, Zion, 2003—05; leader youth group Cornerstone Cmty. Ch., Waukegan, Ill., 2003—05. Mem.: Nat. Sci. Tchrs. Assn. Avocation: sewing. Home: 4118 Greenleaf Court 301 Park City IL 60085 Office: Zion Benton Township High School One Z-B Way Zion IL 60099 Office Phone: 847-731-9576. Personal E-mail: physics_chaquita@hotmail.com. E-mail: fays@zbths.org.

FAY, TERRENCE MICHAEL, lawyer; b. Cleve., Feb. 25, 1953; s. J. Francis and Alice Wilsona (Porter) F.; m. Beverly Ann Luciow, Feb. 25, 1983; children: Robert Michael, Katherine Elizabeth. BA cum laude, Baldwin Wallace Coll., 1974, BS cum laude, 1975; JD, Ohio State U., 1978. Bar: Ohio 1978, U.S. Dist. Ct. (no. dist.) Ohio 1983, U.S. Dist. Ct. (so. dist.) Ohio 1987, U.S. Ct. Appeals (6th cir.) 1987, U.S. Dist. Ct. (no. dist.) Ind. 1992, U.S. Dist. Ct. (ea. dist.) Mich. 1993. Law clk. for chief adminstrv. law judge Ohio Power Siting Commn., Columbus, 1977-78; asst. atty. gen. environ. sect. Ohio Atty. Gen.'s Office, Columbus, 1978-87, chief civil atty., 1987-88; sr. assoc. Smith & Schnacke, L.P.A., Columbus, 1988-89, Benesch, Friedlander, Coplan & Aronoff, Columbus, 1989-90, ptnr., 1992—2001, chair hiring com., 1995—97; of counsel Frost, Brown Todd LLC, Columbus, 2002—. Bd. dirs. Hucksters, Inc., Columbus, 1990. Abrahms scholar, 1975; recipient Book award Lawyers Coop., Inc., 1978, Ohio Gov.'s Spl. Recognition award, 1988. Mem. Phi Alpha Theta, Omicron Delta Kappa, Pi Kappa Delta, Psi Chi. Office: Frost Brown Todd LLC One Columbus Ste 1000 10 W Broad St Columbus OH 43215-3467 Office Phone: 614-559-7213. Business E-Mail: tfay@fbtlaw.com.

FAY, THOMAS A., philosopher, educator; b. Utica, N.Y., July 18, 1927; s. Thomas A. and Theresa A. (Miller) F.; m. Evelyn C. DaCorta, Apr. 6, 1984 BA, Cath. U. Am., 1952; MA, U. Laval, Quebec, 1963; PhD, Fordham U., 1970. Asst. prof. philosophy St. Bernard Coll., 1963-64; mem. faculty St. John's U., Jamaica, N.Y., 1967—, prof. philosophy, 1977—; chmn. dept. philosophy St John's U., Jamaica, N.Y., 1974-80. Vis. prof. Drew U., 1969 Author: Heidegger: The Critique of Logic, 1977, And Smoking Flax Shall He Not Quench: Reflections on New Testament Themes, 1979; mem. editorial bd. Guidebook for Publishing Philosophy, 1977, 2d edit., 1986; contbr. articles to profl. jours. Served with U.S. Army, 1945-46. Mem. Am. Cath. Philos. Assn. (pres. Met. chpt. 1975-81, exec. council 1976-79), Internat. Thomistic Soc. (v.p.), Internat. Soc. Metaphysics, Am. Philos. Assn., Medieval Acad. Am. Home: 20 Melody Ln Kings Park NY 11754-5026 E-mail: tafay@aol.com.

FAY, TONI GEORGETTE, communications executive; b. N.Y.C., Apr. 25, 1947; d. George E. and Allie C. (Smith) Fay. BA, Duquesne U., Pitts., 1968; MSW, U. Pitts., 1972, MEd, 1973; cert., Yale U. Drug Dependence Unit, 1973. Caseworker N.Y.C. Dept. Welfare, 1968-70; regional commr. Gov. Pa. Coun. Drugs and Alcohol, 1973-76; dir. social svcs. Pitts. Drug Abuse Ctr.,

1972-73; dir. planning and devel. Nat. Coun. Negro Women, 1977-79; exec. v.p. D. Parke Gibson Assocs., 1979-82; mgr. cmty. rels. Time Inc. (now Time-Warner Inc.), N.Y.C., 1982-83, dir. corp. cmty. rels. and affirmative action, 1983-93, v.p., corp. officer, 1993-2001; pres. TGF Assocs., Englewood, N.J., 2001—. Bd. dirs. UNICEF, Congl. Black Caucus Found., NAACP Legal Def. Fund Bd., Franklin and Eleanor Inst., Apollo Theatre Found.; apptd. bd. advs. Nat. Inst. Literacy, 1996—, Corp. for Nat. and Cmty. Svc., 2000. Named Woman of Yr., Pitts. YWCA, 1975, N.Y. Women's Forum; recipient Twin award YWCA of USA, 1987; named one 100 Top Women in Bus., Dollars and Sense Mag., 1986. Office: TGF Assocs 233 W Hudson Ave Englewood NJ 07631 Personal E-mail: tonigfay@aol.com.

FAYARD, GARY P., food products executive; BA, U.of Alabama. Ptnr., area dir. audit svcs., manfacturing svcs. Ernst & Young; dep. controller, v.p. Coca-Cola, 1994-99, sr. v.p., CFO, 1999—. Office: Coca Cola Co PO Box 1734 Atlanta GA 30313*

FAYHEE, MICHAEL R., lawyer; b. Canton, Ill., Dec. 18, 1948; m. Janice L. Fayhee. BS summa cum laude, U. Ill., 1970; JD cum laude, U. Mich., 1973. Bar: Ill. 1973. Ptnr., chmn. firm tax dept. McDermott, Will & Emery, Chgo. Former adj. prof. John Marshall Law Sch. Mem. ABA, Ill. State Bar Assn., Chgo. Bar Assn. Office: McDermott Will & Emery 227 W Monroe St Ste 3100 Chicago IL 60606-5096 Office Phone: 312-984-7522. Office Fax: 312-984-7700. Business E-Mail: mfayhee@mwe.com.

FAZAKAS, ART HERSCHEL, writer, educator, editor; b. N.Y.C., Aug. 29, 1952; s. Arpard Albert Fazakas and Sylvia Vivian Siegel; m. Ruth Ann Cunningham, Nov. 7, 1992 (div. Jan. 20, 2000). BA in Math., CUNY, 1977. Sec. East Asia Nat. Coun. Chs., N.Y.C., 1997; tech. writer Eli Lilly & Co., Indpls., 1998; lead writer web content MSN Gaming Zone, Redmond, Wash., 1999; tech. editor Boeing Chem. Equipment, Auburn, Wash., 2000, Microsoft Windows, Redmond, 2000; self-employed home organizer Edmonds, Wash., 2002—. Writing instr. Indpls. Writers Ctr., Discover U, Seattle. Author: Microsoft spl. project Kasparov vs. the World; contbr. articles to mags. and websites. Vol. KCTS-TV Channel 9, Seattle, 2002—; fund raiser Seattle (Wash.) Symphony, 2003, Seattle (Wash.) Chamber Music Festival. Recipient Hon. mention for feature writing, Writers Digest mag., 1996, 1999. Mem.: Soc. for Tech. Comm., The Mountaineers, Hostelling Internat., Sierra Club. Democrat. Avocations: classical piano, hiking, bicycle touring, travel. Home: 103 13th Ave E # 30 Seattle WA 98102 E-mail: northwestart@yahoo.com.

FAZIO, EVELYN M., publisher, writer, agent, editor; b. Hackensack, N.J. BA in History, U. Bridgeport, 1975; MA in History, U. Conn., 1977. Cert. social studies tchr., N.J. Tchr. social studies Cedar Grove (N.J.) High Sch., 1977-79; prodn. editor Prentice-Hall, Inc., Englewood Cliffs, N.J., 1980-82, devel. editor, 1982-83, acquisitions editor, 1983-85; sr. acquisitions editor P-H/Simon & Schuster, Inc., Englewood Cliffs, 1985-88; mng. editor Random House, Inc., N.Y.C., 1988—; exec. editor polit. sci., internat. rels. and policy studies Paragon House Pubs., Inc., N.Y.C., 1989-91; editorial dir. Marshall Cavendish Pubs., N. Bellmore, N.Y., 1992-95; v.p., pub. M.E. Sharpe, Armonk, NY, 1995—2001; v.p. e-content acquisition Baker & Taylor, Bridgewater, NJ, 2001—03; dir. EMF Agy., Hackensack, NJ, 2003—; ptnr. Internat. Lit. Arts, LLC, Hackensack, NJ, 2004—, Moscow, Pa., 2004—. Co-author: (series) Staying Sane When Your Family Comes to Visit, Staying Sane When You're Dieting, Staying Sane When You Quit Smoking. Mem.: ALA (panelist Charleston conf. 2000).

FAZIO, PETER VICTOR, JR., lawyer; b. Chgo., Jan. 22, 1940; s. Peter Victor and Marie Rose (LaMantia) F.; m. Patti Ann Campbell, Jan. 3, 1966; children: Patti-Marie, Catherine, Peter. AB, Coll. of Holy Cross, Worcester, Mass., 1961; JD, U. Mich., 1964. Bar: Ill. 1964, U.S. Dist. Ct. (no. dist.) Ill. 1965, U.S. Ct. Appeals (7th cir.) 1972, U.S. Supreme Ct. 1977, D.C. 1981, U.S. Ct. Appeals (D.C. cir.) 1988, Ind. 1993. Assoc. Schiff, Hardin & Waite, Chgo., 1964-70, ptnr., 1970-82, 84-95, mng. ptnr., 1995—2000, chmn., 2001—; exec. v.p. Internat. Capital Equipment, Chgo., 1982-83, also bd. dirs., 1982-85, sec., 1982-87; exec. v.p., gen. counsel NiSource Inc., 2000—. Bd. dirs. Planmetrics Inc., Chgo., 1984-92, Chgo. Lawyers Commn. for Civil Rights Under Law, 1976-82, co-chmn., 1978-80; bd. dirs. Seton Health Corp. No. Ill., Chgo 1987-90, vice chmn., 1989-90. Trustee Barat Coll., Lake Forest, Ill., 1977-82; bd. dirs. St. Joseph Hosp., Chgo., 1990-95, mem. exec. adv. bd., 1984-89, chmn., 1986-89; vice chmn. bd. dirs. Cath. Health Ptnrs., 1995-99, chmn., 1999—; dir. exec. com. Ill. Coalition, 1994-2005, N.W. Ind. Forum, 1994-98. Mem. ABA (coun. 1991-94, chmn. sect. pub. utility, transp. and comm. law 2000-01), FBA, Ill. Bar Assn., Chgo. Bar Assn., Fed. Energy Bar Assn., Edison Electric Inst. (chmn. legal com. 1999-2001), Am. Gas Assn. (legal com.), Am. Soc. Corp. Secs., Met. Club, Econ. Club Chgo., Comml. Club Chgo. Office: Schiff Hardin LLP 6600 Sears Tower 233 S Wacker Dr Chicago IL 60606-6473 also: NiSource Inc 801 E 86th Ave Merrillville IN 46410 Office Phone: 312-258-5634. E-mail: pfazio@schiffhardin.com.

FAZIO, SERGIO, medical educator, researcher; MD in Medicine summa cum laude, U. Rome, 1983; PhD in Molecular Biology, U. Siena, Italy, 1989. Intern and resident in internal medicine U. Rome, 1983—86; resident svc. of emergency medicine Gen. Hosp. Udine, Italy, 1984—85; fellow in metabolism dept. medicine Univ. Hosp. U. Rome, 1986—88; postdoctoral fellow Gladstone Inst. Cardiovasc. Disease, San Francisco, 1988—91, staff rsch. investigator, 1991—93; rsch. fellow Cardiovasc. Rsch. Inst. U. Calif., San Francisco, 1988—93; asst. prof. medicine and pathology, dir. lipid lab. Vanderbilt U., Nashville, 1993—, assoc. prof. medicine and pathology, co-dir. atherosclerosis rsch. unit. Ad hoc reviewer: Jour. Biol. Chemistry, Biochimica Biophysica Acta, Lipids, Arteriosclerosis and Thrombosis, Jour. of Lipid Rsch., Diabetes; contbr. articles to profl. jours. Recipient Pilot Project and Young Investigator award, CNRU, Established Investigatorship award, Am. Heart Assn., 1996, grant-in-aid, 1995, Joe C. Davies Found. scholarship. Fellow: Am. Heart Assn. (mem. coun. on arteriosclerosis); mem.: Am. Fedn. for Clin. Rsch. Office: Vanderbilt U Sch Medicine Divsn Cardioly 315 Mrb II 2220 Pierce Ave Nashville TN 37232-0001

FAZIO, VICTOR HERBERT, JR., lawyer, former congressman; b. Winchester, Mass., Oct. 11, 1942; m. Judy Kern; children: Dana Fazio, Anne Fazio (dec.), Kevin Kern, Kristie Kern. BA, Union Coll., Schenectady, 1965; postgrad., Calif. State U., Sacramento. Journalist, founder Calif. Jour.; congl. and legis. cons., 1966-75; mem. Calif. State Assembly, 1975-78; mem. 96th -103rd Congresses from Calif. 3rd Dist., 1979-98; former chmn. Dem. Congl. Campaign Com.; chmn. Dem. caucus, house steering policy com.; mem. legis. br. appropriations subcom.; ranking mem. appropriations subcom. energy and water; mem. Ho. budget com. 97th-100th Congress; majority whip-at-large 96th-105th Congress; also co-chmn. Fed. Govt. Svcs. Task Force 96th-101st Congresses, former chmn. bipartisan com. on ethics; mem. approriations com. 105th Congress; sr. ptnr. Clark & Weinstock, Washington, 1999—; sr. advisor Akin Gump Strauss Hauer & Feld LLP, Washington, 2005—. Former mem. Sacramento County Charter and Planning Commns. Bd. dirs. Asthma Allergy Found., Jr. Statesman, Nat. Italian-Am. Found. Coro Found. fellow; named Solar Congressman of Yr. Mem. Air Force Assn. Office: Clark & Weinstock Inc 52 Vanderbilt Ave New York NY 10017-3808

FAZIO, VICTOR WARREN, physician, colon and rectal surgeon; b. Sydney, Australia, Feb. 2, 1940; came to U.S., 1971; s. Victor Warren and Kathleen Eleanor (Hills) F.; m. Carolyn Kisandra Sawyer, Dec. 2, 1961; children: Victor, Jane, David. MB, BChir, U. Sydney, 1965, MS (hon.), 1997; PhD (hon.), U. Lodz, 2003. Diplomate Am. Bd. Colon and Rectal Surgery (pres. 1991-92). Intern and resident St. Vincent's Hosp., Sydney, 1965-67, surgical registrar, 1969-71; lectr. anatomy U. NSW Med. Sch., Sydney, 1967; surg. registrar Repatriation Gen. Hosp., Concord, Australia, 1968; gen. surgeon Australian Surg. Team, Bien Hoa, Vietnam, 1971; fellow gen. surgery Lahey Clinic, Boston, 1972; fellow colorectal surgery Cleve. Clinic, 1973, staff surgeon colorectal surgery, 1974, chmn. dept. colon and rectal surgery, vice chmn. divsn. surgery, 1975—. Bd. govs. Cleve. Clinic Found., 1990-95, 98-99, exec. mem. bd. trustees, 1994-95. Author 320 manuscripts and book chpts.; editor: Current Therapy in Colon and Rectal Surgery, 1989; editor-in-chief Diseases of Colon and Rectum, 1997—. Decorated Order of Australia. Fellow ACS, Royal Australian Coll. Surgeons (hon.), Royal Australasian Coll. Surgeons, Am. Soc. Colon and Rectal Surgery (pres. 1995-96), Royal Coll. Surgeons (Eng., hon.), Royal Coll. Surgeons (Edinburgh, hon.); mem. Soc. Pelvic Surgeons (exec. com. 1980), Soc. for Surgery Alimentary Tract, Ctrl. Surg. Assn., James IV Assn. Surgeons, Ohio Valley Soc. Colon and Rectal Surgeons (past pres.). Roman Catholic. Avocations: naval history, sailing. Office: Cleve Clinic Desk A-111 9500 Euclid Ave Cleveland OH 44195-0001

FAZZOLARI, SALVATORE D., mining products executive; BBA in Acctg., Pa. State U. CPA, Pa.; cert. info. sys. auditor. With Pa. Auditor Gens. Bur. Spl. Audits; sr. auditor Harsco Corp., Camp Hill, Pa., 1980-85, dir. internal audit, 1985-93, sr. v.p., COO, 1993—. Office: Harsco Corp PO Box 8888 350 Poplar Church Rd Camp Hill PA 17011

FEAL, GISELE CATHERINE, foreign language educator; b. Froges, France, July 5, 1939; PhD in Spanish, U. Paris, 1964; PhD in French, U. Mich., 1973. Instr. Ea. Mich. U., Ypsilanti; lectr. U. Mich., Ann Arbor; asst. prof. SUNY Coll., Buffalo, 1974-80, chair dept., 1977-80; assoc. prof. SUNY, Buffalo, 1980—92, assoc. v.p., 1983-88, prof., 1992—2002. Author: Le Théatre de Crommelynck, 1976, La Mythologie Matriarcale, 1993, Ionesco. Un Theatre Onirique, 2001. Mem. Cercle Culturel de Langue Française (bd. dirs. 1980-93). E-mail: fealgc@aol.com.

FEARING, WILLIAM KELLY, art educator, artist; b. Fordyce, Ark., Oct. 18, 1918; s. George David and Frankie (Kelly) F. BA, La. Tech. U., 1941; MA, Columbia U., 1950. Classroom tchr. Windfield Pub. Schs., La., La., 1942-43; prodn. illustrator Consolidated Vultee Aircraft, Fort Worth, 1943-45; prof. art Tex. Wesleyan Coll., Fort Worth, 1945-47, U. Tex., Austin, 1947-87, Ashbel Smith prof., 1983—, Ashbel Smith prof. emeritus, 1987—. Author: (with C.I. Martin and E. Beard) Our Expanding Vision, 1960, The Creative Eye, 1969, 2d edit., 1979, (with E. Beard, N. Krevitsky, C.I. Martin) Art and the Creative Teacher, 1971, (with E.L. Mayton, B. Francis, E. Beard) Helping Children See Art and Make Art, 1982, (with E.L. Mayton and R. Brooks) The Way or Art Inner Vision Outer Expression, 1986; guest editor Tex. Quar., Creativity and the Human Spirit, vol. XVI, 1978; one man shows include El Paso Mus. Art, Esther Bear Gallery, Santa Barbara, 1964, Gallery Visual Arts, La. Tech. U., Ruston, 1966, U. Tex. Art Mus., Austin, 1967, Ft. Worth Art Ctr., 1969, Witte Meml. Mus., San Antonio, 1969, U. Tex. Art Mus., Austin, 1974, Mary Moore Gallery, LaJolla, 1975, Mary Moffett Gallery, La. Tech. U., 1976, DuBose Gallery, Houston, 1977, L and L Gallery, Longview, 1975, 78, Retrospective Spencer Gallery, Fine Arts Ctr., U. Ark.-Monticello, 1981, Mary Moffett Gallery, Sch. Art and Arch., La. Tech. U., 1981, Old Jail Art Ctr., Albany, Tex., 1985, Retrospective Marion Koogler McNay Art Mus., San Antonio, 1986, Valley House Gallery, Dallas, 1992, 96, Robinson Galleries, Houston, 1995, Flatbed Press and Gallery, Austin, 1995, 97, Pascal/Robinson Galleries, Houston, 1999, U. Tex., Austin, 2002, Creative Rsch. Labs., 2002, Sixty Year Retrospective Flatbed Internat. Press Galleries, Austin, 2002, Sixty Year Retrospective Old Jail Art Ctr., 2003, Sixty Year Retrospective Arlington Mus. of Art, 2003; exhibited in group shows at Carnegie Inst., Pitts., 1955, 56, 57, Pa. Acad. Art, Phila., 1954-56, Mus. Fine Arts, Houston, 1956-57, Dallas Mus. Fine Art, 1956-57, Munson-Williams-Proctor Inst., Utica, 1956-57, Edwin Hewitt Gallery, N.Y.C., 1957, Dallas Mus. Fine Art, 1958, Am. Fedn. Art, 1958, Mus. Fine Art of Little Rock, 1961, Colorado Springs Art Ctr., 1961, 63, Philbrook Art Ctr., Tulsa, 1963, Fort Worth Art Ctr., 1963, U. Ill., Urbana, 1955, 59, 63, Denver Art Mus., 1963, U. Ariz. and Ark Art Ctr., 1964-65, N.Y. World's Fair, Tex. Pavillion, 1964, Tex. Pavillion Hemistair, San Antonio, 1968, Tex. Tech U. Mus. Art, Lubbock, 1978, U. Tex.-Austin, 1979, Art Gallery Sch. Art and Architecture, La. Tech. U. Ruston, 1984, Jack S. Blanton Mus. Art (formerly Archer M. Huntington Art Gallery), U. Tex.-Austin, 1963-82, 83-91, 92-98, 99, 2000, 2001, Longview Mus. and Arts Ctr., Tex., 1962, 63, 75, 85, 90, 91, Amarillo Art Ctr., Tex., 1988, Dallas Mus. Fine Arts, 1991, 2003, Robinson Gelleries, Houston, 1993, 94, 96, 97, 98, 99, Valley House gallery, Dallas, 1994-99, 2001, 2004, Flatbed Press and Gallery, Austin, 1996, 97, 98, 99, 2000, 2001, 2004, Ga. Art Mus., U. Ga., Athens, 1997, Marion Koogler McNay Art Mus., San Antonio, 1997, 98, 99, 2000, 2001, Mus. of Big Bend, Sul Ross State U., Alpine, Tex., 1998, Nancy Wilson Scanlon Gallery, Helms Fine Art Ctr., Austin, 1999, Austin Mus. Art, 2000, Pascal Robinson Galleries, 2000, 2001, McKinney Contemporary Art Ctr., Dallas, 2000, Tex. Roots: Arlington Mus. Art, 2000, Ctr. for Visual Arts, Denton, Tex., 2000, Old Jail Art Ctr., Albany, Tex., 2001, San Angelo Art Mus., Tex., 2002, San Angelo (Tex.) Mus. Fine Art, 2002, The Modern Art Mus of Ft. Worth, Tex., 2003, David Dike Gallery, Tex, 2004, Ft. Worth Cmty. Art Ctr., Tex., 2005, Morticello Art Gallery, Ft. Worth, 2005, Valley House Gallery, Dallas, 2005. Mem. Nat. Soc. Lit. and Arts, Austin Mus. of Art, Tex. Fine Arts Assn., Tex. Art Edn. Assn., Phi Kappa Phi. Home: 914 Calithea Rd Austin TX 78746-2716 Office Phone: 512-327-0798.

FEARN, ROBERT MORCOM, retired economics professor; b. Paterson, N.J., Oct. 10, 1928; s. William and Violet Emily (Bray) Fearn; m. Priscilla Anne Southard, Sept. 15, 1951; children: Diane C. Fearn Derosiers, Deborah A. Sears, Priscilla L. Fearn Graham, Robert W. AA, Boston U., 1950; BS in Commerce, Ohio U., 1952; MA in Econs., Wash. State U., 1955; PhD in Econs., U. Chgo., 1968. Intelligence officer CIA, Washington, 1954—63; from asst. to prof. econs. and bus. N.C. State U., Raleigh, 1965—96, dir. grad. programs econs., 1993—96, prof. emeritus, 1996—. Mem. athletics coun. N.C. State U., 1986—89; vis. prof. Duke U., Durham, NC, 1982, Sch. Econs. and Bus., Athens, 1986—87, Liaoning U., 1991; expert witness NLRB, Winston-Salem, NC, 1981—83; cons. Rsch. Triangle Inst., Research Triangle Park, NC, 1968—75; mem. Pres.'s Commn. Income Maintenance, Washington, 1970; mem. techno-econ. rsch. Group on Mideast Labor Problems, 1996—97; mem. Sigma One Ghanaian Labor Code Rev., 1999; mem. econ. study and ad hoc wage bd. City of Raleigh, 1974; mem. edn. video team on Kyrgyzstan, 99. Contbr. articles to profl. jours. Pres., v.p., bd. dirs. West Raleigh Civic Assn., 1968—72; vice chmn. Free Alliance for Improvement of Raleigh, 1968—71; scoutmaster, asst. scoutmaster, committeeman Occoneechee coun. Boy Scouts Am., Raleigh, 1970—80. Served U.S. Army, 1946—48. Mem.: Assn. Comparative Econ. Studies, Ind. Rels. Rsch. Assn., So. Econ. Assn. (mem. bd. editors 1975—77), Am. Econ. Assn., Acad. Outstanding Tchrs., N.C. Faculty Senate (chmn. 1984—85, vice chmn. 1983—84), Raleigh Area Masters Swimming, U. Chgo. Club of N.C. (sec. 1982—83, 1983—84, bd. dirs. 1981—84), Alpha Kappa Lambda, Beta Gamma Sigma, Phi Kappa Phi (pres. 1992—93). Democrat. Unitarian-Universalist. Avocations: swimming, long distance backpacking, camping, sailing, photography. Home: 1032 High Lake Ct Raleigh NC 27606-8064 Office: NC State U Dept Econs PO Box 8110 Raleigh NC 27695-0001 Personal E-mail: BOBFearn@aol.com.

FEARON, LEE CHARLES, chemist; b. Tulsa, Nov. 22, 1938; s. Robert Earl and Ruth Belle (Strothers) F.; m. Wanda Sue Williams, Nov. 30, 1971 (div. June 1998); m. Shirlene Olsen, Dec. 9, 2000. Student, Rensselaer Polytech. Inst., 1957-59; BS in Physics, Okla. State U., Stillwater, 1961, BA in Chemistry, 1962, MS in Analytical Chemistry, 1969. Rsch. chemist Houston process lab. Shell Oil Co., Deer Park, Tex., 1968-70; chief chemist Pollution Engring. Internat., Inc., Houston, 1970-76; rsch. chemist M-I Drilling Fluids Co., Houston, 1976-83; cons. chemist Profl. Engr. Assocs., Inc., Tulsa, 1983-84; chemist Anacon, Inc., Houston, 1984-85; scientist III Bionetics Corp., Rockville, Md., 1985-86; sr. chemist L.A. County Sanitation Dist., Whittier, Calif., 1986; chemist Severn Trent Labs., West Sacramento, Calif., 1986-87; cons. chemist Branham Industries, Inc., Conroe, Tex., 1987-89; chemist 4, Lab Accreditation sect. EAP, Wash. State Dept. Ecology, Manchester, 1989—. Cons. chemist Terra-Kleen, Okmulgee, Okla., 1988—94, Excel Pacific, Inc. & Precision Works, Inc., Camarillo, Calif., 1993—96, 2002—, Precision Works, Inc., 2002—. With U.S. Army, 1962—65. Fellow: Am. Inst. Chemists; mem.: AAAS, Am. Chem. Soc. Achievements include patents for environ. soil remediation tech. Avocations: photography, travel. Home: PO Box 514 Manchester WA 98353-0514 Office: PO Box 488 Manchester WA 98353-0488 Personal E-mail: limafox@wavecable.com. Business E-Mail: lfea461@ecy.wa.gov.

FEARRINGTON, ANN PEYTON, writer, illustrator, news correspondent; b. Winston-Salem, N.C., Aug. 25, 1945; d. James Cornelius Pass Fearrington and Florence Moore (McCanless-Fearrington) Blackwood; m. Hege Hill Russ, Sept. 1967 (div. 1984); children: James Pass Fearrington Russ, Joseph Peyton Fearrington Russ; m. Vance Edwin Cox, Jr., June 17, 1985; 1 stepson, Charles Jonathan Cox. BA in Secondary Edn. and English, U. N.C., 1967; MS in Life Scis., Botany & Horticulture, N.C. State U., 1972. Mid. sch. tchr. Wake County Sch. Sys., Raleigh, 1967-71; landscape designer pvt. practice N.Y.C., Winston-Salem, N.C., 1972-83; corr. Raleigh News & Observer, 1993—. Writer/artist-in-residence Raleigh-Wake County Pub. Schs., 1997-2000. Author, illustrator: Christmas Lights, 1996, Little Green Book-18 Keys to Your Child's Reading Success, 1998 (Southeastern Newspaper Assn. Literacy award 1999), Teacher and Librarian Guide for the Little Green Book, 2000, Pequeño Libro Verde, 2000, Who Sees the Lighthouse?, 2004. Sch. libr. vol. Wake County Sch. Sys., Raleigh, 1985—; Sunday Sch. tchr. Highland United Meth. Ch., Raleigh, 1986-90. Recipient Literacy award, Southeastern Newspaper Assn., 1999. Mem.: N.C. Reading Assn. (James B. Hunt Literacy award 2001), Internat. Reading Assn., Soc. Children's Book Writers and Illustrators, Beatrix Potter Soc., N.C. State Univ. Club. Avocations: gardening, reading, sketching.

FEARS, JESSE RUFUS, historian, educator, academic dean; b. Atlanta, Ga., Mar. 7, 1945; s. Emory Binford Fears. BA summa cum laude, Emory U., 1966; MA, Harvard U., 1967, PhD, 1971. Asst. prof. classical langs. Tulane U., New Orleans, 1971-72; asst. prof. history Indiana U., Bloomington, 1972-75, assoc. prof. history, 1975-80, prof. history, 1980-86; prof., chair classical studies Boston U., 1986-90, assoc. dean Coll. Liberal Arts, 1987-89, dir. humanities found., 1988-90; dir. div. rsch. NEH, 1992—93; dean Coll. Arts and Scis. U. Okla., Norman, 1990-92, prof. Classics, 1990—2004, David Ross Boyd Prof., 2004—, G.T. and Libby Blankenship prof. history of liberty, 1992—, dir. Ctr. for History of Liberty, 1992—. Adj. scholar Okla. Coun. Pub. Affairs, 1996—. Author: Princeps A Diis Electus, 1977, (monographs) The Cult of Jupiter, 1981, The Theology of Victory, 1981, The Cult of Virtues, 1981; books on audio and video tape: A History of Freedom, 2001, Famous Greeks, 2001, Famous Romans, 2001, The Life and Times of Winston Churchill, 2001, Books That Have Made History, 2005; editor: (3 vols.) Selected Writings/Lord Acton, 1985-88; contbr. chpts. to books, numerous articles to profl. jours. Bd. dirs. Okla. Sch. Sci./Math., Oklahoma City, 1990—; pres. Vergilian Soc., 2002-04. Recipient Judah P. Benjamin award, Military Order of Stars and Bars, 1996, Great Plains Region Excellence in Tchg. award, U. Continuing Edn. Assn., 2003; Danforth fellow Danforth Found., 1966-71, CAMWS Award for Excellence in College Tchg, 2005; fellow Am. Acad. in Rome, 1969-71, Guggenheim Found., 1976-77, Howard Found., 1977-78, Alexander Von Humboldt, 1977-78, 80-81, Ctr. for History of Freedom, Wash. U., 1989-90; grantee Am. Philos. Soc., 1972, 79, NEH, 1974, Am. Coun. Learned Soc., 1979, Woodrow Wilson, 1983, Kerr Found., 1994, 99, 2003, Zarrow Found., 2000, 2001, 2002; Sigma Chi Scholar in Residence, Miami U., 2003. Mem. Classical Assn. Middle West and South, Phi Beta Kappa, Golden Key Nat. Honor Soc. Office: U Okla Dept Classics Ctr History of Old Science Hall Norman OK 73019 Personal E-mail: cclfears@aol.com. E-mail: jrfears@ou.edu.

FEARS, LINDA, editor-in-chief; Grad., Cornell Univ. Lifestyle dir. Am. Health for Women; sr. editor, lifestyle dir. Ladies' Home Jour.; editor articles Parents Mag., 1999—2000, dep. editor, 2000—04; editor-in-chief YM Mag., NY, 2004; acting editor-in-chief Family Circle, 2005—. Office: Meredith Corp 375 Lexington Ave 9th Fl New York NY 10017-5514 Office Fax: 212-499-2000.

FEATHERMAN, BERNARD, steel company executive; b. May 3, 1929; m. Sandra Green; children: Andrew C., John James. BS, Temple U., 1951; postgrad., Grad. Bus. Sch., 1951—52, Law Sch., 1952—54, Wharton Sch., U. Pa., 1965—66. Chmn. bd. dirs. Western Metal Bed Co., Phila., 1978-86; with CIATEQ USA, Inc., 1995-98; dir. Pa. Steel and Aluminum Corp. (now Pa. Steel Corp.), Bensalem, 1972—, Wardwell Retirement Complex, Saco, Maine, 1998—, Counselling Svcs., Inc., Saco, 1998-2000, Newsletter Pub. Co., Phila. Contbr. articles to profl. jours.; inventor electronics locking locker. Mem. exec. bd. Southeast chpt. Nat. Found. March of Dimes, 1969-82, vice-chmn., 1978-80; pres. Phila. Assn. for Retarded Citizens, 1975-77, trustee, 1983-96; trustee Phila. Devel. Disabilities Corp., 1991-96, Equity 591 F8AM, 1990-92; chmn. Mayor's Adv. Com. on Mental Health-Mental Retardation, Phila., 1979-92, bd. dirs. 1993; mem. tax policy and budget rev. com. City of Phila., fiscal adv. com., 1990; bd. dirs. Costar, Inc., 1989-92; co-chmn. Mayor's Small Bus. Adv. Com., Phila., 1979-92, mem., 1979-95; del. White House Conf. on Small Bus., 1980, Pa. del., 1995, vice-chmn., 1986; chmn. small bus. coun. Dem. Nat. Com., 1982-84; fin. chmn. Pa. Dem. Orgn., 1985-86; mem. adv. bd. Coll. Liberal Arts and Scis., Temple U., 1982-91, chmn. incubator program, 1989-91, chmn. Entrepreneurial Inst., 1990; co-dir. Enterpreneurial Inst. U. New Eng., 1996-98; adv. bd. West Chester (Pa.) State U. Bus. Sch., 1986-87, Frankford Hosp., 1983—; steering com. entrepreneurial forum Drexel U. Bus. Sch., 1988-91; chmn. 3d Congl. Small Bus. Coun., Phila., 1984-88; bd. dirs. Phila. Citywide Devel. Corp., 1984-96; bd. dirs. Phila. Loan Fund, Inc., 1987-88, ARC, York County, Sanford, Maine. 2004—,corporator So. Maine Med. Ctr., 2005—, York County Econ. Devel.Summit Steering Com., 2004— Recipient award of appreciation Small Bus. Coun., Dem. Nat. Com., 1983; Gold medal of Honor Adult Trainees Found., Phila., 1976; citation White House Conf. on Small Bus., 1980; named Entrepreneur of Yr. Mid Atlantic Region Supporter of Entrepreneurship, 1990, Ea. Pa. Small Bus. Adv. of Yr. SBA, 1991. Mem. Assn. of Steel Distbrs. (nat. pres. 1975-76, 86-87, named Steel Distbr. of Yr. 1976), Inst. Am. Entrepreneurs (life), Shelving Mfrs. Assn. (nat. chmn. 1977-78), Pa. Soc., Assn. Steel Distbrs. (nat. pres. 1975-76, 86-87, Hunting Park-Germantown Bus. Assn. (pres. 1986-96), Biddeford/Saco C. of C. (bd. dirs. 2002—, pres., CEO, 2005—), Rotary, Masons (trustee), B'nai Brith (pres. 1980-82, Nat. Youth Svcs. award Quaker City lodge 1985). Home: PO Box 428A Kennebunkport ME 04046-1728

FEATHERMAN, SANDRA, academic administrator, political science professor; b. Phila., Apr. 14, 1934; d. Albert N. and Rebe (Burd) Green; m. Bernard Featherman, Mar. 29, 1958; children: Andrew Charles, John James. BA, U. Pa., 1955, MA, PhD, U. Pa., 1978. Asst. prof. dept. polit. sci. Temple U., Phila., 1978-84, assoc. prof., 1984-91, asst. to pres., 1986-89, pres. faculty senate, 1985-86, dir. Ctr. Pub. Policy, 1986-91; vice chancellor acad. adminstrn., prof. polit. sci. U. Minn., Duluth, 1991-95; pres. U. New Eng., Biddeford, Maine, 1995—. Commr. New Eng. Assn. Schs. and Coll. Higher Edn. Commn., 2002—; mem. commn. women in higher edn. Am. Coun. Edn., 2005—. Author: Jews, Black and Ethnics, 1979, Race and Politics at the Millenium, 2000; contbr. articles to profl. jours. Nat. bd. Girls Inc., 1971—74; pres. Pa. Fedn. C.C., Girls Inc.; sec. Maine Women's Forum, 2002—; active Maine Compact for Higher Edn., 2003—; commr. Am. Coun. on Edn. Commn. on Women in Higher Edn., 2005—; bur. osteo. edn. Am. Osteo. Assn., 2004—; nat. bd. dirs. Women and Founds.-Corp. Philanthropy, 1986—91; bd. dirs. Citizens Com. Pub. Edn. Phila., 1977—89, pres., 1979—81; trustee C.C. Phila., 1970—92, chmn. bd. trustees, 1984—86; life trustee, v.p. Samuel Fels Found., 1978—; bd. dirs. United Way SE Pa., 1977—89, United Way Pa., 1981—84, U. New Eng., Gulf of Maine Aquarium, Kennebec Girl Scout Coun., Virginia Gildeslove Internat. Fund., 2003—, Vis. Nurse Assn., 2002—03; chair Assembly Pres. Am. Assoc. Coll. Osteopathic Medicine; chmn. Maine Commn. on the State Ceiling on Tax-exempt Bonds, 1999—2000. Named Disting. Daughter Pa., State Pa., 2004; recipient Brooks Graves award, Pa. Polit. Sci. Assn., 1982, Cmty. Svc. award, City of Phila., 1984, Women's Achievement award, YWCA, 1989, Adminstr. of Yr. award, Minn. Women in Higher Edn., 1994, Champion of Econ. Growth award, Maine Devel. Found., 2002, Women Who Make a Difference award, Internat. Women's Forum, 2004, Internat. Women's Forum

Women of Distinction award, 2004. Mem.: AAUW (bd. dirs. Phila. chpt. 1975—78, 1980—91, pres. 1984—86, nat. chair internat. fellowships panel 1987—91, nat bd. dirs. 1993—, Outstanding Woman award 1986), Am. Coun. Edn. (commn. on advancement racial and ethnic equality 2001—), Maine Ind. Colls. Assn. (pres. 1998—2000), Greater Portland Alliance Colls. and Univs. (pres. 1997—98), Nat. Assn. Ind. Colls & Univs. (com. policy analysis & pub. rels. 2001—), Am. Polit. Sci. Assn., Maine Ind. Colls. Assn. Office: U New Eng Hills Beach Rd Biddeford ME 04005-9526 Office Phone: 207-283-0170.

FEATHERS, GAIL M. WRATNY, social worker; b. Gowanda, NY, Nov. 19, 1958; d. Frank John and Elinor Louise (Miller) Wratny; m. Donald James Feathers, May 24, 1980; children: Ryan James, David John, Rachel Marie. BA in English, SUNY, Geneseo, 1982; MSW, Syracuse U., 1992. Cert. social worker. Staff U. Rochester (N.Y.) Med. Ctr., 1992; social worker cmty. of caring program Cath. Family Ctr., Rochester, 1993-95, Cath. Charities of Livingston County, Mt. Morris, N.Y., 1995-97; dir. social work Nicholas H. Noyes Meml. Hosp., Dansville, N.Y., 1997—. Social svcs. adv. com. Livingston County Dept. Social Svcs., Mt. Morris, 1993—, chair, 2000—01; social worker early intervention program Livingston County Dept. Health, 1996—2000; mem. Livingston County Teen Pregnancy Prevention Task Force, Mt. Morris, 1993—99, Livingston County Cmty. Resource Network, Mt. Morris, 1993—, chair, 1994—98; family and consumer edn. com. Cornell Coop. Ext., 1999—2002, bd. dirs.; mem. Wayland Cmty. Chest, 1997—2003, sec., 2001—03. Mem. Livingston-Wyoming Assn. Retarded Citizens, 1986—96, bd. dirs., 1987—96, chairperson advocacy com., 1988—92, children's svcs. com., 1988—91; organizer, mem. parents panel on children who have disabilities SUNY Geneseo and Livingston-Wyoming-Steuben Bd. Coop. Ednl. Svcs., 1988—94; mem. adv. coun. N.Y. State Senate Select Com. for the Disabled, NY, 1990—92; mem. Rochester Sch. Deaf Task Force, 1996; mem. deaf awareness panel SUNY Geneseo and Nat. Tech. Inst. for the Deaf, 1998—99. Mem.: NASW. Avocations: golf, reading. E-mail: gfeathers@noyes-hospital.org, rdfthr3307@aol.com.

FEATHERSTONAUGH, HENRY GORDON, psychologist, health facility administrator; b. Nov. 11, 1917; s. Henry Stuart and Evelyn (Borrow) Featherstonaugh; m. Nancy Ellen Couper, July 28, 1946 (div.); children: Wendy, Rusby. BS, U. Calif., Berkeley, 1939; MS, Lehigh U., 1974; PhD, U. Mo., 1978. Diplomate Am. Bd. Sexology. Chemist H. J. Heinz Co., Berkeley, Calif., 1938—40; dist. mgr. Union Carbide Corp., N.Y.C., 1945—73; geriatric svcs. coord. Ctr. Mental Health, Anderson, Ind., 1979—82; co-founder, pres. Living Skills Inst., Inc., Indpls., 1982—. Health svc. provider Nat. Register Health Svc. Providers Psychology, Ind. State Bd. Examiners Psychology; lectr. in field. Contbr. articles to profl. jours. Exec. bd. Madison County Coun. on Aging, 1979—. Served with U.S. Army, 1941—43 USAAF, 1943—45, ATO, CBI. Decorated Air medal with oak leaf cluster D.F.C.; tchg. asst. and tuition grantee, Lehigh U., 1972—73, rsch. grantee, U. Mo., 1974—78. Mem.: APA, Ind. Counselors Assn. on Alcohol and Drug Abuse, Phi Kappa Phi, Psi Chi. Office: 8204 Westfield Blvd Indianapolis IN 46240-2366

FEATHERSTONE, BRUCE ALAN, lawyer; b. Detroit, Mar. 2, 1953; s. Ronald A. and Lois R. (Bosshart) F.; children: Leigh Allison, Edward Alan, Rex Saunders. BA cum laude with distinction in Econs., Yale U., 1974; JD magna cum laude, U. Mich., 1977. Bar: Ill. 1977, Colo. 1983, U.S. Dist. Ct. (no. dist.) Ill. 1977, U.S. Dist. Ct. Colo. 1983, U.S. Ct. Appeals (5th cir.) 1980, U.S. Ct. Appeals (7th cir.) 1981, U.S. Ct. Appeals (10th cir.) 1983, U.S. Ct. Appeals (9th cir.) 1990, U.S. Ct. Appeals (fed. cir.), U.S. Supreme Ct. 1984, others. Assoc. Kirkland & Ellis, Denver, 1977-83, ptnr., 1983-96, Featherstone & Shea, LLP, Denver, 1996-99, Featherstone DeSisto LLP, Denver, 1999—. Articles editor U. Mich. Law Rev., 1976-77. Mem. ABA (litigation sect., tort and ins. practice sect., prof. liability sect., antitrust sect.), Assn. Trial Lawyers Am., Colo. Bar Assn., Colo. Trial Lawyers Assn., Colo. Def. Lawyers Assn., Denver Bar Assn., Order of Coif. Home: 725 Saint Paul St Denver CO 80206-3912 also: PO Box 1467 Denver CO 80201-1467 Office: Featherstone DeSisto LLP 600-17th St Ste 2400 Denver CO 80202-5402 Office Phone: 303-626-7125. E-mail: bfeatherstone@featherstonelaw.com.

FEAVER, GEORGE ARTHUR, political science professor; b. Hamilton, Ont., Canada, May 12, 1937; arrived in U.S., 1967; s. Harold Lorne and Doris Davies (Senior) F.; m. Nancy Alice Poynter, June 12, 1963 (div. 1978); m. Ruth Helene Tubbesing, Mar. 8, 1986 (div. 1991); children: Catherine Fergusson, Noah George, Anthea Jane, Elysia Beatta. BA with honors, U. B.C., 1959; PhD, London Sch. Econs., 1962. Asst. prof. Mt. Holyoke Coll., South Hadley, Mass., 1962-65; lectr., rsch. assoc. London Sch. Econs. and Univ. Coll., London, 1965-67; assoc. prof. Georgetown U., Washington, 1967-68, Emory U., Atlanta, 1968-71, U. B.C., Vancouver, Canada, 1971-74, prof., 1974—2002, prof. emeritus, 2002—. Vis. fellow Australian Nat. U., Canberra, 1987, London Sch. Econs., 1991-92. Author: From Status to Contract, 1969; editor: Beatrice Webb's Our Partnership, 1975; editor: The Webbs in Asia: The 1911-12 Travel Diary, 1992; co-editor: Lives, Liberties and the Public Good, 1987; contbr. articles to profl. jours., chpts. to books. Fellow Can. Coun., 1970-71, 74-75, Am. Coun. Learned Socs., 1974-75, Social Scis. and Humanities Rsch. Coun. of Can., 1981-82, 86-91. Mem. Can. Polit. Sci. Assn., Am. Polit. Sci. Assn., Am. Soc. for Polit. and Legal Philosophy, Conf. for Study of Polit. Thought, Inst. Internat. de Philosophie Politique, Travellers Club (London). Avocations: rambling, wine appreciation. Home: 4776 W 7th Ave Vancouver BC Canada V6T 1C6 Office: Univ BC Dept Polit Sci Vancouver BC Canada V6T 1Z1 Office Phone: 604-822-2832. Business E-Mail: feaver@politics.ubc.ca.

FEBRES-SANTIAGO, SAMUEL F., retired academic administrator; BA in Secondary Edn.-Hispanic Studies, Inter Am. U. P.R.; MA in Spanish-Am. Literature, MEd in Curriculum and Instrn., Temple U.; MA in Sch. Mgmt., U. P.R.; postgrad., Harvard U.; EdD in Adminstrn. of Ednl. Instns., Seton Hall U. Chancellor Guayama Campus, Interam. U. P.R., 1989-99. Recipient Disting. Alumni award Inter Am. U. Mem. Am. Assn. Higher Edn., Hispanic Assn. Colls. & Univs., Mid. State Assn. Colls. & Univs., Lions (pres. edn. com., bd. dirs.), Phi Delta Kappa. Office: InterAm U PR Guayama Campus PO Box 10004 Guayama PR 00785-4004 E-mail: sffebre@ns.inter.edu.

FECHISIN, WENDY LEIGH, mathematics educator; b. Easton, Pa., Sept. 5, 1950; m. Robert Fechisin; 1 child, Joel Patrick. BS, West Chester State Coll., 1972. Cert. secondary edn. math. Pa. Math. tchr. North Warren Regional H.S., Blairstown, NJ, 1973—. Recipient NJ Gov.'s Tchr. Recognition award, North Warren Regional H.S., 1992. Mem.: NEA, Warren County Edn. Assn., North Warren Regional Edn. Assn. (membership chair, exec. com. 1982—2005), NJ Edn. Assn. Home: 4 Cemetery Rd Blairstown NJ 07825 Office: N Warren Regional HS PO Box 410 10 Noe Rd Blairstown NJ 07825 Office Phone: 908-362-2811.

FECHTEL, VINCENT JOHN, legal administrator; b. Leesburg, Fla., Aug. 10, 1936; s. Vincent John and Annie Jo (Hayman) F.; m. Dixie Davenport, Feb. 1992; children: John, Katherine, Elizabeth D., MaryKatherine. BSBA, U. Fla., 1959. Mem. Fla. Ho. of Reps., 1972-78, Fla. Senate, 1978-80; parole commr. U.S. Dept. Justice, Chevy Chase, Md., 1983-96. Served with USNR and Fla. Nat. Guard. Mem. Alpha Tau Omega. Republican. Methodist. Home: 1414 Park Dr Leesburg FL 34748-6736

FECTEAU, ROSEMARY LOUISE, educational administrator, educator, consultant; b. Niagara, Wis., Aug. 7, 1930; d. Andrew Raymond and Julianna Agnes (Wodenka) Waitrovich; m. Jack Richard Fecteau Sr. (dec. Dec. 1994), June 12, 1954; children: Michele, Julienne, Gervaise, Jack Jr., Andrew, Anne-Marie. BA with high distinction, U. R.I., 1974; MS in Edn., U. Maine, 1976; MS in Ednl. Adminstrn., U. So. Maine, 1979; PhD, Columbia Pacific U., 1999, Columbia Commonwealth U., 2003. Cert. supt. schs. K-12. Sec. A.O. Smith Corp., Milw., 1949-54; sec. to Judge Irving W. Smith, Niagara, 1954-55; asst. tchr. Regional Resource Rm., Yarmouth, Maine, 1974-75; prin. Breakwater Sch., Cape Elizabeth, Maine, 1975-78; tchr. grades 6-8 Wells (Maine) Jr. H.S., 1978-79; dir. spl. svcs. Maine Sch. Adminstrv. Dist. 75, Bowdoin, Bowdoinham, Harpswell, Topsham, Maine, 1979-84; ednl. cons. various states, 1984—; mem. policy adv. group for Maine Gov. John Baldacci, 2002. Owner Serendipity Acres Sheep Farm; secondary handicapped task force State Dept. Edn., Augusta, 1980-81; chairperson nat. insvc. network U. Ind., Topsham, Maine, 1981-84. Author: Discover the Key to Equal Educational Opportunity: Follow the Path of Education Legislation, 2004. Mem. Maine Spl. Edn. Rev. Team; founder Project Co-Step and Project S.E.A.R.C.H.; mem. focus group Casco Bay Estuary Project Maine; brownie leader, girl scout cons. Girl Scouts Am., Erie, Pa., 1965-66; dir. women's Cursillo Movement, Erie, 1967; co-chair publicity St. Vincent Hosp., Erie, 1966-67; chair conservation commn. Town of North Yarmouth, 1987; bd. dirs. Columbia Pacific U.; del. Maine Dem. Conv., 1986. Mem.: State of Main Real Estate Commn., Maine Real Estate Assn., Maine Children's Alliance, Physicians for Social Responsibility, Union of Concerned Scientists, Maine Organic Farmer and Gardener Assn., North Yarmouth Hist. Soc., U. So. Maine Alumni Assn. Avocations: music, arts, nutrition, physical fitness. Home: Serendipity Acres 140 W Pownal Rd North Yarmouth ME 04097-6819 Office Phone: 207-756-5743.

FEDDERS, JOHN MICHAEL, lawyer; b. Covington, Ky., Oct. 21, 1941; s. Aloysius Henry and Mary Margaret (Schmidt) F.; m. Barbara E. Baxter; children: Luke D., Mark A., Matthew C., Andrew M., Peter J. BA in Journalism, Marquette U., 1963; LL.B., Cath. U. Am., 1966. Bar: N.Y. 1967, D.C. 1967. Assoc. Cadwalader, Wickersham & Taft, N.Y.C., 1966-71; exec. v.p. Gulf Life Holding Co., Dallas, 1971-73; with firm Arnold & Porter, Washington, 1973-81; ptnr., 1975-81; dir. Div. of Enforcement, SEC, 1981-85; ptnr. Miller, Cassidy, Larroca & Lewin, 1985-87; sole practice Washington, 1987—. Lectr. corp. securities and fin. Contbr. articles to legal jours. Recipient Service award Marquette U., 1977, Achievement award Cath. U. Am. Alumni Assn., 1982, Chmn.'s award for excellence SEC, 1982, Supervisory Excellence award, SEC, 1983 Mem. ABA, Assn. Bar City N.Y., Sigma Delta Chi, Phi Alpha Delta. Republican. Roman Catholic. Office: 1914 Sunderland Pl NW Washington DC 20036-1608 Office Phone: 202-659-2424. Business E-Mail: jfedders@erols.com.

FEDER, ARTHUR A., lawyer, legal association administrator; b. N.Y.C., Mar. 23, 1927; s. Leo and Bertha (Franklin) F.; m. Ruth Musicant, Sept. 4, 1949; children: Gwen Lisabeth, Leslie Margaret, Andrew Michael. BA, Columbia Coll., 1949; LLB, Columbia U., 1951. Bar: N.Y. 1951. Assoc. Fulton Walter & Halley, 1951-53; rsch. asst. Am. Law Inst. Fed. Income, Estate and Gift Tax Project, 1953-54; assoc., ptnr. Roberts & Holland, N.Y.C., 1954-66; ptnr. Willkie, Farr & Gallagher, N.Y.C., 1966-69, Fried, Frank, Harris, Shriver & Jacobson, N.Y.C., 1970-94, of counsel, 1994—; sr. adv. to exec. com. Herzog, Heine, Geduld Inc., N.Y.C., 1996—2001; counsel Geduld & Co., LLC, N.Y.C., 2002—, Cougar Trading, 2002—. Lectr. in law Columbia U., 1961-63; lectr. Am. Law Inst., NYU Inst. on Fed. Taxation, Practicing Law Inst., various profl. groups. Editor Columbia Law Rev., 1949-51; contbr. articles to profl. jours. With USN, 1945-46. Fellow Am. Coll. Tax Counsel; mem. ABA (taxation sect., chmn. com. on real property tax problems 1964-66, com. on legis. drafting 1968-84), Assn. of Bar of City of N.Y. (various coms.), N.Y. State Bar Assn. (taxation sect., co-chmn. various coms. 1982-86, sec. 1987-88, 2d vice chmn. 1988-89, vice chmn. 1989-90, chmn. 1990-91), Internat. Fiscal Assn. (coun. U.S.A. br. 1984-91), Am. Law Inst. (tax adv. group fed. income tax project), Univ. Club, Phi Beta Kappa. Democrat. Home: 25 W 81st St New York NY 10024-6023 Office: Cougar Trading 375 Park Ave New York NY 10152 Office Phone: 212-702-0690. Personal E-mail: afeder@nyc.rr.com. E-mail: afeder@cougartrading.com.

FEDER, BRUCE, lawyer; b. N.Y.C., May 9, 1950; s. Morton A. and Ruth Leah (Baker) F.; married; two children. BA, U. Ariz., 1972; JD, George Washington U., 1976. Bar: Ariz. 1977, Washington 1982; U.S. dist. Ct. Ariz. 1977, U.S. Ct. Appeals (9th cir.) 1980; U.S. Supreme Ct., 1994. Prin. Feder Law Office PA, Phoenix, 1978—. Mem. Ariz. State Bar (com. on rules of profl. responsibility 1987—, now emeritus), Ariz. Attys. for Criminal Justice (pres. 1993, bd. dirs. 1988-95). Office: 2930 E Camelback Rd Ste 205 Phoenix AZ 85016 Office Phone: 602-257-0135. Personal E-mail: brucefeder@att.net.

FEDER, JUDITH, dean; BA in Polit. sci., Brandeis U., 1968; MA in Polit. sci., Harvard U., 1970, PhD in Polit. sci., 1977. Acting asst. sec. planning & evaluation US Dept. HHS, 1993—95; prof., dean policy studies Georgetown U. Author: Medicare: The Politics of Federal Hospital Insurance, 1977; author: (with John Holahan) Financing Health Care for the Elderly: Medicare, Medicaid and Private Health Insurance, 1979; author: (with Jack Hadley and John Holahan) Insuring the Nation's Health: Market Competition, Catastrophic and Comprehensive Approaches, 1981; editor (with John Holahan and Theodore Marmor): National Health Insurance: Conflicting Goals and Policy Choices, 1980; editor: (with Diane Rowland and Anita Salganicoff) Medicaid Financing Crisis: Balancing Responsibilities, Priorities and Dollars, 1993; contbr. articles to profl. jours., chapters to books. Mem.: Inst. Medicine, 2004. Office: Georgetown Pub Policy Inst 3600 N St NW Ste 200 Washington DC 20007

FEDER, ROBERT, lawyer; b. NYC, Nov. 29, 1930; BA cum laude, CCNY, 1953; LLB, Columbia U., 1953. Bar: N.Y. 1953, U.S. Tax Ct. 1956, U.S. Dist. Ct. (so. dist.) N.Y. 1974. V.p., gen. counsel Presdl. Realty Corp., White Plains, N.Y., 1953-71; ptnr. Cuddy & Feder LLP, White Plains, 1971—. Bd. dirs. Westchester County (N.Y.) Legal Aid Soc., 1972—, pres., 1974—78; adj. prof. sch. bus. Columbia U., N.Y.C., 1988—89; bd. dirs. Presdl. Realty Corp. (Amex), Interplex Industries, Inc., Stellaris Health Network, Inc., vice chmn., 2001—04; adj. prof. Pace U. Law Sch., 1985—87. Pres. White Plains Cmty. Action Program, 1967—69; bd. dir. White Plains Hosp. Ctr., 1978—, also sec., treas., chmn., 1992—97, 2002—05; commr. White Plains Housing Authority, 1984—2002; chmn. White Plains Jud. Rev. Com., 2003; trustee SUNY-Purchase Coll. Found., 1988—, vice-chmn., 1995—. Mem.: ABA, Westchester County Bar Assn., Am. Coll. Real Estate Lawyers, White Plains Bar Assn., N.Y. State Bar Assn. Home: 9 Oxford Rd White Plains NY 10605-3602 Office: Cuddy & Feder LLP 90 Maple Ave White Plains NY 10601-5105 Office Phone: 914-761-1300. Business E-Mail: rfeder@cuddyfeder.com. E-mail: rfeder@pipeline.com.

FEDER, ROBERT, columnist; b. Chgo., May 17, 1956; s. Harold J. and Selma (Reisberg) F.; m. Janet Gail Elkins, June 16, 1985; 1 child, Emily Jacklyn. BS in Journalism, Northwestern U., 1978. Reporter, news editor Lerner Newspapers, Chgo., 1974-78, mng. editor, 1978-80; reporter Chgo. Sun-Times, 1980-83, TV/radio columnist, 1983—. Project cons. (TV documentary) Radio Faces, 1989; contbr. (spl. report) Ency. Brittanica, 1983, World Book Ency., 1996. Recipient Page One award Chgo. Newspaper Guild, 1976; named Best Daily Newspaper Columnist, New City, 1997. Mem. Soc. Profl. Journalists, Chgo. Headline Club, Chgo. Newspaper Guild, Northwestern Club of Chgo., Skokie Hist. Soc. Office: Chgo Sun-Times 350 N Orleans St Chicago IL 60654-1502

FEDER, SAUL E., lawyer; b. Bklyn., Oct. 8, 1943; s. Joseph Robert and Toby Feder; m. Marcia Carrie Weinblatt, Feb. 25, 1968; children: Howard Avram, Fayge Miriam, Tamar Miriam, Michael Elon, David Ben-Zion Aaron, Alexandra Rachel, Evan Daniel, Sarah Lily, Maya Malka, Batsheva, David E., Natan. BS, NYU, 1965; JD, Bklyn. Law Sch., 1968. Bar: N.Y. 1969, U.S. Ct. Appeals (2d cir.) 1969, U.S. Ct. Claims 1970, U.S. Customs Ct. 1972, U.S. Supreme Ct. 1972, U.S. Ct. Customs and Patent Appeals 1974. Mng. lawyer Queens Legal Svcs., Jamaica, N.Y., 1970-71; ptnr. Previte-Glasser-Feder & Farber, Jackson Heights, N.Y., 1972-73, Hein-Waters-Klein & Feder, Far Rockaway, N.Y., 1973-78, Regosin-Edwards-Stone & Feder, N.Y.C., 1979—. Spl. investigator Bur. Election Frauds, Atty. Gen.'s Office, N.Y.C., 1976—77, spl. dep. atty. gen., 1969—70; arbitrator, consumer counsel small claims divsn. Civil Ct. City of N.Y., 1974—. Pres. Young Israel Briarwood, Queens, N.Y., 1978; chmn. polit. affairs com. Young Israel Staten Island, 1985—; rep. candidate State of N.Y. Assembly, Queens, 1976; chmn. Stat Pac Polit. Action Com. Mem.: Com. on Law and Pub. Affairs, Internat. Acad. Law & Sci., Am. Jud. Soc., Soc. Med. Jurisprudence, Am. Arbitration Assn., N.Y. Bar Assn., Queens County Bar Assn., Nassau County Bar Assn., Am. Judges Assn., N.Y. Trial Lawyers Assn., Richmond County Bar Assn. Republican. Home: 259 Ardmore Ave Staten Island NY 10314-4349 Office: Regosin Edwards Stone & Feder 225 Broadway Ste 613 New York NY 10007-3059 Office Phone: 212-619-1990. Business E-Mail: sfeder@resflaw.com.

FEDERER, ROGER, professional tennis player; b. Basel, Switzerland, Aug. 8, 1981; s. Lynette and Robert. Prof. tennis player Assn. Tennis Profls., 1998—; Founder RF- RogerFederer Fragrance Line, 2003—. Mem. Swiss Davis Cup Team, 1999—. Recipient Best Male Tennis Player, ESPY awards, 2005. Achievements include winner, Wimbledon, 2003, 2004, 2005, Australian Open, 2004, U.S. Open, 2004, 2005; 32 Career Singles titles, 7 Doubles titles; became first player since 1988 to win three legs of the Grand Slam in the same year, 2004. Office: Assn Tennis Prof Hdqrs Jeome Jan Strijbis Glarnischstrasse 8 8810 Horgen Switzerland

FEDERING, ERIC K., legislative staff member, public information officer; b. Bronx, N.Y., Feb. 10, 1960; s. Abraham M. and Eileen (Katz) F.; m. Daphne V. Clones, May 2000. BA with distinction, George Washington U., 1982. Aide U.S. Dept. State, Washington, 1979-81; founder, dir. motion picture restoration effort MAD WORLD Campaign, Washington, 1982-91; press sec., speechwriter for mem. of congress Rep. Norman Y. Mineta, Washington, 1987-93; supr. press info. ctr. Dem. Nat. Conv., N.Y.C., 1992, dir. press info. ctr. ops. Chgo., 1996, L.A., Calif., 2000, Boston, 2004; dir. comm. Pub. Works and Transp. Com. U.S. Ho. of Reps., Washington, 1993-94, Dem. dir. comm. Transp. and Infrastructure Com., 1994-97; press sec. Senator Joseph I. Lieberman, Washington, 1997-99; dir. bus. pub. policy, govt. affairs KPMG LLP, 1999—; mem. transition team Sec.-Designate Norman Y. Mineta U.S. Dept. Commerce, 2000. Freelance writer, 1982-87; lit. rep. Larsen-Pomada Lit. Agts., San Francisco, 1984-96, Farber Literacy Agy., N.Y., 1996—; lectr. U. Queensland, Australia, Bond U., Australia, Australian Ctr. Am. Studies, East-West Ctr. Hawaii, 1992, U. Western Australia, Edith Cowan U., Australia, Curtin U., Australia, U. Melbourne, Australia, La Trobe U., Australia, Victoria U., Australia, U.S. Consulate, Melbourne, 1993, U.S. Consulate, Sydney, U.S. Embassy, Canberra, Finders U. So. Australia, 1995; mem. Com. for Econ. Devel. of Australia U. Tasmania, Australian Inst. of Internat. Affairs, James Cook U., 1996, Monash U. Australia, U.S.-Australia Bus. and Trade Coun., Com. for Econ. Devel. of Australia, Flinders U. So. Australia, 1998; congl. liaison to Smithsonian Instn. Bd. Regents, 1995; U.S. dir. Washington internship program The Flinders U. Australia, 1999-2003, U. Queensland, U. Wollongong, U. Western Australia, U. Canberra, Macquarie U., Melbourne U., Deakin U., 2003—; founder, dir. Uni-Capitol Washington Internship Programme, 2003—. Press sec. to nat. co-chair Dukakis-Bentsen Presdl. Campaign, Washington, 1988; prin. Coun. for Excellence in Govt., 2002—; bd. dirs. Nat. Japanese Am. Meml. Found., 2003—; bd. dirs. Nat. Conf. on Citizenship, 2004—. Recipient Commendation for Outstanding Achievement by Sec. of State, 1981. Mem. Phi Beta Kappa. Democrat. Avocations: sound recordings, motion pictures, theater restoration, photography. E-mail: efedering@kpmg.com.

FEDERLE, MICHAEL, publishing executive; married; 2 children. B, Colby Coll., 1981. With Color Computer mag. (bought by Ziff Davis); with Time Inc. People mag., Calif.; with Life mag., NY; assoc. pub. Fortune Mag., NYC, 1997—99, pub., 1999—. Office: Time Inc Time Life Bldg Rockefeller Ctr New York NY 10020-1393*

FEDERLE, THOMAS W., environmental scientist, microbiologist; b. Cin., June 6, 1952; s. Walter E. and Virginia E. Federle; m. Molly Moran Moran; children: Thomas E., Michael C., Megan K. BS, U. Cin., 1974, MS, 1976, PhD, 1981. Postdoctoral scientist Fla. State U., Tallahassee; asst. prof. U. Ala., Birmingham, 1983—85; scientist The Procter & Gamble Co., Cin., 1985—91, prin. scientist, 1991—98, rsch. fellow, 1998—. Participant U.S. Antarctic Rsch. Program, 1983—84; adj. asst. prof. U. Cin., 1986—94, adj. assoc. prof., 1994—. Contbr. articles to profl. jours. Asst. scoutmaster Troop 850 Boy Scouts Am., Cin., 1990—2002. Named Found. Microbiology lectr., Am. Soc. for Microbiology, 1993—95. Fellow: Am. Acad. Microbiology; mem.: Soc. for Environ. Toxicology and Chemistry, Am. Soc. for Microbiology. Roman Catholic. Office: The Procter & Gamble Co PO Box 538707 Cincinnati OH 45253-8707

FEDERMAN, DANIEL DAVID, medical educator, academic administrator, endocrinologist; b. NYC, Apr. 16, 1928; m. Elizabeth Buckley; children: Lise, Carolyn. BA, Harvard U., 1949, MD, 1953. Diplomate Am. Bd. Internal Medicine. Intern Mass. Gen. Hosp., Boston, 1953—54, resident in medicine, 1954—55, fellow in medicine, 1958—60; instr. to prof. Harvard Med. Sch., Boston, 1961—72, dean students and alumni, 1977—89, prof. medicine, 1977—92, dean med. edn., 1989—2000, Carl W. Walter prof. medicine and med. edn., 1992—, sr. dean alumni rels. and clin. tchg., 2000—; chmn. medicine Stanford Med. Sch., Palo Alto, Calif., 1972—77. Author: (med. textbook) Abnormal Sexual Development, 1967; editor: Scientific American Medicine. Recipient Disting. Educator Award, Endocrine Soc., 1999, Abraham Flexner Award for Disting. Svc. to Med. Edn., Assn. Am. Med. Colleges, 2001. Master: ACP (pres. Phila. 1982—83, named Mass. Physician of Yr. 1994, Disting. Tchr. Award 1995); mem.: Inst. Medicine. Office: Harvard Med Sch Office of Dean Bldg A-101 25 Shattuck St Boston MA 02115-6027*

FEDERMAN, RAYMOND, novelist, English and comparative literature educator; b. Paris, May 15, 1928; came to U.S., 1948, naturalized, 1953; s. Simon and Marguerite (Epstein) F.; m. Erica Hubscher, Sept. 13, 1960; 1 child, Simone Juliette. B.A., Columbia U., 1957; M.A., UCLA, 1958, Ph.D., 1963. Asst. prof. U. Calif.-Santa Barbara, 1959-64; assoc. prof. SUNY-Buffalo, 1964-68, prof. English and comparative lit., 1968—, Disting. Faculty prof., 1990—, Melodia E. Jones prof., 1994; vis. prof. U. Montreal, Que., Can., 1969-70, Hebrew U. Jerusalem, 1982-83. Author: Double Or Nothing, 1971 (Frances Steloff prize 1971), Take It or Leave It, 1976, The Voice in the Closet, 1979, The Twofold Vibration, 1982; Smiles on Washington Square, 1985 (Am. Book award 1986), To Whom It May Concern, 1990, Now Then, 1991, Critifiction, 1993, The Supreme Indecision of The Writer, 1996, La Fourrure de Ma Tante Rachel, 1996, Loose Shoes, 1999, The Precipice and Other Catastrophes, 1999. Served with U.S. Army, 1951-54, Korea. Guggenheim fellow, 1966-67; Camargo Found. fellow, Cassis, France, 1977; Fulbright fellow, Israel, 1982-83; Nat. Endowment for Arts fellow, 1985. Mem. Samuel Beckett Soc. (life hon. trustee), PEN Am. Ctr., Fiction Collective (co.-dir. 1978-81), Phi Beta Kappa. Democrat. Jewish. Club: Bernardo Heights Country Club (San Diego). Avocations: golf, tennis, jazz. Office: SUNY Dept English Clemens Hall Buffalo NY 14260

FEDERSPIEL, ULRIK, diplomat; b. Copenhagen, 1943; s. Per and Elin F.; m. Birgitte Hartnack. Degree in polit. sci. cum laude, U. Aarhus, Denmark, 1970; MA in Internat. Rels., U. Pa., 1971. With Danish Fgn. Svc., 1971-77, first sec. London, 1977-81, spl. asst. to permanent sec. state of fgn. affairs Copenhagen, 1981-84, min. Danish Embassy Washington, 1984-89, asst. to fgn. min. and fgn. svc. commn., 1989-91, head fgn. ministry and fgn. svc., permanent sec. state of fgn. affairs, 1991-93, permanent sec. state prime min. office, sec. cabinet, sec. to the Queen coun. mins., chmn. various govt. coms. including European Union-Summit Com., 1993-97, amb. to Ireland, 1997-2000, amb. to U.S., 2000—. Lectr., then sr. lectr. internat. rels. U. Copenhagen, 1971-77, censor, 1990, mem. governing bd., 1993-97; rschr. Danish Fgn. Policy Inst., 1975-76; vis. lectr. George Washington U., Washington, 1985-86. Author: Integration in Theory and Practice, 1985; co-editor yearbook Danish Fgn. Policy Inst., 1981-83, Danish Ct. and Danish Govt., 1993-96. Hon. trustee Crown Prince Frederik Fund; Danish adv. bd. Humanity in Action. With Royal Danish Navy. Decorated comdr. 1st degree Order of Dannebrog, Grand Cross of Belgium, Finland, Iceland, Italy, Lithuania, Norway, Portugal. Office: Royal Danish Embassy 3200 Whitehaven St NW Washington DC 20008-3616 E-mail: wasamb@um.dk.

FEDEWA, LAWRENCE JOHN, management consulting firm executive, entrepreneur; b. Lansing, Mich., Oct. 31, 1937; s. Norman Anthony and Agnes G. (Murphy) F.; m. Theresa Kathryn Goeser, Aug. 18, 1962; children: Kirsten Ann, Eric Christian, Lawrence John Jr. BA, Sacred Heart Sem., Detroit, 1959; postgrad., Mich. State U., 1960-61; PhD, Marquette U., 1969. Cert. high sch. tchr., Colo. Mem. editorial staff Denver Cath. Register, 1962-63; columnist Hi-Time mag., 1963-64; assoc. prof. St. Norbert Coll., De Pere, Wis., 1966-71; prof. philosophy, v.p. Park Coll., Kansas City, Mo., 1971-76, dean of the coll., 1971-74; founder, provost Park Coll./Crown Ctr., Kansas City, Mo., 1974-76; dir. internat. projects Control Data Corp., Washington, 1976-79; pres. Fedewa and Assocs., Washington, 1979-81; co-founder Internat. Inst. for Advanced Tech., Manila, 1978; v.p., sec., bd. dirs. Cordatum Inc., McLean, Va., 1981-90, pres., CEO, bd. dirs., 1990; pres. CEO, chmn. bd. Washington Tech. Group, Fairfax, Va., 1990—; chmn., CFO Washington Inst. Tech., 1990-2000; CFO, chmn. bd. dirs. Internat. Health Corp., 1991-94; mng. exec. K.W. Tunnell Co. Fed. Svcs. Group, Washington, 1994—. Chmn., CEO, bd. dirs. Plowshares Internat., Inc., 1992-95; chmn. Armcoz.com Ltd., 1999-; chmn., pres. Wash. Tech. Capital Group, 2004-; chmn. bd. dirs., CFO Health Interventions, Inc., 1993-95, chmn. WTG Fin. Svcs. Corp., 1995-99; pres. Cedarwood Arabians, 1994—; exec. dir. NEA Ednl. Computer Svc., Washington, 1983-87. Pub. Yellow Book of Computer Products for Edn., 1983-86; author, pub. Guide to the Software Assessment Procedure, 1983-87; author: The Ethics of Ecumenism, 1969, Social Ethics with a Big Beat, 1970, The Design and Development of Computer Interactive Videodisc (CIV) Lessons, 1985; Education in the Information Age, 1986, Safety Training For Railroad Operating Employees: Introduction of Interactive Video Disc Training to the Railroad Industry (A Case Study), 1987, Do Computers Help Teachers Teach?, 1987. Mem. rsch. and devel. com. Met. Washington YMCA, 1986-90; trustee The Dupuy Inst., Washington, 1992. Roman Catholic. Avocations: horseman, racquetball, tennis, history, biography. Office: Washington Tech Group Inc #900 6564 Loisdale Ct Ste 900 Springfield VA 22150-1822 *I have come to believe that perseverance may be the ultimate virtue. Frequently, the ability to keep trying, to stay the course, can be more important to success than talent, luck, contacts, creativity, even purity of heart.*

FEDORCHAK, TIMOTHY HILL, facility planning and program consulting executive; b. Lodi, Calif., Jan. 15, 1958; s. John and Betty Francis (Daugherty) F. Student, San Joaquin Delta Coll., 1976-77, U. Utah, 1977-78; BS in Urban Planning, Calif. State Poly. U., 1981. Pub. works technician City of Lodi, Calif., 1979-80, planner, 1980-81; assoc. Steinmann, Grayson, Smylie, L.A., 1981-87, dir. Sacramento, 1987-89; prin. Daniel C. Smith & Assocs., Sacramento, 1989—2000; CEO, sr. mgmt. cons. Stanislaus County CA, Modesto, Calif., 2000—. Project mgr., cons. Facilities Master Plan, Maricopa County, Ariz., 1982, Corp. Yard Relocation Plan, Scottsdale, Ariz., 1983, Marin County Civic Ctr. Master Plan, San Rafael, Calif., 1984, San Joaquin Human Svcs. Facility Program, Stockton, Calif., 1985-86, over 50 other facility plans and program projects. Pres. Lodi History Hunters, 1972; univ. rep. Calif. State Poly. Univ., 1980-81. Mem. Am. Planning Assn. (charter), Am. Pub. Works Assn., Am. Jail Assn., Calif. State Poly. U. Planning Alumni Assn. (treas. 1986-88), Phi Eta Sigma. Democrat. Avocations: camping, bicycling, photography, model railroading. Office: Stanislaus County Chief Exec Office 1010 10th St Ste 6800 Modesto CA 95354 Home: 1607 Holly Dr Lodi CA 95242

FEDORCHIK, BETTE JOY WINTER, foreign language professional; b. Fairbury, Nebr., Oct. 27, 1953; d. Frederick and Darlene (Groen) Winter; m. Joseph John Fedorchik Jr.; children: Joseph John III, Mikhail Aleksandr, Thomas Francis. BA in German, Mich. State U., 1976. Reservationist Adventure Tours, USA, Dallas, 1977-80; translator Hunt Oil Co., Dallas, 1980-83; adminstrv. asst. Mahle, Inc., Oak Brook, Ill., 1983-86; freelance translator Houston, 1987—. Block capt. Briargrove Park Subdiv., Houston, 1986-87; area rep. Youth for Understanding; pres.-elect Brazos-Robertson County Med. Alliance, 1992-93, pres., 1993-94, sec. 1994-95, historian, 1997-98; chmn. extend-a-hand Jr. League; bd. dirs. Opera and Performing Arts Soc., 1995—, Am. Heart Assn., 1996, 97. Mem. Mich. State U. Alumni Assn. Republican. Roman Catholic. Avocations: piano, ballet, opera, tennis, theater, travel, foreign languages. Home: 3011 Coronado Dr College Station TX 77845-7727

FEDOROCHKO, WILLIAM, JR., retired military officer, military analyst; b. Bayonne, N.J., Sept. 6, 1940; s. William and Helen (Dinis) F.; m. Sandra L. Clements, Dec. 10, 1966; 1 child, Sharon. BA in Econs., Washington and Jefferson Coll., 1962; MA in Econs., U. Pitts., 1971. Commd. 2d lt. U.S. Army, 1962, advanced through grades to brig. gen., 1989; platoon leader, staff officer 14th Armored Cav. Rgt., Fed. Republic Germany, 1962-64; staff officer Dept. Army, Washington, 1973-76; comdr. 1st Armored Div. Materiel Mgmt. Ctr., 501st Supply and Transport Bn., Fed. Republic Germany, 1976-80; student Def. Systems Mgmt. Coll., 1980, Indsl. Coll. Armed Forces, 1981; spl. asst. for joint activities Office of Comdr., Army Materiel Command, Alexandria, Va., 1981-83; chief acquisition and support program analysis div. Office Chief of Staff Army, Washington, 1983-84; comdr. 13th Support Command, Ft. Hood, Tex., 1984-87; spl. asst. Office Under Sec. Def. for Acquisition, Washington, 1987-88, dep. dir. program integration, 1988-90; dep. dir. force structure and resources Joint Staff, J-8, Washington, 1990-93; ret., 1993; sr. policy analyst RAND, Washington, 1993-94; sr. fellow Logistics Mgmt. Inst., McLean, Va., 1994-98; policy analyst strategy, forces and resources divsn. Inst. for Defense Analyses, Alexandria, Va., 1998—. Decorated Legion of Merit with 4 oak leaf clusters, Def. D.S.M. with oak leaf cluster. Mem. Assn. Quartermasters. Baptist. Avocations: golf, tennis. Home: 11404 Stonewall Jackson Dr Spotsylvania VA 22553-4607 Office: Inst for Def Analyses 4850 Mark Center Dr Alexandria VA 22311-1882 Business E-Mail: wfedoroc@ida.org.

FEDOROFF, NINA VSEVOLOD, research scientist, consultant, educator; b. Cleve., Apr. 9, 1942; d. Vsevolod N. Fedoroff and Olga S. (Snegireff) Stacy; children: Natasha, Kyr, James. BS, Syracuse U., 1966; PhD, Rockefeller U., 1972. Asst. mgr. transl. bur. Biol. Abstracts, Phila., 1962-63; flutist Syracuse (N.Y.) Symphony Orch., 1964-66; acting asst. prof. UCLA, 1972-74; postdoctoral fellow UCLA and Carnegie Inst. Washington, Los Angeles and Balt., 1974-78; staff scientist Carnegie Inst. Washington, Balt., 1978-95; dir. Biotechnol. Inst., Pa. State U., 1995—, Willaman prof. of life scis., 1995—, Evan Pugh prof., 2002—; external faculty Santa Fe Inst., 2003—. Dir. Life Scis. Consortium, Pa. State U., 1996—2002; prof. dept. biology John Hopkins U., 1979-95; mem. devel. biology panel NSF, Washington, 1979-80; sci. adv. panel Office of Tech. Assessment, Congress, Washington, 1979-80; recombinant DNA adv. com. NIH, Bethesda, Md., 1980-84; sci. adv. com. Japanese Human Frontier Sci., 1988; sci adv. com. Competitive Rsch. Grants Office, USDA; mem. commn. on life scis., basic biology bd. NRC, NAS, 1984-90; bd. dirs. Genetics Soc. Am.; mem. bd. overseers Harvard U., 1988-91; trustee BIOSIS, Phila., 1990-96; mem. NAS Coun., 1991-94; dir. Internat. Sci. Found., 1992-93; mem. adv. com. Directorate for Biol. Scis., 1994-97; chmn., bd. dirs. Sigma-Aldrich Corp., 1996—. Editor: Gene, 1981—84, Perspectives in Biology and Medicine, 1991—2001, Procs. Nat. Acad. Sci., 1996—2000; editor, bd. rev. editors: Sci., 1985, mem. sci. adv. bd.: The Plant Jour., 1991—98, book editor: various publs.; contbr. chapters to books articles to profl. jours. Recipient Merit award, NIH, 1990, Howard Taylor Ricketts award, U. Chgo., 1990, Arents Pioneer award, Syracuse U., 2003; grantee, NSF and USDA, 1979—84, NIH, 1984—99, NSF, 1992—, NASA, 1997—2000. Mem.: AAAS, NAS (editor procs. 1995—), AAAS (bd. dirs. 2000—03), European Acad. Scis., Am. Acad. Arts and Scis., Nat. Sci. Bd., Sigma Xi (McGovern Sci. and Soc. medal 1997), Phi Beta Kappa (vis. scholar 1984—85, vis. scholar 1984—85). Avocations: chamber music, gardening, tango. Home: 2398 Shagbark Ct State College PA 16803-3367 Office: Huck Insts Life Scis Pa State U University Park PA 16802

FEDOROV, ANDRIY YURI, computer scientist, researcher; b. Berdyansk, Ukraine, May 10, 1980; arrived in U.S., 2001; s. Yuri Fedorov and Tatiana Fedorova. BS, Ternopil Acad. Nat. Economy, Inst. Computer Info. Tech., 2004; MS, Coll. William and Mary, 2003. Rsch. asst. Dept of Comp Sci, Coll. William & Mary, Williamsburg, Va., 2001—. Vis. rschr. computational radiology lab., surg. planning lab. Brigham and Women's Hosp., Harvard Med. Sch., 2005—. Office: Dept of Comp Sci Collg of WM&MARY PO Box 23187-8795 Williamsburg VA 23187-8795 Office Phone: 757-221-3436. E-mail: fedorov@cs.wm.edu.

FEDOROV, SERGEI, professional hockey player; b. Pskov, Russia, Dec. 13, 1969; Forward Detroit Red Wings, 1990—2003, Anaheim Mighty Ducks, 2003—. Founder Sergei Fedorov Found., 1998—. Named to NHL All-Star Game, 1992, 1994, 1996, 2001—03; recipient Hart Trophy, 1994, Selke Trophy, 1994, 1996, Lester B. Pearson award, 1994, Player of Yr. award, Hockey News, 1994, Sporting News, 1999, Hockey Digest, 1994, Silver medal, Olympic Games, Nagano, Japan, 1998. Achievements include mem. of Stanley Cup Champion Detroit Red Wings, 1997, 1998, 2002. Avocations: golf, boating, travel. Office: Detroit Red Wings 600 Civic Center Dr Detroit MI 48226-4419

FEDOSH, MICHAEL STEPHEN, geologist, oceanographer; b. Elizabeth, NJ, Nov. 12, 1955; s. Michael and Mary Fedosh; children: Noel Wood, Karlyn Samantha. BA, Franklin and Marshall Coll., 1977; MA, William and Mary Coll., 1982. Geologist Exploration Logging, Inc., Houston, N.J. Geological Survey, Trenton, Tex., 1977—79; dist. geologist U.S. Army Corps of Engrs., NYC, 1982—89; sr. geologist EcolSciences, Inc., Rockaway, NJ, 1989—. Adv. panel Glynwood Ctr., Cold Springs, NY, 2003; adv. com. Monmouth County Stormwater Task Force, Freehold, NJ, 2004—; grant rev. Nat. Sci. Found., Alexandria, Va., 1999. Recipient Yekel Sedimentology award, Franklin and Marshall Coll., 1976, Vol. award for the environ., N.J. Governor's Office, 2001, Non-profit group award, Middletown Environ. Commn., 1977, U.S. EPA Environ. Commn. award, 2001, Environ. Quality award, 2001. Mem.: Poricy Pk. Nature Conservancy (pres. 2004—, bd. dirs. 1998—2002), Monmouth County Environ. Coun. (chmn. 2004—), Middletown Open Space Com., Middletown Environ. Com. (chmn. 1995—). Avocations: travel, hiking, bicycling, reading, gardening. Home: 3 Church St Middletown NJ 07748 Business E-Mail: mfedosh@ecolsciences.com.

FEDOTOV, IGOR YURIEVICH, music educator, musician; b. Baku, Azerbaijan, June 19, 1959; s. Yuri Vasilievich Fedotov and Galina Alekseevna Fedotova; m. Elina Aleksandrovna Makarova; 1 child, Yuri Igorevich. Undergrad. Degree in Music Performance, Azerbaijan Musical Coll., 1977; M in Music Performance, Azerbaijan State Conservatory Music, Baku, 1986. Soloist Performer, Music Teacher Azerbaijan State Conservatory, 1986. Musician Azerbaijan State Opera And Ballet Theater, Baku, 1977, Azerbaijan State Symphony Orch., Baku, 1980—83, Azerbaijan State Chamber Orch., Baku, 1983—87, Moscow Exptl. Music Theater, 1987—90, European Baroque Orch., Hengelo, Netherlands, 1989—90, Orquesta Simfonica Del Estado de Mex., Toluca, 1990—91, Thouvenel String Quartet, Midland, Tex., 1991—94; prof. U. So. Miss., Hattiesburg, 1994—98, Western Mich. U., Kalamazoo, 1998—; prin. violist Kalamazoo Symphony Orch., 1998—. Bd. dirs. Stulberg Internat. String Competition, Kalamazoo, 2000—. Musician: solo recitals in Europe and US. Cons. Kalamazoo Pushkin Partnership; mem. Stulberg Internat. String Competition, Kalamazoo, 2000. Recipient 1st prize, Internat. Music Competition. Baku, 1986. Mem.: Am. Fedn. Musicians, Am. Assn. U. Profs., Internat. Viola Soc. Office: Western Mich Univ Sch Music 1903 W Michigan Ave Kalamazoo MI 49008-5434 Office Phone: 269-387-4638. Personal E-mail: igor.fedotov@wmich.edu.

FEDUCCIA, J. ALAN, biologist, educator; b. Mobile, Ala., Apr. 25, 1943; m. Margarette Olivia Taylor, Sept. 5, 1947. BS, La. State U., 1965; MA, PhD, U. Mich., 1969. Rsch. assoc. Smithsonian Instn., Washington, 1978—87; S. K. Heninger prof. U. N.C., Chapel Hill, 1994—, chmn. div. natural scis., 1996—97, chmn. dept. biology, 1997—2002. Bd. govs. U. N.C. Press, Chapel Hill, 1999—; Watkins vis. prof. Wichita State U., 2002. Author: Structure and Evolution of Vertebrates, 1975, The Age of Birds, 1980, Catesby's Birds of Colonial America, 1985, Birds of Colonial Williamsburg, 1989, The Origin and Evolution of Birds, 1996 (Excellence in Biol. Sci., Assn. Am. Pubs., 1996); contbr. more than 250 articles to profl. jours.; interview appearances include Nat. Pub. Radio, BBC, Voice of Am., CNN, McNeil/Lehrer Report. Recipient Smithsonian Disting. Lectr., Smithsonian Instn., 2002. Fellow: AAAS (life), Am. Ornithologists' Union (life). Avocations: farming, golf. Home: 704 Wellington Dr Chapel Hill NC 27514 Office: Dept Biology UNC Coker Hall CB # 3280 Chapel Hill NC 27599-3280 Personal E-mail: feduccia@bio.unc.edu.

FEDUNOK, SUZANNE, librarian; b. Pitts., Apr. 23, 1945; d. Yaroslav and Angela S. (Balcius) F. AB, Bryn Mawr (Pa.) Coll., 1967; AM, U. Mich., 1969, AMLS, 1974. Editl., reference libr. Math. Revs., Ann Arbor, Mich., 1969-74, head libr., 1974-77; math, physics libr. Columbia U., N.Y.C., 1977-83, head reference, collection devel. Sci. & Engring Dept., 1983-85, asst. dir., 1985-90, SUNY, Binghamton, 1990-96; head Coles Sci. Libr. NYU, 1996—. Mem. ALA, Spl. Librs. Assn., Internat. Fedn. Libr. Assns. Office: NYU Bobst Libr 70 Washington Sq S New York NY 10012-1091 E-mail: suzanne.fedunok@nyu.edu.

FEE, ELIZABETH, medical historian, administrator; b. Belfast, Northern Ireland, Dec. 11, 1946; d. John Alexander and Deirdre (Carson) F. BA, Cambridge U., Eng., 1968, MA, 1972; PhD, Princeton U., 1978. came to U.S., 1968. Prof. history and health policy Johns Hopkins U., Balt., 1978—; chief history of medicine divsn. Nat. Libr. of Medicine, Bethesda, Md., 1995—. Author: Disease and Discovery, Teaching Quality Assurance and Cost Containment in Health Care: A Faculty Guide, 1982, Women and Health: The Politics of Sex in Medicine, 1983, Disease and Discovery: A History of the Johns Hopkins School of Hygiene and Public Health, 1916-1939, 1987, (with Daniel M. Fox) AIDS: The Burdens of History, 1988 (with Linda Shopes and Linda Zeidman) The Baltimore Book: New Views of Local History, 1991, (with Roy M. Acheson) A History of Education in Public Health: Health That Mocks the Doctors' Rules, 1991, (with Daniel M. Fox) AIDS: The Making of a Chronic Disease, 1992, (with Nancy Krieger) Women's Health, Politcs, and Power: Essays on Sex/Gender, Medicine, and Public Health, 1994, (with Steven H. Corey) Garbage! The History and Politics of Trash in New York City, 1994, (with Esther M. Sternberg, Anne Harrington, Thedore Brown) Emotions and Disease: An Exhibition at the National Library of Medicine, 1997, (with Theodore M. Brown) Making Medical History: The Life and Times of Henry E. Sigerist, 1997, (with Theodore M. Brown) The APHA: 125 Years Old--and Approaching the Millennium, 1997, (with Theodore M. Brown) American Public Health Association. Conflict and Controversy: From Medical Care Policy to the Politics of Environmental Health, 1998, (with Charles S. Marwick) Breath of Life: An Exhibition That Examines the History of Asthma, the Experiences of People with Asthma, and Contemporary Efforts to Understand and Manage the Disease, 2001, (with Susan E. Lederer and Patricia Tuohy) Frankenstein: Penetrating the Secrets of Nature: An Exhibition by the National Library of Medicine, 2002; editor: History of Public Health Education, Making Medical History, AIDS: These Burdens of History; contbr. monographs to profl. jours. Recipient Kellogg Nat. fellowship, Kellogg Found., 1984-87, Golden Apple award, Johns Hopkins U., 1991, NCM Regents award for scholarship, 2000. Mem. Am. Pub. Health Assn. (Viseltear award 1997), Sigerist Circle (chair), Am. Assn. History of Medicine. Avocations: gardening, hiking, theater. Office: Nat Libr Medicine 8600 Rockville Pike Bethesda MD 20894-0001 Office Phone: 301-496-5406. E-mail: elizabeth_fee@nlm.nih.gov.

FEE, WILLARD EDWARD, JR., otolaryngologist; b. Portchester, N.Y., June 10, 1943; s. Willard E. and Jane Frances (Cromwell) F.; m. Caroline Fee, June 13, 1965; children: Heather, Adam. BS cum laude, U. San Francisco, 1965; MD magna cum laude, U. Colo., 1969. Cert. Am. Bd. Otolaryngology, 1974. Intern Harbor Gen. Hosp., Torrance, Calif., 1969-70; resident in gen. surgery Wadsworth VA Hosp., L.A., 1970-71; resident in head and neck surgery UCLA Sch. Medicine, 1971-74; asst. prof. Stanford (Calif.) U. Med. Ctr., 1974-80, assoc. prof. otolaryngology, 1980-86, prof., 1986—, Edward C. & Amy H. Sewall prof., 1996—, chmn. dept., 1980-00. Dir. Am. Bd. of Otolaryngology, Houston, 1985-2003; chmn. med. sch. faculty senate Stanford U., 1992-94. Editl. bd. Archives in Otolaryngology, Chgo., 1984-95; contbr. numerous articles to profl. jours. Mem. Collegium ORLAS-US (chmn. 1995-2001), Paul H. Ward Soc., Inc. (pres. 1988-89), Am. Soc. Head and Neck Surgery (pres. 1989-90), Am. Acad. Otolaryngology and Head and Neck Surgery, Calif. Soc. Otolaryngology (pres. 1995-99), Alpha Omega Alpha. Home: 27299 Ursula Ln Los Altos CA 94022-3222 Office: Stanford U Med Ctr Divsn Otolaryngology Edwards R135 300 Pasteur Stanford CA 94305-5328

FEEHERRY, ANTHONY M., lawyer; b. Worcester, Mass., July 27, 1947; AB magna cum laude, Coll. of Holy Cross, 1969; JD cum laude, Boston U., 1974. Bar: Mass. 1974. Law clk. to Hon. James L. Oakes U.S. Ct. Appeals, 2d cir., 1974-75; ptnr., litig. dept. Goodwin Procter LLP (formerly Goodwin, Procter & Hoar), Boston; co-chair, litig. dept. Goodwin Procter LLP, Boston, 1995—2004. Mem. Zoning Appeals Bd., Wenham, Mass. Mem.: ABA, Boston Bar Assn. Address: Goodwin Procter LLP Exchange Pl 53 State St Boston MA 02109-2803 Office Phone: 617-570-1390. Office Fax: 617-523-1231. Business E-Mail: afeeherry@goodwinprocter.com.

FEELEY, MALCOLM MCCOLLUM, law educator, political scientist; b. North Conway, N.H., Nov. 28, 1942; s. John Aloysious and Mildred (McCollum) F.; divorced; children: Jacob, Miriam, Amin. BA, Austin Coll., 1964; MA, U. Minn., 1966, PhD, 1969. Asst. prof. NYU, N.Y.C., 1968-72; fellow, lectr. Yale U., New Haven, Conn., 1972-77; prof. U. Wis.-Madison, 1977-84; prof. law U. Calif.-Berkeley, 1984—. V.p. Silbert-Feeley Assn., New Haven, 1975-83; editorial advisor Longman Inc., N.Y.C., 1979— Author: The Process is the Punishment, 1979, The Policy Dilemma, 1981, Court Reform on Trial, 1983, Judicial Policy-Making, 1998; Editor: American Constitutional Law, 1985. Recipient Silver Gavel award, ABA, 1980, cert. merit, 1984; fellow Ctr. for Advanced Study, Stanford U., 2001—02. Mem. Law and Soc. Assn. (trustee 1975-80), Am. Polit. Sci. Assn. Democrat. Jewish. Avocations: canoeing, hiking, reading. Office: U Calif Sch Law Boalt Hall Ctr Study Law Society Hl Berkeley CA 94720-0001

FEELISCH, MARTIN, research scientist, consultant; b. Remscheid, Northrhine Westfalia, Germany, June 18, 1959; arrived in U.S., 1999; s. Guenter Max and Hildegard Feelisch; m. Lucia del Pilar Revelo Silva, Jan. 28, 1999; children: Nicolas Constantin, Lucia Gabriela Revelo, Marco Laurenz, Nicole Martina. Pharmacy Technician, Pharmazeutisch-Technische Lehranstalt, Solingen, Germany, 1979—81; BSc, Heinrich-Heine-U., Dusseldorf, Germany, 1985; PhD summa cum laude, Heinrich-Heine-University, Dusseldorf, Germany, 1988. Venia legendi for Pharmacology & Toxicology U. Cologne, Germany, 1997, lic. pharmacist Head Provincial Govt. Dusseldorf, Germany, 1986, cert. specialist for drug info. Apothekerkammer Nordrhein, Germany, 1992, Expert Degree in Pharmacology German Pharmacological Soc., 1992. Vis. rsch. scientist The Wellcome Rsch. Labs., Beckenham, England, 1989—90; head dept. pharmacology Schwarz Pharma AG, Monheim, Germany, 1990—97, dir. pharmacology and internat. project coord., 1991—97; sr. lectr., sci. coord. Wolfson Inst., U. Coll. London, 1997—99; prof. molecular and cellular physiology La. State U. Health Scis. Ctr., Shreveport, 1999—2003; prof. medicine, prof. biochemistry Boston U. Sch. Medicine, 2003—. Co-founder, dir. The Nitric Oxide Soc., 1996—; cons. Lacer S.A., Barcelona, 1997—99; vis. prof. pharmacology U. Florence, Italy, 1999—99; sci. adv. bd. mem. Vasopharm Biotech GmbH, Giessen, Germany, 2000—, NitroMed Inc., Bedford, Mass., 2003—. Author, editor: reference book Method in Nitric Oxide Research, 1996, mem. editl. bd.: Nitric Oxide Chemistry & Biology, 1993—, Endothelium, 1993—, Brit. Jour. Pharm., 2005—; contbr. articles to profl. jours. Named Hon. Sr. Lectureship in Pharmacology, U. Coll. London, 1998—99; fellow, Smith Kline Duaelsberg, 1987—88; grantee, Nat. Heart, Blood and Lung Inst., 2002—. Mem.: Nitric Oxide Soc. (dir. 1996—2003), Soc. for Free Radical Biology and Medicine, German Pharm. Soc., German Soc. for Cardiology, Heart and Circulation Rsch., German Soc. for Exptl. and Clin. Pharmacology and Toxicology (Fritz-Kulz prize 1990), Am. Physiol. Soc., Am. Heart Assn., Am. Chem. Soc. Achievements include patents in field. Office: Boston Univ Sch Medicine Whitaker Cardiovasc Inst 715 Albany St X-305 Boston MA 02118 Office Phone: 617-414-8150. Business E-Mail: feelisch@bu.edu.

FEENEY, DAVID WESLEY, lawyer; b. Phila., Nov. 1, 1938; s. William James McKay and Mary Catherine (Watkins) Feeney; m. Elizabeth Butler Shamel, Aug. 15, 1959; children: Shawn, Shari, David, Darryl. BS, Cornell U., 1960, LLB with distinction, 1963. Bar: U.S. Tax Ct. 1966, U.S. Dist. Ct. (so. dist.) N.Y. 1976, U.S. Ct. Claims 1976, U.S. Ct. Appeals (2d cir.) 1976. Assoc. Cadwalader, Wickersham & Taft, N.Y.C., 1963-64, 66-71, ptnr., 1971—, co-chmn. Tax dept. Served to 1st lt. U.S. Army, 1964-66. Mem. N.Y. State Bar Assn. (tax sect.), Cornell Club of N.Y.C. Republican. Presbyterian. Office: Cadwalader Wickersham & Taft LLP 1 World Fin Ctr New York NY 10281 Office Phone: 212-504-6566. Office Fax: 212-504-6666. Business E-Mail: david.feeney@cwt.com.

FEENEY, DON JOSEPH, JR., psychologist; b. Greenville, N.C., Jan. 17, 1948; s. Don Joseph Sr. and Louise (Saieed) Feeney; 1 child, Kelly Lynn. BA, Colgate U., 1971; MA, Gov.'s State U., 1973; PhD, Loyola U., Chgo., 1979. Registered psychologist Ill., Ind., diplomate Am. Bd. Psychol. Specialties, Am. Bd. Psychology, cert. addictions counselor; profl. coach Grow Tng. Inst., Inc. Clin. dir. Champaign (Ill.) Coun. on Alcoholism, 1976-79; pvt. practice psychology, hypnotherapy, family svcs. Downers Grove, Ill., 1979—, Dangerous Drugs Com., Chgo., 1979-80; psychologist Tri-City Mental Health Ctr., East Chicago, Ind., 1980-82; psychologist alcohol treatment program Christ Hosp., Oak Lawn, Ill., 1982—; cons. Cons. Psychol. Svcs. PC, Downers Grove, 1985—, ceo, 1998—. Chmn. adv. coun. alcoholism Govs. State U., University Park, Ill., 1979—82; devel., presenter self-hypnosis and wellness programs on smoking, weight control and chem. abuse. Author: Entrancing Relationships: Exploring the Hypnotic Framework of Addictive Relationships, 1999, Motif: The Transformative Creation of Self, 2001, Creating Cultural Motifs in the War Against Terrorism, 2003; contbr. articles to profl. jours.; guest cons. (TV series) Oprah Winfrey, Jerry Springer, Jenny Jones, others. Loyola U. fellow, 1976. Mem.: APA, Chgo. Coun. Fgn. Rels., Ill. Psychol. Assn. Roman Catholic. Avocations: chess, tennis, weightlifting, jogging, reading. Office: Cons Psychol Svcs PC 6900 Main St Ste 160 Downers Grove IL 60516-3455 Personal E-mail: drtc11@hotmail.com.

FEENEY, JOAN N., judge; BA in French and Govt., Conn. Coll., 1975; MA, Amherst Coll.; JD, Suffolk Univ. Law Sch., 1978. Law clk. to Judge Harold Lavien U.S. Bankruptcy Ct. Mass., 1978-79, law clk. to Judge James N. Gabriel, 1978-79, 82-86; assoc. Feeney & Freeley, Boston, 1979-82; assoc., then ptnr. Hanify & King P.C., Boston, 1986-92; bankruptcy judge U.S. Bankruptcy Ct. Mass., Boston, 1992—. Mem. Suffolk Univ. Law Review, 1976-78; editor Suffolk Transnational Journal, 1977-78, Suffolk Voluntary Defenders, 1977-78, Volunteer Lawyer's Project. Mem. Mass. Assn. of Women Lawyers, Am. Bankruptcy Inst. Office: Thomas O'Neill Federal Bldg 10 Causeway St Rm 1101 Boston MA 02222-1009

FEENEY, JOHN ROBERT, banker; b. Newark, Feb. 26, 1950; s. P. John and Elizabeth (Podda) F.; m. Judi Tomkowit, June 22, 1974; children—Michael, Ryan, Mark. BS, U. Del., 1972; MBA, Seton Hall U., 1977. Asst. sec., also various other positions Irving Trust Co., N.Y.C., 1972-76; asst. sec., mgr. profit planning Irving Bank Corp., N.Y.C., 1976-78; controller, v.p. Ocean County Nat. Bank, Point Pleasant, N.J., 1978-81, controller, sr. v.p., 1981-83; sr. v.p., CFO, The Summit Bancorporation, N.J., 1983-85, exec. v.p., CFO, 1985-93, sr. exec. v.p., CFO, 1994-96; exec. v.p. Summit Bancorp, NJ, 1996—2001; exec. v.p., CFO Shrewsbury State Bank, 2001—. Republican. Roman Catholic. Avocations: surfing, basketball, golf. Home: 249 Williamsburg Dr Shrewsbury NJ 07702-4564

FEENEY, MARK, journalist; b. Winchester, Mass., July 28, 1957; s. Henry Patrick and Agnes Patricia (Carney) F.; m. Claire Silvers; 1 child, William. BA, Harvard U., 1979. Rschr. The Boston Globe, 1979, data base mgr., 1980, asst. book editor, 1982, book editor, 1993-94; staff writer Boston Globe Mag.,

1993-94; editor Focus sect. The Boston Globe, 1991, Boston Globe Mag., 1994-95, staff reporter, 1995—2004; lectr. Am. studies Brandeis U., 2004—. Author: Nixon at the Movies, 2004; contbr. articles to The New Republic, Commonweal, Washington Monthly, L.A. Times, other publs. Mem. Nat. Book Critics Circle (v.p. 1986-89). Democrat. Roman Catholic. Home: 26 Mead St Cambridge MA 02140-2014 Office: The Boston Globe 135 Morrissey Blvd Boston MA 02125-3338

FEENEY, MARYANN MCHUGH, not-for profit professional; b. Bklyn., July 9, 1948; d. Michael Daniel and Mary Bridget (Hourican) McH.; m. Brian Francis Feeney, Sept. 21, 1974 (dec. Mar. 1992); 1 child, Michael. BA, Marymount Manhattan Coll., 1980; MA, Bklyn. Coll., 2002. Human resources mgr. Muir Cornelius Moore, Inc., NYC, 1977-84; human resources dir. Statue of Liberty-Ellis Island Found., NYC, 1984—88; pres. The Taft Inst., NYC, 1988—97; dir. nat. fundraising Girls Scouts U.S.A., NYC, 1997—99; exec. dir. Bklyn. Tech. H.S. Alumni Assn., 2003—05; dir. instnl. advancement Bishop Louhlin Meml. H.S., 2005—. Exec. prodr. Your Vote Video, 1991 (nominated ACE and Emmy awards 1991). Bd. dirs. Bklyn. Conservatory of Music, 1992-94, SFX-Prospect Park Baseball, Bklyn., 1986—; pres. emeritus, trustee The Taft Inst. at Queens Coll., 1997—. Recipient Cmty. Svc. award SFX-Prospect Park Baseball, 1992, 95, 97. Mem. Ireland House at NYU, Park Slope Civic Coun. (trustee). Democrat. Roman Catholic. Avocations: reading, history, gardening. Office Phone: 718-857-2700. Personal E-mail: mfeeney3@aol.com. Business E-Mail: mfeeney@blmhs.org.

FEENEY, MATTHEW EDWARD, linguist, educator; b. Livermore, Calif., Dec. 24, 1955; s. Martin Edward and Dorothy Ann Feeney. *Great-uncle and namesake, Mathew Rodman, served in the United States Army in Europe in World War II, and in the Battle of the Bulge, and was posthumously awarded the Purple Heart. He was from Manistique, Michigan. Ancestors, the Logsdon and Mattingly families, settled in American Colonies (Colony of Maryland) in the 1600s. They were originally from England. They served in the American Army in the Revolutionary War.* BA, U. Wyo., 1980; MA, SUNY, Albany, 1988; Cert. Advanced Study, 1994; PhD, U. Kans., 2003. Lang. lab. asst. U. Wyo., Laramie, 1989—91, editor English transls. Russian articles, 2004—; grad. asst. SUNY, Albany, 1991—93, dir. study abroad program in Moscow, Russia, 1992—93; tchg. asst. dept. Slavic lang. and lit. U. Kans., Lawrence, 1998—2003, dir. summer study abroad program in Croatia, 2002—03. Presenter Slavic linguistics. Contbr. articles and scholarly papers to profl. jours. and confs.; editor: Russian articles, 2005. Mem.: MLA, Profl. Assn. Edn., Pi Lambda Theta Internat. Honor Soc. Personal E-mail: mef2@hotmail.com.

FEENEY, SEAN PATRICK, lawyer; b. Iowa City, Sept. 13, 1957; s. Thomas J. and Sally P. (Seeker) F.; children: William Shane, Jessica Rose, Jennifer Ann, Ryan Patrick, Emily Marie; m. Eva Marie Mancuso. BA, U. Wis., Eau Claire, 1980; JD magna cum laude, No. Ill. U., 1984. Bar: Wis. 1984, Ill. 1985, R.I. 1989, U.S. Dist. Ct. R.I. 1990. Prosecutor USMC, 1986-88; spl. asst. U.S. atty. Ctrl. Dist. Calif., 1988; spl. counsel City of Providence, 1989-91; assoc. Hamel, Waxler, Allen & Collins, Providence, 1991-96, ptnr., 1996—. Office: Hamel Waxler Allen & Collins 387 Atwells Ave Providence RI 02909-1026

FEENEY, TOM, congressman; b. Phila., May 21, 1958; m. Ellen Stewart. BA in Polit. Sci., Pa. State U., 1980; JD, U. Pitts., 1983. Mem. Fla. Ho. of Reps., 1990—94, 1996—2002, speaker, 2000—02; majority coun. liaison; mem. procedural coun. chair reapportionment com.; mem. econ. impact, govt. responsibility, justice couns.; mem. US Congress from 24th Fla. dist., 2003—; mem. Ho. Judiciary com., Fin. Svcs. com., Sci. com. Rep. nominee lt. gov., 1994; legis. del. chmn. Orange County, 1993, Seminole County, 1996; ambassador to Macedonian Govt., Internat. Rep. Inst., 1995; bd. dir. U. Activity Ctr. Transp. Authority, Mosley's High-Tech Tutoring, Cornerstone Inc. Distbn. Ctr., OIA Kidsway Inc., James Madison Inst., former dir.; mem. bus. leadership coun. City of Light; mem. rep. exec. com. Orange and Seminole County; former Fla. chmn. Empowerment Network; former chmn. edn. task force Am. Legis. Exchang Coun., 1992-94. Recipient Outstanding Legislator of Yr. award Ctrl. Fla. Young Rep., 1991, 92, Am. Legis. Exchange Coun., 1992, So. Coll. Cmty. Svc. award, 1992, Orlando Leadership award, 1993, 40 Under 40 award Orlando Bus. Jour., 1996. Mem. East Orange C. of C., S.W. Volusia, C. of C., Sandord C. of C., Oviedo C. of C. Republican. Presbyterian. Avocations: history, politics, philosophy, reading. Address: 12424 Research Pksy Orlando FL 32826-2109 Office: 323 Cannon House Off Bldg Washington DC 20515

FEENKER, CHERIE DIANE, law librarian; b. Birmingham, Ala., Nov. 14, 1950; d. Marshall Ross and Joy (Martin) F. BA, U. Montevallo, 1971; MLS, U. Ala., 1979; JD with honors, Birmingham Sch. Law, 1989. Periodical libr. sci. and tech. dept. Birmingham Pub. Libr., 1971—73, br. head, 1973—80, reference libr. tech. and bus. dept., 1980—84; law libr. Lange, Simpson, Robinson & Somerville, Birmingham, 1984—2003; libr. Cumberland Sch. Law, Birmingham, 2003—. Firm rep. Exec. Women Internat., 1990—, historian, 1991, bd. dirs., 1993, 96-97, pub. dir., 1993, scholarship dir., 1995, dir. at-large, 1996, sgt.-at-arms, 1997, sustaining mem. liaison, v.p./pres. elect, 1998, pres. 1999, past-pres. 2000. Mem. bd. trustees St. Martin's in the Pines, 1995-2000, bd. dirs. 1999, 2000; vis. allocation team United Way Ctrl. Ala., 1997-2004; mem. vestry St. Andrew's Parish, Birmingham, 1985-87; bd. visitors Coll. Comms. and Info. Scis. U. Ala., 1997— Mem. ABA, Ala. Bar Assn. (faculty CLE 1987), Birmingham Bar Assn. (pub. rels. project com. 1992-93, pub. svc. com. 1994, econ. practice law com. 2002), Ala. Libr. Assn. (law libr. roundtable 1986-88, moderator 1987-88), Am. Assn. Law Librs., Libr. Sch. Assn. (bd. dirs. 1991-94, pres.-elect 1995-97, pres. 1997-2000, past pres. 2000-02, bd. dirs.), Law Libr. Assn. Ala., Spl. Librs. Assn. (pres. Ala. chpt. 2004—), Beta Phi Mu. Episcopalian. Home: 4052 Brentwood Dr Irondale AL 35210-3505 Office: Samford U Law Libr 800 Lakeshore Dr Birmingham AL 35229 Business E-Mail: cdfeenke@samford.edu.

FEESE, SUZANNE, lawyer; b. Danville, Ky. BA with honors, Agnes Scott Col., 1984; JD, Yale Univ., 1987. Bar: Ga. 1988. Law clk. Judge R. Lanier Anderson III, US Ct. Appeals 11th Cir.; ptnr., Tax Practice Group & hiring ptnr., Atlanta King & Spalding, LLP, Atlanta. Trustee Agnes Scott Col.; mem. Chair Council Atlanta Women's Found.; past chairwoman Ga. Ctr. for Children. Mem.: ABA, State Bar Ga. Office: King & Spalding LLP 191 Peachtree St Atlanta GA 30303 Office Phone: 404-572-3566. Office Fax: 404-572-5100. Business E-Mail: sfeese@kslaw.com.

FEEZELL, MARK, music educator; b. San Antonio, Tex. s. John and Judith Feezell; m. Jill Feezell. MusB in Music Theory and Composition, Tex. Christian U., 1997, MusM in Music Theory and Composition, 1999; PhD in Music Composition, U. North Tex., 2003. Adj. instr. of music theory Tex. Christian U., Fort Worth, Tex., 2001; vis. asst. prof. music Claflin U., Orangeburg, SC, 2003—. Composer website. Mem.: Coll. Music Soc. Office: Claflin University 400 Magnolia Street Orangeburg SC 29115 Office Phone: 803-535-5355. E-mail: mfeezell@claflin.edu.

FEFFER, GERALD ALAN, lawyer; b. Washington, Apr. 24, 1942; s. Louis Charles and Elsie (Glick) F.; children: Andrew, John, Keith. BA with honors, Lehigh U., 1964; JD, U. Va., 1967. Bar: N.Y. 1968, D.C. 1980. Assoc. Mudge, Rose, Guthrie & Alexander, N.Y.C., 1967-71; asst. U.S. atty. So. Dist. N.Y., 1971-76, asst. chief criminal div., 1975-76; ptnr. Kostelanetz & Ritholz, N.Y.C., 1976-79; dep. asst. atty. gen. tax div. Dept. Justice, Washington, 1979-81; ptnr. Steptoe & Johnson, Washington, 1981-86, Williams & Connolly, Washington, 1986—. Mem. editl. bd. Busniess Crimes Bulletin: Compliance and Litigation; contbr. articles to profl. jours. Fellow Am. Coll. Tax Counsel, Am. Coll. Trial Lawyers; mem. ABA (criminal justice litigation and taxation sects.), Nat. Assn. Criminal Def. Lawyers, Nat. Inst. on Criminal Tax Fraud (chmn.). Office: Williams & Connolly 725 12th St NW Washington DC 20005-5901 Home: 3000 Garrison St NW Washington DC 20008-1032 Office Phone: 202-434-5007.

FEFFERMAN, CHARLES LOUIS, mathematics professor; b. Washington, D.C., Apr. 18, 1949; s. Arthur Stanley and Liselott Ruth (Stern) Fefferman; m. Julie Anne Albert, Feb. 1975; children: Nina Heidi, Elaine Marie. BS, U. Md., 1966, Doctorate (hon.), 1979; PhD, Princeton U., 1969; Doctorate (hon.), Knox Coll., 1981, Bar-Ilan U., Israel, 1985, U. Madrid (Autonoma), 1990. Asst. prof. U. Chgo., 1970—71, prof. math., 1971—73; lectr. math. Princeton (N.J.) U., 1969—70, prof. math., 1973—84, Herbert Jones U. prof., 1984—, grad. dir. dept. math., 1997—99, dept. chmn., 1999—2002. Vis. prof. U. Md., Calif. Inst. Tech., Courant Inst. Math. Scis., NYU, U. Paris, Mittag-Leffler Inst., Djursholm, Sweden, Weitzmann Inst., Rehovot, Israel, Bar-Ilan U., Ramat-Gen, Israel, U. Madrid (Aútonoma). Author: Reviewing U.S. Mathematics - A Plan for the Nineties, research papers. Recipient Salem prize for outstanding work in fourier analysis by young mathematician, 1978, Alan T. Waterman award, 1978, Fields medal, Internat. Cong. Mathematicians, 1978, 1984; grantee Nat. Sci. Found. Fellowship, 1966—69, Alfred P. Sloan Fellowship, 1970, NATO Postdoctoral Fellowship, 1971. Mem.: Am. Philos. Soc., Am. Acad. Arts and Scis., Am. Math. Soc., Nat. Acad. Scis. Home: 234 Clover Ln Princeton NJ 08540-4051 Office: Princeton U Math Dept 1102 Fine Hall Washington Rd Princeton NJ 08544-1000

FEFFERMAN, HILBERT, government official, lawyer; b. N.Y.C., June 5, 1913; s. Jacob and Sarah F.; m. Helen Libby Relkin, June 16, 1940. BS magna cum laude in philosophy (hon.), NYU, 1934; JD, Harvard U., 1937. Bar: NY 1938, U.S. Supreme Ct. 1953. Pvt. practice, N.Y.C., 1938-41; atty. U.S. Housing and Home Fin. Agy., Washington, 1941-59, asst. gen. counsel for legislation, 1960-62, assoc. gen. counsel for ops., 1962-67; chief legislative counsel HUD, Washington, 1967-72; cons. Housing and Devel. Legislation, Bethesda, Md., 1973—. Lectr., vis. prof. city planning MIT, Cambridge, Mass., 1973-76. Contbr. articles to profl. jours. Recipient Disting. Svc. award, HUD, 1968. Mem.: Phi Beta Kappa. Home and Office: 5661 Bent Branch Rd Bethesda MD 20816-1049

FEGAN, JEFFREY P., airport executive; BS in Geography, Frostburg U.; M in City Planning, Ga. Inst. Tech.; advanced airport mgmt. course, Internat. Aviation Mgmt. Tng. Inst., Montreal. Aviation cons., 1978-83; noise abatement officer Westchester County Airport, N.Y., 1983-84; chief planner Dallas/Ft. Worth Internat. Airport Bd., 1984, asst. dir., dir. planning and engring., 1989-93, dep. exec. dir. fin. and adminstrn., 1993-94, exec. dir., chief adminstr., exec. officer, 1994—. Mem. Airports Coun. Internat.-NA Environ. Affairs Com., Internat. Civil Airports Assn.-Passenger Facilitation World Com., Am. Assn. Airport Execs., Am. Planning Assn., Am. Inst. Cert. Planners. Office: DFW Int'l Airport Adminstrn PO Box 619428 Dallas TX 75261-9428*

FEGLEY, KENNETH ALLEN, systems engineering educator; b. Mont Clare, Pa., Feb. 14, 1923; s. Henry Stanley and Bertha (Malone) F.; m. Virginia Ruth Weaver, Sept. 1, 1951; children: Alan Donald, John David, Paul Andrew. BSEE, U. Pa., 1947, MSEE, 1950, PhD, 1955. Instr. Moore Sch. Elec. Engring., U. Pa., Phila., 1947-53, assoc., 1953-55, asst. prof., 1955-58, assoc. prof., 1958-66, prof. elec. engring., 1966-72; prof. sys. engring. U. Pa., Phila., 1972-90, chmn. dept. sys. engring., 1972-75, chmn. dept. sys., 1986-93, Joseph Moore prof. sys., 1990-93, Joseph Moore prof. emeritus sys., 1993—. Cons. U.S. Army, Phila., Dover, N.J., 1955-85, USN, Phila., 1970-86. Contbr. numerous articles to tech. jours. and chpts. to books. With USN, 1944-46. Fellow IEEE, AAAS; mem. Am. Soc. Engring. Edn., Masons, AAUP, Sigma Xi, Eta Kappa Nu, Tau Beta Pi, Sigma Tau. Democrat. Presbyterian. Office: U Pa Dept Electrical and Systems Engring Philadelphia PA 19104-6315 Personal E-mail: kenfegley@comcast.net.

FEHER, GEORGE, biophysicist, educator; b. Czechoslovakia, May 29, 1924; s. Ferdinand and Sylvia (Schwartz) F.; m. Elsa Rosenvasser, June 18, 1961; children— Laurie, Shoshanah, Paoli BS in Engring. Physics, U. Calif.-Berkeley, 1950, MS in Elec. Engring., 1951, PhD in Physics, 1954; PhD (hon.), Hebrew U. Jerusalem, 1994. Research physicist Bell Telephone Labs., Murray Hill, N.J., 1954-60; vis. assoc. prof. Columbia U., N.Y.C., 1959-60; prof. physics U. Calif.-San Diego, 1960—. Vis. prof. biology MIT, Cambridge, 1967-68; William Draper Hawkins lectr. U Chgo., May 1986; Raymond and Beverly Sackler disting. lectr. U. Tel-Aviv, June 1986; vis. prof. Hebrew U. of Jerusalem, Israel, spring 1989, 93; bd. govs. Weizmann Inst. Sci., Rehovot, Israel, 1988. Author: Electron Paramagnetic Resonance with Applications to Selected Problems in Biology, 1970; contbr. numerous articles to profl. jous., chpts. to books Bd. govs. Technion-Israel Inst. Tech., 1968 Recipient Oliver E. Buckley Solid State Physics prize, 1976, Inaugural Annual award Internat. Electron Spin Resonance Soc., 1991; NSF fellow, 1967-68. Fellow AAAS, Internat. EPR/ESR Soc. (Zavoisky award 1996); mem. Am. Phys. Soc. (prize 1960, biophysics prize, 1982), Biophys. Soc. (nat. lectr. 1983), Nat. Acad. Scis., Am. Acad. Arts and Scis. (Rumford medal 1992), Sigma Xi Office: U Calif Dept Physics 9500 Gilman Dr Dept 319 La Jolla CA 92093-0319 Business E-Mail: gfeher@ucsd.edu.

FEHLBERG, ROBERT ERICK, architect; b. Kalispell, Mont., Apr. 28, 1926; s. Otto Albert Erick and Mary Grace (Nelson) F.; m. LaDonna Karen Rognlie, May 31, 1953; children: Kolby J., Kenje A., Kurt E., Klee J. BS in Architecture, Mont. State U., 1951. Architect in tng. with Gehres D. Weed Architect, Kalispell, 1952-55; partner Weed & Fehlberg Architects, Kalispell, 1955-57; pvt. practice Kalispell, 1957-58; with Cushing Terrell Assos., Billings, Mont., 1958-72, partner, 1960-72; v.p. CTA Architects Engrs., Inc., Billings, 1973-87; ptnr. Collaborative Design Architects, Oakland, Calif., 1987-91, Robert Fehlberg Architects, Pleasanton, Calif., 1991—. Bd. dirs. Yellowstone Art Center Found., 1965-84, 1st pres., 1965; bd. dirs. Mont. Inst. Arts Found., 1976-86, pres., 1976-80, treas., 1980-86. Served with AUS, 1944-46. Recipient (with wife) Gov.'s award for arts, 1983 Fellow AIA (pres. Mont. 1965, nat. dir. 1971-74), Mont. Inst. Arts (pres. 1963-64); mem. Prodn. Systems for Architects and Engrs. (dir. 1971-74, chmn. 1974), East Bay AIA. Home: 7566 Rosedale Ct Pleasanton CA 94588-3762 also: PO Box 2431 Sitka AK 99835-2431

FEHLNER, FRANCIS PAUL, chemist, consultant; b. Dolgeville, N.Y., Aug. 3, 1934; s. Herman J. and Mary E. Fehlner; children: Paul, John, Joseph. BS, Holy Cross Coll., 1956; PhD, Rensselaer Polytechnic Inst., 1959. Research chemist Corning (N.Y.) Inc., 1962-95, cons., 1995—. Adj. prof. dept. materials sci. and engring. Cornell U., 1991—. Author: Low-Temperature Oxidation, 1986; contbr. articles to profl. jours. 1st lt. USAF, 1959-62. Mem. Am. Chem. Soc., Electrochem. Soc., Sigma Xi. Achievements include 15 patents. Home: 227 Watauga Ave Corning NY 14830-3233

FEHR, GREGORY PARIS, marketing and distribution company executive; b. Urbana, Ill., Nov. 10, 1943; s. Orval Joachim and Cuba Lucile (Paris) F.; m. Sharon Louise Burba, Jan. 21, 1965 (div. Jan. 1975); children: Kristina K., Gregory Tyson Howard; m. Kathleen Lorretta Meyers, Aug. 10, 1990. BS in Indsl. Engring., Okla. U., 1967; MBA, Drake U., 1977. Registered profl. mech. engr. Iowa, Okla., Ala.; cert. corrosion technologist, cathodic protection specialist. From engr. to sr. project engr. Fisher Controls Co., Marshalltown, Iowa, 1967-77; fgn. liaison GE, Portland, Maine, 1977-79; gen. mgr. Arabian Am. Oil Co., Dhahran, Saudi Arabia, 1979-81; v.p. Oil Tech. Svcs., Houston, 1981-85; mgr. materials engring. Std. Oil Prodn. Co., Houston, 1985-86; mgr. nuc. products Wyle Labs., Huntsville, Ala., 1986-88; sr. materials engr. Sci. Applications Internat., Las Vegas, Nev., 1988-96; v.p. GPF Mktg. and Distbn., Las Vegas, 1988—; sr. project mgr. Converse Cons. S.W., Inc., Las Vegas, 1996—2002, Terracon Cons. Engrs. and Scientists, 2002—. Cons. task groups Am. Petroleum Inst., 1983-86, Electric Power Rsch. Inst., San Mateo, Calif., 1986-89; chmn. employee adv. coun. Sci. Applications Internat., Las Vegas, 1992. Contbr. articles and tech. papers to profl. jours. Pres. Marshalltown Tennis Assn., 1972-73; head swim coach YMCA/YWCA, Marshalltown, 1973-74; mem. adv. bd. Marshalltown C.C., 1975. Mem. NSPE, ASME, Nat. Assn. Corrosion Engrs., Am. Petroleum Inst., Am. Soc. Nondestructive Testing. Avocations: skiing, scuba diving, sailing, photography. Office: GPF Marketing and Distribution Ste 212 4600 E Sunset Rd Henderson NV 89014

FEHR, JOHN WILL, newspaper editor; b. Long Beach, Calif., Mar. 8, 1926; s. John and Evelyn (James) F.; m. Cynthia Moore, Sept. 4, 1951; children— Michael John, Martha Ann BA in English, U. Utah, 1951. City editor Salt Lake City Tribune, 1964-80, mng. editor, 1980-81, editor, 1981-91. Served to 1st lt. USAF, 1951-53 Mem. Am. Soc. Newpaper Editors, Sigma Chi Home: 468 13th Ave Salt Lake City UT 84103-3229

FEHR, KENNETH MANBECK, retired computer company executive; b. Schuylkill Haven, Pa., Feb. 21, 1937; s. Theodore E. and Eva (Manbeck) F.; m. Jean Alice Greenawalt, June 28, 1952; children: K. Craig, Karen Jean, K. Todd. BS, Pa. State U., 1951; MBA, U. Pitts., 1953. With U.S. Steel Corp., 1951-62, div. controller, 1962; controller Interlake Steel Corp., Chgo., 1962-68; v.p. fin. Hallicrafters Co., 1968-71, E.W. Bliss Co., Salem, Ohio, 1971-74; treas. Alliance Machine Co., Ohio, 1974-86; pres. I.M.S. Corp., Hudson, Ohio, 1986-90, Fehr & Greenawalt Investments, Salem, Ohio, 1990—, Salem Security Storage, LLC, 2002—. Bd. dirs. Fegreen Inc.; night sch. tchr. U. Pitts., 1956—57. Treas. Salem Renaissance. With USNR, 1945—46. Mem.: Nat. Assn. Accts., Fin. Execs. Inst., Salem Hist. Soc., Salem Preservation Soc., Salem-Golf Club, Kiwanis (chpt. pres.), Masons. Home: 725 S Lincoln Ave Salem OH 44460-3709 Office: 1210 So Ellsworth Ave Salem OH 44460 Personal E-mail: fehrken@hotmail.com.

FEHRENBACH, T(HEODORE) R(EED), writer; b. San Benito, Tex., Jan. 12, 1925; s. T.R. and Rose Mardel (Wentz) F.; m. Lillian Breetz, Aug. 22, 1951. BA magna cum laude, Princeton U., 1947. Field supr. Travelers Ins. Co., San Antonio, 1954-56; owner ind. ins. agy. San Antonio, 1956-69; mng. trustee Fehrenbach Trusts, 1970—; pres. Royal Poinciana Corp., San Antonio, 1971-92. Author: This Kind of War, 1963, This Kind of Peace, 1966, Lone Star (PBS TV Series 1985-86), 1968, Fire and Blood, 1973, Comanches, 1974, Seven Keys to Texas, 1983, Texas: A Salute From Above, 1985, others; contbr. numerous articles, stories to mags., U.S. fgn. periodicals. Mem. Tex. 2000 Commn., 1981-82; chmn. Tex. Hist. Commn., 1987-91; mem. design adv. com. Tex. Quarter Dollar, 2001-03. 1st lt. AUS, 1943-46, lt. col., 1950-53, Korea. Recipient Disting. Civilian Svc. medal, Freedoms Found. award, 1965, Evelyn Oppenheimer award, 1968, citations Tex. Ho. of Reps., 1969, 73, Tex. Legislature, 1977, 2003; T.R. Fehrenbach Book awards created in his honor Tex. Hist. Commn., 1986; named Disting. Citizen, San Antonio, 1973, Knight of San Jacinto, Primicerius Order of St. Maurice. Fellow Am. Numismatic Soc., Tex. State Hist. Assn.; mem. Philos. Soc. Tex., Authors Guild, Sci. Fiction Writers Am., Conopus Club, Argyle Club, Torch Club, Princeton Club of N.Y.C., Garden of the Gods Club (Colo.). Republican. Episcopalian. Home: 131 Mary D Ave San Antonio TX 78209-5667 Office: 5108 Broadway St San Antonio TX 78209-5746 Office Phone: 210-824-5511.

FEHRING, MARY ANN, secondary school educator; Secondary tchr. Bishop Noll Inst., Hammond, Ind. Named Outstanding High Sch. tchr. Inland Steel Ryerson Found., 1992. Office: Bishop Noll Inst 1518 Hoffman St Hammond IN 46327-1769

FEI, JAMES ROBERT, engineering executive, consultant; b. Tucson, May 24, 1947; s. Robert Fleming and Barbara Jean (Dukes) F.; m. Patricia Christine Wilson, Aug. 24, 1968; children: Robert Fleming, Christina Kalani. BSME, U. So. Calif., 1969; MS in Ocean Engring., U. Hawaii, 1973. Registered profl. engr., S.C., La., Tex., Ga., Va., N.H., N.C. Design engr. USN, Mare Island, Calif., 1969-70; project mgr. Pearl Harbor (Hawaii) Shipyard, 1970-73; mech. systems engr. Submarine Maintenance Monitoring Systems Office Dept. of the Navy, Washington, 1973-76; chmn., chief exec. officer Life Cycle Engring., Inc., Charleston, S.C., 1977—. Bd. dirs., adv. bd. Nat. Bank of S.C., 1985-92; mem. adv. coun. St. Francis Hosp., 1992-95; mem. pres.'s adv. coun. Med. U. S.C., Charleston, 1995-96; mem. Cold War Submarine Meml. Found., exec. com., bd. Mem. SCSPE, NSPE, ASME, Navy League. Republican. Avocations: golf, boating. Office: Life Cycle Engring Inc 4360 Corporate Rd Charleston SC 29405-7445 Office Phone: 843-744-7110. Business E-Mail: jfei@lce.com.

FEI, JUN, art educator, graphics designer; b. Jingzhou, Hubei, China, Jan. 20, 1970; m. Wei Yang, Oct. 11, 1994. BA, Ctrl. Acad. of Fine Arts, Beijing, 2002; MFA, Alfred (NY) U., 2005. Art editor China Film Press, Beijing, 1992—96; founder & art dir. Beijing Rule Art Svc. Co., LTD., 1996—2002; art dir. Beijing Jianya Advt. Co., 1999—2001, Pooga - Chinese Aviation Tourism Guide Mag., Beijing, 2001—03; vis. prof. Ctrl. Acad. of Fine Arts, Beijing, 2002—03; vis. prof. Sch. of Art and Design Alfred U., 2005—. Interactive installation, Jijizhazha, Transformation, Play you, back; prodr.: (book) New year papers; author: (journal) Art and Design Magazine; art editor, book designer (book) Outstanding folk paper-cuts in China (Golden Prize, The 1st Chinese Design Art Exhbn., 1998); video installation, "init". Recipient First Prize, 4th Nat. Book Design Art Exhbn., Beijing, 1994, 11th Chinese Book Competition, Beijing, 1997, Excellent Prize, 1st Chinese Design Art Exhbn., Chengdu, 1998, 2nd Prize, The 13th No. China Book Design Art Competition and Seminar, Haerbin, 2000, Excellent Prize, The Digital Media Art Competition of Students from Art Academies of China, 2002; scholar, Alfred U., 2003—05. Mem.: Chinese Assn. Book Design (assoc.; beijing, china 1994—2005). Home: Apt 2102 Wangjinghuayuan Chaoyang District, Beijing 100102 China Office: Sch Art & Design NYSCC Alfred Univ 2 Pine St Alfred NY 14802 Office Phone: 607-871-2044. Personal E-mail: feijun70@yahoo.ca.

FEIBEL, ANN, physical therapist, educator; b. Bklyn. d. Carl and Mary Feibel; m. George Nehme. AAS, Kingsborough C.C., Bklyn., 1975; BS in Phys. Therapy, CUNY, 1977; MS, L.I. U., 1988; D in Phys. Therapy, Creighton U., 2003. Staff phys. therapist Cabrini Med. Ctr., N.Y.C., 1979—85; phys. therapy supr. Metro Jewish Geriatric Ctr., Bklyn., 1985—87; dir. rehag. Maimonides Med. Ctr., Bklyn., 1987—90; cons. phys. therapist St. Mary's Hosp. for Children, Queens, NY, 1990—98, East River Child Devel. Ctr., N.Y.C., 1998—; prof. La Guardia C.C., Queens, 1990—. Mem.: Greater NY Phys. Therapy Assn., Am. Phys. Therapy Assn. Office: La Guardia CC 31-10 Thomson Ave Long Island City NY 11101

FEIBEL, FREDERICK ARTHUR, financial consultant; b. Chgo., Oct. 27, 1942; s. Fred and Emma Feibel; m. Marlene Ruth Edwards, Aug. 7, 1965; 1 son, Frederick Curtis. BSEE, Purdue U., 1964; MBA, Northwestern U., 1970. Project engr. Johnson Controls Corp., Milw., 1964-69; sr. mgmt. cons. Arthur Andersen & Co., Chgo., 1970-76; rep. pension fund evaluation A.G. Becker Securities Co., Chgo., 1976-77; spl. agt. Northwestern Mut. Life Ins. Co., Milw., 1977-82; pres. F.A. Feibel Fin. Assocs., Northbrook, Ill., 1982—. Chmn. Village of Northbrook Bicentennial Commn., 1975-76, Boy Scouts Am. Troop 67, 1990—; v.p. Northbrook Civic Found., 1977, pres., 1978, also bd. dirs.; deacon Northfield Cmty. Ch., 1978-81, 95-98, asst. treas., 1986—; trustee Northfield Rural Fire Dist., 2000—. Recipient Disting. Svc. award State of Ill., 1976, Northbrook Civic Found., 1983, 89, Civic Svc. award Northbrook B'nai B'rith, 1981-82, Vol Initiative of Pvt. Sector Recognition award Northbrook C. of C. and Industry, 1985, Vol. Appreciation award Northbrook Park Dist, 1987; named Northbrook Rotary Man of Yr, 1978-79, Hall of Fame III Festival Assn., 1992. Mem. Greater North Shore Estate Planning Coun., Eta Kappa Nu, Tau Beta Pi. Home: 1841 Western Ave Northbrook IL 60062-5041 Office: FA Feibel Fin Assocs PO Box 355 Northbrook IL 60065-0355 Office Phone: 847-272-8152.

FEIDELSON, MARC, advertising executive; b. Aug. 20, 1939; s. Robert and Ceil (Robbins) Feidelson; m. Linda Sarnoff, June 11, 1964; children: Lee, Pamela. BS in Bus. Adminstrn., Boston U., 1961; MA in Psychology, CUNY, 1966. Media rsch. analyst CBS-TV, N.Y.C., 1964—65; sr. media rsch. analyst Ted Bates Advt., N.Y.C., 1966—67; media rsch. dir. Benton & Bowles Advt., N.Y.C., 1967—70; media mgr. RCA Corp., N.Y.C., 1970—72; dir. advt. svcs. Hunt-Wesson Foods, Fullerton, Calif., 1973—79; exec. v.p. Dailey & Assocs. Advt., L.A., 1979—, media dir., 1979—. Guest lectr. UCLA. Editor: Media Decisions Mag., 1983. Mem.: Hollywood Radio & TV Soc., L.A. Media Dirs. Coun. (pres. 1981—82). Jewish. Office: Dailey & Assocs 8687 Melrose Ave West Hollywood CA 90069-5701

FEIFEL, DAVID, neurologist, psychiatrist; MD, MA, BSc, PhD, U. Toronto, 1992. Diplomate Am. Bd. Psychiatry and Neurology, 1997. Assoc. prof. U. Calif., La Jolla, Calif., 1995—, dir., neuropsychiatry program Med. Ctr. San Diego, 1995—. Dir. adult adhd program U. Calif., San Diego, 1995—. Contbr. articles to profl. jours. Grantee, NIH, 1999, 2001, 2002, 2004, Nat. Alliance for Schizophrenia and Depression, 2004. Mem.: Am. Coll. Neuropharmacology (assoc.). Achievements include discovery of animal models of schizophrenia, brain chemistry. Office: University of California San Diego 200 West Arbor Drive San Diego CA 92103-8218 Office Phone: 619-543-2485.

FEIG, BARBARA KRANE, elementary school educator, author; b. Mitchell, S.D., Nov. 8, 1937; d. Peter Abraham and Sally (Gorchow) Krane; m. Jerome Feig, June 8, 1963; children: Patricia Lynn, Lizabeth Ann. Student, Washington U., St. Louis, 1955-58; BE, Nat. Coll. Edn., 1960; postgrad., Northeastern Ill. U. Tchr. various schs., 1960-68, Anshe Emet Day Sch., Chgo., 1966-68, Sacred Heart, Chgo., 1982—, New City Day Sch., Chgo., 1983-90, Chgo. Pub. Schs., 1990—. Pres. J.B. Pal & Co., Inc., Chgo., 1975—; bd. dirs. Barclee Cosmetics, Inc., Chgo., Media Merchandising, Chgo.; meeting planner Ismes, Bergamo, Italy, 1987—, Technica, Chgo., 1987—, Meeting Network, Chgo., 1987—. Author: Now You're Cooking: A Guide to Cooking For Boys and Girls, 1975, The Parents' Guide to Weight Control For Children, 1980; mem. editorial staff Other Voices, 1985—; developer ednl. toy, 1985. Mem. womens bd. Francis Parker Sch., Chgo., 1972—; trustee Chgo. Inst. for Psychoanalysis, 1975—; bd. dirs. Juvenile Diabetes Found., Chgo., 1976—. Mem. Women of the Professions and Trades, Jewish Fedn. Avocations: skydiving, scuba diving, mountain climbing, skiing, marathons. Home: 1340 N Astor St Apt 2906 Chicago IL 60610-8438

FEIG, STEPHEN ARTHUR, pediatrician, educator, preventive medicine physician, hematologist, oncologist; b. N.Y.C., Dec. 24, 1937; s. Irving L. and Janet (Oppenheimer) F.; m. Judith Bergman, Aug. 28, 1960; children: Laura, Daniel, Andrew. AB in Biology, Princeton U., 1959; MD, Columbia U., 1963. Diplomate Am. Bd. Pediat., Am. Bd. Hematology-Oncology. Intern Mt. Sinai Hosp., N.Y.C., 1963-64, resident in pediat., 1964-66; hematology fellow Children's Hosp. Med. Ctr., Boston, 1968-71, assoc. in medicine, 1971-72; asst. prof. pediat. UCLA, 1972-77, chief divsn. hematology and oncology Sch. Medicine, 1977—2005, assoc. prof., 1977-82, prof., 1982—2005, exec. vice chmn. dept. pediat. Sch. Medicine, 1994—2004, prof. emeritus, 2005—. Trustee L.A. chpt. Leukemia Soc. Am., 1978—; bd. trustees, 1984—; chair exec. com. subsect. hemotology/oncology Am. Acad. Pediat.; bd. dirs. Camp Ronald McDonald for Good Times; active numerous other pediatric hosp. and med. sch. coms Reviewer Am. Jour. Pediatric Hematology/Oncology, Blood, Pediat., Pediatric Rsch., Jour. Pediat.; contbr. articles to profl. jours.; editl. bd. Jour. Pediat. Hematology & Oncology. Served with USNR, 1966-68. Mem. Am. Soc. Hematology, Soc. Pediatric Rsch., Am. Pediatric Soc., Internat. Soc. Exptl. Hematology, Am. Assn. Cancer Rsch. Jewish. Avocation: native arts. Office: UCLA Sch Medicine Dept Pediatrics 10833 Le Conte Ave Los Angeles CA 90095-3075 Office Phone: 310-794-4789. Business E-Mail: sfeig@mednet.ucla.edu.

FEIGAL, DAVID W., JR., health science association administrator; BS, U. Minn.; MD, Stanford U. Resident U. Calif., Davis, fellow San Francisco, former assoc. prof.; head divsn. anti-viral drug products Ctr. Drug Evaluation & Rsch. FDA, 1992-97, med. dep. dir. Ctr. Biologics Evaluation & Rsch., 1997-99, dir. Ctr. Devices and Radiological Health, 1999—2004; head of med. devices and biologics NDA Partners, Falls Church, Va., 2004—.

FEIGE, MARY S, literature and language educator; d. George and Mary Rice; m. Thomas Richard Feige, June 19, 1982; children: Thomas, Melissa. BS, So. Conn. State U., 1977—81; MS, So. Conn. state U., 1989—91; 6th Yr., So. Conn. State U., 2003—05, 6th Yr., 1998—99. Intermediate Administrator Conn. State Dept. of Edn./Conn., 2005, Reading and Language Arts Consultant K-12 Conn. State Department of Edn./Conn., 1991, Elementary Education Pre K-8 Conn. State Dept. of Edn./Conn., 1981. Tchr. Seymour Pub. Schools, Seymour, Conn., 1991—2002, reading cons., 2002—04, adminstrv. intern - asst. prin., 2004—. Lang. arts curriculum chairperson Seymour Pub. Schools, 2003—. Mem. St. Michael's Ch., Beacon Falls, Conn., 1983—2005, Seymour Edn. Assn., Conn., 1991—2005. Recipient Tchr. Recognition award, Conn. Assn. of Schools, 1995—96, Writer's Workshop award, 1996—97. Mem.: Internat. Soc. for Tech. in Edn., Assoclatrion for Supervision and Curriculum Devel. (assoc.), Internat. Reading Assn. (assoc.). Home: 4 Pamanata Meadows Beacon Falls CT 06403

FEIGELSON, EUGENE B., dean; Dean SUNY Downstate Med. Ctr. Coll. Medicine, Bklyn., 1996—; interim pres. SUNY-Health Sciences Ctr. Brooklyn Coll. Medicine, 1997—99. Office: SUNY Downstate Med Ctr 450 Clarkson Ave Box 97 Brooklyn NY 11203-2098

FEIGEN, BRENDA S., lawyer, film producer, writer; b. Chgo., July 7, 1944; d. Arthur Paul Feigen and Shirley (Bierman) Feigen Kadison; children: Alexis Feigen Fasteau. BA in Math. cum laude, Vassar Coll., 1966; JD, Harvard U., 1969. Bar: Mass. 1970, N.Y. 1971, Calif. 2001. Chief analyst Boston Redevel. Authority, 1969; assoc. firm Rosenman, Colin, Kaye, Petschek, Freund & Emil, N.Y.C., 1970; pvt. practice NYC, 1974—, LA, 2001—. Founder, coordinating dir. Women's Action Alliance, N.Y.C., 1970—72; co-founder Ms. Mag., 1971; dir. Nat. Women's Rights project ACLU, N.Y.C., 1972—74; ptnr. Fasteau and Feigen, N.Y.C., 1974—80; assoc. Hess, Segall, Guterman, Pelz & Steiner, N.Y.C., 1980—81; atty., motion picture agt. William Morris Agy., N.Y.C., 1982—87; pres. Brenda Feigen Prodns., N.Y.C. and L.A., 1987—97; ptnr. Baxter/Feigen Prodns., 1991—92, Berton & Feigen, Beverly Hills, 1992—94; of counsel Berton & Donaldson, Beverly Hills, 1994—96, Kenoff and Machtinger LLP, 2004—; gen. counsel Feigen/Parrent Lit. Mgmt., Bel Air, Calif., 1995—2004, Reel Life Women Prodn. Co., Bel Air, 1996—2004; chair Nat. Breast Cancer Edn. and Legal Ctr., Bel Air, 2001—04; prof. UCLA Ext., 1990; adv. com. Am. Friends of Israel Mus., 2002—; moderator Harvard Law Sch., Vassar Coll., 2001, Calif. Lawyers Arts, 2003, Lavcender Law Conf., 2004, Tex. Entertainment Law Inst., 2004, Austin Film Festival and Writing Conf., 2004; bd. adv. Am. Screenwriters Assn., 2004—; co-chair confs. and seminars in field; panelist in field. Prodr.: (films) NAVY SEALS, 1990; author: Not One of the Boys: Living Life as a Feminist, 2000; contbr. articles to profl. jours., chapters to books, book reviews. Mem. adv. bd. Working Women United, nat. adv. bd. Take Our Daughters to Work; bd. dirs. Film Forum, 1986-90, N.Y. Women in Film, 1985-86; mem. Pen Ctr. USA West, 1996—, Authors' Guild, 1996—, Harvard Com. Entertainment, Sports and Cyberspace Law, 1997—; candidate for N.Y. State Senate, 1978; panelist L.A. Times Book Festival, 2001 Hon. Pres.'s fellow Columbia U., 1977, 78; participant Exec. Seminar, Aspen Inst., 1979. Mem. ABA (panelist film divsn.), ATLA, NOW (nat. legis. v.p., bd. dirs. 1970-71), Show Coalition (bd. govs. 1990-92), Calif. State Bar Assn., Los Angeles County Bar Assn., N.Y. Civil and Criminal Cts. Bar Assn., Beverly Hills Bar Assn., Women's Action Alliance (co-founder, dir.), Nat. Women's Polit. Caucus (co-founder, nat. adv. com.), Women Lawyers Assn. L.A. Democrat. Office: Kenoff & Machtinger LLP 1901 Ave of Stars Ste 1775 Los Angeles CA 90067 Office Phone: 310-552-0808. Business E-Mail: bfeigen@feigenlaw.com.

FEIGEN, RICHARD L., art dealer, collector, writer; b. Chgo., Aug. 8, 1930; s. Arthur P. and Shirley (Bierman) F.; m. Sandra Elizabeth Canning Walker, Feb. 23, 1966 (div. 1978); children: Philippa Canning, Richard Wood Bliss; m. Margaret Langan Culver, Sept. 12, 1998 (div. 2002). BA, Yale U., 1952; MBA, Harvard U., 1954. Asst. treas. Beneficial Standard Life Ins. Co., LA, 1955—56; mem. N.Y. Stock Exchange, 1956—57; pres., dir. Richard L. Feigen & Co., Inc., NYC, 1957—. Mem. com. works fine art N.Y. State Office Bldg., Harlem; lectr. in field. Author: Tales from the Art Crypt, 2000; contbr. articles to profl. jours. Candidate, del. Dem. Nat. Conv., 1972; trustee John Jay Homestead Assn., Katonah, N.Y., 1979-90, Lincoln U., Pa., 1988-92; mem. pres.'s coun. U. South Fla. Fellow Mpls. Soc. Fine Arts, Met. Mus. Art, Art Inst. Chgo.; mem. Art Dealers Assn. Am. (bd. dirs. 1972-76, 97-99, 2001—), Harvard Bus. Sch. Assn., Century Assn., Arts Club, Casino Club. Home: Cantitoe House Cantitoe Rd Katonah NY 10536-9718 also: 1 rue Allent 75007 Paris France also: 960 Fifth Ave New York NY 10021-1708 Office: 34 E 69th St New York NY 10021-5016 Office Phone: 212-628-0700. Business E-Mail: rfeigen@rlfeigen.com.

FEIGENBAUM, ARMAND VALLIN, systems engineer, information technology executive; b. N.Y.C., Apr. 6, 1920; s. S. Frederick and Hilda (Vallin) F. BS, Union Coll., 1942, DSc (hon.), 1992; MS, MIT, 1948, PhD, 1951; LHD (hon.), U. Mass., 1996; DSc (hon.), Mass. Coll. Liberal Arts, 2003. Engr. test program GE, Schenectady, 1942-45, factory tng. course, 1945-47, sales engr., 1947-48, supr. tng. mfg. personnel Lynn, Mass., 1948-50, asst. to gen. mgr. aircraft gas turbine divsn. Cin., 1950-52, mgr. aircraft nuclear propulsion dept. N.Y.C., 1952, co. mgr. quality control, 1956, co.-wide mgr. mfg. ops. and quality control, 1958-68; pres., CEO Gen. Systems Co., Inc., Pittsfield, Mass., 1968—; Nat. Acad. Engring. U.S., 1992—. Mem. bd. overseers Malcolm Baldridge Nat. Quality Program, Washington, D.C., 1988-91; pres. Internat. Acad. for Quality, 1966-79, chmn. bd. dirs., 1979—; adv. group U.S. Army, 1966—; lectr. MIT, U. Cin., Union Coll., U. Pa. Author: Quality Control-Principles and Practice, 1951, Total Quality Control-Engineering and Management, 1961, Management Programming, 1980, The Organization Process, 1980, Total Quality Control, 3d edit., 1983, Total Quality Control, 40th Anniversary edit., 1991, The Power of Management Capital, 2003; contbr. articles to profl. jours.; articles and speeches included in: Global Leaders in Quality, 2002. Chmn. inst. adminstrn., mgmt. coun. Union Coll., 1963— . Recipient Founders medal, 1977, medaille Georges Borel, Republic of France, 1988, Disting. Svc. award Nat. Inst. for Engring., Mgmt. and Sys., 1991, Disting. Leadership award Quality and Productivity Mgmt. Assn., 1993, Ishikawa/Harrington medal Asia-Pacific Quality Orgn., 1996; Armand V. Feigenbaum Mass. Quality award established by Gov. Mass., 1992, Singapore's Ngee Ann Polytechnic inaugurated the ann. Dr. A.V. Feigenbaum Gold medal award for outstanding quality assurance engring. grad., 1994, Mass. Gov.'s proclamation on 50th anniversary of book, 2001, Feigenbaum Leadership Excellence award, Dubai, UAE, 2005; fellow World Acad. Productivity Sci., 1993; Armand V. and Donald S. Feigenbaum Hall named in his honor Union Coll., 1996, Armand and Donald Feigenbaum Disting. Professorship named in his honor U. Mass. Med. Sch., 1998; recognized with the Outstanding Engring. Alumnus award, 2003. Fellow Am. Soc. Quality Control (pres. 1961-63, chmn. bd. 1963-64, Edwards medal 1966, Lancaster medal 1982, hon. mem. 1986, Feigenbaum award established 1999), World Acad. Productivity Sci.; mem. IEEE (life), NSPE (Disting. Svc. award 1991), ASME (life), AAAS (hon.), Nat. Security Indsl. Assn. (nat. award merit 1965), Inst. Math. Stats., Acad. Polit. and Social Scis., Am. Econ. Assn., Soc. Advancement Mgmt., Indsl. Rels. Rsch. Soc., Coun. Internat. Progress in Mgmt. (chmn. bd. 1968-70), China Assn. Quality Control (hon. advisor), Argentine Inst. Quality (hon.), Philippines Soc. for Quality Control (hon.), NAE. Home: 123 Ann Dr Pittsfield MA 01201-8405 Office: Berkshire Common South St Pittsfield MA 01201-6123 Office Phone: 413-499-2880.

FEIGENBAUM, DAVID LOUIS, lawyer; b. Pitts., Sept. 5, 1947; s. Simon and Pauline (Simon) Feigenbaum; m. Maureen I. Meister, Apr. 28, 1979. BS, Yale Coll., 1969; JD, Harvard U., 1972. Bar: Pa. 1972, Mass. 1982. Assoc. Kirkpatrick & Lockhart, Pitts., 1972—79, ptnr., 1979—80; assoc. Fish & Richardson, Boston, 1980—84, ptnr., 1985—.

FEIGENBAUM, EDWARD ALBERT, retired computer science educator; b. Weehawken, NJ, Jan. 20, 1936; s. Fred J. and Sara Rachman; m. H. Penny Nii, 1975. BEE, Carnegie Inst. Tech., 1956, PhD in Indsl. Adminstrn., 1960; DSc (hon.), Aston U., U.K., 1989. From asst. prof. to assoc. prof. bus. adminstrn. U. Calif., Berkeley, 1960—65; from assoc. prof. computer sci. to prof. Stanford U., 1965—95, prin. investigator heuristic programming project and knowledge sys. lab., 1965—2001, chmn. dept. computer sci., 1976-81, dir. Computation Ctr., 1965-68, Kumagai prof. computer sci., 1995—2001, emeritus, 2001—; pres. Intelli Genetics Inc., 1980—82, mem. tech. adv. bd., 1983-86; chmn., dir. Teknowledge, Inc., 1981-82; dir. IntelliCorp, 1984-90; chief scientist USAF, 1994-97. Computer and biomath. scis. study sect. NIH, 1968-72, adv. com. on artificial intelligence in medicine, 1974-92; mem. Math. Social Sci. Bd., 1975-78; computer sci. adv. com. NSF, 1977-80; mem. Internat. Joint Coun. on Artificial Intellignece, 1973-83; chief scientist, USAF, 1994-97; sci. adv. bd. USAF, 1997-2000; sci. advisor Air Force Office Sci. Rsch., 2000-; cons. in field. Author: (with others) Information Processing Language V Manual, 1961, (with P. McCorduck) The Fifth Generation, 1983; author: (with R. Lindsay, B. Buchanan, J. Lederberg) Applications of Artificial Intelligence to Organic Chemistry: the Dendral Project, 1980; Editor: (with J. Feldman) Computers and Thought, 1963, (with A. Barr and P. Cohen) Handbook of Artificial Intelligence, 1981, 82, 89, (with Pamela McCorduck and H. Penny Nii) The Rise of the Expert Company: How Visionary Companies are using Artificial Intelligence to Achieve Higher Productivity and Profits, 1988, The Japanese Entrepreneur: Making the Desert Bloom, 2002; mem. editorial bd.: Jour. Artificial Intelligence, 1970-88. Trustee Charles Babbage Found. for the History of Info. Processing, U. Minn., 2000—; pres. Feigenbaum-Nii Found., 2000—. Fulbright scholar, 1959-60; Rsch. grant Okawa Found., 2004, award, 2004; recipient Exceptional Civilian Svc. award USAF, 1997, Meritorious Civilian Sci. award USAF, 2000; named Feigenbaum medal in his honor World Congress on Expert Systems, 1991. Fellow AAAI, AAAS, Am. Coll. Med. Informatics, Am. Inst. Med. and Biol. Engring.; mem. NAE, Assn. Computing Machinery (nat. coun. 1966-68, chmn. spl. interest group on biol. applications 1973-76, A.M. Turing award 1994), Am. Assn. Artificial Intelligence (pres. 1980-81, Robert S. Engelmore Meml. award 2004), Am. Acad. Arts and Scis., Cognitive Sci. Soc. (coun. 1979-82), Sigma Xi, Tau Beta Pi, Eta Kappa Nu, Pi Delta Epsilon. Home: 1017 Cathcart Way Palo Alto CA 94305-1048 Office: Stanford U Knowledge Systems Lab Gates Computer Sci Rm 220 Stanford CA 94305-9020 Business E-Mail: feigenbaum@cs.stanford.edu.

FEIGERT, FRANK BROOK, retired political science educator, writer, photographer; b. NYC, Nov. 10, 1937; s. Morris Samuel Feigert and Anna (Frank) Spelke; m. Frances Goodside, June 17, 1961; children: Benjamin, Daniel. BA, Allegheny Coll., 1959; MA, U. Md., 1965, PhD, 1968. Instr. to asst. prof. Knox Coll., Galesburg, Ill., 1966—70; asst. to prof. SUNY, Brockport, 1970—77; from prof. to regents prof. polit. sci. U. North Tex., Denton, 1977—2002, regents prof. emeritus, 2003—. Author: Canada Votes, 1988; co-author: Political Analysis, 1972, 2d edit., 1976, Parties and Politics in America, 1976, Politics and Process of American Government, 1982, American Political Parties, 1984, American Party System and The American People, 1985. Precinct leader Monroe County Dem. Com., NY, 1972—77, registration chmn., 1972; campaign chmn. State Assembly Campaign, Monroe County, 1974; bd. dirs. Participation, 2000—03. Served to capt. USAF, 1959—64. Named Piper Found. prof., Tex., 2002; Fulbright-Hays sr. fellow, 1977—78. Mem.: Art Upstairs Gallery, Dallas Corinthian Yacht Club (Oak Point, Tex.). Jewish. Avocations: reading, travel. Home: 500 Court Sq Apt 404 Charlottesville VA 22902

FEIGH, JOHN EDWARD, music educator; b. Philipsburg, Pa., June 20, 1954; s. Richard Vincent Feigh and Ann Helen Zabinski; m. Mary Jane Crook, Oct. 15, 1977; children: Matthew Thomas, Jason Robert. BS in Music Edn., Pa. State U., 1976. Music instr. Glendale Sch. Dist., Flinton, Pa., 1977—84, Moshannon Valley Sch. Dist., Houtzdale, Pa., 1987—. Firefigther, EMS Glendale Fire Dept., Coalport, Pa., 1972—; choir dir., lector St. Basil The Great Roman Ch., Coalport, 1966—, instr. Fellow: Pa. State Edn. Assn., Music Educators Nat. Conf. (county rep. 1992—), KC. Roman Catholic. Avocations: golf, reading, fishing. Home: 996 Forest St Coalport PA 16627

FEIGIN, BARBARA SOMMER, marketing consultant; b. Berlin, Nov. 16, 1937; arrived in US, 1940, naturalized, 1949; d. Eric Daniel and Charlotte Martha (Demmer) Sommer; m. James Feigin, Sept. 17, 1961; children: Michael, Peter, Daniel. BA in Polit. Sci., Whitman Coll., 1959; cert. of Bus. Adminstrn., Harvard-Radcliffe Program Bus. Adminstrn., 1960. Mktg. rsch. asst. Richardson-Vick Co., Wilton, Conn., 1960-61; market rsch. analyst SCM Corp., N.Y.C., 1961-62; group rsch. supr. Benton & Bowles, Inc., N.Y.C., 1963-67; assoc. rsch. dir. Marplan Rsch. Co., N.Y.C., 1968-69; exec. v.p. worldwide strategic svcs., mem. agy. policy coun. Grey Advt. Inc., N.Y.C., 1969-99. Bd. dirs. VF Corp., Circuit City Stores, Inc.; past chmn. Advert Rsch. Found. Contbr. articles to profl jours. Overseer emeritus Whitman Col; past bd advisors Catalyst. Recipient Women Achievers Award, YWCA, 1987. Mem.: Mkt. Rsch. Hall of Fame.

FEIGIN, RALPH DAVID, medical association administrator, pediatrician, educator; b. N.Y.C., Apr. 3, 1938; s. Jack Bernard and Dorothy Phyllis (Strauss) F.; m. Judith Sue Zobel, June 26, 1960; children: Susan M., Michael E., Debra F. AB, Columbia U., 1958; MD, Boston U., 1962, DHL (hon.), 1998. Diplomate Am. Bd. Pediatrics, sub bd. for infectious diseases. Pediatric intern Boston City Hosp., 1962-63; pediatric resident Boston City Hosp. and Mass. Gen. Hosp., 1963-65; tchg. fellow pediatrics Harvard U. Med. Sch., 1964-65; rschr. U.S. Army Rsch. Inst. Infectious Diseases, Frederick, Md., 1965-67; chief resident children's svc. Mass. Gen. Hosp., 1967-68; from instr. to prof. pediatrics Washington U. Med. Sch., St. Louis, 1968-77, dir. divsn. infectious diseases dept. pediatrics, 1973-77; prof. pediatrics, chmn. dept. Baylor Coll. Medicine, Houston, 1977—, named disting. svc. prof., 1990, sr. v.p., 1992—96, dean med. edn., 1994—96, pres. and CEO, 1996—2003; physician-in-chief Tex. Children's Hosp., 1977—, exec. v.p., 1987-89; chief pediatric svc. Harris County Hosp. Dist., 1977—90; pediatrician-in-chief Methodist Hosp., 1979—; chief pediat. svc. Ben Taub Gen. Hosp., 1990—. Mem. adv. ad hoc study group on spl. infectious disease problems U.S. Army Med. R & D Command, 1974-83; vis. prof., cons. in field; pres. Pediatric Rsch. Found., 1982—. Co-editor: Nutrition and the Developing Nervous System, 1975, Textbook of Pediatric Infectious Diseases, 1981, 5th edit., 2003, Roundsmanship, 1989-93, Oski's Pediatrics: Principles and Practice, 3d edit., 1999; mem. editorial bd. Pediatrics, 1978-90, consulting editor, 1993-94, assoc. editor, 1994—; mem. editorial bd. Jour. Pediatric Infectious Diseases; assoc. editor Jour. Infectious Diseases, 1984-88; editor-in-chief Seminars in Pediatric Infectious Diseases, 1990—; contbr. articles to med. jours., chpts. to books. With M.C., USAR, 1965-67. Recipient Rsch. Career Devel. award USPHS, 1970, Founders Day award Washington U. Med. Sch., 1977, Sr. Class Outstanding Tchr. award Baylor Coll. Medicine, 1978, 80, 81, 82, 83, 84, 85, 86, Minnie Stevens Piper Professorial award, 1984, John McGovern Outstanding Clin. Faculty award Baylor Coll. Medicine, 1986, 94, Disting. Alumnus award Boston U. Sch. of Medicine, 1989, Joseph St. Geme Jr. Leadership award in Pediatrics, Fedn. Pediatric Orgns., 1995, Disting. Faculty award Alumni Assn., Baylor Coll. of Medicine, 1994; named to Baylor Coll. Medicine Outstanding Tchr. Hall of Fame, 1984; Alumni Tchg. scholar Washington U. Med. Sch., 1975, Amer. Acad. Pediatrics Med. Educ. Lifetime Ach. Award. Fellow AAAS, Am. Microbiology; mem. AMA, Am. Pediatric Soc. (pres. 1997-98, Lifetime Achievement award, 1997), Am. Acad. Pediat., Infectious Diseases Soc. Am., Pediatric Infectious Disease Soc. (Disting. Physician award 1996), Inst. Medicine of NAS, N.Y. Acad. Scis., Tex. Med. Assn., Tex. Pediatric Soc., Harris County Med. Soc., Houston Pediatric Soc., Soc. Pediatric Rsch. (pres. 1982-83), Assn. Med. Sch. Pediatric Dept. Chairpersons (pres. 1991-93). Office: Baylor Coll Medicine Dept Pediats One Baylor Plz Houston TX 77030-3411

FEIGL, DOROTHY MARIE, chemistry educator, academic administrator; b. Evanston, Ill., Feb. 25, 1938; d. Francis Philip and Marie Agnes (Jacques) F. BS, Loyola U., Chgo., 1961; PhD, Stanford U., 1966; postdoctoral fellow, N.C. State U., 1965-66. Asst. prof. chemistry St. Mary's Coll., Notre Dame, Ind., 1966-69, assoc. prof., 1969-75, prof., 1975—, chmn. dept. chemistry and physics, 1977-85, bd. regents, 1976-82, acting v.p., dean faculty, 1985-87, v.p., dean faculty, 1987-99, Denise DeBartolo York prof. of chemistry, 2003—. Author: (with John Hill and Erwin Boschmann) General Organic and Biological Chemistry, 1991, (with John Hill and Stuart Baum) Chemistry and Life, 1997; contbr. articles to chem. jours., chpts. to texts. Recipient Spes Unica award St. Mary's Coll., 1973, Maria Pieta award, 1977 Mem. Am. Chem. Soc., Royal Soc. Chemistry, Internat. Union Pure and Applied Chemistry, Sigma Xi, Iota Sigma Pi. Democrat. Roman Catholic. Office: Dept Chemistry Saint Mary's College Notre Dame IN 46556

FEIGL, ERIC OTTO, Physiology educator; s. Herbert and Maria Feigl; m. Polly Bartholomew, July 30, 1957; children: Kurt, Mark H. BA, BS, U. Minn., 1954, MD, 1958. Instr. Med. Sch. U. Pa., Phila., 1959-61; officer Nat. Heart Inst., Bethesda, Md., 1962-64; asst. prof. U. Pa., Phila., 1964—69; from assoc. prof. to prof. physiology U. Wash., Seattle, 1969—72. Assoc. editor Am. Jour. of Physiology, 1981—86, editl. bd., Circulation Rsch. Officer U.S. Pub. Health Svc., 1962—64; mem. com. Am. Physiol. Assn., Am. Heart Assn. Recipient Outstanding Rsch. award Internat. Soc. for Heart Rsch., 1985. Fellow Am. Physiolog. Soc. (chmn. CV sect. 1981-82), Am. Heart Assn. (Louis N. Katz Basic Sci. Rsch. Prize 1969). Home: 2360 43rd Ave E Apt 311 Seattle WA 98112-2701 Office: U Wash Med Sch 357290 Dept Physiology Seattle WA 98195-7290

FEIGON, JUDITH TOVA, ophthalmologist, educator, surgeon; b. Galveston, Tex., Dec. 2, 1947; d. Louis and Ethel Feigon; m. Nathan C. Goldman; children: Michael G., Miriam G. AB, Barnard Coll., Columbia U., 1970; postgrad., Rice U., U. Houston, 1970-71; MD, U. Tex., San Antonio, 1976. Diplomate Am. Bd. Ophthalmology. Intern Mt. Auburn Hosp., Cambridge, Mass.; intern, clin. tchg. fellow Harvard U. Med. Sch., 1976-77; resident in ophthalmology Baylor Coll. Medicine, Houston, 1977-80, fellow in retina, 1980-82, clin. faculty, 1982-95; asst. prof. ophthalmology U. Tex. Med. Br., Galveston, 1982-85, clin. asst. prof., 1985-91, clin. assoc. prof., 1992—; pvt. practice medicine specializing ophthalmology, vitreoretinal diseases, surgery, Houston, 1983—. Physician advisor to Houston br. Tex. Soc. to Prevent Blindness, 1987-89, also bd. dirs.; mem. staff Meth., St. Lukes, Tex. Children's, St. Joseph's Hosp.; clin. faculty Baylor Coll. Medicine, 1982-95. Contbr. articles to profl. publs. Mem. Assn. Am. Physicians and Surgeons, Am. Acad. Ophthalmology, Tex. Med. Assn. Houston Ophthal. Soc., Harris County Med. Soc., U. Tex. San Antonio Alumni Assn., Am. Soc. Retina Specialists, Tex. Ophthalmol. Assn., Houston Ophthal. Soc. (exec. bd. 2000-03). Office: 7515 Main St Ste 650 Houston TX 77030-4599 Office Phone: 713-799-1737. Personal E-mail: itfeigon@sbcglobal.net.

FEIKENS, JOHN, federal judge; b. Clifton, N.J., Dec. 3, 1917; s. Sipke and Corine (Wisse) F.; m. Henriette Dorothy Schulthouse, Nov. 4, 1939; children: Jon, Susan Corine, Barbara Edith, Julie Anne, Robert H. AB, Calvin Coll., Grand Rapids, Mich., 1938; JD, U. Mich., 1941; LLD (hon.), U. Detroit, 1979, Detroit Coll. Law, 1981. Bar: Mich. 1942. Gen. practice law, Detroit; dist. judge Ea. Dist. Mich., Detroit, 1960-61, 70-79, chief judge, 1979-86, sr. judge, 1986—. Past co-chmn. Mich. Civil Rights Commn.; past chmn. Rep. State Central Com.; past mem. Rep. Nat. Com.; mem. com. visitors U. Mich. Law Sch. Past bd. trustees Calvin Coll. Fellow Am. Coll. Trial Lawyers; mem. ABA, Detroit Bar Assn. (dir. 1962, past pres.), State Bar Mich. (commr. 1965-71), U. Mich. Club (com. visitors). Office: US Dist Ct 851 Theodore Levin US Ct 231 W Lafayette Blvd Detroit MI 48226-2700

FEIL, MICHAEL BRUCE, statistician; b. Urbana, Ill., Apr. 30, 1949; s. Richard Anthony and Barbara June Feil; m. Dana Marie Strack, Sept. 6, 1975; children: Margaret Anne, Robert Bruce. BS in Med. Tech., Rutgers U., 1974, MBA, 1979; MS, Georgetown U., 1985; DSc, Canterbury U., 2002. Cert. medical technologist Am. Soc. Clin. Pathologists. Staff technologist North Jersey Blood Ctr., East Orange, NJ, 1974—78, systems analyst, 1979—80; market analyst Am. Blood Commn., Arlington, Va., 1980—81; staff technologist quality control Georgetown U. Hosp., Washington, 1982—86; statistician Dept. Veterans Affairs, Washington, 1986; sr. assoc. Moshman Assoc., Inc., Bethesda, Md., 1986—90; statistician NIMH, Bethesda, 1991—2000; chief statistician Agrl. Mktg. Svc., Washington, 2000—. Contbr. articles to profl. jours. Recipient Pub. Health Spl. Recognition award, US Govt., HHS, 1995, Staff Recognition award, US Govt., HHS, Pub. Health Svc., NIH, 1997. Mem.: Wash. Statis. Soc. (bd. dirs., editor 1995—, Pres. award 1997, 2002), Am. Statis. Soc. Lutheran. Avocations: target shooting, travel. Home: 2361

Emerald Heights Ct Reston VA 20191-1750 Office: Agrl Mktg Svc 1400 Independence Ave SW MS-0223 Washington DC 22050-0223 Office Phone: 202-690-3130. Personal E-mail: pdrule@comcast.net. Business E-Mail: michael.feil@usda.gov.

FEILMEIER, STEVE, energy executive; M in Acctg., Wichita State U. Joined Koch Industries, Wichita, Kans., 1997, v.p. tax, fin. and acctg., sr. v.p., CFO, 2002—, also bd. dirs. Bd. dirs. Big Bros. Big Sisters Sedgwick County, former chmn., treas., 2003. Office: Koch Industries 4111 E 37th St Wichita KS 67220

FEIMAN, RONALD MARK, lawyer; b. NYC, Feb. 28, 1951; s. Richard and Patricia Feiman; m. Hilary J. Ronner, Jan. 7, 1984. BA, Yale U., 1972; JD, MBA, NYU, 1977. Bar: N.Y. 1978., CPA, N.Y. Assoc. Gordon Altman Butowsky Weitzen Shalov & Wein, N.Y.C., 1977-85, ptnr., 1985-99, Mayer, Brown, Rowe & Maw LLP, 1999—. Mem. ABA (bus. law com.), AICPA (fin. svcs. industry taxation com.), Assn. Bar City NY (com. on investment mgmt. regulation), Yale Club. Office: Mayer Brown Rowe & Maw LLP 1675 Broadway New York NY 10019-5889 Office Phone: 212-506-2673. Business E-Mail: ronald.feiman.es.72@aya.yale.edu. E-mail: rfeiman@mayerbrownrowe.com.

FEIMAN, THOMAS E., investment company executive; b. Canton, Ohio, Dec. 21, 1940; s. Daniel Thaviu and Adrienne (Silver) F.; m. Marilyn Judith Miller, June 26, 1966; children: Sheri, Michael. BS in Econs., U. Pa., 1962; MBA, Northwestern U., 1963. CPA, Calif. Staff acct. Arthur Young & Co., L.A., 1963-66; field auditor IRS, L.A., 1966-68; pvt. practice acctg. Thomas Feiman, C.P.A., L.A., 1968-69; ptnr. Wideman & Feiman, C.P.A.s, L.A., 1969-74; pres. Wideman, Feiman, Levy, Sapin & Ko, L.A., 1974-93; investment mgr., v.p. Schroder Wertheim & Co., Inc., 1993-96; CFO Spinal Home Health Systems, Inc., L.A., 1983-85; fin. cons., v.p. Merrill Lynch, 1996—2004, UBS, 2004—; pres., dir. Urol. Scis. Rsch. Found., 1993—. Sr. instr. UCLA Extension, 1967-84. Trustee Temple Israel of Hollywood, Calif., 1981-83, treas., 1983-84. Recipient cert. of award IRS, 1967. Mem. AICPA, Calif. Soc. CPAs, Northwestern Bus. So. Calif. Club (pres. 1977-80), Northwestern Alumni of So. Calif. Club (trustee 1977-92, treas. 1977-90 L.A.). Republican. Jewish. Office: UBS Financial Svcs 31111 Agoura Rd Ste 230 Westlake Village CA 91361-4609 Business E-Mail: thomasfeiman@ubs.com.

FEIN, IRVING ASHLEY, television and motion picture executive; b. Bklyn., June 21, 1911; s. Harry and Fannie (Milstein) F.; m. Florence Kohn, Dec. 25, 1941 (dec.); children: Michael Anthony, Patricia Ann; m. Marion Shepard Schechter, June 21, 1969. Student, U. Balt., 1928-29, U. Wis., 1930-32; LLB, St. Lawrence U., 1936. Publicity and advt. dept. Warner Bros., N.Y.C., 1933-36; dir. exploitation and radio West Coast studios, 1936; asst. publicity dir. Samuel Goldwyn, 1941; dir. exploitation and radio Columbia Pictures, Hollywood, 1942; publicity, advt. dir. Amusement Enterprises, Inc., 1947; with CBS, Inc., 1948-56, dir. exploitation Hollywood, 1950; dir. publicity and exploitation CBS Radio, Hollywood, 1951-53, dir. pub. relations, 1953-55, v.p. sales promotion, advt. and press info. N.Y.C., 1955-56; pres. J & M Prodns., Inc., Beverly Hills, Calif., 1956-65; exec. v.p. J.B. Prodns., 1965-75; producer Jack Benny Programs, 1958-74; pres. TV Prodn. Co. Producer: George Burns TV spls., 1975-96, (films) Just You and Me Kid, Oh God! You Devil, Eighteen Again; author: Jack Benny: An Intimate Biography, 1976. Recipient Emmy award, 1961. Home: 1100 Alta Loma Rd Los Angeles CA 90069-2455 Office Phone: 310-657-5000.

FEIN, MICHAEL R., historian, educator; b. New London, Conn., Apr. 4, 1973; s. Maier Ort and Sonya Esther Fein; m. Marjorie Nan Feld, Oct. 10, 1999; 1 child, Isaac Ellery Feinfeld. BA, Columbia U., 1995; MA, Brandeis U., 1998, PhD, 2003. Tchg. asst. Brandeis U., Waltham, Mass., 1996—98, rsch. asst., 1996—2000, lectr. history, 2003—05; rsch. assoc. Harvard Bus. Sch., Boston, 1998—2001; adj. prof. Lesley U., Cambridge, 2002—; vis. asst. prof. history Babson Coll., Babson Park, 2005—. Fellow, Miller Ctr. for Pub. Affairs, 2001—02; Crown fellow, Brandeis U., 1995—99. Mem.: Orgn. Am. Historians, Am. Hist. Assn. Democrat. Jewish. Home: 26 Ladd St Watertown MA 02472 Business E-Mail: mfein@babson.edu.

FEIN, RASHI, health sciences educator; b. NYC, Feb. 6, 1926; s. Isaac M. and Clara(Wertheim) F.; m. Ruth Judith Breslau, June 19, 1949; children: Alan, Michael, Karen, Bena (dec.). Student, Bridgeport Jr. Coll., 1942—43; BA, Johns Hopkins U., 1948, PhD, 1956; LittD (hon.), SUNY, 1996. Mem. staff Pres.'s Commn. on Health Needs, 1952; from lectr. to assoc. prof. U. N.C., 1952-61; statistician Bur. of Census, 1958-59; sr. staff Pres.'s Coun. Econ. Advisers, 1961-63; sr. fellow Brookings Inst., 1963-68; prof. Harvard U., 1968-99, prof. emeritus, 1999—; Heath Clark lectr. London Sch. Hygiene and Tropical Medicine, 1980; chmn. med. assistance adv. coun. to sec. HEW, 1967-69; mem. adv. com. research and devel. Social Security Adminstrn., 1968-71; mem. Nat. Manpower Policy Task Force, 1967-79, Office Tech. Assessment, Health Adv. Panel, 1981-86. Mem. spl. med. adv. group VA, 1987-91; mem. nat. adv. rsch. resources coun. NIH, 1995-99, emeritus; chair nat. adv. com. Robert Wood Johnson Found. Scholars in Health Policy Rsch. Program; bd. dirs. Ctr. for Child Health Rsch., Am. Acad. Pediat. Author: Economics of Mental Illness, 1958, The Doctor Shortage: An Economic Diagnosis, 1967, (with Gerald Weber) Financing Medical Education: An Analysis of Alternative Policies and Mechanisms, 1971, (with Charles Lewis and David Mechanic) A Right to Health: The Problem of Access to Primary Medical Care, 1976, Alcohol in America: The Price We Pay, 1984, Medical Care, Medical Costs: The Search for a Health Insurance Policy, 1986, 89, (with Julius Richmond) The Health Care Mess: How We Got Into It and What It Will Take To Get Out, 2005. Mem. bd. overseers Beth Israel Deaconess Med. Ctr., Boston; trustee Hebrew Sr. Life, Boston; mem. com. of visitors Goucher Coll.; bd. dirs. Harvard Cmty. Health Plan Found., 1980—87; mem. tech. bd. Millbank Meml. Fund, 1975—78, 1986—90, bd. dirs., 1987—90. Recipient John M. Russell award for advancement knowledge in medicine, 1971; fellow Inst. History Medicine Johns Hopkins U., 1951-52; traveling fellow WHO, 1971. Mem. APHA, AAUP, Inst. Medicine of NAS (Adam Yarmolinsky medal for contbns.), Nat. Acad. Social Ins., Am. Econ. Assn., Am. Adv. Coun. World Orgn. for Ednl. Resources and Tech. Tng. Union. Jewish. Office: Harvard U Sch Medicine Dept Social Medicine 641 Huntington Ave 2d Fl Boston MA 02115-6019 Business E-Mail: rashi_fein@hms.harvard.edu.

FEIN, ROGER GARY, judge; b. St. Louis, Mar. 12, 1940; s. Albert and Fanny (Levinson) F.; m. Susanne M. Cohen, Dec. 18, 1965; children: David I., Lisa J. Student, Washington U., St. Louis, 1959, NYU, 1960; BS, UCLA, 1962; JD, Northwestern U., 1965; MBA, Am. U., 1967. Bar: Ill. 1965, U.S. Dist. Ct. (no. dist.) Ill. 1968, U.S. Ct. Appeals (7th cir.) 1968, U.S. Supreme Ct. 1970. Atty. divsn. corp. fin. SEC, Washington, 1965—67; ptnr. Arvey, Hodes, Costello & Burman, Chgo., 1967—91; ptnr., chmn. adminstrn. and dissolution com. Wildman, Harrold, Allen and Dixon, Chgo., 1992—2003; judge Cir. Ct. Cook County, 2003—. Co-chair Corp., Securities and Tax Practice Group, 1992-99; mem. Securities Adv. Com. to Sec. State Ill., 1973—, chmn., 1973-79, 87-93, vice-chmn., 1983-87, chmn. emeritus, 1994—; spl. asst. atty. gen. State of Ill., 1974-83, 85-99; spl. asst. state's atty. Cook County, Ill., 1989-90; mem. Appeal Bd., Ill. Law Enforcement Commn., 1980-83; mem. lawyer's adv. bd. So. Ill. Law Jour., 1980-83; mem. adv. bd. securities regulation and law report Bur. Nat. Affairs Inc., 1985—; lectr., author on land trust financing, consumer credit and securities law. Mem. Bd. Edn., Sch. Dist. No. 29, Northfield, Ill., 1977-83, pres., 1981-83; mem. Pub. Vehicle Ops. Citizens Adv. coun. City Chgo., 1985-86; mem. Anti-Defamation League Greater Chgo./Upper Midwest Region, Chgo. regional bd., 1975-91, vice chmn., 1980-88, exec. com., 1996—, co-chair pub. affairs com., 1999-2003, assoc. nat. commr., 2000—; chmn. lawyers' com. for ann. telethon Muscular Dystrophy Assn., 1983; past bd. dirs. Jewish Nat. Fund, Am. Friends Hebrew U., Northfield Cmty. Fund. Recipient Pub. Svc. award Sec. State Ill., 1976, Citation of Merit, WAIT Radio, 1976, Sunset Ridge Sch. Cmty. Svc. award, 1984, City of Chgo. Citizen's award, 1986; named one of Leading Ill. Attys., Am. Rsch. Corp., 1997. Fellow Am. Bar Found., Ill. Bar Found. (bd. dirs. 1978-88, v.p. 1982-84, pres. 1984-86, chmn. Fellows 1983-84, chmn., past pres. adv. com. 1988-90, Cert. of Appreciation 1985, 86, Silver fellow 1997), Chgo. Bar Found; mem. ABA (ho. of dels. 1981-85, state regulation of securities com. 1982-2003, Ill. liaison of com., chmn. subcom. liaison with securities adminstrs. and NASD 1998-2003), Ill. State Bar Assn. (bd. govs. 1976-80, del. assembly 1976-88, sec. 1977-78, cert. of appreciation 1980, 88, chmn. Bench and Bar com. 1982-83, chmn. Bench and Bar sect. coun., 1983-84, chmn. bar elections supervision com. 1986-87, chmn. assembly com. on hearings 1987-88, mem. com. on jud. appointments 1987-90), Chgo. Bar Assn. (mem. task force delivery legal svcs. 1978-80, cert. of appreciation 1976, chmn. land trusts com. 1978-79, chmn. consumer credit com. 1977-78, chmn. state securities law subcom. 1977-79), Ill. Judges Assn., Decalogue Soc. Lawyers, Northwestern U. Sch. of Law Alumni Assn. (dir.), Standard Club, The Law Club of the City of Chgo., Tau Epsilon Phi, Alpha Kappa Psi, Phi Delta Phi. Office Phone: 847-470-7200. Business E-Mail: rgfeinz@cookcountygov.com.

FEIN, RONALD LAWRENCE, lawyer; b. Detroit, Aug. 26, 1943; s. Lee Allen and Billie Doreen (Thomas) F.; children: Samantha, Mark. AB with honors, UCLA, 1966; JD with honors, U. San Diego, 1969. Bar: Calif. 1970, U.S. Dist. Ct. (cen. dist.) Calif. 1970. Assoc. Gibson, Dunn & Crutcher, Los Angeles, 1969-75; chief dep. commr. of corps. State of Calif., Los Angeles, 1975-78; ptnr., mem. firmwide adv. com., chmn. corp. fin./mergers and acquisitions sect., chmn. corp. dept. Jones, Day, Reavis & Pogue, Los Angeles, 1978-87; ptnr., mem. exec. com., chmn. gen. bus. dept. Wyman, Bautzer, Kuchel & Silbert, L.A., 1987-91; sr. ptnr. Stutman, Treister & Glatt, 1991—. Bd. dirs. Executours, Inc., Los Angeles, Lottery Info., North Hollywood, Calif., Malibu Grand Prix, Woodland Hills, Calif.; adj. prof. law Loyola U., Los Angeles, 1976; mem. Commr.'s Circle Adv. Com. to the Calif. Commr. of Corps., Fin. Lawyers Conf.; mem. adv. bd. Inst. Corp. Counsel U. S.C Articles editor San Diego Law Rev., 1969; contbr. articles to profl. jours. Co-dir. protocol for boxing Los Angeles Olympic Organizing Com., 1984. Lt. USAF, to 1966-69. Mem. ABA (corp., banking and bus. law sect., mem. ad hoc com. on merit regulation, mem. fed. regulation of securities com., mem. ad hoc com. on the Uniform Limited Offering Exemption, com. on Counsel Responsibility, mem. ad hoc com. on Regulation D, mem. subcom. on Registration Statements—1933 Act, vice chmn. state regulation securities com., chmn. pvt. offering exemption and simplification of capital formation subcom., chmn. NASAA Omnibus guideline subcom.), Calif. Bar Assn. (bus. law sect.), Los Angeles County Bar Assn. (mem. exec. com. bus. and corps. law sect.), Nat. Assn. Securities Dealers, Inc. (mem. subcom. on indemnification, mem. arbitration panel, mem. adv. bd. Prentice-Hall West coast mergers and acquisitions panels), Mountaingate Country Club. Avocations: athletics, reading, theater. Home: 455 N Oakhurst Dr Beverly Hills CA 90210-3911 Office: FL 12 1901 Avenue of the Stars Los Angeles CA 90067-6013 Office Phone: 310-228-5780. Business E-Mail: rfein@stutman.com.

FEIN, RONNIE, writer, journalist; b. N.Y.C., June 5, 1943; d. William and Lily (Hoffman) Vail; m. Edward Fein, Nov. 15, 1969; children: Meredith, Gillian. BA, Northwestern U., 1964; LLB, NYU, 1967. Atty. Chadbourne, Parke, Whiteside & Wolff, N.Y.C., 1967-70, Rosenman, Colin, N.Y.C., 1970-71; dir. Ronnie Fein Sch. Creative Cooking, Stamford, Conn., 1971—; freelance demonstrator cooking, dept. stores various locations, 1971—; journalist Stamford Trader, 1980-81, The Advertiser, New Canaan, 1981-98, Times-Mirror/Tribune newspapers, 1984—, Consumer's Digest Mag., 1989—, Darien Times, 1993—98, Newsday, 1995—, Hersam-Acorn newspapers, 1997—98, L.A. Times Syndicate, 1999—, Westport Mag., 1999—, Greenwich Mag., 1999—. Contbg. editor The New Cook's Catalogue, 2000, Tribune Newspapers, 2001—; talk show host The New WNLK, Norwalk, Conn., 1984. Author: The Complete Idiot's Guide to Cooking Basics, 1995, 3d edit., 2000, The Complete Idiot's Guide to American Cooking, 2002. Alumni admissions dir. Fairfield County, Northwestern U., Evanston, Ill., 1985-98. Fellow Conn. Women's Culinary Alliance (charter, newsletter co-chmn. 1988-89, pres. 1996-97). Home: 32 Heming Way Stamford CT 06903 Personal E-mail: ronnievfein@optonline.net.

FEIN, SEYMOUR HOWARD, pharmaceutical executive; b. N.Y.C., Oct. 28, 1948; s. Abner and Beatrice (Wolkoff) Fein; m. Mary Louise Orizzonto, Apr. 1, 1979; children: Jessica Ann, David Thomas, Renee Elizabeth, Jonathan Parker. BA, U. Pa., 1970; MD, N.Y. Med. Coll., 1974. Intern Dartmouth-Hitchcock Med. Ctr., Hanover, NH, 1974-75, resident in internal medicine, 1975-77; fellow in hematology, oncology Beth Israel Hosp., Harvard Med. Sch., Boston, 1977-80; instr. medicine Harvard Med. Sch., Boston, 1979-80; sr. rsch. physician Hoffmann-LaRoche, Nutley, NJ, 1980-83; dir. med. rsch. Miles Pharmaceuticals, West Haven, Conn., 1983-86, Rorer Pharms., Ft. Washington, Pa., 1986-87; v.p. med. rsch. Greenwich Pharms., Ft. Washington, 1987-88; dir. clin. rsch. and devel. Anaquest, Murray Hill, NJ, 1988-92; v.p. clin. rsch. and biostats. Oxford Rsch. Internat. Corp., Clifton, NJ, 1992-94; pres. Fein Consulting and Rsch. Svcs., New Canaan, Conn., 1994—. Mng. ptnr. CNF Pharma LLC, New City, NY, 2002—; chmn. ChiRhoClin Inc., Burtonsville, Md., 1997—2005. Mem.: AAAS, N.Y. Acad. Scis., Am. Soc. Clin. Oncology. Republican. Jewish. Avocations: reading, cooking, tennis, gardening, travel. Office Phone: 845-639-1820.

FEIN, WILLIAM, ophthalmologist; b. N.Y.C., Nov. 27, 1933; s. Samuel and Beatrice (Lipschitz) F.; m. Bonnie Fern Aaronson, Dec. 15, 1963; children: Stephanie Paula, Adam Irving, Gregory Andrew. BS, CCNY, 1954; MD, U. Calif., Irvine, 1962. Diplomate Am. Bd. Ophthalmology. Intern L.A. County Gen. Hosp., 1962-63, resident in ophthalmology, 1963-66; instr. U. Calif. Med. Sch., Irvine, 1966-69; faculty U. So. Calif. Med. Sch., 1969—, assoc. clin. prof. ophthalmology, 1979—; attending physician Cedars-Sinai Med. Ctr., L.A., 1966—, chief ophthalmology clinic svc., 1979-81, chmn. divsn. ophthalmology, 1981-85; attending physician L.A. County-U. So. Calif. Med. Ctr., 1969—; chmn. dept. ophthalmology Midway Hosp., 1975-78; dir. Ellis Eye Ctr., L.A., 1984—. Mem. editorial bd. CATARACT, Internat. Jour. of Cataract and Ocular Surgery, 1992—; contbr. articles to profl. jours. Chmn. ophthalmology adv. com. Jewish Home for Aging of Greater L.A., 1993—. Fellow Internat. Coll. Surgeons, Am. Coll. Surgeons; mem. Am. Acad. Ophthalmology, Am. Soc. Ophthalmic Plastic and Reconstructive Surgery, Royal Soc. Medicine, AMA, Calif. Med. Assn., L.A. Med. Assn. Home: 718 N Camden Dr Beverly Hills CA 90210-3205 Office: 415 N Crescent Dr Beverly Hills CA 90210-4860 Office Phone: 310-859-0760.

FEINBERG, DAVID ERWIN, publishing executive; b. Mpls., 1922; Grad., U. Minn., 1948. Chmn., chief exec. officer EMC Corp., St. Paul. Sec. bd. dirs., v.p. Paradigm Pub., Inc. Home: 111 Kellogg Blvd E Saint Paul MN 55101-1237 Office: EMC Corp 875 Montreal Way Saint Paul MN 55102-4245

FEINBERG, DENNIS LOWELL, dermatologist; b. Bridgeport, Conn., June 10, 1951; AB, Cornell U., 1973; MD, SUNY, Syracuse, 1976. Diplomat Nat. Bd. Med. Examiners, Am. Bd. Internal Medicine, Am. Bd. Dermatology. Intern U. Miami (Fla.) Affiliated Hosps., 1976-77, resident, 1977-78, Johns Hopkins Med. Inst., Balt., 1978-80; dermatologist pvt. practice, Washington, 1981, Stratford, Conn., 1981—. Sr. attending Bridgeport Hosp., 1981—; attending St. Vincent's Med. Ctr., Bridgeport, 1981—; cons. Milford (Conn.) Hosp., 1982-2000; asst. clin. prof. Yale U. Sch. Medicine, New Haven, 1985—. Fellow Am. Acad. Dermatology; mem. AMA, ACP, Atlantic Dermatol. Soc., New Eng. Dermatol. Soc., Conn. Dermatology and Dermatologic Surgery Soc. (pres.-elect), Conn. State Med. Soc., Fairfield County Med. Assn., Greater Bridgeport Med. Assn., Syracuse Med. Alumni Assn. Office: 2875 Main St Stratford CT 06614-4937

FEINBERG, HERBERT, apparel, real estate, video and beverage executive; b. N.Y.C., June 20, 1926; s. Harry Feinberg and Dorothy (Hurwitz) Goldstein; m. Audrey Frank, Sept. 15, 1948 (div. Mar. 1972); children: Michael(dec.), Mark, Harry; m. Barbara Mays Jones, May 25, 1972 (div. June 1989); 1 child, Candice; m. Sandi Ann Gold, June 1989; 1 child, Tara. BS, U. Ill., 1949. Owner, v.p. Monsieur Henri Wines Ltd., N.Y.C., 1949-72; owner, pres. Hudson Valley Wine Village, Highland, N.Y., 1972—, Regent Champagne Cellars, Highland, N.Y., 1988. With USAF, 1944-46. Republican. Jewish. Avocations: tennis, boating. Home: 472 Mariner Dr Jupiter FL 33477

FEINBERG, JEFFREY ENOCH, religious studies educator, writer; b. Chgo., Mar. 10, 1951; s. Sidney Theodore and Sher Lee F.; m. Patricia Elaine Feinberg, June 15, 1979; children: Avraham David, Zechariah Daniel, Shoshannah Tirzah. BA, Univ. Calif., Berkeley, 1972; MBA, MA, U. Chgo., 1976; MDiv, Trinity Internat. Univ., 1985, PhD, 1988. Instr. Trinity Coll., Deerfield, Ill., 1978-79,82-85; chair of econ./mgmt. Trinity Coll. Sch. of Econ./Mgmt., Deerfield, 1985; educator Adat Hatikvah Congregation, Chgo., 1988-91, interim leader, 1991; rabbi Etz Chaim Congregation, Buffalo Grove, Ill., 1994—; pres. Peniel Cmty. Ctr., Lake Forest, Ill., 1991—, Found. for Leadership and Messianic Edn., Lake Forest, 1988—. Steering com. Union Messianic Jewish Congregations, Albuquerque, 1994—. Recipient Internat. Writer of the Year, Internat. Biog. Ctr., Cambridge, England, 2003. Office: Flame Foundation 234 Surrey Ln Lake Forest IL 60045-3474 E-mail: enoch@flamefoundation.org.

FEINBERG, KENNETH ROY, lawyer, law educator; b. Brockton, Mass., Oct. 23, 1945; s. Martin B. and Dorothy (Rubenstein) F.; m. Diane Shaff, June 29, 1975; children: Michael, Leslie, Andrew. BA cum laude, U. Mass., 1967; JD, NYU, 1970. Bar: NY 1971, DC 1977, Mass. 1980. Law clerk to Chief Judge Stanley H. Fuld NY State Ct. of Appeals, 1970—72; asst. U.S. atty. So. Dist. NY, 1972-75; gen. csl. subcom. on adminstrv. practice and procedure Com. on Judiciary, U.S. Senate, 1975-77; spl. counsel Com. on Judiciary, US Senate, 1979-80; adminstrv. asst. Senator Edward M. Kennedy, 1977-79; mng. ptnr. Kaye, Scholer, Fierman, Hays & Handler, Washington, 1980-92; ptnr., founder The Feinberg Group, Washington, 1993—. Adj. prof. law Georgetown U. Law Ctr., 1979-. Author: What Is Life Worth?: The Unprecedented Effort to Compensate the Victims of 9/11, 2005. Trustee Dalkon Shield Claimants Trust; active Presdl. Adv. Commn. Human Radiation Experiments, Presdl. Commn. Catastrophic Nuclear Accidents, 1989-90, Carnegie Commn. Task Force Sci. and Tech. in Judicial and Regulatory Decision Making, 1989-93, Nat. Judicial Panel, Ctr. Pub. Resources, Marine Spill Response Corp., Spl. Master, Fed. Sept. 11th Victim Compensation Fund, 2001-2005. Named one of 27 Future Leaders of Am. Major Firms, The Am. Lawyer, 1986, one of 100 Most Influential Lawyers in Am., Nat. Law Jour. Mem. Am. Arbitration Assn., Bar Assn. City N.Y., Bar Assn. D.C., Mass. Bar Assn. Office: The Feinberg Group Ste 390 Willard Office Bldg 1455 Pennsylvania Ave NW Washington DC 20004-1008 Office Phone: 202-371-1110. Office Fax: 202-962-9290.*

FEINBERG, LAWRENCE EDWARD, language educator, researcher; b. N.Y., Nov. 13, 1941; s. Samuel and Nettie (Weissman) Feinberg; m. Nana Nikolaishvili, Nov. 24, 1994. BA cum laude, Middlebury Coll., 1962; MA, Harvard U., 1964, PhD, 1969. Asst. prof. U. Colo., Boulder, 1967—70; from asst. prof. to assoc. prof. U. N.C., Chapel Hill, 1970—. Contbr. articles to profl. jour. Mem.: Linguistic Soc. Am., Am. Assn. Tchrs. Slavic and East European Langs., Am. Assn. for Advancement of Slavic Studies. Home: 1506 Halifax Rd Chapel Hill NC 27514 Office: Univ NC Dey Hall 418 CB 3165 Chapel Hill NC 27599-3165

FEINBERG, MARC H., neurologist; b. N.Y., Apr. 1, 1965; s. Harvey and Rochelle Feinberg. BS, SUNY, Binghamton, 1987; MD, SUNY, Bklyn., 1991. Diplomate Am. Bd. Psychiatry and Neurology. Ntern S.I. U. Hosp., 1992; resident Jackson Meml. Hosp., Miami, 1992—95; neurologist South Fla. Neurology Assn., Boca Raton, 1995—. Office: South Fla Neurology Assn 670 Glades Rd Ste 220 Boca Raton FL 33431 Office Phone: 561-392-6446.

FEINBERG, NORMAN MAURICE, real estate company executive; b. Bklyn., Nov. 28, 1934; s. Harry and Beatrice (Soroca) F.; m. Arline S. Itzkoff, Nov. 26, 1960; children: Mitchell, David. BS, NYU, 1956. Exec. Columbia Pictures Corp., NYC, 1956-62; pres. Gateside Corp., Rye, NY, 1965—. Owner, gen. ptnr. 27 cos., Rye. Arbitrator Am. Arbitration Assn., NYC; trustee, vice-chmn. Bklyn. Mus.; bd. dirs. Assn. for Mentally Ill Children, Scarborough, NY; chmn. bd. St. Mary's Health Sys.; mem. adv. bd. Steven L. Newman Real Estate Inst. of Baruch Coll., CUNY. Mem. World Pres. Orgn., Young Pres. Orgn. (chmn.), Chief Exec. Officers Assn. Avocations: art collecting, skiing, tennis, travel, languages. Home: 15 E 69th St New York NY 10021-4905 Office: Gateside Corp 555 Theodore Fremd Ave Rye NY 10580-1451 Office Phone: 914-967-7500.

FEINBERG, PAUL H., lawyer; b. Yonkers, N.Y., Nov. 24, 1938; AB, U. Pa., 1960; LLB cum laude, Harvard U., 1963; LLM, NYU, 1970. Bar: N.Y. 1965, Ohio 1979. Asst. gen. counsel The Ford Found., 1971-77; ptnr. Baker & Hostetler LLP, Cleve. Speaker in field. Contbr. articles to profl. jours. Mem. ABA (mem. sect. taxation, mem. tax exempt orgns. com., co-chair subcom. non C3 organs. 1993-94, co-chair subcom. pvt. founds. 1995—), N.Y. State Bar Assn., Ohio State Bar Assn., Cleve. Bar Assn. (treas. 1996-99). Office: Baker & Hostetler LLP 3200 Nat City Ctr 1900 E 9th St Cleveland OH 44114-3475 Office Phone: 216-861-7498.

FEINBERG, PAUL H., lawyer; b. Newark, Aug. 24, 1951; s. Frederick H. and Ruth S. Feinberg; m. Nancy S. Greenberg, Sept. 3, 1972; children: Jacob L., David R. BA, Rutgers U., 1973; JD, U. Toledo, 1976. Bar: N.J. 1976, U.S. Dist. Ct. N.J. 1976, U.S. Supreme Ct. 1986, U.S. Ct. Appeals (3rd cir.) 1998, cert.: (criminal trial atty.) 1989. Law clk. Superior Ct. Essex County, Newark, 1976—77; atty. Freeman & Bas, Newark, 1977, Leibowitz & Corradino, East Orange, NJ, 1978—79; ptnr. Feinberg & Feinberg, South Orange, NJ, 1979—. Pub. defender Town of South Orange, 1991—. Mem.: ATLA, Essex County Bar Assn., Assn. Criminal Trial Lawyers N.J., Nat. Assn. Criminal Trial Lawyers. Jewish. Office: Feinberg & Feinberg 76 S Orange Ave South Orange NJ 07079 Office Phone: 973-378-8886.

FEINBERG, RICHARD, anthropologist, educator; b. Norfolk, Va., Nov. 4, 1947; s. Isadore and Rose Selma (Hartmann) F.; m. Nancy Ellen Grim, Apr. 15, 1978; children: Joseph Grim Feinberg, Kate Grim-Feinberg. AB, U. Calif., Berkeley, 1969; MA, U. Chgo., 1971, PhD, 1974. Asst. prof. anthropology Kent (Ohio) State U., 1974-80, assoc. prof., 1980-86, prof., 1986—. Mem. editorial bd. Kent State U. Press, 1990-93; chair Kent State U. Faculty Senate, 1997-98; pres. Kent Rsch. Group, 1997-98. Author: Anuta: Social Structure of a Polynesian Island, 1981, Polynesian Seafaring and Navigation, 1988; editor: Politics of Culture in the Pacific Islands, 1995, Seafaring in the Contemporary Pacific Islands, 1995, Leadership and Change in the Western Pacific, 1996, Oral Traditions of Anuta, 1998, The Cultural Analysis of Kinship: The Legacy of David M. Schneider, 2001, (with others) Oceania: An Introduction to the Cultures and Identities of Pacific Islanders, 2002, Anuta: Polynesian Lifeways for the Twenty-first Century, 2004. Kent State Rsch. Coun. grantee, 1983, 88, 00; Wenner-Gren Found. grantee, 1991. Fellow: Assn. for Social Anthropology in Oceania (newsletter editor 1986—90, program coord. 2000—03, exec. bd. mem. 2003—06, chair 2005—), Am. Anthrop. Assn.; mem.: Ctrl. States Anthrop. Soc. (bull. editor 1994—98, 2d v.p. 2002—03, 1st v.p. 2003—04, pres. 2004—05), Am. Ethnological Soc., Polynesian Soc. Avocations: camping, white water kayaking, scuba diving, folk music. Office: Kent State U Dept Anthropology Kent OH 44242-0001

FEINBERG, RICHARD ALAN, clinical psychologist; b. Oakland, Calif., Aug. 12, 1947; s. Jack and Raechel Sacks (Hoff) F. BA, Calif. State U., Hayward, 1969; MA in Clin. Psychology, Mich. State U., 1972, PhD, 1979. Cert. Nat. Register Health Svc. Providers in Psychology. Instr. Merritt Coll., Oakland, 1975-76; clin. psychology Highland Gen. Hosp., Oakland, 1976-79; assoc. Lafayette Ctr. Counseling and Edn., 1978-79; clin. psychology Tri-City Mental Health Ctr., Fremont, Calif., 1979-81, dir., 1981-86; pvt. practice, Fremont, 1976—. Participant profl. conf. USPHS fellow, 1969-71. Mem. APA, Calif. Psychol. Assn. Home: 1684 Decoto Rd #256 Union City CA 94587

FEINBERG, ROBERT S., plastics company executive, marketing professional; b. Newark, May 14, 1934; s. Clarence Jacob and Sabina (Zorn) Feinberg. BA in English, BS in Chemistry, Trinity Coll., Hartford, Conn., 1955; MBA in Mktg., Fairleigh Dickinson U., 1966; diploma in advt., Assn. Indsl. Advt., 1967, NY Inst. Advt., 1967. Pres. Trebor Assocs. and Trebor Plastics Co., Teaneck, NJ, 1961—; mktg. cons. computer software Zettler Softwear Co., Burroughs Corp.; sr. coun. Yankelovich, Skelly and White, Inc.; cons. Greenwich Assocs.; co-chmn., ptnr. Edgeroy Co., Inc., Ridgefield and Palisades Park, NJ, 1973—, LeMont Sales Co., Teaneck, NJ, 1973—. Cons. plastics formulations W. R. Grace, Endicott Johnson, Brown Shoe Co., U.S. Shoe Co., Ciba, Uniroyal. Author: Olympia Shoe Co. (Harvard Case Book Series). Mem.: U.S. Profl. Tennis Assn., Sell Overseas Am., Sporting Goods Mfrs. Assn., Soc. Plastics Engrs. (sr.), Bergen County Tennis League (v.p.), Ahdeek Tennis Club. Achievements include patents in polymer and mechanical engineering fields; co-inventor Edgeroy Ball Press (Internat. Tennis Hall of Fame). Home: PO Box 273 Teaneck NJ 07666-0273

FEINBERG, SHELDON NORMAN, pediatrician, educator; b. N.Y.C., Mar. 16, 1930; m. MaryEllen Wisker, Jan. 2, 1988; children: Lynn Ann, Bette Joan, Barbara Ellen, Paul Howard, John Joseph. MD, N.Y. Med. Coll., 1955. Diplomate Am. Bd. Pediat. Intern Bronx Mcpl. Hosp. Ctr., N.Y.C., 1955-56; resident Met. Hosp., N.Y.C., 1956-57; fellow pediatrics N.Y. Med. Coll., 1959-60; pediat. staff Passack Valley Hosp., Westwood, N.J., 1960-82; emergency physician various hosps., 1982-85; pediat. staff Hackensack (N.J.) U. Med. Ctr., 1985—; clin. asst. prof. pediat. U. Med. & Dentistry N.J., Newark, 1985—. Inventor infant scale guard, simple stool stain. Maj. USAF med. corps., 1957-59. Honor award Bergen County Med. Soc., 1965. Fellow Am. Acad. Pediat.; mem. AMA, N.J. Pediat. Soc. (pres. 1989-91, Honor award 1991). Home: 125 N Country Rd Mount Sinai NY 11766-1503

FEINBERG, WENDIE, producer; BS in Journalism, U. Fla.; MS in Journalism, Boston U. Sr. prodr. Nightly Bus. Report, Miami, Fla. Recipient of three local Emmy Awards for Best Newscast, Best Investigative Reporting, and Best Pub. Affairs Programming, Best News Series/Documentary, Radio & TV News Directors Assn., 1990. Office: NBR Enterprises 14901 NE 20th Ave Miami FL 33181-1121*

FEINBERG, WILFRED, federal judge; b. NYC, June 22, 1920; s. Jac and Eva (Wolin) Feinberg; m. Shirley Marcus, June 23, 1946; children: Susan Stelk, Jack, Jessica Twedt. BA, Columbia U., 1940, LLB, 1946, LLD (hon.), 1985, Syracuse U., 1985; LLD (hon.), Bklyn. Law Sch., 1998. Bar: N.Y. 1947. Law clk. Hon. James P. McGranery U.S. Dist. Ct. (ea. dist.) Pa., 1947—49; assoc. Kaye, Scholer, Fierman & Hays, NYC, 1949—53; ptnr. McGoldrick, Dannett, Horowitz & Golub, NYC, 1953—61; dep. supt. N.Y. State Banking Dept., NYC, 1958; judge U.S. Dist Ct. (so. dist.), NYC, 1961—66, U.S. Ct. Appeals (2nd cir.), NYC, 1966—, chief judge, 1980—88, sr. judge, 1991—. Mem. U.S. Jud. Conf. U.S., 1980—88, chmn. exec. com., 1987—88, mem. Devitt award com., 1989, 90, mem. long-range planning com., 1991—96; Madison lectr. NYU Law Sch., 1983; Sonnett lectr. Fordham U. Law Sch., 1984; Inaugural Howard Kaplan Meml. lectr. Hofstra U. Law Sch., 1986; The Future of Justice lectr. Inst. of Comparative Law, Chuo U., Japan, 1991. Editor-in-chief: Columbia Law Rev., 1946; contbr. to profl. jours. and mags. With U.S. Army, 1942—45. Recipient Learned Hand medal for excellence in fed. jurisprudence, 1982, Gold medal, award for disting. svc. in the law, N.Y. State Bar Assn., 1990, medal for excellence, Columbia Law Alumni Assn., 1990, Pursuit of Justice award, Internat. Assn. Jewish Lawyers and Jurists, 1993, Disting. Pub. Svc. award, N.Y. County Lawyers Assn., 1994, Edward Weinfeld award, 1995, Ann. Wilfred Feinberg prize named in his honor for best student work at Columbia Law Sch. related to fed. cts., 1998, Edward J. Devitt Disting. Svc. to Justice award, 2003. Mem.: ABA, Am. Law Inst., Am. Judicature Soc., N.Y. County Lawyers Assn., Assn. of Bar of City of N.Y., Phi Beta Kappa. Office: US Ct Appeals 2nd Cir Room 2004 US Court House Foley Sq New York NY 10007-1501

FEINER, AVA SOPHIA, public affairs and management consultant, economist; b. Bklyn., Feb. 13, 1950; d. Ignace and Lola (Pasternak) F.; m. Clifford Douglas Stromberg, June 25, 1972; children: Kimberly Greta, Eric George. BA summa cum laude, Yale U., 1971; MA, Harvard U., 1974, PhD in Govt., 1978. Legis. asst. to U.S. Senator Bill Bradley, Washington, 1979-82; dir. internat. trade policy U.S. C. of C., Washington, 1982-83, mgr. internat. policy dept., 1983-85; corp. program dir. IBM, Washington, 1985-87, corp. dir. pub. affairs, trade and investment, 1987; pres. Feiner Pub. Affairs Cons., Washington, 1988—; co-founder, dir. Washington Alive! Inc., 1989-90; pres. Washington Networks, 1990—; mem. campaign and transition team Ehrlich for Gov., 2002; mem. Md. State Ethics Commn., 2003—. Tchg. fellow Harvard U., Cambridge, Mass., 1972-74; lectr. nat. and internat. politics and econs., 1978—; bd. dirs. World Trade Forum, Washington, 1987-89. Co-author: American Excellence in A World Economy, 1987; contbr. articles on econs., trade, fgn. policy to various publs. Del. to Atlantic Coun. Young Leadership Program, Wis. and Can., 1978, 80, Aspen Inst. Exec. Seminar, 1982, Germany-U.S. Young Leadership Conf., San Francisco, 1982, Harbor Sch. Bd., 1992-93; co-chair Holton-Arms Sch. Silent Auction, 1995-96; mem. adv. com. Cmty. Homeowners, 1999—04, chmn., 2001—04; 1st v.p. Potomac Women's Rep. Club., 2002-03. Fgn. Policy fellow Brookings Instn., 1975-76, guest scholar, 1976-77; Carnegie Endowment for Internat. Peace fellow, 1975-76; finalist Photographer's Forum Mag. Mem.: Trade Policy Forum, Coun. Fgn. Rels. (task force on women 1988—91, term membership com. 1988—91, internat. affairs fellows com. 1991—95, Washington program adv. com. 1995—98), Phi Beta Kappa. Avocations: photography, Karate, swimming, bicycling, tennis.

FEINGOLD, DANIEL LEON, anesthesiologist, consultant; b. Boston, May 19, 1958; s. Macey Gerson and Hélène Sultana (Benlolo) F. BS with distinction, U. Ill., Chgo., 1980; MD, U. Health Scis., Chgo. Med. Sch., 1984. Intern Weiss Meml. Hosp., Chgo., 1984-85; resident in anesthesiology U. Ill. Hosps. and Clinics, Chgo., 1986-89; anesthesiologist Hosp. Anesthesia Group, Chgo., 1989—. Contbr. articles to profl. publs. Mem. AMA, AAAS, Am. Soc. Anesthesiologists, Ill. State Med. Soc. Home: PO Box 577429 Chicago IL 60657-7429 Office: PO Box 25678 Chicago IL 60625-0678

FEINGOLD, DAVID SIDNEY, microbiology and biochemistry educator, researcher; b. Chelsea, Mass., Nov. 15, 1922; s. Louis Edward and Miriam F.; m. Batia Babette Haber, Nov. 15, 1949; children: Oded, Anat, Michele. BS, MIT, 1944; PhD, Hebrew U., Jerusalem, Israel, 1956. Chemist Lucidol Corp., Buffalo, 1944; jr. research biochemist U. Calif. at Berkeley, 1957-60; asst. prof. biology U. Pitts., 1960-62, asso. prof., 1962-65, prof., 1965—; prof. microbiology Sch. Medicine, 1966-93, prof. emeritus molecular genetics and biochemistry, 1993—. Contbr. articles to prof. jours. With USNR, 1944—46. Recipient State of Israel prize in natural sci., 1957, Career Devel. award NIH, 1965-75 Fellow Infectious Disease Soc. Am.; mem. Internat. Endotoxin Soc., Am. Soc. for Biochemistry and Molecular Biology. Home: 6420 Bartlett St Pittsburgh PA 15217-1832 Personal E-mail: udpglcdh@juno.com.

FEINGOLD, KENNETH J., artist; b. Pitts., 1952; Studied, Antioch Coll., 1970—76, Calif. Inst. of Arts. Assoc. prof. fine arts Mpls. Coll. Art & Design, 1977—85; adj. assoc. prof. Princeton U., Visual Arts Program, 1989—94, Cooper Union Sch. of Arts, 1993—94; prof. computer art Sch. Visual Arts, NYC, 1993—98. Vis. artist Bard Coll., 2001; guest faculty The Royal U. Coll. Fine Arts, Stockholm, 2002. One-man shows include Whitney Mus., 1979, exhibitions include Signs, The New Mus. Contemporary Art, 1985, Contemporary Art in Context, Mus. Modern Art, 1988, Between Word and Image, 1993, 2002 Biennial Exhibition, Whitney Mus. Am. Art, 2002, Art, Lies, and Videotape: Exposing Performance, Tate Liverpool, 2004, digital works, Subject with Four Footnotes, 1975, Jimmy Charlie Jimmy, 1992, Eros and Thanatos at Sea, 2004; author: New Screen Media: Cinema/Art/Narrative, 2002. Recipient Bonn Videonalle, Videonale-Preis, 1992; fellow Guggenheim Meml. Found., 2004; grantee NEA, 1979, NY Found. for Arts, 1988, Rockefeller Found. Media Arts Fellowship, 2003. E-mail: info@kenfeingold.com.*

FEINGOLD, RUSSELL DANA, senator, lawyer; b. Janesville, Wis., Jan. 2, 1953; s. Leon and Sylvia (Binstock) Feingold; m. Susan Levine, Aug. 21, 1977; children: Jessica, Ellen; m. Mary Speerschneider, Jan. 20, 1991; stepchildren: Sam Speerschneider, Ted Speerschneider. BA with honors, U. Wis.-Madison, 1975; postgrad., Magdalen Coll., Oxford U., Eng., 1975—77; JD with honors, Harvard U., 1979. Bar: Wis. 1979. Assoc. Foley & Lardner, Madison, 1979—82, LaFollette, Sinykin, Anderson & Munson, Madison, 1983—85, Goldman & Feingold, 1985—88; mem. Wis. Senate, 1983—92; US senator from Wis., 1993—; mem. aging com., budget com., fgn. rels. com., judiciary com., senate Dem. policy com. US Senate. Scholar, Wis. Honors scholar, 1971, Rhodes scholar, 1975. Mem.: Phi Beta Kappa. Democrat. Jewish. Office: US Senate 506 Hart Senate Office Bldg Washington DC 20510-0001 also: US Senators Office 1600 Aspen Commons Rm 100 Middleton WI 53562-4626*

FEINGOLD, S. NORMAN, psychologist; b. Worcester, Mass., Feb. 2, 1914; s. William and Aida (Salit) F.; m. Marie Goodman, Mar. 24, 1947; children: Elizabeth Anne, Margaret Ellen, Deborah Carol, Marilyn Nancy. AB, Ind. U., 1937; MA, Clark U., 1940; EdD, Boston U., 1948; LLD, Edward Waters Coll., Saints Coll. Dir. vocat. svc., ednl. and vocat. dir. Hecht. Neighborhood House, Boston, 1940-43; exec. dir. Boston Jewish Vocat. Svc. and Work Adjustment Ctr., 1946-58; nat. dir. B'nai B'rith Career and Counseling Svcs., Washington, 1958-80; pres. Nat. Career and Counseling Svcs., 1980—; pvt. practice, 1980—. Exec. adviser Rehab. Services, Boston, 1953-58; dir. ednl. and vocat. workshop United Cerebral Palsy of Greater Boston, Inc., 1957-58; cons. to Scholarships, Fellowships and Loans News Service, Social Security Adminstrn., 1962—; instr., spl. lectr. Boston U., 1951-58; profl. lectr. Am. U. Rehab. Counseling Adv. Panel, 1963-65; mem. Am. Bd. Counseling Services, 1962-65, 70—. Author: It Pays to Advertise, 1975, Occupations and Careers, 1969, The Vocational Expert in the Social Security Disability Program, 1969, A Counselor's Handbook, 1972, Counseling for Careers in the 80's, 1979, Whither Counseling, 1981, Making It on Your Own, rev., 1991, A Guide to Financial Success, 1981, rev., 1985, Emerging Careers: New Occupations for the Year Two Thousand and Beyond, 1983, The Professional and Trade Association Job Finder, 1983, Getting Ahead: A Woman's Guide to Career Sources, 1983, Scholarships, Fellowships and Loans, Vol. 8, 1987, New Emerging Careers: Today, Tomorrow, and in the 21st Century, 1988, Futuristic Exercises: A Work Book for Emerging Lifestyles and Careers in the 21st Century and Beyond, 1989, Where the Jobs Are: A Comprehensive Directory of 1200 Journals Listing Career Opportunities, 1989, The Complete Job and Career Handbook: 101 Ways to Get from Here to There, 1993; past editor Counselors Information Service. Chmn. Gov.'s Council on Aging, 1956-58, Washington Bus.-Industry Group, 1963-64; mem. Pres.'s Com. on Employment Handicapped, 1950—; adv. com. Nat. Health Council; pres. Greater Boston Persn. and Guidance Assn., 1952-53; mem. Nat. Home Study Accrediting Commn.; chmn. human relations com. Dept. Agr. Grad. Sch.; profl. adv. bd. Epilepsy Found. 1st lt. AUS, 1943-46, ETO and PTO. Recipient Cmty. Svc. award B'nai B'rith, 1957, Brotherhood and Americanization award, 1958, Eminent Career award Nat. Capital Personnel and Guidance Assn. Fellow Am. Psychol. Assn.; mem. Am. Personnel and Guidance Assn. (pres. 1974-75), Mass., Nat. Vocat. Guidance Assn. (pres. 1968-69), Internat. Coun. Psychologists, Nat. Press Club, Nat. Rehab. Assn., Torch Club, New Century Club (bd. dirs. 1954-58), Phi Delta Kappa. Home: 1801 E Jefferson St # 442 Rockville MD 20852-4057 *Any success I may have attained is because of conscientiousness, a love of life, a high energy level, a supportive family, close friends, and being an optimist by temperament and conviction. I believe in people and the tremendous potential of all people. To me, everyone is a Very Important Person, who can make a contribution. My premise is that our most precious resource is people, and everything we do individually or collectively now or in the future depends on that conviction and acting accordingly.*

FEINHANDLER, EDWARD SANFORD, writer, photographer, art dealer; b. Elko, Nev., Jan. 13, 1948; s. Samuel and Sylvia (Manus) F. BA, U. Nev., 1972; BS Elem. Edn., Sierra Nevada Coll., 1997. Supr. underprivileged Washoe County Extension Program, Reno, 1970—71; sports editor, writer Sagebrush Campus newspaper, Reno, 1971—72; internal salesman, mgr. Trigon Corp., Sparks, Nev., 1975—88; owner, operator Art Internat. Gallery Extraordinaire, Reno, 1981—; tennis dir. City of Sparks, 1991—93, 2004, Cmty. Edn. Program, Sparks, 1994, Sparks YMCA, 1995—96; phys. edn. dir., coach 8th grade B boys basketball Clayton Mid. Sch., 2000—01, advisor boys and girls wrestling, 2001; coach freshmen boys basketball Sparks H.S., 2003—05. With nat. news Top Ten radio interviews, U.S., Can. and Eng.; freelance writer and photographer newspapers U.S. and Can.; pres. No. Nev. H.S. Tennis Assn., 1996. Contbr. articles to newspapers and mags.; extra in various movies; TV interviewed AM Chgo., AM L.A., 1979, Afternoon Exchange, Cleve., 1979, To Tell the Truth, 1975, Reno Tonight TV show, 1989, Fox Across America TV show, 1989, Wheel of Fortune, 1995; over 200 radio interviews worldwide including Nat. Examiner, 1999, Nat. Enquirer TV show, 1999-2000, Penthouse Mag., 2000, Reno Gazette Jr., London and New Zealand radio, 2000, Bogota, Colombia and South Africa, 2001, Sydney, Australia, Durban, South Africa, Dublin, Ireland, North Adelaine, Australia, others; contbr. over 30 newspapers, articles to profl. jours. Player, coach Summer Volleyball League, Reno, 1982-85; tennis coach Cmty. Svc. Ctr., Reno, 1986-88, 94; founder Joell Vowell softball event Make-A-Wish Found., Reno, 1985-2004; active U. Nev. Journalism Dept., 1985-2001, UNR Children's Svcs., Reno, 1986-88; basketball coach Little Flower Cath. Sch., 1987-89; head coach girls varsity tennis team Bishop Manogue H.S., 1989-91; coach boys varsity tennis Sparks H.S., 1993-97, 2000-2004, girls varsity tennis, 2001-2004, spl. olympics, 1989, Bishop Monogue girls jr. varsity basketball, 1989-90; head coach freshman boys Sparls H.S., 2003-05; active Ptnrs. in Edn., 1988-2000, Jr. Achievement, 1989-94, Animal Welfare Inst., Statue of Liberty Found., 1984-2001, No. Nev. Cancer Coun., United Blood Svcs., Arthritis Found., Cancer Soc., Sta. KNPB, Ret. Sr. Citizens, Reno Fire Dept. Christmas Basket Delivery, 1991—, Sierra Arts Found.; vol. free tennis lessons, 1993-2005; fundraiser H.L.A. Testing United Blood Svcs., 1991-2000; founder, pres. No. Nev. Youth Opportunistic Tennis program, 1997—, Huey Feinhandler Found., 2001-2005; guest spkr. Rotary Internat., Nev., 1999; guest spkr. Sertoma Club, 2003—, Lions Club, 2003—,blood donor United Blood Svc.; donator Platelet, 1993—; other cmty. activities. Sgt. U.S. Army, 1968-69, Vietnam. Winner Ugly Man contest Make-A-Wish Found., 1999, 2001, 2003-05, No. Nev. Bone Marrow Program, 1991-98, 2000,05. category Ugly Bartender contest Multiple Sclerosis and Make-A-Wish Found., 1989-2005, U. Nev.-Reno Ugly Man, 1967, 70, 71, 72, Krispy Kreme Ugly Necktie winner, ugliest tie in Reno, 2004; Sparks Tennis Club singles, doubles, and mixed doubles Champion B/C divsn., 1994, Singles B Champion, Mixed B Doubles Champion, 1995, 2001, Ladder B Singles Men's Champion, 1996, 97, 3d Ann. B Doubles Champion, 1996; recipient numerous tennis, billiards, volleyball and bowling awards including 1st pl. C divsn. NNCC Tennis Tournament, 1991, RTC C Mixed Doubles Champion, 1992, Sparks Recreation Open Doubles Champion, 1993; world record holder nosedarts and squint, 1972—; recipient Cmty. Svc. award United Blood Svcs., 1995, Svc. Above Self award Rotary Internat., 1995, Joeil Vowell Charity Softball award Make-A-Wish Found., 1997, 98, Cmty. Safety award Associated Builders and Contractors, 1997, Spl. Thank You award Pine Mid. Sch. Students Concerned with Quick Thinking and Great Effort, 1997, Angel award Washoe County Sch. Dist., 1997, USTA Norcal Warren Brown award, 1995-2004, named Vol. of Yr., Sports Articles, 2004. Mem. DAV, Orthodox Jewish Union, Elks (Vol. of Yr. award 2004-05) Democrat. Avocations: bowling, tennis, basketball, baseball, volleyball, billiards, darts. Office: Huey Feinhandler Found PO Box 13405 Reno NV 89507-3405 Office Phone: 775-358-7033. E-mail: mruglyed@yahoo.com, hueyfein@msn.com.

FEININGER, THEODORE LUX, artist; b. Berlin, June 11, 1910; s. Charles Lyonel and Julia (Lilienfeld) F.; m. Patricia Randall, Dec. 17, 1954; children: Lucas, Conrad, Charles. Grad., Bauhaus, Dessau, Germany, 1929. Instr. Sarah Lawrence Coll., 1950-52; lectr. drawing and painting Harvard U., 1953-62; instr. drawing and painting Boston Fine Arts Mus. Sch., 1962-75. Author: Lyonel Feininger: City at the Edge of the World, 1965, Photographs of the 20s and 30s (illustrated catalogue), 1980; exhbns. include Am. Realists and Magic Realists, Mus. Modern Art, N.Y.C., 1943, Revolution and Tradition in Modern Am. Art, Bklyn. Mus., 1951, Whitney Mus. Am. Art Ann., N.Y.C., 1951, Am. Painters, MIT, 1954, Retrospective, Busch-Reisinger Mus., 1962, Wheaton Coll., 1973, Wamsutta Club, New Bedford, Mass., 1974, Prakapas Gallery, N.Y.C., 1980, Sacramento St. Gallery, Cambridge, Mass., 1982, Gallery on the Green, Lexington, Mass., 1986, 88, 90, 92, Achim Moeller Fine Art, N.Y.C., 1954-94, Staatliche Galerie Moritzburg Halle, Saale, Germany, 1998, Städtisches Mus. Karlsruhe, Germany, 2001; represented in permanent collections Mus. Modern Art, N.Y.C., Busch-Reisinger Mus. and Fogg Art Mus., Harvard U., Altonaer Mus., Hamburg, Germany, Schleswig-Holstein Landes Mus., Mus. Folkwang, Essen, Germany, Bauhaus Mus., Weimar, Germany, Getty Mus., Calif., Met. Mus., N.Y., L.A. County Mus., Stedelijk Mus., Amsterdam, Guggenheim Mus., N.Y., Staatliche Galerie Moritzburg, Germany. With U.S. Army, 1942—45. Mem. Westport Art Group. Democrat. Address: 22 Arlington St Cambridge MA 02140-2713 *The practice and teaching of art has shown me that I must seek progress on the basis of understanding and assimilating tradition; that every individual incorporates both revolutionary and conservative tendencies; and that the task of the individual lies in assessing and acting upon his findings, his own proportionate share of these two conflicting trends. I am Society, and Society cannot do without me.*

FEINLAND, ROBERT PHILIP, artist; b. Bklyn., Aug. 18, 1946; s. Irving D. and Ernestine R. Feinland; m. Helene J. Podziba, May 15, 1994. BA, Haverford Coll., 1967; MFA, Bklyn. Coll., 1989. Tchr. The Door, N.Y.C., 1977-81, N.Y. Acad., N.Y.C., 1981-82, Ednl. Alliance Art Sch., N.Y.C., 1986-87. One person show at Nicholas Roerich Mus., N.Y.C., 1986, Chai Gallery, Bklyn., 1996, Vorpal Gallery, N.Y.C., 1997, Civic Ctr. Synagogue, N.Y.C., 2000; exhibited in group shows at A.M. Adler Gallery, N.Y.C., 1985, PS 122 Gallery, N.Y.C., 1988, Provincetown (Mass.) Art Assn. and Mus., 1993, Nat. Acad., N.Y.C., 1994, 96, 98; curator exhibit Police Bldg. Gallery, N.Y.C., 1995, N.Y. Mercantile Exch., N.Y.C., 2002; executed sculpture at All Metal Chocolate Mold Co., Bronx, N.Y. Recipient Founder's prize Clinton Art Soc., 1985, Option prize Art Student League, 1981; grantee Found. for Creative Cmty., 1977, Marine Midland Bank, 1998. Mem. Audubon Artists (Ralph Fabri prize 1995, 97), Michael Ingbar Gallery Archtl. Art, Coll. Art Assn. Home: 153 Ludlow St New York NY 10002-2241

FEINSILVER, DONALD LEE, psychiatry educator; b. Bklyn., July 24, 1947; s. Albert and Mildred (Weissman) Feinsilver. BA, Alfred U., 1968; MD, Autonomous U., Guadalajara, Mexico, 1974. Diplomate Am. Bd. Psychiatry and Neurology, Am. Bd. Forensic Psychiatry. Intern in medicine L.I. Coll. Hosp., Bklyn., 1975—76; resident in psychiatry SUNY-Bklyn., 1977—78, chief resident, 1979; asst. prof. psychiatry and surgery Med. Coll. Wis., Milw., 1980—85, assoc. prof., 1985—; dir. psychiat. emergency svc. Milw. County Mental Health and Med. Complexes, 1980—88; dir. med.-psychiat. unit Milw. Psychiat. Hosp./West Allis Meml. Hosp., 1988—. Contbr. articles to profl. jours.; editor: Crisis Psychiatry: Pros and Cons, 1982; mem. editl. bd.: Psychiat. Medicine Jour., 1983—. Mem.: AAAS, AMA, Acad. Psychosomatic Medicine, Am. Acad. Psychiatry and the Law, Am. Psychiat. Assn. Office: West Allis Psychiat Assocs 2424 S 90th St Milwaukee WI 53227-2455 Office Phone: 414-328-8690. Personal E-mail: DFeinsilver@prodigy.net.

FEINSTEIN, ALLEN LEWIS, lawyer; b. N.Y.C., Apr. 18, 1929; s. Jacob and Kate (Goldberg) F.; m. Charlesa Joan Wolfe, Dec. 14, 1957. AB, CCNY, 1949; LLB, Columbia U., 1952. Bar: N.Y. 1952, U.S. Supreme Ct. 1958, Ariz. 1960, U.S. Dist. Ct. Ariz. 1960, U.S. Ct. Appeals (9th cir.) 1960. Assoc. Proskauer Rose Goetz & Mendelsohn, N.Y.C., 1955-59; law clk. to justice Supreme Ct. Ariz., Phoenix, 1959-61, 1st adminstrv. dir., 1961-64; pvt. practice law Phoenix, 1964-72, 1995—; ptnr. Daughton Feinstein & Wilson, Phoenix, 1972-86; sr. ptnr. Rawlins, Burrus, Lewkowitz & Feinstein, P.C., Phoenix, 1986-95. Mem. Phoenix Housing Code Com., 1968; vice-chmn. adv. com. State Legislative com. on Medicaid; mem. Phoenix Charter Review Com., 1969; mem. exec. com. Phoenix Sister City Commn., 1973-75 Author: First, Second and Third Reports of Courts of Arizona, 1962, 63, 64. Bd. dirs. Meml. Hosp. Phoenix, chmn., 1973-76, Community Coun., 1970-76, Ariz. Jewish Hist. Soc.; chmn. Meml. Hosp. Found., 1980-82; bd. dirs., chmn. coun. trustees, mem. exec. com. Ariz. Hosp. Assn., 1981-87, chmn. 1986-87, Ariz. del. to nat. conf. governing bds.; chmn. PMH Health Resources, Inc., 1983-89, Ariz. Voluntary Hosp. Fedn., 1984-88; chmn. Phoenix chpt. Am. Jewish Com., 1989-91; legal advisor Salt River Pima-Maricopa INdian Cmty. Police Commn., 1997-2002. 2d lt. USAF, 1952-53. Mem. Ariz. Bar Assn., Maricopa County Bar Assn., State Bar Ariz. (chmn. com. civil practice and procedure 1971-74, chmn. long-range com. 1980, peer rev. com., sole practitioner com. sect., alternate dispute resolution sects., mentor-mentee com.), Univ. Club Phoenix (pres. 1971-72), Phi Beta Kappa, Phi Delta Phi. Democrat. Jewish. Address: 2110 Encanto Dr SW Phoenix AZ 85007-1526 Personal E-mail: alfeinstein@cox.net.

FEINSTEIN, DIANNE, senator; b. San Francisco, June 22, 1933; d. Leon and Betty (Rosenburg) Goldman; m. Bertram Feinstein, Nov. 11, 1962 (dec.); 1 child, Katherine Anne; m. Richard C. Blum, Jan. 20, 1980. BA History, Stanford U., 1955; LLB (hon.), Golden Gate U., 1977; D Pub. Adminstrn. (hon.), U. Manila, 1981; D Pub. Service (hon.), U. Santa Clara, 1981; JD (hon.), Antioch U., 1983, Mills Coll., 1985; LHD (hon.), U. San Francisco, 1988. Fellow Coro Found., San Francisco, 1955-56; with Calif. Women's Bd. Terms and Parole, 1960-66; mem. Mayor's com. on crime, chmn. adv. com. Adult Detention, 1967-69; mem. Bd. Suprs., San Francisco, 1970-78, pres., 1970-71, 74-75, 78; mayor City of San Francisco, 1978-88; senator from Calif. U.S. Senate, Washington, 1992—. Mem. exec. com. U.S. Conf. of Mayors, 1983-88; Dem. nominee for Gov. of Calif., 1990; mem. Nat. Com. on U.S.-China Rels.; mem. judiciary com., appropriations com., rules and adminstrn. Com., energy and natural resources com; mem. Coun. Foreign Rels. Mem. Bay Area Conservation and Devel. Commn., 1973-78; mem. Senate Fgn. Rels. Com. Recipient Woman of Achievement award Bus. and Profl. Women's Clubs San Francisco, 1970, Disting. Woman award San Francisco Examiner, 1970, Coro Found. award, 1979, Coro Leadership award, 1988, Pres. medal U. Calif., San Francisco, 1988, Scopus award Am. Friends Hebrew U., 1981, Brotherhood/Sisterhood award NCCJ, 1986, Comdr.'s award U.S. Army, 1986, French Legion of Honor, 1984, Disting. Civilian award USN, 1987; named Number One Mayor All-Pro City Mgmt. Team City and State Mag., 1987; named on of Most Powerful Women, Forbes mag., 2005. Mem. Trilateral Commn., Japan Soc. of No. Calif. (pres. 1988-89), Inter-Am. Dialogue, Nat. Com. on U.S.-China Rels. Democrat. Office: US Senate 331 Hart Senate Office Bldg Washington DC 20510-0001*

FEINSTEIN, FRED IRA, lawyer; b. Chgo., Apr. 6, 1945; s. Bernard and Beatrice (Mines) Feinstein; m. Judy Cutler, Aug. 25, 1968; children: Karen, Donald. BSc, DePaul U., 1967, JD, 1970. Bar: Ill. 1970, U.S. Supreme Ct. 1977. Ptnr. McDermott, Will & Emery, Chgo., 1976—. Lectr. in field. Contbr. articles to profl. jours. Pres. Skokie/Evanston (Ill.) Action Coun., 1981—84; bd. dirs. Temple Judea Mizpah, Skokie, 1982—84, Deborah Goldfine Meml. Cancer Rsch., 1968—, YMCA of Chgo.1985, 1985—. Mem.: Am. Coll. Real Estate Lawyers, Ill. Bar Assn., Blue Key, Union League, Beta Alpha Psi, Beta Gamma Sigma, Lambda Alpha, Pi Gamma Mu. Office: McDermott Will & Emery LLP 227 W Monroe St Ste 4700 Chicago IL 60606-5096 Office Phone: 312-984-7665. E-mail: ffeinstein@mwe.com.

FEINSTEIN, LEONARD, retail executive; Co-founder Bed Bath & Beyond, Union, NJ, 1971, co-CEO, 1971—2003, pres., 1992—99, co-chmn., 1999—. Bd. dir. Bed Bath & Beyond, Union, NJ, 1971—. Office: Bed Bath & Beyond 650 Liberty Ave Union NJ 07083

FEINSTEIN, MARION FINKE, artistic director, dance instructor; b. Nov. 7, 1925; d. Charles and Anne (Krein) Finke; m. Seymour Feinstein, Apr. 2, 1944 (dec.); children: Sandi, Sheree, Lori. Degree in sec. sci., U. S.C., 1944; student, Joffrey Ballet, N.Y.C., Am. Ballet Theatre; studied with Alvin Ailey, N.Y.C. Instr. dance Recreation Dept., Columbia, S.C., 1945; instr. ballet Furman Basketball Team, Greenville, S.C., 1950-55; instr. jazz U. S.C., Spartanburg, 1986-87; dance dir. Carolina Youth Dance Theatre, Spartanburg,

1980—. Tchr. various pageant winners and profl. dancers, including Miss Black Am., Miss World, Miss Am. finalist, Miss Dance Am., 1972, Jr. Miss Dance of S.C., Miss Dance of S.C., 1993, 94, 96, 97. Performed Macy's Thanksgiving Day Parade, N.Y.C., 1999. Mem. USO troupe, Spartanburg, 1942-44; choreographer Spartanburg Little Theatre, 1955-62, Miss Spartanburg Pageant, 1963-72. Recipient Resolution award S.C. Ho. Reps. and Senate, 1988, Cert. Performance Appreciation, City New Orleans, Resolution of Appreciation award Spartanburg County Council, S.C., Cert. Performance Appreciation N.Y.C. com. for entertainment at the Statue of Liberty, Fund Raising award March of Dimes; students performed in opening ceremonies at 1996 Olympic Games, Atlanta. Mem. Dance Educators Am. (regional dir.), Dance Masters Am., So. Coun. Dancemasters (v.p.), Cecchetti Coun. Am., Bus. and Profl. Women, Hadassah Club (Spartanburg), B'nai Israel Sisterhood Orgn. Democrat. Jewish. Office: Miss Marion's Sch Dance 1206 John B White Sr Blvd Spartanburg SC 29306-3930

FEINSTEIN, MARTIN, performing arts educator, consultant, art director; b. N.Y.C., Apr. 12, 1921; BSS, CCNY, 1942; MA, Wayne State U., 1943; MusD (hon.), Cath. U. Am., 1980, Shenandoah Coll. & Conservatory, 1983; LHD (hon.), Am. U., 1991; DFA, U. Md., 1995. Publicity dir. Hurok Concerts, N.Y.C., 1945-50, v.p., 1950-71; vis. prof. Yale U., New Haven, 1971-73; exec. dir. performing arts John F. Kennedy Ctr., Washington, 1972-80; pres., CEO Nat. Symphony, Kennedy Ctr., Washington, 1980-81; gen. dir. Washington Opera, 1980-95, cons., 1995—; sr. cons. U. Md. Performing Arts Ctr., College Park, 1995-2000, artistic dir., 1998-99, adj. prof., 2000—. Panelist, onsite visitor Nat. Endowment of the Arts, 1997—. Decorated commendatore Republic of Italy; cross of officer Order Arts and Letters (France); Grand Decoration of Honor for Svcs. (Austria), officer Order of Merit (Germany); recipient medal Nat. Soc. Lit. and the Arts, 1977, award of Contbns. in Field of Dance Am. Assn. Dance Cos., 1979, Townsend Harris medal CCNY, 1977, John Cranko medal, Stuttgart, 1979, Myrtle Wreath award Washington Hadassah, 1982, Amphion award Memphis Symphony, 1983.

FEINSTEIN, MILES ROGER, lawyer; b. Camden, N.J., June 25, 1941; s. Louis Emory and Sylvia K. (Jacobs) F.; m. Margaret Bott, Oct. 3, 2000; children: Bari, Matthew, Elizabeth. BA, Rutgers U., 1963; JD, Duke U., 1966. Bar: N.J. 1966, U.S. Dist. Ct. N.J. 1966, U.S. Ct. Appeals (3d cir.) 1967, U.S. Ct. Appeals (2d cir.) 1971. Pvt. practice, Clifton, N.J., 1967—. Mem. Passaic Criminal Justice commn.; mem. com. on drugs and cts. N.J. Supreme Ct.; mem. speedy trial com. N.J. Supreme Ct.; expert commentator Nat. Courtroom TV; lectr. N.J. Inst. of Continuing Legal Edn., Trial Lawyers Assn., and other bar groups and civic assns.; appeared on numerous TV and radio shows. Author: Historical Development of Pineys of Southern New Jersey. Trustee Passaic County Heart Fund, 1970-93, Passaic County Cancer Soc.; chmn. Passaic County March of Dimes, 1989. Named Man of Yr., Passaic County Heart Fund, 1976, Passaic County Cancer Soc., 1978, Passaic County coun. Boy Scouts Am., 1978, Passaic County Bad Guys Charitable Orgn., 1974; named one of N.J.'s Super Lawyers N.J. Monthly Mag. and N.J. Super-Lawyers Mag.; recipient award Passaic Civic Orgn., Humanitarian award Unico, 1976, Nationwide Bail Bonds award Policeman's Benevolent Assn., Disting. Svc. award, 1980, 84, 85, History prize Soc. Colonial Wars, PBA Silver Shield; subject of numerous legal and newspaper articles. Mem. ABA, Assn. Trial Lawyers Am., Nat. Assn. Criminal Def. Lawyers, Fed. Bar Assn., N.J. Bar Assn. (criminal law com. 2000-2002), N.J. Assn. Criminal Def. Lawyers (former trustee, treas., v.p., pres. 1990-91; lectr.), N.J. Assn. of Trial Lawyers (bd. govs. 1992-93), Passaic County Bar Assn. (chmn. criminal law com. 1990-93), Phi Beta Kappa, Phi Delta Phi, Phi Alpha Theta (Henry Rutgers scholar). Avocations: sports, theater, collecting stamps. Office: 1135 Clifton Ave Clifton NJ 07013-3642 Office Phone: 973-779-1124. E-mail: mrfeinsteinesq@aol.com.

FEINSTEIN, ROBERT P., dermatologist; b. N.Y.C., July 31, 1941; s. Jerome and May (Wolpin) F.; m. Diane Marla Gutstein, Oct. 25, 1969; children: Steven, Michelle, Suzanne, Gary, Lori. AB in Biology, NYU, 1963, MD, 1967. Diplomate Am. Bd. Dermatology. Intern Kings County Hosp. Ctr., Bklyn., 1967-68; resident in dermatology Columbia U., N.Y.C., 1968-71, assoc. clin. prof. dept. dermatology; chief of dermatology, innoculations and phys. exams. Navy Regional Med. Clinic, Washington, 1971-73; pvt. practice in dermatology Mineola, N.Y., 1973-99, Smithtown, N.Y., 1983-2000. Author: (book) Dermatology, 1975, (monograph) Rosacea, 1998; contbr. articles to profl. jours. Lt comdr. USNR, 1971-73. Fellow Am. Acad. Dermatology (mem. managed care com., 1995-99, mem. com. physician practice, professionalism study group program for dermatology in 21st cent., vice chmn. adv. bd. 2001-04), Am. Soc. for Dermatologic Surgery; mem. AMA, N.Y. State Soc. of Dermatology (pres. 1997-99), L.I. Dermatology Soc. (pres. 1996-98), Suffolk County Dermatology Soc. (pres. 1982-84), Atlantic Dermatology Soc. (bd. dirs. 1995); N.Y. State Med. Soc. (health care delivery sys.). Avocation: golf. E-mail: rfeinstein@pol.net.

FEINSTEIN, ROCHELLE, artist, educator; BFA, Pratt Inst., 1975; MFA, U. Minn., 1978. Represented by Max Protetch Gallery, N.Y.C.; tchr. Bennington Coll., 1979—94; assoc. prof. painting, printmaking Yale U., 1994—98, prof. painting and printmaking, 1998—. Participant pub. arts project CETA/N.Y. Artists Program, 1978—79. Represented in permanent collections Mus. Modern Art. Nat. Endowment for the Arts grantee, 1990, Joan Mitchell Found. grantee, 1994, John Simon Guggenheim Meml. Found. fellow, 1996. Office: Yale U Sch Art PO Box 208339 New Haven CT 06520-8339*

FEINTUCH, HENRY PHILIP, public relations executive; b. Bklyn. BA, Bklyn. Coll. TV and Radio, 1976. Anchorperson, reporter Stas. WMTR and WDHA-FM, N.J.; news editor Sta. WCBS-TV, N.Y.C.; pub. rels. sr. acct. exec. Paul Kaufman Assocs., N.Y.C., Booke and Co., N.Y.C.; dir. corp. comm. Ring Group N.Am., N.Y.C., 1985-86; mng. ptnr. KCSA Pub. Rels., N.Y.C., 1987—. Office: KCSA Pub Rels 800 2nd Ave New York NY 10017-4709 E-mail: hfeintuch@kcsa.com.

FEIR, DOROTHY JEAN, entomologist, educator, physiologist; b. St. Louis, Jan. 29, 1929; d. Alex R. and Lillian (Smith) F. BS, U. Mich., 1950; MS, U. Wyo., 1956; PhD, U. Wis., 1960. Instr. biology U. Buffalo, 1960-61; mem. faculty St. Louis U., 1961—, prof. biology, 1967-99, prof. biology emeritus, 1999—. Mem. tropical medicine and parasitology study sect. NIH, 1980-84 Editor Environ. Entomology, 1977-84; mem. editl. bd. Jour. Med. Entomology, 1995-99, chair editl. bd., 1999. Fellow Entomol. Soc. Am. (pres.-elect 1987-88, pres. 1988-89, Riley Achievement award north ctrl. br. 1993), Mo. Acad. Sci. (v.p. 1987-88, pres.-elect 1988-89, pres. 1989-90, Most Disting. Scientist award 1995); mem. AAAS, Am. Physiol. Soc., N.Y. Acad. Sci., Phi Beta Kappa, Sigma Xi. E-mail: feirdj@slu.edu.

FEIRER, ALAN DAVID, music educator, organizational development consultant; b. Neenah, Wis., Jan. 7, 1969; s. Sally Lynn and David Michael Wilke (Stepfather), David Karl Feirer; m. Julie Lynn Trask, July 12, 1997; 1 child, Mara Lynn. MusB in Edn., Wartburg Coll., Waverly, Iowa, 1991; MusM in Edn., U. of No. Iowa, Cedar Falls, 2003. Band dir. Sumner Cmty. Schs., Iowa, 1995—99, Winterset (Iowa) H.S., 1999—. Orgnl. devel. cons., pub. spkr. Group Dynamic, Winterset, 1998—. Author: (paper) A Review of Research Pertaining to Student Dropout from Instrumental Music Programs; contbr. papers to rsch. publs. (selected for presentation at the Iowa Music Edn. Assn. ann. conf., 2003). Recipient Leadership Inst. fellowship, Iowa Alliance for Arts Edn., 2001. Mem.: Iowa Bandmasters Assn. (Class 1A Honor Band 1997). Democrat. Lutheran. Achievements include research in Only comprehensive literature review on the topic of public school students discontinuing instrumental music instruction. Avocations: competitive Scrabble, running, cooking, travel, trivia. Office: Winterset H S 624 W Husky Dr Winterset IA 50273 Home: 212 N 14th Ave Winterset IA 50273 Office Phone: 515-462-3320. Personal E-mail: alandf@mchsi.com.

FEIRSON, STEVEN B., lawyer; b. Bklyn., June 6, 1950; s. Aaron M. and Gertrude Feirson. BA, U. Pa., 1972; JD, U. Chgo., 1975. Bar: Pa. 1975, U.S. Dist. Ct. (ea. dist.) Pa. 1975, U.S. Dist. Ct. (ea. dist.) Mich. 1996, U.S. Ct. Appeals (3d cir.) 1976, U.S. Ct. Appeals (2d and 9th cirs.) 1990, U.S. Ct. Appeals (8th cir.) 1992, U.S. Ct. Appeals (6th cir.) 1994, U.S. Ct. Appeals (5th cir.) 2003, U.S. Supreme Ct. 1980. Assoc. Dechert LLP, Phila., 1975-83, ptnr., 1983—. Mem.: Phila. Bar Assn. Office: Dechert LLP 4000 Bell Atlantic Tower 1717 Arch St Lbby 3 Philadelphia PA 19103-2713 Office Phone: 215-994-2489.

FEISEL, LYLE DEAN, retired dean, electrical engineer, educator; b. Tama, Iowa, Oct. 16, 1935; s. Clyde Edward and Clara Maria (Ehlers) F.; m. Dorothy Evelyn Stadsvold, June 15, 1957; children: Patricia, Margaret, Kenneth. BSEE, Iowa State U., 1961, MSEE, 1963, PhD in Elec. Engring., 1964. Registered profl. engr., S.D. Engr. Honeywell, Mpls., 1961-62; staff engr. IBM Corp., Poughkeepsie, NY, 1963, Burlington, Vt., 1967; mem. faculty of elec. engring. S.D. Sch. of Mines, Rapid City, 1964-83, head elec. engring. dept., 1975-83; dean Watson Sch. SUNY, Binghamton, 1983—2001. Vis. prof. Cheng Kung U., Tainan, Taiwan, 1969-70; rsch. engr. Northrop Corp., L.A., 1974; Wachmeister prof. engring. Va. Mil. Inst., 1982; mem. engring. accreditation commn. Accreditation Bd. Engring. and Tech., 1987-92, bd. dirs., 1992-97. Nat. Def. fellow, 1961-64; recipient profl. achievement citation Iowa State U., 1984, Ednl. Achievement award N.Y. State Soc. Profl. Engrs., 1989. Fellow IEEE (pres. edn. soc. 1978-79, v.p. ednl. activities 2000-02, Meritorious Svc. award, Ben Dasher award 1983, Centennial medal 1984, Ronald J. Schmitz award 1989, achievement award Edn. Soc. 1999, Third Millennium medal 2000), Nat. Soc. Profl. Engrs. (Achievement award 2002) Am. Soc. Engring. Edn. (bd. dirs. 1982-83, 94-99, pres. 1997-98); mem. S.D. Renewable Energy Assn. (pres. 1979-81, N.Y. State Engr. of Yr. 2000), Tau Beta Pi (Disting. Alumnus award 2002), Eta Kappa Nu Assn. (bd. govs. 2004-). Democrat. Lutheran. Address: PO Box 839 Saint Michaels MD 21663 E-mail: l.feisel@ieee.org.

FEISEL, LYLE DEAN, lawyer; b. Boston, Dec. 14, 1918; s. Edward Barton and Jeannette (Thomas) C.; m. Elizabeth Ann Parker, Sept. 6, 1940; children: Allan M., Elizabeth M. BA, Yale U., 1940; JD, Harvard U., 1943. Bar: Mass. 1943. Of counsel Warner & Stackpole LLP now Kirkpatrick & Lockhart LLP, Boston, 1954—. Chmn. bd. dirs. H.B. Smith Co., Inc.; pres., trustee emeritus Phillips Acad.; chmn. emeritus, trustee Mass. Eye and Ear Infirmary and Found. Hon. dir. Chewonki Found. Inc.; chmn. Yale U. Planned Giving; trustee Sturbridge Village; mem. leadership coun. New Bedford Whaling Mus.; mem. state adv. com. Salvation Army; v.p. Polly Hill Found. Fellow Am. Bar Found., Mass. Bar Found.; mem. ABA, Boston Bar Assn., Mass. Bar Assn., Internat. Bar Assn., Edgartown Yacht Club. Home: 15 Traill St Cambridge MA 02138-4738 E-mail: mchapin@kl.com.

FEIT, BARBERI PAULL, composer, lyricist, psychotherapist, writer; b. N.Y.C., July 27, 1949; d. S. Paull and Alyce (Togniere) Platt; m. Glenn M. Feit, May 24, 1975. Diploma, Juilliard Sch. Music, N.Y.C., 1972; BS, NYU, 1979, MS, 1980. Dir. Barberi Paull Musical Theatre, 1969-75; pvt. practice psychotherapy N.Y.C., 1980—. Studied with Pulitzer prize winning composers Charles Wuorinen and Jacob Druckman; gen. asst. to Mme. Koussevitzky at Tanglewood and asst. condr. to Leonard Bernstein, 1972—74; founder Illumina, Inc.; creator Illumina, Inc. Imprint; co-founder The Barberi Paull Feit and Glenn Martin Feit Charitable Trust; e-newsletter pub. theloveletter-.net. Composer: The American Dream, I Have a Dream, Believe, Celebration, Angel Music, electronic ballets, music for films, A Christmas Carol and Close to the Sky, tours, 1952—63; author: Le Petit Foret, 1999, The Angel Chronicles, 2002, Love and Dreams, 2005, Love for All Time; developer (e-newsletter pub. in print) theloveletter.net, 1990, (e-newsletter pub. online), 1998. Named "Meet the Composer" honoree and internat. tours, 1972—80, scores and memorabilia selected for inclusion in the Am. Heritage Archive, 1975—; recipient Lehman Engles BMI Musical Theatre Workshop fellow, 1972—73, Dellus award, 1979; Nat. Endowment for the Arts fellow, 1982. Mem.: ASCAP (awards 1980—), The Century Assn., Hort. Soc. N.Y. (vice-chmn.), The Met. Opera Club, Mus. City of N.Y. (vice-chmn.), The Doubles Club. Avocations: interior design, yachting, gardening, French culture and language. Home: PO Box 1906 Bridgehampton NY 11932-1906 Office: One Lincoln Plz # 33K New York NY 10023 Office Phone: 212-799-4192, 212-799-4192. Personal E-mail: barberi27@aol.com.

FEIT, GLENN M., lawyer; b. Elizabeth, N.J., Oct. 16, 1929; s. Charles Theodore and Beatrice (Esther) F.; m. Rona F. Gottlieb, June 14, 1953 (div. 1974); children: Glenn M., John Paul, Adam Gibbs (dec.); m. Barberi Platt Paull. BS in Econ., U. Pa., 1951; JD magna cum laude, Harvard U., 1957. Bar: N.Y. 1958, U.S. Dist. Ct. (2d dist.) 1959). Assoc. Cravath, Swaine & Moore, N.Y.C., 1957-64; ptnr. London, Buttenwieser & Chalif, N.Y.C., 1965-70, Feit & Ahrens, N.Y.C., 1970-88, Feit & Shor, N.Y.C., 1988-89, Proskauer Rose LLP, N.Y.C., 1989—. Bd. dirs. Blair Industries, Inc., Scott City, Mo.; sec. Charterhouse Group Internat., Inc., N.Y.C. Mem. editl. bd. Harvard Law Rev., 1955-57. Bd. dirs. Friends of the IDF, N.Y.C. Lt. USN, 1951-54. Mem. ABA, Assn. Bar City N.Y., Aircraft Owners and Pilots Assn., Exptl. Aircraft Assn., Tailhook Assn., Harvard Club, Seaplane Pilots Assn., N.Y. Yacht Club, Doubles. Office: Proskauer Rose LLP 1585 Broadway New York NY 10036-8299 Business E-mail: gfeit@proskauer.com.

FEITH, DOUGLAS JAY, former federal agency administrator; b. Phila., July 16, 1953; s. Dalck and Rose (Bankel) F.; m. Tatyana Belenky, July 8, 1979. AB magna cum laude, Harvard Coll., 1975; JD magna cum laude, Georgetown U., 1978. Bar: D.C. 1978. Assoc. Fried, Frank, Harris, Shriver and Kampelman, Washington, 1978-81; staff mem. NSC, Washington, 1981-82; spl. counsel to asst. sec. def. for internat. security U.S. Dept. Def., Washington, 1982-84, dep. asst. sec. def. for negotiations policy, 1984-86, under sec. for policy, 2001—05; mng. atty. Feith and Zell, P.C., Washington, 1986—2001. Bd. dirs. Ctr. for Security Policy, Washington, 1988—. Mem. Coun. Fgn. Rels.

FEITO, JOSE, architect; b. Havana, Cuba, Jan. 30, 1929; arrived in U.S., 1961; s. Jose and Hermina (Mayo) F.; m. Bertha A. Abascal, Oct. 7, 1995; children: Patricia Maria, Maria Esther, Jose Alfonso, Sergio P. (dec.). MArch, U. Havana, 1954. Registered arch., Fla. Prin. J. Feito Archs., Havana, 1954-60; assoc. J. DeHaro Archs., Madrid, 1960-61; ptnr. Ferendino et al, Miami, Fla., 1966-79; prin. F&F Archs. and Planners, Miami, 1979-80, F&F Fraga and Feito Archs., Miami, 1980—. Pres. Professio Inc., Miami, 1983-84. Bd. dirs. Dade Co. Shoreline Com., 1986—; chmn. Gov.'s com. for Handicapped, Miami, 1973-75; trustee United Way, Miami, 1979-84. Recipient Meritorious Svcs. citation Gov.'s Com. for Handicapped, 1975. Fellow AIA (pres. Miami South chpt. 1977, Honor award 1985); mem. Fla. Assn. AIA (bd. dirs. 1978, Excellence award 1985), Interam. Businessmen's Assn. (pres. 1978-80), Cuba Soc. Archs. (Gold medal 1957), Cuban Mus. Arts and Culture (founder), Greater Miami C. of C. (mem. bd. govs. 1978-83). Republican. Roman Catholic. Avocations: history, tennis, sailing. Office: F&F Fraga & Feito Archs 2151 NW 93rd Ave Doral FL 33172-4804 Office Phone: 305-591-8006. E-mail: ffarchit@bellsouth.net.

FEJER, MARTIN M., physics professor; BA in Physics, Cornell U., 1977; PhD in Applied Physics, Stanford U., 1986. Acting asst. prof. applied physics Stanford (Calif.) U., 1986-89, asst. prof. applied physics, 1989-93, rsch. assoc. phys. sci., 1993-94, assoc. prof., 1994-2000, prof., 2000—, chair applied physics, 2002—, co-dir. Stanford Photonics Rsch. Ctr. Fellow Optical Soc. Am. (W.R. Wood prize 1998); mem. IEEE, Am. Phys. Soc. Achievements include research on nonlinear optical materials and devices, guided waveoptics, microstructured ferroelectrics and semiconductors, photorefractive phenomena, optical characterization of materials and material synthesis processes. Office: Stanford U EL Ginzton Lab 316 Via Pueblo Mall Stanford CA 94305-4085 E-mail: fejer@stanford.edu.

FEJER, T. WILLIAM, musician, composer, architect, furniture designer; b. L.A., Sept. 18, 1940; s. Andrew A. and Edith (Behal) F.; divorced; children: Tony (Stephen), Andrew. BS in Architecture, Ill. Inst. Tech., 1964, MS, 1967. Exhibit designer 20th century Art Inst. Chgo., 1962-67; archtl. draftsman Mies Van de Rohe, Chgo., 1964-66; design architect Skidmore, Owings & Merrill, Chgo., 1966-68; mng. dir. Evanston (Ill.) Art Ctr., 1970-72; instr. architecture Ill. Inst. Tech., Chgo., 1967-74; nat. designer, advt. mgr. Plastofilm, Chgo., 1974-84; creative dir. Design Prodns., Chgo., 1984-87; staff pianist Nordstrom, Schaumburg, Ill., 1993—97; CEO Live From Chgo., 1968—. Co-dir., chief composer Anderson/Fejer Musicals, Round Lake, Ill., 1996—; ofcl. pianist Boy Scouts Am., Chgo., 1990—; entertainment coord. Internat. Press Club Chgo., 1992-96; theme composer Little City Found., Chgo., 1992; founder No One You Know Found., 2005— Designer contemporary furniture; composer: (musical comedy) Menage A Trois, 1997. Spl. occasion pianist Unitarian Ch., Chgo., 1987—97; vol. entertainment chair Woodfield Area Charitable Orgn., Schaumburg, 1994—97; founder No One You Know Found., 2005. Recipient Outstanding Archtl. Design award Women's Archtl. League, 1963. Mem. Internat. Press Club Chgo. (cartoonist), Gulf Jazz Soc., Phi Gamma Delta. Avocations: art collecting, photography, skiing, sailing, golf. Home: 1836 N East Ave Lot 24 Panama City FL 32405-6258 E-mail: ruthswritings@aol.com.

FEKETY, ROBERT, physician, educator; b. Pitts., June 29, 1929; s. Francis Robert and Grace (McShaffery) F.; m. Nancy Jane Baker, June 24, 1954; children: Susan Elizabeth, Sally Jane. AB, Wesleyan U., 1951; MD, Yale U., 1955. Instr. dept. medicine Johns Hopkins U., Balt., 1960-64, asst. prof., 1964-67; assoc. prof. medicine U. Mich., Ann Arbor, 1967-71, chief div. infectious diseases, 1967-95, prof. medicine, 1971-95, prof. medicine emeritus, 1995—; prof. epidemiology, 1987-95; active emeritus prof. medicine U. Mich., Ann Arbor, 1995—. Sr. asst. surgeon USPHS, 1956-58. Fellow ACP, Infectious Diseases Soc. Am. (councillor). Roman Catholic. Home: 812 Berkshire Rd Ann Arbor MI 48104-2631 Office: Univ Mich Hosp 3116 Taubman Ctr Ann Arbor MI 48109 Fax: 734-747-9965. E-mail: rfekety@umich.edu.

FELCH, WILLIAM CAMPBELL, internist, editor; b. Lakewood, Ohio, Nov. 14, 1920; s. Don Harold Willison and Beth (Campbell) Felch; m. Nancy Cook Dean, Aug. 4, 1945; children: Patricia, William Campbell, Robert Dean. BA, Princeton U., 1942; MD, Columbia U., 1945. Diplomate Nat. Bd. Med. Examiners, Am. Bd. Internal Medicine. Intern St. Luke's Hosp., N.Y.C., 1945—46, resident in internal medicine, 1948—51; pvt. practice specializing in internal medicine Rye, NY, 1951—88; chief staff United Hosp., Port Chester, NY, 1975—77; med. dir. Osborn Home, Rye, NY, 1979—88; exec. v.p. Alliance for Continuing Med. Edn., 1978—91. Author: Aspiration and Achievement, 1981, Decade of Decision, 1989, Vision for the Future, 1992, The Secrets of Good Patient Care, Thoughts on Medicine for the 21st Century, 1996, Alliance for Continuing Medical Education: The First 20 Years, 1996; editor: The Internist, 1975—86, ACME Almanac, 1978—91, Jour. of Continuing Edn. in Health Professions, 1992—95; co-editor: Continuing Med. Edn.: A Primer, 2d edit., 1991. Trustee N.Y. Med. Coll., Valhalla, 1971—73. Capt. U.S. Army, 1946—48. Named Internist of Distinction, Internal Medicine Soc. N.Y. County, 1973; recipient award of merit, N.Y. State Soc. Internal Medicine, 1976, Disting. Svc. award, Alliance for Continuing Med. Edn., Founder's medal, 1995. Mem.: AMA (chmn. coun. on legislation 1977—79), ACP, Inst. of Medicine NAS, Am. Soc. Internal Medicine (pres. 1973—74), Alliance for Continuing Med. Edn. (exec. v.p. 1978—91). Home: 8545 Carmel Valley Rd Carmel CA 93923 Personal E-mail: srfelch@comcast.net.

FELD, ALAN DAVID, lawyer; b. Dallas, Nov. 13, 1936; s. Henry R. and Rose (Scissors) F.; m. Anne Sanger, June 1, 1957; children: Alan David, Elizabeth S., John L. BA, So. Methodist U., 1957, LL.B., 1960. Bar: Tex. 1960. Since practiced in Dallas; from ptnr. to chmn. bd. Akin, Gump, Hauer, Strauss & Feld, Dallas, 1960-96, sr. exec. ptnr., 1996—. Lectr. Southwestern U. Med. Sch.; chmn. Tex. State Securities Bd. 1985-1991; bd. dirs. Clear Channel Comms., Inc., Ctr. Point Properties, Inc. Contbr. articles to legal jours. Trustee AMR Advaantage Funds, So. Meth. U.; bd. dirs. Dallas Day Nursery Assn., Timberlawn Found., Dallas Symphony Orch. Mem.: ABA, Dallas Bar Assn., D.C. Bar Assn., Tex. Bar Assn., Dallas Country Club, Royal Oaks Country Club (corr.), Salesmanship Club, Phi Delta Phi. Office: Akin Gump Strauss Hauer & Feld 1700 Pacific Ave Ste 4100 Dallas TX 75201-4675 Office Phone: 214-969-2712. Business E-Mail: afeld@akingump.com.

FELD, CAROLE LESLIE, marketing executive; b. L.A., Nov. 12, 1955; d. Harold Brenman and Phyllis Pearl (Fishman) F.; m. David C. Levy; 1 child, Alexander Wolf Levy. BA, U. Calif., Berkeley, 1979; MBA, U. So. Calif., 1982. Mgr. rsch. Columbia Pictures, L.A., 1982-83; dir. promotion and field pub. Tri-Star Pictures, N.Y.C., 1983-86; dir. promotion and retention mktg. Home Box Office, N.Y.C., 1987-92; v.p. promotion and advt. Pub. Broadcasting Svc., Washington, 1992-97, sr. v.p. advt., promotion and corp. communications, 1995-99, sr. v.p. comms. and brand mgmt., 1999-2000; v.p. brand mktg. The Motley Fool, Washington, 2000—01, mktg. cons., 2002—03; prin. Giving Tree Group, Washington, 2003—. Pres. CINE; cons. New Sch. Beacons in Jazz Program, N.Y.C., 1990—. Named one of Mktgs. Top 100 Advertising Age, 1995. Avocations: skiing, travel, art, film. Business E-Mail: carole@givingtreegroup.com.

FELD, CHARLES S., information technology executive; BA in econ., City Coll. NY. Systems engr. IBM, 1970—81; chief info. officer Frito-Lay, 1981—92; CEO, pres., founder The Feld Group, 1992—2004; chief info. officer Delta Air Lines, 1997—2000; acting chief info. officer First Data Resources, 2000—02; exec. v.p. portfolio mgmt. EDS, Plano, Tex., 2004—. Recipient Chief Info. Officer Yr., State of Ga., 1998, Smithsonian award for Tech. Excellence, 2000. Office: EDS Corp HQ 5400 Legacy Dr Plano TX 75024 Office Phone: 972-604-6000. Office Fax: 972-605-6033.

FELD, ELIOT, dancer, choreographer, performing company executive; b. Bklyn., July 5, 1942; s. Benjamin Noah and Alice (Posner) Feld. Student, High Sch. Performing Arts, N.Y.C., 1954-58; DFA (hon.), Juilliard Sch., 1991. Artistic dir. Ballet Tech, NYC. Dancer child prince The Nutcracker, NYC Ballet, 1954, West Side Story, 1958, Donald McKayle Co., Sophie Maslow Co., Pearl Lang Co., Mary Anthony Co., I Can Get It for You Wholesale, 1962, Fiddler on the Roof, Am. Ballet Theatre, 1963, Les Noces, Wind in the Mountains, Dark Elegies, Fancy Free, Billy the Kid, Helen of Troy, Giselle, choreographer Am. Ballet Theatre, ., Royal Danish Ballet, Nat. Ballet of Can., NYC Ballet, Harbinger, 1967, At Midnight, 1967, Meadowlark, 1968, Intermezzo, 1969, Cortege Burlesque, 1969, Pagan Spring, 1969, Early Songs, 1970, Cortege Parisien, 1970, Consort, 1970, A Poem Forgotten, 1970, Romance, 1971, Theatre, 1971, The Gods Amused, 1971, A Soldier's Tale, 1971, Eccentrique, 1971, Winters Court, 1972, Jive, 1973, Sephardic Song, 1974, Tzaddik, 1974, The Real McCoy, 1974, Mazurka, 1975, Excursions, 1975, Impromptu, 1976, Variations on 'America', 1977, A Footstep of Air, 1977, Santa Fe Saga, 1978, La Vida, 1978, Danzon Cubano, 1978, Half-Time, 1978, Papillon, 1979, Circa, 1980, Anatomic Balm, 1980, Scenes, 1980, Play Bach, 1981, Song of Norway, 1981, Over the Pavement, 1982, Straw Hearts, 1983, Summer's Lease, 1983, Three Dances, 1983, Adieu, 1984, The Jig Is Up, 1984, Moon Skate, 1984, Intermezzo No. 2, 1985, Against the Sky, 1985, The Grand Canyon, 1985, Aurora I, 1985, Aurora II, 1985, Medium: Rare, 1985, Echo, 1986, Bent Planes, 1986, Skara Brae, 1986, Embraced Waltzes, 1987, A Dance for Two, 1987, Shadow's Breath, 1987, Petipa Notwithstanding, 1988, Kore, 1988, The Unanswered Question, 1988, Asia, 1988, Love Song Waltzes, 1988, Ah Scarlatti, 1989, Mother Nature, 1989, Contra Pose, 1990, Charmed Lives, 1990, Ion, 1990, Fauna, 1990, Common Ground, 1991, Savage Glance, 1991, Clave, 1991, Evoe, 1991, Endsong, 1991, Wolfgang Strategies, 1992, To the Naked Eye, 1992, Hello Fancy, 1992, Frets and Women, 1992, Hadji, 1992, Blooms Wake, 1993, The Relative Disposition of the Parts, 1993, Doo Dah Day, 1993, MRI, 1993, Doghead & Godcatchers, 1994, 23 Skidoo, 1994, Gnossiennes, 1994, Ogive, 1994, Chi, 1994, Ludwig Gambits, 1995, Tongue and Groove, 1995,

Meshugana Dance, 1996, Paean, 1996, Paper Tiger, 1996, Shuffle, 1996, Industry, 1996, Evening Chant, 1996, Jukebox, 1997, Re:X, 1997, Yo Shakespeare, 1997, Joggers, 1997, Umbra Rumba, 1997, Yo Johann, 1997, The Last Sonata, 1997, Simon Sez, 1998, Cherokee Rose, 1999, Mending, 1999, Felix: the ballet, 1999, Apple Pie, 1999, Nodrog Doggo, 2000, Coup de Couperin, 2000, Organon, 2001, Pacific Dances, 2001, Skandia, 2002, Pianola: Raven, 2002, Lincoln Portrait, 2002, Behold the Man, 2002, (ballets) Pianola: Indigo, 2002, Mr. XY2, 2003, French Overtures, 2003. Recipient Dance Mag. award, 1990. Office: Ballet Tech 890 Broadway Fl 8 New York NY 10003-1211 Office Fax: 212-353-0936. E-mail: staff@ballettech.org.*

FELD, FRANKLIN FRED, lawyer, accountant; b. Bklyn., July 17, 1923; BBA, CCNY, 1947; LLD, Seton Hall U., 1961. Bar: N.J. 1963, U. S. Dist. Ct. N.J. 1963, U.S. Tax Ct. 1963; CPA, N.J. Pvt. practice acctg., New Brunswick, N.J., 1950-55; ptnr. Feld & Beck, CPAs, New Brunswick, 1955-78; pvt. practice law New Brunswick, 1963-78; pvt. practice law and acctg. Highland Park, 1978-94; ptnr. Feld & Rathjen, 1994—. Asst. law dir. City of New Brunswick, 1968-74; dist. supr. inheritance tax bur. N.J. Dept. Taxation, New Brunswick, 1974-89. Mem. N.J. Bar Assn., Middlesex County Bar Assn. (pres. 1987-88), Am. Assn. Atty. CPAs. Avocations: tennis, swimming, reading. Office: 321 Raritan Ave Highland Park NJ 08904-2701

FELD, JOSEPH, construction executive; b. NYC, June 25, 1919; s. Morris David and Golda (London) F.; m. Doris Rabinor (dec.); 1 child, Elaine Susan; m. Mairuth Hirsch Maloney, July 25, 1999. Student, CCNY, 1946—47. Builder housing, apt. projects, L.I., N.Y.C., N.J., 1948-54; pres. Kohl and Feld, Inc., builder housing devels., Rockland County, N.Y., 1955-57, Feld Constrn. Corp., New City, N.Y., 1957—, Birchland Constrn. Corp., 1957-70, Ramapo Towers, Inc., 1963-83. Vice-chmn. People's Nat. Bank Rockland County, Monsey, N.Y., 1974-85. Mem. Clarkstown Bldg. Code Com., 1959; mem. indsl. devel. adv. com. Rockland County Bd. Suprs., 1969-71; chmn. housing adv. coun. Rockland County Legislature, 1976-86; chmn. Housing Task Force, 1979-80; mem., past pres. Men's Club; mem. Rockland County coun. Jewish War Vets., past commdr. New City post. Staff sgt. AUS, 1941-45. Mem. Rockland County Assn., Inc. (former bd. dir.), Rockland County Home Builders Assn. (past pres., bd. dirs., chmn. rental housing com.), Nat. Assn. Home Builders (past bd. dirs., mem. rental housing com.), N.Y. State Assn. Home Builders (past dir., mem. rental housing com.), Rockland County Apt. Owners Assn. (pres., bd. dirs. 1971-94), Rockland County Bd. Realtors, N.Y. State Assn. Realtors (past dirs.), Masons, Lions (local pres. 1959-60, zone chmn. 1961-62). Home: 901 E Camino Real Apt 6C Boca Raton FL 33432-6344 Personal E-mail: bocamanj@aol.com.

FELD, KAREN IRMA, columnist, journalist, commentator, speech professional; b. Washington, Aug. 23; d. Irvin and Adele Ruth (Schwartz) F. BA, Am. U. Columnist, reporter Roll Call Newspaper, Washington; nat. pub. rels. coord. Ringling Bros./Barnum & Bailey Circus, Washington; publicist Twentieth Century Fox, L.A.; pub. rels. account exec. Harshe, Rotman & Druck, L.A.; freelance writer, broadcaster; corr. People mag., Washington, 1980-85; adj. instr. Kent State U. Pol. Campaign Mgmt. Inst., 1981; broadcaster Voice of Am., 1984; columnist, contbg. editor Capitol Hill mag., Washington, 1980-89; columnist Washington Times, 1986-87, Universal Press Syndicate, 1988-89, Creators Syndicate, 1989-90; syndicated columnist Capital Connections, 1990—; Prodigy polit. columnist, 1990-93. Radio/TV commentator syndicated radio segment Radio America, 1993—; syndicated columnist Nat. Post, 1998-99; Washington editor Delta Shuttle Sheet, 2000-05; columnist Washington Examiner, 2005—; lectr. in field, 1990—. Contbr. articles to Parade mag., People mag., Money mag., Time mag., Vogue mag., George, USA Weekend, Family Circle, others. Recipient Health Journalism award Am. Chiropractic Assn., 1991. Mem. AFTRA/SAG, Nat. Fedn. Press Women (Excellence in Journalism award 1984-2004), Capital Press Women (v.p. 1985-91, Excellence in Journalism award 1984-2004, Entrepreneur/Communicator of Yr. 1995), Am. Soc. Journalists and Authors (award), N.Am. Travel Journalists Assn. (Best Mag. Feature award 2003), Nat. Press Club, Capitol Hill Club, Woodmont Country Club (Rockville, Md.), U.S. Senate Press Gallery, White House Corr. Assn., Soc. Profl. Journalists (bd. dirs., v.p. chpt., Editl. Writing award 2004). Jewish. Office: 1698 32nd St NW Washington DC 20007-2969 Office Phone: 202-337-2044. Personal E-mail: buzz@karenfeld.com.

FELD, MICHAEL STEPHEN, physics professor; b. N.Y.C., Nov. 11, 1940; s. Albert and Lillian R. Norwalk; children: David A., Jonathan R., Alexandra A. SB in Humanities and Sci., SM in Physics, MIT, 1963; PhD in Physics, M.I.T., 1967. Postdoctoral fellow MIT, Cambridge, 1967-68, asst. prof., 1968-73, assoc. prof., 1973-79, prof. physics, 1979—, dir. George R. Harrison Spectroscopy Lab., 1976—, dir. Laser Research Ctr., 1979—; dir. Laser Biomed. Research Ctr., 1985—. Co-editor: Fundamental and Applied Laser Physics, 1973, Coherent Nonlinear Optics, 1980. Alfred P. Sloan rsch. fellow, 1973; recipient Disting. Svc. award MIT Minority Cmty., 1980, Gordon Y. Billard award, 1982, Thompson award Spectrochimica Acta, 1991, Vinci d'Excellence, France, 1995, Disting. Baltzer Colloquim spkr. Princeton U., 1996, Lamb medal Physics of Quantum Electronics Soc., 2003. Fellow: AAAS, Am. Optical Soc., Am. Phys. Soc., Am. Soc. Laser Medicine and Surgery (bd. dirs.), Sigma Xi. Home: 66 Dunster Rd Jamaica Plain MA 02130 Office: MIT George R Harrison Spectroscopy Lab 77 Massachusetts Ave Cambridge MA 02139-4307 Business E-Mail: msfeld@mit.edu.

FELDBAUM, CARL, biotechnologist; B in Biology, Princeton U.; grad. in Law, U. Pa. Asst. spl. prosecutor, Washington, 1973; chief of staff to Senator Arlen Specter (Rep.-Pa.); pres., founder Palomar Corp., Washington; asst. to Sec. of Energy; insp. gen. for def. intelligence U.S. DOD; pres. Biotech. Industry Orgn., Washington. Author: Looking the Tiger in the Eye: Confronting the Nuclear Threat, 1988 (Christopher medal, 1988, N.Y. Times Notable Book of Yr., 1988). Recipient Disting. Civilian Svc. medal, Def. Sec. Harold Brown, 1979. Office: Biotech Industry Orgn Ste 400 1225 Eye St NW Washington DC 20005

FELDBERG, HARLEY, marketing professional; B in history and polit. sci., U. Md. Sales mgr. Time Electronics, Balt., 1982, v.p. sales and mktg.; served as pres. of the interconnect, passive, and electromechanical product bus. group Avnet, Inc., 1996—99, named pres. and dir. Avnet Electronics mktg. Americas' product bus. groups, 1999—2002; corp. v.p. Avnet, Inc., 1999; pres. Avnet Electronics mktg. Asia Avnet, Inc., 2001—02; pres. Avnet Electronics Mktg. Am., Phoenix, 2002—. Office: Avnet Inc 2211 S 47th St Phoenix AZ 85034

FELDBERG, MEYER, investment advisor, university dean emeritus; b. Johannesburg, Mar. 17, 1942; s. Leon and Sarah (Kretzmer) F.; m. Barbara Erlick, Aug. 9, 1965; children: Lewis Robert, Ilana. BA, Witwatersrand U., Johannesburg, 1962; MBA, Columbia U., 1965; PhD, Cape Town (South Africa) U., 1969. Product mgr. B.F. Goodrich Co., Akron, Ohio, 1965-67; dean Grad. Sch. Bus., U. Cape Town, 1968-79; assoc. dean J.L. Kellogg Sch. Mgmt., Northwestern U., Evanston, Ill., 1979-81; prof., dean Sch. Bus., Tulane U., New Orleans, 1981-86; pres. Ill. Inst. Tech., Chgo., 1986-89, chmn. bd. govs. Rsch. Inst.; dean Grad. Sch. Bus. Columbia U., NYC, 1989—2004, Sanford C. Bernstein prof. leadership and ethics, 2003—04; sr. advisor Morgan Stanley, 2004—. Bd. dirs. Federated Dept. Stores, UBS Funds, Revlon, Inc., Primedia Inc., Sappi Ltd.; vis. prof. MIT, 1974, Cranfield Inst. Tech., 1970, 76. Author: Organizational Behaviour: Text and Cases, 1975; contbr. articles to profl. jours. Named Jaycee Young Man of Yr., 1972 Mem. Univ. Club (N.Y.C. and Chgo.), Econ. Club (N.Y.C. and Chgo.). Office: Columbia Bus Sch 33 W 60th St 7th Fl New York NY 10023 Office Phone: 212-761-7400. Business E-Mail: meyer.feldberg@morganstanley.com.

FELDBERG, MICHAEL SVETKEY, lawyer; b. Boston, May 21, 1951; s. Sumner Lee Feldberg and Eunice (Svetkey) Cohen; m. Ruth Lazarus, Sept. 23, 1978; children: Rachel, Jesse, Ben. BA, Harvard U., 1973, JD, 1977. Bar: N.Y. 1978, U.S. Dist. Ct. (ea. and so. dists.) N.Y. 1978, U.S. Ct. Appeals (2d cir.) 1983, U.S. Supreme Ct. 1994. Assoc. Orans, Elsen, Polstein & Naftalis, N.Y.C., 1977—80; asst. U.S. atty. So. Dist. of N.Y., N.Y.C., 1981—84; ptnr. Shea & Gould, N.Y.C., 1985—91, Schulte Roth & Zabel, N.Y.C., 1991—2003; ptnr., head U.S. Litig. Allen & Overy, N.Y.C., 2003—. Dir. Facing History and Ourselves. Bd. dirs. 92d St. YMCA, N.Y.C. Mem. Assn. Bar City N.Y. (criminal law com., com. on the judiciary, com. on profl. responsibility), Facing History and Ourselves Office: Allen & Overy 1221 Avenue of the Americas New York NY 10020 Office Phone: 212-610-6360. E-mail: michael.feldberg@allenovery.com.

FELDBERG, SUMNER LEE, retired retail executive; b. Boston, June 19, 1924; s. Morris and Anna (Marnoy) F.; married; children: Michael S., Ellen R.; stepchildren: Mollye S., Beth, James. BA, Harvard, 1947, MBA, 1949. With New England Trading Corp., 1949-56; treas. Zayre Corp., 1956-73, sr. v.p., 1965-68, exec. v.p., 1969-73, chmn. bd., 1973-87; chmn. exec. com. Zayre Corp. (name now TJX Cos., Inc.), 1987-89; chmn. bd. B.J.'s Wholesale Club, 1989-96, TJX Cos., Inc., Framingham, Mass., 1989-95. Trustee Beth Israel Hosp., Combined Jewish Philanthropies of Greater Boston. Served to 1st lt. USAAF, 1943-46. Office: 770 Cochituate Rd Framingham MA 01701-9175 also: PO Box 9175 Framingham MA 01701-9175

FELDER, FRANKIE OTTOWIESS, academic administrator; b. Nuremburg, Germany, Aug. 19, 1950; d. Tyree Preston and Muriel Diggs Felder; 1 child, Ayesha Chevelle Apryl. EdM, U. of Vt., 1972—74, Harvard U., 1982—84, EdD, 1982—86. Counselor, spl. services Va. Commonwealth U., 1978—79; dir. of upward bound Kans. State U., 1979—82; asst. dir. McKnight Programs in Higher Edn. in Fla., Tampa, Fla., 1984—87; assoc. dean of the grad. sch. Clemson U., SC, 1987—, assoc. dean for internat. programs and services, 1987—2003. Consulting/seminar/presentations on issues related to minorities in higher edn. (mentoring, grantwriting, pursuing grad. edn., univ. rsch.) various universities across the country, 1979—. Author: (poetry book) As a Family Thinketh. Mem. Lions Internat., Clemson, SC, 1987—90; dir., African Heritage Day State Fair of Va., Richmond, 1978—78; pres. (then v.p.) Westside H.S. PTSA, Anderson, SC, 1997—2000; leadership trainer Fifth St. Bapt. Ch., Richmond, Va., 1978—79; mem. Richmond Urban League, Va., 1978—79; chairperson Douglas Cmty. Ctr., Manhattan, Kans., 1981—82; mem. and current chairperson Houston Ctr., Clemson, 1988—2003; initiator Boys Club, Clemson, SC, 1988—90. Recipient Positive Image Award, S.E. Region U.S./Newspaper Group, 1992, Academic Affairs Adminstr. of the Yr. for State of SC, S.E./South Regional Assn. of Academic Affairs Administrators, 1996. Mem.: S.C. Women in Higher Edn. (univ. rep.), Nat. Assn. of State Universities and Landgrant Colleges, Assn. of Internat. Edn. Administrators (editor, newsletter 1989—92), Nat. Assn. of Fgn. Student Affairs (regional rep. 1992—94), Nat. Phys. Sci. Consortium, Coun. of So. Grad. Schools (chair, internat. com. 1998—2000). Baptist. Avocations: reading, writing, art, genealogy, music. Office: Clemson U E106 Martin Hall Clemson SC 29634 E-mail: frankie@clemson.edu.

FELDER, RAOUL LIONEL, lawyer; b. Bklyn., May 13, 1934; s. Morris and Millie (Goldstein) F.; m. Myrna Felder, May 26, 1963; children: Rachel, James. BA, NYU, 1955; JD, NYU, Switzerland, 1959; postgrad., U. Bern, Switzerland, 1955-56; hon. degree of fellow in jurisprudence, Oxford U., 1995. Bar: N.Y. 1959, U.S. Dist. Ct. (so. and ea. dists.) N.Y. 1962, U.S. Ct. Appeals (2d cir.) 1962, U.S. Supreme Ct. 1970. Pvt. practice, N.Y.C., 1959-61, 64—; asst. U.S. atty., 1961-64; of counsel Weiss & Handler, P.A., Boca Raton, Fla. Faculty Practicing Law Inst., 1979, Marymount Coll., 1982-85, Ethical Culture Sch., 1981-82; moderator Nat. Conf. on Child Abuse, 1989; apptd. to NYC Cultural Affairs Adv. Commn., 1995-2001, State Commn. on Child Abuse, 1996; bd. dirs. Kidney and Urology; mem. N.Y. State Commn. Judicial Conduct, 2003—. Author: Divorce: The Way Things Are, Not the Way Things Should Be, 1971, Lawyers Practical Handbook to the New Divorce Law, 1981, Lawyer's Guide to Equitable Distribution, 1988, Raoul Felder's Encyclopedia of Matrimonial Clauses, 1990, updated, 1991, Getting Away with Murder, 1996, Restaurant Guide to Los Angeles and New York, 1996, Survival Guide to New York, 1997, Bare Knuckle Negotiation: Savvy Tips and True Stories From the Master of Give and Take, 2004; columnist Fame mag., 1988-92, Am. Women Mag., 1994, N.Y. Daily News Sundays, 1995; contbr. articles to profl. jours. and popular mags.; columnist Am. Spectator Mag, 1999-2001, Washington Times, 1999-2002, Gotham Mag., 2003—; commentator Cable News Network, 1989, BBC World Wide, 1994-95, 97, Crossing the Line (TV series), 1997-99, The Felder Report (TV series), 1998-99, guest commentator Court TV, 1992, bd. advisors, 1992-95, editl. contbr.; (documentary) Survival Guide to New York, 1998; host (TV series) Metrolaw, 1995-97; host (radio) Felder Report, 1997-2002, TalkAmerica; columnist Gotham Mag., 2003—. Mem. Gov.'s Commn. on Child Abuse, 1989; chmn. Nat. Kidney Found. Auction, N.Y. Fund; chmn. dinner Jerusalem Reclamation Project; bd. dirs. Big Apple Greeters, 1997—99, Cop Care, Hosp. Audiences Inc., Nat. Kidney Found., N.Y.C. Econ. Devel. Corp., 2000—03, Kidney and Urology Found. Am., N.Y. Cops Found.; hon. police commr. N.Y. City Police Comms., 2000—; grand marshall U.S.A. Day Washington, Israel Day Parade, N.Y.C.; apptd. Cultural Adv. Commn., N.Y.C., 1994—2001, 2001—02. Named Man of Yr. Bklyn. Sch. for Spl. Children, Met. Geriatric Ctr., Shield Inst., 1997; recipient Defender of Jerusalem medal, 1990, Crimebusters award Take Back N.Y., 1996, Child Abuse Prevention Svc. award, Child Safety Inst. 1998. Mem. ABA (judge nat. finals client counseling competition), Assn. of Bar of City of N.Y. (spl. com. matrimonial law 1975-77), N.Y. State Trial Lawyers Assn. (mem., matrimonial law com., 1971-76, chmn., 1974-75), Am. Arbitration Assn., N.Y. Women's Bar Assn., Minion of the Stars (chmn. bd. 1993). Office: Raoul Lionel Felder PC 437 Madison Ave New York NY 10022-7001 Office Phone: 212-832-3939. Business E-Mail: raoulfelder@raoulfelder.com.

FELDER-HOEHNE, FELICIA HARRIS, librarian; b. Knoxville, Tenn. d. Henry Thomas and Luvilla Tate Harris. BS in English, Knoxville Coll., 1958; MS in Libr. Sci., Atlanta U., 1966; postgrad., U. Tenn., 1972—78. English tchr. McMinn County Schs., J.L. Cook Sch., Athens, Tenn., 1958—60; adminstrv. asst. Adminstrv. Offices Knoxville (Tenn.) Coll., 1960—63, adminstrv. asst. to the dir. pub. rels., 1963—65; grad. libr. asst. Trevor Arnett Libr., Atlanta U., 1965—66; head circulation and reserve svcs. Alumni Libr. Knoxville Coll., 1966—69; tchr., libr. summer study skills program United Presbyn. Ch., Bd. Nat. Missions, Knoxville Coll., 1967—68; prof., reference libr. John C. Hodges Libr. U. Tenn., Knoxville, 1969—. Founder, dir. LARKS: Librs. Linking with At-Risk Students, Knoxville, 1997—. Author: A Subject Guide to Basic Reference Books in Black Studies; co-author: (online ency.) Project TAPP: Tennessee Authors Past and Present, 1999—; contbr. Notable Black American Women, Book I, Notable Black American Women, Book II, Behavioral & Social Sciences Librarian; author poems; contbr. articles to profl. jours. Adv. bd. Mentoring Acad. for Boys, Knoxville, 1997—; sec. to bd. Ctr. for Neighborhood Devel., Knoxville, 2000—02; dir. pub. rels. Concerned Assn. Residents East, Knoxville, 1988—90; active Tenn. Valley Energy Coalition, Knoxville, 1988—90, Town Hall East, Knoxville, 1988—, Save Our Cumberland Mountains, Tenn., 1988—; religious task force World's Fair, Knoxville Internat. Energy Exposition, 1982; pres. Spring Place Neighborhood Assn., Knoxville, 1980—; pk. vol. Knox County Pk. Vol. Corps., 2003—; land devel. com. Knoxville Farmer's Mkt., 2005; cmty. action com. Leadership Class 2005; active West End Acad. Outreach, 1989—, Solutions to Issues of Concern to Knoxvillians, 1999—, Tribe One, 2000—, Safety City Outreach of Knoxville PD, 2004—, Cmty. Action Com. Leadership Class, 2005, Teen Challenge, 1985—; bd. dirs. Ctr. for Neighborhood Devel., Knoxville, 1998—2002, UT Fed. Credit Union, Knoxville, 1984—89, Knox County Parks and Recreation, 2004—; adv. bd. dirs. Bd. Probation and Parole State of Tenn., Knoxville, 2003—. Named Citizen of Yr., Order of Ea. Star, 2004; named one of Outstanding Young Women of Am., 1967; named to Tenn. African Am. Hall Fame, 1994; recipient Cert. of Merit for Contbns. to Edn., Jack and Jill, Inc., 1976, Plaque of Appreciation, Interdenominational Concert Choir, 1976, Religious Svc. award, Nat. Conf. Christians and Jews, 1976, Citizen of the Yr. award, Order of the Ea. Star Prince Hall Masons, 1979, Cert. of Appreciation, Knoxville's Internat. Energy Exposition, 1982, Pub. Svc. award, U. Tenn. Nat. Alumni Assn., 1984, Habitat for Humanity award, 1992, Merit award for outstanding achievement, City of Knoxville, Mayor Ashe, 1994, The Humanitarian Libr. Spirit award, 1994, Spirit award, The Miles 500 Libr., 1994, 2005, Citation for Svc., Knoxville Police Dept., 1998, Cmty. Cornerstone award, Knoxville News-Sentinel, 1998, Harold B. Love Outstanding Cmty. Involvement award, 2003, The Vol. Spirit award, U. Tenn., 2003, Plaque of Appreciation, U. Tenn. Fed. Credit Union, 2004, Sincerity Disting. Libr. award, Daily Beacon, 2004. Mem.: YWCA, YMCA, ALA, NAACP, Nat. Mus. Women in the Arts (charter), East Tenn. Libr. Assn., Tenn. Libr. Assn., Character Counts Orgn., Dogwood Arts Festival (charter), Beck Cultural Exch. Ctr. (charter), Knoxville Opera Guild (bd. dirs. 1999—), Met. Opera Guild, Citizens Police Acad. Alumni Assn., Alpha Kappa Alpha. Avocations: community service, music, poetry, theater. Office: 152M John C Hodges Libr 1015 Volunteer Blvd Knoxville TN 37996-1000

FELDER-WRIGHT, PAMELA THERESA, education educator; b. Natchez, Miss., Aug. 1, 1956; d. Albert and Yvonne (McMorris) Evans; m. Marion Wright; children: D'Antwanette, Demetric stepchildren: Keon, Crystal. BS, Alcorn State U., 1977, MS, 1980; PhD, Kans. State U., 1982. Resource rm. specialist Jefferson Elem. Sch., Fayette, Miss., 1977-79; GED instr. Alcorn State U., Lorman, Miss., 1980-81; dir. child devel. assn. Rust Coll., Holly Springs, Miss., 1982-84; dir. early childhood ctr. Winston Salem (N.C.) State U., 1984-90; owner Pam's Unique Technique, Winston Salem, 1990-93; coord. Uplift, Inc., Greensboro, N.C., 1993-94; dir. med. ctr. child care N.C. Bapt. Hosp., Winston-Salem, 1994—; assoc. prof. edn., coord. spl. edn. Alcorn State (Miss.) U., 2002—. Pres. Pam's Unique Technique, Natchez, Miss.; mem. Oxford Round Table, London, 2003. Author: (book) Dream...but Dream Big, 1992, I'm Black and Beautiful, 1993, Lupus: How to Beat it One Day at a Time, (poetry) I Looked at You Today (Internat. Poet of the Yr., 2002, 2004), Best Poems, 1996 (Merit, 1996), 2004 (Merit, 2004, Poet of the Year, 2004). Bd. visitors Tech. Assistance Ctr., Winston-Salem, 1996. Recipient Golden Poet award World of Poetry, 1995, Best Poem Nat. Libr. of Poetry, 1995, Internat. Poet of Merit award, 2002, 2004; named Best Poet, 2000, Poet of Merit 2002-03, Poet of Yr., 2002. Mem. ASCD, N.C. Day Care Assn., N.C. Assn. of Educators, So. Assn. for Edn. for Children, Coun. Exceptional Children. Baptist. Achievements include research in Sped Tech SMCET. Avocations: reading, exercising. Office: Dept Edn and Psychology 100 ASU Dr Alcorn State MS 39096-7500

FELDHAUS, STEPHEN MARTIN, lawyer; b. Lawrenceburg, Tenn., Jan. 12, 1945; s. Lawrence Bernard and Margaret Martha (Holthouse) F.; m. Allis Rennie, Aug. 18, 1968 (div. 1980); 1 child, Rennie Elizabeth; m. Marcia Virginia Hughes, Dec. 30, 1980; stepchildren: Matthew Rankin FitzSimmons, Ryan Ford FitzSimmons. AB, U. Notre Dame, 1967; JD, Stanford U., 1973. Bar: Tex. 1973, D.C. 1984. Law clk. to Hon. Eugene A. Wright U.S. Ct. Appeals (9th cir.), Seattle, 1972-73; assoc. Fulbright & Jaworski, Houston, 1973-76, London, 1976-79, ptnr., 1979-81, Washington, 1981—. Bd. dirs. D.C. Downtown Partnership, Washington, 1988-92 Mem.: ABA, D.C. Bar, Internat. Fiscal Assn., Internat. Bar Assn. Republican. Avocations: tennis, squash, skiing, chess, reading. Office: Fulbright & Jaworski 801 Pennsylvania Ave NW Fl 3-5 Washington DC 20004-2623 Office Phone: 202-662-4520. Business E-Mail: sfeldhaus@fulbright.com.

FELDKAMP, JOHN CALVIN, lawyer, educator; b. Milw., Sept. 5, 1939; s. Leroy Lyle and Dorothea Arpke (Reineking) F.; m. Barbara Joan Condon, June 30, 1962; children: John Calvin Jr. (dec. 2004), Stephen Patrick, Amy Genevieve. BA, U. Mich., 1961, JD, 1965. Bar: Mich. 1970, NJ 1980, DC 1983. Asst. to v.p. U. Mich., Ann Arbor, 1964-66, dir. housing, 1966-77; gen. mgr. svcs. Princeton U., NJ, 1977-82; pvt. practice law Ann Arbor, 1970-77, Princeton, NJ, 1977-82; assoc. Caplin & Drysdale, Washington, 1982-85; exec. dir. Brown & Wood, NYC, 1985—2001; exec. dir. NYC office Sidley, Austin, Brown & Wood, 2001—05. Councilman, City of Ann Arbor, 1967-69; hearing referee Mich. Civil Rights Commn., Lansing, 1975-77. Mem. Rotary (bd. dirs. Ann Arbor 1970-77, Princeton 1978-82). Office Phone: 212-839-5560. Office Fax: 212-839-5599. Personal E-mail: jcfeldkamp@comcast.net. Business E-Mail: jfeldkamp@sidley.com.

FELDMAN, ALLAN MAURICE, economist; b. Paterson, N.J., Jan. 9, 1943; s. Jacob and Rachel (Eisen) F.; m. Barbara Ellen Moses, June 19, 1965; children: Paula, Elizabeth, Jacob. BS in Math., U. Chgo., 1965, MA in Anthropology, 1967; PhD in Econs., Johns Hopkins U., 1972. Asst. prof. econs. Brown U., Providence, 1971-78, assoc. prof. econs., 1978—. Cons., expert witness, Providence, 1975—. Author: Welfare Economics and Social Choice Theory, 1980. Treas. Common Sense, Providence, 1983-84. Recipient fellowship, Johns Hopkins U., 1970, Richard D. Irwin fellowship, Richard D. Irwin Found., 1971. Mem. Nat. Assn. Forensic Economists, Am. Economic Assn., Nat. Assn. Watch and Clock Collectors, Phi Beta Kappa (treas. R.I. Alpha chpt. 1999--). Avocations: antique clocks, hiking, nature study. Office: Brown U Dept Econs Providence RI 02912-0001 Office Phone: 401-863-2415. E-mail: allan_feldman@brown.edu.

FELDMAN, ARTHUR M., cardiologist; m. Susan Boochever; children: Emily Kate, Elizabeth Willa. BA, Gettysburg Coll., 1970; MS, U. Md., 1973, PhD, 1974; MD, La. State U., 1981. Diplomate Nat. Bd. Med. Examiners, Am. Bd. Internal Medicine, Sub-Bd. Cardiovascular Disease. Intern, resident, fellow in cardiology Johns Hopkins Hosp., Balt., 1981-86, from asst. prof. to assoc. prof. medicine, 1986-94; Harry S. Tack prof. medicine, prof. cell biology/physiology U. Pitts., 1994—2002, chief divsn. cardiology, dir. Cardiovasc. Inst., 1998—2002; Magee prof., chmn. dept. medicine Jefferson Med. Coll., Phila., 2002—. Mem. editl. bd. Heart Failure, Jour. Cardiac Failure, Jour. Cardivasc. Pharmacology & Therapeutics, Jour. Cardiovasc. Pharmacology, Clin. Cardiology, Jour. Am. Coll. Cardiology, Cardiac Failure. Trustee Gettysburg Coll. Grantee, NIH, 1989—94, 1999—2003. Fellow: Am. Coll. Cardiology, Coun. Clin. Cardiology (exec. com. 1996—2000, basic rsch. coun.), Am. Heart Assn. (heart failure com.); mem.: Assn. Univ. Cardiologists (councilor 1999—2001), Heart Failure Soc. Am. (founding mem. 1995, sec. 1996—98, pres. 1998—2000), Assn. Profs. Cardiology (treas. 2000—01, pres 2002—), Assn. Subsplty. Profs., Internat. Soc. Heart Rsch., Assn. Am. Physicians, Am. Soc. Clin. Investigation. Home: 136 Knightsbridge Wynnewood PA 19096 Office: Jefferson Med Coll Coll Bldg Rm 822 1025 Walnut St Philadelphia PA 19096 E-mail: arthur.feldman@jefferson.edu.

FELDMAN, BERNARD ROBERT, physician; b. Bklyn., July 5, 1934; s. Maurice Sol and Florence (Wagner) F.; m. Clare Elizabeth Krameisen, July 3, 1960; children: David Lawrence, Janet Lynn. BS, Coll. William and Mary, 1955; MD, Chgo. Med. Sch., 1959. Intern Michael Reese Hosp. and Med. Ctr., Chgo., 1959-60, resident in pediatrics, 1960-62, fellow in allergy and immunology, 1962-63, Columbia-Presbyn. Med. Ctr., N.Y.C., 1963-64; asst. prof. clin. pediatrics Columbia Coll. Physicians and Surgeons, N.Y.C., 1964-87, clin. prof. pediatrics, 1996—; assoc. clin. prof. pediatrics Columbia-Presbyn. Med. Ctr., N.Y.C., 1987—. Cons. St. Mary's Hosp. for Children, Queens, N.Y., 1976—. Author: The Complete Book of Childhood Allergies, 1986. V.p. edn. Woodland Community Temple, White Plains, N.Y., 1985-87, trustee, 1983-85. Fellow Am. Acad Allergy and Immunology (cert.), Am. Acad. Pediatrics (cert.); mem. N.Y. Allergy Soc. (past pres., mem. exec. com.), N.Y. State Soc. Allergy and Immunology (treas. 1986-88, pres. 1988-91), Med. Soc. State N.Y. (chmn. sect. allergy and immunology 1982-83), Westchester Allergy Soc. Jewish. Avocations: reading, photography, tennis. Office: Columbia-Presbyn Med Ctr 3959 Broadway Rm 107N New York NY 10032-1551 also: 7 Elmwood Dr New City NY 10956-5136 also: 280 N Central Ave Ste 308 Hartsdale NY 10530-1835 also: Columbia-Presbyn Westside 21 W 86th St New York NY 10024-3616 Office Phone: 212-305-2300. E-mail: bobfmd@cs.com.

FELDMAN, BORIS, lawyer; b. South Bend, Ind., 1955; BA in history summa cum laude, Yale U., 1977; JD, Yale Law Sch., 1980. Law clk. to Judge Abraham D. Sofaer, US Dist. Ct. for So. Dist. NY, 1980—81; assoc. Arnold & Porter, Washington, 1981—85; spl. asst. to legal adviser US Dept. State, 1985—86; atty. Wilson Sonsini Goodrich & Rosati, Palo Alto, Calif., 1986—, mem. exec. mgmt. com., chair policy com. Note & topics editor Yale Law Jour., Vol. 89; mem. Ninth Circuit Lawyer Rep. Coordinating Com.; co-chair lawyer rep. to No. Dist. Calif.; bd. dirs. Silicon Valley Campaign for Legal Svcs.; mem. Santa Clara County Superior Ct. Task Force on Complex Lit.; mem. adv. bd. Securities Regulation Inst. Author: 20 articles on various disclosure topics. Named one of Top 45 Lawyers in Country Under Age of 45, Am. Lawyer, 1995, 100 Most Influential Lawyers in Calif., LA Daily Jour., 2002, Top Ten Lawyers in Bay Area, San Francisco Chronicle. Mem.: Phi Beta Kappa. Office: 650 Page Mill Rd Palo Alto CA 94304 Office Phone: 650-493-9300. Office Fax: 650-493-6811. Business E-Mail: boris.feldman@wsgr.com.

FELDMAN, BRUCE ALLEN, otolaryngologist; b. Washington, Mar. 22, 1941; s. Irvin and Miriam Thelma (Rothstein) F.; m. Sharon Lee Pearlman, Dec. 25, 1966; children: Kathryn Ellen, Michael Aaron. AB, Dartmouth Coll., 1962, B Med. Sci., 1963; MD, Harvard U., 1965. Diplomate Am. Bd. Otolaryngology. Intern Hosp. of U. Pa., Phila., 1965-66, resident in surgery, 1966-67; resident in otolaryngology Mass. Eye and Ear Infirmary-Harvard U., Boston, 1967-70; pvt. practice Washington, 1972—; clin. prof. surgery (otolaryngology), pediatrics George Washington U., Washington, 1990—; clin. prof. otolaryngology Georgetown U. Sch. Medicine, Washington, 1995—. Pres. med. staff Children's Hosp. Nat. Med. Ctr., Washington, 1994-96; vice chmn. bd. dirs. Children's Hosp., Washington, 1994-2004. Contbr. articles to med. jours., chpt. to book. Lt. comdr. M.C., USNR, 1970-72. Mosby scholar, 1963; recipient Physician's Recognition award Children's Hosp. Washington, 1991. Fellow ACS, Am. Laryngol., Rhinol. and Otol. Soc. (Mosher award 1981), Am. Acad. Pediatrics, Am. Acad. Otolaryngology; mem. AMA, Acad. Medicine Washington, Med. Soc. D.C., Jacobi Med. Soc. (pres. 1986-87), Washington Met. Ear, Nose and Throat Soc. (pres. 1978-79), Woodmont Country Club (Rockville, Md.), Phi Beta Kappa, Alpha Omega Alpha, Phi Delta Epsilon (pres. grad. club 1979-80). Jewish. Office: 5454 Wisconsin Ave Chevy Chase MD 20815 Office Phone: 301-652-8847. E-mail: fodm.physician@verizon.net.

FELDMAN, CECILE ARLENE, dean, dental educator; b. N.Y.C., Oct. 8, 1959; d. Melvin and Claire (Halpern) F.; m. Harry Kenneth Zohn, Aug. 19, 1984. BA, U. Pa., 1980, DMD, 1984, MBA, 1985. Asst. prof. U. Pa. Sch. Medicine, 1985—88, NJ Dental School, U. Medicine & Dentistry NJ, Newark, 1988—98, prof. dept. gen. dentistry and cmty. health, 1998—, acting to interim dean, 1999—2001, dean, 2001—. Cons., author in field; leadership inst. fellow Am. Dental Edn. Assn., 1988—; adj. prof. dept. dental care systems U. Pa., sr. adj. fellow Leonard Davis Inst. Health Econs., Wharton Sch. Fellow Acad. Gen. Dentistry, Internat. Coll. Dentists, Am. Coll. Dentists; mem. ADA, Am. Assn. Dental Schs., Internat. Assn. Dental Rsch., Am. Assn. Pub. Health Dentistry, Am. Med. Informatics Assn., N.J. Dental Assn. Office: NJ Dental Sch 110 Bergen St Newark NJ 07103-2400

FELDMAN, CLARICE ROCHELLE, lawyer; b. Milw., Dec. 2, 1941; d. Harry and Beatrice (Hiken) Wagan; m. Howard J. Feldman, July 11, 1965; 1 child, David Lewis. BS, U. Wis., 1963, LL.B., 1965. Bar: Wis. 1965, D.C. 1969, Md. 1984. Appellate atty. NLRB, Washington, 1965—69; co-counsel to Joseph A. Yablonski, Washington, 1969; atty. Washington research project Clark Coll., 1970-72; asso. gen. counsel United Mine Workers Am., Washington, 1972-74; partner Becker, Channell, Becker & Feldman, Washington, 1974-76, Becker & Feldman, 1976-77; gen. counsel Ams. for Energy Independence, Washington, 1978-80; atty. Office of Spl. Investigations, Dept. Justice, 1980-84; pvt. practice law Washington, 1984-98; atty. pro bono, 1999—. Trustee Washington Internat. Sch., 1987-98; advisor Assn. Union Democracy. Mem. Wis., D.C., Md. bar assns. Republican. Jewish. Home: 4455 29th St NW Washington DC 20008-2307

FELDMAN, EDMUND BURKE, art critic; b. Bayonne, N.J., May 6, 1924; s. Lucian Theodore and Bertha (Seldin) F.; m. Lailah G. Link, Mar. 15, 1953; children: Eva Jeanne, Jessica Marion. B.F.A., Syracuse U., 1949; MA, UCLA, 1951; Ed.D., Columbia U., 1953. Curator painting and sculpture Newark Mus., 1953; assoc. prof. art Livingston (Ala.) State U., 1953-56, Carnegie Inst. Tech., 1956-60; head art div. State U. Coll., New Paltz, N.Y., 1960-66; vis. prof. art Ohio State U., 1966; prof. art U. Ga., Athens, 1966-91, Alumni Found. disting. prof. art, 1973-91, prof. emeritus, 1991—. Vis. prof. aesthetic edn. U. Calif., Berkeley, 1974; bd. govs. Pitts. Plan for Art, 1964-66; mem. U.S. Office Edn., Art TV Project, Whitney Mus., 1967, Ednl. Testing Svc., N.Y.C., 1969-70, Coll. Entrance Exam Bd., Princeton, N.J., 1969-70, Nat. Instructional TV Ctr., Bloomington, Ind., 1969-71; editorial cons. art Prentice-Hall, Inc. (arts and humanities Canfield Press subs. Harper & Row); advisor Ga. Coun. for arts, 1973-74, Nat. Faculty for Arts and Humanities, 1986; cons. J. Paul Getty Trust, 1981-85. Author: Art as Image and Idea, 1967, Varieties of Visual Experience, 1971, 4th edit., 1992, The Artist, 1982, 2d edit., 1994, Thinking About Art, 1985, Practical Art Criticism, 1993, Philosophy of Art Education, 1995; editor Art Bull., Ea. Arts Assn., 1957-60, Art in American Institutions, 1970; mem. editorial bd. Rev. Rsch. in Visual Arts Edn., 1975-77; mem. editorial adv. bd. Jour. Aesthetic Edn., 1976-80; chmn. editorial bd. Ga. Rev., 1977. Served with USAAF, 1942-46. Recipient Roswell Hill prize in painting Syracuse U., 1948 Fellow Nat. Art Edn. Assn. (pres. 1981-83, Disting. 1984), Royal Soc. Arts; mem. Coll. Art Assn., U.S. Soc. for Edn. Through Art, Tau Sigma Delta, Kappa Delta Pi, Kappa Pi, Phi Kappa Phi. Jewish. Home: 140 Chinquapin Pl Athens GA 30605-3314 Office: U Ga Sch Art Athens GA 30602

FELDMAN, ELAINE BOSSAK, medical nutritionist, educator; b. N.Y.C., NY, Dec. 9, 1926; d. Solomon and Frances Helen (Fania) Nevler Bossak; m. Herman Black, Dec. 23, 1951 (div. 1957); 1 child, Mitchell Evan; m. Daniel S. Feldman, July 19, 1957 (dec. June 2005); children: Susan, Daniel S. Jr. AB magna cum laude, NYU, 1945, MS, 1948, MD, 1951. Diplomate Am. Bd. Internal Medicine, Nat. Bd. Med. Examiners; cert. in Clin. Nutrition. Rotating intern Mt. Sinai Hosp., N.Y.C., 1951-52, resident in pathology, 1952, asst. resident, 1953, fellow in medicine, resident in metabolism, 1954-55, rsch. asst. in medicine, 1955-58, clin. asst. physician Diabetes Clinic, 1957; asst. vis. physician Kings County Hosp., Bklyn., 1958-66, assoc. vis. physician, 1966-72; asst. attending physician Maimonides Hosp., Bklyn., 1960-68; spl. fellow USPHS Dept. of Physiol. Chemistry U. of Lund, Sweden, 1964-65; attending physician Eugene Talmadge Meml. Hosp., Augusta, Ga., 1972-92, Univ. Hosp., Augusta, 1972-92, cons., 1973; prof. medicine Med. Coll. Ga., Augusta, 1972-92, prof. emeritus, 1992—, chief sect. of nutrition, 1977-92, chief emeritus, 1992—, acting chief sect. of metabolic/endocrine disease, 1980-81, prof. physiology and endocrinology, 1988-92, prof. emeritus physiology and endocrinology, 1992—; instr. medicine SUNY Downstate Med. Ctr., 1957-59, asst. prof. medicine, 1959-68, assoc. prof. medicine, 1968-72. Tchg. fellow dept. zoology U. Wis. Grad. Sch., 1945-46, dept. biology NYU Grad. Sch., 1946-47; cons. N.Y.-N.J. Regional Ctr. for Clin. Nutrition Edn., 1983-92; vis. prof. and Harvey lectr. Northeastern Ohio Sch. Medicine, Youngstown, 1985; cons., vis. prof. U. Nev. Sch. Medicine (NCI grant), 1989-94; mem. nat. adv. com. nutrition fellowship program Nat. Med. Fellowship Inc., 1988-95; dir. Ga. Inst. Human Nutrition, 1978-92, dir. emeritus, 1992—; dir. Clin. Nutrition Rsch. Unit, 1980-86; mem. med. nutrition curriculum initiative adv. bd. U. N.C., Chapel Hill, 1992-2001; advisor ednl. materials Am. Inst. Cancer Rsch., 1997—. Author: Essentials of Clinical Nutrition, 1988; (with others) Conference on Biological Activities of Steroids in Relation to Cancer, 1969, Nicotinic Acid, 1964, The Menopausal Syndrome, 1974, Hyperlipidemia, Medcom Special Studies, 1974, Medcom Famous Teaching in Modern Medicine, 1979, Harrison's Principles of Internal Medicine, 1980, Health Promotion: Principles and Clinical Applications, 1982, The Encyclopedic Handbook of Alcoholism, 1982, The Climacteric in Perspective, 1986, Selenium in Biology and Medicine, Part A., 1987, Medicine for the Practicing Physician, 1988, Clinical Chemistry of Laboratory Animals, 1989, Ency. Human Biology, 1991, Laboratory Medicine: The Selection and Interpretation of Clinical Laboratory Studies, 1993, Modern Nutrition in Health and Diseases, 1994, Nutrition Assessment-A Comprehensive Guide for Planning Intervention, 1995, The Women's Complete Healthbook, 1995, The American Medical Women's Association's Guide to Nutrition and Wellness, 1996, Normal Nutrition and Therapeutics, 1996, Handbook of Nutrition and Food, 2001; editor: Nutrition and Cardiovascular Disease, 1976, Nutrition in the Middle and Later Years, 1983 (paperback edit. 1986), Nutrition and Heart Disease, 1983, Handbook of Nutrition and Food, 2001, Human Nutrient Needs in the Life Cycle, 2001; mem. editl. adv. bd. Contemporary Issues in Clin. Nutrition, 1980-92; mem. edit. bd. Am. Jour. Clin. Nutrition, 1983-91, 92-98, Jour. Clin. Endocrinology and Metabolism, 1984-88, MidPoint: Counseling Women through Menopause, 1984-85, Jour. Nutrition, 1985-89; cons. editor Jour. Am. Coll. Nutrition, 1982-94; mem. edit. bd. Complementary Med. for the Physician, 1996-2000; contbg. editor Nutrition Rev., 1997-2002; mem. editl. bd. Nutrition Today, 1999—; reviewer Jour. Lipid Rsch., Biochm. Pharmacology, Sci., The Physiologist, Jour. Am. Acad. Dermatology, Israel Jour. Med. Scis., N.Y. State Jour. Medicine, Jour. of Nutrition Edn., Jour. Am. Dietetic Assn., Am. Jour. Medicine, Am. Jour. Med. Sci., So. Med. Jour., Jour. AMA, Jour. NCI; contbr. more than 175 articles to profl. jours; presenter in field. Mem. tech. adv. com. for sci. and edn. Rsch. Grants Program, Human Nutrition Grants Peer Panel, USDA, 1982, mem. bd. sci. counselors human nutrition; Community Svc. Block Grant Discretionary Program Panel; vice chmn. Urban and Rural Econ. Devel. Panel, Dept. HHS, 1982, grant reviewer, 1983; mem ad hoc and spl. rev. coms. and groups NIH, 1979-93, mem. nutrition study sect., 1976-80; mem. Rev. Panel Nat. Nutrition Objectives, Life Scis. Rev. Office, Fed. Am. Socs. Exptl. Biology, 1985-86; mem. subcom. Women's Health Trial Nat. Cancer Inst., 1987, mem. bd. sci. counselors cancer prevention and control program, 1990-94; mem. adv. com. Clin. Nutrition Rsch. Unit, U. Ala., 1986-94, Ga. Nutrition Steering Com., 1974-75, Ctrl. Savannah River Area Nutrition Project Coun. 1974-75, ednl. adv. com. Health Central, 1980; mem. geriatrics and gerontology rev. com. Nat. Inst. on Aging, 1986-90; breast cancer initiative peer rev. Dept. of Def., 1997, 98. N.Y. Heart Assn. rsch. fellow, 1955-57. Fellow Am. Heart Assn. Coun. on Atherosclerosis (nominating com. 1978, chmn. nominating com., mem. exec. com. 1979-80, Spl. Recognition award 1995), Am. Inst. Nutrition (grad. nutrition edn. com. 1980-83, 89-93); mem. Am. Coll. Nutrition (chmn. com. pub. affairs), Am. Soc. for Clin. Nutrition (com. on nutrition edn. 1982, chmn. subcom. on nutrition edn. in med. schs. 1983-84, chmn. com. on med./dental residency edn., 1985-87, com. on subsplty. tng. 1988-92, nominating com. 1982, 90, chair nominating com. 1994, com. on clin. practice issues in health and disease 1989-92, Nat. Dairy Coun. award 1991, rep. coun. acad. socs. 1990-96, membership com. 1996-2005, chair 1999, 2000), Fedn. Am. Socs. Exptl. Biology. Am. Oil Chemists Soc., Am. Physiol. Soc., Endocrine Soc., Soc. Exptl. Biology and Medicine, So. Soc. Clin. Investigation, Am. Diabetes Assn., Am. Fedn. Clin. Rsch., Am. Gastroent. Assn., AMA (Joseph B. Goldberger award 1990), Am. Med. Women's Assn. (profl. resources com. 1975-76, med. edn. and rsch. fund com. 1976-79, chmn. 1978-90, chmn. student liaison subcom. of membership com. 1981-84, pres. Br. 51, Augusta 1977-80, treas. 1980-97, Calcium Nutrition Edn. award 1991, CSRA Girl Scout Women of Excellence award 1994), Am. Soc. Parenteral and Enteral Nutrition, Am. Heart Assn. (Ga. affiliate, nutrition com., chmn. sci. session for nutritionists, 1978, chmn. nutrition com. 1979-90, mem. long range planning com. 1980-81, rsch. com. 1980-83, bd. dirs. 1987-90, profl. edn. task force, 1988-89), Richmond Country Med. Assn., Augusta Opera Assn. (bd. dirs. 1973-2002, recording sec. 1973-74, pres. 1974-75, coord. audience devel. 1975-77, at-large exec. com. 1994-96, chair nominating com. 1994-96, corr. sec. 1998-99, 1st v.p. 1999-2000, chair search com., gen. dir. 2002), Augusta Sailing Club (women's com. 1973), Greater Augusta Arts Coun. (Arts Festival Collage 1982 chmn. promotion and publicity com., Festival coms. 1983-86, 89-93, 95, 96, 98, 99, bd. dirs. 1984-94, Vol. of the Yr., 2001), Gertrude Herbert Inst. Art (bd. dirs. 1987-92), Authors Club Augusta, Philomathic Club (sec. 1999-2001), Phi Beta Kappa, Sigma Xi (chpt. sec. 1982-83, pres. elect 1983-84, pres. 1984-85), Alpha Omega Alpha. Avocations: opera, wine tasting, travel. Home: 4275 Owens Rd Apt 1222 Evans GA 30809 Personal E-mail: efeldman17@comcast.net.

FELDMAN, ENRIQUE HANK CANEZ, pre-school educator, composer; b. Tucson, Ariz., July 15, 1966; s. Enrique and Victoria Canez Feldman; m. Marie Ann Altvater, Feb. 28, 1962; children: Samantha Isabel, Nicholas Allan. BS of Music Edn., U. Ariz., 1988; MS of Music Edn., U. Ill., 1989, M in Music Performance, 1990. Cert. K-12 edn. Ariz. Dept. Edn., 1988. Asst. band dir. U. Wis., Madison, 1990—92; assoc. dir. bands, prof. tuba and euphonium U. Ariz., Tucson, 1992—98; composer, performing artist Tubesia, 1992—; dir. Assessment Tech. Inc., 1998—2000; pres., dir. edn. Fostering Arts-Mind Edn. Found., 2000—; dir. Evolved Learning Inc., 2003—; condr., tubist Sky Island Chamber Musicians, 2004—. Dir. Galileo tng. Assessment Tech. Inc., Tucson, 1999—2000; lead trainer Child-Parent Centers, Inc. Head Start, 2003—, Akron Summit Head Start Program, Arkon, Ohio, 2003—, Charles R. Drew U. Medicine Head Start Program, Long Beach and Watts, Calif., 2003—, Early Harris Learning Ctr., Birmingham, Ala., 2004—, Higher Horizons Head Start, Washington DC, 2004—, Tri-County Head Start, Athens, Ohio, 2001—04, KnoHoCo Head Start, Coshocton, 2001—04; keynote spkr. N.J. Child Care Assn., Newark, 2000—00, Ind. Head Start Assn., Indpls., 2000—00; invited presentation Region V Head Start, Detroit, 1999—99; artistic dir. Low Brass Symposium, Tucson, 1993—95; invited jazz improvisation presentation Colo. Music Educators 50th Anniversary State Conf., Colorado Springs, 1996—96; invited composer Wheel Time TV Series, L.A., 2004—; guest condr. So. Ariz. Symphony Orch., Tucson, 2004—; invited presentation/keynote Nat. Assn. Edn. Young Children, Washington, 2005—; keynote spkr. Ariz. Dept. Edn., Phoenix, 2005—, Divsn. Early Childhood, 2005—; invited presentation/keynote spkr. NAEYC, Anaheim, Calif., 2004—04; invited presenter, keynote spkr. Hattie Larlham Rsch. Inst., Cleve., 2004—04. Prodr.: (compact disc) The Tree and the Wind, (performing artist and arranger) (jazz compact disc) Tubesia, (performing artist and composer/arranger) (ethnic jazz compact disc) Vida Rica, (composer and educator) (children's bi-lingual dvd) Watch, Learn, Do; musician (vocalist and composer): (featured jazz soloist) ITEC Brass Conference in Riva Del Garda, Italy; musician: (vocalist and composer/arranger) International Brass Conference (ITEC) Minneapolis, Minnesota, ITEC Brass Conference in Regina, Canada, ITEC Brass Conference in Greensboro, North Carolina, ITEC Brass Conference in Budapest, Hungary. Mem., cons. Early Childhood Consortium, Tucson, 2004. Fellow, U. Ill., Urbana-Champaign, 1998—2000; grantee, NEA and Ariz. Commn. Arts, 2003; scholar, U. Ariz., 1984—88. Mem.: Rotary Internat. (fund raising com. 1993—98), North Am. Reggio Emilia Alliance, Internat. Tuba Euphonium Assn. (coord. jazz coordination 1998—2004). Independent. Achievements include research in Documenting Statistically Validated Outcomes which prove the impact of the Arts and Holistic practices on cognitive development, literacy development, early math development, and social-emotional dev; Artist-in-Residence at the Brevard Music Center; TOURING MUSICIANS with CHICAGO, the Musical 2004; first to Founder of the F.A.M.E. Foundation, www.famefoundation.org; Founder, Evolved Learning Techniques and Conference, www-.evolvedlearning.com; GRAMMY NOMINATION with Ensemble Symphonia for CD Mort De Omp; GRAMMY NOMINATION with Ensemble Symphonia for CD Symphonia Fantastique; Invited as Original member and current member of classical ensemble Symphonia; Excellence in Performing and Teaching at the University of Arizona awarded on March 4 1994; Outstanding Young Executive Award awarded in 1995 to the top 40 Tucson executives under the age of 40; ARTIST-IN-RESIDENCE at Interlochen Center for the Arts. Avocations: travel, gourmet cooking, soccer. Office: FAME Found 4927 N Sabino Gulch Ct Tucson AZ 85750 Office Phone: 520-861-3001. Business E-Mail: info@famefoundation.org.

FELDMAN, ERIC ADAM, law educator, academic administrator; b. NYC, Oct. 18, 1959; s. Saul and Gloria F.; m. Stephanie Cecile Cridelose, June 20, 1997. Student, U. Leeds, 1979-80; BA in History and Philosophy of Sci. cum laude, Vassar Coll., 1982; JD, U. Calif., Berkeley, 1989, PhD in Jurisprudence and Social Policy, 1994; student, Nichibei Kaiwa Gakkuen, Tokyo, 1990-91. Bar: Calif. 1989. Rsch. asst. Hastings Ctr., NYC, 1982-84; tchg. asst. Sch. Journalism Columbia U., NYC, 1984; vis. fellow biomed. ethics Mitsubishi-Kasei Inst. Life Scis., Japan, 1984-85; assoc. LeBoeuf, Lamb, Leiby & MacRae, San Francisco, 1989; fgn. rsch. scholar Inst. Social Scis. U. Tokyo, 1990-91, rsch. scholar faculty law internat. ctr. comparative law and politics, 1991-93; health policy rsch. scholar Instn. Social and Policy Studies Yale U., vis. fellow Sch. Law, 1994-96; assoc. dir. Inst. Law and Soc. NYU, 1996—2001; mem. Ctr. for Asian Studies U. Pa., Phila., 2002—, sr. fellow Ctr. for Bioethics, 2001—, asst. prof. law, 2001—. Cons. Toyota Found., Tokyo, 1993-95, World Health Orgn., 1995-96; vis. prof. Inst. D'Etudes Politiques de Paris, 1999; mem. organizing com. 1999 Law and Soc. Assn. Grad. Student Workshop; prin. investigator various profl. projects; organizer, cons., participant AIDS prevention: bldg. U.S./Japan cooperation and exchange project, 1994-96; chair various profl. meetings; presenter in field. Co-author: AIDS in the Industrial Democracies: Passion, Politics, and Policies, 1992, German transl., 1993, Containing Health Care Costs in Japan, 1996, Comparing Legal Cultures, 1997; guest editor Jour. AIDS and Human Retrovirology, 1997; mem. editl. bd. Law and Soc. Rev., 1998—; contbr. articles to profl. jours.; book reviewer in field; reviewer numerous manuscripts. Vol. Tenderloin Housing Clinic, San Francisco, 1987; bd. dirs. Village Acad. Charter Sch., New Haven, 1997-98. Recipient award U.S.-Japan Culture Ctr. Essay Contest, 1988; Fulbright Grad. Rsch. fellow Japan-U.S. Ednl. Commn./IIE, 1989-93; Toyota Found. Rsch. fellow, 1990; Dissertation grantee Social Sci. Rsch. Coun., Joint Com. Japanese Studies, 1991; Rsch. fellow Japan Soc. Promotion Sci., 1992; Doctoral Dissertation Improvement grantee NSF, 1993; Robert Wood Johnson Found. scholar, 1994-96; Abe fellow Social Sci. Rsch. Coun., Am. Coun. Learned Socs. and Ctr. Global Partnership, 1998—; Stephen Charney Vladeck Jr. Faculty fellow NYU, 1999. Mem. Law and Soc. Assn., Assn. Asian Studies, Japan Policy Rsch. Inst., The Hastings Ctr. Home: 1808 Addison St Philadelphia PA 19146-1403 Office: U Pa Law Sch 3400 Chestnut St Philadelphia PA 19104 Office Phone: 215-573-6400. Fax: 215-573-2025. E-mail: efeldman@law.upenn.edu.*

FELDMAN, EVA LUCILLE, neurology educator; b. N.Y.C., Mar. 30, 1952; d. George Franklin and Margherita Enriceta (Cafiero) F.; children: Laurel, Scott, John Jr. BA in Biology and Chemistry, Earlham Coll., 1973; MS in Zoology, U. Notre Dame, 1975; PhD in Neurosci., U. Mich., 1979, MD, 1983. Diplomate Am. Bd. Neurology; lic. med. practitioner, Mich. Instr. dept. neurology U. Mich., Ann Arbor, 1987-88, asst. prof. neurology, 1988-94, mem. faculty Cancer Ctr., 1992-2000, assoc. prof. neurology, 1994-2000, prof., 2000—, Russell N. DeJong prof. neurology, 2004—. Mem. faculty neurosci. program U. Mich., Mich. Diabetes Rsch. and Tng., Ann Arbor, 1988—; dir. JDRF Ctr. for the Study of Complications in Diabetes. Contbr. chpts. to books, articles to profl. jours. Grantee, NIH, 1989, 1994, 1997, 1998, 2001, 2003, Juvenile Diabetes Rsch. Found., 1994, 1997, 1999, 2001, Am. Diabetes Assn., 2005. Achievements include research on the elucidation of the role of growth factors in the pathogenesis of human disease. Office Phone: 734-763-7274.

FELDMAN, FRANKLIN, retired lawyer, printmaker; b. NYC, Nov. 12, 1927; s. Reuben and Anne (Schulman) F.; m. Naomi Goldstein, June 3, 1956; children: Sarah, Eve, Jacob. BA, NYU, 1948; LLB, Columbia U., 1951. Bar: N.Y. 1952. Mem. office Gen. Counsel, USAF, Dept. Def., Washington, 1951-53; atty. office gen. counsel to gov. State of N.Y., Albany, 1954; assoc. Stroock & Stroock & Lavan, N.Y.C., 1955-64, ptnr., 1965-88, counsel, 1989—2004; ret., 2004. Cons. Temp. N.Y. Commn. on Constl. Conv., 1967; lectr. in law Columbia Law Sch., 1979-2001. Editor-in-chief Columbia U. Law Rev., 1950-51; author: (with Stephen E. Weil) Art Works: Law, Policy and Practice, 1974, Art Law, 1986 (Best Law Book Published in 1986, Scribes); contbr. articles to profl. jours. Trustee Am. Jewish Hist. Soc., Waltham, Mass., 1987-96. 1st lt., USAF, 1951-53. Yaddo Fellow, Saratoga Springs, 1983. Fellow Am. Bar Found. (life); mem. Assn. of Bar of City of N.Y. (chmn. art com. 1968-71), Internat. Found. Art Rsch. (pres. 1971-76, bd. dirs. 1976-96), Ltd., Soc. Am. Graphic Artists, Century Assn., Pvt. Art Dealers Assn., Inc. (counsel, dir. 1993—), Grolier Club. Jewish. Home: 15 W 81st St New York NY 10024-6022 Personal E-mail: ffeldman1@nyc.rr.com.

FELDMAN, GARY JAY, physicist, researcher; b. Cheyenne, Wyo., Mar. 22, 1942; married; 2 children. BS, U. Chgo., 1964; AM, Harvard U., 1965, PhD in Physics, 1971. Research assoc. in physics Stanford Linear Accelerator Ctr., Stanford U., Calif., 1971-74, staff physicist, 1974-79, assoc. prof., 1979-83, prof., 1983-90; prof. physics Harvard U., Cambridge, Mass., 1990-92, Frank B. Baird, Jr. prof. sci., 1992—, chmn. dept. physics, 1994-97. Sci assoc. CERN, Switzerland, 1982-83. Fellow Am. Phys. Soc. (chmn. divsn. particles and fields 1992), Am. Acad. Arts and Scis. Office: Harvard U Lyman Lab Cambridge MA 02138

FELDMAN, GARY MARC, nutritionist, consultant; b. Bklyn., Dec. 3, 1953; m. Debra Lynn Bieler, Sept. 21, 1984. Diploma in Sci. of Nutritional Cons., Am. Nutrition Cons. Assn., 1986. Pres. Steps In Health, Ltd., Douglaston, N.Y., 1986-88, Margate, Fla., 1988-90, Nesconset, N.Y., 1990—. Educator for children in sci. of food and nutritional supplementation. Developer: Steps in Health Ltd.'s Catalogue of Vegetarian Name-Brand Nutritional Supplements and Health Products; author nutrition newsletter. Vol. listen to children program Mental Health Assn. and Vol. Program Broward County (Fla.) Pub. Schs., 1989; arbitration participant Better Bus. Bur. South Fla., 1989-90. Mem. AAAS, Am. Nutrition Cons. Assn., Life Extension Found., Pub. Citizen Health Rsch. Group, People for Ethical Treatment of Animals, Doris Day Animal League, Humane Soc. Broward County, Ctr. for Sci. in the Pub. Interest, Internat. Platform Assn., N.Y. State Sheriffs Assn., L.I. Assn. Inc., Herb Rsch. Found., Vegetarian Resource Group, N.Am. Vegetarian Soc., Nutritionists Health Am. (nutrition edn. program com.), Ctr. Sci. Pub. Interest (edn. com.), Feingold Assn., U.S. Co-op Am. Bus. Network, N.Y. Acad. Scis. Avocations: reading and data collection in health field, bodybuilding. Office: PO Box 220123 Great Neck NY 11022-0123

FELDMAN, H. LARRY, lawyer; b. Tyler, Tex., Apr. 18, 1941; s. Henry and Bess (Booken) F.; m. Janice Kay Asner, June 26, 1960; children: Joseph, Katherine. BA, U. Okla., 1963; JD, So. Meth. U., 1966. Bar: Tex. 1966, U.S. Dist. Ct. (no. dist.) Tex. 1969, U.S. Supreme Ct. 1976. Adj. prof. law U. Dallas, 1967-68; mem. dept. tax Peat, Marwick & Mitchell, 1968-69; atty. Marks, Time & Aranson, 1970; ptnr. Feldman, O'Donnell & Neil, Dallas, 1971; sole practice Dallas, 1971—. Mem. ATLA, Tex. Trial Lawyers Assn., Phi Alpha Delta. Jewish. Personal E-mail: janicedallas@hotmail.com.

FELDMAN, HARRIET RUTH, dean; b. Bklyn., May 5, 1945; d. Mickey and Florence (Gordon) Martin; m. Ronald M. Feldman, Dec. 22, 1973; children: Craig, Jaime. Diploma in nursing, L.I. Coll. Hosp., 1965; BS, Adelphi U., 1968, MS, 1971; PhD, NYU, 1984. Asst. dean Adelphi U., Garden City, N.Y., 1984-87; prof., chairperson dept. nursing Fairleigh Dickinson U., Teaneck, N.J., 1987-93; dean Lienhard Sch. Nursing Pace U., 1993—. Pres. Deans and Dirs. of Nursing Greater NY, 2001—, Strategies for Nursing Leadership, 2001; accreditation site visitor Commn. on Collegiate Nursing Edn., 1999—. Editor: Nursing Leadership Forum, 1998—, Nursing Leaders Speak Out: Issues and Opinions, 2001; co-author: Nurses in the Political Arena: The Public Face of Nursing, 2000; contbr. articles to profl. jours. Fellow: Am. Acad. Nursing; mem.: Am. Assn. Colls. Nursing (mentor Leadership for Acad. Nursing program 1999—2002). Home: 2243 Brody Ln Bellmore NY 11710-5101 E-mail: hfeldman@pace.edu.

FELDMAN, IRVING, poet; b. Bklyn., Sept. 22, 1928; m. Carmen Alvarez del Olmo, 1955; 1 son, Fernando R. Ed., CCNY, Columbia U. Formerly prof. English U. P.R., Rio Piedras, Kenyon Coll., Gambier, O.; disting. prof. English State U. N.Y., Buffalo, 1964—2005, disting. prof. emeritus, 2005—. Author: Works and Days, 1961, The Pripet Marshes, 1965, Magic Papers, 1970, Lost Originals, 1972, Leaping Clear, 1976, New and Selected Poems, 1979, Teach Me, Dear ister, 1983, All of Us Here, 1986, The Life and Letters, 1994, Beautiful False Things, 2000, Collected Poems, 1954-2004; contbr. to periodicals. Recipent poetry prize Jewish Book Coun. Am., 1962, award Nat. Inst. and AAAL, 1973; Ingram Merrill Found. grantee, 1963, N.Y. State Creative Artists Pub. Svc. grantee, 1980; Guggenheim fellow, 1973, Acad. Am. Poets fellow, 1986, MacArthur fellow, 1992; grantee Nat. Endowment for the Arts, 1987. Home: 284 Richmond Ave Buffalo NY 14222 Office: SUNY Dept English Buffalo NY 14260-0001 E-mail: leftyfeldman@hotmail.com.

FELDMAN, JAY NEWMAN, lawyer, communications executive; b. N.Y.C., Nov. 11, 1936; s. Morris Kenneth and Della (Newman) F.; m. Nancy Tobias, Dec. 7, 1963; children— Nina Cheryl, Karen Elise. AB with high honors in History magna cum laude, Colgate U., 1958; JD, Harvard U., 1961. Bar: N.Y. 1962, U.S. Dist. Ct. (so. and ea. dists.) N.Y. 1962. Assoc. Jacobs Persinger and Parker, N.Y.C., 1961-68; sec., treas., gen. counsel Lynch Corp., N.Y.C., 1968-69; counsel Allied Artists Industries, Inc., N.Y.C., 1970-80, sec., 1970-76, v.p., 1975-76, v.p. adminstrn., 1976-77, group v.p., 1977-80, dir., 1973-80; sec. Allied Artists Pictures Corp., 1973-74, dir., 1974-80; v.p., sec., dir. Allied Artists Video Corp., 1978-80; resident counsel Lorimar Prodns., Inc., N.Y.C., 1980-83; gen. corp. atty. NYNEX Corp., White Plains, N.Y., 1983-94; sec. NYNEX Devel. Co., White Plains, N.Y., 1984-87, NYNEX Internat. Co., White Plains, N.Y., 1985-87, Data Group Corp., White Plains, N.Y., 1985-87, NYNEX Info. Solutions Group Inc., White Plains, N.Y., 1987, NYNEX Sci. & Tech., Inc., White Plains, N.Y., 1991, NYNEX Venture Co., White Plains, N.Y., 1992-94. Sec., counsel, dir. PSP, Inc., 1970-76; sec., dir. D. Kaltman & Co., Inc., 1970-79, v.p., 1977-79; sec., dir. Vitabath, Inc., 1970-72, Apollo Motor Homes, Inc., 1970-80, v.p., 1977-80; sec., dir. Westwood Import Co., Inc., 1972-79, v.p., 1977-79; sec., dir. Paul-Marshall Products Inc., 1972-75, Adstat Co., 1972-74; v.p., dir. Palmland Fashions, Inc., 1971-78; mem. com. on criminal cts. Legal Aid Soc., 1969-72. Trustee Temple Beth Israel, Port Washington, N.Y., 1981-83, 87-89, rec. sec., 1983-85, fin. sec., 1985-87. Mem. ABA, N.Y. State Bar Assn., Am. Law Inst., Corp. Bar Assn. Westchester-Fairfield (co-chmn. SEC corp. and fin. com. 1989-90, bd. dirs. 1991-93, chmn. major program com. 1991, co-chmn. 1992-93), Phi Beta Kappa. Home: 61 Roger Dr Port Washington NY 11050-2527 *Dare to be different - the path to success is the road least travelled.*

FELDMAN, JOEL MARTIN, magistrate judge; b. Atlanta, Jan. 2, 1941; s. Louis Aaron and Rosalie (Bach) F.; m. Debora A. Kirkpatrick; children: Lawrence A., Allison R. AB in Law, Emory U., 1962, JD, 1964. Bar: Ga. 1963, U.S. Dist. Ct. (no. dist.) Ga. 1963, U.S. Ct. Mil. Appeals 1964, U.S. Ct. Appeals (5th cir.) 1963, U.S. Ct. Appeals (11th cir.) 1981, U.S. Supreme Ct. 1967. Asst. legis. counsel Gen. Assembly Ga., Atlanta, 1964-66; asst. atty. gen. State of Ga., Atlanta, 1966-68; asst. dist. atty. Atlanta Jud. Cir., 1968-72, 74; legis. asst., legal counsel Sen. Sam Nunn of Ga., 1973-74; magistrate U.S. Dist. Ct. (no. dist.) Ga., Atlanta, 1974—; cert. mil. judge Naval-Marine Corps Trial Judiciary, 1982-92. Former chmn. North Fulton Citizens Mental Health Adv. Coun.; pres. Temple Sinai Synagogue, Atlanta, 1994-96; chmn. Met. Atlanta 50th Ann. WWII Commemorative Cmty. With USAFR, 1964, capt. USNR, 1964-92. Mem. Fed. Bar Assn., State Bar Ga., Atlanta Bar Assn., Naval League U.S. (pres. Atlanta coun. 1985-86), Naval Res. Assn. (pres. 6th Dist. 1982-83), Fed. Magistrate Judges Assn. (dir. 11th cir. 1982-83), Atlanta Lawyers Club, Navy League (Atlanta dir., pres.), Naval Order (Atlanta pres., dir.). Office: 2027 US Courthouse 75 Spring St SW Atlanta GA 30303-3309

FELDMAN, JOEL SHALOM, mathematician; b. Ottawa, Ont., Can., June 14, 1949; s. Keiva and Anna (Ain) F. BS, U. Toronto, Ont., 1970; AM, Harvard U., 1971, PhD, 1974. Rsch. fellow Harvard U., Cambridge, Mass., 1974-75; Moore instr. MIT, Cambridge, 1975-77; prof. U. B.C., Vancouver, Can., 1977—; Aisenstadt chair lectr., Ctr. Rsch. Math. U. Montréal, 1999—2000. Assoc. editor Revs. Math. Physics, 1988—, Can. Jour. Math., 1994-98, Can. Math. Bull., 1994-98, Math Phys. EJ, 1995—, Ann. Henri Poincaré, 2000—, Jour. Math. Physics, 2005—; contbr. articles to profl. jours. Recipient Killam Rsch. prize U. B.C., 1988, Jeffery-Williams prize CMS, 2004, Faculty of Sci. Achievement award for Tchg., U. B.C., 2004; Woodrow Wilson fellow, 1970. Fellow: Royal Soc. Can. (John L. Synge award). Office: U BC Dept Math Vancouver BC Canada V6T 1Z2

FELDMAN, KAYWIN, museum director, curator; BA, U. Mich.; MA in mus. mgmt. and art hist., U. London. Ednl. curator British Mus. Art; dir. Fresno Met. Mus. Art, Hist. and Sci., Calif., 1996—99, Memphis Brooks Mus. Art, Tenn., 1999—. Curator It's Only Rock and Roll. Recipient Ctrl. Calif. Excellence in Bus. award, 1996. Office: Memphis Brooks Mus Art Overton Park 1934 Poplar Ave Memphis TN 38104*

FELDMAN, LARRY, JR., lawyer; b. Shreveport, La., Aug. 7, 1950; BA, La. State U., 1972, JD, 1974. Bar: La. 1974. Atty. Wiener, Weiss & Madison, PC, Shreveport, La. Capt. JAGC U.S. Army, 1974—77. Mem.: ABA, Shreveport Bar Assn., Fedn. Def. and Corp. Counsel, La. Assn. Def. Counsel, La. State Bar Assn. (bd. govs. 1994—97, sec. 1997—99, pres. 2002—03). Office: Wiener Weiss and Madison PO Box 21990 333 Texas St Ste 2350 Shreveport LA 71120-1990 Office Phone: 318-213-9258. E-mail: lfeldman@wwmlaw.com.

FELDMAN, LEONARD CECIL, physicist; b. NYC, June 8, 1939; s. Milton and Minnie (Schulman) F.; m. Elizabeth Gecsey, July 5, 1964; children: Gregory, Dana. MS, Rutgers U., 1963, PhD, 1967. Mem. tech. staff radiation physics rsch. dept. AT&T Bell Labs., Murray Hill, N.J., 1967-83, supr. materials interfaces, 1983-84, dept. head materials interfaces and ceramics, 1984-87, dept. head thin film semicondr. rsch., 1987-90, dept. head silicon device rsch., 1990-92, dept. head silicon materials rsch., 1992-96; Stevenson prof. physics Vanderbilt U., Nashville, 1996—. Guest scientist Aarhus (Denmark) U., 1970-71; vis. prof. Cornell U., Ithaca, N.Y., 1981, 82, 88; cons. Livermore (Calif.) Nat. Lab., 1989—; chmn. Gordon Conf. on Particle Solid Interactions, 1978, Gordon Conf. on Defects in Semicondrs., 1994; chmn. internal sci. coun. Danish Microelectronics Ctr.; mem. adv. com. N.J. Inst. Tech., Colo. Sch. Mines, Livermore Nat. Labs.; disting. vis. scientist Oak Ridge Nat. Lab., 1996—. Co-author: Materials Analysis by Ion Channeling, 1982, Fundamentals of Surface and Thin Film Analysis, 1986 (transl. into Japanese 1988, Russian, 1989), Electronic Thin Film Science, 1992; editor Applied Surface Sci., 1985-96; contbr. over 350 articles on semiconductor interface sci. to sci. jours. Recipient Disting. Merit award in material sci. and engring. U. Ill., 1989, sci. alumni award Drew U., 1995. Fellow AAAS, Am. Phys. Soc. (David Aller award 1999), Am. Vacuum Soc.; mem. IEEE, Materials Rsch. Soc., Am. Ceramic Soc., Danish Acad. Arts and Scis. Achievements include patent on semiconductor heterostructures having GexSi1-x layers, 20 others in thin films; discovery of structure of clean silicon surfaces; first demonstration of preservation of surface structures at buried interfaces; developement of technique of Rutherford Scattering for surface and interface analysis. Home: 510 Belgrave Park Nashville TN 37215-2450 Office: Vanderbilt Univ Dept Physics and Astronomy Nashville TN 37235 Office Phone: 615-343-7273. Business E-Mail: l.c.feldman@vanderbilt.edu.

FELDMAN, LES J., finance educator; b. Miami, Aug. 25, 1946; s. Sidney Feldman and Sophie Suda; children: Joshua, Jessie, Amy. AA, Miami Dade North Jr. Coll., 1969; BS in Sci., Fla. Atlantic U., 1971; MBA, Nova Southeastern U., 1991, Doctorate in Bus. Adminstrn., 1996. Cert. tchr. Fla., purchasing mgr. Purchasing mgr. Motorola, Inc., Ft. Lauderdale, Fla., 1981—; instr. Everglades Coll., Ft. Lauderdale, 2002, Fla. Atlantic U., Ft. Lauderdale, 1996—2001. Contbr. articles to profl. jours., chapters to books. Mem.: Acad. Mgmt. Home: 1780 SW 55th Ave Fort Lauderdale FL 33317

FELDMAN, LEWIS G., lawyer; b. NYC, Feb. 13, 1956; m. Stacey Feldman; children: Jack, Cole. BS with highest honors, Univ. Calif., Santa Cruz, 1978; JD, Univ. Calif., Davis, 1982. Bar: Calif. 1982. Ptnr. Pillsbury Winthrop Shaw Pittman, LA. Arbitrator Am. Arbitration Assn.; bd. mem. City of Hope Real Estate Industry Council; dir. Univ. So. Calif. Lusk Ctr. for Real Estate Devel.; leader pub. fin. practice Pillsbury Winthrop Shaw Pittman, LA, office mng. ptnr. Editor (exec.): UC Davis Law Rev.; contbr. articles to newspapers & profl. jours.; mem. editl. adv. bd. Real Estate So. Calif. Bd. mem. United Way of Greater LA. Mem.: ABA, Nat. Assn. Bond Lawyers, Nat. Assn. Real Estate Investment Trusts, Urban Land Inst., LA Bar Assn., Beverly Hills Bar Assn. Office: Pillsbury Winthrop Shaw Pittman 21st Fl MGM Tower 10250 Constellation Blvd Los Angeles CA 90067-6221 Office Phone: 310-203-1188. Office Fax: 310-286-6672. Business E-Mail: lewis.feldman@pillsburylaw.com.

FELDMAN, MARC D., cardiologist, biomedical engineer, physiologist; b. Washington, Mar. 14, 1955; s. William M. and Gloria M. Feldman; m. Jonquil D. Feldman, June 8, 1981; children: Jake, Nate. BS magna cum laude, Duke U., 1977; MD, U. Pa., 1981. Diplomate Nat. Bd. Med. Examiners, Am. Bd. Internal Medicine, Am. Bd. Cardiovasc. Disease, Am. Bd. Interventional Cardiology. Intern, resident in internal medicine U. Chgo., 1981-83; fellow in cardiology Harvard U., Boston, 1983-87; asst. prof. U. Va., Charlottesville, 1987-94; assoc. prof. U. Pitts., 1994-98, U. Tex., San Antonio, 1998—. Adj. asst. prof. Sch. Biomed. Engring. U. Tex., Austin, 1998—; staff physician South Tex. Vets. Health Care Sys., 1998—; dir. rsch. cardiac catheteriazaion lab U. Va. Sch. Medicine, 1990-94, head com. for clin. referrals dept. cardiology, 1990-94; dir. in-patient cardiology, 1992-94; dir. catheterization lab. Westmoreland Regional Hosp., 1994-95; dir. cardiac catheterization lab. Presbyn. Hosp., U. Pitts. Med. Ctr., 1994-98, coord. cardiac catheterization conf., 1994-98, coord. cardiac didactic and rsch. conf., 1994-98; assoc. dir. cardiac catheterization labs. U. Tex. Health Sci. Ctr., 1998—, dir. interventional rsch., 1998—; lectr. in field; editl. cons. to various med. jours. Co-patentee metabolic catheter, multifrequency conductance system to evaluate cardiac mechanics, method and apparatus for intravascular drug and gene delivery; contbr. numerous articles to profl. publs. Named one of top two physicians in cardiac catheterization in tristate area, Pitts. Mag., 1997; recipient Hon. Sci. award, Bausch and Lomb, 1973, Morton McCutcheon meml. prize, U. Pa. Sch. Medicine, 1979, Young Investigator award, Am. Heart Assn., 1993; fellow, NSF, 1973—74, NIH, 1984—87; grantee, Bayer, 1988—90, Am. Heart Assn., 1988—90, 2002—, Otsuka Pharm., 1992—94, NIH, 1992—97, 2001—02, Merck Pharm., 1992—97, 2000—, Whitby Pharm., 1993—94, Siemens Med. Sys., 1995—96, Millar Instruments, 1999—2001, Mitsubishi Chem. Am., Inc., 1999—2001, Cleve. Clin. Found., 1999—2000, Kronkosky Found., 2000—01, Takeda, 2000—. Fellow Am. Coll. Cardiology; mem. Med. Soc. Va., Cardiovascular Sys. Dynamics Soc. Home: 11 Royal Gardens San Antonio TX 78248 Office Phone: 210-567-2106. E-mail: feldmanm@uthscsa.edu.

FELDMAN, MARC DAVID, psychiatrist; b. Kingston, NY, Sept. 9, 1958; AB, Dartmouth Coll., 1980, MD, 1984. Diplomate Am. Bd. Psychiatry and Neurology, Am. Acad. Pain Mgmt, Nat. Bd. Med. Examiners. Resident in psychiatry Duke U. Med. Ctr., Durham, N.C., 1984-88; chief resident in psychiatry Durham VA Med. Ctr., 1987-88; asst. prof. Duke U. Med. Ctr., Durham, N.C., 1988-90; med. dir. Hill Crest Hosp., Birmingham, Ala., 1990-93; vice chair dept. psychiatry U. Ala., Birmingham, 1993—; med. dir. Ctr. for Psychiat. Medicine-U. Ala., Birmingham, 1993—; dir. divsn. adult psychiatry U. Ala., 1994—; med. dir. United Behavioral Sys., 1996—. Pvt. practice, 1990-93; acting dir. psychosocial support program Duke Comprehensive Cancer Ctr., 1989-90. Contbr. articles to profl. jours. Laughlin fellow Am. Coll. Psychiatrists, 1988; Rufus Choate scholar Dartmouth Coll., 1977-79. Mem. AMA, So. Med. Assn., Am. Psychiat. Assn., Ala. Psychiat. Assn., Phi Beta Kappa. Avocations: movies, computing, collecting contemporary art. Office Phone: 205-529-1500. Personal E-mail: mdf@myself.com.

FELDMAN, MARK B., lawyer; b. Rochester, N.Y., Oct. 3, 1935; s. Edward P. and Grace Feldman; m. Marcia Smith, Nov. 23, 1963; children: Ilana, Rachel. AB, Wesleyan U., 1957; LLB, Harvard U., 1960. Bar: N.Y. 1961, D.C. 1974. Assoc. Kaye, Scholer, Fierman, Hays & Handler, N.Y.C., 1960-65; with Office Legal Adviser, Dept. State, 1965-81, dep. legal adviser, 1974-81, acting legal adviser, 1981; of counsel Donovan, Leisure, Newton & Irvine, Washington, 1981-84, ptnr., 1984-87; mem. Feith & Zell, P.C., 1988—2001; of counsel Garvey, Schubert & Barer, 2002—. Adj. prof. Georgetown U., Washington, 1982—89. Mem.: ABA, Am. Soc. Internat. Law, Coun. Fgn. Rels. Address: 4010 48th St NW Washington DC 20016-2318

FELDMAN, MARK I., lawyer; b. Mar. 15, 1950; BSIE with honors, Univ. Ill., 1971; JD, Georgetown Univ., 1974. Bar: Ill. 1974, US Dist. Ct. (no. dist.) Ill., US Ct. Appeals (7th and Fed. cir.), US Patent and Trademark Off. Sr. trademark counsel G.D. Searle & Co.; ptnr. DLA Piper Rudnick Gray Cary US LLP, Chgo. Mem.: ABA, Am. Intellectual Property Assn. (chair, franchising com. 1997—2000), Intellectual Property Law Assn. Chgo. (bd. mgrs. 1996—97, v.p. 2002—03, pres.-elect 2004, pres. 2005), Internat. Trademark Assn., Brand Names Edn. Found. Office: DLA Piper Rudnick Gray Cary US LLP Ste 1900 203 N LaSalle St Chicago IL 60601-1293 Office Phone: 312-368-7084. Office Fax: 312-236-7516. Business E-Mail: mark.feldman@dlapiper.com.

FELDMAN, MYER, lawyer; b. Phila., June 1917; s. Israel and Bella (Kurland) F.; m. Adrienne Arsht, Sept. 28, 1980; children by previous marriage: Jane Margaret, James Alan. Student, Girard Coll., Phila., 1922-31; BS in Econs., U. Pa., 1935, LL.B. (fellow 1938-39), 1938. Bar: Pa. 1938, D.C. 1965, U.S. Supreme Ct. 1965. Pvt. practice, Phila. and D.C., 1939-42, 65—; spl. counsel, exec. asst. to chmn. SEC, 1946-54; mem. counsel armed svcs. com. U.S. Senate, 1954-55, counsel banking and currency commn., 1955-57; legis. asst. to Senator John F. Kennedy, 1958-61; dep. spl. counsel to Presidents Kennedy and Johnson, 1961-64; counsel to Pres. Johnson, 1964-65; founder, ptnr. Ginsburg Feldman & Bress, Washington, 1965-98; pres. Ardman Broadcasting Corp., 1992—. Pres. S.W. Fla. Broadcasting, KEFCO Apparel Corp.; lectr. law U. Pa., 1941-42; prof. law Am. U., 1955-56; pres. Radio Assocs., Inc., 1959-81; dir. Music Fair Group, Inc.; chmn. bd. Fin. Satellite Corp.; partner Key Stas., 1960-79; chmn. bd. Speer Publs., 1972-77, Capital Gazette Press, Inc., 1972-77, Bay Publs., 1972-77; bd. dirs. Nat. Savs. & Trust Co., Flame Hope, Inc., Media and Art Svcs., Inc., WSSH, Inc., Internat. Fusion Energy Systems Co., Inc., WLLH Broadcasters, WLAM Broadcasters, Capitol Broadcasting Inc., Lazare Kaplan, Inc., Trade Nat. Bank; chmn. bd., CEO Totalbank Corp.; pres. Les Amis Constrn., 1997; v.p. Crystal Galleria LLC, 2000—; dir. Neogenix, 2004—. Author: Standard Pennsylvania Practice, 4 vols., 1958; prodr. various broadway musicals and plays; prodr. Am. Forum TV show; contbr. articles to profl. jours. Pres. N.Y. Art Festival, Inc., 1972-80; del. Democratic Nat. Conv., 1968; pres. McGovern for Pres. Com., 1971-72; vice chmn. Congl. Leadership for Future, 1970; finance chmn. Bayh for Pres. Com., 1975-76; bd. dirs. Weitzman Inst., 1963-84; chmn. exec. com. Spl. Olympics, Inc.; trustee Eleanor Roosevelt Meml. Found., 1963—, Jewish Publ. Soc., 1966-78, Declaration of Independence, House and Library, 1965-75; bd. dirs. Henry M. Jackson Found., 1984-92, trustee; mem. exec. com. Hollings for Pres. Com., 1984; bd. dirs. John F. Kennedy Library, 1983—; bd. overseers V.I. U., 1962—; dir. U. Minn. Freeman Ctr., 1991—. Served with USAAF, 1942-46. Mem. U. Pa. Law Alumni Assn. Washington (pres. 1952-58), Potomac Tennis Club, Tau Epsilon Rho (pres. 1938) Office: 10608 Stapleford Hall Dr Potomac MD 20854-4447 *Using your sense of humor will diffuse any problem.*

FELDMAN, NAN HASS, artist, educator; b. Bklyn., May 6, 1950; d. Samuel Aaron and Marietta (Meshberg) Hass; m. Alan Grad Feldman, Oct. 22, 1972; children: Rebecca Lee, Daniel Gabriel. BFA, SUNY, Buffalo, 1972; MA, Goddard Coll., 1987; MFA, Vt. Coll., 1993. Tchr. art Brophy Pub. Sch., Framingham, Mass., 1972-74; artist tchr. Danforth Mus. Art, Framingham, 1975—2002, Worcester (Mass.) Art Mus., 1982—, DeCordova Mus., Lincoln, Mass., 1985—2005; instr. art Framingham State Coll., 1987—, Worcester State Coll., 1994-96; coord. painting workshops, Provence, France, 1999—2005. Presenter workshops in field; artist-in-resident Babson Coll., 1976, pub. schs., Mass., 1981, 85-86; judge scholastic art awards Boston Globe, 1989-98; artist mentor Art All-State, Worcester, 1994, 96, 98. One-woman shows include Worcester Art Mus., 1990, Jefferson Cutter Gallery, Arlington, Mass., 1994, 1996, Cove Gallery, Wellfleet, Mass., 1994, Waterman Gallery, Wellesley, Mass., 2000—01, Fanning Gallery, Wellfleet, 2001, Galerie de Provence, NYC, 2002—04, Artana Gallery, Framingham, Mass., 2003, 2004, exhibited in group shows at Worcester Art Mus., 1975, 1985, 1987—88, 1990, 1992, 1998, 2001—03, Danforth Art Mus., 1975, 1978, 1982, 1984, 1986, 1988, 1990, 1993, 1997, Fitchburg (Mass.) Art Mus., 1976—77, Mass. Coll. Art, 1981, Newport (R.I.) Mus. Art, 1984, Boston Ctr. Arts, 1989—90, Cove Gallery, 1991—93, 2002, Chase Gallery, Boston, 1991, Arden Gallery, 1991, Powers Gallery, Acton, Mass., 1997—98, 2002—05, Handsel Gallery, Santa Fe, 2000—02, A. Jain Marunouchi Gallery, N.Y.C., 1999—2001, Lyman-Eyer Gallery, Provincetown, Mass., 2003, 2004, 2005, DeCordova Mus., 2004—05, Artana Gallery, Brookline, Mass., 2005, others. Represented in permanent collections Fidelity Investment Corp., Verifine Products, Inc., Warner Bros. Movie Studios, Children's Hosp., Boston, Brigham and Women's Hosp., Mass., Metro West Hosp., St. Elizabeth's Hosp. Recipient Liquitex fine art achievement award, Binney and Smith, Inc., 1987, Basil H. Alkazzi Nat. Acquisition award, 1995, Frances N. Roddy prize, Concord, Mass., 2000, 2001, Frances A. Kinnicutt Fgn. Travel award, Worcester Art Mus., 2005—; grantee Mass. Arts Lottery, 1990, Mass Cultural Coun., 1997. Democrat. Avocations: swimming, reading art continuously, cooking. Home: 399 Belknap Rd Framingham MA 01701-2807 Personal E-mail: nanhassfeldman@aol.com.

FELDMAN, NANCY JANE, insurance company executive; b. Green Bay, Wis., July 6, 1946; d. Benjamin J. and Ellen M. Naze; m. Robert P. Feldman, Aug. 24, 1968; 1 child, Sara J. BA, U. Wis., 1969, MS, 1974. Supr. EPSDT program Minn. Dept. Human Svcs., St. Paul, 1974-80, supr. healthcare programs, 1980-84; team leader human resources budget Minn. Dept. Fin., St. Paul, 1984-87; asst. commr. Minn. Dept. Health, St. Paul, 1987-91; team leader CORE program Minn. Dept. Adminstrn., St. Paul, 1991-93; dir. state pub. programs Medica, Allina Health Sys., Mpls., 1993-95; CEO UCare Minn., St. Paul, 1995—. Bd. chair Minn. Coun. Health Plans, Mpls., 1995—; bd. dir. Stratis Health. Bd. dirs Vols. Am. Health Nat. Svcs., 1994—; vice chair bd. dir. Ctr. for Victims of Torture, 1997-2003, chair, 2004. Mem. Women's Health Leadership Trust, Nat. Inst. Health Policy. Avocations: distance swimming, bicycling, travel. Office: UCare Minn PO Box 52 Minneapolis MN 55440-0052 Home: 4822 Folwell Dr Minneapolis MN 55406 E-mail: nfeldman@ucare.org.

FELDMAN, NOAH, law educator; b. 1970; m. Jeannie Suk. AB summa cum laude, Harvard U., 1992; DPhil in Islamic Thought, Oxford U., 1994; JD, Yale U., 1997. Bar: NY 1998. Law clk. to Hon. Harry T. Edwards US Ct. Appeals DC Cir., 1997—98; law clk. to Hon. David H. Souter US Supreme Ct., 1998—99; jr. fellow Soc. Fellows Harvard U., Cambridge, Mass., 1999—2001; asst. prof. law NYU Sch. Law, 2001—04, assoc. prof., 2004—05, prof., 2005—. Adj. fellow New Am. Found., Washington; vis. prof. Yale U., 2004, Harvard U., 2005. Author: After Jihad: America and the Struggle for Islamic Democracy, 2003, What We Owe Iraq: War and the Ethics of Nation Building, 2004, Divided by God: America's Church-State Problem-and What We Should Do About It, 2005. Rhodes scholar. Office: NYU Sch Law Vanderbilt HallRm 411C 40 Washington Sq S New York NY 10012-1099 Office Phone: 212-998-6711. E-mail: noah.feldman@nyu.edu.

FELDMAN, PHILLIP, lawyer; b. N.Y.C., Apr. 26, 1932; BS, Calif. State U., 1956; MBA, U. So. Calif., 1963, JD, 1966. Bar: Calif., bd. cert. specialist legal malpractice, ABA, ABPLA, CA. Expert witness legal malpractice Law Offices of Phillip Feldman, Sherman Oaks, Calif., 1967—; with Feldman & Haber, Van Nuys, Calif., 1968, Feldman, Golde & Supanic, Van Nuys, Calif., 1970, Feldman, Gordon & Goldstein, Sherman Oaks, Calif., 1980; pvt. practice Sherman Oaks, Calif., 1985; former judge pro tem; former state bar prosecutor; now def. counsel. Fellow Am. Bd. Profl. Liability Attys. (chair cert. com. legal). Office: 15250 Ventura Blvd Ste 610 Sherman Oaks CA 91403-3218 Office Phone: 818-986-9890. E-mail: legmalpexpert@aol.com.

FELDMAN, ROBERT C., public relations executive; b. N.Y.C., Oct. 22, 1956; BA, Syracuse U., 1978. Gen. mgr. Sta. WPNR-FM Utica Coll. Syracuse U., 1976-78; from asst. acct. exec. to sr. v.p., group mgr. Burson-Marsteller, 1978-88; sr. v.p. Ketchum Pub. Rels., N.Y.C., 1988-97; pres., CEO GCI Group, 1997—. Bd. dirs. Thurgood Marshall Scholarship Fund. Mem.: Coun. Pub. Rels. Firms (bd. dirs.), Pub. Rels. Seminar, Pub. Rels. Soc. Am. Office: GCI GROUP INC 777 3rd Ave New York NY 10017-1401

FELDMAN, ROGER DAVID, lawyer; b. N.Y.C., Apr. 7, 1943; s. Louis and Dora (Goldsmith) Feldman; m. Gail Steg, May 31, 1969; children: Rebecca, Seth. AB, Brown U., 1962; LLB, Yale U.; MBA, Harvard U. Bar: N.Y. 1966, DC 1977. Ops. rsch. analyst Office Asst. Sec. Def., Washington, 1967—68; staff asst. Office of U.S. Pres., Washington, 1968—69; assoc. LeBoeuf, Lamb, Leiby, and MacRae, 1969—75; ptnr. Le Boeuf, Lamb, Leiby, and MacRae, 1977—83; dep. asst. adminstr. FEA, Washington, 1975—77; mng. ptnr. project fin. group Nixon, Hargrave, Devans, and Doyle, Washington, 1983—89; head ptnr. project fin. group McDermott, Will, and Emery, Washington, 1989—97; chair project fin. group Bingham McCutchen, LLP, 1997—. Mem. fin. adv. bd. EPA, 1989—92; bd. dirs. R. J. Rudden and Assocs., Inc., Cogeneration Inst., Pub. Pvt. Venture Divsn. Am. Rd. and Transp. Builders, 1991—93, Am. Coun. Renewable Energy, Water Industry Coun.; pres. Nat. Coun. Pub. Pvt. Partnerships, 1983—98, chair, 1998—. Author (with others): Infrastructure Finance: Tools for the Future, 1988, Public-Private Ventures in Transportation, 1990; author: Comprehensive Guide to Water and Wastewater Finance, 1991, Privatization of Public Utilities, 1995, Privatization, 1995; mem. bd. editors Yale Law Jour., 1964—65, Jour. Structured and Project Fin., 1995—, Constrn. Bus. Rev., 1992—; Wash. editor: Cogeneration Monthly Letter, 1987—98, Merchant Power Monthly, 1998—; editor: Strategic Planning for Energy and the Environment, 1992— (Author of the Yr., 1998), Power Marketers Assn. On Line Mag., 1999—, Power Exec., 2002—; contbr. articles to profl. jours. Mem.: ABA (chmn. energy law com. 1980—83, mem. alt. energy sources com. 1981—84, chmn. environ. values com. 1983—89, mem. com. privatization 1985—90, mem. alt. energy sources com. 1986—90, chmn. energy fin. 1990—91, chair renewable energy resources 2003—), Assn. Energy Engr. (Cogeneration Profl. of the Yr. 1990), DC Bar Assn. (chair internat. fin. and investment com. 1998—), N.Y. Bar Assn., Nat. Coun. Pub. and Pvt. Partnerships (Outstanding Contbn. to Privatization award), Fed. Energy Bar Assn. (chmn. cogeneration com. 1981—82), Internat. Pct. Infrastructure Assn. (v.p.), Internat. Pvt. Water Assn. (v.p.), N.E. Energy and Commerce Assn. (bd. dirs., chair reliability and security com.), Phi Beta Kappa. Office: Bingham LLP 1120 20th St NW Ste 800 Washington DC 20036-3406 Office Phone: 202-778-3181. Business E-Mail: r.feldman@bingham.com.

FELDMAN, ROGER LAWRENCE, artist, educator; b. Spokane, Wash., Nov. 19, 1949; s. Marvin Lawrence and Mary Elizabeth (Shafer) Feldman; m. Astrid Lunde, Dec. 16, 1972; children: Kirsten B., Kyle Lawrence. BA in Art Edn., U. Wash., 1972; postgrad., Fuller Theol. Sem., Pasadena, Calif., 1972—73, Regent Coll., Vancouver, B.C., 1974; MFA in Sculpture, Claremont (Calif.) Grad. U., 1977. Tchg. asst. Claremont Grad. U.; prof. art Biola U., La Mirada, Calif., 1989-2000, Seattle Pacific U., 2000—. Adj. instr. Seattle Pacific U., 1979, 80, 82, 83, Linfield Coll., 1978, Edmonds C.C., 1978-80, Shoreline C.C., 1978; guest artist and lectr. One-man shows include Art Ctr. Gallery, Seattle Pacific U., 1977, 83, 84, Linfield Coll., McMinnville, Oreg., 1979, Blackfish Gallery, Portland, 1982, Lynn McAllister Gallery, Seattle, 1986, Biola U., 1989, 93, Coll. Gallery, La. Coll., Pineville, 1990, Gallery W. Sacramento, 1991, 96, Aughinbaugh Gallery, Grantham, Pa., 1992, Riverside Art Mus., 1994, Azusa Pacific U., 1995, Cornerstone '96, Bushnell, Ill., 1996, Davison Gallery, Roberts Wesleyan Coll., Rochester, NY, 1997, Concordia U., Irvine, Calif., 1999, Northwestern Coll., St. Paul, 2000, Union U., Jackson, Tenn., 2001, F. Schaeffer Inst., St. Louis, 2001, G. Fox U., Newberg, Oreg., 2001, Seattle Pacific U., 2002, Suyama Space, Seattle, 2005, Schloss Mittersill, Austria, 2005; group shows include Pasadena Artists Concern Gallery, 1976, Libra Gallery, Claremont, 1977, Renshaw Gallery, McMinnville, 1978, Cheney Cowles Mus., Spokane, 1979, 80, 83, Lynn McAllister Gallery, Seattle, 1985, Bumbershoot, Seattle, 1985, 86, 87, Pacific Arts Ctr., Seattle, 1987, Grand Canyon U., Phoenix, 1990, Connemara, Dallas, 1991, West Bend (Wis.) Gallery, 1992, LA Mcpl. Satellite Gallery, 1990, 93, Greenbelt 93, Northamptonshire, Eng., 1993, Claremont Sch. Theology, 1994, Queens Coll. Cambridge U., Eng., 1994, Jr. Arts Ctr. Gallery, Barnsdall Park, LA, 1994, Bade Mus. Pacific Sch. of Religion, Berkeley, Calif., 1995, Ctrl. Arts Collective, Tucson, 1995, LA Mcpl. Gallery Barnsdall Art Park, 1996, Reconstructive Gallery Santa Ana, Calif., 1997, Guggenheim Gallery, Chapman U., Orange, Calif., 1997, Weaver Art Gallery, Bethel Coll., Mishawaka, Ind., 1998-, Concordia U. Art Gallery, Mequon, Wis., 1999, Palos Verdes Art Ctr., Calif., 1999, Grand Canyon U., Phoenix, 2000, Tryon Ctr. Visual Arts, Charlotte, N.C., 2001, U. Dallas, 2001, Weaver Gallery,

2001, John Brown U., Siloam Springs, Ark., 2001, Sweetwater Ctr. for the Arts, Sewickley, Pa., 2002, Ind. Wesleyan U., Marion, 2002, Tacoma Art Mus., 2004, others; comms. Wheaton, Pasadena, Calif., 1999, Renton Vocat. Tech Inst., 1987-89. Recipient Prescott King County Arts Commn. Individual Artist Project award, Seattle, 1988, Natl. Endowment for the Arts Individual Artist fellowship in Sculpture, 1986, David Gaiser award for sculpture Cheney Cowles Mus., 1980, Disting. award for Harborview Med. Ctr. "Viewpoint", Soc. for Tech. Comm., 1987, Design award for "Seafirst News", Internat. Assn. Bus. Comm., 1987, Pace Setter award, 1987, Prescott Sculpture award CIVA, 2005, others; Connemara Sculpture grant, 1990, Biola U., 1991; Faculty Rsch. grantee Seattle Pacific U., 2001-02, sr. faculty rsch. grantee, 2005—. Office: Seattle Pacific U 3307 Third Ave West Seattle WA 98119 Office Phone: 206-281-3442. Business E-Mail: rfeldman@spu.edu. E-mail: rakfeldman2@comcast.net.

FELDMAN, RONALD ARTHUR, sociologist, educator; b. Buffalo, Jan. 17, 1938; s. David Jacob and Clara (Spector) F.; m. Dina Cohen Feinstein, Dec. 23, 1962; children: Daniel, Deborah, Darrah. BA, U. Buffalo, 1960; MSW, U. Mich., 1963, PhD, 1966. Cert., Acad. Cert. Social Workers. Asst. prof. U. Calif., Berkeley, 1966-68; Fulbright lectr. Social Services Acad., Ankara, Turkey, 1968-69; assoc. prof. Washington U. Sch. Social Work, St. Louis, 1969-72, prof., 1972-86, acting dean, 1973-74; dir. Ctr. for Study of Youth Devel., Boys Town, Nebr., 1974-78, Ctr. for Adolescent Mental Health, St. Louis, 1983-87; assoc. dean Columbia U. Sch. Social Work, N.Y.C., 1985-86, prof., dean, 1986—2001, Ruth Harris Ottman Centennial prof., 1995—, dir. Ctr. for Study of Social Work Practice, 2002—. Cons. NIMH, Rockville, Md., 1980-91; bd. dirs. Ednl. Inst., Jewish Bd. Family and Children's Svcs., N.Y.C., 1986-2004, William T. Grant Found., Bd. Behavior and Mental Disorders, Inst. Medicine. Sr. author: Contemporary Approaches to Group Treatment, 1975, The St. Louis Conundrum: The Effective Treatment of Antisocial Youths, 1983, Children at Risk: In the Web of Parental Mental Illness, 1987; sr. editor: Advances in Adolescent Mental Health, vols. 1-4, 1986—. Citizen leader Clayton (Mo.) Bd. Edn., 1981-82; mem. profl. rev. bd. Mo. Dept. Mental Health, Jefferson City, 1981-86; trustee Wm. T. Grant Found., 1993—. Recipient Disting. Faculty award Washington U., St. Louis, 1984; research grantee NIMH, Rockville, Md., 1970-75, 80-84, Office of Human Devel. Services, Washington, 1983-87. Fellow NASW, Soc. for Rsch. in Child Devel.; mem. Coun. on Social Work Edn. (bd. dirs. 1992-95), Am. Sociol. Assn., Internat. Assn. Child and Adolescent Psychiatry and Allied Professions (v.p. 1995—). Avocations: swimming, tennis. Office: Columbia U Sch Social Work 1255 Amsterdam Ave New York NY 10027 Office Phone: 212-851-2265. Business E-Mail: rafi@columbia.edu.

FELDMAN, SAMUEL MITCHELL, neuroscientist, educator; b. Phila., Sept. 26, 1933; s. Boris and Fannie B. (Shrager) F.; children— Lee Stephen, David Saul. BA, U. Pa., 1954; MA, Northwestern U., 1955; PhD, McGill U., 1959. Fellow in physiology U. Wash., Seattle, 1958-60; from instr. to asso. prof. physiology Albert Einstein Coll. Medicine, 1960-71; prof. psychology N.Y. U., 1971—, head dept., 1972-76, prof. neuroscience, 1988—, dir. grad. studies neural sci., 1989—; mem. psychol. sci. study sect. NIMH, 1968-72, chmn., 1970-72, mem. biol. sci. tng. grant rev. com., 1977-83. Cons. in field. Contbr. articles to profl. jours. Fellow USPHS, 1958-60; recipient Career award, 1969-71, research grantee, 1963— Mem. Am. Physiol. Soc., Soc. Neurosci., Sigma Xi. Home: 336 Ctrl Pk W New York NY 10025 Office: New York Univ Ctr for Neural Science New York NY 10003

FELDMAN, SANDRA, labor union executive; b. N.Y.C., Oct. 14, 1939; m. Arthur Barnes. B, Brooklyn Coll., 1960; M in English Lit., NYU, 1965. Tchr. Pub. Sch. 34, N.Y.C.; field rep. United Fedn. Tchrs., 1966-83, exec. dir., 1983-86, sec., 1983-86, pres. N.Y.C., 1986-97, Am. Fedn. Tchrs., 1997—. Exec. com. Edn. Internat., v.p.; exec. coun. AFL-CIO, 1997—. Active Coun. on Competitiveness, Internat. Rescue Com., Freedom House, A. Philip Randolph Inst., Jewish Labor Com., Coalition Labor Union Women, Nat. Coun. Ams. to Prevent Handgun Violence, N.Y. Urban League, Women's Forum, Women's Commn. on Refugee Children; co-chair Child Labor Coalition; nat. bd. mem. Profl. Tchg. Stds.; chair AFL-CIO Com. on Social Policy; mem. U.S. com. UNICEF Named one of N.Y.C. 75 Most Influential Women, Crain's New York Bus.; recipient Disting. Labor Leadership award, Nat. Urban Coalition, 1989, Labor award, Nat. Jewish Congress, 1997, Robert F. Kennedy-Martin Luther King Jr. award, Coalition to Stop Gun Violence, 2001, Not For Ourselves Alone Outstanding Leadership award, N.Y. State United Tchrs., 2002. Avocations: collecting African art, jazz, reading. Office: Am Fedn Tchrs 555 New Jersey Ave NW Washington DC 20001-2029 E-mail: online@AFT.org.

FELDMAN, STANLEY GEORGE, lawyer; b. NYC, Mar. 9, 1933; s. Meyer and Esther Betty (Golden) F.; m. Norma Arambula; 1 dau., Elizabeth L. Student, UCLA, 1950-51; LL.B., U. Ariz., 1956. Bar: Ariz. 1956. Practiced in, Tucson, 1956-81; ptnr. Miller, Pitt & Feldman, 1968-81; justice Ariz. Supreme Ct., Phoenix, 1982—2002, chief justice, 1992-97; of counsel Haralson, Miller, Pitt Feldman & McAnally. Lectr. Coll. Law, U. Ariz., 1965-76, adj. prof., 1976-81, 2000, 03, 05. Bd. dirs. Tucson Jewish Community Council, U. Ariz. Found., 1999-2005. Mem. ABA, Am. Bd. Trial Advocates (past pres. So. Ariz. chpt.), Ariz. Bar Assn. (pres. 1974-75, bd. govs. 1967-76), Pima County Bar Assn. (past pres.), Am. Trial Lawyers Assn. (dir. chpt. 1967-76), U. Ariz. Law Coll. Assn. Democrat. Jewish. Office: 1 S Church Ave Ste 900 Tucson AZ 85701-1620 Office Phone: 520-792-3836. E-mail: sfeldman@hmpmlaw.com.

FELDMAN, STEPHEN, academic administrator; b. N.Y.C., Sept. 11, 1944; s. Harry and Mae (Morris) F.; m. Constance M. Lerudis, June 1, 1969; children— Jennifer Dawn, Timothy Richard. BBA, CCNY, 1966, MBA, 1968, PhD (fellow), 1971. Chmn. dept. banking, fin. and investments Hofstra U., Hempstead, N.Y., 1969-77, assoc. prof., 1974-77; dean Ancell Sch. of bus. Western Conn. State U., Danbury, 1977-81, pres., 1981-92, Nova Southeastern U., Ft. Lauderdale, Fla., 1992-94; v.p. real estate Ethan Allen Inc., Danbury, 1995-96; v.p. univ. rels., devel. Calif. State U., Long Beach, 1996-99; pres. Astronaut Meml. Found., Kennedy Space Ctr., Fla., 1999—. Bd. dirs. Ethan Allen Inc., Sci. Horizons Inc.; cons. IBM, N.Y. Telephone Co. Editor: Credit Unions, 1974, Handbook of Wealth Management, 1977, Smarter Money, 1985; contbr. articles to profl. jours. Trustee Danbury Hosp., United Way. Mem. Am. Assn. State Colls. and Univs. (chmn. corp. coll. rels.), Greater Ft. Lauderdale C. of C. Office: Astronaut Meml Found Ctr Space Mail Code Amf Kennedy Space Center FL 32899-0001 E-mail: sfeldman@amfcse.org.

FELDMAN, SUSAN ELEANOR, technology analyst; b. N.Y.C., Feb. 14, 1947; d. Bernard and Ruth (Gold) Goodman; m. Robert Larry Feldman, June 25, 1967; children: David, Elana. BA, Cornell U., 1967; AM in Libr. Sci., U. Mich., 1968. Lic. libr., Calif., N.Y. Tech. info. specialist Nat. Tech. Info. Svc., Springfield, Va., 1968-70; audio-visual coord. South Ctrl. Rsch. Libr. Coun., Ithaca, N.Y., 1970-71; young adult svcs. libr. Tompkins County Pub. Libr., Ithaca, 1972-75; adj. prof. Syracuse U. Sch. Info. Studies, 1975; reference libr. Cuesta C.C., San Luis Obispo, Calif., 1976-79, instr., 1977-78, mgmt. intern, 1978-79; asst. to dir. Ithaca Coll. Libr., 1980-81; pres. Datasearch, Ithaca, 1981—2000; rsch. v.p. content mgmt. and retrieval software IDC, Framingham, 2000—. Pres. LAMP, San Luis Obispo, 1978-79; mem. reference com. South Cen. Rsch. Libr. Coun., 1984-89; mem. program. coms. Search Engines, Joint Com. on Digital Librs. Author: The Internet at a Glance, 1993, 94, 95; contbr. articles to profl. publs., chpt. to book. V.p., pres.-elect Children's and Young Adults Svcs. sect. N.Y. Libr. Assn., 1974-75; violist San Luis Obispo Orch., 1976-79, Beaux Eaux Quartet, Ithaca, 1981-2001, Cornell U. Orch., Ithaca, 1989-95, Shir Madness, 2004—; instr. Gifted and Talented Program, 1983-90 Mem. Assn. Ind. Info. Profls. (ethics com. 1986-87, v.p., pres.-elect 1992-93, pres. 1993-94, dir. 1995-2000), Assn. Computing Machinery, Am. Soc. Info. Sci. and Tech Avocations: music, reading, hiking, skiing, travel. Office: IDC 5 Speen St Framingham MA 01701 Office Phone: 508-935-4552.

FELDMAN, TED, cardiologist; b. Lincoln, Nebr., Nov. 3, 1952; BA, Ind. U., 1974, MD, 1978. Diplomate Am. Bd. Internal Medicine, Am. Bd. Cardiology. Intern medicine Rush Med. Coll., 1978-79, resident, 1979-81, chief resident, 1981-82; fellow cardiology U. Chgo., 1982-85, asst. prof. medicine, 1985-92, assoc. prof., 1992-97, prof., 1997—, dir. interventional cardiology, 1988—, dir. cardiac catheterization lab., 1997—. Contbr. articles to profl. jours. Fellow Am. Coll. Cardiology, Soc. for Coronary Angiography and Intervention. Office: U Chgo Hosps 5841 S Maryland Ave Rm 5076 Chicago IL 60637-1463

FELDMAN, WALTER SIDNEY, artist, educator; b. Lynn, Mass., Mar. 23, 1925; s. Hyman and Fradel (Gordon) F.; m. Barbara Rose, June 4, 1950; children— Steven, Mark. B.F.A., Yale U., 1950, M.F.A., 1951; studied with, Willem de Kooning, 1950-51; MA (hon.), Brown U., 1953. Instr. painting Yale U., 1951-53; mem. faculty dept. art Brown U., 1953—, prof., 1961—, John Hay prof. bibliography, 1993—, chmn. studio div., 1973—; founder Ziggurat Press, 1985—; dir. Brown/Ziggurat Press, 1990—. Vis. prof. Harvard U., 1968, U. Calif., Riverside; artist-in-residence Dartmouth Coll., 1978; cons. Providence Lithography Co.; artist-in-residence Rutgers Ctr. for Innovative Printmaking, 1993. One-man shows include Kruaushaar Galleries, N.Y.C., 1958, 61, 63, Obelisk Gallery, Boston, 1965-66, 67, Inst. Contemporary Arts, London, 1967-68, Bristol Mus., 1975, Hopkins Ctr., Dartmouth Coll., 1978; group shows include Mus. Modern Art, 1954, 55, Bklyn. Mus., 1957-58, 60, Corcoran Gallery, Washington, 1959, Butler Inst. Am. Art, Youngstown, Ohio, 1960, Harvard U. Carpenter Ctr. for Visual Arts, 1963, Lowe Art Ctr., Syracuse, 1964, Inst. Contemporary Art, Boston, 1961, 66; represented in permanent collections at Brown U., Fogg Mus., L.A. County Mus., Met. Mus. Art, Mus. Modern Art, Phoenix Art Mus., Princeton U., Yale U. Art Gallery, Lehigh U. Art Collection, U. Mass., Mex.-Am. Inst., U. Florence, Italy, Folger Shakespeare Libr., Washington, Fuller Mus., Brockton, Mass., Victoria and Albert Mus., London and others. Served with U.S. Army, 1943-46. Decorated Purple Heart, Combat Inf. Badge; Alice Kimball English fellow Yale U., 1950, Fulbright fellow, Italy, 1956-57; Eliza Howard fellow Mex., 1961; recipient Gov.'s award for arts, 1980. Home: 107 Benevolent St Providence RI 02906-3154 Office: Brown U 64 College St Providence RI 02912-9021 Office Phone: 401-863-3365. Business E-Mail: walter_feldman@brown.edu.

FELDMANN, EDWARD GEORGE, pharmaceutical chemist, pharmacologist; b. Chgo., Oct. 13, 1930; s. Edward Louis and Vera (Arnesen) F.; stepmother Helen E. Whitney; m. Mary J. Evans, Aug. 30, 1952; children: Ann Marie Whittington, Edward William, Robert George, Karen Lynn Zaragoza. BS in Chemistry, Loyola U., Chgo., 1952; MS in Pharmacy (research fellow Am. Found. Pharm. Edn. 1953-55), U. Wis., 1954, PhD in Pharm. Chemistry-Biochemistry, 1955; postgrad., Northwestern U., 1956, U. Chgo., 1958. Tchg. asst. Loyola U., Chgo., 1951—52; rsch. asst. U. Wis., 1952—53; sr. chemist Am. Dental Assn., 1955—58, dir. divsn. chemistry, 1958—59; assoc. dir. sci. divsn. Am. Pharm. Assn., 1959—60, dir., 1960—85, assoc. editor sci. edit. assn. jour., 1959—60, editor, 1960—97, assoc. exec. dir. sci. affairs, 1970—83, v.p. sci. affairs, 1983—85, project dir. Handbook of Non-Prescription Drugs, 1985—89, mng. editor, 1989—90, project cons. Handbook on Non-Prescription Drugs, 1991—93, mem. adv. panel, 1994—95; exec. sec. Acad. Pharm. Scis., 1983—85; mem. adv. panel Am. Pharm. Assn., 1994—99; pvt. pharm. cons., 1985—; assoc. dir. revision Nat. Formulary, 1959—60; dir. revision Nat. Fomulary, 1960—70. Mem. adv. panel dental drugs Nat. Formulary, 1955-60, Am. Pharm. Assn. Handbook of Non-Prescription Drugs, 1994-95; reviewer Internat. Pharmacopeia, WHO, 1958; spl. lectr. drug standards George Washington U., 1960-64; del. conf. on fellowships Nat. Health Council, 1960; mem. coordinating com. Nat. Conf. Antimicrobial Agts., Soc. Indsl. Microbiology, 1960-63; mem. adv. panel pharm. nomenclature A.M.A.-Am. Pharm. Assn.-U.S. Pharmacopeia, 1961-66, mem. nomenclature com., 1962-66; sec. U.S. Com. Internat. Drug Standards, 1964-65; adv. panel food chems. codex Nat. Acad. Scis.-NRC, 1961-71, liaison rep. to drug research bd., 1968-76; spl. liaison rep. to Commn. of Life Scis., NAS-NRC, 1973-85; mem. lab. com. Am. Pharm. Assn. Found., 1961-75; mem. com. Ebert prize, 1961-75; judge Lunsford-Richardson Pharmacy Awards, 1962-69; cons. Council on Drugs, A.M.A., 1962; vis. scientist Am. Assn. Colls. of Pharmacy, NSF, 1963-66; mem. expert adv. panel on internat. pharmacopeia and pharm. preparation World Health Orgn., 1963-75; drug abuse cons. to Office of US Pres., Lyndon B. Johnson, 1965, drug cons. Office Sec., U.S. Dept. Health, Edn. and Welfare, 1967-70; nomenclature cons. to Commr., U.S. Food and Drug Adminstrn., 1968-71; mem. expert working group Indsl. Devel. Orgn., UN, 1969; mem. organizing com. 31st Internat. Congress Pharm. Scis., 1970-71; mem. NRC, 1971-85; del. U.S. Pharmacopeia, 1970-85, 90-95; mem. Nat. Council on Drugs, 1976-83; mem. scientific adv. bd. Biodecision Labs., Inc., 1987-90; scientific cons. Am. Assn. Pharmaceutical Scientists, 1986-93; pharm. scis. cons. ERGO Sci. Inc., 1992—; mem. steering com. Japan-U.S. Pharmaceutical Scis. Congress, 1987; expert witness congressional drug legis. hearings and civil litigation cases, Drug quality specifications, Fed. legal requirements, Clinical pharmacology and Toxicology, 1965-; lectr. in field. *Dr. Feldmann's professional achievements encompassed four broad areas: conducted laboratory research, most notably to experimentally determine relative duration of action of dental local anesthetic agents; subsequently, coordinated and directed development and adoption of official standards of quality for numerous pharmaceutical products; concurrently, edited leading pharmaceutical research journals broadly fostering major advances in medicinal research, while editing numerous drug reference books thereby facilitating transfer of new pharmaceutical information from research laboratories into clinical practice; lastly, served as frequent consultant to government agencies and Congressional committees, helping to shape public policy, regulations, and legislation on various pharmaceutical issues, e.g., generic drug equivalency.* Assoc. editor Drug Standards, 1959-60, editor, 1960; chmn. (1960-70) Nat. Formulary Bd.; editor Jour. Pharm. Scis., 1961-75, cons. editor, 1975-85, 87-89, interim editor, 1991, editor in chief, 1991-94, emeritus editor 1994-95; editor APS Accd. Reporter, 1983-85; author more than 420 articles in field, editor or co-editor 24 ref. books; mem. editorial adv. bd. Index Chemicus, 1968-71; med. contbr. World Book Ency., 1986-88. Mem. membership com. Ravenwood Park Citizens Assn., Falls Church, Va., 1962, mem. nominating com., 1971-72; mem. Lake Barcroft Community Assn., 1975-97. Recipient Spl. Recognition award U.S. Pres. Lyndon Johnson, 1965, Man of Yr. award Nat. Assn. Pharm. Mfrs., 1970, Disting. citation U. Wis., 1971, Commr.'s citation FDA, 1975, G.A. Bergy Lectr. award U. W.Va., 1975, Pres. award Am. Assn. Pharm. Scis., 1993. Fellow Acad. Pharm. Scis.; mem. Am. Pharm. Assn. (life, Hon. Mem. award 2005), Am. Chem. Soc. (emeritus), Am. Assn. Pharm. Scis. (charter mem., fellow, fellows selection com. 1989, Pres.'s award 1993), N.Y. Acad. Scis., Nat. Soc. Med. Rsch. (coun. 1961-69), Am. Testing Materials, Coun. Biology Editors, AMA (affiliate), Fedn. Internat. Pharm., U.S. Tennis Assn., Mid-Atlantic Tennis Assn., Fla. Tennis Assn., Sleepy Hollow Bath and Racquet Club (Falls Church, Va.), Arlington Tennis and Squash Club, 4-Seasons Tennis Club, Fairfax Golden Racquets Club, Venice (Fla.) Golf and Country Club (bd. mem. tennis assn. 1998—, pres. 2002-2005, mem. sports and health com. 2002—), K.C., Sigma Xi, Rho Chi, Lambda Chi Sigma. Roman Catholic. Home and Office: 316 Wild Pine Way Venice FL 34292-4624

FELDMANN, SHIRLEY CLARK, psychology educator; b. Niagara Falls, N.Y., Apr. 14, 1929; d. Franklin T. and Mildred L. (Payne) Clark; m. Robert Feldmann, June 1952 (dec.); m. Horace S. Bush (dec.). BA, Barnard Coll., 1951; MA, Columbia U., 1952, PhD, 1961. Asst. prof. edn. SUNY, Fredonia, 1958-60; asst. research prof. psychiatry N.Y. Med. Coll., N.Y.C., 1960-63; prof. sch. edn. City Coll., CUNY, N.Y.C., 1963-98; prof., PhD program in ednl. psychology CUNY Grad. Sch., N.Y.C., 1974-98, exec. officer, 1976-85; ret., 1998. Contbr. articles to prof. jours. Mem. APA. Home: 11 Cedar Lake Rd Chester CT 06412-1009

FELDMAN NEBENZAHL, BERNARDO, composer, educator; b. Mexico City, Sept. 28, 1955; s. Jaime Feldman Shtiglick and Felicie Nebenzahl de Feldman; children: Kendahl May Goldwater-Feldman, Gisèle Aliyah Goldwater-Feldman. Advanced Musical Studies, Nat. Conservatory of Music, Mexico City, 1969—78; BA, BS Sci. and Humanities, Mex. Nat. U., Mexico City, 1979; BFA, Calif. Inst. of the Arts, Valencia, 1983; MFA, Calif. Inst. Arts, Valencia, 1985; PhD, UCLA, 1992—2000. Pres. Soc. for Electro-Acoustic Music in the U.S., Los Angeles Chapter, Calif., 1987—90; music faculty Calif. Inst. of the Arts, Valencia, Calif., 1988—99; chmn., dept. of music Coll. of the Canyons, Santa Clarita, Calif., 1989—. Faculty mem. Calif. Inst. of the Arts, Valencia, Calif., 1988—99. Composer (librettist): (electro-rock opera) Fractured Stories (Am. Soc. for Composers, Authors, and Publishers, 2005); composer: (sound designer) (film) Paris is a Woman (Best Short Film at the NY Internat. Ind. Film Festival, 2003); composer: (music producer) (multi-media) Creatures of Habit (Pew Charitable Trust & Lila Wallace-Reader's Digest Award, 1994); composer: (symphonic score) In Red and Black (Am. Soc. for Composers, Authors and Publishers, 1986). Panelist Cultural Affairs Dept., L.A., Calif., 2002—03. Recipient Meet the Composer, Meet the Composer, Inc., 1986, 1988, 1992, 1996. Achievements include Innovative performances involving live musicians interacting with electronics. Avocations: outdoors activities, films, soccer. Home: 121 Strand St Ste #9 Santa Monica CA 90405 Office: Santa Clarita Cmty Coll Dist 26455 Rockwell Canyon Rd Santa Clarita CA 91355 Office Phone: 661-362-3254. Home Fax: 661-259-8302; Office Fax: 661-259-8302. Personal E-mail: bernardo.feldman@canyons.edu.

FELDSHUH, TOVAH S., actress; b. N.Y.C., Dec. 27, 1952; d. Sidney and Lillian (Kaplan) F.; m. Andrew Harris-Levy, Mar. 20, 1977. BA, Sarah Lawrence Coll., Bronxville, N.Y.; McKnight fellow, Guthrie Theatre-U. Minn. Broadway debut in: Cyrano de Bergerac, 1973; starring role in Yentl, N.Y.C., 1974, Yentl Goes to Broadway, 1975; leading lady Am. Shakespeare Festival, Stratford, Conn., 1976, 80, 81; off-Broadway appearance in Three Sisters, 1977; nat. tour in Peter Pan, 1978; starring role in Broadway musicals Sarava, 1978, Lend Me A Tenor, 1989, Golda's Balcony, 2003 (Tony nom. best actress in a play, 2004); one-woman show, Guthrie Theater, 1980, 81; actor (films) Nunzio, 1978, The Idolmaker, 1980, Cheaper to Keep Her, 1980, Daniel, 1983, Brewster's Millions, 1985, Silver Bullet, 1985 (voice), Blue Iguana, 1988, Saying Kaddish, 1991, A Day in October, 1992, Trouble, 1995, Comfortably Numb, 1995, Aaron's Magic Village, 1995, Hudson River Blues, 1997, Montana, 1998, Charlie Hoboken, 1998, A Walk on the Moon, 1999, The Corruptor, 1999, Happy Accidents, 2000, The 3 Little Wolf's, 2001, The Believer, 2001, Kissing Jessica Stein, 2001, Friends and Family, 2001, Noon Blue Apples 2002, The End of the Bar, 2002, Life on the Ledge, 2004, Tollbooth, 2004, The Reality Trap, 2005, Alchemy, 2005; (TV films) Scream Peggy Scream, 1973, The Amazing Howard Hughes, 1977, The World of Darkness, 1977, Terror Out of the Sky, 1978, The Triangle Factory Fire Scandal, 1979, Thief Beggarman, 1979, The Women's Room, 1980, Sexual Considerations, 1991, Citizen Cohn, 1992, Love and Betrayal: The Mia Farrow Story, 1995; (TV series) Ryan's Hope, 1976, Murder Inc, 1981, Mariah, 1987, L.A. Law, 1987, As The World Turns, 1994; (TV mini series) Holocaust, 1978, A Will of Their Own, 1998; guest appearances include Serpico, 1976, The Bob Newhart Show, 1977, Barnaby Jones, 1977, The Love Boat, 1977, 1984, Airwolf, 1984, Law & Order, 1991, 1992, 1994, 1995, 1996, 1998, 2000, 2001, 2002, & 2004, All My Children, 1997, Cosby, 1999, The Education of Max Bickford, 2002 and several others. Recipient Theatre World award, Outer Critics Circle award, Drama Desk award, Israeli Govt. Friendship award, Eleanor Roosevelt Humanitarian award.*

FELDSTEIN, ERIC A., finance company executive; b. Brookline, Mass., June 17, 1959; BA Econ., Columbia College, 1981; MBA, Harvard Bus. Sch., 1985. With treas. office General Motors, 1981-91, regional treas.-Europe, 1991-93; asst. treas., 1993—96; exec. v.p., CFO GMAC and chmn. GMAC Mortgage Group, 1996—97; v.p., treas. General Motors, 1997—2002, GM Group v.p., GMAC chmn., 2002—.

FELDSTEIN, MARTIN STUART, economist, educator; b. N.Y.C., Nov. 25, 1939; s. Meyer and Esther (Gevarter) Feldstein; m. Kathleen Foley, June 19, 1965; children: Margaret, Janet. AB summa cum laude, Harvard U., 1961; MA, Oxford U., 1964, DPhil, 1967; LLD (hon.), Rochester U., 1984; LLD (hon.), Marquette U., 1985. Rsch. fellow Nuffield Coll., Oxford U., 1964—65, ofcl. fellow, 1965—67, lectr. pub. fin., 1965—67; asst. prof. econs. Harvard U., 1967—68, assoc. prof., 1968—69, prof., 1969—, George F. Baker prof., 1984—; pres. Nat. Bur. Econ. Rsch., 1977—82, 1984—; chmn. Coun. Econ. Advisers, 1982—84. Bd. dirs. AIG, HCA, Eli Lilly; mem. internat. adv. coun. J.P. Morgan, Daimler-Chrysler, Robecco. Bd. contbrs.: Wall St. Jour. Hon. fellow, Nuffield Coll. Fellow: Am. Philos. Soc., Nat. Assn. Bus. Economists, Econometric Soc. (coun. 1977—82), Am. Acad. Arts and Scis., Brit. Acad. (corr.); mem.: European Econ. Assn., Nat. Tax Assn. (Daniel Holland medal 2003), Trilateral Commn. (exec. com. 1987—), Coun. on Fgn. Rels. (bd. dirs. 1998—), Inst. Medicine of NAS, Austrian Acad. Scis. (fgn.), Corp. Mass. Gen. Hosp., Am. Econ. Assn. (exec. com. 1980—82, v.p. 1988, pres. 2004, John Bates Clark medal 1977), Phi Beta Kappa. Home: 147 Clifton St Belmont MA 02478-2603 Office: Nat Bur Econ Rsch Inc 1050 Massachusetts Ave Cambridge MA 02138-5317 Office Phone: 617-868-3905. Personal E-mail: mfeldstein@harvard.edu. Business E-Mail: mfeldstein@nber.org.

FELDSTEIN, PAUL JOSEPH, management educator; b. N.Y.C., Oct. 4, 1933; s. Nathan and Sarah Feldstein; m. Anna Martha Lee, Dec. 24, 1968; children: Julie, Jennifer. BA in Econs., CCNY, 1955; MBA in Fin., U. Chgo., 1957, PhD in Econs., 1961. Dir. divsn. rsch. Am. Hosp. Assn., Chgo., 1961-64; prof. Sch. Pub. Health U. Mich., Ann Arbor, 1964-87; prof. Grad. Sch. Mgmt. U. Calif., Irvine, 1987—. Author: Health Care Economics, 6th edit., 2004, Health Policy Issues: An Economic Perspective on Health Reform, 3d edit., 2003, The Politics of Health Legislation, 2nd edit. rev., 2001; contbr. articles to profl. jours. 1st lt. inf. U.S. Army, 1955-57. Mem. Am. Econs. Assn. Avocations: jogging, biking. Office: U Calif Grad Sch Mgmt Irvine CA 92697-0001 Office Phone: 949-824-8157. Business E-Mail: pfeldste@uci.edu.

FELDT, GLORIA A., social service administrator; b. Temple, Tex., Apr. 13, 1942; m. Alex Barbanell; 3 children; 3 stepchildren. BA in Sociology and Speech with honors, U. Tex. Permian Basin, 1974; postgrad., Ariz. State U., Western Behavioral Scis. Inst., La Jolla, Calif. Broadcast operator Sta. KOIP-FM, Odessa, Tex., 1965-67; substitute tchr. Ector County Ind. Sch. Dist., Odessa, Tex., 1967-68; tchr., spl. projects dir. head start Greater Opportunities of the Permian Basin, Odessa, Tex., 1968-73; exec. dir. Planned Parenthood of West Tex., Odessa, 1974-78; exec. dir., CEO Planned Parenthood Ctrl. and Northern Ariz., Phoenix, 1978-96; pres. Planned Parenthood Fedn. Am., Planned Parenthood Action Fund, N.Y.C., 1996—2005; also bd. dirs. Planned Parenthood Fedn. Am. Mem. steering com. Pro-Choice Ariz.; founder Planned Parenthood Fedn. Am. Leadership Inst.; cons. in leadership and strategic planning for non-profit orgns. Spkr. in field; Author: Behind Every Choice Is a Story, 2003, The War on Choice:The Right-Wing Attack on Women's Rights and How to Fight Back, 2004. Mem. exec. bd. Ariz. Affordable Health Care Found.; bd. dirs. Pro-Choice Resource Ctr., Hospice of the Valley; mem. cmty. adv. bd. Jr. League of Phoenix; mem. adv. bd. UN Assn.; charter mem. Ariz. Women's Town Hall; active Charter 100, World Affairs Coun., Ariz. Acad. Town Halls. Recipient Women of Achievement award, 1987, Ruth Green award Nat. Exec. Dirs. Coun., 1990, award Women Helping Women, 1989, 94, Golden Apple award Sun City chpt. NOW, 1995, City of Phoenix Martin Luther King, Jr. Living the Dream award City of Phoenix Human Rels. Commn., 1996. Mem. APHA, Nat. Family Planning and Reproductive Health Assn., Ariz. Pub. Health Assn.

FELDT, LEONARD SAMUEL, academic administrator, educator; b. Long Branch, New Jersey, Nov. 2, 1925; s. Harry and Bessie (Doris) F.; m. Natalie Ruth (Fischer), Aug. 29, 1954; children: Sarah Feldt Roach, Daniel C. BS in Edn., Rutgers Univ., 1950, EdM, 1951; PhD, U. Iowa, 1954. Asst. prof. to prof. U. Iowa, Iowa City, 1954-94, dir. testing programs, 1981-94, Lindquist prof. ednl. measurement, 1981-94, prof. emeritus, 1994. Pres. Iowa Measurement Rsch. Found., Iowa City, 1978-2004; editor standardized tests, Iowa Tests Ednl. Devel., 1960—. With U.S. Army, 1943—46. Recipient Disting. Svc. Award Rutgers U., 1999; Disting. Achievement Award, Nat. Ctr. for

Rsch. on Evaluation Stds. and Student Testing, 1999. Mem.: Am. Stats. Assn., Psychometric Soc., Nat. Coun. on Measurement in Edn. (Career Contbns. award 1994), Am. Ednl. Rsch. Assn. (E.F. Lindquist award 1995), Sigma Xi, Phi Beta Kappa. Avocation: golf. Home: 810 Willow St Iowa City IA 52245-5438 Office: Univ Iowa Lindquist Ctr Iowa City IA 52242 Business E-Mail: leonard-feldt@uiowa.edu.

FELGAR, RAYMOND EUGENE, pathologist, educator; b. Mt. Pleasant, Pa., Mar. 2, 1963; s. Samuel Hurst and Anna June (Stull) F. BS in Microbiology with honors, Pa. State U., 1985; PhD in Pathology, U. Pitts., 1990, MD, 1992. Diplomate Am. Bd. Pathology in Anatomic and Clin. Pathology, Am. Bd. Pathology, cert. subspecialty in Hemotology Am. Bd. Pathology. Resident in anatomic and clin. pathology U. Pa. Med. Ctr., Phila., 1992—96; fellow in hematopathology dept. pathology Vanderbilt U., Nashville, 1996—98; dir. hematopathology and clin. flow cytometry Hahnemann Hosp., Phila., 1998; asst. prof. dept. pathology and lab medicine MCP-Hahnemann Sch. Medicine, Phila., 1998; dir. clin. flow cytometry lab., hematopathologist, dir. hematopathology Strong Meml. Hosp., Rochester, NY, 1998—; asst. prof. Dept. Pathology & Lab. Medicine U. Rochester Sch. Medicine & Dentistry, 1998—2004, assoc. prof. Dept. Pathology & Lab Medicine, 2004—. Co-dir. Course on T-cell lymphomas, ASCP Nat. Meeting; mem. sci. adv. bd. Bioreference Labs. Inc., Elmwood Park, N.J.; mem. med. adv. bd. Med-Well Group, West Lake Village, Calif. Contbr. articles to profl. jours., chpt. to book. NIH med. scientist tng. fellow, 1987-92. Mem. AMA, Coll. Am. Pathologists, Am. Soc. Clin. Pathologists (co-dir. course t-cell lymphomas nat. mtg.), Am. Soc. Hematology, U.S. and Can. Acad. Pathology, Soc. for Hematopathology, European Assn. for Hematopathology, Eastern Coop. Oncology Group (pathology com.), Southwestern Oncology Group, Children's Oncology Group, Pa. State U. Alumni Assn., Phi Beta Kappa.

FELGER, RALPH WILLIAM, education educator, retired military officer; b. Hamilton, Ohio, Oct. 14, 1919; s. Edward Lewis and Blanche Esther (House) F.; m. Bernice Regina Moeller, Dec. 28, 1944 (dec.); 1 child, Mary Karen. BA, Whitworth Coll., 1950; MBA, U. Denver, 1952; MS, Trinity U., 1954. Cert. instr. bus. and psychology Calif. Commd. 2d lt. U.S. Army, advanced through grades to 1st lt., pers. tng. officer, 1942—46, relieved from active duty, 1946; commd. 1st lt. USAF, 1951, advanced through grades to col., edn. and pers. officer, 1951—67, ret., 1967; asst. prof. Bakersfield Coll., Calif., 1967—68; dean continuing edn. Lincoln Land C.C., Springfield, Ill., 1968—72; dir. corp. tng. Sangamo Electric Co., West Union, SC, 1972—74; asst. campus dir. Ohio State U., Marion, 1974—79, asst. to v.p. Columbus, 1979—83; exec. v.p. Internat. Mgmt. Inst., Westerville, Ohio, 1983—84; dir. continuing edn. N.Mex. Inst. Mining and Tech., Socorro, 1984—85; part-time cons. edn. and mktg. Midwest Human Resource Sys., Columbus, 1985—89; acad. counselor Franklin U., Columbus, 1990—91; mgr. edn. program Jr. Achievement of Ctrl. Ohio, Columbus, 1991—92; v.p. Career Mgmt. Ctrs., Inc., Columbus, 1991—92; ret., 1992. Chmn. Ill. divsn. United Way, Springfield, 1972; mem. Police Human Rels. Com., Springfield, 1970-72; bd. dirs. ARC, Oconee, S.C., 1973; edn. chmn. Marion (Ohio) Econ. Coun., 1975-79, Marion County chpt. Am. Heart Assn., 1975-79. Decorated Legion of Merit, U.S. Joint Chiefs of Staff Badge, 3 USAF Commendation medals; recipient 2 commendations United Way Cmty. Svc. Mem.: U.S. Ret. Mil. Officers Assn., Pers. Mgrs. Club (v.p. 1972—74), Delta Sigma Pi (life). Avocations: fishing, camping, travel, cooking, reading. Home: 1300 O Ave #106 Anacortes WA 98221 Office Phone: 360-588-9778.

FELGRAN, STEVEN DAVID, economist, educator; b. N.Y.C., July 1, 1953; s. Howard H. and Ilse H. (Sturm) F.; m. Hilary Ann Macht, June 13, 1999; children: Harry, Samuel BA, U. Pa., 1975; MA in Econs., MPhil in Econs., Yale U., 1978, PhD in Econs., 1982. Analyst Congl. Budget Office, Washington, 1975-76; cons. Arthur D. Little, Inc., Cambridge, Mass., 1981-83; economist Fed. Res. Bank Boston, 1983-89; prof. Coll. Bus. Adminstrn. Northeastern U., 1989-93; sr. mgr. Economic and Valuation Svcs./KPMG, N.Y.C., 1993-97, ptnr., 1997—. Contbr. articles to profl. jours. Mem. ABA, Am. Econ. Assn., Internat. Fiscal Assn., Phi Beta Kappa. Avocations: theater, musical comedy, historic preservation and restoration, civil war era, travel. Office: 99 High St Boston MA 02110 Office Phone: 617-988-1042. E-mail: sfelgran@kpmg.com.

FELICETTI, DANIEL A., academic administrator; b. N.Y.C., Apr. 25, 1942; s. Ernest and Rose (DiAdamo) F.; m. Barbara D'Antonio, July 13, 1969. BA in Polit. Sci., Hunter Coll., 1963; MA in Polit. Sci., NYU, 1966, PhD in Polit. Sci., 1971. From asst. to assoc. prof. Fairfield (Conn.) U., 1967-77, chmn. dept. politics, 1973-76, spl. asst. to pres., 1977; acad. v.p., acad. dean Wheeling (W.Va.) Coll., 1977-80; sr. v.p. for acad. affairs Coll. New Rochelle, N.Y., 1980-81, Southeastern U., Washington, 1982-84; v.p. acad. affairs U. Detroit, 1984-89; pres. Marian Coll., Indpls., 1989-99, Capital U., Columbus, Ohio, 1999-2001; founder Higher Edn. Leadership Projects Consulting Svc., 2001—. Participant Am. Coun. on Edn., Washington, 1976-77, vis. assoc., 1984-85; intern Inst. for Ednl. Mgmt. program Harvard U., 1981; cons. Coun. for Ind. Colls., Washington, 1986. Trustee Am. Heart Assn., Mich.; bd. dirs. Am. Heart Assn., Ind., Mental Health Assn. Marion County, Econ. Club Indpls., Coun. Ind. Colls.; mem. health and substance abuse com. New Detroit, Inc., 1986-89; mem. Greater Indpls. Progress Com.; mem. Pub. Safety Task Force Ind.; mem. Colls. Ind. Found.; mem. Indpls. delegation to Pres.'s Summit for Am.'s Future, 1997. Trustee Am. Heart Assn., Mich.; bd. dirs. Am. Heart Assn., Ind., Mental Health Assn. Marion County, Econ. Club Indpls., Coun. Ind. Colls.; mem. health and substance abuse com. New Detroit, Inc., 1986-89; mem. Greater Indpls. Progress Coml; mem. Pub. Safety Task Force Ind.; mem. Colls. Ind. Found.; mem. safety vision coun. United Way Columbus. Named to Hunter Coll. Hall of Fame, Hunter Coll. Alumni Assn., 1986; recipient Cert. of Recognition Sen. Lugar, 1994; Lilly Found. vis. faculty fellow Yale U., 1975; named Sagamore of the Wabash Gov. of Ind., 1990. Mem. Indpls. Athletic Club, received hon. doctoral degree from Marian Coll., 1999, Columbus C. of C. (pub. rels. com.), Rotary, Alpha Sigma Nu (hon.), Beta Gamma Sigma (hon.). Democrat. Roman Catholic. Avocations: baseball, reading, antiques. Office Phone: 410-571-7777.

FELICIANO, JOSÉ, entertainer; b. Larez, P.R., Sept. 10, 1945; s. Jose and Hortencia (Garcia) F.; m. Susan Feliciano; children: Melissa, Jonathan, Michael. DHL (hon.), 2001. Pres. Feliciano Enterprises. Folk singer in Greenwich Village, N.Y.C., 1962, rec. artist for Universal Records; TV appearances Feliciano—Very Special, 1969, Monsanto Night Presents Jose Feliciano, 1972, Statue of Liberty Celebration, 1984, Absolutely the Best, 2000, Feliciano, A Legend in Concert, 2000, over 100 others; has performed with major symphonies worldwide; composer some of own material including: Affirmation, Rain, Chico and the Man, Feliz Navidad, Ay Carino, Como tu Quieres; composer: guitar concerto Concerto de Paulinho, Mozartean Influence. Recipient 6 Grammy awards, including award in 1990, 16 Grammy nominations, Best Folk Guitarist award Guitar Player Mag. 1973, Best Pop Guitarist award 1973-77; more than 40 Gold and Platinum recotds; star in his name implanted on Hollywood Blvd., 1987. Achievements include having José Feliciano Sch. Performing Arts, East Harlem, N.Y., dedicated in his honor, 1987; being Amb. before the UN for Internat. Immigrants Found., 2003. Address: Feliciano Enterprises 606 Post Rd # Ste 880 Westport CT 06880 *The greatest tragedy for many so-called handicapped people is that they let others convince them that there are limits to what they can accomplish. It's just not so.*

FELISKY, BARBARA ROSBE, artist; b. Chgo., Mar. 24, 1938; d. Robert Lee and Margaret (Black) Rosbe; m. Timothy Felisky, Oct. 6, 1962; children: Kendra, Marc, Kyra. BA in Edn., U. Mich., 1960. Tchr. Peekskill (N.Y.) Sch. Dist., 1960-61; asst. to edn. dir. Simplicity Pattern Co., N.Y.C.; tchr. Anaheim (Calif.) Sch. Dist. Contbr. articles to mags. Bd. guilds Orange County Performing Arts Ctr., Costa Mesa, Calif., 1983-85. Mem. Laguna Beach Art Mus., L.A. County Mus. Art, Gamma Phi Beta, Calif. Art Club. Avocations: travel, photography. Home: 2942 E Lake Hill Dr Orange CA 92867-1910

FELIX, ARTHUR MARTIN, chemistry educator, researcher; b. N.Y.C., June 15, 1938; s. Barney and Beatrice (Thaler) F.; m. Maureen A. Kopelson, Oct. 28, 1967; children: Alison, Stephan. BA, NYU, 1959; PhD, Poly. U. N.Y., 1964. Rsch. assoc. Harvard U., Cambridge, Mass., 1964-66; sr. scientist Hoffmann-La Roche Inc., Nutley, N.J., 1966-75, rsch. fellow, 1976-80, rsch. group chief, 1980-83, asst. dir., 1983-85, dept. head, 1985-95; asst. prof. chemistry William Paterson Coll., Wayne, N.J., 1995-97, Ramapo Coll., Mahwah, NJ, 1998—2003, assoc. prof. chemistry, 2003—. Adj. asst. prof. Fairleigh Dickinson U., Teaneck, N.J., 1967-79, Hunter Coll., CUNY, 1974-75; adj. prof. U. of Medicine and Dentistry of N.J., 1992—; guest investigator Rockefeller U., N.Y.C., 1968-69. Contbr. more than 180 articles mainly on peptide synthesis to sci. jours. Bd. dirs. Big Bros.-Big Sisters Bergen-Passaic, N.J., 1980-82; pres. Washington Sch. Home Sch. Assn., West Caldwell, N.J., 1980-82. Mem. Am. Chem. Soc., Am. Peptide Soc. (sec. 1990-93), N.J. Inst. Chemists (coun. 1983-84), Sigma Xi (chpt. pres. 1980-81, 2000-01). Achievements include 30 patents related to drug discovery; synthesis of biologically important peptides including immunotropics, vaccines and growth factors. Office Phone: 201-684-7793. Personal E-mail: artfelix@verizon.net. Business E-Mail: afelix@ramapo.edu.

FELIX, CHERYL A., air transportation executive; b. St. Paul, Aug. 31; d. Lawrence J. and Beverly J. McGuinn; m. Guy J. Felix, May 20, 2000. AA, Normandale C.C., Bloomington, Minn.; AAS in Exec. Secretarial, Inver Hills C.C., Inver Grove Heights, MN; BA in Polit. Sci., BA in Pub. Adminstrn., St. Cloud State U., 2000; postgrad., Embry-Riddle Aero. U., 2001—03. Customer svc., tech. support adminstr. Shadin Co., Inc., St. Louis Park, Minn., 1995—98; materials mgr. Dallas Airmotive, Mpls., 2000—01; engring. adminstr./master planner/scheduler Shadin Co., Inc., St. Louis Park, Minn., 2001—03; purchasing, inventory analyst Wipaire, Inc., South St. Paul, Minn., 2004—. Grad. rsch. asst. Embry-Riddle Aero. U. Mem.: Am. Soc. Pub. Adminstrn., Women Aviation, Internat., Exptl. Aircraft Assn., Aircraft Owners and Pilots Assn., Internat. Aerobatic Club. Avocations: aerobatics, politics, pool. Personal E-mail: Little_scrapper@msn.com.

FELIX, OTTO J.F., actor, film producer, film director, scriptwriter, photographer; b. Pitts., Dec. 31; s. Jack David Felix and Juanita Felix Lewis; m. Jan Thompson; children: Kenneth, Jessica. Student, U. Pitts., 1962—63, Cambridge Coll., Boston, 1964—65; lic., Fla. Engring. Inst., 1967. Disc jockey WCSB, WAMR, WYND, 1964—68; actor over 300 TV commls., Calif., 1968—, TV series, L.A., 1970—94; prodr. 3 films, 24 variety shows, L.A., 1976—2004; writer, dir. 14 films, L.A., 1990—2004. Bd. dirs., tchr. Performing Arts for the Handicapped, Hollywood, 1980—82; founder, dir. Handicapped Artists & Performers, Ptnrs., Inc., 1986—2004, Film Actors Shop, Westwood, Calif. Author: 10 books of poetry and photography, 1976—2004. Mem. Beverly Glenn Traffic Com. Staff sgt. USAR, 1960—65. Recipient Best Black and White Photo award, N.Y.C., 1989, Rollings Meml. award, Roll-On Prodns., Hollywood, 1992. Mem.: Disability Awareness Assn., Calif. Assn. Motorcyclists (founder). Avocations: motorcycles, antique and classic cars. Office: Off Prodns 11000 Wilshire Blvd PO Box 24225 Los Angeles CA 90024 E-mail: ottoffelix@aol.com.

FELKNOR, BRUCE LESTER, publishing executive, consultant, writer; b. Oak Park, Ill., Aug. 18, 1921; s. Audley Rhea and Harriet (Lester) F.; m. Joanne Sweeney, Feb. 8, 1942 (div. Jan. 1952); 1 child, Susan Harriet Felknor Pickard; m. Edith G. Johnson, Mar. 1, 1952; children: Sarah Anne Felknor Ragland, Bruce Lester II. Student, U. Wis., 1939-41. Reporter Dunn County News, Menomonie, Wis., 1937-39; freight brakeman Pa. R.R., N.Y.C., 1941, asst. yardmaster, 1942; prodn. coordinator Hwy. Trailer Co., Edgerton, Wis., 1943; radio officer U.S. Maritime Service, 1944-45; flight radio officer Air Transport Command, 1945; mem. pub. relations dept. Am. Airlines, 1945; writer pub. relations dept. ITT, 1946; Southeast regional pub. relations dir. Ford Motor Co., Chester, Pa., 1946-48; free lance pub. relations N.Y.C., 1948-49; pub. relations exec. Foote, Cone & Belding, Inc., N.Y.C., 1950-53; v.p. Market Relations Network, N.Y.C., 1954-55; exec. dir. Fair Campaign Practices Com., Inc., N.Y.C., 1956-66; asst. to William Benton (chmn. and pub. Ency. Brit.), 1966-70; dir. mktg. info. internat. div. (Ency. Brit.), 1970-73, dir. advt. and promotion, 1973, dir. pub. info., 1974-76, exec. editor, 1977-83; dir. yearbooks Ency. Brit., 1983-85; editorial cons., 1985—. Vis. lectr. Hamilton Coll., 1966, 75, 82; history editor Mcht. Marine internet web site www.usmm.org, 1999—. Author: Fair Play in Politics, 1960, State-by-State Smear Study, 1956, You Are They, 1964, (with C.P. Taft) Prejudice & Politics, 1960, Dirty Politics, 1966, reprinted, 1975, 2001, (with Frank Jonas et al) Political Dynamiting, 1970, How to Look Things Up and Find Things Out, 1988, Political Mischief: Smear, Sabotage, and Reform in U.S. Elections, 1992, The Highland Park Presbyterian Church: A History 1871-1996, 1996 (Robert Lee Stowe award 1997), The U.S. Merchant Marine at War 1775-1945, 1998, The Great Witch Hunt of the Presbyterian Left, 2001, Of Clubbable Nature: Chicago's Tavern Club at 75, 2005; editor: The U.S. Government: How and Why it Works, 1978; also various newspaper, jour. and yearbook articles on politics; contbg. editor (with Clifton Fadiman) The Treasury of the Encyclopaedia Britannica, 1992; contbr. Encyclopedia of the American Presidency, 1993. Chmn. Citizens Com. for Sch. Centralization in Armonk, N.Y., 1957-61; ruling elder, chmn. com. religion and race Presbytery Hudson River, 1963-67, mem. nat. coun. on ch. and soc., 1966-72; bd. dirs., mem. exec. com. Fair Campaign Practices Com.; mem. nat. adv. bd. Amigos de las Americas, 1982-89, Am. U., Washington, 1982—; mem. Ill. Literacy Coun., 1984-86; mem. bd. advisors, acad. adv. coun. Nat. Strategy Forum, 1987—; mem. bd. edn. Lake Forest (Ill.) H.S. Dist., 1989-93. Republican. Presbyterian. Home and Office: 509 Trinity Ct Evanston IL 60201-1908 E-mail: bruce_felknor@yahoo.com. *Man's greatest gifts are empathy and the ability to penetrate balderdash.*

FELL, JAMES FREDERICK, lawyer; b. Toledo, Ohio, Nov. 18, 1944; s. George H. Fell and Bibianne C. (Hebert) Franklin; children from a previous marriage: Jennifer A., Brian F.; m. Betty L. Wenzel, May 23, 1981. BA, U. Notre Dame, 1966; JD, Ohio State U., 1969. Bar: N.Y. 1970, Calif. 1972, Idaho 1978, Wash. 1981, Oreg. 1984, U.S. Ct. Appeals (9th cir.) 1983, U.S. Dist. Ct. Idaho 1978. Assoc. Breed, Abbott & Morgan, N.Y.C., 1969-72; ptnr. McKenna & Fitting, L.A., 1972-78; atty. Office Atty. Gen., State of Idaho, Boise, 1978-79; dir. policy and administrn. Idaho Pub. Utilities Commn., Boise, 1979-81; gen. counsel, dep. dir. Northwest Power Planning Coun., Portland, Oreg., 1981-84; ptnr. Stoel Rives LLP, Portland, 1984—. Mem. ABA (pub. utility law sect.), Oreg. State Bar (pub. utility law sect.). Office: Stoel Rives LLP 900 SW 5th Ave Ste 2600 Portland OR 97204-1268

FELL, M. ANN, publishing executive; BA in Comm., Boston U., 1980; graduate pub. program, N.Y.U., 1982. Asst. mktg. mgr. Time Warner Inc., N.Y.C., 1981-83; mktg. rsch. mgr. Conde Nast Inc., N.Y.C., 1983-86; sales rep. Spy Mag., N.Y.C., 1986-87, Forbes Mag., N.Y.C., 1987-88, Venture Mag., N.Y.C., 1988-90; pres., group pub. SCENE Pub. Inc., N.Y.C., 1990—. Office: SCENE Publishing Inc 930 5th Ave New York NY 10021-2651

FELL, SAMUEL KENNEDY (KEN FELL), infosystems executive; b. Wilmington, Del., Oct. 6, 1944; s. S. Kennedy and Anna Elizabeth (Alford) F.; m. Diana Marie Dickson, May 8, 1965; children: Melissa Ann, Michael Kennedy. BSBA, Oklahoma City U., 1983; postgrad. in bus., John F. Kennedy U.; grad. exec. mgmt. program, Duke U., 1991. Mgmt./data processing sys. designer/implementor Gen. Motors Corp., Detroit and Oklahoma City, 1967-81; v.p. info. systems Totco Divsn. Baker Internat., Norman, Okla., 1981-85; v.p. computer info. Cleve. Pneumatic subs. Pneumo Abex Corp. div. IC Industries, 1985-88; sr. dir. systems devel. Sprint, Kansas City, Mo., 1988-95; exec. v.p. product devel., exec. bd. mem. SynQuest, Inc., A Warburg Pincus Co., 1995-2000; CIO NYISO, Schenectady, N.Y., 2000—. Mem.: Data Processing Mgrs. Assn., Soc. Info. Mgrs., Oracle Users Group. Office: NY ISO 3890 Carman Rd Schenectady NY 12303

FELLA, MARIE ANN, intelligence analyst, drug enforcement administration; b. New London, Conn., Dec. 9, 1956; d. Rosario Joseph and Mildred Mae (Carlins) F.; m. Thomas Boles, Sept. 10, 1975 (div. 1979). Associate's, U. Cinti and No. C.C., Annandale, Va., 1997. Clk., stenographer Gen. Svcs. Adminstrn., Cin., 1978-79, Drug Enforcement Adminstrn., Cin., 1979-82, office asst. V.p. Joint Task Force Miami, Fla., 1982-83, adminstrv. support specialist Marseille, France, 1983-93, chief sec. Arlington, Va., 1993-95, program analyst internal affairs, 1995-99, intelligence analyst, 1999—. Mem. World View Internat. T.V., Kennedy Ctr. Roman Catholic. Avocations: golf, tennis.

FELLEGI, IVAN PETER, statistician; b. Szeged, Hungary, June 22, 1935; immigrated to Can., 1957. s. Andor and Barbara (Partos) F.; m. Marika Gulyas, Dec. 27, 1958; children— Nicolette, Vivien. BSc, U. Budapest, Hungary, 1956; MSc, Carleton U., Ont., Can., 1958, PhD, 1961; PhD (hon.), Simon Fraser U., 1995; LLD (hon.), McMaster U., 1997; PhD (hon.), Carleton U., 1999; D (hon.), U. Que., 2001, U. Montreal, 2002. With Statistics Can., Ottawa, Ont., 1957—, asst. chief statistician, 1973-84, dep. chief statistician, 1984-85, chief statistician of Can., 1985—. Contbr. articles to profl. jours. Bd. govs. Carleton U., 1989—, chmn. bd. govs., 1995-97; chair Conf. European Statisticians, 1993-97. Decorated officer Order of Can., Order of Merit of the Hungarian Republic; recipient Robert Schuman medal, European Cmty., 1997, Outstanding Achievement award, Pub. Svc. Can., 2002. Fellow AAAS, Am. Statis. Assn., Royal Statis. Soc. (hon.); mem. Internat. Statis. Inst. (hon., pres. 1987-89), Statis. Soc. Can. (pres. 1982), Internat. Assn. Survey Statisticians (pres. 1985-87). Home: 16 Larchwood Ave Ottawa ON Canada K1Y 2E3 Office: Statistics Canada RH Coats Bldg Tunney's Pasture Ottawa ON Canada K1A 0T6

FELLER, BENJAMIN E., actuary; b. Bronx, N.Y., Mar. 4, 1947; s. Morris and Beatrice (Wolff) F.; m. Debra May Morane, June 1973 (div. 1983); children: Amy; m. Sue Ann Kaufman, Sept. 23, 1984; children: Meredith; stepchildren: Stefanie McCoy, Alison McCoy. BS in Math., Clarkson U., Potsdam, N.Y., 1968; MA in Math., Ind. U., 1971. Enrolled actuary. Actuarial asst. U.S. Life Ins. Co., N.Y.C., 1971-75; assoc. actuary The Wyatt Co., Washington, 1975-76; cons. actuary Buck Cons., N.Y.C., 1976-85; ptnr. Chernoff Diamond & Co., Williston Park, N.Y., 1985-92; pres. Pension Rev. Svcs., Plainview, N.Y., 1992—. Contbr. articles to profl. jours. Fellow Soc. Actuaries; mem. Am. Soc. Pension Actuaries, Am. Acad. Actuaries, Bklyn. Tech. H.S. Alumni Assn. (dir.). Republican. Jewish. Home: 10 Allison Dr Old Bethpage NY 11804-1602 Office: Pension Rev Svcs 45 Executive Dr Plainview NY 11803-1737 Office Phone: 516-349-5500. Business E-Mail: bfeller@pensionreviewservices.com.

FELLER, LLOYD HARRIS, lawyer; b. New Brunswick, N.J., Aug. 27, 1942; s. Alexander and Freda (Kaminsky) F.; m. Susan Sydney Weinberg, Aug. 6, 1967; children: Jennifer, Andrew. BS in Econs., U. Pa., 1964; LLB, NYU, 1967. Bar: N.Y. 1967, D.C. 1980. Assoc. Rubin, Wachtel, Baum & Levin, 1967—70; trial atty. organized crime sect., divsn. enforcement SEC, Washington, 1970—72, legal asst. Commr. A. Sydney Herlong, Jr., 1972—73, legal asst. Commr. A.A. Sommer, Jr., 1973—76; chief counsel Office of the Chief Acct., 1976—77; assoc. dif. divsn. market regulation Office of Market Structure and Trading Practices, 1977—79, of counsel, 1979—81; ptnr. Morgan, Lewis & Bockius LLP, Washington, 1981—99, mem. governing bd., 1996—99, mem. exec. com., 1989—99, mem. allocations com., 1999—; sr. v.p., sec., gen. counsel SoundView Tech. Group, Inc., San Francisco, 1999—. Office: SoundView Tech Group Steuart Twr One Market Plaza San Francisco CA

FELLER, MILLICENT (MIMI) A., newspaper publishing executive; BA cum laude, Creighton U., 1970; JD, Georgetown U. Asst. dir. congl. rels. Gen. Svcs. Adminstrn., 1975-77; legis. asst. Environ. and Pub. Works Com. U.S. Senate, 1977-81; from legis. dir. to Washington chief of staff Sen. John Chafee (Rep.), R.I., 1981-83; dep. asst. sec. legis. affairs U.S. Dept. Treasury, 1983-85; from v.p. to sr. v.p. pub. affairs and govt. rels. Gannett Co., 1985—. Bd. dirs. Nat. Ct. Apptd. Spl. Advs. Assn. Bd. dirs. Creighton U. Recipient Disting. Alumnus award Creighton U., 1987. Office: Gannett Co Inc 7950 Jones Branch Dr Mc Lean VA 22107

FELLER, ROBERT LIVINGSTON, chemist, art conservation scientist; b. Newark, Dec. 27, 1919; s. William Henry and Edna (Buckelew) F.; m. Ruth M. Johnston, Mar. 31, 1975 (dec. 2000). AB, Dartmouth Coll., 1941; MS, Rutgers U., 1943, PhD, 1950. Sr. fellow Nat. Gallery Art Research Project, Mellon Inst., Pitts., 1950-76; dir. Research Ctr. on Materials of Artist and Conservator, Carnegie-Mellon Rsch. Inst., Pitts., 1976-88, dir. emeritus, 1988—. Vis. scientist Conservation Ctr., Inst. Fine Arts, NYU, 1961; pres. Nat. Conservation Adv. Council, 1975-79 Co-author: On Picture Varnishes and their Solvents, 2d rev. edit., 1985, Evaluation of Cellulose Ethers for Conservation, 1990; author: Accelerated Aging: Photochemical and Thermal Aspects, 1994; editor: Artists' Pigments: A Handbook of Their History and Characteristics, Vol. I, 1986. Served with USN, 1944-46. Recipient Coll. Art Assn.-Nat. Inst. for Conservation Joint award, 1992, Univ. Products award for disting. achievement in conservation of cultural property, 2000. Fellow Internat. Inst. Conservation Hist. and Artistic Works (hon.), Am. Inst. Conservation Hist. and Artistic Works (hon.), Illuminating Engring. Soc.; mem. AAAS, Am. Chem. Soc. (Pittsburgh award 1983), Internat. Coun. Museums (pres. conservation com. 1969-78), Fedn. Socs. Coatings Tech., Inter-Soc. Color Coun., Am. Inst. Conservation. Clubs: Cosmos (Washington); Univ. (Pitts.). Achievements include research on deterioration of varnishes, paper, pigments and dyes used by artists. Office: Carnegie Mellon U Artists Materials Rsch Ctr 700 Technology Dr Pittsburgh PA 15219-3124

FELLER, ROBERT WILLIAM ANDREW, public relations executive, retired professional baseball player; b. Van Meter, Iowa, Nov. 3, 1918; s. William and Lena (Forrett) F.; m. Anne Morris Gilliland, Oct. 1, 1974. Pub. rels. exec. Cleveland Indians Baseball Team, 1936-56. Played first major league game Cleve. vs. St. Louis Browns, 1936; pitched 3 no-hitters Cleve. vs. Chgo., 1940, Cleve. vs. N.Y., 1946, Cleve. vs. Detroit, 1951; member 9 all-star teams. Author: Strikeout Story, 1947, How to Pitch, 1948, Now Pitching Bob Feller, 1990, Bob Feller's Little Black Book of Baseball Wisdom, 2000. CPO USNavy, 1941-45, PTO. Inducted to Baseball Hall of Fame, Cooperstown, N.Y., 1962; named Greatest Living Right-Hand Pitcher Profl. Baseball Centennial Celebration, 1969. Mem. Green Berets (hon.). Republican. Episcopalian. Avocation: restoring caterpiller tractors. Home Fax: 440-423-3248.

FELLHAUER, AMANDA MICHELE, elementary school educator; b. San Diego, Sept. 10, 1978; d. Manuel Frank and Joanie Louise Pia; m. Nathan James Fellhauer, May 25, 2002. BA, San Diego State U., 2001. Cert. tchr. San Diego State U., 2003. 1st grade tchr. San Diego Unified Sch. Dist., 2002—. Mem.: Calif. Tchrs. Assn. Avocation: reading.

FELLHAUER, DAVID E., bishop; b. Kansas City, Mo., Aug. 19, 1939; Student, Pontifical Coll. Josephinum; D in Canon Law, PhD, St. Paul U., Ottawa, Can. Ordained priest Roman Cath. Ch., 1965. Former prof. Holy Trinity Sem., Dallas; judicial vicar Diocese of Dallas, 1990; bishop of Victoria Tex., 1990—. Bd. govs. Canon Law Soc. Am. Recipient Role of Law award, Canon Law Soc., 1998. Office: PO Box 4070 Victoria TX 77903-4070*

FELLIN, JO ANN, mathematics professor; d. Peo and Anna Millie Fellin. PhD, U. Ill., 1970. Prof. emerita math. Benedictine Coll., Atchison, Kans., 1970—2004. Kansas City regional coord. Women and Math, Kans., 1984—92; nat. treas. Kappa Mu Epsilon, 1987—95. Pres. Mount Cmty. Senate, 2005—, Mt. Cmty. Ctr., Atchison, Kans., 1999—2003. National Disting. Educator, Benedictine Educator; recipient Disting. Mem. award, Kappa Mu Epsilon, 1981, George R. Mach Disting. Svc. award, 2001, Outstanding Alumni award, Springfield Cath. H.S., 1996. Mem.: Math. Assn. of Am. (Kans. sect. chairperson 1981—82, gov. 1982—85, chairperson-elect 2003—04, chairperson 2004—05). Office: Mt St Scholastic Monastery 801 South 8th Atchison KS 66002

FELLIN, OCTAVIA ANTOINETTE, retired librarian, historical researcher; b. Santa Monica, Calif. d. Otto P. and Librada (Montoya) F. Student, U. N.Mex., 1937—39; BA, U. Denver, 1941; BS in L.S., Dominican U., River Forest, Ill., 1942. Asst. libr. instr., libr. sci. St. Mary-of-Woods Coll., Terre Haute, Ind., 1942-44; libr. U.S. Army, Bruns Gen. Hosp., Santa Fe, 1944-46, Gallup (N.Mex.) Pub. Libr., 1947-90; post libr. Camp McQuaide, Calif., 1947; freelance writer, 1950—. Libr. cons.; N.Mex. del. White House Pre-conf. on Librs. & Inof. Svcs., 1978; dir. Nat. Libr. week for N.Mex., 1959. Author: Yahweh the Voice that Beautifies the Land, 1975; A Chronicle of Mileposts a Brief History of the University of New Mexico, Gallup Campus, 1968. Chmn. Gallup St. Naming Com., 1958—59; organizer Gt. Decision Discussion groups, 1963—85; chmn. Aging Com., 1964—68, Gallup Mus. Indian Arts and Crafts, 1964—78, Gallup Sr. Citizens Ctr., 1965—68; publicity com. Gallup Inter-Tribal Indian Ceremonial Assn., 1966—68; active Gov.'s Com. 100 on Aging, 1967—70; bd. dirs., sec., co-organizer Gallup Area Arts Coun., 1970—78; bd. dirs. Gallup Opera Guild, 1970—74; chmn. adv. bd. Gallup Sr. Citizens, 1971—73; active N.Mex. Libr. Adv. Coun., 1971—75, vice chmn., 1974—75; mem. Eccles. Conciliation and Arbitration Bd., Province of Santa Fe, 1974; chmn. pledge campaign Rancho del Nino San Huberto Empalme, Mexico, 1975—80; chmn. hist. com. Gallup Diocese Bicentennial, 1975, steering com., 1975—78; active Cathedral Parish Coun., 1980—83, v.p., 1981; cmty. edn. adv. coun. U. N.Mex., Gallup, 1981—82; pres. Rehoboth McKinley Christian Hosp. Aux., 1983; chmn. Red Mesa Art Ctr., 1984—88; Diocese of Gallup rep. to nat. convocation on laity concerns with Pope John Paul II, San Francisco, 1987; pres. Gallup Area Arts Coun., 1988; century com. Western Health Found., 1988; cultural bd. Gallup Multi-Model Cultural Com., 1988—95; chmn. aux. scholarship com. Rehoboth McKinley Christian Hosp. Aux., 1989—; co-organizer, v.p. chair fund raising com. Gallup Pub. Radio com., 1989—95; active McKinley County Recycling Com., 1990—; local art selection com. N.Mex. Art Dirs., 1990; N.Mex. organizing chmn. Rehoboth McKinley Christian Hosp. Aux., chmn. cmty. edn. loan selection com., 1990—; com. mem. Rio Grande Hist. Collection, NMSU, 1991—96; bd. dirs., corr. sec. Rehoboth McKinley Christian Hosp. Aux., 1991—94; chmn. Trick or Treat for UNICEF, Gallup, 1972-77, Artists Coop, 1985-89; active Network: Nat. Cath. Social Justice Lobby; mem. N.Mex. Humanities Coun., 1979, Gallup Centennial Com., 1980-81; 35th anniversary com. U. N.Mex., Gallup, 2001—02; adv. coun. US Cath. Bishops, 1969—75; active N.Mex. ACLU, 2001—; mem. adv. coun. to U.S. Cath. Bishops, 1969—74; chmn. Gamp Sr. Citizen Ctr., 1974—77. Recipient Dorothy Canfield Fisher Libr. award, 1961, Outstanding Cmty. Svc. award Gallup C. of C., 1968, 70, Outstanding Citizen award, 1974, Benemerenti medal Pope Paul VI, 1977, Celibrate Literacy award Gallup Internat. Reading Assn., 1983-84, Woman of Distinction award Soroptimists, 1985, N.Mex. Disting. Pub. Svc. award, 1987, Edgar L. Hewitt award Hist. Soc. N.Mex., 1992, Gov.'s award as Outstanding N.Mex. Woman, 1988, Cmty. Svc. award U. N.Mex., 1993; Octavia Fellin Pub. Libr. named in her honor, 1990. Mem.: NAACP, LWV (v.p. 1953—56), AAUW (v.p. co-organizer Gallup br., chmn. com. on women), ALA, N.Mex. Gallup Film Soc. (v.p. 1950—58, co-corgnizer), N.Mex. Mcpl. League (pres. libr.'s divsn. 1979), Gallup C. of C. (organizing chmn. women's div. 1972, v.p. 1972—73), N.Mex Archtl. Found., Plateau Scis. Soc., N.Mex. Libr. Assn. (hon.; chmn. hist. materials com. 1964—66, pres. 1965—66, chmn. com. to extend libr. svcs. 1969—73, chmn. local and regional history roundtable 1978, v.p., sec., salary and tenure com., nat. coord. N.Mex. Legis. com., Libr. of Yr. award 1975, life, Cmty. Achievement award 1983, Lifetime Membership award 1994), Nat. New Deal Preservation Assn., Habitat for Humanity, Call to Action Nat. Ca. Renewal Org., Pax Christi U.S.A., Hist. Soc. N.Mex., Gallup Hist. Soc., Women's Ordination Conf. Network, N.Mex. Women's Polit. Caucus, N.Mex. Foklore Soc. (pres. 1958), Alpha Delta Kappa (hon.). Roman Catholic. Home and Office: 513 E Mesa Ave Gallup NM 87301-6021

FELLMAN, GERRY LOUIS, lawyer, arbitrator; b. Omaha, May 22, 1932; s. Charles and Rose Mae Fellman; m. Jane Hallock, July 25, 1964. BS in Law, U. Nebr., 1954, JD, 1956; MA, U. Minn., 1959. Bar: Nebr. 1956, Calif. 1964, U.S. Supreme Ct. 1982; cert. Mediator. Field atty. NLRB, L.A., 1959-63; atty. div. labor law enforcement State of Calif., L.A., 1964-66; sole practice L.A., 1967-83; assoc. Ibanez & Fellman, L.A., 1968-75; sole practice Pasadena, Calif., 1984—. Arbitrator labor-mgmt. disputes Am. Arbitration Assn., 1967—, Fed. Mediation and Conciliation Svc., 1968—, Calif. State Mediation and Conciliation Svc., 1967—, UCLA, 1977-89, L.A. City Employee Rels. Bd., 1973—, E.E.O.C. Mediation Panel, 1996—. Contbr. numerous articles to legal jours. Bd. dirs. Legal Aid Found. L.A., 1974-83, pres., 1981-82. With U.S. Army, 1956-58. Mem. Nat. Acad. Arbitrators (chmn. So. Calif. region 1980-82, bd. dirs. 1997-2000), Indsl. Rels. Rsch. Assn. (past pres. So. Calif. chpt. 1976-77), ABA, Calif. Bar Assn., L.A. County Bar Assn. (exec. com. labor and employment sect.), Nebr. Bar Assn., Soc. for Profl. in Dispute Resolution, So. Calif. Mediation Assn. Jewish.

FELLNER, ERIC, film producer; b. Oct. 10, 1959; Formed Working Title Films (with Tim Bevan), 1982-; Prodr. (films) Sid & Nancy, 1986, Straight to Hell, 1987, Pascali's Island, 1988, Hidden Agenda, 1990, Liebestraum, 1991, Wild West, 1992, Romeo is Bleeding, 1993, No Worries, 1993, The Hawke, 1993, Four Weddings and a Funeral, 1994, French Kiss, 1995, Moonlight & Valentino, 1995, Fargo, 1996, Bean, 1997, The Matchmaker, 1997, The Borrowers, 1997, The Hi-Lo Country, 1998, Elizabeth, 1998 (Alexander Korda Awd, ALFS Awd, 1999), What Rats Won't Do, 1998, Solo, 1999, Plunkett & MacCleane, 1999, Bridget Jones Diary, 2001, Captain Corelli's Mandolin, 2001, 40 Days and 40 Nights, 2002, About A Boy, 2002, The Guru, 2002, Johnny English, 2003, Love Actually, 2003, The Calcium Kid, 2003, Thunderbirds, 2004, Wimbledon, 2004; exec. prodr.: The Rachel Papers, 1989, Year of the Gun, 1991, A Kiss Before Dying, 1991, Posse, 1993, Romeo is Bleeding, 1993, The Hawk, 1993, Four Weddings and a Funeral, 1994, The Hudsucker Proxy, 1994, Panther, 1995, Dead Man Walking, 1995, Loch Ness, 1995, Fargo, 1996, The Big Lebowski, 1998, Notting Hill, 1999, O Brother, Where Art Thou?, 2000, The Man Who Cried, 2000, The Man Who Wasn't There, 2001, Long Time Dead, 2002, My Little Eye, 2002, Thirteen, 2003, The Shape of Things, 2003, Ned Kelly, 2003, The Italian Job, 2003, Mickeybo & Me, 2004, Shaun of the Dead, 2004; prodr. TV; Frankie's House, 1992, Underbelly (exec.). Recipient ShowEast's Kodak award for excellence in filmmaking (with Tim Bevan), 2003.

FELLOWES, JAMES, manufacturing executive; BA, Denison U. Chmn., CEO Fellowes Mfg., Itasca, Ill. Named Entrepreneur of Y., Ernst & Young, 1997. Office: Fellowes Manufacturing 1789 Norwood Ave Itasca IL 60143-1095

FELLOWS, ALICE COMBS, artist; b. Atlanta, Sept. 14, 1935; d. Andrew Grafton III and Wilhelmina Drummond (Jackson) Combs; m. Robert Ellis Fellows Jr., Aug. 20, 1957 (div. 1978); children: Ariadne Elisabeth Fellows-Mannion, Kara Suzanne Fellows. BFA, Syracuse U., 1957; M in Clin. Psychology, Antioch U., 1992. Guest artist Yaddo, Saratoga Springs, N.Y., 1991; artist-in-residence Dorland Colony, Temecula, Calif., 1983; guest lectr. psychology seminar UCLA, 1990. Exhibited works in numerous group and one-woman shows including The True Artist, di Rosa Preserve, Napa, 2004, Shakespeare As Muse, Schneider Mus., Ashland, Oreg., 2004, di Rosa Preserve, Napa, 2003, 04, Hiromi Gallery, Santa Monica, Otis Gallery, Otis Coll. Art and Design, L.A., 2000, L.A. Mcpl. Art Gallery, C.O.L.A. Fellows Exhbn., 1998, El Camino Coll., 1997, Hunsaker-Schlesinger Gallery, 1996, The Armory Ctr. at Pasadena, 1996, Barnsdall Mcpl. Gallery, 1995, Claremont Grad. Sch. Gallery, 1991, Saxon-Lee Gallery, L.A., 1989, Santa Monica Coll. Gallery Art, 1988, J. Rosenthal Gallery, Chgo., 1986, The Biennial at the Hirshhorn Mus. and Sculpture Garden, Washington, 1986, Kirk de Gooyer Gallery, L.A., 1984, 85, many others; works represented in numerous collections including The Norton Collection, Santa Monica, Broad Found., Santa Monica, Mint Mus., Charlotte, N.C., N.C. Mus. Raleigh, N.C., Security Pacific Corp., L.A., Ft. Lauderdale Mus.; others. Arts commr. City of Santa Monica Arts Commn., 1995—99; mem. Pub. Art Com., Santa Monica, 1996—2000; mem. artists adv. bd. L.A. Mcpl. Art Gallery at Bransdall, 1998—2001. Recipient Durfee Found. award; grantee Dale Chihuly grant for Srs. Making Art Workshops, 1996; painting fellow Western States Arts Fedn./NEA, 1990, painting fellow Getty Trust, 1990, NEA fellow in painting, 1991, City of L.A. Individual Artist's fellow, 1998. Home: 18880 Melvin Ave Sonoma CA 95476 E-mail: alice@alicefellows.com.

FELLOWS, ESTHER ELIZABETH, musician, music educator; b. Miami, Ariz., Nov. 5, 1952; d. John Wilmont and Flora Elizabeth (Eyestone) Walker; m. James Michael Fellows, Aug. 20, 1976; children: Joy Christine, Rachel Lindsay, Daniel Matthew, Jessica Grace. B in Music Edn., U. Colo., 1975. Co-dir. Children's Piano Lab. U. Colo., Boulder, 1975-76; instr. So. Calif. Conservatory Music, Sun City, 1976-78; pvt. instr. Ft. Lauderdale, 1978-84; instr. Ft. Lauderdale Christian Sch., 1981-83; sect. violinist Signature Symphony Tulsa Ballet, 1984—, Bartlesville (Okla.) Symphony, 1990—; pvt. instr. Broken Arrow, Okla., 1984—. Pvt. instr. Ft. Lauderdale, 1978-84; sec. orch. com. Signature Symphony. Mem. Music Tchrs. Nat. Assn. (cert. piano, violin and viola), Am. String Tchrs. Assn., Am. Viola Soc., Okla. Music Tchr. Assn., Suzuki Assn. Am., Hyechka Music Club Tulsa, Tulsa Accredited Music Tchrs. Assn. (chmn. scholarship com., pres.). Avocation: biking. Home: 19821 S Harvard Ave Mounds OK 74047-5049

FELLOWS, JERRY KENNETH, lawyer; b. Madison, Wis., Mar. 19, 1946; s. Forrest Garner and Virginia (Witte) F.; m. Patricia Lynn Graves, June 28, 1969; children: Jonathon, Aaron, Daniel. BA in Econs., U. Wis., 1968; JD, U. Minn., 1971. Bar: U.S. Dist. Ct. (no. dist.) Ill. 1971. Ptnr. McDermott, Will & Emery, Chgo., 1971—2002; with Bell, Boyd & Lloyd LLC, Chgo., 2002—. Speaker Bur. Nat. Affairs, Washington, 1985—. Contbr. articles to profl. jours. Bd. dirs. Midwest Benefits Coun., 1998. Mem. U. Minn. Law Alumni Assn. (bd. visitors), Gamma Eta Gamma. Avocations: coaching track, basketball, baseball. Home: 4541 Middaugh Ave Downers Grove IL 60515-2761 Office: Bell Boyd & Lloyd LLC 70 West Madison St Ste 3100 Chicago IL 60602-4207 Office Phone: 312-807-4358. Business E-Mail: jfellows@bellboyd.com.

FELLOWS, JOHN, delivery service executive; Grad. in engring., Dalhousie U., Nova Scotia Tech. Coll. With Canadian Nat. Railways; v.p., corp. strategy and devel. Canada Post Corp., Ottawa, Canada; chmn., CEO DHL Holdings Inc., Plantation, Fla., 2001—. Office: DHL Holdings 1200 S Pine Island Rd Ste 600 Plantation FL 33324

FELLOWS, ROBERT ELLIS, medical educator, medical scientist; b. Syracuse, NY, Aug. 4, 1933; s. Robert Ellis and Clara (Talmadgie) F.; m. Karlen Kiger, July 2, 1983; children: Kara, Ari, Thomas, Gregory, Jamey. AB, Hamilton Coll., 1955; MD, CM, McGill U., 1959; PhD, Duke U., 1969. Intern NY Hosp., NYC, 1959—60, asst. resident, 1960—61, Royal Victoria Hosp., Montreal, Canada, 1961—62; asst. prof. dept. medicine Duke U., Durham, NC, 1966—76, asst. prof. dept. physiology and pharmacology, 1966—70, assoc. prof. dept. physiology and pharmacology, assoc. dir. med. scientist tng. program, 1970—76; prof., chmn. dept. physiology and biophysics U. Iowa Coll. Medicine, 1976—2002, dir. med. sci. tng. program, 1976—97, dir. physician sci. program, 1984—88, dir. neurosci. program, 1984—88. Mem. Nat. Pituitary Agy. Adv. Bd.; mem. NIH Population Rsch. Com., 1981-86, VA Career Devel. Rev. Com., 1985-88; cons. NIH, NSF, March of Dimes. Mem. editl. bd.: Endocrinology, Am. Jour. Physiology. Mem. AAAS, Am. Chem. Soc., Am. Fedn. Clin. Rsch., Am. Physiol. Soc., Am. Soc. Biol. Chemists, Am. Soc. Cell Biology, Assn. Chmn. Depts. Physiology, Biochem. Soc., Biophys. Soc., Endocrine Soc., Internat. Soc. Neuroendocrinology, NY Acad. Scis., Soc. for Neurosci., Assn. Neurosci. Depts. and Programs (pres. 1995-96), Sigma Xi, Alpha Omega Alpha. Home: 135 Pentire Cir Iowa City IA 52245-1575 Office: 5-660 Bowen Sci Bldg Iowa City IA 52242 Office Phone: 319-335-7804. Business E-Mail: robert-fellows@uiowa.edu.

FELLS, CHARLES DAYTON, civil engineer, educator; b. Everett, Wash., June 29, 1933; s. Everett Orrin and Isabel Helen Fells; m. Patricia Anne Campbell, Jan. 9, 1993; 1 child, Donald Kevin; m. Audrey Carol Morgan, Sept. 29, 1962 (div. Mar. 1992). BS, Mont. State U., Bozeman, 1983. Gen. mgr. Constrn. Assist, Bothell, Wash., 1984—89; quality evaluator USN, Pearl Harbor, Hawaii, 1989—90; quality control engr. Kiewit Constrn. Co., Princeville, Hawaii, 1990—91; project engr. Engrs., Surveyors, Hawaii, Honolulu, 1991—93; compliance inspector cons. Honolulu, 1994—96; project engr. G.W. Murphy Constrn., Honolulu, 1995—96; mem. faculty U. N.Mex., Los Alamos, 1996—2000; ret., 2000. Continuing edn. lectr. C.C. Beaver County, Monaca, Pa., 2002—03. Contbr. articles and papers to profl. jours. Mem.: VFW (master of ceremonies for Vets. Day, Los Alamos 1997), U.S. Naval Inst., Am. Legion. Avocations: historical writing and research, public speaking, long distance running, military history. Home: 216 Pine Rd Sewickley PA 15143 Personal E-mail: chuckfells@aol.com.

FELOS, KIMBERLY, humanities educator; b. Bryn Mawr, Pa., Feb. 14, 1953; d. Kenneth Joseph and Virginia (Rosborough) Andrasko; 1 child, Alexander James. BA, Boston U., 1977, MA, 1978. Prof. St. Petersburg Coll., Tarpon Springs, Fla., 1980—. Fulbright Found. grantee, Pakistan, 1984.

FELS, JAMES ALEXANDER, lawyer; b. Chgo., Nov. 13, 1944; s. William Frederick and Rosemary (Budasi) Fels; m. Nancy Ann Dugan, July 15, 1967; children: Jeffery Scott, Scott Thomas, Thomas Jeffery. BS, Butler U., 1970; JD magna cum laude, Ind. U., 1974. Assoc. atty. Wilson & Tabor, Indpls., 1974-76, Wilson, Tabor & Holland, Indpls., 1976-81; mng. atty. Holland & Tabor, Indpls., 1981-87; ptnr. Tabor, Fels & Tabor, Indpls., 1987-2000, Mediation Group LLC, Indpls., 2000—. With U.S. Army, 1967—72. Mem.: ABA, Assn. Conflict Resolution, Indpls. Bar Assn., Ind. Trial Lawyers Assn., Ind. Bar Assn., Am. Coll. Civil Trial Mediators. Republican. Roman Catholic. Home: 8136 Rush Pl Indianapolis IN 46250-4266 Office: 8888 Keystone Xing Ste 1500 Indianapolis IN 46240-4614 Office Phone: 317-569-3000. E-mail: jfels@comcast.net, jfels@mede8.com.

FELS, NICHOLAS WOLFF, lawyer; b. White Plains, NY, Mar. 19, 1943; s. Lawrence P. and Fredricka (Gaines) F.; m. Susan T. McEwan, Dec. 28, 1968; 1 child, Sarah. BA magna cum laude, Harvard U., 1964; MA, U. Calif., Berkeley, 1965; LLB cum laude, Harvard U., 1968. Bar: NY 1968, Calif. 1970, US Dist. Ct. (cen. dist.) Calif. 1970, DC 1971, US Dist. Ct. DC 1971, US Ct. Appeals (10th cir.) 1976, US Ct. Appeals (DC cir.) 1977, US Supreme Ct. 1978, US Ct. Appeals (4th cir.) 1979, US Ct. Appeals (8th cir.) 1981, US Ct. Appeals (5th cir.) 1982. Law clk. to Hon. John Minor Wisdom U.S. Ct. Appeals, New Orleans, 1968-69; atty. OEO Legal Services, Los Angeles, 1969-70; assoc. Covington & Burling, Washington, 1970-76, ptnr., Energy Practice Group, 1976—. Mem. Nat. Com. on US-China Relations, NYC, 1982—. Contbr. articles to profl. jours. Bd. dirs. Pub. Edn. Partnership Fund, 2003—. Mem. Energy Bar Assn., DC Appleseed Ctr. (bd. dirs. 1994—, pres. 1996-2000). Office: Covington & Burling 1201 Pennsylvania Ave NW Washington DC 20004-2401 Office Phone: 202-662-5648. Office Fax: 202-662-6291. Business E-Mail: nfels@cov.com.

FELS, RENDIGS, economist, educator; b. Cin., June 11, 1917; s. Clifford George and Estella Luella (Rendigs) F.; m. Beatrice Carmichael Baker, Dec. 27, 1941, (dec.); children: Charles Wentworth Baker, Carmichael (dec.); m. Marilyn W. Whiteman, July 15, 2001. AB, Harvard U., 1939, PhD, 1948; AM, Columbia U., 1940. Mem. faculty Vanderbilt U., 1948—, prof. econs., 1956-82, prof. emeritus, 1982—, dir. grad. program econ. devel., 1956- 57, chmn. dept. econs. and bus. adminstrn., 1962-65, 77-79. Chmn. Univs.-Nat. Bur. Com., 1962-67. Author: American Business Cycles, 1865-1897, 1959, Challenge to the American Economy, an Introduction to Economics, 1961, 2d edit, 1966, (with C. Elton Hinshaw) Forecasting and Recognizing Business Cycle Turning Points, 1968; Editor: (with Stephen Buckles) Casebook of Economic Problems and Policies, 5th edit, 1981. Served with USAAF, 1942-46. Mem. Am. Econ. Assn. (sec.-treas. 1970-75, treas. 1976-87), Midwest Econ. Assn. (pres. 1984-85), So. Econ. Assn. (pres. 1967-68) Personal E-mail: rendigsf@aol.com.

FELSBURG, DAVID F., engineering executive, educator; b. Wilmington, Del., July 3, 1946; s. Francis Edward and Alice Jenny (Biscoe) F.; children: Michelle A., David W., Daniel E., Darrell B., Darren T. BS in Electronics Engring., N.Mex. State U., Las Cruces, 1975; M in Engring., U. Utah, 1980; grad., So. Bapt. Sem. Ext., Colorado Springs, 1985; postgrad. in Ministry, Luther Rice Sem., 2002—. Ordained pastor So. Bapt. Ch., 1981. Chief technician, sys. trainer 1961 Comm. Squadron, Clark AFB, The Philippines, 1969-73; dir. plans and programs 4754 Radar Evaluation Squadron, Hill AFB, Utah, 1976-79; dir. USAF/FAA Joint Ops. for Atmospheric Def. Hdqs. N.Am. Aerospace Def. Command, Colorado Springs, 1979; comdr., dir. comms. sys. 47 Comms. Group, Cheyenne Mountain AFB, Colo., 1979-81; dept. head math., football defensive line coach USAF Acad., Colorado Springs, 1981-85; sr. program mgr., dir. ops. CTA Inc., Boston, 1985-89; v.p., dir. ops. CTA Inc. Northeastern Region, Boston, 1989-97; exec. v.p., COO, co-founder Paloma Sys., Inc., Alexandria, Va., 1997—. Author: New Christians Everyday, 1987; author, editor 24 tech. bus. proposals, 1985—; lectr. in field. Interim pastor Faith Evangelical Ch., Melrose, Mass., 1996-97; pastor, tchr., evangelist, seminar leader Bapt. Chs., N.Mex., Tex., Miss., Utah, Colo., Mass., N.H., Maine, Conn., R.I., Vt., Va., 1973—; pastor Bon Air Bapt. Ch., Arlington, Va, 2004—; founder Eton Park Home Owners Assn., Alexandria, 1998; founder, pastor Alexandria Bible Chapel, 1997, Wilmington Bible Chapel, Mass., 1990; platinum mem. Rep. Nat. Com., Washington, 1993—. Mem. IEEE, Nat. Def. Indsl. Assn. (chpt. pres. 1995-98, pres. award 1996-97), Air Force Comms. Electronics Assn. and Air Force Assn., Assn. of Old Crows. Republican. Southern Baptist. Avocations: preaching and teaching bible, golf. Home: 11506 Sperrin Cir Ste 402 Fairfax VA 22030-8595 Office: Paloma Sys Inc 7002 Evergreen Ct Annandale VA 22003-3227 Fax: 703-591-0987. Office Phone: 703-563-2060. Business E-Mail: dave.felsburg@palomasys.com.

FELSEN, LEOPOLD B., engineering educator; DEE, Polytechnic Inst. Bklyn., 1952; D (hon.), Tech. U. Denmark, 1979, U. Sannio, Italy, 2003, Tech. U., Munich, 2004, Poly. U., 2005, Dogus U., Istanbul, Turkey, 2005. Prof. Polytechnic Inst. N.Y., 1961-78, dean engring., 1975-78, inst. prof., 1978-85; Univ. prof. Polytechnic U., 1985-94, Univ. prof. emeritus, 1994—; prof. dept. aerospace and mech. engring. Boston U., 1994—. Vis. disting. prof. Northeastern U., 1991-94; vis. lectr. Soviet Acad. Sci., 1967, 71, 88; fellow Guggenheim Meml. fellow, 1973-73; vis. mem. Faculty Math & Physics Charles U., Prague, 1984; vis. Sackler fellow Tel Aviv U., 1985; vis. scholar Acoust Inst., Academia Sinica, Beijing, 1985; vis. prof. Nat. Defense Acad., Japan, 1985. Recipient citation Sigma Xi, Van der Pol Gold medal Internat. Union Radio Sci., 1975. Fellow IEEE (Heinrich Hertz medal 1992, Ant. and Propag. Soc. Disting. Achievement award 1998, Electromagnetics award 2003), Internat. Union Radio Science, Optical Soc. Am., Acoustic Soc. Am.; mem. Nat. Acad. Engring. Home: Brook House 33 Pond Ave Brookline MA 02445-7163

FELSENTHAL, CAROL JUDITH, writer; b. Chgo., Apr. 25, 1949; d. Louis H. and Ruth (Glass) Greenberg; m. Steven A. Felsenthal, June 14, 1970; children: Rebecca Elizabeth, Julia Alison, Daniel Louis Altus. BA, U. Ill., 1971; MA, Boston Coll., 1972. Editor F.W. Faxon Co., Westwood, Mass., 1973-74; reporter Northbrook (Ill.) Star, 1974-76; editor About Books ALA, Chgo., 1976-78; freelance writer Chgo., 1978—. Instr. creative writing U. Chgo. Author: Sweetheart of the Silent Majority, 1981, Cry for Help, 1983, Alice Roosevelt Longworth, 1988, Power, Privilege and the Post: The Katharine Graham Story, 1993, Citizen Newhouse, 1998; contbr. articles to numerous mags. Recipient Peter Lisenger award for in depth reporting, 2005. Office: 30 N La Salle St Ste 3000 Chicago IL 60602-2506 Office Phone: 312-944-2180. E-mail: cfelsenthal@att.net.

FELSENTHAL, STEVEN ALTUS, lawyer, educator; b. Chgo., May 21, 1949; s. Jerome and Eve (Altus) F.; m. Carol Judith Greenberg, June 14, 1970; children: Rebecca Elizabeth, Julia Alison, Daniel Louis Altus. AB, U. Ill., 1971; JD, Harvard U., 1974. Bar: Ill. 1974, U.S. Dist. Ct. (no. dist.) Ill. 1974, U.S. Ct. Claims 1975, U.S. Tax Ct. 1975, U.S. Ct. Appeals (7th cir.) 1981. Assoc. Levenfeld, Kanter, Baskes & Lippitz, Chgo., 1974-78; ptnr. Levenfeld & Kanter, Chgo., 1978-80, Levenfeld, Eisenberg, Janger, Glassberg & Lippitz, Chgo., 1980-84; sr. ptnr. Sugar, Friedberg & Felsenthal, Chgo., 1984—. Lectr. Kent Coll. Law, Ill. Inst. Tech., Chgo., 1978-80. Mem. ABA, Ill. Bar Assn., Chgo. Bar Assn., Chgo. Coun. Lawyers, Harvard Law Soc. Ill., Standard Club, Harvard Club, Phi Beta Kappa. Office: Sugar Friedberg & Felsenthal 30 N La Salle St Ste 3000 Chicago IL 60602-3327 Office Phone: 312-704-9400. Business E-Mail: saf@sff-law.com.

FELSKI, RITA, language educator; b. Birmingham, Eng., Apr. 15, 1956; BA, Cambridge U., Eng., 1979; MA, Monash U., 1982, PhD, 1987. Asst. prof. Murdoch U., Perth, Australia, 1987-93; prof. U. Va., Charlottesville, 1994—. George A. Miller vis. prof. U. Ill., 1998. Author: Beyond Feminist Aesthetics, 1989, The Gender of Modernity, 1995, Doing Time. 2000, Literature After Feminism, 2003. Fellow Soc. for Humanities, 1988-89, Commonwealth Ctr., 1991; grantee Australian Rsch. Coun., 1993; Inst. for Human Scis. fellow, Vienna, 2000. Office: U Va Dept English Bryan Hall Charlottesville VA 22903

FELSTED, CARLA MARTINDELL, librarian, writer, editor; b. Barksdale Field, La., June 21, 1947; d. David Aldenderfer Martindell and Dorthe (Hetland) Horton; m. Robert Earl Luna, Aug. 24, 1968, (div. 1972); m. Hugh Herbert Felsted, Nov. 2, 1974. BA in English, So. Meth. U., 1968, MA in History, 1974; MLS, Tex. Woman's U., 1978. Cert. secondary tchr., Tex.; cert. learning resources specialist, Tex. Tchr. Bishop Lynch High Sch., Dallas, 1968-72, Lake Highlands Jr. High Sch., Richardson, Tex., 1973-75; instr. Richland Coll., Richardson, Tex., 1973-76; library asst. So. Meth. U., Dallas, 1977-78; librarian Tracy-Locke Advt., Dallas, 1978-79; corp. librarian Am. Airlines, Inc., Ft. Worth, 1979-84; research librarian McKinsey & Co., Dallas, 1984-85; reference librarian St. Edward's U., Austin, Tex., 1985—2002, assoc. prof., 1994—2002; libr. Sedona (Ariz.) Pub. Libr., 2003—. Ptnr. Southwind Info. Svcs. and Southwind Bed-Breakfast, Wimberley, Tex., 1985-92. Editor, compiler: Youth and Alcohol Abuse, 1986; co-editor Mexican Meanderings, 1991-99; contbr. Frommer's travel guides, 1991-96. Mem. adv. bd. Sch. Libr. and Info. Scis., Tex. Women's U., Denton, 1982-84; mem. curriculum com. Wimberley Ind. Sch. Dist., 1986; bd. dirs. Hays-Caldwell Coun. on Alcohol and Drug Abuse, San Marcos, Tex., 1986-88, Inst. Cultures for Wimberley Valley, 1989-91, Tex. Alliance Human Needs, 1992-96; Tex. Team Survivor, Danskin Triathlon, 1995-2002, co-capt. 1997-99; vol. Breast Cancer Resource Ctr., 1998-2000, Sedona Cultural Pk., 2003-04, Sedona Pub. Libr., 2003, Sedona Gt Decisions, 2003-. Grantee St. Edward's U., 1986-89, 96. Mem. ALA, Tex. Libr. Assn. (dist. program com., membership com. 1986-88, Tex.-Mex. rels. com. 1992-2002), REFORMA, Wimberley C. of C. (bd. dirs. 1987-88). Unitarian Universalist. Avocations: health issues research and advocacy, regional and ethnic cooking, physical fitness, art history, travel.

FELSTINER, MARY LOWENTHAL, history educator; b. Pittsburgh, Feb. 19, 1941; d. Alexander and Anne Lowenthal; m. John Felstiner, Feb. 19, 1966; children: Sarah Alexandra, Aleksandr. BA, Harvard U., 1963; MA, Columbia U., 1966; PhD, Stanford U., 1971. Prof. history San Francisco State Univ., 1972—. Author: To Paint Her Life, 1994, Out of Joint, 2005. Mem.: Phi Beta Kappa. Office: San Francisco State Univ History Dept 1600 Holloway Ave San Francisco CA 94132-1722

FELTENSTEIN, HARRY DAVID, JR., chemicals executive; b. St. Joseph, Mo., Nov. 6, 1920; s. Harry David and Isabel (Rosenbaum) F.; m. Rosalie Goldstein, Jan. 18, 1945 (dec. Sept. 1977); children: Andrew, Martha; m. Carmen Archabala Fernandez, Aug. 24, 1979; 1 son, Henry. BS, Harvard U., 1942. Engaged in book pub., 1946-50; with Merrill Lynch, Pierce, Fenner & Smith, 1951-57, Lithium Corp., Am. Inc., N.Y.C., 1957-69, fin. v.p., treas., 1957-58, exec. v.p., treas., 1958-60, pres., treas., 1960-69; pres., dir. Beryllium Metals & Chems. Corp., 1962-69, Gt. Salt Lake Minerals and Chems. Corp., 1967-69; exec. v.p., dir. Gulf Resources & Chem. Corp., 1967-69; pres., bd. dirs. Fuel Mgmt. Corp., Washington, 1970-94, chmn., 1995—; pres., bd. dirs. Internat. Wine Investors, Ltd., 1972-86, Wildenstein & Co.,

1972-74; European rep. C & K Coal Co. divsn. Gulf Resources & Chem. Corp., 1981-82; cons. to Spanish govt. cos., 1990—. Author: Dreamworlds, 2004. Served with USNR, 1942-46. Address: Calle Lerez 4 Madrid 2 Spain Personal E-mail: harry8@teleline.es.

FELTER, JOHN KENNETH, lawyer; b. Monmouth, N.J., May 9, 1950; s. Joseph Harold and Rosanne (Bautz) F. BA magna cum laude, MA in Econs., Boston Coll., 1972; JD cum laude, Harvard U., 1975. Bar: Mass. 1975, D.C. 2002, N.Y. 2003, U.S. Dist. Ct. Mass. 1976, U.S. Ct. Appeals (1st cir.) 1977, U. S. Ct. Appeals (2d cir.) 2002, U.S. Supreme Ct. 1982, U.S. Tax Ct. 1993. Assoc. Goodwin Procter LLP, Boston, 1975-83, ptnr., 1983—. Spl. asst. gen. Commonwealth of Mass., 1982-84, 94-95; spl. counsel Town of Plymouth, Mass., Town of Salisbury, Mass., Town of Edgartown, Mass.; spl. outside counsel City of Boston, 1990-92; mem. devel. com. Greater Boston Legal Svcs., 1980-99, bd. dirs., 1982—, mem. exec. com., 1989-93; mem. faculty Mass. Continuing Legal Edn., Inc., Boston. Mem. adv. com. The Boston Plan for Excellence in Pub. Schs.; mem. elem. edn. com. Blue Ribbon Commn. on Cmty. Learning Ctrs.; VIP panelist Easter Seals Telethon, Boston, 1978-79. Named one of Am.'s Leading Lawyers for Bus., Chamber's USA. Fellow: Am. Coll. Trial Lawyers; mem.: ABA (litigation sect., mem. personal rights litigation com., mem. ABA-Am. Law Inst. com. on cont. edn.), Greater Boston C. of C. (mem. edn. com., mem. health care com.), Boston Bar Assn. (bd. dirs. law firm resources project 1985—, mem. coll. and univ. law com. 1986—, chmn. fed. rules com. litigation sect. 1994), Mass. Bar Assn., Am. Arbitration Assn. (comml. arbitrator). Office: Goodwin Procter LLP Exchange Pl 53 State St Ste 17 Boston MA 02109-2881 Office Phone: 617-570-1211. Business E-Mail: kahuna@goodwinprocter.com.

FELTER, JUNE MARIE, artist; b. Oakland, Calif., Oct. 19, 1919; m. Richard Henry Felter, Feb. 7, 1943; children: Susan, Tom. Student, San Francisco Art Inst., 1960, student, 1961, Oakland Art Inst., 1937—40. Instr. San Francisco Mus. Art, 1965—78, San Francisco State U., 1970—78, U. Calif., 1979—80, Santa Rosa Jr. Coll., Calif., 1981, Elaine Badgley-Arnoux Sch. Art, San Francisco, 1982, Elaine Badgley-Amoux Sch. Art, San Francisco, 1983, U. Calif., San Francisco, 1979—80, 1984—85. One-woman shows include Kennedy Gallery, 2001, Holy Names U., Oakland, 2001, Oakland Mus. Calif. Art, 2002, Gumps Gallery, San Francisco, 1965-66, Linda Ferris Gallery, Seattle, 1971, Richmond Art Gallery, 1971-74, Dana Reich Gallery, San Francisco, 1978, 80-81, 871 Fine Arts Gallery, San Francisco, 1987, 89, 90, 92; exhibited in group shows at San Francisco Mus. Art., 1960-79, Civic Arts Gallery, Walnut Creek, Calif., 1983, U.S. Art, San Francisco, 1990, Oakland Art Mus., 1991, Wiegand Gallery, 1992, Jack London Square Oakland, 1993, U.S. Embassy, Vienna, Austria, 1995; represented in permanent collections at Nat. Mus. Art, Washington, Oakland Mus. Calif. Art, San Jose (Calif.) Mus. Art, Achenbach Found. Mus. Fine Arts, San Francisco, Yale U. Art Gallery, New Haven. Home and Office: 1046 Amito Dr Berkeley CA 94705-1502

FELTHEIMER, JON, entertainment company executive; B in Economics, Washington Un. Pres. Columbia Tristar TV; pres., CEO New World Entertainment, 1989—97; exec. v.p. Sony Pictures Entertainment Inc., 1997—99; CEO Lions Gate Entertainment, 2000—, co-chmn. bd. dirs. Office: Lions Gate Entertainment Inc 2700 Colorado Blvd Santa Monica CA 90404*

FELTHOUSE, PATRICIA MAE AVRIT, librarian; b. Tillamook, Oreg., Mar. 28, 1924; d. Roy Calvin and Louise (Morgan) Avrit; m. James Whitman Felthouse, May 10, 1944; children: Timothy Roy, Daphne Diane. Student, Oreg. State U., 1941—44; BA in Elem. Edn., U. Wash., 1960. With Fed. Land Bank, Berkeley, Calif., 1945—51; libr. Tehama County Libr., Red Bluff, Calif., 1965—85; organist United Meth. Ch., Red Bluff, 1985—. Contbr. articles to profl. jours. Bd. dirs. Tehama County Mus. Found., 1980—. Mem. AAUW (pres. Red Buff-Tehama County 1974-75), Calif. Conf. Hist. Socs. (regional v.p. 1981-84). Assn. No. Calif. Records and Rsch. (bd. dirs. 1983-86), Colusi County Hist. Soc. (bd. dirs. 1983-90, pres. 1984-85), Bus. and Profl. Women's Club (pres. 1977-78, Woman of Yr. 1987), Tehama County Geneal. and Hist. Soc. (pres. 1986-90). Republican. Methodist. Avocation: quilting. Home: 1140 Wetter Way Red Bluff CA 96080-4123

FELTMAN, JEFFREY D., ambassador; b. Greenville, Ohio; BS, Ball State U., 1981; M in Law and Diplomacy, Tufts U., 1983. Consular officer U.S. Embassy, Port-au-Prince, Haiti, 1986—88, econ. officer Budapest, Hungary, 1988—91; spl. asst. to dep. asst. sec. Larry Eagleburger US Dept. State, Washington, 1991—93, fgn. svc. officer bur. near ea. affairs, 1993—95; econ. offier U.S. Embassy, Tel Aviv, 1995—98, spl. asst. on peace process issues, 2000—01, chief polit. and econ. sect. Tunis, Tunisia, 1998—2000; dep. prin. officer U.S. Consulate-Gen., Jerusalem, 2001—02, acting prin. officer, 2002—03; vol. Coalition Provisional Authority, Irbil, Iraq, 2004; U.S. amb. to Lebanon US Dept. State, Beirut, 2004—. Office: Am Embassy Beirut 6070 Beirut Pl Washington DC 20521-6070*

FELTON, JOHN WALTER, public relations executive; b. Grundy, Va., Mar. 21, 1929; s. John S. and Mary (Williams) F.; m. Ann Reynolds, June 26, 1954; children: J. Frerderick, David Alan, MariAnn Reynolds (Mrs. James Seybold). BA in Journalism, U. Mich., Ann Arbor, 1951, MA, 1952. With U.S. Steel, various locations, 1957-69; dir. pub. relations Interstate Brands Corp., Kansas City, Mo., 1969-75; v.p. corp. communications McCormick & Co., Inc., Sparks, Md., 1977-95; pres., CEO Inst. for Public Relations Rsch. and Edn., 1996—. Vis. prof. in pub. rels. U. Fla. Playwright: Peace is an Olive Color; With No Reservations; The Star Gazer; Touch of a Shadow; Christmas at Checkpoint Charlie; Soliloquy on Sounds of Easter; author: (film) The Bread Winners (George Washington medal for Freedoms Found.), 1974. Bd. dirs. Balt. Symphony; trustee Ind. Coll. Fund of Md. Served with USAF, 1952-56. Named Freedom Forum Disting. Vis. Prof. of Public Relations U. Fla., 1995—. Mem. NAM (chmn. pub. relations council 1980-85), Found. Public Relations Research and Edn. (trustee), Am. Spice Trade Assn., Balt. Wine and Food Soc. (bd. govs. 1977), Pub. Relations Soc. Am. (bd. dirs. 1983-85, pres. elect 1986, pres. 1986-87), Internat. Pub. Rels. Assn. (bd. dirs.), Nat. Press Found. (bd. dirs.), Advt. Assn. Balt., Nat. Press Club. Clubs: Hunt Valley Golf, Capitol Hill, Center, N.Y. Publicity, Haile Plantation Golf & Country. Republican. Presbyterian. Home: 4318 SW 91st Dr Gainesville FL 32608-4173 Office: U Fla Coll of Journalism 3601 Weimer Hall Gainesville FL 32611-2084

FELTON, JULE WIMBERLY, JR., lawyer; b. Macon, Ga., July 22, 1932; s. Jule Wimberly and Mary Julia (Sasnett) F.; m. Kate Gillis, May 15, 1965; children— Jule Wimberly III, Mary Katherine, Laura Borden Student, Emory U., Atlanta, 1949-50; AB, U. Ga., Athens, 1954, LL.B, 1955. Bar: Ga. 1954. Assoc. Hansell & Post, Atlanta, 1955-59, mng. ptnr., 1959-89; sr. of counsel Jones Day Reavis & Pogue, Atlanta, 1989-92; ptnr. Ford & Felton, 1993-95, Proctor, Felton & Atkinson, Atlanta, 1995-96, Proctor, Felton & Chambers, Atlanta, 1996-99. Bd. dirs. dept. cmty. affairs Ga. State, chair, 2003—. Mem. Ga. Gen. Assembly, Atlanta, 1969-72; mem. ofcl. bd. dirs. Northside United Meth. Ch., Atlanta, 1974-85, 88; mem. U. Ga. Bd. Visitors, 1986, 87, 91, chmn., 1987-88, 93-94; bd. dirs. Ga. Dept. Cmty. Affairs Bd., 1999-2003, chair, 2002-03. 1st lt. JAGC, U.S. Army, 1955-56. Recipient Disting. Svc. award, U. Ga. Law Sch. Fellow Am. Bar Found.; mem. ABA, Ga. Bar Assn. (pres. 1973-74), Nat. Conf. Bar Pres., Am. Coll. Trial Lawyers, Ga. Bar Found., Am. Judicature Soc., U. Ga. Law Sch. Assn. (pres. 1984-85), Lawyers Club Atlanta, Old War Horse Lawyers Club (pres. Atlanta chpt. 1983), Piedmont Driving Club, Capital City Club. Avocations: piano, golf, boating. Home: 1061 Arbor Trce NE # 34 Atlanta GA 30319-5381 Office Phone: 404-239-0750. Business E-Mail: jwf@petersonharris.com.

FELTS, JOAN APRIL, retired elementary school educator; b. Tulsa, Apr. 8, 1940; d. John Hickland and Dorris Retha (Finley) Matlock; m. Wayne Keith Felts, Aug. 19, 1962; children: David Wayne, Michael Scott, Steven Doyle. BS in Edn., Northeastern State U., Tahlequah, Okla., 1962. Cert. tchr., Okla. Tchr. Ruby Ray Swift Elem. Sch., Arlington, Tex., 1962-64; co-owner Felts Family Shoe Store, Muskogee, Okla., 1966-79; tchr. Hilldale Elem. Sch., Muskogee, 1979—2000; ret., 2000. Leader Neosho dist. Boy Scouts Am., 1969-78, trainer, 1978-88. Recipient Dist. award of merit Boy Scouts Am., 1982, Wood Badge tng. award Nat. coun., 1983, Silver Beaver award Tulsa coun., 1985; Tchr. of Yr. award Hilldale Ind. Schs., 1988. Mem. Hill Assn. Classroom Tchrs. (chmn. staff devel. 1985-89, newsletter editor 1988-90), Northeastern State U. Alumni Assn (bd. dirs. 1976-95, pres.-elect 1990-91, pres. 1991-93), Beta Sigma Phi (pres. Xi Zeta Zeta chpt. 1993-95, Woman of Yr. award Muskogee chpt. 1987), Kappa Kappa Iota. Republican. Methodist. Avocations: writing, reading, researching trivia, nostalgia radio shows, sewing. Home: 109 Grandview Blvd Muskogee OK 74403-8608

FELTS, MARGARET CLEMEN, environmental engineer, consultant; b. Ft. Worth, Tex., Dec. 16, 1950; d. Arthur Taylor and Jane Jolliffe Clemen; m. Robert Louis Felts; children: Shane, Jonathan, Julia. BA Orgn. Communications, Eckerd Coll., St. Petersburg, Fla., 1973; BS Petroleum Engring., La. Tech., Ruston, La., 1977; MS Energy Engring., LaSalle U., 1989; JD, U. Pacific, 2000. Registered environ. assessor II, Calif.; registered environ. mgr., Nat. Registered Environ. Profls.; lic. gen. contractor, Calif. Engr. AMOCO Oil Co. Refinery, Yorktown, Pa., 1977-80; process engr. Celanese, Vernon, Tex., 1980-82; energy spl. Calif. Energy Commn., Sacramento, 1982-84; energy cons., owner Clemen Co., Sacramento, 1984-89; chief engring. divsn. Environ. Mgmt., McClellan AFB, Sacramento, 1985-89; owner, mgr. Clemen Environ. Svcs., 1989-92; pres. Invictus Corp., Wilton, Calif., 1992—; dir. Calif. Superfund Program Calif. Dept. Toxic Substances Control, 1993-95; chmn. bd., CEO, M.C. Felts Corp., 1995—; pres., CFO Calif. Tel. Assn., 2002—. Litigation cons. Pvt. Attys. in Calif.; CEO Oil-Gasoline.com., Inc., 1999—; expert witness FERC; expert witness natural resources and utilities coms. Calif. State Assembly; cons., expert witness Calif. Pub. Utilities Commn., Calif. Energy Commn. Author: Studies and Testimonies for Calif. Pub. Utilities Com., FERC, Citizen's Energy Coun., 1984-89; article, Oil & Gas Jour., 1985; paper, Soc. of Petroleum Engring., 1986. Recipient Lee Community Leadership Award, Eckerd Coll., 1973. Mem. Soc. Petroleum Engrs. (assoc.), Calif. Telephone Assn. (pres.). Presbyterian. Office: MCFelts Corp 9156 Tavernor Rd Wilton CA 95693-9659 also: Calif Tel Assn 1851 Heritage Ln Ste 255 Sacramento CA 95815 Office Phone: 916-567-6702.

FELTS, MARGARET JEAN, secondary school educator; b. Richmond, Va., Aug. 7, 1965; d. Benjamin R. and Jean Felts. BA, Mary Wash. Coll., 1987. Cert. tchr. secondary social studies Va. Admissions counselor Mary Wash. Coll., 1987—88; tchr. Va. Beach City Pub. Schs., Va. Beach, Va., 1988—. Cheerleading coach Kempsville HS, 1990—95, asst. student activities coord., 1997—2001; chmn. Safe Schs. Action Team, Kempsville HS, 2003—; scholarship com. mem. Kempsville HS, 2003—. Stage mgr.: Arts Guild of Christ and St. Lukes Espisc. Ch., 1997—2000. Tchr. coord. CEL Voting Precinct, Va. Beach, Va., 2004; vol. Boardwalk Art Show, Va. Beach Art Ctr., Va. Beach, Va., 1995—; usher Bayside Presbyn. Ch., Va. Beach, Va., 1999—. Mem.: Parent Tchr. Student Assn. Avocations: travel, theater, reading, movies, Nascar. Office: Kempsville HS 5194 Chief Trail Virginia Beach VA 23464 Office Phone: 757-474-8400. Office Fax: 757-474-8404. E-mail: margaret.felts@vbschools.com.

FELTUS, ALAN EVAN, artist; b. Washington, May 1, 1943; s. John Randolph Feltus and Anne Eve Winter; m. Toni Travis, May 1968 (div. 1974); m. Lani Helena Irwin, Dec. 10, 1978; children: Tobias, Joseph. Student, Tyler Sch. Fine Arts, Phila., 1961-62; BFA, Cooper Union, 1966; MFA, Yale U., 1968. Instr. painting and drawing Sch. of Dayton Art Inst., 1968-70; asst. prof. art dept. Am. U., Washington, 1972-84; artist, 1984—. One-person shows include Forum Gallery, NYC, 1976, 80, 83, 85, 87, 91, 94, 96, 98, 2002-03, Ann Nathan Gallery, Chgo., 1994, 98, 2000, 03, Huntington (W.Va.) Mus. Art, 2000, Wichita (Kans.) Art Mus., 1987, Hemphill Fine Arts, Washington, DC, 2001. Mem.: NAD (nat academician 1994—). Avocations: lectures, workshops. Office: Forum Gallery 745 Fifth Ave New York NY 10151 Fax: 212-355-4547. Office Phone: 212-355-4545. E-mail: alan@alanfeltus.com.

FENCHEL, GERD HERMANN, psychoanalyst; b. Berlin, Mar. 29, 1926; arrived in U.S., 1940; s. Eric Otto and Rosa (Goldschmidt) F.; children: Karen Fenchel Spiler, Erich; m. Leslie Spitz, June 30, 1991. BSS, CCNY, 1949, MS in Edn., 1950; PhD, NYU, 1959; cert., Washington Sq. Inst., 1970. Cert. psychologist, N.Y., Pa. Pvt. practice psychoanalysis, N.Y.C., 1949—; asst. dean Alfred Adler Inst., N.Y.C., 1955-73; psychotherapist, supr. and dir. group psychotherapy L.I. Cons. Ctr., Forest Hills, N.Y., 1953-60; mem. faculty Inst. for Analytic Psychotherapy, N.J., 1960-71; exec. dir., dean Washington Sq. Inst., N.Y.C., 1960—. Author: Psychoanalytic Reflections on Love and Sexuality, 2005; co-author: Development of Ego and Emergence of the Self in Group Psychotherapy, 1979; editor: Psychoanalysis at 100, 1994, The Mother-Daughter Relationship, 1998; contbr. articles to profl. jours. Fellow Coun. Psychoanalysts and Psychotherapists (pres. 1966-67), Am. Group Psychotherapy Assn., Pa. Psychol. Assn.; mem. APA. Avocations: travel, stamps, photography. Office: Washington Sq Inst 41 E 11th St Fl 4 New York NY 10003-4678 Office Phone: 212-477-2600. E-mail: ghfenchel@hotmail.com.

FENDLER, JANOS HUGO, chemistry professor; b. Budapest, Hungary, Aug. 12, 1937; came to U.S., 1964; s. Janos and Vilma (Csiky) F.; m. Eleanor Johnson, june 15, 1965 (div. 1975); children: Michael, Lisa; m. Ann Fendler, Feb. 15, 1976 (div. 1997); children: Peter, Monika; m. Eliza Hutter, Sept. 15, 1997; children: Veronika Isabelle, David Viktor. BSc, U. Leicester, Eng., 1960; Diploma in Radiochemistry, Leicester Coll. Tech., 1961; PhD, U. London, 1964, DSc, 1978; DSc (hon.), U. Szeged, Hungary, 1999. Postdoctoral fellow U. Calif., Santa Barbara, 1965-66; fellow Mellon Inst., Pitts., 1966-70; assoc. prof. chemistry Tex. A&M U., College Station, 1970-75, prof., 1975-81; prof. chemistry Clarkson Coll., Potsdam, N.Y., 1982-85; disting. prof. chemistry, dir. Ctr. Membrane Engring. & Sci. Syracuse U., 1985-97; disting. Camp prof. chemistry Clarkson U., 1997—. Adj. prof. U. Montreal, 1967—94; indsl. cons., vis. prof., Japan, 1975, Switzerland, 79, Sweden, 81, France, 85, Germany, 92, Israel, 97, Paris, 2001—. Author: Catalysts in Micellar and Macromolecular Systems, 1975, Membrane Mimetic Chemistry, 1982, Membrane Mimetic Approach to Advanced Materials, 1994; rsch., numerous publs. in field; N.Am. editor Colloid and Polymer Sci.; mem. editl. bd. Jour. Organic Chemistry, 1978-82, jour. Colloid and Interface Sci., 1981-87, Langmuir, 1985-87, Bull. Chem. Soc. France, 1986-92, Magyar Kèmiai Folyoirat, 1992—, Advanced Materials, 1994—, Chemistry of Materials, 1997—. Recipient Sr. Humboldt Rsch. award, 1992. Mem. Am. Chem. Soc. (Kendall award 1982), Royal Chem. Soc., Internat. Assn. Colloid and Interface Scientists. Home: 608 Swan St Potsdam NY 13676-1147 Office: Clarkson U Ctr Adv Material Processing PO Box 5814 Potsdam NY 13699-0001 E-mail: fendler@clarkson.edu.

FENDRICH, ROGER PAUL, lawyer; b. Newark, Dec. 27, 1943; s. Howard and Elsie (Zahler) F.; m. Renee Madeleine Obestein, July 10, 1965; children: Howard Joseph, Alexander Daniel. AB, U. Miami, Coral Gables, Fla., 1965; PhD, U. Tex., 1971; JD, Yale U., 1980. Bar: D.C. 1980, U.S. Ct. Appeals (D.C. cir.) 1981, U.S. Supreme Ct. 1987, U.S. Ct. Appeals (4th cir.) 1987, U.S. Ct. Appeals (9th cir.) 1991, U.S. Ct. Appeals (3rd cir.) 1992, U.S. Ct. Appeals (2nd cir.) 1993. Assoc. prof. Beloit (Wis.) Coll., 1969-77; acting asst. gen. counsel Yale U., New Haven, 1980; assoc. Hughes, Hubbard & Reed, Washington, 1980-88; ptnr. Arnold & Porter, Washington, 1988—. Spl. master U.S. Dist. Ct., New Haven, 1985; barrister Am. Inns Ct., Washington, 1985-88; cons. Fed. Cts. Study Com., Washington, 1989-90. Contbg. author The Individual and Society, 1978; contbr. philosophy articles to profl. jours. Spl. master U.S. Dist. Ct. Conn., New Haven, 1985; barrister Am. Inns Ct., Washington, 1985-88. Woodrow Wilson fellow, 1966; NEH rsch. grantee, 1976, 77. Mem. ABA, D.C. Bar Assn. Office: Arnold & Porter 555 12th St NW Washington DC 20004-1206

FENDRICK, ALAN BURTON, retired advertising executive; b. Bronx, N.Y., Mar. 22, 1933; s. Louis and Esther (Silberberg) F.; m. Beverly R. Schoenfeld, June 12, 1960; children: Sarah Shifrin, Lisa Rubinstein. AB with honors in Econs, Columbia U., 1954; MBA, Harvard U., 1958. Asst. sales mgr. splty. divsn. Hankins Container Co., 1958-60; mgr. bus. adminstrn., ops. and engring. NBC, 1960-67; exec. v.p., sec., treas. Grey Advt. Inc., N.Y.C., 1967-89, exec. v.p., chmn. fin. com., 1990-93. Trustee Woodlands H.S. Scholarship Fund, Greenburgh, N.Y., pres., 1977-78; trustee Jewish Child Care Assn. N.Y., 1985-97, hon. trustee, 1997—; trustee SAG Producers Pension and Health Plans, 1993—; mem. sch. bd. Mt. Plesant Cottage Sch., 1985-99; bd. dirs. Columbia Coll. Alumni Assn., 1989-96. With AUS, 1954-56. Mem. Am. Assn. Advt. Agys. (chmn. com. on fiscal control 1979-81), Advt. Agy. Fin. Mgmt. Group (chmn. exec. com. 1980-82, pres. 1982-84), Otis Woodlands Club Inc. (bd. dirs. 1985-89, treas. 1984-88), Columbia U. Alumni Club of Sarasota (pres. 1997—). Jewish (trustee temple). Home: 5880 Midnight Pass Rd Sarasota FL 34242-4106 Personal E-mail: bevalan711@verizon.net.

FENECH, CRAIG E., lawyer; b. 1947; BA in econ. with honors, U. Notre Dame, 1969; JD, Boalth Hall Sch. Law, U. Calif., Berkeley, 1973. Bar: Calif. 1973. Staff atty. IBM Corp.; atty. Fed. Defenders San Diego, Inc.; atty. representing athletes and media figures, 1980—. Adj. prof. bus. of sports Mgmt. Inst., NYU. Mem.: Sports Lawyers Assn. (bd. mem.).

FENECH, DANIEL THOMAS, cartoonist; b. Garden City, Mich., 1957; s. Carmel John and Elizabeth Frances (Borg) Fenech; m. Linda M. Speegle, Dec. 7, 1992. BA, U. Mich., 1979. Coll. intern WXYZ-TV, ABC, Southfield, Mich., 1978—79; tech. on-air dir. WEYI-TV, Flint, Mich., 1979—80; cartoonist Daniel Fenech Prodns., Saline, Mich., 1980—. Contbr. to over 90 newspapers including USA Today, Best Editorial Cartoons of the Year, 2001-05. Pres. bd. of trustees Saline Dist. Libr., 1998—2001. Avocations: reading encyclopedias, reading, swimming, running, travel.

FENECH, JOSEPH CHARLES, lawyer; b. London, May 28, 1950; came to U.S., 1953; s. Carmel John and Elizabeth Frances (Borg) F.; m. Cynthia A. Rennie, June 14, 1980 (div. 1998); children: Paul C., Peter J., Elizabeth F. BA with hons., Mich. State U., 1972; JD, U. Mich., 1975. Bar: Mich. 1975, U.S. Dist. Ct. (ea. dist.) Mich. 1975, U.S. Ct. Appeals (6th cir.) 1977, Ill. 1980, U.S. Dist. Ct. (no. dist.) Ill. 1980, U.S. Dist. Ct. (ctrl. dist.) Ill. 1993, U.S. Dist. Ct. (ea. dist.) Wis. 1993, U.S. Ct. Appeals (7th cir.) 1980, U.S. Supreme Ct. 1993, U.S. Tax Ct. 1993. Law clk. Washtenaw Cir. Ct., Ann Arbor, Mich., 1975-76; asst. atty. gen. State of Mich., Detroit, 1976-80; labor rels. counsel McDonald's Corp., Oak Brook, Ill., 1980-82, sr. internat. atty., 1982-84; sr. mem. Fenech, Pachulski & Welgat, P.C., Oak Brook, Ill., 1985—. Contbr. articles to profl. jours. Bd. dirs. Cath. Charities Diocese of Joliet, Ill.; active Family Focus, Mich., 1979-80, Internat. Found. Employee Benefit Plans, Brookfield, Wis., 1980-83, Chmns. Club Ctrl.; mem. bd. govs. DuPage Hosp., Ctrl. DuPage Hosp. Tree Life, Ctrl., Glen Oaks Med. Ctr., Tree of Life, Rep. Campaign Coun., 1995; supt. adv. com. Naperville Cmty. Sch. Dist. 203; improvement com. Mill St. Sch., Naperville; charter mem. Marklund Children's Home Endowment; bd. govs. Ctrl. DuPage Hosp. Named Regents scholar U. Mich., 1973, 74, 75, Trustees scholar Mich. State U., 1969-72. Mem. ABA, Ill. State Bar Assn., Mich. Bar Assn., DuPage Estate Planning Coun., U. Mich. Lawyers Club, Ill. Bankers Assn., Ill. Mortgage Bankers Assn., Internat. Platform Assn., Am. Hosp. Assn. (sr. mem.), Am. Acad. Healthcare Attys. (sr. mem.), Mich. State U. Pres. Club. Office: Fenech Pachulski & Welgat PC 1656 Imperial Cir Ste 100 Naperville IL 60563-0129 Office Phone: 630-510-8600.

FENG, CHANGJIAN, biochemist, chemist; s. Weiqun Feng and Zhongfang Li; m. Danping Liao, Jan. 28, 1998; 1 child, Daniel L.; 1 child, David J. PhD, Nanjing U., 1998. Fellow Zhejiang U., Hangzhou, China, 1998—2000; rsch. scientist U. Ariz., Tucson, 2000—. Contbr. articles to profl. jours. Recipient Disting. Svc. award, Asia-Pacific Electronic Paramagnetic Resonance/Electronic Spin Resonance Soc., 1999. Mem.: Am. Chem. Soc., Sigma XI. Office: Dept Chem Univ Ariz 1306 E University Blvd Tucson AZ 85721

FENG, CHUNG-CHIANG, music educator; s. Tai-Ping and Ji-Chee Feng. B Engring., Chun-Yuan Christian U., Chun-Li, Taiwan, 1991; MusB, Berklee Coll. Music, 1997; MusM, U. Miami, 1999. Cert. music tchr. Fla., tchr. Yamaha Music Found., Japan. Music instr. Yamaha Music Found., Taipei, Taiwan, 1993—94; music tchr. Miami Dade County Pub. Schs., Miami, Fla., 1999—2000, Sagemont Sch., Weston, 2000—. Judge performing art cmopetition Miami Dade County Youth Fair, Miami, 2000; judge all state chorus audition Fla. Music Educator Assn., Ft. Lauderdale, 2003. Arranger piano music: The Best Hits of Love Songs, 1997, music arranger: Key West Music Festival, 1998. With Taiwan armed forces, 1991—93. Named Rookie Tchr. of Yr., Amelia Earhart Elem., Miami Dade Pub. Sch., 2000; recipient 2d pl. organ competition, Technic Inc., 1991. Mem.: Music Tchrs. Nat. Assn., Nat. Assn. Music Edn., Internat. Cake Exploration Soc. Avocations: cake decorating, growing orchids, early childhood music and movement. Office Phone: 954-729-7129. Personal E-mail: jcfeng@hotmail.com.

FENG, GEN-SHENG, medical educator, researcher; b. Sept. 8, 1961; BSc in Biology, Hangzhou U., China, 1981; MSc in Immunology, 2d Med. Sch. of Army, Shanghai, China, 1984; PhD in Molecular Biology, Ind. U., 1990. Rsch. assoc. in molecular genetics 2d Med. Sch. of Army, Shanghai, 1985—86; assoc. instr. dept. biology Ind. U., Bloomington, 1987—90; postdoctoral fellow in molecular biology U. Toronto, 1990—94; with Rsch. Inst. The Hosp. for Sick Children, Toronto, 1990—91, Rsch. Inst. Mt. Sinai Hosp., Toronto, 1991—94; asst. prof. dept. biochemistry and molecular biology, dept. med. and molecular genetics, asst. mem. Walther Oncology Ctr. Ind. U., Indpls., 1994—; assoc. prof. oncogenes and tumor suppression program Burnham Inst., 2000—. Ad hoc reviewer: Jour. Biol. Chemistry, Jour. Cell. Sci., Oncogene, Leukemia; contbr. articles to profl. jours.; reviewer of rsch. grants: Internat. Human Frontier Sci. Program, 1994, 1995, U.S. Vets. Affairs Med. Rsch. Sys., 1996; spkr. in field. Recipient Silver prize for Achievement of Health Sci. and Tech., China, 1986, Carrie E. Wolff award, Am. Heart Assn. Ind. Affiliate, Inc., 1995. Mem.: AAAS, Soc. Chinese Biologists Am., Am. Soc. Microbiology, Am. Diabetes Assn. (career devel. award 1995—). Office: Ind U Sch Medicine Dept Biochemistry and Molecular Biology 1044 W Walnut St Rm 302 Indianapolis IN 46202-5254 also: The Burnham Inst 10901 N Torrey Pines Rd La Jolla CA 92037-1005

FENG, PAUL YEN-HSIUNG, lawyer, chemist; s. Chih-Chung and Pao-Ru Hu Feng; m. Marie Rose Rysiejko, Feb. 14, 1976; m. Mary Stella Pao-Ching Pai, Oct. 2, 1947 (dec. May 25, 1975); children: Joseph, Dorothy Feng Hamamura, Alphonso. BS, Fu-Jen Cath. U., 1947; grad. fellow, Nat. Beijing U., 1947—48; PhD, Wash. U., 1954; JD, DePaul U., 1986; MBA, U. Chgo., 1991. CPA U. of Ill. Bd. Examiners, 1996; bar: U. S. Dist. Ct. (no. dist.) Ill. 1986, U. S. Tax Ct. 1994, U. S. Patent and Trademark Office 1989, U. S. Ct. Appeals (7th cir.) 1986, U. S. Supreme Ct. Tchr. Wen-Hua H.S., Beijing, 1945—47; tech. dir. Manu-Mine R & D Co., Reading, Pa., 1953—55; mgr. IIT Rsch. Inst. (formerly Armour Rsch. Found.), Chgo., 1955—66; sci. advisor IIT Rsch. Inst., Chgo., 1962—66; assoc. prof. Marquette U., Milw., 1966—70, prof., 1970—88; of counsel Lamet Kanwit & Davis, Brezina & Ehrlich, Chgo., 1990—2000; Fulbright lectr. Nat. Taiwan U., Taipei, 1965; NRC prof. and dean Nat. Tsinghua U., Hsinchu, Taiwan, 1973—74; pvt. practice Wilmette, Ill., 1986—. Tech. advisor U. S. Del. to 2nd UN Conf. Peaceful Uses Atomic Energy, Geneva, 1958; cons. U.S. Army Natick Labs., Natick, Mass., 1966—74, Apollo Program - NASA, Washington, 1968, Chung Shan Inst. Tech., Taoyuan, Taiwan, 1970—74; sr. advisor NRC, Taipai, Taiwan, 1973—74; pres. North Suburban Bar Assn., Glenview, Ill., 1996—97. Contbr. articles, chapters to books; author: (book) Dividend Reinvestment Handbook. Dir. Chinese Refugee Relief, Washington, 1962; mem. Chinese Adv. Com. Cultural Rels. in Am., Washington; dir. Neighborhood Assistance Found., Chgo., 1992—96. Recipient Achievement award, Nat. Youth Commn., Taiwan, 1971; Rsch. grantee, USAF, U. S. Army, U.S. AEC, 1955 - 74. Mem.: Phoenix Soc., ACS (career cons. 1992—), Overture Soc., Elliott Soc. (life), Sigma Xi (pres., marquette chpt. 1973—74). Achievements include patents for method of making fluorinated compounds; a hot-atom cation defixation method for the production of high specific activity isotopes; research in method for specific tritiation of organic compounds. Avocations: linguistics, musicology, geographic archaeology. Mailing: PO Box 424 Kenilworth IL 60043 Office Phone: 847-271-3953. Personal E-mail: paulfeng@att.net.

FENG, TSE-YUN, computer engineering educator; b. Hangchow, China, Feb. 26, 1928; s. Shih-ching and Lin Shao; m. Elaine Hu, Jan. 28, 1965; children: Wu-chun, Wu-chi, Wu-che, Wu-chang. BS, Nat. Taiwan U., 1950; MS, Okla. State U., 1957; PhD, U. Mich., 1967. Asst. engr. Taiwan Power Co., 1950-56; sr. designer Ebasco Services, N.Y.C., 1957-60; teaching fellow U. Mich., 1962-65, research asst., 1965-66, asst. research engr., 1966, research asso., 1967; asst. prof. elec. and computer engring. Syracuse U., 1967-71, asso. prof., 1971-75; prof. elec. and computer engring. Wayne State U., Detroit, 1975-79; prof. computer sci. Wright State U., Dayton, Ohio, 1979-80, chmn. dept., 1979-80; prof. computer and info. sci. Ohio State U., 1980-84; Binder prof. computer engring. Pa State U., University Park, 1984—, dir. computer engring. program, 1984-88; program dir. NSF, Arlington, Va., 1993—97, 2000—02. Cons. Transidyne Gen., Syracuse U., Pattern Analysis and Recognition Corp., N.Y. State Bd. Edn., NSF, Arlington, Va., 2000; chmn. Internat. Conf. on Parallel Processing, 1975—, Internat. Conf. on Computers and Applications, 1983-87; dir. N.E. Consortium for Engring. Edn., 1976-80; participant U.S. Technol. Policy Conf., 1978; leader del. U.S. Sr. Experts to China, 1985; cons. USAF. Contbr. numerous articles to others; patentee in field Recipient ABCD award NSF, 2001. Fellow Assn. Computing Machinery, IEEE (chmn. computer soc. standards com. 1974-78, mem. numerous other coms., presiding officer computer soc. governing bd. 1979-80, computer soc. disting. visitor 1973-78, pres. 1979-80, chmn. nominations com. 1981-83, chmn. disting. visitors program, 1987-93, Best Paper award 1975, Honor Roll award 1978, Spl. award 1981, Centennial medal 1984, Richard E. Merwin Disting. Service award 1985, Meritorious Service award, 1986, 2000, Millennium medal 2000, mem. del. to Chinese Electronics Soc. 1978, leader del. 1980, del. to Popov Soc. Congress, USSR 1978, editor-in-chief Trans. on Computers 1982-86, Trans. on Parallel and Distributed Systems, 1989-93, Tech. Achievement award and Outstanding Contbn. award, 1991); mem. Am. Fedn. Info. Processing Socs. (dir. 1979-80, 82-87, nominating com. 1979-80, 83-85, chmn. publs. com. 1984-86, exec. com. 1986-87, mem. numerous other coms.), Am. Nat. Standards Inst. (info. systems standards mgmt. bd. 1974-78), Sagamore Computer Conf. (chmn., editor proc. 1972-75), Pa. State Engring. Soc. (Outstanding Rsch. award 1989), Internat. Assn. Computers and Comms. (pres. 1995—), Hon. Order of Ky. Cols., Sigma Xi, Phi Kappa Phi, Tau Beta Pi, Eta Kappa Nu, Phi Tau Phi. Home: 319 Christopher Ln State College PA 16803-1261 Office: U Pa Dept Computer Sci & Engring Pond Lab University Park PA 16802 E-mail: feng@cse.psu.edu, t.feng@computer.org.

FENG, Z. L., artist, art educator; b. Shanghai, Oct. 23, 1954; arrived in U.S., 1986; s. Fu Yaun Feng and Lian-Bi Zhao; m. Mei Xu, Jan. 8, 1984; children: Ping-Ping, Jason J., Jeff L. MFA, Radford U., 1989; BFA, Shanghai Tchrs.' U., 1982. Prof. art Radford (Va.) U., 1989—. Recipient more than 300 state, regional, nat. and internat. awards, including Best in Show, Internat. Pastel Exhbn., Wichita, Kans., Internat. Watercolor Exhbn., Houston, Adirondacks Nat. Exhbn. Am. Watercolors, NY, Audubon Artists, N.Y.C., Nat. Exhbn. Watercolor Socs., Miss., Mont., Ga., Calif., Mid-Atlantic Watercolor Exhbn., Balt., Acad. Artists Assn., Mass., Western Colo. Watercolor Soc., Va. Watercolor Soc. Master: Pastel Soc. Am. (life); mem.: Nat. Watercolor Soc. (life Artists' Mag. award 2000), Allied Artist Am. (life Am. Artists Profl. League award 2004), Am. Watercolor Soc. (life Clara Stroud Meml. award 2000). Home: 1006 Walker Dr Radford VA 24141 Office: Radford University Art Dept PO Box 6965 Radford VA 24142 Office Phone: 540-831-6622. Personal E-mail: zfeng@radford.edu.

FENICHELL, STEPHEN CLARK, writer; b. N.Y.C., Apr. 22, 1956; s. Stephen Sidney and Lois Elizabeth (Forde) F.; m. Carol Goodstein, Mar. 4, 1995; children: Loisa Anna, Aaron Forde. AB, Harvard U., 1977. Author: Daughters at Risk: A Personal Des History, 1980, Other Peoples Money, 1985, Plastic: The Making of a Synthetic Century, 1996; (with Mark Mobius) Passport to Profits, 1999, (with J. Hollender) What Matters Most, 2004 Home: 523 Hudson St Apt 2rs New York NY 10014-6119

FENIGER, JEROME ROLAND, JR., broadcast executive; b. Peoria, Ill., June 16, 1927; s. Jerome Rol and Marie Dorothy (Miller) F.; m. Marian Laura Schwartz, June 24, 1951; children: Robin Jean, Bruce David. BA, U. Iowa, 1948; postgrad., Columbia U., 1948, N.Y. U., 1949-50; D.Bus. in Sci. (hon.), St. John's U., 1984. Advt. account exec. Biow Co., N.Y.C., 1949-50; chief advt. time buyer Cunningham & Walsh, N.Y.C., 1950-51, v.p., 1954-60; sales exec. CBS, N.Y.C., 1952-54; exec. Cowles Comm. Co., N.Y.C., 1960-65; v.p. Grey Advt. Inc., N.Y.C., 1965-70; pres. Horizons Comm. Corp., N.Y.C., 1970-83; mng. dir. Sta. Reps. Assn., Inc., N.Y.C., 1983—2002; life bd. dirs. Advt. Coun., 1984—2002. Pres. Louise Wise Svcs., 1986-89; mem. pvt. sector commn. USIA/Voice of Am. Trustee Columbia Grammar and Prep Sch., 1965-77, treas., 1970-77; bd. dirs. UJA Fedn. on Domestic Affairs. Sgt. USAF, 1946—47. Recipient Disting. Alumnus award, U. Iowa, 2002. Mem. Internat. Radio and TV Soc. (pres. 1975-77), Friars Club, Dutch Treat Club, Yale Club of N.Y.C. Democrat. Home: 16 W 77th St New York NY 10024-5126

FENIGER, SUSAN, chef, television personality, writer; Former mem. staff Le Perroquet, Chgo., Ma Maison, L.A., L'Oasis, France; formerly chef, co-owner City Cafe, L.A.; chef, co-owner CITY, L.A., 1985—94, Border Grill, L.A., 1985—91, Santa Monica, 1990—. Co-host (TV series) Too Hot Tamales, 1995—, Tamales' World Tour, (radio show) Good Food; co-author: City Cuisine, 1989, Mesa Mexicana, 1994, Cantina, 1996, Cooking with Too Hot Tamales, 1997. Active Scleroderma Rsch. Found. Named Chef of Yr., Calif. Restaurant Writers, 1993. Mem.: Chef's Collaborative 2000, Women Chefs and Restaurateurs. Office: Border Grill 1445 4th St Santa Monica CA 90401

FENIMORE, GEORGE WILEY, management consultant; b. Bertrand, Mo., 1921; BBA in Fin., Northwestern U., 1941; LLB, Harvard U., 1947; postgrad., UCLA, 1955; LLD (hon.), Southwestern U., 1992. Bar: Mich. 1948. Asst. to dir. planning Ford Motor Co., Dearborn, Mich., 1947-48; exec. to v.p. and gen. mgr. Hughes Aircraft Co., Culver City, Calif., 1948-53; adminstrv. mgr. tech. products Packard Bell Electronics Co., 1954-55; with TRW, Inc., L.A., 1955-64; v.p., gen. mgr. TRW Internat., L.A., 1959-64; v.p. internat. ops. Bunker Ramo Corp., L.A., 1964-65; dir. pub. rels., then corp. sec. Litton Industries, Inc., Beverly Hills, Calif., 1965-73, v.p., corp. sec., 1973-81, sr. v.p., corp. sec., 1981-86, mgmt. cons., 1986—; sr. v.p. Peck Jones Constrn., Beverly Hills. Past chmn. bd. Southwestern U. Sch. Law; mem. Calif. Tchrs. Retirement Bd.; cons. JCM Group. Bd. dirs. Children's Bur. L.A., Child Shelter Homes a Rescue Effort; sec. French Found. for Alzheimer's Rsch.; past mem. Calif. Fair Polit. Practices Commn., 1986-91; mem. United Way Emergency Food Sys. Study Task Force; elder, chmn. fin. com. Westwood Presbyn. Ch.; past trustee Sheldon Jackson Coll., Sitka, Alaska; mem. Beverly Hills Mayor's Econ. Adv. Com. and MOVE com., Calif. Fraud Assessment Commn. Maj. USAAF, WW II. Recipient Citizen of Yr. award, Beverly Hills Lions Club, 1976, Spirit Honoree, Beverly Hills Edn. Found., 1986, Beverly Hills YMCA, 1988, Brentwood/San Vicente C. of C., 1987, Hon. Citizen award, Beverly Hills City Coun., 1986, Guardian Angel award, Child S.H.A.R.E., 1989, Lifetime Achievement award, 2001, Highest award for Lifetime Svc. to Cmty., Key to City of Beverly Hills, 1990, State Gold award, Calif. Tchrs. Assn., 1993. Mem. Am. Soc. Corp. Secs. (dir., past nat. dir., past pres. L.A. Group), Beverly Hills C. of C. (past pres., Citizen of Yr. award 1979, chmn. edn. com., bd. dirs., David Orgell Meml. award 1990), Mandeville Canyon Assn. (past pres.), Bar Assn. Mich., L.A. Country Club, Rotary (past pres. Beverly Hills, Paul Harris fellow, William C. Ackerman trophy 1986), Shriners. Presbyterian. Office Phone: 310-472-9264. Personal E-mail: fenimore98@aol.com.

FENING, M. BRADY, lawyer; b. Middletown, Ohio, May 21, 1969; s. Walter and Wanda Lee (Lewis) F. BA, Miami U., Oxford, Ohio, 1991; JD, U. Toledo, 1994. Bar: Ohio 1994, U.S. Dist. Ct. (so. dist.) Ohio 1995. Lawyer Bryant & Sanzone, Middletown, 1994—. Instr. paralegals Rets-Tech. Sch., Centerville, Ohio, 1996—. Trustee Big Bros./Big Sisters, Middletown, 1996-97. Roman Catholic. Avocations: sports, computers. Home: 14 N Marshall Rd Middletown OH 45042-3820 Office: Bryant & Sanzone 11 S Sutphin St Middletown OH 45044-4640

FENINGER, CLAUDE, food service executive; b. Cairo, Jan. 15, 1926; came to U.S., 1960; s. Paul and Therese (DeRogatis) F.; m. Jill Ellis, Nov. 26, 1986; children from previous marriage: Paul Gordon, Eric. Student, Lausanne (Switzerland) Sch. Hotel Mgmt., 1948, Am. U., Cairo, 1945, Lincoln Sch., 1943, Lycee Francais, 1935. With Hilton Internat., 1955-67; product line mgr. ITT, 1967-68; pres. Sheraton Internat., 1968-74; chmn. bd., chief exec. officer Omni Internat. Hotels, Inc., Atlanta, 1974-80; pres. Aramark Internat., Phila., 1980—. Cons. in field, 1960—; dir. VS Services, Can., Traulsen Refrigeration Co., N.Y.C. Mem. Am. Mgmt. Assn., Am. Hotel Assn. Home: 2045 Yellow Springs Rd Malvern PA 19355-8702 Office: Aramark Corp ARA Svcs Inc 1101 Market St Ste 45 Philadelphia PA 19107-2988 E-mail: cfeninger@aol.com.

FENN, JOHN BENNETT, chemist, educator; b. NYC, June 15, 1917; s. Herbert Bennett and Jeanette Clyde (Dingman) F.; m. Margaret Elizabeth Wilson, June 6, 1939; children: Margaret Marianne, Barbara Leigh, John Bennett. AB, Berea Coll., 1937; PhD, Yale U., 1940. Research chemist (Monsanto Chem. Co.), Anniston, Ala., 1940-43, Sharples Chems., Inc., Wyandotte, Mich., 1943-45; v.p. Experiment, Inc., Richmond, Va., 1945-52; dir. Project SQUID, Princeton, 1952-62, prof. mech. engring., 1959-63, prof. aerospace scis., 1963-66; prof. applied sci. and chemistry Yale U., 1967—80; pres. Relay Devel. Corp., 1975—; prof. of engineering Yale U., 1980—87, prof. emeritus, 1987—93; prof. of analytical chem. Virginia Commonwealth U., 1993—. Vis. scientist N.Am. Aviation Sci. Center, 1965-66; vis. prof. U. Trento, Italy, 1976, U. Tokyo, 1979, U. of China, 1987; dir. Thermal Research & Engring. Corp., 1952-59; sci. liaison officer Office Naval Research, London, 1955; dir. Aero Chem. Research Labs., 1956-60; cons. UN; vis. prof. Indian Inst. Sci., Bangalore. Author: Engines, Energy and Entropy, 1982; editor: (with A.B. Cambel) Transport Properties in Gases, 1958, Dynamics of Conducting Gases, 1960. Recipient Sr. Scientist award Alexander von Humboldt Found., 1983-84, Disting. Alumnus award Berea Coll., 1987, Nobel Prize in Chemistry, 2002. Mem. Am. Chem. Soc., AAAS, Am. Inst. Chem. Engrs., Internat. Soc. Mass Spectrometry (sec. 2000), Sigma Xi. Office: VCU Dept of Chemistry 1001 W Main St PO Box 842006 Richmond VA 23284-2006*

FENN, ORMON WILLIAM, JR., furniture company executive; b. Tyler, Tex., Mar. 13, 1927; s. Ormon William and Madonna (Muphree) Fenn; m. Lucille Adrianne Kelley (dec.); children: Andrea Lee, Miles Linton, Kelly Sue, Michael Thomas. Student, U. Minn., 1945, Okla. U., 1945, Imperial U., 1946; BS, Yale U., 1949. Asst. dist. mgr. Armsrong Cork Co., Lancaster, Pa., 1949-59, asst. gen. sales mgr., 1959-70; v.p., gen. sales mgr. Thomasville (N.C.) Furniture Industries, Inc., 1970-74, sr. v.p., gen. sales mgr., 1974-77; exec. v.p. sales and mktg. Stanley Furniture Co. Mead Corp., Stanleytown, Va., 1977-78, pres., 1978-79; pres. CEO Stanley Furniture Co., 1979-82; vice chmn. LADD Furniture Co., High Point, N.C., 1982-92, dir., 1982-98. Chmn. emeritus N.C. furnishings export coun. N.C. Dept. Commerce, High Point, 1993—; chmn. N.C. Home Furnishing Coun., 1995-97; past chmn. bd. govs. Western Mdse. Mart, San Francisco; past chmn. market adv. bd. High Point So. Furniture Market Center; past dir. N.C. Furniture Export Office; past chmn. Internat. Home Furnishings Mktg. Assn.; past bd. dirs. Furniture Info. Coun.; past bd. dirs./exec. com. Home Furnishing Coun.; bd. dirs. Am. Furniture Mfrs. Hall of Fame; apptd. by Gov. of N.C. to nat. adv. bd. HandMade in Am.; bd. dirs. Vaughn Bassett Funriture Co., Galax, Va. Past adv. bd. Bryan Sch. Bus. and Econs., U. N.C., Greensboro; appt. hon. consul gen. Japan, 1999-2004. 1st lt. U.S. Army, 1944-52, PTO. Recipient The Order of the Long Leaf Pine award (NC) Gov. Hunt (N.C. highest civilian honor), 1995. Mem. String and Splinter Club (bd. dirs.), High Point Country Club (mem. sr. bd. dirs.). Episcopalian. Avocations: golf, hunting, physical fitness. Home: 510 Emerywood Dr High Point NC 27262-2812 Personal E-mail: billfennoo@hotmail.com.

FENN, PATRICK B., lawyer; b. Atlanta; BA with honors, Univ. Va., 1977, JD, 1982. Bar: NY 1983. Ptnr., head tax practice group and mem. mgmt. com. Akin Gump Strauss Hauer & Feld LLP, NYC. Articles editor Va. Tax Rev., 1981—82. Named one of World's Leading Tax Advisers, Euromoney, 2003. Mem.: ABA. Office: Akin Gump Strauss Hauer & Feld LLP 590 Madison Ave New York NY 10022-2524 Office Phone: 212-872-1040. Office Fax: 212-872-1002. Business E-Mail: pfenn@akingump.com.

FENN, SANDRA ANN, programmer, analyst; b. Sugar Land, Tex., Oct. 31, 1953; d. William Charles and Helen Maxine (Kyle) F.; m. Jimmie Dan Watts, May 21, 1973 (div. June 1988); children: Gabriel Nathaniel Watts, Lindsay Nichelle Garza. AA in Gen. Studies summa cum laude, Alvin (Tex.) C.C., 1994; BS in Computer Info. Sys., U. Houston, Clear Lake, 2000. Shampoo asst. LaVonne's Salon of Beauty, Houston, 1972-73; coding clk. Prudential Ins. Co., Houston, 1974-75; word processing operator MacGregor Med. Assn., Houston, 1983-85; computer applications analyst Computer Scis. Corp., Houston, 1987-92; program support adminstr. Sci. Applications Internat. Corp., Houston, 1992-95, programmer/analyst, 1995-98; software developer astronaut office Johnson Space Ctr., 1998-2000; info. tech. analyst El Paso Corp., Houston, 2000—03, Williams Bailey Law Firm, Houston, 2003—. Mem. Am. Bus. Women's Assn. (newsletter chair 1995-2001, 1999 Woman of Excellence), Phi Theta Kappa. Avocations: horseback riding, camping, biking, volleyball, reading. Home: 1619 Newcomb Way Houston TX 77058-2264 Personal E-mail: safenn@orbitworld.net.

FENNEBRESQUE, JOHN C., lawyer; b. Oyster Bay, NY, Apr. 25, 1947; s. John Drouet and Frances (Campbell) Fennebresque; m. Frances Woltz, June 6, 1970; children: John C. Jr., Amy W., Frances C., William T. BA, U. NC, 1970; JD, Vanderbilt U., 1973. Bar: NC 1973. From assoc. to ptnr. Moore & Van Allen, Charlotte, NC, 1973—93; ptnr. Fennebresque, Clark, Swindell & Hay, Charlotte, 1993—98; mng. ptnr. Charlotte office McGuireWoods LLP, 1998—. Bd. governors, U. NC, 1995-2003; bd. dirs. New Arena Com., Charlotte, Mint Mus. Art. Republican. Presbyterian. Avocations: golf, reading. Office: McGuireWoods LLP Bank of Am Corp Ctr 100 N Tryon St Ste 2900 Charlotte NC 28202-4011 Office Phone: 704-373-8989. Office Fax: 704-353-6180. Business E-Mail: jfennebresque@mcguirewoods.com.

FENNELL, DIANE MARIE, marketing professional, process engineer; b. Panama, Iowa, Dec. 11, 1944; d. Urban William and Marcella Mae (Leytham) Schechinger; m. Leonard E. Fennell, Aug. 19, 1967; children: David, Denise, Mark. BS, Creighton U., Omaha, 1966. Process engr. Tex. Instruments, Richardson, 1974-79; sr. process engr. Signetics Corp., Santa Clara, Calif., 1979-82; demo lab. mgr. Airco Temescal, Berkeley, Calif., 1982-84; field process engr. Applied Materials, Santa Clara, 1984-87; mgr. product mktg. Lam Rsch., Fremont, Calif., 1987-90; dir. sales and mktg. Ion & Plasma Equipment, Fremont, Calif., 1990-91; pres. FAI, Half Moon Bay, Calif., 1990-96; v.p. mktg. Tegal Corp., Petaluma, Calif., 1997-99; v.p. mktg. and sales Semicaps, Inc., Santa Clara, Calif., 1999—2001; exec. dir. Ctr. for Internat. Devel., Santa Clara, 2001—03; pres. World Info., Menlo Park, Calif., 2003—. Founder, coord. chmn. Plasma Etch User's Group, Santa Clara, 1984-87; tchr. computer course Adult Edn., Half Moon Bay, Calif., 1982-83. Founder, bd. dirs. Birth to Three program Mental Retardation Ctr., Denison, Tex., 1974-75; fund raiser local sch. band, Half Moon Bay, 1981-89; community rep. local sch. bd., Half Moon Bay, 1982-83. Mem. Am. Vacuum Soc., Soc. Photo Instrumentation Engrs., Soc. Women Engrs., Material Rsch. Soc., Commonwealth Club. Avocations: hiking, reading, gardening. Home: 441 Alameda Ave Half Moon Bay CA 94019-5337

FENNELL, STEPHEN A., lawyer; BA magna cum laude, U. Md., 1974; JD magna cum laude, Georgetown U., 1978. Bar: DC 1980, Md. 1987. Law clk. for Judge Edward S. Northrop US Dist. Ct. (Dist. Md.), 1978—79; ptnr., litig. dept. Steptoe & Johnson LLP, Washington, mem. exec. & profl. advancement com., chmn. hiring & pro bono com. Editor: Georgetown Law Jour.; contbr. articles to profl. jour.; spkr. in field. Mem.: Phi Beta Kappa. Office: Steptoe & Johnson LLP 1330 Connecticut Ave NW Washington DC 20036 Office Phone: 202-429-8082. Office Fax: 202-429-3902. Business E-Mail: sfennell@steptoe.com.

FENNELLY, JANE COREY, lawyer; b. N.Y.C., Dec. 12, 1942; d. Joseph and Josephine (Corey) F. BA, Cornell U., 1964; MLS, UCLA, 1968; JD, Loyola U., L.A., 1974. Bar: Calif. 1974, U.S. Dist. Ct. (ctrl. and so. dists.) Calif. 1974, U.S. Dist. Ct. (ea. dist.) Calif. 1977, U.S. Dist. Ct. (no. dist.) Calif. 1980, N.Y. 1982, Colo. 1993, Ariz. 1995. Ptnr. Graham & James, 1976-83; with legal dept. Bank of Am., L.A., 1973-76, Wyman, Bautzer, Kuchel & Silbert, L.A., 1983-87, Dennis, Shafer, Fennelly & Creim (merged with Bronson & McKinnon), L.A., 1987-96; with Squire, Sanders & Dempsey, Phoenix, 1996—98; prin. Jane C. Fennelly, P.C., Phoenix, 1998—; of counsel Creim, Macias & Koenig LLP, L.A., 1999—. Mem. ABA, Am. Bankruptcy Inst., Calif. Bankruptcy Forum, L.A. County Bar Assn. (bd. dirs., mem. exec. com. comml. law and bankruptcy sect. 1989-92), Maricopa County Bar Assn., Fin. Lawyers Conf. (pres. bd. dirs. 1983-84, mem. bd. govs. 1984—). Home: 15356 W Pasadena Dr Surprise AZ 85374 Office: #610 Ste 101 15508 W Bell Rd Surprise AZ 85374 Office Phone: 602-909-1855. E-mail: jane.fennelly@azbar.org.

FENNELLY, WILLIAM, basketball coach; b. Davenport, Iowa., May 14, 1957; m. Deborah Fennelly; children: Billy, Steven. BBA and Econs., William Penn Coll., 1979. Women's basketball coach William Penn Coll., Fresno State U., Notre Dame (Ind.) U.; head women's basketball coach U. Toledo, Ohio, Iowa State U., Ames, 1994—. Office: Iowa State Univ Jacobson Athletic Bldg 1800 S 4th St Ames IA 50011-0001

FENNEMA, OWEN RICHARD, food chemistry educator; b. Hinsdale, Ill., Jan. 23, 1929; s. Nick and Fern Alma (First) F.; m. Ann Elizabeth Hammer, Aug. 22, 1948; children: Linda Gail, Karen Elizabeth, Peter Scott. BS, Kans. State U., 1950; MS, U. Wis., 1951, PhD, 1960; PhD of Agrl. and Environ. Scis. (hon.), Wageningen Agrl. U., The Netherlands, 1993. Project leader for R&D, Pillsbury Co., Mpls., 1953-57; asst. prof. food sci. dept. U. Wis., Madison, 1960-64, assoc. prof., 1964-69, prof., 1969-96, chmn. dept., 1977-81, interim chmn. dept. landscape architecture, 1994-96, prof. emeritus, 1996—. Cons. Grand Metropolitan, Mpls., 1979-99; pub. mem. Internat. Life Scis. Inst.-Nutrition Found., 1987-90; mem. food adv. com. U.S. FDA, 1995-99, mem. sci. bd., 2000-02. Author: Low Temperature Preservation of Foods, 1973; editor: Principles of Food Science, 2 vols., 1976, Proteins at Low Temperatures, 1979, Food Chemistry, 3d edit., 1996; mem. editl. bd. Cryobiology, 1966-82, Internat. Jour. Food Sci. and Nutrition, Jour. Food Sci., 1975-77, Jour. Food Processing Preservation, 1977-2002, Jour. Food Biochemistry, 1977-80, Nutrition Rsch. Newsletter, 1983-98, Acta Alimentaria (Budapest, Hungary), 1990-98, South African Jour. Food Sci. and Nutrition, 1991-2002; editor-in-chief Jour. Food Sci., 1999-2003, Jour. Food Sci. Edn., Comprehensive Revs. in Food Sci., Food Safety. Served to 2d lt. U.S. Army, 1951-53. Recipient Excellence in Tchg. award U. Wis., Madison, 1977, Dir.'s Spl. Citation award Ctr. Food Safety and Nutrition, FDA; Fulbright disting. lectr., Spain, 1992. Fellow Am. Chem. Soc. (Agrl. and Food Chemistry Divsn. award 1995), Inst. Food Technologists (pres. 1982-83, treas. 1994-99, Excellence in Tchg. award 1978, Carl R. Fellers award 1988, Nicholas Appert award 1988); mem. Internat. Union Food Sci. and Tech. (del. 1983-88, exec. com. 1988-99, v.p. 1992-95, founding fellow Internat. Acad. Food Sci. and Tech. 1997, pres. 1999-2001. Office: U Wis 1605 Linden Dr Madison WI 53706-1519 Fax: 608-262-6872. E-mail: ofennema@facstaff.wisc.edu.

FENNER, SUZAN ELLEN, lawyer; b. Grand Junction, Colo., Dec. 5, 1947; d. Harry J. and Louise (Bain) Shaw; m. Michael Lee Riddle, Apr. 24, 1969 (div. Feb. 1976); m. Peter R. Fenner, Nov. 24, 1978; children: Laura Elizabeth, Adam Kyle. BA, Tex. Tech U., 1969, JD, 1971. Bar: Tex. 1972, U.S. Dist. Ct. (no. dist.) Tex. 1972. Assoc. Smith & Baker, Lubbock, Tex., 1971-72; law clk. to presiding judge U.S. Dist. Ct., Dallas, 1972-73; assoc. Gardere Wynne Sewell LLP, Dallas, 1973-78, ptnr., 1978—, chair retirement com., 1973—, chair tax practice., 2001—, mem. ptnrs. bd., 1991—94. Bd. dirs. Tex. Lawyers Ins. Exch., 1983—, S.W. Benefits Assn. (formerly S.W. Pension Conf.), 1987—92, pres., 1990—91. Bd. dirs. East Dallas Devel. Ctr., 1982—91; Lone Star coun. Camp Fire USA, 1995—2001, v.p. outdoor programs, 1996—98, pres.-elect, 1997, pres., 1998—2000; bd. dirs. Episcopal Ch. Women of the Diocese of Dallas, 1992—2002, pres., 1996—2000; del. to triennial nat. conv. Episcopal Diocese of Dallas, 1994, 1997, 2000, asst. chancellor, 1994—2004, exec. coun., 1995—2000, standing com., 2001—04; pres. Episcopal Ch. Women for Episcopal Ch. of Ascension, 1992, bd. dirs., 1992—94; pres. Province VII Episcopal Ch. Women, bd. dirs., 1999—2002; exec. coun. Province VII of the Episcopal Ch., 1999—2002; mem. vestry Episcopal Ch. of the Ascension, 1996—99, 2005—. Mem. ABA, Tex. Bar Assn. (chmn. bar. jour. com. 1982-88), Dallas Bar Assn. (treas. employee benefits com. 1998, sec. 1999, v.p. 2000, pres. 2001), Dallas Bus. League (pres. 1986), Episcopal Ch. of the Ascension (vestry 1996-99, 2005-). Avocation: sailing. Home: 600 Goodwin Dr Richardson TX 75081-5603 Office: Gardere Wynne Sewell LLP 1601 Elm St Ste 3000 Dallas TX 75201-4761 Office Phone: 214-999-4576. E-mail: sfenner@gardere.com.

FENNESSEY, PAUL VINCENT, pediatrics and pharmacology educator, researcher; b. Oct. 3, 1942; m. Susan Blackwell; children: Shirley, Karl, Shaun. BS in Chemistry, U. Okla., 1964; PhD of Organic Analytical Chemistry, MIT, 1968. Rsch. asst. U. Okla., Norman, 1963-64; predoctoral fellow MIT, Cambridge, 1964-69; asst. prof. pediat. and pharmacology U. Colo. Health Sci. Ctr., Denver, 1975-81, co-dir. mass spectral ctr., 1980, assoc. prof. pediat. and pharmacology, 1981-90, prof. pediat. and pharmacology, 1990—, vice chair pediat., 1991—. Contbr. articles to profl. jours. Asst. program scientist Viking Project, Martin Marietta Corp., Denver, 1969-72, program scientist, 1972-74. Recipient NSF Undergrad. Rsch. award, 1963-64, Merck award in Organic Chemistry, 1963; fellow Woodrow Wilson, 1964-65, NIH, 1964-68. Mem. Am. Chem. Soc., Am. Soc. Mass Spectrometry, Nat. Acad. Clin. Biochemists, Soc. Inherited Metabolic Diseases, Am. Soc. Pharmacology and Exptl. Therapeutics, Internat. Soc. Study Xenobiotics, Sigma Xi. Home: 13009 S Parker Ave Pine CO 80470-9617 Office: U Colo Health Sci Ctr 4200 E 9th Ave # C232 Denver CO 80220-3706 Office Phone: 303-315-7286. Business E-Mail: paul.fennessey@uchsc.edu.

FENNESSY, JAMES GERARD, retired engineer; b. Limerick, Ireland, July 10, 1927; arrived in U.S., 1949; s. James and Ellen Noonan Fennessy; m. Jean Frances McMahon, Jan. 6, 1951; children: James, Michael, Maryellen, Jeanne, Kathleen, Carolyn, Kevin, Colleen. Student, Christian Brothers Sec. Coll. and Limerick Tech. Inst., 1940—45, Rutgers U., 1957, Brookdale Coll., 2002. Cert. quality engineer, Am. Soc. for Quality, Milw.,Wis. Planning and develop. engr. Western Electric Co. Inc., Kearny, NJ, 1956—83; mem. tech. staff Bell Comm. Rsch., Piscataway, NJ, 1983—92. Author: (book) The Domestics, 1999, The Professionals, 2004. Mem. and chmn. Old Bridge Township Planning Bd., NJ. Mem.: Soc. of Irish Playwrights, Irish Writers Union, Am. Soc. for Quality, Telephone Pioneers of Am. (life), Order of Friendly Sons of Shillelagh (pres. 1975—77). Republican. Cath. Avocations: writing, golf, bridge. Home: Limclare House 69 Bennett Rd Matawan NJ 07747 Personal E-mail: himself@bellatlantic.net.

FENNING, LISA HILL, lawyer, mediator, retired judge; b. Chgo., Feb. 22, 1952; d. Ivan Byron and Joan (Hennigar) Hill; m. Alan Mark Fenning, Apr. 3, 1977; 4 children. BA with honors, Wellesley Coll., 1971; JD, Yale U., 1974. Bar: Ill. 1975, Calif. 1979, U.S. Dist. Ct. (no. dist.) Ill., U.S. Dist. Ct. (no., ea., so. & cen. dists.) Calif., U.S. Ct. Appeals (6th, 7th & 9th cirs.), U.S. Supreme Ct. 1989. Law clk. U.S. Ct. Appeals 7th cir., Chgo., 1974-75; assoc. Jenner and Block, Chgo., 1975-77, O'Melveny and Myers, L.A., 1977-85; judge U.S. Bankruptcy Ct. Cen. Dist. Calif., L.A., 1985-2000; mediator JAMS,

Orange, Calif., 2000-01; ptnr. Dewey Ballantine LLP, L.A., 2001—. Bd. govs. Nat. Conf. Bankruptcy Judges, 1989-92; pres. Nat. Conf. of Women's Bar Assns., N.C., 1987-88, pres.-elect, 1986-87, v.p., 1985-86, bd. dirs.; lectr., program coord. in field; bd. govs. Nat. Conf. Bankruptcy Judges Endowment for Edn., 1992-97, Am. Bankruptcy Inst., 1994-2000; mem., bd. advisors Nat. Jud. Edn. Program to Promote Equality for Women and Men in the Cts., 1994—. Mem., bd. advisors: Lawyer Hiring & Training Report, 1985-87; contbr. articles to profl. jours. Durant scholar Wellesley Coll., 1971; named one of Am's. 100 Most Important Women Ladies Home Jour., 1988, one of L.A.'s 50 Most Powerful Women Lawyers, L.A. Bus. Jour., 1998, named one of So. Calif. Superlawyers, L.A. Mag., 2005. Fellow Am. Bar Found., Am. Coll. Bankruptcy (bd. regents 1995-98); mem. ABA (standing com. on fed. jud. improvements 1995-98, mem. commn. on women in the profession 1987-91, Women's Caucus 1987—, Individual Rights and Responsibilities sect. 1984—, bus. law sect. 1986—, bus. bankruptcy com.), Nat. Assn. Women Judges (nat. task force gender bias in the cts. 1986-87, 93-94), Nat. Conf. Bankruptcy Judges (chair endowment edn. bd. 1994-95), Am. Bankruptcy Inst. (nominating com. 1994-95, bd. steering com. stats. project 1994-96), Calif. State Bar Assn. (chair com. on women in law 1986-87), Women Lawyers' Assn. L.A. (ex officio mem., bd. dirs., chmn., founder com. on status of women lawyers 1984-85, officer nominating com. 1986, founder, mem. Do-It-Yourself Mentor Network 1986-96), Phi Beta Kappa. Democrat. Office: Dewey Ballantine LLP 333 S Grand Ave 26th Fl Los Angeles CA 90071 Office Phone: 213-621-6000. Business E-Mail: Lfenning@deweyballantine.com, lfenning@dbllp.com.

FENNINGER, LEONARD DAVIS, medical educator, consultant; b. Hampton, Va., Oct. 3, 1917; s. Laurence and Natalie Ayers (Bourne) F.; m. Jane Thomas, Mar. 20, 1943; children: David McClure, Anne Randolph. AB, Princeton U., 1938; MD, U. Rochester, 1943. Diplomate: Am. Bd. Internal Medicine. Asso. dean, prof. health services, chmn. dept., prof. medicine U. Rochester; also physician, med. dir. Strong Meml. Hosp., 1961-67; dir. Bur. Health Manpower, USPHS, 1967-69; asso. dir. health manpower NIH, 1969-73; dir. dept. grad. med. edn. AMA, Chgo., 1973-76, group v.p. med. edn., 1976-80, v.p. med. edn. and sci. policy, 1981-84; lectr. in medicine Northwestern U. Med. Sch., Chgo., 1985—; attending physician emeritus Northwestern Meml. Hosp., Chgo. Home: 1020 Grove St Apt 901 Evanston IL 60201-4236

FENNO, RICHARD FRANCIS, JR., political scientist, educator; b. Winchester, Mass., Dec. 12, 1926; s. Richard Francis and Mary Brooks (Tredennick) Fenno; m. Nancy Davidson, Sept. 10, 1948; children: Mark Richard, Craig Pierce. Student, Williams Coll., 1944-46; AB, Amherst Coll., 1948, LLD (hon.), 1986; PhD, Harvard U., 1956; LHD (hon.), Union Coll., 1989. Instr. govt. Wheaton (Mass.) Coll., 1951-53; instr. polit. sci. Amherst Coll., 1953-56, asst. prof., 1956-57; mem. faculty U. Rochester, NY, 1957—, prof., 1964—, Don Alonzo Watson prof. polit. sci., 1971-78, William R. Kenan prof. polit. sci., 1978—, Disting. Univ. prof., 1985—. Author: (book) The President's Cabinet, 1959, The Power of the Purse, 1966, Congressmen in Committees, 1973, Home Style: U.S. House Members in Their Districts, 1978 (Woodrow Wilson Found. award, 1979, D. B. Hardeman prize, 1980); author: (with F. Munger) National Politics and Federal Aid to Education, 1962; author: The Making of a Senator: Dan Quayle, 1989, The Presidential Odyssey of John Glenn, 1990, Watching Politicians, 1990, The Emergence of a Senate Leader: Pete Domenici and the Reagan Budget, 1991, Learning to Legislate: The Senate Education of Arlen Specter, 1991, When Incumbency Fails: The Senate Career of Mark Andrews, 1992; editor: The Yalta Conf., 1956, 1973, (book) Senators on the Campaign Trail: The Politics of Representation, 1996, Learning to Govern: An Institutional View of the 104th Congress, 1997, Congress at the Grassroots: Represntational Change in the South, 1970-1998, 2000, Going Home: Black Representatives and Their Constituents, 2003. With USNR, 1944—46. Rockefeller Found. fellow, 1963—64, Ford fellow, 1971—72, Guggenheim fellow, 1976—77, Russell Sage Found. grantee, 1978, 1980—85. Mem.: Am. Philos. Soc., Am. Acad. Arts and Scis., Social Sci. Rsch. Coun. (dir. 1973—75, fellow 1960—61), Nat. Acad. Scis., Am. Polit. Sci. Assn. (coun. 1971—73, v.p. 1975—76, pres. 1984—85), Phi Beta Kappa. Home: 108 Farm Brook Dr Rochester NY 14625-1519

FENSCH, THOMAS CHARLES, journalism educator, writer; b. Ashland, Ohio, Nov. 29, 1943; s. Edwin August and Heloise (Moore) F.; m. Jean Robinson, Dec. 27, 1977 (dec. July 1991); children: William Robinson, Susan Robinson Schwartz, Lynn Robinson Marrable; m. Sharon Wanslee, June 14, 1994; 1 child, Morris Johnson. AB in Psychology, History, Ashland Coll., 1965; MA in Journalism, U. Iowa, 1967; PhD in Comm., Syracuse U., 1977. Faculty mem. Shippensburg (Pa.) State U., 1970-71; asst. prof. journalism Ohio State U., Mansfield, 1971-73; assoc. prof. journalism U. Tex., Austin, 1977-91; Warner prof. journalism Sam Houston State U., Huntsville, Tex., 1991-97. Lectr. in field. Author: The Lions and the Lambs, 1970, Alice in Acidland, 1970, Films on the Campus, 1970, Smokeys, Truckers, CB Radios & You, 1976, Steinbeck and Covici: The Story of a Friendship, 1979 (Biographical Book of Yr., Ohioana Libr. Assn. 1980), paperback edit., 1984, Skydiving, 1980, The Hardest Parts: Techniques for Effective Non-Fiction, 1984, Conversations with John Steinbeck, 1988, The Sports Writing Handbook, 1988, 2d edit. 1995, Writing Solutions: Beginnings, Middles & Endings, 1988, Conversations with James Thurber, 1989, Best Magazine Articles: 1988, 1989, Associated Press Coverage of a Major Disaster: The Crash of Delta Flight 1141, 1990, Nonfiction for the 1990s, 1991, Television News Anchors, 1993, Oskar Schindler and His List, 1995, Of Sneetches and Whos and the Good Dr. Seuss: Essays on the Writings and Life of Theodor Geisel, 1997; photographs have appeared in 6 books; contbr. over 115 articles to profl. jours. and mags. Mem. Am. Soc. Journalists and Authors, Nat. Book Critics Circle. Home: 692 Elkins Lk Huntsville TX 77340-7317 Office: Sam Houston State Univ Dept Journalism Huntsville TX 77341

FENSELAU, CATHERINE CLARKE, chemistry professor; b. York, Nebr., Apr. 15, 1939; d. Lee Keckley and Muriel (Thomas) Clarke; m. Allan Herman Fenselau, 1962 (div. 1980); children: Andrew Clarke, Thomas Stewart; m. Robert James Cotter, 1984. AB, Bryn Mawr Coll., 1961; PhD, Stanford U., 1965. Research scientist U. Calif.-Berkeley, 1965-67; instr. to prof. Johns Hopkins U., Balt., 1967-87; chmn. chemistry, biochemistry U. Md., Balt. County, 1987-98, prof. dept. chemistry and biochemistry College Park, 1998—; chmn. dept. chemistry and biochemistry, 1998-2000. Cons. NIH, NSF, USDA, U.S. Army, FDA, others. Editor: Biomed. Environ. Mass Spectrometry, 1973—89; editor: (assoc. editor) Analytical Chemistry, 1990—; contbr. articles to profl. jours. Recipient Hillebrand prize, Chem. Soc. Washington, 2005. Fellow: AAAS; mem.: U.S. Human Proteomic Orgn. (pres. 2004—), Am. Soc. Pharmacology and Exptl. Therapeutics, Am. Chem. Soc. (Garvan medal 1985, Md. Chemist award Md. sect. 1989), Am. Soc. Mass Spectrometry (pres. 1980—82). Office: U Md Dept Chemistry Biochemistry College Park MD 20742-0001

FENSIN, DANIEL, diversified financial service company executive; b. 1943; BS in Acctg., DePaul U., 1965. Ptnr. Topel, Forman & Co., 1965-74; ceo, mng. ptnr. Blackman Kallick Bartelstein, L.L.P., Chgo., 1974—. Office: Blackman Kallick Bartelstein 10 S Riverside Plz Ste 900 Chicago IL 60606-3770

FENSKE, JERALD ALLAN, minister; b. Wausau, Wis., Sept. 29, 1960; s. Martin W. and Whynona B. (Ramthun) F.; m. Kay A. Lang, Aug. 17, 1985; children: Kiersten, Deena. BA, Lakeland Coll., 1983; MDiv, United Theol. Sem. of the Twin Cities, 1988. Ordained to ministry United Ch. of Christ, 1991. Pastor Congl. Ch. of Excelsior United Ch. of Christ, Excelsior, Minn., 1998—. Mem. Excelsior Masons, Western Clergy Cluster United Ch. of Christ, Excelsior Ministerial Assoc. Mem. Lakeland Coll. Alumni Assn. (Zeta Chi chpt.). Home: 17411 Creek Ridge Pass Minnetonka MN 55345-6230 Office: Congl Ch Excelsior United Ch Christ 471 3rd St Excelsior MN 55331-1945 Office Phone: 952-474-5919.

FENSKE, MARISA LYNN, elementary school educator; b. Columbus, Ohio, Aug. 20, 1976; d. Fred G. Fenske and Mary Ellen Pizzino. B of Edn., Ohio U., 1998; M of Adminstrn., Ashland U., 2002. Tchr. 4th grade United Elem. Sch., Hanoverton, Ohio, 1998—. Bd. dirs. YWCA, Salem, Ohio, 2005—. Mem.: United Edn. Assn. (v.p. sch. union 2005—, sec. union 2003—05), Elks. Roman Catholic. Avocation: walking. Office Phone: 330-223-8001.

FENSTER, ALBERT M., lawyer; b. 1952; AB with distinction, U. Mich., 1973; JD cum laude, Harvard U., 1976. Bar: NY 1977, US Dist. Ct. (so. and ea. dists.) NY 1977. Ptnr. Corp. & Fin. Dept. Kay, Scholer LLP, NYC. Office: Kaye Scholer LLP 425 Park Ave New York NY 10022 Office Phone: 212-836-8205. E-mail: afenster@kayescholer.com.

FENSTER, HERBERT LAWRENCE, lawyer; b. N.Y.C., Mar. 29, 1935; s. Oscar Samuel and Bessie Estelle (Schafran) Fenster; m. Gail Frances Meier, Apr. 18, 1964; children: Christopher Lawrence, Jennifer Gail, Jonathan Adam; m. Jane Porter Elam Allen, Dec. 31, 1993. AB, U. Pa., 1957, MA, 1958; JD, U. Va., 1961. Bar: Va. 1961, D.C. 1962, U.S. Supreme Ct. 1967, Colo. 1993. Assoc. Sellers, Conner & Cuneo, Washington, 1961—66, ptnr., 1967—78, sr. ptnr., 1978—80, McKenna, Conner & Cuneo, Washington, 1980—90, McKenna & Cuneo, Washington, 1990—2002, McKenna, Long & Aldridge, Washington, 2002—. Bd. dirs. Nat. Chamber Litig. Ctr., Washington, Keewaydin Found., Middlebury, Vt., trustee, corp. dir.; litig. counsel Reagan-Bush Campaign Com., Washington, 1980—83; mem. pres.'s pvt. sector survey Grace Commn., Washington, 1982—. Fellow: ATLA; mem.: ABA (treatise Anti Deficiency Act 1979), Am. Law Inst., D.C. Bar Assn., Fed. Bar Assn., Univ. Club, Met. Club. Republican. Episcopalian. Home: 845 6th St Boulder CO 80302-7418 Address: 1875 Lawrence St Denver CO 80202-1370

FENSTER, MARVIN, lawyer, department store executive; b. Bklyn., Jan. 19, 1918; s. Isaac and Anna (Greenman) F.; m. Louise Rapoport, Nov. 13, 1953; children: Julie, Mark. AB, Cornell U., 1938; LLB, Columbia U., 1941. Bar: N.Y. 1942. Assoc. Lauterstein, Spiller, Bergerman & Dannett, N.Y.C., 1941-42, 46-48; atty., asst. gen. atty. R.H. Macy & Co., Inc., N.Y.C., 1948-60, sr. v.p., gen. counsel, sec., 1960-84, sr. v.p. spl. counsel, sec., 1984-87, dir., sr. v.p., spl. counsel, sec., 1987—; pres., dir. Macy's Bank, 1981—; sr. v.p., sec. Macy Credit Corp., N.Y.C., 1961-86, pres., dir., chief exec. officer, 1986—; pres., chief exec. officer Macy Receivables Funding Corp., N.Y.C., 1989—. 1st lt. U.S. Army, 1943-46. Mem. Assn. of Bar, City of New York (corp. law depts. post-admission legal edn., council jud. adminstrn. 1983), Am. Coll. Real Estate Lawyers, Harmonie Club, Beach Point Club, Phi Epsilon Pi. Jewish. Office: R H Macy & Co Inc 151 W 34th St New York NY 10001-2180

FENSTER, SAUL K., university president emeritus; b. N.Y.C., Mar. 22, 1933; s. Samuel and Rose (Glass) F.; m. Roberta Schamis, Jan. 11, 1959; children: Deborah, Lisa, Jonathan. Student, Bklyn. Coll., 1949-51; B of Mech. Engring., CUNY, 1953; MS, Columbia U., 1955; postgrad., NYU, 1955-56; PhD, U. Mich., 1959; LLD, Rutgers U., 2002, William Paterson U., 2002; DHL (hon.), N.J. Inst. Tech., 2002. Lectr. mech. engring. CUNY, 1953-56; teaching fellow engring. mechanics U. Mich., 1956-57, with univ. Rsch. Inst., 1957-58; rsch. engr. Sperry-Rand Corp., 1959-62; prof. engring. Fairleigh Dickinson U., Teaneck, N.J., 1962-78, chmn. dept. physics, 1962-63, chmn. dept. mech. engring., 1963-70, grad. adminstrv. asst. to dean, 1965-70, assoc. dean, 1970-71, exec. asst. to pres., 1971-72, provost Rutherford campus, 1972-78; pres. N.J. Inst. Tech., Newark, 1978—2002, N.J. Inst. Tech. (Found.), 1978—2002. Bd. dirs. various Prudential Mut. Funds, IDT Corp.; vice-chmn. Bus.-Higher Edn. Forum, 1992; cons., 1962—. Author: (with Wallace Arthur) Mechanics, 1969, (with A. Cahit Ugural) Advanced Strength and Applied Elasticity, 1975, 87, 94; contbr. chpts. to books, tech. papers. Mem. Hudson River Waterfront Study and Planning Commn., 1979-80; bd. dirs. N.J. Assn. Colls. and Univs., 1980-2002, N.J. Alliance for Action, 1982-2002, R&D Coun. N.J., 1994-2002, Regional Bus. Partnership, 1994-95, Prosperity N.J., Inc., Soc. Mfg. Engrs. Edn. Found., 1998—; trustee Newark Boys Chorus Sch., 1980-84, Newark Acad., 1984-86; mem., vice chmn. N.J. Water Supply Authority, 1981-88; mem. N.J. Commn. on Sci. and Tech., 1985—; bd. govs. Union County Coll.; mem. Commn. Def. Conversion and Cmty. Assistance, 1993; mem. Commn. on Jobs, Growth and Econ. Devel., 2003—; mem. N.J. Coun. on Job Opportunities; bd. visitors Air U., 1993-98. Shell fellow U. Mich., 1957-58. Fellow ASME, Am. Soc. Engring. Edn., Soc. Mfg. Engrs.; mem. AAAS, Assn. Ind. Colls. and Univs. N.J. (chmn. bd. 1978-80, bd. dirs. 1980-96), Greater Newark C. of C. (bd. dirs. 1980-91), N.J. State C. of C. (bd. dirs. 1987-2002), Coun. on Competitiveness, Sigma Xi, Tau Beta Pi, Omicron Delta Kappa, Pi Tau Sigma. Office: NJ Inst Tech Office of Pres Emeritus University Heights Newark NJ 07102 Home: 477 Ocean Ave N Long Branch NJ 07740 Business E-Mail: fenster@njit.edu.

FENSTERSHEIB, MARTIN, city health department administrator; b. Pitts., 1949; MD, U. Autonoma de Guadalajara, 1975. Internist MC Pa. Hosp., Phila., 1975—77; resident, pediat. Milw. Children's Hosp., 1977—79; fellow, preventive medicine U. Calif., Berkeley, 1981—82; clin. practice Ira Greene Positive PACE Clinic; health officer, pub. health med. dir. Santa Clara Co. Pub. Health Dept., San Jose, Calif., 1994—. Chair, dept. cmty. health and preventive medicine Valley Med. Ctr. Mem.: Santa Clara Co. Med. Assn. (v.p., cmty. health), Calif. Conf. of Local Health Officers (past pres.). Office: Santa Clara Co Pub Health Dept 976 Lenzen Ave San Jose CA 95124

FENSTERSTOCK, BLAIR COURTNEY, lawyer; b. NYC, Aug. 20, 1950; s. Nathaniel and Gertrude (Isaacson) Fensterstock; children: Michael Bayard, Evan Steele, Laurel Sage. AB summa cum laude, Bowdoin Coll., 1972; JD, Columbia U., 1975. Bar: Ind. 1976, N.Y. 1976, U.S. Dist. Ct. (so., ea. and no. dists.) 1976, U.S. Ct. Appeals (2d cir.) 1976, U.S. Customs Ct. 1976, U.S. Ct. Internat. Trade 1976, U.S. Supreme Ct. 1980, U.S. Ct. Appeals (5th cir.) 2004. Assoc. Simpson, Thacher & Bartlett, N.Y.C., 1975-79, Dewey, Ballantine, Bushby, Palmer & Wood, N.Y.C., 1979-83; v.p., assoc. gen. counsel, asst. sec. Reliance Group Holdings, Inc., N.Y.C., 1983-91; sr. v.p., gen. counsel, sec. Frank B. Hall & Co., Inc., 1987-92; ptnr. Sutherland, Asbill & Brennan, 1993-95, Brock, Fensterstock, Silverstein & McAuliffe, LLC, N.Y.C., 1995-98, Fensterstock & Ptnrs., LLP, N.Y.C., 1998—. Bd. visitors Columbia U. Sch. Law, 1988—2004. Bd. dirs. Safety Nat. Casualty Corp., 1990—93; vice chmn. regents Ctr. Security Policy, 2003—04. Harlan Fiske Stone scholar, Columbia U., 1975. Master: N.Y. Inn of Ct.; mem.: ABA, Am. Arbitration Assn. (panel arbitrators), Coun. N.Y. Law Assocs. (bd. dirs. 1979—82), Assn. Bar City of N.Y., N.Y. State Bar Assn., Internat. Peace Acad. (sec. 1977—79), Lawyers Com. Internat. Human Rights (bd. dirs. 1979—80), Pinehurst Country Club (N.C.), Palmas del Mar Country Club (P.R.), Aspetuck Valley Country Club (Weston, Conn.) (bd. govs. 1993—97), Univ Club. (N.Y.C.), Phi Beta Kappa. Republican. Jewish. Home: 10 West St New York NY 10004- Office: Fensterstock & Ptnrs LLP 30 Wall St New York NY 10005-2201 Office Phone: 212-785-4100. Business E-Mail: bfensterstock@fensterstock.com.

FENTON, CLIFTON LUCIEN, investment banker; b. Bryan, Ohio, May 11, 1943; s. Gibson Lucien and Elizabeth (Newcomer) F.; m. Judith Todd Wallis, June 23, 1973; children: Gregory, Eric, Alyssa. AB, Princeton U., 1965; JD, Ohio State U., 1968; MBA, Columbia U., 1970; grad., Kellog Grad. Sch. Mgmt., 2001. Bar: Ohio 1968. Assoc. Bank N.Y., N.Y.C., 1970-72, Morgan Guaranty Trust Co., N.Y.C., 1972; v.p. Kidder, Peabody, N.Y.C., 1972-84; mng. dir. Prudential-Bache Securities, N.Y.C., 1984-89; v.p., nat. mgr. John Nuveen & Co., Chgo., 1989-95, v.p. and mgr. Investment Banking Divsn., 1995-99; mng. dir. and co-head pub. fin. U.S. Bancorp Piper Jaffray, Chgo., 1999-2000. Bd. mem. Ravinia Festival, Associated Colls. of Ill. Rotaryone and Good City. Mem. Met. Club (N.Y.C.), Univ. Club Chgo. Avocations: water and snow skiing, sailing, piano. Home: 130 N Garland Ct Chicago IL 60602 E-mail: cliffenton@comcast.net.

FENTON, DONALD MASON, retired oil company executive; b. L.A., May 23, 1929; s. Charles Youdan and Dorothy (Mason) F.; m. Margaret M. Keehler, Apr. 24, 1953; children: James Michael, Douglas Charles. BS, U. Calif., L.A., 1952, PhD, 1958. Chemist Rohm and Haas Co., Phila., 1958-61; sr. rsch. chemist Union Oil Co., Brea, Calif., 1962-67, rsch. assoc., 1967-72, sr. rsch. assoc., 1972-82, mgr. planning and devel., 1982-85; mgr. new tech. devel. Unocal, Brea, 1985-92. Cons. AMSCO, 1967-73; co-founder, 1st chmn. Petroleum Environ. Rsch. Forum; chmn. bd. dirs. Calif. Engring. Found., 1991-92. With U.S. Army, 1953-55. Inventor in field. Fellow Am. Inst. Chemists, Alpha Chi Sigma; mem. Am. Chem. Soc. Achievements include more than 100 patents in field; co-invention of unisulf process. Home: 2861 E Alden Pl Anaheim CA 92806-4401

FENTON, ELLIOTT CLAYTON, lawyer; b. Oklahoma City, Nov. 26, 1914; s. Edgar R. and Mary (Gaddo) F.; m. LeNoir Massey, July 6, 1939; children: Mike, Ann Wallis; m. Ruby L. Simpson, Aug. 21, 2002. BA, U. Okla., 1935, LLB, 1937. Bar: Okla. 1937, U.S. Dist. Ct. (no., ea. and we. dists.) Okla., U.S. Ct. Appeals (10th cir.), U.S. Supreme Ct., U.S. Ct. Mil. Appeals. Atty. Looney & Fenton, Oklahoma City, 1937—38; atty., claims rep. Nat. Mut. Casualty Co., Tulsa, 1938-40, Hartford Ins. Group, Oklahoma City, 1940-47; atty. Fenton & Fenton, Oklahoma City, 1947—. Chmn. bd. trustees United Meth. Found., Oklahoma City, 1973-83; chancellor United Meth. Found., Oklahoma City, 1983-89. Ret. comdr. USNR. Fellow Am. Bar Found; mem. Internat. Assn. Def. Counsel, Def. Research Inst. (state chmn. 1978-83), Okla. Assn. Def. Counsel (pres. 1972), Okla. County Bar Assn. (bd. dirs.). Republican. United Methodist. Avocation: golf. Home: 14901 N Penn Ave Duplex 4A Oklahoma City OK 73134-6079 Office: Fenton Fenton Smith et al 1 Leadership Sq Ste 800 Oklahoma City OK 73102 Office Phone: 405-235-4671. E-mail: elbeau88@cox.net, ecfenton@fentonlaw.com.

FENTON, HOWARD NATHAN, III, lawyer, educator; b. Toledo, May 6, 1950; s. Howard Nathan, Jr. and Maxine Claire (LaFountaine) F.; children: William Carl, Margaret Claire, Andrew Scimeca, Julie Marie, Christopher Howard; m. Beth Anne Kostic, Mar. 9, 2001. BS with honors, U. Tex., 1971, JD with honors, 1975. Bar: Tex. 1975, D.C. 1976, Ohio 1990, U.S. Dist. Ct. D.C. 1976, U.S. Ct. Appeals (D.C. cir.) 1976. Assoc. Williams & Jensen PC, Washington, 1975-77; ptnr. Swift & Swift PC, Washington, 1978; supervisory compliance officer office antiboycott compliance Internat. Trade Adminstrn./U.S. Dept. Commerce, Washington, 1979-80, dir. compliance policy, 1981-84; assoc. prof. Miss. Coll. Sch. Law, Jackson, 1984-87, prof., 1987-88, Ohio No. U. Coll. Law, Ada, 1988—, assoc. dean, 1988-93, interim dean, 1995—96. Cons. adminstrv. law reform to govts. of Bosnia Herzegovina, Ukraine, Georgia, Armenia, Uzbekistan, 1996—; chief of party US AID Rule of Law Project, Tbilisi, Georgia, 2001-02; cons. Adminstrv. Conf. U.S., 1989-91, 93-94; fellow Nat. Ctr. for Export/Import Studies, Georgetown U., Washington, 1983-86; adj. faculty Cath. U. Law Sch., Washington, spring 1984; mem. U.S.-Can. Free Trade Agreement Dispute Panel, 1993-94, N.Am. Free Trade Agreement Dispute Panel, 1994—. Contbg. editor: Boycott Law Bull, 1984—92. Fellow Ohio State Bar Found.; mem. ABA, Ohio State Bar Assn. (chmn. internat. law com. 2002-05), Am. Soc. Internat. Law. Democrat. Office: Pettit Coll of Law Ohio Northern U Ada OH 45810 Office Phone: 419-772-2233. Personal E-mail: fentonhoward@hotmail.com. Business E-Mail: h-fenton@onu.edu.

FENTON, LAWRENCE JULES, pediatric educator; b. Chgo., June 1, 1940; s. Arthur S. Fenton and Dorothy (Schochet) Wade; m. Gayle Ann Yeager, Apr. 10, 1965; children: Lori Ann Novak, Scott L. BS, U. Mich., 1962; MD, U. Cin., 1966. Diplomate Am. Bd. Pediatrics, Sub-bd. Neonatal and Perinatal Medicine. Intern U. Cin. Med. Ctr., 1966-67, jr. and sr. resident, 1967-69, chief pediatric resident, 1969-70, fellow neonatal, perinatal medicine, 1972-74; asst. prof. pediatrics U. Ariz. Health Scis. Ctr., Tucson, 1974-78; assoc. prof. pediatrics U. S.D. Sch. Medicine, Sioux Falls, 1978-84, head sect. of neonatal, perinatal medicine, 1979-88, prof. pediatrics, 1984—, chmn. dept. pediatrics, 1988—. Dir. newborn intensive care unit Sioux Valley Hosp., 1980-88; chmn. pharmacy and therapeutics com. Sioux Valley Hosp., 1982-97, bd. dirs., 1997—2002; v.p. children's med. svcs. Sioux Valley Hosp. and U. S.D. Med. Ctr., 2000-02. Author: (with others) Current Therapy in Neonatal and Perinatal Medicine, 1989, Conn's Current Therapy, 1989, 90; contbr. articles to profl. jours. Chmn. rsch. funding group Am. Heart Assn., Dakota Affiliate, 1986-88; mem. allocations com. Childrn's Miracle Network Telethon, Sioux Falls, 1986-87; bd. dirs. Childrens Miracle Network, 1996-99; chmn. Health Svcs. Adv. Com., State of S.D., 1991-93. Maj. U.S. Army, 1970-72. Rsch. grantee Nat. Inst. Child Health and Human Devel., Tucson, Sioux Falls, 1976-79, Am. Heart Assn., Sioux Falls, 1984; recipient Army Commendation medal, 1991-93, Pioneer award S.D. Perinatal Assn., 1993; inductee Hall of Honor Children's Hosp. U. Cin. MEd. Ctr., 1993. Fellow Am. Acad. Pediatrics; mem. Society for Pediatric Rsch., Midwest Soc. for Pediatric Rsch., Assn. Med. Sch. Pediatric Dept. Chmn., S.D. States Med. Assn. Avocations: water-skiing, boating, hiking, scuba diving, classical music. Office: 1305 W 18th St Sioux Falls SD 57117-5039 Office Phone: 605-333-7197. Business E-Mail: ijfenton@usd.edu.

FENTON, NOEL JOHN, venture capitalist; b. New Haven, May 24, 1938; s. Arnold Alexander and Carla (Mathiasen) F.; m. Sarah Jane Hamilton, Aug. 14, 1965; children: Wendy, Devon, Peter, Lance. BS, Cornell U., 1959; MBA, Stanford U., 1963. Research asst. Stanford (Calif.) U., 1963-64; v.p. Mail Systems Corp., Redwood City, Calif., 1964-66; v.p., gen. mgr. products div. Acurex Corp., Mountain View, Calif., 1966-72, pres., chief exec. officer, dir., 1972-83, Covalent Systems Corp., Sunnyvale, Calif., 1983-86; mng. gen. ptnr. Trinity Ventures Ltd., 1986—. Bd. dirs. Requisite Tech., Inc., LoopNet, Inc., SciQuest, Inc., Fuego, Inc., ID Analytics, Inc. Mem. adv. coun. resource Ctr. for Women, chmn. bd. dirs. 1987-88; mem. San Jose Econ. Devel. Task Force, 1983, Young Pres.'s Orgn., 1976-88, Pres. Reagan's Bus. Adv. Panel; mem. World Pres.'s Orgn., 1988—, dir., 1994-2000; mem. athletic bd. Stanford U., 2003—. Lt. (j.g.) USN, 1959-61. Mem. Am. Electronics Assn. (chmn. 1978-79, dir. 1976-80), Santa Clara County Mfrs. Group (dir. 1980-83), Chief Execs. Orgn., Stanford Bus. Sch. Alumni Assn. (pres. 1976-77, dir. 1971-76), Stanford Alumni Assn. (exec. bd. 1985-89). Republican. Episcopalian. Home: 247 Mapache Dr Portola Valley CA 94028-7354 Office: Trinity Ventures Bldg 4 3000 Sand Hill Rd Ste 160 Menlo Park CA 94025-7113 Business E-Mail: noel@trinityventures.com.

FENTON, ROBERT EARL, electrical engineering educator; b. Bklyn., Sept. 30, 1933; s. Theodore Andrew and Evelyn Virginia (Brent) F.; m. Alice Earlyn Gray, Dec. 13, 1934; children: Douglas Earl, Andrea Leigh. BEE, Ohio State U., 1957, MEE, 1960, PhD in Electrical Engring., 1965. Registered profl. engr., Ohio. Engr. rsch. N. Am. Aviation, Columbus, Ohio, 1957; instr. electric engring. Ohio State U., Columbus, 1960-65, prof., 1965-95, prof. emeritus, 1995—. Cons. transp. sys. divsn. GM, Warren, Mich., 1974-80, Battelle Meml. Inst., Columbus, Ohio, 1991-93. Inventor kinesthetic-tactile display; contbr. articles to profl. jours. Capt. USAF, 1957-60. Recipient Outstanding Tchr. award Eta Kappa Nu, 1963, Neil Armstrong award Ohio Soc. Profl. Engrs., 1971, Pioneering Rsch. award Nat. Automated Hwy. Systems Consortium, 1997, Significant Achievement award Intelligent Vehicle Hwy. Sys. Ohio, 1993. Fellow IEEE (IEEE Millennium medal 2000), Radio Club Am., IEEE Vehicular Tech. Soc. (pres. 1985-87, v.p. 1983-85, treas. 1981-83, prize paper 1980, Avant Garde award, 1982, Stuart F. Meyer Meml. award 1998), NAE, Sigma Xi. Avocations: bicycling, swimming, classical music. Home: 2177 Oakmount Rd Columbus OH 43221-1229 Office: Ohio State Univ Dept Elec Engring 2015 Neil Ave Dept Elec Columbus OH 43210-1210 Office Phone: 614-292-4310. E-mail: fenton.2@osu.edu.

FENTON, ROBERT LEONARD, lawyer, writer, film producer; b. Detroit, Sept. 14, 1929; s. Ben B. and Stella Frances (Saffir) F.; children: Robert L. Jr., Cynthia R. AB, Syracuse U., 1952; LLB, U. Mich., 1955. Bar: Mich. 1955. Asso. Marks, Levi, Thill & Wiseman, Detroit, 1955-60; ptnr. Fenton, Nederlander, Tracy & Dodge, Detroit, 1960-85; pvt. practice Detroit, 1985—. Adj. prof. U. Mich. Law Sch., Marygrove Coll., Detroit, 2002-03; lectr. Flint and Lansing Real Estate Bds., 1966-68; spl. counsel Detroit Fire Dept.,

1975—, Mich. Motion Picture and TV Commn., 1978-82; producer Universal Studios, Calif., 1983-86, 20th Century Fox, 1986-87; guest lectr. U. Mich. Law Sch., 1998; presenter entertainment law seminar, U. Mich., Apr. 1998, writers workshop Holland Am. Cruise Lines, Feb. 1999; condr writers workshops. Author: (novels) Black Tie Only, 1990, Blue Orchids, 1992, Royal Invitation, 1995; producer NBC movie of week Double Standard, 1988, Woman on the Ledge, 1993. Treas. Oakland County Dem. Com., 1960-64; mem. Dem. State Fin. Com., 1966-69, Nat. Fin. Com., 1962-74, Dem. Pres.'s Club, 1962-74; fin. adviser to Mayor Roman S. Gribbs, 1969-73, Mayor Coleman A. Young, 1974-94; chmn. State of Mich. Film and TV Commn.; bd. dirs. Detroit Bicentennial Commn., Rivers and Harbour Congress of U.S.; mem. adv. bd. NAACP, U. Mich. Pres.'s Club. Served with USAF, 1950-52. Recipient Distinguished Pub. Service medal City of Detroit, 1973, Letter of Commendation USAF, 1953; named Man of the 60's City of Detroit, 1964; decorated Order of St. Johns of Jerusalem, 1980. Mem. ABA, Mich., Detroit bar assns., Econs. Club, Acad. Magical Arts, Soc. Preservation Variety Arts, Franklin Hills Country Club, Variety Club of Detroit (bd. dirs.), Variety Clubs Internat., Recess Club (Detroit), St. James Club (L.A., N.Y.C., London, Paris), Mt. Kenya Safari Club (Nairobi), Masons, Shriners. Office: Village Park Bldg 31800 Northwestern Hwy Ste 204 Farmington Hills MI 48334-1604 Office Phone: 248-855-8780. Personal E-mail: fenent@msn.com.

FENTON, THOMAS TRAIL, journalist; b. Balt., Apr. 8, 1930; s. Matthew Clark and Beatrice (Trail) F.; m. Simone France Marie Lopes-Curval, Jan. 10, 1959; children: Ariane France, Thomas Trail. AB, Dartmouth Coll., 1952; PhD (hon.), U. Balt., 1999. Mem. staff Balt. Sun, 1961-70, chief Rome bur., 1966-68, chief Paris bur., 1968-70; reporter-producer Rome bur. CBS News, 1970-73, corr. Tel Aviv bur., 1973-77, corr. Paris bur., 1977-79, chief European corr. London, 1979-94, Moscow, 1994-96, London, 1996—2004. Assignments include 1967 Middle East War, 1968 Paris Peace Talks, 1971 Indo-Pakistan War, 1973 Middle East War, 1979 takeover of the Am. Embassy in Tehran, 1985 Geneva Summit, 1989-90 Revolution in Ea. Europe, 1990 Gulf Crisis, Moscow Coup, 1991, Collapse of Communism and the Soviet Union, 1992, War in Former Yugoslavia, 1992, War in Chechnya, 1995, Persian Gulf War, 1991, Balkans War, 1999, Death of Princess Diana, 1997, War Against Terrorism Pakistan, 2001, Afghanistan, 2002, War in Iraq, 2003; author: Bad News: the Decline of Reporting, the Business of News and the Danger to Us All, 2005. Served with USN, 1952-61. Recipient Overseas Press Club awards for articles from Paris, 1968, for coverage Indo-Pakistan War, 1971, Mid. East War, 1973, Sadat visit to Jerusalem, 1977, Mountbatten funeral, 1980, hunger in Africa, 1981, radio documentary series, 1992, Emmy awards NATAS for bombing of Marines in Beirut, 1983, for assassination in Indira Gandhi, 1984, 2 Emmy awards for death of Princess Diana, 1998, DuPont award, 1990, Weintal award Georgetown U., 1999. Mem. Soc. the Cin., Internat. Inst. Strategic Studies, Assn. Am. Corrs. London, Assn. de la Presse Presdl. Paris. Personal E-mail: ttfenton@yahoo.com.

FENTON, TIM, food service executive; LLB, U. We. Ont., Can., 1986. With McDonald's Corp., 1973—, various restaurant and ops. pos., including ops. mgr. South Fla. region, field svc. mgr. Kansas City region, others, dir. Asia Pacific, 1990—92, mng. dir. McDonald's Poland, v.p. McDonald's Ctrl. Europe North, 1992—95, v.p., mng. dir. Middle East Devel. Co., sr. v.p., Southeast Asia/Middle East/Africa, pres., East Divsn., McDonald's USA Oak Brook, Ill., pres., McDonald's Asia, Pacific, Middle East and Africa, 2005—. V.p. Am. C. of C., Warsaw, 1992—95; bd. dirs. Friends of Luetefska Children's Hosp., Warsaw, 1994—95. Office: McDonald's Corp McDonald's Plz Oak Brook IL 60523*

FENTON, WAYNE S., psychiatrist; b. Mar. 24, 1953; BA in Exptl. Psychology, Bard Coll., 1975; MD, George Washington U., 1979. Cert. Am. Bd. Medical Examiners, 1980; cert. Md., Conn., Va.; Diplomate in Psychiatry. Rotating internship, dept. internal medicine Norwalk Hosp., Conn., 1979-80; resident, post doctoral fellow psychiatry Yale U., 1980-83; fellow Inst. Social and Policy Studies, Yale U., 1983-84; staff psychiatrist Yale Psychiat. Inst., Yale U., New Haven, 1983-84, Chestnut Lodge, Rockville, Md., 1984-85; rsch. assoc. Chestnut Lodge Rsch. Inst., Rockville, Md., 1984-90; clin. adminstrv. psychiatrist Chestnut Lodge Hosp., Rockville, Md., 1985-90; dir. rsch. Chestnut Lodge Rsch. Inst., Rockville, Md., 1990—99; asst. clin. dir. Chestnut Lodge Hosp., Rockville, Md., 1990—94, med. dir., 1994—98, CEO, 1994—96; assoc. clin. prof., psychiatry and behavior scis. George Washington U., D.C., 1990—; mem. faculty Washington Sch. Psychiatry, 1991—; dep. dir. clin. affairs NIMH, 1999—, acting dep. dir. Bethesda, 2001—02, associate dir., clinical affairs, 2003—. Cons. Montgomery County Pub. Defender, Md., 1984—, McAuliffe House, Md., 1990—. Editl. cons. Schizophrenia Bulletin, 1986—, assoc. editor, 1994—; editl. cons. Jour. of Nervous and Mental Disease, 1986—, Am. Jour. Psychiatry, 1989—; contbr. to profl. jours. Recipient nat. rsch. svc. award USPHS, 1983-84, young investigator award NIH, 1989, Nat. Alliance for Rsch. in Schizophrenia and Depression, 1989, Gralnick award Am. Suicide Found., 1992, Md. Schizophrenia Sci. award, 1995. Mem. Am. Psychiat. Assn., Wash. Psychiat. Sopc., Nat. Alliance for Mentally Ill (exemplary psychiatrist 1996), NAPPH.

FENTRESS, CURTIS WORTH, architectural firm executive; b. N.C., 1947; m. Barbara Hochstetler Fentress. BArch, N.C. State U., 1972. Founding ptnr. CW Fentress JH Bradburn & Assoc. PC, Denver, 1980—; with I.M. Pei, Kohn Pedersen Fox, N.Y.C.; founder C.W. Fentress & Assocs. (now Fentress Bradburn), Denver, 1980—. Co-author: Civic Builders, 2002; prin. works include Denver Internat. Airport. Mem.: AIA (former pres. Colo. chpt.), Urban Land Inst., Western Mus. Assn., New Eng. Mus. Assn., MidAtlantic Assn. Mus., Assn. Midwest Mus., Southeastern Mus. Assn., Mountains-Plains Mus. Assn., Colo.-Wyo. Assn. Mus., Am. Assn. Mus. Office: Fentress Bradburn 421 Broadway Denver CO 80203

FENVES, GREGORY L., engineering educator; PhD, U. of Calif. Berkeley. Prof. civil engring. U. Calif. Berkeley, T.Y. and Margaret Lin Prof. Engring., chair, dept. civil and environmental engring. Asst. dir. industry programs Pacific Earthquake Engring. Rsch. Ctr. U. of Calif. Berkeley; mem. Ctr. for Information Technol. Rsch. in the Interest of Society. Recipient Walter L. Huber Civil Engring. Rsch. prize ASCE, 1995. Office: U Calif Berkeley Dept Civil Engring MC 1710 Berkeley CA 94720-1710

FENWICK, JAMES HENRY, editor; b. South Shields, Eng., Mar. 17, 1937; came to U.S., 1965; s. James Henry and Ellen (Tinmouth) F.; m. Suzanne Helene Hatch, Jan. 27, 1968. BA, Oxford U., Eng., 1960. Freelance lectr., writer, 1960-65; assoc. editor Playboy mag., Chgo., 1965-71; planning and features editor Radio Times, BBC, London, 1971-77, U.S. rep. N.Y.C., 1978-87; sr. editor Modern Maturity mag., Lakewood, Calif., 1987-90, exec. editor, 1990-91, editor, 1991-98; contbg. editor Get Up and Go!, Age Wave Comm., Lakewood, Calif., 1998-99; editor Next Mag., Palm Springs, Calif., 2000—01, Desert Mag., Palm Springs, 2002—.

FENYK, JULIET MELISSA, management consultant, educator; d. John Raymond and Dianne Curry Fenyk; m. Todd Michael Billadeau, Aug. 10, 2002. MA, U. Minn., 2005. Cons. Fenyk Consulting, Minnetonka, Minn., 2003—; adj. faculty DeVry U., Edina, Minn., 2005—. HIV/AIDS task force City of Hopkins, Minn., 1998—2001; mem. United Way's Success By 6 NW, Minneapolis, Minn., 1997—99; alumna adv. bd., sec. Kappa Kappa Gamma, Mpls., 1997—2000; strategic planning com. mem. Annex Teen Clinic, Robbinsdale, Minn., 2004—05; cmty. mgmt. bd., com. chair Jr. League of Mpls., Mpls., 2004—05; alumna assn. bd. social and philanthropic advisor Kappa Kappa Gamma, Mpls., 2002—03. Mem.: APA, Am. Ednl. Rsch. Assn., Soc. for the Psychol. Study of Social Issues, Jr. League of Mpls. (com. chair 2004—05), Phi Kappa Phi, Kappa Kappa Gamma. Personal E-mail: feny0003@umn.edu.

FENZL, TERRY EARLE, lawyer; b. Milw., Mar. 19, 1945; s. Earle A. and Elaine A. (Chandler) F.; m. Barbara Louise Pool, June 24, 1967; children: Allison, Andrew, Ashley. BBA, U. Wis., 1966; JD, U. Mich., 1969. Bar: Ariz. 1970, U.S. Dist. Ct. Ariz. 1970, U.S. Ct. Claims 1970, U.S. Ct. Appeals (9th cir.) 1973, U.S. Supreme Ct. 1973, U.S. Dist. Ct. (no. dist.) Calif. 1983. Assoc. Brown & Bain, P.A. and predecessor firms, Phoenix, 1969-74; ptnr. Perkins Coie Brown & Bain, P.A. and predecessor firms, Phoenix, 1975—. Mem. ABA, Ariz. State Bar Assn., Maricopa County Bar Assn., Ariz. Town Hall. Democrat. Mem. United Ch. of Christ. Home: 6610 N Central Ave Phoenix AZ 85012-1014 Office: Perkins Coie Brown & Bain PA PO Box 400 Phoenix AZ 85001-0400 Office Phone: 602-351-8205. Business E-Mail: tfenzl@perkinscoie.com.

FEOLA, DAVID CRAIG, secondary school administrator; b. Akron, Ohio, Oct. 14, 1954; s. Thomas and Mary (Koci) F.; m. Shellie Feola. BA in Edn., U. Akron, 1976, MA in Edn., 1979, PhD, 1999. Tchr. math. Akron Pub. Schs., 1976-86, asst. prin., 1986-95, Revere H.S., Richfield, Ohio, 1995-2001; prin. Buckeye Jr. High, Medina, Ohio, 2001—. Part-time prof. U. Akron, 1997-2000; math./computer cons. Assocs.: Programs for Learning, Akron, 1991—. Interviewer People to People, Akron, 1994—; vol. for homeless Gennesaret, Inc., Akron, 1997. Named Top Asst. Prin., Akron Edn. Assn., 1995. Mem. ASCD, Nat. Assn. Secondary Sch. Prins., Ohio Assn. Secondary Sch. Prins., Akron Adminstrs. Assn. (treas. 1986-95), Akron City Club, Pi Lambda Theta. Democrat. Congregationalist. Avocations: travel, computers, woodworking, reading, outdoor sports. Home: 4101 Timber Trl Medina OH 44256 Office: Buckeye Jr HS 3024 Columbia Rd Medina OH 44256

FERAN, RUSSELL G., sales executive; b. New Orleans, Oct. 1, 1948; s. Fred and Jean (Zyslina) F.; m. Phyllis Sobel, 1973; 1 child, Leslie. BS in Indsl. Engring., La. State U., 1973. Cert. audio cons.; cert. technician Nat. Assn. Bus. and Ednl. Radio. Audio engr. WIBR Radio, Baton Rouge, 1970—71; broadcast engr. WWL-TV (CBS), New Orleans, 1971—73; engr. South Cen. Bell. Telephone Co., New Orleans, 1973-75; SMIA mgr. Tandy Corp., Fort Worth, 1975-87; regional sales mg. Internat. Union Police Assns., Alexandria, Va., 1987-93; regional mgr. S.W. Pub., Phoenix, 1993—. Bd. dirs. Book Rack Metairie, La., Crohn's & Colitis Found. Am.; cons. Vietnam Vets. Am., Washington, 1987—; arbitrator Better Bus. Bur. New Orleans, 1984-90. With HMM-767, NAS, USMC, 1967-70. Mem. Am. Philatelic Soc., Vietnam Vets. Am., Patrolman's Assn. New Orleans (hon. life 1988), Westside Amateur Radio Club (pres. 1983-85), JWV-USA (post # 580), Am. Radio Relay League (DCXX award 1971), Delta DX Assn., B'nai B'rith (pres. lodge # 182 1986-88, 93-95, v.p. New Orleans coun. 1990-92, election commr. criminal dist. ct., Orleans Parish, La., 2002—). Avocations: stamp collecting/philately, amateur radio (w5rgf, ex-wa5oxk). Home: 101 Fairway Dr New Orleans LA 70124-1016 Office: RGF Enterprises Inc 2305 Metairie Rd Metairie LA 70001-5533 E-mail: w5rgf@arrl.net, w5rgf@aol.com.

FERBEL, THOMAS, physicist, educator; b. Radom, Poland, Dec. 12, 1937; arrived in U.S., 1949, naturalized, 1955; s. Joseph and Natalie (Gotfryd) F.; m. Barbara G. Goolnick, Apr. 20, 1963; children: Natalie, Peter Jordan. BS, Queens Coll., 1959; MS, Yale U., 1960, PhD, 1963. Research staff physicist Yale U., New Haven, 1963-65; asst. prof. physics U. Rochester, N.Y., 1965-69, assoc. prof., 1969-73, prof., 1973—, assoc. dean grad. studies, 1989-91; sci. assoc. CERN, Geneva, 1980-81. Vis. scientist cen. design group Superconducing Supercollider, Lawrence-Berkeley Lab., U. Calif., 1988-89; vis. prof. LAL, Orsay, France, 1995, U. Mainz, Germany, 2001, U. Freiburg, Germany, 2002; mem. program adv. com. Stanford Linear Accelerator Ctr., Calif., 1974-76, Brookhaven Lab., Upton, N.Y., 1981-84; exec. com. Users' Orgn. of Brookhaven Lab., 1972-74; exec. com. Fermi Nat. Accelerator Lab., 1973-75, chmn., 1986-87; sci. dir. Biennial Advanced Study Inst. on High Energy Physics, St. Croix, 1980-2000; mgr. U.S. LHC rsch. program CERN, 2004—. Author: (with A. Das) Introduction to Nuclear and Particle Physics, 1993, second edit., 2004; editor: Techniques and Concepts of High Energy Physics, Vol. 1-X, Silicon Detectors in High Energy Physics, 1982, Experimental Techniques in High Energy and Nuclear Physics, 1991; mem. editl. bd. Phys. Rev., 1978-80, Zeitschrift fur Physik, 1981-85, Internat. Jour. Modern Physics, 1995—. Recipient Alexander von Humboldt prize, 1995; Alfred P. Sloan fellow, 1970, John S. Guggenheim fellow, 1971; Particle Physics and Astronomy Rsch. Coun. sr. fellow Imperial Coll., London, 2002-03. Fellow Am. Phys. Soc. (sec.-treas. divsn. particles and fields 1983-85, chmn. com. on internat. freedom of scientists 1990-92, mem. com. on internat. sci. affairs 1999-2001). Office: U Rochester Dept Physics Rochester NY 14627

FERBER, LEONARD, lawyer; b. Albany, NY, July 19, 1957; AB with high distinction, U. Mich., 1979; JD, U. Pa., 1983. Bar: Ill. 1983. Ptnr., co-char Tech. Practice Katten Muchin Zavis Rosenman, Chgo. Mem.: ABA, Internet Exec. Club, Chgo. Software Assn., Chgo. Bar Assn., Phi Beta Kappa. Office: Katten Muchin Zavis Rosenman 525 W Monroe St, Ste 1600 Chicago IL 60661 Office Phone: 312-902-5679. Office Fax: 312-577-8806. E-mail: leonard.ferber@kmzr.com.

FERBER, LINDA S., museum director; BA cum laude, Barnard Coll., 1966; MA, Columbia U., 1968, PhD in Art History, 1980. Curator Am. Painting and Sculpture The Bklyn. Mus., 1970-97, chief curator, 1985-99, Andrew W. Mellon curator Am. Art, 1997—2005; v.p., dir. NY Hist. Soc. Mus., 2005—. Author: William Trost Richards (1833-1905): American Landscape and Marine Painter, 1980, Tokens of a Friendship: Miniature Watercolors by William T. Richards, 1982, (with others) The New Path: Ruskin and the American Pre-Raphaelites, 1985, Never at Fault: The Drawings of William T. Richards, 1986, (with others) Albert Bierstadt: Art and Enterprise, 1991, (with others) Masters of Color and Light: Homer, Sargent and the American Watercolor Movement, 1998, Pastoral Interlude: William T. Richards in Chester County, 2001, (with others) In Search of a National Landscape: William T. Richards in the Adirondacks, 2002; contbr. articles on 19th and 20th century Am. art history. Wyeth Endowment for Am. Art fellow, 1976-77; recipient Disting. Alumna award Barnard Coll., 2001, Fleischman award Smithsonian Archives of Am. Art, 2002. Mem. Coll. Art Assn., Am. Assn. Mus., Am. Studies Assn., Assn. Art Mus. Curators, Century Assn., Phi Beta Kappa. Office: NY Hist Soc 170 Ctrl Pk W New York NY 10024 Office Phone: 212-873-3400. Business E-Mail: lferber@nyhistory.org. E-mail: lferber@bnyhistory.org.

FERBER, MARIANNE ABELES, economics professor; b. Mirkov, Bohemia, Czechoslovakia, Jan. 30, 1923; came to U.S., 1944; d. Karl and Elsa (Ornstein) Abeles; widowed; children: Don R., Ellen J. BA, McMaster U., 1944; MA, U. Chgo., 1946, PhD, 1954; LHD (hon.), Ea. Ill. U., 2002. Economist Standard Oil (N.J.), N.Y.C., 1944-46; lectr. Hunter Coll., N.Y.C., 1945-46; dir. women's studies U. Ill., Urbana, 1980-83, 91-93, from vis. lectr. to full prof., 1954—. Matina S. Horner Disting. Vis. prof. Radcliffe Coll., 1993—95. Pres. LWV, Champaign County, Ill., 1954; chair Univ. YWCA, Urbana, 1957. Named Disting. Alumna, McMaster U., 1996; recipient Carolyn Shaw Bell award, Com. on Status of Women in Econs. Profession, 2002. Mem. Am. Econ. Assn. (com. status women 1975-78), Midwest Econ. Assn. (pres. 1987-88), Am. Stats. Assn. (chair com. status women 1979-80), Indsl. and Labor Rels. Assn., Internat. Assn. Feminist Economists (pres. 1995-96). Jewish. Avocations: swimming, cooking. Home: 101 W Windsor Rd #.4105 Urbana IL 61802 Office Phone: 217-333-4599. Business E-Mail: m-ferber@uiuc.edu.

FERBER, NORMAN ALAN, retail executive; b. N.Y.C., Aug. 25, 1948; m. Rosine Abergel; children: Robert, Lauren, Richard. Student, Bklyn. Coll., 1965-68, L.I.U., 1968-70. Buyer, mdse. mgr. Atherton Industries, N.Y.C., 1976-79; v.p., mdse. mgr. Raxton Corp., N.Y.C., 1979-82; v.p. Fashion World, N.Y.C., 1982; v.p merchandising, mktg. and distbn. Ross Stores Inc., Newark, Calif., 1984-87, pres., COO, 1987-88, pres., CEO, 1988-93, chmn., CEO, 1993-96, chmn., 1996—. Office: Ross Stores Inc 4440 Rosewood Dr Pleasanton CA 94588*

FERBER, ROBERT RUDOLF, retired physics researcher, educator, science administrator; b. June 11, 1935; s. Rudolf F. and Elizabeth J. (Robertson) F.; m. Eileen Merhaut, July 25, 1964; children: Robert Rudolf, Lynne C. BSEE, U. Pitts., 1958; MSEE, Carnegie-Mellon U., 1966, PhD in Semiconductor Physics, 1967. Registered profl. engr., Pa. Mgr. engring. dept. WRS Motion Picture Labs., Pitts., 1954-58, sec., 1959-76, v.p., 1976-79; sr. engr. Westinghouse Rsch. Labs., Pitts., 1956-67; mgr. nuclear effects group Westinghouse Elec. Corp., Pitts., 1967-71, mgr. adv. engr. energy projects East Pittsburgh, 1971-77; photovoltaic materials and collector rsch. mgr. Jet Propulsion Lab., Pasadena, Calif., 1977-85, SP100 Project contract tech. mgr., 1985-90, asst. project mgr. Spaceborne Imaging Radar, 1990-96, Earth Observing Sys. microwave limb sounder radiometer, 1995-99, mgr. Herschel HIFI project amplifier devel. task mgr., 2000—04, ret., 2004. V.p. Executaire Inc., Pitts., 1960-64; pres. Tele-Cam Inc., Pitts., 1960-78. Editor: Transactions of the 9th World Energy Conf. 1974, Digest of the 9th World Energy Conf., 1974. Contbr. articles to profl. jours.; patentee in field. Mem. Franklin Regional Sch. Dist. Bd., Murrysville, Pa., 1975-77. Fellow Buhl Found., 1965-66, NDEA, 1976-77. Mem. IEEE (sr.), ASME (chmn. 1986 Solar Energy divsn. conf.). Republican. Lutheran. Home: 5314 Alta Canyada Rd La Canada Flintridge CA 91011-1606 Personal E-mail: rrferber@sbcglobal.net.

FERBER, SAMUEL, publishing executive; b. NYC, June 6, 1920; s. Isidore and Sadie (Irgang) F.; m. Beatrice Ruth Ziman, June 18, 1944; children: Bruce Joseph, Joel David. BBA, CCNY, 1941; postgrad., Columbia U., 1946-48. Promotion dir. Nat. Advt. Service, Inc., N.Y.C., 1946-50, Boys' Life mag., N.Y.C., 1950-52; promotion dir. Esquire mag., N.Y.C., 1952-58, advt. mgr., 1959-65, sr. v.p., assoc. pub., 1965-70, advt. dir., 1970-74, pub., 1974-76; co-dir. Esquire mag. (Bus. and the Arts awards program), 1966-74; dir. Esquire mag. (Corp. Social Responsibility awards program), 1972-75; sr. v.p., prin. Altman, Stoller, Weiss Advt., 1976-80, exec. v.p., 1980-82; v.p. Nadler & Larimer Advt., 1982-84; owner Sam Ferber, Pub. Cons., 1984—. Faculty econs. and advt. Latin Am. Inst., NYC, 1946-49; bd. advisors Alliance Resident Theatres, NYC, 1987—; lectr. in fied. Mem. Leader Gt. Books Discussion Group, Bd. Art/N.Y. Served with Adj. Gen.'s Dept. AUS, 1942-46. Home: 2210 Rutland Pl Thousand Oaks CA 91362 *I have always subscribed to the philosophy of my former colleague, Arnold Gingrich, that one should "never leave well enough alone" . When things are progressing smoothly is the precise moment to plan the evolutionary change that insures progress and vitality. In my time, I have seen pillars of industry and publishing fall by the wayside because their emphasis has been on self-preservation rather than innovation.*

FERDERBER-HERSONSKI, BORIS CONSTANTIN, process engineer; b. Craiova, Romania, May 17, 1943; came to U.S., 1980; s. Boris Modest and Anetta (Mihail) F.; m. Alexandra Ionescu; children: Boris Constantin Jr., Alexandru Vlad. MS in Process Engring., Poly. Inst., Bucharest, Romania, 1968; diploma fgn. trade, Romanian U., Bucharest, 1975. Registered profl. engr., Romania. Plant engr. Pham. Complex, Bucharest, 1968-69, plant mgr., 1969-73; prin. engr. Indsl. Export Import, Bucharest, 1973-75, fgn. trade diplomate, 1975-80; sr. process engr. Foster Wheeler Corp., Livingston, NJ, 1980-85; projects mgr. CPC Internat., Fairfield, 1985-91; project mgr., engring. mgr. Aqualytics, Inc., Morristown, 1991-99; engr., mgr., tech. dir. Ameridia, Tokuyama, Japan, Eurodia, France, 1999—2000; dir. fuel cell. devel. HPower Co., 2000—. Founder, pres. B.F.H. Design Corp., 1984—. Inventor in field. Mem. Rep. Nat. Com., Washington, 1981. Mem. AIChE, Instrument Soc. Am., Am. Rowing Assn. Avocations: electronic applications, water and snow skiing. Home: 122 Dupont Ave Hopatcong NJ 07843-1705

FERDINANDI, V. MICHAEL, retail executive; B in Indsl. Edn., M in Indsl. Edn., Rhode Island Coll.; PhD, Boston U. Various positions Ford Motor Co.; dir. human resources PepsiCo, Inc., 1994—96, v.p. ops. Can., 1996—99; v.p. human resources and orgnl. devel. CVS Pharmacy, Inc., Woonsocket, RI, 1999—2002, sr. v.p. human resources and corp. comms., 2002—. Bd. trustees William M. Davies, Jr. Career & Tech. H.S. Office: CVS Corporation Corporate HQs One CVS Drive Woonsocket RI 02895*

FEREBEE, STEPHEN SCOTT, JR., architect; b. Detroit, July 30, 1921; s. Stephen Scott and Caroline (Cheatham) F.; m. Mary Elizabeth Cooper, July 7, 1945; children: Scott III, John, Caroline. BArch in Engring., N.C. State U., 1948; DFA (hon.), U. N.C., Charlotte, 1992. Job capt. A.G. Odell, Jr. & Assocs. (Architects), Charlotte, NC, 1948-53; ptnr. Higgins & Ferebee (Architects), Charlotte, 1953-59, Ferebee & Walters (Architects), 1959-64; pres. Ferebee, Walters & Assos. (Architects/Planners), Charlotte, 1964-86; chmn., CEO FWA Group (Architects & Planners), Charlotte, 1987-90. Dir. AIA Found., Washington, 1986-87, Prodn. Systems for Architects and Engrs., Inc., Washington, 1969-71, 77-78, Republic Bank & Trust Co., Charlotte, 1971-91, John Crosland Co., Charlotte, 1973-83. Prin. projects include Southpark Mall, Colonial Heights, Va., 1989, Tech. Ctr. for Union Carbide Agrl. Products Co., Inc, Research Triangle Park, N.C., 1982, Coll. Vet. Medicine, N.C. State U., Raleigh, 1983, Charlotte Conv. Ctr., 1994, Coll. Architecture bldg., U. N.C., Charlotte, 1990. Bd. dirs. United Cmty. Svcs., Charlotte, 1977—82, Opera Carolina, Charlotte, 1988—91, Aldersgate, Charlotte, 1995—2004, 2005—, Habitat for Humanity, Charlotte, 1999—2002; pres. N.C. Design Found., 1966—68, 1978—79. Capt. 101st Airborne Divsn. AUS, 1942—46, maj. gen. Res. (ret.). Decorated D.S.M., Bronze Star, Purple Heart, Croix de Guerre France and Belgium, Order of the Long Leaf Pine State of N.C.; recipient Watauga medal, N.C. State U., 2001. Fellow: AIA (pres. N.C. 1964, chmn. commn. profl. practice 1971, nat. pres. 1973, chancellor Coll. of Fellows 1987, Deitrick medal N.C. chpt. 1995, F. Carter Williams Gold medal N.C. chpt. 2004), Internat. Union Architects (coun. 1975—81), Royal Archtl. Inst. Can. (hon.); mem.: Mex. Soc. Architects (hon.), N.C. State U. Alumni Assn. (pres. 1980—81), Charlotte C. of C. (v.p. 1975—76, bd. dirs. 1989—91), Rotary (pres. Charlotte East 1997—98), Phi Kappa Phi. Methodist. Home: 5334 Sandtrap Ln Charlotte NC 28226-7978 Personal E-mail: sferebee@bellsouth.net.

FERENCZ, BENJAMIN BERELL, lawyer; b. Soncuta Mare, Romania, Mar. 11, 1920; arrived in U.S., 1921, naturalized, 1933; s. Joseph Ferencz and Sarah (Legman) Ferencz Schwartz; m. Gertrude Fried, Mar. 29, 1946; children: Carol, Robin Eve, Donald Martin, Nina Dale. BSS, CCNY, 1940; JD, Harvard U., 1943. Bar: N.Y. 1943, U.S. Supreme Ct. 1943, U.S. Dist. Ct. (so. and ea. dists.) N.Y. 1958. Exec. counsel U.S. Chief Counsel War Crimes, Nuremberg, Germany, 1946—48; dir. gen. Jewish Restitution Orgn., Franfurt, Germany, 1948—56; ptnr. Taylor, Ferencz & Simon, N.Y.C., 1956—. Adj. prof. Pace U. Sch. Law, N.Y.C.; dir. United Restitution Orgn., London, Frankfurt, N.Y.C., 1948—. Author: Less than Slaves, 1979 (Nat. and Present Tense Lit. awards, 1980), Defining International Aggression, 2 vols., 1975, An International Criminal Court, 2 vols., 1980, Enforcing International Law, 2 vols., 1983, Common Sense Guide to World Peace, 1985, New Legal Foundations for Global Survival, 1994. Mem. Human Rights Commn., New Rochelle, NY, 1975—. With inf. U.S. Army, 1943—45, ETO. Mem.: Internat. Law Assn., Am. Soc. Internat. Law (v.p. 1979—80), World Peace Through Law Ctr., Amnesty Internat., Internat. League Human Rights, Harvard Club (N.Y.C.), B'nai B'rith (local pres. 1960, counsel supreme lodge 1966—70). Democrat. Jewish. Home: 14 Bayberry Ln New Rochelle NY 10804-3402 Personal E-mail: benferen@aol.com.

FERENCZ, CHARLOTTE, pediatrician, epidemiologist, preventive medicine physician, educator; b. Budapest, Hungary, Oct. 28, 1921; came to U.S., 1954; d. Paul Ferencz and Livia deFekete. BSc, McGill U., 1944, MD, CM, 1945; MPH, Johns Hopkins U., 1970. Cert. pediatrics Royal Coll. Physicians and Surgeons, Can., pediatric cardiology Am. Bd. Pediatrics. Demonstrator McGill U., Montreal, 1952-54; asst. prof. pediatrics Johns Hopkins U., Balt., 1954-58, U. Cin., 1959-60; asst. prof. SUNY, Buffalo, 1960-66, assoc. prof., 1966-73; assoc. prof. epidemiology and preventive medicine U. Md. Sch. Medicine, Balt., 1973-74, prof., 1974-98, prof. pediatrics, 1985—, prof. emeritus, 1998—. Prin. investigator population based study Etiology of Congenital Heart Disease, 1981-89; mem. epidemiology and disease control study sect. NIH, 1984-88; pres. Delta Omage Alpha chpt. Pub. Health Soc., 1990-92. Recipient M.E.S. Abbott scholarship McGill U., 1943-45, M.E.R.I.T. award Nat. Heart, Lung & Blood Inst., 1987, Fogarty Internat. Ctr. Health Sci. Exchange award NIH, 1988, Helen B. Taussig award Am. Heart Assn. Md. Affiliate, 1991, Achievement award Univ. Ctr. Life Scis., Balt., 1993, Johns Hopkins U. Disting. Alumnus award, 2001. Fellow Am. Acad.

Pediatrics (Spl. Achievement award Md. chpt. 1994), Am. Coll. Cardiology; mem. Teratology Soc. Democrat. Office: U Md Sch Medicine 660 W Redwood St Baltimore MD 21201-1541

FERENCZ, ROBERT MARK, mechanical engineer; b. Cleve., Mar. 28, 1957; s. Bruce Joseph Ferencz and Catherine Rose Wheeler; 1 child, Stephen. BSCE, Case Western Res. U., 1980, MSCE, 1981; MSME, Stanford U., 1984, PhD in Mech. Engring., 1989. Engr., analyst Lawrence Livermore (Calif.) Nat. Lab., 1980-83, engr., code developer, 1984-89, project leader, 1998—2002, leader methods devel. group, 2002—; mgr. quality assurance Centric Engring. Sys., Inc., Stanford, Calif., 1990-93, dir. software devel. Santa Clara, Calif., 1994-96, v.p. R & D Sunnyvale, Calif., 1996-98. Contbr. chpt. to textbook and handbook in field. Coach youth soccer league, Livermore, 1997-2000. Mem. AIAA, ASME, Am. Acad. Mechanics, Soc. Indsl. and Applied Math., Sigma Xi, Tau Beta Pi. Unitarian Universalist. Avocations: performing arts, history. Home: 25278 Gold Hills Dr Castro Valley CA 94552- Office: Lawrence Livermore Nat Lab PO Box 808 L-125 Livermore CA 94551-0808 Fax: 925-423-4096. Business E-Mail: ferencz1@llnl.gov.

FERENS, DANIEL VINCENT, civilian military employee; b. Oswego, NY, Feb. 26, 1948; s. Walter Frank and Sophie (Longeski) F.; m. Marcella Jean Spinner, Apr. 28, 2001. BS, Rensselaer Poly. Inst., 1969, MSEE, 1970; MBA, U. No. Colo., 1976. Satellite sys. engr. air def. co. USAF, Denver, 1971-75, computer software engr. Aeronaut. Sys. Ctr. Dayton, Ohio, 1976-77, program mgr. Aeronaut. Sys. Ctr., 1977-78; engring. cost analyst civil svc. USAF Avionics Lab., Dayton, 1978-83; assoc. prof. civil svc. USAF Inst. Tech., Dayton, 1984-97; program dir., 1995-97; adj. assoc. prof. civil svc. USAF Inst. Tech., Dayton, 1998-2000; corp. affordability officer civil svc. USAF Rsch. Lab., Dayton, 1998-00, directorate rep. Corp. Affordability Coun., 1999—2001; tchr. software mgmt. NATO Officers, Belgium, 2000; program mgr. USAF Rsch. Lab., Rome, NY, 2001—. Software estimating cons. Aeronautics Sys. Ctr., Dayton, 1984—2000, Electronic Sys. Ctr., Boston, 2000—02; adj. instr. SUNY Inst. Tech., Utica, 2003—. Author: Mission Critical Computer Software Management, 1987, Defense System Software Project Management, 1990; guest editor: Engineering Cost and Production Economics, 1988; contbr. 35 articles to profl. jours. Tchr. adult Sunday sch. Kirkmont Presbyn. Ch., Beaver Creek, Ohio, 1987—2000, chmn. edn. com., 1992; adult Sunday sch. tchr. Abiding Christ Luth. Ch., Fairborn, Ohio, 2000—01; mem. Christian edn. com. First Presbyn. Ch., Rome, NY, 2002—, adult Sunday Sch. tchr. Capt. USAF, 1969—78. Decorated USAF Commendation medal. Mem. Internat. Soc. Parametric Analysts (bd. dirs. 1979-80, 2004—, pres. Midwest chpt. 1993-94, Internat. Parametrician of the Yr. award 1990, Freiman Lifetime Achievement award 1999, keynote spkr. European Symposium, 1999, life), Internat. Function Point Users Group (univ. mem., mem. edn. com. 1999-2000), Soc. Cost Estimating and Analysis (mem. edn. com. 1992—), Soc. Logistics Engrs. (assoc. editor newsletter 1993), Toastmasters Internat. (Area Gov. of Yr. 1987, pres. 2003-04, area gov. 2003, 2004-2005, Disting. Toastmaster 2004), Polish Legion Am Vets. Avocations: computers, church activities, travel, games, reading. Mailing: PO Box 386 Rome NY 13442-0386 Office: Air Force Rsch Lab (AFRL/IFEA) 525 Brooks Rd Rome NY 13441-4505 Office Phone: 315-330-4098. Business E-Mail: ferensd@rl.af.mil.

FERENTZ, KEVIN SCOTT, physician; b. New York, NY, Apr. 26, 1958; s. Leslie Benjamin and Sylvia F.; m. Lisa Roslyn Ettinger, Nov. 13, 1983; children: Jacob Avi, Zachary Daniel, Noah Samuel. MD, SUNY, Buffalo, 1983. Diplomate Nat. Bd. Med. Examiners, cert. Am. Bd. Family Practice. Assoc. prof. dept. family medicine U. Md. Sch. of Medicine, Balt., 1993—. Residency dir. Dept of Family Medicine, Balt., 1993—. Contbr. articles; host (weekly nat. radio show) Sunday Rounds. Mem. adv. bd. Tova Ho., Balt., 2002. Recipient Resident rsch. award, North Am. Primary Care Rsch. Group Nat. Meeting, 1986. Mem.: Soc. Tchrs. Family Medicine, Md. Acad. Family Physicians (pres. 1997—98), Am. Acad. Family Physicians (chair, com. on pub. rels. and mktg. 1995—96, Exemplary Tchr. of Yr. 1981, Pub. Rels. award 1991, Outstanding Program Dir. 2004). Democrat. Jewish. Achievements include organized smoking cessation program for Baltimore County High Schools, using medical students and residents as group leaders. Avocations: theater, music. Office: U Md Sch Medicine Lower Level 29 South Paca St Baltimore MD 21201 Office Phone: 410-328-8792. Business E-Mail: kferentz@som.umaryland.edu.

FERGENSON, ARTHUR FRIEND, lawyer; b. N.Y.C., Dec. 9, 1947; s. A. Leon and Constance Elinor (Friend) F.; m. Jeannette Emma Festa, Nov. 23, 1974; children: Leah F., Nina E. Festa, Micah F. AB, Dartmouth Coll., 1969; JD, Yale U., 1972. Bar: N.Y. 1973, U.S. Dist. Ct. (so. dist.) N.Y. 1973, D.C. 1975, U.S. Ct. Appeals (2d cir.) 1975, U.S. Dist. Ct. Md. 1984, U.S. Ct. Appeals (4th cir.) 1984, Md. 1985, U.S. Supreme Ct. 1986. Law clk to Hon. Thomas P. Griesa U.S. Dist. Ct., N.Y.C., 1972-73; law clk. to U.S. Chief Justice Warren E. Burger U.S. Supreme Ct., Washington, 1973-74; atty. Covington & Burling, Washington, 1974-76; asst. prof. Ind. U. Sch. Law, Bloomington, 1976-79; assoc. prof. U. Md. Sch. Law, Balt., 1979-81; gen. counsel Action Agency, Washington, 1981-82; cons. Nat. Inst. Justice, Washington, 1982-83; asst. U.S. atty. U.S. Atty.'s Office, Balt., 1983-85; ptnr., of counsel Weinberg and Green, Balt., 1985-95; of counsel Ballard Spahr Andrews & Ingersoll, Balt., 1995—2001; ptnr. DLA Piper, 2001—. Mem. adv. coun. Atlantic Legal Found., Inc., 1997—. Editl. bd. mem. Bus. Law Today, 2001—. Trustee Center Stage, Balt., 1987—. Republican. Jewish. Avocations: theater, film, politics, political theory. Home: 507 Edgevale Rd Baltimore MD 21210-1901 Office: 6225 Smith Ave Baltimore MD 21209 Office Phone: 410-580-4438. Business E-Mail: arthur.fergenson@dlapiper.com.

FERGUS, GARY SCOTT, lawyer; b. Racine, Wis., Apr. 20, 1954; s. Russell Malcolm and Phyl Rose (Muratore) F.; m. Isabelle Sabina Beekman, Sept. 28, 1985; children: Mary Marckwald Beekman Fergus, Kirkpatrick Russell Beekman Fergus. AB, Stanford U., 1976; JD, U. Wis., 1979; LLM, NYU, 1981. Bar: Wis. 1979, Calif. 1980. Assoc. Brobeck, Phleger & Harrison, San Francisco, 1980-86, ptnr., 1986—2001, mng. ptnr. products liability, ins. coverage, environ. and antitrust/appellate practices, 1996-2000, sr. ptnr. e-commerce anti-trust group, 2000—01; founder law firm Fergus, San Francisco, 2002—. Mem. ABA. Home: 3024 Washington St San Francisco CA 94115-1618 Office: Fergus a law firm 595 Market St Ste 2430 San Francisco CA 94105 Office Phone: 415-537-9032. Business E-Mail: gfergus@ferguslegal.com.

FERGUS, PATRICIA MARGUERITA, English language educator, writer, editor; b. Mpls., Oct. 26, 1918; d. Golden Maughan and Mary Adella (Smith) Fergus. BS, U. Minn., 1939, MA, 1941, PhD, 1960. Various pers. and editing positions U.S. Govt., 1943-59; mem. faculty U. Minn., Mpls., 1964-79, asst. prof. English, 1972-79, coord. writing program conf. on writing, 1975, dir. writing centre, 1975-77; prof. English and writing, dir. writing ctr., assoc. dean Coll. Mt. St. Mary's Coll., Emmitsburg, Md., 1979-81; dir. writing seminars Mack Truck, Inc., Hagerstown, Md., 1979-81; writer, 1964—. Editor, 1997—; vocal soloist, 1997—; editl. asst. to pres. Met. State U., St. Paul, 1984—85; coord. creative writing, writer program notes for Coffee Concerts The Kenwood, 1992—94; dir. Kenwood Scribes Presentation, 1994; spkr., cons. in field; dir. 510 Groveland Assocs.; bus. mgr. Eitel Hosp. Gift Shop; freelance manuscript editor, 1997—99; writer, reviewer Whittier Pubs., Long Beach, NY, 1997; instr. Elderlearning Inst., 1999—2000, Univ. Coll., U. Minn., 1999—2000; poetry and prose reading, retirement cmtys., 2002—05; pres., resident coun. Walker Tree Tops, Mpls., 2003—04, spl. events dir., master of ceremonies, dir., spkr., 2003—05. Author: Spelling Improvement, 5th edit., 1991; contbr. to Downtown Cath. Voice, Mpls., Mountaineer Briefing, ABI Digest, Women in the Arts The Penletter; contbr. poems to Minn. English Jour., Women in the Arts, Decatur Area Arts Coun. Newsletter, Mpls. Muse, The Moccasin, Heartsong and Northstar Gold, The Pen Woman, Midwest Chaparral, Rhyme Time, The Best of Rhyme Time, 1998, Fantasy, 1998; contbr. short stories to anthologies, including Seeking the Muses, Inspired Works of Creativity, 2000; musical works performed at St. Olaf Ch., 1997, Nat. League Am. Pen Women, 1998. Mem. spl. vocal octet St. Olaf Ch. Choir, 1977-79, 81-92, St. Olaf Parish Adv. Bd., 1982-84, Windmore Found. for the Arts., 1996. Recipient Outstanding Contbn. award U. Minn. Twin Cities Student Assembly, 1975, Horace T. Morse-Amoco Found. award, 1976; Golden Poet award World of Poetry, 1992; Ednl. Devel. grant U. Minn., 1975-76, Mt. St. Mary's Coll. grant, 1980; 3d prize vocal-choral category Nat. Music Composition Contest, Nat. League Am. Pen Women, poetry prize No. Dist. Women's Club, Va., 1996. Mem.: Midwest Fedn. Chaparral Poets (poetry judge, numerous poetry prizes including 1st prize 1998, 1999, 2001, 2003), Mpls. Poetry Soc. (pres. 2000—02, numerous poetry prizes including 1st prize 1999, 2d prize 2003, 1st prize 2005), World Lit. Acad., Nat. League Am. Pen Women (Minn. br. and state past pres., 1st pl. Haiku nat. poetry contest 1992), Minn. Coun. Tchrs. English (chmn. career and job opportunities comm., spl. com. tchr. licensure, sec. legis. com.), Nat. Coun. Tchrs. English (regional judge 1974, 1976—77, state coord. 1977—79), Mpls. Woman's Club (critic writers group). Roman Catholic. Home and Office: # 612 3535 Bryant Ave S Minneapolis MN 55408-4134 Office Phone: 612-827-4867.

FERGUSON, BRADFORD LEE, lawyer; b. Ottumwa, Iowa, May 29, 1947; s. G. Wendell and Virginia Sue (Baker) Ferguson. BA, Drake U., 1969; JD, Harvard U., 1972. Bar: Minn. 1972, Ill. 1980. Assoc. Dorsey, Marquart, Windhorst, West & Halladay, Mpls., 1972-75; legis. asst. Senator Walter F. Mondale, Washington, 1975-77; spl. asst. to asst. sec. tax policy U.S. Treasury Dept., Washington, 1977-78, assoc. tax legis. counsel, 1978-80; ptnr. Hopkins & Sutter, Chgo., 1980-96, Sidley & Austin, Chgo., 1996-2001. Fellow Am. Coll. Tax Counsel; mem. ABA (taxation sect., chair com. formation tax policy 1991-93, mem. coun. 1994-97), Chgo. Bar Assn., Nat. Tax Assn. (bd. dirs. 1994-97).

FERGUSON, BRUCE A., construction executive, contractor; b. 1944; BA, Colo. State U. With Gerald H. Phillips Co., Denver, 1966—, now pres. Office: Gerald H Phillips Inc 1530 W 13th Ave Denver CO 80204-2402

FERGUSON, CATHY LYNNE, elementary school educator; b. Jefferson City, Mo., June 4, 1956; d. William Thomas and Rometta Pearl Ferguson. BS in Edn., Ctrl. Mo. State U., 1978; MA in Reading Edn., U. Mo., Kansas City, 1984, Edn. Specialist in Reading Edn., 1987. Cert. elem. tchr. Mo., reading tchr. Mo., jr. high English tchr. Mo. Elem. tchr. 5th grade Chillicothe (Mo.) Pub. Schools, 1978—79; elem. tchr. 4th grade Houston Mo. Pub. Schs., 1979—82; substitute tchr. Mountain Grove (Mo.) Pub. Schs., 1982—83, Hickman Mills Schs., Kansas City, 1983—84, Grandview (Mo.) Consol. Sch. Dist., 1983—84; elem. accelerated reading tchr. Grandview Consol. Sch. Dist. No. 4, Grandview, Mo., 1984—; substitute pub. libr. clk. Mid-Continent Pub. Libr., Grandview, 1992—. Mem. tchr. support team Butcher-Greene Elem. Sch., Grandview, 1999—. Vol. Kans. City Cares, 1997—2005; mem. Christian Women's Fellowship, Kansas City, 1992—2005; elders' cabinet Hickman Mills Cmty. Christian Ch., Kansas City, 2004—05, Sunday sch. and vacation bible sch. tchr., deaconess, 1985—2002, mem. worship, church-in-society, nominating, and meml. coms., elder, 2002—05. Mem.: Butcher-Greene Parent Tchr. Assn., Grandview Cmty. Tchrs.' Assn. (bldg. rep. 1989—99), Mo. State Tchrs.' Assn. (Mini-grantee 1995, 1998, 2000, 2002), Kans. City Cares (24 Hour Club 1999—2003). Office: Butcher-Greene Elem Sch 5302 E 140th St Grandview MO 64030-3904 Office Phone: 816-316-5400.

FERGUSON, CHARLES AUSTIN, retired newspaper editor; b. New Orleans, Mar. 16, 1937; s. Austin and Josephine Hayes (Gessner) F.; m. Jane Pugh, Dec. 21, 1961; children: Elizabeth Hayes, Caroline Pugh. BA, Tulane U., 1958, LL.B., 1961; DLitt (hon.), Dillard U., New Orleans, 1996. Bar: La. bar 1961. From reporter to editor States-Item, New Orleans, 1961-80; editor Times-Picayune/States-Item, New Orleans, 1980-90. Anchor TV program City Desk, New Orleans, 1971-78 Trustee Dillard U., New Orleans, 1972—2005, chmn. exec. com., 1978—2005, chmn. bd. trustees, 1992—2005, emeritus, 2005—; mem. adv. bd. Nieman Found., Harvard U., 2004—; co-chmn. Louis Armstrong Meml. Park Com., New Orleans, 1971-79. Recipient Torch of Liberty award Anti-Defamation League of B'nai B'rith, 1981; Nieman fellow, 1965-66 Mem. La. Bar Assn., Internat. Lawn Tennis Club U.S.A., New Orleans Lawn Tennis Club, Harvard Club (N.Y.C.). Home: 1448 Joseph St New Orleans LA 70115-4263

FERGUSON, CLEVE ROBERT, lawyer, educator; b. Long Beach, Calif., Dec. 31, 1938; s. Frank H and Ruth S Ferguson; m. Kathryn Jane Weaver, Apr. 10, 1965 (div. June 25, 1995); children: Sharon Anne, Robert Timothy; m. Peggy Burke Daniell, Nov. 19, 1995. Attended, U. Vienna, 1960—61; AB in Econs., U. So. Calif., 1961, JD, 1965. Bar: Calif 1966, U.S. Dist. Ct. (cen. dist.) Calif. 1966, U.S. Ct. Appeals (9th cir.) 1987, U.S. Supreme Ct. 1975. Assoc. Musick, Peeler & Garrett, L.A., 1965—69, Hayes & Hume, Beverly Hills, Calif., 1969—74; pvt. practice Pasadena/Claremont, Calif., 1974—; adj. prof. physics and astronomy U. La Verne, Calif., 1993—; pres., CEO Mars Manned Mission Corp.; pres. Hyde Mountain Mktg. Co., 2004—; adj. prof. Coll. Law U. La Verne, 1994—2001. Mem. alcohol and drug abuse com. Calif. State Bar, 1990—91; instr. astronomy and bus. law Chapman U., 1992—93; arbitrator Am. Arbitration Assn.; lectr. in field; instr. telescope use and telescope optics UCLA, U. Calif., Irvine. Editor (rschr.): Quarter Circle 81, Prescott and Camp Wood, Arizona, 1883-1912, 2004; columnist Claremont Inst. Mem. Stony Ridge Obs., 1985—, pres., 1994—97; co-founder, bd. trustees Mt. Wilson Inst., Calif., 1987—; lectr., cons. Mcpl. Officers for Redevel. Reform, Calif., 1996—; mem. L.A. Opera League; bd. dirs. Clan Fergusson Soc. N.Am., 1987—2000. With U.S. Army, 1961—62. Decorated Knights Templar of Jerusalem, Grand Priory of the Scots. Fellow: Soc. Antiquaries Scotland; mem.: Sons of the Revolution, Univ. Club Pasadena, Beta Theta Pi. Avocations: astronomy, dry fly fishing, skiing, mountaineering. Office: C Robert Ferguson Atty at Law 237 W 4th St Claremont CA 91711-4710 Office Phone: 909-482-0782. E-mail: crflawyer@earthlink.net, crf@marsmannedmission.org.

FERGUSON, DIANA S., food products executive; b. 1963; M in Mgmt., Northwestern U.; Bachelor's, Yale U. With Eaton, Fannie Mae, First Nat. Bank Chgo., IBM, US Fort James Corp.; v.p., treas. Sara Lee Corp., 2001—. Fellow: Leadership Greater Chgo. Office: Sara Lee Corp 3 First Nat Plaza Chicago IL 60602-4260

FERGUSON, DOUGLAS EDWARD, finance company executive; b. Bronx, Apr. 21, 1940; s. Lawrence and Claire (Billingheimer) Ferguson; m. Cynthia L. Kords, Jan. 29, 1966; children: Elisabeth, Keith, Jonathan. AB, Columbia Coll., 1962. CFA. Security analyst Heritage Securities/Nat. Securities and Rsch. Corp., N.Y.C., 1963-68; asst. v.p. John W. Bristol & Co., Inc., N.Y.C., 1968-74; v.p. Van Cleef, Jordan & Wood, Inc., N.Y.C., 1974-75; portfolio mgr. Trustees of Columbia U., N.Y.C., 1975-76; mgr. investment svcs. Trascott, Alyson, Craig, Inc., Teaneck, N.J., 1977-84; v.p. portfolio mgmt. Swiss Bank Corp., N.Y.C., 1984-88; chmn. Ferguson Investment Cons., Inc., Sleepy Hollow, 1988—. Contbr. articles to profl. jours. and newspapers. Pres. Weschester ARC, 1991—95; mem. Estate Planning Coun., Westchester County; bd. dirs. HERO, Inc. Mem.: N.Y. Soc. Security Analysts, Rotary. Home and Office: Ferguson Investment Cons 528 Bellwood Ave Sleepy Hollow NY 10591-1336 Office Phone: 914-631-7188.

FERGUSON, EARL WILSON, cardiologist, medical executive, telemedicine consultant; b. Lebanon, Pa., Aug. 29, 1943; s. Warren Earl and Norma Laura (Wilson) F.; m. Sun Hye Paik, May 1, 1998; children: Steven Mark, Matthew Earl, Erin Lee. BA in Chemistry, Baylor U., 1965; MD, PhD in Physiology, U. Tex., Galveston, 1970. Diplomate Am. Bd. Internal Medicine, Cardiovasc. Disease, Am. Bd. Preventive Medicine. Grad. tchg. asst. dept. physiology U. Tex. Med. Br., Galveston, 1967-70, intern medicine, 1970-71; resident medicine, then fellow cardiology Duke U. Med. Ctr., Durham, NC, 1971-75, mem. assoc. faculty dept. medicine, 1974-75; research assoc. cardiology VA Hosp., Durham, 1974-75; commd. lt. USAF, 1966, advanced through grades to col., 1984-95; staff cardiologist, dir. coronary care Wilford Hall USAF Med. Ctr., Lackland AFB, Tex., 1975-76, chief cardiology, dir. cardiology tng. program, 1983-84; asst. prof. biochemistry, medicine and mil. medicine Uniformed Svcs. U. Health Scis., Bethesda, Md., 1976-80, assoc. prof. physiology, medicine and mil. medicine, 1980-84, asst. comdt., 1977-82, mem. faculty senate, 1979-80, adj. prof. physiology, 1984-93; dir. hosp. svcs. USAF Med. Ctr., Scott AFB, Ill., 1984-86; comdr. USAF Hosp., Little Rock AFB, Ark., 1986-88; dep. command surgeon Mil. Airlift Command, Scott AFB, 1988-90; dir. Aerospace Medicine and Occupl. Health NASA, Washington, 1993-96; comdr. USAF Med. Ctr., Wiesbaden, Germany, 1990-93; CEO Sun Biomed. Techs., 2000—. Cons. to surgeon gen. for cardiology, medicine and physiology USAF, 1980—95; cons. N.J. State Police and N.J. Atty. Gen.'s Office, 1984—90, Ind. Atty. Gen's Office, 1985—87, NASA, 1997—, mem. life scis. subcom., 1989—93; interagency working group on telemedicine, 1994—96; adj. assoc. prof. preventive medicine Uniformed Svcs. U. Health Scis., Bethesda, Md., 1993—96; physician So. Sierra Med. Clinic, Ridgecrest, Calif., 1996—; advisor House/Senate Com. on telemedicine and health care, 1994—96; corp. bd. Ridgecrest Regional Hosp., 1997—, bd. dirs., 1998—2004, Calif. Telemedicine and eHealth Ctr., 1997—, chair bd. dirs., 2002—04; chief of medicine Ridgecrest Regional Hosp., 2001—04; CEO Sun Biomedical Tech., 2000—; chief of staff Ridgecrest Regional Hosp., 2005—. Mem. editl. bd.: Telemedicine and e-Health Jour., 1996—2003; contbr. articles to profl. jours. Rsch. grantee VA, 1974-75, Dept. Def., 1976-82, NASA, 1982-84, Cooperative R&D Agreement, Naval Air Warfare Ctr., China Lake, Calif., 2000—, Dept. Def. SBIR, 2002—, NSF, 2004—; Cardiovasc. Health fellow Health Forum/Am. Hosp. Assn., 1999-2000. Ashbel Smith Disting. Grad., 1993. Fellow Am. Coll. Cardiology (bd. govs. 1985-88), ACP, Am. Coll. Preventive Medicine, Nat. Rep. Congl. Com. Bus. Adv. Coun., 2002-. Unitarian Universalist. Avocations: physical fitness activities, flying. Office Phone: 760-446-6404.

FERGUSON, EMMET FEWELL, JR., surgeon; b. DeSoto, Ga., Mar. 28, 1921; s. Emmet Fewell Sr. and Emma Ruth (Smith) F.; Edith Geraldine Strozier, Nov. 26, 1954; children: Berrylin, Joann, Virginia, Fran, Emmet III. Student, U. Ga., 1938-40; BS in Elec. Engring., US Naval Acad., 1943; MD, Med. Coll. Ga., 1950. Diplomate Am. Bd. Surgery, Am. Bd. Colon-Rectal Surgery. Rsch. assoc. U.S. Naval Hosp., St. Albans, N.Y., 1950-51; surg. resident U. Fla., Jacksonville, 1951-53, 54-55, U. Ala., Brimingham, 1953-54; pvt. practice Jacksonville, 1955-93; pres. staff Meth. Hosp., Jacksonville, 1958-60, U. Hosp., Jacksonville, 1972-73; chief colon rectal surgery Bapt., Meth., and St. Vincents Hosps. Clin. prof. surgery coll. medicine U. Fla., 1960-93; mem. med. missions to Honduras, Costa Rica, Nicaragua, Ecuador; del., speaker Pan Am. Med. Meeting, Buenos Aires, 1967; mem. adv. com. coll. medicine U. Fla., Gainesville, 1976-82; chmn. bd. dirs. N.E. Fla. Health Svc. Agy., 1980-2000; mem. Statewide Health Coun., 1980-89, chair, 1980-82. Author: Commonly Memorized Verse, 1991, The Five Most Important Numbers in our World, 1995, Guide to the Major and Minor Springs of Florida, 1997; contbr. articles to profl. jours. Del., speaker from Jax C. of C. to Internat. Exhbn., Moscow, 1959; tchr. Sunday sch. Riverside Bapt. Ch., 1955—, deacon, 1960, 90; del. from Am. Cancer Soc. to Internat. Cancer Soc., Tokyo, 1966; mem. United Way Bd., Jacksonville, 1970-80, chmn. profl. divsn., 1980; chmn. Fla. host com. Pres. Carter's Inauguration, Washington, 1977; life mem. Jacksonville Hist. Soc., pres., 1986-88; mem. Jacksonville Indigent Care Com.; bd. regents Nat. Libr. Medicine, Washington, 1977-81; founder bd. dirs. Bapt. Towers, 1970—; trustee, pres. bd. trustees Riverside Bapt. Day Sch., 1971-75; trustee health sci. ctr. libr. U. Fla., 1972-93; trustee Bartram Sch., 1974-84, pres., 1976-77; mem. exec. com., mem. office state commn. rsch., profl. svc. Am. Cancer Soc. With USN, 1940-46, 50-51, capt. M.C. res. Decorated Am. Def. medal, Naval Res. medal; recipient Disting. Svc. award Fla. divsn. Am. Cancer Soc., Tampa, 1972, 75, Silver Beaver award Boy Scouts Am., 1986, Emmet Ferguson award U. Fla. Health Sci. Ctr. Fellow ACS (pres. Fla. chpt. 1968), Am. Soc. Surgery Alimentary Tract, Am. Soc. Colon Rectal Surgeons, Piedmont Soc. Colon Rectal Surgeons (pres. 1996-97), Fla. Soc. Colon Rectal Surgeons (pres. 1972-74, 76-78); mem. AMA, Fla. Med. Assn. (life), So. Med. Assn., Southeastern Surg. Congress (Best Motion Picture award 1975), Duval County Med. Soc. (life, editor bull. 1970-73, pres. 1975-76), Navy League (life, pres. Jacksonville coun. 1983-84, Commendation award 1984), Sons Confederate Vets., Rotary (bd. dirs. 1978-80, chmn. com. polio plus 1987-88, Commendation award 1989, Adm. Kaufman award 2004), St. John's Dinner Club (pres. 1975-78, Commendation award 1978), Fla. Yacht Club (life), River Club, Kappa Sigma. Democrat. Avocations: hunting, fishing, tennis, sailing, sculpting. E-mail: effjo@aol.com.

FERGUSON, ESTHER B., volunteer; b. Sumter, S.C., Jan. 24, 1943; d. Norwood Fleming Baskin and Nan Richardson Rickenbaker; m. George William Moore (div.); m. James Larnard Ferguson. BA in Polit. Sci./Art History, U. S.C.; LLD, William Penn Coll., 1983; DHL, Dominican Coll., 1987, U. Pacific, 1990, Johnson and Wales U., 1996, Coker Coll., 1996. Founder Nat. Drop-Out Prevention Fund & Ctr., Clemson U., 1985—, Study Abroad Program, Trujillo, Spain, 1995; bd. dirs. Charleston Symphony Orchestra, S.C., 1990-2000; vice-chmn. Young Concert Artists, N.Y.C., 1982-2000; bd. dirs. Spoleto U.S.A., Charleston, 1983-2000, Internat. Found. for Edn. and Self-Help, Phoenix, 1980—, Monmouth (N.J.) Coll., 1985-89, Coke Coll., Hartsville, S.C., 1993-96; founder, chair Am. Mental Health Resources, 1999—. Contbr. articles to profl. publs. and newspapers. Episcopalian. Republican. Avocations: reading, skiing, international travel. Office: PO Box 1457 Charleston SC 29402

FERGUSON, GARY WARREN, retired public relations executive; b. Stockton, Kans., May 5, 1925; s. Richard and Nelle (McBee) F.; m. Doris Drisler, Oct. 2, 1948; children: Arthur Richard, Frances (Mrs. Gregory H. Gebhart), Robert Warren, Scott William. AB, Yale U., 1946; MS in Journalism, Columbia U., 1948. Reporter Providence Jour. Bull., 1948-49, Richmond (Va.) News Leader, 1949-52, St. Louis Post-Dispatch, 1954-55, spl. writer, 1955-60; counselor Fleishman-Hillard, Inc., St. Louis, 1961-62, sr. ptnr., 1962-71; pres. Gary Ferguson Assocs., Inc., 1971-93. Vice-chmn. Dorf and Stanton Comm., Inc., 1988-93; editorial cons., 1993-99. Mem. founding bd. Greater St. Louis Coun. Alcoholism, 1965, pres., 1966-69; pres. mental Health Assn., St. Louis, 1980-81; trustee World Affairs Coun. St. Louis, 1990-95. Recipient Bishop's award Episcopal Diocese Mo., 1965. Mem.: Press Club Met. St. Louis. Home: 1 Colonial Village Ct Apt D Saint Louis MO 63119-2722

FERGUSON, GLENN WALKER, writer, educator, retired ambassador; b. Syracuse, N.Y., Jan. 28, 1929; s. Forrest Erwin and Mabel Gertrude (Walker) F.; m. Patricia Lou Head, June 22, 1950; children: Bruce Walker, Sherry Lynn, Scott Sherwood. BA, Cornell U., 1950, MBA, 1951; grad., U. Santo Tomas, Manila, 1953; student, U. Chgo. Law Sch., 1955-56; JD, U. Pitts., 1957; D.S. (hon.), Worcester Poly. Inst., 1973; LL.D. (hon.), Sacred Heart U., 1974; DHL (hon.), Am. U. Paris, 1995. Staff assoc. Govtl. Affairs Inst., Washington, 1954—55; asst. editor, asst. sec.-treas. Am. Judicature Soc., Chgo., 1955—56; asst. to chancellor and asst. dean Grad. Sch. Pub. Affairs, U. Pitts., 1956—60; with McKinsey & Co. (mgmt. cons.), Washington, 1960—61, Peace Corps, 1961—64, rep. Thailand, 1961—63, assoc. dir. Washington, 1963—64; dir. Vols. in Svc. to Am., Washington, 1964—66; U.S. ambassador to Kenya, 1966—69; chancellor L.I. U., 1969—70; pres. Clark U., 1970—73, U. Conn., 1973—78, Radio Free Europe/Radio Liberty, Munich, 1978—82, Lincoln Ctr. Performing Arts, N.Y.C., 1983—84, Equity for Africa, 1985—92, Am. U. Paris, 1992—95. Cons. govt. agys., 1959-64, TV moderator fgn. affairs, Pitts., 1957-60; USIS lectr. India, Sudan, Uruguay, Argentina, 1984-92; vis. prof. fgn. policy Conn. Coll., U. R.I., 1990-91; cons. Internat. Exec. Svc. Corps., Uruguay, 1992. Author: (aphorisms) Unconventional Wisdom, 1999, (essays) Americana Against the Grain, 1999, Tilting at Religion, 2003, Sports in America, 2004; contbr. articles to profl. jours. Human rights commr. City of Worcester, Mass., 1971-72; trustee Cornell U., 1972-76, former mem. corp. bds.; mem. French-Am. Commn. for Ednl. Exch., 1992-95. 1st lt. USAF, 1951-53, Korea. Recipient Arthur S. Flemming award, 1968; Asso. fellow Timothy Dwight Coll., Yale U. Mem.: Am. Birding

Assn., ABA, Coun. Am. Ambs. (bd. dirs. 1996—2003), Fgn. Policy Assn. (bd. dirs. 1974—83), Coun. Fgn. Rels., Fed. Bar Assn., Nat. Press Club, Phi Delta Phi, Psi Upsilon, Phi Beta Kappa. Address: 1060 Governor Dempsey Dr Santa Fe NM 87501-1078

FERGUSON, J. BRIAN, chemicals executive; b. Lubbock, Tex., June 16, 1954; B in Chem. Engring., Ariz. State U., 1977. Rsch. and devel. staff Eastman Kodak Co., Longview, Tex., 1977, various mfg. and staff pos., various bus. and strategic planning pos. Kingsport, Tenn., 1989, Washington, 1992—94; v.p. industry and fed. affairs Eastman Co., Washington, 1994, mng. dir. for Gtr. China Hong Kong; mng. dir. Eastman Chem. Asia Pacific Pte., Ltd., Singapore; pres. Eastman Co. Polymers Group, 1999, Eastman Co. Chems. Group, 2001; chmn., CEO Eastman Chem. Co., Kingsport, Tenn., 2002—. Office: Eastman Chem Co PO Box 511 100 N Eastman Rd Kingsport TN 37662-5075

FERGUSON, J. SCOTT, music educator, director; b. Newton, Mass., Sept. 13, 1957; s. W. Eugene and Kathryn Deal Ferguson; m. Eva Mazanovska Ferguson, July 29, 1995; children: Filip, Eva. MusB in Organ Performance, Oberlin (Ohio) Conservatory Music, 1979; MFA in Choral Conducting, U. Calif., Irvine, Calif., 1981; MusD in Choral Conducting, U. Wis., 1987. Dir. choral activities Plymouth (N.H.) State U., 1987—90, Hope Coll., Holland, Mich., 1990—94; dir. opera State Conservatory Music, Bratislavia, Slovakia, 1994—96; dir. choral activities Ill. Wesleyan U., Bloomington, Ill., 1996—. Pvt. music, voice instr., 1982—; dir. chapel choir, asst. organist Second Presbyn. Ch., Bloomington, 1996—; organist, cantor St. Joseph Cath. Ch., Chenoa, Ill., 2002—; vis. condr. Cantus, Bratislava, 1995; organist Wentworth (N.H.) Congl. Ch., 1987—90; dir. music Bel Canto Chamber Singers, Hanover, NH, 1987—89; asst. to condrs. Wis. Youth Orchs., 1985—87; dir. music many chs., 1977—; presenter in field; various coms. Ill. Wesleyan U. Editor: Europa Cantat, 2004—; singer: (albums) Ye Shall Have A Song, 1993, Choirmaster, Bratislava Conservatory Choir, with Academy of Music Orchestra, 1995, Polyphonic Poetry: the Ars Antiqua Motet and the Gothic Spirit, 2000, IWU Collegiate Choir, Live on Tour, 1997-2000, 2001, IWU Collegiate Choir: Live on Tour, 1998-2004, 2004, IWU Choral Sampler, 2004, 2003 Christmas Choral Concert: IWU, 2004, 13th-c, 2004, Selections from 2003 Christmas Choral Concert, 2004; contbr. articles to profl. jours.; performer (condr.): numerous performances nationally and internationally, 1993—. Grantee, Ill. Wesleyan U., 1998, 2004. Mem.: Nat. Assn. Tchrs. Singin, Music Educators Nat. Conf., Internat. Fedn. Choral Music, Am. Choral Dirs. Assn., Pi Kappa Lambda (pres. chpt. 2004—, 1998—2000), Phi Beta Delta, Phi Mu Alpha. Avocations: hiking, gardening. Home: 16 Inverness Dr Bloomington IL 61701-2046 Office: Sch Music Ill Wesleyan Univ PO Box 2900 Bloomington IL 61702-2900

FERGUSON, JAMES CLARKE, mathematician, algorithmist; b. Spokane, Wash., June 23, 1938; s. James Forsythe and Dorothy Eileen (Dillon) F. MS in Math., U. Wash., 1963; PhD in Math., U. N.Mex., 1984. Sci. programmer Boeing, Seattle, 1960-64; staff mem. GE Tech. Mil. Planning Office, Santa Barbara, Calif., 1964-66; mathematician TRW, Inc., Redondo Beach, Calif., 1966-71, Teledyne-Ryan Aero., San Diego, 1971-77; staff mem. Los Alamos (N.Mex.) Nat. Lab., 1977-85; sr. scientist Tektronix, Beaverton, Oreg., 1985-87, BBN Systems and Techs. Corp., Bellevue, Wash., 1987-92; with Point Control, Eugene, 1993-94, Camax Mfg. Technologies, Eugene, 1994-95; mathematician SDRC/Camax, Eugene, 1995-2000, consulting mathematician, 2001—. Cons. in field, 1975-87. Co-author: Key Works in Geometric Modeling, 1991, Fundamental Developments of Computer Aided Geometric Modeling, 1992; contbr. articles to profl. jours. Recipient advanced study fellowship, Los Alamos Nat. Lab., 1981. Mem. Assn. Computing Machinery, Soc. Indsl. and Applied Math. Achievements include introduction of parametric curve and surface techniques into computer aided geometric design field; complete classification of parametric planar cubics; application of parametric curve techniques to problem of shape preservation. Home: PO Box 1783 Hillsboro OR 97123-1783 E-mail: dddjim@earthlink.net.

FERGUSON, JO MCCOWN, retired lawyer; b. Central City, Ky., Apr. 5, 1915; s. Jo Marvin and Willie Mae (Cain) F.; m. Margarita Hauser, July 12, 1947; children— Rita, Diane, Jo Frances. AB, U. Ky., 1937, LL.B., 1939. Bar: Ky. 1938. Practiced in, Central City, 1939-42; asst. atty. gen. Ky., 1948-56; atty. gen., 1956-60; commr. econ. security, 1960-61; partner firm Harper, Ferguson & Davis.; ret. Mcpl. bd. counsel, 1961-91. Chmn. Gov.'s Com. on Constl. Revision, 1961-62; chmn. Gov.'s Task Force on Fin., 1976-77; pres. Ky. Hist. Soc., 1988-90; chief Property Control br. Mil. Govt., Bavaria, 1946-47. Capt. AUS, 1944-47, ETO. Decorated Brigadier d'Honneur 3eme Regiment Anjou, French Army. Mem. ABA, Ky. Bar Assn., VFW, So. Attys. Gen. (chmn. 1957-58). Democrat. Episcopalian. Home: 403 Duff Ln Louisville KY 40207-1524

FERGUSON, JOHN DUNCAN, medical research educator; b. Saskatoon, Sask., Can., Aug. 20, 1929; s. George Alexander and Urdine (LeValley) F.; m. Tamara van den Bergh, Sept. 12, 1958. MA, U. Toronto, Ont., Can., 1956; PhD, Columbia U., 1966. Project dir. Bur. Applied Social Rsch., Columbia U., N.Y.C., 1958-64; asst. prof. Northeastern U., Boston, 1966-68; from assoc. prof. to prof. U. Windsor, Ont., 1968—; mem. assoc. med. staff Harper Hosp., Detroit, 1982-2000, rsch. cons., 2000—. Author reports in field. Grantee Ont. Cmty. and Social Svcs. Ministry, 1991-93. Presbyterian. Home: 1516 Iroquois Ave Detroit MI 48214-2747 Office: U Windsor Windsor ON Canada N9B 3P4 E-mail: tamjackferg@worldnet.att.net.

FERGUSON, JOHN LEWIS, state historian; b. Nashville, Ark., Mar. 1, 1926; s. Clarence Walter and Nannye Nell (McCrary) F.; m. Oris Brandon, June 9, 1956; children— Clay Walt, Ora Lee. B.A., Henderson State Tchrs. Coll., 1950; M.A., U. Ark., 1952; Ph.D., Tulane U., 1960. Head dept. social studies Conway Bapt. Coll., Ark., 1952-58; asst. prof. history Ark. Poly. Coll., Russellville, 1958-60; state historian Ark. History Commn., Little Rock, 1960— . Editor: Arkansas and the Civil War, 1965; author: Arkansas Lives, 1965; co-author: Historic Arkansas, 1966. Baptist. Home: 12 Pilot Point Pl Little Rock AR 72205-2856 Office: Ark History Commn 1 Capitol Mall Little Rock AR 72201-1049

FERGUSON, JOHN PATRICK, health facility administrator; b. Weehawken, NJ, Jan. 22, 1949; s. Donald George and Margaret (Rienzo) F.; m. Gene Marie Promersperger, Jan. 16, 1971; children: Adam, David, Kate. BS in Econs., St. Peter's Coll., 1970; MBA in Hosp. Adminstrn., George Washington U., 1973; LHD (hon.), Felician Coll., 2005. Sr. v.p. St. Vincent's Hosp., N.Y.C., 1972-81; v.p. ops. Hackensack (N.J.) Univ. Med. Ctr., 1981-85, sr. v.p., 1985, acting pres., chief exec. officer, 1985-86, pres., chief exec. officer, 1986—. Pres. Met. Health Adminstrs., N.Y.C., 1977—78; adj. faculty New Sch. for Social Rsch. Grad. Sch. Mgmt. and Urban Professions, N.Y.C., 1978—84; chmn. bd. trustees Univ. Health Sys. (now N.J. Coun. Tchg. Hosps.), Trenton, 1999—2001, vice chmn., 2002—03; trustee UMDNJ, 2002—, sec. bd. trustees, 2003—. Trustee Garden State Arts Found., 2004—; mem. jobs growth and econ. devel. commn. State of N.J., 2002—; co-chmn. health transition team Gov.-elect Jim McGreevey, 2001; trustee Molly Found. for Diabetes Rsch., 1995—; commr. Econ. Devel. Commn. of City of Hackensack, 1996—2002; founding commr. Bergen County Econ. Devel. Corp., 1996—; mem., bd. govs. Greater N.Y. Hosp. Assn., 2000—; trustee St. Peter's Coll., 2000—, Martha's Vineyard Hosp., Inc., 2000—; chmn. bd. dirs. Martha's Vineyard Hosp., 2002—; mem. exec adv. com. State of N.J. Commn. on Cancer Rsch., 2000. Named One of Top 12 Up and Coming Healthcare Execs., Modern Healthcare mag., 1988, One of 50 Bus. People to Watch for the 1990's, N.J. Bus. Jour., 1990, Citizen of Yr., Meadowlands Regional C. of C., 1993, Man of Yr., Nat. Burn Victim Found., 1994, Humanitarian of Yr., Make A Wish Found., 1996, Disting. Citizen of N.J., Ramapo Coll. Found., 1998, Humanitarian of Yr., Boys' Towns of Italy, 1999; named one of 100 Most Powerful People in Healthcare in US, Modern Healthcare Mag., 2004, NJ 50 Most Influential Players in Polit. Healthcare Arena, Healthsense, Inc., 2005; named to, Found. for Free Enterprise Hall of Fame, 2002; recipient Man of Yr. award, Tomorrow's Children's Fund, 1989, Medallion award, Bergen C.C., 1993, Disting. Cmty. Svc. award, Anti-Defamation League, 1995, Disting. Citizen award, Hackensack C. of C., 1995, Disting. Cmty. Health Svc. award, Bergen County Bd. of Chosen Freeholders, 1996, Pres.'s award, N.J. State Nurses Assn., 1999, Med. Exec. award, Acad. Medicine N.J., 2000, Good Scout award, No. N.J. Coun. Boy Scouts Am., 2000, Ellis Island medal of honor, 2002, Disting. Alumni award for profl. achievement, St. Peter's Coll., 2002, Humanitarian award, Nat. Conf. for Cmty. and Justice, 2003, Disting. Alumni award, George Washington U. Health Sci. Mgmt. and Policy, 2004. Fellow: Am. Coll. Healthcare Execs. (regent, gov. dist. II 1994—99, Regents Recognition award 2004); mem.: Met. Health Adminstrn. Assn. (Distinction award 1997), Am. Fedn. for Aging Rsch. (bd. dirs. 1997—2000), Commerce and Industry Assn. N.J. (bd. dirs. 1996—, chmn.'s award for Outstanding Leadership 1997), Am. Heart Assn. (pres. Mid-Bergen divsn. 1992—93, bd. dirs. 1993—94), Cath. Hosp. Assn., Am. Hosp. Assn. Office: Hackensack U Med Ctr 30 Prospect Ave Hackensack NJ 07601-1912

FERGUSON, KINGSLEY GEORGE, retired psychologist; b. Newcastle-on-Tyne, Eng., Apr. 13, 1921; emigrated to Can., 1927; s. William George and Isobel (Finnegan) F. BA in English and French, U. Western Ont., 1943; MA in Psychology, U. Toronto, 1951, PhD, 1956. Diplomate Am. Bd. Profl. Psychology. Staff psychologist Sunnybrook Vets. Hosp., Toronto, Ont., Can., 1949-50; chief psychologist Westminster Vets. Hosp., London, Ont., Can., 1950-61, Montreal Gen. Hosp., Que., Can., 1961-68; psychologist-in-chief Clarke Inst. Psychiatry, Toronto, 1968-86. Chmn. Ont. Bd. Examiners in Psychology, Toronto, 1972-77. Served to lt. Can. Navy, 1942-45 Fellow Can. Psychol. Assn.; mem. Am. Psychol. Assn., Ont. Psychol. Assn. (pres. 1959-60; Lifetime Achievement award 1994-97). Address: 694 Sammon Ave Toronto ON Canada M4C 2E4 Personal E-mail: geordie614@sympatico.ca.

FERGUSON, LAURA COBB, music educator; b. Starkville, Miss., Aug. 1, 1951; d. W. J. and Marjorie Raye Cobb; m. Frank Howard Ferguson, Sept. 4, 1971; children: Adam Howard, Gary Stuart. BME, Delta State U., 1971. Music tchr. Scott Ctrl. Pub. Sch., Forest, Miss., 1971—73, Hermitage Pub. Sch., Hermitage, Ark., 1985—89; music tchr., choir dir. Warren Pub. Sch., Warren, Ark. Mem.: SE Region Ark. Choral Dirs. Assn. (assoc.; jr. region chmn. 1995—2005, dir. yr. 1995, 1998, 2001, Dir. Yr. 1995, 1998), Ark. Choral Dirs. Assn. (assoc.), Am. Choral Dirs. Assoc. (assoc.), Monticello Music Club (assoc.; pres.), Delta Kappa Gamma (assoc.). Avocations: reading, travel, gardening. Office Phone: 870-226-6736.

FERGUSON, LISA BERYL, accountant; b. L.A., Apr. 17, 1958; d. Harry Alfred Abramson and Dolores Gloria Cohen; m. Jeffrey Monroe Ferguson, June 23, 1984 (div. Oct. 1992); children: Kate Emily, Colin James; m. Michael Jonathan Miqdadi, May 17, 2003. BSBA, U. Phoenix, 1997. CPA Calif., 2000; notary pub. Calif., 1979. Acct. Neal Levin and Co., Beverly Hills, Calif., 1978—2002; acct., mng. ptnr. Premier Bus. Mgmt. Group, 2003—. Democrat. Office: Premier Bus Mgmt Group 15260 Ventura Blvd # 1700 Sherman Oaks CA 91403 Office Phone: 818-933-2600.

FERGUSON, LLOYD ELBERT, retired manufacturing engineer; b. Denver, Mar. 5, 1942; s. Lloyd Elbert Ferguson and Ellen Jane (Schneider) Romero; m. Patricia Valine Hughes, May 25, 1963; children: Theresa Renee, Edwin Bateman. BS in Engring., Nova Internat. Coll., 1983. Cert. hypnotherapist, geometric tolerance instr. Crew leader FTS Corp., Denver, 1968-72; program engr. Sundstrand Corp., Denver, 1972-87, sr. assoc. project engr., 1987-90, sr. liaison engr., 1990-93; sr. planning engr. Hamilton Sundstrand Corp., Denver, 1990-2000; ret., 2000. V.p. Valine Corp. Lic. practitioner of religious sci. United Ch. of Religious Sci., L.A.; team capt. March of Dimes Team Walk, Danver, 1987; mem. AT&T Telephone Pioneer Clowns for Charity. Recipient recognition award AT&T Telephone Pioneers, 1990 Mem. Soc. Mfg. Engrs. (chmn. local chpt. 1988, zone chmn. 1989, achievement award 1984, 86, recognition award 1986, 90, appreciation award 1988), Nat. Mgmt. Assn. (cert., program instr. 1982—, honor award 1987, 90), Am. Indian Sci. and Engring. Soc., Colo. Clowns. Mem. United Ch. of Religious Sci. Home: 10983 W 76th Dr Arvada CO 80005-3481

FERGUSON, MARGARET ANN, tax specialist, consultant; b. Steuben County, Ind., Mar. 24, 1933; d. Leo C. and Ruth Virginia (Engle) Wolf; m. Billy Hugh Ferguson, Feb. 15, 1955 (dec. Oct. 1971); children: Theresa Ruth, Scott Earl, Wade Leo, Luke, Angela, Cynthia, Brenda. AA in Psychology/Social Svs., Palomar Coll., San Marcos, Calif., 1977; BA in Behavioral Sci., Nat. U., Vista, Calif., 1980. Enrolled agt. Office mgr., adminstr. asst. Better Bus. Bur., San Diego, 1979-82; tax technician IRS, Oceanside, Calif., 1982-84, problem resolution tax specialist, 1985-87, revenue agt., 1987-90; pvt. cons. Vista, Calif., 1991—. Instr. adult edn. Vista Unified Sch. Dist., 1990-99; mem. adv. com. of nat. cemetery sys. Dept. Vet. Affairs, 1991-98, adv. coun. IRS, 1999-2001. Mem. AAUW (treas.), Calif. Assn. Ind. Accts., Calif. Soc. Enrolled Agts. (dir. Palomar chpt. 1993-95, 2000-01, 1st v.p. 1998-2000), Inland Soc. Tax Cons., Assn. Homebased Bus., Gold Star Wives Am., Inc. (regional pres. 1989-90, chpt. pres. 1992-93, 96-97, nat. pres. 1993-95, chmn. nat. bd. dirs. 2004—). Avocations: lace making, needle work, gardening, writing. Home and Office: 1161 Tower Dr Vista CA 92083-7144 Office Phone: 760-724-2343. Personal E-mail: gswtax@aol.com.

FERGUSON, MARK KENDRIC, surgeon, educator; b. Mpls., Jan. 10, 1951; s. David Lee and Shirley (Mark) F.; m. Phyllis Marie Young, July 8, 1989; 1 child, Benjamin. AB, Harvard U., 1973; MD, U. Chgo., 1977. Diplomate Am. Bd. Surgery, Am. Bd. Thoracic Surgery. Resident U. Chgo., 1977-81, chief resident gen. surgery, 1981-82, fellow cardiothoracic surgery, 1982-84, asst. prof., 1984-88, assoc. prof., 1988—97, prof., 1998—; chief thoracic surgery U. Chgo. Med. Ctr. Fellow ACS, Am. Assn. Thoracic Surgery, Soc. Thoracic Surgeons, Soc. Surg. Oncology, Am. Surg. Assn. Office: U Chgo Med Ctr MC 5040 5841 S Maryland Ave Chicago IL 60637-1463 Office Phone: 773-702-3551.

FERGUSON, MICHAEL A., congressman; b. Ridgewood, NJ, July 22, 1970; m. Maureen Ferguson; 3 children. BA in govt., U. Notre Dame; M in pub. policy, Georgetown U. Founder, pres. ednl. con. firm; history tchr. Mount St. Michael Acad., Bronx; mem. U.S. Ho. Reps. from 7th N.J. dist., 2001—. Mem. Congress Energy & Commerce com., adj. prof. Brookdale Cmty. Coll., Lincroft, NJ; exec. dir. Better Sch. Found., Catholic Campaign for Am. Mem. Nat. Fedn. Independent Bus., NJ Chamber Commerce, Epilepsy Found. NJ, Delbarton Sch., Friendly Sons of St. Patrick, Nat. Italian-Am. Found., Sierra Club, KC. Republican. Office: 214 Cannon House bldg Washington DC 20515-3007 also: 792 Chimney Rock Rd, Ste E Martinsville NJ 08836*

FERGUSON, MICHAEL JOHN, electronics educator, communications educator; b. Toronto, Ont., Can., May 7, 1941; s. John Albert and Dorothy (Bracewell) F.; m. Virginia Louise Boardman, June 15, 1969; 1 child, Margaret Elizabeth. BASc, U. Toronto, 1962; MS, Calif. Inst. Tech., 1963; PhD, Stanford U., 1966. Engring. specialist Ford Aerospace Co., Palo Alto, Calif., 1966-68; prof. McGill U., Montreal, Que., Can., 1968-76; rsch. assoc., mgr. Aloha system U. Hawaii, Honolulu, 1974-76; rsch. scholar Internat. Inst. Applied Systems Analysis, Laxenburg, Austria, 1976-78; mgr. systems analysis Bell Northern Rsch., Montreal, Que., 1978-82; Cyrille Duquet prof. comm. software INRS-Telecomm., Verdun, Que., 1985-98; prof. emeritus INRS Telecomms., 2001—. Recipient Erskine fellowship, U. Canterbury, 2001. Fellow IEEE; mem. Assn. for Computer Machinery (chmn. spl. interest group on communications 1985-87), Tex User Group (bd. dirs. 1991-96), Sigma Xi. Avocation: bicycle touring. Home: 4336 King Edward Ave Montreal PQ Canada H4B 2H5 E-mail: mjf_ferguson@yahoo.ca.

FERGUSON, MILTON CARR, JR., lawyer; b. Washington, Feb. 10, 1931; s. Milton Carr and Gladys (Emery) F.; m. Marian Evelyn Nelson, Aug. 21, 1954; children: Laura, Sharon, Marcia, Sandra. BA, Cornell U., 1952; LL.B., 1954; LL.M., N.Y. U., 1960. Bar: N.Y. State 1954. Trial atty. tax div. Dept. Justice, Washington, 1954-60, asst. atty. gen., 1977-81; asst. prof. law U. Iowa, 1960-62; assoc. prof. N.Y.U., 1962-65; prof. N.Y. U., 1965-77; vis. prof. law Stanford (Calif.) U., 1972-73; of counsel Wachtell, Lipton, Rosen & Katz, N.Y.C., 1969-76; ptnr. Davis Polk & Wardwell, N.Y.C., 1981—2001, sr. counsel, 2002—. Spl. cons. to Treasury Dept., Commonwealth P.R., 1974 Author: (with others) Federal Income Taxation Legislation in Perspective, 1965, Federal Income Taxation of Estates and Beneficiaries, 1970, 2d edit., 1994. Trustee NYU Law Ctr. Found., Lewis and Clark Coll. Mem. ABA (chmn. tax sect. 1993-94), N.Y. State Bar Assn., Soc. Illustrators. Home: 32 Washington Sq W New York NY 10011-9156 Office: Davis Polk & Wardwell 450 Lexington Ave New York NY 10017-3982

FERGUSON, NIALL CAMPBELL, historian; b. Glasgow, Scotland, Apr. 18, 1964; s. James Campbell Campbell and Molly Archibald Ferguson; m. Susan Margaret Douglas, 1994; 3 children. BA, PhD, Magdalen Coll., Oxford U., 1981—89; Hanseatic Scholar, U. Hamburg, 1986—88. Rsch. fellow Christ's Coll., Cambridge U., 1989—90; official fellow and lectr. Peterhouse, Cambridge, 1990—92; fellow & tutor modern history Jesus Coll., Oxford U., 1992—2000, sr. rsch. fellow, 2003—; prof. polit. & fin. history Oxford U., 2000—02; John E. Herzog prof. fin. history Leonard N. Stern Sch. Bus. NYU, NYC, 2002—04; prof. history Harvard U., 2004—. Judge Samuel Johnson Prize for Non-Fiction, 2001; writer & presenter TV documentaries on modern history; vis. prof. modern European history Oxford U., 2003—. Contbr. articles to newspapers including Sunday Times, Daily Telegraph, Financial Times; author: Paper and Iron: Hamburg Business and German Politics in the Era of Inflation 1897-1927, 1995, The World's Banker: A History of the House of Rothschild, 1998, The Pity of War: Explaining World War I, 1998, The Cash Nexus: Money and Power in the Modern World 1700-2000, 2001, Empire: The Rise and Demise of the British World Order and the Lessons for Global Power, 2002, Colossus: The Price of America's Empire, 2004. Recipient Wadsworth Prize for Bus. History, 1998; Houblon-Norman fellowship, Bank of England, 1998—99. Mem.: German Hist. Soc. (sec. 1991—97). Office: Harvard U Ctr European Studies 27 Kirkland St Cambridge MA 02138

FERGUSON, PAUL-THOMAS, history professor, writer; BA summa cum laude, Western Ill. U., 1996; MA, postgrad., Marquette U., 1998. Tchg. fellow Marquette U., Milw., 1999—2000; history instr. Black Hawk Coll., Moline, Ill., 2001—. Contbr. articles to profl. jours. Recipient Tom Batell scholarship, Black Hawk Coll., 1993, History scholarship, Western Ill. U., 1996; Tchg. fellowship, Marquette U., 1999-2000, Rsch. fellowship, Arthur J. Schmitt Found., 2000-2001. Mem.: Urban History Assn., Orgn. of Am. Historians, Milw. Country Hist. Soc., Am. Hist. Assn., Phi Kappa Phi, Phi Beta Kappa, Phi Alpha Theta. Avocations: fiction writing, film study. Office: Black Hawk Coll 6600 - 34th Ave Moline IL 61265 Office Phone: 309-796-5425. Business E-Mail: fergusonp@bhc.edu.

FERGUSON, R. BRIAN, anthropologist, educator; b. N.Y.C., July 19, 1951; s. Frank C. and Joan Ferguson; m. Leslie E. Farragher, Nov. 24, 1979; 1 child, Elise. BA, Columbia U., 1974, MA, 1976, PhD, 1988. Instr. Rutgers U., Newark, 1983—85, asst. prof., 1985—91, assoc. prof., 1991—99, prof. anthropology, 1999—. Mem.: NY Acad. Scis. (mem. bd. govs. 2002—). Office: Rutgers U Dept Sociology and Anthropology 360 Martin Luther King 603 Hill Newark NJ 07102

FERGUSON, R. NEIL, computer scientist, consultant; b. Dallas, June 22, 1952; s. Roy and Hellon Ferguson; m. L. Jean Ferguson, Aug. 12, 1977; 1 child, Rheachel Claire. BA in Psychology, U. Tex., 1976; grad., Winfield Sch. Race Driving, 1984. Systems engr. EDS, Dallas, 1976-77; systems programmer Collins Radio/Rockwell Internat., Richardson, Tex., 1977-78; systems programmer/analyst Moore Bus. Systems, Denton, Tex., 1978-79; supr., computer graphics Atlantic Richfield Co., Dallas, 1979-85; software engring. specialist E-Systems, Inc., Garland, Tex., 1986-90; dir. product mgmt., graphics and database systems MPSI, Inc., Irving, Tex., 1990-92; pvt. practice computer cons. Lewisville, Tex., 1990—; owner Computer Sys. Svc. & Cons. Co. Tech. program dir. Internat. Microcomputer Exposition, Dallas, 1978. Vol. computer sys. adminstr. Trinity Presbyn. Ch., 1997-2000. Recipient Golden Eagle award Am. Acad. Achievement, Tymshare award Tymshare Corp., Panasonic Sci. Achievement award Matsushita Electric Corp. of Am. and Jr. Engring. Tech. Soc., NASA award, Dallas County Med. Soc. award, 1st Place award in math. and computers 21st Internat. Sci. Fair; featured in Grolier's Sci. Ency. supplement, 1967; named Regional Class Champion, Sports Car Club of Am. Mem. Assn. for Computing Machinery, Spl. Interest Group on Computer Graphics, Am. Congress Surveying and Mapping, Am. Soc. Photogrammetry and Remote Sensing. Avocations: exotic sportscar restoration, stamp collecting/philately, scale model car construction, wrist and pocket watch collecting and restoration, jewelry design. Home and Office: 1097 Holly Ln Lewisville TX 75067-5711

FERGUSON, ROBERT A., law educator; AB, Harvard U., 1964, JD, 1968, PhD, 1974. Lectr. Am. history Harvard U., 1974—75; asst. prof. to prof. English U. Chgo., 1975—89, assoc. chmn. Dept. of English, 1978—84, Andrew W. Mellon prof., 1987—89; George Edward Woodberry prof., Dept. English Columbia U., NYC, 1989—2000, George Edward Woodberry prof., Sch. Law, 2000—. Author: The American Enlightenment, 1750-1820, 1997, Reading the Early Republic, 2004. Fellow: Am. Acad. Arts & Scis. Office: Columbia U Sch Law Mailbox B-23 435 W 116th St New York NY 10027-7297 Office Phone: 212-854-7992. E-mail: ferguson@law.columbia.edu.*

FERGUSON, ROGER W., JR., bank executive, federal agency administrator; b. Washington, Oct. 28, 1951; m. Annette L. Nazareth; two children. BA in Econs. magna cum laude, Harvard U., 1973, JD cum laude, 1979, PhD in Econs., 1981; PhD (hon.), Lincoln Coll., Webster U. Bar: N.Y. 1983. Atty. Davis Polk & Wardwell, N.Y.C., 1981-84; assoc. and ptnr. McKinsey & Co., Inc., N.Y.C., 1984-97; mem. bd. govs. Fed. Res. Sys., Washington, 1997—, vice chmn. Wash., 1999—. Chmn. Joint Yr. 2000 Council, 1998—2000, Group of Ten Working Party on Financial Sector Consolidation, 1999—2001, Comm. on the Global Financial System, 2003—, Financial Stability Forum, 2003—; bd. trustees Inst. Advanced Study, 2004—. Past treas. Friends of Edn.; trustees' com. Mus. Modern Art, N.Y.C.; bd. overseers Harvard U., 2003—. Hon.fellow Pembroke Coll., Cambridge U., 1973-74, 2004-. Office: Fed Res Sys Office of the Vice Chmn 20th & C Sts NW Washington DC 20551-0001

FERGUSON, RONALD EUGENE, reinsurance company executive; b. Chgo., Jan. 16, 1942; s. William and Elizabeth F.; m. Carol Jean Chapp, Dec. 27, 1964; children: Brian, Kristin. BA, Blackburn Coll., 1963; MA, U. Mich., 1965. Statistician Lumbermans Mut. Casualty Co., Long Grove, Ill., 1965-69; actuary Gen. Reins. Corp., Greenwich, Conn., 1969-70, asst. v.p, 1972-74, v.p., 1974-77, sr. v.p., 1977-82, exec. v.p., 1982, dir., 1983, chmn., 1985—, CEO, bd. dirs., 1987—2002; ret., 2002. V.p., group exec. Gen. Re Corp., Stamford, 1981, pres., COO, 1983—87, chmn., pres., CEO, 1987—2002; chmn., bd. dirs. Colgate-Palmolive Co.; bd. dirs. Hartford Fin. Svcs. Group, Cologne Re Corp. Contbr. articles to profl. jours. Served with USPHS, 1966-68. Fellow Casualty Actuarial Soc. (bd. dirs. 1978-81); mem. Am. Acad. Actuaries (dir. 1981—). Clubs: Patterson. Congregationalist. Office: Gen Re Corp Financial Ctr PO Box 10351 Stamford CT 06904-2351

FERGUSON, RONALD STEVEN, artist, educator; b. Galesburg, Ill., Dec. 30, 1947; s. Conley and Dorothy Willadee Ferguson; m. Jeannette Yvonne Brooks, July 14, 1982; children: Amy Martha Haag, Ellen Margaret Aldus, Sean David Kistler. BFA, We. Ill. U., 1971. Car foreman Burlington-Northern RR, Cicero, Ill., 1977—82; art tchr. Ctrl. Unified Sch. Dist. 205, Galesburg, Ill., 1985—. Achievements include patents for a golfcar storage shelf. Home: 1018 Park Side Hill Dr Galesburg IL 61401 Office: Galesburg CUSD 205 1135 W Fremont St Galesburg IL 61401 Office Phone: 309-343-4146. Personal E-mail: fergs@grics.net.

FERGUSON, SARAH, The Duchess of York; b. London, Oct. 15, 1959; d. Ronald Ivor Ferguson and Susan Mary (Fitzherbert Wright) Barrantes; m. Andrew, Duke of York, July 23, 1986 (div. 1996); children: Beatrice Elizabeth Mary, Eugenie Victoria Helena. Student, Hurst Lodge, Sunningdale, Eng., Queen's Secretarial Coll., London. Author: Budgie the Little Helicopter, 1989, Budgie at Bendick's Point, 1989, Budgie Goes to Sea, 1991, Budgie and the Blizzard, 1991, Victoria and Albert-Life at Osborne House, Travels with Queen Victoria, My Story, 1996. Recipient Mother Hale award, 1996. Address: Simon & Schuster Publicity Dept Ste C3A 1230 Avenue Of The Americas Fl Concl New York NY 10020-1586

FERGUSON, STANLEY LEWIS, lawyer; b. Evanston, Ill., Aug. 2, 1952; m. Mary M. Pyle, Aug. 16, 1980; children: Kate, Brooke. BA, Northwestern U., 1975; JD cum laude, Boston U., 1978. Bar: Ill. 1978, US Dist. Ct. No. Dist. Ill. 1978, US Ct. Appeals 6th and 7th circuits. Assoc. Kirkland & Ellis, Chgo., 1978-85, ptnr., 1985-87; named asst. gen. counsel USG Corp., Chgo., 1987, assoc. gen. counsel litig., v.p., assoc. gen. counsel, 1999—2000, v.p., gen. counsel, 2000—01, sr. v.p., gen. counsel, 2001—04, exec. v.p., gen. counsel, 2004—. Mem. ABA, Ill. Bar Assn., Legal Club Chgo. Office: USG Corp 125 S Franklin St Chicago IL 60606-4678 Office Phone: 312-606-5387.

FERGUSON, SYBIL, retired franchise business executive; b. Barnwell, Alta., Can., Feb. 7, 1934; came to U.S., 1938, naturalized, 1976; d. Alva John and Xarissa (Merkley) Clarke; m. Roger N. Ferguson, July 10, 1952; children: Debra Kay, Michael David, Wade Clarke, Lois Christine, Julie Xarissa. Ed. pub. schs. Founder Diet Ctr. Inc., Pitts., 1970—. Co-owner Golden Eagle Ranches. Author: The Diet Center Program, Lose Weight Fast and Keep It Off Forever, 1983, Diet Center Cookbook. Charter mem. women's aux. Madison Meml. Hosp., Rexburg; founding sponsor Children's Miracle Network Telethon; past mem. nat. adv. coun. Brigham Young U., adv. bd. Ricks Coll., Boise State U.; mem. Rexburg Civic Assn. Charter mem. women's aux. Madison Meml. Hosp., Rexburg; founding sponsor Children's Miracle Network Telethon; past mem. nat. adv. coun. Brigham Young U., adv. bd. Ricks Coll., Boise State U.; mem. Rexburg Civic Assn. Mem. Internat. Franchise Assn., Am. Entrepreneur Assn., Rexburg C. of C. (program dir. 1976), Com. of 200 (founder). Mem. LDS Ch. Lodge: Soroptimists (v.p. Rexburg chpt. 1975, award 1979). Office: PO Box 519 Rexburg ID 83440-0519

FERGUSON, THOMAS CROOKS, lawyer; b. Nov. 27, 1933; s. Thomas C. and Grace (Crooks) F.; children: Leslie Mead, Ian Thomas. AB, Vanderbilt U., 1955, JD, 1959; cert., Hague Acad. Internat. Law, 1958; postgrad., Kenney Sch. Govt., Harvard U., 1985. Bar: Ill. 1960, Ky. 1961, D.C. 1993; D.C. Ct. Appeals, 1995, US Supreme Ct., 1995. Bd. mem. Mead Johnson Found., 1960-70, Taylor Energy, Taylor Found.; mktg. mgr. Pharmaseal Labs., 1962-75; pres. Atlantic Salvage Corp., 1975-78, Brevard Marina, 1977-82; dir. Eastern Caribbean Peace Corps, 1982-84; dep. commr. Immigration and Naturalization Service Dept. Justice, 1984-87; U.S. amb. to Brunei Darussalam, 1987-89; pres. Airscan Internat., Indialantic, Fla., 1989-91; pvt. practice Washington, 1991—. With U.S. Army, 1955-58. Recipient Comdr.'s medal for civilian svc. Grenada, 1983. Mem. ABA, Fed. Bar Assn. Clubs: Offshore Cruising of Calif., Eau Gallie Yacht, Epping Forest Yacht Club. Avocations: sailing, tennis, diving. Home: 1306 Oak Haven Rd Jacksonville FL 32207-2219 E-mail: hetf1@comcast.net.

FERGUSON, THOMAS GEORGE, retired healthcare advertising agency executive; b. Newark, Oct. 14, 1941; s. George Francis and Dorothy Marie (Stinson) F.; m. Roberta Chiaviello, Jan. 27, 1967; children: Thomas, Jr., Michael, Cathleen, Margaret. BS in Bus. Mgmt., Fairleigh Dickinson U., 1965. Product mgr. Bard-Parker div. Becton Dickinson & Co., Lincoln Park, N.J., 1965-70; acct. exec. L.W. Frolich, Inc., 1970-71; v.p., acct. group supr. Sudler & Hennessey, Inc., N.Y.C., 1971-74; chmn., pres. Thomas G. Ferguson Assocs., Inc., Parsippany, N.J., 1974—; chmn. Ferguson Common Health USA. Mem. Hemophilia Assn. N.J., 1981-98, ret., 1998; bd. dirs. Tri-County Scholarship Fund, Paterson, N.J., 1982—; pres., bd. trustees Epilepsy Found. N.J., Trenton, 1982—; past pres., bd. mem. Delbarton Sch. Fathers & Friends, Morristown, N.J. Served with USNG, 1971. Recipient Humanitarian award Hemophilia Assn. N.J., 1985, Disting. Svc. award Epilepsy Found. N.J., 1987. Mem. Pharm. Advt. Club, Pharm. Mfrs. Assn., Midwest Pharm. Advt. Club, Nat. Wholesale Druggists' Assn., Bus. Publication Audits, Fairleigh Dickinson U. Alumni Assn. Republican. Roman Catholic. Clubs: Morris County Golf (bd. dirs. 1975—), Baltusrol Golf. Avocation: golf. Office: Ferguson Common Health USA 30 Lanidex Plz W Parsippany NJ 07054-2717

FERGUSON, TIM WAYNE, editor, journalist; b. Santa Ana, Calif., May 23, 1955; s. Harold Lee and Patricia (Shepard) F. BA in Econs., Stanford (Calif.) U., 1977. News reporter, editor Orange County Register, Santa Ana, 1977-81, editorial pages editor, 1981-83; corr. Sta. KOCE-TV, Huntington Beach, Calif., 1979; editorial features editor Wall Street Jour., N.Y.C., 1983-90, bus. world columnist, mem. editorial bd. L.A., 1990—95; west coast bureau mgr. Forbes, 1995—98, asst. mng. editor, 1998—2002, editor, Forbes Global, 2002—. Contbr. articles to political jours. Office: Forbes Mag 60 5th Ave New York NY 10011

FERGUSON, TIMOTHY HOWARD, music educator; b. Tupelo, Miss., Feb. 12, 1975; s. Merle Morris and Mary Ruth Ferguson; m. Jennifer Lynn Cook, Dec. 16, 1997; 1 child, Sarah. MusB Edn., U. Miss., Miss., 1999. Cert. Music Edn. 1999. Dir. of bands Hatley H.S., Amory, Miss., 1999—2001; asst. dir. of bands Saltillo High, Guntown Mid. Schs., Saltillo, Miss., 2001—. Mem.: Miss. Bandmasters Assn. (mem. 1999—2002). Conservative. Meth. Home: 409 Highway 6 West Pontotoc MS 38863 Office: Guntown Middle Sch Band Saltillo H P O Drawer 8 Guntown MS 38849 Personal E-mail: tjferguson@watervalley.net.

FERGUSON, TOM C., music educator, department chairman; s. Thomas C. and Bertha E. Ferguson; m. Trude McMahon, Apr. 5, 2003; children: Shari Paris, Terry Shade. BME, Murray (Ky.) State U., 1954; MusM, Eastman Sch. Music, 1957, PhD, 1972. With U.S. Naval Sch. Music U.S. Army, Washington, 1957—59; dir. bands U. Memphis, 1960—73; dir. jazz studies Ariz. State U., Tempe, Ariz., 1973—77; chmn. Dept. Performing Arts C.C. So. Nev., North Las Vegas, 1978—. Commentator KOOC TV, Phoenix, 1976—78. Co-author: The Jazz-Rock Ensemble; contbr. articles to mags. Mem.: NEA (mem. jazz panel 1975—77), ASCAP, Am. Fedn. Musicians, Internat. Assn. Jazz Edn. (pres. 1977—79). Republican. Meth. Avocation: songwriting. Home: 3001 Hartsville Rd Henderson NV 89053 Office: CCSN 3200 East Cheyenne Ave North Las Vegas NV 89030

FERGUSON, WARREN JOHN, federal judge; b. Eureka, Nev., Oct. 31, 1920; s. Ralph and Marian (Damele) Ferguson; m. E. Laura Keyes, June 5, 1948; children: Faye F., Warren John, Teresa M., Peter J. BA, U. Nev., 1942; LLB, U. So. Calif., 1949; LLD (hon.), Western State U., San Fernando Valley Coll. Law. Bar: Calif. 1950. Mem. firm Ferguson & Judge, Fullerton, Calif., 1950—59; city atty. for cities of Buena Park, Placentia, La Puente, Baldwin Park, Santa Fe Springs, Walnut and Rosemead, Calif., 1953—59; mcpl. ct. judge Anaheim, Calif., 1959—60; judge Superior Ct., Santa Ana, Calif., 1961—66, Juvenile Ct., 1963—64, Appellate Dept., 1965—66; U.S. dist. judge Los Angeles, 1966—79; judge U.S. Circuit Ct. (9th cir.), Los Angeles, 1979—86; sr. judge U.S. Ct. Appeals (9th cir.), Santa Ana, 1986—; faculty Fed. Jud. Ctr., Practising Law Inst., U. Iowa Coll. Law, N.Y. Law Jour. Assoc. prof. psychiatry (law) Sch. Medicine, U. So. Calif.; assoc. prof. Loyola Law Sch. With U.S. Army, 1942—46. Decorated Bronze Star. Mem.: Orange County Bar Assn., Calif. Bar Assn., ABA, Theta Chi, Phi Kappa Phi. Democrat. Roman Catholic. Office: US Courthouse 411 W 4th St Ste 10080 Santa Ana CA 92701-4500 Office Phone: 714-338-4680. E-mail: judge_ferguson@ca9.uscourts.gov.

FERGUSON, WENDELL, private school educator; b. Sandersville, Ga., May 6, 1954; d. Isadore and Willie Mae (Roberts) Jordan; m. Larry Brown Sr., May 28, 1971 (div. Dec. 1985); children: Larry Brown Jr., Dwyne Lamont Brown, Anthony Patrick Brown; m. Jerry Lang Ferguson, Sept. 28, 1992 (div.). Diploma, Alphena C.C., 1972; student, Ga. State U., 1983-87. Sales clk. U.S. NAS, Albany, Ga., 1972-74, 76-77; substitute tchr. Ga. Dept. Edn., Houston County, 1976-77; nutritionist (nursery) Howard AFB, Panama Canal, 1980; joined Sweet Adelines, Inc., Tulsa, 1981; data entry operator dept. budget mgmt. Atlanta City Hall, 1982; mgr., operator Atlanta Connections, 1982-83; asst. supr. micro-film Ga. Dept. Revenue, Atlanta, 1986-88; loan broker Cherokee Funding Inc., Thomaston, Ga., 1989—; promotional sales rep. RG Clothier/L.B. Holyfield, Atlanta, 1992-95; substitute tchr. Old Nat. Christian Acad., College Park, Ga., 1995—; owner, wholesale dist. Dells' Clevor Enterprises, 2000. Libr. YWCA, Rochester, N.Y., 1999; co-prodr., writer, owner Jeri-Del Prodns., Atlanta; asst. to owner New Dimension Realistate & Mortgage co., 2005—; with Mass Entertainment Group, 2005—. Actress, singer, dancer various prodns. (Irving Berlin award 1982); author: Times In Life, 1996. Vol. persona bus. broker Asst. Sec. of State, Atlanta, 1994, J.D. Sims Recreation Ctr., 2000, Atlanta; Gospel Fest judge, 1995, coord. nominees judgeship position Fayette, Pike, Upson & Spaulding Counties, Ga., 1992; surveyor for st. lights, Atlanta, 1982; vol. Fulton County Dept. Parks and Recreation, Burdett Gym, 1996—; active We Are Today and Tomorrow; founder Steadfast Children Learning Systems Atlanta Coalition of Chs., 1997. Recipient Gold Citizens Acheivement award Mayor William Campbell, 1997. Democrat. Avocations: horseback riding, chess, painting, cooking, tennis. Personal E-mail: dellthangs@aol.com.

FERGUSON, WHITWORTH, III, pastor; b. Buffalo, Aug. 16, 1954; s. Whitworth and Elizabeth Ferguson Jr.; m. Patricia Pierson, May 5, 2000. BA in Econs., St. Lawrence U., Canton, N.Y., 1976; MBA in Fin., U. Pa., 1978; JD, Cornell U., 1981; MDiv, Princeton Theol. Sem., 1999. Bar: Ill. 1981, N.Y. 1983. Assoc. McDermott, Will & Emery, Chgo., 1981—82, Damon & Morey, Buffalo, 1982—84; officer fin. planning Key Trust Co., Buffalo, 1984—86; pres. Alpine Sports, Ltd., Williamsville, NY, 1986—90, Buffalo Consulting Co., Buffalo, 1990—94; editor The Economist Intelligence Unit, N.Y.C., 1994—96; pastor The First Presbyn. Ch., 2000—. Mng. dir. The NORAM Group, Ltd., Buffalo, 1990-94. Contbg. editor Knowledge@Wharton, 1999—2004. Bd. dirs. Senecare Corp., 1983-88, YMCA Greater Buffalo, 1985-94, vice chmn., 1988-90; ho. of dels. United Way Buffalo and Erie County, 1984-94; chmn. campaign for creativity Creative Edn. Found.; advisor ctr. entrepreneurial leadership Sch. Mgmt., SUNY, Buffalo, 1991-94; dir. Western N.Y. Venture Assn., 1991-94; mem. Westminster Presbyn. Trustees, 1989-91, ruling elder, 1992; advisor Ctr. for Entrepreneurship, Canisius Coll., 1992-94; bd. gov.'s Stony Point Conf. Ctr., 2001-04.

FERGUSON, WILLIAM MCDONALD, rancher, writer, banker, retired lawyer, former state official; b. Wellington, Kans., Dec. 2, 1917; s. William McDonald and May (Deems) F.; m. Harriet Shelden, Sept. 12, 1939; children— Joan, William McDonald III. AB, U. Kans., 1938; LLB, Harvard U., 1941. Bar: Kans. 1946. City atty., Wellington, 1948—57; gen. practice law, 1948—73; atty. gen., 1961—65; pres. Security State Bank, Wellington, 1958—74, chmn. bd., 1974—85, chmn. emeritus, 1985—. Co-mgr. Ferguson Ranch, Ferguson Cattle Co., 1965—, Spur Cattle Co., 1980-96; pres. Ferguson Ranch, Inc., 1993—. Author: (with John Q. Royce) Maya Ruins of Mexico in Color, 1977, Maya Ruins in Central America in Color, 1984; (with Arthur H. Rohn) Anasazi Ruins of the Southwest, 1986, Mesoamerica's Ancient Cities, 1990, 2d edit. (with R.E.W. Adams), 2001, revised edit., 2004, Anasazi of Mesa Verde and the Four Corners, 1996. Mem. Kans. Ho. of Reps. 69th Dist., 1949-57. Served to lt. (s.g.) USNR, 1942-46. Mem. ABA (ho. dels. 1961-62), Kans. Bar Assn. (exec. coun. 1952-61, v.p. 1961, pres. 1963), Am. Legion, Elks, Sigma Alpha Epsilon Republican. Home: PO Box 236 101 N Washington Wellington KS 67152-3813 E-mail: wmferg@frontier.net.

FERGUSON, YALE HICKS, political scientist, educator; b. Austin, Tex., May 28, 1940; s. Phil Moss and Marion (Hicks) Ferguson; m. Kitty Gail Vetter, Aug. 26, 1961; children: Colin Yale, Duff Christopher, Caitlin Christiana. BA magna cum laude, Trinity U., 1960; PhD, Columbia U., 1967. Lectr. CUNY, Bklyn., 1965; instr. Rutgers U., Newark, 1966-67, from asst. prof. to assoc. prof. polit. sci., 1967—77, prof., 1977-98, prof. II, 1998—, chmn. dept. polit. sci., 1985-90, 96-01, co-dir. Ctr. for Global Change and Governance, 2002—. Hon. prof. U. Salzburg, Austria, 2002—; rschr. Fgn. Svc. Inst. U.S. Dept. State, Washington, 1979. Author (with R.W. Mansbach): The Web of World Politics: Nonstate Actors in the Global System, 1976, The Elusive Quest: Theory and International Politics, 1988, The State Conceptual Chaos and the Future of International Relations Theory, 1989, Polities: Authority, Identities and Change, 1996, The Elusive Quest Continues: Theory and Global Politics, 2003, Remapping Global Politics: History's Revenge and Future Shock, 2004; contbg. editor: Handbook L.A. Studies, 1979—86; co-editor: Continuing Issues in International Politics, 1973, Political Space: Frontiers of Change and Governance in a Globalizing World, 2002; editor: Contemporary Inter-American Relations, 1972; contbr. articles to profl. jours., chpts. to books; mem. adv. bd. European Jour. Internat. Rels., 1995—2000, Internat. Studies Quar., 1998—2003, Internat. Studies Rev., 2003—, Global Governance, 2005—. Named Fulbright prof., U. Salzburg, 1992—93; recipient Bd. Trustees award Excellence in Rsch., Rutgers U., 1999; fellow, Norwegian Nobel Inst., 1996; scholar, U. Padova, 2001—02; Ctr. Internat. Studies fellow, Cambridge U., 1986—87, 1991. Mem.: AAUP, Commn. of History Internat. Rels., Mid Atlantic Coun. L.Am. Studies (exec. com. 1988—90), Brit. Internat. Studies Assn., Internat. Studies Assn. (NE bd. dirs. 1996—2000), Clare Hall (life). Episcopalian. Avocations: tennis, swimming, photography. Office: Rutgers U Ctr for Global Change and Governance 123 Washington St Ste 510 Newark NJ 07102 Office Phone: 973-353-5585. Business E-Mail: yhfergus@andromeda.rutgers.edu.

FERGUSSON, DIANNE SMITH, secondary school educator; b. Laurinburg, N.C., July 20, 1945; d. Carson O'Kella and Dottie (Gause) Smith; m. W.E. Fergusson III, July 31, 1971 (div. Mar. 1987); 1 child, Molly Eleanor. BS in Edn., Western Carolina U., 1966; MA in English, U. S.C., 1971, PhD in English, 1974. Tchr. English Union Pines High Sch., Carthage, N.C., 1966-67; vol. U.S. Peace Corps, Burkina Fasso, Africa, 1967-69; tchr. English Scotland County Schs., Laurinburg, N.C., 1969; reporter, feature writer Laurinburg Exchange, 1969-70; teaching asst. U. S.C., Columbia, 1970-74; rsch. analyst Dept. Youth Svcs., Columbia, 1974-76; adj. instr. Midlands Tech. Coll., Columbia, 1976-79, chmn. dept., 1979-84; tchr. advanced placement English Irmo High Sch., Columbia, 1985—98, chair dept. English, 1994—98; dir. grad. regional studies U. S.C., Columbia, 1998—2000; tchr. Dorman H.S., 2000—02, English tchr., testing coach, 2005—; tchr. specialist office tchr. quality SC Dept. Edn., 2002—05. Adj. instr. Newberry (S.C.) Coll., 1976-79; cons. Skills Devel. Systems, Columbia, 1986—; adj. prof. mgmt. comm. Webster U. Grad. Sch., 1990-98, faculty coord., 1994-98, acad. advisor, 1987-93; freelance writer. Co-author: Internal Audit Training Program, 1982; copy editor Y'all Mag., 2004—. Mem.: Foothills Artisan Guild (stained glass artist).

FERGUSSON, FRANCES DALY, academic administrator, educator; b. Boston, Oct. 3, 1944; d. Francis Joseph and Alice (Storrow) Daly. BA, Wellesley Coll., 1965; MA, Harvard U., 1966, PhD, 1973; DLitt, U. Hartford, 2000, U. London, 2001. Asst. prof. Newton Coll., Mass., 1969—75; assoc. prof. U. Mass., Boston, 1974—82, asst. chancellor, 1980—82; provost, prof. Bucknell U., Lewisburg, Pa., 1982—86; pres. Vassar Coll., Poughkeepsie, NY, 1986—. Bd. dirs. HSBC Bank USA, Wyeth Pharms.; trustee Mayo Found., 1988—2002, chmn., 1998—2002; trustee Ford Found., 1989—2001, Hist. Hudson, 1990—99. Bd. overseers Harvard U., 2002—; bd. dirs. Noguchi Found., 2004—. Recipient Founder's award Soc. Archtl. Historians, 1973, Eleanor Roosevelt at Val-Kill medal, 1998, Centennial medal Harvard Grad. Sch. of Arts and Scis., 1999. Fellow: Am. Acad. Arts and Scis.; mem.: Fgn. Policy Assn. (bd. dirs. 2003—). Avocation: piano. Office: Vassar Coll PO Box 1 Poughkeepsie NY 12604-0001

FERHOLT, J. DEBORAH LOTT, pediatrician; b. New Rochelle, N.Y., Aug. 27, 1942; d. Sidney and Rose Lott; m. Julian Ferholt, June 19, 1963; children: Beth, Sarah. BS in Biology, U. Rochester, 1963, MD, 1967. Diplomate Am. Bd. Pediatrics. From instr. to assoc. prof. Yale Sch. Nursing, New Haven, 1969-90, lectr., 1990—2001, clin. assoc. prof. pediatrics, 1987—2003; pvt. practice pediatrics New Haven, 1982—. Author: (book) Health Assessment of Children, 1980 (Best Pediatric Book award 1981). Fellow Am. Acad. Pediatrics. Office: 303 Whitney Ave New Haven CT 06511-7204 Office Phone: 203-776-1243.

FERLAND, BRENDA L., state representative; b. Lebanon, N.H., Oct. 23, 1949; d. Wilbur Fred Snelling and Lorraine Latouche; m. Daniel Edward Ferland; children: Lisa Marie, James Daniel. State rep. N.H. Ho. of Reps., Concord, 1997-98, 2001—. Treas. Charlestown (N.H.) Econ. Assn. Tourism, 1996-, Jesse Farwell Sch. Trust, 1990-95; mem. Charlestown Bd. of Select, 2000—, N.H. Traffic Safety Commn., 1998-, VFW Ladies Aux., 1999. Office: NH State Legis State House Concord NH 03301

FERLAND, E. JAMES, electric power industry executive; b. Boston, Mar. 19, 1942; s. Ernest James and Muriel (Cassell) F.; m. Eileen Kay Patridge, Mar. 9, 1964; children: E. James, Elizabeth Denise. BS in Mech. Engring., U. Maine, 1964; MBA, U. New Haven, 1979; postgrad., Harvard U. Grad. Sch. Bus. Adminstrn. Electric utility engr. HELCO, New London, Conn., 1964-67; supt. nuclear ops. NNECO, Waterford, Conn., 1967-78; dir. rate regulation N.E. Utilities, Berlin, Conn., 1978-79, v.p., CFO, 1980-83, pres., COO, 1983-86; chmn., pres., CEO Pub. Svc. Enterprise Group Inc., Newark, 1986—; pres. Pub. Svc. Electric & Gas Co., 1986—91, chmn., CEO, 1986—. Former dir. Vermont Yankee Nuclear Power Corp., Yankee Atomic Electric Co., Maine Yankee Atomic Power Co.; former chmn. NJ State Chamber of Commerce, Metro Newark Chamber of Commerce, Public Affairs Rsch. Inst. of NJ, Inst. of Nuclear Power Ops., Electric Power Rsch. Inst.; bd. dirs. subcoms. Pub. Svc. Enterprise Group. Mem.: com. for econ. devel. Office: Pub Svc Enterprise Group Inc 80 Park Plz # 4B Newark NJ 07102-4194*

FERLINGHETTI, LAWRENCE, poet; b. Yonkers, N.Y., 1919; s. Charles and Clemence (Mendes-Monsanto) F.; children: Julie, Lorenzo. AB, U. N.C.; MA, Columbia U., Doctorat de l'Université, mention très honorable, Sorbonne, 1950. Founder (with Peter D. Martin) first all paperbound bookstore in U.S., City Lights Books, San Francisco, 1955-, City Lights Rev., firm also publishes works of modern poets and writers; widely traveled poetry reader, also painter; participant (with Allen Ginsberg), Pan Am. cultural conf., U. Concepcion, Chile, 1960; participant, One World Poetry Festival, Amsterdam, 1981, Internat. Poetry Festival of Rome, 1979-85, World Congress of Poets, Florence, Italy, 1986, U.N. World Poetry Day, Delphi, Greece, 2000; author: poetry Pictures of the Gone World, 1955, A Coney Island of the Mind, 1958, Starting from San Francisco, 1961, The Secret Meaning of Things, Open Eye, Open Heart, 1973, Who Are We Now?, 1976, Landscapes of Living and Dying, 1979, Endless Life: Selected Poems, 1981, Over All the Obscene Boundaries, 1984, These Are My Rivers: New and Selected Poems, 1955-1993, 1993; novel Her, 1960, Routines; plays Back Roads to Far Places; (poetry) A Far Rockaway of the Heart, 1997; poetry and prose jour. Northwest Ecolog, 1978, (with Nancy J. Peters) Literary San Francisco: A Pictorial History, 1980; Seven Days in Nicaragua Libre, 1984, novel Love in the Days of Rage, 1988, How to Print Sunlight, 2001, Americus: Book One, 2004; performed in literary events Winter Olympic Games, Calgary, 1988; one-man exhbns., paintings: Butler Inst. Am. Art, Youngstown, Ohio, 1993, Retrospective Painting Exhbn. Palazzo delle Esposizioni, Rome, 1996. Lt. comdr. USNR, World War II, Normandy. A San Francisco street named in his honor, 1994; recipient poetry prize City of Rome, 1993; Premio Internazionale Flaiano, Italy, 1999, di Ostia, Italy, 99, Premio Internazionale di Camaiore, Italy, 1999, Premio Cavour, Italy, 2000, Poet Laureate of San Francisco, 1998-2000, L.A. Times Book Festival Lifetime Achievement award, 2001, Am. Civil Liberties Union award, 2001, elected to the Am. Acad. of Arts and Letters, 2003, Authors Guild Lifetime Achievement award, 2003, Robert Frost medal Poetry Soc Am, 2003; Curtis Benjamin award for creative publishing, 2005. Address: City Lights Booksellers and Pubs 261 Columbus Ave San Francisco CA 94133-4519 Office Phone: 415-362-1901.

FERLINZ, JACK, cardiologist, medical educator; b. Marburg, Austria, Feb. 18, 1942; came to U.S., 1957. s. Anthony and Maria (Nachtigall) F. AB, Harvard U.; MBA, Northeastern U., 1965; MD, Boston U., 1969; doctorate (hon.), U. Maribor, Slovenia, 1990. Diplomate Am. Bd. Internal Medicine, Am. Bd. Cardiovascular Diseases. Intern. U. Hosp. Boston U., 1969-70; jr. resident M. Hitchcock Hosp. Dartmouth Med. Sch., Hanover, N.H., 1970-71; sr. resident Jackson Meml. Hosp., U. Miami, 1971-72; NIH rsch. fellow cardiology P.B. Brigham Hosp., Harvard U., Boston, 1972-74; dir. cardiac cath. lab., asst. chief cardiology V.A.M.C., Long Beach, Calif., 1974-82; asst. prof. medicine U. Calif., Irvine, 1975-81, assoc. prof. medicine, 1981-82; chmn. adult cardiology Cook County Hosp., Chgo., 1982-88; prof. medicine Chgo. Med. Sch., North Chicago, Ill., 1984-88; chmn. dept. of internal medicine Providence Hosp., Southfield, Mich., 1988-92; clin. prof. medicine Wayne State U. Sch. Medicine, Detroit, 1989-92; dir. med. edn. & rsch., prof. medicine & cardiology Hamad Med. Ctr., Doha, Qatar, 1992-94; chief dept. medicine Aleda E. Lutz VA Med. Ctr., Saginaw, Mich., 1994—; clin. prof. medicine Mich. State U. Coll. Human Medicine, 1994—. Vis. prof. numerous U.S., Canadian and European med. schs., 1980—. Mem. editl. bds. Am. Jour. Cardiology, 1989—, Am. Jour. Noninvas Cardiology, 1987—, Jour. Am. Coll. Cardiology, 1984-88, 89-93; contbr. over 300 book chpts. and sci. papers. Named to Begg's Soc. Boston U. Sch. Medicine, 1969. Fellow Am. Coll. Cardiology, Am. Coll. Chest Physicians (chmn. coronary sect. 1983-85), Am. Heart Assn., Am. Coll. Physicians, Am. Coll. Angiology; mem. Am. Fedn. Clin. Rsch., Am. Soc. Clin. Pharm. Therapy. Avocations: mountain climbing, skiing, tennis, scuba diving. Office: VA Med Ctr 1500 Weiss St Saginaw MI 48602-5251 Office Phone: 989-497-2500 x3520. Business E-Mail: jack.ferlinz@med.va.gov.

FERM, LOIS ROUGHAN, retired religious organization administrator; b. Buffalo, Feb. 5, 1918; d. Laurence Roughan and Bertha Margaret Lucy (Jopp) R.; m. Robert O. Ferm, June 28, 1941 (dec. Mar. 1994); children: Lois Esther, Rebecca Ann, Paul Robert, Stephen John. BA, Houghton Coll., 1939; MA, U. Mich., 1955; PhD, U. Minn., 1972. Cert. tchr., N.Y. Tchr. Rushford (N.Y.) Cen. Sch., 1939-41; instr. library, sociology John Brown U., Siloam Springs, Ark., 1949-51; librarian Cuba (N.Y.) Cen. Schs., 1953-55; chmn. dept. edn. Houghton (N.Y.) Coll., 1955-57; instr. edn. U. Minn., Mpls., 1959-61, mgr. Coll. Edn. Library, 1961-64; personal asst. rsch., resource coord. Billy Graham Evangel. Assn., Mpls., 1973—2005; ret., 2005. Pres. Riceville Property Owners Assn., Asheville, N.C., 1982, 83, 87, 88; bd. dirs. N.C. Arboretum, 1992-96. Mem. Soc. Am. Archivists, Oral History Assn., Pi Lambda Theta. Republican. Baptist. Avocations: sewing, gardening, walking. Home: 200 Tabernacle Rd J226 Black Mountain NC 28711

FERM, ROBERT LIVINGSTON, religion educator; b. Wooster, Ohio, Jan. 2, 1931; s. Vergilius Ture Anselm and Nellie Agnette (Nelson) F.; m. Fleur Kinney, June 28, 1952 (div. 1968); children: Eric, Alison; m. Sonja Olson. BA, Coll. Wooster, 1952; BD, Yale U., 1955, MA, 1956, PhD, 1958. From instr. to assoc. prof. religion Pomona Coll., Claremont, Calif., 1958-67, prof., 1967-69, acting chmn. dept. religion, 1960-63, chmn. dept. religion, 1963-69; prof., chmn. dept. religion Middlebury (Vt.) Coll., 1969-94, Pardon E. Tillinghast prof. religion, 1988-2000, Tillinghast prof. religion emeritus, 2000. Author: Jonathan Edwards The Younger 1745-1801: A Colonial Pastor, 1976, Piety, Purity Plenty: Images of Protestantism in America, 1991; editor Readings in the History of Christian Thought, 1964, Issues in American Protestantism, 1969. Mem. Am. Acad. Religion. Presbyterian. Home: PO Box 752 Middlebury VT 05753-0052

FERMANIS, ERNEST GEORGE, urological surgeon; b. N.Y.C., May 15, 1944; s. George Anastasios and Georgia Martha Fermanis; m. Pauline Angelique Papageorgopoulos Moore, Feb. 20, 1982; children: Nicole Elaine, Alexis Georgette. BS cum laude, CUNY, 1966; MA cum laude, Columbia U., 1969; MD, Vanderbilt U., 1974. Diplomate Am. Bd. Urology, Nat. Bd. Med. Examiners. Intern Albert Einstein Med. Sch. Montefiore Med. Sch., N.Y.C.; resident NYU Med. Ctr.; assoc. clin. prof. urology, urologic surgeon Crawford Long Hosp. of Emory U., Atlanta, 1982—. Columbia U. scholar, 1966-69. Mem. AMA, AMA Southeastern Sect., Am. Urol. Assn., Am. Urol.

Assn. Southeastern Sect., Ga. Urol. Assn., Med. Assn. Ga., Atlanta Urol. Assn., Med. Assn. Atlanta, Am. Hellenic Ednl. Progressive Assn., Lions Club, Phi Beta Kappa. Greek Orthodox. Avocations: reading, pets. Home: 3056 Slaton Dr NW Atlanta GA 30305-2007

FERN, ALAN MAXWELL, art historian, retired museum director; b. Detroit, Oct. 19, 1930; s. Martin and Rose F.; m. Lois Ann Karbel, Mar. 17, 1957. AB, U. Chgo., 1950, MA, 1954, PhD, 1960. Asst., instr., asst. prof. humanities The Coll., U. Chgo., 1952-61; asst. curator prints and photographs divsn. Libr. of Congress, Washington, 1961, curator fine prints, 1962-64, asst. chief, 1964-73, chief, 1973-76, dir. rsch. dept., 1976-78, dir. spl. collections, 1978-82; dir. Nat. Portrait Gallery, 1982-2000; ret., 2000. Author: A Note on the Eragny Press, 1957, (with others) Art Nouveau, 1960, (with M. Constantine) Word and Image, 1968, Leonard Baskin, 1970, (with M. Constantine) Revolutionary Soviet Film Posters, 1974; introductory essay Lasansky: Printmaker, 1975, Eichenberg, The Wood and the Graver, 1977, People and Power, 1985, Arnold Newman's Americans, 1992, (with H. Wright) Prints at the Smithsonian, 1996; contbr. articles to profl. jours. Bd. dirs. Smart Mus. Art, Chgo., Washington; active U.S Senate Curatorial Adv. Bd., State Md. Commn. on Artistic Property. Decorated chevalier Ordre de la Couronne (Belgium), Ordre des Arts et Lettres (France), comdr. Royal Order of Polar Star (Sweden); Fulbright scholar Courtauld Inst., U. London, 1954-55. Mem. Print Coun. Am. (past pres.), Coll. Art Assn., Am. Antiquarian Soc., AIA (hon.), Double Crown Club (hon.), Cosmos Club (bd. dirs.), Grolier Club (NYC). Home: 3605 Raymond St Chevy Chase MD 20815-4151

FERNALD, HAROLD ALLEN, publishing executive; b. Haverhill, Mass., June 1, 1932; s. Harold Allen and Leona Swan (Horton) F.; m. Sally Camilla Carroll, June 23, 1956; children: Robert Arthur, Melissa Anne, Thomas Allen. BA in Psychology, U. Maine, 1954; MBA, NYU, 1964; PhD, U. Maine, 2002. Trainee Nat. Shawmut Bank, Boston, 1954—55; sales Carter's Ink Co., Cambridge, Mass., 1955—56; sect. chief Western Electric Co., Andover, Mass., 1956—60, buyer N.Y.C., 1960—64; corp. devel. Holt Rinehart & Winston, N.Y.C., 1964—66, pers. dir., 1966—68, mgr. adminstrn., 1968—70; v.p. adminstrn. CBS, Inc. Pub. Group, 1970—77, v.p., gen. mgr. coll. pub. divsn., 1971—77; pub. Down East mag., Fly Rod and Reel mag., Fly Tackle Dealer Mag., Shooting Sportsman Mag., Fishing Tackle Trade News; pres. Down East Enterprise, Inc., Camden, Maine, 1977—2002, chmn., 2002—; pres. Twin City Printery, Inc., Lewiston, Maine, 1978—80, Fernald-Spahn Enterprise, Inc., Rockport, Maine, 1978—80; pres., treas. Hanson Energy Products, Inc., Newcastle, Maine, 1981—85; co-chmn., treas. Global Info. Inc., N.Y.C., 1987—95; pub., CEO Fishing Tackle Trade News, 1995—99. Bd. dirs. John Wiley & Sons., Inc., N.Y.C., 1978-2003, United Publs., Inc., Foreside Co., Inc., Sun Jour., Inc., U. Maine Press; chmn. Performance Media, LLP, 2000—. Vice chmn. Maine Gov.'s Coun. Vacation Travel, 1979-81; bd. dirs. N.E. Health Found., 1982-89, 91-99; bd. dirs. U. Maine-Orono Devel. Found., 1982—, vice chair, 1991, chmn., 1992-93; mem. U. Maine Pres.'s Coun., 1995-97, bd. visitors, vice chmn., 2000-2002, chmn., 2003—; bd. dirs. Maine Cmty. Found., 1989-99, Bay Chamber Concerts, Inc., 1981-85, U. Maine Alumni Coun.; v.p. Farnsworth Mus., 1985-88, pres., 1988-93; chair Knox County Fund, 1996-99, Expansion Arts Fund, 1995-99; mem. Maine Gov.'s Bus. Adv. Com., 1985-86; v.p. Maine Tourism Commn., 1981-89; pres. 1st Congl. Ch., Camden, 1985-86; dir. The Camden Conf., 1987-92. Mem. Assn. Am. Pubs., Internat. Regional Mag. Assn. (dir., pres. 1988-89), Camden-Rockport C. of C. (dir. 1977-85), Alpha Tau Omega, Sigma Mu Sigma. Clubs: Camden Outing (dir. 1979). Lodges: Masons, Rotary (Camden pres. 1986).

FERNANDER, KAREN GENEINE, secondary school educator; b. Ft. Lauderdale, Fla., Feb. 18, 1957; d. Wilbur Franklin and Gloria Elaine (Chunn) Fernander. BA, Wesleyan Coll., Macon, Ga., 1978; MS, Nova U., Ft. Lauderdale, Fla., 1987. Cert. tchr. Fla. Author: (book) Hired Help, 1996. Charter mem. Dem. Women's Club of Ctrl. Broward, Ft. Lauderdale, 1990—91; mem. Dem. Exec. Com., Broward County, 1995—96; bd. dirs. Gwen Cherry Polit. Caucus, Ft. Lauderdale, 1988—90. Recipient Plaque for Svc./MAC chair, Broward Tchrs. Union, Tamarac, Fla., 1990. Mem.: Fla. Edn. Assn. (minority leadership cert. trainer 2001—), Broward Tchrs. Union (area v.p. 1985—, mem. exec. bd. 1985—). Democrat. Baptist. Avocations: travel, snorkeling, theater. Home: 27 SW 7th Ave Dania FL 33004

FERNANDES, DAVID RICHARD, physician; b. N.Y.C., Oct. 28, 1946; m. Donna Marie Catapano, July 21, 1991; children: Justin, Rachel, Julia, Brandon. BS, Fordham U., 16658; MPA, NYU, 1980; MD cum laude, SUNY, Bklyn., 1972. Intern in pediats. and pediatric pathology to resident Kings County Hosp., Bklyn., 1972-74; chief resident Northshore Univ. Hosp., Manhasset, N.Y., 1974-75; fellow in pediatric ambulatory care Bellevue (N.Y.) Hosp., 1975-76; dir. ambulatory care N.Y.C. Dept. Health, 1976-78; tchr. SUNY, Bklyn., 1978-81; physician pvt. practice, Bklyn., 1980—. Mem. Am. Acad. Pediatrics, Brooklyn Pediatric Soc. Avocations: magic, music. Office: 126 95th St Brooklyn NY 11209-7203

FERNANDES, EDWARD F., lawyer; b. Carver, Mass. BA, Dartmouth Coll., 1980; JD, Columbia U., 1983. Bar: Mass., Tex., U.S. Dist. Ct. Tex., Mass., Ariz., U.S. Ct. Appeals, First & Fifth cir. Ptnr. Weil, Gotshal & Manges, LLP, Houston, Solar & Fernandes LLP; mng. ptnr. Brobeck, Phleger & Harrison LLP, Austin, Tex., 2000—03; ptnr., litig. and energy Akin Gump Strauss Hauer & Feld LLP, Austin, 2003—. Former dir. Houston Bar Assn.; former pres. Houston Referral Svc.; former adj. prof. U. Houston Sch. Law; mem. steering com. State Bar Tex. Minority Counsel Prog. Mem Econ. Devel. Council Greater Austin C. of C. Named a Tex. Super Lawyer, Texas lawyers, 2004; named one of Nation's Top Litigators, Nat. Law Jour., 2004, Top Comml. Litig. in Austin, Austin Bus. Jour., 2004. Office: Akin Gump Strauss Hauer & Feld LLP Ste 2100 300 W 6th St Austin TX 78701 Office Phone: 512-499-6265. Office Fax: 512-499-6290. Business E-mail: efernandes@akingump.com.*

FERNANDES, JANE, academic administrator, educational consultant, sign language professional; b. Worcester, MA, Aug. 21, 1956; d. Richard Paul and Mary Kathleen (Cosgrove) Kelleher; m. James John Fernandes; children: Sean William, Erin Frances. BA comparative lit., Trinity Coll., Hartford, CT, 1978; MA comparative lit., U of Iowa, Iowa City, IA, 1980, PhD comparative lit., 1986. Acting dir. (ASL prog.) Northeastern U., Boston, 1986—87; chmn. (sign comm.) Gallaudet U., Wash., DC, 1987; coord. (interp. tng.) Kapiolani C.C., Honolulu, 1988—90; dir. Statewide Ctr., Dept. of Ed., Honolulu, 1990—95; VP Gallaudet U, Wash., DC, 1995—2000, provost, 2000—. Edit. rev. bd. Perspectives in Ed. & Deafness, Wash., DC, 1994—97. Co-author: (novels) Signs of Eloquence, 2003. Chair State Commn. Persons with Disabilities, Honolulu, 1993—95, mem., 1988—95; mem. (bd. of dir.) Goodwill Indust. of Honolulu, Honolulu, 1992—95; joint com. Am. Annuls of the Deaf, 2005—. Recipient Alice Cogswell, Gallaudet U, 1993; fellow alumni, U of Iowa/ IA, 2001. Mem.: Nat. Assoc. of the Deaf. Office: Gallaudet Univ 800 Florida Ave NE Washington DC 20002-3695

FERNANDEZ, ANTONIO S., investment company executive; BBA, Pace U., NY. Sys. engring. mgr. Electronic Data Sys.; v.p. duPont Glore Forgan; dir. ops., treas. Thompson McKinnon; founder, former head, internat. investment banking dept. Oppenheimer & Co., Inc., several positions including: exec. v.p., dir. ops., treas., CFO, dir., 1979—99. Bd. dir. Banco Latinoamericano de Exportaciones, 1992—99, Terremark Worldwide, Inc., 2003—, Spanish Broadcasting Sys. CL A, 2004—. Trustee Mulenberg Coll.*

FERNANDEZ, FERDINAND FRANCIS, federal judge; b. 1937; BS, U. So. Calif., 1958, JD, 1963; LLM, Harvard U., 1963. Bar: Calif. 1963, U.S. Dist. Ct. (cen. dist.) Calif. 1963, U.S. Ct. Appeals (9th cir.) 1963, U.S. Supreme Ct. 1967. Elec. engr. Hughes Aircraft Co., Culver City, Calif., 1958-62; law clk. to dist. judge U.S. Dist. Ct. (cen. dist.) Calif., 1963-64; pvt. practice law Allard, Shelton & O'Connor, Pomona, Calif., 1964-80; judge Calif. Superior Ct. San Bernardino County, Calif., 1980-85, U.S. Dist. Ct. (cen. dist.) Calif., L.A., 1985-89, U.S. Ct. Appeals (9th cir.), L.A., 1989—2002, sr. judge, 2002—. Lester Roth lectr. U. So. Calif. Law Sch., 1992. Contbr. articles to profl. jours. Vice chmn. City of La Verne Commn. on Environ. Quality, 1971-73; chmn. City of Claremont Environ. Quality Bd., 1972-73; bd. trustees Pomona Coll., 1990—. Fellow Am. Coll. Trust and Estate Counsel; mem. ABA, State Bar of Calif. (fed. cts. com. 1966-69, ad hoc com. on attachments 1971-85, chmn. com. on adminstrn. of justice 1976-77, exec. com. taxation sect. 1977-80, spl. com. on mandatory fee arbitration 1978-79), Calif. Judges Assn. (chmn. juvenile cts. com. 1983-84, faculty mem. Calif. Jud. Coll. 1982-83, faculty mem. jurisprudence and humanities course 1983-85), L.A. County Bar Assn. (bull. com. 1974-75), San Bernardino County Bar Assn., Pomona Valley Bar Assn. (co-editor Newsletter 1970-72, trustee 1971-78, sec.-treas. 1973-74, 2d v.p. 1974-75, 1st v.p. 1975-76, pres. 1976-77), Estate Planning Coun. Pomona Valley (sec. 1966-76), Order of Coif, Phi Kappa Phi, Tau Beta Pi, Eta Kappa Nu. Office: US Ct Appeals 9th Cir 125 S Grand Ave Ste 602 Pasadena CA 91105-1621

FERNANDEZ, FERNANDO LAWRENCE, aeronautical engineer, research and development company executive; b. N.Y.C., Dec. 31, 1938; s. Fernando and Luz Esther (Fortuno) F.; m. Carmen Dorothy Mays, Aug. 26, 1962; children: Lisa Marie, Christopher John (dec.). ME, Stevens Inst. Tech., 1960, MS in Applied Mechanics, 1961; PhD in Aeronautics, Calif. Inst. Tech., 1969. Engr. Lockheed Missiles & Space Co., Sunnyvale, Calif., 1961-63; div. mgr. The Aerospace Corp., El Segundo, Calif., 1963-72; program mgr. R & D Assocs., Santa Monica, Calif., 1972-75; v.p. Phys. Dynamics, Inc., San Diego, 1975-76; pres. Arete Assocs., San Diego, 1976-93, AETC Inc., San Diego, 1994-98; dir. Def. Advanced Rsch. Projects Agy., Arlington, Va., 1998-2001; disting. rsch. prof., dir. inst. tech. initiatives Stevens Inst. Tech., Hoboken, NJ, 2001—05; pvt. cons., 2005—. Mem. Chief Naval Ops. Exec. Panel, Washington, 1983-98; chair Def. Sci. Bd. Tech. Panel on Role of DOD in Homeland Security, 2003; mem. Naval Rsch. Adv. Coun., 2004-. Editor Jour. AIAA, 1970; contbr. articles to Fluid Mechanics. Mem. Naval Rsch. Adv. Coun., 2004—. Office Phone: 858-922-2546. Personal E-mail: frankdarpa@yahoo.com.

FERNANDEZ, FRANK L., lawyer, retail executive; BBA, St. Bonaventure U.; JD, Albany Law Sch.; LLM in Taxation, NYU. CPA; bar: NY. Acct. Haskins & Sells, N.Y.C.; ptnr. Fernandez Burstein Tuczinski & Collura, P.C., Albany, NY, 1982—2001; sec., gen. counsel, exec. v.p. Home Depot, Inc., Atlanta, 2001—. Mem. legal adv. com. NYSE; dir. MS Tax Program, SUNY Albany. Pres. Saratoga Equine Sports Ctr.; bd. dir. Woodruff Arts Ctr., Atlanta. Mem.: ABA, Am. Inst. CPAs, NY State Bar Assn., NY State Soc. CPAs. Office: Home Depot Inc 2455 Paces Ferry Rd Atlanta GA 30339-4024*

FERNANDEZ, HAPPY CRAVEN (GLADYS FERNANDEZ), academic administrator; b. Scranton, Pa., Mar. 3, 1939; d. Orvin William and Florence (Waite) Craven; m. Richard Ritter Fernandez, June 10, 1961; children: John Ritter, David Craven, Richard William. BA, Wellesley Coll., 1961; MA in Teaching, Harvard U., 1962; MA, U. Pa., Phila., 1970; EdD, Temple U., 1984. Social studies tchr. various pub. schs., 1961-64; from vis. asst. prof. to prof. Sch. Social Adminstrn. Temple U., Phila., 1974—92; exec. dir. Parents Union for Pub. Sch., Phila., 1980-82; dir. The Child Care and Family Policy Inst., Phila., 1988-92; city councilwoman Phila., 1992-98; candidate for mayor City Phila., 1998-99; pres. Moore Coll. of Art and Design, Phila., 1999—. Cons. Nat. Com. for Citizens in Edn., Columbia, Md., 1982—87, Phila. Youth Study Ctr., 1988—90; commr. Phila. Gas Comm, 1992—97; trustee Edn. Law Ctr., Phila., 1983—; bd. dirs. Cultural Fund, 1996—98; chair Select Com. on Bus. Taxes, 1992—98, Select com. on Land Reuse, 1997—98; pres. Delaware Valley Child Care Coun., 1988—90. Author: Parents Organizing to Improve Schools, 1976, The Child Advocacy Handbook, 1980, Elder Care and Child Care Policies of Philadelphia Area Businesses, 1991. Chair bd. dirs. Am. for Dem. Action, Phila., 1980—92; chair Children's Coalition, 1982—86; bd. dirs. Phila. Citizens for Children and Youth, 1986—93; founder Parents Union for Pub. Schs., 1972—, chair Phila., 1972—75, 1978—80; trustee Phila. Award, 2003—; del. Dem. Nat. Conv., 1988, 1992, 1996; bd. dirs. Greater Phila. Cultural Alliance, 2000—, chmn. bd., 2004—, Pa. Women's Forum, 2000—. Recipient Women in Edn. award Women's Way, 1989, Pub. Citizen of Yr. award NASW, 1991, Local Elected Ofcl. award Pa. Citizens for Better Librs., 1993, Pub. Svc. award Homeowners Assn. Phila., 1994 Phila. Op. Smile award, 1999, Woman of Yr.-Ivy Willis award, 2000, Fleisher Art Meml. Founders award 2001, Woman of Achievement award AAUW, 2005; named Outstanding Advisor, Health Promotions Coun., 1994, 2002, Disting. Dau. of Pa., 2002; Wellesley Coll. scholar, 1961. Mem.: Nat. Assn. Ind. Colls. and Univs. (bd. dirs. 2003—), Assn. Ind. Schs. of Art and Design (nat. sec. 2001—04, vice chmn. nat. bd. dirs. 2004—). Mem. United Church Of Christ. Avocations: tennis, gardening. Home: 3400 Baring St Philadelphia PA 19104-2076 Office: Moore College 20th & Parkway 4 Philadelphia PA 19103 Office Phone: 215-568-4515 x1100.

FERNANDEZ, JACK EUGENE, lawyer; b. Washington, Aug. 23, 1956; s. Jack Eugene and Sylvia Knapp Fernandez; m. Carin Carr, Aug. 25, 1979; children: Marina, Jack, Abbey. BS, U.S. Naval Acad., 1978; JD magna cum laude, Cornell U., 1989. Fighter pilot USN, Virginia Beach, 1982-86; law clk. 4th Cir. Ct. Appeals, Richmond, Va., 1989-90; atty. Holland & Knight, Tampa, Fla., 1990-92, U.S. Atty.'s Office, Tampa, 1992-96; ptnr. Bavol, Bush & Sisco, Tampa, 1996—. Editor-in-chief Cornell Law Rev., 1988. Mem. Rotary (bd. dirs. Ybor City chpt. 1995-97), Order of the Coif. Democrat. Roman Catholic. Home: 529 Severn Ave Tampa FL 33606 Office: Zucherman Spaeder LLP 101 E Kennedy Blvd Tampa FL 33602 E-mail: jfernandez@zuckerman.com.

FERNANDEZ, JAMES, anthropology educator; b. Chgo., Nov. 27, 1930; m. Renate Helene Lellep, Oct. 18, 1958; children: Lisa Oyana, Luke Oliver, Andrew McClintock. BA, Amherst Coll., 1952; postgrad. in cultural anthropology, Northwestern U., 1953—54; postgrad., U. Madrid, 1954—55, Museo Etnologico Barcelona, 1955; PhD, Northwestern U., 1962. Tchg. asst. Northwestern U., 1955—57, grad. rsch. fellow in program of African studies, 1956—57; instr. sociology and anthropology Smith Coll., 1961—62, asst. prof. anthropology, 1962—64; area program dir. Gabon Peace Corps trainees, 1962—63; cons., lectr. Fgn. Svc. Inst., Washington, 1964—70; prof. anthropology Dartmouth Coll., 1969—75, chmn. dept. anthropology, 1971—75; prof. anthropology Princeton U., 1975—86, chmn. dept. anthropology, 1978—82; prof. anthropology U. Chgo., 1982—. Lectr. and cons. in field. Recipient Guggenheim fellowship, 2003, Carnegie Fund Grant for African Rsch., 1955, Ford Found. fellowship, 1957, Ford Found. Ext. fellowship, 1959, Social Sci. Rsch. Coun.-Am. Coun. Learned Socs. African Rsch. fellowship, 1965, NSF grant, 1970, 1971, Spanish-N.Am. Joint Com. fellowship, 1977, NEH grant, 1988—89. Fellow: African Studies Assn., Am. Anthropol. Assn., Am. Acad. Religion, Am. Acad. Arts and Scis.; mem.: Northeastern Anthropol. Assn. (pres. 1973), Sigma Xi. Office: U Chgo Dept Anthropology 1126 E 59th St Chicago IL 60637 E-mail: jwf1@uchicago.edu.

FERNANDEZ, JAMES, retail products executive; m. Dolores Fernandez; 2 children. MBA, Fordham, 1982. CPA. Mem. fin. staff Avon; various positions in fin. planning and mgmt. Tiffany, 1983—89, sr. v.p.-CFO, 1989—97; exec. v.p.-CFO, 1998—. Bd. dir. Dun & Bradstreet Corp. Office: Tiffany & Co 727 5th Ave New York NY 10022*

FERNANDEZ, KATHLEEN M., cultural organization administrator; b. Dayton, Ohio, Oct. 8, 1949; d. Norbert Katzen and Yenema Vermeda (Bermingham) F.; m. James Robert Hillibish, Oct. 1, 1977. BA, Otterbein Coll., 1971. Edn. asst. Ohio Hist. Soc., Columbus, 1971, vol. coord., 1971-74, interpretive specialist Zoar, 1975-88; site mgr. Village State Meml., Zoar, 1988—2004; freelance mus. cons. Canton, Ohio, 2004—. Author: A Singular People: Images of Zoar, 2003. Bd. dirs., newsletter editor Ohio & Erie Canal Corridor Coalition, Akron, 1989—. Mem. Am. Assn. State and Local History, Nat. Trust Hist. Preservation, Zoar Cmty. Assn., Communal Studies Assn. (pres. 1981, editor newsletter 1981-86, 1997-2004, bd. dirs. 1995—, exec. sec. 2004—), Am. Assn. Mus. (surveyor mus. assistance program 1999—). Office: 221 18th St NW Canton OH 44703 Office Phone: 330-456-3611.

FERNANDEZ, LISA, softball player; b. Long Beach, Calif., Feb. 27, 1971; m. Mike Lujan. Grad., UCLA, 1995. Mem. Calif. Commotion Amateur Softball Assn.; pitching and hitting coach UCLA Softball Team, 1995—. Pitcher U.S. Olympic Softball Team, Atlanta, 1996, Sydney, 2000, Athens, 04. Recipient Gold medal Pan Am. Games, 1991, 1999, ISF Women's World Championship, 1990, 94, 1998, 2002, Women's World Challenger Cup, 1992, Intercontinental Cup, 1993, South Pacific Classic, 1994, Superball Classic, 1995, Atlanta Olympics, 1996, Sydney Olympic Games, 2000, Athens Olympic Games, 2004, Honda award, 1991-93; named All-Am. Amateur Softball Assn., 1990-1993, 1995-1999, Sports Woman of Yr., 1991-92, MVP ASA Women's Major National, 1992, 1996-1999, mem. ASA Women's Major National Championship teams, 1990-92, 1996-99, NCAA Championship teams, 1990, 1992 Office: USA Softball 2801 NE 50th St Oklahoma City OK 73111-7203 also: TPS Hdqs care Lisa Fernandez PO Box 35700 Louisville KY 40232-5700

FERNANDEZ, RAUL J., data processing executive; BA in Economics, U. Md. Dir. emerging techs. govt. contracting firm, Bethesda, Md.; founder, pres., CEO, chmn. bd. Proxicom, 1991-2000; founder, CEO, chmn. bd. Proxicom (acquired by Dimension Data North America), 2000—01; CEO Dimension Data North America, 2001—02, chmn. emeritus, 2002; chmn. ObjectVideo, 2002—, CEO, 2004—. Bd. dirs. No. Va. Tech. Coun, Liz Claiborne, Critical Path, Internosis; mem. President's Coun. of Advisors on Sci. and Tech.; special advisor Gen. Atlantic Partners; co-owner Wash. Capitals, 2000—, Wash. Wizards, 2000—, Wash. Mystics, 2000—, MCI Ctr., 2000—. Office: ObjectVideo 11600 Sunrise Valley Dr Ste 290 Reston VA 20191 Office Phone: 703-654-9300. Office Fax: 703-654-9399.

FERNANDEZ, YANIRIS M., dean; b. N.Y.C., July 4, 1970; d. Basilio and Esmeralda Fernandez; m. Alberto M. Morales, July 5, 1997; children: Alberto Morales-Fernandez III, Lucas Morales-Fernandez. BA, Ithaca Coll., N.Y., 1992; MS, U. Mass., Amherst, 1994, ABD, 1996. Asst. to pres. Hampshire Coll., Amherst, Mass., 1995—98, asst. dean faculty, 1998—2004, assoc. dean faculty, 2004—. Mem. exec. and pers. bd. A Better Chance, Amherst, Mass., 2004; chair Hampshire Coll. Children's Ctr., Amherst, Mass., 2000. Roman Catholic. Home: 3 Carriage Ln Amherst MA 01002 Office: Hampshire Coll 893 West St Amherst MA 01002 Office Phone: 413-559-5781. Home Fax: 413-559-6081; Office Fax: 413-559-6081. E-mail: yfernandez@hampshire.edu.

FERNANDEZ-POL, BLANCA DORA, psychiatrist, researcher; b. Buenos Aires, Mar. 5, 1932; came to U.S., 1967; d. Balbino Fernandez and Maria Remedios van Pol. MD, U. Buenos Aires, 1958. Diplomate Am. Bd. Psychiatry and Neurology. Intern N.Y. Polyclinic Med. Sch., 1967-68; resident in psychiatry UCLA/Brentwood Hosp., 1968-69, NYU/Bellevue Hosp., 1969-71; gen. practitioner Hosp. Espanol, Buenos Aires, 1959-62; forensic psychiatrist Criminoloy Inst., Buenos Aires, 1963-65; clin. attending psychiatrist Bellevue Psychiat. Hosp., N.Y.C., 1971-75; pvt. practice St. Petersburg, Fla., 1976-78; chief psychiat. svcs. USAF Hosp. Yokota, Tokyo, 1980, USAF Hosp., Homestead, Fla., 1981; chief continuing treatment program dept. psychiatry Bronx-Lebanon Hosp., Bronx, 1983-2000. Prof. psychology U. Moran, Buenos Aires, 1962-67; asst. prof. psychiatry N.Y. Med. Coll., N.Y.C., 1972-74; clin. asst. prof. psychiatry Albert Einstein Coll. Medicine, Bronx, 1982—. Contbr. articles to profl. jours. Maj. USAF, 1978-81. Mem. Am. Psychiat. Assn., N.Y. Acad. Scis., Am. Acad. Psychiatrists in Alcoholism and Addictions, Res. Officers Assn. U.S., Assn. Mil. Surgeons U.S. Avocations: travel, painting, sculpture. Home: PO Box 21644 Brooklyn NY 11202-1644 Office: Bronx Lebanon Hosp 1285 Fulton Ave Bronx NY 10456-3401

FERNANDEZ-VELAZQUEZ, JUAN RAMON, university chancellor; b. San Juan, PR, Aug. 9, 1936; s. Ramon Fernández-Serrano and Elena Velazquez; m. Norah Moran, 1960 (div. 1967); children: Lynnette, Yasmin; m. Sonia M. Ramirez, Aug. 12, 1971 (div. 1992); 1 child, Juan Ernesto. BS, U. P.R., 1957, M in Pub. Adminstrn., 1963; PhD, CUNY, 1978; D honoris causa, U. Nacional, Piura, Peru, 1987. Adminstrv. tech. II Dept. Labor, San Juan, 1960; asst. to dir., lectr. Sch. Pub. Adminstrn., U. P.R., Río Piedras Campus, 1961-64, asst. prof., 1969-72, 79-80, assoc. prof., 1980-85, prof., 1984—, also chancellor, 1985-92; acad. senator faculty of social scis. U. P.R., 1983-85, mem. univ. bd., rep. Río Piedras Campus Acad. Senate, 1984-85; spl. asst. to Gov. of P.R., 1965-68; prof. Bklyn. Coll., CUNY, 1973-76; prof. sch. of pub. affairs Baruch Coll., CUNY, 1994—. Vis. assoc. rschr. Bildner Ctr. CUNY Grad. Sch., 1993-95; participant Fifth Ann. Conf. Caribbean Studies Assn., Curacao, 1980 and ann. meeting, 1981, seminar P.R. Planning Bd., 1979, symposium P.R. Found. for the Humanities, 1979, panel discussion Inst. Policy Scis. Ctr. for Study of State Policy, Duke U., 1981, seminar for grad. students Grad. Sch. Edn., Harvard U., 1981, Fifth Hispanic-Am. Conf., U. Mich., Ann Arbor, 1983, other confs., seminars; lectr. in field, 1975—; cons. Tchr.'s Assn., Hato Rey, P.R., 1984; hon. prof. U. Iberoamericana Sto. Do., Dominican Republic; lectr., bd. dirs. Ralph Bunche Inst. on the UN, 1986; vis. scholar, Bildner Ctr. for Western Hemisphere Studies, CUNY, 1993, adv. to the pres., Interam. U. P.R., 1996-97; founder Consenso Nacional Puertorriqueno, 1999; coodr. Com. for Devel. of Vieques Island, P.R., 1999; spl. commr. for Vieques and Culebra, Gov. P.R., 2001-04. Contbr. chpts. to books and articles to profl. jours. Mem. Puerto Rico's delegation to UNESCO World Conf. on Higher Edn., Paris, 1998; del. to Internat. Sem. on Evaluation and Accreditation Models for Higher Edn. Instns. in Latin Am. and the Caribbean/sponsored by IESALC-UNESCO, San Juan, 1999 Named Most Disting. Grad. Class 1953, Ctrl. High Sch. P.R.; Ford Found. grantee, 1981; recipient Disting. Alumni award CUNY, 1988. Mem. Acad. Arts, History and Archeology of P.R., Acad. for the Humanities and Scis., Caribbean Studies Assn.

FERNANDO, CHRISTOPHER G., engineering educator; s. Joseph and Thresa M. Fernando; m. Chitra Dissanayake Fernando, July 2, 1999; 1 child, Anuk. BSc, U. Peradeniya, Sri Lanka, 1995; MSc, Ohio U., 1999, PhD, 2003. Asst. lectr. U. Peradeniya, 1995—97; rsch. asst. Ohio U., Athens, 1997—2001, instr., 2001—02; asst. prof. W.Va. U. Tech., Montgomery, 2002—. Cons. Dana Corp., Maccoysville, Ohio, 2001—02. Mem.: IEEE, Am. Soc. Engring. Edn., ASME. Avocations: reading, travel, movies, computers. Office: WVa Univ Tech 413 Davis Hall Montgomery WV 25136

FERNBACH, HARVEY, psychiatrist; b. N.Y.C., July 4, 1944; BA, Kenyon Coll., 1966; MD, MPH, Yale U., 1971. Diplomate Am. Bd. Psychiatry and Neurology. Resident in gen. psychiatry SUNY-Downstate, Bklyn., 1974; clin. assoc. NIMH, Bethesda, Md., 1974—76; pvt. practice Lanham, Md., 1976—. Health care advocate Physicians for a Nat. Health Program, Chgo. Lt. comdr. USPHS, 1974—76. Named Outstanding Physician, Washington Consumers' Guidebook, 1998; named one of Top Drs., Washingtonian Mag., 1999, 2002, Top Psychiatrists, Consumers' Rsch. Coun. Am., 2004—05. Mem.: Am. Psychiat. Assn., Md. Med. Soc. (legis. com. 1988—), Washington Psychiat. Soc. (coun. 1995—). Office: 7726 Finns Ln Lanham MD 20706

FERNBERGER, MARILYN FRIEDMAN, not-for-profit developer, consultant, volunteer; b. Phila., Aug. 13, 1927; d. David and Edith (Rosen) Friedman; m. Edward Fernberger, June 21, 1947; children: Edward Jr., Ellen, James. BA, U. Pa., 1948. Promoter, developer, executor major events for cmty. orgns. and instns. on local, nat. and internat. basis. Co-chmn. U.S. Pro Indoor Tennis Championships, 1967-92; co-chmn. Phila. Women's Tennis Championships, 1970-79; cons. tennis promoters throughout U.S., creates new events and expands markets for existing events; staged profl. women's tennis tournament, Phila., 1970-79; cons. Internat. Mgmt. Group for Advanta Women's Tennis Championships; cons. on fundraising and art adminstrn.; former event coord. U. Pa. Inaugural Centenary Tennis Hall of Fame dinner; bd. dirs. Phila. Internat. Indoor Tennis Corp., Nat. Jr. Tennis League, Am. Tennis Assn., Phila. Tennis Patrons Assn., Phila. Youth Tennis & Edn. Benefit, Arthur Ashe Youth Tennis and Edn. Bd.; bd. dirs. Group of Four representing Wimbledon Mus., London, Roland Garros Mus., Paris, Tennis Australia Mus., Melbourne, and Internat. Tennis Hall of Fame, Newport, R.I.; v.p. Middle States Patrons Assn.; chmn. Middle States Devel. Com., chmn. membership com.; chmn. Nat. Arthur Ashe Day; publ. com. U.S. Tennis Assn.; mem. Phila. Women's Interclub Bd.; founder, mgr. Ea. Pa. Boy's Championships; active Phila. Gold Cup; founder, chmn. People to People Sports Jr. Exhbns. Contbr. to nat. and internat. publs., including World Tennis mag., Tennis South Africa, Tennis Italiano, Tenis Espanol, Algeman Dagblad, Royal Tennis, Japan, Tennis Australia, Tennis de France, Brit. Lawn Tennis Jour. of Lawn Tennis Assn., Eng. Trustee Phila. Mus. Art; lifetime bd. mem., mem. adv. com. Phila. Mus. Art Assocs.; past pres. Rodin Mus., mem. bd. or officer United Way, Nat. Coun. Jewish Women, Fairmount Park Assn. for Hist. Sites, Phila. Sports Congress, Nat. Art Mus. Sport, Internat. Tennis Hall of Fame and Mus.; sec. treas. Tennis N.Am., Internat. Tennis Tournamet Dirs. Assn.; pres., Women's Tournament Dirs. Assn.; active Pa. Ballet, Emergency Aid, Albert Einstein Med. Ctr., Drama Guild, Ctr. for Internat. Visitors, Festival Theatre New Plays, U. Arts, Inst. Contemporary Art; mem. assocs. com., past chmn., life mem., pres. Rodin Mus.; bd. dirs. Phila. Mus. Art; life trustee Internat. Tennis Hall of Fame and Mus.; mem. mus. devel. gala 2004 50th anniversary celebration, mus. com. dir., long range planning com., accreditation com., ann. fund com.; chmn. Phila. City of Yr. 1996 Dinner, Internat. Tennis Hall of Fame. Recipient Marlboro award, Humanitarian Svc. award Phila. Bd. Edn., Kelly award Pa. Parks and Recreation Commn., Cmty. Svc. award Big Bros.-Big Sisters, Police Athletic League, Coren award Nat. Jr. Tennis League Phila., YWCA, Phila., Mangan Svc. award USTA/Mid. States, Pub. Svc. award City of Phila., 8 times, Appreciation award Orange Bowl Com. Rotary Club, Phila., Phila. Bd. Edn., Chmn.'s award Internat. Tennis Hall of Fame and Mus., Pres.'s award Internat. Tennis Hall of Fame, 2002; named to USTA/Mid. States Hall of Fame; enshrined in Phila. Jewish Sports Hall of Fame, 2005. Mem. U.S. Tennis Writers Assn. (bd., officer), Internat. Tennis Tournament Dirs. Assn. (bd., officer), Assn. Tournament Dirs. (bd., officer), U. Pa. Alumni Assn. (bd., officer), Internat. Tennis Club USA (hon.). Home and Office: 1112 Penmore Pl Rydal PA 19046-1239

FERNELIUS, NILS CONRAD, physicist; b. Columbus, Ohio, Nov. 10, 1934; s. Willis Conard and Anna Naomi (Baker) F. AB, Harvard U., 1956; student, Oxford U., 1956—57; MS, U. Ill., 1959, PhD, 1966. Rsch. assoc. dept. physics U. Ill., Urbana, 1966—67; asst. physicist Materials Sci. Divsn., Argonne, Ill., 1968—71; v.p. Rsch. Cons., Oak Ridge, Tenn., 1971—72; sr. fellow Nat. Rsch. Coun. Aerospace Rsch. Lab., Wright-Patterson AFB, Ohio, 1973—75; vis. scientist Universal Energy Sys., Dayton, Ohio, 1975—76; physicist U. Dayton Rsch. Inst., 1977—82; sr. rsch. assoc. Nat. Rsch. Coun. Materials Lab., Wright-Patterson AFB, 1982—85; vis. scientist Systran Corp., Dayton, 1985, 1987—88; physicist Stolle Corp., Sidney, Ohio, 1985—86, Materials Directorate Air Force Rsch. Lab., Wright-Patterson AFB, 1988—. Contbr. articles to profl. jours. NSF fellow, 1959-62. Mem. IEEE (sr.), SPIE, Optical Soc. Am., Am. Phys. Soc. (life), Am. Assn. Physics Tchrs., Lasers and Electro-Optics Soc., Soc. Applied Spectroscopy (George Rappoport Meml. award 1995), Materials Rsch. Soc., Sigma Xi. Avocations: genealogy, stamp collecting/philately, travel, photography. Home: 1528 Sussex Rd Troy OH 45373-2446 Office: AFRL/MLPSO Materials Directorate Air Force Rsch Lab Wright Patterson Afb OH 45433 Office Phone: 937-255-4474 3246.

FERNHOLZ, ERHARD ROBERT, investment executive; b. Princeton, NJ, Mar. 27, 1941; s. Erhard and Mary (Briganti) F.; m. Luisa Turrin, June 4, 1970; children: Daniel, Ricardo. AB, Princeton U., 1962; PhD, Columbia U., 1967. Rsch. dir. Met. Securities, N.Y.C., 1980-87; chief investment officer, founder Enhanced Investment Techs., Princeton, 1987—; founder, trustee Minerva Rsch. Found., 1993—. Author: Stochastic Portfolio Theory, 2002; contbr. articles to profl. jours.; patentee in field. NSF grantee, 1963-69. Home: 12 Dogwood Ln Princeton NJ 08540-5629 Office: Enhanced Investment Techs One Palmer Sq Princeton NJ 08542 Business E-Mail: bob@enhanced.com.

FERNQUIST, ROBERT, sociology educator; PhD in Sociology, Ind. U., 1996. Prof. sociology Cen. Mo. State U., Warrensburg, 1997—. Adj. prof. sociology Mont. State U., Bozeman, 1993—96. Contbr. articles to rsch. jours. Mem.: Internat. Acad. for Suicide Rsch. (assoc.). Office: Cen Mo State U Wood Hall 203 Warrensburg MO 64093 E-mail: fernquist@cmsu1.cmsu.edu.

FERNSLER, JOHN PAUL, lawyer; b. Lebanon, Pa., Dec. 24, 1940; s. K. Paul and Elizabeth M. (Snyder) F.; m. Christine Joan Chester, July 31, 1965; children: Euan, Scott. AB, Dickinson Coll., 1962; JD, U. Mich., 1965. Bar: Pa. 1965, U.S. Dist. Ct. (ea. and we. dists.) Pa., U.S. Ct. Appeals (3d cir.). Assoc. Snyder, Balmer & Kershner, Reading, Pa., 1965-66; dep. atty. gen. Commonweatlh of Pa., Harrisburg, 1968-70; chief counsel HUD, Pitts., 1970-81; ptnr. Reed Smith Shaw & McClay, Pitts., 1981-97; corp. counsel Weis Markets, Inc., Sunbury, Pa., 1997—2002; prof. bus. law Bucknell U., Lewisburg, Pa., 2003—. Lectr., spl. cons. Mortgage Bankers Assn., 1985-92; solicitor Mt. Lebanon Parking Authority, 1990-91; mem. Mt. Lebanon Commn., 1992-96, pres. 1993; bd. dirs., treas. Med./Rescue Team South Authority, 1995-97; bd. dirs. Rail Authority, 2004—; chair land preservation subcom. of real property adv. com. Pa. Joint State Govt. Commn., 2004—. Contbr. articles to profl. jours. Mem. Mt. Lebanon Zoning Hearing Bd., 1981—88, sec., 1982—82, chmn., 1983—88; bd. dirs. or pres. Linn Conservancy, 2001—; chmn. Mt. Lebanon Rep. Com., 1990—92; bd. dirs., counsel Coun. for Luth. Campus Ministry in Gt. Pitts., 1979—82. Decorated Commendation medal; recipient Spl. Cert. Pa. Dept Community Affairs, 1970. Mem. ABA (urban state and local law sect. coun. 1984-87), Pa. Bar Assn., Allegheny County Bar Assn. (real property sect., chmn., 1988), Am. Coll. Real Estate Lawyers (elected). Republican. Episcopalian. Avocations: bicycling, walking, photography. Home: 20 Brown St Lewisburg PA 17837-2104 Office: Bucknell Univ Management Dept Lewisburg PA 17837 Office Phone: 570-577-1560. E-mail: jjfern@jdweb.com, jfernsle@bucknell.edu.

FERNSTROM, JOHN DICKSON, psychiatry educator, researcher; b. N.Y.C., July 9, 1947; s. Karl Dickson and Dorothy Weston (Bond) F.; m. Madelyn Jill Hirsch; children: Aaron, Lauren. SB, MIT, 1969, PhD, 1972. Research fellow Roche Inst. of Molecular Biology, Nutley, N.J., 1972-73; asst. prof. MIT, Cambridge, Mass., 1973-77, assoc. prof., 1977-82, U. Pitts. Sch. of Medicine, 1982-87, prof. psychiatry, behavioral neurosci., 1987—; prof. pharmacology U. Pitts. Sch. Medicine, 1992—. Mem. Nat. Inst. Neurol. and Communicative Disorders and Stroke/NIH Program Project Rev., Bethesda, Md., 1978-82, chmn., 1981-82; mem. NASA Life Scis. Adv. Commn., Washington, 1980-86, NIMH Neurosci. Br. Evaluation Panel, Rockville, Md., 1983, Nat. Adv. Coun., Monell Chem. Senses Ctr., Phila., 1987—; mem. nutrition program rsch. evaluation panel Nat. Inst. Childhood Diseases, 1989; Burroughs-Wellcome vis. prof. basic med. scis., 1993; mem. com. on mil. nutrition rsch., food and nutrition bd. NAS, 1994-2001, com. dietary ref. intake, 1997-2003. Contbr. articles to profl. jours. Recipient Rsch. Scientist Devel. award NIMH, Rockville, 1979-88, Alfred P. Sloan fellowship in neurochemistry A.P. Sloan Found., N.Y.C., 1974-76, Predoctoral fellowship NIH, Bethesda, 1970-72, Rsch. Scientist award NIMH, Rockville, 1989-94. Mem. Am. Soc. for Neurochemistry, Am. Soc. for Pharmacology and Exptl. Therapeutics, Am. Physiol. Soc., Am. Inst. Nutrition (chmn. nervous system sect., mem. publ info. com., mem. coun., Mead-Johnson award 1980), Endocrine Soc. Office: U Pitts Dept Psychiatry 3811 Ohara St Pittsburgh PA 15213-2593 Office Phone: 412-246-5297.

FERNSTRUM, DAVID ROSS, lawyer; b. Detroit, Mar. 24, 1950; s. Richard Franklin and Margaret Elizabeth (Mehlhope) F.; m. Marilyn Jeanne Waite, June 3, 1972; children: Megan, Tait. BA, Ohio Wesleyan U., Delaware, 1972; JD, Wayne State U., Detroit, 1975. Bar: Mich. 1975, U.S. Dist. Ct. (we. dist.) Mich. 1975, U.S. Dist. Ct. (ea. dist.) Mich. 1977, U.S. Dist. Ct. (no. dist.) Ky. 1981. Clk. Mich. State Appellate Defender's Office, Detroit, 1974-75; assoc. Clary, Nantz, Wood, Hoffius, Rankin & Cooper, Grand Rapids, Mich., 1975-81; shareholder Clary, Nantz, Grand Rapids, 1981-83; ptnr. Mika, Meyers, Beckett & Jones, Grand Rapids, 1984; v.p. Atmosphere Processing, Inc., Holland, Mich., 1985; ptnr. Mika, Meyers, Beckett & Jones, Grand Rapids, 1986—. Lectr. Grand Valley State U., Allendale, Mich., 1989-92. Mem. Planning Commn., East Grand Rapids, Mich., 1987-88. Mem. ABA (chair subcom. rights of union mems. and non mems., com. on state and local govt., bargaining and employment law, sect. labor and employment law 1984—), Grand Rapids Bar Assn. (sec. labor and employment law, chair 1999). Avocations: boating, golf, photography.

FEROZ, EHSAN HABIB, accounting educator, researcher, writer; b. Chittagong, Bangladesh, Jan. 9, 1952; came to U.S., 1979, permanent resident, 1983, naturalized, 1990; s. Mohammad Obaidul and Sabera (Begum) Hakim; m. Kishwar Sultana Beg, Oct. 16, 1982; children: Rubens, Jonas, Amran. BA with honours, U. Dacca, 1972, MA first class first, 1974; MA, Carleton U., 1978; PhD, U. Chgo., 1982. Cert. fraud examiner; cert. govt. fin. mgr. Asst. prof. acctg. SUNY, Buffalo, 1983-86; asst. prof. acctg. CUNY, Baruch, 1986-89; vis. asst. prof. acctg. Carlson Sch. of Mgmt. U. Minn., 1989-91, assoc. prof. acctg., assoc. mem. grad. faculty, 1991-93, prof. acctg., assoc. mem. grad. faculty, 1993—. Invited guest Ctr. For Internat. Studies, MIT, 1979; disting. faculty mentor U. Minn., 1990, 91; faculty mentor sch. bus. and econs., mem. honors and awards com., dean search com., outcome measures com., student behavior judiciary com., libr. policy com. U. Minn., Duluth, spl. project assoc. of vice-chancellor for acad. adminstrn., spring, 1995; invited presenter Jour. Acctg. Rsch. Conf., 1991; invited nominator Seidman Disting. Award in Polit. Economy, 1991, 92. Contbr. numerous articles to profl. jours., including Advances in Acctg., Acctg. Horizons, Australian Jour. Mgmt., Acctg. Orgns. and Soc., Acctg. Rev., Jour. Acctg. Rsch., Jour. Bus. Fin. and Acctg., Pub. Adminstrn. Quarterly, Fin. Accountability and Mgmt., Jour. Acctg. Abstracts, IEEE Transactions on Neural Networks, Encyclopedic Dictionary of Acctg.; mem. editl. bd. Internat. Jour. Acctg., Internat. Jour. Acctg. and Bus. Soc., Rsch. in Govtl. and Non Profit Acctg. Bd. dirs. Duluth Children's Mus., 1996—; mem. affirmative action rev. com. Minn. Edn. Assn., 1996-98. Mem. Assn. Govt. Accts., Assn. Cert. Fraud Examiners, Acad. Internat. Bus., Am. Acctg. Assn. (rsch. com. GNP sect. 1982-93, fin. com. 1992), Minn. Coun. Acctg. Educators. Avocations: walking, swimming, classical music.

FERRAND, LOUIS GEORGE, lawyer; b. East Grand Rapids, Mich., Apr. 12, 1942; s. Louis George and Margaret Louise (LaBour) F.; m. Mary Eleanore Braseth, Oct. 25, 1969; children: Anne Elizabeth, Gregory Louis, Jacqueline Louise. BA, Alma Coll., 1964; JD, U. Mich., 1971. Bar: Mich. 1971, D.C. 1974, U.S. Supreme Ct. Pres., co-founder Cornerstone Project, Inc., Bklyn., 1966; vol. Peace Corps., Dominican Republic, 1966-68, trainer, 1968; dir. manpower programs Grand Rapids CAP, Mich., 1969-70; trial atty. Dept. Justice, Washington, 1971-76; counsel for civil rights Dept. Labor, Washington, 1976-81, dep. assoc. solicitor for civil rights, 1981-87, dep. assoc. solicitor for mine safety and health, 1987-88; of counsel Newman & Newell, 1988-89; sr. atty. OAS, 1990-94, prin. atty., 1994—2004, dir. Office of Gen. Legal Svcs., dep. gen. counsel, 2004—05, legal advisor to the OAS sec. gen., 2005—. Bd. dirs. Ayuda, Inc., 1988—2003, hon. trustee, 2003—, chair legal affairs and pers. coms., exec. com.; officer at large, bd. dirs. Parklawn Recreation Assn., Alexandria, Va., 1982—84, No. Va. Meml. Soc., 1991—95, Arlington Retirement Housing Corp., 1988—93; co-founder, bd. dirs. Fondo Quisqueya Found., Inc., 1993—, treas., 1993—2005, pres., 2005—; co-founder, bd. dirs. Friends of Williamsburg Rowing, Inc., 1993—97, treas., 1993—95; leader cub scout pack George Washington dist. Boy Scouts Am., 1984—86; basketball coach Recreational League, 1983—89; bd. dirs. T.C. Williams H.S. Track Boosters, 1992—97, treas., 1992—95, co-pres., 1995—96; chmn. social responsibilities com. Unitarian Ch., Arlington, Va., 1981, co-chmn. capital fund dr., 1993—94; trustee Unitarian Ch. of Arlington, 1984—87, chmn. bd. trustees, 1986—87; bd. dirs. MOAS Found., 1997—, treas., 1999—; bd. dirs. I-A Bar Found., 1995—2005; incorporator, bd. dirs. Young Americas Bus. Trust, Inc., 1999—, vice chair, 1999—; incorporator, bd. dirs. The Am.'s Endowment, Inc., 2003—. Mem.: Am. Law Inst., Fed. Am. Inns of Ct. (co-founder, charter mem., master 1989—, program chmn. and counselor 1998—99, pres. 1999—2000), Inter-Am. Bar Assn. (co-chmn. labor law sect. 1986—91, asst. sec. 1989—91, asst. treas. 1993—94, sec. gen. 1995—2004, mem. exec. com. 1995—2004, coun. mem. 1995—, mag. editor 1999—2004), Mich. Bar Assn., D.C. Bar Assn., Fed. Bar Assn. (bd. dirs. D.C. chpt. 1986—, officer 1988—94, co-chmn. nat. conv. com. 1989, pres. 1993—94, nat. cir. officer 1993—97, nat. coun. mem. 1993—99, chair fed. career svc. divsn. 1996—99, nat. coun. mem. 2003—05), Fed. Bar Found. (adv. 1994—99). Avocations: reading, hiking, swimming, bicycling, travel. Office: Orgn of Am States Office of Gen Legal Advisor to Sec-Gen Washington DC 20006 Office Phone: 202-458-3903. E-mail: lferrand@oas.org.

FERRANDO, JONATHAN P., retail executive; b. Kalamazoo, Mich., 1966; BA in Econs., U. Mich., 1988; JD, Harvard U., 1991. Atty. Skadden, Arps, Slate, Meagher & Flom, Chgo.; sr. v.p., gen. counsel automotive retail group AutoNation, Inc., Fort Lauderdale, Fla., 1996—2000, sr. v.p., gen. counsel, corp. sec., 2000—. Office: AutoNation Inc 110 SE 6th St Fort Lauderdale FL 33301

FERRANTE, JOAN MARGUERITE, language educator, literature educator, writer; b. N.Y.C., Nov. 11, 1936; d. Nicholas Henry and Josephine (Pisacane) Ferrante; m. R. Carey McIntosh. Student, Brearley Sch., 1950-54, Radcliffe Coll., 1954-55; BA, Barnard Coll., 1958; MA, Columbia U., 1959, PhD, 1963. Asst. prof. English and comparative lit. Columbia U., N.Y.C., 1966-70, assoc. prof., 1970-74, prof., 1974—, chmn. English and comparative lit., 1988-91, dir. Ctr. Italian Studies, 1977-80. Lectr. modern langs. Swarthmore (Pa.) Coll., 1968; lectr. medieval studies Fordham U., N.Y.C., 1976; Andrew Mellon prof. humanities Tulane U., 1984. Author: (book) The Conflict of Love and Honor, 1973, Guillaume d'Orange, Four Twelfth Century Epics, 1974, Woman as Image in Medieval Literature from the Twelfth Century to Dante, 1975; author: (with Robert Hanning) The Lais of Marie de France, 1978; author: The Political Vision of the Divine Comedy, 1984, To the Glory of Her Sex: Women's Roles in the Composition of Medieval Texts, 1997; editor (with George Economou): In Pursuit of Perfection, Courtly Love in Medieval Literature, 1975; editor: (with Robert hanning) The Challenge of the Medieval Text, 1985; editor: Database: Epistolae, Correspondence of Medieval Women, Texts and Translations; mem. adv. bd. Speculum, 1975—78, cons. editor Records of Civilization, 1975—. Am. Coun. Learned Socs. fellow, 1969—70, NEH fellow, 1980—81. Fellow: Medieval Acad. Am. (councillor, 2d v.p. 1998—99, 1st v.p. 1999—2000, pres. 2000—01); mem.: MLA (exec. coun. 1986—90), Dante Soc. Am. (councillor, v.p. 1978—83, pres. 1985—91), Phi Beta Kappa (senator 1979—97, v.p. 1988—91, pres. 1991—94). Office: Columbia U 614 Philosophy Hall New York NY 10027 Business E-Mail: jmf2@columbia.edu.

FERRARA, ANNETTE, editor, educator; MA, Sch. of the Art Inst. Founding editor, writer TENbyTEN, Chgo., 1999—. Guest lectr. Columbia Coll., DePaul, SAIC; tchr. art history Mus. of Contemporary Art. Co-author: Xtreme Interiors, 2003; contbr. writings to Artforum, zingmagazine, provinceton Arts. Mem.: Chgo. Art Critics Assn. Office: TENbyTEN 22 S Morgan 3E Chicago IL 60607 Office Phone: 312-421-0480. Office Fax: 312-421-0491. Business E-Mail: contact@tenbyten.net.*

FERRARA, CHARLES THOMAS, II, music educator; b. Valley Stream, N.Y., Jan. 27, 1975; s. Charles Thomas Ferrara and Roberta Marie Sorge; 1 child, Virginia Casey. BA in Music Edn., Miami U., Oxford, Ohio, 1997; postgrad., U. Ghana. Band dir. Turpin H.S., Cin., 1998—. Pvt. trumpet instr., Cin., 1995—. Recipient World Music Program award, Key Bank, Cin., 2000, Nat. Tchr. Appreciation award, Congl. Youth Leadership Coun., Washington, 2001, Cultural Diversity Through Music award, Learning Links, Cin., 2002. Mem.: Ohio Music Edn. Assn. (sec./treas. 2002). Avocations: music performance, travel. Home: 976 Ludlow Ave Cincinnati OH 45220 E-mail: cferrara@foresthills.edu.

FERRARA, JAMES LAWRENCE MICHAEL, pediatrician, oncologist, educator; b. N.Y.C., Dec. 17, 1952; s. Lawrence Andrew and Mary Theresa (Fichter) F.; m. Flora Eleanor Viola Watson, June 27, 1981; children: Andrew, David, Michael. Diploma d'etudes, La Sorbonne, Paris, 1973; AB summa cum laude with honors, Xavier U., 1974; MA, Oxford U., 1976; MD cum laude, Georgetown U., 1980. Diplomate Am. Bd. Pediat. Intern in pediatrics Children's Hosp., Boston, 1980, resident in pediatrics, 1981; fellow pediatric hematology/oncology Children's Hosp. and Dana-Farber Cancer Inst., Boston, 1982, rsch. fellow pediatric hematology/oncology, 1983; rsch. fellow pediatrics Harvard Med. Sch., 1982, clin. instr. pediatrics, 1980, 85, asst. prof. pediatrics, 1987, assoc. prof. pediatrics, 1993; pediat. oncologist Dana Farber Cancer Inst., 1985-98; prof. medicine and pediatrics U. Mich. Med. Sch., 1998; dir. bone marrow transplant program U. Mich. Cancer Ctr., 1998. Lectr. Sydney, 1992, Munich, 1993, Chustchuch, New Zealand, 1993, Okayama, Japan, 1996, Innsbruck, Austria, 1997, Geneva, 1997, Bologna, 2000, Stockholm, 2001, Beijing, 2001, Seoul, 2002, Rio de Janiero, 2002, Tokyo, 2003, Osaka, 2003, Istanbul, 2003, Melbourne, 2004, Paris, 2004. Author (with others): Graft Versus Host Disease, 1990, 2nd edit., 1996; editor Hematology Revs. and Comm., 1985, Transplantation, 1988, Jour. Immunology, 1993, Transplantation Immunology, 1993, Bone Marrow Transplantation, 1994; contbr. numerous articles to profl jours., chpts. to books. Recipient Physician Sci. award NIH, 1985, Stohlman scholar Leukemia Soc. Am., 1997, Alexander von Humoldt award, 1998, Doris Duke Disting. Clin. Scientist award, 2002; Am. Cancer Soc. Rsch. grantee, 1991, NIH grantee, 1992, 93; sr. fellow Mich. Soc. of Fellows, 2004. Mem. NIH (study sect. 1996), Am. Assn. Immunologists, Am. Soc. Hematology, Am. Soc. Clin. Investigation, Soc. Pediat. Rsch., Transplantation Soc., Am. Acad. Pediat., Am. Assn. Physicians. Avocations: opera, antique books and maps. Office: U Mich Cancer Ctr 1500 E Medical Center Dr Ann Arbor MI 48109-0005 E-mail: ferrara@umich.edu.

FERRARA, JEAN THERESE, church administrator; b. Kansas City, Mo., Feb. 19, 1949; d. Richard Eugene Carroll, Sr. and Mary Therese (Sheil) Carroll; m. Dominic Aldon Ferrara, Nov. 21, 1970; children: Marisa, Devon, Antonia, Gavin. BS Edn., St.Mary Coll., Leavenworth, Kans., 1995; MEd Adminstrn., Benedictine U., Atchinson, Kans., 2002. Tchr. St. John Sch., Kans. City, Mo., 1989—90, Holy Cross Sch., Kans. City, Mo., 1990—93, Holy Family Sch., Independence, Mo., 1993—95, Visitation Sch., Kans. City, Mo., 1995—2001, St. Mary's H.S., Independence, Mo., 2001—02; pastoral assoc. St. Mary Ch., Independence, Mo., 2002—. Liturgist, cantor, dir. religious edn. Holy Rosary Ch., Kans. City, Mo., 1983—2001; devel. curriculum for computer innovation and drama dept. Visitation Sch., Kans. City, Mo., 1998—2001. Mem. Sheffield Neighborhood Assn., Kans.City, Mo., 1985—. Grantee, Diocese of Kansas City, St. Joseph, 1996, 2000, K.C. Independence Chpt., 2005. Avocations: interior decorating, flower arranging, gardening, writing. Office: St Mary Cath Ch 600 N Liberty Independence MO 64050

FERRARA, LEE, graphics designer, artist, educator; b. Somerville, Mass. d. Joseph Charles and Mary Rose (Macalini) F. BFA, Mass. Coll. Art, 1951; postgrad., Yale U., 1951; MFA in Visual Comms., Syracuse U., 1976. Sr. designer Montgomery Ward, Chgo., 1956-61; graphic designer Raymond Loewy and Assocs., Chgo., Chapman, Goldsmith, and Yamasaki, Chgo., 1961-63; design dir. Family Products, Inc., Tyngsboro, Mass., 1972—82; founder, graphic designer Lee-Graphics, Santa Monica, Calif. Sr. designer Container Corp. Am., Boston, Walter Dorwin Teague, N.Y.C., 1971-72; mem. Winc Arts Coun., 1997-2000; freelance designer cos. including Max Factor of Hollywood, Pacific Air Inc., Metric Sys., Pacific Game Co., Chicken Delight, Joyce Chen, Sunbeam Corp., Teladyne, numerous others. Exhibns. include New Eng. Watercolor Soc., 1994, 95, 2002, 2003, Plymouth Art Assn., 1996, Dedham Art, 1996, Haverhill Art, 1997, Andover Art, 1997, Sharon Art Ctr., N.H., Copley Soc., Boston, 1996, Concord Art Assn., 1997, Lexington Arts and Crafts, Springfield (Mass.) Art League, 1998, Captured Wildlife 5th Annual, 1998, Andover Art in the Park, 1998, Internat. Nature Fine Arts Competition Bennington Art Complex, 1998, Arts Coun. S.E. Mo., Faulkner Centennial U. Mus., Acad. Artists Assn., 1998, Nat. Park Acad. Arts Top 200, 1998, Catharine Lorillard Wolfe Nat. Arts Club, 1998, 2001, Cambridge Art Assn., numerous others; author poems; contbr. articles to mags. publication, Art Of Color Printing On Pressure-Sensitve Lables. Participant advanced project mentor program Lincoln Sch., 1993, mem. arts lottery coun., 1998-2000; bd. dirs. Civic Symphony, 1982-88 Recipient Cert. of Appreciation, Lincoln Sch., 1993, Editor's Choice award Nat. Libr. Poetry, 1994, awards 3 categories Dedham Art, 1996, 2nd Place award Haverhill Art, 1997, 2nd Place award Andover Art, 1997, 1st prize mixed media Andover Art in the Park, 1998, Wilkins Art Cons. award Acad. Artists Assn. Nat. 1998, 2nd Place 25th Annual Winter Show Duxbury Art Assn. Mem. Am. Inst. Graphic Arts (N.Y.C.), Am. Artists Profl. League (signature mem.), New Eng. Watercolor Soc. (sig. mem.), Soc. Typographic Art (exhibn. chmn.), Artists Guild (Chgo.), Art Dirs. Club L.A., Concord Art Assn. (Mixed Media Collage award, Watercolor award 1999, 2002, Disting. Artist 2002), Copley Soc. (past bd. dirs.), North Shore Art Assn. (bd. dirs.), Allied Artists Am., Lexington Arts and Crafts (Rogowitz award, Most Creative award 2001, 2002). Achievements include pioneer design of fabric overlay for plastic cap; Clio finalist. Avocations: acting, writing, tennis, folk music, mycology. Home: 41 Franklin Rd Winchester MA 01890 Personal E-mail: leeferraradesigns@yahoo.com.

FERRARA, RALPH C., lawyer; b. Gloversville, NY, June 16, 1945; s. Rufus Ferrara and Clara F. Riccitiello. BSBA, Georgetown U., 1967; JD, U. Cin., 1970; LLM in Corp. Law, George Washington U., 1972. Bar: D.C. 1970, N.Y., 1982, Fla., 1990, Colo., 1993, U.S. Ct. Appeals, U.S. Supreme Ct. Profl. asst. to law libr. Nat. Law Ctr., Washington, 1970-72; mem. faculty George Washington U. Nat. Law Ctr., Washington; atty. divsn. enforcement SEC, Washington, 1971-72, trial atty. divsn. trading and markets, 1972-73, spl. counsel to chief enforcement atty., 1973-74, supervisory trial atty., 1974-75, spl. counsel to chmn., 1975, asst. gen. counsel, 1975-76, exec. asst. to legal counsel, 1976-77, exec. asst., 1977-78, gen. counsel, 1978-81; mng. ptnr. Debevoise & Plimpton LLP, Washington, 1981—2004; ptnr., litig. dept. LeBoeuf, Lamb, Greene & MacRae LLP, Washington, 2005—. Faculty, National Law Center, George Washington University, 1970-1972; gen. counsel, bd. of visitors, U. Cin. Coll. Law; bd. advisors, The Center for Corporate Law, U. Cin. Coll. Law, 1987-; mem. adv. bd. Securities Regulation and Law Report and The Review of Financial Services Regulation, 1987-; mem. "e Securities", bd. advisors, 1998-; mem. Washington, D.C. Panel of Distinguished Neutrals, CPR Inst. for Dispute Resolution, 1996-, administrv. conf. of the U.S., 1982-85, Ray Garrett Inst. advisory com., 1982-84, securities law advisory com., Practising Law Institute, 1981-; co-chair, Annual Institute on Securities Regulation, 1994-98, Sweeping Reform: Litigating and Bespeaking Caution Under the New Securities Law, 1996; mem. legal advisory com., N.Y. Stock Exchange Bd. Dirs. Chairman, Center for Public Resources, Inc., 1992-94, Securities Dispute Com., 1988-1989; bd. advisors, D & O Advisor, 2003—; dir. Park Pl. Entertainment. Author: Takeovers II: A Strategists' Manual for Business Combinations in the 1990s, 1993, Shareholder Derivative Litigation: Beseiging the Board, 1995, Ferrara on Insider Trading the Wall, 1995, Managing Marketeers: Supervisory Responsibilities of Broker-Dealers and Investment Advisors, 2000, Takeovers: A Strategic Guide to Mergers and Acquisitions, 2001; contbr. articles on topics related to fed. securities law to profl. jours. With USAR. Recipient John L. Sayler award, Am. Jurisprudence award, Judge Alfred Mack award. Mem. ABA (mem. sect. on corp., banking and bus. law, fed. regulation of securities com., task force on insider trading controls, 1985-, task force SEC settlements, 1987-1989, task force on sect. 15 (c) (4) Proceedings, 1987-, task force on securities arbitration, 1987-, sect. planning and Review, 1986-, vice-chmn. civil liabilities and litig. subcommittee, 1981-, chmn., task force on broker-dealer compliance, 1988-, chmn., market structures working group of the task force on review of federal securities laws), FBA (exe. coun. securities law com. 1978-, nat. coun., gen. counsels' com. 1978-81), Southwestern Legal Found. (adv. com.), Insurance Marketplace Standards Assn. (Independent Assessor Certification Market Conduct Program, 1997), Am. Law Inst. Address: 919 3rd Ave New York NY 10022 Office: LeBoeuf Lamb Greene & MacRae LLP 1875 Connecticut Ave NW Ste 1200 Washington DC 20009-5728

FERRARI, GIANNANTONIO, electronics executive; Diploma in acctg., U. Milan. With Gavazzi SpA, 1960, Honeywell Italia, 1965; gen. mgr. Honeywell Iran, Honeywell Greece; dir. fin., adminstrn., and human resources

Honeywell Mid. E.; controller Honeywell Europe, 1981-85, v.p. fin. and adminstrn., 1985-88, pres., 1992-97; v.p. Western Europe, Mid. E., Africa Honeywell, Inc., Italy, 1988-92, pres., COO, 1997—. Bd. dirs. No. State Power Co., Nat. Assn. Mfrs.; bd. govs. Nat. Elec. Mfrs. Assn. Office: 1985 Douglas Dr N Minneapolis MN 55422-3992

FERRARI, LEONARDO, small business owner; b. Mendoza, Argentina, Nov. 14, 1952; s. Celestino Alejandro Ferrari and Ana Gonzalez; 1 child, Diana Christina. PhD, Nat. U. Cuyo, Mendoza, 1978; cert. parapsychology asst., Am. Inst. Parapsychology, Buenos Aires, 1982. RN Argentina. Owner The Shoe Svc., Miami, Fla., 1989—. Avocations: photography, reading, walking, writing, meditation. Office: The Shoe Svc 115 South Miami Ave Miami FL 33130 Personal E-mail: leonardo_ferrari330@hotmail.com.

FERRARI, RAFFAELE, oceanographer, educator; s. Attilio Ferrari and Gabriella Mortara; m. Anna Leonova, Apr. 15, 1999. Diploma, Med. Sch. San Govannini, Turin, Italy, 1981; grad. in classics, Liceo Classico Val Salice, Turin, 1986; MS in Physics, U. Turin, 1994; PhD in Fluid Dynamics, Poly. Turin, 1999; PhD in Oceanography, Scripps Inst. Oceanography, 2000. Rsch. asst. Politecnico di Torino, Torino, Italy, 1994—97, Scripps Instn. of Oceanography, La Jolla, 1995—2000; postdoctoral scholar Woods Hole Oceanog. Instn., Mass., 2000—01; asst. prof. MIT, Cambridge, Mass., 2002—. Recipient Victor P. Starr Career devel. Chair, MIT, 2003; grantee Climate Process Team Leader, NSF, 2004; Killian and Lee scholar, MIT, 2004, Woods Hole Postdoctoral scholar, Woods Hole Oceanog. Instn., 2001. Mem.: Am. Meteorol. Soc. Office: 54 1920 MIT 77 Massachusetts Ave Cambridge MA 02139 Office Phone: 617-253-7762. Office Fax: 617-253-4464.

FERRARI, ROBERT JOSEPH, finance educator, retired bank executive; b. Bklyn., Dec. 3, 1936; m. Patricia A. Cantalupo, Sept. 6, 1958 (dec. Jan. 1991); children: Robert Joseph, James G., Judith A., Thomas A. BS in Econs., Villanova U., 1958; MBA, NYU, 1962; grad. certificate, Brown U., 1969, Henry George Sch. Social Sci., 1961; DSc, London Inst., 1973. With arbitrage dept. Goodbody & Co., 1957-60; bank auditor Fed. Res. Bank, N.Y.C., 1960-65; v.p. fin. Am. Savs. Bank, N.Y.C., 1965-81; prof., chair dept. econs. and bus. Marymount Coll. of Fordham U., Tarrytown, 1981—. Cons. LaCorte Agy., Inc., 1963—65. Office: Marymount Coll of Fordham Univ 100 Marymount Ave Tarrytown NY 10591-3704 Home: 425 River Rd Pipersville PA 18947 Office Phone: 914-332-7461. E-mail: rferrari@fordham.edu.

FERRARI, VICTOR STEVEN, surgeon; b. Buenos Aires, Aug. 31, 1961; came to U.S., 1964; BS, Davidson Coll., 1983; MD, U. N.C., 1987. Diplomate Am. Bd. Surgery, Am. Bd. Plastic Surgery. Intern U. Kans., Kansas City, 1987-88, resident in gen. surgery, 1988-92; resident in plastic surgery U. Miami, Fla., 1993-94, fellow in craniofacial surgery, 1995; pvt. practice. Med. dir. Impact Internat. Fgn. Mission Orgn., Boca Raton, Fla., 1996—. Mem. AMA, Christian Med. Soc. Office: Plastic Surgery Assocs Miami 8940 N Kendall Dr Ste 903 Miami FL 33176-2151

FERRARO, BETTY ANN, retired state senator; b. Newport, Vt., Mar. 3, 1925; d. Clarence John and Mauretta Rowena (Potter) Morse; m. Dominic Thomas Ferraro, Oct. 8, 1964; children: Deborah, David, Susan, Barbara. Student, Mary Hitchcock Hosp. Sch. Nursing, Coll. St. Joseph, Rutland, Vt. Exec. sec. to asst. treas. Ctrl. Vt. Pub. Svc. Corp., Rutland, 1943-44; sec. to dean N.Y. Med. Coll., N.Y.C., 1944-46; model G. Fox Co., Hartford, Conn., 1947; corp. sec., office mgr. John Russell Corp., Rutland, 1970-80; exec. dir. Rutland Area Coordinated Child Care Com., Washington, 1977-79; adminstrv. asst. Hilinex of Vt., Rutland, 1981-83; owner Classic Connection Gift Shop, Rutland, 1983-87; adminstr. Vicon Recovery Sys., Inc., Rutland, 1987-90. Owner, operator nursery sch., 1973—77; mgr. Day Care Ctr., 1978—80; mem. Rutland City Bd. Aldermen, 1984—86, 2001—03; resource dir. Rutland City Emergency Mgmt. Team for State of Vt., 1984—90; mem. Vt. State Cmty. Devel. Commn., 1986. Chmn. Rutland City Rep. Com., 1991-93; county committeewoman State Rep. Com., 1984-86, rep.; rep. Rutland County Rep. Com.; state del. Rep. Nat. Conv., 1992; Rep. campaign coord. State of Vt., 1997-98; county co-chair Jim Douglas for Gov., 2001-02; mem. Vt. Ho. Reps., 1990-92; mem. Vt. Senate, 1992-94, 95-97; mem. jud. nominating bd. Human Resource Investment Com., 1995-96, Vt. Student Assistance Corp. Bd.; mem. Amtrak Study Commn., 1995-96; bd. dirs. Vt. Physicians Coun., 1997—, Coll. St. Joseph, 1996-2000, Marble Valley Transit, 1996—, sec. bd. dirs.; mem. adv. bd. Paramount Theatre, 1997—; sec., receptionist Orton Family Found., 1999-2000; sec., receptionist Eddy Enterprises, Inc., 2000-01; county co-chair Jim Douglas for Gov., 2002; hon. chair Kevin Mullin for Sen. Campaign, 2004—; mem. Vt. State Transp. Bd, 2003-05; devel. coord. Neighbor Works We. Vt., 2002-05 Fleming Inst. fellow, 1995; named Woman of Yr. Green Mt. Coun. of Boy Scouts Am. Mem. Nat. Assn. Women in Constrn. (chartered, past pres.), Rutland County Rep. Women. Republican. Roman Catholic. Avocation: flower arranging. Home and Office: Condo 17 155 Dorr Dr Rutland VT 05701-3853 E-mail: b.m.ferraro@verizon.net.

FERRARO, JOHN FRANCIS, investment banker; b. N.Y.C., Jan. 3, 1934; s. John Anthony and Angelina (Figliola) F.; children: Elizabeth Ann, John Robert, Laura Marie, Rosemary. BS in Indsl. Engring. with honors and distinction, NYU, 1962. With United Technologies Corp., Windsor Locks, Conn., 1962-66; sr. project engr. United Techs. Corp., Windsor Locks, Conn., 1962-64, chief research and devel. promotion, 1964-66; founding ptnr. P.M.C. Corp., 1966-78; chmn. bd., chief exec. officer Thermodynetics, Inc.; pres. Spectrum Inc., 1966—, also dir.; pres. Pioneer Capital Corp.; mng. dir. Pioneer Ventures Assocs. L.P., Capital Mgmt. Ptnrs. LLC. Bd. dirs. Turbotec Products, Inc., Xtec Corp. Contbr. numerous articles on bus., fin. and stock market to fin. publs., 1966-81; contbg. editor: Handbook of Wealth Management, 1977. Trustee Birth Right, Conn., 1970—80; chmn. Congl. Com. for Apointees USAF Acad., 1980; commr. Develop Agy., Enfield, Conn., 1981; mem. Gov.'s task force for mfg. State of Conn., 1989—91; mem. exec. com. Holy Family Retreat League, 1984—88; mem. bd. advisors St. Joseph's Residence, Conn., 1991—; trustee Suffield Acad., Conn., 1980—93, chair budget and fin. com., 1987—92; trustee Western New Eng. Coll., 1997—2003. 1st lt. USAF, 1954—58. Decorated Meritorious Service medal. Mem. Psi Upsilon, Suffield Country Club. Home: 86 Berkshire Ave Southwick MA 01077-9642 Office: 651 Day Hill Rd Windsor CT 06095-1719 E-mail: jigfox@earthlink.net.

FERRARO, KAREN L., marketing professional; m. Lloyd John Ferraro, Jan. 11, 1951. Assocs. in Computer Sci., L.A. Wilson Tech., 1970. Cert. computer science 1970. Dir. MIS Exxon Enterprises, N.Y.C., 1976—79; dir. customer tng. Binary Sys., Plainview, N.Y., 1979—82; sr. dir. mktg. Nortel Networks, Bohemia, N.Y., 1982—2001; v.p. mktg. Misys Healthcare Sys., Raleigh, N.C., 2001—03; pres. Aklyn & Co., Bellport, NY. Editor: (client newsletter) PeriGram; author: The Guide to Voice Processing. Founder PACE, Bohemia, 1995—2000. Recipient Pres.'s award, Periphonics Corp., 1990. Mem.: L.I. Assn., L.I. Ctr. Bus. and Profl. Women, Internat. Assn. Bus. Communicators, Assn. Info. Technology Profls., LISTnet. Office: Aklyn & Co PO Box 513 Bellport NY 11713 Office Fax: 631-294-5686. Business E-Mail: karen@aklyn.com.

FERRAZ, FRANCISCO MARCONI, neurological surgeon; b. Floresta, Pernambuco, Brazil, Aug. 14, 1951; arrived in U.S., 1976; Student, Colegio Nobrega, Recife-Brazil, 1967—69; MD, Faculdade de Medicine da Universidade Federal de Pernambuco-Brazil, 1975. Diplomate Am. Bd. Neurol. Surgery. Intern Jamaica Hosp., N.Y.C., 1976—77; resident Georgetown U. Med. Ctr. and Affiliated Hosps., Washington, 1977—82; pvt. practice medicine specializing in neurol. surgery Washington, 1982—; mem. staff Georgetown U. Hosp., 1982—, Arlington Hosp., 1982—; chief divsn. neurosurgery, faculty clin. instr. Georgetown U. Sch. Medicine, 1982—; faculty clin. assoc. prof. George Washington Sch. Medicine, 1994—. Cons. in health care fin., internat. health care. Contbr. articles to profl. jours. Fellow: ACS, Internat. Coll. Surgeons; mem.: AMA, Congress of Neurol. Surgery, Washington Acad. Neurosurgery, Neurosurg. Soc. of D.C., Arlington Med. Soc., Am. Assn. Neurol. Surgeons. Office: 611 S Carlin Springs Rd Ste 105 Arlington VA 22204-1061 Office Phone: 703-845-1552. Business E-Mail: fferraz@starpower.net.

FERRÉ, MAURICE ANTONIO, entrepreneur; b. Ponce, P.R., June 23, 1935; s. Jose Antonio and Florence (Salichs) F.; m. Maria Mercedes Malaussena; children: Mary Isabel, Jose Luis, Carlos Maurice, Maurice Raymundo, Florence, Francisco Antonio. BS in Archtl. Engring., U. Miami, 1957. Mem. Fla. Ho. of Reps., 1967; commr. City of Miami, 1973—85, mayor, 1968-85; prin. Ferré Holdings, Miami. Author: Metro-Miami Destination 2000, 1996. Vice chmn. Miami Dade County Commn., 1993—96; bd. dirs. ICARE Bay Point Schs. Roman Catholic. Home: 3900 Poinciana Ave Coconut Grove FL 33133-6424 Office: Ferré Holdings 2655 Le Jeune Rd #511 Miami FL 33134 Office Phone: 305-779-3051. Personal E-mail: maferre2002@aol.com.

FERREE, JOHN NEWTON, JR., fundraising specialist, consultant; b. Wadesboro, N.C., Nov. 21, 1946; s. John Newton and Mary Cleo Ferree. AA, Bluefield (Va.) Coll., 1966; BA, Baylor U., 1968; JD, Cumberland Sch. Law, Samford U., 1975. Bar: Ala. Contr. Aetna Life Ins. Co., Seattle, 1972; atty. Ferree & Armstrong, Alabaster, Ala., 1975-82; exec. dir. Northwest Bapt. Found., Portland, Oreg., 1982-84; asst. v.p. Harris Trust Co. of Ariz., Scottsdale, 1984; v.p. Bapt. Found. of Ariz., Phoenix, 1985-89; dir. planned giving Phoenix Children's Hosp., 1989-91; pres. Scottsdale (Ariz.) Healthcare Found., 1991—; bd. dir. Nat. Com. Planned Giving, 1994-96. Bd. dirs. FBI Citizen's Acad. Found., 1994—, v.p. 1994-96, 98-99, Charitable Accord, v.p., 1996-1998; instr. Cannon Sch. Found. Mgmt., 1995-2000; adj. prof. Ariz. State U., 1998-2000; cons. in field. Named Ariz. Profl. Fundraiser of Yr., 1996. Mem. Assn. Fundraising Profls. (pres. greater Ariz. chpt. 1991), Planned Giving Roundtable of Ariz. (pres. 1992, 97), Assn. for Healthcare Philanthropy. Republican. Baptist. Office: Scottsdale Healthcare Found 10001 N 92d St Ste 121 Scottsdale AZ 85258-4530 Office Phone: 480-882-4516. Business E-Mail: jferree@shc.org.

FERREIRA, ALEXANDRE C., medical educator; b. Fortaleza, Ceara, Brazil, Sept. 3, 1966; s. Jose Carlos and Cleomar Aguiar Ferreira; m. Jacqueline V. Leite, Dec. 27, 1990; children: Gabriela V. Gondim, Isabela V., Felipe V. MD, Universidade Fed. do Ceara, Fortaleza, Brazil, 1990. Assoc. prof. clin. medicine U. Miami, 1998—; dir. interventional cardiology tng. program Jackson Meml. Hosp., Miami, 1999—2005. Dir. Jackson Meml. Hosp., Miami, 2004—. Author: (medical textbook) Interventional Cardiology Secretes. Recipient Eric Reiss Award for Outstanding Tchr., U. Miami, 1994. Fellow: Am. Coll. Cardiology (assoc.). Office: Univ Miami 1611 NW 12 Ave Miami FL 33136 Office Phone: 305-585-5527. Office Fax: 305-585-7089. Personal E-mail: aferreir@med.miami.edu.

FERREIRA, ARMANDO THOMAS, sculptor, educator; b. Charleston, W.Va., Jan. 8, 1932; s. Maximiliano and Placeres (Sanchez) F.; children: Lisa, Teresa. Student, Chouinard Art Inst., 1949—50, Long Beach City Coll., 1950—53; BA, UCLA, 1954, MA, 1956. Asst. prof. art Mt. St. Mary's Coll., 1956-57; mem. faculty dept. art Calif. State U., Long Beach, 1957—, prof., 1967—, chmn. dept. art, 1971-77, assoc. dean Sch. Fine Arts, acting dean Coll. Arts. Lectr., cons. on art adminstrn. to art schs. and univs., Brazilian Ministry Edn. One-man shows include, Pasadena Mus., 1959, Long Beach Mus., 1959, 69, Eccles Mus., 1967, Clay and Fiber Gallery, Taos, 1972; exhibited in group shows at L.A. County Art Mus., 1958, 66, Wichita Art Mus., 1959, Everson Mus., 1960, 66, San Diego Mus. Fine Arts, 1969, 73, Fairtree Gallery, N.Y.C., 1971, 74, L.A. Inst. Contemporary Art, 1977, Utah Art Mus., 1978, Bowers Mus., Santa Ana, Calif., 1980, No. Ill. U., 1986, Beckstrand Gallery, Palos Verdes (Calif.) Art Ctr., 1987, U. Madrid, 1993; permanent collections include Utah Mus. Art, Wichita Art Mus., Long Beach (Calif.) Mus. Art, State of Calif. Collection, Fred Jones Jr. Mus. Art U. Okla., U. Okla. Art Mus.; vis. artist, U. N.D., 1974. Fulbright lectr. Brazil, 1981. Fellow: Nat. Assn. Schs. Art and Design (bd. dirs.). *I suppose much of my own life has been shaped by my experience as a first generation American. What modest success I may have had in my work is considerably due to that sense of ambition with which immigrant parents imbue their children. My vision as an artist is also shaped by the strong sense of Spanish culture that was part of my upbringing.*

FERREIRA, FERNANDA L, language educator; b. Olinda, Brazil, July 26, 1965; d. Iracema Lima Pires and Eraldo Pires Ferreira. BA French Translation, Universidade Fed. de Pernambuco, 1992; MA Portuguese, U. Ill., 1996; PhD Spanish & Portuguese, U. N.Mex., 2001. Asst. prof. Bridgewater State Coll., Mass., 2001—. Grantee travel & rsch. grant, Latin Am. and Iberian Inst., 1999, travel grant, Grad. and Profl. Student Assn., 1999. Mem.: Linguistic Assn. of the SW, Soc. for Pidgin and Creole Languages, Am. Assn. of Teachers of Spanish and Portuguese, Linguistic Soc. of Am. Office: Bridgewater State College Tillinghast Hall 317 Bridgewater MA 02325 Business E-Mail: fferreira@bridgew.edu.

FERRELL, ALLEN F., law educator; b. Lankenan, Pa., Jan. 23, 1970; BA in Philosophy, MA in Philosophy, Brown U., 1992; JD, Harvard U., 1995. Law clk. to Hon. Laurence H. Silberman US Ct. Appeals DC Cir., 1995—96; law clk. to Justice Anthony M. Kennedy US Supreme Ct., 1996—97; Olin Fellow in Law, Economics, and Bus. Harvard Law Sch., Cambridge, Mass., 1997—99, named asst. prof. law, 1999, John M. Olin Rsch. Prof. in Law, Economics, and Bus., 2000—01, prof., 2005—. Bd. econ. advisors NASD. Office: Harvard Law Sch 1563 Massachusetts Ave Cambridge MA 02138 Office Phone: 617-495-8961. Office Fax: 617-496-4863. Business E-Mail: fferrell@law.harvard.edu.

FERRELL, CATHERINE KLEMANN, sculptor, painter; b. Detroit, Apr. 27, 1947; d. Robert Byron and Elizabeth (Crapo) Klemann; m. William Barksdale Ferrell Jr., Nov. 4, 1987; children: Adrienne Elizabeth, Peter Klemann. Student, U. Mich., 1966-67; BA in Sculpture, Fla. Atlantic U., 1969; MA in Sculpture, U. Miami, Fla., 1972. Asst. to sculptor Luis Montoya Montoya Art Studios, West Palm Beach, Fla., 1983; pres., sculptor Art Equities, Inc., Vero Beach, Fla., 1986—. One-woman shows include Musee Universale, Montreal, Can., 1985, Elliott Mus., Stuart, Fla., 1985, Lighthouse Gallery Inc., 1991, J. Sexton Gallery, Vero Beach, Fla., 1996, McCreeless Fine Arts Gallery, Asbury Coll., Lexington, Ky., 1996, U. Mich., Flint, Mich., 1996, Cornell Mus., Delray Beach, Fla., 1999, Pen Brush, Inc., NY, 2002, Pen and Brush Inc., NYC, 2002, Cheryl Newby Gallery, SC, 2003; represented in permanent collections: Norton Mus. Art, West Palm Beach, Fla., Bennex Internat., Oslo, Norway, Brevard Mus. Art, Melbourne, Fla., Gunter Schultz-Franke, Arch., Osnabruch, West Germany, dr. Paul Gingras, Palm Beach, Fla.; numerous pvt. collections Recipient Silver medal, Audubon Artists Am. Fellow Nat. Sculpture Soc. (colleague); mem. Am. Acad. Women Artists, Am. Artists Profl. League, Knickerbocker Artists, Allied Artists (assoc.), Profl. Artists Guild, Artists Forum, Pen and Brush, Inc. (award 1992), S.E. Sculptors Assn., Catherine Lorillard Wolfe Art Club, Salmagundi Club (Cert. of Merit, Elliot Liskin Meml. award 1993, Pres. award 1994) Home: 12546 Highway A1A Vero Beach FL 32963-9411 Personal E-mail: tcferrell@aol.com.

FERRELL, CHARLES MADISON, nuclear engineer, physicist; b. Clarksburg, W.Va., Apr. 30, 1928; s. Benjamin Franklin and Mary Ethlyn (Selby) F.; m. Donnie Sue Thompson, Aug. 30, 1957; children: Donald Franklin, Jeffrey Madison, Kimberly Marilyn. BS, Salem (W.Va.) Coll., 1950; postgrad., Vanderbilt U., 1954-55, W.Va. U., 1955-56, U. Md., 1959-61. Phys. scientist U.S. Army Chem. Corps, Edgewood, Md., 1951-52, physicist Frederick, Md., 1953-54; radiol. physicist U.S. AEC, Oak Ridge, 1956-57, Germantown, Md., 1957-74; nuc. engr. U.S. NRC, Bethesda and Rockville, Md., 1974-95; cons., 1995—. Co-author 5 U.S. Nuc. Regulatory publs. Dist. advancement chmn., unit commr. Seneca Dist. and Forest Oak coun. Boy Scouts Am., 1993-2005. With U.S. Army, 1950-52. U.S. AEC radiol. physics fellow, 1954-55; recipient Silver Beaver award Boy Scouts Am., 1998, numerous vol. svc. awards including Nat. Assn. of Ret. Fed. Employees State of Md. award, 1997, City of Gaithersburg, Md. People of Character award, 1997; named to Md. Sr. Citizens Hall of Fame, 2001, City of Gaithersburg Disting. Citizen Outstanding Cmty. Svc., 2004. Mem. Health Physics Soc., Shriners. Methodist. Achievements include design of instrumentation to measure thermal radiation from nuclear tests; evaluation of radioactive sealed sources and devices for AEC licenses; evaluation of shipping casks for spent reactor fuel; tech. asst. to AEC office of Hearing Examiner on Contract Appeal cases and nuclear power reactor licensing; evaluation of power reactor site safety and design basis accidents. Home: 227 Rolling Rd Gaithersburg MD 20877-2041

FERRELL, CONCHATA GALEN, actress, performing arts educator; b. Charleston, W.Va., Mar. 28, 1943; d. Luther Martin and Mescal Loraine (George) F.; m. Arnold A. Anderson; 1 dau., Samantha. Student, W.Va. U., 1961-64, Marshall U., 1967-68. Actor: (NY theater appearances) The Hot L Baltimore, 1973, The Sea Horse, 1973—74 (OBIE award and Drama Desk award, 1974), Battle of Angels, 1975; (plays) Getting Out, 1978, Here Wait, 1980, Picnic, 1986; (TV series) The Hot L Baltimore, 1975, B.J. and the Bear, 1979, McClain's Law, 1981, E.R., 1984, A Peaceable Kingdom, 1989, L.A. Law, 1991, Hearts Afire, 1993—94, Townies, 1996, Teen Angel, 1997, Push, Nevada, 2002, Two & 1/2 Men, 2003—, (movies) Network, 1975, Dangerous Hero, 1975, Heartland, 1981, Where the River Runs Black, 1986, For Keeps, 1987, Mystic Pizza, 1987, Witches of Eastwick, 1987, Chains of Gold, 1990, Edward Scissorhands, 1990, Family Prayers, 1993, True Romance, 1993, Samurai Cowboy, 1993, Heaven and Earth, 1993, Freeway, 1995, Touch, 1996, My Fellow Americans, 1996, Erin Brokovich, 2000, Crime and Punishment-High School, 2000, Stranger Inside, 2001, K-Pax, 2001, Mr. Deeds, 2002, (TV movies) A Girl Called Hatter Fox, 1977, A Death in Canaan, 1977, The Orchard Children, 1978, Before and After, 1979, Bliss, 1979, Reunion, 1980, The Rideout Case, 1980, The Great Gilley Hopkins, 1981, Life of the Party, 1982, Emergency Room, 1983, Nadia, 1984, Miss Lonely Hearts, 1985, Samaritan, 1986, Northbeach and Rawhide, 1986, Picnic, 1986, Eye on the Sparrow, 1987, Runaway Ralph, 1987, Goodbye Miss Liberty (Disney Channel), 1988, Running Mates, 1990, Deadly Intentions, Again, 1990, Back Field in Motion, 1991, 120 Volt Miracle, 1992, Forget Me Not, 1996, Sweetdreams, 1996, Amy and Isabelle, 2001. Recipient Wrangler award Nat. Cowboy Hall of Fame, 1981, Most Promising Newcomer award Theatre World, 1974, Emmy award nomination, 1991-92, 2004-2005. Mem. AFTRA, ACLU, NOW, Actors Equity Assn., Screen Actors Guild, Women in Films, Circle West. Democrat. Office: 360 N Crescent Pl North Bldg Beverly Hills CA 90210

FERRELL, DAVID STANLEY, aerospace transportation executive; b. South Charleston, W.Va., Nov. 24, 1946; s. Erastus Carden and Ella Belle (Stanley) F.; m. Lynda Ann Snodgrass, Jan. 25, 1969; children: Holley Elizabeth, Eric Carden. BA, Marshall U., Huntington, W.Va., 1969; MA, Webster U., St. Louis, 1983. Lic. comml. pilot. Commd. lt. U.S. Army, Washington, 1969-94, mgr. digitization, 1994-98; mgr., dir. Aviation Activities, Washington, 1998-2000; mgr. Washington ops. Sys. Studies and Simulations, Washington, 2000—. Recipient Bronze Star, U.S. Army, 1971, Legion of Merit, 1994, Combat Air Medals for Valor, 1971, others. Mem. Am. Helicopter Soc. (pres. 1994—), AHS Internat. (pres. membership 2000—), Crystal City Rotary (sec. 1994-96), Assn. U.S. Army (v.p. at large 1995-97). Lutheran. Avocations: outdoor activities, reading, computers.

FERRELL, ELIZABETH ANN, lawyer; b. Morgantown, W.Va., Feb. 10, 1957; BA magna cum laude, U. SC, 1979, JD, 1982. Bar: SC 1982, DC 1985. Law clk. to Hon. Sol Blatt, Jr. US Dist. Ct. Dist. SC, 1982—84; assoc. Pierson Ball & Dowd, Washington, Piper & Marbury, Washington, 1988—91, ptnr., 1991; ptnr., govt. contracts group Sonnenschein Nath & Rosenthal LLP, Washington, 1991—. Office: Sonnenschein Nath & Rosenthal LLP Ste 600, E Tower 1301 K St NW Washington DC 20005 Office Phone: 202-408-6420. Office Fax: 202-408-6399. Business E-Mail: eferrell@sonnenschein.com.

FERRELL, HEATHER A., curator; b. Boise, Idaho, Aug. 15, 1970; d. Christine Louise and Michael Claude Kenyon (Stepfather); m. Nathan Gary Niederhauser, May 14, 1994 (div. Jan. 2, 2003). BFA, Utah State U., 1988—94; MA, Case Western Res. U., 1995—97. Director-adj. art faculty Roland Dille Ctr. for the Arts Gallery, U. of Minn., Moorhead, Minn., 1998—99; collections mgr./registrar Plains Art Mus., Fargo, ND, 1997—99; assoc. curator of art Boise Art Mus., 1999—2005; dir. Salina Arts Ctr., Salina, Kans., 2005—. Bd. mem., newsletter editor Museums in ND, 1998—99; bd. mem., exec. com. Western Museums Assn., Berkeley, Calif., 2003—; bd. mem. Idaho Assn. of Museums, Boise, Idaho, 2003—; grad. Getty Leadership Inst., Los Angeles, 2004. Dir.(project director and artist): Snapshots: Lives in Transition; exhibitions include The Allegorical Figure, CWRU Mather Gallery; author: (museum brochure) Lucinda Parker: New Paintings, Ron Jude: 45th Parallel. Recipient Best of Boise: Arts Profl., Boise Weekly, 2004; Museums Leaders the Next Generation, Getty Leadership Inst., 2004, 1997 Dorothy Zieburtz Buckhold Tchg. Asst., Case Western Res. Univ., 1997. Mem.: Idaho Assn. of Museums (bd. mem. 2003—05), Western Museums Assn. (bd. mem. 2003—05), Am. Assn. of Museums. Avocations: running, photography, travel. Office: Salina Art Ctr 242 South Santa Fe Salina KS 67402-0743 Office Phone: 208-345-8330 ext. 20. Office Fax: 208-345-2247. Business E-Mail: heather@boiseartmuseum.org.

FERRELL, HENRY CLIFTON, JR., historian, educator; b. Greensboro, N.C., July 28, 1934; s. Henry Clifton and Mary Louise Ferrell; m. Martha Smith, Sept. 6, 1958; children: Mary Elizabeth, Martha Ann, Henry Clifton Ferrell III. AB, Duke U., 1956, MA, 1957; PhD, U. Va., 1964. Prof. History East Carolina U., Greenville, NC, 1961—. Planner East Carolina U., Greenville, 1980—85, univ. historian, 2001—. Author: Claude A. Swanson of Virginia, 1986. Spec 4 U.S. Army, 1959—65. Democrat. Methodist. Home: 2010 Fern Dr Greenville NC 27858

FERRELL, JAMES EDWIN, energy company executive; b. Atchison, Kans., Oct. 17, 1939; s. Alfred C. and Mabel A. (Samson) F.; m. Elizabeth J. Gillespie, May 10, 1959; children: Kathryn E., Sarah A. BS in Bus. Adminstrn., U. Kans., 1963. Pres. Ferrell Cos., Inc., Liberty, Mo., 1965—; chmn., chief exec. officer Gas Service Co., Kansas City, Mo., 1983-85; chmn., pres., CEO Ferrellgas Partners, Liberty, Mo. Bd. dirs. United Mo. Bancshares, Kansas City, Ferrell Cos., Inc. Bd. dirs. Coun. Ind. Colls., 1988-91; trustee Kansas City Symphony, 1987—. Served to 1st lt. U.S. Army, 1963-65. Republican. Lutheran. Office: Ferrell Cos Inc 1 Liberty Plz Liberty MO 64068 Office Fax: 816-792-7985.*

FERRELL, JANICE RENE, music educator; b. Ft. Worth, Mar. 18, 1946; d. Thomas Benton Dewett and Fanny Kathleen Martin-Bean; 1 child, Shannon Michelle. BFA, U. Tex., Tyler, 1979, MA, 1981; PhD, U. North Tex., 2003. Tchr. gen. music Tyler Ind. Sch. Dist., Tex., 1977—80; choral dir. Athens High Sch., 1986—90; asst. prof. music Nebr. Wesleyan U., Lincoln, 1993—97, Calif. State U., Bakersvield, 1999—. Organist, choirmaster Christ Epsicopal Ch. Girls Choir, Tyler, 1975—80; condr. adult choir Cedar St. United Meth. Ch., 1982; condr. Nebr. Suzuki Camp Festival Chorus, 1994; condr. women's chorus Nebr. Wesleyan U., 1993—97; condr. children's choir St. John's Epsicopal Ch., Ft. Worth, 1998—99; condr. Calif. State U., Bakersfield, 2004—05; guest condr. region IV All-Region Honor Choir Paris Tex. Mid. Sch., 1987; guest condr. Singing Youth Nebr. Choral Festival, 1994, Sing Around Nebr. Choral Festival, 1996, 98, Norfolk Invitational Trebel Choral Festival, Va., 1994, 95, 96, 97, 98, 98, 99, 2000, 01; guest condr. honor choir Kern County Jr. High Sch., Calif., 2001; guest condr. Bakersfield High Sch., 2005; tchr. treble chorus Bell Elem. Sch., Tyler, 1977—80; condr. treble chorus,. tchr. voice New Eng. Music Camp, Waterville, Maine, 1989—91; presenter and cons. in field. Bd. dirs., clinician Tex. Conf. Choir Clinic and Camp, 1984—94; bd. dirs. Tyler Civic Chorale, 1979—82. Fellow, U. North Tex., Denton, 1991—93. Mem.: Calif. Coun. Music Tchr. Edn., Coll. Music Soc., Music Educators Nat. Conf., Calif. Choral Dirs. Assn., Am. Choral Dirs. Assn., Am. Orff-Schulwerk Assn. (nat. adv. coun. 1995—97), Kern County

Music Educators Assn., Calif. Music Educators Assn., Kolady Assn. So. Calif., Orgn. Am. Kolady Educators (Svc. award 1996), Internat. Kodaly Soc., Mu Phi Epsilon, Phi Delta Kappa, Pi Kappa Lambda. Address: 8717 Heely Ct Bakersfield CA 93311-1924

FERRELL, JOSEPH STEVENS, law educator; b. Elizabeth City, N.C., Sept. 11, 1938; s. Joseph Franklin and Bertie Virginia (Morgan) F. BS, U. N.C., 1960, JD with honors, 1963; LLM, Yale U., 1964. Prof. pub. law and govt. U. N.C., Chapel Hill, 1964—, disting. prof., 1989—, sec. of faculty, 1997—. Prin. cons. N.C. Local Govt. Study Commn., 1967-73; cons. N.C. Constitution Study Commn., 1969. Autor: Suggested Rules of Procedure for the Board of County Commissioners, 1990, The General Assembly of North Carolina: A Handbook for Legislators, 7th edit., 1997; co-author: (with Bonnie E. Davis) Handbook for North Carolina County Commissioners, 1998; contbr. articles to profl. jours., including N.C. Law Rev., Popular Govt.; editor: North Carolina Legislation, 1986-96. Mem. Diocesan Coun., Diocese of N.C., 1984-87, 89-91, 93-96, mem. standing com., 1999—. Recipient Disting. Svc. award N.C. Assn. County Commrs. Mem. N.C. Bar Assn., Phi Beta Kappa, Order of Coif. Democrat. Episcopalian. Home: 1 Iris Ln Chapel Hill NC 27514-4208 Office: U NC Office Fac Governance 204 Carr Blvd Chapel Hill NC 27599-0001

FERRELL, MICHAEL J., lawyer; b. Detroit, Mar. 27, 1951; BS in History & Polit. Sci., Mercy Coll. of Detroit, 1973; JD, George Mason U., 1979. Bar: DC, Va. Various legislative positions US Ho. of Reps. & US Senate, Washington; gen. ptnr. O'Connor & Hannon, Washington; sr. staff v.p., legislative counsel Mortgage Bankers Assn. of Am.; founder Potomac Partners; ptnr., legislative & govt. affairs, trade & professional assn. Venable LLP, Washington, 2002—, former co-chair, homeland security practice group, former chair, legislative practice. Office: Venable LLP 575 7th St NW Washington DC 20004 Office Phone: 202-344-8588. Office Fax: 202-344-8300. Business E-Mail: mjferrell@venable.com.

FERRELL, MILTON MORGAN, JR., lawyer; b. Coral Gables, Fla, Nov. 6, 1951; s. Milton M. and Annie (Blanche) Bradley; m. Lori R. Sanders, May 22, 1982; children: Milton Morgan III, Whitney Connolly. BA, Mercer U., 1973, JD, 1975. Bar: Fla. 1975. Asst. state's atty. State's Atty.'s Office, Miami, 1975-77; ptnr. Ferrell & Ferrell, Miami, 1977-84; sole practice Miami, 1985-87; ptnr. Ferrell & Williams, P.A., Miami, Fla., 1987-90, Ferrell & Fertel, P.A., Miami, 1990-98, Ferrell Schultz Carter & Fertel P.A., 1999-2000, Ferrell Schultz Carter & Fertel, P.A., 2000—; pvt. practice, 2005—. Mem. Ambs. of Mercy, Mercy Hosp. Found., Inc., 1985—94; trustee Greater Miami and the Keys chpt. ARC, mem., 2001—, bd. dirs., 2001—; trustee, mem. legal. com., chair com. Project to Cure Paralysis U. Miami, 1985—94; trustee Mus. Sci. and Space Transit Planetarium, 1977—82; bd. trustees Eaglebrook Sch., 1995—98, Mercer U., 2004—; bd. dirs. Performing Arts Ctr. Found., 1998—, Jackson Meml. Found., 1999—2004, chmn., 2004—; bd. dirs. Robinson Charitable Found., 1993—; bd. dirs. The Founders Mount Sinai Med. Ctr. Found., 2002—; trustee United Way of Miami-Dade, 2000—. Mem. ABA (grantee 1975), Am. Bd. Criminal Lawyers (bd. dirs. 1982-83, sec. 1983-85, v.p. 1985-86, pres. 1986-87), Nat. Assn. Criminal Def. Lawyers, Am. Bar Found., Fla. Bar Assn. (jury instrns. com. 1987-89, chmn. grievance com. L 1987-90), Internat. Bar Assn., Dade County Bar Assn. (bd. dir. 1977-80), Assn. Trial Lawyers Am., Bath Club (bd. gov. 1992-95), Miami City Club, Univ. Club, Banker's Club, Cat Cay Yacht Club, Inc. (bd. dir. 1997-2000, treas. 1998-99, pres. 1999-2000), Indian Creek Country Club, LaGorce Country Club, Fisher Island Club, GlenArbor Golf Club, Farmington Country Club Home: Bay Point 4511 Lake Rd Miami FL 33137-3372 Office: 201 S Biscayne Blvd Fl 34 Miami FL 33131-4325 Business E-Mail: mmf@ferrellworldwide.com.

FERRELL, PAUL CLEVELAND, writer; b. Morehouse, Mo., Aug. 17, 1943; s. Sherman Gentry and Virginia Irene (Brawley) F.; m. Wanda Darlene Jones, Nov. 27, 1963. Student, Mineral Area Jr. Coll., Flat River, Mo., 1965—66, U. Mo., S.E. Mo. State U. Registered technologist Am. Radiol. Soc. Head radiology dept. Madison Meml. Hosp., Fredericktown, Mo., 1965-66; ambulance attendant Pub. Emergency Svc., Sikeston, Mo., 1970-73; tchr. math. Sikeston Pub. Schs., 1978-80, vocat. instr., 1980-85; ghost writer Sikeston, 1981-84; author Bloomfield, Mo., 1985—. Mem. adv. bd. Vocat. Edn., Sikeston, 1980—85; lectr. in math., health and philosophy. Author: Diet and the Cardiovascular Condition, 1995, The Utopian Cause, 1996, Night Reader I, 1997, Night Reader II, 1997, Art-Mail, 1997, Morehouse Missouri, 1997, vol. 3, 2001, Night Reader III, 1998, Good Son/Bad Son, 1999, The Songs and Dreams of the Iconoclast and the Misanthrope, 2000, others; ghost writer, editor: The Headlee Anthology, 1984; author (cultural newsletter) The Plow and the Stars, 1992-93; inventor game Choice and Chance, 1992. Served with USN, 1966—70, Vietnam. Mem.: Am. Registry Radiol. Technologists. Avocations: local history, visual and performing arts. Office: The Plow and the Stars 21212 County Road 510 Bloomfield MO 63825-8500 Personal E-mail: starplow@hotmail.com.

FERRELL, RICHARD BRADLEY, neuropsychiatrist; b. South Bend, Ind., Aug. 13, 1943; s. Rupert Tyler and Beatrice Bradley Ferrell; m. Melanie A. Ferrell; children: Catherine Lynn Ferrell de Correa, Elisabeth Jane Ferrell Horan, Anne Christine. AB, DePauw U., 1961—65; MD, Ind. U., 1965—69. Diplomate Am. Bd. of Psychiatry and Neurology, Inc., 1975, Am. Bd. of Psychiatry and Neurology, Inc., 2001. Assoc. prof. of psychiatry Dartmouth Med. Sch., Hanover, NH, 1975—, asst. prof. of psychiatry, 1975—81. Contbr. articles to profl. jours. Girls basketball coach Hanover Recreation Dept., Hanover, NH, 1982—2005; bd. mem. Opera North, Lebanon, NH, 1991—97. Recipient Alpha Omega Alpha Mem., Alpha Omega Alpha, 1969. Fellow: Am. Psychiatric Assn. (disting. fellow); mem.: Am. Neuropsychiatric Assn. Office: Dartmouth-Hitchcock Med Ctr One Medical Ctr Dr Lebanon NH 03756 Office Phone: 603-650-2887.

FERRELL, ROBERT HUGH, historian, educator; b. Cleve., May 8, 1921; s. Ernest Henry and Edna Lulu (Rentsch) F.; m. Lila Esther Sprout, Sept. 8, 1956 (dec. Jan. 2002); 1 dau., Carolyn Irene. BS in Edn., Bowling Green State U., 1946, BA, 1947, LLD (hon.), 1971; MA, Yale U., 1948, PhD, 1951. Intelligence analyst U.S. Air Force, 1951-52; lectr. in history Mich. State U., 1952-53; asst. prof. history Ind. U., 1953-58, asso. prof., 1958-61, prof., 1961-74, Disting. prof., 1974-88, emeritus, 1988—. Vis. prof. Yale U., 1955-56, Am. U. at Cairo, 1958-59, U. Conn., 1964-65, Cath. U. Louvain, Belgium, 1969-70, Naval War Coll., 1974-75, U.S. Mil. Acad., 1987-88. Author: Peace in Their Time, 1952, American Diplomacy in the Great Depression, 1957, American Diplomacy: A History, 1959, 4th edit., 1987, Frank B. Kellogg and Henry L. Stimson, 1963, (with M.G. Baxter and J.E. Wiltz) Teaching of American History in High Schools, 1964, George C. Marshall, 1966, (with R.B. Morris and W. Greenleaf) America: A History of the People, 1971, (with others) Unfinished Century, 1973, Harry S. Truman and the Modern American Presidency, 1983, Truman: A Centenary Remembrance, 1984, Woodrow Wilson and World War I, 1985, Harry S. Truman: His Life on the Family Farms, 1991, Ill-Advised, 1992, Choosing Truman: The Democratic Convention of 1944, 1994, Harry S. Truman: A Life, 1994, The Strange Deaths of President Harding, 1996, The Dying President: Franklin D. Roosevelt, 1998, The Presidency of Calvin Coolidge, 1998, Truman and Pendergast, 1999, Harry S. Truman, 2003, Collapse at Meuse-Argonne, 2004, Five Days in October: The Lost Battalion of World War I, 2005; editor: (with H.H. Quint) The Talkative President: The Off-the-Record Press Confreences of Calvin Coolidge, 1964, Off the Record: The Private Papers of Harry S. Truman, 1980, The Autobiography of Harry S. Truman, 1980, The Eisenhower Diaries, 1981, Dear Bess: The Letters from Harry to Bess Truman, 1983, (with Samuel Flagg Bemis) American Secretaries of State and Their Diplomacy, 10 vols., 1963-85, Banners in the Air: The Eighth Ohio Volunteers and the Spanish-American War, 1988, Monterrey is Ours!, 1990, Truman in the White House: The Diary of Eben Ayers, 1991, (with L.E. Wikander) Grace Coolidge: An Autobiography, 1992, Holding the Line: The Third Tennessee Infantry 1861-64, 1994, Truman and the Bomb, 1996, (with Joan Hoff) Dictionary of American History Supplement, 2 vols., 1996, FDR's Quiet Confidant: The Autobiography of Frank C. Walker, 1997, The Kansas City Investigation, 1999, A Youth in the Meuse-Argonne: A Memoir of World War I, 1917-1918, 2000, A Colonel in the Armored Divisions: A Memoir 1941-1945, 2001, In the Philippines and Okinawa: A Memoir 1945-1948, 2001, Meuse-Argonne Diary, 2004, Trench Knives and Mustard Gas, 2004, A Soldier in World War I, 2004. Served with USAAF, 1942-45. Mem. Soc. Historians, Am. Fgn. Rels. Orgn. Am. Historians, Am. Hist. Assn. Home: 3496 Daleview Ann Arbor MI 48105

FERRELL, WILL (JOHN WILLIAM FERRELL), actor; b. Irvine, Calif., July 16, 1967; s. Lee and Kay Ferrell; m. Viveca Paulin, Aug. 2000; 1 child, Magnus Paulin. Degree in Sports Info., U. So. Calif. Comedian with group The Groundlings. Actor: (films) Men Seeking Women, 1997, Austin Powers-International Man of Mystery, 1997, The Thin Pink Line, 1998, The Suburbans, 1999, Austin Powers: The Spy Who Shagged Me, 1999, Dick, 1999, Superstar, 1999, Drowning Mona, 2000, The Ladies Man, 2000, Jay and Silent Bob Strike Back, 2001, Zoolander, 2001, Old School, 2003, Elf, 2003, Melinda and Melinda, 2004, The Wendell Baker Story, 2005, Kicking & Screaming, 2005, Bewitched, 2005, Wedding Crashers, 2005; (TV films) Bucket of Blood, 1995; actor, writer (films) A Night at the Roxbury, 1998, Anchorman: The Legend of Ron Burgundy, 2004, (video) Wake Up, Ron Burgundy: The Lost Movie, 2004; actor: (TV series) Saturday Night Live, 1995—2002; voice (TV series) Cow and Chicken, The Oblongs, King of the Hill, 1999, Family Guy, 2000, 2001, guest appearances Grace Under Fire, 1995, Living Single, 1995. Named one of 100 Most Powerrful People in Hollywood, Premiere mag., 2004—05. Office: c/o Jason Heyman Creative Artists Agy 9830 Wilshire Blvd Beverly Hills CA 90212*

FERREN, JOHN MAXWELL, judge; b. Kansas City, Mo., July 21, 1937; s. Jack Maxwell and Elizabeth Anne (Hansen) Ferren; m. Ann Elizabeth Speidel, Sept. 4, 1961 (div.); children: Andrew John, Peter Maxwell; m. Linda Jane Finkelstein, June 17, 1994. AB magna cum laude, Harvard U., 1959, LLB, 1962. Bar: Ill. 1962, Mass. 1967, D.C. 1970. Assoc. Kirkland, Ellis, Hodson, Chaffetz & Masters, Chgo., 1962—66; dir. Neighborhood Law Office Program Harvard U. Law Sch., Cambridge, Mass., 1966—68; tchg. fellow, dir. Legal Svcs. Program Harvard Law Sch., Cambridge, 1968—69, lectr. law, dir. Legal Svcs Program, 1969—70; ptnr. Hogan & Hartson, Washington, 1970—77; assoc. judge D.C. Ct. Appeals, 1977—97; corp. counsel D.C., 1997—99; sr. judge D.C. Ct. Appeals, 1999—, disciplinary bd., 1972—76; fellow Woodrow Wilson Internat. Ctr. for Scholars, 2000—01; exec. com., bd. dirs. Council on Legal Edn. for Profl. Responsibility, 1970—80. Exec. com. Washington Lawyers Com. for Civil Rights Under Law, 1970—77. Author: Salt of the Earth, Conscience of the Court: The Story of Justice Wiley Rutledge, 2004; contbr. articles to profl. jours. Exec. com. of legal adv. com. Nat. Com. Against Discrimination in Housing, 1974—77; steering com. Nat. Prison Project ACLU Found., 1975—77; legis. subcom. on consumer credit Chgo. Commn. on Human Rels. Com. on New Residents, 1964—66; originator, chmn. Neighborhood Legal Advice Clinics, Ch. Fedn. Greater Chgo., 1964—66; treas., bd. dirs. Firman Neighborhood House, Chgo., 1964—66; bd. dirs. Frederick B. Abramson Meml. Found., 1991—97, People's Devel. Corp., Washington, 1970—74, George A. Wiley Meml. Fund, 1974—84, Nat. Resource Ctr. for Consumers of Legal Svcs., 1973—77, Ctr. for Law and Edn., Cambridge, Mass., 1989—94. Fellow: Am. Bar Found.; mem.: ABA (commn. on nat. inst. justice 1972—80, consortium on legal svcs. and pub. 1972—73, 1976—79, chmn. 1979—82, chmn. spl. com. on pub. interest practice 1976—78), Am. Law Inst., Phi Beta Kappa. Presbyterian. Office: Dist Columbia Ct Appeals 500 Indiana Ave NW Washington DC 20001-2131 Office Phone: 202-879-2772. E-mail: jferren@dcca.state.dc.us.

FERRER, MIGUEL ANTONIO, brokerage house executive; b. Ithaca, NY, May 18, 1938; s. Miguel and Conchita (Bolivar) F.; m. Suzan Nudelman, Aug. 1962 (div. 1973); children: Miguel Antonio, Ilena Christine; m. Lizette Gratacos, Sept. 4, 1980 (div. 2000); children: Alejandro Miguel, Augusto Miguel. BA, Cornell U., 1959, MBA, 1961. Account exec. Merrill Lynch Pierce Fenner Smith, San Juan, P.R., 1961-65; br. mgr. Eastman Dillon Union Securities, San Juan, 1965-71, ptnr., 1971-73; sr. v.p. Blyth Eastman Dillon & Co., Inc., San Juan, 1973-80, PaineWebber Inc., San Juan, 1980—; pres., CEO UBS Fin. Svcs., Inc. of P.R., Hato Rey, 1983—; chmn. PaineWebber Latin Am., 1993-98; pres., CEO UBS Trust Co. of P.R., 1997—. Bd. dirs. P.R. Investors Tax Free Fund, Alianza para el Desarrollo de Puerto Rico, Comision Pro Sede ALCA; dir. consultive bd. U. P.R., Rio Piedras, 1989-92; mem. governing bd. P.R. Strategy Project. Bd. dirs. P.R. Aqueducts and Sewer Authority, San Juan, 1986-88, P.R. Pub. Broadcasting Corp., 1990-92, P.R. Mus. Arch., San Juan; Rafael Hernández Colon Found., 1993-2000, U. P.R. Found., 1995, 2001; pres. fund raising ARC, Rio Piedras, 1990-91; bd. dirs., treas. Casa del Libro, San Juan; founding dir. Found. Friends of P.R. Acad. of Spanish Lang., 1996—; trustee Cornell U. Recipient Top Mgmt. award in fin. Sales and Mktg. Execs. Assn., 1980. Mem. Securities Industry Assn. (founding mem., bd. dirs., past pres.), P.R. Fin. Analysts Assn. (founding mem., past pres.), Alianza el Desarrollo PR (founder, bd. dirs.), Com. Pro Sede ALCA (founder, bd. dirs.), Banker's Club. Avocations: gymnasiums, art collecting, philanthropy. Home: Cond Millenium PH 8 San Juan PR 00901-2316 Office: UBS Financial Svcs Inc of PR American International Plz Penthouse Fl Hato Rey PR 00918*

FERRERA, ARTHUR ROCCO, food distribution company executive; b. Boston, Feb. 1, 1916; s. James F. and Mary (Mangini) F.; m. Mildred Grace Rugg, Sept. 9, 1944; children: Kenneth Grant, James Howard. AB, Harvard U., 1938. Co-founder James Ferrera & Sons, Inc., 1945—, pres., 1945-57, chmn. bd., 1957-89, chmn. emeritus, cons., 1989-91, ret., 1991. Chmn. emeritus, cons. James Ferrera & Sons, Inc.; dir. Commonwealth Bank of Boston, 1966-70; past dir. Romi Foods, Toronto; chmn. food divsn. CD, Mass., 1966. Served with AUS, 1942-46; to lt. col. USAFR (ret.) Name to Mass. Food Assn. Hall of Fame, 1993; recipient Cert. of Recognition, U.S. Dept. Def., 2000. Mem. New Eng. Wholesale Food Distbrs. Assn. (dir., past pres.), Nazareth Food Assn. (dir.), Mass. Food Assn. (Hall of Fame 1993), DAV (life). Clubs: Officers (Bedford, Mass.). Republican. Roman Catholic. Home: 5 Longfellow Rd Winchester MA 01890-2209 Personal E-mail: murugg@att.net.

FERRERE, RITA L., band director, music educator; b. Grove City, Pa., Feb. 19, 1965; d. Regis R. and Anna F. Ferrere. BS summa cum laude in Edn., Clarion U., 1987; M in Music Edn., Dana Sch. Music, Youngstown State U., 1992. Cert. instrnl. level II tchg. Pa., 1991. Instrumental music /band tchr. Elk County Christian H.S., St. Marys, Pa., 1988—94; instrumental music/band dir. Kane Area Sch. Dist., 1994—95, Brookville Area H.S., Pa., 1995—2001; instrumental music tchr. Chartiers Valley Intermediate Sch., Pitts., 2001—02; instrumental music/band dir. Moniteau Sch. Dist., West Sunbury, Pa., 2002—. Jazz band dir./founder Jazz Transitions Big Band, Pa., 1990—95; band dir. Harrisville Cmty. Band, Pa., 1994—98. Recipient Band Dir. Distinction award, Fiesta-Val Band Festival, Va. Beach, 2001. Mem.: Phi Beta Mu (Nu chpt.), Pa. Music Educators Assn. (life), Women Band Director's Internat. Assn. (life), Music Educators Nat. Conf. (life). Avocation: music. Home: 272 Boyers Rd PO Box 55 Forestville PA 16035 Office: Moniteau HS 1810 West Sunbury Rd West Sunbury PA 16061 Personal E-mail: rferrere@moniteau.k12.pa.us.

FERRERI, MICHAEL VICTOR, optometrist; b. Park Ridge, Ill., May 15, 1967; s. Samuel Joseph and Dolores Jean (Liebich) F.; children: Christopher, Anthony. BS in Biol. Scis., U. Calif., Irvine, 1989; OD, So. Calif. Coll. Optometry, 1993. Cert. therapeutic optometrist, Calif., Tex. Extern Ctr. for the Partially Sighted, Santa Monica, Calif., 1992-93; pvt. practice, Long Beach, Calif., 1993—; assoc. optometrist Antelope Mall Vision Ctr., Palmdale, Calif., 1995-99. Color vision analysis cons. Dept. Health and Human Svcs., Long Beach, 1994-97; participating doctor Vision USA, Long Beach, 1995-2000. Contbr. articles to profl. jours. Mem. Rep. Nat. Com., 1991—; v.p. congregation Grace Luth. Ch., Long Beach, 1996-99, also elder. Recipient Corning Low Vision award Corning Optics, Anaheim, Calif., 1993, Vision Therapy Enhancement cert. So. Calif. Coll. Optometry, Fullerton, 1993, appreciation cert. for outstanding contbns. to Save Your Vision Week, U.S. Senate, 1997, gov.'s letter of commendation for organizing coloring and essay contest for sch. children State of Calif., 1997, appreciation certificate Calif. Optometric Assn., 1998, Svc. award Kaiser Permanente Optometry Dept., 2003, Cert. of Recognition, Nat. Campaign for Tolerance, 2004, Eisenhower Commn., 2005. Mem. Am. Optometric Assn. (contact lens sect.), Calif. Optometric Assn., Fellowship of Christian Optometrists, Optometric Ext. Program (clin. assoc.), Rio Hondo Optometric Soc. (treas. 1997-99). Avocations: camping, golf, watersports. Home: PO Box 217 Corona CA 92878-0217 Office: SCPMG 9985 Sierra Ave Bldg 4 Mod 1 Fontana CA 92335

FERRERO, JUAN CARLOS, professional tennis player; b. Onteniente, Valencia, Spain, Feb. 12, 1980; s. Eduardo and Rosario. Profl. tennis player ATP Tour, 1998—; owner Equalite J.C. Ferrero tennis sch., Villena, Spain, 2001—. Named ATP Newcomer of Yr., 1999. Achievements include Winner 11 career single titles: Mallorca, 1999, Barcelona, 2001, Dubai, 2001, Estoril, 2001, Rome TMS, 2001, Hong Kong, 2002, Monte Carlo TMS, 2002, Madrid TMS, 2003, Monte Carlo TMS, 2003; Roland Garros, 2003, Valencia, 2003. Office: ATP Tour Internat Hdqrs 201 ATP Blvd Ponte Vedra Beach FL 32082

FERRETTI, DANTE, display designer; b. Macerata, Italy, Feb. 26, 1943; m. Francesca LoSchiavo; 1 child, Edoardo. Prodn. designer: (films) The Working Class Goes to Heaven, 1971, (with Nicola Tamburro) Medea, 1971, The Decameron, 1971, Sbatti il Mostro in Prima Pagina, 1972, The Canterbury Tales, 1972, Storie Scellerate, 1973, Il Fiore della Mille e una Notte, 1974, Crime of Love, 1974, The Night Porter, 1974, Salo: One Hundred Days of Sodom, 1975, Todo Modo, 1976, Bye Bye Monkey, 1978, Il Gatto, 1978, Eutanasia di un amore, 1978, Orchestral Rehearsal, 1979, Till Marriage Do Us Part, 1979, Arabian Nights, 1980, Il Minestrone, 1980, City of Women, 1980, La Pelle, 1981, Oltra la Porta, 1982, Desire, 1983, La Nuit de Varennes, 1983, Tales of Ordinary Madness, 1983, And the Ship Sails On, 1983, Pianoforte, 1984, Il Futuro e Donna, 1984, Le Bon Roi Dagobert, 1984, The Name of the Rose, 1986, Il Secreto del Sahara, 1987, The Adventures of Baron Munchausen, 1989 (Academy award nomination best art direction 1989), The Voice of the Moon, 1990, Hamlet, 1990 (Academy award nomination best art direction 1990), (with Francesca LoSchiavo) The Sleazy Uncle, 1991, (with Wolfgang Hundhammer) Club Extinction, 1991, The Age of Innocence, 1993 (Academy award nomination best art direction 1993), Interview with the Vampire, 1994 (Academy award nomination best art direction 1994), Casino, 1995, Kundun, 1997, Meet Joe Black, 1998, Bringing Out the Dead, 1999, Titus, 1999, Gangs of New York, 2002, Cold Mountain, 2003, The Aviator, 2004 (Academy award for best art direction, 2005); prodn. designer, set designer: (films) Ginger and Fred, 1986. Office: Sandra Marsh Mgt 9150 Wilshire Blvd Ste 220 Beverly Hills CA 90212-3429*

FERRETTI, MADDALENA FUNICIELLO, humanities educator; d. Luigi Funiciello and Carmela Minozzi; m. Aldo Ferretti, Oct. 6, 1956; children: Victoria Monica Ferretti-Aceto, Louise Emily Ferretti-Ohrbach. AA in Classics, Lyceum Giulio Cesari, Rome, 1947; PhD in Chemistry, U. Rome, 1947—53. Asst. prof. U. Milan, 1956—57; rsch. asst. State Water Survey, Urbana, Ill., 1958—59; instr., Italian Internat. Ctr. for Lang. Studies, Washington, 1975—85, Casa Italiana, Cultural Ctr. of Italian-Americans, Washington, 1975—88, Fgn. Svc. Inst., U.S. Dept. Sch. Langs., Rosslyn, Va., 1976—78; lectr., inorganic chemistry and toxicology Am. U., Washington, 1982—85; Italian instr. for editl. bd. Wash. Post, 1982—90; adj. prof., Italian Montgomery Coll., Rockville, Md., 1985—90; frp, lectr. to asst. prof. George Wash. U., Washington, 1984—2001, asst. prof., 2001—. Dir., Italian program George Wash. U., Washington, 1993—; mem. Comites Italia, 2004—. Sec. Italian Cultural Soc., Washington, 2001—03. Fellow: Coun. for Promotion of Italian Lang. in Am. Schs. (assoc.; sec. 1998); mem.: MLA, Nat. Italian Am. Found., Am. Assn. Tchrs. Italian, Order of Sons of Italy (hon.). Roman Catholic. Avocations: travel, swimming, cooking. Home: 8516 Howell Rd Bethesda MD 20817 Office: George Washington Univ Dept Romance Lang and Lit 801 22nd St NW Washington DC 20052 Office Phone: 202-994-6300. Business E-Mail: ferretti@gwu.edu.

FERREY, MARK LAURENCE, environmental scientist, researcher; b. St. Paul, Minn., Jan. 14, 1958; s. Gregory M. and Audrey E. Ferrey; m. Tory Maureen Arfstrom, Sept. 4, 1982; children: Seth Laurence, Nathan Douglas. BS in Microbiology cum laude, U. Minn., 1982, MS in Soil Microbiology, 1992. Cert. Profl. Soil Scientist Minn., 2004. Rsch. scientist U. Minn., Mpls., 1992—93; environ. scientist Minn. Pollution Control Agy., St. Paul, 1993—. Tech. reviewer Lindbergh Found., Anoka, Minn., 2003—, Environ. Sci. and Tech. Jour., 2004; editl. adv. bd. Remediation Jour., 2004—. High adventure scout leader Boy Scouts Am., White Bear Lake, Minn., 1999—; baseball coach, 1997—; sci. curriculum rev. panel Mahtomedi Sch. dist., Minn., 2004—05. Recipient Eagle Scout award, Boy Scouts of Am., 1976. Mem.: Minn. Ground Water Assn. (assoc.), Am. Soc. of Microbiology (assoc.). Achievements include In 1993, published the first report that a microbial isolate can mineralize the aromatic ring carbon of the widely-used herbicide alachlor; In 2004, published the first report that dichloroethylene isomers break down abiotically in ground water and is a significant factor in the remediation of solvent contaminated aquifers; In 1997, authored Minnesota's policy and technical guidelines for evaluating natural attenuation remedies for contaminated ground water; 1999-2005, Collaborative research with the Environmental Protection Agency on the contribution of abiotic processes in the removal of chlorinated solvents in ground water; In 1987, researched microbial microcalorimetry as a method to rapidly measure concentrations of carbohydrates and assess the biodegradability of lignin-like compounds in aqueous solution; Demonstrated that intrinsic reductive dechlorination of solvents in ground water can be inhibited by oxidative remedial technologies; Implemented a panel discussion on ground water remediation issues in a professional journal format. Avocations: swimming, running, camping. Office: Minn Pollution Control Agy 520 Lafayette Rd Saint Paul MN 55155 Office Phone: 651-296-7775. Office Fax: 651-296-9707. Personal E-mail: mark_ferrey@email.msn.com. E-mail: mark.ferrey@pca.state.mn.us.

FERRI, KAREN LYNN, lawyer; b. McKeesport, Pa., Aug. 15, 1956; d. Edward James and Carole Elizabeth (Petterson) Ferri. BA, Duquesne U., 1977, JD, 1981. Bar: Pa. 1981, U.S. Dist. Ct. (we. dist.) Pa. 1981, U.S. Supreme Ct. 1986. Law clk. Weiler & Dolfi, Pitts., 1980-81, assoc., 1981-84; of counsel Stokes, Lurie & Cole, Pitts., 1984-90; sole practice Murrysville and Pitts., 1984—. Weekend mgr. Ferri Supermarkets Inc., Murrysville, Pa., 1977-90; atty. Ferri Enterprises, 1981-96. Bd. dirs. Crisis Ctr. North, Pitts., 1986-89, vol., 1986-2001; bd. dirs. planned parenthood, 1998—. Recipient Sr. Leaders award Duquesne U., 1977, Am. Jurisprudence award Joint Pubs. Total Client-Service Library Pitts., 1978-79. Mem.: ABA (family law commn. 2003—), Pa. Bar Found., Pa. Bar Assn. (family law sect.), Duquesne U. Alumni Assn., Am. Inns of Ct. (Pitts. chpt. 1992—95), Westmoreland County Bar Assn. (family law com, fee dispute com.), Women's Bar Assn. Roman Catholic. Home: 3319 Carriage Cir Export PA 15632-9214 Office: 3950 William Penn Hwy Ste 2 Murrysville PA 15668 Office Phone: 724-733-4666.

FERRICK-ROMAN, KAREN L., journalist; d. Paul E. and Catherine M. Ferrick; m. R. Daniel Roman, Apr. 16, 1983; children: Theodore P. Roman, Christopher M. Roman. BA in Journalism and Sociology, Indiana U. of Pa., 1977; postgrad., Western Ill. U., Macomb, Ill., 1980; MA in Journalism and Comm., Point Park U., Pitts., 1991. News reporter Beaver County Times, Pa., 1980—82, feature writer, 1982—91, projects editor, 1988—91, copy editor, 1991—95, feature writer, 1995—97, edn. reporter, 1997—99, features writer, 1999—2002, staff reporter, 2002—. Adj. prof. Robert Morris U., Coraopolis, Pa., 1995; memoirs writing instr. Kent State Univ.-East Liverpool, Ohio, 2003. Editor (travel columnist): GoPlaces, 1997—2000; contbr. articles to mags. and jours. Bd. of rev. Boy Scouts, Troop 407, Beaver Falls, Pa., 1999—2004. Recipient Silver Gavel award, ABA, 1983, Schnader Meml. award, Pa. Bar Assn., 1983, Women in Comm. award, Pitts. Chpt., 1983, Disting. Achievement award, Ednl. Press Assn., 1997, Outstanding Edn. Writing award, Nat. Benjamin Fine, 1997, Mng. Editor's award, AP, 1998, Governor's Traffic Safety award, 1983, Robert L. Vann award, Pitts. Black Media Fedn., 2003, Keystone award, Pa. Newspaper Pubs. Assn., 2003, 2001,

2000, 1998, 1997, 1983, runner-up, travel, Preservation Found., 2004; fellow, Hechinger Inst., 1999. Avocation: travel. Office: Beaver County Times 400 Fair Ave Beaver PA 15009 Business E-Mail: kroman@timesonline.com.

FERRIER, DOUGLAS M., librarian; b. Dallas, Oct. 12, 1943; s. David M. and Ima R. Ferrier; m. Marie H. McKenna, Dec. 28, 1968; children: Kathleen Marie, Thomas J.M. BA, U. Tex., 1971; MA, U. Tex., Arlington, 1972; MLS, U. North Tex., 1978. Spl. coll. cataloger, archivist U. Tex., Arlington, 1975—78; aquisition/serials libr. U. Ark., Little Rock, 1979—82; head tech. svcs. St. Mary's U. Law Libr., San Antonio, 1982—85; dean libr. Tex. Wesleyan U., Ft. Worth, 1985—95; dir. libr., info. resources, dist. edn./media U. Tex./Tex. Southmost Coll., Brownsville, 1995—. Archivist Tex. State Libr.-Archives Divsn., Austin, 1973—75. Vol. Vista, Okeechobee, Fla., 1965—66, Peace Corps, Sierra Leone. Mem.: ALA, Tex. Libr. Assn. Home: Rt 3 Box 67A Los Fresnos TX 78566 Office: Univ Tex Brownsville 80 Fort Brown Brownsville TX 78520

FERRIER, RICHARD BROOKS, architect, educator; b. Ft. Worth, Mar. 29, 1944; s. Samuel Foster and Opal Birtha (Brooks) F.; m. Lynna Gail Elmore Mindlin; 1 child, Sean Brooks. BA, Tex. Tech U., 1968; MA in Art, U. Dallas, Irving, Tex., 1973. With planning dept. City of Lubbock, Tex., 1962-63; with Atcheson, Atkinson and Cartwright: Architects, Lubbock, 1963-65, Engring. Assocs., Lubbock, 1966-68; mem. faculty U. Tex., Arlington, 1968—, prof. architecture, assoc. dean, 1980-95; prin. Richard B. Ferrier, AIA, architect, Arlington, 1982-91, Firm X Richard B. Ferrier, FAIA, architect, Arlington, 1991—. With Ralph Kelman, architects, Dallas, 1969-70; assoc. William S. Austin, Architect, Arlington, 1976-80; with Comm. Cons., Arlington, 1970-82; mem. architecture adv. bd. Dallas County C.C., 1983-88; architecture critic Ft. Worth Star Telegram, 1989; lectr., juror in field. Contbr. articles and revs. to profl. jours.; prin. works includeNat. Compact House Design Competition, 1990 (First Place), EML House, 1991, Nat. Cowboy Hall of Fame Addition, 1992, DMA Tower, 1993, Nara Toto, 1994, Bar K R Ranch, 1994, Compact House III, 1996, New Lighthouse Ch., 1997; exhibited in numerous group shows, 1968—, including Dallas Mus. Art, 1991-99, Arlington Mus. Art, 1992-2002, Tex. Fine Arts Assn., Austin, 1992-98, Archtl. Gallery, Chgo., 1994. Named Alumni of Yr., Tex. Tech U. Coll. Architecture, 1993; recipient numerous awards Am. Soc. Archtl. Illustrators, 1986—, 12 awards Tex. Architect Graphics Competition, 1988—, amateur animated film award Cannes Internat. Film Festival, 1973, Romieniec award Tex. Soc. Archs., 1997. Mem. AIA (elected to Coll. Fellows 1993, recipient 12 Dallas design awards 1991-2005, 50 Dallas graphic awards 1980—, including 17 honor awards). Democrat. Episcopalian. Home: Firm X 1628 Connally Ter Arlington TX 76010-4516 Office: U Tex Sch Arch PO Box 19108 Arlington TX 76019-0001 Fax: 817-469-1856. Office Phone: 817-469-8605. Personal E-mail: firmx@aol.com.

FERRILLO, PATRICK J., JR., dean, endodontist; b. St. Louis, Mar. 4, 1941; s. Patrick J. Ferrillo Sr. BS in biology, Georgetown U., 1973; DDS, Baylor U., 1976, cert., 1978. Instr. Baylor Coll. of Dentistry, Dallas, 1976-78; clin. asst. prof. So. Ill. U. Sch. Dental Medicine, Alton, 1978-79, asst. prof., 1979-84, sect. head, 1979-87, dir. current affairs, 1982-87, acting chmn., 1984-85, chairperson, 1985-87, acting dean, 1986-87, dean, assoc. prof., 1987—2002; dean Sch. Dental Medicine Univ. of Nevada, Las Vegas, 2002—, vice provost divsn. health sciences, 2002—. Pres. Am. Assn. Dental Schs., Washington, DC, 1999—2000. Fellow Am. Coll. Dentists, Internat. Coll. Dentists; mem. Omicron Kappa Upsilon (v.p. 1988-89, pres. 1989-91), Phi Kappa Phi. Office: Univ Nevada Sch Dentistry 4505 Maryland Pkwy Box 453055 Las Vegas NV 89154

FERRINI, JAMES THOMAS, lawyer; b. Chgo., Jan. 14, 1938; s. John B. and Julia (Marre) F.; m. Jeanne Marie Fontana, June 8, 1963; children: Anthony, Mary Caren, Emily, Joseph, Danielle. JD, Loyola U., 1963. Bar: U.S. Supreme Ct. 1963, U.S. Ct. Appeals (7th cir.) 1967, U.S. Ct. Appeals (8th cir.) 1969, U.S. Ct. Appeals (3d cir.) 1975, U.S. Ct. Appeals (6th cir.) 1982, U.S. Ct. Appeals (10th cir.) 1984, U.S. Ct. Appeals (4th cir.) 1987, U.S. Ct. Appeals (9th cir.) 1989. Sr. ptnr. Clausen Miller Gorman Caffrey & Witous, P.C., Chgo., 1963—. Mem. pattern jury instructions Ill. Supreme Ct. Commn., Chgo., 1978-94. Contbr. articles to profl. jours. Mem. Mary Seat of Wisdom Parish, Park Ridge. Fellow Am. Acad. Appellate Lawyers; mem. ABA, Ill. Bar Assn., Chgo. Bar Assn. (chmn. civil practice com.), Ill. Assn. Def. Trial Counsel, Appellate Lawyers Assn. (pres. Chgo. chpt. 1978, 79), Justinian Soc. Roman Catholic. Avocations: handball, sailing, skiing, cooking. Office: Clausen Miller PC 10 S La Salle St Ste 1600 Chicago IL 60603-1098 Office Phone: 312-606-7597. Business E-Mail: jferrini@clausen.com.

FERRINI-MUNDY, JOAN, mathematician, educator, education educator; PhD, U. N.H. Instr. math. Mount Holyoke coll., 1982—83; faculty mem. math. U. N.H., 1983—95; dir. Math. Scis. Edn. Bd. Nat. Rsch. Coun. for Sci., Math., and Engring. Edn., 1995—99; prof. tchr. edn. and math. Mich. State U., East Lansing, 1999—2002, assoc. dean math. and sci. edn. Coll. Natural Scis., 2002—. Vis. scientist NSF, 1989—91. Recipient Louise Hay award, Assn. for Women in Math., 2000. Mem.: Nat. Rsch. Coun. (assoc. exec. dir. Ctr. for Sci., Math., and Engring. Edn.), Math. Scis. Edn. Bd. (bd. dirs.), Assn. for Women in Math. (Louise Hay award 2000), Nat. Coun. Tchrs. Math. (chair Writing Group for Stds. 2000 1999—, chair Rsch. Adv. com.). Office: Dept Math A343 WH Mich State Univ 211 Kedzie Hall East Lansing MI 48824-1027

FERRIS, ARTHUR DAVID, musician, educator; b. Port Arthur, Tex., Dec. 16, 1960; s. George Washington and Edna Mae Ferris; m. Renate Brigitte Elisabeth Urban, Sept. 6, 1991; children: Sascha Oliver Rentschler, Yvonne Gerda Rentschler, David Philippe Alexandre. MusB, Lamar U., Beaumont, Tex., 2000—04. Bandman U.S. Army, Tex., 1980—98; band dir. West Orange - Stark H.S. Band, Orange, Tex., 2004—05. Cmty. band dir. Orange Cmty. Concert Band, Tex., 2003—05. Staff sgt. (ret.) US Army, 1980—98. Decorated Army Good Conduct Medal U.S. Army, Army Commendation Medal, Nat. Def. Svc. Medal, Army Achievement Medal, Meritorious Svc. Medal. Mem.: IAJE (corr.), ATSSB (corr.), TMEA (corr.). Conservative. Protestant. Avocation: travel. Personal E-mail: arthur.d.ferris@us.army.mil.

FERRIS, CHARLES DANIEL, lawyer, former government official; b. Boston, Apr. 9, 1933; s. Henry Joseph and Mildred Mary (MacDonald) F.; m. Patricia Catherine Brennan; children: Caroline, Sabrina. AB, Boston Coll., 1954, JD, 1961, LL.D. (hon.), 1978; grad. advanced mgmt. program, Harvard U., 1971. Bar: Mass. Supreme Jud. Ct. bar 1961, D.C. bar 1969. Research physicist Sperry Gyroscope Co., Gt. Neck, N.Y.C., 1954-55; asst. prof. naval sci. Harvard U., 1958-60; trial atty. Dept. Justice, Washington, 1961-63; gen. counsel U.S. Senate Democratic Policy Com., U.S. Senate Majority Counselor; also chief counsel to U.S. Senate Majority Leader Mansfield, 1963-76; gen. counsel U.S. Ho. of Reps. Speaker Thomas P. O'Neil, 1977; chmn. FCC, Washington, 1977-81; sr. ptnr. Mintz, Levin, Cohn, Ferris, Glovsky & Popeo, Washington and Boston, 1981—, chmn., Fed. Law Sect. Bd. dirs. Cablevision, Woodbury, N.Y., KIDSNET, Washington. Author: Cable Television Law-A Video Communications Practice Guide, 3 vols., 1983, rev., 1984-87. Mem. steering com. Clearinghouse for Children's TV, Washington, 1982-86; trustee Boston Coll., Chestnut Hill, Mass., 1987—. Served to lt. USN, 1955-58. Mem. Mass. Bar Assn., D.C. Bar Assn. Democrat. Roman Catholic. Office: Mintz Levin Cohn Ferris Glovsky & Popeo PC Ste 900 701 Pennsylvania Ave NW Washington DC 20004 Office Phone: 202-434-7301. Office Fax: 202-434-7400. Business E-Mail: cdferris@mintz.com.

FERRIS, GEORGE MALLETTE, JR., investment banker; b. Washington, Mar. 11, 1927; s. George Mallette and Charlotte (Hamilton) F.; m. Nancy Strouce, Jan. 25, 1964; children: George Mallette III, Willard Bradley, Kimberly Anne, David Hamilton. BS in Engring. magna cum laude, Princeton U., 1948; MBA, Harvard U., 1950. Chmn. Ferris, Baker Watts, Inc., Washington, 1971—. Commr. Md. Aviation Commn.; past bd. govs. NY Stock Exch.; past chmn. Pres.'s Commn. on Mgmt. Aid Programs; past pres. Washington Soc. Investment Analysts. Past gen. campaign chmn. United Givers Fund, 1966; past gen. chmn. sustaining fund drive Nat. Symphony Orch.; past mem. Pres.'s Task Force Internat. Pvt. Enterprise; past chmn. investment adv. bd. AID. Recipient Princeton in Nations's Svc. award, Washingtonian award Jaycees, Order Red Triangel award YMCA Greater Washington, Silver Beaver award Boy Scouts Am. Mem. Harvard Bus. Sch. Club Washington (past pres.), Met. Club, Chevy Chase Club (Md.), Burning Tree Club (Md.), The Ctr. Club (Balt.), Phi Beta Kappa, Tau Beta Phi. Home: 5601 Kirkside Dr Bethesda MD 20815-7113 Office: Ferris Baker Watts Inc 1700 Pennsylvania Ave NW Washington DC 20006-4704 Office Phone: 202-661-9501. Business E-Mail: g.ferris@fbw.com.

FERRIS, JAMES LEONARD, academic administrator; b. Bellingham, Wash., Jan. 15, 1944; s. Gerald Durward and Esther Evelyn (Larson) F.; m. Virginia Marie Dowde, June 23, 1972; children: Eric, Heidi. BSChemE, U. Wash., 1966; MS in Pulp and Paper Sci., Lawrence U., Appleton, Wis., 1969, PhD in Pulp and Paper Sci., 1974; Advanced Mgmt. Program, Harvard Bus. Sch., 1992. Mill engr. Weyerhaeuser Paper Co., Everett, Wash., 1966-67, scientist R & D dept., 1974-75, mgr. tech. svcs. pulp div. Tacoma, 1975-80, dir. R & D, 1980-85, mgr. mfg. pulp div., 1985-88, v.p. rsch., 1988-96; pres. Inst. Paper Sci. and Tech., Atlanta, 1996—. Bd. dirs. Albany Internat. Corp.; dir. Atlanta Consortium for Higher Edn., 1998—. Lt. (j.g.) USN, 1970-72, Vietnam. Mem. TAPPI. Office: Inst Paper Sci and Tech 500 10th St NW Atlanta GA 30318-5794

FERRIS, JAMES PETER, chemist, educator; b. Nyack, N.Y., July 25, 1932; s. Richard B. and Mabel G. (Collier) F.; m. Joan E. Herrlich, Sept. 3, 1955 (div. 1985); children: Alison R., Laura J.; m. Susan Shipherd, Mar. 7, 1992. BS, U. Pa., 1954; PhD, Ind. U., 1958. Postdoctoral researcher MIT, 1958-59; asst. prof. Fla. State U., 1959-64; research assoc. Salk Inst., 1964-67; assoc. prof. chemistry Rensselaer Poly. Inst., Troy, N.Y., 1967-73, prof., 1973-97, chmn. dept. chemistry, 1980-83, rsch. prof., 1997—. Dir. N.Y. Ctr. for the Study of the Origins of Life, a NASA NSCORT, 1998—; vis. prof. Lab. Organic Chemistry, Swiss Fed. Inst. Tech., Zurich, 1985-86, Salk Inst., 1995; mem. life scis. adv. com. NASA, 1987-88, chair adv. panel on exobiology, 1995—; mem. task force on life scis. of space sci. bd. NRC, 1984-86, past vice chair subcommn. F3 com. space rsch., sci. com. oceanic rsch. working group on hydrothermal sys., 1989-92, mem. space studies bd., 1990-94, com. planetary and lunar exploration, 1998; mem. panel on exobiology Am. Inst. Biol. Scis., 1984-90. Mem. editl. bd. Biosystems. Recipient Career Devel. award USPHS, 1969-74; NRC fellow, 1976 Fellow AAAS; mem. Am. Chem. Soc., Internat. Soc. for Study Origins of Life (treas. 1980-89, editor Origins Life and Evolution of Biosphere 1982-99, pres. 1993-96, Oparin medal 1996, exec. coun. 2005—), Univ. Space Rsch. Assn. (bd. trustees 1999-2005), Clay Minerals Soc., Inter-Am. Photochem. Soc Home: 10 Saddlehill Rd Wynantskill NY 12198-7616 Office: Rensselaer Poly Inst Dept Chemistry Troy NY 12180 Office Phone: 518-276-8493. Business E-Mail: ferrij@rpi.edu.

FERRIS, ROBERT ALBERT, lawyer, venture capitalist; b. NYC, May 11, 1942; s. Albert Gerard and Helen Elizabeth (Jones) F.; m. Evelyn T. Jarvis; children: Robert C., Kathleen J. AB, Boston Coll., 1963; JD, Fordham U., 1966; grad. Advanced Mgmt. Program, Harvard U., 1974. Bar: NY 1967, Calif. 1973. Assoc. Carter Ledyard & Milburn, N.Y.C., 1966-71; v.p., sec. Arcata Corp., Menlo Park, Calif., 1972-82; ptnr. Sequoia Assocs., Menlo Park, 1982-98; mng. dir. Caxton-Iseman Capital Inc., N.Y.C., 1998—. Bd. dirs. Buffets, Inc., Anteon Corp., Ply Gem Industries, Inc., N.Am. Health Plans, Inc.; bd. overseers Hooven Instn., Stanford U.; bd. trustees Fordham U. Served with AUS, 1966-67. Home: 77 Elena Ave Atherton CA 94027-4025 E-mail: raferris@comcast.net.

FERRIS, ROGER PATRICK, architect; b. Buffalo, Jan. 3, 1952; s. Herbert Parkhill and Dolores (Murphy) F.; m. Yvonne DeHaas, May 20, 1995; children: Wren, Georgia. BA, La Salle Coll., 1974; postgrad., Columbia U., 1977-78; M in Design, Harvard U., 1982. Registered arch., Conn., N.Y., Mass., Vt., Maine, N.H., Ill., Tex., N.Mex., Washington, Va., N.C., Pa., R.I., N.J., Fla., S.C., N.C.; cert. Nat. Coun. archtl. Registration Bds. Arch. Victor Christ-Janer & Assocs., new Canaan, Conn., 1974-78; prin. Landworks Assocs., Southport, Conn., 1978-80, Ferris Franzen Assoc., Southport, 1980-82, Ferris Architects, Westport, Conn., 1982-98, Roger Ferris & Ptnrs., Westport, Conn., 1998—. Co-editor: Architectural Practices in the Nineties, 1996. Recipient Progressive Architecture Citation award, 1991, Outstanding Design award James Beard Found., 1997; Loeb fellow in advanced environ. design Grad. Sch. Design Harvard U., 1991, 92. Mem.: AIA (New Eng. regional award excellence in arch. 1985, Design award Conn. 1985—86, Builders Nat. Design and Planning award 1988, 1988—92, Design award Conn. 1989, 1993—94, New Eng. regional award excellence in arch. 1994, Builders Nat. Design and Planning award 1994, Design award Conn. 1996—98, New Eng. regional award excellence in arch. 1997, Builders Nat. Design and Planning award 1998, New Eng. regional award excellence in arch. 1999, 2000, 2001, Design award Conn. chpt. 2002, 2003, Residential Architect Design award 2004, cert., New Eng. regional award excellence in arch. (2) 2005), Conn. Trust Hist. Preservation (Conn. Preservation Design award 1994), Royal Inst. Brit. Archs., Am. Planning Assn. Office: Roger Ferris & Ptnrs 90 Post Rd E Westport CT 06880-3409 Business E-Mail: ferris@ferrisarch.com.

FERRIS, RONALD CURRY, bishop; b. Toronto, Ont., Can., July 2, 1945; s. Herald Bland and Marjorie May (Curry) F.; m. Janet Agnes Waller, Aug. 14, 1965; children: Elisa, Jill, Matthew, Jenny, Rani, Jonathan. Grad., Toronto Tchrs. Coll., 1965; BA, U. Western Ont., London, 1970; MDiv, Huron Coll., London, 1973, DD (hon.), 1982; DMin, Pacific Sch. of Religion, Calif., 1995; STD (hon.), Thorneloe U., 1995. Ordained to ministry Anglican Ch., 1970. Tchr. Pape Ave. Sch., Toronto, 1965-66; prin. Carcross Elem. Sch., Y.T., 1966-68; incumbent St. Luke's Ch., Old Crow, Y.T., 1970-72; rector St. Stephen's Ch., London, Ont., 1973-81; bishop Diocese of Yukon, Whitehorse, 1981-95, Diocese of Algoma, Sault Sainte Marie, Can., 1995—. Author: (poems) A Wing and a Prayer, 1990. Home: 134 Simpson St Sault Sainte Marie ON Canada P6A 3V4 Office: Diocese of Algoma Box 1168 Sault Sainte Marie ON Canada P6A 5N7 E-mail: dioceseofalgoma@on.aibn.com.

FERRIS, RUSSELL JAMES, II, writer; b. Rochester, NY, June 11, 1938; s. Russell James and Phyllis Helen (Breheny) F.; m. Ilma Maria dos Santos, June 29, 1968. Student, St. Bonaventure U., 1956-59; BS, U. Rochester, 1967; MS, Emerson Coll., 1989; PhD, Universal Life Ch., 1983. Cert. social worker. Film inspector City of Rochester, 1962-67; social worker Tulare County, Visalia, Calif., 1967-69, Alameda County, Oakland, Calif., 1969-71; ghostwriter self-employed, San Francisco, 1971—. Author: Crescendo, 1972 and 14 other novels. With USAR, 1956-68. Botany fellow, Emerson Coll., 1989. Mem.: Blue Army, KQED-TV Pub. Broadcasting System, United Macanese Assn., Inc., Air Force Assn., Assn. U.S. Army, Res. Officers Assn. (life), Mil. Officers Assn. Am. (life). Libertarian. Roman Catholic. Avocation: aviculture. Home and Office: 202 Font Blvd San Francisco CA 94132-2404

FERRIS, WILLIAM MICHAEL, lawyer; b. Jackson, Mich., May 1, 1948; s. Franklyn C. and Betty J. (Dickerson) F.; m. Cynthia L. Muffitt, June 26, 1970 (div.); 1 child, Christina M.; m. Kathleen S. Santacroce, Mar. 21, 1987; stepchildren: Michael W. Santacroce, Megan D. Santacroce. BS with distinction, U.S. Naval Acad., 1970; JD summa cum laude, U. Balt., 1978, LLM in Taxation, 1994. Commd. ensign USN, 1970, advanced through grades to lt., 1974, resigned active duty, 1977; staff atty. Md. Legis., Annapolis, 1977-78, 80-81; assoc. Semmes, Bowen & Semmes, Balt., 1978-80; ptnr. Ferris & Robin, Annapolis, 1981-83, Krause & Ferris, Annapolis, 1983-87, Michaelson, Krause & Ferris, PA, Annapolis, 1987-91, Krause & Ferris, Annapolis, 1991—. Adj. faculty Anne Arundel C.C., 1988—, U. Balt. Sch. Law, 1997-2004 Author: Maryland Style Manual for Statutory Law, 1985; article supr. Md. Annotated Code, 1981-84. Elder Woods Meml. Presbyn. Ch., Severna Park, Md., 1980—; temporary zoning hearing officer Anne Arundel County, Annapolis, 1984—87; hearing officer Anne Arundel County Bd. Edn., Annapolis, 1990—98; pres. Md. Bd. Dental Examiners, Balt., 1987—88; mem. inquiry com. Md. Atty. Grievance Commn., 1987—2001; mem. Md. Commn. on Jud. Disabilities, 1995—2005; treas. Bay Hills Cmty. Assn., 1990—96. Comdr. USNR, 1984—91. Mem. ABA, Md. State Bar Assn., Maritime Law Assn., Anne Arundel County Bar Assn. Republican. Avocations: golf, running, tennis, Bocce. Home: 115 Terrapin Ln Stevensville MD 21666 Office: Krause & Ferris 196 Duke Of Gloucester St Annapolis MD 21401-2515 Office Phone: 410-263-0220. Business E-Mail: wferris@krauseferris.com.

FERRIS, WILLIAM PAUL, finance educator, consultant; b. Long Beach, Calif., Feb. 16, 1945; s. Theodore Vincent and Doris Donaghue Ferris; m. Cheryl Tromley, Jan. 13, 2004; children: Laura Ferris Anderson, Ellen. BA, Dartmouth Coll., Hanover, NH, 1962—66; M, Trinity Coll., 1970; PhD in Communication, Rensselaer Poly. Inst., 1975; vis. fellow, Yale U., New Haven, CT, 1985—86. Tchr., dept chair, acting vice prin., prin. Longmeadow H.S., Mass., 1966—79; prof. mgmt., asst. dean Western New Eng. Coll. Sch. Bus., Springfield, Mass., 1979—. Mgmt. cons. Various Cos. and Orgns., 1975—; pres., dir. Ea. Acad. Mgmt., 1988—99; chmn. Mgmt. Edn. & Devel. Divsn. Acad. Mgmt., 1999—2000; pres. Acad. of Bus. Edn., 2002—04; founding pres. A Better Chance, Longmeadow, Inc., 1972—76; mem., bd. of dirs. Inst. for Cmty. Econs., 1999—; pres. of club officers assn. world-wide Dartmouth Coll. Alumni, 1983—84. Editor various national conference proceedings; contbr. articles to profl. jours. Home: 11 Howard Ave Branford CT 06405 Office: Western New England Coll 1215 Wilbraham Rd Springfield MA 01119 Office Phone: 413-782-1629. Personal E-mail: bferris@wnec.edu.

FERRIS, WILLIAM REYNOLDS, humanities organization administrator, folklore educator; b. Vicksburg, Miss., Feb. 5, 1942; s. William Reynolds and Shelby Gibbs (Flowers) F.; 1 child, Virginia Louise. BA, Davidson (N.C.) Coll., 1964; MA in English, Northwestern U., 1965; MA in Folklore, U. Pa., 1967, PhD in Folklore, 1969. Asst. prof. English Jackson State U., 1970-72; assoc. prof. Am. and Afro-Am. Studies Yale U., 1972-79; prof. anthropology U. Miss., University, 1979-97; chmn. Nat. Endowment for Humanities, Washington, 1997—2001; prof. of history, adj. prof. in folklore curriculum, sr. assoc. dir. Ctr. for Study of Am. South Univ. N.C., Chapel Hill, NC, 2002—. Dir. Ctr. for Study So. Culture, U. Miss., Oxford, 1979-2001; nat. advisor U. Pa. Black Lit. Ctr., Phila., 1989—; mem. history and memory group DuBois Inst., Harvard U., Cambridge, Mass., 1987—; vis. fellow Stanford U. Humanities Ctr., Palo Alto, Calif., 1989-90; pub. policy fellow Woodrow Wilson Internat. Ctr. for Scholars, 2002—. Author: Local Color, 1982, Blues from the Delta, 1984; editor Afro-Am. Folk Arts and Crafts, 1983; co-editor Ency. of Southern Culture, 1989, You Live and Learn, And Then You Die and Forget It All, Ray Lum's Tales of Horses, Mules, and Men, 1992. Decorated chevalier des arts et des lettres (France), 1985, Officer in Order of Arts and Letters, 1994; named Disting. Alumnus, Rotary Found., 1989, One of Top 10 Tchrs. in Nation, Rolling Stone, 1991; recipient Charles FRankel prize in the Humanities, 1995. Mem. Am. Folklore Soc. (exec. bd. 1987—), Am. Studies Assn. (nat. coun. 1991). Office: Univ NC Dept History CB #9127 Chapel Hill NC 27599-9127

FERRISS, JOHN ALDEN, III, medical educator; b. Erie, Pa., Sept. 7, 1951; s. John Alden II and Helen Ritchie (Collison) F.; m. Mary Elizabeth (Maloney), June 20, 1981; children: Katherine, John IV, Elizabeth. BS in Biology, Nasson Coll., Springvale, Maine, 1973; MD in Medicine, Thomas Jefferson U., Phila., 1977. Diplomate Am. Bd. Internal Medicine, Am. Bd. Rheumatology. Battalion surgeon 2d Battalion, 12th Marine Regiment, Okinawa, Japan, 1978—79; chief primary care clinic U.S. Navy Hosp., Groton, Conn., 1980—82; cons. in rheumatology Cen. Vt. Hosp., Montpelier, 1986—88; asst. prof. medicine Pa. State U., Hershey, 1988—94, assoc. prof. medicine, acting chief rheumatology, 1994—96, chief rheumatology, 1996—99; assoc. prof. medicine U. Mass. Med. Sch., 1999—. Vice chmn. Ctrl. Pa. Chpt. Arthritis Found., Camp Hill, 1995-97, chmn., 1997-98; treas. Ch. of the Redeemer, Hershey, Pa., 1995; comdr. USNR, 1978-91. Fellow: ACP, Am. Coll. Rheumatology. Office: U Mass Meml Wing 40 Wright St Palmer MA 01069 Office Phone: 413-284-5400. Business E-Mail: Ferrij01@ummhc.org.

FERRITOR, DANIEL E., chancellor emeritus; b. Kansas City, Mo., Nov. 8, 1939; m. Patricia Jean Ferritor; children: Kimberly Ann, Kristin Marie, Sean Patrick. BA, Rockhurst Coll., 1962; MA, Washington U., St. Louis, 1967, PhD, 1969. Tchr. grade sch., Raytown, Mo., 1962-64; program assoc., asst. dir. Nat. Program on Early Childhood Edn., 1970-71; asst. program dir. CEMREL Inc., St. Ann, Mo., 1969-70, assoc. dir. instrnl. systems program, 1970-71; asst. prof. sociology U. Ark., Fayetteville, 1967-68, assoc. prof., 1973-79, prof., 1979-85, chmn. dept., 1973-85, vice chancellor for acad. affairs, provost, 1985-86, chancellor, 1986-97, prof., 1997—, chancellor emeritus, 1998—. Author: (with Robert L. Hamblin, D. Buckholdt, M. Kozloff and L. Blackwell) The Humanization Processes, 1971; contbr. articles to profl. jours. Office: Dept Sociology Social Work Criminal Justice U Ark Fayetteville AR 72701 E-mail: def@uark.edu.

FERRO, THOMAS LOUIS, lawyer, publishing executive; b. Paterson, N.J., Dec. 26, 1947; s. Alphonse Rinaldi and Mary (Sachs) F.; m. Patricia M. Jacobs, July 5, 1970 (div. Jan. 1983); 1 child, Amanda. BS, NYU, 1969; JD, Rutgers U., 1973. Bar: N.J. 1973. Profl. musician various bands, 1961-86; asst. pros. atty. County of Passaic, Paterson, 1975-79; sole practice Ridgewood, N.J., 1979—. Owner Hot Rod Prodns., Ridgewood, 1987—. Composer (songs) Hot Rod, 1987, You Taught Me, 1989. Fundraiser Big Bros./Big Sisters, Wayne, N.J., 1987, March of Dimes, Muscular Dystrophy Assn. Mem. N.J. State Bar Assn. Republican. Avocations: playing keyboards, politics, bicycling. Office Phone: 201-444-3000.

FERRO, WALTER, artist; b. N.Y.C., Oct. 6, 1925; s. Joseph Salvador and Mary Elizabeth (Potezna) F.; m. Lore Gausmann, Sept. 20, 1966; children—Elizabeth, Paula. Certificate, Bklyn. Mus. Art Sch., 1952. Art cons. One-man exhbns. include Wakefield Gallery, N.Y.C., 1960, Dominican Coll., Racine, Wis., 1962, Kings Coll., Briarcliff, N.Y., 1967, Hiram Malle Meml. Library, Pound Ridge, N.Y., 1988, Gallery L 9, Oberursel, Fed. Republic Germany, 1991; group exhbns. include Bklyn. Mus., 1953, U. Okla., 1959, Jersey City Mus., 1966, Phila. Mus., 1966; represented in permanent collections Met. Mus. Art, Nat. Mus. Am. Art, Smithsonian Instn. Served with USNR, 1942-44. Recipient Kenneth Hayes Miller Meml. award Audubon Artists, 1953; Kate W. Arms Meml. award Soc. Am. Graphic Artists, 1959; Guggenheim fellow, 1972 Address: PO Box 304 Pound Ridge NY 10576-0304

FERRUA, PIETRO MICHELE STEFANO, foreign language educator, writer; b. San Remo, Italy, Sept. 18, 1930; came to U.S., 1969; s. Libero and Anita Libera (Taggiasco) F.; m. Diana Jane Lobo Filho, June 24, 1957; children: Anna Piera, Franco Dorian. MA, U. Geneva, Switzerland, 1957, Cath. Pontifical U., Rio de Janeiro, 1966; postgrad., U. Fed., Rio de Janeiro, 1969; PhD, U. Oreg., 1973. Prof. Italian Ecole Internat., Geneva, 1958-62; prof. French Alliance Française, Rio de Janeiro, 1964-69; asst. prof. French Pontifícia U. Cath., Rio de Janeiro, 1966-68; lectr. Italian U. Gâmafilho, Rio de Janeiro, 1968-69; asst. prof. Portuguese Portland (Oreg.) State U., 1970-73; prof. French Lewis and Clark Coll., Portland, 1970-87, prof. emeritus, 1987—. Cons. Nat. Endowment for the Humanities; chmn. Luso-Brazilian sect. 24th Pacific N.W. Conf. on Fgn. Lang; sec. workshop 8th INternat. Congress Comparative Lit., Budapest, 1976. Author: Gli Anarchici nella Rivoluzione Messicana: Praxedis G. Guerrero, 1976, Eros Chez Thanatos, 1979, Avanguardia Cinematografica Lettrista, 1984, Appunti Sul Cinema Nero Americano, 1987, Italo Calvino A San Remo, 1992, INI Art USA, Individual Expressions within the International Group, Espressioni individuali in seno al gruppo internazionale, 1996, L'Obiezione di Coscienza Anarchica in Italia, 1997, Conversations About Letterism, 1998, Ifigenia in Utopia, 2000. Founder Ctr. Internat. de Rsch. sur L'Anarchisme, Ctr. Brasileiro de Estudos Internats. Recipient Cittadino Benemerito, Municipality of San Remo, Italy, 1984; Chmn. grantee Oreg. Com. for the Humanities, Portland, 1983, Travel grantee Am. Coun. Learned Socs., 1979. Mem. Am. Assn. Tchrs. of French, Am. Assn. Tchrs. of Italian, Am. Assn.

Tchrs. of Spanish and Portuguese, Internat. Assn. Comparative Lit., Romanian Study Group, Latin Am. Studies Assn. Avocation: multimedia creations. Office: Lewis and Clark Coll Palatine Hill Rd Portland OR 97219 Home: PO Box 4077 Portland OR 97208-4077

FERRUOLO, STEPHEN CARL, lawyer, historian; b. Providence, July 26, 1949; s. Anthony Frank and Virginia (DePetrillo) F.; m. Karen McLaughlin, Feb. 23, 1974 (div. 1981); m. Carolyn Elisabeth Springer, Aug. 27, 1988. BA magna cum laude, Wesleyan U., Middletown, Conn., 1971; MPhil, Oxford (Eng.) U., 1973; MA, Princeton U., 1975, PhD, 1979; JD with distinction, Stanford U., 1990. Bar: Calif. Lectr. Bennington (Vt.) Coll., 1977-79; asst. prof. Stanford (Calif.) U., 1979-87; judicial clk. to Hon. Bruce M. Selya U.S. Ct. Appeals (1st cir.), Providence; atty. Heller, Ehrman, White, & McAuliffe, LLP, San Francisco, 1993—. Author: Origins of the University, 1985; co-author: University and the City, 1988; contrbr. articles to profl. jours. Rhodes scholar, 1971; Danforth fellow, 1971. Mem. Order of the Coif. Home: 85 Cavalcade Blvd Warwick RI 02889-1604 Office: U S Courthouse 311 Federal Providence RI 02903-1454

FERRY, DAVID KEANE, electrical engineering educator; b. San Antonio, Oct. 25, 1940; s. Joseph Jules and Elizabeth (Keane) F. m. Darleen Heitkamp; Aug. 25, 1962; children: Lara Annette, Linda Renee. BSEE, Tex. Tech U., 1962, MSEE, 1963; PhD, U. Tex., 1966. Lectr. U. Tex., Austin, 1966; postdoctoral fellow U. Vienna, 1966-67; asst. prof., then assoc. prof. Tex. Tech. U., Lubbock, 1967-73; sci. officer Office Naval Rsch., Arlington, Va., 1973-77; prof., head elec. engring. Colo. State U., Ft. Collins, 1977-83; Regent's prof., dir. Ctr. for Solid State Electronics Rsch. Ariz. State U., Tempe, 1983-89, Regent's prof., chair elec. computing engring., 1989-92, Regent's prof., 1992—. Mem. microelectronics panel NRC, Washington, 1977-79; mem. materials rsch. coun. Def. Advanced Rsch. Projects Agy., Arlington, 1982-98; mem. supercomputer adv. group NSF, Washington, 1984-87. Author (with D.R. Fannin): Physical Electronics, 1971; author: (with L.A. Akers and E.W. Greeneich) Ultra Large Scale Integrated Microelectronics, 1988, Semiconductors, 1991; author: (with R.O. Grondin) Physics of Submicron Devices, 1991, Quantum Mechanics, 1995, 2d edit., 2000; author: (with S.M. Goodnick) Transport in Nanostructures, 1997, Semiconductor Transport, 2000; author: (with J.P. Bird) Electronic Materials and Devices, 2001, Semiconductor Transport, 2001; numerous pub. sci. articles; editor: GaAs Technology, 1985, GaAs Technology II, 1989; editor: (with J.R. Barker and C. Jacoboni) Physics of Nonlinear Transport in Semiconductors, 1979, Granular Nonelectronics, 1991; editor: (with C. Jacoboni) Quantum Transport in Semiconductors, 1992; editor: (with C. Jacoboni, A.P. Jauho, H.L. Grubin) Quantum Transport in Ultrasmall Devices, 1995; editor: (with S. Ode) Silicon Nanoelectronics, 2005; patentee in field. Fellow IEEE (Cledo Brunetti prize for advancements in nanoelectronics 1999), Am. Phys. Soc.; mem. Sigma Xi. Avocations: photography, skiing. Office: Ariz State U Elec Dept Tempe AZ 85287

FERRY, JAMES ALLEN, physicist, electrostatics company executive; b. Sept. 9, 1937; s. Darwin J. and Eleanor J. (Irwin) F.; m. Karen A. Greenwood, Feb. 8, 1964; children: Thomas E., Jennifer J. BS in Physics, U. Wis., 1959, MS in Physics, 1962, PhD in Physics, 1965. Rsch. assoc. U. Wis., Madison, 1965-66; exec. v.p., COO Nat. Electrostatics Corp., Middleton, Wis., 1967-95, pres., CEO, chmn. bd., 1995—. Patentee in field. Mem. Am. Phys. Soc. Home: 4105 Teal Ct Middleton WI 53562-5266 Office: Nat Electrostatics Corp Graber Rd PO Box 620310 Middleton WI 53562-0310 E-mail: nec@pelletron.com.

FERRY, JOAN EVANS, school counselor; b. Summit, N.J., Aug. 20, 1941; d. John Stiger and Margaret Darling (Evans) F. BS, U. Pa., 1964; cert., Coll. of Preceptors, London, 1966; EdM, Temple U., 1967; postgrad., Villanova U., 1981. Cert. elem. sch. tchr., elem. sch. counselor; cert. vol. Dale Carnegie; cert. cash flow cons. Indsl. photographer Bucksco Mfg. Co., Inc., Quakertown, Pa., 1958-59; math. and German tutor St. Lawrence U., Canton, N.Y., 1959-61; research asst. U. Pa., Phila., 1963; tchr. elem. sch. Pennridge Schs., Perkasie, Pa., 1964—77, elem. sch. counselor, 1981—2001; pvt. practice counselor, real estate partnership Perkasie, 1981—; chair child study team Perkasie Elem. Sch., 1988-94; editor Princeton (NJ) Pub. Group, 2000—; self-employed as cash flow cons., 2004—. Tutor math., German, St. Lawrence U., Canton, N.Y., 1959-61; supervisory tchr. East Stroudsburg U., Pennridge Schs., 1971-74; research asst. U. Pa., Phila., 1963; mem. acad. coms. for Pennridge Schs.; adj. faculty Bucks County Community Coll., 1983—; instr. Am. Inst. Banking, 1982—; notary pub., 1986—; mcpl. auditor, sec. bd. auditors, 1984-90, mcpl. auditor 1990—, chmn. bd. auditors 1990—; cons. in field. Author (with others) Life-Time Sports for the College Student: A Behavioral Objective Approach, 1971, 3d rev. edit. 1978, Elementary Social Studies as a Learning System, 1976. Vol. elem. sch. counselor Perkasie, 1979-81; mem. Hilltown Civic Assn., 1965-70, 92—; chair exec. com. Hilltown PTO, 1965-73; soloist Good Shepherd Episcopal Ch. Choir, Hilltown, 1964-77, mem. choir, 2000—; mem. steering com. Perkasie Sch., 1989-95; poll watcher, 1993; med. vol. Olympics, Atlanta, 1996; vol. Dublin Ambulance Squad, 1996—, House Rabbit Soc., Chadds Ford, Pa., 1998—, Spl. Olympics World Games, Summer, N.C., 1999, Silverdale Quick Responsë Med. Svc., 1999-2001, Chalfont Ambulance Squad, 2000—; mem. Dublin Vol. Fire and Ambulance Co., Silverdale (Pa.) Fire Co.; mem. prin.'s round table Perkasie (Pa.) Sch., 1997; vol. House Rabbit Soc. Southeastern Pa./Del. Foster Home and Sanctuary, Chadds Ford, Pa., 1998—; vol. marshal First Union US Pro Championship Cycling Race, Phila., 1999-2003; vol. spl. driver Bush Family and Friends at Rep. Nat. Conv., Phila., 2000, Bucks County Crisis Response Team, 2001—; mem. Chalfont Chem. Fire Engine Co. No. 1; mem. Nat. Arbor Day Found., Best Friends Animal Sanctuary. NSF grantee, Washington, 1972-73, Philanthropic Edn. Orgn. grantee, Doylestown, Pa., 1982; recipientJudith Netzky Meml. Fellowship award B'nai B'rith, Phila., 1979; Durning scholar Delta Delta Delta, Arlington, Tex., 1981, Am. Mgmt. Assns. scholar, N.Y.C., 1983, Achievement award Women's Inner Circle, 1990, Golden Acad. award for lifetime achievement, 1991; named to Women's Internat. Hall of Fame, 2003, Internat. Tennis Hall of Fame, 2000, Cmty. Leaders of Am. Hall of Fame, 1990, Internat. Bus. and Profl. Women's Hall of Fame, 1994, Millennium Hall of Fame, 1999; recipient Lifetime Achievement Acad. Humane Soc. U.S., Internat. Honor Soc. In Edn., Cert. of appreciation Atlanta Olympics Med. Team, 1997, Hon. Educator cert. St. Joseph's Indian Sch., 1996, ARC, 1986, Cert. Achievement in Recognition of Contbn. as Med. Svcs. Vol. at Centennial Olympic Games, 1996, Honor Award for Svc. to Edn. and Tchg. Profession, 1996, 99, award for Outstanding Svc. to Edn. Pennridge Schs., 1999, Cert. of appreciation Spl. Olympics World Summer Games, 1999, World Lifetime Achievement award, Raleigh, 2003, 21st Century award for Achievement, Internat. Bio. Ctr., 2004. Mem. AAUW, NEA, NAFE, Humane Soc. U.S., Pa. State Edn. Assn. (polit. action com. for edn., chair Pennridge Schs. 1986—, del. leadership conf. 1987, 89, Honor award for svc. to edn. and tchg. profession, 1996, 99), Pennridge Edn. Assn. (faculty rep. 1986-88, exec. coun. 1986—, negotiations resource com. 1987-89, 1990-93, steering com. Perkasie Sch. 1989-95, chair Child Study Team, 1988-94, Instructional Support Team, 1992—), Am. Inst. Banking (chair 1987), U.S. Tennis Assn. (hon. life), Pa. and Mid. States Tennis Assn. (hon. life), U.S. Profl. Tennis Registry, Mid. States Profl. Tennis Registry, Women's Internat. Tennis Assn., Nat. Ski Patrol (Svc. Recognition award 1994), Spring Mountain Ski Patrol, Pa. Elected Women's Assn., Bucks County Assn. Twp. Ofcls., Bucks County Sch. Counselors Assn., Pa. Sch. Counselors Assn., Pa. Assn. Notaries, Am. Soc. Notaries, Internat. Fedn. Univ. Women, Internat. Platform Assn., Rails-to-Trails Conservancy, World Wildlife Fund, Bucks County Sch. Counselors Assn., Highpoint Athletic Club, Pennridge Cmty. Rep. Club. (rec. sec. 1986-91, publicity chmn. 1991-92, Pen care chmn. 1992—), Assn. Tennis Profls. Tour Tennis Ptnrs., Sierra Club, The Nature Conservancy, Nat. Wildlife Fedn., John Wayne Found., Mediterranean Club, Phila. Sports Club, Delaware Valley Jaguar Club, Jaguar Clubs N.Am., Nockamixon Boat Club, Peace Valley Yacht Club, Kappa Delta Pi. Episcopalian. Avocations: land and water sports, flying, music, parasailing, photography. Home and Office: 834 Rickert Rd Perkasie PA 18944

FERRY, JOHN DOUGLASS, retired chemist, educator; b. Dawson, Can., May 4, 1912; s. Douglass Hewitt and Eudora (Bundy) F.; m. Barbara Norton Mott, Mar. 25, 1944; children: Phyllis Leigh, John Mott. AB, Stanford U., 1932, PhD, 1935; student, U. London, 1932-34. Pvt. asst. Hopkins Marine Sta., Stanford, Calif., 1935-36; instr. biochem. scis. Harvard U., 1936-38; mem. Soc. Fellows, 1938-41; assoc. chemist Woods Hole Oceanographic Inst., 1941-45; research assoc. Harvard U., Cambridge, Mass., 1942-45; asst. prof. chemistry U. Wis., 1946, assoc. prof., 1946-47, prof., 1947-82, prof. emeritus, 1982—, Farrington Daniels Research prof., 1973-82, chmn. dept., 1959-67. Chmn. Internat. Com. on Rheology, 1963-68; vis. lectr. Kyoto U., Japan, 1968, Ecole d'Ete, U. Grenoble, France, 1973 Author: Viscoelastic Properties of Polymers, 1961, 2d edit., 1970, 3d edit., 1980; co-editor: Fortschritte der Hochpolymeren Forschung, 1958-85. Recipient Eli Lilly award Am. Chem. Soc., 1946, Bingham medal Soc. Rheology, 1953, Kendall Co. award Am. Chem. Soc., 1960, Witco award, 1974, Colwyn medal Instn. Rubber Industry, U.K., 1972, Tech. award Internat. Inst. Synthetic Rubber Producers, 1977 Fellow Am. Phys. Soc. (high polymer physics prize 1966), Am. Acad. Arts and Scis.; mem. Nat. Acad. Sci., NAE, Am. Chem. Soc. (Goodyear medal Rubber div. 1981, Polymer div. award 1984), Am. Soc. Biol. Chemists, Soc. Rheology (pres. 1961-63), Internat. Soc. Hematology, d'Honneur Groupe Francais Rheologie, Soc. Rheology Japan (hon.), Phi Beta Kappa, Sigma Xi, Phi Lambda Upsilon, Alpha Chi Sigma Lodges: Rotary. Home: 6175 Mineral Point Rd Madison WI 53705-4457

FERRY, MARTHA MORTON, non-profit executive; b. Amherst, Mass., Apr. 5, 1945; d. Edward Morrison and Dorothy Mae (Beck) F. AB, Mt. Holyoke Coll., 1966; MBA, Harvard U., 1968. Asst. mgmt. sci. officer Bankers Trust Co., N.Y.C., 1968-71; v.p. Am. Express Internat. Bank Corp., N.Y.C., 1971-82; sr. v.p. Nat. Westminster Bank USA, N.Y.C., 1982-88; CFO Cmty. Svc. Soc. of N.Y., 1989—2002; dir. fin. and adminstrn. Assn. Jr. Leagues Internat., 2002—. Bd. dirs. NY Women's Found., 2001—, treas., 2002—04, bd. dirs., NYC YWCA, 1987-99, bd. trustees, 1st Presbyn. Ch., NYC, 1997-2000, session, 2000-02, 04-05. Mem. Fin. Womens Assn. N.Y., Alumnae Assn. Mt. Holyoke Coll. (treas. 1983-86), Harvard Club, Mt. Holyoke Club (pres. 1974-75, bd. dirs. 1988-98). Democrat. Presbyterian. Avocations: travel, reading, performing arts. Office: 90 William St New York NY 10038 Office Phone: 212-951-8364.

FERRY, MILES YEOMAN, state legislator; b. Brigham City, Utah, Sept. 22, 1932; s. John Yeoman and Alda (Cheney) F.; m. Suzanne Call, May 19, 1952; children: John, Jane Ferry Stewart, Ben, Helen, Sue Ferry Thorpe. BS, Utah State U., 1954. Rancher, Corinne, Utah, 1952; pres. J.Y. Ferry & Son, Inc.; mem. Utah Ho. of Reps., 1965-66, Utah Senate, 1967-84, minority whip, 1975-76, minority leader, 1977-78, pres. senate, 1979-84; mem. presdl. advisor commn. on intergovtl. affairs, 1984; mem. governing bd. Council State Govts., 1983-84. V.p. Legis./Exec. Consulting Firm, 1994—; chmn. Corinne Cemetery Dist., 1989—. Pres. Brigham Jr. C. of C., 1956-61, Nat. Conf. of State Legislators, 1984, v.p., 1982, pres.-elect, 1983, pres., 1984; v.p. Utah Jr. C. of C., 1960-61; nat. dir. Utah Jaycees, 1961-62; pres. Farm Bur. Box Elder County, 1958-59; food and agr. commr. USDA, commr. agr. State of Utah, 1985-93. Recipient award of merit Boy Scouts Am., 1976, Alumnusi of Yr. award Utah State U., 1981, award of merit Utah Vocat. Assn., 1981, Friend of Agr. award Utah Farm Bur., 1988, Cert. Appreciation USDA, 1988, Contbn. to Agr. award Utah-Idaho Farmers Union, 1989, Disting. Svc. award Utah State U., 1993, 94; named Outstanding Young Man of Yr., Brigham City Jr. C. of C., 1957, Outstanding Nat. Dir. U.S. Jaycees, 1963, Outstanding Young Man in Utah, Utah Jr. C. of C., 1961, Outstanding Young Farmer, 1958, One of 3 Outstanding Young Men of Utah, 1962, Rep. Legislator of Yr., 1984, One of 10 Outstanding Legislators of Yr., 1984. Mem. SAR, Sons Utah Pioneers, Gov.'s Cabinet, Utah Commn. Agr., Fed. Rsch. Com., Nat. Assn. State Depts. Agr. (bd. dirs. 1989), Western Assn. of State Depts. of Agr. (v.p. 1990-91, pres. 1991-92), Western U.S. Agr. Trade Assn. (sec. treas- elect 1987-88, pres. 1989-90), Utah Cattlemen's Assn., Nat. Golden Spike Assn. (dir. 1958—), Phi Kappa Phi, Pi Kappa Alpha. Republican. Address: 815 N 6800 W Corinne UT 84307-9737 E-mail: leg.ex.con@worldnet.att.net.

FERRY, RICHARD MICHAEL, retired executive recruiter; b. Ravenna, Ohio, Sept. 26, 1937; s. John D. and Margaret M. (Jeney) F.; m. Maude M. Hillman, Apr. 14, 1956; children: Richard A., Margaret L., Charles Michael, David W., Dianne E., Ann Marie. BS, Kent State U., 1959. CPA. Cons. staff Peat, Marwick, Mitchell, L.A., 1965-69, ptnr., 1969; founder chmn. Korn/Ferry Internat., L.A., 1969—2004, ret., 2004. Bd. dirs. Mellon/1st Bus. Bank, L.A., Avery Dennison, Pasadena, Calif., Dole Food Co., Calif., Pacific Life Ins. Co., Newport Beach, Calif. Trustee St. John's Health Ctr., Santa Monica, Calif.; bd. dirs. Calif. Cmty. Found., Hugh O'Brian Youth Leadership; pres. Cath. Edn. Found., L.A. Republican. Roman Catholic. Office: Korn/Ferry Internat 1900 Ave of the Stars Ste 2600 Los Angeles CA 90067

FERSTANDIG ARNOLD, GAIL, research scientist, educator; m. Edward Arnold, 1981; children: Lizzie, Emmie. Assoc. mem. graduate program, molecular genetics and microbiology Rutgers U., Piscataway, NJ; co-established Rutgers U., Ctr. of Advanced Biotechnology and Medicine, Piscataway, NJ, 1987—, sr. rsch. scientist, 1987—. Partnered (with husband Edward Arnold) in 1987 to form laboratory at Rutgers University, Center of Advanced Biotechnology and Medicine that is working with a 30 member research team to develop a trio of drugs that are believed to destroy HIV, the virus that causes AIDS, tenifovir, or the DAPY (diarylpyrimidine). The team is working to develop and apply structure-based drug and vaccine designs for the treatment and prevention of serious human diseases. Office: Rutgers U Ctr Advanced Biotechnology & Medicine 679 Hoes Ln Rm 020 Piscataway NJ 08854 Office Phone: 732-235-4343. Office Fax: 732-235-5788. Business E-Mail: gfarnold@cabm.rutgers.edu.*

FERTIG, HOWARD, publishing executive; b. N.Y.C. s. Benjamin and Rose (Mallman) F.; children: Paul, Daniel; m. Ana-Maria Daranga, 2004. BA, NYU. Asst. editor Commentary mag., N.Y.C., 1960; editor Alfred A. Knopf, Inc., N.Y.C., 1961-62; chief editor Univ. Library Paperbacks, Grosset & Dunlap, Inc., N.Y.C., 1962-65; pres., editor-in-chief Howard Fertig, Pub., N.Y.C., 1966—. Mem. MLA, P.E.N., Am. Hist. Assn., Friends of Columbia Library. Home: 49 E 10th St New York NY 10003-6153 Office: Howard Fertig Pub 80 E 11th St New York NY 10003-6000 Office Phone: 212-982-7922.

FERTITTA, ANGELA, dean; BFA, MFA, U. Colo. Dean academic affairs Art Inst. Boston at Lesley U., Boston, adj. prof. drawing & painting/foundation. Exhibitions include Faculty Honorarium Exhbn. Office: Art Institute of Boston at Lesley University 700 Beacon St Boston MA 02215-2598 Office Fax: 617-585-6600.*

FERTUCK, ERIC ANDREW, psychologist, researcher; b. Detroit, Feb. 6, 1970; s. Douglas A. and Lorraine E. Fertuck. BS with honors, Mich. State U., 1992; PhD, Adelphi U., 1998. Lic. psychologist N.Y., 1999. Postdoctoral rsch. fellow dept. psychiatry Columbia U. Coll. P&S, N.Y.C., 2003—. Glass fellow, Columbia U. Ctr. for Psychoanalytic Tng. and Rsch., 2000—02. Mem.: APA. Achievements include research in severe psychopathology and borderline personality disorder. Office: New York State Psychiatric Institute Dept Neurosci Unit 42 Ste 2917 1051 Riverside Dr New York NY 10032 E-mail: ef304@columbia.edu.

FERVENZA, FERNANDO C., nephrologist, educator; b. Livramento, R.S., Brazil, Nov. 21, 1958; s. Fernando E. and Lorena C. Fervenza; m. Ivete Martinez; 1 child, Sophia. MD, PUCRS, 1982; PhD, Oxford U., 1991. Diplomate Am. Bd. Internal Medicine and Nephrology. Sr. house officer, sr. registrar Renal Unit Oxford U., England, 1986—91; asst. prof. Medicine PUCRS, Porto Alegre, Brazil, 1991—93; fellow Nephrology divsn. Stanford U., Calif., 1993—97; resident Internal Medicine Mayo Clinic, Rochester, Minn., 1997—99; asst. prof. Mayo Med. Sch., Rochester, Minn., 1999—2004; assoc. prof. Mayo Clinic Coll. Medicine, Rochester, Minn., 2004—. Cons. Nephrology Mayo Clinic, Rochester, 1999—. Fellow: Am. Soc. Nephrology. Office: Mayo Clinic 200 First St SW Rochester MN 55905 Office Phone: 507-266-7361. Business E-Mail: fervenza.fernando@mayo.edu.

FERZLI, GEORGE SALEM, surgeon; b. Lebanon, Jan. 10, 1955; came to U.S., 1979; s. Salem and Milia Ferzli; m. Berthe Ferzli, Aug. 25, 1983; children: Georgina, Christina, George Jr., Christopher. MD, St. Joseph U., Beirut, 1979. Lic. physician, France, N.J., N.Y.; diplomate Am. Bd. Gen. Surgery, Am. Bd. Surg. Critical Care. Resident gen. surgery S.I. (N.Y.) U. Hosp., 1979-84, dir. surg. ICU, assoc. dir. surgery, 1984—90, dir. laparoendoscopic surgery, 1991—2003; prof. surgery SUNY Health Sci. Ctr., Bklyn., 1999—; dir. laparoendoscopic surgery Luth. Med. Ctr., Bklyn., 2004—, chmn. dept. surgery, 2005—. Vis. and oper. surgeon NYU, Cornell U., Columbia Presbyn. Hosp., Beth Israel Hosp., Maimonides Med. Ctr., Montefiore Hosp., L.I. Coll. Hosp., St. Mary's Hosp., Valley Hosp., St. Peter's Hosp., U. Medicine and Dentistry N.J. Children's Hosp., Newark, Overlook Hosp., L.I. Coll. Hosp., China, South Africa, France, Russia, Bahrain, Kuwait, Kazakhstan, Greece, Egypt, Lebanon, Uzbekistan Portugal, Belgium, Can., Japan, Singapore, Italy, Dominican Republic; vis. prof. Spain, Portugal, Norway, Singapore, Italy, Belgium, Turkey, Japan, France, Can., Scotland, Poland. Reviewer Jour. ACS, Surg. Endoscopy, Am. Jour. Surgery, Archives of Surgery, Jour. Laparoendoscopic Surgery, contbr. over 100 articles to profl. jours., chpts. to books; patentee in field. Fellow ACS, Am. Coll. Gastroenterologists; mem. Soc. for Surgery Alimentary Tract, Am. Soc. Bariatric Surgery, N.Y. Surg. Soc., Soc. Internat. de Chirurgie, Soc. Am. Gastrointestinal Endoscopic Surgeons, Assn. Francaise de Chirurgie, Soc. Critical Care Medicine, Am. Soc. Parenteral and Enteral Nutrition, Richmond County Med. Soc., Med. Soc. State N.Y., European Assn. Endoscopic Surgery, Internat. Fedn. Surg. Colls. Office: 65 Cromwell Ave Staten Island NY 10304-3933 Office Phone: 718-667-8100. E-mail: info@drferzli.com.

FESHBACH, MURRAY, demographer, educator; b. N.Y.C., Aug. 8, 1929; s. Benjamin and Lilly (Harfenist) F.; m. Muriel Joan Schreiner, Dec. 30, 1956; children: Michael Lee, David Steven. AB in History, Syracuse U., 1950; MA in History, Columbia U., 1951; PhD in Econs., Am.U., 1974. Rsch. asst. Nat. Bur. Econ. Rsch., N.Y.C., 1955-56; economist U.S. Bur. Census, Washington, 1957-67; chief USSR population, employment, rsch. and devel. br., 1967-81; sr. rsch. scholar Georgetown U., Washington, 1981-84, rsch. prof. demography, 1984-2000; sr. scholar Woodrow Wilson Internat. Ctr. for Scholar, Smithsonian Instn., Washington, 2000—. Rsch. emeritus prof., 2000—; bd. dirs. Internat. Rsch. and Exch. Bd., program com., 1975-94; cons. Rand Corp., Santa Monica, Calif., 1981-90, U.S. Dept. Def., 1981-90, U.S. Dept. State, 1982-83, NSF, 1987, World Bank, 1992-93, Health Found. of Russia, 1992, Russian Winter Campaign, 1992; sr. advisor CH2M Hill on Environ. Policy and Tech. in Russia; vis. prof. Columbia U., N.Y.C., 1983-84; Sovietologist-in-residence Office of Sec. Gen., NATO, Brussels, 1986-87; internat. adv. bd. Fernand Braudel Inst. World Econs., Sao Paulo, Brazil; disting. vis. lectr. U.S. Dept. State. Author: Ecological Disaster: Cleaning Up the Hidden Legacy of the Soviet Regime, 1995, Russian Population Meltdown, 2001; (with Alfred Friendly Jr.) Ecocide in the USSR: Health and Nature Under Siege, 1992; editor-in-chief Environmental and Health Atlas of Russia, 1995; editor National Security Issues in the USSR, workship held at NATO, Nov. 6-7, 1986, Brussels, Dordrecht, Nijhoff, 1987; contbr. articles to profl. jours. Mem. Coun. on Fgn. Rels. Served to sgt. U.S. Army, 1951-55. Recipient Silver medal Dept. Commerce, Washington, 1979; Woodrow Wilson Internat. Ctr. for Scholars fellow Smithsonian Instn., 1979. Mem. Assn. Comparative Econ. Studies (pres. 1985), Am. Assn. for Advancement of Slavic Studies (pres. Washington chpt. 1974-78, bd. dirs. 1979-82, v.p. 1984-85, nat. pres. 1985-86), Internat. Union for Sci. Study of Population, Internat. Instn. Strategic Studies, Ctr. for Strategic and Internat. Studies (adv. coun.), Cosmos Club. Democrat. Jewish. Home: 11403 Fairoak Dr Silver Spring MD 20902-3136 Office: Woodrow Wilson Internat Ctr for Scholar Smithsonian Instn 1300 Pennsylvania Ave NW Washington DC 20004-3027

FESKO, COLLEENE, art appraiser; B, Bucknell Univ. Tchr., art hist. Mount Ida Coll.; appraiser Childs Gallery, Boston; cons. Vespi Corp.; joined Skinner, Inc., Boston, 1987, now v.p., and dir., Am., European paintings & prints dept. Appraiser Antiques Roadshow, WGBH-PBS; founder, Firewall Gallery Skinner, Inc. Lectr., writer in field. Mem.: Art Table women in arts orgn. Office: Skinner Inc 63 Park Plz Boston MA 02116 Office Phone: 617-350-5400. Office Fax: 617-350-5429. Business E-Mail: tvappraisers@skinnerinc.com.*

FESKOE, GAFFNEY JON, management consultant; b. N.Y.C., Feb. 21, 1949; s. George Jon and Mary Margaret (Gaffney) F.; children: Gregory, Alexandra, Julia, Elizabeth. BS, Boston Coll., 1971; MBA, Fordham U., 1976. With Mfrs. Hanover Trust, N.Y.C., 1971-75; asst. treas. European-Am. Bank, N.Y.C., 1975-77; asst. v.p. Citibank, N.A., N.Y.C., 1977-80; asst treas. U.S. Filter Corp., N.Y.C., 1980-82; v.p. Bank of N.Y., N.Y.C., 1982-84; cons. Arthur D. Little, Inc., N.Y.C., 1986-88; exec. v.p. Madison One Group, N.Y.C., 1988-93; mng. ptnr. Horton Group Internat., N.Y.C., 1994-95; pres. Halifax Assocs., LLC; ptnr. Handy Assocs. Corp., N.Y.C. Advisor Halifax Ship Yard, 1997-99. Trustee Yale Libr. Assocs., 1983—; mem. Darien (Conn.) Cable TV and Comm. Commn., 1985-87; mem. steering com. Friends of Yale Ctr. for Brit. Art, 1989-95; mem. London Libr. Mem. Bibliog. Soc. (London), Bibliog. Soc. Am., Boston Athenaeum (propr.), Can. Soc. N.Y., Club of Odd Vols. (Boston), Mass. Hist. Soc. Roman Catholic. Office: 420 Lexington Ave New York NY 10168-0002 E-mail: gfeskoe@handypartners.com.

FESSEL, ROBIN D., lawyer; b. Glen Cove, NY, 1956; BA, Univ. Conn., 1980; JD, Columbia Univ., 1989. Bar: NY 1990, Conn. 1990. Assoc. litig. group Sullivan & Cromwell, NYC, 1989—98, ptnr. litig. and dep. coord. labor and employment practice area, 1998—. Mem.: ABA. Office: Sullivan & Cromwell 128 Broad St New York NY 10004-2498 Office Phone: 212-558-4000. Office Fax: 212-558-3588. Business E-Mail: fesselr@sullcrom.com.

FESSEL, WALFORD JEFFREY, rheumatologist; b. London, June 20, 1932; came to U.S., 1957; s. Jack Isaac and Alma (Yarmolinski) F.; m. Nicole J. Noble, Sept. 11, 1957; 1 child, Jason N. MB, BS, U. London, 1955. Diplomate Am. Bd. Internal Medicine. Intern U. Coll. Hosp., London, 1955; resident Can. Red Cross Hosp., Taplow, England, 1956, U. Calif., San Francisco, 1963, 64; rheumatologist Kaiser-Permanente, San Francisco, 1965—, chief of medicine, 1979-89, dir. internal medicine residency tng. program, 1979-89, dir. HIV rsch. unit, 1989—; clin. prof. medicine U. Calif., San Francisco, 1983-97, mem. clin. faculty promotion com., 1986—, emeritus clin. prof. medicine, 1997—. Chmn. regional chiefs of medicine No. Calif. Permanente Med. Group, 1980-89. Contbr. articles to profl. jours. Fellow ACP, Royal Coll. Physicians, Am. Coll. Rheumatology (founder). Jewish. Avocations: gardening, art, music, travel, languages. Office: Kaiser Permanente 2238 Geary Blvd San Francisco CA 94115-3394 Office Phone: 415-833-2854. Business E-Mail: jeffrey.fessel@kp.org.

FESSLER, RAYMOND R., metallurgical engineering consultant; b. St. Nazianz, Wis., May 6, 1939; BS, Carnegie Inst. Tech., 1961; PhD in Metallurgy, MIT, 1965. Staff mem. Battelle Columbus Divsn., 1965-68, assoc. mgr. ferrous metallurgy sect., 1968-77, mgr. phys. metallurgy sect., 1977-82, assoc. dir. programs corp. tech. devel., 1982-83, mgr. transp. and structure dept., 1983-85, mgr. advanced materials dept., 1985-86; dir. basic indsl. rsch. lab. Northwestern U., Evanston, Ill., 1987-96; prin. cons. BIZTEK Cons., Inc., Evanston, Ill., 1997—. Fellow Am. Soc. Metals Internat. Achievements include research in physical metallurgy of steels, high temperature alloys and nonferrous metals; fracture toughness; metal physics; optical and electron metallography; advanced ceramics; process and physical metallurgy; polymers; corrosion; electrochemistry; mechanics. Address: 820 Roslyn Ter Evanston IL 60201-1724

FESTA, FRED E. (ALFRED E. FESTA), chemicals executive; BS magna cum laude, SUNY, Oswego. With General Electric, 1981—93; fin. & mgmt. positions through v.p., gen. mgr. Allied Signal, 1993—2000; pres., CEO ICG

Commerce, 2000—02; ptnr. Morgenthaler Private Equity, 2002—03; pres., COO W.R. Grace & Co., Columbia, Md., 2003—05, pres., CEO, 2005—. Office: WR Grace & Co 7500 Grace Dr Columbia MD 21044*

FESTA, ROGER REGINALD, chemist, educator; b. Norwalk, Conn., Sept. 6, 1950; s. Reginald and Rosemary (Chappa) F. BA in Biology and Chemistry magna cum laude, St. Michael's Coll., 1972; MA in Agr., U. Vt., 1979; cert. in Adminstrn., Fairfield U., 1981; PhD in Edn., U. Conn., 1982. Tchr. Cen. Cath. High Sch., Norwalk, 1975-79, Brien McMahon High Sch., Norwalk, 1979-82; asst. prof. chemistry Truman State U. (formerly N.E. Mo. State U.), Kirksville, 1983-89, dir. Chem. Comm. Devel. Ctr., 1983-90, assoc. prof., 1989-97, prof., 1997—, coach men's volleyball, 1991-2000, dean frats., 1991-92. Adj. prof. U. Conn., 1983. Author: National Curriculum Development Programming for Teachers of High School Chemistry, 1981, Fairfield County High School Chemistry Curriculum Handbook, 1982. Sec. Diocese Bridgeport (Conn.) Edn. Assn., 1978-79, sci. cons. schs. office, 1979, exec. adminstr., 1979; bd. dirs. Norwalk Community Services Agy., 1980-81. Named one of Ten Outstanding Young Men of Mo., Mo. Jaycees, 1986. Fellow Am. Inst. Chemists (pub. edn. com. 1980-83, edn. editor The Chemist Jour. 1981-95, mem. editl. bd. The Chemist 1986-91, bd. dirs. 1982-99, chmn. nat. meetings com. 1982-91, 94-95, history com. 1982-99, archivist 1983-2002, sec. 1991-93, pres.-elect 1994-95, pres. 1996-97), Am Inst. Chemists Found. (trustee 1992-); mem. Am. Chem. Soc. (founding editor The Fairfield Chemist 1978-79, assoc. editor Jour. Chem. Edn. 1980-89, vice chmn. edn. com. Western Conn. sect. 1979-81, chmn. elect Mark Twain sect. 1985, chmn. 1986, exec. bd. 1984-95, program chair 1984-95), St. Louis Inst. Chemists (founder 1984, pres. 1985-87, sec.-treas. 1987—), Coun. Scientific Soc. Pres. (mem. 1996-97, emeritus 1998-), Acad. Sci. St. Louis, Assn. Frat. Advisors, Coll. Frat. Editors' Assn., Kirksville Jaycees (bd. dirs. 1983-86, sec. 1984-85, chair ret. sr. vols. com. 1985-87), Order of Omega, Delta Epsilon Sigma, Alpha Chi Sigma (assoc. editor The Hexagon 1984-99), Sigma Phi Epsilon (advisor Truman State U. chpt. 1991—), Sigma Phi Epsilon Ednl. Found. Democrat. Roman Catholic. Home: 114 E Mcpherson St Kirksville MO 63501-3570 Office: Truman State U 100 E Normal Ave Kirksville MO 63501-4200 Office Phone: 660-785-4524. Business E-Mail: rrf@truman.edu.

FETCHERO, JOHN ANTHONY, JR., otolaryngologist; b. Jeannette, Pa., June 4, 1951; s. John Anthony Sr. and Cleda (Byerly) F.; m. Wynona Ann Kestler, Feb. 26, 1982; children: John Anthony III, Christopher Jason, Dominic Vincent, Victor Thomas. BS in Biology, St. Vincent Coll., 1973; DO, Coll. Osteo. Medicine, Des Moines, 1976. Intern Des Moines Gen. Hosp., 1976-77; Flight surgeon Naval Aero. Med. Inst., Pensacola, Fla., 1977-78; resident Nat. Naval Med. Ctr., Bethesda, Md., 1980-84; otorhinolaryngologist, oro-facial plastic surgeon Am. Co. Osteo. Opthalmology and Otorhinolaryngology, 1987; otolaryngologist Am. Coll. Otolaryngology, 1988; pvt. practice, Orange Park, Fla., 1988—. Capt. USNR, 1973—2001, ret. Med. Sch. scholar USN, 1973-76. Mem. Fla. Osteo. Assn., Osteo. Acad. Otorhinolaryngology, Am. Acad. Otolaryngology, Am. Osteo. Assn., Fla. Med. Assn., Clay County Med. Soc. Republican. Roman Catholic. Avocations: running, photography, boating, bowling. Home: 2862 Country Club Blvd Orange Park FL 32073-5728 Office Phone: 904-278-3820. Personal E-mail: johnjr@dnamail.com.

FETHKE, GARY C., dean; m. Carol Fethke. BA in econ., U. Iowa, 1964, PhD in econ., 1968. Faculty mem. Bradley U., U. Iowa, 1976; dean, prof. mgmt. scis. and econs. Henry B. Tippie Coll. Bus., U. Iowa, 1994—2003, dean, Leonard A. Hadley prof. leadership, 2003—. Office: Univ Iowa Henry B Tippie Coll Bus 21 E Market St C120D John Pappajohn Bldg Iowa City IA 52242-1000 Business E-Mail: gary-fethke@uiowa.edu.

FETLER, ANDREW, author, educator; b. Riga, Latvia, July 24, 1925; came to U.S., 1939, naturalized, 1944; s. Basil Andreyevitch and Barbara (Kovalevski) Fetler-Malof; m. Carol J. McMahon, Aug. 29, 1960; 1 son, Jonathan. Student, U. Chgo., 1946-48; BA, Loyola U., Chgo., 1959; M.F.A., U. Iowa, 1964. Tchr. Master Fine Arts Program in English, U. Mass., Amherst, 1964-89. Author: The Travelers, 1965, To Byzantium, 1976, Norton Anthology of Short Fiction, 5th edit., 1994; contbr. fiction to lit. quars. Served with AUS, 1944-46. Recipient grants for fiction writing Iowa Industries, 1962-63; grantee Mass. Arts and Humanities Found., 1976, Nat. Endowment for Arts, 1976-77, 83-84, Guggenheim Found., 1978-79; recipient O. Henry awards, 1977, 84 Home: 46 Arnold Rd Pelham MA 01002-9789

FETLER, PAUL, retired composer; b. Phila., Feb. 17, 1920; s. William Basil and Barbara (Kovalevski) Fetler-Malof; m. Ruth Regina Pahl, Aug. 13, 1947; children: Sylvia, Daniel, Beatrix. MusB, Northwestern U., 1943; MusM, Yale U., 1948; PhD, U. Minn., 1956. From instr. to prof. music theory and composition U. Minn., Mpls., 1948—91, ret., 1992. Vis. composer, condr. and lectr. various colls. and univs. Composer: Symphonic Fantasia, 1941, Passacaglia for orch., 1942, Sextet for string quartet, clarinet and horn, 1942, Dramatic Overture, 1943, Prelude for orch., 1946, Orchestral Sketch, 1949, A Comedy Overture for Orchestra, 1952, Gothic Variations for Orchestra, 1953, Impromptu for piano, 1953, Contrasts for orch., 1958, Sing Unto God for mixed voices, 1958, Nothing but Nature for mixed voices and orchestra, 1961, Soundings for orch., 1962, Jubilate Deo for voices and brass, 1963, Te Deum for mixed voices, 1963, Four Symphonies, 1948-67, Cantus Tristis for orch., 1964, Five Pieces for guitar, 1964; opera Sturge Maclean, 1965, A Contemporary Psalm for chorus, organ and percussion, 1968, Prayer for Peace for mixed voices, 1969, Hosanna for mixed voices, 1970, Cycles for percussion and piano, 1970, The Words From the Cross for mixed voices, 1971, First Violin Concerto, 1971, Four Movements for guitar, 1972, Dialogue for flute and guitar, 1973, Six Pastoral Sketches for guitar, 1974, Lamentations for chorus, narrator, percussion and flute, 1974, Three Venetian Scenes for guitar, 1974, Dream of Shalom for mixed voices, 1975, Songs of the Night for voices, narrator and flute, 1976, Three Poems by Walt Whitman for narrator and orch., 1975, Pastoral Suite for piano trio, 1976, Celebration for orch., 1976, Three Impressions for guitar and orch., 1977, Five Piano Games, 1977, Sing Alleluia, 1978, Song of the Forest Bird for voices and chamber orch., 1978, Six Songs of Autumn for guitar, 1979, Second Violin Concerto, 1980, Missa de Angelis for three choirs, orch., organ and handbells, 1980, Serenade for chamber orch., 1981, Rhapsody for violin and piano, 1982; song cycle The Garden of Love for voice and orch., 1983, Piano Concerto, 1984; Capriccio for chamber orch., 1985; Frolic for Flute, Winds and Strings, 1986, Three Excursions, A Concerto for Percussion, Piano and Orchestra, 1987, String Quartet, 1989, Toccata for Organ, 1990, numerous sacred and secular choral works, 1949-93, Twelve Sacred Hymn Settings, 1993, Divertimento for Flute and Strings, 1994, December Stillness for Flute, Harp and Voices, 1994, Suite for Woodwind Trio, 1995, Up the Dome of Heaven, Three Pieces for Mixed Voices and Flute, 1996; The Raven for basso, clarinet, percussion and string, 1998, Saraband variations for guitar, Folia Lirica, 1999 . Served with AUS, 1943-45. Recipient Guggenheim awards, 1953, 60, Soc. for Publ. Am. Music award, 1953, Yale U. Alumni Assn. cert. of merit, 1975, NEA award, 1975, 77, 87; Ford Found. grantee, 1958. Mem. ASCAP (ann. award 1962—), Sigma Alpha Iota (nat. arts assoc.) Home: 174 Golden Gate Pt Apt 32 Sarasota FL 34236-6602 Office: U Minn 100 Ferguson Hall Minneapolis MN 55455 E-mail: paulfetler@webtv.net. *Ultimately there is no way to explain a new work of art if it does not explain itself.*

FETNER, ROBERT HENRY, radiobiologist; b. Savannah, Ga., Feb. 22, 1922; s. William Westcott and Lucille Fedora (Goodrich) F.; m. Mary Carolyn Guiney, July 8, 1972; 1 dau., Amber. BS, U. Miami, Fla., 1950, MS, 1952; PhD, Emory U., 1955. Mem. faculty Ga. Inst. Tech., Atlanta, 1955—, prof. radiation biology, 1963—; dir. Ga. Inst. Tech. (Sch. Biology), 1964-70. Cons. in field. Contbr. articles in field to profl. jours.; patentee computer digitizer. Served with AUS, 1942-45. Decorated Combat Inf. badge. Mem. Ga. Acad. Sci. (editor bull. 1960-64), Sigma Xi, Phi Kappa Phi. Presbyterian. Address: 2219 Walker Dr Lawrenceville GA 30043-2473 Office Phone: 770-943-6118. Personal E-mail: robertf308@aol.com. *My most rewarding career experience has been as a participant in the search for knowledge in science.*

FETRIDGE, BONNIE-JEAN CLARK (MRS. WILLIAM HARRISON FETRIDGE), civic volunteer; b. Chgo., Feb. 3, 1915; d. Sheldon and Bonnie (Carrington) Clark; m. William Harrison Fetridge, June 27, 1941; children: Blakely (Mrs. Harvey H. Bundy III), Clark Worthington. Student, Girls Latin Sch., Chgo., The Masters Sch., Dobbs Ferry, N.Y., Finch Coll., N.Y.C. Bd. dirs. region VII com. Girl Scouts U.S.A., 1939-43, nat. program com., 1966-69, nat. adv. bd., 1972-85, internat. commr.'s adv. panel, 1973-76, Nat. Juliette Low Birthplace Com., 1966-69; bd. dirs. Girl Scouts Chgo., 1936-51, 59-69, sec., 1936-38, v.p., 1946-49, 61-65, chmn. Juliette Low world friendship com., 1959-67, 71-72; mem. Friends Our Cabana Com. World Assn. Girl Guides and Girl Scouts, Cuernavaca, Mexico, 1969—, vice chmn., 1982-87; founder, pres. Olave Baden-Powell Soc. of World Assn. Girl Guides and Girl Scouts, London, 1984-93, bd. dirs., 1984—, hon. assoc., 1987; asst. sec. Dartnell Corp, Chgo., 1981-91, sec., 1991-98, bd. dirs. 1989-98; vice chmn. Dartnell Found., 1990-2000, Ravenswood Found., 2001—; bd. dirs. Jr. League of Chgo., 1937-40, Vis. Nurse Assn. Chgo., 1951-58, 61-63, asst. treas., 1962-63; women's bd. dirs. Children's meml. Hosp., 1946-50; v.p. parents coun. Latin Sch. Chgo., 1952-54, bd. dirs. alumni assn., 1964-69; Fidelitas Soc., 1979, 96; mem. women's bd. U.S.O., 1965-75, treas., 1969-71, v.p., 1971-73; mem. women's svc. bd. Chgo. Area coun. Boy Scouts Am., 1964-70, mem. nat. exploring com., 1973-76; staff aide and ARC Motor Corps, World War II. Recipient Citation of Merit Sta. WAIT, Chgo., 1971, Juliette Low World Friendship medal Girl Scouts U.S.A., 1989; 1st recipient Medal of Recognition World Assn.Girl Guides and Girl Scouts, London, 1993; Baden-Powell fellow World Scout Found., Geneva, 1983. Mem. Nat. Soc. Colonial Dames Am. (life, Ill. bd. mgrs. 1962-65, 69-76, 78-82, v.p. 1970-72, corr. sec. 1978-80, 1st v.p. 1980-84, state chmn. geneal. info. svcs. com. 1972-76, corr. sec. 1978-80, hist. activities com. 1979-83, mus. house com. 1980-83, house gov. 1981-82), Chgo. Dobbs Alumnae Assn. (past pres.), Nat. Soc. DAR, Conn. Soc. Genealogists, New Eng. Hist. Geneal. Soc., N.Y. Geneal. and Biog. Soc., Newberry Libr. Assocs., Chgo. Hist. Soc. (life), Casino Club, The Racquet Club Chgo., Onwentsia Club, Union League Club. Republican. Episcopalian. Home: 1100 Pembridge Dr Apt 215 Lake Forest IL 60045

FETRIDGE, CLARK WORTHINGTON, publishing executive; b. Chgo., Nov. 6, 1946; s. William Harrison and Bonnie-Jean (Clark) F.; m. Jean Hamilton Huebner, Apr. 19, 1980; children: Clark Worthington II, William Hamilton. BA, Lake Forest Coll., 1969; MBA, Boston Coll., 1971. Money market specialist Continental Ill. Nat. Bank, Chgo., 1971-73; with Dartnell Corp., Chgo., 1973-98, sr. v.p., 1977-78, pres., CEO Chgo., 1978-98, chmn. bd., CEO, 1995-98; pres. The Ravenswood Corp., Chgo., 1998—2002; mng. ptnr. Michigan Ave. Ventures, Chgo., 2002—. Bd. dirs. Clin. Resources Internat., Inc., M.R. Mead & Co. LLC., Old People's Home of Chgo. Author: Office Administration Handbook, 1975. Trustee Lake Forest Coll., 1977-85, 91-95, Jacques Holinger Meml. Found., 1983-95; pres. Dartnell Found., 1989—; trustee Latin Sch. Chgo., 1990-94, Newcomen Soc. U.S.; internat. commr. Boy Scouts Am., 1992-95, mem. nat. exec. bd., 1986-96, mem. internat. com., mem. Chgo. coun.; pres. U.S. Found. Internat. Scouting 1991-95; chmn. 1200 Club Ill., 1975-84; Rep. candidate for Congress, 1972; del. Rep. Nat. Conv., 1976; bd. dirs. Rep. Fund of Ill.; mem. pres.'s coun. Mus. Sci. and Industry, Chgo., 1986-94. Mem. Ill. Mfrs. Assn. (bd. dirs. 1990-96), Latin Sch. Chgo. Alumni Assn., St. Andrews Soc. (bd. dirs. 1994-97, 98—), Nat. Eagle Scout Assn. (chmn. 1985-88), Chgo. Pres. Orgn. (bd. dirs. 1998-2001), Tau Kappa Epsilon. Republican. Episcopalian. Office: Michigan Avenue Ventures 30 N Michigan Ave Ste 1412 Chicago IL 60602-3404 Office Phone: 312-236-1332. Office Fax: 312-236-1343.

FETTER, ALEXANDER LEES, theoretical physicist, educator; b. Phila., May 16, 1937; s. Ferdinand and Elizabeth Lean Fields (Head) F.; m. Jean Holmes, Aug. 4, 1962 (div. Dec. 1994); children: Anne Lindsay, Andrew James; m. Lynn Bunim, Sept. 10, 2004. AB, Williams Coll., 1958; BA, Balliol Coll., Oxford U., 1960; PhD, Harvard U., 1963. Miller rsch. fellow U. Calif., Berkeley, 1963-65; mem. faculty dept. physics Stanford U., 1965—, prof., 1974—, chmn. dept. physics, 1985-90, assoc. chmn. dept. physics, 1998-99, asso. dean undergrad. studies, 1976-79, assoc. dean humanities and sci., 1990-93, dir. Hansen Exptl. Physics Lab., 1996-97, dir. lab. for adv. materials, 1999—2002; vis. prof. Cambridge U., 1970-71; Nordita vis. prof. Tech. U., Helsinki, Finland, 1976. Author: (with J.D. Walecka) Quantum Theory of Many Particle Systems, 1971, Theoretical Mechanics of Particles and Continua, 1980. Alumni trustee Williams Coll., 1974-79. Rhodes scholar, 1958-60; NSF fellow, 1960-63; Sloan Found. fellow, 1968-72; Recipient W.J. Gores award for excellence in teaching Stanford U., 1974 Fellow Am. Physics Soc. (chmn. div. condensed matter physics 1991), AAAS; mem. Sigma Xi. Home: 904 Mears Ct Palo Alto CA 94305-1029 Office: Stanford U Physics Dept Stanford CA 94305-4045

FETTER, JEFFREY MICHAEL, lawyer; b. Elmira, N.Y., Feb. 8, 1955; s. William and Mary Fetter; m. Anne Fetter; children: Jennifer, Joseph, Daniel. BS, SUNY, Geneseo, 1977; JD, Ohio No. U., 1983. Bar: NY 1984, Pa. 1992. Assoc. Moot Sprague Law Firm, Buffalo, 1982-85; ptnr. Scolaro, Shulman, Cohen, Fetter & Burstein, P.C., Syracuse, NY, 1985—. Pres. Onondaga County Cultural Resources Coun., 2000-01; mem. bus. adv. coun. Sch. Bus., SUNY-Geneseo, 1997—; parish coun. St. Charles Borromeo Ch., 1992-93. Fellow N.Y. Bar Found. Assn., ABA, Am. Agrl. Law Assn.; mem. ABA, N.Y. State Bar Assn. (ho. of dels. 1993-94, 2000-02, chair young lawyers sect. 1991-92, chair gen. practice, solo and small firm section, membership com. 1996—), Pa. Bar Assn., Onondaga County Bar Assn., N.Y. State Bar Found. Office: Scolaro Shulman et al 507 Plum St Ste 300 Syracuse NY 13204 E-mail: Jfetter@scolaro.com.

FETTER, ROBERT BARCLAY, retired administrative sciences educator; b. Berwyn, Ill., May 6, 1924; s. Russell M. and Dorothy (Dupuis) F.; m. Audrey Louise Lillard, Feb. 7, 1951; children: Sarah Anne, Robert Alan, Martha Sue. BS, Va. Poly. Inst., 1947; MBA, Ind. U., 1949, DBA, 1952; MA (hon.), Yale U., 1963. Instr., asst. prof. Ind. U., 1949-53; asst. prof. Mass. Inst. Tech., 1953-58; asso. prof. Yale U., 1958-63, prof. adminstrv. scis., 1963-86, Harold H. Hines Jr. prof. health care mgmt., 1986-89, chmn. adminstrv. scis., 1969-72; dir. Health Systems Mgmt. Group, Sch. Orgn. and Mgmt., 1976-89, Instn. Social and Policy Studies, 1969-89. Cons. Rand Corp., 1963-71, E.I. duPont de Nemours & Co., Inc., 1960-72, McKinsey & Co., Inc., 1960-89, 3M, 1990-97; cons. editor R.D. Irwin, Inc., Homewood, Ill., 1960-90, WHO, 1972-73; v.p. Puter Assocs., Inc., 1971-77, chmn., 1977-82; v.p., dir. Health Systems Internat. Inc., 1982-90; dir. Dead River Co., 1984-94. Served with USNR, 1944-46. Recipient Baxter Found. prize Assn. Univ. Programs in Health Adminstrn., 1992; Ford Found. fellow, 1964. Fellow Acad. of Mgmt., Decision Scis. Inst.; mem. Ops. Research Soc. Am., Inst. Mgmt. Scis. (Franz Edelman prize 1990). Home: 427 Indies Dr Vero Beach FL 32963-9552 E-mail: BobFet@aol.com.

FETTER, TREVOR, healthcare industry executive; b. San Diego, Jan. 16, 1960; married; 2 children. BS in Econs., Stanford U., 1982; MBA, Harvard U., 1986. With investment banking divsn. Merrill Lynch Capital Mkts.; sr. v.p. MGM/UA Comm. Co., 1988; exec. v.p., CFO Metro-Goldwyn-Mayer, Inc.; exec. v.p. Tenet Healthcare Corp., Dallas, 1995—96, exec. v.p., CFO, 1996—2000; chmn., CEO Broad Ln., Inc., San Francisco, 2000—02; pres. Tenet Healthcare Corp., Dallas, 2002—03, pres., acting CEO, 2003, pres., CEO, 2003—. Chmn. bd. Santa Catalina Island Conservancy; trustee Santa Barbara Zool. Garden. Office: Tenet Healthcare Corp 13737 Noel Rd Dallas TX 75240*

FETTERLY, BARBARA LOUISE, artist; b. Painesville, Ohio, May 28, 1930; d. Ralph Frances and Claire Louise (Marquis) Fetterly; m. Henry Joseph Hargis Jr., June 4, 1955 (dec.); children: Ben William, William John, Glenn D. AA, Citrus Coll., 1985. Artist Art Gallery, La Puente, Calif., 1984-94; gallery owner Hargis Chim Gregg Art Gallery, Pomona, Calif., 1994—. Grantee Millenn Prodn., Pomona, Calif., 1994-97. Mem. Carlsbad Oceanside Art League (life), DA Gallery Non Profit, Pomona Valley Art (dir. 1988, life), Corona Art Assn. (life), Women in Arts Mus. (charter mem.), Covina Arts and Crafts, Parks and Recreation (life). Republican. Baptist. Avocations: amateur radio, tennis, swimming, sewing, pool. Studio: BHUA El Cerrito CA 92881 Office: Gallery SoHo 300 A South Thomas St Pomona CA 91766 Office Phone: 951-340-1060. E-mail: FINEART28@aol.com.

FETTERMAN, DAVID MARK, anthropologist, educator; b. Danielson, Conn., Jan. 24, 1954; s. Irving and Elsie (Blumenthal) F.; m. Summer Fetterman; 1 child, Sarah Rachel BA, BS, U. Conn., 1976; MA in Anthropology, Stanford U., 1977, MA in Edn., 1979, PhD in Anthropology, 1981. Cert. tchr. Calif., Conn. Tchr. Richard C. Lee High Sch., New Haven, 1975-76; dir. Office of Econ. Opportunity Anti-Poverty, Danielson, 1976; tchr. Beth Am and Beth David, Cupertino and Palo Alto, Calif., 1976-78; sr. assoc., project dir. RMC Rsch. Corp., Mountain View, Calif., 1978-82; prin. rsch. scientist Am. Insts. Rsch., Stanford, Calif., 1982-91; dir. MA policy analysis and evaluation Stanford U., 1991-93, dir. evaluation tng. program, 1993—, dir. evaluation, career devel. and alumni rels., 2003, dir. evaluation Sch. Medicine, 2005—; dir. rsch. and evaluation Calif. Inst. Integral Studies, San Francisco, 1993—. Mem. adv. bd. Ednl. Leadership, U.S. Dept. Edn., Washington, 1987—, mem. adv. bd. Nat. Rsch. Ctr. Gifted & Talented; trustee Nueva Learning Ctr., Hillsborough, Calif., 1990—; chair accreditation team Calif. Inst. Integral Studies, San Francisco, 1994—. Author: Empowerment Evaluation Principles in Practice, 2005, Excellence and Equality, 1988 (Mensa award 1990), Ethnography: Step by Step, 1989, (G. & L. Spindler award Am. Anthropol. Assn., 1990), 2d edit., 1998, Foundations of Empowerment Evaluation, 2002 (Paul Lazarsfeld award for contbns. to evaluation theory, Am. Evaluation Assn. 2002); editor: Speaking the Language of Power, 1993, Empowerment Evaluation, 1995. Pres. Mini-Infant Day Care Ctr., Palo Alto, 1992-93. Fellow Am. Anthrop. Assn. (bd. dirs. 1993), Soc. Applied Anthropology (liaison 1989); mem. Am. Evaluation Assn. (pres. 1992-94, Myrdal award 1999), Coun. Anthropology and Edn. (life, pres. 1988-92, Ethnographic Evaluation award 1988), Collaborative, Participatory, and Empowerment Group (chair 1995—, Pres.'s prize 1984). Avocations: computers, internet. Home: 520 Barron St Menlo Park CA 94025-3593 Office: Stanford U Sch Medicine Stanford CA 94305 Office Phone: 650-269-5689. Personal E-mail: profdavidf@yahoo.com.

FETTERMAN, ROBERT EUGENE, music educator; m. Melissa Davis, July 14, 1973; children: Joshua Davis, Christopher Davis. BS, Mansfield State Coll. (now U.), 1972; EdM, Pa. State U., 1976. Cert. music edn. Pa., 1972. Elem. band dir. Tamaqua (Pa.) Area Sch. Dist., 1972—77; H.S. band dir. Tamaqua Area Sch. Dist., 1977—82; elem. band dir. and instrumental music dept. chair East Stroudsburg (Pa.) Area Sch. Dist., 1982—. Pres. Borough Coun., Weissport, Pa., 1978—86. Mem.: Pa. Music Educators Assn. (adjudication chair 1995—2003). Home: 805 Orioles Dr Lehighton PA 18235 Office: JT Lambert Intermediate School 2000 Milford Rd East Stroudsburg PA 18301 Office Phone: 570-424-8430. Personal E-mail: bobfett@esasd.net.

FETTEROLL, EUGENE CARL, JR., human resources professional; b. Hartford, Conn., Mar. 8, 1935; s. Eugene Carl and Gladys Marion (Crilley) F.; m. Barbara Ann Meeker, June 15, 1957; children: Eugene Carl III, Douglas Alan, Steven Joseph, Gary Michael. BA, U. Conn., 1957; MEd, Suffolk U., 1973. Supt. customer svc., mgr. pers. svcs., dir. tng. Boston Gas Co., 1957-76; dir. Ea. Enterprises, Boston, 1977-81, Associated Industries of Mass., Boston, 1981-87, v.p. human resources, 1987-89; pres. Fetteroll Assocs., South Portland, Maine, 1989—. Tng. cons. Associated Industries of Mass., Boston. Author: Growing Teams, 1993, The Sage's Secrets of Successful Supervision, 2004; editor: Trainer's Resource, 1989. Vol. United Way, Mass. and R.I., 1965—; vice-chmn. bd. trustees Medfield (Mass.) Pub. Libr., 1966-70; chmn. Sch. Land Acquisition Com., Medfield, 1963-65; bd. dirs. Growth Opportunity Alliance Lawrence/Quality Productivity Competitiveness, Salem, N.H. Mem. ASTD (pres. Mass. chpt. 1972-73, Bay Colonies chpt. 1981-82, nat. ethics com. 1986—, Torch award 1979), Mass. Coalition for Adult Edn., Mass. Arms Collectors. Republican. Roman Catholic. Avocations: collecting antique powder flasks, photography, travel. Home and Office: Fetteroll Assocs PO Box 2887 South Portland ME 04116 Office Phone: 207-741-9030. E-mail: genefett@maine.rr.com.

FETTERS, NORMAN CRAIG, II, retired banker; b. Pitts., Aug. 27, 1942; s. Karl Leroy and Hazel (Lower) F.; m. Linda Wood, Aug. 14, 1965; children— Eric Craig, Kevin Edward, Brian Allan AB, Westminster Coll., 1964; MBA, U. Pitts., 1965. Various positions to v.p. Security Pacific Nat. Bank, Los Angeles, 1965-66, 69-74, v.p., 1974-82; sr. v.p. Security Pacific Bank Washington, Seattle, 1982-92, SeaFirst Bank, Seattle, 1992-93; sr. v.p., dir. Security Pacific Savs. Bank, Seattle, 1993-94; v.p. Key Bank of Wash., Seattle, 1994-96, sr. v.p., 1996-99; v.p., credit officer Fed. Home Loan Bank Seattle, 1999—2003, v.p., credit analysis mgr., 2003—05, ret., 2005. Served to lt. U.S. Army, 1966-69 Mem. Risk Mgmt. Assocs., Lions Club (pres. 1988-89, 05-06, Melvin Jones fellow). Presbyterian (elder). Avocations: cross country skiing, travel, hiking, photography. Personal E-mail: ncfetters@aol.com.

FETTIG, JEFF M., manufacturing executive; BA in Fin., MBA, Ind. U. Mem. fin. ops. Whirlpool Corp., 1981, various mgmt. positions, 1981-89, v.p. mktg. KitchenAid, 1989-90; v.p. mktg., Philips Whirlpool Appliance Group Whirlpool Europe B.V., 1990—92; v.p., group mktg. and sales North Am. Appliance Group/Whirlpool, 1992—94; exec. v.p. Whirlpool Corp., 1994; pres. Whirlpool Europe & Asia, 1994; pres., COO Whirlpool Corp., 1999—2004, CEO, 2004—, also bd. dirs. Bd. dirs. Dow Chemical Co., 2003—. Office: Whirlpool Corp 2000 N M 63 Benton Harbor MI 49022-2692*

FEUER, BRADLEY SCOTT, lawyer, physician; b. Mineola, N.Y., June 29, 1960; s. Jerome Solomon and Celia (Dank) F.; m. Ileana Cepeda, June 17, 1984; children: Benjamin Samuel, Tracy Lynn. BS in Chemistry, U. Miami, Coral Gables, Fla., 1980, JD, 1990; DO, N.Y. Coll. Osteo. Medicine, 1986. Diplomate Am. Bd. Forensic Examiners, Am. Bd. Forensic Medicine, Nat. Bd. Osteo. Med. Examiners; lic. med. practitioner, Fla., N.Y.; bar: Fla., 1991; cert. health care risk mgr.; CLIA master cruise counselor. Chief intern medicine and surgery Humana Hosp. Palm Beaches, West Palm Beach, Fla., 1986—87; asst. to dir. U. Miami Health Svcs., Coral Gables, 1988—90; pvt. practice legal medicine Lake Worth, Fla., 1991—2002; ptnr. Brennan, Manna & Diamond, PLC, 2002—; dir. med. edn., physician advisor Humana Hosp., Palm Beaches, 1991—92; dir. med. and acad. affairs Columbia Hosp., 1992—; police surgeon Fla. Hwy. Patrol, 2003—. Physician advisor Humana Med. Plan, Inc., Miami, 1987-91; pres. Pace Travel, Inc., 1990—; chmn. ethics com. Columbia Hosp., 1993—; med. expert WPBF-Channel 25, West Palm Beach, 1996-97. Prodr. and host: For Your Health, WPBR Talk 1340 AM, Palm Beach, 1993-95; prodr. and announcer For Your Health Minute, WRLX 92.1 FM, Palm Beach, 1993-95; host Doctor to Doctor, WPEC-Ch. 12, West Palm Beach, 1998-2000. Founder Coral Gables Police Student Security Patrol Program, U. Miami, 1979; mem. Senate Health Adv. Bd. to Hon. Connie Mack; assoc. clin. prof. family medicine, Nova Southeastern U.; dir. Palm Beach Regional Acad. Tng. Ctr., Nova Southeastern U. Fellow: Am. Coll. Forensic Examiners, Am. Coll. Legal Medicine; mem.: AMA, Palm Beach County Bar Assn. (chmn. legal/med. com. 1998—99), Palm Beach County Med. Soc. (treas. 1996—97, 1st v.p. 1998—99, pres. 2000—01, treas., chmn. med.-legal com.), Fla. Osteo. Med. Assn., Fla. Med. Assn. (del.), Am. Osteo. Assn., Am. Coll. Family Practitioners. Office: 6910 Lake Worth Rd Lake Worth FL 33467-2903 Office Phone: 561-798-7326. E-mail: cruiseox@pca.net.

FEUER, CY, film producer, director, theater producer; b. N.Y.C., Jan. 15, 1911; s. Herman and Ann (Abrams) F.; m. Posy Greenberg, Jan. 20, 1946 (dec. 2005); children: Robert, Jed. Student, Inst. Mus. Art Juilliard Found., 1928-32. Head music dept. Republic Pictures, 1938-42, 45-47; partner Feuer and Martin Prodns., N.Y.C., 1947—; mgr., dir. San Francisco & LA Civic Light Opera Assn., 1975-80. Pres. The League of Am. Theatres and Producers, 1989—. Theatrical prodns. include Where's Charley, 1948, Guys and Dolls, 1950, Can-Can, 1953, The Boy Friend, 1954, Silk Stockings, 1955, Whoop-Up, 1958, How To Succeed in Business Without Really Trying, 1961 (Pulitzer prize for drama), Little Me, 1962, Skyscraper, 1965, Walking Happy,

1966, The Goodbye People, 1968, The Act, 1977; producer: motion pictures Cabaret, 1972 (winner 8 Acad. awards), Piaf, 1975, Chorus Line, 1985; author: (autobiography) I Got the Show Right Here, 2003. Inducted into the Theater Hall of Fame, 1994. Office: League Am Theaters and Producers 226 W 47th St New York NY 10036

FEUER, HENRY, retired chemist; b. Stanislau, Austria, Apr. 4, 1912; arrived in U.S., 1941, naturalized, 1946; s. Jacob and Julia (Tindel) Feuer; m. Paula Berger, Jan. 19, 1946. MS, U. Vienna, Austria, 1934, PhD, 1936. Postdoctoral fellow U. Paris, 1939; with dept. chemistry Purdue U., Lafayette, Ind., 1943-79, prof. chemistry, 1961-79, prof. emeritus, 1979—. Vis. prof. Hebrew U., Jerusalem, 1964, Indian Inst. Tech., Kanpur, India, 1971, Peking (China) Inst. Tech., 1979. Pres., contbr. Organic Electronic Spectral Data, Inc., 1962—89; mng. editor: Organic Nitro Chemistry Series, 1982—; mem. adv. bd. Turkish Jour. Chemistry, mem. editl. bd. Chimica Acta Turcica. Fellow: AAAS; mem.: Royal Soc. Chemistry, Am. Chem. Soc., Sigma Xi, Phi Lambda Upsilon. Achievements include research in organic nitrogen compounds; discovery of new methods for syntheses nitro compounds, cyclic hydrazides; research in mechanism of nitro compounds reactions. Home: 1700 Lindberg Rd Apt 219 West Lafayette IN 47906-2036 Office: Purdue U Dept Chemistry Lafayette IN 47907

FEUER, MARSHALL ZEV, import/export company executive; b. N.Y.C., Dec. 13, 1941; s. Menkes and Rose Feuer; m. Judith Fern Rosenberg, Dec. 18, 1966; children: Menachem (Matthew), Ronald. BS, Columbia U., 1963; MS in Ops. Rsch., Johns Hopkins U., 1965. Engr. Martin-Marietta Corp., Balt., 1965; sr. engr. Ford Instrument Co. div. Sperry Rand Corp., N.Y.C., 1965—66, Lockheed Electronics Co.-Lockheed Aircraft Corp., Plainfield, NJ, 1965—68; tech. support Chamy Tan Processing Corp., Gloversville, NY, 1968—71; leather mcht. Trans-Am. Leather Co. Inc., Gloversville, 1971—77; leather mcht., pres. Interamerica Leather Co. Inc., Gloversville, 1977—90; dir. Safety Leather Co., Johnstown, NY, 1991—. Mem. B'nai Brith, N.Y.C., 1985—2002; hon. state chmn. Nat. Rep. Congl. Com., N.Y.C., 2002; congregant Knesseth Israel Synagouge, Gloversville, 1968—2002. Recipient Walter M. Rautenstrauch award, Columbia U., 1963; fellow, Rockefeller Inst., 1959; NASA fellow, Johns Hopkins U., 1963—65. Mem.: Alpha Pi Mu, Tau Beta Pi. Conservative. Jewish. Avocations: physical fitness, travel, sailing.

FEUER, MARVIN C., government affairs, educator; b. Cleve., Oct. 15, 1950; s. Henry and Gita Feuerwerger; m. Debra S. Lichtman, Dec. 1, 1974; children: David Feuerwerger, Rachel Feuerwerger, Danny Feuerwerger. BA, Columbia U., 1971; MA, Harvard U., 1974, PhD, 1977. Dep. sr. advisor to pres. and sec. of state Carter Adminstrn., Washington, 1978-80; dir. for policy planning Office of Asst. Sec. of Def. for Internat. Security Affairs, Washington, 1984-85; dep. asst. sec. of def. for policy analysis Office of Sec. of Def., Washington, 1985-86; first sec. Am. Embassy, Tel Aviv, 1986-89; prof. lectr. in internat. rels. The Johns Hopkins U. Sch. of Advanced Internat. Studies, Washington, 1990—; asst. dep. undersec. for policy analysis Office of the Sec. of Def., Washington, 1990; sr. strategic fellow Washington Inst. for Near East Policy, 1990-92; dir. for def. and strategic issues Am. Israel Pub. Affairs Com., Washington, 1992—. Cons. Nat. Pub. Radio, Washington, 1991. Author: Congress and Israel, 1979, Restoring the Balance: U.S. Strategy and the Gulf Crisis, 1991, The Arrow Next Time?, 1992. Mem. nat. adv. coun. Am. Jewish Com., Washington, 1992—, Johns Hopkins U. Strategoi, Washington, 1996—. Recipient Alumni Achievement award, Am. Friends of Hebrew U., Jerusalem, 1996; Found. fellow, Nat. Found. Jewish Culture, 1975—76. Office: AIPAC 440 1st St NW Ste 600 Washington DC 20001-2028 Office Phone: 202-639-5200. E-mail: marvin_feuer@aipac.org.

FEUER, MICHAEL, venture capitalist, former office products executive; Various positions to sr. v.p. Fabri-Centers Am., Cleveland, Ohio, 1970—88; co-founder, chmn., CEO OfficeMax, Shaker Heights, Ohio, 1988—2003; CEO, co-founder Max-Ventures LLC venture fund, 2004—. Adv. coun. Case We. Reserve Univ. Weatherhead Bus. Sch., Univ. Pitts. Katz Bus. Sch. Office: Max-Ventures Ste 3200 1900 E 9th St. Cleveland OH 44114*

FEUERMAN, CAROLE A., sculptor, artist; b. Hartford, Conn., Sept. 21, 1945; d. Milton and Doris Sue Ackerman; div.; m. Ron Cohen; children: Lauren, Craig, Sari Gibson; stepchildren: Adam, Aurielle, Leah Cohen. Student, Hofstra U., 1963, Temple U., 1964, Sch. Visual Arts, 1967. Pres. Feuerman Studios, Inc., N.Y.C., 1967—. One-woman shows include Art 10 '79 Basel Art Fair, Switzerland, 1979, O.K. Harris, Scottsdale, Ariz., 1982, Ackland Art Mus., Chapel Hill, N.C., 1985, Queens Mus., Flushing, N.Y., 1987, Arnesen Gallery, Vail, Colo., 1990, Internat. Swimming Hall of Fame, Ft. Lauderdale, Fla., 1993, So Alleghenies Mus. Art, Loretto, Pa., 2000 (award, 2002), Lobby Gallery The Durst Orgn., N.Y.C., 2001, Queensborough C.C. Mus. and Art Gallery, CUNY, Bayside, N.Y., 2003, Frederick R. Weisman Mus. Art, Malibu, Calif., 2003, Pepperdine U., 2003, exhibited in group shows at The State Hermitage, St. Petersburg, Russia, Isetan Mus. Art, Tokyo, ACA Gallery, Harkone Open-Air Mus., Parrish Art Mus., Whitney Mus. Am. Art, Nat. Sculpture Soc., Riverside Art Mus., West Chelsea Arts Festival, N.Y.C., 1998, Frederick R. Weisman Mus. Art, Pepperdine U., Malibu, Calif., 1998, Biennale Internat. dell'ARTE Contemporanea, Florence, Italy, 2001 (Lorenzo di Medici award, 2001), So. Alleghenies Mus. Art, 2002, Queensborough C.C. Mus. and Art Gallery, 2002, Nat. Biennale fur Bildende Kunst, 2002 (Honor prize), Austria Biennale (Honor prize, 2002), Boca Raton (Fla.) Mus., Chelsea (Mass.) Art Mus., Bass Art Mus., Represented in permanent collections Lowe Art Mus., Fla., Tampa Mus. Art, So Alleghenies Mus. Art, Brandeis U., Queensborough CC at CUNY, Bayside, Bass Mus., Miami, Fla., Sen. Hilary Rodham Clinton, Pres. Bill Clinton, Dr. Henry Kissinger, Bass Mus., Fla., Ft. Lauderdale (Fla.) Mus. Art, Boca Raton Mus., Fla., Caldic Collection, Rotterdam, The Netherlands, Pres. Mikael S. Gorbachov, Moscow, Lowe Art Mus., U. Miami, Tampa Mus. Art, Apollon Art Rsch. Found., others. Recipient Betty Parsons Sculpture award 1970, Charles D. Murphy Sculpture award 1981, Amelia Peabody award for sculpture 1982, 1st prize U.S. Nat. Fine Arts Competition 1984. Mem.: Internat. Women's Forum (N.Y.), Solomon R. Guggenheim Mus., Met. Mus. Art, Mus. Modern Art, Internat. Sculpture Ctr., Nat. Assn .Women Artists, Am. Women's Econ. Devel. Corp., Pro Arts, Nat. Women Caucus for Art, Woman's Leadership Forum, Sch. Visual Arts Alumni Assn., UNESCO. Home: 200 Mercer St Apt 1F New York NY 10012-1510 Studio: Feuerman Studios Inc 200 Mercer St Ste 1F New York NY 10012 Business E-Mail: caroljf@mindspring.com.

FEUERSTEIN, DONALD MARTIN, lawyer; b. Chgo., May 30, 1937; s. Morris Martin and Pauline Jean (Zagel) F.; m. Dorothy Rosalind Sokolsky, June 3, 1962 (dec. Mar. 1978); children: Eliza Carol, Tony David; m. Summer Donnamarie Berben, May 25, 1987; 1 child, Ashley Paul. BA magna cum laude, Yale U., 1959; JD magna cum laude, Harvard U., 1962. Bar: N.Y. 1962. Assoc. firm Cleary, Gottlieb, Steen & Hamilton, N.Y.C., 1962-63; law clk. to U.S. dist. judge N.Y.C., 1963-65; assoc. firm Saxe, Bacon & Bolan, N.Y.C., 1965; asst. gen. counsel, chief counsel instl. investor study SEC, Washington, 1966-71; ptnr., counsel Salomon Bros., N.Y.C., 1971-81, mng. dir., sec., 1981-91; exec. v.p., chief legal officer Salomon, Inc., 1991; spl. asst. U.S. Dept. Edn., Washington, 1993-94, sr. advisor, 1994-99; pres. New Am. Schs., Arlington, Va., 1999-2000, sr. advisor, 2000-2001, Imaging Acceptance Corp., 2001—02, Nat. Coun. Accreditation of Tchr. Edn., Washington, 2001—. Spl. cons. Intersch. Group, N.Y.C., 1991-93; mem. bus. policy coun. com. on excellence in edn. Nat. Alliance of Bus., 2000-2001. Editor Harvard Law Rev., 1960-62; mem. editl. adv. bd. Securities Regulation Law Jour., 1973-90; bd. editors Nat. Law Jour., 1978-90. Mem. vis. com. Northwestern U. Law Sch., 1975—78; bd. dirs. 1st All Children's Theatre, 1976—85, chmn., 1976—82; mem. long-range planning and capital campaign coms. Brearley Sch., N.Y.C., 1981—83; mem. adv. bd. Solomon R. Guggenheim Mus., 1984—91, chmn. bus. com., 1988—91, mem. internat. coun., 1991—; bd. dirs. Arts and Bus. Coun., 1980—85, v.p., 1985—88; trustee, v.p., mem. exec. com. Dalton Sch., 1983—89, 1990—93; mem. dean's adv. coun. Harvard U. Law Sch., 1988—95, mem. steering com. and capital campaign, 1991—95; mem. com. on univ. resources Harvard U., 1988—; mem. vis. com. Harvard Grad. Sch. Edn., 1993—99, mem. tech. adv. coun., 1996—2001; chmn. tech. com. Georgetown Day Sch., 1997—2000, trustee, 1997—2003, mem. exec. com., 2001—02, chmn., trusteeship commn., 2001—02, chmn. fin. aid com., 2002—03, mem. investment subcom., 2003—; mem. Brookings Coun., 1998—2001. Mem. ABA, Phi Beta Kappa, Pi Sigma Alpha. Home: 6430 Bradley Blvd Bethesda MD 20817-3246 Office Phone: 202-466-7496. E-mail: dfeuer13@cs.com.

FEUERSTEIN, HOWARD M., lawyer; b. Memphis, Sept. 16, 1939; s. Leon and Lillian (Kapell) F.; m. Tamra Lynn Saperstein, May 19, 1968; children: Laurie, Leon. BA, Vanderbilt U., 1961, JD, 1963. Bar: Tenn. 1963, Oreg. 1965. Law clk. to justice U.S. Ct. Appeals (5th cir.), Montgomery, Ala., 1963-64; teaching fellow Stanford U., 1964-65; assoc. Davies, Biggs et al (now Stoel Rives LLP), Portland, Oreg., 1965-71; ptnr. Stoel Rives LLP, Portland, 1971—. Mem. Oreg. Gov.'s Task Force on Land Devel. Law, 1974; bd. realtors Condominium Study Com., Oreg., 1975-76. Editor-in-chief Vanderbilt Law Rev., 1962-63. Trustee Congregation Beth Israel, Portland, 1977-83; bd. dirs. Jewish Family & Child Service, Portland, 1975-81, Young Musicians and Artists Inc., 1991-96. Recipient Founder's medal Vanderbilt Law Sch., 1963. Mem. ABA, Oreg. State Bar, Community Assn. Inst. (bd. dirs. Oreg. chpt. 1980-86), Am. Coll. Real Estate Lawyers. Office: Stoel Rives LLP 900 SW 5th Ave Ste 2600 Portland OR 97204-1268 Office Phone: 503-294-9215. E-mail: hmfeuerstein@stoel.com.

FEUERSTEIN, SANDRA JEANNE, judge; b. N.Y.C., Jan. 21, 1946; m. Albert Feuerstein, June 5, 1966; children: Adam, Seth. BS, U. Vt., 1966; JD, Benjamin Cardozo U., 1979. Bar: N.Y. 1980, U.S. Dist. Ct. (so. and ea. dists.) N.Y. 1983, U.S. Ct. Mil. Appeals, 1988, U.S. Tax Ct. 1988, U.S. Supreme Ct. 1988. Sr. law asst. NY State Supreme Ct., Mineola, 1980-86, matrimonial referee, 1985-86; judge Nassau County Dist. Ct., Hempstead, NY, 1987—93; assoc. justice NY State Supreme Ct. (10th judicial dist.), 1994—99, NY State Supreme Ct. (Appellate div., 2d dept.), 1999—2003; judge U.S. Dist. Ct. (ea. dist.) NY, 2003—. Law sec. to adminstrv. judge Leo J. McGinity, Mineola, 1985-87; lectr. Trial Def. Bar of Nassau County, 1984, Town and Village Justice Continuing Jud. Edn., 1987; mem. discovery oversight com. U.S. Dist. Ct. (ea. dist.) N.Y., 1983-86; mem. Nassau County Exec.'s Blue Ribbon Panel on Domestic Violence, 1989; mem. com. on civil litigation U.S. Dist. Ct. (ea. dist.) N.Y. 1989-91. Assoc. editor Nassau Lawyer, 1984-87, editor, 1987-89; contbr. numerous articles to profl. jours. Counsel Merrick Sr. Citizens Ctr., 1980-87; life mem. Hadassah, Long Beach Meml. Hosp. Aux.; bd. dirs. L.I. Arts Coun.; life mem., bd. dirs. Am. Cancer Soc.; dir., Benjamin N. Cardozo Sch. Law, Yeshiva U. Recipient Mesivta Torah award, 1985. Mem. Women's Bar Assn. of N.Y. State (v.p. 1990, pres. Nassau County chpt. 1988-89, founder pro bono project, judiciary com., spl. matrimonial com. 1985-86, v.p. 1986-87, 87-88, 90, chmn. judiciary com. 1984), Nassau County Bar Assn. (bd. dirs. 1988, Pro Bono Recognition award 1990), Franklin D. Roosevelt Inns of Ct. (master), Bus. and Profl. Women of Nassau County, L.I. Ctr. for Bus. and Profl. Women, Yeshiva U. Alumni Assn. (founding bd. dirs.), Acad. of Law (pub. edn. com.). Office: Dist Ct 1014 Federal Plaza Central Islip NY 11722*

FEUER-STERN, BARBIE SHNIDER, elementary and secondary school educator; b. Cin., Mar. 27, 1949; d. Edward and Nilda Ruth (Ostrovsky) Shnider; children: Courtney, Jennifer, Brian; m. Geoffrey Stern, 1985. Student, U. Tel Aviv, 1968-70; BS in Edn., Ohio State U., 1972; MS in edn., U. Dayton, 1989, EDd, 1999. Cert. tchr., Ohio. Adminstr., prin. Ashland U. Bd. mem. advisor Interdisciplinatry Coun., Columbus, Ohio, 1991-92; tribes leader Columbus Pub. Schs., 1989-90, 2001-2002; speaker Ohio Edn. Assn. Mid. Eastern Women Assn. Author: You and Your Sexuality, 1973, Famous Black American Personalities, 1988, Guide for New Teachers in Urban Schools, 2002, Parental Involvement in Urban Schools, 2003, Teaching Diversity in the Urban School, 2004; contbr. articles to various ednl. publs. Mem. discipline coun. Ohio State Tchrs., Columbus, 1988-90, leader com., 2001-05. Recipient Aspiring Women Adminstr., Ashland U. Mem. Hadassah (life), Nat. Assn. of Profl. Women Adminstrs., Aspiring Women Adminstrs. Achievements include development of mid. sch. program for gays/lesbians in mid. and high sch.

FEUERWERKER, ALBERT, historian, educator; b. Cleve., Nov. 6, 1927; s. Martin and Gizella (Feuerwerker) F.; m. Yi-tsi Mei, June 11, 1955; children: Alison, Paul. AB, Harvard U., 1950, PhD, 1957. Lectr. history U. Toronto, Ont., Can., 1955-58; rsch. fellow Harvard U., Cambridge, Mass., 1958-60; assoc. prof. history U. Mich., Ann Arbor, 1960-63, prof., 1963-96, chmn. dept., 1984-87; dir. U. Mich. Ctr. for Chinese Studies, Ann Arbor, 1961-67, 72-83; A.M. and H.P. Bentley prof. of history U. Mich., Ann Arbor, 1986-96, prof. emeritus, 1996—; dir. d'études École des Hautes Etudes en Scis. Sociales, Paris, 1981; vis. scholar Acad. Social Scis., Shanghai, China, 1981, 88, Sichuan U., Chengdu, China, 1988. Joint com. on contemporary China, Social Sci. Research Council-Am. Council Learned Socs., 1966-78, 80-83, chmn., 1970-75; mem. com. on scholarly comm. with the People's Republic of China, Nat. Acad. Scis.-Social Sci. Rsch. Coun.-Am. Council Learned Socs., 1971-78, 81-83, vice-chmn., 1975-78 Author: China's Early Industrialization, 1958, History in Communist China, 1968, The Chinese Economy 1870-1911, 1969, Rebellion in 19th Century China, 1975, The Foreign Establishment in China, 1976, Economic Trends in the Republic of China, 1977, Chinese Social and Economic History from the Song to 1900, 1982, Studies in the Economic History of Late Imperial China, 1996, The Chinese Economy, 1870-1949, 1996; co-editor: Cambridge History of China, vol. 13, 1986; mem. editl. bd. Am. Hist. Rev., 1970-75, The China Quar., 1967-91, Comparative Studies in Soc. and History, 1964-2001. Served with AUS, 1946-47. Fellow NEH, 1971-72, Social Sci. Research Council-Am. Council of Learned Socs., 1962-63, Guggenheim Found., 1987-88. Fellow AAAS; mem. Assn. for Asian Studies (v.p. 1990, pres. 1991), Nat. Com. on U.S.-China Rels. Home: 827 Asa Gray Dr Apt 356 Ann Arbor MI 48105 Office: U Mich Ctr for Chinese Studies 1080 S University Ave Ste 3668 Ann Arbor MI 48109-1106 E-mail: afeuer@umich.edu.

FEUERWERKER, ELIE, biologist, educator; b. Paris, Dec. 2, 1948; arrived in U.S., 1989, naturalized, 1999; s. David Feuerwerker and Antoinette Gluck; m. Anne Esther Ackermann, Dec. 28, 2004. BSc in Biology, U. Montreal, Que., Can., 1971, MSc in Biology, 1976, PhD in Biology, 1983. Postdoctoral fellow Harvard U., Cambridge, Mass., 1985—87; rsch. assoc. Boston U., 1987—88; rsch. fellow McGill U., Montreal Neurol. Inst., 1987—89; mem. I-V team The Mount Sinai Med. Ctr., N.Y.C., 1990—94; tchr. biology Lycee Français de N.Y., 1994—2000; tchr. N.Y.C. Bd. Edn., 2000—. Presenter in field. Contbr. articles to profl. jours. and newspapers. Grantee, The Hannah Inst. for the History of Medicine, NSF, The Rockefeller U. Mem.: N.Y. Acad. Scis. Jewish. Avocation: photography. Home: 1617 Cherry St Highland Park NJ 08904-3716

FEUERZEIG, HENRY LOUIS, lawyer; b. Chgo., Dec. 12, 1938; s. Samuel Alexander Feuerzeig and Esther Fleeger; m. Penny Zweigenhaft, Apr. 8, 1967; children: Paul Lawrence, Darcy Elizabeth. BS, U. Wis., 1962; JD, George Washington U., 1970. Bar: D.C., V.I., Fla., Md. Reporter various newspapers, Dubuque, Iowa, Chgo., Madison, Wis., Cin. and Washington, 1962-64, 65-67; assoc. Sachs, Greenebaum, Frohlich & Tayler, Washington, 1970—72; asst. atty. gen. V.I. Dept. Law, St. Thomas, 1972-73, chief civil and adminstrv. law divsn., 1973-74, 1st asst. atty. gen., 1974; ptnr. Feuerzeig & Zebedee, St. Thomas, 1974-76; judge Territorial Ct. V.I., St. Thomas, 1977-87; del., chmn. jud. powers and functions com. 4th V.I. Constl. Conv., 1981; ptnr. Dudley, Topper and Feuerzeig, St. Thomas, 1987—. Mem. supervisory bd. V.I. Law Enforcement Planning Commn., 1978—87, Juvenile Justice and Delinquency Prevention, 1988—; mem. V.I. Juvenile Code Revision Task Force, 1978—83, V.I. Criminal Code Revision Task Force, 1978—87. Mem. Montgomery County (Md.) Dem. State Ctrl. Com., 1970-72; mem. V.I. Indsl. Devel. Commn., 1976; bd. dirs. Environ. Studies Program, St. Thomas, 1977-80, United Way, 1986-92; bd. reps. Hebrew Congregation of St. Thomas, 1983-90, 96-2002, co-chair Bicentennial Campaign com., 1993-97; trustee Antilles Sch., St. Thomas, 1983-91; mem. adv. coun. Youth Multi-Svc. Ctr., 1989-94; dir. Cmty. Found. of V.I., 1990-2003, pres., 1993-94, emeritus dir., 2003-. Sigma Delta Chi scholar, 1962; Congressional fellow Am. Polit. Sci. Assn., 1964-65; named Person of Yr. Hebrew Congregation of St. Thomas, 2003, St. Thomas & St. John C. of C. Cmty. Svc. award, 2004. Mem. ABA (lawyers conf. jud. performance and conduct com. 1984—), D.C. Bar Assn., Fla. Bar Assn., V.I. Bar Assn. (pres. 1976), Am. Law Inst. (life, cons. group for principles of family dissolution, 1992-2000, cons. group for restatement of law governing lawyers, 1992-99), Am. Judicature Soc., Assn. Trial Lawyers Am., Internat. Soc. of Barristers, Order of Coif, Rotary, Harmonic Lodge No. 356, Sigma Delta Chi, Phi Delta Phi. Jewish. Office: Dudley Topper and Feuerzeig 1A Frederiksberg Gade PO Box 756 Charlotte Amalie VI 00804-0756 Office Phone: 340-715-4443. E-mail: hfeuerzeig@dtflaw.com, hfeuer@attglobal.net.

FEUILLE, RICHARD HARLAN, lawyer, director; b. Mexico City, June 10, 1920; s. Frank and Margaret (Levy) F.; m. Louann Johnston Hoover, Oct. 20, 1948; children: Louann H., Richard H., Robert R., Joseph L. (dec.), James M., Patrick F. (dec.), Margaret J. BA, U. Va., 1947, LLB, 1948; JD, 1970. Bar: Tex. 1948. Assoc. Jones, Hardie, Grambling & Howell, El Paso, Tex., 1948-53; ptnr. Hardie, Grambling, Sims & Feuille, El Paso, 1953-57; sr. ptnr. Scott, Hulse, Marshall & Feuille, El Paso, 1957—. Bd. dirs. El Paso Nat. Bank (now known as JPMorgan Chase Bank), 1964—93. Active United Fund El Paso, 1963—, founder, v.p. trust fund, 1969—, pres., 1968, 75—, bd. dirs., 1966-72; pres. El Paso Cmty. Concert Assn., 1961-67; mem. adv. coun. U. Tex. at El Paso, 1968—, mem. exec. com., 1968-70; bd. dirs. Providence Meml. Hosp., 1986-92; bd. dirs. St. Clement's Episcopal Parish Sch., El Paso, pres., 1993-95; trustee YWCA, El Paso; bd. dirs. El Paso Cmty. Found., 1980—, pres., 1983-84, chmn. bd., 2004. Served to maj. USAAF, 1941-46, PTO, participant in invasion of Iwo Jima. Decorated bronze star; recipient Disting. Svc. award City of El Paso and Rotary Club, 2002. Mem. ABA (estate and gift tax com.), El Paso County Bar Assn. (pres. 1972-73), Tex. Bar Assn., Greater El Paso Tennis Assn. (bd. dirs.), Rotary Club of El Paso, Order Coif, Phi Beta Kappa, Omicron Delta Kappa. Episcopalian (vestryman, sr. warden). Clubs: Coronado Country (El Paso), El Paso Tennis (El Paso) (pres. 1973). Home: 1021 Broadmoor Dr El Paso TX 79912-2003 Office: Scott Hulse Marshall et al 201 East Main Dr 1100 Chase Tower El Paso TX 79901 Office Phone: 915-546-8212. Business E-Mail: bfeu@scotthulse.com.

FEULNER, EDWIN J., JR., research foundation executive; b. Chgo., Aug. 12, 1941; s. Edwin John and Helen J. (Franzen) F.; m. Linda C. Leventhal, Mar. 8, 1969; children: Edwin John III, Emily V. BS, Regis Coll., 1963; MBA, U. Pa., 1964; PhD, U. Edinburgh, 1981; degree (hon.), Nichols Coll., 1981, Universidad Francisco Marroquin, Guatemala City, 1982, Hanyang U., Seoul, Korea, 1982, Bellevue Coll., Nebr., 1987, Gonzaga U., 1992, Grove City Coll., 1994, Pepperdine U., 2000, St. Norbert Coll., 2002, Hillsdale Coll., 2004, Thomas More Coll., 2005. Richard Weaver fellow London Sch. Econs., 1965; fellow Ctr. for Strategic and Internat. Studies, 1965—66; pub. affairs fellow Hoover Instn., 1966—68; rsch. analyst Rep. Conf. U.S. Ho. of Reps., 1968-69; confidential asst. to sec. def. Melvin Laird, 1969-70; campaign mgr. Crane for Congress Com., 1972; adminstrv. asst. to U.S. Congressman Philip M. Crane, 1970-74; exec. dir. Rep. Study Com., Ho. of Reps., 1974-77; pres. Heritage Found., Washington, 1977—; chmn. Inst. European Def. and Strategic Studies, 1977-96; counselor to v.p. candidate Jack Kemp, 1996. US del. IMF/World Bank, 1974—76; mem. exec. com. Presdl. Transition Pres.'s Commn. White House Fellows, 1980—81, mem., 1981—83; pub. del. UN 2nd Spl. Session on Disarmament, 1982; chmn. USIA, 1982—91, U.S. adv. com. pub. diplomacy, 1982—94; mem. Carlucci Comm. Fgn. Assistance, 1983; disitng. fellow mobilization concepts Devel. Ctr. Nat. Def. U., 1983—89; White House cons. on domestic policy, 1987; mem. US Com. Improving Effectiveness of UN, 1989—93; mem. adv. com. Am. Polit. Channel, 1994—96; vice-chmn. Nat. Com. Econ. Growth and Tax Reform, 1995—96; mem. Congrl. Policy Adv. Bd., 1997—2001, Internat. Fin. Inst. Adv. Com., 1999—2000; disting. vis. prof. Hanyang U., Seoul, 2001—; mem. Gingrich/Mitchell Task Force on UN Reform, 2005; nat. adv. bd. Ctr. Edn. and Rsch. in Free Enterprise Tex. A&M U. Author: Congress and the New International Economic Order, 1976, Looking Back, 1981, Conservatives Stalk the House, 1983, The March of Freedom, 1998, Intellectual Pilgrims, 1999, Leadership for America, 2000; pub. Policy Rev., 1977-2001; contbr. articles to profl. jours., newspapers, chpts. to books. Sec. Korea-U.S. Exch. Coun.; chmn. Citizens for Am. Edn. Found., 1985—89; mem. coun. advisors Bryce Harlow Found.; trustee Nat. Chamber Found., 1998—; mem. exec. coun. Am.'s Future Found., 1998—; trustee Lehrman Inst., 1981—90, Sarah Scaife Found., 1988—, St. James Sch., 1990—98, Sequoia Nat. Bank, 1987—99, Regis U., 1991—2001, 2005—, Internat. Rep. Inst., 1995—2001, Acton Inst., 1995—2002; vice-chmn. bd. Aequus Inst., 1989—, Intercollegiate Studies Inst., 1979—, chmn., 1989—93, 2003—; vice-chmn. bd. dirs. Roe Found., 1983—; mem. exec. com. Coun. Nat. Policy, 1993—2001; trustee Am. Coun. Germany, NY, 1982—92, Found. Francisco Marroquin, Inst. Rsch. Econs. Taxation, 1980—87; vice chmn., trustee Manhattan Inst. Policy Studies, 1977—86; mem. bd. visitors George Mason U., 1996—2004; mem. Multimedia Supercorridor Internat. Adv. Coun., Malaysia, 2001—. Decorated Order of Brilliant Star with Grand Cordon Republic of China, Order of Diplomatic Svc. Merit-Gwanghwa medal Republic of Korea; named Free Enterprise Man of Yr., Tex. A&M U., 1985, Man of Yr., Wharton Sch., 1993; recipient Washington award, Freedom Found., 1979, 1980, Am. Eagle award, Invest-in-Am. Nat. Coun., 1983, Disting. Alumni award, Regis U., 1985, Superior Pub. Svc. award, Dept. of Navy, 1987, Presdl. Citizens medal, 1989, Dir.'s Svc. award, USIA, 1992, Thomas Jefferson Servant Leadership award, Coun. Nat. Policy, 1996, Walter Judd Freedom award, Fund for Am. Studies, 2004. Mem. Am. Econs. Assn., Internat. Inst. Strategic Studies, U.S. Strategic Inst., Inst. d'Etudes Politques, Phila. Soc. (treas. 1964-79, pres. 1982-83), Mont Pelerin Soc. (treas. 1979-96, 2000-, pres. 1996-98, sr. v.p. 1998-2000), Internat. Com. of the G.K. Chesterton Soc. (chmn. 1989-92), Belle Haven Country Club, Union League (N.Y.C.), Met. Club, Reform Club (London), Bohemian Club (San Francisco), Old. Dominion Boat Club (Alexandria, Va.), Knights of Malta, Knights of the Holy Sepulchre, Alpha Kappa Psi. Republican. Roman Catholic. Office: The Heritage Found 214 Massachusetts Ave NE Washington DC 20002-4958 Office Phone: 202-546-4400. E-mail: ed@feulner.us.

FEUSS, LINDA ANNE UPSALL, lawyer; b. White Plains, NY, Dec. 9, 1956; d. Herbert Charles and Edna May (Hart) Upsall; m. Charles E. Feuss, Aug. 16, 1980; children: Charles Herbert, Anne Hart. BA in French lit., Colgate U., 1978; JD, Emory U., 1981. Bar: Ga. 1981, SC 1981, Minn. 2000. Assoc. Rainey, Britton, Gibbes & Clarkson, Greenville, SC, 1981-83; counsel Siemens Energy & Automation, Atlanta, 1983-91, Siemens Corp., Atlanta, 1991-93, sr. counsel, 1993-94, assoc. gen. counsel, 1994-98; v.p., gen. counsel Pillsbury Co., Mpls., 1998-2000; v.p., gen. counsel to exec. v.p. legal and human resources PEMSTAR Inc., Rochester, Minn., 2001—03; v.p., gen. counsel, sec. C.H. Robinson Worldwide Inc., Eden Prairie, Minn., 2003—. Rep. law coun. II Mfr.'s Alliance, Washington, 1995-98; rep. law com. Nat. Elec. Mfr.'s Assn., Washington, 1995-98. Bd. dirs. Am. Heart Assn., Greenville, 1981-83, Success with Children, 1999, CityLights, 1999; mem. leadership com. Woodruff Arts Ctr. Campaign, Atlanta, 1985-90; vol. High Mus. Art, Atlanta, 1993-99, Ga. 100 Mentor Exch., 1998. Mem. ABA, Am. Corp. Coun. Assn. (dir. Ga. chpt. 1995-98, v.p. Ga. chpt. 1996, pres. 1997), State Bar Ga., SC Bar, Minn. Bar Assn., Colgate Club Atlanta (pres. 1986-88, bd. dirs. 1989-98). Office: CH Robinson Worldwide Inc 8100 Mitchell Rd Eden Prairie MN 55344-2248

FEWEL, JOHN GERRARD, government agency administrator, director; b. Chickasha, Okla., Aug. 20, 1944; s. Kenneth Jack and Cleo LaRue Fewel; m. Vicki Ann Huber, May 26, 2000; children: Jeffrey Scott Pickens, Sean Allen. BA in Microbiology, U. Tex., Austin, 1966; MS in Mgmt., U. Tex., San Antonio, 1980. Rsch. asst. U. Ky. Med. Ctr., Lexington, 1966—69; rsch. assoc. N.J. Coll. Medicine, Newark, 1969—75; dir. cardiothoracic rsch. lab VA Med. Ctr., San Antonio, 1975—82, adminstrv. officer trainee Memphis, 1982—83; adminstrv. officer rsch. VA Outpatient Clinic, Boston, 1983—84, VA Med. Ctr., Boston, 1984—84, Dallas, 1984—2003; exec. dir. Dallas VA Rsch. Corp., Dallas, 1990—2002; ret., 2003; pres., CEO Miracle Wish Orgn. for Multidimensional Healing, LLC. Rsch. coord. U. Tex. Southwestern Med. Ctr., Dallas, 1984—90. *Founder and president of Miracle Wish Organization* *for Multidimensional Healing, LLC. This organization provides pro bono alternative therapy to indigents and children everywhere who suffer from life threatening illness and injury. Patients from around the globe receive treatment that is complimentary to professional Western and Eastern medical care. This organization provides support to not-for-profit foundations to assist them with patients who have developed life threatening illnesses such as heart and vascular disease, HIV and AIDS, hepatitis, neurological disease and injury, cancer, respiratory disease, and genetically induced illness.* Author: Reflections from the Shaman's Tear; contbr. articles to profl. jours. Recipient Unsung Hero award, VA Med. Ctr. at Dallas, 1989. Mem.: Soc. of Rsch. Adminstrs. (pres. govt. divsn. 1997—98). Achievements include securing millions of dollars in funding to support scientific and administrative equipment purchases for the support of hundreds of research investigators; development of quantitative analytical technique measuring variety of metabolites in tissue biopsies; establishment and operation of non-profit foundation; contributed to the understanding of the underlying biochemistry of hemorrhagic/endo-toxia shock and cardio pulmonary bypass resulting in improvements in surgical techniques and treatment regimens. Home and Office: 1307 High Ridge Drive Duncanville TX 75137

FEX, CECILIA, lawyer; b. Stockholm, Dec. 23, 1957; d. Jorgen and Harriet (Carlson) Fex; m. Dane Galloway, June 7, 1997. AD, Montgomery Coll., Sch. Nursing, Takoma Park, Md., 1982; BA summa cum laude, U. Md., College Park, 1988; JD, Harvard Law Sch., Cambridge, 1991. Bar: Md., D.C. Assoc. Koonz McKenney, Washington, 1991—94; tchr. The Cath. U. Law Sch., Washington, 1994—96; assoc. Proskauer Rose, Washington, 1996—98; mem. The Ackerson Group, Washington, 1998—2002; dir. Sommer Barnard Ackerson, PC, Washington, 2002—. Contbr. articles to profl. jours. Mem.: ABA, Wash. Agrl. Roundtable, Supreme Ct. Hist. Soc., U.S. Ct. Appeals for Fed. Cir. Bar Assn., Assn. Trial Lawyers of Am., U.S. Ct. of Fed. Claims Bar Assn., Harvard Law Sch. Assn. Avocations: running, movies, reading, painting. Office: Sommer Barnard Ackerson PC 1666 K St NW Ste 1010 Washington DC 20006

FEY, JOHN THEODORE, retired insurance company executive; b. Hopewell, Va., Mar. 10, 1917; s. Raymond B. and Ruth (Fultz) F.; m. Jane K. Gerber, Apr. 5, 1947 (dec.); 1 child, John Theodore; m. Deborah F. Fitzgerald, Dec. 6, 1986. Student, Washington and Lee U., 1935-37, LL.D., 1978; LL.B., U. Md., 1940; MBA, Harvard U., 1942; J.S.D., Yale U., 1952; LL.D., Middlebury Coll., Alma Coll., 1961, U. Vt., 1967, Washington and Lee U., 1980, St. Augustine Coll., 1981. Bar: Md. 1940, D.C. 1953, Vt. 1959, N.Y. 1977. County atty., Md., 1947-49; faculty Law Sch., George Washington U., 1949-53, dean, 1953-56, professorial lectr., 1956; clk. Supreme Ct. U.S., 1956-58; pres. U. Vt., 1958-64, U. Wyo., 1964-66, Nat. Life Ins. Co., 1966-74, also dir., 1966-74; chmn. bd. Equitable Life Assurance Soc. U.S., N.Y.C., 1974-82, Nat. Westminster Bank U.S.A., N.Y.C., 1982-85, Fidelity Union Life Ins. Co., Dallas, 1982-85. Bd. dirs. Sara Lee Corp., Certain-Teed Co., Norton Corp.; chmn. bd. dirs. Saint-Gobain Corp.; mem. Md. Legislature, 1946-50 Trustee Getty Mus., Malibu, Calif., 1979-92. Served to col. USMCR, 1942-46. Mem. Am. Coll. Life Underwriters, Order of Coif. Office Phone: 520-795-6624. Personal E-mail: fitzfey@cox.net.

FEY, TAMMEY LYNN, elementary school educator; b. Ashland, Pa., May 26, 1973; d. Roger Eugene and Donna Suzanne Grose; m. Wayne Raymond Fey, Aug. 9, 1997; children: Colton James, Ciara Elizabeth. BS in Edn., Bloomsburg U., 1995; M in Classroom Tech., Wilkes U., 2005. Substitute tchr. various sch. dists., Pa., 1995—96; summer camper, presch. tutor Trinity Ctr. Children, Pottsville, Pa., 1996—98; substitute tchr. Minersville Pine Grove Sch. Dist., Pa., 1998—2000, N. Schuylkill Sch. Dist., Pa., 1998—2002, tchr. Ashland, Pa., 2000—05. Summer camp tchr., pre-sch. tchr. Minersville, Pine Grove, 1998—2005. Mem.: Pa. State Edn. Assn. Republican. Avocations: reading, gardening. Home: 5 Fey Ln Hegins PA 17938 Office: North Schuylkill Sch Dist 15 Academy Ln Ashland PA 17921

FEY, TINA, actress; b. Upper Darby, Penn., May 18, 1970; m. Jeff Richmond, 2001; 1 child, Alice. BA in drama, U. Va., 1992. Head writer Saturday Night Live, 1997—. Writer: TV series Saturday Night Live: 25th Anniversary, 1999, The Colin Quinn Show, 2002, NBC 75th Anniversary Special, 2002, writer, composer: films Mean Girls, 2004; actor: (films) Mean Girls, 2004; writer Saturday Night Live, 1997—, head writer, 1999—; actor: (TV series) Saturday Night Live, 2000—, (guest appearances) Upright Citizens Brigade, 1999, The Real World/Road Rules Extreme Challenge, 2001; guest appearances Film 72, 2004, 60 Minutes, 2004. Named Entertainer Yr., Entertainment Weekly, 2001.*

FEY, WILLARD, global environmental researcher, educator; b. Cin., Ohio, June 29, 1935; s. Russell Richard and Irene Emma Fey; m. Mary Elizabeth Foley, June 21, 1958 (div. July 18, 1974); children: Lorenne Elizabeth, Leanne Susan, Erik Richard. BSEE, MIT, 1953—57, BS in Mgmt., 1957, MSEE, 1961. Instr. Sloan Sch. Mgmt. MIT, Cambridge, Mass., 1961—64; lectr. indsl. engring. dept. Northeastern U., Boston, 1963—68; asst. prof. Sloan Sch. Mgmt. MIT, Cambridge, 1964—67, dir. undergrad. sys. program, 1964—67; tech. staff The MITRE Corp., Bedford, Mass., 1967—68; assoc. prof. Indsl. and Sys. Engring. Sch. Ga. Inst. Tech., Atlanta, 1969—99; CEO Ecocosm Dynamics Ltd., Tucker, Ga., 2000—. Cons. The MITRE Corp., Bedford, 1962—67, Reynolds, Smith & Hills, Jacksonville, Fla., 1969—71, Guyana Mining, Ltd., Georgetown, Guyana, 1980—83, Coca Cola Co. USA, Atlanta, 1981—83; prin. rsch. investigator U.S. Law Enforcement Assistance Adminstrn., Washington, 1972—74, USAF, Tyndall AFB, Panama City, Fla., 1979—80, U.S. Forest Svc., U. Ga. Office, Athens, Ga., 1981—88. Contbr. book Some Theories of Organization, 1972; co-author (Luis Gutierrez): (book) Ecosystem Succession, 1980; co-prodr. Ann Lam: (video presentation) Pie in the Sky: A System Dynamics Perspective of Sustainability, 1998; co-prodr. The Bridge to Humanity's Future, 2000; contbr. reports and articles to profl. publs. Voting dep. Episcopal Ch., Detroit, 1988; bd. dirs. Episcopal Diocese Atlanta, 1983—85; mem. standing com. Episcopal Diocese, Atlanta, 1986—88; sr. warden Holy Cross Episcopal Ch., Decatur, Ga., 1986—88. Named to Leadership Atlanta, 1977. Mem.: Soc. Christian Ethics, Am. Schs. Oriental Rsch., Internat. Soc. for Sys. Scis., Sys. Dynamics Soc. (charter mem.), Bibl. Archaeology Study Group of Greater Atlanta, Inc. Episcopalian. Achievements include research in system dynamics philosophy and practice; dynamics of higher education, dynamics of Atlanta criminal justice system, forest management dynamics; development of environmental research that identified Ecocosm Paradox. Avocations: Biblical research, classical music, opera, sustainable architectural design, gardening. E-mail: fey@ecocosmdynamics.org.

FIALA, THOMAS G.S., plastic surgeon; b. Montreal, Que., Aug. 6, 1965; s. George J. and Maureen A. Fiala; m. Sandra L. Cooper, Sept. 21, 2002. BA, Queen's U., Can., 1984, MD, 1988; ARCT, Royal Conservatory Music, Toronto, 1986. Diplomate Am. Bd. Plastic Surgery, cert. gen. and plastic surgery Royal Coll. Physicians and Surgeons Can. Med. dir. Preferred Plastic Surgery, Orlando, Fla., 2000—. Contbr. multiple jour. articles. Bd. mem. Lake Marion Restoration Com., Altamonte Springs, Fla., 2003—04. Fellow: Royal Coll. Physicians and Surgeons Can., ACS; mem.: Fla. Med. Soc., Fla. Soc. Plastic Surgeons, Reed Dingman Surg. Soc., Am. Soc. Aesthetic Plastic Surgery, Am. Soc. Plastic Surgeons. Avocations: music, scuba diving, travel. Office: Preferred Plastic Surgery Orlando 220 E Central Pkw Ste 2020 Altamonte Springs FL 32701 Office Phone: 407-339-3222. Office Fax: 407-339-3085. E-mail: info@drfiala.com.

FIBICH, HOWARD RAYMOND, retired newspaper editor; b. Oak Park, Ill., Jan. 6, 1932; s. Raymond Clarence and Vivian (Barrie) F.; m. Carrol Jean Anderson, June 5, 1954; children: Linda, Steven, Barbara. BS, Northwestern U., 1954, MS, 1955; postgrad., Columbia U., 1966. Reporter Kokomo (Ind.) Tribune, 1955-56; copy editor Milw. Jour., 1956-64, telegraph editor, 1964, asst. news editor, 1964-67, news editor, 1967-84, asst. mng. editor, 1984-86, dep. mng. editor, 1986-93; ret., 1994. Freelance writer, 1959-63; chmn. Mid-Am. Press Inst.; producer, host Jazz for the Quiet Hours, WYMS, Milw. Bd. dirs. Friends of WYMS; mem. Brookfield Greenway Corridor Com., 2003. Named Milw. Media Hall of Fame, 1994. Mem. Mid.-Am. Press Inst. (bd. dirs. 1976-86, chmn. 1980-81), Wis. History Found., AP Mng. Editors Assn. (new tech. com.), Milw. Press Club, Kappa Tau Alpha. Home: 17800 Caribou Pass Unit B Brookfield WI 53045-2041

FIBIGER, JOHN ANDREW, life insurance company executive; b. Copenhagen, Apr. 27, 1932; came to U.S., 1934, naturalized, 1953; s. Borge Rottboll and Ruth Elizabeth (Wadmond) F.; m. Barbara Mae Stuart, June 22, 1956; children: Karen Ruth McCarthy, Katherine Louise. BA, U. Minn., 1953, MA, 1954; postgrad., U. Wis. With Lincoln Nat. Life Ins. Co., Ft. Wayne, Ind., 1956-57; with Bankers Life Ins. Co. Nebr., Lincoln, 1959-73, sr. v.p. group, 1972-73; with New Eng. Mut. Life Ins. Co., Boston, 1973-89, vice chmn., pres., chief operating officer, 1981-89; with Transam Life Cos., 1991-94; exec. v.p., CFO, then pres. Transamerica Occidental Life Ins. Co., L.A., 1994-95, chmn., 1995-97. Past vice chmn. Actuarial Bd. for Counseling and Discipline; bd. dirs. Fidelity Life Assn., Genworth Pvt. Asset Mgmt., Contra Fund. Life trustee, past chmn. Mus. Sci., Boston, 1989-91; past overseer New Eng. Med. Ctr., Boston Symphony Orch.; past bd. dirs. Menninger Found., past v.p.; mem. fin. com., strategic planning com. L.A. Chamber Orch.; past chmn. Menninger Fund; past bd. dirs. U. So. Calif. Sch. Gerontology; bd. dirs. Austin Symphony Orch.; past trustee Calif. Mus. Sci. and Industry; bd. visitors Menninger Baylor Meth. Found Fellow Soc. Actuaries (past bd. dirs.); mem. Nat. Acad. Social Ins. (founding mem.), Am. Acad. Actuaries (past pres.), Assn. Calif. Life Cos. (past bd. chmn.). Personal E-mail: fibij@aol.com.

FICCAGLIA, LESLIE M., psychologist, portrait artist; b. Huntington, NY, Oct. 3, 1943; d. Sewall M. and L. Lillian (Bartok) Pastor; m. Anthony W. Ficcaglia, Nov. 4, 1968; children: Jeremy Clinton, Linnet Kyung. BA in Psychology, NYU, 1965; MA in Psychology, Western Wash. U., Bellingham, 1971; cert. sch. psychologist, Rowan Coll., Glassboro, N.J., 1984. Cert. sch. psychologist. Clin. psychologist Eastern Diagnostic and Evaluation Ctr., Phila., 1968; staff clin. psychologist Vineland State Sch., NJ, 1970—74; staff psychologist Cumberland County Hosp., Hopewell Twp., NJ, 1974—81; sch. psychologist Downe Twp. Bd. Edn., Newport, NJ, 1981—2000, grantswriter, 1990—2000; portrait artist Minnamuska Creek Studio, Port Elizabeth, NJ, 1995—. Devel. ecotourism website; author newspaper articles. Mem. Maurice River Twp. Planning Bd., 1979-98, chair, 1990-98; mem. Cumberland County Planning Bd., Bridgeton, NJ, 1982—, vice chair, 1988—; mem. NJ State Pinelands Commn., New Lisbon, 1996—; trustee Assn. NJ Environ. Commns., Mendham, 1995-99, adv. bd., 2000—; trustee Citizens United to Protect the Maurice River and Its Tributaries, 1999—; mem. Del. Bayshore adv. bd. Nature Conservancy, 1998—; founding chmn. Riverfront Renaissance Ctr. Arts, Millville, NJ, bd. dir., 1999-2004. Recipient Outstanding Svc. award Cumberland County Bd. Freeholders, 1991; EPA Region 2 Environ. Qualtiy Award for Individuals, 2003. Mem.: Portrait Soc. Am., Nat. Assn. Sch. Psychologists, N.J. Planning Ofcl., Phi Delta Kappa. Avocations: land use planning, environmental issues. Home: Minnamuska Creek Farm and Studio Box 27 Port Elizabeth NJ 08348

FICHANDLER, ZELDA, director; m. Thomas C. Fichandler (separated); children: Hal, Mark. BA in Russian Lang. and Lit., Cornell U., 1945; MA in Theater Arts, George Washington U., 1950, Doctor in Humane Letters (hon.), 1974, Smith Coll. Co-founder, producing dir. Arena Stage, Washington, 1950—90. Former vis. prof. U. Tex.; former prof. theater arts Boston U.; former artistic cons. Huntington Theater Co.; former artistic dir. The Acting Co.; chmn. grad. acting program Tisch Sch. of the Arts, NYU. Dir. at Arena Stage: (plays) A Doll House, The Three Sisters, Death of a Salesman, An Enemy of the People, Six Characters in Search of an Author, Duck Hunting, Ascent of Mt. Fuji, Screenplay, Inherit the Wind, After the Fall, The Crucible. Recipient Artistic Founder award Cultural Alliance of Greater Washington, 1989, Common Wealth award, John Houseman award The Acting Co., The Margo Jones award, Washingtonian of the Yr. award, Brandeis U. Creative Arts award, Tony award, 1976, Nat. Medal of Arts award, 1997;Inducted to The Theatre Hall of Fame, 1999.

FICHTEL, RUDOLPH ROBERT, retired association executive; b. N.Y.C., Dec. 12, 1915; s. Paul Gotthard and Helen (Szapka) F.; m. Elsie E. Terebesy, Dec. 24, 1942; children: Nancy Lynn, Robert Paul, Richard John. BBA cum laude, Coll. City N.Y., 1938; cert., Am. Inst. Banking, 1941; diploma fin. pub. relations, Northwestern U., 1950; MBA, NYU, 1951; diploma banking, Rutgers U. Stonier Grad. Sch. Banking, 1954. Tchr. N.Y.C. Pub. Schs., 1938-39; adminstr. East River Savs. Bank, 1939-42; dir. pub. relations, editor, asst. sec. Savs. Banks Assn. N.Y. State, 1945-53; dir. pub. relations council, savs. and mortgage div. Am. Bankers Assn., N.Y.C. and Washington, 1953-64; nat. dir. Am. Inst. Banking, 1964-78; regional v.p. United Student Aid Funds, Inc., N.Y.C., 1978-87. Mem. lender relations com. Higher Edn. Loan Programs; mem. faculty Am. Inst. Banking, Stonier Grad. Sch. Banking; contbg. editor Am. Inst. Banking textbooks; speaker. Contbr. articles to profl. jours. Vol. tutor Literacy Program, N.Y.C.; income tax counsellor Am. Assn. Retired Persons. Served to capt. AUS, 1942-45, ETO. Recipient highest award citation Internat. Council Indsl. Editors, 1948, Dr. Marcus Nadler award for excellence in finance; N.Y. U., 1951 Mem. Beta Gamma Sigma. Home: 65-19 170th St Flushing NY 11365-1949 *Success in my life has been the result of hard work, continuing search for knowledge, constant effort to understand and relate to people, and total dedication to excellence in full partnership with a loving family.*

FICHTENHOLTZ, PHYLLIS SANDRA, retired English educator; b. Bklyn., May 31, 1942; d. Samuel and Sarah (Gendel) F.; life ptnr. Sheila Cooney Swigert. BS, NYU, 1963; MA, Kean Coll., 1975. English tchr. Intermediate Sch. 246, Bklyn., 1963-68, Curtis H.S., Staten Island, N.Y., 1968-96, dropout prevention coord., 1993-96. Mem. Nat. Coun. Tchrs. English, AAUW. Avocations: travel, reading, computers, writing, photography. Home: 50 Fort Pl Apt B2E Staten Island NY 10301-2418

FICHTNER, MARGARIA, journalist; b. Lakeland, Fla., May 4, 1944; d. August Albert and Margaret Louise (Kelly) Fichtner. BA, Fla. So. Coll., 1966. Feature writer, fashion editor Miami Herald, 1968—92, book editor, 1992—2001, book critic, 2001—03, sr. feature writer, 2003—. Recipient First Pl. Criticism award, Am. Assn. Sunday and Feature Editors, 1996, Fla. Soc. Newspaper Editors, 1997, First Pl. Criticism Green Eyeshade award, Soc. Profl. Journalists, 2000, First Pl. Critical Writing Sunshine State award, 2003. Office: The Miami Herald Pub Co One Herald Plz Miami FL 33132-1693 Office Phone: 305-376-3630. Business E-Mail: mfichtner@herald.com.

FICK, GARY WARREN, agronomist, educator; b. O'Neill, Nebr., July 10, 1943; s. Walter Henry and Doris Marie (Parks) F.; m. Mae Ellen Ruddell, June 29, 1969; children— Joseph, David, Charles BS, U. Nebr., 1965; diploma Agr. Sci., Massey U., 1968; PhD, U. Calif., Davis, 1971. Asst. prof. Cornell U., Ithaca, N.Y., 1971-76, assoc. prof., 1976-84, prof., 1984—, acting chair dept. soil crop and atmospheric scis., 1993, 95, tchg. leader soil crop and atmospheric scis., 1994—99; vis. scientist Lincoln Coll., N.Z., 1977-78; tchg. leader crop and soil scis. Cornell U., Ithaca, NY, 2002—. Assoc. editor Agronomy Jour., 1978—81. Assoc. editor Jour. of Prodn. Agr., 1987-93; mem. edit. bd. Jour. of Sustainable Agr., 1996—; contbr. articles to profl. jours. and monographs. Fellow Crop Sci. Soc. Am., Am. Soc. Agronomy (tchg. award N.E. br. 1991); mem. Am. Forage and Grassland Coun. (Merit cert. 1989), Sigma Xi, Gamma Sigma Delta (Cornell pres. 1992-93), SUNY Chancellor's tchg. award 1995. Office: Cornell U Dept Crop and Soil Scis Ithaca NY 14853 Office Phone: 607-255-1704. Business E-Mail: gwf2@cornell.edu.

FICKE, GREGORY C., utilities executive; m. Carol Ficke; children: Lisa, Lindsay. BS, Miami U.; degree in Engring., The Ohio State U.; MBA, U. Cin.; JD, No. Ky. U.; grad. Adv. Mgmt. Program, Harvard Bus. Sch. Registered profl. engr., Ohio; bar: Ohio. With Bechtel Power Corp., Ann Arbor, Mich.; from mem. staff to pres. The Cin. (Ohio) Gas & Electric Co. Cinergy Corp., Cin., 1978—2001, pres. The Cin. (Ohio) Gas & Electric Co., 2001—. Bd. trustees Clovernook Ctr. Blind, Ohio Found. Ind. Colls. Mem.: Greater Cin. (Ohio) C. of C. (bd. trustees), Ohio C. of C. (bd. trustees). Office: Cinergy Corp 139 E 4th St Cincinnati OH 45202*

FICKENSCHER, GERALD H., chemicals company executive; b. Buenos Aires, 1943; Graduate, Cath. U. Argentina, Buenos Aires, 1967; Post-Graduate, Cath. U. Argentina, 1970. V.p., CFO Uniroyal Chem. Corp., Middlebury, Conn.; v.p.-Europe, corp. officer Crompton Corp., Middlebury, 1994—. Home: 3200 Park Ave Unit 6b1 Bridgeport CT 06604-1147 Office: 199 Benson Rd Middlebury CT 06749 E-mail: gerald_fickenscher@cromptoncorp.com.

FICKERT, KURT JON, writer, retired language educator; b. Pausa, Saxony, Germany, Dec. 19, 1920; came to U.S., 1926; s. Kurt Alfred and Martha Elsa (Searchinger) F.; m. Madlyn Barbara Janda, Aug. 6, 1946; children: Linda Mosbacher, Jon, Chris. AB, Hofstra U., 1941; MA, NYU, 1947, PhD, 1952. Instr., then asst. prof. Hofstra U., Hempstead, N.Y., 1948-53; asst. prof. Fla. State U., Tallahassee, 1953-54, Kans. State U., Ft. Hays, 1954-56; assoc. prof., then prof. Wittenberg U., Springfield, Ohio, 1956-86, ret., 1986. Chairperson dept. langs. Wittenberg U., 1969-75. Author: To Heaven and Back, 1972, Hermann Hesse's Quest, 1978, Kafka's Doubles, 1979, Signs and Portents, 1980, Franz Kafka: Life, Work, Criticism, 1987, Neither Left Nor Right, 1987, End of a Mission, 1993, Dialogue with the Reader, 1996; contbr. articles and poetry to lit. publs. Fullbright grantee, Germany, 1957, NEH grantee, U. Calif., Irvine, 1981; Fickert Lang. award established in his honor Wittenberg U., 1986. Lutheran. Home: 33 S Kensington Pl Springfield OH 45504-1030

FICKETT, EDWARD HALE, architect, educator, arbitrator; b. L.A., 1923; s. George Edward and Marguerite (Hale) F.; m. Joyce Helen Steinberg, Apr. 8, 1982. BArch, grad. studies in engring and archaelogy, U. So. Calif.; M in City Planning, M in City Planning, M in Arch, MIT. Registered architect, 50 states. Pvt. practice architecture, L.A., 1950—. Archtl. advisor to Pres. Dwight D. Eisenhower, 1957-60; cons. to Federal Govt. on Housing; wrote guidelines and specifications for HUD, VA, FHA; Calif. Housing Bd. under Gov. Edmund G. Pat Brown; honored with fellowship in AIA, 1969; archtl. commr. City of Beverly Hills, Calif., 1977-86, chmn. Archtl. Commn., 1979-82; guest lectr., vis. prof. UCLA, U. Calif., Berkeley, MIT, Stanford U., U. So. Calif., U. Fla., Calif. Poly. State U.-San Luis Obispo, Rensselaer Poly. Inst., N.Y., U. Chgo.; arbitrator Nat. Panel Arbitrators, 1961—, Am. Arbitration Assn., 1963—. Archtl. works include L.A. Harbor (Port of L.A.) Cargo and Passenger Terminals, San Pedro, Sands Hotel, Las Vegas, Nev., La Costa Resort and Condominiums, Carlsbad, Calif., Las Cruces Resort Hotel, La Paz, Mex., Hacienda Hotel, Cabo San Lucas, Mex., Ocotillo Lodge Hotel, Palm Springs, Calif., Mammoth Mountain Inn, Mammoth, Calif., Murietta Hot Springs Resort, Murietta, Calif., Stallion Springs Resort, Tehachapi, Calif., Bistro Gardens Restaurant, Beverly Hills, Calif., Spago Restaurant, Beverly Hills, Scandia Restaurant, West Hollywood, Calif., Nicks Fishmarket Restaurant, West Hollywood, Univ. High Sch., UCLA Faculty Ctr., L.A. Police Acad., L.A., master plans for Edwards AFB, Calif., Norton AFB, Calif., Murphy Canyon Heights Naval Base, Calif., Los Alametos Naval Base, Calif., San Pedro Naval base, Calif., L.A. City Hall Hist. and Seismic Renovation, Nethercutt Antique Car Mus., Dodger Stadium, others; comml. devels., master planned communities, office bldgs., restaurants, resorts, hotels, homes, condominiums, shopping ctrs., air force bases, naval bases, schs., renovation of hist. bldgs.; historic & seismic rehab, designed over 60,000 homes. Mem. Gov. Pat Brown's Housing Bd. for Calif.; U.S. del. to Internat. Congress of Archs. Lt. comdr. Sea Bees, USN. Recipient Merit of Honor award by Pres. of U.S., L.A. Conservancy Preservation Arch. award, 1999, National Progressive Architecture Design awards, city beautification awards from L.A., Beverly Hills, Reno, Seattle, numerous Nat. Assn. Home Builders awards, Sunset Magazine and House and Home awards, Better Homes and Gardens House of Yr. awards, Nat. Assn. Home Builders awards, Los Angeles Conservancy Archtl. Design Award, 1999, Nat. Hist. Monuments Archtl. Design Award, 1999, Housing Hall of Fame, other awards. Fellow AIA (AIA First Honor Awards, numerous AIA merit of honor awards, pres. So. Calif. chpt. 1958-62, pres. Calif. chpt. 1962, chmn. Nat. Ethics Com., featured speaker nat. convs., lectr., formulated and participated in AIA Univ. Lecture series, fellow 1969, U.S. del. internat. congress archs.), Nat. Comm. for Bldg. Industry (chmn. 1962-72), Nat. Assn. Home Builders (speaker nat. convs.), Calif. Coun. Architects (sec. 1960), Am. Archtl. Found. Octagon Soc. (charter mem.), U. So. Calif. Archtl. Guild (charter mem.). Avocations: tennis, golf. Office: 7421 Beverly Blvd Los Angeles CA 90036-2703 Fax: 323-935-4144. Office Phone: 323-939-7476.

FICKLER, ARLENE, lawyer; b. Phila., Apr. 21, 1951; BA cum laude, U. Pa., 1971, JD cum laude, 1974. Bar: Pa. 1974, D.C. 1980, U.S. Supreme Ct. 1989. Ptnr. Hoyle Fickler Herschel & Mathes LLP, Phila. Staff atty. Commn. on Revision of Fed. Ct. Appellate System, 1974-75; exec. asst. Bicentennial Com. Jud. Conf. of U.S., 1975-76. Comment editor U. Pa. Law Rev., 1973-74; co-reporter American College of Trial Lawyers Mass Tort Litigation Manual; contbr. chpt. to book and articles to law jours. Pres. U. Pa. Law Sch. Alumni Bd. Mgrs., 1997-99; trustee Jewish Fedn. of Greater Phila., 1981-88, 89-93, 94-98, 99—. Phila. Bar Found., 1993-98, Jewish Cmty. Rels. Coun. Greater Phila., 1983-94, 98-00; trustee Jewish Cmty. Ctrs. of Phila., 1997—, chair, 2003—; trustee HIAS Immigration Svcs. Phila., 1998—, treas., 1999-2003; mem. United Jewish Appeal Nat. Young Women's Leadership Cabinet, 1982-87; v.p. Phila. chpt. Am. Jewish Congress, 1995-2001; co-chmn. Phila. Maccabi Games, 2001. Recipient Mrs. Isidore Kohn Young Leadership award Jewish Fedn. Greater Phila., 1981, Next Generation Leadership award Jewish Cmty. Ctrs. Assn., 2000, award of merit U. Pa. Law Sch. Alumni, 2001. Mem. ABA, Am. Law Inst., Am. Bar Found., Pa. Bar Assn., D.C. Bar, Phila. Bar Assn. (chmn. fed. cts. com. 1992), Fed. Bar Coun. of Second Cir., U. Pa. Am. Inn of Ct. Office: Hoyle Fickler Herschel & Mathes LLP One South Broad St 1500 Philadelphia PA 19103 Office Phone: 215-981-5850. Business E-Mail: afickler@hoylelawfirm.com.

FIDDICK, PAUL WILLIAM, municipal official, broadcast executive; b. St. Joseph, Mo., Nov. 20, 1949; s. Lowell Duane and Betty Jean (Manring) F.; m. Julie Hanna Lorms, July 31, 1983; children: Lea Elizabeth, Hanna Manring. BJ, U. Mo., 1971. Account exec. Sta. KCMO-KFMU, Kansas City, Mo., 1971-72, Sta. WEZW, Milw., 1972-74, dir. sales mktg., 1974-76, v.p., gen. mgr., 1976-81; sr. v.p. Multimedia Broadcasting Co., Milw., 1981; pres. Multimedia Radio, Cin., 1982-86, Radio Group, Heritage Communications, Inc., Des Moines, 1986-87, Radio Group, Heritage Media Corp., Dallas, 1987-98; dir, vice chmn. RadioWave.com, Inc., Schaumburg, Ill., 1998-99, acting pres., 1999; asst. sec. USDA, Washington, 1999-2001, dir. USDA Grad. Sch., 2000—; dir. Nat. Assn. of Broadcasters, Washington, 1994-98; pres. Emmis Internat., Wash., 2002—; dir. pres. Democracy Radio Inc., Wash., 2002—. Dir. Radio Advt. Bur., N.Y.C., 1983—99, chmn., 1993—94; trustee Washington Chorus, 2000—05; mem. acad. staff U. Wis., Milw., 1978—81; mem. adv. bd. Advanced Microbial Solutions LLC, Pilot Point, Tex., 2002—; mem. adv. coun. Bus. for Diplomatic Action, San Francisco, 2004—; mem. adv. bd. Siena Holdings LLC, Bethesda, Md., 2005—. Elder Westminster Presbyn. Ch., Dallas, 1997-99, Western Presbyn. Ch., Washington, 2004—. Named one of 40 Most Powerful People in Radio, Radio Ink Mag., 1996, Fifth Estater, Broadcasting Mag., 1990, Up and Coming Radio Exec. of Yr., Radio Only mag., 1983, Pub.'s Profile, Radio and Records mag., 1998. Mem. Phi Eta Sigma, Kappa Tau Alpha.

FIDDLER NICHOLS, BARBARA DILLOW, sales and marketing professional; b. Decatur, Ill., Sept. 2, 1940; s. N. Eugene and Ruth (Kirchhoff) Dillow; children: John Eugene, Thomas Crawford stepchildren: J. C., Danielle, Morgan, Kathryn. BA, U. Vt., 1963. Grad. registrar Troy State U., European divsn., Wiesbaden, W. Ger., 1977-79; adminstrv. asst. Mt. Mansfield Co. Mktg. Dept., Stowe, Vt., 1980-84; asst. dir. promotions and advt. Rossignol Ski Co., Tennis divsn., Williston, Vt., 1984-85; project mgr. Birch Hill Devel. Co., Stowe, 1985-86; asst. to dir. of devel. Johnson State Coll., Johnson, Vt., 1986-89; asst. dir. devel. The Trustees of Reservations, Beverly, Mass., 1989-91; adminstr. Epsilon Inc., Burlington, Mass., 1991-94; group sales mgr. Topnotch at Stowe, Vt., 1994-98. Bd. dirs., pres. Robert Alden Ellsworth Trust, Johnson, Vt., 1991—. Trustee Fund Johnson State Coll.; bd. dirs., chmn. fin. and fundraising com. Johnson Friends of Arts, 1986—88; bd. dirs. United Way Lamoille County, Hyde Park, 1988—92, 1994—2000, pres., 1998—99; mem. Stowe (Vt.) Planning Commn., 1988—92; regional trustee Vt. Symphony Orch., 1995—2000. Mem.: Lamoille Valley C. of C. (bd. dirs.), Women in Devel. Greater Boston. Republican. Episcopalian. Avocations: skiing, knitting, reading, creative cooking. Home and Office: 227 Upper Baird Rd Stowe VT 05672-4203 Office Phone: 802-253-7501. E-mail: bfiddler@aol.com.

FIDEL, RAYA, information science educator; b. Tel Aviv, Jan. 18, 1945; came to U.S., 1977; BSc, Tel Aviv U., 1970; MLS, Hebrew U., Jerusalem, 1976; PhD, U. Md., 1982. Tchr. Adult Edn. Ctr., Jerusalem, 1971-72; br. libr. Hebrew U., Jerusalem, 1972-77; asst. prof. libr. sci. U. Wash., Seattle, 1982-87, assoc. prof. libr. sci., 1987-2000, prof. Info. Sch., 2000—, head Ctr. Human-Info. Interaction The Info. Sch., 2003—. Vis. libr. Duke U. Libr., Durham, N.C., 1992-93. Author: Database Design, 1987; editor Advances in Classification, 1991-94 (award 1992-94); contbr. articles to profl. publs. Recipient Research award Am. Society for Information Science, 1994 Mem. AAUP (chair U. Wash. chpt. 1990-92, pres. state conf. 1992-97), Assn. Computing Machinery, Am. Soc. Info. Sci. (dir.-at-large 2000-02). Home: 5801 Phinney Ave N Seattle WA 98103-5862

FIEBACH, H. ROBERT, lawyer; b. Paterson, N.J., June 7, 1939; s. Michael M. and Silvia Irene (Nadler) F.; m. Elizabeth D. Carlton, Mar. 17, 1984; children: Michael, Emma; children by previous marriage: Jonathan, Rachel. BS, U. Pa., 1961, LLB cum laude, 1964. Bar: Pa. 1965, U.S. Supreme Ct. 1971. Law clk. to Chief Judge Biggs U.S. Ct. Appeals for 3d Cir., 1964-65; assoc. Wolf, Block, Schorr and Solis-Cohen, Phila., 1965-71, ptnr., 1971-79, sr. ptnr., 1979-95; sr. mem., shareholder Cozen O'Connor, Phila., 1995—. Permanent mem. U.S. Jud. Conf. for 3d cir., 1967—; mem. Pa. Supreme Ct. Adv. Com. on Appellate Rules, 1987-93, Commn. on Jud. Elections, 1997-98; arbitrator, mediator U.S. Dist. Ct. (ea. dist.) Pa., 1966—, Commerc Ct., Phila., Pa., 1999—; lectr. Nat. Legal Malpractice Seminar, 2003, 04; course planner, lectr. PBI Litigating the Legal Malpractice Case Seminar, 2004. Contbg. author: Business and Commercial Litigation in the Federal Courts, 1998; rsch. editor U. Pa. Law Rev., 1964-65; contbr. articles to legal jours. Past mem. Phila. adv. bd. Anti-Defamation League of B'nai Brith, Greater Phila. Regional Commn. on Law and Social Action, Am. Jewish Congress; bd. dirs. Greater Phila. chpt. ACLU, past chmn. criminal justice and police practices com.; past bd. dirs. Pa. chpt. ACLU; bd. dirs., sec. Rodeph Shalom Synagogue; mem. mayor's task force on gaming Pub. Interest Law Ctr. of Phila.; mem. Mayor's Task Force on Gaming, 2005. Fellow: Am. Coll. Trial Lawyers; mem.: ABA (past chmn. jud. performance and conduct com., jud. adminstrn. divsn. 1986—91, nat. conf. bar pres. 1991—95, pres. nat. caucus state bar assns. 1994—95, chmn. standing com. on lawyers profl. liability 1994—95, bd. govs. 1997—2000, ho. of dels. 2001—, nat. conf. bar pres. 2001—, state del. 2001—, litigation sect., 1988 and 2002 midyear meeting host com., state chair), Bd. Div. Pa. Bar Found., Am. Bar Found., Soc. of Fellows (state chair 2003—, state co-chmn. 2003—), Phila. Trial Lawyers Assn. (bd. dirs. 1989—90, past chmn. bus. litig. com.), Am. Judicature Soc. (state membership chmn. 1988), Defender Assn. Phila. (bd. dirs.), Pa. Bar Inst. (pres. bd. dirs. 1984—90, 2000—01), Phila. Bar Assn. (chmn. spl. com. on ins. 1983—84, bd. govs. 1983—87, past chmn. fed. cts. com., spkr. various panels, past vice-chmn. arbitration com., civil jud. procedures com., past mem. spl. com. to study appellate cts.), Pa. Bar Assn. (past vice-chmn. jud. selection com., chmn. jud. retention election com 1980—83, chmn. polit. action com. for merit retention of judges 1980—83, ho. of dels. 1983—, chmn. com. on profl. liability 1984—87, bd. govs. 1987—95, pres.-elect 1992—93, pres. 1993—94, Pa. Bar Trust 1996—2004, chair 1999—2004, Spl. Achievement award 1986), Order of Coif (past dir. U. Pa. chpt.). Home: 301 Delancey St Philadelphia PA 19106-4208 Office: Cozen & O'Conner 1900 Market St Fl 3 Philadelphia PA 19103-3572 Office Phone: 215-665-4166. Business E-Mail: rfiebach@cozen.com.

FIEBERT, MARTIN STEPHEN, research and development company executive; b. NYC, June 6, 1939; s. Max and Grace F.; m. Paula Barbara Schwartz, June 1, 1963 (div. 1999); children: Bryan, Deirdre; m. Margo Law Kasdan, Dec. 22, 1999. PhD, U. Rochester, 1965. Lic. psychologist, Calif. Prof. psychology Calif. State U., Long Beach, Calif., 1965—. Contbr. articles to profl. jours. Mem.: Calif. Faculty Assn. (immediate past pres. chpt.), Am. Psychol. Soc. Avocations: tennis, travel, sculpting, meditation. Office: Calif State U 1250 Bellflower Blvd Long Beach CA 90840 Fax: 562-985-8004. E-mail: mfiebert@csulb.edu.

FIEDEROWICZ, WALTER MICHAEL, lawyer; b. Hartford, Conn., Aug. 23, 1946; s. Michael and Sylvia Christine (Ramunno) F.; m. Gerry Prattson, June 1, 1968; children: Michael, Catherine. BA, Yale U., 1968; JD (DuPont fellow), U. Va., 1971. Bar: Conn. 1971, U.S. Supreme Ct. 1977. Mem. firm Cummings & Lockwood, Stamford, Conn., 1971-76, ptnr. firm, 1979-88, of counsel, 1989-91; pres. Covenant Mut. Ins. Co., Hartford, 1985-92; White House fellow U.S. Dept. Justice, Washington, 1976-77; spl. asst. to Atty. Gen., Dept. Justice, Washington, 1976-77; assoc. dep. Atty. Gen., 1977-79. Bd. dirs. Photronics, Inc., First Albany Corp., Hematech; chmn. CDT Corp., Meacock Capital, Omega Underwriting Holdings, Ltd. Mem. editl. Va. Law Rev., 1969-71. Grad. coun. Loomis-Chaffee Sch. Bd.; trustee Conn. Trust for Hist. Preservation; comr. Conn. Commn. Arts and Tourism. Mem. ABA, Conn. Bar Assn., Order of the Coif, Hartford Golf Club, Univ. Club. Roman Catholic. Home: 102 North St PO Box 939 Litchfield CT 06759-0939 Office Phone: 860-567-9828. Personal E-mail: fiederowicz@juno.com.

FIEDLER, FRED EDWARD, retired organizational psychology educator, consultant; b. Vienna, July 13, 1922; arrived in US, 1938; s. Victor and Hilda (Schallinger) F.; m. Judith Joseph, Apr. 14, 1946; children: Decky, Ellen Victoria, Carol Ann. AM, U. Chgo., 1947, PhD, 1949. Clin. psychol. trainee US VA, Chgo., 1947-50; rsch. assoc., instr. U. Chgo., 1949-51; asst. prof. psychology to prof. U. Ill., Urbana, 1951-69; prof. U. Wash., Seattle, 1969-93, prof. emeritus psychology, 1993—. Vis. prof. U. Amsterdam, 1958-59; guest prof. U. Louvain, Belgium, 1963-64; vis. rsch. fellow Templeton Coll., Oxford, 1986; cons. State of Wash., 1981-84, King County, Wash., 1970-80; cons. various govt., mil., pvt. orgns., U.S., Europe, 1953—; apptd. to SLA Marshall chair U.S. Army Rsch. Inst., 1988-89. Author: Boards, Management and Company Success, 1959; A Theory of Leadership Effectiveness, 1967; Improving Leadership Effectiveness, 1976; Leadership and Effective Management, 1974; New Approaches to Effective Leadership—Cognitive Resources and Organizational Performance, 1987; contbr. numerous articles to profl. jours. Mem. Wash. Gov.'s Transition Team, 1980, Task Force on Pers. Selection of Apptd. Ofcls; co-chmn. Tech. Transfer, State of Wash., 1980-81; pub. mem. State Med. Disciplinary Bd., 1981-85. With Med. Dept. and Mil. Govt. br. U.S. Army, 1942-45. Recipient Outstanding Rsch. award Am. Pers. and Guidance Assn., 1953, Stogdill award for disting. contbns. to leadership, 1978, award Outstanding Sci. Contbns. to Mil. Psychology, 1979; named Disting. Bicentennial lectr. U. Ga., 1985; Claremont Grad. Sch. and Claremont-McKenna Coll. 1991 Leadership Conf. dedicated to him. Fellow APA (Rsch. award in cons. psychology 1971), Soc. for Indsl./Orgnl. Psychology (Disting. Sci. Contbns. award 1996), Am. Psychol. Soc. (James McKeen Caltell award 1999), Am. Acad. Mgmt. (Disting. Educator award), Internat. Assn. Applied Psychology (Disting. Contrbns. award 2002), Internat. Assn. Applied Psychology (past pres. orgnl. psychology divsn.), Soc. Orgnl. Behavior. Office: Univ Wash Dept Psychology # 351525 Seattle WA 98195-0001 E-mail: fiedler@u.washington.edu.

FIEDLER, JAY, professional football player; b. Dec. 29, 1971; Postgrad in engring. sci., Dartmouth Coll. Quartback Minn. Vikings, 1998—99, Miami Dolphins, 2000—04, New York Jets, 2005—. Mem. bd. dirs. Reach for the Stars Found. Recipient Dick Steinberg Good Guy award. Office: 1000 Fulton Ave Hempstead NY 11550

FIEDLER, JOHN F., automotive executive; b. 1938; B in Chemistry, Kent State U., 1960; M in Bus., MIT, 1979. Joined The Goodyear Tire & Rubber Co., Akron, Ohio, 1964, various positions including pres. Retread Sys. Co. divsn., pres. Kelly Springfield Tire Co. divsn., exec. v.p. N.Am. tire divsn.; pres., COO Borg-Warner Automotive, Inc., Chgo., 1994—, also bd. dirs. Office: Borg Warner 200 S Michigan Ave Chicago IL 60604

FIEDLER, JOSEPH ROBERT, mathematician, educator; b. Dayton, Ohio, Aug. 26, 1948; s. Otto E and Winifred Cochran Fiedler. AB in Math., Harvard U., Cambridge, Mass., 1970; MS in Math., The Ohio State U., 1972, PhD in Math., 1988. Program assoc. Dept. of Math., The Ohio State U., Columbus, 1980—85; asst. prof. Dept. of Math., Calif. State U., Bakersfield, 1989—93, assoc. prof., 1993—99, prof., 1999—. Vis. assoc. prof. math. Ohio State U., 1995; co-dir. math. preparation initiative Calif. State U. Co-author (textbook) Calculus Laboratories with Maple: A Tool, not an Oracle, Calculus: Mathematics and Modeling. Grantee Prin. Investigator, Math. Profl. Devel. Inst., U. of Calif., 1001—, 2002—. Mem.: Am. Math. Assn. of Two Yr. Colls. (referee, amatyc rev. 1988), Assn. for Women in Math., Calif. Math. Coun. of Cmty. Colls., Bakersfield Math. Coun. (interim pres. 2000—02, Tchr. of the Yr. 2002), Calif. Math. Coun., Nat. Coun. Tchrs. Math., Teachers Tchg. with Tech. (coll. short course instr.), Am. Math. Assn. of Two Yr. Colleges, Nat. Coun. of Teachers of Math. (mem. math. tchr. adv. panel 2001—02), Math. Assn. of Am. (chair subcom. on svc. courses 1995—98). Home: 6513 S Half Moon Dr Bakersfield CA 93309 Office: California State University Bakersfield 9001 Stockdale Hwy Bakersfield CA 93311-1099 Office Phone: 661-664-2058. Business E-Mail: jfiedler@csub.edu.

FIEDLER, MARC, lawyer, advocate; b. New Haven, May 4, 1955; s. Ernest and Evelyn (Zimmerman) F. BA, Harvard U., 1978, JD, 1984. Bar: Mass. 1985, U.S. Ct. Appeals (D.C. cir.) 1987, D.C. 1988, U.S. Dist. Ct. D.C. 1988, U.S. Ct. Appeals (4th cir.) 1988, U.S. Supreme Ct. 1988. Law clk. to assoc. judge D.C. Ct. Appeals, Washington, 1984-85; assoc. Koonz, McKenney & Johnson P.C., Washington, 1985-93; ptnr. Koonz, McKenney, Johnson, DePaolis & Lightfoot LLP, Washington, 1994—. Co-founder, chmn. Disability Rights Coun. of Greater Washington; pres. NE Independent Living Program, Lawrence, Mass., 1982-84; v.p. Disability Law Ctr., Boston, 1982-84. Founder, assoc. dir. Mass. Office Handicapped Affairs, Boston, 1979-81. Recipient Lawyer of Yr. award Trial Lawyers Assn., 1989, Trailblazer award DC Cts., 2002, Alfred McKenzie award Washington Lawyers Com. for Civil Rights and Urban Affaris. Mem. ABA, ATLA (co-chmn. Amicus Com. 1996-98), D.C. Bar Assn. (trustee rsch. found. 1992-95, young lawyers sect., civil jury instrn. com. 1988-91), Trial Lawyers Assn. Metro Washington (chmn. Amicus Com. 1987-2001, pres. 2001-02). Office: Koonz McKenney Johnson DePaolis & Lightfoot LLP 2001 Pennsylvania Ave NW Ste 450 Washington DC 20006 E-mail: mfiedler@koonz.com.

FIEDLER, TOM, editor-in-chief; Degree in engring., Merchant Marine Acad.; M in Journalism, Boston U., 1971. Fellow profl. journalism Duke U., 1984—85; polit. editor, columnist, White Ho. corr., war corr. Miami Herald, editl. page editor, 1999—2001, v.p., exec. editor, 2001—. Author: Florida Institute of Government's Almanac of Florida Politics. Recipient Bronze Medallion, Soc. Profl. Journalists, 1988, Pulitzer prize reporting polit. influence extremist group, 1991, Pulitzer prize coverage Hurricane Andrew disaster, 1993. Office: Miami Herald One Herald Plz Miami FL 33132

FIEGELMAN, RICHARD PAUL, sales consultant, freelance writer; b. Phila., Pa., Nov. 5, 1957; s. Marvin Louis and Beverly Jane Fiegelman; m. Ruthann Claudia Brink, Aug. 2, 1992; children: Zachary, Derek, Alexander, Jared. BS in comm., Northeastern U., Boston, Mass., 1980, Lic. Real Estate Pa. Corp. sales cons. Legion Industries, Dallas, Pa., 2000—; land devel., sales Eagle Rock Resort, Valley of Lakes, Pa., 1999—; sales cons. Colo. Prime Foods, Wilkes-Barre, Pa., 1993—99. Author short story, numerous poems; contbr. articles to jours. Vol. Defend Our Watershed, Wyoming Valley, Pa., 2001—, ALS Found., 2002—. Recipient outstanding achievement, Nat. Libr. of Poetry, Maryland, 1995. Home: 19 Country Pine Dallas PA 18612 E-mail: rsiegelman@epix.net.

FIEGER, GEOFFREY NELS, lawyer; b. Detroit, Dec. 23, 1950; s. Bernard Julian and June Beth (Oberer) F.; m. Kathleen Janice Podwoiski, June 25, 1983. BA, U. Mich., 1974, MA, 1976; JD, Detroit Coll. Law, 1979. Bar: Mich. 1979, U.S. Dist. Ct. (ea. dist.) Mich. 1979, Fla. 1980, U.S. Dist. Ct. (mid. dist.) Fla. 1980, Ariz. 1980. Ptnr. Fieger Fieger Kenney & Johnson, P.C., Southfield, Mich., 1979—. V.p. Orgn. United to Save Twp., West Bloomfield, Mich., 1987; dem. nominee for gov. of Mich., 1998. Mem. ABA, Detroit Bar Assn., Assn. Trial Lawyers Am. Unitarian Universalist. Avocations: running, swimming. Office: Fieger Fieger Kenney & Johnson PC 19390 W 10 Mile Rd Southfield MI 48075-2463

FIEL, MAXINE LUCILLE, journalist, behavior analyst, educator; Student in psychology and humanities, NYU. Nat. columnist, contbg. editor Mademoiselle Mag., NYC, 1972—2001; nat. columnist Women's World, Englewood, NJ, 1979-89; contbg. editor Overseas Promotions, NYC, 1979—; articles and features editor Japanese Overseas Press, 1976—; feature editor N.Y. Now, NYC, 1980-91; contbg. editor Woman's World mag., 1979-89, Bella mag., England, 1987-89; nat. columnist First mag. for women, 1989-91; founder Starcast Astrological Svcs., Floral Park, NY, 1993—; columnist Borderland Mag., Japan, 1995—2000, IM Mag., Japan, 1997—2000; pres. GemEssence Co., 2002—. Cons. legal profession jury selection, 1984—; mktg. cons. Imperial Enterprises, Tokyo and Princeton, NJ, 1983—; cons. spokesperson Rowland Co., NYC, 1972-81, Allied Chem. Co., NYC, 1972-75; lectr., cons. Atlanta and Fla. Bar Assns., 1986—; creator Touch Game Parker Bros., Salem, Mass., 1971-76; behavior analyst and comm. advisor multi-nat. bus. corps.; cons. Chesebrough-Ponds, Footwear Coun., Grand Marnier Liquor; founder Starcast Astrological Svcs., 1993; pres. Interglobal Mktg. Co., 1999. Pioneer field of polit. body lang., 1969; author: Lovescopes, 1998, The Little Book of Body Language, 1998; contbr. articles to Wireless News Flash, News Am., LA Times, Newhouse News Svc., Newspaper Enterprise Assocs., King Features, Borderland Mag., Glamour, Redbook, Cosmopolitan, others; adv. bd. mem. Writers Digest Mag., 2002; TV appearances on morning and afternoon shows including A Current Affair, The Regis Philbin Show, Eyewitness News, Cable News Networks, Tonight Show, Today Show, Good Morning Am., Joan Rivers Show, Jenny Jones, Entertainment Tonight, Hard Copy, Inside Edition, BBC Breakfast Show, Good Morning Japan, Fox News Channel, MSNBC, many others; appears in daily segment Good Morning Japan; own daily TV show on Nippon Network, Japan, 1989-2004. Active Sister Cities, Tokyo and NYC; charter mem. Elem. Sch. Cultural Exch., Toyko and NYC, Ctr. Environ. Edn.; bd. dirs. Periwinkle Prodns. Anti-Drug Abuse, NYC, Adirondacks Save-A-Stray. Recipient Achievement award field behavioral sci. and photojournalism, Tokyo, 1974, Outstanding Rsch. award field psychology of gesture, Tokyo, 1976, Outstanding Achievement award Internat. Conf. Soc. Para-Psychology, 1974-75, award for contbn. to Asand Inst. for Humanistic Psychology; honored guest at award dinner for involvement and support in the merging of Eye Rsch. Inst. Boston and Harvard Med. Sch., 1991. Mem. AFTRA, Internat. Found. Behavioral Rsch. (past v.p.), Nat. Writers Assn. (profl.), Profl. Writers Assn., Authors Guild, Authors League, World Wildlife Fund, Whale Protection Fund, Environ. Def. Soc., Nature Conservancy, Greenpeace, People for Ethical Treatment Animals, Humane Assn. U.S., Sea Shepherd Conservation Soc., Defenders of Wildlife, Guiding Eyes for Blind, Braille Camps for Blind Children, Save the Children, Lotos Club (NYC), East End Yacht Club (Freeport, NY). Office: 338 Northern Blvd Ste 3 Great Neck NY 11021-4808 Office Phone: 516-482-3700. E-mail: interglobal@verizon.net.

FIELD, ALEXANDER JAMES, economics professor, dean; b. Boston, Apr. 17, 1949; s. Mark George and Anne (Murray) F.; m. Valerie Nan Wolk, Aug. 8, 1982; children: James Alexander, Emily Elena. AB, Harvard U., 1970; MS, London Sch. Econs., 1971; PhD, U. Calif., Berkeley, 1974. Asst. prof. econs. Stanford (Calif.) U., 1974-82; assoc. prof. Santa Clara (Calif.) U., 1982-88, acad. v.p., 1986-87, prof., chmn. dept. econs., 1988-93, assoc. dean Leavey Sch. Bus. and Adminstrn., 1993-96, dean, 1996-97, Michel and Mary Orradre prof. econs., 1992—. Mem. bd. trustees Santa Clara U., 1988-91. Author: Educational Reform and Manufacturing Development in Mid-Nineteenth Century Massachusetts, 1989, Altruistically Inclined: The Behavioral Sciences, Evolutionary Theory and the Origins of Reciprocity, 2001; assoc. editor: Jour. Econ. Lit., 1981—2004; editor: Rsch. in Econ. History, 1993—; mem. editl. bd.: Explorations in Econ. History, 1993—, Jour. Econ. History, 2001—04; contbr. articles to profl. jours. Recipient Nevins prize Columbia U., 1975; NSF rsch. grantee, 1989. Mem. Econ. History Assn. (exec. dir. 2004—), Phi Beta Kappa, Beta Gamma Sigma. Home: 3762 Redwood Cir Palo Alto CA 94306-4255 Office: Santa Clara Univ Dept Econs Santa Clara CA 95053-0001 Office Phone: 408-554-4348.

FIELD, ANDREA BEAR, lawyer; b. New London, Conn., Nov. 30, 1949; d Geurson Donald and Lorraine (Solomon) Silverberg; m. Thornton Withers Field, May 17, 1984; children: Benjamin, Geoffrey. Student, Wellesley Coll., 1967-69; BA, Yale U., 1971; JD, U. Va., 1974. Bar: Va. 1974, D.C. 1978, U.S. Ct. Appeals (3d, 4th, 5th, 7th, 8th and D.C. cirs.). Assoc. Hunton & Williams LLP, Washington and Richmond, Va., DC, 1974-81, ptnr. Washington, 1991—, mng. ptnr., resources, regulatory & environ. law, and mem. exec. com. Mem. ABA (chair sect. natural resources, energy and environ. law 1989-90, coun. 1984-87, 90-91, chair com. air quality 1982-84, vice chair teleconf. com. 1990—, environ. controls bus. law sect. 1990-91, vice chair com. environ. law, real property, probate and trust law sect. 1990-91; chair standing com. on natural conf. groups 1993-94, nat. conf. lawyers and scientists 1990-93, sect. ad hoc com. nat. insts. 1989-90, coun. sect. sci. and tech. 1991-92), Va. Bar, DC Bar. Office: Hunton & Williams 1900 K St NW Washington DC 20006-1109 Office Phone: 202-955-1558. Office Fax: 202-778-2201. Business E-Mail: afield@hunton.com.

FIELD, ARTHUR NORMAN, lawyer; b. NYC, Sept. 28, 1935; s. Harry and Rose (Lemberg) F.; m. Doris Helen Rabbiner, Sept. 1, 1957; children: Michael, Karen. BBA, CCNY, 1955; LLB, Harvard U., 1958. Bar: (NY) 1959, (Fla.) 1975. Assoc. Shearman & Sterling, NYC, 1959-68, ptnr., 1968-2000; pres. GXG Mgmt., LLC, NYC, 2000—; mem. Field Cons. LLC. Co-author (with Jeffrey M. Smith): Legal Opinions in Business Transactions, 2003; co-editor (with M. Moskin): Transactional Lawyers Deskbook, 2001. Chmn., bd. dirs. Community Action Legal Svcs., 1972-77 (chair 78-79); bd. dirs. Brookdale Found., 1983—, Wave Hill Inc., NYC, 1968-80, Washington Square Legal Svcs., 1979-95, Historic House Trust NY, 2000-; trustee Ramapo Trust, 1983; bd. dirs. Preservation League NY, 2003—; mem. adv. bd. N.E. Bus. Law Ctr. Fellow Am. Bar Found., NY Bar Found., NY County Lawyers Assn. (pres. 1990-92); mem. ABA (ho. of dels. 1990-92, mem. bus. sect. coun. 2004—), NY State Bar Assn. (v.p. 1992-97), Assn. Bar City NY, Am. Law Inst., Assn. of Arbitrators, NYC, (dir. 1998-2002), chair Tribar Opinion Com.1985-90, chair ABA Bus. Sect. Opinion Com. 2002-04). E-mail: anfield@igxg.com.

FIELD, BARRY ELLIOT, internist, gastroenterologist; b. Hartford, Conn., Apr. 21, 1947; s. Arnold and Selma (Nechrich) F.; m. Julie Farr, Jan. 6, 1991; children: Rachel Elizabeth, Hannah Margaret, Miles Jay. BA (scholar), Harvard U., 1968; MD, Albert Einstein Coll. Medicine, 1972. Intern in pediat. Montefiore Hops., Bronx, N.Y., 1972-73; intern in medicine Met. Hosp., N.Y.C., 1973-74, resident in medicine, 1974-76; fellow in gastroenterology Harbor Gen. Hosp., Torrance, Calif., 1976-78; pvt. practice in internal medicine and gastroenterology North Tarrytown, N.Y., 1978—. Dir. medicine Phelps Meml. Hosp., North Tarrytown. Mem. Am. Gastroenterol. Assn., Alpha Omega Alpha. Office: 777 N Broadway Ste 305 Tarrytown NY 10591-1040 Office Phone: 914-366-6120.

FIELD, CAROL HART, writer, news correspondent, journalist; b. San Francisco, Mar. 27, 1940; d. James D. and Ruth (Arnstein) Hart; m. John L. Field, July 23, 1961; children: Matthew, Alison. BA, Wellesley Coll., 1961. Contbg. editor, assoc. editor, asst. editor City Mag., San Francisco, 1974-76; contbg. editor New West/Calif. Mag., San Francisco, L.A., 1975-80, San Francisco Mag., 1980-82; fgn. corr. La Gola, Milan, 1990-94, Il Sole 24 Ore, Milan, 2001—03. Lectr. Smithsonian Inst., Washington, 1991, 95, Schlesinger Libr., Radcliffe Coll., 1995; TV appearances with Lorenza de Medici, 1992, Julia Child, 1995, Mario Batali, 2004; bd. dirs. U. Calif. Press. Author: The Hill Towns of Italy, 1983 (Commonwealth Club award 1984), new edit., 1997, The Italian Baker, 1985 (Internat. Assn. Culinary Profls. award 1986), Celebrating Italy, 1990 (Commonwealth Club award Internat. Assn. Culinary Profls. award 1991), paperback, 1997, Italy in Small Bites, 1993 (James Beard award), new edit., 2004, Focaccia: Simple Breads from the Italian Oven, 1994, In Nonna's Kitchen: Traditional Recipes and Culture from Italian Grandmothers, 1997 (main selection Good Food Club, Book of the Month Club), Mangoes and Quince, 2001, paperback, 2002; mem. editl. bd. Gastronomica; contbr. articles to profl. jours. Lit. jury Commonwealth Club Calif., San Francisco, 1987-88, 92; bd. dirs. Women's Forum West, San Francisco, 1990-92, Bancroft Libr. U. Calif., Berkeley, 1991-97, Headlands Inst., San Francisco, 1992-93; bd. dirs. Mechanics' Inst., San Francisco, 1987-92, pres., 1990-92, Arion Press/Lyra Corp., 1998—; mem. Food Runners, San Francisco, 2000—. Decorated cavaliere Italian Govt., 2004; recipient Internat. Journalism prize Maria Luigia Duchessa di Parma, Italy, 1987, Barbi Colombini prize Tuscany, 1991, Nat. Journalism prize Vanghetto d'Oro, 1997, Gold Medal World Media awards Australia, 1999; named Alumna of Yr. Head Royce Sch, Oakland, Calif., 1991, Honoree of Yr. Bread Bakers Guild of Am., 1999. Mem. Accademia Italia della Cucina, Authors Guild, Les Dames d'Escoffier, Internat. Assn. Culinary Profls., Pen Ctr. USA West, Internat. Women's Forum. Home and Office: 2561 Washington St San Francisco CA 94115-1818

FIELD, DAVID ANTHONY, lawyer; b. N.Y.C., Mar. 25, 1934; s. Arthur N. and Rose F.; m. Ellen J. Hirshon, Apr. 1, 1958; children: Mitchell, Lawrence. BA, Tufts U., 1955; JD, Columbia U., 1958; LLM, NYU, 1965. Bar: N.Y. 1958, U.S. Dist. Ct. (so. and ea. dists.) N.Y., U.S. Tax Ct., U.S. Supreme Ct. Ptnr. Field, Florea & Field, N.Y.C., 1959-62, DiFalco, Field, Lomenzo & Turret, N.Y.C., 1962-78, Field, Lomenzo & Turret, N.Y.C., 1978—. Exec. com. Five Young Dem. Club, Woodmere, N.Y., 1964-66; pres. Hewlett Park Civic Assn., Woodmere, 1963-64. Mem. N.Y. State Trial Lawyers Assn., N.Y.C. Bar Assn. Avocations: golf, boating. Office: Field Lomenzo Turret 205 Lexington Ave Fl 17 New York NY 10016-6070

FIELD, FRANCIS EDWARD, electrical engineer, educator; b. Casper, Wyo., Nov. 20, 1923; s. Jesse Harold and Persis Belle (St. John) F.; m. Margaret Jane O'Bryan, Oct. 13, 1945; children: Gregory A., Christopher B., Sheridan Diane. BSEE, U.S. Naval Acad., 1945; MA in Internat. Affairs, George Washington U., 1965; AMP, Harvard U., 1970. Master cert. graphoanalyst; comml. pilot. Owner Field Lumber Co., Lander, Wyo., 1948-50; commd. ensign U.S. Navy, 1945, advanced through grades to capt., 1966, ret., 1975; rsch. engr. George Washington U., Washington, 1975-90, adj. faculty, 1977-90. Pres. EXTANT, cons. firm, McLean, Va., 1981—; program dir. NSF, Washington, 1982-90. Author: Chronicle of a Workshop, 1977. Trustee Fremont County Mus. Bd., 1998—2003. Mem. Internat. Graphoanalysis Soc. (award of merit 1984), Mayflower Soc., Masons, Sigma Xi. Republican. Home: 280 S 3rd St Lander WY 82520-3109 E-mail: vacquero@bresnan.net.

FIELD, HENRY AUGUSTUS, JR., lawyer; b. Wisconsin Dells, Wis., July 8, 1928; s. Henry A. and Georgia (Coakley) F.; m. Patricia Ann Young, Nov. 30, 1957 (dec. 1980); children: Mary Patricia (dec. 1992), Thomas Gerard, Susan Therese (Mrs. Thomas Hempel); m. Molly Kelly Martin, Apr. 13, 1985. Student, Western Mich. Coll., 1946-47; PhB, Marquette U., 1950; LLB (cum laude), U. Wis., 1952. Bar: Wis. 1952, U.S. Dist. Ct. (we. and ea. dists.) Wis. 1952, U.S. Ct. Appeals (7th cir.) 1957, U.S. Supreme Ct. 1980. Asst. U.S. atty. Western Dist. of Wis., 1956-57; assoc. Roberts, Boardman, Suhr, Bjork & Curry, 1957-62; jr. ptnr. Roberts, Boardman, Suhr & Curry, 1962-70; ptnr. Boardman, Suhr, Curry & Field, Madison, Wis., 1970—, chmn. exec. com., 1985-95; mem. Wis. Jud. Council, 1974-79. Dir. Family Service Soc., 1969-75, treas., 1971-72, pres., 1973-74; trustee Dane County Bar Pro Bono Trust Found., 1995-99. Served with C.I.C., AUS, 1952-55. Fellow: Wis. Bar Found., Am. Bar. Found., Am. Coll. Trial Lawyers (state chmn. 1982—83);

mem.: ABA (Wis. chmn. legis. com. 1975—76), Wis. Law Found. (trustee 2003, treas. 2005), Wis. Bar Assn. (chmn. litigation sect. 1971—72), Milw. and Dane County Bar Assn. (pres. 1971—72), 7th Fed. Cir. Bar Assn., Madison Club, Order of Coif, Sigma Tau Delta, Phi Delta Phi. Republican. Roman Catholic. Home: 3310 Valley Creek Cir Middleton WI 53562-1988 Office: Boardman Suhr Curry & Field 1 S Pinckney St Madison WI 53703-2892 Office Phone: 608-257-9521. Business E-Mail: hfield@boardmanlawfirm.com.

FIELD, JAMES BERNARD, internist, educator; b. Fort Wayne, Ind., May 28, 1926; s. Abraham and Clara (Ridner) F.; m. Dorothy Spivey, Sept. 25, 1954; children: Carolyn, Nancy, Douglas, Susan. Student, Harvard Coll., 1944, student, 1946—47; MD cum laude, Harvard Med. Sch., 1951. Diplomate: Am. Bd. Internal Medicine. Intern internal medicine Mass. Gen. Hosp., Boston, 1951-52, asst. resident internal medicine, 1952-53, resident internal medicine, 1953-54; practice medicine specializing in endocrinology Pitts., 1962-78, Houston, 1978-89. Med. officer USPHS, Nat. Inst. Arthritis and Metabolic Diseases, Bethesda, Md., 1954, sr. asst. surgeon, 1954-58, sr. investigator, 1958-60, surgeon, 1958-60, sr. surgeon, 1960-61; asst. in medicine diabetic dept. Kings Coll. Hosp., London, 1957-58; med. officer Nat. Inst. Metabolic Disease, Bethesda, Md., 1961-62; head divsn. endocrinology and metabolism U. Pitts. Sch. Medicine, 1962-78, assoc. prof. medicine, 1962-66, prof. medicine, 1966-78, dir. clin. research unit, 1962-78; Rutherford prof. medicine Baylor Coll. Medicine, Houston, 1978-89, head div. endocrinology and metabolism, 1978-87; vis. prof. dept. exptl. medicine Univ. Coll. Med. Sch., London, 1985-86; dir. Diabetes and Endocrinology Rsch. Ctr., Baylor Coll Medicine, 1980-89; med. adv. bd. Nat. Pituitary Agy., 1967-69; research collaborator Brookhaven Nat. Lab., 1972-85; mem. nat. diabetes adv. bd. HEW, 1977-85, chmn., 1982-85; mem. endocrinology study sect. USPHS, 1965-69, chmn., 1968-69, endocrinology and metabolism tng. grant com., 1970-74, gen. clin. rsch. ctr. rev. com., 1976-79; mem. panel clin. scis. com. study nat. needs biomed. and behavioral rsch. pers. Nat Rsch. Coun., 1976-80; mem. VA merit rev. com. on endocrinology and metabolism, 1982-85; lectr. medicine Harvard Med. Sch., 1992—; mem. honors com. Harvard Med. Sch., 1993-2001. Editor (assoc. editor): Metabolism, 1959—69; editor: (editor-in-chief), 1969—; editor: (contbg.) Clin.Thyroidology, 1988—2000; contbr. numerous research articles on endocrinology to profl. jours. Bd. dirs. Gen. Clin. Research Centers, 1977-79; mem. Physician Vols. in Medicine, Hilton Head Island, S.C., 2001—. Served with U.S. Army, 1944-45. Decorated Purple Heart, Bronze Star; recipient Van Meter prize award Am. Goiter Assn., 1961, Prize Boylston Soc., 1951. Mem. Assn. Am. Physicians, Endocrine Soc. (mem. coun. 1972-75, internat. liaison com. 1972-75, mem. pub. affairs com. 1972-75, mem. awards com. 1972-75, chmn. 1974-75, nominating com. 1982-84, chmn. 1984), Am. Diabetes Assn. (dir. 1968-74, vice chmn. com. on rsch. 1972-73, chmn. com. rsch. 1975-77, mem. established investigator rev. bd. 1975-77, Eli Lilly award 1958), Am. Fedn. Clin. Rsch., Am. Clin. and Climatol. Assn., Am. Physiology Soc., Am. Soc. Clin. Investigation, Mass. Med. Soc. (chmn. com. on ret. physicians 1993-2002, Prize 1951, Vol. of Yr. 2001), Quechee Lakes Club (Quechee, Vt.), Harvard Med. Alumni Assn., (treas. 1997-2000), Sea Pines Country Club (Hilton Head), Alpha Omega Alpha. Home: 50 Stoney Creek Rd Hilton Head Island SC 29928

FIELD, JOHN LOUIS, architect; b. Mpls., Jan. 18, 1930; s. Harold David and Gladys Ruth (Jacobs) F.; m. Carol Helen Hart, July 23, 1961; children: Matthew Hart, Alison Ellen. BA, Yale U., 1952, MArch, 1955. Individual practice architecture, San Francisco, 1959-68; v.p. firm Bull, Field, Volkmann, Stockwell, Architects, San Francisco, 1968-83; ptnr. Field/Gruzen, Architects, San Francisco, 1983-86, Field Paoli Architects, San Francisco, 1986—. Guest lectr. Stanford, 1970; chmn. archtl. council San Francisco Mus. Art, 1969-71; mem. San Francisco Bay Conservation and Devel. Commn., Design Rev. Bd., 1980-84; founding chmn. San Francisco Bay Architects Review, 1977-80 Co-author, producer, dir.: film Cities for People (Broadcast Media award 1975, Golden Gate award San Francisco Internat. Film Festival 1975, Ohio State award 1976); film The Urban Preserve (Calif. Council AIA Commendation of excellence 1982); co-design architect: design for New Alaska Capital City (winner design competition). Recipient Archtl. Record award, 1961, 1972; AIA, Sunset mag. awards, 1962, 64, 69; No. Calif. AIA awards, 1967, 82; Calif. Council AIA award, 1982; certificate excellence Calif. Gov.'s Design awards, 1966; Homes for Better Living awards, 1962, 66, 69, 71, 77; Albert J. Evers award, 1974, Best Bldg. award Napa (Calif.) C. of C., 1987, Design award Internat. Council Shopping Ctrs., 1988, Stores of Excellence award Nat. Mall Monitor, 1989, 92, 93, Pacific Coast Builders Gold Nugget award, 1989, 91, Urban Design award Calif. Coun. AIA, 1991, 93; Density Myth and Competition winner Boston Soc. Architects, 2003. Fellow AIA (com. on design, Lifetime Achievement award, 2005); mem. Nat. Coun. Archtl. Registration Bds., Urban Land Inst. (Design award 1995), Yale Club, Lambda Alpha. Office: Field Paoli Architects 150 California St 7th Fl San Francisco CA 94111-1315 Office Phone: 415-788-6606. Business E-Mail: jlf@fieldpaoli.com.

FIELD, KATHLEEN COTTRELL, lawyer; b. Honolulu, Dec. 30, 1955; d. Harold Everett Cottrell and Ann (Pappenhagen) Reimann; m. Harold B. Field, June 20, 1981; children: Lydia Elizabeth, Russell Ellsworth. BA, Coll. of Idaho, 1978; JD, U. Wash., 1981, MA, 1982. Bar: Wash. 1982, U.S. Dist. Ct. (we. dist.) Wash. 1984. Dep. prosecutor Snohomish County, Everett, Wash., 1982-88; pvt. practice Lynnwood, Wash., 1988—. Judge pro tem. City of Edmonds, 1989—, City of Lynnwood, 1990—; mem. Nat. Task Force on Juvenile Sexual Offending, Denver, 1987-94; mem. Gov.'s Juvenile Justice Adv. Com., 1987-93; bd. dirs. Columbia Legal Svcs. Bd. dirs. Open Door Theatre, 1984-94, pres., 1988-89; bd. dirs. Wash. Assn. Child Abuse Couns., 1985-91, co-chair advocacy com., 1985-87; bd. dirs. Snohomish County Child Abuse Coun., 1984-87, chair legis. com.; active Snohomish County Children's Commn., 1986-87, Pathways For Women/Snohomish County Legal Svcs., 2001; founder A Better Way Mediation & Arbitration Svcs., Inc., 1996—. Recipient Award for Extraordinary Pro Bono Svc. Hours Snohomish County Legal Svcs., Everett, 1992, Pro Bono Lawyer of Yr. award, 1994, Lawyer of Yr. award Snohomish County Bar Assn., 1999. Mem. Wash. State Bar Assn. (hearings examiner 1998), Wash. Women Lawyers Assn. (Passing the Torch award 1995), Wash. State Trial Lawyers Assn., Soc. Profls. Dispute Resolution. Office: 5800 236th St SW Mountlake Terrace WA 98043-5120 Fax: 425-774-2034. E-mail: abetterwaynow@aol.com.

FIELD, LARRY, paper company executive; b. June 2, 1939; BS, U of Illinois. CEO Field Container, Elk Grove Village, Ill. Named to Chgo. Area Entrepreneurship Hall of Fame. Office: Field Container 1500 Nicholas Blvd Elk Grove Village IL 60007-5575

FIELD, MARGARET M., retired librarian; b. Washington, Sept. 16, 1928; d. Samuel Weis and Catherine Reel (Hawley) Mendum; m. Rodney Wayne Lancaster, Aug. 12, 1950 (div. Jan. 1969); children: Barbara Lynn, Margaret Susan; m. Jack Field, Jan. 26, 1980. BA, U. Wis., 1950; MLS, Rutgers U., 1971. Hazlet br. libr. Monmouth County Libr., Manalapan, NJ, 1971-73, br. libr., Ocean Twp., 1973-79, br. coord., 1980-93, asst. dir., 1993—2002, ret., 2002. Mem. Monmouth Librs. Assn. (pres. 1979-80). Unitarian Universalist. Avocations: medieval times, repair work, sewing, exploring, local history.

FIELD, MARSHALL, retail executive; b. Charlottesville, Va., May 13, 1941; s. Marshall IV and Joanne (Bass) F.; m. Joan Best Connelly, Sept. 5, 1964 (div. 1969); 1 child, Marshall; m. Jamee Beckwith Jacobs, Aug. 19, 1972; children: Jamee Christine, Stephanie Caroline, Abigail Beckwith. BA, Harvard Coll., 1963. With N.Y. Herald Tribune, 1964-65; pub. Chgo. Sun-Times, 1969-80, Chgo. Daily News, 1969-78; dir. Field Enterprises, Inc., Chgo., 1965-84, dir., mem. exec. com., 1965-84, chmn. bd., 1972-84, The Field Corp., 1984—, Cabot, Cabot & Forbes, 1984—, chmn. exec. com., 1985-89, sr. dir., chief exec. officer, 1989—; pub. World Book-Childcraft Internat. Inc., 1973-78, dir., 1965-80. Trustee Art Inst. Chgo., Rush-Presbyn.-St. Lukes Med. Ctr., Chgo. Cmty. Trust; chmn. bd. trustees Chgo. Pub. Libr. Found.; chmn. bd. Terra Mus. Am. Art; chmn. bd. trustees Field Mus. Natural History; adv. bd. Brookfield Zoo; mem. charitable adv. coun. Office of Atty. Gen. of State of Ill.; active Chgo. Orchestral Assn.; mem. bd. visitors, vice chair Nicholas Sch. of the Environment, Duke U.; bd. dirs. First Nat. Bank Chgo., 1970—85, Field Found. Ill., Lincoln Park Zool. Soc.; chmn. Nat. Coun. of the World Wildlife Fund; bd. dirs. Atlantic Salmon Fedn., Openlands Project. Mem. Nature Conservancy, River Club, Chgo. Club, Harvard Club, Racquet Club, Onwentsia Club, Jupiter Island Club, Shore Acres Club. Office: 225 W Wacker Dr Ste 1500 Chicago IL 60606-1235

FIELD, MARTHA AMANDA, law educator; b. Boston, Aug. 20, 1943; d. Donald T. and Adelaide (Anderson) Field; children: Maria Adelaide, Gabriel Hartry, Lucas Anthony. BA in Chinese History, Radcliffe Coll., 1965; JD, U. Chgo., 1968. Bar: DC 1969. Law clk. to Justice Abe Fortas, US Supreme Ct., 1968-69; asst. prof. U. Pa. Law Sch., Phila., 1969—72, prof., 1973—78; prof. law Harvard Law Sch., Cambridge, Mass., 1979—, Langdell prof. law, 1998—. Vis. prof. law Harvard Law Sch., 1978—79. Author: Surrogate Motherhood, 1991; co-author: Equal Treatment for People with Mental Retardation, 2000, Legal Reform in Central America: Dispute Resolution and Property Systems, 2001. Office: Harvard Law Sch 1563 Massachusetts Ave Cambridge MA 02138 Office Phone: 617-495-2962. Office Fax: 617-496-4947. Business E-Mail: mfield@law.harvard.edu.*

FIELD, PATRICIA, apparel designer; Fashion designer. Costume designer (TV series) Crime Story, 1986, L.A. Takedown, 1989, Spin City, 1996—2002, Sex and the City, 1998—2004, Big City Blues, 1999. Recipient Award for Excellence for Costume Design for TV (contemporary), Sex in the City, Costume Designers Guild, 2000, 2004, Emmy Award for Outstanding Costumes for Series, Sex and the City, 2002. Office: Hotel Venus 382 W Broadway New York NY 10012

FIELD, ROBERT EDWARD, lawyer; b. Chgo., Aug. 21, 1945; s. Robert Edward and Florence Elizabeth (Aiken) F.; m. Jenny Lee Hill, Aug. 5, 1967; children: Jennifer Kay, Kimberly Anne, Amanda Brooke. BA, Ill. Wesleyan U., 1967; MA, Northwestern U., 1969, JD, 1973. Bar: Ill. 1973, U.S. Dist. Ct. (no. dist.) Ill. 1974, U.S. Supreme Ct. 1979. Exec. dir. Winnetka (Ill.) Youth Orgn., 1969-73; assoc. Seyfarth, Shaw, Fairweather & Geraldson, Chgo., 1973-79, ptnr., 1979-93, Field & Golan, Chgo., 1993—. Bd. dirs. Gt. Lakes Fin. Resources, Matteson, Ill., 1983—, vice chmn., 1988-91, chmn. 1991—; bd. dirs. Gt. Lakes Trust Co., 2001--, chmn., 2001--; bd. dirs. Chgo. chpt. Ill. Wesleyan U. Assocs., Great Lakes Ins. Svcs., Alsip, Ill., 2001--; chmn. bd. dirs. 1st Nat. Bank of Blue Island, 1989-2001, Great Lake Bank, 2001—, Bank of Homewood, 1988-2001; bd. dirs. Winchester Mfg. Co., Wood Dale, Ill., Ludell Mfg. Co., Milw., Comml. Resources Corp., Naperville, Ill., 1984-93; dir., sec. Ellis Corp., Itasca, Ill., 1980—; chmn. bd. dirs. Cmty. Bank of Homewood-Flossmoor, Ill., 1983-92, Bank of Matteson, Ill., 1992-99; bd. dirs. Grand Prairie Svcs., Inc., 1999--, sec., 2001--; mem. State Banking Bd. Ill., 1993-97. Bd. dirs. Ctr. for New Beginnings, 1997—, Svcs. Exch., 1998—, Family Svc. Ctrs. Cook County, Matteson, 1979-99, treas., 1981-82, pres., 1986-88, chmn., 1988-93; pres. Lakes of Olympia Condominium Assn., 1987-89; trustee Village of Olympia Fields, Ill., 1981-89, pres., 1991-97; trustee Ill. Wesleyan U., 1990—, treas., 1994—; bd. dirs. Northwestern U. Sch. Law Alumni Assn., 1990-94. Mem. ABA, Ill. Bar Assn., Am. Bankers Assn., Ill. Bankers Assn., United Meth. Bar Assn. (v.p. Chgo. chpt. 1989), Chgo. Bar Assn., Bankers Club Chgo., Union League Club Chgo., Calumet Country Club. Office: Field & Golan Ste 1500 3 1st National Plz Chicago IL 60602 Office Phone: 312-263-2300. Business E-Mail: refield@fieldgolan.com.

FIELD, ROBERT W., epidemiologist, health physicist, educator; b. Lancaster, Pa., Jan. 31, 1954; BS in Biology, Millersville (Pa.) U., 1977, MS in Biology, 1985; PhD, U. Iowa, 1994. Health physicist U. Calif., Berkeley, 1983—87; assoc. prof. U. Iowa, Coll. Pub. Health, Iowa City, 1994—. Cons., Iowa City, 1987—94. Editor numerous scientific journals; contbr. articles to profl. jours. Grantee, Nat. Cancer Inst., Nat. Inst. Environ. Health Sci., EPA. Office: Dept Epidemiology 104 IREH Univ Iowa Iowa City IA 52242 E-mail: bill-field@uiowa.edu.

FIELD, ROBERT WARREN, chemistry professor; b. Wilmington, Del., June 13, 1944; s. Edmund Kay Huebsch (Field). AB, Amherst Coll., 1965, DSc (hon.), 1997; MA, Harvard U., 1971, PhD, 1972. Adj. asst. prof. chemistry U. Calif.-Santa Barbara, 1974; asst. prof. chemistry M.I.T., Cambridge, 1974-78, assoc. prof. phys. chemistry, 1978-82, prof., 1982—, Haslam and Dewey prof. chemistry, 1998—. Mem. editorial bd. Jour. Molecular Spectroscopy, contbr. articles to profl. jours. Alfred P. Sloan fellow, 1975-77. Fellow AAAS, Am. Acad. Arts and Scis., Am. Phys. Soc. (H.P. Broida prize 1980, E.K. Plyler prize 1988), Optical Soc. Am. (E. Lippincott award 1990, W. Meggers award, 1996); mem. Am. Chem. Soc. (Nobel Laureate Signature award to Y. Chen, co-preceptor with J.L. Kinsey 1990). Office: MIT Dept Chemistry Rm 6-219 Cambridge MA 02139 E-mail: rwfield@mit.edu.

FIELD, SALLY MARGARET, actress; b. Pasadena, Calif., Nov. 6, 1946; m. Steve Craig, Sept. 1968 (div. 1975); children: Peter, Eli; m. Alan Greisman, Dec. 1984 (div. 1994); 1 son, Samuel. Student, Actor's Studio, 1973-75. Starred in TV series Gidget, 1965, The Flying Nun, 1967-70, The Girl With Something Extra, 1973, The Court, 2002; film appearances include The Way West, 1967, Stay Hungry, 1976, Heroes, 1977, Smokey and the Bandit, 1977, Hooper, 1978, The End, 1978, Norma Rae, 1979 (Cannes Film Festival Best Actress award 1979, Acad. award 1980), Beyond the Poseidon Adventure, 1979, Smokey and the Bandit II, 1980, Back Roads, 1981, Absence of Malice, 1981, Kiss Me Goodbye, 1982, Places in the Heart, 1984 (Acad. award for best actress 1984), Murphy's Romance (also exec. producer), 1985, Surrender, 1987, Punchline, 1987 (also prodr.), Steel Magnolias, 1989, Soapdish, 1991, Not Without My Daughter, 1991, Homeward Bound: The Incredible Journey, 1993 (voice), Mrs. Doubtfire, 1993, Forrest Gump, 1994, Homeward Bound II: Lost in San Francisco, 1996 (voice)(also prodr.), Eye for an Eye, 1996 (also prodr.), Where the Heart Is, 2000, Say It Isn't So, 2001, Legally Blonde 2: Red, White & Blonde, 2003; TV movies include Maybe I'll Come Home In the Spring, 1971, Marriage: Year One, 1971, Home for the Holidays, 1972, Bridger, 1976, Sybil, 1976 (Emmy award 1977), All the Way Home, 1981, Merry Christmas George Bailey, 1997 (also prodr.), A Cooler Climate, 1999 (also prodr.), David Copperfield, 2000; TV mini series David Copperfield, 1986, A Women of Independent Means, 1995 (also exec. prodr.), From the Earth to the Moon, 1998 (also dir.); exec. prodr. The Christmas Tree, 1996 (also writer, dir.), The Lost Children of Berlin, 1997; prodr. Dying Young, 1991; dir. Beautiful, 2000; guest appearances include The Hollywood Squares, 1966, Rowan & Martin's Laugh-In, 1968, Carol Burnett & Co., 1979, Saturday Night Live, 1993, King of Hill (voice), 1997, Murphy Brown, 1998, ER, 2000-2003 (several episodes), and several others.*

FIELD, STEVEN PHILIP, medical educator; b. Newark, Feb. 21, 1951; s. Irving and Florence (Engel) F. BA, Yale U., 1973; MD, NYU, 1977, cert. in Bioethics and Med. Humanities, 2003. Diplomate Am. Bd. Internal Medicine, Am. Bd. Gastroenterology; cert. psychodynamic psychotherapy NYU Psychoanalytic Inst., Bioethics, Montefiore, NYU. Intern in internal medicine Bellevue Hosp., N.Y.C., 1977-78, resident in internal medicine, 1978-81; instr. in medicine Mt. Sinai Hosp., N.Y.C., 1981-83, NYU Sch. of Medicine, N.Y.C., 1983—, clin. asst. prof. medicine, 1991—. Contbr. articles to med. jours., chpts. to med. textbooks. Recipient John Addison Porter Prize Yale U., 1973. Mem.: ACP, Crohn's and Colitis Found. Am. (sci. adv. coun.), N.Y. State Med. Soc., N.Y. Acad. Gastroenterology (v.p. 1995—96), Am. Gastroent. Assn., Yale Club Ctrl. N.J. (alumni schs. com.), Alpha Omega Alpha. Office: 245 E 35th St New York NY 10016-4283 Office Phone: 212-686-9477.

FIELD, TED (FREDERICK FIELD), film and record industry executive; b. Chgo. s. Marshall Field IV and Katherine W. Fanning; 8 children. Student, U. Chgo., Pomona Coll. Former race car driver; chmn., CEO Radar Pictures, 2002—; chmn. Artistdirect, Inc.; chmn., CEO Artistdirect Recs.; founder Interscope Communications, Interscope Records; former co-owner Field Enterprises, Chgo.; owner Panavision, 1985-87. Co-prodr. (films) Critical Condition, 1987, Outrageous Fortune, 1987, Three Men and a Baby, 1987, Revenge of the Nerds II, 1987, Cocktail, 1988, The Seventh Sign, 1988, An Innocent Man, 1989; co-exec. prodr. (films) Bill and Ted's Excellent Adventure, 1989, Renegades, 1989; prodr. Revenge of the Nerds, 1984, Turk 182, 1985, Three Men and a Little Lady, Class Action, Jumanji, 1995, Mr. Holland's Opus, 1996, Runaway Bride, 1999; exec. prodr. The First Power, 1990, Bird on a Wire, 1990, The Hand That Rocks the Cradle, 1992, What Dreams May Come, 1998, Very Bad Things, 1998, Pitch Black, 2000, Texas Chainsaw Massacre, 2003, The Last Samurai, 2003, Le Divorce, 2003, The Amityville Horror, 2005; co-exec. prodr. (TV films) The Father Clements Story, Everybody's Baby: The Rescue of Jessica McClure, A Mother's Courage. Avocations: chess, martial arts. Office: Radar Pictures 10900 Wilshire Blvd Ste 1400 Los Angeles CA 90024-6532

FIELDEN, C. FRANKLIN, III, academic administrator, consultant; b. Gulfport, Miss., Aug. 4, 1946; s. C. Franklin and Georgia (Freeman) F.; children: Christopher Michaux (dec.), Robert Michaux, Jonathan Dutton. Student, Claremont Men's Coll., 1964-65; AB, Colo. Coll., 1970; MS, George Peabody Coll. Tchrs., 1976, EdS, 1979. Tutor Proyecto El Guacio, San Sebastian, P.R., 1967-68; asst. tchr. GET-SET Project, Colorado Springs, Colo., 1969-70, co-tchr., 1970-75, asst. dir., 1972-75; tutor Early Childhood Edn. Project, Nashville, 1975-76; pub. policy intern Donner-Belmont Child Care Ctr., Nashville, 1976—77; asst. to urban min. Nashville Presbytery, 1977; intern to prin. Steele Elem. Sch., Colorado Springs, 1977-78, tchr., 1978-86; resource person Office Gifted and Talented Edn. Colorado Springs Pub. Schs., 1986-87; tchr. Columbia Elem. Sch., Colorado Springs, 1987-92; tchr., pre-sch. team coord. Helen Hunt Elem. Sch., Colorado Springs, 1992-93; validator Nat. Acad. Early Childhood Programs, 1992—, mentor, 1994—, commr., 1996-2000, 2001—; cons. Colo. Dept. Edn., Denver, 1993—96, sr. cons., 1996—2001, state coord. Even Start Family Literacy Program, 1997—, prin. cons., 2001—. Lectr. Arapahoe C.C., Littleton, Colo., 1981-82; instr. Met. State Coll., Denver, 1981; cons. Jubail Human Resources Devel. Inst., Saudi Arabia, 1982; mem. governing bd. GET-SET Project, 1969-79, 91-93. Mem. ad hoc bd. trustees Tenn. United Meth. Agy. on Children and Youth, 1976-77; mem. So. Regional Edn. Bd. Task Force on Parent-Caregiver Relationships, 1976-77; day care com. Colo. Commn. Children and Their Families, 1981-82; active Nashville Children's Issues Task Force, 1976-77, Tenn. United Meth. Task Force on Children and Youth, 1976-77, Citizens' Goals Leadership Tng., 1986-87, Child Abuse Task Force, 4th Jud. Dist., 1986-87, FIRST IMPRESSIONS (Colo. Govs. Early Childhood Initiative) Task Force, 1987-88, El Paso County Placement Alternatives Commn., 1990-96, White Ho. Summit on Early Childhood Cognitive Devel., 2001; proposal rev. team Colo. Dept. Edn., 1992—; co-chair City/County Child Care Task Force, 1991-92; charter mem. City/County Early Childhood Care and Edn. Commn., 1993-96; bd. dirs. Colo. Office of Resource and Referral Agys., 1996-99; appeals panel Divsn. Child Care, Colo. Dept. Human Svcs., 2002—; bd. dirs. Colo. Parents as Tchrs., 2004—. Recipient Arts/Bus./Edn. award, 1983, Innovative Tchg. award, 1984; fellow NIMH, 1976-77. Mem.: ASCD, Pikes Peak Assn. Edn. Young Children, Nat. Assn. Early Childhood Specialists in State Depts. of Edn. (v.p. 1997—99, pres. 1999—2001, past. pres. 2001—03), Colo. Assn. Edn. Young Children (legis. com. 1979—84, governing bd., sec., exec. com. 1980—84, rsch. conf. chmn. 1982, tuition awards com. 1983—86, governing bd. 1985—86, chmn. tuition awards com. 1985—86, governing bd. 1989—95, pub. policy com. 1989—96, exec. com., treas. 1993, primary grades conf. chmn. 1994), Nat. Assn. Edn. Young Children (founding mem. primary-grades caucus 1992—2001, co-chair Western States Leadership Network 1993, Membership Action Group grantee 1993, panel profl. ethics in early childhood edn. 1993—97, nominating panel 2000—02, co-facilitator primary-grades interest forum 2001—05), Nat. Trust Hist. Preservation, Huguenot Soc. Gt. Britain and Ireland., Phi Delta Kappa. Presbyterian. Home: PO Box 7766 Colorado Springs CO 80933-7766 Office: 201 E Colfax Ave Denver CO 80203-1704

FIELDER, CHARLES ROBERT, retired oil industry executive; b. Lubbock, Tex., Mar. 9, 1943; s. Clarence Daniel and Ola Marie (Sewell) F.; m. Mary Ruth Wills, May 31, 1964; 1 child, Sara Elizabeth. BBA, Tex. Tech. U., 1965, MS in Acctg., 1972. C.P.A., Tex. Staff acct. Peat, Marwick, Mitchell & Co., Dallas, 1965-66, Arthur Andersen & Co., Dallas, 1968-69; treasury acct. Halliburton Co., Dallas, 1969-71, treasury supr., 1971-72, asst. treas., 1972-78, treas., 1978-89, v.p., treas., 1990-96; ret., 1997. Mem. AICPA, Fin. Execs. Inst., Tex. Soc. CPAs, Phi Eta Sigma, Beta Alpha Psi, Beta Gamma Sigma, Phi Kappa Phi. Republican. Mem. Ch. of Christ. Office: PMB 189 6757 Arapaho Rd Ste 711 Dallas TX 75248-4073

FIELDING, ALLEN FRED, oral and maxillofacial surgeon, educator; b. Paterson, N.J., Jan. 22, 1943; s. Fred W. and Emily Claire (Boehm) F. BS, Fairleigh Dickinson U., 1959, DMD, 1963; postgrad. in oral surgery, N.Y. U., 1965-66; MD, U. Health Sci. Antigua, 2001; MBA, U. Phoenix, 2003. Diplomate Am. Bd. Oral and Maxillofacial Surgery (adv. bd. 1983-86), Am. Bd. Forensic Medicine, Dental Nat. Anesthesia Bd. Intern in oral surgery Roosevelt Hosp., N.Y.C., 1966-67; resident in oral surgery Phila. Gen. Hosp., 1967-69; practice dentistry specializing in oral-maxillo facial surgery Phila., 1969—; prof., chmn. dept. oral and maxillofacial surgery Temple U., Phila., 1983-88, staff prof., chief dept. oral and maxillofacial surgery univ. hosp., 1982-87. Cons. VA Hosp., Wilmington, Del.; staff St. Christopher's Hosp. for Children, Phila., Northeatern Hosp.; staff, chief divsn. oral and Maxillofacial surgery Epics. Hosp.; sect. chief oral and maxillofacial surgery Quakertown (Pa.) Hosp., Lawndale Hosp., Phila.; cons. Gt. Lakes Naval Hosp., Ill., Brandywine Hosp.; lectr. in field. Contbr. articles to profl. jours. Mem. Chapel of Four Chaplains, Valley Forge, Pa.; amb. People To People, 2004. Served to capt. USAF, 1963-65. Fellow Am. Dental Soc. Anesthesiology, Royal Soc. Health, Am. Soc. Oral and Maxillofacial Surgeons (Pa. del.), World Affairs Coun. (Phila. chpt.), Am. Coll. Dentistry (editor local chpt.), Internat. Coll. Dentists, Internat. Assn. Oral and Maxillofacial Surgeons, Am. Assn. Oral and Maxillofacial Surgeons, Am. Coll. Oral and Maxillofacial Surgeons, Internat. Assn. Oral Maxillofacial Surgery; mem. AAUP, ADA, Pa. Dental Soc., Phila. County Dental Soc. (bd. govs.), Assn. Mil. Surgeons, Am. Assn. Dental Schs., Del. Valley Soc. Oral Surgeons (com. resident tng. 1973-85, exec. com., pres. 1985), Am. Assn. Hosp. Dentists (sec.-treas. Del. County chpt. 1972-74, v.p. 1974, pres. 1976), Great Lakes Soc. Oral Maxillofacial Surgeons, Mid-Atlantic Soc. Oral Maxillofacial Surgeons, Temple U. Oral Surgery Honor Soc. (advisor), Pa. Soc. Oral and Maxillofacial Surgeons (exec. com., govt. affairs com., pres. 1995-96), Coll. Physicians and Surgeons Phila., Dental Assts. Nat. Bd. (adv. bd.), Internat. Assn. Oral Implantologists, Del. Valley Acad. Osseointegration, Pierre Fauchard Soc. (elected mem.), Omicron Kappa Upsilon (pres. 1985, Temple chpt.). Home: 1203 Rodman St Philadelphia PA 19147-1129 Office: Temple Univ Hospital 3223 N Broad St Philadelphia PA 19140-5007 also: County Line Med Ctr Lincoln Hwy Gap PA 17527 Office Phone: 717-442-9537.

FIELDING, FRED FISHER, lawyer; b. Phila., Mar. 21, 1939; s. Fred P. and Ruth Marie (Fisher) F.; m. J. Maria Dugger, Oct. 21, 1967; children: Adam Garrett, Alexandra Caroline. AB, Gettysburg Coll., 1961; LL.B, JD, U. Va., 1964; LittD (hon.), U. Detroit, 1986; LLD (hon.), Pepperdine U., 1986, Mich. State U., 1986. Bar: Pa. 1965, D.C. 1974. Assoc. Morgan, Lewis & Bockius, Phila., 1964-65, 67-70, ptnr. Washington, 1974-81; asst. counsel to Pres. of U.S. The White House, Washington, 1970-72, dep. counsel, 1972-74, counsel to Pres. of U.S., 1981-86; sr. ptnr., corp. svcs., govt. affairs, crisis mgmt./white collar litig. Wiley, Rein & Fielding LLP, Washington, 1986—; pres. Gilmore Broadcasting Corp., 1988-90. Mem. Jud. Conf. D.C. Cir. Ct., 1976—; internat. adv. bd. Credit Internat. Bank, 1990-96; bd. dirs. Gilmore Broadcasting Corp., Coun. for Excellence in Govt.; spl. counsel Adminstrv. Conf. U.S., 1982-86, pub. mem., 1987-94, chmn. spl. com. on ethics in govt., 1988-92, com. on regulation, 1992-94; presdl. appointment to panel arbitrators Internat. Ctr. for Settlement Investment Disputes, 1987-95, 2002—; CPR panel Disting. Neutrals, 2000—: standing com. Fed. Judiciary ABA, 1996-2002; bd. dirs., vchmn. Nat. Legal Ctr. for Pub. Interest, 2002—; clearance counsel Bush-Cheney transition team, 2000-2001; commr., The Nat. Commn. on Terrorist Attacks Upon the U.S.(The 9-11 Commn.), 2002-04. Mem. Commn. on White House Fellowships, 1981-86, Pres.'s Commn. for German-

Am. Tricentennial, 1983-84; presdl. del. to observe Philippine presdl. elections, 1986, pres.'s personal rep. Australia/Am. Friendship Week, 1986; spl. counsel to Rep. vice presdl. campaign, 1988, sr. legal advisor Bush-Quayle campaign, 1992; conflict-of-interest counsel Office of Pres.-Elect, 1980; gen. counsel 50th presdl. inaugural, 1984-85; dep. dir. presdl. transition, 1988-89; mem. Pres.'s Commn. on Fed. Ethics Law Reform, 1989; U.S. designated arbitrator Arbitration Tribunal on U.S.-U.K. Air Treaty Dispute, 1989-94, Sec. of Transp. Task Force on Air Disaster Victims, 1996-98; bd. vis. Sch. Law Pepperdine U., 1989-92; bd. dirs. Coun. for Excellence in Govt., 1989-95, Pediat. AIDS Found., 1998-2002; bd. fellows Gettysburg Coll., 1992—, trustee; bd. dirs. USAir Shuttle, 1992-97, Ethics Resource Ctr., 1993; sec.-treas., bd. dirs. Arlington Va. Hosp. Found., 1994—; mem. commn. on selection fed. judges U. Va. Miller Ctr., 1994-97; bd. dirs. Washington Scholarship Fund, 1994-97, Ctr. Democracy, 1995-98, vice-chmn. 1996-97, chmn., 1997. Capt. AUS, 1965-67. John McKee Found. fellow; recipient Gettysburg Coll. Disting. Alumni award, 1982; named Lawyer of Yr. Bar Assn. DC, 2004. Fellow ABA (life, standing com. on fed. judiciary CEELI), FBA, DC Bar Assn. (bd. govs. 1996-98), Pa. Bar Assn., Am. Arbitration Assn. (nat. panel, bd. dirs.), Law Initiative, Lawyers Club of Washington, Beachview Country Club, Washington Golf and Country Club, Met. Club, Phi Gamma Delta (Disting. Fiji 1987), Pi Delta Epsilon, Omicron Delta Kappa, Pi Lambda Sigma, Phi Delta Phi. Republican. Lutheran. Home: 1602 Maddux Ln Mc Lean VA 22101 Office: Wiley Rein & Fielding LLP 1776 K St NW Washington DC 20006-2304 Office Phone: 202-719-7320. E-mail: ffielding@wrf.com.

FIELDING, HELEN, writer; b. Yorkshire, Eng., Feb. 19, 1958; BA English, St. Anne's Coll., U. Oxford, Eng., 1979. Prodr. BBC-TV, England, 1979—89; freelance writer, 1989—; former columnist The Daily Telegraph; columnist The Independent of London, 2005—. Columnist London Ind., 1995—. Author: (novels) Cause Celeb, 1995, Bridget Jones's Diary, 1996, Bridget Jones: The Edge of Reason, 1999, Bridget Jones's Guide to Life, 2001, Olivia Joules and the Overactive Imagination, 2004; exec. prodr., screenwriter: (films) Bridget Jones's Diary, 2001 (London Critics Circle Film award for best screenwriter, 2002, Evening Standard British Film award for best screenplay, 2002); Bridget Jones: The Edge of Reason, 2004. Avocations: hiking, swimming, reading, movies. Office: c/o Viking Publicity 375 Hudson St New York NY 10014*

FIELDING, JONATHAN EVAN, pediatrician; b. Oct. 4, 1942; BA, Williams Coll., 1964; MA, MD, Harvard Coll., 1969, MPH, 1971; MBA, U. Pa., 1977. Diplomate Am. Bd. Pediats., Am. Bd. Preventive Medicine. Josiah Macy fellow Harvard U., Cambridge, Mass., 1969; intern, resident Boston Children's Hosp., 1969-71; fellow Harvard U., Boston, 1971; resident in pediats. Georgetown U. Med. Ctr., Washington, 1971-72, prin. med. svcs. nat. officer Job Corps, 1971-73; commr. pub. health Commonwealth of Mass., 1975-79; prof. health svcs. & pediats. UCLA, 1979—; dir. pub. health L.A. County, 1997—. Spl. asst. to dir. Bur. Cmty. Health Svcs. Health Svcs. & Mental Health Adminstrn. HEW, 1971-73; co-dir. Ctr. Health Enhancement Edn. & Rsch., 1979-84; co-dir. Ctr. for Healthier Children, Families & Cmtys., 1995—; lectr. Harvard U., Boston, 1973-75, Boston U., 1975-79, Brandeis U., 1975-79, Northwestern U., 1975-79; vis. lectr. UCLA, 1977; rsch. assoc. Urban Rsch. Ctr. Hunter Coll. CUNY, 1978; vis. prof. Nordic Sch. Pub. Health, Sweden, 1980, 83, 93. Editor: Ann. Revs. Pub. Health, 1995—; asst. editor Mercy-Rosenau Pub. Health and Preventive Medicine 1992-98, 14th edit. Vice-chair Partnership for Prevention, 1997—; chmn. U.S. Cmty. Preventive Svcs. Task Force, 2001—. Fellow Assn. Health Svcs.; mem. NAS Inst. Medicine, Am. Acad. Pediats., Am. Assn. Pub. Health Physicians, Am. Med. Peer Rev. Assn., Am. Pub. Health Assn., Assn. Health Svcs. Medicine, Am. Heart Assn., Am. Coll. Preventive Medicine (pres. 1997-99). Office: UCLA Sch Pub Health Ctr Health Sci 61 253A Los Angeles CA 90095-0001

FIELDING, PEGGY LOU MOSS, writer; b. Davenport, Okla., Oct. 28, 1928; d. John Richard and Hazel (Matlock) Moss; B.S., Central State U., 1949, M.A., U. Santo Tomás, 1971. Tchr. various U.S. govt. overseas schs., Japan, Cuba and Philippines, 1955-71; owner Partners in Pub., Tulsa, 1975—; instr. writing Tulsa C.C., 1976— . Mem. Okla. Writers Fedn., NE Okla. Romance Writers, Tulsa Night Writers Club, Romance Writers Am. Democrat. Baptist. Office: PO Box 50347 Tulsa OK 74150-0347

FIELDING, STUART, psychopharmacologist; b. Bronx, N.Y., Oct. 31, 1939; s. Harry and Ethel (Weisberg) Feinblatt; m. Maralyn J. Lowy, Aug. 26, 1962; children: Kimberly Ellen, Bradford Scott. BA, Monmouth Coll., 1962; MS, Howard U., 1964; PhD, U. Del., 1968. Mgr. psychopharmacology rsch. Ciba-Geigy Corp., Summit, N.J., 1967-75; assoc. dir. pharmacology Hoechst-Roussel Pharms., Inc., Somerville, N.J., 1975-76, assoc. dir. biol. sci., mgr. pharmacology, 1977-84, dir. pharmacology, 1984-86, dir. biol. rsch., 1987-89; v.p. R & D, dir. Interneuron Pharms., Inc., Lexington, Mass., 1989-92; chmn., CEO Bio-Enhancement Systems Corp., Morris Plaines, N.J., 1992—. Editor: (book) Psychopharmacology of Clonidine, 1981, (book series) Industrial Pharmacology: A Monograph Series, 1974-79, (jour.) Drug Devel. Rsch., 1980-92; contbr. articles to profl. publs. Fellow Am. Psychol. Assn.; mem. Am. Chem. Soc., Am. Soc. Pharmacology and Exptl. Therapeutics, Soc. Neurosci. Home and Office: 16 Bromleigh Way Morris Plains NJ 07950-1642 Office Phone: 973-292-3492.

FIELDS, ANTHONY LINDSAY AUSTIN, health facility administrator, oncologist, educator; b. St. Michael, Barbados, Oct. 21, 1943; arrived in Can., 1968; s. Vernon Bruce and Marjorie F.; m. Patricia Jane Stewart, Aug. 5, 1967. MA, U. Cambridge, 1969; MD, U. Alta., 1974. Diplomate Am. Bd. Internal Medicine. Sr. specialist Cross Cancer Inst., Edmonton, Alta., Can., 1980-85, dir. dept. medicine, 1985-88, dir., 1988-2000; v.p. med. affairs and cmty. oncology Alta. Cancer Bd., 2000—. Asst. prof. medicine U. Alta., Edmonton, 1980-84, assoc. prof., 1984-98, prof., 1998—, dir. divsn. med. oncology, 1985-89, dir. divsn. oncology, 1988-93; v.p. Nat. Cancer Inst. Can., 2000-02, pres., 2002-04. Fellow ACP, Royal Coll. Physicians and Surgeons Can. (specialist cert. med. oncology, internal medicine); mem. Can. Assn. Med. Oncologists (pres. 1994-96), Am. Soc. Clin. Oncology, Am. Fedn. Clin. Rsch., Can. Soc. for Clin. Investigation, Can. Med. Assn. Avocation: photography. Office: # 1220 10405 Jasper Ave Edmonton AB Canada T5J 3N4

FIELDS, BARRY E., lawyer; b. Feb. 6, 1966; BA in chem., Bellarmine Coll., 1988; JD, U. Chgo., 1991. Bar: Ill. 1991. Law clk. U.S. Dist. Ct. Appeals Sixth Cir.; ptnr., pro bono Kirkland & Ellis LLP, Chgo. Mem.: Rules Adv. Com. U.S. Dist. Ct. N. Dist. Ill., ABA. Office: Kirkland & Ellis LLp 200E Randloph Dr Chicago IL 6006I Home: 506 Thatcher Ave River Forest IL 60305 Office Phone: 312-861-2081. Office Fax: 312-861-2200. Business E-Mail: bfields@kirkland.com.

FIELDS, BERTRAM HARRIS, lawyer; b. LA, Mar. 31, 1929; s. H. Maxwell Fields and Mildred Arlyn (Ruben); m. Lydia Ellen Minevitch, Oct. 22, 1960 (dec. Sept. 1986); 1 child, James Eldar; m. Barbara Guggenheim, Feb. 21, 1991. BA, UCLA, 1949; JD magna cum laude, Harvard U., 1952. Bar: Calif. 1953. Practiced in, LA, 1955—; assoc. firm Shearer, Fields, Rohner & Shearer, and predecessor firms, 1955—57, mem. firm, 1957—82; ptnr. Greenberg, Glusker, Fields, Claman, Machtinger and Kinsella, 1982—. Mem. edit. bd.: Harvard Law Rev., 1953—55; author (as D. Kincaid): The Sunset Bomber, 1986; author: The Lawyer's Tale, 1992; author: (as B. Fields) Royal Blood Richard III and the Mystery of the Princess, 1998, Players-The Shakespeare Mystery, 2005. 1st lt. USAF, 1953—55, Korea. Mem.: ABA, Coun. Fgn. Rels., LA County Bar Assn. Achievements include being the subject of profiles Calif. Mag., Nov. 1987; Avenue Mag., Mar. 1989; Am. Film Mag., Dec. 1989; Vanity Fair Mag., Dec. 1993; Harvard Law Sch. Bull., spring 1998; London Sunday Telegraph, June 1999; Sunday New York Post, July 1999; W Mag., Apr. 2002; L.A. Times, Apr. 2003; London Sunday Times, Apr. 2003; NY Times, May 2005. Office: Greenberg Glusker Fields Claman Machtinger & Kinsella Ste 2000 1900 Avenue Of The Stars Los Angeles CA 90067-4590 Business E-Mail: bfields@ggfirm.com.

FIELDS, DOUGLAS PHILIP, building supply wholesale company executive; b. Jersey City, May 19, 1942; s. M. Emanuel and Priscilla (Wagner) F.; m. Paulette Susan Titko, Dec. 15, 1970 (div. Feb. 1990); children: Douglas Philip, Priscilla Wagner, Jessica Elizabeth; m. Maureen Virginia Hanmer, June 12, 1993; 1 child, Jacob Wagner. BS summa cum laude, Fordham U., 1964; MBA with distinction, Harvard U., 1966. Investment analyst Lehman Bros., N.Y.C., 1966-67; asst. to pres. Talley Industries Inc., Mesa, Ariz., 1967-69; CEO, pres. TDA Industries Inc., N.Y.C., 1969—; founder Unimet Corp., N.Y.C., 1970-73; pres., chmn. Westcalind Corp., R.I., 1971-87; CEO Acqueren, Inc., 1995-98. Chmn. bd. TDA Industries, Inc., N.Y.C., 1970—, Westco Corp., Boston, 1970—79, Cooper Flooring Internat., Inc., Miami, 1972—98; chmn. bd. dirs., CEO Eagle Supply, Inc., Tampa, Fla., 1973—2004; CEO JEH/Eagle Supply, Inc., Dallas, 1997—2004; CEO, chmn. MSI/Eagle Supply Inc., Dallas, 1998—2000, Eagle Supply Group, Inc. (NASDAQ:EEGL), N.Y.C., 1996—2004; chmn. Northeastern Plastics, Inc., NY, 1986—98; cons. U.S. Office Edn., 1973—74, Fed. Energy Adminstrn., 1974—75. Outside dir. NYU Grad. Sch. Bus., Mgmt. Decision Lab., 1973-78; mem. N.Y. State adv. com. U.S. Civil Rights Commn., 1974-85; bd. dirs. YMHA-YWHA of So. Westchester, Mt. Vernon, N.Y., 1981-92, Associated YMHA-YWHA of N.Y.C., Inc., 1989-91; mem. Young Pres.'s Orgn., 1973-92; road commr. Deer Park Assn., Greenwich, Conn., 2001-04, pres., 2005—. Mem. Chief Execs. Orgn., Met. Pres. Orgn., World Pres. Orgn., Deer Park Assn. (rd. commr. 2001-04, pres. 2005-), Belle Haven Club, Midtown Tennis Club (pres. 1969—). E-mail: dpfeagle@msn.com.

FIELDS, HENRY MICHAEL, lawyer; b. N.Y.C., Feb. 11, 1946; s. Jack and Sylvia (Eggert) F.; m. Barbara Ann Schinman, June 20, 1971; children: Alexandra Wynne, Matthew Wyatt. BA magna cum laude, Harvard U., 1968; JD, Yale U., 1972. Bar: N.Y. 1973, N.J. 1974, Calif. 1981. Law clk. to presiding judge U.S. Dist. Ct. N.J. and U.S. Ct. Appeals (3d cir.), Newark, 1972-73; assoc. Cleary, Gottlieb, Steen & Hamilton, N.Y.C. and Paris, 1973-80, Morrison & Foerster, L.A., 1980—81, ptnr., 1981—, mem. exec. com. Lectr. banking law various orgns. Mng. editor Yale U. Law Rev., 1971-72; contbr. articles to profl. jours. Tower fellow Harvard U., 1968. Mem. ABA, Internat. Bar Assn., Calif. Bar Assn. (chmn. fin. insts. com. bus. law sect. 1985-86), Los Angeles County Bar Assn., Union Internationale des Avocats, French-Am. C. of C., Phi Beta Kappa. Clubs: Harvard-Radcliffe So. Calif, University (Los Angeles). Avocations: tennis, photography. Office: Morrison & Foerster LLP 555 W 5th St Ste 3500 Los Angeles CA 90013-1024 Office Phone: 213-892-5275. Office Fax: 213-892-5454. Business E-Mail: hfields@mofo.com.

FIELDS, HENRY WILLIAM, college dean; b. Cedar Rapids, Iowa, Sept. 25, 1946; m. Anne M. Fields; children: Benjamin Widdicomb, Justin Riley. AB in Psychology, Dartmouth, Hanover, N.H., 1969; DDS in Dentistry, Univ. Iowa, Iowa City, 1973, MS in Pedodontics, 1975; MSD in Orthodontics, Univ. Wash., Seattle, 1977. Cert. dentistry Iowa 1973, N.C. 1978, Ohio 1991. Staff, Dept. Hosp. Dentistry Univ. Iowa Hosps., Iowa City, 1973; grad. supr. Muscatine (Iowa) Migrant Program, 1974; grad. instr. Univ. Iowa, 1974—75; AFDH tchr. tng. fellow Dept. Orthodontics Univ. Wash., 1975—77, clin. asst., 1977; Dental Faculty Practice Sch. Dentistry Univ. N.C., 1977—91, asst. prof. Depts. of Pediatric Dentistry and Orthodontics, 1977—82; with N.C. Meml. Hosp., 1978—91; assoc. prof., Depts. of Pediatric Dentistry and Orthodontics Univ. N.C., 1982—87, grad. program dir., Dept. Pediatric Dentistry, 1984—89, prof., Dept. Pediatric Dentistry and Orthodontics, 1987—91, acting dir. grad. studies Sch. Dentistry, 1989, asst. dean acad. affairs, Sch. Dentistry, 1990—91; chair, Dept. Dentistry OSU Hosps., Columbus, Ohio, 1991—2001; Faculty Practice OSU Coll. Dentistry, 1991—, prof. Dept. Orthodontics, 1991—, dean, 1991—2001; staff Columbus Children's Hosp., 1992—. Mem. human subjects com. Sch. Dentistry, Univ. N.C., 1989-91, chmn. curriculum com., 1990-91, chmn. dirs. com. adv. edn. program, 1989-91, health promotion disease prevention task force, 1990-91; deans coun. computerization com. The Ohio State Univ., 1991-1993; bd. dirs. IADR-AADR Craniofacial Biology Group, 1988-90; cons. Callahan award commn., 1992-2001; external examiner BDS and MDS programs Dept. Pediatric Dentistry and Orthodontics Univ. Hong Kong, 1991-93. Contbr. chpts. to books, articles to profl. jours. Recipient NIDR grantee, 1980-83, NIDR Inst. grantee, 1985-86, 1988-93. Home: 4066 Fenwick Rd Columbus OH 43220-4870 Office: Ohio State U Coll Dentistry 4088F Postle Hall Columbus OH 43210-1241 E-mail: fields31@osu.edu.

FIELDS, HOWARD LINCOLN, neurologist, physiologist, educator; b. Chgo., Dec. 12, 1939; s. Charles and Mae (Pinkert) F.; m. Carol Margaret Felts, Dec. 31, 1966; children: Rima Tamar, Gabriel Charles. Research neurologist Walter Reed Research Inst., Washington, 1967-70; clin. fellow Harvard Med. Sch., Boston, 1970-72; asst. prof. U. Calif., San Francisco, 1973-78, assoc. prof., 1978-82, prof., 1982—; vice chmn. neurology, 1993—; dir. Wheeler Ctr. for Neurobiology of Addiction. Cons. NIH, Bethesda, Md., 1979-84; vis. fellow Clare Hall Coll., Cambridge (Eng.) U., 1979; vis. prof. Royal Soc. Medicine, 1988. Editor: (book) Recent Advances in Pain Research and Therapy, 1985, Core Curriculum for Professional Education in Pain, 1991, 2d edit., 1995; author: Pain, 1987, Pain Syndromes in Neurology, 1990, Pharmacotherapy of Pain, 1994; contbr. 200 articles to profl. jours. Recipient rsch. career devel. award NIH, merit award Nat. Inst. Drug Abuse, Kerr award Am. Pain Soc., 1997. Mem. Internat. Assn. Study of Pain (program chmn. 1981-84, sec. 1990-93, editor-in-chief IASP Press 1993—2003), Am. Soc. Clin. Investigation, Am. Acad. Neurology (Cotzias lecture award 2000), Am. Neurol. Assn. (councillor 1991, program com. 1991), Soc. for Neurosci., Inst. Medicine of NAS. Office: U Calif Dept Neurology 5858 Horton St Ste 200 Emeryville CA 94608 Business E-Mail: hlf@phy.ucsf.edu.

FIELDS, JAMES PERRY, dermatologist, dermatopathologist, allergist, pharmacologist, pharmacist; b. Sherman, Tex., July 30, 1932; s. John Galloway and Alma (Goff) F.; m. Linda Hensley, May 30, 1958; children: Timothy Austin, Amy Elizabeth. BS, U. Tex., 1953, MS, 1957; MD, U. Tex., Galveston, 1958. Diplomate Am. Bd. Dermatology, Am. Bd. Allergy and Immunology, spl. competence cert. in dermatopathology. Dir. dept. dermatology USPHS, S.I., N.Y., 1964-78; assoc. prof. medicine and pathology Vanderbilt U. Sch. of Medicine, Nashville, 1978-88; pvt. practice, Nashville, 1988—; dir. dermatopathology Lab. of the Mid-South, Nashville, 1988—. From instr. to assoc. clin. prof. dermatology and pathology Columbia-Presbyn. Hosp. and Coll. of Physicians and Surgeons, N.Y.C., 1968-88; assoc. clin. prof. medicine Vanderbilt U. Sch. Medicine, Nashville, 1988—. Author (with others): Mycobacterial Diseases, 1991, 2d edit., 2000; contbr. articles to profl. jours. Bd. dirs. Am. Leprosy Missions Internat., Greenville, S.C., 1974—; vol. med. missionary, United Meth. Vols. in Mission, 1984—. Capt. USPHS, 1958-79. Recipient citation for meritorious svcs. President's Com. on Employment of Handicapped, 1970, Meritorious Svc. medal USPHS, 1978, Good Samaritan award Nashville Acad. Medicine, 2002. Fellow ACP (Volunteerism and Cmty. Svc. award in Medicine, Tenn. chpt. 2000), Am. Acad. Allergy and Immunology, Am. Acad. Dermatology, Am. Coll. Allergy and Immunology, Am. Soc. Dermatopathology, Am. Soc. for Dermatologic Surgery, N.Y. Acad. Medicine (sec. 1976-77, chmn. sect. on dermatology 1977-78). Home: 411 Lynwood Blvd Nashville TN 37205-3434 Office: 4301 Hillsboro Rd # 222 Nashville TN 37215-3314 Office Phone: 615-386-9719. Personal E-mail: jpfields@earthlink.net.

FIELDS, JANICE L., food service executive; m. Doug Wilkins. From crew mem. to regional v.p. Pitts. McDonald's Corp., 1978—94, v.p Pitts. region, 1994—2000, v.p. Great Lakes divsn., 2000, sr. v.p. SE divsn., sr. v.p. ctrl. divsn., 2000—03, pres. ctrl. divsn., 2003—. Bd. dirs. Ronald McDonald House Charities, Urban League. Recipient WON award, Women's Operator Network, 1988, Women's Leadership award, Women's Network, 2002. Office: McDonald's Corp McDonald's Plz Oak Brook IL 60523*

FIELDS, JERRI LYNN, foundation administrator; b. Sept. 1965; d. Larry and Janice Fields; m. David Burgess. B in English, M in Coll. Student Pers. Adminstrn., Western Ill. U. Positions at De Paul U., Chicago; dir. youth svcs. Horizons Cmty. Svcs., Chicago, anti-violence project dir., dir. programs; exec. dir. Rape Victim Adv., Chicago, 1998—2001; devel. and comm. dir. Fund for City of N.Y., 2001, V-Day: Until the Violence Stops, N.Y.C., 2001—02, exec. dir., 2002—. Past pres. Ill. Coalition Against Sexual Assault; mem. leadership com. Rape Victim Advs.; mem. adv. coun. RAINN Nat. Sexual Assault Hotline.

FIELDS, JON W., writer; b. Columbia, Mo., Nov. 29, 1968; s. Thomas Allen and Elizabeth Schumacher (Craig) Fields. Writer Transfromation, Reno, 2001—, Current News, Kansas City, Mo. Show dir. Club Spark, Kansas City, 2000—01. Musician: Refusion, 2001. With USN, 1987—90. Office: Jolie Moore Productions 3915 Booth #2 Kansas City KS 66103 Personal E-mail: moorejollie@hotmail.com. Business E-Mail: moorejollie@netzero.net.

FIELDS, MARK, automotive executive; b. 1961; Grad., Rutgers Univ.; MBA, Havard Univ., 1989. Joined Ford Motor Co., Dearborn, Mich., 1989, served in a variety of sales and mktg. positions, 1990—96, mng. dir. Argentina, 1997; sr. adviser Mazda Motor Corp., 1998, sr. mng. dir. of mktg., sales, and customer svc., 1998, rep. dir. and pres., 1999—2002; group v.p., Premier Automotive Group Ford Motor Co., 2002—04, exec. v.p., Ford of Europe, 2004—, exec. v.p., premier automotive group, 2004—. Recipient Global Leader of Tomorrow, World Economic Forum, 2000, Innovator of the Year, CNBC's Asian Business Leader, 2001. Office: Ford Motor Co One American Rd Dearborn MI 48126-1899

FIELDS, MARVIN LEON, secondary school educator; b. Mahanttan, N.Y., May 27, 1965; s. Ella Nora Fields. BS in Comm., U. New Haven, 1991; MS in Edn., Hamilton U., 2000. Mail carrier U.S. Postal Svc., Ridgewood, NJ, 1992—93; stockbroker trainee Gruntal and Co., N.Y.C., 1993—95; prodr. ind. TV U.S. Cable, Paterson, NJ, 1993—; tchr. PAterson Pub. Schs., 1998—. Pres. Dolphn Sports, Paterson, 2000—. Youth advvisor NAACP, Paterson, 1993—97; mem. Athletics in Action Men's Basketball Team, 1991; founder Kids Without Parents Found., Joella Field Scholarship Fund. Recipient Achievement award, Christ Temple Bapt. Ch., Paterson, 2001. Mem.: Fellowship of Christian Athletes Assn., Phi Delta Kappa, Kappa Alpha Psi. Home: 376 E 28th St Paterson NJ 07514 Office Phone: 973-321-0140. E-mail: mlfields0@lycos.com.

FIELDS, POLLY STEVENS, humanities educator, researcher, writer; b. Tenn. BA, Vanderbilt U., 1978; PhD, La. State U., 1992. Cert. tchr., Tenn. Tchr. U. Sch. Nashville, 1978—84, Miami Valley Day Sch., Dayton, Ohio, 1984—87; tchg. grantee U. Ala., Tuscaloosa, Ala., 1993—95; from asst. prof. english to prof. Lake Superior State U., Sault Ste. Marie, Mich., 1995—2003, prof. english, 2003—. Vis. scholar UCLA, 2000-01. Co-author (with others): Compendious Conversations: Methods of Dialogue in the Early Enlightenment, 1993, Eighteenth-Century Anglo-American Women Novelists, 1998, A Pilgrimage for Love: New Essays in Early Modern Literature, 2000; contbr. essays New Dictionary of Nat. Biography, 2004; contbr. articles to profl. jours. Recipient Faculty award, Mich. Assn. Governing Bd., 1998; grantee Tchg. grant, U. Ala., 1993—95; rsch. fellow, La. State U., 1990, 1991, 1992, UCLA, 1997—98, William Andrews Clark Libr., 2000—01, NEH, 2002. Fellow: MLA, Rocky Mountain MLA, Seventeenth Century Soc., Shakespeare Soc., Mich. Acad. Arts, Scis. and Letters, Milton Soc., John Donne Soc., Ireland Soc., Early Modern Studies Assn., Brit. and Am. Women Writers, Assn. Lit. Scholars and Critics, Nat. Coun. Tchrs. English, The Voltaire Soc., The Brit. Soc. Eighteenth-Century Studies, Can. Soc. Eighteenth-Century Studies, Am. Soc. Eighteenth-Century Studies, Aphra Behn Soc. Avocations: opera, exercise, yoga. Office: Lake Superior State U 650 West Easterday Ave Sault Sainte Marie MI 49783 Fax: 906-635-6678. E-mail: pfields@gw.lssu.edu.

FIELDS, RICHARD CHARLES, lawyer; b. Waterloo, Iowa, Jan. 10, 1931; s. George H. and Emily H. Fields; m. Shirley Izawa, Nov. 25, 1957; children: Stephanie, Diana, Deborah (dec.), Steven. AB magna cum laude, Harvard U., 1952; JD, U. Denver, 1964. Bar: Colo. 1964, Idaho 1966, U.S. Dist. Ct. Colo. 1964, U.S. Dist. Ct. Idaho 1966, U.S. Ct. Appeals (10th cir.) 1965, U.S. Ct. Appeals (9th cir.) 1968. Reporter, editor AP, Boise, Idaho and Helena, Mont., 1952-60; editor, supr. The Martin Co., Littleton, Colo., 1960-64; staff atty. NLRB, Denver, 1964-66; ptnr. Moffatt, Thomas, Barrett, Rock & Fields, Boise, 1966—. Sec. Boise Indsl. Found., 1970-99; sec./past pres. Greater Boise Rotary Found., 1980-96; mem. adv. bd. Learning Lab, Boise, 1995-98, bd. dirs., 1999-04; lawyer rep. 9th Cir. Jud. Conf., 1983-86. Dir., chmn. Ada County Paramedics, Boise; commr. Boise City Civil Svc. Commn., 1995—; pres. Boise Philharmonic Assn., 1993-95; mem. Salvation Army Adv. Bd., Boise, 1973-03. 1st lt. USAF, 1952-57. Recipient William Booth award Salvation Army, Boise, 1999. Mem. Idaho State Bar (commr. 1980-83, pres. 1982, Outstanding Svc. award 1990, Profl. award 1992, Disting. Lawyer award 2000), Am. Health Lawyers Assn., Am. Bd. Trial Advs. (state chmn.), Am. Coll. Trial Lawyers (state chmn.), Am. Employment Law Coun., Western States Bar Conf. (past pres.), Jackrabbit States Bar (past chancellor), Rotary (Boise club pres., dist. gov.), Order of St. Ives. Methodist. Avocations: fishing, photography, travel, music, golf. Home: 3800 Mountain View Dr Boise ID 83704-3548 Office: Moffatt Thomas Barrett Rock and Fields PO Box 829 Boise ID 83701-0829 E-mail: rcf@moffatt.com.

FIELDS, RUTH KINNIEBREW, secondary and elementary educator, consultant; b. Notasulga, Ala. d. Lee Wesley and Olivia S. (Scruggs) Kinniebrew; m. Benjamin Belton Fields, Dec. 24, 1950; children: Ivan W., Benjamin B. Jr. BS, Tuskegee Inst., 1949, MEd, 1954, postgrad., 1971—75. Cert. vocat. home econs. tchr., Ala.; cert. supt. edn., Ala. Prin., tchr. Choctaw County Bd. Edn., Butler, Ala., 1950-56; dietician, tchr. home econs. Hale County Bd. Edn., Greensboro, Ala., 1957-62; prin., tchr. Tuscaloosa (Ala.) County Bd. Edn., 1962-64, tchr. home econs., 1964-67, home sch. worker, 1967-76, tchr. kindergarten, early childhood edn., 1976-85. Supervising tchr. of students Ala. A&M U., Normal, U. Ala., Tuscaloosa, 1976-85; sec./treas. Dist. II Attendance Suprs., Ala., 1974-75. Bd. dirs. ARC, Tuscaloosa, 1967-73, Girl Scouts, Tuscaloosa, 1967-73, ARC, Tuscaloosa, 1968-74, LWV, Tuscaloosa, Black Warrior coun. Boy Scouts Am.; treas. Planned Parenthood, Tuscaloosa, 1967-76, Cmty. Svc. Programs, Tuscaloosa, 1968-74, Tuscaloosa City Bd. Edn.; advisor Chpt. 2/Title II Adv. Coun., Tuscaloosa, 1985-89. Recipient Presdl. Assoc. award Tuskegee U., 1990; named to Nat. Women's Hall of Fame, 1995. Mem. NEA, AAUW, LWV (dir. Greater Tuscaloosa chpt. 2003), Ala. Edn. Assn. (Excellence in Edn. 1982), Tuscaloosa County Edn. Assn., Nat. Women's History Mus., The Links, Inc., Delta Kappa Gamma, Alpha Kappa Alpha, Gamma Sigma Sigma. Democrat. Baptist. Avocations: reading, working puzzles, walking, cooking, travel. Home: PO Box 1755 Tuscaloosa AL 35403-1755

FIELDS, SARA A., travel company executive; With Boeing Aircraft, Renton, Wash.; flight attendant UAL Corp., Elk Grove Village, Ill., 1963, various positions including mgr. flight attendant training, mgr. indsl. rels., dir. inflight svc internat., dir. employee rels., 1963—94, sr. v.p. onboard svc., 1994—. Office: UAL Corp 1200 E Algonquin Rd Arlington Heights IL 60005-4712 also: PO Box 66100 Chicago IL 60666-0100 Fax: 847-700-4899.*

FIELDS, STEPHEN P., music educator; b. Las Vegas, Aug. 14, 1978; s. Joe and Kathy Fields. MusB in Edn., Miss. State U., 2001. Cert. tchr. music Ga., 2001. Asst. band dir. Starr's Mill H.S., Fayetteville, Ga., 2001—. Mem.: Nat. Band Assn., Music Educators Nat. Conf., Ga. Music Educators Assn., Golden Key, Phi Mu Alpha. Office Phone: 770-486-2710.

FIELDS, STUART HOWARD, labor relations specialist; b. Chgo., Dec. 15, 1943; s. Albert B. and Cecelia (Kessler) Fields; m. Birgit Willeke, Dec. 5, 1971; children: Jessica N., Jascha D. BS, UCLA, 1965; MS, U. Calif., Northridge, 1968. Cert. tchr. and instr. Calif. Labor rels. specialist Hughes Tool Co., Culver City, Calif., 1970, Dept. of the Navy, Point Mugu, Calif., 1971-76; employee rels. specialist Agrl. Rsch. Svc., Hyattsville, Md., 1976-81, labor rels. specialist, 1981-84, Pub. Health Svc., Rockville, Md., 1985-86; employee rels. specialist Def. Nuclear Agy., Bethesda, Md., 1986-88, Consumer Product Safety Commn., Bethesda, 1988-89, U.S. Dept.

Commerce, Washington, 1989-97; sr. paralegal Gagliardo & Zipin, Attys. at Law, Silver Spring, Md., 1997—; labor rels. specialist IRS, Washington, 1997—2004. Presdl. classroom instr.; cons. in field. Author: Requirements for Top Positions in Personnel Administration, 1968. Lt. U.S. Army, 1968—70. Mem.: Soc. Fed. Labor Rels. Profls., Mensa, Jewish Cmty. Ctr. Democrat. Avocations: classical music, coin collecting/numismatics, tax law, basketball. Home: 9449 Reach Rd Potomac MD 20854-2853 Office: Fed Election Commn 999 E St NW Washington DC 20463 Office Phone: 202-694-1085. Personal E-mail: stuarthfields@aol.com.

FIELDS, SUZANNE BREGMAN, syndicated columnist; b. Washington, Mar. 7, 1936; d. Samuel Holiday and Sadie (Hurwitz) Bregman; m. Theodore Martin Fields, June 16, 1957; children: Alexandra, Miriamne, Tobias. BA, George Washington U., 1957, MA, 1964; PhD, Cath. U., 1971. Freelance writer, Washington, 1965-71; editor Innovations Mag., Washington, 1971-79; columnist Vogue mag., Washington, 1982; author Like Father, Like Daughter (Little Brown), 1983; columnist Washington Times, 1984—; syndicated columnist L.A. Times Syndicate, Washington, 1988-2001, Chgo. Tribune Media Svcs., 2001—05, Creators Syndicate, 2005—. TV commentator, regular panelist CNN & Co. Mem. Phi Beta Kappa. Jewish. Home: 1934 Biltmore St NW Washington DC 20009-1510 Office: The Washington Times 3600 New York Ave NE Washington DC 20002-1996

FIELDS, WARREN C., music educator, minister; b. York, Ala., Mar. 12, 1936; s. Travis Edward and Ada Beatrice Fields; m. Bobbie R. Richards; children: Karen Byrd, Kristi Warden. B in Music Edn., Samford U., 1958; MusM, Baylor U., 1963; PhD, U. Iowa, 1973. Tchr. Ensley H.S., Birmingham, Ala., 1958—66; prof. Ga. So. U., Statesboro, 1966—85; state missionary, dept. dir. Ga. Bapt. Conv., Atlanta, 1986—99; adj. prof. Atlanta Christian Coll., East Point, Ga., 2000—; min. of music Pky. Bapt. Ch., Duluth, Ga., 2000—. Conf. leader Lifeway Christian Resources, Nashville, 1986—99. Mem.: So. Bapt. Ch. Music Conf., Am. Choral Dirs. Assn., The Hymn Soc., Soc. for Am. Music. Avocations: woodworking, travel. Home: 2152 Plantation Ct Lawrenceville GA 30044-3743 Office: Atlanta Christian Coll 2605 Ben Hill Rd East Point GA 30344-1999

FIELDS, WILLIAM ALBERT, lawyer; b. Parkersburg, W.Va., Mar. 30, 1939; s. Jack Lyons and Grace (Kelley) F.; m. Prudence Brandt Adams, June 26, 1964. BS magna cum laude, Ohio State U., 1961; postgrad., Harvard Law Sch., 1961-64. Bar: Ohio bar 1964. Since practiced in, Marietta; city prosecutor, 1964-65; acting Judge Marietta Mcpl. Ct.; dir. elections Washington County, 1967-74; profl. bass-baritone soloist. Bd. dirs. Bank One, Marietta, N.A.; lectr. on estate planning and probate matters. Mem. editl. bd. Probate Law Jour. of Ohio. Chmn. Washington County Heart Assn., 1965-67; mem. dist. exec. com. Boy Scouts Am., 1967-74; Treas. County Republican Exec. Com., 1966—; trustee YMCA, Salvation Army; pres. bd. trustees Washington State Community Coll., Marietta; exec. com., trustee Coll. Adminstrv. Scis., Ohio State U.; trustee Appalachian Bible Coll., Bradley, W.Va., 1974-77, Marietta Meml. Hosp., also treas.; bd. dirs. Ohio Valley Port Authority. Recipient Wall St. Jour. award, 1961; named Outstanding Young Man of Marietta, 1968, Outstanding Citizen of Marietta, 1992; named to Ohio Valley Sports Hall of Fame, 2001. Fellow Am. Coll. Trust and Estate Counsel; mem. Ohio Bar Assn. (chmn., bd. govs., probate and trust law sect., mem. splty. bd. Ohio Supreme Ct., splty approval bd. trust, probate, and best planning), Washington County Bar Assn., Marietta Area C. of C. (v.p., trustee), Am. Mensa, Nat. Soc. of Arts and Letters (bd. trustees), Sigma Chi, Beta Gamma Sigma. Clubs: Rotarian (pres. 1970-71), Marietta Country (trustee). Home: 129 Hillcrest Dr Marietta OH 45750-9321 Office: 217 2nd St Marietta OH 45750-2916 Personal E-mail: wafpaf@charter.net. *Without the light of Christ, all is darkness and vain machination.*

FIELDS-GOLD, ANITA, retired dean; b. Amarillo, Tex., Oct. 29, 1940; d. Dera and Mamie Maureen (Craig) Bates; m. Maurice Gold; 1 child, William Kyle. Grad. nursing, Jefferson Davis Hosp., 1962; BSN, Tex. Christian U., 1966; MSN, Northwestern State U. La., 1974; PhD, Tex. Women's U., 1980. C.E. coord., asst. prof. Northwestern State U., Shreveport; prof., dean McNeese State U., Lake Charles, La., ret., 2000. Gov.'s appointee, chmn. S.W. La. Hosp. Dist. Commn., 1989—91. Mem. allocations com. and loaned exec. United Way, 1991—92, Am. Heart Assn.; Am. Cancer Soc.; ARC. Recipient Ben Taub award, 1962, Ann Magnussen award, ARC, 1977. Mem.: ANA (del.), Lake Charles Dist. Nurses Assn. (bd. dirs., Nurse of Yr. award 1972, 1980), La. Nurses Assn. (past pres. and 1st v.p., Spl. Recognition award 1993, Nightingale Hall of Fame award 2002), Phi Kappa Phi, Delta Kappa Gamma, Sigma Theta Tau (Image of Nursing award 1993). Home: 2339 21st St Lake Charles LA 70601-7946 Personal E-mail: amgold@cox-internet.com.

FIELED, ADAM, poet, musician; b. N.Y.C., Feb. 7, 1976; d. Robert Sydney Field and Susan Lee Wallack. Cert., Carnegie Mellon U., 1992; BA magna cum laude, U. Pa., 2004; postgrad., New Eng. Coll., 2004—. Part-time bookseller Barnes & Noble, Phila., 1999—2004; founder, dir., performer This Charming Lab., Phila., 1999—2003, Philly Free Sch., Phila., 2004—. CDs, Partyr Sooner, 2000, Raw Rainy Fog, 2002, Ardent, 2004; contbr. poetry to books and jours.; actor: 13th St. Repertory Theater Co.; author: 4 one-act plays. Polit. commentator The Phila. Ind., 2003. Democrat. Jewish. Avocations: film, art history, modern novels, jazz. Home and Office: Philly Free Sch 154 N 21st St Apt 2A Philadelphia PA 19103 Office Phone: 610-608-2094.

FIELEKE, NORMAN SIEGFRIED, economist, educator; b. Kankakee, Ill., Aug. 22, 1932; s. Lessly and Catharine M. (Nicholson) F.; m. Carol A. Curtiss, June 16, 1962 (div. Dec. 1985); children: Andrew, Eric, Michael. BA summa cum laude, Amherst Coll., 1954; AM, Harvard U., 1955, PhD, 1969. Economist, budget examiner Office Mgmt. and Budget, Washington, 1959—64; industry economist Office U.S. Trade Rep., Exec. Office Pres., 1964—65; v.p., economist Fed. Res. Bank of Boston, 1967—97. Dir. econ. rsch. U.S. Internat. Trade Commn., Washington, 1980; cons. IMF, Washington, 1993; adj. prof. Boston U., 1975-76, Brandeis U., 1988-90, Duke U., Durham, NC, 1998-2000; lectr. Duke Inst. for Learning in Retirement, 2001—. Author: The Welfare Effects of Controls over Capital Exports from the United States, 1971, The International Economy under Stress, 1988; contbr. articles to profl. jours. Lt. USAF, 1955-57. Littauer fellow, NSF fellow Harvard U., 1969. Home: 101 Dundalk Dr Chapel Hill NC 27517-6583

FIELO, MURIEL BRYANT, interior designer; b. Brooklyn, Dec. 11, 1921; d. Harry and Minnie (Dick) Bryant; m. Julius Fielo, June 17; one child, Michael Kenneth. Student, Rutgers U., 1965—69; cert., N.Y. Sch. Interior Design, 1970. Gen. mgr. Fidelity Discount Corp., Irvington, NJ; advt. supr. Lincoln Loan Co., Essex County, NJ, 1941—49; interior designer Alex Fielo Interior Decorators, Newark, 1942—49, prin., 1949—69, owner, 1969—. Designer, cons., space engr. Mudge Interior Design Studios, East Orange, N.J., 1969-; mem. adv. panel Interior Design mag., 1977-. Clk. Essex County Bd. Freeholders, 1972-76; commr. East Orange Bus. Devel. Authority, 1977-86; mem. U.S. adv. coun. SBA-Region II, 1980-811 active LWV, 1950-55; organizer, first pres. South Orange chpt. Women's Am. ORT, 1952-54, mem. nat. speakers bur., 1952-65, parliamentarian No. N.J. coun., 1955-65; pres. Amity chpt. B'nai B'rith, Newark, 1946-48, v.p. No. N.J. coun., 1948-49, various nat. and state positions, 1948-80; mem. nat. com. on sect. fund raising Nat. Coun. Jewish Women, 1979-81, nat. tour chmn., 1979-81; trustee cmty. svc. coun. Oranges and Maplewood, United Way Essex and West Hudson, 1981-83; bd. dir. East Orange Ctrl. Ave. Mall Assn., 1979-83, chmn. new voter registration drive East Orange 2d Ward, 1955, entire city, 1969; pres. East Orange Dem. Club, 1957-58, campaign coord. for Dem. mayoral candidate, 1969; calendar coord. Essex County Dem. Com., 1970-76; mem. N.J. Bipartisan Coalition for Women's Appoinments, 1981. Named Outstanding Entrepreneur of 1984, Gov. of N.J., Outstanding Orgn. Pres., Kean Coll. Profl. Women's Assn., 1985, Wonder Woman of 1986, Bus. Jour. N.J., One of Eight Women To Watch, Jersey Woman mag., 1987, Bus. Person of Yr., East Orange C. of C., 1988; recipient various awards for civic svc. Mem. Internat. Soc. Interior Designers (bd. dir. 1981-85), Nat. Home Fashions League (N.J. membership chmn. N.Y. chpt. 1981-82), Interior Design Soc., Internat. Interior Design Assn. (charter), N.J. Assn. Women Bus. Owners (state bd. dir. 1979-82), Women Entrepreneurs N.J. (pres. 1981-85, CEO 1987—), N.J. Home Furnishings Assn. (bd. dir. 1981-84, 86—), Constrn. Specifications Inst., N.J. Soc. AIA profl. affiliate), Guild Designer Woodworkers, Women Bus. Ownership Ednl. Coalition (N.J. pres. 1985-87, CEO 1987—, mem. steering com. interior designers for licensing in N.Y. 1985—), East Orange C. of C. (bd. dir. 1977—, v.p. 1981-85), Bus. and Profl. Women's Club Oranges (bd. dir. 1958-66). Jewish. Home and Office: Mudge Interior Design Studio 185 S Clinton St East Orange NJ 07018-3099 Fax: 973-672-7287. Office Phone: 973-673-6008. Personal E-mail: mbfielo@erols.com.

FIENNES, RALPH NATHANIEL (RALPH NATHANIEL TWISLETON-WYKEHAM FIENNES), actor; b. Ipswich, Suffolk, Eng., Dec. 22, 1962; s. Mark and Jini (Jennifer Lash) Fiennes; m. Alex Kingston, 1993 (div. 1997). Student, Chelsea Coll. Art and Design, Royal Acad. Dramatic Art. Actor (theatre prodns.) with Royal Shakespeare Co., Broadway debut in Hamlet, 1995 (Tony award Lead Actor in a Play), Ivanov, 1997, Richard II and Coriolanus, 2000, The Talking Cure, 2002, Brand, 2003, Julius Caesar, 2005; (TV films) Prime Suspect, 1991, A Dangerous Man: Lawrence After Arabia, 1992, Wuthering Heights, 1992, The Baby of Macon, (films) Schindler's List, 1993 (Academy award nomination best supporting actor 1993, New York Film Critics Circle award best supporting actor 1993), Quiz Show, 1994, Strange Days, 1995, The English Patient, 1996 (Academy award nominee, Golden Globe award nominee), Oscar & Lucinda, 1997, The Avengers, 1998, Spider, 2002, The Good Thief, 2002, Red Dragon, 2002, Maid in Manhattan, 2002; exec. prodr.Taste of Sunshine, 1999, End of the Affair, 1999; voice Prince of Egypt, 1998, actor, prodr. Onegin, 1999*

FIER, ELIHU, lawyer, educator; b. N.Y.C., Mar. 25, 1931; s. Charles H. and Helen N. (Nadel) F.; m. Jane Lee Saltser, Jan. 10, 1956 (dec. Jan. 1964); children— Jennifer, Michael, Carlyn. BA, Dartmouth Coll., 1952; LL.B., Harvard U., 1958. Bar: N.Y. 1959, U.S. Dist. Ct. (so. and ea. dists.) N.Y. 1960 U.S. Tax Ct. 1961, U.S. Ct. Appeals (2d cir.) 1961, Fla. 1997. Ptnr. Weil, Gotshal & Manges, N.Y.C., 1969-80, Morgan, Lewis & Bockius, N.Y.C., 1980-83, Finley, Kumble, Wagner, Heine, Underberg, Manley & Casey, Beverly Hills, Calif., 1983-88, N.Y.C., 1983-88; of counsel Pryor, Cashman, Sherman & Flynn, N.Y.C., 1988-93, Blum & Fier P.C., N.Y.C., 1993-97, Gillespie & Allison, P.A., Boca Raton, Fla., 1995-97; mgr. Realty Cons. LLC. Adj. assoc. prof. NYU, N.Y.C., 1969-76; lectr. N.Y. Law Jour., Law and Bus., Practicing Law Inst. Served to lt. (j.g.) USNR, 1952-60 Mem.: ABA (com. creditors' rights in real estate financing 1983—90). Home: 240 NW 70th St Boca Raton FL 33487-2391 E-mail: efier13@bellsouth.net.

FIERHELLER, GEORGE ALFRED, communications executive; b. Toronto, Can., Apr. 26, 1933; s. Harold Parsons and Ruth Hathaway (Bauld) F.; m. Glenna E. Fletcher, Apr. 17, 1957; children: Vicki Elaine, Lori Ann BA, U. Toronto, 1955; LLD, Concordia U.; DSLitt, Trinity Coll., U. Toronto. With IBM, Toronto, 1955-58, account mgr., 1962-65, mktg. mgr., 1966-68; founder, pres. Sys. Dimensions Ltd., Ottawa, Ont., 1968-79; pres., CEO Rogers Cable TV Broadcasting Co. Ltd., Vancouver, B.C., Can., 1979-85, Cantel Inc., Toronto, 1985-90; chmn., CEO Rogers Cantel Mobile, Inc., 1990-93; vice chair Rogers Comm., Inc., Toronto, 1993-96; pres. Four Halls Inc., Toronto, 1997—. Bd. dirs. Extendicare Inc., Can. Inst. Advanced Rsch.; pres. Bd. of Trade of Met. Toronto, 1996-97. Contbr. articles to profl. jours. Gen. chmn. United Appeal Campaign, Ottawa, 1972; chmn. campaign Carleton U., 1975-77, also chmn. bd. govs., 1977-79; mem. adv. com. Norman Paterson Sch. Internat. Affairs; bd. dirs., v.p. United Way Ottawa, 1975-79 (United Way of Can. highest award 1998); Opera Ottawa, 1970-71; trustee, mem. exec. com. Nat. Arts Ctr., 1973-79; trustee Royal Ottawa Hosp., 1978-79, Vancouver Gen. Hosp. Found., 1981-85, Can. Ctr. for Advanced Rsch, 2001—; mem. Vancouver Centennial Commn., 1983-84; bd. govs. Simon Fraser U., Vancouver, 1981-84; chmn. United Way Vancouver, 1981, B.C. Coun. of 80's, 1980-83, Vision 2000, 1990-91; chair United Way Met. Toronto, 1994-96, chmn. gen. campaign, 1991; trustee Sunnybrook Hosp. Found., 1993-99, chair Sunnybrook and Women's Health Scis. Ctr. campaign, 1999—; McMichael Can. Art Collection, 1993-99; chair Trinity Coll. Campaign, 1996-99. Decorated mem. Order of Can.; recipient Award of Merit, City of Toronto, 1991, Award of Excellence, Can. Wireless Ind. Assn., 1996, Queen's Golden Jubilee medal, 2002, Salute to City award Toronto, 2002; named to Can. Info. Tech. Hall of Fame, 1998, Outstanding Vol. of Yr., Assn. Fundraising Profls., 2001; named to Sigma Chi Hall of Fame, 2005. Mem. Can. Info. Processing Soc. (pres. 1970-71), World Pres. Orgn., Chief Execs. Orgn., Can. Assn. Data Processing Svc. Orgns., Assn. Cert. Computer Profls. (founding com.), Can. Ctr. for Philanthropy (bd. dirs. 1987-91), Bus. Coun. on Nat. Issues, Coun. for Bus. and the Arts in Can. (bd. dirs. 2003--), Cellular Telecom. Industry Assn. (bd. dirs. 1986-94), Smart Toronto (chmn. 1996), Greater Toronto Mktg. Alliance (chair 1997-2003), Vancouver Club, Rideau Club, Granite Club, Nat. Club, Rosedale Golf Club, Toronto (Can.) Adventurers Club (chmn. 2003—). Home: 24 Pearwood Crescent Toronto ON Canada M3B 2C2 Office: Four Halls Inc 77 King St W Ste 4545 Toronto ON Canada M5K 1K2 Office Phone: 416-861-1351. Home Fax: 416-443-9360. Personal E-mail: fierhel@attglobal.net.

FIERO, PETRA SCHUG, language professional, educator; b. Oberwinkling, Bavaria, Germany, June 4, 1962; came to U.S., 1985; d. Alfred and Edda (Baarmann) Schug; m. David Brian Fiero, May 25, 1989. BA, U. Regensburg, Germany, 1984; MA, U. Nebr., 1989, PhD, 1994. Tchg. asst., lectr. U. Nebr., Lincoln, 1985-94; assoc. prof. German and Spanish Western Wash. U., Bellingham, 1995—. Author: Schreiben gegen Schweigen: Grenzerfahrungen in Jean Amérys autobiographischem Werk, 1997. Mem. Am. Assn. Tchrs. Germans, Modern Lang. Assn., Wash. Assn. Fgn. Lang. Tchrs., Women in German, Delta Phi Alpha. Avocations: playing piano, reading. Office: Western Washington Univ Dept Modern Classical Lang HU 241 Bellingham WA 98225

FIERRO, MARCELLA FARINELLI, forensic pathologist, educator; b. Buffalo, May 24, 1941; d. Marcello Francis and Lena Louise (Luppino) Farinelli; m. Robert J. Fierro, May 30, 1966. BA in Biology (cum laude), D'Youville Coll., NY, 1962; MD in Forensic Pathology, SUNY, Buffalo, 1966. Cert. Am. Bd. Pathology. Intern, resident Ottawa Civic Hosp., Ontario, Canada; resident, pathology Cleve. Clinic Ednl. Found., Ohio, 1973—74, Va. Commonwealth Univ., 1973—74; chief resident, pathology with fellowship in forensic pathology, dept. legal medicine Med. Coll. Va./Va. Commonwealth Univ., Richmond, Va., 1973—74; deputy chief med. examiner, city med. examiner State of Va., Richmond, 1975-92; staff pathologist Richmond Med. Coll. Va. Hosp., 1975—92; clin. prof., pathology Univ. Va., Charlottesville, 1983—92, 1999—2002; prof. pathology East Carolina Sch. Medicine, Greenville, NC, 1992—94; designated med. exam. and forensic pathologist Med. Exam Sys., NC, 1992-94; chief med. examiner State of Va., Richmond, 1994—. Chmn. forensic pathology com. CAP, 1996-2001; co-dir. Vir. Inst. of Forensic Sci. and Medicine; cons. FBI task force on Nat. Crime Investigation Ctr., unidentified Persons and Missing Person Files, Washington, DC, 1983-; presenter and lectr. for profl. orgns. Bd. editors, reviewer Am. Journal of Forensic Medicine and Pathology, 1979—; contbr. articles to peer-reviewed jours.; guest appearances (TV series) New Detectives, Discovery Channel, BBC. Recipient Lifetime Achievement award, Sch. Medicine and Biomedical Scis. Med. Alumni Assn., State Univ., Buffalo, 2001. Mem. AMA, Internat. Assn. for Identification, Am. Med. Women's Assn., Med. Soc. Va., Richmond Acad. Medicine, Va. Soc. Pathology, Nat. Assn. Med. Examiners (bd. dirs. 1993-95, mem. exec. com. 1995, pres. 1991), Am. Acad. Forensic Sci., Coll. Am. Pathologist; fellow Am. Soc. Clin. Pathologist (mem. forensic pathology coun. 1992-96). Office: Office Chief Med Examiner 400 E Jackson St Richmond VA 23219

FIERRO, ROBERT, JR., librarian; s. Robert L. and Avelica Fierro; m. Jane Stephanie Garcia, Feb. 14, 1993; children: Hisser, Randal Maurice Harvell, Juanito, Socks, Anna Belle, John, Pepper. BBA, Angelo State U., San Angelo, Tex., 2000. Employment interviewer Tex. Employment Commn., Houston, 1995—96; client mgmt. specialist Harris County Pvt. Industry Coun., Houston, 1996—99; family preservation specialist II Tex. Dept. Protective and Regulatory Svcs., Houston, 1999—2002; libr. br. supr. Harris County Pub. Libr., Houston, 2002—. Dep. comdr. CAP #42023, San Angelo, 1997; vol. M.D. Anderson Cancer Ctr., Houston, 2004; mem. policy coun., cmty. ptnr., fin. liason Early Childhood Ctr., Galena Park, Tex., 2004; instnl. head, chartered rep. Boy Scouts of Am., Galena Park; dist. scout exec. Concho Valley coun. Boy Scouts Am., San Angelo, 1999, Sam Houston Area coun. Boy Scouts Am., Houston, 1992—94; treas. East Side Mobile Resources Collaborative, Inc., Galena Park, 2004. Recipient Order of Condor, InterAm. Scout Found., 2004; James E. West fellow, Nat. Coun. Boy Scouts Am., 2001. Mem.: League Latin Am. Citizens. Mem. Determination Party. Roman Catholic. Avocations: swimming, travel, reading. Office: Harris County Pub Libr 1500 Keene St Galena Park TX 77547-2400 Office Phone: 713-450-0982. Office Fax: 713-451-1131. E-mail: rfierro@hcpl.net.

FIERSTEIN, HARVEY FORBES, playwright, actor; b. Bklyn., June 6, 1954; s. Irving and Jacqueline Harriet (Gilbert) F. Acting debut in Andy Warhol's Pork, N.Y.C., 1971; author: (plays) In Search of the Cobra Jewels, 1973, Freaky Pussy, 1975, Flatbush Tosca, 1976, Cannibals Just Don't Know Better, 1978, Spookhouse, 1984, Safe Sex, 1987, Forget Him, 1988; (book of musical) La Cage Aux Folles, 1983 (Tony award best book of musical 1984, Tony award best musical 1984, L.A. Drama Critics Circle award 1984, Dramatists Guild award 1984), (with Peter Allen and Charles Suppon) Legs Diamond, 1989; author and star: The International Stud, 1978, Fugue in a Nursery, 1979 (Villager award 1980), Widows and Children First!, 1979, (all three one-acts compiled into) Torch Song Trilogy, 1981 (Obie award 1982), (on Broadway), 1982 (Tony award best play 1982, Tony award best actor 1982, Drama Desk award best play 1982, Drama Desk award best actor 1982, George Oppenheimer-Newsday Playwrighting award 1982, Theatre World award 1983), (in London's West End), 1985 (Olivier Best Play award nominee 1985), Hairspray, 2002-2004 (Tony award best actor in a musical, 2003); screenwriter and star: Tidy Endings, 1988 (ACE award best dramatic special 1988, ACE award writing 1988); actor: (off-Broadway) The Haunted Host, 1991, (films) Garbo Talks, 1984, The Harvest, 1992, Mrs. Doubtfire, 1993, White Lies, 1993, Bullets Over Broadway, 1994, Dr. Jekyl and Ms. Hyde, 1995, The Celluloid Closet, 1996, Independence Day, 1996, Everything Relative, 1996, Kull The Conqueror, 1997, Safe Men, 1998, Legend of Mulan, 1998, Playing Mona Lisa, Death to Smoochy, 2002, Duplex, 2003; (TV guest star appearances) Miami Vice, 1985, The Simpsons, Murder She Wrote, 1992, Cheers, 1992 (Emmy award nomination 1992), (narrator) The Times of Harvey Milk, (Sesame Street spl guest star) Elmo Saves Christmas, 1996, (spl. project) Am. Film Inst. TV or Not TV (Guest star HBO) Larry Sanders Show, 1996; audio CD This Is Not Going to Be Pretty, 1995, (Live Performance Plump Record) 1996; (wrote and starred in productions) (HBO's children's specials) The Sissy Duckling, 1999, (Showtime special film) Common Ground, 2000; returned to Broadway in Hairspray, 2002 (Drama Desk award, 2003, Tony award, 2003); monthly commentator POS' In the Life, 2002. Recipient Theater World award for Broadway debut, 1983, Fund for Human Dignity award, 1983. Avocations: aids activist, gay rights activist, painting, gardening, cooking. Home: RF Entertainment 29 Haines Rd Bedford Hills NY 10507 Office Phone: 914-241-4400 x 102.

FIESS, STEPHEN CHARLES EDWARD, musician, music educator; b. Stratford, Ont., Sept. 10, 1956; s. Philip Louis and Grace Phyllis Fiess. BMus with honors, U. Western Ont., 1978; MMus, Ind. U., 1980; D of Mus. Arts, U. Colo., 1989. Accompanist, composer-in-residence Ballet Images Studio, Boulder, Colo., 1983—88; piano continuing edn. instr. U. Colo., Boulder, 1985—88, part-time instr. piano, 1988—89; pvt. piano instr. Highlands Ranch Piano Instr., Highlands Ranch, Colo., 1989—. Organist Prince of Peace Luth. Ch., Denver, 1989—98, Good Shepherd Episc. Ch., Centennial, Colo., 1998—; accompanist Columbine Chorale, Denver, 1992—2001. Author: (book) The Piano Works of Serge Prokofiev, 1994; composer: (piano sonata) Sonata in Ragtime, 1985, (organ composition) Variations on Twas in the Moon of Wintertime, 1995, (piano composition) Northern Wilderness Suite, 2002. Recipient Rosie Robinow prize for piano, U. Western Ont., 1977, 3d prize sr. Kronek divsn., Joanna Hodges Internat. Piano Competition, 1989; fellow Postdoctoral fellow, U. Colo.-Boulder, 1987—88. Mem.: Music Tchrs. Nat. Assn., Nat. Guild of Piano Tchrs., Pi Kappa Lambda. Lutheran. Home and Office: 1837 W Mountain Daisy Ct Highlands Ranch CO 80129-6279

FIETZER, WILLIAM HAROLD, librarian, writer; b. Clintonville, Wis., July 3, 1948; m. Christine Fietzer; children: Alexander, Nicholas. MA, U. Wis., 1974, MLS, 1989. Cataloging libr. U. N.C., Charlotte, 1991—97; classics and African studies selector/digital resources & humanities cataloger U. Minn., Mpls., 1997—2003. Author: (novel) Penal Fires, 2002, (scholarly non-fiction) The Best Books for Academic Libraries: Political Science, Law, Education, 2003, The Best Books for Academic Libraries: Language & Literature, 2003, Libraries, the Internet, and Scholarship: Tools and Trends Converging, 2002, Cataloging the Web: Metadata, AACR, and MARC 21, 2002. Mem. newletter bd., bus. feature writer Standish-Erickson Neighborhood Assn., Mpls., 2003—05. Mem.: ALA (assoc.; chair networked resources and metadata com. 2000—01), Metrolina Libr. Assn. (pres. 1996). Personal E-mail: wfietzer@mn.rr.com.

FIFE, EDWARD H., landscape architecture educator; b. Mass., Oct. 18, 1942; s. Edwin Kenneth and Yvonne Barbara F.; children: Sarah Rodman and Mike Malcolm. BS in Landscape Architecture, R.I. Sch. Design, Providence, 1965; M in Landscape Architecture, Harvard U., 1967. Registered landscape architect, Ont. Designer Sasaki, Strong Assoc., Toronto, Ont., Can., 1964-66; asst. prof. landscape architecture Ohio State U., Columbus, 1967-69, U. of Toronto, 1969-73, assoc. prof., 1973—, asst. chmn., 1983-85, chmn. program in landscape architecture, 1985-89, 92-96; dir. Ctr. for Landscape Rsch. U. Toronto, 1987—89, 2001—03; prin. E. H. Fife Landscape Architecture, Toronto, 1979—. Mem. roster vis. educators Landscape Archtl. Accreditation Bd., 1986-96. Bd. dirs. Koffler Gallery, Toronto, 1986-95, Landscape Architecture Can. Found., 1987-88, 94—; mem. adv. com. Restoration of Monserrate Park, Portugal, 1988-90; mem. sci. and edn. com. Royal Bot. Garden, 1988-91, mem. property com., 1991-93; mem. acad. bd. governing coun. U. Toronto, 1988-89. Fellow Can. Soc. Landscape Architects; mem. Internat. Fedn. Landscape Architects, Can. Soc. Landscape Architects (roster vis. educators), Ont. Assn. Landscape Architects (pres. 1987-88, bd. dirs. 1983-89, 2000-02). Avocations: painting, organic farming, canoeing, hiking. Home: 269 Waverley Rd Toronto ON Canada M4L 3T5 Office Phone: 416-946-3077. Office Fax: 416-971-2094. Business E-mail: fife@clr.utoronto.ca.

FIFE, ELAINE HARNER, lawyer, mediator; b. Apr. 22, 1950; d. Orville David and Anna Louise (Mathews) Harner; m. Thomas N. Biehl, June 13, 1971 (div. Sept. 1982); 1 child, Brandon Thomas; m. David Mack Fife, Oct. 9, 1983; 1 child, David Mackie. BA, Ohio State U., 1972; JD, Loyola U., L.A., 1975. Bar: Ohio 1975; U.S. Dist. Ct. (so. dist.) Ohio 1975. Atty. Clinton County Pub. Defender's Office, Wilmington, 1976-77, dir.-atty., 1977-98; pvt. practice Wilmington, 1979-83; ptnr. Fife and Fie, Wilmington, from 1983. Pres., Clinton County Council on Alcoholism, Wilmington, 1985-86; bd. trustees program com. Leadership Clinton, 1986-87; bd. dirs. Ohio Criminal Justice Supervisory Com., 1978-83, Clinton County Cmty. Supervision Program, 1996—; adj. prof. of English So. State Cmty. Coll. Recipient Ohio Pub. Defender award, 1996. Mem. Clinton County Bar Assn. (sec. 1979-80, 86-87, treas. 1985-86, pres. 1988-89), Acad. Family Mediators, Ohio State Pub. Defender Assn. 9bd. dirs. 1977-81), AAUW (pres. 1993-95), Beta Sigma Phi, recipient Silver Beaver Award, Tecumseh Council, B.S.A. Mem. Soc. Of Friends. Died May 25, 2005.

FIFE, JONATHAN DONALD, education educator; b. Washington, Nov. 9, 1941; s. G. Donald and Marie (Wall) F.; m. Janice McKenna, Aug. 10, 1968 (div.); children: Patrick McKenna, Timothy Kingston, Brendan Martin; m. Ann Ferren, 1996. BBA, U. Mass., 1965; MS, SUNY, Albany, 1970; postgrad, U. Cin., 1965-67; EdD, Pa. State U., 1975. Asst. dir. student activities State U. Coll., Buffalo, 1967-69; rsch. asst. Pa. State U. Ctr. for Study Higher Edn., State College, 1970-72; assoc. dir. ERIC Clearinghouse on Higher Edn., George Washington U., Washington, 1972-77, dir., 1977-98, prof. edn., 1977-98; vis. prof. Va. Poly. Inst. and State U., Blacksburg, 1998—2005;

adminstrv. Am. U. Bulgaria, 2005—. Edn. pilot team evaluator Malcolm Baldridge Nat. Quality Award, 1994, sr. evaluator, 1995-96, bd. examiners, sr. examiner, 1996-97, alumni examiner, 1999-2000, examiner, VA Sen. Productivity & Quality Award, 2002-04. Mng. editor Rev. Higher Edn., 1980-86; cons. editor Change, 1981-2001. Bd. dirs. Nat. Ctr. for Higher Ednl. Mgmt. Systems, Boulder, 1980-82; cons. Rosenberg Commn., Md., 1975; pres., Wheaton Sq. East Condominium, Wheaton, Md., 1973-78; pres. High Meadows Owners' Master Assn., Radford, Va., 2000-05. Mem. Assn. Study Higher Edn. (exec. sec. treas. 1978-87), Am. Ednl. Rsch. Assn. (sec. treas. spl. interest group postsecondary edn. 1977-81), Higher Edn. Group Washington (sec. 1979-81, v.p., 1997-98, pres. 1998-99), Assn. Instl. Rsch., Phi Kappa Phi. Avocations: tennis, golf, boating. Business E-Mail: jfife@vt.edu.

FIFE, WILLIAM FRANKLIN, retired drug company executive; b. Buffalo, W.Va., Nov. 6, 1921; s. Alfred Charles and Grace (Pitchford) F.; m. Frances H. Rosi, 2003; children: Scott Franklin, Susan Elizabeth, Cindy Francine. AB, Berea Coll., 1949; MS, U. Wis., 1950. Operating mgr. McKesson & Robbins, Chgo. and Kansas City, Mo., 1950-56, Cleve. Wholesale Drug Co., 1956-58; with Owens, Minor & Bodeker, Inc., 1958-91; pres., exec. v.p., sr. v.p. Owens & Minor, Inc., Richmond, Va., 1981-87, chief oper. officer, 1987-91, exec. v.p., 1989-91, ret., 1991—, now cons., bd. dirs.emeritus, 1998—. Capt. C.E. U.S. Army, 1942-46. Office: Owens & Minor Inc 4800 Cox Rd Glen Allen VA 23060-6294

FIFE, WILMER KRAFFT, retired chemistry professor; b. Wellsville, Ohio, Oct. 19, 1933; s. Wilmer George and Lourene Elizabeth (Krafft) F.; m. Betsy Louise Jones, Dec. 26, 1959; children: Kimberly, Julia, Steven. B.Sc. in Chemistry, Case Inst. Tech., 1955; PhD in Organic Chemistry, Ohio State U., 1960. Applications chemist Monsanto Chem. Co., Dayton, Ohio, summers 1955, 57; instr. Muskingum (Ohio) Coll., 1959-60, asst. prof., 1960-64, asso. prof., 1964-70, prof., 1970-71, chmn. dept. chemistry, 1966-71; prof. chemistry Ind. U.-Purdue U. at Indpls., 1971—, chmn. dept., 1971-80; ret. NIH postdoctoral fellow Harvard U., 1965-66; NIH postdoctoral fellow Columbia U., 1968-69; NSF fellow, 1955-56; Sinclair Oil Co. fellow, 1958-59; DuPont fellow, 1960; Danforth assoc., 1969—; others; vis. scholar in chemistry Louis Pasteur U., Strasbourg, France, 1994, U. San Francisco, 1999; named Outstanding Rschr. in Sci. Ind. U.-Purdue U., Indpls. Mem. Am. Chem. Soc., AAAS, Sigma Xi, Tau Beta Pi, Phi Lambda Upsilon. Home: 7102 Dean Rd Indianapolis IN 46240-3626 Office: IUPUI Chemistry 402 N Blackford St Indianapolis IN 46202-3217 E-mail: fife@chem.iupui.edu.

FIFFIE PROCTOR, JOANN, media and technology specialist; b. New Orleans; d. Joseph Paul Sr. and Elouise Marie Fiffie. BA in Comm., U. Southwestern, Lafayette, La., 1980; EdM, Minot State U., 1992; M of Libr. and Info. Sci., U. So. Miss., 1997. Tchr. St. James Sch. Bd., Lutcher, La., 1992-93, tchr. computers, 1994-96; spl. edn. tchr. Calif. Sch. Dist., Sacramento, 1993-94; instr. Southwestern U., Lafayette, La., 1997-98; media/tech. specialist St. John Sch. Bd., Reserve, La., 1998—; rschr. Lyndon Baines Johnson Presdl. Libr., 1996—2000. Dir. sta. WJLO-TV Magnet Sch., LaPlace, La., 2000. Founder mag. Tender Times, 2000. Active Parent-Tchr., St. James, La., 1994-96; pres./CEO House Hands & Hugs, Vacherie, La.; mem. adv. bd. Big Brothers & Sisters, Lafayette. Houma-Terabone grantee, 1998; Metrovision Sch.-To-Career grantee, 2002. Mem. ALA, AAUW, NEA, Libr. Info. Tech. Assn., Nat. Assn. Female Execs., Mothers of 21st Century Leaders. Office: John L Ory Magnet Sch 182 W 5th St La Place LA 70068-4501

FIFIELD, RICHARD DELMAGE, lawyer; b. Elizabeth, N.J., Dec. 29, 1946; s. George Henry and Virginia Louise (Bogart) F.; m. Maureen Ann Dooley, June 10, 1978; children: Teresa, Amanda, Meghann. BA, U. Conn., 1968; JD, Temple U., 1971. Bar: N.J. 1971. Law sec. Hunterdon County Ct., Flemington, N.J., 1971-72; assoc. Arthur L. Alexander, Washington, N.J., 1972-83; sole practice, Washington, N.J., 1983-94; assoc. Mulligan & Mulligan, Hackettstown, N.J., 1994—. Committeeman Warren County Republican Com., 1982—, Washington Twp. Com., 1983—; Mayor Washington Twp., 1985. Mem. Warren County Bar Assn.

FIFIELD, WILLIAM O., lawyer; b. Crown Point, Ind., May 25, 1946; BS with honors and distinction (hon.), Purdue U., 1968; JD cum laude (hon.), Harvard U., 1971. Bar: Ill., 1971; Tex., 1998, US Ct. of Appeals (7th and 11th circuits), US Dist. Ct. (no. dist.) Ill. Assoc. Sidley and Austin (now Sidley Austin Brown & Wood LLP), Dallas, 1971-77; ptnr. Sidley Austin Brown & Wood LLP, Dallas, 1977—, mng. ptnr. Dallas office, 1996—, and mem. exec. com. bd. dirs. Kimberly-Clark Corp., 1995—2003. Mem.: ABA, Chgo. Bar Assn. Office: Sidley Austin Brown & Wood LLP Ste 3400 717 N Harwood St Dallas TX 75201-6534 Office Phone: 214-981-3333. Office Fax: 214-981-3400. Business E-Mail: wfifield@sidley.com.

FIFLIS, TED JAMES, lawyer, educator; b. Chgo., Feb. 20, 1933; s. James P. and Christine (Karakitsos) F.; m. Vasilike Pantelakos, July 3, 1955; children: Christina Eason, Antonia Fowler, Andreanna Lawson. BS, Northwestern U., 1954; LLB, Harvard U., 1957. Bar: Ill. 1957, Colo. 1975, U.S. Supreme Ct. 1984. Pvt. practice law, Chgo., 1957-65; mem. faculty U. Colo. Law Sch., Boulder, 1965—, prof., 1968—. Vis. prof. NYU, 1968, U. Calif., Davis, 1973, U. Chgo., 1976, U. Va., 1979, Duke U., 1980, Georgetown U., 1982, U. Pa., 1983, Am. U., 1983, Harvard U., 1988; Lehmann disting. vis. prof. Washington U., St. Louis, 1991; cons. Rice U.; arbitrator AT&T divesture disputes, 1984-87. Author: (with Homer Kripke, Paul Foster) Accounting for Business Lawyers, 1970, 3rd edit., 1984, Accounting Issues for Lawyers, 1991; editor-in-chief Corp. Law Rev., 1977-88; contbr. articles to profl. jours. Mem. ABA, Am. Assn. Law Schs. (past chmn. bus. law sect.), Colo. Bar Assn. (mem. coun. sect. of corp., banking and bus. law 1974-75), Am. Law Inst. (chmn. com. on rsch. proposed fed. securities code), Colo. Assn. Corp. Counsel (pres. 1998-99). Greek Orthodox. Home: 1602 Columbine Ave Boulder CO 80302-7832 Office: Univ Of Colo Law Sch Boulder CO 80309-0001 Office Phone: 303-492-6049. E-mail: ted.fiflis@colorado.edu.

FIFTY CENT See JACKSON, CURTIS

FIGA, PHILLIPS., judge; b. Chgo., July 27, 1951; BA, Northwestern U., 1973; JD, Cornell U., 1976. Assoc. Sherman & Howard, Denver, 1976-80; ptnr. Burns & Figa, P.C., Denver, 1980-90, pres., 1988-90; pres., shareholder Burns, Figa & Will, PC, Englewood, Colo., 1991—2003; judge US Dist. Ct. for Dist. of Colo., 2003—. Instr. U. Denver Law Sch., 1984, 86, Nat. Inst. Trial Advocacy, Rocky Mountain Region, 1992, 94; mem. model rules of profl. conduct Colo. Supreme Ct., 1987-92, com. lawyer regulation to revise Colo. discipline rules, 1997-98, com. group legal svcs. and advt., 1982-86; mem. US Dist. Ct. Justice Reform Act. Adv. Com., 1994-97; mem. Colo. Commn. on Jud. Discipline, 1995-2003; chair nominating com. Faculty Fed. Advs., 1999-2000; mem. bd. vis. Wienberg Coll., 2004— Articles editor: Cornell Internat. Law Rev., 1975—76. Bd. dirs. B'nai B'rith Anti-Defamation League, 1984-2003, regional bd. chair, 1996-98, co-chmn. civil rights com., 1988-90; trustee Rose Med. Ctr., 1987-95, exec. com., 1990-95, AMC Cancer Rsch. Ctr., 1993-95; trustee Rose Cmty. Found., 2002-03, Jewish Life Com., 2001-03, co-chmn., 2002-03. Evans scholar, 1969-73. Fellow Internat. Soc. Barristers, Am. Bar Found., Colo. Bar Found. (trustee 1999-2003, pres. Colo. Bar. Fellows 2001-03); mem. ABA (standing com. on profl. discipline 1997-99), Am. Judicature Soc., Colo. Bar Assn. (mem. ethics com. 1978-93, chair ethics com. 1984-85, bd. govs. 1986-88, 89-91, pres. 1995-96, chair awards com. 1998-99, chair nominating com. 1999-2000), Denver Bar Assn., Arapahoe County Bar Assn., Federalist Soc., Phi Beta Kappa, Phi Eta Sigma. Office: Alfred A Arraj Courthouse Chambers A-635 901 19th St Denver CO 80294-3589 Office Phone: 303-335-2174. Business E-Mail: figa_chambers@cod.uscourts.gov.

FIGARI, ERNEST EMIL, JR., lawyer, educator; b. Navasota, Tex., Feb. 18, 1939; s. Ernest Emil and Louise (Campbell) F.; children: Alexandra Caroline, Audrey Elizabeth. BS, Tex. A&M U., 1961; LLB, U. Tex., 1964; LLM, So. Meth. U., 1970. Bar: Tex. 1964, U.S. Ct. Appeals (5th cir.) 1965, U.S. Dist. Ct. (no. dist.) Tex. 1964, U.S. Supreme Ct. 1967. Law clk. to judge U.S. Dist. Ct. (no. dist.) Tex., Dallas, 1964-65; assoc. Coke & Coke, Dallas, 1965-70, ptnr., 1970-75, Johnson & Swanson, Dallas, 1975-86, Figari & Davenport, Dallas, 1986—. Adj. prof. law So. Meth. U., Dallas, 1974-79, 81-82, U. Tex., 1980. Contbr. articles to profl. jours. Fellow ABA Found., Tex. Bar Found., Dallas Bar Found.; mem. State Bar Tex. Roman Catholic. Office: Figari & Davenport Bank of Am Plz 901 Main St Ste 3400 Dallas TX 75202-3796 Office Phone: 214-939-2001.

FIGLEY, MELVIN MORGAN, radiologist, physician, educator; b. Toledo, Dec. 5, 1920; s. Karl Dean and Margaret (Morgan) F.; m. Margaret Jane Harris, Mar. 16, 1946; children: Karl Porter, Joseph Dean, Mark Thompson. Student, Dartmouth, 1938-41; MD magna cum laude (John Harvard fellow), Harvard, 1944. Diplomate: Am. Bd. Radiology (trustee 1967-72). Intern, then resident internal medicine Western Res. U., 1944-46; resident radiology U. Mich., 1948-51, instr., asst. prof., asso. prof. radiology, 1950-58; practice specializing in radiology Seattle, 1958-86; prof. radiology, chmn. dept. U. Wash., 1958-78, prof. radiology and medicine, 1979-85, emeritus prof. radiology and medicine, 1986—. Mem. radiation study sect. NIH, 1963-67; mem. com. on radiology Nat. Acad. Scis.-NRC, 1964-69, chmn., 1968-69 Editor: Am. Jour. Roentgenology, 1976-85; contbr. articles profl. jours. Bd. dirs. James Picker Found., 1970-80. Served to capt. M.C. AUS, 1946-48. John and Mary R. Markle scholar, 1952-57 Fellow Am. Coll. Radiology (Gold medal 1987), Royal Coll. Radiologists (hon., London), Royal Australian Coll. Radiologists (hon.); mem. Royal Soc. Medicine (hon.), Assn. Univ. Radiologists (pres. 1966, Gold medal 1983), Am. Roentgen Ray Soc. (exec. council 1970-88, pres. 1983-84, Gold medal 1986), N. Am. Soc. Cardiac Radiology (pres. 1974), Fleischer Soc. (pres. 1986-87), Radiol. Soc. N.Am. (Gold Medal 1986), AMA, Boylston Med. Soc., Wash. Heart Assn. (past trustee), Soc. Chmn. Acad. Radiology Depts. (exec. council 1969-71), Phi Beta Kappa, Sigma Xi, Alpha Omega Alpha, Sigma Alpha Epsilon. Home: PO Box 859 Grantham NH 03753-0859

FIGLIN, ROBERT ALAN, hematologist, oncologist; b. Phila., June 22, 1949; s. Jack and Helen Figlin; 1 child, Jonathan B. BA in Chemistry, Temple U., 1970, postgrad., 1972; MD, Med. Coll. Pa., 1976. Diplomate Am. Bd. Internal Medicine, sub-bd. Med. Oncology; diplomate Nat. Bd. Med. Examiners; lic. physician, Calif. Med. intern, resident in medicine Cedars-Sinai Med. Ctr., L.A., 1976-79, chief resident in medicine, 1979-80; fellow in hematology-oncology UCLA, 1980-82, asst. prof. medicine Sch. Medicine, 1982-88, assoc. prof. Sch. Medicine, 1988-94, prof. medicine Sch. Medicine, 1994—, chmn. instnl. rev. bd., human rsch. policy bd., 1998—; dir. Bowyer Oncology Ctr., dir. outpatient clin. rsch. unit Jonsson Comprehensive Cancer Ctr., 1990-92, dir. clin. rsch. unit, 1993-98, dir. hematology/oncology fellowship program, 1995—2003; prof. urology, Sch. Medicine UCLA, 2001—, Henry Alvin and Carrie L. Meinhardt chair in urol. oncology, 2001—. Med. dir. thoracic oncology program Johnson Comprehensive Cancer Ctr., 1994—, genito uninary program, 1994—, solid tumor program, 1997—99, solid tumor translational rsch. program, 1999—2002, co-dir. GU oncology, 2004—; co-dir. Lung Cancer Rsch. Program; prin. investigator UCLA S.W. Oncology Group, 1992—2000; sci. founder Agensys, 1996—; co-prin. investigator, clin. dir. NCI Specialized Program of Rsch. Excellence, Lung Cancer, 2000—, NCI Bladder Cancer Prevention, 2003—. Editor: Interferons in cytokines, 1988—90, Kidney Cancer Jour., 1993—94, Current Clin. Trials, 1992—96; UCLA Cancer Trials Newsletter, 1990—96, Seminars on Oncology-Kidney Cancer, 1995, Cancer Therapeutics, 1997, Cancer Biotherapy and Radio Pharms., 1997; contbr. articles and revs.; editor: Renal & Adrenal Tumors, 2002, Kidney Cancer Jour., 2003—. Mem. med. adv. bd. Nat. Kidney Cancer Assn., 1993—; FDA cons., 1990-92. Recipient numerous awards. Fellow ACP; mem. Am. Soc. Clin. Oncology, Am. Fedn. Clin. Rsch., Am. Assn. for Cancer Rsch., Soc. for Biologic Therapy (chmn. ann. scientific meeting 1997, pres. cancer panel 1997, S.W. Oncology Group, Assn. Subsplty. Profs., Internat. Assn. for Study of Lung Cancer. Office: UCLA 10945 Le Conte Ave Ste 2333 Los Angeles CA 90024-2828 Office Phone: 310-825-5788.

FIGNER, WILLIAM JAMES, computer engineer; b. Cheverly, Md., Feb. 5, 1968; s. James Alexander and Eleanor Rose Figner; m. Amelia Elizabeth Figner, Oct. 20, 1997. BA in History, U. Ctrl. Fla., Orlando, 1992—94, BA in Liberal studies, 1992—95, MA in Instrnl. Sys. Design, 1992—96. Florida Professional Educator's Certificate Fla. Dept. of Edn., 1997. Instrnl. designer Carley Corp., Orlando, Fla., 1997—98; lead instrnl. designer Jardon & Howard Technologies, Inc., 1998—2001; quality assurance dir. EDO Corp. PSD, 2001—, lead instrnl. designer, 2001—. Ofcl. town historian Mt. Dora Hist. Soc., Mount Dora, Fla., 1995—96. E-5 USAR, 1985—99, Eustis, FL. Decorated Meritorious Svc. Ribbon U.S. Army, Fla. N.G.; recipient Cold War Cert. of Recognition, U.S. Sec. of Def., 2000. Mem.: Army Aviation Assn. Am. Home: 26509 State Rd 19 Howey In The Hills FL 34737 Office: EDO Corp PSD 11315 Corporate Blvd Ste 100 Orlando FL 32817 Office Phone: 407-382-6446. Personal E-mail: bfigner@msn.com. E-mail: bill.figner@edocorp.com.

FIGUEROA, JOSE DE JESUS, communications executive; b. Mexico City, Mex., Nov. 9, 1964; children: Zacnite, Atl. BSEE, Autonomus U. of Morelos State, Cuernavaca, Mex., 1994. Math & sci. tutor Ho. of Sci., Cuernavaca, Mexico, 1985—87; advanced math prof. Colegio Morelos de Cuernavaca, Cuernavaca, Mexico, 1995—2001; interpreter/translator Henderson County Pub. Schs., Hendersonville, NC, 2003—. Bd. chmn. Latino Advocacy Coalition El Centro, Hendersonville, NC, 2004—. Pres. Latino Advocacy Coalition, Hendersonville, NC, 2004. Personal E-mail: atlzacnite@yahoo.com.

FIGUERRES, CYRIL IWAMURA AMOROZO, research psychologist, educator; b. Lahaina, Maui, Hawaii, July 10, 1948; s. Cirilo Amorozo and Kimiko (Iwamura) F.; m. Aileen Chizuko Shitamoto, Jan. 14, 1972; children: Dawn Ayumi, Derek Shitamoto, Kevin Shitamoto. Student, U. Hawaii, 1966-69, 71; BS, Brigham Young U., 1972, MA, 1974; PhD, Purdue U., 1977. Cert. tchr., Utah. Rsch. assoc. Ch. of Jesus Christ of Latter-day Saints, Salt Lake City, 1978, mgr. rsch. and evaluation, 1979—. Adj. prof. ednl. psychology U. Utah, Salt Lake City, 1979-91; mem. aux. faculty psychology Brigham Young U., Salt Lake City, 1979-83; talent group cons., 1994-98. Contbr. rsch. articles to profl. jours. Active Boy Scouts Am., 1976-79; Bishopric Ch. Jesus Christ of Latter-day Saints, West Lafayette, Ind., 1976-78, high counselor, Salt Lake City, 1978-84, Bishopric, Salt Lake City, 1986-91; mission pres. Japan Fukuoka Mission, 1991-94; mem. sch. bd. Fukuoka Internat. Sch., 1992-93. Ethnic minority doctoral fellow Purdue U., 1975-77; named Outstanding Young Man Am., U.S. Jaycees, 1980. Avocations: martial arts, reading. Home: 2111 Terra Linda Dr Salt Lake City UT 84124-2733 Office: Church of Jesus Christ of Latter-Day Saints 50 E North Temple Salt Lake City UT 84150-0002 E-mail: figuerresci@ldschurch.org.

FIJOLEK, RICHARD M., lawyer; b. Oak Park, May 31, 1958; AB with honors, Stanford (Calif.) U., 1979; JD, Columbia U., 1982. Bar: Ill. 1982, Tex. 1986. Assoc. Katten, Muchin and Zavis, Chgo., 1982-86, Haynes and Boone LLP, Dallas, 1986-89, ptnr., Bus., 1990—. Author: Complying with FIRPTA, 1989. Named one of best lawyers in Dallas, D Magazine, 2003. Fellow: Am. Coll. Tax Counsel; mem.: Tex. Bar Assn., Internat. Fiscal Assn., ABA (chmn. Internat. Real Estate Com.). Office: Haynes and Boone 901 Main St Ste 3100 Dallas TX 75202-3789 Office Phone: 214-651-5570. Office Fax: 214-200-0442. Business E-Mail: rick.fijolek@haynesboone.com.

FIKE, EDWARD LAKE, newspaper editor; b. Delmar, Md., Mar. 31, 1920; s. Claudius Edwin and Rosa Lake (Pegram) F.; m. Rosa Amanda Drake, Apr. 1, 1952; children: Rosa, Evelyn, Amy, Melinda. *Remarkably, Edward and his three siblings are all represented in Who's Who in America. Brother Dr. Claude E. Fike (deceased) was a Professor of History and Dean of Arts and Sciences at Mississippi Southern University, Hattiesburg, Miss. Sister Evelyn's Husband Dr. William Laupus was the founding first Dean of the Medical School at Eastern Carolina University, Greenville, N.C. Sister Ruth's husband Robert Pittman was editor, Editorial Page at the St. Petersburg, Fla. Times.* BA, Duke U., 1941; postgrad., U. Cin., 1941-42. Editor, co-pub. Nelsonville (Ohio) Tribune, 1945-48; dir. bur. pub. info. Duke U., Durham, N.C., 1948-52; mem. U.S. del. N. Atlantic Council, Paris, 1952-53; assoc. editor Rocky Mount (N.C.) Evening Telegram, 1953-57; editor, pub. Fike Newspapers, Lewistown and Glendive, Mont., 1957-62, also Wilmington and Tujunja, Calif., 1957-68; assoc. editor Richmond (Va.) News Leader, 1968-70; dir. news and editorial analysis Copley Newspapers, 1970-77; editor editorial pages San Diego Union, 1977-90. Lectr. journalism San Diego State U., San Diego Evening Coll. Parole commr. San Diego County, 1993-94, pres. adv. coun. San Diego State U., 1988-93; bd. dir. Hubbs Seaworld Rsch. Inst. and Midway Aircraft/Carrier Mus. Grossmont Hosp. Found., Armed Svc. YMCA. Lt. USNR, 1942-45. Recipient George Washington award Freedoms Found., 1969-71, 73, 78, Editorial Writing awards N.C. Press Assn., 1954-55, Va. Press Assn., 1969, Calif. Newspaper Pubs. Assn., 1969, 80; Hoover Inst. Media fellow Stanford U., 1990-91. Mem. Omicron Delta Kappa. Republican. Methodist. Home: 17369 Plaza Maria San Diego CA 92128-2251

FIKES, JAY COURTNEY, anthropology educator, art dealer; b. San Luis Obispo, Calif., June 14, 1951; s. J.C. and Virginia Lee (Roberts) F.; m. Lebriz N. Tosuner, Apr. 17, 1979; 1 child, Leyla Tupina. BA in Comparative Culture, U. Calif., Irvine, 1973; MEd in Bilingual Edn., U. San Diego, 1974; MA in Anthropology, U. Mich., 1977, PhD in Anthropology, 1985. Tutor Palomar Coll., Pala Indian Reservation, Calif., 1974; instr. anthropology Allan Hancock Coll., Santa Maria, 1975—76; land use planner Navajo Nation, Windowrock, Ariz., 1983; instr. anthropology U.S. Internat. U., Oceanside, Calif., 1985; instr. rsch. methods soc. sci. Marmara U., Istanbul, 1985—87; prof. anthropology Yeditepe U., 1998—. Owner Cuatro Esquinas Traders, Carlsbad, Calif., 1979—; adj. prof. anthropology Highlands U., Las Vegas, N.Mex., 1989; lobbyist Friends Com. on Nat. Legislation, 1990—91; pres. Inst. Inter-cultural Issues, 1993—98. Author: Huichol Indian Identity and Adaptation, 1985, Step Inside the Sacred Circle, 1989, Carlos Castaneda, Academic Opportunism and the Psychedelic Sixties, 1993, Reuben Snake, Your Humble Serpent, 1996, Huichol Indian Ceremonial Cycle, 1997, Huichol Mythology, 2004; contbr. articles on edn. and anthropology to profl. jours. Coord. Fiestas Patrias, Carlsbad Bicentennial Com., 1975. Anthropology teaching fellow U. Mich., Ann Arbor, 1976-79, Postdoctoral fellow Smithsonian Instn., Washington, 1991-92, 95; acad. scholar dept. anthropology, U. Mich., 1981-82; doctoral dissertation grantee Rackham Grad. Sch. U. Mich., 1981. Mem. Internat. Platform Assn., Am. Anthropol. Assn., N.Y. Acad. Scis., Rotary (dir. internat. svc. 1982-83). Mem. Religious Soc. Friends. Home: 2421 Buena Vista Cir Carlsbad CA 92008-1601 Office: PO Box 517 Carlsbad CA 92018 Business E-Mail: cfikes@yeditepe.edu.tr. E-mail: jayfikes2004@yahoo.com.

FIKRIG, EROL, rheumatologist, medical educator; b. Dec. 15, 1959; BA in Chemistry cum laude, Cornell U., 1981, MD, 1985. Diplomate Am. Bd. Internal Medicine, Am. Bd. Infectious Diseases. Resident in internal medicine Vanderbilt U. Hosp., 1985—88; fellow in infectious diseases and immunobiology Yale U., 1988—92, assoc. rsch. scientist in immunobiology, 1992, asst. prof. medicine sect. of rheumatology, 1992—96, assoc. prof. medicine sect. of rheumatology, 1996—. Contbr. articles to profl. jours.; ad hoc reviewer NIH study sect.: Bacteriology and Mycology I, 1994; spkr. in field. Recipient Young Investigator award, Nat. Found. Infectious Disease, 1991, award in vaccine devel., Infectious Disease Soc. Am., 1992, Young Investigator award, Am. Heart Assn., 1993, Investigator award, Arthritis Found., 1993, Apollo Kinsley award, State of Conn., 1993, NIH First award, 1994, Goodyear award, State of Conn., 1994, Established Investigator award, Am. Heart Assn., 1996; fellow NIH Clin. Investigation, 1990, Daland, Am. Philos. Soc., 1990; scholar Pew, 1993. Mem.: Phi Beta Kappa. Office: Yale U Sch Medicine Dept Rheumatology 333 Cedar St New Haven CT 06510-3289*

FILA, JOHN CHARLES, psychoanalyst; b. Boston; s. John F. and Marion L. Fila. AB, Harvard U., 1992; PhD, U. Berkeley, Mich., 1995. Diplomate Am. Coll. Profl. Mental Health Practitioners. Pvt. practice, Wellesley, Mass., 1997—2000, Santa Monica, Calif., 2000—. Nat. bd. dirs. Internat. Acad. Philosophy, N. Hollywood, Calif. Contbr. articles to profl. jours. Vol. mentor for disadvantaged, 1995—; ombudsman/officer The Prometheus Soc. Internat.; mem. Nat. Com. on Am. Fgn. Policy, N.Y.C., Nat. Campaign for Tolerance, Montgomery, Ala. Mem.: AAAS, Royal Overseas Soc., N.Y. Acad. Scis., Menninger Soc., Harvard Club (Boston, So. Calif., Palm Beach). Republican. Episcopalian. Achievements include research in post traumatic stress disorder and its comorbid relationship to a syndrome of mental health issues. Avocations: eclectic reading, sports, travel, theater, films. Home: Apt 40 2928 4th St Santa Monica CA 90405 Office: Ste 1215 5155 Rosecrans Ave Hawthorne CA 90250 Office Phone: 310-491-3680. E-mail: psychdr721@hotmail.com.

FILARDI, ELDONNA MARIE, music educator, accompanist; b. South Bend, Ind., July 19, 1957; d. Frank Dominick Massa and Emalou (Harshman) Massa; m. Robert Joseph Stephen Filardi, Nov. 9, 1996. BS in Music, Nyack Coll., 1980; postgrad., Westminster Choir Coll., Princeton, N.J., 1985-87. Cert. ESL tutor. Pvt. tchr. piano, Bergen County, N.J., 1973—. Music dir. Vacation Bible Sch., Oakland, NJ, 1991-93, Curtain Up, Ridgewood, NJ, 1992; tchr. music St. Alban's Presch., Oakland, 1991-92, Saddle River (NJ) Day Sch., 1992-93; music dir., Christian edn. asst. St. Alban's Ch., Oakland, 1991-93; dir. handbell choir Congl. Ch., Park Ridge, NJ, 1993-94; accompanist Canticum Sacrum, Wyckoff, NJ, 1993-94, Royal Acad. Dance classes and exams Robin Horneff Performing Arts Ctr., Waldwick, NJ, 1991-96; adj. faculty music dept. William Paterson Coll., Wayne, NJ, 1994-96; asst. Summer Choir Sch., Ridgewood; mem. Pro Arte Festival Chorus, 1987-92. Performance with Bergen Philharm., John Harms Ctr., Englewood, 2001; accompanist Ridgewood Choral, 2004- . Accompanist benefit concert Christ Ch., Pompton Lakes, NJ, 1996, Leukemia and Lymphoma Soc., 2003; choir St. Paul's Episcopal Ch., Englewood, NJ, 2000-01; tutor Literacy Vol. Am., 2004—; interim organist Zion Luth. Ch., Maywood, N.J., 2005; mem. NJ Choral Soc., 1986-87 Avocations: cross stitch, crocheting, crafts, watercolor painting, writing. Home: 326 Faller Dr Apt C New Milford NJ 07646-5265

FILARDO, THOMAS WESLEY, physician; b. Alton, Ill., June 15, 1945; s. Vincent and Carmen Irene (Clagg) F.; m. Nora L. Zorich, Mar. 22, 1984; children: N.V. Wesley, T. Daniel. BS cum laude, U. Notre Dame, 1967; MD, U. Ill., Chgo., 1971. Diplomate Am. Bd. Family Practice. Asst. prof. U. Ill. Coll. Medicine, Urbana, 1978-87, dir. intro. to clin. medicine, 1979-87; new terms editor, chief lexicographer Stedman's Med. Dictionary, 1995—. Author: (with others) Chronic Disease Management in the Homeless in Health Care of Homeless People, 1985, Medical Aspects of Homelessness in the Homeless Mentally Ill, 1984; contbr. articles to profl. jours. Founder Champaign-Urbana Physicians for Social Responsibility, Champaign, Ill., 1981. Lt. comdr. USPHS, 1975-78. Named Provider of Yr., Champaign County Health Care Consumers, 1986. Mem. Am. Acad. Family Practice, Alpha Epsilon Delta.

FILARSKI HASSELBECK, ELIZABETH, television host/personality; b. Cranston, RI, May 28, 1977; d. Kenneth J. Filarski and Elizabeth A. DelPadre; m. Tim Hasselbeck, July 6, 2002. Degree in Art, Boston Coll., 1999. Tchr., Belize, 1997; contestant, finished fourth Survivor: The Australian Outback, 2001; judge Miss Teen USA Pageant, 2001; shoe designer Puma; host The Look for Less, The Style Network, 2001—; co-host The View, ABC, 2003—. Office: The View ABC 320 W 66th St New York NY 10023-6304 also: Babette Perry Internat Creative Mgmt 8942 Wilshire Blvd Beverly Hills CA 90211

FILBERT, MICHELE LEE, music educator; b. Hays, Kans., Sept. 20, 1954; d. Vernon C. and Joan Kathleen (Beedy) Henry; m. Dwight Edward Filbert, Aug. 12, 1978; children: Kelli, Courtney, Casey. BME, Fort Hays State U., Hays, Kans., 1976; MS, Ft. Hays State U., Hays, Kans., 1993. Music instr. Unifed Sch. Dist. 304, Bazine, Kans., 1976—82, Unified Sch. Dist. 303, Ness City, Kans., 1985—97; dir. of bands Unified Sch. Dist. 489, Hays, Kans., 1997—. Profl. performer, Hays, 1976—. Mem. B us. and Profl. Women, Ness City, 1978—. Named Woman of Yr., B.P.W., 1990. Mem.:

KMEA/MENC, NEA, Sigma Sigma Sigma (nat. music dir. 1996—), Sigma Alpha Theta (editor 1976—). Avocations: reading, football, watersports, camping. Home: 1702 Wheatland Dr Hays KS 67601-2753 E-mail: filbert@gbta.net.

FILBY, IVAN LEONARD, academic administrator; b. King's Lynn, Eng., Apr. 20, 1962; s. Leonard William and Mary Elizabeth (Day) Filby; m. Kathie Susanne Taggart, July 26, 1991; children: Samuel, Katie. BS in Mgmt. and Adminstrv. Scis., Aston U., Birmingham, Eng., 1984, PhD, 1990; MA, Dublin (Ireland) U., 1993, Sheffield U., 2002. Lectr. bus. studies Trinity Coll., Dublin, 1989-99, dir. internat. student affairs, 1999—2004, chair Irish Coun. Internat. Students, 2000—03; prof. mgmt., chair mgmt. dept., assoc. faculty moderator Greenville Coll., Ill., 2005—. Vis. prof. U. Anahuac, Mexico City, 1999—, U. del Mayab, Merida, Mexico, 2002—04; expert European Commn., Brussels, 1994—2004. Contbr. articles to profl. jours.; mem. internat. editl. bd. Internat. Jour. Strategic Change Mgmt., Anahuac Jour. Dir. Cornerstone Christian Ch., Dublin, 1993. Office: Greenville Coll Greenville IL 62246 Office Phone: 618-664-6827. Business E-Mail: ivan.filby@greenville.edu.

FILCHOCK, ETHEL, education educator; BS in Edn., Kent State U. Tchr. Cleve. Pub. Schs.; with EFC Creations, Solon, Ohio. Author: Voices in Poetics: Vol. 1, 1985 (Merit award), Hall of Fame, Ethel Filchock, Vol. 1, 1991, (book of poetry) Softer Memories Across a Lifetime, 1989, (poetry chapbook) A Glimpse of Love, 1991; composer: Praise God, The Lord is Coming; lyricist (numerous songs including most recently) (Harmonious Honor award, Award for Excellence, 2000), (songs) Beautiful Lady of Medugorje, 1993, This Holy Morning, 1998, Theatre of the Mind, 2003, Only The Faces Change, 2003, Amerecord, 2003, My Beautiful America, 2003, this Holy Child, 2003, What About Tomorrow, 2003, Rolling On For Freedom, 2003, Something About You, 2003, Santa's Ho-Ho-Ho, 2003, Hilltop, 2003, Holiday Blues Circle of Life, 2003 (named into Nat. Lib. Poetry, 03). Chmn. sch. United Way, 1985-86. Recipient Cert. of Achievement N.Y. Profl./Amateur Song Jubilee, 1986, Editor's Choice award Disting. Poets of Am., Outstanding Achievement in Poetry, Nat. Libr. Poetry, 1993, Outstanding Poets of 1994, Interregnum Nat. Libr. Poetry, Best Poets of 1995, Transformation, Nat. Libr. of Poetry, Editor's Choice award Outstanding Achievement in Poetry, 1996, 2000-02, Nat. Libr. Poetry, 1995-96, 2001, Outstanding Poets of 1998 for Magnanimous Beauty, Nat. Libr. Poetry, 1998, Editor's Choice award, 1998. Mem. NAFE, Am. Fedn. Tchrs. Clubs: Akron Manuscript. Roman Catholic. Avocations: painting, travel, dance, fishing.

FILE, JOSEPH, retired research physics engineer; b. Lecce, Italy, May 6, 1923; s. Carlo and Laura (Nuzzi) F.; m. Dorothy Richards, Sept. 2, 1944; children: Joseph C., Laurel M., Jeannette. BME, Cornell U., 1944; MS, Columbia U., 1958, PhD, 1967; D in Physics, U. Lecce, Italy, 1978. Design engr. Petro Chem. Devel. Co., N.Y.C., 1946-56; rsch. sr. Princeton (N.J.) U., 1956—. Advisor N.E. region Fed. Lab. Consortium, 1992—; ofcl. U.S. rep. 2nd Atoms for Peace Conf., Geneva, 1958; Def. Dept. appointee Employer Support for the Guard and Res., 1995. Contbr. articles to profl. jours. Pres. Marine Corps Scholarship Found., 1965-75, chmn. bd. dirs., 1975-94, chmn. emeritus. Col. USMCR, 1942-74; PTO, Korea. Decorated comdr. Order of Italian Republic; Fulbright fellow, 1978. Roman Catholic. Achievements include patent on bending free D, shaped magnetic coils for fusion reactors, and fabrication and operation of world's first sixth order superconducting magnet now used on MRI imaging devices. Office: PPPL Princeton U Princeton NJ 08543

FILER, TOM HANFORD, writer, educator; b. NYC, Dec. 27; s. William LeVerne Filer and Florence Georgette Meeker. Student, Cornell U., 1943—44, Rochester U., 1944, UCLA, 1949—52. Travel agt. Haley Corp, N.Y.C., Washington and San Francisco, 1946—49; lobster diver Filer/Cunningham Inc., Malibu, Calif., 1954—56; vis. lectr. U. Iowa, Iowa City, 1963—64, Scripps Coll., Claremont, Calif., 1973—74; lectr. writers' program UCLA, 1970—97. Dir. Goat Alley Writers' Workshop, Santa Monica, Calif., 1970—2004; dealer Harrah's Club and Harvey's Wagon Wheel Casino, 1960—65; 1st mate albacore boat Patrita, 1956—59. Author: The Last Voyage, 1957 (O'Henry prize, 1959), reprint, 1962, The Man on Watch, 1961, The Box Man, 1968, The Love Makers, 1968, The Fall of Casa Malvado, 1968, The Man They Called My Wife, The Strangest Game, 1968, The Reluctant Couple, 1969, (novel trilogy) Finding Mahmoud, 2001, numerous short stories, articles, (plays) The Puritan Spirit, 1951, The Orangoutan, 1951, First Blood, 1951, Marge Moon, 1957; actor: (films) Ride the Whirlwind, 1966; author: (short stories) Treasury of America, 1981. Ensign USNR, 1945—46, PTO. Fellow, Huntington Hartford Found., Pacific Palisades, Calif., 1957—61, Montalvo, Saratoga, Calif., 1963, MacDowell Colony, Peterborough, NH, 1961—82, Yaddo Found., Saratoga Springs, NY, 1962—73, Wurlitzer Found., Taos, N.Mex., 1966, 1997; sr. fellow, Provincetown Fine Arts Ctr., 1999. Democrat. Avocations: skin diving, mountain hopping, swimming, nature.

FILERMAN, GARY LEWIS, health science association administrator, educator; b. Mpls., Nov. 16, 1936; s. Joseph H. and Bonnie (Kobrin) F.; m. Jane Harding, Sept. 15, 1962; children: Amy Beth, Joseph Harding, Suzanne Louise. BA, U. Minn., 1959, M.Health Adminstrn. (Phillips Found. fellow 1959-60), 1961, MA (W.K. Kellogg fellow 1961-64), 1963, PhD (Milbank travel grantee 1964, Orgn. Am. States fellow 1964), 1970. Adminstrv. resident Johns Hopkins Hosp., 1961-62; acting dir. Minn. Hosp. Assn., 1965; pres. Assn. Univ. Programs in Health Adminstrn., Washington, 1965-93; exec. sec. Accrediting Commn. Edn. Health Services Adminstrn., 1968-80; assoc. dir. PEW Health Professions Commn., Washington, 1993-95; dir. David A. Winston Fellowship, 1986—, pres., 1998—2003. Mem. faculty George Washington U., chmn., prof. dept. health mgmt. and policy, 1998-2000, prof., chmn. health sys., Georgetown U., 2000—; guest scholar Brookings Instn., 1962; sr. health advisor Acae. Edml. Devel., 1998-2000; cons. in field. Author: A Future of Consequence, 1989;, editor Jour. Health Adminstrn. Edn., 1982-93; author articles in field.; mem. editl. bds. profl. jours. Mem. nat. health professions adv. coun. HHS, 1983-87, coun. agy for health care policy and rsch., 1990-92; bd. dirs. Am. Refugee Commn., 1982-2004, Fairfax Audubon, 1989-93, Am. Internat. Health Alliance, Companion Care Assn., 2005; chmn. Planned Parenthood Metro Washington, 1990-91, bd. dirs. 1989-92; bd. dirs. Ctr. for Transformational Leadership, 2000-02; internat. adv. bd. Vols. of Am., 2003—. Recipient Silver medal Leuven (Belgium) U., 1972, Disting. Contbn. award Assn. U. Programs Health Adminstrn., 1979, Outstanding Achievement award Regents of U. Minn., 1982, Outstanding Achievement award Ohio State U., 1992, Humanitarian award, Am. Refugee Com., 2005; Salzburg Seminar fellow, 2000. Fellow APHA, Am. Acad. Med. Adminstrn. (hon.), hon. alumni, Univ. Chgo.,1992, diplomate Am. Coll. of Health Care Execs., 1990—; mem. Royal Soc. Health, Assn. Am. Med. Colls., Assn. Acad. Health, Cosmos Club (Washington), Phi Beta Kappa. Home: 1322 Banquo Ct Mc Lean VA 22102-2707

FILERMAN, MICHAEL HERMAN, television producer; b. Chgo., May 4, 1938; s. Arthur Joseph and Anne Leah (Greenfield) F. BS in Communications, U. Ill., 1960. Gen. program dir. Sta. WGN-TV, Chgo., 1962-67; gen. program dir., dir. daytime programs CBS TV Network, N.Y.C., 1967-72; dir. series devel. Paramount TV, 1972-74; v.p. series devel. Lorimar Prodns., 1976-83; with 20th Century Fox, 1983-85, NBC Prodns., 1985-88. Exec. prodr.: Knots Landing, Falcon Crest, Flamingo Road, Secrets of Midland Heights, King's Crossing, Sisters, John Grisham's The Client, Four Corners, (Movie of the Week) Christmas Eve, Peyton Place: The Next Generation, A Letter to Three Wives, Assault and Matrimony, The Child Saver, Take My Daughters, Please, Turn Back the Clock, Coins in the Fountain, The Story Lady, The Return of Eliot Ness, Roommates, Deadly Family Secrets, Once You Meet a Stranger, Knots Landing: Back to the Cul-de-Sac, When Andrew Came Home; prodr.: (theatre) 24th Day, I Love You!, You're Perfect!, Now Change!, Lypsinska: The Boxed Set, Our Lady of 121st Street, Tea At Five, Frozen, Sin: A Cardinal Deposed.

FILES, MARK WILLARD, business and financial consultant; b. Bartlesville, Okla., Dec. 5, 1941; s. Francis Marion and Alice Wade (Webb) F.; m. Elizabeth Kay Maltby; children: Patrick, Jennifer Leigh. BBA, U. Okla., 1963, MA, 1964; postgrad., Stanford U. CPA, Okla., La. From asst. acct. to ptnr. Peat, Marwick, Mitchell & Co., Tulsa, Okla., 1964-80; vice chmn., dir. Braeloch Holdings, Inc., Covington, La., 1980-93; ptnr. Graham Ptnrs. Fin. Cons. and Investments, Covington, La., 1993—; dir. Petrocorp Inc., 2000—. Exxon Corp. fellow U. Okla., 1964. Trustee Christ Episc. Sch., Covington, 1993—, Ctr. for Devel. and Learning. Exxon Corp. fellow U. Okla., 1964. Mem. AICPA, Okla. Soc. CPAs (chmn. ethics com. 1975-76), La. Soc. CPAs, Am. Petroleum Inst., Beau Chene Golf and Racquet Club (Mandeville, La.), Phi Eta Sigma, Beta Gamma Sigma, Pi Kappa Alpha. Republican. Episcopalian. Home: 40 Green Hills Dr Covington LA 70435-8417

FILICIA, THOM, television personality, interior designer; b. 1969; BA in Interior Design, Syracuse U. With Parish Hadley Assocs., Robert Metzger Interiors, Bilhuber Inc.; founder Thom Filicia Inc., 1998—; design specialist TV series Queer Eye for the Straight Guy, 2003—. Spokesperson Pier 1 Imports, 2004—. Co-author: Queer Eye for the Straight Guy: The Fab 5's Guide to Looking Better, Cooking Better, Dressing Better, Behaving Better, and Living Better, 2004; design work featured in House & Garden, W, City, Details, New York, N.Y. Times. Named one of House Beautiful's Top 100 Am. Designers. Office: William Morris Agy One William Morris Pl Beverly Hills CA 90212

FILI-KRUSHEL, PATRICIA, media company executive; b. Nov. 12, 1953; BA, St. John's U., Jamaica, NY, 1975; MBA, Fordham U., Bronx, NY, 1982. Various positions including program contr. ABC Sports ABC, 1975—79; dir. sports adminstrn. HBO, 1979—80, dir. sports and spls. program budgeting, 1980—81, dir. of prod., 1981—83, v.p. business affairs, 1984—88; senior v.p. programming & prod. Lifetime Television, 1988—89; group v.p. Hearts/ABC-Viacom Entertain. Services, 1990—93; pres. of ABC Daytime Walt Disney Co., 1993—98, pres., ABC TV, 1998-2000; pres., CEO Web MD Health, 2000—01; exec. v.p., admin. AOL Time Warner Inc. (now Time Warner Inc.), 2001—. Bd. dirs. Oxygen Media, Inc. Co-chair child care initiative Mayor Bloomberg's Commn. on Women's Issues; bd. dirs. Second Stage Theater, The Ctrl. Pk. Conservancy; mem. bd. comm., trustee Fordham U. Named Woman of Yr., Police Athletic League; named one of 50 Most Powerful Women, Fortune mag., 1998; recipient Muse award, Women in Film, 1993, Vision award, 1996, Women of Achievement award, Women's Project and Prodns., 1999, Matrix award, N.Y. Women in Comm., Inc., Crystal Apple award, City of N.Y. Mem.: Acad. TV Arts and Scis. (exec. com., bd. govs.), N.Y. Women in Film (past pres.). Office: Time Warner Inc 75 Rockefeller Plz New York NY 10012*

FILINSON, RACHEL, sociology educator; b. Chgo., Aug. 25, 1956; d. Herman Charles and Ediene Edith Filinson; m. Darek Niklas, Jan. 7, 1984; children: Melanie Hope Niklas, Valerie Tina Niklas. PhD, U. Aberdeen, Scotland, 1982; BA, U. Ill., 1977; MSc, U. Stirling, Scotland, 1979. Rsch. fellow Inst. of Med. Sociology, Aberdeen, Scotland, 1979—82; postdoctoral NIMH fellow U. Mo., Columbia, 1982—84; asst. prof. Purdue U., Hammond, Ind., 1984—87; prof. and chair RI Coll., Providence, 1987—. Cons. Providence Dept. of Sr. Svcs. Needs Assessment, Providence, 2004—. Contbr. articles various profl. jours. V.p. New Eng. Gerontology Acad., Cranston, RI, 2002—. Mem.: Assn. for Gerontology in Higher Edn., Gerontol. Soc. of Am. Avocations: travel, cooking. Home: 540 Lloyd Ave Providence RI 02906 Office: Rhode Island Coll 600 Mt Pleasant Ave Providence RI 02908 Office Phone: 401-456-8732. Office Fax: 401-456-8665. Business E-Mail: rfilinson@ric.edu.

FILIPACCHI, DANIEL, publishing executive; b. Paris, Jan. 12, 1928; s. Henri Filipacchi. French corr. Ebony Mag., Paris; photographer Paris Match mag.; jazz disc jockey, radio prodr. Europe 1, Paris, 1955-60; chmn., prin. owner Publs. Filipacchi, Paris, 1960—; founder, owner, editor various mags., France, 1963—; chmn., CEO Warner-Filipacchi Music, S.A., Paris, 1970-85; chmn. Hachette Filipacchi Mags., NYC, 1990—; co-artistic dir. Sidney Bechet Centennial, New Orleans, 1997; prodr. Musisoft/Masters of Jazz. Chmn., prin. owner Paris Match, other French consumer mags. Editor: Surrealism: Two Pvt. Eyes, The Nesuhi Ertegun & Daniel Filipacchi Collections, 1999. Trustee S.R. Guggenheim Mus. Named one of Top 200 Collectors, ARTnews Mag., 2004. Avocation: collector modern art, especially surrealism. Address: Hachette Filipacchi Mags 1633 Broadway 40th Floor New York NY 10019-6708 Office: Hachette Filipacchi 149-151 rue Anatole France 92300 Levallois-Perret France*

FILIPIC, MATTHEW VICTOR, academic administrator; b. Cleve., Oct. 12, 1945; s. Henry M. and Norma (Grady) Filipic; m. Louise Hutter Filipic, Mar. 16, 1974; children: Kristen, Katherine, Anne. AB in History, John Carroll U., 1967; MA in Polit. Sci., Ohio State U., 1975, PhD in Polit. Sci., 1977. CPA Ohio. Budget analyst, sr. analyst, dep. dir., asst. dir. Office Budget Mgmt., Columbus, Ohio, 1977-82; legis. budget officer Ohio Gen. Assembly, 1983-85; dir. budgets Ohio Bd. Regents, 1985-89, vice chancellor adminstrn., 1990-98, sr. vice chancellor, 1998—2000. Bd. dirs. Ohio Tuition Trust Authority, Columbus, Ohio, 1991—2000, Ohio Higher Edn. Facilities Commn., 1993—2000; v.p., bus. fiscal affairs Wright State Univ., 2000—; mem., chair funding for success com. Blue Ribbon Task Force on Financing Student Success, 2003—04. Lt. (j.g.) USNR, 1968—71. Recipient Elijah Watts Sells award, AICPA, Columbus, Ohio, 1984. Mem.: Am. Soc. Pub. Adminstrn. (pres. Ctrl. Ohio chpt. 1987). Office: Wright Street University 3640 Colonel Glenn Highway Fairborn OH 45435-0001 Home: 2934 White Water Ct Dayton OH 45431-5677

FILIPPINE, EDWARD LOUIS, federal judge; b. 1930; AB, St. Louis U., 1951, JD, 1957. Bar: Mo. 1957. Pvt. practice law, St. Louis, 1957—77; spl. asst. atty. gen. State of Mo., 1963—64; dist. judge U.S. Dist. Ct. (ea. dist.) Mo., St. Louis, 1977—, chief judge, 1990—95; U.S. sr. dist. judge U.S. Dist. Ct. for Ea. Dist. Mo., 1995—. Served with USAF, 1951-53 Mem. ABA, Mo. Bar Assn., Bar Assn. Met. St. Louis, Lawyers Assn. of St. Louis. Office: US Dist Ct Thomas F Eagleton US Cthse 111 S 10th St Rm 10.137 Saint Louis MO 63102 Office Phone: 314-244-7640. E-mail: edward_filippine@moed.uscourts.gov.

FILISKO, FRANK EDWARD, physicist, researcher; b. Lorain, Ohio, Jan. 29, 1942; s. Joseph John and Mary Magdalene (Cherven) F.; m. Doris Faye Call, Aug. 8, 1970; children: Theresa Marie, Andrew William, Edward Anthony. BA, Colgate U., 1964; MS, Purdue U., 1966; PhD, Case Western Res. U., 1969. Post doctoral fellow Case Western Res. U., Cleve., 1968-70; prof. materials sci. engrng. and macromolecular sci. U. Mich., Ann Arbor, 1970—, acting dir. macromolecular sci. and engring., 1987-96. Dir. Polymer Lab., U. Mich. Editor: Progress in Electrorheology, 1995; contbr. more than 125 articles to profl. jours. Mem. Am. Phys. Soc., Am. Chem. Soc., KC, Soc. of Rheology. Roman Catholic. Achievements include patents for Electric field dependent fluids and Electric dependent fluids-CIP. Office: U Mich Materials Sci & Engring Ann Arbor MI 48109 Office Phone: 734-763-2240. Business E-Mail: fef@umich.edu.

FILKINS, DEXTER PRICE, newspaper reporter; b. Cin., May 24, 1961; s. Cedric Eugene and Helen Jean (Samp) F. BA in Polit. Sci. with high honors, U. Fla., 1983; MPhil in Internat. Rels., U. Oxford, Eng., 1986. Legis. aide to U.S. Sen. Lawton Chiles, Washington, 1983-84; reporter The Miami Herald, 1986—95, LA Times, 1995—97, bur chief New Delhi, 1997—2000; reporter NY Times, 2000—. Recipient George B. Polk award for Iraq war coverage, 2005. Mem. Phi Beta Kappa. Office: Newsroom NY Times 229 W 43rd St New York NY 10036*

FILLAFER, RICHARD, music educator; b. Fargo, ND, May 16, 1955; s. Harry and Phyllis Fillafer; m. Carol Enger, June 20, 1987; children: Jonathan, Sarah. BA, Concordia Coll., 1977; MEd, Coll. St. Scholastica, 2000. Cert. tchr. ND, Minn. Music educator Golden Valley (ND) Sch. Dist., 1977—78, Newfolden (Minn.) Ind. Sch. Dist., 1978—82, Big Lake (Minn.) Ind. Sch. Dist., 1984—, music dept. chair, 1994—. Pres. region V sub-sect. II Music Educators, Minn., 1997—98; pres. Comprehensive Arts Planning Program, Big Lake, 1995—98; asst. condr. - norway tour Lincoln H.S., Thief River Falls, Minn., 1984—84; soloist Northland Cmty. Band - European Tour, Thief River Falls, 1990—90; exec. officer Therco, Inc., Thief River Falls, 1980—82. Recipient Leadership in Ednl. Excellence award, Ctrl. Minn. Ednl. Coop. Svc. Unit, 1994. Mem.: Comprehensive Arts Planning Program, Big Lake Edn. Minn., Edn. Minn., Minn. Music Educators, Music Educators Nat. Conf. Office: Ind Sch Dist 727 501 Minnesota Avenue Big Lake MN 55309

FILLBROOK, THOMAS GEORGE, telephone company executive; b. Detroit, Jan. 3, 1949; s. John Moyle and Marie Evelyn (Pelto) F. BA, Wayne State U., 1970. Cert. tchr., Mich. Substitute tchr. Van Dyke Pub. Schs., Warren, Mich., 1971-73; mgr. Ameron, Okemos, Mich., 1973-74; salesman F&E Check Protector, Detroit, 1974-76; ops. mgr. Loss Prevention Inc., Royal Oak, Mich., 1976-78; svc. rep. SBC Global Markets, Pontiac, Mich., 1979—; actor/clown Clowning Around Entertainment, Romeo, Mich., 1958—. Actor Holy Cow Show, WGPR Channel 62, Detroit, 1988; dir. Winter Magic, Harron Cable, Rome, 1991; on air analyst "Hockeytime" WBRW Channel 6, 1998—2004. Polit. and hist. columnist, polit. editor Mill Creek View Newspaper, Washington; mem. City of Hope 1994 Com. Mem. Rep. Nat. Com., Washington, Founders Soc., Detroit Inst. Arts. Recipient commendation Macomb County Bd. Commrs., 1991, 1st Place Clown Costume Competition and Group Act award Mich. State Fair and Exposition, 1995, Top Individual Fund Raiser City of Hope, 1997, 98, 99, 2000. Mem. Internat. Platform Assn., Finnish Ctr. Assn., Detroit Zool. Soc., Citizens Against Government Waste (charter), Elks (chmn. 1985). Episcopalian. Avocation: poetry. Home: 54723 Shelby Rd Shelby Township MI 48316-1441 E-mail: fillbrookme@aol.com.

FILLER, RONALD HOWARD, lawyer; b. St. Louis, Apr. 11, 1948; s. Leon Isaac and Jeanette Frances (Sanofsky) F.; m. Paula; children: Stephen Paul, Lindsay Ann. BS, U. Ill., 1970; JD, George Washington U., 1973; LLM in Taxation, Georgetown U., 1976. Bar: D.C. 1973, Ill. 1976, N.Y. 1993. Atty. SEC, Washington, 1973-76; assoc. Abramson & Fox, Chgo., 1976-77; assoc. counsel Conti Cmty. Svc., Chgo., 1977-78, dir. mgmt. accounts, 1978-80; mng. ptnr. Filler Zaner & Assocs., Chgo., 1980-85; ptnr. Vedder, Price, Kaufman & Kammholz, Chgo., 1985-93, corp. practice leader, 1989-91, mem. exec. com., 1991-93; dir. futures adminstrn. Lehman Bros., Inc., 1993—. Dir. Commodities Law Inst., Ill. Inst. Tech./Chgo-Kent Law Sch., 1978-97, adj. prof. law, 1977-93, bd. overseers, 1982-97; lectr. Commodities Ednl. Inst., 1977-89; adj. prof. law Bklyn. Law Sch., 1994-96; vice chmn. Broker Tec Clearing Corp., 2002-04. Contbr. articles to jours. and futures mags. Named one of top 315 lawyers State of Ill., 1991. Mem. ABA (chmn. sub futures commn. mchts. 1986-1995), Nat. Futures Assn. (bd. dirs. 1984-87), Am. Arbitration Assn. (arbitrator), Mid Am. Commodity Exch. (bd. dirs. 1984-86), Chgo. Bar Assn. (chmn. commodities law com. 1981-82, vice chmn. fin. and legal svcs. com. 1988-89, co-vice chmn. large law firm com. 1991-92), Nat. Assn. Futures Traders Assn., Futures Industry Assn. (bd. dirs. 1990-92, exec. com. Chgo. divsn. 1986-88, exec. com. Law and Comp. divsn. 1985-90, 92—, sec. 1995-98, pres. 1998-2000), N.Y. State Bar Assn., Ill. State Bar Assn. Democrat. Jewish. Office: Lehman Brothers Inc 745 7th Ave 3d Fl New York NY 10019 Home: 100 Warren St #1915 Jersey City NJ 07302 Office Phone: 212-526-0236. Business E-Mail: rfiller@lehman.com.

FILLEY, CHRISTOPHER MARK, neurologist, researcher; b. Saranac Lake, N.Y., July 31, 1951; s. Giles Franklin and Mary Brown (Klinefelter) F. BA, Williams Coll., 1973; MD, Johns Hopkins U., 1979. Diplomate Am. Bd. Psychiatry and Neurology. Intern U. Conn., Farmington, 1979—80; resident in neurology U. Colo., Denver, 1980—83; behavioral neurology fellow Boston U., 1983—84; from instr. to asst. prof. neurology U. Colo. Sch. Medicine, Denver, 1984—91, assoc. prof. neurology, 1991—97, prof. neurology, 1997—. Prin. investigator studies in Alzheimers Disease NIH, Bethesda, Md., 1991-94. Author: Neurobehavioral Anatomy, 1995, Neurobehavioral Anatomy, 2d edit., 2001, The Behavioral Neurology of White Matter, 2001; contbr. articles to profl. jours. Health com. Denver Found., 1995-98. Fellow Am. Acad. Neurology; mem. Am. Neurol. Assn., Internat. Neuropsychol. Soc., Soc. for Behavioral and Cognitive Neurology, Colo. Soc. Clin. Neurologists. Avocations: piano, hiking, reading, guitar, skiing. Office: Univ Colo Behavioral Neurology Sect 4200 E 9th Ave Denver CO 80220-3700 Office Phone: 303-315-6461. Business E-Mail: christopher.filley@uchsc.edu.

FILLEY, WARREN VERNON, allergist; b. Topeka, Kans., Oct. 27, 1950; MD, U. Kans. Sch. Medicine, 1976. Diplomate Am. Bd. Allergy and Immunology, Am. Bd. Internal Medicine. Intern U. Okla., 1976-77, resident in internal medicine, 1977-79; fellow allergy and immunology Mayo Clin., Rochester, Minn., 1979-81; with Presbyn. Hosp., Oklahoma City; clin. prof. medicine U. Okla. Mem. AMA, Am. Acad. Allergy, Asthma and Immunology, Am. Coll. Allergy, Asthma and Immunology, Okla. Med. Assn. Office: Okla Allergy and Asthma Clin 750 NE 13th St Oklahoma City OK 73104-5051 Office Phone: 405-235-0040. Business E-Mail: wfilley@oklahomaallergy.com.

FILLINGER, MARK F., vascular surgeon, researcher; b. Columbus, Ohio, Oct. 7, 1957; s. Robert J. and Charlotte A. Fillinger; m. Mary C. Pawlinga, Jan. 1, 1989. BS in Mech. Engring., Ohio State U., 1979, MD, 1984. Diplomate Am. Bd. Surgery (Added Qualifications in Vascular Surgery), Nat. Bd. Med. Examiners; registered vascular technologist; lic. physician, N.Y., N.H. Resident in gen. surgery SUNY Health Sci. Ctr., Syracuse, 1984-91, rsch. fellow dept. surgery, 1987-89; fellow in vascular surgery Dartmouth-Hitchcock Med. Ctr., Hanover, NH, 1991—93, asst. prof. vascular surgery, 1993—99, assoc. prof., 1999—. Contbr. chpts. to books, articles to profl. jours. Recipient Peter B. Samuels award Soc. Clin. Vascular Surgery, 1989, Ralph A. Deterling award New Eng. Soc. for Vascular Surgery, 1993. Fellow ACS, Soc. Vascular Surgery, European Soc. Vascular Surgery, Internat. Soc. Endovascular Specialists; mem. AMA, Internat. Soc. for Applied Cardiovascular Biology, Soc. for Vascular Tech., Am. Inst. Ultrasound in Medicine, N.H. Med. Soc., Pi Tau Sigma. Avocations: golf, skiing, tennis, horseback riding. Home: 17 Mulherrin Farm Rd Hanover NH 03755-4907 Office: Dartmouth-Hitchcock Med Ctr Sect Vascular Surgery One Medical Ctr Dr Lebanon NH 03756

FILLION, THOMAS JOHN, lawyer; b. Detroit, Apr. 21, 1953; s. George Joseph and Patricia Vera (Roy) F. B in Gen. Studies with distinction, U. Mich., 1975, JD, 1980. Bar: Mich. 1981, U.S. Dist. Ct. (ea. dist.) Mich. 1981. Pvt. practice, West Bloomfield, Mich., 1981—. Mem. ABA. Home and Office: 1814 Henbert West Bloomfield MI 48324

FILLIOS, LOUIS CHARLES, retired science educator; b. Boston, July 1, 1923; s. Charles Louis and Pagona (Kefalas) F.; m. Iphigenia Loomis, June 15, 1947; children: Despena Fillios Billings, Diana Fillios Downey, Hilary Fillios Grant. AB, Harvard, 1948, MS, 1953, ScD, 1956. Rsch. assoc., then assoc. Harvard U., 1956-60; asst. prof. physiol. chemistry MIT, 1961-64, assoc. prof., 1964-66; assoc. rsch. prof. biochemistry and pathology Boston U. Sch. Medicine, 1966-68; prof. nutritional sci. Boston U., 1968-94; prof. biochemistry Boston U. Sch. Medicine, 1970-94; dir. divsn. basic sci. Boston U. Sch. Medicine (Sch. Grad. Dentistry), 1970-75, chmn. dept. nutritional scis., 1973-94; prof. biochemistry emeritus Boston U., 1994—. Chmn. Mass. Task Force Nutrition and Aging, 1970-71; cons. Mass. Office of Elder Affairs, 1971-73; co-chmn. nutrition sect. White House Conf. Aging, 1971-72; cons. VA, Bedford, Mass., 1982-87; mem. pres.'s adv. coun. Hellenic Coll., 1968-73. Author numerous research articles fields biochemistry, pathology and nutrition; contbr. sci. and profl. jours. 1st lt. USAAF, 1943-45. Decorated D.F.C., Air Medal with 3 oak leaf clusters (7 battle stars); recipient Outstanding Educator of Am. award Boston U., 1972, Spl. Honor, 1995. Fellow AAAS, Am. Heart Assn. (established investigator 1961-66); mem. Am. Inst. Nutrition (chmn. fellow award com. 1978-81), Am. Soc. for Nutritional Scis., Sigma Xi (Harvard chpt.), Omicron Kappa Upsilon (hon.). Home: 19 Eliot Rd Lexington MA 02421-5630

FILLMORE, JOHN DILLON, artist; b. Canoga Park, Calif., Nov. 24, 1951; s. Herbert Peter and Patricia Louise (Dillon) F. BFA, Art Ctr. Coll. Design, Hollywood, Calif., 1973. Fine artist, designer Chris O'Connell Inc./Ancient Echoes/Martex, Santa Fe, N.Mex., 1989-95; freelance fine artist Santa Fe, Tarzana, 1974—. Recipient Hubbard Art award for excellence, 1991. Republican. Roman Catholic. Avocations: art history, collecting art and books.

FILLMORE, PETER ARTHUR, mathematician, educator; b. Moncton, N.B., Can., Oct. 28, 1936; s. Henry Arthur and Jeanne Margaret (Archibald) F.; m. Anne Ellen Garvock, Aug. 6, 1960; children: Jennifer Anne, Julia Margaret, Peter Alexander. B.Sc., Dalhousie U., 1957; MA, U. Minn., 1960, PhD, 1962. Instr. U. Chgo., 1962-64; asst. prof. math. Ind. U., 1964-67, assoc. prof., 1967-71, prof., 1971-72; vis. assoc. prof. U. Toronto, Canada, 1970-71; prof. math. Dalhousie U., Halifax, Canada, 1972-2001; Killam sr. fellow Dalhousie U., Halifax, 1972-73, Killam rsch. prof., 1973-78, chmn. dept. math., stats. and computer sci., 1987-91, prof. emeritus, 2001—. Sr. vis. fellow U. Edinburgh, 1977; mem. Math. Scis. Rsch. Inst., Berkeley, Calif., 1984-85, Fields Inst. Rsch. Math. Sci., 1994-95; vis. prof. U. Copenhagen, 1990. Author: Notes on Operator Theory, 1970, A User's Guide to Operator Algebras, 1996; mem. editl. bd. Jour. Integral Equations and Operator Theory, C.R. Math. Rep. Acad. Soc. Can.; contbr. articles to profl. jours. Fellow Royal Soc. Can.; mem. Can. Math. Soc. (council 1973-75, 77-79, v.p. 1975-77, pres. 1994-96), Am. Math. Soc. (council 1982-84). Office: Dalhousie U Math Dept Halifax NS Canada B3H 3J5 Office Phone: 902-494-2572. Business E-Mail: fillmore@mathstat.dal.ca.

FILLMORE, ROBERT M., lawyer; b. Wichita, Kans., 1953; BGS, Univ. Kans., 1975, JD, 1977. Bar: Kans. 1977, Tex. 1986, lic.: US Supreme Ct. 1980. Asst. atty. gen., litig. divsn. State of Kans., 1979—80, spl. asst. atty. gen., 1981—85; ptnr., co-head, regulated industries, govtl. rels. team; head, regulated utilities practice area Hunton & Williams LLP, Dallas. Adj. faculty, law Univ. Kans, 1981—82. Mem.: ABA (chmn., spl. com. on restructuring elec. industry 2003—), State Bar of Tex. (mem., vice chmn., pub. utility law section 1997—2001), Ctr. Am. and Internat. Law (mem. exec. com, chmn., power energy trading and mktg. com. 2002—04). Office: Hunton & Williams Energy Plz 30th Fl 1601 Bryan St Dallas TX 75201-3402 Office Phone: 212-979-3092. Office Fax: 214-880-0011. Business E-Mail: bfillmore@hunton.com.

FILLPOT, BOB G., architecture educator; BArch, Tex. Tex., 1967; M in Design Studies, Harvard U., 1997. With Lloyd Jones Fillpot Assocs. (formerly Lloyd, Morgan and Jones, Archs.), Houston, 1967, pres., 1984—96; prof. arch. U. Okla. Coll. Arch., Norman, dean, 1998—. Named Disting. Alumnus, Tex. Tech. U. Coll. Arch.; recipient Citation of Recognition, Tex. Soc. Archs. Fellow: AIA. Office: Univ Okla Divsn Arch 830 Van Vleet Oval Norman OK 73019

FILNER, BOB, congressman; b. Pitts., Sept. 4, 1942; m. Jane Merrill; children: Erin, Adam. BA in Chemistry, Cornell U., 1963; MA in History, U. Del., 1969; PhD in History, Cornell U., 1973. Prof. history San Diego State U., 1970-92; legis. asst. Senator Hubert Humphrey, 1974, Congressman Don Fraser, 1975; spl. asst. Congressman Jim Bates, 1984; city councilman 8th dist. City of San Diego, 1987-92, dep. mayor, 1992; mem. U.S. Congress from 51st Calif. dist. (formerly 50th), 1993—; mem. transp. and infrastructure com., vets. affairs com. Pres. San Diego Bd. Edn., 1982, mem.-elect 1979-83; chmn. San Diego Schs. of the Future Commn., 1986-87. Democrat. Office: US Ho of Reps 2428 Rayburn House Office Bldg Washington DC 20515-0001 also: 333 F St Ste A Chula Vista CA 91910 Address: 1101 Airport Rd Ste D Imperial CA 92251 Office Phone: 619-422-5963, 760-355-8800. Office Fax: 619-422-7290, 760-355-8802.*

FILO, DAVID, Internet company executive; b. Moss Bluff, La. BS in Computer Engring., Tulane U.; MSEE, Stanford U., 1990, PhD studies in Elec. Engring. Co-creator online navigational guide Yahoo!, Calif., 1994—; co-founder, chief Yahoo! Inc., Calif., 1995—. Co-author (with Jerry Yang, Karen Heyman): (books) Yahoo! Unplugged: Your Discovery Guide to the Webb, 1995; co-author: (with Richard Raucci, Elizabeth Crane, Jerry Yang) Yahooligans!: Way Cool Web Sites, 1996. Named one of 400 Richest Americans (#74), Forbes mag., 2004. Named company YAHOO! (acronym for Yet Another Hierarchical Officious Oracle). Office: Yahoo! Inc 701 First Ave Sunnyvale CA 94089

FILORAMO, DOROTHY CHRISTINE, academic administrator; d. John Michael Filoramo and Lillian Cecilia Bracken; m. William Thomas Byrnes, Sept. 8, 1962 (div. Jan. 0, 1985); children: Christa Regina Brynes-O'Brien, John Anthony Byrnes, William Thomas Byrnes, Meghan Rita Byrnes-Coyle. BA, Marymount Manhattan Coll., N.Y.C., 1962. Dir. of mktg. Gurney's Inn Resort and Internat. Spa, Montauk, NY, 1983—89, Deer Run Ski Resort, Stamford, NY, 1989—90; mktg. cons. NY, 1990—93; dir. of mktg. Catskill Advt. Agy., Arkville, NY, 1991—92; v.p. for instl. advancement Dominican Coll., Orangeburg, NY, 1993—. Mem. Westchester Devel. Orgn., 1997—; mem. adv. bd. S.C.O.R.E.; bd. dirs. Leadership Rockland, Inc., NY, 2002—; pres. Leadership Rockland Alumni, NY, 2002—04; pres., bd. dirs. People-To-People, Nyack, NY, 2005; chair of the bd. of trustees Dominican Acad., N.Y.C., 1998—2000, trustee, 1994—2000; first pres., founding mem. East End Women's Network, Riverhead, NY, 1981—83; chair New Directions for Women, Riverhead, NY, 1983—85; first pres. and founder Catskill Women's Network, Roxbury, NY, 1991—93; exec. bd. dir. Rockland Devel. Coun., NY. Named Woman of the Yr., East End Women's Network, 1990; recipient Nat. Silver award for mktg., ARRDA, 1985, 1987. Mem.: Women in Devel., Fund Raising Profls. Roman Catholic. Home: 18 Bon Aire Cir Suffern NY 10901 Office: Dominican College 470 Western Hwy Orangeburg NY 10962 E-mail: dorothy.filoramo@dc.edu.

FILOSA, GARY FAIRMONT RANDOLPH V., II, columnist, theater producer, film producer; b. Wilder, Vt., Feb. 22, 1931; s. Gary F.R. de Marco de Varra and Rosaline M. (Falzaran) F.; m. Catherine Moray Stewart (dec.); children: Marc Christian Bazire de Villadon III, Gary Fairmont Randolph de Varra III. Grad., Mt. Hermon Sch., 1950; PhB, U. Chgo., 1954; BA, U. Americas, Mex., 1967; MA, Calif. Western U., 1968; PhD, U.S. Internat. U., 1970. Sports reporter Claremont Daily Eagle, Rutland Herald, Vt. Informer, 1947-52; pub. The Chicagoan, 1952-54; account exec., editor house publs. Robertson, Buckley & Gotsch, Inc., Chgo., 1953-54; account exec. Fuller, Smith & Ross, Inc., N.Y.C., 1955; prodr./host Weekend KCET Channel 13, N.Y.C., 1955-67; editor Apparel Arts mag. (now Gentlemen's Quar.), Esquire, Inc., N.Y.C., 1955-56; chmn. bd., CEO, pres. Filosa Publs. Internat., N.Y.C., 1956-63; pub. Teenage, Rustic Rhythm, Teen Life, Mystery Digest, Top Talent, Rock & Roll Roundup, Celebrities, Stardust, Personalities, Campus monthly mags.; pres., chmn. bd. Teenarama Records, Inc., N.Y.C., 1956-62; chmn. bd., pres. Produciones Mexicanes Internationales (S.A.), Mexico City, 1957-68; assoc. pub. Laundromatic Age, N.Y.C., 1958-59; ptnr. with Warner LeRoy purchase of Broadway plays for Hollywood films, N.Y.C., 1958-61; pres. Montclair Sch., 1958-60, Pacific Registry, Inc., L.A., 1959-61; exec. prodr. Desilu Studios, Inc., Hollywood, Calif., 1959-61; exec. asst. to Benjamin A. Javits, 1961-62; propr. Gino's of Hollywood, 1961-70; dean adminstrn. Postgrad. Ctr. for Mental Health, N.Y.C., 1962-64; chmn. bd., CEO Filosa Films Internat., Beverly Hills, Calif., 1962—; pres. Amateur Athletes Internat., Iowa City, Iowa, 1996-2000; chmn. bd., pres. Cinematografica Americana Internationale (S.A.), Mexico City, 1964-84; pres. Casa Filosa Corp., Palm Beach, Fla., 1982-87; dir. Cmty. Savs., North Palm Beach, Fla., 1982-87. V.p. acad. affairs World Acad., San Francisco, 1967-68; asst. to provost Calif. Western U., San Diego, 1968-69; assoc. prof. philosophy Art Coll., San Francisco, 1969-70; v.p. acad. affairs, dean of faculty Internat. Inst., Phoenix, 1968-73; chmn. bd. dirs., pres. Universite Universelle, 1970-73, 2000—; bd. dirs., v.p. acad. affairs, dean Summer Sch., Internat. C.C., L.A., 1970-72; chmn. bd., pres. Social Directory Calif., 1967-75, Am. Assn. Social Registries, L.A., 1970-76; pres. Social Directory U.S., N.Y.C., 1974-76; pres. Herbert Hoover Forum, Iowa City, 1996-2000; chmn. bd. dirs. Internat. Soc. Social Registers, Paris, 1974—; surfing coach U. Calif. at Irvine, 1975-77; v.p. Xerox-Systemic, 1979-80; CEO Internat. Surfing League, Palm Beach, 1987-95, Santa Barbara, Calif., 1996—; chmn., CEO Filosa Harrop Internat., Phoenix, 1987-89; pres. Amateur Athletes Internat., Iowa City, 1996-2000; nationally syndicated columnist Conservations with Am., 1997-. Editor: Sci. Digest, 1961-62; composer: (lyrics) The Night Discovers Love, 1952, That Certain Something, 1953, Bolero of Love, 1956; author: (stage play) Let Me Call Ethel, 1955, The Bisexual, 1961, Technology Enters 21st Century, 1966, (mus.) Feather Light, 1966, No Public Funds for Nonpublic Schools, 1968, Creative Function of the College President, 1969, The Surfers Almanac, 1977, The Filosa Newsletter, 1986-92, The Sexual Continuum, 1990, Traveltalk, 1991, God's Own Prince, 1995, Holy Hawai'i, 1996, (biography) A Plague on Paradise, 1994, (TV series) Danny Thomas Show, 1963, Surfing USA, 1977, Payne of Florida, 1985, Honolulu, 1991, The Gym, 1992, Sales Pitch, 1992, 810 Ocean Avenue, 1992, One Feather, 1992, Conversations with America, 1989, All American Beach Party, 1989, Riding High, 2000, Dreamsport, 2000, Icons, 2000; contbr. numerous articles, editorials, to profl. jours., newspapers, and encys., including Life, Look, Sci. Digest, Ency. of Sports, World Book Ency., New York Times, Cedar Rapids Gazete, L.A. Times, others. Trustee Univ. of the Ams., Pueblo, Mex., 1986-2000; candidate for L.A. City Coun., 1 959; chmn. Educators for Re-election of Ivy Baker Pirest, 1970; mem. So. Calif. Com. for Olympic Games, 1977-84. With AUS, 1954-55. Recipient DAR Citizenship award, 1959, Silver Conquistador award Am. Assn. Social Registers, 1970, Ambassador's Cup U. Ams., 1967, resolution Calif. State Legis., 1977, Duke Kahanamoku Classic surfing trophy, 1977, gold pendant Japan Surfing Assn., 1978, Father of Olympic Surfing award Internat. Athletic Union, 1995, Father of Surfing trophy Amateur Athletes Internat., 1997, Father of Surfing trophy Internat. Surfing Fedn., 2000; inducted into Rock & Roll Mus. & Hall of Fame, Cleve., 1995. Mem. NAACP, NCAA (bd. dels. 1977-82), AAU (gov. 1978-82), Am. Acad. Motion Picture Arts and Scis., Internat. Surfing Com., U.S. Surfing Com. (founder 1960—), Internat. Surfing League (founder, chmn., CEO 1988—), Internat. Surfing Fedn. (pres. 1960—), Am. Assn. UN, Authors League, Authors Guild, Alumni Assn. U. Ams. (pres. 1967-70), Surf Club of the Palm Beaches (pres. 1983-94), Sierra Club, Surfing Hui of Hawaii, Internat. Soc. Bibliotherapists (Paris, pres. 1997—), Lords Corybantes (Berlin) (life pres. 1966—), Commonwealth Club (San Francisco), Town Hall (L.A.), Calif. Club (L.A.), Palm Beach Surf Club, Sigma Omicron Lambda (founder, pres. 1965-92). Episcopalian. Office: PO Box 299 Beverly Hills CA 90213-0299 Personal E-mail: garyfilosa@att.net. Business E-Mail: ffilms@att.net.

FILPI, ROBERT ALAN, lawyer; b. Chgo., Oct. 8, 1945; s. John Andrew and Eunice Lorraine (Taylor) F.; m. Janice Elizabeth Crusoe, June 24, 1967; children: Jennifer Anne, Christopher Alan, Emily Elizabeth. BA in History, magna cum laude, Harvard U., 1967; JD, Northwestern U., 1970. Bar: Ill. 1970, U.S. Dist. Ct. (no. dist.) Ill. 1971, U.S. Ct. Appeals (7th cir.) 1971, U.S. Supreme Ct. 1975. Asst. U.S. atty. No. Dist. Ill., Chgo., 1971-75; dep. chief U.S. atty. No. Dist. Ill., Civil Divsn., Chgo., 1975-76; ptnr. Stack & Filpi, Chgo., 1976—. Assoc. editor Jour. Criminal Law, Criminology and Police Sci., 1969-70. Coach, Spring Lake Sports League, Lincolnshire, Ill. 1984-91; mem. Village of Lincolnshire Plan Commn., 1984-94. Recipient Hyde prize Northwestern U. Sch. Law, 1967. Mem. ABA, Chgo. Bar Assn., Union League, Harvard Club. Office: 140 S Dearborn St Ste 411 Chicago IL 60603-5201

FILSON, RONALD COULTER, architect, educator, dean; b. Chardon, Ohio, Dec. 11, 1946; s. Clifford Coulter and Mae Alice (Foster) F.; m. Susan Virginia Saward, Dec. 14, 1973 (div. May 1996); children: Timothy Coulter, Lily Virginia; m. Lea Ann Sinclair, Oct. 9, 1999. Diploma, Am. Acad. in Rome, 1970; B.Arch., Yale U., 1970. Registered arch., Calif., La., Mass., Ohio, Miss., Nat. Coun. Archtl. Registration Bds. Architect Atelier d'Etudes, Ghardaia, Algeria, 1971-73; asst. prof., asst. dean Sch. of Architecture UCLA, 1974-80; dean sch. architecture Tulane U., New Orleans, 1980-92, prof. sch. architecture, 1980—; prin. Ronald Filson, FAIA, Architects, New Orleans. Prin. works include Piazza d'Italia, New Orleans, 1978 (award 1976), Eola Hotel, 1980, Lee House, 1984, Hyatt Hotel, Poydras Plaza, 1987-88, Nat. Pk. Svc. Edn. Ctr., Nat. D-Day Mus., Trump Casino, L.A. Artists Guild, Natchez Visitors Ctr. Pres. Friends of the Schindler House, L.A., 1978-80; bd. dirs. New Orleans Arts Coun., 1980-93, pres., 1989-92, Contemporary Arts Ctr., New Orleans, 1980-84, New Orleans Planning Commn., 1985-87. Recipient design citations Progressive Architecture mag., 1969, 76, Rome prize Am. Acad. in Rome, 1969 Fellow AIA (Design awards 1980, 81, 85, 87, 89, 92, 94, 98, 99, 2000, 01, Richardson medal 1992); mem. AIA La. (pres. 1998), New Orleans AIA (pres. 1994), Yale Alumni Assn. La. (pres. 1992-94), So. Yacht Club, New Orleans Lawn Tennis Club (bd. govs. 1998—). Avocations: watercolors, sailing. Office: 1750 St Charles Ave 204 New Orleans LA 70130 Office Phone: 504-412-0060, 504-865-5389. Business E-Mail: rfilson@tulane.edu.

FILSTON, HOWARD CHURCH, pediatrician, surgeon, educator; b. NYC, Dec. 29, 1935; s. Howard Samuel and Marion (Church) F.; m. Nancy Lee Jameson, June 3, 1961 (dec. Nov. 2002); children: Scott Jameson (dec.), Timothy Howard, Megan Lee Johnson; m. Sandra Kay Stoutt, May 7, 2005. AB, Harvard U., 1958; MD, Case Western Res. U., 1962. Diplomate Am. Bd. Med. Examiners. Intern in gen. surgery Univ. Hosps., Cleve., 1962-63, asst. resident in gen. surgery, 1963-64, 66-68, chief resident, 1968-69; asst. chief resident pediatric surgery Children's Hosp. Phila., 1969-70; instr. pediatric surgery U. Pa. Sch. of Medicine, Phila., 1969-71, chief resident pediatric surgery, 1970-71; asst. prof. pediatric surgery Case Western Res. U. Hosp., Cleve., 1971-76; assoc. prof. pediatric surgery and pediatrics Duke U. Med. Ctr., Durham, NC, 1976-82, chief pediatric surgery, 1976-90, prof. pediatric surgery and pediats., 1982—90, prof. pediatric surgery and pediatrics, U. Tenn. Med. Ctr., Knoxville, 1990-2000, chief pediatric surgery, 1990-2000, vice chmn. dept. surgery, 1992-2000; emeritus prof.of pediat. surgery, 2000—. Specialist site visitor, pediatric surgery, Accreditation Coun. Grad. Med. Edn., 1982-90, 1995—. Author: Surgical Problems in Children, 1982; author: (with others) The Surgical Neonate, 1978, rev. 1985; assoc. editor, Jour. Pediatric Surgery, 1985-2000; mem. editorial bd. Pediatrics, 1990-97; contbr. articles to profl. jours. Bd. dirs. Pediatric Family Ctr. of N.C. (Ronald McDonald House), Durham, 1980-90, Surgeon Gen.'s Workshop on Drunk Driving, chmn. Citizens Adv. Panel, 1988; mem. exec. bd. Met. Drug Commn., Knoxville, 1993-2000, v.p., 1997-2000, chair DUI task force, 1994-99. Served to capt. U.S. Army, 1964-66. Nat. scholar Harvard U., 1954-58. Fellow ACS (gov. 1992-98), Am. Acad. Pediatrics (surg., exec. com. 1984-91, chmn. 1989-90), Am. Pediatric Surg. Assn. (edn. com. 1984-90, sec., bd. govs. 1994-97), Am. Surg. Assn., So. Surg. Assn.; mem. Alpha Omega Alpha. Republican. Presbyterian. Avocations: family activities, water sports, sailing. Office: Univ of Tenn Med Ctr Dept Surgery Box U-11 1924 Alcoa Hwy Knoxville TN 37920-6900 Personal E-mail: hnfilston@earthlink.net.

FILTER, TERRANCE ANDERSON, clinical psychologist; b. Celina, Ohio, Aug. 15, 1950; s. Donald Francis and Elizabeth Jane (Anderson) F.; m. Patricia Ann Green, Aug. 21, 1971 (div. 1986); m. Sara Bahar, Apr. 22, 1988 (dec. 1999). BA, Ohio State U., 1972; MA, U. Mich., 1976, PhD, 1978. Lic. psychologist, Mich. Fellow psychol. clinic U. Mich., Ann Arbor, 1975-78, rsch. assoc. med. ctr.; pvt. practice clin. psychology Birmingham and Ann Arbor, Mich., 1979—; dir. psychol. svcs. Detroit Psychiat. Inst., 1982-86; program dir. Woodside Med. Ctr., Pontiac, Mich., 1986-89; dir. chem. dependency programs Wyandotte (Mich.) Hosp. and Med. Ctr., 1989—, faculty program for advanced psychotherapy, 1990-96; adj. prof. psychology U. Detroit, Mich., 1983—; founder, pres. Vital Connections, PLLC, Detroit, 1999—. Cons. Detroit Osteo. Hosp., Highland Park, Mich., 1982-83, Wyandotte (Mich.) Gen. Hosp., 1984—, Bloomfield Inst. Sleep Disorders, Pontiac, 1986—, Ctr. for Forensic Psychiatry, Ypsilanti, Mich., Mich. Dept. Corrections Bur. Forensic Svcs., 1998—; dir., v.p. and treas. edn. and research fund Detroit Psychiat. Inst., 1983-87; dir. Downriver Addiction Network div. Henry Ford Healthcare Corp., 1992—, ctrl. diagnostic and referral svcs and Downriver Psychiat. Assessment Ctr. Henry Ford Wyandotte Hosp., 1996—. Mem. Am. Psychol. Assn., Mich. Psychol. Assn. (pub. service com. 1986), Mich. Soc. Psychoanalytic Psychologists, Alliance for Mental Health Services. Office: 380 N Old Woodward Ave Ste 156 Birmingham MI 48009-5307 E-mail: terryfilter@comcast.net.

FILTON, STEVE G., corporate financial executive; Grad., U. Pa., 1979. CPA. With audit divsn. Arthur Andersen, 1979—85; dir. corp. acctg. Universal Health Svcs., King of Prussia, Pa., 1985—91, v.p., contr., 1991—2003, v.p., CFO, 2003—. Office: Universal Health Svcs PO Box 61558 King Of Prussia PA 19406-0958

FINA, PAUL JOSEPH, lawyer; b. Chgo., Mar. 1, 1959; s. Paul Emil and Vera Christiane (Mutzbauer) F.; m. Robyn Leann Hughes, May 24, 1986; 1 child, Paul George. BA in Econs., U. Ill., 1982, MA, 1983; JD, DePaul U., Chgo., 1987; postgrad. in Internat. Bus. and Trade Law, U. Ill., 2003—. Bar: Ill. 1988, U.S. Dist. Ct. (no. dist.) Ill. 1990, U.S. Ct. Appeals (7th cir.) 1990, U.S. Supreme Ct. 1991, U.S. Ct. Internat. Trade 2004. Assoc. Haskin, Taylor & McDonough, Wheaton, Ill., 1988-90, Komessar & Wintroub, Chgo., 1990-94; pvt. practice Law Offices of Paul J. Fina, Chgo., 1994—2001, Law Offices of Fina & Hunner, Chgo., 2001—. Mem. bus. faculty Coll. of DuPage, Glen Ellyn, Ill., 1986—, Aurora (Ill.) U., 1997—. Gen. counsel Housing Helpers, Inc., Riverside, Ill., 1991—. DePaul law grantee, 1985. Fellow Internat. Biog. Assn. (named Man of Yr. 2004); mem. ATLA, ABA, Internat. Bar Assn., Ill. Bar Assn., DuPage County Bar Assn. (civil practice com.), Million Dollar Advocates Forum (life), Phi Alpha Delta. Roman Catholic. Avocations: music performance, athletics. Home: 509 Bent Tree Ct Oswego IL 60543-8734 Office: 940 W Adams St Ste 300 Chicago IL 60607 Office Phone: 312-733-4455. Personal E-mail: pjfinalawyer@aol.com.

FINALE, FRANK LOUIS, retired elementary school educator, writer; b. Bklyn., Mar. 10, 1942; s. Ralph and Mary (Guidone) F.; m. Barbara Ann (Long), Oct. 20, 1973; children: Michael, Alan, Steven. BS in edn., Ohio State U., 1964; MA in human devel., Fairleigh Dickinson U., 1976. Tchr. Toms River Regional Sch., NJ, 1964—2002; retired, 2002; editor-in-chief Jersey Shore Publs., 1996—. Presenter, Young Authors Conf., 1985—, voted tchr. of the yr., 2002-2003, East Dover Elementary and named to the State of New Jersey's 2002 Governor's Tchr. Program. Author: To the Shore Once More, 1999, To the Shore Once More Vol. II, 2001, A Gull's Story, 2002, Without Halos, 1985-95; poetry editor: the new renaissance, 1996—; co-editor: Under A Gull's Wing, 1996; author poems and essays. Recipient: Exemplary Svc. Award, Internat. Reading Assn. and Ocean County Reading Coun., 1993; Nominated for Excellence in Edn. Award, 2002 Mem. NEA, Acad. Am. Poets, N.J. Edn. Assn., Ocean County Poets Collective (founding mem.). Avocations: reading, films, music, comedians. Office Phone: 732-892-1276. E-mail: ffinale@aol.com.

FINAN, MARCEL BASSIL, mathematics professor, researcher; s. Bassil Michel Finan and Therese Tarazi; m. Pallavi Subhash Ketkar, June 1, 1999. PhD, U. of North Tex., 1998. Vis. asst. prof. U. of Tex., San Antonio, 1998—99, vis. scholar Austin, 1999—2001; asst. prof. math. Ark. Tech U., Russellville, 2001—. Referee Electronic Jour. of Differential Equations, Tex., 1998—2000. Author: (manuscript) Fundamentals of Linear Algebra, Lecture Notes in Discrete Math., A Calculus Approach to Math. Modeling, A Problem Solving Approach to Coll. Algebra; contbr. articles to profl. jours. Mem.: Math. Assn. of Am., Am. Math. Soc. Office: Ark Tech U Dept of Math Corley 244 Russellville AR 72801 Personal E-mail: marcel.finan@mail.atu.edu.

FINAURI, GRACIELA MARIA, foreign service official; b. Buenos Aires, June 18, 1956; d. Gerardo and Norma Mercedes (Burich) F. Student in law, Cath. U. Buenos Aires, 1985. Adminstr. protocol dept. Ministry of Fgn. Affairs, Buenos Aires, 1979-85, pvt. sec. min., 1985-87; pvt. sec. amb. Embassy of Argentina, Rome, 1987-91; pvt. sec. min. Ministry of Internal Affairs, Buenos Aires, 1993-95; chief of protocol Senate of Argentina, Buenos Aires, 1995-98; pvt. sec. to v.p. Argentine Republic, Buenos Aires, 1995-98; attaché Mission of Argentina to UN, N.Y.C., 1998—2003; consular agt. Consulate Gen. and Promotion Ctr. Argentine Republic in N.Y., N.Y.C., 2003—05. Named Cavalier of Hon. and Merit, Haiti Republic, 1983, Officer of Order of Merit, Italian Republic, 1985; recipient Insignia award, Mex. Order of Aztec Eagle, 1984. Roman Catholic. Office: Consulate Gen and Promotion Ctr Argentine Republic NY 12 W 56th St New York NY 10019 Office Phone: 212-603-0412. Business E-Mail: gmf@mrecic.gov.ar.

FINBERG, BONNY, psychologist, writer; b. Bronx, N.Y., Mar. 7, 1948; d. Robert and Marcella (Efrus) Finberg; m. Jerry Orter, June 9, 1973 (div. 1990); 1 child, Reuben Wood Orter. BA, NYU, 1978, MA, 1983. Intern child & adolescent psychiatry dept. St. Vincent's Hosp. and Med. Ctr., NY, 1982—83; with Educational Records Bureau, 1983—86, 1994; counselor Grand St. Settlement, 1984—86; psychotherapist New Hope Guild for Mental Health, Brooklyn, 1984—88, Fifth Ave. Ctr. for Psychotherapy, 1988—91; with Mental Health Providers of Western Queens Psychol. Assessment Svcs., 1986—88; psychologist N.Y.C. Bd. of Ed. Com. on Spl. Edn., Dist. 2, 1988—.

FINBERG, JAMES MICHAEL, lawyer; b. Balt., Sept. 6, 1958; s. Laurence and Harriet (Levinson) Finberg; m. Melanie Piech; children: Joseph, John. BA, Brown U., 1980; JD, U. Chgo., 1983. Bar: Calif. 1984, U.S. Dist. Ct. (no. dist.) Calif. 1984, U.S. Dist. Ct. (ea. dist.) Calif. 1987, U.S. Ct. Appeals (9th and fed. cirs.) 1987, U.S. Dist. Ct. Hawaii, 1988, U.S. Supreme Ct. 1994. Law clk. to assoc. justice Mich. Supreme Ct., 1983-84; assoc. Feldman, Waldman and Kline, San Francisco, 1984-87, Morrison and Foerster, 1987-90; ptnr. Lieff, Cabraser, Heimann & Bernstein, L.L.P., San Francisco, 1991—. Lawyer rep. to 9th Jud. Conf., 1999-2001 (chair No. Calif. del. 2000-01); adv. com. local rules for securities cases U.S. Dist. Ct., Calif., 1996. Exec. editor U. Chgo. Law Rev., 1982-83. Mem.: ACLU (bd. dirs. No. Calif. chpt. 1995), ABA (chmn. securities subcom. class and derivative action com. 1998—, plaintiff's program chair equal employment opportunity com. 1999—2001), Lawyers Com. for Civil Rights of San Francisco Bay Area (fin. chmn. 1992—95, bd. dirs. 1992—98, sec. 1996, co-chmn. 1997—98), Calif. Bar Assn. (mem. standing com. on legal svcs. to poor 1990—94, vice-chmn. 1993—94), Bar Assn. San Francisco (jud. evaluation com. 1994, bd. dirs. 1999—2000, sec. 2001—02, treas. 2002—03, pres. 2004—05). Office: Lieff Cabraser Heimann & Bernstein LL 275 Battery St Fl 30 San Francisco CA 94111-3305 Office Phone: 415-956-1000. Business E-Mail: jfinberg@lchb.com.

FINBERG, KAAREN B., mathematician, educator; d. Joseph P. Baltin and Helen S. Reis; children: Dana Beth, Jodi Michelle. MS in Pure/Applied Math., Montclair (N.J.) State U., 1999. Supr. acad. learning ctr. Union County Coll., Cranford, NJ, 1993—96; mem. adj. faculty math. Montclair State U., 1997—2000; instr. math. Seton Hall U., South Orange, NJ, 1998—2001, Middlesex County Coll., Edison, NJ, 2001—02, Ocean County Coll., Toms River, NJ, 2003—. Author: The Wonder of Math, 2002. Recipient Gold medal, U.S. Figure Skating Assn., 1967, Silver medal in dance, 1971. Mem.: Assn. Women in Math., Am. Math. Soc., Profl. Skaters Guild (master rating in figures/free 1970). Office Phone: 732-255-0400 2205. Personal E-mail: baltin@optonline.net.

FINBERG, LAURENCE, pediatrician, educator, dean; b. Chgo., May 20, 1923; s. Joseph and Anne (Malkow) F.; m. Harriet Levinson, June 17, 1945 (dec. Jan. 1994); children: Robert, Jeanne, James; m. Joann Quane, Mar. 17, 1995. BS, U. Chgo., 1944, MD, 1946. Diplomate: Am. Bd. Pediatrics (examiner 1969-94, bd. dirs. 1974-79, 82-88, pres. 1978, chmn. 1987). Intern U. Chgo. Clinics, 1946-47; asst. resident pediatrics Balt. City Hosps., 1949-50, resident in pediat., 1950-51; practice medicine specializing in pediat. Balt., 1951-63, N.Y.C., 1963-94; asst. chief pediatrician Balt. City Hosps., 1951-61, dir. pediatric out-patient dept., 1951-63, dir. premature nursery, 1951-59, assoc. chief pediatrics, 1961-63; pediatrician Harriet Lane Home, 1951-63; chmn. dept. pediatrics Montefiore Hosp. and Med. Center, Bronx, N.Y., 1963-80, prof., 1995—; chmn. dept. pediatrics SUNY Health

Sci. Ctr., Bklyn., 1982-95, prof. pediatrics, 1982-95, prof. emeritus, 1995—, dean, 1988-91; prof. clin. pediat. U. Calif., San Francisco, 1995—, Stanford U. Sch. Med., 1997—. Instr. pediatrics Johns Hopkins U., 1951-56; asst. prof., 1956-63; prof. pediatrics Albert Einstein Coll. Medicine, Yeshiva U., Bronx, 1963-82, chmn., 1968-80; cons. in field; mem. pediatric adv. com. N.Y.C. Dept. Health, 1970-94. Mem. editl. bd. Jour. Pediat., 1973-83, Am. Jour. Diseases of Children, 1984-94, named changed to Archives of Pediat. and Adolescent Medicine, 1994-2002, editor nutrition sect., 1995-2002; editor Saunders Manual of Pediat. Practice, 1997, 2002. Served with USPHS, 1947-49. Recipient Bela Schick medal, 1992, Nutrition award Am. Acad. Pediatrics, 1992. Mem. AAAS, AMA (Goldberger Clin. Nutrition award 1993), Am. Pediatric Soc., Soc. Pediatric Research, Am. Acad. Pediatrics (com. on environ. hazards 1968-83, chmn. 1979-83, com. nutrition 1983-89—, chmn. 1984-89), Am. Coll. Nutrition, Am. Soc. for Nutritional Scis., Nat. Cholesterol Edn. Program Coordinating Com. (panel on children and adolescents 1989-93), Ambulatory Pediatric Assn., Am. Soc. Clin. Nutrition, Am. Fedn. Clin. Research, Sociedad Peruana de Pediatria, Sociedad Dominica De Peditria, Harvey Soc., N.Y. Acad. Medicine (past chmn. pediatric sec.), Phi Beta Kappa, Sigma Xi, Alpha Omega Alpha. Achievements include research in electrolyte physiology. Home: 152 Lombard St Apt 602 San Francisco CA 94111-1134 Office Phone: 415-398-6205. Personal E-mail: finberg@itsa.ucsf.edu.

FINCH, EDWARD RIDLEY, JR., lawyer, educator, retired diplomat, ambassador; b. Westhampton Beach, N.Y., Aug. 31, 1919; AB with Atwater honors, Princeton U., 1941; JD, NYU, 1947; LLD (hon.), Mo. Valley Coll., 1963; DSc (hon.), Cumberland Coll., 1985. Bar: N.Y. 1948, U.S. Supreme Ct. 1953, D.C. 1978, Fla. 1980, Pa. 1992. Ptnr. Finch & Schaefler, N.Y.C., 1950-85; of counsel Le Boeuf, Lamb, Leiby & MacRae, N.Y.C., 1986-88; commr. City of N.Y., 1955-58. V.p. gen. counsel, dir. St. Giles Found., 1964—, Am. Internat. Petroleum Corp., 1988-92; U.S. del. 4th UN Congress, Geneva, 1970, 5th UN Congress, Japan, 1975; U.S. spl. ambassador to Panama, 1972; legal advisor, mem. U.S. Del. UNISPACE II, 1982, UNISPACE III, Vienna, Austria, 1999; lectr. in field. Author: Holes in Your Pockets, 3rd edit., Astro Business-A Guide to Commerce and Law of Outer Space, Judicial Politics; contbr. articles to profl. jours. Pres., bd. dirs. St. Nicholas Soc. N.Y., 1948—; past pres. N.Y. Inst. Spl. Edn., 1950—; bd. govs. Nat. Space Soc., 1984—; mem. faculty adv. com. dept. politics Princeton U.; bd. dirs., treas. Jessie Ridley Found., N.Y.C., Finch Trusts; pres. Adams Meml. Fund Inc.; v.p. St. Giles Found.; trustee St. Andrew's Dune Ch., Southampton, Cathedral of St. John the Divine, 1989-92, Whittell Trust, Am. Found. Cancer Rsch.; life trustee Met. Mus. of Art, N.Y.C.; mem. Coun. Am. Ambs. Col. JAG, USAFR, 1941-72. Decorated U.S. Legion of Merit with oak leaf cluster; order Brit. Empire; Knight Order St. John; comdr. French Legion of Honor, Disting. Eagle Scout, Coun. of Am. Ambs Fellow Am. Bar Found. (chmn. aerospace coun. sect. sci. and tech 1986-92); mem. ABA (ho. of dels. 1971-72, chmn. corp. lawyers sr. lawyer divsn., chmn. aerospace law divsn. internat. law sect.1973-79), AIAA (sr.), FBA, Inter-Am. Bar Assn. (Hallgartern telecommunications award 1991), N.Y. State Bar Assn. (internat. law and practice sec., chmn. arms control and nat. security com.), Pa. Bar Assn., Fla. Bar Assn., Assn., Bar City of N.Y., Internat. Bar Assn., Judge Advs. Assn. U.S. (past pres.), Am. Law Inst., Am. Judicature Soc. (sr.), Internat. Astronautical Acad. (full elected mem.), Internat. Inst. Space Law (Lifetim Disting. Svc. award 1997), Nat. Space Soc. (bd. dirs.), Am. Arbitration Assn. (panelist), Univ. Clubs of Wash. and N.Y., Union League Club, Union Club, Princeton Club (bd. govs. 1982—), L.I. Club, Bathing Corp. of Southampton, Westhampton Country Club, Hillsboro Club (sr.). Office: 862 Park Ave New York NY 10021-1831 Office Phone: 212-327-0493. Office Fax: 212-327-0593. Personal E-mail: erfinchjr@aol.com.

FINCH, EVELYN VORISE, financial planner; b. Marietta, Ohio, Jan. 20, 1930; d. Richard Raymon Juantzee and Oreatha Fay (Carnes) Metcalf; m. Herman Frederick Ahrens, May 13, 1948 (div. Nov. 1957); children: Erick K.F. Ahrens, Hilda Kate Ahrens(dec.), Nicole Schwartz; m. James Derwood Finch, June 29, 1973 (dec. Oct. 1993). BS in Music Edn., Concord U., 1961; postgrad., U. Md., Am. U., Northeastern U., 1990. Registered Health Underwriter, Boston. Music tchr. Prince George's County Pub. Schs., 1961—72; pvt. piano tchr. Washington, 1961—73; sales rep. china and crystal Quality Products Co., Washington, 1973—80; ins. agt. Mut. of Omaha Cos., Washington, 1980—92, Memphis, 1992—94; pvt. practice Alamo, Tenn., 1994—; tax specialist H&R Block Inc., Jackson, Tenn., 2002—. Ind. assoc. Pre-Paid Legal Svcs., Inc., 2000—. Supporting mem. Nat. Mus. Women in Arts, Washington, 1990—, Women's Philharm., San Francisco, 1993—. Mem.: LWV (Memphis br.), AAUW (br. pres. 1994-96, Tenn. chair ednl. found. 1996-98, Nat. Diversity Resource Team 1997-2000), Internat. Assn. Fin. Planners, Nat. Assn. Health Underwriters (registered health underwriter), Nat. Assn. Ret. Fed. Employees, Chesapeake Bay Yacht Clubs Assn. (commodore 1982), Prince George's Yacht Club (commodore 1978), Potomas River Yacht Clubs Assn. (legis. chair 1978-87), Nat. Boating Fedn. (pres. 1985), Kappa Delta Pi, Pi Mu. Home and Office: 208 Finch Rd Alamo TN 38001-5923 Personal E-mail: EvelynFinch@msn.com.

FINCH, JAMES STUART, lawyer; b. Boston, Oct. 23, 1948; s. Stuart C. and Patricia (O'Brien) F.; m. Deborah Jane Roller, June 15, 1974; 1 child, Alexander Stuart. BA with distinction, Dartmouth Coll., 1971; JD, U. Calif., Hastings, 1974. Bar: Vt. 1974, D.C. 1980, N.Y. 1980. Lawyer Vt. Legal Aid, Springfield, 1974-75, Aghayan and Assoc., Tehran, Iran, 1975-79, Russin & Vecchi, N.Y.C., 1979-84, ptnr. N.Y.C. and Santo Domingo, 1988-95, Hanoi, Vietnam, 1995-96, Yangon, Myanmar, 1996—; fgn. svc. officer U.S. State Dept., Guayaguil, Ecuador, 1984-86. Author: Dominican Republic Contract Manual, 1990; contbr. articles to profl. jours., chpts. to books. Mem. N.Y. Bar Assn., Assn. of Bar of City of N.Y. Avocations: photogrpahy, wind surfing, skiing. Home: care Roller 125 Captains Walk Milford CT 06460-6517

FINCH, JANET BUSWELL, musician; b. Columbus, Ohio, Aug. 26, 1955; d. Delbert LeRoy and Marjorie Rose Buswell; m. Monte Gene Finch; children: Stephanie Elise, Randall James. Student, Am. Inst. Musical Studies, 1977; MusB, Ohio State U., 1978; postgrad., U. Cin., 2000—. Staff, profl. accompanist Murray State U., Ky., 1996—99; instr. U. Cin., 2002. Profl. accompanist Murray State U., Murray, Ky.; adjudicator Murray Woman's Club Sophomore Scholarship Auditions, Murray, 1987, Ohio Music Tchr.'s Assn., Cin., 2003, Murray Music Tchr.'s Assn., 2005; accompanist U. Cin., 2000—03; rehearsal accompanist Dayton Opera Assn., Ohio, 1983; part-time faculty U. Akron, 1982—83. Sec. exec. bd. Murray Civic Music Assn., 2004; mem. Murray State U. Parent Orgn.; com. First Bapt. Ch., Murray, 2004, Fellowship of Christian Women, 2004; grant rev. bd. U. Cin. Grad. Student Governance Assn.; adult learning com. Nat. Pedagogy Conf., Princeton, NJ, 2001—03; monitor MTNA, Murray, 1999—; membership bd. Stuart Poston Wellness Ctr., 2003—04. Recipient Grad. Student of Yr., U. Cin. Grad. Student Governance Assn., 2000—03; scholar, U. Cin., Coll. Conservatory Music, 1999—, Dept. Secondary Piano and Pedagogy, 2002. Mem.: Ky. Music Tchr.'s Assn., Sigma Alpha Ipsilon (hon. Hon. Patroness Mem. 1999). Republican. Baptist. Avocations: exercise, reading, bible study, writing, travel.

FINCH, JENNIE, softball player; b. La Mirada, Calif., Sept. 3, 1980; d. Doug and Bev Finch. Degree in Comm., U. Ariz., 2002. Color commentator Women's Coll. World Series, ESPN, 2003; mem. U.S.A. Women's Softball Team, Athens Olympics, 2004. Co-host This Week in Baseball, ESPN. Co-recipient Ruby award for Most Outstanding Female Sr. Student Athlete, U. Arizona; named First Team All American, Nat. Fastpitch Coach's Assn., 2000, 2001, 2002; recipient Honda award for Nation's Best Softball Player, 2001, 2002. Achievements include winning a NCAA-record 60 consecutive games as a pitcher over three seasons; number retired at the U. Ariz. on May 9, 2003; member of the U. Ariz. NCAA Championship Team in 2001; mem. of the U.S.A. Women's Softball Gold medal Team, Internat. Softball Fedn. World Championships in 2002, Athens Olympic games, 2004.

FINCH, RAYMOND LAWRENCE, federal judge; b. Christiansted, St. Croix, V.I., Oct. 4, 1940; s. Wilfred Christopher and Beryl Elaine (Bough) Finch; m. Anne Marie Mohammed, May 8, 1996; children: Alison, Mark, Jennifer. AB, Howard U., 1962, JD, 1965. Bar: V.I. 1971, Ct. Appeals (3d cir.) 1976. Law clk. Judge's Municipal Ct. V.I., 1965-66, Hodge, Sheen Finch & Ross, 1969—70; ptnr. Hodge, Sheen, Finch & Ross, Christiansted, 1970-75; judge Territorial Ct. V.I., Charlotte Amalie, 1975-86, Ct. Appeals, V.I., Charlotte Amalie, 1986-94, US Dist. Ct. V.I., 1994—, chief judge, 1999—. Instr. grad. divsn. Coll. V.I., Am. Inst. Banking, 1976—. Bd. dirs. Boy Scouts Am., Boys Club Am. Served to capt. U.S. Army, 1966—69. Decorated Commendation medal U.S. Army, Bronze Star. Mem.: ABA, Internat. Assn. Chiefs Police, Nat. Bar Assn., Am. Judges Assn. Democrat. Lutheran. Office: PO Box 24051 Christiansted VI 00824-0051 Office Phone: 340-773-5021. Business E-Mail: rfinch@vitelcom.net.

FINCH, ROBERT JONATHAN, communications engineer, consultant; b. Chgo., Sept. 21, 1955; s. Herman Manuel and Frances (Gutlow) Finch; m. Gayle Deborah Falk, Mar. 28, 1991; children: Layla Michelle, Grant Dillon. BA in Broadcast Mgmt., U. So. Calif., 1977. Engr.-in-charge LFI Prodns., Inc., Lafayette, Ind., 1990—92; comm. engring. cons. L.A., 1978—90, Lafayette, 1992—. Developer ABC Hollywood's 1st satellite video-tape ctr., Saudi Arabia's 1st color TV studio; contbr. articles to profl. jours. Mem.: Hollywood Magic Castle, Tippecanoe Amateur Radio Assn. (trustee), Pasadena Casting Club (instr.). Achievements include development of 1st digitally based pub. transponder in a 2-way radio service in continental U.S; 1st large volume, pub. access and radio accessed computer database in U.S. Avocations: fly fishing, close-up magic. Home: 10436 Calle Perdiz NW Albuquerque NM 87114-1311

FINCH, ROGERS BURTON, association management consultant; b. Broadalbin, N.Y., Apr. 16, 1920; s. Cecil Clement and Olga Ulrika (Lofgren) F.; m. Barbara Ellen Hine, Jan. 3, 1942; children: David Rogers, John Richard, Steven Alan, Kathryn Ann, Elizabeth Gale. BS, Mass. Inst. Tech., 1941, MS, 1947, Sc.D., 1950. Prof. Mass. Inst. Tech., 1946-53; dir. U.S. Fgn. Aid Mission, Rangoon, Burma, 1953-54; dir. research Rensselaer Poly. Inst., Troy, N.Y., 1954-61, v.p. planning, 1963-72; dir. univ. relations Peace Corps, Washington, 1961-63; exec. dir. ASME, N.Y.C., 1972-81; cons., 1987—; exec. v.p. Illuminating Engineering Soc. N.Am., 1982-87. Contbr. articles profl. jours. Served to maj. AUS, 1941-46; to brig. gen. U.S. Army Res.; ret. 1975. Decorated Army Commendation medal, Legion of Merit. Fellow ASME (life), AAAS; mem. Am. Soc. Assn. Execs. (life), Am. Soc. Engring. Edn. (life), Council Engring. and Sci. Soc. Execs. (emeritus past pres.), Illuminating Engring. Soc. N.Am., Sigma Xi, Tau Beta Pi. Home: 202 Brooksby Village Dr Apt 304 Peabody MA 01960

FINCH, SPENCER, artist; Attended, Doshisha U., Kyoto, Japan, 1983—84; BA in Comparative Lit., magna cum laude, Hamilton Coll., NY, 1985; MFA in Sculpture, RI Sch. Design, 1989. One-man shows include with Paul Ramirez Literal Truth, Real Art Ways, Hartford, Conn., 1993, one-man shows include, Postmasters Gallery, NY, 1994, 1995, 1997, 1998, 2000, 2002, 2004, Matrix 133, Wadsworth Atheneum, Hartford, Conn., 1997, Rhona Hoffman Gallery, Chgo., 2001, Artpace, San Antonio, Tex., 2003, exhibited in group shows at Home for June, Home of Contemporary Theater & Art, NY, 1991, Vacation Show, Four Walls, Bklyn., 1992, Part II, Sandra Gering Gallery, NY, 1994, Four Views From Earth, Ctr. Arts, San Francisco, 1995, Between the Acts, Ice Box, Athens, Greece, 1996, Paradise 8, Exit Art, 1999, Conceptual Art As Neurobiological Praxis, Thread Waxing Space, NY, 1999, Made You Look, Austin Mus. Art, Tex., 2000, Art on Paper, Weatherspoon Art Gallery, NC, 2000, NY Paper Sculpture Show, Sculpture Ctr., NY, 2003, Indivisible Cities, Bill Maynes Gallery, NY, 2004, Nothing Compared to This, Contemporary Arts Ctr., Cin., 2004, Whitney Biennial, Whitney Mus. Am. Art, 2004. Mailing: c/o Postmasters Gallery 459 West 19th St New York NY 10011*

FINCH, TIMOTHY ROBERT, historian; b. Charles City, Iowa, Sept. 15, 1953; s. Randall Blaine and Laurel Rae Finch; m. Jayne Ann Richardson, Apr. 22, 1978; children: Graham Reed, Hillary Ann. AA, Cypress Coll., Calif., 1973; BA, Calif. State U., 1977, MA, 2004. Working lead Disneyland, Anaheim, Calif., 1973—89; realtor Century 21, Mission Viejo, Calif., 1989—91; merch. coord. Mervyn's, Mission Viejo, Calif., 1992—2000. Mem.: Soc. for History of Authorship, Reading and Pub., Am. Hist. Assn., Phi Alpha Theta.

FINCHER, CAMERON LANE, psychology professor; b. Douglas County, Ga., Nov. 4, 1926; s. Andrew Jackson and Ada (Swafford) F.; m. Mary Frances Cutts, June 15, 1957; children: Marcel Andriette, Matthew Donnellan, Ada Amanda, Melissa Lane. B.C.S., Ga. State U., 1950; MA, U. Minn., 1951; PhD, Ohio State U., 1956. Lic. psychologist, Ga. Dir. testing and counseling Ga. State U., Atlanta, 1956-65; assoc. dir. Inst. Higher Edn., U. Ga., Athens, 1965-69, dir. Inst., 1969-99, prof. higher edn. and psychology, 1965—, Regents prof. higher edn. and psychology, 1981—. Cons. various indsl. and comml. cos., also state governing bds. colls. and univs., La., S.C., Ala., Tenn.; mem. Gov.'s Com. on Postsecondary Edn., Ga., 1978-83; mem. rsch. panel So. Edn. Found., 1978-86. Author: A Preface to Psychology, 1972, Challenge of Reform in Higher Education, 1991, Historical Development of the University System of Georgia, 1991, 2d edit., 2003, Administrative Leadership in Academic Governance and Management, 2003; co-author: One Hundred Classic Books in Higher Education, 2001; contbg. columnist: Athens Banner-Herald, 1970-90; editor: Planning Imperatives for the 1990s, 1989, Assessing Institutional Effectiveness in Higher Education, 1989, Defining and Assessing Quality, 1994, IHE Perspectives, 1999—; contbg. editor: Greenwood Dictionary of Education, 2003; contbg. editor Rsch. in Higher Edn., 1978—; contbr. articles to profl. jours. Served with USNR, 1944-46. Recipient Disting. Achievement in Public Service medallion U. Ga., 1980, 2000, Ben W. Gibson award So. Regional Council, Coll. Bd., 1982; Ga. Ho. of Reps. and Senate Resolution recognizing contbns. to higher edn. and State of Ga., 1986, Abraham Baldwin award U. Ga. Alumni Assn., 1991. Mem. APA, Ga. Assn. Instnl. Rsch., Planning, Assessment and Quality (1st recipient Cameron Lane Fincher outstanding svc. award 1997), Assn. Study of Higher Edn. (Howard Bowen Disting. Career award 1991), So. Assn. Instl. Rsch. (James R. Montgomery award 1991), Am. Assn. Higher Edn., Assn. Instnl. Rsch. (Disting. Mem. 1983, Outstanding Svc. award 1980, AIR/Suslow award, 1995), So. Assn. Instnl. Rsch. (disting.), Alpha Kappa Psi, Phi Delta Kappa, Golden Key Office: U Ga Inst Higher Edn Meigs Hall Athens GA 30602 E-mail: cfincher@uga.edu.

FINCHER, DAVID, film director, film producer; b. Denver, Colo., May 10, 1962; m. Donya Fiorentino. With Industrial Light & Magic, 1981—83; co-founder Propaganda Films, 1986. Dir. videos for Don Henley, Sting, The Wallflowers, Paula Abdul, Aerosmith, Madonna, Michael Jackson, Rolling Stones (Grammy award for best music video Love is Strong 1995), Wallflowers; dir.:(films) Alien 3, 1992, Seven, 1995, The Game, 1997, The Fight Club, 1999, The Panic Room, 2002; prodr. Ambush, 2001, Chosen, 2001, The Follow, 2001, Star, 2001, Power Keg, 2001, The Ticker, 2002. Office: Propaganda Films 1746 Ivar Ave Los Angeles CA 90028

FINCHER, RUTH MARIE EDLA, medical educator, dean; b. Hartford, Conn., Dec. 16, 1949; d. Wilber Roe and Hannah Camilla (Andersen) Griswold; m. Michael Edward Fincher, June 26, 1977. BA, Colby Coll., 1972; BMS, Dartmouth U., 1974; MD, Emory U., 1976. Diplomate Am. Bd. Internal Medicine. Intern then resident internal medicine Emory Hosps., Atlanta, 1976-79; practicing internist Pub. Health Svc., Ludowici, Ga., 1979-81; pvt. practice internal medicine Hinesville, Ga., 1981-82; staff physician Am. Lake VA Med. Ctr., Tacoma, Wash., 1982-84; asst. prof. medicine Med. Coll. Ga., Augusta, 1984-89, assoc. prof., 1989-94, prof. medicine, 1994—, vice dean acad. affairs, 1994—. Pres. Clerkship Dirs. in Internal Medicine, Washington, 1992—93; com. chair Nat. Bd. Med. Examiners, Phila., 1995—96, bd. mem., 2005—; co-chair rsch. in med. edn. com. Assn. Am. Med. Colls., Washington, 1995—96, chair group on ednl. affairs, 1996—97. Co-editor: Clinical Medicine 2nd Edit., 1995; contbr. articles to profl. jours.; editl. bd. Am. Jour. Medicine, Birmingham, Ala., 1994-98, Jour. Gen. Internal Medicine, 1998—. Bd. mem. Nat. Bd. Medical Examiners at Large, 2005—. Fellow: ACP (gov. Ga. chpt. 2003—, bd. dirs. ACP Found., J. Willis Hurst Tchg. award 1994, Disting. Tchg. award 1996); mem.: Alpha Omega Alpha (bd. dirs. 2003—, Robert J. Glaser Disting. Tchg. award 1996, Daniel S. Tostesen award for leadership in med. edn. 2003, Inaugural inductee U. Sys. Ga. Hall of Fame 2004). Avocations: woodworking, gardening, running. Office: Med Coll Ga CB 1843 1457 Laney Walker Blvd Augusta GA 30912 Office Phone: 706-721-3529. Business E-Mail: rfincher@mail.mcg.edu.

FINCK, BARRY RUSSELL, lawyer; b. Warwick, R.I., Oct. 2, 1969; s. Keith Barry and Mary Anne Ryan F. BA, Boston Coll., 1991; JD, U. Denver, 1995. Bar: Colo. 1995. Atty. pvt. practice, Denver, 1995—. Mem. Colo. Bar Assn., Colo. Criminal Def. Assn. Office: 1490 Lafayette St Ste 407 Denver CO 80218-2394

FINCK, KEVIN WILLIAM, lawyer; b. Whittier, Calif., Dec. 14, 1954; s. William Albert and Ester (Gutbub) F.; m. Kathleen A. Miller, Oct. 7, 1989. BA in History, U. Calif., Santa Barbara, 1977; JD, U. Calif., San Francisco, 1980. Bar: Calif. 1980. Ptnr. Ord and Norman, 1985—88; pvt. practice San Francisco, 1989—. Lectr. Internat. Bar Assn., Learning Annex. Author: California Corporation Start Up Package and Minute Book, 1982, 10th edit., 2005; contbr. articles to various profl. jours. Avocations: hiking, golf, travel. Office: Ste 1670 Two Embarcadero Ctr San Francisco CA 94111 Office Phone: 415-296-9100. Personal E-mail: kevin@kevinfinck.com.

FINCKE, EDWARD MICHAEL (MIKE), astronaut; b. Pitts., Pa., Mar. 14, 1967; s. Edward and Alma Fincke; m. Renita Saikia; 1 child. BSc in Aero. & Astronautics, BSc in Earth, Atmospheric & Planetary Sci., MIT, 1989; MSc in Aero. & Astronautics, Stanford U., 1990; Msc in Physical Sci. (Planetary Geology), U. Houston, 2001. Commd. 2d lt. USAF, 1989, advanced through grades to col., various assignments, 1990—94, lt. col., mem. 39th flight test squadron, flight test engineer Eglin AFB, Fla., 1994—96; flight test liaison USAF, Gifu Test Ctr., Gifu Air Base, Japan, 1996; astronaut NASA, Houston, 1996—. Astronaut Internat. Space Sta. Expedition, 2001. Decorated two Commendation medals USAF, Achievement medal. Mem.: British Interplanetary Soc., Geological Soc. Am. Achievements include technical duties in the Astronaut Office Station Operations Branch serving as an International Space Station Spacecraft Communicator (ISS CAPCOM); a member and flight engineer of the Crew Test Support Team in Russia; and as the ISS crew procedures team lead and flight engineer. Avocations: hiking, flying, travel, geology, astronomy, reading, learning new languages. Office: Astronaut Office CB NASA Lyndon B Johnson Space Center Houston TX 77058

FINDAKLY, HANI K., investment company executive; BSc in Civil Engrng. magna cum laude, Baghdad U., 1966; MSc in Computer Simulation, MIT, 1971, DSc in Decision Theory, 1972. Prof. & rschr. decision theory and systems analysis MIT, 1972—75; various positions including dir, investment dept. & chief investment officer World Bank, Washington, 1975—86; mng. dir., global risk mgmt. PaineWebber Inc., NYC, 1986—88; dir., internat. div. Drexel Burnham Lambert, NYC, 1988—90; pres. Potomac Babson, Inc., NYC, 1990—99; vice chmn., dir. Clinton Group, Inc., NYC, 1999—. Visiting prof. Catholic U., Rio de Janeiro, 1973; mem. Council on Foreign Relations. Office: Clinton Group 9 W 57 St 26th Fl New York NY 10019*

FINDER, ALAN ELIOT, forensic economist; b. Washington, Pa., Apr. 16, 1952; s. Sanford Sidney and Saranne (Weiner) F.; m. Patricia Lee Hale, Aug. 7, 1977; children: Benjamin David, Matthew Aaron. BA, Coll. of William and Mary, 1974; MA, Ind. U., Bloomington, 1979, PhD in Econs., 1985. Commonwealth intern Commonwealth of Va., Richmond, 1974-75; rsch. specialist Commonwealth of Ky., Frankfort, 1975; spl. asst. Coun. of State Govts., Lexington, Ky., 1976-77; assoc. instr. Ind. U., Bloomington, 1978-83; pub. utility economist State of Mo., Jefferson City, 1983-85; sr. analyst Nat. Econ. Rsch. Assocs., White Plains, N.Y., 1985-87; sr. cons. Arthur D. Little, Inc., Cambridge, Mass., 1988-94; unit mgr. Arthur D. Little Inc., Cambridge, Mass., 1993-94; mgr. Arthur D. Little, Inc., Cambridge, Mass., 1995—96; sr. mgr. Arthur Andersen, Boston, 1996—2002; mem. Global Regulatory Advisors LLC, Winchester, 2002; sr. mgr. Deloitte Touche Tohmatsu Emerging Markets, Washington, 2003, KPMG LLP, Balt., 2004—. Contbr. articles to profl. jours. Mem. Am. Econ. Assn. Office Phone: 410-949-8864.

FINDER, JOSEPH ALAN, writer; b. Chgo., Ill., Oct. 6, 1958; s. Morris and Natalie Finder; m. Michele Souda, Aug. 27, 1989; 1 child, Emma Josephine Souda Finder. BA summa cum laude, Yale Coll., 1980; MA, Harvard U., 1984. Writer, novelist, Boston, 1982—; writing faculty Harvard Coll., John F. Kennedy Sch. Govt., Harvard U., Cambridge, Mass., 1988, Harvard Coll./Harvard Ext. Sch., Cambridge, 1984—90. Author: (nonfiction book) Red Carpet: The Connection Between the Kremlin and America's Most Powerful Businessmen, 1983, (novels) The Moscow Club, 1991, Extraordinary Powers, 1993, The Zero Hour, 1996, High Crimes, 1998, Paranoia, 2004, Company Man, 2005; contbr. book revs. and articles to newspapers and publs. Mem.: SAG, PEN New Eng. (bd. dirs.), Boston Athaenaeum, Harvard Club Boston, Yale Club Boston, Phi Beta Kappa. E-mail: joe@josephfinder.com.

FINDER-STONE, PATRICIA ANN, nursing educator, volunteer; b. Platteville, Wis., Jan. 27, 1929; d. Arthur Charles and Marcella Mary Finder; m. Mark Henry Stone, Dec. 28, 1953 (dec. Nov. 1997); children: Teresa Kay Stone Gulyas, Susan Elizabeth Stone Crane, Mark Henry Jr., Matthew Riley. Grad., Columbia Sch. Nursing, 1950; BS, U. Wis., Green Bay, 1973; MS, U. Wis., Madison, 1975. RN; cert. in pub. health, Wis. DON San Luis Manor, Green Bay, Wis., 1967-68; asst. head nurse Bellin Meml. Hosp., 1968-69; instr. nursing Bellin Coll. Nursing, 1969-79; dir. Bellin Hospice Program, 1979-80; staff and adminstrv. nurse, 1980-95; instr. ADN program N.E. Wis. Tech. Coll., Green Bay, Wis., 1980-96; nursing cons. local law firms, 1984—87, 1999—2001. Past chair Brown County Bd. of Health; ethics com. St. Mary's Hosp., Green Bay, Wis., 1987—, adv. bd., 1998—, chair legis. com., 1999—; mem. Wis. ethics com. network Med. Coll. Wis., Milw., 1988—; assoc. mem. Hastings Ctr. Inst. Soc., Ethics and Life Scis., N.Y., 1975—. Bd. dirs. Wis. divsn. Am. Cancer Soc., 1975-99, Midwest divsn., 1998-2000, pub. issues chair Wis. divsn., 1983-91, sec. bd. dirs. 1990-91, chair bylaws, 1994-96, chair bd. dirs., 1996-97, chair advocacy com. 1998-2000, mem. midwest tactical team, 2000-2001; mem. Midwest Regional Leadership Group, 2001—; bd. dirs., pres., pub. affairs chair Brown County unit Am. Cancer Soc., 1976-2000; bd. dirs. Greater Green Bay Cmty. Found., 1991-97; bd. dirs. Bay Area Cmty. Coun., 1992—, chmn., 2001-03; bd. dirs. Bay Area Cmty. Health Partnership, chair pub. policy, 2001-04; bd. dirs. ASPIRO, 1996—, pres., 2002-05, chair legis. com., 1998—; mem. Brown County Women's Cancer Coalition, 1994—; memm. adv. bd. Brown County Planning Commn., 1992-98; mem. planning divsn. United Way, 1992-99, chair cmty. edn. com., 1997-2000, mem. planned givers adv. com., 2001-02, mem. health and wellness impact coun., 2002—; bd. dirs., legis. chair Start Smart, 1997-2002; past bd. dirs. Northeastern Wis. Health Systems Agys., Wis. Health Policy Coun.; mem. Brown County Tobacco-Free Coalition, 1996—, chair, 1996-99; mem. Wis. Tobacco Control Bd., 2000-03; mem. Wis. Supreme Ct. Commn. on Jud. Ethics and Elections, 1997-2000; mem. Wis. Bd. on Aging and Long Term Care, 2003—, sec., 2004—; bd. dirs. Brown County Commn. on Aging/Aging Resource Ctr., 1997—2004, Scholarships, Inc., 1998-2004, Wis. Dept. Health and Family Svcs. Turning Point, 1998-2002; mem. Bay Area Agy. on Aging, 2002-04, chair legis. com., 2001-04; mem. AARP State Coord. Coun., 2001—; mem. exec. coun. AARP-Wis., 2002—, pres., 2005—; mem. adv. com. Wis. Pub. TV Creating Health, 1999-2000; mem. WNA Coalition to Improve Palliative Care; bd. dirs. Coalition of Wis. Aging Groups, 1999-2005, v.p., 2003-2005; chair palliative care com. Wis. Comprehensive Cancer Control Program, 2004-2005. Lt. Nurse Corps. USAF, 1950—53, with reserves USAF, 1953—57. Named Woman of the Yr. Green Bay YWCA, 1977, Vol. of Yr., Greater Green Bay, 1997; recipient Tchr. of the Yr. award Wis. Vocat. Assn., 1983, J.C. Penney Golden Rule award for volunteerism, 1997, nominee Heart of Gold, Wis. Pub. Svc., 2004, Disting. Svc. award U. Wis.-Green Bay Alumni Assn., 1998, Zonta award Sci. and Tech., 1999, Outstanding Cmty. Vol. award

United Way, 1999, Woman of Vision award YWCA, 2002, St. George award Am. Cancer Soc., 1999; grantee NEH, Marquette U., 1992-93; fellow Advocacy Inst., Washington, 1999. Mem. LWV (bd. dir. Greater Green Bay chpt. 1992—, pres. 1989-92, action chair 1992—, bd. dirs. Wis. chpt. 1993-94, mem. legis. com. Wis. chpt. 1994—), AAUW (pres. Greenbay area 1997-98, pub. policy chair 1998—, v.p. 2004-2005, bd. dir. 1995—, Wis. chpt. bd. dir., voter edn. chmn. 1999-2000), Am. Cancer Soc. (nat. divsn. St. George award 1999), Wis. Nurses Assn. (chair legis. commn. 1985-94, ethics commn. 1994-2001, pub. policy commn. 1995—, chair 2000-02, Polit. Nurse of Yr. 1996), N.E. Wis. Dist. Nurses Assn. (bd. dir., pres. 1992-94, co-chair legis. com. 1994-2001, Nurses Leadership award 1992), Pi Lambda Theta, Sigma Theta Tau (past v.p.), Phi Delta Kappa. Avocations: hiking, cross country skiing, world travel. E-mail: stone@netnet.net.

FINDLAY, DONALD CAMERON, lawyer, former federal agency administrator; b. Chgo., Sept. 7, 1959; s. Donald C. and Judith R. (Lilly) F.; m. Amy Scalera, July 9, 1988; children: Alexander B., James M. BA summa cum laude, Northwestern U., 1982; MA 1st class, Oxford U., Eng., 1984; JD magna cum laude, Harvard U., 1987. Bar: Ill. 1987, D.C. 1988. Law clk. to Judge Stephen Williams US Ct. Appeals D.C. cir., Washington, 1987-88; law clk. to Justice Antonin Scalia US Supreme Ct., Washington, 1988-89; counselor to sec. US Dept. Transp., Washington, 1989-91; dep. asst. to pres. and counselor to chief of staff The White House, Washington, 1991-92; assoc. Sidley Austin Brown & Wood, Chgo., 1992-95, ptnr., 1995—2001; dep. sec. US Dept. Labor, Washington, 2001—03; exec. v.p., gen. counsel Aon Corp., Chgo., 2003—. Adj. prof. Northwestern U., Evanston, Ill., 1994-96. Trustee Northwestern U. Office: Aon Corp 200 E Randolph St Chicago IL 60601 Business E-Mail: cameron_findlay@aon.com.

FINDLAY, MICHAEL ALISTAIR, art dealer, poet; b. Innellan, Scotland, May 13, 1945; came to U.S., 1964; s. Robert John Findlay and Mary Beatrice (Duffy) Collins; m. Naomi Sims, Aug. 4, 1973 (div. Jan. 1990); children: Bob, Beatrice; m. Victoria Wolfe, July 24, 1999. BA, York U., Toronto, Ont., Can., 1963. V.p., dir. exhbns. Richard L. Feigen and Co., Ltd., N.Y.C., L.A., Chgo., 1964-70; founder, owner, dir. J.H. Duffy and Sons, Ltd., N.Y.C., 1970-77; dir. William Beadleston Gallery, N.Y.C., 1977-84; sr. v.p., sr. dir. Christie, Manson and Woods, N.Y.C., 1984-94, sr. dir., 1994-97, internat. dir., 1997—; dir. fin., 1997-2000; dir. Acquevella Galleries, N.Y.C., 2000—. Lectr. Moore Coll. Art, Phila., 1970-80; find arts advisor N.Y.C. Parks Dept., 1979-84; mem. art adv. panel GSA, N.Y.C., 1985; keynote spkr. Oxford U. Alumnae Assn., N.Y.C., Rotary Clubs Internat., Taipei, Taiwan, Credit Suisse, Singapore, Young Pres.'s Orgn., N.Y.C., 1993-96; sr. faculty Christie's Edn., 1994-2000; bd. dirs. Christie's Internat.; mem., bd. dirs. Christie's Fine Art, Inc. Contbr. poetry and articles on art criticism to Arts, Artnews, mags. Bd. dirs. Peacemaker Found., Inc., Santa Fe, 1975—, Lacoste Sch. Arts, Vaucluse, France, Christie's Internat. Fine Arts, 1998—; hon. sec., v.p. for grants Brit. Sch. and Univs. Found., Inc., N.Y.C., 1975-85, bd. dirs., 1985—; trustee Parrish Mus., Southampton, N.Y., 1993-95; mem. adv. coun. Shanghai Mus., China, 1996; mem. scholarship com. Jade Found., N.Y.C., 1999—. Mem. ACLU, Amnesty Internat. Roman Catholic. Office: Acquavella Galleries 18 E 79th St New York NY 10021-0106

FINDLEY, CARTER VAUGHN, historian, educator; b. Atlanta, May 12, 1941; s. John Clarke and Elizabeth (Steed) F.; m. Lucia LaVerne Blackwelder, Aug. 31, 1968; children: Madeleine Vaughn, Benjamin Carter. BA, Yale U., 1963; PhD, Harvard U., 1969. Asst. prof. Ohio State U., Columbus, 1971-79, assoc. prof., 1979-87, prof. Middle East and world history, 1987—. Vis. mem. Inst. for Advanced Study, Princeton U., 1981-82; enseignant invité Ecole des Hautes Etudes en Scis. Sociales, Paris, 1994. Author: Bureaucratic Reform in the Ottoman Empire: The Sublime Porte, 1789-1922, 1980, Ottoman Civil Officialdom, 1989 (Book award Ohio Acad. of History 1990, Turkish Studies Assn. 1990), An Ottoman Occidentalist in Europe: Ahmed Midhat Meets Madame Gulnar, 1889, 1998; co-author: Twentieth-Century World, 1986, 3d edit., 1994; contbr. articles to profl. publs. Capt. USAR, 1969-71. Joint Com. on Near and Middle East/Am. Coun. Learned Socs./SSRC fellow, 1976-77, 79, 85-86; Fulbright grantee, 1983, 94, Inst. Turkish Studies grantee, 1986. Fellow Middle East Inst., Middle East Studies Assn.; mem. ACLU, Am. Hist. Assn., Am. Oriental Soc., Ohio Acad. History, Turkish Studies Assn. (pres. 1990-92), World History Assn. (exec. coun. 1991-94). Home: 2515 Sherwin Rd Columbus OH 43221-3623 Office: Ohio State U Dept History 106 Dulles Hall 230 W 17th Ave Columbus OH 43210-1361 E-mail: findley.1@osu.edu.

FINDLEY, DON AARON, manufacturing executive; b. Gadsden, Ala., June 11, 1926; s. Royal Guy and Hattie Elizabeth (Walden) F.; m. Mary Elizabeth Abernathy, Oct. 22, 1947; children: Elizabeth Jane Findley Dever, David Walden. BS, Auburn U., 1950. Acct. Buckeye Cellulose Corp. Augusta, Ga., 1950-51; acct. Tenn. Eastman Co., Kingsport, 1951-59, gen. supr. standard cost and analysis dept., 1959-64, gen. mgmt. staff, 1964-67, asst. comptroller, 1971-73, comptroller, 1975-79, v.p. fin. and adminstrn., 1979-88; mng. dir. Ectona Fibres Ltd., Cumberland, Eng., 1967-71; asst. comptroller Eastman Chem. Products, Eastman Chem. Internat. Ltd., Kingsport, 1971-73, comptroller, 1975-79, v.p. fin. and adminstrn., 1979-88; asst. comptroller Eastman Chem. Internat. Co., Kingsport, 1971-73, comptroller, 1975-79, Holston Def. Corp.; asst. v.p. Ark. Eastman Co., Carolina Eastman Co., Tex. Eastman Co. Dir. 1st Am. Nat. Bank, Kingsport Bd. dirs. Holston Valley Hosp. and Med. Ctr., Kingsport, 1978-90, treas., 1978-83; dir. United Way of Kingsport, 1994-97. Recipient Achievment award Ala. Soc. C.P.A.s, 1950, Outstanding Acctg. Alumnus award Auburn U., 1981 Fellow Inst. Dirs. (U.K.); mem. Nat. Assn. Accts. (pres. East Tenn. chpt. 1963-64), Tenn. Mfrs. and Taxpayers Assn. (bd. dirs. 1978-86), Delta Sigma Pi, Phi Kappa Phi, Beta Alpha Psi, Greater Kingsport C. of C. (bd. dirs. 1975-77) Clubs: Ridgefields Country (Kingsport) (bd. dirs. 1984-86). Republican. Methodist. Avocations: photography, coin collecting/numismatics, gardening, golf. Home: 524 Lakewood Rd Kingsport TN 37660-3420

FINDLEY, JOHN ALLEN, JR., publishing executive; b. Fulton, Mo., Feb. 25, 1951; s. John Allen and Naomi Joan (Reker) F.; m. Oneida Lynn Blackwell, Dec. 4, 1993; children: John III, Hugh. AB, Westminster Coll., 1973. Sales rep. Kingdom Daily News, Fulton, 1973-74; advt. dir. Colo. Daily, Boulder, 1973-74; advt. sales rep. Dallas Times Herald, 1976-77, advt. sales mgr., 1977-80, dir. consumer mktg., 1981-83, dir. circulation, 1983, dir. retail advt., 1983-84; regional sales mgr. Times Mirror Nat. Mktg., 1984-86; v.p. mktg. So. Conn. Newspapers, Stamford, 1986-88, sr. v.p. mktg. and prodn., 1989-93; pres. Charleston (W.Va.) Newspapers, 1993-97; pub., CEO Long Beach (Calif.) Press-Telegram, 1998—2001; v.p. newspaper rels. Parade Mag., L.A., 2002—03, sr. v.p., 2003—. Bd. govs. Calif. State U., Long Beach; bd. dirs. Long Beach Found., Long Beach Venture Forum, Nat. Conf. Cmty. and Justice. Mem. Newspaper Assn. Am., Internat. Newspaper Promotion Assn., Sigma Chi. Office: 6300 Wilshire Blvd Los Angeles CA 90048

FINDLEY, PAUL, former congressman, author, educator; b. Jacksonville, Ill., June 23, 1921; s. Joseph S. and Florence Mary (Nichols) F.; m. Lucille Gemme; children: Craig Jon, Diane Lillian. AB, Ill. Coll., 1943, LLD, 1972; LHD (hon.), Lindenwood Coll., 1969, Lincoln U., 1988, MacMurray Coll., 1997; LLD, Sana'a U., Yemen, 1997. Mem. 87th-97th Congresses from 20th Ill. dist., mem. Fgn. Affairs com., mem. Agr. com.; chmn. factfinding mission to Paris, 1965; chmn. Rep. NATO Task Force, 1965-68; chmn. com. to investigate internat. problems caused by agrl. support policies Ditchley (Eng.) Conf., 1973; del. N. Atlantic Assembly, 1965-70, 72-79, Munich Conf. German Rels., 1969-71; Ditchley Conf. Atlantic Trade, 1967; European Parliament, 1974-76; mem. 7th Congl. Del. to People's Republic China, 1975; chmn. Ill. Trade Mission to, USSR, 1972, 1978. Internat. food and agrl. devel. bd. AID, 1983-94; vis. prof. MacMurray Coll., 1994-96. Author: Abraham Lincoln: The Crucible of Congress, The Federal Farm Fable, They Dare to Speak Out: People and Institutions Confront Israel's Lobby, Deliberate Deceptions: Facing the Facts About the U.S.-Israel Relationships, Silent No More: Confronting America's False Images of Islam; contbr. numerous articles on fgn. policy and agr. to periodicals. Trustee emeritus Ill. Coll.; lectr. leadership program UN Leadership Acad., Amman, Jordan, 1987-88; chmn. Coun. for the Nat. Interest, 1989-2000. Lt. (j.g.) USNR, WWII. Named laureate Lincoln Acad., 1980; decorated Grand Cross Order of Merit Fed. Republic of Ger.; recipient Outstanding Svc. to Agr. citation So. Ill. U., Kefauver award for promoting Fedn. of Atlantic Nations; Hon. Am. Farmer degree FFA, Outstanding Achievement award FFA Alumni Assn., citation Nat. Assn. State Univs. and Land-Grant Colls., EAFORD Humanitarian award, 1986, Alex Odeh Human Rights award Am. Arab Anti-Discrimination Com., 1992, Disting. Svc. award Assn. for Internat. Agr. and Rural Development, 1995; Malcolm X award Muslim Assn., 2000. Mem. Assn. to Unite Democracies (bd. dirs.), Am. Legion, Phi Beta Kappa. Republican. Presbyterian. Home and Office: 1040 W College Ave Jacksonville IL 62650-2306 Office Phone: 217-243-8444.

FINDLEY, SALLY E., public health educator; b. Cleve., Nov. 20, 1948; d. Robert Morton Evans and Elizabeth Vanderbeek Leutner; m. Richard E. Glass, Nov. 6, 1930; children: Molly Katherine, Peter William. PhD, Brown U., 1985. Project officer Rockefeller Found., NYC, 1988—90; prof. Mailman Sch. Pub. Health, Columbia U., NYC, 1990—. Com. mem. Am. Friends Svc. Com., NYC, 1990—2005. Mem.: APHA, Internat. Union for Sci. Study of Population, Am. Thoracic Soc., Population Assn. Am. Liberal. Quaker. Achievements include research in child health promotion programs in NYC and Africa. Avocations: swimming, cross-country skiing, hiking, bicycling, birding. Office: Columbia Univ 60 Haven Ave B2 New York NY 10032 Office Phone: 212-304-5790.

FINE, ANNE, writer; b. Leicester, Eng., Dec. 7, 1947; d. Brian and Eileen Mary (Baker) Laker; m. Kit Fine, Aug. 3, 1968 (div. 1991); children: Ione, Cordelia. BA with honors, U. Warwick, Eng., 1968. Tchr. Cardinal Wiseman Secondary Sch., Coventry, U.K., 1968-69; info. officer Oxfam, Oxford, England, 1969-71; tchr. Saughton Prison, Edinburgh, Scotland, 1971-72. Author: (children's fiction) The Summer-House Loon, 1978, The Other Darker Ned, 1979, The Stone Menagerie, 1980, Round Behind the Ice House, 1981, The Granny Project, 1983, Scaredy-Cat, 1984, Anneli the Art Hater, 1986, Madame Doubtfire, 1987, Crummy Mummy an Me, 1987, A Pack of Liars, 1988, Goggle-Eyes, 1989, Bill's New Frock, 1989, The Book of the Banshee, 1991, Flour Babies, 1992, Step By Wicked Step, 1995, The Tulip Touch, 1996, Charm School, 1999, Bad Dreams, 2000, Up on Cloud Nine, 2002, Stories of Jamie and Angus, 2002, The True Story of Christmas, 2003, Frozen Billy, 2004, others; (adult fiction) The Killjoy, 1986, Taking the Devil's Advice, 1990, In Cold Domain, 1994, Telling Liddy, 1998, All Bones and Lies, 2001, Raking the Ashes, 2005. Decorated Order Brit. Empire; named Children's Author of Yr., Brit. Book Awards, 1990, 1993, U.K. nominee for Hans Christian Andersen Author award, 1998, Children's Laureate, 2001—03; recipient Children's Lit. award, The Guardian, 1990, Carnegie medal, Brit. Libr. Assn., 1990, 1993, Whitbread Children's Novel award, 1993, 1996, Horn Book award, Boston Globe, 2003; fellow, Royal Soc. Lit., 2003. Avocations: reading, walking. Office: David Higham Assocs 5-8 Lower John St Golden Sq London W1R 4HA England

FINE, ARTHUR I., philosopher, educator; b. Lowell, Mass., Nov. 11, 1937; s. David Fine and Rae (Silverberg) Mintz; m. Helene S. Feldberg, June 16, 1957 (div. May 1980); children: Dana S., Sharon D.; m. Micky Forbes, July 11, 1980. Student, Harvard U., 1955-56; BS, U. Chgo., 1958; MS, Ill. Inst. Tech., 1960; PhD, U. Chgo., 1963. Asst. prof. math and philosophy Ill. Inst. Tech., Chgo., 1961—63; asst. prof. philosophy U. Ill., Urbana, 1963—65; assoc. prof. philosophy Cornell U., Ithaca, NY, 1967—71, prof. philosophy, 1971—72, U. Ill., Chgo., 1972—82, Northwestern U., Evanston, Ill., 1982—85, John Evans prof. philosophy, 1985—2001; prof. philosophy U. Wash., Seattle, 2001—, adj. prof. physics, 2003—, adj. prof. history, 2003—. Mem. nat. com. Internat. Union History and Philosophy of Sci. Nat. Acad. Sci., 1973-77; mem. adv. panel History and Philosophy of Sci. Nat. Sci. Found., 1975-77, 87-88, 92-93. Author: The Shaky Game, 1986, 2d edit., 1996; co-editor: Philosophical Review, 1969-71; editor: (with others) PSA: 1986, 88, 90, vols. I and II; subject editor: Philosophy of Science Routledge Encyclopedia of Philosophy, 1993-98; contbr. articles to profl. jours. NSF fellow, 1966-67; NSF grantee 1968, 73, 78, 80, 89; sr. fellow NEH, 1974-75; Guggenheim fellow, 1982-83; fellow Ctr. Advanced Study in Behavioral Scis. Stanford, 1985-86; vis. fellow Dibner Inst., MIT, 1996. Mem. Philosophy of Sci. Assn. (pres. 1986-88), Am. Philos. Assn. (ctrl. divsn. pres. 1997-98). Office: U Wash Philosophy Dept Box 353350 Seattle WA 98195-3550

FINE, A(RTHUR) KENNETH, lawyer; b. N.Y.C., June 29, 1937; s. Aaron Harry and Rose (Levin) F.; m. Ellen Marie Jensen, July 11, 1964; children: Craig Jensen, Ricki-Barie, Desiree-Ellen. AB, Hunter Coll., 1959; JD, Columbia U., 1963; CLU, Coll. Ins., 1973; diploma, Command and Gen. Staff Coll., 1978. Bar: N.Y. 1974; registered rep. and limited prin. Nat. Assn. Securities Dealers, Inc. Joined U.S. Army N.G., 1955, advanced through grades to maj., 1973, ret., 1980. Cons. U.S. Life Ins. Co., N.Y.C., 1970-74, atty., 1975-78, asst. gen. counsel, 1978; asst. counsel USLIFE Corp., N.Y.C., 1978-79, assoc. counsel, 1979-93; v.p., sr. counsel Western Res. Life Assurance Co. Ohio, Clearwater, Fla. Mem. ABA, Soc. Fin. Svc. Profls., N.Y. State Bar Assn., N.G. Assn. U.S., Militia Assn. N.Y. (chmn. vet. officers com. 1981-90), Am. Legion (7th regt. post), Mil. Officers Assn. of Am. (St. Petersburg chpt.). Republican. Lutheran. Home: 5953 36th Ave N Saint Petersburg FL 33710-1835 Office: Western Res Life Assurance Co of Ohio PO Box 5068 Clearwater FL 33758-5068 Office Phone: 727-299-1743. Business E-Mail: kfine@aegonusa.com.

FINE, CHARLES LEON, lawyer; b. Waukegan, Ill., Jan. 30, 1932; s. David M. and Henrietta (Goodman) F.; m. Penny J. Haines, Aug. 30, 1958; children: Karen L., Andrew H. BS, U. Wis., 1955; LLB, JD, Am. U., 1961. Bar: Mich. 1962, Ariz. 1981, U.S. Supreme Ct. 1971. Newscaster, news editor WKOW Radio and TV, Madison, Wis., 1953-58; editor, writer U.S. Bur. Pub. Roads, Washington, 1958-61; trial, staff atty. U.S. NLRB, Washington, Detroit, 1961-63; atty., assoc. Griffith & Griffith law firm, Detroit, 1963-69; atty., ptnr. Clark, Hardy, Lewis & Fine, Detroit, Birminghan, 1969-81; assoc. prof. law U. Detroit Sch. Law, 1976-80; ptnr. O'Connor, Cavanagh, et al, Phoenix, 1981-96, Streich Lang, 1996-2000, Littler Mendelson, 2000—. Cons. Met. Detoit Bur. Sch. Studies, 1970-80, Employer's Assn. Detroit, 1970-80. Assoc. editor Washington Coll. Law Rev., 1960; co-editor, author: Ariz. Employment Law Handbook, 1994; contbr. articles to legal jours. and chpts. to books. Mem. Ariz. Supreme Ct. Commn. on Minorities, 1996-2000; pres. Meadowlake Homeowners Assn., Birmingham, Mich., 1972-73; bd. dirs. Sch. Law Inst., Detroit, 1976-77; atty., advisor Gov.'s Office, Mich., 1979-80; cons. Cmty. Legal Svcs., Phoenix, 1986—. 1st lt. U.S. Army, 1955-57. Recipient Best Advocate award Nat. Moot Ct. Competition, Washington, 1960, Order of Barristers award Nat. Honor Soc., 1978; scholarship fund in his name U. Detroit Sch. of Law, 1979. Fellow Coll. Labor and Employment Lawyers; mem. Am. Employment Law Coun., Ariz. Bar Assn., Mich. Bar Assn., Am. Arbitration Assn. (arbitrator, employment arbitration panelist 1995—), Ariz. Insl. Rels. Assn. Avocations: badminton, hiking, swimming, reading. Home: 9041 N 33rd Way Phoenix AZ 85028-4968 Office: Littler Mendelson 2425 E Camelback Rd Ste 900 Phoenix AZ 85016 E-mail: CFINE@Littler.com.

FINE, CORY R., education educator, consultant; b. Queens, N.Y., Oct. 25, 1961; s. Roslyn Fine; m. Lisa C. Augustine, Jan. 24, 1993; 1 child, Tyler Marcus. M in Pub. Adminstrn., U. of N.Mex, 1992—94; PhD in Indsl. Rels., U. of Leeds, Eng., 1995—98. Prof. of mgmt. U. of North Fla., Jacksonville, 2000—. Mgmt. cons. www.LaborWise.com, Jacksonville, Fla., 2000—; vis. prof. Warsaw U., Poland, 2001—. Author: (rsch. article) Employee Rights and Responsibilities Jour., (book chapter) Ann. Editions: Mgmt.; member, editorial board (rsch. jour.) Mgmt. Devel. Forum; author: (rsch. article) Jour. of Intellectual Capital, Jour. of Labor Rsch., Labor Law Jour., Labor Studies Jour., Jour. of Collective Negotiations in the Pub. Sector, East European Quart., Pub. Adminstrn. Rev., Dispute Resolution Jour. Grantee Assoc. Sr. Rsch. Fellowship, Hungarian Acad. of Sci., Inst. of Polit. Sci., 2002-Present, Sr. Rsch. Assoc., U. of North Fla. Ctr. for Internat. Bus. Studies, 2002-Present. Mem.: Indsl. Rels. Rsch. Assn., Internat. Indsl. Rels. Assn., Soc. for Human Resource Mgmt., Acad. of Mgmt., River Club, Jacksonville. Avocations: travel, antiques. Home: 5336 Heronview Dr Jacksonville FL 32257 Office: U of North Fla CCB-MML 4567 St John's Bluff Rd South Jacksonville FL 32224

FINE, DAVID A., lawyer; b. Mar. 1, 1956; BA magna cum laude, Brandeis Univ., 1978; JD, Duke Univ., 1981. Bar: Mass. 1981. Law clk. Supreme Judicial Ct. Mass., 1981—82; assoc. Ropes & Gray, Boston, 1982—90, ptnr. corp. dept., 1990—, co-head securities & public companies practice group. Mem.: ABA, Mass. Bar Assn., Boston Bar Assn., Order of the Coif. Office: Ropes & Gray 1 International Pl Boston MA 02110-2624 Office Phone: 617-951-7473. Office Fax: 617-951-7050. Business E-Mail: david.fine@ropesgray.com.

FINE, DAVID JEFFREY, hospital executive, educator, consultant, lecturer; b. Flushing, N.Y., Oct. 10, 1950; s. Arnold and Phyllis F.; m. Susan Gory, Dec. 29, 1985; children: Jeffrey Jacob, Christopher Lee. BA, Tufts U., 1972; MHA, U. Minn., 1974. Asst. to dir. U. Calif. Hosp. and Clinics, San Francisco, 1974-76, asst. dir., 1976-78; sr. assoc. dir. U. Nebr. Hosp. and Clinic, Omaha, 1978-83; adminstr. W.Va. Univ. Hosp., Morgantown, 1983-84; pres. W.Va. Univ. Hosps., Inc., Morgantown, 1984-87, Houston, 2004—; pres., chief oper. officer Health Net, Inc., Charleston, 1985-87; vice provost for health affairs, chief exec. officer U. Cin. Health System, 1987-90; pres. U. Cin. Med. Assocs., 1988-90; vice chancellor Tulane U. Med. Ctr., New Orleans, 1990-95, emeritus vice chancellor, 1995—; prof., chmn. dept. health sys. mgmt. Sch. Pub. Health and Tropical Medicine Tulane U., New Orleans, 1990—99; pres., CEO New Orleans Region Columbia/HCA Healthcare Corp., 1995—96, St. Luke's Episcopal Health Systems, 2004—; pres. Columbia Health Edn. and Rsch. Found., 1996—97, S.E. Med. Alliance, 1998—99; CEO U. Ala. Birmingham Health Sys., 1999—2004. Chmn. bd. dirs. Allied Health Svcs., Morgantown, W.Va.; prof. med. econ. and pharmacy U. Cin., 1987-90; vice chair Nat. Ctr. Healthcare Leadership; vis. fellow King Fund Coll.; prof. Dept. Health Svcs. Adminstrn. Sch. Health Related Professions, UAB, 1999-2004, Dept. Health Care Org. and Policy Sch. Pub. Health, 2003-04; Regents prof. Dept. Health Sys. Mgmt., Tulane U. Sch. Pub. Health and Trop. Medicine, 1996-99; prof. mgmt. policy and cmty. health, U. Tex. Sch. Pub. Health, 2004-, Baylor Coll. Med., 2005-; cons. in field. Mem. editl. bd. Hospital Formulary, 1982-87, Health Adminstrn. Press, 1991-94, Jour. Health Adminstrn. Edn., 1991-2001; contbr. jour. articles, book chpts. and films. Trustee Monongalia Arts Coun., 1984-86, Cin. Chamber Orch., 1987-91; sec.-treas. Internat. Found. for Pharmacy Edn. Recipient James A. Hamilton prize, U. Minn., 1974; W. K. Kellog fellow. Fellow Am. Coll. Healthcare Execs. (Robert S. Hudgens Young Adminstr. of Yr. award 1985, mem. com. on awards and testimonials), Royal Coll. Medicine; mem. Am. Hosp. Assn. (mem. regional policy bd., mem. ho. of dels., mem. governing coun. sect. on met. hosps.), Am. Assn. Med. Coll. (coun. tchrs. hospis administrv. bd, 2005), Assn. U. Programs in Health Adminstrn. (chmn. 2000-02), Coronado Club, Omicron Delta Epsilon, Delta Omega. Roman Catholic. Office: St Luke Episcopal Health System 6624 Fannin Ave Houston TX 77030 Office Phone: 832-355-7661.

FINE, DAVID R., lawyer; b. Toledo, Ohio, Mar. 10, 1965; s. Burnl B. and Marilynn (Abramson) F.; m. Beth Campbell, Sept. 1, 1990; 1 child, Kenneth Campbell. BS, Cornell U., Ithaca, N.Y., 1987; MS in Journalism, Northwestern U., 1988; JD, U. Toledo, 1992. Bar: Pa. 1992, U.S. Ct. Appeals (3d cir. 1993), U.S. Dist. Ct. (mid. dist.) Pa. 1993. Anchor/reporter WUTR-TV, Utica, N.Y., 1988-89; law clk. U.S. Dist. Ct., Mid. Dist. Pa., Harrisburg, 1992-94; assoc. to ptnr. Kirkpatrick & Lockhart, Harrisburg, 1994—2004; ptnr. & pro bono coord. Kirkpatrick & Lockhart Nicholson Graham LLP, Harrisburg, 2005—. Mem. Lawyers Adv. Com. of US Dist. Ct. Middle Dist. Pa., 1999—, chmn., 2003—. Co-author The Middle District Manual (5th edit. 2003); contbr. articles to profl. jours.; editor-in-chief U. Toledo Law Rev., 1991-92. Bd. dir. Ctrl. Pa. Autism Edn. & Resource Ctr.; mem. Pa. Autism Task Force, 2003—. Named a Pa. Super Lawyer, Phila. Mag. & Law & Politics mag., 2004; named one of 30 Pa. Lawyers on the Fast Track, Am. Lawyer Media, 2004. Fellow Fed. Bar Found.; mem. ABA, Fed. Bar Assn. (pres. Middle Dist. Pa. chptr. 2001-02, mem. nat. resolutions com. 2002-), Pa. Bar Assn. (mem. Council of Civil Litigation sect. & Appellate Adv. Com. 2003-), Dauphin County Bar Assn., Order of the Coif. Office: Kirkpatrick & Lockhart Nicholson Graham LLP 240 N 3rd St Harrisburg PA 17101-1507 Office Phone: 717-231-5820. Office Fax: 717-231-4501. Business E-Mail: dfine@klng.com.

FINE, DEBORAH, publishing executive; V.p., advt. dir. Family Cir. Mag., 1991—93; v.p., assoc. pub. Mary Emmerling's Country, 1993—94; advt. dir. Glamour, 1994—95, assoc. pub., 1995—96; pub. Bride's Mag., 1996—99; v.p., pub. Glamour, 2000—01; pres. Avon Future, 2001—05; chief exec. of Pink, Limited Brands, Inc., 2005—. Office: Limited Brands Inc 3 Limited Pkwy Columbus OH 43216

FINE, DREW S., lawyer; b. Newark, 1962; BS, Georgetown Univ., 1984; JD, Northwestern Univ., 1987. Bar: N.Y. 1988. Ptnr. Global Transp. Fin. Group & mem. recruiting com. Milbank Tweed Hadley & McCloy, N.Y.C. Contbr. articles to profl. jours. Office: Milbank Tweed Hadley & McCloy 1 Chase Manhattan Plz New York NY 10005-1413 Office Phone: 212-530-5940. Office Fax: 212-530-5219. Business E-Mail: dfine@milbank.com.

FINE, EDWARD JAY JUDAH, neurologist, educator; b. Cin., Jan. 18, 1941; s. Archie and Anne Fine; m. Debra Lee Kleiman, May 19, 1969. AB cum laude, Ohio U., 1962; MD, Ohio State U., 1966. Diplomate Am. Bd. Psychiatry and Neurology, additional qualification in clin. neurophysiology; Am. Bd. Clin. Neurophysiology. Asst. prof. neurology Rutgers Med. Sch., Piscataway, N.J., 1974-78; fellow clin. neurophysiology Harvard Med. Sch., Boston, 1978-80; assoc. clin. prof. neurology Robert W. Johnson Med. Sch., New Brunswick, N.J., 1980-83; dir. clin. neurophysiology SUNY, Buffalo, 1983—, assoc. prof. neurology, 1995. Med. dir. Niagara C.C., Sandbourn, N.Y., 1984-2005. Inventor in field; contbr. articles to profl. jours. Cmdr. USN, 1968-70. Fellow Am. Acad. Neurology, Am. Assn. Electrodiagnostic Medicine, Internat. Soc. History of Neurosci. (pres. 2004), Sigma Xi, Phi Delta Epsilon. Jewish. Avocations: swimming, sailing, photography. Office: SUNY Neurology Dept 3495 Bailey Ave Buffalo NY 14215-1129 E-mail: efine@buffalo.edu.

FINE, ELAINE SARAH, composer, musician; b. Cleve., Apr. 30, 1959; d. Burton Davis and June Lois Fine; m. Michael James Leddy, Sept. 30, 1984; children: Rachel Anne Leddy, Benjamin Nathan Leddy. MusB, Juilliard Sch. Music, N.Y.C., 1980; MusM, Eastern Ill. U., 2002. Classical music dir. Sta. WEIU-FM, Charleston, Ill., 1987—2000; violist LeVeck String Quartet, Charleston, 1994—2004; program annotator New Philharm. DuPage County, Glenn Ellyn, Ill., 2002—; faculty mem. Lake Land Coll., Mattoon, Ill. Reviewer: Am. Record Guide, 1993—; editor: Practice for Performance (Daniel Morganstern), 2002; co-author: Classical Music: The Third Ear, 2002; contbr. articles to profl. jours.; composer: (large works) Five Pieces for String Quartet on Classidic Melodies, 1995, Introit a 4, 2002, Prologue and Lachrimae for String Quartet, 2003, Sonata for Oboe, Viola, Percussion and Mallet Instruments, 2003, Flute Quartet, 2003, The Happy Family, 2004, The Snail and the Rosebush, 2004, (chamber music) Essay for Chamber Orchestra, 2001, The Snow Queen, 2002, Tenor, Baritone, Violin and Piano, 2003, Sister Beatrice, 2004, Emma, 2005, Duo for Clarinet and Piano, 2000, The Solitary Cello, 2001, Tango Mariposa, 2002, Sonata for Trumpet and Piano, 2002, Sonata for Horn and Piano, 2002, Sonata for Viola and Piano, 2003, Four Greek Myths, 2004, Oh to be an Angel, 2004, Four Movements for Violin and Piano, 2004, Inventions and Creations: Five Very Short Pieces for Piano, 2004, others. Pres. Coles County Arts Coun., Charleston, 2002—04. Recipient Spl. commendation, Nancy Van De Vate Competition, 2003, award, ASCAP, 2003. Home: 2409 Terrace Ln Charleston IL 61920 Office Phone: 217-345-4310.

FINE, FREDERICK L., computer company executive, health products executive; BA in Econ., U. Ga. Founder, pres., CEO InfoCure Corp. (name changed to VitalWorks, Inc. in 2001), Atlanta; chmn., sr. advisor VitalWorks, Inc., 2001; co-founder Rialto Capital Partners, LLC, Atlanta. Mem. adv. bd. Asset Mgmt. Advisors. Office: Rialto Capital Partners LLC 3343 Peachtree Rd NE Ste 530 East Tower Atlanta GA 30326 Office Fax: 404-256-0272, 404-442-2426. Business E-Mail: rick@rialtocapitalpartners.com.*

FINE, GLENN A., federal agency administrator; AB magna cum laude, Harvard Coll., 1979; BA, MA, Oxford U.; JD magna cum laude, Harvard U., 1985. Asst. states atty. U.S. States Attys. Office, Washington, Del., 1986—89; atty. Washington, Del.; spl. counsel Dept. Justice Office Inspector Gen., Alexandria, 1995—96, dir. spl. investifations and rev. unit, 1996—2000, inspector gen., 2000—. Rhodes scholar. Office: US Dept Justice 950 Pennsulvania Ave NW Washington DC 20530-0001*

FINE, HOWARD ALAN, management consultant; BS, NYU, 1961, MBA, 1964. Internat. sales mgr. Pfaff, A.G., Fed. Republic of West Germany, 1964-67; regional sales dir. Brit. Transport Hotels, London, Eng., 1967-70; dir. internat. mktg. Sonesta Internat. Hotels, N.Y.C., 1970-71; dir. Pacific mktg. Forte Hotels, L.A., 1971-74, dir. Atlantic area and Latin Am. mktg. N.Y.C, 1974-75, v.p. sales and mktg., 1975-78, exec. v.p., 1978-81; pres. Norwegian Am. Cruise Line, N.Y.C, 1981-83; pres., chief exec. officer Costa Cruise Line, Miami, Fla., 1983-87; chmn., chief exec. officer Tourism Devel. Internat., Miami, 1987—; internat. mgmt. cons., advisor to corp. bds. and heads of state worldwide. Bd. dirs. Bahamas Devel. Found., Nassau, Traveling Times, L.A.; spkr., presenter Young Pres.'s Orgn, World Pres.'s Orgn., 1987—. Contbr. articles to profl. jours. Mem. mayors adv. bd. City of Los Angeles, 1972-74; mem. senatorial commn. Rep. Senatorial Inner Circle, Washington, 1984—, Presdl. task force to Pres. Bush, 1989—; bd. dirs. Calif. Dept. Agr. Wine Bd., 1974-75, Ptnrs. for Liveable Places, Washington, 1978-83, NYU Ctr. for Study of Foodservice, 1978-83, Fla. Crime Prevention Commn., 1984—, Boys Town of Italy, 1986—. Served to capt. USAR, 1961-66. Named Hon. Order Ky. Cols., 1986; named Man of Yr. Am. Jaycees, 1983, Man of Yr. Internat. Hotel Industry, 1980; recipient Disting. Marker of Yr. Sales and Mktg. Mgmt. Mag., 1979, Christopher Columbus award Nat. Columbus Day Com., 1986, Spirit of Life Humanitarian award City of Hope, 1987; numerous hotel and travel industry awards and citations from fgn. govts., 1972-87. Fellow Inst. Cert. Travel Agts.; mem. Young Pres.'s Orgn. (chmn. 1978—), World Pres.'s Orgn., Hotelier of World Com. (bd. dirs.), Italian C. of C. (bd. dirs.), Brit. C. of C. (bd. dirs.), Norwegian C. of C. (bd. dirs.), South African C. of C. (bd. dirs.), Greater Ft. Lauderdale C. of C. (bd. govs. 1986—), NYU Alumni Fedn., Sigma Alpha Mu, NYU Club (N.Y.C.), 110 Tower Club (bd. dirs.), Harbor Beach Club (bd. dirs.). Avocations: boating, travel, gardening, photography, flying. Office: Tourism Devel Internat PO Box 22323 Fort Lauderdale FL 33335-2323

FINE, J(AMES) ALLEN, insurance company executive; b. May 2, 1934; s. Samuel Lee and Ocie (Loflin) F.; m. Marie Nan Morris, Sept. 1, 1957 (dec. Apr. 1989); children: James A(llen), William. Student, Pfeiffer Coll., 1957—58; BS, U. N.C., 1961, MBA, 1965. Sr. acct. Haskins & Sells, CPAs, Charlotte, NC, 1961—62, Watson, Penry & Morgan, Asheboro, NC, 1962—64; instr. U. N.C., Chapel Hill, 1964—65; asst. prof. Pfeiffer Coll., Misenheimer, NC, 1956—66; treas., v.p. adminstrn. Nat. Lab. for Higher Edn. (formerly Regional Edn. Lab. Carolinas and Va.), Durham, NC, 1966—72; organizer, CEO, treas., dir. Investors Title Ins. Co., Inc., Chapel Hill, 1972—, Cpres., dir., 1976—; developer Carolina Forest Subdivsn., Chapel Hill, 1970—78, Springhill Forest Subdivsn., 1977—80, Stonycreek Subdivsn., 1978—. Lectr. acctg. U. N.C., Chapel Hill, 1967—70. Area officer ann. alumni giving U. N.C., Chapel Hill, 1968—69, 1971—73, 1975—; mem. Chapel Hill Downtown Econ. Devel. Corp.; trustee N.C. Mus. Art, 2003—. With USN, 1953—57. Recipient Haskins & Sells Found. award for excellence in accounting, 1961, N.C. Assn. CPAs award for most outstanding accounting student, U. N.C., 1961. Mem.: AICPA, NC Museum of Art (bd. trustees), CEDAR Bus. Mgrs. (chmn. nat. exec. com. 1971), U. N.C. Nat. Devel. Com., Nat. Assn. Ins. Commrs. (liaison com. 1987—88, 1994—), Am. Land Title Assn. (rsch. com. 1983—2003, membership com. 1984—85, recruitment, retention subcom. 1985, exec. com. underwriters sect. 1986, 2002—), Am. Acctg. Assn., N.C. Assn. CPAs, Phi Beta Kappa, Beta Gamma Sigma (treas. 1961). Home: 112 Carolina First Chapel Hill NC 27516-9033 Office: 121 N Columbia St Chapel Hill NC 27514-3502

FINE, JAMES STEPHEN, physician; b. St. Paul, June 14, 1946; s. Ralph Irving and Beverlee Lois (Rockler) F.; m. Meredith Ann Blehert, June 20, 1970; children: Zachary, Esther, Gabriel. BA in Math., U. Minn., 1968, MD, 1972, MS in Biometry, Health Info. Systems, 1977. Intern in medicine St. Paul-Ramsey Hosp., 1972-73; residency U. Minn., Mpls., 1973-77; assoc. prof., dir. info. and specimen processing div. U. Wash. Hosp., Seattle, 1977-94, chmn. lab. medicine, 1994—. Mem. Am. Assn. Clin. Chemistry, Acad. Clin. Lab. Physicians and Scientists (Gerald T. Evans award 2001), Computer Soc. IEEE, Assn. Pathology (chmn.), Am. Med. Informatics Assn., Wash. State Med. Assn., King County Med. Soc. Office: U Wash Hosp Box 357110 1959 NE Pacific Ave NW 120 Seattle WA 98195 Office Phone: 206-598-6151. Business E-Mail: jsfine@u.washington.edu.

FINE, JANE MADELINE, visual artist; b. N.Y.C., Sept. 25, 1958; d. Arnold and Cecile (Glassen) F. BA, Harvard U., 1980; MA, Tufts U., 1982; postgrad., Skowhegan Sch. Painting, 1989. One-woman show Casey M. Kaplan, N.Y., 1995; exhibited in group shows at Bard Coll., 1991, Marymount Coll., 1990, PS 122 Gallery, 1989, The Drawing Ctr., 1988, Soho Ctr. for Visual Artists, 1988, White Columns, N.Y., 1992, Jack Tilton Gallery, N.Y., 1993, Leo Tony Gallery, N.H., 1994, Art in Gen., N.Y., 1994, Petzel/Borgmann Gallery, N.Y., 1994, Marymount Manhattan Coll., 1995, Arena, Bklyn., 1995, E.S. Vandam, N.Y., 1995. Fellow Millay Colony for the Arts, 1990, Yaddo, 1990, NEA, 1989, Visual Artists fellow N.Y. Found. for the Arts, 1994.

FINE, JEFFREY LOUIS, psychologist, educator, writer; b. NYC, Mar. 2, 1941; s. Joseph Fine and Helen Bloomfield; m. Dalit Kamerman Fine, Apr. 5, 1998; 1 child, Kesem Joseph. BS in biology, NYU, NYC, 1966; MS in health edn., New Sch. for Social Rsch., 1968; PhD in psychology, U. London, 1974. Cert. eating disorder specialist (CEDS), bd. cert. diplomate Internat. Assn. Eating Disorders, 1993. Clinical assoc. Acad. Orthomolecular Psychiatry, Manhasset, NY, 1976—77; rsch. cons. in psychodietitrics Coun. Nutrition, Am. Chiropractice Assn., NYC, 1976—77; dir. Shangi-La Natural Health Inst., Bonita Springs, Fla., 1977—80; mng. dir. Bay Harbour Health Inst., Stuart, Fla., 1980—81; owner, clinical dir. Fineway House Clinic and Spa, Palm Beach, Fla., 1981—86; pvt. practice NYC, 1986—2001, Bal Harbour, Fla., 2001—. Spkr. in field for TV and radio, 1980—94; adv. bd. Birthing the Future, Bayfield, Colo., 2003—04; dir. Am. Found. for Conscious Parenting, Miami, 2004; pres. Carlebach Synagogue, NYC, 1991—94. Editor, writer (jour.) Alternatives mag., 1976—77; author: (jour.) Jour. Energy Medicine, 1980—82, (weekly column) "Ask Dr. Fine", 1995—97, The New Parenting, 2004. Recipient TV Emmy award for costume design, Nat. Acad. TV Arts and Scis., 1970, Rsch. award, Am. Holistic Health Sci. Assn., Milw., 1983. Achievements include identifying and naming the "Night Eating Disorder Syndrome" (NEDS), 1992; advancing the application and understanding the use of "consciousness itself" in the psychotherapeutic process, 1997; founder/dir. NYC chpt. "The Mankind Project" and "New Warrior Training Adventure", 1994. Avocations: music, scuba diving, bodybuilding, antiques, clothing design. Office: Am Found Conscious Parenting Box 546020 Miami FL 33154 E-mail: drfine@the-beach.net.

FINE, JO RENÉE, management executive; b. June 19, 1943; d. Ruby Arthur and Tillie Fern (Goldman) F.; m. Edward Trieber, Apr. 12, 1981; 1 child, Jessica. BA, Smith Coll., 1965; MA, NYU, 1968, PhD, 1973. Probation officer N.Y.C. Office Probation, 1966; rsch. asst. NYU, N.Y.C., 1966-68; assoc. rsch. scientist Inst. Devel. Studies, N.Y.C., 1968-73, rsch. scientist, 1973-77; program analyst N.Y. State Dept. Mental Health, N.Y.C., 1977-78; pvt. practice psychotherapy N.Y.C., 1978-81; pres. CVM Prodns., Inc., N.Y.C., 1978-92; dir. Ctr. for Diversity and Quality Mgmt. Cicatelli Assocs., N.Y.C., 1992-96; exec. v.p., dir. tng. Harris Rothenberg Internat., N.Y.C., 1996—. Adj. asst. prof. dept. ednl. psychology, NYU, 1973-76, adj. asst. prof. ednl. comm. and tech., 1988-95; cons. to bds. edn., N.Y.C., also greater met. area, 1973-92, tng. cons., 1990-96. Co-author: The Synagogues of New York's Lower East Side, 1978. Co-chair bd. dirs. Project People Found. Mem. APA, ASTD, Am. Jewish Com. (v.p. N.Y. chpt., nat. bd. govs.). Home: 55 W 16th St New York NY 10011-6305 Office: Harris Rothenberg Internat 99 Wall St Fl 8 New York NY 10005-4389

FINE, JO-DAVID, dermatologist; b. Louisville, Apr. 9, 1950; s. Lewis and Bernice Rhea (Friedman) F.; m. Catherine Miles Evans, June 3, 1972; children: David, Jeffrey, Kenneth. BS in Chemistry, Yale Coll., 1972; MD with distinction, U. Ky., 1976; MPH in Epidemiology, U. N.C., 1992. Diplomate Am. Bd. Internal Medicine, Am. Bd. Dermatology (gen. and immunologic dermatology). Intern and jr. asst. resident Duke U. Med. Ctr., Durham, N.C., 1976-78; resident dermatology Harvard Med. Sch. and Mass. Gen. Hosp., Boston, 1978-80; sr. resident dermatology Harvard Med. Sch. and Lahey Clin. Found., Boston, 1980-81; med. staff fellow dermatology br. Nat. Cancer Inst./NIH, Bethesda, Md., 1981-83; asst. prof. dermatology U. Ala. Sch. of Medicine, Birmingham, 1983-85, assoc. prof. dermatology, 1985-90, U. N.C. Sch. Medicine, Chapel Hill, 1990-92, prof. dermatology, 1992—. Clin. prof. epidemiology U. N.C. Sch. of Pub. Health, Chapel Hill, 1993—; prin. investigator Nat. Epidermolysis Bullosa Registry, Chapel Hill, 1986—; trustee Dystrophic Epidermolysis Bullosa Rsch. Assn. of Am., Inc., N.Y.C., 1989—; mem. med. sch. admission com. U. N.C. Sch. of Medicine, Chapel Hill, 1990-96; ad hoc reviewer grants NIH, 1986—. Editl. bd.: Clinical and Experimental Dermatology, London, 1994—; dep. editor: Jour. of Investigative Dermatology, 1992-93; editor/author: (book) Bullous Diseases, 1993; contbr. approximately 125 articles to profl. jours. Vice-pres. Yale Club of Ala., Birmingham, 1989; dir. cen. N.C. alumni schs. com., Yale U., New Haven, Conn., 1994—. Recipient Disting. Svc. award Dystrophic Epidermolysis Bullosa Rsch. Assn. of Am., N.Y.C., 1984, New Investigator Rsch. award, NIH, Bethesda, 1985, rsch. grants, 1985—, rsch. grants Vet. Adminstrn., Washington, 1984-88. Fellow ACP, Am. Acad. Dermatology, Royal Soc. of Medicine (London); mem. Soc. for Investigative Dermatology, Am. Fedn. for Clin. Rsch., Am. Pub. Health Assn., Am. Dermatol. Assn., So. Soc. for Clin. Investigation. Jewish. Avocations: golf, photography. Office: Univ NC Dept Dermatology 3100 Thurston Clb # 7287 Chapel Hill NC 27599-0001

FINE, LAWRENCE B., lawyer; b. June 20, 1951; BA, BS, U. Pa., 1973; JD, U. Va., 1976. Bar: Pa. 1976. Ptnr. Morgan, Lewis & Bockius, Phila. Office: Morgan Lewis & Bockius 1701 Market St Philadelphia PA 19103-2903 Office Phone: 215-963-5246. Business E-Mail: lfine@morganlewis.com.

FINE, MICHAEL JOSEPH, publishing company executive; b. NYC, Jan. 30, 1937; s. William and Rosa F.; m. Marlene Rosen, Apr. 4, 1959; children: Anton Adeus, Kaethe Elizabeth. Student, U. Fla., 1953—54; BA, Bklyn. Coll., 1957; postgrad., State U. Iowa, 1959—60. Propr. Paper Place Bookstore, Iowa City, 1960-63; v.p. Paperback Affiliates, Inc., N.Y.C., 1963-74; mgr., co-owner The Paperback Forum Bookstore, N.Y.C.; mgr. The Manhattanville Book Forum, Manhattanville Coll., Purchase, N.Y.; asst. to pres. Simon & Schuster, Inc., N.Y.C., 1964-65, v.p. Assoc. Ednl. Svcs., 1966, assoc. dir. Washington Square Press N.Y.C., 1967-69, mem. editl. bd., 1968; founder, pub. trade paperback divsn. Simon & Schuster Clarion Books, N.Y.C., 1967-69; founder, exec. v.p. Bookthrift, Inc., 1971-78; pres. Bookthrift, Inc. div. Simon & Schuster, 1978-81; sr. v.p., exec. com. mem. Ingram Book Co., Nashville, 1981-83; pres., chief exec. officer Ingram Ventures, Inc., N.Y.C., 1981-83; chief exec. officer Feeling Fine Programs, Inc., 1984-86; co-founder, pres. Lynx Communications, Inc., N.Y.C., 1987-90; founder, pres. Fine Creative Media, Inc., N.Y.C., 1991—. Pub. MJF Books, Prod. Barnes and Noble Classics. Contbr. articles to profl. jours. Past chmn. bd. dirs. St. Michaels Montessori Sch., NYC; bd. dirs. Morningside Area Alliance, Inc., 1974-83, Labyrinth Theater Co., 2003 Mem. N.Y. Acad. Scis. (mem. publs. com. 1984-88), Nat. Arts Club. Office: Fine Comm MJF Books 322 8th Ave New York NY 10001 *The older I become the more I am struck by how uniquely independent each of us is, one from the other and, at the same time, how urgently connected we all are, one to each other. To publish is to navigate the time and the space between the two .*

FINE, MILTON, hotel company executive, lawyer; b. Pitts., May 18, 1926; s. Samuel and Ida (Krimsky) F.; m. Sara Mariam Fogel, June 15, 1952 (div. 1971); children: Carolyn Francis Fine Friedman, Sibyl Ann Fine King, David Jeremy; m. Sheila Dianne Cook, Nov. 24, 1989. BA magna cum laude, U. Pitts., 1949, JD, 1950. Bar: Pa. 1951. Pvt. practice, 1951-55; ptnr. Fine, Perlow & Stone, Pitts., 1955-75; co-chmn. Interstate Hotels Corp., Pitts., 1960-88, chmn., CEO, 1988-96, chmn. bd. dirs., 1996-98; chmn. FCC Hotel Devel. Corp., 1998—. Mem. adv. bd. Greenwich St. Capital Ptnrs., Inc., 1996—; bd. dirs. Wyndham Internat., Inc., Dallas. Lifetime trustee Carnegie Inst., Pitts., 1983—; chmn. bd. dirs. Carnegie Mus. Art, 1992—; trustee U. Pitts., 1997—; mem. bd. dirs. Warhol Mus., Pitts., 1989—. Recipient Bicentennial Medallion of Distinction, U. Pitts., 1987, Cultural award Pitts. Ctr. for the Arts, 1995. Mem. Pa. Bar Assn., Duquesne Club. Republican. Jewish. Avocations: golf, collecting contemporary art. Office: Interstate Hotels Corp Foster Plz 10 680 Andersen Dr Pittsburgh PA 15220-2700 *With all the unexpected turns in my life, the thing which has been most predictable has been change. What remains constant is the need to be flexible and resilient, the need to take advantage of change rather than being overwhelmed by it, and, most importantly, the need to remain a student throughout one's life.*

FINE, MORRIS EUGENE, materials engineer, educator; b. Jamestown, N.D., Apr. 12, 1918; s. Louis and Sophie (Berrington) F.; m. Mildred Eleanor Glazer, Aug. 13, 1950; children: Susan Elaine, Amy Lynn. B.Metall. Engring. with distinction, U. Minn., 1940, MS, 1942, PhD, 1943. Instr. U. Minn., 1942-43; mem. tech. staff Bell Telephone Labs., Murray Hill, N.J., 1946-54; prof. emeritus Northwestern U., Evanston, Ill., 1954—, prof., chmn. dept. metallurgy Tech. Inst., 1955-57, chmn. dept. materials sci., 1958-60, prof. and chmn. materials research center, 1960-64, Walter P. Murphy prof. materials sci., 1963-89, tech. inst. prof., 1985-89, dir. Am. Iron and Steel Inst. steel resource ctr., 1986-93, assoc. dean grad. studies and research Tech. Inst., 1973-85, prof. emeritus, 1989, mem. grad. faculty, 1989—. Vis. prof. dept. materials sci. Stanford U., 1967-68; JSPS vis. scholar, Japan, 1979; chmn., vis. prof. materials sci. and engring. U. Tex., Austin, 1984-95; assoc. engr. Manhattan Project, U. Chgo. and Los Alamos, N.Mex., WWII; mem. materials adv. bd. NRC, 1963-68; mem. com. geol. and materials scis. NRC, 1979-82; chmn. adv. bd. program on modular methods for tchg. materials Pa. State U., 1973-77; chmn. vis. com. metallurgy and materials Sci. and Materials Rsch. Ctr., Lehigh U., 1965-75; mem. vis. com. Lawrence Berkeley Lab., 1978-81, chmn., 1981, mem. vis. com. Ames Dept. Energy Lab., 1976-80, Materials Rsch. Ctr., Pa. State U., 1988-91, Colo. Sch. Mines, 1991-96; chmn., organizer numerous confs. in field. Author numerous tech. and sci. articles on mech. properties of metals and ceramics, fatigue of metals, phase transformations, high temperature alloys, and other subjects.; author: Introduction to Phase Transformation in Condensed Systems. Recipient Gilbert Speich award Iron and Steel Soc., 1993; named Chicagoan of Year in Sci., 1961 Fellow AAAS, Am. Phys. Soc., Japan Soc. Metals (hon.), Am. Soc. Metals (chpt. chmn. 1963, Campbell lectr. 1979, chmn. seminar com. 1979, hon. mem. com. 1993-96, gold medal 1986), Am. Acad. Arts and Scis., Metall Soc. of AIME (chmn. inst. metals divsn. 1966-68, bd. dirs. 1968-71, bd. dirs. inst. 1972-75, mem. Bardeen gold medals com. 1992-96, chmn. 1995-96, Mathewson gold medal for rsch. 1981, James Douglas gold medal 1982, Educator award 1993, hon. mem.), Am. Ceramic Soc. (keynote lectr. electronic materials div. 1972); mem. NAE (astronautics space engring. bd. 1973-77, membership com. 1974-79, chmn. 1977-78, mem. membership adv. com. 1991-94), Scripta Met et Mat (Outstanding Paper award 1991), The Metals, Materials, Minerals Soc. (inst. metals lecture and R.F. Mehl gold medal 1996), Sigma Xi, Tau Beta Pi, Alpha Sigma Mu, Sigma Alpha Sigma. Home: 1101 Manor Dr Wilmette IL 60091-1026 Office: Dept Materials Sci and Engring Northwestern U Evanston IL 60208-3108 E-mail: m-fine@northwestern.edu.

FINE, PAMELA B., newspaper editor; Grad., U. Fla. Reporter Daytona Beach News, 1979; several editl. positions with Atlanta Journal-Constitution, 1982—94; mng. editor, v.p. Mpls. Star Tribune, 1994—2002; mng. editor The Indianapolis Star, 2003—. Nat. conf. chair Associated Press Mng. Editors Assn., 2000; juror for Pulitzer Prize. Office: The Indianapolis Star PO Box 145 Indianapolis IN 46206-0145 Office Phone: 317-444-6168. Business E-Mail: pam.fine@indystar.com.*

FINE, RANA ARNOLD, chemical and physical oceanographer; d. Joseph and Etta (Kreisman) Arnold; m. Shalle Stephen Fine, June 20, 1965 (div. 1979); m. James Stewart Mattson, Jan. 5, 1983. BA, NYU, 1965; MA, U. Miami, 1973, PhD, 1975. Systems analyst Svc. Bur. Corp. subs. IBM, Miami, 1965-69; rsch. assoc. Rosenstiel Sch. U. Miami, 1976-77, rsch. asst. prof., 1977-80, rsch. assoc. prof., 1980-84, assoc. prof., 1984-90, prof. marine and atmospheric chemistry, 1990—, chair divsn. marine and atmospheric chemistry, 1990-94; assoc. program dir. NSF, Washington, 1981-83. Mem. div. polar programs adv. com. NSF, Washington, 1987-90, geophys. study com. NAS, Washington, 1989-92, ocean studies bd., 1992-98, adv. panel Tropical Ocean/Global Atmosphere Program, 1990-93, chair adv. panel major ocean programs, 1996-98; mem. UCAR Bd Trustees 2005-, Inter-Am. Inst. for Global Ch. SSC, 2004-. Contbr. articles to profl. jours. Vol. guide Vizcaya Mus., Miami, 1967-78, adv. panel mem. methane hydrade rev. 2003-04. Grantee NSF, 1977—, NOAA, 1986—, Office of Naval Rsch., 1983-88, NASA, 1990-97. Fellow: AAAS (chair-elect atm and hydrospheric sci. sect. 2001—04), Am. Meteorol. Soc. (coun. mem. 2001—04), Am. Geophys. Union (sec. oceanography sect. 1986—88, pres.-elect oceanography sect. 1994—96, pres. 1996—98); mem.: Oceanography Soc. Avocations: sailing, scuba diving, fishing, tennis, reading. Office: RSMAS/MAC/U Miami 4600 Rickenbacker Cswy Miami FL 33149-1031 Office Phone: 305-421-4722. Business E-Mail: rfine@rsmas.miami.edu.

FINE, RICHARD ISAAC, lawyer; b. Milw., Jan. 22, 1940; s. Jack and Frieda F.; m. Maryellen Olman, Nov. 25, 1982; 1 child, Victoria Elizabeth. BS, U. Wis., 1961; JD, U. Chgo., 1964; PhD in Internat. Law, U. London, 1967, cert., 1965, 66; cert. comparative law, Internat. U. Comparative Sci., Luxembourg, 1966; diplôme supérieur, Faculté Internat. pour l'Enseignment du Droit Comparé, Strasbourg, France, 1967. Bar: Ill. 1964, D.C. 1972, Calif. 1973. Trial atty. fgn. commerce sect. antitrust divsn. U.S. Dept. Justice, 1968-72; chief antitrust divsn. L.A. City Atty.'s Office, also spl. counsel gov. efficiency com., 1973-74; prof. internat., comparative and EEC antitrust law U. Syracuse (N.Y.) Law Sch. (overseas program), 1970-72; individual practice Richard I. Fine and Assocs., L.A., 1974—; mem. antitrust adv. bd. Bur. Nat. Affairs, 1981—. Bd. dirs. Citizens Island Bridge Co., Ltd., 1992—; vis. com. U. Chgo. Law Sch., 1992-95; hon. consul gen. Kingdom of Norway, 1995—. Contbr. articles to legal publs. Bd. dirs. Retinitis Pigmentosa Internat., 1985-90. Mem. ABA (chmn. subcom. internat. antitrust and trade regulation, internat. law sect. 1972-77, co-chmn. com. internat. econ. orgn. 1977-79), ATLA, Am. Soc. Internat. Law (co-chmn. com. corp. membership 1978-83, exec. coun. 1984-87, budget com. 1992-97, regional coord. for L.A. 1994—, 1995 ann. program com. 1994-95, corr. editor Internat. Legal Materials 1983—), Am. Fgn. Law Assn., Internat. Law Assn., Brit. Inst. Internat. and Comparative Law, State Bar Calif. (chmn. antitrust and trade regulation law sect. 1981-84, exec. com. 1981-87), L.A. County Bar Assn. (chmn. antitrust sect. 1977-78, exec. com. sect. internat. law 1993—, treas. 1997, chmn. 2003-04), Ill. Bar Assn., Am. Friends London Sch. Econs. and Polit. Sci. (bd. dirs. 1984—, chmn. So. Calif. chpt. 1984—, chmn. L.A. adv. com.), L.A. World Affairs Coun. (internat. cir. 1990—), Phi Delta Phi. Office: Ste 200 468 N Camden Dr Beverly Hills CA 90210 Office Phone: 310-277-5833. E-mail: rifinelaw@earthlink.net.

FINE, ROGER SETH, pharmaceutical executive, lawyer; b. Bklyn., Sept. 22, 1942; s. Jack F. and Mildred (Perlmutter) F.; m. Rebecca Gold, June 14, 1964; children: David, Adam. BA, Columbia Coll., 1963; LLB, NYU, 1966. Bar: NY 1966, U.S. Dist. Ct. (so. dist.) NY 1967, U.S. Ct. Appeals (2d cir.) 1967. Assoc. Cahill, Gordon & Reindel, NYC, 1966-74; gen. atty. Johnson & Johnson, New Brunswick, NJ, 1974-78, asst. gen. counsel, 1978-84, assoc. gen. counsel, 1984-91, v.p. adminstrn., mem. exec. com., 1991-95, v.p., gen. counsel, mem. exec. com., 1996—. Mem. ABA. Office: Johnson & Johnson 1 Johnson And Johnson Plz New Brunswick NJ 08933-0002

FINEBERG, GERALD, real estate company executive; m. Sandra Fineberg. Founder The Fineberg Companies, Fine Hotels Corp., 1990—, chmn., 1990—; ptnr. Frontier Capital Mgmt. LLC. Friend of Rose Art Mus., Brandeis U., 1990—, mem. bd. overseers, 1997—, chmn. bd. overseers, 2000—. Named in his honor Gerald S. & Sandra Fineberg Gallery, Rose Art Mus. of Brandeis U., 2005; named one of Top 200 Collectors, ARTnews Mag., 2004. Avocations: squash, golf, collector modern & contemporary art. Address: 5 Byron St Boston MA 02108 Office: The Fineberg Companies 1 Washington St Ste 402 Wellesley MA 02481 Office Phone: 781-239-1480. Office Fax: 781-239-1439.*

FINEBERG, HARVEY VERNON, medical institute administrator; b. Pitts., Sept. 15, 1945; s. Saul and Miriam (Pearl) F.; m. Mary Elizabeth Wilson, May 16, 1975. AB, Harvard U., 1967, MD, M.P.P., Harvard U., 1972, PhD, 1980. Intern Beth Israel Hosp., Boston, 1972—73; asst. prof. Sch. Pub. Health, Harvard U., Boston, 1973—78; physician East Boston Health Ctr., 1974—76, Harvard Street Health Ctr., 1976—84; assoc. prof. Harvard U., Boston, 1978—81, prof., 1981—2002, dean Sch. Pub. Health, 1984—97, provost Cambridge, Mass., 1997—2001; pres. Inst. of Medicine, Washington, 2002—. Jr. fellow Harvard U., 1974—75; Mellon fellow, 1976. Co-author: Clinical Decision Analysis, 1980, The Epidemic That Never Was, 1983, Adverse Effects of Pertussis and Rubella Vaccines, 1991, Society's Choices: Social and Ethical Decision Making in Biomedicine, 1995, Innovators in Physician Education: The Process and Pattern of Reform in North American Medical Schools, 1996. Trustee Newton Wellesley Hosp., Mass., 1981-86; study sect. chmn. Nat. Ctr. Health Services Research, Rockville, Md., 1982-85; active Pub. Health Council, Mass., 1976-79; bd. dirs. Am. Found. AIDS Rsch., 1986-97, William and Flora Hewlett Found., 2003—. Mem.: Soc. Med. Decision Making (pres. 1980—81), Inst. Medicine. Jewish. Office: Inst Medicine 500 5th St NW Washington DC 20001-2721

FINEGOLD, AMY BETH, elementary school educator, consultant; b. Bklyn., June 10, 1968; d. Ira and Barbara May Finegold. BA, Univ. Miami, 1990; MA, Ind. State U., 1992, N.Y.U., 1999. Cert. tchr. N.Y. Tchr. ESL N.Y. Bd. Edn., N.Y.C., 1997—. New tchr. staff devel. tchr.; elem. lang. trainer; geography cons. N.Y. Geographic Alliance; mem. spl. interest group N.Y. State Tchrs. Eng. to Spkrs. Other Langs., 1997—2001; presenter in field. Contbr. articles to newsletters. Vol., chair events for entertainment United Jewish Appeal Fedn. Young Leadership, 1995—98; mem. Make A Wish Found., NY, 1997. Grantee, Excell, N.Y., 1998, United Fedn. Tchrs., 1998; scholar, NYU, 1996—97. Mem.: Manhattan Soc., Kappa Delta Pi, Pi Lambda Theta (membership chair, historian). Republican. Jewish. Avocations: reading, dance. Home: 309 East 49th St Apt 5B New York NY 10017

FINEGOLD, MAURICE NATHAN, architect; b. Providence, Sept. 6, 1932; s. Samuel R. and Ruth (Marks) F.; m. Muriel Ann Savitz, Apr. 30, 1964; Jordan, Daniel Warren, Jonathan Eric, Michael Andrew. AB, Harvard Coll., 1954; MArch, Harvard U., 1958. Lic. architect, Mass., and 15 other states. Prin. Maurice N. Finegold & Assocs., AIA, Architect, Boston, 1964-69; ptnr. Finegold & Bullis, Architects, Boston, 1969-74; prin. Notter Finegold & Alexander, Boston, 1974-92; pres. Finegold Alexander & Assocs., Inc., Boston, 1992—. Chair Mass. Bd. of Registration of Architects, Boston, 1989-91. Bd. dirs. Downtown North Assn., Boston, 1990—, pres. 1997-99; mem. New Eng. Holocaust Meml. Com., Boston, 1990—; chair presdl. search com. Boston Archtl. Ctr., 1990-91, 96-97, bd. dirs., 1994—, vice chair bd. dirs., 1995-99, chair, bd. dirs., 1999-2003. Sgt. U.S. Army, 1958-64. Fellow AIA (numerous local and nat. design awards, Frey award 2002), Soc. for Arts, Religion and Contemporary Culture; mem. ALA, Boston Soc. Architects (chmn. several coms. 1961—), Soc. Coll. and Univ. Planning, Nat. Trust for Hist. Preservation, League Hist. Am. Theaters. Democrat. Jewish. Avocations: sailing, skiing, travel. Office: Finegold Alexander & Assocs Inc 77 N Washington St Boston MA 02114-1908 Office Phone: 617-227-9272. Business E-Mail: mnf@faainc.com.

FINEGOLD, SYDNEY MARTIN, microbiology educator; b. N.Y.C., Aug. 12, 1921; s. Samuel Joseph and Jennie (Stein) F.; m. Mary Louise Saunders, Feb. 8, 1947 (dec. June 1994); children: Joseph, Patricia, Michael; m. Gloria Weiss, Feb. 18, 1996. AB, UCLA, 1943; MD, U. Tex., 1949. Diplomate: Am. Bd. Med. Microbiology (mem. bd. 1979-85), Am. Bd. Internal Medicine. Intern USPHS, Galveston, Tex., 1949-50; fellow in medicine U. Minn. Med. Sch., 1950-52, research fellow, 1951-52; resident medicine Wadsworth Hosp., VA Ctr., Los Angeles, 1953-54; instr. medicine U. Calif. Med. Ctr., Los Angeles, 1955-57, asst. clin. prof., 1957-59, asst. prof., 1959-62, assoc. prof., 1962-68, prof., 1968—2000, emeritus, 2000—, prof. microbiology and immunology, 1983—2000, emeritus, 2000—; chief chest and infectious disease sect. Wadsworth Hosp., 1957-61, chief infectious disease sect., 1961-86, assoc. chief staff for research and devel., 1986-92; staff physician infectious disease sect. VA Med. Ctr., L.A., 1992—. Mem. pulmonary disease rsch. program com. VA, 1961-62, infectious disease rsch. program com., 1961-65, merit rev. bd. (infectious diseases), 1972-74, med. rsch. program specialist, 1974-76, adv. com. on infectious disease, 1974-87; mem. NRC-Nat. Acad. Sci. Drug Efficacy Study Group, 1966-69; mem. subcom. on gram-negative anaerobic bacilli Internat. Com. on Nomenclature Bacteria, 1966—, chmn., 1972-78; mem. adv. panel U.S. Pharmacopoeia, 1970-75; chmn. working group on anaerobic susceptibility test methods Nat. Com. Clin. Lab. Standards, 1987-97, advisor, 1998-2002. Mem. editl. bd. Calif. Medicine, 1966-73, Applied Microbiology, 1973-74, Western Jour. Medicine, 1974-77, Am. Rev. Respiratory Disease, 1974-76, Jour. Clin. Microbiology, 1975-85, Infection, 1976—, Jour. Infectious Disease, 1979-82, 84-85, Antimicrobial Agts. Chemotherapy, 1980-89, Diagnostic Microbiology and Infectious Diseases, 1982-90; editor Revs. of Infectious Diseases, 1990-91, Clin. Infectious Diseases, 1992-2000; sect. editor: infectious diseases vols. Clin. Medicine, 1978-82, Microbiol. Ecology in Health and Disease, 1987-90; assoc. editor, consulting editor Anaerobe, 1994—. editor-in-chief, 1998—. Vice chmn. UCLA Acad. Senate, 1986-87, chair, 1987-88. Served with USMCR, with USNR, 1943-46, to 1st. lt. AUS, 1952-53. Co-recipient V.A. William S. Middleton award for biomed. rsch., 1984; recipient Profl. Achievement award UCLA, 1987, Mayo Soley award Western Soc. Clin. Investigation, 1988, Disting. Alumnus award U. Tex. Med. Br., 1988, UCLA Med. Alumni Assn. Med. Scis. award, 1990, Hoechst Roussel award Am. Soc. Microbiology, 1992, medal Helsinki U., Finland, 1996, Lifetime Achievement award Infectious Disease Assn. Calif., 1995, Wm. H. Oldendorf Lifetime Achievement awrd VA Med. Ctr., 1996, Lifetime Achievement award Internat. Soc. Anaerobic Bacteriology, 1998, Becton Dickinson award in Clin. Microbiology, 1999; organism named Finegoldia magna, 1999; new species named Alistipes finegoldii, 2003. Master ACP; fellow APHA, AAAS, Am. Acad. Microbiology, Infectious Diseases Soc. Am. (councilor 1976-79, pres.-elect 1980-81, pres. 1981-82, exec. com. 1980-83, Bristol award 1987, Soc. citation 1999); mem. Assn. Am. Physicians, Am. Soc. Microbiology (chmn. subcom. on taxonomy of Bacteroidaceae 1971-74, 1st annual Alex Sonnenwirth award 1986), Am. Thoracic Soc., Western Soc. Clin. Rsch., Western Assn. Physicians, Wadsworth Med. Alumni Assn. (past pres.), Anaerobe Soc. of the Ams. (interim pres. 1992-94, pres. 1994-96), Soc. Intestinal Microbiology Ecology and Disease (interim pres. 1982-83, pres. 1983-87), Va. Soc. Physician in Infectious Diseases (pres. 1986-88), Am. Fedn. Clin. Rsch., Sigma Xi, Alpha Omega Alpha. Democrat. Jewish. Office: Infectious Disease Sect VA Med Ctr Wilshire & Sawtelle Blvds Los Angeles CA 90073 Home: 13082 Mindanao Way #17 Marina Del Rey CA 90292 E-mail: sidfinegol@aol.com.

FINELSEN, LIBBI JUNE, lawyer; b. Encino, Calif., Apr. 14, 1968; BA in Polit. Sci. summa cum laude, U. Nev., 1990; JD magna cum laude, Lewis and Clark Coll., 1993. Bar: D.C. 1996, U.S. Ct. Appeals (9th, 11th and D.C. cirs.) 1996, U.S. Ct. Appeals (4th cir.) 1999, U.S. Ct. Appeals (fedl. cir.) 2001, Ct. Fed. Claims 2001. Jud. law clk. Gen. Svcs. Bd. Contract Appeals, Washington, 1993-94; assoc. McAleese & Assocs. P.C., McLean, Va., 1994-96; atty. USDA, Washington, 1996-99; trial atty. U.S. Dept. Air Force, Wright Patterson AFB, Ohio, 2000—01; atty./adv. U.S. Dept. Air Force, L.A. AFB, 2001—. V.p. edn. Hadassah Young Profls. Group, Washington, 1998-99; mem. hospitality com. Kesher Israel Synagogue, Washington, 1998-99. Mem. ABA, Phi Alpha Delta, Phi Kappa Phi. Avocations: cooking, handicrafts, travel, art exhibitions.

FINEMAN, GERALDINE GOTTESMAN, artist; b. Phila., Mar. 8, 1920; d. Harry and Bessie Gottesman; m. Al I. Fineman, Nov. 28, 1943 (dec. Nov. 2002); children: Samuel, Lawrence. BS in Edn., N.J. State Tchrs. Coll., 1941; MEd, Temple U., 1949. Tchr. elem., Blackwood, NJ, 1941—43, Phila., 1943—45; tchr. deaf, 1960—70; watercolorist, 1970—. Vol. tchr. sign lang., Boca Raton, Fla., 2000—. Represented in permanent collections Gallaudet U., Kellogg, Battle Creek, Mich., Nat. Deaf Inst., Fla. Mem. bd. assocs. Jewish Found. for Group Homes, Rockville, Md., 1992—; aux. mem. bd. assocs. Gallaudet U., Washington, 1985—2002; vol. sec. Rogers East Condominium Assn., 1989—; established program for developmentally disabled deaf adults Rockville. Fellow: Artist Guild Boca Mus. (numerous awards), Palm Beach Watercolor Soc. (numerous awards), Women in Visual Arts (numerous awards); mem.: Fla. Watercolor Soc. (signature). Avocations: swimming, sewing, travel, reading. Home: 900 NE Spanish River Blvd Boca Raton FL 33431 Personal E-mail: jerrigf@aol.com.

FINEMAN, HOWARD DAVID, news correspondent; b. Pitts., Nov. 17, 1948; s. Charles Morton and Jean (Lederman) F.; m. Amy Lee Nathan, Apr. 21, 1984; children: Meredith Claire, Nicholas Lowell. AB, Colgate U., 1971; MS, Columbia U., 1973; JD, U. Louisville, 1980. Reporter The Courier-Journal, Louisville, 1973-79; correspondent Newsweek, Washington, 1980-84, chief polit. corrs., 1984—, dep. bur. chief, 1994—, sr. editor, 1996—. Panelist "Washington Week in Review" PBS, Arlington, Va., 1982-95, "Capital Gang Sunday", CNN, Washington, 1995-98; contbr. MSNBC, CNBC, Fox News Network, 1996-98; news analyst NBC, 1998—. Recipient Front Page award N.Y. Newspaper Guild, 1983, Silver Gavel award ABA, 1990, Nat. mag. award 1983, 92, 98, 2001, 03, 04, award Deadline Club, 2003; Pulitzer Traveling fellow Columbia U., 1976, Watson fellow Thomas J. Watson Found., 1971. Mem.: Phi Beta Kappa. Office: Newsweek Ste 1220 1750 Pennsylvania Ave NW Washington DC 20006-4578

FINEMAN, S. DAVID, lawyer; b. Phila., Oct. 23, 1945; BA, Am. U., 1967; JD with honors, George Washington U., 1970. Bar: Pa. 1971, U.S. Dist. Ct. (ea. dist.) Pa., U.S. Ct. Appeals (3d cir.) Pa. 1980. Trial atty. Defender Assn., Phila., 1971-72; law clk. Superior Ct. Commonwealth, Pa., 1972-73; mng. ptnr. Fineman Krekstein & Harris, P.A., Phila., 1981—, 1987—. Instr. bus. law Temple U., 1974-83; mem. Phila. Planning Commn., 1989-91, Industry Policy Adv. Com. to Advise Sec. of Commerce on Internat. Trade Issues, 1994-98. Bd. govs. U.S. Postal Svc., 1995—2005, chmn. compensation com., 1997-2000, vice chmn., 2001-03, chmn., 2003-05, chmn. strategic planning com., 2001-03. Mem. ABA, Phila. Bar Assn., Pa. Bar Assn., Pa. State Trial Lawyers Assn., Def. Rsch. Inst. Home: 335 Woodley Rd Merion Station PA 19066-1430 Office: 30 S 17th St 18th Fl Philadelphia PA 19103-5443 Office Phone: 215-893-8701. Business E-Mail: sdfineman@finemanlawfirm.com.

FINEMAN, STEVEN E., lawyer; b. LA, Feb. 13, 1963; BA, U. of California, San Diego, 1985; JD, University of California, Hastings College of the Law, 1988. Bar: California 1989, D.C., New York, U.S. Dist. Ct. 1995, U.S. Ct. of Appeals, Ninth Circuit 1995, U.S. Ct. of Appeals, Fifth Circuit 1996, No., Ea., Ctrl. Districts of California. Managing ptnr. Lieff Cabraser Heimann & Bernstein, LLP. Mem.: Lawyers Comm. for Human Rights, Supreme Ct. Historical Soc., Assoc. of Trial Lawyers of Am., Assoc. of the Bar for the City of N.Y., Trial Lawyers for Public Justice, D.C. Bar Assoc., Calif. Bar Assoc., N.Y. Bar Assoc., Am. Bar Assoc. Office: Lieff Cabraser Heimann & Bernstein LLP 780 Third Avenue 48th Floor New York NY 10017

FINER, WILLIAM A., lawyer; b. Bklyn., Nov. 10, 1942; s. Samuel and Rachel Finer; 1 child, Jessica Rose. AB in Econs., Calif. State U., Long Beach, 1969; JD, Loyola U., L.A., 1972. Bar: Calif. 1972, U.S. Dist. Ct. (cen. dist.) Calif. 1972. Sole practitioner, Palos Verdes Estates, Calif., 1973-76, Torrance, Calif., 1977-85; mng. dir. Bell, Fainsbert & Finer, El Segundo, Calif., 1985-87, Finer, Kim & Stearns, Torrance, 1988—. Counsel Palos Verdes Art Ctr., Rolling Hills Estates, Calif., 1988-92, pres.-elect, 1992-94, pres. 1994-95; counsel, bd. dirs. Palos Verdes Beach and Athletic Club, Palos Verdes Estates, 1990-94, South Bay Svc. Ctr., Torrance, 1978-92. Mem. City Coun. of Palos Verdes Estates, 1994—, mayor pro tem, 1995-96, mayor, 1996-97. With USN, 1960-63. Mem. ABA, Los Angeles County Bar Assn., South Bay Bar Assn., Kiwanis (pres. 1988-90). Republican. Avocation: bicycling. Office: 3424 W Carson St Ste 500 Torrance CA 90503-5723 also: 78-845 via Ventana La Quinta CA 92253 Office Phone: 310-214-1477. E-mail: waf@finerkimstearnslaw.com.

FINERTY, MARTIN JOSEPH, JR., military officer, researcher, association executive; b. Wilmington, Del., July 22, 1936; s. Martin Joseph and Jane Morris (McClenaghan) F.; m. Joan Eddleman, Dec. 3, 1960; children: Nancy Jane, Laura Tourison. BSE, U.S. Naval Acad., 1959; MS in Phys. Oceanography, U. Miami, Coral Gables, Fla., 1966; MS in Indsl. Mgmt., Coll. of the Armed Forces, 1979. Commd. ensign USN, 1959, advanced though grades to capt., 1985; head, polar programs Office of Oceanographer of Navy, Alexandria, Va., 1975-76; spl. asst. submarines Office of Asst. Sec. of Navy, Washington, 1976-77; spl. asst. ocean environ. Office of Chief of Naval Ops., Washington, 1977-78; commdg. officer Naval Polar Oceanography Ctr., Washington, 1982-85; program officer NAS, Washington, 1985-87; asst. dir. rsch. ASME, Washington, 1987-88; exec. dir., COO Marine Tech. Soc., Washington, 1988-99; sr. cons. editor Compass Publs., Arlington, Va., 1999—. Expert in ocean and hydro survey ops., polar programs and assn. mgmt. Author/editor tech. publs. Fellow Marine Tech. Soc.; mem. AAAS, Assn. of U.S. Naval Acad. Class of 1959 (sec. 1971-74), The Army Navy Club. Lodges: Masons. Avocations: reading, gardening. Home: 1841 Northbridge Ln Annapolis MD 21401-6576 Personal E-mail: mjfjef@erols.com.

FINESTEIN, RUSSELL MARK, lawyer; b. Bklyn., Jan. 10, 1956; s. Norman and Claire M. (Bogitsh) F.; m. Eve F. Ozimek, Aug. 20, 1978; children: Sara, Daniel, Lauren. BS in Commerce with distinction, U. Va., 1978; JD cum laude, U. Mich., 1981. Bar: N.J. 1981, N.Y. 1988, U.S. Dist. Ct. N.J. 1981, Fla. 1984, Ct. Appeals (3d cir.). Assoc. McCarter & English, Newark, 1981-85; ptnr. Nochimson, Schablik, Kessler & Finestein, Livingston, N.J., 1985-87, Schablik, Kessler & Finestein, Livingston, N.J., 1987-90, Stern, Dubrow & Marcus, Maplewood, N.J., 1990-97, Edwards & Angell, Short Hills, N.J., 1997-2000, Finestein & Malloy L.L.C., Chatham, N.J., 2000—. Bd. dirs. Advantage Leasing Corp., Media, Pa.; lectr. N.J. Land Title Inst. Coach soccer Woodbridge (N.J.) Little League, 1982, Westfield (N.J.) Little League, 1988-96—; v.p., bd. dirs., Aspen Manor Condominium Assn., Woodridge, 1982-83; d. dirs. Builders Assn. No. N.J., 1990-92—, Housing and Redevel. Partnership J Inc., 1990-92 Habitat for Humanity Newark Inc., 1991-93, Edn. Fund of Westfield, 2000—; atty. Westfield Planny Bd., 2003—. Echols scholar U. Va., 1975. Mem. ABA, N.J. Bar Assn., Essex County Bar Assn., N.J. Builders Assn., Cmty. Assns. Inst., N.J. Land Title Assn., Optimist Club of Westfield (bd. dirs. 1995-05, pres. 1995-1996), Beta Gamma Sigma. Republican. Jewish. Avocations: tennis, skiing. Home: 751 Knollwood Ter Westfield NJ 07090-3418 Office: 26Main St Chatham NJ 07928 E-mail: rfinestein@fmnj.law.com.

FINESTONE, SHEILA, senator, retired legislator; b. Montreal, Que., Can., Jan. 28, 1927; d. Monroe and Minnie Abbey; m. Alan Finestone, June 9, 1947; children: David, Peter, Maxwell, Stephen. BS in Edn., McGill U. M.P. to Ho. of Commons for Mount Royal, 1984, 1988, 1993—99; critic for commn. and culture, 1985—93; Sec. of State Multiculturalism and the Status of Women, 1993—96; appt. Senate of Can., Ottawa, Canada, 1999—. Advisor to Parliament on eliminating anti-personal land mines; mem. transp. and comm., statutes and regulations; vice chair human rights; mem. spl. com. custody and access in divorce, constitution amendments edn.; past pres. La Fed. des Femmes du Quebec; mem. Quebec Referendum Organizer Les Yvettes, 1980; vice chair Amendment Equality Rights Can. Constn., 1985; min. of state Status of Women; leader Can. Delegation to Beijing World Conf. on Women's Rights, 1995; mem. exec. com. Can. Assn. Former Parliamentarians, Can. Land Mines Found., Adopt a Minefield Can. Pres. (hon.) Young Men and Young Women's Hebrew Assn.; ret. sec. Parliamentarian Assoc.; guide Canadian Mus. of Civilization; exec. World Exec. of Inter Parliamentary Union; mem. Nat. Coun. Jewish Women; hon. gov. Jewish Gen. Hosp.; mem. exec. com. Orgn. Jewish Parliament. Named Person of the Yr., McGill U., 2001; recipient Jackie Robinson Leadership award, 1996, Samuel Bronfinan Leadership award, 1995, O.R.T. Sophie Benett award, 1996. Mem. Orgn. Rehab. and Tng. Liberal.

FINGAR, THOMAS, federal agency administrator; AB, Cornell U., 1968; MA, Stanford U., 1969, PhD, 1977. Co-dir. U.S.-China Edn. Clearinghouse NAS; adv. Congl. Office Tech. Assessment; various positions including sr. rsch. assoc., dir. U.S.-China Rels. Program Stanford U., 1975—86; chief China divsn. U.S. Dept. State, 1986—89, dir. office of analysis E. Asia and Pacific, 1989—94, dep. asst. sec. analysis, 1994—2000, prin. dep. asst. sec., 2001—03, acting asst. sec. bur. intelligence and rsch., 2000—01, 2003—04, asst. sec. bur. intelligence and rsch., 2004—05; dep. dir. nat. intelligence for analysis Office Nat. Intelligence, 2005—; chmn. Nat. Intelligence Coun., 2005—. Editor: (book) Higher Education in the People's Republic of China: Report of the Stanford University Delegation, 1980, China's Quest for Independence: Policy Evolution in the Nineteen Seventies, 1980; author: Modernizing China's Electronics Industry: Prospects for U.S. Business, 1985; co-author: Education in the People's Republic of China and U.S.: China Educational Exchanges, 1989, American Studies of Contemporary China, 1993; contbr. articles to profl. jours. German linguist, intellegence analyst U.S. Army, 1969—72.*

FINGARETTE, HERBERT, philosopher, educator; b. Bklyn., Jan. 20, 1921; m. Leslie J. Swabacker, Jan. 23, 1945; 1 dau., Ann Hasse. BA, UCLA, 1947, PhD, 1949; LHD, St. Bonaventure U., 1993. Mem. faculty U. Calif.-Santa Barbara, 1948—, Phi Beta Kappa Romanell prof. philosophy, 1983—; William James lectr. religion Harvard U., 1971; W.T. Jones lectr. philosophy Pomona Coll., 1974; Evans-Wentz lectr. Oriental religions Stanford U., 1977; Gramlich lectr. human nature Dartmouth Coll., 1978; cons. NEH; Raphael Demos lectr. Vanderbilt U., 1985. Disting. tchr. U. Calif.-Santa Barbara, 1985, faculty rsch. lectr., 1977. Author: The Self in Transformation, 1963, On Responsibility, 1967, Self Deception, 1969, Confucius: The Secular as Sacred, 1972, The Meaning of Criminal Insanity, 1972, Mental Disabilities and Criminals Responsibility, 1979, Heavy Drinking: The Myth of Alcoholism as a Disease, 1988, Rules, Rituals, and Responsibility: Essays Dedicated to Herbert Fingarette, 1991, Death; Philosophical Soundings, 1996, Mapping Responsibility, 2004. Washington and Lee U. Lewis law scholar, 1980; fellow NEH, NIMH, Walter Meyer Law Rsch. Inst., Battelle Rsch. Ctr., Addiction Rsch. Ctr., Inst. Psychiatry, London; fellow Ctr. for Advanced Studies in Behavioral Sci., Stanford, 1985-86. Mem. Am. Philos. Assn. (pres. Pacific divsn. 1977-78). Home: 1507 APS Santa Barbara CA 93103 Office: U Calif Dept Philosophy Santa Barbara CA 93106

FINGER, HAROLD B., nuclear energy industry executive, consultant; b. N.Y., Feb. 18, 1924; s. Beny and Anna (Perlmutter) F.; m. Arlene Karsch, June 11, 1949; children: Barbara Lynn Korengold, Elyse Sue Camozzo, Sandra Ruth Ciccarelli. BME, CCNY, 1944; MS in Aero Engring., Case Inst. Tech., 1950. With NASA and predecessor NACA, 1944-69; mgr. AEC-NASA Space Nuc. Propulsion Office, 1960-67; dir. nuc. sys. NASA, 1958-64, dir. space power and nuclear sys., 1964-67; dir. space nuc. sys. divsn. AEC, 1965-67; assoc. adminstr. for orgn. and mgmt. NASA, 1967-69; asst. sec. for rsch. and tech. HUD, 1969-72; mgr. electric utility engring. oper. GE, Schenectedy, N.Y., 1972-74, gen. mgr. Ctr. for Energy Sys. Washington, 1972-80; staff exec. Power Sys. Strategic Planning and Devel., Fairfield, Conn., 1980-83; pres., CEO U.S. Com. for Energy Awareness, Washington, 1983-87, U.S. Coun. for Energy Awareness, Washington, 1987-91; energy, space, nuc. energy, housing, urban affairs, govt. mgmt. Recipient Manley Meml. award Soc. Automotive Engrs., 1958. Fellow: AIAA (James H. Wyld Propulsion award 1968), Nat. Acad. Pub. Adminstrn.; mem.: AAAS, AIA (hon.), Am. Astronautical Soc., NASA Alumni League (pres.), Nat. Housing Conf. (life trustee), Am. Nuc. Soc., Am. Soc. Pub. Adminstrn., Cosmos Club.

FINGER, STANLEY, psychology educator; b. Bronx, N.Y., May 11, 1943; s. Harry Finger and Beatrice Kaplowitz; m. Wendy Zien; children: Robert, Bradley. BA, Hunter Coll., 1964; MA, Ind. U., 1966, PhD, 1968. Prof., psychology dept. Washington U., St. Louis, 1968—; visiting prof. U. Gothenberg, Sweden, 1972, Clark U., Worcester, Mass., 1979, Cambridge U., Eng., 1987. Author: Brain Damage and Recovery, 1982, Origins of Neuroscience, 1993, Minds Behind the Brain, 2000; editor: Early Brain Damage, 1984, Brain Injury and Recovery, 1988. Recipient Prin. Investigator award NIH, 1966-82, Miles Labs., 1986-93. Mem. Soc. Neurosci., Internat. Soc. Hist. Neurosci. Avocations: antique clocks and barometers, art, fishing, travel. Office: Wash U Psychology Dept Saint Louis MO 63130 E-mail: sfinger@artsci.wustl.edu.

FINGERMAN, MILTON, biologist, educator; b. Boston, May 21, 1928; s. Irving and Rose Lillian (Goodman) F.; children: Stephen Whitsell, David Clay; m. Maria Esperanza Espinosa, Dec. 17, 1994. BS, Boston Coll., 1948; MS, Northwestern U., 1949, PhD, 1952. Instr. Tulane U., New Orleans, 1954-56, asst. prof., 1956-60, assoc. prof., 1960-63, prof. dept. ecology, evolution and organismal biology, 1963—, chmn. dept., 1990-99, chmn. dept. ecology, evolution and organismal biology, 1990-99, prof. emeritus, 2000—. Mem. univ. senate Tulane U., 1995-96, pres.'s faculty adv. com., 1995-96; instr. invertebrate zoology Marine Biol. Lab., Woods Hole, Mass., 1958-60; Petrie chair vis. prof. Technion, Haifa, Israel, 1986; mem. adv. panel for regulatory biology NSF, 1966-69; mem. com. on marine invertebrates Inst. Lab. Animal Resources of NRC, 1976-81; cons. Food and Agr. Orgn. of UN, Cochin, India, 1986, U.S. Office Naval Rsch. project on biofouling, Goa and Aurangabad, India, 1990-97, Inst. Wood Sci. & Tech., Bangalore, India, 1997—; Ming Yu vis. scholar Chinese U. Hong Kong, 1997. Author: The Control of Chromatophores, 1963, Animal Diversity, 1969; assoc. editor Jour. Crustacean Biology, 1980-85, Pigment Cell Rsch., 1986-91; mem. editorial bd. Physiol. Zoology, 1976-84, Trends in Life Scis., 1986—, Indian Jour. Invertebrate Zoology and Aquatic Biology, 1999, 1998—; co-editor Recent Advance in Marine Biotech., 1997-2004. Served with U.S. Army, 1952-54 Recipient Excellence in Rsch. award The Crustacean Soc., 2000; NSF grantee, 1956-85; named to Hon. Order Ky. Cols. Fellow AAAS; mem. Am. Inst. Biol. Scis., Am. Soc. Zoologists (exec. com. 1981-95, mng. editor Am. Zoologist 1981-95), Sigma Xi (pres. chpt. 1972-73), Delta DX Assoc. (pres. 1983-84, 96-97, sec. 2002-03). Democrat. Jewish. Avocation: amateur radio. Home: 1730 Broadway St New Orleans LA 70118-5304 E-mail: miltonf@tulane.edu.

FINGLETON, THOMAS D., retail executive; b. Kokomo, Ind. m. Kathleen L. Wentland; children: Rebecca, Elizabeth, Stephanie. Degree in bus., Ind. U. Acct. Arthur Andersen & Co., 1977; from dir. corp. acctg. to sr. v.p fin. May Dept. Stores Co., St. Louis, 1978—84, exec. v.p., CFO, 2000—; from sr. v.p. fin., CFO to chmn. Hecht's, Washington, 1985—2000. Office: May Dept Stores Co 611 Olive St Saint Louis MO 63101

FINIZIO-BASCOMBE, JAMIE JULIA, lawyer; b. Phila., Jan. 29; d. Rick Finizio; m. Timothy Paul Bascombe, Nov. 5, 1994. BSBA in Fin., U. Fla., 1989; JD, Nova Law Sch., 1993. Clk. English Solicitors, London, 1992; pvt. practice Ft. Lauderdale, Fla., 2000—. Bd. dirs. PACE Girls Ctr. Mem. Broward County Bar Assn. (bd. dirs. young lawyers divsn.), Women's Bar Assn. (past pres.) Republican. Roman Catholic. Avocations: water-skiing, travel, languages. Office Phone: 954-767-6000. Business E-Mail: jamie@Finiziolaw.com.

FINK, ALMA, retired elementary school educator; b. Missoula, Mont., Sept. 2, 1934; d. Frederick James and Annabelle (Pearson) Gariepy; m. Millard Allen Fink, June 18, 1955 (dec. Sept. 1980); children: Melanie Ann, Laurie Jean. Diploma, Western Mont. Coll., Dillon, 1954; BA, U. Mont., 1968, MA, 1992. Cert. elem. and reading tchr., Mont. Tchr. 1st grade Granite County Elem. Sch., Phillipsburg, Mont., 1954-55, Missoula County Pub. Schs., Missoula, 1955-56, 68-99; ret. Mem. Five Valleys Reading Coun., MIssoula. Editor state newsletter Chit Chat. Named Gold Star Tchr., KECI-TV, 1998. Mem. NEA (life), Missoula Elem. Edn. Assn. (polit. action com. for educators, mem. exec. bd.), Alpha Delta Kappa (Mont. state pres. 1988-90, pres. chpt., regional chmn., Violet award). Roman Catholic. Avocations: sewing, crafts, sports, reading, travel. E-mail: fink@rigsky.net.

FINK, CHARLES AUGUSTIN, behavioral systems scientist; b. McAllen, Tex., Jan. 1, 1929; s. Charles Adolph and Mary Nellie (Bonneau) F.; m. Ann Heslen, June 1, 1955 (dec. June 1981); children: Patricia A., Marianne E., Richard G., Gerard A. AA, Pan-Am. U., 1948; BS, Marquette U., 1950; postgrad., George Washington Med. Ctr., Walter Reed Army Med. Ctr., 1969-70, No. Va. C.C., 1973, George Mason U., 1974; MA, Cath. U. Am., 1979. Journalist UP and Ft. Worth Star-Telegram, 1950-52; commd. 2d lt. U.S. Army, 1952, advanced through grades to lt. col., 1966, various positions telecommunications, 1952-56, instr., 1956-58, exec. project mgmt., 1958-62, def. analysis and rsch., 1962-65, fgn. mil. rels., 1965-67, def. telecommunications exec., 1967-69, chief planning, budget and program control office Def. Satellite Communications Program, Def. Communications Agy., 1969-72, ret., 1972; pvt. practice cons. managerial behavior Falls Church, Va., 1972-77; pres. Behavioral Systems Sci. Orgn. (and predecessor firms), Falls Church, 1978—. Leader family group dynamics, 1958-67; home hemodialysis technician, 1969-81; pub (jour.) Circle, 1985—; computer program cons. Hubble Space Telescope Servicing Mission, NASA, 1993. Developer hierarchial theory of human behavior, 1967—, uses in behavioral, social and biol. sci. and their applications, 1972—, behavioral causal modeling research methodology, 1974—, computer-aided behavior systems coaching for persons and orgns., 1982—, telecoaching, 1989; microbiol. chromatographic profiling, 1989—; public domain Portable Personal Health Record, 1994; adv. for copyrighting computer graphics displays and multi-media communications in scis. Adv. bd. Holy Redeemer Roman Cath. Ch., Bangkok, Thailand, St. Philip's Ch., Falls Church, Va., 1971-73. Decorated Army Commendation medals, Joint Services Commendation medal; named to Fink Hall of Fame, 1982; recipient Behavior Modeling award Internat. Congress Applied Systems Rsch. and Cybernetics, 1980, Mission Pin award NASA, 1993. Mem. AAAS, SAR, Nat. Genealogical Soc., Internat. Soc. Systems Scis., Am. Soc. Cybernetics, Internat. Assn. Cybernetics, Internat. Network Social Network Analysis, Assn. U.S. Army, Ret. Officers Assn., Finks Internat. (v.p. 1981—), KC. Home: 3305 Brandy Ct Falls Church VA 22042-3705 Office: PO Box 2051 Falls Church VA 22042-0051

FINK, CONRAD CHARLES, journalist, educator, communications executive, consultant; b. Marquette, Mich., Sept. 16, 1932; s. Donald Ellsworth and Mary Ruth (Fox) F.; m. Sue Carol Henry, Sept. 4, 1954; children: Karen Sue, Conrad Stephan. BS, U. Wis., 1954. Reporter Bloomington (Ill.) Daily Pantagraph, 1956-57; various positions to night city editor AP, Chgo., 1957-60, writer fgn. desk N.Y.C., 1961, fgn. corr. Tokyo Bur., 1961-64, bur. chief South Asia New Delhi, 1964—67; dir. AP-Dow Jones Econ. Report, London, 1967-70; asst. to pres. AP, N.Y.C., 1970, v.p., 1971-77, sec., 1974-77; 1st v.p., dir. Wide World Photos, Inc.; v.p. Press Assn., Inc.; v.p., dir. AP (Can.), Ltd.; sec., dir. N.Y.C. News Assn., Inc., 1974-77; exec. v.p. adminstrn., dir. Park Broadcasting, Inc., Ithaca, N.Y., 1977-81, Park Newspapers, Inc., 1977-81; disting. lectr. U. Ga. Sch. Journalism, Athens, 1982, prof. newspaper mgmt., 1983—; dir. James M. Cox Jr. Inst. for Newspaper Mgmt. Studies, Athens, 1990—, William S. Morris prof. newspaper strategy and mgmt., 1995—, Josiah Meigs disting. tchg. prof., 2004—. Sr. fellow emeritus U. Ga., Univ. Tchr. Acad., 2000—. Author: Strategic Newspaper Management, 1988, Media Ethics, 1988, Inside the Media, 1990, Introduction to Professional Newswriting, 1992, Introduction to Magazine Writing, 1993, Writing Opinion for Impact, 1999, Bottom Line Writing, 2000, Sports Writing: The Lively Game, 2001, Writing to Inform and Engage, 2003. Served to 1st lt. USMCR, 1954-56. Named Nat. Journalism Tchr. of year, Freedom Forum, 2002; recipient Disting. Svc. award, U. Wis., 1969, Regents Tchg. Excellence award, 2004. Home: 116 S Stratford Dr Athens GA 30605-3024 Office: U Ga Sch Journalism Athens GA 30602 Office Phone: 706-542-5031. Business E-Mail: CFink@uga.edu.

FINK, DANIEL JULIEN, management consultant; b. Jersey City, Dec. 13, 1926; s. Joseph and Dorothy (Weisberger) F.; m. Tobie E. Weiss, June 24, 1951; children: Kenneth Wayne, Betsy Ilene, Karen Patrice. BS, MIT, 1948, MS, 1949. Registered profl. engr., Mass. Aeromechanics engr. Cornell Aero. Lab., 1948; chief aircraft dynamics Bell Aircraft Corp., Buffalo, 1949-52; v.p. Allied Rsch. Assocs., Inc., Concord, Mass., 1952-63; asst. dir. def. rsch. and engring. (def. systems) Dept. Def., 1963-65, dep. dir. def. rsch. and engring. (strategic and space sys.), 1965-67; with Gen. Electric Co., 1967-82, v.p., gen. mgr. space divsn., 1969-77, v.p., group exec. aerospace group Phila., 1977-79, sr. v.p. corp. planning and devel. Fairfield, Conn., 1979-82; pres. D.J. Fink Assocs., Inc., 1982—. Bd. dirs. Titan Corp., Orbital Scis. Corp.; def. sci. bd. Dept. Def., 1968—72, sr. cons., 1979—98; nat. indsl. adv. coun. Opportunities Industrialization Ctrs., 1977—79; sci. adv. panel Dept. Army, 1971—74; adv. coun. NASA, 1978—79, chmn. adv. coun., 1982—88; corp. vis. dept. aero. and astronautics MIT, 1972—82, Sloan Sch., 1982—85; chmn. dept. adv. bd. dept. mech. engring. Rensselaer Poly. Inst., 1981—84; mem. Vice Pres.'s Space Policy Adv. Bd., 1992. Patentee vibration isolation, weapon systems mgmt., aerospace mgmt. and corp. planning. Recipient Disting. Pub. Svc. award Dept. Def., 1967, NASA Disting. Svc. medal, 1986, NASA medal for Outstanding Leadership, 1988; Collier trophy, 1974 Hon. fellow AIAA (pres. 1974-75, von Karman lectr. 1980); fellow AAAS; mem. NAE (chmn. space applications bd. 1976-81, chmn. telecomms. and computer applications bd. 1984-87, chmn. com. on U.S.-Japan linkages in transport aircraft 1993, chmn. com. on space facilities 1994), Cosmos Club.

FINK, DAVID LEONARD, surgeon; b. St. Louis, June 6, 1936; s. Sidney Fink and Estelle Esses Goldstein; m. Frances Carole Bower, June 13, 1965; children: Dana Lynne, Denise Lysette. BA, Columbia Coll., 1957; MD, Cornell U., N.Y.C., 1961. Diplomate Am. Bd. Surgery. Resident in surgery St. Luke's Hosp. Med. Ctr., N.Y.C., 1961-64, U. Wis. Med. Ctr., Madison, 1964-66; pvt. practice, Paterson, N.J., 1970—; chief exec. officer Gen. Surgeons North Jersey, P.A., Paterson, 1970—. Chief surgery Barnert Meml. Hosp., Paterson, 1982-86, 2003—, pres. med. staff, 1988; assoc. clin. prof. surgery Seton Hall Postgrad. Sch. Medicine; asst. clin. prof. surgery U. Medicine and Dentistry of N.J. Maj. U.S. Army, 1966-70. Decorated Army Commendation medal. Fellow ACS, Soc. of Surgeons of N.J.; mem. Vascular Soc. N.J., Ea. Vascular Soc., Southeastern Surg. Soc., Cornell U. Med. Alumni Assn. (bd. dirs. 1986-89), Stuyvesant Yacht Club. Avocation: sailing. Office: Gen Surgeons North Jersey 707 Broadway Paterson NJ 07514-1425 Office Phone: 973-742-3371.

FINK, HOLLY BERMAN, elementary school educator; b. Louisville, Ky., June 24, 1952; d. Lee Harris and Joan Barbara Berman; m. Joel Aaron Fink, Aug. 19, 1973. BA in elem. edn., U. Louisville, 1978, MEd, 1983. Tchr. Spencer County Schs., Taylorsville, Ky., 1979, Oldham County Schs., Crestwood, Ky., 1979—. Inservice trainer Louisville Writing Project, Louisville, 1990—92; writing cons. State BOE, Frankfort, Ky., 1990—91. Editor: Wordswork, 1984—86. Tutor in writing Oldham County Schs., Crestwood, Ky., 1995—, drama workshops tutor, 1979—. Recipient Dean's Honor scholar, U. Louisville, 1978. Mem.: Nat. Coun. Tchrs. of English, Kappa Delta Pi, Phi Kappa Phi, Phi Delta Kappa. Achievements include design of Spanish buddy program at Crestwood Elem. Sch; elementary Shakespeare program, award-winning writing program. Avocations: writing, reading, art. Office Phone: 502-241-8401.

FINK, JEROLD ALBERT, lawyer; b. Dayton, Ohio, July 16, 1941; s. Albert Otto and Marjorie Carolyn (Scheidt) F.; m. Mary Jo McHone, Dec. 31, 1961 (div. July 1978); children: Marjorie, Kathryn, Erick; m. 2d, Deborah Lynn Bailey, Dec. 25, 1980 (div. Oct. 1986); 1 child, Justin. AB, Duke U., 1963, LLB, 1966. Bar: Ohio 1966. Assoc. Taft, Stettinius & Hollister, Cin., 1966-73, ptnr., 1973—. Bd. dirs. The Wm. Powell Co., Cin., 1974—, Great Trails Broadcasting Co., Cin., 1974-79. Co-author: (with Judy Cohn) Power Defensive Carding, 1988, (with Joe Lutz) The American Forcing Minor Bidding System, 1995, (with Joe Lutz) Defensive Carding in the 21st Century, 2001. Pres. Cin. Musical Festival Assn., 1978-79; trustee Cin. Playhouse, 1976-95, New Life Youth Svcs., Cin., 1971—. Republican. Presbyterian. Office: 1800 Firstar Tower 425 Walnut St Cincinnati OH 45202-3923 E-mail: fink@taftlaw.com.

FINK, JORDAN NORMAN, allergist, educator; b. Milw., Oct. 13, 1934; s. Jack and Ruth Fink; m. Phyllis Mechanic, Aug. 26, 1956; children: Leslie, Rosanne, Robert. BS, U. Wis.-Madison, 1956, MD, 1959. Diplomate Am. Bd. Internal Medicine, Am. Bd. Allergy and Immunology. Inst. Med. Coll. Wis., Milw., 1965-68, asst. prof. medicine, 1968-70, assoc. prof. medicine, 1970-73, prof., chief allergy and immunology, 1973—98, prof. medicine and pediats, 1994—. Chmn. adv. com. on pulmonary allergy FDA, Rockwell, Md., 1980-81, cons., 1983— Contbr. articles to profl. jours., chpt. to book Chmn. Camp Interlaken Com., Milw., 1978-81 bd. dirs. Jewish Community Ctr., Milw., 1977-81 Grantee NIH, 1982, VA, 1984 Fellow ACP, Am. Acad. Allergy (pres. 1984-85); mem. Assn. Am. Physicians, Am. Soc. Clin. Investigation, Am. Assn. Immunologists, Alpha Omega Alpha, Phi Delta Epsilon Avocations: swimming, travel. Home: 2829 W Golf Cir Mequon WI 53092-2446 Office: Med Coll Wis 9000 W Wisconsin Ave Milwaukee WI 53226-3518

FINK, JOSEPH ALLEN, lawyer; b. Lexington, Ky., Oct. 4, 1942; s. Allen Medford and Margaret Ruth (Draper) F.; m. Marcia L. Horton; children: Alexander Mentzer, Justin McGranahan. Student, Wayne State U., 1960-61; BA, Oberlin Coll., 1964; JD, Duke U., 1967. Bar: Mich. 1968, U.S. Dist Ct. (ea. dist.) Mich. 1968, U.S. Dist. Ct. (we. dist.) Mich. 1974, U.S. Ct. Appeals (6th cir.) 1987, U.S. Supreme Ct. 1998. Assoc. Dickinson, Wright, McKean & Cudlip, Detroit, 1967—72, Lansing, Mich., 1972—75; ptnr. Dickinson Wright PLLC, Lansing, 1976—. Instr. U.S. Internat. U. Grad. Sch. Bus., San Diego, 1971; adj. prof. trial advocacy Thomas M. Cooley Law Sch., Lansing, 1984-85; mem. com. on local rules U.S. Dist. Cts., 1985; chmn. trial experience subcom. U.S. Dist. Ct. (we. dist.) Mich., 1981. Contbg. author: Construction Litigation, 1979, Legal Considerations in Managing Problem Employees, 1988, Michigan Civil Procedure During Trial, 2d edit., 1989; contbr. articles to profl. jours. Bd. dirs. Lansing 2000 Inc., 1985-92, Professionals Direct, Inc., Universal Holding Co.; bd. trustees Olivet (Mich.) Coll., 1985-94; mem. bd. advisors Mich. State U. Press, 1993-96. Lt. JAGC, USNR, 1968-72. Fellow: Mich. State Bar Found.; mem.: State Bar of Mich. (chmn. local disciplinary com. 1983—, com. for US Cts. 1984), Assn. Life Ins. Counsel, Internat. Assn. Ins. Receivers. Episcopalian. Avocations: writing, reading, golf. Office: Dickinson Wright PLLC 215 S Washington Sq Ste 200 Lansing MI 48933-1816 Office Phone: 517-487-4711. Business E-Mail: jfink@dickinsonwright.com.

FINK, JOSEPH RICHARD, academic administrator; b. Newark, Mar. 20, 1943; s. Joseph Richard and Jean (Chorazy) F.; m. Donna Gibson, 1965 (div. 1986); children: Michael, Taryn; m. Christine Gaudenzi, oct. 4, 1992 (div. 2003); children: Madison, Joseph. AB, Rider U., 1963; PhD in Am. History, Rutgers U., 1971; DLitt (hon.), Rider U., 1982, Coll. of Misericordia, 1992, Golden Gate U., 1994. Asst. then assoc. prof history Immaculata (Pa.) Coll., 1964-72, adminstrv. asst. to pres., 1969-72; dean of Arts & Scis. City Colls. Chgo., 1972-74; pres. Raritan Valley Coll., Somerville, N.J., 1974-79, Coll. Misericordia, Dallas, 1979-88, Dominican U of Calif, San Rafael, 1988—. Pres. Regional Planning Coun. Higher Edn., Region 3/Northeastern Pa., 1986-88. Mem. exec. com. Philharm. Soc. Northeastern Pa., 1986-89; bd. dirs. Marin Symphony, 1989-2004, San Francisco Ballet, 1994-97, Ind. Coll. No. Calif., 1992—, Marin Forum, 1991—, Guide Dogs for the Blind, 1994-97; bd. dirs. Am. Land Conservancy, 1995—, exec. com.; mem. campaign cabinet United Way San Francisco, 1990; bd. dirs. North Bay Coun., 1993—, chmn., 1996, exec. com. Mem. Nat. Assn. Ind. Colls. and Univs. (secretariat 1986), Nat. Assn. Intercollegiate Athletics (pres.'s adv. coun. 1986), Am. Coun. on Higher Edn. (commn. leadership devel. higher edn. 1978-82, commn. on internat. edn. 1993-96, acad. adminstrn. fellow 1974-75), Assn. Mercy Colls. (pres. 1985-87, exec. com. 1981-87), Coun. for Ind. Colls. (bd. dirs. 1989-92), Am. Hist. Assn., World Affairs Coun. No. Calif. (bd. dirs. 1990-96), Commonwealth Club Calif. (quar. chmn. 1989, chmn. Marin County chpt. 1989—, bd. dirs. 1992—, exec. com. 1997—, pres., 2003). Office: Dominican U Calif 50 Acacia Ave San Rafael CA 94901-2230 Business E-Mail: jrf@dominican.edu.

FINK, LAURENCE D., diversified financial services company executive; BA in Polit. Sci., U. Calif., LA, Calif., 1974, MBA in Real Estate, 1976. Mng. dir., mem. mgmt. com., head mortgage & real estate products group, co-head taxable fixed income div. First Boston Corp., 1976—88; chmn. & CEO BlackRock Inc., 1988—; chmn. Nomura BlackRock Asset Mgmt. Mem. bd. executives NYSE, 2003—; bd. dirs. PNC Asset Mgmt. Group Inc. Trustee, mem. exec. com., chmn. fin. affairs com. NYU; co-chmn. bd. trustees, mem. exec. com. Mount Sinai NYU Health; co-chmn. bd. trustees NYU Hosp. Ctr. Office: BlackRock Inc 40 East 52nd St New York NY 10022

FINK, MARK J., chemistry educator; b. Athens, Ga., Feb. 26, 1957; s. Edward Jason and Barbara (Donehoo) F. ScB, Brown U., 1978; PhD, U. Wis., 1983. Asst. prof. chemistry Tulane U., New Orleans, 1983-89, assoc. prof. chemistry, 1989—2004, prof., 2004—. Contbr. articles to profl. jours. Mem. ACS, AAAS, Sigma Xi. Office: Dept Chemistry Tulane U New Orleans LA 70118 Office Phone: 504-862-3568. Business E-Mail: fink@tulane.edu.

FINK, MATTHEW POLLACK, retired trade association administrator, lawyer; b. N.Y.C., Jan. 8, 1941; s. Harry L. and Helen (Pollack) F.; m. Ellanor Thompson Stengel, June 22, 1945; children: Emily Pollack, Owen Thompson, Nina Pepper BA summa cum laude, Brown U., 1962; LLB cum laude, Harvard U., 1965. Asst. gen. counsel Investment Co. Inst., Washington, 1971-77, gen. coun., 1977-82, sr. v.p., 1982-91, pres., 1991—2004; ret. Mem. adv. coun. SEC Hist. Soc.; bd. dirs. Oppenheimer Mut. Funds; trustee Com. for Econ. Devel. Bd. dirs. ICI Edn. Found. With U.S. Army, 1967-68. Mem. Met. Club. E-mail: mainsail@earthlink.net.

FINK, RAYMOND, medical educator; b. N.Y.C., Apr. 21, 1927; s. William and Yetta (Rales) F.; m. Ruth Ursula Gebhard, May 28, 1961 (div. 1982); children: William D., David S.; m. Louise Berenson, Jan. 27, 1983. BBA, CCNY, 1947; MA, U. Denver, 1949; PhD, Cornell U., 1956. Statistician Opinion Rsch. Ctr. U. Denver, 1949; survey statistician U.S. Bur. Census, Suitland, Md., 1949-50, 56; rsch. assoc. human resources rsch. George Washington U., Washington, 1952-53; rsch. assoc. Bur. Social Sci. Rsch., Washington, 1957-60; assoc. dir. drinking practices study Calif. State Dept. Pub. Health, Berkeley, 1960-62; v.p. rsch. and stats. Health Ins. Plan Greater N.Y., N.Y.C., 1962-78; prof. community and preventive medicine N.Y. Med. Coll., Valhalla, 1978-2000, dir. health policy mgmt., 1982-90, dir. health svcs. rsch., 1990-2000; dir. rsch. Mid-Hudson Family Health Inst., New Paltz, N.Y., 1999—. Chmn. social sci. adv. com. Planned Parenthood Fedn. Am., N.Y.C., 1966-71; chair task force on HMOs Nat. Inst. Mental Health, Rockville, Md., 1971-72. Contbr. articles to profl. jours. Trustee Health Svcs. Improvement Fund, N.Y.C., 1986-2000. Sgt. U.S. Army, 1950-52. Grantee Nat. Inst. Mental Health, 1968-72, Nat. Cancer Inst., 1972-78, Social Sci. Rsch. Coun., 1982-83, Robert Wood Johnson Found., 1990-94. Mem. APHA, Am. Assn. Public Opinion Rsch. (co-editor 1968-69), Med. and Health Rsch. Assn. (chair 1975-2002), Assn. for Health Svcs. Rsch., Herman Biggs Soc. (pres. 1994-98). Jewish. Office: Med Health Rsch Assn NYC 40 Worth St Rm 720 New York NY 10013-2904 E-mail: raymond.fink@att.net.

FINK, RICHARD DAVID, chemist, educator; b. N.Y.C., July 14, 1936; s. Merwin Jesse and Claudia (Lowenthal) F.; m. Alice Christine Hovenden, Sept. 8, 1961; children: Rebecca Elisabeth, Johanna Hovenden. AB, Harvard U., 1958; PhD, MIT, 1962; MA (hon.), Amherst Coll., 1971; LHD (hon.), Doshisha U., Kyoto, 1988. NSF fellow in chemistry Yale U., 1962-63; NIH fellow, 1963-64; asst. prof. chemistry Amherst (Mass.) Coll., 1964-67, assoc. prof., 1967-71, prof., 1971—, Mellon prof., 1977-80, chmn. dept., 1970-73, 79-82, dean of faculty, 1983-88. Vis. prof. U. London, 1972-73, 76-77, 96-97, 99-2000; vis. scholar U.S. Army War Coll., 1992, MIT, 1988-90, 93-95; cons. Edn. Assocs., Inc. Contbr. articles to profl. jours. NSF fellow U. London, 1968-69, Sloan Found. fellow, 1970-74; Dreyfus Found. tchr.-scholar prize, 1971; NSF Profl. Devel. award, 1979 Mem. Am. Phys. Soc., Am. Chem. Soc., AAAS, Sigma Xi. Home: 30 Orchard St Amherst MA 01002-2516 Office: Amherst Coll Amherst MA 01002

FINK, ROBERT RUSSELL, music educator, retired dean, music theorist; b. Belding, Mich., Jan. 31, 1933; s. Russell Foster and Frances (Thornton) F.; m. Ruth Joan Bauerle, June 19, 1955; children: Denise Lyn, Daniel Robert. B.Mus., Mich. State U., 1955, M.Mus., 1956, PhD, 1965. Instr. music SUNY, Fredonia, 1956-57; instr. Western Mich. U., Kalamazoo, 1957-62, asst. prof., 1962-66, assoc. prof., 1966-71, prof., 1971-78, chmn. dept. music, 1972-78; dean Coll. Music U. Colo., Boulder, 1978-93; retired, 1994. Prin. horn Kalamazoo Symphony Orch., 1957-67; accreditation examiner Nat. Assn. Schs. Music, Reston, Va., 1973-92, grad. commr., 1981-89, chmn. grad. commn., 1987-89, assoc. chmn. accreditation commn., 1990-91, chmn., 1992. Author: Directory of Michigan Composers, 1972, The Language of 20th Century Music, 1975; composer: Modal Suite, 1959, Four Modes for Winds, 1967, Songs for High School Chorus, 1967; contbr. articles to profl. jours. Bd. dirs. Kalamazoo Symphony Orch., 1974-78, Boulder Bach Festival, 1983-90. Mem. Coll. Music Soc., Soc. Music Theory, Mich. Orch. Assn. (pres.), Phi Mu Alpha Sinfonia (province gov.), Pi Kappa Lambda. Home: 643 Furman Way Boulder CO 80305-5614 E-mail: Robert.Fink@colorado.edu.

FINK, ROBERT STEVEN, lawyer, writer, educator; b. Bklyn., Dec. 7, 1943; s. Samuel Miles and Helen Leah (Bogen) F.; m. Abby Deutsch, Mar. 20, 1980; children: Juliet Leah, Robin Rachel. *Father, Samuel Miles Fink, also an attorney, was founder and senior partner of the Fink & Pavia law firm, now known as Paria & Harcourt. He was counsel to the Italian embassy in Washington, DC and the Consul General in New York City. Samuel was decorated by the Italian government as Commander of the Order of the Italian Republic and was president of the Consular Law Society. Mother, Helen Leah Fink, taught English in the New York City school system. Wife, Abby Fink, is an internationally recognized jewelry designer, known under the trade name Abigail Sands.* Diploma, U. Vienna, 1962; BA, Bklyn. Coll., 1965; JD, NYU, 1968, LLM, 1973. Bar: N.Y. 1969, U.S. Dist. Ct. (so. and ea. dists.) N.Y. 1970, U.S. Tax Ct. 1970, U.S. Ct. Appeals (2d cir.) 1970, U.S. Supreme Ct. 1972, U.S. Dist. Ct. (we. dist.) N.Y. 1975, U.S. Ct. Claims 1984, U.S. Dist. Ct. (no. dist.) N.Y. 1985, U.S. Ct. Appeals (fed. cir.) 1990, U.S. Ct. Internat. Trade 1998. Assoc. Kostelanetz & Ritholz, N.Y.C., 1968-75, ptnr., 1975-87, Kostelanetz, Ritholz, Tigue and Fink, N.Y.C., 1987-94, Kostelanetz & Fink LLP, N.Y.C., 1994—. Lectr. in field; expert witness IRS; adv. com. tax divsn. Dept. Justice; chmn. IRS/Bar Liaison Com. N.E. Region, 1996-99; adj. prof. law NYU. Author: Tax Controversies: Audits, Investigations, Trials, 2 vols., 1980, 25th rev. edit., 2005; co-author: How to Defend Yourself Against the IRS, 1987, 2nd rev. edit., 1988; dept. editor Jour. Taxation, contbr. numerous articles to profl. jours. Fellow Am. Coll. Tax Counsel; mem. ABA (chmn. com. civil and criminal tax penalties 1983-85, chmn. task force for revision of tax penalties 1982, Jules Ritholz Meml. Merit Lifetime Achievement award 2003), N.Y. State Bar Assn. (chmn. com. criminal and civil tax penalties 1982-85, 88-90, chmn. compliance and unreported income 1985-87, chmn. commodities and fin. futures 1987-88, chmn. com. compliance and penalties 1991-93, chmn. com. compliance practice and procedure 1993-2003, mem. ho. of dels. 1995-97), Fed. Bar Assn., N.Y. County Lawyers Assn. (chmn. com. taxation 1988-92, 96-97, bd. dirs. 1989-95), Assn. of Bar of City of N.Y., Am. Arbitration Assn. (arbitrator). Office: Kostelanetz & Fink LLP 530 5th Ave New York NY 10036-5101 Office Phone: 212-808-8100. Business E-Mail: rfink@kflaw.com.

FINK, SCOTT ALAN, lawyer; b. Aurora, Ill., Sept. 18, 1953; s. Harold Lawrence and Lois (Franch) F.; m. Kathy Ellen Klein, May 14, 1978; children: Lindsay Klein, Anna Klein. AB, Stanford U., 1974; JD, U. Mich., 1978. Bar: Calif. 1978, U.S. Dist. Ct. (no. dist.) Calif. 1978, U.S. Ct. Appeals 9th cir.) 1981, U.S. Supreme Ct. 1985. Assoc. Heller, Ehrman, White & McAuliffe, San Francisco, 1978-84, ptnr., 1985-87, Gibson, Dunn & Crutcher, San Francisco, 1987—. Office: Gibson Dunn Crutcher 1 Montgomery St Fl 31 San Francisco CA 94104-4505 Office Phone: 415-393-8200. Business E-Mail: sfink@gibsondunn.com.

FINK, WILLIAM JAMES, retired surgeon; b. Washington, June 24, 1917; s. Gale J. and Elizabeth (Thomas) F.; m. Frances Kay Kerlin, Mar. 1945 (dec. Aug. 1985); children: Robert, Barbara, Barry; m. Arline Peeler, Jan. 1992. AB, DePauw U., 1939; MD, George Washington U., 1944. Diplomate Am. Bd. Surgery. Intern George Washington Hosp., Washington, 1944-45, resident in anesthesiology, 1948; resident in surgery Sibley Meml. Hosp., Washington, 1945-46, VA Hosp., Coral Gables, Fla., 1948-51, chief surg. svc. Fayetteville, Ark., 1951-79; advanced clin. assoc. prof. surgery to clin. prof. surgery U. Ark, 1967-80; ret., 1979. Pres. Universal Tongs, Inc., Fayetteville, 1979-90. Contbr. numerous articles to med. jours. Capt., M.C., AUS, 1946-48. Fellow ACS, S.W. Surg. Congress, Western Surg. Assn.; mem. Sigma Nu, Phi Chi. Republican. Methodist. Home: 1412 E Elmwood Dr Fayetteville AR 72703-3002

FINK, WILLIAM ORMAN, retired federal agency administrator, management consultant; b. Washington, Mar. 21, 1948; s. Orman S. and June B. Fink; m. Barry Elizabeth Brown, Aug. 7, 1970; children: Sara M., Jennifer L. BA in Polit. sci., U. Denver, 1970. Various nat. pk. ranger jobs Nat. Pk. Svc., 1971—80, site mgr. Friendship Hill Nat. Hist. Site Point Marion, Pa., 1980—85, supt., Ft. Necessity Nat. Battlefield and Friendship Hill Nat. Hist. Site Farmington, Pa., 1985—90, supt. Isle Royale Nat. Pk. Houghton, Mich., 1990—92, supt. Keweenaw Nat. Hist. Pk. Calumet, Mich., 1992—96, asst. regional dir. strategic planning and performance mgmt. Midwest region Houghton, Mich., 1996—2004. Mgmt. cons. Bill Fink Comm., Houghton, Mich., 2001—. Contbr. articles to profl. publs. Leadership vol. Am. Nat. Red Cross, Washington, 1994—2005. Recipient Disting. Grad. award, Fed. Law Enforcement Tng. Ctr., 1973, Gov.'s award for tourism, State of Mich., 1994, Gold award, Upper Peninsula Travel and Recreation Assn., 2001. Mem.: Keweenaw Indsl. Coun., George Wright Soc., Assn. Nat. Pk. Rangers, Inst. Mgmt. Cons., Keweenaw C. of C. (life). Unitarian Universalist. Avocations: skiing, photography, canoeing. Home: 22083 Royalewood Rd Houghton MI 49931 Office: Bill Fink Comm LLC 616 Shelden Ave Rm 201 Houghton MI 49931 Office Phone: 906-370-9597. Personal E-mail: billfink@chartermi.net.

FINK, YOEL, science educator, researcher; BSc in Chem. Engring., Israel Inst. Tech.(Technion), 1994, BA in Physics, 1995; PhD in Materials Science, Mass. Inst. Tech., 2000. Rsch. asst. Israel Inst. Tech. (Technion), 1991—95, part-time instr. physics advancement project, 1993—95, lab instr. chemistry and physics track project, 1993—95; postdoctoral assoc. dept. physics Mass. Inst. Tech., Cambridge, Thomas B. King assist. prof. materials sci., 2000—. Co-founder, pres. OmniGuide Comm., 2000—. Contbr. articles to profl. jours. Achievements include research in optical materials synthesis, optical characterization, simulation and theory; design of novel optical structures and devices; development of processing method for photonic band gap fibers. Office: Mass Inst Tech Rm 13-5013 77 Massachusetts Ave Cambridge MA 02139 Office Phone: 617-258-6113. Fax: 617-452-3432. Business E-Mail: yoel@mit.edu.

FINKBEINER, CARLTON S. (CARTY FINKBEINER), radio personality, former mayor; b. Toledo, 1939; BA, Dennison U. Tchr., football coach Maumee Valley Country Day Sch., St. Francis De Sales H.S., U. Toledo; city councilman City of Toledo, vice-mayor, mayor, 1994—2002; founder Toledo's Cmty.-Oriented Drug Enforcement program; co-sponsor City-wide Curfew; chair Coun.'s Housing, Neighborhood Revitalization and Natural Resources Com., Toledo; host Carty & Co., Toledo; weekly commentator WTVG-ABC, Toledo, 2002—. Mem. Econ. Opportunity Planning Assn. of Greater Toledo, Presidential Scholars Commn., U.S. Small Bus. Adminstrn. Adv. Commn. Northeastern and Northwestern Ohio, Internat. Gt. Lakes St. Lawrence Mayors Conf.; mem. Toledo-Lucas County Port Authority, 2003—. Achievements include being appointed to the Presidential Scholars Commission by President Gerald Ford, 1975. Office: WTVG 13 ABC 4247 Dorr St Toledo OH 43607

FINKE, LEONDA FROEHLICH, sculptor, educator; b. NYC; d. Herman and Evelyn (Praeger) Froehlich; m. Arnold I. Finke; children: David, Erica, Rachel. Student, Art Students League, N.Y.C., 1945. Instr. large bronze figure sculpture and samll art medals, Roslyn, N.Y., 1969-95; academician NAD, 1994—. One-woman shows include Oxford Gallery, Rochester, NY, Stonybrook U., 2005, others; exhibited in group shows at L.I. Mus., Stonybrook, NY, 2003, others; represented in permanent collections at Smithsonian Nat. Portrait Gallery (portrait of Georgia O'Keefe), Brit. Mus., Century Assn., Chrysler Mus., Butler Inst. Am. Art, CUNY, Bates Coll. Mus. Art, (outdoor sculpture) Brookgreens Gardens, S.C., Grounds for Sculpture, N.J., Stonybrook U., 2005; commd. works include 3 life-size bronzes for park in Altlanta, Max Som medal for Albert Einstein Med. Coll., 1991, Brit. Art Med. Soc. commn. of Virginia Woolf medal, 1989, Royal Philharm. Orch. commn. for medal, 1995, Aiken award poetry, Sewanee Rev., Tenn.; exhibited medals FIDEM, Helsinki, 1990, Brit. Mus., London, 1992; slide talk FIDEM, London, 1992, Germany, 2000; guest lectr., exhibitor Brit. Art Medal Soc., Loughborough U., Eng. Recipient medal of Honor Nat. Assn. Women Artists, 1972, Alex Ettl award NAD, 1990, J. Sanford Saltus award Am. Numismatic Soc., 1997. Fellow Nat. Sculpture Soc. (sec. 1987—, Gold medal 1989, Bas Relief award 1991, Maurice Hexter award 1992, Agop Agapoff award 1993, Silver medal and John Cavanaugh prize 1994, Sculpture House Annual award in recognition of a strong body of work throughout lifetime, 2005, Sculpture House Annual award, 2005, Kenan Master Sculptor in Residence, 2004), Sculptors Guild, (sculptors guild exhbn. in Kyoto, Japan 1993), Medallic Sculpture Assn., Audubon Artists (pres. 1984-85, medal of honor 1979), Kenan Master Scuptor in Residence Brookgreen Gardens, SC, 2004. Jewish. Home: 10 The Locusts Roslyn NY 11576-1724 Office Phone: 516-484-5415.

FINKE, ROBERT FORGE, lawyer; b. Chgo., Mar. 11, 1941; s. Robert Frank and Helen Theodora (Forge) Finke. AB, U. Mich., 1963; JD, Harvard U., 1966. Bar: Ill. 1966, U.S. Dist. Ct. (no. dist.) Ill. 1966, U.S. Ct. Appeals (7th cir.) 1966, U.S. Supreme Ct. 1970, U.S. Ct. Appeals (9th cir.) 1980, U.S. Ct. Appeals (4th and 6th cirs.) 1982, (8th cir.) 1998. Law clk., 1966—67; assoc. Mayer, Brown Rowe & Maw LLP, Chgo., 1967—71, ptnr., 1972—. Pres., bd. dirs. Lyric Opera Guild; trustee Rush U. Med. Ctr.; bd. dirs. Chgo. Bot. Garden. Mem. ABA (sects. litigation, bus., antitrust, legal edn. and admissions to the bar, vice chmn. 1974-75), Lawyers Club Chgo., Univ. Club, Econ. Club. Office: Mayer Brown Rowe & Maw 71 S Wacker Dr Chicago IL 60606-4637 Office Phone: 312-701-7110. Business E-Mail: rfinke@mayerbrownrowe.com.

FINKEL, DAVID, advertising executive; Grad., Wharton Sch.; MBA, NYU. With Am. Express; v.p. O&M Direct; gen. mgr. Brann Worldwide, Wilton, Conn., 1992—2001, sr. v.p., dir. client services, 1989—92, pres., eastern region of North America, 2000, pres., 2000—01, CEO Wilton, Conn., 2001—.

FINKEL, EUGENE JAY, lawyer; b. Phila., June 21, 1931; BA, Swarthmore (Pa.) Coll., 1952; MA, George Washington U., 1961, JD, 1965. Bar: U.S. Dist. Ct. D.C. 1966, U.S. Ct. Appeals (D.C. cir.) 1972, U.S. Supreme Ct. 1980. Various positions U.S. Dept. Treasury, Washington, 1952-74; dep. dir.

Office Internat. Fin. Policy Coordination and Ops., Washington, 1963-67; dir. Office Latin Am., Washington, 1967-70, Multilateral Instns. Program Office, 1970-74, Developing Nations Fin., 1974-75; asst. exec. sec. World Bank-IMF Devel. Com., 1975-77; alt. U.S. exec. dir. Inter-Am. Devel. Bank, Washington, 1977-81; ptnr. Porter Wright Morris & Arthur, Washington, 1981—. Lt. comdr. USNR ret. Office: Porter Wright et al 1919 Pennsylvania Ave NW Washington DC 20006-3434 Office Phone: 202-778-3033. Business E-Mail: jfinkel@porterwright.com.

FINKEL, EVAN, lawyer; b. Bklyn., Oct. 7, 1956; BS, Harpur Coll., SUNY, Binghampton, 1978; JD, Univ. Calif., Hastings, 1981. Bar: Calif. 1981, US Patent & Trademark Office, US Dist. Ct., (Calif. & Mich. dists.), US Ct. Appeals (9th, Fed. cir.), US Supreme Ct. 1988. Ptnr., chmn. LA Intellectual Property group Pillsbury Winthrop Shaw Pittman, LA. Named a So. Calif. Super Lawyer, LA Mag., 2004. Mem.: Intellectual Property Assn., Phi Beta Kappa, Order of the Coif, Thurston Soc. Office: Pillsbury Winthrop Shaw Pittman Suite 2800 725 S Figueroa St Los Angeles CA 90017 Office Phone: 213-488-7307. Office Fax: 213-629-1033. Business E-Mail: evan.finkel@pillsburylaw.com.

FINKEL, GARY SAMUEL, elementary school educator; b. L.A., Oct. 10, 1957; s. Harold Weiner and Shari Ann Finkel; m. Karen Jane McKay, Apr. 11, 1987; children: Sean, Kelli. BS, San Diego State U., 1979; MA, Calif. State U., Dominguez Hills, 1990. Cert. tchr., Calif. Tchr. 99th St. Sch., L.A. Unified Sch. Dist., 1985-89, sci. resource tchr., 1989-91; tchr. Ambler Gifted Magnet Sch., L.A. Unified Sch. Dist., 1991—. Staff developer Calif. Sci. Implementation Network. Mem. Calif. Sci. Tchrs. Assn., Nat. Sci. Tchrs. Assn., Sigma Chi. Avocations: skiing, hiking, bicycling. Office: LA Unified Sch Dist Ambler Gifted Magnet Sch 319 E Sherman Dr Carson CA 90746-1158

FINKEL, GERALD MICHAEL, lawyer; b. N.Y.C., July 29, 1941; s. Abraham B. and Elizabeth B. (Michaels) F.; m. Beverly Lynne Jaffee, Aug. 26, 1962; children: Bruce Daniel, Judith Michelle. BA, NYU, 1962; JD, U. S.C., 1970. Bar: S.C. 1970, U.S. Dist. Ct. S.C. 1970, U.S. Ct. Appeals (4th cir.) 1973, U.S. Supreme Ct. 1973, D.C. 1973. Prin. Finkel & Altman, L.L.C. and predecessor firm, Columbia, S.C., 1970—. Adj. prof. trial advocacy and ins. law U. S.C.; mem. faculty fed. trial practice AM. Law Inst., ABA; lectr. S.C. Bar, S.C. Trial Lawyers Assn., Richland County Bar and Profl. Insts.; instr. S.C. Dept. Pub. Safety/Criminal Justice Acad.; spl. judge Richland County Family Ct., 1974-78, Ct. Gen. Sessions 5th Jud. Cir., 1976 Author: (with Ralph C. McCullough II) A Guide to South Carolina Torts, 1st edit., 1981, 2d edit., 1986, 3d edit., 1990, 4th edit., 1995, (with Elizabeth Rhodes) South Carolina Legal and Business Forms, Vols. 1 and 3, 1997. Hearing officer S.C. Dept. Health and Environ. Control, 1979-82; mem. S.C. Appellate Def. Commn., 1982-83, Gov.'s Sentencing Guidelines Commn., 1982-83. Served to capt. U.S. Army, 1962-67. Recipient Outstanding Alumni cert. Phi Alpha Delta, 1972 Mem. ABA, S.C. Bar Assn. (bd. govs. 1985-88, profl. responsibility com. and ethics adv. com.), Richland County Bar Assn., Assn. Trial Lawyers Am., Am. Law Inst. (consultative group for restatement of the law 3d unfair competition, consultative group restatement law 3d torts), S.C. Trial Lawyers Assn. (exec. bd. 1978-81, pres. 1982-83), Phi Alpha Delta (dist. justice 1976-78). Democrat. Jewish. Home: 156 Pelzer Dr Summerville SC 29485-9703 Office: Finkel & Altman 1201 Main St Ste 1800 Columbia SC 29201-3294 E-mail: jfinkel@finkellaw.com.

FINKEL, MARION JUDITH, internist, pharmaceutical administrator; b. N.Y.C., Nov. 2, 1929; d. Israel and Bella (Stillman) Finkel; m. Simon V. Manson, Sept. 12, 1954. Student, L.I. U., 1945-48; MD (Howard Sloan Meml. scholar), Chgo. Med. Sch., 1952. Intern Jersey City Med. Ctr., 1952-53; resident in internal medicine Bellevue Hosp., N.Y.C., 1954-56; med. editor Merck and Co., 1957-61; pvt. practice specializing in internal medicine, N.Y.C., 1956-57, N.J., 1961-63; with FDA, 1963-85, dir. divsn. metabolic and endocrine drugs, 1966-70, dep. dir. bur. drugs, 1970-71, 72-74, dir. office new drug evaluation, 1971-72, 74-82, dir. office orphan products devel., 1982-85; exec. dir. R&D Berlex Labs., Inc., 1985-88; v.p. drug registration and regulatory affairs Sandoz Pharms., Inc., 1988-94, v.p. corp. regulatory compliance, 1994-95, cons. regulatory affairs, clin. R&D, 1995—. Contbr. chpts. to books, numerous articles to profl. jours. Recipient award of merit FDA, 1972, Superior Svc. award USPHS, 1976, 84, Fed. Woman's award Fed. Govt., 1976, Meritorious Exec. award, 1980; named Disting. Alumnus, Chgo. Med. Sch., 1977, L.I. U., 1980. Office: 21 Squirrel Run Morristown NJ 07960-6411

FINKEL, SANFORD NORMAN, lawyer; b. Troy, N.Y., Oct. 19, 1946; s. Max and Mildred (Fares) F.; m. Amy Lynn Gordon, Oct. 13, 1974 (div. July 1984); children: Marcy Jennifer, Melanie Gordon. BA, SUNY, Buffalo, 1968; JD, Union U., 1974. Bar: N.Y 1975, U.S. Dist. Ct. (no. dist.) N.Y. 1975. Tchr. sci. Enlarged City Sch. Dist. of Troy, N.Y., 1968-71; pvt. practice Troy, 1975—; counsel to dem. study group N.Y. State Assembly, Albany, 1977-78; instr. paralegal studies Jr. Coll. Albany divsn. Russell Sage Coll., 1977-81; dep. corp. counsel City of Troy, 1990-94. Mem. Rensselaer County Bar Assn. Avocations: reading, coin collecting/numismatics, stamp collecting/philately, travel. Home: 19 Capitol Pl Rensselaer NY 12144-9658 Office: 68 2nd St Troy NY 12180-3932 Office Phone: 518-272-2300. E-mail: sanfordonfinkel@aol.com.

FINKELPEARL, TOM, museum director; m. Eugenie Tsai; 1 child. BA, Princeton U.; MFA, Hunter Coll. Curator, dir. P.S. 1's Clocktower Gallery, 1982—90; exec. dir. Percent for Art Prog., Dept. Cultural Affairs, NYC, 1990—96; dir. artist colony Maine, 1996—99; dep. dir. P.S. 1 Contemporary Art Ctr., Long Island City, 1999—2002; exec. dir. Queens Mus. Art, 2002—. Office: Queens Mus Art New York City Bldg Flushing Meadows Corona Park Corona NY 11368*

FINKELSON, ALLEN, lawyer; b. NYC, June 23, 1946; BA magna cum laude, St. Lawrence Univ., 1968; JD, Columbia Univ., 1971. Bar: NY 1972. Assoc. Cravath Swaine & Moore LLP, NYC, 1971—77, ptnr., 1977—83, ptnr., trusts, estates, 1985—; mng. dir., mergers, acquisitions Lehman Brothers, NYC, 1983—85. Editor: Columbia Law Rev. Mem.: Assn. of Bar of City of NY, Phi Beta Kappa. Office: Cravath Swaine & Moore LLP Worldwide Plz 825 Eighth Ave New York NY 10019-7475 Office Phone: 212-474-1262. Office Fax: 121-474-3700. Business E-Mail: afinkelson@cravath.com.

FINKELSTEIN, ALLEN LEWIS, lawyer; b. N.Y.C., Mar. 19, 1943; s. David and Ella (Miller) F.; m. Judith Elaine Stutman, June 20, 1964 (div. Mar. 1980); children: Jill, Jennifer; m. Shelley Gail Barone, June 15, 1980; 1 child, Amanda. BS, NYU, 1964; JD, Bklyn. Law Sch., 1967; MBA, L.I. U., 1969. Bar: N.Y. 1968, U.S. Dist. Ct. (ea. and so. dists.) N.Y. 1973, U.S. Ct. Appeals (2d cir.) 1973, U.S. Supreme Ct. 1976, U.S. Tax Ct. 1979. Ptnr. Finkelstein, Bruckman, Wohl, Most & Rothman, N.Y.C., 1974-97; sr. ptnr. Pressman Finkelstein, N.Y.C., 1997-99; ptnr. Ganfer & Shore LLP, N.Y.C., 1999—. Asst. prof. L.I. U., N.Y.C., 1969-73, adj. assoc. prof., 1973-74; chmn. bd. dirs. Amyotrophic Lateral Sclerosis Assn., 2004-05. Mem. ABA (bus. law and family law sect.), N.Y. State Bar Assn., Assn. of Bar of City of N.Y., Queens County Bar Assn., Masons. Jewish. Home: 425 E 63rd St New York NY 10021-7804 Office: Ganfer & Shore LLP 360 Lexington Ave New York NY 10017-6502 Office Phone: 212-922-9250. Business E-Mail: afinkelstein@ganshore.com.

FINKELSTEIN, BERNARD, lawyer; b. N.Y.C., Jan. 21, 1930; s. Irving and Sadie (Katz) F.; m. Adele S. (Levine), June 29, 1952; children: Sharon Ann, Marcia Lyn. BA, NYU, 1951; LLB, Yale U., 1954. Bar: N.Y. 1954, D.C. 1970. Assoc. Paul, Weiss, Rifkind, Wharton, and Garrison, LLP, N.Y.C., 1956—64, ptnr., 1965—95, of counsel, 1966—. Trustee, mem. Altman Found., N.Y.C., 1985—. Named one of Best Lawyers in N.Y. Mag., 1995. Fellow Am. Coll. of Trust and Estate Counsel (estate and gift tax com. 1987-93); mem. ABA (com. on pre-death planning, probate and trust div. of sect. on real property, probate and trust law 1985-88), N.Y. State Bar Assn. (chmn. gift and tax com. of tax sect. 1978-80), Assn. of Bar of City of N.Y. (trusts, estate and surrogate's ct. com. 1986-89), N.Y. Bar Found., Yale Law Sch. Assn. (exec. com. 1983-86), Phi Beta Kappa, Phi Alpha Delta, Order of Coif. Home: 1 Tory Ln Scarsdale NY 10583-2314 Office: Paul Weiss Rifkind Wharton and Garrison LLP 1285 Ave of the Americas New York NY 10019-6064 Office Phone: 212-373-3380.

FINKELSTEIN, CLAIRE, law educator; BA magna cum laude, Harvard U., 1986; MA in Philosophy, U. Paris, Sorbonne, 1987; JD, Yale U., 1993; PhD in Philosophy, U. Pitts., 1996. Acting prof. law U. Calif., Berkeley, 1995—2000, prof., 2000—01; vis. faculty U. Pa. Law Sch., Phila., 2000—01, prof. law and philosophy, 2001—, dir. Inst. for Law and Philosophy, 2003—04. Contbr. articles to law jours. Office: U Pa Law Sch 3400 Chestnut St Philadelphia PA 19104 Office Phone: 215-898-5798. Office Fax: 215-573-2025. E-mail: cfinkels@law.upenn.edu.*

FINKELSTEIN, DAVID RITZ, physicist, educator, consultant; b. NYC, July 19, 1929; s. Isidore and Esther (Rubinstein) F.; m. Helene Cooper, 1948 (div.); children: Daniel, Beth, Eve; m. Shlomit Ritz, 1981; 1 child, Aria. BS, CCNY, 1949; PhD, MIT, 1953. Asst., then assoc. prof. physics Stevens Inst. Tech., 1954-60; assoc. prof. Yeshiva U., then prof., chmn., dean, 1960-79; prof. physics Ga. Inst. Tech., 1979—2003, prof. emeritus, 2004—. Vis. prof. Tougaloo Coll., 1965, Hebrew U. Jerusalem, 1974 Author: Quantum Relativity, 1996; editor Internat. Jour. Theoretical Physics; mem. editl. bd. Jour. Math. Physics, 1991-93. Co-chmn. Miss. Project Parents Com., 1965. Ford Found. fellow, 1958; NSF grantee, 1954-96. Fellow Lindisfarne Assn.; mem. AAAS, Am. Phys. Soc., Internat. Quantum Structures Assn. (sec. 1990-93). Jewish. Achievements include research in black holes, high energy physics, space-time quanta, topological physics, gravity, quantum logic and set theory, Clifford algebra. Office: Ga Inst Tech Physics Dept Atlanta GA 30332-0430 E-mail: david.finkelstein@physics.gatech.edu.

FINKELSTEIN, DAVID S., lawyer; b. NYC, July 14, 1972; BA cum laude, Harvard Univ., 1994; JD magna cum laude, Fordham Univ., 1998; LLM, NYU, 2000. Bar: NY 1999. Assoc. Cravath Swaine & Moore LLP, NYC, 1998—2005, ptnr., trusts, estates, 2005—. Mem.: ABA. Office: Cravath Swaine & Moore LLP Worldwide Plz 825 Eighth Ave New York NY 10019-7475 Office Phone: 212-474-1304. Office Fax: 212-474-3700. Business E-Mail: dfinkelstein@cravath.com.

FINKELSTEIN, HENRY, artist; BFA, Cooper Union, 1980; MFA, Yale School of Art, 1983. Painting instructor Cooper Union, NYC, 1979—80; teaching asst. Yale School of Art, 1982; vis. asst. prof. Pratt Institute, Brooklyn, NY, 1986—87; vis. artist The College of William and Mary, 1989; asst. prof. U. of Hartford, 1984—92, Chmn., Painting dept., 1988—90; drawing instructor NY Studio School, 1999; vis. artist Washington Studio School, 1998—99; drawing, painting instructor Nat. Acad. of Design, 1996—; vis. artist Lyme Acad. College of Fine Arts, Old Lyme, Conn., 2003. Exhibitions include Prince St. Gallery, New York, 1986, 1988, 1991, Andrews Gallery, Williamsburg, VA, 1989, Parkerson Gallery, Houston, TX, 1989, Wash. Art Assoc., Washington Depot, CT, 1991, Musee du Chateau de Rochefort En Terre, France, 1992, Bengert MacRae Gallery, Wycoff, NJ, 1993, Gleason Fine Art Gallery, Portland, ME, 1993, Between the Muse Gallery, Rockland, ME, 1999, Simon Gallery, Morristown, NJ, 1999, Kraushaar Galleries, New York, 2001, 2003, 2005, Valley House Gallery, Dallas, TX, 2002, 2004, exhibited in group shows at Nat. Arts Club Annual Exhibitions, New York, 1979, Houghton Gallery, Cooper Union, 1982, MFA Thesis Show, Yale School of Art, New Haven, CT, 1983, Faculty Exhibitions, Joseloff Galler, West Hartford, CT, 1984—91, Young Masters I, Ingber Gallery, New York, 1988, Cranberry Island Artists, Maine Coast Artists, Rockport, ME, 1988, Young Masters II, Ingber Gallery, New York, 1989, The Winter Landscape, Wyckoff Gallery, Wyckoff, NJ, 1989, On the Edge: 40 Years of Maine Painting, Maine Coast Artists, Rockport, ME, 1992—93, Mostly Maine, Tibor de Nagy Gallery, New York, 1993, Ice Gallery, 1997, Nat. Acad. of Design, 1988—2003, 2003, NJ Landscapes, Rider U. Art Gallery, Lawrenceville, NJ, 1999, The Art of the Garden, College of the Atlantic, Bar Harbor, ME, 2000, Still Life, Kraushaar Galleries, New York, 2001, Beyond the Apple and Bottle: Still Life Invitational, Valley House Gallery, Dallas, TX, 2002, Musee du Chateau de Rochefort en Terre, France, 2003, Foliage, Kraushaar Galleries, New York, 2004. Named National Academician, Nat. Acad. of Design, 1994; recipient Ethel Cram Mem. Prize, Cooper Union, 1980, Julius Hallgarten Prize, Nat. Acad. of Design, 1988, Carnegie Prize, 2003; fellow Fulbright Fellowship, Painting, Italy, 1983—84, Alfred and Trafford Klots Residency Fellowship, Chateau du Rochefort en Terre, France, 1992, Chateau de Rocefort en Terre, France, 2000, Residency Fellowship, Dorland Mountain Arts Colony, 1994; grantee Ford Found. Materials Grant, 1980. Office: 46 W 22nd St New York NY 10010*

FINKELSTEIN, JAMES A., media executive; b. NYC; s. Jerry and Shirley Finkelstein; m. Pamela Gross, Feb. 1, 1998; children: Alexander, Gregory, Zachary, Jennifer, Eliza. BA, NYU, NYC, 1970; LLD honoris causa (hon.), Hofstra U., 1984. Pres. and CEO Nat. Law Pub. Co, NYC, 1971—98; pres. JAF Comm. Inc., NYC, 1998—2001, News Comm., Inc., NYC, 2001—, Marquis Who's Who, New Providence, NJ, 2003—; exec. chmn. Thompson Pub. Group, Washington, 2004—; Chmn. Global Media Ptnrs. Credit Suisse First Boston, NYC, 2004—05; Partner, Avista Capital Holdings, LP, 2005—. Media consultant DB Capital Ptnrs., NYC, 2001—03, Veronis Suhler Stevenson, NYC, 2002; bd. dirs. Advanstar Comm. Past bd. mem. Faculty Arts and Sci.- bd. overseers NYU; past bd. mem. Legal Aid Soc., NYC. Mem.: Yale Club, Harvard Club (assoc.). Avocations: tennis, chess. Office: 2 Park Ave Suite 1405 New York NY 10016 Office Phone: 212-689-1470.

FINKELSTEIN, JAMES ARTHUR, management consultant; b. NYC, Dec. 6, 1952; s. Harold Nathan and Lilyan (Crystal) F.; m. Lynn Marie Gould, Mar. 24, 1984; children: Matthew, Brett. BA, Trinity Coll., Hartford, Conn., 1974; MBA, U. Pa., 1976. Cons. Towers, Perrin, Forster & Crosby, Boston, 1976-78; mgr. compensation Pepsi-Cola Co., Purchase, N.Y., 1978-80; mgr. employee info. systems Am. Can. Co., Greenwich, Conn., 1980; mgr. bus. analysis Emery Airfreight, Wilton, Conn., 1980-81; v.p. Meidinger, Inc., Balt., 1981-83; prin. The Wyatt Co., San Diego, 1983-88; pres., chief exec. officer W. F. Corroon, San Francisco, 1988-95; founder, CEO FutureSense, Inc., 1995—97, chmn., CEO, 2001—; founder TallyUp Software, 1996—98; dir. En Wisen, Inc., 1996-98; ptnr. Andersen LLP, San Francisco, 1997-2001. Mem. regional adv. bd. Mchts. and Mfrs. Assn., San Diego, 1986-88; instr. U. Calif., San Diego, 1984-88. Mem. camp com. State YMCA of Mass. and R.I., Framingham, 1982-86; pres. Torrey Pines Child Care Consortium, La Jolla, Calif., 1987-88, Marin Football Club, Inc., 2003—; vice chmn. La Jolla YMCA, 1986-88; chmn. fin. com. YMCA, San Francisco, 1992-95, vice chmn., 1993-95, chmn., 1995-97, bd. dirs., 1988-2004; bd. dirs. San Domenico Sch., 1994-2000; trustee World Affairs Coun., 1998-2004; bd. dirs. Becket Chimney Corners YMCA, 1999—2003; treas. Ctrl. Marin Competitive Soccer Club, 2000-05. Avocations: soccer coaching and refereeing, music, theater, sports, camping. Home: 17 Bracken Ct San Rafael CA 94901-1587 Office: FutureSense Inc 369 B 3d St # 181 San Rafael CA 94901-3581 Personal E-mail: futuresense@yahoo.com.

FINKELSTEIN, JAMES DAVID, physician, educator; b. N.Y.C., Oct. 16, 1933; s. Harry and Sylvia Z. (Bernstein) F.; m. Barbara Joan Eisenberg, Dec. 12, 1959; children: Donna Ilene, Laura Helene. AB, Harvard U., 1954; MD, Columbia U., 1958. Diplomate Am. Bd. Internal Medicine. Intern, resident in medicine Presbyn. Hosp., N.Y.C., 1971-73; chief med. svc. VA Med. Ctr., Washington, 1979-99, chief gastroenterology, 1970-79, assoc. chief staff for rsch., 1975-79, med. investigator, 1970-75, clin. investigator, 1965-68, chief biochemistry rsch. lab., 1965—, sr. clinician, 1999—. Cons. Children's Hosp., Washington, 1968-85; prof. medicine George Washington U., 1969—; clin. prof. medicine Georgetown U., 1981—; prof. medicine Howard U., Washington, 1983—; mem. Nutrition Study sect. NIH, 1972-78; hon. pres. 2d Internat. Conf. on Homocysteine Metabolism, Nijmegen, Netherlands, 1998. Contbr. articles on biochemistry and nutrition of methionine to profl. jours. Served as surgeon USPHS, 1963-65. Recipient F.P. Gay Rsch. award Columbia U., N.Y.C., 1956, Arthur S. Fleming award Jr. C. of C., Washington, 1971, Disting. Rschr. medal George Washington U., 1999; NIH grantee, 1966-95. Mem. Am. Soc. for Clin. Investigation, Am. Gastroent. Assn., Assn. of Am. Physicians, Am. Inst. Nutrition, Am. Soc. Clin. Nutrition (Robert H. Herman award 2001), Am. Fedn. Clin. Rsch., Harvard Club. Office: VA Med Ctr 50 Irving St NW Washington DC 20422-0001 Office Phone: 202-745-8373. E-mail: james.finkelstein@med.va.gov.

FINKELSTEIN, JOEL S., physician; b. Columbus, Ohio, Sept. 10, 1954; BA, MS in Biol. Scis., Northwestern U., 1976; MD, Washington U., St. Louis, 1980. Internal medicine intern Northwestern U. Hosp., Chgo., 1980-81, resident in internal medicine, 1981-83; clin. fellow in endocrinology Mass. Gen. Hosp., Boston, 1983-84, rsch. fellow in endocrinology, 1984-88; instr. medicine Harvard Med. Sch., Boston, 1986-89, asst. prof. medicine, 1989-99, assoc. prof. medicine, 1999—; clin. asst. in medicine Mass. Gen. Hosp., 1989-90, asst. in medicine, 1990-95, asst. physian, 1995-99, assoc. physician, 1999—; cons. in medicine Mass. Eye and Ear Inst., 1985—. Contbr. chpts. to textbooks, numerous articles to profl. jours. Recipient Govs. award ACP, 1987. Mem. Endocrine Soc., Am. Soc. for Bone and Mineral Rsch., Internat. Soc. for Clin. Densitometry, Am. Soc. for Clin. Investigation, Phi Beta Kappa. Office: Mass Gen Hosp Endocrine Unit Bulfinch 327 55 Fruit St Boston MA 02114

FINKELSTEIN, JOSEPH SIMON, lawyer; b. Vineland, N.J., Feb. 28, 1952; s. Absalom and Goldie (Cukier) Finkelstein; m. Sara M. Green, May 30, 1976; children: Adam, Julia, Seth. BA, Rutgers U., 1973; JD, U. Pa., 1976. Bar: Pa. 1976, N.J. 1976, U.S. Supreme Ct. 1982. Assoc. Wolf, Block, Schorr and Solis-Cohen, Phila., 1976-85, ptnr., 1985—. Pres. Perelman Jewish Day Sch., 1996—99, chmn. bd. trustees, 2005—; mem. Wexner Heritage Found., 1991—95; mem. exec. com., bd. dirs., chair funds distbn. United Way Southeastern Pa., 1997—99; exec. bd. young leadership coun. bd. Fedn. Jewish Agys., Phila., 1986—88; mem. nat. young leadership cabinet United Jewish Appeal, 1987—91; bd. dirs. Temple Beth Hillel Beth El; v.p., treas. Beth Am Israel; trustee Jewish Fedn. Greater Phila., 1996—2000; bd. dirs. State of Israel Bonds, Phila., SCRUB Found. Recipient New Life/New Leadership award, State of Israel, 1989, Hearts of Gold award, United Way Southeastern Pa., 1999. Mem.: ABA, Pa. Land Title Assn., Phila. Bar Assn., N.J. Bar Assn., Pa. Bar Assn., Internat. Coun. Shopping Ctrs. Home: 716 Oxford Rd Bala Cynwyd PA 19004-2112 Office: Wolf Block Schorr & Solis-Cohen LLP 1650 Arch St Fl 22D Philadelphia PA 19103-2097 Office Phone: 215-977-2082. Business E-Mail: jfinkelstein@wolfblock.com.

FINKELSTEIN, NORMAN HENRY, retired librarian, writer; b. Chelsea, Mass., Nov. 10, 1941; s. Sydney and Mollie (Fox) F.; m. Rosalind Brandt, July 4, 1967; children: Jeffrey, Robert, Risa. BS, Boston U., 1963, MEd, 1964; MA, Hebrew Coll., 1986. Dir. edn. Hebrew Coll. Sch. & Camp, Northwood, N.H., 1982-87; instr. Hebrew Coll., Brookline, Mass., 1982—; libr./media specialist Brookline Pub. Schs., 1970—2005. Author: Remember Not to Forget: A Memory of the Holocaust, 1985, The Other 1492: Jewish Settlement in the New World, 1989, The Emperor General: A Biography of Douglas MacArthur, 1989, Theodor Herzl: Architect of a Nation, 1991, Captain of Innocence: France and the Dreyfus Affair, 1991, Sounds in the Air: The Golden Age of Radio, 1993, Thirteen Days/Ninety Miles: The Cuban Missile Crisis, 1994, With Heroic Truth: The Life of Edward R. Murrow, 1997, Heeding The Call, 1997, Friends Indeed, 1998, The Way Things Never Were, 1999, Forged in Freedom, 2002, Ariel Sharon, 2005. Recipient study award, Kennedy Presdl. Libr., 1987, Ford Presdl. Libr., 1996, Golden Kite Honor award, 1997, Nat. Jewish Book award, 1998, 2002; CBE/NEH fellow, Washington, 1992, Study grantee, Brookline Found., 1987. Mem. Mass. Sch. Libr./Media Assn. (com. chair 1977-82), Wayfarer's Club, Phi Delta Kappa. Office: Hebrew Coll 160 Herrick Rd Newton Center MA 02459 Business E-Mail: nfinkelstein@hebrewcollege.edu. E-mail: biowriter@hotmail.com.

FINKELSTEIN, PHIL, retail executive; BS economics, Wharton School, U. Penn; MBA, Harvard Business School. With Glemby Internat., 1966—81; chmn., Beauty Div. Seligman & Latz (S&L), 0191—1984; CEO Turner Hall Corp., 1984—87; sr. v.p. Revlon, 1987; exec. v.p. Regis Corp., 1987—88, pres., COO, 1988—96, pres., 1996—2004, CEO, 1996—, chmn., 2004—. Mem. World Pres. Org., Chief Executives Org. Office: c/o Regis Corp 7201 Metro Blvd Edina MN 55439*

FINKELSTEIN, RICHARD ALAN, retired microbiology educator, consultant; b. N.Y.C., Mar. 5, 1930; s. Frank and Sylvia (Lemkin) F.; m. Helen Rosenberg, Nov. 30, 1952; children: Sheri, Mark, Laurie; m. Mary Boesman, June 20, 1976; 1 dau., Sarina Nicole. BS, U. Okla., 1950; MA, U. Tex., Austin, 1952, PhD, 1955. Tchg. fellow, rsch. scientist U. Tex., Austin, 1950-55; fellow, instr. U. Tex. Southwestern Med. Sch., Dallas, 1955-58; chief bioassay sect. Walter Reed Army Inst. Research, Washington, 1958-64; dep. chief, chief dept. bacteriology and mycology U.S. Army Med. Component, SEATO Med. Research Lab., Bangkok, 1964-67; assoc. prof. dept. microbiology U. Tex. Southwestern Med. Sch., Dallas, 1967-73, prof., 1973-79; prof., chmn. dept. microbiology Sch. Medicine U. Mo., Columbia, 1979-93, Curators' prof., 1990-2000, Millsap Disting. Prof., 1985-2000, prof. emeritus, 2000—. Mem. Nat. Com. for Coordination Cholera Rsch., Ministry for Pub. Health, Bangkok, 1965-67; cons. WHO, 1970—, commdg. gen. U.S. Army Med. R&D Command, 1975-79, Schwarz-Mann Labs., 1974-79, ICN Biomeds., 1979—, Wyeth-Ayerst, 1992—, Amgen, 1992, Molecular Pharms., 1993—; Microbiolog. and Infectious Diseases Rsch. Com. Nat. Inst. Allergy and Infectious Diseases, NIH, 1994-98; vis. assoc. prof. U. Med. Scis., Bangkok, 1965-67; vis. prof. U. Chgo., Med. Sch., 1977; vis. scientist Japanese Sci. Coun., 1976, Ciba-Geigy lectr. Waksman Inst., Rutgers U., 1975; vis. lectr. Nat. Sci. Coun., Taipei, Taiwan, 1995, others. Contbr. articles on cholera, enterotoxins, gonorrhea, and role of iron in host-parasite interactions to profl. jours. Recipient Robert Koch prize Bonn, Fed. Republic Germany, 1976; Chancellor's award for outstanding faculty rsch. in biol. scis. U. Mo.-Columbia, 1985, Sigma Xi Rsch. award U. Mo.-Columbia, 1986. Fellow Am Acad. Microbiology (bd. govs. 1990-93), Am. Soc. for Microbiology (pres. Tex. br. 1974-75, hon. Tex. br. divsn. councilor, chmn. program com. 1979-82, sec.-treas. Mo. br. 1985-87, v.p. 1987-89, pres. 1989-91, councillor, 1991-92, coun. policy com. 1992-95, Disting. Svc. award 1998), Am. Assn. Immunologists, Infectious Diseases Soc. of Am., Soc. Gen. Microbiology, Pathol. Soc. Gt. Britain and Ireland, Sigma Xi. Achievements include first purification of cholera enterotoxin; first purification of heat-labile enterotoxin from Escherichia coli; patent for living attenuated candidate cholera vaccine. Home: 3861 S Forest Acres Dr Columbia MO 65203-8608 Office: U Mo Sch Medicine Dept Molecular Microbiol Columbia MO 65212-0001 Office Phone: 573-882-4117. Business E-Mail: finkelsteinr@health.missouri.edu.

FINKELSTEIN, STUART M., lawyer; b. N.Y., 1960; BBA with distinction, U. Mich., 1982, JD cum laude, 1985. Bar: N.Y. 1986. Assoc. Skadden, Arps, Slate, Meagher & Flom LLP, N.Y.C., 1985-93, ptnr., 1993—. Office: Skadden Arps Slate Meagher & Flom LLP 4 Times Sq New York NY 10036-6595 Office Phone: 212-735-2841. E-mail: sfinkels@skadden.com.

FINKELSTEIN, WILLIAM BERNDT, lawyer; b. Austin, Tex., June 19, 1949; s. Willard Casper and Doris Jean (Frennesson) F.; m. Jeri Helen Goldberg, Feb. 6, 1972; children: Robin, Lisa, Shana. BA, U. Tex., 1971; JD cum laude, Baylor U., 1974. Bar: Tex. 1974. Law clk. to assoc. justice Supreme Ct. Tex., Austin, 1974-75; from assoc. to ptnr. Hughes & Luce, Dallas, 1975—. Lectr. in field. Mem. Young Leadership Cabinet of United Jewish Appeal; co-chair lawyers divsn. Jewish Fedn. Greater Dallas, 2002. Named one of Best Lawyers in Dallas, D Mag., 2003, Tex. Super Lawyers, Tex. Monthly, 2004—05. Mem. ABA, State Bar Tex., Dallas Bar Assn., Assn. Comml. Fin. Attys., Am. Bankruptcy Inst., Masons, Shriners, Inn of Ct. (master). Office: Hughes & Luce 1717 Main St Ste 2800 Dallas TX 75201-4685 Home: 11544 Valleydale Dr Dallas TX 75230-2402 E-mail: bfinkelstein@hughesluce.com.

FINKLE, JEFFREY ALAN, professional association executive; b. Newark, Ohio, Apr. 22, 1954; s. Richard James and Margery (Orr) F.; m. Diane Elizabeth Letchford, Aug. 20, 1983 (div. July 1989). BSc cum laude, Ohio U., 1976; postgrad., Ohio State U., 1978-80. Legis. dir. Ohio Rep. Party, Columbus, 1976-78; legis. liason Ohio Dept. Mental Health, Columbus, 1978-80; mktg. dir. Systems 80, Bethesda, Md., 1980-81; exec. asst. HUD, Washington, 1981-83, dep. asst. sec., 1983-86; pres., CEO Coun. for Urban Econ. Devel., Washington, 1986—2001; pres, CEO Internat. Econ. Devel. Coun., 2001. Mem. adv. com., Ohio U. Inst. for Local Govt. Adminstrn. and Rural Devel., 1986—. Bd. dirs., pres. Bollinger Found., 1989—, Arlington County Va. Econ. Devel. Corp., 1999—, D.C. Mktg. Ctr., 1998-2000. Mem. Housing Rehab. Assn. (bd. dirs. 1986-90), Nat. Assn. Ind. Living Ctrs. (nat. adv. bd. 1987-89), Sr. Living Choices (bd. dirs. 1991-98), Ohio U. Alumni Assn. (past pres. Washington chpt., past bd. dirs. nat. assn.). Republican. Roman Catholic. Avocations: golf, genealogy. Office: Internat Econ Devel Coun 734 15th St NW Ste 900 Washington DC 20005 E-mail: jfinkle@iedconline.org.

FINKS, ROBERT MELVIN, paleontologist, educator; b. Portland, Maine, May 12, 1927; s. Abraham Joseph and Sarah (Bendette) F. BS magna cum laude, Queens Coll., 1947; MA, Columbia U., 1954, PhD, 1959. Lectr. Bklyn. Coll., 1955-58, instr., 1959-61; lectr. Queens Coll., CUNY, 1961-62, asst. prof., 1962-65, acting chmn., 1963-64, assoc. prof. geology, 1966-70, prof., 1971—2002, prof. emeritus, 2002—; geologist U.S. Geol. Survey, 1952-54, 63—; rsch. assoc. Am. Mus. Natural History, 1961—77, Smithsonian Instn., 1968—; rsch. assoc. in paleontology N.Y. State Mus.; rsch. prof. dept. geology Union Coll., Schenectady, NY. Doctoral faculty CUNY, 1983—; cons. in field. Author: Late Paleozoic Sponge Faunas of the Texas Region, 1960; Editor: Guidebook to Field Excursions, 1968; Contbr. articles profl. jours. Queens Coll. Scholar, 1947. Fellow AAAS, Geol. Soc. Am., Explorers Club; mem. AAUP, Paleontol. Soc. (vice chmn. Northeastern sect. 1977-78, chmn. 1978-79), Paleontol. Assn. Britain, Soc. Econ. Paleontologists and Mineralogists, Internat. Palaeontol. Assn., Geol. Soc. Vt. (charter mem.), Planetary Soc. (charter), Phi Beta Kappa (v.p. Sigma chpt. N.Y. 1993-95, pres. 1995-99), Golden Key (hon.), Sigma Xi (exec. sec. Queens Coll. chpt. 1982-85). Office: Queens Coll CUNY Sch Earth and Environ Scis Flushing NY 11367 Address: Geology Dept Union Coll Schenectady NY 12308 Business E-Mail: Finksr@union.edu. *Be humble in studying nature.*

FINLAY, JAMES CAMPBELL, retired museum director; b. Russell, Man., Can., June 12, 1931; s. William Hugh and Grace Muriel F.; m. Audrey Joy Barton, June 18, 1955; children: Barton Brett, Warren Hugh, Rhonda Marie. BSc, Brandon U., 1952; MSc in Zoology, U. Alta., Can., 1968. Geophysicist Frontier Geophys. Ltd., Alta., 1952-53; geologist, then dist. geologist Shell Can., Ltd., 1954-64; chief park naturalist and biologist Elk Island (Can.) Nat. Pk., 1965-67; dir. hist. devel. and archives, dir. hist. and sci. svc., dir. Nature Ctr., dir. interpretation and recreation City of Edmonton, Alta., 1967-92; ret., 1992; founder Fedn. Alta. Naturalists, 1969. Author: A Nature Guide to Alberta, Bird Finding Guide to Canada; (with Joy Finlay) Ocean to Alpine-A British Columbia Nature Guide, A Guide to Alberta Parks. Recipient Order of the Bighorn, Govt. of Atla., 1987, Heritage award Environment Can., 1990, Loran Goulden award Fedn. Alta. Naturalists, 1991, Can. 125th Anniversary award, 1993, Greenways Achievement award, B.C. Province Capital Commn., 2001; named to Edmonton Hist. Hall of Fame, 1976. Mem. Can. Mus. Assn. (pres. 1976-78), Alta. Mus. Assn. (founding mem., past pres.), Am. Mus. Assn. (past coun.), Am. Ornithol. Union. Home: 270 Trevlac Pl RR 3 Victoria BC Canada V9E 2C4 Personal E-mail: joyandcamfinlay@shaw.ca. *I will walk but once on this earth. In this short time I hope to help my fellow man come to a greater awareness, appreciation and understanding of the world environment of which we are very much a part. I am trying to ensure that our descendants have a fit planet on which to live.*

FINLAY, ROBERT DEREK, food company executive; b. U.K., May 16, 1932; s. William Templeton and Phyllis F.; m. Una Ann Grant, June 30, 1956; children: Fiona, Rory, James. BA with honors in Law and Econs, Cambridge (Eng.) U., 1955, MA, 1959. With Mobil Oil Co. Ltd., U.K., 1955-61; assoc. McKinsey & Co., Inc., 1961-67, prin., 1967-71, dir., 1971-79; mng. dir. H.J. Heinz Co. Ltd., U.K., 1979-81; sr. v.p. corp. devel. world hdqs. H.J. Heinz Co., Pitts., 1981-93, chief fin. officer world hdqrs., 1989-92, sr. v.p. corp. devel., area v.p., 1992-93. Chmn. Dawson Internat., 1995-98; mem. Inst. Mktg., 1976-2004. Mem. London com. Scottish Coun. Devel. and Industry, 1979-03; trustee Mercy Hosp., Pitts., 1983-93; bd. dirs. Pitts. Symphony Soc., 1989-92, U.S.-China Bus. Coun., 1984-92, Pitts. Pub. Theater, 1988-92; gov. Kingston Grammar Sch., 1997-2002. Capt. Gordon Highlanders, 1950-61. Fellow Inst. Dirs., Royal Soc. Arts; mem. Highland Brigade Club, Leander Club, Annabel's, Caledonian Club, Three Rivers Rowing Assn. (gov.).

FINLAY, SUSAN SPARLING, education educator; b. Sarasota, Fla., Sept. 5, 1963; d. Gerald Walker and Joan Highleyman Sparling; m. John Michael Finlay, Sept. 5, 1987; 1 child, Logan Spencer. BA, Eckerd Coll., 1981—85; MA, U. of South Fla., 1988—90. Assoc. prof. sociology Suffolk C.C., Selden, NY, 1992—95, Manatee C.C., Venice, Fla., 1995—. Mem.: Profl. Orgnl. Devel. Network in Higher Edn., Nat. Coun. Staff Program and Orgnl. Devel., Am. Sociology Assn., Am. Assn. of Women in Cmty. Colleges (corr.). Office: Manatee CC 8000 South Tamiami Trail Venice FL 34293 Office Phone: 941-408-1473. E-mail: finlays@mccfl.edu.

FINLAY, TERENCE EDWARD, retired archbishop; s. Terence John and Sarah (McBryan) F.; m. Alice-Jean Cracknell, 1962; 2 daus. BA, U. We. Ont., London; BTh, Huron Coll., London, Ont.; MA, U. Cambridge, Eng.; DD (jure dignitatis), Huron Coll., 1987. Ordained deacon Anglican Ch., 1961, priest, 1962. Dean of residence Renison Coll., Waterloo, Can.; incumbent All Saints, Waterloo, 1964-66, St. Aidan's, London, Can., 1966-68; rector St. John the Evangelist, London, 1968-78; archdeacon of Brant, 1978-82; incumbent Grace Ch., Brantford, Can., 1978-82, St. Clement's, Eglinton, Toronto, Can., 1982-86; suffragan bishop Diocese of Toronto, 1986, coadjutor bishop, 1987, bishop Toronto, 1989—2004; archbishop Met. of Ecclesiastical Province of Ont. Anglican. Avocations: music, skiing, travel. Office: Diocese of Toronto 135 Adelaide St E Toronto ON Canada M5C 1L8

FINLAYSON, ALISTAIR JAMES REID, psychology professor; b. Glasgow, Scotland, Sept. 23; arrived in US, 2001; s. Alexander and Margaret Isobel (Nee Reid) Finlayson; children: James Drew, Heather Alway. MD, U. Western Ontario, Canada, 1969. Lectr. McMaster U., Hamilton, Canada, 1992—99; asst. prof. U. Western Ontario, London, Canada, 1980—89; assoc. prof. U. Ottawa, Ottawa, Canada, 1990—93, McMaster U., Hamilton, Canada, 1994—2001; asst. prof. Vanderbilt U., Nashville, 2001—. Med. dir. Ctr. for Profl. Excellence, Nashville, Vandervbilt Comprehensive Assessment Program, Founds. Assoc., Nashville. Recipient Dist. Fellow, Am. Psychiatric Assn., 1990. Mem.: Can. Med. Assn., Am. Psychiat. Assn. Avocations: theater, skiing, running, travel. Office: Vanderbilt U 1601 23rd Ave S Nashville TN 37212 Office Phone: 618-322-4567. Office Fax: 615-322-7526. E-mail: reid.finlayson@vanderbilt.edu.

FINLAYSON, BRUCE ALAN, chemical engineering professor; b. Waterloo, Iowa, July 18, 1939; s. Rodney Alan and Donna Elizabeth (Gilbert) F.; m. Patricia Lynn Hills, June 9, 1961; children: Mark, Catherine, Christine BA, Rice U., 1961, MS, 1963; PhD, U. Minn., 1965. Asst. prof. to assoc. prof. U. Wash., Seattle, 1967-77, prof. dept. chem. engring. and applied math., 1977-82, Rehnberg prof. dept. chem. engring., 1983—, chmn. dept. chem. engring., 1989-98. Vis. prof. Univ. Coll., Swansea, Wales, U.K., 1975-76, Denmark Tekniske Hojskole, Lyngby, 1976, Universidad Nacional del Sur, Bahia Blanca, Argentina, 1980; Gulf vis. prof. Carnegie Mellon U., 1986; trustee Computer Aids to Chem. Engring. Edn., Austin, Tex., 1980-92; mem. bd. on chem. sci. and tech. NRC, 1990-92. Mem. editorial bd. Internat. Jour. Numerical Methods in Fluids, Swansea, 1980—, Numerical Heat Transfer, 1981-2002, Numerical Methods for Partial Differential Equations, 1984—, Chem. Engring. Edn., 1991—; author: The Method of Weighted Residuals and Variational Principles, 1972, Nonlinear Analysis in Chemical Engineering, 1980, Numerical Methods for Problems with Moving Fronts, 1992. Lt. USNR, 1965-67. Recipient Undergrad. Computational Engring. and Sci. award, U.S. Dept. Energy, 1996, Dow Lectureship award, ASEE, ChE divsn., 2005. Fellow AIChE (CAST divsn. programming 1981-85, William H. Walker award 1983, bd. dirs. CAST divsn. 1984-86, vice chmn. 1987-88, chmn. 1989, bd. dirs. 1992-94, editorial bd. 1985-91, v.p. 1999, pres. 2000, past pres. 2001); mem. Am. Chem. Soc. (bd. dirs. Petroleum Rsch. Fund 1998-2004), Am. Soc. Engring. Edn. (dir. Summer Sch. for Chem. Engring. Faculty 1997, Martin award Ch.E. divsn. 1994, Dow Lectureship award, 2005), Soc. Indsl. and Applied Math., Soc. Rheology, Nat. Acad. Engring., N.Am. Alliance of Chem. Engrs. (pres. 2001). Home: 6315 22nd Ave NE Seattle WA 98115-6919 Office: U Wash Dept Chem Engring PO Box 351750 Seattle WA 98195-1750 Office Phone: 206-685-1634. Personal E-mail: bafinlayson@mindspring.com. Business E-Mail: finlayson@cheme.washington.edu.

FINLAYSON, JOHN SYLVESTER, retired biochemist; b. Phila., Sept. 19, 1933; s. Alexander Smeillie and Anna Eva (Sylvester) F.; m. Rasma Irēne Bramane; children: Mark Lars, Siglinda Erika Finlayson Beyeler. BA summa cum laude, Marietta Coll., 1953; MS, U. Wis., 1955, PhD, 1957. Rsch. fellow Inst. Radiophysics, Stockholm, 1957-58; biochemist NIH, Bethesda, Md., 1958-72; rsch. chemist FDA, Bethesda, 1972-75, chief Lab. Plasma Derivatives, 1975-86, chief Lab. Hepatitis, 1986-89, chief Lab. Hemostasis & Thrombosis, 1988-89, acting dir. divsn. hematology, 1990-92, assoc. dir. sci. office blood rsch. and review, 1993—2003, ret., 2003, guest worker, 2004—. Vis. prof., scientist Protein Rsch. Inst., Osaka, Japan, 1976; lectr. in biochemistry Found. Advanced Edn. in Sci., Bethesda, 1961-76, 86-96. Author: Basic Biochemical Calculations, 1969; co-editor: Immunoglobulins, 1980; contbr. articles to profl. jours. With USPHS, 1958-61. Mem. Internat. Soc. Thrombosis and Haemostasis (charter, emeritus), Soc. Exptl. Biology and Medicine, Sr. Biomed. Rsch. Svc. Office: FDA Ctr Biol Eval & Rsch HFM-330 1401 Rockville Pike Rockville MD 20852-1448

FINLEY, BRUCE BISSELL, journalist; b. Palo Alto, Calif., Mar. 30, 1962; s. David Dewees and Judy Reid F.; m. Claire Martin, Sept. 22, 1993; children: Cordelia, Tessa. B in Am. Studies, Stanford U., 1984; M in Internat. Rels., U. Lancaster, Eng., 1985; M in Journalism, Northwestern U., 1987. Freelance Africa corr., Zimbabwe, 1991-92; internat. affairs writer Denver Post, 1992—. Recipient Human Rights award U.N. Assn., 2000, Best of West award Soc. profl. Journalists, Pulitzer Prize Denver Post team coverage Columbine H.S. massacre; Fulbright scholar U. Lancaster, 1984-85; Mich. Journalism fellow U. Mich., 1993-94. Mem. Denver Coun. Fgn. Rels. (v.p. 1999—). Avocations: mountain climbing, skiing, soccer. Office: Denver Post Denver CO 80202

FINLEY, GEORGE ALVIN, III, wholesale executive, oil industry executive; b. Aurora, Ill., Apr. 25, 1938; s. George Alvin, II, and Sally Ann (Lord) F.; m. Sue Sellors, June 20, 1962 (dec. 1995); m. Phyllis Ann Finley; children: Valerie, George Alvin IV (dec. 2005). BBA, So. Meth. U., 1962; postgrad. Coll. Grad. Program, Ford Motor Co., 1963. Rep. for Europe Finco Internat., 1959-61; trainee Ford Motor Co., Dearborn, Mich., 1962-63; v.p. mktg. Internat. Motor Cars, Oakland, Calif., 1963-64, Sequoia Lincoln lease mgr., 1965; regional mgr. Behlen Mfg. Co., Dallas, 1965-67; pres. C C Distbrs., Corpus Christi, Tex., 1967—. Guest instr. Sch. Bus., So. Meth. U., pres., 1986-91, Nueces River Authority, 1975-2001; bd. dirs. Contract Svcs. Assn. Am. Sec. Bd. Washington, MD Anderson Hosp. U. Tex., Christus-Spohn Health Sys., McDonald Obs., U. Tex., exec. com.; mem. Del Mar Coll. Found. Mem. pres.'s coun. Tex. A&M U., Corpus Christi; bd. mem. Coastal Bend Alcohol and Drug Rehab. Ctr., 1973—97, 2005—. Mem. Tex. Wholesale Hardware Assn. (pres. 1991-92), Nat. Assn. Wholesalers, Am. Supply Assn., Wholesale Distbrs. Assn. (bd. dirs. 1994—), Impact Industries Inc. (chmn. bd. Sandwich, Ill. 1986-93), N.Am. Bldg. Material Distbn. Assn., Rotary Internat., State Bar of Tex. (grievance com. 1995-2001), Phi Delta Theta. Democrat. Episcopalian. Achievements include assisted in design, engineering, production, and marketing of the Apollo Automobile, 1963-64. Home: 3360 Ocean Dr Corpus Christi TX 78411-1457 Office: PO Box 9153 210 Mcbride Ln Corpus Christi TX 78408-2338 Office Phone: 361-289-0200.

FINLEY, GLENNA, writer; b. Puyallup, Wash., June 12, 1925; d. John Ford and Gladys De Ferris (Winters) F.; m. Donald MacLeod Witte, May 19, 1951; 1 child, Duncan MacLeod. BA cum laude, Stanford U., 1945. Prodr. internat. divsn. NBC, 1945-49; film libr. March of Time, 1949; with news bur. Life Mag., 1950; publicity and radio writer Seattle, 1950-51; freelance writer, 1951-57; contract writer New Am. Libr. Inc., N.Y.C., 1970—. Author numerous books including Master of Love, 1978, Beware My Heart, 1978, The Marriage Merger, 1978, Wildfire of Love, 1979, Timed for Love, 1979, Love's Temptation, 1979, Stateroom for Two, 1980, Affairs of Love, 1980, A Business Affair, 1983, Wanted for Love, 1983, A Weekend for Love, 1984, Love's Waiting Game, 1985, A Touch of Love, 1985, Diamonds for My Love, 1986, Secret of Love, 1987, The Marrying Kind, 1988, Island Rendezvous, 1990, Stowaway for Love, 1992, The Temporary Bride, 1993. Named Matrix Table Woman of Achievement, 1976. Mem. Mem.: Women's Univ. Club (Seattle). Republican. Anglican. Home: 7868-F Rea Rd #312 Charlotte NC 28277 *I have always made a point of writing pleasant books that "turn out right"-believing that after readers have opened their wallets to purchase a book all suffering should cease.*

FINLEY, HARRY, artist, museum director; b. Long Branch, N.J., July 18, 1942; s. George and Marjorie Finley. BA, Johns Hopkins U., 1964; postgrad., U. Fla., 1966, U. Fla., 1969—71. Graphic designer Dept. Army, Washington and Germany, 1971—2004; mus. founder, dir. Mus. Mestruation, New Carrollton, Md., 1994—; artist, 1971—. Portraits. With U.S. Army, 1964—66, with U.S. Army, 1971—74. Decorated Commendation medal for Civilian Svc. Dept. Army; recipient Keith L. Ware award, 1974, Thomas Jefferson award, Dept. Def., 1974. Mem.: ACLU, Am. Assn. History Medicine, Soc. Menstrual Cycle Rsch. Democrat. Avocations: foreign languages, astronomy, cultural history.

FINLEY, JULIE HAMM, ambassador, former political party official; Nat. co-chmn. Fin. Dole for Pres., 1995—96; asst. secy. 1996 Rep. Nat. Conv.; co-chmn. D.C. Republican Party, Team 100, 1997—2005; nat. committee-woman D.C. Republican Com., 1999—2005; US amb. to Orgn. for Security & Cooperation in Europe, 2005—. Founding bd. mem. US Com. on NATO. Office: Orgn for Security & Cooperation in Europe Kaerntner Ring 5-7 1010 Austria*

FINLEY, KATHERINE MANDUSIC, professional society administrator; b. Mansfield, Ohio, Nov. 8, 1954; d. Sam and Ann Julia (Konves) Mandusic; m. Edwin D. McDonell, Aug. 18, 1979 (div. Dec. 1994); m. Jeffrey A. Finley, June 12, 1999. BA, Ohio Wesleyan U.; MA in History and Mus. Studies, Case Western Res.; MBA, Ind. U. Rschr. Conner Prairie Mus., Fishers, Ind., 1978-82; exec. dir., rsch. historian Ind. Med. History Mus./Ind. Hist. Soc., Indpls., 1982-91; asst. dir. comm. and mktg. Ind. U. Ctr. Philanthropy, 1991-93; exec. dir. Roller Skating Assn. Internat., Indpls., 1993-2000, Assn. Rsch. Nonprofit Orgns. and Voluntary Action (ARNOVA), 2000—; mem. faculty philanthropic studies Ind. U.-Purdue U., Indpls., 2001—; rsch. dir. William E. Smith Inst. for Assn. Rsch., 2004—. Rsch. dir. William E. Smith Inst. Assn. Rsch., 2004—. Author: (book) The Journals of William A. Lindsay, 1989; contbg. editor: The Encyclopedia of Indianapolis, 1994; contbr. articles to profl. jours. Pres. Altrusa Internat. Indpls., 1995—97, treas., 1998—99, chmn. svc. com., 1999—2000; pres. Altrusa Found. Indpls., 2001—03; bd. dirs. Nat. Mus. Roller Skating, Lincoln, 1994—2000. Mem.: Assn. Fund Raising Profls. (bd. dirs. Ind. chpt. 2003—), Ind. Soc. Assn. Execs. (chair edn. com. 1997—98, chair conv. com. 1999—2000, bd. dirs. 1999—2001, chair found. 2000), Nat. Soc. Fund Raising Execs. (cert.), Am. Soc. Assn. Execs. (mem. ethics com. 2004—, Assn. Exec. of Yr. 2002, cert. meeting planner 2003), MINI Cooper Car Club Ind. (club advisor 2003—04), Toastmasters (v.p. edn. 1998—99, v.p. pub. rels. 2000, v.p. edn. 2000—02, gov. area 18 2001—02), Rotary Internat. of Indpls., Phi Beta Kappa, Sigma Iota Epsilon, Beta Gamma Sigma. Avocations: reading, walking, gourmet cooking. Office: ARNOVA Ste 301 550 W North St Indianapolis IN 46202 E-mail: kmfinley@iupui.edu.

FINLEY, KAY THOMAS, chemistry educator, researcher; b. Elmira, N.Y., Aug. 29, 1934; s. Thomas Wolf and Helene Grace (Kennedy) F.; m. Patricia J. Siegel, July 10, 1978; children: John Michael, Sarah Marie, Moira Elizabeth. BS, Rochester Inst. Tech., 1959; PhD, U. Rochester, 1963. Assoc. prof. Rochester (N.Y.) Inst. Tech., 1962-66; sr. rsch. chemist Eastman Kodak Co., Rochester, 1966-70; dean sci. and maths. SUNY, Brockport, 1970-76, prof., 1970—. Author: Fundamental Organic Chemistry, 1970, Triazoles: 1,2,3, 1980, Women in the Scientific Search (with P.J. Siegel), 1985. With USN, 1952-55. Named Outstanding Alumnus Rochester Inst. Tech., 1976. Roman Catholic. Avocations: stamp collecting/philately, writing popular science, history and biography in science. Home: 57 Heather Rdg Rochester NY 14626-1085 Office: SUNY 350 New Campus Dr Brockport NY 14420-2914 E-mail: kfinley@brockport.edu.

FINLEY, LEWIS MERREN, financial consultant; b. Reubens, Idaho, Nov. 29, 1929; s. John Emory and Charlotte (Priest) Finley; m. Virginia Ruth Spousta, Feb. 23, 1957; children: Ellen Annette Finley Guldenzopf, Charlotte Louise Finley Kinney. Student pub. schs., Spokane. With Household Fin. Co., Portland, Oreg. and Seattle, 1953-56, Doug Gerow Fin., Portland, 1956-61; pres. Family Fin. Planners Inc., Portland, 1961—. Assoc. broker Peoples Choice Realty, Inc., Milwaukie, Oreg., 1977-82, Lewis M. Finley, Real Estate Broker, Inc., 1982—; standing trustee Chpt. 13, Fed. Bankruptcy Ct., Dist. of Oreg., 1979. Author: The Complete Guide to Getting Yourself Out of Debt, 1975. With U.S. Army, 1951-53. Mem. Oreg. Assn. Credit Counselors (past pres.), N.W. Assn. Credit Counselors (past treas.), Am. Assn. Credit Counselors (v.p. 1982-85), Authors Guild, Nat. Assn. Realtors, Masons (past master), Scottish Rite (32d degree), Shriners. Republican. Methodist. Home: 3015 SE Riviere Dr Portland OR 97267-5548 Office: PO Box 12287 Portland OR 97212-0287 Personal E-mail: yelnif@msn.com.

FINLEY, LUCY LAYNE, artist; b. Sanford, N.C., Jan. 31, 1937; d. James Oscar and Vera Jane (Banner) Layne; m. William Ronald Finley, Apr. 11, 1959; children: Peggy Ann, James Lloyd, Thomas Lee. AA in Fine Art magna cum laude, No. Va. C.C., 1981. Gallery artist The Art League, Alexandria, Va., 1991—, White Hill Gallery, Carthage, NC, 2003—. Recipient Gold from the Guilds award Fairfax County Coun. of the Arts, 1981, Arschile Gorky award Waterford Found., 1983. Mem. The Art League (Exemplary award 1991), Manassas Art Guild (pres. 1981-82), Torpedo Factory Art Ctr. Home: 13100 Ginger Ct Manassas VA 20112-4618

FINLEY, MARGARET MAVIS, retired elementary school educator; b. Jackson, Mich., Dec. 2, 1927; d. Allen Aaron and Minnie Mavis (Graham) Lincoln; m. Duane Douglas Finley, Aug. 23, 1952; 1 child, Linda Louise. BS, Ea. Mich. U., 1960; postgrad., Pepperdine U., 1968-72. Cert. tchr., Mich., Calif. Tchr. Jackson (Mich.) Sch. Dist., 1960-67, Pomona (Calif.) Sch. Dist., 1967-88; ret., 1988. Contbr. poetry and articles to profl. jours. Mem.: NEA, DAR (historian (Los Cerritos chpt.), libr. (Los Cerritos chpt.)), Calif. Tchrs. Assn., Calif. Ret. Tchrs. Assn. (editor divsn. 82 newsletter). Avocations: writing, reading, hiking, travel, theater. Home: 1072 Cypress Point Dr Banning CA 92220-5404

FINLEY, MICHAEL C., writer, poet; b. Flint, Mich., July 4, 1950; s. Paul William and Mary (Mulligan) Finley; m. Rachel M. Frazin, June 25, 1981; children: Daniele, Jonathan. BA, U. Minn., Mpls., 1972. Editor, tv prodr. U. Minn., Mpls.; editor Worthington (Minn.) Daily Globe, 1978—80; proprietor Future Shoes, Mpls., 1985—; head writer The Masters Forum, Mpls., 1992—2000. Contbg. editor Computer User Mag., Mpls., 1988—. Author: The Movie under the Blindfold, 1976, Home Trees, 1976, Lucky You, 1976, Water Hills, 1985, Looking for China, Poems 1976-1990, 1990, Why Change Doesn't Work, 1996, Transcompetition: Moving from Competition to Collaboration, 1997, The New Why Teams Don't Work, 2000 (Best Mgmt. Book, Fin. Times Global Bus., 1996); contbr. Masters of the Wired World, 2000. Pres. Minn. Folk Festival, St. Paul, 1999—2000. Named Am. Reporter Corres. of Yr., Am. Reporter, 2000; recipient Pushcart prize, Pushcart Found., 1985; fellow Wis. Arts fellow, Wis. State Arts Bd., 1985; scholar, Nat. Coun. Tchrs. English, 1964. Office: Future Shoes 1841 Dayton Ave Saint Paul MN 55104 Personal E-mail: mf@mfinley.com. Business E-Mail: mfinley@mfinley.com.

FINLEY, MICHAEL VALTON, foundation executive; b. Medford, Oreg., Apr. 8, 1947; s. Valton Austin and Anne Elsie (Huebner) F.; m. Lillie Eiteneir, June 14, 1969; children: Devon, Laura. BS in Biology, So. Oreg. State Coll., 1969. With Nat. Park Service, 1970-2001; park ranger Big Bend (Tex.) Nat. Park, 1970, Pinnacles Nat. Monument, Paicines, Calif., 1972-73, Yosemite (Calif.) Nat. Park, 1974-76; exchange ranger Calif. State Park System-Big Bas State Park, 1973-74; law enforcement specialist Grand Teton Nat. Park, Moose, Wyo., 1976-78; staff park ranger, Washington, 1978-80; legis. affairs specialist Washington, 1980-81; supt. Assateague Island Nat. Seashore Berlin, Md., 1981-83; assoc. regional dir. Anchorage, 1983-86; supt. Everglades Nat. Pk., Homestead, Fla., 1986-89, Yosemite Nat. Pk., Mammoth Hot Springs, 1989-94; pres. Turner Found., Atlanta, 2001—. Served to sgt. U.S. Army, 1968-70. Mem. Assn. Nat. Park Rangers (pres. 1980-82). Lodges: Rotary. Lutheran. Avocations: fishing, scuba, photography, hiking, skiing. Office: Turner Found Inc 133 Luckie St NW 2nd Fl Atlanta GA 30303

FINLEY, PATRICIA ANN, psychologist, artist; b. Phoenix, Oct. 30, 1936; d. Richard Edward and Ethel Buck Finley; m. William M. Larson, Aug. 31, 1957 (div. June 5, 1978); children: Sabin Lynne Larson, Shura Lee McGraw, Sean William Larson. BFA Graphic Design, Univ. Ariz., Tucson, Ariz., 1958; MS Art Edn., Univ. Oreg., Eugene, Oreg., 1981, PhD Art Edn., 1984; PhD Psychology, Walden Univ., Mpls., 2002. Cert. basic tchg. Oreg., 1982, lifetime tchg. in C.C. Ariz., 1987. Coll. instr. Ariz. State Univ./Columbia Coll., Phoenix, 1985—95; psychotherapist Sexual Assault Recovery Inst., Phoenix, 1990—94, Westside Social Svc., Phoenix, 1994—97; clin. specialist ProtoCall Crisis Line, Portland, 1997—2000; sex offender therapist New Horizons Wellness Svc., Portland, Oreg., 2000—01; Psychologist, owner, dir. Lake Oswego (Oreg.) Counsel Ctr., 2001—. Exec. dir. Phoenix Festivals, Phoenix, 1987—90; bd. cert. expert Am. Acad. Trauma Svc., Portland, Oreg., 1997—. Media coord. John Denver Ariz. Windstar Connection Group, Phoenix, 1989; mem., planning com. Very Spl. Arts, Scottsdale, Ariz., 1993. Fellow: Kappa Kappa Gamma; mem.: Milton H. Erickson Found., Eye Movment Desensitisation & Reprocessng, Am. Psychol. Assn., Am. Mental Health Assn. (Oreg. chpt.), Psi Chi. Independent. Unitarian. Avocations: running, swimming, reading, cooking, antiques. Office: Lake Oswego Counseling Ctr Inc 15110 SW Boones Ferry Rd #248 Lake Oswego OR 97035 Office Phone: 503-675-2830.

FINLEY, ROBERT VAN EATON, minister; b. Charlottesville, Va., May 2, 1922; s. William Walter and Melissa (Hoover) Finley; m. Ethel Drummond, Dec. 23, 1949; children: Deborah Ann, Ruth Ellen. BA, U. Va., 1944; postgrad., U. Chgo. Div. Sch., 1946-47; LittD, Houghton Coll., 1952. Ordained to ministry Bapt. Ch., 1957. Evangelist Youth for Christ Internat., Chgo., 1945-46, Inter-Varsity Christian Fellowship, Chgo., 1945-46, overseas, 1948-51; pastor Evang. Free Ch., Richmond, Calif., 1951-52; minister to fgn. students 10th Presbyn. Ch., Phila., 1952-55; founder, gen. dir. Christian Aid Mission, Charlottesville, 1953-70, chmn., CEO, 1970—; founder, gen. dir. Overseas Students Mission, Ft. Erie, Canada, 1954-68, pres., 1969-85; pastor Temple Bapt. Ch., Washington, 1965-66. Pres. Bharat Evang. Fellowship, Washington, 1973—87; founder, pres. Christian Aid Mission Can., 1985—88, chmn. bd. dirs., 1989—2003; pres. Internat. Congress Indigenous Missions, Harrisburg, Pa., 1988—. Author: The Future of Foreign Missions, 2002, Reformation in Foreign Missions, 2005; editor: Conquest for Christ mag., 1954—74, Christian Mission mag., 1974—. Founder, pres. Internat. Students, Inc., Colorado Springs, 1952—67, chmn., 1968—70. Mem.: Assn.

Christians Ministering Internats. (bd. dirs. 1995—99), Omicron Delta Kappa. Office: Christian Aid Mission PO Box 9037 Charlottesville VA 22906-9037 *To indulge myself, beyond actual need, with the benefits of material wealth leaves me the poorer. But when my surplus resources are used to uplift those who lack opportunity, I am enriched.*

FINLEY, SARA CREWS, medical geneticist, educator; b. Lineville, Ala., Feb. 26, 1930; m. Wayne H. Finley; children: Randall Wayne, Sara Jane. BS in Biology, U. Ala., 1951, MD, 1955. Diplomate Am. Bd. Med. Genetics; cert. clin. geneticist; cert. clin. cytogeneticist. Intern Lloyd Noland Hosp., Fairfield, Ala., 1955-56; NIH fellow in pediatrics U. Ala. Med. Sch., Birmingham, 1956-60; NIH trainee in med. genetics Inst. Med. Genetics, U. Uppsala, Sweden, 1961-62; mem. faculty U. Ala. Med. Sch., 1960-96, co-dir. lab. med. genetics, 1966-96, prof. pediatrics, 1975-96, occupant Wayne H. and Sara Crews Finley chair med. genetics, 1986-96, prof. emeritus, 1996—; Disting. Faculty lectr. Med. Ctr., U. Ala. at Birmingham, 1983; mem. staff Univ. U. Ala. Hosp., Children's Hosp. Ala. Mem. ad hoc com. genetic counseling Children's Bur., HEW, 1966; mem. ad hoc rev. panel for genetic disease and sickle cell testing and counseling programs, 1980; mem. genetic diseases program objective rev. panel Bur. Maternal and Child Health and Resources Div., HHS, 1989, mem. adv. group on lab. quality assurance, 1989. Birmingham Author papers on clin. cytogenetics, human congenital malformations, human growth and devel. Mem. White House Conf. Health, 1965; mem. rsch. manpower rev. com. Nat. Cancer Inst., 1977-81; mem. Sickle Cell Disease Adv. Com., NIH, 1983-87; chairperson physician's campaign bd. dirs. United Way, 1993-95. Recipient Disting. Alumna award U. Ala. Sch. Medicine Alumni Assn., 1989, Med. award Ala. Assn. for Retarded Children, 1969, Turlington award Planned Parenthood of Ala., 1982, Nat. Outstanding Alumnae award Zeta Tau Alpha, 1992, Disting. Alumna award U. Ala. Nat. Alumni Assn., 1994, Brother Bryan Prayer Point award Birmingham Women's Com. of 100, 2001, Gardner award Ala. Acad. Sci., 2002, Local Legend award Am. Med. Women's Assn. Nat. Libr. Medicine, 2004, Lifetime Achievement award Birmingham Bus. Jour., 2003; co-recipient Will Holmes award Children's Aid Soc. Birmingham, 1999; named Top Ten Women in Birmingham, 1989, Top 31 Most Outstanding Alumnae U. Ala., Tuscaloosa, 1993, Ala. Health Hall of Fame, 2001, named to Birmingham Bus. Jour. Healthcare Hall of Fame, 2002, Finley-Compass Bank Genetics Conf. Ctr. with portrait opened, 2001. Fellow AMA (founding), Am. Coll. Med. Genetics; mem. Am. Soc. Human Genetics, Med. Assn. Ala. (Samuel Buford Word award 2003, Fifty Year Club 2005), Ala. Assn. Retarded Children (Ann. Med. awad 1969), Ala. Acad. Sci., Jefferson County Med. Soc. (pres. 1990), Jefferson County Pediatric Soc., Rotary Club of Birmingham, Phi Beta Kappa, Sigma Xi, Alpha Omea Alpha, Alpha Epsilon Delta, Omicron Delta Kappa, Phi Kappa Phi, Zeta Tau Alpha. Office: U Ala Kaul Bldg 210E Birmingham AL 35294

FINLEY, SARAH MAUDE MERRITT, retired social worker; b. Atlanta, Nov. 19, 1946; d. Genius and Willie Maude (Wright) Merritt; m. Craig Wayne Finley, Aug. 10, 1968; children: Craig Wayne Jr., Jarret Lee. *Father, Genius Merritt, served as a NCO in the United States Army in World War II. Genius served as pastor of the Bethsaida Baptist Church in Stone Mountain, Georgia. While a career employee with the Communicable Disease Center in Atlanta, Georgia, Genius was lauded for inventing a gadget to restrain small laboratory animals while simultaneously decreasing their trauma during experiments. Sarah's parents served as foster parents in Fulton County, Georgia. After Genius's death, Willie Maude remained a foster parent. After completing high school and/or post secondary education, her foster children maintain steady employment as paraprofessionals in Metropolitan Atlanta.* BA, Spelman Coll., 1968; postgrad., Atlanta U., 1968-69. Cert. GPS/MAPP leader 2001. Job placement advisor Marsh Draughton Bus. Coll., Atlanta, 1971-72; child attendant Fulton County Juvenile Ct., Atlanta, 1972; social worker Fulton County Dept. Family and Children Svcs., Atlanta, 1972-2000, casework supr., 1976-98, Title VI customer svc. coord. Ctrl. City/North Area office, 1990-98; RTD Fulton County Govt., 1996—2005, State of Ga., 2004—05; counselor/asst. to the project dir. Right Way Home Project N.W. Area Office, 1998-99; social svcs. case mgr. Placement Resource Devel. N.W. Area Office, 2000; social worker Clayton County Dept. Family and Children Svcs., Jonesboro, Ga., 2000—05; co-leader GPS/MAPP, 2001—05; ret. Supr. Count on Me video Ga. Dept. Human Resources, 1987. Vol. coord. family support program Family Support Group of Atlanta Detachment of 2d Army Maneuver Tng. Command.; vol. family support coun. 87th Maneuver Area Command (now 4th Brigade, 87th Divsn.), 1991-93; del. Ft. McPherson (Ga.) Army Family Symposium, 1992, 3d ann. worldwide USAR Family Support Conf., St. Louis, 1992. Mem.: Fulton County Ret. Employees Assn., Ga. County Welfare Assn., Nat. Alumnae Assn. Spelman Coll., Womens Aux. Ga. VFW. Baptist. Avocations: poetry, reading, volunteer work, stress mgmt. Personal E-mail: maudngen@aol.com.

FINLEY, SKIP, media consultant, communications executive; b. Ann Arbor, Mich., July 23, 1948; s. Ewell W. and Mildred Virginia (Johnson) F.; m. Karen Michele Woolard, May 6, 1971; children: Kharma I., R. Kristin. Student, Northeastern U., 1966-71. Owner Skifin Gallery, Boston, 1970-71; floor dir. Sta. WHDH-TV, Boston, 1971; floor mgr., asst. dir., producer Sta. WSBK TV, Boston, 1971-72; account exec. Sta. WRKO-AM, Boston, 1972-73; account mgr. Humphrey, Browning, MacDougall Advt., Boston, 1973-74; sales mgr. Sta. WAMO-AM-FM Sheridan Broadcasting Corp., 1974-75, gen. mgr. Sta. WAMO-AM-FM, 1975-76, v.p. radio div. Pitts., 1976-77; dir. of sales Sheridan Broadcasting Network, 1977-79, exec. v.p., gen. mgr., 1979-81, pres., 1981-82; gen. ptnr. Sta. KEZO AM-FM, Omaha, 1983-88, Sta. KDAB-FM, Salt Lake City and Ogden, Utah, 1985-90; pres., gen. mgr. Sta. WKYS-FM, Washington, 1988-95; pres., CEO, Albimar Communications, Washington, 1982-95; CEO, COO Am. Urban Radio Networks, Pitts., 1995-98; pres., CEO Answers, Solutions, 1999—2003; v. chmn. Inner City Broadcasting Corp., 2003—. Contbr. numerous articles on media-related subjects to various publs. Testimony to House subcom. on Communications, 1977, Congl. Black Caucus, 1990; mem. bd. overseers, trustee Vineyard Open Land Found. Recipient Excellence in Media award Nat. Assn. Media Women, 1981, Communicator of Yr. award Washington Area Media Orgn., 1982, New Horizons award D.C. Gen. Hosp., Washington, 1990, Advocacy in Edn. award D.C. Pub. Schs., Washington, 1990, Radio Wayne award as best overall broadcaster Radio Ink Mag., 1994. Mem. Nat. Assn. Black Owned Broadcasters (bd. dirs. 1977-95), Radio Advt. Bur. (bd. dirs. 1990—, chair 1997-98), Nat. Assn. Broadcasters (bd. dirs., vice chair radio bd. 1990-94), Nat. Thespian Soc., The Advt. Coun., Inc. (bd. dirs. 1998—99), Martha's Vineyard Rod and Gun Club, Lowes Island Golf Club (founding adv. bd. govs. 1992-97). Avocations: computers, model trains, shooting, automobiles, yoga, fishing. Office: Inner City Broadcasting Corp 3 Pk Ave 40th Flr New York NY 10016-4244 Office Phone: 212-592-0406.

FINLEY, STEVEN R., lawyer; b. Apr. 25, 1946; BA cum laude, Yale U., 1968; JD, Harvard U., 1973. Bar: NY 1974. Ptnr. corp. transactions practice group Gibson, Dunn & Crutcher, NYC. Mem. exec. com. Gibson Dunn & Crutcher. Mem. ABA, Assn. of Bar of City of NY Office: Gibson Dunn & Crutcher 200 Park Ave Fl 47 New York NY 10166-0193 Office Phone: 212-351-3920. Office Fax: 212-351-5226. Business E-Mail: sfinley@gibsondunn.com.

FINLEY, WAYNE HOUSE, medical educator; b. Goodwater, Ala., Apr. 7, 1927; s. Byron Bruce and Lucille (House) F.; m. Sara Will Crews, July 6, 1952; children: Randall Wayne, Sara Jane. BS, Jacksonville State U., 1948; MA, U. Ala., 1950, MS, 1955, PhD, 1958, MD, 1960; postgrad., U. Uppsala, Sweden, 1961-62. Cert. clin. cytogenetics Am. Bd. Med. Genetics, 1983. Sci. tchr. High Sch., Tuscaloosa, Ala., 1949-51; intern U. Ala. Hosps. and Clinics, 1960-61; from asst. prof. to assoc. prof. pediat. U. Ala. Sch. Medicine, 1962-70, prof., 1970-96, asst. prof. biochemistry, 1965-75, prof., 1975-96, asst. prof. physiology and biophysics, 1968-75, assoc. prof., 1975-96, chmn. med. student rsch. day, 1965-75, dir. Lab. Med. Genetics, 1966-96, prof. epidemiology, pub. health and epidmiology, 1975-96, prof. emeritus, 1996—, adj. prof. biology, 1980-96, chmn. faculty coun. Sch. Medicine, 1977-78, 84-87. Dir. med. genetics grad. program U. Ala. at Birmingham, 1983-96, dir. Am. Bd. Med. Genetics approved tng. program, 1978-96, dir. med. genetics residency program, 1995-98; chmn. Carey Phillips Travel Fellowship, 1972—; mem. com. on genetic counseling Children's Bur., Dept. HEW, 1966-67; nat. adv. rsch. resources coun. NIH and HEW, 1977-80; sr. scientist Comprehensive Cancer Ctr., Cystic Fibrosis Rsch. Ctr., Ctr. for Health Risk Assessment and Disease Prevention, 1982-96; bd. dirs. Southeastern Regional Genetics Group, 1982-2000, editor newsletter, 1997-2000; chmn. steering com. Reynolds Hist. Libr. Assocs., 1981—, Com. on Future Needs in Med. Genetics, Genetics Svc. Br., USPHS, 1987, Carmichael Fund for Grad. Students, 1989—; faculty rep. U. Ala. Sys. Bd. Trustees, 1995-96; senator U. Ala. at Birmingham Faculty Senate, 1995-96; mem. adv. and nominating com. Ala. Healthcare Hall of Fame, 1998—. Contbr. articles on human malformations and clin. cytogenetics to tech. jours. Deacon Dawson Meml. Bapt. Ch., 1994—. With AUS, 1945-46, 51-53; lt. col. Res.; ret. Recipient Med. award Ala. Assn. Retarded Children, 1969, Outstanding Educators of Am., 1971, Turlington award, 1982, Disting. Faculty Lectr. award U. Ala. Med. Ctr., 1983, Wayne H. and Sara C. Finley chair in med. genetics U. Ala., Birmingham, 1986, Alumnus of Yr. award Jacksonville State U., 1989, Portrait Reynolds Libr., 1991, Will Gaines Holmes award Childrens Aid Soc., 1999, Brother Bryan Humanitarian award, 2001, Gardner award Ala. Acad. Sci., Samuel Buford Word award Med. Assn. State of Ala., 2003, Lifetime Achievement award Birmingham Bus. Jour., 2003, Disting. Svc. award U. Ala. Med. Alumni, 2005; named to Ala. Healthcare Hall of Fame, 2001; Finley-Compass Bank Genetics Conf. Ctr. established at U. Ala. Birmingham, 2001. Fellow Am. Coll. Med. Genetics (founder, edn. com. 1993-97, program dir. 1996), Royal Soc. Medicine; mem. AMA (Physicians Recognition award 1971, 75, 81, 84, 87, 90, 93, 96), AAAS, N.Y. Acad. Scis., Soc. Exptl. Biology and Medicine, Am. Inst. Chemists, Am. Fedn. Clin. Rsch., Am. Soc. Human Genetics, So. Med. Assn., So. Soc. Pediat. Rsch., Med. Assn. Ala. (counsellor 1990—), Jefferson County Med. Soc. (maternal and child health com. 1975-79, chmn. 1976-77, pres. 1983), Jefferson County Pediat. Soc., Ala. Acad. Sci. (trustee 1991—), Caduceus Club (pres. 1984-86), NIH Alumni Assn., U. Ala. Sch. Medicine Alumni Assn. (pres. 1974-75, Disting. Alumni award 1978, Disting. Svc. award 2005), Greater Birmingham Area C. of C. (bd. dirs. 1983-86), Newcomen Soc., Kiwanis (pres. Shades Valley 1973-74), Rotary, SAR, Sigma Xi (pres. U. Ala. Birmingham chpt. 1972-73), Kappa Delta Pi, Phi Delta Kappa, Alpha Omega Alpha, Phi Beta Pi, Omicron Delta Kappa. Baptist. Home: 3412 Brookwood Rd Birmingham AL 35223-2023 Office: U Ala Dept Genetics Univ Station Birmingham AL 35294-0017 Office Phone: 205-934-4983. Personal E-mail: wfinley1942@charter.net.

FINLEY, YVONNE SMITH, retired social worker; b. St. Louis, Sept. 10, 1936; d. Walter Edward and Carenthia Springfield Smith; children: Benjamin Tai, Cicely Y. Taylor. BS, St. Louis (Mo.) U., 1958, MSW, 1962. LCSW Ill., 1994. Social worker Ill. Dept. Children and Family Svcs., Chgo., 1962—67, 1971—75; social work coord. Family Care Ill., Chgo., 1978—99; clin. dir. Cabrini-Green Youth and Family Svcs., Chgo., 2001—05; ret., 2005. Named Outstanding Social Worker, St. Louis (Mo.) U., 1987; recipient Tolton award, St. Philip Neri Parish, 1993. Home: 9351 S Cregier Chicago IL 60617 Office Phone: 312-377-4735 230.

FINN, A. MICHAEL, corporate communications specialist; b. Trenton, N.J., Oct. 4, 1929; s. Charles and Blanche (Englander) Finn; m. Antoinette Mary DiLeo, Feb. 2, 1957; children: Tracey Maureen, Alison Mary Finn Davis, Christopher Charles. Student, U. Pa., 1947-49; BA in Journalism, U. Md., 1952. Reporter Balt. Sun, 1947-54; sports editor Prentice Hall, Inc., N.Y.C., 1955-57; dir. advt. and pub. rels. Cypress Gardnes, Winter Haven, Fla., 1957-58; account supr. Hill & Knowlton, Inc., N.Y.C., 1958-64; v.p. PR Assocs., N.Y.C., 1964-70; pres. Michael Finn Assocs., N.Y.C., 1970-77; v.p. pub. affairs STP Corp., Ft. Lauderdale, Fla., 1977-78; dir. pub. rels. Esmark Inc., Chgo., 1978-79; sr. v.p., nat. dir. pub. rels. divsn. Cunningham & Walsh, Inc., N.Y.C., 1979-87; chmn., CEO E.B. Wilson Pub. Rels., 1987-88; CEO FCS Comms. Inc., N.Y.C., 1988—90; cons. mgmt. comm., 1990—. Guest lectr. numerous colls. and univs. Editor, author: books on sports, recreation, self help, 1955—57; contbr. articles to publs. Mem. various coms. Bronxville PTA, 1970—76, pres., 1976—77; mem. Bronxville Adult Edn., 1980—81; bd. dirs. Cath. Comm. Found., 1987—2000; vol. Colonial Williamsburg Found., 1995—; mem. Williamsburg Land Conservancy, 1997—. With Intelligence U.S. Army, 1952—55. Mem.: Pub. Rels. Soc. Am. (accredited), Ford's Colony Country Club. Home: 100 Eagle Williamsburg VA 23188-7428

FINN, ALBERT FRANK, JR., physician; b. Huntington, N.Y., Sept. 30, 1956; s. Albert F. and Margaret F. (May) F.; m. Anna M. Cannella, July 19, 1982; children: Anastasia, Alexandria, Abigail. BS cum laude, St. John's U., 1980; MD cum laude, SUNY, Syracuse, 1984. Diplomate Am. Bd. Internal Medicine, Am. Bd. Pathology, Am. Bd. Allergy and Immunology. Intern gen. medicine SUNY, Stony Brook, 1984-85, resident clin. pathology, 1985-88, resident internal medicine, 1988-89, allergy and clin. immunology fellow, 1989-91, clin. assoc. instr., 1985-91, cons. divsn. lab. medicine Med. Ctr., 1988-91, clin. asst. prof. medicine, 1991-92, head sect. on allergy, 1991-92; clin. assoc. prof. medicine, microbiology and immunology Med. U. S.C., Charleston, 1992—. Adj. asst. prof. St. John's U., N.Y.C., 1991-92 Contbr. articles to profl. jours. Mem. com. on advanced cardiac life support Am. Heart Assn., Nassau County, NY, 1988—92; mem. Am. Lung Assn., SC, 1992—94, pres. Coastal br. Nassau County, SC. Mem. ACP (bd. rev. course allergy and immunology sect. 1992), Am. Acad. Allergy and Immunology (task force 1994), Am. Soc. Clin. Pathology (course dir. lyme borreliosis 1989-92), S.C. Soc. Allergy & Immunology (pres. 1998-2000), Dorchester County Med. Soc. (pres. 1997-98), Rho Chi (pres.), Alpha Omega Alpha. Avocations: fishing, antique collecting, boating, skiing. Office: Allergy & Asthma Ctrs of Charleston PA 9165 University Blvd Charleston SC 29406-9120

FINN, BRIAN D., financial services executive; b. 1960; BS in econ., Wharton Sch., U. Pa., 1982. Previous mng. dir. and co-head- mergers and acquisitions Credit Suisse First Boston, 1982—97; prin. Clayton, Dubilier & Rice, 1997—2002; co-pres. instl. securities Credit Suisse First Boston, NYC, 2002—04, pres., 2004—, also mem. Office Chmn., 2002—, also mem. exec. bd. and oper. com., 2002—; mem. exec. bd. Credit Suisse Group, 2003—. Mem. undergraduate exec. bd. Wharton Sch., U. Pa.; bd. dirs. City Kids Found. Office: Credit Suisse First Boston 11 Madison Ave New York NY 10010-3629

FINN, CHESTER EVANS, retired lawyer; b. Dayton, Ohio, July 13, 1918; s. Samuel Lawrence and Lillian Rose (Evans) F.; m. Phyllis Muriel Kessel, Apr. 29, 1942 (dec. Oct. 30, 1987); children: Chester E. Jr., Natalie K., Samuel J.; m. Theodora K. Wilks, Sept. 18, 1988. BA, Yale U., 1940; LLB, Harvard U., 1946. Bar: Ohio 1947, U.S. Dist. Ct. (so. dist.) Ohio 1949, U.S. Ct. Claims 1949, U.S. Ct. Appeals (6th cir.) 1966, U.S. Supreme Ct. 1975, U.S. Ct. Internat. Trade 1984. Assoc. Estabrook, Finn & McKee, Dayton, 1947-53, ptnr., 1953-83, Porter, Wright, Morris & Arthur, Dayton, 1983-92, of counsel, 1992-99; ret., 1999. Pres. Dayton United Way, 1969; trustee various civic groups. Lt. USNR, 1942-45, PTO. Mem. ABA, Ohio Bar Assn., Dayton Bar Assn. (pres. 1969), Dayton Bicycle Club, Belfair Golf Club (Bluffton, S.C.). Avocations: golf, travel. Home: 501 Tidepointe Way Apt 5101 Hilton Head Island SC 29928

FINN, EDWIN A., JR., publishing executive; BA in English and Polit. Sci., Tufts U.; MA in Internat. Banking and Fin., Columbia U. Asst. mng. editor Blackstone Valley Tribune, 1970; mng. editor Southbridge (Mass.) Daily News, 1970; nat. copyreader The Wall St. Jour., N.Y.C., 1980—81, editor fgn. desk, 1981—84, banking and fin. reporter Dallas bur., 1984—85; sr. editor internat. bus. and fin. Forbes Mag., 1986—89, asst. mng. editor, 1989—90; editor Am. Banker, 1990—92; mng. editor Barron's, The Dow Jones Bus. and Fin. Weekly, NYC, 1993—95, editor, 1995—, pres., 1998—, pub., 2000—01. Chmn., editor-in-chief SmartMoney, 2002—. Office: Barron's 200 Liberty St New York NY 10281-1003

FINN, GERALD C., real estate company executive; m. Norma Finn. Chmn., CEO, founder New Am. Internat., Hightstown, NJ, 1978—. Lectr. in field; bd. mem. First Washington State Bank; mem. adv. bd. Comml. Property World; founding mem. U. Pa. Wharton Real Estate Ctr. Mem.: Indsl. Devel. Rsch. Coun., Internat. Assn. Corp. Real Estate Execs., Internat. Coun. Shopping Ctrs. Office: New Am Internat Inc PO Box 950 572 US Route 130 Hightstown NJ 08520

FINN, JEFFREY M., real estate company executive; m. Cherie Finn; 2 children. Grad. cum laude, Boston U. Lic. real estate broker N.J. Pres., COO New Am. Internat., Inc., Hightstown, NJ. Mem. editl. adv. bd.: Shopping Ctr. World mag., Nat. Real Estate Investor mag. Trustee The Peddie Sch.; founding mem. U. Pa. Wharton Real Estate Ctr. Named one of 40 Stars of Tomorrow, Nat. Real Estate Investor, Top Execs. to Watch, Real Estate Forum. Mem.: Internat. Assn. Corp. Real Estate Execs. (v.p. N.J. chpt.), Indsl. Devel. Rsch. Coun., Internat. Coun. Shopping Ctrs. Office: New Am Internat INc PO Box 950 572 US Rte 130 Hightstown NJ 08520

FINN, PETER, public relations executive; b. N.Y.C., Mar. 31, 1954; s. David and Laura (Zeisler) F.; m. Sarah Duncan; children: Noah J., Emily M. BA, Brown U., 1976; MA, Columbia U., 1977. Researcher Research & Forecasts Inc., N.Y.C., 1977-79, dir. ops., 1979-81, chmn., 1981-84; chmn. fin. com. Ruder-Finn, Inc. (formerly Ruder, Finn & Rotman, Inc.), N.Y.C., 1984—, CFO, 1985-94, exec. v.p., 1986-87, chmn. exec. com., 1988—2001, CEO, 2001—. Chmn. Catskill Mt. Found., Inc., 1998—; bd. dirs. Hunter Found., Inc., 1998—. Office: Ruder-Finn Inc 301 E 57th St New York NY 10022-2900*

FINN, PETER MICHAEL, broadcast executive; b. Milton, Mass., Feb. 19, 1936; s. Matthew Charles and Mary Germaine (Ireland) F.; m. Judith Mary Barry, Sept. 7, 1957 (div. Aug. 1996); children: Pamela Ann, Mary Kathryn, Matthew Ireland; m. Debra Jo McGraw, Oct. 18, 1997. AB, Holy Cross Coll., 1956; MBA, George Washington U., 1962; A.M.P., Harvard U., 1980. Account exec. J. Walter Thompson Co., N.Y.C., 1962-64, account supr., 1966-67; account exec. Foote Cone & Belding, N.Y.C., 1964-66, v.p., account supr., 1967-68, Doyle Dane Bernbach, N.Y.C., 1968-70; sr. v.p., dir. F.W. Free, N.Y.C., 1970-74; pres. Henderson Advt., Greenville, S.C., 1974-80, Bozell & Jacobs, Dallas, 1980-85, also dir.; sr. ptnr., div. pres. Whittle Communications, Knoxville, Tenn., 1985-92; pres., CEO Peter Matthew Prodns., NYC, 1992—. Mem. Greater Greenville Planning Council, 1976-79, Dallas Citizens Council. Served to lt. USNR, 1957-62. Mem. Am. Assn. Advt. Agys. (bd. govs.), Am. Advt. Fedn., Am. Mktg. Assn. Office: Peter Matthew Prodns 523 W 45th St New York NY 10036

FINN, ROBERT, writer, educator; b. Boston, July 13, 1930; s. Edward Anthony and E. Caroline (Seifert) F.; m. Mary Pacana, Oct. 12, 1957; children: Laurence, Elaine. BA, Boston U., 1952. Staff reporter, music-drama critic New Bedford (Mass.) Standard-Times, 1956-59, Akron (0hio) Beacon Jour., 1959-64; music critic Cleve. Plain Dealer, 1964-92. Mem. guest faculty Rockefeller Found. project for tng. music critics, 1965, 66 Author: Exploring Classical Music, 2000, A Musical Journey, Con Amore, 2003; contbr. to Opera News mag., Am. Record Guide. Served with AUS, 1953-56. Co-recipient ASCAP-Deems Taylor award for, 1972, 74, 78, 80 Mem. Music Critics Assn. (life, exec. bd. 1975-83, v.p. 1983-85, pres. 1985-89). Roman Catholic. Home: 1211 Blanchester Rd Cleveland OH 44124-1325 E-mail: robertfinn@aol.com.

FINN, ROBERT W., bishop; b. St. Louis, Mo., Apr. 2, 1953; s. Theodore and Betty (Schneider) Finn. Grad., St. Louis Preparatory Sem. North, 1971; BA in Philosophy, Cardinal Glennon Coll., 1975; M in Theology, Angelicum U., Rome, 1979; MEd, St. Louis U., 1989. Ordained priest, St. Louis, 1979; assoc. pastor Diocese of St. Louis; mem. faculty St. Francis Borgia Regional H.S., Washington, 1983—89; adminstr. St. Dominic H.S., O'Fallon, Mo., 1989—96; named dir. continuing formation of priests Archdiocese of St. Louis, Mo., 1996, editor St. Louis Review, 1999—2004; ordained bishop, 2004; Coadjutor Bishop of Kansas City-St. Joseph, 2004—05; Bishop of Kansas City-St. Joseph, Mo., 2005—. Roman Catholic. Office: Diocese of Kansas City-St Joseph PO Box 419037 300 E 36th St Kansas City MO 64141-6037*

FINN, STEPHEN MARTIN, film producer; b. Indpls., June 21, 1949; s. Martin Joseph and Theresa Diane (Mervar) F.; children: Shawn Marie, Stephanie Michelle, Rhyan Linthicum, Raimie Catherine (dec.). Pres. Equinox Systems, Grand Rapids, Mich., 1975-77, Solstice, Lake Helen, 1978—. Photographer Equitable Gallery, N.Y.C., 1978; contbr. articles profl. mags. Recipient Kinsa award Kodak Internat., N.Y.C., 1978. Mem. Am. Film Inst., Profl. Photographers Am., Aircraft Owners and Pilots Assn., Mensa, Fla. Motion Picture Theater Assn. Home and Office: PO Box 129 Lake Helen FL 32744-0129

FINN, TERRENCE M., lawyer; b. Mpls., Feb. 13, 1948; BA, Yale U., 1970; JD, U. Pa., 1973. Bar: R.I. 1973, U.S. Dist. Ct. R.I. 1973, U.S. Ct. Appeals (1st. cir.) 1982, Mass. 1984. Mng. ptnr. Edwards & Angell, LLP. Mem. R.I. Bar Assn., Mass. Bar Assn., Fla. Bar., Boston Bar Assn. Office: Edwards & Angell 101 Federal St Fl 23 Boston MA 02110-1800

FINNARN, THEODORE ORA, lawyer; b. Greenville, Ohio, Aug. 20, 1949; s. Theodore Lincoln and Jeannie (Kelman) F.; m. Holly C. Bankson, Sept. 15, 1973; children: Shawn April, Theodore O., Thomas A., Alexander H., Alison C. B.Ed., Miami U., 1972; JD cum laude, U. Toledo, 1976. Bar: Ohio 1976, U.S. Dist. Ct. (so. dist.) Ohio 1978. Acting dir. Preble County Cmty. Action Com., 1973, program developer, 1972-73; chief agrl. engr. Finnarn Farms, Greenville, Ohio, 1976—; individual practice law Greenville, 1976—; sec.-treas. Finnarn Devel. Corp., 1977—. Editor articles in legal jours. Bd. dirs. Darke County Ctr. for Arts; active Greenville Friends of Libr., 1977—. Mem. Assn. Trial Lawyers Am., Ohio Acad. Trial Lawyers Am., Ohio, Darke County bar assns., Ohio Farmers Union, Darke County Farmers Union (sec.-treas.), Scribes, Phi Alpha Delta. Democrat. Presbyterian. Home: 3153 Us Route 127 Greenville OH 45331-9717 Office: 201 E 5th St Greenville OH 45331-1937

FINNBERG, ELAINE AGNES, psychologist, editor; b. Bklyn., Mar. 2, 1948; d. Benjamin and Agnes Montgomery (Evans) Finnberg; m. Rodney Lee Herndon, Mar. 1, 1981; 1 child, Andrew Marshal Herndon. BA in Psychology, L.I. U., 1969; MA in Psychology, New Sch. for Social Rsch., 1973; PhD in Psychology, Calif. Sch. Profl. Psychology, 1981. Diplomate Am. Bd. Forensic Examiners, Am. Bd. Forensic Medicine, Am. Bd. Med. Psychotherapists and Psychodiagnosticians, Am. Bd. Disability Analysts (profl. adv. coun.), Am. Bd. Psychol. Specialties, Prescribing Psychologists Register (fellow), lic. psychologist Calif. Rsch. asst. med. sociology Cornell U. Med. Coll., NYC, 1969-70; med. abstractor USV Pharm. Corp., Tuckahoe, NY, 1970-71, Coun. Tobacco Rsch., NYC, 1971-77; editor, writer Found. Thanatology Columbia U., NYC, 1971-76, 1973-74; dir. grief psychology and bereavement counseling San Francisco Coll. Mortuary Scis., 1977-81; rsch. assoc. dept. epidemiology and internat. health U. Calif., San Francisco, 1979-81, asst. clin. prof. dept. family and cmty. medicine, 1985-93, assoc. clin. prof., dept. family and cmty. medicine, 1993—; active med. staff Natividad Med. Ctr., Salinas, Calif., 1984—2002, 2004—, chief psychologist, 1984—96. Asst. chief psychiatry svc. Natividad Med. Ctr., 1985—96, acting chief psychiatry, 1988—89, vice-chair medicine dept., 1991—93, sec.-treas. med. staff, 1992—94; cons. med. staff Salinas Valley Meml. Hosp., 1991—2003, Mee Meml. Hosp., 1996—97; dir. tng. Monterey Psychiat. Health Facility, 1996—97, chief clin. staff, 1996—97; expert cons. Calif. Bd. Psychology; cons. psychologist Calif. Forensic Med. Group, 1984—, Calif. Dept. Mental Health Sexually Violent Predator Program, 1996—. Editor: Jour. Thanatology, 1972—76, Cahtexis, 1976—81, Calif. Psychologist, 1988—95. Mem. Gov.'s adv. bd. Agnews Devel. Ctr., San Jose, Calif., 1988—96, chair, 1989—91, 1994—95. Mem.: APA, Internat. Soc. Police Surgeons, Internat. Rorschach Soc., Soc. Personality Assessment, Assn. Treatment Sexual Abuses, Am. Med. Writers Assn., Assn. Advancement Behavior Therapy, Western Psychol. Assn., Forensic Mental Health Assn. Calif., Mid-Coast Psychol. Assn. (sec. 1985, treas. 1986, pres. 1987, Disting. Svc. to Psychology award 1993), Soc. Behavioral Medicine, Calif. Psychol. Assn. (Disting. Svc. award 1989), Nat. Register Health Svc. Providers Psychology. Personal E-mail: finnberg@sbcglobal.net.

FINNEGAN, CYRIL VINCENT, retired university dean, zoology educator; b. Dover, N.H., July 17, 1922; emigrated to Can., 1958; s. Cyril Vincent and Hilda A. (McClintock) F.; children: Maureen A., Patrick S., Cathaleen C., Kevin S., Eileen D., Gormlaith R., Michaeleen S., Mairead B., Conal E. BS, Bates Coll., Lewiston, Maine, 1946; MS, U. Notre Dame, 1948, PhD, 1951. From instr. to asst. prof. St. Louis U., 1952-56; asst. prof. U. Notre Dame, South Bend, Ind., 1956-58; from asst. prof. to prof. zoology U. B.C., Vancouver, 1958-88, emeritus, 1988—, assoc. dean sci., 1972-79, dean sci., 1979-85, dean emeritus, 1988—, assoc. acad. v.p., 1986-88. Contbr. articles to sci. jours. Served to sgt F.A. and C.E. AUS, 1942-45, NATOUSA, CBI. Postdoctoral research fellow NIH, 1952-53; Killum sr. fellow, 1968-69 Mem. Soc. Devel. Biology, Can. Soc. Cell Biology, Tissue Culture Assn., Internat. Soc. Develop. Biology, Sigma Xi Roman Catholic. Office: U BC Dept Zoology Faculty of Science Vancouver BC Canada V6T 1Z4

FINNEGAN, BROTHER JAMES A., educational administrator, consultant; b. Buffalo; s. Paul and Ruth (Murray) F. BA in Classical Langs., Iona Coll., 1966; MA in Student Pers. Svcs., Montclair State Coll., 1973. Joined Congregation Christian Bros., Roman Cath. Ch., 1962; cert. English and Latin tchr., dir. student svcs., prin., supr., supt. schs., N.J. Tchr. Cath. Meml. High Sch., West Roxbury, Mass., 1966-68; dir. guidance, counselor, tchr. Essex Cath. High Sch., Newark, 1968-73; dir. guidance Iona Prep. Sch., New Rochelle, N.Y., 1973-84; vice prin. Essex Cath. High Sch., East Orange, N.J., 1984-86; prin. Notre Dame-Bishop Gibbons High Sch., Schenectady, 1986-87; assoc. supt. schs. Archdiocese of Newark, Irvington, N.J., 1987—, mem. ednl. endowment bd. Newark, 1991—. Chmn. province long range planning Congregation Christian Bros., New Rochelle, 1989—; cons. Diocese of Metuchen, Perth Amboy, N.J., 1990-92; presenter Archdiocese of Indpls. Archbishop's Summit Cath. Edn., 1992; mem. com. Archdiocese of Newark Catechetical Congress, 1994; chair com. Christian formation & life long edn. Newark Archdiocesan Synod, 1993-94, del. archdiocesan synod, 1993-94; mem. mayor's adv. bd. on health concerns City of Elizabeth, 1993-94; chair prin. evaluation com. Bishop Kearney High Sch., Rochester, N.Y., 1994; mem. mid. states vis. team Mt. St. Mary Acad., Newburgh, N.Y., St. Mary's Boys High Sch., Manhasset, N.Y., Trinity Sch., N.Y.C. Named to Alumni Hall of Fame, Iona Prep. Sch., 1984. Mem. Nat. Cath. Ednl. Assn., Chief Adminstrs. Cath. Edn., Nat. Assn. Bds. Edn., Christian Bros. Ednl. Assn. Office: Office Supt Schs 100 Linden Ave Irvington NJ 07111-2560

FINNEGAN, JOHN D., insurance company executive; b. Jersey City; m. Kathleen Finnegan; 2 children. BA in Polit. Sci., Princeton U., 1971; JD, Fordham U., 1975; MBA, Rutgers U., 1976. Mem. tax. dept. GMAC, 1976—86, dir. strategic planning, 1985; CFO GMAC Mortgage Corp., 1986; asst. treas. worldwide benefits compensation GM, 1987—89, asst. treas. internat. financing ops., 1989—92; exec. v.p., CFO GMAC, 1992—95; v.p., treas. GM, 1995—97; pres. GMAC, 1997—99, chmn., pres., 1999—2002; exec. v.p. GM, 1999—2002; pres., CEO, dir. Chubb Corp., 2002—, chmn., 2003—. Bd. dirs. Merrill Lynch & Co.; mem. Bus. Council, Bus. Roundtable, Fin. Services Roundtable. Office: Chubb Group Ins Cos 15 Mountain View Rd Warren NJ 07059*

FINNEGAN, MICHAEL J., lawyer; b. LA, Dec. 14, 1962; BA cum laude, Loyola Marymount Univ., 1985; JD with honors, Loyola Law Sch., 1988. Bar: Calif. 1988. Ptnr., Litigation practice, mem. mng. bd. Pillsbury Winthrop Shaw Pittman, LA. Bd. dir. Public Counsel. Mem.: ABA, Am. Arbitration Assn., LA Bus. Trial Lawyers Assn., LA County Bar Assn. Office: Pillsbury Winthrop Shaw Pittman Suite 2800 725 S Figueroa St Los Angeles CA 90017 Office Phone: 213-488-7272. Office Fax: 213-629-1033. Business E-Mail: michael.finnegan@pillsburylaw.com.

FINNEGAN, NEAL FRANCIS, retired banker; b. Boston, Mar. 28, 1938; s. Neal Francis and Mary Theresa (McNeil) F.; children: Theresa, Lynn, Neal, Wayne. BS, Northeastern U., 1961; MBA, Babson Coll., 1969. With Shawmut Bank of Boston, 1961-80, sr. v.p. in charge of OIC comml. banking, 1977-80; pres., chief exec. officer Worcester Bancorp Inc., Mass., 1980-82; chmn., chief exec. officer Worcester County Nat. Bank, 1980-82; sr. exec. v.p. Shawmut Corp., Boston, 1982-83, vice-chmn., 1983-86, dir., 1982-86; exec. v.p. Shawmut Bank of Boston, N.A., 1983-86; pres., chief operating officer, dir. Bowery Savs. Bank, N.Y.C., 1986-88; exec. v.p. Bankers Trust Co., N.Y.C., 1988-93; chmn., CEO USTrust, Boston, 1993-99; chmn. Citizens Bank of Mass., Boston, 2000—04. Bd. dirs. Citizens Capital, Inc. Vice chmn. exec. com., trustee, former chmn. bd. trustees Cath. Charities; vice chmn. Mass. chpt. Multiple Sclerosis Soc.; chmn. bd. trustees Northeastern U., Boston, 1998; bd. dirs. Ireland C. of C. Office: Citizens Bank 28 State St Boston MA 02109 Office Phone: 617-725-5775.

FINNEGAN, PATRICK, dean, military officer, lawyer; b. Fukuoka, Japan; BS, U.S. Mil. Acad., West Point, 1971; MPA, Kennedy Sch. Govt., Harvard Univ.; JD, Univ. Va. Bar: Va., U.S. Supreme Ct. Commd. 2d lt. U.S. Army, advanced through grades to brig. gen.; dep. dir. & criminal law instr. JAG Sch., Charlottesville, Va.; staff judge advocate MacDill AFB, Fla.; legal adv. joint spl. ops. command, U.S. European command; staff judge advocate U.S. Mil. Acad., West Point, 1998—99, prof., head dept. law, 1999—2005, dean of academic bd., 2005—. Editor: Va. Law Rev.; contbr. articles to profl. legal jours. Mem.: Phi Kappa Phi, Order of the Coif. Office: USMA Office of the Dean Bldg 600 West Point NY 10996

FINNEGAN, SARA ANNE (SARA F. LYCETT), publisher; b. Balt., Aug. 1, 1939; d. Lawrence Winfield and Rosina Elva (Huber) F.; m. Isaac C. Lycett, Jr., Aug. 31, 1974. BA, Sweet Briar Coll., 1961; MLA, Johns Hopkins U., 1965; exec. program, U. Va. Grad. Sch. Bus., 1977. Tchr., chmn. history dept. Hannah More Acad., Reisterstown, Md., 1961-65; redactor Williams & Wilkins Co., Balt., 1965-66, asst. head redactory, 1966-71, editor book div., 1971-75, assoc. editor-in-chief, 1975-77, v.p., editor-in-chief, 1977-81, pres. book div., 1981-88, group pres., 1988-94; editor Kalends, 1973-78, 89-92; exec. sponsor jour. Histochemistry and Cytochemistry, 1973-77. Dir. Passano Found., 1979—91. Editor: Visions, Friends of Art of Sweet Briar Coll. Mag., 2001—03. Trustee St. Timothy's Sch., Stevenson, Md., 1974—83; mem. adv. bd. Balt. Ind. Schs. Scholarship Fund, 1977—81; mem. adv. coun. grad. study Coll. Notre Dame of Md., 1983; mem. bd. overseers Sweet Briar Coll., 1987—88, bd. dirs., 1988—2000, chmn.-elect, 1994, chmn., 1995—2000, dir. emerita, 2003—; docent The Walters Art Mus., 1994—; v.p. The Walters Art Mus. Docents, 2000—01, pres., 2001—02; bd. trustees The Walters Art Mus., 2001—02; bd. dirs. The Woman's Indsl. Exch., Balt., 1997—2000, v.p., 1998—2000; bd. dirs. Friends of Art of Sweet Briar Coll., 2000—, The Hamilton St. Club, 2003—, The Art Seminar Group, 2004—. Mem. Assn. Am. Pubs. (exec. coun. profl. and scholarly pub. divsn. 1984-85), Internat. Sci., Tech. and Med. Pubs. Assn. (group exec. 1986-93, chmn.-elect 1988, chmn. 1989-92). Republican. Lutheran.

FINNELL, JOHN T., emergency physician, educator; b. Stamford, Conn., Sept. 10, 1965; s. Joe Ann and John T. Finnell; m. Maria E. Lof, Feb. 2, 2002. BS, U. Vt., Burlington, 1983—87. Asst. prof., emergency medicine U. Minn., Mpls., 1995—2002; asst. prof., clin. emergency medicine Ind. U. Sch. Medicine, Indpls., 2002—. Fellow: Am. Coll. Emergency Physicians. Office: Regenstrief Inst 1050 Wishard Blvd RG5 Indianapolis IN 46278 Office Phone: 317-630-7400. Office Fax: 317-630-6962. E-mail: jtfinnell@gmail.com.

FINNELL, MICHAEL HARTMAN, mining executive; b. LA, Jan. 27, 1927; s. Jules Bertram and Maribel Hartman (Schumacher) F.; m. Grace Vogel, Sept. 11, 1954 (div. June 1964); children: Lesley Finnell Blanchard, Carter Hartman, Hunter Vogel. BA, U. Toronto, 1950; MBA, Harvard U., 1952; HHD (hon.), Capital U., Columbus, Ohio, 1980. Sec.-treas. Triad Oil Co. Ltd., 1952-62, v.p., dir., 1962-65; pres. Devon-Palmer Oils Ltd., 1966—70; v.p., dir. Can. Hydrocarbons, Ltd., 1970, pres., 1970—71, Montreal River Internat. Silver Mines Ltd., 1972—. Trustee Capital U., Columbus, 1982—94; life trustee Columbus Mus. of Art. Mem. Calif. Club, Annandale Golf Club, Ranchmen's Club, Calgary Petroleum Club, Calgary Golf and Country Club, Nantucket Yacht Club. Home: 724 Holladay Rd Pasadena CA 91106-4115 Office: 625 Fair Oaks Ave Ste 288 South Pasadena CA 91030-2668 Office Phone: 626-403-9588.

FINNERAN, JOHN G., JR., lawyer; b. Feb. 1950; m. Catherine A. Cotter; 2 children. BA in history, Pa. State U., 1972; JD, Georgetown U. Bar: Va. 1981. Atty. Cleary, Gottlieb, Steen & Hamilton, Washington, 1981—91; assoc. gen. counsel resolutions Fed. Deposit Ins. Corp., 1991—94, acting dep. gen. counsel, 1994; sr. v.p., gen. counsel, corp. sec. Capital One Fin. Corp., McLean, Va., 1994, now exec. v.p., gen. counsel, corp. sec. Bd. dirs. Local Initiatives Support Corp., NYC, chmn. local adv. com. Richmond, Va. Recipient Outstanding Liberal Arts Alumni Award, Pa. State U. Coll. Liberal Arts, 2003. Office: Capital One Fin Corp 1680 Capital One Dr Mc Lean VA 22102

FINNERAN, JOHN PATRICK, JR., finance company executive, educator; b. N.Y.C., Sept. 11, 1959; s. John Patrick and Mary Elenor (McCorry) F.; m. Dena Jo Golden, Mar. 19, 1983; children: John Patrick III, Meagan E., Brendan R., Ryan E., Katelyn J. BBA, Siena Coll., 1981; M Acctg., George Washington U., 1983. CPA, D.C., Va. Staff auditor Price Waterhouse, Washington, 1983-84; staff cons. KMG Peat Marwick (Main Hurdman), Washington, 1984-85; mgr. fin. analysis Finalco Group, Inc., McLean, Va., 1985-87; investment analyst Potomac Capital Investment Corp., Washington, 1987-89, mgr. fin. planning and investments, 1989-91, treas., 1991—, v.p., 1994—. Adj. lectr. acctg. and bus. No. Va. C.C., Annandale, 1984—. Named Team Leader of Yr., Dale Carnegie Ctr. Excellence, 1993. Mem. AICPA, D.C. Inst. CPAs, Va. Inst. CPAs, Nat. Assn. Corp. Treas., Fin. Execs. Inst., KC (3d degree). Republican. Roman Catholic. Avocations: golf, reading, children's sporting events, new york giants. Office: Potomac Capital Investment Corp 900 19th St NW Ste 600 Washington DC 20006-2105

FINNERAN, KATIE (KATHLEEN FINNERAN), actress; b. Chgo., Jan. 22, 1971; Actor: (Broadway plays) On Borrowed Time, 1991—92, Two Shakespearean Actors, 1992, My Favorite Year, 1992—93, In the Summer House, 1993, The Heiress, 1995, Neil Simon's Proposals, 1997—98, The Iceman Cometh, 1999, Cabaret, 2000—01, Noises Off, 2001—02 (Tony award for Best Performance by a Featured Actor in a Play, 2002, Outer Critics Circle award, Drama Desk award nomination); (films) Night of the Living Dead, 1990, You've Got Mail, 1998, Liberty Heights, 1999, Live at Five, 2005, Bewitched, 2005; (TV films) Plainsong, 2004; (TV series) Bram and Alice, 2002, Wonderfalls, 2003, The Inside, 2005—, (guest appearance) Sex and the City, 1998, Frasier, 1999, All My Children, 1999, Oz, 2001.*

FINNERTY, FRANCES MARTIN, medical administrator; b. Asheville, N.C., Dec. 23, 1936; d. Robert James and Elizabeth Howerton (Babbitt) Martin; m. Richard Phillip Caputo, Sept. 23, 1961 (div. 1974); m. Frank A. Finnerty Jr., July 26, 1975; children: Jonathan, Robert, Richard. Student, Mary Washington Coll., 1954-55, Croft Coll., 1955-57. Dist. mgr. Bus. Census Dept. Commerce, Suitland, Md., 1969-71; program coord. Georgetown U. D.C. Gen. Hosp., Washington, 1972-76; clin. mgr. Hypertension Ctr. Washington, 1976-82; project dir. PharmaKinetic Clin. Rsch. Labs., Balt., 1983; dir. mktg. Classic Glass, Alexandra, Va., 1984-86; office adminstr. Frank A. Finnerty Jr., M.D., Washington, 1987—. Cons. U.S. Census, U.S. Army, The Pentagon, Washington, 1969-70; cons. mapping ops. U.S. Census, Prince Georges County, Md., 1970; cons. paramedics pers. Merck Sharpe & Dohme, West Point, Pa., 1974. Contbr. articles to profl. jours. Recipient Cmty. Svc. award Dist. of Columbia, 1980. Mem. Am. Art League (Disting. Artist award 1993), Nat. Assn. Women in Arts, Dist. Med. Soc. Wives. Avocations: artist, landscape artist, reading. Home: 5 Eagle Circle Brevard NC 28712-4205 Office Phone: 828-883-8407.

FINNERTY, JOSEPH GREGORY, JR., lawyer; b. Balt., Jan. 25, 1937; s. Joseph Gregory and Sara Virginia (Porter) F.; m. Alice Ann Fannon, Sept. 14, 1958 (div. May 1989); children: Sara F. Kelly, Joseph G. III, Alice Ann Martin, Thomas P., Kathleen F. Curtis, Eileen F. McCoy; m. Deborah Barrett, Oct. 20, 1989; 1 child, Bridget P. BS in Physics, Loyola Coll., 1958; JD, U. Md., 1963. Bar: Md. 1963, D.C. 1981, N.Y. 1993. Law clk. Supreme Bench, Balt., 1960-63; assoc. Piper & Marbury, Balt., 1963-66; ptnr. Gallagher, Evelins & Finnerty, Balt., 1966-71; gen. counsel The Ryland Group, Columbia, Md., 1971-72; ptnr. Piper & Marbury, NYC, 1972-99; mng. ptnr. NY office Piper Rudnick LLP (now DLA Piper Rudnick Gray Cary), NYC, 1999—. 2nd lt. U.S. Army, 1958-59. Fellow Am. Coll. Trial Lawyers, Am. Bar Found.; mem. ABA, N.Y. State Bar Assn., Md. State Bar Assn. Avocation: farming. Office: DLA Piper Rudnick Gray Cary 1251 Avenue Of The Americas New York NY 10020-1104 Office Phone: 212-835-6110. Office Fax: 212-835-6001. Business E-Mail: joseph.finnerty@dlapiper.com.

FINNERTY, JOSEPH GREGORY, III, lawyer; b. Balt., Apr. 25, 1960; s. Joseph Gregory Jr. and Alice Ann (Fannon) F.; m. Amy Caroline Shull, Nov. 12, 1988 (div. 1999); life ptnr. Donna Paparella; children: Katherine Pagett, Alice Olivia, Samuel Joseph. AB in English Lit., Hamilton Coll., 1982; JD, U. Md., Balt., 1987. Bar: N.Y. 1988, US Dist. Ct. (so., ea., no., we. NY, Ariz., ea., we. Ark., Colo., Nebr. dist.), US Ct. Appeals (2d cir.). Assoc. Rogers & Wells, N.Y.C., 1988-94; prin. ptnr. McCarrick, Finnerty & Mayer, N.Y.C., 1994-96; ptnr. Piper & Marbury, L.L.P., N.Y.C., 1996-99, Piper & Rudnick LLP, 1999—2004; ptnr. head of NY Litigation DLA Piper Rudnick Gray Cary, NYC, 2005—. Contbr. articles to profl. jours. Trustee Bklyn. Mus. Mem. ABA, Assn. Bar City N.Y. Office: DLA Piper Rudnick Gray Cary 1251 Ave of Americas New York NY 10020-1104 Office Phone: 212-835-6260. Office Fax: 212-835-6001. Business E-Mail: joseph.finnertyIII@dlapiper.com.

FINNERTY, LOUISE HOPPE, food products executive; b. Alexandria, Va., Jan. 19, 1949; d. William G. and Ruth A. (Ehren) Hoppe; m. John D. Finnerty, May 21, 1988; 1 child, William Patrick Taylor. BA, Va. Commonwealth U., 1971; postgrad., Am. U., 1972—73. Staff asst. to Dr. Henry Kissinger NSC, Washington, 1971-73; adminstrv. asst. Nat. Petroleum Coun., Washington, 1973-75; profl. staff mem. Senate Armed Svc. Com., Washington, 1976-81; spl. asst. Office Legis. Affairs, U.S. Dept. State, Washington, 1981-84, dep. asst. sec. of state, 1984-88; mgr. govt. affairs PepsiCo, Inc., Purchase, NY, 1988-91; dir. govt. affairs PepsiCo Foods and Beverages Internat., Somers, NY, 1991-95; v.p. internat. govt. affairs PepsiCo., Inc., Purchase, 1995—2003, v.p. global health and wellness policy, 2004—. Mem. Spring Lake Bath and Tennis Club, Coveleigh Club. Republican. Lutheran. Avocations: reading, gardening, cooking. Home: 400 Park Ave Rye NY 10580-1213 also: 506 2nd Ave Spring Lake NJ 07762-1107 Office: PepsiCo Inc 700 Anderson Hill Rd Purchase NY 10577-1444 Business E-Mail: louise.finnerty@pepsi.com.

FINNEY, ALBERT, actor, director; b.Manchester, England, May 9, 1936; m. Jane Wenham, 1957 (div. 1961); 1 child; m. Anouk Aimee, Aug. 7, 1970 (div. 1978). Litt.D. (hon.), Sussex U., 1965, Salford U., 1979. Assoc. artistic dir. English Stage Co., 1972—; appearances include: The Party, New, London, 1958; Cassio in Othello, and Lysander, Stratford-on-Avon, 1959; The Lily White Boys, Royal Court, 1960; Billy Liar, Cambridge Theatre, 1960; Luther, in Luther, Royal Court Theatre and Phoenix Theatre, 1962-62, N.Y., 1963; Armstrong, in Armstrong's Last Goodnight, Miss Julie and Black Comedy, Chichester, 1965, Old Vic, 1966; A Day in the Death of Joe Egg, N.Y., 1968; Alpha Beta, Royal Court and Appollo, 1972; Krapp's Last Tape, Royal Court, 1973; Cromwell, Royal Court, 1973; Chez Nous, Globe, 1974; Uncle Vanya, and Present Laughter, Royal Exchange, Manchester, Eng., 1977, J.J. Farr, 1987; Nat. theatre appearances include: Love for Love, 1965, Much Ado About Nothing, 1965, A Flea in Her Ear, 1966, Hamlet, 1975, Tamburlaine, 1976, The Country Wife, 1977, The Cherry Orchard, Macbeth, Has "Washington" Legs?, 1978; stage dir. The Freedom of the City, Royal Court, 1973; Loot, Royal Court, 1975; dir. and appeared in The Biko Inquest, 1984, Serjeant Musgrave's Dance, 1984; films include: The Entertainer, 1960, Saturday Night and Sunday Morning, 1960, Tom Jones, 1963, The Victors, 1963, Night Must Fall, 1964, Two for the Road, 1967, Charlie Bubbles, 1967 (also dir.), The Picasso Summer, 1969, Scrooge, 1970, Gumshoe, 1971, Alpha Beta, 1973, Murder on the Orient Express, 1974, The Duellists, 1977, Wolfen, 1981, Loophole, 1981, Looker, 1981, Shoot the Moon, 1982, Annie, 1982, The Dresser, 1983, Under the Volcano, 1983, Orphans, 1987, Miller's Crossing, 1990, The Playboys, 1992, Rich in Love, 1992, The Browning Version, 1994, A Man of No Importance, 1994, The Run of the Country, 1995, Washington Square, 1997, Breakfast of Champions, 1999, Simpatico, 1999, Erin Brockovich, 2000, Traffic, 2000, Hemingway, the Hunter of Death, 2001, Delivering Milo, 2001, Big Fish, 2003, Ocean's Twelve, 2004, (voice) Corpse Bride, 2005; (TV films) Lights, Camera, Annie!, 1982, The Biko Inquest, 1984 (also dir.), Pope John Paul II, 1983, A Simple Man, 1987, The Green Man, 1990, The Wall: Live in Berlin, 1990, The Image, 1990, The Endless Game, 1990, A Rather English Marriage, 1998, The Gathering Storm, 2002, My Uncle Silas II, 2003; (TV series) Emergency Ward 10, 1957; (TV mini series) Cold Lazarus, 1996, Nostromo, 1997. *

FINNEY, CLIFTON DONALD, publishing executive; b. Dubuque, Iowa, Apr. 7, 1941; s. Clifton Monroe and Violet Irene (Snyder) F.; m. Kazuko Akiyama, Aug. 17, 1968; 1 child, Ann. BA in Chemistry, Austin Coll., 1964; PhD in Phys. Chemistry, Kans. State U., 1970. Postdoctoral fellow U. Toronto, Ont., Can., 1969-71; asst. prof. chemistry Drake U., Des Moines, 1971-75; pres. Natural Dynamics, Des Moines and Houston, 1975-86, Golf Physics Co., Baton Rouge, 1986-94, DeerStats, Houston and Baton Rouge, 1996—. Assoc. Ames (Iowa) Lab., U.S. AEC, 1971-75; instr. computer sci. U. Houston, 1984-86. Contbr. articles to Phys. Chemistry, Sci., Computers and Edn. Recipient energy rsch. grant Iowa Energy Policy Coun., 1975, USERDA, 1976. Mem. Am. Chem. Soc., N.Y. Acad. Scis. Achievements include patents in Inertial Weighting Systems for Golf Clubheads and a Superventuri Power Source. Home and Office: 17732 Glenn Knoll Ave Baton Rouge LA 70817-9567

FINNEY, GRAHAM STANLEY, management consultant; b. Greenwich, Conn., Sept. 6, 1930; s. William Stanley and Sarah Margaret (Boswell) F.; m. Katharine Pillsbury Becker, June 22, 1957; children: Sarah Boswell Finney Johnston, Martha Becker, Samuel Warner, Garrett Stevens. Student, Washington and Lee U., 1948-49; BA, Yale U., 1952; MPA, Harvard U., 1954. Planning dir. City of Portland, Maine, 1957-60; asst. exec. dir. Phila. City Planning Commn., 1961-65; exec. dir. Phila. Coun. for Cmty. Advancement, 1965-66; dep. supt. schs. Phila., 1966-69; commr. addiction svcs. agy. City of N.Y.; mng. ptnr. Greater Phila. Partnership, 1975-76; dir. Phila. Partnership, 1973-75; pres. Corp. for Pub./Pvt. Ventures, Phila., 1977-80; sr. ptnr. The Conservation Co., Phila., 1980-87, pres., 1988-95; mgmt. cons.; pres. 21st Century League, 1997-2000. Trustee Seybert Instn., Phila., 1978; dir. Mastery High Charter Sch., Phila., 2001—. Author: Administering Catastrophe, 1975; (with others) Philadelphia: 1776-2076, 1975. Vol. exec. Internat. Exec. Svc. Corps., 2001—; chair Nat. Ctr. on Adult Literacy; bd. dirs. Phila. Parks Alliance, 2003—, Awbury Arboretum. With U.S. Army, 1954-56. Recipient The Phila. award, 1998. Mem.: Yale Club (N.Y.C.). Democrat. Presbyterian. Avocations: gardening, tennis, hiking. Home: 615 W Hortter St Philadelphia PA 19119-3650 Personal E-mail: gkfinney@aol.com.

FINNEY, JOHN EDGAR, III, food products executive; b. Hominy, Okla., Oct. 13, 1943; s. John Edgar and Ella Frances (Beckett) F.; m. Claudia Maddalena, Aug. 29, 1965 (div. Nov. 1979); children: Kristen, Eric; m. Tiare Richert, Oct. 18, 1980; children: Thomas Beckett, Elizabeth Stuart. BA, Okla. State U., 1965; JD, Stanford U., 1968. Bar: Colo. 1969, Hawaii 1969, U.S. Dist. Ct. Hawaii 1970, U.S. Ct. Appeals (9th cir.) 1970, Calif. 1974. Assoc. law Carlsmith, Carlsmith, Wichman Case, Honolulu, 1970-73; ptnr. law Augustine & Delafield, San Diego, 1973-75; pres., chief exec. officer Pentagram Corp., Honolulu, 1976-90; pres. Indsl. Income Property Inc., Honolulu, 1992—, also bd. dirs. Bd. dirs. Offshore Holdings Inc. Bd. dirs., bd. visitors Stanford (Calif.) U. Law Sch., 1986-93, USAF Pacific Adv. Bd., Hickam AFB, Honolulu, 1987-89, Hawaii Maritime Ctr., Honolulu, 1988-90. Capt. USMC, 1968-75. Named Okla. Ambassador, State of Okla., 1989; recipient Community Svc. award Aloha United Way, Honolulu, 1988, Community Svc. award Burger King Corp., San Francisco, 1987. Mem. Young Presidents' Orgn. (chmn. 1983-84), World Presidents' Orgn., Okla. Cattlemen's Assn., Stanford Univ. Assocs., Outrigger Canoe Club. Avocations: literature, canoe racing, rugby, skiing. Home: 155 Dowsett Ave Honolulu HI 96817-1109 Office: Indsl Properties Inc 6 Marin Lane Honolulu HI 96813-3107 E-mail: jefinneyhi@hotmail.com.

FINNEY, PAUL, acupuncturist, Chinese herbologist, entrepreneur; b. Humboldt, Kansas, Apr. 19, 1944; s. Robert Arthur and Gertrude (Leitzbach) F. BS in Indsl. engring., Stanford U., 1968; diploma in Acupuncture, Medicina Alternativa, Colombo, Sri Lanka, 1988; cert. Chinese herbalist, Herbal Traditions, Boston, 1993. Mgmt. asst. Signet Sci. Co., Burbank, Calif., 1971; pres. Atlantic Coastal Cmty., Cocoa Beach, Fla., 1972-81; lobbyist Am. Legion, Washington, 1982-83; legis. dir. Nat. Tax Limitation Com., Washington, 1983-84; pres. League for Ltd. Govt., Washington, 1985-86; intern Xi Yuan Hosp., Beijing, 1990; pvt. practice acupuncturist Humboldt, Kans., 1989—. Propr. Finney Enterprises, Humboldt, 1994—, India Tours Internat., Humboldt, 1996—, Bailey Hotel, Humboldt, 1997—, Finney Outdoor Advertising, Humboldt, 2004—. Mem. staff Reagan for Gov., San Francisco, 1966; founding pres. Humboldt Hist. Preservation Alliance, 1992-97, 99-2003; founder Sathya Sai Baba Ctr. of Humboldt, pres., 1998—. Lt. Signal Corp USAR, 1968, comm. officer 2/12 Arty. Bn., 23d Arty. group U.S. Army, 1969—70, Vietnam. Decorated Bronze Star. Mem.: VFW (life), Acupunture Assn. Kans. (polit. dir. 1998—), Lotus Life Car Club, Humboldt Rotary Club (Paul Harris Fellow). Libertarian. Presbyterian. Office: Finney Acupuncture Clinic 714 Bridge St Humboldt KS 66748-1708

FINNEY, ROY PELHAM, JR., urologist, surgeon, inventor; b. Gaffney, S.C., Dec. 7, 1924; s. Roy P. Finney Sr. and Mary Frances (Cannon) Woodard; m. Kay Harkness, Apr. 5, 1963; children: Wright C., James L., Joella R., Gray, Kevin. MD, Med. U. S.C., 1952. Diplomate: Am. Bd. Urology. Resident in urology Johns Hopkins U., Balt., 1952-57; prof. surg. urology U. South Fla., Tampa, 1972-84, dir. div. urology, 1972-84; ret. Designer and inventor implantable prostheses incontinence device inflatable penile prostheses treatment impotence, Double J ureteral stent, developer new surg. procedures treatment impotence; patentee in field. Fellow ACS; mem. Am. Urology Assn., Soc. Internationale D'Urologie, Internat. Continenece Soc., Urodynamic Soc. Republican. Home: 4382 Cortez Blvd Weeki Wachee FL 34607-1209

FINNIGAN, ROBERT EMMET, retired small business owner; b. Buffalo, May 27, 1927; s. Charles M. and Marie F. (Jacobs) F.; m. Bette E. van Horn, Apr. 1, 1950; children: Michael, Patrick, Robert E. Jr., Joan, Shawn, Thomas, Matthew. BS, U.S. Naval Acad., 1949; MS, U. Ill., 1954, PhD, 1957. Commd. lt. USAF, 1949, advanced through grades to capt., 1954; sr. scientist Livermore Lab., U. Calif., 1959, U. Calif. Lawrence Livermore Lab., 1957-62; sr. rsch. scientist Stanford Rsch. Inst., Menlo Park, Calif., 1962-63; dir. Electronic Assocs. Inc., Palo Alto, Calif., 1963-67; founder, vice chmn., sr. v.p., chief strategic officer Finnigan Corp., San Jose, Calif., 1967-92, vice chmn. emeritus, cons., 1992—. Mem. panel NAS, Washington, 1986—89; bd. dirs. Pacific Nanotechnology, Inc., Santa Clara, Calif. Author: Identification and Analysis of Organic Pollutants in Water, 1976, Advances in Identification and Analysis of Organic Pollutants in Water, 1981. Chmn., co-founder U.S. Nat. Working Group on Pollution, Internat. Orgn. for Legal Metrology, Washington, 1982-87; mem. pres.'s coun., U. Ill., Urbana, 2002—. Recipient Alumni Honor award Coll. of Engring., U. Ill., 1980, Winston Churchill medal of wisdom, 1999; named Pioneer in Analytical Instrumentation-Mass Spectrometry, Soc. for Analytical Chemists of Pitts. and Pitts. Conf. on Analytical Chemistry, 1994, Instrumentation Hall of Fame, Pitts., Conf. on Analytical Chemistry and Analytical Chem. Soc., 1999; named to Wisdom Hall of Fame, 1999; recipient Disting. Alumnus award, U. Ill. Dept. Elec. Engring. 1975; Robert Finnigan professorship established Keck Grad. Inst.

Applied Life Sci., Claremont, Calif., 2002. Mem. IEEE (sr.), Am. Soc. for Mass Spectrometry (bd. dirs.), Am. Electronic Assn. (bd. dirs. 1982-84, 87, chmn., co-founder environ. and occupational health com.), U.S. Naval Acad. Alumni Assn. (pres.'s cir. 1996—). Avocations: wine, hiking, snowshoeing.

FINO, MARIE GEORGETTE KECK, retired real estate broker; b. Greenville, Pa., Jan. 30, 1923; d. Harvey I. and Winifred L. (Fuller) Keck; m. Alex F. Fino, Sept. 27, 1947; children: Timothy A., Jeffrey J. Cert. in real estate, Pa. State U., 1980; grad., Realtors Inst., Harrisburg, Pa., 1981. RN, Pa.; lic. real estate broker, Pa. Broker, owner 305 Realty, North Warren, Pa., 1983-96; instr. Pa. State U., 1985-96, ret., 1996. Treas. Warren County Bd. Realtors, 1981-84, v.p., 1984-86, pres., 1988. Patentee fuel storage vent. Treas. Northwestern Pa. Regional Planning Commn., 1985-92, exec. com., 1988-92, treas., 1991; bd. dirs. Warren County Devel. Assn., Warren County Crime Stoppers, 1989-96. Named Woman of Yr. in Bus. and Industry, County of Warren, 1986, Citizen Amb. to China, 1994. Mem. Nat. Assn. Realtors, Pa. Assn. Realtors (bd. dirs. 1984-88, vice-chair comml.-indsl. com. 1984-88, bd. dirs. 1992-93), Soc. Indsl. and Office Realtors (nat. bd. dirs. 1992-95, dist. v.p. 1993-95), Warren County C. of C., Philomel Club (bd. dirs. 1978-80), Conewango Valley Country Club (Warren), Conewango Valley Kennel Club. Republican. Roman Catholic. Avocations: golf, bridge, showing and breeding maltese dogs. Personal E-mail: marief@mmca.com.

FINOCCHIARO, ALFONSO G., bank executive; b. Catania, Italy, Aug. 20, 1932; came to U.S., 1960; s. Giovanni and Giuseppina (Cavalieri) F.; m. Diana Louise Cavagnolo, Jan. 19, 1936; children: John Paul, Carol Anne. D in Polit. Sci., U. Catania, 1958; MBA in Internat. Fin., Pace U., 1967. V.p. Chem. Bank, N.Y.C., 1966—77; pres., gen. mgr. Conn. Bank Internat., N.Y.C., 1977—78; exec. v.p., regional dir. Banco Portugues do Atlantico, N.Y.C., 1978—95; dir. BPA Futures Cayman, 1989—96, Internat. Strategy Svcs., 1990—96; vice-chmn. BPA Brazil, 1993—96; dir. BPA Overseas Ltd., 1993—96; advisor to bd. dirs. Banco Portugues do Atlantico, Lisbon, Portugal, 1996—97; chmn., CEO FINAB Internat. Corp. Svc. Ltd., 2000—; chmn. BPD Bank, N.Y.C., 2005—. Bd. dirs. BPD Internat. Bank, N.Y.C., 1997-2005; Alfie Internat., Inc., IMAG, N.Y.C., So. Fin. BAnk, Va., 1997-2004; advisor to bd. dirs. Banco Internat. do Funchal, Lisbon, Portugal, 1997—. Mem. Friends of Queen Catherine, Inc., chmn. fin. com., trustee, 1988-2001. Decorated comdr. Order Infante D. Henrique (Portugal). Fellow: Internat. Mgmt. and Devel. Inst. (Leadership award); mem.: European-Am. C. of C. in the U.S. (bd. dirs. 1991—98, v.p.), Internat. Mgmt. and Devel. Inst., Global Leadership Inst. (bd. dirs. 1991—2001), Am. Portuguese Soc. (v.p., bd. dirs. 1979—), Portugal C. of C. (bd. dirs., pres. 1978—98). Republican. Roman Catholic. Avocations: piano, music, travel, foreign affairs. Personal E-mail: alfie333@yahoo.com.

FINS, JOSEPH JACK, internist; b. NYC, Nov. 16, 1959; s. Herman and Ruth (Lovett) F.; m. Amy B. Ehrlich, July 2, 1989. BA with deptl. hons., Wesleyan U., 1982; MD, Cornell U., 1986. Diplomate Am. Bd. Internal Medicine. Intern in psychiatry N.Y. Hosp. Payne Whitney Clinic, N.Y.C., 1986—87; resident in medicine N.Y. Hosp., N.Y.C., 1987—89; instr. Cornell U. Med. Coll., N.Y.C., 1990; fellow in medicine N.Y. Hosp. Cornell Med. Ctr., N.Y.C., 1990—92; vis. assoc. for medicine Hastings Ctr., Briarcliff Manor, NY, 1990—92; instr. Cornell U. Med. Coll., N.Y.C., 1992—93; assoc. for medicine Hastings Ctr., Garrison, 1992—; asst. attending physician N.Y. Hosp., 1992—98; asst. prof. medicine Cornell U. Med. Coll., N.Y.C., 1993—98; assoc. attending physician N.Y. Presbyn. Hosp., 1998—2003; assoc. prof. medicine and assoc. prof. medicine in psychiat. Weill Med. Coll. Cornell U., N.Y.C., 1998—2003; assoc. prof. program clin. epidemiology/health sci. rsch. Weill Grad. Sch. Med. Scis. Cornell U., N.Y.C.; assoc. prof. of pub. health Weill Med. Coll. of Cornell U., N.Y.C., 2001—03, chief divsn. med. ethics, 2001—, prof. medicine in psychiatry, 2003—, prof. public health, 2003—, prof. medicine, 2003—; attending physician NY Presbyn. Hosp., 2003—. Vis. scholar Hastings Ctr., Briarcliff Manor, 1989; ethics com. dept. medicine N.Y. Hosp., N.Y.C., 1991-94; dir. med. ethics The N.Y. Hosp., chmn. com., 1994-2002; physician, ethicist in residence The Healthcare Chaplaincy, N.Y., 1994-2002; temp. advisor Regional Bioethics Ctr. of Pan Am. Health Orgn., 1995; vis. fellow Woodrow Wilson Found., 1998—; faculty scholar Open Soc. Inst. Project on Death in Am., 1997-2000; bd. dirs. Fund for Modern Cts., 2003-, mentor, adj. facutly, Rockefeller U., 2003-; attending physician N.Y Presby. Hosp.; bd. dirs. N.Y. Organ Donor Network, 2003-05; bd. trustees Wesleyan U., 2004—. Mem. editl. bd. Jour. Am. Geriatrics Soc., 1991-92, The Oncologist; editor Bioethics, Cancer Investigation 1995-2000, Jour. Pain and Symptom Mgmt., 1997—; contbr. articles to profl. jours. Presdl. appt. commr. to White Ho. Commn. on Complementary and Alternative Medicine Policy, 2000—02; nat. adv. com. Woodrow Wilson Nat. Fellowship Found., 2003—; mem. quality care at the end of life commn. N.Y. State Atty. Gen.'s Office, 1997—98; bd. dirs. Partnership for Caring, 1999—2003. Fellow: ACP (chair 2003—, chmn. health and pub. policy com. N.Y. chpt., councilor at large), N.Y. Acad. Medicine; mem.: Am. Geriat. Soc. (vice chair ethics com. 1994—96), Assn. Bar of City of N.Y. (adj.). Office: Weill Med Coll Cornell U Divsn Med Ethics 435 East 70th St ste 4-J New York NY 10021

FINSTER, JAMES ROBERT, library media specialist; b. Milw., Sept. 29, 1947; s. Milton Robert Finster and Eleonore B. (Worgull) Helvey; children: James Andrew, Nicholas William. BS in Edn., Dr. Martin Luther Coll., 1971; BS in Resource Mgmt., U. Wis., Stevens Point, 1976; MS in Edn. Media, U. Wis., LaCrosse, 1987. Cert. libr. media specialist, Wis., Minn. Ski instr. various ski clubs, resorts, Wis. and Colo., 1971—; elem. tchr. pvt. and pub. schs. Wis., 1971-73, 78-81; teaching asst. U. Wis., Stevens Point, 1975; park ranger Nat. Park Svc., various locations, 1976-77; ski. sch. dir. Whitecap Mountain, Montreal, Wis., 1982-83, Coffee Mill Ski Area, Wabasha, Minn., 1983-84; grad. asst. U. Wis., LaCrosse, 1986-87; libr. media specialist Chilton (Wis.) High Sch., 1987-93; libr. media specialist K-12 Rib Lake (Wis.) Pub. Schs., 1993-94, Elcho (Wis.) Pub. Sch., 1994-96; ski instr. Trollhaugen, 1997—. Mem. Wis. Ednl. Media Assn. Republican. Lutheran. Avocations: downhill skiing, travel, sports, games, music. Home: 200 Seminole Ave Lot 78 Osceola WI 54020-8076

FINUCANE, ANNE M., communications and marketing executive; married; 4 children. BA with honors, U. N.H. Pub. info. officer Mayor of City of Boston; dir. creative svcs. Sta. WBZ-TV, Boston; head creative svcs. Hill, Holliday, Connors, Cosmopulos, Inc., Boston, dir. account mgmt., dir. corp. devel.; prin. Anne Finucane Mktg. and Telecomm., Boston; sr. v.p., dir. corp. mktg. and comm. Fleet Fin. Group, Boston, 1995—. Bd. dirs. Internat. Ctr. for Journalists. Bd. dirs. Urban Improv, Emerson Coll., New Eng. Coun., Mass. Women's Forum; co-chmn. tech. divsn. United Way of Mass. Bay Campaign, 1995, 96; mem. adv. coun. Children's Defense Fund, Washington, Conservation Law Found. Office: Fleet Fin Group Corp Mktg & Comm One Federal St Boston MA 02110 Fax: 617-346-4740.

FINZEN, BRUCE ARTHUR, lawyer; b. Mpls., Mar. 11, 1947; s. Floyd Arthur and Lorraine Jeannette (Offerdahl) F.; children: Margaret, Sara, Stephanie. BA, U. Minn., 1970; JD, U. Kans., 1973. Bar: Minn. 1973, U.S. Dist. Ct. Minn. 1973, Calif. 1988, U.S. Ct. Appeals (8th cir.) 1973, U.S. Ct. Appeals (7th cir.) 1983, U.S. Ct. Appeals (2d cir.) 1986, U.S. Ct. Appeals (4th cir.) 1994, U.S. Ct. Appeals (9th cir.) 1994, U.S. Supreme Ct. 1996. D.C., 2002, U.S. Dist. Ct. D.C. 2003. Law clk. to presiding justice Minn. Supreme Ct., St. Paul, 1973-74; assoc. Robins, Kaplan, Miller & Ciresi, Mpls., 1974-79; ptnr. Robins, Kaplan, Miller & Ciresi LLP, Mpls., 1979—. Mem. adv. bd. Ctr. for Pub. Integrity, 2001—; trustee Ho. of Hope Presbyn. Ch., 1988—94; bd. dirs. Union Gospel Mission, St. Paul, 1983—89; sec. bd. dirs. Boys and Girls Clubs St. Paul, 1984—91. Mem. ABA, Minn. Bar Assn., ATLA, Minn. Trial Lawyers Assn., Consumer Attys. Calif., Assn. Personal Injury Lawyers. Avocations: hunting, fishing. Office: Robins Kaplan Miller & Ciresi LLP 2800 LaSalle Plz 800 Lasalle Ave Ste 2800 Minneapolis MN 55402-2015 Office Phone: 612-349-8500.

FIOCK, SHARI LEE, economics development executive; b. Weed, Calif., Oct. 25, 1941; d. Webster Bruce and Olevia May (Pruett) Fiock; children from previous marriage: Webster Clinton Pfingsten, Sterling Curtis. Cert., Art Instrn. Sch., Mpls., 1964. Copywriter Darron Assocs., Eugene, Oreg., 1964—68; staff artist Oreg. Holidays, Springfield, 1966—69, 1971; co-owner, designer Artre Enterprises, Eugene, 1969—74; design entrepreneur Shari & Assocs., Yreka, Calif., 1974—99; exec. dir. Siskiyou County Econ. Devel. Coun., Yreka, Calif., 1999—2005. Cons., devel. sec. Cascade World Four Season Resort, Siskiyou County, Calif., 1980—86; owner Coyote pub., 1991—99; adminstrv. asst., coord. regional catalog Gt. Northern Corp. U.S. Dept. Commerce and Econ. Devel., 1994—96; local cons. CalEnergy Co., Inc., 1998—99. 5 ton chain saw sculpture, Oreg. Beaver, 1967, Holiday Fun Book, 1978; author, illustrator: Family Reunions and Clan Gatherings, 1991, Blue Goose Legend, 1995, Blue Goose Legend, rev. edit., 1998; editor: Choo and Moo Cookbook, 1998. Counselor Boy Scouts Am., 1983—91; co-creator Klamath Nat. Forest Interpretive Mus., 1979—91; residential capt. United Way, Eugene, 1972; rschr. Beaver Ofcl. State Animal, Eugene, 1965—71. Mem.: Siskiyou Writers Club (co-founder, past pres.). Home and Office: 406 Walters Ln Yreka CA 96097-9704 Office Phone: 530-842-7279. E-mail: sharifiock@snowcrest.net.

FIOL MATTA, LIANA, state supreme court justice; Grad., Trinity Coll.; M., Columbia U., 1988, JSD, 1996; JD, U. P.R. Prof. Inter-Am. U., 1978—88, Pontifical Catholic U.; judge PR Ct. of Appeals, 1992—2003; justice PR Supreme Ct., 2004—. Author numerous articles in professional journals. Mem.: P.R. Bar Assn. Office: PR Supreme Ct PO Box 9022392 San Juan PR 00902-2392

FIORAVANTI, JEFF, artist; b. Saugus, Mass., Feb. 21, 1958; s. Richard and Anne Fioravanti; m. Cathleen Martin, May 12, 1984; 1 child, Nicole. BSBA in Bus. Mgmt., Salem State Coll., 1982. Cert. graphics arts/web designer; cert. webmaster. Sr. materials planner Teradyne, Inc., Boston, 1984-96; prodn. scheduler Compensated Devices, Inc., Melrose, Mass., 1997-99; web specialist Attunity, Inc., Burlington, Mass., 2000-01; graphic designer, advt. copywriter T.K. Keith Co., Wakefield, Mass., 2001—; prin., owner Fioravanti Fine Art, 2003—. Tchg. asst. Clark U., Woburn, Mass., 2000. Exhibited in group shows at Art 3 Gallery, Manchester, N.H., 1996, Art Rsch. Assocs. Gallery, South Hamilton, Mass., 1997, Gallery 30, Gettysburg, Pa., 2003, Cape Cod Mus. Fine Art, 2003. Coach Saugus Youth Hockey, 1977-81, 93-94, Saugus Youth Soccer, 1977-79. Inducted into Saugus H.S. Athletic Hall of Fame, 1992; recipient Olympian Corp. award Pastel Soc. W. Coast Internat. Open Exhbn., 2000, Best in Show award Conn. Pastel Soc. Mem. Pastel Soc. Am. (signature), Degas Pastel Soc., Pastel Soc. Oreg., Conn. Pastel Soc. (signature), Pastel Painters Soc. Cape Cod (Dakota Art Store award 1999), North Shore Art Assn., Soc. of Civil War Historians, Civil War Preservation Trust, Gettysburg Battlefield Preservation Assn., Blue and Gray Edn. Soc Avocations: American Civil War reenacting, collecting sports memorabilia, walking, U.S. history. Home: 49 Pennybrook Rd Lynn MA 01905 Office: TK Keith Co 15 Edgewater Dr Wakefield MA 01880 Office Phone: 781-245-0531. E-mail: jfiorava@concentric.net, jfioravanti@tkkeithco.com.

FIORE, CARMEN ANTHONY, writer; b. Trenton, N.J., Sept. 19, 1932; s. Ernest and Margaret Fiore; m. Catherine Marie Butera, Oct. 4, 1958; children: David, Lisa Fiore Childs. BS, Rider U., Trenton, N.J., 1954; MEd, Rutgers U., 1963. Cert. tchr. N.J., lic. real estate appraiser N.J. Social caseworker State of N.J., Trenton, 1957—60; tchr. Trenton Pub. Schs., 1960—61; with State of N.J., Trenton, 1961—87. Author: (novels) The Barrier, 1964, 1986, Little Oscar, 1988, Vendetta Mountain, 1987, (juvenile novel) The Snakeskin, 1991, (young adult hist. nonfiction) Young Heroes of the Civil War, 2005, (nonfiction) Voices of the Daughters, 1989, (novels) Searching, 2002, (screenplays) Vendetta Mountain, 1992, Manipulators, 1994, Little Oscar, 1993, Mixed Doubles, 2000, A Case in Principle, 1998, Avarice Can Be Deadly, 2000, Till Death Do Us Part, 1999, The Colored Kid, 1996, Italian Interlude, 1999, Prisoners of Love, 1999, Sweepstakes, 2000; contbr. short stories to lit. and comml. mags., articles and essays to newspapers and online mags. With U.S. Army, 1955—57. Mem.: Assn. Writers and Writing Programs, Fla. Writers Assn., Space Coast Writers Guild, Poets and Writers, Creative Screenwriting, Civil War Round Table of Ctrl. Fla., Greater Orlando Civil War Round Table, Civil War Preservation Trust, Camp Olden Civil War Round Table. Roman Catholic. Home and Office: 1682 Keys Gate Dr Melbourne FL 32940-6317 E-mail: bigcarm@cfl.rr.com.

FIORE, JAMES LOUIS, JR., accountant, educator; b. Jersey City, Oct. 7, 1935; s. James Louis and Rose (Perrotta) F.; m. Alberta W. Pope, July 21, 1957; children: Carolyn Leigh, James Louis III, Toni Lynn. BS in Acctg., Seton Hall U., 1957; MBA, We. Colo. U., 1972; PhD, Calif. We. U., 1979. Lic. acct. Pa., N.J. Field auditor State of N.J., Trenton, 1958-60; supr. internal auditing Ronson Corp., Woodbridge, N.J., 1960-64; surp. gen. acctg. Electronic Assocs., West Long Branch, N.J., 1964-65; pvt. practice acctg., 1965—. Pres. Bucks County Rsch. Inst., Inc., 1972-79; mem. adj. faculty Allentown Coll. St. Francis de Sales, Ctr. Valley, Pa., 1979-81, Pa. Coll. Chriopractic, 1986-94, Holy Family Coll., Phila., 1995; sec.-treas. Gordian Group Internat., Inc. Bus. Cons., 2001—. Author: Comparative Bioavailability of Doxycycline, 1974, Non-Absorption of Nitrofurazone from the Urethra in Men, 1976, Shareholder Loans, The National Public Accountant, 1988, Financial Problems and Your Profession, 1989, The Tactical Entrepreneurial Manual For Running Your Business, 2005; contbr. articles to profl. jours Founder Brick Twp. (N.J.) Scholarship Fund, 1963-67; mem. adv. coun. Inst. for Accts., Pa. State U.; trustee Pa. Coll. Chiropractic, 1986-94; founder, treas. Cath. Acad. Sci. in U.S.A., Washington. Lt. U.S. Army, 1957. Named Jayce of Yr., 1962; recipient Legion of Honor, Chapel of Four Chaplains, 1979. Mem. Calif. We. U. Alumni Assn., We. Colo. U. Alumni Assn., Seton Hall U. Alumni Assn. (Crest and Centrury Clubs), Masons, Shriners, Scottish Rite, Liberty Bell Chpt. Nat. Spkrs. Assn. (pres. 1993-94) Home: 265 Thompson Mill Rd Newtown PA 18940-3105 Office Phone: 215-598-3481. Personal E-mail: jim@gordianintl.com.

FIORE, JOSEPH ALBERT, artist; b. Cleve., Feb. 3, 1925; s. Salvatore Emmanuel and Gemma Marie (Cominelli) F.; m. Mary Falconer Fitton, Oct. 10, 1952; children: Thomas, Susanna. Student, Black Mountain Coll., 1946—48, student, 1949, San Francisco Sch. Art Inst., 1948—49. Instr. painting, drawing Black Mountain (N.C.) Coll., 1949-56, chmn. art dept., 1951-56; free lance designer N.Y.C., 1958-61; instr. painting Phila. Coll. Art, 1962-70, Md. Inst. Coll. Art, Balt., 1970-75; instr. landscape painting Nat. Acad. Design, N.Y.C., 1979, Parson's Sch. Design Summer Program, Dordogne, France, 1980. Vis. artist-critic Artists for Environment Found., Walpack Center, N.J., 1972-83, Vt. Studio Sch., Johnson, Vt., 1987. One-man shows include Ten-Thirty Gallery, Cleve., 1944, 48, 50, Galerie Parnass, Wuppertal, Germany, 1955, Round Top Ctr. for Arts, Damariscotta, Maine, 1997, 2002, Cathedral of St. John the Divine, N.Y.C., 1997, Black Mountain Coll. Mus. and Arts Ctr. at Zone One Contemporary, Asheville, N.C., 1995-96, Staempfli Gallery, N.Y.C., 1960, Robert Schoelkopf Gallery, N.Y.C., 1965, 69, Green Mountain Gallery, N.Y.C., 1973, John Bernard Myers Gallery, N.Y.C., 1974, Fischbach Gallery, N.Y.C., 1977, 81, Caldbeck Gallery, Rockland, Maine, 1988, Le Va-Tout Gallery, Waldboro, Maine, 1991, River Gallery, Damariscotta, Maine, 2002, Rider U. Art Gallery, Lawrenceville, N.J., 2004, Ctr. for Maine Contemporary Art, Rockport, 2004; exhibited in group shows Stable Gallery, N.Y.C., 1954, 55, Whitney Mus. Am. Art, 1959, U. Ill., Urbana, 1961, Am. Fedn. Art Travelling Exhbn., 1964, Corcoran Gallery Art, Washington, 1975, State Mus., Augusta, 1976, Cape Split Place, Addison, Maine, 1977, Am. Acad. Arts and Letters, N.Y.C., 1981, Landmark Gallery, N.Y.C.,•1981, Jersey City Mus., 1982, Farnsworth Mus., Rockland, Maine, 1983, Artist's Choice Mus., 1983, Black Mountain Connection, Gilliam and Peden Gallery, Raleigh, 1987, Black Mountain Coll., Blum Art Inst., Bard Coll., N.Y.C., 1987, N.C. State Mus., Raleigh, 1987, Grey Art Ctr., NYU, 1987, Snyder Fine Arts, N.Y.C., 1992, Station Gallery, Katonah, N.Y., 1992, Anita Shapolsky Gallery, N.Y.C., 1997, Hofstra Mus., Hempstead, N.Y., 2001 Black Mountain Coll.: Experiment in Art Museo Nacional Centro De Arte Renia Sofia, Madrid, 2002-03, numerous others; represented in permanent collections Whitney Mus. Am. Art, N.Y.C., N.C. State Mus. Art, Raleigh, Corcoran Gallery, Art, Washington, Colby Art Mus., Waterville, Maine, Weatherspoon Gallery, Greensboro, N.C., NAD, N.Y., Chase Manhattan Collection, N.Y.C., Asheville Mus. of Art, N.C., Black Mountain Coll. Mus. and Art Ctr., Housatonic Mus. Art, Bridgeport, Conn., Farnsworth Mus., Rockland, Maine, 2004. Served with AUS, 1943-46. Recipient prize for painting San Francisco Mus. Ann., 1949, 1st prize Met. Young Artists 1st Ann. Nat. Arts Club, N.Y.C., 1958, Adolph and Clara Obrig Prize, NAD 178th Ann., 2003, Obrig prize Nat. Acad., 2005; Artists for Environment Found. residence grantee, 1976; Nettie Marie Jones fellow Ctr. Music, Drama and Art, Lake Placid, N.Y., 1983, purchase award Am. Acad. Arts and Letters, 1998. Mem. NAD (cert. of merit 168th Ann. Exhbn. 1993, Edwin Palmer Meml. prize 170th Ann. 1995, Cannon prize 175th Ann. 2000, Andrew Carnegie prize 176th Ann. 2001, Adolph and Clara Obrig prize 178th Ann. 2003), Artists Equity Assn. N.Y. Office Phone: 212-362-8897.

FIORE, NICHOLAS FRANCIS, metal products executive; b. Pitts., Sept. 24, 1939; s. William H. and Margaret (Scinto) F.; m. Sylvia M. Chinque, Aug. 13, 1960; children: Maria L., Nicholas F., Kristin M., Anthony T. BS, Carnegie-Mellon U., 1960, MS, 1963, PhD, 1964. Asst. prof. metall. engring. and materials sci. U. Notre Dame, Ind., 1966-69, prof., 1969-81, chmn. dept., 1969-72, 80-81; v.p. Cabot Corp., Boston, 1982-89; mng. dir. materials and applied physics Arthur D. Little, Inc., Cambridge, Mass., 1989-90; v.p. Carpenter Tech. Corp., Reading, Pa., 1990-93, sr. v.p., 1993-2000; CEO Walsin USA, Henderson, Nev., 2000—. Vis. scientist Argonne (Ill.) Nat. Labs., 1974-75. Co-author: Binding of Solute to Dislocations, 1967, Hydrogen Related Embrittlement of High Temperature Materials, 1975; editor: (with B.J. Berkowitz) Advanced Techniques for Characterizing Hydrogen in Metals, 1982; contbr. articles to profl. jours. Trustee Albright Coll.; sci. and tech. edn. com. New Eng. Coun. Capt. U.S. Army, 1964-66. Fellow Am. Soc. Metals (trustee); mem. AIME, Alpha Sigma Mu. Home: 2294 Feathertree Ave Henderson NV 89052 Office: Walsin USA 701 N Green Valley Ste 200 Henderson NV 89074 Office Phone: 702-379-8654. Personal E-mail: nffsr@aol.com. Business E-Mail: fiore@walsinusa.com.

FIORE, PETER MARIO, artist, educator; b. Teaneck, NJ, Dec. 15, 1955; s. Mario Rosario and Rose Fiore; m. Barbara Lynne Meyer, Sept. 23, 2000; children: Lisa Emily, Paul Michael. Student, Pratt Inst., 1977. Artist Red Oak Studios, Matamoras, Pa., 1973—; instr. Pratt Inst., Bklyn., 1979—88, Syracuse (N.Y.) U., 1985—91, Sch. of Visual Arts, N.Y.C., 1992—. Exhibitions include Painting Light, Places Near and Far, children's book, Lynne Cheney's When Washington Crossed the Delaware. Mem.: Oil Painters Am. (assoc.), Am. Artists Profl. League (assoc.), Soc. of Illustrators (life; pres., vp 1991, Silver Medal). Avocation: photography. Office Phone: 570-491-2610.

FIORE, ROBERT J., lawyer; b. Miami, Fla., Apr. 22, 1961; s. Robert Victor and Angela (Vaccaro) F. BA, Biscayne Coll., 1983; JD, U. Fla., 1986. Bar: Fla. 1986, U.S. Dist. Ct. 1987. Assoc. Floyd Pearson et al, Miami, Fla., 1986-94, ptnr., 1994-96, Russomanno Fiore & Borrello, Miami, Fla., 1996-98; sole practitioner Miami, 1998—. Spkr. Acad. Fla. Trial Lawyers, Dade County Trial Lawyers Assn.; program chair The Stephen R. Covey Professionalism Program for Lawyers, Judges & Staff. Mem. steering com., com. of 100 Big Bros./Big Sisters of Greater Miami, 1994; co-organizer Halloween for Hurricane Kids, 1992. Mem. ATLA (chair new lawyers divsn. 1995-96, vice chair 1994-95, bd. govs. 1996—, Most Dedicated Pub. Servant award 1994, Nat. Pub. Svc. award 1994, Most Outstanding Young Lawyers Sect. Nat. award 1995), Acad. Fla. Trial Lawyers (chair young lawyers sect. 1994-95, chair elect 1993-94, sec. 1993, program chair ultimate trial notebook seminar 1994, bd. dirs. 1993—), Dade County Trial Lawyers Assn. (bd. dirs. 1992—, sec. 1993-94, treas. 1994-95, pres. elect 1995-96, pres. 1996-97, Exceptional Svc. and Leadership award 1996), Dade County Bar Assn. (bd. dirs. 1997—, chair meetings and luncheons com. 1993-94, exec. com. 1990—, treas. 2000-01). Democrat. Roman Catholic. Avocations: exercise, nutrition, health, art and wine collector. Office: 22 W Flagler St Miami FL 33130-1802

FIORELLA, RUSSELL MICHAEL, pathologist; s. Russell and Flora Fiorella; children: Alex, Anna, Max. BA, Tulane U., 1977; MD, U. of Mo., Kansas City, 1982; MBA, Avila Coll., Kansas City, Mo., 1996. Diplomate cytopathology Am. Bd. of Pathology, anatomic and clin. pathology Am. Bd. of Pathology, Nat. Bd. of Med. Examiners. Clin. instr. of pathology U. of Kans. Med. Ctr., Kansas City, Kans., 1986—87; asst. prof. of pathology U. of Mo., Kansas City, 1991—95; dir. cytopathology dept. of pathology Truman Med. Ctr., Kansas City, Mo., 1991—93, dir. surg. pathology dept. of pathology, 1993—94; assoc. prof. of pathology U. of Mo., Kansas City, 1995—99; dir. anatomic pathology dept. of pathology Truman Med. Ctr., Kansas City, Mo., 1995—98, vice-chair dept. of pathology, 1996—98, interim chair, dept. of pathology, 1998—99; prof. of pathology U. of Mo., Kansas City, 1999—; chair dept. of pathology Truman Med. Ctr., Kansas City, Mo., 1999—. Pres., med. and dental staff Truman Med. Ctr., Kansas City, Mo., 2002—, mem. search com. for chief med. officer, 1999—2000, bd. of dirs., exec. com., 1999—2001; mem. legal com. Hosp. Hill Health Svcs. Corp., Kansas City, Mo., 1999—2001, mem. bd. nominating com., 1999—2002, mem. fin. com., 1999—2002, mem. compensation com., 1999—2002, mem. bylaws com., 1999—2002, bd. dirs.; mem. coun. on grad. med. edn. U. of Mo. Sch. of Medicine, Kansas City, 1999—, mem. acad. chairs, 1999—; bd. dirs. Truman Med. Ctr., Kansas City, Mo., pres.-elect med. and dental staff, 1998—2001, mem. coun. of chairs, 1998—, mem. joint profl. stds. com., 1998—2000, dir. pathology residency program, 1998—2002, sec.-treas. med. and dental staff, 1995—2002, mem. utilization com., 1994—98, mem. tissue com., 1994—96, dir. Sch. of Cytotechnology, 1993—96, mem. med. records com., 1993—94, mem. grievance com., 1992—93, mem. joint conf. and quality com., 2002—; dir. pathology course U. of Mo. Sch. of Medicine, Kansas City, 1991—98, mem. search com. for dean, 2003—03; mem. search com. for exec. dir. Hosp. Hill Health Svcs. Corp., Kansas City, Mo., 2001; mem. search com. for chief nursing officer Truman Med. Ctr., Kansas City, Mo., 2000; mem. search com. for med. dir. TMC Hosp. Hill Med. Pavillion, Kansas City, Mo., 2000—01; chair strategic planning com. Hosp. Hill Health Svcs. Corp., Kansas City, Mo., 2000—01; mem. med. and dental staff fin. com. Truman Med. Ctr., Kansas City, Mo., 2000—02, mem. info. svcs. bd. com., 1999—2001. Author: (book chpt.) Cytopathology in Laboratory Test Handbook; contbr. book rev. Cytopathology of malignant effusions in Modern Pathology, book rev. Guides to clinical aspiration biopsy restroperitonseum & intestine in Modern Pathology, articles and abstracts to profl. jours.; jour. reviewer: Diagnostic Cytopathology. Fellow: Coll. of Am. Pathologists; mem.: Kans. City Soc. of Pathologists, Am. Coll. of Physician Execs., Am. Soc. of Cytology, Internat. Acad. of Pathologists, Nat. Com. for Clin. Lab. Stds., Am. Soc. of Clin. Pathologists, Assn. of Pathology Chairs. Office: Truman Med Ctr 2301 Holmes Kansas City MO 64108

FIORENZA, FRANCIS P., religion educator; b. Bklyn., Feb. 27, 1941; married, 1967; 1 child. AB, St. Mary's U., 1961, STB, 1963; ThD, U. Münster, Fed. Republic of Germany, 1972. Asst. prof. theology U. Notre Dame, Ind., 1971-77, Villanova (Pa.) U., 1977-79; assoc. prof. theology Cath. U. Am., Washington, 1979-87; now Charles Chauncey Stillman prof. Roman Cath. theol. studies Harvard U., Cambridge, Mass. Vis. scholar Union Theol. Sem., N.Y.C., 1974-75; vis. prof. Yale U., 1995. Author: Critical Social Theory and Christology, 1975, Political Theology as Foundational Theology, 1977, Religion und Politik, Christliche Glaube, 1982; translator: Schleiermacher: Open Letters on the Glaubenslehre, 1981, Foundational Theology: Jesus and Church, 1984; editor: Systematic Theology, Roman Catholic Perspectives, 2 vols., 1991; co-editor: (with Don Browning) Habermas, Modernity and Public Theology, 1992, Handbook of Catholic Theology, 1995, (with James Livingston) Modern Christian Thought: Vol. 2 The Twentieth Century, 2000; contbr. articles to religious jours. Fellow Div., U. Chgo., 1978-79; rsch. fellow Am. Assn. Theol. Schs., 1982-83, 89, Henry Luce III fellowship, 2005-2006. Mem. Am. Acad. Religion, Cath. Theol. Soc. Am. (pres. 1985-86), Soc. Values Higher Edn., Coll. Theol. Soc., Hegel Soc. Roman Catholic. Office: Harvard U Div Sch 45 Francis Ave Cambridge MA 02138-1911 Office Phone: 617-495-4518.

FIORENZA, JOSEPH A., archbishop; b. Beaumont, Tex., Jan. 25, 1931; s. Anthony and Grace (Galiano) Fiorenza. Grad., St. Anthony HS, Beaumont, Tex., 1947. Ordained priest Sem. Chapel, St. Mary's Sem., La Porte, Tex., 1954; asst. pastor Queen of Peace Ch., Houston, 1954—57; prof. med. ethics Dominican Coll., Houston, 1957—59; adminstr. Sacred Heart Co-Cathedral, Houston, 1959—67; pastor St. Augustine Ch., Houston, 1967—69, St. Benedict Ch., Houston, 1969—72, Assumption Ch., Houston, 1972—73; named Prelate of Honor to his Holiness, 1973; vice chancellor Diocese of Galveston-Houston, Tex., 1972—73, chancellor, 1973—79; consecrated bishop Sacred Heart Cathedral, San Angelo, Tex., 1979; bishop Diocese of San Angelo, 1979—85, Diocese of Galveston-Houston, 1985—2004; archbishop Archdiocese of Galveston-Houston, 2004—. Bd. dirs. U. St. Thomas, Houston, Cath. Near East Welfare Assn., US. Mem.: US Conf. Cath. Bishops (adminstrv. com. 1995—, v.p. 1995—98, pres. 1998—2001). Roman Catholic. Office: Archdiocese of Galveston-Houston 1700 San Jacinto Houston TX 77001*

FIORI, PAMELA, publishing executive, writer; b. Newark, Feb. 26, 1944; d. Edward and Rita (Rascati) F.; m. Colton Givner. BA cum laude, Jersey City State Coll., 1966. Tchr. English Gov. Livingston High Sch., Berkeley Heights, N.J., 1966-67; assoc. editor Holiday Mag., N.Y.C., 1968-71, Travel & Leisure Mag., N.Y.C., 1971-74, sr. editor, 1974-75, editor-in-chief, 1975-80; editor-in-chief, exec. v.p. Am. Express Pub. Corp. (Travel & Leisure/Food & Wine), N.Y.C., 1980-89, editorial dir., exec. v.p., 1989-93; editor-in-chief Town & Country, N.Y.C., 1993—. Columnist: Travel & Leisure, 1976—89, Town & Country, 1993—; contbr. articles to periodicals. Founding chmn. UNICEF Snowflake Project. Recipient Chevalier de l'Ordre du Merite, 1985, Melva C. Pederson award for disting. travel journalism Am. Soc. Travel Afts., 1992, Outstanding Woman of the 90s award Found. for Neurosurg. Rsch., 1994, Bus. award Nat. Italian Am. Found., 1996, Fashion Oracle of Yr., Coun. Fashion Designers, 2004. Office: Town & Country 1700 Broadway New York NY 10019-5905 Office Phone: 212-903-5334.

FIORI-BLANCHFIELD, JOAN, artist, art historian; b. Tuxedo, N.Y., May 26, 1942; d. Anthony Justus Fiori and Janet Cynthia Pohl; m. William Charles Blanchfield; children: Lyn, Mark. BA, Coll. New Rochelle, 1964; MA in Studio Art, SUNY, Albany, 1972; MA in Art History with high honors, Syracuse U., 1999; postgrad., CUNY, 2001—02, SUNY, Albany, 2004—. Tutor in fine arts Empire State Coll., Saratoga Springs, N.Y., 1974-75; instr. in art Jewish Cmty. Ctr., Utica, N.Y.; adj. instr. Mohawk Valley C.C., Utica, 1976-83; instr. in art and fine art Herkimer (N.Y.) County C.C., 1979-80; dir. cultural exch. to Italy Utica Coll. of Syracuse U., Utica, 1988-89, lectr. in fine art, 1973, 82-93, dir. Edith Barrett Art Gallery, 1983-96; ind. scholar, artist, cons. Utica, 1996—. Contbr. articles to profl. publs.; executed sculpture at Museo d'Arte Moderna, Italy, Mostra Internazionale di Sculture all'Aperto, Italy, 1978, 79. Bd. dirs. Art Discovery Consortium, Herkimer, Madison, Oneida Counties, N.Y., 1985-87; dir. art-in-edn. program for Oneida, Herkimer and Madison Counties, N.Y. State Coun. on Arts, N.Y.C., 1985-96; art judge Munson Williams Proctor Inst. Art, Utica, 1992, Utica Pub. Libr., 1992-95; curator women's unit exhbn. Women's History Mus., Seneca Falls, N.Y., 1984; mem. upstate N.Y. com. Nat. Mus. Women in Arts, Washington, 1989-90. Recipient 1st prize Albany Inst. Art, 1966, Hon. Mention award Albany Inst. Art, 1967, Best in Show award Cooperstown Art Mus., 1981, 1st prize in sculpture, 1979, 80; Rettore's medal Università dell'Aquila, Italy, 1989; grantee Utica Coll. Syracuse U., 1988-91, N.Y. State Coun. Arts, 1983-89, N.Y. Coun. Humanities, 1984-85, others. Mem.: NOW, Assn. Historians Am. Art, Coll. Art Assn., Chamber Mus. Soc. Utica (sec. 2002—, bd. dirs.), Southeastern Medieval Assn. (sec., treas. 1989—96), Medieval Acad. Am. Avocations: piano, jogging. Home: 2610 Sunset Ave Utica NY 13502-6009 E-mail: jfioriblanchfield@adelphia.net.

FIORILLA, JOHN LEOPOLDO, lawyer, finance company executive; b. Paterson, N.J., July 1, 1965; s. Giovanni and Maria Giuseppina (Mazzara) Fiorilla; m. Annie Carla Matilde Maria Borello, Sept. 27, 2003. BS, Seton Hall U., 1987; JD, U. Pitts., 1990; LLM in Internat. Legal Studies, NYU, 1999. Bar: N.J. 1990, N.Y. 1991, D.C. 1991, U.S. Supreme Ct. 1995; master lic. USCG. Assoc. Sullivan & Cromwell, N.Y.C., London, 1990-94, Brosio, Casati e Associati, Milan, 1992—93; prin., gen. counsel Elysium Group Inc., N.Y.C., 1994—; of counsel Studio Legale Vassalli, Milan, 1994-2001, Studio Legale Caffi-Maroncelli & Associati, Bergamo and Milan, Italy, 1994—. Adviser to the nunciature, Permanent Observer Mission of the Holy See to the UN, 1997—, mem. Holy See Del. to the Gen. Assembly and other UN bodies, 1997—. Pres. standing com. Young Friends Save Venice, 1998-; bd. dirs. Internat. Cath. Orgns. Info. Ctr., 1999-, Save Venice Inc., 2001-; hon. usher St. Patrick's Cathedral, 2003-; mem. adv. bd. Peggy Guggenheim Collection, 2004-. Decorated Knight Order Merit Rep. Italy (motu proprio), Knight Sovereign Mil. Order Malta, Grand Officer Equestrian Order Holy Sepulchre Jerusalem, Knight with Star Sacred Mil. Constantinian Order St. George (moto proprio), Knight Officer Order Merit Savoy, Silver Cross of Merit, Red Cross of the Republic of San Marino, Knight Order of St. Maurice and Lazarus, Savoy, Grand Officer Order of Prince Danilo I of Montenegro; recipient Silver medal of Merit, Italian Red Cross. Fellow: Fgn. Policy Assn.; mem.: Assn. Bar City N.Y., Met. Opera Club, Racquet Club Phila., Met. Club, Econ. Club NY, Down Town Assn., Circolo del Golf di Roma. Roman Catholic. Home: 555 Park Ave New York NY 10021-8166 Office: Elysium Group Inc 641 Lexington Ave 26th Fl New York NY 10022-4503 Also: Via degli Omenoni 2 20121 Milan Italy Office Phone: 212-661-6222. E-mail: jlf@fiorilla.com.

FIORILLO, JOHN A., engineering educator; b. N.Y.C., Aug. 18, 1947; s. Jack and Theresa Fiorillo; m. Linda Hansen Fiorillo, June 30, 1973; 1 child, Steven John. AAS, Acad. Astronautics, Flushing, N.Y., 1968; MS, N.Y. Inst. Tech., 1970, L.I. U., 1974; PhD, NYU, 1980. Electronics engr. Optics Tech., Flushing, NY, 1969—73; asst. prof. Acad. Astronautics, Flushing, NY, 1973—75; prof. Farmingdale State U., NY, 1975—. Contbr. articles to profl. jours. Mem. adv. bd. L.I. Tech. Edn. Coun., Farmingdale, NY, 1997—. Grantee NSF, 2000, 2001. Mem.: IEEE, Am. Soc. for Engrng. Edn., Tau Alpha Pi.

FIORINA, CARLY (CARLETON SNEED FIORINA), former computer company executive; b. Austin, Tex., Sept. 6, 1954; d. Joseph and Madelon Sneed; m. Frank J. Fiorina. BA in Medieval History and Philosophy, Stanford U., 1976; MBA, Robert H. Smith Sch. Bus. U. Md., College Park, Md., 1980; MSc, MIT, 1989; postgrad., UCLA. Account exec. Long Lines AT&T, 1980, sr. v.p. Global Mktg., pres., AT&T network systems, N. Am., 1994—95; exec. v.p. corp. ops. Lucent Technologies, Murray Hill, NJ, 1995—96, pres., consumer products bus., 1996—97, group pres. Global Svc. Provider bus., 1997—99; pres. Hewlett-Packard Co., Palo Alto, 1999—2000, CEO, 1999—2005, chmn. bd. dirs., 2000—05. Bd. dirs., PowerUp, Hewlett-Packard, 1999-2005, Merck & Co. Inc., 1999-2001, Revolution Health Group, 2005-; mem., US China Bd. Trade.; appointed to US Space Commn. by the White House Named one of Fortune Mag. Most Powerful Women in Am. Bus., Hon. Fellow London Bus. Sch., 2001; recipient Appeal of Conscience award, 2002, Concern Worldwide "Seeds of Hope" award, 2003, Leadership award, Private Sector Coun., 2004. Business E-Mail: csfiorina@sbcglobal.net.

FIORITO, EDWARD GERALD, lawyer; b. Irvington, N.J., Oct. 20, 1936; s. Edward and Emma (DePascale) F.; m. Charlotte H. Longo (widowed 2-3-2004); children: Jeanne C., Kathryn M., Thomas E., Lynn M., Patricia A. BSEE, Rutgers U., 1958; JD, Georgetown U., 1963. Bar: U.S. Patent and Trademark Office 1960, Va. 1963, N.Y. 1964, Mich. 1970, Ohio 1975, Tex. 1984. Patent staff atty. IBM, Armonk, N.Y., 1958-69; v.p. patent and comml. relations Energy Conversion Devices, Troy, Mich., 1969-71; mng. patent prosecution Burroughs Corp., Detroit, 1971-75; gen. patent counsel B.F. Goodrich Corp., Akron, Ohio, 1975-83; dir. patents and licensing Dresser Industries, Inc., Dallas, 1983-93. Alt. mem. Dept. Commerce Adv. Commn. on Patent Law Reform, 1991-92; spl. master, arbitrator, neutral evaluator, expert providing opinion testimony in intellectual property litigation, 1986—; U.S. del. to World Intellectual Property Orgn. Diplomatic Conf., 1991. Bd. dirs. Akron's House Extending Aid on Drugs, 1976. Mem. ABA (chmn. sci. and tech. sect. 1984-85, chair intellectual property law sect. 2000-2001), IEEE, Tex. Bar Assn. (chmn. intellectual property law sect. 1990-91), Internat. Assn. for Protection Indsl. Property (exec. bd. 1989—), Assn. Corp. Patent Counsel (exec. com. 1982-84), Tau Beta Pi. Roman Catholic. Avocations: music, flying. E-mail: ipconsulting@msn.com. *Those of you who have received gifts in great abundance at the beginning of your journey here, should remember to use them before your journey ends in the service of your creator who gave them to you.*

FIRCHOW, EVELYN SCHERABON, German language and literature educator, writer; b. Vienna; came to U.S., 1951, naturalized, 1964; d. Raimund and Hildegard (Nickl) Scherabon; m. Peter E. Firchow, 1969; children: Felicity (dec. 1988), Pamina. BA, U. Tex., 1956; MA, U. Man., 1957; PhD, Harvard U., 1963. Instr. coll. math. Balmoral Hall Sch., Winnipeg, Man., Can., 1953-55; tchg. fellow in German Harvard U., Cambridge, Mass., 1957-58, 61-62; lectr. German U. Md. in Munich, 1961; instr. German U. Wis., Madison, 1962-63, asst. prof., 1963-65; assoc. prof. German U. Minn., Mpls., 1965-69, prof. German and Germanic philology, 1969—, McKnight rsch. prof., 2004—; vis. prof. U. Fla., Gainesville, 1973; Fulbright rsch. prof. Iceland, 1966-67, 80, 94; vis. rsch. prof. Nat. Cheng Kung U., Tainan, Taiwan, 1982-83; permanent vis. prof. Jilin U., Changchun, China, 1987—. Vis. prof. U. Graz, Austria, 1989, Austria, 91, Austria, 2002—03, U. Vienna, Austria, 1995, U. Bonn, 1996, Nat. U. Costa Rica, 2000. Editor and author: (under name E.S. Coleman) Taylor Starck-Festschrift, 1964, Stimmen aus dem Stundenglas, 1968, (under name E.S. Firchow) Studies by Einar Haugen, 1972, Studies for Einar Haugen, 1972, Was Deutsche lesen, 1973, Deutung und Bedeutung, 1973, Elucidarius in Old Norse Translation, 1989, The Old Norse Elucidarius: Original Text and English Translation, 1992, Notker der Deutsche von St. Gallen: De interpretatione, 1995, Categoriae, 2 Vols., 1996, De nuptiis Philologiae et Mercurii, 2 Vols., 1999, Notker der Deutsche von St. Gallen (950-1022): Ausführliche Bibliographie, 2000, De consolatione Philosophiae, 3 vols., 2003, Reluctant Modernists, Festschrift Peter Firchow, 2002, Gottfried von Strassburg: Tristan und Isolde, 2004; translator: Einhard: Vita Caroli Magni, Das Leben Karls des Grossen, 1968, 84, 95, Einhard: Vita Caroli Magni, The Life of Charlemagne, 1972, 85, Icelandic Short Stories, 1974, 87, East German Short Stories, 1979, (with P.E. Firchow) Alois Brandstetter, The Abbey, 1998; dir., editor Computer Clearing-House Project for German and Medieval Scandinavian, to 2000; assoc. editor Germanic Notes and Revs., Am. Linguistics, Germanic Linguistics; contbr. articles and book revs. to profl. jours. Fulbright scholar Tex., 1951-52; fellow Alexander von Humboldt-Stiftung, Munich, 1960-61, Tuebingen, 1974, Marburg, 1981, Goettingen, 1985, Tokyo, 1991, Marburg and Berlin, 1993, Bonn, 2001, Fulbright Found., Iceland, 1967-68, 80, 94, Austrian Govt., 1977, NEH, 1980-81, Am. Inst. Indian Studies, 1988, BUSH fellow, 1989, Thor Thors fellow, 1994, Faculty summer fellow and Mc Knight summer fellow, 1995, 96, 99, 2004, Deutscher Akademischer Austausdienst (DAAD) rsch. fellow, 2000; elected hon. mem. Multilingual Rsch. Ctr., Brussels, 1986. Mem. AAUP, MLA (chmn. divsn. German lit. to 1700 1979-80, 93-96, vice chmn. pedagogical seminar for Germanic philology 1979-86, 91-93, chair 1994), Medieval Acad. Am., Soc. German-Am. Studies (chair Linguistics I 1992), Internat. Comparative Lit. Assn., Soc. for Advancement Scandinavian Studies (chmn. Germanic philology 1979, text editing 1980, linguistics 1984, computers and Old Norse 1985), Assn. for Lang. and Linguistic Computing (founding mem.), Am. Comparative Lit. Assn., Midwest Modern Lang. Assn. (chmn. German I 1965-66, chmn. Scandinavian 1979), Am. Assn. Tchrs. German, Mediävisten Verband, Soc. for Germanic Philology, Österreichische Germanisten-Gesellschaft, Assn. Lit. Scholars and Critics. Office: U Minn 205 Folwell Hall 9 Pleasant St SE Minneapolis MN 55455 Business E-Mail: firch001@umn.edu.

FIRCHOW, PETER EDGERLY, language professional, educator, writer; b. Needham, Mass., Dec. 16, 1937; s. Paul Karl August and Marta Loria (Montenegro) F.; m. Evelyn Maria Scherabon Coleman, Sept. 18, 1969; 1 dau., Pamina Maria Scherabon. BA, Harvard Coll., 1959; postgrad., U. Vienna, Austria, 1959—60; MA, Harvard U., 1961; PhD, U. Wis., 1965. Asst. prof. English U. Mich., 1965-67; asst. prof. English and comparative lit. U. Minn., Mpls., 1967-69, assoc. prof., 1969-73, prof., 1973—, chmn. Comparative Lit. Program, 1972-78. Disting. vis. prof. Nat. Cheng Kung U., Taiwan, 1982-83, Jilin U., Peoples Republic China, 1987, U. Munich, 1988, U. Graz, Austria, 1989, 2003; Fulbright prof. U. Bonn, Germany, 1995-96, Nat. U. Costa Rica, 2000. Author: Friedrich Schlegel's Lucinde and the Fragments, 1971, Aldous Huxley, Satirist and Novelist, 1972, The Writer's Place: Interviews on the Literary Situation in Contemporary Britain, 1974; (with E.S. Firchow) East German Short Stories: An Introductory Anthology, 1979; The End of Utopia: A Study of Huxley's Brave New World, 1984; The Death of the German Cousin: Variations on a Literary Stereotype, 1986; translator (with E.S. Firchow) The Abbey (Alois Brandstetter), 1998, Envisioning Africa: Racism and Imperialism in Conrad's "Heart of Darkness", 2000, W.H. Auden: Contexts for Poetry, 2002, Reluctant Modernists: Aldous Huxley and Some Contemporaries, 2002; contbr. articles on modern lit. subjects to profl. jours. Fellow Inst. Advanced Studies in Humanities, Edinburgh, 1977. Mem. Midwest Modern Lang. Assn. (v.p. 1977, pres. 1978), Am. Comparative Lit. Assn., Assn. Lit. Scholars and Critics, Internat. Aldous Huxley Soc. Home: 135 Birnamwood Dr Burnsville MN 55337-6814 Office: U Minn Dept English 310D Lind Hall 207 Church St SE Minneapolis MN 55455-0134 Office Phone: 612-625-3363. E-mail: pef@tc.umn.edu.

FIRE, ANDREW Z., pathologist, educator, geneticist; b. Santa Clara, Calif., 1959; BA in Math., U. Calif., Berkeley, 1978; PhD in Biology, MIT, 1983; postdoctoral studies, Med. Rsch. Coun. Lab., Cambridge, U.K., 1983—86. Microbiologist, dept. embryology Carnegie Instn., Washington, 1986—2003; adj. prof., biology Johns Hopkins U., Balt., 2000—; prof., depts. pathology and genetics Stanford U. Sch. Medicine, Calif., 2003—. Recipient Maryland Disting. Young Scientist award, 1997, medal, Genetics Soc. Am., 2002, Dr. H.P. Heinken prize in biochemistry and biophysics, Netherlands Acad. Arts and Sci., 2004. Fellow: Am. Acad. Arts and Scis.; mem.: NAS (award in Molecular Biology 2003). Achievements include discovery of process now known as RNAi (with Craig C. Mello). Office: Stanford Univ Sch Medicine 300 Pasteur Dr L235 Stanford CA 94305-5324*

FIREBAUGH, FRANCILLE MALOCH, academic administrator; b. El Dorado, Ark., July 15, 1933; d. Delton Verdis and Dorothy Lucille (Measeles) Maloch; m. John David Firebaugh, Dec. 28, 1970. BS, U. Ark., 1955; MS, U. Tenn., 1956; PhD, Cornell U., 1962. Instr. U. Tex., Austin, 1956-58; asst. prof. home econs. Ohio State U., Columbus, 1962-65, assoc. prof., 1965-69, prof., 1969-88; dir. Sch. Home Econs., 1973-82; acting v.p. agrl. adminstrn.; exec. dean of agr., home econs., natural resources, 1982-83; assoc. provost Office Acad. Affairs, 1983-84; vice provost for internat. affairs, 1984-88; acting provost, v.p. acad. affairs, 1985-86; dean coll. human ecology Cornell U., Ithaca, NY, 1988-99, dir. spl. projects office of pres. and provost, 2000—01, vice provost for land grant affairs, spl. asst. to the pres., 2001—05, sr. consultant to provost, 2005—. Mem. joint com. on agrl. research and devel. Bd. Internat. Food and Agr., 1982-87. Author: Home Management: Context and Concepts, 1975, Family Resource Management, 1981, 88. Bd. dirs. Columbus Coun. on World Affairs, 1987-88, Boyce Thompson Inst. for Plant Rsch., 1991-97; moderator First Baptist Ch., 1981-83; bd. dirs. Cayuga Med. Ctr., 1992-2001, Panamerican Agr. Sch., Zamorano, Honduras, 1994—, Kendal at Ithaca, 1995-2003; Families and Work Inst., N.Y.C., 1995—; trustee Ithaca (N.Y.) Coll., 2000—, Cmty. Found. of Tompkins County, 2000-02. Mem. Nat. Coun. Family Rels., AAAS, Am. Home Econs. Found. (bd. dirs. 1987-90), Am. Assn. of Family and Consumer Scis., Ohio State U. Faculty Club (pres. 1988), Assn. Women in Devel. (sec. 1988-89), Sigma Xi, Sigma Delta Epsilon, Kappa Omicron Nu, Phi Upsilon Omicron, Gamma Sigma Delta, Phi Kappa Phi, Epsilon Sigma Phi. Office: Cornell U Office of Provost 449 Day Hall Ithaca NY 14853-2801 Business E-Mail: fmf1@cornell.edu.

FIREMAN, PAUL B., footwear and apparel company executive; b. Cambridge, Mass., Feb. 14, 1944; m. Phyllis Fireman; 3 children. Student, Boston U. Pres., chmn., CEO Reebok Internat. Ltd., Stoughton, Mass., 1979—. Founder The Reebok Found.; founder Paul & Phyllis Fireman Found.; co-founder One Family, Inc., 1998—. Recipient numerous industry awards., Honored by Human Rights Law Group, private-sector achievement award, Nat. Alliance to End Homelessness, 2005. Office: Reebok Internat Ltd 1895 JW Foster Blvd Canton MA 02021*

FIREMAN, PHILIP, pediatrician, allergist, immunologist; b. Pitts., 1932; MD, U. Chgo., 1957. Diplomate Am. Bd. Allergy and Immunology (chmn. 1992-93). Intern Phila. Gen. Hosp., 1957-58; resident in pediatrics Children's Hosp., Pitts., 1958-60; fellow in allergy and immunology NIH, Bethesda, Md., 1960-62; fellow allergist, immunologist Harvard Children's Hosp., Boston, 1962-64; prof. pediatrics, internal medicine U. Pitts. Med. Sch. Chmn. Am. Bd. Allergy & Immunology, 1990—91. Mem.: Am. Acad. Allergy, Asthma and Immunology (pres. 1997—98). Office: Childrens Hosp 3705 5th Ave Pittsburgh PA 15213-2583 Office Phone: 412-692-5103. Business E-Mail: philip.fireman@chp.edu.

FIRESIDE, HARVEY FRANCIS, political scientist, educator; b. Vienna, Dec. 28, 1929; came to U.S., 1940, naturalized, 1945; s. Norbert and Frances F.; m. Bryna Joan Levenberg, Dec. 12, 1959; children: Leela Ruth, Douglas Leonard, Daniel Ephraim. BA magna cum laude, Harvard U., 1952, MA, 1955; PhD, New Sch. Social Research, 1968. Info. specialist AEC, 1957-58; editor Palmerton Publishing Co., N.Y.C., 1959-60, Am. Cyanamid Co., N.Y.C., 1960-61, Fgn. Policy Assn., N.Y.C., 1961-62; freelance editor, 1962-64; asst. prof. polit. sci. N.Y. Inst. Tech., 1964-68; Charles A. Dana prof. politics Ithaca (N.Y.) Coll., 1968-96, prof. emeritus, 1998. Fulbright advisor Cornell U., 2003—04, vis. prof. Einaudi Ctr. Internat. Studies, 2003-; cons. in field. Author: Icon and Swastika: The Russian Orthodox Church under Nazi and Soviet Control, 1971, Soviet Psychoprisons, 1979, Brown vs Board of Education, 1994, Young People from Bosnia Talk About War, 1996, Plessy vs. Ferguson, 1997, The Fifth Amendment, 1998, New York Times vs. Sullivan, 1999, Nuremberg Trials of Nazi War Criminals, 2000, The Mississippi Burning Civil Rights Murder Conspiracy Trial, 2002, Separate and Unequal: Homer Plessy and the Supreme Court Decision That Legalized Racism, 2004; also articles. Group leader Amnesty Internat., Ithaca, 1973-80; co-chmn. Socialist Studies Com., NY, 1977-83, Working Group Against Psychiat. Abuse, 1980-83; bd. dirs. Tompkins County chpt. ACLU, 1968-71, Ithaca Sanctuary Com., 1986-92, Tompkins County Mental Health Assn., 1986-89, 93-95, pres., 1995-96; bd. dirs. Com. on U.S.-Latin Am. Rels., 1990-92, Hillel Found., Ithaca Coll., 1991-93; coord. The Border Fund, 1989—, Bosnian Student Project, 1994-2000; Citizenship Project, 1997-99, Eleanor Roosevelt Loan Fund, 2000—, Ithaca City of Asylum, 2001-03. Recipient Tompkins County Human Rights award, 1992, 98, Carter G. Woodson award Nat. Coun. Social Studies, 2003; Harvard U. Russian Rsch. Ctr. fellow, summers 1975, 80; fellow Harvard U. Ukrainian Rsch. Inst., summer 1976; fellow Cornell U. Inst. for European Studies, 1995-98, 2004-05, Peace Studies Program, 1998-01, Cornell Law Sch., 2001-03; grantee N.Y. Dept. Edn., 1965; vis. scholar Russian Inst., Columbia U., 1966; Nat. Endowment Humanities fellow, summer, 1983, 94. Mem. Am. Polit. Sci. Assn. Democrat. Jewish. Home: 202 Eastwood Ave Ithaca NY 14850-6239 Personal E-mail: hfireside@juno.com. Business E-Mail: hff1@cornell.edu.

FIRESTONE, CHARLES MORTON, lawyer, educator; b. St. Louis, Oct. 16, 1944; s. Victor and Betty (Solomon) F.; m. Pattie Winston Porter, Apr. 19, 1975; children: Laurel, Asa. BA, Amherst Coll., 1966; JD, Duke U., 1969. Bar: D.C. 1969, U.S. Ct. Appeals (D.C. cir.) 1970, U.S. Ct. Appeals (5th cir.) 1972, U.S. Ct. Appeals (9th cir.) 1973, U.S. Ct. Appeals (2d cir.) 1975, U.S. Ct. Appeals (3d cir.) 1976, U.S. Ct. Appeals (8th cir.) 1977, U.S. Supreme Ct. 1977, Calif. 1983. Litigation atty. FCC, Washington, 1969-73; dir. litigation Citizens Comm. Ctr., Washington, 1973-77; adj. prof. law, dir. comm. law program UCLA, 1977-86; counsel Mitchell, Silberberg & Knupp, L.A., 1983-90; vis. lectr. UCLA Sch. Law, 1986-90; exec. dir. comm. and society program Aspen Inst., 1989—, exec. v.p. policy programs and internat. activities, 1998-2000. Vis. prof. Duke U., Stanford Ctr. Pub. Policy, 2003; faculty adviser Fed. Comm. Law Jour., L.A., 1977-86; counsel statewide TV debates LVW Calif., 1978-90, counsel Calif. media Dukakis-Bentsen Com.; co-cmmn. adv. com. LWC Calif. Speak Out 1988 Election Project; pres. Bd. Telecom. Commrs., City of L.A., 1984-86; mem. nat. adv. bd. Privacy and Am.Bus., 1993-2000; mem. Commn. on Radio and Tv Policy, 1996. Author: (with Ellen Mickiewicz) Television and Elections, 1992, (with Donald R. Browne and Mickiewicz) Television/Radio News and Minorities, 1994, (with Robert Entman, Dee Reid and Mickiewicz) Television, Radio & Privatization, 1998, (with Craig L. Lamay and Mickiewicz) Television Autonomy & the State, 1999, (with Mickiewicz Browne LaMay) Democracy on the Air, 2000; editor: Television for the 21st Century: The Next Wave, 1993, (with Jorge Reina Schement) Toward An Information Bill of Rights and Responsibilities, 1995, (with Amy Korzick Garmer) Creating a Learning Society: Initiatives for Education and Technology, 1996, (with Anthony Corrado) Elections in Cyberspace: Toward A New Era in American Politics, 1996, (with Garmer) Digital Broadcasting and the Public Interest, 1998; mem. editl. bd. Aspenia, 2000-04; contbr. articles to profl. jours., chpts. to books. Bd. dirs. Corp. for Disabilities and Telecom., L.A., 1980-82; bd. dirs. KCRW Found., Santa Monica, Calif., 1982-90, vice chmn., 1987-90; trustee Ctr. for Law in Pub. Interest, 1988-89; mem. adv. com. campaign Mondale for Pres., L.A., 1984; mem. adv. com. Ctr. for Govtl. Studies, 2003-; Campaign Legal Ctr., 2004-. Recipient cert. of commendation Mayor of L.A., 1986, resolution commendation award City Coun. L.A., 1986; Luther Ely Smith scholar and Andrew Laurie scholar Amherst Coll., 1965-66; Glocom fellow Japanese Inst. Global Comms., 2001—. Mem. ABA (chmn. broadcast and spectrum use com., sect. sci. and tech. 1981-83, chmn. electronic campaigning com. 1984-86), Fed. Comm. Bar Assn., Soc. Satellite Profls. (sec. bd. dirs. So Calif. chpt. 1984-87), Coun. Fgn. Rels., Cosmos Club. Jewish. Office: 1 Dupont Cir NW Ste 700 Washington DC 20036-1133 Office Phone: 202-736-5818. Business E-Mail: firestone@aspeninstitute.org.

FIRESTONE, MORTON H., finance company executive; b. Chgo., Feb. 4, 1935; s. William and Lillian (Kliot) F.; m. Roberta (Bobbie) Schwartz, Feb. 3, 1957; children: Jeffrey, Scott, Dan. BS, U. Calif., Davis, 1957; MBA, U. So. Calif., 1971. V.p. Security Pacific Nat. Bank, Los Angeles, 1957-77; chmn. bd., chief fin. officer, corp. sec. Elixir Industries, 1977-87, also dir.; pres. Garden Ins., 1978-87, Club Wholesale Concepts, Inc., 1986-87; chmn. bd., chief exec. officer Rondure Industries, 1987-90; pres. Lin Mor Corp., Woodland Hills, Calif., 1990—. Bd. dirs. Robert Burns & Sons, Inc. Past chmn. Los Angeles-Eilat Sister City Com. Mem. Fin. Execs. Inst., Beta Gamma Sigma. Lodges: Optimist (past pres. Hollywood), Kiwanis (past pres. West Hollywood). Office: Lin Mor Corp PO Box 571025 Tarzana CA 91357-1025 E-mail: mort@linmorcorp.com.

FIRESTONE, NANCY B., federal judge; b. Manchester, N.H., Oct. 17, 1951; d. Albert and Bernice (Brown) F. BA, Washington U., St. Louis, 1973; JD, U. Mo., 1977. Bar: Mo. 1977, U.S. Ct. Appeals (2nd, 4th, 5th, 6th, 9th, 8th and 10th cirs.). Trial atty. U.S. Dept. Justice, Washington, 1977-84, asst. chief, 1984-85, dep. chief environ. enforcement, 1985-89, dept. asst. atty. gen., environment & natural resources div., 1995—98; assoc. dep. adminstr. EPA, 1989-92, adminstrv. judge, 1992-95; judge US Ct. of Fed. Claims, 1998—. Adj. prof. Georgetown U. Law Ctr., 1986—. Mem. ABA.*

FIREY, WALTER IRVING, JR., retired sociologist; b. Roundup, Mont., Aug. 13, 1916; s. Walter Irving and Marie (Oveson) F.; m. Mary Lou Powell, Aug. 23, 1952; children: Paul, John. BA, Univ. Wash., 1938, MA, 1940; PhD, Harvard U., 1945. Asst. prof. Mich. State U., East Lansing, 1945-46; from asst. prof. to prof. emeritus Univ. Tex., Austin, 1946-85, prof. emeritus, 1985—. Author: Land Use in Central Boston, 1947, 3d edit., 1975, Man, Mind & Land, 1960, 3d edit., 1999, Law & Economy in Planning, 1965; contbr. numerous articles to profl. jours. Ctr. for Advanced Study in Behavioral Scis. fellow Stanford, Calif., 1959-60. Mem. Am. Sociological

Assn., Rural Sociological Assn. (award of merit 1983), Sociological Rsch. Assn. (pres. 1972), Phi Beta Kappa. Presbyterian. Avocation: reading. Home: 1307 Wilshire Blvd Austin TX 78722 Personal E-mail: fireyma@aol.com.

FIRMIN, MICHAEL WAYNE, psychology professor; b. New Orleans, July 28, 1961; s. Lloyd John and Betty L. (Shepherd) F.; m. Karen Sue Tuttle, Aug. 4, 1984; children: Ruth, Sarah. BA, Calvary Bible Coll., 1983; MA, Calvary Theol. Sem., 1985; MS, Bob Jones U., 1987, PhD, 1988; MA, Marywood U., 1992; PhD, Syracuse U. Nat. cert. counselor; lic. psychologist, Ohio. Dir. counseling svcs. Bapt. Bible Coll. of Pa., Clarks Summit, 1988-98, assoc. prof., 1988-98, chmn. divsn. grad. studies, 1995-97; resident in psychology TCN: Behavioral Health Svcs., 2000—01; assoc. prof. psychology Cedarville (Ohio) U., 1998—2004, prof. psychology, 2004—, chmn. dept. psychology, 2000—. Cons. for psychol. svcs. Assn. Bapts. for World Evangelism, Harrisburg, Pa., 1991—94, 1999—; clin. assessment cons. Keystone City Residence, 1994—2000. Pastor Faith Fellowship Bapt. Ch., Danbury, Conn., 1991-94. Mem. Psi Chi. Republican. Home: 84 E Elm St Cedarville OH 45314-8513 Office: Cedarville Univ 251 N Main St Cedarville OH 45314-0601

FIRMINGHAM, KELLY ANN, writer, poet; b. Flint, Mich., Oct. 23, 1959; d. Daniel Sawczyn and Bonnie Emily O'Dell; 1 child, Kim Marie Sawczyn. Student, Harcourt/Inenrat., Scranton, Pa., 1990. Game clk., ride assembler J & R Shows/ Carnival, Mich., 1980; janitorial/stock clk. Sweet Mornings Bakery, Flint, 1986; cashier, mem. staff Shoppin-Sort Market, Flint, 1987; auto parts handler Genesee County Cmty. Industries, Flint, 1989; personal care aide Arvo-Care Takers, Flint, 1990—2000; direct mail distributor Flint, 2002. Author: Collective Works of Poetry, 2001; lyricist: J.C. and Thee, 1990. Presenter person centered plan Cmty. Mental Health, Ann Arbor, Mich., 1999. Mem.: Psychosocial/Rainbow Coalition, Friends of the Flint Pub. Libr., Assertive Cmty./The Next Step. Democrat. Avocations: woodworking, music, puzzles, handcrafts. Home: 1737 Davison Rd Apt 1 Flint MI 48506-4427

FIRSCHEIN, SYLVIA, librarian, elementary education educator; b. Belleville, N.J., Apr. 8, 1933; d. Louis and Sonia (Osheroff) Haft; m. Hilliard E. Firschein, Apr. 12, 1964; children: Merry, Warren. BA, Brandeis U., 1955. Cert. K-8 tchr., ednl. media specialist, N.J., Calif., Mass. Tchr. Nutley (N.J.) Bd. Edn., 1959-65; tchr. learning disabled Wayne (N.J.) Bd. Edn., 1972-78, media specialist, 1986—97; libr. dir. YM & YWHA of North Jersey, Wayne, 1977-86, chair Judaica Libr., trustee, 1988—97, ret., 1997. Trustee Akiba Acad., L.A., 1969-72, Am. Labor Mus., Haledon, N.J., 1985-1997; libr. Idelson Adult Libr. Temple Beth Shalom, 2005— Coun. mem. Assn. Jewish Libraries, chair, membership recruitment, 1984-1992; pres. Sch. Synagogue, Ctr. Divsn., 1984-86; founder, 1st pres. N.J. Assn. Jewish Libraries. Mem. Jewish Geneal. Soc., Pi Lambda Theta, Hadassah. Avocations: storytelling, genealogy.

FIRST, HARRY, law educator; b. 1945; BA, U. Pa., 1966, JD, 1969. Bar: Pa. 1969, NY 1979. Law clk. to Justice Samuel J. Roberts Supreme Ct. Pa., 1969-70; atty. antitrust divsn. US Dept. Justice, Washington, 1970-72; asst. prof. U. Toledo Coll. Law, 1972-76; vis. assoc. prof. NYU Sch. Law, NYC, 1976-77, assoc. prof., 1977-79, prof., 1979—, now Charles L. Denison prof. law, dir. trade regulation program; counsel Loeb & Loeb, NYC & LA, 1985-99; chief antitrust bur. NY State Office of Atty. Gen., NYC, 1999-2001. Vis. prof. faculty law Sophia U., Tokyo, 1983—84; adj. prof. faculty law U. Tokyo, 1992—93. Fulbright Rsch. Fellow, Tokyo, 1983—84, 1992—93. Mem. Order of Coif, Phi Beta Kappa. Office: NYU Sch Law Vanderbilt Hall Rm 327 40 Washington Sq S New York NY 10012-1099 Office Phone: 212-998-6211. E-mail: hf3@nyu.edu.*

FIRST, MICHAEL BRUCE, psychiatrist, educator; b. Phila., Nov. 25, 1956; s. E. David and Reda Bell (Dissin) F. BS in Engring., Princeton (N.J.) U., 1978; MS in Computer Sci., U. Pitts., 1981, MD, 1983. Diplomate Am. Bd. Psychiatry and Neurology. Intern in medicine Shadyside Hosp., Pitts., 1983-84; resident in psychiatry Columbia-Presbyn. Hosp., N.Y.C., 1984-87; fellow in biometrics N.Y. State Psychiat. Inst., N.Y.C., 1986-88, rsch. psychiatrist, 1988—; pvt. practice Columbia-Presbyn. Hosp., 1987—. Prof. clin. psychiatry Columbia U., 1997—. Author: The Structured Clinical Interview for DSM-IV (SCID), 1994, DSM-IV Guidebook, 1995, DSM-IV Handbook, 1995, (computer software) DTREE: The DSM-IV Expert, 1997, Am I OK? A Layman's Guide to the Psychiatrist's Bible, 1999; editor: DSM-IV Text and Criteria, 1990—. Mem. AMA, Am. Psychiat. Assn. Office: NY State Psychiat Inst 1051 Riverside Dr New York NY 10032-1013 Office Phone: 212-543-5531. Business E-Mail: mbf2@columbia.edu.

FIRSTENBERG, JEAN PICKER, film institute executive; b. N.Y.C., Mar. 13, 1936; d. Eugene and Sylvia (Moses) Picker; m. Paul Firstenberg, Aug. 9, 1956 (div. July 1980); children: Debra, Douglas BS summa cum laude, Boston U., 1958. Asst. producer Altman Prodns., Washington, 1965-66; media advisor J. Walter Thompson, N.Y.C., 1969-72; asst. for spl. projects Princeton (N.J.) U., 1972-74, dir. publs., 1974-76; program officer John and Mary R. Markle Found., N.Y.C., 1976—80; dir., CEO Am. Film Inst., L.A., Washington, 1980—; mem. Citizens' Stamp Advisory Com. U.S. Postal Svc., 2002—. Bd. dirs. Trans-Lux Corp.; former chmn. nat. adv. bd. Peabody Broadcasting Awards; bd. dirs. Trans-Lux Corp. Former trustee Boston U.; mem. adv. bd. Will Rogers Inst., N.Y.C.; chmn., bd. advisors Film Dept. N.C. Sch. of Arts. Recipient Alumni award for disting. service to profession Boston U., 1982; seminar and prodn. chairs at directing workshop for women named in her honor Am. Film Inst., 1986 Mem. Women in Film (Crystal award 1990), Trusteeship for Betterment of Women, Acad. Motion Picture Arts and Scis. Office: Am Film Inst 2021 N Western Ave Los Angeles CA 90027-1657 Office Phone: 323-856-7677.*

FIRTH, EVERETT JOSEPH, timpanist; b. Winchester, Mass., June 2, 1930; s. Everett Emanuel and Rosemary (Scandura) F.; m. Olga Kwasniak, June 22, 1960; children— Kelly Victoria, Tracy Kimberly. Mus.B. with distinction, 1952. Faculty head New Eng. Conservatory, 1950—; mem. faculty Berkshire Music Center, 1956—. Pres., CEO Vic Firth Inc. (mfr. and distbr. worldwide drum sticks and mallets); CEO Vic Firth Mfg., Newport, Maine. Solo timpanist, Boston Symphony Orch., 1952—2002, Boston Pops Orch., 1952—2002, with, Boston Symphony Chamber Players; Recs. with, RCA Victor, Mercury, Columbia, Cambridge, Deutsche Grammophon. Mem. ASCAP, Phi Kappa Lambda, Phi Mu Alpha Sinfonia. Home: 3 Pinewood Rd Dover MA 02030-2521 Office: Vic Firth Inc 65 Commerce Way Dedham MA 02026-2953 Office Phone: 781-326-3455. Business E-Mail: vic@vicfirth.com.

FISCH, JOSEPH, lawyer; b. N.Y.C., Apr. 7, 1939; s. Israel Ben Zion and Esther Leah (Spielvogel) F.; m. Norma Potter, Aug. 7, 1960; children: Adam Jeffrey, Jennifer Anne, Rachel Lynne. BA, Tufts U., 1960; JD, NYU, 1963, LLM in Taxation, 1969. Bar: N.J. 1964, U.S. Dist. Ct. N.J. 1964, U.S. Tax Ct. 1966, U.S. Supreme Ct. 1969, U.S. Ct. Appeals (3d cir.) 1971. Law clk. to judge N.J. Superior Ct., Jersey City, 1963-64; assoc. Hannock, Wiseman, Stern and Besser, Newark, 1964-65, Blume and Kalb, Newark, 1965-66; pvt. practice Somerset, NJ, 1966-87, Kendall Park, NJ, 1987—2005. Asst. prof. Rutgers U., New Brunswick, N.J., 1971-81; arbitrator Am. Arbitration Assn., 1969-97, N.J. Superior Ct., Somerville, 1985-89; atty. Franklin Twp. Rent Leveling Bd., Somerset, 1980-91; mem. malpractice panel N.J. Supreme Ct., 1980-84; atty. Franklin Twp. Bd. Adjustment, Somerset, 1991-2001. Contbr. articles to law jours. Pres. Franklin Twp. Jaycees, 1967-68, Franklin Housing and Neighborhood Devel. Corp., Somerset, 1975-78, Temple Beth El Men's Club, Somerset, 1971-72, trustee, 1970, 1997-2004. Mem. ABA, N.J. Bar Assn. (chair gen. practice sect. 1990-91, Gen. Practitioner of Yr. 1992), Somerset County Bar Assn., Rotary (Franklin Twp. bd. dirs. 1987-88), Franklin Twp. Rep. Club (pres. 1999-2001). Republican. Jewish. Avocations: tennis, golf, skiing, sailing. Office: PO Box 5321 838 Easton Ave Somerset NJ 08875-5321 E-mail: fischjos@aol.com.

FISCH, NATHANIEL JOSEPH, physicist; b. Montreal, Quebec, Can., Dec. 29, 1950; s. Mandel and Helene (Greenfield) F.; m. Tobe Michelle Mann, Aug. 12, 1984; children: Jacob, Benjamin, Adam. BS, MIT, 1972, MS, 1975, PhD, 1978. Researcher Princeton (N.J.) Plasma Physics Lab., 1978-91, assoc. dir. for acad. affairs, 1993—; dir. program in plasma physics Princeton U., 1991—, prof. astrophys. scis., 1991—. Cons. Exxon Rsch. and Engring., Clinton, N.J., 1981-86; vis. scientist IBM, Yorktown Heights, N.Y., 1986. Recipient fellowship Guggenheim Found., 1985, 1992 APS award for Excellence in Plasma Physics, Am. Phys. Soc., 1992, Bronze medal for Outstanding Mentor, US Dept. Energy, 2002, E.O. Lawrence award, US Dept. Energy, 2004, James Clerk Maxwell Prize winner, 2005. Fellow Am. Phys. Soc. (vice chair divsn. of plasma physics 1996, chair-elect 1997, chair 1998). Achievements include patents in new ways to produce current in plasmas. Office: Princeton U Forrestal Campus PO Box 451 MS30 Princeton NJ 08543-0451 E-mail: fisch@princeton.edu.

FISCH, ROBERT OTTO, medical educator; b. Budapest, Hungary, June 12, 1925; came to U.S., 1957. s. Zoltan and Irene (Manheim) F.; 1 dau., Rebecca A. Med. diploma, U. Budapest, 1951; study art, Acad. Fine Arts, Budapest, 1943, Mpls. Coll. Arts and Design, 1970-76. Gen. practice medicine, Hungary, 1951-55; pub. health officer, 1955; pediatrician Hosp. for Premature Children, Budapest, 1956; intern Christ Hosp., Jersey City, 1957-58; intern pediatrics U. Minn. Hosps., 1958-59, researcher, 1959-60, research fellow, 1961; instr. U. Minn. Sch. Medicine, 1961-63, asst. prof., 1963-72, assoc. prof., 1972-79, prof., 1979—, dir. phenylketonuric clinic, 1961-97. Author: Respiratory Diseases; PKU, Child Development (Best Cover Minn. Med. 1975), Light from the Yellow Star: A Lesson of Love from the Holocaust, 1994, The Metamorphosis to Freedom, 2000, Dear Dr. Fisch: Children's Letters to a Holocaust Survivor, 2004; contbr. articles to profl. jours.; exhibited art works in various one-man and group shows. Mem. Soc. Pediatric Rsch., Am. Physician Art Assn. (Best of Show award 2002, numerous others). Home: 1201 Yale Pl 2301 Minneapolis MN 55403 Personal E-mail: fisch001@umn.edu.

FISCH, SANFORD MICHAEL, lawyer; b. Newark, July 27, 1955; s. Theodore W. and Iris Fisch. BA magna cum laude, Boston U., 1977; JD, U. San Diego, 1980; M of Law-Tax, Georgetown U., 1982. Tax specialist Coopers & Lybrand, San Diego, 1982-84; ptnr. Rosenberg and Fisch, San Diego, 1984-88, Armstrong, Fisch & Tutoli, PLC, San Diego, San Francisco and Santa Clara, Calif., 1988—. Tchr. Am. Coll., Bryn Mawr, Pa., 1983; co-founder Am. Acad. Estate Planning Attys., 1992. Co-founder San Diego Sr. Olympics, 1988; mem. law review U. San Diego, 1979-80. Recipient Program of Yr. award San Diego Jewish Community Ctr., 1988. Mem. Nat. Mortar Bd. Office: Armstrong Fisch & Tutoli PLC 9360 Towne Centre Dr La Jolla CA 92037 also: Am Acad Estate Planning Attys Ste 850 4365 Executive Dr San Diego CA 92121 Office Phone: 858-453-2128. Office Fax: 858-535-8241. Business E-Mail: sandyf@aaepa.com.

FISCH, WILLIAM BALES, law educator; b. Cleve., May 11, 1936; s. Max Harold and Ruth Alice (Bales) F.; m. Janice Heston McPherson, Sept. 2, 1961 (dec. 1987); m. Suzanne Fischer Good, June 19, 1993 (dec. 1998); children: Katherine Emily, Stephen McPherson. AB, Harvard Coll., 1957; LLB, U. Ill., 1960; M.Comparative Law (univ. fgn. law fellow), U. Chgo., 1962; JUD, U. Freiburg, Germany, 1972. Bar: Ill. 1961, Mo. 1982. Assoc. firm Kirkland & Ellis, Chgo., 1962-65; asst. prof. law U. N.D., 1965-68, assoc. prof., 1968-70, U. Mo., Columbia, 1970-74, prof., 1974—, Isador Loeb prof. law, 1977—. Author: Die Vorteilsausgleichung im amerikanischen und deutschen Recht, 1974; co-author: Problems, Cases and Materials on Professional Responsibility, 1985, 2d edit., 1995; bd. editors: Am. Jour. Comparative Law; contbr. articles, revs. to law jours. Alexander von Humboldt-Stiftung Rsch. fellow, 1968-69, 89-90; Fulbright-Hays Rsch. scholar Hamburg, Germany, 1980-81, 89-90; Max Planck Soc. Rsch. fellow, Hamburg, 1992. Mem. ABA, AAUP, Am. Law Inst. Office: U Mo Law Sch Columbia MO 65211-0001

FISCHBACH, CHARLES PETER, rail transportation executive, consultant, lawyer, arbitrator, mediator; b. Apr. 3, 1939; s. Howard C. and Pauline Lillian (Wasserman) F.; m. Paula Rae Steinhorn, July 15, 1973. BS, U. Wis., 1960, JD, 1967; MA, Rutgers U., 1962. Bar: Wis. 1967, U.S. Supreme Ct. 1974. Pvt. practice, Madison, Wis., 1967-68; labor rels. rsch. analyst and cons. N.Y.C., 1968-70; asst. to exec. officer labor rels. and pers. N.Y.C. Transit Authority, 1970; labor rels. rsch. analyst N.Y.C., 1970-72; exec. dir. Classified Mcpl. Employees Assn. Balt. City, 1972-74; labor rels. cons./arbitrator Balt., 1974-77; dir. labor rels., chief labor rels. officer, spl. labor counsel Chgo., Rock Island and Pacific R.R. Co., 1977-81, dir. pers. and employee rels., spl. labor counsel Chgo., 1981-84; dir. adminstrn. and human resources Chgo. Pacific Corp., 1984-85. V.p. Rock Island Improvement Co., 1984—85; dir. Peoria and Bur. Valley R.R. Co., 1984—85; arbitrator, mediator, 1985—; lectr. Am. Mgmt. Assn., Am. Arbitration Assn. Collective Bargaining Inst. Contbg. editor: The Railway Labor Act, 1995; mem. editl. adv. panel Labor Rels. Bull. Aspen Pubs., Inc., 1999-2003; contbr. articles to profl. jours. Mem. Acad. Poli. Sci., Columbia U., 1972—75; advisor Balt. City Commn. on Aging, 1973—74; pub. sector labor rels. conf. bd. U. Md., 1973—77; advisor Balt. City Charter Revision Commn., 1974—75; landlord-tenant law study commn. State of Md., 1976—77; active Ill. Econ. Bd., 1988—90; coll. edn. adv. coun. Roosevelt U., 1990—93; gov.'s commn. on sci. and tech. State of Ill., 1990—98; Chgo. postal customer adv. coun. U.S. Postal Svc., 1994—95; Chgo. workforce bd. City of Chgo., 1999—2004, mayor's taskforce on employment of people with disabilities, 2002—05; tax increment financing works adv. com. Mayor's Office of Workforce Devel., 2005—; bd. visitors dept. polit. sci. and LaFolette Sch. Pub. Affairs U. Wis., Madison, 2001—, vice chair, 2002—05; chair Com. on Support for Tchg. and Rsch., 2002—, Employment Barriers and Model City Work Group, City of Chgo., 2002—05; referee Nat. R.R. Adjustment Bd., Ill. State Bd. Edn. Panel Hearing Officers; arbitration panel Herzog Transit Svcs./Transp. Workers Union; neutral mem. mediation and arbitration Warner-Lambert Arbitration Panel, Montgomery Ward Holding Corp. and Loewen Group Internat. Alternative Dispute Resolution Panels; neutral mem. ADR Sys. Am., Nat. Arbitration and Mediation Panel; commr. Chgo. Commn. on Human Rels., 2005—. Recipient Am. Jurisprudence prize in corp. law Joint Pubs. of Annotated Reports Sys., 1966, cert. for encouragement of vol. dispute settlement procedures Am. Arbitration Assn., 1981-84; Hon. fellow Harry S. Truman Libr. Inst., 1976 Fellow: Coll. of Labor and Employment Lawyers; mem.: ACLU, ABA, So. Poverty Law Ctr., Labor and Employment Rels. Assn., Am. Arbitration Assn. (chmn. Chgo. regional office labor adv. com. 1998—2001), Nat. Hist. Soc., State Bar Assn. Wis., Am. Found. Automation and Employment, Ill. Pub. Employee Arbitration Mediation Panel, Nat. Mediation Bd. Register of Arbitrators, Fed. Mediation and Conciliation Svc. Roster of Arbitrators, Art Inst. Chgo., Nat. Assn. R.R. Referees (regional v.p. 1996—2000), Am. Airlines and Air Line Pilots Assn. (sys. bd. adjustments), United Airlines and Internat. Assn. Machinists and Aerospace Workers (sys. bd. adjustments), U.S. Holocaust Meml. Mus., Rutgers Alumni Assn., Wis. Alumni Assn., Friends of the Nat. Baseball Hall of Fame and Mus., Soc. Am. Baseball Rsch., Statue of Liberty -Ellis Island Found. (charter). Avocations: coin collecting/numismatics, stamp collecting/philately, reading, baseball, art. Office: 1122 N Clark St Ste 2303 Chicago IL 60610-2866 also: Ste 305-PMB 110 3455 Peachtree Industrial Blvd Duluth GA 30096-6501 Office Phone: 312-664-3415. Personal E-mail: cpfischbach@adelphia.net.

FISCHBACH, DONALD RICHARD, lawyer; b. Ventura, Calif., Sept. 26, 1947; s. Richard A. and Ruth (Blevins) F.; m. Linda Say, Nov. 22, 1986; children: Amy, Sara, Andrea, Sean. BS in Bus. adminstrn. with honors, Calif. State Poly. Coll., 1969; JD, U. Calif., San Francisco, 1972. Bar: Calif. 1972. Assoc. Baker, Manock & Jensen, Fresno, Calif., 1972-75, ptnr., 1976—. Adj. asst. prof. San Joaquin Coll. Law., Fresno, 1980-82; commr. jud. State Bar Calif., 1983; lectr. in field Vol. atty. Fresno County Legal Services, 1973-79; chmn. fund raising United Way, 1979, Am. Cancer Soc., 1980-81, bd, dirs. 1980-82; bd. dirs. Fresno Met. Mus., 1982, Rally for Ratcliffe, 1983; bd. dirs. Valley Childrens Hosp., 1986, trustee, 2000—; trustee Fresno County Legal Svcs., 1976-79; bd. govs. Fresno Regional Found., 1997—, pres., 2000-01. Mem. ABA (del. young lawyers div. 1977-79), Calif. Bar Assn. (treas. young lawyers assn. 1978, 1st v.p. 1979, bd. dirs. 1976-79, Pres.'s Pro Bono Svc. award 1988), Fresno County Bar Assn. (pres. 1985, v.p. 1984, bd. dirs. 1975, 78-81, 1983—), State Bar Calif. (bd. govs., pres. 1994-95), Assn. Trial Lawyers Am., Calif. Trial Lawyers Assn., Fresno County Young Lawyers Assn. (pres. 1975, bd. dirs. 1975-79), No. Calif. Def. Counsel Assn., So. Calif. Def. Coun. Assn., Fresno Trial Lawyers Assn. (bd. dirs., officer 1978-82), Def. Rsch. Inst. Home: 520 E Summerdale Ct Fresno CA 93720-0893 Office: Baker Manock & Jensen 5260 N Palm Ave Ste 421 Fresno CA 93704-2222

FISCHBACH, GERALD D., dean, neurobiology educator; b. New Rochelle, N.Y., Nov. 15, 1938; children: Elissa, Peter, Neal, Mark. AB, Colgate U., 1960; MD, Cornell U., 1965; MA (hon.), Harvard U., 1978. Intern U. Washington Hosp., Seattle, 1965-66; sr. surgeon, Pub. Health Svc., Lab. of Neurophysiology, Nat. Inst. Neurol. Diseases and Stroke NIH, Bethesda, Md., 1966-69; fellow Behavioral Biology Br. Nat. Inst. Child Health, 1969-73; assoc. prof. pharmacology Harvard Med. Sch., Boston, 1978-81, prof., 1978-81; Edison prof. neurobiology, chmn. dept. anatomy and neurobiology Washington U. Sch. Med., St. Louis, 1981-90; Nathan Marsh Pusey prof. neurobiology, chair dept. neurobiology Harvard Med. Sch., Mass. Gen. Hosp., Boston, 1990-98; dir. Neurol. Disorders and Stroke NIH, Bethesda, Md., 1998—2001; exec. v.p. for health and biomed. sciences, dean, faculty medicine Columbia U. Coll. of Physicians and Surgeons, NY, 2001—. Mem. exec. com. Program in Cell and Devel. Biology, Harvard Med. Sch., 1974-81; nonresident tutor Leverett House, Harvard Coll., 1974-77; clk. of corp. Marine Biol. Lab., Woods Hole, Mass, 1978-81, trustee, 1982—, exec. com., 1984-89; master Fuller Albright Acad. Soc., Harvard Med. Sch., 1979-81, faculty coun., 1980-81; chmn. Gordon Conf. on Molecular Pharmacology, 1983; dir. Ctr. for Cellular and Molecular Neurobiology, Washington U. Sch. of Med., 1983-90, dir. Jacob Javits Ctr. for Excellence in Neurosci., 1985-90, dir. Ctr. for Higher Brain Function, 1988-90, mem. Med. Ctr. Bd., 1989-90; dir. Neurosci. Ctr., Mass. Gen. Hosp., 1990—; mem. adv. bd. Nat. Spinal Cord Injury Assn., 1978—, Neurology B Study Sect., NIH, 1978-80, Alfred P. Sloan Found., 1984-89, Dept. Biology Adv. Coun., Princeton U., 1984-88, Fidia Rsch. Found., 1986—, McKnight Neurosci. Rsch. Awards Rev. Com., 1986—, Howard Hughes Med. Inst., 1988—, SUNY Health Sci. Ctr. at Bklyn, 1988—, Helen Hay Whitney Found., 1991, Children's Hosp., Boston, 1991; vis. prof. Dept. Pharmacology U. Calif. at San Francisco, 1978; lectr. Disting. Lecture Series in Pharmacology, U. Md. Sch. Medicine, 1978, 25th Ann. Bishop Lecture, Washington U. Sch. Medicine, 1980, Disting. Lecture Series, Dept. Zoology, U. Tex., 1981; invited speaker 5th Ann. Meeting European Neurosci. Assn., 1981; Alden Spencer lectr. Coll. Physicians and Surgeons, Columbia, U., 1981, Stephen W. Kuffler lectr. Harvard Med. Sch., 1990, numerous others; assoc. Neurosci. Rsch. Program, 1981—. Editor Jour. Cell Biolog, 1985-86; assoc. editor Devel. Biology, 1974-78, Jour. Neurophysiology, 1975-81, 1989—, Jour. Neurobiology, 1986—; corr. editor Proc. Royal Soc., Series B, London, 1989—; contbr. articles to profl. jours. Recipient Polk award Cornell U., 1965, Mathilde Solowey award Found. for Advanced Edn. in the Scis., NIH, 1975, W. Alden Spencer award Coll. Physicians and Surgeons, Columbia U., 1981; N.Y.State Regents scholar, 1956-60, N.Y. State med. scholar, Cornell U., 1962-65; Salk Inst. non-resident fellow, 1990. Mem. Soc. for Neurosci. (llth ann. lectr., pres.-elect 1982-83, pres. 1983-84), Soc. Gen. Physiologists, Am. Soc. Cell Biology, NAS (mem. governing coun. 2005-), Phi Beta Kappa. Office: Columbia U Coll Physicians and Surgeons 630 West 168th St P&S 2-401 New York NY 10032*

FISCHBACH, ROBERT, lawyer, musician; b. Havre de Grace, Md., Dec. 22, 1953; s. Joseph W. and Beatrice (Eckstein) F. AA, Sullivan County C.C., Loch Sheldrake, N.Y., 1973; BA, SUNY, Utica/Rome, 1977; Cert. in Basic Electronics, Cleve. Inst. Electronics, 1994; JD, Pace U., 1996. Bar: Conn. 1996, Mass. 1997, N.Y. 1997. Prin. office asst. New Rochelle (N.Y.) City Ct., 1986-92; ct. asst. Mt. Vernon (N.Y.) City Ct., 1992-94; sole practitioner Mt. Vernon, 1996—. Mem. IEEE, ABA, N.Y. State Bar Assn., Am. Mensa, Golden Key, Alpha Beta Kappa. Avocations: fitness activities, running, bodybuilding, electronics, music performance. Home: 539 New Rochelle Rd Mount Vernon NY 10552-1520

FISCHBEIN, CHARLES ALAN, pediatrician; b. Newark, June 5, 1945; s. Martin and Naomi (Litzky) F.; m. Ellen Ruth Niemtzow, Aug. 10, 1969; children: Melissa Paige, Neil Todd. BA in Biology, Case Western Reserve U., 1966; MD, SUNY, Buffalo, 1970. Diplomate Am. Bd. Pediatrics. Resident in pediatrics Children's Hosp. Med. Ctr., Cin., 1970-72, fellow in pediatric cardiology Boston, 1972-74; pvt. practice pediatrics, 1974—; pres. Pediatric Assocs. of Conn., Waterbury, 1982—; asst. clin. prof. U. Conn. Med. Sch., Farmington, Conn., 1974—, Yale U. Sch. Medicine, New Haven, Conn., 1974—; acting co-chief dept. pediatrics St. Mary's Hosp., Waterbury, Conn., 1995-97. Fellow Am. Acad. Pediatrics; mem. AMA, Am. Coll. Sports Medicine. Avocation: mountain biking. Office: Pediatric Assocs Conn PC 160 Robbins St Waterbury CT 06708-2652 Office Phone: 203-755-2999.

FISCHEL, DANIEL NORMAN, publishing consultant; b. Bklyn., N.Y., Apr. 13, 1922; s. Joseph Louis and Liza (Herman) F.; m. Maxine Friedman, May 9, 1943; children: Anne, Jonathan, Lisa. BA, N.Y. U., 1943. Mng. editor Am. Water Works Assn., N.Y.C., 1946-55; editor Dodge Books, N.Y.C., 1955-61; with McGraw-Hill Book Co., N.Y.C., 1962-78, v.p., gen. mgr. profl. and reference books div., 1970-78; pres. Elsevier North-Holland, Inc., N.Y.C., 1978-81, Gordon & Breach Sci. Pubs., N.Y.C., 1982-85; pub. cons., 1981—. Mem. exec. com. tech., sci. and med. div. Am. Assn. Pubs., 1972-78, 79-81 Author: A Practical Guide to Writing and Publishing Professional Books: Business, Technical, Scientific, Scholarly, 1984 Served with AUS, 1943-45. Home and Office: 2200 N Central Rd Fort Lee NJ 07024-7557

FISCHEL, DANIEL R., law educator; b. 1950; BA in Am. History, Cornell U., 1972; MA in Am. History, Brown U., 1974; JD cum laude, U. Chgo., 1977. Bar: Ill. 1977. Law clk. to Judge Thomas E. Fairchild US Ct. Appeals 7th Cir., Chgo., 1977-78; law clk. to Assoc. Justice Potter Stewart US Supreme Ct., Washington, 1978-79; atty. Levy & Erens, Chgo., 1979-80; asst. prof. law Northwestern U. Sch. Law, 1980-81, assoc. prof., 1981-82, prof., 1982-84, U. Chgo. Law Sch., 1984—, Lee and Brena Freeman prof. law & bus., 1989—, dir. law & economics program, 1984—91, dean, 1999—2001; prof. law & bus. U. Chgo. Grad. Sch. Bus., 1987—90. Vis. prof. law U. Chgo. Law Sch., 1982—83; Jack N. Pritzker disting. vis. prof. law Northwestern U. Sch. Law, 2002. Co-author (with F.H. Easterbrook): The Economic Structure of Corporate Law, 1991; author: Payback: The Conspiracy to Destroy Michael Milken and His Financial Revolution, 1995. Mem.: Am. Fin. Assn., Am. Econ. Assn. Office: U Chgo Law Sch 1111 E 60th St Chicago IL 60637 Office Phone: 773-702-9495. E-mail: daniel_fischel@law.uchicago.edu.*

FISCHEL, EDWARD ELLIOT, internist, educator; b. N.Y.C., July 29, 1920; s. Joseph L. and Lisa (Herman) F.; m. Pauline Dunieff, Dec. 26, 1943; children: Robert, Janet. BA, Columbia U., 1941, MD, 1944, Sc.D. in Medicine, 1948. Diplomate: Am. Bd. Internal Medicine. Intern Presbyn. Hosp., N.Y.C., 1944-45, asst. resident medicine, 1945-46; asst. in medicine Columbia U. Coll. Physicians and Surgeons, N.Y.C., 1947-50, asso. medicine, 1950-55, assoc. clin. prof. medicine, 1969-72, lectr. medicine, 1972-87; practice medicine specializing in internal medicine and rheumatology; asst. physician Presbyn. Hosp., N.Y.C., 1947-55; asso. clin. prof. medicine Albert Einstein Coll. Medicine, Yeshiva U., N.Y.C., 1957-69, prof. medicine, 1972-80, vis. prof. medicine, 1980-81; dir. dept. medicine Bronx-Lebanon Hosp. Center, Bronx, N.Y., 1954-80; chief dept. medicine Mt. Sinai Hosp., Hartford, Conn. and prof. medicine U. Conn., 1980-83; chief of staff VA Med. Ctr., Northport, N.Y., 1983-91; prof. medicine, assoc. dean vet. affairs SUNY, Stony Brook, 1983-91, prof. medicine emeritus, 1991—. Mem. exec. com. Health Rsch. Coun. City N.Y., 1966-75, chmn. allergy and infectious disease panel, 1968-75; mem. N.Y. State Coun. on Grad. Med. Edn., 1991-94. Contbr. articles to med. jours. Recipient Disting. Svc. award The Arthritis Found., 1978, Silver Medallion Bicentennial Awd., Columbia Univ., Coll. of Physicians, 1967. Fellow ACP, AAAS (past mem. coun.), N.Y. Acad. Medicine (past v.p., trustee 1972-80, plaque 1981); mem. Am. Soc. Clin. Investigation, Am. Assn. Immunologists, Am. Coll. Rheumatology (past pres.), Assn. Am.

Med. Colls., Infectious Diseases Soc., Harvey Soc., Soc. Exptl. Biology and Medicine, Am.Fedn. Clin. Rsch., AMA, Bronx County Med. Soc., Am. Heart Assn. (past mem. rsch. com.), N.Y. TB and Health Assn. (past dir.), Phi Beta Kappa, Alpha Omega Alpha. Achievements include research in rheumatic fever—pathogenesis, treatment and prevention; effect of cortisone on antibody production and inflammation, serum complement in nephritis and non-specific (and nonimmunologic) inflammatory conditions, antiinflammatory and antirheumatic effects of aspirin. Home: 220 Little Neck Rd Centerport NY 11721-1145 E-mail: eefischel@aol.com.

FISCHEL, RICHARD JEFFREY, thoracic surgeon; b. L.A., Oct. 19, 1959; s. Maarna Rae Fischel; m. Lulu Fischel, July 18 1987; children: Rachel Marissa, Christina Jenelle, Ricky Jr. BS summa cum laude, U. Calif., Riverside, 1981; MD, UCLA, 1984; PhD, U. Minn., Mpls., 1995. Diplomate Am. Bd. Thoracic Surgery, Am. Bd. Surgery. Intern in gen. surgery U. Minn., Mpls., 1984, resident in gen. surgery, 1985—92, fellow in thoracic surgery, 1992—95; dir. Lung Ctr. Chapman Med. Ctr., Orange, Calif., 1995—, attending thoracic surgeon, 1995—; assoc. dir. Lung Ctr. Cedars Sinai Med. Ctr., L.A., 1996—, attending thoracic surgeon, 1996—; clin. asst. prof. thoracic surgery UCLA, 1995—, U. Calif. Irvine, 1997—; chief surgery Chapman Med. Ctr., Orange, Calif., 2003—. Kolf young investigator ASAIO. Editor Video Assisted Surgery, 1995—; contbr. articles to profl. jours., chpts. to books; patentee in field. Dir. Chapman Found., Irvine, 1997—; vol. soccer ref. AYSO, Irvine, 1996, 97, 98, 99. Fellow in thoracic rsch. U. Minn., Mpls., 1987. Fellow ACS, Soc. Thoracic Surgeons, Am. Coll. Chest Physicians; mem. ACS Oncology Group, Am. Soc. Artificial Internal Organs, 21st Century Surg. Soc., Am. Soc. Artificial Internal Organs, Orange County Med. Assn., L.A. Med. Assn., Am. Youth Soccer Org. Avocations: skiing, snorkeling, hiking, biking, tennis. Office: 2601 E Chapman Ave Orange CA 92869 E-mail: cmclungctr@aol.com.

FISCHEL, WILLIAM ALAN, economics professor; b. Bethlehem, Pa., Apr. 10, 1945; s. John Jacob and Lois T. (Yerger) F.; m. Janice M. Goldberg, Aug. 5, 1973; 1 child, Joshua. BA, Amherst Coll., 1967; PhD, Princeton U., 1973. Prof. Dartmouth Coll., Hanover, N.H., 1973—, dept. chair, 2000—02, Patricia F. and William B. Hale prof. in arts and sci., 2002—. Vis. assoc. prof. U. Calif., Davis, 1980-81; vis. prof. U. Calif., Santa Barbara, 1985-86, U. Wash., Seattle, 1998-99; adj. prof. Vt. Law Sch., South Royalton, 1985, 87-92. Author: Economics of Zoning Laws, 1985, Regulatory Takings, 1995, Homevoter Hypothesis, 2001; mem. editl. bd. Land Econs. Jour., 1984—, Ea. Econ. Jour., 1992—. Mem. Zoning Bd., Town of Hanover, N.H., 1987-97, chmn., 1993-97. Olin fellow U. Calif., Berkeley, 1991-92. Mem. Phi Beta Kappa, Psi Upsilon. Home: 2 Read Rd Hanover NH 03755-1909 Office: Dartmouth Coll Dept Of Econs Hanover NH 03755 Office Phone: 603-646-2940. Business E-Mail: Bill.Fischel@Dartmouth.Edu.

FISCHELL, ROBERT ELLENTUCH, physicist; b. N.Y.C., Feb. 10, 1929; s. Philip and Julia (Ellentuch) Fischell; m. Marian Standard; children: David R., Tim A., Scott J.S. BSMechE cum laude, Duke U., 1951; MS in Physics, U. Md., 1953, ScD (hon.), 1996. Physicist U.S. Naval Ordnance Lab., Silver Spring, Md., 1951—56; prin. staff engr. Emerson Rsch. Labs., Silver Spring, 1956—60; various staff positions Applied Physics Lab., Johns Hopkins U., Laurel, Md., 1959—97, prin. profl. physicist, 1962—, chief engr. space dept., 1972—80, chief tech. transfer space dept., 1978—88; pres., chmn. bd. MedInnovations, Inc., Dayton, Md., 1988—90; chmn. bd. MedInTec, Inc., Dayton, Md., 1990—; pres. Fischell Biomed. LLC, 2000—; prof. practice of engring. U. Md., 2003—. Chmn. bd., v.p R & D Cathco, Inc., 1991—; pres., chmn. bd. IsoStent, Inc., Dayton, Md., 1993—; chmn. emeritus NeuroPace, Inc., Dayton, 1997—; cons. Cordis, a J&J Co., 1998—; expert witness Brown and Bain, Palo Alto, Calif., 1992—93; rsch. assoc. in medicine Johns Hopkins U. Sch. Medicine, 1983—95, Yale U. Sch. Medicine, 1988—95; mem. exec. panel Chief of Naval Ops., Washington, 1983—87; expert witness Fish and Neave, N.Y.C., 1986—92; field reviewer for orphan products FDA, 1984—90; mem. rsch. com. Md. affiliate Am. Heart Assn., 1985—87; mem. tech. com. on space guidance and control AIAA, 1972—75, chmn. nat. conf., 1973; mem. space com. Internat. Fedn. Automatic Control, 1970—75; mem., chmn. photovoltaic specialities com. IEEE, 1959—72; chmn., pres. Angel Med. Sys., Inc., 2001—, Neuralieve, Inc., 2002—; dir. U. Sys. Md. Author over 50 tech. publs.; assoc. editor: AIAA Jour. Spacecraft and Rockets, 1972—75; holder 110 patents in field of biomed. engring., biomed. devices and spacecraft. Bd. visitors U. Md., 1997—; trustee U. Md. Found., 2000—. Named Disting. Citizen of Yr., "M" Club U. Md., 1984; named to Space Tech. Hall of Fame, U.S. Space Found., 1988; recipient Tech. Achievement award, ASME, 1962, Outstanding Young Engr. award, Washington Capitol area, 1963, awards for most significant inventions, Indsl. Rsch. mag., 1967, 1970, 1973, Inventor of Yr. award, Intellectual Property Owners Assn., 1984, Gold medal for contbn. to aerospace sci. and tech., N.Y. Acad. Sci., 1987, Exceptional Engring. award for MAGSAT satellite, NASA, 1980, Individual Achievement award for human tissue stimulator, 1982, Exceptional Engring. medal, 1984, Space Act prize, 1984, Disting. Engring. Alumnus award, Duke U., 1992, Tech. for Humanity award, Discover Mag., 1993, TED prize, Tech., Entertainment, Design Conf., 2004. Mem.: NAE, N.Y. Acad. Scis., Internat. Soc. for Artificial Organs, Beta Omega Sigma, Pi Tau Sigma, Sigma Pi Sigma, Pi Mu Epsilon, Tau Beta Pi, Phi Beta Kappa. Avocations: tennis, sailing. Office: MedInTec Inc 14600 Viburnum Dr Dayton MD 21036-1247 Office Phone: 410-988-9509. Personal E-mail: mfischell@aol.com.

FISCHER, A. CHARLES, pharmaceutical executive; Grad., Tex. A&M U. With Dow Chem. Co., 1967—, global bus. ops. mgr., herbicides bus. mgr.; Brazil v.p. and gen. mgr. Dow Brazil Agrl. Chems., 1984—87; v.p., gen. mgr. Europe Dow Chem. Co., 1987—89; v.p., gen. mgr. DowElanco Europe, 1989—92; v.p. N.Am. DowElanco, 1992; global leader agrl. chems. and urban pest bus. platform Dow AgroScis. LLC, 1997—99; pres., CEO Dow Agroscis., Indpls., 1999—2004; chmn. Dow Agroscis. Mem. Committee, 2004—. Trustee Farm Found.; bd. dirs. Jr. Achievement of Ctrl. Ind.; past found. chair Nat. FFA. Named Agribusiness Leader of the Year, National Agri-Marketing Association, 2002. Mem.: Am. Crop Protection Assn. (exec. com., chair strategic planning com.).

FISCHER, ALFRED GEORGE, geology educator; b. Rothenburg, Germany, Dec. 10, 1920; came to U.S., 1935; s. George Erwin and Thea (Freise) F.; m. Winnifred Varney, Aug. 26, 1939; children: Joseph Fred, George William, Lenore Ruth. Student, Northwestern Coll., Watertown, Wis., 1935-37; BA, U. Wis., 1939, MA, 1941; PhD, Columbia U., 1950. Instr. Va. Poly. Inst. and State U., Blacksburg, 1941-43; geologist Stanolind Oil & Gas Co., Kans. and Fla., 1943-46; instr. U. Rochester, N.Y., 1947-48; from instr. to asst. prof. U. Kans., Lawrence, 1948-51; sr. geologist Internat. Petroleum, Peru, 1951-56; prof. geology Princeton (N.J.) U., 1956-84, U. So. Calif., Los Angeles, 1984—. Co-Author: Invertebrate Fossils, 1952, The Permian Reef Complex, 1953, Electron Micrographs of Limestone, 1967; editor: Petroleum and Global Tectonics, 1975. Recipient Verrill medal Yale U. Fellow Geol. Soc. Am. (Penrose medal 1993), Geol. Soc. London (hon., Lyell medal 1992), Soc. Econ. Paleontologists (hon., Twenhofel medal); mem. AAAS, NAS, U.S. Nat. Acad. Sci., Am. Assn. Petroleum Geologists, Paleontol. Soc. (medal 1995), German Geol. Soc. (Leopold von Buch medal), Geol. Union (Gustav Steinmann medal 1992), Mainz Acad. Sci. Lit. (corr.), Lincei Acad. Rome (fgn.), U.S. Nat. Acad. Sci., Sigma Xi. Home: 1736 Perch St San Pedro CA 90732-4218 Office: U So Calif Dept Earth Scis Univ Park Los Angeles CA 90089-0001

FISCHER, ANGELA BROWN, real estate company executive, volunteer; b. Providence, Mar. 8, 1938; d. John Nicholas and Anne (Kinsolving) Brown; m. Edwin Garvin Fischer, May 4, 1963; children: Olivia Fischer Fox, Edwin Garvin Jr., Chad B. BA, Harvard-Radcliffe Coll., 1960. Clk., dir., co-founder The Boston Cookery, Inc., 1979-84; dir. Le Dioyte Land Co., Omaha, 1978-88, Manisses Comms. Group, Providence, 1992-99, van Liew Capital, Providence, 1984—; mng. ptnr. Brown Land Co., Providence, 1979—; pres. Brown & Fischer Corp., Providence, 1979—. Trustee Hope Found., Providence, 1988—; v.p. Preservation Soc. Newport County, 1988—; dir. steering com. chair Redwood Libr. and Athenaeum, Newport, 1993—; treas., co-founder The J.N. Brown Ctr. for the Study of Am. Civilization, Providence, 1985-94; chair Gov.'s Commn. for Preserving the State House, Providence, 1993—; bd. govs. R.I. Commodores, Providence, 1987—; corp. mem. Brown U., Providence, 1980-93; bd. dirs., chair numerous coms. Preserve R.I., Inc., Providence, 1979-95, 97—. Recipient John H. Chaffee Meml. Svc. award R.I. Hist. Soc., 2000. Avocations: sailing, travel, reading.

FISCHER, ASHLEY MCKINNEY, lawyer; b. Chgo., Feb. 27, 1974; d. Peter and Donna McKinney; m. Patrick Spencer Fischer, June 18, 2005. BA cum laude, Georgetown U., 1996; JD, Northwestern U., 2000. Bar: Ill. 2000. Assoc. Gardner Carton & Douglas LLP, Chgo., 2000—. Co-editor: (publication) ABA Antitrust Health Care Chronicle. Co-pres. Andover/Abbott Alumni Assn. Ill., Chgo., 2003—; guild bd. mem. Boys and Girls Club Chgo., 2004—; alumni interviewer Georgetown U., Chgo., 1996—, Northwestern U. Sch. Law, Chgo., 2000—, alumni student mentor, 2004—. Mem.: ABA, Am. Health Lawyers Assn., Lawyer's Club Chgo. Office: Gardner Carton & Douglas LLP Ste 3700 191 N Wacker Dr Chicago IL 60606 Office Phone: 312-569-1266. Office Fax: 312-569-3266. Business E-Mail: amckinney@gcd.com.

FISCHER, BRUCE DOUGLAS, management consultant; b. Shelby, Mich., July 3, 1944; s. Henry and Dorothy (Prill) F.; 1 child, Laura Van Zoest. BS in Engring., Western Mich. U., 1967; MBA, U. Chgo., 1972; PhD, Northwestern U., 1987. Mgf. engr. Parker-Hannifin Corp., Des Plaines, Ill., 1969-70; mgmt. trainee Borg-Warner Corp., Chgo., 1972-73; assoc. A.T. Kearney, Inc., Chgo., 1973-76; cons. Bruce D. Fischer: Mgmt. Cons., Chgo., 1976—; asst. prof. Coll. Bus. and Mgmt. Northeastern Ill. U., Chgo., 1983-88; asst. prof. Coll. Engring. and Applied Scis. Western Mich. U., Kalamazoo, 1988-90; prof. Coll. Bus. and Pub. Adminstrn. Govs. State U., University Park, Ill., 1990-97. Bd. dirs. Naylor Pipe Co., Chgo. Contbr. articles to profl. jours. With U.S. Army, 1966-69. Mem. Internat. Modapts Assn. (bd. dirs.), Northwestern U. Alumni Assn., Chgo. Grad. Sch. Bus. Club. Home and Office: 1744 N Wood St Chicago IL 60622-1356

FISCHER, BRUCE G., gas industry executive; BS, Drexel U., 1976, MBA, 1983. Logistics and sys. mgr. Sunoco Inc., 1989—95; gen. mgr. Sunoco MidAmerica Mktg. and Refining, 1995—99, v.p., gen. mgr., 1999—2000; v.p. Sunoco Chems., 2000—02; sr. v.p. Sunoco Inc., Phila., 2002—. Office: Sunoco Inc Ten Penn Ctr 1801 Market St Philadelphia PA 19103-1699*

FISCHER, CARL, photographer, graphics designer, actor; b. NYC, May 3, 1924; s. Joseph Albert and Irma (Schwerin) F.; m. Marilyn Wolf, Oct. 30, 1949; children: Kim Alison Lloyd George, Douglas James, Kenneth Lee. BFA, Cooper Union Sch. Art, 1948; postgrad., Ctrl. St. Martins Coll. Art & Design, London, 1952. Designer Columbia Records, 1948, Look mag., 1949-51; asst. art dir. William H. Weintraub & Co., 1952-54; art dir. Sudler & Hennessey, 1954-56, Grey Advt., 1956-58; owner Carl Fischer Photography Inc., N.Y.C., 1960—. Adj. prof. art Cooper Union; TV, film dir.; William A. Reedy Meml. lectr. Rochester Inst. Tech. Exhibited Mus. Modern Art, 1965, Whitney Mus. Am. Art, 1974, Pentagram Gallery, London, 2004, Galleria Carla Sozzani, Milan, 2004, Gallerie Colette, Paris, 2004, Nat. Portrait Gallery, London, 2005; represented in permanent collections, Met. Mus. Art, NYC, Rose Art Mus., Amherst, Mass., Internat. Ctr. Photography, NYC, Internat. Mus. Photography at George Eastman House, Rochester, Spencer Mus. Art, Lawrence, Kans.; contbg. editl. photographer various mags. including London Observer, London Sunday Times, Time, Life, Fortune, Esquire, N.Y. With AUS, 1942-45, PTO. Fulbright grant, 1951; recipient Profl. Achievement citation Cooper Union, 1966, St. Gaudens medal, 1969, Mark Twain Jour. award, 1971, Cleo award, 1980. Mem. Actors Equity Assn., SAG, Dirs. Guild, Art Dirs. Club (past pres., gold and silver medals), Century Assn. Office: 121 E 83d St New York NY 10028-0821 Office Phone: 212-794-0400. E-mail: fischerny@mac.com.

FISCHER, CARL ROBERT, retired health facility administrator; b. Rahway, N.J., Nov. 15, 1939; s. Robert Carlton and Elsie Marie (Wolfarth) F.; m. Lynn Elaine Ekstrand, Mar. 12, 1966; children: Kristen, Leslie, Meredith, Kelly. BSN, Wagner Coll., 1964; MS, SUNY-Buffalo, 1966; MPH, Yale U., 1968. With Yale-New Haven Hosp., 1968-77, assoc. dir., 1975-77; exec. assoc. adminstr. U. Cin. Med. Ctr., 1977-80; exec. dir. clin. programs U. Ark. for Med. Scis., Little Rock, 1980-86; assoc. v.p. health scis., CEO Med. Coll. of Va. Hosps., Richmond, 1986-99; exec. v.p. corp. functions VCU Health Sys., 1999—2002; ret., 2003. Bd. dirs. Univ. Health Systems Consortium, exec. com. 1994-2000, chmn. bd. dirs. 1997-98, chmn. supply and svcs. divsn., 1988-89, 95-96; mem. exec. com. Nat. Assn. Pub. Hosps., 1999-2002. Pres. Ctrl. Va. Health Planning Agy., 1991-93, mem.-at-large, 1997-2002, exec. com., 2000-2002; bd. dirs. Richmond Luth. Home, 2000-01. Mem. Am. Assn. Med. Colls., Am. Hosp. Assn., Va. Hosp. Assn. (bd. dirs. 1986-91, 99-2000, chmn. coun. on adminstrn. and health planning 1988, coun. on assn. devel. 1987-88, physician liaison com. 1989-90, chmn. ctrl. Va. regional planning coun. 1997-99).

FISCHER, CHARLOTTE FROESE, research scientist, educator; b. Nikolajevka, Bachmut, Ukraine, Sept. 21, 1929; arrived in Can., 1930; came to U.S., 1974; d. John David and Helen (Thiessen) F.; m. Patrick Carl Fischer, Apr. 2, 1967; 1 child, Carolyn. BA, U. B.C., Vancouver, Can., 1952, MA, 1954; PhD, Cambridge U., England, 1957. Instr. math. to prof. U. B.C., 1957-68; prof. applied analysis, computer sci., & applied math. U. Waterloo, Ont., Can., 1968-75; prof. computer sci. Pa. State U., 1974-79; prof. computer sci., math., physics & astronomy Vanderbilt U., Nashville, 1980-96, rsch. prof. computer sci., 1996—2003; prof. emeritus, 2003. Cons. Pacific Oceanographic Group, Nanaimo, B.C., Can., 1960-62; rsch. fellow Harvard Coll. Obs., Cambridge, 1963-64. Author: Introduction to Programming the IBM 1620, 1964, The Hartree-Fock Method for Atoms, 1977, Computational Atomic Spectroscopy, 1997, Douglas Rayner Hartree: His Life in Science and Computing, 2003; contbr. articles and papers to profl. jours.; editor Computing Reviews, 1968-78, Computer Physics Comm., 1968-2000. Fellow Alfred Sloan Found., 1964-68, Fulbright Found., 1998-99; grantee U.S. Dept. Energy, 1978-2005 Fellow Am. Phys. Soc.; mem. Royal Physiographical Soc. Lund., Lithuanian Acad. Scis. Business E-Mail: Charlotte.F.Fischer@Vanderbilt.edu.

FISCHER, CRAIG LELAND, physician; b. Bklyn., Feb. 17, 1937; s. Emil Carl and Ruth Barbara (Minarcik) F.; m. Sandra Lucile Canfield, Feb. 17, 1962; children: Craig L. Jr., Emil Lewis, Lisa Anne. BS, Kans. State U., 1958; MD, U. Kans., 1962. Diplomate Nat. Bd. Med. Examiners, Am. Bd. Family Practice; cert. anat. and clin. pathology, nuclear medicine. Intern in anatomic pathology Kansas U. Med. Ctr., 1962-63, resident in anatomic pathology, 1963-64, rsch. fellow in pathology (pub. health svc.), nuclear medicine, 1962-64, 1965-66; resident in clin. pathology, Meth. Hosp. Baylor U. Coll. Medicine, 1967-68; rsch. med. officer Manned Spacecraft Ctr., NASA, Houston, 1965-68, pathologist, chief clin. labs., 1968-71; chief med. ops. Johnson Space, NASA, Houston, 1980-82; assoc. dir. labs. to dir. labs. Eisenhower Med. Ctr., Rancho Mirage, Calif., 1971-78, dir. nuclear med., 1975-78; gen. practice medicine Palm Desert, Calif., 1978-80; pathologist, co-dir. Valley Clin. Labs., Palm Desert, Calif., 1982-99; gen. practice medicine Indio, Calif., 1982-99; dir. post grad. edn. J.F. Kennedy Hosp., 1982-92; dir. Fischer and Yao Cons. Pathologists, Indio, 1987-89; pres. Fischer Assocs., Cons. in Pathology, Indio, 1989-95; ptnr. Fischer and Starke Assocs., Indio, 1995-99; aviation med. examiner FAA, 1991-99; asst. dir. space medicine NASA Johnson Space Ctr., 1999—2001, assoc. dir. clin. lab., 1999—, chief, Space Medicine & health Care Systems Office, 2001—03, asst. dir. internat. space medicine, 2003—. Clin. prof. dept. preventive medicine and cmty. health U. Tex. Med. Br., Galveston, 2002-; asst. clin. prof. U. Calif., Irvine, 1986-99; mem. sci. adv. bd. Dept. Air Force, Washington, 1986-90, NAE, NRC; mem. Air Force Studies Bd., Washington, 1987-93; mem. aerospace med. adv. com. Office Space Scis. and Applications, NASA Hdqrs., Washington, 1988-93, chmn. operational medicine discipline working group, Life Scis. Directorate, 1988-92, mem. Shuttle-Mir Joint Sci. Working Group, 1993-94, mem. Adv. Coun. Task Force on the Shuttle-Mir Rendezvous and Docking Missions, 1995; mem. Mir Sci. Program Rev. Panel, 1993-98; mem. Internat. Space Sta. Task Force (Stafford Commn.), 1998—; chmn. multinat. med. ops. panel Internat. Space Sta., 2000-04, chmn. Space Medicine Ops. Team, 2000-04, co-chmn. crew safety working group, 2004—; cons. lab. medicine project tektite U.S. Dept. Interior, 1969-70. Contbr. numerous articles to profl. jours. Capt. USAR, 1964-66; lt. col. USAFR, 1983-97. Recipient Group Achievement award NASA Manned Spacecraft Ctr., 1966, 69, 70, Group Achievement award Gemini support team NASA Manned Spacecraft Ctr., Apollo 7 Flight Ops. Team award NASA Manned Spacecraft Ctr., 1969, Sustained Superior Achievement award NASA Manned Spacecraft Ctr., 1969, Superior Achievement award, 1969, Skylab Group Achievement award NASA Johnson Space Ctr., 1974, Presdl. medal of Freedom Apollo 13 Mission Ops. Team, 1970, Group Achievement award NASA Space Shuttle Launch and Ops. Team NASA Manned Spacecraft Ctr., 1982, Meritorious Civilian Svc. award Dept. of Air Force, 1990, Spl. Profl. Achievement award, STS-107 Columbia Contingency Support Team, 2003. Fellow Am. Coll. Preventive Medicine, Am. Coll. Nuc. Physicians, Coll. Am. Pathologists, Am. Soc. Clin. Pathologists (CCE Commr.'s medal 1989), Aerospace Med. Assn., Riverside County Med. Assn. (councilor 1984-89, pres. 1990-91, alt. delegate 1991-96, councilor 1996-99, Outstanding Contbn. to Medicine award 1996), Palm Springs Acad. Medicine (pres. 1988-89). Republican. Avocations: sailing, tennis, flying. Home: 2330 Lidston # 8 Seabrook TX 77586 Office: Bldg 1 Mail Code SA 2101 NASA Pkwy Houston TX 77058 Office Phone: 281-483-3378. Business E-Mail: craig.l.fisher@nasa.gov.

FISCHER, DAVID HACKETT, historian, educator; b. Balt., Dec. 2, 1935; s. John Henry and Norma (Frederick) Fischer; m. Judith Hummel, Nov. 23, 1960; children: Susanna, Anne. AB, Princeton U., 1958; PhD, Johns Hopkins U., 1962; MA (hon.), Oxford U., 1985. Mem. faculty Brandeis U., Waltham, Mass., 1962—, prof. history, 1970—, Earl Warren prof., 1971—, chmn. Am. history program, Univ. prof., 2002—. Vis. lectr. Harvard U., 1964-65; vis. prof. U. Wash., Seattle, 1975, U. Otago, New Zealand, 1999, U. Waikato, 1995; Harmsworth prof. Oxford U., 1985-86; Fulbright lectr., New Zealand, 1994. Author: Revolution of American Conservatism, 1965, Historians Fallacies, 1970, Growing Old in America, 1977, Albion's Seed: Four British Folkways in America, 1989, Paul Revere's Ride, 1994, The Great Wave: Price Movements in Modern History, 1996, Bound Away: Virginia and the Westward Movement, 2000, Washington's Crossing, 2004 (Nat. Book Award finalist, 2004, Pulitzer Prize for history, 2005); contbr. (with James McPherson) Times Atlas of World History, 1978; editor: Concord: A Social History of a New England Town, 1983, Brookline: A Social History of a Boston Suburb, 1985. Fellow Queens Coll., Oxford, 1985 Mem. Am. Hist. Assn., Hakluyt Soc., Orgn. Am. Historians, Soc. Am. Historians, Am. Antiquarian Soc., St. Botolph Club (Boston), Princeton Club (N.Y.). Democrat. Lutheran. Office: Brandeis U MS 036 415 South St Waltham MA 02453-2728 Office Phone: 781-736-2270. E-mail: fischer@brandeis.edu.

FISCHER, DAVID J., retired mayor; b. Evanston, Ill., July 24, 1933; m. Margo Fischer; children: Susan, David, James, Allison. BA in Bus. Adminstrn., Duke U., 1955. Chartered mcpl. fin. advisor, mcpl. bond dealer, 1958-90; pres., owner Fischer Johnson, Inc., 1977-86; mayor City of St. Petersburg, Fla., 1991—2001. Pres. Fla. Mcpl. Bond Coun., 1982-83, mem., 1975-90. Vice mayor St. Petersburg City Coun., 1978-79, mem., 1975-79; pres. Lakewood H.S. Parent Coun., 1973-74; chmn. Environ. Devel. Commn., 1972-75, Bayfront Ctr. Found. and Adv. Coun., 1989, mem., 1989-91; chmn. United Way Allocations and Admissions Com., 1967, treas., 1968-70; co-chmn. Cmty. Alliance, 1970-71; chmn. bd. trustees Eckerd Coll., 1985-87, trustee, 1979—; pres. Neighborhood Housing Svcs., 2003-; CEO, pres. Community Found. of Tampa Bay, 2004-; Served to capt. USAF, 1956-58. Recipient Leadership award St. Petersburg Alumni Assn., 1979, Disting. Citizen award U. So. Fla., 1994. Dist. committeeman Nat. Assn. Securities Dealers, 1980-83; pres. C. of C., 1982 (Outstanding Contbns. to Community award 1986). Office Phone: 813-282-1975.

FISCHER, DUNCAN KINNEAR, neurosurgeon; b. Chapel Hill, N.C., Sept. 14, 1957; s. Newton Duchan and Janet (Jordan) F.; m. Anne Holmes Billington, Sept. 10, 1983; children: Luke Duncan, Kent Billington, Duncan Newton II. AB, Princeton U., 1979; MPhil, Yale U., 1982, MD, PhD, 1986. Cert. in neurosurgery. Intern in surgery Baylor Coll. Medicine Affiliated Hosps., Houston, 1986-87, resident in neurosurgery, 1987-92; rsch. assoc. Baylor Coll. Medicine, Houston, 1988-92; neurosurgeon San Angelo (Tex.) Cmty. Med. Ctr. and Neurosurg. Ctr., 1992—. Contbr. numerous articles to profl. publs. Med. Scientist Tng. Program scholar NIH, ACS scholar. Fellow ACS; mem. Harvey Cushing Soc., Am. Assn. Neurol. Surgeons, Sigma Xi, Phi Beta Kappa. Republican. Episcopalian. Achievements include extensive experience in outpatient spinal microsurgery. Office: 3515 Executive Dr San Angelo TX 76904-6883 Office Phone: 325-947-2525.

FISCHER, EDMOND HENRI, biochemistry educator; b. Shanghai, Apr. 6, 1920; arrived in U.S., 53; s. Oscar and Renée (Tapernoux) Fischer. Lic. es Sciences Chimiques et Biologiques, U. Geneva, 1943, Diplome d'Ingenieur Chimiste, 1944, PhD, 1947; D (hon.), U. Montpellier, France, 1985, U. Basel, Switzerland, 1988, Med. Coll. of Ohio, 1993, Ind. U., 1993, U. Bochum, Germany, 1994. Pvt. docent biochemistry U. Geneva, 1950—53; research assoc. biology Calif. Inst. Tech., Pasadena, 1953; asst. prof. biochemistry U. Wash., Seattle, 1953—56, assoc. prof., 1956—61, prof., 1961—90, prof. emeritus, 1990—. Mem. exec. com. Pacific Slope Biochem. Conf., 1958—59, pres., 1975; mem. biochemistry study sect. NIH, 1959—64; symposium co-chmn. Battelle Seattle Rsch. Ctr., 1970, 73, 78; mem. sci. adv. bd. Biozentrum, U. Basel, Switzerland, 1982—86, Weizmann Inst. Sci., Rehovot, Israel, 1998—, bd. govs., 1997—; mem. sci. adv. bd. Principe Felipe Sci. Mus., Valencia, Spain, 1998—, Friedrich Miescher Inst., Ciba-Geigy, Basel, 1976—84, chmn., 1981—84; mem. bd. sci. govs. Scripps Rsch. Inst., La Jolla, Calif., 1987—; mem. scientific adv. bd. Basel Inst. for Immunology, 1996—2001; bd. sci. govs. Scripps Rsch. Inst., La Jolla, Calif. Contbr. numerous articles to sci. jours. Mem. sci. council on basic sci. Am. Heart Assn., 1977—80; sci. adv. com. Muscular Dystrophy Assn., 1980—88. Recipient Lederle Med. Faculty award, 1956—59, Guggenheim Found. award, 1963—64, Disting. Lectr. award, U. Wash., 1983, Laureate Passano Found. award, 1988, Steven C. Beering award, 1991, Nobel prize in physiology or medicine, 1992. Fellow: Am. Acad. Arts and Scis.; mem.: AAUP, NAS, AAS, Am. Chem. Soc. (editl. adv. bd. Biochemistry 1961—66, adv. bd. biochemistry divsn. 1962, assoc. editor 1966—91, exec. com. divsn. biology 1969—72, monograph adv. bd. 1971—73), fgn. acads. (hon.), Korean Acad. Sci. and Tech. (hon.), Japanese Biochem. Soc. (hon.), Spanish Royal Acad. Scis. (assoc.; fgn.), Venice Inst. Sci., Arts and Letters (assoc.; fgn.), Royal Acad. Medicine and Surgery (hon.; Cadiz, Spain), European Acad. Scis. (hon.), Am. Soc. Biol. Chemists (coun. 1989—93). Achievements include cellular regulation by phosphorylation/dephosphorylation cycle. Office: U Washington Med Sch PO Box 357350 Seattle WA 98195-7350 E-mail: efischer@u.washington.edu.

FISCHER, ELIZABETH (BETSY), television producer; b. New Orleans, Feb. 17, 1970; d. George Julius and Sally (Ford) Fischer; m. Gene Robert Raineri, Oct. 21, 1995; 1 child, Ella Elizabeth Raineri. BA cum laude, Am. U., 1992, MA, 1996. Polit. rschr. NBC News Meet the Press and Polit. Unit, Washington, 1992-94, assoc. prodr., 1995-96, prodr., 1997, sr. prodr., 1998—2002, exec. prodr., 2002—. Term mem. Coun. Fgn. Rels. Mem. Jr. League Washington, mem. coun. fgn. rels. Nominee Emmy, Nat. Acad. TV Arts and Scis., 1997; recipient Walter Cronkite/USC Annenberg award. Mem.: Am. Women Radio and TV, Radio and TV News Dirs. Assn., Nat. Press Club, Am. New Women's Club, Delta Gamma. Presbyterian. Avocations: racquetball, genealogy, reading, tennis. Home: 6525 Orland St Falls Church VA 22043-1865 Office: NBC News Meet the Press 4001 Nebraska Ave NW Washington DC 20016-2733 Office Phone: 202-885-4752.

FISCHER, ERIC ROBERT, lawyer, educator; b. N.Y.C., Aug. 22, 1945; s. Maurice and Pauline (Pilcer) F.; m. Anita Ellen Cohen, July 31, 1977; children: Joshua, Lauren BA, U. Pa., 1967; MBA, JD, Stanford U., 1971; LLM in Taxation, Boston U., 1982. Bar: N.Y. 1975, Mass. 1977. Assoc. Fried, Frank, Harris, Shriver & Jacobson, N.Y.C., 1971-76; v.p., asst. gen. counsel, asst. sec. First Nat. Bank of Boston, 1976-86; exec. v.p., gen. counsel, corp. sec. UST Corp., Boston, 1986-2000; sr. counsel Goodwin Procter LLP, Boston, 2000—02, ptnr., 2002—. Lectr. on law Boston U. Law Sch., 1984— Trustee Boston Lyric Opera, Inc., 1989-2001; bd. dirs. Boston Area Youth Soccer, 1989-90, Spirit of Mass. Boys Soccer Club, 1991-97. Mem. ABA (banking law com., chmn. cmty. banking subcom., banking law com.), Bank Capital Markets Assn. (chmn. banking law subcom. 1984-90), UN Assn. Boston (treas. 1978-91), New Eng. Legal Found. (bd. dirs. 1990-92). Jewish. Home: 205 Waban Ave Waban MA 02468-2101 Office: Goodwin Procter Exchange Pl Boston MA 02109 E-mail: efischer@goodwinprocter.com. *The pursuit of an objective which you believe is meaningful and constructive (whether you are right or wrong) gives definition to your life and allows you to accept your own limitations.*

FISCHER, FRED WALTER, physicist, engineer, educator; b. Zwickau, Germany, June 26, 1922; s. Fritz and Louiska (Richter) F.; m. Yongja Kim, Oct. 1, 1970. BS in Mech. Engring., Columbia U., 1949, MS, 1950; MS in Physics, U. Wash., 1957; D in Elec. Engring., Tech. U. Munich, 1966. Analyst Boeing Co., Seattle, Germany, 1950—84, cons., 1984—88; owner Fischer Cons., 1984—88. Instr. physics, math., and engring. North Seattle Community Coll., 1973-93; guest tchr. Perkins Sch. Author: Analysis for Physics and Engineering, 1982, Renaissance Mathematics, 1992. First v.p., trustee Wedgwood Cmty. Coun., 1994-2000; mem. Wedgwood Elem. Sch. Site Coun., Eckstein Middle Sch. Site Coun. With AUS, 1943-46. Boeing scholar Max Planck Inst. Plasma Physics, 1964-65. Mem. AAAS, N.Y. Acad. Sci., Mercedes Benz Club (Seattle sect. bd. dirs.), Sigma Xi (life). Office: North Seattle CC 9600 College Way N Seattle WA 98103-3514

FISCHER, JOEL, social work educator; b. Chgo., Apr. 22, 1939; s. Sam and Ruth (Feiges) F.; m. Renee H. Furuyama; children: Lisa, Nicole. BS, U. Ill., 1961, MSW, 1964; D in Social Welfare, U. Calif., Berkeley, 1970. Prof. sch. social work U. Hawaii, Honolulu, 1970—. Vis. prof. George Warren Brown Sch. Social Work, Washington U., St. Louis, 1977, U. Wis. Sch. Social Welfare, Milw., 1978-79, U. Natal, South Africa, 1982, U. Hong Kong, 1986; cons. various orgns. and univs. Author: (with Harvey L. Gochros) Planned Behavior Change: Behavior Modification in Social Work, 1973, Handbook of Behavior Therapy with Sexual Problems, vol. I, 1977, vol. II, 1977, Analyzing Research, 1975, Interpersonal Helping: Emerging Approaches for Social Work Practice, 1973, The Effectiveness of Social Casework, 1976, (with D. Sanders and O. Kurrem) Fundamentals of Social Work Practice, 1982, Effective Casework Practice: An Eclectic Approach, 1978, (with H. Gochros) Treat Yourself to a Better Sex Life, 1980, (with H. Gochros and J. Gochros) Helping the Sexually Oppressed, 1985, (with Martin Bloom) Evaluating Practice: Guidlines for the Helping Professional, 1982, (with Kevin Corcoran) Measures for Clinical Practice, 1987, (with Daniel Sanders) Visions for the Future: Social Work and Pacific-Asian Perspectives, 1988, (with Martin Bloom and John Ormel) Evaluating Practice, 2nd edit., 1995, (with Kevin Corcoran) Measures for Clinical Practice, 2nd edit., vol. 1, 1994, Couples, Children, Families, vol. 2, 1994, Adults, 1994, East-West Connections: Social Work Practice Traditions and Change, 1992, (with Martin Bloom and John Orme) Evaluating Practice, 3d edit., 1999, (with Martin Bloom and John Orme) Instructor's Manual for Evaluating Practice, 1999; (with Kevin Corcoran) Measures for Clinical practice, 3d edit, vol. 1, 2000, Couples, Children and Families, Adults, vol. 2, 2000, (with Martin Bloom and John Orme) Evaluating Practice, 4th edit., 2003, Instructor's Manual for Evaluating Practice, 2d edit., 2003, (with Martin Bloom and John Deme) Evaluation Practice, 5th edit., 2005, Instructor Manual for Evaluation Practice, 3d edit., 2005, (with W.K. Corcoran) Measures for Clinical Practice and Research, vol. 1, 2005, Couples, Children and Families, vol. 2, 2005; mem. editl. bd. 12 profl. jours.; contbr. over 150 articles to profl. jours. Bd. dirs. U. Hawaii Profl. Assembly, Hawaii Peoples' Fund; precinct pres. Dem. Party. With U.S. Army, 1958. Mem. NASW (Social Worker of Year, 2005), ACLU, Hawaii Com. for Africa, Coun. Social Work Edn., Acad. Cert. Social Workers, Nat. Conf. Social Welfare, AAUP, Unity Organizing Com., Hawaii People's Legis. Coalition, Bertha Reynold Soc., Amnesty Internat. Democrat. Office: U Hawaii Sch Social Work Henke Hall Honolulu HI 96822-2217 Business E-Mail: jfischer@hawaii.edu.

FISCHER, KAREN, librarian; b. St. Paul, Minn. BA in History, Hamline University, St. Paul, Minn., 1969; MLS, University of Minnesota, Minneapolis MN, 1969—71; MA in Hist. of Sci., Mont. State U., 1980. Cataloger U. Iowa, Iowa City, 1971—73; head tech. svcs. Coll. St. Benedict, St. Joseph, Minn., 1973—76; cataloger and reference libr. Mont. State U., Bozeman, 1976—86; dir. libr. Ctrl. Oreg. C.C., Bend, 1986—93, U. Minn. Morris Campus, 1993—2000; head reference and instrn. Gould Libr., Carleton Coll., Northfield, Minn., 2000—03; dir. libr. U. Puget Sound, 2003—. Mem.: ALA, Minn. Libr. Assn., Assn. Coll. and Rsch. Librs. Office: Libr U Puget Sound 1500 N Warner St Tacoma WA 98416 Home: 1208 Buena Vista Ave Fircrest WA 98466

FISCHER, KURT WALTER, education educator; b. Balt., June 9, 1943; s. Kurt Wilhelm and Irmgaard Louise (Funke) Fischer; m. Sandra Pipp (div.); 1 child, Seth; m. Jane Haltiwanger, Dec. 7, 1986; children: Johanna, Lukas, Kara. BA in Psychology summa cum laude, Yale U., 1965; MA in Soc. Rels., Harvard U., 1968, PhD in Soc. Rels., 1971. Asst. prof. Univ. Denver, 1972-78, assoc. prof., 1978-85, prof., 1985-87; prof. edn. Harvard U., Cambridge, Mass., 1986—, Charles Bigelow prof., chair human devel., 1989—92, 1994—95, 1999—2000, dir. mind, brain and edn., 1999—. Vis. scholar Univ. Geneva, 1978—79; vis. prof. U. Pa., Phila., 1985—86; master lectr. U. Groningen, The Netherlands, 1996; vis. prof. Nanjing Normal U., China, 2000. Author: Cognitive Development, 1981, Levels and Transitions in Cognitive Development, 1983; co-author: Psychology Today: An Introduction, 2d and 3d edits., 1972, 75, Human Development from Conception to Adolescence, 1984, Development in Context, 1993, Human Behavior and the Developing Brain, 1994, Self Conscious Emotions, 1995, Development and Vulnerability in Close Relationships, 1996, Socioemotional Development across Cultures, 1998; contbr. articles to profl. jours. Fellow James McKeen Cattell Fund, 1985-86, Ctr. for Advanced Study, Palo Alto, Calif., 1992-93; grantee Carnegie Found., Nat. Inst. Child Health and Devel., 1994—2004, Sloan Found., Spencer Found., Rose Found., 1995—. Mem. Jean Piaget Soc. (pres. 1988-91), Internat. Mind Brain Edn. Soc. (founding pres. 2004-), Phi Beta Kappa, Sigma Xi. Home: 29 Vincent Ave Belmont MA 02478-4418 Office: Harvard U Human Devel Grad Sch Edn Cambridge MA 02138 Office Phone: 617-495-3446. E-mail: kurt_fischer@harvard.edu.

FISCHER, LEROY HENRY, historian, educator; b. Hoffman, Ill., May 19, 1917; s. Andrew LeRoy and Effie (Risby) F.; m. Martha Gwendolyn Anderson, June 20, 1948; children: Barbara Ann, James LeRoy, John Andrew. BA, U. Ill., 1939, MA, 1940, PhD, 1943; postgrad., Columbia U., 1941. Grad. asst. history U. Ill., 1940-43; asst. prof. history Ithaca (N.Y.) Coll., 1946, Okla. State U. at Stillwater, 1946-49, assoc. prof. history, 1949-60, prof. history, 1960-73, Oppenheim Regents prof. history, 1973-78, Oppenheim prof. history, 1978-84, Oppenheim prof. emeritus, 1984—. Exec. sec. honors program, 1959-61; exec. coun. Emeriti Assn., 2000-02. Author: Lincoln's Gadfly, Adam Gurowski, 1964; (with Muriel H. Wright) Civil War Sites in Oklahoma, 1967, The Civil War Era in Indian Territory, 1974, The Western States in the Civil War, 1975, Territorial Governors of Oklahoma, 1975, The Western Territories in the Civil War, 1977, Civil War Battles in the West, 1981, Oklahoma's Governors 1907-1979, 3 vols., 1981-85, Oklahoma State University Historic Old Central, 1988; co-author: A History of Governance at Oklahoma State University, 1992; editor: The History of the Oklahoma State University Centennial Histories Project, 1993; contbr articles to profl. jours. Vice chmn. Honey Springs Battlefield Park Commn., 1968-92, Okla. Civil War Centennial Commn., 1958-65; chmn. Old Ctrl. com. Okla. State U., 1971-98; mem. Okla. State Hist. Preservation Rev. Commn., 1978—, vice chmn., 1978-81, chmn., 1981-83, 1997-2004; bd. dirs. Nat. Indian Hall of Fame, 1969-2002, YMCA, 1951-54, 83-85, 91—; bd. dirs. Assocs. Western History Collections, U. Okla., 1981-2002, pres., 1989-90; bd. dirs. Stillwater Mus. Assn., 1987-93, pres., 1990-91; mem. Okla. Chisholm Trail Centennial Commn., 1967-68; bd. dirs. Friends of Honey Springs Battlefield Park, 1991—, pres., 1994-97, sec. 1997-2000. With Signal Corps, AUS, 1943-45. Recipient Lit. award Loyal Legion U.S., 1963; named tchr. of Yr., Okla. State U.-Okla. Edn. Assn., 1969; inducted in Okla. Historians Hall of Fame, 1995, Centralia (Ill.) Hall of Fame, 1997, Okla. Higher Edn. Hall of Fame, 2002. Mem. Am. Hist. Assn., Southern Hist. Assn., Western History Assn., Am. Assn. State and Local History, AAUP, Okla. Heritage Assn. (Disting. Svc. award 1989), Okla. Hist. Soc. (bd. dirs. 1966—, treas. 1984-87), Ill. Hist. Soc., Orgn. Am. Historians, Omicron Delta Kappa, Pi Gamma Mu, Phi Alpha Theta, Alpha Kappa Lambda. Methodist (chmn. various coms. 1946—, adminstrv. bd. 1950-77, chmn. 1976-77, lay leader 1970-71). Home: 1010 W Cantwell Ave Stillwater OK 74075-4603

FISCHER, MARK DAVID, lawyer; b. Manhasset, NY, May 2, 1961; s. Martin Joseph and Greta Priscilla Fischer; m. Marlene Kern, Aug. 16, 1987; children: Eric, Jonah, Isaac. BA, Brandeis U., 1983; JD, Boston U., 1987. Bar: Mass. 1987, N.Y. 1988, U.S. Dist. Ct. (so. and ea. dists.) N.Y. 1988. Assoc. Nixon. Hargrave, Devans & Doyle, N.Y.C., 1987—89, Rosenman & Colin, N.Y.C., 1989—96, ptnr., 1996—99; v.p., gen. counsel, sec. Phllips-Van Heusen Corp., N.Y.C., 1999—. V.p. Whippoorwill Hills Home Owners Assn., Armonk, NY, 2001—02; mem. nat. alumni bd. Brandeis U., Waltham, Mass., 2001—; coach Am. Youth Soccer Assn., Armonk, 1998—. Mem.: ABA, Am. Soc. Corp. Secs. (mem. securities law com. 2001—), Am. Corp. Counsel Assn. Office: Phillips-Van Heusen Corp 200 Madison Ave New York NY 10016-3903 E-mail: markfischer@pvh.com.

FISCHER, MICHAEL JOHN, computer science educator; b. Ann Arbor, Mich., Apr. 20, 1942; s. Carl Hahn and Kathleen (Kirkpatrick) F.; m. Alice Edna Waltz, June 1, 1963; children: Edward Michael, Robert Patrick, David Frederick. BS, U. Mich., 1963; MA (NSF fellow), Harvard U., 1965, PhD, 1968. Teaching fellow Harvard U., 1965-67; asst. prof. computer sci. Carnegie-Mellon U., 1968-69; asst. prof. math. MIT, 1969-73, assoc. prof. elec. engring., 1973-75; prof. computer sci. U. Wash., 1975-81, dir. Computer Sci. Lab., 1976-79; prof. computer sci. Yale U., New Haven, 1981—, dir. grad. studies in computer sci., 1992-99. Program chmn. IEEE Symposium on Founds. Computer Sci., 1976, 11th Assn. Computing Machinery Symposium on Theory Computing, 1979, Assn. Computing Machinery Symposium on Principles of Distributed Computing, 1982; sr. vis. fellow U. Warwick, Coventry, Eng., summer 1972; vis. assoc. prof. U. Toronto, spring, 1974; guest professor U. Frankfurt, Germany, summer 1974, ETH, Zurich, summer 1975; vis. scientist U. Saarbrücken, Germany, fall 1988; mem. adv. com. for math. and computer scis NSF, 1978-81; mem. com. on recommendations for U.S. Army Basic Sci. Rsch., 1978-81; cons. Xerox Palo Alto Research Ctr., 1982; co-organizer Oberwolfach Confs. on Math. Methods of VSLI and Distributed Computing, 1983, 87, 91; founding mem. subcom. on status women in computer sci. Computing Rsch. Assn., 1990-93; chmn. internat. sci. adv. bd. Max-Planck-Inst. for Informatik, Saarbrücken, 1993—; guest prof. Wuhan Univ. and mem. acad. com. State Key Lab. Software Engring., Wuhan, 2001-2004. Grantee NSF, 1974-92, 2000—; recipient Edsger W. Dijkstra prize in Distributed Computing, 2001. Fellow Assn. Computing Machinery (sec.-treas. spl. interest group on programming langs. 1971-73, local arrangements chmn. conf. 1973); mem. Am. Math. Soc., Soc. Indsl. and Applied Math., European Assn. Theoretical Computer Sci., Yale Figure Skating Club (pres. 1989-91, 1997-2001), Phi Beta Kappa, Phi Kappa Phi. Office: Yale U Dept Computer Sci PO Box 208285 New Haven CT 06520-8285

FISCHER, MICHAEL LUDWIG, environmental executive; b. Dubuque, Iowa, May 29, 1940; s. Carl Michael and Therese Marie (Stadler) F.; m. Jane Pughe Rogers; children: Christina Marie, Steven Michael. BA in Polit. Sci., Santa Clara U., 1964; M in City and Regional Planning, U. Calif., Berkeley, 1967; grad. exec. program in environ. mgmt., Harvard U., 1980. Planner City of Mountain View, Calif., 1960-65; planner assoc. Bay Area Govts., 1966-67; planner County of San Mateo, Calif., 1967-69; assoc. dir. San Francisco Planning and Urban Rsch. Assn., nonprofit civc orgn., 1969-73; exec. dir. North Cen. region Calif. Coastal Zone Conservation Commn., San Rafael, 1973-76; chief dep. dir. Gov.'s Office Planning and Rsch., Sacramento, 1976-78; exec. dir. Calif. Coastal Commn., San Francisco, 1978-85; sr. assoc. Sedway Cooke Assocs., environ. cons., San Francisco, 1985-87; exec. dir. Sierra Club, San Francisco, 1987-93; resident fellow John F. Kennedy Sch. Govt., Inst. Politics, Harvard U., Cambridge, Mass., 1993; sr. cons. Natural Resources Def. Coun., San Francisco, 1993-95; exec. officer Calif. Coastal Conservancy, Oakland, 1994-97; program dir. environ. William & Flora Hewlett Found., Menlo Park, Calif., 1997—2002, sr. fellow, 2002—03, environ. and mgmt. cons., 2003—. Lectr. dept. city and regional planning U. Calif., Berkeley, 1984; mem., co-chair environ. com. adv. coun. Calvert Social Investment Fund, 1989-2005; mem. Harvard Commn. Global Change Info. Policy, 1993-95; mem. com. on impact of maritime facility devel. NAS/NRC, 1975-78; mem. nat. sea grant review panel NOAA, 1998-01; bd. dirs. High Country News Found., 2000—05, Resources for Cmty. Collaboration, 1999-; mem. adv. bd. Sustainable Conservation, 2003-; mem. steering com. Indigenous Cmtys. Mapping Initiative, 2000-05. Co-author Calif. state plan, An Urban Strategy for Calif., 1978, Building a New Municipal Railway, 1973, Oral History, Coastal Commn. Yrs., 1973-85, Oral History, Sierra Club Yrs., 1987-93; author intro. Ansel Adams: Yosemite, 1995; contbr. papers to profl. publs. Recipient Life Achievement award Assn. Environ. Profls., 1986, Disting. Leadership award. Am. Soc. Pub. Adminstrn., 1987, Outstanding Nat. Leadership award Coastal States Orgn., 1990, Exemplary Pub. Svc. award San Francisco Bay Conservation and Devel. Commn., 1997, Spl. Recognition award Calif. State Legis., 1998, Coastal Champion award, Calif., 2003., Coastal Hero award, 2005. Fellow Inst. Journalism & Nat. Resources; Mem. Calif. Planning and Conservation League (bd. dirs. 1970-76), Alliance Ethnic and Environ. Orgn. (founding bd. dirs. 1991-93), The Oceanic Soc. (bd. dirs. 1983-88), Sierra Club, Friends of the Earth (bd. dirs. 1988-94), Am. Youth Hostels, Inc. (bd. dirs. 1985-87), Yosemite Restoration Trust (bd. dirs. 1990-97, pres. 1995-97), Lambda Alpha. E-mail: fischer@igc.org.

FISCHER, MICHELLE K., lawyer; BA in Econs., Yale U., 1986; JD with honors, U. Chgo., 1989. Bar: Ohio 1989, D.C. 1991. With Jones Day, Cleve., 1989—, ptnr., 1999—. Mem.: ABA (antitrust law sect.), Cleve. Bar Assn., Ohio State Bar Assn. (bd. govs. antitrust law sect.). Office: Jones Day North Point 901 Lakeside Ave Cleveland OH 44114-1190

FISCHER, PAMELA SHADEL, public relations executive; b. Harrisburg, Pa., Feb. 28, 1959; d. Richard Lee and Pauline Louise (Nies) S.; m. Charles J. Fischer Jr., June 11, 1983; 1 child, Zachary Joseph. BA in English, Lebanon Valley Coll., Annville, Pa., 1981. Cert. child passenger safety technician AAA. Pub. rels. coord. Pa. Optometric Assn., Harrisburg, 1981-83; pub. rels. dir. Morris Ctr. YMCA, Cedar Knolls, NJ, 1983-85; pub. rels. coord. Delta Dental Plan of N.J., Parsippany, 1985-86; pub. rels. mgr. AAA N.J. Automobile Club, Florham Park, NJ, 1986-91, mgr. mem. svcs. and pub. affairs, 1991-94, asst. v.p. pub. rels. & safety, 1994-96, asst. v.p. pub. affairs and fin. svcs., 1996—2002, v.p. pub. affairs and fin. svcs., 2002—. Corp. capt. United Way of Morris County, Cedar Knolls, 1985—90, chmn. publs. com., 1989—90, chmn. mktg. com., 1991—95, v.p. mktg., 1996, mem. women's leadership initiative exec. com., 1999—, vice chmn., 2002—03, chmn., 2003—04; career counselor Lebanon Valley Coll., 1983—90, alumni amb., 2004—; mem. hwy. traffic safety policy adv. com. Gov.'s Office, 1998—; chair legis. com. Gateway Tourism Coun., 1997—2000; mem. Driver Edn. Commn. N.J., 1999—2005; bd. dirs. First Night of Morris County, 1999—2002, chmn., 2004; mem. NJ Motor Vehicle Commn., 2003—, vice chmn., 2004; mem. N.J. Child Passenger Safety Coalition, 2003—; mem. corp. leadership coun. Family Svc. Morris County, NJ, 2005—; trustee Trans Options, 2005—; bd. dirs. Morris Ctr. YMCA, 1992—94, Hist. Morris County Visitors Ctr., 1999—, bd. pres., 2001—04. Rotary Found. scholar, 1981; recipient Gold award United Way of Morris County, 1988, Traffic Safety award Gov.'s rep., 2004. Mem. Pub. Rels. Soc. Am. (bd. dirs. 1995), N.J. Press Assn., N.J. Travel Industry Assn., N.J. Comm. Regional Plan Assn., Internat. Assn. Bus Communicators, Y's Club of Cedar Knoll (pres. 1986-91), Long Valley Ice Hockey Club (dir. media rels. 2003—). Republican. Roman Catholic. Avocations: stenciling, reading, writing, photography. Office: AAA NJ Automobile Club 1 Hanover Rd Florham Park NJ 07932-1888 Office Phone: 973-245-4858. Personal E-mail: aaanjacpr@aol.com.

FISCHER, PAUL, corporate financial executive; BA in Acctg., Loyola U.; MBA, Creighton U. CPA. Staff auditor Amsted Industries, 1980—92; controller Am. Steel Foundries, 1992—97, v.p. mgr., 1997—2000, v.p. end-of-car ops., 2000; controller Amsted Industries, 2000—03; chief operating officer ASF-Keystone, Ind. and Keystone Europe, 2001—03; v.p. fin., chief fin. officer Amsted Industries, 2003—. Office: Amsted Industries 205 N Michigan Ave 44th Fl Chicago IL 60601

FISCHER, R. M., sculptor; b. N.Y.C., Mar. 21, 1947; s. Bernard and Alva (Sherman) F.; m. Patti Paige, June 22, 1986; 1 child, Dena Paige. BA, L.I. U., 1971; MFA, San Francisco Art Inst., 1973. Numerous one-man shows, including Musee Ville Toulon, France, 1984, Whitney Mus. Am. Art, N.Y.C., 1984, Inst. Contemporary Art, Boston, 1985, Jay Gorney Modern Art, N.Y.C., 1989, Donald Young Gallery, Chgo., 1988, Sidney Janis Gallery, N.Y.C., 1991, Deitch Projects, N.Y.C., 1998, Sandra Gering Gallery, N.Y.C., 2002; exhibited in numerous group shows, including Mus. Modern Art, 1984, Whitney Mus. Am. Art, 1985, 88, 91, Aldrich Mus. Contemporary Art, 1988, Vienna (Austria) Seccession, 1990; represented in permanent collections Cin. Art Mus., Whitney Mus. Modern Art., Mus. Modern Art, Dallas Mus. Art, Carnegie Mus. Fine Arts, Pitts., Fundacao de Serrales Found., Oporto, Portugal; permanent pub. artworks include Kansas City Convention Ctr., Cleve. Gateway Plaza, Battery Park City, N.Y., Mass. State House, Boston, Seattle Tower, Sony Studios Fountain, Union Square, San Francisco. Studio: 390 Wythe Ave # 101 Brooklyn NY 11211

FISCHER, RICHARD SAMUEL, lawyer; b. Buffalo, July 31, 1937; s. Richard D. and Isabel B. (Van Dorn) F.; m. Malinda Berry, June 3, 1960; children: Richard B., Van D. AB, Harvard U., 1959, JD, 1963. Bar: N.Y. 1963, Okla. 1996. Law clk N.Y. Ct. Appeals, Albany, 1963-65; assoc. Nixon, Hargrave, Devans & Doyle, Rochester, N.Y., 1965-71, ptnr., 1972-95, mem. policy com., 1991-95, head Rochester office, 1992-95; mem. faculty Okla. State U., Stillwater, 1997—2002. Past chair, trustee Highland Hosp.; past pres. Harley Sch.; past bd. dirs. Rochester Area Hosp. Corp., Primary Mental Health Project, United Way, Stillwater; past pres. Friends of Music and Allied Arts, 2000-01; mem. CHES exec. com. Okla. State U. Mem. ABA, N.Y. State Bar Assn. (past chmn. com. ins. programs and retirement plans), Monroe County Bar Assn., NYU Inst. Fed. Taxation (adv. com.), Okla. Bar Assn. Clubs: Genessee Valley, Country Club of Rochester (N.Y.), Stillwater Country Club, Karsten Creek Golf Club. Office: PO Box 1897 Stillwater OK 74076-1897

FISCHER, ROB, sculptor; b. Mpls., 1968; Degree, Escuela Salmintina, Spain, 1989; degree Interdisciplinary Studies Honors Program, Mpls. Coll. Art & Design, 1993. One-man shows include Hiding Places for a Dense City, Art in Gen., NY, 1999, New Work, Conductor's Hallway Gallery, London, 1999, Light/ House, Franklin Art Works, Mpls., 2000, My Winnebago Travels, Vox Populi Gallery, Phila., 2000, Mirrored Boat, Macalester College Art Gallery, St. Paul, 2000, In Site, Madison Art Ctr., Wis., 2000, Dee/ Glasoe, NY, 2001, Elizabeth Dee Gallery, NY, 2002, Mary Goldman Gallery, LA, 2004, Cohan and Leslie, NY, 2005, exhibited in group shows at Five Jerome Artists, Mpls. Coll. Art & Design, 1996, Reimaging the Landscape, Katherine E. Nash Gallery, Mpls., 1997, One Hundred Years of Sculpture, Walker Art Ctr., Mpls., 1998, Interval, Sculpture Ctr., NY, 1999, Door as Metaphor in Contemporary Art, NJ Ctr. Visual Art, 2002, Druid: Wood as a Superconductor, Space 101, Bklyn., 2003, Soft Cell, Foxy Productions, Bklyn., 2003, Whitney Biennial, Whitney Mus. Am. Art, NY, 2004, I Feel Mysterious Today, Palm Beach Inst. Contemporary Art, Fla., 2004. Grantee Visual Arts Fellowship, Minn. State Arts Bd., 1996; Jerome Found. Fellowship, 1995, Visual Arts Fellowship, Bush Found., 1999. Mailing: c/o Cohan and Leslie 138 Tenth Ave New York NY 10011*

FISCHER, ROBERT BLANCHARD, university administrator, researcher; b. Hartford, Conn., Oct. 24, 1920; s. Charles Albert and Matilda (Nylen) F.; m. Mary Ellen Mitchell, June 29, 1946; children: Lois, Marcia, Philip, Vivian, Valerie. BS, Wheaton Coll., 1942; PhD, U. Ill., 1946. Rsch. chemist U.S. Army Atomic Bomb Project, Chgo., 1944-46; instr. chemistry U. Ill., Urbana, 1946-48; prof. chemistry Indiana U., Bloomington, 1948-63; dean sch. of sci. Calif. State U.-Dominguez Hills, Carson, 1963-79, dean emeritus, 1979—; provost, sr. v.p. Biola U., La Mirada, Calif., 1979-88, disting. prof., 1988-89, provost, disting. prof. emeritus, 1989—. Research assoc. Calif. Inst. Tech., Pasadena, 1959-60; cons. in field. Contbr. articles to profl. jours. Fellow AAAS, Am. Sci. Affiliation (nat. pres. 1965-66); mem. Am. Chem. Soc. (sect. and region chmn.). Republican. Avocations: theology, amateur radio, sports. Home: 860 Morningside Dr C302 Fullerton CA 92835

FISCHER, RUSSELL LEONARD, public relations executive; b. East Orange, NJ, Feb. 4, 1958; s. Harold Martin and Annette Carol Fischer. BA, Boston U., 1980; JD, Antioch U., Washington, 1984. Importer, retailer, owner Fendi of Short Hills, N.J., 1982-92; pub. rels. dir., v.p. IME-Xaminations, Elizabeth, N.J., 1994—. Vol. World Trade Orgn., NYC, battered wives Unity Group, Short Hills, 1995-98; del. reform coun. Am. Jewish Congress, N.Y.C., 1991; adv. bd. Am. Assn. Reform Judaism, Washington, 1995-99; alumni advisor, pres. South Fla. chpt. Boston U. Alumni Assn., 2000-02; active Heritage Soc. Congregation Emanu-El, NYC. Recipient Meritorious and Outstanding Cmty. Svc. award Am. Nat. Red Cross, 1976. Mem.: N.J. Improters Assn., Ocean Point Beach Club, World Trade Ctr. Club, Williams Island Club, Crestmont Country Club. Avocation: sculpture.

FISCHER, STANLEY, bank executive; b. Lusaka, Zambia, Oct. 15, 1943; came to U.S., 1966, naturalized, 1976; s. Philip and Ann (Kopelowitz) F.; m. Rhoda Keet, Dec. 12, 1965; children: Michael Adam, David Benjamin, Jonathan Philip. BSc, London Sch. Econs., 1965, MSc, 1966; PhD, MIT, 1969. Fellow U. Chgo., 1969-70, asst. prof. econs., 1970-73; assoc. prof. MIT, 1973-77, prof., 1977—98, Killian prof., 1992-94; chief economist, v.p. devel. econs. World Bank, 1988-90; 1st dep. mng. dir. IMF, 1994—2001; vice chmn. Citigroup, N.Y.C., 2002—, head sect. client group, 2004—. Vis. sr. lectr. Hebrew U. Jerusalem, 1972; fellow Ctr. for Advanced Studies Hebrew U., 1976-77; vis. fellow Hoover Instn., Stanford U., 1981-82; cons. on Israeli economy Dept. State, 1984-87, 91-94; cons. IMF, 1991-92. Author: Indexing Inflation and Economic Policy, 1986, (with R. Dornbusch and R. Schmalensee) Economics, 1988, (with O. Blanchard) Lectures in Macroeconomics, 1989, (with R. Dornbusch and R. Startz) Macroeconomics, 9th edit., 2004, IMF Essays From a Time of Crisis, 2004; editor Nat. Bur. Econ. Rsch. Macroecons. Ann., 1986-94; contbr. articles to profl. jours. Guggenheim fellow. Fellow Econometric Soc.; mem. Am. Acad. Arts and Scis., Coun. on Fgn. Rels. Home: 181 E 65th St #23A New York NY 10021-6607 Business E-Mail: fischers@citigroup.com.

FISCHER, THOMAS COVELL, law educator, consultant, writer; b. May 2, 1938; s. Vilas Uber and Elizabeth Mary (Holland) Fischer; m. Katherine Brenda Andrew, Sept. 29, 1972. AB, U. Cin., 1960; postgrad., U. Wash., 1960-62, Loyola U., Chgo., 1964-66; JD, Georgetown U., 1966. Asst. dir. U. Ill., Chgo., 1964-66; asst. dean Georgetown U. Law Ctr., 1966-72; cons. Antioch Sch. Law, 1972-73; asst. exec. dir. Am. Bar Found., Chgo., 1974-76; assoc. dean, prof. law U. Dayton, 1976-78; dean, prof. law New Eng. Sch. Law, Boston, 1978—81, prof., 1981—2003, prof. emeritus, 2003—; disting. acad. in residence Seattle U. Law Sch., 2003—. Vis. scholar, Cambridge, 1991, Exeter, 91, Edinburgh, 91, Konstanz U., 1993, Muenster U., 1993, U. Auckland, 1996; fellow Inst. Advanced Legal Studies, U. London, English Inns of Court, 1997; vis. fellow Wolfson Coll., Cambridge, England, 1997; sr. vis. fellow, LLM program U. Southampton Law Faculty, 2001, sr. vis. tutor, 02; cons. in field. Author: Due Process in the Student/Institutional Relationship, 1970; author: (with Duscha) The Campus Press: Freedom and Responsibility, 1973; author: (with Zenhle) Introduction to Law and Legal Reasoning, 1977, Legal Education, Law Practice and the Economy: A New England

Study, 1990, The Europeanization of America: What Americans Need to Know About the European Union, 1996, The United States, the European Union, and the Globilization of World Trade: Allies or Adversaries?, 2000; author: (with Cox) Quick Review of Conflict of Laws, 4th edit., 2001. Project dir. Commn. Legal Edn. and Practice and Econ. New Eng. Recipient Elaine R. Maham award, U. Cin., 1960; Pi Kappa Alpha Meml. scholar, 1960—62. Fellow: Inns of Ct.; mem.: Phi Alpha Theta, Pi Delta Epsilon, Delta Theta Phi. Roman Catholic. Office: 755 Brookcliff Ln NE Bainbridge Island WA 98110 Office Phone: 206-398-4034. E-mail: fischert@seattleu.edu. *Every one of us is a teacher in some way; we are also students. May we teach truthfully, and learn well.*

FISCHER, VIOLETA PÈREZ CUBILLAS, Spanish literature and linguistics educator; b. Havana, Cuba, Nov. 20, 1923; came to U.S., 1959; d. Josè M. and Carmen (Reyes Pizey) Pèrez Cubillas; m. Rolando F. Fischer, Dec. 27, 1947 (dec. May 1994); 1 child, Violet Fischer Pack. PhD in Law, U. Havana, 1949; postgrad., U. N.C., 1967-68, MA in Romance Langs., 1975. Prin. Spl. Ctr. for English Teaching, Havana, Cuba, 1945—59; lawyer Havana, Cuba, 1949—59; asst. prof. East Carolina U., Greenville, NC, 1962—66; prof. Spanish lit. and linguistics Coastal Carolina Community Coll., Jacksonville, NC, 1970—96; ret., 1996. Speaker various civic, mil., ednl. assns., and community colls., 1963—. Bd. dirs. Onslow County Community Concerts, Jacksonville, N.C., 1987; chmn. CCCC Women's Assn., 1972-73. Recipient Josè de la Luz y Caballero award Cruzada Educativa Cubana Assn., 1987, Juan J. Remos award Cruzada Educativa Cubana, 1987, N.C. State Svc. award for 30 yrs. of svc., 1994; Paul Harris fellow Rotary Internat., 1996. Mem. MLA, Nat. Assn. Cuban Lawyers, Havana Bar Assn. in Exile, Nat. Cuban Tchrs. Assn., Nat. Assn. Cuban-Am. Educators, Count of Galvez Hist. Soc., Sigma Delta Mu (co-founder, state rep.), Delta Kappa Gamma (chmn. world fellowship com. 1982-84, 96-98, Wreath of Excellence ednl. award 1989, 2d v.p. Upsilon chpt. Jacksonville 1994-96). Roman Catholic. Home: 2107 Perry Dr Jacksonville NC 28546-1642

FISCHER, WILLIAM SAMUEL, composer, lecturer; b. Shelby, Miss., Mar. 5, 1935; s. Robert A. and Willye (Samuels) F.; m. Dolores Labrie, Feb. 14, 1934; children: Darius, Marc, Bryan, Paul. BS in Mus. Edn., Xavier U., 1956; postgrad., Vienne Acad. Music, 1965—66; studied in Music Theory and Composition, U. S.W. La., 1961; MA in Music Theory and Composition, Colo. Coll., 1962. Dir. band, choir Christianburg Inst., Cambria, Va., 1957-58, St. Landry Parish, Opelousas, La., 1958-62; faculty music Xavier U., 1962-66, High Sch. of Music and Art, N.Y.C., 1969-76; dir. music Atlantic Rec. Co., N.Y.C., 1967-71, record prodr., 1975—, Fantasy Rec. Co., Berkeley, Calif., 1976-79; freelance composer, arranger N.Y.C., 1967—. Lectr. N.Y.C.; cons. bd. of Edn., N.Y.C. Composer: (operas) Jesse, 1965-66, Simone, 1970, Touch Kiss, 1971, Dong Film opera, 1977, Choral Music for Mass Saint in honor of Katharine Drexel, 1988, Gospel Spirit, 1973, choirs concerto Grosso in D soloists and orch., 1969, Mass for a Saint, Vatican, Rome, 1988-2000, Cross Bronx Concerto violin concerto music saxophone, 1997, Experience in E orch. and jazz quintet, 1970; author: Music Theory, 2000, Mind to Music, 2001, Private Hours Trilogy and Meditation and Trance, LeBeau Mass, 1997. Mem. The LeBeau Mass com. for celebration 100 years of ch. established 1897 Immaculate Conception, St. Landry Parish, La. Served to corp. USMC, 1956-57. Recipient Deutsches Akademische Austaudienst award Fed. Republic of Germany, 1966; grantee Fulbright Found., 1965-66, Austrian govt., 1965, Pan Am. grantee, 1965, Tulane U., New Orleans. Mem. ASCAP., Internat. Platform Assn. Roman Catholic. Avocation: astronomy.

FISCHHOFF, BARUCH, psychologist, educator; b. Detroit, Apr. 21, 1946; s. Henry and Shirley (Levine) F.; m. Andrea Marks, Dec. 22, 1968; children: Maya, Ilya, Noam. BS in Math., Wayne State U., 1967; MA in Psychology, Hebrew U., Jerusalem, 1972, PhD in Psychology, 1975. Rsch. assoc. Oreg. Rsch. Inst., Eugene, 1974-76, Decision Rsch., Eugene, 1976-85, Applied Psychology Unit Med. Rsch. Coun., Cambridge, Eng., 1981-82, Eugene Rsch. Inst., 1985-87; prof. Carnegie-Mellon U., Pitts., 1987—, Univ. prof., 1998—, Howard Heinz prof., 2002—. Vis. prof. U. Stockholm, 1982-83; mem. panels NRC; mem. sci. adv. bd. EPA; cons. in field. Author: Acceptable Risk, 1981, Mental Models, 2001; mem. editl. bd. Jour. Risk Uncertainty, Decision Analysis, Risk Analysis, also others; contbr. numerous articles to profl. jours . Mem. Eugene Commn. on Rights of Women, 1975-81; pres. Eugene Human Rights Coun., 1979-81; mem. sci. adv. bd. EPA, 2003—; mem. sci. tech. adv. com. Dept. Homeland Security, 2004—. Fellow APA (Disting. Sci. award 1981, psychology in Pub. Interest award 1991), Soc. for Risk Analysis (pres. 2004, Disting. Achievement award 1991), Soc. Judgment and Decision-Making (mem. coun. 1988-91, pres. 1990-91), Inst. Medicine, Phi Beta Kappa. Home: 1437 Denniston Ave Pittsburgh PA 15217-1332 Office: Carnegie Mellon U Dept Engring and Pub Policy Pittsburgh PA 15213-3890 Office Phone: 412-268-3246. Business E-Mail: baruch@cmu.edu.

FISCHL, ERIC, artist; b. N.Y.C., 1948; BFA, Calif. Inst. Arts, 1972. Exhibitions include Dalhousie Art Gallery, Halifax, Canada, 1975, Studio, 1976, Galerie B., Montreal, Canada, 1976, 1978, Edward Thorp Gallery, New York, 1980, 1981—82, Emily Davis Art Gallery, Akron, OH, 1980, Sable-Castelli Gallery, Toronto, Canada, 1981—82, 1985, 1987, Sir George Williams Gallery, Montreal, Canada, 1983, Saidye Bronfman Centre, 1983, Larry Gagosian Gallery, Los Angeles, 1983, 1986, Mario Diacono Gallery, Rome, 1983, Boston, 1985, 1999, Multiples/Marian Goodman Inc., New York, 1983, Nigel Greenwood Gallery, London, 1983, Mendel Art Gallery, Saskatoon, Cananda, 1985, Stedelijk Van Abbe Museum, The Netherlands, 1985, Kunsthalle Basel, Basel, Switzerland, 1985, Institute of Contemporary Art, London, 1985, Art Gallery of Ontario, Toronto, Canada, 1985, Whitney Museum of Am. Art, New York, 1986, Mary Boone Gallery, 1984, 1986—88, 1990, 1992, 1994, 1996, 1999—2000, Daniel Weinberg Gallery, Los Angeles, 1986, Galerie Michael Werner, Koln, West Germany, 1988, Waddington Galleries, London, 1989, Akademie der Bildenden Kunste, Vienna, Austria, 1990, Musee Cantonal des Beaux-Arts de Lausanne, Lausanne, Switzerland, 1990, Aarhus Kunstmuseum, Aarhus, Denmark, 1991, Louisiana Museum of Modern Art, Humlebaek, Denmark, 1991, Michael Kohn Gallery, Santa Monica, CA, 1992, Center for the Fine Arts, Miami, FL, 1992, Galeria Soledad Lorenzo, Madrid, Spain, 1993, Galerie Daniel Templon, Paris, France, 1994, 1999, Daniel Weinberg Gallery, San Francisco, CA, 1994, Michael Nagy Fine Art, Potts Point, Australia, 1995, Baldwin Gallery, Aspen, CO, 1997, Gagosian Gallery, New York, 1998, London, 2000, Galleria Lawrence Rubin, Milan, Italy, 1998. Named National Academician, Nat. Acad. of Design, 1994. Office: c/o Baldwin Gallery 209 S Galena St Aspen CO 81611 also: c/o Mary Boone Gallery 745 Fifth Ave New York NY 10151 Office Phone: 970-920-9797, 212-752-2929. Office Fax: 970-920-1821, 212-752-3939.*

FISCHLER, ABRAHAM SAUL, retired academic administrator, educator; b. Bklyn., Jan. 21, 1928; s. Morris and Esther P. Fischler; m. Shirley Balter, Apr. 9, 1949; children: Bruce Evan, Michael Alan, Lori Faye. BS in Soc. Sci., CUNY, 1951; MA in Sci. Edn., NYU, 1952; EdD, Columbia U., 1959; DSc (hon.), N.Y. Inst. Tech., 1981; LLD (hon.), Nova U., 1992. Sci. tchr., supr. Ossining (N.Y.) Pub. Schs., 1952-58; instr. Columbia U., N.Y.C., 1958-59; asst. prof. edn. Harvard U. Grad. Sch., Cambridge, Mass., 1959-62; assoc. prof. then prof. edn. U. Calif., Berkeley, 1962-66; dean grad. studies Nova U., Ft. Lauderdale, Fla., 1966-70, James Donn prof., 1966—, exec. v.p., 1969-70, pres., 1970-92; pres. emeritus, univ. prof., 1992—; mem. Broward County Sch. Bd., 1994-98, chair, 1996-97. Vis. prof. nat. and internat. univs., 1963-65; cons. numerous sch. dists., Calif., 1962-67; advisor ednl. pubs.; mem. bus.-edn. adv. com. Alameda-Contra Costa Counties, Calif.; mem. Calif. Elem. Sci. Adv. Com., Sacramento; mem. Overseas Tchrs. Examining Team, Berkeley; bd. dirs. Cardio-Metrics, Inc., Inst. Learning Techs., Inc., Hollywood Med. Ctr., Fla. Med. Ctr., 2000— Author: Modern Science, Grades 7,8,9, 1963; (with others) Science: A Modern Approach, 1966, Modern Science, 1967, Modern Elementary Science: Grades 1 through 8, 1971, Nova U.'s Three National Doctoral Degree Programs: An Analysis and Formative Evaluation, 1977; contbr. numerous articles to profl. jours., author monograph and rsch. reports. Pres. United Way Broward County (Fla.), 1984-85, bd. dirs., 1973-2000, chmn. budget com., 1976-81; chmn. Broward County Overall Econ. Devel. Com., 1980-88, Broward Edn. and Tng. Coun., 1989—; pres. S.E. Fla. Holocaust Meml. Ctr., 1985-87, Temple Beth El, Hollywood, 1988-90; adv. bd. Leadership Broward; mem. 17th Jud. Nominating Commn., Broward County, 1982-86, Ft. Lauderdale Mus. Art, Fla. Philharm., Broward County Crime Commn., Broward Workshop Edn. Task Force, Town of Davie, Fla. Econ. and Indsl. Devel. Bd.; bd. dirs. Hollywood (Fla.) Med. Ctr., 1982—, chmn. bd. dirs., 1985—; pres. Health Care Rsch. and Edn. Found., 1988-89, United Ways Fla., 1990-91; bd. govs. Fla. Bar, 1991-95, Fla. Bar Found., 1996-01; chmn. Hollywood City Master Plan; mem. Broward Ctr. Performing Arts Authority, 1998; co-chair Sun Sentinel Diversity Fund, 2000—; chair Broward Edn. Found., 2002, South Fla. Cmty. Blood Ctrs., 2002. With USN, 1945-47. Recipient Outstanding Mgmt. and Leadership award Sales and Mktg. Execs., Ft. Lauderdale, 1978, Leader of Yr. award Leadership Broward, 1991, Humanitarian of Yr. award E.A.S.E. Found., 1991, Disting. Educator award Assn. Ind. Schs. Fla., 1992, Tree of Life award Jewish Nat. Fund, 1993, Spirit of Broward award, 1994, Lifetime Achievement award Urban League, 1994; named Broward Educator of Yr., Women's Am. ORT, 1997, Disting. Pub. Svc. award ADL, 1998, Sun Sentinel Cmty. Leader of the Yr., 1999, Sun Sentinel Cmty. Svc. award, 2000, Fla. Bar medal of Hon., 2005; DuPont fellow UCLA, 1958, Sci. Manpower fellow Columbia U., 1958-59. Fellow AAAS, Phi Delta Kappa; mem. ASCD, NSTA, Assn. for Edn. Tchrs. Sci. (past pres.), Nat. Assn. Research in Sci. Teaching, Soc. Advancement Edn., Soc. Research Adminstrs., Am. Assn. Higher Edn., Nat. Council Univ. Research Adminstrs., Com. of 100, Hollywood, Hundred Club Broward County (pres. 1985-86), Tower Club, Woodmont Country Club, Kappa Delta Pi. Avocations: running, golf, travel. Office: Nova U Office Pres Emeritus 3301 College Ave Fort Lauderdale FL 33314-7796 Office Phone: 954-262-5375. Business E-Mail: fischler@nova.edu.

FISCHLER, SANDY LYNN, charitable and informational organization executive; b. Anchorage, Alaska, Dec. 28, 1962; d. Joseph Michael Fischler and Sharon Leigh (Blodgett) Smith. Student, U. Alaska, 1980-83, Circle in Square Theatre Sch., 1983. Spl. event coord. Universal Studios Fla., Orlando, 1993-95; prodn. mgr. Headdress Ball, Orlando, 1994; assoc. prodr. Nickelodeon "Guts", Orlando, 1994; event mgr. First Night Providence, 1995; prodr. bike stunt segment 1997 Holiday Bowl Halftime Show, San Diego, 1997; event prodr. ESPN X Games, San Diego, 1995-98; ptnr. Avalanche Events Group, 1998—; owner 4th Wall Events, 1998—; event mgr. NFL Experience, Super Bowl XXXIII, 1999; broadcast mgr. NFL Experience, Super Bowl XXXIV, XXXV, XXXVI, XXXVII; exec. dir., founder The Pilonidal Support Alliance, 2005—. Vol. Feral Cat Coalition, San Diego, 1998, Kisses for Kats Pet Rescue, 2000-01, Cat's Meow Cat Rescue, 2002--. Mem. Women in Sports and Events, Internat. Festival and Events Assn., Calfest, Nat. Sports Mktg. Network. Avocations: gardening, stained glass. Home: 5911 Cerritos Ave Long Beach CA 90805

FISCHMAN, MYRNA LEAH, accountant, educator; d. Isidore and Sally (Goldstein) Fischman. BS, Coll. City N.Y., 1960, MS, 1964; PHD, NYU, 1976. CPA N.Y. Asst. to contr. Sam Goody, Inc., N.Y.C.; tchr. accounting Ctr. Comml. H.S., N.Y.C., 1960—63, vicat. adviser, 1963—66; instr. acctg. Borough of Manhattan C.C., N.Y.C., 1963—66; self-employed acct. N.Y.C., 1960—; chief acct. investigator rackets Office Queens Dist. Atty., 1969—70, cmty. fels. coord., 1970—71; adv. prof. L.I. U., 1970—79, prof. acctg. taxation and law, 1979—, coord. grad. capstone courses, 1982—86, dir. Sch. Profl. Accountancy Bklyn. Campus, 1984—, dir. Ctr. Acctg. and Tax Edn., 1986—, chmn. acctg. dept. Editor: Ea. Bus. Educators Jour., 1988. Rsch. cons. pre-tech. program N.Y.C. Bd. Edn., mem., 1992—; acct.-advisor Inst. for Advancement of Criminal Justice; acct.-cons. Coalition Devel. Corp., Interracial Coun. for Bus. Opportunities; treas. Breakfree Inc., Lower East Side Prep. Sch.; mem. ednl .task force Am. Jewish Com., 1972—; mem. Chancellor Com. Against Discrimination in Edn., 1976—97; chmn. supervisory com. Fed. Credit Union # 1532, N.Y.C., 1983—; chmn. consumer coun. Astoria Med. Ctr., 1980—92; mem. subcom. on bus. edn. to the econ. devel. and mktg. com. Bklyn. C. of C., 1984—; mem. adv. bd. acctg. dept. burough of Manhattan C.C., 1997—; mem. Bus. Edn. Adv. Coun.; mem. steering com., youth div. N.Y. Dem. County Com., 1967—68; del. to Nat. Conv. Young Dems. Am., 1967, rep. assigned to women's activities com., 1967; mem. legis. adv. bd. N.Y. State Assemblyman Dennis Butler, 1979—97. Recipient award for meritorious svc., Cmty. Svc. Soc., 1969, Lifetime Achievement award, Soroptimist Internat. Bklyn., 1997. Mem.: NEA (bus. edn. assns.), AAUP, AICPA, Inst. Mgmt. Accts. (dir. N.Y. chpt. 1983—, dir. profl. devel. 1986—87, dir. pub. rels. 1987—88, dir. manuscripts 1991—92, dir. univ. rels. 1993—94), Tax Inst. L.I. U. (dir. Blyn. chpg. 1984—), N.Y. State Soc. CPAs (mem. com. on recruitment for CPA careers 1981—, auditing com. 1991—, gen. com. on edn. in colls. and univs. 1991—, pub. rels. com. 1992—, pres. Bklyn. chpt. 2001—02, Dr. Emanuel Saxe Outstanding CPA in Edn. award 1994—95), Fed. Credit Union (chmn. supervisory com. # 1532 n.Y.C. 1983—), Young Alumni Assn., Am. Assn. Jr. Colls., Doctorate Assn. N.Y. Educators (v.p. 1975—97), Assn. Govt. Accts. (dir. N.Y. chpg. 1983—, pres. elect n.Y. chpg. 1989—90, pres. N.Y. chpt. 1990—91), Fin. Execs. Inst., Grad. Students Orgn. NYU (treas. 1971—73), Internat. Soc. Bus. Edn., Nat. Eastern (co-chmn. ann. meeting 1967), Am. Acctg. Assn., Govt. Accts. (v.p. 1973—74, dir. rsch. and manuscripts 1985—, pres. elect N.Y. chpt. 1989—90, pres. 1990—91, bd. dirs. N.Y. chpt. 1994—), Emanu-El League Congregation Emanu-El, N.Y. (chmn. cmty. svcs. com. 1967—68), Jewish Guild for Blind, Jewish Braille Inst., Cmty. Welfare Com. Assn., Friends Met. Mus. Art, Friends Am. Ballet Theatre, Women's City Club (N.Y.), Delta Pi Epsilon (treas. 1976). Democrat. Jewish. Achievements include development of new bus. machine course and curriculum Borough Manhattan Bus. C.C. Office: LI U Sch Bus 1 University Plz Rm 700 Brooklyn NY 11201-5301

FISCHMAR, RICHARD MAYER, resort executive, financial consultant; b. N.Y.C., Apr. 11, 1938; s. John B. and Sylvia (Moosnick) F.; m. Sandra P. Fensin, July 3, 1967; children: Brian, Laura. BS, U. Ill., 1959, MA, 1962. CPA, Ill. Sr. auditor L.K.H.&H., Chgo., 1962-66; contr. Lake States Engr., Park Ridge, Ill., 1966-68, New Communities Enterprises, Park Forest South, Ill., 1968-70; dep. dir. Ill. Drug Abuse Program, Chgo., 1970-71; dir. internal audit Ill. Dept. Labor, Chgo., 1971-73; contr. Ill. Dept. Employment Security, Chgo., 1973-78, D.L. Pattis Real Estate, Lincolnwood, Ill., 1978-86, Goodman Realty Group, Inc., Chgo., 1986-90, Harold J. Carlson, Rosemont, Ill., 1990-92; CFO L.J. Sheridan & Co., Chgo., Ill., 1992-94, Am. Resorts Internat., Oakbrook, Ill., 1994—. Guest lectr. Mich. State U., Gov.'s State U. Author: (booklet) Bibliography of Management Services, 1972; contbr. articles to profl. jours. Mem. Ill. Soc. CPAs (real estate com., mgmt. adv. svcs. and constrn. com., entertainment and leisure industries coms.).

FISCUS, LINDA KAY, music educator; b. Blackwell, Okla., Sept. 22, 1950; d. Howard Orris and Ella May Reusser; m. Terry Ray Fiscus, June 24, 1972; children: Sarah Elaine, Seth Howard. BA, Northwestern Okla. State U., 1972, ME, 1995. Vocal music instr. Freedom (Okla.) H.S., 1972—74, Lone Wolf (Okla.) Schs., 1974—76; choral accompanist Blackwell H.S., 1983—87; vocal music instr. Huston Elem., Blackwell, 1987—93, Deer Creek-Lamont (Okla.) Schs., 1993—97; prof. music No. Okla. Coll., Tonkawa, 1997—. Judge various piano contests, 1972—; pianist Victory Fellowship, Blackwell, 1981—. Active Music Boosters, Blackwell, 1993—, Basketball Boosters, Blackwell, 1999—; hostess Miss NOC Pageant, Tonkawa, 1998—. Avocations: sewing, reading, interior decorating. Office: No Okla Coll PO Box 310 Tonkawa OK

FISCUS, PHILIP WAYNE, underwriter; b. Hastings, Nebr., Nov. 8, 1955; BA, Calif. State U., Northridge, 1978. CPCU. Underwriter St. Paul Fire and Marine Ins. Co., 1978-80, sr. underwriter, 1980-84, underwriter dir., 1984-92; v.p. Reliance Nat., N.Y.C., 1992-94; sr. v.p. Minet, Inc., N.Y.C., 1994-95; v.p. Chubb Group of Ins. Cos., Warren, NJ, 1995—2002, sr. v.p., 2002—. Mem. adv. bd. Biolaw & Bus. Publ. Contbr. articles to profl. jours. Mem. AAAS, Biotechnology Industry Assn., Risk and Ins. Mgmt. Soc. (assoc.). Office: Chubb & Son Inc 202 Hall's Mill Rd PO Box 1650 Whitehouse Station NJ 08889 Business E-Mail: pfiscus@chubb.com.

FISCUS, THOMAS J., former judge, career military officer; BSc in Computer Sci., USAF Acad., 1972; JD, Ohio State U., 1975; MSc in Nat. Security Strategy, Nat. War Coll., 1994. Bar: Iowa, U.S. Dist. Ct. (no. dist.), U.S. Court of Appeals (5th, 10th, 11th cir.), U.S. Ct. Appeals (fed. cir.), U.S. Ct. Appeals (armed forces), U.S. Supreme Ct., U.S. Ct. Fed. Claims. Advanced through ranks to maj. gen. USAF, 2000; asst. staff judge advocate, 1975—76; dep. staff judge advocate Zaragosa Air Base, Spain, 1976—78; chief appellate review divsn. Ramstein Air Base, Germany, 1978-80; litigation atty. office JAG USAF, Washington, 1980—83, asst. exec. JAG, 1983—85; staff judge advocate Mather AFB, Sacramento, 1985-88; chief preventive law and legal aid group USAF, 1988—91, exec. JAG, 1991—93, staff judge advocate Travis AFB, Calif., 1994-96, Hickam AFB, Hawaii, 1996-99, Langley AFB, Va., 1999—2000, dep. JAG, 2000—02, JAG, 2002—04. Decorated Legion of Merit with oak leaf cluster, Meritorious Svc. medal with two oak leaf clusters, Nat. Defense Svc. medal with bronze star, Vietnam Svc. medal with bronze star, Disting. Svc. medal, SW Asia Svc. medal. Mem. Judge Advocates Assn. (past pres.).

FISH, CHESTER BOARDMAN, JR., retired editor; b. Worcester, Mass., June 30, 1925; s. Chester Boardman and Mary Elizabeth Ada (Sheehan) F.; m. Claire Margaret Commo, Sept. 10, 1948; children: Craig Michael, Scott Kevin, Maribeth Ann, Andrea Dawn, Brian John. BA, Syracuse U., 1950, MA, 1952. Asst. editor Boys' Life mag., N.Y.C., 1951-53; assoc. editor Sports Afield mag., N.Y.C., 1953-55; copy chief Am. Home mag., N.Y.C., 1955-57; assoc. editor Outdoor Life mag., N.Y.C., 1957-63, article editor, 1963-67, mng. editor, 1967-73, editor in chief, 1973-76; sr. editor David McKay Co., Inc. book pubs., N.Y.C., 1976-80, Charles Scribner's Sons (pubs.), N.Y.C., 1980-81; pub. cons. The Competitive Edge, Greenlawn, N.Y., 1981-83; editorial dir. Stackpole Books, Harrisburg, Pa., 1983-85, exec. v.p., 1986-89, Stackpole Inc., Harrisburg, Pa., 1989-90; pub. Harness Horse mag., Harrisburg, 1989-91; pub. cons. and freelance writer Carlisle, Pa., 1990-94. Served with USNR, 1943-46, PTO. Mem. Carlindian Barbershop Chorus, Phi Beta Kappa. Republican. Roman Catholic. Home: 709 Sutton Dr Carlisle PA 17013-3546

FISH, DAVID EARL, insurance company executive; b. Port Jervis, N.Y., Sept. 22, 1936; s. William Earl and Elizabeth Dorthea (Schleer) F.; m. Patricia Ann Reilly, June 14, 1958 (dec.); children: Nancy S., Susan L., Brian D. BSBA, Muhlenberg Coll., 1958. Claims adjuster Liberty Mut. Ins., East Orange, N.J., 1961-65, claims supr. Pitts., 1966-68, claims examiner Boston, 1969-70, claims mgr. Buffalo, Syracuse, Balt., Phila., 1971-80, asst. divsn. claims mgr. Phila., 1980-81, asst. v.p. Chgo., 1981-86, divsn. claims mgr., asst. v.p., 1986-87, v.p. Boston, 1988-94, sr. v.p., 1994—. Bd. dirs. Arbitration Forums, Tampa, Fla., Nat. Ins. Crime Bur., Palos Hills, Ill. Avocations: golf, spectator sports. Home: 13 Chandler Dr East Sandwich MA 02537-1729 Office: Liberty Mut Ins Co Riverside Office Park 13 Riverside Rd Weston MA 02493-2249

FISH, HOWARD MATH, aerospace transportation executive; b. Melrose, Minn., Aug. 1, 1923; s. Nathaniel and Louise Margaret (Gaetz) Fish; m. Jamie Katherine Tom, May 15, 1948; 1 child, Howard Math Jr. Student, Air Command and Staff Coll., 1954; MBA, U. Chgo., 1957; postgrad., Armed Forces Staff Coll., 1960, Air War Coll., Montgomery, Ala., 1964; MAIA, George Washington U., 1964. Enlisted USAF, 1942, commd. 2d lt., 1944, capt., 1950, col., 1965, advance through grades to lt. gen., 1974, ret., 1979; deputy asst. sec. defense internat. security affairs Dept. Defense, Washington; asst. vice chief of staff USAF, Washington; chmn. U.S. Mil. Delegation to UN; v.p. internat. LTV Aerospace and Defense Co., 1980—82, Loral Corp., 1992—96; sr. advisor Internat. Lockheed-Martin Missiles and Fire Control, Dallas, La., 1996—2005. Mem. Def. Policy Adv. Com. Trade, Washington, 1987—94; chmn. Am. League Exports and Security Assistance, Washington, 1986—94. Decorated Def. DSM, Air Force DSM, Legion of Merit, DFC, Air medal, Purple Heart, POW medal. Mem.: Washington Inst. Fgn. Affairs, Am. Def. Preparedness Assn. (chmn. internat. divsn. 1984—94), Air Force Assn., Army Navy Club, Beta Gamma Sigma. Roman Catholic. Avocations: tennis, fishing. Personal E-mail: genhmfish@aol.com.

FISH, JANET ISOBEL, artist; b. Boston, May 18, 1938; d. Peter and Florence (Voorhees) F. BA, Smith Coll., 1960; postgrad., Skowhegan (Maine) Art Sch., summer 1961; BFA, MFA, Yale U., 1963; DFA (hon.), Lyme Acad., 2000. Represented by D.C. Moore Gallery, N.Y.C. One-woman shows D.C. Moore Gallery, N.Y.C., Columbus (Ga.) Mus., Ogunquit Mus. Am. Art, Maine, also others; represented in permanent collections Whitney Mus. Am. Art, N.Y.C., Met. Mus. Art, N.Y.C., Cleve. Mus. Art, Dallas Mus. Fine Arts, Am. Fedn. Arts, Am. Acad. Inst. Arts and Letters, Art Inst. Chgo., Kemper Mus., Kansas City, Albright-Knox Gallery, Buffalo, N.Y., Newark Mus., Mpls. Mus. of Art, Nat. Gallery of Victoria, Melbourne, Australia, Powers Inst., Sydney, Australia, Colby Coll., Waterville, Maine, Mus. of Fine Arts, Houston Art Ctr., RISD, Providence, Mus. Art, Providence, Va. Mus. Fine Arts, Richmond, Yale U., New Haven, Smith Coll. Mus. Art, Northampton, Mass., Albrecht Art Mus., St. Joseph, Mo., Milw. Art Mus., Hunter Mus. Art, Chattanooga, others. Bd. govs. Skowhegan Sch. Painting and Sculpture, Marie Walsh Sharpe Art Found. Recipient Harris award Chgo. Bienale award, 1974, Outstanding Woman Artist award Aspen Mus., 1992, Am. Acad. Arts and Letters award, 1994, Henry Ward Ranger Purchase prize NAD, 2001, William A. Patton prize, 2005; MacDowell fellow, 1968, 70, 72; Yale scholar, Australian Coun. for Arts grantee, 1975. Mem. NAD, Am. Acad. and Inst. Arts and Letters. Office Phone: 212-966-0616. E-mail: jfcp1@earthlink.net.

FISH, JEANNE SPENCER, artist, retired lawyer; b. Sedan, Ks., Jan. 15, 1921; d. Charles William and Lena (Hall) Spencer; m. Robert Irwin Fish, Jan. 6, 1947. BA, U. Kans., 1942, JD, 1945; BA in Art, Humboldt State U., 1974. Bar: Ks. 1945. Assoc. C.W. Spencer, Atty. at Law, Sedan, 1945-47; city atty. City of Sedan, 1947; asst. gen. counsel Ks. State Corp. Commn., Topeka, 1948-51; artist Eureka, Calif., 1974—. One-woman shows include oil paintings, 1977, 1986, 2004. Mem. AAUW (Edn. Found. award 1980, pres. local chpt. 1964-65), P.E.O. (pres. local chpt. 1972-73, 95-96, 99-01, pres. Humboldt Reciprocity Bur. 1996), Redwood Art Assn. (pres. 1979-81, Best of Show award 1973), Humboldt Docent Coun. (pres. 1977-79), Humboldt Arts Coun. (pres. 1982-83), Humboldt Sponsors, Phi Kappa Phi. Republican. Episcopalian. Avocations: flute, chamber music, golf, travel.

FISH, LAWRENCE KINGSBAKER, banker; b. Chgo., Oct. 9, 1944; s. Alvin Kingsbaker and Beatrice (Brown) F.; m. Atsuko Toko, June 29, 1980; children: Leah Okajima, Edward Takezo, Emily Takako. BA, Drake U., Des Moines, Iowa, 1966; MBA, Harvard Bus. Sch., Cambridge, 1968. U.S. aid officer U.S. Agy. Internat. Capital Devel., 1970-72; internal officer Bank of Boston, Brazil, 1972, dir. internat. ops., 1972-74, asst. v.p., gen. mgr., 1974-75, v.p., dep. gen. mgr., 1975, v.p., 1975, v.p., gen. mgr. Tokyo, 1978-79, 1st v.p., 1979-80; 1st v.p., head Pacific Asia divsn., Bank of Boston, Hong Kong, 1980-81, sr. v.p., 1981-82, exec. v.p., 1982-83, exec. v.p., head of trust function Boston, 1983-84, exec. v.p, head New Eng. Group, 1984-88; pres., chief oper. officer Columbia Savs. & Loan Assn., Beverly Hills, Calif., 1988-90; chmn., chief exec. officer Bank of New Eng., Boston, 1990-92; Chmn., CEO and pres. Citizens Fin. Group, Inc., Providence. Bd. dirs. Mastercard Internat. Mem. exec. com. Children's Museum, Boston, 1984-85; pres. Boston/Kyoto Sister City Found., 1984-85; bd. dirs. Japan Soc. of Boston, 1984-85, Inst. Contemporary Art of Boston; mem. exec. bd. USAID Pvt. Enterprise, Washington, 1984-88; overseer New Eng. Conservatory Music. Woodrow Wilson Found. fellow, 1984 Mem.: Longwood (Brookline, Mass.). Office: Citizens Financial Grp One Citizens Plaza Providence RI 02903-4689

FISH, MARY MARTHA, economics professor; b. Albert Lea, Minn., July 17, 1930; d. Charles H. and Olga (Stennes) Thomassen; m. Donald C. Fish, Oct. 1954 (dec.); children: Jill S., Lynn M., Jason M. BBA, U. Minn., 1951; MBA in Econs, Tex. Tech. Coll., 1957; PhD (AAUW fellow 1960), U. Okla., 1963. Statis. asst. Iowa Bd. Control, 1951-53; pub. health analyst State of Calif., 1953-54; analytical statistician 46th Med. Gen. Lab., U.S. Army Forces, Tokyo, 1954-57; instr. econs. and bus. Odessa (Tex.) Coll., 1957-58;

asst. prof., then assoc. prof. West Tex. State U., 1961-66; prof. econs. U. Ala., 1966-99, prof. emeritus, 1999—; prof. econs. Landegg Internat. U., Wienacht, Switzerland, 2000—02. Fulbright lectr. U. Liberia, 1974-75, Gambian Govt., 1978-79; cons. in field. Co-author: Convicts, Codes and Contraband, 1974; contbr. articles to profl. jours. Founding mem. Nat. Campaign for Tolerance. Grantee U. Ala., 1967-68, 87-89, Dept. Labor, 1978-79; Fulbright rsch. fellow, Taiwan, 1995; Phifer Faculty Scholar, 1998. Mem. Am. Econ. Assn., So. Econ. Assn. Mem. Baha'i faith. Home: 1405 High Forest Dr N Tuscaloosa AL 35406-2153 Business E-Mail: mfish@cba.ua.edu.

FISH, PAUL WARING, lawyer; b. Ligonier, Pa., Apr. 12, 1933; s. Edmund R. and Catherine (McGuiggan) F.; m. Jacquelyn A. Shea, Sept. 19, 1959; children: Charles M., Edmund J., Catherine G., John H., Jacquelyn A. BS in Elec. Engring, Cath. U. Am., 1959, M.E.E., 1961; LL.B., George Washington U., 1965. Bar: D.C. 1965, N.Y. 1966, Mich. 1967, Wis. 1976, Ill. 1983, Pa. 1993. Patent agt., atty. Xerox Corp., Rochester, N.Y., 1965-66; patent atty., asst. dir. patent div. Burroughs Corp., Detroit, 1969, dir. patents, to 1976; asst. gen. counsel Jos. Schlitz Brewing Co., Milw., 1976-79, v.p., gen. counsel, sec., 1979-83; v.p., gen. counsel. Comdisco, Inc., Rosemont, IL, 1983-86, sr. v.p., gen. counsel, 1986-91, cons., 1991-93; of counsel Mason, Fenwick and Lawrence, Washington, 1992-94, Christie, Parker & Hale, Pasadena, Calif., 1994-97, Rader, Fishman & Grauer, Bloomfield Hills, Mich., 1997—. Mem. adj. faculty Cath. U. Am. Columbus Sch. of Law, 1994-99. With USN, 1951-55. Mem. Am. Intellectual Property Law Assn., D.C. Bar Assn., Pa. Bar Assn., Wis. Bar Assn., Ill. Bar Assn., Mich. Bar Assn. Roman Catholic. Home and Office: PO Box 239 Jones Mills PA 15646-0239 Fax: 724-593-6250. Office Phone: 724-593-6244. E-mail: fish@westol.com, pwf@raderfishman.com.

FISH, RAYMOND RICHARD, elementary school educator; b. Pittsfield, Mass., Sept. 26, 1950; s. Richard Raymond and Katherine Mary Fish. AS, Becker Jr. Coll., 1970; MA, Wadhams Hall, 1973, Coll. St. Joseph, 1978. Tchr. mid. sch. Christ the King Sch., Rugland, Vt., 1977—78; tchr. grade 6 Arlington Elem. Sch., 1978—80; tchr. mid. sch. lang. arts Leland & Gray Mid. Sch., Townsend, 1980—86, Proctor Jr./Sr. High Sch., 1986—97, Otter Valley High Sch., Brandon, 1997—. Athletic dir. Proctor & Leland & Gray Sch. Dist. Mem.: SAR, Italian-Am. Club, Elks. Avocations: reading, sports, horseback riding, golf. Home: 3 Jan Ave Rutland VT 05701 Office: Otter Valley Union High Sch 2997 Franklin St Brandon VT 05733

FISH, STANLEY EUGENE, dean, language educator; b. Providence, Apr. 19, 1938; s. Max and Ida Dorothy (Weinberg) F.; m. Adrienne A. Aaron, Aug. 23, 1959 (div. 1980); 1 dau., Susan.; m. Jane Parry Tompkins, Aug. 7, 1982. BA, U. Pa., 1959; MA, Yale U., 1960, PhD, 1962. Instr. U. Calif., Berkeley, 1962-63, asst. prof., 1963-67, assoc. prof., 1967-69, prof., 1969-74; Kenan prof. English and Humanities Johns Hopkins U., Balt., 1978-85, chmn. dept., 1983-85; Arts and Sci. Disting. prof. English and prof. law Duke U., Durham, N.C., 1985-98, chmn. dept., 1986-92; exec. dir. Duke U. Press, Durham, 1994-98; dean U. Ill. Coll. Liberal Arts and Scis., Chgo., 1999—2004; Davidson-Kahn Disting. Univ. Prof. humanities and Law Fla. Internat. U. Coll. Law, Miami, 2005—. Author: John Skelton's Poetry, 1965, Surprised by Sin: The Reader in Paradise Lost, 1967, 97 (Hanford Book award 1998), Seventeenth Century Prose: Modern Essays in Criticism, 1971, Self-Consuming Artifacts, 1972, The Living Temple: George Herbert and Catechizing, 1978, Is There a Text in This Class?, 1980, Doing What Comes Naturally, 1989, There's No Such Thing as Free Speech...And It's a Good Thing Too, 1994 (PEN/Spielvogel-Diamonstein award 1994), Professional Correctness: Literary Studies and Political Change, 1995, The Trouble with Principle, 1999, How Milton Works, 2001; mem. editl. bd. Milton Studies, Milton Quar. Recipient 2d place, Explicator prize, 1968; Am. Council Learned Socs. fellow, 1966; Guggenheim fellow, 1969 Mem. MLA, Am. Acad. Arts and Scis., Milton Soc. (hon. scholar 1991), Spenser Soc. Office: Fla Internat U Coll Law Univ Park Campus Green Library Ste 484 Miami FL 33199

FISHBACK, DENNIS, information technology executive; Mgmt. Va. Power; with Calif. Ind. Sys. Operator; sr. v.p. & chief info. officer Calpine Corp., San Jose, Calif., 2001—. Named one of the Premier 100 IT Leaders, Computerworld mag., 2004, one of top tech. innovators, Info. Week mag., 2004. Office: SVP & CIO Calpine Corp 50 W San Fernando St San Jose CA 95113

FISHBEIN, MARTIN, psychologist, educator; b. N.Y.C., Mar. 2, 1936; s. Sydney and Gloria (Nadelstein) F.; m. Deborah Louise Kaplan, Dec. 26, 1959. AB, Reed Coll., Portland, Oreg., 1957; PhD, UCLA, 1961. Mem. faculty U. Ill., Urbana, 1961—, prof. psychology, 1970—, head social-orgnl.-indsl. div., 1979-87, also rsch. prof. Inst. Communications Rsch., 1970—, exec. com. Survey Rsch. Lab., 1964-72, 81-86, assoc. mem. Ctr. Advanced Studies, 1974-75, 88-89. Vis. scholar London Sch. Econs. and Polit. Sci., 1967-68, 74-75; cons. NIMH AIDS Rsch. Program, 1988-89, mem. AIDS adv. subcom., 1987-90; guest researcher Ctrs. for Disease Control, 1992—. Author: (with Steiner) Current Studies in Social Psychology, 1965, Readings in Attitude Theory and Measurement, 1967, (with Ajzen) Belief, Attitude, Intention and Behavior: An Introduction to Theory and Research, 1975, Progress in Social Psychology, vol. 1, 1980, (with Ajzen) Understanding Attitudes and Predicting Social Behavior, 1980; contbr. articles to profl. jours. Guggenheim fellow, 1967-68; inducted into Am. Mktg. Assn. Attitude Rsch. Hall of Fame, 1981, recipient Paul D. Converse award for disting. contbns. to theory and sci. in mktg., 1981, Spl. Recognition award Nat. Assn. Recording Merchandisers, 1981; Internat. prize Interam. Psychol. Soc., 1987. Fellow APA, Soc. Consumer Psychology (pres. 1991-92), Am. Psychol. Soc.; mem. Midwestern Psychol. Assn., Am. Sociol. Assn., Psychonomic Soc., Interam. Psychol. Soc. (pres. 1993—). Home: 2218 Saint James St Philadelphia PA 19103-5502 Office: U Ill 603 E Daniel St Champaign IL 61820-6232

FISHBEIN, MICHAEL CLAUDE, physician, pathologist; b. Brussels, May 25, 1946; came to U.S., 1949; s. Fred F. and Celia (Feldman) F.; m. Astrid Lorette du Mortier, Aug. 11, 1974; children: Danielle Renee, Gregory Andrew. BS, U. Ill., 1967; MD, U. Ill., Chgo., 1971. Diplomate Coll. Am. Pathologists; cert. anatomic and clin. pathology. Intern UCLA/Harbor Gen. Hosp., 1971-72, resident, 1972-75; asst. prof. pathology Harvard U. Sch. Medicine, Boston, 1975-78; assoc. pathologist Peter Bent Brigham Hosp., Boston, 1975-78, Cedars-Sinai Med. Ctr., L.A., 1978-97, UCLA Med. Ctr., 1997—. Cons. Beth Israel Hosp., Boston, 1975-78, mem. faculty Harvard U.-MIT program in health scis., Boston, 1975-78; prof. UCLA Sch. Medicine, 1978—. Achievements include research in heart disease; contbr. over 300 articles to profl. jours. and 13 chpts. to books. Piansky scholar anatomy rsch.award, 1997—. Mem. Phi Beta Kappa, Alpha Omega Alpha. Jewish. Avocation: tennis. Office: UCLA Med Ctr A7-149 CHS 10833 Le Conte Ave Los Angeles CA 90095-3075 E-mail: mfishbein@mednet.ucla.edu.

FISHBEIN, PETER MELVIN, lawyer; b. NYC, June 20, 1934; s. Arthur L. and Lotta (Chary) F.; m. Bette Klinghoffer, June 16, 1957; children: Stephen, Bruce, Gregory. BA magna cum laude, Dartmouth Coll., 1955; JD, Harvard U., 1958. Bar: N.Y. 1959, U.S. Supreme Ct. 1973. Note editor Harvard Law Rev., Cambridge, Mass., 1956-58; law clk. to Justice William J. Brennan, Jr. U.S. Supreme Ct., Washington, 1958-59; dep. sec. gen. Internat. Peace Corps., Washington, 1962-64; ptnr. Kaye, Scholer LLP, N.Y.C., 1967—2002, mng. ptnr., 1984-91; chief counsel N.Y. State Constl. Conv., Albany, 1967; mem. Presdl. Commn. to Nominate Candidates for Fed. Ct. of Appeals, N.Y.C., 1980. Adj. prof. constl. law NYU Law Sch., 1970-84. Contbr. articles to profl. jours. Trustee Goddard Coll., 1967—75, Fedn. Jewish Philanthropies, N.Y.C., 1975—81, Citizen's Budget Comm., 1995—99; mem. N.Y. State Gov.'s Bd. Pub. Disclosure, Albany, 1975—77; mgr. Justice Arthur J. Goldberg's Campaign for Gov., 1970; bd. dirs. Health Care Chaplaincy, 1993—99, Brennan Ctr. for Justice, 1995—, I Have A Dream Found., 2001—, White Plains Hosp., 2002—, Friends of the Supreme Ct. of Israel, 2003—, Purchase Coll., SUNY, 2005—. Recipient Disting. Cmty. Svc. award Brandels U., Jurisprudence award Am. Ort. Fellow Am. Coll. Trial Lawyers, Am. Bar Found.; mem. ABA, Assn. of Bar of City of N.Y., Harvard Club (N.Y.), Beach Point Club (bd. govs. 1981-86), Phi Beta Kappa Home: 101 Woodlands Rd Harrison NY 10528-1423 Office: Kaye Scholer LLP 425 Park Ave New York NY 10022-3506 Business E-Mail: pfishbein@kayescholer.com.

FISHBEIN, WILLIAM, psychologist, neuroscientist; b. Feb. 28, 1938; BS, NYU, 1961, MA, 1964; PhD, U. Colo., 1969; post-doct. fellow, U. Calif., 1970. Prof. psychology CCNY, N.Y.C., 1970—. Office: 150 E 93d St New York NY 10128-3727 Office Phone: 212-410-9499. Business E-Mail: wfishbein@ccny.cuny.edu.

FISHBERG, GERARD, lawyer; b. Bronx, NY, May 23, 1946; s. Alfred and Sarah (Goldberg) F.; m. Eileen Taubman, Dec. 23, 1972; children: David, Dana. BA, Hofstra U., 1968; JD, St. John's U., Bklyn., 1971. Bar: N.Y. 1972, U.S. Dist. Ct. (ea. and so. dists.) N.Y. 1973, U.S. Ct. Appeals (2d cir.) 1975, U.S. Supreme Ct. 1976. Assoc. Cullen & Dykman, Garden City, NY, 1972-79, ptnr., 1980—. Assoc. editor St. John's U. Law Rev., 1970-71. Legis. com. N.Y. Conf. of Mayors and Mcpl. Ofcls., Albany, 1976—; bd. dirs. Am. Heart Assn. L.I. region, 1995—, treas. 1997-98, vice chair, 1998-2000, chair, 2000-02; bd. dirs. Heritage Affiliate 1999-2005. Capt. USAR, 1968-77. St. Thomas Moore scholar St. John's U. Sch. Law, 1969-71. Mem.: Nassau County Bar Assn. (chmn. mcpl. law com. 1981—83, 1985—87, chmn. labor law com. 1991-92 1991—92, bd. dirs. 1999—2002), N.Y. State Bar Assn. (mem. exec. com. 1978—, labor law sect. 1985, sec. 1985—87, mcpl. law 1985—, 1st vice chmn. 1989—91, chmn. 1991—93, mem. ho. of dels. 1993—), Rotacare (bd. dirs. 1992—, pres. 1993—99), Rotary (bd. dirs. 1988—94, treas. 1990—91, pres. 1992—93), Garden City C. of C. Jewish. Home: 1 Bucknell Dr Plainview NY 11803-1801 Office: Cullen & Dykman LLP 100 Quentin Roosevelt Blvd Garden City NY 11530-4850 Office Phone: 516-357-3703. Business E-Mail: gfishberg@cullenanddykman.com.

FISHBUNE, ROBERT, food products executive; CFO Specialty Foods Corp., Deerfield, Ill., US Food Service, Columbia, Md., 2004—. Office: US Foodservice 9755 Patuxent Woods Dr Columbia MD 21046 Office Phone: 410-312-7100. Office Fax: 410-312-7149.*

FISHBURN, JANET FORSYTHE, dean; m. Peter Clingerman Fishburn, 1958; children: Susan, Katherine, Sally. BA magna cum laude, Monmouth Coll., 1958, LHD (hon.), 1984; PhD, Pa. State U., 1978. Ordained to ministry Presbyn. Ch., US, 1988. Dir. Christian edn. 1st United Presbyn. Ch., Cleveland Heights, Ohio, 1958-60; lectr. Pa. State U., 1977-78; asst. prof. Christian edn. Theol. Sch., Drew U., Madison, N.J., 1978-83, assoc. prof., 1983-90, asst. prof. Am. ch. history, 1982-83, assoc. prof., 1983-95, prof. tchg. ministry, 1990-95, prof. emeritus, 1995—, acting dean Theol. Sch., 1994-95. Parish assoc. Mt. Freedom Presbyn. Ch., 1991—94; manuscript reviewer Scholars Press, Fairleigh Dickinson Press, U. Pa. Press; lectr. in field, 1982—; panelist, spkr. profl. confs. and religious orgns.; cons. books for Pastors Series Abingdon Press, 1987; mem. social justice com. Newton Presbytery, 1989—95, mem. coun., 1995—2001, 2004—, mem. com. on ministry, 2001—04. Author: (book) The Fatherhood of God and the Victorian Family: The Social Gospel in America, 1982, Confronting the Idolatry of Family: A New Vision for the Household of God, 1991, Parenting is for Everyone: Living Out Our Baptismal Covenant, 1996; editor: Drew Gateway, 1989—93; contbr. articles and revs. to profl. jours., clergy jours. and encys; editor: People of a Compassionate God: Creating Welcoming Congregations, 2003. Leader weekly bible study Madison Presbyn. Ch., 1985—89, mem. chancel choir, 1982—90, Morristown United Meth. Ch., 1992—96, co-leader spiritual growth group, 1990—; spkr. clergy confs.; tchr. adult edn. Mem.: Am. Soc. Ch. History, Presbyn. Profs. Social Witness Policy (panel coord. 1994), United Meth. Assn. Scholars Christian Edn. (chmn. rsch. com. 1995—97). Office Phone: 908-630-8787. E-mail: jfishbur@drew.edu.

FISHBURNE, BENJAMIN P., III, lawyer; b. South Bend, Ind., Nov. 14, 1943; s. Benjamin Postell and Peggy (Gahan) F.; m. Edith E., Aug. 5, 1983. BA cum laude, U. Notre Dame, 1965; JD, U. Va., 1968. Bar: U.S. Ct. Mil. Appeals 1968, U.S. Army Ct. Mil. Rev. 1968, D.C. 1971. Capt. JAG Corps US Army, 1968-72; atty. Surrey & Morse, Washington, 1968, ptnr., 1975, mng. ptnr. Washington, 1981-84; ptnr. Jones, Day, Reavis & Pogue, 1986, ptnr.-in-charge Hong Kong office, 1986-91, ptnr., 1991-93, Winston & Strawn, Washington, 1993—. Gen. counsel Nat. Coun. U.S.-China Trade, 1981—87, assoc. coun., 1987—89, chmn. legal com., 1994—2001; mem. adv. com. China-U.S. Conciliation Ctr., 1993—; mem. Am. Arbitration Assn. spl. corp. com. East-West trade arbitration, 1973—79; mem. nat. coun. U.S.-China Trade Investment Del. to China; alt. mem. UN Assn.'s Nat. Policy panel study U.S.-China Rels., 1979; spkr. in field. Contbr. articles to profl. jours. Co-chmn. Am. C. of C. Hong Kong legal com., 1990, mem. bd. govs., 1991; mem. bd. advisors Johns Hopkins Nanjing Ctr., 1986-97. Mem.: Order of Coif. Home: 5535 Nevada Ave NW Washington DC 20015-1768 Office: Winston & Strawn LLP 1700 K St NW Washington DC 20006 Office Phone: 202-282-5792. Business E-Mail: bfishbur@winston.com.

FISHBURNE, JOHN INGRAM, JR., obstetrician/gynecologist, educator; b. Charleston, S.C., Aug. 18, 1937; m. Jean Crawford, June 10, 1971; children: John Ingram III, Barron Crawford, Virginia Heyward. AB, Princeton U., 1959; MD, Med. Coll. S.C., 1963. Diplomate Am. Bd. Ob-Gyn. (sub. specialty maternal-fetal medicine), Am. Bd. Anes. Surg. intern Duke U. Hosp., Durham, N.C., 1963-64; resident in ob-gyn U. N.C., Chapel Hill, 1966-70, resident in anesthesiology, 1970-72, instr. dept. ob-gyn., 1970-71, asst. prof., 1971-74, assoc. prof., 1974-75, asst. prof. dept. anesthesiology, 1972-75; assoc. prof. dept. ob-gyn. Bowman Gray Sch. Medicine, Wake Forest U., Winston-Salem, N.C., 1975-78, prof., 1978-83, assoc. prof. anesthesiology, dept. anesthesiology, 1975-83; prof., chmn. dept. ob-gyn. U. Okla. Health Scis. Ctr., Oklahoma City, 1983-97, adj. prof. dept. anesthesiology, 1983-97, chmn. search com. for chair pathology dept., 1987-88, chmn. search com. for chair family medicine dept., 1993-94; residency program dir. dept. ob-gyn. Maricopa Med. Ctr., Phoenix, 1997—2001, chair dept. ob-byn., 1997—2000, vice chmn. dept. ob-gyn., 2000—04, assoc. program dir. dept. ob-gyn., 2001—04; prof. clin. ob-gyn. U. Ariz. Coll. Medicine, 1997—. Dir. maternal-fetal medicine dept. ob-gyn. Forsyth Meml. Hosp., Winston-Salem, 1977-83; vis. prof. U. W.I., Kingston, Jamaica, 1973-74, African-Health Tng. Instns. Project Nairobi, Kenya, 1975; cons. devel. mission U.S. AID, Dacca, Bangladesh, 1980, Assn. Vol. Surg. Contraception World Fedn. Health Agys., Manila, 1984, Singapore, 1986, Zhordania Inst., Tbilisi, Republic of Georgia, 1992, 93, 97, Ivanovo, Russia, 1994, Almaty, Kazakhstan, 1994, St. Petersburg, Russia, 1995, Khojand, Tahjikistan, 1995, Odessa, Ukraine, 1995, Chechenov, Moldova, 1996, L'viv Ukraine; oral examiner Am. Bd. Ob-Gyn, 1980—2002; chmn. Gov.'s Task Force on Perinatal Care, 1984-86; mem. steering com. Robert Wood Johnson Healthy Futures of Okla., 1988-92; trustee Am. Assn. for Gynecologic Laparascopists, 1980-81; presenter numerous sci. papers and lectures local, nat. and internat. profl. meetings. Author: (with others) The Prostaglandins, 1972, Endocrine-Metabolic Drugs, 1974, Gynecologic Laparoscopy: Principles and Techniques, 1974, Laparoscopy, 1977, Endoscopy in Gynecology, 1978, Clinics in Perinatology, 1982, Obstetric Anesthesia, 1982, Clinical and Diagnostic Procedures Obstetrics and Gyncecology, Part B, 1984, Advances in Clinical Obstetrics and Gynecology, Medical Economics Books, 1985, Clinical Obstetrics, 1987, Danforth's Obstetrics and Gynecology, 1994, 98, Bonica's Obstetric Analgesia and Anesthesia, 1995; contbr. update series Am. Coll. Obstetricians and Gynecologists; editorial bd. Obstetrics and Gynceology, 1985-89; author self instructional programs in field; contbr. numerous articles to profl. jours. Capt. USAFR, 1964—66. Clin. fellow Am. Cancer Soc. U. N.C., 1968-69, clin. fellow obstet. anesthesia Pub. Health Svc. U. Hosps. Case Western Res. U., 1969; tng. rsch. grantee NIH Med. U. S.C., 1961-62. Fellow Am. Coll. Ob/Gyn (spl. interest rep. for obstet. anesthesia 1974-78, learning resource commn. 1981-82, mem. personal rev. of learning in ob-gyn. task force for obstetrics 1981-82, chair obs. IV, 1996-98, chair edn. commn. Accreditation Coun. for Grad. Med. Edn. (residency rev. com. ob/gyn 1991-93, chair 1994-96, dir.), Accreditation Coun. for Grad. Med. Edn. (exec. com. 2001-02, vice chair coun. of residency rev. com. chairs 1996, chair accreditation coun. for grad. med. edn. coun. res. rev. com. chairs, 1997-98, oral examiner 1980-2002), Am. Bd. Ob/Gyn, Am. Coll. Anesthesiologists (assoc. examiner 1974); mem. Am. Soc. Anesthesiologists, Soc. Maternal and Fetal Medicine (rep. liaison com. ob.-gyn. 1983-89, bd. dirs. 1981-84), South Atlantic Assn. Obstetricians and Gynecologists (assoc.), Internat. Soc. Advancement Humanistic Studies in Medicine (pres. 1997). Episcopalian. Avocations: golf, movies, reading, home repair. Home: 7060 N Hillside Dr Paradise Valley AZ 85253-2813 Office: Maricopa Med Ctr Dept Ob-Gyn 2601 E Roosevelt St Dept Ob Phoenix AZ 85008-4973 Office Phone: 602-344-5119.

FISHBURNE, LAURENCE, III, actor; b. Augusta, Ga., July 30, 1961; s. Laurence John Jr. and Hattie Bell Crawford F.; m. Hajna O. Moss, July 1, 1985 (div.); children: Langston Issa, Montana Isis; m. Gina Torres Sept. 20, 2002. Appearances include (theatre) Section D, 1975, Eden, 1976, Short Eyes, 1984, Loose Ends, 1988, Urban Blight, 1988, Two Trains Running, 1992 (Best Featured Actor Tony award 1992), (films) Cornbread, Earl and Me, 1975, Apocalypse Now, 1979, Fast Break, 1979, Willie and Phil, 1980, Death Wish II, 1982, Rumble Fish, 1983, The Cotton Club, 1984, The Color Purple, 1985, Band of the Hand, 1986, Quicksilver, 1986, Gardens of Stone, 1987, A Nightmare on Elm Street 3: Dream Warriors, 1987, School Daze, 1988, Red Heat, 1988, King of New York, 1990, Cadence, 1991, Class Action, 1991, Boyz N the Hood, 1991, Deep Cover, 1992, What's Love Got To Do With It, 1993 (Academy award nominee, Best Actor, 1993), Searching For Bobby Fischer, 1993, Higher Learning, 1995, Bad Company, 1995, Just Cause, 1995, Othello, 1995, Fled, 1996, Hoodlum, 1997, Event Horizon, 1997, The Matrix, 1999, Once in the Life, 2000 (also dir., writer, prodr.), Osmosis Jones, 2001, Biker Boyz, 2003, The Matrix Reloaded, 2003, Mystic River, 2003, The Matrix Revolutions, 2003, Assault on Precinct 13, 2005, (TV movies) A Rumor of War, 1980, I Take These Men, 1983, 1983, The Father Clements Story, 1987, Decoration Day,1990, Miss Ever's Boys, 1997, Always Outnumbered, 1998; prodr. Miss Evers' Boys, 1997, Hoodlum, 1997, Always Outnumbered, 1998, dir., writer, prodr., actor: Once in the Life, 2000; TV guest appearances M*A*S*H, 1972, Hill Street Blues, 1981, Miami Vice, 1984, Spenser: For Hire, 1985, The Equalizer, 1985. Recipient Emmy award, 1993, 97, Image award, 1996, 98. Mailing: Landmark Artist & Mgmt 4116 W Magnolia Blvd, Ste 101 Burbank CA 91505*

FISHEL, ANDREW S., commissioner, director; b. Apr. 7, 1948; married, 1969. BA, Am. U., 1969; EdD of Am. Politics and Edn., Columbia U., 1975; MEd, Am. U., 1970. Legis. planning coord. U.S. Dept. HEW, Washington; mgmt. dir. Office for Civil Rights U.S. Dept. Edn., Washington; dir. fin. and resource mgmt. EEOC, Washington, 1982-89; mng. dir. FCC, Washington, 1989—. Co-author: (with Jan Pottker) Sex Bias in the Schools: The Research Evidence, 1977, National Politics and Sex Discrimination in Schools, 1977. Recipient Quality Improvement Prototype award Office Mgmt. and Budget, 1987, Outstanding Mgr. award ASTD, 1992, Disting. Svc. medal FCC, 1992. Office: Fed Comm Commn 445 12th St SW Washington DC 20554

FISHEL, JAMES JOSEPH, lawyer; b. Allentown, Pa., July 23, 1959; s. Joseph John and Barbara (Boyer) F.; m. Suzyn Elizabeth Card, 1989. BA, Am. Univ., 1981; JD, U. Fla., 1985. Bar: U.S. Dist. Ct. (mid. dist.) Fla. 1986, U.S. Dist. Ct. D.C. 1986, Calif. 1990. Assoc. Subin Shams Rosenbuth & Morg., Orlando, Fla., 1985; pvt. practice Washington, 1986-90, San Francisco, 1990—. Mem. ABA, Fla. Bar Assn., D.C. Bar Assn., Calif. Bar. Office: James J Fishel Atty at Law 110 Blue Ridge Dr Ste 1 Martinez CA 94553-6102

FISHEL, PETER LIVINGSTON, finance company executive; b. Chgo., Apr. 25, 1935; s. Philip W. and Dorothy B. (Livingston) F.; m. Donna Swift, Dec. 17, 1961; children: Pamela Leslie Fishel Saccocio, Patricia Jane Fishel, Françoise Suzanne. BS, U. Pa., 1959. CPA, Pa., Fla. Agt.-in-charge investigation and civil rights divsn. Commonwealth of Pa. Dept. Justice, 1961-62; contr. Internat. Playtex Corp., 1962-70, BVD Knitwear, 1970-71; corp. contr. BVD Co., Inc., N.Y.C., 1971-73; v.p. fin. BVD Co., Inc. (BVD divsn.), N.Y.C., 1973; chief fin. officer Colebrook Mills, divsn. Bobbie Brooks, Inc., Hialeah, Fla., 1973-77; owner Gen. Bus. Svcs., 1978-86, regional dir. S.E. Fla., 1982-86; pvt. practice acctg., 1987—; mem. adv. com. Oceanmark Fed. Savs. & Loan, 1983-88. Mem. Andover Civic Assn., 1973—2001; mem. citizens adv. com. Met. Dade Police, Miami, Fla., 1981—, treas., 1985—; mem. fin. com. Metro-Dade Pig Bowl, 1985; v.p. Andover Civic Assn., 1986—91; mem. NMB Pride, 1989—93, bd. dirs., 1991—93, Dade Alumni Club, U. Pa., 1991—; chmn. Bus. Devel. Com., 1995—; mem., treas. Coalition Improvement N.W. Dade, 1996—; bd. dirs. Rolling Hills Home Owners Assn., treas., 2003—; mem. Aventura Mktg. Coun., 1991—. With M.P. U.S. Army, 1954—56. Mem. AICPA, Pa. Inst. CPAs, Fla. Inst. CPAs, Nat. Assn. Tax Practitioners, Mensa, N. Dade C. of C. (bd. dirs. 1978-97, v.p., Businessman of Yr. 1990, Mem. of Month, 1987, 91), N. Miami Beach C. of C., Rolling Hills HOA (bd. dirs., treas. 2003-). Home: 8119 S Savannah Cir Davie FL 33328-3033 Office: 2396 NE 172nd St Aventura FL 33160-2923 Office Phone: 305-944-0040. Personal E-mail: plfishel@aol.com.

FISHELL, JOHN CHRISTOPHER, music educator; s. Wallace George and Suzanne Marie (Odiorne) Fishell. Cert. recording engr., Omega Sch. Applied Rec. Arts, Rockville, Md., 1989; MusM in Theory/Composition, James Madison U., 1993. Instr., program mgr. Ala. State U., Montgomery; lectr. music tech. U. Durban-Westville, South Africa, 1994—96; instr. James Madison U., Harrisonburg, Va., 1996—2000; asst. prof. Mid. Tenn. State U., Murfreesboro, 2000—04, U. Colo., Denver, 2004—. Prodr.: (music) Beyond the Line (Grammy nomination, 2004). Office: Univ Colo Dept of Music and Ent Industry Studies Denver CO 80204 Office Phone: 303-352-3866. Office Fax: 303-556-2335. Business E-Mail: john.fishell@cudenver.edu.

FISHENFELD, GRACE, artist, educator; b. Bklyn., July 31, 1932; d. Joseph and Jean (Lipofsky) Goldberg; m. Bernard Fishenfeld, May 28, 1953; children: Keith, Randi. AAS, N.Y. State U. Applied Arts, 1952; BS, Molloy Coll., 1972; MA, CW Post, 1976. Cert. art tchr., N.Y. Layout advt. designer Denhardt & Stewart, N.Y.C., 1952-53; art dir. Mid Island YMYWHA, Wantagh, N.Y., 1964-72; art tchr. Brentwood (N.Y.) H.S., 1972-92. Pub. rels. chmn., edn. chmn., designer, organizer Wonderful World of Art Tchg. Manual, 1996. Exhibited in group shows Natan D. Rosen Art Gallery and Mus., 1992 (Best in Show award), Artist Guild of Norton Gallery, Fla., 1995 (award of distinctive merit), Lake Worth (Fla.) Art League, 1997 (1st prize for graphic image, Best in Show award 1999). Dir. spring celebration of H.S. art exhbn., Palm Beach County, Fla., 1996-97. Named One of 8 Emerging Women Artists, Rosen Gallery Nat. Search, Boca Raton, Fla., 1993; recipient Award Coral Springs Mus., 1999; recipient Best in Show award, Great Neck Ctr. Arts nat. art competition, 1999, 1st prize in painting, Fla. Art Show, 2000. Mem. Women in Visual Arts (bd. dirs., pub. rels. com. 1992—, edn. chmn. 1996-98), Profl. Artist Guild of Boca Raton Mus., Nat. Assn. Women Artists (Sara Winston award 1996), Women in Visual Arts (bd. dirs. 1993-95, scholarship fundraiser 199798, chmn. vol. art program 1997-98, Best in Holiday Art Show competition award 1998). Avocations: jazz and classical music. Home: 75 Knightsbridge Rd Apt 1C Great Neck NY 11021 E-mail: fishenfeld@aol.com.

FISHER, ADA MARKITA, physician, health services administrator, writer, poet; b. Durham, N.C., Oct. 21, 1947; d. Miles Mark and Ada Virginia (Foster) Fisher; children: Shevin Michael, Charles Malvern. BA, U. N.C., Greensboro, 1970; MD, U. Wis., 1975; MPH, Johns Hopkins U., 1981. Resident in family medicine U. Rochester (N.Y.), Highland Hosp., 1975-78; chief med. officer, med. dir. Plain View Health Svcs., Inc., Greenevers, N.C., 1978-80; residency supr., employee health supr., physician, program dir. Alcohol Detoxification Unit John Umstead Hosp., Butner, N.C., 1981-85; indsl. physician Martin Marietta Energy Sts., Inc., Oak Ridge, Tenn., 1985-89; dir. occupl. medicine, med. dir., mgr. med. policies and practices Amoco Corp., Chgo., 1989-95; assoc. program dir. occupl. and environ. medicine program Healthline Corp. Health Svcs., St. Louis, 1995-96; occupl. health physician, OWCP cons. VA Hosp., Salisbury, N.C., 1996—, chief occupl. health, safety and wellness, Office Workers Compensation Program cons., 1996—. Participant, med. rep. Am. Petroleum Inst.; lectr. in field. Author: How to Survive a Terrorist Attack Citizens Advisory, 2003. Mem sch. reform/local sch. coun. Chgo. Pub. Schs., 1989-94; treas. Alliance of Black Jews, 1995—; bd. dirs. Salisbury Rowan Symphony Soc., Inc.; trustee Barber

Scotia Coll., Concord, N.C., 1997-99; mem. Rowan Salisbury Bd. Edn., 1998-2002, bd. Preservation N.C., Salisbury Symphony bd.; candidate U.S. Senate, 2002, U.S. 12th Congl. Dist. for 2004; mem. NMA, NRA, ACOEM; advocate children at-risk. Named one of Ten Outstanding Young Women in Am., 1984, Outstanding Alumni, Hillside High Sch.; recipient Alumni Disting. Svc. award U. N.C. Greensboro Alumni Assn., 1985. Mem. AAUW, NAFE, AMA, APHA, NAACP (life), APA (occupl. heath psychology adv. bd.), Rowan County C. of C. (bd. dirs. 1997—). Jewish. Avocations: restoring buildings and furniture, student recruitment for black colleges and universities. Home: PO Box 777 Salisbury NC 28145-0777

FISHER, ALAN HALL, guidebook writer; b. Evanston, Ill., July 16, 1945; s. Howard Taylor and Marion Ethel (Hall) F.; m. Margaret Ellen Williams, July 3, 1974; children: Ellen Williams, Howard Williams. BA, Harvard U., 1967; JD, Boston U., 1977. Bar: Md. 1977. English tchr. Trinity-Pawling (NY) Sch., 1967-68, Acton (Mass.)-Boxborough H.S., 1968-70; rsch. asst. Grad. Sch. Design Harvard U., Cambridge, Mass., 1971-72; assoc. Venable, Baetjer and Howard, Balt., 1977-80; guidebook writer Balt., 1980—. Author: Country Walks Near Boston, 1976, 3rd edit., 2000, Country Walks Near Baltimore, 1981, 4th edit., 2001, Country Walks Near Philadelphia, 1983, Country Walks Near Washington, 1984, 2d edit., 1996, Country Walks Near Chicago, 1987, Day Trips in Delmarva, 1992, 2d edit., 1998, Country Walks and Bikeways in the Philadelphia Region, 1994, Country Walks in the Chicago Region, 2003. Home and Office: 1430 Park Ave Baltimore MD 21217-4230 Office Phone: 410-523-5257. Business E-Mail: ramblerbooks@aol.com.

FISHER, ALAN WASHBURN, historian, educator; b. Columbus, Ohio, Nov. 23, 1939; s. Sydney Nettleton and Elizabeth E. (Scipio) F.; m. Carol L. Garrett, Aug. 24, 1963; children: Elizabeth, Ann Christy, Garrett. BA, DePauw U., 1961; MA, Columbia U., 1964, PhD, 1967. Instr. history Mich. State U., East Lansing, 1966-67, asst. prof., 1967-70, assoc. prof., 1970-78, prof. Russian and Turkish history, 1978—2003, assoc. dean grad. studies and research, Coll. Arts and Letters, 1987-89, dir. Ctr. for Integrative Studies in Arts and Humanities, 1989-97, emeritus prof., 2003—. Author: Russian Annexation of the Crimea, 1772-1783, 1970, The Crimean Tatars, 1978, revised edit., 1987, Ottoman Studies Directory, I, 1979, II, 1981, III, 1983, Between Russians, Ottomans, and Turks: Crimea and Crimean Tatars, 1998, A Precarious Balance: Conflict, Trade and Diplomacy on the Russian-Ottoman Frontier, 1999. Am. Rsch. Inst. in Turkey fellow, 1969, 73, 76; Am. Coun. Learned Socs. grantee, 1976-77 Fellow Royal Hist. Soc., Turkish Hist. Assn. (corr.), Am. Rsch. Inst. Turkey (mem. bd. dels. 1990-99, v.p. 1995-99), Mid. East Studies Assn., Turkish Studies Assn. (pres. 1982-84, editor bull. 1984-87), Inst. Turkish Studies (dir. 1995-97, chmn. 1997-99). Office: Mich State U Dept History 301 Morrill Hall East Lansing MI 48824-1036 Office Phone: 517-355-7500. Business E-Mail: fishera@msu.edu.

FISHER, ANDREW, management consultant; b. Richmond, Va., Dec. 17, 1920; s. Marion Nimmo and Sarah Randolph (Talcott) F.; m. Cornelia Johnson, Oct. 10, 1942; children: Peter R., Carolyn, Andrew R. BA, Amherst Coll., 1943; MBA, Harvard U., 1947; D.Sc. (h.c.), Albany Med. Coll. Dir. indsl. relations Internat. Braid Co., Providence, 1947; with N.Y. Times, 1947-71, v.p., 1963-70, exec. v.p., 1971; mgm. cons., 1972-76; chmn., pres., pub. News Jour. Co., 1976-78. Mgmt. cons. Trustee emeritus Albany Med. Coll. Capt. AUS, 1943-46. Mem. Moorings Club. Home: 1780 Cedar Ln Vero Beach FL 32963-2621

FISHER, ANDREW, IV, newswriter, television producer; b. Richmond, Va., Jan. 15, 1944; s. Andrew III and Dorothy Dale (Crannis) Fisher; m. Sharon Mary Cozza, Aug. 16, 1969. BA, Columbia U., 1965. News anchor Sta. WIP Radio, Phila., 1965, investigative reporter, 1968-69; writer, editor WNEW News, N.Y.C., 1969-74; overnight news anchor Sta. WNEW-AM, N.Y.C., 1974-79; morning news anchor Sta. WNEW-FM, N.Y.C., 1979-81; radio news corr. NBC News, N.Y.C., 1981-89, prin. news writer Today Show, 1990-99; fin. journalist CNBC, Englewood Cliffs, NJ, 1999—. Guest lectr. NYU, 1978, 80, Rutgers U., New Brunswick, NJ, 1984, Ramapo Coll., Mahwah, NJ, 2002; adj. prof. journalism Columbia U., N.Y.C., 1989—90; judge TV Emmy Award, 2002, 04; panelist Nat. Publicity Summit, N.Y.C., 2005. Reporter, prodr. Sunday News Closeup, 1969—79, corr. Source Report, 1981—88, host, prodr. Catch of the Day, 1985—88, Andy Fisher Reporting on Religion, 1986—89, network radio anchor Winter Olympics, Calgary, Can., 1988, Summer Olympics, Seoul, Republic of Korea, 1988; consulting editor: Joyful Noiseletter, 1988—, contbg. writer: Marketplace, Am. Publ. Radio, 1989, More Holy Humor, 1997, Dick Clark's American Bandstand: An Anniversary Celebration of Music and Dance, 1997, Holy Hilarity, 2000; writer (TV spl.) Christmas in Rockefeller Center, 1999, Attack on America, 2001, Wall St. Responds, 2001, The U.S. vs. Martha Stewart, 2004. Clk. vestry St. Peter's Ch., Morristown, NJ, 1979; mem. various coms. Episcopal Diocese, Newark, 1982—87; lay reader Ch. of Saviour, Denville, NJ, 1982—87; founding patron Flying Boat Mus., Foynes, Ireland, 1990—; mem. Denville Hist. Soc. With U.S. Army, 1965—68, spl. agt. Army Intelligence U.S. Army, 1966—68. Decorated Disting. Mil. Svc. medal; recipient Headliner Reporting award, Nat. Headliners Club, 1985, Media award, Am. Women in Radio & TV, 1985, N.Y. State Bar Assn., 1985, Gold medal, Internat. Radio Festival, 1989. Mem.: AFTRA, Writers Guild Am., N.Y. Acad. Scis., Actors Fund (life), Albany Acad. Alumni Assn., Boston St. Rlwy. Assn., Fellowship Merry Christians, Nat. Rlwy. Hist. Soc., N.Y.C. Transit Mus. (sustaining), Indian Lake Cmty. Club. Office: CNBC 1 CNBC Plaza 900 Sylvan Ave Englewood Cliffs NJ 07632 Office Phone: 201-735-3098. Business E-Mail: andrew.fisher@nbcuni.com.

FISHER, ANITA JEANNE (KIT FISHER), retired language educator; b. Atlanta, Oct. 22, 1937; d. Paul Benjamin and Cora Ozella (Wadsworth) Chappelear; m. Kirby Lynn Fisher, Aug. 6, 1983; 1 child from previous marriage, Tracy Ann. Postgrad., Stetson U., 1961, postgrad., 1987; BA, Bob Jones U., 1959; postgrad., U. Fla., 1963, 87, 90; MAT, Rollins Coll., 1969; PhD in Am. Lit., Fla. State U., 1975; postgrad., U. Ctrl. Fla., 1978, NEH Inst., 1979, U. Ctrl. Fla., 1987, Disney U./U. Ctrl. Fla., 1996, Jacksonville U., 1996, Agnes Scot Coll. AP Inst., 1998, Duke U., 1999. Cert. English, gifted and adminstrn. supr., in ESOL. Chairperson basic learning improvement program secondary sch. Orange County, Orlando, Fla., 1964-65; chmn. composition Winter Park (Fla.) HS, 1978-80; chmn. English depts. Orange County Pub. Schs., Fla., 1962, 71; reading tchr. Woodland Hall Acad., Reading Rsch. Inst., Tallahassee, 1976; instr. edn., journalism, reading, Spanish, thesis writing Bapt. Bible Coll., Springfield, Mo., 1976-77; prof. English S.W. Mo. State U., Springfield, 1980-84, instr. continuing edn. music and creative writing, 1981-82, editor LAD Leaf; tchr. Volusia County Schs., Fla., 1984-88, 95-97, gifted students, 1986-88; tchr. Lee County Schs., 1988-95; gifted students Lake Mary HS, 1997; tchr. Seminole Pub. Schs., 1997—2004; ret., 2004. Instr. Seminole CC; adj. prof. Edison CC, 1989—95, U. So. Fla., 1990—95, Barry U., 1993; steering com. So. Assn. Colls. and Schs.; active Fla. Coun. Tchrs. English; assessor tchr. performance Nat. Bd. Profl. Tchg. Stds.; panel mem. PSAT/NMSQT Descriptive Score Report Ednl. Testing Svc.; chair advanced placement vertical team Lake Mary HS, 2000—01, chair dept. English, chair vertical team curriculum implementation, 2001—; spkr., presenter in field. Co-editor: Fla. English Jour., 1998—2000; contbr. articles to profl. jours. Vol. Green County Action Com., 1977, Heart Fund, 1982; book reviewer Voice Youth Advs. Writing Program fellow U. Ctrl. Fla., 1978; mem. Rep. Nat. Com., 1994—; active Rep. Presdl. Task Force, 1998—2000. Named Lee County Tchr. of Distinction, 1994—95. Mem.: Seminole County Tchrs. English (chartered, pres. 1998—2000), Volusia Coun. Tchrs. English (pres. 1997), Fla. Coun. Tchrs. English (chair commn. ESL 1997—99, sch. adv. coun.), Nat. Count. Tchrs. English, Phi Delta Kappa (historian). Presbyterian.

FISHER, ANN, business executive, lawyer; b. N.Y.C., Apr. 5, 1939; d. William Parker and Dorothy Howe (Douglas) Fisher; m. William J. Danaher, Feb. 22, 1958 (div. 1963); children: Dorothy Lynn Danaher, Jo Ann Danaher Chitty. MBA, U. Miami, 1976, JD, 1981. Bar: Fla. 1981. Sales promotion mgr. Aristar Mgmt. Corp., Miami, 1965-71, dir. instl. sales Terner's of Miami Corp., Miami, 1971-80; assoc. Stinson, Lyons et al, Miami, 1981-83; co-owner Now Courier, Inc., Hialeah, Fla., 1983-84; pres. Cannon & Fisher Corp., 1984-86; prin. Ann Fisher, P.A., 1986—; owner Corp. Records, Inc., 1986—. Mem. Fla. Bar Assn., Coral Gables Bar Assn. (v.p. 1989-90), U. of Miami Sch. of Bus. Alumni Assn. (pres. 1990-91), South Miami Bus. Network (pres. 1988-89), Entrepreneurial of South Fla. Club (pres. 1988-89, bd. dirs.), Rotary (pres, 1994-95), Beta Gamma Sigma. Republican. Home: 1514 Zuleta Ave Miami FL 33146-2318 Office Phone: 205-665-5944.

FISHER, ANN BAILEN, lawyer; b. N.Y.C., Oct. 15, 1951; d. Eliot and Elise (Thompson) Bailen; m. John C. Fisher, Apr. 6, 1980. BA magna cum laude, Radcliffe Coll., 1973; JD, Harvard U., 1976. Bar: N.Y. 1977. Assoc. Sullivan & Cromwell, N.Y.C., 1976-80, 82-84, ptnr., 1984—, assoc. Paris, 1980-82. Mem. ABA, N.Y. State Bar Assn. Clubs: Cosmopolitan, Harvard (N.Y.C.). Episcopalian. Office: Sullivan & Cromwell 125 Broad St Fl 32 New York NY 10004-2400

FISHER, ARON BAER, physiology and medicine educator; b. Phila., Apr. 20, 1936; m. Joan C. Fisher, 1957; children: Marc L., Steven A., Eric R., Mara E. BS in Chemistry summa cum laude, Dickinson Coll., 1956; MD, U. Pa., 1960. Diplomate Am. Bd. Internal Medicine; diplomate Nat. Bd. Med. Examiners. Intern and resident in medicine U. Hosps., Cleve., 1960-61, 64-65; resident in pulmonary medicine Hosp. U. Pa., 1965-66; fellow dept. physiology U. Pa., 1966-68, assoc. in medicine, assoc. in physiology, 1968-70, from asst. prof. to assoc. prof. medicine, 1970-80, prof. medicine, 1980—, from asst. prof. to assoc. prof. physiology, 1970-1980, prof. physiology, 1980—, prof. environmental medicine, 1986—; staff physician VA Hosp., Phila., 1968-73, clin. investigator, 1973-76, cons. in pulmonary medicine, 1976-82; mem. med. staff Hosp. U. Pa., 1976—, dir. hyperbaric medicine clin. practice, 1985—; dir. Inst. Environ. Medicine U. Pa., 1985—. Mem. Am. Heart Assn. student rsch. fellowship adv. com. U. Pa., 1983-97, mem. diabetes ctr. adv. com., 1985—, mem. teaching awards com., 1989-92, chmn. animal care com. 1982-84, 87-89, chmn. com. for animal facility planning, 1985-86, chmn. transgenic mouse facility com., 1989, chmn. instnl. animal care and use com., 1989-92, mem. bioengring. grad. group, 1988—, chmn. biochemistry grad. group rev. com., 1989-90, others, supr. grad. students; fellow dept. biophysics and phys. chemistry U. Pa., 1971-72; mem. study sect. Pa. Coal Worker's Respiratory Disease Program, 1976-78; mem. cardiovascular study sect. A NIH, 1979-81, mem. respiratory and applied physiology sect., 1981-83; mem. adv. panel U.S. Army Med. R&D Command, 1980-85; mem. VA Merit rev. com. for respiration, 1998—. Editor: (with others) Handbook of Physiology: The Respiratory System (Section 3), vol. 1, 1980-85; mem. editorial bd. Exptl. Lung Rsch. 1979-88, Am. Rev. Respiratory Diseases, 1981-87, Jour. Applied Physiology, 1984-87, Am. Jour. Physiology, 1988—; guest editor Symposium on Lung Surfactant Apoproteins, 1984; contbr. numerous articles and revs. to profl. jours., chpts. to books. With USPHS, 1958, 59-61; capt. MC USAR, 1961-65. Grantee NIH, 1986-91, 1988—; recipient Clin. Investigator award VA Res. Svc., 1973-76, Established Investigator award Am. Heart Assn., 1977-82, Christian R. and Mary F. Lindback Found. award for Disting. Teaching, 1984. Mem. AAAS, ACP, Am. Physiol. Soc. (chmn. respiration dinner 1991, councillor respiratory sect. 1991-95), Am. Thoracic Soc. (sec. assembly on structure, function and metabolism 1973-74, chmn. 1981, sec. sect. on pulmonary circulation 1979, councillor ea. sect. 1973-77, chmn. ann. meeting program com. 1976, pres. 1983), Am. Fedn. Clin. Rsch., Am. Soc. Clin. Investigation, Am. Heart Assn. (cardiopulmonary coun.), Am. Soc. Cell Biology, Undersea and Hyperbaric Med. Soc., Oxygen Soc., Aerospace Med. Assn., John Morgan Soc. U. Pa., Laennec Soc. Phila., Pa. Thoracic Soc. (chmn. rsch. com. 1985-87), Phi Beta Kappa, Alpha Omega Alpha. Achievements include co-determination that lung lamellar bodies maintain an acidic internal pH, that phospholipids co-isolated with rat surfactant protein-C account for the apparent protein-enhanced uptake of liposomes into lung granular pneumocytes, that secretogues for lung surfactant increase lung uptake of alveolar phospholipids, that cAMP increases synthesis of surfactant-associated protein A by perfused rat lung; research on secretory granule calcium loss after isolation of rat alveolar type II cells, on alveolar uptake of lipid and protein components of surfactant, on oxygen-dependent peroxidation during lung ischemia, on choline transport by lung epithelium, and on role of acidic compartment in synthesis of disaturated phosphatidylcholine by rat granular pneumocytes; isolation and molecular cloning of a new calcium-independent phospholipase A2. Home: 239 E Gowen Ave Philadelphia PA 19119-1021 Office: U Pa Inst Environ Medicine One John Morgan Bldg 36th St and Hamilton Walk Philadelphia PA 19104-6068

FISHER, ARTHUR, magazine editor; b. N.Y.C., Mar. 10, 1931; s. Abraham G. and Sadie (Gold) F.; m. Liliane E. Kowarsky, Aug. 18, 1951; 1 child, Anthony E. BA, NYU, 1951. Sr. rsch. aide NYU, 1954-56; mng. editor Dodge Books, 1957-62, Sci. World & Sr. Sci., 1962-68; sci. and tech. editor Popular Sci., N.Y.C., 1969-94, exec. editor, 1994-96, sci. editor emeritus, 1996—. Author: The Healthy Heart, 1981; co-author: (with Ernest V. Heyn) Century of Wonders, 1972, Fire of Genius, 1976; contbr. articles to mags. Recipient citations for excellence in sci. writing Deadline Club, 1973, 74, Claude Bernard Sci. Journalism award Nat. Soc. Med. Rsch., 1978, Sci. Writing award Am. Heart Assn., 1981, Am. Inst. of Phys. Sci. Writing award, 1985, Sci. Writing award AAAS, 1986, Grady-Stack Sci. Writing award Am. Chem. Soc., 1988, Writing award Ednl. Writers Assn., 1993, Journalism award Engring. Found., 1997. Mem. Nat. Assn. Sci. Writers, Coun. for Advancement of Sci. Writing (bd. dirs. 1989—). Home: 120 Cabrini Blvd New York NY 10033-3438

FISHER, BARBARA A., former broadcast executive; b. 1954; m. Michael Scott; children: Kyle, Zachary. BA, Oberlin Coll., Ohio. Publicist A&M Records; prodr. Dave Bell Assoc.; v.p. creative affairs New World Pictures, MCA TV Entertainment; dir. movies and miniseries Universal TV Entertainment, 1987—91, pres., 1991—99; exec. v.p. Lifetime Entertainment Svcs., 2002—04.*

FISHER, BART STEVEN, lawyer, educator, investment banker; b. St. Louis, Feb. 16, 1943; s. Irvin and Orene (Moskow) F.; m. Margaret Cottony, Mar. 1, 1969; 1 child, Ross Alan. AB, Washington U., 1963; MA, Johns Hopkins Sch. Advanced Internat. Studies, 1967, PhD, 1970; JD, Harvard U., 1972. Bar: D.C. 1972. Assoc. Patton, Boggs & Blow, Washington, 1972—78, ptnr., 1978—94, Arent Fox Kintner Plotkin & Kahn, Washington, 1994—95; mng. ptnr. Capital House, LLC, 1995—, JJ & B, LLC, 2003—, Law Office of Bart S. Fisher, 2004—; of counsel Porter Wright Morris & Arthur, 1996—2001, Bryan Cave, 2002—03, Dorsey & Whitney, 2003—04. Adj. prof. internat. rels. Georgetown U. Sch. Fgn. Svc., Washington, 1974-82, 97; profl. lectr. internat. rels. Johns Hopkins U. Sch. Advanced Internat. Studies, 1983-96, George Mason U., 1991, 93, George Washington U., 2002-04. Author: The International Coffee Agreement, 1972, (with John H. Barton) International Trade and Investment: Regulating International Business, 1986; editor: Regulating the Multinational Enterprise, 1983, Barter in the World Economy, 1985. Pres. Aplastic Anemia Found. Am. Inc., Balt., 1983—92, pres. emeritus, 1993; bd. dirs. Marrow Found.; vice chmn. The Inst. at Mars Hill Coll.; chmn. Give Life Found., 2003—; ex-officio bd. govs. Internat. Practice sect. Bar Va.; participating mem. Internat. Trade Working Group, Pres. Coun. on Year 2000 Conversion. Recipient Dean's Cert. Appreciation Georgetown U. Sch. Fgn. Svc., Washington, 1984. Mem. ABA, Internat. Bar Assn., Am. Soc. Internat. Law (rapporteur, panel trade policy and insts. 1974-77), Va. State Bar (bd. govs. internat. law sect.), Parkville Post Am. Legion, Great Falls Swim and Tennis Club Va. Jewish. Home: 9009 Potomac Forest Dr Great Falls VA 22066-4110 Office: 700 12th St NW Ste 700 Washington DC 20005 Office Phone: 202-659-2979. Personal E-mail: bart_fisher2002@yahoo.com.

FISHER, BENJAMIN CHATBURN, lawyer; b. Coos Bay, Oreg., Feb. 6, 1923; s. Benjamin S. and Catherine Selina (Chatburn) F.; m. Jean L. Whiting, June 30, 1951; children: John, Richard, Robert. AB with honors, U. Ill., 1948; JD magna cum laude, Harvard U., 1951. Bar: D.C. 1951. Law clk. to Hon. Learned Hand U.S. Ct. Appeals 2d cir., N.Y.C., 1951-52; with Fisher, Wayland, Cooper, Leader & Zaragoza, Washington, 1952-2000; sr. counsel Pillsbury Winthrop Shaw Pittman, Washington, 2000—. Mem. edn. appeal bd. U.S. Office Edn., 1973-83; mem. Adminstrv. Conf. U.S., 1970-76; U.S. del. Plenipotentiary Conf. Internat. Telecomm. Union, Nice, France, 1989, Geneva, 1992, Kyoto, Japan, 1994, Mpls., 1998, Marrakesh, Morocco, 2002; mem. U.S. del. World Radio Conf., Torremolinos, Spain, 1992, Geneva, 1995, 97; mem. nat. com. radio comm. sect., 1989—; chmn. bd. dirs. U.S. Internat. Telecomm. Union Assn., 2000—. Bd. dirs. Boys and Girls Clubs of Greater Washington, 1990—; bd. govs. Sigma Chi Found., 1991—. Mem. ABA (chmn. sect. adminstrv. law 1968-69, mem. ho. of dels. 1970-72, 73-75), Fed. Commn. Bar Assn. (pres. 1967-68), D.C. Bar Assn., Am. Law Inst., Soc. Satellite Profls. (chmn. 1983-85, bd. dirs. 1986-93, gen. counsel 1993—), Rotary (bd. dirs. Washington Club 1980-85, pres. 1983-84), Phi Beta Kappa, Phi Kappa Phi. Home: 5118 Cammack Dr Bethesda MD 20816-2902 Office: 2300 N St NW Washington DC 20037-1128 Office Phone: 202-663-8154. Business E-Mail: ben.fisher@pillsburylaw.com.

FISHER, BERNARD, surgeon, educator; b. Pitts., Aug. 23, 1918; s. Reuben and Anna (Miller) F.; m. Shirley Kruman, June 5, 1947; children: Beth, Joseph, Louisa. BS, U. Pitts., 1940, MD, 1943; DSc (hon.), Mt. Sinai Sch. Medicine, CUNY, 1986; HHD (hon.), Carlow Coll., Pitts., 2003; DMS (hon.), Yale U., 2004. Diplomate Am. Bd. Surgery. Intern Mercy Hosp., Pitts., 1943—44, resident in surgery, 1944—48; fellow in surg. research, resident in gen. surgery Harrison Dept. Dept. Surg. Research U. Pa., Phila., 1950—52; fellow London Postgrad. Med. Sch. Hammersmith Hosp., 1955—56; tchg. fellow in pathology U. Pitts., 1944—45, 1945—47, assoc. prof., 1956—59, prof. surgery, 1959—86, Disting. Svc. prof., 1986—; Fulbright Commn. award appointee to Peru, 1965; med. surg. staff Presbyn.-Univ. Hosp., 1953—98. Past mem. cons. staff Children's Hosp., Pitts.; mem. cons. staff Magee-Women's Hosp., VA Hosp., Pitts.; chmn. Nat. Surg. Adjuvant Breast and Bowel Project, 1967—94, sci. dir., 1995—; chmn. Adjuvant Therapy Ctr., 1973—94, Breast Care and Diagnostic Ctr., 1980—93, Pitts. Cancer Inst., 1985—, Comprehensive Breast Care Ctr., 1992—98; mem. spl. del. to China, 1977; mem. President's Cancer Panel, 1979—82, Nat. Cancer Adv. Bd., 1986—92, Inst. Medicine of NAS. Mem. editl. bd.: Transplantation, 1966—71, Cancer, 1969—71, 1975, Year Book of Cancer, 1973—85, Internat. Jour. Radiation Oncology Biology Physics, 1975—78, Cancer Clin. Trials, 1977, Invasion and Metastis, 1981—85, Cancer Metastasis Revs., 1981—85, Jour. Clin. Oncology, 1982—87, Internat. Jour. Breast and Mammary Pathology, 1982—84, Cancer Rsch., 1976, Seminars in Oncology, 1979, Breast Cancer Rsch. and Treatment, 1980, 1992—, Clin. and Exptl. Metastasis, 1980—94, Breast Diseases: Yr. Book Quar., 1989—95, Annals Surg. Oncology, 1993—94, Internat. Jour. Oncology, 1993—94, Advances in Oncology, 1992—96, Breast Disease: Internat. Jour., 1993—96, Cancer Jour., 1994—, Internat. Jour. Cancer, 1993—94, European Jour. Cancer, 1995—97; contbr. more than 550 articles to med. jours. Recipient Man of Yr. award in medicine, Pitts. Jr. C. of C., 1966, Philip Hench Disting. Alumnus award, U. Pitts. Sch. Medicine, 1976, McGraw medal, Detroit Surg. Assn., 1978, Lucy Wortham James Clin. Rsch. award, 1981, Heath Meml. award, 1982, Joseph H. Morton Meml. award, 1983, Julia Hudson Freund Meml. award, 1983, Albert Lasker Med. rsch. award, 1985, Hammer Cancer prize, 1988, Am. Cancer Soc. Medal of Honor, 1986, Susan Komen Found. Sci. Distinction award, 1988, Milken Med. Found. Ctr. Rsch. award, 1989, Assn. Commn. Cancer Ctrs. award, 1990, Chancellors Dist. Rsch. award U. Pitts., 1992, Nat. Health Couns. Med. Rsch. award, 1992, Brinker Internat. Breast Cancer award, 1992, Durham N.C. City of Medicine award, 1992, Dr. Josef Steiner Cancer Rsch. prize, 1992, GM Cancer Rsch. Found. Kettering prize, 1993, Bristol-Myers Squib award, 1993, James Ewing Lectr. award SSO, 1993, Gottlieb Meml. award, 1993, Sheen award, 1993, Claude Jacquillet award, 1995, Lifetime Achievement award in Breast Cancer Rsch., Senologic Internat. Soc., 1996, Health Care Lifetime Achievement award, Pitts. Bus. Times, 1998, Potamkin Found. award for breast cancer rsch., Pa. Breast Cancer Coalition, 1999, Celebrating Survival: A Century of Advancements in Early Breast Cancer award, 2000, Am. Surg. Assn. Medallion for Sci. Achievement, 2000, Flance-Karl award for contbns. to sci. of clin. surgery, 2001, St. Gallen Internat. Breast Cancer award, 2003, AstraZeneca Hist. Milestone Excellence Clin. Rsch. award, 2003, Jill Rose award, Breast Cancer Rsch. Fond., 2003, Internat. Spirit of Life Rsch. award, 2003, C. Chester Stock award, Meml. Sloan Kettering Cancer Ctr., 2004, Breast Cancer Awareness Month award, 2004; Markle scholar in med. sci., John and Mary Markle Found., 1953—58, Fisher Breast Cancer lectureship established in his honor, U. Pitts., 1989. Fellow: AAAS, Am. Coll. Radiology (hon.); mem.: ACS, AAUP, Am. Italian Fedn. Cancer Rsch., Internat. Assn. Breast Cancer Rsch., Assn. Italiana per la Divulgaxione Sci. della Cancerologia Clinica, Italian Surg. Rsch. Assn., Pitts. Surg. Soc. (pres. 1979), Pitts. Acad. Medicine, Allegheny County Med. Soc. (Man of Yr. award 1983), Pa. Med. Soc., Am. Socs. for Exptl. Biology, Soc. Univ. Surgeons, Soc. Surg. Oncology, N.Y. Acad. Scis., Am. Surg. Assn. (v.p. 1996), Cell Kinetic Soc., Assn. Am. Med. Colls., Am. Physiol. Soc., Am. Soc. Clin. Oncology (pres. 1992-93, bd. dirs., Karnofsky award 1980, Disting. Svc. award for sci. achievement 1999), Am. Assn. Cancer Research (bd. dirs., 3d Jos. H. Burchenal Clin. Rsch. award 1998), Assn. Cancer Edn., Oncology Nursing Soc. (hon.), Peruvian Acad. Surgery (hon.), Am. Soc. Therapeutic Radiology and Oncology (hon.), Phi Beta Kappa, Alpha Omega Alpha. Office: 4 Allegheny Ctr Ste 602 Pittsburgh PA 15212-5234

FISHER, BRUCE DAVID, elementary school educator, education educator; b. Long Beach, Calif., Dec. 24, 1949; s. Oran Wilfred and Irene (May) F.; m. Mindi Beth Evans, Aug. 15, 1976; 1 child, Jenny Allison Viola. BA, Humboldt State U., 1975, standard elem. credential, 1976, learning handicapped credential, 1977. Instrnl. svcs. specialist Blue Lake (Calif.) Elem. Sch.; resource specialist Fortuna (Calif.) Union Sch. Dist., tchr. 3d grade, tchr. 5th grade, 1988—; prof. Humboldt State U., 1996—, disting. tchr.-in-residence, 1999—. Sci. cons. Pitsco, 1995; cons. Newton's Apple, 1995-97, NASA, 1995; site leader tchr., cons., 1998-99, curriculum writer Calif. Sci. Internet, 1995-97; cons. U.S. Forest Svc., 1999; mem. J.P.L./NASA/Johns Hopkins U. Core Curriculum Devel. Team Project KidSat and CASOE; mem. ednl. adv. bd. Calif. Dairy Coun., 1998-99, advisor, 1998; rep. Calif. Tech. Assistance Project, 1998; mem. Calif. Ski Industry and U.S. Forest Svc. Vice chmn. Tchrs. Edn. and Cmty. Helpers, Arcata, Calif., 1990—; v.p. Sequoia Pk. Zool. Soc., Eureka, 1989-90, chmn. Whale Fair, 1989—; mem. selection com. Christa McAuliffe Fellowship; bd. dirs. Redwood Environ. Edn. Fair, Eureka, 1990—, Family Wellness Project, 1991; apptd. to Calif. Curriculum and Supplemental Materials Commn.; commr. Calif. Curriculum Commn., 1992-95; chairperson math. assessment Calif. Dept. Edn., 1995; cons. PITSCO Sci., 1995, NASA/JPL, 1995-97; mem. NASA/JPL and Johns Hopkins U. CORE Curriculum Devel. Team, 1995-96; lead tchr. KidSat and CASDE projects Calif. Sci. Internat. Site. Named Calif. Tchr. of Yr. Dept. Edn., 1991, Favorite Tchrs. ABC-TV, 1991, Humboldt County Tchr. of Yr., 1991, Disting. Alumni, Humboldt State U., 2000; recipient Leadership Excellence award Calif. Assn. Sci. Specialists, 1990, Masonic Meritorious Svc. award for Pub. Edn., 1991, Profl. Best Leadership award Learning Mag., Oldsmobile Corp., and Mich. State U., 1991, Nat. Educator award Miliken Found. Calif. State Dept. Edn., 1991, NASA/NSTA Newest award, 1993, Newton's Apple Multimedia Inst., 1995, Lifetime Achievement award Humboldt County Bd. Edn., 1996. Mem. Calif. Tchrs. Assn., Calif. Sci. Tchrs. Assn., Calif. Assn. Health, Phys. Edn., Recreation, and Dance. Democrat. Avocations: whale watching, curriculum development, photography, sports, aviation, travel. Home: 4810 14th St Arcata CA 95519-9778 Office: Fortuna Elem Sch 843 L St Fortuna CA 95540-1997

FISHER, CALVIN DAVID, food manufacturing company executive; b. Nerstrand, Minn., June 10, 1926; s. Edward and Sadie (Wolf) F.; m. Patricia Vivian Capriotti, July 28, 1950; children: Cynthia, Nancy Joann, Michael. BS, U. Minn., 1950. Dairy specialist U.S. Dept. Agr., Mpls., 1950-54, chemist and dairy specialist Omaha, 1954-58; with Roberts Dairy Co., Omaha, 1958-80, sr. v.p., chief operating officer, 1967-70, pres., chief exec. officer, 1970-80, owner, chief exec. officer, 1975-80, Fisher Foods Ltd., Lincoln, Nebr., 1980—; pres., dir. Master Dairies, Indpls., 1968-80; bd. dirs. Internat. Assn. Ice Cream Mfrs. Milk Industry Found., 1973-80. Patentee spray-dried ice cream mix, pasteurized egg products. Bd. dirs., v.p. Omaha Safety Council,

1981; bd. dirs. Arthritis Found., 1972-81; mem. adv. council SBA; bd. dirs. Nebr. State Patrol Found., 1990—. With USN, 1944-47. Mem. Omaha C. of C. (pres.'s coun. 1976, 78), Internat. Food Scientists Assn., Inst. Food Tech., Nat. Ind. Dairies Assn., Rotary, Univ. Club (Lincoln), Firethorn Country Club. Republican. Methodist. Home: 18940 E Via Hermosa Rio Verde AZ 85263 Office: Fisher Foods Ltd 220 S 20th St Lincoln NE 68510-1007

FISHER, CARRIE FRANCES, actress, writer; b. Beverly Hills, CA, Oct. 21, 1956; d. Eddie Fisher and Debbie Reynolds; m. Paul Simon, 1983 (div. 1984); 1 child, Billie Catherine. Ed. high sch., Beverly Hills, Calif.; student, London Cen. Sch. Speech and Drama. Mem. chorus in Broadway musical Irene, 1972, also in Broadway prodn. Censored Scenes from King Kong; appeared in films Shampoo, 1975, Star Wars, 1977, Mr. Mike's Mondo Video, 1979, The Blues Brothers, 1980, The Empire Strikes Back, 1980, Under the Rainbow, 1981, Return of the Jedi, 1983, Garbo Talks, 1984, The Man with One Red Shoe, 1985, Hannah and Her Sisters, 1986, Hollywood Vice Squad, 1986, Amazon Women on the Moon, 1987, Appointment With Death, 1988, When Harry Met Sally..., 1989, The 'Burbs, 1989, Loverboy, 1989, She's Back, 1989, Sibling Rivalry, 1990, Drop Dead Fred, 1991, Soapdish, 1991, This Is My Life, 1992, Austin Powers: International Man Of Mystery, 1997, Scream 3, 2000, Famous, 2000; TV movies include Come Back, Little Sheba, (spl.) 1977, Leave Yesterday Behind, 1978, Liberty, Sunday Drive, 1986, Sweet Revenge, 1990; TV series Leaving L.A., 1997; author: Postcards from the Edge, 1987, (also screenplay, 1990), Surrender the Pink, 1990, Delusions of Grandma, 1994.

FISHER, CHARLES HAROLD, chemistry educator, researcher; b. Hiawatha, W.Va., Nov. 20, 1906; s. Lawrence D. and Mary (Akers) F.; m. Elizabeth Dye, Nov. 4, 1933 (dec. 1967); m. Lois Carlin, July 1968 (dec. June 1990); m. Elizabeth Snyder Kiser, Nov. 29, 1991. BS in Chemistry, Roanoke Coll., 1928, ScD (hon.), 1963; MS in Chemistry, U. Ill., 1929, PhD, 1932; DSc (hon.), Tulane U., 1953. Tchg. asst. in chemistry U. Ill., Urbana, 1928—32; instr. Harvard U., 1932—35; leader rsch. group U.S. Bur. Mines, Pitts., 1935—40; head carbohydrate divsn. Ea. Regional Rsch. Ctr. USDA, 1940—50; dir. So. mktg. and nutrition rsch. divsn. So. Regional Rsch. Ctr., USDA, New Orleans, 1950—72. Adj. rsch. prof. Roanoke Coll., Salem, Va., 1972—; established Elizabeth Snyder Fisher Scholarship, Roanoke Coll., 1992. Co-author: Profiles of Eminent American Chemists, 1988; contbr. over 200 articles to profl. jour. Co-inventor 72 patents. Pres. New Orleans Sci. Fair, 1967-69; bd. dir. Salem Hist. Soc., 1982-85, Salem Ednl. Found., 1991-99; established Lawrence D. and Mary A. Fisher Scholarship Roanoke Coll., 1978, Lois Carlin Fisher Scholarship, 1991. Recipient So. Chemists award, 1956, Herty medal, 1959; named Polymer Science Pioneer, 1981, Roanoke Coll. medal, 1996; named to Hall of Fame, Salem Ednl. Found., 1996; Charles H. Fisher Lectures established in his honor Roanoke Coll., 1990; Laboratory of Organic Chem. named in his honor Roanoke Coll., 2002. Mem. AAAS, Am. Inst. Chemists (hon., pres. 1962-63, chmn. bd. dir., Chem. Pioneer award 1966, Presdl. citation of merit 1986), Oil Chem. Soc., Am. Chem. Soc. (dir. region IV 1969-71), Chemurgic Coun. (dir.), Am. Assn. Textile Chemists and Colorists, Hidden Valley Country Club (Salem, Va.), Cosmos Club (Washington), Internat. House, Round Table Club (New Orleans); Chemists Club (NYC). Achievements include co-inventor of acrylic rubber. Office: Roanoke Coll Dept Chemistry 221 College Ln Salem VA 24153-3742 Business E-Mail: fisher@roanoke.edu. *I have worked hard as a physical scientist and research administrator because research is fun and offers the best way of benefiting humankind.*

FISHER, CHARLYN SEWELL, academic administrator, researcher; b. Balt., May 11, 1951; d. Charles Smith and Phoebe Louise (McFadden) Sewell; m. Stephen James Fisher, May 23, 1998. BA, Salem Coll., 1973; MS, The Johns Hopkins U., 1977, MS, 1988; PhD, Gonzaga U., 2001. Cert. elem. sch. tchr., Md. Tchr., adminstr. Harford County Pub. Schs., Bel Air, Md., 1973-2000; mgr. instnl. rsch. Hood Coll., 2000—04; dir. instnl. rsch. and assessment York Coll. Pa., 2004—. Fulbright exchange tchr. Foothills Sch. Divsn., High River, Alta., Can., 1990-91; adminstrv. intern Gonzaga U., Spokane, Wash., 1998, Salem Coll., Winston-Salem, N.C., 1998-99. The Tidball Ctr. for Study of Ednl. Environments fellow Hood Coll., 1999-2000. Mem. Nat. Assn. Elem. Sch. Prins., Md. Assn. Elem. Sch. Adminstrs., Assn. Instnl. Rsch., Md. Assn. Instnl. Rsch. Methodist. Avocations: travel, gardening, baking, quilting, flower arranging.

FISHER, D. MICHAEL, federal judge; b. Pitts., Nov. 7, 1944; s. C. Francis and Dolores (Darby) Fisher; m. Carol Hudak, Aug. 15, 1973; children: Michelle Lynn Fisher Reyes, Brett Michael. AB, Georgetown U., 1966; JD, Georgetown Law Ctr., 1969. Bar: Pa. 1970. Asst. dist. atty. Allegheny County, Pitts., 1970—74; assoc. Brenlove & Fisher, 1970—75; rep. Pa. Ho. of Reps., Harrisburg, 1974—80; assoc. Fisher & McGinley, 1975—80; mem. Pa. Senate, Harrisburg, 1980—97; ptnr. Fisher & Flynn, 1981—83, Houston Harbaugh, Pitts., 1984—97; atty. gen. Commonwealth of Pa., Harrisburg, 1997—2003; judge U.S. Circuit Ct. Appeals (3rd cir.), Pitts., 2003—. Chmn. House Subcom. on Crime and Corrections, 1979—80, Senate Environ. Resources & Energy, 1981—90, Senate Majority Policy Com., 1988—90, Senate Rep. Caucus, 1991—92; vice-chmn. Senate Jud. Com., 1981—90; Majority Whip, 1990—96. Contbr. articles to profl. jours. Active Environ. Quality Bd., 1980—90, Pa. Commn. on Crime and Delinquency, 1979—2003; mem. Pa. Security Task Force, 2001—03; chmn. Office of Nat. Drug Control Policy's Phila./Camden High Intensity Drug Trafficking Area, 2003—; mem. exec. working group for fed., state and local prosecutorial rels. U.S. Dept. Justice, 2001—03; v.p. Nat. Assn. Attys. Gen. Exec. Bd., 2000—01; Rep. candidate for lt. gov. State of Pa., 1986; active Pa. Gov.'s Energy Coun., 1981—86, Pa. Energy Devel. Authority, 1984—86; del. Rep. Nat. Conv., 1988, 1992; Rep. nominee for gov. State of Pa., 2002; bd. dirs. Am. Legacy Found., 2003—04. Named Man of Yr., Upper St. Clair Rep. Club, 1980, Vector's Law & Govt., 1991; named one of Outstanding Young Men Am., 1977—79. Mem.: Fed. Bar Assn., Allegheny County Bar Assn., Pa. Bar Assn., Rotary, Am. Legion, Elks. Republican. Roman Catholic. Avocations: golf, hockey, football, baseball. Office: US Circuit Ct Appeals 3rd Cir 5360 US PO & Courthouse 700 Grant St Pittsburgh PA 15219

FISHER, DALE DUNBAR, animal scientist, dairy nutritionist; b. Lewisburg, Pa., Feb. 13, 1945; s. Glenn Murray and Elsie May (Bryson) F.; divorced; children: Elsie Maria, Maria Vanessa. BS in Animal Sci., Pa. State U., 1967, MS in Animal Industry, 1978, PhD in Animal Industry, 1980. Vol. animal husbandry Peace Corps, Ciudad Quesada, Costa Rica, 1967-71; area animal husbandry-pasture specialist Costa Rican Ministry of Agr., Ciudad Quesada, 1971-73; vis. scientist Internat. Ctr. for Tropical Agr., Cali, Colombia, 1973-75; animal nutritionist Co-op. Feed Dealers, Inc., Chenango Bridge, N.Y., 1981—. Contbr. articles to profl. jours. Eva B. and G. Weidman Groff Meml. scholar Pa. State U., 1979. Mem. Am. Soc. Animal Sci., Am. Dairy Sci. Assn., Am. Soc. Agronomy, Am. Acad. Vet. Nutrition, N.Y. Acad. Scis., Am. Coll. Nutrition, Sigma Xi, Phi Kappa Phi, Gamma Sigma Delta. Democrat. Avocations: jogging, reading. Office Phone: 607-651-9078 x 312. Business E-Mail: nutrition@co-opfeed.com.

FISHER, DALE JOHN, retired chemist, medical investigator; b. Omro, Wis., June 4, 1925; m. Ruth J. Laird, Apr. 27, 1957; 1 child, Shelley Dale. BS, U. Wis., Oshkosh, 1947; PhD (Univ. fellow), Ind. U., 1951. Staff mem. Inst. Paper Chemistry, Appleton, Wis., summer 1945; chemist City of Oshkosh, Wis., summers 1946-48; chemist ionic analyses group Oak Ridge Nat. Lab., 1951-52, group leader analytical instrumentation group, 1952-72, mem. dir.'s staff, 1972-73; physicist (nuclear medicine) VA Hosp., Gainesville, Fla., 1973-74, tech. dir. nuclear medicine, 1974-76; grad. studies faculty U. Fla., Gainesville, 1974-76; physicist FDA, 1976-91, physicist divsn. in vitro diagnostic device standards, 1976-83, physicist Office Sci. and Tech., divsn. life scis., health scis. br., 1983-91; ret., 1991. Recipient Disting. Alumni award U. Wis., Oshkosh, 1982. Mem. ASTM (sr.), Am. Chem. Soc. (emeritus; nat. award chem. instrumentation), U. Wis. Oshkosh Alumni Assn. (life), Sigma Xi (emeritus), Phi Lambda Upsilon. Achievements include design and new applications of instrument systems and methods for analysis, process monitoring and research; creation electronic and mechanical designs and administration of research. Patentee in field. Research with computer-based nuclear medicine imaging instrumentation for the improvement of patient care. Development of med. device standards and performance requirements. Establish sci. basis for med. diagnostic and clin. lab. instruments. Improve safety and effectiveness of medical devices through toxicology and statistics research. Home: 6319 Golden Hook Columbia MD 21044-3710

FISHER, DEENA KAYE, social studies education administrator; b. Elk City, Okla., Dec. 20, 1950; d. Earl Dean and Rosa Lee (Stone) Music; m. Mike Fleck, May 29, 1970 (div. June 1988); children: DeeAnna Michelle, Carrie Denise, William Michael; m. Tom Fisher, Nov. 13, 1993; 1 stepchild, Eleni. BA in Edn.-Social Sci., Southwestern Okla. State U., 1979, MEd in Social Sci., 1983, MEd in Sch. Counseling, 1987; EdD, Okla. State U., 2004. Instr. in social sci. Cordell (Okla.) H.S., 1979-85, El Reno (Okla.) C.C., 1985-88, Upward Bound guidance and career counselor, instr., 1987-89; instr. Am. History Yukon (Okla.) H.S., 1986-87; instr. polit. sci. and Am. history Southwestern Okla. State U., 1987-89; chair dept. Am. history, instr. Am. govt. Woodward (Okla.) H.S., 1989-96; instr. social studies Northwestern Okla. State U., Alva, 1989—, assoc. prof., 2004; dean Northwestern Okla. State U., Woodward Campus, 2002—. Author ednl. materials in field. Del. Dem. Nat. Conv., Okla. Dem. Party, Chgo., 1996; law day coord. Okla. Bar Assn., Woodward, 1990-96; regional coord. Citizen Bee, Tulsa World, 1994-97; panelist U.S. History Nat. Assessment of Ednl. Progress, St. Louis, 1994. Recipient Outstanding Am. History Tchr. award Okla. Soc. DAR, 1993, Tchr. of Yr. award Okla. Supreme Ct., 1992; Bill of Rights Edn. Collaborative grantee, 1991. Mem. Nat. Coun. for Social Studies (ho. dels., co-chmn. resolution com. 1996), Okla. Social Studies Suprs.' Assn. (membership bd. 1997), Okla. Coun. for Social Studies (del.-at-large 1996, pres. 1994-96), Woodward Edn. Assn. (pres. 1996), Woodward C. of C. (mem. edn. com. 1997), Delta Kappa Gamma (pres. Psi chpt. 1996-98), Phi Delta Kappa. Mem. Christian Ch. (Disciples Of Christ). Avocations: reading, chess. Home: 3308 Bent Creek Dr Woodward OK 73801-6931 Office: Northwestern Okla State U Woodward Campus PO Box 1046 Woodward OK 73802-1046 Office Phone: 580-256-0047.

FISHER, DELBERT ARTHUR, pediatric endocrinologist, educator, health facility administrator; b. Placerville, Calif., Aug. 12, 1928; s. Arthur Lloyd and Thelma (Johnson) Fisher; m. Beverly Carne Fisher, Jan. 28, 1951; children: David Arthur(dec.), Thomas Martin, Mary Kathryn. BA, U. Calif., Berkeley, 1950; MD, U. Calif., San Francisco, 1953. Diplomate Am. Bd. Pediat., Sub Bd. Pediatric Endocrinology. Intern, resident in pediat. U. Calif. Med. Ctr., San Francisco, 1953—55; resident in pediat. U. Oreg. Hosp., Portland, 1957—58; Irwin Meml. fellow in pediatric endocrinology, 1958—60; from asst. prof. to assoc. prof. pediat. Med. Sch. U. Ark., Little Rock, 1960—67, prof. pediat., 1967—68, UCLA, 1968—73, prof. pediat. and medicine Med. Sch., 1973—91, prof. emeritus, 1991—; chief, pediat. endocrinology Harbor-UCLA Med. Ctr., 1968—75, rsch. prof. devel. and perinatal biology, 1975—85, chmn. pediat., 1985—89, sr. scientist Rsch. and Edn. Inst., 1991—, chmn. bd. Rsch. and Edn. Inst., 2001—02; dir. Walter Martin Rsch. Ctr., 1986—91; pres. Nichols Inst. Reference Labs, San Juan Capistrano, Calif., 1991—93; pres. acad. assocs., chief sci. officer Nichols Inst., San Juan Capistrano, Calif., 1993—94, Quest Diagnostics-Nichols Inst., San Juan Capistrano, Calif., 1994—97, sr. sci. officer, 1997—98, chief sci. officer, 1998—99; v.p. sci. and innovation Quest Diagnostics Inc., 1999—2005, sr. sci. and med. officer, 2005—. Cons. genetic disease sect. Calif. Dept. Health Svcs., 1978—98; mem. organizing com. Internat. Conf. Newborn Thyroid Screening, 1977—88; examiner Am. Bd. Pediat., 1971—80, mem. subcom. on pediat. endocrinology, 1976—79. Co-editor: Pediatric Thyroidology, 1985, 9 other books; editor-in-chief: Jour. Clin. Endocrinology and Metabolism, 1978—83, Pediat. Rsch., 1984—89; contbr. over 400 articles to profl. jours., over 100 chpts. to books. Capt. M.C. USAF, 1955—57. Named to Hall of Honor, NICHHD, NIH, 2003; recipient Career Devel. award, NIH, 1964—68. Mem.: Am. Assn. Clin. Chemistry (So. Calif. sect. 2004, Albert L. Nichols award 2005), Clin. Ligand Assay Soc. (Disting. Scientist award 2001), Western Soc. Pediat. Rsch. (pres. 1982—83), Lawson Wilkins Pediatric Endocrine Soc. (pres. 1982—83), Assn. Am. Physicians, Am. Soc. Clin. Investigation, Am. Thyroid Assn. (pres. 1988—89, Disting. Lectr. 1982), Endocrine Soc. (pres. 1983—84, Leadership award 1998), Am. Pediat. Soc. (pres. 1992—93, John Howland medal 2001), Soc. Pediat. Rsch. (v.p. 1973—74), Am. Acad. Pediat. (Borden award 1981), Nat. Acad. Clin. Biochemistry, Inst. Medicine of NAS, Alpha Omega Alpha, Phi Beta Kappa. Home: 24582 Santa Clara Ave Dana Point CA 92629-3031 Office: Quest Diagnostics-Nichols Inst 33608 Ortega Hwy San Juan Capistrano CA 92675-2042 Office Phone: 949-728-4235. Business E-Mail: delbert.a.fisherd@questdiagnostics.com.

FISHER, DONALD G., retail executive; b. 1928; m. Doris Fisher. BS, U. Calif., 1950. With M. Fisher & Son, 1950-57; former ptnr. Fisher Property Investment Co.; co-founder Gap Stores, San Bruno, Calif., 1969; chmn. Gap Inc., San Bruno, Calif., 1969—2004, pres., 1969—83. Mem. adv. coun. Office of US Trade Rep., 1987—98. Dir Schwab Charles Corp.; trustee Presidio Trust, 1997—; bd. mem. Calif. State Bd. Ed. Named one of Top 200 Collectors, ARTnews Mag., 2004. Avocation: collector of contemporary art, especially German & Am. Office: Gap Inc 2 Folsom St San Francisco CA 94105 Address: 3456 Washington St San Francisco CA 94118*

FISHER, DONALD WAYNE, medical association administrator; b. Pitts., Mar. 2, 1946; s. David H.W. and Jean K. F.; children by previous marriage: Kimberly Elizabeth, Jeffrey Wayne. AA, Hinds Jr. Coll., 1966; BS in Biology and Chemistry, Millsaps Coll., 1968; MS in Anatomy, U. Miss., 1970, PhD in Anatomy, 1973; postgrad. in assn. mgmt., U. Md., 1977-79. Cert. assn. exec. Instr. dept. chemistry and biology Hinds Jr. Coll., Raymond, Miss., 1968-74; instr. dept. anatomy U. Miss. Sch. Medicine, Jackson, 1973-74, co-dir. and exec. officer physician asst. program, 1972-74; asst. professorial lectr. George Washington U. Sch. Medicine, 1974—; exec. dir. Assn. Physician Asst. Programs, Arlington, Va., 1974-80, Am. Acad. Physician Assts., Arlington, 1974-80; pres., CEO Am. Med. Group Assn., Alexandria, Va., 1980—; chmn. Am. Med. Group Corp., Inc., Anceta, 2001—; pres., CEO Am. Med. Group Data Warehouse; treas. polit. action com. Am. Med. Group, 1980—. Mem. Nat. Commn. on Allied Health Edn., 1977-80; mem. adv. com. for tng., devel. and utilization of physician extenders Systems Scis., Inc., 1975-80; pres. Am. Acad. Physician Assts. Ednl. and Rsch. Found., 1977-80; sec., treas. Am. Med. Group Found., 1980—; mem. Am. Express Health Care Faculty, 1985-88. Robert Wood Johnson Found. grantee, 1973-80 Mem. Am. Soc. Assn. Execs. (govt. rels. com. 1980—), Assn. Am. Med. Colls., AAAS, Am. Internat. Health Alliance (bd. dirs. 1992—, treas. 1995-2003, chair 2004--), Greater Washington Soc. Assn. Execs., Fairfax County Hosp. Assn., Asian Mgmt. assn. Am. (bd. dirs. 2004—), Arlington (Va.) C. of C, Am. Internat. Alliance (chair, 2004—). Home: 3814 Ivanhoe Ln Alexandria VA 22310-2170 Office: Am Med Group Assn 1422 Duke St Alexandria VA 22314-3430 Office Phone: 703-838-0033.

FISHER, DORIS, retail executive; m. Donald G. Fisher; 1 child, Robert J. Co-founder Gap, Inc., 1969, merchandiser, 1969—2003, bd. dir., 1969—. Trustee Stanford U. Named one of most powerful women, Forbes mag., 2005. Office: Gap Inc Two Folsom St San Francisco CA 94105 Office Phone: 650-952-4400.*

FISHER, DOUGLAS HOWARD, state legislator; b. Bridgeton, N.J., Apr. 28, 1947; BBA, Bryant Coll., Smithfield, R.I., 1969. Supermarket operator, 1971—2000; pres. Bridgeton Meat Co., 1971—2000; freeholder dir. N.J. Cumberland County, 1996—2000; mem. N.J. State Assembly, 2001—. Trustee Woodland Country Day Sch.; sec. South Jersey Transp. Planning Orgn., 1996-2000. Served as sgt. N.J. N.G., 1970-76. Mem. Nat. Assn. Splty. Food Mchts. (charter). Jewish. Home: 421 Marlboro Rd Bridgeton NJ 08302-6716 Office: Rouner Realty 117 W Broad St Bridgeton NJ 08302

FISHER, EDWARD ABRAHAM, cardiologist, educator; b. Honolulu, Apr. 30, 1958; s. Hyman Wendell and Rosalie (Joseph) F.; m. Vivian Degenszejn, Mar. 27, 1993; children: Rebecca, Alexander, Oliver. BA in Econs., U. Va., 1980; MD, Ea. Va. Med. Sch., 1984. Diplomate Nat. Bd. Med. Examiners, Am. Bd. Internal Medicine, Am. Bd. Cardiovascular Disease; lic. physician, N.Y. Intern Lenox Hill Hosp., N.Y.C., 1984-85, resident, 1985-87, adj. attending physician dept. medicine, 1987—; cardiology fellow Mt. Sinai Med. Ctr., N.Y.C., 1987-89, cardiology rsch. fellow, 1989-90, clin. asst. dept. medicine, 1990, asst. dir. echocardiography dept. medicine divsn. cardiology, 1990-98; asst. attending Mt. Sinai Sch. Medicine, N.Y.C., 1990-92, asst. clin. prof., 1992-97, assoc. clin. prof., assoc. attending, 1997—. Co-author: Effects of Estrogen and Progesterone on Blood Vessels, 1991, Restrictive Cardiomyopathy, 2002, Native Aortic Valve Endocarditis, 2003; author numerous articles concerning transthoracic and transesophageal echocardiography. Fellow ACP, Am. Coll. Cardiology, Am. Heart Assn. Avocation: marathon running. Office: 45 East 85th St New York NY 10028 Office Phone: 212-472-7370.

FISHER, EDWIN R., pathologist; b. Pitts., Sept. 2, 1923; s. Reuben and Anna (Miller) F.; m. Carole Levy; children: Marjorie, Abbe Dava. BS, U. Pitts., 1945, MD, 1947. Staff pathology Cleve. Clin., 1953-54; prof. pathology U. Pitts., 1954; chief pathology VA Hosp., Pitts., 1954-70, Shadyside Hosp., Pitts., 1970-95. Mem. editorial bd. Breast Cancer Research and Treatment, European Cancer; chief pathologist Nat. Surg. Adj. Breast Project. Contbr. articles to profl. jours. Sr. surgeon USPHS, 1951-53. Recipient Parke-Davis award Soc. Exptl. Pathology, 1963. Mem. Am. Assn. Cancer Research, Am. Soc. Clin. Pathologists, Internat. Acad. Pathologists, Am. Thoracic Soc., Coll. Am. Pathology. Republican. Jewish. Avocations: golf, landscaping. Office: Allegheny Gen Hosp Human Oncology Cancer Ctr 320 E North Ave Pittsburgh PA 15212

FISHER, ERIC O'NEILL, economist; b. N.Y.C., Feb. 9, 1954; s. Leonard and Lora (Segall) Porter; m. Kathryn G. Marshall, June 15, 1991; children: Jane Marshall, Marshall Havard. AB, Princeton (N.J.) U., 1974; MA, Johns Hopkins U., 1979; PhD, U. Calif., Berkeley, 1985. Economist bd. of govs. FRS, Washington, 1984-87; asst. prof. Cornell U., Ithaca, N.Y., 1987-93; asst., assoc. prof. econs. Ohio State U., Columbus, 1993—. Vis. fellow Inst. for Internat. Econ. Studies, Stockholm, 1987, Australian Nat. U., Canberra, 1994; vis. prof. U. Sao Paulo, 1990, Va. Polytech. Inst., 2004, U. Calif., Santa Barbara, 2005—; vis. asst. prof. U. Chgo., 1990-91; vis. fellow Tinbergen Inst., Rotterdam, 1993; vis. fgn. scholar Inst. Social and Econ. Rsch., Osaka, Japan, 1998; Associazione Generale di Italiana Petrol prof. Johns Hopkins U., 2002-03; Jean Monnet fellow European U. Inst, 2002-03; rsch. assoc. Fed. Res. Bank, Cleve., 2003—; mem. editl. coun. Rev. Internat. Econs., 1994—; mem. editl. bd. Jour. Econ. Integration, 1994-2000; mem. COTA Legacy Coun., 2000-04; assoc. editor Jour. Internat. Econs., 2004—, Jour. Money, Credit and Banking, 2005—. Contbr. articles to profl. jours. Vol. Peace Corps, Morocco, 1975-77; mem. City of Ithaca Rep. Com., 1991-93; village coun. Riverlea, Ohio, 2000-02; mem. staff Amnesty Internat./USA, 1978. Mem. Econometric Soc., Am. Econ. Assn., Internat. Econs. and Fin. Soc. (sec. 1998-2000). Republican. Episcopalian. Avocation: fly fishing. Home: 5801 Carrington Ct Worthington OH 43085-3802 Office: Ohio State U Dept Econs Columbus OH 43210 Business E-Mail: fisher.244@osu.edu.

FISHER, EUGENE, marketing professional; b. Sept. 30, 1927; s. Morris and Sarah (Edelstein) Fisher; m. Joline Cobb, July 28, 1956 (dec.); children: Robin Downing, Amy Homer, Douglas; m. Penny Blanchard, Dec. 18, 1988. PhB, U. Chgo., 1945, MBA, 1948. With Brunswick Corp., Lake Forest, Ill., 1955-95, dir. mktg. planning bowling divsn., 1955-72, dir. corp. mktg. rsch., 1972-87, corp. mktg. dir., 1987-95; pres. Fisher Mktg. Intelligence, Inc., 1982—; chmn. Conf. Bd. Mktg. Rsch. Coun., 1988-89, mem. exec. com., 1989-95. Guest lectr. in field. Mng. editor: Profile Mag., 1988—98; prodr.: Maritime Festival, 1988—91, Brunswick 150th Anniversary Exhbn., 1995. Civic planning com. Ill. State Hist. Soc., 1994—2002; exec. dir. Diversey Harbor Lakeview Assn., 2000—; chmn., pres. Diversey Harbor Lakeview Preservation Assn., 2001—; bd. dirs. Park West Cmty. Assn., 2001—04, pres., 2003—04; bd. dirs. 2626 Lakeview Condominium Assn., 1995—2000, 2004—, pres., 1996—2000, 2004—; 50th reunion dinner chmn. U. Chgo. Alumni Assn., 1995; 55th reunion program chmn. U. Chgo. Class of 1945, 2000, vice chmn. emeritus, 2002—03; mem. cmty. rels. com. Children's Meml. Hosp., 2003—. Mem.: Nat. Bowling Coun. (mktg. com. 1975—83), Chgo. Maritime Soc. (bd. dirs. 1991—95), Am. Mktg. Assn., Phi Sigma Delta. Home and Office: Apt 4103 2626 N Lakeview Ave Chicago IL 60614-1832 Office Phone: 773-388-9103. E-mail: Fishermarketing@aol.com.

FISHER, FARAH LEE, education educator; b. Albany, Oreg., Jan. 25, 1947; d. William John and Iva Glocile Peters; m. Scott Fjeldstad Fisher, Aug. 15, 1970; children: Allen Scott, Christopher David, William RIchard. BA in Edn., Pacific Luth. U., 1969; MS, Calif. State U., Long Beach, 1979; EdD, U. So. Calif., 1986. Assoc. prof. L.A. Harbor Coll., Wilmington, Calif., 1975—91; prof. grad. edn. Calif. State U. Dominguez Hills, Carson, 1991—. Author: Teaching with Technology. Recipient award for tech. use, McLuhan Found., 1984, Nat. Tchg. Excellence award, U. Tex., Austin, 1987. Mem.: Coun. for Exceptional Children, Am. Ednl. Rsch. Assn., Phi Kappa Phi. Office: Calif State U Dominguez Hills 1000 E Victoria St Carson CA 90747 Office Phone: 310-243-3926. Business E-Mail: ffisher@csudh.edu.

FISHER, FENIMORE, business development consultant; b. NYC, 1926; s. Benn and Sadie (Cohan) F.; m. Marcia Obler, Nov. 9, 1952; children: Bennett G., Alan L., Karen Soo. BS in Physics, Columbia U., 1951; MBA, U. Pa., 1952. Staff physicist USN Rsch. Lab., Phila., 1951-52; ops. mgr., chief engr. instrument divsn. Thomas A. Edison Industries, West Orange, N.J., 1952-60; pres. Analogue Controls Inc., Hicksville, N.Y., 1960-67; corp. v.p. IMC Magnetics Corp., Jericho, N.Y., 1967-77, pres., CEO, 1977-89, also bd. dirs. Chmn. bd. Hansen Mfg. Co. Inc., Princeton Ind., IMC Ariz. Divsn., Tempe, IMC Fla. Divsn., Miami Lakes, IMC Tenn. Divsn., Camden, IMC Tex. Divsn., Mexia, IMC Western Divsn., Cerritos, Calif., New Eng. Alloys Inc., Lawrence, Mass., Pacific Propeller Inc., Kent Washington, Universal Magnetics Corp., Cerritos, 1989—; exec. v.p. Synergy Gas Corp., 1989-93; bus. devel. cons., 1993-96; v.p. bus. and fin. Dowling Coll., Oakdale, N.Y., 1996-98; exec. dir. Action Long Island, 1999—2001. Contbr. numerous articles on bus. econs., tech. edn., relation with the Far East. Bd. dirs. L.I. Philharm., West Suffolk YM & YWHA, United Way L.I.; chmn. L.I. Forum for Tech., Suffolk Cmty. Planning Coun., Old Westbury Coll. Found.; trustee Dowling Coll. Served to 1st lt. U.S. Army, 1944-46, PTO. Mem.: Eastpoint Golf and Racquet Club (West Palm Beach, Fla.). Home: 6451 Woodthrush Ct West Palm Beach FL 33418-1429 Office Phone: 561-801-0100. E-mail: ff1570@aol.com.

FISHER, FREDERICK HENDRICK, oceanographer emeritus; b. Aberdeen, Wash., Dec. 30, 1926; s. Sam (Sverre) and Astrid K. Fisher; m. Julie Gay Saund, June 17, 1955 (dec. 1993); children: Bruce Allen, Mark Edward, Keith Russell, Glen Michael; m. Shirley Mercedes Lippert, Oct. 10, 1994 (div. 2003). BS, U. Wash., 1949, PhD, 1957. Tchg. asst. U. Wash., 1949-53; rsch. asst. UCLA, 1954-55; grad. rsch. physicist Marine Phys. Lab., Scripps Inst. Oceanography, 1955-57, rsch. physicist, rsch. oceanographer, 1958-91, assoc. dir., 1975-87, dep. dir., 1987-93, acting assoc. dir., 1993-94, rsch. oceanographer emeritus, 1997—; rsch. fellow acoustics Harvard U., 1957-58. Dir. rsch. in reverse osmosis and desalination Havens Industries, San Diego, 1963-64; prof., chmn. dept. physics U. R.I., Kingston, 1970-71; mem. governing bd. Am. Inst. Physics, 1984-90. Assoc. editor: Jour. Oceanic Engring., 2001—. Mem. San Diego County Dem. Ctrl. Com., 1956-57, 60-62. Midshipman U.S. Naval Acad., 1945-47, with USNR, 1945. NCAA nat. tennis doubles champion, 1949; named to U. Wash. Athletic Hall of Fame, 1989; recipient Disting. Svc. award IEEE Oceanic Engring. Soc., 1991, Disting. Tech. Achievement award IEEE/OES, 1996, 3d Millennium Medal IEEE, 2000. Fellow: Acoustical Soc. Am. (assoc. editor jour. 1969—76, v.p. 1980—81, pres. 1983—84, emeritus); mem.: IEEE (life; sr. editor Jour. Oceanic Engring. 1988—91, emeritus editor 2001—), Am. Geophys. Union, The Oceanographic Soc., Marine Tech. Soc., Seattle Tennis Club. Achievements include co-designer and project scientist ocean research platform FLIP, 355' long manned spar buoy with 300' draft in vertical position, 1960-62; co-discoverer of boric acid as cause of low frequency sound absorption in the ocean; measured effect of pressure on sound absorption and electrical conductivity of magnesium and calcium sulfate and other salts related to high frequency sound absorption in the ocean; conducted sound propagation measurements at long range 30-800 miles in the ocean. Home: # 106 291 Rosecrans St San Diego CA 92106 Office: Scripps Instn Oceanography Marine Phys Lab La Jolla CA 92093-0701 E-mail: fhf@mpl.ucsd.edu.

FISHER, GARTH (DONALD GARTH FISHER), plastic surgeon; b. Sacto, MS, May 24, 1958; s. Donald Fisher.m. Brooke Burke, 2001 (separated 2005); 2 children. BA in Biology, U. Miss., Oxford, 1980; MD, U. Miss., Jackson, 1984. Diplomate Am. Bd. Plastic Surgery, Am. Bd. Surgery. Intern in gen. surgery U. Calif., Irvine, 1984-85, resident in gen. surgery, 1985-89, resident in plastic surgery, 1989-91; fellow in aesthetic plastic surgery Santa Ana, Calif., 1991; pvt. practice Beverly Hills, Calif., 1991—. Instr. dept. surgery U. Miss. Sch. Medicine, 1980, dept. anatomy, 1980; lectr. in field; consulted extensively for many TV, news and magazine interviews. Author: (5 part ednl. video series) The Naked Truth About Plastic Surgery, The Informed Patient; contbr. articles to sci. and profl. jours.; appeared in: (TV series) Extreme Makeover. Fellow ACS; mem. AMA, Calif. Med. Assn., Los Angeles County Med. Assn., L.A. Soc. Plastic Surgeons. Achievements include first plastic surgeon selected to appear on ABC's hit show ″Extreme Makeover″. Office: 120 S Spalding Dr Ste 222 Beverly Hills CA 90212-1840 Office Phone: 310-273-5995. Personal E-mail: garthmd@earthlink.net.*

FISHER, GENE JORDAN, retired chemical company executive; b. Quitman, Miss., Mar. 26, 1931; s. Ira R. and Gertrude (Jordan) F.; m. Christine Ann Hodges, May 28, 1954; children— Denise, Darrell BS, U. Tex., 1952. From research chemist to sr. research chemist Celanese Chem. Co., Corpus Christi, Tex., 1952-59, group leader, 1959-67, research mgr., 1967-77, dir. research, 1977-83, tech. dir., 1983-85, ret., 1985; tech. and mgmt. cons., 1985—. Contbr. articles to profl. jours.; patentee in field. Baptist. Home: PO Box 1944 Rockwall TX 75087-2044 E-mail: genefisher@sbcglobal.net.

FISHER, GENE LAWRENCE, financial executive; b. Chillicothe, Ill., Nov. 15, 1929; s. Lawrence Hubert and Alyce Anne (Niggemeyer) F.; m. Sandra Kay Burns, Sept. 19, 1959; children— Kyle Butler, Kelley Anne. B.S., U. Ill., 1957. Staff acct. Inland Container Corp., Indpls., 1957-63, mgr. corp. acctg., 1964-65, asst. corp. controller, 1966-78, dir. fin. systems, 1979-93; ret., 1993. Chmn. fin. com.-exec. com. Winona Meml. Hosp., Indpls., 1979-81, chmn. bd. dirs., 1982-83. Served with U.S. Army, 1951-53. Mem. Beta Alpha Psi, Sigma Iota Epsilon. Republican. Avocations: fishing, swimming. Home: 5427 N Washington Blvd Indianapolis IN 46220-3027 E-mail: genofish@aol.com.

FISHER, GEORGE, law educator; b. 1959; AB summa cum laude, Harvard U., 1982, JD magna cum laude, 1986. Law clk. to Hon. Stephen G. Breyer US Ct. Appeals 1st Cir., 1986—87; asst. dist. atty. Middlesex Co. Dist. Atty.'s Office, Mass., 1987—91; asst. atty. gen. civil rights divsn. Mass. Atty. Gen's Office, 1991—92; asst. clin. prof. law Boston Coll. Law Sch., 1992—95; assoc. prof. law Stanford Law Sch., 1995—99, prof., 1999—, Judge John Crown prof., 2004—, Robert E. Paradise faculty scholar, 2003—04, academic assoc. dean rsch., 2003—04. Adj. instr. Northeastern U., 1991; vis. prof. law Yale Law Sch., 2000, Harvard Law Sch., 2000. Author: Cases and Materials on Evidence, 2002, Plea Bargaining's Triumph: A History of Plea Bargaining in America, 2003; co-editor: The Crime Conundrum: Essays on Criminal Justice, 1997. Recipient John Bingham Hurlbut Award for Excellence in Teaching, Stanford U., 1999, 2003. Office: Stanford Law Sch Crown Quadrangle 559 Nathan Abbott Way Stanford CA 94305-8610 Office Phone: 650-723-2578. Business E-Mail: fisherg@stanford.edu.*

FISHER, GEORGE MYLES CORDELL, retired photographic imaging company executive, mathematician, engineer; b. Anna, Ill., Nov. 30, 1940; s. Ralph Myles and Catherine (Herbert) Fisher; m. Patricia Ann Wallace, June 18, 1965; children: Jennifer, Barcy, William. BS in Engring., U. Ill., 1962; MS in Engring., Brown U., 1964, PhD in Applied Maths., 1966. Mem. tech. staff Bell Tel Labs., 1965—76; sr. exec. v.p. Motorola Corp., Schaumburg, 1986—88, pres., CEO, 1988—90, chmn., CEO, 1990—93; chmn., pres., CEO Eastman Kodak Co., Rochester, NY, 1993—97, chmn., CEO, 1997—99, chmn., 1997—2000; ret., 2000. Bd. dirs. GM, Eli Lilly & Co.; chmn. Nat. Acad. Engring., 2000—04; former mem. Pres.'s Adv. Com. for Trade Policy and Negotiation. Contbr. articles on continuum physics. Recipient M. Eugene Mcht. Mfg. medal, ASME, 1994. Mem.: IEEE, Internat. Acad. Astronautics. Achievements include patents for optical wave guides and digital communications.

FISHER, GEORGE ROSS, III, physician, educator; b. Erie, Pa., May 8, 1925; s. George Ross and Margaret (Schwitay) F.; m. Mary Stuart Blakely; children: George Ross IV, Miriam Schaefer, Margaret Fisher-Rosenthal, Stuart Blakely. BS, Yale U., 1945; MD, Columbia U., 1948. Diplomate Am. Bd. Internal Medicine. Intern Pa. Hosp., Phila., 1948-50, med. resident, 1953-54, dir. house staff, 1954-56; fellow in endocrinology Jefferson Hosp., Phila., 1950-51; surgeon endocrinology br. Nat. Cancer Inst., NIH, Bethesda, Md., 1951-53; from instr. to asst. prof. clin. medicine Jefferson U., Phila., 1955—; asst. prof. clin. medicine U. Pa., Phila., 1960—. Pres. Phila. Profl. Standards Rev. Orgn., 1981-84; med. dir. Heritage Health Systems, King of Prussia, Pa., 1986—; chmn. Ross and Perry, Inc. Book Pubs., Haddonfield, NJ; cons. in field. Author: The Hospital That Ate Chicago, 1980; contbr. articles on endocrinology and med. econs. to profl. jours. Served as sr. asst. surgeon USPHS, 1951-53. Fellow ACP, Phila. Coll. Physicians; mem. AMA (ho. of dels. 1978—), Pa. Med. Soc. (ho. of dels. 1969-89, chmn. coun. of med. econs. 1985-88, trustee 1989—), Phila. County Med. Soc. (bd. dirs. 1969-81), Pa. Soc. Internal Medicine (pres. 1980), Am. Soc. Internal Medicine (ho. of dels. 1974—), Union League (life), Republican. Mem. Soc. Of Friends. Avocations: computer science, Phila. history. Home: 203 Chews Landing Rd Haddonfield NJ 08033-3837 Office: 829 Spruce St Philadelphia PA 19107-5752 Office Phone: 856-427-6135. Business E-Mail: gfisher@rossperry.com.

FISHER, HARRY, lawyer, theologian, writer; b. Grand Forks, ND, June 15, 1931; s. George DeFoldessy and Evelyn Sarah (Korroll) Fisher; m. Arden Irene Mueller, June 18, 1981; m. Joy Marilyn Waltke, Nov. 12, 1955 (dec. Dec. 1980); children: Hal, Diane. AB, U. Chgo., 1950; JD, U. Chgo. Law Sch., 1953. Bar: Iowa 1953, Mo. 1957. Assoc. Stolar Partnership, St. Louis, 1957—59; acct. exec. Lemoine Skinner P.R., Inc., St. Louis, 1959—63; prin. Stemmler, Fisher & Assocs., St. Louis, 1963—80; editor St. Louis Regional Commerce Mag., 1980—87; freelance rschr., 1987—. Res. scholar Ecumenical Inst. for Theol. Rsch., Jerusalem, 1977; adv. bd. Cmty. Music Sch. of Webster U., 1999—; reader Talking Tapes for the Blind and Disabled, 1988—. Author: Luke-Acts is a Legal Brief, A Unified Commentary, hymns, poems and plays. Trustee Trinity Presbyn. Ch., 1963. Capt. USAF, 1953—57, Tex., Calif. Independent. Avocations: chess, piano, travel. Home: 6 Godwin Lane Saint Louis MO 63124

FISHER, IRENE B., lawyer; b. Odessa, Russia, July 20, 1965; BA summa cum laude, Yale U., 1987; JD cum laude, Harvard U., 1990. Bar: N.Y. 1990. Assoc. Milbank, Tweed, Hadley & McCloy, 1990—94; v.p., assoc. gen. counsel Triarc Co., Inc., 1994—96; dep. gen. counsel Big Flower Holdings, Inc., 1996—2002; gen. counsel Lane Capital LLC, 1996—2002, NBTY Inc., 2002—. Mem.: Phi Beta Kappa. Office: NBTY Inc 90 Orville Dr Bohemia NY 11716 Office Phone: 631-567-9500.

FISHER, JACOB ALEXANDER SHULTZ, retired clergyman; b. Wichita Falls, Tex., Apr. 22, 1925; s. Hiram Herbert Fisher and Mary Elizabeth Shultz; m. Nell Davidson, Aug. 13, 1949 (dec. June 2001); children: Michael D., Kelly Paige Fisher Matthews; m. Adelaide Boggs, Apr. 12, 2003. BA, Centenary Coll., 1950; MDiv, S.W. Bapt. Theol. Sem., 1953. Ordained to ministry Bapt. Ch., 1951. Commd. ensign USN, 1953, advanced through grades to lt. comdr., 1959, chaplain, 1953-72, ret., 1972; dir. pastoral care La. State U. Med. Ctr. (formerly Confederate Meml. Med. Ctr), Shreveport, 1972-95; ret., 1995. Founding pres. Ret. Srs. Vol. Program, Shreveport, 1976-78. With USNR, 1943-46, 47-55. Decorated Navy Letter of Commendation with combat star. Mem.: Greater Shreveport Ministerial Assn. (pres. 1980), La. Chaplains Assn. (pres. 1982, 1983), Assn. Profl. Chaplains, Masons. Democrat. Avocation: jogging. Home: 305 Baycliff Ln Shreveport LA 71105-4815 Personal E-mail: jasfisher1@aol.com.

FISHER, JAMES AIKEN, marketing professional, consultant; b. Pitts., Mar. 15, 1920; s. Chester G and Margaret R (Aiken) Fisher; m. Edith C Hall, June 12, 1955; children: George S, Chester G III, James Aiken. BA, Yale, 1942. Engr. Alcoa Niagara Works, 1942-44; with Fisher Sci. Co., Pitts., 1944-85, sales staff, 1945-50, advt. staff, 1950-60, sr. v.p., dir., 1963-81; asst. to pres., 1981-85; chmn., pres. Kipling Corp., mktg. cons., 1985—. Trustee Carnegie Inst, Carnegie Mus Art, Carnegie Sci Ctr. Mem.: Am Mkt Asn, Sci Apparatus Makers Asn (past pres), Am Chemical Soc, Pittsburgh Golf Club, Rolling Rock Club, Duquesne Club, HYP-Pittsburgh Club. Home: 5414 Kipling Rd Pittsburgh PA 15217-1038 Office: 622 Oliver Bldg Pittsburgh PA 15222-2304

FISHER, JAMES LEE, lawyer; b. Akron, Ohio, Apr. 10, 1944; s. James Lee and Maxine (Sumner) F.; m. Nancy Lorenz, Dec. 20, 1980. BSCE, U. Akron, 1968, JD, 1971. Bar: Ohio 1971. Staff atty. Brunswick Mgmt. Co., Akron, 1972-77; prin. James L. Fisher Co., L.P.A., Akron, 1977-88, Buckingham, Doolittle & Burroughs, Akron, 1988—. City planner City of Akron, 1968-71, community devel. atty., 1971-73; mem. Metro Regional Transit Authority Bd., 1992—; sec.-treas. Summit County Planning Commn., 1978-99. Mem. ABA, Ohio Bar Assn., Akron Bar Assn., Home Builders Assn., Am. Planning Assn., Ohio Planning Conf., Copley Lions (pres. 1982). Republican. Mem. United Ch. of Christ. Home: 1135 Forest Pool Rd Akron OH 44333-1509 Office: Buckingham Doolittle & Burroughs PO Box 1500 Akron OH 44309-1500

FISHER, JAMES R., lawyer; b. South Bend, Ind., Apr. 15, 1947; s. Russell Humphries and Virginia Opal (Maple) F.; m. Cynthia Ann Winters, Aug. 14, 1971; children: Gabriel Christopher, Cory Andrew. AB in Psychology, Ind. U., 1969, JD summa cum laude, 1972. Bar: Ind. 1972, U.S. Dist. Ct. (so. dist.) Ind. 1972. Ptnr. Ice Miller, Indpls., 1971—. Co-author: Personal Injury Law and Practices vol. 23 of Indiana Practice series; contbr. articles to legal publs. Mem. ATLA, Ind. Bar Assn., Ind. Trial Lawyers Assn., Order of Coif. Office: Ice Miller 1 Am Sq PO Box 82001 Indianapolis IN 46282 E-mail: james.fisher@icemiller.com.

FISHER, JAMES WILLIAM, pharmacologist, medical educator; b. Tucapau (now Startex), S.C., May 22, 1925; s. Ernest Amaziah and Mamie V. (Turner) F.; m. Carol Barbara Brodarick, June 5, 1947; children: Candis Loreen Fisher Rush Smith, Patricia Eileen Fisher Valladares, Richard W., William E., John C., Elaine Marie Fisher Spurr. BS, U. S.C., 1947; PhD in Pharmacology (USPHS fellow), U. Louisville, 1958. Devel. chemist Armour Pharm. Rsch. Labs., Chgo., 1950-53, Ayerst Pharm. Labs., Rouses Point, NY, 1953—54; pharmacologist Lloyd Bros. Pharm. Co., Cin., 1954-56; instr. pharmacology U. Tenn., 1958-60, asst. prof., 1960-62, assoc. prof., 1962-66, prof., 1966-68; prof., chmn. dept. pharmacology Med. Sch., Tulane U., 1968-96; Regents prof., chmn. pharmacology Tulane U., 1987—96, James W. Fisher Disting. Lectureship in Pharmacology, 1991—, Regents prof. emeritus, chmn., 1999—. Vis. prof. U. Zambia, Lusaka, 1987, Keio U., Tokyo, 1987, U. Nairobi, 1993; external examiner U. W.I., Trinidad, 1992; vis. scientist Christie Hosp. and Holt Radium Inst., Manchester, Eng., 1963-64; dir. Tulane-Universidad Nacional del Nordeste, Corrientes, Argentina, Pan Am. Health Orgn. Physiol. Scis. Tng. Program, 1972-77; lectr. in field; mem. Nat. Heart, Lung and Blood Inst. (erythropoietin com. 1971-74), mem. NIH hematology tng. grants com., 1977; mem. Cooley's Anemia Nat. Rsch. Com., 1974; pres. So. Blood Club, 1975-77; mem. Wellcome Professorships Com., 1976, 93, 94, 95; mem. pharmacology com. Nat. Bd. Med. Examiners, 1988-92; mem. ad hoc group med. rsch. funding AAMC, 1990-93. Author: Readings on the History of Pharmacology; editor: Kidney Hormones, Vol. I, 1971, Vol. II, 1977, Vol. III, 1986, Renal Pharmacology, 1971, Handbook of Pharmacology: Blood and Blood Forming Organs, 1992; co-editor: Erythropoiesis, 1975, Erythropoietin and Erythropoiesis, 1981; cons. editor: Erythropoletin, 1968; mem. editl. bd. Proc. Soc. Exptl. Biology and Medicine, 1971-86; contbr. articles to profl. jours. Served to lt. (j.g.) USNR, 1943-46, PTO. Recipient rsch. career devel. award USPHS, 1960-65, Purkinje medal Czechoslovakia Med. Soc., 1975, Golden Sovereign award, 1976, Aspet Exptl. Therapeutics award, 1992, U. Louisville Med. Sch. Alumni award, 1999; named Disting. faculty AOA Honor Med. Soc., 1993; Ann. Tulane Fisher Lectureship established in his honor, 1992. Mem. AAAS, AAUP, Am. Soc. Pharmacology and Exptl. Therapeutics (Sollman awards com. 1981, exptl. therapeutics award com. 1982, 94, alerting network 1986-90, ednl. affairs com. 1986-89, Krayer awards com. 1990, Exptl. Therapeutics award 1992, nominating com. 1997), Soc. Exptl. Biology and Medicine, Am. Soc. Nephrology, Am. Soc. Hematology (sci. affairs com. 1973-74, chmn. eythropoietin subcom. 1973), Assn. Med. Sch. Pharmacology (exec. com. 1979-82, nominating com. 1975, 86, 94, 96, 99, chmn. essential knowledge base in pharmacology com. 1984-95, pres. 1990-92), N.Y. Acad. Scis., Sigma Xi. Home: 4025 S Pin Oak Ave New Orleans LA 70131-8449 Business E-Mail: jfisher@tulane.edu. *Creativity and brilliance are very important in science but in order to test one's ideas these qualities must be adequately supplemented by the necessary amount of work at the bench.*

FISHER, JANET WARNER, secondary school educator; b. San Angelo, Tex., July 7, 1929; d. Robert Montell and Louise (Buckley) Warner; m. Jarek Prochazka Fisher, Oct. 17, 1956 (div. May 1974); children: Barbara Zlata Harper, Lev Prochazka, Monte Prochazka. BA, So. Meth. U., 1950, M of Liberal Arts, 1982; student various including, Columbia U., U. Dallas, U. Colo., U. London and others. Cert. English, German and ESL tchr., K-12, Tex., N.Y. Bd. dirs., sec. Masaryk Inst., N.Y.C., 1968-71; with orphan sect. Displaced Persons Commn., Washington, 1950; fgn. editor Current Digest of the Soviet Press, N.Y.C., 1953-55; cable desk clk. Time, Inc., N.Y.C., 1955-56; tchr. of English and reading, langs. Houston Ind. Sch. Dist., 1975-80; tchr. Carmine Ind. Sch. Dist., Round Top, Tex., 1980-82; tchr. German Region IV Interactive TV, 1983-85; adj. prof. English U. Houston, 1983-87; tchr. Royal Ind. Sch. Dist., Brookshire, Tex., 1989-92, Hempstead Ind. Sch. Dist., Waller County, Tex., 1992-94. Adj. prof. English, U. Houston, Houston C.C., 1983-87, 1997—; tchr. Amnesty Program, Houston, 1988-90; adj. prof. English Blinn Coll., Brenham, Tex., 1995-97. Candidate sch. bd., South Orangetown, N.Y., 1962, state rep., Houston, 1980; del. Houston Tchrs. Assn., 1975-80; officer LWV, Nyack, N.Y., 1960-62; trustee, chair adminstrn. bd. Shepherd Drive United Meth. Ch., Houston, 1994-2003; del. Tex. ann. conf. United Meth. Ch., 1994-2001; del. Tex. State Dem. Conv., 1996, 2000, 02. Recipient award for Svc. to Missions, United Meth. Ch., Houston, 1985. Mem. AAUW, NOW, WILPF, Harris County Women's Polit. Caucus. Avocations: Russian and German literature, real estate development.

FISHER, JEFF, professional football coach; b. Culver City, Calif., Feb. 25, 1958; m. Juli; children: Brandon, Trenton, Tara. Student, U. Southern California. Professional football player Chicago Bears, 1981-85; defensive backs coach Philadelphia Eagles, 1986-88, defensive coordinator, 1989-90, Los Angeles Rams, 1991; defensive backs coach San Francisco 49ers, 1992-93; defensive coordinator Tenn. Titans, 1994; head coach Tenn. Oilers (now Titans), 1995—; exec. v.p. Tenn. Titans, 2000—. Avocations: fly-fishing, golf, sushi, travel. Office: Tennessee Titans Baptist Sports Park 460 Great Circle Rd Nashville TN 37228-1404*

FISHER, JEFFREY L., lawyer; BA in English, Duke U., 1992; JD, U. Mich. Law Sch., 1997. Bar: Wash. 2000. Law clk. to John Paul Stevens U.S. Supreme Ct., Washington; law clk. to Hon. Stephen Reinhardt U.S. Ct. Appeals (9th cir.); assoc. Davis Wright Tremaine LLP, Seattle, 1999—2004, ptnr., 2005—. Vis. lectr. U. Wash. Law Sch.; vice chair, amicus com., co-chair supreme ct. oral argument com. Nat. Assn. Criminal Def. Lawyers; spkr. in field. Contbr. articles to profl. jours. Named one of Top 40 Lawyers Under 40, Nat. Law Jour., 2005; recipient Professionalism award, Wash. Young Lawyers Divsn., Wash. State Bar, 2004. Mem.: Wash. State Bar Assn., ACLU of Washington (mem. legal com.). Office: Davis Wright Tremaine LLP 2600 Century Sq 1501 Fourth Ave Seattle WA 98101-1688 Office Phone: 206-622-3150. Business E-Mail: jefffisher@dwt.com.*

FISHER, JEROME, apparel executive; m. Anne Fisher; children: Marc, Jodi. Founder Nine West Group, chmn. emeritus. Jerome & Anne C. Fisher Charitable Found.; overseer Wharton Sch., U. Pa.; trustee U, Pa. Named one of Top 200 Collectors, ARTnews Mag., 2004; recipient Humanitarian Award, 1997, Humanitarian of Yr., Shoes on Sale, 2003. Mem.: Acad. of U. Pa., Coll. House Adv. Bd. Avocation: collector modern art. Office: Nine West Group 1129 Westchester Ave White Plains NY 10604*

FISHER, JIMMIE LOU, state official; b. Delight, Ark., Dec. 31, 1941; Student, Ark. State U.; grad. John F. Kennedy Sch. Govt., Harvard U., 1985. Treas. Greene County, Ark., 1971-78; auditor State of Ark., Little Rock, 1979, treas., 1981—. Sec. Ark. State Bd. Fin. Trustee, ex-offico mem. Ark. Pub. Employees Retirement System, Ark. Tchr. Retirement System; trustee Ark. State Hwy. Retirement System; former vice chair Dem. State Com.; former mem. Dem. Nat. Com.; del. Dem. Nat. Conv., 1988; past pres. Ark. Dem. Women's Club; mem. Ark. Devel. Fin. Authority. Mem. State Bd. Fin. (sec.), State Bd. Election Commrs., Nat. Assn. State Treas. (pres.). Office: Treasurer of State 1401 W Capitol Ave #275 Little Rock AR 72201-2936

FISHER, JOEL MARSHALL, political scientist, educator, legal association administrator, consultant; b. Chgo., June 24, 1935; s. Dan and Nell (Kolvin) F.; children: Sara Melinda, Matthew Nicholas. AB, U. So. Calif., 1955; LLB, MA, U. Calif.-Berkeley; PhD in Govt., Claremont Grad. U., 1968. Orgn. dir. Republican Citizens Com. of U.S., Washington, 1964-65; dir. arts and scis. state legis. divs. Rep. Nat. Com., Washington, 1968-69; asst. dep. counsel to pres. U.S. White House, 1969-70; dep. asst. sec. econ. and social affairs U.S. Dept. State, Washington, 1969-71; vis. prof. comparative and internat. law Loyola U. Sch. Law, L.A., 1972-73; dir. World Bus. Inst., L.A., 1974-75; prof. constl. law Southwestern U. Sch. Law, L.A., 1974-76; dir. World Trade Inst. So. Calif., 1976-84; prof. internat. law, asst. dean Whitter Coll. Sch. Law, L.A., 1977-80; prin. Ziskind, Greene and Assocs., 1980-83; v.p. Wells Internat., 1983-84; pres. LawSearch Inc., 1984-91; v.p. Clarke Cos., 1991-93; pres. Fisher Group, 1993—; adj. prof. Calif. Internat. U., L.A., 1993-99. Spl. projects Hollywood Palace, 1998-2002, pub. affairs, 2002--; ofcl. visitor The European Communities, 1974, 76, wine instr., AILA/culinary arts, 1999—; mem. U.S. dels. UN confs., 1969-71; chmn. Strategy for Peace Conf. Panel on U.S. and UN, 1972—; coord. Series on the Contemporary Am. Presidency, 1972-73; cons. Robert Taft Inst., 1977-82, World Trade Inst. N.Y., 1977-80; chair Bid Renewal Steering Com., Hollywood Entertainment Dist.; pres. Hollywood United Neighborhood Coun.; chair Security Com., 2001-03, 2003—, bd. dirs., treas. Hollywood Bus. Improvement Dist., 2001—, v.p., 2003—. Co-author three books; contbr. articles to profl. jours. Steering com. Calif. Com. Reelection of Pres., 1972; nat chmn. Cmty. Leaders Ford, 1976; trustee Rep. Assocs., 1978—, exec. com., 1986—; mem. vestry, sr. warden St. Michael and All Angeles Ch., Studio City, Calif., 1983-86, 89-93, mem. diocesan coun. L.A., 1986-88, chmn. budget com. 1987; bd. dirs. Corp. of the Cathedral, 1988-91, com. on constn. and canons, 1993—; mem. bd. dirs. Hollywood-Wilshire YMCA, 2005-. Fellow Nobel Found., 1958; Falk fellow, 1961-62 Mem. Am. Polit. Sci. Assn. (state legis. fellow 1970-73). Home: 4358 Mammoth Ave Unit 26 Sherman Oaks CA 91423-3692 Office: 1735 Vine St Hollywood CA 90028-5248 Office Phone: 818-429-6770. Personal E-mail: jmfisher@aol.com.

FISHER, JOHN E, research scientist; b. Brookline, Mass., Sept. 14, 1947; s. Philip Edward and Mimi M Fisher; 1 child, Benjamin David. BSc magna cum laude, U. Mass., 1981; PhD, Drexel U., 2000. Rsch. assoc. Merck Rsch. Labs., West Point, Pa., 1997—2000, rsch. fellow, 2000—. Contbr. articles to profl. jours. Bd. dirs. Jenkintown Libr., Pa., 1996—2002. Mem.: Endocrine Soc., Am. Soc. for Bone and Mineral Rsch. Achievements include contributions to understanding of molecular mechanism of action of N-bisphosphonates, role of cell adhesion molecules in osteoclast biology and biological activity of PTHrP. Avocations: hiking, music, literature. Home: 609 Harper Ave Jenkintown PA 19046 Office: Merck Rsch Labs 26A-1000 West Point PA 19486 E-mail: john_fisher@merck.com.

FISHER, JOHN MORRIS, association official, business executive, educator; b. Fairhaven, Ohio, Apr. 20, 1922; s. Marion Hays and Bessie (Morris) F.; m. Thelma Ison, Feb. 2, 1947; children: Steven, Roger, Linda Lucille. AB, Miami U., Oxford, Ohio, 1947; postgrad., Bklyn. Law Sch., 1950-51, Northwestern U., 1954-55; LLD (hon.), Nasson Coll., 1972. With Belden Mfg. Co., Richmond, Ind., 1941; spl. agt. FBI, 1947—53; exec. staff asst. to v.p. personnel and employee rels. Sears Roebuck & Co., Chgo., 1953—57, chmn. corp. security com., 1957—61; chmn., CEO, oper. dir. Am. Security Coun., 1956—2002, pres., 1957—2002. Pres. Am. Rsch. Found., 1961-90; pres., CEO Am. Security Coun. Found., 1962-87, CEO, 1987-2002, chmn., 1992-2002; pres. Comm. Corp. Am., 1972-80, chmn., 1980—; pres. Am. Coalition Patriotic Socs., 1978-91; adminstrv. chmn. Coalition for Peace Through Strength, 1978-2002; dir. Ctr. for Internat. Security Studies, 1977-83; organizer, pres. Fidelifax, Inc., 1956-57; chmn. merc. divsn. Nat. Safety Coun., 1959-60, 1st vice chmn. trades and svcs. sect., 1961-62. Chmn. Chgo. Retail Safety Conf., 1959-60; spl. adviser Ill. Supt. Pub. Instrn., 1963-64; cons. to Gov. Fla.; cons. to chmn. com. cold war edn. Nat. Gov.'s Conf., 1962-65, Ill. CD Adv. Coun., 1965-68; pres. Am. Coun. World Freedom, 1971-72; mem. exec. com. Nat. Captive Nations Com., 1968-70; bd. visitors Freedoms Found., 1964-65; bd. dirs. Am. Fgn. Policy Inst., 1976-84, Security and Intelligence Fund, 1976-84, James Monroe Libr., 1977-85; pres. Culpeper Meml. Hosp. Found., 1984-86; exec. chmn. U.S. Congl. Adv. Bd., 1982-2002; chmn. Nat. Security Caucus Found., 1997-2002. 1st lt. USAAF, 1943-45. Decorated Air medal with clusters; recipient 10th Anniversary medal and scroll Assembly Captive European Nations, Order Lafayette Freedom award, 1973, Disting. Svc. award Chapel of 4 Chaplains, 1979, Pres. Eagle, Pres. Reagan, 1982, others. Mem. Am. Soc. Indsl. Security (dir. 1959-62), Phi Kappa Tau. Republican. Presbyterian. Office: Comms Corp Am 13195 Freedom Way Boston VA 22713 Home: 1210 S Blue Ridge Ave Culpeper VA 22701 Office Phone: 540-547-1700. E-mail: johnf@cca.net, johnmfisher@adelphia.net.

FISHER, JOHN RICHARD, engineering consultant, retired military officer; b. Columbus, Ohio, Dec. 28, 1924; s. Don Alfred and Katherine Buchanan (Galigher) F.; m. Kitson Overmyer, Oct. 2, 1946; children: Scott Owen, Lani Kitson. BS, U.S. Naval Acad., 1946; BCE, MCE, Rensselaer Poly. Inst., Troy, N.Y., 1950; grad. Advanced Mgmt. Program, Harvard, 1971. Registered profl. engr., S.C. Commd. ensign U.S. Navy, 1946, advanced through grades to rear adm., 1972; service in North Africa, Cuba, The Philippines, Antarctica, Vietnam, Australia; comdr. 30th Seabee Rgt., Vietnam, 1968-69; dep. comdr. Naval Facilities Engring. Command; also comdr. Chesapeake divsn. constrn. facilities U.S. Naval Acad. and Omega Nav. System, 1969-73; comdr. Pacific divsn. Naval Facilities Engring. Command, Constrn. Facilities Diego Garcia, 1973-77; ret., 1977; v.p. Raymond Internat., Inc., 1977-81, sr. group v.p., 1981-83, exec. v.p., 1983-86. Pres. Cmty. Hosp. Assn. Mid-Am., Scottdale, Ariz., 1985-96; past sr. warden St. Anthony Episcopal Ch. Decorated DSM, Legion of Merit with combat V (2). Fellow Am. Soc. Mil. Engrs.; mem. ASCE, Navy League U.S. (nat. pres. 1999-2001), The Moles, Outrigger Canoe Club (Honolulu), Army-Navy Country Club (Arlington, Va.), Tau Kappa Epsilon (nat. pres. 1993-95), Navy League of U.S. (nat. pres. 1999-2001), Tau Beta Pi. Office: PO Box 5585 Scottsdale AZ 85261-5585 Home: 16455 E Ave of The Fountains #A249 Fountain Hills AZ 85268 E-mail: jFisher1947@aol.com.

FISHER, JOHN W., insurance company executive; With Auto-Owners Ins., Lansing, Mich., 1978—, pres., 1993—. Pres., bd. dirs. Lake Country Corp.; dir. Mut. Reinsurance Bur. Mem.: Nat. Assn. Mut. Ins. Cos. (chmn. 2002—03). Office: Auto Owners Ins PO Box 30660 6101 Anacapri Blvd Lansing MI 48917

FISHER, JOHN WELTON, II, lawyer, educator, academic administrator; b. Fisher, W.Va., Dec. 11, 1942; s. John Welton and Orrie (Shobe) F.; m. Susan Carol Vass, June 6, 1964; children: John Welton III, Jennifer Lynn. BA, W.Va. U., 1964, JD, 1967. Bar: W.Va. 1967, U.S. Dist. Ct. (no. and so. dists.) W.Va. 1967, U.S. Ct. Appeals (4th cir.) 1969. Law clk. to chief judge U.S. Dist. Ct. (no. dist.) W.Va., 1967-68; assoc. Farmer & Farmer, Morgantown, W.Va., 1968-71; mem. faculty W.Va. U. Coll. Law, 1971—, prof. law, 1977—, acting dean, 1981-82, 92-93, 97-98, dean, 1998—, exec. officer univ., 1982-86; magistrate judge U.S. Dist. Ct. No. Dist. W.Va., 1977-98. Reporter Speedy Trial Planning Group, No. Dist. W.Va. Reporter: Local Rules of Practice, Northern District of West Virginia, 1980. Fellow Am.Bar Found., W.Va. Bar Found.; mem. W.Va. State Bar, W.Va. Bar Assn., Fourth Cir. Jud. Conf., Order of Coif. Office: PO Box 6130 Morgantown WV 26506-6130 Office Phone: 304-293-3199. Business E-Mail: John.Fisher@mail.wvu.edu.

FISHER, JOHN WESLEY, manufacturing executive, director; b. Walland, Tenn., July 15, 1915; s. Arthur Justin and Rachel (Malott) F.; m. Janice Kelsey Ball, Aug. 10, 1940; children: Joan Fisher Woods, Michael J., James A., Jeffrey E., Judith Fisher Oetinger, John Wesley III, Jerrold M. BS, U. Tenn., 1938; MBA, Harvard U., 1942; LLD (hon.), Ball State U., 1972, Butler U., 1977, DePauw U., 1981, Ind. U., 1985. Field sec. Delta Tau Delta Frat., Indpls., 1938-40; trainee, various mfg., sales and adminstrv. positions Ball Corp., Muncie, Ind., 1941-70, pres., chief exec. officer, 1970-78, chmn. bd., chief exec. officer, 1978-81, chmn. bd., 1981-86, also dir., chmn. emeritus, 1986—. Bd. dirs. Kindel Furniture Co., Grand Rapids, Mich.; ptnr. Blackwood & Nichols Corp., Oklahoma City; chmn. CID Equity Ptnrs., Indpls., Old Nat. Trust Co., Muncie; pres. Nature's Catch, Inc., Clarksdale, Miss., Fisher Properties of Ind., Inc. State del. Rep. Party, Ind., 1950-70; mem. Rep. State Fin. Com., 1952-56, del. nat. conv., 1952, 54, 64, 68; chmn. Cardinal Health Sys.; chmn., pres. Ball Bros. Found. Mem. NAM (chmn. 1979-80, bd. dirs.), Glass Packaging Inst. (trustee 1962-68, pres. 1965-67), Grocery Mfrs. Assn. (bd. dirs.), Ind. C. of C. (dir. 1959—, pres. 1966-68), Muncie C. of C. (past pres.), Conf. Bd., Ind. Acad., Delaware Country Club, Columbia Club (Indpls.), Royal Poinciana Country Club, Naples (Fla.) Yacht Club, Rotary, Naples Nat. Golf Club, Delta Tau Delta. Republican. United Methodist. Home: PO Box 832 Muncie IN 47308-0832 Office: Ball Assocs PO Box 1408 Muncie IN 47308-1408 Office Phone: 765-741-5515.

FISHER, JOHN WILLIAM, civil engineering educator; b. Ancell, Mo., Feb. 15, 1931; s. Nevan August and Nettie (Miller) Fisher; m. Nelda Rae Adams, Oct. 11, 1952; children: John Timothy, Christopher Lee, Elizabeth Renee, Nevan Andrew. BSCE, Washington U., St. Louis, 1956; MS, Lehigh U., 1958, PhD, 1964; PhD (hon.), Swiss Fed. Inst. Tech., Lausanne, Switzerland, 1988. Registered Ill. Asst. bridge rsch. engr. Nat. Acad. Scis., Ottawa, Ill., 1958—61; from rsch. instr. to assoc. prof. Lehigh U., Bethlehem, Pa., 1961—69, prof. civil engring., 1969—, Joseph T. Stuart prof., 1988—2002, prof. emeritus, 2002—, assoc. dir. Fritz Engring. Lab., 1971—85, co-chmn. civil engring., 1984—85, dir. advanced tech. large structural sys. Engring. Rsch. Ctr, 1986—99, co-dir., 1999—2001. Civil col. eminent overseas spkr. Inst. Engrs. Australia, 1983; vis. prof. Swiss Fed. Inst. Tech., Lausanne, Switzerland, 1982, Lausanne, 99; sr. vis. scholar, China, 85; exec. com. Transp. Rsch. Bd., 1997—2000; cons. in field; lectr. in field. Author: Guide to Design Criteria for Bolted Joints, 1974, 2d edit., 1987, Bridge Fatigue Guide, 1977, Fatigue and Fractures in Steel Bridges, 1984, A Fatigue Primer for Structural Engineers, 1998; co-author: Structural Steel Design, 1974; contbr. articles to profl. jours. Directory council mem. Southside Ministries, Bethlehem, 1983—98; bd. dirs. New Bethany Ministries, Bethlehem, 1985—90. 2d lt. U.S. Army, 1951—53. Named Constrn. Man of Yr., ENR, 1987, Engr. of Yr., Rsch. Inst. for Bridge Integrity and Safety, 1989; recipient Alumni Achievement award, Washington U., 1987, John A. Roebling medal, Engrs. Soc. We. Pa., 1987, Frank P. Brown medal, Franklin Inst., 1992, Roy W. Crum Disting. Svc. award, Transp. Rsch. Bd., 2001. Mem.: NSPE, NAE (chmn. NAE/NRC com. internat. constrn. study 1987—88, internat. affairs adv. com. 1988—92, program adv. com. 1992—94, awards com. 2002—), ASCE (hon.; world trade ctr. bldg. performance study team 2001—02, Huber Rsch. prize 1969, Ernest E. Howard award 1979, R.C. Reese Rsch. prize 1981, Cleve. sect. G. Brooks Earnest award 1997, United Engring. Found. John Fritz medal 2000), Am. Assn. State Hwy. Trans. Officials Fed. Hwy. Adminstrn. (Chmns. Lecture award 2004, Blue Ribbon Bridge and Tunnel Security 2002—03), Am. Inst. Steel Constrn. (specification com. 1976—, T.R. Higgins lectr. 1977, Lifetime Achievement Educator award 2001), Internat. Assn. Bridge and Structural Engrs. (Laureate of Internat. Merit award 2001), Am. Welding Soc. (Adams mem.), Am. Ry. Engring. Assn. (emeritus mem. 2003—, steel structures com.), Am. Soc. Engring. Educators. Republican. United Methodist. Avocations: hiking, photography. Office: Lehigh U 117 Atlas St Bethlehem PA 18015-4728 Office Phone: 610-758-5537. Business E-Mail: jwf2@lehigh.edu.

FISHER, JULIA KATHLEEN, library media specialist; b. Tribune, Kans., July 2, 1951; d. Lyle Lee and Ella Louise (Kinlund) Griffin; m. James Dale Fisher Jr., Aug. 11, 1977 (div. Jan. 1991); children: Sarah Kathleen, Benjamin James. BS in Edn., U. Colo., 1973; MS in Edn., Ft. Hays State U., Hays, Kans., 1976, Libr. Media Specialist, 1991. Cert. libr. media specialist K-12, cert. in elem. edn., lang. arts, social sci. and natural sci., Kans. Kindergarten screening coord. Greeley County Schs., Tribune, 1973-88, kindergarten tchr., 1973-89, libr. media specialist, 1990—. Libr. media practicum supr. Ft. Hays State U., 1991, 96. Pianist for children's choir United Meth. Ch., Tribune, 1980—, sec., 1994-96. Named Ch. Woman of Yr., United Meth. ch., 1988; recipient scholarships. Mem. NEA, ALA, Kans.-NEA, Kans. Assn. Sch. Librs., Delta Kappa Gamma (all offices). Avocations: reading, stamp art, gardening, skiing, water-skiing. Home: 3427 Woods Dr Manhattan KS 66503-2166 Office: Manhattan H S East Campus 901 Poyntz Ave Manhattan KS 66502-5456

FISHER, KENNETH LAWRENCE, investment management firm executive; b. San Francisco, Nov. 29, 1950; s. Philip Arthur and Dorothy (White) F.; m. Sherrilyn Ellis, Nov. 4, 1970; children: Clayton, Nathan, Jesse. AB in Econs., Humboldt State U., 1972. Rsch. assoc. Fisher & Co., San Francisco, 1972-73; sole proprietor K.L. Fisher & Co., San Francisco, 1973-76; ptnr. Fisher Investments, San Francisco, 1976-78; chief exec. Fisher Investments, Inc., Burlingame, Calif., 1978-85, Woodside, Calif., 1985—, now chmn., chief investment officer. Mem. adv. bd. Investment Co. Inst., Washington, 1989-92. Author: Super Stocks, 1984, The Wall Street Waltz, 1987, 100 Minds That Made the Market, 1992; outside columnist Forbes Mag., 1984—. Mem. bd. San Mateo County Hist. Assn., San Mateo, Calif., 1990-92. Mem. The Kings Grove, Sons of Norway, Bohemian Club. Republican. Avocation: history of 19th century redwood lumbering. Office: Fisher Investments Inc 13100 Skyline Blvd Woodside CA 94062-4542

FISHER, KIM, artist; b. 1973; BFA, UCLA, 1996; MFA, Otis Coll. Art & Design, 1998. One-woman shows include, China Art Objects, LA, 1999, 2001, Midway Contemporary Art, St. Paul, 2003, John Connelly Presents, NYC, 2004, Shane Campbell, Oak Park, Ill., 2004, Modern Inst., London, 2005, exhibited in group shows at LA-LV-LA, Donna Beam Fine Art Gallery, U. Nev., 1997, The Comestible Compost, Gallery 207, West Hollywood, Calif., 1998, Young & Dumb, ACME, LA, 2000, Platypus, Lawrence Rubin Greenberg Van Doren Fine Art, NY, 2001, Selections, Bolsky Gallery, Otis Coll. Art & Design, LA, 2001, Cancelled Art Fair!, China Art Objects, LA, 2001, The Stray Show, boom, Chgo., 2002, 21 Paintings from LA, Robert V. Fullerton Art Mus., San Bernardino, Calif., 2002, Fair, Royal Coll. Art, London, 2002, Works for Giovanni, China Art Objects, LA, 2003, Still or Sparkling?, John Connelly Presents, NY, 2003, A Red Letter Day, Fredericks Freiser Gallery, NY, 2003, such things I do just to make myself more attractive to you, Peres Projects, LA, 2004, Whitney Biennial, Whitney Mus. Am. Art, 2004. Mailing: c/o John Connelly Presents 526 West 26th St Ste 1003 New York NY 10001*

FISHER, LAURA LANI, physician, medical educator; b. East Orange, NJ, July 13, 1959; d. Hyman Wendell and Rosalie Jane (Joseph) F.; m. Adi Raviv; children: Micaela Sara, Jessica Alana, Gabriella Noa. BA in Biology and Biomed. Ethics, Brown U., 1981, MD, 1984. Intern in internal medicine N.Y. Hosp., 1984-85, resident in internal medicine, 1985-87, chief resident in medicine, 1989-90, dir. Lyme Disease Ctr., 1990—; from clin. to rsch. fellow in infectious diseases Mass. Gen. Hosp., Boston, 1987-89; dir. student health svc. Cornell Med. Coll., N.Y.C., 1990-93, asst. prof. medicine, 1990—. Contbr. articles to profl. jours. Mem. nat. cabinet Israel Bonds-Young Leadership, U.S., 1992-94, mem. city bd. dirs., 1993-94; mem. Anti-Defamation League, N.Y.C., 1993-94. Recipient Rsch. Scientist award NIH, 1988-89. Fellow ACP; mem. AMA, N.Y. Med. Soc., Mass. Med. Soc., Brown Med. Soc., Infectious Disease Soc. Am. Democrat. Jewish. Avocations: painting, sports, sculpture, reading, travel. Office: 1385 York Ave New York NY 10021-3904 Office Phone: 212-717-5920.

FISHER, LAWRENCE EDGAR, market research executive, anthropologist; b. Los Alamos, N.Mex., Jan. 13, 1946; s. Leon H. and Phyllis (Kahn) F.; m. Valerie Joseph, Mar. 25, 1979; children: Lael Sharon, Jonathan Daniel, Matthew Joseph. AB, U. Calif., Berkeley, 1968; MA, Northwestern U., 1969, PhD, 1973; postdoctoral fellow, U. Chgo., 1973—74; postgrad. in bus. adminstrn., U. Pa., 1982. Asst. prof. U. Ill., Chgo., 1974-83; dir. Ethnographic Field Sch. Northwestern U., Evanston, Ill., 1975-78, adj. assoc. prof., 1984-86; dir. client svc. MRCA Info. Svc., Northbrook, Ill., 1983—88; group mgr. Test Mktg. Group, Control Data Corp., Chgo., 1988-89; dir. client svc. Info. Resources, Inc., Chgo., 1989-90, v.p., 1991—94, sr. v.p., 1994—2000, NFO WorldGroup, Chgo., 2000—04; sr. v.p., dir. Global Online Strategy, Synovate, Inc., 2004—. Vis. scholar Stanford U., 1978; vis. asst. prof. U. Mich., Ann Arbor, 1979—80; mem. external adv. bd. A.C. Nielsen Ctr., Grad. Sch. Bus. U. Wis., Madison, 1991—, chmn. bd., 1998—99; founding bd. govs. Interactive Market Rsch. Orgn., 2000—. Author: Colonial Madness, 1985; also numerous articles; mem. editl. rev. bd., Jour. Online Rsch., 2001—. Fellow Woodrow Wilson Found., 1972-73, NIH, 1973-74, NEH, 1975. Mem.: Mktg. Rsch. Assn., Market Rsch. Assn. (annual conf. program com. mem. 2005), Am. Anthrop. Assn., Am. Mktg. Assn. (EXPLOR award com. 2001—, conf. com. Exec. Insights Forum 2003, mem. program com., Mktg. Rsch. Summit 2004). Home: 324 S Euclid Ave Oak Park IL 60302-3508 Office: Synovate Inc 222 S Riverside Plz Chicago IL 60606 E-mail: larry.fisher@synovate.com.

FISHER, LAWRENCE N., lawyer, engineering company executive; BA, U. So. Calif., 1965, JD, 1968. Bar: Calif. 1969. Assoc. ptnr. Hahn & Han, 1969-74; tax counsel Fluor Corp., Calif., 1974-76; sr. tax counsel Fluor Corp., Calif., 1976-78; v.p. adminstrn. Fluor Arabia Ltd., 1978-79; v.p., corp. law and asst. sec. Fluor Corp., Calif., 1984—96, sr. v.p. law, corp. sec., chief legal officer, 1996—. Office: Fluor Corp 1 Enterprise Aliso Viejo CA 92656-2606

FISHER, LEONARD EVERETT, artist, educator, writer; b. NYC, June 24, 1924; s. Benjamin M. and Ray Mera (Shapiro) F.; m. Margery Meskin, Dec. 21, 1952; children: Julie Anne, Susan Abby, James Albert BFA, Yale U., 1949, MFA, 1950. Dean Whitney Art Sch., New Haven, Conn., 1951-53; mem. faculty Paier Art Sch., Hamden, Conn., 1966-78; acad. dean Paier Coll. of Art, Hamden, 1978-82, dean emeritus, 1982—, vis. prof., 1982-87, Fairfield U., Conn., 1983-85. Del. at large White House Conf. Libr. and Info. Svcs., Washington, 1979; lectr. in field, 1957-; mem. adv. bd. MFA program Western Conn. State U., Danbury. Author 90 childrens books; illustrator approximately 260 childrens books; author, illustrator: A Russian Farewell (Nat. Jewish Book award), 1981; designer 10 U.S. postage stamps including 1972 and 1977 U.S. Bicentennial Commemorative issues; paintings and illustrations represented in permanent collections Butler Art Inst., Youngstown, Ohio, Mt. Holyoke Coll., Mass., Union Coll., Schenectady, N.Y., Housatonic Mus., Bridgeport, Conn., New Britain Mus. Am. Art, Conn., Columbus Musuem of Art, Columbus, Ohio, U. Conn., Storrs, U. Minn., Mpls., U. Oreg., Eugene, U. So. Miss., Hattiesburg, Brown U., Providence, Libr. of Congress, Washington, N.Y. Pub. Libr., Mus. Am. Illustration, N.Y.C., Norwalk (Conn.) Transp. Ctr. Trustee Westport Pub. Library, Conn., 1982-89, v.p., 1985-86, pres. 1986-89; founding mem. Westport-Weston Arts Coun., 1969, pres., bd. dirs., 1973-74, trustee, 1969-76; mem. Lowe com. New Britain Mus. Modern Art, Conn. With U.S. Army, 1942-46, NATOUSA, PTO, ETO. Recipient Premio Grafico Internat. Book Fair, Italy, 1968, Medallion, U. So. Miss., 1979, Christopher medal, 1980, Non-Fiction award Childrens Book Guild Washington and the Washington Post, 1989, Regina medal Cath. Libr. Assn., 1991, Kerlan award U. Minn., 1991, Arbuthnot Honor Lectr. citation ALA, 1995, New Eng. Booksellers award for children's lit., 2002, Westport Arts Heritage award, 2003, Pulitzer Art scholarship, 1950; Winchester fellow Yale U., 1949. Mem. Soc. Illustrators, Silvermine Guild (life, trustee 1970-74), Authors Guild N.Y., P.E.N. Home: 7 Twin Bridge Acre Rd Westport CT 06880-1028 Studio: Landmark Sq Ste 204 8 Knight St Norwalk CT 06851 Office Phone: 203-855-8778. E-mail: l.efisher@sbcglobal.net.

FISHER, LESTER EMIL, retired zoo administrator; b. Chgo., Feb. 24, 1921; s. Louis and Elizabeth (Vodicka) F.; m. Wendy Fisher, Jan. 23, 1981; children: Jane Serrita, Katherine Clark. MDV, Iowa State U., 1943. Supr. animal care program Northwestern U. Med. Sch., 1946-47; attending veterinarian Lincoln Park Zoo, Chgo., 1947-62, zoo dir., 1962-92, dir. emeritus, 1992—; owner, dir. Berwyn (Ill.) Animal Hosp., 1947-68. Producer, moderator ednl. closed circuit TV for nat. vet. meetings, 1949-66; asso. prof. dept. biology DePaul U., 1968-98; adj. prof. zoology U. Ill., from 1972 Editor: Brit. Small Animal Jour. and Small Animal Clinician, 1958-72. Mem. citizens com. U. Ill.; chmn. zoo and wildlife div. Morris Animal Found. Served to maj., Vet. Corps AUS, 1943-46. Recipient Alumni Merit award Iowa State U., 1968, Stange award Iowa State U., 1988, Chgo. Superior Pub. Svc. award Chgo. Park Dist., 1973, 92, Laureate Ill. Lincoln Acad., 1993. Mem. Am. Animal Hosp. Assn. (regional dir., outstanding Service award 1969), Am. Vet. Med. Assn., Nat. Recreation and Park Assn., Internat. Union Dirs. Zool. Gardens (v.p. 1980-83, pres. 1983-86), Am. Assn. Zoo Veterinarians (pres. 1966-69), Am. Assn. Zool. Parks and Aquariums (pres. 1972-73, chmn. gorilla species survival plan 1982-92), Chgo. Geographic Soc. (v.p.), Adventures Club (pres. 1971-72), Execs. Club of Chgo. (bd. dirs. 1968-71), Arts Assoc., Chgo. Econs. Club (membership com.), Theta Xi. Home: 3180 N Lake Shore Dr Apt 17H Chicago IL 60657-4868 Home (Summer): PO Box 656 Alexandria Bay NY 13607-0656

FISHER, LINDA ALICE, physician; b. Plainfield, NJ, Dec. 27, 1947; d. Alvin Edwin and Bertha Sophie (Steigmann) F. BA, Douglass Coll., New Brunswick, N.J., 1970; M in Med. Sci., Rutgers U., 1972; MD, Harvard U., 1975; MPH, St. Louis U., 1996. Diplomate Am. Bd. Internal Medicine, Am. Bd. Preventive Medicine. Intern, then resident Jewish Hosp. St. Louis, 1975-78; dir. ambulatory care St. Luke's Hosp., St. Louis, 1978-84; chief med. officer St. Louis County Dept. Health, Clayton, 1984-97, dir. rsch., 1997-2000; project dir. St. Louis STD/HIV Prevention Tng. Ctr., 1995-2000. Chief physician St. Louis Met. Police Dept., 1978-88; clin. instr. medicine Washington U., St. Louis, 1978-94, asst. clin. prof., 1994-2000; asst. clin. prof. medicine St. Louis U., 1979-95, assoc. clin. prof., 1996-2000; adj. faculty health svcs. mgmt. U. Mo., Columbia, 1996, St. Louis U. Sch. Pub. Health, 1993-2000; bd. overseers St. Louis Regional Med. Ctr., 1985-95; cons. Ill. Local Govtl. Law Enforcement Officers Tng. Bd., 1988; dir. Fairfax County Health Dept., 2000-2001. Author short stories; contbr. articles to profl. jours. Chmn. licensure com. Mo. Bd. Registration for Healing Arts, 1983-86; adv. coun. Greater St. Louis Coun. Girl Scouts U.S., 1986-2000. Recipient Disting. Alumni award Douglass Coll., 1992, Publ. award Mo. Pub. Health Assn., 1994, St. Louis Woman of Achievement award KMOX Radio and Suburban Jours., 1995. Fellow ACP; mem. AMA, APHA, Am. Med. Women's Assn. (chpt. pres. 1982-85, Cmty. Svc. award 1992), Am. Med. Writers Assn., Nat. Assn. Med. Communicators (Ken Alvord Cmty. Svc. award 1998), St. Louis Met. Med. Soc. (councilor 1982-84, sec. 1986, editor 1989-90), Med. Soc. No. Va., Internat. Women's Forum, Assn. Documentary Editing. Lutheran. Office: Box 3927 Fairfax VA 22038-3927 Personal E-mail: laf314@earthlink.net. E-mail: lfisher2@cox.net.

FISHER, LINDA J., former federal agency administrator; b. Saginaw, Mich., June 26, 1952; BA, Miami U., Oxford, Ohio, 1974; MBA, George Washington U., 1978; JD, Ohio State U., 1982. Legis. asst. to Hon. Clarence J. Brown, Ohio, 1974-75, Hon. Ralph S. Regula, Ohio, 1976-80; special asst. to asst. adminstr. solid waste and emergency response EPA, 1983-84, chief staff to adminstr., 1985-87, asst. adminstr. policy and evaluation, 1988, asst. adminstr. pesticides and toxic substances Washington, 1989—93, dep. adminr., 2001—03; of counsel Latham & Watkins, 1993—95; v.p. govt. and pub. affairs Monsanto, 1995—2000.

FISHER, LLOYD EDISON, JR., lawyer; b. Medina, Ohio, Oct. 23, 1923; s. Lloyd Edison and Wanda (White) F.; m. Twylla Dawn Peterson, Sept. 11, 1949 (dec. Apr. 1996); children: Karen S., Kirk P. BS, Ohio State U., 1947, JD, 1949. Bar: Ohio 1950. Mem. gen. hearing bd. Ohio Dept. Taxation, 1950-53; trust officer Huntington Nat. Bank, Columbus, 1953-62; ptnr. Porter, Wright, Morris & Arthur and predecessor firm, Columbus, 1962—. Adj. prof. law Ohio State U., Columbus, 1967—69, Columbus, 1984—91. Bd. dirs Wesley Glen Retirement Ctr., 1974-80, 88-95; bd. dirs. Grant/Riverside Hospice, 1997—. Served with AUS, 1943-45. Fellow Am. Coll. Trust and Estate Counsel; mem. ABA, Ohio Bar Assn., Columbus Bar Assn., Order of Coif. Home: 6478 Strathaven Ct E Worthington OH 43085-2985 Office: 41 S High St Columbus OH 43215-6101 Office Phone: 614-227-2285. Business E-Mail: lfisher@porterwright.com.

FISHER, LUCY, film producer; b. N.Y.C., Oct. 2, 1949; d. Arthur Bertram and Naomi (Kislak) F.; m. Douglas Z. Wick, Feb. 16, 1986; children: Sarah, Julia, Tessa. BA, Harvard U., 1971. V.p. prodn. 20th Century Fox, L.A., 1979-80; v.p. worldwide prodns. Zoetrope Studios, Burbank, Calif., 1980-81; v.p., sr. prodn. exec. Warner Bros. Pictures, Burbank, 1981-87, sr. v.p., 1987-89, exec. v.p. prodn., 1989-96; vice chmn. Columbia Tristar Motion Picture Co., Culver City, Calif., 1996-2000; producer Red Wagon Productions, Culver City, Calif., 2000—. Office: Red Wagon Entertainment Hepburn West 10202 Washington Blvd Culver City CA 90232-3119

FISHER, MARGARET CATHARINE, pediatrician, epidemiologist, educator; b. York, Pa., Mar. 1, 1949; d. Robert Foster Fisher and Miriam Arlene (Miller) Coryell. BA summa cum laude, Susquehanna U., 1971; MD, UCLA, 1975. Diplomate sub-bd. pediat. infectious disease Am. Bd. Pediats. Resident in pediat. St. Christopher's Hosp. Children, Phila., 1975—78, fellow pediat. infectious disease, 1978—80, mem. staff, 1980—2000, hosp. epidemiologist, 1980—99; asst. prof. pediat. Temple U., Phila., 1980—86, assoc. prof., 1986—94; assoc. prof. pediat. Drexel U. Coll. Medicine, Phila., 1994—97, prof., 1997—; mem. staff, chmn. dept. pediat. Monmouth Med. Ctr., Long Branch, NJ, 2000—. Cons. Temple U. Hosp., Phila., 1985—95; pres. St. Christopher's Hosp. for Children Med. Staff, 1995—97. Contbr. articles to profl. jours. Fellow: Infectious Diseases Soc. Am., Pediat. Infectious Disease Soc., Am. Acad. Pediat. (editl. bd. Pediatric UPDATE 1993—, com. on infectious diseases 1996—2002, com. on continuing med. edn. 2004—, exec. bd. infectious diseases sect. 2004—); mem.: Infectious Disease Soc. N.J. Avocations: reading, jigsaw puzzles. Office: Monmouth Med Ctr Dept Pediatrics 300 Second Ave Long Branch NJ 07740 Business E-Mail: mfisher@sbhcs.com.

FISHER, MARK JAY, neurologist, neuroscientist, educator; b. Bklyn., Aug. 23, 1949; s. Ralph Aaron and Dorothy Ann (Weissman) F.; m. Janeth Godeau, Aug. 5, 1994. BA in Polit. Sci., UCLA, 1970; MA in Polit. Sci., U. S.D., 1972; MD, U. Cin., 1975; JD, Loyola U., 1997. Diplomate Am. Bd. Psychiatry and Neurology. Intern UCLA Sepulveda VA Hosp., 1975-76; resident UCLA Wadsworth VA Med. Ctr., 1976-79, chief resident, 1979-80; faculty mem., dir. stroke rsch. program U. So. Calif. Sch. of Medicine, L.A., 1980-98, prof. neurology, 1995-98; dir. residency tng. program U. So. Calif. Sch. Medicine, L.A., 1992-96; chmn. dept. neurology U. Calif. at Irvine, Orange, 1998—, prof. neurology and anatomy and neurobiology, 1998—, prof. polit. sci., 2003—; dir. U. Calif. at Irvine Stoke Ctr., 2002—. Editor: Medical Therapy of Acute Stroke, 1989. Recipient Tchr. Investigator award NIH, Bethesda, Md., 1984-89, Program Project grantee, 1994-99. Mem. Am. Acad. Neurology, Am. Neurol. Assn., Am. Heart Assn. (stroke coun.), Am. Polit. Science Assn., Internat. Soc. for Thrombosis and Haemostasis, State Bar of Calif., Am. Polit. Sci. Assn. Office: U Calif Irvine Dept Neurology 101 The City Dr S Orange CA 92868-3201

FISHER, MARK ROBERT, sales and management executive; b. Denver, Oct. 8, 1950; s. Robert James and Louise (Bokan) F.; m. Katherine Elizabeth Hess, May 6, 1978; 1 child, Zachariah Mark. Profl. musician and entertainer pvt. practice, Denver, 1962-82, owner and mgr. thoroughbred horses, 1975-81; sales engr. Pipe Products Co., Denver, 1971-73, v.p., 1973-80, Excellent Sales Co., Denver, 1980-81; territory mgr. Keystone Sales, Denver, 1981-86; distributor sales mgr., regional mgr. Keystone Valve U.S.A., Houston, 1986-87; br. mgr. Keystone Sales, Lenexa, Kans., 1987-91; sales mgr. Midwest region Keystone Internat., Lenexa, Kans., 1991-95; regional mgr. Performance Valve & Controls (now Harley Valve & Instrument), Broken Arrow, Okla., 1995-2000, Flowserve (formerly Harley Valve & Instrument), Broken Arrow, 2000—03; pres. Excellent Sales Co., Lenexa, Kans., 2003—. Bd. mem., Excellent Sales, Denver, 1981-84; owner/mem., Colo. Racing Commn., Denver, 1977-80; mem., Rocky Mt. Plumbing & Heating Assn., Denver, 1971-83. Author: (book) Champagne Canyons, 1968; writer songs, poems. Mem. Oak Hill Homes Assn., Lenexa, Kans., 1988—; charter mem. Sons of Am. Legion, Golden, Colo., 1956-84. Mem. Nat. Space Soc., Instrumentation, Sys., and Automation Soc. (sr., chpt. v.p. 1985-86, show chmn. 1983-85, membership chmn. 2004—, mktg. chmn. 2004—), 10-K Club, Club France, PGA Tour Ptnrs., U.S. Golf Assn., BMW Car Club Am., Smithsonian Inst., Spotlighters (pres. 1997-98), Planetary Soc., Nat. Writer's Union, Internat. Press Assn., Film Soc. Greater Kansas City, Halfway to Hollywood, Oak Country Club. Avocations: golf, music, reading, computers, travel. Fax: 913-894-1480. Office Phone: 913-894-1470. E-mail: mark@excellentkc.com.

FISHER, MICHAEL D., retail executive; Bachelors Degree, Univ. Fla. With Maas Brothers Dept. Stores, Robinson's Dept. Stores, The May Co.; exec. vice-pres. Stein Mart Stores, 1993; pres., CEO Stein Mart, Inc., 2003—. Office: Stein Mart Inc 1200 Riverplace Blvd Jacksonville FL 32207 Office Phone: 904-398-9945.*

FISHER, MICHAEL ELLIS, physicist, educator, chemist; b. Trinidad, W.I., Sept. 3, 1931; m. Sorrel Castillejo; children: Caricia J., Daniel S., Martin J., Matthew P.A. BS with 1st class honors in Physics, King's Coll., London, 1951, PhD, 1957; DSc (hon.), Yale U., 1987, Tel Aviv U., 1992. Lectr. math. RAF, 1952-53; lectr. theoretical physics King's Coll., 1958-62, reader physics, 1962-64; prof. physics U. London, 1965-66; prof. chemistry and math. Cornell U., 1966-73, Horace White prof. chemistry, physics and math., 1973-89, chmn. dept. chemistry, 1975-78; Disting. prof. Inst. for Phys. Sci. and Tech. U. Md., 1987—, Regents prof. Inst. for Phys. Sci. & Tech., 1993—. Guest investigator Rockefeller Inst., 1963-64; vis. prof. applied physics Stanford U., 1970-71; Buhl lectr. theoretical physics Carnegie-Mellon U., 1971; Richtmyer Meml. lectr. Am. Assn. Physics Tchrs., 1973; S. H. Klosk lectr. NYU, 1975; 17th F. London Meml. lectr. Duke U., 1975; Walker-Ames prof. U. Wash., Seattle, 1977; Loeb lectr. physics Harvard U., 1979; vis.prof. physics MIT, 1979; Welsh Found. lectr. in physics U. Toronto, Ont., Can., 1979; 21st Alpheus Smith lectr. Ohio State U., 1982; Fairchild scholar Calif. Inst. Tech., 1984; Cherwell-Simon lectr., vis. prof. Oxford U., 1985; Schlapp scholar Edinburgh U., 1987; Marker lectr. Pa. State U., 1988, Nat. Sci. Coun. lectr., Taiwan, 1989; Hamilton Meml. lectr. Princeton U., 1990, 65th J. W. Gibbs lectr. Am. Math. Soc., 1992; E. U. Condon lectr. U. Colo., 1992; M. S. Green Meml. lectr. Temple U., 1992; R&B Sackler Disting. lectr. in solid state physics Tel Aviv U., 1992; 1st Lars Onsager lectr., Norway, 1993; Phi Beta Kappa vis. scholar, 1994; Lennard-Jones lectr. Royal Soc. Chemistry, 1995; Joseph O. Hirschfelder Prize lectr. U. Wis., 1995; Gilbert Newton Lewis Meml. lectr. U. Calif., Berkeley, 1995; George Fisher Baker lectr. chemistry Cornell U., 1997; distng. lectr. in theoretical Physics, The Techniron, 2004. Author (with D.M. MacKay): Analogue Computing at Ultra-High Speed,

1962; author: The Nature of Critical Points, 1964, The Theory of Equilibrium Critical Phenomena, 1967; assoc. editor Jour. Math. Physics, 1965—68, 1972—75, 1986—89, mem. adv. bd. Jour. Theoretical Biology, 1969—82, Chem. Physics, 1972—84, Discrete Math., 1971—78, Jour. Statis. Physics, 1978—81, mem. editl. bd. Comms. Math. Phys., 1984—2000. Recipient award in phys. and math. scis. N.Y. Acad. Scis., 1978, Guthrie medal and prize Inst. Physics, London, 1980, Wolf prize in physics, 1980, Michelson-Morely award Case Western Res. U., 1982, Boltzmann medal IUPAP, 1983, Hirschfelder prize U. Wis., 1995; Guggenheim fellow, 1970-71, 78-79. Fellow: AAAS, Kings Coll. London, Am. Phys. Soc., Phys. Soc. London, Am. Acad. Arts and Scis., Royal Soc. Edinburgh (hon.), N.Y. Acad. Scis. (hon.), Royal Soc. London (regional editor 1989—93, v.p. 1993—95); mem.: NAS (fgn. assoc.), Royal Norwegian Soc. Scis. and Letters (fgn. assoc.), Indian Acad. Scis., Brazilian Acad. Scis. (fgn. assoc.), Math. Assn. Am., Soc. Indsl. and Applied Math., Am. Philos. Soc., Am. Chem. Soc. Office: U Md Inst Phys Sci & Tech College Park MD 20742-0001 Office Phone: 301-405-4819. E-mail: xpectnil@ipst.umd.edu.

FISHER, MILES MARK, IV, education educator, religious studies educator, minister; b. Huntington, W.Va., Sept. 25, 1932; s. Miles Mark and Ada Virginia (Foster) F. BA, Va. Union U., 1954, M.Div., 1959; MA, N.C. Central U., 1968; D.Min., Howard U., 1978. Ordained to ministry Baptist Ch., 1961; tchr. pub. schs. Durham, N.C., 1959-67; assoc. min. White Rock Bapt. Ch., Durham, N.C., 1959-65; asst. prof. edn., counselor Norfolk (Va.) State U., 1967-69; cons. Model Cities Area of Recreation, Norfolk, 1968-69; exec.-sec., CEO Nat. Assn. Equal Opportunity in Higher Edn., Washington, 1969-78; spl. cons. Inst. for Services to Edn., Washington, 1969-70; vis. asst. prof. Sch. Divinity Howard U., 1978-80; staff dir., com. clk. Com. of Whole, Council of D.C., Washington, 1979-83; spl. asst. to v.p. acad. affairs U. D.C., Washington, 1983-84, dir. policy rev. and analysis Office of the Bd. of Trustees, 1985-88, exec. dir. Office of the Bd. of Trustees, 1989-90, interim pres., 1990-91, disting. U. prof., 1991—. Chaplain counselor Lincoln Hosp. Sch. Nursing, Durham, N.C., 1962-67; chaplain Fisher Funeral Parlor, Durham, 1963-67; mem. task force employment of minority populations Nat. Recreation and Park Assn., 1970-71; mem. task force on edn. and Vietnam Era vet. VA, 1971-72; mem. steering com. U.S. Office of Edn. Common Core Data for the 70's, 1971-78, Congl. Black Caucus Nat. Policy Conf. on Black Edn., 1972; mem. Nat. task force on Student Financial Aid Problems, 1974-75; bd. trustees Consortium of U. of the Washington Met. Area, 1990-91; bd. dirs. Washington Rsch. Libr. Consortium, 1990-91. Bd. dirs. Cooperative Coll. Registry, 1973-75; mem. adv. bd. Four-Year Servicemen's Opportunity Coll., 1974-77; mem. adv. com. to bd. dirs. Nat. Student Ednl. Fund, 1974-78; v.p. bd. dirs. Reading is Fundamental Program, 1977-79, Vis. Nurse Assn., 1974-80; bd. dirs. D.C. Citizens for Better Public Edn., 1977, pres., 1981-83; bd. dirs. Voice Informed Community Expression, pres., 1982-84; trustee Va. Union U., 1983-85, Shaw U. Div. Sch., 1982-88. Mem. ACA, Am. Assn. Higher Edn., Am. Acad. Polit. and Social Scis., Am. Acad. Religion, Assn. Multicultural Counseling and Devel., Assn. Spiritual Ethical and Religious Values in Counseling, Am. Soc. Ch. History, Internat. Alumni Assn. Va. Union U. (pres. 1983-85), Am. Tennis Assn. (life), Assn. for Study of Afro-Am. Life and History (life), Assn. for Study of Higher Edn., U.S. Tennis Assn. (life). Home: 4444 Connecticut Ave NW Apt 402 Washington DC 20008-2319 Office: PO Box 2340 Washington DC 20013-2340 Office Phone: 202-744-8141. Personal E-mail: milesmfisher@yahoo.com.

FISHER, MORTON POE, JR., lawyer; b. Balt., Aug. 17, 1936; s. Morton Poe Sr. and Adelaide (Block) F.; m. Ann P. Fisher, Aug. 12, 1962; children: Stephen N., Marjorie P. AB, Dartmouth Coll., Hanover, N.H., 1958; LLB, Yale U., 1961. Bar: Md. 1961, D.C. 1961. Law clk. to presiding justice U.S. Dist. Ct. Md., Balt., 1961-62; assoc. Piper & Marbury, 1962-68; asst. gen. counsel Rouse Co., 1968-73; ptnr. Frank, Bernstein, Conaway & Goldman, Balt., 1973-92; mng. ptnr. Ballard Spahr Andrews & Ingersoll, Balt., 1992—2004. Faculty mem. U. Md. Law Sch., 1978-87. Mem. Balt. County Econ. Devel. Commn., 1988-90, Mayor's Adv. Commn., Balt. City, Risk Mgmt. Com. Balto City, 1999; bd. dirs. Balt. Downtown Partnership, 1998-2004, Johns Hopkins U. Real Estate Inst., 2004; dean U. of Shopping Ctrs., 1998-99; trustee U. Md. Balt. Found., 2003—. Mem. ABA (vice chmn. real property divsn 1990-92, chmn. sect. real property, probate and trust law 1993-94), Am. Coll. Real Estate Lawyers (pres. 1988-89), Am. Coll. Constrn. Lawyers, Am. Law Inst., Anglo-Am. Real Property Inst., Internat. Coun. Shopping Ctrs. (co-chmn. law conf. 1995-97). Office: Ballard Spahr Andrews & Ingersoll LLP 300 E Lombard St Ste 1800 Baltimore MD 21202-6739 Office Phone: 410-528-5615. Business E-Mail: fisher@ballardspahr.com.

FISHER, NANCY DEBUTTS, library director; b. Pitts., Apr. 10, 1945; d. Jacob John DeButts and Marie Christine Grills; m. Bruce C. Fisher, May 29, 1971. BS, Cleve. State U., 1968; MSLS, Case Western Res. U., 1973. Reference libr. Cleveland Heights-University Heights Pub. Libr., 1968-79; mgr. Beachwood (Ohio) br. Cuyahoga County Pub. Libr., 1980-90; dir. Wickliffe (Ohio) Pub. Libr., 1990—. Mem. adv. coun. Wickliffe United Way, 1991—2001; key communicator Wickliffe City Schs., 1992; mem. comm. com. Lake County United Way, 2002—, mem. cabinet, 2003—04; mem. Wickliffe Cmty. Adv. Panel, 1995—; grad. Leadership Lake County, 2003; bd. dirs. Wickliffe Civic Ctr., Inc., 1999—, pres. bd. dirs., 2004—; mem. adv. com. Holden Aboretum Warren H. Corning Libr., 1999—2002; mem. alumni planning com. Case Western Res. U. Libr. Sci., 1997—; mem. Lake Hosp. Sys., women's health adv. bd., 1999—. Mem.: ALA, Cleve. Area Met. Libr. Sys. (bd. dirs. 1994—96, mem. pers. com. 2003—), Ohio Libr. Coun., Lake County C. of C. Bd., Wickliffe C. of C. (v.p. 1998—99, pres. 2001—03, Civic Leader of Yr. 1999), Rotary (pres. 1992—94, chair charity ball 2002—03). Home: 939 Stuart Dr South Euclid OH 44121-3425 Office: Wickliffe Pub Libr 1713 Lincoln Rd Wickliffe OH 44092-2499 Office Phone: 440-944-6010. Business E-Mail: nfisher@wickliffe.lib.oh.us.

FISHER, NANCY LOUISE, pediatrician, geneticist, retired nurse; b. Cleve., July 4, 1944; d. Nelson Leopold and Catherine (Harris) F.; m. Larry William Larson, May 30, 1976 (div. Oct. 2000); 1 child, Jonathan Raymond. Student, Notre Dame Coll., Cleve., 1962-64; BSN, Wayne State U., 1967; postgrad., Calif. State U., Hayward, 1971-72; MD, Baylor Coll. of Medicine, 1976; M in Pub. Health, U. Wash., 1982, certificate in ethics, 1993. Diplomate Am. Bd. Pediatrics, Am. Bd. Med. Genetics. RN coronary care unit and med. intensive care unit Highland Gen. Hosp., Oakland, Calif., 1970-72; RN coronary care unit Alameda (Calif.) Hosp., 1972-73; intern in pediatrics Baylor Coll. of Medicine, Houston, 1976-77, resident in pediatrics, 1977-78; attending physician, pediatric clinic Harborview Med. Ctr., Seattle, 1980-81; staff physician children and adolescent health care clinic Columbia Health Ctr., Seattle, 1981-87, founder, dir. of med. genetics clinic, 1984-89; maternal child health policy cons. King County div. Seattle King County Dept Pub. Health, 1983-85; dir. genetic svcs. Va. Mason Clinic, 1986-89; dir. med. genetic svcs. Swedish Hosp., 1989-94; pvt. practice Seattle, 1994-97; med. cons. supr. office of managed care Wash. State Dept. Social and Health Svcs., Olympia, 1996-97; med. dir. Medicaid Dept. of Social and Health Svcs., Wash., 1997-99; assoc. med. dir. Govt. Programs Regence Blue Shield, 1999; med. dir. Regence Blue Shield, 2000—02; chief med. officer Wash. State Health Care Authority, 2003—. Nurses aide psychiatry Sinai Hosp., Detroit, 1966—67; charge nurse Women's Hosp., Cleve., 1967; rsch. asst. to Dr. Shelly Liss, 76; with Baylor Housestaff Assn., Baylor Coll. Medicine, 1980—81; clin. asst. prof. grad. sch. nursing U. Wash., Seattle, 1981—85, clin. asst. prof. dept. pediat., 1982—92, clin. assoc. prof. dept. pediat., 1992—; com. appointments include Seattle CCS Cleft Palate Panel, 1984—97; bd. dirs., first v.p. King County Assn. Sickle Cell Disease, 1985—86, acting pres., 1986, pres., 1986—87; hosp. affiliation include Childrens Orthopedic Hosp. and Med. Ctr., Seattle, 1981—, Virginia Mason Hosp., Seattle, 1985—89, Harborview Hosp., Seattle, 1986—89. Contbr. articles to profl. jours. Active Seattle Urban League, 1982-96, 101 Black Women, 1986-94; bd. dirs. Seattle Sickle Cell Affected Family Assn., 1984-85, Am. Heart Assn., 2001—; mem. People to People Citizen Ambassador Group; sec. Health and Human Svcs. Com. on Infant Mortality, 1993—2003; mem. Twins Com. Inst. of Medicine, 1995-2000; Evaluation, Rsch. and Planning Group Ethical Legal and Social Implications Nat. Human Gerome Rsch. Inst., 1997-2000. Served to lt. USN Nurse Corps, 1966-70. Fellow Am. Coll. Medicine Genetics (founder); mem. Am. Acad. Physician Execs., Student Governing Body and Graduating Policy Com. Baylor Coll. Medicine (founding mem. 1973-76), Loans and Scholarship Com. Baylor Coll. Medicine (voting mem. 1973-76), Am. Med. Student Assn., Student Nat. Med. Assn., Admission Com. Baylor Coll. Medicine (voting mem. 1974-76), AMA, Am. Med. Women's Assn., Am. Acad. Pediatrics, Am. Pub. Health Assn., Am. Soc. Human Genetics, Nat. Speakers Assn., Wash. State Assn. Black Providers of Health Care, Soc. Health and Human Values, Wash. State Soc. Pediatrics, Seattle C. of C. (mem. Leadership Tomorrow 1988—), Wash. State Med. Assn. (women in medicine com., interspity. coun., fin. com.), Sigma Gamma Rho, Phi Delta Epsilon. Office: Wash State HCA 676 Woodland Sq Loop SE MS-42701 Olympia WA 98504-2701 Office Phone: 360-923-2709. Business E-Mail: nfis107@hca.wa.gov.

FISHER, NEAL FLOYD, religious organization administrator; b. Washington, Ind., Apr. 4, 1936; s. Floyd Russell and Florence Alice (Williams) F.; m. Ila Alexander, Aug. 18, 1957; children: Edwin Kirk, Julia Bryn. AB, DePauw U., 1957, LHD (hon.), 1982; MDiv, Boston U., 1960, PhD, 1966; STD, MacMurray Coll., Jacksonville, Ill., 1991; DD, Coe Coll., 1994. Ordained to ministry United Meth. Ch., 1958; pastor 1st United Meth. Ch., Revere, Mass., 1960-63, North Andover, Mass., 1963-68; planning assoc. United Meth. Bd. Global Ministries, N.Y.C., 1968-73, dir. planning, 1973-77; assoc. dean, asst. prof. theology and society Boston U. Sch. Theology, 1977-80; pres., prof. theology and society Garrett-Evang. Theol. Sem., Evanston, Ill., 1980-2001, pres. emeritus, sr. scholar, 2001—. Mendenhall lectr. DePauw U., Greencastle, Ind., 1982, Willson lectr., Nashville, 1983, Voigt lectr. McKendree Coll., 1984, McKendree Blair lectr. MacMurray Coll., 1986, Henry Martin Loud lectr. U. Mich., Ann Arbor, 1987; Wright lectr. Morningside Coll., 1991, Bransford lectr., 1999; chaplain, preacher, Chautauqua, N.Y., 1984, 88, Lakeside, Ohio, 1996; mem. theol. edn. commn. United Meth. Ch., 1992-2000, former mem. univ. senate; mem. bd. of ordained ministry No. Ill. Conf. United Meth. Ch.; chmn. com. on acad. affairs DePauw U. Bd. Trustees. Author: Parables of Jesus: Glimpses of the New Age, 1979, rev. edit., 1990, Context for Discovery, 1980, Parables of Jesus: Glimpses of God's Reign, 1990; contbg. editor: Truth and Tradition: A Conversation about the Future of United Methodist Theological Education, 1995. Trustee DePauw U., Greencastle, Ind, 1996-2000; mem. bd. visitors Boston U. Sch. Theology, 2002—. Recipient Disting. Alumnus award Boston U. Sch. Theology, 1985, Disting. Alumni citation DePauw U., 1993; Jacob Sleeper fellow, 1960-61. Mem. Assn. United Meth. Scis., Assn. Chgo. Theol. Schs. (pres. 1985-87, 95-97). Mem. United Methodist Ch. Home: 2008 Elmore Pond Road Wolcott VT 05680 E-mail: nfisher@garrett.edu.

FISHER, NEAL FOSTER, artist, writer; b. Indpls., Oct. 20, 1929; s. Willard Farmer and Ann Mae Mabbitt. Author, artist self employed, Canon City, Colo., 1966—97. Author: (book) Before the Dawn, 2003. Vol. Fremont Ctr. Arts, Canon City, Colo., 1968—2003. Pvt. U.S. Army, 1951. Avocations: painting, photography. Home: 431 Macon Ave 208 Canon City CO 81212 Office: Farmer's Nymph Prodns 431 Macon Ave 208 Canon City CO 81212 Office Phone: 719-269-1468. E-mail: nealfisher@msn.com.

FISHER, ORA T., lawyer; BS in Econ., Univ. Pa., 1984; JD cum laude, Univ. Mich., 1991. Bar: Calif. 1991. Internal cons. and public fin. banking officer JPMorgan, NYC; atty. Latham & Watkins LLP, San Francisco, 1991—97, atty., Silicon Valley office Menlo Park, 1997—2004, mng. ptnr. Silicon Valley office, 2004—, and co-chair, venture & tech. practice group. Mem.: ABA, San Francisco Bar Assn., State Bar of Calif. Office: Latham & Watkins LLP Silicon Valley Office 135 Commonwealth Dr Menlo Park CA 94025

FISHER, PAUL CARY, writing supplies company executive; b. Lebanon, Kans., Oct. 10, 1913; s. Carey A. Fisher and Alice Bales-Fisher; children: Terry Hough, Cary Fisher, Pomm Hepner, Marteen Moore, Morgan Fisher, Scott Fisher. BS, Kans. State U., 1939. Gen. mgr. Butter-Nut Bakery, Cedar Rapids, Iowa, 1936-38, Aetna Ball Bearing Co., Chgo., 1942—45; pres. Fisher-Armour Mfg. Co., Chgo., 1945-50; owner Fisher Space Pen Co., Boulder City, Nev., 1950—. Dem. presdl. candidate, N.H. Primary, 1960. Named Small Bus. Person of Yr., State of Nev., U.S. Small Bus. Adminstrn., 1980, Exporter of Yr., Gov.'s Office State of Nev., 1995, 97, Inventor of Yr. Nev. Tech. Coun., 1998, Pres.'s Inventor award, Nev. Desert Rsch., 2001. Mem. Boulder city Rotary, Phi Kappa Phi. Achievements include invention of pressurized space pen for NASA. Avocations: handball, tennis, chess. Office: Fisher Pen Co 711 Yucca St Boulder City NV 89005-1905 Office Phone: 702-293-3100. E-mail: fisher@spacepen.com.

FISHER, PETER R., investment company executive, former federal agency administrator; b. 1956; 2 children. BA in History, Harvard U., 1980, JD, 1985. With Bank for Internat. Settlements, Basle, Switzerland, 1989—90; sr. v.p. fgn. exch. Fed. Res. Bank N.Y., N.Y.C., 1993—94, exec. v.p., 1994—2001; under sec. domestic fin. US Dept. Treasury, Washington, 2001—03; mng. dir. BlackRock, Inc., N.Y.C., 2004—. Bd. dirs. Securities Investor Protection Corp.; chair Advanced Counterfeit Deterrence Steering Com. Recipient Disting. Svc. award, Bond Market Assn., 2004. Office: BlackRock Inc 40 E 52nd St New York NY 10022

FISHER, PHILIP J., English language educator, literature educator; b. Pitts., Oct. 11, 1941; s. Leo and Anna (Walker) F.; 1 child, Mark. BA, U. Pitts., 1963; AM, Harvard U., 1966, PhD, 1970. Asst. prof. U. Va., Charlottesville, 1970-72, Brandeis U., Waltham, Mass., 1973-80, assoc. prof. English and Am. lit., 1980-87; Reid prof. English and Harvard U. Coll. prof., Cambridge, Mass., 2005—; prof. Brandeis U., Waltham, Mass., 1987—; chair dept. English Harvard U., Cambridge, Mass., 1990-93, prof., 2005—. Asst. prof. Andrew Mellon Harvard U., 1976-77; vis. prof. Free U. Berlin, 1981, Yale U., 1985-86, U. Konstanz, W.Ger., 1986, Harvard U., 1986-87; adv. bd. Inst. Advanced Study, Berlin, 1994—. Author: Making Up Society, 1981, Hard Facts: Setting and Form in the American Novel, 1984 (finalist Nat. Book Critics Circle prize for criticism), Making and Effacing Art: Modern American Art in a Culture of Museums, 1991, The New American Studies, 1991, Wonder, the Rainbow and the Aesthetics of Rare Experiences, 1998, Still The New World, American Literature in a Culture of Creative Destruction, 1999 (Truman Capote prize for literary criticism, 2000), The Vehement Passions, 2002. Recipient Howard Mumford Jones prize, Harvard U., 1971; fellow, Inst. Advanced Study, Berlin, 1987—88, Stanford Ctr. for Advanced Study in Behavioral Scis., 2003—04; Nat. Endowment Humanities fellow, 1972—73, Mellon fellow, 1976—77, Exxon fellow program in sci., tech. and soc., MIT, 1984—85, Guggenheim fellow, 1996—97, sr. fellow, Getty Mus., 1998—99. Office: Harvard U Dept English Barker Ctr Cambridge MA 02138 Business E-Mail: PJFisher@fas.harvard.edu.

FISHER, PIERRE JAMES, JR., physician; b. Chgo., Oct. 29, 1931; s. Pierre James and Evelyn F.; m. Carol Ann Walton, Mar. 16, 1951; children: James Walton, David Alan, Steven Edward, Teresa Ann. Student, Taylor U., 1949-51, Ball State U., 1951-52; MD, Ind. U., 1956. Diplomate Am. Bd. Surgery. Intern U.S. Naval Hosp., San Diego, 1956-57, resident in surgery, 1957-61; pvt. practice specializing in surgery Surgeons Inc., Marion, Ind., 1965—, pres., 1977—; mem. staff Marion Gen. Hosp., chief staff, 1970. Trustee Meth. Hosp., Indpls., 1972-94; bd. dirs. Charlotte County Cultural Ctr. Served with USN, 1956-65. Recipient Physicians Recognition award AMA, 1974, 77, 80, 83, 89. Fellow ACS; mem. AMA, Grant County Med. Soc. (pres. 1980), Marion Area C. of C. (v.p. 1979-81), N.Am. Med. Golf Assn. (v.p. 1989-90, pres. 1991-93), Rotary (pres. Marion 1983-84, Dist. 656 Disting. Svc. award 1989), Kingsway Country Club (bd. dirs., pres. 1997-99), Royal Order of Ponce de Leon Conquistadors (treas. 2000-). Methodist. Home: 11250 SW Essex Dr Lake Suzy FL 34269 Office: Surgeons Inc 330 N Wabash Ave Ste 450 Marion IN 46952-2600 Office Phone: 765-662-8303. E-mail: fpjfisher@aol.com.

FISHER, RAYMOND CORLEY, federal judge; b. Oakland, Calif., July 12, 1939; s. Raymond Henry and Mary Elizabeth (Corley) Fisher; m. Nancy Leigh Fairchilds, Jan. 22, 1961; children: Jeffrey, Amy. BA, U. Calif., Santa Barbara, 1961; LLB, Stanford U., 1966. Bar: Calif. 1967, U.S. Supreme Ct. 1967. Law clk. to Hon. J. Skelly Wright U.S. Ct. Appeals (D.C. cir.), Washington, 1966—67; law clk. to Hon. William J. Brennan U.S. Supreme Ct., Washington, 1967—68; ptnr. Tuttle & Taylor, L.A., L.A., 1968—88, Heller, Ehrman, White & McAuliffe, L.A., 1988—97; assoc. atty. gen. U.S. Dept. of Justice, Washington, 1997—99; judge U.S. Ct. Appeals (9th cir.), 1999—. Pres.: Stanford Law Rev., 1965—66. Dir. Constl. Rights Found., L.A., 1978—, pres., 1983—87, L.A. City Bd. Civil Svc. Commn., 1987—88; dep. gen. counsel Christopher Commn., L.A., 1991—92; pres. L.A. City Bd. Police Commrs., 1996—97; dir. Western Justice Ctr. Found., 2000—; spl. asst. to Gov. of Calif., 1975. With USAR, 1957—64. Fellow: Am. Bar Found., Am. Coll. Trial Lawyers; mem.: ABA, Am. Law Inst., L.A. County Bar Assn., Calif. State Bar, Fed. Bar Assn. (exec. com. 1990—96), Chancery Club, Order of Coif. Office: US Ct Appeals 125 S Grand Ave Rm 400 Pasadena CA 91105

FISHER, RICHARD FORREST, research scientist, editor-in-chief; b. Champaign, Ill., May 15, 1941; S. Richard Forrest Fisher and Hannah Elizabeth Ponath; m. Karen Dangerfield, Sept. 4, 1959; children: William Forrest, Marilu, Kevin Royden. BS, U. Ill., 1963; MS, Cornell U., 1967, PhD, 1968. Rsch. scientist Can. Forestry Svc., Sault Sainte Marie, Ont., 1968-69; asst. prof. forestry U. Ill., Urbana, 1969-72; assoc. prof. U. Toronto, Ont., 1972-77; prof. U. Fla., Gainesville, 1977-82; prof., head dept. forest resources Utah State U., Logan, 1982-90; prof., head dept. forest sci. Tex. A&M U., 1990-96, prof., 1996-99; dir. rsch. Temple-Inland, Diboll, Tex., 1999—. Author: (with others) Ecology and Management of Forest Soil, 3d edit.; contbr. articles to profl. jours. Fellow Soc. Am. Foresters, Soil Sci. Soc. Am. (co-editor in chief Forest Ecology and Mgmt.); mem. Internat. Soc. Tropical Foresters, Ecol. Soc. Am., Nat. Assn. Profl. Forestry Schs. and Colls. (pres. 1994-96), Internat. Assn. Round Dance Tchrs. (gen. chmn. 1997-99). Democrat. Avocations: round dance cuer, tchr. Home: 1004 Augusta Dr Lufkin TX 75901-7412 Office: Temple-Inland Forest PO Drawer N Diboll TX 75941 Office Phone: 936-829-1475. Business E-Mail: dickfisher@templeinland.com.

FISHER, RICHARD N., lawyer; b. LA, Oct. 28, 1943; BA, U. Redlands, 1965; MA, U. Wis., 1966; JD, U. Calif., Berkeley, 1969. Bar: Calif. 1970. Ptnr. O'Melveny & Myers, L.A., 1969—2003; ret., 2003. Editor, Calif. Law Rev., 1967-69. Mem. and chmn. bd. trustees U. Redlands. Office: O'Melveny & Myers 400 S Hope St Los Angeles CA 90071-2899 Office Phone: 213-430-7222. E-mail: Dick.Fisher@OMM.com.

FISHER, RICHARD PAUL, chemist; b. Alameda, Calif., Feb. 10, 1948; s. George Paul and Mary Augusta (Caldeira) F.; m. Melinda Ruth Maledy, June 2, 1973. BS, U. Calif., Berkeley, 1970; PhD, U. Calif., Davis, 1974. Rsch. chemist U.S. Borax Rsch. Corp., Anaheim and Boron, Calif., 1974-79, sr. rsch. chemist Boron, 1979-87, asst. mgr., 1987-91, mgr. chem. rsch. Anaheim, Valencia, Calif., 1991-93, rsch. fellow Valencia, Boron, 1993—. Contbr. articles to profl. jours. Kiwanis scholar, 1966-70; U. Calif. Berkeley Alumni scholar, 1966; NDEA fellow, 1971-73. Mem. Am. Chem. Soc. Home: 8850 Hickory Ave Hesperia CA 92345-3845 Office: US Borax Inc Pilot Plant Ctr 14486 Borax Rd Boron CA 93516-2017 Office Phone: 760-762-7167. E-mail: richard.fisher@borax.com.

FISHER, RICHARD S., lawyer; b. Bklyn., Oct. 1, 1937; s. Morris S. and Fanny (Saidel) F.; m. Rosalea S. Sandler, Feb. 4, 1968; children: Jodi A., Michael B. BS, Pa. State U., 1959; JD, Cornell U., 1962; LLM in Taxation, George Washington U., 1968. Bar: Pa. 1964, Conn. 1971, U.S. Tax Ct. Tax law specialist IRS, Washington, 1965-68; tax atty. Crucible Steel Corp., Pitts., 1968, Colt Industries Inc, N.Y.C., 1968-70; ptnr. Hirschberg, Pettengill, Strong & Nagle, Greenwich and Stamford, Conn., 1970-78, Whitman & Ransom, N.Y.C., Greenwich and Stamford, Conn., 1978-79, Woyke, Fisher & Field, Stamford, Conn., 1979-81, Copelon, Schiff & Zangari, New Haven, Conn., 1981-83; sole practice Stamford, 1983-87; ptnr. Fisher & Stein, Stamford, 1987-96; sole practice Stamford, 1996-98; ptnr. Cacace, Tusch & Santagata, Stamford, 1998—. Pres. Jr. Achievement S.W. Conn., 1978-80; v.p. Stamford Symphony Soc., 1986-91; v.p. Estate Planning Coun., Lower Fairfield County, 1989-93, pres., 1993-94; bd. dirs. Alzheimer's Assn., Fairfield County, 1991-2000, v.p., 1994-96, pres., 1996-98; bd. dirs. Alzheimer's Assn. So. Conn. chpt., 2000-2002, Conn. chpt., 2002-, sec., 2004-; bd. dirs. Jewish Home for the Elderly, Fairfield County, 1992—, rec. sec., 1994-96, vice-chmn., 1996-2002. 1st lt. U.S. Army, 1962—64, capt. USAR, 1964—68. Mem. ABA (taxation sect. 1968-97, real property, probate and trust law sect. 1995—), Conn. Bar Assn. (vice chmn. tax sect. 1991-94, chmn. 1994-96, exec. com. elder law sect. 1991—, exec. com. estates and probate sect. 1998—), Nat. Acad. Elder Law Attys. Office: Cacace Tusch and Santagata 777 Summer St Stamford CT 06901-0859 Office Phone: 203-327-2000. E-mail: rfisher@lawcts.com.

FISHER, RICHARD WELTON, investor, ambassador, bank executive; b. LA, Mar. 18, 1949; s. Leslie Welton and Magnhild (Fisher; m. Nancy Collins, Sept. 8, 1973; children: Andersen, Alison, James, Texana. BA cum laude, Harvard U., 1971; student, Oxford (Eng.) U., 1972-73; MBA, Stanford U., 1975. Asst. to Robert Roosa Brown Bros. Harriman & Co., N.Y.C., 1975-77, sr. mgr., 1983-87; exec. asst. to sec. U.S. Treasury, Washington, 1977-79; mng. ptnr. Fisher Capital Mgmt., Dallas, 1987-98, Fisher Ewing Ptnrs. (Value Ptnrs., Ltd.), Dallas, 1989-98; dep. U.S. trade rep. Exec. Office of the Pres., Washington, 1998-2001; vice-chmn. Kissinger McLarty Assocs., Washington, 2002—05; pres., CEO Fed. Res. Bank Dallas, 2005—. Chmn. Stanford U. Sch. Bus. Trust, Palo Alto, Calif., 1982-84, Am. Assembly, N.Y., 2003—; adj. prof. L.B.J. Sch., U. Tex., 1996-98; Weatherhead fellow Harvard U., 2001. Bd. dirs., mem. exec. com. Dallas Mus. Art, 1985-89; bd. dirs. Goodwill Industries Dallas, 1989-98, treas., 1991-93, chmn., 1993-95; bd. dirs. Boys Club Dallas, 1984-84, Dallas Assembly, 1983-97, Russian Am. Enterprise Fund, 1993-98; active Dallas Com. Fgn. Rels., chmn., 1987-98; trustee Brookings Instn., 2001-05, Eisenhower Fellowships, 2001-2003, Pacific Coun., 2002—; mem. Trilateral Commn., 2002-; Dem. candidate U.S. Senate, 1994. Decorated gran oficial Order of Bernardo O'Higgins (Chile); U.S.-Japan leadership fellow Japan Soc., 1989; recipient Outstanding Achievement award Stanford U. Assocs., 1986; hon. fellow Hertford Coll., Oxford U., 2002; named Admiral of Tex. Navy, 1987. Fellow Am. Acad. Arts and Scis.; mem. Inst. Ams. (chmn. 1987-93), Inter-Am. Dialogue (exec. com. 1992), Am. Coun. on Germany (bd. dirs. 1985-94, 2004—), Philos. Soc. Tex., Harvard Club, Petroleum Club, Met. Club (Washington). Presbyterian. Office: Fed Res Bank Dallas Dallas TX 75201

FISHER, ROBERT, gastroenterologist, health facility administrator; b. Bklyn., July 28, 1939; married. BSE, Princeton U., 1960; MD, U. Pa., 1964. Intern Chgo. Wesley Meml. Hosp., 1964-65; resident in internal meedicine Temple U. Hosp., Phila., 1967-70; fellow in gastroenterology Hosp. U. Pa., 1970-72; from asst. prof. to assoc. prof. Temple U. Sch. Medicine, 1972-80, prof. medicine, 1980—; dir. Functional Gastrointestinal Disease Ctr. Temple U. Hosp., Phila., 1984—, chief gastroenterology sect., 1985—. Mem. Am. Coll. Gastroenterology, Am. Gastroent. Assn., Am. Soc. Gastrointestinal Endoscopy, Am. Fedn. Clin. Rsch., Rsch. Soc. Alcoholism. Office: Temple Univ 3400 N Broad St Philadelphia PA 19140-5104 Office Phone: 215-707-3433. E-mail: robert.fisher@temple.edu.

FISHER, ROBERT, retail executive; MBA, Stanford U. Store mgr. The Gap, Inc., 1980-85, exec. v.p., mdse., Banana Republic, 1985-89, pres., Banana Republic, 1989-90, bd. dirs., 1990—, exec. v.p., 1992—, COO, 1992-93, 95-97, CFO, 1993-95, chmn., 2004—. Dir. Sun Microsystems Inc. Office: The Gap Inc 1 Harrison St San Francisco CA 94105-1602*

FISHER, ROBERT ALAN, laser physicist; b. Berkeley, Calif., Apr. 19, 1943; s. Leon Harold and Phyllis (Kahn) F.; children: Andrew Leon, Derek Martin. AB, U. Calif., Berkeley, 1965, MA, 1967, PhD, 1971. Programmer

Stanford (Calif.) linear accelerator Stanford U., 1965; staff mem. Granger Assocs., Palo Alto, Calif., 1966; lectr. U. Calif., Davis, 1972-74; physicist Lawrence Livermore Lab., Calif., 1971-74; laser physicist Los Alamos (N.Mex.) Nat. Lab., 1974-86. Cons. R.A. Fisher Assocs., Santa Fe, 1986—; instr. Engring. Tech., Inc., 1982—; mem. Air Force ABCD Panel, 1982; program com. mem. Internat. Quantum Electronics Conf., 1982, 86, Program Com. CLEO Conf., 2002—, mem. architecture panel, 2003—04, chair subcommittee nonlinear optics, 2005; vice chmn. Gordon Conf. on Lasers and Non-linear Optics, 1981; chmn. Soc. Photo-Optical Instrumentation Engrs. Conf. on Optical Phase Conjugation/Beam Combining/Diagnostics, 1987—; mem. Air Force Red Team for Space-Based Laser, 1983—86, HEDS II SDI Red Team, 1986, U.S. Ballistic Missile Office Options Team, 1986; mem. secretariat SDI Red/Blue Sensor Teams, 1986, SDI GBL Red/Blue Team Interaction, 1987—88; mem. architecture panel SDI SDS Phase I, 1990, Air Force Laser 21 Working Group, 1990. Assoc. editor Optics Letters, 1984-86, Applied Optics, 1984-91, Topical Edit. Optics Letters, 2002-04; editor: Optical Phase Conjugation, 1973; contbr. articles to profl. jours. Vol. coach elem. sch. chess team Pojoaque Elem. Sch. (winner nat. elem. championship 1984), Santa Fe, 1984. Fellow Optical Soc. Am. (guest editor jour. spl. issue on optical phase conjugation, mem. Engring. Excellence award com. 2003, chmn. 2004), SPIE (bd. dirs. 2002-04, scholarship com. 2001-04, edn. com. 2004-); mem. IEEE (sr.). Avocation: bluegrass music. Home and Office: 2996 Plaza Blanca Santa Fe NM 87507-5340 Office Phone: 505-992-3930. Business E-Mail: bob@rafisher.com.

FISHER, ROBERT BRUCE, priest; b. Paragould, Ark., Feb. 6, 1937; s. Lawrence Bruce Fisher and Georgia M. (Paris) Kasper. BA, Divine Word Seminary, Techny, Ill., 1961, MA, 1965; STB, STL, Gregorian Univ., Rome, 1966; STD, Pont. Ateneo di Sant' Anselmo, Rome, 1969. Ordained priest Roman Cath. Ch., 1965. Adminstrv. attache Nunciature of Holy See, Accra, Ghana, 1982-83; pastor Good Shepherd Ch., Tema, Ghana, 1984-86; asst. pastor St. Matthias Ch., New Orleans, 1990-94; pastor St. Martin de Porres Ch., Prairie View, 1996-2000, St. Anthony's Ch., Lafayette, La., 2000—03, St. Bartholomew Ch., Little Rock, 2003—04; dir. William J. Kelley, SVD Retreat Ctr., Bay St. Louis, Miss., 2004—. Asst. prof. Xavier U., New Orleans, 1988—95; dir. studies A. Tolton Ho. of Studies, New Orleans, 1991—96; dist. superior Divine Word Soc., New Orleans, 1990—96; promoter New African Cinema film series; instr. ethics and critical thinking Prairie View (Tex.) A&M U., 1998—2000, adj. prof., 1997—2000. Author: West African Religious Traditions: Focus on the Akan of Ghana, 1998; editor: (liturgical ordo) Ordo for the Philippines, 1972. Co-chmn. Cath. Returnee Crisis Com., Accra, 1982-83; active Cmty. Oriented Govt. Program, Lafayette, 2002-03 Mem. Am. Soc. Missiology, Coll. Theology Soc., Am. Acad. Religion, KC (chaplain Met. chpt. 1993-96, chaplain Bay St. Louis chpt. 2004—), African Assn. for Study of Religions, Divine Word Soc. (dist. coun.). Democrat. Mailing: 510 N Second St Bay Saint Louis MS 39520 Office Phone: 228-467-9837. E-mail: africoco@aol.com, office@wjkretreatcenter.org.

FISHER, ROBERT CHARLES HARU, publishing executive, editor; b. Burlington, Iowa, Mar. 3, 1930; s. Ray Erwin and Blanche Columbia (Brolin) Fisher. BA cum laude, Harvard U., 1955; postgrad., Columbia U. Law Sch., 1955-56, Tokyo U., 1957-59. Analyst, adjutant gen's. office U.S. Army, Kansas City, Mo., 1949-50, Washington, 1950-51; adv. Prime Minister Takeo Miki of Japan, 1957-64; Far Eastern rep. Fodor Travel Guides, Tokyo, 1959-64, exec. editor N.Y.C., 1964-66, 75-77, exec. v.p., 1975-77, pres., 1977-80, exec. editor London, 1966-74; v.p. David McKay Co., N.Y.C., 1976-80; pres. Fisher Travel Guides, 1980-88; gen. editor Crown Insider's Travel Guides, 1988-89; editl. dir. Gault Millau Guides, 1989-90; cons. Simon & Schuster, N.Y.C., 1990-92; editl. dir. Maco Comm., N.Y.C., 1992-94; exec. editor Arthur Frommer, Inc., N.Y.C., 1995—2000; exec. editor, columnist www.frommers.com, N.Y.C., 2000—; U.S. nat. student assn. Tokyo, 1956—59. Founder, dir. Kansas City Open Forum, 1949—50; bd. dirs. Internat. Assn. Med. Assistance to Travelers, 1972—, v.p., 1985—; chmn. Hotel and Restaurant Unsafe Food Labeling Action com., 1995—; pres. Fisher Publs. Inc., 1997—; founder Key West Travel Writers Workshop, 1991—; T. Author: Picasso, 1967, Klee, 1967, Guide to Japan, 1981, Insider's Guide to Japan, 1986; co-author: Off-Season Riviera, 1997, Off-Season London, 1999. Served with CIC U.S. Army, 1952—54, Korea. Grantee for study in Japan, Balt. Scholarship Fund, 1956—59. Mem.: Soc. Am. Travel Writers Found. (pres. 1985—90), Brit. Guild Travel Writers (vice-chmn. 1970—71), N.Y. Travel Writers Assn. (pres. 1979—81), Soc. Am. Travel Writers (dir. 1978—80, v.p. 1981—83, pres. 1983—84), Internat. House of Japan, Japan Soc.N.Y., Am. Club of Japan, Harvard Club N.Y.C. Personal E-mail: BobHaru@aol.com.

FISHER, ROBERT DALE, stockbroker, retired naval officer; b. Memphis, July 30, 1924; s. Hollis Welton and Anna Sue (Parrish) F.; m. Joy Lee Chandler, Mar. 30, 1946. BS, Am. U., 1957. Commd. ensign USN, 1944, advanced through grades to comdr., 1963; tng. officer Polaris Missile program, 1955-58, comdr. destroyer, 1959-61, ret., 1963; stockbroker, 1963—; v.p. investments Smith Barney, Washington, 1979—. Mem. Mil. Order Carabao, Kiwanis (pres. Falls Church, Va. 1969, McLean, Va. 1979-80), Army-Navy Club, Masons, Shriners, Jesters. Republican. Methodist. Home: 6033 Chesterbrook Rd Mc Lean VA 22101-3213 Office: 1850 K St NW Ste 900 Washington DC 20006-2222 Office Phone: 202-862-2866. E-mail: robert.d.fisher@smithbarney.com.

FISHER, ROBERT DARRYL, cardiovascular and thoracic surgeon, lawyer; b. Wewoka, Okla., Sept. 18, 1939; s. R. D. and Lurine (Weir) F.; m. Orpha Lou Morrison, Aug. 19, 1961; children: Eric Scott, Laura Elizabeth. BS, East Cen. U., 1960; MD, U. Okla. Health Scis. Ctr., 1964; JD, Oklahoma City U., 1989. Diplomate Am. Bd. Surgery, Am. Bd. Thoracic Surgery. Surgical intern then resident Johns Hopkins Hosp., Balt., 1964-66, sr. and chief resident, 1969-73; clin. assoc. NIH, Bethesda, Md., 1966-68; rsch. fellow Harvard Med. Sch., Boston, 1968-69; assoc. prof. Sch. Medicine Vanderbilt U., Nashville, 1973-78; pvt. practice Oklahoma City, 1978—. Chmn. bd. dirs. Pontotoc County Bank, Roff, Okla., 1989—; bd. dirs. Granite Reins. Co., Oklahoma City, 1988—. Contbr. articles to profl. jours. Recipient Disting. Alumnus award East Cent. U., 1980; Nat. Med. Scis. Tng. grantee., 1969-73. Mem. AMA, ABA, Am. Assn. for Thoracic Surgery, Soc. for Thoracic Surgery, So. Thoracic Surg. Soc., Soc. Univ. Surgeons, Okla. Med. Assn., Alpha Omega Alpha. Presbyterian. E-mail: fisherok@cox.net.

FISHER, ROBERT HENRI, physician; b. Auburn, NY, Jan. 5, 1955; s. Egon Fisher; children: Laura, Jessica, Deborah. BA, Haverford Coll., 1977; MD, U. Rochester, 1981; MS in Med. Adminstrn., U. Wis., 2000. Med. resident Washington U., St. Louis, 1981-84; instr. of medicine Deaconess Hosp., St. Louis, 1984-85; fellow clin. immunology Johns Hopkins U., Balt., 1985-88; asst. prof. medicine East Carolina U. Sch. Medicine, Greenville, N.C., 1988-93, Med. Coll. Wis., Milw., 1993-95; dir. allergy sect. Med. Assocs. Health Ctr., Menomonee Falls, Wis., 1995-2001; v.p. med. affairs Comty. Meml. Hosp., Menomonee Falls, Wis., 2001—05. Chmn. subspecialty medicine Med. Assn. Health Ctrs., 1997—2001; clin. asst. prof. Med. Coll. of Wis., 1995—. Pres. Allergy Rsch. and Care, S.C. Rsch. grantee Am. Lung Assn. Wis., 1994-96; Davis fellow Am. Lung Assn. N.C., 1989-90. Fellow Am. Coll. Allergy and Immunology, Am. Acad. Allergy and Immunology; mem. ACP, Am. Thoracic Soc., Wis. State Med. Soc. (CME coun. 2000—, chmn. CME sect.) Achievements include 2 patents for method of treating asthma using IL-8 and other cytokines; discovered that a group of protein cytokines improve bronchial hyperresponsiveness and symptoms associated with asthma. Office: Allergy Rsch & Care 2355 W Sueclare Rd Glendale WI 53209 Office Phone: 262-784-5431. Business E-Mail: rhfisher@allergy-research.com.

FISHER, ROBERT I., lawyer; b. Bklyn., July 10, 1939; s. Sidney B. and Jeanette (Talisman) F.; m. Debra Kram Fisher, June 30, 1974; children: Daniel I., Elizabeth R. BA, Columbia U., 1960; JD cum laude, Harvard U., 1963; LLM, N.Y.U., 1967. Bar: N.Y. 1964. Assoc. Dewey, Ballantine, Bushby, Palmer & Wood, N.Y.C., 1964-67, Sullivan & Cromwell, N.Y.C., 1967-72; ptnr. Greenbaum, Wolff & Ernst, N.Y.C., 1972—82, Katten Muchin Roseman LLP, N.Y.C., 1982—. Lectr. Practicing Law Inst. Fulbright fellow, Israel, 1963-64. Mem. ABA, N.Y. State Assn. Home: 150 Factory Pond Rd Locust Valley NY 11560-1416 Office: Katten Muchin Rosenman LLP 575 Madison Ave Fl 11 New York NY 10022-2585 Office Phone: 212-940-8827. E-mail: robert.fisher@kattenlaw.com.

FISHER, ROBERT MORTON, foundation administrator, academic administrator; b. St. Paul, Minn., Oct. 15, 1938; s. S.S. and Jean Fisher; m. Elinor C. Schectman, June 19, 1960; children: Laurie, Jonathan. AB magna cum laude, Harvard Coll., 1960; JD, Harvard U., 1963; PhD, London Sch. Econs, Polit. Sci., 1967; LLD, West Coast U., L.A., 1981; DHL, Profl. Sch. Psychology, San Francisco, 1986; DPS, John F. Kennedy U., Orinda, Calif., 1988. Rsch. assoc. Mass. Mental Health Ctr., Cambridge, 1957-62; rsch. asst. Ctr. Study Juvenile Delinquency, Cambridge, 1961-63; spl. asst. to chief psychologist British Prison Dept. Home Office, London, 1963-67; prof. Sch. Criminology U. Calif., Berkeley, 1965-71; profl. race car driver, 1972-77; pres. John F. Kennedy U., Orinda, Calif., 1974-85; exec. dir. 92d St. YMHA, N.Y.C., 1984-85; dir., CEO The San Francisco Found., 1987-97; pres. non-profit edn. and founds. Rusher, Loscavio & LoPresto Exec. Search, San Francisco, 2005—. Mayor, councilman Lafayette, Calif., 1968-76; mem. Minn. and Calif. Bar Specialty: charitable gift planning; CEO Fisher Cos., 1997—; exec. dir. Alonzo King's Line Ballet, 2002; prin. cons. Robert Fisher Assocs. Non-Profit Cons., 2003—. Scholar-in-residence Rockefeller Found., Bellagio, 1994; Polit. Sci. vis. fellow London Sch. Econs. and Polit. Sci., 1994; named Outstanding Fundraising Exec. Nat. Soc. Fund Raising Execs. Home: 85 Southwood Dr Orinda CA 94563-3026 Office: Rusher Loscavio and LoPresto Exec Search 100 Spear St # 935 San Francisco CA 94105 Office Phone: 415-765-6584. E-mail: rmfisher@earthlink.net.

FISHER, ROBERT PERRY, environmental scientist, researcher; b. Houston, May 30, 1945; s. George Robert and Brownie (Perry) F.; m. Cari Patrice Guritz, Sept. 6, 1969; children; William Robert, Jay Kenneth. BS in Chemistry cum laude, Centenary Coll., 1967; PhD in Analytical Chemistry, U. Fla., 1971. Postdoctoral rsch. assoc., asst. prof. U. Fla., Gainesville, 1971-72; rsch. chemist Nat. Coun. for Air and Stream Improvement, Gainesville, 1972-83, investigative programs mgr., 1983-88, regional mgr., 1988-92, program dir., 1992-95, v.p., 1995—. Chmn. methods com. APHA-Standard Methods, Washington, 1980—; co-chair, mem. tech. com. EPA Gulf of Mexico Program, 1999—. Contbr. articles to Analytical Chemistry, Jour. Tech. Assn. Pulp and Paper Industry, Pulp and Paper Canada and chpt. to ASTM Quality Assurance Monitoring. Leader Cub Scouts Boy Scouts Am., Gainesville, 1985-95. Recipient Teaching award DuPont, U. Fla., 1969. Fellow Am. Inst. Chemists (Outstanding Chemistry Student 1967), Mem. ASTM (methods com. 1980—), Am. Chem. Soc., Am. Indsl. Hygiene Assn. Achievements include methodology for controlling sulfur gas releases from kraft pulp mills; 2 patents for methods of generating chlorine dioxide gas. Office: Nat Coun Air/Stream Improve PO Box 13318 Research Triangle Park NC 27709 E-mail: rfisher@ncasi.org.

FISHER, ROGER DUMMER, negotiation expert, law educator; b. Winnetka, Ill., May 28, 1922; s. Walter Taylor and Katharine (Dummer) F.; m. Caroline Speer, Sept. 18, 1948; children: Elliott Speer, Peter Ryerson. AB, Harvard U., 1943, LLB magna cum laude, 1948; LHD, Conn. Coll., 1994; DHL, Bay Path Coll., 1999. Bar: Mass. 1948, D.C. 1950. Asst. to gen. counsel, then asst. to dep. U.S. spl. rep. ECA, Paris, 1948-49; with firm Covington & Burling, Washington, 1950-56; asst. to solicitor gen. U.S., 1956-58; lectr. law Harvard Law Sch., Cambridge, Mass., 1958-60, prof. law, 1960-76, Samuel Williston prof. law, 1976-92, dir. Harvard negotiation project, 1980—, prof. emeritus, 1992—. Vis. prof. internat. rels. dept. London Sch. Econ., 1965-66; cons. pub. affairs editor WGBH-TV, Cambridge, 1969; tech. advisor Found. for Internat. Conciliation, Geneva, 1984-87; sr. advisor Mercy Corps'; lectr. in field. Originator, 1st exec. editor: (pub. TV series) The Advocates, 1969-70, moderator, 1970-71; co-originator, exec. editor: (pub. TV series) Arabs and Israelis, 1975; author: International Conflict for Beginners, 1969, Dear Israelis, Dear Arabs, 1972, International Mediation: A Working Guide, 1978, International Crises and the Role of Law: Points of Choice, 1978, Improving Compliance with International Law, 1981; co-author: Getting to Yes: Negotiating Agreement Without Giving In, 1981, 2d edit., 1991, Getting Together: Building Relationships as We Negotiate, 1988, Beyond Machiavelli: Tools for Coping with Conflict, 1994, Getting Ready to Negotiate: The Getting to Yes Workbook, 1995, Coping with International Conflict: A Systematic Approach to Influence in International Negotiation, 1997, Getting It Done: How to Lead When You're Not in Charge, 1998, (with Daniel Shapiro) Beyond Reason: Using Your Emotions as You Negotiate, 2005; co-author, editor: International Conflict and Behavioral Science--The Craigville Papers, 1964; contbr. articles to profl. jours. Bd. dir. Coun. for Livable World; trustee Hudson Inst., 1962-95. 1st lt. USAF, 1942-46. Recipient Sziland Peace award 1981, Peace Advocate award Lawyers Alliance for Nuclear Arms Control, 1988, Spl. Contbn. award Ctr. Pub. Resources, 1993, Steve Brutschè award Assn. Atty. Mediators, 1994, D'Alemberte-Raven Outstanding Achievements and Contributions to Dispute Resolution award, 1995, Honorato Vasquez Nat. Order Insignia Great Cross Republic Ecuador, 1999, helping settle in 1998 the fifty-yr. boundary war between Ecuador and Peru, Lifetime Achievement award Am. Coll. Civil Trial Mediators, 1999, Pioneer award New Eng. Soc. Profls. Dispute Reolution, 1999, St. Thomas More award St. Mary's U. Law Sch., 1999; named Guggenheim fellow 1965-66. Fellow Am. Acad. Arts and Sci.; mem. ABA (sect. dispute resolution), Am. Soc. Internat. Law (exec. coun. 1961-64, 66-69, v.p. 1982-84), Mass. Bar Assn., Commn. to Study Orgn. of Peace, Coun. Fgn. Rels., Phi Beta Kappa. Clubs: Metropolitan (Washington); Harvard (NYC). Office: Harvard U Law Sch Harvard Negotiation Project Pound Hall # 525 Cambridge MA 02138 Address: Mercy Corps Conflict Mgmt Group 9 Waterhouse St Cambridge MA 02138-3607 Office Phone: 617-495-7786. Business E-Mail: rfisher@law.harvard.edu.

FISHER, RUSSELL D, insurance company executive; B in econ., Westminster Coll. Various sales and mgmt. positions Aetna Inc., 1970—90, head of nat. field sales mgmt., 1991—96; joined Aetna U.S. Healthcare Nat. Accounts Mgmt. Team, 1996—98; sr. v.p., nat. accounts and Aetna global benefits Aetna Inc., 1998—. Office: Aetna Inc 151 Farmington Ave Hartford CT 06156

FISHER, SEYMOUR, psychologist, educator; b. N.Y.C., Nov. 4, 1925; s. George and Fannie (Hesselson) F.; m. Carmen Eldridge, June 20, 1959; children: Mark, Andrew. BA, NYU, 1948; PhD, U. N.C., 1952; postgrad., Washington Sch. Psychiatry, 1954-55. Diplomate Am. Bd. Examiners in Psychol. Hypnosis. Clin. psychologist trainee VA Hosp., Roanoke, 1950, psychology trainee, 1952; intern Psychol. Clinic, U. N.C., Chapel Hill, 1950-51; supervising clin. psychologist Walter Reed Army Inst. Rsch., Washington, 1952-58; rsch. psychologist Psychopharmacology Svc. Ctr., NIMH, Bethesda, Md., 1958-60; chief spl. studies unit Psychopharmacology Rsch Br., NIMH, Bethesda, 1960-63; prof. psychiatry (psychology), dir. rsch. tng., dir. psychopharmacology lab., divsn. psychiatry Boston U. Sch. Medicine, 1963-78; prof. dept. psychiatry and behavioral scis., U. Tex. Med. Br., Galveston, 1978—, prof. emeritus, 2000—, assoc. chmn. for rsch., 1978-80, rsch. advisor to chmn. dept., 1980-91, dir. Ctr. for Medication Monitoring, 1987-2000. Vis. prof. Harvard U., Boston U., May to Nov., 1988; cons. NIMH, Chevy Chase, Md., 1964-66, mem. clin. psychopharmacology rsch. rev. com., 1973-77, mem. treatment devel. and assessment rsch. rev. com., 1979-83; cons. Office Naval Rsch., Washington, 1964-66, Mass. Dept. Mental Health, 1969-78, FDA, 1973-77; pres. Boston Mental Health Found., Inc., 1970-72; mem. Commn. on Cmty. Care of Mentally Ill, chmn. tech. com. Hogg Found., 1987-90, planning com. for 50th anniversary rsch. conf., 1988-89 Mem. editl. bd. Psychopharmacology Svc. Ctr. Bull., 1959-63; assoc. editor Psychol. Record, 1960-66; sr. editor vol. on clin. and biobehavioral aspects of cocaine, Oxford U. Press, 1987; mem. adv. bd. Internat. Jour. Methods Psychiatry, 1998-2000; contbr. numerous articles to profl. jours., chpts. in books. Recipient Disting. Alumnus award U. N.C., 1981, Donald E. Francke award for best paper Drug Info. Jour., 1987. Fellow APA (mem. exec. coun. divsn. psychopharmacology 1979-82), Am. Coll. Neuropsychcopharmacology (life, pres. 1984, asst. sec.-treas. 1974-77, chmn. hon. awards com. 1985-87, mem. other coms. 1973-87, emeritus), Soc. Clin. and Exptl. Hypnosis, Internat. Coll. Psychosomatic Medicine, Collegium Internat. Neuro-Psychopharmacologicum (emeritus); mem. Am. Psychopathol. Assn. (exec. coun. 1970-72), Psi Chi, Sigma Xi, Beta Lambda Sigma. Office: U Tex Med Br 1310 Harbor View Dr Galveston TX 77550 Business E-Mail: sfisher@utmb.edu. *The difference between intelligence and wisdom: intelligence is knowing that half of what you hear or read is garbage; wisdom is knowing which half.*

FISHER, SHARON MARY, musician; b. Orange, N.J., Sept. 29, 1944; d. Stanley and Veronica Shirley (Conway) Cozza; m. Andrew Fisher IV, Aug. 16, 1969. B Music Edn., Westminster Choir Coll., 1966; postgrad., Acad. Vocal Arts, 1966—67, Temple U., 1967—69. Cert. music tchr., N.J. Chorister Westminster Choir, Princeton, N.J., 1964-66; music tchr. Phila. Pub. Schs., 1967-69; sect. leader Phila. Boys' Choir, 1969; performer Manhattan Light Opera Co., N.Y., 1969-70; soprano soloist St. Peter's Ch., Morristown, N.J., 1975-79; organist Ch. of the Saviour, Denville, N.J., 1981-84; performer, lectr., 1986—. Performer Scottish Games, Millington, N.J. Albums include Concert Memories, 1991, Ireland: Land of Harp and Song, 1998. Grand marshal Holiday Parade, Denville C. of C., 1991. Recipient Marietta MacLeod award An Comunn Gaidhealach, 1989, Scots award Scottish Club of Twinstates, 1988-89, Harp/Voice trophy O'Carolan Harp Festival, Keadue, Ireland, 1988, Merit award Passaic County Irish Am. Cultural Soc., 1995. Mem. Clarsach Soc. (Edinburgh), Scottish Harp Soc. Am. (Ellice MacDonald grantee 1987), Am. Harp Soc., Nat. Assn. Tchrs. Singing, Nat. Assn. Pastoral Musicians, Internat. Soc. Folk Harpers and Craftsmen, Comhaltas Ceoltoiri Eireann. Avocations: gardening, language study, study of pain management through music. Home: 46 W Shore Rd Denville NJ 07834-1520 Personal E-mail: harpvoice@msn.com.

FISHER, SOLOMON, lawyer; b. Phila., Apr. 4, 1935; s. Samuel and Ethel (Chernicoff) F.; m. Alice M. Rosenthal, June 30, 1963; children: Emil Eric, Suzanne Ruth. BS, Temple U., 1957, JD, 1960. Bar: Pa. 1960, D.C. 1964, U.S. Ct. Fed. Claims 1963, U.S. Tax Ct. 1964, U.S. Supreme Ct. 1964. Trial atty. tax divsn. U.S. Dept. Justice, Washington, 1960-64; assoc. Dilworth, Paxson, Kalish & Kauffman, Phila., 1964-68, ptnr., 1968-84, Horvitz, Fisher, Miller & Sedlack, Phila., 1984-93, Reed Smith LLP and predecessor, Phila., 1993—2001, counsel, 2002—. Lectr. tax practice Grad. Tax Law program Temple U., Phila., 1976—; lectr. civil and criminal penalties, 1986-93; adj. assoc. prof. Grad. Sch. Mgmt., Widener U., 1993. Pres. Phila. chpt. Am. Jewish Com., 1970-72, chmn. 1972-74, nat. bd. govs. 1976-83, nat. bd. trustees, nat. exec. coun.; pres. Jewish Cmty. Rels. Coun. Phila., 1977-79, mem. exec. com. adv. coun. 1978-81; bd. trustees Fedn. Jewish Agys. 1976-84, 86-95, 97--; pres. Congregation Adath Jeshurun, 1983-86, Auerbach Ctrl. Agy. for Jewish Edn., 1996-98. Mem. ABA, Pa. Bar Assn., Fed. Bar Assn., Phila. Bar Assn., (former sec.-treas. tax sect.), Am. Coll. Tax Counsel, Tau Epsilon Rho (chancellor Phila. chpt. 1983-84, chancellor 1985-86). Office: Reed Smith LLP 2500 One Liberty Pl 1650 Market St Fl 25 Philadelphia PA 19103-7394 E-mail: sfisher@reedsmith.com.

FISHER, STEPHEN TODD, retired military officer, health science association administrator, consultant; b. Little Falls, N.Y., Apr. 7, 1941; s. Edwin Morgan and Lillian Wing (Burrell) F.; m. Myra Halcomb, May 15, 1971; children: Arlie, Abby, Ann, Alexandra. BA, Washington and Jefferson U., 1963; MBA, Cornell U., 1965; MA, Cath. U., 1985. Commd. ens. USN, 1965, advanced through grades to rear adm.; pers. officer Naval Hosp., Newport, R.I.; dir. mgmt./XO Naval Sch. Health Scis., USN, Bethesda, Md., 1972-82, enlisted cmty. mgr. chief naval ops. Washington, 1982-84, med. adminstrn. officer HQ, Fleet Marine Force Pacific Hawaii, 1984-87, cmdg. officer Naval Med. Clinic Washington, 1987-88; dep. asst. chief pers. mgmt. Bur. Medicine and Surgery, Washington, 1988-92, med. insp. gen., 1992-93, dir. med. svc. corps, 1993-95, asst. chief health care ops., 1993-95, dep. surgeon gen. Navy, 1995-2000, dep. chief, 1995-2000; CEO, Martin & Assocs. Healthcare Cons. Firm, Washington, 2000—03; interim CIO, TriWest Healthcare Alliance, Phoenix, 2003, v.p. leadership devel. and tng., 2003—. Office Phone: 602-644-8283.

FISHER, STEVEN KAY, neurobiology educator; b. Rochester, Ind., July 18, 1942; s. Stewart King and Hazel Madeline (Howell) F.; m. Dinah Dawn Marschall, May 2, 1971; children: Jenni Dawn, Brian Andrew, Steven William. BS, Purdue U., 1964, MS, 1966; postgrad., Johns Hopkins U., 1967—69; PhD, Purdue U., 1969. Postdoctoral fellow Johns Hopkins U., Balt., 1969-71; prof. U. Calif., Santa Barbara, 1971—, dir. Inst. Environ. Stress, 1985-88, dir. Neurosci. Rsch. Inst., 1989-2001. Cons. Ultrastructure Tech., Goleta, Calif., 1984—, Regeneron Pharms., Inc., 1993, 94, Amgen, Inc., 1994, 95; mem. NIH Visual Scis. A2 Study Sect. Contbr. numerous articles to profl. jours. Recipient Devel. award, NIH, 1980—84, M.E.R.I.T. award, 1989—99, Ludwig von Sallmann prize for vision rsch., 2002; grantee, NIH, 1971—, NSF, 2003. Mem. Assn. Rsch. in Vision and Ophthalmology (mem. program com. 1979-80, K-12 edn. com. 1997-2001), Internat. Soc. for Eye Rsch., Soc. Neurosci. Avocations: music, gardening, guitar, literature, weightlifting. Home: 6890 Sabado Tarde Rd Goleta CA 93117-4305 Office: U Calif Neurosci Rsch Inst Santa Barbara CA 93106-5060 E-mail: fisher@lifesci.uscb.edu.

FISHER, THOMAS GEORGE, lawyer, media specialist; b. Debrecen, Hungary, Oct. 2, 1931; came to U.S., 1951; s. Eugene J. and Viola Elizabeth (Rittersporn) F.; m. Rita Knisley, Feb. 14, 1960; children: Thomas G. Jr., Katherine F. Vaaler. BS, Am. U., 1957, JD, 1959; postgrad., Harvard U., 1956. Bar: D.C. 1959, Iowa 1977. Atty. FCC, Washington, 1959-61, 65-66; pvt. law practice, 1961-65, 66-69; asst. counsel Meredith Corp., N.Y.C., 1969-72, assoc. gen. counsel Des Moines, 1972-76, gen. counsel, 1976-80, v.p. gen. counsel, 1980-94, corp. sec., 1988-94, ret., 1994. Comml law liaison ABA Ctr. and East European Law Initiative, Krakow, Poland, 1994—95; atty. Iowa Legal Aid, 1996—. Contbr. articles to profl. jours. Bd. dirs. Des Moines Met. Opera Co., Indianola, 1980-94, pres., 1990-91; bd. dirs. Civic Music Assn., Des Moines, 1982-92, pres., 1987-88; chmn. legis. com. Greater Des Moines C. of C., 1976-77; bd. dirs. Legal Aid Soc. Polk County, 1986-93, pres., 1993. With U.S. Army, 1952-54. Mem. ABA, Iowa State Bar Assn. (chmn. corp. counsel subcom. 1979-82), Polk County Bar Assn., Embassy Club. Office: Iowa Legal Aid Ste 230 1111 9th St Des Moines IA 50314-2527 Office Phone: 515-243-1198 ext. 1687.

FISHER, THOMAS GEORGE, JR., lawyer; b. Washington, June 1, 1961; s. Thomas George and Rita (Knisley) F.; m. Susan Jane Koenig, June 23, 1990. BA, Iowa State U., 1983; JD with high distinction, U. Iowa, 1986. Bar: Iowa 1986, U.S. Dist. Ct. (so. dist.), Iowa 1987, U.S. Ct. Appeals (8th cir.) 1987, U.S. Dist. Ct. (no. dist.) Iowa 1993. Jud. clk. Iowa Supreme Ct., Davenport, 1986-87; assoc. Duncan, Jones, Riley & Finley, P.C., Des Moines, 1987-91; asst. atty. gen. State of Iowa, Justice Dept., Des Moines, 1991-95; counsel Am. Mut. Life Ins. Co., Des Moines, 1995-96; ptnr. Hogan & Fisher, PLC, Des Moines, 1997—2003, Whitfield & Eddy, P.L.C., Des Moines, 2003—04; atty. in pvt. practice, 2004—. Precinct chair Polk County Dem. Party, Des Moines, 1988-90, 94-96, 98-2000, 02--; candidate Iowa Ho. of Reps. Dists. 73, 1994; mem. Des Moines Leadership Inst., 1998-99; bd. dirs., chair Metro Arts Alliance of Greater Des Moines; bd. dirs. Des Moines Emergency Food Pantry. Mem. Blackstone Inn of Ct. Democrat. Roman Catholic. Office: PO Box 12277 Des Moines IA 50312 E-mail: fisher@dwx.com.

FISHER, THOMAS JEFFREY, art educator; b. San Fernando, Calif., May 7, 1946; s. Harry Joseph and Jeanne Elois Fischer; m. Sharon Louise Miner, Dec. 1967; children: Matthew Brady, Ethan Robert. BA, Calif. State U., 1972; MFA, Stanford (Calif.) U., 1987. Instr. Lucia Man United Sch. Dist., Arrdyo Grande, Calif., 1987—90; prof. photography Savannah (Ga.) Coll. Art and Design, 1997—99, 2002—, dean Sch. Media Arts, 1999—2002; prin., owner Tom Fisher Photography, Savannah, 1998—. Lectr. art Stanford (Calif.) U., 1986—88; instr. Cuesta C.C., San Luis Obispo, Calif., 1988—89; cons. in field; peer reviewer So. Assn. Colls. and Schs., 1999—2002. Dir.(photographer): (films) Fourth WardSchool Project, 2001; Western Environmental Law Control, 2001; dir.: (films) The Lacoste (France) Documentary Project, 2003; exhibitions include more than 20 exhbns., more than 50 group shows, more than 100 pub. and pvt. collections. Sgt. U.S. Army, 1966—69. Recipient Cultural Olympiad award, 1996 Olympics, award, Carnegie Found., 2004; James Borelli fellow, 1983—87, G.B. Canter fellow, 1983—87. Mem.: Soc. Photographic Edn., Coll. Art Assn., Sierra Club. Avocations: fishing, sculpting, woodworking. Home: 307 Washington Ave Savannah GA 31405-2209 Office: Savannah College Art and Design PO Box 3140 Savannah GA 31408-3140

FISHER, THOMAS LEE, gas industry executive; b. 1944; Grad., Purdue U., 1966, U. Chgo., 1983. Pres. No. Ill. Gas Co. (now Nicor Gas Co.), Naperville, Ill., 1988—2002, CEO, 1988—2003, chmn. bd. dirs., 1996—; pres. Nicor Inc., Naperville, Ill., 1994—2002, CEO, 1995, chmn. bd. dirs., 1996—2005, non-exec. chmn. bd., 2005—. Dir. Gas Rsch. Inst. Address: Nicor Gas and Nicor Inc 1844 Ferry Rd Naperville IL 60563 Mailing: Nicor Gas PO Box 190 Aurora IL 60507-0190*

FISHER, THOMAS SCOTT, army officer, broadcasting network executive; b. Madison, Wis., June 24, 1963; s. Gale Eugene Fisher and Claudia Jane Clodfelter Killinger; m. Andreina Louisa Zanier Fisher, Aug. 4, 1989; children: Thomas Junior, Maximilian Andreas. BA, U Minn., 1987; MA in Journalism, Marshall U., 1995. Commd. 2d lt. U.S. Army, advanced through grades to maj., 1998; airborne ranger A Co. 2d Bn., 75th Inf., Tacoma, Wash., 1981-83; platoon leader Canadian Army Trophy Team, 7th Corps, Bavaria, 1987-89; exec. officer B Co. 2-64 ARMOR, Schweinfurt, Germany, 1989-90, bn. maintenance officer HQ, 1990; brigade asst. ops. officer 1st Brigade, 3 I.D., Schweinfurt, Germany, 1990-91; co. comdr. A Co. 2-64 ARMOR, Schweinfurt, Germany, 1991-93; ops. officer Am. Forces Network, Frankfurt, Germany, 1996; comdr. AFN-North, Frankfurt, 1997-98, AFN-Balkans, Tuzla, Bosnia, 1998—. Co-author: (book) ...So Are They All, All Honorable Men, 1996, (screenplay) Storm In The Desert, 1995, Reoccurence, 1996. Decorated Army Achievement medal with 4 oak leaf clusters, 1983, Army Good Conduct medal, 1984, Nat. Def. Svc. medal, 1990, Army Commendation medal, 1992, Meritorious Svc. medal, 1993, Armed Forces Svc. medal, 1996, NATO medal, 1997, Joint Svc. Achievement medal, 1998, Def. Superior Svc. medal, 1999. Mem. U.S. Armor Assn., Order of St. George (knight, bronze medallion 1993), World Martial Arts Fedn. (black belt). Baptist. Avocations: golf, skiing, Karate.

FISHER, WILLIAM LAWRENCE, geologist, educator, dean; b. Marion, Ill., Sept. 16, 1932; s. Henry Adam and Madge Lenora (Moore) F.; m. Marilee Booth, Dec. 18, 1954; children: Leah, Karl, Peter. BS, So. Ill. U., 1954, DSc, 1986; MS, U. Kans., 1958, PhD, 1961; DEng, Colo. Sch. Mines, 2002. Cert. Profl. Geologist Am. Inst. Profl. Geologists, Petroleum Geologist Am. Assn. Petroleum Geologists, Profl. Earth Scientist Soc. Ind. Profl. Earth Scientists. Rsch. scientist Tex. Bur. Econ. Geology, Austin, 1960-68, assoc. dir., 1968-70, dir., 1970-75, 77-94, John A. and Katherine G. Jackson Sch. Geoscis., 2001—05; asst. sec. for energy and minerals Dept. Interior, Washington, 1976—77; prof. dept. geol. scis. U. Tex., Austin, 1969—, dep. asst. sec. energy, 1975—76, Morgan J. Davis prof. petroleum geology, 1984-86, Leonidas T. Barrow chair in mineral resources, 1986—, participating faculty LBJ sch. pub. affairs, 1977—81, chmn. dept. geol. scis., 1984-90, dir. Geology Found., 1984—; dean John A. & Katherine G. Jackson Sch. Geoscis., 2005—. Vis. prof. dept. geology So. Ill. U., 1967; bd. dirs. Pogo Producing Co.; geology assoc. bd. U. Kans., 1972-74, 83—; adv. coun. Gas Rsch. Inst., Tex. Energy and Natural Resource; mem. Tex. Sci. Adv. Coun., Gov.'s Energy Coun., White House Sci. Coun., Nat. Petroleum Coun., Pres.' Coun. of Advisors on Sci. and Tech. Panel on Energy R & D and Sec. Energy Adv. Bd.; mem. Tex. 2000 Commn.; bd dir. Diamond Shamrock, 1987-98. Trustee Am. Assn. Petroleum Geologists Found., Southwest Rsch. Inst., Am. Geol. Inst. Found. With AUS, 1954—56. Shell fellow, 1961; recipient Hedberg medal Inst. for the Study of Earth and Man, 1995, Robert Earll McConnell award Am. Inst. Mining, Metall. and Petroleum Engrs., 2004. Fellow AAAS, Soc. Econ. Geology, Geol. Soc. Am. (councillor); mem. NRC (commn. on geoscis., environ. and resource, chmn. bd. mineral and energy resources, US nat. com. on geology, chmn. bd. on earth scis. and resources, bd. on energy and environ. sys.), Nat. Acad. Engring., Nat. Assoc., Nat. Academies (nat. assoc. 2003), Am. Inst. Profl. Geologists (pres. Tex. sect. 1979, pres. 1993, Galey Pub. Svc. award, 1985, Parker medal, 1996), Assn. Am. State Geologists (hon. pres. 1981-82), Am. Assn. Petroleum Geologists (hon., pres. 1985-86, Sidney Powers Meml. medal award, 1994), Am. Geol. Inst. (pres. 1991, Campbell medal, 1991, Heroy award, 1997), Austin Geol. Soc. (hon., pres. 1973-74), Gulf Coast Assn. Geol. Scis. (hon. 1986, pres. 1994, Boyd medal, 2002), Tex. Ind. Prodrs. and Royalty Owners (Hats Off award, 2002), Tex. Acad. Medicine, Engring. and Sci., Acad. Medicine, Engring. Sci. Tex. (founding mem., 2004), Soc. Sedimentary Geology (Twenhofel medal, 2001), Soc. Petroleum Engrs., Soc. Ind. Profl. Earth Scientists, Brazilian Assn. Petroleum Geologists. Republican. Achievements include first to introduce the concept of depositional systems linking modern depositional environments to ancient counterparts in 1967; introduce the concept of additional mobile oil recovery and its significance to oil and gas reserves growth. Home: 8705 Ridgehill Dr Austin TX 78759-7342 Office: Univ Tex Dept Geological Scis Austin TX 78712 Office Phone: 512-471-5600. Business E-Mail: wfisher@mail.utexas.edu.

FISHER, WILLIAM THOMAS, business administration educator; b. Central Falls, R.I., Mar. 15, 1918; s. William L. and Sarah (Foley) F.; m. Mary Rowena Donnelly, Dec. 26, 1949; 1 son, William Thomas. BS with high honors, Am. Internat. Coll., 1949; MEd in Econs. and Edn., Boston U., 1951; PhD, U. Conn., 1956; postgrad., Clark U., 1954, Columbia U., 1957, St. Thomas Sem., Bloomfield, Conn., 1970-73. Prodn. planner local industry, Putnam, Conn., 1938-42; prin. Templeton (Mass.) Sch., 1949-50, Tourtellotte High Sch., Thompson, Conn., 1950-57; instr. Becker Jr. Coll., Worcester, Mass., 1955-57; assoc. prof. State U. N.Y. at, Albany, 1957; asst. dean Sch. Ins., U. Conn., 1957-76; asst. dean adminstrn. U. Conn. Sch. Bus. Adminstrn., 1976-77; adminstrv. dir. (Hartford MBA program), 1957-64; vis. prof. Ohio U., summer 1962; dir. (IBM Advanced Ins. Industry Sch.), 1960-70; ednl. cons. IBM Corp., 1960-80; adminstr., asst. dir. Ctr. for Ins. Edn. and Rsch., Hartford, 1976-81; assoc. prof. mgmt. and adminstrv. scis. dept. Sch. Bus. Adminstrn., U. Conn., Storrs, 1976-81, assoc. prof. mgmt. and orgn. dept., 1981-89, prof. emeritus, 1989—, adj. prof., 1989-90, 92; ordained permanent deacon Roman Cath. Ch. for Archdiocese of Hartford, 1973; assigned St. Joseph Cathedral, Hartford, part-time 1973-83; rsch. fellow Divinity Sch. Yale U., New Haven, 1989-91, Theol. Opportunities Program Harvard U., Cambridge, Mass., 1994-95. Vis. scholar Divinity Sch., Duke U., Durham, N.C., 1995, 96, 98, 99, Divinity Sch., Vanderbilt U., Nashville, 1996-97, Emory U., Candler Sch. Theology, Atlanta, 1997; real estate broker, 1973-93; mem. Conn. State Ins. Com. and Conn. State Ins. Purchasing Bd., 1963-73, 75-91, chmn. bd., 1971-73; past pres., dir. Conn. Assn. Mcpl. Devel. Commns., 1963-91; mem. Conn. adv. coun. SBA, 1964-70, chmn., 1967; chmn. various coms. Greater Hartford Coun. Econ. Edn., 1958-81; mem. Thompson Bd. Fin., 1963-75; chmn. Thompson Indsl. and Devel. Com., 1964-70, 71-80, 81-91. Editor: Selective Readings in Human Resources Management, 1985, 87, 89; contbr. articles to profl. jours. Pres. Thompson Indsl. Found., 1965-66; mem. Gov.'s Conf. on Human Rights and Opportunities, 1967, Gov.s Conf. on Innovation, 1989; Organizer Conn. small bus. divsn. Businessmen for V.P. Humphrey, 1968; alumni dir. Am. Internat. Coll., 1961-63, 89-93, trustee, 1963-71, mem. corp., 1972—; chmn. adv. bd. govs. Conn. Libr. Svc. Ctr., Willimantic, 1964-68; bd. dir., sec. Edn. and Rsch. Found. IMA-PIA for States N.Y., N.J. and Conn., Glenmont, N.Y., 1973-83; past trustee, past pres. Thompson Libr.; corporator Day Kimball Hosp., Putnam, Conn.; mem. region 3 adv. and planning coun. Conn. Dept. Mental Retardation, 1987-92; trustee Annhurst Coll., Woodstock, Conn., 1977-84; active Conn. Small Bus. Devel. Ctr., summer 1982, 83, 84, 85; bd. dir. Norwich-Quinebaug unit Am. Cancer Soc. Served with AUS, 1942-45, 39.5 months continuous overseas svc. Recipient Yr. award Hartford Assn. Ins. Women, 1969; Presdl. Appreciation cert. Conn. Assn. Mcpl. Devel. Commns., 1968, Alumni Achievement award Am. Internat. Coll., 1999. Mem. NEA (life), AAUP, KC (hon. life), Am. Risk and Ins. Assn. (fellowship 1960, 62), Risk and Ins. Mgmt. Soc., Am. Soc. Personnel Adminstrn., Am. Acad. Mgmt., Am. Acad. Religion, Northeastern Indsl. Developers Assn., Conn. Hist. Soc., Nat. Trust Historic Preservatio, Am. Legion, Phi Delta Kappa, Delta Pi Epsilon.: Loomis Village Apt A310 20 Bayon Rd South Hadley MA 01075

FISHER, WILLIAM W., III, law educator; b. Portland, Maine, Oct. 12, 1953; BA in Am. Studies, summa cum laude, Amherst Coll., 1976; JD magna cum laude, Harvard U., 1982, PhD in History Am. Civilization, 1991. Teaching fellow history and lit. dept. Harvard Coll., 1978—82; law clk. to Judge Harry T. Edwards US Ct. Appeals DC Cir., 1982—83; law clk. to Justice Thurgood Marshall US Supreme Ct., 1983—84; asst. prof. Harvard Law Sch., Cambridge, Mass., 1984—90, prof., 1990—, Hale and Dorr prof. intellectual property law, 2003—, dir. legal history program, 1988—2002, dir. Berkman Ctr. for Internet & Soc., 2002—. Co-author: American Legal Realism, 1993, Legal Reform in Central America: Dispute Resolution and Property Systems, 2001; author: Promises to Keep: Technology, Law, and the Future of Entertainment, 2004. Danforth Postbaccalaureate Fellowship, 1978—82, postdoctoral fellowship, Ctr. for Advanced Study in the Behavioral Sciences, Stanford, Calif., 1992—93. Office: Harvard Law Sch 1563 Massachusetts Ave Cambridge MA 02138 Office Phone: 617-495-0957. Office Fax: 617-496-4947. Business E-Mail: tfisher@law.harvard.edu.

FISHMAN, ALFRED PAUL, physician; b. N.Y.C., Sept. 24, 1918; s. Isaac Fishman and Anne (Tinter) Fishman; m. Linda Fishman, Oct. 7, 1984; children: Mark, Jay, Hannah Rae. AB, U. Mich., 1938, MS, 1939; MD, U. Louisville, 1943; MA (hon.), U. Pa., 1971. Diplomate Am. Bd. Internal Medicine, Nat. Bd. Med. Examiners. Intern Jewish Hosp., Bklyn., 1943—44; Dazian Found. fellow pathology Mount Sinai Hosp., N.Y.C., 1946—47, asst. resident, resident medicine, 1947—48; Dazian Found. fellow cardiovascular physiology Michael Reese Hosp., Chgo., 1948—49; Am. Heart Assn. rsch. fellow Bellevue Hosp., N.Y.C., 1949—50, established investigator Am. Heart Assn. cardiopulmonary lab., 1951—55; Am. Heart Assn. rsch. fellow in physiology Harvard U., Boston, 1950—51; instr. physiology NYU, 1951—53; assoc. in medicine Columbia Coll. Physicians and Surgeons, N.Y.C., 1953—55, asst. prof., 1955—58, assoc. prof., 1958—66; prof. medicine U. Chgo., 1966—69; dir. Inst. and Divsn. Cardiovasc. Disease Michael Reese Hosp., Chgo., 1966—69; prof. medicine U. Pa., Phila., 1969—72, William Maul Measey prof. medicine, 1972—, assoc. dean Sch. Medicine, 1969—99, dir. cardiovasc.-pulmonary divsn., 1969—90, chmn. dept. rehab. medicine, 1990—97; steering com. of dept. chmn. U. Pa. Med. Ctr., 1992; assoc. dean program devel. U. Pa., 1998—99, sr. assoc. dean program devel., 1999—; mem. coun. on grad. med. edn. U. Pa. Med. Ctr., 1992—93. Dir. Robinette Found., Clin. Cardiovascular Rsch. Ctr., U. Pa. Med. Ctr., 1969—82; mem. steering com. dept. chmn. U. Pa. Med. Ctr., 1992, coun. on grad. med. edn., 1992—93; dir. Specialized Ctr. of Rsch. (Lung), 1973—81; attending physician Hosp. U. Pa., 1969—, Presbyn. Hosp. Phila., 2000—; sr. attending physician Phila. Gen. Hosp., 1970—78; physician Mass. Gen. Hosp., 1979; cons. to chancellor U. Mo., Kansas City, 1973—78; vis. prof. Harvard U., 1970, Oxford (Eng.) U., 1972, Washington U., St. Louis, 1973, Johns Hopkins U., 1974, Ben Gurion U., 1975, Emory U., Atlanta, 1976, U. Porto Alegra, Brazilia, Brazil, 1976, U. Zurich, Switzerland, 1978, Duke U., 1986, U. N.C., 1986; vis. scientist for NIH to Peking, China, 1980, to USSR, 1985; cons. Exec. Office Pres., 1961—69, U. Athens, Greece, 1980; mem. WHO Expert Panel, Geneva, 1973—76, Nat. Adv. Heart and Lung Council, NIH, 1968—71, 1979—83, Steering Com. of Dept. Chmn U. Pa. Med. Ctr., 1992, Coun. on Grad. Med. Edn. U. Pa. Med. Ctr., 1992—93; coun. mem. Coll. of Physicians of Phila., 1993—; chmn. Gov.'s Com. for Rsch. on Respiratory Diseases in Coal Miners, 1974—90, Internat. Conf. on Lung, Titisee, Germany, 1976, Florence, Italy, 84, Prague, Czech Republic, 86, Prague, 89, NIH Conf. Proliferative & Obliterative Vascular Disease; chair steering com. Nat. Emphysema Treatment Trial, 1996—; U.S. chief del. Internat. Union of Physiol. Scis., Helsinki, Finland, 1989; cons. N.Y. State Bd. Health, 1987—91, Cleve. Found., 1984—; vis. com. Case Western Res. Sch. Medicine, Cleve., 1989—, Rsch Inst., Lankenau Hosp., Phila., 1990; chmn. Scientific Edn. Partnership U. Mo.-U. Kans.-Merrill Dow, 1989—2001. Editor (with D.W. Richards): Circulation of The Blood-Men and Ideas, 1964; editor: (with H.H. Hecht) The Pulmonary Circulation and Interstitial Space, 1969; editor: Handbooks of Respiratory Physiology, Am. Physiol. Soc., 1967—72, 1979—87, Physiology in Medicine, New Eng. Jour. Medicine, 1969—79, Jour. Applied Physiology, 1981—89, 1989—99; editor: (with D.W. Richards) Circulation of the Blood Men and Ideas, 1982; editor: Merck Manual, 1972—80, Ann. Rev. Physiology, 1977—81, Heart Failure, 1979; editor: (with E. M. Renkin) Pulmonary Edema, 1979; editor: Pulmonary Diseases and Disorders, 1979, 2d edit., 1988, Classics in Biology and Medicine, 1989—97, The Pulmonary Circulation: Normal and Abnormal, 1990;: 3d edit., 1998, Pulmonary Rehabilitation, 1994, Fishman's Pulmonary Diseases and Disorders, 3rd edit., 1998—, Fishman's Manual of Pulmonary Diseases and Disorders, 2002; contbr. articles to profl. jours.; reviewer Health Care Financing Adminstrn., 1995—97, Washington Adv. Group, 2000—. Bd. dirs. Polachek Found., Phila. Zool. Soc.; mem. Kansas City Life Scis. Inst., 2000—01. Recipient Disting. Alumni award, U. Louisville, 1984, Disting. award in nephrology, A.N. Richards, 1998. Fellow: ACP, Royal Coll. Physicians, Am. Coll. Chest Physicians (hon.); mem.: AAAS, NAS (com. on sci., edn. and pub. policy 1987—90, policy bd. complementary/alternative medicine 2003), Am. Thoracic Soc. (Trudeau medal 2001), Heart Assn. Southeastern Pa. (bd. dirs.), Coll. of Physicians of Phila. (coun. 1993—, pres.-elect 1994, pres. 1996—97), N.Y. County Med. Soc., Nat. Space Biomed. Rsch. Inst. (bd. dirs. 1999—), Health Care Financing Adminstrn. (mem. lung transplant ctr. rev. com. 1996—, NIH-HCFA nat. emphysema treatment trial 1996—, chair steering com.), Am. Coll. Cardiology (A.N. Richards Disting. Achievement award 1997), Fedn. Am. Socs. for Exptl. Biology (exec. bd. 1983—85), Internat. Union Physiol. Scis. (U.S. Nat. Com. 1982—89, chmn. 1986—89), N.Y. Heart Assn. (pres. 1965—67), Am. Heart Assn. (chmn. coun. on cardiopulmonary disease 1972—74, rsch. coun. 1974—79, sci. pub. com. 1986—88, bd. dirs. 1988—92, chmn. 1988—94, sci. adv. com. 1992—98, founder, Disting. Achievement award 1980, Merit award 1989, Gold Heart award 1992, Sr. Rsch. award 2003), Assn. Am. Physicians, Royal Soc. Medicine (London), Am. Acad. Arts and Scis., Am. Soc. Clin. Investigation, Am. Physiol. Soc. (chmn. publs. bd. 1974—81, pres. 1983, chmn. centennial celebration com. 1985—87, editor handbook 1986, Ray G. Daggs award 2004, Trudeau medal 2005), Inst. Medicine of NAS (chmn. health scis. bd. 1990—95, com. on social and ethical impact of advances in biomedicine 1992—94, com. on use of CAM by the pub. 2004—), Interurban Clin. Club, Alpha Omega Alpha. Home: 2401 Pennsylvania Ave Apt 20a7 Philadelphia PA 19130-3004 Office: Hosp U Pa 3400 Spruce St Philadelphia PA 19104-4206

FISHMAN, BERNARD, mechanical engineer; b. Bklyn., June 26, 1920; s. Max and Mollie (Greenberg) F.; m. Sara Fishman, July 3, 1947; 1 dau., Carol Beth. Student, Bklyn. Coll., 1937-39; B.M.E., CCNY, 1942; M.M.E., Bklyn. Poly. Inst., 1951. Instr. CCNY Sch. Tech., 1942-44; design and mfg. engr. Star Auto Radio, 1944-45; rocket propulsion engr. M.W. Kellogg Co., 1946-53; chief hydro-mech. engr. Simmonds Precision Products, 1953-65; engring. specialist Reaction Motors div. Thiokol Corp., 1965-67; dir. research, dir. ops. exec. office ASME, N.Y.C., 1967-89; freelance consulting engr., 1989—. Contbr. articles to profl. jours.; patentee in field. Mem. Bd. Edn., Ft. Lee, N.J., 1968-72. Served with USAF, 1945-46. Fellow ASME; mem. Nat. Soc. Profl. Engrs., Tau Beta Pi, Pi Tau Sigma. Business E-Mail: fishmanb@asme.org.

FISHMAN, BERNARD PHILIP, museum director; b. N.Y.C., July 25, 1950; m. Elizabeth Andersen, Jan. 8, 1983; 1 child, Philip. BA summa cum laude, Columbia U., 1972; MA, U. Pa., 1982. Rsch. fellow Mus. Applied Sci. Ctr. for Archaeology, U. Pa., Phila., 1976-79; Egyptologist Epigraphic Survey Oriental Inst., U. Chgo., Luxor, Egypt, 1979-82; dir. Fenster Mus. Art, Tulsa, 1982-85, Jewish Mus. Md., Balt., 1985-98, Lehigh County Hist. Soc., Allentown, Pa., 1998—2002, R.I. Hist. Soc., Providence, 2002—. Tchr., lectr. in field. Author, co-author, editor numerous books, exhibit catalogues, jours., articles; art critic World newspaper, Tulsa. Participant Getty Mus. Leadership Inst. Fellow R.I. Found.; mem. Phi Beta Kappa. Home: 499 Seven Mile Rd Hope RI 02831 Office: The RI Hist Soc 110 Benevolent St Providence RI 02906 Office Phone: 401-331-8575 ext. 36. Business E-Mail: bfishman@rihs.org. *Without the study of history there can be no civilization; without the cultivation of the arts there can be no immortality.*

FISHMAN, ELLEN BETH, lawyer; b. Bklyn., May 19, 1953; d. Stanley Irving and Elizabeth Flynn Fishman. BA summa cum laude, MA, Tufts U., 1974; JD, U. Pa., 1978. Bar: N.Y. 1979. Asst. corp. counsel N.Y.C. Law Dept., 1978—86, asst. chief. appeals divsn., 1986—2000, sr. coun. appeals divsn., 2000—03; ptnr., appellate coun. Martin Clearwater & Bell LLP, N.Y.C., 2003—. Pres. Epiphany Parish Coun., N.Y.C., 1988—89. Mem.: N.Y. Cir. Translators, N.Y. County Lawyers Assn., N.Y. State Bar Assn. (chair com. on appellate cts. 1992—94), Phi Beta Kappa. Democrat. Roman Catholic. Office: Martin Clearwater & Bell LLP 220 E 42nd St New York NY 10017 Office Phone: 212-697-3122.

FISHMAN, FRED NORMAN, lawyer; b. N.Y.C., Aug. 21, 1925; s. Arthur Elihu and Frederica (Greenspan) F.; m. Claire S. Powsner, Sept. 19, 1948; children: Robert J., Nancy K. S.B. summa cum laude, Harvard U., 1946, LL.B. magna cum laude, 1948; postgrad., Yale U., 1945-46. Bar: N.Y. State 1950, U.S. Supreme Ct. 1954. Law clk. to Chief Judge Calvert Magruder, U.S. Ct. Appeals, 1st Circuit, Boston, 1948-49; to Asso. Justice Felix Frankfurter, Supreme Ct. U.S., 1949-50; assoc. firm Dewey Ballantine LLP (and predecessors), N.Y.C., 1950-57; with Freeport Minerals Co., N.Y.C., 1957-61, asst. sec., 1958-59, asst. v.p., 1959-61; partner firm Kaye Scholer LLP, N.Y.C., 1962-92, mem. exec. com., 1970-87, chmn. exec. com., 1981-83, spl. counsel, 1993-95. Editor, officer: Harvard Law Rev. Chmn. Harvard Law Sch. Fund, 1977—79; mem. bd. overseers' com. to visit Harvard Law Sch., 1975—81, 1988—94, mem. dean's adv. bd., 2001—; chmn. com. Harvard Law Sch. Class of 1948 Twenty-Fifth Anniversary Gift, Forty-Fifth Anniversary Gift; mem. bd. overseers' com. to visit Grad. Sch. Edn., Harvard U., 1971—77, bd. overseers' Com. on Univ. Resources, 1991—, permanent class com. Harvard Coll. Class of 1946; mem. bd. overseers' com. to visit Med. Sch. and Sch. of Dental Medicine Harvard U., 1997—2003; trustee Pub. Edn. Assn., N.Y.C., 1956—73, chmn. bd., 1970—71; dir. Harvard Alumni Assn., 1981—83; trustee Hosp. for Joint Diseases and Med. Ctr., 1971—73, Lawyers' Com. for Civil Rights under Law, 1979—2004, bd. dirs., 1983—2004, co-chmn., 1983—85, hon. lifetime trustee, 2005—; mem. steering com. Campaign for Harvard Law Sch., 1991—95; mem. leadership coun. Harvard Sch. Pub. Health, 2003—. Recipient Alumni award, Harvard Alumni Assn., 2004. Fellow: Am. Bar Found.; mem.: ABA, Harvard Law Sch. Assn. (coun. 1978—82, exec. com. 1980—82, 1st v.p. 1984—86, pres. 1986—88, exec. com. 1988—90), Legal Aid Soc. (bd. dirs. 1991—94), Am. Law Inst. (adviser corp. governance project 1980—92), Assn. Bar City N.Y. (chmn. com. fed. legis. 1963—66, exec. com. 1966—70, chmn. com. corp. law 1980—82, treas. 1993—94), N.Y.C. Harvard Law Sch. Assn. (trustee 1966—69, pres. 1988—89, v.p. 1974—75), Harvard Club N.Y.C., Phi Beta Kappa. Home: 650 Park Ave Apt 3D New York NY 10021-6115 Office: Kaye Scholer LLP 425 Park Ave New York NY 10022-3598 Office Phone: 212-836-8348. Business E-Mail: ffishman@kayescholer.com.

FISHMAN, GEORGE MAYER, historian, educator; b. Phila., Jan. 6, 1917; s. Morris Fishman and Rose Schwartz; m. Edie Bartman; 1 child, Joelle. BS in Edn., Temple U., 1938; MA in History, U. Pa., 1941; PhD in History, Temple U., 1990. Tchr. social sci., histry, math. Phila. Pub. Schs., 1946—52, 1969—84; tchr. N.J. Pub. Schs., 1960—69, ret., 1984. Author: The African American Freedom Struggle in New Jersey History, 1997, For a Better World: A Miscellany, 2002; contbr. articles to pubs. Candidate gov. Communist Ticket, NJ, 1985. With USNR, 1943—45, WW II. Co-recipient Ida B. Wells Cmty. Activist award, NAACP, 1994; scholar African Am. and Labor studies. Mem.: NAACP, ACLU, Pa. Labor hist. Assn., Social Studies Coun. N.J., World History Assn., Orgn. Am. Historians, Am. Hist. Assn., Am. Fedn. Ret. Tchrs. Phila. and New Haven, Alliance Ret. Ams., Sierra Club. Avocations: walking, music.

FISHMAN, IRA, lawyer; b. Chgo., Nov. 6, 1957; BA magna cum laude, Yale Univ., 1979; JD cum laude, Harvard Univ., 1982. Bar: DC 1982. Assoc. to ptnr. Patton Boggs LLP, Washington, 1983—93; v.p. Congl. & External Affairs Import-Export Bank, Washington, 1993—95; dep. asst. Legis. Affairs to Pres. of U.S., Washington, 1995—96; spl. counsel & dir. Task Force on Edn. FCC, Washington, 1996; founder & past bd. chmn. NetDay, Irvine, Calif.; ptnr., Public Policy, Edn. practices Patton Boggs LLP, Washington, 2001—, COO, 2004—. Trustee KIPP Key Acad. Office: Patton Boggs LLP 2550 M St NW Washington DC 20037-1350 Office Phone: 202-457-6330. Office Fax: 202-457-6315. Business E-Mail: ifishman@pattonboggs.com.

FISHMAN, JAY STEVEN, financial services executive; b. NYC, Nov. 4, 1952; s. Edward and Shirley (Cantor) F.; m. Randy Lee Chapman, Sept. 25, 1976; children: Jordan Elliot, Scott Martin. BS in Econs. magna cum laude, MS in Acctg., U. Pa., 1974. CPA, N.Y. Audit supr. Coopers & Lybrand, NYC, 1974-79; dir. mergers and acquisitions Am. Can Co., Greenwich, Conn., 1979-83; sr. v.p. Goergen & Sterling, Greenwich, 1983-86; sr. v.p. mcht. banking Shearson Lehman Bros., NYC, 1986-89; exec. v.p., CFO Comml. Credit Co., NYC, 1989-91; sr. v.p., treas. Primerica Corp., NYC, 1991-94; sr. v.p. Travelers Group, NYC, 1994; vice chmn., CFO ins. group Travelers Inc., Hartford, Conn., 1994, pres., CEO, 1998—2004, chmn., 2000—04; pres., dir., CEO St. Paul Travelers Cos., Inc., Minn., 2004—. Mem. Wharton Club. Avocations: golf, running, skiing. Office: St Paul Travelers 385 Washington St Saint Paul MN 55102*

FISHMAN, JERALD G., semiconductor executive; BSEE, CCNY; MSEE, Northeastern U.; MBA, Boston U.; JD, Suffolk Law Sch. Mgr. in product mktg., ops., strategic planning Analog Devices, Norwood, Mass., 1971-79, gen. mgr. semicondr. divsn., 1979-80, v.p., 1980-82, group v.p., 1982-88, exec. v.p., 1988-91, pres., COO, 1991-96, pres., CEO, 1996—. Bd. dirs. Xilinx, Lahey Clinic, Cognex Corp. Office: Analog Devices 1 Technology Way Norwood MA 02062

FISHMAN, JOSHUA AARON, sociolinguist, educator; b. Phila., July 18, 1926; s. Aaron S. and Sonia (Horwitz) F.; m. Gella Jeanne Schweid, Dec. 23, 1951; children: M. Manuel, David Elliot, Avrom Avi. BS, MS (Mayor Phila. competitive scholar 1944-48), U. Pa., 1948; PhD, Columbia U., 1953; Ped.D. (hon.), Yeshiva U., 1968; LittD (hon.), Free U. Brussels, 1986. Tchr. elem. and secondary Yiddish secular schs., 1945-50; ednl. psychologist, sr. research asso. dept. research and experimentation Jewish Edn. Com. N.Y., 1951-54; from lectr. to vis. prof. psychology CCNY, 1955-58; research assoc. to dir. research Coll. Entrance Exam. Bd., 1955-58; assoc. prof. human relations and psychology U. Pa., 1958-60; prof. psychology and sociology, dean Grad. Sch. Edn. Yeshiva U., 1960-66, disting. univ. research prof. social scis. Ferkauf Grad. Sch. Psychology, 1966-88, emeritus, 1988—, univ. v.p. acad. affairs, 1973-76; vis. rschr., vis. prof. Stanford (Calif.) U., 1990—. Cummings lectr. McGill U., 1979; Linguistics Soc. Am. prof. Linguistics Inst., 1980; disting. vis. prof. Monash U., Melbourne, Australia, summers 1985, 2000; mem. com. on sociolinguistics Social Sci. Rsch. Coun.; adviser, cons. Am. Jewish Congress, Nat. Scholarship Svc. and Fund for Negro Students, Coll. Entrance Exam. Bd., Am. Assn. Jewish Edn., Ministry of Fin., Republic of Ireland; cons. Ctr. for Applied Linguistics, Internat. Rsch. Ctr. on Bilingualism, Secretariat Linguistic Policy Basque Govt., 1986—, Maori Lang. Commn., 1995—; vis. prof. linguistics L.I. U., 2000, NYU, 1998—, Grad. Ctr. CUNY, 1999—; bd. dirs. Consortium for Study of Lang. Problems, 2001—. Author: Studies on Polish Jewry, 1974, Sociology of Bilingual Education, 1976, The Spread of English, 1977, Advances in the Study of Societal Multilingualism, 1978, Never Say Die: A Thousand Years of Yiddish in Jewish Life and Letters, 1981, Bilingual Education for Hispanic Students in the U.S., 1982, The Rise and Fall of the Ethnic Revival, 1985, Readings in the Sociology of Jewish Languages, 1985, Ethnicity in Action, 1985, The Fergusonian Impact (2 vols.), 1986, Ideology, Society and Language, 1987, Language and Ethnicity in Minority Sociolinguistic Perspective, 1988, Yiddish: Turning to

Life, 1991, Reversing Language Shift, 1991, The Earliest Stage of Language Planning, 1993, Post-Imperial English, 1996, In Praise of the Beloved Language, 1997, The Multilinges Apple: Languages in New York City, 1997, Handbook of Language and Ethnic Identity, 1999, Can Threatened Languages Be Saved?, 2000, Llengua i identitat, 2001, Test Construction for Students of the Behavioral and Social Sciences, 2003, Spanish for Native Speakers: Community Perspectives, 2005, Do Not Leave Your Language Alone, 2005, also numerous profl. publs. including Afn shvel, 1980—, Forverts, 1996—; assoc. editor: Jour. Ednl. Sociology, 1963-65, Yivo Ann., 1970-77, Yidishe Sprakh, 1970—; editor: Yivo Bleter, 1974-77; editor Jour. Social Issues, 1964-69; editor: (series) Contributions to the Sociology of Lang., 1971—, Internat. Jour. Sociology of Lang., 1973—, (series) Contributions to the Sociology of Jewish Languages, 1985-88. Pres.'s scholar E.C. Morris fellow Columbia Tchrs. Coll., 1952-53, postdoctoral rsch. tng. fellow Social Sci. Rsch. Coun., 1954-55, fellow Ctr. Advanced Study Behavioral Scis., 1963-64, Princeton Inst. Advanced Study fellow, 1975-76, fellow Netherlands Inst. Advanced Study, 1982-83, Israel Inst. Advanced Studies, 1983, Nat. Fgn. Lang. Ctr., 1995-96; NSF European Conf. grantee, 1960, Office of Edn. grantee, 1960-63, 66-68, 72-74, 79-80, Social Sci. Rsch. Coun. European Conf. grantee, 1961, NIMH grantee, Latin Am., 1963, 66, NSF grantee, Europe, 1966, 79-83, Ford Found. grantee, 1969-72, 75-76, Meml. Found. Jewish Culture grantee, 1970-71, 78-79, 82-83, Nat. Inst. Edn. grantee, 1978-79, 79-81; sr. specialist Inst. Advanced Projects, East-West Ctr., 1968-69; sr. assoc. Multicultural-Bilingual divsn. Nat. Inst. Edn., 1976-77. Fellow APA, Am. Sociol. Assn., Am. Anthrop. Assn.; mem. AAAS, Am. Ednl. Rsch. Assn., Linguistic Soc. Am., Yivo Inst. Jewish Rsch., Nat. Assn. Bilingual Edn. (Man of Yr. 1992), TESOL, Terralingua. Personal E-mail: joshuaafishman@aol.com. *I have had the incredible good fortune to be exposed simultaneously to modern Western as well as both classical and modern Jewish thought, to secular and religious values, beliefs and ideals, and theoretical and applied emphases, to the comforts of a language of wider communication (English) and a language of ethnic intimacy (Yiddish), to the infinite world of science, the eternal land of my ancestors and the new world of democracy, opportunity and pluralism to which my parents came as immigrants. I have tried to combine all of these forces within myself and to contribute to them. I consider both the tensions and the creativity resulting from these varied stimuli to be a unique heritage: an American-Jewish heritage to be treasured, cultivated, improved and handed on.*

FISHMAN, LAWRENCE MARTIN, endocrinologist; b. Bklyn., Dec. 20, 1933; s. Matthew and Ruth Janet (Frank) F.; m. Suzanne Marian Rubenstein, Oct. 16, 1955; children: Matthew Edward, Charles Neal, Betsy Rachel, Andrew Klein. AB magna cum laude, Harvard Coll., 1955; MD, Harvard U., 1960. Diplomate Nat. Bd. Med. Examiners, Am. Bd. Internal Medicine, subsplty. in endocrinology and metabolism. Intern Peter Bent Brigham Hosp., Boston, 1960-61, asst. resident in medicine, 1961-62; clin. assoc. endocrinology Nat. Cancer Inst., NIH, Bethesda, Md., 1962-65; fellow in diabetes and endocrinology Vanderbilt U. Sch. Medicine, Nashville, 1965-67; asst. prof. medicine U. Miami Sch. Medicine, 1967-72, assoc. prof., 1972-75, prof., 1975—. Chief endocrinology and metabolism sect. VA Med. Ctr., Miami, 1967-99, assoc. chief of staff for rsch., 1975-2003; rsch. subject adv. program U. Miami Gen. Clin. Rsch. Ctr., 2004— Contbr. chpts. to books and articles to profl. jours. Fellow ACP; mem. Am. Fedn. Clin. Rsch., Endocrine Soc., So. Soc. Clin. Investigation, Phi Beta Kappa, Sigma Xi, Alpha Omega Alpha.

FISHMAN, LEN, state commissioner; BA in Polit. Sci., Antioch Coll., 1975; JD with honors, U. Md., 1981. Gen. counsel N.J. Assn. Non-profit homes for the Aging, 1991-94; commr. Dept. Health and Sr. Svcs., Trenton, NJ, 1994—99; CEO Am. Assn. Home and Svcs. for the Aging, Washington, 1999—2000; pres., CEO Hebrew Rehab. Ctr. for Aged, Boston, 2000—. Chair N.J. Health Care Financing Authority Recipient Disting. Citizen award N.J. Health Decisions, 1998; named Person of Yr. Med. Soc. N.J., 1996. Achievements: created first cabinet-level dept. for srs.; initiated Worlds Aids Day of Learning for Youth, electronic birth cert. in hosps; developed consumer-oriented HMO rules, first report on mortality rates following coronary artery bypass surgery; expanded assisted living and alternate family care for elderly; published HMO report card. Office: Hebrew Rehab Ctr for Aged 1200 Centre St Boston MA 02131

FISHMAN, LOUIS, physicist, researcher; b. Washington, Feb. 17, 1948; s. Fabius Samuel and Miriam (Helfand) F.; m. Ingrid Celeste Palmer, Aug. 18, 1974 (div. 1979); m. Shi Di, June 28, 1992; 1 child, Michael Di Fishman. BS in Chemistry, U. Rochester, 1969; AM in Chem. Physics, Harvard U., 1971, PhD in Physics, 1977. Postdoctoral fellow dept. chemistry U. Colo., Boulder, 1976-77; postdoctoral fellow dept. physics Villanova State Lab., Cath. U. Am., Washington, 1978, sr. rsch. fellow dept. civil engring., 1978-83; prof. math. dept. math. and computer scis. Colo. Sch. Mines, Golden, 1987-93; sr. scientist Applied Math. Scis., Ames DOE Lab., Iowa State U., Ames, 1994-96; prof. physics U. New Orleans, 1997—2001; sr. scientist Naval Rsch. Lab., Stennis Space Ctr., Miss., 1997—2001. Adj. assoc. prof. dept. civil engring., The Cath. U. Am., Washington, 1983-87; vis. scientist in applied math. scis., Iowa State U., Ames DOE Lab., 1990; summer faculty fellow Naval Underwater Systems Ctr., New London, Conn., 1991; vis. prof. math. S.N. Bose Ctr. for Basic Scis., Calcutta, 1992; vis. Erskine fellow dept. math. and stats., U. Canterbury, Christchurch, New Zealand, 1999; pres. MDF Internat., 2001—; vis. prof. math. City U. of Hong Kong, 2002, Växjö (Sweden) U., 2002, 05, Univ. Calgary, Alberta, Can., 2004; Disting. chair Univ. Calgary, Alerbat, Can., 2005; nat. and internat. presenter in field. Co-editor: Wave Splitting and Inverse Problems, 1999, Mathematical Methods in Wave Phenomena, 2004; editl. bd. Jour. Computational Acoustics, 1990—, Jour. Applied Sci. and Computation, 1992—; reviewer multiple jours. including Applied Mecsh. Rev., Jour. Acoustical Soc. Am., Jour. Optical Soc. Am., numerous others; contbr. numerous articles to sci. and profl. jours. Mem. AAAS, Am. Math. Soc., Math. Assn. Am., Soc. Indsl. and Applied Math., Am. Geophys. Union, N.Y. Acad. Scis., Acoustical Soc. Am., Internat. Union Radio Scientists, Electromagnetics Acad., Internat. Soc. for Analysis, its Applications and Computation (bd. dirs. 1997-2002). Office: MDF Internat Slidell LA 70461 Office Phone: 985-781-0713. Personal E-mail: shidi53@aol.com.

FISHMAN, MARK BRIAN, computer scientist, educator; b. Phila., May 17, 1951; s. Morton Louis and Hilda (Kaplan) F.; m. Alice Faber, Feb. 20, 1977 (div. 1986); m. E. Alexandra Baehr, Apr. 13, 1992 (div. 1994). AB summa cum laude, Temple U., 1974; postgrad., Northwestern U., 1974-76; MA, U. Tex., 1980. Bilingual tchr. Wilmette Pub. Schs., 1974; rsch. assoc., programmer, asst. instr. U. Tex., Austin, 1976-80; instr. computer and info. scis. U. Fla., Gainesville, 1980-85; asst. prof. computer sci. Eckerd Coll., St. Petersburg, Fla., 1985-90, dept. coord., 1988-90, 91—, assoc. prof. computer sci., 1991—; instrnl. cons. to IBM, 1980—. Cons. artificial intelligence Battelle Corp., 1987-89, USN Naval Tng. Sys. Ctr., 1997—, Advanced Techs., Inc., 1988—, LBS Capital Mgmt., 1990—. Series editor: Advances in Artificial Intelligence Rsch., Vol. I, 1989; editor: Proc. of the First Florida Artificial Intelligence Rsch. Symposium, 1988, Proc. of the Second Florida Artificial Intelligence Rsch. Symposium, 1989, Advances in Artificial Intelligence Rsch., vol. I, 1989, vol. II, 1992, Proc. of the Third Florida Artificial Intelligence Rsch. Symposium, 1990, Proc. of the Fourth Florida Artificial Intelligence Rsch. Symposium, 1991, Proc. of the Fifth Artificial Intelligence Rsch. Symposium, 1992; guest editor: International Jour. of Expert Systems, Vol. 5, no. 2; steering com. First Internat. Conf. Human and Machine Cognition; contbr. articles to profl. jours.; presenter in field. U. Tex. fellow, 1978-80; F.C. Austin scholar, 1975, Nat. Def. Fgn. Lang. fellow, 1974. Mem. Assn. Computing Machinery (Tchr. of Yr. award U. Fla. 1984), IEEE Computer Soc., Am. Assn. Artificial Intelligence, Assn. Computational Linguistics, Fla. Artificial Intelligence Rsch. Soc. (proc. chair 1988—, sec. 1988-89, v.p. 1989-91, pres. 1991—), Am. Soc. Engring. Edn. (faculty rsch. fellow summer 1986, 91), Internat. Soc. Philosophical Enquiry, Sigma Xi, Phi Beta Kappa, Phi Kappa Phi, Upsilon Pi Epsilon. Office: Eckerd Coll Dept Computer Sci Saint Petersburg FL 33733 Home: # 132 10460 Roosevelt Blvd St Petersburgh FL 33716 Business E-Mail: fishman@eckerd.edu.

FISHMAN, MARSHALL LEWIS, chemist; b. Phila., July 2, 1937; s. Harvey Abraham and Rose (Needleman) Fishman; m. Nanette Doris Hoffman, July 3, 1966 (dec. Sept. 1997); children: Harvey Abraham, Amy Lisa; m. Anne Austin, Oct. 14, 2001. AB, Temple U., 1959; MS, Villanova U., 1961; PhD, Poly. Inst. Bklyn., 1968. Postdoctoral fellow Poly. Inst. Bklyn., 1968-69; NRC/NAS postdoctoral fellow USDA, Phila., 1969-71; rsch. chemist R.B. Russel Ctr. USDA, Athens, Ga., 1971-80, USDA, Phila., 1980—. Editor: Chemistry and Function of Pectins, 1986, Polymers from Agricultural Coproduct, 1994; contbr. 70 articles to profl. jours. Mem. Am. Chem. Soc. (sec. Phila. sect. 1980, chmn. nutrition and food biochem. 1990-91, Agr. and Food divsn. fellow 1991), Chromatography Forum Delaware Valley (pres. 1985-86, exec. bd. 1983—, award 2000). Avocations: tennis, bicycling. Office: East Regional Rsch Ctr USDA 600 E Mermaid Ln Wyndmoor PA 19038 E-mail: mfishman@arserre.gov.

FISHMAN, MARVIN ALLEN, pediatric neurologist, educator; b. Chgo., Feb. 16, 1937; s. Joseph and Mary (Schneider) F.; m. Gloria Brenda Greenberg, Dec. 20, 1959; children: Bradley Steven, Patricia Ann. BS, U. Ill., 1959, MD, 1961. Diplomate Am. Bd. Pediatrics, Am. Psychiatry and Neurology. Intern, then resident in pediatrics Michael Reese Hosp. and Med. Center, Chgo., 1961-64; resident in neurology Mass. Gen. Hosp., Boston, 1966-67; fellow in pediatric neurology St. Louis Children's Hosp., 1967-70, dir. Birth Defects Ctr., 1971-79; prof. pediatrics, neurology and preventive medicine Washington U. Med. Sch., St. Louis, 1970-79, dir. Irene Walter Johnson Inst. Rehab., 1974-79; prof. pediatrics and neurology, dir. pediatric neurology tng. program Baylor Coll. Medicine, Houston, 1979—2004, vice chmn. dept. pediatrics, 1992—; chief neurology service Tex. Children's Hosp., Houston, 1979—2004, chief Blue Bird Clinic for Child Neurology. Mem. residency rev. com. for neurology Accreditation Coun. for Grad. Med. Edn., 1991-96, chmn., 1995-96; bd. dirs. Am. Bd. Psychiatry and Neurology, 1991-97, exec. com., 1995-97, v.p., 1996, pres., 1997, cons., 1999—; cons. Am. Bd. Pediat., 1999—. Conbr. articles in field, chpts. in books; mem. editorial bd. Jour. Pediatrics, 1980-87, Jour. Child Neurology, Pediatric Neurology, Annals of Neurology; editor textbook. With USAR, 1964-66. Grantee HEW, Grant Found., Ga. Warm Springs Found., Nat. Found.-March of Dimes. Mem. Am. Soc. Neurochemistry (councilor 1977-79), Child Neurology Soc. (exec. com., councillor 1980-82, sec.-treas. 1984-86, pres.-elect 1986-87, pres. 1987-89, past pres. 1989-90, John B. Hower award 1999), Houston Neurol. Soc. (pres.-elect 1989-90, pres. 1990-91), Am. Acad. Pediatrics, Am. Acad. Ncurology, Am. Neurol. Assn., Am. Pediatric Soc., Soc. for Pediatric Rsch., Soc. for Neuroscis. Home: 1523-B Potomac Dr Houston TX 77057-1925 Office: Tex Children's Hosp 6621 Fannin Houston TX 77030 Business E-Mail: mfishman@bcm.tmc.edu.

FISHMAN, MITCHELL STEVEN, lawyer; b. N.Y.C., July 27, 1948; s. Abraham and Sylvia (Sher) F.; m. Alison Rivard, Sept. 7, 1980 (div.) children: Danielle, Matthew, Jeremy; m. Mary Ellen Spiegel, Sept. 21, 2003. BA cum laude, Harvard U., 1970, JD cum laude, 1973; LLM in Taxation, NYU Law Sch., 2005. Bar: N.Y. 1974, D.C. 1984. Assoc. Breed, Abbott & Morgan, N.Y.C., 1973-74, Paul, Weiss, Rifkind, Wharton & Garrison, N.Y.C., 1975-81, ptnr., 1981-99. Exec. dir. Temp. State Commn. on Banking, Ins. and Fin. Svcs., N.Y., 1983-84; cons. Sirius Satellite Radio, Inc., N.Y.C., 2000-01. Mem. ABA, N.Y. State Bar Assn., Assn. of Bar of City of N.Y. (com. on corp. law 1976-79, mem. com. on securities regulation 1998-01). Democrat. Home: 10 Barnes Rd PO Box 1443 Washington CT 06793-0443 E-mail: mitchell_fishman@hotmail.com.

FISHMAN, ROBERT ALLEN, retired neurologist, educator, department chair; b. N.Y.C., May 30, 1924; s. Samuel Benjamin and Miriam (Brinkin) F.; m. Margery Ann Satz, Jan. 29, 1956 (dec. May 29, 1980); children: Mary Beth, Alice Ellen, Elizabeth Ann.; m. Mary Craig Wilson, Jan. 7, 1983. AB, Columbia U., 1944; MD, U. Pa., 1947. Mem. faculty Columbia Coll. Physicians and Surgeons, 1954-66, asso. prof. neurology, 1962-66; asst. attending neurologist N.Y. State Psychiat. Inst., 1955-66, Neurol. Inst. Presbyn. Hosp., N.Y.C., 1955-61, asso., 1961-66; co-dir. Neurol. Clin. Research Center, Neurol. Inst., Columbia-Presbyn. Med. Ctr., 1961-66; prof. neurology U. Calif. Med. Ctr., San Francisco, 1966-94, chmn. dept. neurology, 1966-92, prof. emeritus, 1994—; ret., 2005. Cons. neurologist San Francisco Gen. Hosp., San Francisco VA Hosp., Letterman Gen. Hosp.; dir. Am. Bd. Psychiatry and Neurology, 1981-88, v.p., 1986, pres., 1987 Author: Cerebrospinal Fluid in Diseases of the Nervous System, 1992; chief editor Annals of Neurology, 1993-97; contbr. articles to profl. jours. Nat. Multiple Sclerosis Soc. fellow, 1956-57; John and Mary R. Markle scholar in med. sci., 1960-65; recipient Disting. Alumnus award U. Pa. 1996. Mem. Am. Neurol. Assn. (pres. 1983-84), Am. Fedn. for Clin. Research, Assn. for Research in Nervous and Mental Diseases, Am. Acad. Neurology (v.p. 1971-73, pres. 1975-77), Am. Assn. Physicians, Am. Soc. for Neurochemistry, Soc. for Neurosci., N.Y. Neurol. Soc., Am. Assn. Univ. Profs. Neurology (pres. 1972-73), AAAS, Am. Epilepsy Soc., N.Y. Acad. Scis., AMA (sec. sect. on nervous and mental diseases 1964-67, v.p. 1967-68, pres. 1968-69), Alpha Omega Alpha (hon. faculty mem.), NAS Insts. Medicine. Home: 205 Paradise Dr Belvedere Tiburon CA 94920-2534 Personal E-mail: raf530@comcast.net.

FISHMAN, STEVEN T., psychologist; b. St. Louis, Sept. 19, 1941; s. Paul Leon and Frances Fishman; m. Cheryl Dee Sheinberg, Nov. 23, 1972; 1 child, Cohen; 1 child, Stephanie Carie. BA, Washington U., 1963; MA, PhD, U. Mo., 1970. Cert. behavioral psychology Am. Bd. Profl. Psychology, 1987, clin. psychology Am. Bd. Profl. Psychology, 1985. Intern VA, Palo Alto, Calif., 1967—68, Stanford U., Palo Alto, 1967—68; postdoctoral fellow SUNY, Stony Brook, 1970—71; founder and dir. Inst. For Behavior Therapy, N.Y.C., 1971—. Vis. clin. faculty Columbia U., N.Y.C., 1971—72; vis. assoc. prof. Grad. Sch. Applied Profl. Psychology, Rutgers U., New Brunswick, NJ, 1975—85; adj. grad. faculty Yeshiva U., N.Y.C., 1983—, Hofstra U., Hempstead, NY, 1989—2000. Author: (audiotape series) Agoraphobia:multiform Behavioral Treatment; contbr. chapters to books, articles to profl. jours. Mem. Mental Health Commn., Rockland County, NY, 1983—89. Fellow clin. psychology, USPHS, 1968—69. Mem.: APA (com. mem.), Assn. for the Advancement of Behavior Therapy (chairperson numerous coms. 1971—2005, Outstanding Svc. award 2002), Behavior Soc. N.Y. (pres. 1975—80), Am. Acad. Behavioral Psychology (pres. 1998—2001), Am. Bd. Behavioral Psychology (dir., sec./treas. 1985—2001). Office: Institute For Behavior Therpay Ste 206 104 East 40th St New York NY 10016 Office Phone: 212-692-9288. Office Fax: 212-692-9305. Personal E-mail: sfishman@ifbt.com.

FISHWICK, JOHN PALMER, retired lawyer, automotive executive; b. Roanoke, Va., Sept. 29, 1916; s. William and Nellie (Cross) F.; m. Blair Wiley, Jan. 4, 1941 (dec. June 1987); children: Ellen Blair (Mrs. Guyman Martin III), Anne Palmer (Mrs. Wesley Posvar), John Palmer Jr.; m. Doreen Allton, Nov. 17, 1989. AB, Roanoke Coll., 1937, DHL (hon.), 1971; LL.B., Harvard U., 1940; DL (hon.), Washington & Lee Univ., 2000. Bar: Va. 1939. Assoc. Cravath, Swaine & Moore, N.Y.C., 1940-42; asst. to gen. solicitor N. & W. Ry., Roanoke, Va., 1945-47, asst. gen. solicitor, 1947-51, asst. gen. counsel, 1951-54, gen. solicitor, 1954-56, gen. counsel, 1956-58, v.p., gen. counsel, 1958-59, v.p. law, 1959-63, sr. v.p., 1963-70, pres., chief exec. officer, 1970-80, chmn., chief exec. officer, 1980-81, also dir.; ptnr. Windels, Marx, Davies & Ives, N.Y.C., 1981-84; of counsel Fishwick, Jones and Glenn, Roanoke, Va., 1984-95; ret. Chmn., chief exec. officer Erie Lackawanna Ry. Co., 1968-70; pres., chief exec. officer Del. and Hudson Ry. Co., 1968-70; pres., dir. Dereco, Inc., 1968-81; chmn. investment com., bd. dirs. Norfolk So. Corp., 1981-89. Trustee Roanoke Coll., 1964-72; trustee Va. Theol. Sem.; former chancellor Diocese S.W. Va.; former bd. dirs. Va. Found. Humanities; former trustee Va. Mus. Fine Arts, Richmond. Served as lt. comdr. USNR, 1942—45. Mem. Met. Club (Washington). Episcopalian. Office: 110 Franklin Rd SE Roanoke VA 24042-0002 Personal E-mail: fish87@cox.net.

FISK, CATHERINE LAURA, law educator, lawyer; m. Erwin Chemerinsky. AB summa cum laude, Princeton Univ., 1983; JD, Univ. Calif., Berkeley, 1986; LLM, Univ. Wis., Madison, 1995. Bar: Calif. 1986, D.C. 1988. Staff atty. U.S. Ct. Appeals 9th cir., San Francisco, 1986—87, law clerk, 1987—88; assoc. Rogovin Huge & Schiller, Washington, 1988—90; atty. Appellate Staff, Civil Div., U.S. Dept. of Just., Washington, 1990—91; lectr. Univ. Wis. Law Sch., Madison, 1991; assoc. prof. Loyola Marymount Univ., 1992—96, prof., 1996—2003; vis. prof. Univ. Calif., Los Angeles, 1997—2002, Duke Univ., 2002; prof. Univ. Calif., Los Angeles, 2003—04, Duke Univ., 2004—. Contbr. articles prof. law jour. Vice-chair spec. comm. Investigative Oversight, City of Los Angeles, 1998; bd. dir. ACLU So. Calif., 1996—2004, exec. comm., 1998—2000, 2003—04, v.p., 2000—04; mem. nat. comm. commercial speech ACLU, 2003—; chair Willard Hurst Prize comm., Law & Society Assn., 2003—04. Recipient Pro Bono Svc. award, ACLU So. Calif., 2004, Distinguished Law Prof., 2003, Excellence in Education award, Indsl. Relations Rsch. Assn., 2000. Mem.: Am. Soc. Legal Hist. (mem. comm. membership 1997—99), Labor Law Group. Office: Duke Univ Sch Law Sci Dr & Towerview Rd Durham NC 27708-0360

FISK, CHARLES JOHN, meteorologist, researcher, consultant; s. Everett Vincent Fisk and Florence Linnea Carlson. BSBA, U. Minn., 1968; MS in Meteorology, U. Wis., 1984; MBA, Mankato State U., 1973. Meteorologist/climatologist Naval Base Ventura County, Point Mugu, Calif., 1986—; fin. analyst IBM Corp., Rochester, 1974—79. Cons. long-range forecasting of so. Calif. temperatures and precipitation, 1996—2000. Author: The First Fifty Years of Continuous Recorded Weather History In Minnesota (1820-1869) - A Narrative Chronology; contbr. articles to profl. jours.; author procs. Pvt. U.S. Army, 1968—69. Mem.: Am. Statis. Assn., Am. Meteorol. Soc. Avocations: reading, travel, web publishing. Home: 590 Gilbert Street Newbury Park CA 91320 Office: Point Mugu CA 91342 Personal E-mail: cjfisk@worldnet.att.net.

FISK, EDWARD RAY, retired civil engineer, author, educator; b. Oshkosh, Wis., July 19, 1924; s. Ray Edward and Grace O. (Meyer) Barnes; married, Oct. 28, 1950; children; Jacqueline Mary, Edward Ray II, William John, Robert Paul. BCE, Marquette U., 1949; student, Fresno (Calif.) State Coll., 1954, UCLA, 1957-58. Registered profl. engr., Ariz., Calif., Colo., Fla., Idaho, Ky., La., Mont., Nev., Oreg., Utah, Wash., Wyo.; lic. land surveyor, oreg., Idaho; lic. gen. engring. contractor, Calif.; cert. arbitrator Calif. Constrn. Contract Arbitration Com. Engr. Calif. Div. Hwys., 1952-55, Bechtel Corp., Vernon, Calif., 1955-59; project mgr. Toups Engring. Co., Santa Ana, Calif., 1959-61; dept. head Perliter & Soring, Los Angeles, 1961-64; Western rep. Wire Reinforcement Inst., Washington, 1964-65; cons. engr. Anaheim, Calif., 1965; assoc. engr. Met. Water Dist. So. Calif., 1966-68; chief specification engr. Koebig & Koebig, Inc., Los Angeles, 1968-71; mgr. constrn. svcs. VTN Consol., Inc., Irvine, Calif., 1971-78; pres. E.R. Fisk Constrn., Orange, Calif., 1978-81; corp. dir. constrn. mgmt. James M. Montgomery Cons. Engrs., Inc., Pasadena, Calif., 1981-83; v.p. Lawrance, Fisk & McFarland, Inc., Santa Barbara and Orange, 1983—; pres. E.R. Fisk & Assocs., Orange, 1983—, Gleason, Peacock & Fisk, Inc., 1987-92. V.p. constrn. svcs. Wilsey & Hamm, Foster City, Calif., 1993-94; adj. prof. engring., constrn. Calif. State U., Long Beach, 1987-90, Orange Coast Coll., Costa Mesa, Calif., 1957-78, Calif. Poly. State U., Pomona, 1974; instr. U. Calif., Berkeley, Inst. Transportation Studies, 1978—, engring. prof. programs U. Wash., 1994—2003, internationally for ASCE Continuing Edn. Author: Machine Methods of Survey Computing, 1958, Construction Project Administration, 1978, 82, 88, 92, 97, 2000, Construction Engineers Complete Handbook of Forms, 1981, 92, Resident Engineers Field Manual, 1992; co-author: Contractor's Project Guide, 1988, Contracts and Specifications for Public Works Projects, 1992, Introduction to Engineering Construction Inspection, 2004. With USN, 1942-43, USAF, 1951-52. Fellow ASCE (life, past chmn. exec. com. constrn. divn., past chmn. nat. com. inspection 1978—), Nat. Acad. Forensic Engrs. (diplomate); mem. Orange County Engring. Coun. (past pres.), Calif. Soc. Profl. Engrs. (past pres. Orange County), Structural Engrs. Assn. Calif. (engrs. joint contracts documents com. 1993-95), U.S. Com. Large Dams, Order Founders and Patriots Am. (past gov. Calif.), Soc. Colonial Wars (dep. gov. gen. Calif. chpt.), S.R. (past dir.), Engring. Edn. Found. (trustee), Tau Beta Pi. Home: 1792 N Ridgewood St Orange CA 92865-4454 Office Phone: 714-321-7200. Personal E-mail: erfiskpe@worldnet.att.net.

FISK, ELIOT H., musician; b. Phila., Aug. 10, 1954; s. George and Neva Hamilton Fisk; m. Zaira Meneset; 1 child, Raquel. BA summa cum laude, Yale U., 1976, MusM with honors, 1977. Lectr. Yale U., New Haven, 1977—82; prof. Hochschule für Musik, Köln, Germany, 1982—89, Universität Mozarteum, Salzburg, Austria, 1989—, New Eng. Conservatory, Boston, 1996—. Bd. dirs. Internat. Guitar Festival, Granada, Spain, 1998—99. Asst. editor: Guitar Rev. Founder Guitar and Friends, Salzburg, 1996. Named Best Classical Guitarist, Guitar Player Mag., 1996. Office: 90 Peter Robles Vantage Artists 131 Varicle # 937 New York NY 10013

FISK, HAYWARD DAN, lawyer, computer company executive; b. Las Vegas, Mar. 5, 1943; BS, U. Kans., 1965, JD, 1968; LLM, U. Mo., 1971. Bar: Kans. 1968, Pa. 1972, DC 1986, US Dist. Ct. Dist. Kans. 1968, US Ct. Appeals 5th Cir. 1970, US Supreme Ct. 1971. V.p., gen. counsel, sec. United Telephone Sys. Ea. Group, Carlisle, Pa., 1971—82; v.p., Wash. counsel Sprint Corp., Washington, 1982—88, v.p., assoc. gen. counsel Kansas City, 1988—89; v.p., gen. counsel, sec. Computer Sciences Corp., El Segundo, Calif., 1989—. Bd. dirs. Atlantic Legal Found., 1971—, chmn., 1997—; legal adv. bd. Nat. Legal Ctr. for Pub. Interest, 1991—; editl. bd. The Computer and Internet Lawyer, 1989—; Common Carrier and Emergency Preparedness Adv. Com. FCC, 1985—; Govt. and Regulatory Affairs Com. US C. of C., 1985—. Mem.: Am. Soc. Corp. Secretaries (bd. dirs.), Am. Corp. Counsel Assn. (bd. dirs., pres. So. Calif. Chpt. 1999, Excellence in Corp. Practice Award 2000), DC Bar, Pa. Bar Assn., Kans. Bar Assn., ABA. Office: Computer Scis Corp 2100 E Grand Ave El Segundo CA 90245-5024

FISK, IRWIN WESLEY, financial investigator; b. Byers, Kans., Nov. 20, 1938; s. Walter Roleigh Fisk and Mae Pearle Irwin; m. Susie Bea Walters, Sept. 9, 1973; children: Mark Christopher, Paul Steven. Student, LA City Coll., 1958—60, Calif. State U., LA, 1960—64, Pasadena C.C., 1987—88. Lic. pvt. investigator, Calif. Asst. exec. dir. Stores Protective Assn., L.A., 1962-66; sr. spl. investigator Calif. Dept. Corps., L.A., 1966-83, chief investigator, 1983-94; pres. Bus. and Fin. Investigations, Inc., La Crescenta, 1994—. Mem. Multi-State Law Enforcement Task Force of Fraudulent Telemarketing, LA, 1987—94, Nat. Coun. Policy Advisors, 1994—2004; mem. criminal justice adv. bd. Bethany Coll., 2002—. Contbr. articles to profl. publs. (Cramer journalism award 2004). Recipient Cramer Journalism award, 2004. Mem. U.S. Chess Fedn. (life), Am. Radio Relay League (DXCC award 1993, Cramer Journalism award 2004), Authors Guild, So. Calif. Fraud Investigators Assn., Masons, Nat. Coun. Policy Adv. for Inst. Law and Econ. Policy, 1994-2004, Criminal Justice Adv. Bd. Bethany Coll., 2002-. Republican. Avocations: chess, amateur radio. Home: 701 Emerald Dr Lindsborg KS 67456-2004 Office Phone: 888-438-4121. E-mail: iwfisk@yahoo.com.

FISK, MERLIN EDGAR, judge; b. Great Falls, Mont., Mar. 18, 1921; s. Edgar Anson and Eleanor Sybil (Worden) F.; m. Margery Anne Hall, May 27, 1942 (dec. Feb. 1999), m. Helen Ruth Freeman, Sept. 16, 2000; children: Mary Dana, Catherine, Anne, Elizabeth. BSChemE, Mont. State U., 1942. Tech. adminstr. Lago Oil & Transport Co., Ltd. subsidiary Exxon Corp., Aruba, Aruba Netherlands Antilles, 1942-62; v.p., gen. mgr. Antilles Chem. Co. subsidiary Exxon Corp., 1962-64; dir. mfg. Esso Pappas Indsl. Co., Athens, Greece, 1964-67; gen. mgr. Essochem, S.A. subsidiary Exxon Corp., Madrid, 1967-69, mgr. ops. and planning Brussels, 1969-71, ret., 1971; judge probate div. State of Conn., Newtown, 1979-91; ret., 1991. Pres. judge Conn. Probate Assembly, 1990-91. Mem. Commn. on Aging, Newtown, 1987-99; trustee Cyrenius H. Booth Libr., Newtown, 1975-95, 97-2003; bd. dirs. Newtown Meals on Wheels, Inc., 1974-93, Recording for the Blind, Inc. Conn. chpt., New Haven, 1975-92, Waterbury (Conn.) Ballet Co., 1987-97. Mem. Am. Arbitration Assn. (comml. panel 1991-98), Men's Literary and Social Club of Newtown (pres. 1984-85). Republican. Episcopalian. Avocations: golf, gardening, reading.

FISKE, EDWARD B., editor, educator, journalist, consultant; b. Phila., June 4, 1937; s. Edward R., Jr. and Jean B.; m. Dale Alden Woodruff, July 12, 1963 (div. May 1997); children: Julia F. Hogan, Suzanna F. Wilson; m. Helen F. Ladd, June 29, 1997. BA, Wesleyan U., Middletown, Conn., 1959; MA, Princeton Theol. Sem., 1963, Columbia U., 1965; LL.D. (hon.), Occidental Coll., 1991; and others. Religion reporter and editor N.Y. Times, 1964-74, edn. editor, 1974-91. Cons. Pew Forum on Edn. Reform, 1991-92, Bus. Roundtable Edn. Initiative, 1991-92, Dana Found., 1992-99, UNICEF Edn. Mission to Bangladesh, 1993, Internat. Rescue Com. in Cambodia, 1993-94, Acad. Ednl. Devel., 1993—, World Bank, 1995—, UNESCO, 1996—, USAID, 2003-; edn. analyst Asian Devel. Bank, 1994; vis. scholar Victoria U. Wellington, New Zealand, 1998, U. Cape Town, South Africa, 2002. Author: Fiske Guide to Colleges, (annual) Smart Schools, Smart Kids, 1990, (with Bruce Hammond) Fiske Guide to Getting into The Right College, 1997, 3d edit., 2004, (with Hammond) When Schools Compete, 2000, (with Helen Ladd) Fiske What to Do When for College, 2004, (with Hammond) Fiske New SAT Insider's Guide, 2004, (with Hammond) Elusive Equity, 2004; contbr. articles to nat. periodicals. Trustee Found. for Excellent Schs., 2000—, N.C. Ctr. for Internat. Understanding, 2001—, Central Park Sch. for Children, Durham, 2002—. Wolynsky-Joukowsky fellow Brown U., 1990, Montgomery fellow Dartmouth Coll., 1991. Mem.: Phi Beta Kappa. Home: 1723 Tisdale St Durham NC 27705-5631 E-mail: efiske@aol.com.

FISKE, JORDAN JAY, lawyer, retired prosecutor; b. Bklyn., Apr. 4, 1943; s. George Vlatofe and Pearl (Kalker) F.; m. Sandra Joyce Rappaport, June 22, 1974. BA, Brandeis U., 1963; JD, Fordham U., 1966. Bar: N.Y. 1967. Spl. agt. USAF Office of Spl. Investigations, Washington, 1966-71; trial atty. Dept. of Justice, N.Y.C., 1971-73; spl. asst. atty. gen. N.Y. State Office of the Spl. Prosecutor, N.Y.C., 1973-76; chief asst. dist. atty. Onondaga County Dist. Attys. Office, Syracuse, NY, 1976—2002; assoc. Syracuse Office of McGraw Law Firm, 2003—. Adviser Dist. Attys. Adv. Coun., Syracuse, 1976-2002; mem. Criminal Justice Adv. Bd., Syracuse, 1991. Capt. USAF, 1970-71, Vietnam. Mem. Jewish War Vets., Disabled War Vets., Vietnam Vets. Am. Office: 333 E Onondaga St Syracuse NY 13202 Office Phone: 315-422-7725.

FISKE, NEIL S., retail executive; Degree in Polit. Economy, Williams Coll.; MBA, Harvard U. Bus. cons. Boston Consulting Group, 1989—99, mng. ptnr., 2000—02; CEO Bath & Body Works, Reynoldsburg, Ohio, 2003—. Author: Trading Up: The New American Luxury, 2003. Past legis. adv. Congressman and Senator Timothy E. Wirth. Office: Bath & Body Works Inc Seven Ltd Pkwy Reynoldsburg OH 43068*

FISKE, ROBERT BISHOP, JR., lawyer; b. NYC, Dec. 28, 1930; s. Robert Bishop and Lenore (Seymour) F.; m. Janet Tinsley, Aug. 21, 1954; children: Linda Goucher, Robert Bishop, Susan Williams. BA, Yale U., 1952; JD, U. Mich., 1955, LLD (hon.), 1997. Bar: Mich. 1955, NY 1956, U.S. Ct. Appeals (2nd cir.) 1957, U.S. Supreme Ct. 1961. Assoc. Davis, Polk, Wardwell, Sunderland & Kiendl, 1955-57; asst. U.S. atty. So. Dist. N.Y., 1957-61; assoc. Davis Polk & Wardwell, 1961-64, ptnr., 1964—76, 1980—2002; U.S. atty. So. Dist. N.Y., N.Y.C., 1976-80; ind. counsel for Whitewater, Little Rock, 1994. Chmn. N.Y. State Jud. Commn. on Drugs and the Cts., 1999—2000; mem. Commn. for the Rev. of FBI Security Programs, 2001—02. Fellow Am. Coll. Trial Lawyers (pres. 1991-92); mem. ABA (chmn. standing com. on fed. judiciary 1984-87), Assn. of Bar of City of N.Y., Fed. Bar Coun. (pres. 1982-84), N.Y. State Bar Assn., Noroton Yacht Club, Wee Burn Country Club. Republican. Congregationalist. Office: 450 Lexington Ave New York NY 10017-3911 Office Phone: 212-450-4090.

FISKIN, JUDITH ANNE, artist, educator; b. Chgo, Apr. 1, 1945; d. Fred Albert and Cecile (Citron) Bartman; m. Jeffrey Allen Fiskin, Jan. 1, 1967 (div. Apr. 1975); m. Jonathan Marc Wiener, Jan. 17, 1987. BA, Pomona Coll., 1966; postgrad., U. Calif., Berkeley, 1966-67; MA, UCLA, 1969. Assoc. dean Calif. Inst. Arts, Valencia, 1977-84, faculty, 1977—. One-woman shows include Castelli Graphics, N.Y.C., 1976, Asher-Faure, L.A., 1991, Mus. Contemproary Art, L.A., 1992, Curt Marcus Gallery, N.Y.C., 1994, Patricia Faure Gallery, Santa Monica, Calif., 1994; exhibited in group shows at Internat. Ctr. for Photography, NYC, San Francisco Mus. Modern Art, Corcoran Gallery Art, Washington, LaJolla (Calif.) Mus. Art and Mus. in Richmond, Va., Miami, Fla., Chgo., Akron, Ohio, also in Copenhagen, Geneva, Verona; video: Diary of a Midlife Crisis, 1998 (San Francisco and Houston Internat. film festivals awards); videos shown at San Francisco Internat. Film Festival, Atlanta Film and Video Festival, Houston Internat. Film Festival, U.S. Super-8 Festival, Mus. Contemporary Art, LA, Brisbane (Australia) Internat. Film Festival, Kassel Film Video Festival, Germany; videos My Getty Center at Getty Mus. and Paris, Berlin, Utrecht and Toronto, What We Think About When We Think About Ships at L.A. County Mus. Art, 2002-03, 50 Ways To Set The Table Mus. Modern Art N.Y.C., 2004, Anthology Film Archives, N.Y.C., 2004, Angles Gallery, Santa Monica, 2004. Cmty. funding bd. mem. Liberty Hill Found., LA, 1994. Recipient Lifetime Achievement award in photography LA Ctr. for Photographic Studies, 1995, Silver Spire award San Francisco Internat. Film Festival, award Houston Internat. Film Festival, Bronze award Houston Internat. Film Festival; grantee Nat. Endowment for Arts, 1979, 90, Logan, 1986. E-mail: jfiskin@judyfiskin.com.

FISS, OWEN M., law educator; b. 1938; BA, Dartmouth Coll., 1959; BPhil, Oxford U., 1961; LLB, Harvard U., 1964. Bar: N.Y. 1965. Law clk. to Judge Thurgood Marshall US Ct. Appeals 2d Cir., 1964—65; law clk. to Justice Brennan US Supreme Ct., 1965; spl. asst. atty. gen. civil rights divsn. US Dept. Justice, Washington, 1966—67; acting dir. Office of Planning Coordination, 1968; prof. U. Chgo. Law Sch., 1968—74, Yale Law Sch., New Haven, 1974—84, Alexander M. Bickel prof. pub. law, 1984—92, Sterling prof., 1992—. Vis. prof. Stanford U., 1972; mem. Harvard Law Rev. Author: Injunctions, 1972, The Civil Rights Injunction, 1978; author: (with R.M. Cover) The Structure of Procedure, 1979; author: (with D. Rendleman) Injunctions 2d edit., 1984; author: (with Cover and J. Resnick) Procedure, 1988; author: (with Cover and Resnick) The Fed. Procedural Sys., 1988, The Fed. Procedural Sys. 3d edit., 1991, Holmes Devise Hist. of the Supreme Ct.: Troubled Beginnings of the Modern State, 1888-1910, 1993, Liberalism Divided, 1996, The Irony of Free Speech, 1996, A Cmty. of Equals, 1999, A Way Out, 2003; mem. edtl. bd.: Philosophy and Pub. Affairs and Found. Press, Yale Jour. Criticism, Yale Jour. Law and Humanities, Law, Econs. and Orgns. Office: Yale Law Sch PO Box 208215 New Haven CT 06520 E-mail: owen.fiss@yale.edu.

FISTER, MICHAEL J., computer company executive; b. Savannah, Ga. m. Teresa Fister; children: Allison, Sarah. BSEE, U. Cin., 1977, MSEE, 1978. Various exec. and engring. mgmt. positions Wyse Tech., Machine Vision Internat., Cin. Milacron; ops. mgr. 8-bit focus group Intel Corp., Chandler, Ariz., 1987—88, engring. mgr. application-specific integrated circuit group, 1988—90, mgr. microcomputer engring. group, 1990—91, gen. mgr. end user components divsn., 1991—95, gen. mgr. microprocessor divsn., 1995—99, v.p., 1996—2000, gen. mgr. enterprise server group, 1999—2000, gen. mgr. enterprise platform group, 2000—04, corp. v.p., 2000—02, sr. v.p., 2002—04; pres., CEO Cadence Design Systems, Inc., San Jose, Calif., 2004—, also bd. dirs. Bd. dirs. Autodesk Corp., San Rafael, Calif. Office: Cadence Design Systems Inc 2655 Seely Ave San Jose CA 95134*

FISZEL, GEOFFREY LYNN, investment banker, investment advisor; b. NYC, Aug. 9, 1942; s. John Henry and Rebecca (Wexman) F.; m. Barbara Ann Foohey, Jan. 30, 1970; children: Sharon Lynn, Morgan Bernard, Austin Tyler, Alexander William. BS in Mgmt. and Ops. Rsch., NYU, 1974; MS in Acctg. and Tax (Seminar award), U. Hartford, 1976; grad. scholar program econs. of fin., Trinity Coll., 1980. Registered securities rep., gen. securities prin., investment adviser. Cost acct. O'Malley Cos., Phoenix, 1974; regional acct., asst. regional contr. Sanitas Svc. Corp., Hartford, Conn., 1974-75; asst. to corp. contr. Bristol (Conn.) Brass Corp., 1975-76; asst. contr. Security Ins. Co. of Hartford, 1976-80; contr. Chase Enterprises, 1980-81, v.p., contr., 1981, sr. v.p., contr., 1985, sr. v.p. corp. and real estate devel., banking, ins., telecom., and mergers and acquisitions, 1988-89; CEO, pres., chmn. Equity Investors Holding Co., Glastonbury, Conn., 1989—; v.p. investments Advest, Inc., Hartford, 1993-94, Tucker Anthony, Inc., Hartford, 1994-2000, first v.p. investments, 2000—01; v.p., fin. advisor Morgan Stanley, Hartford, 2001—. Tax and fin. cons. U. Conn.; lectr., cons. in field. Author: How to Start Your Own Private Investment Partnership, 1997; pub., author investment adv. newsletter Continuing Walks On The Wild Side. Mem. Juvenile Diabetes Found. Served with USMC, 1959-63. Mem. Real Estate Bd. N.Y., Fin. Execs. Inst. (mem. corp. fin. and taxation coms.), The Nature Conservancy. Home: 245 Farmcliff Dr PO Box 578 Glastonbury CT 06033-0578 Office: Morgan Stanley One City Pl Hartford CT 06103 Office Phone: 860-275-6592. Personal E-mail: geoffrey_fiszel@msn.com.

FISZER-SZAFARZ, BERTA (BERTA SAFARS), research scientist, researcher; b. Feb. 1, 1928; m. David Safars; children: Martine, Michel. MS, U. Buenos Aires, 1955, PhD, 1956. Lab. chief Cancer Inst. Villejuif, France, 1961—67; vis. scientist Nat. Cancer Inst., Bethesda, Md., 1967—68; lab. chief Institut Curie, Orsay, France, 1696—. Vis. scientist Ins. Applied Biochemistry, Mitake, Gifu, Japan, 1986; gen. sec. dep. French-Israel Assn. Sci. Rsch. and Tech., 1994. Contbr. articles to profl. jours. Mem.: French Soc. Cell Biology, European Cell Biology Orgn., European Assn. Cancer Rsch., Am. Assn. Cancer Rsch. (corr.). Office: Institut Curie-Biologie Bat 110 Centre Universitaire 91405 Orsay France

FITCH, BLAKE, museum director, photographer, curator; b. Greensboro, NC, 1971; BFA, Pratt Inst., 1994; attended, Art Inst. Chgo., 1998; MS in arts adminstrn., Boston U., 2001. Exec. dir. Griffin Museum of Photography, Winchester, Mass. Curator Photobooth, Jan Staller: A Retrospective. Office: Griffin Mus Photography 67 Shore Rd Winchester MA 01890 E-mail: blake@griffincenter.org.*

FITCH, COY DEAN, internist, educator; b. Marthaville, La., Oct. 5, 1934; s. Raymond E. and Joey (Youngblood) F.; m. Rachel Farr, Mar. 31, 1956; children: Julia Anne, Jaquelyn Kay. BS, U. Ark., 1956, MS, MD, U. Ark., 1958. Diplomate Am. Bd. Internal Medicine and Endocrinology. Intern U. Ark. Sch. Medicine, 1958-59, resident, 1959-62, instr. biochemistry, 1959-62, asst. prof. medicine and biochemistry, 1962-66, asso. prof., 1966-67; dir. U. Ark. Sch. Medicine (Honors Med. Student Research Program), 1965-67; asso. prof. internal medicine and biochemistry St. Louis U. Sch. Medicine, 1967-73, prof. internal medicine, 1973—, prof. biochemistry, 1976—, head sect. metabolism, 1969-76, dir. div. endocrinology and metabolism, 1977-85; chief med. service St. Louis U. Hosps., 1976-77, vice-chmn. dept. internal medicine, 1983-85, acting chmn. dept. internal medicine, 1985-88, chmn. dept., 1988-2000; practice medicine, specializing in internal medicine Little Rock, 1962-67, St. Louis, 1969—. Dir. Diabetic Clinic, U. Ark. Med. Ctr., 1962-67, head sect. metabolism and endocrinology, 1966-67; mem. nutrition study sect. div. research grants NIH, 1967-71 Assoc. editor: Nutrition Revs., 1964; contbr. articles to profl. jours. Served from capt. to lt. col., M.C. AUS, 1967-69. Recipient Lederle Med. Faculty award, 1966-67; Russell M. Wilder-Nat. Vitamin Found. fellow, 1959-62. Master ACP (gov. Mo. chpt. 1995-99); mem. Am. Inst. Nutrition, Am. Soc. Biol. Chemists, Ctrl. Soc. Clin. Rsch., Phi Beta Kappa. Office: 1402 S Grand Blvd Saint Louis MO 63104-1004 Office Phone: 314-577-8759. Business E-Mail: fitchcd@slu.edu.

FITCH, DIANE K., human services administrator; b. Afton, Okla., Oct. 18, 1954; d. Everett Leroy Gray and Patricia Dean Bailey; 1 child, Christopher Michael. AS, Butler County C.C., Eldorado, Kans., 1988; BS, Friends U., 1991. Advanced dispute resolution State of Kans., 2000. Intake counselor Salvation Army, Wichita, Kans., 1989—92, youth counselor, 1989—91, Sedgwich County, Wichita, 1990—91; human svc. specialist Social and Rehab. Services, Wichita, 1991—. Equal employment officer Social and Rehab. Svcs., Wichita, 1991—2000. Rep. United Way of the Plains, Wichita, 1989—2005; v.p. Social and Rehab. Kans., Wichita; treas. Lunch Bunch, Wichita, 1998—2005. Named Legal Eagle, State of Kans., 1992; recipient Outstanding Recognition in Philosophy and Religion, Nat. Collegiate Awards Acad., 1988, Kans. Quality Mgmt. Award of Excellence, State of Kans., 1998; scholar, Friends U., 1989—91. Mem.: Gen. Fedn. of Women's Clubs Internat. (Delta Hypatia chpt.) (assoc.). Democrat. Avocations: gardening, landscaping. Office: Social and Rehabilitation Services PO Box 1620 320 East William Wichita KS 67201 Office Phone: 316-337-7157. Business E-Mail: dkf@srskansas.org.

FITCH, DONALD EVERETT, librarian; b. Miles City, Mont., Apr. 9, 1928; s. Everett Willis and Teresa Helen (Sagaser) F.; m. Dorothy Ann Lamb, June 19, 1954; children: Stephen, Charles, Robert, Jane, Alan, Hugh. BA in English, Gonzaga U., 1953; MA in English, UCLA, 1954; MLS, U. Calif., Berkeley, 1959. Tchr. Coeur d'Alene (Idaho) High Sch., 1954-56, Santa Monica (Calif.) Coll., 1958; libr. U. Calif., Santa Barbara, 1959—, head reference dept., 1963-84, asst. coll. devel. officer, 1984—. Author: Blake Set to Music, 1990; composer choral works include Ye Sons and Daughters, 1991; editor: Soundings Jour., 1969—; contbr. articles to profl. jours. Home: 7281 Butte Dr Santa Barbara CA 93117-1335

FITCH, FRANK WESLEY, pathologist, educator, immunologist, dean; b. Bushnell, Ill., May 30, 1929; s. Harold Wayne and Mary Gladys (Frank) F.; m. Shirley Dobbins, Dec. 23, 1951; children— Mary Margaret, Mark Howard. MD, U. Chgo., 1953, S.M., 1957, PhD, 1960; MD (hon.), U. Lausanne, Switzerland, 1990. Postdoctoral research fellow USPHS, 1954-55, 57-58; faculty U. Chgo., 1957—, prof. pathology, 1967—, Albert D. Lasker prof. med. sci., 1976—, emeritus prof., 1996, assoc. dean med. and grad. edn. div. biol. scis., 1976-85, dean acad. affairs, 1985-86, dir. Ben May Inst., 1986-95. Vis. prof. Swiss Inst. Exptl. Cancer Research, Lausanne, Switzerland, 1974-75. Editor-in-chief The Jour. of Immunology, 1997-2002; contbr. chpts. to books, articles to profl. jours. Recipient Borden Undergrad. Research award, 1953, Lederle Med. Faculty award, 1958-61; Markle Found. scholar, 1961-66; Commonwealth Fund fellow U. Lausanne (Switzerland) Institut de Biochimie, 1965-66; Guggenheim fellow, 1974-75 Mem. Fedn. Am. Socs. for Exptl. Biology (pres. 1993-94), Am. Assn. Immunologists (pres. 1992-93), Am. Soc. for Investigative Pathology, Am. Assn. for Cancer Rsch., Chgo. Path. Soc., Transplantation Soc., Sigma Xi, Alpha Omega Alpha. Business E-Mail: ffitch@uchicago.edu.

FITCH, JANET, writer; b. L.A. Grad., Reed Coll. Mng. editor Am. Film mag.; editor The Mancos Times Tribune; book reviewer Speak mag., San Francisco. Author: Kicks, 1996, White Oleander, 1999, short stories. Office: c/o Heather Rizzo Little Brown and Co 1271 Avenue of the Americas New York NY 10020

FITCH, MARK, mathematics professor; b. Mpls., Sept. 26, 1972; s. Philip and Anne Fitch; m. Kamilla Fitch. BS, Bob Jones U., 1994; PhD, Clemson U., 2001. Asst. prof. math. U. Alaska, Anchorage, 2001—. Fulbright scholar, Fulbright Commn., 1997—98. Office: U Alaska Anchorage 3211 Providence Dr Anchorage AK 99508 Office Phone: 907-786-1656. E-mail: afmaf@uaa.alaska.edu.

FITCH, MARTHA JEAN, minister; b. Tulsa, May 30, 1960; d. Wallace Lee and Helen Jean (Ruth) Spleth; m. Gregory Scott Fitch, Aug. 6, 1983; children: Mary Christine, David Lee, Nathaniel Mark. BA, Tex. Christian U., 1982; MDiv, Brite Div. Sch., 1985. Ordained to ministry Christian Ch. (Disciples of Christ), 1986. Min. to children South Hills Christian Ch. (Disciples of Christ), Ft. Worth, 1982-88; co-pastor 1st Christian Ch. (Disciples of Christ), Sterling, Colo., 1988—97, Allen, Tex., 1997—2003, Galesburg, Ill., 2003—. Moderator elect Cen. Rocky Mountain Region of Christian Chs. (Disciples of Christ), Colo., Wyo., 1990-92; moderator Ctrl. Rocky Mt. Region of Christian Ch., Colo., Wyo., 1992-94. Mem.: AAUW, Galesburg Ministerial Assn. (sec. 2005—), Coop Ministry (sec., bd.dirs. 1990, vice chair 1991—93, chair 1996). Republican. Office: 301 N Broad St Galesburg IL 61401

FITCH, NANCY ELIZABETH, historian, educator; b. White Plains, N.Y., June 17, 1947; d. Robert Franklin and Nancy Elizabeth (Harvey) F. BA in Polit. Sci./English Lit., Oakland U., Rochester, Mich., 1969; MA in History, U. Mich., 1971, PhD in History, 1981. Danforth tchg. intern dept. history U. Mich., Ann Arbor, 1970; asst. prof. history and lit. Sangamon State U., Springfield, Ill., 1972-74; sr. social sci. rsch. analyst The Congl. Rsch. Svc. of Libr. of Congress, Washington, 1975-78; asst. to the chmn./historian U.S. EEO Commn., Washington, 1982-89; asst. prof. history Lynchburg Coll. of Va., 1989-91; asst. prof. African Am. studies Temple U., Phila., 1991-92; Jesse Ball Dupont vis. scholar Randolph-Macon Woman's Coll., Lynchburg, Va., 1992-93; assoc. prof. history U. N.C. at Asheville, 1993-95; assoc. prof. history and English Coll. New Rochelle, NY, 1995—, chair dept., 1999—2003. Chmn.'s rep. White House Inst. on Hist. Black Colls. and Univs., U.S. Dept. Edn., 1985-89, EEO com.; pub. rels. vol. S. Africa Exhibit Project, Washington, 1986-88; mem. adv. com. DuPont Vis. Scholars Project, Va. Found. Ind. Colls., 1990-91; adj. prof. in history Shaw U., Asheville, 1994; lectr. Jesse Ball DuPont Found. Coll. Confs. on Diversity, The Aspen Inst., Queenstown, Md., 1995, 96; participating historian, spkr. Schomburg Ctr. for Rsch. in Black Culture, N.Y.C., 1994, Booker T. Washington Jr. Anniversary Commemoration. Anthology Editor: How Sweet the Sound: The Spirit of African American History, 1999; editl. assoc.: Jour. South Asian Lit., 1969-79; co-editor: Diversity: A Jour. of Multicultural Issues, 1995-98; mem. editl. adv. bd. Kente Cloth: African Am. Voices in Tex.; contbr. book reviews to Jours.; author: (series) Essays on Liberty, 1988; contbr. articles to profl. jours. Organizer, producer Ann. Dr. Martin Luther King Jr. Celebration prog., Washington, 1986-88; guest lectr. on history of Am. music Blue Ridge Music Festival, Lynchburg, 1991; participant Radio America African-Am. contbrs. to art and lit., 1990; vol./cons. The Holiday Project, Washington, 1986-88; mem. Widening Horizons Prog. of D.C. Pub. Schs., 1986-88; trustee Sister to Sister Internat, 2004. Recipient Achievement award Mt. Vernon Day Care Ctr., 1983, Spl. Commendation, U.S. EEO Commn., 1985-89, Ft. Drum Sgt. Maj.'s medal for svc. 10th Mountain div. Light Inf., Ft. Drum, N.Y., 1992; fellow Ford Found., 1971-72, Nat. Def. Fgn. Lang., 1970, U. Mich., 1970-71, 78-79, John Hay Whitney Found., 1969-70; Faculty summer seminar fellowship Nat. Endowment for the Humanities, U. Kans., Lawrence, 1996; Alden B. Dow creativity fellow Northwood U., 1998; Millennium writer Westchester Libr. Sys. Inc., 2000. Fellow Soc. Values in Higher Edn.; mem. Assn. for Study African Am. Life and History, Orgn. Am. Hists., Phi Alpha Theta (faculty advisor 1990-91). Republican. Episcopalian/Buddhist. Avocation: photography. Home: 267 Bedford Ave Mount Vernon NY 10553-1517 Office: Coll New Rochelle 29 Castle Pl New Rochelle NY 10805-2338

FITCH, RACHEL FARR, claims consultant; b. July 27, 1933; d. Allen Edward and Rosie Leola (Jones) Farr; m. Coy Dean Fitch, Mar. 31, 1956; children: Julia Anne, Jaquelyn Kay. Student, Little Rock U., 1965-67; BS, St. Louis U., 1974, MS, 1976, PhD, 1983. RN, Mo. Psychiat. staff nurse VA Ft. Root Hosp., North Little Rock, Ark., 1954-57; surg.-med. staff nurse St. Vincent Infirmary, Little Rock, Ark., 1957-65; acute care nurse Georgetown U. Hosp., Washington, 1968-69; pub. health nurse to adminstr. South office Vis. Nurse Assn. Greater St. Louis, 1970-73; cons. in edn. St. Louis City Health Dept., 1977-80; rsch. specialist Sen. John C. Danforth, St. Louis, 1980; owner RFF Assocs., 1983-86. Project dir. study of infant mortality in city of St. Louis, 1978. Mem. community health edn. com. Am. Heart Assn., 1977-87; bd. dirs. LWV of Mo., 1984-2001, editor newspaper, 1984-87, dir. health issues, 1987-99, 1st v.p. 1999-2001, 2003—; chmn. Mo. Consumer Health Care WATCH, 1996-2002; mem. adv. com. Mo. Medicaid Consumer, 1996-97; mem. Mo. Welfare Coord. Com., 1997-99; mem. healthcare mgmt. and policy adv. com. Maryville U., 2002—04; mem. Mo. Found. for Health Advocates steering com., 2003—04; sec. St. Louis U. Hosp. Aux. Mem. APHA, Acad. Polit. Sci., Grand Jury Assn. St. Louis (bd. dirs.), Woman's Club St. Louis U. Sch. Medicine (past pres., bd. dirs., 2004—), Jr. League St. Louis, Sigma Theta Tau, St. Louis U. Hosp. Aux. (sec). Address: 23 Lenox Pl Saint Louis MO 63108-1901 Office Phone: 314-961-6869. E-mail: rachel.farr.fitch@sbcglobal.net.

FITCH, ROBERT MCLELLAN, manufacturing executive, consultant; b. Shanghai, Apr. 30, 1928; came to U.S., 1937; s. George A. and Geraldine (Townsend) F.; m. Reta Peck, Aug. 21, 1955; children: David H.A., Douglas G., Christopher M. AB, Dartmouth Coll., 1949; PhD, U. Mich., 1954. Prof. U. Conn., Storrs, 1962-83; v.p. corp. rsch. SC Johnson Wax, Racine, Wis., 1983-85, sr. v.p. R & D, 1985-89; pvt. practice cons., 1990—. Author: Polymer Colloids, A Comprehensive Introduction, 1997; editor: Polymer Colloids, 1971, Polymer Colloids II, 1980; contbr. over 100 articles to profl. jours.; patentee in field. Mem. adv. bd. Nat. Sci. Resources Ctr., Smithsonian Inst. and Nat. Acad. Science, 1992-96, chmn., 1994-96; mem. adv. team Nat. Inst. for Sci. Edn., 1995-2000; chmn. Taos Talking Pictures, 1998-2000; bd. dirs. Taos Chamber Music group, 2001—. Recipient Disting. Svc. award Am. Chem. Soc., 1987; named to S.E. Wis. Educators Hall of Fame, 1992. Fellow AAAS. Avocations: skiing, scuba diving, photography.

FITCH, VAL LOGSDON, physics professor; b. Merriman, Nebr., Mar. 10, 1923; s. Fred B. and Frances Marion (Logsdon) Fitch; m. Elise Cunningham Fitch, June 11, 1949 (dec. 1972); children: John Craig(dec.), Alan Peter; m. Daisy Harper Sharp, Aug. 14, 1976. Bin Engring., McGill U., 1948; PhD, Columbia U., 1954; PhD (hon.), Princeton, 2000. Instr. Columbia, 1953; instr. physics Princeton, 1954—56, asst. prof., 1956—59, assoc. prof., 1959—60, prof., 1960—94, Class 1909 prof. physics, 1968—76, Cyrus Fogg Bracket prof. physics, 1977—84, James S. McDonnell Distinguished Univ. prof. physics, 1984—94, prof. emeritus, 1994—. Mem. Pres.'s Sci. Adv. Com., 1970—73. Trustee Assoc. Univ., Inc., 1961—67. Served with USAR, 1943—46. Recipient Rsch. Corp. award, 1967, E.O. Lawrence award, 1968, Wetherill medal, Franklin Inst., 1976, Nobel prize in Physics, 1980, Grad. Alumnus award, Am. Assn. State Colls. and Univs., 1984, Nat. medal of Sci., 1993; fellow Sloan, 1960. Fellow: Am. Assn. for Advancement of Sci., Am. Phys. Soc. (pres. 1987—88); mem.: NAS, Am. Philos. Soc., Am. Acad. Arts and Scis. Office: Princeton U Dept Physics 391 Jadwin Hall Princeton NJ 08544-0001

FITCHEN, ALLEN NELSON, publisher; b. Syracuse, Aug. 8, 1936; s. John Frederick and Mary (Nelson) F. III; m. Jane Cady, June 13, 1959 (div. Feb. 1986); children— Anne Wheeler, Christopher Hardy, William Mills; m. Shirley Bergen, May 23, 1991. BA in English cum laude, Amherst Coll., 1958; MA in English, Cornell, 1960. Coll. traveler Macmillan Co., N.Y.C., 1960-62, editor, 1962-67; humanities editor U. Chgo. Press, 1968-82, sr. editor, 1971-82; dir. U. Wis. Press, 1982-98, ret., 1998. Mem.: Psi Upsilon. Home: 603 Eugenia Ave Madison WI 53705-3404 E-mail: afitchen@wiscmail.wisc.edu.

FITCHEN, DOUGLAS BEACH, physicist, researcher; b. N.Y.C., June 8, 1936; s. Paul R. and Eleanor B. Fitchen; m. Janet Mathews (dec. 1995); children: John, Katherine, Sylvia; m. Nancy Mathews, 1996 (dec. 2000); m. Karen Brazell, 2002. AB, Harvard U., 1957; PhD, U. Ill., 1962. Asst. prof. physics Cornell U., Ithaca, N.Y., 1962-65, assoc. prof., 1965-71, prof., 1971—, chmn. dept. physics, 1977-82, 86-91, 94-99. Vis. prof. Oxford U., 1968, U. Paris, Orsay, 1975 Alfred P. Sloan fellow, 1964-68 Achievements include research in optical studies of solids, Raman spectroscopy. Office: Cornell U Clark Hall Ithaca NY 14853

FITCHETT, TAYLOR, law librarian; b. 1947; BA, Kans. State U., 1970; MLS, U. Ala., 1979. Acting dir., Law Libr. U. Ala., 1981—83; assoc. libr., Law Libr. Tulane U., 1983—86; dir., Law Libr. U. Cin., 1986—98; assoc. libr., Law Libr. U. Va., 1998—2000, dir. Law Libr. and Lectr. Gen. Faculty, 2000—. Mem.: Va. Assn. Law Libr. (chmn., publications com.), Am. Libr. Assn., Am. Assn. Law Libr. Office: Office of Law Libr Dir U Va 580 Massie Rd Charlottesville VA 22903-1789 Office Phone: 434-924-7725. Business E-Mail: tf2u@virginia.edu.

FITHIAN, SHARON, artist, consultant; b. Pitts., Nov. 29, 1944; d. William and Verne Fields; m. David Fithian; 1 child, Steven Reichert. BFA, No. Ill. U., 1966. Dir. pub. rels. Crealde Sch. Art, Winter Park, Fla., 1979—82, Maitland

(Fla.) Art Ctr., Fla., 1982—84, Richard Stone and Assocs., Orlando, 1984—85; computer mgr. Paula Hawkins for U.S. Senate, Winter Park, 1985—87; gen. mgr. Fla. Audubon Soc., Maitland, 1987—88; asst. to dirs. Arts United Ctrl. Fla., Orlando; owner Fithian Studios, Orlando, 1991—2000, Fithian Studios Fine Arts, DeLand, Fla., 2001—. Workshop instr. Fithian Studios, 1990—; art cons. Fithian Studios Fine Arts, DeLand, 1999—2001. Exhibitions include Artscape '90, 1990 (First Place, 1990), Mixed media painting, 1999 (2nd Place, 1999). Bd. dirs. Center Stage Mag., Maitland, 1983—90, Eureka Springs Assn. Artists and Craftspersons, Eureka Springs, 1992—94. Mem.: Nat. Mus. Women in Arts (founding mem., mem. Fla. com.). Avocations: sailing, travel, meditation. Home: 116 1/2 N Woodland Blvd Deland FL 32720 Office: Fithian Studios 219 N San Souci Ave Deland FL 32720-4220 E-mail: fithian1@bellsouth.net.

FITOUSSI, JEAN-PAUL SAMUEL, economist, educator; b. Aug. 19, 1942; s. Joseph and Mathilde (Cohen) F.; m. Annie Krief, July 11, 1964; children: Lisa, David. Student, U. Paris, 1961-63; licencie in Econs., U. Strasbourg, 1966, D d'Etat in Econs., 1971, Agrege in Econs., 1973; D honoris causa, U. Buenos Aires. From asst. to hon. dean Louis Pasteur U., Strasbourg, France, 1968-77, hon. dean, 1977—; prof. European U. Inst., 1979-83, Inst. d'Etudes Politiques de Paris, 1983—. Cons. EEC, 1978-82, 84—; dir. Bur. Theoretical and Applied Econs., U. Strasbourg, 1974-82, rsch. dept. Observatoire Francais des Conjonctures Econs., 1982-89, pres. 1990—; adv. com. Econ. and Social Scis. Rsch. Coun., U.K., 1986; mem. French Nat. Com. Sci. Rsch., 1987-90; bd. dirs. GAN Ins. Co; hon. prof. U. Trento; mem. exec. com. Aspen Inst. Italia, 2001—; mem. rsch. coun. European U. Inst., Florence, Italy, 2003—; mem. com. nationel d'évaluation politique ville, 2002—, d'initiative et de proposition par la recherche, 2004—; mem. sci. bd. Austrian Inst. Econ. Rsch., 2004—; hon. prof. U. Trento. Author: Inflation, Equilibre et Chômage, 1973, Le Fondement microéconomique de la theorie Keynésienne, 1974; co-author: (with Edmond Malinvaud) Unemployment in Western Countries, 1980, (with Pierre-Alain Muet) Macrodynamic et Déséquilibres, 1987, (with S. Phelps) The Slump in Europe, 1988, Al' Est. En Europe, 1990, (with Pierre Rosanvallon) Le débat interdit, 1995, Le Nouvel Age des Inégalitès, 1996, (with Oliver Blanchard) Croissance et Chômage, 1998 (dir. Jean-Paul Fitoussi) Rapport sur l'État de l'Union Européenne, 1999-2000, 02-04, L'enseignement supérieur de l'économie en question, 2001, La Regle et le choix, 2002, (with J. Creel) How to Reform the ECB, 2002, Il dittatore benevolo, 2003, EDF, le marche et l'Europe, 2003, Rapport sur l'etat de l'union europeene 2004, 2003, l'ideologue du monde, 2004, (with Eloi Laurent e Joël Naurice) Ségrégation urbaine et intégration sociale, 2004, (with Eloi Laurent e Joël Naurice) Nacioeconomic theory and Economic Policy Essay in honor of J.P. Fitoussi, 2004, (with Eloi Laurent e Joël Naurice) La démocratie et le marché, 2004, La politique de l'impuissance, 2005. Mem. Econ. Commn. of the Nation, 1996—, Coun. Econ. Analysis of the Prime Min., 1997—; pres. sci. coun. Inst. d'Etudes Politiques de Paris, 1997—; expert Commn. of the European Parliament, 2000—; mem. adv. bd. inst. rsch. UN Social Develop., 2001-; adminstrv. coun. mem. Ecole Normale Supérieure, 2004-; adv. bd. mem. Ctr. Capitalism Soc., Columbia U., 2004. Decorated chevalier Order of Nat. Merit, chevalier Legion of Honor (France); recipient prize Acad. Scis. Morales et Politiques, 1974. Mem. Internat. Assn. Applied Econometrics, Internat. Econ. Assn. (gen. sec. 1984, European chpt., French chpt. prize 1972, Am. chpt.). Office: Observatoire Francais des Conjonctures Economiques 69 quai d'Orsay 75007 Paris France Office Phone: 0144185400. Business E-Mail: presidence@ofce.sciences-po.fr.

FITTON, HARVEY NELSON, JR., former government official; b. Washington; s. Harvey Nelson and Ada Hortense (Marshall) F.; m. Bernice Jeanette Sutton, Jan. 8, 1946 (dec. Sept. 1998). Student, Nat. Acad. Theater, 1940; degree in Am. Studies, George Washington U., 1949, MA in Am. Lit. and Cultural History, 1956; postgrad., Am. U., 1963. Editor, rsch. asst. Nat. Acad. Scis., Nat. Rsch. Coun., Washington, 1949-56; med. writer and editor NIH, Bethesda, Md., 1956-58; info. specialist farmer cooperative svc. USDA, Washington, 1958-61, publs. editor office of info., 1961-63, chief editorial br. office of info., 1963-66, head pub. divsn. office govtl. and pub. affairs, 1966-84, dep. dir. of info., office govt. and pub. affairs, 1984. Instr. USDA Grad. Sch., Washington, 1962-92, chmn. editl. adv. com., 1976-85, mem. comm. skills adv. com., 1986-97. Editor, rsch. asst. Atlas of Tumor Pathology, 1949-56; editor NIH Record, 1956-58; contbr. articles to profl. jours. Pres. Clermont Woods Community Assn., Fairfax County, Va., 1968, No. Va. Family Svc., Falls Church, 1972-73; elder local Presbyn. Ch. With USN, 1942-45. Recipient Horace Hart award Edn. Coun. of Graphic Arts Industry, 1980; inductee Internat. Poetry Hall of Fame, 1996. Fellow Soc. for Tech. Comm. (pres. Washington chpt. 1972-73, asst. to pres. for recognition programs 1976-77); mem. Acad. Am. Poets, Internat. Soc. Poets, Haiku Soc. Am., Agrl. Communicators in Edn. (pres. Washington chpt. 1968, Spl. Achievement award 1986), Nat. Assn. Govt. Communicators (pres. Washington chpt. 1979, nat. pres. 1980, mem. editl. bd. Govt. Comm., 1994—, Communicator of Yr. 1984), St. Andrews Soc., Nat. Assn. Scholars, Assn. Lit. Scholars and Critics, Toastmasters (pres. Alexandria chpt. 1959-60), SAR. Avocations: gardening, tap dancing and singing, book collecting, poetry. Home and Office: 5624 Glenwood Dr Alexandria VA 22310-1323 E-mail: hnfitton@aol.com.

FITTON, TOM J., lawyer; Editor and publisher Opinion Inc.; pres. Judicial Watch Inc.; political analyst America's Voice (TV Network). Mailing: Judicial Watch Inc PO Box 96234 Washington DC 20077-7480

FITTS, CATHERINE AUSTIN, investment advisor; b. Phila., Dec. 24, 1950; d. William Thomas Jr. and Barbara Kinsey (Willits) Fitts. AA, Bennett Coll., 1970; student, Chinese U., Hong Kong, 1971; BA, U. Pa., 1974, MBA, 1978; postgrad., MIT. With Dillon, Read & Co., Inc., N.Y.C., 1978-89, sr. v.p., 1984-86, mng. dir., 1986-89, also bd. dirs.; asst. sec. housing, urban devel., fed. housing commr. HUD, Washington, 1989-90; pres., chmn. Hamilton Securities Group, Inc., Washington, 1990-97, Solari, Inc., Tenn., 1998—. Adv. bd. Fedn. Nat. Mortgage Assn. Fannie Mae, 1992—93; emerging markets adv. com. SEC, 1990—93; mem. Gold Anti-Trust Action Com. Columnist: Mapping the Real Deal, Scoop Media. Bd. dir. Student Loan Mktg. Assn. Sallie Mae, 1991—94; mem. grad. adv. bd. Wharton Sch., U. Pa., Phila., 1986—95. Office Phone: 731-764-2515. Business E-Mail: catherine@solari.com.

FITTS, DONALD DENNIS, chemist, educator; b. Concord, N.H., Sept. 3, 1932; s. Russell P. and Elisabeth (Reille) F.; m. Beverly Hoffman, July 11, 1964; children: Robert K., William R. AB, Harvard U., 1954; PhD, Yale U., 1957. NSF postdoctoral fellow U. Amsterdam, Netherlands, 1957-58; research fellow Yale U., 1958-59; mem. faculty U. Pa., 1959—, assoc. prof. chemistry, 1964-69, prof. chemistry, 1969—, asst. chmn. dept., 1965-72, assoc. dean grad. studies faculty arts and scis., 1978-82, 83-94, acting dean arts and scis., 1982-83. Cons. Am. Cyanamid Co., 1959-63 Author: Nonequilibrium Thermodynamics, 1962, Vector Analysis in Chemistry, 1974, Principles of Quantum Mechanics, 1999; also articles. Mem. Am. Phys. Soc. Achievements include research on theory of optical activity, statis.-mech. theory of transport processes, nonequilibrium thermodynamics, molecular quantum mechanics, theory of liquids, intermolecular forces, surface phenomena. Home: 634 Revere Rd Merion Station PA 19066-1008 Office: Dept Chemistry U Pa Philadelphia PA 19104-6323 E-mail: dfitts@sas.upenn.edu.

FITTS, MICHAEL ANDREW, dean, law educator; b. Phila., Mar. 1, 1953; s. William Thomas Jr. and Barbara Kinsey (Willits) F.; m. Renee Judith Sobel, Jan. 2, 1982; children: Alexis, Whitney. AB, Harvard Coll., 1975; JD, Yale U., 1979; MA (hon.), U. Pa., 1991. Law clk. Hon. A. Leon Higginbotham, Jr., U.S. Ct. Appeals (3d cir.), Phila., 1979-81; atty. office legal counsel Dept. of Justice, Washington, 1981-85; asst. prof. law U. Pa., Phila., 1985-90, assoc. prof., 1990-92, prof., 1992—, assoc. dean acad. affairs, 1996-98, Robert G. Fuller Jr. prof. law, 1996-2000, Bernard G. Segal prof. law, 2000—, dean Sch. of Law, 2000—. Vis. prof. dept. polit. sci. Swarthmore Coll., 1999; adv. com. Weseda Law Sch.; bd. dirs. World Affairs Coun.; adv. bd. Reinvestment Fund. Editor Yale Law Jour., 1978-79; contbr. articles to profl. jours. and chpts. to books. Harvard U. scholar, 1971. Mem. Am. Polit. Sci. Assn. (law and polit. process working group), Pa. Bar Assn., Com. of Seventy, Phi Beta Kappa. Mem. Soc. Of Friends. Office: U Pa Law Sch 3400 Chestnut St Philadelphia PA 19104-6204 Office Phone: 215-898-7061. Office Fax: 215-573-2025. Business E-Mail: deanfitts@law.upenn.edu.

FITZ, LAWRENCE VONDRAKE, foundation administrator, musician; b. Los Angeles, Aug. 14, 1971; s. Patricia Ann Morris and Hamp Morris, Jr. (Stepfather). BSc, U. of Phoenix, 1997—99. Administrative & Teaching Credentials Calif. Commn. on Tchr. Credentialing, 1997. Instrnl. supr./tchr. East San Gabriel Valley Regional Occupl. Program/Tech. Ctr., West Covina, Calif., 1999—; exec. dir./founder Celebration Entertainment Acad., Inc., La Verne, Calif., 1999—; assoc. dir. of music Glendora H.S., Glendora, 1997—99; student affairs coord. Calif. State Poly. U., Pomona, 1991—97; dir. of music activities Diamond Bar Congl. Ch., Diamond Bar, Calif., 1997—98. Pres./chmn. Celebration Entertainment Acad., Inc., La Verne, Calif., 1999—2005. D-Conservative. Avocations: travel, media. Office: Celebration Entertainment Acad Inc 2355 Foothill Blvd Ste 240 La Verne CA 91750 Home Fax: 951-582-9450. Personal E-mail: lvfitz@cs.com.

FITZALAN-HOWARD, BENNETT-THOMAS HENRY ROBERT, news analyst, consultant, political scientist, theologian; b. Geneva, Oct. 10, 1955; came to U.S., 1959; s. S. and A. (Argyle-Campbel) FitzA.-H. BA, BS, Union Coll., Albany, N.Y., 1973; BA, Union Coll., 1973; MDiv, NBTS, 1978; MS, Rutgers U., 1980; MA, Russell Sage Coll., 1987; postgrad., NYU, 1989, Yale U., 1989. Cert. fin. analyst, broker, contractor in Nigeria, 1993-98; cert. min. Bride in the Light New Testament Ministry. Adminstrv. analyst Todd Logistics, Inc., NJ, Saudi Arabia, 1980—81; owner, cons. Fitz Co., Internat., Albany, 1981—; contractor Nigeria, 1988—98. Mem. N.Y. Merc. Exch.; instr. Gaton Sch., Yale U., 1987-89, NYU, 1987-89. Author: Expropriation Predictability and Politics, 1979, The Politics of the U.S. Budget, 1987, The Courts in a Democratic System, 1987, White House-Wall Street: The October 87 Crash and the Post Regan Persidency, 1987, The Politics of Deficits, 1988, Enemyless: Can We Survive?, 1989, Responsibility and Accountability: The Forgotten Cornerstones of Democracy, 1990, The Eagle and the UN: Is the US Mature Enough to be the Sole Super-Power?, 1998: contbg. author: Toward a Global Government, 1972, Conservetism: New World Order?, 1990, Tory vs. Labour: Tory: The New English Order, 1992, Hyperinflation, 1992, Eschatology Now, 1992, Eschatology and Current Events, 1992, Bride in the Light: New Testament Church, The Opened Seals of Revelation, How Bush Ambushed America, 2002. Active local ARC, RP Found. With U.S. Army, 1974-77. Mem. AIGA, AAAS, APA, SAR, VFW, Acad. Polit. Sci. (life), Am. Philatelic Soc. (life). Am. Vietnam Vets. Assn., Audubon Soc., Am. Numismatic Assn. (life), Fin. Analysts Fedn. (at large), Fin. Execs. Inst. (at large), Nat. Assn. Securities Dealers (at large), N.Y. Mercantile Exchange, Am. Enterprise Inst., Brookings Inst., Am. Legion, MENSA, Am. Soc. Internat. Law, Am. Bach Found., Am. Soc. Info. Sci., Blind Vets. Assn. (life), Am. Conservative Union, Nat. Press Club, Equestrian Club, Gideons, Mus. Modern Art, Barons of Magna Carta. Avocations: oriental antiques and silver, british stamps and coins, photography, reading, piano and cello. E-mail: Norfolk90@aol.com.

FITZ-CARTER, ALEANE, elementary school educator, composer; b. Council Bluffs, Iowa, July 24, 1929; d. Andrew Wilburt and Beatrice Mildred (Maddox) Fitz; m. James Benny Carter, Dec. 10, 1958 (wid. Aug. 1964); children: Angel Beatrix, Angel Sherrie. BSEd, U. Nebr., 1956. Elem. sch. tchr. Omaha Pub. Schs., 1956—69; instr. Black history and music U. Nebr., Omaha, 1970—74; nat. faculty mem. Gospel Music Workshop Am. Inc., 1986—2005; tchr. music Ascension Luth. Sch., L.A., 1990—94; min. music Messiah Luth. Ch., L.A., 1996—2003; ch. musician Tamarind Seventh Day Adventist Ch., Compton, Calif., 1997—2003; performing artist Nebr. Arts Coun., Omaha, 1980—, Iowa Arts Coun., Des Moines, 1998—; tchr. adult edn. L.A. Unified Schs., 1998—; ednl. cons. Torrance Unified Schs., Calif., 1997—99; ret., 2005. Min. music Olivet Luth. Ch., Hawthorne, 2003-05; program prodr. KETV TV, Omaha, 1970-73; talk show host, Radio Sta. KOWH, Omaha, 1973-74; comm. cons. Mayor's Human Rels. Bd., Omaha, 1970-73; midwest bd. rep. Nat. Black Media Coalition, Washington, 1973-76, others; tchr. Black Awareness Opportunities Industrialization Ctr., 1969-74; instr. history of jazz, Oasis, L.A., 1997-2001; arranger, librettist, lyricist, elocutionist, storyteller, lectr. in field Recs. include I Love Jesus, 1965, A Mighty Fortress, 1986; performer: (one-woman show) Rosa Parks, 1979—, Omaha Junior Theater, 1980—85; actress: I Elvis; Hard Copy, 1992; Ice Cube video Dead Homie MTV, 1990; (films) A Man Apart, 2003; music dir. (stage) One Last Look, Marla Gibbs Theater, 1990; contbr. articles to profl. jours.; composer: One Child, 1993, (sacred hymns) Psalm 91, 1993—97, Children's TV workshop, Strawberry Square II: Take Time, NETV, 1983; performer: South African Chs. of KwaZulu Natal and African Enterprises, 1995. Presentation Visiting With Huell Howser, KCET; rschr. soul food history and cooking; amb. storytelling programs Dwight D. Eisenhower's People to People, to South Africa, 2004. Nominee Best Supporting actress, Great White Hope Ctr. Stage, Omaha, Nebr., 1982; recipient Comty. Christian Leadership award, Salem Baptist Ch., Omaha, Nebr., 1987, Woman in Fine Arts award, Alyce Wilson Womens Ctr., Omaha, 1987, 5 yr. ACT-SO award, NAACP, Omaha, 1986, Outstanding Songwriter award, 1987—88, Psalm 91 Song of Yr. award, Thurston Frazier Chorale, 1987, Nebr. Chpt. GMWA award, 1987—88, Fine Arts award, Bethesda Seventh Day Adventist Ch., 1988, Comty. Guest Day, Bethesda Seventh Day Ch., Omaha, Nebr., 1988, Outstanding Svc. award, L.A. Union Seventh Day Acad., 1992, Creativity in music award, Thurston Frazier Chorale, Gospel Music Workshop Am., 1993, Svc. comty. award, Salem Baptist Mission, Norfolk, Nebr., 1995; grantee, L.A. Dept. of Cultural Affairs. Mem.: ASCAP, SAG, Nat. Storytelling Network, Rec. Acad., Profl. Musicians Union - Local 47, Nebr. Congress of Parents and Tchrs. (hon. life), Gold Star Wives Am., L.A. Pianist Club, VFW Ladies Aux., Sigma Gamma Rho (Gamma Beta Sigma chpt.). Adventist. Avocations: walking, swimming, cooking. Mailing: PO Box 90087 Los Angeles CA 90009 Home: 200 E Hyde Pk Blvd #1 Inglewood CA 90302 Personal E-mail: Psalm91@mymailstation.com.

FITZ-ENZ, DAVID G., retired military officer, television producer; b. Aurora, Ill., Oct. 18, 1940; s. John Arthur and Kathryn M. Fitz-Enz; m. Carol J. Fitz-Enz, Aug. 12, 1961; children: David Scott, Timothy Robert, Jonathan Gregory. BA, Marquette U., 1963; postgrad., Command and Gen. Staff Coll., Ft. Leavenworth, Kans., 1974-75, U.S. Army War Coll., Carlisle, Pa., 1985-86. Comd. 2d lt. U.S. Army, 1963, advanced through grades to col.; ret., 1993; v.p. Cannonade Filmworks, Plattsburgh, N.Y., 1994—. Lectr. Brit. Nat. Army Mus., London, Eng., 2000—, U.S. Army War Coll. Author: Why a Soldier?, 2000, The Final Invasion, 2001, Nineteenth Century U.S. Army History, 2001 (Disting. Writing award Am. Hist. Found.), Eagle of the Sea, 2004; script writer: (films) The Final Invasion, 1999. Trustee Francis Scott Key Found., Frederick, Md., 1979-83, Battle of Plattsburgh Assn., 1999—. Named Knights Templar, Sovereign Mil. Order of Temple of Jerusalem, 2003. Mem. Am. Mil. Retirees (nat. pres. 1994-98), Mil. Order St. Louis, Naval and Mil. Club (Eng.). Office Phone: 518-891-6792. E-mail: coldfitzenz@earthlink.net.

FITZGEORGE, HAROLD JAMES, former oil and gas company executive; b. Trenton, N.J., June 15, 1924; s. George T. and Cecilia M. (Jansen) Fitzgeorge; m. Bette M. Weidel, June 23, 1945 (dec. May 1987); children: Barbara Marsh, Virginia Fisher, Patricia Boyle, Elizabeth Brown; m. Roberta Tefft, July 23, 1999. AB, Princeton U., 1948; M.B.M., MIT, 1964. Geologist Magnolia Petroleum Co., Oklahoma City, 1948; numerous positions with petroleum cos., 1948-60; with Mobil U.S. Exploration, N.Y.C., 1960-63; v.p. Mobil Exploration Can., 1964-66; mgr. Mobil Fgn. Exploration, N.Y.C., 1966-68; pres. Mobil de Venezuela, 1968-73; gen. mgr. Western U.S. Exploration & Prodn., Mobil Oil, Denver, 1973-77; cons. in field, 1977-78; pres. Pennzoil Exploration and Prodn., Houston, 1978-84, adv. dir., 1984—; now ret. Served with USMC, 1943-46, 50-52. Decorated Purple Heart, Bronze Star Combat V; Sloan fellow, 1963-64 Mem. Am. Assn. Petroleum Geologists, Assn. Profl. Engrs. and Geologists of Alta., Am. Petroleum Inst. Clubs: Princeton (N.Y.); Moorings; Hawksnest (Vero Beach, Fla.), Vero Beach Yacht Club. Republican. Roman Catholic. Home: 4800 Hwy A1A Apt 509 Vero Beach FL 32963-1235

FITZGERALD, CAROL J., foundation administrator, association executive; b. Chgo., July 2, 1950; d. Lucien W. and Dian (Gorgas) F.; m. Douglas Paul Becknell, July 10, 1971; 1 child, Rachel Fitzgerald Becknell. BS in Edn., No. Ill. U., 1973; MA in French, Ill. State U., 1976. Tchr. Prophetstown (Ill.) High Sch., 1976-77; dir. program Sterling-Rock Falls YWCA, Ill., 1977-80; county coord. Highland Coll. CETA, Freeport, Ill., 1980-81; tchr. Sauk Valley Coll., Dixon, Ill., 1981-82; planner N. Cen. Ill. Coun. Govts., Princeton, 1982-83; exec. asst. Sterling C. of C., 1985; exec. dir. YWCA Sauk Valley, 1985—. Dir. Lincoln Land Chpt. ARC, 1986-91; adv. bd. Whiteside County Health Dept., Morrison, 1985-89; founder Sauk Valley Chpt. NOW, Sterling, 1978, pres. 1978-79, 81-82; sec. Sterling-Rock Falls Ministerial Assn., 1986-87; steering com. mem. Daily Bread Food Co-op, 1980—; treas. Rock Valley Nuclear Freeze Coalition, 1982, Ill. Coalition Against Sexual Assault, Springfield, 1988—, Rock Falls Fire and Police Commn., 1997—, chmn., 2004—; mem. Whiteside Bd. Health, 2001—. Mem. Coun. Ill. and St. Louis YWCAs (pres. 1995, 2004), Rock River Valley Human Resource Profl. Assn., Twin Cities Sunrise Rotary Club (pres. 2002-03). Unitarian Universalist. Office: YWCA 412 1st Ave Sterling IL 61081-3603

FITZGERALD, CHRISTINE ANN, clinical social worker; b. Norwalk, Conn., Oct. 2, 1952; d. Christopher and Evelyn Marie (Brennan) Fitzgerald; m. Barry Jay Toiv; children: Daniel, Nora. BS, Va. Commonwealth U., 1974; MS, Fordham U., 1975; MSW, Catholic U., 1982. Lic. clin. social worker Md., D.C. Spl. edn. tchr. Fairfax (Va.) County Pub. Schs., 1976-80; social worker Johns Hopkins Hosp., Balt., 1981-83, Arlington (Va.) Pub. Schs., 1983—. Pvt. practice social work, Takoma Park, Md., 1985—. Adv. bd. Neighborhood Assn., Md., 1992-93; mem. Com. of 100, Prince George's County, Md., 1990-93, boundary com. Montgomery County, 1993-96; coord. girls' soccer Takoma Park Soccer League, 1994-2003; organizer One Takoma, 1994-97. Named Counselor of Yr., Arlington County, 2005. Mem. NEA, Nat. Assn. Social Workers, Takoma Found. (bd. mem. 2004—). Democrat. Avocations: coaching soccer, playing soccer, reading, swimming, volunteering. Home: 7110 Central Ave Takoma Park MD 20912-6452

FITZGERALD, COLLEEN, physician; b. Evergreen Park, Ill., Dec. 18, 1969; d. William James and Patricia Ann Fitzgerald; 1 child, Mary Rose. BS with honors, Loyola U., Chgo., 1992; MD, Northwestern U., 1996. Intern Northwestern U., Chgo., 1996—97, resident, 1997—2000, clin. instr., 2000—; attending physician Rehab. Inst. Chgo., 2000—; med. dir. Rehab. Inst. Chgo., Women's Health Rehabilitation. Asst. prof.; presenter in field. Mem.: Am. Congress Rehab. Medicine, Assn. Acad. Psysiatrists (bd. cert. in phys. medicine and rehab.), Am. Acad. Phys. Medicine and Rehab. Office: Rehab Inst Chgo 345 E Superior St Rm 1134 Chicago IL 60611 Office Phone: 312-238-6030.

FITZGERALD, DENNIS D., federal agency administrator; b. New Haven, Conn., Feb. 28, 1943; m. Deborah Fitzgerald; 2 children. BS, Fairfield U., 1964; four Master's degrees, John Hopkins U. Cert. Profl. Engr., NY, Va.; lic. Master Electrician Va. Field engr. Sperry Gyroscope, 1964—66, Vitro Labs., 1966—74; various positions with directorate of sci. and tech., office of devel. and engring. and nat. reconnaissance office CIA, 1974—, assoc. dir. Nat. Photographic Interpretation Ctr.; dep. dir. Nat. Reconnaissance Office, 2001—, acting. dir., 2005. Avocation: running. Office: Nat Reconnaissance Office Office of Inspector Gen 14675 Lee Rd Chantilly VA 20151-1715*

FITZGERALD, EDMUND BACON, electronics executive; b. Milw., Feb. 5, 1926; s. Edmund and Elizabeth (Bacon) F.; m. Elisabeth McKee Christensen, Sept. 6, 1947; children: Karen, Kathleen, Edmund Greer, Rogers Christensen. BSEE, U. Mich., 1946. With Cutler-Hammer, Inc., Milw., 1946-78, v.p. in charge engring., 1959-61, adminstrv. v.p., 1961-63, pres., CEO, 1964-69, chmn., chief exec. officer, 1969-78; vice chmn. Eaton Corp., Cleve., 1978-79; mng. dir. Hampshire Assocs., Milw., 1979-80; pres., dir. No. Telecom, Inc., Nashville, 1980-82; pres. No. Telecom Ltd., 1982-84, chmn. bd. dirs. Mississauga, 1985-90; mng. dir. Woodmont Assocs., Nashville, 1990—. Adj. prof. mgmt. Vanderbilt U., Nashville, 1990—; former chmn., bd. dirs. Milw. Brewers Baseball Club, Inc.; former chmn. Com. for Econ. Devel.; mem. President's Nat. Security Telecom. Adv. Com. Capt. USMCR, 1943-46, 51-52. Named Man of Yr., Milw. Jr. C. of C., 1956 Mem. Nat. Elec. Mfrs. Assn. (pres. 1968). Office: Woodmont Assocs 3434 Woodmont Blvd Nashville TN 37215-1422

FITZGERALD, EDWIN ROGER, physicist, researcher; b. Oshkosh, Wis., July 14, 1923; s. James C. and Edwina (Brown) F.; m. Carolyn H. Johnson, Aug. 30, 1946; children: Lucia Edwina, Margaret Mary, William Maurice, Alice Ann, Roger Edwin, Douglas Brendan, Thomas Michael, Jane Carolyn. BS in Elec. Engring, U. Wis., 1944, MS in Physics, 1950, PhD in Physics, 1951. Registered profl. engr., Md. Physicist Phys. Research Lab., B.F. Goodrich Co., 1944-46; Project asso. chemistry U. Wis., 1951-52; faculty Pa. State U., 1953-61, prof. physics, 1959-61; prof. dept. mechanics Johns Hopkins U., 1961—99, dr. of u., 1999—; ret., 1999. Vis. prof. chemistry U. Wis., Madison, 1981. Author: Particle Waves and Deformation in Crystalline Solids, 1966; contbr. articles to profl. jours., sects. in books; patentee in field. Fellow: Am. Phys. Soc. (exec. com., chmn. high polymer physics 1958—59); mem.: Am. Chem. Soc. (poly. materials divsn.), Materials Rsch. Soc., Acoustical Soc. Am., Tau Beta Pi, Eta Kappa Nu, Sigma Xi, Phi Beta Kappa. Achievements include research in mechanical and dielectric properties solids including dynamic mechanical properties of violin wood in relation to tone qualities of violins and viscoelastic properties of marine mammal tissues, dynamic mechanical measurements during freezing and thawing of ice. Home: 2445 Traceys Store Rd Parkton MD 21120-9642

FITZGERALD, EUGENE FRANCIS, management consultant; b. Jersey City, Mar. 15, 1925; s. Arthur Gregory and Anna (O'Rourke) F.; m. Ellen M. O'Connor, Sept. 1, 1951; children— Timothy, Mary Ellen, Eugene Francis, Maura, John, Ann, Katherine. BS in Bus. Adminstrn, Georgetown U., 1949. Spl. agt. FBI, 1951-52; mgr. Prudential Ins. Co. Am., Newark, 1953-65; agy. v.p. K.C., New Haven, 1965-67; v.p. Minn. Mut. Life Ins. Co., St. Paul, 1967-70; pres., dir. North Star Equities Co., St. Paul, 1969-70; exec. v.p. Southland Life Ins. Co., Dallas, 1970-72, also dir.; exec. v.p. Equitable Life Ins. Co., Washington, 1972-73, also trustee; v.p. Liberty Life Ins. Co., Greenville, S.C., 1974-81; pres. Mountain View Orchard, Inc., 1981-85; mgmt. cons. Phillips Resource Group, Greenville, S.C., 1986—. Dir. Nathan Hale Life Ins. Co.; cons. Phillips Resource Group; bd. dirs. Nat. Peach Council, 1984-85 Chmn. bd. United Ministries, Greenville Free Med. Clinic; chmn. Greenville County Human Rels. Commn., 1991—; bd. dirs. Catholic Charities, Diocese of Charleston. Served with USMCR, 1943-45. Decorated Bronze Star. Mem. Nat. Assn. Life Underwriters, Sales and Mktg. Execs. Internat., Newcomen Soc. Clubs: Green Valley Country. Roman Catholic. Home: 305 Aberdare Ln Greenville SC 29615-2406 Office: Phillips Resource Group PO Box 5664 Greenville SC 29606-5664 E-mail: dadfitz@aol.com.

FITZGERALD, GARRET ADARE, medical educator; b. May 11, 1950; married; three children. MBBCh with honors, Univ. Coll., Dublin, 1974, MD, 1980; Diploma in Stats., Trinity Coll., Dublin, 1977; MS in Stats., U. London, 1979. FRCP/Ireland, FACP, RCP/U.K. Intern gastroenterology/therapeutics St. Vincent's Hosp., Dublin, 1974, intern, urology, 1975, intern, gen. surgery, 1975, sr. house officer, hematology/oncology, 1975-76; sr. house officer endocrinology/diabetes mellitus Mater Hosp., Dublin, 1976-77, rsch. register, endocrinology/diabetes mellitus, 1977; rsch. fellow Royal Postgrad. Med. Sch., London Clin. Pharmacology, 1977-79; rsch. fellow dept. internal medicine II U. Cologne, 1979-80; rsch. fellow to assoc. dir. Rsch. Ctr. Grant in Pharm. Scis. Vanderbilt U. Sch. Medicine, Nashville, 1980-91, chief. Divsn. Clin. Pharmacology, 1988-91, William Stokes prof. exptl. therapeutics, 1989-91; dir. Ctr. Cardiovascular Sci. U. Coll. Dublin/Mater Hosp.,

1991-94, prof., chmn. dept. medicine and exptl. therapeutics, 1991-94; prof. medicine, pharmacology U. Pa., 1994—, chair dept. pharmacology, 1996—, dir. Clin. Res. Ctr., 1994—, clin. Robinette Found. prof., dir. Ctr. Exptl. Therapeutics/Rsch., cardiovasc. divsn., 1994—. Lectr. in field, including vis. prof. Harvard U., U. London, Duke U., Wash. U., numerous others; served numerous coms. and advisory groups in field. Mem. editl. bd. Jour. of Pharmacology and Exptl. Therapeutics, Trends in Cardiovascular Medicine, 1990—, Atherosclerosis Thrombosis, and Vascular Biology, 1990-96, Jour. Biol. Chemistry, Circulation, 1993—; contbr. numerous articles to profl. jours. and publs. Fellowship Nat. U. Ireland, 1977-80, Wellcome Clin. Rsch. fellow, 1977-79, Alexander von Humboldt Stiftung fellow, Germany, 1979-80; grantee in field, PhRMA Found award of Excellence, 2004. Mem. Assn. Physicians of Gt. Britain and Ireland, Assn. Am. Physicians, Am. Soc. Clin. Investigation, Am. Fedn. Clin. Rsch., Am. Heart Assn. (exec. and long-range planning com. Thrombosis Coun. 1987-91, program dir. 1996, vice chair coun. arterio and vascular biology 1997—), Am. Soc. Pharmacology and Exptl. Therapeutics, Am. Soc. Clin. Pharmacology and Therapeutics, AAAS. Office: 153 Johnson Pavillion 3620 Hamilton Walk Philadelphia PA 19104-6013

FITZGERALD, HAROLD KENNETH, social work educator, consultant; b. Lakewood, Ohio, Apr. 28, 1921; s. Edward James and Julia Florence (Klell) F.; m. Caroline Lee Graham, May 31, 1951; children: Mark, Matthew, Mary, Maura, Kristin. AB, John Carroll U., 1942; MSSW, Cath. U. of Am., 1948, PhD, 1953. Social worker ARC, Cin., 1950-53; exec. dir. Cath. Social Svcs., Atlanta, 1953-56; dir. social services Muscular Dystrophy Assn. of Am., N.Y.C., 1957-58; regional cons., survey dirs. Am. Found. for the Blind, N.Y.C., 1958-66; assoc. dir. Commn. on Standards and Accreditation for the Blind, N.Y.C., 1963-66; prof. social work Syracuse (N.Y.) U., 1966-88, prof. emeritus, 1988—. Dir. internat. projects Coun. on Social Work Edn., N.Y.C., 1956-67; bd. dirs. Lighthouse, Syracuse, 1967-90, Ctrl. N.Y. Assn. for Hearing Impaired, Syracuse, 1976-90, Support, 1990-96, Aurora, 1991—; cons. Nat. Conf. Cath. Charities, Washington, 1966-80, UN, Teheran, Iran, 1975-76. Contbr. articles to profl. jours. Mem. Commn. on Peace and Social Justice, Diocese of Syracuse, 1989-91. Lt. USN, 1943-46. Mem. NASW, AAUP, N.Y. State Assn. Human Svcs. (bd. dirs. 1980-93), Internat. Assn. Schs. Social Work, Inter Univ. Consortium Internat. Social Devel. Roman Catholic. Avocation: swimming. Home and Office: 301 Greenwood Rd Syracuse NY 13214-2327 Personal E-mail: hkenfitz1@msn.com.

FITZGERALD, HELEN TERESA, social worker, writer; b. Jackson, Minn., Nov. 12, 1938; d. John Raymond and Mayme Mary (Benes) Cihak; m. Richard Carl Olson; stepchildren: Mark Albert Olson, Thomas Parker Olson, Jeffrey Paul Olson, Melissa Karen Franger; m. Jerald Charles Fitzgerald (dec. Apr. 1, 1974); children: Patti Ann Rauld, Sarah Jane Turosak, Charles Edwin, Mary Elizabeth. Diploma, Jackson HS, Jackson, MN, 1956. Cert. in thanatology Assn. for Death Edn. and Counseling, 2003. Creative therapist Fairfax Hosp., 1972—82; coord. grief program Mt. Vernon Ctr. for Cmty. Mental Health, Alexandria, Va., 1977—2000; dir. tng. Am. Hospice Found., Washington, 1996—. Mem. adv. bd. Haven of No. Va., Annandale, Va. Author: (Book) The Grieving Child, 1992, 2003, The Mourning Handbook, 1994, The Grieving Teen, 2000, (tng. manual) Grief At School, 1998, Grief At Work, 1999. Recipient Outstanding Performance award, Cmty. Svcs. Bd. Fairfax County, 1998, Cmty. Svc. award, Social Work Assn. Fairfax County, 1999. Mem.: Assn. for Death Edn. and Counseling (bd. dirs. 1993—96, Clin. Practices award 1999). Avocation: painting. Home: 3601 Devilwood Ct Fairfax VA 22030 Office: Am Hospice Found Ste 200 2120 L St NW Washington DC 20037 Office Phone: 703-273-3454. Personal E-mail: helen38@cox.net.

FITZGERALD, JAMES FRANCIS, cable television executive; b. Janesville, Wis., Mar. 27, 1926; s. Michael Henry and Chloris Helen (Beiter) F.; m. Marilyn Field Cullen, Aug. 1, 1950; children: Michael Dennis, Brian Nicholas, Marcia O'Loughlin, James Francis, Carolyn Jane, Ellen Putnam. BS, Notre Dame U., 1947; LLD, U. Wis., Whitewater, 1999; LHD, Baldwin-Wallace U., 2001. With Std. Oil Co. (Ind.), Milw., 1947-48; pres. F.-W. Oil Co., Janesville, 1950—, Total TV, Inc. (cable TV Systems), Wis., 1965-86. Bd. dirs. Milw. Ins. Co., Bank One, Janesville N.A.; chmn. bd. Golden State Warriors, Oakland, Calif., 1986-95, Total TV Calif., 1987-96. Bd. govs., chmn. TV com. NBA; chmn. bd., pres. S.P.A.C.E. Inc. subs. Milw. Bucks NBA team, 1976-85; chmn. Greater Milw. Open PGA Tournament, 1985, Notre Dame Bus. Adv. Coun., 1989—. Lt. (j.g.) USNR, 1944-46, 51-53. Named to Wis. Sports Hall of Fame, 1999, Wis. Bus. Hall of Fame, 2001. Mem. Chief Execs. Forum, World Bus. Coun., Wis. Petroleum Assn. (pres. 1961-62), Janesville Country Club, Vintage Club (pres. 1989-91), San Francisco Golf Club, El Dorado Country Club. Roman Catholic. Home and Office: PO Box 348 Janesville WI 53547-0348

FITZGERALD, JAMES PATRICK, lawyer; BA, U. Nebr., 1968; JD, Creighton U., 1974. Bar: Nebr. 1974, U.S. Dist. Ct. Nebr. 1974, U.S. Ct. Appeals (8th cir.) 1974. Law clk. U.S. Dist. Ct. Nebr., Omaha, 1974-76; atty. McGrath, North, Mullin & Kratz, P.C., Omaha, 1976—. With U.S. Army, 1968-71. Mem. ABA, Nebr. Bar Assn., Assn. Trial Lawyers Am., Nebr. Assn. Trial Attys., Def. Rsch. Inst. Home: 16728 Jones Cir Omaha NE 68118-2711 Office: McGrath North Mullin & Kratz 1601 Dodge St Ste 3700 Omaha NE 68102 Office Phone: 402-341-3070.

FITZGERALD, JANET ANNE, philosophy educator, academic administrator; b. Woodside, N.Y., Sept. 4, 1935; d. Robert W. and Lillian H. (Shannon) F. BA magna cum laude, St. John's U., 1965, MA, 1967, PhD, 1971, LLD (hon.), 1982. Joined Sisters of St. Dominic of Amityville, Roman Catholic Ch., 1953; NSF postdoctoral fellow Cath. U. Am., summer 1971; prof. philosophy Molloy Coll., Rockville Centre, NY, 1969—, pres., 1972-96, pres. emerita, 1996—. Trustee L.I. Regional Adv. Coun. on Higher Edn., 1972-96, chmn., 1981-84; trustee Commn. on Ind. Colls. and Univs., 1981-84, 89-92, Cath. Charities, Diocese of Rockville Centre, 1979-82; trustee Fellowship of Cath. Scholars, 1977—, v.p., 1977-80; invited expert peritus Vatican Internat. Conf. on Cath. Higher Edn., Rome, 1989; prof. S. John Neumann, Archdiocese of N.Y.; invited auditor St. Thomas Aquinas Pontifical U., Rome, 1999. Author: Alfred North Whitehead's Early Philosophy of Space and Time, 1979. Mem. bd. advisors Sem. of Immaculate Conception, 1975-80; mem. adv. bd. pre-theology program Dunwoodie Sem., Archdiocese of N.Y.; mem. pub. policy com. N.Y. State Cath. Conf., 1992-94; mem. N.Y. State Edn. Dept.-Blue Ribbon Panel on Cath. Schs., 1992-93; 1st woman grand marshal St. Patrick's Day Parade, Glen Cove, 1992. Recipient Disting. Leadership award L.I. Bus. News, 1988, plaque of recognition L.I. Women's Coun. for Equal Edn. Tng. and Employment, 1989, Pathfinder award Town of Hempstead, 1990, Disting. Long Islander in Edn. award Epilepsy Found. L.I., 1991, Educator of Yr. award Assn. Tchrs. N.Y., 1980, Spl. award for arts in edn. L.I. Arts Coun., 1994; honored by L.I. Cath. League for Religious and Civil Rights, 1989; named L.I.'s 100 Influentials, L.I. Bus. News, 1992, 93, 94, 95, 96. Mem. Soc. Cath. Social Scis. (bd. advisors). Office: Molloy College PO Box 5002 Rockville Centre NY 11571-5002 Office Phone: 516-678-5000 6362. Business E-Mail: jfitzgerald@molloy.edu.

FITZGERALD, JANICE S., public relations executive, academic administrator; b. Poughkeepsie, N.Y., Nov. 2, 1948; d. Lloyd Raymond and Emily Mae (Anderson) Spinner; m. David R. Davis. BA magna cum laude, Cheyney U. Pa., 1972, MEd, 1973; MA, Villanova U., 1980; postgrad., Carnegie Mellon U., 1979, Harvard U., 1992. Prof. Cheyney U. Pa., 1972-74, dir. pub. rels. Cheyney, 1974-83, Pa. State System of Higher Edn., Harrisburg, 1983—, exec. assoc. to chancellor, dir. communications, 1985-90, exec. deputy, 1990—2001; dep. chancellor, chief staff Minn. State Colls. and Univs., St. Paul, 2001—. Pres. Correct Correspondence; free lance writer. Former bd. mem. Allied Arts Fund, Inst. for Cultural Partnerships, Friends of the State Mus.; pub. rels. coun. State System of Higher Edn.; bd. dirs. Kesher Israel Congregation. Named one of Outstanding Women in Am., 1981, named Alumnus of Yr. Nat. Assn. Equal Opportunity, 1985; recipient award Chapel of Four Chaplains, 1982, Valedictory and Alumni Key award Cheyney U. Pa., 1972. Mem. Am. Coun. Edn. (mem. nat. identification program for advancement of women, state planning com.), Coll. and Univ. Pub. Rels. Assn. of Pa., Pub. Rels. Soc. of Am., Edn. Writers Assn., Nat. Assn. Women in Edn. Office: Minn State Colls and Univs Wells Fargo Pl Ste 350 30 Seventh St E Saint Paul MN 55101 Office Phone: 651-297-2057. Business E-Mail: janice.fitzgerald@so.mnscu.edu.

FITZGERALD, JOHN CHARLES, JR., investment banker; b. Sacramento, May 23, 1941; s. John Charles and Geraldine Edith (McNabb) F.; m. Mildred Ann Kilpatrick, June 26, 1965; children: Geraldine Kathrine, Erec John. BS, Calif. State U., Sacramento, 1964; MBA, Cornell U., 1965. Dir. corp. planning Bekins Co., L.A., 1966-73; mgr. corp. planning Ridder Publs., Inc., L.A., 1973-75; CFO City of Inglewood, Calif., 1975-77; treas./contr. Inglewood Redevel. Agy., 1975-77; v.p. mcpl. fin. White, Weld & Co., Inc., L.A., 1977-78; v.p. pub. fin. paine Webber Jackson & Curtis, L.A., 1978-79; v.p. and mgr. for Western region, mcpl. fin. dept. Merrill Lynch Capital Markets, L.A., 1979-82, mng. dir. Western region, mcpl. fin. dept., 1982-86; mng. dir. Seidler-Fitzgerald Pub. Fin., L.A., 1986—2002; sr. v.p. The Seidler Cos., Inc., L.A., 1986—2002; mng. dir. John C. Fitzgerald & Assocs. (Divsn. Wulff, Hansen & Co.), 2002—. Instr. fin./adminstrn. El Camino Coll., Torrance, Calif., 1977-80. Chmn. bd. dirs., exec. com., treas., chmn. fund-raising com. L.a. chpt. Am. Heart Assn., 1977—; bd. dirs. Daniel Freeman Hosps. Inc., Corondelet Health Care corp.; trustee Mt. St. Mary's Coll., L.A., 1992-2001, regent, 2004—; bd. dirs. Tau Kappa Epsilon Ednl. Found., Indpls., 1995-2003; bd. dirs. Calif. Soc. for Biomed. Rsch., 1998; alumni coun. mem. Johnson Grad. Sch. Mgmt. Cornell U., real estate coun. Mem. Fin. Execs. Inst., Mcpl. fin. Officers, League Calif. Cities, So. Calif. Corp. Planners Assn. (past pres.), L.A. Bond, Lido Isle Yacht Club, Jonathan Club, The Calif. Club, Lake Arrowhead Country Club, Rotary, Beta Gamma Sigma. Address: PO Box 765 27447 Bayshore Dr Lake Arrowhead CA 92352 Office Phone: 213-955-5977.

FITZGERALD, JOHN EDMUND, retired civil engineering educator; b. Revere, Mass., Sept. 29, 1923; s. John Valentine and Gertrude Margaret (Doyle) F.; m. Elaine Louise Ohlson, Feb. 24, 1945; children: Deborah Lee, Christine Louise, David John, John Paul (dec.). Student, Tufts U., 1941-42, 46; MCE, Harvard U., 1947; MS in Math.-Physics, Nat. U. Ireland, Cork, 1970, DSc, 1972. Registered profl. engr., Utah, N.D.; chartered physicist, U.K. Regional constrn. engr. Liberty Mut. Ins. Co., Dallas, 1947-48; assoc. prof. N.D. State U., Fargo, 1948-51; supr. structures and dynamics Armour Rsch. Found., Chgo., 1951-53; mgr. applied mechanics and med. physics Rsch. divsn. Am. Machine & Foundry Corp., Chgo., 1953-56; mgr. applied math. and mechanics Borg-Warner Ctr. Rsch. Labs., Des Plaines, Ill., 1956-59; dir. devel. br. Lockheed Propulsion Co., Redlands, Calif., 1959-66; prof. civil engring., chmn. dept. U. Utah, Salt Lake City, 1966-74, prof., assoc. dean, 1973-74; prof., dir. Sch. Civil Engring. Ga. Inst. Tech., Atlanta, 1975-89, prof. emeritus, 1991—, assoc. dean, 1989-91; ret., 1991. Cons. numerous aerospace cos., govt. agys., 1966—; guest lectr. Trinity Coll., Dublin, Ireland, U. Bristol, U.K., U. Marseilles, France, NATO Advanced Study Inst., Italy, others., 1968—; bd. dirs. EFM Corp., Dublin. Author: Engineering Structural Analysis of Solid Propellants, 1971; editor Structural Integrity Handbook, 1972; contbr. over 100 articles to profl. jours.; 27 patents. Served with submarine service USN, 1942-46, ETO. Recipient U.S. Sr. Scientist award for teaching and research Alexander von Humboldt Found., 1973-74. Fellow Inst. Physics U.K., ASCE, AIAA (assoc., Outstanding Achievement in Solid Propulsion award 1987); mem. Soc. Rheology, Am. Acad. Mechanics, Structural Engring. Inst., Am. Phys. Soc., Irish Sailing Assn. Clubs: Royal Cork Yacht (Crosshaven, Ireland). Roman Catholic. Avocations: swimming, bicycling, sailing. Home: 2318 Ventana Crossing Marietta GA 30062-7747 Office Phone: 770-565-3392. Personal E-mail: jedmund72@aol.com.

FITZGERALD, JOHN EDWARD, III, lawyer; b. Cambridge, Mass., Jan. 12, 1945; s. John Edward Jr. and Kathleen (Sullivan) FitzGerald. BCE, U.S. Mil. Acad., West Point, N.Y., 1969; JD, M in Pub. Policy Analysis, U. Pa., 1975. Bar: Pa 1975, NY 1978, Calif 1983, US Supreme Ct 1991. Commd. 2d lt. U.S. Army, 1969, advanced through grades to capt., 1971, resigned, 1972; assoc. Saul Ewing Remick & Saul, Phila., 1975-77, Shearman & Sterling, N.Y.C., 1977-78; atty., dir. govt. rels. and pub. affairs Pepsico, Inc., Purchase, N.Y., 1978-82; sr. v.p., dept. head Security Pacific Corp., Los Angeles, 1982-83; ptnr. Schlesinger, FitzGerald & Johnson, Palm Springs, Calif., 1983-87; mng. ptnr. FitzGerald & Mulé, Palm Springs, 1987—. Judge pro tem Desert Jud. Dist., 2000—. Chmn., pres. United Way Desert, 1998—; trustee, v.p. Palm Springs Desert Mus., 1998—; past pres. exec. bd. Coachella Valley coun. Boy Scouts Am, 2000; bd. dirs., past chmn. Palm Springs Boys and Girls Club, 1990—; treas. Desert Youth Found., 2000; bd. dirs., vice chair Desert Regional Med. Ctr., 2004—. Named Palm Springs Disting. Citizen of Yr., 1999; recipient Friend of Youth award, Boys and Girls Clubs, 1998, Disting. Eagle award, Boy Scouts Am., 1999, Jefferson Bronze Medallion award, 2004. Mem.: Am. Arbitration Assn. (arbitrator), Desert Bar Assn. (pres. 2003—04), Calif. Bar Assn., Lincoln Club of the Coachella Valley (vice chmn. bd. dirs.), Desert Bus. Roundtable. Office: 1111 E Tahquitz Canyon Way Ste 110 Palm Springs CA 92262 Personal E-mail: jackfitzgerald3@aol.com.

FITZGERALD, JOHN T., JR., lawyer; b. Worcester, Mass., 1947; AB magna cum laude, Harvard Coll., 1969; JD cum laude, U. Pa., 1972. Bar: NY 1973, Fla. 1986, US Tax Ct. Ptnr., pvt. clients group leader Nixon Peabody LLP, Rochester, NY. Chmn., bd. govs. Hillside Family of Agencies; trustee U. Rochester Med. Ctr. Mem.: Estate Planning Coun. of Rochester, Monroe County Bar Assn., NY State Bar Assn. Office: Nixon Peabody LLP 1100 Clinton Square Rochester NY 14604 Office Phone: 585-263-1357. Office Fax: 866-947-0918. E-mail: jfitzgerald@nixonpeabody.com.

FITZGERALD, JOHN THOMAS, JR., religious studies educator; b. Birmingham, Ala., Oct. 2, 1948; s. John Thomas and Annie Myrtle (Walters) Fitzgerald; m. Karol Bonneaux, May 23, 1970; children: Kirstin Leigh, Kimberly Anne. BA, Abilene Christian U., 1970, MA, 1972; MDiv, Yale U., 1975, PhD, 1984. Instr. Yale Coll., New Haven, 1979, Yale Div. Sch., New Haven, 1980—81; from instr. to asst. prof. U. Miami, Coral Gables, Fla., 1981—88, assoc. prof., 1988—, dir. honors program, master Hecht Residential Coll., 1987—91. Vis. assoc. prof. Brown U., Providence, 1992, Yale Div. Sch., New Haven, 1998—99, New Haven, 2004. Author: Tabula of Cebes, 1983, Cracks in an Earthen Vessel, 1988; editor: Christian Origins sect. Religious Studies Rev., 1994—2002, Friendship, Flattery and Frankness of Speech, 1996, Greco-Roman Perspecitves on Friendship, 1997, Early Christianity and Classical Culture, 2003, Philodemus and the New Testament World, 2004; contbr. articles to profl. jours. Judge for Silver Knight awards Miami (Fla.) Herald, 1988, 1990. Named Two Bros. fellow, Yale Div. Sch., 1974—75; recipient Max Orvitz Summer Rsch. award, U. Miami, 1985, 1987, 1994, 1995, 1998, 2002; fellow, Rotary, Tuebingen, Germany, 1975—76. Mem.: Soc. Bibl. Lit. (chmn. com. 1989—96, editor Texts and Translations Series: Greco-Roman Religion 1993—2000, editor Writings from the Greco-Roman World Series 2001—, chmn. com. 2003—04, coun. 2003—, sec. 2003—, rsch. grantee 1997—99), Golden Key Nat. Honor Soc., Iron Arrow Hon. Soc., Omicron Delta Kappa, Phi Kappa Phi (chpt. pres. 1988—89). Home: 15215 SW 78 Ct Palmetto Bay FL 33157-2349 Office: U Miami PO Box 248264 Coral Gables FL 33124-4672 Office Phone: 305-284-3698. Business E-Mail: john.fitzgerald@miami.edu.

FITZGERALD, JOHN WARNER, law educator; b. Grand Ledge, Mich., Nov. 14, 1924; s. Frank Dwight and Queena Maud (Warner) F.; m. Lorabeth Moore, June 6, 1953; children: Frank Moore (dec.), Eric Stiles, Adam Warner. BS, Mich. State U., 1947; JD, U. Mich., 1954. Bar: Mich. 1954. Practiced in Grand Ledge, 1955-64; chief judge pro tem Mich. Ct. Appeals, 1965-73; justice Mich. Supreme Ct., 1974-83, dep. chief justice, 1975-82, chief justice, 1982; prof. law Thomas M. Cooley Law Sch., Lansing, Mich., 1982—. Mem. Mich. Senate from 15th Dist., 1958-64 Served with AUS, 1943-44. Mem. ABA, State Bar Mich. (bd. commrs. 1985-90), Am. Judicature Soc.

FITZGERALD, JUDITH KLASWICK, federal judge; b. Spangler, Pa., May 10, 1948; d. Julius Francis and Regina Marie (Pregno) Klaswick; m. June 5, 1971 (div. Dec. 1982); 1 child; m. Barry Robert Fitzgerald, Sept. 20, 1986; 1 child. BSBA, U. Pitts., 1970, JD, 1973. Legal rschr. Assocs. Fin., Pitts., 1972-73; law clk. to pres. judge Beaver County (Pa.) Ct. Common Pleas, 1973-74; law clk. to judge Pa. Superior Ct., Pitts., 1974-75; asst. U.S. atty. U.S. Dist. Ct. (we. dist.) Pa., Pitts. and Erie, 1976-87, U.S. bankruptcy judge Pitts., Erie and Johnstown, 1987—, U.S. Dist. Ct. (ea. dist.) Pa., U.S. Dist. Ct. U.S. V.I., U.S. Dist. Ct. Del. Adj. prof. law U. Pitts., 2003-04. Co-author: Bankruptcy and Divorce, Support and Property Division, 1991; editor: Pennsylvania Law of Juvenile Delinquency and Deprivation, 1976; contbr. articles to profl. jours. Mem. Pitts. Camerata, 1978-80, Allegheny County Polit.-Legal Edn. Project, 1980, Mendelssohn Choir Pitts., 1982—; mem. coun. Program to Aid Citizen Enterprise, 1985-87. Recipient Spl. Achievement awards Dept. Justice, Spl. Recognition award Pittsburgh mag., Operation Exodus Outstanding Performance award Dept. Commerce, 1986. Mem. Internat. Women's Insolvency and Restructuring Conf., Allegheny County Bar Assn., Women's Bar Assn. of Western Pa., Nat. Conf. Bankruptcy Judges, Am. Bankruptcy Inst., Nat. Conf. Bankruptcy Clks., Comml. Law League of Am., Fed. Criminal Investigators Assn. (Spl. Svc. award 1988), Zonta. Republican. Lutheran. Avocations: singing, reading, travel. Office: US Bankruptcy Ct 600 Grant St Ste 5490 Pittsburgh PA 15219-2805

FITZGERALD, KEVIN C., lawyer; b. Redlands, Calif., 1962; BA, George Washington Univ., 1985, MA, 1988, JD, 1991. Bar: Mass. 1991, DC 1994, Supreme Ct. 2001. Assoc. Reid & Priest, 1991—95; of counsel Troutman Sanders LLP, 1995—97, ptnr., energy, project develop., fin., 1997—, mng. ptnr., Washington office, 1999—. Adv. coun. Cath. Charities, Archdiocese, Washington. Mem.: ABA, Mass. Bar Assn., Energy Bar Assn., DC Bar Assn. Office: Troutman Sanders LLP Ste 1000 401 Ninth St NW Washington DC 20004-2134 Office Phone: 202-274-2955. Office Fax: 202-654-5600. Business E-Mail: kevin.fitzgerald@troutmansanders.com.

FITZGERALD, MARY EILEEN, museum program director; b. Dayton, Ohio, Dec. 21, 1944; d. William McAvoy and Irene Ann (Dougherty) F. BA in Studio Art, U. Dayton, 1966; MA in Art History, Ohio State U., 1970; PhD in Humanities, Syracuse U., 1986. Lectr. Colgate U., Hamilton, N.Y., 1984-85; asst. prof. Ithaca (N.Y.) Coll., 1987-89, Syracuse (N.Y.) U., 1989-90, Roanoke Coll., Salem, Va., 1990-96; curator of edn. Maier Mus. of Art, Lynchburg, Va., 1996—2002; head of edn. Art Mus. Western Va., Roanoke, 2002—. Vis. prof. Ohio U., Athens, 1986-87; adj. asst. prof. Sweet Briar (Va.) Coll., 2001—. Mem. editl. bd. Artemis, 1994-95. Grantee St. James Ch. (Italy), 1983, NEH, 1994; Mednick fellow Va. Found. Ind. Coll., 1991, Florence fellow Syracuse U., 1977-79. Mem. Artemis (pres. bd. dirs. 1994-98). Avocations: photography, hiking, yoga. Home: 2571 Brambleton Ave SW Roanoke VA 24015-4303 Office: Art Mus Western Va Roanoke VA 24011-1436 E-mail: mfitzgerald@artmuseumroanoke.org.

FITZGERALD, MAURA, public relations executive; b. 1949; Former freelance writer AP, UPI, Electronic Bus., Boston Globe, USA Today; former reporter Ft. Lauderdale News, Quincy Patriot Ledger; v.p. Sterling Hager, Inc.; sr. account exec. Miller, 1986, account supr., 1986-88, v.p., 1989-90, sr. v.p., 1990-91; ptnr. Cunningham Comm., Santa Clara, Calif., 1991-93; founder, pres. Fitzgerald Comm., Cambridge, Mass., 1993—. Office: Fitzgerald Comm Inc 855 Boylston St Boston MA 02116-2622

FITZGERALD, PATRICK J., prosecutor; b. 1960; BA, Amherst Coll., 1982; JD, Harvard U., 1985. Litigation assoc. Christy & Viener, 1984—87; asst. U.S. atty. (So. dist.) NY U.S. Dept. Justice, 1988—2001, chief narcotics unit, 1994, co-chief organized crime-terrorism unit, 1995—2001, nat. security coord., 1996—99, U.S. atty. (No. dist.) Ill., 2001—. Spl. prosecutor investigating government leak in the identification of Valerie Plame as a CIA operative US Dept. Justice, 2005. Recipient Atty. Gen.'s award for Exceptional Service, 1996, Stimson Medal, NY Bar Assoc., 1997, Atty. Gen.'s award for Dist. Svc., 2002. Office: 219 S Dearborn St 5th Fl Chicago IL 60604

FITZGERALD, PAUL A., endocrinologist, educator; b. N.Y.C., Apr. 9, 1946; s. Paul F. and Jessica M. Fitzgerald; m. Kathryn Morgan, Dec. 28, 1973; children: Brent, Erin. BA, Dartmouth Coll., 1968; MD, Jefferson Med. Coll., Phila., 1972. Diplomate Am. Bd. Internal Medicine, Am. Bd. Endocrinology and Metabolism. Resident in medicine Presbyn. Med. Ctr. & Hosp., Denver, 1977; fellow in endocrine U. Calif., San Francisco, 1978, attending physician, clin. prof., 1979—, mem. exec. med. bd. Med. Ctr., 1993—95. Editor: Handbook of Clinical Endocrinology, 1986, 1992; author: Basic & Clinical Endocrinology; contbr. articles to profl. jours. Recipient Charlotte Bier Meml. award, U. Calif. San Francisco, 1990. Mem.: Calif. Med. Assn., San Francisco Med. Soc., Endocrine Soc. (mem. coun. 1994—97), Am. Diabetes Assn. Office: U Calif San Francisco 350 Parnassus Ave Ste 710 San Francisco CA 94117

FITZGERALD, PETER GOSSELIN, former senator, lawyer; b. Elgin, Ill., Oct. 20, 1960; s. Gerald Francis and Marjorie (Gosselin) F.; m. C. Nina Kerstiens, July 25, 1987; 1 child, Jake Buchanan. AB, Dartmouth Coll., 1982; cert. of attendance, Aristotelian U., Salonica, Greece, 1983; JD, U. Mich., 1986. Bar: Ill. 1986, U.S. Dist. Ct. (no. dist.) Ill. 1986. Assoc. Isham, Lincoln & Beale, Chgo., 1986-88; ptnr. Riordan, Larson, Bruckert & Moore, Chgo., 1988-92; mem. Ill. Senate, 1993-98, chmn. state govt. ops. com., 1997-98; U.S. senator from Ill., 1999—2005; chmn. Subcom. Consumer Affairs and Product Safety of U.S. Senate Com. on Commerce, Sci. and Transportation, Subcom. Fin. Mgmt., Budget, and Internat. Security of U.S. Senate Com. on Govt. Affairs, 2003—05. Counsel Harris Bankmont, Inc., 1992-96. Rotary Found. internat. grad. scholar, 1982-83. Mem. Econ. Club Chgo., Union League Club. Republican. Roman Catholic. E-mail: dgumino@fitzgeraldpeter.com.

FITZGERALD, ROBERT HANNON, JR., orthopedic surgeon; b. Denver, Aug. 25, 1942; s. Robert Hannon and Alyene (Webber) Fitzgerald Anderson; m. Lynda Lee Lang, Apr. 27, 1968 (div. 1984); children: Robert III, Shannon, Dennis, Katherine, Kelly; m. Jamie Kathleen Dent, Mar. 9, 1985; children: Brian, Steven. BS, U. Notre Dame, 1963; MD, U. Kans., 1967; MS, U. Minn., 1974; Magistri Artivum, U. Pa., 1995. Cert. Am. Bd. Othropaedics, 1975, Am. Bd. Othropaedics, 1995. Instr. orthop. surgery Mayo Med. Sch., Rochester, Minn., 1974-77, cons. orthop. surgery, 1974-89, asst. prof., 1977-82, assoc. prof., 1982-86, prof., 1986-89, chief adult reconstructive surgery, 1987-89, dir. orthop. rsch., 1988-89; prof. chmn. dept. orthop. surgery Wayne State U. Sch. Med., 1989-95; chief orthop. surgery Hutzel Hosp., 1989-95, Detroit Receiving Hosp., 1989-95; orthopedist-in-chief Detroit Med. Ctr., 1989-95, chmn. coun., specialist-in-chief, 1993-95; chmn. dept. orthop. surgery U. Pa. Sch. Med., Phila., 1995-99; chief orthop. surgery Hosp. U. Pa., Phila., 1995—2000; P.B. Magnuson prof. bone and joint surgery U. Pa. Sch. Med., Phila., 1996—2001; chief orthop. surgery Phila. Veterans Med. Ctr. Dir. Penn. Orthop. Inst., U. Pa. Health Sys., 1997—2001; cons. CDC, Atlanta, 1981—, NIH, 1987—93, chmn. orthop. study sect., 1989—91; cons. health care financing adminstrn. Ctr. of Excellence Program, 2001; cons. MMS, 2001, CMS, 2002—; chief orthop. surgery Bell Meml. Hosp., 2001—04, Adams County Meml. Hosp., 2004—. Mem. editl. bd. Jour. Orthop. and Traumatology, 1978—, Jour. Bone Joint Surgery, 1982—88, Clin. Orthop. and Related Rsch., 1988—, Jour. Long Term Results Biomed. Devices, 1990; editor: Seminars in Arthoplasty, 1993—, Am. Acad. of Orthop. Surgery Ortho Knowledge Online, 2000—03; trustee Jour. Bone Joint Surgery, 1987—92, sec., 1988—92. Mem. bd. devel. Mayo Clinic, 1984—86, St. John's Ch., 1988—89; mem. bd. edn. St. John's Grade Sch., Jr. H.S., Rochester, 1983—87; trustee Hutzel Hosp., 1989—95; bd. dirs. Adams County ARC, 2004—, ARC; trustee Lourdes H.S. Devel. Bd., Rochester, 1982—88. Capt. USAF, 1968—70. Decorated Air Commendation medal; Traveling fellow AOA N.Am., 1974, Am. Brit. Can., 1981; recipient Kappa Delta award, 1983. Fellow Am. Acad. Orthop. Surgeons, Phila. Coll. Physicians; mem. AMA, Am. Orthopedic Assn., Rsch. Soc., Assn. Bone and Joint Surgeons, Interurban Ortho Soc., Internat. Soc. Microbiology, Zumbro County Med. Soc., Min-

Da-Man Orthop. Soc., Minn. Orthopedic Soc., Am. Soc. Microbiology, NY Acad. Scis., Am. Hip Soc. (Stinchfield award 1985, Charnley award 1986, 95, pres. 1993-94), Internat. Hip Soc., Am. Orthop. Assn. (N.Am. traveling fellow 1974, Am. Brit. Can. traveling fellow, 1981), Surg. Infection Soc. (charter mem.), Clin. Orthop. Soc., Internat. Soc. Orthop. Surgery and Traumatology, Mid-Am. Orthop. Soc. (bd. dirs. 1989-93, 94—, pres. elect 1994, pres. 1996), Detroit Acad. Orthop. Surgery, Mich. Orthop. Soc., Mich. State Med. Soc., Detroit Acad. Med., Pa. Orthop. Soc., Phila. Orthop. Soc. (bd. dirs. 1998-2001), Phila. Acad. Med., Ind. State Med. Assn., Interurban Club, Sigma Xi, Kappa Delta, Alpha Epsilon Delta. Republican. Roman Catholic. Avocation: cross-country and downhill skiing. Home and Office: Fitzgerald Orthopaedics PC 203 N 12th St Decatur IN 46733 Office Phone: 260-728-3849. Business E-Mail: rhfitz@mchsi.com.

FITZGERALD, ROBERT MAURICE, financial executive, retired bank executive; b. Chgo., Jan. 8, 1942; s. James Patrick and Catherine (McNulty) Fitzgerald; children: Stephen, Peter, Susan, Martin. BS, Loyola U., Chgo., 1971; postgrad., U. Wis., 1974-76, Northwestern U., 1980. Sr. v.p. Fed. Reserve Bank, Chgo., 1979-85; pres. Chgo. Clearing House Assn., Chgo., 1985—. Cons. Currency Bd., Abu Dhabi, United Arab Emirates, 1979; past bd. dirs. Nat. Automated Clearing House Assn., Washington; advisor U.S. Coun. on Internat. Banking, N.Y.C. Pres. Coun. on Alcoholism, Ann Arbor, Mich., 1978, Diocesan Bd. Edn., Joliet, Ill., 1981—84; former dir. Frances Xavier Warde Sch.; vice chair. Chgo. Crime Commn.; trustee Union League Boys and Girls Clubs; sec. Civic and Arts Found.; former mem. adv. bd. St. Mary of Nazereth Hosp.; past pres., bd. dirs., vice chmn. exec. com. LaLalle St. Coun.; former chair, bd. trustees Old St. Patrick's Ch., Chgo.; bd. dirs. Concern Worldwide (U.S.), Inc. Mem.: City Club Chgo., Bankers Club Chgo. (sec., treas., exec. com.), Union League Club Chgo. (past pres.), Econ. Club Chgo., Execs. Club of Chgo. (bd. dirs., treas.). Democrat. Roman Catholic. Office: Chgo Clearing House Assn 230 S La Salle St Ste 700 Chicago IL 60604-1410 E-mail: fitz@chgo.org.

FITZ-GERALD, ROGER MILLER, lawyer; b. NYC, July 13, 1935; s. Gerald Hartpence and Rovenia Francis (Miller) F.-G.; m. Martha Ann Odell, 1967 (div. 1985); children: Kathleen Odell, Maureen Roxanne, Arthur Thomas; m. Janice Evens, 1993. BS with honors, U. Ill., 1957, JD with honors, 1961. Bar: Ill. 1961, U.S. Dist. Ct. (no. dist.) 1961, U.S. Patent and Trademark Office, 1965, U.S. Ct. Customs and Patent Appeals, 1978, U.S. Ct. Appeals (fed. cir.) 1982, U.S. Dist. Ct. (so. dist.) Ill. 1992, U.S. Dist. Ct. (cen. dist.) Ill. 1994. Assoc. Kirkland, Ellis, Hodson, Chaffetz & Masters, Chgo., 1961-64; assoc. specializing in fgn. patent law Fitch, Even, Tabin & Luedeka, Chgo., 1964-72; patent atty. Bell & Howell Co., Chgo., 1972-74, sr. patent atty., 1974-75, group patent atty., 1975-76, group patent counsel, 1976-82, sr. patent counsel, 1982-85, sr. tech. law counsel, 1985-86, chief tech. law counsel, 1986-90; pvt. practice Urbana, Wilmette, Belleville, Ill., 1990—, St. Louis, 1990—. Author: (with Ferdinand J. Zeni) Precinct Captain's Guide, 1968; contbg. author: Materials on Legislation (Read, MacDonald, Fordham and Pierce), 1973 Constl. revision chmn. Ill. Young Republican Orgn., 1968-70. Served with AUS, 1957 Mem. ABA, Ill. Bar Assn., Chgo. Bar Assn., Champaign County Ill. Bar Assn., Intellectual Property Law Assn. Chgo., Am. Intellectual Property Law Assn., Assn. Corp. Patent Counsel, Computer Law Assn., Order of Coif, Phi Beta Kappa, Phi Eta Sigma, Phi Delta Phi, Delta Upsilon (province gov. 1969-75). Office: 1104 S Orchard St Urbana IL 61801-4852 Personal E-mail: rogerthebrave@juno.com.

FITZGERALD, THOMAS JOE, psychologist; b. Wichita, Kans., July 8, 1941; s. Thomas Michael and Pauline Gladys (Zink) FitzGerald. BA, San Francisco State U., 1965; MA, U. Utah, 1969, PhD, 1971. Dir. behavioral svcs. programs VA Hosp., Topeka, 1971—73; pvt. practice Topeka, 1973—74; pres. Psychol. Svcs. Corp., Prairie Village, 1974—. Clin. instr. Menninger Sch. Psychiatry, Topeka, 1972—74; v.p. Preferred Mental Health Care Mgmt., Inc., 1986—90; pres. Preferred Mental Health, Inc., 1990—; sec.-treas. Kans. Bd. Psychologist Examiners, 1976—80, chmn., 1980—, chmn. psychology examining com.; mem. Behavioral Scis. Regulatory Bd., 1980—82. Active Gov.'s Commn. on Criminal Adminstrn., 1974—76, Mid-Am. Health Sys. Agy., 1979—82; vice-chmn. Gov.'s Com. on Med. Assistance, 1978—80; com. on utilization rev. orgn. Kans. Ins. Commr. Adv. Com., 1994—. With USMC, 1958—61. Mem.: Kans. Assn. Profl. Psychologists (pres. 1981—82, Outstanding Psychologist award 1979—82), Greater Kansas City Soc. Clin. Hypnosis (pres. 1978—85), Kans. Psychol. Assn. (pres. 1980—81). Office: Preferred Mental Health Inc PO Box 4404 Overland Park KS 66204-0404

FITZGERALD, THOMAS ROBERT, state supreme court justice; b. Chgo., July 10, 1941; s. Thomas Henry and Kathryn (Touhy) Fitzgerald; m. Gayle Ann Aubry; 5 children. Attended, Loyola U., Chicago, 1959—63; JD, John Marshall Law Sch., Chicago, 1968. Bar: Ill. 1968. Trial asst. State Atty. Office Cook County, 1968—72, asst. state atty., 1968—76, felony trial supr., 1973—76; judge criminal div. Circuit Ct. Cook County, 1976—2000; justice Ill. Supreme Ct., 2000—. Adj. prof. law Kent Coll. Law, 1977—2000. Served in USN. recipient Outstanding Jud. Performance award Chgo. Crime Commn., Herman Kogan Media award for excellence in broadcast jour.; named Celtic Man of Yr. Celtic Legal Soc.; fellow Ill. Bar Found. Office: Ill Supreme Ct 160 N LaSalle St Rm N-2013 Chicago IL 60601*

FITZGERALD, TIMOTHY K., writer, political organizer, non-profit administrator; b. San Jose, Calif., Jan. 3, 1946; *Tim is single, the oldest of three brothers. His grandfather Fitzgerald found his fortune as a baker in Nome, Alaska, during the Klondike gold rush. His mother's family date themselves to the Battle of King's Mountain in the American Revolution and further back to the early founding of Jamestown, Virginia in 1612. Tim himself pioneered first ascents in Yosemite Valley in its golden era of the sixties.* BA in Econs., San Jose State Coll., 1971; BA in History, San Jose State U., 1980, MA in Social Sci., 1985, MA in History, 1997. Treas. Associated Students San Jose State Coll., 1969-70; camp bus. mgr. Boy Scouts Am., Sonora, Calif., 1973; co. budget analyst Allstate Equity Investments, 1980; adminstrv. asst. Summer Employment of Youth program CETA, San Jose, 1981; pres. Corp. for Shared Responsibility, San Jose, 1983-84; rschr. San Jose, 1992-96; owner/operator Raccoon Pubs., San Jose, 1991-92; freelance writer San Jose, 1986—; rschr., 1992-96; realtor Mammoth Lakes, Calif., 2004. Sec. Discovery, Inc, 1991-93; adminstrv. trustee Inst. for Social Orgnl. Rsch., 1992-94, 98-2001, exec. dir., 2001-; instr. Cerro Coso C.C., Mammoth Lakes, Calif., 1998-2000, Columbia C.C., Sonoma Calif., 2004; staff writer David Cobb Campaign for U.S. pres., 2004. *Tim has been a civic leader in his community since his undergraduate days in the mid-sixties. As a student activist, he was first elected to office on a ticket with a militant black civil rights spokesperson in a campus party of ethnic pluralism in 1969. His first writings were published as letters in the campus daily. An advocate of issues of poverty, the disabled and disadvantaged, he has since become a facilitator in national and State issues in Green Party politics.* Author: Trail to Black Mountain, 1978, Impressions from Idle Rock, 1981, Essays in Capitalism, 1986, Inner City, 1993, Twilight in the Afternoon, 1997, Challenge To America, 1998, (triology) The Quest: The Cut of the Diamonds, 2001—03, Statecraft and War, 2004; corr.: Mono County Rev. Herald, 1997—98; talk show host KSJS Radio, San Jose, 1995—97. Mgr., candidate for State Assembly, San Jose, 1994, for San Jose City Coun., 1982, for Mono County Bd. Edn., 1998; nat. del. Green Party of U.S. Coordinating Com., delegate Green Party Nat. Conv., 2000, 04; co-coord. State Green Party Platform, Calif., 1993, State Green Party campaigns and candidates, Calif., 1995-97; elected mem. Green Party County Coun., Santa Clara County, Calif., 1992-94, Mono County, 2000-03; staff writer David Cobb Campaign for U.S. Pres., 2004; elector Electorial Coll., 2004, vol. Cmty. Companions, Inc., San Jose, 1990-91; commr. City of San Jose Disability Adv., 1993-97, vice chair, 1997; mem. task force on poverty Santa Clara County, 1995-97; mem. Mono County Mental Health Adv. Bd., 1998-2002, chair, 1999-2000; coord. com. Nat. Green Party, 2005—. Advanced cadet U.S. Army ROTC, 1966-67 Mem. Am. Acad. Poets, Nat. Writers Union, Amnesty Interant., Fellowship of Reconciliation, Ams. for Dem. Action, Commonwealth Club, Sierra Club, Tau Delta Phi. Lutheran. Avocations: hiking, wilderness photography, chess, bridge. Office: Inst for Social Organizational Rsch 1750 Sokes St 118 San Jose CA 95126 Personal E-mail: timkf@hotmail.com.

FITZGERALD, WARREN FRANKLIN, lawyer; b. Methuen, Mass., Feb. 4, 1955; s. Donald Franklin and Ruth Elizabeth (Mann) F.; m. Lisa Christine Prokowich; children: Sara Elizabeth, Christopher David, Dillon Charles. BA magna cum laude, Boston U., 1976, JD, 1979. Bar: Mass. 1979, U.S. Dist. Ct. Mass. 1980, U.S. Ct. Appeals (1st cir.) 1985. Assoc. Hutchins & Wheeler, Boston, 1979-84, Parker, Coulter, Daley & White, 1984-85, Meehan, Boyle & Cohen, P.C., 1985—; ptnr. Meehan, Boyle, Black & Fitzgerald, P.C. Mem. ABA, Assn. Trial Lawyers Am., Mass. Acad. Trial Attys., Mass. Bar Assn. (pres.-elect 2004), Boston Bar Assn., Fed. Bar Assn., Phi Beta Kappa. Avocations: skiing, scuba diving, reading. Home: Fosters Pond Andover MA 01810 Office: Meehan Boyle Black & Fitzgerald Ste 600 2 Center Plz Boston MA 02108

FITZGERALD, WILLIAM ALLINGHAM, savings and loan association executive, director; b. Omaha, Nov. 18, 1937; s. William Frances and Mary (Allingham) F.; m. Barbara Ann Miskell, Aug. 20, 1960; children— Mary Colleen, Katherine Kara, William Tate. BSBA in Fin., Creighton U., 1959; grad. Savs. and Loan League exec. tng. program, U. Ga., 1962, U. Ind., 1969. With Comml. Fed. Savs. & Loan Assn., Omaha, 1959—, v.p., asst. sec., 1963-68, exec. v.p., 1968-73, pres., 1974-82, CEO, 1983—, chmn., CEO, 1994—. Trustee Ind. Coll. Found.; vice chmn. bd. dirs. Creighton U.; bd. dirs. Coll. of St. Mary, United Way of Midlands; trustee Archbishop's com. for ednl. devel. Roman Catholic Ch. Served to lt. Fin. Corps, U.S. Army. Chmn. Am. Cmty. Bankers, 1998—. Clubs: Omaha Country, Kiewit Plaza. Lodges: Knights of Ak-Sar-Ben (gov.).*

FITZGERALD, WILLIAM HENRY G., diplomat; b. Boston, Dec. 23, 1909; s. William Joseph and Mary Ellen (Smith) F.; m. Annelise Petschek, July 2, 1943; children: Desmond, Anne. BS, U.S. Naval Acad., 1931; postgrad., Harvard Law Sch., 1934-35; DSc (hon.), Adelphi U., 1962; LLD (hon.), Cath. U. Am., 1990; D in Pub. Svc. (hon.), Regis U., 1999. With Borden Co., N.Y.C., 1936-41; personal bus. interests Mexico, 1946-47; organized Metall. Research & Devel. Co., Washington, 1947, v.p., treas., 1947-56, pres., 1956-58, 60-82, chmn., 1960-82; chmn. bd. Nat. Metallizing Corp., Trenton, N.J., 1956-58; organizer FitzGerald Corp., 1959, pres., 1980—; chmn. bd. The Cottages, Ltd., Jamaica, 1960-70, Linden Corp., Washington, 1962-70, N.Am. Housing Corp., Washington, 1971-88; chmn. Supramar, Ltd., Lucerne, Switzerland, 1963-69, dir., 1970-75; pres. Nat. Media Analysis, Inc., Washington, 1968-70, chmn., 1970-72; ptnr. Hornblower & Weeks, Hemphill-Noyes, Inc., 1970-72, 1st v.p., 1972-77; vice chmn., dir., exec. com. Fin. Gen. Bankshares, Inc., 1977-82; vice chmn. African Devel. Found., 1990-92; U.S. amb. to Ireland, 1992-93. Dir., mem. exec. com. First Am. Bank (N.A.), Washington, 1977-83; dir., mem. exec. com., chmn. investment com. Avemco Corp., Washington, Frederick, Md., 1970-89; Cosmadent, Ltd., Zurich, Switzerland, 1964-75, Chase Fund of Boston, Chase Convertible Fund, Income & Capital Shares Inc., 1970-75, Pyrotector, Inc., Hingham, Mass., 1963-76; cons. to dir. ICA, Washington, 1957; dep. dir. for mgmt. ICA, Dept. State, 1958-60; U.S. conciliator Internat. Center for Investment Disputes, 1975-82; dir. Inst. Inter Am. Affairs, 1958-60; mem. President's Adv. Bd. on Internat. Investments, 1976-78; treas. Presdl. Inaugural Com., 1981; trustee Presdl. Inaugural Trust, 1981-89; mem. nat. adv. com. Internat. Edn., 1982-85. Trustee Fed. City Coun., 1962-90, Wash. Inst. Fgn. Affairs, 1966—; bd. dirs. Atlantic Coun. U.S., 1976—, treas., 1979-92, mem. exec. com., 1980—, vice chmn., 1993—; trustee Fgn. Student Svc. Coun., 1963—, Oblate Coll. (Cath. U.), 1966—; trustee Corcoran Gallery Art, 1977-90, also mem. exec. com., chmn. devel. com.; pres. Soc. for a More Beautiful Nat. Capital, Inc., 1974-77; bd. dirs., mem. exec. com., sr. v.p. Internat. Tennis Hall of Fame, 1964-92, 94—, hon. chmn., 2000—; nat. chmn. Yorktown Internat. Bicentennial Com., 1981; dir., mem. exec. com. Washington Tennis and Ednl. Found., 1987—; U.S. del. Atlantic Treaty Assembly, Reykjavik, Iceland, 1977, Washington, 1979, Rome, 1983, Istanbul, Turkey, 1987, Brussels, 1989, Rome, 1996, sofia, 1997; grand officer Confrèrie des Chevaliers du Tastevin, 1979—; grand senechal Sous Commanderie de Washington, 1980-90; trustee White House Preservation Fund, 1979-89, chmn., 1982-89, chmn. emeritus, 1989-90; mem. Nat. Task Force on Prison Industries; trustee, mem. nominating com. U.D.C., 1982-87; mem. nat. com. Vatican Judaica Exhbn., 1987-89; mem. Bretton Woods com., 1992—; mem., dir. Coun. of Am. Ambassadors, 1992—. Ensign USN, 1931-34; from lt. (j.g.) to comdr., 1941-46. Decorated Orden Militar de Ayacucho Peru, knight grand cross honor & devotion in obedience Order Malta, knight grand cross Sovereign Mil. Order Malta, Equestrian Order Holy Sepulchre, Sacred Mil. Constantinian Order St. George; named to Mid-Atlantic Tennis Hall of Fame, 1997. Mem. Fed. Assn. in U.S.A. Sovereign Mil. Order of Malta (pres. 1975-79), Assn. for Diplomatic Studies and Tng. (dir. 1993—), Army-Navy Country Club (Washington), Univ. Club (Washington), Harvard Club (Washington), River Club (N.Y.C.), Met. Club (Washington), Essex Country Club (Manchester, Mass.), Portmarnock Golf Club (Dublin, Ireland), FitzWilliam Lawn Tennis Club (Dublin). Roman Catholic. Home and Office: 2305 Bancroft Pl NW Washington DC 20008-4005 Office Phone: 202-332-5401.

FITZGIBBON, DANIEL HARVEY, lawyer; b. Columbus, Ind., July 7, 1942; s. Joseph Bales and Margaret Lenore (Harvey) FitzGibbon; m. Joan Helen Meltzer, Aug. 12, 1973; children: Katherine Lenore, Thomas Bernard. BS in Engring., U.S. Mil. Acad., 1964; JD cum laude, Harvard U., 1972. Bar: Ind. 1972, U.S. Dist. Ct. (so. dist.) Ind. 1972, U.S. Tax Ct. 1977. Commd. 2d lt. U.S. Army, 1964, advanced through grades to capt., 1967, served with inf. in West Berlin and Vietnam, resigned, 1969; assoc. Barnes & Thornburg, Indpls., 1972-79, ptnr., 1979-99, of counsel, 2000—. Spkr. various insts.; comml. law liaison ABA-CEELI, Moscow, 1998—99. Author: To Bear any Burden, A Hoosier Green Beret's Letters Home from Vietnam, 2005. Mem. sch. bd. Met. Sch. Dist. Lawrence Twp., 1988—96, pres., 1990—91, 1994—95; bd. advs. Eiteljorg Mus. Am. Indian and Western Art, 1993—2003. Fellow: Am. Bar Found., Am. Coll. Tax Counsel; mem.: ABA (internat. law sect.), Indpls. Bar Assn. (chmn. tax sect. 1982—83, coun. 1982—86), Ind. State Bar Assn. (tax sect.), Am. Law Inst., Woodstock Club, Lawyers Club. Home: 6460 Lawrence Dr Indianapolis IN 46226-1035 Office: Barnes & Thornburg 1313 Merchants Bank Bldg Indianapolis IN 46204-3506 Office Phone: 317-231-7247. Business E-Mail: dfitzgib@btlaw.com.

FITZHARRIS, JOSEPH CHARLES, history educator; b. Mpls., Oct. 12, 1946; s. Maurice E. and Gertrude I. (McBride) F.; m. Mary Helen Schreiner, Aug. 30, 1969; children: Scott J., Keith R. BA, Coll. St. Thomas, 1968; MA, U. Minn., 1969; PhD, U. Wis., 1975. Part-time instr. history U. St. Thomas, 1971-72, instr. history, 1972-75, asst. prof., 1975-81, assoc. prof., 1981—2004, acting chmn. history dept., 1982; rsch. fellow in agrl. and applied econs. U. Minn., 1972-75, rsch. assoc., 1975-79, part-time rsch. assoc., 1979-80; prof. U. St. Thomas, 2004—. Project evaluator Minn. Humanities Com., 1979-80; reader advance placement Ednl. Testing Svc.; cons. Ramsey County Hist. Soc.; bd. dirs. St. Thomas Coll. Fed. Credit Union; mem. at large Bd. Edn., Archdiocese of St. Paul and Mpls., 1988-91; guest lectr. Air War Coll., Maxwell AFB, 2003; vis. assoc. prof. U. Minn. Dept. of Soil Sci., Twin Cities Campus, St. Paul, Minn., 1990-1991, v.p., dir., 1998-99, 2003-04, pres., dir., 99-2001, past pres., dir., 01-03 Contbr. articles to profl. jours. Mem. Mpls. Aquatennial Parades Com., 1972-87; mem. coordinating com. St. Paul Campus Ministry, 1975-77, vice-chmn., 1977; vol. scouter Indianhead coun. Boy Scout Am., 1984—; chair, coord We. Soc. Sci. Assn., 1991-1993; appointed to bd. dirs. H-RURAL; organizer Soc. for Mil. History Sessions, No. Great Plains History Conf, 2000—; judge Minn. Book awards, 2001, 2003; mem. planning com. Minn. On-Line Encyclopedia, 2001-2003; great plains regional coord Soc. for Mil. History, 2004—. Recipient Certs. Appreciation, Coll. St. Thomas, 1977, 81, medallion, 1982, grantee 1982, Cub Scouter medal Boy Scouts Am., 1989, Dist. award of merit, 1996, Ford Found. fellow, 1970-71; grantee Rockefeller Found. 1972-75, U. Minn. Agrl. Expt. Sta., 1975-79; recipient Tng. Award medals Boy Scouts Am., 1987, 91, Silver Beaver award, Boy Scouts Am., 2001. Mem. Orgn. Am. Historians, Internat. Econ. History Assn., Soc. Mil. History, Phi Alpha Theta. Roman Catholic. Home: 13645 Elkwood Dr Saint Paul MN 55124-8773 Office: U St Thomas 412 John Roach Ctr 2115 Summit Ave Saint Paul MN 55105-1048

FITZHUGH, DAVID MICHAEL, lawyer; b. San Francisco, Nov. 24, 1946; s. William DeHart and Betty Jean (Jeffries) F.; m. Jenny Lu Conner, Dec. 22, 1967; children: Ross DeHart, Cameron Hyatt, Michael Jeffries. Student, Carleton Coll., 1964-67; BA, Coll. William and Mary, 1972; JD, U. Va., 1975. Bar: D.C. 1975, U.S. Dist. Ct. D.C. 1979, U.S. Dist. Ct. Md. 1987, U.S. Ct. Claims 1980, U.S. Ct. Appeals (fed. cir.) 1982, U.S. Ct. Appeals (D.C. cir.) 1987, U.S. Ct. Appeals (4th cir.) 1989, U.S. Supreme Ct. 1982. Assoc. McKenna & Cuneo, Washington, 1975-80, ptnr., 1980-98, chmn. litigation dept., 1984-94; assoc. counsel Office of Counsel Naval Air Systems Command, 1999—. Mem. editl. bd. Nat. Contract Mgmt. Assn. Jour., 1975-2000; contbr. articles to legal pubs. Capt. USMC, 1967-71, Vietnam. Home: 11140 Beacon Way Lusby MD 20657-2442 Office: AIR-11 1 NAVAIRSYSCOM HQ Office Counsel Bldg 2272 Ste 257 47123 Buse Rd Unit Moffett Patuxent River MD 20670-1547 Office Phone: 301-757-6005. Business E-Mail: david.fitzhugh@navy.mil.

FITZHUGH, WILLIAM, IV, curator; b. NYC, Feb. 1, 1943; BA in Anthropology, Dartmouth U., 1964; MA in Anthropology, Harvard U., 1967, PhD in Anthropology, 1970. Assoc. curator dept. anthropology Nat. Mus. Natural History/Smithsonian Instn., 1970—75, chmn. dept. anthropology, 1975—80, 2002—, curator dept. anthropology, 1980—; dir. Smithsonian Arctic Studies Ctr., Washington, 1988—. Robert L. Stigler lectr. U. Ark., 1988. Recipient Casebook award, 1984, Cine-Golden Eagle 2d prize for film Secrets of the Lost Red Paint People, Coun. on Internat. Non-theatrical Events, 1988, Smithsonian Disting.Lecture award, 2003.*

FITZMAURICE, DEANNE, photojournalist; BFA in Photography, Acad. Art Coll., San Francisco. Photographer San Francisco Chronicle, 1989—. Contbr. photog. to Day in the Life books. Named Photographer of the Yr., Bay Area Press Photographers Assn., 2002; recipient Pulitzer Prize for feature photography, 2005, Soc. Prof. Journalists award, Nat. Press Photographers Assn. award, Calif. Press Photographers Assn. award. Office: Photo Dept San Francisco Chronicle 901 Mission St San Francisco CA 94102 Office Phone: 415-777-7100.*

FITZMYER, JOSEPH AUGUSTINE, theology studies educator, priest; b. Phila., Nov. 4, 1920; s. Joseph Augustine and Anna Catherine (Alexy) F. AB, Loyola U., Chgo., 1943, AM, 1945; Licentiate in Sacred Theology, Facultés St. Albert de Louvain, Belgium, 1952; PhD, Johns Hopkins U., 1956; Licentiate in Sacred Scripture, Pontifical Bibl. Inst., 1957. Joined S.J., 1938, ordained priest Roman Cath. Ch., 1951. Asst. prof. N.T. and Bibl. langs. Woodstock (Md.) Coll., 1958-59, assoc. prof., 1959-64, prof., 1964-69; prof. Aramaic and Hebrew dept. Nr. Ea. langs.-civilizations U. Chgo., 1969-71; prof. N.T. and Bibl. langs. dept. theology Fordham U., Bronx, NY, 1971-74, Weston Jesuit Sch. Theology, Cambridge, Mass., 1974-76; prof. dept. Bibl. studies Cath. U. Am., Washington, 1976—2004, prof. emeritus, 2004—. Tchr. Gonzaga H.S., Washington, 1945-48; Spkr.'s lectr. Bibl. studies Oxford (Eng.) U., 1974-75. Author: Essays on the Semitic Background of the New Testament, 1971, The Genesis Apocryphon of Qumran Cave I, 1966, 3d edit., 2004; editor (with R.E. Brown and R.E. Murphy) The New Jerome Biblical Commentary, 1990; The Gospel According to Luke (Anchor Bible), vol. 28, 1981, vol. 28A, 1985, Romans (Anchor Bible), vol. 33, 1993, The Acts of the Apostles, vol. 31, 1998, The Letter to Philemon, vol. 34C, 2000. Mem. Cath. Bibl. Assn. (pres. 1970, editor Quar. 1980-84), Soc. Bibl. Lit. (pres. 1978-79, editor Jour. 1971-76), Studiorum Novi Testamenti Societas (pres. 1992-93). Home: Georgetown U Jesuit Cmty PO Box 571200 Washington DC 20057-1200 E-mail: fitzmyja@georgetown.edu.

FITZPATRICK, AL W., secondary school educator; b. Wash., Jan. 14, 1962; BS in Polit. Sci., So. Oreg. State Coll., 1974, MS in Social Sci., 1975. Tchr. Mazama High Sch., Klamath Falls (Oreg.) City Schs., 1975-78; govt. and law tchr. Newport (Oreg.) High Sch., 1978—. Presenter in field. Del. Republican Nat. Conv., New Orleans, 1988, Houston, 1992, San Diego, 1996, Phila., 2000; advisor YMCA Youth & Govt., Salem, Oreg., 1989-1991; selected for German marshall insvc. Nat. Coun. Social Studies, 1991; mem. Nat. Coun. Social Studies Textbook Com., 1990-1995, Nat. St. Law Conv., Washington, 1996. Recipient Leavey award Freedom Found., Levey award of Excellence in private Enterprise Edn., Arrid Tchr. Recognition award Carter-Wallace, Inc., Golden Apple award; Keizai Koho fellow Japanese C. of C., Tokyo; grantee law studies Oreg. Law Related Edn. Project; James Madison Meml. fellowship. Mem. Oreg. Theatre Arts Assn., Oreg. Speech Tchrs. Assn. (workshop presenter), Oreg. Thespians Conf. (workshop presenter), Yaquina Bay Optimists Club (dir. youth activities, pres.). Avocations: photography, bodysurfing, swimming, waterpolo, travel. Office: Newport H S 322 NE Eads St Newport OR 97365-2819 Home: 1080 NE 7th Dr Newport OR 97365

FITZPATRICK, BRIAN, Canadian legislator; b. Assiniboia, Can., Nov. 18, 1945; m. Zinaida Fitzpatrick; 2 children. BA in History, Bemidji (Minn.) State U.; LLB, U. Saskatchewan, Can. Cert. tchr. Can. Mem. 37th parliament House of Commons, Ottawa, Canada, mem. 38th parliament, mem. standing com. on pub. accounts. Trustee Nipawin Bd. Edn.; mem. Reform's Nat. Task Force on Criminal Justice, Dem. Populism and Provincial Party Involvement. Office: House of Commons Justice Bldg Ste 402 Ottawa ON K1A 0A6 Canada Address: 201 118 12th St E Prince Albert SK S6V 1B6 Canada Office Phone: 613-995-3295. Business E-Mail: fitzpb@parl.gc.ca.

FITZPATRICK, CHRISTOPHER, music educator, musician; s. Paul Fitzpatrick and Mary Kay Kauth. BA, Clarke Coll., 1984; MusM, New Eng. Conservatory, 1989. Cert. Music, K-12 Fla., Music 5-12 Mass., Music, K-9 Mass. Dir. music The Pingree Sch., S. Hamilton; faculty The Boston Conservatory, 2001—04; head performing arts Pine Crest Sch., Ft. Lauderdale, Fla., 2004—. Instr. Miami Dade Coll. Music Learning Ctr., Fla., 2004—; musical dir., instr. North Shore Music Theatre, Beverly, Mass., Camp Broadway, NYC; singer Cantata Singers and Ensemble, Boston; arts outreach Provincetown Theatre Co.; instr. North Shore Music Theatre, Beverly. Author: (vh1 music studio) Lesson Plans; singer: (choral) Cantata Singers and Ensemble; musical director/composer (education department) North Shore Music Theatre, musical director (performance), accompanist. Recipient Connolly Music award; Horace Mann grantee. Mem.: Am. Choral Dirs. Assn., Am. Fedn. Musicians (assoc.), Theater League South Fla. (assoc.), Coll. Music Soc. (assoc.), Fla. Vocal Assn. (assoc.), Fla. Music Educators Assn. (assoc.). Personal E-mail: christopherfitzpatrick@musician.org.

FITZPATRICK, DANIEL M., trust company executive, lawyer; b. Plattsburgh, N.Y., Mar. 5, 1958; s. James A. and Joan M. FitzPatrick; m. Helen Ix, Aug. 24, 1985; children: Whitney G., Caroline I., John R. A.B., cum laude, Dartmouth Coll., Hanover, New Hampshire, 1980; J.D., Vanderbilt U. Sch. of Law, Nashville, Tennessee, 1983. Bar: NY 1984. Atty. Davis Polk & Wardwell, New York, NY, 1983—92; mng. dir. J.P. Morgan & Co., Inc., New York, NY, 1992—2000, Goldman, Sachs & Co., New York, NY, 2000—; chmn., pres. & ceo The Goldman Sachs Trust Co., N.A., New York, NY, 2000—. Trustee The Health Care Chaplaincy, New York, NY, 2005—; bd. mem. Greenwich Emergency Med. Svc., Inc., Greenwich, Conn., 2004—. Editor-in-chief Vanderbilt Journal of Transnational Law. Knight of magistral grace Am. Assn. of the Sovereign Mil. Order of Malta, New York, NY, 1992—2005. Mem.: Assn. of the Bar of the City of NY, NY State Bar Assn., ABA, Trust & Investment Divsn., NY Bankers Assn. (exec. com. mem. 2002—04), Trust Mgmt. Assn. (exec. com. mem. 2002—05), The Anglers Club, NY, NY, The Preston Mountain Club, Kent, CT, The Belle Haven Club, Greenwich, CT, The U. Club, NY, NY. Roman Catholic. Office: The Goldman Sachs Trust Company NA One New York Plaza 40th Floor New York NY 10004 Office Phone: 212-902-9996. Personal E-mail: fitz500@optonline.net. E-mail: daniel.fitzpatrick@gs.com.

FITZPATRICK, DAVID J., electronics executive; b. 1954; BS in Acctg., U. Ill.; M in Mgmt., Northwestern U. CPA, Ill. With GM, 1977, chief acctg. officer; group v.p. fin. and adminstn. GMAC; contr., v.p. Eastmas Kodak Co., 1995; sr. v.p., CFO United Technologies Corp., Hartford, Conn., 1998—2002; exec. v.p., CFO Tyco Internat., 2002—. Bd. dirs. GMAC, GMAC Mortgage.

FITZPATRICK, ELLEN F., historian, educator; BA, Hampshire Coll., 1974; PhD, Brandeis U., 1981. Vis. asst. prof. history Wellesley (Mass.) Coll., 1984—87, MIT, Cambridge, Mass., 1988—89; asst. prof. history Harvard U., Cambridge, Mass., 1989—93, assoc. prof. history, 1993—97; prof. history U. N.H., Durham, 1997—. Mem. governing coun. Rockefeller Archive Ctr., Tarrytown, NY, 1999—2005. Author: Endless Crusade: Women Social Scientists and Progressive Reform, 1990, History's Memory: Writing America's Past, 1880-1980, 2002; co-author (with Alan Brinkley): America in Modern Times, 1997; editor: Muckraking: Three Landmark Articles, 1994, Century of Struggle, 1994. Chair Newtonville Local Hist. Dist. Commn., Newton, Mass., 2002—05. Grantee, The Spencer Found., 1987, Ford Found., 1999; Irving and Rose Crown fellow, Brandeis U., 1975—80, Andrew Mellon Faculty fellow, Harvard U., 1983, Charles Warren Ctr. fellow, 1987, 1993. Mem.: Orgn. Am. Historians, Am. Hist. Assn. Democrat. Office Phone: 603-862-1234.

FITZPATRICK, J. MICHAEL, chemicals executive; m. Jean Fitzpatrick. BS in Chemistry, U. New Orleans, 1969; PhD in Organic Chemistry, Rice U., 1973. NIH fellow Harvard U., 1973—75; from sr. scientist rsch. divsn. to mktg. specialist Rohm and Haas Co., Phila., 1975—80, from product mgr. to mktg. mgr. agrl. chemicals Brazil, 1981—84, bus. mgr. agrl. chemicals, 1985—87, gen. mgr., 1988—89, mng. dir. UK and Europe, 1990—92, from v.p., dir. rsch. to chief tech. officer, 1993—97, pres., COO Phila., 1999—; also bd. dirs. Bd. dirs. Carpenter Tech. Corp., McCormick & Co., Inc., Green Chemistry Inst. Bd. trustees Franklin Inst. and Sci. Mus. Mem.: Am. Cancer Soc. (chmn. Pa. divsn.). Office: Rohm and Haas Co 100 Independence Mall W Philadelphia PA 19106-2399

FITZPATRICK, JAMES A., JR., lawyer; b. Plattsburgh, N.Y., July 1, 1949; BA cum laude, Dartmouth Coll., 1971; JD, Albany Law Sch., Union Univ., 1974. Bar: N.Y. Ptnr., chmn. corp. dept. & chmn. hiring com. Dewey Ballantine LLP, N.Y.C., 1989—. Dir. Ultimate Software Group. Mem.: ABA. Office: Dewey Ballantine LLP 1301 Ave of the Americas New York NY 10019-6092 Office Phone: 212-259-6220. Office Fax: 212-259-6333. Business E-Mail: jfitzpatrick@dbllp.com.

FITZPATRICK, JAMES DAVID, lawyer; b. Syracuse, N.Y., Oct. 21, 1938; s. William Francis and Margaret Mary (Shortt) F. BS, Holy Cross Coll., Worcester, Mass., 1960; JD, Syracuse U., 1963. Bar: N.Y. 1963, U.S. Dist. Ct. (no. dist.) N.Y. 1965. Assoc. Bond, Schoeneck & King, Syracuse, N.Y., 1963-76, mem., 1976-88, ptnr., 1988—. Pres. Hiscock Legal Aid Soc., Syracuse, 1975-76; faculty Nat. Bus. Inst., Eau Claire, Wis., 1990—; del. Russian Conf. on Banking-The Kremlin, Moscow, 1992, 93; spkr. Internat. Conf. on Terrorism, Madrid, 2002. Mem. Presdl. Roundtable, Washington, 1991-92; founding mem. pres.'s task force Nat. Coalition Against Pornography, Common Cause; chmn. adv. bd. Rep. Nat. Coms., 1994; mem. The Studio Mus. in Harlem, Am. Mus. Nat. History; founding mem. Am. Air Mus.; nat. adv. coun. USN Meml. Found. Recipient Afghanistan Freedom Fighter award Afghan Mercy Fund, 1989, Rep. Senatorial Medal of Freedom, Honored Friend of El Salvador award, 1991, Wisdom award of Honor, Wisdom Soc. for Advancement of Knowledge, Learning and Rsch. in Edn., named to Wisdom Hall of Fame, 1999. Mem. ABA, NAACP, N.Y. State Bar Assn., Onondaga County Bar Assn. (chmn. real estate com. 1990-96), Internat. Bar Assn., Am. Land Title Assn., UN Assn. of U.S.A., Habitat for Humanity Internat., Amnesty Internat. U.S.A., Nat. Audubon Soc., Ctr. for Nat. Independence in Politics, Smithsonian Nat. Assocs., Nat. Trust for Hist. Preservation, Navy League U.S., World Future Soc., Ams. Guild, Internat. Platform Assn. (spkr. Internat. Youth Ctr., New Delhi), Inst. Global Ethics, World Jurist Assn. Republican. Roman Catholic. Avocations: housing education, reading, walking. Home: 201 Croyden Rd Syracuse NY 13224-1917 Office: Bond Schoeneck & King 1 Lincoln Ctr Fl 18 Syracuse NY 13202-1324 Office Phone: 315-218-8000. Business E-Mail: jfitzpatrick@bsk.com.

FITZPATRICK, JAMES FRANKLIN, lawyer; b. Bluffton, Ind., Jan. 18, 1933; s. Raymond North and Evelyn (Baughman) F.; m. Sandra McNear, July 22, 1961; children: Michael, David, Benjamin. AB, Ind. U., 1955, JD, 1959; postgrad., Cambridge U., 1956. Law clk. to chief judge U.S. Ct. Appeals, Chgo., 1959-61; assoc. Arnold & Porter, Washington, 1961-67, ptnr., 1967—. Adj. prof. law Georgetown U., Washington, 1971-75, 2003-05; acad. visitor. London Sch. Econs., 1978-79, Trinity Coll., Dublin, Ireland, 1987-88; chmn. Global Rights, 1999—; vis. prof. law U. N.Mex., 1998, 2005. Author: Law and Roadside Hazards, 1975. Bd. dirs. ACLU, 1983-85, pres. Nat. Capital chpt., Washington, 1982-83; pres. Washington Project for the Arts, 1984-90; dir. Ctr. for Auto Safety, 1984—, The Phillips Collection, 1990—, The Shakespeare Theatre, 1991—, Site Santa Fe, 1997—, Ctr. for Arts and Culture, 1998—, Brit. Am. Arts Assn., 1999—; nat. chmn. Young Citizens for Johnson, 1964. Mem. ABA, Phi Beta Kappa Democrat. Presbyterian. Office: Arnold & Porter 555 12th St NW Washington DC 20004-1206 Office Phone: 202-942-5878.

FITZPATRICK, JAMES WARD, JR., engineering educator; b. Birmingham, Ala., June 17, 1921; s. James Ward and Ellen Barbara (Vogtle) Fitzpatrick; m. Ruth Bertha Horn, June 19, 1948; 1 child, James Ralph (dec.). BS in Indsl. Engring., Auburn (Ala.) U., 1942, BSME, 1947; student, MIT, 1949—50, Auburn (Ala.) U., 1951—52. Registered profl. engr., Ala. Indsl. engr. O'Neal Steel, Birmingham, 1947-48; plant engr. Stockham Valves & Fittings, Birmingham, 1948-49; instr. mech. engring. Auburn U., 1950-53; structural engr. Decatur (Ala.) Iron & Steel Co., 1953-56, chief engr. jail and prison equipment, 1956-64; engring. and project mgr. Monsanto Co., St. Louis, 1964-72, engring. supt., 1972-82; v.p. personnel and ops. Continental Commodities, Inc., Charlotte, N.C., 1982-83; instr. York Tech. Coll., Rock Hill, SC, 1986—98, dept. mgr., indsl. and engring. tech. and constrn. trades, continuing edn. divsn., 1999—2001, cons. continuing edn. divsn., 2002—. Cons. in field. Author: (software) Workplan, 1984. Capt. U.S. Army, 1942—46, ETO. Decorated Bronze Star. Mem.: Charlotte Philatelic Soc. (pres. 1985—89). Republican. Presbyterian. Avocations: fantasy baseball, stamp collecting/philately. Home: 5006 Gamton Ct Charlotte NC 28226-7920 E-mail: ogoytc@att.net.

FITZPATRICK, JOHN, poet; s. William Harry Fitzpatrick and Cecelia Schmidt. BA, U. Notre Dame, 1959; MS, Hofstra U., 1972; PhD, NYU, 2000. Cert. secondary edn., supr. secondary edn., secondary sch. prin. N.Y. English tchr. Hicksville (N.Y.) H.S., 1962—64, George W. Hewlett (N.Y.) H.S., 1964—94, coach speech-debate team, 1964—94. Pres. George W. Hewlett H.S. Faculty, 1968—70, L.I. Forensic Assn., 1976—78; sec., v.p. Hewlett-Woodmere (N.Y.) Faculty Assn. Retirees, 1994—99, 1999—2000. Author poetry. Dist. coord. Bicentennial Youth Debates Nassau County, L.I., 1975—76; bd. mem., officer Theatre Five, Dix Hills, NY, 1962—70, prodr., actor, publicity chairperson, 1962—70. Recipient Outstanding Educator award, U. Notre Dame, 1998. Mem.: Kappa Delta Pi, Pi Lambda Theta (Rho chpt.). Avocations: gardening, hiking. Home: 44 Creekside Rd Red Hook NY 12571-9155

FITZPATRICK, JOHN CHARLES, humanities educator, curator; b. Streator, Ill., July 17, 1947; s. Eileen Veronica Leber and John Bernard Fitzpatrick. BA, Principia Coll., Elsah, Ill., 1965—69; EdS, U. Iowa, Iowa City, 1969—79; postgrad., UCLA, 1986. Cert. tchr. State of Iowa, 1980. Grad. asst., asst. varsity swim coach U. Iowa, Iowa City, 1969—73; lectr., health and phys. edn. Cornell Coll., Mount Vernon, Iowa, 1973—78; art history chmn. Kirkwood CC, Cedar Rapids, Iowa, 1977—78; tchr. and coach Iowa City Cmty. Sch. Dist., 1978—80; curriculum program facilitator Cedar Rapids Cmty. Sch. Dist., Iowa, 1981—82. We. regional dir. for supervision and adminstrn. Nat. Art Edn. Assn., Washington, 2003—05; pres. Humanities Iowa, Iowa City, 2004—; art tchr. Polk Elem. Sch., Cedar Rapids, 2002—03; adj. art edn. methods Coe Coll., 2001—03. Contbr. anthology, educational programming (NEH Swartz Award, 2002). Mem. Iowa Old Capitol restoration com., 1976; judge Cmty. Betterment Programs, Iowa Devel. Commn., 1976-77; bd. mem. Friends of the Jeffrey Ballet, N.Y.C., 1985-89; bd. mem. Dance Focus of Iowa, 1986-90, pres. 1988-90; mem. arts com. Iowa City C. of C., 1986-91; mem. Iowa Arts Festival Com., 1988-90; chmn. Grant Wood Centennial Celebration State Com., 1991; mem. Cedar Rapids Literary Club, Cedar Rapids Country Club, 1992-96; spkr. Nat. Endowment for the Arts in ednl. programs with Kitty Carlisle Hart, Lincoln Ctr., U.S. Senate subcom., 1993; presenter, Lt. Gov.'s Conf. on Diversity, 1995; mem. Am. Theatre Organ Soc., 1966-, Nat. Edn. Com., 1994-96; mem. arts advisory bd., Grant Wood Edn. Agy., 1991-; mem. design com., Regional Arts Facility-Ctr. Space, 1991-98; mem. City of Cedar Rapids Visual Arts Com., 1994-2001, v.p., 1998, chmn., 1999, 2000; mem. Art in State Bldgs. Com., U. Iowa Hosps. & Clinics, 1996-2003; events chair U. Iowa Mus. Art, 1997; bd. mem. Cedar Rapids Opera Theater, 1998-2004; mem. River Way Design Team, City of Cedar Rapids, 1998-2001; mem. exhbns. com., the History Ctr., 1999-; cons. Humanities Iowa, Born Again project, 2001-02, treas. and chair programming and grants com., 2002-03, v.p., 2003-04, pres., 2004-05; mem. fundraising com. Friends of the Paramount Theatre, 2001-04; bd. dirs. Cedar Rapids Oak Hill Cemtery, 2001-; Performance Pavilion chair, band commn. City of Cedar Rapids, 2001- Named Arts Adminstr. of the Yr., Iowa Art Edn. Assn., 2001; recipient Arts Edn. Award, Rockefeller Bros. Fund, 1982, John Fitzpatrick Day, City of Cedar Rapids, 2001. Mem.: Nat. Art Edn. Assn. (we. region dir., adminstrn. and supervision 2003, Nat. Educator of the Yr. 2002). Avocations: travel, reading, swimming, jogging. Home: 721 North Linn Iowa City IA 52245-1937 Office: Cedar Rapids Cmty Schs 346 Second Ave SW Cedar Rapids IA 52404-2099 Office Phone: 319-558-1132. Office Fax: 319-558-2900. Personal E-mail: historicphillips@aol.com. Business E-Mail: jfitzpatrick@cr.k12.ia.us.

FITZPATRICK, JOHN DAVID, lawyer; b. Boston, July 17, 1961; s. Robert A. and Genevieve A. (Manfredonia) F.; children: Katharine Lasell, Timothy Sumner. BSEd, U. Mich., 1983; JD, Harvard U., 1987. Bar: Mass. 1987, U.S. Dist. Ct. Mass., U.S. Ct. Appeals (1st cir.). Law clk. Supreme Jud. Ct. of Maine, Auburn, 1987-88; atty. Com. for Pub. Counsel Svcs., Brockton, Mass., 1988-89, Cambridge, Mass., 1989-93; assoc. Looney & Grossman, Boston, 1993-94; atty., sole practitioner Boston, 1994-97; ptnr. Fitzpatrick & Warrenbrand LLP, Boston, 1997—. Clerical instr. Harvard Law Sch., 1998—. Office: Fitzpatrick & Warrenbrand LLP 1 Mckinley Sq Boston MA 02109-2603

FITZPATRICK, JOHN J., bishop; b. Trenton, Ont., Can., Oct. 12, 1918; s. James John and Lorena (Pelkey) F. Student, Propaganda Fide Coll., Italy, Our Lady of Angels Sem.; BA, Niagara U., 1941. Ordained priest Roman Catholic Ch., 1942. Titular bishop of Cenae and Aux. of Miami, Fla., 1968—71; bishop of Brownsville, 1971—91; bishop emeritus, 1991—. Roman Catholic. Office: 1904 Barnard Rd Brownsville TX 78520-8247

FITZPATRICK, KATHLEEN G., education educator, accountant; b. Nashua, New Hampshire, July 7, 1955; d. Joseph Leo and Gertrude Meunier; m. Thomas Joseph Fitzpatrick, Dec. 29, 1978; children: Brendan, Kyle, Rachel. BS in Acctg., Syracuse U., 1977; MBA in Computer Sys., U. of Toledo, 1983. Cert. mgmg. acct., cert. fin. mgmt., Inst. of Mgmt. Accountants. Staff acct. U. Engineers Cons., Seabrook, NH, 1977—79; fiscal officer Criminal Justice Coordinating Coun., Toledo, Ohio, 1979—84; acctg. supr. Omni Source Corp., Toledo, 1984—85; asst. contr. Bostwick Braun Co., Toledo, 1985—87; part-time instr. U. of Toledo, 1988—98, vis. prof., 1998—2000, asst. prof., 2000—. Mem.: Inst. of Mgmt. Accountants.

FITZPATRICK, KATHLEEN GAIL, music director, soprano; d. Shirley Prath and John Thomas Fitzpatrick; children: Thomas Francis Napack, Joseph Timothy Napack, Daniel William Napack, William James Lantry. BA cum laude, Barnard Coll., Columbia U.; postgrad, Cath. U. Am.; student, La Schola Cantorum, Paris. Soprano solist, cantor St. Jane Francis de Chantal Ch., Bethesda, Md., Holy Cross Ch., Garrett Park; dir. liturgical music St. Dominic's Cath. Ch., Washington, 2002—03, St. Catherine Laboure Ch., Wheaton, 2003—. Workshop presenter NPM, DC, Internet2; condr. St. Catherine Laboure Liturgical Choir Concert Series, Wheaton, Md. Recipient Natalie Bogardus Vocal award, Schubert Club. Mem.: Nat. Assn. Pastoral Musicians. Office: St Catherine Laboure Ch 11801 Claridge Rd Wheaton MD 20902 Office Phone: 301-946-8080.

FITZPATRICK, LOIS ANN, library administrator; b. Yonkers, N.Y., Mar. 27, 1952; d. Thomas Joseph and Dorothy Ann (Nealy) Sullivan; m. William George Fitzpatrick, Jr., Dec. 1, 1973; children: Jennifer Ann, Amy Ann. BS in Sociology, Mercy Coll., 1974; MLS, Pratt Inst., 1975. Clk. Yonkers Pub. Libr., 1970-73, libr. trainee, 1973-75, libr. I, 1975-76; reference libr. Carroll Coll. Libr., Helena, Mont., 1976-79, acting dir., 1979, dir., 1980—; asst. prof. Carroll Coll., Helena, 1979-89, assoc. prof., 1989-99, prof., 2000—. Bd. dirs. Mont. Shares; chmn. arrangements Mont. Gov.'s Pre White House Conf. on Libraries, Helena, 1977-78; mem. steering com. Reference Point coop. program for librs., 1991; mem. adv. com. Helena Coll. of Tech. Libr., 1994—; adv. coun. Mont. Libr. Svcs., 1996-2000; mem. Networking Task Force, 1998-2003, Laws Revision Task Force, 1998-2001, Not Ready for Prime Time Freedom Fighters; pres. elect Helena Area Health Sci. Libraries Cons., 1979-84, pres., 1984-88; bd. dirs. Mont. FAXNET; mem. cancer comprehensive cancer plan State Mont., 2004—. Co-chmn. interst group OCLC; chmn. local arrangements Mont. Gov.'s Pre White House Conf.; mem. Mont. Race for the Cure, 1998-2004; bd. dirs. ACLU-MT, 2000—, pres., 2005-2007; mem. adv. com. Am. Cancer Soc. Lewis and Clark County. Mem. Mont. Libr. Assn. (task force for White House conf. 1991, chair govt. affairs com. 1997-2003, EdLINK-MT 1997-99, 2000-01), Soroptimist Internat. of Helena (2d v.p. 1984-85, pres. 1986-87). Home: 1308 Shirley Rd Helena MT 59602-6635 Office: Carroll Coll Jack & Sallie Corette Libr 1601 N Benton Ave Helena MT 59625-0001 Office Phone: 406-447-4341. Business E-Mail: lfitzpat@carroll.edu.

FITZPATRICK, M. LOUISE, dean, nursing educator; b. South River, N.J., May 24, 1942; d. John Francis and Bettina (Galassi) F. Diploma in nursing, Johns Hopkins U., 1963; BSN, Cath. U. Am., 1966; MA, Columbia U., 1968, MEd, 1969, EdD, 1972; cert., Harvard U., 1985. Former assoc. prof., dept. nursing edn. Tchrs. Coll., Columbia U., N.Y.C.; dean, prof. Villanova (Pa.) U. Coll. Nursing, 1978—. Cons. Mid. States Assn., Phila.; cons. to numerous univs., also univs. in Morocco, Egypt, Jordan, West Bank, Sultanate of Oman; cons., reviewer USPHS; bd. dirs. Nurses Ednl. Funds, Inc., N.Y.C. Author: The National Organization for Public Nursing, Development of a Practice Field, 1975; editor: Present Realities/Future Imperatives, 1977, Historical Studies in Nursing, 1978, Nursing in Society: A Historical Perspective, 1983; also 21 articles in profl. jours. Recipient Disting. Alumni award Columbia U. Tchrs. Coll., 1966, Cath. Univ. McManus medal, 1992; WHO fellow, Scandinavia and U.K., 1974; Am. Acad. Nursing fellow, 1978. Mem. Am. Nurses Assn. (past chmn. cabinet on nursing edn.), Am. Assn. Colls. Nursing, Nat. League for Nursing (bd. of govs.). Democrat. Roman Catholic. Avocations: music, theater, cooking, international travel. Home: 80 Woodstone Ln Villanova PA 19085-1425 Office: Villanova U Coll Nursing Villanova PA 19085

FITZPATRICK, MICHAEL G. (MIKE), congressman, lawyer; b. Phila., Pa., June 28, 1963; m. Kathleen Fitzpatrick; 6 children. BA, St. Thomas Univ., Miami, Fla., 1985; JD, Pa. State Univ., 1988. Bar: Pa., NJ. Spl. counsel Saul Ewing LLP, Phila.; commr. Bucks County, Pa., 1995—2004; mem. U.S. Ho. Reps., 109th Congress, 8th Dist. Pa., 2005—. Past pres. Bucks County Council, Boy Scouts Am.; bd. mem. Temple Lower Bucks County Hosp.; mem. bd. adv. Conwell Egan Catholic High Sch. Mem.: ABA, Pa. State Bar Assn., Bucks County Bar Assn., Brehon Law Soc., Ancient Order of Hibernians, Levittown Bristol Kiwanis, KC. Republican. Roman Catholic. Office: 1516 Longworth House Office Bldg Washington DC 20515-3808 Office Phone: 202-225-4276.*

FITZPATRICK, MICHELLE LYNN, music educator; b. Middletown, Ohio, Feb. 20, 1967; d. Leonard Junior and Ruth Mary Denniston; m. Andrew Patrick Fitzpatrick, Dec. 18, 1993; children: Miranda Alyse, Natalie Michelle, Brendan Andrew. MusB in Edn., Morehead State U., Ky., 1989; MusM, Miami U., Oxford, OH, 1992. Cert. tchg. permanent Ohio. Gen. music tchr. Carlisle (Ohio) Intermediate Sch., 1990—. Mem.: Sigma Alpha Iota.

FITZPATRICK, NANCY HECHT, editor; b. Dec. 29, 1942; d. Ira Youngwood and Bettie Jane (Van Cleave) Hecht; m. Alan Rush Fitzpatrick, Dec. 15, 1973 (dec.); m. Thomas H. Gervais, May 17, 2003. Student, Upsala Coll., 1960-62, New Sch. Social Rsch., 1962-64, Johns Hopkins U., summer 1987, Bennington Coll., summer 1988; MFA in writing, Union Inst., 2005. Asst. copy editor Am. Home mag., N.Y.C., 1964-68; v.p. Creative Comms. Assocs., Newark, 1968-70; sr. editor Family Circle mag., N.Y.C., 1970-77; corp. sec., v.p. mktg. Alternative Telecom. Corp., N.Y.C., 1977-92; exec. editor Meeting News mag., N.Y.C., 1993-95; assoc. news editor, book and art reviewer The Vineyard Gazette, 1997—2001; archivist and publs. editor Wampanoag Tribe of Gay Head/Aquinnah, 2002—04; editor Spice Arts and Entertainment Guide, 2005—. Editor various publs. Mem.: LWV, NOW, Eastern Bedford Environ. Assn. (treas.), Empire women in Telecom. (pres.), N.Y. Women in Comms.

FITZPATRICK, ROBERT JOHN, museum director; b. Toronto, Ont., Can., May 18, 1940; came to U.S., 1952, naturalized, 1962; s. John and Maxine (Dunn) F.; m. Sylvie M. Blondet, Jan. 1966; children: Joel Denis, Michael Sean, Claire Valerie. BA magna cum laude, Spring Hill Coll., 1963, MA magna cum laude, 1964; student (Woodrow Wilson fellow), Johns Hopkins U., 1964-65. Asst. prof. French U. Maine, 1965-68; mem. staff McCarthy Nat. Campaign Hdqrs., 1968; staff asst., campaign aide to Sen. Joseph D. Tydings, Washington, 1970; chmn. dept. modern langs. Gilman Sch., Balt., 1968-72; dean of students Johns Hopkins U., 1972-75; pres. Calif. Inst. of Arts, Valencia, 1975-87, Euro Disneyland, Burbank, Calif., 1987—93; CEO RFC, Paris, 1993—95; dean Sch. of the Arts Columbia U., N.Y.C., 1995—2001; Pritzker dir., CEO Museum of Contemporary Art, Chicago, 2001—. Mem. Balt. City Council, 1971-75; v.p. Mayor's Com. on Cultural Affairs, Los Angeles, 1976-79, Calif. Confedn. of Arts, 1977-79; dir. Olympic Arts Festival, Los Angeles, 1984, Los Angeles Festival, 1985-87; mem. Md. Democratic State Central Com., 1970-74; mem. adv. com. Next Wave Festival, Bklyn. Coll.; trustee Craft and Folk Art Mus., Los Angeles, 1976-82; bd. dirs. Los Angeles Chamber Orch., 1977-81; trustee Dunn Sch., Los Olivos, Calif., 1980-84, Bennington Coll., Vt. Democrat. Office: Museum of Contemporary Art 220 E Chicago Ave Chicago IL 60611*

FITZPATRICK, SANDRA MARLENE, lawyer; b. East St. Louis, Ill., Jan. 21, 1940; d. Clottis F. and Louise (Campbell) Gray; m. Lorenzo Fitzpatrick, May 5, 1961; children: Andre Renard, Eric D'Wayne. BA, U. Tex., 1973, JD, 1976. Bar: Tex. 1977, U.S. Dist. Ct. (we. dist.) Tex. 1980, U.S. Ct. Appeals (5th and 11th cirs.) 1981, U.S. Supreme Ct. 1982. Appeals referee Tex. Employment Commn., Austin, 1976-78; hearings examiner Tex. Water Commn., Austin, 1978-83; pvt. practice Austin, 1983-89, 2002—; prosecutor City of Austin, 1989-91; staff atty. Tex. State Bd. Med. Examiners, 1991-94, Tex. Dept. Protective and Regulatory Svcs., 1994-98, State Bd. Educator Cert., Tex., 1998—2002. Assoc. judge City of Austin, 1991—98, City of Round Rock, 2005—. Mem.: Austin Black Lawyers Assn. Democrat. Baptist. Office: 14313 Mowsbury Dr Austin TX 78717-4427 Office Phone: 512-310-0894. Personal E-mail: sandyfitz@sbcglobal.net.

FITZPATRICK, SUSAN, biochemist, neurologist, foundation executive; married. Grad., St. John's U.; PhD in Biochemistry and Neurology, Cornell U. Postdoctoral tng. Yale U., New Haven; dir. edn. Miami Project To Cure Paralysis, Miami, Fla., assoc. exec. dir.; adminstr. grants program Brain Trauma Found., Miami; program dir. James S. McConnell Found., St. Louis. Office: James S McDonnell Found Ste 1850 1304 S Brentwood Blvd Saint Louis MO 63117

FITZPATRICK, THOMAS MARK, lawyer; b. Anaconda, Mont., June 12, 1951; s. Marcus Leo and Natalie Stephanie (Trbovich) F. BA, U. Mont., 1973; JD, U. Chgo., 1976. Bar: Ill. 1976, Wash. 1978. Asst. to pres.-elect ABA, Chgo., 1976-77, asst. to pres., 1977-78; assoc. Karr, Tuttle, Campbell, Seattle, 1978-85, ptnr., 1985-89, Stafford, Frey, Cooper, Seattle, 1989-99; asst. chief civil divsn. Snohomish County Prosecuting Atty.'s Office, Everett, Wash., 1999—2005; exec. dir. Snohomish County County Exec. Office, Everett, 2005—. Editor: ABA: A Century of Service, 1979. Fellow Am. Bar Found.; mem. ABA (chmn. lawyer and media conf. 1985-88, profl. discipline com. 1988-94, LRIS com. 1994-97, ethics com. 2001-04, chmn. nat. conf. groups 1982-85, ho. of dels. 1990—, state del. 1993-98, bd. govs. 1998-2001), Wash. Bar Assn. (pres. young lawyer divsn. 1986-87), Snohomish County Bar Assn., Seattle-King County Bar Assn., U. Chgo. Law Sch. Alumni Assn. (bd. dirs., Seattle regional pres. 1980-86). Roman Catholic. Home: 7345 13th Ave NW Seattle WA 98117-5306 Office: Snohomish County Exec Office MIS 407 3000 Rockefeller Ave Everett WA 98201-4046 Office Phone: 425-388-3123. Business E-Mail: tfitzpatrick@co.snohomish.wa.us.

FITZPATRICK, TIM (THOMAS J. FITZPATRICK), finance company executive; b. Waterbury, Conn., Jan. 7, 1949; s. Thomas James and Blanche (Confrancesco) F.; m. Joan M. Mancini Fitzpatrick, Mar. 1, 1976; children: T.J., Leah Joan, Brian. BS in Bus., La Salle U., 1972, MBA, 1981; Advanced Mgmt. Program, Harvard U., 1985. Staff acct. UniRoyal, Inc., Waterbury, Conn., 1972-74; acct. First Pa. Corp., Phila., 1974-78, asst. contr., 1974-76; contr. Fin. Services, Phila., 1978-80; CFO Mfrs. Hanover consumer Services, Huntingdon Valley, Pa., 1980-84, pres., COO, 1984—88; vice chmn. Consumer Credit Co., 1988—89; pres., CEO, founder Equity One Inc., 1989—98; exec. v.p. SLM Corp. (Sallie Mae), Reston, Va., 1998—2000, pres., chief mktg. & adminstrv. officer, 2000—01, pres., COO, 2001—05, CEO, vice chmn., 2005—. Bd. dirs. SLM Corp., BanPonce Fin. Corp., M.A. Bruder & Sons Inc.; bd. trustees Manor Jr. Coll. Asst. coach Voorhees (N.J.) Soccer Assn., 1984-85; coach Voorhees Basketball Assn., 1986; bd. trustees Manor Jr. Coll.; mem., Voorhees County Edn. and Recreation Program. Mem. Am. Fin. Services Assn., La Salle U. Council of Pres.'s Assocs., La Salle U. Alumni Assn. (80's campaign. com.). Office: SLM Corp 12061 Bluemont Way Reston VA 20190

FITZPATRICK, WHITFIELD WESTFELDT, lawyer; b. New Orleans, Jan. 31, 1942; s. William Harry and Frances (Westfeldt) F.; m. Jean Phipps, July 6, 1984. BA, Washington & Lee U., 1964; JD, Tulane U., 1967; LLM, Grenoble U., France, 1969, Doctorate, 1972. Bar: La. 1967, Va. 1972, N.Y. 1974, U.S. Dist. Ct. (ea. dist.) La. 1974, D.C. 1975, U.S. Dist. Ct. (we. dist.) La. 1975, U.S. Ct. Appeals (5th cir.) 1975. Law clk. Supreme Ct. Commonwealth of Va., Norfolk, 1969-70; assoc. Coudert Bros., N.Y.C., 1972-74; sr. assoc. Phelps, Dunbar, Marks, Claverie & Sims, New Orleans, 1974-76; counsel Mobil Oil Corp., New Orleans, 1976-79, Mobil North Sea Ltd., London, 1979-82; gen. counsel Mobil, The Hague, Netherlands, 1982—87; sr. counsel, asst. sec. Mobil Exploration and Producing U.S., Inc., Midland, Tex., 1987-89; asst. sec. Mobil Producing Tex. and N.Mex., Inc., Midland, 1987-89; with direction juridique Elf Aquitaine, Europe and U.S. coord., 1989-94; spl. advisor to dir. of comml. and lic. adminstrn. divsn. ELF Petroleum Norge, 1994-97; exec. v.p. and gen. counsel Fountain Oil Inc., 1997—99; of counsel The Silecky Firm, 1999—; ptnr., gen. counsel Scandinavian Bus. Ptnrs., 2005—. Contbr. articles to profl. pubs. Dir. Am. Coordinating Coun. of Norway, 1990—92. Named Mem. Soc. of the Friends of the Legion of Honor, Ordres de Chevalerie; Grenoble U. Law Sch. scholar, 1967-69; fellow Govt. of France, 1970-72. Mem. ABA, Maritime Law Assn., Internat. Bar Assn., La. Bar Assn., Va. Bar Assn., N.Y. Bar Assn., D.C. Bar Assn., Boston Club of New Orleans, Racquet and Tennis Club of N.Y., Royal Auto Club of London, Soc. Colonial Wars, Societé des Amis du Musée National de la Légion d'Honneur. Avocations: golf, skiing, reading, tennis. Home: Camilla Collets vei No 8 0258 Oslo Norway also: 2206 Nealy Ave Midland TX 79705 Office Phone: 432-684-9055, 47-22-56-1837. Personal E-mail: whitfitzpatrick@yahoo.com.

FITZSIMMONS, ELLEN MARIE, lawyer; b. May 1960; BS, Va. Poly. Inst. & State Sch.; JD, Georgetown U. Sr. gen. counsel CSX Corp., Richmond, asst. gen. counsel, 1995-97, gen. counsel, 1997—. Office: CSX Corp 901 E Cary St Richmond VA 23219-4031

FITZSIMONDS, GENEVA MAE, director, music educator; b. Northfield, Minn., July 17, 1966; d. Donald Joseph and Alice Leona (Gruber) Langer; m. Scott David Fitzsimonds, Dec. 22, 1989; children: Bram Joseph, Berit Laura. MusB in Music Edn., Concordia Coll., 1988; MA, St. mary's U., 2002. Cert. tchr. Minn. Band dir. Babbitt (Minn.) Pub. Sch., 1988—89, Anne Arundel County Pub. Sch., Annapolis, Minn., 1989—91, Cromwell (Minn.) Pub. Sch., 1991—93, Lake Superior Pub. Sch., Two Harbors, Minn., 1993—2000, Albert Lea (Minn.) Pub. Sch., 2000—; bassoonist Duluth (Minn.)-Superior Orch., 1999—2001. Dir. Two Harbors City Band, 1994—2001, Albert Lea Cmty. Band, 2001—. Recipient Golden Apple award, Sta. KITL-TV, 2002. Mem.: Minn. Music Educators Assn., Minn. Band Dirs. Assn. (bd. dirs.), Am. Sch. Band Dirs. (officer, sec.).

FITZSIMONS, DENNIS JOSEPH, broadcasting and publishing executive; b. N.Y.C., June 26, 1950; s. Genevieve Theresa (English) F.; m. Ann Christie, Sept. 27, 1980; children: Matthew, Christine. BA, Fordham U., 1972. Account exec. Blair TV, N.Y.C., 1975-77; sales mgr. TeleRep, Inc., Chgo., 1977-78, N.Y.C., 1979-81, dir. spl. projects, 1978-79; dir. advt. sales Viacom Internat., N.Y.C., 1981; dir. sales and mktg. Sta. WVIT-TV, Hartford, Conn., 1981-82; dir. sales Sta. WGN-TV, Chgo., 1982-84, v.p., gen. mgr., 1987—92, Sta. WGNO-TV, New Orleans, 1984-85; v.p. ops. Tribune Broadcasting Co., Chgo., 1985-87; pres. Tribune Television, 1992—94, Tribune Broadcasting Co., 1994—2003; exec. v.p. Tribune Co., 2000—01, bd. dirs., 2000—, COO, 2001—03, pres., 2001—, CEO, 2003—, chmn., 2004—. Vice chmn. United Negro Coll. Fund of Chgo. With U.S. Army, 1970-76. Mem. Ill. Assn. Broadcasters (bd. dirs.), INTV (bd. dirs.). Roman Catholic. Office: Tribune Co 435 N Michigan Ave Chicago IL 60011

FITZSIMONS, GEORGE KINZIE, bishop; b. Kansas City, Mo., Sept. 4, 1928; Student, Rockhurst Coll., Immaculate Conception Sem. Ordained priest Roman Cath. Ch., 1961. Aux. bishop, Kansas City-St. Joseph, Kans., 1975—84; bishop Salina, Kans., 1984—. Office: Chancery Office PO Box 980 Salina KS 67402-0980 E-mail: chancery2@salinadiocese.org.*

FITZSIMONS, SHARON RUSSELL, international consumer goods, financial and treasury executive; b. Toronto, Ont., Can., June 25, 1945; d. Leslie and Winifred; m. John Henry Fitzsimons, Jan. 4, 1969; children: Luke, Michael. BA, U. So. Calif., 1968; MA, Calif. State U., 1971; MS in Bus. Adminstrn., U. Calif., Irvine, 1978; grad. internat. bus. ISMP program, Harvard Bus. Sch., 1990. Mgr. rsch. William Pereira Assocs., Newport Beach, Calif., 1970-71; asst. mgr. interior design Concept Environment Inc. subs. Ford Motor Co., Orange County, Calif., 1971-72; v.p. Urban Interface Group, Orange County, 1972-74; cons. in field, 1975-76; mgr. strategic planning Mission Viejo Co., Orange County, 1976-80; mgr. fin. Philip Morris Internat., N.Y.C., 1980-82, asst. treas., 1983-84, ops., strategic mktg. and logistics exec. PM Australia Ltd., Melbourne, 1984-86, dir. U.S. export logistics and customer svc., N.Y.C., 1987-90, internat. fin. dir. treas., N.Y.C., 1990—; chmn., CEO, Internat. Intrigues, 1997—, pres., CEO, co-trustee Pamco Historic Property Mgmt. Co., Phoenix, Ariz. CEO trustee Mem. Harvard Women's Alumnae Network Assn. (bd. dirs.), Women in Mgmt., Harvard Club Greater N.Y., The Internat. Alliance.

FIUMEFREDDO, CHARLES A., brokerage house executive; b. Bayonne, N.J., May 12, 1933; s. Charles F. and Alice (Guiliana) F.; m. Joan Kuczynski, June 18, 1955; children— Joanne Fiumefreddo Lewicki, Charles M. BS, St. Peter's Coll., Jersey City, 1955; postgrad., NYU Sch. Bus. Adminstrn., 1955-57. Asst. v.p. First Jersey Nat. Bank, Jersey City, 1953-65; asst. v.p. investment mgmt. Anchor Corp., Elizabeth, N.J., 1965-69; from v.p. to pres., CEO Standard & Poor's/InterCapital, N.Y.C., 1969—77; pres. Morgan Stanley Investment Advisors Inc., N.Y.C., 1977—84, treas., 1977—82, chmn., 1982—98, CEO, 1977—98; pres. Morgan Stanley Investment Cos., N.Y.C., 1982—99, dir., trustee, 1991—, chmn., 1992—; exec. v.p., bd. dirs. Dean Witter Reynolds Inc., until 1998. Chmn. Morgan Stanley Trust FSB, Jersey City, 1989-98; bd. dirs., mem. exec. com. Investment Co. Inst., Washington, 1983-98; mem. investment co. com. SIA, N.Y.C., 1984-86. Bd. dirs. Bayonne Hosp., N.J., 1983-89. Mem.: K.C. (Bayonne, N.J.). Avocations: stamp collecting/philately, fishing.

FIVEL, STEVEN EDWARD, lawyer; b. Aug. 26, 1960; Atty. Melvin Simon & Assoc., Inc., 1988—93, Simon DeBartolo Group, Inc., 1988—97, Simon Property Group, Inc., 1993—97; exec. v.p., gen. counsel Brightpoint, Inc., Plainfield, Ind., 1997—. Lectr. in field. Office: Brightpoint Inc 501 Airtech Pky Plainfield IN 46168 Office Phone: 317-707-2355. Office Fax: 317-707-2514.

FIVENSON, DAVID PAUL, physician; b. Alpena, Mich., Nov. 4, 1958; s. Morton Fivenson, Lois Fivenson; m. Mara Miles; children: Daniel, Elayne. MD, U. Mich. Med. Sch., 1984. Dir. med. dermatology, clinical rsch. and wound care svcs. Henry Ford Health Sys., Detroit, 1989—2003. Office: 25 Research Dr Ann Arbor MI 48103 Personal E-mail: dfivenson@comcast.net.

FIX, DOUGLAS MARTIN, electrical engineer; b. Lincoln, Nebr., Oct. 20, 1953; s. Raymond Harold and Juliana Marie (Spatz) F. BSEE, BSCS, U. Colo., 1979; MSEE, Southern Meth. U., 1983. Registered profl. engr. Tex. Computer ops. Seismograph Svc. Corp., Denver, 1974—78, seismic analyst, 1978—80; design engr. Tex. Instruments, Dallas, 1980—85, sr. engr., 1985—88, lead engr., 1988—. Adj. prof., Eastfield Coll., Mesquite, Tex., 1983—; cons. Computers U2, Allen,Tex., 1990—. Contbr. article to profl. jours.; patentee digital video monitor interface arch., hardware ind. device interface. Elder, tchr. Zion Luth. Ch., Dallas, 1992—; crime watch coord. Neighborhood Homeowners, Dallas, 1988. Recipient Sundstrand scholarship Sundstrand Corp., 1978. Mem. IEEE, Eta Kappa Nu (sec. 1978), Soc. Info. Display, Mensa, Tau Beta Pi. Republican. Lutheran. Achievements include electrical design of several types of consumer calculators, research in digital pll clocking for TV synch signal processor and preprocessor designs for 4 classified military projects. Home: 761 Livingston Dr Allen TX 75002-5229 Office: Texas Instruments 13510 N Central Expy Dallas TX 75243-1108 Office Phone: 972-344-3640. E-mail: dmfix@swbell.net.

FIX, JOHN NEILSON, banker; b. Evanston, Ill., Apr. 10, 1937; s. John Leonard and Margaret (Neilson) F.; m. Linda Harris, Dec. 21, 1961; children: John, Christopher, David, Wendy. BS, U. Ill., 1959; grad., Stonier Sch. Banking, Rutgers U., 1971. Asst. cashier, v.p. No. Trust Co., Chgo., 1962-77; v.p., divsn. head Continental Ill. Nat. Bank & Trust Co., Chgo., 1977-80; sr. v.p., group head Continental Bank N.A., Chgo., 1980-83, sr. v.p., dept. head, 1983-94; sr. v.p, dir. corp. devel. global payment svcs. Bank of Am. N.T.S.A., Chgo., 1994-95, ret., 1995; mng. dir. Fixco, Inc., 1996—; prin. Treasury Strategies, Inc., Chgo., 1997—, dir., 2001—. Bd. dirs. Kenilworth Dist. 38 Sch. Bd., Ill., 1969-75; trustee, pres. Kenilworth Park Bd., 1981-89; mem. exec. com. Chgo. Area Boy Scouts, 1981-89; pres., treas. Kenilworth Baseball Assn., 1976-85; trustee Kenilworth Union Ch., 1988-93; bd. dirs. Western Golf Assn., 1989—, audit com., 1992—. Lt. U.S. Army, 1959-61. Recipient George Huff award U. Ill., Champaign, 1955; Good Scout award Chgo. Area Boy Scouts Am., 1982 Mem. Bankers Club of Chgo., Ill. State C. of C. (bd. dirs., treas. 1980-82), Exec. Club of Chgo., Econ. Club of Chgo., U. Ill. Alumni Assn. (mem. bd. trustees 1987, exec. com. 1990-93, chmn. investment com. 1992-93), Nat. Corp. Cash Mgmt. Assn. (mem. publs. com. 1987-91, strategic planning com.), Indian Hill Club (bd. govs. 1984-87, 98-02, sec. 1999-2001, pres. 2001-03), Old Elm Club (Highland Park, Ill.), Western Golf Assn. (exec. com., par club chmn. 2000—). Clubs: Chicago; Minneapolis; Indian Hill (bd. govs. 1984-87). Avocations: golf, skiing, paddle tennis. E-mail: fixco@earthlink.net.

FIXMAN, MARSHALL, chemist, educator; b. St. Louis, Sept. 21, 1930; s. Benjamin and Dorothy (Finkel) F.; m. Marian Ruth Beatman, July 5, 1959 (dec. Sept. 1969); children: Laura Beth, Susan Ilene, Andrew Richard; m. Branka Ladanyi, Dec. 7, 1974. AB, Washington U., 1950; PhD, MIT, 1954. Jewett postdoctoral fellow chemistry Yale U., 1953-54; instr. chemistry Harvard U., 1956-59; sr. fellow Mellon Inst., Pitts., 1959-61; prof. chemistry, dir. Inst. Theoretical Sci., U. Oreg., 1961-64, prof. chemistry, research asso. inst., 1964-65; prof. chemistry Yale U., New Haven, 1965-79; prof. chemistry and physics Colo. State U., Ft. Collins, 1979-2000, prof. emeritus, 2000—. Mem. editorial bd. Jour. Chem. Physics, 1962-64, Jour. Phys. Chemistry, 1970-74, Macromolecules, 1970-74, Accounts Chem. Rsch. 1982-85, Jour. Polymer Sci. B, 1991-93; assoc. editor Jour. Chem. Physics, 1994—. Wwith U.S. Army, 1954-56. Fellow Alfred P. Sloan Found., 1961-63; recipient Governor's award Oreg. Mus. Sci. and Industry, 1964 Mem. NAS, Am. Acad. Arts and Scis., Am. Chem. Soc. (award pure chemistry 1964, award polymer chemistry 1991), Am. Phys. Soc. (high polymer physics award 1980), Fedn. Am. Scientists. Office: Colo State U Dept Chemistry Fort Collins CO 80523-0001 Business E-Mail: mf@fibm.mfbl.colostate.edu.

FJORDBOTTEN, ALF LEE, language educator; b. Camrose, Alta., Can., Apr. 26, 1952; arrived in U.S., 1960, naturalized, 1987; s. Alf Lee and Helene Josephine (Hansen) Fjordbotten; m. Beverly Elaine Lee, Oct. 22, 1983. BA in Religion, St. Olaf Coll., 1974; MDiv, Luther Theol. Sem., 1978; MA in English and Comparative Lit., Fairleigh Dickinson U., 1989; PhD in English Lang. and Lit., Fordham U., 1999. Ordained to ministry Evang. Luth. Ch. Am., 1978. Vicar, chaplain Grace Luth. Ch., Good Shepherd Home, Allentown, Pa., 1976-77; pastor St. Mark's Luth. Ch., Ridge, NY, 1978-83, Holy Spirit Luth. Ch., Leonia, NJ, 1983—2002, Grace Luth. Ch., North Arlington, NJ, 2002—, First Luth. Ch., Kearny, NJ, 2002—; sr. editor Bishop Books, NYC, 2000—02; freelance editor, 2002—. Tchg. fellow Fordham U., 1989—92, adj. instr., 2003—, Fairleigh Dickinson U., 1994—, St. Peter's Coll., 2004—, Felician Coll., 2004—. Recipient Charles J. Donahue prize, Fordham U., 1990; Presdl. scholar, 1989—92. Home: 580 Gail Ct Teaneck NJ 07666-4128 Personal E-mail: aleefjord@aol.com. E-mail: drfjord@optonline.net.

FJORTOFT, NANCY FAY, univeristy administrator, educator; b. Osseo, Wis., Sept. 20, 1953; d. Willard c. and Rachel M. (Hubbard) Schmidt; m. Jon M. Fjortoft, May 10, 1986. BA, Blackburn Coll., 1975; MA, DePaul U., 1980; PhD, U. Ill., Chgo., 1994. Circulation mgr. DePaul U., Chgo., 1977-84; registrar, bus. mgr. Chgo. Sch. of Profl. Psychology, 1984-88; asst. to dean U. Ill., Chgo., 1988-93, asst. dean, 1993-97; asst. dean, assoc. prof. Coll. Pharmacy Midwestern U., Downers Grove, Ill., 1997-2000, assoc. dean, assoc. prof., 2000—. Lay leader First United Meth. Ch., Oak Park, Ill., 1993-98. Recipient Lyman award Am. Assn. of Colls. of Pharmacy, 1994. Office: Midwestern Uo 555 31st St Downers Grove IL 60515-1235 E-mail: nfjort@midwestern.edu.

FLACH, FREDERIC FRANCIS, psychiatrist; b. NYC, Jan. 25, 1927; s. George Raymond and Margaret (Donovan) F.; m. Patricia Anne Kane, June 23, 1951 (div. 1966); children: Frederica, Christopher, Geraldine, Andrew, Winifred; m. Joyce Elizabeth Rasmussen, Sept. 9, 1971. BA summa cum laude, St. Peter's Coll., Jersey City, 1947; MD, Cornell U., 1951. Diplomate Am. Bd. Psychiatry Neurology. Intern second med. div. Bellevue Hosp., NYC, 1951-52; resident, chief resident psychiatry Payne Whitney Clinic, NYC, 1953-58; pvt. practice NYC, 1958—; attending psychiatrist NY Presbyn. Hosp., NYC, 1962—, St. Vincent's Hosp., NYC, 1974—. Adj. assoc. prof. psychiatry Cornell U. Med. Coll., NYC, 1962—; program dir. Directions in Psychiatry, NYC, 1981—; chmn. Hatherleigh Co., Ltd., 1990—. Author: The Secret Strength of Depression, 1974, Choices, 1976, Fridericus, 1980, Resilience, 1988, Rickie, 1990, Take Command, 1994, The Secret Strength of Angels, 1998, Faith, Healing, and Miracles, 2000, others. Lt. (j.g.) USNR, 1945-46. Decorated knight comdr. Equestrian Order Holy Sepulchre Jerusalem. Fellow Am. Psychiat. Assn. (life). Roman Catholic. Avocations: travel, swimming, reading. Office: 420 E 51st St New York NY 10022-8014 Office Phone: 917-363-0457, 212-355-4757. E-mail: january@c4.net.

FLACHMANN, MICHAEL CHARLES, English language educator; b. St. Louis, Nov. 3, 1942; s. Charles Randall and Charlotte W. (Widen) F.; m. Josephine Kumbera Marschel, June 30, 1969; children: Christopher Michael, Laura Marschel. BA, U. of the South, 1964; MA, U. Va., 1965; PhD, U. Chgo., 1972. Asst. prof. English So. Ill. U., Edwardsville, 1965-68; from asst. prof. to prof. English Calif. State U., Bakersfield, 1972—. Dir. univ. honors programs Calif. State U., 1985—; dir. Camp Shakespeare Utah Shakespeare Festival, 1986—, company-dramaturg, 1985—; vis. prof. Calif. Inst. Arts, Valencia; mem. Western Region Adv. Coun. Shakespeare Globe Ctr., 1983—; mem. Internat. Com. for the Bibliography of Shakespeare Quarterly, 1985—. Author: Shakespeare's Lovers, 1983, Teaching Excellence, 1998, Shakespeare: From Page to Stage, 2005, Shakespeare's Women, 1986, The Prose Reader, 1986, 7th edit., 2004, Beware the Cat, 1988; editor: Image of Idleness, 1990, Teaching Excellence, 1998; contbr. articles to profl. jours. Named CSU System-Wide Outstanding Prof., 1993, Carnegie Found. U.S. Prof. of Yr., 1995; recipient Wang Tchg. Excellence award Calif. State U., 2001. Mem. MLA, Shakespeare Assn. Am., Early English Text Soc., Renaissance Soc. Am., Assn. for Theatre in Higher Edn., So. Calif. Ednl. Theatre Assn. Avocations: judo, tennis, antiques, kids. Avocations: Judo (black belt), tennis, antiques. Home: 1236 Fairway Dr Bakersfield CA 93309-2422 Office: Calif State Univ Dept English 9001 Stockdale Hwy Bakersfield CA 93311-1099 Office Phone: 805-664-2121. E-mail: mflachmann@csub.edu.

FLACK, CHARLES HAYNES, lawyer; b. Macomb, Ill., June 15, 1927; s. Charles Earl and Mary Helen (Gesler) F.; m. Barbara Joan Hull, Sept. 14, 1952; 1 child, Teresa Flack Hillyer. Student Western Ill. U., 1946; BS, Northwestern U., 1951, JD, 1954. Bar: Ill. 1954. Ptnr., Flack & Kerman, Macomb, 1954-59, Flack & Flack, 1959-62, Flack & Dye, 1963-72, Flack & Kwacala, 1975-79, Flack, Kwacala & Murphy, 1979-85, Flack, Kwacala, Murphy & Ashenhurst, 1986-90, Flack, McRaven & Stephens, 1990-97; spl. asst. Ill. Atty. Gen., 1983-94. Bd. dirs. Western Ill. U. Found. Served with USNR, 1945-46. Fellow Am. Coll. Trust and Estate Counsel; mem. ABA, Ill. Bar Assn., McDonough County Bar Assn. Democrat. Presbyterian. Clubs: Macomb Country, Masons, Elks, Am. Legion. Office: PO Box 359 Macomb IL 61455-0359

FLACK, ROBERTA, singer; b. Black Mountain, N.C., Feb. 10, 1939; d. Laron and Irene F.; m. Stephen Novosel, 1966 (div. 1972). BA in Music Edn., Howard U., 1958. Tchr. music and English lit. pub. schs., Farmville, N.C., Washington, 1959-67; rec. artist Atlantic Records, 1968—. Star ABC TV spl. The First Time Ever, 1973; composer: (with Jesse Jackson and Joel Dorn) Go Up, Moses; albums include: First Take, 1969, Chapter Two, 1970, Quiet Fire, 1971, Killing Me Softly, 1973, Feel Like Makin' Love, 1975, Blue Lights In The Basement, 1977, Roberta Flack, 1978, The Best of Roberta Flack, 1981, I'm The One, 1982, Born To Love, 1983, Hits and History, 1984, Roberta Flack, 1985, Oasis, 1989, Set the Night to Music, 1991, Roberta, 1994; writer TV theme song Valerie. Recipient Gold Record for The First Time Ever I Saw Your Face, 1972; Grammy awards for best record, best song (The First Time Ever I Saw Your Face), 1972, best record, best female vocalist (Killing Me Softly With His Song), 1973, best pop vocal duo (Where Is The Love), 1972; winner Downbeat's reader poll as best female vocalist, 1971-73; City of Washington celebrated Roberta Flack Human Kindness Day, 1972; Star on the Hollywood Walk of Fame,2000. Mem. Sigma Delta Chi. Office: care Atlantic Records 75 Rockefeller Plz New York NY 10019-6908

FLACK, RONALD DAVID, diplomat, public service educator, banker; b. Cloquet, Minn., Feb. 3, 1934; s. John and Marian Gladys (Steidl) F.; m. Danièle Guigard, Mar. 11, 1961; children: Jean-Marc, Claire-Paule. BA, U. Minn., 1960. Joined Fgn. Svc., Dept of State, Washington, 1962; 3rd sec. Am. Embassy, Athens, Greece, 1963-65, 2nd sec. Manila, 1965-69, Abidjan, Ivory Coast, 1969-70, 1st sec. Paris, 1970-73, Algiers, Algeria, 1973-75, counselor Athens, 1976-80; permanent rep. UN, Geneva, 1983-87; dep. amb. Am. Embassy, Copenhagen, 1987-90; min. counselor U.S. Mission to OECD, Paris, 1990-95; diplomat in residence NYU, N.Y.C., 1995-97; vice chmn. Taylor Cos., Washington, 1998—, sr. vice chmn. Paris, 2001—. Bd. dirs. Internat. YMCA, N.Y.C., 1997. Mem. Danish Am. Soc., Scandinavian Am. Soc. Home: 5 rue Leo Delibes 75116 Paris France Office: Taylor Cos 7 Pl d'Iena 75116 Paris France

FLACKE, JOAN WAREHAM, physician, anesthesiologist, educator; b. Evanston, Ill., Dec. 16, 1931; d. Loyal Delbert and Alice (Cummings) Wareham; m. Werner E. Flacke, Aug. 7, 1957; children: Christopher, Gary, Timothy. BA, Scripps Coll., 1953; MD, Harvard U., 1959. Rsch. fellow Med. Sch., Harvard U., Boston, 1964-67, rsch. assoc., 1967-69, instr., 1969-70; asst. prof. med. sci. U. Ark., 1972-75, assoc. prof. med. sci., 1975-76; adj. assoc. prof. UCLA, 1977-82, adj. prof., 1982-89, prof.-in-residence, 1989-95, prof. emeritus, 1995—. Cons. to FDA, 1989-93; assoc. examiner Am. Bd. Anesthesiology, L.A., 1974-76; program chmn. Anesthesia Ednl. Found., La.A., 1986-91; dir. cardiovascular anesthesiology UCLA Hosp., 1990-91. Contbr. numerous articles to profl. jours. Mem. Am. Soc. Anesthesiologists, Assn. Univ. Anesthesiologists, Internat. Anesthesia Rsch. Soc., Soc. Cardiovascular Anesthesiologists, Calif. Soc. Anesthesiologists, Mass. Med. Soc. Roman Catholic. Avocations: reading, skiing, needlecrafts, horseback riding. Home and Office: PO Box 308 Wolcott CO 81655-0308 E-mail: flacke@colorado.net.

FLADELAND, BETTY, historian, educator; b. Grygla, Minn., Jan. 18, 1919; d. Arne O. and Bertha (Nygaard) F. BS, Duluth State Coll., 1940; MA, U. Minn., 1944; PhD (Rackham fellow), U. Mich., 1952. Mem. faculty Wells Coll., Aurora, N.Y., 1952-55, Central Mich. U., 1956-59, Central Mo. State Coll., 1959-62; mem. faculty So. Ill. U., Carbondale, 1962—, prof. history, 1968—, distng. prof., 1985, disting. prof. emerita, 1986—. Vis. prof. U. Ill., summer 1966 Author: James Gillespie Birney: Slaveholder to Abolitionist, 1955, Men and Brothers: Anglo-American Antislavery Cooperation, 1972, Abolitionists and Working Class Problems in the Age of Industrialization, 1984, also articles. Recipient Anisfield-Wolf award in race relations, 1972, Queen award, 1984; grantee Am. Philos. Soc., 1963, 75, Lilly Found., 1962; NEH teaching grantee, 1984 Mem. Am. Hist. Assn., So. Hist. Assn. (exec. council), Orgn. Am. Historians (exec. bd.), Assn. Study Afro-Am. Life and History, Norwegian-Am. Hist. Soc., Soc. Historians Early Am. Republic (adv. bd., bd. editors, pres.), ACLU, NAACP, Phi Beta Kappa, Phi Kappa Phi. Home: Liberty Village 2950 West Ridge Pl #230 Carbondale IL 62901-7135 Office: So Ill Univ Dept Of History Carbondale IL 62901

FLADUNG, THOM, managing editor; b. Canton, Ohio; m. Jeanette Meyer-Fladung; 2 children. Grad., Univ. Dayton, 1982. Various ed. positions Detroit Free Press, Mich., 1994—2000; mng. ed. Akron Beacon Journal, Ohio, 2000—02, Detroit Free Press, 2002—. Office: Detroit Free Press 600 W Fort St Detroit MI 48226

FLAGG, MICHAEL JAMES, communications and graphics company executive; b. N.Y.C., Aug. 14, 1958; s. Wilbor Thomas and Sylvia (Kobitz) F. BA with highest distinction, U. Va., 1980. Intern, internat. economist U.S. Customs, Washington, 1979; mgmt. assoc. First Nat. Bank Atlanta, 1980-81, cash mgmt. officer, 1981-83, asst. v.p., group mktg. mgr., 1983-84; treasury mgr., asst. to chief exec. officer Contel Corp., Atlanta, 1984-89; v.p. fin. Contel Office Communications, Inc., St. Louis, 1989-91; v.p., treas. Am. Internat., Inc., Chgo., 1991-94; v.p. fin. Alliance Capital, N.Y.C., 1994; sr. v.p. corp. bus. devel. USL Capital, San Franciso, 1995; CFO InterCall, Chgo., 1995, COO, 1996-97; cons. Heidrich & Struggles, Inc., 1997—99, ptnr., 1999—2000, ptnr.-in-charge, 2000—. Instr. Am. Inst. Banking, 1982-83; chmn. Contel Profl. Devel. Assn., Atlanta, 1986. Assoc. editor Cash Mgmt. Forum, 1982-84; co-founder, co-editor First Word newsletter, 1983-84. Chmn. fundraising unit United Way, Atlanta, 1985—88, Atlanta unit Am. Cancer Soc., 1985—88, Atlanta Coll. Arts, 1985—88; governing mem. Brookfield Zoo, Chgo., 1992—99. Mem. Nat. Corp. Cash Mgmt. Assn. (bd. dirs. 1987-91, exec. com. 1988-91), Fin. Execs. Inst., Treasury Mgmt. Assn. Chgo., St. Louis Zoo Friends Assn. (bd. dirs. 1990-91). Avocations: sports, art, travel. Office: 1750 Tysons Blvd Ste 300 Mc Lean VA 22102 E-mail: mflagg@heidrick.com.

FLAGG, RAYMOND OSBOURN, retired medical products executive; b. Martinsburg, W.Va., Jan. 31, 1933; s. Dorsey Slemons and Dorothy (Hobbs) F.; m. Ann Quinlan Birmingham, May 19, 1956; children: Richard Matthew, Elizabeth Ann, Catherine Garnett. BA with honors, Shepherd Coll., 1957; PhD in Biology, U. Va., 1961; diploma in advanced mgmt. program, U. N.C., Chapel Hill, 1994. Math tchr. Boonsboro (Md.) High Sch., 1957; rsch. asst. Blandy Exptl. Farm, Boyce, Va., 1957-61; rsch. assoc. U. Va., Charlottesville, 1961-62; dir. botany Carolina Biol. Supply Co., Burlington, NC, 1962-80, v.p., 1980-2000, exec. v.p., 2001—03; v.p. Wolfe Sales Corp., Burlington, 1985-97. Head Cabisco Biotech., Burlington, 1988-91; v.p. Found. for Ednl. Devel., Research Triangle Park, N.C., 1983-85; vice chmn. N.C. Plant Conservation Bd., Raleigh, 1984-88. Contbr. articles to profl. jours. Chmn. Beautification Commn., Burlington, 1976-80, Hist. Dist. Commn., 1981-82; bd. dirs. United Way of Alamance County, Burlington, 1984-88; vice chmn. Tree Adv. Com., Burlington, 1993-2000. Rsch. grant Am. Cancer Soc., 1960, rsch. equipment grant Va. Acad. Sci., 1961; recipient Community Leadership award No. Piedmont Devel. Assn., 1977. Mem. AAAS, Assn. Southeastern Biologists (pres. 1978-79), N.C. Acad. Sci. (pres. 1983-84), Va. Acad. Sci., Rotary (pres. Alamance A.M. 1988-89). Democrat. Presbyterian. Achievements include invention of instant drosophila medium, Carosafe, FlyNap, Sterigel, Planoslo, Vitachrome, Alga-Gro. Office: Carolina Biol Supply 2700 York Rd Burlington NC 27215-3398 E-mail: ray.flagg@carolina.com.

FLAGG, RONALD SIMON, lawyer; b. Milw., Dec. 3, 1953; s. Arnold and Marian (Levy) F.; m. Patricia Sharin, June 20, 1982; children: Laura Sharon, Emily Rachel, Naomi Erica. AB, U. Chgo., 1975; JD, Harvard U., 1978. Bar: Wis. 1978, US Dist. Ct. (ea. dist.) Wis. 1978, US Ct. Appeals (7th cir.) 1979, DC 1980, US Dist. Ct. DC 1980, US Ct. Appeals (DC cir.) 1980, US Ct. Appeals (3d cir.) 1984, US Supreme Ct. 1986, US Ct. Appeals (5th cir.) 1987, US Ct. Appeals (8th cir.) 1989. Law clk. to presiding judge U.S. Dist. Ct. (ea. dist.) Wis., Milw., 1978-80; atty., adv. office of intelligence policy and rev. U.S. Dept. Justice, Washington, 1980-82; assoc. Sidley & Austin, Washington, 1982-85, ptnr., 1986—2001; ptnr. comml. and adminstrv. litig. Sidley Austin Brown & Wood LLP, Washington, 1986—, and chair pro bono and public interest law com. Bd. dirs. Nat. Vets. Legal Svcs. Program, chair, Legal Counsel for the Elderly. Mem. ABA, DC Bar Assn. (chair), Phi Beta Kappa. Office: Sidney Austin Brown & Wood LLP 1501 K St NW Washington DC 20005-1401 Office Phone: 202-736-8171. Office Fax: 202-736-8711. Business E-Mail: rflagg@sidley.com.

FLAGG DAVIS, VIVIAN ANNETTE, librarian, researcher, public information officer; b. Milledgeville, Ga., July 18, 1960; d. Rufus and Sandra Ann (Seals) F.; m. Joe H. Davis Jr., Jan. 16, 1993. BA, Ga. State U., 1982, MPA, 1988. Purchasing and sales clk. Reed Drugs, Atlanta, 1980-81; libr. assoc. Atlanta Jour. & Constn., 1981-84, libr. asst., 1984-89, assoc. libr., rsch. supr., 1989-91, systems libr., 1991—. Tutor Lit. Action, Atlanta, 1981-83, Alonzo Herndon Elem. Sch., 1999-2001; bd. dirs. Odyssey Family Counseling Ctr., Hapeville, Ga., 1983-85; adv. coun. Vol. Atlanta, 1984-87, pres., 1983-85; vol. spl. projects Changed Living Recovery, 1994—; svc. coun. Youth Devel. Allocations and Evaluation Com., Atlanta, 1987—, planning and allocations com. United Way, Atlanta, 1987—, co-chair Task Force for Homeless and Hungry, 1992-1996; chmn. social action com. social svcs. and human resources dir. Greater Piney Grove Bapt. Ch.; mem. Atlanta Ballet Assocs.; bd. dirs. Higher Plain Ministries, 1994—, chair adminstrn. com., 2003; co-chair edn. com. AJC in Action; founder reading program Will You Read To Me?, 2003. Recipient Outstanding Leader award Vol. Ga., 1984, Vol. of Yr. Golden Link, 2004. Mem. ASPA, Nat. Young Profls. Forum, NAACP, Am. Soc. Info. Sci., Spl. Librs. Assn. Democrat. Avocations: piano, sewing, tennis, gardening, travel. Home: 3735 Landgraf Cv Decatur GA 30034-4775 Office: Atlanta Jour Constn 72 Marietta St NW Atlanta GA 30303-2804

FLAHERTY, DAVID THOMAS, JR., lawyer; b. Boston, June 17, 1953; S. David Thomas Sr. and Nancy Ann (Hamill) F.; children: Alexandra Lynn, David Thomas III. BS in Math., German, U. N.C., 1974, JD, 1978. Bar: Mass. 1979, N.C. 1979, U.S. Dist. Ct. (we. dist.) N.C. 1979, U.S. Dist. Ct. (mid. dist.) N.C. 1981, U.S. Ct. Appeals (4th cir.) 1981, U.S. Tax Ct. 1982, U.S. Supreme Ct., 1987, U.S. Ct. Claims, 1992. Assoc. Wilson & Palmer, Lenoir, N.C., 1979-80, Ted West P.A., Lenoir, 1980-82; ptnr. Robbins, Flaherty & Lackey, Lenoir, 1982-85, Robbins & Flaherty, Lenoir, 1985-88, Delk, Flaherty, Swanson & Hartshorn, P.A., Lenoir, 1988-89, Delk, Flaherty, Robbins, Swanson & Hartshorn, P.A., Lenoir, 1989-90, Flaherty, Robbins, Swanson & Hartshorn, P.A., 1990-95; dist. atty. 25th prosecutorial dist. Office Dist. Atty., Lenoir, 1995—. Mem. N.C. Ho. of Reps., Raleigh, 1988-94, N.C. Cts. Commn., 1989—, N.C. Jud. Adv. Commn., 1997—. Mem. exec. com. Caldwell County Reps., Lenoir, 1985-86, 88—. Mem. N.C. Bar Assn., N.C. Conf. Dist. Attys., 25th Jud. Dist. Bar Assn. (mem. exec. com. 1987-88), Reps. Men's Club, Blue Key. Methodist. Avocations: water and snow skiing, motorcycling. Home: 228 Pennton Ave SW Lenoir NC 28645-4316 Office: 202 1/2 Main St NW Lenoir NC 28645

FLAHERTY, FRANCIS XAVIER, state supreme court justice; b. Providence, Jan. 8, 1947; son of Eugene and Gertrude (Strong) F.; married Donna Marie Anderson, 1969; children: Nicole, Michael, Brendan. BA, Providence Coll., 1968; JD, Suffolk U. Sch. of Law, 1975. Dir. Warwick Drug Abuse Program, RI, 1971—73, Federal Program, 1973—75; labor relations administr. City of Warwick, 1975—78, asst. city solicitor, city prosecutor, 1975—87, councilman ward 6, 1978—84, mayor, 1985—90; litigation partner Edwards & Angell; mnging partner Wynn & Wynn, Flaherty, Orton, and Flaherty, 1995—2003; justice RI Supreme Ct., 2003—. chmn. Warwick Community Action Program; bd. dirs. Warwick Boys and Girls Club; mem. R.I. Nat. League Cities. Served to 1st lieutenant U.S. Army, 1968—70. Decorated 3 Bronze Stars, 3 Air medals, Vietnam Campaign medal, Vietnamese Cross for Gallantry, Combat Infantryman's award, Vietnamese Civic Action award, Vietnamese Service medal. Member VFW, Am. Legion, ABA, R.I. Bar Assn., Kent County Bar Assn., Kent County Bd. Realtors. Office: Frank Licht Judicial Complex 250 Benefit St Providence RI 02903

FLAHERTY, JOHN JOSEPH, quality assurance company executive; b. Chgo., July 24, 1932; s. Patrick J. and Mary B. Flaherty; m. Norrine Grow, Nov. 20, 1954 (dec. Sept. 1995); children: John, Bridgette, George, Eileen, Daniel, Mary, Michael, Amy; m. Rosemarie Clausen, Dec. 27, 2001. BEE U. Ill., 1959. Design engr. Admiral Corp., Chgo., 1959—60; project engr. Magnaflux Corp., Chgo., 1960—79, v.p., mgr. rsch. and engring., 1979—84, v.p., mgr. mktg. and sales, 1984—86, v.p., gen. mgr. electronic products, 1986—88; pres. Flare Tech., Chgo., 1988—. Served with AUS, 1951—53. Fellow: Am. Soc. Non-Destructive Testing; mem.: IEEE, Am. Soc. Metals. Roman Catholic. Achievements include patents and publications on nondestructive testing, including medical ultrasonic; laser scanning. Office: 401 Meadow Lark Rd Bloomingdale IL 60108 Home: 401 Meadowlark Rd Bloomingdale IL 60108-1331 Office Phone: 630-980-4537. Personal E-mail: johnflare@aol.com.

FLAHERTY, JOHN PAUL, JR., retired judge; b. Pitts., Nov. 19, 1931; s. John Paul and Mary G. (McLaughlin) F.; m. Linet Flaherty; 7 children, 2 stepchildren. BA, Duquesne U., 1953; JD, U. Pitts., 1958; LLD (hon.), Widener U., 1993. Bar: Pa. 1958. Pvt. practice, Pitts., 1958-73; mem. faculty Carnegie-Mellon U., 1958-73; judge Ct. Common Pleas Allegheny County, 1973-79, pres. judge civil divsn., 1978-79; justice Supreme Ct. Pa., 1979-96, chief justice, 1996—2001, chief justice emeritus. USIA speaker in Far East, 1985-86. Mem. Pa. Hist. Soc.; chair Pa. County Records Com. Recipient Medallion of Distinction U. Pitts., 1987, Judicial award Pa. Bar Assn., 1993, Pres. award Pa. Bar Assn., 1999; Chief Justice John P. Flaherty award, Pa. Bar Assn. Conf. of Bar Leaders, 2001; named Man of Yr. in law and govt., Greater Pitts. Jaycees, 1978, named to Century Club of Disting. Alumni, Duquesne U., 1994. Mem. Pa. Acad. Sci. (chmn. hon. exec. bd. 1978-89, Disting. Alumnus award 1977), Am. Law Inst., Pa. Soc., Pa. Bar Assn. (award 2001), Mil. History Soc. Ireland, Friendly Sons St. Patrick, Am. Legion. Office: Pa Supreme Ct Rm 810 City County Bldg Pittsburgh PA 15219 *The law is the energy of the living world, and although developed and defined by the judiciary in our Anglo-American society, it is applied and is derived by and from the people. It exists only to protect one person from being hurt, physically or economically, by another. Serious problems face our age. In the final analysis, the judiciary must accomodate the various solutions which will be forthcoming. I hope that my brothers have the foresight and the stamina to accommodate what might be quite novel innovations in the law, which is the living energy, to make this world a place in which it's worth living, since that is the function of the law. Every case involves people. There is no such thing as a small case.*

FLAHERTY, KATHLEEN RUTH, telecommunications company executive; b. Boston, May 19, 1951; d. John P. and Annette (Baker) Flaherty; m. Kenneth D. Davis, Dec. 30, 1973. BA, Northwestern U., 1973, MS, 1975, PhD in Indsl. Engring., 1979. Policy analyst US Dept. Commerce, Gaithersburg, Md., 1976-79; sr. mgr. sales programs Gen. Electric Info. Services Co., Rockville, Md., 1979-80; sr. mgr. network planning MCI, Washington, 1981-82, dir. network engring., 1982-84, v.p. fin. ops., 1984-86; v.p. communications network services MCI N.E., Rye Brook, NY, 1986—90; v.p. product mktg. MCI, 1990, named sr. v.p., 1993; sr. v.p. worldwide sales & mktg. Concert Services (joint venture of MCI & Brit. Telecom), 1993—95; sr. v.p., marketing dir. nat. bus. communications Brit. Telecom, 1995—97; sr. v.p. global product architecture MCI, 1997—98; pres., COO WinStar Europe SA, 1998—99, WinStar Internat., 1999—2001; chief mktg. officer AT&T bus. services AT&T Corp., 2004—. Dir. CMS Energy Corp., 1995—2004; mem. Industry Adv. Coun. McCormick Sch. Engring., Northwestern U. Coordinator Cmty. Garden Program, Washington, 1983; treas. Woodbine Condominium Assn., Washington, 1979-81. Named one of Outstanding Young Women of Am., Jaycees, 1982; Walter P. Murphy Fellow, 1973. Mem. Sigma Xi. Avocations: reading, camping, gardening, swimming. Office: AT&T Bus Services One AT&T Way Bedminster NJ 07921*

FLAHERTY, LOIS TALBOT, editor, psychiatrist, educator; b. Nashville, Apr. 28, 1942; BA, Wellesley Coll., 1963; MD, Duke U., 1968. Diplomate Nat. Bd. Med. Examiners. Intern D.C. Gen. Hosp., 1968-69; resident in psychiatry Georgetown U. Hosp., 1969-71; resident in child psychiatry Johns Hopkins Hosp., 1971-73; pvt. practice Cross Keys, Md., 1973-81; dir. tng. divsn. child and adolescent psychiatry U. Md., 1981-89, assoc. prof. med. sch. divsn. child and adolescent psychiatry, 1982-93, dir. divsn. child and adolescent psychiatry, 1984-92, adj. assoc. prof., 1994—; clin. assoc. prof. psychiatry U. Pa., 1997-2000; pvt. practice Blue Bell, Pa., 1994-99; editor Adolescent Psychiatry, 2000—. Instr. depts. psychiatry and pediatrics Johns Hopkins U. Sch. Medicine, 1973-92; attending staff psychiatrist family, child and adolescent divsn. Sinai Hosp. Balt., 1974-77; staff child psychiatrist Walter P. Carter Ctr., 1977-78, dir. child and adolescent svcs., 1978-92, acting dir. inpatient adolescent unit, 1979-80; clin. asst. prof. U. Md., 1977-81; lectr. psychiatry Harvard U., 2002—; cons. Northwest Drug Alert Sinai Hosp. Balt., 1971-72, St. Vincent's Child Care Ctr., 1973-78, Children's Guild, Inc., 1975-82, SSA, Balt., 1985, many others. Contbr. chpts. to books, articles and book revs. to profl. jours. NIMH grantee, 1983-86. Fellow: Am. Soc. for Adolescent Psychiatry, Am. Psychiat. Assn. (disting.); mem.: Group for Advancement of Psychiatry, Am. Coll. Psychiatrists, Am. Acad. Child Psychiatry. Office: 4 Charlesgate East #605 Boston MA 02215-2369 Personal E-mail: lflaher770@aol.com.

FLAHERTY, SISTER MARY JEAN, dean; Dean, prof. Sch. Nursing, Cath. U. Am., Washington. Office: Cath U Am Sch Of Nursing Washington DC 20064-0001

FLAHERTY, PAMELA POTTER, bank executive; b. Jefferson City, Mo., July 1, 1944; d. Reese H. and Mary Jane (Stagg) Potter; m. Peter A. Flaherty, Nov. 28, 1970; children: Jonathan Peter, David Alexander. BA, Smith Coll., 1966; MA in internat. rels., Johns Hopkins U., 1968. Various positions internat. banking Citicorp, N.Y.C., 1968-76, various position consumer banking, 1976-85, head of human resources, 1985-89, head of consumer banking in N.E., 1989—95, senior v.p., dir. community rels., 1995—98; senior v.p., global community rels. Citigroup Inc. (formerly Citicorp), N.Y.C., 1998—. Bd. dirs. Rockefeller Fin. Svcs., Inc., N.Y.C.; mem. adv. coun. Bass plc U.S., 1990—; bd. dirs., mem. exec. com. Am. Women's Econ. Devel. Corp., N.Y.C., 1987—. Bd. trustees Johns Hopkins Medicine, 2000—. Named one of Women Who Make a Difference by Smith Coll. Club of N.Y., 1991. Mem. Com. of 200. Office: Citigroup 399 Park Ave New York NY 10043

FLAHERTY, SERGINA MARIA, ophthalmic medical technologist; b. Düsseldorf, Germany, Nov. 22, 1958; came to U.S., 1962; d. Austin W. and Evelyn (Kähl) F. Cert. ophthalmic med. technologist. Ophthalmic asst. U.S. Army, Ft. Rucker, Ala., 1978-82; ophthalmic technician Wiregrass Total Eye Care Clinic, Enterprise, Ala., 1983-86, Straub Hosp. and Clinic, Honolulu, 1986-90; ophthalmic technologist Eye Cons. of San Antonio, San Antonio, 1993-96, Stone Oak Ophthalmology, San Antonio, 1996—. Founder, owner, CEO Ophthalmic Seminars of San Antonio, 1996—. Mem. Assn. Tech. Pers. in Ophthalmology, Ophthalmic Photographer Soc., Hawaii Ophthalmic Assts. Soc. (founding mem., sec. 1987-89, pres. 1989-90), Ophthalmic Pers. Soc. San Antonio (program dir. 1994-95, 2001—, pres. 1996-2000). Avocation: shin shin toitsu aikido. Office: Stone Oak Ophthalmology 325 Sonterra Blvd Ste 100 San Antonio TX 78258-3932 Office Phone: 210-490-6759. E-mail: ophthsem@gvtc.com.

FLAHERTY, TIMOTHY THOMAS, radiologist; b. Fond du Lac, Wis., 1933; m. Joan Flaherty; 4 children. MD, Marquette U., 1959. Diplomate Am. Bd. Radiology. Intern St. Marys Hosp., Milw., 1959-60; resident in radiology, chief resident U. Wis., Madison, 1963—66; fellowship U. Wis. Hosps., Madison, 1964-65; pvt. practice. Bd. dirs., sec. Nat. Patient Safety Found.; founding dir. Physicians Ins. Co.-Wis., exec. com. and underwriting com., chair investment com., chmn. bd. dirs.; mem. Govs. task force on health reform, Wis.; founding dir. SMS Svcs., Inc.; bd. dirs. Bank One of Appleton, N.A.; chair Profl. Svcs. Network, Inc.; trustee Novus Health Group Inc., Appleton, Wis., 1988-94; mem. med. exec. com., bd. trustees dept. radiology Theda Clark Regional Med. Ctr., Neenah, Wis., chmn. dept. radiology, 1980-95; clin. prof. dept. radiology U. Wis. Ctr. for Health Scis., Madison, Med. Coll. of Wis., Milw. Maj. gen. USAF, ret. Fellow Am. Coll. Radiology (councilor); mem. AMA (exec. com. 1995—, chair fin. com., chair com. on membership 1996-97, chair com. on orgn. and operation, mem. compensation com., commr. to joint commn. on accreditation of healthcare orgns. 1994, dir. Commn. on Office Lab. Assessment, 1996—, bd. trustees 1994—, chair bd. trustees, 2001-02, sec.-treas. exec. com.), AMPAC (bd. dirs.), State Med. Soc. of Wis. (vice chair bd. dirs., commn. chair), Wis. Radiol. Soc. (past pres.), Radiol. Soc. of N.Am. (counselor 1991-97), Soc. of Med. Cons. of the Armed Forces, Aerospace Med. Assn., Assn. of Mil. Surgeons, Soc. of Air Force Flight Surgeons. Office: AMA 515 N State St Chicago IL 60610-4325 Address: Radiology Assoc Fox Valley 54 E Wisconsin Neenah WI 54956-2966

FLAHERTY, TINA SANTI, corporate communications executive, writer; b. Memphis; d. Clement Alexander and Dale (Pendergrast) Santi; m. William Edward Flaherty, Feb. 22, 1975. BA, U. Memphis, 1961; hon. doctorate, St. John's U., 1979. Commentator host interview program Sta. WMC-TV, Memphis, 1960-61; newscaster, commentator Sta. WHER, Memphis, 1961-62; cmty. rels. specialist Western Electric Co., N.Y.C., 1964-66; v.p. pub. rels. divsn. Grey Advt., N.Y.C., 1966-72; dep. dir. corp. rels. Colgate-Palmolive Co., N.Y.C., 1972-75, dir. corp. rels., 1975-76, corp. v.p., v.p. in charge of communications, 1976-84; v.p. pub. affairs GTE Corp., Stamford, Conn., 1984-86; pres., chief exec. officer Image Mktg. Internat., N.Y.C., 1986—. Author: The Savvy Woman's Success Bible, 1997 (one of Top Motivational Books of Yr., Books for a Better Life 1997), Talk Your Way to the Top, 1999, What Jackie Taught Us: Lessons from the Remarkable Life of Jacqueline Kennedy Onassis, 2004. Former chmn. Bus. Coun. of UN Decade for Women; bd. dirs. Nat. Jr. Achievement, 1978—; mem. The White House Pub. Affairs Advisors, 1981-84; nat. bd. dirs. Animal Med. Ctr. Recipient Jr. Achievement Meml. award, 1984; named One of N.Y.C.'s Outstanding Women of Achievement, NCCJ, One of 100 Top Corp. Women, Bus. Week, One of 73 Women Ready to Run Corp. Am., Working Woman, Woman of Distinction, Birmingham So. Coll., One of 100 Amazing Ams., Am.'s Elite, 2000. Mem. DAR, Com. of 200, Internat. Women's Forum, Daughters of the American Revolution (DAR). Home and Office: Image Mktg Internat 1040 Fifth Ave New York NY 10028-0137 Office Phone: 212-535-0025. Personal E-mail: imi1040@aol.com. *Persistence alone is omnipotent.*

FLAHERTY, WILLIAM E., chemicals and metals company executive; b. 1933; m. Tina Santi. Formerly with GM Overseas Corp., Reynolds Metals Co.; with Gulf & Western, 1974-81, past COO zinc and chems. divsn.; past chmn. bd., CEO Horsehead Industries, NYC.

FLAITZ, CATHERINE M., dean, dental educator; B in psychology, DDS, Creighton U.; MS in pediat. dentistry, U. Iowa. Bd. cert. oral and maxillofacial pathology. With Creighton U., U. Iowa, U. Colo.; pvt. practice pediat. dentistry Denver; prof., chair diagnostic sci. Dental Branch, U. Tex., Houston, dir. oral and maxillofacial pathology residency program, 2001—02, interim dean, 2002—04, dean, 2004—. Prof. pediat. dentistry Dental Branch, U. Tex., 1992; mem. editl. bd. Pediat. Dentistry, Jour. Dentistry Children, Am. Jour. Dentistry; cons. commn. dental accreditation advanced specialty edn. programs ADA. Mem. editl. bd.: Archives of Pathology and Laboratory Medicine. Recipient George W. Teuscher Silver Pen award, Jour. Dentistry Children, 2001. Fellow: Am. Acad. Pediat. Dentistry (mem. grants and fellowship com., mem. pres. circle); mem.: ADA, Omicron Kappa Upsilon, Tex. Dental Assn., Internat. Assn. Dental Rsch., Am. Assn. Dental Rsch., Am. Acad. Oral Medicine (mem. clinical investigation and abstract com.), Greater Houston Dental Soc., Am. Acad. Oral and Maxillofacial Pathology (exec. coun.), Am. Dental Edn. Assn., Am. Coll. Dentists. Office: Univ Tex Health Sci Ctr Dental Branch 6516 M D Anderson Blvd Rm 147 Houston TX 77225-0068 Office Phone: 713-500-4021. Business E-Mail: catherine.m.flaitz@uth.tmc.edu.

FLAKE, FLOYD HAROLD, former congressman; b. LA, Jan. 30, 1945; m. M. Elaine McCollins; children: Aliya, Nailah, Rasheed, Hasan. BA in Psychology, Wilberforce U., 1967; D in Ministry, United Theol. Sem., Dayton, Ohio, 1995; postgrad., Northeastern U. Social worker, 1968-69; sales rep. Reynolds Tobacco Co., 1969; mktg. analyst Xerox Corp., 1969-70; assoc. dean students, dir. student activities Lincoln U., Pa., 1970-73; dean students, univ. chaplain, dir.Martin Luther King Jr. Afro-Am. Ctr. Boston U., 1973-76; mem. 101st-105th Congresses from 6th N.Y. dist., Washington, 1987-97, mem. banking and fin. svcs. com., mem. domestic & internat. monetary policy subcom., mem. small bus. com.; pastor Allen A.M.E. Cathedral, Jamaica, N.Y., 1976—; pres. Edison Charter Schs. Pres., Edison Charter Sch. 2000; sr. fellow Manhattan Inst., 1998—; pres., Wilberforce U., 2002-present, bd. dir. Fannie Mae Found. Columnist N.Y. Post, 1999; author: The Way of the Bootstrapper: Nine Action Steps For Achieving Your Dreams, co-author, Practical Virtues. Pastor Allen A.M.E. Ch., Jamaica, N.Y., past chmn. affiliate corps. including Allen Sr. Citizen Complex, Allen Christian Sch. and Multi-Purpose Ctr., Allen Home Care Agy., Allen Housing Corp., So. Jamaica Multi-Svc. Ctr. Alfred Sloan fellow Northeastern U., Danforth fellow Payne Theol. Sem.; Gilbert H. Jones scholar Wilberforce U. 1986, Ebony Mag. Black Achievement award in Religion. Office: Allen AME Cathedral 11031 Merrick Blvd Jamaica NY 11433-3440 Office Phone: 718-206-4600.

FLAKE, JEFF, congressman; b. Snowflake, Ariz., Dec. 31, 1962; m. Cheryl, 15 yrs.; 5 children. BA in Internat. Rels., Brigham Young U., 1986, MA in Polit. Sci., 1987. Worked in pub. rels., Wash., DC, 1987; exec. dir. Found. Democracy, Nambia, Goldwater Instit., Ariz., 1992; mem. U.S. Ho. Reps. from 1st Ariz. dist., 2001—. Mem. House Judiciary com.; serving on House Internat. Rels. com. Republican. Mem. Lds Ch. Office: 424 Cannon House Office Bldg Washington DC 20515-0306

FLAKE, L. GORDON, think-tank executive; b. Rehoboth, N.Mex. m. Pakayvanh Sisoutham; 5 children. BA in Korean, MA, Brigham Young U. Dir. rsch. and acad. affairs Korea Econ. Inst. Am.; assoc. dir. program on conflict resolution The Atlantic Coun. of the U.S., 1997—99, sr. fellow program on conflict resolution, 1999; interim exec. dir. Mansfield Ctr. for Pacific Affairs, 1999; exec. dir. The Maureen and Mike Mansfield Found., Washington, 1999—. Conf. participant and lectr. in field. Author: Patterns in Inter-Korean Economic Relations, 1999, Inter-Korean Economic Relations Under the 'Sunshine Policy', 1999, North Korea and Northeast Asian Regional Integration: Strategic Implications for Future Economic Relations, 1998, Trading Places: U.S. and ROK Policy on Economic Engagement of the DPRK, 1998. Office: Mansfield Found Ste 740 1401 New York Ave NW Washington DC 20005-2102

FLAKES, LARRY JOSEPH, civil engineer; b. Birmingham, Ala., Jan. 27, 1947; s. John W. and Lurlene (Patton) F. BS in Civil Engring., Howard U., 1969; cert. Transp. Inst., Northwestern U., 1970. Registered profl. engr., Ga. Ala. Structural mass properties engr. Lockheed Ga. Co., Marietta, Ga., 1969-70; traffic engr. I, City of Atlanta, 1970-71; contract engr. Ala. Power Co., Birmingham, 1972-74; property tax engr. So. Ry. Co., Atlanta, 1976-81; project engr. Norfolk So. Corp., 1981-89; pres. Flakes Engring. Co., cons. engrs., 1983—. Mem. NAACP. Recipient Presdl. Merit award, 1982; Howard U. scholar, 1964-65. Mem. ASCE (Student Newsletter award 1967), Nat. Soc. Profl. Engrs., Am. Ry. Engrs. Assn. Baptist. Home and Office: 48 18th Ct S Birmingham AL 35205-6331

FLAKES, SUSAN, playwright, scriptwriter, theater director; b. San Diego, July 9, 1943; d. Herbert Franklin and Dorothy Jean (Loafman) Barrows; m. Donald Lewis Flakes, Dec. 31, 1964; 1 child, Daniel Keith. BA, U. N.Mex., 1965; MA, San Diego State U., 1969; PhD, U. Minn., 1973. Asst., then assoc. prof. Tisch Sch. Arts N.Y. U., N.Y.C., 1973-76, dept. chair Tisch Sch. Arts, 1973-76; founder, artistic dir. Blue Tower Theatre, Stockholm, 1977-80, Strindberg's Intima Teater, Stockholm, 1981-83, Source Prodns., N.Y.C., 1984-90. Instr. U.S. Internat. Univ., San Diego, 1972-73; founder, artistic dir. 1st Strindberg Festival, Stockholm, 1977; mem. Women's Project and Prodns., N.Y.C., 1984-90; v.p. Ibsen Soc. Am., N.Y.C., 1986-99; coord. writers unit W. Coast Ensemble Theatre, Hollywood, Calif., 1991-93. Author: (plays) The Woman Will Play Strindberg's Christina, Laura, Silent Star, And Immortality, Marilyn's Rose, Portrait of Psyche, Daddy's Eyes, To Take Arms, Cafe L.A., Café Heaven, (with Shirl Hendryx) 4F; (libretto with Galt MacDermot) Take It Higher, Maid of Lorraine; (with Gabe Green) Any Saints Out There?, It Girls; (screenplays) To Take Arms, Stand the Storm, Hometown, Inc., Café L.A., Francois Poet/Thief, Lifetime Achievement, Immortality, The Sacred Garden; (with Stephane Haskell) Immortalité: Daddy's Eyes, The Sacred Garden; dir. Hughie, 1989, Mother Love, 1994; contbr. articles to profl. jours., chpts. to books; creator Exptl. Theatre Wing, U.G. Drama Tisch Sch. Arts, NYU, 1975-76; contbr. play And Immortality to Baltic Seasons Mag., Russia, 2003. Ensign USN, 1965-67. Recipient winner 10-minute play festival, Fire Rose Productions, 2004, Fullerton Coll. Playwriting Festival, Resident Theater Co., 2004, Alliance of L.A. Playwrights New Works Lab 2004 at the Co. of Angels, LA, Lamia Ink Internat. competition, 1991; fellow Am. Film Inst., 1990; grantee Nat. Endowment for Arts, 1972, Travel grantee Am. Scandinavian Found., Norwegian and Swedish Govts., 1985-86, 89, 94, 2001. Mem. Dramatists Guild, Actor's Studio (playwright/dirs. unit), Am. Film Inst. (finalist directing workshop for women 2003), Alliance L.A. Playwrights, Phi Beta Kappa. Address: 7552 Amazon Dr #1 Huntington Beach CA 92647 Office Phone: 714-848-1893. E-mail: sflakes@socal.rr.com.

FLAM, JACK DONALD, art historian, educator; b. Paterson, NJ, Apr. 2, 1940; s. Max and Rose Leila (Silverberg) F.; m. Bonnie Suzanne Burnham, Oct. 7, 1972 (div.); 1 child, Laura Rose. BA, Rutgers U., 1961; MA, Columbia U., 1963; PhD, NYU, 1969. Instr. Rutgers U., Newark, N.J., 1962-66; asst. prof. U. Fla., Gainesville, 1966-69; assoc. prof., 1969-72, Bklyn. Coll., 1975-80, prof. grad. ctr., 1980-90, disting. prof., 1991—. Author: Matisse on Art, 1973, Bread and Butter, 1977, Robert Motherwell, 1983, Matisse, the Man and His Art, 1986, Motherwell, 1991, Richard Diebenkorn: Ocean Park, 1992, Matisse: The Dance, 1993, Western Artists/African Art, 1994, Robert Smithson: The Collected Writings, 1996, Judith Rothschild: An Artist's Search, 1998, Frankenthaler, 1999, The Modern Drawing, 1999, Matisse in the Cone Collection, 2001, Matisse and Picasso: The Story of Their Rivalry and Friendship, 2003, Primitivism and Twentieth-Century Art: A Documentary History, 2003, Manet: Un Bar Aux Folies Bergere Ou L'abysse Du Miroir, 2005; art critic Wall St. Jour., 1984-92. Guggenheim Found. fellow, 1979, NEH, 1986. Mem. Internat. Art Critics Assn., Internat. PEN, Coll. Art Assn. Am. Office: Bklyn Coll Art Dept Bedford Ave # H Brooklyn NY 11210-2889

FLAMER, MARGARET CHASE, elementary school educator; b. Vienna, Md., July 2, 1949; d. Robert Fulton and Missouri Exfelt (Hill) Chase; m. Walter William Flamer, Sept. 23, 1972; children: Shirelle Etoria, Damon Scott. BS, Bowie State Coll., 1971; MEd, Johns Hopkins U., 1978. Cert. tchr. Md. Tchr. elem. Anne Arundel County Schs., Annapolis, Md., 1974—. Vol. Am. Cancer Soc., Am. Diabetes Assn., Md. MADD; tchr. mentor, grade group chairperson, vol. United Negro Coll. Fund; mem. Inroads/Greater Wash. Parent Support Group, First Generation Coll. Bound, Inc. Nominee Human Rels. Edn. award, Mills King, 1999; recipient Excellence Minority Achievement award, Md. State Dept. Edn., 2000. Mem.: NAACP, NEA, Md. State Tchrs. Assn., Tchrs. Assn. Anne Arundel County, Nat. Coun. Negro Women, Alpha Kappa Alpha (life Silver Star 1998). Democrat. Methodist.

FLANAGAN, BARBARA, journalist; b. Des Moines; d. John Merrill and Marie (Barnes) F.; m. Earl S. Sanford, 1966. Student, Drake U., 1942-43. With promotion dept. Mpls. Times, 1945-47; reporter Mpls. Tribune, 1947-58; women's editor, spl. writer Mpls. Star and Tribune, 1958-65; columnist Mpls. Star, 1965—. Author: Ovation, Minneapolis. Active Junior League Mpls., Womans Club Mpls. Mem. Mpls. Soc. Fine Arts (life), Mpls. Inst. Arts (founding mem. Minn. Arts Forum), Mpls. Club, Minikahda Club, Kappa Alpha Theta, Sigma Delta Chi. Episcopalian. Office: Mpls Star Tribune 5th And Portland Sts Minneapolis MN 55488-0001

FLANAGAN, CHRISTIE STEPHEN, lawyer; b. Port Arthur, Tex., June 28, 1938; s. Christie John and Rita Catherine (Hancock) F.; m. Gretchen Dowling Neuhoff; children: Mary Eileen, Margaret, Christopher, Michael. BBA, U. Notre Dame, 1960; LLB, U. Tex., Austin, 1962. Bar: Tex. 1962. Assoc. Hutchenson & Grundy, Houston, 1962-68; ptnr. Jenkens & Gilchrist, Dallas, 1968-88, mgr. ptnr., 1982-87, mem., 1988—. Active Dallas Citizens Coun., 1982-92; trustee Hockaday Sch., 1980-86, St. Marks Sch. Tex., 1986-92, Sierra Internat. Found., 1984-88. Mem. ABA, Tex. Bar Assn., Dallas Bar Assn., Salesmanship Club, Serra Club Dallas, Fishers Island Club, Brook Hollow Gold Club, Coon Creek Club. Office: Jenkens & Gilchrist PC 1445 Ross Ave Ste 3200 Dallas TX 75202-2785

FLANAGAN, CLYDE HARVEY, JR., psychiatrist, psychoanalyst, educator; b. Louellen, Ky., Aug. 21, 1939; s. Clyde H. Sr. and Ruby M. Flanagan; m. Gloria Kay Glymph, June 1, 1961 (div. Feb. 1974); children: Clyde H. III, Christopher Shane; m. Carol Anne Ross, Apr. 13, 1974; children: Patrick Ross, Colleen Helen. BS, Maryville Coll., 1962; MD, U. Tenn. Med. Unit, Memphis, 1966. Cert. Am. Bd. Psychiatry and Neurology in Adult, Child, Adolescent Psychiatry; diplomate Nat. Bd. Med. Examiners. Commd. 2d lt. U.S. Army, 1965, advanced through grades to col. MC, 1980; rotating med. intern U.S. Army Tripler Gen. Hosp., Honolulu, 1966-67; gen. psychiatry resident U.S. Army Walter Reed Gen. Hosp, Washington, 1967-69; child psychiatry resident Walter Reed Hosp., Washington, 1969-71; asst. chief child guidance svc. Walter Reed Army Med. Ctr., Washington, 1971-80; chief Cmty. Mental Health Activity, Ft. Belvoir, Va., 1980-86; asst. head tri-svc. alcohol rehab. dept. Nat. Navy Hosp., Bethesda, Md., 1986-88; dir. gen. psychiat. residency program W.S. Hall Psychiat. Inst., Columbia, S.C., 1988-92; prof. psychiatry dept. of psychiatry/behavioral sci. Sch. Medicine U. S.C., Columbia, 1988—, dir. divsn. psychoanalysis dept. psychiat./behavioral sci., 1992—. Candidate in psychoanalysis Washington Psychoanalytic Inst., 1978-88; tng. and supervising analyst U. N.C./Duke PSA Ednl. Program, Chapel Hill, 1991—. Contbr. chapters to books. Recipient Tchr. Yr. award Resident's Gen. Psychiat. Rsch. Program William S. Hall Psychiat. Inst., 1995, Spl. Alumni citation Maryville Coll., 2000. Fellow: Am. Coll. Psychiatrists (com. pub. edn. 1998—99, Laughlin fellow selection com. 2000—03, membership devel. com. 2003—05), Am. Psychiat. Assn. (disting. life fellow), Am. Acad. Child and Adolescent Psychiatry (life Franklin Robinson award 1975); mem.: Am. Assn. Child Psychoanalysis, Internat. Psychoanalytic Assn., Am. Group Psychotherapy Assn. (founder, cert. group psychotherapist), S.C. Psychiat. Soc. (membership chmn. 1991—), N.C. Psychoanalytic Soc. (councilor 1989—98), Am. Psychoanalytic Assn. (councilor 1989—, cert. in adult, adolescent, and child psychoanalysis Bd. Profl. Stds. 1991). Avocations: fishing, boating. Office: U SC Sch Medicine Dept Neuropsychiatry 3555 Harden St Ext Ste 104A Columbia SC 29203-6894 Office Phone: 803-434-4250. Business E-Mail: cflanagan@medpark.sc.edu.

FLANAGAN, FIONNULA MANON, actress, writer, theater director; b. Dublin; came to U.S., 1968; d. Terence Niall and Rosanna (McGuirk) F.; m. Garrett O'Connor, Nov. 26, 1972; 2 stepchildren. C.I.H.E., U. Fribourg, Switzerland, 1962; student, Abbey Theatre Sch., Dublin, 1964-66. Pres. The Rejoycing Co., 1978—. Stage appearances include: Ulysses in Nighttown, N.Y.C., 1974, Lovers, 1968, Ghosts, 1989, Happy Days, 1991, Unfinished Stories, 1992, Countess Cathleen, 1992, Summerhouse, 1994; author, actress one-woman shows: James Joyce's Women, 1977 (L.A. Drama Critics award, San Francisco Theatre Critics award, Drama-Logue award); films include: Ulysses, 1967, In the Region of Ice, 1980, Mr. Patman, 1980, James Joyce's Women, 1984, Reflections, 1984, Chain Reaction, 1985, Death Dreams, 1992, Mad at the Moon, 1992, Money for Nothing, 1993, Some Mother's Son, 1996, Waking Ned Devine, 1998, With or Without You, 1999, The Others, 2000, Divine Secrets of the Ya-Ya Sisterhood, 2002, Tears of the Sun, 2003, One of the Oldest Con Games, 2004, Blessed, 2004, Man About Dog, 2004, Transamerica, 2005, Four Brothers, 2005; TV appearances include: The Picture of Dorian Gray, 1973, The Legend of Lizzie Borden, 1975, Rich Man Poor Man, 1976 (Emmy award for most outstanding support role 1976), How the West Was Won, 1977-79 (Emmy nominee 1978), A Winner Never Quits, 1986, White Mile, 1994, Kings in Grass Castles, 1998, To Have and To Hold, 1998, For Love or Country: The Arturo Sandoval Story, 2000, Murder She Wrote: The Celtic Riddle, 2003, Revelations, 2005; dir. Freedom of the City, Theatre West L.A., 1988 (Dramalogue award), Faith Healer, 1989, Away Alone, Court Theatre, L.A., 1991, Abbey Theatre, Dublin, 1992, A Secret Affair, 1999, Havana Nocturne, 2000; TV guest appearances include: Chicago Hope, 1999, Enterprise, 2002, Law & Order: Special Victims Unit, 2003, Nip/Tuck, 2004. Mem. AFTRA, Actors' Equity, Screen Actors' Guild, Irish Actors Equity. Office: Don Buchwald & Assocs 6500 Wilshire Blvd Ste 2200 Los Angeles CA 90048-4942*

FLANAGAN, JAMES LOTON, electrical engineer, researcher, engineering educator; BSEE, Miss. State U., 1948; SMEE, MIT, 1950, ScDEE, 1955; PhD (hon.), U. Madrid, 1992, U. Paris, 1996. Elec. engring. faculty Miss. State U., 1950-52; tech. staff Bell Labs., Murray Hill, N.J., 1957-61, head dept. speech and auditory rsch., 1961-67, head dept. acoustics rsch., 1967-85, dir. info. prins. rsch. lab., 1985-90; dir. ctr. for advanced info. processing Rutgers U., Piscataway, NJ, 1990—, v.p. for rsch. Piscataway, NJ, 1993—. Evaluation panel Nat. Bur. Standards/NRC, 1972—77; adv. panel on White House tapes U.S. Dist. Ct. for D.C., 1973—74; sci. adv. bd. Callier Center, U. Tex., Dallas, 1974—76; sci. adv. panel on voice comm. Nat. Security Agy., 1975—77. Author: Speech Analysis, Synthesis and Perception, 1972; contbr. articles to profl. jours. Recipient Disting. Svc. award in sci., Am. Speech and Hearing Assn., 1977, L.M. Ericsson Internat. prize in telecomms., 1985, Nat. Medal Sci., Nat. Medal Sci. Com., Pres. Clinton, 1996, N.J. R&D Coun. Sci. and Tech. medal, 2000; fellow, Marconi Internat., 1992. Fellow: IEEE (selection com. 1979—81, Edison medal 1986, Honor medal 2005), Am. Acad. Arts and Scis., Acoustical Soc. Am. (assoc. editor Speech Comm. 1959—62, exec. coun. 1970—73, v.p. 1976—77, pres. 1978—79, Gold medal 1986); mem.: NAS (chmn. engring. sect. 1996—99), NAE, Acoustics, Speech and Signal Processing Soc. (v.p. 1967—68, pres. 1969—70, Achievement award 1970, Soc. award 1976), Eta Kappa Nu. Achievements include patents in field. Office: Rutgers U Advanced Info Processing Piscataway NJ 08854-8088 Business E-Mail: jlf@caip.rutgers.edu.

FLANAGAN, JOE, principal, conductor, music adjudicator; b. Lawrenceburg, Tenn., Mar. 8, 1958; s. Bill and Marci Flanagan; m. Brenda Siltzer, June 6, 1981; children: Matt, Tyler. MusB in Edn., Troy State U., 1981; MEd, Ga. So. U., 1986. Fla. Ednl. Cert. Fla. Dept of Edn., 1988. Dir. of bands Vidalia Comprehensive H.S., Ga., 1981—87, South Fork H.S., Stuart, Fla., 1988—2000; prin. Dizzy Gillespie Sch. of Fine and Performing Arts, 2000—01; asst. prin. Crystal Lake Elem. Sch., Stuart, Fla., 2001—. Dir.(conductor): (musical performances) Conductor, South Fork HS Wind Ensemble (Superior Performances award, 1994). Achievements include Highest achievements in Musical Performances for Marching Band, Concert Band, Jazz Band, and Flag/Dance Corps. Home: 315 SW Indian Grove Dr Stuart FL 34994-7147 Office: Crystal Lake Elem 2065 96th St Stuart FL 34997-2601 Office Phone: 772-219-1525. Personal E-mail: bjflan315@aol.com. E-mail: flanagj@martin.k12.fl.us.

FLANAGAN, JOSEPH PATRICK, advertising executive; b. Chgo., Jan. 6, 1938; s. Charles Larkin and Helen Mary (Sullivan) F.; children: Charlotte Ahern, Joseph P. Jr., Michael S., Larkin S., Brian A.; m. Carol Perkins, Nov. 6, 1999. BA, Mich. State U., 1959; MBA, U. Chgo., 1961. Dist. mgr. sales Time mag., Pitts. and Chgo., 1961-69; gen. mgr. Ctr. Advanced Research in Design, Chgo., 1969-75; v.p., dir. client services BBDO, Chgo., 1975-77; sr. v.p. IMPACT subs. Foote, Cone & Belding Comm. Co., Chgo., 1977-85, pres., 1985-99; corp. dir. sales promotion Foote, Cone & Belding Comm. Co., Chgo., 1987-99; pres. Flanagan Mktg., 1999—. Pres. Coun. of Sales Promotion Agys., 1986-89, also bd. dirs. Mem. governing bd. Chgo. Symphony Orch., 1974; v.p. Lyric Opera Guild, Chgo., 1974; trustee Loyola Acad.; bd. dirs. Count Theater; dir. arts and letters bd. Nat. Adv. Coun., Mich. State U.; bd. dirs. Total Focus Leo Burnett, Root-Lowell Mfg; client relationship exec. Diamond Cluster Internat., 1999—. Named Sales Promotion Profl. of Yr., Coun. Sales Promotion Agys., 1989; recipient Disting. Alumni award Mich. State U., 1991. Mem. Am. Assn. Advt. Agencies (chmn. sales promotion com.), Assn. of Promotion Mktg. Agys. Worldwide (Hall of Fame award 1998), Creek Club (Locust Valley, N.Y.), Centre Island, Seawanahaka Yacht Club (Oyster Bay, N.Y.). Roman Catholic. Avocations: classical music, opera. Home and Office: Flanagan Mktg 369 South Lake Dr Palm Beach FL 33480 Home (Summer): 334 Yacht Club Rd Oyster Bay NY 11771 Office Phone: 561-833-1607. E-mail: jpflanagansr@aol.com.

FLANAGAN, JOSEPH PATRICK, JR., retired lawyer; b. Wilkes-Barre, Pa., Sept. 18, 1924; s. Joseph P. and Grace B. Flanagan; m. Mary Elizabeth Mayock, Aug. 5, 1950; children: Maureen Elizabeth, Joseph P. III. BS, U.S. Naval Acad., 1947; JD, U. Pa., 1952. Bar: Pa. 1953, U.S. Dist. Ct. (ea. dist.) Pa. 1953, U.S. Ct. Appeals (3d cir.) 1953, U.S. Supreme Ct. 1997. Assoc. Saul, Ewing, Remick & Saul, Phila., 1952-56; ptnr. Ballard, Spahr, Andrews & Ingersoll, Phila., 1956-94, chmn. pub. fin. dept., 1961-90; ret., 1994. Editor: Practicing Law Inst., Health Facilities Financing, 1976; co-author: In Search of Capital-A Trustee's Guide to Hospital Financing; reviewing editor: Disclosure Roles of Counsel in State and Local Government Securities Offerings, editor-in-chief: U. Pa. Law Rev., 1951—52; contbr. articles to profl. jours. Bd. dirs. Phila. Com. 70, 1952—56; former trustee Wyo. Sem., Kingston, Pa.; mem. adv. coun. federalism Nat. Govs. Assn., 1988; former mem. bd. visitors U. Pa. Law Sch.; bd. dirs. John Bartram Assn., 1993—2003, v.p., 2000—03. Served to lt. (j.g.) USN, 1946—49. Fellow: Am. Bar Found.; mem.: ABA (past chmn. urban, state and local govt. sect.), Pa. Bar Inst. (chmn. curriculum and course planning com. 1976—88, pres. 1983), Pa. Bar Assn., Phila. Bar Assn. (past chmn. bus. law sect., bd. govs., past founding chmn. tax exempt fin. com., past chmn. profl. edn. com., mem. client's security fund com., mem. fee disputes com.), Nat. Assn. Securities Dealers (arbitrator 1998—), Army Navy Country Club Va., Chesapeake Bay Yacht Club, Phila. Cricket Club, Racquet Club, Phila. Club. Republican. Roman Catholic. Office: Ballard Spahr Andrews & Ingersoll 1735 Market St Fl 49 Philadelphia PA 19103-7501

FLANAGAN, JUDY, corporate communications specialist, marketing professional; b. Lubbock, Tex., Apr. 28, 1950; d. James Joseph II and Jean (Breckenridge) F. BS in Edn., Memphis State U., 1972; postgrad., Disney U., 1975—81, Valencia C.C., 1977—79, Rollins Coll., 1979; MS in Comm., U. Tenn., 2004. Area/parade supr. entertainment divsn. Walt Disney World, Orlando, Fla., 1972—81; parade dir. Gatlinburg (Tenn.) C. of C., 1981-85; entertainment prodn. mgr. The 1982 World's Fair, Knoxville, 1982; cons. Judy Flanagan Prodns./Spl. Events, Gatlinburg, 1982—, Miss U.S.A. Pageant, Knoxville, 1983; prodn. coord. Nashville Network, 1983; dir. sales River Terr. Resort, Gatlinburg, 1985-86; account exec. Park Vista Hotel, Gatlinburg, 1986-88; project coord. Universal Studios, Fla., 1988-90; dir. spl. events U. Tenn., Knoxville, 1990—. Dir. Neyland Stadium Expansion Dedication, 1996—; U. Tenn. Bicentennial Events, 1994, 21st Century Campaign Major Events; prodn. mgr. 1984 World's Fair Parades and Spl. Events, New Orleans, Neil Sedaka rock video, Days of Our Lives daytime soap opera. Recipient Gatlinburg Homecoming award, 1986, World Lifetime Achievement award, 1993. Mem.: ASPCA, Tenn. Festivals and Events Assn. (bd. dirs.), Internat. Festivals and Events Assn. (cert. festival and events exec., found. bd.), Internat. Spl. Events Soc., Doris Day Animal League, Defenders of Wildlife, Humane Soc. U.S., U. Tenn. Soc. Pres. Club. Roman Catholic. Home: 350 Bruce Rd Gatlinburg TN 37738-5612 Office Phone: 865-974-5028. E-mail: judy-flanagan@tennessee.edu.

FLANAGAN, L. MARTIN, lawyer; b. Greenville, S.C., Jan. 22, 1932; s. Leon Smith and Eloise (Martin) F.; m. Mary Georgie deSaussure, Feb. 5, 1955; children: Patrick B.; Michael C., Georgiana M., M. Kathleen. AB, The Citadel, 1953; LLB, U. Va., 1958, JD, 1970. Bar: S.C. 1958, Fla. 1959, U.S. Supreme Ct. 1971, U.S. Dist. Ct. S.C. 1958, U.S. Dist. Ct. (so. dist.) Fla. 1959, U.S. dist. Ct. (mid. dist.) Fla. 1989, U.S. Ct. Appeals (5th cir.) 1965, U.S. Ct. Appeals (11th cir.) 1988; cert. circuit ct. mediator. Clerk Jones, Adams, Paine & Foster, West Palm Beach, Fla., 1958-59, assoc., 1959-64, partner, 1964-75; shareholder Jones, Paine & Foster, P.A., West Palm Beach, 1975-80, Jones & Foster, P.A., West Palm Beach, 1980-89, Jones, Foster, Johnston & Stubbs P.A., West Palm Beach, 1989-91, of counsel, 1991—, Flanagan & Maniotis P.A., 1993—. Founder: Trial Advocate Quarterly, 1982, editorial bd. mem., 1982-91. Judge Palm Springs (Fla.) Municipality, 1960-65, Lake Clarke Shores (Fla.) Municipality, 1967; councilman Lake Clarke Shores, 1964-66; committeeman Rep. Exec. Com., Palm Beach County, 1964-74. Capt. U.S. Army, 1953-55. Recipient Execptional Performance citation Def. Rsch. Inst., 1982. Mem. ABA, Am. Bd. Trial Advocates (diplomate 1981-92). Fedn. Ins. and Corp. Counsel, Product Liability Adv. Coun., Fla. Def. Lawyers Assn. (pres. 1982), Fla. Bar, Palm Beach County Bar Assn., The Acad. of Fla. Trial Lawyers, Assn. Trial Lawyer Am. Republican. Presbyterian. Avocations: presidential political buttons, vintage fountain pens, vintage autos. Home: 115 Russlyn Dr West Palm Beach FL 33405-3355 Office: Flanagan & Maniotis 2586 Forest Hill Blvd West Palm Beach FL 33406-5929

FLANAGAN, MARIANNE, music educator; d. William James and Catherine Theresa Flanagan. B in Music Edn., N.E. La. U., 1984; M in Music Edn., U. So. Miss., 1998. Cert. Nat. Bd. Cert. Tchr. Early and Young Adolscent Music, 2000. Band dir. Bastrop (La.) Jr. HS, 1988—89; dir. band Bastrop HS, 1989—91, Lakeview Mid. Sch., Winter Garden, Fla., 1991—92, Colonial HS, Orlando, Fla., 1992—. Mem.: Internat. Assn. Jazz Educators, Music Educators Nat. Conf., Fla. Bandmasters Assn. (adjudicator 1995—, mem. profl. resource com. 1996—). Office: Colonial HS 6100 Oleander Dr Orlando FL 32807 Business E-Mail: flanagan@ocps.net.

FLANAGAN, MARTHA LANG, publishing executive; BS in Fine Arts, U. Cin., 1978. Various exec. secretarial positions, 1960-75; corp. sec., asst. to pres. Cin. Enquirer, 1973—. Mem. adv. com. to Cin. Police Chief, 1976-85; mem. Cin. Music Hall Centennial Com., 1976-78; mem. adv. bd. U. Cin. Coll. Design, Art, Architecture and Planning, 1988-91; trustee Neediest Kids of All, 1980—, Women's Fund Greater Cin. Found., 2000—, St. Ursula Acad., 2002—05. Office: The Cincinnati Enquirer 312 Elm St Fl 20 Cincinnati OH 45202-2739 Office Phone: 513-768-8094. E-mail: mflanagan@enquirer.com.

FLANAGAN, MICHAEL BRENDAN, obstetrician, gynecologist; b. Ireland, 1917; s. Thomas Flanagan and Bridgid Conway; m. Vera Doreen Payne, Nov. 7, 1947; children: Michael Ashley, Amanda Jane, Veronica Margaret. MBBCh, Trinity Coll., 1942, MD, 1952. Diplomate Am. Bd. Ob-Gyn. Intern St. Mary's Hosp., San Francisco, 1953-54; resident in ob/gyn. Middlesex County Hosp., London, 1948-52; staff St. Mary's Hosp., San Francisco, 1955-81, ret. honorary staff, 1981—. With Royal Navy, 1943-46. Fellow ACS, Am. Coll. Ob-Gyn., Royal Coll. Obs-Gyn.; mem. AMA. Home: 26317 Camino Real Carmel CA 93923-9241 E-mail: Flangan2@pacbell.net.

FLANAGAN, MICHAEL P., school system administrator; m. Anna Flanagan; children: Mike, Brian, Christa. Degree, Notre Dame U., Ea. Mich. U. Supt. Farmington/Farmington Hills Sch. Dist., Mich., Wayne Regional Ednl. Svcs. Agency, Mich.; exec. dir. Mich. Assn. of School Adminstrs. (MASA), 2001—05; edn. adv. to Gov. Jennifer M. Granholm, 2003; state supt. pub. instrn. Mich. Dept. Edn., 2005—. Chair Edn. Alliance of Mich. Past mem. Mich. Commn. on Asia in Schs.; bd. mem. Ready to Succeed Partnership, North Ctrl. Assn. State Com., Detroit Regional C. of C. Bus. and Edn. Training Alliance, Mich. Leadership Inst., Botsford Hosp. Recipient PTA-PTO Lifetime Achievement Award, Crystal Apple Award, Mich. State U. Mem.: Mich. Sch. Bus. Officials, Mich. Liquid Asset Fund, Nat. County Supts. Assn. Office: Mich Dept Edn 608 W Allegan St PO Box 30008 Lansing MI 48909 Office Phone: 517-373-3324.*

FLANAGAN, NORMAN PATRICK, lawyer; b. Pitts., Feb. 3, 1953; s. Norman Patrick and Janice (Smith) F.; m. Caroline E.E. Reverdin, Aug. 2, 1975; children: Erin Elizabeth, Sean Patrick. BS in Edn., Duquesne U., 1975; JD, Calif. Western U., 1978. Bar: Pa., Nev., U.S. Dist. Ct. Nev., U.S. Ct. Appeals (9th cir.), U.S. Supreme Ct. Dep. pub. defender Washoe County Pub. Defender's Office, Reno, 1979-81; asst. pub. defender Pub. Defender's Office, Reno, 1982—90; atty. Hale, Lane, Peek, Dennison & Howord, 1990—. Mem. Nev. State Bar Assn. (continuing legal edn. sect., pres-elect, 2002-03), Legal Def. Fund (capital litigation sect.). Republican. Roman Catholic. Avocations: tennis, cross country skiing. Office: 100 W Liberty St 10th Fl Reno NV 89505 E-mail: pflanagan@halelane.com.

FLANAGAN, ROBERT JOSEPH, economics professor; b. New Haven, Dec. 16, 1941; s. Russell Joseph and Anne (Macauley) F.; m. Susan Rae Mendelsohn, Aug. 23, 1986. BA, Yale U., 1963; MA, U. Calif., 1966, PhD, 1970. Economist U.S. Dept. Labor, Washington, 1963-64; asst. prof. labor econs. Grad. Sch. Bus. U. Chgo., 1969-75; assoc. prof. labor econs. Grad. Sch. Bus. Stanford (Calif.) U., 1975-86; sr. staff economist Coun. of Econ. Advisors, Washington, 1978-79; sr. fellow The Brookings Instn., Washington, 1983-84; prof. labor econs. Grad. Sch. Bus., Stanford (Calif.) U., 1987-92, Matsushita prof. internat. labor econs. and econ. policy, 1993—, assoc. dean, 1996-99. Cons. OECD, Paris, 1988, U.S. Civil Rights Commn., Washington, 1982-83, NOAA, Washington, 1981; vis. scholar IMF, 1994, Australian Nat. U., 1990, 2000. Author: Labor Relations and Litigation Explosion, 1987; (with others) Unionism, Economic Stabilization and Income Policy, 1982, Economics of the Employment Relationship, 1989, numerous others; contbr. articles to profl. jours. Mem. Am. Econs. Assn., Indls. Rels. Rsch. Assn., Soc. Labor Economists. Office: Stanford U Grad Sch Bus Palo Alto CA 94305

FLANAGAN, SEAN PATRICK, publishing executive; b. Oct. 16, 1963; m. Donna; children: Riley, Owen. BA, Villanova U., 1985. Territory mgr. Playboy, Nat. Geographic Traveler, Am. Bar Assn. Journal, N.Y. mgr.; advertising dir. Men's Health Mag., N.Y.C., 1993-96, assoc. publisher, 1996-97, publisher, 1997—2000; eastern ad. dir. Yahoo! Internet Life, 2000—01; assoc. pub. Nat. Geographic Mag., N.Y.C., 2001—03, U.S. pub., 2003—. Mem. AAAA, ACNY, BPAA, CTFA, MPA, NACDS, TFA, Fragrance Found., Beacon Hill Country Club. Avocations: family, irish music, golf, landscape horticulture. Office: Nat Geographic 711 Fifth Ave New York NY 10022

FLANAGAN, STEPHEN THOMAS, humanities educator; b. Danbury, Conn., Oct. 21, 1954; s. Thomas Gerard and Elizabeth Mary F.; m. Joyce Luongo; 1 child, Kevin. BA in History, Western Conn. State U., 1978, MA in History, 1984; MA in Govt. & Polit., St. Johns U., 1997. Cert. tchr., Conn. History tchr. New Milford (Conn.) H.S., 1985—. Adj. lectr. history Western Conn. State U., Danbury, 1987—. Councilman Common Coun., Danbury, 1983-89 Named Tchr. of Yr., New Milford Tchr. of Yr. Com., 1996-97. Democrat. Roman Catholic.

FLANAGAN, SUSAN MARIE, special education educator; d. John Bresnahan Flanagan and Marguarite McKenna; m. Norman Christian Kristoff, 1981 (div. 1983). MS, Johns Hopkins U., 2001; BS, Wheelock Coll., 1979. Meyers Briggs Cert. Md., 1990, cert. State Dept. Edn. Md., 1997, Pvt. Pilot Fla., 1995. Dir. pediat. play therapist Dartmouth Hitchcock Med. Ctr., Hanover, NH, 1979—81; pediat. play therapist Meml. Sloan Kettering Hosp., New York City, 1981—83. Recruiter Cosmopolitan, New York, 1983—88; real estate developer Foxmoore Assocs. Ltd. Partnership, Annapolis, Md., 1988—97; child adv.- entreprenuer Susan Flanagan, M.S., LLC, Annapolis, 1997. Author (designer): Phlanagan Phonics Reading Program (Amb. Award, 2003). Bd. mem. Jr. League of Annapolis, 1988—2003. Clara E. Cade Scholarship, Quincy Sch., 1974. Mem.: Learning Disabilities Assn., Coun. For Exceptional Children, Johns Hopkins Alumni Assn., Pvt. Pilots Assn. (pvt. pilot). Achievements include design of Created a remedial reading program for students with disabilities. Avocations: collector of movie memorabilla, fitness training, long distance runner, gourmet cook. Office: Susan Flanagan MS LLC 2315 Forest Drive Annapolis MD 21401

FLANAGAN, TIMOTHY JAMES, criminal justice educator, university official; b. Pitts., May 16, 1951; s. Norman Patrick and Dorothy Helen (Hoffmann) F.; m. Nancy Ann Rosenbaum, Aug. 4, 1973; children: Erin E., Kevin C. BA, Gannon U., 1973; MA, SUNY, Albany, 1974, PhD, 1980. Asst. prof., then assoc. prof. Sch. Criminal Justice, SUNY Rockefeller Coll. Pub. Affairs and Policy, 1982—91; prof. criminal justice, dean Coll. Criminal Justice Sam Houston State U., Huntsville, Tex., 1991—98; provost SUNY, Brockport, 1998—. Presenter numerous papers to profl. meetings, also panel convenor, chmn., discussant; exec. dir. Michael J. Hindelang Criminal Justice Rsch. Ctr., Inc., Albany, 1981-83. Co-editor: Sourcebook of Criminal Justice Statistics - 1978-92; editor: Jour. Criminal Justice Edn., 1989-93; contbr. articles and book revs. to profl. jours., chpts. to books. Recipient Disting. Alumnus award SUNY Rockefeller Coll. Pub. Affairs and Policy, 1992. Fellow: Acad. Criminal Justice Scis.; mem.: Harvard U. Inst. for Ednl. Mgmt., Am. Coun. on Edn. (coun. fellows, leadership devel. fellow 1988—89), Am. Soc. Criminology, Pi Gamma Mu, Blue Key, Golden Key. Roman Catholic. Avocations: photography, bicycling, computers, sports, reading. Office: SUNY Brockport Brockport NY 14420-2914 Office Phone: 585-395-2524. Business E-Mail: flanagan@brockport.edu.

FLANAGAN, VAN KENT, journalist; b. San Antonio, Sept. 20, 1945; s. Marquiss Monroe and Nina Louise (Fowler) F.; m. Janet Dorothy Robinson, Dec. 16, 1972. BA, Angelo State U., 1968. Reporter, editor San Angelo Standard-Times, Tex., 1966-68; copy editor Fort Lauderdale News, Fla., 1973-74; from news editor to editor Sun. Express-News, San Antonio, 1974-79; from newsman to bur. chief AP, Phila., 1979-80, Columbia, S.C., 1980-82, Bismarck, N.D., 1982-83, Nashville, 1983—2004; editor, adj. instr. Freedom Forum First Amendment Ctr., Vanderbilt U., Nashville, 2005—. Served with U.S. Army, 1968-72, Vietnam. Decorated Bronze star. Mem.: Tenn. Coalition for Open Govt. (founding mem., sec. 2004—), Soc. Profl. Journalists (pres. Mid. Tenn. chpt. 1986—87, 2000—03). Presbyterian. Avocations: walking, hiking, reading novels and non-fiction. Home: 613 Riverview Dr Franklin TN 37064-5514 Personal E-mail: flanag_k@bellsouth.net.

FLANAGAN KELLY, ANNE MARIE, academic administrator; b. North Kingstown, RI, Apr. 13, 1954; d. John James Flanagan and Margaret Mary Ortstein; children: Timothy Kelly, Brigid Kelly. Cert. advanced studies, BA, SUNY; MEd, Pa. State U. Cert. sch. dist. adminstr., sch. adminstrv. supr., nursery, kindergarten and grades 1-6, spl. edn. K-12. Grade 4 tchr. Narrowsburgh Ctrl. Sch. Dist., Narrowsburgh, NY, 1976; spl. edn. tchr. Tompkins-Seneca-Tioga BOCES, Ithaca, NY, 1977—80; learning disabilities specialist Ithaca City Sch. Dist., Ithaca, NY, 1980—81; head tchr. Adolescent Day Sch./Cmty. Treatment Ctr., Worcester, Mass., 1981—83; resource/cons./remedial tchr. Onteora Ctrl. Sch. Dist., Boiceville, NY, 1986—93; supr. spl. edn. Ulster BOCES, New Paltz, NY, 1993—. Adv. bd. 21st Century Grant- Ulster BOCES and Ellenville CSD, New Paltz, NY, 2001—; mem. NY State Coun. of Admstrs. Spl. Edn., NY; student success mgr. SUNY-Ulster, Stone Ridge. Religious edn. tchr. St. Joseph's Ch., Kingston, NY, 1989—2000, eucharistic min., 1996—2003; merit badge counselor Boy Scouts of Am. Troop 20, Hurley, NY, 1999—2003; mem. Kingston H.S. Alumni Choir, 2002—, St. Joseph's Music Ministry, Kingston. Fellow Spl. Edn., US Office Edn., 1976-1977; grantee VATEA, NY State Edn. Dept., 1995—97. Mem.: Regional Bd. N.Y. State Parent Tchr. Assn. (scholarship chairperson 1993—95, Hudson Valley chpt.), N.Y. State United Tchrs., SUNY Cortland Alumni Assn., SUNY New Paltz Alumni Assn., Penn State U. Alumni Assn., Coun. for Exceptional Children, Assn. Supervision and Curriculum Devel. Roman Catholic. Avocations: reading, singing, church activities, athletic events. Home: 28 Village Ct Kingston NY 12401 Office: Ulster BOCES 175 Route 32 N New Paltz NY 12561 Personal E-mail: kellya@sunyulster.edu. Business E-Mail: akelly@mhric.org.

FLANARY, DONALD HERBERT, JR., lawyer; b. Texarkana, Ark., July 27, 1949; s. Donald Herbert and Tenney-Margaret (Webb) Flanary; m. Gina Lynn Rexrod; children: Donald Herbert III, Shannon Gail, Lauren Paige, David Tyler, John Paul, Noah Toliver. BS with honors, Tex. A&M U., Commerce, 1971; JD, U. Houston, 1974. Bar: Tex. 1974, U.S. Dist. Ct. (no. dist.) Tex. 1975, U.S. Dist. Ct. (ea. dist.) Tex. 1976, U.S. Tax Ct. 1982, U.S. Ct. Appeals (5th cir.) 1976, U.S. Supreme Ct. 1983. Law clk. Hon. Mary Lou Robinson U.S. Dist. Ct., Amarillo, Tex., 1974—75; asst. dist. atty. Dallas County, Tex., 1975—76; ptnr. Henderson Bryant & Wolfe, Sherman, Tex., 1976—87, Vial Hamilton Koch & Knox, Dallas, 1988—99, Arter and Hadden, Dallas, 1999—2002, Flanary & Carter, Dallas, 2002—04, The Flanary Group, Dallas, 2004—. Lectr. for bar assns. on tort law, 1981—84. Bd. dirs. Texoma Valley coun. Boy Scouts Am., Cancer Soc., Sherman. Named one of Outstanding Young Men Am., Jaycees, 1981. Fellow: Tex. Bar Found. (life); mem.: Am. Bd. Trial Advocates (cert.), Am. Bd. Profl. Liability Attys. (cert.), State Bar Assn. Tex. (bd. dirs. 1986—89, pres.-elect 1999), Nat. Bd. Trial Adv., Bd. Legal Specialization (civil trial law), Internat. Assn. Ins. Counsel (bd. cert. personal jury trial law), Grayson County Bar Assn. (pres. 1983—84), Tex. Assn. Def. Counsel (bd. dirs. 1981 1984, bd. dirs. 1986—88). Democrat. Roman Catholic. Office Phone: 214-397-0333. Business E-Mail: dflanary@theflanarygroup.com.

FLANDERS, ELEANOR CARLSON, community volunteer; b. Spearville, Kans., Mar. 27, 1916; d. Carl Edward and Laura Rebecca (Pine) Carlson; m. Laurence Burdette Flanders, Jr., June 6, 1941; children: Laurel F. Umile, John C., Lynette F. Moyer, Paul L. BA, cert. journalism, U. Colo., 1938; family inst. cert., Vassar Coll., 1958. Examiner of credits U. Colo., Boulder, 1938-41; stock market analyst trust dept. First Nat. Bank, Longmont, Colo., 1970-85; landlady Historic Library Hall Apt. House. V.p. St. Vrain Valley Sch. Bd., 1978—84. Contbr. articles to profl. jours. Precinct worker, del. Rep. Party, Longmont and Boulder, 1941—; club leader 4-H Boulder County, 1947-63; pres., charter mem. Boulder County Mental Health Clinic, 1947-60; mem. PEO Sisterhood, 1948—; trustee, investment com. First Congl. Ch., Longmont, 1960-2001; North Colo. area rep. Am. Field Svc., Longmont, 1965-70;

coord. tutoring program Boulder County Juvenile Ct., 1965-81; trustee, farm mgr. Carl and Laura Carlson Trust, Oberlin, Kans., 1971-85; trustee, dir. Colo. 4-H Youth Fund, Ft. Collins, 1973-86; trustee, investment counsel Am. Mothers Endowment Fund, N.Y.C., 1979-90; founder, pres. St. Vrain Edn. Found. Endowment Fund, Longmont, 1985—2004; trustee, bd. dirs. Longmont Cable Trust, 1986-88; nat. treas. Am. Mothers, N.Y., 1988-90; elected 2-term dir. St. Vrain Valley Sch. Bd., 1978-86. Mem.: AAUW (charter), St. Vrain Hist. Soc. (dir., pres. 1970—), Sunshine Club, U. Colo. Alumni Assn. (dir., sec. 1950—58), Delta Kappa Gamma (hon.). Avocations: gardening, travel, duplicate bridge, reading, writing. Home: Covenant Village 9153 Yarrow St #1418 Broomfield CO 80021

FLANDERS, RAYMOND ALAN, dentist, governmental health agency administrator; b. Bangor, Maine, Jan. 4, 1929; s. Carroll Benjamin and Mary (Watson) F.; m. Anne-Liss Teisen; children: Molly Olivia and Michael Benjamin (twins), Katherine Todd Mohan, James C. Todd. Student, Colgate U., 1948-50; BS, U. Miami, Fla., 1955; DDS, U. Md., 1959; MPH, U. Mich., 1979. Mem. faculty W.Va. U., Morgantown, 1964-65; program dir. Project Hope, Brazil, 1976-78; mem. faculty Coll. Dentistry U. Alagoas, Maceio, Brazil, 1976-78; regional dental dir. Va. State Health Dept., Richmond, 1970-76, 79-85; mem. faculty Med. Coll. Va., Richmond, 1980-85; state dental dir. Ill. Dept. Health, Springfield, 1985-96; mem. faculty Coll. Dental Medicine So. Ill. U., Alton, 1985-96; mem. faculty Coll. Dentistry Sch. Pub. Health U. Ill., Chgo., 1990-96; dental cons. Aetna U.S. Healthcare, 1998—. Cons. Project Esperanca, Amazon River, Brazil, 1981, Project HOPE/U.S.A.I.D., Grenada, West Indies, 1984, Project HOPE, Honduras, 1986, Am. Dental Assn., Brazil and Guyana, 1992. Contbr. articles to profl. jours. Served to capt. U.S. Army, 1946-47, 50-51, 60-63. Recipient Sec's Excellence in Health Promotion Award, 1990, Ranking 5th, Age Group 60-65, Western Tennis Assn., 1989, Gold Medal, Singles and Doubles Tennis, Ranked 4th Nat., Age Group 65-70, Sr. Olympics, 1994, Gold Medal, Singles Tennis, Age Group 70-75, 1999; fellow USPHS fellow, 1978—79. Mem. ADA (Preventive Dentistry award 1983, Cmty. Preventive Dentistry award 1990, 95), Va. Dental Assn., Assn. State Territorial Dental Dirs. (exceptional achievement award 1998), Am. Assn. Pub. Health Dentists, Ill. Pub. Health Assn., Va. Dental Assn. Home: 5 Whittakers Mill Williamsburg VA 23185 E-mail: rafalt@aol.com.

FLANDERS, ROBERT G., JR., lawyer, educator, legal association administrator; b. Freeport, N.Y., July 9, 1949; m. Ann I. Walls, May 29, 1971; children: Danielle, Heather, Zachary. AB magna cum laude, Brown U., 1971; JD, Harvard Law Sch., 1974. Bar: N.Y. 1975, Mass. 1976, R.I. 1976, U.S. Ct. of Appeals (1st and 2d. cir.), U.S. Dist. Ct. (so. dist., ea. dist.) N.Y., R.I., Mass. Assoc. Paul, Weiss, Rifkind, Wharton & Garrison, N.Y.C., 1974-75; ptnr., chmn. litig. dept. Edwards & Angell, Providence, 1975-87; founding ptnr. Flanders & Medeiros Inc., 1987-96; assoc. justice R.I. Supreme Ct., 1996—2004; ptnr. Ainckley, Allan & Snyder, 2004—; disting. visiting prof. Roger Williams U. Sch. of Law, 2004—. Mem. Am. Law Inst., 2000—; bd. dirs. Rsch. Engring. and Mfg., Inc., Nestor, Inc. Contbr. articles to profl. publ. Bd. dirs. Brown Sports Found., 2000, Greater Providence YMCA, 1995—, Providence Performing Arts Ctr., 1997—, Vets. Meml. Auditorium, 1999—, Women and Infants Hosp., 1996—. Mem. ABA, Phi Beta Kappa. Avocations: tennis, clarinet, jazz, poetry, cigars. Office: Roger Williams U Sch Law 10 Metacom Ave Bristol RI 02809 Office Phone: 401-457-3775, 401-457-5184. Business E-Mail: rflanders@haslaw.com.

FLANIGAN, JAMES J(OSEPH), journalist; b. N.Y.C., June 6, 1936; s. James and Jane (Whyte) F.; m. Patricia Quatrine, Nov. 28, 1997; children: Michael, Siobhan Jane. BA, Manhattan Coll., 1961. Fin. writer N.Y. Herald Tribune, 1957-66; bur. chief, asst. mng. editor Forbes Mag., 1966-86; bus. columnist, sr. econs. editor L.A. Times, 1986—. Office: LA Times 202 W 1st St Los Angeles CA 90012 Office Phone: 213-237-7167. E-mail: jim.flanigan@latimes.com.

FLANIGAN, MATTHEW C., manufacturing executive; Degree, U. Mo. Formerly with Society Gen., Dallas, InterFirst Bank, Dallas; with Leggett & Platt, 1997—, pres. Office Furniture Components Group, 1999—2003, v.p., CFO, 2003—. Office: Leggett & Platt No 1 Leggett Rd Carthage MO 64836

FLANNAGAN, WILLIAM PATRICK, music educator; b. Bristol, Va., Dec. 25, 1952; s. Charles Bascom and Margaret Moore Flannagan; m. Della Elizabeth Luffman, Aug. 24, 1974; children: Mary Margaret, Charles Grady. BA in Psychology, King Coll., 1974; MusB in Ch. Music, Westminster Choir Coll., 1977, MusM in Choral Conducting, 1978; PhD in Musicology, Cath. U. Am., 1995. Min. music First United Meth. Ch., Ozark, Ala., 1978—82; prof. King. Coll., Briston, 1982—. Tenor soloist The Sophisticates, Johnson City, Tenn., 1999—; chorus master Kingsport Symphony Chorus, Tenn., 2001; music dir. Bristol Concert Choir, 2002—. Contbr. articles to profl. jours. Vol. Little League Baseball, Bristol, 1990—. Mem.: Am. Choral Dir. Assn., Rotary (Paul Harris fellow 1991). Avocations: bridge, reading, sports. Office: King Coll 1350 King College Rd Bristol TN 37620 E-mail: wpf@3wave.com.

FLANNERY, ELLEN JOANNE, lawyer; b. Bklyn., Dec. 13, 1951; d. William Rowan and Mary Jane (Hamilla) Flannery. AB cum laude, Mount Holyoke Coll., 1973; JD cum laude, Boston U., 1978. Bar: Mass. 1978, DC 1979, US Ct. Appeals (DC cir.) 1979, US Dist. Ct. DC 1980, US Ct. Appeals (4th cir.) 1981, US Supreme Ct. 1983. Spl. asst. to commr. of health Mass. Dept. Pub. Health, Boston, 1973-75; law clk. US Ct. Appeals DC cir., Washington, 1978-79; assoc. Covington & Burling, Washington, 1979-86, ptnr., 1986—, co-chmn., Food & Drug Regulatory Practice Group. Lectr. ins. U. Va. Sch. Law, 1984—90, Boston U. Sch. Law, 1993, bd. visitors, 1995—; lectr. ins. U. Md. Sch. Law, 1994; mem. Nat. Conf. Lawyers and Scientists, AAAS-ABA, 1989—92; chair Fellows Adv. Rsch. Commn., 2002—. Contbr. articles to profl. jour. Fellow: Am. Bar Found. (chair fellows adv. rsch. com. 2002—, sec. fellows 2005—); mem.: ABA (chmn. life scis. divsn. 1982—84, chmn. com. med. practice 1987—88, chmn. life scis. divsn. 1988—91, vice chair food and drug law com. 1991—97, chmn. sect. sci. and tech. 1992—93, del. of sci. and tech. sect. to ho. of dels. 1993—, chmn. coordinating group on bioethics and the law 1998—2000, vice chair Ho. Tech. Com. 2002—04, chmn. conf. sect. and divsn. dels. 2003—), Cosmos Club. Office: Covington & Burling 1201 Pennsylvania Ave NW Washington DC 20004-2401 Office Phone: 202-662-5484. Office Fax: 202-662-6291. Business E-Mail: eflannery@cov.com.

FLANNERY, JAMES WILLIAM, performing arts educator, theater director, singer; b. Hartford, Conn., Nov. 8, 1936; s. James Joseph and Eileen Cotter Flannery; m. Ildiko Elizabeth Pokoly, Sept. 7, 1964; 1 child, Ciaran Pokoly. BA, Trinity Coll., 1958; MFA, Yale Sch. Drama, 1961; PhD, Trinity Coll., Dublin, 1970; DLitt (hon.), Trinity Coll., 1994, U. Ulster, Derry, Ireland, 2001. Dir. Eng. theater U. Ottawa, Canada, 1961—76; chair dept. theater U. R.I., Kingston, 1976—79, Emory U., Atlanta, 1982—89, prof. performing arts, 1989—, Winship prof. arts and humanities, 2001—. Prodr. Yeats Internat. Theatre Festival, Abbey Theatre, Dublin, 1989—93; founder, dir. W. B. Yeats Found., Atlanta, 1989—; prodr., lectr. concerts, symposia, exhbns. Emory U., Atlanta, 1992—. Author: (book) W. B. Yeats and the Idea of Theatre; author/singer (book-recording) Dear Harp of My Country: The Irish Melodies of Thomas Moore. Named one of Top 100 Irish Americans, Irish-America Mag., NY, 1990—93, 1998; recipient Wild Geese Award for Outstanding Contbn. to Irish Culture, 1994, Gov.'s Award in the Humanities, Ga. Humanities Coun., Atlanta, 2002; Disting. Fulbright fellow, Fulbright Commn., UK, 2001. Mem.: Phi Beta Kappa. Roman Catholic. Home: 1342 Harvard Rd NE Atlanta GA 30306 Office: Emory Univ 1463 S Oxford Rd Atlanta GA 30322

FLANNERY, JOHN PHILIP, lawyer; b. N.Y.C., May 15, 1946; s. John Philip and Agnes Geraldine (Applegate) F.; 1 child by a previous marriage: Diana Elizabeth; m. Holly Lynne Smith, Mar. 1, 2003; 1 stepchild, Alexandra Elizabeth. BS in Physics, Fordham Coll., 1967; BS in Engring., Columbia U., 1969, JD, 1972; student, Art Students League, 1972-73; MS in Info. Sci., George Washington U., 2002. Bar: N.Y. 1973, U.S. Dist. Ct. (so. dist.) N.Y. 1973, U.S. Ct. Appeals (2d cir.) 1973, Va. 1983, U.S. Ct. Appeals (4th cir.) 1985, U.S. Ct. Appeals (D.C. cir.) 1985, U.S. Dist. Ct. (ea. dist.) Va. 1985, U.S. Supreme Ct. 1985. Mem. staff Ford Found. Project to Restructure Columbia U., N.Y.C., 1968; news rep. nat. press rels. IBM, 1970; law clk. Adminstrv. Conf. U.S., 1971, U.S. Ct. Appeals (2d cir.), 1972-74; asst. U.S. atty. Narcotics and Ofcl. Corruption units, So. Dist. N.Y., N.Y.C., 1974-79; sr. assoc. Poletti Freidin Prashker Feldman & Gartner, N.Y.C., 1979-82; spl. counsel U.S. Senate Judiciary Com., 1982, U.S. Senate Labor Com., 1982-83; Dem. candidate U.S. Congress from Va. 10th Dist., 1983-84; pvt. practice in civil and criminal litigation, 1984—. Spl. counsel Sen. Howard Metzenbaum, 1985-87; asst. dist. atty., Bronx, N.Y., 1986-87; counsel, bd. dirs. Washington Internat. Horse Show Assn., 1989-91; legal expert "Crime in D.C.", Fox TV, 1993, "Crime Bill" Wis. Pub. Radio, 1994, "People vs. O.J. Simpson" ABC Network Radio, 1994-95, "Va.'s No Parole" Larry King Live CNN, 1994, "Imprisonment" CBS Morning Show, 1994, Habeas Reform Court TV, 1996, Terrorism, 1996, O'Reilly Factor, Fox News, "Torture", 2004, Fox News "Supreme Court," 2004-05; spl. counsel U.S. House Judiciary Com., 1996-97; project dir., spl. counsel U.S. Edn. and Work Force Com., 1997-98; spl. counsel (impeachment proceedings) U.S. Rep. Zoe Lofgren, 1998-99, Washington staff chief, spl. counsel, 1999-2001; vis. exec. George Washington U. Sch. Bus. and Pub. Mgmt., 2002-04; of counsel, Campbell, Miller, Zimmerman, P.C., 2002— lectr. in field. Author: Commercial Information Brokers, 1973, Habeas Corpus Bores Hole in Prisoners' Civil Rights Action, 1975, Pro Se Litigation, 1975, Prison Corruption: A Mockery of Justice, 1980, Conspiracy: A Primer, 1988, Is Innocence Relevant to Execution? If Not, Isn't that Murder?, 1994, Equal Justice For All, 1995, Virginia Governor Allen's No-Parole Plan: A Billion Dollar Wasteland of Prisons, 1995; tech. columnist, Loudoun Times Mirror, May 2002-04; contbg. columnist Loudoun Times Mirror, 2004—; on-air commentator O'Reilly Factor, Fox News, Chris Matthews' Hardball, MSNBC, 2004-2005. Mem. legis. commn. Citizen's Union, 1971—72; mem. Arlington Transp. Commn., 1983—85; chmn. bus. coun. Va. Gov.'s War on Drugs Task Force, 1983—84; pres. Franklin Soc., 1979—80; committeeman Dem. Party N.Y. County, 1979—80, Dem. Party Arlington County, 1983—84; coord. N.Y. State Lawyers Com. for Sen. Edward M. Kennedy, 1979—80; dir. Citizens for Sen. M. Kennedy, 1980; del. Dem. Nat. Conf., 1988, Va. Assembly Univ. W.Va., 1990; committeeman Loudoun County Dem. Com., 1995—, sec., 1995—, chmn., 1995—97; del. 10th Congress and Dist. Com., 1997—; mem. Ctrl. State (Va.) Com., 1997—; del. Dem. Nat. Conv., 2000, 2004; v.p. Loudoun County Dem. Com., 2001; Va. coord. Kerry for Pres., 2003—04. Recipient U.S. Justice Dept. award for Outstanding Contbns. in Field of Drug Law Enforcement, 1977, U.S. Atty. Gen.'s Spl. Commendation for Outstanding Svc., 1979, FLEOA award, Fed. Law Enforcement Officer's Assn., 1984, NACDL's Marshall Stern award Outstanding Legis. Achievement, 1997. Mem. ABA, Assn. Bar City N.Y., N.Y. County Lawyers Assn., Arlington County Bar Assn., Loudon County Bar Assn., Nat. Assn. Criminal Def. Lawyers (chair briefbank com. 1990-91, legis. co-chair 1991-96, dir. 1993-97, President's commendation 1991, 92, 95), Acad. Polit. Sci., Va. Coll. Criminal Def. Attys. (bd. dirs. 1993-96), London Restoration and Preservation Soc. (bd. dirs. 2004—), Leesburg Rotary (bd. dirs. 2005—). Democrat. Home: Ithaca Manor 38469 Triticum Ln Lovettsville VA 20180 Office Phone: 703-771-8344. E-mail: jonflan@aol.com.

FLANNERY, JOSEPH PATRICK, manufacturing executive, director; b. Lowell, Mass., Mar. 20, 1932; s. Joseph Patrick and Mary Agnes Egan F.; m. Margaret Barrows, June 1957; children: Mary Ann, Diane, Joseph, James, David, Elizabeth. BS in Chemistry, Lowell Tech. Inst., 1953; MBA, Harvard U., 1955; PhD, U. Lowell, Mass., 1981. Pres. Uniroyal Chem. Co., Naugatuck, Conn., 1975-77; exec. v.p. Uniroyal, Inc., Middlebury, Conn., 1977, pres., 1977—, chief exec. officer, 1980—, chmn. bd., 1982—; chmn., pres., chief exec. officer Uniroyal Holding, Inc., Naugatuck, Conn., 1986—. Bd. dirs. The Scotts Co., ArvinMeritor. Mem.: Country Club of Fla., Oyster Harbors (Mass.), Vesper Country Club (Lowell), Country Club of Waterbury (Conn.), Knights of Malta. Roman Catholic. Office: Uniroyal Holding Inc 70 Great Hill Rd Naugatuck CT 06770-2224

FLANNERY, MICHAEL ALLEN, librarian, historian; b. Cin., May 30, 1953; s. Gerald (Stepfather) and Helen Elizabeth Perry; m. Dona Joy Kuhns. BA, No. Ky. State Coll., 1974; MLS, U. Ky., 1989; MA, Calif. State U., Dominguez Hills, 1994. Dir. Lloyd Libr. and Mus., Cin., 1994—99; assoc. dir. hist. collections U. Ala., Birmingham, 1999—. Libr. cons., coord. rsch. Ghana Christian U., Dodowa, 2003—. Author: John Uri Lloyd: The Great American Eclectic (Kremers Award for outstanding pharm. scholarship by an American, 2001); author: (with Alex Berman) America's Botanical Medical Movements: Vox Populi (Choice award for outstanding academic title, 2002); author: (with Dennis B. Worthen) Pharmaceutical Education in the Queen City: 150 Years of Service, 1850-2000; author: Civil War Pharmacy: A History of Drugs, Drug Supply and Provision, and Therapeutics for the Union and Confederacy. Fellow: Academie internationale d'histoire de la pharmacie (life; mem. 1999—2005); mem.: Am. Inst. History of Pharmacy (exec. coun. 2005—), Med. Libr. Assn. (sec./treas. 2004—, Gottleib prize 2002). Home: 200 Lake Forest Way Maylene AL 35114 Office: U Ala Birmingham 1530 Third Ave S Birmingham AL 35294-0013 Office Phone: 205-934-4475. Office Fax: 205-975-8476. Personal E-mail: dflann@bellsouth.net. E-mail: flannery@uab.edu.

FLANNERY, MICHAEL SIDNEY, environmental scientist; b. Logan, W. Va., Sept. 11, 1952; s. Wilbur Elmer and Mildred Davis Flannery; m. Terrie Mackin Lee, Nov. 24, 1984; children: Lauren Lee, Brian Mackin. *Father, W. E. Flannery, was Speaker of the House of Delegates in the West Virginia State Legislature for five terms. Mother, Mildred Flannery, taught in the Florida and West Virginia public school systems for forty-five years.* MS, U. Fla., 1984, BS in forestry, 1975. Biologist U. Fla., Gainesville, Fla., 1975—81; biologist, botanist Northwest Fla. Water Mgmt. Dist., Havana, Fla., 1984—85; sr. environ. scientist Southwest Fla. Water Mgmt. Dist., Brooksville, Fla., 1985—2005. Office: SW Fla Water Mgmt Dist 2379 Broad St Brooksville FL 34604-6899

FLANNERY, REBECCA R., harpist; b. Hartford, Conn., Jan. 27, 1952; MusB, SUNY, Stony Brook, 1975; MusM, Yale U., 1978; cert., Am. Ctr. for the Alexander Technique Tchr. Tng., 1987. Mem. N.Y. Harp Ensemble, tours U.S., Can. and Europe, 1970-73; mem. flute and harp duo Chrysolith, tours U.S. and Can., 1976—. 2nd harp New Haven Symphony; instr. harp Hartt Sch. Music, U. Hartford, U. Conn.; founder Conn. Harp Festival. Rec. artist (album) Dreams and Fantasies, (CD) This Son So Young. Recipient Sprague-Woolsey Hall Competition award, 1978; named one of Outstanding Young Women in Am., 1981. Mem. Am. Harp Soc. (pres. Conn. chpt.).

FLANNERY, SUSAN MARIE, library administrator; b. Newark, Feb. 18, 1953; d. John Patrick Flannery and Assunta (Lardieri) Ege; m. Stephen A. Coren, Oct. 6, 1984. BA in History of Art, U. Pa., 1974; MLS, Simmons Coll., 1975. Dir. of libr. Newton Country Day, 1975-77, Am. Sch. in Switzerland, Montagnola, 1977-78; young adult libr. Somerville (Mass.) Pub. Libr., 1979-81; reference libr. Cary Meml. Libr., Lexington, Mass., 1981-83; asst. dir. Lucius Beebe Libr., Wakefield, Mass., 1983-87; dir. Reading (Mass.) Pub. Libr., 1987-91; assoc. dir. Cambridge (Mass.) Pub. Libr., 1991-1993, dir., 1993—. Steering com. Mass. delegation to White Ho. Conf. on Librs., 1990; corporator East Cambridge Savs. Bank. Reviewer Sch. Libr. Jour.; contbr. articles to profl. jours. Incorporator Cambridge (Mass.) Family YMCA, 1991—93; bd. dirs. Guidance Ctr., Inc., Cambridge, 1994—2000, sec., 2001—. Recipient Friend to Writers award, PEN New Eng., 2004, Leading Role award, Cambridge Cmty. TV, 2005. Mem. ALA (Mass. councilor 1993-97, John Cotton Dana award 1989, Outstanding Libr. Adv. 20th Century 2000), ACLU Mass. (adv. bd. 1994-96, bd. dirs. 1996—2004), Mass. Libr. Assn. (pres. 1985-87, v.p. 1983-85), Rotary (bd. dirs. Cambridge 1993-99, v.p. 1995-96, pres. 1997-98, pres. Reading club). Office: Cambridge Pub Libr 359 Broadway Cambridge MA 02139 Office Phone: 617-349-4032. E-mail: sflannery@cambridgema.gov.

FLANSBURGH, EARL ROBERT, architect; b. Ithaca, N.Y., Apr. 28, 1931; s. Earl Alvah and Elizabeth (Evans) F.; m. Louise Hospital, Aug. 27, 1955; children: Earl Schuyler, John Conant. BArch, Cornell U., 1954; MArch, MIT, 1957; S.C.M.P., Harvard U. Sch. Bus., 1982. Job capt., designer The Architects Collaborative, Cambridge, Mass., 1958-62; partner Freeman, Flansburgh & Assos., Cambridge, 1961-63; prin. Earl R. Flansburgh & Assocs., Cambridge, 1963-69, pres., dir. design, 1969—. Bd. dirs. daka, Inc.; exec. v.p. Environment Systems Internat., Inc.; vis. prof. archtl. design Mass. Inst. Tech., 1965-66; instr. art Wellesley Coll., 1962-65, lectr. art, 1965-69; cons. Arthur D. Little, Inc., Cambridge, 1964-70. Archtl. works include Weston (Mass.) High Sch. Addition, 1965-67, Cornell U. Campus Store, 1967-70, Cumnock Hall, Harvard U. Bus. Sch, 1973-75, Acton (Mass.) Elementary schs, 1966-68, 69-71, Wilton (Conn.) High Sch, 1968-71, 14 Story St. Bldg, 1970, Boston Design Ctr., 1985-86, Glenwood Sch., Dallas, 1985-88, New Univ. No. B.C., Prince George, Can., 1991—, Boston Coll. Law Sch., 1992—; exhibited works Light Machine I, IBM Gallery, N.Y.C., 1958, Light Machine II, Carpenter Center, Harvard, 1965, 5 Cambridge Architects, Wellesley Coll., 1969, Work of Earl R. Flansburgh and Assos, Wellesley Coll., 1969, New Architecture in New Eng, DeCordova Mus., 1974-75, Residential Architecture, Mead Art Gallery, Amherst Coll., 1976, works represented in, 50 Ville del Nostro Tempo, 1970, Nuove Ville, New Villas, 1970, Vacation Houses, 1970, Vacation Houses, 2d edit., 1977, Interior Design, 1970, Drawings by American Architects, 1973, Interior Spaces Designed by Architects, 1974, New Architecture in New England, 1974, Great Houses, 1976, Architecture Boston, 1976, Presentation Drawings by American Architects, 1977, Architecture, 1970-1980, A Decade of Change, 1980, Old and New Architecture, A Design Relationship, 1980, 25 Years of Record Houses, 1981, School Ways: The Planning and Design of American Schools, 1992, Elem. and Secondary Schs., 2001; Author: (with others) Techniques of Successful Practice, 1975. Chmn. architecture com. Boston Arts Festival, 1964, Downtown Boston Design adv. com.; bd. dirs. Cambridge Ctr. Adult Edn.; pres. Downtown North Boston, 1994—; trustee Cornell U., 1972—; chmn. bldgs. and properties com., 1976-87; mem. exec. com. acad. affairs com.; class sec. SCMP VII Harvard Bus. Sch., 1982-89. 1st lt. USAF, 1954-56. Recipient design awards Progressive Architecture, design awards Record Houses, design awards AIA, design awards City of Boston, design awards Mass. Masonry Inst., spl. design citations Am. Assn. Sch. Adminstrs., spl. 1st prize Buffalo-Western N.Y. chpt. AIA Competition., Walter Taylor award Am. Assn. Sch. Adminstrs., 1986, William Candill award Am. Coll. & Univ. Mag., 1993, Award of Honor, Boston Soc. Archs., 1999; Fulbright Rsch. grantee Bldg. Rsch. Sta., Eng., 1957-58. Fellow AIA, Nat. Acad. Design; mem. Royal Inst. Brit. Architects, Boston Soc. Architects (chmn. program com., 1969-71, commr. pub. affairs 1971-73, commr. design 1973-74, dir. 1971-74, pres. 1980-81), Boston Found. Architecture (treas. 1984-89), Cornell U. Coun., Quill and Dagger Soc., St. Botolph Club, Tau Beta Pi. Home: 3 Old Conant Rd Lincoln MA 01773 Office: 77 N Washington St Boston MA 02114-1908*

FLASTRUP, ASGER, information technology executive; B in Bus. Mktg., Copenhagen Bus. Coll. Sales mgr. Tex. Instruments, 1980; co-founder Datateam Group Cos. (now Ingram Micro), 1984; v.p. Nordic region Ingram Micro Denmark, mng. dir.; v.p. Ingram Micro Europe; pres. Ingram Micro Can., 2000—01; sr. v.p., pres. L.Am. Ingram Micro, Inc., Santa Ana, Calif., 2001—. Office: Ingram Micro Inc 1600 E St Andrew Pl PO Box 25125 Santa Ana CA 92799

FLATER, MORRIS EUGENE, lawyer; b. Augusta, Ga., Sept. 1, 1943; s. Morris E. Flater and Sue (Ransom) Bell; m. Susanne R. Flater (div. 1987); children: Lara, Morris E. III. BS, Tulane U., 1966; JD magna cum laude, Washington and Lee U., 1973; LLM, Georgetown U., 1997. Bar: Va. 1973, Mass. 1991. Of counsel Hunton and Williams, Norfolk, Va., 1973-84; pres. Channel Labs., Ltd., Norfolk, 1984-85, Hub Express Airlines, Boston, 1986-91; exec. dir., gen. counsel Am. Helicopter Soc., Alexandria, Va., 1991—. Pub. Vertiflite mag. Capt. USMC, 1966-70. Recipient Helicopter Assn. Internat. Excellence in Comm. award. Fellow Royal Aeronautical Soc., Order of Coif, Omicron Delta Kappa. Office: Am Helicopter Soc 217 N Washington St Alexandria VA 22314-2520 E-mail: rflater@vtol.org.

FLATO, WILLIAM ROEDER, JR., software development company executive; b. Apr. 20, 1945; s. William Roeder and Juanita Flato; m. Beatrice Pesl, Aug. 22, 1974; children: Amanda Leigh, William Roeder III. BBA, U. Houston, 1967. CPA, Tex. Acct. Hughes Tool Co., Houston, 1966-67, Milchem, Inc., Houston, 1967-72, accounting mgr., asst. contr., corp. contr., 1972-78; v.p. fin., sec., treas. Baker Performance Chems. Inc. (formerly magna Corp.), Houston, 1978-82, exec. v.p. fin. and planning, sec.-treas., 1982-93; CFO, v.p. fin. CoToCo Techs., Inc., Houston, 1993-97; founder, CFO, v.p. fin. Connective Techs., Inc., Houston, 1996—2001, CEO, pres., chmn. bd. dirs., 2001—. Active Country Village Civic Assn.; state chmn. Young Ams. for Freedom, 1964; precinct chmn. Harris County Rep. Exec. Com., 1966-67. With U.S. Army, 1968-69. Decorated Army Commendation medal. Mem. Tex. Soc. CPA, Mensa. Presbyterian. Home: 11931 Drexel Hill Dr Houston TX 77077-3009 Office: 7676 Hillmont St Ste 120 Houston TX 77040-6468 Office Phone: 713-690-6789. Personal E-mail: bflato@houston.rr.com. Business E-Mail: bflato@connective-edi.com.

FLATT, ADRIAN EDE, surgeon; b. Frinton, Eng., Aug. 26, 1921; came to U.S., 1956, naturalized, 1960; s. Leslie Neeve and Barbara F.; m. Judith Johnson. BA, Cambridge U., 1942, MA, 1945, MBBchir., 1946, MD, 1953, M. chir., 1972. Diplomate: Am. Bd. Orthopedic Surgery. Rotating intern, then resident in gen., plastic and orthopaedic surgery London (Eng.) Hosp., 1946-54, 55-56; mem. faculty U. Iowa Med. Sch., 1956-79; prof. orthopaedic surgery and anatomy, dir. div. hand surgery, chmn. dept. surgery Norwalk (Conn.) Hosp., 1979-82; clin. prof. Yale U. Med. Sch., 1979-82; chief dept. orthopaedics Baylor U. Med. Ctr., Dallas, 1982-92, coord. rsch. Tom Landry Sports Medicine Ctr., 1992-94, dir. edn. dept. orthopaedics, 1995—. Hunterian prof. Royal Coll. Surgeons, 1962; McIlrath guest prof. Royal Prince Alfred Hosp., Sydney, Australia, 1972; Sir R. Watson-Jones lectr. Brit. Orthopaedic Assn., 1986; cons. in hand surgery to surg. gen. U.S. Air Force, 1962— Editor in chief Jour. Hand Surgery, 1981-91; author textbooks, papers in field; patentee artificial wrist and finger joints. Served as officer RAF, 1948-50. Recipient Kappa Delta award Am. Acad. Orthopaedic Surgeons, 1972 Mem. Am. Soc. Surgery Hand, Brit. Hand Soc., Brit. Assn. Plastic Surgery (hon.), Group Etude de la Main, Am. Orthopaedic Assn., Am. Acad. Orthopaedic Surgeons, Am. Soc. Plastic and Reconstructive Surgery. Office: Baylor U Med Ctr George Truett James Orthopedic Inst 3500 Gaston Ave Dallas TX 75246-2096 Office Phone: 214-820-1989.

FLATTÉ, MICHAEL EDWARD, physicist, researcher; b. Walnut Creek, Calif., Apr. 14, 1967; s. Stanley Martin and Renelde Marie (Demeure) F.; m. Jennifer Beatrice Kirsch, Aug. 20, 1989; children: Devra Tamar, Shecharya Nathaniel. AB, Harvard U., 1988; PhD, U. Calif., Santa Barbara, 1992. Teaching asst., rsch. asst. dept. physics U. Calif., Santa Barbara, 1989-92, postdoctoral rsch. assoc. Inst. Theoretical Physics, 1992-93; postdoctoral rsch. fellow divsn. applied scis. Harvard U., Cambridge, Mass., 1993—. NSF fellow, 1988, Russell and Sigurd Varian fellow Am. Vacuum Soc., 1991. Mem. Am. Phys. Soc. Office: Harvard U Divsn Applied Scis Pierce Hall 204C Cambridge MA 02138

FLATTÉ, STANLEY MARTIN, physicist, researcher; b. LA, Dec. 2, 1940; s. Samuel and Henrietta (Edelstein) Flatté; m. Renelde Marie Demeure, June 26, 1966; children: Michael, Anne. BS, Calif. Inst. Tech., 1962; student, NYU, 1960-61; PhD, U. Calif.-Berkeley, 1966. Rsch. particle physicist Lawrence Berkeley Lab., Calif., 1966-71; asst. prof. physics U. Calif., Santa Cruz, 1971-73, assoc. prof., 1973-78, prof., 1978—2004, prof. emeritus, 2004—; dir. Ctr. Studies Nonlinear Dynamics La Jolla Inst., 1982-86, dept. chmn., 1986-89. Cons. phys. oceanography and underwater sound U.S. Govt.; vis. rschr. Cern, Geneva, 1975, Scripps Inst. Oceanography, 1980, Cambridge (Eng.) U., 1981. Author (with others): Sound Transmission Through a Fluctuating Ocean, 1979; contbr. articles to profl. jours. Woodrow Wilson fellow, 1962, NSF fellow, 1962—66, Guggenheim Found. fellow, 1975.

Fellow: AAAS, Optical Soc. Am., Acoustical Soc. Am., Am. Phys. Soc.; mem.: Am. Geophys. Union, Sigma Xi (pres. Santa Cruz chpt. 1999—2000). Achievements include discovery of cusp phenomenon in particle physics; development of methods for using sound and light waves to probe statistical atmosphere, ocean and earth processes. Office: Univ Calif Physics Dept Santa Cruz CA 95064 Business E-Mail: sflatte@ucsc.edu.

FLATTERY, THOMAS LONG, lawyer, legal administrator; b. Detroit, Nov. 14, 1922; s. Thomas J. and Rosemary (Long) F.; m. Gloria M. Hughes, June 10, 1947 (dec.); children: Constance Marie, Carol Dianne Lee, Michael Patrick, Thomas Hughes, Dennis Jerome, Betsy Ann Sprecher m. Barbara J. Balfour, Oct. 4, 1986; children: Laura B. Lundquist, Linda B. Flint, William D. Balfour III. BS, U.S. Mil. Acad., 1947; JD, UCLA, 1955; LLM, U. So. Calif., 1965. Bar: Calif. 1955, U.S. Patent and Trademark Office 1957, U.S. Customs Ct. 1968, U.S. Supreme Ct. 1974, Conn. 1983, N.Y. 1984. With Motor Products Corp., Detroit, 1950, Equitable Life Assurance Soc., Detroit, 1951, Bohn Aluminum & Brass Co., Hamtramck, Mich., 1952; mem. legal staff, asst. contract adminstr. Radioplane Co. (divsn. Northrop Corp.), Van Nuys, Calif., 1955—57; gen. counsel, asst. sec. McCulloch Corp., L.A., 1957—64; sec., corp. counsel Technicolor, Inc., Hollywood, Calif., 1964—70; v.p., sec. and gen. counsel Amcord, Inc., Newport Beach, Calif., 1970—72; v.p., sec., gen. counsel Schick Inc., L.A., 1972—75; counsel, asst. sec. C.F. Braun & Co., Alhambra, Calif., 1975—76; sr. v.p., sec., gen. counsel Automation Industries, Inc. (now PCC Tech. Industries Inc. a unit of Penn Ctrl. Corp.), Greenwich, Conn., 1976—86; v.p., gen. counsel G&H Tech., Inc. (a unit of Penn Ctrl. Corp.), Santa Monica, Calif., 1986—93; temp. judge Superior Ct. Calif. L.A. Jud. Dist. and Santa Monica Unified Cts., 1987—; settlement officer L.A. Superior Ct., 1991—; pvt. practice Palisades, Calif., 1993—. Panelist Am. Arbitration Assn., 1991—; jud. arbitrator and mediator Alternative Dispute Resolution Programs L.A. Superior Ct., 1993—, Calif. Ct. Appeals 2d Appellate Dist., 1999—; mem. L.A. Supr. Ct. Alternative Dispute Resolution com., 2001—. Contbr. articles to profl. jours. Served to 1st lt. AUS, 1942-50. Mem. ABA, Nat. Assn. Securities Dealers (bd. arbitrators 1996, bd. mediators 1997), State Bar Calif. (co-chmn. corp. law dept. com. 1978-79, lectr. continuing legal edn. program, mandatory fee arbitrator 2001—), L.A. County Bar Assn. (chmn. corp. law dept. com. 1966-67, dispute resolution svcs. atty.-client fee dispute arbitrator and mediator 1993—), Century City Bar Assn. (chmn. corp. law dept. com. 1979-80), Conn. Bar Assn., Santa Monica Bar Assn. (trustee 1999-2003, chmn. alt. dispute resolution sect. 2000—, atty.-client fee dispute arbitrator and mediator), N.Y. State Bar Assn., Am. Soc. Corp. Secs. (L.A. regional group pres. 1973-74), L.A. Intellectual Property Law Assn., L.A. West Am. Inns Court, Irish-Am. Bar Assn. Calif., Am. Ednl. League (trustee 1988—, sec. 1998—), Am. Legion (life), West Point Alumni Assn., Army Athletic Assn., Friendly Sons St. Patrick, Jonathan Club (dir. 1996-99), Phi Alpha Delta. Roman Catholic. Home and Office: 439 Via De La Paz Pacific Palisades CA 90272-4633 Personal E-mail: flatterytl@earthlink.net.

FLATTMANN, ALAN RAYMOND, artist, educator; b. New Orleans, Aug. 6, 1946; s. Louis Eusabe and Julia Margaret (Kastner) Flattmann; m. Rebecca Regina Price, Oct. 6, 1972. Cert., John McCrady Art Sch., New Orleans, 1968. Tchr. John McCrady Art Sch., New Orleans, 1967—82; instr. painting workshops coll. and art socs., 1970—. Lectr., travel art tour leader Hellenic Arts Soc., New Orleans, 1987, Webster's World, Falls Church, Va., 1993—2005. Author: The Art of Pastel Painting, 1987; subject of book: The Poetic Realism of Alan Flattmann, 1981, Alan Flattman's French Quarter Impressions, 2002; one-man shows include Lauren Rogers Mus. Art, Laurel, Miss., 1970, 1975, 1981, Okla. Arts Ctr., Oklahoma City, 1975, Bryant Galleries, New Orleans, Jackson, Birmingham, Atlanta, Palm Beach, 1975—, exhibited in group shows at Columbus Club, N.Y.C., 1981, Represented in permanent collections New Orleans Mus. Art, Miss. Mus. Art, Okla. Art Ctr., Lauren Rogers Mus. Art, Meriden Art Ctr., Longview Mus. Art, Ogden Mus. So. Art. Named Best of Show, Biennial Nat. Exhbn., Pastel Soc. North Fla., 2004; recipient Tchr. award, Am. Artist Art Masters, 1996; grantee Study, Elizabeth T. Greenshields Found., 1973; scholar, New Orleans Art Assn., 1964. Mem.: Southeastern Pastel Soc. (award 1993—96), Pastel Soc. Am. (award 1979, 1986, 1991, 1998, 2002), Degas Pastel Soc. (founder, pres. 1999—, award 1987—88, 1990, 1993—95, 1997—2000, 2002). Avocations: photography, travel. Office: 1202 Main St Apt A Madisonville LA 70447-9742 E-mail: art@alanflattmann.com.

FLATTO, DAVID, social worker, consultant; b. N.Y.C., Sept. 4, 1947; s. Eve Kaufmann. BA, SUNY, Brockport, 1965—69; MSW, Boston U., 1973—75. Cert. clin. social worker State of N.Y. Vol. Vols. in Svc. to Am., Carrolton, Ga., 1969—71; recreational therapist Jewish Child Care Assn., Pleasantville, NY, 1971—73; coord., instl. svcs. Greer Children's Svcs., Millbrook, NY, 1977—82; supr., social work Vassar Hosp., Poughkeepsie, NY, 1982—84; chief psychiat. social worker Westchester County Dept. Health, White Plains, NY, 1982—92; supr., psychiat. social work Westchester County Mobil Crisis Team, Valhalla, NY, 1992—94, Westchester County Med. Ctr., Valhalla, NY, 1994—95; psychotherapist pvt. practice, White Plains, NY, 1995—97; cons., writer. Contbr. articles to profl. jours. Named Commonwealth fellow, Mass., 1974, Employee of Month, Westchester County, 1987. Avocations: singing, music. Home: 250 Mamaroneck Ave White Plains NY 10605 Office Phone: 646-258-5964.

FLAUM, JOEL MARTIN, federal judge; b. Hudson, NY, Nov. 26, 1936; s. Louis and Sally (Berger) Flaum; m. Delilah Brummet, June 4, 1989. BA, Union Coll., Schenectady, 1958; JD, Northwestern U., 1963, LLM, 1964; LLD, John Marshall Law Sch., 2002. Bar: Ill. 1963. Asst. state's atty. Cook County, Ill., 1965—69, 1st asst. atty. gen. Ill., 1969—72; 1st asst. U.S. atty. Chgo., 1972—75; judge U.S. Dist. Ct. (no. dist.) Ill., Chgo., 1975—83, U.S. Ct. Appeals (7th cir.), 1983—, chief judge, 2000—. Mem. Ill. Law Enforcement Commn., 1970—72; cons. U.S. Dept. Justice, Law Enforcement Assistance Adminstrn., 1970—71; lectr. DePaul U. Coll. Law, 1987—88; adj. prof. Northwestern U. Sch. Law, 1993—2000. Mem.: Northwestern U. Law Rev., 1962—63; contbr. articles to legal jours. Mem. vis. com. U. Chgo. Law Sch., 1983—86; law bd. Northwestern U. Sch. Law, 1983—; mem. adv. com. USCG Acad., 1990—93. Lt. comdr. JACG USNR, 1981—92. Fellow Ford Found., 1963—64. Fellow: Chgo. Bar Found. (licentiate), Am. Bar Found. (licentiate); mem.: FBA, ABA, Am. Judicature Soc., Navy-Marine Corps Ret. Judges Advs. Assn., Maritime Law Assn., Chgo. Bar Assn., Chgo. Inn of Ct., 7th Cir. Bar Assn., Ill. Bar Assn., Naval Res. Assn., Lawyers Club Chgo. Jewish. Office: US Ct Appeals 7th Ct 219 S Dearborn St Chicago IL 60604-1702 Office Phone: 312-435-5626.

FLAUM, MARSHALL ALLEN, television producer, writer, director; b. Bklyn. s. Mayer and Ethel (Lamkay) P.; m. Gita Faye Miller; children: Erica, Seth Baruch. BA, U. Iowa, 1948; DFA (hon.), So. Ill. U., Edwardsville, 1974. Story editor, writer, assoc. producer TV series for 20th Century, 1957-62; producer, writer, dir. TV spls. for Wolper Prodns., 1962-65; founder Flaum-Grinberg Prodns., 1966; v.p. Metromedia Producers Corp., 1968-76; pres. Marshall Flaum Prodns., Inc., 1976—. Prodr., writer, dir.: TV spls. Day of Infamy, 1963, Hollywood: The Great Stars, 1963, The Yanks Are Coming, 1964, Battle of Britain, 1964, Berlin: Kaiser to Kruschev, 1964, Let My People Go, 1965 (Ohio State award, George Foster Peabody award), Miss Goodall and the Wild Chimpanzees, 1966 (Edinburgh Festival award), Bogart, 1967 (Melbourne Festival award) Hollywood: The Selznick Years, 1969 (Silver Lion award Venice film Festival), The Time of Man, 1969 (Silver Hugo award Chgo. Internat. Festival), Yabba Dabba Doo! The Happy World of Hanna-Barbera, 1977, Bing Crosby: His Life and Legend, 1978 (Christopher award), Playboy's 25th Anniversary Celebration, 1979, A Bing Crosby Christmas...Like the Ones We Used to Know, 1979, Bob Hope's Texaco Star Theatre, Life's Most Embarrassing Moments, 1984, Portrait of Dorothy Stratten, 1985, A Yabba Dabba Doo Celebration, 50 Yrs. of Hanna Barbera, 1989, Arts and Entertainment's Ancient Mysteries, 1996, Celebrate the Century, 1998-99, The Desilu Story, 1999-2000; prodr., writer TV spls. Killy Le Champion, 1969; exec. prodr., co-writer: (TV series) Undersea World of Jacques Cousteau, 1970-76, Jane Goodall and The World of Animal Behavior, 1972-76, The Wild Dogs of Africa, 1973 (Emmy award best documentary, Chgo. Internat. Festival Gold Hugo award), Baboons of Gombe, 1974, Hyena, 1975, Lions of Serengeti, 1976; prodr. Am. Film Inst. Salute to Bette Davis, 1977; prodr., co-writer (with others): TV spls. Ripley's Believe It or Not, 1982, Bob Hope's Who Makes the World Laugh, 1983. Recipient Emmy award as best documentary for A Sound of Dolphins, 1972, The Unsinkable Sea Otter, 1972, George Foster Peabody award for TV spls. for Miss Goodall and The Wild Chimpanzees, 1966, Monte Carlo Internat. TV Festival Golden Nymph award for TV spl. The Yanks are Coming, 1964, Silver medal Atlanta Film Festival for Wild Dogs of Africa, 1973, Octopus, Octopus, 1972, Chgo. Internat. Film Festival Silver Hugo award for Tragedy of the Red Salmon, 1971, Oscar nomination sfor best documentary feature for The Yanks Are Coming, 1964, Let My People Go, 1966, Golden Globe nomination for The Fogotten Mermaids, 1972, Writers Guild of Am. nomination for The Time of Man, 1969, 16 Emmy award nominations. Mem. Writers Guild Am., Dirs. Guild Am., Acad. Motion Picture Arts and Scis., Acad. TV Arts and Scis. Address: 301 S Rodeo Dr Beverly Hills CA 90212-4206

FLAUM, SANDER ALLEN, advertising and marketing executive; b. Apr. 5, 1937; s. Joseph and Rose (Deutsch) F.; children: Pamela, Jonathon; m. Mechele Plotkin, Apr. 25, 1990. BA, Ohio State U., 1958; MBA, Fairleigh Dickinson U., 1970. Mktg. dir. Lederle Labs. divsn. Am. Cyanamid Co., Wayne, NJ, 1964-84; exec. v.p. Klemtner Advt., N.Y.C., 1984-88; chmn., CEO Robert A. Becker, Inc., N.Y.C., 1988-98, 1998—. Vice chmn. Euro RSCG, Healthcare; chmn. Fordham Grad. Sch. Bus., NYU Stern Sch. Bus. Author: The Shortest Road to Success, Focusing Is for Tough Guys, The Leader's Edge, There's a Little Consumer in Every M.D., Great Is Better than Good, Hocus Focus, Darwin 2000; Survival of Fastest, Focus on the Future Direction: Outward. Trustee Hollins Coll. Comms. Rsch. Inst.; bd. mem. Atrix Labs., Neopharm Corp. With U.S. Army, 1959—61. Mem. Am. Mktg. Assn. Avocations: running, golf. Office: Robertr A Becker Euro Rscg 75 9th Ave Frnt 2 New York NY 10011-7029

FLAVER, JOHN ANTHONY, retired music educator; b. Rome, NY, May 15, 1948; s. John F. and Conchetta M. Flaver; m. Lorraine M. Montalbano, Feb. 16, 1974; children: John A. Jr., Celia Claire. MusB, Temple U., 1970; MusM, Cath. U. Am., 1973. Music tchr. Vernon-Verona-Sherrill Ctrl. Schs., 1973—78, 1981—85, Fayetteville-Manlius (NY) Schs., 1978—80, Lafayette (NY) Ctrl. Schs., 1985—88, Westhill Ctrl. Schs., Syracuse, NY, 1988—2005; ret., 2005. Adj. instr. clarinet Le Moyne Coll.; music dir. Jr. Summerfame; pvt. instr. clarinet; vis. lectr. Ithaca Coll.; mem. U.S. Army Band, Washington, Syracuse Symphony Orch., Lake Placid Ctr. Orch.; presenter clarinet clinics. With U.S. Army, 1970—73. Recipient Citation of Excellence, Nat. Band Assn., Outstanding Instrumental Music Educator award, Syracuse Symphony Orch., 1996. Mem.: NY State Band Dirs. Assn., Onondaga County Music Educators Assn., NY State Sch. Music Assn. Avocation: swimming. Home: 208 DeForest Rd Syracuse NY 13214

FLAVIN, CHRISTOPHER, think-tank executive; b. Monterey, Calif. Grad. cum laude, Williams Coll. V.p. rsch. Worldwatch Inst., Washington, sr. v.p., pres., 2000—. Participant Earth Summit, Rio de Janeiro, 1992, Climate Change Conf., Kyoto, 1997, World Summit on Sustainable Devel., Johannesburg, 2002; founding mem. bd. dirs. Bus. Coun. for Sustainable Energy; spkr. in field. Author: Power Surge: Guide to the Coming Energy Revolution, 1994, Rising Sun, Gathering Winds: Policies to Stabilize the Climate and Strengthen Economies, 1997; contbr. articles to profl. jours. Mem.: NAS (bd. on energy and environ. sys.), Environ. and Energy Study Inst., Climate Inst. Office: Worldwatch Inst 1776 Massachusetts AVe NW Washington DC 20036-1904

FLAVIN, FRANCIS E., history professor; BS in Computer Sci., U. Mass.; MA in History, PhD in History, Ind. U. Faculty U. Tex., Dallas, 2002—05. Mem.: Western History Assn., Am. History Assn.

FLAWS, JAMES B., technology executive; B in Engring., Tufts U.; Masters degree, Dartmouth Coll. Fin. analyst internat. divsn. Corning (N.Y.) Inc., 1973-83, dir. fin. and adminstrn. for consumer products divsn., 1983-89, v.p. planning and bus. devel., 1989-92, v.p., CFO Corning Consumer Products Co., 1992-97, asst. treas., 1993—97, v.p., contr., fin., treas., 1997, sr v.p., treas., CFO, 1997—99, exec. v.p., CFO, 1999—2002, vice chmn., CFO, 2002—. Bd. dirs. Dow Corning Corp., Corning Mus. Glass. Bd. mem. United Way, bd. chmn., treas.; bd. dirs. Cmty. Found. Office: Corning Inc 1 Riverfront Plz Corning NY 14831-0002

FLAX, HERSCHEL, surgeon; b. Capetown, South Africa, Feb. 9, 1941; came to U.S., 1974; s. Alexander Elliah and Mary Freda (Pasvolsky) F.; m. Elana Yehudith Matzkin; children: Joshua, Daniel, Rachel, Alexander. MB ChB, U. Capetown, 1964; ChM, U. Capetown Med. Sch., 1974; MA, NYU, 1978. Diplomate Am. Bd. Surgery. Intern Groote Schuur Hosp., Cape Town, South Africa, 1965-66; surg. registrar U. Cambridge, London, Birmingham, Eng. and Cape Town, 1966-72; chief resident Albert Einstein Coll. of Medicine, Bronx, N.Y., 1974-75, attending surgeon, asst. clin. prof., 1975—, attending surgeon, 1975—, assoc. clin. prof. surgery, 1989-97, prof. clin. surgery, 1997—; attending surgeon, specializing in diseases of the breast Mt. Sinai Hosp., N.Y.C., 1999—. Contbr. articles to profl. jours. Recipient Frank Forman prize, Moffat Meml. prize, Sir Abe Bailey Travel Bursar, Paul Martini European prize, Bronte-Stewart Rsch. prize. Fellow ACS, Royal Coll. Surgeons (Eng.); mem. Med. Soc. State N.Y., N.Y. Surg. Soc., N.Y. Met. Breast Cancer Soc. Avocations: piano, photography, politics, travel, skiing. Office: 9 E 63rd St New York NY 10021 Office Phone: 212-755-3833. E-mail: hflax@hotmail.com.

FLAX, MARTIN HOWARD, pathologist, retired educator; b. N.Y.C., Jan. 19, 1928; s. Abraham and Sadie (Finkel) F.; m. Ann E. Brockway, June 26, 1955; children: Adam, Jonathan, Elizabeth. AB, Cornell U., 1946; AM, Columbia U., 1948, PhD, 1951; MD, U. Chgo., 1955; MS in Health Mgmt., MIT, 1979. Intern Mt. Sinai Hosp., N.Y.C., 1955-56; fellow pathology U. Chgo., 1956-57; chief biophysics br. Armed Forces Inst. Pathology, Washington, 1957-59; clin. fellow Mass. Gen. Hosp., Boston, 1959-61, asst. pathology, 1961-66; fellow pathology Harvard U. Med. Sch., 1959-61, instr. pathology, 1961-63, assoc. pathology, 1961-66, asst. prof., 1966-69; prof., chmn. pathology dept. Tufts U. Sch. Vet. Medicine, 1970-97, chmn. pathology dept., 1985-96; pathologist-in-chief New Eng. Med. Ctr. Hosp., Boston, 1970-97; emeritus prof. pathology Tufts U., 1998—. Cons. pathology B study sect. NIH, 1970-74. Vol. Peabody Mus. Anthropology and Ethnology, Cambridge, Mass., 1998-2005, George Eastman House, Rochester, N.Y., 2001-2005. Capt. M.C., USAF, 1957-59. Recipient Rsch. Career Devel. award NIH, 1966-69; Nat. Cancer Inst. fellow, 1959-61, Med. Found. fellow, 1963-65, Sloan fellow MIT, 1979. Mem.: Sigma Xi, Phi Beta Kappa. Home: 32 Gate House Rd Chestnut Hill MA 02467-1335 Personal E-mail: martinflax@earthlink.net.

FLAX, ROBERT LEONARD, lawyer; b. Richmond, Va., July 2, 1953; s. Herbert Bruce and Rhoda (Merrin) F.; m. Marilyn R. Lipsitz, June 13, 1999. BA, Antioch Coll., Balt., 1975; JD, U. Richmond, 1977. Assoc. Steingold & Steingold, Richmond, 1977; sole practice Richmond, 1977—. Mem. state adv. council Nat. Legal Svcs. Corp., 1982-85, 87—; bd. govs. gen. practice sect. Va. State Bar, 1988—. Mem. planning com. MOVE United Way, 1981-83; mem. Leadership Metro Richmond, 1984-85; chmn. 3d Dist. Young Dems., Richmond, 1980; pres. Richmond Young Dems., 1978-80; mem. state cen. com. Va. Dems., 1985—; v.p. Richmond Chamber Players, 1985—. Mem. Va. Bar Assn. (legal aid com. 1983—, chmn. 1986-87, bd. govs., chmn. gen. practice sec. 1992—, lawyer referal svc. com.), Va. State Bar (vice-chmn. gen. practice sect. 1991-92, chmn. legal aid com. 1984-85), Richmond Bar Assn. (exec. com., young lawyers com. 1983—, bankruptcy sect.), Va. Trial Lawyers Assn., Richmond Trial Lawyers Assn., Richmond Jaycees (bd. dirs. 1980-83), Richmond C. of C. (exec. com., small bus. com. 1981-83, legis. affairs com. 1987—). Lodges: B'nai Brith (pres. Richmond chpt. 1985-87, Most Outstanding Mem. 1987). Jewish. Avocations: bicycling, reading, performing arts. Home: 4814 W Franklin St Richmond VA 23226-1218 Office: 8 S Sheppard St Richmond VA 23221-3028

FLAY, BOBBY, food service executive; m. Stephanie March, 2005. Diploma, French Culinary Inst., 1984. Exec. chef Miracle Grill, N.Y.C., 1984—91; chef, ptnr. Mesa Grill, N.Y.C., 1991—; ptnr. Bolo, N.Y.C., 1993—, Mesa Grill Las Vegas, Caesar's Palace, 2004—. Celebrity judge Wickedly Perfect TV series, 2005. Author: (cookbook) Bold American Food, 1994 (IACP award for design, 1995), From My Kitchen to Your Table, 1998, Boy Meets Grill, 1999, Bobby Flay Cooks American, 2001, Bobby Flay's Grilling for Life: 75 Healthier Ideas for Big Flavor from the Fire, 2005; host (TV series) Grillin' & Chillin', The Main Ingredient, Hott Off the Grill. Named Rising Star Chef of Yr., James Beard Found., 1993; recipient Outstanding Graduate award, French Culinary Inst., 1993. Office: Mesa Grill 102 Fifth Ave New York NY 10011

FLAYHART, MARTIN ALBERT, lawyer; b. Williamsport, Pa., Mar. 1, 1950; s. William Henry and Naomi (Laux) F. BA with hons., U. Va., 1971; JD, U. Pa., 1974. Bar: Pa. 1974, U.S. Dist. Ct. (mid. dist.) Pa. 1976, U.S. Ct. Appeals (3rd cir.) 1985, U.S. Supreme Ct. 1986. Assoc. Smith & Williamson, Lock Haven, Pa., 1974-76; ptnr. Saxton & Flayhart, Lock Haven, 1977-83; dist. atty. Clinton County, Lock Haven, 1979; pvt. practice Jersey Shore, Pa., 1983-84; ptnr. Carpenter, Harris & Flayhart, Jersey Shore, 1984—. Lectr. Lock Haven U., 1981-85, 90, 2005, Lycoming Coll., Williamsport, Pa., 1993-94, State U. of Chernivtsi Law Sch., Ukraine, 1993. Pres. Jersey Shore Area C. of C., Pa., 1990, 2001-02; com. Lycoming County Dem. Party, 1988—. Mem. ABA, Lycoming County Bar Assn., Pa. Bar Assn., Rotary (pres. Lock Haven club 1991, Rotarian of Yr. 1990), Phi Beta Kappa. Methodist. Avocation: rare book collecting. Office: Carpenter Harris & Flayhart PO Box 505 128 S Main St Jersey Shore PA 17740-1810 Office Phone: 570-398-1071.

FLECHTNER, HARRY MARSHAL, law educator; b. Fostoria, Ohio, Apr. 8, 1951; s. August Marshall and Dorothy Mary (Reardon) F.; m. Joan Patricia Kammer, Aug. 5, 1978; children: Emily Lora, Andrew Robert. AB, Harvard U., 1973, AM, 1975, JD, 1981. Bar: D.C. 1981. Assoc. Wilmer Cutler and Pickering, Washington, 1981-84; asst. prof. law U. Pitts., 1984-88, assoc. prof. law, 1988-94, prof. law, 1994—. Faculty adviser Journal Law and Commerce Sch. Law U. Pitts., 1986—. Contbr. articles to profl. jours. Mem. ABA, Assn. Am. Law Schs., Am. Bankruptcy Inst. Office: U Pitts Sch of Law Pittsburgh PA 15260 Business E-Mail: flechtner@law.pitt.edu.

FLECK, ALBERT HENRY, JR., retired insurance agency executive; b. Jasper, Ind., Aug. 4, 1929; s. Albert J. and Emily M. (Hopf) F.; m. LaVern C. Sermersheim, Oct. 8, 1953 (dec. 1980); children: Steven L., Jeffery E., Patrick J., Gregory K., Lisa A., Christopher A., Douglas G. Grad. high sch., Jasper. With Jasper Turning Co., 1952-56; pres. A.H. Fleck Agy., Inc., Jasper, 1956-98; retired. Clk. cir. ct. Dubois County, Jasper, 1971-78; councilman County of Dubois, Jasper, 1982-94. With U.S. Army, 1948-52, Korea. Mem. K.C., Jasper Civitan (pres. 1972-74), Am. Legion, Ind. Guard Res. (capt. 1987—). Democrat. Roman Catholic. Home and Office: AH Fleck Agy Inc 309 E State Road 164 Jasper IN 47546-9305

FLECK, BELA, country musician; Albums Deviation, 1985, Bela Fleck and The Flecktones, 1989, Drive, Places, Flight of the Cosmic Hippo, 1991, UFO Tofu, 1992, Three Flew Over the Cuckoo's Nest, 1993, Tabula Rosa, 1994, Tales from the Acoustic Planet, 1995, Live Art, 1996, Left of Cool, 1998, Outbound, 2000, Perpetual Motion, 2001, Live at the Quick, 2002, Little World, 2003, 2004. Recipient Grammy award Best Country Instrumental Performance, 1996. Office: Warner Bros Records 20 Music Sq E Nashville TN 37203-4344*

FLECK, RAYMOND ANTHONY, JR., retired academic administrator; b. Bklyn., Mar. 9, 1927; s. Raymond Anthony and Dorothy (Canavan) F.; m. Dorothy Marie Rossow, Aug. 22, 1970; children: Andrew Jerome, Casey Thomas. Student, Manhattan Coll., 1946-48; BS, U. Notre Dame, 1951, PhD, 1954; student Ins. Coll. and Univ. Adminstrs., Harvard U., 1959. Brother of Holy Cross, 1949-70. Prof. chemistry St. Edward's U., 1954-69, pres., 1957-69; assoc. research chemist dept. environ. toxicology U. Calif. at Davis, 1969-72; pres. Marygrove Coll., Detroit, 1972-79; acting dir. Food Protection and Toxicology Center, U. Calif., Davis, 1979-83; dir. research Calif. State Poly. U., Pomona, 1983-95; assoc. Anver Biosci. Design, Inc., Sierra Madre, Calif., 1995—. Cons. EPA, La. Bd. Regents, U. Wis., Eau Claire, NSF; dir. Monterey Basin Pilot Monitoring Project, 1971-72; pres. Our Lady of the Assumption Conf., St. Vincent de Paul Soc., Claremont, Calif., 1999-05. Vice pres., bd. dirs. Harmony Village Home Corp. N.W., Detroit, 1977-79. Served with USN, 1945-46. NSF fellow, 1952, 1969; recipient U. Notre Dame Centennial of Sci. medal, 1965; sci. bldg. at St. Edward's U. named Fleck Hall. Home: 4273 Guava St La Verne CA 91750-3010 E-mail: raymonda2@aol.com.

FLEDER, ROBERT CHARLES, lawyer; b. New London, Conn., Aug. 31, 1948; s. Samuel and Pearl (Perelman) F.; m. Laura Louise Waltuch, Dec. 19, 1971; children: Daniel, Anna, Michael. BA, Columbia U., 1969, MA, 1971, LLB, 1973. Bar: N.J. 1974, N.Y. 1977, D.C. 1991. Law clk. to presiding justice N.J. Supreme Ct., Trenton, 1973-74; assoc. Stryker, Tams & Dill, Newark, 1974-75, Kramer, Levin, Nessen, et al, N.Y.C., 1976-80, ptnr., 1981-86, Paul, Weiss, Rifkind, Wharton & Garrison, N.Y.C., 1986—. Contbr. articles to profl. jours. Mem. ABA, N.Y. State Bar Assn. Office: Paul Weiss Rifkind Wharton & Garrison Rm 202 1285 Avenue Of The Americas Fl 21 New York NY 10019-6028

FLEEGER, DAVID CLARK, colon and rectal surgeon; b. Neubrucke, Germany, July 11, 1959; s. James Elliott and Madge Ellen (Iseminger) F.; m. Jamie Greenstreet, Aug. 16, 1984; 1 child, Lauren Ann. BS, Baylor U., 1981; MD, Tex. A&M U., 1985. Diplomate Am. Bd. Surgery, Am. Bd. Colon and Rectal Surgeons. Resident in gen. surgery Mayo Clinic, Rochester, Minn., 1985-90; fellow in colon and rectal surgery La. State U., Shreveport, 1990-91; ptnr. Austin (Tex.) Colon and Rectal Clinic, 1991—; chief surgery Columbia St. Davids. S. Hosp., 1996-97; chair Cancer Ctr. St. Davids Med. Ctr., 1997—, co-chair Pain Mgmt. Ctr., 2000—, chair dept. surgery, 2004—. Fellow ACS, Am. Soc. Colon and Rectal Surgeons (socioecons. com. 2000-02), Tex. Soc. Colon and Rectal Surgeons (pres-elect 1994, pres. 1994-95); mem. AMA (alt. mem. ho. of dels.), Am. Soc. Gastrointestinal Endoscopy Surgeons, Soc. Am. Gastrointestinal Endoscopy, Tex. Med. Assn. (chmn. young physician sect., mem. governing coun. 1992-99, chmn. com. on physician distbn. 1999-2002). Avocations: fishing, hunting, photography, kayaking. Office: 4208 Medical Pkwy Austin TX 78756-3310 Office Phone: 512-452-9551.

FLEENER, TERRY NOEL, marketing professional; b. Ottumwa, Iowa, May 26, 1939; s. Lowell F. and Freda B. (Sparks) F.; m. Jane A. Bacon, Dec. 9, 1969; children: Clinton Todd, Clayton Scott. BSME, U. Iowa, 1963. Engr. Bendix Corp., Davenport, Iowa, 1963-67, Ball Aerospace, Boulder, Colo., 1967-74, bus. mgr., 1974-78; v.p. gen. mgr. Entropy Ltd., Boulder, 1978-80; pres. Energy Bank, Inc., Golden, Colo., 1980-82; program mgr. Ball Aerospace, Boulder, 1982-84, dir. mktg., 1984-99; mng. gen. ptnr. The Montane Group LLLP, 1999—. Pres. U.S. Rugby Assn., Colorado Springs, 1987-89, Pam-Am. Rugby Assn., Miami, 1991-93, 97-98. Mem. ASME, AIAA, Am. Astron. Soc., Cryogenic Soc. Am. Office: The Montane Group 2122 Montane Dr E Golden CO 80401-9126

FLEENOR, GENEVA LUCILLE, retired elementary school educator; b. Kokomo, Ind., Mar. 25, 1923; d. Howard Burton and Jennie Pauline (Henderson) Benjamin; m. Gerald Howard Fleenor, Mar. 27, 1945; children: Sherri Lynn Fleenor Sebring, Roger Lee, Regina(dec.). BA in Edn., Ariz. State U., 1962, MA in Edn., 1964. Cert. edn. Ariz., 1962. Weather-map plotter U.S. Weather Bur., Washington, 1944—45; elem. sch. tchr. Roosevelt Dist.,

Phoenix, 1962—85; ret., 1985. Co-author (and co-editor): How Arizona Came to Life, 1968 (Thank You award, 1972). Vol. Women's Help of Ariz., Phoenix, Fountain of Hope, Phoenix; tchr., com. mem. Forest Lakes (Ariz.) Cmty. Ch., cmty. bible study leader. Recipient Golden Rule Cert., State of Ariz., 2003. Conservative. Home: 2234 W Vista Ave Apt 11 Phoenix AZ 85021-6925

FLEER, KEITH GEORGE, lawyer, retired film company executive; b. Feb. 28, 1943; s. Samuel Robert and Sophia M. (Scherer) Fleer. BA in Govt., Am. U., 1964, JD, 1967. Bar: N.Y. 1968, D.C. 1968, Calif. 1976. Asst. dir. athletics Fordham U., 1967—68; assoc. Gettinger, Gettinger & Manheimer, N.Y.C., 1968—72, Kaye, Scholer, Fierman, Hays & Handler, N.Y.C., 1972—75; sr. counsel Avco-Embassy Pictures, Hollywood, Calif., 1976; assoc. Schiff, Hirsch & Schreiber, Beverly Hills, Calif., 1977; sr. v.p. bus. and legal affairs Melvin Simon Prodn., Inc., Beverly Hills, 1978—81; exec. v.p. Simon, Reeves, Landsburg Prodns., Beverly Hills, 1982—84; v.p. bus. affairs Warner Bros., Beverly Hills, 1984—88; ptnr. Denton Hall Burgin and Warrens, Beverly Hills, 1987—88, Sinclair Tenenbaum & Emanuel & Fleer, Beverly Hills, 1989—98, Loeb & Loeb, Century City, Calif., 1998—. Guest lectr. U. West LA Law Sch., 1979—80; legis. counsel N.Y. State Assemblyman, 1969—70; adj. prof. Law Ctr. U. So. Calif., 1995. Bus. editor: Am. U. Law Rev., 1966—67. Bd. trustees Am. U., 0920—1997. Recipient Bruce Hughes award, Am. U., 1964, Alumni award, Am. U. Law Sch., 1967, Stafford H. Cassell award, 1979. Mem.: ABA, Acad. Motion Picture Arts and Scis., LA Copyright Soc. (trustee 1983—90, pres. 1988—89), Beverly Hills (Calif.) Bar Assn. Office: 10100 Santa Monica Blvd Los Angeles CA 90010

FLEETWOOD, CLIFFORD GENE, recording industry executive, publishing executive, lawyer; b. Tulsa, Okla., Mar. 25, 1961; PhD in Philosophy, So. Calif. Coll., Chula Vista, 1996; J.S.D. in Law, Northwestern Internat. U., 2005. Chmn., CEO Bluegrass and Cadillacs Record and Pub. Corp., Nashville, 1992—; pres., bur. chief Rio Grande Pub. S.W. Inc., Santa Fe, 2001—. Mem. physician's adv. bd. Nat. Rep. Congl. Com., Washington, 2003—, mem. bus. adv. coun., 2003—; controlling shareholder Bluegrass and Cadillacs Record and Pub. Corp., Fleetwood Master Art Works Co., Sir Lloyd of London Films Co., Coupe DeVille Broadcasting Co., Emerson C. Winchester and Co., Rio Grand Pub. S.W., 2006. Author, composer, lawyer, philosopher: lit. works The Presidential Collection, for President George W. Bush, Jr. & Family (placed in Smithsonian Mus., 2004); author: The Vatican Prayers and Passages, for: Pope John Paul II, 2003 (letter of acceptance from Pope John Paul II, 2003), Royal Family Collection for Queen Elizabeth and The Royal Family, 2005, The Tri-Angular Equation, 2005; composer: 207 catalogued top 40 country music hit songs; record prodr.: The Ballad of Jacob Wright, 1990, Hank Sr. Died With the Blues, 1990, Highways, Bluegrass & Cadillacs, 1990, The Indian and the Cowboy, 1990, From Texas to Dixie, 1990, Big Timber Cowboy, 1992, Dancin' Across Texas, 1993, Southern Style, 1993, Calling All Hearts, 1994, The Blues Cadillac, 2000, Watermelon Mountain, 2001, Your Quarter Bar and Griddle, 2003, 58 Freight Shaker, 2005. Mem. Nat. Rep. Party, Washington, 2002—. With US Army and USCG, 1981—87. Named Businessman of Yr., Nat. Rep. Congl. Com., 2003, Rep. of Yr., 2003; named to Colo. Country Music Hall of Fame, 1999; recipient Congl. Order of Merits, US Congress and US Pres. George W. Bush, Jr., 2003, 2005. Mem.: ASCAP, ABA (assoc.), United Press Internat., Pub. Rels. News Wire, Associated Press Mng. Editors, Music Broadcast Inc., Am. Conductors and Composers, Am. Soc. Law Medicine, and Ethics, Rep. Nat. Lawyers Assn., Nat. Lawyer's Assn., Internat. Law Assn., Internat. Bar Assn., Country Music Assn. Conservative. Avocations: walking, chess, writing, shipwatching, music. Office: Clifford Fleetwood Cos Inc PO Box 9022 Fort Lauderdale FL 33310 Office Phone: 1-800-675-3259, 954-567-8447. Business E-Mail: drcliffordgfleetwoodphd@lawyer.com.

FLEETWOOD, DANIEL MARK, physicist; b. Seymour, Ind., Aug. 3, 1958; s. Louis Edmond and Dorothy Ruth (Otte) F.; m. Betsy Eileen Fox, June 9, 1984; children: Aaron Daniel, Zachary Evan, Nathan Bartholomew. BS in Physics and Math., Purdue U., 1980, MS in Physics, 1981, PhD in Physics, 1984. Sr. tech. staff Sandia Nat. Labs., Albuquerque, N.M., 1984-90, disting. tech. staff, 1990—. Radiation hardness working group Defense Threat Reduction Agy., Alexandria, Va., 1987—; exec. com. Semiconductor Interface Specialists Conf., 1997—. Editor (special issues) IEEE Transactions on Nuclear Sci. jour., 1988-90, 96; contbr. papers to IEEE Nuclear and Space Radiation Effects Conf., 1985—, Hardened Electronics and Radiation Technology Conf., 1985-95. Recipient Lark-Horovitz award Purdue U. Physics Dept., W. Lafayette, Ind., 1984, R & D 100 award, 1997, Industry Week award, 1997, Discover Mag. award, 1998; Internat. Corr. Chess Master title, 1997. Fellow IEEE (vice-chmn publs. 1994-97); mem. Am. Phys. Soc., Phi Beta Kappa. Republican. Lutheran. Achievements include invention (with others) of a protonic nonvolatile memory chip; development of internat. stds. for predicting radiation effects on electronics in space; demonstrated dependence of low-frequency noise in metal-oxide-semiconductor devices and metals on defect densities; developed new terminology for border traps in microelectronics. Avocations: corr. chess, golf, investing. Office: Sandia Nat Labs PO Box 5800 Albuquerque NM 87185-0100

FLEETWOOD, M. FREILE, psychiatrist, educator; b. Valparaiso, Chile, Nov. 20, 1915; d. Alfonso Larrea and Berta (Cordovez) Freile; children: Harvey Blake, Francis Freile. MD, U. Chile, 1941; PhD, Pedagogic Inst., Santiago, Chile, 1947; MD, U. of State of N.Y., 1950. Instr. biochemistry to asst. in pub. emergencies U. Chile, Santiago, 1937-41, resident in neurology at neurol. clinic, 1941-42, head of rsch. lab. in psychiatry, 1944-48; resident in psychiatry Henry Phipps Clinic, John Hopkins U., Balt., 1942-44; provisional asst. in psychiatry to out-patient psychiatrist N.Y. Hosp., N.Y.C., 1948-61; attending psychiatrist Gracie Square Hosp., N.Y.C., 1961—; clin. asst. prof. psychiatry Cornell Univ., N.Y. Hosp., N.Y.C., 1970-88, emeritus status, 1988—. Instr. psychiatry, Payne Whitney Clinic, Cornell U., N.Y. Hosp., N.Y.C., 1950-63; cons. Family Svc. of Patterson, N.J., 1955-56, East Harlem Project Community Svc. Soc., N.Y.C., 1960-61, Manhattan Family Svc. Ctr. Community Svc. Soc., N.Y.C., 1960-61; asst. psychiatrist NYU, U. Hosp., Bellevue Med. Ctr., N.Y.C., 1954, psychiatrist 1954-55, and others. Contbr. articles to profl. publs. Recipient Rockefeller Found. grantee, 1942-43, 43-44, 44-45, Sagin Fund grantee, 1952-53, Squibb Fund grant, 1952-53. Mem. AAAS, Med. Soc. State and County of N.Y., Am. Med. Soc. on Alcoholism and Other Drug Dependencies, Am. Psychiat. Assn. (N.Y. county dist. br.), N.Y. Acad. Sci., Spanish Am. Med. Soc., Pan Am. Med. Soc., N.Y. Soc. for Adolescent Psychiatry, The N.Y. County Review Orgn., Women's Med. Assn. N.Y., Am. Med. Women's Assn. Office: PO Box 1955 28 Central Ave Amagansett NY 11930 Home: 5 West 86th St 12E New York NY 10024

FLEGLE, JIM L., lawyer; b. Paducah, Ky., Dec. 3, 1951; s. J.L. and Alice M. (Goodman) F.; m. Ophelia Flegle Camina; children: Lauren Tyler, Brittanie Len, James Brendan, Alexandra Carlisle, James Armand. BA, U. Ky., 1974; JD, U. Va., 1977. Bar: Tex. 1977, U.S. Dist. Ct. (so. dist.) Tex. 1977, U.S. Dist. Ct. (no. dist.) Tex. 1984, U.S. Dist. Ct. (we. dist.) Tex. 1988, U.S. Dist. Ct. (ea. dist.) Tex. 1989, U.S. Dist. Ct. Colo. 2002, U.S. Ct. Appeals (5th and 11th cirs.) 1981, U.S. Ct. Appeals (9th cir.) 1991, U.S. Ct. Appeals (7th cir.) 2004, U.S. Ct. Appeals (fed. cir.) 1994, U.S. Supreme Ct. 1994. Assoc. Bracewell & Patterson, Houston, 1977-83, ptnr., 1983-89, Dallas, 1989—2002, head Dallas office, 1992-98; adv. com. Bracewell & Patterson, Dallas, 1996-98; ptnr. Loewinsohn & Flegle, LLP, 2002—. Mem. Coll. of the State Bar of Tex., 2003-, criminal justice act vol. atty. panel U.S. Dist. Ct. (no. dist.) Tex. Vol. Houston Pro Bono Program; active Tex. Lawyers and Accts. for Arts, Houston, 1982-85, St. Paul's Chamber Music Soc.; mem. corp. campaign com. Dallas Mus. Art, 1994-95, Dallas Hist. Soc., 1991-92. Named Tex. Super Lawyer, Tex. Monthly Mag., 2004, 2005. Mem. ABA, Tex. Bar Assn. (grievance com. 1996-99, advt. rev. com. 2003-), Houston Bar Assn., Dallas Bar Assn., Houston Bar Found. (life fellow), Tex. Bar Found., Dallas Bar Found., Am. Bd. Trial Advocates (assoc.), Higginbotham Inn of Ct. (barrister), Raven Soc., Phi Beta Kappa, Omicron Delta Kappa, Sigma Nu. Methodist. Office: Loewinsohn & Flegle 18383 Preston Rd ste 100 Dallas TX 75252-5476 Office Phone: 214-572-1701. Business E-Mail: jimf@texasverdict.com.

FLEHARTY, MARY SUE, government agency administrator; b. Lincoln, Nebr., Aug. 13, 1962; d. Joseph Patrick and Joy Lou (Harnish) Huntley; m. Bradley Daryle Osborne, Mar. 26, 1983 (div. June 1988); m. Terry Lester Fleharty, Aug. 13, 1990. Student, Lincoln Sch. Commerce, 1996-97; student in sign lang., S.E. C.C., 2003—. Loan processor Am. Charter Fed. Savings and Loan, Lincoln, 1981-84; pub. broadcast exchange operator, sec. Lincoln Clinic, P.C., 1989-91; PBX operator, sec. Woods Park Med. Mgmt. Inc., Lincoln, 1991-93; data reporting asst. Harris Tech. Group, Lincoln, 1993; lease coord. Progressive Lease, Inc., Lincoln, 1993; PBX comms. specialist Branker Buick, Lincoln, 1994-97; sec., receptionist Reel Quick, Inc., Lincoln, 1997-98; case mgmt. sec. Madonna Rehab. Hosp., Lincoln, 1998-2000; exec. adminstrv. asst. Nebr. Heart Inst., Lincoln, 2000; office clk. Nebr. Dept. Labor, Lincoln, 2000—01, staff asst. I, 2001—. Sec. Lincoln Police Citizen Acad., 2001—03. Vol. ARC, Lincoln, 1977—, chmn., 1983-84, pres. Lincoln Fire Dept. Aux., 1993; cert. EMT; notary public Nebr., 1993. Named Outstanding Vol. ARC, 1985. Mem. NAFE, Benevolent Patriotic Order of Does (inner guard 1999, sec. 2000-01, chaplain 2000-02, flag bearer 2003—), Lancaster County Emergency Mgmt., Internat. Assn. Workforce Profls. (state chpt. pres. 2004—). Republican. Presbyterian. Avocations: church handbell ringing, shuffleboard, playing pool, bowling, gardening. Office: Nebr Dept Labor 550 S 16th St Lincoln NE 68508 Office Phone: 402-471-9962. Personal E-mail: msfleharty@earthlink.net.

FLEISCHAKER, DANIEL TEMPLETON, music educator, school system administrator; b. Louisville, Nov. 6, 1972; s. Jon Leopold Fleischaker and Jennifer Kay Wild; m. Rachael Lynn Wilds, Nov. 29, 1996; children: Emma Jane, Abram Mark. B in Music Edn., Coll. Wooster, 1994; postgrad., Kent State U., 2003—. Tchr. Bruce Mid. Sch., Louisville, 1994—96, Perry Local Schs., Massillon, Ohio, 1996—2002; tchr., dist. supr. Barberton (Ohio) City Schs., 2002—. Mem.: NEA, Ohio Music Edn. Assn. Avocations: music, reading, exercise. Home: 2530 Dogwood Dr NE Massillon OH 44646 Office: Barberton HS 555 Barber Rd Barberton OH 44203 Office Phone: 330-753-1084 5010.

FLEISCHAKER, GORDON HENRY, JR., pediatrician; b. Louisville, July 1, 1928; s. Gordon H. and Agnes Rose (Shatzen) F.; m. Barbara Lorraine Draeger, Aug. 15, 1954 (dec. 1998); children: Rachel, Judith, James. BA in Zoology, U. Louisville, 1949, MD, 1953. Diplomate Am. Bd. Pediatrics, 1960. Intern Univ. Hosp., Madison, Wis., 1953-54; resident in pediat. The Children's Hosps., Denver, 1956-58; fellow in pediatric rheumatology State U. Iowa, Iowa City, 1958-60; practice medicine specializing in pediat. Denver, 1960—. Assoc. clin. prof. pediat. U. Colo. Sch. Medicine, Denver, 1960—; mem. active med. staff The Children's Hosp., Denver. Served to capt. MC, USAF, 1953-56. Fellow Am. Acad. Pediat.; mem. AMA, AAAS, Colo. Med. Soc., Clear Creek Valley Med. Soc. (pres. 2002-03). Office: G H Fleischaker MD 4485 Wadsworth Blvd Wheat Ridge CO 80033-3318 Office Phone: 303-421-0194. E-mail: PeeDaTrx@aol.com.

FLEISCHAKER, MARC L., lawyer; b. Cin., Feb. 22, 1945; s. Leopold and Betty Jane (Spritz) F.; m. Phyllis S. Schmidt, June 16, 1969; children: Deborah, Julia. BS in Econs., Wharton Sch. U. Pa., 1967; JD, George Washington U., 1971. Bar: D.C. 1971, U.S. Dist. Ct. D.C. 1971, U.S. Supreme Ct. 1974, U.S. Ct. Mil. Appeals, U.S. Ct. Appeals D.C., U.S. Ct. Appeals (3d cir.) 1986, U.S. Ct. Appeals (4th, 5th and 11th cirs.). From assoc. to chmn. Arent Fox PLLC, Washington, 1971—, head environ. practice, 1978—2000, interim mng. ptnr., 1993, mng. ptnr., 2002, exec. com., 1983—, vice chmn., 1986—96, chmn., 1997—, non-profit initiative chair, 2004—. Exec. com. Washington Lawyers Com. for Civil Rights and Urban Affairs, 1989—, co-chmn., 1990-91, 99—, chair fin. com. 1992-93; bd. dirs. Coun. for Ct. Excellence, 2002—, Nat. Lawyers Com. Civil Rights Under Law, co-chmn. 1996-98; chmn. tech. com. legal sect. Am. Soc. Assn. Execs., 1995-96, bd. dirs. tchg., learning and tech. group; mentor U. Md. Sch. Pub. Affairs, 2002—. Contbr. articles to profl. jours. Mem. Fed. City Coun., 2000—; bd. dirs. The Appleseed Found., 2004, co-chair, 2005—. With USNG, 1969-75. Recipient Triangle award, Motor and Equipment Mfrs. Assn., 1976. Mem.: ABA, Fed. Bar Assn., Econ. Club Washington. Avocations: politics, competitive running, golf, tennis. Home: 6308 Broad Branch Rd Bethesda MD 20815-3342 Office: Arent Fox 1050 Connecticut Ave NW Washington DC 20036-5339 E-mail: fleischaker.marc@arentfox.com.

FLEISCHER, ALAN BERNARD, JR., dermatologist, educator; b. St. Louis, June 6, 1961; s. Alan Bernard and Eileen Barbara (Meyer) F.; m. Anne Bridget Fitzsimmons, Aug. 12, 1989; 1 child, Gerrit James. AB, U. Mo., 1982, MD, 1987. Diplomate Am. Bd. Dermatology, Nat. Bd. Med. Examiners. Internal medicine intern U. N.C., Chapel Hill, 1988, resident in dermatology, 1988-91; asst. prof. dermatology Bowman Gray Sch. Medicine, Winston-Salem, N.C., 1991-96, assoc. prof. dermatology, 1996—. Contbr. 2 chpts. to books, numerous articles to profl. jours. Med. Found. Teaching scholar, 1993. Mem. Am. Acad. Dermatology, So. Med. Assn., European Acad. Dermatology, Soc. for Investigative Dermatology, Internat. Dermatoepidemiology Assn. (bd. dirs. 1996—), Phi Beta Kappa, Sigma Xi, Alpha Omega Alpha. Office: Bowman Gray Sch Medicine Dept Dermatology Medical Center Blvd Winston Salem NC 27157-0001

FLEISCHER, ARTHUR, JR., lawyer; b. Hartford, Conn., Jan. 27, 1933; s. Arthur and Clare Lillian (Katzenstein) F.; m. Susan Abby Levin, July 6, 1958; children: Elizabeth, Katherine. BA, Yale U., 1953, LLB, 1958. Bar: NY 1959. Assoc. Strasser, Spiegelberg, Fried & Frank, NYC, 1958-61; legal asst. SEC, Washington, 1961-62, exec. asst. to chmn., 1962-64; assoc. Fried, Frank, Harris, Shriver & Jacobson, NYC, 1964-67, ptnr., 1967—, chmn., 1989-97, sr. ptnr., 1997—. Vis. lectr. law Columbia U., NYC, 1972-73; adviser to adv. com. Fed. Securities Code Project, Am. Law Inst., 1970-78; adviser to com. to consider new issue proposals Nat. Assn. Securities Dealers, 1973-75, mem. com. corp. financing, 1976-80; bd. dirs. Haleakala Inc. (The Kitchen), NY, 1987-2002; chmn. Ann. Inst. on Securities Regulation, Practising Law Inst., 1969-81; mem. indsl. issuers adv. com. SEC, 1972-73; mem. adv. com. corp. disclosure, 1976-77; bd. govs. Am. Stock Exch., 1977-83; legal adv. com, bd. dirs. NY Stock Exch., 1987-91 Co-author: Tender Offers, 1978, 6th edit., 2002, Board Games, 1988; co-editor: Annual Institute on Securities Regulation, 1970-81; contbr. articles to profl. jours. Mem. adv. coun. Ctr. for study of fin. instns. U. Pa.; trustee, mem. photography com. of Whitney Mus.; trustee Ind. Curators Internat., 1990-2002. Recipient Disting. Cmty. Svc. award Brandeis U., 1983, Judge Learned Hand Human Rels. award Am. Jewish Com., 1983, Harold P. Seligson award Practicing Law Inst., 1988, Judge Joseph W. Proskauer award UJA Fedn., 1994. Mem. ABA (mem. com on fed. regulation of securities regulation 1969—), Assn. Bar City NY (mem. spl. com. on lawyers role in securities transactions 1973-77, chmn. com. securities regulation 1972-74), Century Country Club (NYC). Office: Fried Frank Harris 1 New York Plz Fl 27 New York NY 10004-1980 Office Phone: 212-859-8120. Business E-Mail: fleisar@friedfrank.com.

FLEISCHER, ARTHUR C., medical educator, radiologist; b. Miami, Fla., May 15, 1952; s. Eugene and Lucille Fleischer; m. Leona Fleischer, May 25, 1975; children: Braden, Jared, Amy. BS in Biology, Emory U., 1973; MD, Med. Coll. Ga., 1976. Diplomate Am. Bd. Radiology. Prof. radiology Vanderbilt U. Med. Ctr., Nashville, 1987—, prof. ob-gyn., 1988—. Author: Principles and Practice of Ultrasonography in Ob/Gyn, 2004, 20 books on diagnostic sonography. Recipient Frank H. Bochum tchg. award for continuing med. edn., Vanderbilt U. Sch. Medicine, 2005. Fellow: Am. Inst. Ultrasound in Medicine (bd. govs. 1989—91, William Fry award 1999), Am. Coll. Radiology, Soc. Radiologists in Ultrasound (Larry Mack award 1999). Office: Vanderbilt Univ Med Ctr 1161 21st Ave S Nashville TN 37232

FLEISCHER, BARBARA JANE, organizational psychologist, consultant, researcher; b. NYC, July 10, 1948; d. Francis Joseph and Dolores (Pietri) F. AB cum laude, St. Louis U., 1970, MS, 1975, PhD, 1978. Lic. in indsl. and orgnl. psychology, La. Evaluation cons. Change in Liberal Edn., Washington, 1974-75; evaluation coord. St. Louis CETA office, 1975-76; dir. rsch. svcs. U. So. Miss. Sch. Nursing, Hattiesburg, 1976-78; orgnl. cons. South Miss. Home Health, Hattiesburg, 1979-80; dir. tng. Associated Cath. Charities, New Orleans, 1980-86; staff psychologist Wellness Inst., New Orleans, 1981-84; dir. Loyola U. Inst. for Ministry, 1995—2002. Cons. New Orleans, 1980—; assoc. prof. psychology and pastoral studies Loyola U., New Orleans. Author: Facilitating the Growth; contbr. articles to profl. jours. Grantee Nat. Ret. Tchrs. Assn.-Am. Assn. Ret. Persons Andrus Found., 1977, German Protestant Orphan Asylum, 1984, Lilly Found., 1991. Mem. APA, Am. Assn. Tng. Dirs. Roman Catholic. Avocations: music, church service, tennis. Office: Loyola U Inst for Ministry 6363 Saint Charles Ave # 67 New Orleans LA 70118-6195 Office Phone: 504-865-3728. Business E-Mail: fleishe@loyola.edu.

FLEISCHER, CARL AUGUST, law educator, consultant; b. Oslo, Aug. 26, 1936; s. Carl Johan and Marie (Mathiesen) F.; m. Eva Sylvia Funder, Sept. 15, 1967. Legal exam. laudabilis, U. Oslo, 1960, LLD, 1964. 1st sec. legal divsn. Ministry Fgn. Affairs, 1960-61; spl. cons. internat. law, 1962—. Lectr. law U. Oslo Faculty Law, 1961-69, prof., 1969—; adviser in internat. law Ministry Fgn. Affairs, 1986—; lectr., cons., mem. dels. internat. confs.; mem. Internat. Council Environ. Law, Norwegian Petroleum Soc., Norwegian Soc. Int. Law. Author: Jurisdiction on Fisheries, 1963, International Law, 7th edit., 2000, Constitutional Limitations, 1969, The Law on Building and Regulation of Property, 4th edit., 1983, Commentary to the Act of Expropriation and Compensation, 1974, The Economic Zone, 1976, The Law of Expropriation, 1978, Expropriation Procedure, 1980, Application and Interpretation of Judgements, 1981, Petroleum Law, 1983, La pêche (The Fisheries), 1985; co-author: Traitê du Nouveau Droit de la Mer, 1985, Compensation to Fisheries for Offshore Devel. Report, 1986, The New Regime of Maritime Fisheries, 1989, Environment and Resources Management, 1991, 99; co-author: A Handbook on the Law New of the Sea, 1991, Environmental Law, 1992-96, Planning Building Law, 1992, Land-lease Contracts, 1992, Sources of Law, 1995, Private Law Subjects, 1995, Studies in International Law, 1997, Sources of Law and Legal Method, 1998; contbr. articles to profl. jours. Home: 13 Thomas Heftyes Oslo 2 Norway Office: U Oslo Karl Johans gt 47 Oslo N-0162 Norway

FLEISCHER, EVERLY BORAH, academic administrator; b. Salt Lake City, June 5, 1936; s. Arthur and Clare (Katzenstein) F.; m. Harriet Eve Perlysky, June 14, 1959; children: Deborah, Adam Joseph. BS, Yale U., 1958, MS, 1959, PhD, 1961. Asst. prof., then assoc. prof. chemistry U. Chgo., 1961-69; prof. U. Calif., Irvine, 1970-80, dean phys. sci., 1975-80; prof. chemistry, dean Coll. Arts and Scis. U. Colo., Boulder, 1980-88; exec. vice chancellor, prof. chemistry U. Calif., Riverside, 1988-94; program exec. Am. Acad. Arts and Scis., Western Ctr., 1996; project dir. NSF Math. Sci. Partnership Focus! grant, 2003—. Author articles on metalloporphyrins, bioinorganic chemistry. NSF fellow, 1959-61; Alfred P. Sloan fellow, 1962-66; recipient Univ. Svc. award U. Calif., Irvine, 1980. Fellow AAAS; mem. Am. Chem. Soc., Sigma Xi, Alpha Chi Sigma. Home: 8 Tivoli Ct Newport Beach CA 92657-1533 Office: Univ California Dept Chemistry Irvine CA 92697-0001 E-mail: ebfleisc@chem.ps.uci.edu.

FLEISCHER, GERALD ALBERT, industrial engineer, educator; b. St. Louis, Jan. 7, 1933; s. Louis Saul and Rita Bashkow F.; m. Ann Ivancic, Dec. 17, 1960 (div. 1992); children: Laural Andrea, Adam Steven; m. Carolyn M. Boyum, Apr. 13, 1993. BS, St. Louis U., 1954; MS, U. Calif., Berkeley, 1959; PhD, Stanford U., Calif., 1962. Ops. analyst Consolidated Freightways, Menlo Park, Calif., 1959-60; instr. Stanford U., Calif., 1961-63; asst. prof. U. Mich., Ann Arbor, 1963-64; assoc. prof. engring. U. So. Calif., Los Angeles, 1964-71, prof. engring., 1971-97, univ. marshal, 1981-87, pres. faculty senate, 1986-87, prof. emeritus, 1998—. Author: Capital Allocation Theory, 1969, Risk and Uncertainty, 1975, Contingency Table Analysis, 1981, Engineering Economy, 1984, Introduction to Engineering Economy, 1994; contbr. to Handbook of Industrial Engineering, 2001, Industrial Engineering Handbook, 2001, Manufacturing Engineering Handbook, 2004. Served to lt. (j.g.) USN, 1954-57 Ford Found. fellow, 1960-62, Fulbright sr. lectr. Ecuador, 1974; fellow Inst. Advancement of Engring., 1976 Fellow Inst. Indsl. Engrs. (region v.p. 1984-86); mem. Am. Soc. Engring. Edn., Inst. Mgmt. Scis. Home: 4449 Chateau Dr Loveland CO 80538-1591 Business E-Mail: fleische@usc.edu.

FLEISCHER, HUGH WILLIAM, lawyer; b. Riverside, Calif., Aug. 14, 1938; s. Frederick John and Helen Marie (Bendorf) F.; m. Lanie Lacey, May 31, 1960; children: Robin, Erin, Ian. BA, Washington U., St. Louis, 1961; JD, U. Denver, 1964. Bar: Colo. 1964, U.S. Supreme Ct. 1970, Alaska, 1971, Mo. 1972. Atty. U.S. Dept. Justice, Washington, 1964-70, Alaska Legal Svcs. Corp., Anchorage, 1971-72; atty., adviser St. Louis Legal Aid Soc., 1972; ptnr. Hedland, Fleischer, Friedman, Brennan & Cooke, Anchorage, 1972-96. Co-dir., McGovern for Pres. campaign, Anchorage, 1972; pres. Bartlett Dem. Club, Anchorage, 1987; bd. dirs. Alaska Pub. Interest Group, 1974—, Out North Theater, 1988-94; pres. Anchorage Friends of Libr., 1989-92; bd. dirs. Alaskans Against the Dealth Penalty, 1993—, pres., 2003—. Avocations: reading, mountain climbing. Home: 1401 W 11th Ave Anchorage AK 99501-4248 Office: 310 K St Ste 200 Anchorage AK 99501-2064 Office Phone: 907-264-6635.

FLEISCHER, NORMAN SAMUEL, endocrinology administrator, medical educator; b. Springfield, Tenn., Jan. 24, 1936; s. Paul and Eva (Cohen) F.; m. Eva Lessy, Apr. 7, 1966; children: Deborah, Arlene. AB, Vanderbilt U., 1958, MD, 1961. Med. resident Albert Einstein Coll. of Medicine, Bronx, 1961-64; fellow in endocrinology Vanderbilt U., Nashville, 1964-66; dir. endocrinology Albert Einstein Coll. of Medicine, Bronx, 1976—, prof., 1978—; fellow in endocrinology Sch. of Medicine Vanderbilt U., Nashville, 1964-66; asst. prof. Coll. of Medicine Baylor U., Houston, 1966-71, assoc. prof. Sch. of Medicine, 1971-73; assoc. prof. Albert Einstein Coll. of Medicine, Bronx, 1973-77. Author chpts. in books; contbr. numerous articles to profl. jours. NIH grantee, 1966—. Fellow ACP; mem. Am. Fedn. Clin. Rsch., Am. Soc. Clin. Investigation, Am. Assn. Physicians, Am. Diabetes Assn., Endocrine Soc. Office: Yeshiva U Albert Einstein Coll Medicine 1300 Morris Park Ave Bronx NY 10461-1926

FLEISCHER, PETER, research geologist, oceanographer, educator; b. Coburg, Germany, Sept. 10, 1941; came to U.S., 1948; s. Heinrich Rudolf and Else Antonie (Kellersch) F.; m. Virginia Ann Thomas, Dec. 27, 1972. BA, U. Minn., 1963; PhD, U. So. Calif., 1970. Lectr. UCLA, 1970; postdoctoral fellow Marine Lab. Duke U., Beaufort, NC, 1970—71; asst. prof. Inst. Oceanography Old Dominion U., Norfolk, Va., 1971—78; geologist Naval Ocean R&D Activity Naval Oceanog./Atmospheric Rsch. Lab., Stennis Space Ctr., Miss., 1978—91; geologist Naval Rsch. Lab., Stennis Space Ctr., 1992—99; oceanographer Naval Oceanog. Office, Stennis Space Ctr., 1999—. Contbr. articles to profl. jours. Mem. Am. Assn. Petroleum Geologists, Soc. for Sedimentary Geology, Sigma Xi. Achievements include research in marine sediments, side scan sonar applications, geoacoustics, clay mineralogy, coastal oceanography, marine geology. Home: 971 E 2nd St Pass Christian MS 39571-4719 Office: Naval Oceanog Office Code N541 Stennis Space Center MS 39522-0001 Office Phone: 228-688-4215. E-mail: mudbug@sigmaxi.org, peter.fleischer@navy.mil.

FLEISCHER, ROBERT LOUIS, geology professor; b. Columbus, Ohio, July 8, 1930; s. Leo H. and Rosalie (Kahn) F.; m. Barbara L. Simons, June 10, 1954; children: Cathy Ann, Elizabeth Lee. AB, Harvard U., 1952, AM, 1953, PhD, 1956. Asst. prof. metallurgy MIT, 1956—60; physicist GE Rsch. Lab., Schenectady, 1960—92; rsch. prof. earth and environ. scis. Rensselaer Poly. Inst., Troy, NY, 1992—97; rsch. prof. geology Union Coll., Schenectady, 1997—. Sr. rsch. fellow physics Calif. Inst. Tech., 1965-66; adj. prof. physics and astronomy Rensselaer Poly. Inst., 1967-68; adj. prof. geol. sci. SUNY, Albany, 1982-87; cons. U.S. Geol. Survey, 1967-70, GE R&D Ctr., 1992-93; vis. scientist Nat. Ctr. for Atmospheric Rsch., NOAA, 1973-74; adj. prof. applied physics and mech. engring. Yale U., 1984; vis. scientist Materials Rsch. Soc., 1995. Author: Nuclear Tracks in Solids, 1975, Tracks to Innovation, 1998; co-editor: Intermetallic Compounds: Principles and Practice, vols. 1 and 2, 1995, vol. 3, 2002, Crystal Structures of Intermetallic Compounds, Basic Mechanical Properties of Intermetallic Compounds, Magnetic, Electrical and Optical Properties, and Applications of Intermetallic

Compounds, 2000, others; assoc. editor: 1st-4th Lunar Sci. Conf. Procs., 1970-73. Pres. Zoller Sch. PTA, 1968-69; mem. com. on candidates Schenectady Citizens Conv. for Sch. Bd., 1969-72, 82-83, chmn., 1969-70, 71-72, vice chmn. conv., 1977-78, chmn., 1978-79; mem. com. on priorities Schenectady Sch. Bd., 1974-75; bd. dirs. Schenectady Citizens' League, Freedom Forum, Inc; mem. Mayor's Com. on Transp. and Infrastructure, 2000. Recipient awards Indsl. Rsch., 1964, 65, 72, Spl. award Am. Nuc. Soc., 1964, Ernest O. Lawrence award AEC, 1971, Gen. Elec. Silver medallion Inventor's award, 1971, Gold Medallion Inventor's award, 1991, Golden Plate award Am. Acad. Achievement, 1972, Coolidge award Gen. Electric Rsch. and Devel. Ctr., 1972; NASA Exceptional Sci. Achievement award, 1973, spl. recognition, 1979; Disting. Career award Hudson-Mohawk chpt. AIME, 1991. Fellow: NAE, AAAS, Am. Soc. Metals, Health Physics Soc., Am. Geophys. Union, Am. Phys. Soc., Am. Acad. Arts and Scis.; mem.: Sigma Xi. Achievements include research in charged particle tracks in solids and their use in several fields, including cosmic ray and meteorite sci., geochronology, nuclear physics, radiobiology, environmental radon, personal radon dosimetry, Hiroshima neutron dosimetry, mineral exploration; defects in solids and their effects on mech. properties and superconducting properties, high temperature materials. Office: Union Coll Dept Geology Schenectady NY 12308 Office Phone: 518-388-6985. Business E-Mail: fleischr@union.edu.

FLEISCHER, ROLAND EDWARD, art history professor; b. Balt., Feb. 12, 1928; s. Edward Charles and Freda Anna (Denker) Fleischer; children: Edward Brandt, Frederick Roland. BA, Western Md. Coll., 1952; MA, Johns Hopkins U., 1954, PhD, 1964; DFA, Western Md. Coll., 1993. Instr. art history Johns Hopkins U., Balt., 1955—56; assoc. prof. U. Miami, Coral Gables, Fla., 1956—66; prof. art history George Washington U., 1966—74, Pa. State U., State College, 1974—96, prof. emeritus, 1996—. Cons. in field. Author (editor): The Age of Rembrandt, 1988; author: Ludolf de Jongh, 1989. Recipient Fulbright award, U.S. Govt., 1954—55; fellow, Pa. State U., 1989; scholar, 1990. Mem.: Found. Corelis Hofstate de Groot, Am. Assn. Netherlandic Studies, Coll. Art Assn., Moose. Democrat. Lutheran. Avocations: theater, acting, singing, fishing, travel. Home: 30355 Falcon Ln Big Pine Key FL 33043

FLEISCHER-RIEVESCHL, ELLEN, real estate agent; b. Cin., Dec. 15, 1945; d. Leo Simon and Janet Fleischer; m. George Rieveschl, Jr. BA in Mgmt. Econs., U. Cin., 1968. Pub. rels. Cin. Gas and Electric CO., 1968-71; campaign coord. Taft for Senate, Cin., 1971-72; new bus. devel. profl. Fifth Third Bank N.A., Cin., 1973-77; mktg. mgr. Williamsburg Mgmt., Cin., 1984-86; real estate agt. Sibcy Cline Realtors, Ft. Mitchell, Ky., 1986-91, Re/Max Affiliates, Ft. Mitchell, 1992—. Artist, Cin., 1978-85; mem. Kenton Boone Bd. Realtors, Northern Ky. Exhibitor watercolor abstracts various galleries in Cin., Naples and Coral Gables, Fla., N.Y.C.; author essay, Congl. Record, 1st pl. award, 1968. Mem. steering com. Emery Soc. Childrens Hosp.; bd. dirs. Carnegie Arts Ctr.; bd. dirs. family practice dept. U. Cinty Coll. of Musicians; bd. dirs. Cinti May Festival. Mem. Ky. Assn. Realtors, Nat. Assn. Realtors, Million Dollar Club, Friends of Covington, No. Ky. Heritage League, Cin. Art Mus., Cin. Symphony Com., Forward Quest of Covington, Omicron Delta Epsilon. Avocations: horseback riding, walking, swimming, travel, painting. Home: 100 Riverside Pl Covington KY 41011-1718

FLEISCHHAKER, KARIN, insurance agent; b. Warren, Minn., Oct. 8, 1947; d. William Valentine and Margaret Mary (Staloch) Gerszewski; 1 child, Tamara Lynn. Student Gen. Bus., U. Minn., St. Paul, 1988. CPCU Ins. Inst. Am., 1987. V.p. comml. mktg. Lee F. Murphy, Inc., St. Paul/ Mpls., 1979—84; account exec. Corroon & Black of Minn., Mpls., 1984—86; mktg. rep comml. lines The Drew Agy., Inc., St. Paul, 1986—89; producer, inst. First Am. Ins. Agy., Crookston, Minn., 1989—90; comml. mktg. rep. Hendrickson Agy/Bus. Ins. Brokers, Bloomington, Minn., 1990—94; large acct. mktg. rep. A and H Ins., Inc., Reno, 1995—98; comml. and personal lines agt. Farmers Ins. Group, Sparks, Nev., 1998—2000; comml. acct. mgr., contract specialist A and H Ins. Inc./ Western Ins. Co., Reno, 2000—04; welding robot operator Artic Cat Inc., Thief River Falls, Minn., 2004—. Comml. lines underwriter, artist, rschr. Minn. Mutual Fire and Casualty Co., Mpls., 1965—74; loss prevention engring. clk. The St. Paul Cos., 1974—75; dept. mgr. personal lines. Alexander & Alexander, St. Paul, 1975—79. Author (Pen Name Kathryn Weiss): (novels) The Dance of a Lifetime. Vol. Mpls. Aquatenniel, 1979—86; chmn, Crookston Ox Cart Days, 1989—90. Avocations: painting, sculpting. Office: Artic Cat Inc 601 Brooks Ave Thief River Falls MN 56701

FLEISCHMAN, AARON I., lawyer; b. Chgo., Jan. 8, 1939; BA with honors, Trinity Coll., Conn., 1960; LB, Harvard Law Sch., 1963. Bar: DC 1965. Sr. ptnr. Fleischman & Walsh LLP, 1976—, mng. ptnr.; dir. Citizen's Comm. Co. Dir. Citizen's Comm. Co., So. Union Co., 1990—2002. Named one of Top 200 Collectors, ARTnews Mag., 2004. Mem.: Fed. Comm. Bar Assn., DC Bar, Miami Art Mus. (trustee), Nat. Gallery Art, DC (trustee coun.), Whitney Mus. Am. Art (bd. mem.), Pi Gamma Mu, Phi Beta Kappa. Avocation: collector modern & contemporary art. Office: Fleischman & Walsh LLP Ste 600 1919 Pennsylvania Ave NW Washington DC 20006 Office Phone: 202-939-7940. Business E-Mail: afleischman@fw-law.com.*

FLEISCHMAN, ALBERT SIDNEY (SID FLEISCHMAN), writer; b. Bklyn., Mar. 16, 1920; s. Reuben and Sadie (Solomon) F.; m. Beth Elaine Taylor, Jan. 25, 1942; children— Jane, Paul, Anne. BA, San Diego State Coll., 1949. Newspaper reporter San Diego Daily Jour., 1949-50; freelance screenwriter. Lectr. fiction writing UCLA. Author: (children's books) Mr. Mysterious & Company, 1962, By the Great Horn Spoon!, 1963, The Ghost in the Noonday Sun, 1965, Chancy and the Grand Rascal, 1966, McBroom and the Great Race, 1970, Longbeard the Wizard, 1970, Jingo Django, 1971, Kate's Secret Riddle Book, 1977, Me and the Man on the Moon-Eyed Horse, 1977, Jim Bridger's Alarm Clock and Other Tall Tales, 1978, Humbug Mountain, 1978, McBroom and the Beanstalk, 1978, The Hey Hey Man, 1979, McBroom and the Great Race, 1980, The Bloodhound Gang in the Case of the Cackling Ghost, 1981, The Bloodhound Gang in the Case of the Flying Clock, 1981, The Bloodhound Gang in the Case of the Princess Tomorrow, 1981, The Bloodhound Gang in the Case of the Secret Message, 1981, The Bloodhound Gang in the Case of the 264-Pound Burglar, 1982, McBroom's Zoo, 1982, McBroom's Ear, 1982, McBroom and the Big Wind, 1982, The Bloodhound Gang's Secret Code Book, 1983, McBroom's Almanac, 1984, The Whipping Boy, 1986 (John Newbery medal 1987), The Scarebird, 1988, The Midnight Horse, 1990, Jim Ugly, 1992, Here Comes McBroom, 1992, McBroom's Wonderful One-Acre Farm, 1992, The 13th Floor, 1995, The Abracadabra Kid, A Writer's Life, 1996, Mr. Mysterious & Company, 1997, Chancy and the Grand Rascal, 1997, The Ghost on Saturday Night, 1997, Bandit's Moon, 1998, McBroom's Ghost, 1998, McBroom Tells the Truth, 1998, McBroom the Rainmaker, 1999, McBroom Tells a Lie, 1999, A Carnival of Animals, 2000, Bo and Mzzz Mad, 2001, Disappearing Act, 2003, The Giant Rat of Sumatra, 2005; (screenplays) Blood Alley, 1955, Goodbye, My Lady, 1956, Lafayette Escadrille, 1958, The Deadly Companions, 1973, Scalawag, 1973, Prince Brat and the Whipping Boy, 1995. Served with USNR, 1941-45. Recipient Spur award Western Writers Am., Commonwealth Club award, Lewis Carrol Shelf award, Mark Twain award, Calif. Young Reader award, John and Patricia Beatty award. Mem. Writers Guild Am., Authors Guild, Soc. Children's Book Writers. Democrat. Jewish. Office: care Greenwillow Books 1350 Avenue Of The Americas New York NY 10019-4702

FLEISCHMAN, BARBARA GREENBERG, public relations consultant; b. Detroit, Mar. 20, 1924; d. Samuel J. and Theresa (Keil) Greenberg; m. Lawrence A. Fleischman, Dec. 18, 1948; children: Rebecca, Arthur, Martha. BA, U. Mich., 1944. Tchr. Detroit Pub. Schs., 1944-45; psychoanalyst's sec., 1947-49; sec. Greenberg Ins. Agy., 1947-49; customer/pub. rels. cons. Kennedy Galleries, N.Y.C., 1976—. Bd. dirs. Detroit Artists Market, 1958-66, Planned Parenthood, N.Y.C., 1970-80, Craft Coun., 1980-83, Friends of Channel 13, 1968-80, pres., N.Y.C., 1975-79, chmn. auction, 1975, trustee, 1975-84; mem. women's com. Detroit Inst. Arts, 1957-66; pres. Friends of N.Y. Pub. Libr., 1979-84, trustee, 1980—, v.p., bd., 1987-2002; trustee The Acting Co., 1986-89, pres., 1988-89; mem. gov. bd. Off the Record Luncheons, Fgn. Policy Assn., 1978-85; assoc. prodr. Channel 13 Auction, 1978-80; trustee Mus. TV and Radio, 1988-92, Archives of Am. Art, 1997—, caryatids chmn., 1998-2003; vis. com. Am. Wing, Met. Mus., 1998—; commr. Art Commn. of the City of N.Y., 1995-98; hon. patron Brit. Mus., 1996—, Caryatids com., pres., 1998—2003, chmn.; v.p. Archives of Am. Art, pres.; mem. trustees com. Libr. Mus. Modern Art, 1998—; pres. Archives of Am. Art, 1998—; mem. Coun. Am. Mus. Nat. History, 1999—; mem. devel. trust Brit. Mus., 1999—2003; treas. Assocs. of Art Commn., 1999—; trustee The J. Paul Getty Museum, 2000—. Mem. Cosmopolitan Club. Office: 870 United Nations Plz New York NY 10017 E-mail: bgf324@aol.com.

FLEISCHMAN, EDWARD HIRSH, lawyer, consultant; b. Cambridge, Mass., June 25, 1932; s. Louis Isaac and Jean (Grossman) F.; m. Joan Barbara Walden, Dec. 27, 1953 (dec. 1993), m. Judy Vernon, Sept. 27, 1998. BA, Harvard U.; LLB, Columbia U., 1959. Bar: N.Y. 1959, U.S. Supreme Ct. 1980. Assoc. Beekman & Bogue, N.Y.C., 1959-67, ptnr., 1968-86; commr. SEC, Washington, 1986-92; ptnr. Rosenman & Colin, 1992-94; sr. counsel Linklaters, N.Y.C., 1994—. Bd. dirs. Soundview Tech. Group, Inc. (formerly Wit Capital Corp.), 1998—2003; bd. govs. Security Traders Assn., 1997—2000; chmn. exec. com. Corps., Secs. and AntiTrust Practice Group. Federalist Soc., 2004—. Served with U.S. Army, 1952-55. Mem.: ABA (chmn. bus. law subcom. rule 144 1970—72, subcom. broker-dealer matters 1973—78, subcom. model simplified indenture 1980—83, adminstrv. law com. on securities, commodities and exchs. 1981—84, bus. law com. on devels. in bus. financing 1987—91, com. on counsel responsibility 1995—99, internat. law com. on internat. securities transactions 1999—2002), Internat. Law Assn. (chmn. com. on internat. securities regulation 1998—), Internat. Bar Assn., Am. Soc. Corp. Secs., Am. Coll. Investment Counsel (pres. 1990—91), Am. Law Inst. Republican. Jewish. Office: Linklaters 1345 6th Ave New York NY 10105-0302 Home: 897 Franklin Lake Rd Franklin Lakes NJ 07417-2115 Office Phone: 212-424-9011. Business E-Mail: edward.fleischman@linklaters.com, edward@fleischman.org.

FLEISCHMAN, GARY FRANKLIN, acupuncturist; s. Edward Norman and Lillian Ruth Fleischman; 1 child, Wayne. MD in Podiatry, Ohio Coll. of Podiatric Medicine, 1966; OMD, China Inst. of Acupuncture, 1998. Bd. cert. acupuncturist Conn. Resident St. Lukes Hosp. and Children's Med. Ctr., Phila., 1966—67; position in pathology Mt. Sinai Hosp., Hartford, Conn., 1967—68; pvt.practice podiatric medicine and surgery, 1968—72; instr. So. Conn. State U., New Haven, 1985—, Quinnipiac U., Hamden, Conn., 1996—97; clin. tng. Guangdong Provincial Hosp. of Traditional Chinese Medicine, 1998. Author: Acupuncture: Everything You Ever Wanted To Know, 1998. Recipient Cert. of Appreciation award, Conn. Student Nurses Assn., 1999. Mem.: Am. Med. Writers Assn., Connection for Health Network (pres. 1997—2000). Office: Acupuncture Health Svcs New Haven 116 Anthony St New Haven CT 06515

FLEISCHMAN, JOSEPH JACOB, lawyer; b. Jersey City, Mar. 10, 1946; s. Benjamin Emanuel and Esther (Robfogel) F.; m. Gloria Damast, May 31, 1975; children: Michael, Richard. BA with highest honors, Rutgers U., 1968; JD, Columbia U., 1972. Bar: N.J. 1972, U.S. Dist. Ct. N.J. 1972, U.S. Ct. Appeals (3d cir.) 1983, U.S. Ct. Appeals (9th cir.) 1986, U.S. Ct. Appeals (2d cir.) 1994, U.S. Supreme Ct. 1983. Assoc. Hannoch Weisman, Roseland, N.J., 1972-77, ptnr., 1977-99, Norris, McLaughlin & Marcus, P.A., Somerville, N.J., 1999—. Contbr. articles to legal publs. Mem. ABA, N.J. Bar Assn., Essex County Bar Assn., Phi Beta Kappa. Avocations: reading, golf. Home: 209 Lyncrest Rd Englewood Cliffs NJ 07632-2020 Office: Norris McLaughlin & Marcus PO Box 1018 Somerville NJ 08876-1018 Office Phone: 908-252-4265. Personal E-mail: jjfleisch@aol.com. Business E-Mail: jjfleischman@nmmlaw.com.

FLEISCHMAN, PAUL, children's author; BA, Univ. of N.Mex., 1977. Author: The Birthday Tree, 1979, The Half-a-Moon Inn, 1980 (Silver medal Commonwealth of Calif. 1980, Golden Kite honor book Soc. Children's Book Writers 1980), Graven Images: Three Stories, 1982 (Newbery honor book 1983), The Animal Hedge, 1983, Finzel the Farsighted, 1983, Path of the Pale Horse, 1983 (Golden Kite honor book Soc. Children's Book Writers 1983, Parents' Choice award Parents' Choice Found. 1983), Phoebe Danger, Detective, in the Case of the Two-Minute Cough, 1983, Coming-and-Going Men: Four Tales, 1985, I Am Phoenix: Poems for Two Voices, 1985, Rear-View Mirrors, 1986, Rondo in C, 1988, Joyful Noise: Poems for Two Voices, 1988 (John Newbery medal 1989), Saturnalia, 1990, Shadow Play, 1990, Time Train, 1991, The Borning Room, 1991, Townsend's Warbler, 1992, Copier Creations, 1993, Bull Run, 1993 (Scott O'Dell award), Dateline: Troy, 1996, A Fate Totally Worse than Death, 1997, Seedfolks, 1997, Whirligig, 1998, Weslandia, 1999 (Pen West Lit. award, Calif. Young Readers medal), Mind's Eye, 1999, Cannibal in the Mirror, 2000, Big Talk: Poems for Four Voices, 2000, Lost!: A Story in String, 2000, Seek, 2001, Sidewalk Circus, 2003, 04, Animal Hedge, 2003, Breakout, 2003 (Nat. Book award finalist), Zap, 2005. Office: Candlewick Press 2067 Mass Ave Cambridge MA 02140 also: PO Box 646 Aromas CA 95004 Business E-Mail: pf@redshift.com.

FLEISCHMAN, PAUL ROBERT, psychiatrist, writer; b. Newark, N.J., Aug. 4, 1945; s. Martin L. and Etta G. Fleischman; m. Susan K., June 15, 1974; 1 child, Forrest. BA, U. Chgo., 1967; MD, Albert Einstein Coll. Medicine, 1971. Diplomate Am. Bd. Psychiatry and Neurology. Seminar leader in psychiatry and religion Yale U., New Haven, 1981-87; pvt. practice psychiatry Amherst, Mass., 1975—. Keynote spkr. Highland Hosp., Asheville, NC, 1992, Albany Med. Coll., Coll. St. Rose, Albany Jewish Family Svcs., 1993, Values in Psychotherapy conf. Nashville Inst. Psychotherapy, 1995; 31st Williamson lectr. in religion and medicine U. Kans., 1995; cons. in psychiatry, Amherst, 1975—; lectr., spkr. U. Mass., Amherst, Hampshire Coll., Smith Coll., Amherst Coll., 1989—98, Med. Group Rounds Albany Med. Coll., 1990, Beth Israel, Boston, 1994; cons. Western Mass. Psychiat. Soc., 1994, Jaipur Med. Coll., India, 1994, Smith Coll. Chapel, 1995, Bombay Psychiat. Soc., India, 1996, Smith Sch. for Social Work, 1998, Antioch Coll., Seattle, 1998, U. Wash. Health Svc., 1998, N.W. Rehab. Facility, Seattle, 1998, Mich. Psychoanalytic Found., 1999, Vipassana in Prisons, 1999, Gujarati Sanagi South Mich., 1999, Vipassana, Addictions, Psychotherapy & Mental Health, 1999, U. Mass. Dept. Counseling, 1999, First Ch., Springfield, Mass., Unitarian Meeting, Amherst, Mass., Korf Found., N.Y.C., Johnson Meml. Hosp., Stafford Springs, Conn., 1999, Ctr. for Behavioral Health Holyoke Hosp., 1999, Biennial Jain Conf., Phila., 1999, Theosophical Soc., Seattle, 1999, Vancouver Pub. Libr., 1999, East Asian Studies, Wesleyan U., 2000, Barre Ctr. for Buddhist Studies, 2000, Medicine, Sci. and Spirtuality Conf., 2000, Brattleboro Retreat, 2001, MacAllister Coll., St. Paul, 2001, U.S. Psychiat. and Mental Health Congress, Boston, 2001, Dept. Religious Studies, McGill U., Montreal, 2001, CoPlanet Conf., Oaxaca, Mexico, 2002, Foros Univs., Oaxaca, Mexico, 2002, UNAM, Toluca, Mexico, 2002, Mex. City Hosp., 2002, Dharma Study Group, Mass., 2002, Wesleyan Coll., Conn., 2002, U. Mass. Sch. Nursing, Amherst, 2002, Evergreen State Coll., Olympia, Wash., 2002, U. Wash. Sch. Social Work, Seattle, 2002, U. Wash. Health Care Svcs., Seattle, 2002, Open Mind Forum, Mumbai, India, 2003, World Pres. Assn., Mumbai, 2004, Harvard U., 2004, Evergreen State Coll., Olympia, Wash., 2004, Smith Coll. Chapel, 2005, 2nd Congl. Ch., Greenfield, 2005, Jones Libr., Amherst; numerous others, 2005. Author: Therapeutic Action of Vipassana Meditation, 1986, The Experience of Impermanence, 1990, The Healing Spirit, 1990, Spiritual Aspects of Psychiatric Practice, 1993, Cultivating Inner Peace, 1997, 2d edit., 2004, Karma & Chaos, Collected and New Essays, 1999, Snowstorm in a Cabin in the Woods, 2001, Tapas, 2001, The Buddha Taught Nonviolence, Not Pacifism, 2002, Cultivating Inner Peace, rev. edit., 2004, You Can Never Speak Up Too Often, 2004; contbr. articles to profl. jours. Recipient Oskar Pfister award for important contbns. to spiritual and humanistic side of psychiatry Am. Psychiat. Assn., 1993. Mem. Phi Beta Kappa, Alpha Omega Alpha. Office: 1394 S East St Amherst MA 01002-3030

FLEISCHMAN, PHIL, radio news executive; b. Saxonburg, Pa., Jan. 8, 1965; Student, U. Pitts., 1984-86. News dir. WPIT, Pitts., 1988—92; prodr., editor Std. News, Washington, 1992—97, sr. editor, newsroom supr., religion editor; bur. chief SRN News, Washington, 1997—. Office: SRN News 1901 N Moore St Ste 201 Arlington VA 22209-1706 Business E-Mail: pfleisch@srnnews.com.

FLEISCHMANN, DENNIS C., lawyer; BA, Fordham U., 1971, JD, 1975. Mng. ptnr., mem. exec. com. Bryan Cave LLP, NYC. Office: Bryan Cave LLP 1290 Ave of the Americas New York NY 10104 Office Phone: 212-541-2000. E-mail: dcfleischmann@bryancave.com.

FLEISCHMANN, ERNEST MARTIN, performing arts association administrator; b. Frankfurt, Germany, Dec. 7, 1924; came to U.S., 1969; s. Gustav and Antonia (Koch) F.; children: Stephanie, Martin, Jessica. B of Commerce, U. Cape Town, South Africa, 1950, MusB, 1954; postgrad., South African Coll. Music, 1954-56; MusD (hon.), Cleve. Inst. Music, 1987. Gen mgr. London Symphony Orch., 1959-67; dir. Europe CBS Masterworks, 1967-69; exec. v.p., mng. dir. L.A. Philharm. Assn. and Hollywood Bowl, 1969-98; artistic cons. L.A. Philharm. Assn., 1998—; pres. Fleischmann Arts, Intl. Arts Mgmt. Cons. Svc., 1998—. Mem. French Govt. Commn. Reform of Paris Opera, 1967-68; steering com. U.S. nat. commn. UNESCO Conf. Future of Arts, 1975; artistic dir. Ojai Festival, 1998-2003. Debut as condr. Johannesburg (Republic of South Africa) Symphony Orch., 1942; asst. condr. South African Nat. Opera, 1948-51, Cape Town U. Opera, 1950-54; condr. South African Coll. Music Choir, 1950-52, Labia Grand Opera Co., Cape Town, 1953-55; music organizer Van Riebeeck Festival Cape Town, 1952; dir. music and drama Johannesburg Festival, 1956; contbr. to music publs. Decorated officier Ordre des Arts et Lettres (France), comdrs. cross Order of Merit (Germany), knight 1st class Order of the White Rose (Finland); recipient award of Merit, L.A. Jr. C. of C., John Steinway award, Friends of Music award, Disting. Arts Leadership award U. So. Calif., 1989, L.A. Honors award, L.A. Arts Coun., 1989, Live Music award Am. Fedn. Musicians Local 47, 1991, Disting. Authors/Artists award U. Judaism, 1994, Treasures of L.A. award, Ctrl. City Assn. L.A., 1996, Los Amigos de Los Angeles award, L.A. Conv. and Vis. Bur., 1996; honored Mayor and City Coun. as First Living Cultural Treasure of L.A., 1998, Gold Baton award Am. Symphony Orch. League, 1999. Mem. Assn. Calif. Symphony Orchs., L.A. Philharm. Assn. (bd. dirs. 1984—), Salzburg Seminar/Alberto Vilar Conf. on Orch. Mgmt. (co-chmn. 2002). Office: Fleischmann Arts 2225 Maravilla Dr Los Angeles CA 90068 Office Phone: 323-851-5822. Personal E-mail: artsernest@aol.com. Business E-Mail: efleischmann@laphil.org. *Progress in the arts involves taking risks. Safety and blandness go hand in hand and should be banished from the artistic experience: better to stick your neck out and fail than to err on the side of correctness and caution.*

FLEISCHMANN, JOHN, academic administrator; b. Miami, Fla., Sept. 24, 1946; s. George Adam and Mary Lucille Fleischmann; m. Valerie Lynne Smith, July 3, 1975; children: Bryanne Leigh, Kelley Lynne. BBA in Mgmt., Ga. State U., 1972, MPA, 1975, MBA in Mgmt., 1979; EdD in Higher Edn., U. Ga., 1990; diploma, U.S. Army Gen. Staff Coll., 1991. With Ga. State U., Atlanta, 1970-86, dir. personnel svcs., 1977-79, dept. mgr. bus. svcs., 1974-82, mgr. payroll and dispersements dept., 1982-86, asst. comptroller, 1986; dir. faculty rsch. and info. systems, dir. faculty pers. U. System of Ga., Atlanta, 1986-99; coll. adminstrv. officer Ga. State U., 1999—2004, chief adminstrv. officer Coll. Edn. Atlanta, 2004—; campus exec. offiver Ga. Campus -Phila. Coll. of Osreopathic Medicine, Gwinnett County, Ga., 2004—. Maj. adjutants gen. corps. U.S. Army Personnel Command, Alexandria, Va., 1979; adjutant 1036th Mil. Support Civil Def., Atlanta, 1979—. Contbr. articles to profl. jours. Mem. fin. com. St. John Neumann Cath. Ch., Lilburn, Ga., 1986-87; coach Mountain Pk. Athletic Asn., Gwinnett County, Ga., 1989—. With U.S. Army, 1967-68. Mem. Assn. for Instnl. Rsch., Foxmoor Community Club (community action chair Lilburn chpt. 1989—), Beta Kappa of Kappa Delta Pi. Roman Catholic. Avocations: horticulture, running, swimming, scuba diving, racquetball. Office: Ga State U Coll of Edn University Plz SE Atlanta GA 30303

FLEISCHMANN, MARC W., semiconductor company executive; MS in Bus. Engring., U. Karlsruhe, Germany. Various positions Hewlett-Packard Labs., 1993—98; sr. dir. software and corp. program mgr. Transmeta, 1998—2002; v.p., gen. mgr. media processor bus. unit Pixelworks, Inc., Tualatin, Oreg., 2002, sr. v.p., 2002—. Office: Pixelworks Inc Ste 300 8100 SW Nyberg Rd Tualatin OR 97062

FLEISCHMANN, PAUL, religious organization administrator, minister; b. June 20, 1946; s. Leonard and Viola (Tyler) F.; m. Antoinette Jordan, June 14, 1973; children: Todd Paul, Tyler Jonathan. BA, Seattle Pacific Coll., 1968; MDiv, Western Bapt. Sem., Portland, Oreg., 1975; postgrad., Internat. Christian Grad. U., San Bernardino, Calif. Ordained to ministry, Conservative Bapt. Assn., 1981. Youth pastor Ballard Bapt. Ch., Seattle, 1965-67; campus staff Seattle Youth for Christ, 1967-68; high sch. ministry staff Campus Crusade for Christ, various locations, 1968-88; pres. Nat. Network of Youth Ministries, San Diego, 1982—. Home missionary, 1968—; youth ministry cons., 1974—; officer Bd. Deacons, 1980—82, 1988—93; mem. Bd. Christian Edn., 1980—82; ch. planter, 1988—93; adj. prof. Christian edn. Western Bapt. Sem., Portland, Oreg., 1981—83; chmn. Youth Ministry Exec. Coun., 1992—, Atlanta 96 Youth Leaders Conf., 1993—96, Campus Alliance. Author: Where to Turn for Help in Youth Ministry, 1996; contbg. author: Working with Youth, 1982, Magnet Effect, 1995—, Reaching a Generation for Christ, 1997, exec. editor: Insight for Student Discipleship, 1979—83, Network Mag., 1983—; editor: Discipling the Young Person, 1985; contbr. articles to profl. jours. Dir. Continental Singers Choir and Orch., 1977, Nat. Conv. on High Sch. Discipleship, 1979-83; asst. dir. Youth Congress '85, Washington. Recipient Gold Medallion, Evang. Christian Pubrs. Assn., 1986. Baptist. Office: Nat Network of Youth Min 12335 World Trade Dr Ste 16 San Diego CA 92128-3791

FLEISCHMANN, THOMAS JOSEPH, lawyer; b. Saginaw, Mich., Oct. 6, 1947; s. Clarence W. and Catherine L. (Byrne) F.; m. Mary E. Walker, Dec. 29, 1973. BS, U. Dayton, 1969; JD, Boston U., 1972. Bar: Ohio, 1972, Mich., 1972, U.S. Dist. Ct. (ea. dist.) Mich. 1973, Ill. 1979, U.S. Ct. Appeals (6th and 7th cir.) 1980, U.S. Dist. Ct. (no. dist.) Ill. 1982, U.S. Supreme Ct. 1985. Asst. Prosecuting Atty., Jackson, Mich., 1972-73; atty. Adams, Goler & Boham, Jackson, Mich., 1973-75, Aymond, Sullivan & Schwartz, Jackson, Mich., 1975-78; spl. atty. criminal divsn. U.S. Dept. Justice, Chgo., 1978-80; ptnr. Rooks, Pitts & Poust, Chgo., 1980-85; atty., founding owner Gessler, Flynn, Fleischmann, Hughes & Socol, Ltd., Chgo., 1985-95; pvt. practice Chgo., 1995—. Lectr. Ill. Inst. Continuing Edn.; spl. teaching faculty, lectr. Jackson (Ill.) C.C., 1972-74. Bd. dirs. Fox River chpt. ARC, 1995—. Recipient Meritorious award U.S. Dept. Justice, 1979. Mem. ABA, Kane County Bar Assn., Abraham Lincoln Marovitz Inn of Ct. (founding officer, recording officer 1994-95). Office: 2580 Foxfield Rd Ste 101 Saint Charles IL 60174 Office Phone: 630-584-5555. E-mail: tjfleisch@aol.com.

FLEISHER, DAVID, research scientist, educator; b. Rochester, Ny, Oct. 1, 1944; s. Gerald and Eunice; m. Barbara Houle Stewart; children: Laurie, Lisa, Lucas, Cybil. BS, SUNY, Buffalo, 1967; MS, U. Rochester, 1977; PhD, U. Wisc., 1983. Registered Pharmacist NY. Pharmacist U. Rochester Hosp., NY, 1969—79; post doctoral fellow U. Mich., 1983—85, asst. prof., 1985—93, assoc. prof., 1993—. Cons. Pharm. Inst., 1985—, FDA, Rockville, Md., 1997; expert witness State Mich., 1999—. Co-editor: Pharmaceutical Research Journal, 1990—93; contbr. articles in field. Mem.: Am. Assn. Pharm. Scientists. Avocations: music, tennis. Office: U Mich 428 Church St Ann Arbor MI 48109 Business E-Mail: fleisher@umich.edu.

FLEISHER, ERIC WILFRID, retired foreign service officer; b. Washington, Jan. 31, 1926; s. Wilfrid and Greta Agda (Sundberg) F.; m. Elizabeth Fredrikson, Dec. 22, 1948 (div. 1974); children: Emily Susanne, Eric Torsten; m. Thale Gunneng, Aug. 5, 1974 (dec. Feb. 2000); 1 child, Arne Ericsson.

Cert., U. Stockholm, 1948; BA, George Washington U., 1950; PhD, U. Lund, Sweden, 1953. Orientation officer U.S. Displaced Persons Commn., French Zone, Germany, 1950-51; program and ops. officer Refugee Relief Dept. State, Washington, 1954-55, intelligence rsch. analyst, 1955-58; polit. officer Am. Embassy, Copenhagen, 1959-63; consul Faroe Islands, 1959-63; polit. counselor Helsinki, Finland, 1964—69; dep. country dir., then dir. Nordic countries Washington, 1969—73; press attache Am. Embassy, Stockholm, 1974—76; spl. asst. human rights and refugee affairs Washington, 1977-80; fgn. affairs cons., sr. cons., 1980—. Author: Viking Times to Modern, 1953; translator, editor: Scandinavia in Great Power Politics, 1905-1908, 1958; contbr. articles to various publs. 1st lt. U.S. Army, 1944-47, Tokyo. Mem. Am. Fgn. Svc. Assn., Diplomatic and Consular Officers Ret., Am. Scandinavian Found. Avocations: hiking, hunting, photography. Home: 8300 Thoreau Dr Bethesda MD 20817-3164 Office: Rm 7000 SA2 Dept State Washington DC 20522-6001 E-mail: flycatcher26@comcast.net.

FLEISHER, JERRILYN, financial planner; b. Phila., May 7, 1952; d. Earl D. and Bette (Romisher) F.; m. Steven M. Bierman, May 28, 1978; 1 child, Emily Larissa. BA, Dickinson Coll., 1973; MBA, Wharton Sch. U. Pa., 1975. Promotion analyst Gillette Co., Boston, 1975-77; product mgr. Chesebrough Ponds Co., Greenwich, Conn., 1977-80, Loreal Co., N.Y.C., 1980-81; account exec. Futterman Orgn., N.Y.C., 1981-83; fin. cons. Shearson Lehman Bros., Greenwich, 1983-92; pres. Fin. Views, Greenwich, 1992—. Mem. Internat. Bd. CFPs, Phi Beta Kappa. Home: 216 Millertown Rd Greenwich CT 06830 Personal E-mail: shanaraisa@aol.com.

FLEISHER, PAUL, retired elementary school educator; BA, Brandeis U., 1970; MEd, Va. Commonwealth U., 1975. Tchr., coord. Providence Free Sch., 1970-72; tchr. corps intern Va. Commonwealth U., Richmond, 1973-75; 6th grade tchr. Petersburg (Va.) Pub. Schs., 1975-76, Williamsburg (Va.) Pub. Schs., 1976-78; tchr. programs for gifted Richmond Pub. Schs., 1978—2005, trainer computer programming and applications, 1983-85; ret., 2005. Instr. div. continuing studies Va. Commonwealth U., 1981-86; instr. adult continuing studies U. Richmond, 1998—; adj. faculty Ctr. for Talented Youth, Johns Hopkins U., Balt., 1989-90; leader workshops in field. Author: Secrets of the Universe, 1987, Understanding the Vocabulary of the Nuclear Arms Race, 1988, Write Now!, 1989, (with Patricia Keeler) Looking Inside, 1991, Changing the World: A Handbook for Young Activists, 1992, The Master Violinmaker, 1993, Ecology A-Z, 1994, Our Oceans, 1995, Life Cycles of a Dozen Diverse Creatures, 1996, Webs of Life: Tide Pool, Coral Reef, Saguaro Cactus, Oak Tree, 1997, Brain Food: Games That Teach Kids to Think, 1997, Webs of Life: Salt Marsh, Pond, Alpine Meadow, Mountain Stream, 1998, Tanglers Too, 1998, Gorilla, 2000, Secrets of the Universe, (5 vols.), 2001, Ice Cream Treats: The Inside Scoop, 2001, Ants, 2002, 21st Century Writing, 2003; also computer software in field; contbr. articles to profl. jours.; editor: Va. Educators for Peace newsletter, 1982-86 Mem. adv. bd, Chespeake Bay Found. CLEAN, 1996—97; faculty advisor S.T.O.P. Nuclear War, 1982—86; bd. dirs. ACLU of Va., 2002—. Recipient Award for Peace and Internat. Rels., Va. Edn. Assn., 1988, Thomas Jefferson medal for outstanding contbns. to nat. sci. edn., Va. Mus. Nat. History, 1999; finalist R.E.B. awards for Teaching Excellence, 1995, Pub. Schs. Tchr. of Yr., Richmond, 1997. Mem. NEA (editor Peace Caucus News 1987-88), Va. Edn. Assn.(award for peace and internat. rels., 1988), Richmond Edn. Assn. (faculty rep., del. to convs., editor REAlworld and Actionline, 1980-85). Home: 2781 Beowulf Ct Richmond VA 23231-7366 E-mail: pfleishe@earthlink.net.

FLEISHER, THOMAS ARTHUR, physician; b. Rochester, Minn. s. Gerard and Gisela Fleisher; m. Mary Fleisher; children: Jeffrey, Jeremy, Matthew. BS, U. Minn., 1969, MD, 1971. Diplomate Am. Bd. Pediats., Am. Bd. Allergy and Immunology. Staff physician bone marrow transplant svc. Naval Med. Rsch. Inst., Bethesda, Md., 1975—77; commd. lt.comdr. USNR, 1975—77; commd. USPHS, 1977—80, advanced through grades to capt., 1983—2001; ret., 2001; clin. assoc. metabolism br. Nat. Cancer Inst., NIH, Bethesda, 1977—80; asst. chief allergy clin. immunology svc. Walter Reed Army Med. Ctr., Washington, 1980—83; chief immunology svc. Warren G. Magnuson Clin. Ctr., NIH, Bethesda, 1983—, chief dept. lab. medicine, 1998—. Tng. program dir. clin. lab. immunology NIH, Bethesda, 1992—; bd. dirs. Am. Bd. Allergy and Immunology, Phila., 1991—2001, chair, 1996. Editor Clin. Immunology, 1985—89, 1993—, Immunology, 1983—86, Clin. Diag. Lab. Immunology, 1993—, Cytometry, 1996—, contbr. numerous articles to sci. jours., —. House capt. Christmas in April, Montgomery County, Md., 1991—2000; deacon, elder St. Mark Presbyn. Ch., Rockville, Md., 1983—88; bd. dirs. Bethesda Soccer Club, 1987—95. Fellow: Am. Acad. Allergy, Asthma and Immunology (bd. dirs. 2003—); mem.: Clin. Immunology Soc. (pres. 2004—), Clin. Cytometry Soc., Soc. for Pediat. Rsch., Am. Assn. Immunologists. Avocations: travel, skiing, woodworking. Office: NIH 10/2C306 9000 Rockville Pike Bethesda MD 20892-1508 E-mail: tfleisher@nih.gov.

FLEISHHACKER, DAVID, school administrator; b. San Francisco, May 30, 1937; s. Mortimer and Janet (Choynski) F.; m. Victoria Escamilla, Aug. 1965; children: William, Eleanor, Jeffrey. AB, Princeton U., 1959; MA, U. Calif., 1965. Tchr. Lick-Wilmerding High Sch., San Francisco, 1959-61, Peace Corps, Afghanistan, 1962-64, Marin Country Day Sch., Corte Madera, Calif., 1965, Town Sch., San Francisco, 1965-70; headmaster Katherine Delmar Burke Sch., San Francisco, 1970-95; ret.; interim head Hillbrook Sch., Los Gatos, 1997-98, South Peninsula Hebrew Day Sch., 1998-99. Pvt. ednl. cons. Author: (book) Lessons from Afghanistan, 2002; contbr. articles to profl. jours. Trustee Internat. Ho., Berkeley, Calif., 1987—95; pres. Fleishhacker Found., San Francisco, 1990—; bd. dirs. St. Joseph's Hosp./Queen of Angels, L.A., 1976—, San Francisco Youth Orch., 1981—, San Francisco Boys Chorus, 1997—2003, Booker T. Washington Cmty. Ctr., 1995—2004, Educating Girls Globally, 2002—; pres. Music in Sch. Today, 2002—. Mem. Nat. Assn. Prins. Schs. Girls. (bd. dirs. 1979-82), Elem. Sch. Heads Assn., Calif. Assn. Ind. Schs. (treas. 1978-81). Home: #8 1958 Vallejo St San Francisco CA 94123 Personal E-mail: trampc@aol.com.

FLEISHMAN, PHILIP ROBERT, internist; b. Hartford, Conn., Apr. 17, 1935; s. Morris and Anna Lillian (Farber) Fleishman; m. Anita Rose Coopersmith, Oct. 18, 1964; children: David, Beth, Rachael. BS, Trinity Coll., Hartford, 1957; MD, SUNY, Bklyn., 1961. Diplomate Am. Bd. Internal Medicine. Practice specializing in internal medicine East Islip, N.Y., 1967—; attending physician, dir. medicine Southside Hosp., Bay Shore, N.Y., 1993—; attending physician Good Samaritan Hosp., W. Islip, N.Y.; v.p. med. bd. Southside Hosp., 1986-89; pres., 1989—; clin. asst. prof. SUNY Med. Sch., Stony Brook, 1967—; asst. dir. medicine, 1988—; dir. med. sch., 1993—; founder, co-dir. diabetic clinic Southside Hosp.; also bd. dirs., 1999—; med. intern Bklyn. Jewish Hosp., 1961—62, med. resident, 1962—65. Bd. dirs. Southlake Hosp. Contbr. articles to profl. jours. Co-author, chmn. constn. and bylaws Pro-Arts Group Islips, 1979; asst. basketball coach Police Athletic League, 1979; v.p., trustee Bay Shore Jewish Ctr., 1979—, pres., 1988—90. Capt. M.C. U.S. Army, 1965—67. Fellow: ACP; mem.: AMA, Suffolk County Med. Soc., N.Y. State Soc. Internal Medicine (past chpt. pres.), N.Y. State Med. Soc., Am. Diabetes Assn. Office Phone: 613-967-7373.

FLEISHMAN, SUSAN NAHLEY, film company executive; b. Charlottesville, Va., Sept. 26, 1960; d. Richard and Mary Daniels Nahley; m. Eric Philip Fleishman, Dec. 28, 1995; 1 child, Henry Richard. BA Am. Lit., Middlebury Coll., Middlebury, Vt., 1978—82. Copywriter Macy's, New York, NY, 1984—86; dir. Interbrand, New York, NY, 1986—87; asst. v.p. Continental Ins., New York, NY, 1987—93; dir., pub. affairs Sony Corp. of Am., New York, NY, 1993—95; v.p. corp. comm. & pub. affairs Universal Studios, Los Angeles, Calif., 1995—2000, sr. v.p. corp. comm. & pub. affairs, 2000—. Bd. mem. Workplace, Hollywood, Los Angeles, Calif., 2001—, St. Joseph's Hosp., Burbank, Calif., 2002—. Office: Universal Studios LRW-14 100 Universal City Plaza Universal City CA 91608

FLEISZIG, SUZANNE MARIANE JANETE, optometry educator; b. Melbourne, Australia, Sept. 5, 1960; came to U.S., 1990; d. Kornel Fleiszig and Judith Mary (Falus) Fleiszig-Farkas. BSc in Optometry, U. Melbourne, 1983, MSc in Optometry, 1985, PhD, 1990. Lic. optometrist, Victoria, Australia. Rsch. asst. Victorian Eye and Ear Hosp., Melbourne, 1983-85; demonstrator U. Melbourne, 1983-84, clin. instr., 1984-90; vis. rsch. assoc. Harvard U. Med. Sch., Boston, 1989, rsch. fellow in medicine, 1990-93, instr., 1993-94; assoc. microbiologist Brigham and Women's Hosp., Boston, 1993-94; asst. prof. optometry U. Calif., Berkeley, 1994—. Cons. to contact lens industry, 1993—. Contbg. author: Clinical Contact Lens Practice, 1992; contbr. articles to Investigtive Ophthalmology and Vision Sci., Jour. Clin. Microbiology, Infection and Immunity. Postdoctoral fellow Nat. Soc. To Prevent Blindness, 1991, C.J. Martin fellow Nat. Health and Med. Rsch. Coun. Australia, 1992; rsch. grantee NIH, 1995; recipient Borish award, 1997. Mem. Am. Soc. for Microbiology, Assn. for Rsch. in Vision and Ophthalmology (v.p.), Internat. Soc. for Contact Lens Rsch. (v.p.). Achievements include discovery that contact lens wear enhances bacterial binding to human corneal cells, discovered that Pseudomonas aeruginosa invades corneal cells. Home: 6745 Sobrante Rd Oakland CA 94611-1126 Office: U Calif 688 Minor Hall Optometry Berkeley CA 94720-0001

FLEIT, MARTIN, lawyer; b. Bklyn., Apr. 5, 1926; s. Samuel and Nellie (Greenfield) Fleit; m. Lois Lenefsky, Dec. 29, 1979; children: Julie, Pam, Douglas, Lauren, David. At, Tufts U., 1944—45; BSChemE, U. N.H., 1948; JD, Georgetown U., 1952. Bar: D.C. 1952, Fla. 1974, N.Y. 1980. Ptnr. Stevens, Davis, Miller & Mosher, Washington, 1948—69; sr. ptnr. Fleit, Jacobson, Cohn & Price, Washington, 1969—92; of counsel Keck, Mahin & Kate, Washington, 1992—97, Evenson, McKeown, Edwards & Lenahan, 1997—99, Fleit, Kain, Gibbons, Gutman & Bongini, 2000—; pres. Martin Fleit P.A., Miami, Fla., 1992—. Mem. adv. bd. Patent, Trademark and Copyright Jour., Bur. Nat. Affairs, Inc. With USNR, 1943—46. Mem.: ATLA, ABA, Internat. PAT-GOT Assn. (founder), Fedn. Internat. Des Conseils en Propriete Industrielle, Inter-Am. Assn. Indsl. Property, Internat. Assn. Protection Indsl. Property, Patent and Trademark Inst. Can., Am. Intellectual Property Law Assn., FBA. Home and Office: 520 Brickell Key Dr Ste 201 Miami FL 33131-2607 Office Phone: 305-416-4490. E-mail: mfleit@focusonip.com.

FLEMING, BLANCHE MILES, educational administrator; d. William Alford and Mary Blanche (Cottman) Miles; m. Daniel Edward Fleming II, Apr. 12, 1952 (dec. Mar. 1970); 1 child, Daniel Edward III. BS, Del. U., 1939; MA, Columbia U., 1947; PhD, Union Grad. Sch., Yellow Springs, Ohio, 1976. Cert. profl. edn., Del.; lic. bus. cert., Del. Tchr. English Wilmington (Del.) Bd. Edn., prin. Bayard Jr. H.S., supr. social studies, intern to supt. of schs., 1974-75; coord. undergrads. Del. State U., Dover, 1971; exec. dir. Nat. Tchr. Corps U. Del., Newark, 1970-72; dir. secondary edn. Del. Bd. Edn., Wilmington, 1980-83; pres. B.M. Fleming & Assocs. Charter mem. Helping Hands Cmty. Svc., Inc., Wilmington, 1996—; bd. dirs. Common Cause of Del., Wilmington, 1984—, Housing Opportunity of No. Del., Wilmington, 1987—, Del. state adv. com. U.S. Commn. on Civil Rights, Washington, 1991—; chair housing com. LWV, Wilmington, 1997—. Recipient Legacy from Del. Women award Chesapeake Bay Girl Scouts, Wilmington, 1987. Mem. Nat. Assn. Univ. Women (pres. 1990-94, cert. of appreciation 1994), Wilmington Women in Bus. (bd. dirs. 1983-85), Delta Kappa Gamma Internat. (corr. sec. 1991-93), Phi Delta Kappa, Kappa Delta Pi, Pi Beta Lambda. Avocations: photography, painting, poetry. Office: Fleming & Assocs 2806 W 5th St Wilmington DE 19805-1824

FLEMING, DOUGLAS RILEY, journalist, publishing executive, consultant; b. Fairmont, W.Va., Jan. 25, 1922; s. Douglas Riley and Sarilda Artemes (Short) F.; m. Irene Stachowicz, Oct. 28, 1944 (dec. 1979); m. Nancy Evelyn Kincaid, May 30, 1992. BS, Georgetown U., 1953. Commd. ensign U.S. Navy, 1944, advanced through grades to comdr.; naval aviator; chief protocol NATO, Naples, Italy, 1962-67; ret. U.S. Navy, 1967; with Francis I. DuPont & Co., Investment Banking, Rome, 1968-70; exec. editor, gen. mgr. Daily American, Rome, 1970-75; pres. Stampa Generale, S.R.L., Pubs., Naples, 1975—80; mng. dir. Italo-Am. Assn., Naples; dir. Am. Studies Ctr., Naples, 1975-80; pres. Gen. Press Svcs., Washington, 1979—. Dir. Va. Winery Coop., Inc., Culpeper, 1985-93; propr., operator Campicello Vineyards, Madison, Va., 1982-92. Active Nat. Trust Hist. Preservation, Smithsonian Assocs., Assn. Naval Aviation. Mem. Associazione della Stampa Estera in Italia, The Cogswell Soc., The Murray Clan Soc., St. Andrew's Soc. of Washington D.C., Georgetown U. Alumni ASsn. (pres. Italy 1972-80), Am. C. of C. in Italy, Military Officers Assn., Navy League of U.S., Nat. Press Club, Vinifera Wine Growers Assn., Jeffersonian Wine Grape Growers Soc., Va. Vineyards Assn., Naval and Mil. Club, Steering Wheel Club, Royal Aero Club (London), Circolo Canottieri (Naples), N.Y. Athletic Club, Dist. Yacht (Washington). Address: 400 Madison St Apt 1408 Alexandria VA 22314-1724

FLEMING, FRANCINE FAYE, legal nurse consultant; b. Houston, Apr. 17, 1947; d. Francis Elmer Turner and Evelyn Frances Fieseler; m. Garrel Vern Fleming, Dec. 23, 1995. Diploma, Brackenridge Hosp. Sch. Nursing, 1968; BS, Southwest Tex. State Coll., 1989. RN. Staff nurse Brachenridge Hosp., Austin, Tex., 1968—70, Galveston County Meml. Hosp., Texas City, 1970—72, Seton Med. Ctr., 1979—84; staff nurse, head nurse St. David's Hosp., Austin, 1972—78; office nurse Med. Pk. Orthop. Group, 1982—83; rsch. nurse Biomed. Rsch. Group, 1983—84; paralegal Brown McCarroll LLP, 1984—2005. Chair Concepts Care Adv. Com., Austin, 1989—90, vice chair, 1991—93, 1995. Mem. Vol. Assistance Program, Austin, 1984, ARC, 1965—; bd. dirs. Windermer Homeowners Assn., Pflugerville, Tex., 1986. Mem.: Am. Assn. Legal Nurse Cons. (pres. 1990—92, 1997, co-founder), State Bar Tex. (paralegal divsn.), Capital Area Paralegal Assn,., Alpha Chi. Mem. Ch. Of Christ. Avocations: genealogy, gardening, music, singing, birdwatching. Office: Brown McCarroll LLP 111 Congress Ave #1400 Austin TX 78701 E-mail: ffleming@mailbmc.com.

FLEMING, GEORGE ROBERT, psychologist; 1 child, Maisha Amira. BA, Hillsdale Coll., 1969; MA in Clin. Psychology, Mich. State U., 1972, PhD in Clin. Psychology, 1975. Lic. psychologist Mich., Am. Bd. Profl. Disability Cons., Psychol. Am. Coll. Forensic Examiners, Emergency Crisis Response, Am. Acad. Experts in Traumatic Stress, cert. Profl. Qualification in Psychology, Assn. State and Provincial Bd. Staff mem. Allied Health-Detroit Med. Ctr.; staff dept. psychiatry and behavioral neuroscis. Harper Hosp. and Detroit Receiving Hosp., 1990—; ind. psychiatric examiner mental divsn. Wayne County Probate Ct., 1991—; psychologist risk mgmt. divsn. Detroit Police Dept., 1997—; psychologist dept. behavioral medicine St. John Detroit Riverview Hosp., 1998—; prof. med. staff Detroit Riverview Hosp. St. John Health Sys., 1998—; clin. dir. Wayne County Juvenile Assessment Ctr., Mich., 2000—03. Cons. Sacred Heart Rehab. Ctr., Inc., Detroit, 1981-84, Detroit Pub. Schs., 1981, 1986, Southgate Regional Ctr. for Devel. Disabilities, Mich. Dept. Mental Health, 1989-90, 1995; cons., facilitator Morehouse Rsch. Inst., Morehouse Coll., Atlanta, 1990-92; advisor African Am. Males at Risk, Rockefeller Found., NYC, 1989-90; workshop panelist Congl. Black Caucus Found., Washington, 1988; asst. prof. dept. cmty. medicine Wayne State U., 1991-. Bd. trustees Optometric Inst. and Clinic of Detroit, 1995—, pres., 1998—2001. Named one of Outstanding Young Men in Am., U.S. Jaycees, 1982; recipient Spirit of Detroit award, 1986; fellow Nat. Inst. Mental Health, Mich. State U., 1974—75. Fellow Am. Orthopsychiatric Assn.; mem. Am. Psychol. Assn., Assn. Black Psychologists (past pres. Mich. chpt., 1981-82), Nat. Register Health Svc. Providers in Psychology, Am. Bd. Profl. Disability Cons., Am. Coll. Forensic Examiners (diplomate 1997—), Nat. Black Child Devel. Inst., Am. Acad. of Experts in Traumatic Stress (diplomate 1999-), Internat. Soc. for Traumatic Stress Studies, Soc. Cmty. Rsch. and Action. Office: 243 W Congress Ave Ste 350 Detroit MI 48226 Office Phone: 313-567-2234. Personal E-mail: gpsychdet@sbcglobal.net.

FLEMING, GREGORY J., finance company executive; BA in Econ. summa cum laude, Colgate U., 1985; JD, Yale U., 1988. Prin. Booz-Allen & Hamilton; co-head global fin. instns. group Merrill Lynch & Co., Inc., NYC, 1992, from mng. dir. to COO global investment banking, 1998—2003, exec. v.p., pres. global mkts. and investment banking, 2003—. Office: Merrill Lynch & Co Inc Four World Financial Ctr New York NY 10080

FLEMING, JAMES EDWARD, JR., information scientist, educator; s. James Edward Fleming, Sr. and Dolores Fleming; m. Lynda Mullen Fleming, July 8, 1995; children: James, Joshua, Destin. BA in Psychology, Saint Leo Coll., 1982—86; MS in Mgmt., Nat. Louis U., 1993—95; D in Info. Sys., Argosy U., 1997—2004. Dir. academic affairs National Louis U., Tampa, Fla., 1993—98; campus registrar St. Petersburg Coll., Clearwater, Fla., 1998—99; dir. info. resources Beacon Coll., Leesburg, Fla., 1999—. Adj. instr. Nat. Louis U., 1996—, U. Tampa, 1997—98, Springfield Coll., Tampa, 1998—99. Mem.: Am. Assn. of Univ. Profs., Fla. Alliance for Assistive Svcs. and Tech., Learning Disablilities Assn. of Am., Rehab. Engring. and Assistive Tech. of Am. Roman Cath. Avocations: motorcycling, golf, computers.

FLEMING, JAMES RODGER, science historian, educator; b. Windber, Pa., May 28, 1949; s. James Thomas and Ellen Jane (Rodger) Fleming; m. Miyoko Yamato, July 1, 1982; children: Jamitto, Jason Thomas. BS in Astronomy, Pa. State U., 1971; MS in Atmospheric Sci., Colo. State U., 1973; MA in History of Sci., Princeton U., 1984, PhD in History of Sci., 1988. Grad. rsch. asst. Colo. State U., 1971—73; meteorologist cloud physics divsn. U. Wash., 1973—74, Nat. Ctr. Atmospheric Rsch., 1973; cons. meteorologist pvt. practice, Fla. and NY, 1974—82; hist. cons., history editor Bull. Am. Meteorol. Soc., 1987—88; prof. sci., tech. and soc. program Colby Coll., Waterville, Maine, 1988—, chair interdisciplinary studies divsn., 1997—99; vis. scholar dept. history sci. Harvard U., 1999—2000. Vis. prof. Pa. State U. Ctr. Global Change Sci., 1994; vis. scholar MIT Program Sci., Tech. and Soc., 1992—94; rsch. assoc. dept. history of sci. Harvard U., 1992—93; founder, pres. Internat. Commn. on History of Meteorology, 2000—; spkr. in field. Author: (book) Meteorology in America, 1800-1870, 1990, Science, Technology and the Environment: Multidisciplinary Perspectives, 1994, International Bibliography of Meteorology: From the Beginning of Printing to 1889, 1994, Historical Essays on Meteorology, 1919-1995, 1996, Historical Perspectives on Climate Change, 1998, Weathering the Storm: Sverre Petterssen, the D-Day Forecast, and the Rise of Modern Meteorology, 2001; guest editor: Hist. Studies in the Phys. and Biol. Scis., 2000, Studies in the History and Philosophy of Modern Physics, 2000, editor and pub.: History of Meteorology, 2004—; contbr. chapters to books, articles to profl. jours. Recipient Bausch-Lomb Sci. award, 1967; grantee Rsch. and Course Devel., Colby Coll., 1988—, NSF, 2001—05; Predoctoral fellow, Smithsonian Instn., 1985—87, Mellon Rsch. fellow, Am. Philos. Soc., 1991, Frederick W. Beinecke fellow, Yale U., 1992, NEH fellow, 1992—93, Undergrad. scholar, Pa. State U., 1968—71, Ritter Meml. fellow, Scripps Instn. Oceanography, 2003. Fellow: AAAS (mem. nominating com. 2003—05); mem.: Nat. Air and Space Mus. (Charles A. Lindbergh chair), History of the Earth Scis. Soc. (assoc. editor Earth Scis. History 2002—, program officer), Soc. History Tech., History of Sci. Soc. (spkr., adv. editor Isis, Schuman prize com.), Brit. Soc. History of Sci., Am. Meteorol. Soc. (chair history com. 1996—2003, hist. cons. 1996—, keynote spkr. 1999, history editor, Rsch. grantee 1987—88), Am. Geophys. Union (numerous offices), Internat. Union History and Philosophy Sci. Office: Colby Coll Sci Tech and Soc Program Waterville ME 04901 E-mail: jfleming@colby.edu.

FLEMING, JAMES WILLIAM, ceramics engineer; b. St. Louis, May 23, 1947; s. James and Mary Fleming; children: Melissa Lynn, Gregory James, Alena Ione. BS in Ceramic Engring., U. of Mo., 1970, MS in Ceramic Engring., 1971; PhD in Ceramic Sci., Rutgers U., New Brunswick, N.J., 1981. Registered profl. engr., Mo., 1999. Rsch. assoc. U. of Mo., Rolla, 1971—72; mem. of tech. staff Bell Labs., Murray Hill, NJ, 1972—89, disting. mem. tech. staff, 1989—2000, ofs Labs., 2000—. Contbr. articles to profl. jours. Recipient Disting. Alumnus, U. of Mo., 1984; fellow Am. Ceramic Soc. fellow, 1989, Bell Labs. fellow, 2001, Optical Soc. of Am. fellow, 2003. Fellow: Optical Soc. of Am., Am. Ceramic Soc.; mem.: Optimist Club of Westfield (pres. 1997—98). Achievements include patents for Over 90 domestic and foreign patents. Avocations: wine making, bicycling, sailing, astronomy, photography. Home: 245 Tuttle Pkwy Westfield NJ 07090 Office: ofs Laboratories 600 Mountain Ave Murray Hill NJ 07974 Office Phone: 908-582-4499. Personal E-mail: jwf1@verizon.net. E-mail: jwf@ofsoptics.com.

FLEMING, JANE WILLIAMS, retired elementary school educator, writer; b. Bethlehem, Pa., May 26, 1926; d. James Robert and Marion Pauline (Melloy) Groman; m. George Elliott Williams, July 2, 1955 (div. July 1965); children: Rhett Dorman, Santee Stuart, Timothy Cooper; m. Jerome Thomas Fleming, Sept. 25, 1980 (dec. 2002). BS, UCLA, 1951; MA, Calif. State U., Long Beach, 1969. Tchr. San Diego Unified Sch Dist., 1951-55, Costa Mesa (Calif.) Sch. Dist., 1955-56, Long Beach (Calif.) Sch. Dist., 1956-58, 62-87, 90-92; ret. Author: Why Janey Can't Teach, 2001. Mem. Phi Kappa Phi, Ret. Tchrs. Assn., UCLA Alumni Assn., Planetary Soc. (charter), Red Hat Soc., Mus. of Tolerance. Avocations: theater, travel. Address: PO Box 13053 Long Beach CA 90803-8053 Personal E-mail: jwilli5687@aol.com.

FLEMING, JENNIE M, retired education educator; b. Elba, Ala., Aug. 8, 1948; d. Amie Junior Fleming and Lessie Mae Broxton-Burrows-Fleming; children: Jenna Helena Fleming-Matthews, Bashiri Phillips, Nia Dafina Diggs-Evans. Graduate, Herbert H. Lehman Coll., Bronx; Battaliton Mgmt., BMTS, Ft. Taylor Harding, Montgomery, Ala., 1985; Pastorial Counseling, Speak the Word Sch. of Ministry-Dothan, Dothan, Ala., 2002—04; Adminstrv. Specialist, Civilian Acquired Skills Program, Ft. McClellan, Ala., 1975; Logistics Exec. Devel. Course, The Army Logisitcs Manangement Coll., Ft. Lee, Va., 1999—99; BS in Early Childhood Edn., Troy State U., Dothan, Ala., 1980; MS- ECE Specialist, Troy State U., Ala., 1993; Adj. Gen. Corps- Basic Officer Course, Ft. Benjamin Harrison, Lawrence, Ind., 1978—79; Advanced Officer Course, Adj. Gen. Corps, Lawrence, Ind., 1981—82; Clergy Leadership Tng., Fla. Bapt. Sem., Graceville, Fla, 1997—99; Family Support Tng., 81st RSC (Reserve Service Components), Birmingham, Ala. Congregational Elder Northview Christian Ch., 1999; Early Childhood Specialist Troy State U., 1995. Early childhood educator Geneva County Schools Sys. - Samson Elem., Samson, Ala., 1975—2001; ceo/ founder Angelic Cultural Ctr., Inc., Dothan, Ala., 1974—; sec./ cmty. liaison Seven Loaves Cmty. Arts Coalition, East Village, New York, NY, 1972—74; spl. staff officer USAR Control Group (REINF), St. Louis, 1987; founder, CEO Beacon Produztions Unlimited, Dothan, Ala., 2003. Coord. Student Mock Election, Samson, Ala., 1998—99. Participant Family Action Plan Symposium, Fort Rucker, Ala., 1987, Centennial Commn., Enterprise, Ala., 1992; coord. and cultural cons. African-American History Celebration, Fort Rucker, Ala., 1992; founder Angelic Cultural Ctr., Inc, Dothan, Ala., 1974; coord. and ednl. cons. Northview Christian Ch.- Learning With Dignity Program, Dothan, Ala., 2003. Served Army Nat. Guard, Ala. Scholar TSU tuition, Kappa Delta Pi, 1979, Tech. Scholarship, Ala. State Dept. of Edn., 1993. Mem.: SE Ala. Arts Alliance (assoc.; CEO Angelic Cultural Ctr., Inc. 1974), Kappa Delta Pi, Gamma Delta Pi. Democrat. Achievements include being the first African-Native Am. to graduate from Ala. Military Acad. Avocations: gospel singing, writing, performing arts, interior decorating, landscaping. Home: 102 Montrose Ctt Apt 6 Dothan AL 36305 Office: Angelic Cultural Ctr Inc 909 S St Andrews St Dothan AL 36302 Personal E-mail: jfleming07@comcast.net. E-mail: www.seartsalliance.org.

FLEMING, JILL LOUISE, education educator; b. Phila., Apr. 3, 1950; d. William Davidson and Janice Hirst Middleton; m. Gary Lee Fleming (div.). BS, Shippensburg U., Pa., 1972; MEd., Kutztown U., Pa., 1975; Reading Recovery tchr., Oakland, U., Rochester Hills, Mich, 1994; tchr. leader, Oakland U., 2001. Cert. Eng. Language Arts Nat. Bd., 94, Nat. Bd. Renewal, 2004. Tchr. Topton Cmty. Sch., Pa., 1972—75; reading EdS. Bucks County Sch. Dist., Doyelstown, Pa., 1975—76, Romulus Pub. Sch., Romulus, Mich., 1978—90; reading EdS. to reading recovery tchr. Farmington (Mich.) Pub. Sch., 1990—2005, reading recovery tchr., 2000—. Grad. instr. Oakland U., 2001—03; cons. Pontiac (Mich) Pub. Sch., 2001—02; mem. tchr. adv. panel Mich. Dept. Edn., 2005. Pres. Reading Coun. of Mich., 2003—04; parent leader Church Youth Group, Farmington, Mich., 1994—2002, AG Bell, Mich., 1982—, Secondary Literacy Com., Lansing, Mich., 1988—95; tchr. rep. Early Literacy Com., Lansing, 1995—2000. Recipient Disting. Educator award, Nat. Bd. for Profl. Tchg. Standards, 2004. Mem.: Mich. Reading Assn.,

Internat. Reading Assn., Reading Recovering Council North Am. (pres. 2003—05). Avocations: reading, cooking, sports, dance, camping. Home: 2049 Maedow Ridge Walled Lake MI 48390 Office: Woodcreek Elementary 28400 Harwich Dr Farmington MI 48334 Office Phone: 248-478-2077.

FLEMING, JON LEE, gastroenterologist; b. Charles City, Iowa, Sept. 7, 1952; s. Gilbert and Rose (Basuk) F. BS with distinction, Iowa State U., 1975; MD, U. Iowa, 1979. Diplomate Am. Bd. Internal Medicine, Am. Bd. Gastroenterology. Intern U. Kans. Hosps. and Clinics, Kansas City, 1979-80; resident in internal medicine U. Kans., Kansas City, 1980-83; fellow in gastroenterology Mayo Clinic, Rochester, Minn., 1983-86; gastroenterologist McFarland Clinic, Ames, Iowa, 1986—. Comprehensive rev. com. Iowa Found. for Med. Care, 1994-96, quality assessment com., 1990-93; adv. bd. Iowa Jewish Sr. Life Ctr., Des Moines, 1996—2002, Iowa State U. Athletic Dept., Ames, 1994-2000, corp. bd. dirs. Theta Chi, 1990—, devel. bd. dirs. WOI radio, 1997—, devel. bd. dirs. parks libr., 1991-96. Named Greek Alumnus of Yr., Iowa State U. Greeks, 1991, 97, Theta Chi Alumnus of Yr., 1996-97; Coll. Sci. and Humanities scholar, 1975. Fellow ACP, Am. Gastroenterology Assn.; mem. Iowa Crohns-Colitis Assn. (physicians adv. bd. 1990—), Phi Beta Kappa, Phi Kappa Phi, Phi Eta Sigma, Pi Mu Epsilon. Democrat. Jewish. Avocations: jogging, golf, sports, reading. Home: 401 Pearson Ave Ames IA 50014-7033 Office: McFarland Clinic PO Box 3014 Ames IA 50010-3014

FLEMING, JOSEPH CLIFTON, JR., dean, law educator; b. Atlanta, July 24, 1942; s. Joseph Clifton Sr. and Claudia Leola (Duncan) F.; m. Linda Wightman, May 27, 1964; children: Allison, Erin, Anne, Matthew Clifton, Stephen Joseph, Michael Grant. BS, Brigham Young U., 1964; JD, George Washington U., 1967. Bar: Wash. 1967, U.S. Dist. Ct. (we. dist.) Wash. 1967, U.S. Tax Ct. 1969, U.S. Ct. Appeals (9th cir.) 1970, Utah 1979. Assoc. Bogle & Gates, Seattle, 1967-73; assoc. prof. Law Sch. U. of Puget Sound, Tacoma, 1973-74, Brigham Young U., Provo, Utah, 1974-76, prof. Law sch., 1976-98, assoc. dean Law Sch., 1986—2004, Ernest L. Wilkinson prof. Law Sch., 1998—; Fulbright prof. faculty law U. Nairobi, Kenya, 1977-78; prof. in residence Office of Chief Counsel IRS, Washington, 1985-86. Vis. prof. U. Queensland, Brisbane, Australia, 1997, 99, Ctrl. European U., Budapest, Hungary, 2001—04; James J. Freeland eminent vis. scholar U. Fla. Law Sch., 2002. Author: Estate and Gift Tax, 1975, Tax Aspects of Buying and Selling Corporate Businesses, 1984, Tax Aspects of Forming and Operating Closely Held Corporations, 1992, Federal Income Tax: Doctrine, Structure and Policy, 1995, 3d edit., 2004; notes editor George Washington U. Law Rev., 1966-67; contbr. numerous articles to scholarly and profl. jours. Bishop Ch. of Jesus Christ of LDS, Orem, Utah, 1981-85. Mem. ABA (subcom. chair tax sect. corp. tax com. 1979-83, chair tax sect. com. on teaching taxation 1992-94), Am. Law Inst. (tax adv. group 1988-94, 98-2001). Office: Brigham Young U J Reuben Clark Law Sch Provo UT 84602-8000

FLEMING, JUANITA WILSON, nursing educator, academic administrator; BS, Hampton Inst., 1957; MA, U. Chgo., 1959; PhD, Cath. U. Am., 1969; D Pub. Svc., Berea Coll., 1994. From staff nurse to head nurse med.-surg. pediat. unit Children's Hosp., Washington, 1957-58; pub. health nurse Bur. Pub. Health Nursing, 1959-60; instr. nursing children Sch. Nursing Freedmen's Hosp., Washington, 1962-65; cons. pub. health nursing dept. pediat. Child Devel. Clin., Howard U., 1965-66; from asst. prof. to assoc. prof. U. Ky. Coll. Nursing, Lexington, 1969-73; prof. U. Ky., Lexington, 1973—, spl. asst. to pres. for acad. affairs, 1991—2001, prof. emeritus, 2001—03; provost v.p. acad. affairs Ky. State U., Frankfort, 2003—. Mem. grad. faculty Coll. Nursing, U. Ky, 1971—, asst. dean grad. edn., 1975-81, assoc. dean, dir. grad. edn., 1982-86; prof. Coll. Edn. Edpt. Edn. Policy Studies and Evaln., 1979—; assoc. vice-chancellor acad. affairs Med. Ctr., 1984-91; prin. investigator nursing care high risk infants State Maternal and Child Health Divsn., 1972; project dir. advanced nurse tng. grant divsn. nursing Dept. Health Edn. and Welfare, 1977-80, prin. investigator high tech home care chronically ill children Bur. Maternal Child Health, 1989-93; prin. investigator healthcare and devel. status Children and Their Families MIRT Fogarty Ctr., 2001-2002; vis. prof. Case We. Res. U., Cleve., 1984, West Chester U., 1997; Martin Luther King/Rosa Parks/Cesar Chavez vis. prof. U. Mich., Ann Arbor, 1989, Elizabeth Carnegie endowed vis. prof. Howard U., 1995; Houston Endowed Minority Health and Rsch. Disting. vis. prof. Prairie View U., 1998; prin. investigator Am. Nurses Found., 1970-71; Faville lectr. Wayne State U., 1998. Recipient Ky. Nurses Assn. award, Marion E. McKenna leadership award, 1988, Disting. Svc. award ANA, 1994; Olhson scholar U. Ill., 1999, Robert A. Zumwinkle Student Rights award U. Ky. Student Govt. Assn., 2001, Diversity award, U. Ky. Inst. Medicine, 2005; named Living Legend, Am. Acad. Nursing, 2004. Mem.: Ky. Inst. Medicine (Diversity award 2005), Am. Acad. Nursing (Named Living Legend 2003), Nat. Acad. Scis., Inst. Medicine. Office: Provost Ky State Univ Frankfort KY 40601 Office Phone: 502-597-6395. Business E-Mail: jfleming@gwmail.kysu.edu.

FLEMING, JULIAN DENVER, JR., lawyer; b. Rome, Ga., Jan. 12, 1934; s. Julian D. and Margaret Madison (Mangham) F.; m. Sidney Howell, June 28, 1960; 1 dau., Julie Adrianne. Student, U. Pa., 1951-53; BChemE, Ga. Inst. Tech., 1955, PhD, 1959; JD, Emory U., 1967. Bar: Ga. 1966, D.C. 1967; registered profl. engr., Ga., Calif. Rsch. engr., prof. chem. engring. Ga. Inst. Tech., 1955-67; ptnr. Sutherland, Asbill & Brennan, Atlanta, 1967—. Contbr. articles to profl. jours.; patentee in field. Bd. dirs. Mental Health Assn. Ga., 1970-80; bd. dirs. Mental Health Assn. Met. Atlanta, 1970-80, pres., 1974-75; mem. coun. legal advisors Rep. Nat. Com., 1981-85. Fellow: Am. Bar Found., Am. Coll. Trial Lawyers, Am. Inst. Chemists; mem.: AIChE, AAAS, ABA (coun. sect. sci. and tech. 1980—, vice chmn. 1982—84, chmn. 1985—86, ho. dels. 1990, bd. govs. 1994—95, ho. dels. 1994—96, chmn. spl. citation issues com. 1995—96, coord. commn. legal tech. 1995—97, standing com. tech. and info. sys. 1997—2001), Bleckley Inn of Ct. (master of bench), Nat. Conf. Lawyers and Scientists (chmn. ABA del. 1988—90, standing com. nat. conf. groups 1990, ABA liaison 1990—93, chmn. 1992—93). Achievements include patent for data apparatus. Home: 1248 Oxford Rd NE Atlanta GA 30306-2610 Office: Sutherland Asbill & Brennan 999 Peachtree St NE Ste 2300 Atlanta GA 30309-3996

FLEMING, KEVIN J., academic administrator, educator; s. John and Janet Fleming. BA in Psychology and Philosophy, Loyola Marymount U., 2000; MA in Higher Edn., The Ohio State U., 2002; MBA, U. Redlands, 2005. Adminstr. U. Redlands, Calif., 2002—. Cons. CAMPUSPEAK, Inc, Colo.; spkr. in field. Mem.: Sigma Phi Epsilon (vol.).

FLEMING, KEVIN JONATHAN, psychologist, musician; b. Springfield, Mass., Sept. 11, 1972; s. David John and Barbara Teresa Fleming; m. Frannie Elizabeth Biolchini, Jan. 15, 2005; 1 child, Paul. BA, U. Notre Dame, 1994, MA, 1996, PhD, 1999. Resident U. Wyo., Laramie, 2000; clin. psychologist Psychol. and Behavioral Health Ctr., Toms River, NJ, 2000—01; dir. tng. Trestletree, Inc., Fayetteville, Ark., 2001—04; consulting psychologist Jackson Hole, Wyo., 2004—. Exec. coach, corp. psychologist, const., 2004—. Musician (singer, songwriter): (CD) Glimpse, 2003. Mem.: ASTD, APA. Roman Catholic. Avocations: outdoor activities, sports, recording/playing drums and guitar. Office: Kevin J Fleming PhD, PC 555 E Broadway Ste 229 Jackson WY 83002

FLEMING, LEE VIRGINIA, writer, art critic, curator; b. Phila., Jan. 26, 1952; d. Ralph Daniel and Helen Haymond (Wolfe) F. B.A. in English Lit., Yale U., 1972; M.A. in English Lit., U. Toronto, 1974. Visual arts editor Washington Rev., 1979—; Washington corr. ARTnews, N.Y.C., 1982—, Washingtonian, 1980—; galleries art critic, Washington Post; writer Washington Art Review; freelance writer; contbr. Beaux Arts mag., Paris, Smithsonian Mag., Images & Issues, 1980—; reporter visual arts Nat. Pub. Radio (WAMV) morning edit., Washington, 1985, WETA TV show 'Around Town"; curator, organizer, cons., lectr. to schs. and mus. including R.I. Sch. Design, Corcoran Sch. Art, Balt. Mus., Md. Inst., Washington Project for Arts, Md. Art Place, 1979— . Author: Someone Special, 1983. Scriptwriter for performance arts, 1981— . Author art catalogues, 1981— . Contbr. articles and revs. to numerous cultural publs. D.C. Commn. Arts fellow, 1981, 84; UCross Found. resident, 1985. Mem. Washington Rev. of Arts (trustee 1980-85, sec. 1981). Club: Elizabethan (Yale U.). Home and Office: 1924 Park Rd NW Washington DC 20010-1021 Address: WETA TV 2775 S Quincy St Arlington VA 22206*

FLEMING, LORA E., physician, researcher; BA, Radcliffe Coll., Harvard U., Cambridge, Mass., 1978; MSc, Imperial Coll., London U., London, Eng., 1979; MD, Harvard Med. Sch., Boston, Mass., 1984; MPH, Harvard Sch. of Pub. Health, Boston, Mass., 1984; PhD, Yale U. Sch. of Medicine, Pub. Health, New Haven, Conn., 1997. Diplomate Am. Bd. of Family Physicians, 2005, cert. Family Medicine Am. Bd. of Family Medicine, 1987, Occupl. and Environl. Medicine Preventive Medicine Boards, 1989. Prof. U. Miami Sch. of Medicine and Rosenstiel Sch. of Marine and Atmospheric Sci., Miami, Fla., 1989—2005. Achievements include research in Aerosolized red tide interdisciplinary rsch. in humans. Office: Univ Miami 1801 NW 9th Ave Ste 200 Miami FL 33136 Office Phone: 305-243-5912. Office Fax: 305-243-3384. Business E-Mail: lfleming@med.miami.edu.

FLEMING, LUCINDA MARIE, secondary school educator; b. Kenton, Ohio, July 20, 1970; d. Edwin L. and Anita M. Green; m. David Andrew Fleming, July 31, 1999; 1 child, Samuel Alan. BA, Cedarville (Ohio) U., 1992; MEd, Wright State U., 2001. Substitute tchr. Benjamin Logan H.S., Rushsylvania, Ohio, 1992—2000; test car driver Transp. Rsch. Ctr. Ohio, East Liberty, Ohio, 1996—99; tchr. english Riverside H.S., DeGraff, Ohio, 2000—. Handbell choir Calvary Bapt. Ch., Bellefontaine, 1997—2005; sec. Hillcrest Bapt. Ch., Bellefontaine, Ohio, 1997—2000. Office: Riverside High School 2096 County Road 24 South DeGraff OH 43318 Office Phone: 937-585-5981 250. Personal E-mail: lfleming@riverside.k12.oh.us.

FLEMING, MAC ARTHUR, retired labor union administrator; b. Walnut Grove, Miss., Sept. 22, 1945; s. Austin J. and Dorothy (Downey) F.; m. Phyllis Jean Tatro, May 18, 1984; children: Vaughn L. Voth, Vaughn L. Voth II AA, Jones County Jr. Coll., Laurel, Miss., 1967; student, So. Colo. State Coll., Pueblo, 1967-68; student in trade union program, Harvard U., 1979. System organizer Atchison, Topeka & Santa Fe System Fedn., Pueblo, 1972, asst. gen. chmn. San Bernardino, Calif., 1972-73, asst. chmn., sec.-treas. Newton, Kans., 1974-75, vice chmn., 1975-80, gen. chmn., 1980-86; grand lodge sec.-treas. Brotherhood Maintenance Ways Employees, Detroit, 1986-90; pres. Brotherhood Maintenance of Way Employees, Detroit, 1990—2004; v.p. AFL-CIO, 1995—2004, ret., 2004. Democrat. Avocations: tennis, golf. Home: 39921 Urbana Dr Sterling Heights MI 48313-5678

FLEMING, MACKLIN, judge, author; b. Chgo., Sept. 6, 1911; s. Ingram Macklin Stainback and Hazel (Caldwell) Fleming; m. Polly Naething, May 17, 1941; children: Penelope, Frances, Ingram. BA, Yale U., 1934, LLB, 1937; LLD, Pepperdine U., 1968. Bar: N.Y. 1938, Calif. 1946. Assoc. Sullivan & Cromwell, N.Y.C., 1937-39; atty. Bituminous Coal divsn. U.S. Govt., Washington, 1939-41; pvt. practice San Francisco, 1946-49; asst. U.S. atty. U.S. Atty.'s Office, San Francisco, 1949-53; assoc. Mitchell, Silberberg & Knupp, L.A., 1954-59; judge Superior Ct., L.A., 1959-64; justice Calif. Ct. Appeal, L.A., 1964-81; of counsel Troy and Gould, L.A., 1981-91; assigned judge Superior Ct., L.A., 1992-98. Author: The Price of Perfect Justice, 1974, Of Crimes and Rights, 1978, Lawyers, Money, & Success, 1997, Perfect Justice, 2001. Chmn. Far Eastern Art Coun., L.A. County Mus., 1967-69; v.p. Ctr. Theater Group, L.A., 1970. Pvt. to Capt. U.S. Army, 1941-46. Fellow Am. Bar Found.; mem. ABA, L.A. County Bar Assn., Bar of City of N.Y., Inst. of Jud. Adminstrn., Selden Soc. Democrat. Episcopalian. Avocations: skiing, tennis, gardening. Home: 331 N Carmelina Ave Los Angeles CA 90049-2701

FLEMING, MARJORIE FOSTER, freelance writer, artist; b. Phila., Sept. 12, 1920; d. Major Bronson and Helen Margaret (Vertner) Foster; m. John Joseph Hundermark, Sept. 24, 1949 (div. Sept. 1955); children: John Foster Hundermark, David Laurence Hundermark; m. Paul Stewart Fleming, May 6, 1961. BA, Ursinus Coll., 1942; studied painting with Morris Blackburn, Pa. Acad. Fine Arts and Cheltenham Ctr. for Arts; with Robert Goldman, Cheltenham Twp. Ctr. Arts; studied painting with Paul Wieghardt, Chgo. Art Inst. and Cheltenham Twp. Ctr. for Arts. Cert. tchr. Cost acct. Philco Corp., Phila., 1942-43; asst. bank auditor Liberty Title and Trust, Phila., 1943-44; asst. dept. spl. events Phila. Evening Bulletin, 1945-47; asst. stage TV and radio show prodr. Phila., 1947-49. Appeared on Wit's End (live pilot TV show), 1948, guest Poetry Today, Sta. WRTN radio, N.Y.C., 1997. Author: Whispers of Escaped Thoughts, 2003; Whispers of Escaped Thoughts, 2003; contbr. poetry to local newspapers. Vol. occupl. therapist ARC; spl. duty hostess for Purple Heart and Stage Door Canteen, WWII. Mem. Internat. Poetry Mus., Internat. Libr. Poetry, Internat. Soc. Poets (inducted into Hall of Fame Mus.), Poetry Guild, Am. Diabetes Assn., Cheltenham Ctr. Arts, Kappa Chi Delta, Omega Chi. Republican. Methodist. Avocations: sculpture, photography, creative needlework, pianist, collecting sheet music, art, creative writing. Home: 82 Holly Dr Crystal Lake IL 60014-5022

FLEMING, MARTIN, economist, strategist; b. Lowell, Mass., Mar. 19, 1953; s. M. Brendan and Bernice (Kenney) F.; m. Patricia Marie Magnan; children: Brian Martin, Katherine Mary. BS, Lowell (Mass.) Tech. Inst., 1974; MA, Tufts U., 1976; PhD, Tufts U., 1980. Tech. dir. MIT, Cambridge, 1974-75; project dir. Tufts U., Medford, Mass., 1978-81; v.p. strategy Reed Elsevier Inc., Newton, Mass., 1982-95; prin. cons. Abt Assocs. Inc., Cambridge, Mass., 1995-99; v.p. strategy IBM Corp., White Plains, NY, 1999—. Mem. Am. Econ. Assn., Nat. Assn. Bus. Economists (bd. dirs. 1990), Boston Assn. Bus. Economists (pres., various offices 1984-86), N.Y. Assn. of Bus. Economists Roman Catholic. Home: 38 Oval Ave Greenwich CT 06878-2128

FLEMING, MATTHEW BASIL, education educator; b. Redwood City, Calif., May 2, 1970; s. Basil Aubrey and Sharon Ann Fleming; m. Suzanne Michelle Reed, Aug. 17, 1991; children: Aidan, Hannah, Andrew. BA in journalism, Point Loma Nazarene U., 1992; MA, Western Seminary, 2004. Ordained Minister Assembly of God, 2005; Calif. Teaching Credential 1996, cert. Trauma Responder 2005. Dist. exec. Boy Scouts Am., San Diego, 1992—93; tchr. Escondido Christian Sch., Calif., 1995—97, Bret Harte Union H.S., 1997—; assoc. pastor Angels Assembly of God, 2004—. Sec. Calif. Fire Chaplain Corps., 2004—. Commdr. Royal Rangers, 2004—; chaplain Calveras County Sheriff's Office, 2001—, Calif. Dept. of Fire and Forestry, 2001—. Recipient Quarter Master award, Boy Scouts Am., Sea Explorers, 1989. Mem.: Assn. of Traumatic Stress Specialists, Calif. Assn. of English Teachers, Nat. Eagle Scout Assn. Avocations: music, trumpet, guitar, bagpipes, mountain biking. Home: 5831 E Highway 4 Murphys CA 95247 Office: Bret Harte Union H S P O Box 7000 Angels Camp CA 95222

FLEMING, MICHAEL O., physician; b. Monroe, La., June 16, 1950; m. Sally Fleming; 4 children. MD, La. Med. Ctr., 1975. Intern Confederate Meml. Med. Ctr., Shreveport, 1975—76; resident LSU Med. Ctr., Shreveport, 1976—78; asst. clinical prof. Dept. Family Medicine, LSU Health Sci. Ctr. Mng. sr. ptnr. The Family Doctors. Mem.: Northwest La. Soc. Family Physicians, Shreveport Med. Soc., La. Acad. Family Physicians, La. State Med. Soc., Am. Acad. Family Physicians (pres. 2003—). Office: Am Acad Family Physicians PO Box 11210 Shawnee Mission KS 66207-1210

FLEMING, NORMAN PATRICK, information scientist; s. Lindsey Fleming, Sr. and Laura D. Fleming; m. Yolanda Elisa Rocio, June 5, 1993. BS, So. Ill. U., 1986; MBA, Devry U., Oak Brook Terrace, Ill., 1999. Div. mgr. Chgo. Tribune Co., 1988—99; dir. client svcs. NY Times, NYC, 1999—2000; sys. leader Kraft Foods, Inc., Northfield, Ill., 2000—04; vaccine div. leader Merck & Co., Inc., West Point, Pa., 2004—. Specialist Army Nat. Guard, 1986—87, Ill. Recipient Spec Req, 1989, 1991, Pres.'s award, Chgo. Tribune Co., 1994, ABCD award, Kraft Foods, Inc., 2003. Mem.: MML, NAIC (life), Am. Mgmt. Assn., Am. Mktg. Assn., Nat. Black MBA Assn. Inc. (life; chmn. 2001—03), Mu Mu Lambda (dir. edn. found. 1998—2003, pres. 2002—03), Alpha Phi Alpha (life; chap. pres. 2002—04, proect mgmt. inst. 2000—). Republican. Roman Catholic. Office: Merck Co Inc WP97-A369 PO Box 4 West Point PA 19486 Office Phone: 215-652-1614. Personal E-mail: nfleming@msn.com. Business E-Mail: norman_fleming@merck.com.

FLEMING, PATRICIA STUBBS (PATSY FLEMING), artist; b. Phila., Mar. 17, 1936; d. Fredrick Douglass Stubbs and Marion Turner Stubbs Thomas; m. Harold S. Fleming, June 1958 (div. Feb. 1971); children: Douglass, Craig, Gordon. BA, Vassar Coll., 1957; postgrad., NYU, 1958-60, U. Pa., 1957-58, Pa. Acad. Fine Arts, 1957-58. Legis. asst. to reps. U.S. Ho. of Reps., Washington, 1971-77; asst. to sec. HEW, Washington, 1977-78, dir. intergovtl. and legis. affairs Office Civil Rights, 1979-80; asst. to sec. U.S. Dept. Edn., Washington, 1979-80, dep. asst. sec. legis., 1980-81; sr. pub. policy assoc. James H. Lowry & Assocs., Washington, 1981-83; chief staff Rep. Ted Weiss U.S. Ho. of Reps., Washington, 1983-86, profl. staff mem. subcom. human resources & intergovtl. rels, 1986-93; spl. asst. to sec. HHS, Washington, 1993-94; dir. Office Nat. AIDS Policy The White House, Washington, 1994-97, cons. on govt. rels. and AIDS policy and programs, 1997—. Washington rep. Joint Co-sponsored UN Programme on HIV/AIDS, 1997-99; mem. bd. Prevention Works Needle Exch. Program in the Nation's Capitol. One-person shows include NYU, Foundry Gallery, Washington, Anne C. Fisher Gallery, Washington; exhbns. include NYC, Washington and St. Petersberg, Russia, New Delhi and numerous others. Democrat. Episcopalian. Avocations: travel, music, reading. Home and Studio: 6009 Massachusetts Ave Bethesda MD 20816-2041 Office Phone: 301-320-5420. E-mail: pfleming@erols.com.

FLEMING, PETER EMMET, JR., lawyer; b. Atlantic Highlands, N.J., Aug. 18, 1929; s. Peter Emmet and Anna (Sullivan) F.; m. Jane Breed, June 2, 1956 (dec.); children— Peter Emmet III, James M., William B., David W., Jane H. AB, Princeton U., 1951; LL.B., Yale U., 1958. Bar: N.Y. 1959, U.S. Dist. Ct. (so. and ea. dists.) N.Y. 1960, U.S. Ct. Appeals (2d cir.) 1963, U.S. Ct. Appeals (4th cir.) 1979, U.S. Supreme Ct. 1985. Assoc. Davis, Polk & Wardwell, N.Y.C., 1958-61; asst. U.S. atty. U.S. dist. Ct. (so. dist.) N.Y., N.Y.C., 1961-70; mem. Curtis, Mallet-Prevost Colt & Mosle, N.Y.C., 1970—. Home: 122 Old Church Rd Greenwich CT 06830-4821 Office: Curtis Mallet-Prevost Colt & Mosle 101 Park Ave Fl 34 New York NY 10178-0061 Office Phone: 212-696-6008. Business E-Mail: pfleming@cm-p.com.

FLEMING, RENÉE L., opera singer; b. Indiana, Pa., Feb. 14, 1959; d. Edwin Davis Fleming and Patricia (Seymour) Alexander; m. Richard Lee Ross, Sept. 23, 1989 (div. 2000). BM in Music Edn., Potsdam State U., 1981; MM, Eastman Sch. Music, 1983; student, Juilliard Am. Opera Ctr., N.Y.C., 1983—84, Juilliard Am. Opera Ctr., 1985—87; PhD (hon.), Juilliard, 2003. Exclusive rec. artist Decca Records, London, 1995—. Debut engagements include Spoleto Festival, Charleston and Italy, 1986-90, Houston Grand Opera & N.Y.C. Opera, 1988, 89, San Francisco Opera, 1991, Met. Opera, Paris Opera at the Bastille, 1991, Covent Garden, London, 1989, Teatro Colon Buenos Aires, 1991, Vienna State Opera, 1993, La Scala, 1993, Lyric Opera of Chgo., 1993, Paris Opera at Palais Garnier, 1996; author: The Inner Voice (also German and Japanese transl.), 2004. Bd. trustees Carnegie Hall Corp., 2004—; mem. adv. bd. White Nights Found. Am., 2005—, Louise T. Blouin Found., 2005—. Decorated comdr. Order Arts and Letters (France); winner Met. Opera Nat. Auditions, 1988; recipient George London prize, 1988, Richard Tucker award, 1990, Solti prize l'Acad. du Disque Lyrique, 1996, Prix Maria Callas, Academie due Disque Lyrique, 1997, Prize l'Acad. du Disque Lyrique, 1998; Fulbright scholar, Frankfurt, Germany, 1984-85, Classical Brits award for outstanding contbn. to music, 2004; named Vocalist of Yr. Mus. Am., 1997, Female Artist of the Yr., Classic Brits Awards, 2003, Prix Maria Callas, Acad. du Disque Lyrique, 2005; nominated 8 Grammy awards, 1997-2003; recipient 2 Grammy awards, 1999, 2003; 3 gramophone awards, 1999, Record of yr., Opera award, Recital award, Gift of Music award Orch. of St. Luke's, 2000; named one of top 10 classical singers of the 90s, AP, 2000; La Diva Renée dessert named in her honor by chef Daniel Boulud, 1999; Commandeur de l'Ordre des Arts et des Lettres, France, 2002; Renee Fleming iris introduced, 2004. Mem.: Royal Acad. Music (hon.). Office: care ML Falcone Pub Rels 155 W 68th St Apt 1114 New York NY 10023-5817

FLEMING, RENEE RIZZO, pharmacist; d. Ralph Charles and Mary Ann Rizzo; m. Donald William Fleming, May 19, 1984; children: Matthew, Lauren, Mark. BS in Nuc. Medicine Tech., SUNY, Buffalo, 1980, BS in Pharmacy, 1983, MBA, 1985. Cert. nuc. medicine tech., registered pharmacist N.Y. Pharmacist Sisters of Charity Hosp., Buffalo, 1984—90; mgr. pharmacy Blue Cross Blue Shield of Western N.Y., Buffalo, 1988—97; corp. dir. of pharmacy HealthNow N.Y., Buffalo, 1997—2000, v.p. corp. pharmacy svcs., 2000—. Cons. Mary Ann King & Assocs., Buffalo, 1991—92; mem. adv. bd. various pharm. cos. Com. chair Maple East Elem. Sch. PTSA, Williamsville, NY, 1998—2004. Recipient award for outstanding CME collaboration, Internat. Soc. CME Profls., 2003, BCBSA Best of Blues award in medical and pharmacy mgmt., 2004. Mem.: Nat. Coun. Physician Execs., Blue Cross Blue Shield Assn. (pharmacy adv. bd. 2003—), Am. Soc. Health Systems Pharmacists, Acad. Managed Care Pharmacy (ednl. affairs com. 2002—), SUNY Buffalo Pharmacy Alumni Assn. (bd. dirs. 1995—). Avocations: exercise, tennis. Office: HealthNow NY 1901 Main St Buffalo NY 14208

FLEMING, REX JAMES, meteorologist; b. Omaha, Apr. 25, 1940; s. Robert Leonard and Doris Mae (Burrows) F.; m. Kathleen Joyce Ferry, Sept. 3, 1969; children: Thane, Manon, Mark, Noel. BS, Creighton U., 1963; MS, U. Mich., 1968, PhD, 1970. Commd. lt. U.S. Air Force, 1963, advanced through grades to capt., 1972; research scientist Offutt AFB, Nebr., 1963-67; sci. liaison to Nat. Weather Service for Air Weather Service, Suitland, Md., 1970-72; resigned, 1972; mgr. applications mktg. advanced sci. computer Tex. Instruments, Inc., Austin, 1972-75; dir. U.S. Project Office for Global Weather Expt., NOAA, Rockville, Md., 1975-80, Spl. Research Projects Office, 1980-82, Office of Climate and Atmospheric Research, 1983-84, Internat. Tropical Ocean and Global Atmosphere Project Office and Nat. Storm Program Office, 1984-86; pres. Tycho Tech. Inc., Boulder, Colo., 1986-87, Creative Concepts, Boulder, Colo., 1987-91; sr. mgr., coord. FAA rsch. Nat. Ctr. for Atmospheric Rsch., 1991-92, vis. scientist, 1987-88; NOAA, Boulder, 1993-2001; program mgr. U. Corp. for Atmospheric Rsch., 2001—04; pres. Global Aerospace, LLC, Boulder, Colo., 2005—. Contbr. articles to profl. jours. Recipient Gold Medal award Dept. Commerce, 1980 Fellow AAAS; mem. Am. Meteorol. Soc. (chmn. probability and statistics com. 1976-77), The Planetary Soc., Am. Geophys. Union (sec. atmospheric scis. sect. 1984-86). Republican. Home: 7225 Spring Dr Boulder CO 80303-5115 Office: NCAR PO Box 3000 Boulder CO 80307-3000 *One need only be inspired by its spring-morning freshness, stimulated by its magnificent variety of color and form, and humbled by the power of its ever-present energy, to be driven to unveil the secrets of our life-sustaining atmosphere.*

FLEMING, RHONDA, actress, singer; b. L.A. d. Harold Cheverton and Effie (Graham) Louis; m. Darol W. Carlson; 1 child, Kent Lane. Student, pub. and pvt. schs., L.A., Beverly Hills. Appeared in 40 motion pictures, including Spellbound, 1945, Spiral Staircase, 1945, Out of the Past, 1947, A Connecticut Yankee in King Arthur's Court, 1949, The Great Lover, 1949, The Eagle and the Hawk, 1950, Cry Danger, 1951, Last Outpost, 1951, Hong Kong, 1952, Tropic Zone, 1953, Tennessee's Partner, 1955, Gunfight at OK Corral, 1956, Slightly Scarlett, 1956, Home Before Dark, 1958, Pony Express, 1953, The Nude Bomb, 1980; Broadway debut in The Women, 1973; appeared in musical and plays, including The Boyfriend, 1975, Marriage Go Round, 1960, Bell, Book and Candle, 1962, Kismet at Music Center, 1976; sang Gershwin concert in; 10-week tour, 1963; starred in Las Vegas, Nev., 1959, one-woman concert at Hollywood Bowl, 1964, numerous guest appearances on TV series and talk shows including MacMillan and Wife, Love Boat; TV movies include The Last Hours Before Morning, 1975; NBC's Legends of the Screen, 1980, Metromedia Spl. Road to Hollywood, 1983, Wildest West Show of the Stars, 1986. Founder Rhonda Fleming Mann Clinic and Resource Ctr. for Women's Comprehensive Care at UCLA, PATH (People Assisting the Homeless) Rhonda Fleming Family Ctr.; benefactor Music Ctr.; supporter Childhelp USA, Achievement Rewards Coll. Scientists; life assoc. Pepperdine U.; founding mem. French Found. for Alzheimer Rsch.; adv. bd. Olive

Crest Treatment Ctrs. for Abused Children; supporter Freedoms Found. at Valley Forge, City of Hope, Excellence in Media, SPCA, Humane Soc. USA; patron of the arts Music Ctr. Blue Ribbon; bd. dirs. World Opportunities Internat., St. John's Med. Ctr.; mem. nat. adv. cabinet Guideposts. Recipient award NCCJ, Gold Angel award Excellence in Media, Woman of the World award Childhelp, USA, Eve award Mannequins of the Assistance League, 1986, Our Lady of Perpetual Inspiration award; named Woman of Year City of Hope, Oper. Children, 1991, honoree of the Music Ctr. Club 100, 1992, UCLA Alumni Assn. Disting. Contbns. award to UCLA Cmty., 2000; Rhonda Fleming Rsch. fellowship for women's cancer established at City of Hope, 2000.

FLEMING, RICHARD H., finance executive; b. Milw., July 22, 1947; s. David M. and Mildred (Codere) F.; m. Diana Loane, Mar. 21, 1970; children: Douglas Codere, Petria Anne. BA, U. Pacific, 1969; MBA, Dartmouth, 1971. Fin. analyst Graco, Inc., Mpls., 1971-72, mgr. banking and fgn. exchange, 1972-73; fin. analyst Masonite Corp., Chgo., 1973-74, mgr. capital investment, 1974-77, asst. treas., 1977-82, treas., 1982-84, v.p. fin., chief fin. officer, 1985-89; dir. corp. fin. and asst. treas. USG Corp., Chgo., 1989-90, v.p., treas., 1991-94, v.p., CFO, 1994-95, sr. v.p., CFO, 1995-99, exec. v.p., CFO, 1999—. Trustee USG Found., 1989—; bd. dirs. Columbus McKinnon Corp. Bd. dirs. Family Care Services Met. Chgo., 1977—, pres. 1983-86; bd. dirs. Child Welfare League Am., Washington, 1987—, pres. 1999-2000. Alumni fellow U. Pacific Sch. Bus. Adminstrn. and Pub. Policy, 1990. Office: USG Corp PO Box 6721 125 S Franklin St Chicago IL 60680-6721 Home: Apt 2802 195 N Harbor Dr Chicago IL 60601-7532

FLEMING, RONALD A., lawyer; b. May 24, 1967; BA summa cum laude, JD, Columbia Univ., 1991. Bar: NY 1992. Ptnr., co-chmn. Emerging Growth & Tech. practice Pillsbury Winthrop Shaw Pittman, NYC. Harlan Fiske Stone scholar. Mem.: Phi Beta Kappa. Office: Pillsbury Winthrop Shaw Pittman 1540 Broadway New York NY 10036 Office Phone: 212-858-1143. Office Fax: 212-858-1500. Business E-Mail: ronald.fleming@pillsburylaw.com.

FLEMING, RONALD LEE, urban planner, consultant; b. LA, May 13, 1941; s. Ree Overton and Elizabeth Ann (Ebner) F.; m. Renata von Tscharner, Nov. 9, 1978 (div. Nov. 1999); children: Severine von Tscharner, Siena Antonia von Tscharner, Reynolds Lombard von Tscharner BA cum laude, Pomona Coll., 1963; M of City Planning, Harvard U., 1967. Urban planner in Boston office of Marshall, Kaplan, Gans and Kahn, San Francisco, 1969-71; townscape designer Cambridge, Mass., 1971-78; pres. Townscape Inst., Cambridge, 1979—. Cons., lectr. townscape and planning issues throughout U.S. Author: Saving Face: How Corporate Franchise Design can Respect Community Identity, 1994, 2d edit., 2002, Place Makers, 1981, 2d rev. edit. 1987, On Common Ground, 1982, Facade Stories, 1982; co-author: New Providence: A Changing American Cityscape, 1987; editor: Censored Laughter, 1976; contbr. articles to profl. jours. Founder, chmn. Cambridge Arts Coun., 1975-79; chmn. for Pub. Art, 1980-87; mem. adv. and standing com. Trustees of Reservations, Beverly, Mass., 1985-97; chmn. Boston chpt. Save Venice, 1993-96; chmn. bd. overseers Strawbery Banke, Portsmouth, N.H., 1980-84; bd. dirs. Victorian Soc. Phila., 1983-89; gov.'s appointee Mass. Hist. Com., 1986-90; co-founder Fleming Fellowships and Lecture Program on the built environment, Claremont Colls., 1985. Capt. Intelligence, U.S. Army, 5th Spec. Forces Group, 1966-68, Vietnam. State Dept. grantee, 1975; fellow Salzburg Seminars Am. Studies, Austria, 1978; recipient 1st prize Architecture and Planning, Columbia U. Urban Film Competition for Newburyport, A Measure of Change, 1975, Merit award Am. Soc. Landscape Architects, 1981, commendation NEA/Dept. Transp., 1981; nominated for Pulitzer prize Mass. Hist. Soc., 1982; winner EDRA/Places award for Urban Design, W. Radnor, Pa. Project, 1998, BSA award for urban design Radnor Pa. project, 1999. Fellow Royal Soc. Arts (London); mem. Mass. Hist. Soc., Soc. for Preservation New England Antiquities (past trustee), Mass. Hort. Soc. (past trustee), Inst. for Urban Design, Am. Inst. City Planners, Soc. Archtl. Historians, Scenic America (bd. dirs., sec. 1985-2002, 2004—), Preservation Soc. Newport County (trustee 2004-). Clubs: Somerset, Union Boat, Harvard (Boston), Club of Odd Volumes, Tavern (Boston); Century Assn., Knickerbocker (N.Y.C.), S.R.B.A. Newport Reading Room. Unitarian Universalist. Home and Office: 8 Lowell St Cambridge MA 02138-4726 Home: Bellevue House 304 Bellevue Ave Newport RI 02840-3518 Office Phone: 617-491-8952. E-mail: rfleming@townscape.org.

FLEMING, SCOTT MICHAEL, art educator, artist; b. Fresno, Calif., Dec. 17, 1958; s. Robert Keith Fleming and Josephine Frances Pira-Fleming; m. Cheryl Jean Reistetter, Feb. 16, 2002; 1 child, Angelina. AS in Indsl. Tech., Fresno City Coll., Fresno, 1982; BA in Indsl. Tech., Calif. State U., Fresno, 1988. Profl. clear single subject tchg. credential Commn. on Tchr. Credentialing, Calif., 1989, supplementary authorization-art Commn. on Tchr. Credentialing, Calif., 1997, supplementary authorization-social studies Commn. on Tchr. Credentialing, Calif., 1999. 7th & 8th indsl. tchr. Tioga Mid. Sch., Fresno Unified Sch. Dist., Calif., 1989—97; tchr. 7th grade art Sequoia Mid. Sch., Fresno Unified Sch. Dist., 1997—; counselor for kids at risk Fresno Unified Sch. Dist., 1990—93. Mem.: Alpha Gamma Sigma. Avocations: hiking, camping, travel, cartooning, painting. Office Phone: 559-457-3000.

FLEMING, SUZANNE MARIE, academic administrator, freelance/self-employed writer; b. Detroit, Feb. 4, 1927; d. Albert T. and Rose E. (Smiley) F. BS, Marygrove Coll., 1957; MS, U. Mich., 1960, PhD, 1963. Joined Congregation of Sisters Servants of Immaculate Heart of Mary, Roman Catholic Commn., 1945. Chmn. natural sci. div. Marygrove Coll., Detroit, 1970-75, v.p., dean, 1975-78, acad. v.p., 1978-80; asst. v.p. acad. affairs Eastern Mich. U., Ypsilanti, 1980-82, acting assoc. v.p. acad. affairs, 1982-83; provost, acad. v.p. Western Ill. U., Macomb, 1983-86; vice chancellor U. Wis., Eau Claire, 1986-89; freelance writer, 1989—. Vis. scholar U. Mich., 1989-2001; pres. Mich. Coll. Chemistry Tchrs. Assn., 1975; councilor Mich. Inst. Chemists, 1973-77; bd. dirs. Nat. Ctr. for Rsch. to Improve Postsecondary Teaching and Learning, 1988-90. Contbr. articles to profl. publs. NIH rsch. grantee, 1966—69. Home and Office: 2888 Cascade Dr Ann Arbor MI 48104-6659

FLEMING, SYLVIA SHACKELFORD, secondary school educator, writer; b. Philadelphia, Miss., Feb. 1, 1943; d. John William and Annie Ruth (Fulton) Shackelford. BS, U. So. Miss., 1973; MEd, Miss. State U., 1985, postgrad., 1985—86. Cert. libr. sci. tchr., English edn., educationally handicapped elem. edn., supervision, adminstrn., provisional educator evaluator, Miss. Adj. tech. Am. lit., short story and essay, novel classic Columbia City Schs., Miss., 1973—77, chmn. English dept., 1974—76; resource tchr. sr. English, composition and rsch. Leake County Schs., Edinburg, Miss., 1982—83; resource tchr., spl. edn., H.S. English, K-8 Bur. Indian Affairs, Philadelphia, Miss., 1983—85; tchr. spl. edn. English at jr. h.s. Neshoba County Schs., Philadelphia, 1985—93, tchr. English, 10th grade and 10th accelerated, 12th advanced placement, 1993—2005; tchr. sr. and AP English Philadelphia Mcpl. H.S., 2005—; instr. freshman English composition East Ctr. C.C., Decatur, Miss., 1991—92. Tchr., cons. Miss. Writing and Thinking Project, Starkville, 1984-97; lit. dir. Winston Bapt. Assn., Louisville, Miss., 1992-93; presenter in field. Columnist Neshoba Dem., 1999-2000, Cook-of-the-Week column, 1999; writer Sunday sch. curriculum The Bapt. Record, 1995, 99; STAR tchr., Neshoba Co. Schs., 1998, 99, 2003. Tchr. Sunday sch. Bapt. Ch., Philadelphia and Louisville, Miss., 1982-2005; tchr. Bible study Ladies Home Bible Study, Philadelphia and Louisville, 1990-97; assoc. interfaith witness Bapt. Conv. Home Mission Bd., Atlanta, 1986-97; dir. interfaith witness Winston County Bapt. Assn., Louisville, 1992-93. Grantee Allies for Edn., 1995, 96, 97, 98, 99, Weyerhaeuser, 1996, BellSouth, 1996, 97, 99. Fellow Miss. Writing and Thinking Inst.; mem. Nat. Coun. Tchrs. English, Miss. Coun. Tchrs. English (presenter). Republican. Avocations: piano, reading, baking. Office Phone: 601-656-3391. E-mail: sylvia2girls@bellsouth.net.

FLEMING, THOMAS J., editor, publishing executive; b. Superior, Wis., 1945; BA in Greek, Charleston Coll., 1967; PhD in Classics, U. N.C., 1973. Prof. classics Miami U., Charleston (S.C.) Coll., Shaw U., Raleigh, NC. Founding editor The Southern Partisan, 1979—83; mng. editor Chronicles, Rockford, Ill., 1984—85, editor, 1985—, pres., 1997—. Author: The Politics of Human Nature, 1987. Office: The Rockford Inst Chronicles 928 N Main St Rockford IL 61103-7061 E-mail: tri@rockfordinstitute.org.

FLEMING, THOMAS JAMES, writer; b. Jersey City, July 5, 1927; s. Thomas James and Katherine (Dolan) F.; m. Alice Mulcahey, Jan. 19, 1951; children: Alice, Thomas, David, Richard. AB, Fordham U., 1950; postgrad., Sch. Social Work, 1950-51. Reporter Yonkers (N.Y.) Herald Statesman, 1951; asst. to Fulton Ourslег, 1951-52, lit. executor estate, 1953; asso. editor Cosmopolitan mag., 1954-58, exec. editor, 1959-61; writer, 1961—. Author: (book) Now We Are Enemies, 1960, All Good Men, 1961, The God of Love, 1963, Beat the Last Drum, 1963, One Small Candle, 1964, King of the Hill, 1966, A Cry of Whiteness, 1967, West Point, The Men and Times of the U.S. Military Academy, 1969, The Man from Monticello, 1969, Romans Countrymen Lovers, 1969, The Sandbox Tree, 1970, The Man Who Dared the Lightning, 1971, The Forgotten Victory, 1973, The Good Shepherd, 1974, 1776: Year of Illusions, 1975, Liberty Tavern, 1976, Rulers of the City, 1977, New Jersey, 1977, Promises to Keep, 1978, A Passionate Girl, 1979, rev. edit., 2004, (book) The Officers' Wives, 1981, Dreams of Glory, 1983, rev. edit., 2001, (book) The Spoils of War, 1985, Time and Tide, 1987, Downright Fighting: The Story of Cowpens, 1988, Over There, 1992, Loyalties: A Novel of World War II, 1994, Remember The Morning, 1997, Liberty! The American Revolution, 1997, The Wages of Fame, 1998, Lights Along the Way, 1998, Hours of Gladness, 1999, Duel: Alexander Hamilton, Aaron Burr and the Future of America, 1999, The New Dealers' War: FDR and the War Within World War II, 2001, When This Cruel War is Over, 2001, Conquerors of the Sky, 2003, The Illusion of Victory, America World War I, 2003, The Louisiana Purchase, 2003, Mysteries of My Father: An Irish-American Memoir, 2005, Washington's Seal of War The Hidden Story of Valley Forge, 2005; editor: Affectionately Yours, George Washington, 1967, Benjamin Franklin, A Biography in His Own Words, 1972, The Living Land of Lincoln, 1980, The Secrets of Inchon, 2002; contbr. book Reader's Companion to American History, 1991, book Young Reader's Companion to American History, 1991, book Past Imperfect: History According to the Movies, 1995, book Forgotten Heroes, 1997, book What If, 1999, book To The Best of My Ability: The American Presidents, 2000, also various TV scripts, articles, short stories, book What If, 2001; cons. (movie) The American Revolution The History Channel, 1994, prin. commentator Long Journey Home - The Irish in America, 1998, (TV films) In Depth, 2004. Chmn. N.Y. Am. Revolution Round Table, 1970-81, Sr. scholar, Nat. Ctr. for the Am. Revolution of Valley Forge. Recipient achievement award in comm.arts Fordham U., 1961, Encaenia award, 1965, Mass Media award NCCJ, 1965, Christopher award, 1970, Colonial Dames Am. ann. book award, 1970, 72, award of merit Am. Assn. for State and Local History, 1974, fiction award Nat. Cath. Press Assn., 1974, Best Book award Am. Revolution Round Table, 1975, 97, 99, award of recognition N.J. Hist. Commn., 1992, Burack award for lifetime achievement Boston U., 2001, Best Mag. Article award Army Hist. Found., 2002, Abraham Lincoln Lit. award Union League Club, 2003. Fellow N.J. Hist. Soc., Soc. Am. Historians; mem. Am. PEN (pres. 1971-73), The Century Assn. Personal E-mail: tflem37048@aol.com.

FLEMING, THOMAS MICHAEL, artist, educator; b. Phila, May 12, 1951; s. Thomas Joseph and Eleanor Virginia (Huston) F.; m. Kristin Karen Wigley, Oct. 29, 1977 (dec. Jan. 1980); m. Beverly Jean Folgert, Sept. 25, 1987. AA with honors, Harrisburg (Pa.) Community Coll., 1972; BFA with honors, Pa. State U., 1975; MFA, U. Minn., 1978. Art instr. U. Wis., Wausau, 1978-84, asst. prof., 1985-89, assoc. prof., 1990-97, prof., 1998—. Dir., co-founder SoHo Studio Ctr., N.Y.C.; pres. Art Shoot, N.Y.C.; artistic program cons. Anglo-American Workshops, N.Y.C., 1988-89; art. dir.:W/Co., Wis.; founder Art NYC .com, 1996. Represented in permanent collections Musee Des Arts, Lausanne, Switzerland, Corning (N.Y.) Mus., Internat. Glasmuseum, Ebeltoft, Denmark. One of 100 Art Judges U.S. News and World Report's Best of America, 1990. Grantee U. Wis., 1981, 82, 84, 86, 87, 91, Wis. Arts Bd. Madison, 1985, 91. Mem. Glass Art Soc., Wis. Acad. Scis. Arts and Letters, Internat. Sculpture Assn., Wis. Painters and Sculptors, Artist Space N.Y. Home: 518 S 7th Ave Wausau WI 54401-5362

FLEMING, WENDELL HELMS, mathematician, educator; b. Guthrie, Okla., Mar. 7, 1928; s. James Lucian and Helen (Helms) F.; m. Florence Tatum, Apr. 4, 1948; children: Randall, Daniel, William. BS, Purdue U., 1948, MS, 1949, D honoris causa, 1991; PhD, U. Wis., 1951. Mathematician RAND Corp., 1951-55, cons., 1960-65; asst. prof. Purdue U., 1955-58; mem. faculty Brown U., 1958—, prof. math., 1963—, prof. applied math., 1969-95, chmn. dept., 1965-68, 82-85, 1991-94; prof. emeritus, 1995—. Author: Functions of Several Variables, 1965, (with R.W. Rishel) Deterministic and Stochastic Optimal Control, 1975, (with H.M. Soner) Controlled Markov Processes and Viscosity Solutions, 1992; editor SIAM Rev. NSF fellow, 1968-69; Guggenheim fellow, 1976-77 Mem. Am. Math. Soc. (chmn. com. on employment and ednl. policy 1975-77, Steele prize 1987), Soc. Indsl. and Applied Math. (Reid prize 1994), Am. Acad. Arts and Sci. Home: 9 Dolly Dr Bristol RI 02809-1578 Office: Brown U Div Applied Math Providence RI 02912-0001 E-mail: whf@cfm.brown.edu.

FLEMING, WILLIAM CARY, retired physician, retired consultant; b. Lee Hall, Va., Jan. 16, 1918; s. Thomas Hayes and Martha (Kirby) F.; m. Mabel Clare Green, Mar. 19, 1944; children: Martha Frances, Sharon Anne, Joan Marie. BS in Chemistry, U. Va., 1942, MD, 1945. Diplomate: Am. Bd. Phys. Medicine and Rehab. Intern Del. Hosp., Wilmington, 1945-46; gen. practice Glasgow, Va., 1948-49; mem. staff student health U. Kans., 1949-51; indsl. physician E.I. duPont de Nemours & Co., Inc., Waynesboro, Va., 1951-53; resident phys. medicine and rehab. VA Hosp.-Med. Coll. Va., Richmond, 1953-56; phys. medicine and rehab. physician VA hosps., Richmond, 1956-58, Pitts., 1959, Coral Gables, Fla., 1959-64, VA Hosp., Birmingham, Ala., 1970-78, cons. 1978-88, ret., 1988; prof. phys. medicine and rehab. U. Ala. Med. Sch., 1964-88, chmn. dept., 1964-70; physiatrist in chief Univ. Hosp. Birmingham, 1964-70. Med. dir. Spain Rehab. Ctr., Birmingham, 1964-69, physiatrist, 1969-88, ret.; dir. U. Ala. Rehab. Research and Tng. Ctr., 1966-69,; med. staff, chmn. med. bd. Lakeshore Rehab. Hosp., 1973—88; cons. staff Children's and St. Vincent's Hosps., 1965—88; cons. rehab. pavillion, courtesy staff Druid City Hosp., Tuscaloosa, Ala., 1984—88; courtesy staff Med. Ctr. East, Birmingham, 1989—90, med. dir. rehab. St. Francis Hosp., Topeka, 1989-91; dir. chronic illness project, Dade County, Fla., 1962-63; mem. med. adv. bd. Birmingham Vis. Nurse Assn., 1965-86, Central Ala. chpt. Nat. Multiple Sclerosis Soc., 1966—93, chmn., 1976, 85-87; bd. dirs. N. Central Ala. Occupational Rehab. Ctr., 1966-70, 73-79, chmn. bd., 1978-79; surveyor Commn. on Accreditation Rehab. Facilities, 1984—93; mem. State Profl. Adv. Council for Home Health Service, 1986-88. Bd. dirs. Birmingham Civic Ballet, 1971-77. Served to capt. M.C. AUS, 1946-48. Mem. AMA, So. Med. Assn. (chmn. sect. 1966-67), Ala. Med. Assn., Am. Acad. Phys. Medicine and Rehab., So. Soc. Phys. Medicine (founding mem., chmn. 1970-72), Ala. Soc. Phys. Medicine and Rehab. (founding mem., v.p., pres.), Assn. Acad. Physiatrists, Raven Soc. (v.p. 1942-43), Assn. Med. Rehab. Dirs. and Coordinators (cert. bd. 1964—87), Alpha Chi Sigma, Nu Sigma Nu. Clubs: Poinsettia Men's (founding mem. 1970, pres. 1971-72), Shoal Creek, The Club (Birmingham, Ala.). Lodges: Rotary (Paul Harris fellow). Spl. research rehab. aspects stroke, emphysema, kidney disease, heart disease, spinal cord injury, electromyography. Home: 3528 Belle Meade Way Birmingham AL 35223-1522

FLEMING, WILLIAM SLOAN, energy executive, computer company executive; b. Long Beach, Calif., Aug. 13, 1937; s. William Sloan and Helen Jean (Disler) Fleming; m. Jacquline M. Carrio, Mar. 9, 1960; children: Katherine A., Kimberly A. BSME, Calif. Maritime Acad., 1958; MBA, Syracuse U., 1970. Commd. ensign USN, 1958, advanced through grades to lt., 1967, attack pilot, 1958—67, disabled in the line of duty, ret., 1967; mech. engr. Carrier Corp., Syracuse, NY, 1967—70; regional sales mgr. Rheem Mfg., Atlanta, 1970—71; market devel. supr. Owens Corning Fiberglas, Toledo, 1971—73; pres. W. S. Fleming & Assocs., Inc., Syracuse, 1975—86, Fleming Group, Syracuse, 1986—87, CEO, chmn. bd., 1987—94; bus. devel. mgr., energy systems group Sci. Applications Internat. Corp. SAIC/Fleming Group, Syracuse, 1994—96; bus. devel. mgr. Sci. Applications Internat. Corp./Energy Sys. Group, 1996—97; exec. v.p. Jacwill Svcs. Inc., Cazenovia, NY, 1997—2000, pres. St. Petersburg, Fla., 2000—. Pres. Enterlog Sys., Inc., Syracuse, 1985—94; chmn. bd. Assn. Intelligent Sys. Tech., Inc., Syracuse, 1986—90. Contbr. articles to profl. jours.; author: singer energy simulation computer program. Recipient Energy awards, Ctrl. N.Y., 1981. Fellow: ASHRAE (life; chmn. tech. com. 9.6, sys. energy utilization 1981—83, chmn. ad hoc com. 90, energy stds. 1983—84, chmn. tech. com. 6.7, solar energy utilization 1984—86, chmn. nat. program com. 1985—86, mem. edn. coun. 1989—90, rsch. and tech. com. 1991—95, chmn. spl. publs. com. 1998—99, rsch. adminstrn. com. 2000—01, mem. handbook com. 2001—05, chmn. handbook fund subcom. 2004—05, chmn. handbook com. 2005—); mem.: DAV, Assn. Energy Engrs. (charter, 1 of 34 in Hall of Fame), Mil. Officers Assn., Am. Legion. Roman Catholic. Avocations: skiing, boating, homework. Office: JacWil Svcs Inc PO Box 8249 Saint Petersburg FL 33738-8249

FLEMING, WILLIAM WRIGHT, JR., pharmacology educator; b. Washington, Jan. 30, 1932; s. William Wright and Esme (Reeder) F.; m. Dolores D. Atchison, Sept. 1, 1952; children: Lisa Marie, Jennifer Amelia, David William. AB cum laude, Harvard U., 1954; PhD (Procter fellow), Princeton U., 1957. Mem. faculty W.Va. U. Med. Ctr., Morgantown, 1960—, prof. pharmacology, 1966—, chmn. dept., 1966-86, Mylan Chmn. of Pharmacology and Toxicology, 1986-99, prof. emeritus, 1999—. Vis. prof. U. Melbourne, Australia, 1969, St. George's Hosp. Med. Sch. U. London, 1978, Flinders U., Adelaide, Australia, 1985, 87, U. Adelaide, 1987; adj. prof. pharmacology U. Pitts. Sch. Medicine, 2005—; cons. Mead Johnson Rsch. Ctr., Evansville, Ind., 1970-77, Spriggs & Hollingsworth Law Firm, Washington, 2004—; mem. pharmacology-toxicology rsch. program. Nat. Inst. Gen. Med. Scis., NIH, 1973-77, chmn., 1975-77; mem. drug abuse rsch. rev. com. Nat. Inst. Drug Abuse, 1985-89; mem. pharmacology study sect., div. rsch. grants NIH, 1990-94. Mem. editl. bd. Jour. Pharmacology and Exptl. Therapeutics, 1966-85, Life Scis., 1978-90; contbr. articles to profl. jours. USPHS postdoctoral fellow Harvard U., 1957-60; Fogarty sr. internat. fellow, 1978; recipient P.L. MacLachlan award excellence in teaching W.Va. U. Med. Sch., 1964, 67, 78, 89, 92, 97, 99; named Outstanding Tchr., W.Va. U. Found., 1978. Mem. AAAS, Am. Soc. Pharmacology and Exptl. Therapeutics (councilor 1975-78, pres. 1981-82, chmn. bd publs. trustees 1984-90, Otto Krayer award 1986, Croker Meml. lectr. 1988, Torald Sollman award 1999), Assn. Med. Sch. Pharmacology (councilor 1977-79, treas. 1977-78, pres. 1986-88), Fedn. Am. Socs. for Exptl. Biology (dir. 1980-83), Internat. Union Pharmacology (del. 1980-83, 91-94, mem. internat. adv. com. for Congress of Pharmacology 1987, exec. com. 1994-98, 2002—, pres. 1998-2002, past pres. 2002—). Home: HC 3 Box 22 A Tionesta PA 16353 Office: WVa U Health Scis Ctr Dept Physiology & Pharmacology Morgantown WV 26506 Personal E-mail: wfle216184@aol.com.

FLEMING-RIFE, ANITA L., communications educator, consultant; b. Des Moines, Iowa; d. Guy A. Fleming and Fannie J. West, Charles R. and Mary C. Finney; m. Donald LeRoy Rife, Sr., Mar. 13, 1964 (div. Aug. 7, 1971); children: Donnyta Kameco Rife-Alexander, Donald LeRoy Rife, II, Charles Christopher Rife. BA, U. No. Colo., 1979, MA, 1988; PhD, So. Ill. U., 1997. Lic. practical nurse, Iowa Bd. Practical Nursing, 1967. Project mgr., pub. info. officer UN Secretariat, N.Y., 1992—93; asst. prof. U. No. Colo., Greeley, Colo., 1995—98, Pa. State U., State College, Pa., 1998—2003; cons. Fleming-Rife Cons., State College, 2003—04; assoc. prof. Lock Haven U. of Pa., Lock Haven, Pa., 2004—. Bd. dirs. Adventures in Health, Edn. and Agr. Devel., Rockville, Md.; exec. prodr., dir. Fleming-Rife Productions, State College, Pa., 1998—; rsch. cons. Fleming-Rife Cons., State College, 1998—. Prodr.: (films) I, Too, Sing America: The Public School Education of African-American Children Before and After Brown v. The Board of Education (Hon. Mention award Black Filmmakers' Hall of Fame, 2003), Lest We Forget the Teachers' story (Freedom Forum Professors Rsch. grant, 2000); contbr. articles to profl. jours., chapters to books. Vice-chmn. Pa. and Del. Nat. Summit on Africa, Washington, 2000; co-chmn. pub. rels. com. Adventures in Health Edn. and Agr. Devel., Rockville, Md., 2004—. Fellow, Freedom Forum, 1997, The Am. Soc. Newspaper Editors, 2001; scholar, So. Ill. U., 1990. Mem.: Assn. Edn. in Journalism and Mass Comms. (chmn. rsch. paper competition 1999—2001), Nat. Soc. Collegiate Scholars (Disting. Mem. award 2003). Protestant. Avocations: travel, reading.

FLEMINGS, MERTON CORSON, engineering educator, materials scientist; b. Syracuse, N.Y., Sept. 20, 1929; s. Merton C. and Marion (Dexter) F.; m. Elizabeth Goodridge, Sept. 7, 1956 (div. 1976); children: Anne, Peter; m. R. Elizabeth ten Grotenhuis, Feb. 20, 1977; children: Cecily, Elspeth. SB, MIT, 1951, SM, 1952, ScD, 1954; PhD (hon.), Swiss Fed. Inst. Tech., Lausanne, 2004. Mem. faculty MIT, Cambridge, 1956—70, ABEX prof. Metallurgy, 1970—75, Ford prof. engring., 1975—81, dir. materials processing ctr., 1979—82, Toyota prof. materials processing, 1981—94, dept. head materials sci. and engring., 1982—95; dir. MIT-Singapore Alliance, 1999—2001, Lemelson-MIT Program, 2001—. Vis. prof. U. Tokyo, 1989, Ecole des Mines de Paris, 1996; bd. dirs. Hitchiner Corp., Metal Casting Tech., Inc., Silk Road Project, Inc. Author: Foundry Engineering, 1959; Solidification Processing, 1974. Contbr. numerous articles on metallurgy to profl. jours. Mem. Mass. Gov.'s Coun. Econ. Growth and Tech., 1994-2000. Recipient Simpson Gold medal Am. Foundrymen's Soc., 1961, Henri Sainte-Claire Deville medal Soc. Francaise de Metallurgie, 1977, Herbert J. Holloman award Acta Metallurgica, 1997, David Turnbull lectureship Materials Rsch. Soc., 1997. Fellow Metall. Soc. (Leadership award 1990, Bruce Chalmers award 1993, Educator award 1999), ASM Internat. (bd. trustees 1994-97, Henry Marion Howe medal 1973, 90, Edward DeMille Campbell Meml. lectr. 1990); mem. Am. Inst. Metall. Engrs. (Mathewson Gold medal 1969), Am. Acad. Arts and Scis., Japan Foundrymen's Soc. (hon.), Iron and Steel Inst. Japan (hon., Yukawa Meml. lectr. 1985, Tawara award 2000), Italian Metall. Assn. (Luigi Losana Gold medal 1986), Japan Inst. Metals (hon., Gold medal 2005), Nat. Acad. Engring., Fed. Materials Socs. (Nat. Materials Advancement award 1999), Korean Acad. Sci. and Tech. Home: 975 Memorial Dr Apt 605 Cambridge MA 02138-5803 Office: Dept Materials Sci and Engring MIT 4-415 Cambridge MA 02139 Office Phone: 617-253-3233. Business E-Mail: flemings@mit.edu.

FLEMMING, DAVID PAUL, biologist; b. Kittanning, Pa., Oct. 23, 1953; s. Paul Ross and Jeanne Marie (Seaton) F.; m. Diane Frances MacKenzie, Sept. 17, 1983; children: Daniel Robert, Peter David. BS in Biology, Grove City Coll., 1975; MS in Biology, Bowling Green State U., 1977. Child care worker George Jr. Rep., Grove City, Pa., 1978-79; park naturalist State of Pa.-McConnell's Mill State Park, Portersville, 1979; biologist sect. 7 U.S. Fish & Wildlife Svc., Washington, 1979-80, Atlanta, 1980-83, recovery coord. Denver, 1983-87, biologist endangered species Vero Beach, Fla., 1987-88, chief divsn. endangered species Atlanta, 1988-96, chief ecol. svcs., 1997-98, ecol. svcs. supr., 1998—. Contbg. author: Conservation and Resource Management, 1993. Asst. coach T-ball and soccer YMCA, Lawrenceville, Ga., 1991—92, premier soccer coach Snellville, Ga., 1995—2001; USS Ofcl., 1996—2003.

FLEMMING, STANLEY LALIT KUMAR, family practice physician, mayor, state legislator; b. Rosebud, S.D., Mar. 30, 1953; s. Homer W. and Evelyn C. (Misra) F.; m. Martha Susan Light, July 2, 1977; children: Emily Drisana, Drew Anil, Claire Elizabeth Misra. AAS, Pierce Coll., 1973; BS in Zoology, U. Wash., 1976; MA in Social Psychology, Pacific Luth. U., 1979; DO, Western U., 1985. Diplomate Am. Coll. Family Practice; cert. ATLS. Intern Pacific Hosp. Long Beach (Calif.), 1985-86; resident in family practice Pacific Hosp. Long Beach, 1986-88; fellow in adolescent medicine Children's Hosp. L.A., 1988-90; clin. preceptor Family Practice Residency Program Calif. Med. Ctr., U. So. Calif., L.A., 1989—; clin. instr. Sch. Medicine U. So. Calif., L.A., 1989-90; clin. instr. Western U. Health Sci., Pomona, Calif., 1989-90, clin. asst. prof. Family Medicine, 1987—; exam. commr., expert examiner Calif. Osteo. Med. Bd., 1987-89; med. dir. Cmty. Health Care Delivery System Pierce County, Tacoma, Wash., 1990—; mayor City of University Place, Wash. Clin. instr. U. Wash. Sch. Medicine, 1990—; bd. dirs.

Calif. State Bd. Osteo. Physicians Examiners, 1989—, cons., 1989. Mayor, City of University Place, Wash. Col. M.C., U.S. Army, 1976—, Named one of Outstanding Young Men of Am., U.S. Jaycees, 1983, 85, Intern of Yr. Western U. Health Sci. Coll., 1986, Resident of Yr., Greater Long Beach Assn., 1988, Alumnus of Yr., Pierce Coll., 1993, 97; recipient Pumerantz-Weiss award, 1985. Mem. Fedn. State Bds. Licensing, Am. Osteopathic Assn., Am. Acad. Family Practice, Soc. Adolescent Medicine, Assn. Military Surgeons U.S., Assn. U.S. Army (chpt. pres.), Soc. Am. Military Engrs. (chpt. v.p.), Calif. Med. Assn., Wash. Osteopathic Med. Assn. (Physician of Yr. 1993), Calif. Family Practice Soc., Long Beach Med. Assn. (com. mem.), N.Y. Acad. Sci., Calif. Med. Review Inc., Sigma Sigma Phi, Am. Legion. Episcopalian. Home: 7619 Chambers Creek Rd W University Place WA 98467-2015 Office: Family Health Ctr University Place WA 98466

FLESHER, DALE LEE, accounting educator, dean; b. Albany, Ind., June 27, 1945; s. Myron Lee and Deloris Rachel (Wright) F.; m. Tonya Kay Maloney, June 6, 1970; children: Flyn Lee, Felicity Kay. BS, Ball State U., 1967, MA, 1968; PhD, U. Cin., 1975. CPA, Cert. Govt. Fin. Mgr. Asst. mgr. Price's Food Market, Albany, 1960—66; asst. prof. Ball State U., Muncie, Ind., 1968—71; instr. U. Cin., 1971—73; assoc. prof. Appalachian State U., Boone, NC, 1973—77; prof. accountancy U. Miss., Oxford, 1977—, assoc. dean, 1993—. Controller Am. Wicker, Inc., Boone, 1973-77; auditor Arthur Andersen & Co., New Orleans, 1978. Author 41 books, including: Accounting for Advertising Assets, 1978, CMA Examination Rev., 1984, 11th edit., 2004, 50 Years of Progress Through Sharing, 1991, The Third Quarter Century of the AAA, 1991, Auditing the Marketing Function, 1993, Internal Auditing Standards and Practices, 1996, Accountancy at Ole Miss, 1997, 60 Years of Progress, 2002; contbr. over 400 articles to profl. publs. Treas. Oxford-Univ. Meth. Ch., 1985-2004, mem. fin. com., 1985-2004; mem. sch. bd. Oxford-Univ. Sch., 1993-97, 1998-2002; pres. Meth. Men's Club, Oxford, 1980-81; treas. Oxford-U. Sch.-Parent Support Group, Oxford, 1989-90. Mem.: Acad. Acctg. Historians (pres. 1988, trustee), Miss. Soc. CPA (Outstanding Educator award 1998), Assn. Cert. Fraud Examiners (cert. examiners), Inst. Internal Auditors (Leon Radde award 1990, cert. mgmt. acct., cert. internal auditor), Am. Acctg. Assn., Ind. Hist. Soc., Inst. Mgmt. Accts. (nat. bd. dirs. 1984—86, Cert. of Merit 1993, 1994, 1995, 1996, 2005), AICPA Found. (bd. dirs. 2002—, bd. dirs. 2002—05), Miss. Hist. Soc. (life). Avocations: softball, scripophily, writing, fishing, basketball. Office: U Miss Sch Accountancy University MS 38677 Office Phone: 662-915-7623. Business E-Mail: acdlf@olemiss.edu.

FLESHER, GAIL A., lawyer; b. 1960; BA, Wharton Sch., U. Pa., 1983; JD, Hastings Coll. Law, 1988. Bar: N.Y. 1989, Conn. 1989. Assoc. Davis, Polk & Wardwell, N.Y.C., 1988—96, pntr., 1996—, hiring ptnr. & mem. firm recruitment com. Mem.: NALP Found. Law Career Research & Edn. (chmn. 2000—02, bd. trustees 1992—), ABA. Office: Davis Polk & Wardwell 450 Lexington Ave New York NY 10017 Office Phone: 212-450-4469. Office Fax: 212-450-3469. Business E-Mail: gail.flesher@dpw.com.

FLESHMAN, JAMES W., medical association administrator; b. New Orleans, Aug. 2, 1954; MD, Wash. U., St. Louis, 1980. Surgery residency Jewish Hosp., St. Louis, 1980—86; fellowship colon & rectal surgery U. Toronto, 1986—87; now assoc. prof. surgery Wash. U. Sch. of Medicine, St. Louis. Mem.: Am. Bd. Colon & Rectal Surgery ((former v.p., pres., 2004-)). Office: Am Bd Colon & Rectal Surgery 20600 Eureka Rd Ste 600 Taylor MI 48180 also: Wash U Sch of Medicine Box 8109 660 S Euclid Campus Saint Louis MO 63110

FLESSNER, PAUL, information technology executive; b. Roberts, IL, Jan. 1959; m. Sue Flessner; children: Andy, Jonathan. BS in Computer Sci. & Bus. Adminstrn., Ill. State U., 1981. With Microsoft, 1994—, sr. v.p. .NET enterprise servers divsn. Redmond, Wash., sr. v.p., server platform div. Mem. bus. leadership team Microsoft, leader devel. & coord. combined enterprise bus. strategy plan. Office: One Microsoft Way Redmond WA 98052-6399

FLETCHER, ALPHONSE, JR., financial analyst; BA, Harvard Univ.; masters environ. mgmt., Yale Univ. Vice-pres. Bear, Stearns & Co., Inc.; sr. vice-pres. Kidder, Peabody & Co. Benefactor Alphonse Fletcher Fund Yale Univ. Lieutenant Inactive Reserve USAF. Office: Fletcher Asset Mgmt 425 Fifth Ave New York NY 10018 Office Phone: 212-221-0543.*

FLETCHER, ANTHONY C., artist, graphics designer; s. Wilbert G. and Betty Jane Fletcher. Student, Sch. of Visual Art, N.Y.C., 1999, Phila. Inst. Art, 1975—76, Fla. A&M U., 1974—78. Graphic designer J.C. Penney Co., N.Y.C., 1981—86, U. Del., Newark, 1986—89; art dir., graphic designer Sachs Finley Entertainment, 1989—2000; art dir. Bahia Entertainment Co., N.Y.C., 1993; graphic designer K-lll Press/K-lll Info. Corp., N.Y.C., 1992—94; graphic designer, illustrator Happy Kids, N.Y.C., 1997—98, Mamiye Sales, Inc., N.Y.C., 1998—99, Group 3 Design, N.Y.C., 1999—2000, Signal-Tahiti, N.Y.C., 2000, Nautica Internat., N.Y.C., 2000—01, Farm Boys, Parigi Group Ltd., 2002—03. Exhibited in group shows at N.C. Art Mus., 1997, Cordoza Law Sch., Yeshiva U., N.Y.C., 1996, Tanqueray's Underground Gallery, Orlando, Fla., 1991, AC-BAW Gallery, Mt. Vernon, N.Y., 1987, Ariel Gallery, N.Y.C., 1987, one-man shows include Clinton Hill Simply Art Gallery, Bklyn., 1994, many others, Represented in permanent collections Sony Records, J.C. Penney Co., Inner-City Broadcasting Co., October Gallery, London, Henry Holt & Co., N.Y.C., many individual collections. Recipient Gold Record for mktg. design, Epic Records, 1984. Home and Office: 2600 John F Kennedy Blvd 3-L Jersey City NJ 07306-4715 Office Phone: 201-433-1813. E-mail: anthony.fletcher@verizon.net.

FLETCHER, ANTHONY L., lawyer; b. Washington, Dec. 12, 1935; s. Robert J. and Lyndell (Pickett) F.; m. Juliana Schump, Sept. 3, 1960 (div. 1977); children: Leigh Anne Grinstead, Kristin Marie Giffin, Julie Bowen Cimino; m. Zelda L. Fletcher, Mar. 30, 1986. BA, Princeton U., 1957; JD, Harvard U., 1962. Bar: NY 1963, U.S. Ct. Appeals (2d cir.) 1966, U.S. Ct. Appeals (7th cir.) 1966, U.S. Supreme Ct. 1966, U.S. Ct. Appeals (3d cir.) 1969, U.S. Ct. Appeals (fed. cir.) 1972, U.S. Ct. Appeals (5th cir.) 1973, U.S. Ct. Appeals (1st cir.) 1981, U.S. Ct. Appeals (9th cir.) 1983. Assoc. Simpson Thacher & Bartlett, NYC, 1962-71, Conboy, Hewitt, O-Brien & Boardman, NYC, 1971-74, ptnr., 1974-86, Hunton & Williams, NYC, 1986-97; prin. Fish & Richardson P.C., NYC, 1997—2002, sr. counsel, 2003—. Editor-in-chief Trademark Reporter, 1982-84; contbr. articles to profl. jours. With infantry U.S. Army, 1957—59. Mem. Internat. Trademark Assn. (bd. dirs. 1983-85, Pres.'s award 2003). Episcopalian. Office: Fish & Richardson PC 153 E 53d St New York NY 10022 Business E-Mail: fletcher@fr.com.

FLETCHER, BETTY BINNS, federal judge; b. Tacoma, Mar. 29, 1923; BA, Stanford U., 1943; LLB, U. Wash., 1956. Bar: Wash. 1956. Mem. firm Preston, Thorgrimson, Ellis, Holman & Fletcher, Seattle, 1956—79; judge U.S. Ct. Appeals (9th cir.), Seattle, 1979—, sr. judge, 1998—. Mem.: ABA (Margaret Brent award 1992), Fed. Judges Assn. (past pres.), Am. Law Inst., Wash. State Bar Assn., Phi Beta Kappa, Order of Coif. Office: US Ct Appeals 9th Cir 1200 6th Ave 21st Fl Seattle WA 98101

FLETCHER, BILL, JR., not-for-profit fundraiser; Undergraduate, Harvard Univ. Organizer Dist. 65-united Auto Workers; org. sec., admin. dir. Nat. Postal Mail Handlers Union; vice-pres. internat. trade unit devel. prog. George Meany Ctr./ Nat. Labor Coll. AFL-CIO; edn. dir., pres. asst. AFL-CIO. Adj. faculty Univ. Mass.-Boston. Office: TransAfrica Forum 1426 21st St NW Washington DC 20036 Office Phone: 202-223-1960. Office Fax: 202-223-1966.*

FLETCHER, BRADY JONES, vocational education career specialist; b. Natchitoches, La., Apr. 17, 1928; d. Louis Benjamin and Isadore Hannah (Stephens) Jones; m. Donald Greene Fletcher, Aug. 13, 1950; children: Donald Bruce, Nathan Louis, Debra Patrice. BA, Clark Coll., 1950; MA (fellow), Howard U., 1953; postgrad. (NDEA fellow), Ind. U., 1965; EdS in Guidance, George Washington U., 1967, EdD, 1977. Tchr. math. and sci. Fairmont Heights (Md.) High Sch., 1951-54; tchr. math. and sci. Douglas High Sch., Upper Marlboro, Md., 1955-57, Prince George's County (Md.) Pub. Schs., 1951-59, Banneker Jr. High Sch., Washington, 1959-63; chmn. guidance dept. Garnet/Patterson Jr. High Sch., 1963-67; counselor Lincoln Jr. High Sch., D.C. pub. schs., 1967-69, Kensington (Md.) Jr. High Sch., 1969-73, Banneker Jr. High Sch., 1975-77; career edn. specialist Montgomery County (Md.) Schs., 1973-75; counselor Frederic Douglass Middle Sch., Indpls., 1999—. Cons. Md. State Dept. Edn., 1973, Balt. City Pub. Schs., 1973, Balt. County Pub. Schs., 1973, D.C. Pub. Schs.; mem. adv. com. for spl. needs population Montgomery Coll., Rockville, Md., Am. Coll. Testing Bd., Washington, 1987—; project dir. InterAmerica Rsch. Assoc., Inc., Rosslyn, Va., 1977. Editor: Career Edn., 1973-75; Increasing Collaboration in Career Education (2 vols.). Rep. to Cmty. Action Bd. for Montgomery County Edn. Assn.; dir. D.C. Summer Youth Job Program, 1981; tech. cons., del. to Russia, Czech Republic and Poland with citizen amb. program People to People Internat., 1993. Inst. Ednl. Leadership fellow, summer 1984, Montgomery County Vocat. Assessment Ctr. (recipient dedicated service award 1987); recipient Educators award Clinton A.M.E. Ch., 1988, Multicultural Counseling award Founders of Orgn., 1987, award Montgomery County Coun., 1990; resolution in her honor Md. State Senate, 1990; Adminstr. of Yr. for I-Star Program, Ind. Say No to Drugs, 1994; named Alumnus of Yr. George Washington U., 1999, keynote spkr. opening conf. edn. and tech.; inducted into Hall of Fame, Englewood H.S., Chgo., 1999. Mem. AACD (Nat. award for govt. rels.), Am. Pers. and Guidance Assn. (Human Rels. Com. award 1974, editor conv. newsletter 1983), Am. Assn. Specialists in Group Work (nat. chairperson human rels. 1993, Recognition award 1993), Md. Pers. and Guidance Assn. (award 1975), Nat. Capital Pers. and Guidance Assn. (award 1975-76), Ind. Counseling Assn. (v.p. ctrl. chpt. 1992), Ind. Sch. Counselors Assn., Ind. Career Devel. Assn. (Ind. sch. counselor), Ind. Multicultural Assn., D.C. Assn. Counseling and Devel. (pres. 1986-87, del. to North Atlantic region assembly, recipient award disting. profl. leadership 1987, award for profl. devel. of assn. 1986, trustee 1988-89, co-chairperson govt. rels. com., Nat. awards Govt. Rels. Com. Boston 1989 and Cin. 1990), Nat. Vocat. Guidance Assn., Assn. Non-White Concerns, Nat. Assn. Career Edn., Nat. Sch. Counselor Assn., Internat. Platform Assn., Indpls. Urban League, Alpha Kappa Alpha, Phi Delta Kappa. E-mail: dgflet1098@prodigy.net.

FLETCHER, CATHY ANN, auditor; b. Barnesville, Ga., Aug. 23, 1949; d. John James and Dorothy Lee (Banks) Fletcher; 1 child, Lisa Faye. Student, Ohio State U., 1969—70; AS, Mass. Bay C.C., 1982; BS, AS, Northeastern U., 1984; MA in Human Resources Mgmt., Emmanuel Coll., Boston, 1993. Mail clk. Fed. Res. Bank, Boston, 1971-72; office mgr. Breckenridge Sportswear, Boston, 1973-74; asst. dir. Whittier Street Health Ctr., Boston, 1974-81; sec. to dir. Northeastern U., 1981-84; auditor Def. Contract Audit Agy. N.E. Region, Boston, 1984—. Sec., bd. dirs. Boston Tenant Policy Coun., 1977-79; mgr. northeastern region Fed. Women's Program, 1989—, mgr. northeastern region Black Employment program, 1999—; mem. adv. bd. DCAA EEO, 1989—. Author: Softball Team Book, 1975. V.p., bd. dirs. Bromley Heath Tenant Mgmt. Corp., Jamaica Plain, Mass., 1976-91, bd. dirs., 1997-2000; apptd. fed. women program coord. State of Mass., 1988; mem. women's opportunity com. Boston Fed. Exec. Bd., 1990—, mem. women's coun., 1994—, mem. diversity com., 1997—; with Women's Ednl. Indsl. Union, 1993-99; mem. Fed. Spl. Emphasis Program Coalition, 2000—. Mem. NAFE, Profl. Coun., Nat. Tenants Orgn., Assn. Govt. Accts. (cert. govt. fin. mgr.), Federally Employed Women (treas. Greater Boston chpt. 1992-93, pres. 1994—; New Eng. Regional mgr. 1995—, rep. 1996—), Hawkettes Social (pres., past. mem. profl. coun.), Blacks in Govt., Sigma Epsilon Rho. Avocations: reading, bible studies, cooking, walking, travel. Office: Def Contract Audit Agy Boston Br Office 101 Merrimac St Ste 820A Boston MA 02114-4724 Business E-Mail: cfletcher@dcaa.mil.

FLETCHER, CHARLES, secondary school educator; Instr. music dept. Fernley (Nev.) H.S. Mem. Nev. Commn. on Profl. Stds. in Edn., 1996—99. Recipient Marna Zachry award for disting. svc., Lyon County Edn. Assn., 1999. Mem.: No. Zone Nev. Music Educators Assn. (sec.-treas. 1989—99), Nat. Bd. for Profl. Tchg. Stds. (bd. mem.). Office: Fernley High Sch Music Dept 1300 Hwy 95A Fernley NV 89408

FLETCHER, COURTNEY VANCE, pharmacologist, educator; b. Greybull, Wyo., Mar. 25, 1955; s. John Cullen and H. Christene Fletcher; m. Jean Stanius Fletcher, Oct. 14, 1983. AS, Northwestern C.C., Powell, Wyo., 1975; BS in Pharmacy, Univ Wyo., Laramie, Wyo., 1978; DPharm, U. Minn., Mpls., 1982. Prof. and chmn. Dept of Clin. Pharmacy, Univ Colo. Health Sciences Ctr., Denver, Colo., 2002—; prof. Univ of Minn., Minneapolis, Minn., 1989—2001. Mem. antiviral drug adv. com. FDA, Rockville, Md.; mem. panel on clin. practices for treatment of HIV infection U.S. Dept. Health and Human Svcs., Washington. Contbr. articles to profl. jours. (Highest impact paper in clin. pharmacy infectious diseases, 1999). Fellow: Am. Coll. Clinical Pharmacy; mem.: ASM, AAAS, Am. Soc. for Clin. Pharm and Therapeutics, Soc. of Infectious Diseases Pharmacists. Office: U Colo Health Scis Ctr 4200 East 9th Ave C-238 Denver CO 80262 E-mail: courtney.fletcher@uchsc.edu.

FLETCHER, DENISE KOEN, strategic and financial consultant; b. Istanbul, Turkey, Aug. 31, 1948; came to U.S., 1967, naturalized, 1976; d. Moris and Kety (Barkey) Koen; m. Robert B. Fletcher, Nov. 11, 1969; children—David, Kate. AB (Coll. scholar), Wellesley Coll., 1969; M in City Planning, Harvard U., 1972. Analyst Ea. div. Getty Oil Co., N.Y.C., 1972-73, sr. analyst, 1973-74, cash mgmt. and bldg. supr., 1974-76, Getty Oil Co. (Eastern), 1976; asst. treas. N.Y. Times Co., N.Y.C., 1976-80, treas., 1980-88; pres. Fletcher Assocs. Inc., Larchmont, N.Y., 1988-96; CEO Comm. Venture Group, Ltd., N.Y.C., N.Y., 1989-90; v.p., CFO Bowne & Co., 1996-98, sr. v.p., CFO, 1998—2000; exec. v.p., CFO Mastercard, 2000—03; sr. v.p. Davita, Inc., 2004—, sr. adv. to CEO, 2004—, CFO, 2004—. Bd. dirs. Unisys Corp., Orbitz, Inc., Sempra Energy. Bd. dirs. Overseas Edn. Found. Internat., 1989-90, Boy Scouts Am., Exploring, 1991-93; bd. dirs., trustee and v.p. bd. dirs., exec. com. YWCA, N.Y., 1987-2002, Girl Scouts USA, 2000-02; mem. budget com. City of Larchmont, N.Y., 1981-83, chmn. zoning bd. appeals, 1987—, mem. selection com., 1985-87; mem. alumni exec. coun. Harvard U. Sch. Govt., 1982-87. Mellon scholar, 1970 Mem. Academy of Women Achievers, The Business Leadership Coun., Fin. Execs. Internat., Fin. Women's Assn., Women's Forum, Treasurers Club N.Y., Harvard Club (N.Y.C.), Phi Beta Kappa.

FLETCHER, DONALD RODGERS, writer, religious studies educator; b. Ventnor, NJ; s. Archibald Grey and Jessie Rodgers Fletcher; m. Martha Clayton Bradway, May 19, 1942; children: Donna Poole, Sylvia, Marilyn Keith, Alan, Lawrence, Thomas. BA in english, Princeton U., 1939; MDiv, Princeton Theol. Seminary, 1943; PhD in english, Princeton U., 1951. Fgn. missionary Presbyn. Ch., Chile, 1944—56, field rep. Caribbean, 1956—60; biblical studies tchr. U. Tex., Austin, 1960—65; chair, divsn. of humanities Stillman Coll., Tuscaloosa, Ala., 1965—67; sec. of continuing edn. Presbyn. Bd. of Christian Edn., Phila., 1967—73; English tchr. Cherry Hill H.S. West, Cherry Hill, NJ, 1973—86; sr. pastor Rossmoor Cmty. Ch., Monroe, NJ, 1993—99; ret. Interim pastor St. Paul's Presbyn. Ch., Laurel Springs, NJ, 1978—79; organizing pastor Bethel Presbyn. Ch., 1981—83; supply pastor First Presbyn. Ch., Janvier, NJ, 1987—93. Author: (book) I, Lukas Wrote the Book, 2003, View from the Playroom Floor, 2005. Elected mem. Sch. Bd., Cherry Hill, NJ, 1970—73; mem. and officer Kiwanis Club of Rossmoor, Monroe, NJ, 1998—; dir. Mutual 15, Rossmoor, Monroe, 2003—; ordained mem. Presbyn. of Monmouth, 1994. Recipient Disting. Alumnus, Princeton U., 1979. Mem.: U.S. Croquet Assn. Democrat. Presbyn. Avocations: writing, poetry, watercolor. Personal E-mail: donmarflet@aol.com.

FLETCHER, DOUGLAS CHARLES, lawyer; b. Rockford, Ill., Mar. 5, 1943; s. Fred Leland and Dorothy Edwards Fletcher; children: Adrian, Lauren, Robin. BA in Econs. and Engring., U. Nev., Reno, 1969, MBA in Fin. cum laude, 1972; JD, U. of Pacific, 1975; postgrad., Colo. State U., 1976. Bar: Nev. 1975, U.S. Ct. Appeals (9th cir.) 1976. Exec. v.p. PanWorld Engring., 1967-68; design engr. Nev. Bell, 1968-70; economist Sierra Pacific Power Co., 1970-72, gen. counsel, 1975-78; operating trustee William Lear Motors Co., 1978-79; ptnr. Leslie Gray & Assocs., 1979-81; oper. trustee Horseshoe Club Casinos, 1981-82, Mapes Hotel and Money Tree Casinos, 1982-85; owner, ptnr. Douglas C. Fletcher, Ltd., 1985—; operating receiver Echo Summit Tahoe Ski Resort, 1989-92. Advisor U. Nev. Grad. Bus. Sch., Reno, 1976-85; mem. U.S. Trustee Panel, 1978-95; judge pro tem Reno Mcpl. Ct., 1980-82. Author: Bond Reverse Yield Gaps of Public Utilities, 1972. Mem. ctrl. planning com. Republican Party of Washoe County, 1978-82; bd. dirs. Washoe County Youth Found., Reno, 1983-92, Eagles Nest Assn., Reno, 1998; founder, bd. dirs. Sierra League, Reno, 1989-99; bd. dirs., pres. ski team advisors U. Nev., Reno, 1982—. Mem. No. Nev. Bankruptcy Bar Assn. (founding mem.), Washoe County Bar Assn., State Bar Nev. (environ. law com. 1975—), Reno Tennis Club (pres., bd. dirs.), U.S. Ski Coaches Assn. (cert.), Reno Ski and Recreation Club (bd. dirs., pres. 1982—), Prospectors Club (bd. dirs.), Prof. Ski Instr. of Am. (cert.), Sigma Nu, Phi Kappa Phi, Beta Gamma Sigma. Office: 20 Sharps Cir Reno NV 89509-8009 Personal E-mail: fletchlaw1@aol.com.

FLETCHER, DUNCAN MCARTHUR, athletic institute director; s. Tom and Nancy Fletcher. BA in Polit. Sci., U. B.C., Vancouver, 1998; MBA, Quinnipiac U., 2002. Dir. Profl. Athlete Transition Inst. Quinnipiac U., Hamden, Conn., 2002—. Office: Professional Athlete Transition Inst 275 Mt Carmel Ave New Haven CT 06518 Business E-Mail: duncan.fletcher@quinnipiac.edu.

FLETCHER, EDWARD ABRAHAM, engineering educator; b. Detroit, July 30, 1924; s. Morris and Lillian (Protes) F.; m. Roslyn Silber, June 15, 1948; children— Judith Ellen, Deborah Gail, Carolyn Ruth. BS, Wayne State U., 1948; PhD (DuPont fellow, AEC fellow), Purdue U., 1952. Head propellant chemistry and flame mechanics sects. NASA, Cleve., 1952-59; assoc. prof. U. Minn., Mpls., 1959-60, prof., 1960—, dir. grad. studies, 1965-86, prof. emeritus, 2001. Vis. scientist Byellorussian Acad. Scis., 1964; vis. Fulbright prof. U. Poitiers, 1968; sr. Fullbright lectr. Weizmann Inst., Israel, 1989; vis. scientist, prof. Weizmann inst., 1991-97; cons. U.S. Dept. Commerce Study Waste Heat Mgmt., Minn. Energy Agy., No. States Power Co., Pub. Systems Rsch. Corp.; co-chmn. com. on fire resistant hydraulic fluids NRC-Nat. Acad. Scis. Nat. Materials Adv. Bd., 1977-78; Participant adv. group for aero. rsch. and devel. NATO Confs. on supersonic combustion, 1960, 61. Editor: Isotopes, 1958-59. Bd. dirs. Minn. Com. for Technion, New Friends of Chamber Music. Served with USNR, 1943-46. Recipient NASA Tech. Devel. award, 1961; Outstanding Ski Patrolman of Western Region award Nat. Ski Patrol, 1969-70 Mem. Combustion Inst. (bd. advisers, sec. Central States sect. 1967-78, vice chmn. 1978-79, chmn. 1979-82), Am. Chem. Soc., AAAS, Internat. Solar Energy Soc., Am. Solar Energy Soc., Sigma Xi, Tau Beta Pi, Pi Tau Sigma, Phi Lambda Upsilon. Home: 3909 Beard Ave S Minneapolis MN 55410-1042 Office Phone: 612-625-0532. Personal E-mail: fletcher@umn.edu.

FLETCHER, ERNIE (ERNEST L. FLETCHER), governor, former congressman; b. Mt. Sterling, Ky., Nov. 12, 1952; m. Glenna Foster; children: Rachael, Benjamin. BS, U. Ky., 1974, MD with distinction, 1984. Physician, Lexington, Ky., 1984—96; CEO St. Joseph Med. Found., Lexington, 1997—99; state rep. Ky. Ho. Reps. from 78th dist., 1994—96; mem. U.S. Congress from 6th Dist. Ky., 1998—2003; governor State of Ky., 2003—. Mem. Ho. Budget Com., Agr. Com., Com. on Edn. and the Workforce (vice chmn. subcom. on Employer-Employee Rels.); elected freshman liaison to the Ho. Leadership; chmn. bd. So. States Energy; bd. dirs. Achieve, Inc. Served on numerous coms. including the Ky. Commn. on Poverty and the Task Force on Higher Edn.; chosen by gov. to play an important leadership role in reforming Ky.'s ailing health care sys.; lay min. Porter Meml. Baptist Ch.; vol. in cmty. With USAF, 1974—80. Republican. Baptist. Office: 700 Capitol Ave Ste 100 Frankfort KY 40601

FLETCHER, GEORGE P., law educator; b. 1939; BA, U. Calif.-Berkeley, 1960; JD, U. Chgo., 1964, M.C.L., 1965. Bar: Calif. 1970. Grad. fellow U. Freibur, Fed. Republic Germany, 1964-65; asst. prof. U. Fla. Law Sch., 1965-66, U. Wash., Seattle, 1966-69; acting prof. UCLA Law Sch., 1969-70, prof., after 1971; Charles Keller Beekman prof. law Columbia U., NYC, 1983—; Cardozo prof. jurisprudence Columbia U. Sch. Law, NYC. Vis. assoc. prof. Boston Coll., 1968-69; acting prof. UCLA, 1969-71; vis. prof. Hebrew U., Jerusalem, 1972-73, Harvard U., 1973-74, Yale U., 1977, U. Frankfurt, 1980; Guggenheim fellow, 1986-87 Author: Rethinking Criminal Law, 1978, A Crime of Self-Defense: Bernhard Goetz and the Law on Trial, 1988 (ABA Silver Gavel Award, 1989), Loyalty: An Essay on the Morality of Relationships, 1992, With Justice for Some: Victim's Rights in Criminal Trials, 1995, Basic Concepts of Legal Thought, 1996, Basic Concepts of Criminal Law, 1998. Fellow: Am. Acad. Arts and Scis. Home: 404 Riverside Dr New York NY 10025-1861 Office: Columbia U Sch Law 435 W 116th St New York NY 10027-7297 E-mail: fletch@law.columbia.edu.*

FLETCHER, HARRELL, filmmaker; BFA in Photography, San Francisco Art Inst., 1990; MFA, Calif. Coll. Arts & Crafts, 1994; Cert. in Ecol. Horticulture & Sustainable Food Systems, U. Southern Calif., 1996. Co-founder Gallery HERE, Oakland, Calif., 1993—94; guest lectr. Calif. Coll. Arts & Crafts, 1994, San Francisco Art Inst., 1994; video & mag. co-coord. Creativity Explored, San Francisco, 1994—98; guest lectr. U. Calif.- Berkeley, 1998; instr. Beginning Sculpture Stanford U., 1998, instr. Interdisciplinary Seminar, 1999; guest lectr. Calif. Coll. Arts & Crafts, San Francisco, 1999, Henry Art Gallery, Seattle, 1999; Salon Lecture Series Programmer Headlands Ctr. Arts, 1999; guest lectr. Calif. Coll. Arts & Crafts, San Francisco, 2000, San Francisco State U., 2000, White Chapel Gallery, London, 2001, Yale U., 2002, Pratt Inst., Bklyn., 2002, Otis Sch. Art & Design, LA, 2003, U. Calif.-Irvine, 2003; instr. sculpture Cooper Union, NYC, 2004; asst. prof. Portland State U., Oreg., 2004. Exhibitions include Garage Sale, Gallery Here, Calif., 1993, Some People We Met..., Richmond Art Ctr., Va., 1996, Anthony, McBean Project Room, San Francisco Art Inst., 1997, Wanderings & Observations, Bedford Gallery, Walnut Creek, Calif., 1998, The Boy Mechanic, Yerba Buena Ctr. Arts, San Francisco, 1999, Saying I Love You or Something Like That, Institution, San Francisco, Calif., 2000, Every Sunshine, Portland Inst. Contemporary Art, 2001, The Sound We Make Together, DiverseWorks, Houston, 2003, Now Its A Party, Hartford, Conn., 2003, A Moment of Doubt, Christine Burgin, NY, 2004, Happiness Follows Us Like a Shadow, New Langton Arts, San Francisco, 2004, Tender Feelings, Gas Works, London, 2005, exhibited in group shows at Urban Renewal Laboratory, Southern Exposure, San Francisco, 1998, Mus. Pieces, M. H. de Young Meml. Mus., San Francisco, 1999, Yes, We're Excerpts, Andrew Kreps Gallery, NY, 2002, Street Selections, The Drawing Ctr., NY, 2003, Whitney Biennial, Whitney Mus. Am. Art, NY, 2004; curator (exhibitions) Whipper Snapper Nerd, Yerba Buena Ctr. Arts, San Francisco, 1998, Survivalist, Southern Exposure, San Francisco, 1999, A Love For All Animals, San Francisco Art Commn. Gallery, 2001, Hello There Friend, Christine Burgin, NY, 2003. Recipient Post-Grad. Studio Award, Headlands Ctr. Arts, 1994, Headlands Ctr. Arts Residency, 1998; Residency Grant, Calif. Arts Coun., 1994, Creative Work Fund Grant, 1996, 2000, Artists & Communities Millenium Grant, 1999, Creative Capital Grant, 2002, Artslink Grant, 2003, Gunk Grant, 2003. E-mail: hfletcher@earthlink.net.*

FLETCHER, HARRY GEORGE, III, library director; b. Bklyn., Mar. 25, 1941; s. Harry G. and Helen T. (Dawson) F.; m. Toni A. Owen, 1966 (div. 1987); children: Alexandra, Thomas; m. 2d, Florence Sussman, 1987. AB, Fordham Coll., 1962, MA, 1970. Asst. editor, editor, dir. Fordham U. Press, 1966-91; Astor curator of printed books and bindings Pierpont Morgan Libr., N.Y.C., 1991-98; Brooke Russell Astor dir. spl. collections N.Y. Pub. Libr., N.Y.C., 1998—, acting dir. Humanities and Social Scis. Libr., 2003—04. Adj. assoc. prof. NYU, 1996—. Author: Gutenberg and the Genesis of Printing, 1994, New Aldine Studies, 1988, In Praise of Aldus Manutius, 1995, Izaak Walton's The Complete Angler 1653-2003, 2003; co-author: Art Deco Bookbindings: the work of Pierre Legrain and Rose Adler, 2004; editor: The Heritage of New York, 1970, A Miscellany for Bibliophiles, 1979, The Wormsley Library, 1999; co-editor: Paradosis, 1976; contbr. articles to profl.

jours., chpts. to books. Served with AUS, 1963-66. DAAD fellow, 1962-63. Mem. Baker Street Irregulars. Clubs: Grolier. Office: NY Pub Libr Fifth Ave and 42d St New York NY 10018-2788 E-mail: hgfletcher@nypl.org.

FLETCHER, HOMER LEE, librarian; b. Salem, Ind., May 11, 1928; s. Floyd M. and Hazel (Barnett) F.; m. Jacquelyn Ann Blanton, Feb. 7, 1950; children— Deborah Lynn, Randall Brian, David Lee. BA, Ind. U., 1953; MS in L.S, U. Ill., 1954. Librarian Milw. Pub. Library, 1954-56; head librarian Ashland (Ohio) Pub. Library, 1956-59; city librarian Arcadia (Cal.) Pub. Library, 1959-65, Vallejo (Calif.) Pub. Library, 1965-70, San Jose, Calif., 1970-90; ret., 1990. Contbr. articles to profl. jours. Pres. S. Solano chpt. Calif. Assn. Neurol. Handicapped Children, 1968-69; mem. Presbyn. Ch. Sunnyvale, 1997. Served with USAF, 1946-49. Mem. ALA (intellectual freedom com. 1967-72), Calif. Library Assn. (pres. pub. libraries sect. 1967), Phi Beta Kappa. Democrat. Presbyterian. Home: 7921 Belknap Dr Cupertino CA 95014-4973 *Standing up for what I believe regardless of the consequences. Accepting all human beings as important regardless of their circumstances. Emphasizing honest and forthright behavior in personal and professional life. Retaining a sense of humility and thankfulness.*

FLETCHER, KEITH MERRIL, mathematics educator; b. Baton Rouge, La., May 15, 1969; s. Billy Merril and Judy Ann (Low) Fletcher. BSc, Northwestern State U., 1991. Cert. Math Teacher La. Dept. of Edn. Math tchr. Winn Parish Sch. Bd., Winnfield, La., 1992—94, 1994—98, St. Charles Parish Sch. Bd., Luling, La., 1998—99, Rapides Parish Sch. Bd., Alexandria, La., 1999—2000, math tchr., dept. chair, 2002—; math tchr. Winn Parish Sch. Bd., 2000—01. Recipient State-runner up coaches award, La. H.S. Athletic Assn., 1998, Tchr. of the Yr., Atlanta H.S., 1997, Coach of the Yr., Dist. 3-C Girls Basketball, 1994. Republican. Bapt. Avocations: sports, travel. Home: 949 Mars Hill Church Rd Atlanta LA 71404 Office: Peabody Magnet HS 2727 Jones St Alexandria LA 71302 Business E-Mail: fletcherk@rapides.k12.la.us.

FLETCHER, LEROY STEVENSON, mechanical engineer, educator; b. San Antonio, Oct. 10, 1936; s. Robert Holton and Jennie Lee F.; m. Nancy Louise McHenry, Aug. 14, 1966; children: Laura Malee, Daniel Alden. BS, Tex. A&M U., 1958; MS, Stanford U., 1963, Engr., 1964; PhD, Ariz. State U., 1968. Registered profl. engr., Ariz., N.J., Va., Tex., Australia; chartered engr., U.K. Rsch. scientist NASA-Ames Rsch. Ctr., Moffett Field, Calif., 1958-62, dir. aeronautics/aerospace, 1999—; instr. Ariz. State U., Tempe, 1964-68; prof. aero., engrng. Rutgers U., New Brunswick, N.J., 1968-75, assoc. dean, 1974-75; prof., chmn. dept. mech. and aero. engrng. U. Va., Charlottesville, 1975-80; dir. Ctr. Energy Analysis, 1979-80; assoc. dean Tex. A&M U., College Station, 1980-88, assoc. dir. Tex. Engrng. Expt. Sta., 1985-88, Dietz prof. mech. engring., 1988—, Regents prof., 1998—. Vis. prof. Tokyo Inst. Tech., 1993; hon. prof. Ruhr U.-Bochum, Germany, 1988—; disting. vis. prof. Am. U., Cairo, 1998, Am. U. Sharjah, U.A.E., 2000—; cons. to various industries, govt. labs. and univs.; mem. exec. com. Internat. Ctr. for Heat and Mass Transfer, Ankara, Turkey, 1994—, chmn., 1999-2003, fellow, 1998; disting. vis. scholar Hong Kong Polytechnic U., 2002. Author: Introduction to Engineering Including FORTRAN Programming, 1977, Introduction to Engineering Design with Graphics and Design Projects, 1979; editor: Aerodynamic Heating and Thermal Protection, 1978, Heat Transfer and Thermal Control Systems, 1978. Served to capt. USAF, 1958-61. Recipient Disting. Alumni award Ariz. State U., 1985, Exceptional Achievement medal NASA-Ames, 2002, Outstanding Leadership medal NASA, 2005. Fellow ASME (bd. govs. 1983-87, pres. 1985-86, Charles Russ Richards award 1982, Heat Transfer Meml. award 1996, hon., medal 2002), AAAS (chair sect. M-engring. 1988-89, Internat. Scientific Coop. award 2003), Accreditation Bd. Engrng. and Tech. (dir. 1979-89, 1991-94, 2003-, Linton Grinter award 2002), Am. Astron. Soc. (bd. dirs. 1993-96), Inst. Engrs. Australia, Inst. Mech. Engrs. U.K (James Watt Internat. Gold medal 2005), Royal Aeronautical Soc. U.K., Am. Soc. Engrng. Edn. (dir. 1974-77, v.p. 1978-80, George Westinghouse award 1982, Ralph Coats Roe award 1983, Donald E. Marlowe award 1986, Leighton W. Collins award 1993, Benjamin Garver Lamme award 2001), AIAA (dir. 1981-84, 1992-98, v.p. edn. 1992-95, pres. 1996-97, Lee Atwood award 1982, Energy Sys. award 1984, Thermophysics award 1992, Disting. Svc. award 2002, hon. fellow, 2004), Internat. Astro. Fedn. (Frank J. Malina award 1997), Union Panamericana de Asociaciones de Ingenieros (Vector de Oro award 2000), Pan Am. Acad. Engring., Internat. Acad. Astronautics; mem. Sigma Xi, Tau Beta Pi, Pi Tau Sigma, Sigma Gamma Tau, Phi Kappa Phi. Office: Tex A&M Univ Dept Mech Engring College Station TX 77843-3123

FLETCHER, MARK, entrepreneur; BS in Computer Sci., U. Calif., San Diego. Sr. software engr. Diba (acquired by Sun Microsystems), Menlo Park, Calif., 1997; started ONElist (acquired eGroups), 1997—99; CEO ONElist and eGroups, 1999; chief tech. officer ONElist and eGroups (acquired by Yahoo and renamed at that time eGroups, now Yahoo! Groups), 1999—2000; founder, CEO Bloglines (acquired by Ask Jeeves), 2003—05; v.p., gen. mgr. of Bloglines Ask Jeeves, Oakland, Calif., 2005—. Lectr. in field; lectr. U. San Francisco. Appeared on ZDTV, featured in Wall Street Journal, San Jose Mercury News, Time Magazine, Red herring Magazine, Upside Magazine, Industry Standard, Salon, PC World, NY Times, & Business Week. Named Best Blog/Feed Search Engines (Bloglines), Search Engine Watch awards, 2005; named one of Top 50 Web Sites (Bloglines), Time Mag., 2004; recipient Rave award in Technology, WIRED, 2005. Office: Ask Jeeves Inc 555 12th St Ste 500 Oakland CA 94607

FLETCHER, NORMAN S., state supreme court justice; b. July 10, 1934; s. Frank Pickett and Hattie Sears Fletcher; m. Dorothy Johnson, 1957; children: Mary Kiker, Elizabeth Coan. BA, U. Ga., 1956, LLB, 1958; LLM, U. Va., 1995. Assoc. Matthews, Maddox, Walton and Smith, Rome, Ga., 1958-63; pvt. practice LaFayette, Ga., 1963-90; city atty. City of LaFayette, 1965-89; county atty. County of Walker, 1973-88; spl. asst. atty. gen. State of Ga., Atlanta, 1979-89; justice Ga. Supreme Ct., Atlanta, 1990—2005, chief justice; ret., 2005. Mem. State Disciplinary Bd., 1984-87, chair investigative panel, 1986-87. Ruling elder Peachtree Presbyn. Ch., Atlanta; former officer First Presbyn. Ch. of Rome, Ga., LaFayette Presbyn. Ch., Cherokee Presbytery; former commr. Presbyn. Ch. USA Gen. Assembly, 1984, 85; bd. visitors U. Ga. Sch. Law, 1992-95, chmn., 1994-95. Master Joseph Henry Lumpkin Inn of Ct.; fellow Am. Bar Found., Ga. Bar Found.; mem. State Bar Ga. (chair local govt. sect. 1977-78), U. Ga. Law Sch. Alumni Assn. (pres. 1977), Rotary. Office Phone: 404-656-3477. Business E-Mail: fletchen@gasupreme.us.

FLETCHER, RAYMOND RUSSWALD, JR., lawyer; b. Schenectady, N.Y., June 7, 1929; s. Raymond Russwald and Elsie Dorothea (Hovemeyer) F.; m. Elsa Ellen Tillema, Dec. 20, 1949 (div. 1973); children— Raymond Russwald III, Nicholas H., Pamela L., William E., Catherine A. B.Ch.E., Rensselaer Poly. Inst., 1949; LL.B., Harvard U., 1956. Bar: N.Y. 1956. Vice-pres., gen. counsel Trans World Airlines, Inc., N.Y.C., 1969-78; ptnr. Chadbourne, Parke, Whiteside & Wolff, N.Y.C., 1978-84; counsel Gilbride, Tusa, Last & Spellane, N.Y.C., 1984—2004. Vice chmn. legal com. Internat. Air Transport Assn., Geneva, Switzerland, 1976-77 Served as lt. (j.g.) USN, 1949-53; Korea Decorated Air medal Mem. Harvard Club. Democrat. Presbyterian. Home and Office: 453 Albany Hill Rd Rensselaerville NY 12147-2705 Office Phone: 518-797-3863.

FLETCHER, RICHARD WESLEY, music educator, musician; b. Little Rock, Oct. 22, 1945; s. Robert Lee Fletcher and Eleanor May Hurlbut; m. Kristine Sue Klopfenstein, May 28, 1972; 1 child, Evan Paul. BA in Music Edn., Ark. Tech U., 1967; MusM, U. So. Ill., 1968; D of Musical Arts, U. Iowa, 1974. Band dir. Benton (Ark.) Jr. High Schs., 1968—69; woodwind instr. City H.S., Iowa City, 1970—73; assoc. prof. music Ark. Tech U., Russellville, 1973—82; prof. music U. Wis., Eau Claire, 1982—. Vis. fellow Tokyo Nat. U. Fine Arts and Music, 1988; prof. music Wis. in Scotland, Dalkeith, 1994. Musician: (CD) Zodiac, 1998, Eau Claire Chamber Orchestra Live, 2002, Clearly Three: Trios from the Twentieth Century, 2005, Music of Allan J. Segall; contbr. articles to profl. jours. Mem.: N.Am. Saxophone Alliance, Nat. Assn. Coll. Wind and Percussion Instructors, Internat. Clarinet Assn., Phi Mu Alpha. Office: U Wis-Eau Claire Dept Music and Theatre Arts Eau Claire WI 54702 Office Phone: 715-836-2405. Office Fax: 715-836-3952.

FLETCHER, ROBERT, retired lawyer; b. Birmingham, Ala., May 4, 1920; s. Robert Hall and Beatrice (Skelding) Jones; m. Florence K. Szuba, Sept. 12, 1942; children— Andrew R., William Alan. B.F.A., Ohio U., Athens, 1943; LL.B., JD, Case Western Res U., 1948. Bar: Ohio 1948. Asst. gen. counsel Cleve. Transit System, 1951-56; with firm Jamison, Ulrich, Johnson & Burt, Cleve., 1956-59, Meyers, Stevens & Rea, Cleve., 1959-61; pvt. practice Cleve., 1961-82; horologist Parma, Ohio, 1982—. Lectr. Am. Heart Assn. Served with AUS, World War II, Korea. Recipient Speakers Bur. award Am. Heart Assn., 1973-76 Mem.: Rosicrucian Order, Masonic Order. Republican. Presbyterian. Home: 5801 Hollywood Dr Cleveland OH 44129-5220

FLETCHER, ROBERT HILLMAN, medical educator; b. Abington, Pa., Mar. 26, 1940; s. Stevenson Whitcomb and Wanda (Moss) F.; m. Suzanne Wright, June 15, 1963; children: John Wright, Grant Selmer BA, Wesleyan U., Middletown, Conn., 1962; MD, Harvard U., 1966; MSc, Johns Hopkins U., 1973. Diplomate Am. Bd. Internal Medicine. Intern, resident in medicine Stanford U. Hosp., Palo Alto, Calif., 1967-68; resident in medicine Balt. City Hosp., 1971-73; asst. prof. faculty of medicine McGill U., Montreal, Canada, 1973-78; assoc. prof. medicine Sch. Medicine U. N.C., Chapel Hill, 1978-83, prof. medicine, clin. prof. epidemiology, 1983-90, dir. Robert Wood Johnson Clin. Scholars Program, 1983-90, co-dir. Clin. Epidemiology Resource and Tng. Ctr., Internat. Clin. Epidemiology Network, 1986-90; assoc. exec. v.p. ACP, Phila., 1990-92, sr. v.p., 1992-93; prof. Harvard Med. Sch., Boston, 1994—; assoc. med. dir. clin. edn. Harvard Pilgrim Health Care, Boston, 1998, dir. tchg. ctr., dept. ambulatory care and prevention, 1992—2002. Bd. dirs. INCLEN Inc., chmn., 1993-97. Sr. author: Clinical Epidemiology, The Essentials, 1982, 2d edit., 1988, 3d edit., 1996; co-editor: Jour. Gen. Internal Medicine, 1984-89, Annals of Internal Medicine, 1990-93; primary care editor UpToDate, 1997-. Served to maj. M.C., U. S. Army, 1968-71. Master ACP; mem. Am. Pub. Health Assn., Soc. Gen. Internal Medicine (pres. 1991-92), Phi Beta Kappa, Sigma Xi. Democrat. Mem. Soc. Of Friends. Home: 208 Boulder Bluff Chapel Hill NC 27516 Office: Dept Ambulatory Care/Prevention 133 Brookline Ave 6th Fl Boston MA 02215-3920 E-mail: robert_fletcher@hms.harvard.edn.

FLETCHER, STEPHEN L., art appraiser; Ptnr., exec. v.p., chief auctioneer & appraiser Skinner, Inc., Boston, 1975—, and dir., Am. Furniture and Decorative Arts. Appraiser Antiques Roadshow, WGBH-PBS. Contbr. writer Art & Antiquities in Estates, lectr. in field. Mem.: Provincetown Art Assn., Mus. (bd. trustees), Mus. Fine Arts, Boston. Office: Skinner Inc 63 Park Plz Boston MA 02116 Office Phone: 617-350-5400. Office Fax: 617-350-5429. Business E-Mail: tvappraisers@skinnerinc.com.*

FLETCHER, SUZANNE WRIGHT, epidemiologist, medical educator, editor; b. Jacksonville, Fla., Nov. 14, 1940; d. Robert Dean and Helen (Selmer) Wright; m. Robert H. Fletcher; children: John Wright, Grant Selmer. BA, Swarthmore Coll., 1962; MD, Harvard Med. Sch., 1966; MSc, Johns Hopkins U., 1973. Diplomate Nat. Bd. Med. Examiners, Am. Bd. Internal Medicine. Intern Stanford (Calif.) U. Med. Ctr., 1966—67, resident, 1967—68; physician 22nd med. detachment U.S. Army, New Ulm, Germany, 1969—70; asst. prof. epidemiology and health Mc Gill U., Montreal, Canada, 1974—77, assoc. prof., 1977—78, asst. prof. medicine, 1973—78; dir. med. clinic dept. medicine NC Meml. Hosp., 1978—82; assoc. prof. medicine U. NC, 1978—83, co-chief divsn. gen. medicine and clin. epidemiology dept. medicine, 1978—86, rsch. assoc. health svcs. rsch. ctr., 1978—90, vice chmn. clin. svcs., 1981—90, prof. medicine, clin. prof. epidemiology, 1983—90, program dir. faculty devel. gen. medicine and gen. pediatrics, 1985—90, co-dir. internat. clin. epidemiology network program Rockefeller Found., 1986—90; prof. ambulatory care and prevention Harvard Med. Sch., 1994—; editor Annals of Internal Medicine, Phila., 1990—93. Adj. prof. medicine U. Pa., Phila., 1990—93, Jefferson Med. Coll., 1991—93, U. NC, 1994—; physician internal medicine; chmn. NIH Tech. Assessment Conf., 1992, Nat. Cancer Inst. Internat. Workshop, 1993; active World Bank Seminar on Preventive Strategies in Med. Edn., Hangzhou, China, 1986, Ad Hoc NCI Com. on BSE Cancer Detection Rsch. and Applications, 1986. Author: Clinical Epidemiology—The Essentials, 1982, 4t edit., 2005; contbr. chapters to books, articles to profl. jours. Named rsch. grantee, Conseil de la Recherche en Sante du Quebec, 1975—77; recipient Can. Nat. Health Rsch. Scholar award, Can. Govt., 1975—78; grantee, Health and Welfare Can., 1976—78, Robert Wood Johnson Teaching Hosp. Gen. Medicine Group Practice Program, 1980—84, Nat. Ctr. Health Scis. Rsch. and Health Tech., 1985—89, Rockefeller Found. Clin. Epidemiology Resource and Tng. Ctr., 1986—90, NIH, 1987—90, 1997—. Master: ACP (med. knowledge self assessment program 1984—85, clin. practice subcom. 1987, pub. policy subcom. 1988—89); fellow: Coll. Physicians Phila., Am. Coll. Epidemiology (bd. dirs. 1990—93, chmn. pub. com. 1992—94); mem.: APHA, Am. Bd. Internal Medicine (bd. govs. 1981—87), NCI Bd. Sci. Advisors, World Assn. Med. Editors (v.p. 1997—2001), Internat. Clin. Epidemiology Network (bd. dirs.), Inst. Medicine (coun. 1993—96, exec. com. 1993—96), Soc. Gen. Internal Medicine (counsellor 1978—81, pres.-elect 1982—83, pres. 1983—84, co-editor Jour. Gen. Internal Medicine 1984—89, mem. publs. com. 1990—, chmn. Glaser award com. 1991). Unitarian Universalist. Office: 208 Boulder Bluff Chapel Hill NC 27516 Business E-Mail: Suzanne_Fletcher@hms.harvard.edu.

FLETCHER, THOMAS HARVEY, chemical engineer, educator; married. BSChemE, Brigham Young U., 1979, MSChemE, 1980, PhD, 1983. Sr. mem., tech. staff Sandia Nat. Labs., Livermore, Calif., 1984—91; prof. chem. engring. Brigham Young U., Provo, Utah, 1991—2005. Mem.: ACS, ASME, Combustion Inst.

FLETCHER, WILLIAM A., federal judge, law educator; b. June 6, 1945; BA, Harvard U., 1968, Oxford U., 1970; JD, Yale U., 1975. Law clk. to presiding justice U.S. Dist. Ct. Calif., San Francisco, 1975—76; law clk. to Justice William J. Brennan U.S. Supreme Ct., Washington, 1976—77; acting prof. law U. Calif., Berkeley, 1977—84, prof. law, 1984—98; judge U.S. Ct. Appeals (9th cir.), San Francisco, 1998—. With Office of Emergency Preparedness, Exec. Office of the Pres., 1970—72; prof. Salzburg Seminar on Am. Legal Institutions; mem. Am. Law Inst. Lieutenant USN, 1970—72. Mem.: Calif. Bar Assn. Office: 95 7th St San Francisco CA 94103*

FLETCHER, WINONA LEE, theater educator; b. Nov. 25, 1926; m. Joseph Grant; 1 child, Betty. BA, Johnson C. Smith U., 1947; MA, U. Iowa, 1951; PhD, Ind. U., 1968. Prof. speech and theatre Ky. State U., Frankfort, 1951-78; prof. theatre and afro-Am. studies Ind. U., Bloomington, 1978-94, prof. emeritus, 1994; assoc. dean COAS, 1981-84. Costumer, dir. summer theatre, U. Mo., Lincoln, 1952-60, 69. Sr. editor: Community Memories: A Glimpse of African American Life in Frankfort, Ky., 2003. Recipient Lifetime Achievement award, 1993; Am. Theatre fellow, 1979. Mem. Am. Theatre for Higher Edn., Black Theatre Network, Ky. Hist. Soc., Nat. Assn. Dramatic and Speech Arts, Nat. Theatre Conf., Alpha Kappa Alpha. Home: 317 Cold Harbor Dr Frankfort KY 40601-3011

FLETTNER, MARIANNE, opera administrator; b. Frankfurt, Germany, Aug. 9, 1933; d. Bernhard J. and Kaethe E. (Halbritter) F. Bus. diploma, Hessel Bus. Coll., 1953. Sec. various cos., 1953-61, Pontiac Motor Div., Burlingame, Calif., 1961-63, Met. Opera, N.Y., 1963-74, asst. co. mgr., 1974-79; artistic adminstr. San Diego Opera, 1979—. Avocations: travel, hiking, swimming, cooking. Home: 4015 Crown Point Dr San Diego CA 92109-6270 Office: San Diego Opera 1200 Third Ave 18th Fl San Diego CA 92101-4112 Office Phone: 619-232-7636, 619-533-7004. Business E-Mail: marianne.flettner@sdopera.com.

FLEURY, PAUL AIMÉ, dean, physicist; b. Balt., July 20, 1939; m. Carol Anne Moss, Aug. 22, 1964; children: Ellen, Laura, Jennifer. BS in Physics, John Carroll U., 1960; PhD in Physics, MIT, 1965. Mem. tech. staff AT&T Bell Labs., Murray Hill, N.J., 1965-70, head condensed state physics rsch., 1970-79, dir. materials rsch., 1979-84, dir. phys. rsch., 1984-92; v.p. rsch. Sandia Nat. Lab., Albuquerque, 1992-93; dir. materials & process rsch. AT&T Bell Labs., Murray Hill, NJ, 1993-96; dean engrng. U. N.Mex., Albuquerque, 1996-2000, Yale U., New Haven, 2000—. Editor: Coherence and Energy Transfer in Glasses, 1983; contbr. over 120 articles to Phys. Rev., Sci., others. Fellow AAAS, NAE, NAS, Am. Acad. Arts and Scis., Am. Phys. Soc. (Michaelson Morley prize 1985, Frank Isakson prize for optical effects in solids 1992). Achievements include 5 patents for optical devices, lasers, optical fibers; research in laser spectroscopy. Office Phone: 203-432-4220. E-mail: paul.fleury@yale.edu.

FLEURY, WILBERT LEIGH, musicologist, educator; b. Columbus, Oct. 17, 1971; s. Wilbert Joseph and Joyce Elizabeth Fleury; m. Tacy Susanna Gray, July 1, 2000. BA in Music, The Ohio State U., 1994; MusM, U. of Cin.-Conservatory of Music, 1996; doctorate candidate, U. Cin. Conservatory of Music, 2005. Prin. organist and pianist St. Elizabeth Ann Seton Parish, Pickerington, Ohio, 1986—94; asst. organist St. Joseph's Cathedral, Columbus, Ohio, 1994—96; music dir., organist St. John's United Ch. of Christ, Cin., 1996—2000; assoc. for music ministries, organist 1st Presbyn. Ch., Winston-Salem, 2000—. Recipient Dosogne award, Nat. Pastoral Musicians, 1992, Ann. Scholarship prize, 1993. Mem.: Am. Choral Dir.'s Assn., Am. Guild of Organists. Presbyterian. Avocations: painting, hiking, travel, reading, composing. Home: 290 Village Creek Cir Apt G Winston Salem NC 27104 Office: First Presbyterian Church 300 N Cherry St Winston Salem NC 27101 Office Phone: 336-723-1621 288. Personal E-mail: wlfleury@juno.com. E-mail: leighf@1stpres.com.

FLEXNER, JOSEPHINE MONCURE, musician, educator; b. Marion, Va., Oct. 11, 1919; d. Walter Raleigh Daniel and Harriet Ashby (Ogburn) Moncure; m. Kurt Fisher Flexner, Dec. 20, 1942; children: Thomas Moncure, Peter Wallace. BA, Univ. Richmond, 1941; tchr. cert. in piano, Peabody Conservatory, 1945; MS in piano, Juilliard Sch. Music, 1950. Class piano tchr. Balt. Pub. Sch., 1945-46; mem. piano faculty Peabody Conservatory Prep., Balt., 1945-46, Pius X Sch. Manhatanville Coll. Sacred Heart, N.Y.C., 1946-50, Henry Street Settlement Sch., N.Y.C., 1949-50; piano tchr. Bronxville, N.Y., 1950-54; mem. piano faculty Rhodes Coll., Memphis, Tenn., 1970-82; piano tchr. St. Mary's Episcopal Sch., Memphis, 1982-87. Judge for Tenn. piano auditions, 1980—85; judge Tenn. Nat. Guild Auditions, 1983—84. Contbr. articles to profl. jours. Den mother Boy Scouts Am., 1963-65, vice chmn., 1964-65; precinct worker, capt. Nat. Elections, Memphis, 1972, 74; mem. Memphis Arts Coun., 1977-79; area chmn. Westchester Soc. Performing Arts, 1964-66, chmn. cultural activities Sch. No. 8, Yonkers, N.Y., 1963-66; vice chmn. music dept. Bronxville Women's Club, 1964-66; pres. chancel choir Dutch Reformed Ch., Bronxville, 1963-66; program chmn. Seoul Internat. Women's Assn., Seoul, Korea, 1967-68, chmn. cultural activities Seoul Am. Schs., 1966-68, chmn. culutral seminars Am. Women's Club, Seoul, 1967-68; treas., pres. Greater Memphis Music Tchrs. Assn., 1975-79; bd. dirs. Young Peoples Piano Concerto Competition, 1979-85, Tenn. Music Tchrs. Assn., 1977-79. Named Tchr. of Yr., Greater Memphis Music, 1983, Tenn. Music Tchrs. Assn., 1985. Democrat. Presbyterian. Avocations: writing, reading, playing piano. Home: The Fountains at Millbrook 17 Crestview Rd Millbrook NY 12545

FLEXNER, KURT FISHER, economist, educator; b. Vienna, Sept. 26, 1915; arrived in U.S., 1928; s. Otto Gerard and Wilhelmine (Fisher) Flexner; m. Josephine Moncure, Dec. 20, 1942; children: Thomas Moncure, Peter Wallace. BS in Econs., Johns Hopkins U., 1946; PhD in Econs., Columbia U., 1954. From asst. prof. to prof. econs. NYU Grad. Sch. Arts and Scis., U. Coll. and Sch. Commerce, 1946-59; chief economist, dep. mgr. The Am. Bankers Assn., 1959-66; adj. prof. banking and fin. NYU, 1965-66, prof., chmn. dept. econs., 1968-78; prof. econs. U. Memphis, 1978-87, prof. emeritus, 1987—. Cons. U.S. Savs. and Loan League, 1955—59, N.Y. State Savs. and Loan League, 1955—59; P. K. Seidman vis. distin. prof. Christian Bros. U., Memphis, 1990—94; lectr. intergenerational seminars Bard Coll., Annandale on the Hudson, NY, 1987—, Ctr. for Life Studies, Marist Coll., Poughkeepsie, NY, 1995—; chief fin. instns. advisor U.S. Agy. for Internat. Devel., Seoul, Republic of Korea, 1966—68; spkr. in field; adv. com. to Chancellor Franz Vranitzky Prime Minister of Austria, 1991—93; guest lectr. Inst. USA and Can. Acad. Sci., Moscow, 1991—95; advisor to coun. Pres. Mikhail Gorbachev, 1990—91, Pres. Boris Yeltsin, 1991—94. Author: The European Payments Union 1950 to 1954, 1957, The Savings and Loan Associations in the State of New York, 1958, Mortgage Lending by Commercial Banks, 1964, The Enlightened Society: The Economy with a Human Face, 1989, The 21st Century-The Best or the Last, 2005; columnist Memphis Daily News, 1986—90, Comml. Appeal, 1980—87; contbr. articles to profl. jours. Trustee M. L. Seidman Town Hall Meml. Lecture Series, 1968—87; mem. Gov. Alexander's Action Team, 1980—85. With U.S. Army, 1944—45. Mem.: Econ. Club Memphis (exec. dir. 1973—85, pres. 1985—92). Home and Office: The Fountains at Millbrook 17 Crestview Rd Millbrook NY 12545 E-mail: kandjflexner@aol.com.

FLEYSHMAN, BENTSION, physicist, researcher, retired mathematician; b. Moscow, Nov. 21, 1923; s. Shimon and Nehama Fleyshman; m. Mira Etingof, June 19, 1955; 1 child, Simon. MS in Math., Moscow State U., 1947; PhD in Physics & Math., Russian Acad. of Sci., 1958, D in Physics & Math., 1966. Scientist Mil., Moscow, 1947—54; sr. scientist inst. radiotechnics & electronics Russian Acad. of Sci., Moscow, 1955—68, prin. scientist inst. oceanology, 1968—96; ind. cons. in risk analysis Bklyn., 1996—. Mem. of the interdisciplinary com. hon. pres. World Cultural Coun., Monterrey, NY, 1987—. Author: Constructive Methods of Optimal Coding for Channels with Noize (in Russian), 1963, Elements of Theory of Potential Efficiency of Complex Systems (in Russian), 1971, Fundamentals of Systemology (in Russian), 1982; contbr. Complex Ecology, 1995; author: The Choice is Yours (in Russian), 2000. Recipient Exceptional Work During WWII medal, Soviet Gov., 1945, City Com. Environ. Protection medal, Sofia, Bulgaria, 1991. Mem.: Soc. of Risk Analysis. Home and Office: 3093 Brighton 4th St Apt 5D Brooklyn NY 11235

FLICK, ARNOLD L., retired physician, political organization worker; b. LA, May 1, 1930; s. Samuel and Pearl Flick; m. Nancy Flick; children: Susan, Rachel, Sarah. BS, UCLA, 1950; MD, U. Chgo., 1954. Cer. Am. Bd. Internal Medicine, Am. Bd. Gastroenterology. Ret. clin. prof. medicine U. Calif., San Diego, 1968-91; med. dir. Smoking Rsch., San Diego, 1966-68; pvt. practice San Diego, 1961-98; cmty. activist Citizens for Fully Informed Vote, San Diego, 1999—. Jewish. Avocations: biking, hiking, tennis, violin. E-mail: alf96@san.rr.com.

FLICK, CARL, electrical engineer, consultant; b. Vienna, June 22, 1926; came to U.S., 1939; s. Henry Chaim Ber and Sofie (Dornhelm) F.; m. Frances Ethel Berman, July 4, 1954; children: Lawrence David, Susan Naomi, Jack Bennet. BEE, Poly. U. of N.Y., 1951; MEE, Poly. U., 1953. Registered profl. engr., Fla., Pa. Various engring. positions, adv. engr. Westinghouse Electric Corp., East Pittsburgh, Pa., 1952-84, adv. engr., Orlando, Fla., 1984-89; cons. Techno-Lexic, Orlando, 1989—. Co-author: Handbook of Electric Machines, 1987; contbr. articles to profl. jours.; patentee in field. With U.S. Army, 1945-47, PTO. Fellow IEEE (life; various coms., Centennial medal 1984, Outstanding Engr. award Orlando sect. 1989, Fla. coun. 1989, Region 3 1990, Nikola Tesla award 1994), Power Engring. Soc. (com. Disting. Svc. award, Millenium medal 2000); mem. B'nai B'rith. Democrat. Jewish. Avocations: writing, photography, painting.

FLICK, CONNIE RUTH, real estate agent, real estate broker; d. Hugh D and Lenore Violet Myers; children: Kendra A Merriman, Tonya L Moore, Charity I Risley. Lic. Ind. Real Estate Broker Ind. Profl. Licensing Agy., 1968. Plant mgr. USPS, Terre Haute, Ind., 1993—, quality specialist Lafayette, Ind., 1986—93; owner, realtor, broker Flick Realty, Crawfordsville, Ind., 1968—;

ins. agt. Met. Ins. Co., Lafayette, Ind., 1981—82; supr. mail processing USPS, Lafayette, Ind., 1985—86; hq test team mem. USPS, Equipment Devel., Merrifield, Va., 1989—92. Priority mail improvement team USPS, Indpls., 1995—96, activation coord., Inpls., Ind., 2000—02, mgr., air mail facility, 1995—96, acting postmaster (officer in charge), Lafayette, Ind., 1995—96, internat. svc. ctr. activation coord., Chgo., 1999—2000. Mem. Sch. Bd. Nominating Com., Crawfordsville, Ind., 1983—85; fund raising chmn. Hose PTO, Crawfordsville, Ind., 1980—81; vice precinct committeeman Rep. Party, Crawfordsville, Ind., 1980—85. Recipient Gold Sales award, Met. Ins. Co., 1981, Cert. of Appreciation, US Postal Svc., 1991, U.S. Postal Svc., 2001. Mem.: MIBOR, Past Presidents Bus. and Profl. Women (pres. 1979—80), Nat. Assn. of Realtors, Montgomery County Bd. of Realtors (sec. 1969—72), Ind. Realtors Assn., Ea. Star, Faternal Order of Women of the Eagles, Women of the Moose. Independent-Republican. Baptist (Brownsvalley Missionary Baptist Church). Avocations: swimming, reading, birdwatching, puzzles, genealogy. Home: 300 Covington St Crawfordsville IN 47933-1332 Office: United States Postal Service 150 West Margaret Dr Terre Haute IN 47802-9997 Personal E-mail: cflick@tctc.com. E-mail: cflick@usps.gov.

FLICK, JOHN EDMOND, lawyer; b. Franklin, Pa., Mar. 14, 1922; s. Edmond Leroy and Mary M. (Weaver) F.; m. Lois Anna Lange, Apr. 20, 1946; children: Gregory Allan, Scott Edmond, Lynn Ellen, Ann Elizabeth. Student, Northwestern U., 1941-44, U. Pa., 1945; LLB, Northwestern U., 1948. Bar: Ill. 1948, Calif. 1971, U.S. Dist. Ct. (ctrl. dist.) Calif. 1971, U.S. Ct. Appeals (9th cir.) 1971, U.S. Supreme Ct. 1974. Commd. 1st lt. Judge Adv. Gen. Corps U.S. Army, 1950, advanced through grades to lt. col. Res., 1968; ret., 1972; faculty U.S. Mil. Acad., 1954-57, Judge Adv. Gen. Sch., U. Va., 1960-61; counsel Litton Industries, 1963-67; sr. v.p., sec., gen. counsel, dir. Bangor Punta Corp., 1967-69; sr. v.p., gen. counsel Times Mirror Co., Los Angeles, 1970-87, cons., 1987-88, ret., 2004. Past chmn. Los Angeles adv. bd. Salvation Army; past mem. nat. adv. bd. Salvation Army. Recipient Am. Bar Assn. Acad. award, 1961 Mem. State Bars Calif. and Ill., Wigmore Club (life benefactor, Northwestern U. Law Sch.).

FLICK, THOMAS MICHAEL, mathematician, educator, educational association administrator; b. Covington, Ky., July 14, 1954; s. Thomas Lawrence and Crystel (Moore) F.; m. Jeanine M. Moran, Nov. 23, 1991. BS, No. Ky. U., 1976, MA, 1981; MEd, Xavier U., 1977; PhD, Southeastern U., 1979; EdD, U. Sarasota, 1989. Cert. secondary tchr., Ohio, Ky. Assoc. vice prin., dean, chmn. math., prin. summer sch. Purcell Marian High Sch., Cin., 1977-89; asst. prof. Xavier U., Cin., 1989-95, assoc. prof., 1995—2004, prof., 2004—, dir. Ctr. Excellance in Edn., 2004—. Lectr. astronomy Wilmington Coll., Ohio, 1977-78, engring. and nat. sci., U. Cin., 1979—. Author: Guidelines for Astronomy Courses, 1976, 1978; author: (with J. Ventre & J. Boothe) Astronomy Teaching Handbook, 1992; author: Introduction to the Universe, 1991, 1993, 2002, Eclipses: Presentations for Educators, 1999; author: (with J. Ventre, J. Boothe and L. Rutherford) Handbook for Astronomy Educators, 2004; contbr. articles to profl. jours. Guest lectr. Cin. Nature Ctr., Milford, 1976—; chmn. edn. Astron. League, Washington; tchr. Super Saturday Program for Gifted and Talented., Cin., 1983; commn. mem. Archdiocese Cin., 1986. Recipient Ohio NSF Presdl. Award for Excellence in Math. Edn., 1986, Greater Cin. Found./GE grantee, 1987. Mem. Ohio Coun. Tchrs. Math. (contest coord. 1983—, Outstanding Math. Tchr. award 1982), Nat. Astron. League (v.p. 1980-82, chmn. edn. 1975—), Nat. Coun. Tchrs. Math., Math. Assn. Am., Ohio Acad. Sci. (Jerry Acker Outstanding Math. Tchr. award 1986-87), Sigma Xi (Outstanding Math. Tchr. award 1985), Pi Mu Epsilon. Clubs: Midwestern Astronomers. Roman Catholic. Avocations: golf, piano, bicycling, model railroading. Office: Xavier U Dept Edn 3800 Victory Pkwy Dept Edn Cincinnati OH 45207-1035 Office Phone: 513-745-3477. Business E-Mail: flick@xavier.edu.

FLICKER, JOHN, foundation executive; b. Minnesota; Grad., U. Minnesota, William Mitchell Coll. of Law. With The Nature Conservancy, Great Plains dir., gen. counsel, chief legal officer, exec. v.p., Fla. state dir.; pres. Nat. Audubon Soc., N.Y.C., 1995—. Office: National Audubon Soc 700 Broadway New York NY 10003-9536

FLICKINGER, CHARLES JOHN, anatomist, educator; b. Bethlehem, Pa., July 13, 1938; s. Wilbur James and Verna (Diehl) F.; m. Agnes Elizabeth Dickel, Feb. 23, 1963; children: Laura Jill, David Paul. AB, Dartmouth Coll., 1960; MD, Harvard U., 1964. Rsch. fellow dept. anatomy U. Colo., Denver, 1964-65, Harvard Med. Sch., Boston, 1965-66; rsch. assoc. Inst. Devel. Biology, U. Colo., Boulder, 1966-67, asst. prof., 1967-70; assoc. prof. dept. anatomy Sch. Medicine, U. Va., Charlottesville, 1971-75, prof., 1975—, Harvey E. Jordan prof. anatomy, 1982—2002, chmn. dept. cell biology, 1982—2002. Mem. reproductive biology study sect. NIH, 1979-83; mem. anatomy test com. Nat. Bd. Med. Examiners, 1981-84. Author: (with Brown, Kutchai, Ogilvie) Medical Cell Biology, 1979; contbr. articles to profl. jours.; assoc. editor: Jour. Andrology, 1989-92; adv. editor: Internat. Rev. Cytology, 1974-98; mem. editl. bd. Biology of Reprodn., 1986-89, 2002-04, Jour. Andrology, 1986-89, Anatomical Record, 1972-98. NIH rsch. career devel. award grantee, 1968-70. Mem. Am. Soc. Cell Biology, Am. Assn. Anatomists, Soc. Study Reproduction, Am. Soc. Andrology, Phi Beta Kappa, Alpha Omega Alpha. Home: 2009 Meadowbrook Rd Charlottesville VA 22903-1247 Office: University of Virginia Dept Cell Biology PO Box 800732 Charlottesville VA 22908-0732 Office Phone: 434-924-1916. Business E-Mail: cjf@virginia.edu.

FLICKINGER, HARRY HARNER, management consultant; b. Hanover, Pa., July 27, 1936; s. Harry Roosevelt and Goldie Anna (Harner) F.; m. Hsin Yang, May 30, 1961; children: Audrey Mae, Deborah Lynn. BS in Psychology, U. Md., 1958. Investigator U.S. Civil Service Commn., Washington, 1962-64; personnel specialist U.S. Naval Ordinance Lab., Silver Spring., Md., 1964-66; from asst. dir. to dir. personnel U.S. OMB, Washington, 1966-73; asst. dir. personnel AEC and Dept. Energy, Washington, 1973-78; dir. personnel U.S. Dept. Justice, Washington, 1978-79, dep. asst. atty. gen. adminstrn., 1979-85, assoc. asst. atty. gen., 1985-87, asst. atty. gen., 1987-92; exec. dir. Am. Consortium for Internat. Pub. Adminstrn., Washington, 1993; pres. Flickinger Enterprises, Gaithersburg, Md., 1994—2003. Recipient Presdl. Disting. Exec. Rank award, 1988.

FLICKINGER, JOE ARDEN, telecommunications educator; b. Cadillac, Mich., Feb. 4, 1949; s. Arden Henry and Stella Frances (Hurst) F.; m. Judith Marie Gardner, Sept. 18, 1971; children: Jan Elsa, Jill Kimberly. BA, Kalamazoo Coll., Mich., 1971; MA, U. So. Calif., 1975; AS, Clatsop Community Coll., 1985; PhD, U. Oreg., 1993. Asst. chief engr. Sta. KUSC-FM, L.A., 1972-74; sta. engr. Sta. KAST-AM-FM, Astoria, Oreg., 1974-75; studio operator, instr. Clatsop Community Coll., Astoria, 1975-88; grad. teaching fellow in telecommunications U. Oreg., Eugene, 1988-90; sr. mktg. cons. RKM Corp., Vancouver, Wash., 1990-93; vis. asst. prof. communications Lewis and Clark Coll., Portland, Oreg., 1991-92; assoc. prof. media studies Radford (Va.) U., Va., 1992—, dir. grad. program, corp. and profl. comm., 1996-98, chair media studies dept., 1998—. Session organizer on high definition TV, Northcon, 1989, IEEE and ERA Tech. Conf., 1989. Dir. TV muscular dystrophy telethon Astoria Jaycees, 1980, 81; canvasser Friends of Coll., Astoria, 1982; pres. bd. dirs. Sta. KMUN-FM Tillicum Found., Astoria, 1983-84. Mem. IEEE, IEEE Computer Soc., IEEE Comm. Soc., Am. Radio Relay League (life), Pacific Telecomm. Coun., Northcom Inner Circle, N.Y. Acad. Scis., Nat. Model R.R. Assn., Sunset Empire Amateur Radio Club (sec. 1978-81), Lions Club (region chair dist. 24-E 1999-2002). Democrat. Presbyterian. Avocations: amateur radio, golf, fishing, astronomy, cooking. Office Phone: 540-831-6039. Business E-Mail: jflickin@radford.edu.

FLIER, JEFFREY S., endocrinologist; b. N.Y.C., 1948; BS in Biology, CCNY, 1968; MD, Mt. Sinai Sch. Medicine, 1972; MD (hon.), U. Athens, 1997. Diplomate Am. Bd. Internal Medicine. Intern Mt. Sinai, N.Y.C., 1972—73, resident in internal medicine, 1973—74; fellow in endocrinology NIH, Bethesda, Md., 1974—77; asst. prof. medicine Harvard Med. Sch., Boston, 1978—82, assoc. prof. medicine, 1982—93, prof. medicine, 1993—; chief diabetes unit Beth Israel Hosp., Boston, 1978—90, chief divsn. endocrinology, 1990—2000; vice chair for rsch. dept. medicine Beth Israel Deaconess Med. Ctr., Boston, 1998—2002, chair rsch. strategy com., 1999—, chief acad. officer, 2002. Vis. scientist Whitehead Inst., MIT, Cambridge, Mass., 1985—86; lectr. in field; Smith Kline Beecham vis. prof. U. Cambridge, 1998. Contbr. articles to profl. jours. Recipient Eli Lilly award for outstanding sci. achievement, Am. Diabetes Assn., 1991. Fellow: Am. Acad. Arts and Scis., AAAS; mem.: Assn. of Am. Physicians, Inst. Medicine, 2004 (life; pres. 2001), Inter Urban Clin. Club. Avocations: golf, skiing. Office: Beth Israel Deaconess Med Ctr Research North 325 330 Brookline Ave Boston MA 02215-5400

FLIER, MICHAEL STEPHEN, Slavic languages educator; b. L.A., Apr. 20, 1941; s. Albert and Bonnie Flier; m. Glenn Patton Wright, Sept. 19, 2004. BA, U. Calif., Berkeley, 1962, MA, 1964, PhD, 1968. Acting vis. asst. prof. Slavic langs. and lits. U. Calif., Berkeley, 1968; asst. prof. Slavic langs. and lits. UCLA, 1968-73, assoc. prof., 1973-79, prof., 1979-91, chmn. dept., 1978-84, 87-89. Vis. prof. Slavic langs. Columbia U., fall 1988, Harvard U., fall 1989; Oleksandr Potebnja prof. Ukrainian Philology Harvard U., 1991—, chmn. dept. Linguistics, 1994-99, chmn. dept. Slavic langs. and lits., 1999—2005, acting chmn. dept. linguistics, 2002; acting dir. Harvard Ukrainian Rsch. Inst., 2001, dir., 2004-. Author: Aspects of Nominal Determination in Old Church Slavic, 1974, Say It In Russian, 1982; editor: Slavic Forum: Essays in Slavic Linguistics and Literature, 1974, Am. Cont. to the Intl. Congress of Slavists, 1983, Ukrainian Philology and Linguistics, 1994; co-editor: Medieval Russian Culture, 1984, Issues in Russian Morphosyntax, 1985, The Scope of Slavic Aspect, 1985, Language, Literature, Linguistics, 1987, Medieval Russian Culture, vol. 2, 1994, For SK: In Celebration of the Life and Career of Simon Karlinsky, 1994, The Language and Verse of Russia: In Honor of Dean S. Worth on His Sixty-fifth Birthday, 1995, Francis J. Whitfield, Old Church Slavic Reader, 2004; mem. editl. bd. Slavic and East European Jour., 1989—, Movoznavstvo, 1991—, Harvard Ukrainian Studies, 1991—, Russkii iazyk v nauchniom osveshchenii, 2000—. Vice chmn. Am. Com. Slavists, 1989-94, chmn., 1994—. Internat. Rsch. and Exchs. Bd. travel grantee Russia, Czechoslovakia, 1966-67, 71, 78, 93, 96; U. Calif. Pres.'s fellow, 1990, John Simon Guggenheim Meml. Found. fellow, 1990-91. Mem. Linguistics Soc. Am., Am. Assn. Tchrs. Slavic and East European Langs., Am. Assn. Advancement Slavic Studies, Western Slavic Assn., Coll. Art Assn., Am. Assn. for Ukrainian Studies (sec.-treas. 1989-93, bd. dirs.). Home: 76 Fresh Pond Ln Cambridge MA 02138-4641 Office: Harvard U Dept Slavic Langs and Lits Barker Ctr, 12 Quincy St Cambridge MA 02138 Office Phone: 617-495-4065. Business E-Mail: flier@fas.harvard.edu.

FLIGGE, JÖRG, librarian, library director; b. Königsberg, Germany, Dec. 1, 1940; s. Armin and Ursula (Schroeter) F.; m. Gabriele Edner, July 6, 1968; children: Christina, Claudia. PhD, U. Bonn, Germany, 1972. Cert. sci. libr. Jr. libr. U. Libr., Bonn, 1972-74, libr. adminstr. Duisburg, Germany, 1974-77, head libr. adminstr., 1978-79, dep. dir., 1979, libr. dir., 1980; dep. dir. City Libr., Duisburg, 1983-90; dir., ltd. libr. dir. Bibliothek der Hansestadt Lübeck, Germany, 1990—. Head commn. AV-media in librs. German Libr. Inst., Berlin, 1980-90; mem. German-Russian Libr. Commn. Restitution, Berlin, and St. Petersburg, Russia, 1993—. Author: Herzog Albrecht von Preussen und der Osiandrismus, 1972; author: (editor) Bibliotheca Baltica, 1994, Stadt und Bibliohek, 1997, Die Wissenschaffliche Stadtbibliothek, 2001; contbr. articles to profl. jours. Active Assn. zur Beförderung gemeinnütziger Tätigkeit, Lübeck, 1991—. Mem. Verein Deutscher Bibliothekare, Verein der Bibliothekare an Öffentlichen Bibliotheken, Rotary. Lutheran. Avocations: music, studying cultural history. Home: Hermann-Lönsweg 24 23562 Lübeck Germany Office: Bibliothek der Hansestadt Lübeck Hundestr 5-17 23552 Lübeck Germany Office Phone: 49 (0) 451 122 4111.

FLINCHBAUGH, DAVID EDWARD, physicist; b. Poughkeepsie, N.Y., Oct. 11, 1934; s. Louis David and Lolita Mildred (Hook) F.; m. Heidi Maria Rose, June 15, 1957; children: William David, Laura Jean, Karen Marie, Karl Louis. BS in Physics and Math., Union Coll., 1957; MS in Physics, U. Conn., 1960, PhD in Modern Physics, 1964; cert. computer database mgmt., Harvard U., 1979. Registered profl. engr., Fla., Pa.; cert. tchr., Fla. Rsch. physicist IBM Corp., Poughkeepsie, 1956-57; rsch. assoc. Argonne Nat. Labs., Lemont, Ill., 1958; rsch. scientist United Techs. Rsch. Labs., East Hartford, Conn., 1959-60, 63-65; mgr. R&D Andersen Labs., Bloomfield, Conn., 1965-68; dir. R&D Orlando (Fla.) Rsch. Corp., 1968-69; v.p. R&D Control Laser Corp., Orlando, 1968-71; staff cons. Martin Marietta Aerospace Corp., Orlando, 1971-73, 86-87, Internat. Laser Corp., Orlando, 1975; sr. staff cons. Sperry Microwave Electronics Corp., Clearwater, Fla., 1977-78; program mgr., P.I. Planning Rsch. Corp., Kennedy Space Center, 1978-80; cons. team leader Westinghouse Electric Corp., Pitts., 1980-81; systems engring. mgr. McDonnell Douglas Astronautics Co., Titusville, Fla., 1982-86; v.p., dir. mfg. UroSolutions, Orlando. Chief cons., chief exec. officer Aerobeam Corp., Orlando, 1971—. Patentee refractive acousto-optic modulators, robotic manipulator system, urinary drainage control valve, others. Vol. instr. ARC, Orlando, 1968-90; lead counselor Boy and Girl Scouts Am., Orlando, 1968—; mem. Nat. Dem. Policy Com., 1984-86. Named Engr. of Yr. Fla. Engring. Soc., Tallahassee, 1984, Fla. Inventor of Yr. Palm Beach Soc. Am. Inventors, 1986—, Nat. Inventor of Yr. Inventor's Soc. South Fla., Ft. Lauderdale, 1988; recipient Environ. Award, Orange Co., Fla., 1998, DaVinci Award, 2002, Albert M. Sargent Progress Award, Soc. Mfg. Engrs., 2003. Fellow IEEE (Engr. of Yr. Orlando sect. 1982, 83, Entrepreneur of Yr. 1998), Optical Soc. Am., Soc. Mfg. Engrs./Robotics Internat.; mem. AIAA, NSPE, Laser Inst. Am. (bd. dirs. 1975-79), Fla. Coun. Engring. Socs. (exec. com., pres. 1985-86), Inventors Coun. Cen. Fla. (exec. com., pres. 1984—). Presbyterian. Achievements include invention of the UroCycler®. Avocations: music, photography, aviation, swimming, boating. Home: 4855 Big Oaks Ln Orlando FL 32806-7826 Office: UroSolutions, Inc Ste A 5509 Commerce Drive Orlando FL 32839 E-mail: davidf@urosolutions.com.

FLINN, CHARLES GALLAGHER, lawyer, priest; b. Ft. Lauderdale, Fla., Feb. 22, 1938; s. Robert Galloway and Gertrude (Gallagher) F. AB, Princeton U., 1959; LLB, U. Va., 1962; BD, U. London, 1980; ThM, Westminster Theol. Sem., 1994; MA, Cath. U., 2001. Bar: Fla. 1962, Va. 1962, U.S. Supreme Ct. 1966, D.C. 1970; ordained to ministry Episcopal Ch. as deacon, 1991, as priest, 1992. Assoc. Charles B. Fulton, Esq., West Palm Beach, Fla., 1962-63; asst. counsel Office Gen. Counsel U.S. Dept. Navy, Washington, 1963-71; asst. commonwealth's atty. County of Arlington, Va., 1971-72, asst. county atty., 1972-75, dep. county atty., 1975-81, county atty., 1981-93; atty. Arlington Sch. Bd., 1981-93; curate Grace Episcopal Ch., Brunswick, Md., 1991-93; vicar Trinity Episcopal Ch., Monmouth, Ill., 1994-96; vice-chancellor Episcopal Diocese, Quincy, Ill., 1996—. Vis. lectr. in bibl. lang. Reformed Theological Seminary, Orlando, Fla., 1997-2000; adj. faculty Protestant Episcopal Theol. Sem., Alexandria, Va., 1999-2000; pres. Nathanael Inst., 2001—. Mem. Va. Local Govt. Attys. Assn. (bd. dirs. 1988-92), Va. Coun. Sch. Bd. Attys. (dir.-at-large 1988-93). Business E-Mail: cgflinn@alumni.princeton.edu.

FLINN, DAVID LYNNFIELD, financial consultant; b. Atlanta, Aug. 6, 1943; s. William Adams and Caroline Elizabeth (Blackshear) F.; divorced; children: Raymur Elizabeth, Marion Orme. BA, Ga. State U., 1967. With Citizens & So. Nat. Bank, Atlanta and Miami, Fla., 1967-70; asst. to pres. Panelfab Internat. Corp., Miami, 1970-72; v.p. Citibank, Miami, 1972-76; ind. fin. cons. Miami, 1976—; CFO, Aljoma Lumber, Inc., Miami, 1990—. Cons. various fgn. corps., 1981—; bd. dirs. Aljoma Lumber, Inc., Medley, Fla., Continental Trust Mortgage Corp., Miami, Grand Lakes Devel. Corp. Bd. dirs., former pres. La Gorce Island Assn., 1974-89; bd. dirs. Children's Home Soc., Miami, 1980-83. Mem. La Gorce Country Club (Miami Beach, Fla.), Fisher Island Club (Miami), Com. of 100 (Miami). Republican. Episcopalian. Home: 1717 N Bayshore Dr Apt 1231 Miami FL 33132-1150 Office: 10300 NW 121st Way Miami FL 33178-1003

FLINN, MICHAEL DE VLAMING, investment company executive; b. Durham, N.C., June 15, 1941; s. Lawrence and Marion (de Vlaming) Flinn; m. Elizabeth Jamison Folk, Aug. 3, 1962 (div. Mar. 1985); children: William III, Michael de Vlaming, T. Rex, Randall E.; m. Ann G. Hanes, Feb. 14, 1993. BA magna cum laude, Yale U., 1962; JD, Harvard U., 1965. Bar: Conn. 1968. Ltd. ptnr. Ingalls & Snyder, 1970-96; mem. Conn. Ho. of Reps., Hartford, 1983-86; v.p. Spears, Benzak, Salmon & Farrell, Inc. (name now Victory, N.Y.C., 1996—2005, mng. dir., 1997, Tocqueville Asset Mgmt. LP, N.Y.C., 2005—. Mng. dir. Victory SBSF Capital Mgmt. Active Town Meeting, Greenwich, Conn., 1970—82; pres., bd. dirs. Greenwich Boys Club Assn., 1977—92, Round Hill Assn., 1972—81, Boys and Girls Club Greenwich, 1993—94; trustee Green-Wood Cemetery, 1983—; bd. dirs. Coldwater Conservation Fund, 2002—; mem. Conn. Rep. Fin. Com., 1972, Greenwich Rep. Town Com., 1980—85, mem. exec. com., 1982—84. Capt. U.S. Army, 1966—68. Mem.: ABA, Greenwich Bar Assn., Conn. Bar Assn., Yale Alumni Assn. Greenwich (gov. 1982—85), Hotchkiss Alumni Assn. (gov. 1979—83), Burning Tree Club, Links. Home: PO Box 1309 Greenwich CT 06836-1309 Office: Tocqueville Asset Mgmt 40 West 57th St 19th Fl New York NY 10019 Office Phone: 212-698-0803. Business E-Mail: mflinn@tocqueville.com.

FLINN, MICHAEL JAMES, lawyer; b. Pitts., June 9, 1949; s. George E. and Iris R. (Schartl) F.; m. Eileen McGrady, Aug. 7, 1971; children: Erin, Kevin. BA, U. Notre Dame, 1971; JD, U. Pitts., 1974. Bar: Pa. 1974, U.S. Dist. Ct. (we. dist.) Pa. 1974. Assoc. Moorhead & Knox, Pitts., 1974-81; ptnr. Buchanan Ingersoll, P.C., Pitts., 1981—. Pres. Nat. Aviary, 1992-97; mem. adv. bd. The Salvation Army, Southwestern Pa., 1993—; mem. Bd. Nat. Aviary, 1998—. Home: 728 Harden Dr Pittsburgh PA 15229-1107 Office: Buchanan Ingersoll PC 301 Grant St Ste 21 Pittsburgh PA 15219-1408 Office Phone: 412-562-1027. E-mail: flinnmj@bipc.com.

FLINN, PAUL ANTHONY, materials scientist; b. N.Y.C., Mar. 25, 1926; s. Richard A. and Anna M. (Weber) F.; m. Mary Ellen Hoffman, Aug. 20, 1949; children: Juliana, Margaret, Donald, Anthony, Patrick. AB, Columbia Coll., 1948, MA, 1949; ScD, MIT, 1952. Asst. prof. Wayne U., Detroit, 1953-54; research staff Westinghouse Research Lab., Pitts., 1954-63; prof. Carnegie-Mellon U., Pitts., 1964-78; sr. staff scientist Intel Corp., Santa Clara, Calif., 1978-95; cons. prof. dept. material sci. and engring. Stanford (Calif.) U., 1985—. Vis. prof. U. Nancy, France, 1967-68, U. Fed. do Rio Grand du Sol, Porto Allegro, Brazil, 1975, Argonne (Ill.) Nat. Lab., 1977-78, Stanford (Calif.) U., 1984-85. Contbr. sci. articles to profl. jours. Served with USN, 1944-46, PTO. Fellow Am. Phys. Soc.; mem. Metall. Soc., Materials Rsch. Soc., Phi Beta Kappa, Tau Beta Pi. Office: Stanford U Dept Material Sci & Engring Stanford CA 94305-2205 Business E-Mail: pflinn@stanford.edu.

FLINN, ROBERTA JEANNE, management and computer applications consultant; b. Twin Falls, Idaho, Dec. 19, 1947; d. Richard H. and Ruth (Johnson) F. Student, Colo. State U., 1966-67. Cert. Novell netware engr. Ptnr. Aqua-Star Pools & Spas, Boise, Idaho, 1978—, mng. ptnr., 1981-83; IT architect IBM Global Services, 2000—. Ops. mgr. Polly Pools, Inc., Canby, Oreg., 1983-84, br. mgr. Polly Pools, Inc., A-One Distributing, 1984-85; comptr., Beaverton Printing, Inc., 1986-89; mng. ptnr. Invisible Ink, Canby, Oreg., 1989—2000. Mem. Nat. Appaloosa Horse Club, Oreg. Dressage Soc., British Computer Soc Home: 24687 S Central Point Rd Canby OR 97013-9743 E-mail: rjflinn@invisibleink.net.

FLINNER, BEATRICE JEFFREYS ALLAYAUD, retired library and media sciences educator; b. Uledi, Pa., Feb. 8, 1924; d. Charles Robert and Esther Marjorie (Sickles) Jeffreys; m. Donald Allayaud, May 18, 1944 (dec.); 1 child, Donald Allayaud; m. Lyle P. Flinner, June 27, 1947; 1 child, Carol Jean Flinner Dorough. AB summa cum laude, So. Nazarene U., 1974; MLS, U. Okla., 1977; MA in Social Studies, So. Nazarene U., 1978, MA in Early Childhood, 1981. Cataloging dept. Asbury Theol. Sem., Wilmore, Ky., 1949-52; aquisitions Geneva Coll., Beaver Falls, Pa., 1959-62, audio visual coord., 1965-68; assoc. prof., head pub. svcs. So. Nazarene U., Bethany, Okla., 1968-96, adj. prof. grad. edn., 1980-2000; ret., 1996. Adv. bd. Bethany Libr., rep. to bd. trustees, 1986-87. Book reviewer The Christian Librarian, 1980-94; indexer Christian Periodical Index, 1988-96; contbr. articles to profl. jours., short stories to lit. publs. Mem. AAUW (directory), Assn. Christian Librs. (life, v.p. 1991-93, program chair internat. conf. 1992), Univ. Women's Club, U. Okla. Sch. Libr. Info. Sci. Alumni Assn., Assn. Christian Librs. (conf. coord. 1992-95), Rsch. Interest Group, Acad. Sr. Profls. (libr. resources columnist, named one of 2000 Notable Am. Women), Phi Delta Lambda (faculty advisor), Delta Kappa Gamma. Republican. Nazarene. Personal E-mail: lylebeaflinner@aol.com.

FLINSPACH, URSULA R., pharmacy technician, mathematics educator; b. Washington, Pa., Jan. 22, 1950; d. Albert M. Sr. and Rose K. Jackson; m. Donald A. Flinspach, Jr., May 20, 1972; 1 child, Donald A. III. BS in Math., So. Ill. U., Carbondale, 1975; AA in computer sci., John Wood C.C., Quincy, Ill., 1985; cert. in pharmacy tech., Harcourt Learning Direct, 2001. Cert. tchr. math., sci., computer sci. Ill., 1974, Mo., 1975, pharmacy technician Ill., 1997, Nat. Bd. Pharmacy Technician Cert., 1998, Mo., 2000. Math. instr. Highland HS, Ewing, Mo., 1975—76; math. and computer sci. instr. Notre Dame HS, Quincy, Ill., 1977—85; math. instr. Homer HS, 1986—88; math./physics instr. Mt Zion HS, 1989—92; math. instr. Routt HS, Jacksonville, 1993—95, Unity HS, Mendon, 1995—98; cert. pharmacy technician ShopKo Stores, Inc., Quincy, 1998—. Golf coach Notre Dame HS, Quincy, Ill., 1978—85; coach Mt Zion HS, 1989—92, Unity H.S., Mendon, 1996—98. Neighborhood chairperson Mother's Mar. of Dimes, Quincy, Ill., 2003—03; vol. runner Hannibal Regional Hosp., Hannibal, Mo., 1996—2003; vol. coach Little People's Golf Tournament, Quincy, 1979—85; team leader Shopko store #2139 United Way, 1999—99; mayoral candidate Ind. Party, Quincy, Ill., 1995—96. Tradevman 2d class WAVES USN, 1969—72. Decorated Nat. Def. Medal USN; nominee Hero of the Year award, Champaign County, 1989; recipient Above and Beyond Tchg., Homer Cmty. Consol. Sch. Bd., 1986—88, 5-10k Bronze medal, Hannibal Regional Hosp., 2001. Mem.: Quincy Soc. Fine Arts, Pharmacy Technician Certification Bd., Am. Pharmacists Assn. Roman Catholic. Achievements include first female from 1967 Trinity High School to enlist in the military WAVES during Vietnam; first female Mayoral candidate Quincy Illinois. Avocations: reading, continued education, walking/hiking, music, biking. Home: 1608 Madison Quincy IL 62301 Office: ShopKo Stores Inc 3200 Broadway Quincy IL 62301 Personal E-mail: uflin@hotmail.com.

FLINT, DOUGLAS J., investment company executive; b. July 8, 1955; s. David and Dorothy (Jardine) Flint. Articled clerk KPMG (formerly Peat Marwick Mitchell & Co.), 1977—80, chartered acct., 1980—88, ptnr., 1988-95; group fin. dir. HSBC Holdings plc, London, 1995—. Bd. dirs. HSBC Holdings plc, HSBC Bank Malaysia Berhad. Office: HSBC Holdings plc 8 Canada Square London E14 5HQ England

FLINT, GEORGE SQUIRE, lawyer; b. Ft. Wayne, Ind., Oct. 28, 1930; s. A. Verne and Alberta (Minor) F.; m. Emily Gregg McLees, Nov. 23, 1968; 1 son, Alexander C.; children by previous marriage: Julia M., Melissa A., Anthony E. AB, U. Mich., 1952, JD, 1955. Bar: N.Y. 1956. Assoc., then sr. assoc. Fulton, Walter & Duncombe, N.Y.C., 1955-65; ptnr. Fulton, Duncombe and Rowe, 1983-89; with Tenneco Chems., Inc., 1965-82, v.p., sec., gen. counsel, 1969-82; counsel Jackson & Nash, N.Y.C., 1989—2002. Arbitrator Small Claims Part. Civil Ct., N.Y.C. With USN, 1955-57. Mem. N.Y. State Bar Assn., Assn. Bar City N.Y., Order of Coif. Clubs: Indian Harbor Yacht, Wadawanuck, Stonington. Home: 1185 Park Ave New York NY 10128-1308

FLINT, H. HOWARD, II, printing company executive; b. Apr. 17, 1939; MBA, U of Penn Wharton Sch. With Flint Ink Corp., Detroit, 1960—, pres., 1985—92, chmn. bd., CEO, 1992—. Office: Flint Ink Corp 4600 Arrowhead Dr Ann Arbor MI 48105-2773

FLINT, JAMES OLIVER, retired electronics engineer, retired accountant; b. Augusta, Ga., July 6, 1931; s. Ollie Benjamin Flint and Ruby Inez Glenn; m. Susanne Rosemarie Pofandt, Dec. 22, 1968; children: Dianne Elizabeth Ellis, Rosemarie Gundela Petersen, Ollie Benjamin, Claire Francesca Brandon. AA in acctg., New River C.C., 1962; AA in electronics, Tidewater C.c., 1981. Tech. AT&T, Burlington, NC, 1960—61, MCS, Fairlawn, Va., 1999—. Home: 419 Short Rd Nw Riner VA 24149

FLINT, JOHN E., retired historian; b. Montreal, May 17, 1930; s. Alfred Edgar and Sarah (Pickup) F.; m. Nezhat Sepanj, Sept. 19, 1975; children: Helen Sarah, Richard John. BA, U. Cambridge, 1952, MA, 1954; PhD, U. London, 1957. Asst. lectr., lectr., reader colonial history King's Coll., U. London, 1954-67; vis. prof., Fulbright fellow U. Calif., Santa Barbara, 1960-61; vis. prof., head history dept. U. Nigeria, Nsukka, 1963-64; prof. history Dalhousie U., 1967—, dir. African Studies Centre, 1967-92; prof. emeritus, 1993—. Mem. acad. panel Can. Council, 1967-68, Social Scis. and Humanities Research Council Can. Author: Sir George Goldie and the Making of Nigeria, 1960, Nigeria and Ghana, 1966, Cecil Rhodes, 1974; co-author: Oxford History of the British Empire, Vol. V, 1999; editor: Cambridge History of Africa, Vol. V, 1790-1870, 1977. Fellow Royal Hist. Soc., Royal Soc. Can.; mem. Canadian Assn. African Studies, Canadian Hist. Assn., Nigerian Hist. Assn., African Studies Assn. U.K. Personal E-mail: johnflint@rogers.com.

FLIPSE, JOHN EDWARD, naval architect, mechanical engineer; b. Montville, N.J., Feb. 4, 1921; SB, MIT, 1942; MME, NYU, 1948. Registered profl. engr., NY, Va., Tex. Sr. engr., ship stabilization dept. head, marine div. Sperry Gyroscope Co., Great Neck, N.Y., 1955-57; rsch. engr., dir. rsch., mgr. systems dept., asst. to pres. Newport News (Va.) Shipbuilding and Dry Dock Co., 1957-68; chmn., pres., chief exec. officer Deepsea Ventures, Inc., Gloucester, Va., 1968-77; pres., chief exec. officer Tex. A&M Rsch. Found., College Station, 1983-84; dep. dir. Tex. Engring. Experiment Sta., 1985-88; disting. prof. civil and ocean engring. Tex. A&M U., 1982-92, assoc. dean engring. College Station, 1984-88, assoc. dep. chancellor for engring., 1984-89, Wofford Cain prof. engring., 1988-91, dir. Offshore Tech. Rsch. Ctr., 1988-91, dir. emeritus, 1991—2000. Chmn. Nat. Adv. Com. on Oceans and Atmosphere, 1985-86; mem. marine bd. Nat. Rsch. Coun., 1979-84, chmn., 1982-84; mem. marine facilities panel U.S./Japan Coop. Program in Natural Resources, 1980-96; mem. marine petroleum and minerals adv. com. Dept. Commerce, 1974-75; expert mem. U.S. delegation to Law of the Sea Conf., UN, 1975-76; cons., lectr. in field. Contbr. articles to profo. publs., patentee in field. Mem. dean's adv. coun. Sch. Engring. & Applied Sci., U. Va., 1995-98. Fellow Marine Tech. Soc. (pres. 1985-87), Soc. Naval Architects and Marine Engrs. (past chmn. tech. and rsch. steering com.); mem. Nat. Acad. Engring. (membership policy com. 1987-90, membership com. 1987-90, peer rev. com. 1985-86), Va. Inst. Marine Sci. (vice chmn. bd. dirs. 1968-76).

FLITCRAFT, RICHARD KIRBY, II, former chemical company executive; b. Woodstown, N.J., Sept. 5, 1920; s. H. Milton and Edna (Crispin) F.; m. Bertha LeSturgeon Hitchner, Nov. 14, 1942; children: Alyce, Anne, Elizabeth, Richard. BS, Rutgers U., 1942; MS, Washington U., 1948. With Monsanto Co., St. Louis, 1942—, dir. inorganic rsch., 1960-65, dir. mgmt. info. and systems dept., 1965-67, asst. to pres., 1967-68, group mgr. electronics enterprises, 1968-69, gen. mgr. electronic products div., 1969-71; v.p. Monsanto Rsch. Corp., 1971-75; dir. Mound Lab., 1971-75, v.p. ops., 1975-76; pres. Monsanto Resh. Corp., Dayton, 1976-82, ret., 1982. Past chmn., bd. dirs. United Way, Dayton; bd. dirs. City-Wide Devel. Corp.; former trustee and chmn. bd. Miami Valley Hosp.; past bd. dirs. Pvt. Industry Coun., Srs., Inc.; chmn. bd. Headstart program Miami Valley Child Devel., Inc. Mem. AAAS, AICE, Am. Chem. Soc., Am. Inst. Chemists, Am. Mgmt. Assn., N.Y. Acad. Scis., Ohio Acad. Scis. (past exec. com.), Dayton C. of C. (past bd. dirs., chmn. small bus. adv. bd., mil. affairs com.), Engrs. Club of Dayton (past bd. dirs.), Engrs. Club Dayton Found. (bd. trustees, chmn.), Moraine Country Club, Dayton Racquet Club. Presbyterian.

FLITTIE, CLIFFORD GILLILAND, retired petroleum company executive; b. Brookings, S.D., Mar. 10, 1924; s. Theodore Ignatius and Grace Eliza (Gilliland) F.; m. Dawn Marie Lee, May 22, 1954. Student, Okla. State U., 1944, Colo. Sch. Mines, 1946; BS (Nat. scholar Am. Inst. Mining and Metall. Engrs.), S.D. Sch. Mines and Tech., 1948. Geologist Arabian Am. Oil Co., Dhahran, Saudi Arabia, 1948-57; v.p. exploration Conorada Petroleum Corp., N.Y.C., 1958-63, dir., 1963-65; v.p., mgr. Amerada Petroleum Corp. of U.K., London, 1964-65, Amerada Petroleum Corp. of Australia, Brisbane, 1966-69; exploration supr. Amerada Hess Corp., N.Y.C., 1970-73; v.p. Shaheen Natural Resources Co., Inc., N.Y.C., 1974-75, Macmillan Oil Co., N.Y.C., 1975-82, Natomas Co., San Francisco, 1982-86. Dir. Amerada Exploration Ltd., 1964-65 Served with USNR, 1944-46. Mem. Am. Assn. Petroleum Geologists, Soc. Exploration Geophysicists, Theta Tau, Sigma Tau. Episcopalian. Home: 46 San Jacinto Way San Francisco CA 94127-2033

FLOCCO, BARBARA A., music educator; b. Springfield, Pa., Mar. 30, 1948; d. Norman Edward Griffiths and Mildred Rose Hoffman-Griffiths; m. James Lee Flocco, Oct. 17, 1970; children: Christine, Michael, Thomas. BS summa cum laude in music, West Chester U., 1970; MEd in adminstrn., U. NH, 1995. Music dir. St. Clair Regional Schs., St. Clair, Pa., 1972—73; organist, dir. music Air Force Base Chapels, Plattsburgh, Portsmouth, NH, 1973—78; dir. music Sanborn Regional Schs., Newton, Kingston, NH, 1991—92, Lincoln Akerman Sch., Hampton Falls, NH, 1992—97; dir. music, organist First Bapt. Ch., Hampston Falls, NH, 1979—2004; vocal coach Gordon Coll., Wenham, Mass., 1999—2004; music dir., organist Bedford Presbyn. Ch., Bedford, NH, 2004—05; choral accompanist, asst. Phillips Exeter Acad., Exeter, NH, 2001—04. Dir. NH Children's Choir Fest., Hampton Falls, NH, 1985, Youth Chamber Music Program, Stratham, NH, 1979; pedagogist self employed, 1970—2000. Pianist: various chamber music. Recipient Piano Concerto Competition, West Chester U., 1970. Mem.: Am. Guild of English, Am. Guild of Organists, Handbell Ringers. Avocations: hiking, snowshoeing, bicycling. Home: 69 River Rd Springfield PA 19064 E-mail: weddingorganist@hotmail.com.

FLOCK, HOWARD, psychology professor; b. Phila., Nov. 24, 1924; s. Salomon and Della (Buschel) F. BA, Yale U., 1944; MA, Harvard U., 1958; PhD, Cornell U., 1962. Asst. prof. CUNY, 1961-64; assoc. prof. Dartmouth Coll., 1964-65, York U., Toronto, Ont., Can., 1965-70, prof. psychology, 1970—. Contbr. articles to profl. publs., chpts. to books, also to films. Lt. (j.g.) USN, 1943-45, ETO. Grantee NSF, NSERC, NRC Can., 1964-82. Fellow APA; mem. Psychonomic Soc., Ea. Psychol. Assn., Harvard Club. Avocations: skiing, travel, films, photography. Home: 20 W 64th St New York NY 10023-7180 Office: York U Dept Psychology North York ON Canada M3J 1P3 Office Phone: 212-595-2895. E-mail: hrflock@aol.com.

FLOCKHART, CALISTA, actress; b. Freeport, Ill., Nov. 11, 1964; d. Ronald and Kay F. BA in acting, Rutgers U. Actress Ally McBeal Twentieth Century Fox, L.A. Appeared in Broadway plays, including The Glass Menagerie, The Three Sisters; television work includes; The Guiding Light, 1978, Darrow, 1991, Ally McBeal, 1997-2002; film work includes; Quiz Show, 1994, Getting In, 1994, Naked in New York, 1994, Pictures of Baby Jane Doe, 1996, The Birdcage, 1996, Milk and Money, 1997, Drunks, 1997, Telling Lies in America, 1997, A Midsummer Night's Dream, 1999, Like a Hole in the Head, 1999, Jane Doe, 1999, The Last Shot, 2004. Recipient Best Actress award Golden Globes, 1998 for her work on Ally McBeal. Office: Ally McBeal c/o David E Kelly Productions c/o Twentieth Century Fox 10201 W Pico Blvd Bldg 80 Los Angeles CA 90064-2606

FLOERSCH, RICHARD, human resources specialist; BS, MBA, State U. NY. Cons. human resources Meredith Assocs., Conn.; with human resources mgmt. Internat. Playtex, Conn.; joined General Foods, 1984; v.p. compensation Kraft Foods N.Am.; v.p. corp. compensation Philip Morris; v.p. human resources Kraft Foods Internat., Rye Brook, NY, 1998—2003; exec. v.p. worldwide human resources McDonalds, Oak Brook, Ill., 2003—. Bd. dirs. AIESEC Yale. Office: McDonalds One Kroc Dr Oak Brook IL 60523*

FLOHRE, KYLE ANTHONY, music educator, director; s. Ralph Anthony and Brenda Kay Flohre. MusB in Edn., James Madison U., 2002. Dir. bands Colonial Heights (Va.) H.S. and Mid. Sch., 2002—. Mem.: Va. Band and Orch. Dirs. Assn., Nat. Assn. Music Edn. Roman Cath. Avocations: exercise, tennis, computers.

FLOM, EDWARD LEONARD, retired metal products executive; b. Tampa, Fla., Dec. 10, 1929; s. Samuel Louis and Julia (Mittle) F.; m. Beverly Boyett, Mar. 31, 1956; children— Edward Louis, Mark Robert, Julia Ruth. B.C.E., Cornell U., 1952. With Fla. Steel Corp., Tampa, 1954-93, v.p. sales, 1957-64, pres., dir., 1964-93, ret., 1993. Bd. dirs., mem. exec. com. Com. of 100, Tampa, United Fund Tampa; mem. adv. com. St. Joseph's Hosp., Tampa; bd. dirs. Family Svc. Assn. Tampa, Jewish Welfare Fedn. Tampa; bd. dirs. temple. With C.E., U.S. Army, 1952-54. Mem. Am. Iron and Steel Inst. (bd. dirs.), Fla. Engring. Soc., Young Pres. Orgn., Univ. Club, Palma Ceia Golf and Country Club, Tampa Yacht Club, Gasparilla Krewe, Rotary (bd. dirs. Tampa). Home: 4936 Saint Croix Dr Tampa FL 33629-4831

FLOM, GERALD TROSSEN, lawyer; b. Neenah, Wis., Feb. 6, 1930; s. Russell Craig and Lois Eva (Trossen) F.; m. Martha Herrington Benton, Aug. 21, 1954 (div. June 25, 1980); children— Katherine Simmons, Sarah Elizabeth Kiecker, Russell Craig. BA magna cum laude, Lawrence U., 1952; JD, Yale U., 1957. Bar: Minn. 1957, U.S. Dist. Ct. Minn. 1957. Assoc. Faegre & Benson LLP, Mpls., 1957-64, ptnr., 1964-95; retired, 1995. Adj. asst. prof. Law Sch., U. Minn., Mpls., 1966, bd. dirs., Old Republic Natl. Title Holding Co. and Old Republic Natl. Title Ins. Co., 1977-99. Mem. editorial bd. Yale Law Jour. Trustee Mpls. Soc. Fine Arts, 1970-76, Lawrence U., 1974-81, Plymouth Congl. Ch., 1978-81, William Mitchell Coll. Law, St. Paul, 1983-89; bd. dirs. Met. Med. Ctr. Research Found., Mpls., 1975-85. Served with U.S. Army, 1952-54. Mem. ABA, Minn. State Bar Assn., Hennepin County Bar Assn., Assn. Bar City of N.Y., Mace, Mpls. Club, Interlachen Country Club (Edina, Minn.), Phi Beta Kappa, Phi Delta Theta, Phi Alpha Delta. Congregationalist. Home: 3434 Zenith Ave S Minneapolis MN 55416-4663 Office: Faegre & Benson LLP 2200 Wells Fargo Ctr 90 S 7th St Minneapolis MN 55402-3901

FLOM, JOSEPH HAROLD, lawyer; b. Balt., Dec. 20, 1923; s. Isadore and Fannie (Fishman) Flom; m. Claire Cohen, Nov. 14, 1958; children: Peter Leslie, Jason Robert. Student, CCNY, 1948; LLB cum laude, Harvard U., 1948; LHD (hon.), Queens Coll., 1984; LLD (hon.), Fordham U., 1990. Bar: NY 1949. Joined Skadden Arps Slate, NYC, 1948—; now ptnr. Skadden Arps Slate Meagher & Flom LLP, NYC. Spl. counsel subcom. on admisntrn. of internal revenue laws House Ways and Means Com., 1951—52; mem. SEC Com. on Tender Offers, 1983—85; trustee Petrie Stores Liquidating Trust, 1996—; adv. bd. RRE Investors, LLC, 1999—; bd. dirs. Wm. Wrigley Jr. Co., 1977—94, Revlon Group Inc., 1990—96, Warnaco Group Inc., 1997—2000, Urban Am., LLC, 1998—. Editor Harvard Law Rev., 1947—48; co-editor: Disclosure Requirements of Public Corporations and Insiders, 1967, Texas Gulf Sulphur-Insider Disclosure Problems, 1968, Lawyer's Conflicts-The Evolving Case Law, 1991. Trustee Fedn. Jewish Philanthropies NY, 1977—89, Mt. Sinai-NYU Med. Ctr. Health Sys., 1978—99, Barnard Coll., 1983—93, NY Hist. Soc., 1989—94, Skadden Fellowship Found., Constl. Edn. Found., 1989—93; mem. NYC Commn. on Status of Women, 1975—76, NYC Holocaust Meml. Commn., 1982—87, Mayor's Coun. Econ. Advisors, NYC, 1990—93, Mayor's Mgmt. Adv. Task Force, 1991—93; bd. dirs. United Way NYC, 1991—97, Am.-Israel Friendship League, 1996—2000; co-chair task force on capital fin. and constrn. NYC Bd. Edn., 1987—89; co-chair NYC Commn. on Bicentennial of US Constn., 1986—89, NYC Operation Welcome Home Commn., 1991; chair Woodrow Wilson Internat. Ctr. for Scholars, 1994—98; chair adv. com. Export-Import Bank of US, 1995; adv. coun. Bologna Ctr. of the Paul H. Nitze Sch. Advanced Internat. Studies Johns Hopkins U., 2000—03; mayor's rep. Met. Mus. Art, 1990—93; mem. Woodrow Wilson Coun., Archdiocesan Task Force on Crime Prevention and Youth, 1982—87. Recipient Servant of Justice Award, Legal Aid Soc., 1986, Whitney North Seymour Jr. Award, Fed. Bar Coun., 1989, Disting. Svc. Medal, Dept. Def., 1992, Lifetime Achievement award, The Am. Lawyer, 2004. Mem.: Coun. on Fgn. Rels., Assn. Bar City NY. Office: Skadden Arps Slate 4 Times Sq Fl 41 New York NY 10036-6522 Office Phone: 212-735-3100. Business E-Mail: jflom@skadden.com.

FLOOD, ANGELA, interior designer, artist; b. NYC, Jan. 22, 1945; d. Americo Montes and Candace M. Hansen; m. Oscar William Rocafort, June 2, 1963 (div.); 1 child, Angélique Rocafort-Ward; m. Steven Arthur Flood, June 12, 1988. Student, NYU, 1965—66, Pace U., 1973—76; AAS, Suffolk C.C., 1992. Artist, curator F.O.R.E., Bedford, NY, 1976—86; owner, designer A&S Interiors, Westhampton Beach, NY, 1992—; owner design and art exhbns. Exhibitions include Easthampton (NY) Town Hall, 2001, Westhampton Beach Libr., 2002, Southampton RML Gallery, 2003, Easthampton Guild Hall Mus., 2004, 2005, Easthampton Artist Alliance Hall, 2005. Counselor ARC, White Plains, NY, 1974—77. Republican. Avocations: horseback riding, kayaking, canoeing, sailing, skiing. Office: A&S Interiors PO Box 413 Westhampton Beach NY 11978 E-mail: lilly11967@yahoo.com.

FLOOD, ANNMARIE ELIZABETH, librarian; b. Budapest, Hungary, Mar. 7, 1949; came to U.S., 1957; d. Antal Kartsoke and Clara G. (Gatska Kartsoke) Kerr; m. Donald James Flood, May 31, 1975; 1 child, Lisa Eileen. BA in English/Edn., Notre Dame Coll. Ohio, 1972. Field tng. Gesu Sch. Libr., University Heights, Ohio, 1972; children's asst. Maple Heights (Ohio) Regional Libr., 1972-75; asst. to children's libr. Sandusky (Ohio) Libr. Assn., 1975-80; office mgr. High Water Enterprises, Sandusky, 1989—; daycare provider Kiddie Korral, Sandusky, 1997; substitute tchr. Cold Creek Ducklings Enrichment Ctr., 1997-98. Sales assoc. Elder Beerman Dept. Stores. Treas. St. Mary's Ctrl. Cath. H.S. Band Boosters, Sandusky, 1996-97; mem. Old House Guild, Sandusky; tour guide E. Cooke House, Sandusky. Recipient Woman of Excellence award Providence Hosp., 1998. Mem. AAUW (pres. 1990-92, 96-98). Roman Catholic. Avocations: reading, knitting, needlepoint.

FLOOD, H. GAY (HULDA GAY FLOOD), editor, consultant; b. Plainfield, N.J., Aug. 14, 1935; d. William Edward and Lucy (Dycker) Flood. BA, Smith Coll., 1957. With picture dept. Sports Illustrated, Time Inc., N.Y.C., 1957-58, with letters dept., 1958-59, reporter, 1959-60, writer-reporter, 1960-71, assoc. editor, 1971-85, sr. editor, 1985-90. Mem. Greater Consistory First Reformed Ch., Nyack, NY; assoc. mem. The Ch. of the Pilgrimage, Plymouth, Mass. Mem.: Smith Coll. Students Aid Soc., Alumnae Assn. Smith Coll., Boston Smith Coll. Club, Garden Club Nyack (chair cmty. flower show 2001), Smith Coll. Club N.Y. Office: 7 Sampson Commons Plymouth MA 02360

FLOOD, JAMES TYRRELL, broadcasting executive, public relations executive; b. L.A., Oct. 5, 1934; s. James Joseph and Teresa (Rielly) F.; m. Bonnie Carolyn Lutz, Mar. 25, 1966; children: Hilary C., Sean L. BA in Liberal Arts, U. Calif., Santa Barbara, 1956; MA in Comms., Calif. State U., Chico, 1981. Publicist Rogers & Cowan, 1959-60, Jim Mahoney & Assocs., 1960-61, ABC-TV, San Francisco, Hollywood, Calif., 1961-64; cons. pub. rels. Beverly Hills, Calif., 1964-72; pub. rels. and advt. dir. Jerry Lewis Films, 1964-72; dir. pub. rels. MTM Prodns., 1970-72; pub. rels. cons. Medic Alert Found. Internat., 1976-83; owner mgr. Sta. KRIJ-FM, Paradise, 1983-88; instr. Calif. State U. Sch. Comms., Chico, 1982-89; gen. mgr. KIXE-TV (PBS), Redding-Chico, Calif., 1991-92; media cons., 1993—. Represented numerous artists including Pearl Bailey, Gary Owens, Ruth Buzzi, Allen Ludden, Betty White, Celeste Holm, Jose Feliciano, Tom Kennedy, Shirley Jones, David Cassidy, others; pub. rels. dir. Warren Miller Prodns., 1967—, Mary Tyler Moore Prodns., 1971. Calif. media cons. Carter/Mondale campaign, 1976; mem. Calif. Dem. Fin. Com., 1982-83. Served with USNR, 1956-58. Mem. Calif. Broadcasters Assn. (bd. dirs. 1986-88). Personal E-mail: xsh2oj@earthlink.net.

FLOOD, RICHARD SIDNEY, curator; b. Nov. 10, 1943; BA, St. Joseph's Coll., Phila., 1965; MA Annenberg Sch. Comm., U. Pa., 1967. Tchr. film, video & English Phila. pub. schools; dir. Cmty. Sch. Phila.; co-founder, editor Art Exchange mag., Phila., 1976—79; mng. editor to books editor ArtForum Mag., 1980—83; dir. Barbara Gladstone Gallery, NYC, 1983—94; chief curator Walker Art Ctr., Mpls., 1994—2005, New Mus. Contemporary Art, NYC, 2005—. Advisor grad. sculpture dept. RI Inst. Art & Design, Providence, 1981—83. Office: New Mus Contemporary Art 556 W 22nd St New York NY 10011 Office Phone: 212-219-1222. Office Fax: 212-431-5328.*

FLOOR, RICHARD EARL, lawyer; b. Lynn, Mass., Aug. 3, 1940; s. Albert C. and Blanche (Goldthwait) F.; m. Elizabeth Wilson, Apr. 19, 1969; children: Amy, Lucy, Rebecca. AB, Fairfield U., 1962; JD, Harvard Law Sch., 1965. Bar: Mass. 1965, N.Y. 2001. Law clk. to Hon. C.P. O'Sullivan U.S. Ct. Appeals (6th cir.), 1965-66; assoc. Goodwin, Procter & Hoar, Boston, 1966-74; ptnr. Goodwin Procter LLP (formerly Goodwin, Procter & Hoar), Boston, 1974—; mem. mgmt. com. & exec. com. Goodwin, Procter & Hoar, Boston, 1987-93; mem. mgmt. com., co-chair corp. dept. Goodwin Procter LLP, Boston. Lectr. Harvard Bus. Sch., Cambridge, 1988-92; bd. dirs. Affiliated Mgrs. Group, Inc., New Am. High Income Fund, NYSE. Contbr. articles to profl. jours. Co-chmn. reverse investment com. internat. trade adv. bd. Commonwealth Mass., 1994; organizer Inst. Mgmt. Edn. Thailand; trustee Regis Coll., Wellesley, Mass., 1990-97, 99-; chmn. Harvard Ctr. Eating Disorders, 2000-01. Mem. ABA, Boston Bar Assn. Office: Goodwin Procter LLP Exchange Pl 53 State St Boston MA 02109-2881 Office Phone: 617-570-1260. E-mail: rfloor@goodwinprocter.com.

FLOR, CLAUS PETER, conductor; b. Leipzig, Saxonia, Germany, Mar. 16, 1953; adopted s. Richard and Sigrid (Langer) F.; m. Sabine Winni Niedziella, Mar. 15, 1984; 1 child, Claus Peter Jr. Grad., Music Sch., Weimar, Germany, 1971; Diploma, High Sch. Music, Weimar/Leipzig, 1971-77; grad. in conduction, High Sch. Music, Leipzig, 1975-78. Chief condr. Philarm. Orch., Suhl, Germany, 1981-84; chief condr., gen. music dir. Berliner Sinfonie Orchester, 1984-92; prin. guest coord. Dallas Symphony Orch. Prin. guest condr. Dallas Symphony Orch., 1998—. Guest condr. numerous symphonic orchs. including Munich and Berlin Philarm. Orchs., various famous London, Paris, Vienna orchs., L.A. Philarm., N.Y. Philarm., and many others, also various opera houses in Munich, Berlin, Hamburg; prin. guest condr. Zurich Tonhalle Orch., 1991-96; prin. guest condr. Philharmonia Orch., 1991-94. Avocations: collecting red wines, history and genealogy of the european nobility, horses, sailing. also: Intermusica Artists Mgmt 16 Duncan Terr London N18BZ England Office Phone: 1712785455. E-mail: swflor@AOL.com.*

FLORA, BETHANY HOPE, academic administrator; b. Abingdon, Va., Dec. 14, 1974; d. Linda Diane and Phil Cecil Crane (Stepfather), Leon Isham Alder and Kate Jacob-Alder (Stepmother); m. William Francis Flora, Dec. 19, 2004; children: Jonah Washington Fullen, Jack Samuel, Faith Wyndham Fullen, Carty Breese. BA in Bus. Adminstrn., U. Va.'s Coll., Wise, 1993—96; MA in Orgnl. Mgmt., Tusculum Coll., Greeneville, Tenn., 1998—99. Ednl. dir. Boys & Girls Club, Bristol, Va., 1996—97; prodn. control specialist Ball Corp., Bristol, Va., 1997—2001; adj. prof. Tusculum Coll., Greeneville, Tenn., 2001—03; acct. Sugar Hollow Med., Inc., Bristol, Va., 2002—04; site dir., S.W. Va. higher edn. ctr. Radford U., Va., 2003—04, dir., grad. recruiting & retention, 2004—. V.p. Fairmount Elem. Parent-Teacher Assn., Bristol, Tenn., 2003—04. Home: 308 7th Ave Radford VA 24141 Office: Radford Univ Box 6928 Radford VA 24142 Office Phone: 540-831-5023. E-mail: bhfullen@radford.edu.

FLORA, JAIRUS DALE, JR., statistician; b. Northfield, Minn., Mar. 27, 1944; s. Jairus Dale and Betty Ruth (Garvin) F.; m. Sharyl Ann Hughes, Aug. 18, 1967; 1 child, Edward Hughes BS magna cum laude, Midland Luth. Coll., 1965; postgrad., Tech. U. Karlsruhe, Fed. Republic Germany, 1965-66; MS, Fla. State U., 1968, PhD, 1971. Asst. prof. biostats Sch. Pub. Health U. Mich., Ann Arbor, 1971-73, asst. prof., asst. rsch. scientist Hwy. Safety Rsch. Inst., 1973-76, assoc. rsch. scientist Hwy. Safety Rsch. Inst., 1976-81, assoc. prof. biostats. Sch. Pub. Health, 1976-81, prof. biostats. Sch. Pub. Health, rsch. scientist Transp. Rsch. Inst., 1981-84; prin. statistician Midwest Rsch. Inst, Kansas City, Mo., 1984-90; sr. advisor for stats. Midwest Rsch. Inst., Kansas City, Mo., 1991-99, pres. coun. prin. scientists, 1986; clin. prof. biostats. Sch. Medicine U. Mo., Kansas City, 1984—; prin. statistician Ken Wilcox Assocs., Inc., Grain Valley, Mo., 1999, statis. cons., 1999—. Cons. statistician Nat. Burn Info. Exchange, 1971-76 Editl. collaborator Annals of Thoracic Surgery, Mathematical Bioscis., Biometrics, Accident Analysis and Prevention, 1979-90; contbr. articles to profl. jours.; patentee in field. Mem. adminstrn. bd. Valley View U. Meth. Ch., 1989-92; vol. leader Boy Scouts Am. Recipient CPS Enterprise award, 1985, Dir.'s award, 1987; German Acad. Exch. Svc. fellow, 1965-66; NASA trainee, 1966-69; NIH trainee, 1969-71; Nat Hwy. Traffic Safety Adminstrn. rsch. grantee, 1974-81. Mem. Am. Statis. Assn., Biometric Soc., Inst. Math. Stats., Masons (area dep. Grand Master 2003-05), Scottish Rite, Masonic Societas Rosiercruciana in Civitatibus Foederatus, Blue Key, Sigma Xi (pres. Kansas City chpt. 1990-91, v.p. 1994-96). Republican. Home: 9921 Foster St Shawnee Mission KS 66212-2452 Personal E-mail: jdflora@swbell.net.

FLORA, JOSEPH M(ARTIN), language educator; b. Toledo, Feb. 9, 1934; s. Raymond D. F. and Frances (Ricica) Neumann; m. Glenda Christine Lape, Jan. 30, 1959; children: Ronald James, Stephen Ray, Peter Joseph, David Benjamin. BA, U. Mich., 1956, MA, 1957, PhD, 1962. Instr. U. Mich., Ann Arbor, 1961-62, U. N.C., Chapel Hill, 1962-64, asst. prof., 1964-66, assoc. prof., 1966-77, prof. English, 1977—, Atlanta prof. so. culture, 2001—, acting chmn. dept. English, 1980-81, chmn., 1981-91, asst. dean grad. sch., 1967-72, assoc. dean grad. sch., 1977-78. Author: Vardis Fisher, 1965, William Ernest Henley, 1970, Frederick Manfred, 1974, Hemingway's Nick Adams, 1982 (Mayflower Cup award 1982), Ernest Hemingway: A Study of the Short Fiction, 1989, Vardis Fisher: Centennial Essays, 2000; editor: The English Short Story, 1880-1945, 1985; co-editor: Southern Writers, 1979, Fifty Southern Writers Before 1990, 1987, Fifty Southern Writers After 1900, 1987, Contemporary Fiction Writers of the South, 1993, Contemporary Poets, Dramatists, Essayists, Novelists of the South, 1994, The Companion to Southern Literature, 2001, The New Southern Writers: A Biographical Dictionary, 2006; editorial bds. Mem. MLA, South Atlantic MLA (v.p. 1997-98, pres. 1998-99), Western Lit. Assn. (bd. dirs. 1978-81, 83-86, v.p. 1990, pres. 1992), Soc. for Study So. Lit., Thomas Wolfe Soc. (v.p. 1993-95, pres. 1995-97), Phi Beta Kappa, Phi Eta Sigma. Home: 505 Caswell Rd Chapel Hill NC 27514-2705 Office: UNC Dept Of English Chapel Hill NC 27599-0001 Office Phone: 919-962-2503. Business E-Mail: jflora@email.unc.edu.

FLORA, KATHLEEN M., retired state representative; b. Dearborn, Mich., Nov. 10, 1952; m. James A. Flora; two children. BA, Mich. State U., 1975, MA, 1977. State rep. N.H. Ho. of Reps., 1996—2002. Mem. Bedford Rep. Com., 1996— Vol. adv. bd. VNA Hospice, 1996-97. Mem. ASTD. Office: NH State Legis State House Concord NH 03301 Office Phone: 941-907-6063. E-mail: kflora@tampabay.rr.com.

FLORA, KENT ALLEN, small business owner; b. Urbana, Ill., Jan. 7, 1944; s. Loyal Lee and Ercel Hannah (Puzey) F.; m. Sharon Jean Bray, Dec. 31, 1974; children: Donald William, William Christopher, Brent Allyn. BS, U. Ill., 1966. Prodn. mgr. Flora Farms, Fairmount, Ill., 1961—70, owner, operator, 1970—89; nat. sales mgr. Marketmatic Ltd., Champaign, Ill., 1990—91; owner AmeriSpec Home Inspection Svc., Champaign, 1994—96; tech. staffing specialist Snelling Search, Champaign, 1996; tech. staffing specialist dept. agri-bus. quality assurance Grossman & Assocs., Savoy, Ill., 1997—2002; mem. global surveillance team Vestas Americas, Champaign, 2003—05; asst. shipping superintendent Clifford-Jacobs Forging Co., Champaign, Ill., 2004—. Bd. dirs. Vermilion County Agrl. Extension Adv. Council, 1967-69; nat. pres. Am. Shropshire Registry Assn., 1972-73, nat. bd. dirs., 1965-73; pres. Ill. Shrophire Assn., 1970-72; bd. dirs. Ill. Purebred Sheep Breeder's Assn., 1965-70. Mem. Jamaica Unit Dist. #12 Bd. Edn., Sidell, Ill., 1981-90, v.p. bd. dirs., 1987-90, pres. citizen's adv. council, 1978-82; trustee Vance Twp., Fairmount, 1967-75, mem. Park Bd., 1977-81; mem. exec. com. Vermilion County Rep. Cen. Com., 1986-89; v.p. Vermilion County Merit

Commn. for Law Enforcement, 1986-88, pres. 1988-89; pres. Vermilion County Chmn. Unit Am. Cancer Soc., 1972-73; Vermilion County campaign coordinator Mike Houston for Ill. State Treas., 1986; Ill. 19th Congl. Dist. del. Jack Kemp for Pres., 1988. Served to sgt. USAR. Named Outstanding Young Farmer Jaycees, Danville, Ill., 1972, Hon. Chpt. Farmer Jamaica Future Farmers Assn., 1985; recipient Centennial Farm award State of Ill., 1970. Mem. U. Ill. Alumni Assn., Chi Phi, Masons, Shriners. Presbyterian. Avocations: family genealogy, collecting coca-cola memorabilia, travel. Home: 3206B Halifax Dr Champaign IL 61822-5216

FLOREEN, JOHN ERIC, music educator; b. Jersey City, Oct. 11, 1943; m. Susan Ellen Meadoo. MusB, Gustavus Adolphus Coll., 1965; M in sacred music cum laude, Sch. Sacred Music, 1967; D in conducting, U. Iowa, 1980; prof. music (hon.), Sichuan Conservatory of Music, Chengdu, China, 2002. Instr. music Becker Coll., Worcester, Mass., 1972—73, U. Delaware, Newark, 1973—76; tchg. asst. U. Iowa, 1976—79; prof. music Rutgers U., 1979—. Chmn., music dept. Rutgers U., 1989—92, coord., music program, 2001—. Composer (and arranger): Arise, oh ye Servants of God, Clap Your Hands, Angels We Have Heard on High, O Come, O Come, Emmanuel. Trustee Rainbow Lakes Commn. Assn., Denville, NJ, 1992—97. Recipient Fulbright award, Fulbright Assn., 1985, 1986, 1992; fellowships, Nat. Endowment for the Humanities, 1983, 1984, 1986. Mem.: Am. Choral Directors Assn. Avocation: cooking. Office: Rutgers U Bradley Hall 254 Newark NJ 07102

FLORENCE, ERNEST ESTELL, JR., special education educator; b. Grayson, Ky., Feb. 19, 1954; s. Ernest Estell Florence and Margaret Jean (Tittsworth) Ikemire; m. Ginger Lynn Miller, Apr. 19, 1980; children: Ashley Michelle, Charles Todd. BS in Edn., Ea. Ill. U., 1975; MS in Edn., No. Ill. U., 1980. Behavior disorder tchr. Project Advocate Northwestern Ill. Assn., Geneva, 1976-80; behavior disorder tchr. O'Donnell Elem. Sch. Dist. 131, Aurora, Ill., 1980-85, behavior disorder/learning disability tchr. Bardwell Elem., 1985-93; behavior disorder tchr. Prairie Elem. sch. Dist. 203, Naperville, Ill., 1993—, mem. Spl. Edn. Inst. Day com., 1998-2000. Vol. Spl. Olympics, Aurora, 1990-93; com. mem. Just Say No Com., City of Aurora, 1991-95; com. mem. Aurora 2000 Com., 1993; chmn. scholarship com. Boulder Hill Sch. PTA, Montgomery, Ill., 1992—, reflections chmn., 1995-98; vol. bell ringer Salvation Army, 1995—; vol. Prairie Sch. Market Day, 1995—; mem. Prairie Sch. Bldg. Leadership Team, 1995-98. Named Tchr. of Yr., Bardwell Sch. PTA, 1989, Educator of Yr., Ill. Learning Disabilities Assn., 1989; recipient Chpt. Recognition award Ill. Learning Disabilities Assn., 1992. Mem. NEA (local sch. rep. 1998-2000), Coun. for Exceptional Children, Learning Disabilities Assn. Am. (chmn. Proud Projects 1997-98, state pres. rep. to Nat. Bd. 1998-99, affiliate support com. 1998-2000), Learning Disabiities Assn. Ill. (regional dir. 1991-94, pres.-elect 1994-96, pres. 1996-98, chmn. scholarship 1992-96, chmn. prin. scholarship programs 1992—, chair nominations com. 1999-2000), Ill. Coun. for Children with Behavior Disorders, Kane Kendall Learning Disabilities Assn. (v.p. 1987—, Kane Kendall Recognition award 1994), Ill. br. Orton Dyslexia Soc., Aurora Moose. Democrat. Avocations: travel, reading, music. Home: 113 Circle Dr W Montgomery IL 60538-2725 Office: Naperville Comty Unit Sch Dist 203 203 W Hillside Rd Naperville IL 60540-6500

FLORENCE-HOUK, AMANDA S., psychologist; b. Elizabethtown, Ky., Jan. 30, 1979; d. Sam E., Jr. and Nancy L. Florence; m. Brandon L. Houk, Sept. 2, 1997. BS in Psychology, Morehead State, 2001; MS in Family Studies, U. Ky., 2004, postgrad. Tchg. asst. U. Ky., Lexington, rsch. asst. Editor: Young Women in Sciences; author: ANDY: Another New Dad-less Year, 2004. Co-coord. Lexington Wellspsonor Found., 2002—. Jane Venable Coroan scholar, U. Ky., 2002. Mem.: Nat. Family Caregivers Assn., Phi Upsilon (pres. Iota chpt. 2004—). Avocation: writing.

FLORES, AMY CLAIRE CATRON, music educator, musician; d. Clell Dexter and Shirley Ann Catron; m. Ricardo Flores, July 11, 1998. MusB in cello performance, Eastman Sch. Music, Rochester, NY, 1989—93; MusM in cello performance, U. Akron, Ohio, 1993—96. Cello prof. Millikin U., Decatur, Ill., 2000—; prin. cello Ill. Symphony Orch., Springfield, 2000—. Cellist Naples Philharm. Orch., Fla., 1996—2004; acting prin. Sinfonic da Cameno, 2000—. Mem.: Am. String Tchrs. Assn. Office: Millikin U 1184 W Main St Decatur IL 62522-2084 Business E-Mail: aflores@mail.millikin.edu.

FLORES, GEORGE ANTHONY, physicist, researcher; s. George Armendariz and Stella Flores. BS in physics, Calif. State U., Long Beach, 1996; AA in French, Long Beach City Coll., 2002. Physics rschr. Calif. State U., Dept. Physics, Long Beach, 1993—2003. Cons. U. Toledo, Mech. Indsl. and Materials Engring. Dept., 2000. Contbr. articles to jour. Personal E-mail: floresg1@netzero.net.

FLORES, GEORGE H., obstetrician, gynecologist; b. Garapan, Saipan, Northern Marianas, Jan. 7, 1937; s. Francisco Aguon and Maria (Pangelinan) F.; m. Ursa Damian Flores, Aug. 27, 1960; children: George Jr., Nina June, Marybeth, Linda, Debra Jean. BS, St. Louis U., 1960, MD, 1964. Diplomate Am. Bd. Obstetrics and Gynecology. Commd. U.S. Army, 1965, advanced through grades to col., 1979, ret., 1985, chief ob-gyn. 5th Gen. Hosp. Stuttgart, S, Germany, 1971-73, Ft. Knox, Ky., 1973-75, chief dept. surgery, 1975-79, chief ob-gyn. Gorgas Army Hosp. Panama Canal Zone, 1982-84; med. dir. Jefferson County Health Dept., Louisville, 1985-90; chief ob-gyn. dept. Hardin Meml. Hosp., Elizabethtown, Ky., 1994-95; pvt. practice ob-gyn. Elizabethtown, 1990—97; ret. Chmn. parish coun. St. Christopher Ch., Radcliff, Ky., 1977-81. Rotary Club of Guam scholar, 1957-60, Govt. of Guam Med. Sch. scholar, 1960-64. Fellow ACOG; mem. AMA, K.C. Republican. Roman Catholic. Avocation: volunteer work with church. Home: 884 Martin Ln Radcliff KY 40160 E-mail: geofloresmd@aol.com.

FLORES, JANICE A. H., medical technician; b. N.Y.C., Nov. 14, 1940; d. Dominick and Anna Gasparo; m. Beryl D. Hamilton (div.); children: Beryl D. Hamilton, Christopher Hamilton, Janice A. Hamilton Harnett, Lawrence Hamilton; m. Rony A. Flores, Dec. 4, 1974; 1 child, Amalita M. AS in Med. Tech., Nassau CC, N.Y., 1972. Med. technician Mid Island Hosp., Bethpage, NY, 1973—. Religious edn. tchr. Our Lady of Lourdes, Massapequa Park, NY, 1978—, St. Rose of Lima, Massapequa Park, 1988—90. Recipient 25 Yr. watch, New Island Hosp., 1993. Office: New Island Hosp 4295 Hempstead Turnpike Bethpage NY 11714

FLORES, JUAN P., school system administrator; BA in Biology, Colgate U., 1980; EdM, cert. in Ednl. Leadership, U. Portland, 1998; student in Leadership Studies. Tchr. Bedford Jr. HS, Westport, Conn., 1980—81, The Field Sch., Washington, 1981—83; asst. dir. alumni programs Franklin and Marshall Coll., Lancaster, Pa., 1983—84; asst. dean admissions Colgate U., Hamilton, NY, 1984—86; tchr. St. Stephen's Episc. Sch., Austin, Tex., 1986—89; assoc. dir. admissions Choate Rosemary Hall, Wallingford, Conn., 1989—94; tchr. Guam Dept. Edn., 1994—98; program specialist Applied R&D Program Pacific Resources Edn. and Learning, Honolulu, 1998—2000; dean students Acad. Pacific, Honolulu, 2000—01; lectr. U. Portland, 2001—03; dir. edn. Dept. Edn., Hagatna, 2003—. Office: Guam Dept Education PO Box DE Hagatna Guinea

FLORES, LYDIA, retired Spanish educator; b. L.A., Sept. 1, 1929; d. Francisco Gomez and Anita Guadalupe (Perez) F.; children: William Francis, Naomi Lynn, Stephanie, Carl Christopher, Kristin, Gretchen. BA, Immaculate Heart Coll., 1951; MEd, Long Beach State U., 1970. Cert. secondary, gen. elem., bilingual edn. tchr., Calif.; cert. lang. devel. specialist. Primary tchr. St. Eugene's Elem. Sch., L.A., 1952-53, Torrance (Calif.) Unified Sch. Dist., 1953-60, mid. grade tchr., 1965-68; bilingual resource tchr. Madera (Calif.) Unified Sch. Dist., 1979-89; Spanish tchr., limited English proficient resource tchr. Fresno (Calif.) Unified Sch. Dist., 1992-97; ret. Mem. bilingual adv. com., Madera, 1989-89, Fresno, 1992-97. Unitarian Universalist. Avocations: bicycle riding, gardening, organizing, massage, travel. Home: 8316 N Raisina Ave Fresno CA 93720-2083

FLORES, ROBIN ANN, social worker, social services administrator; b. Allentown, Pa., Oct. 6, 1949; d. Norman Henry and Ann May (Huff) F. BS in Edn., Kutztown U., 1971; MS in Adminstrn., U. Scranton, 1983. Exec. dir. Lehigh County Aging and Adult Svcs., Allentown, 1996—2004; pvt. cons. in geriatric and cmty. programs, 2004—. Lectr. cmty. svcs., family care giving and on aging process, utilization cmty. resources, Lehigh County; co-dir. The Ethics Inst., Inc., Allentown Mem. adv. bd. Cmty. Action Com. Lehigh Valley, 1979-82, Elder Well, 1987-90; Pa. del. White House Conf. on Aging, Hershey, Pa., 1981; bd. dirs. Vis. Nurse Assn. Lehigh County, 1982-98, Women Inc., 1983-87; mem. adv. bd. Homecare, Inc., 1982-91, Geriatric Edn. Modules, Allentown Osteo. Hosp., 1979; mem. profl. adv. com. Lehigh Valley Hospice, 1984-98; mem. utilization and rev. bd. Vis. Nurse Assn., 1979-98; consumer rep. Pa. Power and Light Co.; co-chmn. Human Svcs. Tng. Coop., 1975-81; bd. assocs. Lehigh Valley Hosp.; trustees Ethics Inst., Inc. Mem.: NAFE, United Way Alliance Aging, Nat. Assn. Area Agys. on Aging, Am. Soc. Aging, Allentown Art Mus., Quota Internat. Home: 2206 Overlook Ln Fogelsville PA 18051-1812 Office Phone: 610-248-5064, 610-794-5155. E-mail: robina6@msn.com.

FLORESCUE, LEONARD GEORGE, lawyer; b. Rochester, N.Y., Nov. 29, 1946; s. Harold M. and Sarah (Miller) F.; m. Susan Thypin, Aug. 13, 1972 (dec. 1975); m. Marilyn Cronenberg, Apr. 10, 1976; 1 child, Heather. BA, U. Rochester, 1967; JD, NYU, 1972. Bar: N.Y. 1973, U.S. Dist. Ct. (so. and ea. dists.) N.Y. 1974, U.S. Ct. Appeals (2d cir.) 1974. Assoc. Fried Frank Harris Shriver & Jacobson, N.Y.C., 1972-83; ptnr. Ruskin Schlissel Moscou Evans & Faltischek, Mineola, N.Y., 1983-91; counsel Tenzer Greenblatt LLP (now Blankhome LLP), N.Y.C., 1991-96; ptnr. Blank Rome LLP, N.Y.C., 1997—. Adj. prof. Fordham Law Sch., Benjamin Cardozo Sch. Law, N.Y.C.; lectr. in field. Co-author: Tax Aspects of Divorce and Separation, 1989; contbr. columns to N.Y. Law Jour., 1983—. Office: Blank Rome LLP 405 Lexington Ave New York NY 10174-0208 Office Phone: 212-885-5396. Business E-Mail: lflorescue@blankrome.com.

FLORETH, FREDERICK DENNIS, lawyer; b. Litchfield, Ill., Mar. 24, 1956; s. Nelson Keiser and Victoria Jane (Swartz) F.; m. Lauren Jean Pashayan, Sept. 3, 1983. BS, So. Ill. U., Edwardsville, 1979; JD, St. Louis U., 1982. Bar: Ill. 1982, U.S. Dist. Ct. (cen. dist.) Ill. 1983; cert. master guardian. Sole practice, Litchfield, 1983—. Pub. adminstr., guardian Montgomery County, Ill., 1984—; rep. precinct committeeman Montgomery County, 1984-90; mem. Litchfield Unit 12 Community Schs. Bd. Edn., 1985-93, pres., 1989-93; rep. candidate for state legislature, 1992. Mem. Ill. Bar Assn., Montgomery County Bar Assn. (pres. 1985-86), Ill. Assn. Sch. Bds. (bd. dirs. 1989-93), Guardianship and Protective Svcs. Assn. Ill. (bd. dirs. 1990-93, corr. sec. 1991-92), Ill. Guardianship Assn. (pres. 2000). Home: 520 S 2d St Apt 1200 Springfield IL 62701 Office: PO Box 246 Litchfield IL 62056-0246 Office Phone: 217-324-5986. Business E-Mail: freddfloreth@consolidated.net.

FLOREY, KLAUS GEORG, chemist, pharmaceutical consultant; b. Dresden, Germany, July 4, 1919; came to U.S., 1947, naturalized, 1952; s. Friedrich Georg and Margarethe Käthe (Pick) F.; m. Anne Major, Nov. 22, 1956; children: Peter, Andrea. Ed., U. Munich, U. Heidelberg, Germany; PhD, U. Pa., 1954. Research asst. Bayer, Leverkusen, Germany, 1944-45; research asso. Merck & Co., Rahway, N.J., 1949-50; research chemist Squibb Inst. Med. Research, New Brunswick, N.J., 1954-59, dir. analytical research and devel., 1959-84, cons., 1984-90. Mem. com. revisions U.S. Pharmacopeia, 1970-95, hon. mem., 2000; mem. WHO Expert Adv. Panel Internat. Pharmacopeia, 1976-93; docent The Princeton U. Art Mus., 1991--. Editor: Analytical Profiles of Drug Substances, 22 vols., 1971—; contbr. articles to profl. jours.; patentee in field. Recipient Justin L. Powers award, 1987. Fellow AAAS, Acad. Pharm. Scis. (chmn. pharm. analysis and control sect. 1967-68, pres. 1980-81); mem. Am. Chem. Soc., Soc. Nuclear Medicine, Am. Assn. Pharm. Scientists (Disting. Svc. award 1990), Coun. Sci. Soc. Pres. (chmn. 1983) Home: 151 Loomis Ct Princeton NJ 08540-3438

FLORI, ANNA MARIE DIBLASI, nurse anesthetist, educational administrator; b. Amsterdam, N.Y., Oct. 29, 1940; d. Tony and Maria (Macario) DiBlasi; children: Tammy, Tina, Toni; m. Gilberto Flori, May 24, 1986. Grad., Albany Med. Ctr. Sch. Nursing, 1962, Fairfax Hosp. Sch. Nurse Anesthetists, Va., 1972; BS in Anesthesia, George Washington U., 1979; M. in Bus. and Pub. Adminstrn., Southeastern U., Washington, 1982; PhD, Columbia Pacific U., 1983. Cert. registered nurse anesthetist. Staff nurse West Seattle Gen. Hosp., 1962-64; office nurse Filmore Buckner, M.D., Seattle, 1964-66; staff nurse anesthetist Fairfax Hosp., 1972-73; staff nurse anesthetist Potomac Hosp., Woodbridge, Va., 1973, chief nurse anesthetist, 1973—; dir. Potomac Hosp. Sch. for Nurse Anesthetists and Sch. for Nurse Anesthesia; faculty mem. Columbia Pacific U., 1973-90; chief nurse anesthetist No. Va. Anesthesia Assn., 1988—; guest lectr. No. Va. Community Coll., Inservice Potomac Hosp., George Washington U.; coord. Free Clinic Prince William County, Woodbridge, Va. Contbr. books on anesthesia. Mem. Am. Assn. Nurse Anesthetists, Va. Nurse Anesthesia Assn., Nat. Italian Am. Found. Home: 12954 Pintail Rd Woodbridge VA 22192-3831 Office Phone: 703-490-5496.

FLORIAN-LACY, DOROTHY, social worker, educator; b. Dearborn, Mich., Oct. 27, 1958; d. Raymond Joseph and Dorothy Mae Florian; m. Bill George Lacy, July 25, 1981; children: Jason M., Miles, Anderson. BS in Psychology and Edn., Eastern Mich. U., 1978, MA in Guidance and Counseling, 1979; EdD in Counselor Edn., Tex. Southeastern U., 1998. Lic. profl. counselor, Tex. Realtor Century 21, Ann Arbor, Mich., 1978—79; tchr. Adult Exception Ctr., Compton, Calif., 1979—81; owner, dir. Village Learning & Play Ctr., Houston, 1982—94; dept. chair spl. edn. Milby Sr. H.S., Houston, 1994—2000; therapist Houston Achievement Place, 1998—. Author: Fundamentals of Mathematics I, Fundamentals of Mathematics II, Consumer Math; co-author: Reference Manual for Special Education Department Chairpersons. Vol. Child Abuse Prevention, Houston, 1989-91, vol. coach YMCA, Houston, 1987-90. Recipient Adaptor grant Impact II, 1997, Study Group grant Impact II, 1998. Mem. ACA, Children's Mus Avocation: golf coach. Office: Houston Achievement Place 236 W 17th St Houston TX 77008-4002 Office Phone: 713-868-2909 272. Personal E-mail: dflorian@houstonisd.org.

FLORIDA, RICHARD LOUIS, finance educator; b. Newark, Nov. 26, 1957; s. Louis and Eleanor F. BA, Rutgers Coll., 1979; MPh, Columbia U., 1984, PhD, 1986. Prof. Ohio State U., Columbus, 1984-87; H. John Heinz III prof. regional econ. devel. Carnegie Mellon U. Sch. Pub. Policy and Mgmt., Pitts., 1987, dir. Software Industry Ctr., 2001—; now Hirst prof., sch. pub. policy George Mason Univ.; and non-resident sr. fellow Brookings Inst. Vis. prof. MIT, John F. Kennedy Sch. Govt. Harvard U.; adv. White House Office of Sci. and Tech.Policy, U.S. Dept. Commerce, U.S. Congress, state and local govts., Govt. of Can., EU, Govt. of Japan, multinat. corps. Author: Beyond Mass Production, 1993, The Breakthrough Illusion, 1990, Rise of the Creative Class, 2002 (Washington Monthly Polit. Book award), Flight of the Creative Class, 2005, (editor)Industrializing Knowledge: University-Industry Linkages in Japan and the United States, 1999; contbr. 75 articles to profl. jours., newspapers including The N.Y. Times, The Wall St. Jour., Washington Post; commentator on PBS documentaries about U.S. economy, global competitiveness, future of jobs. Active Cooun. Gt. Lakes Govs.; bd. dirs. TeamPa., Pa.'s 21st Century Environ. Commn. Office: Richard Florida Creative Group 115 Valley Dr Pittsburgh PA 15215 also: Public Policy Dept George Mason Univ 4400 University Drive Arlington VA 22201 Office Phone: 412-782-5211, 703-993-2280. Business E-Mail: florida@gmu.edu.*

FLORIN, SHARON, artist; b. Bklyn., Feb. 16, 1952; d. Lawrence and Blanche Ina (Title) F. BA cum laude, Adelphi U., 1973; postgrad., Art Students League, 1969-77. Freelance artist, 1973—. Solo exhbns. at Noho Gallery, N.Y.C., 1982, 83, 85, 86, 89, 91, 2003, 05, The Wall Gallery, John Jay Coll., N.Y.C., 2002, The Interchurch Ctr. Gallery, N.Y.C., 2002; group exhbns. include Queens Mus., Flushing, N.Y., 1984, Hoyt Inst. Fine Arts, New Castle, Pa., 1990, Butler Inst. Am. Art, Youngstown, Ohio, 1991, 2003, 05, Hudson River Mus., Yonkers, N.Y., 1982, 83, 91, Chautauqua (N.Y.) Instn., 1992, Alexandria (La.) Mus. Art, 1992, Michael Ingbar Gallery, N.Y.C., 1993-98 N.Y. Transit Mus., N.Y.C., 97, N.J. Ctr. for Visual Arts, Summit, 98, Hudson Waterfront Mus., N.Y.C., 98, Mus. of City of N.Y., 99, Fraser Gallery, Bethesda, Md., 2001, Hopper House Art Ctr., Nyack, N.Y., 2002. Recipient Hon. Mention award Butler Inst. Am. Art, 1991. Mem. Nat. Assn. Women Artists (Awards, 90, 92, 95, 96, 98, 2001, 04, Medal of Honor, 2000), Women in the Arts, Inc., Artists Equity, Orgn. Ind. Artists, Catharine Lorillard Art Club (Award 98, 2000, 04), Pen and Brush Club (Award 2002) Home: 339 E 19th St New York NY 10003-2825 Studio: 12-23 Jackson Ave Long Island City NY 11101-5501 Office Phone: 718-786-9896. E-mail: sjfstudio@aol.com.

FLORINSKI, VLADIMIR, physicist; b. St. Petersburg, Russia, July 21, 1971; s. Anatoly Florinski and Tamara Florinskaia; m. Lioubov Florinskaia, Jan. 10, 1997; 1 child, Andre. MS, St. Petersburg State Tech. U., 1988—94; PhD, U. of Ariz., 1995—2001. Rsch./tchg. asst. U. of Ariz., 1995—2001; postdoctoral rschr. U. of Calif., 2001—03, asst. rsch. physicist, 2003—. Editor: (book) Physics of the Outer Heliosphere; contbr. articles to profl. jours. Recipient Gerard P. Kuiper Meml. award, U. of Ariz., 2001, Young fellow of the IGPP, U. of Calif., 2004. Mem.: Am. Geophys. Union. Office: IGPP Univ of Calif 900 University Ave Riverside CA 92521 Office Phone: 951-827-3943. Office Fax: 951-827-4509. E-mail: vflorins@ucr.edu.

FLORIO, STEVEN T., magazine executive; b. NYC, Apr. 19, 1949; s. F. Steve and Sophia (Masciale) F.; m. Marianne McNeill, June 1, 1974; children: Steven John, Kelly Anne. AA, NYU, 1970, BS, 1972. Rschr. Esquire mag., NYC, 1972-73, New Eng. mgr., 1974-76, advt. dir., 1976-79, v.p., 1979-80; pub. Gentlemen's Quar., NYC, 1980-85; pres., CEO New Yorker mag., NYC, 1985-94, pub., 1985-88; pres. Condé Nast Publs., Inc., NYC, 1994—2004, CEO, 1996—2004; vice chmn., Advanced Mag. Group Conde Nast Publs., Inc., NYC, 2004—. Guest spkr. lecture series Harvard U., Rice U., NYU, Yale U. Chmn. Namesake Com. USS N.Y.C. USN. Mem.: Mag. Pubs. Assn. (chmn. conf. 1989), Men's Fashion Assn. Office: Conde Nast Publ 4 Times Sq New York NY 10036-6561

FLORIO, THOMAS A., magazine publisher; Formerly advt. dir. Conde Nast Traveler, N.Y.C., pub., 1990-94; pres. The New Yorker, N.Y.C., 1994-99; v.p., pub. Gentleman's Quarterly, N.Y.C., 1999—2002; v.p. Vogue, 2002—, pub., 2002—. Office: Vogue 4 Times Sq New York NY 10036-6522*

FLORMAN, SANDER SCOTT, transplant surgeon; b. N.Y.C., Sept. 20, 1967; s. Larry David and Phyllis Ehrlich Florman; m. Toby Jill Florman, June 28, 1998; children: Zachary, Frankie. BA, Brandeis U., 1989; MD, U. Louisville, 1994. Cert. bd. cert. gen. surgeon. Gen. surgery resident Tulane U., New Orleans, 1994—2000, assoc. prof., 2005; transplant fellow Mt. Sinai, N.Y.C., 2000—02, asst. prof., 2002—05. Adminstrv. chief resident Tulane Surgery, New Orleans, 1999—2000; rsch. resident Mt. Sinai Liver Transplant, N.Y.C., 1996—97. Author: (book chpt.) Mastery of Surgery, 2000, American College of Surgeons Surgery, 2002, Textbook of Endocrine Surgery, 2004, Liver Transplantation, 2005; contbr. articles to profl. jours. Mem.: ACS, Am. Soc. Transplant Surgeons (40 under 40 2004, Vanguard prize 2005, Charity Hosp. Resident of the Year 1998), Soc. for Surgery of the Alimentary Tract, Am. Soc. Transplantation. Office: Tulane Ctr for Abdominal Transplantation TW-35 1415 Tulane Ave New Orleans LA 70112 Office Phone: 504-988-7867. E-mail: sflorman@tulane.edu.

FLORSHEIM, RICHARD STEVEN, lawyer; b. Milw., Apr. 2, 1949; s. Ernst Frederick and Ingeborg Miriam Florsheim; m. Neena B. Florsheim; children: Ali Brynn, David Ira, Rebecca Lynn. BS, MIT, 1971; JD magna cum laude, Marquette U., 1974. Bar: Wis. 1974, Fla. 1983. Assoc. Foley & Lardner, Milw., 1974-81, ptnr., 1981—, leader intellectual property litigation group, 1987-97, chair intellectual property dept., 1997—. Co-author: Biotechnology Patent Practice, 1994, Inside the Minds: Leading Intellectual Property Lawyers, 2001. Pres. North Shore Libr., Milw., 1985-87, Jewish Found. Econ. Opportunity, Milw., 1992-96; bd. dirs. Milw. Jewish Fedn., 1987-93, 96-2002, NCCJ Wis. region, 1990—; bd. dirs. Ohr Hatorah Jewish Heritage Ctr., 2002—, pres., 2002—. Mem. ABA, Am. Intellectual Property Law Assn. (subcom. chmn. 1992-97), Fed. Cir. Bar Assn., Wis. Bar Assn., Milw. Bar Assn., Marquette Law Alumni Assn. (pres. 1985-86). Office: Foley & Lardner LLP 777 E Wisconsin Ave Ste 3800 Milwaukee WI 53202-5367 Office Phone: 414-297-5515. Business E-Mail: rflorsheim@foley.com.

FLORY, CURT ALAN, research physicist; BS in Physics with distinction, Stanford U., 1975; MS in Physics, U. Wash., 1977; PhD in Physics, U. Calif., Berkeley, 1981. R&D fellow, rsch. physicist Agilent Technologies, Palo Alto, Calif., 1984—; postdoc. SLAC, 1981-84. Recipient Indsl. Physics prize Am. Inst. Physics, 1993-94. Fellow Am. Phys. Soc. Office: Agilent Technolgies 3500 Deer Creek Rd # 26M Palo Alto CA 94304-1317 E-mail: curt_flory@agilent.com.

FLORY, PETER CYRIL WYCHE, federal agency administrator; BA, McGill U.; JD, Georgetown U. Spl. asst. to under sec. for policy US Dept. Def., Washington, 1989—92; assoc. coord. counter-terrorism US Dept. State, Washington, 1992—93; atty. Hughes, Hubbard & Reed LLP, Washington, 1993—97; chief investigative counsel, select. com. on intelligence U.S. Senate, Washington, spl. counsel select com. on intelligence; prin. dep. asst. sec. internat. security affairs US Dept. Def., Washington, 2002—05, asst. sec. def. internat. security policy, 2005—. Office: US Dept Def 2000 Defense Pentagon Rm 4E817 Washington DC 20301-2000 Office Phone: 703-697-7728.*

FLOSS, HEINZ G., chemistry educator, scientist; b. Berlin, Aug. 28, 1934; s. Friedrich and Annemarie F.; m. Inge Sauberlich, July 17, 1956; children: Christine, Peter, Helmut, Hanna. BS in Chemistry, Technische Universitat, Berlin, 1956, MS in Organic Chemistry, 1959; PhD in Organic Chemistry, Technische Universitat, Munich, W. Ger., 1961, Habilitation in Biochemistry, 1966; DSc (hon.), Purdue U., 1986; Dr. (h.c.), U. Bonn, 2001. Hilfsassistent Technische Universitat, Berlin, 1958-59; hilfsassistent Technische Hochschule, Munich, 1959-61, wissenschaftlicher asst. and dozent, 1961-66; on leave of absence at dept. biochemistry and biophysics U. Calif.-Davis, 1964-65; assoc. prof. Purdue U., 1966-69, prof., 1969-77, Lilly Disting. prof., 1977-82, head dept. medicinal chemistry, 1968-69, 74-79; prof. chemistry Ohio State U., Columbus, 1982-87, chmn. dept. chemistry, 1982-86; prof. chemistry U. Wash., Seattle, 1987—, adj. prof. medicinal chemistry and microbiology, 1988—, adj. prof. biochemistry, 1988-99, prof. emeritus, 2001—. Vis. scientist ETH Zurich, 1970; vis. prof. Tech. U. Munich, 1980, 86, 95; mem. bio-organic and natural products study sect. NIH, 1989-93; mem. internat. adv. Natural Product Reports, 1997—. Mem. editorial bd. Lloydia-Jour. Natural Products, 1971—2002, BBP-Biochemie und Physiologie der Pflanzen, 1971-84, Applied and Environ. Microbiology, 1974-84, Planta Medica, 1978-83, Jour. Medicinal Chemistry, 1979-83, Applied Microbiology and Biotech., 1984-88, Jour. Basic Microbiology, 1989—. Recipient Lederle faculty award, 1967, Mead Johnson Undergrad. Rsch. award, 1968, rsch. career and devel. award USPHS, 1969-74, Volwiler award, 1979, Humboldt sr. scientist, 1980, Newby-McCoy award 1981, award in microbial chemistry Kitasato Inst. and Kitasato U., 1988, White Magnolia Commemoration award and medal, Shanghai, 1995. Fellow Acad. Pharm. Scis. (Research Achievement award in natural products 1976), AAAS; mem. Am. Chem. Soc., Am. Soc. Biol. Chemistry and Molecular Biology, Am. Soc. Microbiology, Am. Soc. Pharmacognosy (Rsch. award 1988), Phytochem. Soc. N.Am., Sigma Xi (Faculty Research award 1976) Office: Univ Wash Box 351700 Seattle WA 98195-1700

FLOTEN, BARBARA JEAN, educational dean; b. Mt. Clemens, Mich., Aug. 21, 1946; d. Joseph Michael and Dorothy Winston (Bowles) Sarto; m. Frederick Floten, Sept. 10, 1971. BA, Portlant State U., 1968; MA, Portland State U., 1970. Social worker Multnomah County, Portland, 1970—71; instr. Mt. Hood CC, Gresham, Oreg., 1971—74; dir. student programs Edmonds

CC, Lynnwood, Wash., 1974—77, dean students, 1977—. Chair or mem. various profl. groups, 1971—; bd. dirs. Planned Parenthood, Snobomish County, 1978; mem. Joint Action Coun. Edn., Seattle, 1979. Named Honorary Triton, ASEdCC, 1975—78; recipient numerous profl. recognitions. Mem.: LWV, Am. Assn. of Univ. Women, Nat. Assn. Student Pers. Adminstrn., Wash. CC Adminstrs., Seattle Wash. Athletic Club. Office: Edmonds Community Coll 20000 68th Ave W Lynnwood WA 98036-5912 also: Bellevue Community Coll 3000 Landerholm Cir SE Bellevue WA 98007-6406

FLOTTE, TERENCE ROBIN, pediatrician, pulmonologist; b. New Orleans, Dec. 4, 1961; s. Arthur Victor and Marie Therese (Indest) F.; children: David Edward, Lindsay Hanna, Jesse Cole. BS summa cum laude, U. New Orleans, 1982; MD, La. State U., 1986. Diplomate Am. Bd. Pediatrics, subspecialty in pulmonary pediatrics. Pediatric resident Johns Hopkins Hosp., Balt., 1986-89; pediatric pulmonary fellow Johns Hopkins U., Balt., 1989-92, instr., 1992-93, asst. prof., 1993-96; postdoctoral rsch. fellow NIH, Bethesda, Md., 1989-92; asst. prof. pediats. and molecular genetics 1998U. Fla., Gainesville, 1996—98; co-dir. Powell Gene Therapy Ctr. U. Fla., Gainesville, 1996—2000; dir. Powell Gene Therapy Ctr., 2000—02, UF Genetics Inst., 2000—02; prof., chmn. pediat., 2002—. Contbr. articles to profl. jours. Recipient Leroy Mathews Physician Scientist award Cystic Fibrosis Found., 1991, Chancellor's award La. State U. Sch. Medicine, 1986, E. Mead Johnson award, 2005; NIH CF Gene Therapy Ctr. Rsch. grantee, 1993; Nemours Eminent scholar. Mem. AMA, Am. Thoracic Soc., Alpha Omega Alpha. Roman Catholic. Achievements include research on first NIH recombinant DNA advisory committee - approved gene therapy protocol using an adeno-associated virus vector in humans; inventor 2 patents of AAV-Vectors for cystic fibrosis gene therapy and production process for these vectors. Office: Univ Fla Pediat Gene Therapy Ctr PO Box 100296 Gainesville FL 32610-0296

FLOURNOY, JOHN CHARLES, SR., retired civilian military employee, retired military officer; b. Florala, Ala., Nov. 30, 1936; s. Q. P. and Alice Ruby (Cope) Flournoy; m. Charlene Reneé Lett, June 7, 1957; children: Jamie Lynn, John Charles Jr., Jeffrey Allan. BS, Auburn U., 1959. Commd. 2d lt. USAF, 1959, advanced through grades to col., dep. chief of staff for ops. 23rd Air Force Scott AFB, 1983—88; site mgr., tng. mgr. Raytheon Sys., Kirkland AFB, N.Mex., 1988-98, tng. analyst, Air Force Rsch. Lab. Albuquerque, 1998—99; training cons. Air Force Rsch Lab, Mesa, 2003—. Decorated Legion Merit; recipient German Gratitude medal, Fed. Republic of Germany, 1962. Mem.: Pedro Rescue Helicopter Assn. (member at large), Air Rescue Assn. (pres.), Air Commando Assn., USAF Helicopter Pilot Assn., Tanker/Airlift Assn., Jolly Green Assn. (1st v.p. 1983—84, pres. 1985—86), Order of Daedalians (former flight capt.). Republican. Avocations: fishing, walking, coin collecting/numismatics, NASCAR. Home: 6817 Medinah Ln NE Albuquerque NM 87111-6419 Personal E-mail: jflournoy2@comcast.net.

FLOURNOY, JOHN CRAIG, journalism educator; b. Shreveport, La., June 26, 1951; s. Camp Rogers and Carolyn (Clay) F.; m. Nina Planchard, May 21, 1977; children: Kathryn Helene, Louise, Emma. BA in History with honors, U. New Orleans, 1975; MA in History, So. Meth. U., 1986; PhD in Mass. Comm., La. State U., 2003. Freelance writer, landscaper The Courier, New Orleans, 1975; polit. reporter Houma (La.) Daily Courier, 1976; polit. reporter, columnist Shreveport Jour., 1977-78; investigative reporter Dallas Morning News, Dallas, 1978-2000; journalism prof. So. Meth. U., 2002—. Recipient First pl. Investigative Reporting Dallas Press Club, 1981-83, 85, 93, Pub. Svc. award Assn. Press Managing Editors Assn., NYC, 1986, Silver Gavel award ABA, NYC, 1986, Pulitzer prize, NYC, 1986, Outstanding Investigative Reporting award Investigative Reporters and Editors, 1989, Worth Bingham prize for investigative reporting, 1993, Edward Meeman award for environ. reporting, 1993. Avocation: gardening. Office Phone: 214-768-3395. Business E-Mail: cflourno@smu.edu.

FLOURNOY, LINDA WESLEY, minister, educator; b. Minden, La., Aug. 29, 1957; d. John Henry and Lillie Anderson Wesley; m. Connell Flournoy, Feb. 14, 1975; children: Adrian Connell, Amber Nicole. AA, La. Tech. U., 1994, BA, 1996, postgrad., 1998. Ordained elder 1995. Prescription tutor Eckerd Drug Stores, Minden, 1982—84; accounts receivable clk. City of Minden, 1984—90; office mgr. Custom Windows and Glass, Shreveport, La., 1991; pastor, tchr. Christian Meth. Ch., Shreveport, 1991—, Hattiesburg, Miss., 1998—2002. Established youth and young adult outreach ministry, Bassfield, Miss., 1999. Recipient Devoted and Invaluable Svc. award, Webster Parish Penal Farm Ministry, Minden, 1992, 1994—95, Invaluable Svc. award, Town & Country Nursing Home Ministry, Minden, 1992. Democrat. Avocations: interior decorating, homebuilding, reading. Home: 137 Flournoy Dr Minden LA 71055 Office: Christian Meth Ch Holcomb Dr Shreveport LA 71103

FLOURNOY, NANCY, statistician, educator; b. Long Beach, Calif., May 4, 1947; d. Carr Irvine Flournoy and Elizabeth Flournoy-Rivera; m. Leonard B. Hearne, Aug. 28, 1978. BS, UCLA, 1969, MS, 1971; PhD, U. Wash., 1982. Dir. clin. stats. Fred Hutchinson Cancer Rsch. Ctr., Seattle, 1974-86; dir. stats. and probability NSF, Washington, 1986—; prof. stats. American U., Washington, 1988—2002; chmn., prof. stats. U. Mo., Columbia, Mo., 2002—. Mem. of corp. Nat. Inst. Statis. Scis., Research Triangle Park, N.C., 1990-97, coun. Inst. Math. Stats., 2004—. Editor Multiple Stats. Integration, 1991, Adaptive Designs, 1995, New Developments and Applications in Experimental Designs, 1998, Adaptive Designs in Clinical Trials, 2005; assoc. editor Jour. Statis. Planning and Inference, 1998-2004. Grant reviewer AAUW, NSF, NIH, Nat. Security Agy USPHS fellow, 1969-71; Nat. Cancer Inst. grantee, 1975-86, NSF grantee, 1989-90, 96-2001, Am. Math. Soc./Inst. of Math. Stats./Soc. of Indsl. Applied Math. grantee, 1989, 92, EPA grantee, 1994-2000; recipient Elizabeth Scott award Com. of Pres. of Statis. Socs., 2000. Fellow AAAS, Inst. Math. Stats., Am. Statis. Assn. (chair coun. sects. 1994), World Acad. Art & Sci., Washington Acad. Sci.; mem. AAUW, Caucus for Women in Stats., Internat. Stats. Inst., Internat. Biometric Soc., Internat. Assn. for Statis. Computing. Democrat. Achievements include development of new statistical procedures for clinical trials and response-driven experimental designs; research on bone marrow transplantation, on graft versus leukemia, on infectious diseases in immuno-compromised hosts, on information management. Office: U Mo Dept Stats 146 Middlebush Columbia MO 65211-4100 Office Phone: 573-882-6376.

FLOURNOY, WILLIAM LOUIS, JR., landscape architect; b. Raleigh, NC, May 6, 1945; s. William Louis and Flossie (Combs) F. Student, Gardner-Webb Jr. Coll., 1964-66; BS in Recreation and Parks Adminstrn., N.C. State U., 1969, M of Landscape Architecture, 1972. Cons. to City of Raleigh N.C. State U. Sch. Design, 1971—72; community planner Wake County Planning Dept., Raleigh, N.C., 1972-80; environ. analysis program mgr. Office Legis. & Intergovtl. N.C. Dept. Environment and Natural Resources, Raleigh, 1980—2002; sr. conservation specialist Office Conservation and Cmty. Affairs NC Dept. Environ. and Natural Resources, Raleigh, 2002—. Mem. alumni adv. bd. dept. landscape architecture N.C. State U., 1999—, chair, 2003—. Contbr. articles to profl. jours. Bicycle com. NC Dept. Transp., 1974—83, chair, 1974—76, 1978—79; mem. nat. recreational trails adv. com. U.S. Dept. Transp., 1992—94; steering com. Wake County Cmty. Assessment, 1992—94; organizing com. NC Greenways Conf., 1986—95, conf. chair, 1992; active Triangle Open Space Network, 1997—99; bd. dirs. Southeastern U.S. Masters Track and Field, Inc., Raleigh, 1976—82, Triangle Land Conservancy, Rsch. Triangle Pk., NC, pres., 1991—94; bd. dirs. Triangle Greenways Coun., pres., 1989—91; bd. dirs. People for Parks, Wake County, NC, pres., 2002—04. Fellow Am. Soc. Landscape Architects (treas. N.C. chpt. 1982-86, v.p. 1978-79, awards 1978, 86, 90, 95), N.C. Trails Assn. (bd. dirs. 1977-82, acting pres. 1977), Landscape Architecture Founds., Landscape Architecture Urban Parks Honor Roll, others. Democrat. Methodist. Avocations: trail construction/maintenance, jogging, canoeing, hiking, bicycling. Home: 520 Polk St Raleigh NC 27604-1960 Office: NC ENR Office Conservation and Cmty Affairs 512 N Salisbury St Raleigh NC 27604-1170 E-mail: bill.flournoy@ncmail.net.

FLOWE, CAROL CONNOR, lawyer; b. Owensboro, Ky., Jan. 3, 1950; d. Marvin C. Connor and Ethel Marie (Thorn) Smith; children: Samantha Kathleen, Andrew Benjamin. BME magna cum laude, Murray State U., 1972; JD summa cum laude, Ind. U., 1976. Bar: Ohio 1977, D.C. 1981, U.S. Dist. Ct. (so. dist.) Ohio 1977, U.S. Dist. Ct. Md. 1983, U.S. Dist. Ct. D.C. 1981, U.S. Supreme Ct. 1987, U.S. Ct. Appeals (2d, 3d, 4th, 5th, 7th, and D.C. cirs.). Assoc. Baker & Hostetler, Columbus, Ohio, 1976-80, Arent Fox Kintner Plotkin & Kahn, Washington, 1980-87; dep. gen. counsel Pension Benefit Guaranty Corp., Washington, 1987-89, gen. counsel, 1989-95; ptnr. Arent Fox, PLLC, 1995—. Mem. ABA, D.C. Bar Assn., Order of Coif, Alpha Chi, Phi Alpha Delta. Avocations: computers, reading. Home: 8608 Aqueduct Rd Potomac MD 20854-6249 Office: Arent Fox PLLC 1050 Connecticut Ave NW Ste 500 Washington DC 20036-5339 Office Phone: 202-857-6054. Business E-Mail: flowe.carol@arentfox.com.

FLOWER, RENÉE BEVILLE, artist; b. Chgo., Oct. 22, 1950; d. Milton Oliver and Doris Lea (Beville) F.; m. Victor Allan Spiegel, June 22, 1975 (div. June 1981); m. James Anderson MacKenzie, July 31, 1982. BA in Studio Art, U. Calif., Santa Cruz, 1979. Lectr. in field. Ilustrator: (books) The Complete Sylvie & Bruno, 1991, City Noise, 1994, School Supplies, 1996; one-woman shows include Eloise Pickard Smith Gallery, 1993; exhibited in group shows at Ste 311, Pacific Grove, 1985, Zaner Gallery, Rochester, N.Y., 1986, San Francisco Mus. Modern Art Rental Gallery, 1987, The Art Mus. Santa Cruz County, 1988, Christopher Grimes Gallery, Carmel, 1989, Susan Cummins Gallery, Mill Valley, Calif., 1990, One Market Plaza, San Francisco, 1991, Gallery 500, Elkins Park, Pa., 1992, Yummy! Eating Through A Day, 2000, and others.

FLOWER, WALTER CHEW, III, investment counselor; b. New Orleans, Mar. 3, 1939; s. Walter Chew Flower II and Anne Elisa (lusk) Flower; m. Ella Smith Montgomery, Dec. 21, 1966; children: Anne Stuart, Lindsey Montgomery. BA in Econs., Tulane U., 1960; MBA in Fin., Harvard U., 1964. Cons. AID State Dept., 1964—65; fin. analyst Delta Capital Corp., New Orleans, 1965—66; v.p., mng. ptnr. Loomis Sayles & Co. Inc., New Orleans, 1967—78; pres., investment counsel Walter C. Flower & Co., New Orleans, 1978—. Dir. Starmount Cos. Chmn. Tulane U. Health Scis. Ctr.; bd. govs. Longue Vue Found., 1983—; dir. GPOA Found., 1985—; dir., fin. adv. Jr. League New Orleans, 1978—82; fin. adv. Beauregard House, 1979—2002, Metairie Park Country Day Sch., 1991—, New Orleans Mus. Art, 1998—; vestryman, mem. parish coun. Trinity Ch., 1978—. Lt. USNR, 1960—62. Mem.: Confrerie Des Chevalier Du Tastevin Club, N.Y. Yacht Club, Wyvern Club, Stratford Club, So. Yacht Club New Orleans, Pickwick Club, Boston Club, La. Club, New Orleans Lawn Tennis Club, Fishers Island Yacht Club, Lakeshore Club, Phi Beta Kappa. Office: 408 Magazine St New Orleans LA 70130-2435 E-mail: wcf@wfco.net.

FLOWERREE, ROBERT EDMUND, retired forest products company executive; b. New Orleans, Jan. 4, 1921; s. Robert E. and Amy (Hewes) F.; m. Elaine Dicks, Sept. 22, 1943; children: Ann D., John H., David R. BA, Tulane U., 1942. Vice pres. Georgia-Pacific Corp., 1956-63, exec. v.p. pulp, paper and chem. ops., 1963-75, pres., 1974-76, chmn., chief exec. officer, 1976-83, chmn., 1983-84, ret., 1984, Kilgore Corp. Past bd. dirs. Ga. Gulf Corp. Emeritus adminstr. Tulane U., New Orleans; life trustee Lewis and Clark Coll., Portland, Oreg. Served to lt. USNR, 1942-46. Recipient Disting. Alumnus award Tulane U., 1978; inducted into Paper Industry Internat. Hall of Fame, 2001. Mem.: Knights of Malta; Arlington (Portland), Waverley Country (Portland); Boston (New Orleans); Links (N.Y.C.). Office: 805 Broadway Ste 2290 Portland OR 97205

FLOWERS, CREOLE DUANE, publishing executive; b. Vandalia, Ill., Dec. 16, 1942; s. Creole Udell Flowers and Genevieve Eileen Beeson; m. Linda Kay Mollett, Aug. 5, 1966; 1 child, John Curtis. BS in Bus., Greenville Coll., 1965. Quality analyst Allis-Chalmers, Springfield, Ill., 1965-66, quality engr., 1967; jr. ptnr. Bass-Mollett Pubs., Springfield, 1969-72, sales v.p. Greenville, Ill., 1972-76, pres., 1976—, also bd. dirs. Adv. dir. Mercantile Bank, St. Louis, 1997—; bd. dirs. Masters Engraving Co., Virden, Ill. Trustee bd. Lindenwood U., St. Charles, Mo., 1995—; committeeman Rep. Party, Bond County, 1976-82; trustee 1st Meth. Ch., Greenville, 1974-77; mem. parents adv. com. Rhodes Coll., Memphis, 1993-95. With Ill. Air N.G., 1966-72. Mem. Ill. Funeral Supply Assn. (pres. 1973-76), St. Pats Investment Syndicate (sgt. at arms 1997—), Greenville C. of C., Mo. Athletic Club, Oaks Country Club. Republican. Presbyterian. Avocations: hunting, fishing, golf. Office: Bass-Mollett Pubs 507 Monroe St Greenville IL 62246-2033

FLOWERS, JUDITH ANN, marketing and public relations director; b. Oxford, Miss., Feb. 21, 1944; d. Woodrow Coleman and Ola Marie (Harding) Haynes; m. Sayles L. Brown Jr., Apr. 20, 1963 (div. Apr. 1974); children: Sayles L. III, Gregory A., Matthew C., Stephen W.; m. Taylor Graydon Flowers Jr., Apr. 27, 1979. Grad. high sch., Clarksdale, Miss. Office mgr. The KBH Corp., Clarksdale, 1964-69; office mgr., estimator Willis & Ellis Constrn., Clarksdale, 1969-75; with advt. prodn. Farm Press Pub., Clarksdale, 1975-79, advt. mgr., 1979-86, dir. advt. svcs., 1986-93; dir. mktg. and pub. rels. Cotton Club Casino, Greenville, Miss., 1992-95; dir. spl. projects C. of C., Clarksdale, Miss., 1996—; pres. JF Designs, Inc., 1999—. Counselor County Youth Ct., Clarksdale, 1985—; sec. Keep Clarksdale Beautiful, 1990-92; bd. dirs. Delta Arts Coun., 1994-95, Miss. Tourism Promotion Assn., 1996—; co-chair Tennessee Williams Festival, 1996, chair, 1999, 2000, 01; pres. Clarksdale Heritage Found., 1997—, founding mem. Mem. NAFE, Bus. and Profl. Women (corr. sec. 1987-88, 1st v.p. 1989-90, pres. 1992-93), Agri-Women Am., Nat. Agri-Mktg. Assn. (v.p. mid-south chpt. 1989-90, pres. 1990-91, nat. dir. 1991-93), Clarksdale C. of C. (chmn. agri-bus. commn. 1989-92, bd. dirs. 1989-92), So. Garden History Soc. (bd. dirs. 1992-95), The Garden Conservancy (city beautification 1996—), Miss. Tourism Promotion Assn. (bd. dirs. 1996—), Miss. Delta Arts Coun. (bd. dirs. 1996—), Clarksdale Women's Club (1st v.p. 2001-02). Republican. Baptist. Avocations: genealogy, gardening. Home: PO Box 26 Dublin MS 38739-0026 Office: JF Designs Inc PO Box 26 Dublin MS 38739-0026

FLOWERS, LANGDON STRONG, foods company executive; b. Thomasville, Ga., Feb. 12, 1922; s. William Howard and Flewellyn Evans (Strong) Flowers; m. Margaret Clisby Powell, June 3, 1944 (dec. Nov. 22, 1003); children: Margaret Flowers Rich, Langdon Strong, Elizabeth Powell, Dorothy Howard Flowers Swinson, John Howard. BS, MIT, 1944, MS, 1947; H.H.D., Presbyn. Coll., 1984. Engr., Douglas Aircraft, Los Angeles, 1947; supr. Flowers Baking Co., Thomasville, 1947-50, sales mgr., 1950-58, v.p. sales, 1958-65; pres., chief operating officer Flowers Industries, Inc., Thomasville, 1965-76, vice chmn. bd., chief exec. officer, 1976-80, chmn. bd., 1980-85, ret., 1985. Past pres. Thomasville YMCA, 1958-62; past trustee Presbyn Coll., Clinton, S.C., Archbold Meml. Hosp., Thomasville. Served as lt. (j.g.) USNR, 1943-46. Named Man of Year, Thomas County C. of C., 1974 Mem. Am. Bakers Assn. (exec. com. 1974-75, chmn. 1975-76), So. Bakers Assn. (chmn. bd. 1969-70), NAM (dir., exec. com.), Thomasville C. of C. (pres. 1953-54), Sigma Alpha Epsilon. Presbyterian (chmn. bd. deacons 1952-56, elder 1956—, rep. Gen. Assembly 1966). Club: Rotarian. Home: 207 Fairways Dr Thomasville GA 31792-7626 Office: PO Box 997 Thomasville GA 31799-0997

FLOWERS, ROBERT B., engineering company executive, retired career military officer; b. Pa., July 9, 1947; m. Lynda F.; 4 sons. Grad., Va. Mil. Inst., 1969; M in Civil Engring., U. Va., 1976; grad., Command & Gen. Staff Coll., Nat. War Coll. Registered profl. engr., Va. Commd. 2nd lt. US Army, 1969, advanced through grades to lt. gen., 2000, various positions, 1969-85, comdr. 307th Engr. Battalion, 1985-87, joint staff Nat. Mil. Command Ctr./Counternarcotics Divsn. Washington, 1987-90, comdr. 20th Engr. Brigade (Combat) (Airborne Corps) Ft. Bragg, NC, 1990-92; dep. asst. commandant US Army Engr. Sch., 1992-93, asst. commandant Ft. Leonard Wood, 1993-95; dep. commdg. gen. US Army Engring. Ctr., 1993-95; asst. divsn. comdr. 2nd Inf. Divsn. (Mechanized) Eighth US Army; dep. chief staff engring. US Army Europe, 1996; pres. Miss. River Commn. US Army, comdr. Miss. Valley Divsn.; commandant US Army Engr. Sch.; commdg. gen. US Army Engr. Ctr. and Ft. Leonard Wood, 1997—2000; chief of engineers/commanding gen. US Army Corps of Engineers, 2000—04; CEO HNTB Fed. Svcs, Corp., Va., 2004—. Joint task force engr. Joint Task Force, Somalia. Office: HNTB Fed Svcs Corp Ste 200 2900 S Quincy St Arlington VA 22206

FLOWERS, TAIRIA MIMS, softball player, Olympic athlete; b. Tucson, Ariz., Jan. 9, 1981; m. Jason Flowers, Aug. 23, 2003. Grad., UCLA, 2003. Mem. U.S.A. Women's Softball Team, Athens Olympics, Greece, 2004. Named First Team All American, Nat. Fastpitch Coach's Assn., 2003. Achievements include member of the UCLA NCAA Championship Team in 2003; memb. of the U.S.A. Women's Softball Gold medal Team, Internat. Softball Fedn. World Championships in 2002, Athens Olympic games, 2004.

FLOWERS, V. ANNE, retired academic administrator; b. Dothan, Ala., Aug. 29, 1928; d. Kyrie Neal and Annie Laurie (Stewart) Flowers. BA, Fla. State U., 1949; MEd, Auburn U., 1958; EdD, Duke U., 1963. Teaching asst. Duke U., Durham, NC, 1963; elem. and secondary sch. tchr., adminstr. Dothan, Dalton, Ga., 1949-61; from assoc. prof. to prof. edn., head dept. Columbia (S.C.) Coll., 1963-68, from assoc. dean to dean, 1969-72; prof. edn. Va. Commonwealth U., 1968-69; tchg. asst. Duke U., 1963, assoc. dean, asst. provost, acting dean, vice provost Trinity Coll. Arts and Scis., 1972-74, prof. edn., chmn. dept., asst. provost ednl. program devel., 1974-80; dean Sch. Edn. Ga. So. Coll., Statesboro, 1980-85; asst. vice chancellor acad. affairs Univ. Sys. Ga., Atlanta, 1985-88, vice chancellor, 1988-90, ret., 1990, vice chancellor emerita, 1990—. Mem. coun. aging and human devel. Duke U., 1974—80; cons. in field. Co-author: Law and Pupil Control, 1964, Readings in Survival in Today's Society, 2 vols., 1978; mem. editl. bd. Ednl. Gerontology, 1979, Jour. Tchr. Edn., 1980—82; contbr. articles to profl. jours. Bd. dirs., mem. exec. com. Learning Inst. N.C., 1976—80; vice chmn. continuing commn. study black colls. related to United Meth. Ch., 1973—76; pres. univ. senate Bd. Higher Edn. and Ministry United Meth. Ch., 1977—80; adv. trustee Queens Coll., Charlotte, NC, 1976—78; mem. bd. visitors Charleston So. U., 1992—93. Delta Kappa Gamma scholar, Duke U., 1963, State of Fla. scholar, Fla. State U., 1949. Mem.: NEA, Nat. Orgn. Legal Problems Edn., Am. Assn. Colls. Tchr. Edn. (pres. 1983—84, bd. dirs., mem. exec. com. 1979—84), Am. Assn. Higher Edn., So. Assn. Colls. and Schs. (mem. commn. colls.), Am. Ednl. Rsch. Assn., Phi Delta Kappa, Kappa Delta Pi. Home and Office: 41 Williamsburg Pl Dothan AL 36305

FLOWERS, WILLIAM HAROLD, JR., lawyer; b. Chgo., Ill., Mar. 22, 1946; s. William Harold Sr. and Ruth Lolita (Cave) Flowers; m. Pamela Ann Mays, Sept. 13, 1980. BA, U. Colo., 1967, JD, 1971. Bar: Colo. 1973, U.S. Ct. Appeals (10th cir.) 1973, U.S. Dist. Ct. Colo. 1973, U.S. Supreme Ct. 1985, U.S. Ct. Appeals (4th cir.) 1994. Atty. Pikes Peak Legal Svcs., Colorado Springs, Colo., 1973; ptnr. Tate, Tate & Flowers, Denver, 1973-76; dep. dist. atty. Office Adams County Dist. Atty., Brighton, Colo., 1977-78; ptnr. Taussig & Flowers, Boulder, 1978-81; pvt. practice Boulder, 1981-89; ptnr. Holland & Hart, LLP, Denver, 1989-97, Hurth Yeager, Sisk & Blakemore LLP, Boulder, 1997—. Mem. Boulder County Cmty. Corrections Bd., 1985—90. Mem. Boulder Bd. Zoning Adjustment, 1973-78, chmn., 1977-78; mem. Boulder Growth Task Force, 1980-82; mem. exec. bd. Longs Peak coun. Boy Scouts Am., 1983-98; bd. dirs. Sta. KGNU, Boulder County Broadcasting, 1981-84, Coloradans Against the Death Penalty, 2001-04; trustee Nat. Coll. Advocacy, 2002—. Mem.: ATLA (chair Coun. of Pres. 2001—02, exec. com. 2001—03, chair state dels. 2002—03, bd. govs. 2002—04), Colo. Bar Assn. (bd. govs. 2000, v.p. 2002—03), U. Colo. Found. (bd. dirs. 1995—2002), U. Colo. Boulder Alumni Assn. (bd. dirs. 1987—96, pres. 1994—95), Sam Cary Bar Assn. (pres. 1987), Boulder County Bar Assn. (civil litigation com. 1978—, criminal law com. 1979—, bd. dirs. 2003—, sec.-treas. 2005—), Colo. Trial Lawyers Assn. (bd. dirs. 1989—, exec. com. 1996—2005, pres. 1999—2000), Colo. Criminal Def. Bar (bd. dirs. 1982—83), Nat. Bar Assn. (regional dir. 1983—86, bd. govs. 1983—96, v.p. 1990—91). Democrat. Methodist. Office: Hurth Yeager Sisk & Blakemore LLP PO Box 17850 4860 Riverbend Rd Boulder CO 80308 Office Phone: 303-443-7900.

FLOYD, ALTON DAVID, cell biologist, consultant; b. Henderson, Ky., July 17, 1941; s. Frank and Queen Tina (Melton) F.; m. Barbara Wilson, Aug. 18, 1962; children: Fara Alison, Heather Lynn. BS, U. Ky., 1963; PhD, U. Louisville, 1968. From lectr. to asst. prof. U. Mich., Ann Arbor, 1967-72; from asst. to assoc. prof. Sch. of Medicine Ind. U., Bloomington, 1972-83, assoc. prof. Sch. of Medicine Indpls., 1983-84; sect. head cell biology Miles Sci., Inc., Naperville, Ill., 1984-85; sr. staff scientist Miles, Inc., Elkhart, Ind., 1985-89; pvt. practice cons. Edwardsburg, Mich., 1989—; assoc. dir. Ctr. Light Microscope Imaging and Biotech. Carnegie Mellon U., Pitts., 1991. Bd. dirs. Endotech Corp., Indpls.; mem. subcom. immunohistochem. stains NCCLS, 1995-96; industry rep. adv. panel hematology and pathology devices FDA, 1996-99; trustee Biol. Stain Commn., 1997—. Mem. Am. Assn. Anatomists, Tissue Culture Assn., Soc. Analytical Cytology, Histochem. Soc., Soc. Quantitative Morphology, Soc. Histotech. Avocations: sailing, reading, wood and metal shopwork, computing. Home and Office: 23126 S Shore Dr Edwardsburg MI 49112-8502 Personal E-mail: al.floyd@juno.com.

FLOYD, DAISY HURST, dean, law educator; BA, MA in Polit. Sci., Emory U., 1977; JD cum laude, U. Ga., 1980. Bar: Ga., TEx. Dir. Legal Rsch. and Writing Prog. U. Ga. Sch. Law; atty. Alston, Miller & Gaines, Atlanta; prof. law Tex. Tech U. Sch. Law, assoc. dean academic affairs; dean Walter F. George Sch. Law, Mercer U., 2004—. Faculty mem. Nat. Inst. Trial Advocacy (NITA), Nat. Jud. Coll., Tex. Jud. Acad., Tex. Ctr. for Judiciary. Mem. bd. dirs. Lubbock Legal Aid Soc. Named Phi Alpha Delta Prof. of Yr., 2001, Carnegie Scholar, 2001; recipient New Prof. Excellence in Tchg. Award, 1995. Fellow: Am. Bar. Found.; mem.: Tex. Bar Found. Office: Mercer U Sch Law 1021 Georgia Ave Macon GA 31207-0001 Office Phone: 478-301-2602. E-mail: floyd_dh@mercer.edu.

FLOYD, GARY LEON, plant cell biologist; b. Moline, Ill., Dec. 23, 1940; s. Leland L. and Zenta (Henderson) F.; m. Myrna A. Floyd, Aug. 18, 1963. BA, U. No. Iowa, 1962; MS, U. Okla., 1966; PhD, Miami U., Oxford, Ohio, 1971. Sci. tchr. Grinnell (Iowa) Jr. High Sch., 1962-65; instr. Miami U., 1966-68; asst. prof. Rutgers U., New Brunswick, N.J., 1971-75; asst. prof. plant biology Ohio State U., Columbus, 1975-78, assoc. prof., 1978-83, prof., 1983-96, assoc. dean biol. scis., 1986-88, dean, 1989-96, prof. and dean emeritus, 1996—. Dir. TEM facility plant biology dept. Ohio State U., Columbus, 1978-86. Contbr. articles to profl. jours. NSF scholar, 1965-66; recipient Alumni Teaching award Ohio State U., 1980, Disting. Rsch. award, 1982, Darbaker prize Bot. Soc. Am., 1993, award of excellence Phycological Soc. Am., 2003; Phycological Soc. Am. nat. lectr., 1983-85. Avocation: golf. Home: 936 Kendale Rd S Columbus OH 43220-4148 Business E-Mail: floyd.1@osu.edu.

FLOYD, ISRAEL J., lawyer, chemicals executive; BA, Lincoln U., Nebr., 1969; MBA in fin., Temple U., 1973; JD, Villanova U., 1973. From atty. to corp. sec., gen. counsel Hercules Inc., Wilimington, Del., 1973—2001, gen. counsel, corp. sec., 2001—. Office: Hercules Inc 1313 N Market St Wilmington DE 19894 E-mail: ifloyd@herc.com.*

FLOYD, JACK WILLIAM, lawyer; b. Columbia, S.C., May 14, 1934; s. Edward Immanuel and Edith Fletcher (Herlong) F.; m. Ruth Parker Matthews, Jan. 10, 1957; children: Connie, Cindy, Jay. BS, U. N.C., 1958, JD with honors, 1961. Bar: N.C. 1961, U.S. Supreme Ct. 1971. Assoc. Smith, Moore, Smith, Schell & Hunter, Greensboro, NC, 1961-67, ptnr., 1967-87, Floyd, Greeson, Allen & Jacobs, Greensboro, 1988-90, Floyd, Allen & Jacobs, Greensboro, 1991-97, Floyd & Jacobs, Greensboro, 1998—. Lectr. acctg. U. N.C., 1960-61; lectr. bus. law Guilford Coll., 1962-64; spkr. on jury trials ABA, Am. Patent Law Assn.; arbitrator U.S. Dist. Ct. Annexed Arbitration Program. Bd. editors N.C. Law Rev., 1960—61. Mem. parents' bd. dirs. Meredith Coll., Raleigh, NC, 1977—79, chmn., 1980—81. Served with USN, 1951—55. Mem. ABA, N.C. Bar Assn. (panelist on family law), Am. Law Inst., N.C. Assn. Trial Lawyers, Elks Club, Order of Coif. Democrat. Baptist.

Home: 1404 Valleymeade Rd Greensboro NC 27410-3938 Office: Floyd & Jacobs 401C N Eugene St Greensboro NC 27401-2644 Office Phone: 336-273-1797. Personal E-mail: jwf1404@aol.com. E-mail: jackfloyd@bellsouth.com.

FLOYD, JAMES M., JR., adult education educator; s. James M. and Carolyn S. Floyd; m. Linda J. Mosier, Feb. 12, 1999. AS in Liberal Arts, U. State N.Y., Albany; BFA in Visual Comm., postgrad., Am. Intercontinental U. Mem. adj. faculty Ivy Tech State Coll., Indpls., 2001—. Mem.: Cognitive Sci. Soc.

FLOYD, JOHN ALEX, JR., marketing professional, director, horticulturist; b. Selma, Ala., Feb. 21, 1948; s. John Alex Sr. and Louise (Johnson) F.; m. Pamela Lorene Billups, Aug. 14, 1982; children: Ryan Thomas, James Alex. BS, Auburn (Ala.) U., 1970; MS, Clemson (S.C.) U., 1972, PhD, 1975. Instr. Jefferson State Jr. Coll., Birmingham, Ala., 1975-77; sr. horticulturist So. Living Mag., Birmingham, 1977-84; editorial dir. Classics-So. Accents, Birmingham, 1985-87, Creative Ideas and Cooking Light, Birmingham, 1987-88; dir. mktg. svcs., editor So. Progress Corp, Birmingham, 1988-91; v.p., editor So. Living, 1991—. Author: (with others) Southern Living Trees & Shrubs, 1980, Southern Living Garden Guide, 1982, Southern Living Vegetable & Herbs, 1984. Mem. adv. com. Landscape Architecture Adv. Coun., Auburn U., 1988-93; bd. dirs. U. N.C. Bot. Gardens, Chapel Hill, 1988-90; program com. Brookgreen Gardens; bd. dirs. Ea. Health Found., Trussville Tree Commn.; vis. com. Longwood Gardens; bd. dirs., co-chair steering com. Trussville Schs. Ency. of Ala. Grantee NSF, 1977. Mem. Am. Soc. Hort. Sci., Garden Writers Am., Birmingham Bot. Soc. (pres. 1981, trustee 1984—), Am. Hort. Soc. (bd. dirs. 1991-94), Gamma Sigma Delta, Pi Alpha Xi. Methodist. Home: 369 Palace Dr Trussville AL 35173-1067 Office: So Progress Corp 2100 Lakeshore Dr Birmingham AL 35209-6721 Office Phone: 205-445-6365. E-mail: john_floyd@timeinc.com.

FLOYD, JOHN DAVID, theology studies educator, minister; b. Lockesburg, Ark., Sept. 28, 1934; s. William Chaney Floyd and Alice Thadine (Park) Trammell; m. Helen Nutt, June 3, 1955; children: Elizabeth Ann Stivers, John Paul. BA, Ouachita Bapt. U., 1952-56; BD, Southwestern Bapt. Theol. Sem., 1962, M in Div., 1969; PhD, Mid-Am. Bapt. Theol. Sem., 1976; post doctoral studies, Fuller Theol. Sem., 1980-81. Ordained to ministry Bapt. Ch., 1952. Pastor various So. Bapt. Chs., 1952-65; missionary Fgn. Mission Bd. So. Bapt. Conv., Philippines, 1965-75; v.p. adminstrn., prof. missions Mid-Am. Bapt. Theol. Sem., Memphis, 1975-84; dir. missionary enlistment Fgn. Mission Bd. So. Bapt. Conv., Richmond, Va., 1984-85; v.p., dir. ministry program Mid-Am. Bapt. Theol. Sem., Memphis, 1985-93; dir. fgn. mission bd. for Europe The Southern Baptist Convention, 1993-2000; v.p., chmn. missions dept. Mid-Am. Bapt. Theol. Sem., 2000—. Head Missions Dept. Mid-Am. Bapt. Theol. Sem., Memphis, 1977-84, cons. ch. growth, 1979-84, dir. sch. world missions, 1982-84. Editor: Inductive Bible Study Series, 1970, 1971 Church Growth Survey in the Philippines, 1972, Modern Cults, 1979; editor numerous articles Mid-Am. Bapt. Theol. Jour., 1976-86; editor Jour. Evangelism and Missions. Campaigner Rep. Party in Va., Richmond, 1984-85. Served as 1st lt. inf. US Army, 1957-59. Recipient Eye of the Eagle award 101st Airborne Div. Ft. Campbell, 1984, Key to the City award Booneville City Govt., 1982. Mem. Am. Assn. Missiologists, Assn. Mission Profs., Internat. Missiological Soc., Nat. Planned Giving Assn., Am. Mgmt. Assn. Home: 2533 Brotherwood Cv Collierville TN 38017-8972 Office: Mid-Am Bapt Theol Sem 2216 S Germantown Rd Germantown TN 38138-3804 Office Phone: 901-751-8453. E-mail: jdfloyd@mabts.edu.

FLOYD, JOHN TAYLOR, electronics executive; b. Quincy, Mass., Jan. 17, 1942; s. John Taylor and Virginia Marie (Watts) Floyd; m. Denise Angela Dufault, Oct. 4, 1969; children: Jennifer, Aimee. BA, Northeastern U., 1965; MBA in Fin., Boston Coll., 1972. Product group controller Tex. Instruments, Attleboro, Mass., 1972-75; asst. to v.p. fin. Waters Assocs., Milford, Mass., 1975-76; group fin. mgr. Digital Equipment Corp., Maynard, Mass., 1976-82; v.p. mfg. Computer Devices, Burlington, Mass., 1982-83; dir. fin. and adminstrn. Wang Labs., Lowell, Mass., 1984-85; v.p. ops. Charleswater Products, Newton, Mass., 1985-90; v.p. Devon Group, Waltham, Mass., 1991—, also bd. dirs. Served to capt. U.S. Army, 1965—70, Vietnam. Mem.: Fin. Execs. Inst., Treas.' Club Boston, Am. Legion. Independent. Office: Devon Group 800 South St Waltham MA 02453-1478

FLOYD, JUDY LOUISE CASBURN, anesthesiologist, political scientist; b. Graham, Tex., May 13, 1939; d. William Robert and Bessie (Bep) Pearl (Slay) Casburn; m. John Scales Floyd, 1960 (div. 1975); children: Tracey Lynn, Cinda Gale, Leann Renee. BS in nursing, psychology, Tex. Christian U., 1962; M in polit. Sci. internat. affairs, Ctrl. State U., 1989. Registered nurse Tex, Okla, Tenn., Miss. Pub. health svc. Ft. Worth Health Dept., 1962—63; asst. head nurse All Saints Episcopal Hosp., Ft. Worth, 1963—64, surpr. surgery, 1964—65; anesthetist tng. Harris Hosp., Ft. Worth, 1965—67; anesthetist Graham Gen. Hosp., Ft. Worth, 1967—69, freelance, Tex., 1969—74, Deaconess Hosp., Okla. City, Okla., 1975—89, Bapt. Meml. Hosp., Memphis, 1989—2003; retired, 2003. Expert witness in anesthesia, 2000—03. Vol. to project Huesteco to give anesthia to repair cleft lips/palates, Mexico, 1975; vol. gave anesthia to children with cataracts Christian Med. Soc., Dominican Republic, 1985—87; tchr. Sunday Sch., 1968—69. Mem.: Acad. Polit. Sci., Am. Hist. Assn., Soc. for Intercultural Tng. and Rsch., Am. Assn. Nurse Anesthetists, Am. Polit. Sci. Assn., Tex. Christian U. Alumni Assn. (life). Republican. Avocations: travel, history. Home: 4248 Oak Pk Ct Fort Worth TX 76109 Office Phone: 817-691-2746. Home Fax: 817-928-8475. Personal E-mail: jcfloyd44@charter.net.

FLOYD, KIMBERLY HAYES, lawyer; b. Greensboro, NC, Jan. 10, 1958; d. Joe Don and Bonita Jean (Hayes) F. BS, Campbell U., 1980, JD, 1983; postgrad., London Sch. Econs., 1982. Bar: N.C. 1985, U.S. Dist. Ct. (mid. dist.) N.C. 1986, U.S. Dist. Ct. (ea. dist.) N.C. 1994, U.S. Supreme Ct. 1991. Ptnr. Joe D. Floyd, PA, Law Firm, High Point, N.C., 1985—. Presdl. adv. bd. Campbell U., 2002—. Co-chmn. Guilford County Dole for Pres. Campaign, N.C., 1995-96; del. Rep. Nat. Convention, 1996; mem. Jr. League of High Point, 1990—; pub. spkr. childwatch com. in coop. with Guilford County Dept. Social Svcs., 1992-94, mem. legis. action/pub. policy com., 1994-98, asst. chmn., 1996-97, chmn., 1997-98; del. N.C. Pub. Affairs Com., 1996-98; spkr. Green St. Bapt. Ch. Women's Conf., 1995. Named one of Outstanding Young Women of Am., 1988, 91; recipient Disting. Alumna award Campbell U., 1997. Mem. N.C. Bar Assn., N.C. Acad. Trial Lawyers, N.C. Assn. Women Attys. (gov. bd. dirs. 1992-94), Guilford County Bar Assn. (sec.-treas. 1992-93), High Point Bar Assn. Republican. Baptist. Office: Joe D Floyd PA Law Firm 401 S Main St High Point NC 27260-6634 Office Phone: 336-886-5031. E-mail: kfloydatty@northstate.net.

FLOYD, MICHAEL O'S., lawyer; b. Woodbury, NJ, 1939; AB, St. Joseph's Coll., 1961; student, Hague Acad. Internat. Law, 1963; LLB cum laude, Univ. Pa., 1964. Bar: NJ 1965, Pa. 1967. Of counsel, co-chair, products liability practice group Drinker Biddle & Reath LLP, Phila. Co-founder Phila. Chamber Ensemble; former v.p., dir. Navy League of US, Phila. Chapter. Mem.: ABA, NJ Bar Assn., Pa. Bar Assn., Phila. Bar Assn., Def. Rsch. Inst. Office: Drinker Biddle & Reath LLP One Logan Sq 18th & Cherry Sts Philadelphia PA 19103-6996 Office Phone: 215-988-2941. Office Fax: 215-988-2757. Business E-Mail: michael.floyd@dbr.com.

FLOYD, OTIS HENRY, retired military officer, adult education educator; b. York, S.C., June 4, 1951; s. John Mason Barnette and Mozelle Phillips Lindsay; m. Shirley Jane Sims, Feb. 6, 1955; 1 child, Nashara Yvette Hopkins. AAS, C.C. of Air Force, Maxwell, AFB, Ala., 1988; BS, Gardner-Webb U., Boiling Springs, N.C., 2000; MS, N.C. Agrl. and Tech. State U., Greensboro, 2000; post grad., U. N.C., Charlotte, 2001—. Aircraft maintenance technician US Air Force, Washington, 1969—90; cmty. devel. instr. Ctrl. Piedmont C.C., Charlotte, NC, 2001—. V.p. Gaston Cmty. Action Inc., Gastonia, NC, 2004—. Decorated Vietnam Gallantry Cross US Air Force, Vietnam Svc. medal, 4 commendation medals; named to Nat. Deans List, Gardner-Webb U., 2000. Mem.: Am. Assn. Adult and Continuing Edn. (assoc.), Am. Mil. Soc., Kappa Delta Pi. Office Phone: 704-330-7646. E-mail: otis_floyd@cpcc.edu.

FLOYD, RAYMOND LORAN, professional golfer; b. Ft. Bragg, NC, Sept. 4, 1942; s. Loren B. and Edith (Brown) F.; m. Maria; children: Raymond Loran, Robert Loran, Christina Loran. Student, U. N.C., 1960. Profl. golfer PGA, 1961-92; profl. golfer Sr. PGA, 1992—; mem. Ryder Cup team, 1969, 75, 77, 81, 83, 85, 89, 91, 93; capt. Ryder Cup Team, 1989. Winner 2000 Ford Sr. Players Championship, Doral Ryder Open, 1992, GTE North Classic, 1992, Northville Long Island Classic Senior PGA, 1993, Sr. Tour Championship, 1994, Ford Sr. Players Championship, 2000; named Rookie of Year Golf Mag., 1963, 77, Player of Yr., 1976. Winner PGA tournament, 1969, 82 St. Petersburg Open, 1963, St. Paul Open, 1965, Jacksonville Open, 1969, Am. Golf Classic, 1969, Kemper Open, 1975, Masters, 1976, World Open, 1976, Byron Nelson Golf Classic, 1977, Pleasant Valley Golf Classic, 1977, Brazilian Open, 1978, Greater Greensboro Open, 1979, Canadian PGA, 1981, Vardon Trophy, 1983, Ryder Cup, 1969, 75, 77, 81, 83, 85, Doral Ea. Open, 1980, 81, Tournament Players Championship, 1981, Westchester Classic, 1981, Meml. Tournament, 1982, Memphis Classic, 1982, PGA Championship, 1982, $1Million Sun City Challenge, 1982, Houston Open, 1985, Chrysler Team Championship, 1985, U.S. Open, 1986, Walt Disney/Oldsmobile Classic, 1986, Skins Game, 1988, RMCC Invitational, 1990, Doral-Ryder Open, 1992, GTE North Classic, 1992, Ralph's Sr. Classic, 1992, Sr. Tour Championship, 1992, Thailand Srs., 1992, Northville L.I. Classic, 1993, The Tradition, 1994, Sr. Skins Game, 1994, 95, 96, 97, 98, Las Vegas Srs. Classis, 1994, Sr. Tour Championship, 1994, PGA Srs. Championship, 1995, Burnet Sr. Classic, 1995, Ford Sr. Players Championship, 1996; capt. Ryder Cup, 1989; inducted in PGA/World Golf Hall of Fame, 1989, winner father-son tourn. w/son Raymond Jr., 1995, 96, 97, w/son Robert, 2000, 01, winner Par 3 Shootout, 2000. Office: 505 S Flagler Dr West Palm Beach FL 33401

FLOYD, TIM, men's college basketball coach, former professional basketball coach; b. Hattiesburg, Miss. m. Beverly Floyd; 1 child, Shannon. BS, La. Tech. Univ., 1977. Coach Univ. El Paso, 1977-86, Idaho Univ., 1986-88, Iowa State Univ., 1994-98; head coach Chgo. Bulls, 1999—2001, New Orleans Hornets, 2003—04, U. of So. Calif., 2005—. Named Coach of Yr. Office: c/o USC Athletic Dept 3501 Watt Way HER 203 A Los Angeles CA 90089

FLOYD, WILLIAM R., health facility administrator; BA, U. Pa.; MBA, U. Pa., Wharton Sch. Bus. With Gillette; various positions to v.p. mktg. Bennigan's chain Pillsbury, 1975; exec. v.p., gen. mgr. Safeguard Business Systems, Inc.; Northeast brand mgr. PepsiCo, COO, Ky. Fried Chicken, 1994, COO, Taco Bell, 1995—96; CEO Choice Hotels Internat., 1997—98; pres., COO Beverly Enterprises Inc., 2000—, CEO, chmn., 2001—. Bd. trustees Valley Forge Military Academy. Office: 1000 Beverly Way Fort Smith AR 72919*

FLUG, JANICE, librarian; b. Mpls., Oct. 19, 1949; d. Albert William and Elberta Edna (Kimball) F.; m. William Raymond LeFevre, Jan. 2, 1982 (dec. June 1986). BA, Hamline U., St. Paul, 1971; MLS, U. Md., 1975; MPA, Am. U., 1980. Acquisitions searcher Am. U. Libr., Washington, 1972-75, asst. to the univ. libr., 1975-91, acquisitions libr., 1991—. Chmn. U. Libr. Faculty Coun., 1999—2003; mem. faculty senate Am. U., 2003—, chmn. com. on instrl. budget and benefits, 2003—. Mem. bd. editors The Pub. Mgr., 1996—. Exec. bd. Libr. Orgn. Mgmt., 1997—99. Mem.: ALA (exec. bd. 1997—99), Libr. Adminstrn. Mgmt. Assn. (exec. bd. 1997—99, mem. leadership devel. com. 1999—2003, chmn. leadership devel. com. 2001—03, budget and fin. com. 2003—, chmn. 2005—), Am. Soc. Pub. Adminstrn. (pres. Md. chpt. 1994—95, nat. coun. 1995—99, chair policy issues com. 1998—99, fin. com vice chair 1999—2000, chair 2000—01, bd. ins. trustees 2001—, vice chair steering group 2002—03, chmn. steering group 2003—04, past chair 2004—05, fin. com. vice-chair 2005—, fin. com. fin. vice chair 2005—). Democrat. Lutheran. Avocations: swimming, church activities. Home: 2927 Mozart Dr Silver Spring MD 20904-6802 Office Phone: 202-885-3211. Personal E-mail: jflug@earthlink.net. Business E-Mail: jflug@american.edu.

FLÜGELMAN, MAXIMO ENRIQUE, financier, composer; b. Buenos Aires, Nov. 2, 1945; s. Cirilo and Matilde (Rhein) F. Lic. es Sci. Econ., U. Geneva; diploma in econ. policy, Cath. U., Buenos Aires; MBA, Harvard U.; BM, Manhattan Sch. Music; M in Composition, Juilliard Sch. Credit officer Citibank, Buenos Aires and N.Y.C., 1970; sr. investment officer World Bank Group Internat. Fin. Corp., Washington, 1972-77; internat. mgr., chief external funding, negotiator Nat. Devel. Bank, Buenos Aires, 1981-84; v.p. banker 1st Chgo. Internat. Capital Markets Group, Chgo. and N.Y.C., 1985-89; v.p., exec. com. Inter-Am. Investment Corp., Washington, 1989—94; prin. Corfina Global Advisors, LLC, 1995—. Mem. ofcl. Argentine del. to IMF/World Bank meetings, Inter Am. Devel. Bank gen. assemblies; lectr. Buenos Aires Nat. U., Cath. U., Washington. Author: Argentina and the Debt Crisis; composer: Symphonic Variants for orch., Concertino for woodwinds and orch., Sea Sonnets for soprano and orch., Sonatina for chamber orch., Rhapsody for Cello and Orch., Concerto for Piano and String orch., Dialogues for Orchestra, chamber works performed at Aspen Festival, Latin Am. Chamber Music Festival, Quinteto Rego, orchestral works performed Indpls. Symphony, Seattle Symphony, Puerto Rico Symphony, Interam. Festival Orch., Kennedy Ctr., Carnegie Hall, Northwestern U. Orch., Nat. Argentine Symphony, Buenos Aires Philharm. at Teatro Colon, Conn. Chamber Orch., Fla. Philharm., Am. Composers Orch., Orchestre de la Cité; contbr. articles. Bd. dirs. Am. Composers Orch. Recipient 14th ann. contemporary orchestral composition award Ind. State U./Indpls. Symphony; 1st prize LRA Argentine State Radio Chamber Orch. composition contest, Outstanding Young Musician of Yr. award Argentine Jr. C. of C.; Amigos de la Musica composition contest; finalist Nissim Orchestral Composition Competition, Plymouth Music Series award; fellow Bunge and Born Found. Mem. ASCAP, Am. Composers Orchestra (dir.), Argentine Coun. on Fgn. Rels., Teatro Colón Found. (trustee, founding), A. Ginastera Found. (dir.), Soc. Argentina de Autores y Compositores, Soc. Rural Argentina, Cosmos Club (Washington), Doubles, Harvard Club (N.Y.C.), Club Nautico San Isidro (Buenos Aires). Home: 2817 Dumbarton St NW Washington DC 20007-3366

FLUHARTY, DAVID ARTHUR, automotive executive, statistician, consultant; b. Steubenville, Ohio, Feb. 28, 1951; s. Ralph Osborn and Grace Elaine (Martin) Fluharty; m. Mary Margaret Reiter, Nov. 25, 1978; 1 child, Margaret Rose Elaine Fluharty-Reiter (dec.). BA, Wheeling (W.Va.)Jesuit U., 1973; MBA, U. Chgo., 1975, MA, 1978; grad. in applied stats., Oakland U., Rochester, Mich., 1992; postgrad., Wayne State U., Detroit, Michigan, 1995. Loan guarantee analyst Maritime Adminstrn. U.S. Dept. Commerce, Washington, 1976—77; fin. analyst Ford Motor Co., Dearborn, Mich., 1977—85, statistician, 1985—88; program mgr., warranty/reliability mgr. Alcoa Fujikura Ltd., Allen Park, Mich., 1988—99, sr. statistician, 1999—2001; mgr. reliability and warranty adminstrn. Continental Teves, Auburn Hills, Mich., 2001—03, statistician, 2003—. Assoc. editor Stats Mag.; contbr. Statistical Case Studies: A Collaboration Between Academe and Industry. Mem. math. steering com. Macomb Intermediate Sch. Dist., Clinton Township, Mich., 1998; participant program Ignatian spirituality Manresa SJ Retreat Ho., Bloomfield Hills, Mich., 1999. Mem.: Am. Statis. Assn. (various officer positions in the detroit chpt. 1990—2002, com. on tchr. enhancement 2000—, chpt. svc. recognition award 1999). Roman Catholic.

FLUHR, HOWARD, consulting firm executive; b. Bklyn., Feb. 20, 1943; s. Morton and Evelyn (Cohen) F.; m. Margaret Appel, Sept. 7, 1963; children: Lisa Metaxas, Allison Kaufman. BS in Math. and Philosophy cum laude, NYU, 1964. Various actuarial positions Guardian Life Ins. Co., 1964-66, Eastern Life Ins. Co., 1966-69; various actuarial and mgmt. positions The Segal Co., N.Y.C., 1969-73, v.p., 1973-76, sr. v.p., 1976-87, exec. v.p., 1987-93, pres., CEO, 1994—. Contbr. articles to profl. jours.; speaker in field. Fellow Soc. Actuaries, Conf. Cons. Actuaries (bd. dirs. 1990-96, v.p. 1991-96), Can. Inst. Actuaries; mem. Internat. Actuarial Assn., Am. Acad. Actuaries (bd. dirs. 1989-95, v.p. 1993-95), Employee Benefit Rsch. Inst. (trustee 1994—, chmn. 2000-2002). Office: The Segal Co 1 Park Ave New York NY 10016-5895 E-mail: hfluhr@segalco.com.

FLUKE, JOHN MAURICE, JR., electrical equipment manufacturing company executive; b. 1942; s. John Maurice Sr. and Lyla (Schram) F. BS in elec. engring., Univ. of Wash., 1964; MS in elec. engring., Stanford Univ., 1966. With John Fluke Mfg. Co. Inc., 1966—, gen. mgr. Central Products Group, 1978-82, gen. mgr. Indsl. Measurement & Control Div., 1982, vice-chmn., 1982-84, chief exec. officer, 1983-88, chmn., 1984—. Bd. dirs. PACCAR, Inc., U.S. Bank Wash., John Fluke Mfg. Co., Inc. Mem. engring. vis. com. U. Wash., 1983—; mem. engring. adv. bd. Stanford U., 1985—. Mem. Greater Seattle C. of C. (chmn. 1990—), Wash. Bus. Roundtable (bd. dirs. 1984—), Am. Electronics Assn. (bd. dirs. 1987—), Nat. Assn. Mfrs. (bd. dirs. 1989—). Office: FCM 11400 SE 6th St Bellevue WA 98004-6423

FLUKE, LYLA SCHRAM (MRS. JOHN M. FLUKE SR.), publisher; b. Maddock, ND; d. Olaf John and Anne Marie (Rodberg) Schram; m. John M. Fluke, June 5, 1937 (dec. 2002); children: Virginia Fluke Gabelein, John M. Jr., David Lynd. BS in Zoology and Physiology, U. Wash., Seattle, 1934, diploma tchg., 1935. H.S. tchr., 1935-37; tutor Seattle schs., 1980-84; pub. Portage Quar. mag. Hist. Soc. Seattle and King County, 1980-84. Hon. mem. Rsch. on Nanotechnology, 2000. Contbr. articles to profl. jours. Co-founder N.W. chpt. Myasthenia Gravis Found., 1953, Wash. Tech. Ctr., 1996, pres., 1960-66; obtained N.W. artifacts for Navy destroyer Tender Puget Sound., 1966; mem. Seattle Mayor's Com. for Seattle Beautiful, 1962; sponsor Seattle World's Fair, 1962; charter and founding mem. Seattle Youth Symphony Aux., 1974; benefactor U. Wash., 1982-01, sponsor first chair mfg., U Wash., 1982, nat. chmn. ann. giving campaign, 1983-84; benefactor Cascade Symphony, Salvation Army, Sterling Cir. Stanford U., MIT, 1984, Seattle Symphony, 1982-2002, Wash. State Hist. Soc., Pacific Arts Coun., Pacific Sci. Ctr., 2003-04, Twenty-Twelve Club, 1962-2002; mem. condr.'s club Seattle Symphony, 1978—; mem. U. Wash. Campaign Exec. Com., 2003—, hon. mem. Campaign Com. NSF Grant to Nat. Nanotechnology Infrastructure Network; hon. exec. com. on nanotech. U. Wash. Coll. Engring., 2003-; benefactor Seattle Symphony, 2004, Univ. Wash., 2004; chmn. mfg. Recipient Crystal plaque Coll. Engring. U. Wash., 2002; Seattle Pacific U. fellow, 1972; Lyla and John M. Fluke chair in mfg. U. Wash., 1982. Mem. IEEE Aux. (chpt. charter mem., pres. 1970-73), Wash. Trust for Hist. Preservation, Nat. Trust for Hist. Preservation, N.W. Ornamental Hort. Soc. (benefactor, life, hon.), Nat. Assn. Parliamentarians (charter mem., pres. N.W. unit 1961-64), Wash. Parliamentarians Assn. (charter), Seattle C. of C. (women's divsn. 1965-66), Seattle Symphony Women's Assn. (life, charter, sec. 1982-84, pres. 1985-87), Hist. Soc. Seattle and King County (exec. com. 1975-78, pres. women's mus. league 1975-79, pres. Moritz Thomsen Guild of Hist. Soc., 1978-80, 84-87), Highlands Orthopedic Guild (life), Wash. State Hist. Soc., Antiquarian Soc. (v.p. 1986-88, pres. 1988-90, hon. mem. John Fluke Mfg. Co. 20 Year Club 1987—), Rainier Club, Seattle Golf Club, U. Wash. Pres.'s Club, Twenty Twelve Club Republican. Lutheran. Achievements include sponsorship of the Fluke Chair in Coll. of Engring. U Wash. Address: 1206 NW Culbertson Dr Seattle WA 98177-3942 also: Vendovi Island PO Box 703 Anacortes WA 98221-0703 Office Phone: 425-453-4590.

FLUMENBAUM, MARTIN, lawyer; b. Bronx, July 22, 1950; AB summa cum laude, Columbia Coll., 1971; JD cum laude, Harvard Law Sch., 1974. Bar: NY 1975, DC 1985, admitted to practice: US Dist. Ct. (So. Dist.) NY 1975, US Dist. Ct. (Ea. Dist.) NY 1975, US Ct. Appeals (2nd Cir.) 1975, US Ct. Appeals (5nd Cir.), US Supreme Ct. 1986, US Dist. Ct. (DC). Clk. to Hon. Whitman Knapp US Dist. Ct., (So. Dist.) NY; asst. U.S. Atty. US Dist. Ct. (So. Dist.) NY, 1972—82; with Paul, Weiss, Rifkind, Wharton & Garrison, 1975—, ptnr. NYC, 1983—, co-chair. Litigation Dept. Monthly columnist Second Cir. Rev., NY Law Jour. Mem.: DC Bar, Assn. Bar City NY, ABA, Fed. Bar Coun. Office: Paul Weiss Rifkind Wharton & Garrison Ste 4200 1285 Avenue Of The Americas Fl 21 New York NY 10019-6065 Office Phone: 212-373-3191. Fax: 212-373-2226. E-mail: mflumenbaum@paulweiss.com.

FLUMMERFELT, JOSEPH, retired music director; b. Vincennes, Ind., Feb. 24, 1937; s. John Ross and Mavorette N. Flummerfelt. BMus, DePauw U., 1958; MusM, Phila. Conservatory Music, 1962; D in Musical Arts, U. Ill., 1971; MusD (hon.), DePauw U., Ursinus Coll., Vincennes U.; DHL (hon.), Purdue U. Dir. choral activities DePauw U., Greencastle, Ind., 1964—68, Fla. State U., Tallahassee, 1968—71; maestro del coro Spoleto Festival, Italy, 1971—93; artistic dir. Westminster Choir Coll., Princeton, NJ, 1971—2004; choral dir. NY Philharm., N.Y.C., 1971—; artistic dir. Spoleto Festival USA, Charleston, SC, 1978—; music dir. Singing City, Phila., 1996—2000. Vis. prof. U. Ind., Bloomington, 1988; vis. disting. prof. DePauw U., Greencastle, 2005. Musician: over 45 recordings. Nominee Grammy award (2); named Condr. of Yr., Musical Am., 2004; recipient Pegasus 'Oro, Mobil Oil Italiano, 1975, Gran Prix du Bisque, Disting. Alumni award, DePauw U. Avocations: reading, travel. Home: 61 Shirley Ln Lawrenceville NJ 08648

FLUSSER, PETER R., retired mathematics educator; b. Vienna; s. Rudolf J. and Blanka M. (Lipiner) F.; m. Virginia A. Huber, June 3, 1958; children: Kathy, Karen, David, Lora. BA, Ottawa U., 1958; MA, U. Kans., 1960; EdD, Okla. State U., 1971. Asst. prof. to prof. math. Ottawa U., Kans., 1960-78; asst. prof. Hays (Kans.) State U., 1978-82; prof. math. Iowa Wesleyan U., Mt. Pleasant, Iowa, 1982-86, Kans. Wesleyan U., Saline, from 1986. Health physicist Oak Ridge Nat. Lab., Tenn., 1958-63; physicist Tech/Ops, Burington, Mass., 1964, 65. Mem. editl. bd. The Math Teacher, 1997-2000; contbr. articles to profl. jours. Mem. site-com. Sunset Sch., Salina, 1995-98. Grantee Eisenhower grant, Salina, Kans., 1993. Mem. Am. Math. Soc., Nat. Coun. Tchrs. Math., Math. Assn. of Am. Avocations: chess, classical music, history, bridge. Home: Salina, Kans. Died Nov. 25, 2002.

FLUTH, JOHN ADAM, educational administrator; b. Beeville, Tex., May 19, 1954; s. John and Elouise (Perdue) F.; m. Martye René Glenn, June 22, 1991; children: Craig, Kent, Chad. PhD, Tex. A&M U., 1986; computer technician, Apple Computer, Inc., Culpertino, Calif., 1994. Cert. edni. adminstr., Tex. Surrogate parent Coastal Bend Youth City, Driscol, Tex., 1977-78, dir. halfway house Corpus Christi, Tex., 1978; tchr. spl. edn. Robstown, Tex., 1978-81; grad. asst. Tex. A&M U., College Station, Tex., 1981-86; coord. assistive tech. Region 5 Edn. Svc. Ctr., Beumont, Tex., 1986-97; dir. Tex. Acad. Leadership in the Humanities, Beaumont, 1997-98. Peer reviewer US Dept. Edn., Washington, 1995—; grant reviewer Entergy, Inc., Beaumont, Tex., 1995-98; fellow Perkins Sch. Theology So. Methodist U., Dallas, 1998—. Pres. Ptnrs. Resource Network, Tex., 1994-96, Cerebral Palsy Rehab. Ctr., 1994-96; mem. exec. bd. Boy Scouts Am., Beaumont, Tex., 1996-98; chaplain Tex. Dept. Pub. Safety Critical Incident Response Team, 2003. Olympic Torch Bearer Atlanta Com. for The Olympic Games, 1996; named Cmty. Hero, United Way, Beaumont, Tex., 1996; recipient Perkins-Prothro fellowship, Perkins Sch. of Theology, Dallas, 1998. Mem. Order of Eastern Star (worthy patron), Masons (worshipful master). E-mail: john@fluth.com.

FLY, EMERSON H., academic administrator; b. Milan, Tenn. m. Catherine Fly; 4 children. B in Acctg., U. Tenn., 1961. CPA 1962. Jr. acct. Price Waterhouse and Co., 1961—62; asst. auditor U. Tenn., Knoxville, 1962—68, internal auditor, 1968—73, vice chancellor for fin. Chattanooga, 1973—75, v.p. for bus. and fin., 1977—91, exec. v.p. Knoxville, 1991—2001, acting pres., 2001—. Past pres. So. Assn. Coll. and Univ. Bus. Officers; past higher edn. rep., adv. com. Govtl. Acctg. Stds. Bd.; charter mem., pres. East Tenn. chpt. Inst. Internal Auditors; past chair exec. com., Coun. Bus. Affairs Nat. Assn. State Univs. and Land Grant Colls.; past adv. coun. chair Tchrs. Ins. and Annuity Assn./Coll. Retirement Equities Fund. Pres. U. Tenn. Found.; past pres., treas. Jr. Achievement, Inc.; active ARC, Knoxville; bd. dirs. U. Tenn.-Battelle, Univ. Health Sys. Inc. Pilot USN, comdr. USNR. Mem.: Nat. Assn. Coll. and Univ. Bus. Officers (acctg. principles com., Disting. Bus. Officer award). Office: Office of Pub Rels Ste 107 Communications Bldg Knoxville TN 37996

FLYE, M. WAYNE, surgeon, immunologist, educator, writer; b. Tarboro, N.C., June 23, 1942; s. Charlie A. and Martha E. (Bullock) F.; m. Phyllis Webb, June 7, 1964; children: Christopher Warren, Brandon Reid. BS, U. N.C., 1964, MD, 1967; MA in Immunology, Duke U., 1972, PhD in Immunology, 1980; MA (hon.), Yale U., 1985. Diplomate Am. Bd. Surgery, Am. Bd. Thoracic Surgery, Am. Bd. Vascular Surgery. Intern. surg. Case-We. Res. U., Cleve., 1967-68, res. gen. and cardio-thoracic surgery, 1968-75; instr., teaching scholar, vascular and transplantation surgery Duke U. Med. Ctr., Durham, N.C., 1975-76; sr. investigator, chief thoracic surg. svc. NIH, Bethesda, Md., 1977-79; chief vascular surgery U. Tex. Med. Br., Galveston, 1979-82, assoc. prof. surgery and microbiology, 1980-82; dir. div. organ transplantation and immunology, prof. transplantation, dir. sect. gen. surgery Yale U. Sch. Medicine, New Haven, 1983-85; prof. surgery, molecular microbiology and immunology Washington U. Med. Sch., St. Louis, 1985—, prof. radiology, 2000—, mem. admissions com., 2000—. Trustee New Eng. Organ Bank, Boston, 1984-85; com. mem. United Network Orgn. Sharing, Richmond, Va., 1986-89; mem. anesthesiology and trauma study sect. NIH Surgery, 1991-95; merit rev. com. for surgery VA, 1994-96, chmn., 1996—; merit rev. com. Am. Heart Assn. study sect., 2001-; chief of surgery St. Louis Regional Hosp., 1996; chief thoracic surgery St. Louis VA Hosp., 1996—. Editor: Principles of Organ Transplantation, 1989, The Thymus: Regulator of Cellular Immunity, 1993, Atlas of Organ Transplantation, 1994; mem. editl. bd. Clin. Transplantation, 1986—, Prospectives in Gen. Surgery, 1988-94, Transplantation, 1989-2000, Xanthus Intelligence Unit Reports, 1990—, Shock: Molecular, Cellular and Systemic Pathobiology of Injury, 1993-99, Transplantation Sci., 1993—, Jour. Surg. Rsch., 1995-2000, Surgery, 1997—, Graft, Jour. Organ and Cellular Transplantation, 1998—, New Surgery, 2000—; assoc. editor Jour. Immunology, 1996-99, Hepatology, 2003—. Lt. col. U.S. Army, 1976-78. Recipient James W. McLaughlin medal U. Tex.-Galveston, 1982. Fellow ACP, So. Thoracic Surg. Assn. (Best Sci. Paper award 1980); mem. Am. Assn. Immunologists, Internat. Cardiovascular Soc., N.Y. Acad. Sci., Soc. Thoracic Surgeons, Am. Soc. Transplant Physicians, Am. Soc. Transplant Surgeons (program com. 1984-86, Ethics Com. 1994-95), Brit. Soc. Immunology, Transplantation Soc., Mid-Am. Transplant Assn. (bd. dirs. 1986-89), Am. Fedn. Clin. Rsch., Royal Soc. Medicine, AAAS, Surg. Infection Soc. (edn. and fellowship com. 1998-2002), Reticuloendothelial Soc., Soc. Univ. Surgeons, Soc. Clin. Vascular Surgery, Brit. Transplantation Soc., So. Assn. Vascular Surgery, Am. Coll. Chest Physicians, Soc. Surg. Oncology, Am. Assn. Thoracic Surgery, Surg. Biology Club I, Am. Assn. Study Liver Diseases, Am. Surg. Assn., So. Surg. Assn., Cen. Surg. Assn., Soc. Internat. de Chirurgie, Midwestern Vascular Surg. Soc., Soc. Vascular Surg., World Ann. Hepato-Pancreato-Bilary Surg., Soc. Surgery of Alimentary Tract, Shock Soc., Gen. Thoracic Surgery Club, Soc. Thoracic Surg., St. Louis Surg. Soc. (v.p. 2002-03, treas. 2003—), Sigma Xi, Alpha Omega Alpha., Chi Psi, Young Republicans N.C. Episcopalian. Avocations: sports, geneology, medical history. Home: 585 Coeur De Royale Dr Apt 402 Saint Louis MO 63141-6915 Office Phone: 314-362-7145. Business E-Mail: flyew@msnotes.wustl.edu.

FLYER, MICHAEL R., lawyer; b. Brooklyn, NY, Nov. 13, 1937; AB, U. Mich., 1959; JD, U. Mich. Law Sch., 1962. Bar: DC 1963. Atty. IRS, 1962—69, section chief, corp. reorganization branch, 1968—69; co-founder, ptnr. Tucker Flyer, 1969—99; (Tucker Flyer PC merged with Venable LLP, 1999); ptnr., tax & business law Venable LLP, Washington, 1999—. Adjunct prof. George Washington U. Law Sch., 1972—2001; former mem., steering com. DC Div. of Taxation; lecturer U. Mich. Law Sch. Inst. of Continuing Legal Ed., Great Plains Federal Tax Inst., Tenn. Tax Inst., Federal Bar Assn. Inst. on Federal Taxation, NYU Tax Inst. Bd. dirs. Jewish Social Service Agency, Jewish Federation of Washington. Mem.: ABA (mem. corp. tax com., taxation section), DC Bar Assn. Office: Venable LLP 575 7th St NW Washington DC 20004 Office Phone: 202-344-8520. Office Fax: 202-344-8300. Business E-Mail: mrflyer@venable.com.

FLYGARE, RICHARD ANDREW, physician assistant; s. Grant and Joan Flygare; m. Adriana Nunes, Jan. 25, 1991; children: Erica, Andrew. BS, Brigham Young U., 1994; MPAS, U. of Iowa, 1996; postgrad., Touro Coll., N.Y.C., 2001—. Cert. physician asst. Nat. Commn. on Cert. of Physician Assts., lic. ACLS ARC. Med. staff 92nd Med. Ops. Squadron USAF, Fairchild AFB, Wash., 1996—2000, med. liaison officer 92nd ARW, 1997—2000; sr. physician asst. North Idaho Dermatology, Coeur D'Alene, Idaho, 2000—. Capt. USAF, 1996—2000. Recipient Burgener Health Sci. scholarship, Brigham Young U., 1993. Fellow: Idaho Acad. Physician Assts., Soc. Dermatology Physician Assts., Am. Acad. Physician Assts. (BTLS, lectr. 2001); mem.: Idaho Med. Soc. (assoc.). Avocations: audio engineering, video editing, travel, art (pen and ink, pencil), medical photography. Office: North Idaho Dermatology Ste 370 700 Ironwood Dr Coeur D Alene ID 83814 Personal E-mail: richardflygare@hotmail.com.

FLYNN, DANIEL RICHARD, elementary school educator; b. Kenmore, N.Y., May 22, 1975; s. James Michael and Susan Jane Flynn; m. Kelly Ann Zuch, July 30, 2005. B, Buffalo State Coll., 1998, M, 2003. Cert. elem. edn. tchr. N.Y. Tchr. 4th grade Starpoint Intermediate Sch., Lockport, NY, 2001—. Co-chair report card commn. Starpoint Intermediate Sch., 2003—04, co-chair English lang. arts commn., 2002—05. Wegman's scholar, Amherst, N.Y., 1995. Avocations: golf, music, reading. Office: Starpoint Intermediate Sch 4363 Mapleton Rd Lockport NY 14094

FLYNN, DUANE JAMES, entomologist; b. Pontiac, Mich., May 26, 1949; s. Eugene Robert and Helen Elizabeth Flynn; m. Shirley Sue Barker, Sept. 12, 1969 (div. Sept. 1977); children: David Paul, Andrew Douglas; m. Pamela Ann Moyer, May 8, 1978. BA in Biology cum laude, Olivet Coll., 1971; MS in Entomology, U. Ga., 1974; postgrad., Mich. State U., 1975-80. Tech. advisor Boland Bonded Pest Control, Athens, Ga., 1973; med. entomologist Ga. Dept. Human Resources, Atlanta, 1974-75; asst. curator entomology collection Mich. State U., East Lansing, 1975-78, teaching asst. biology & entomology depts., 1975-81; rsch. asst. Lee County Mosquito Control, Ft. Myers, Fla., 1981; pest & termite inspector Orkin Exterminating, Hampton, Va., 1983-84, Charlotte, NC, 1984; curator life scis. Schiele Mus. Natural History, Gastonia, NC, 1997—. Bd. dirs. Gaston County Humane Soc., 1985—89; vol. Crowder's Mountain State Pk., Kings Mountain, NC, 1985—. Mem.: Coleopterists Soc., Entomol. Soc. Am., Gaston Audubon Soc. (pub. chmn. 1985, field trips chmn. 1987, 1993, 1994, v.p. 1986, pres. 1989, conservation chair 1990—94, chpt. rep. N.C. Audubon coun. 1987—94), Gaston County Birding Club (founder, pres. 2002—), Phi Sigma Kappa, Sigma Zeta, Alpha Chi. Democrat. Achievements include research in arthropod biodiversity, treehopper taxonomy (Hemiptera: Membracidae). Avocations: birding, insect collecting, nature walks, reading. Home: 209 Wrentree Ln Gastonia NC 28056 Office: Schiele Mus Natural History 1500 E Garrison Blvd Gastonia NC 28054 Office Phone: 704-869-1913. Business E-Mail: duanef@cityofgastonia.com.

FLYNN, GARY L., pharmaceutical executive; b. Columbus, Ohio, Oct. 8, 1949; BBA, Franklin U. Various fin. and mgmt. positions Abbott Labs., Abbott Park, Ill., 1971—, divisional v.p., contr. Ross Products divsn., 1993, v.p., contr., sr. v.p. Ross Products, 2001—. Mem. bd. dirs. Columbus Children's Hosp. Rsch. Inst.; bd. trustees Franklin U. Office: Abbott Labs 100 Abbott Park Rd Abbott Park IL 60064-6400

FLYNN, GEORGE RICHARD, poet; b. Bklyn., Aug. 14, 1926; s. Francis Joseph and Mary Josephine Flynn; m. Catherine Mary Regan, Oct. 31, 1945 (div. 1975); children: Margaret, Christine, William. BS in English Edn., NYU, 1951. Ins. claims adjuster Gt. Am. Ins. Co., N.Y.C., 1951—59; poet, 1959—72. Author: Selected Poems, 1965, The High Ground: New Poems, 1972, Zingers: 25 Poems, 1978. Served with USN, 1943—45. Avocations: physical therapy, softball, swimming, films, theater. Home: 303 W 66th St Apt 8CE New York NY 10023

FLYNN, HARRY JOSEPH, archbishop; b. Schenectady, N.Y., May 2, 1933; BA in English, MA in English, Siena Coll., Loudonville, N.Y.; ed., Mt. St. Mary's Coll., Emmitsburg, Md. Ordained priest Roman Cath. Ch., 1960. Assoc. pastor, pastor, teacher, retreat master, and spiritual leader Diocese of Albany; dean, vice rector then rector Mount St. Mary's Seminary, 1965—79; coadjutor bishop Diocese of Lafayette, La., 1986—89, bishop, 1989—94; coadjutor archbishop Archdiocese of St. Paul and Minneapolis, Minn., 1994—95, archbishop, 1995—. Chmn., bd. of trustees St. Paul Seminary, U. St. Thomas; pres. of bd. St. John Vianney Seminary; mem. com. for Black Catholics US Catholic Conference of Bishops. Address: Archdiocese of St Paul and Minneapolis 226 Summit Ave Saint Paul MN 55102-2121*

FLYNN, JOHN J., museum curator; b. Wilkes-Barre, Pa., Aug. 10, 1955; s. John J. and Phyllis B. Flynn; m. Alison L. Flynn; children: Rachel, Peter. BS cum laude, Yale U., 1977; MA, Columbia U., 1979, MPhil, 1980, PhD, 1983. Lectr. dept. geology and geophysics Yale U., New Haven, 1982; asst. prof. geol. scis. Rutgers U., New Brunswick, N.J., 1982-88; assoc. curator dept. geology Field Mus. Natural History, Chgo., 1988-92, curator dept. geology, 1992—2004, chmn. dept. geology, 1993-2000, MacArthur curator dept. geology, 1995—2004; Frick curator Am. Mus. Natural History, N.Y.C., 2004—. Co-chair Earth History and Global Change com. Systematics Agenda 2000, 1991-96; lectr. Com. on Evolutionary Biology, U. Chgo., 1990-2005, assoc. chair, 1995-2004; adj. prof. dept. biol. scis. U. Ill., Chgo., 1994-2004. Co-editor: Vertebrate Paleontology in the Neotropics: The Miocene Fauna of La Venta, Colombia, 1997, Mesozoic/Cenozoic Vertebrate Paleontology: Classic Localities, Contemporary Approaches, 1989; assoc. editor Jour. Vertebrate Paleontology, 1988-91, Systematic Paleontology, 2001—; contbr. articles to profl. jours. Grantee in field; recipient William R. Belknap prize, 1977, Best Mus. Curator award Chgo. Mag., 1995, Premio Roberto Araya award Sociedad Geologica de Chile, 2002; John S. Guggenheim fellow, 2001-02. Mem. Soc. Vertebrate Paleontology (chair affiliated soc. liaison 1986-93, mem. devel. com. 1987-89, 2002—, chair collections computerization com. 1990-93, sec. 1993-96, v.p. 1996-98, pres. 1998-2000, past pres. 2000-02, Alfred Sherwood Romer prize 1982), Geol. Soc. Am., The Paleontological Soc., Soc. Systematic Biologists. Achievements include discovery of oldest S.Am. rodent, oldest well-preserved S.Am. monkey skull, exceptional triassic vertebrates from Madagascar, work on geologic time scales. Office: Am Mus Natural History Divsn Paleontology Central Park W at 79th St New York NY 10024

FLYNN, LAURIE M., social worker; Exec. dir. Nat. Alliance for the Mentally Ill, Arlington, Va., 1984—. Bd. trustees Found. for Accountability; mem. adv. com. Johns Hopkins U. Health Svcs. Ctr., interdisciplinary adv. bd. Jour. Psychiat. Svcs., Am. Psychiat. Assn.; apptd. by Pres. Clinton to White House Nat. Bioethics Adv. Commn.; past co-chair Md. Commn. Women's Health; past mem. Nat. Task Force on Homelessness and Mental Illness; past bd. dirs. Child Welfare Inst.; mem. nat. adv. bd. Ctr. Rsch. Orgn. and Financing of Care for the Severely Mentally Ill, Rutgers U. Co-author: Care of the Seriously Mentally Ill: A Rating of State Programs, Criminalizing the Seriously Mentally Ill: The Abuse of Jails as Mental Hospitals; co-editor: Using Clinet Outcomes Information to Improve Mental Health and Substance Abuse Treatment; mem. editl. bd. Assn. Health Svcs. Rsch.; contbr. articles to profl. jours., chpts. to books. Recipient Presdl. Commendation award Am. Psychiat. Assn., 1994, Patient Advocacy award, 1995, Mental Health Sect. award APHA, McLean Hosp. award, Disting. Svc. award NAPHS and Am. Hosp. Assn., Pub. Svc. award Am. Assn. Psychosocial Rehab., 1996; Hon. fellow Academia, Medicinae & Psychiatriae Found. Office: Columbia Univ - Carmel Hill Ctr for Early Diagnosis & Treatment 1775 Broadway Ste 715 New York NY 10019

FLYNN, MARIE COSGROVE, portfolio manager, corporate financial executive; b. Honolulu, Jan. 1, 1945; d. John Aloysius and Emeline Frances Cosgrove; m. John Thomas Flynn, Jr., June 3, 1968; children: Jamie Marie, Jacqueline Elizabeth. BA, Trinity Coll., 1966. CFP, CFA. Analyst U.S. Govt., Washington, 1967-70; coord. nat. reading coun. F.X. Doherty Assocs., N.Y.C., 1970-71; security analyst Corinthian Capital Co., N.Y.C., 1971-73; portfolio mgr. Clark Mgmt. Co., Inc., N.Y.C., 1973-78; 1at v.p., sr. portfolio mgr. Lexington Mgmt. Corp., Saddle Brook, NJ, 1978-96; pres. Corinthian Capital Mgmt. Co., Inc., Morristown, NJ, 1996-99; 1st v.p., mng. dir., sr. portfolio mgr. Glenmede Trust Co., 1999—. Bd. dirs., v.p. First Call for Help, 1996—2000; bd. trustees N.J. Pension and Annuity Fund, 1996—; elected mem. Somerset County Rep. Com., 1994—98; treas. Bernardsville Rep. Com., 1996—98, Bernardsville Planning Bd., 1996—98; elected to Bernardsville Borough Coun., 1998—; mayor Bernardsville, 2002—04; commr. Bernardsville Police Commn., 2000—04; pres. Women's Polit. Caucus NJ, 2001—03; bd. dirs. Soc. Women's Health Rsch., 2004. Recipient Tribute to Women award, Patriots' Path Coun., 2002, Somerset Commn. on Women, 2004. Mem. Fin. Analysts Fedn., Inst. Chartered Fin. Analysts, N.Y. Soc. Security Analysts. Home: 50 Pickle Brook Rd Bernardsville NJ 07924-1909 Office: Carriage Ct II 264 South St Morristown NJ 07960-6078

FLYNN, MEGAN ALICE, librarian; b. Bronxville, N.Y., Oct. 30, 1967; d. Joseph Thomas and Dorothy Alice (Flood) F.; m. William D. Chura, Apr. 30, 2005. BA, Boston Coll., 1988; MS, Simmons Coll., 1991. Ref. libr. Thomas Crane Pub. Libr., Quincy, Mass., 1993-97; ref. and collection devel. libr. Wellesley (Mass.) Free Libr., 1997—. Mem. ALA. Home: 9 Bower St Medford MA 02155 Office: Wellesley Free Libr 530 Washington St Wellesley MA 02482-5916 Fax: 781-237-1354. Business E-Mail: mflynn@minlib.net.

FLYNN, MICHAEL J., real estate executive; Chmn., pres. Slattery Assocs., Inc., N.Y.C., 1988-96; pres., vice chmn. Kimco Realty Corp.; chmn. Blue Ridge Real Estate Co. Mem. Urban Land Inst. (Coun. Comml. and Retail Devel.), Internat. Coun. Shopping Ctrs. (bd. trustees). Office: Kimco Realty Corp 3333 New Hyde Rd New Hyde Park NY 11042

FLYNN, NORMA JEAN, librarian; b. Fitzhugh, Okla., Sept. 17, 1934; d. Marion Alfred and Rosa Lee (Brady) Sorrels; m. Robert L. Flynn, June 1, 1953; children: Deirdre Siobhan, Brigid Erin (dec.). BA, Baylor U., 1962; MLS, Our Lady of Lake U., 1976. Tchr. Waco (Tex.) Pub. Schs., 1962-63, Holmes High Sch., San Antonio, 1963-67, 71-76, Ursuline Acad., San Antonio, 1967-71; libr. Thunderbird Hills Elem., San Antonio, 1976-84, Sam Rayburn Mid. Sch., San Antonio, 1985-93. Libr. cons., presenter workshops, 1976—; guest speaker in schs., 1982—. Author: Jim Bowie: A Texas Legend, 1980, Stephen F. Austin: The Father of Texas, 1981, William Barret Travis: Victory or Death, 1982, James Walter Fannin: Remember Goliad, 1983, James Butler Bonham: The Rebel Hero, 1985, Lady: A Biogrpahy of Claudia Alta (Lady Bird) Johnson, 1992, Anson Jones: Last President of the Republic of Texas, 1997, Annie Oakley: Legendary Sharpshooter, 1998, Texas Women Who Dared to Be First, 1999, Henry B. Gonzalez: A Rebel With a Cause, 2004; ednl. videos: Heroes of the Texas Revolution, 1995, The Spanish Mission of Texas, 1996. Vol. Dem. Party Campaigning, San Antonio, 1990; mem. San Antonio Conservation Soc. Named Woman of Yr. in Svc., San Antonio Express-News Corp., 1987. Mem. Tex. Libr. Assn., Bexar Libr. Assn., Tex. Folklore Soc. Democrat. Baptist. Avocations: travel, walking, reading. Home: 101 Cliffside Dr San Antonio TX 78231-1510

FLYNN, OWEN V., information technology executive; Sr. v.p. & CTO Equifax, Inc., Atlanta. Named one of top tech. innovators, Info. Week mag., 2004. Avocation: running. Office: CTO Equifax Inc 1550 Peachtree St NW Atlanta GA 30309

FLYNN, PATRICIA M., director, special education educator, gifted and talented educator; b. East Cleveland, Ohio, Sept. 11, 1952; d. Harry L. and Eleanore (Mahon) Flynn. BS in Edn. magna cum laude, St. John Coll., Cleve., 1974, MS in Edn., 1975; cert., Notre Dame Coll., 1992, Ursuline Coll., 2001. Cert. elem. edn., prin., edn. handicapped Ohio Detp. Edn. Reading specialist East Cleveland City Schs., 1974—98, reading coord., 1998—2000, curriculum specialist, 2000—01; dir. pupil svcs. Fairview Park (Ohio) Schs., 2001—. Local coord. Reading Is Fundamental Project, East Cleveland, 1996—2000; coord. East Cleveland Elem. Acad., East Cleveland, 1999. Scholar, St. John Coll., 1974. Mem.: Nat. Assn. Fed. Edn. Program Adminstrs., Internat. Reading Assn., Ohio Assn. Adminstrs. State and Fed. Edn. Programs, Ohio Assn. Pupil Svcs. Adminstrs., Irish Am. Club, City Club Cleve., Kappa Gamma Pi. Roman Catholic. Office: Fairview Park City Schs 20770 Lorain Rd Fairview Park OH 44126 E-mail: pflynn@leeca.org.

FLYNN, PAUL BARTHOLOMEW, foundation executive; b. Quincy, Mass., Sept. 17, 1935; s. Bartholomew Joseph and Katherine Marie (Coleman) F.; m. Aline Therese Nicholson, Feb. 11, 1961; children: Bonnie Marie, Laureen P., Elizabeth A., Bernadette J. AB, Stonehill Coll., 1957; LL.D. (hon.), Allentown Coll., 1985. Sportswriter The Patriot Ledger, Quincy, 1955-63, cmty. rels. dir., 1963-65; dir. pub. rels. Mass. Tchrs. Assn., Boston, 1965-66; asst. dir. pub. svc. Rochester (N.Y.) Democrat and Chronicle and The Times-Union, 1966-71, dir. pub. svc. and rsch., 1971-72; dir. advt. Huntington (W.Va.) Herald-Dispatch and Advertiser, 1972-74, Binghamton (N.Y.) Press and Sun-Bulletin, 1974-76; dir. mktg. services Gannett Co., Rochester, N.Y., 1976-77; gen. mgr. Jour.-News, Nyack, N.Y., 1977; pres., pub. Fort Myers (Fla.) News-Press, 1977-84; S.E. regional v.p. Gannett Co., 1981-83; exec. v.p. USA Today, Washington, 1983-84, pres., 1984; pres., pub. Pensacola News-Jour., Fla., 1984-87; v.p. Gannett South Newspaper Group, 1985-87; exec. v.p. Foster's Daily Democrat, Dover, N.H., 1989-93; dir. mktg. and pub. rels. Strawbery Banke Mus., Portsmouth, N.H., 1993-95; mktg. cons. Jour.-Transcript Newspapers, N.H., Maine, 1995-96; v.p. Susan Bennett Mktg. & Media, Fort Myers, Fla., 1996-97; exec. dir. Southwest Fla. Community Found., Ft. Myers, Fla., 1997—2004, pres., CEO, 2004—. V.p. Gannett Newspaper Advt. Sales, N.Y.C., 1976-77 Author: You Can Make News, 1996; co-editor: Promoting the Total Newspaper, 1977. Pres. Lend-A-Hand Fund S.W. Fla., S.W. Fla. coun. Boy Scouts Am., 1981, adv. bd., 1997—, commr. Daniel Webster coun., 1989-96, v.p., 1995-96; bd. dirs. Lee County United Way, 1979-84, campaign chmn., 1981; bd. dirs. Edison C.C. Endowment Fund, 1978-83, Sr. Friendship Ctrs., Inc., 1981-83, United Way Pensacola, Sacred Heart Hosp. Found., Pensacola Jr. Coll. Found.; mem. adv. bd. Stonehill Coll., 1984, trustee, 1987-92. With U.S. Army, 1957-58. Recipient Disting. Service award B'nai B'rith of Cape Coral, Fla., 1979; Gold medal for good citizenship SAR, 1980; disting. alumni award Stonehill Coll., 1984; Patriotism citation Freedom's Found., 1986, Legacy award ARC, 2003. Mem. Internat. Newspaper Promotion Assn. (bd. dirs. 1977-78), Fla. Fedn. Cmty. Founds. (treas. 2003—), Greater Dover C. of C. (bd. dirs. 1989-93), Stonehill Coll. Alumni Assn., Rotary Ft. Myers. (bd. dirs. 2000-02, 05-). Roman Catholic.

FLYNN, PETER ANTHONY, judge; b. Bronxville, N.Y., July 23, 1942; s. Ralph Harold and Caroline (Lindberg) F. BA magna cum laude, Harvard U., 1963; LLB, Yale U., 1966. Bar: Ill. 1969, U.S. Dist. Ct. (no. and so. dists.) Ill. 1969, U.S. Ct. Appeals (7th cir.) 1969, U.S. Supreme Ct. 1976, U.S. Dist. Ct. (ea. dist.) Wis. 1980, U.S. Ct. Appeals (2d and 5th cirs.) 1980, U.S. Ct. Appeals (9th cir.) 1987. Asst. lect. law U. Ife, 1967-69; assoc. Jenner & Block, Chgo., 1969-75; ptnr. Cherry & Flynn, Chgo., 1976-99; judge Cir. Ct. of Cook County, Ill., 1999—; adj. prof. The John Marshall Law Sch., 2002—. Mem. Olympia Fields Plan Commn., Ill., 1979-83, chmn., 1983-85; trustee Village of Olympia Fields, 1985-89; pres. Touchstone Theatre, 1990-93; active U.S. Peace Corps, 1967-69. Mem. ABA, Ill. Bar Assn., Am. Law Inst., Yale Law Sch. Assn. (nat. exec. com. 2002-05), Chgo. Lincoln Inn of Ct., Chgo. Bar Assn. (vice chair comml. litigation com. 2003-04). Avocations: theater, piano, poetry, guitar, choral music, sailing, history.

FLYNN, SARAH CHAPIN, editor; b. Washington, July 28, 1950; d. John Patrick and Hulda Rees Flynn; m. David Mark Prosten, Nov. 7, 2003. Student, Sarah Lawrence Coll., 1967—69; BA, Rutgers U., 1971. Assoc. editor Real Paper, Cambridge, Mass., 1975—80; manuscript editing supr. Houghton Mifflin Co., Boston, 1986—88, manuscript editor, 1982—86; freelance book editor, cons. Annapolis, Md., 1988—. Co-chair adv. com. Writers' Rm. Boston, Boston, 1989—90. Author (with H. Hampton and S. Fayer): Voices of Freedom: An Oral History of the Civil Rights Movement from the 1950s to the 1980s; editor: numerous books for general readers. Bd. dirs. Friends of Quiet Waters Pk., Annapolis, 1997—2000. Mem.: Nat. Writers Union, Washington Ind. Writers, Pen Am. Ctr., Dem. Club (pres. dist. 30 2005—). Democrat. Avocations: reading, cooking, travel. Personal E-mail: sarahflynn@comcast.net.

FLYNN, SCOTT D., lawyer; b. Washington, Iowa, Mar. 2, 1971; s. Daniel D. and Vickie L. Flynn. BS in Agrl. Engring., Iowa State U., 1994; JD, U. Iowa, 2000. Bar: Iowa, 2000. Rsch. asst. engring. ext. Iowa State U., Ames, 1991-92; laboror Carriage House Meats, Ames, 1993; tax asst. Neuzil & Sanderson, Iowa City, 1998-2000; legal clk. Garst Seed Co./Advanta USA, Inc., Slater, Iowa, 1998; assoc. Davis, Brown, Koehn, Shors & Roberts, P.C., Des Moines, 1999—; ptnr. Flynn Farms, Keota, Iowa. Reader, min. Newman Cath. Student Ctr., Iowa City, 1999-2000. Mem. ABA, Am. Numismatic Assn., Am. Farm Bur., Am. Agrl. Law Assn., Am. Soc. Agrl. Engrs., Iowa Numismatic Assn., Iowa Farm Bur., Iowa Bar Assn., Coun. for Agrl. Sci. and Tech., Polk County Bar Assn., Washington County Farm Bur., Ctrl. Iowa Alpha Gamma Rho Chpt., Iowa State U. Alumni Assn., Crohn's & Colitis Found. Am., Phi Delta Phi, Alpha Gamma Rho Ednl. Found. Eta Chpt. (sec. 2000-01, v.p. 2001-02, pres. 2002-03, treas. 2003-), Eta Alumni Corp. Alpha Gamma Rho (sec. 2000-01, v.p. 2001-02, pres. 2002--03, treas. 2003—). Avocations: coin collecting/numismatics, model trains. Home: 1917 NW Third St Ankeny IA 50021 Office: Davis Brown Koehn Shors & Roberts PC Ste 2500 666 Walnut St Des Moines IA 50309 E-mail: Scott.Flynn@lawiowa.com.

FLYNN, TIMOTHY P., finance company executive; m. Susan Flynn; children: Laura, Tyler. BA in Acctg., U. St. Thomas. With KPMG LLP, NYC, 1988—, various positions including vice chair audit and risk advisory svcs., vice chair human resources; chmn., CEO, 2005—. Mem. dean's advisory coun. Coll. Commerce and Fin. Villanova U.; mem. fin. com. Most Blessed Sacrament parish, Franklin Lakes, NJ; bd. dirs. YMCA, NY. Office: KPMG LLP 345 Park Ave New York NY 10154-0102 Office Phone: 212-909-5029. Office Fax: 212-758-9819.

FLYNN, WILLIAM JOSEPH, insurance company executive; b. N.Y.C., Sept. 6, 1926; s. William and Anne (Connors) F.; m. Margaret M. Collins, Mar. 21, 1952; children: William, Maureen, James, Robert. MA in Econs., Fordham U., 1951. V.p. group ops. Equitable, N.Y.C., 1953-71; pres. Mut. Am. Life Ins., N.Y.C., 1971-72, pres., CEO, 1972-82, chmn. bd., CEO, 1982—. Bd. dirs. Richmond Hill Savs. Bank, Floral Park, N.Y. Pres. bd. dirs. N.Y. Foundling Hosp., N.Y.; bd. dirs. U.S. Cath. Hist. Soc., S.I., N.Y., United Student Aid Funds, Indpls., Coll. Constrn. Loan Ins. Assn., Washington, Elie Wiesel Found. for Humanity, N.Y.C., Williamsburg Charter Found., Washington, United Student Aid Fund, N.Y.C., United Way Internat., Alexandria, Va; past chmn. adv. com. U.S. Holocaust Meml. Council, Bd. Life Ins. Council N.Y., St. Vincent's Svcs. Served with USAF, 1951-53, Korea. Recipient Disting. Community Service award Brandeis U. 1980, Ubi Cantas Deus Ibi award Cath. Charities 1983, Nat. Profl. Leadership award United Way Am. 1984, Brotherhood award NCCJ, 1984, Disting. Service award United Way Bergen County, 1985. Mem. Am. Council Life Ins. Clubs: University (N.Y.C.); Garden City (N.Y.) Country. Avocations: golf, reading. Home: 69 2nd St Garden City NY 11530-4322 Office: Mutual of Am Life 680 5th Ave New York NY 10019-5429

FLYNN-CONNORS, ELIZABETH KATHRYN, editor; b. Chgo., Aug. 17, 1939; d. Timothy Carver Flynn and Elizabeth Eleanor (Tait) Scanlon; m. Gerald Martin Connors, Dec. 30, 1978; children: Andrew, Kathryn, Elizabeth. Student, Monmouth Coll., Ill., 1957-59; BA in Journalism, U. Wis., 1961, postgrad., 1965-66. Cityside reporter Mpls. Tribune, 1961-62, Chgo. Daily News, 1962-66, UN/N.Y. corr., 1966-75, Washington corr., 1968; writer, press officer UN, N.Y.C., 1975-82; sr. writer UN Chronicle, N.Y.C., 1982-85, editor-in-chief, 1985-96; chief editor Yearbook of UN, N.Y.C., 1996-99; chief UN pubs., N.Y.C., 1999—. Troop leader Girl Scouts U.S., Tarrytown, N.Y., 1993-95. Russell Sage fellow U. Wis., 1965-66; recipient Investigative Reporting award Sigma Delta Chi, 1962, 1st Pl. Spot News award AP, 1970. Mem. UN Corrs. Assn. (alumni), Sleepy Hollow Sr. Citizens Club (sec.),

White Plains Garden Club, Phi Beta Kappa, Kappa Delta. Avocations: reading, watching old movies. Home: 238 Hunter Ave Sleepy Hollow NY 10591-1317 E-mail: betty1153@aol.com.

FLYNT, CANDACE LAMBETH, writer; b. Greensboro, NC, Mar. 12, 1947; d. Ralph MacAulay Lambeth, Dorothea Elaine Patterson, James Hoyt Bray (Stepfather), Helen Marie Craven (Stepmother); m. John Franklin Kime; children: MacAulay, Charles, Elizabeth, Stuart Kime, Jordan Kime, Katherine Kime; m. Charles Homer Flynt (div. Dec. 3, 1991). BA, Greensboro Coll., 1969, DLitt, 2004; MFA, U. N.C., Greensboro, 1974. Reporter Greensboro (NC) Record, 1969—73. Pres., CEO Lambeth Enterprises Inc., 2005—. Author: (novel) Mother Love, 1987, Sins of Omission, 1984, Chasing Dad, 1980. Trustee Greensboro Coll., 1985—; pres. Lambeth Enterprises Inc., 2005. Episcopalian. Avocation: photography. Home: 2005 Madison Avenue Greensboro NC 27403

FOARD, DOUGLAS W., educational association administrator; b. Balt., Oct. 23, 1939; s. George Winfield and Anna (Herrmann) F.; m. Janet Hess, Aug. 26, 1961; children: Wendy Lynn, Scott Douglas. BA, Randolph-Macon Coll., 1961; MA, U. Va., 1965; PhD, Washington U., 1972; LHD (hon.), Randolph-Macon Coll., 1992, Hampden Sydney Coll., 2001. Asst. to dir. pub. rels. Ferrum (Va.) Coll., asst. prof. history, 1965-70, chair social sci., 1970-79, prof. history, 1972-85, assoc. dean, 1979-81; program officer NEH, Washington, 1985-89; exec. sec. Phi Beta Kappa, Washington, 1989-2001; dir. Loudoun (Va.) County Mus., 2001—. Adj. prof. history George Mason U., Fairfax, Va. Author: The Revolt of the Aesthetes, 1989; contbr. articles to profl. jours.; guest editor Mag. of History, 1991. Bd. dirs. Nat. Humanities Alliance, 1994-2001, mem. exec. com., 1997-2000; bd. dirs. Nat. History Day, Washington, 1987-2001; bd. dirs. Va. Found. for Humanities and Pub. Policy, 1990-96, chmn., 1995-96; trustee Randolph-Macon Coll., 2001—. Grantee Ford Found. 1969-70; James Still fellow U. Ky. 1983, Nat. Defense Act fellow Washington U., 1967-70, Philip DuPont fellow U. Va., 1961-62, Ford Found. fellow Asian Studies, 1967, Nat. Meth. scholar Randolph-Macon Coll., 1960-61; NEH summer seminar Vanderbilt U., 1976. Mem. Soc. Spanish & Portuguese Hist. Studies (newsletter editor 1982-85) Va. Soc. History Tchrs. (pres. 1981-83), Phi Beta Kappa. Address: 38998 Bolington Rd Lovettsville VA 20180

FOARD, SUSAN LEE, editor; b. Asheville, NC, Aug. 1, 1938; d. Carson Cowan and Anne (Brown) F. AB, Salem Coll., 1960; MA, William and Mary Coll., 1966. Asst. editor Inst. Early Am. Hist. and Culture, Williamsburg, Va., 1961-66, assoc. editor, 1966; editor U. Va. Press, Charlottesville, 1966—2004.

FOCER-RICHARDS, LINDA JEAN, library director; b. Pitts., Oct. 24, 1935; d. Samuel Walter Focer and Mary Isabelle Murphy; m. Daniel Taddeo, Aug. 6, 1956 (div. Sept. 1984); children: Laurie Lane, Dana Belkot, Christian Focer Taddeo; m. George S. Richards, Feb. 24, 1998. BA in English, Geneva Coll., 1958; M Info. Sci., U. Pitts., 1982. Elem. sch. tchr. Avon (Ohio) Pub. Schs., 1967-70, Sweickley (Pa.) Presch., 1974-78; children's librarian Beaver (Pa.) Meml. Libr., 1978-81; dir. Carnegie Free Libr., Beaver Falls, Pa., 1983—. Mem. adv. bd. Big Bros./Big Sisters, Beaver County, Pa., 1990-92, Adult Literacy Project, Beaver County, 1992-94, Pride, Beaver Falls; mem. Beaver County Tourist Promotion Agy., Monaca, Pa., 1993-95; treas. Beaver Falls Bus. Dist. Authority, 1995—. Recipient cert. of merit CCBC Prevention Project, 1997. Mem. Afro-Am. Folk History Assn. (bd. dirs.), Outlook Club (com. chair 1985—), Merrick Art Gallery. Avocations: little theater work, writing, boating, travel. Office: Carnegie Free Libr 1301 7th Ave Beaver Falls PA 15010-4219

FOCH, NINA, actress, creative consultant, film director, educator; b. Leyden, The Netherlands, Apr. 20, 1924; came to U.S. 1927; d. Dirk and Consuelo (Flowerton) F.; m. James Lipton, June 6, 1954; m. Dennis de Brito, Nov. 27, 1959; 1 child, Dirk de Brito; m. Michael Dewell, Oct. 31, 1967 (div.). Grad., Lincoln Sch., 1939; studies with Stella Adler. Adj. prof. drama U. So. Calif., Grad. Sch. Cinema & TV, L.A., 1966—68, 1978—80, adj. prof. film, 1987—; creative cons. to dirs., writers, prodrs. of all media. Artist-in-residence U. N.C., 1966, Ohio State U., 1967, Calif. Inst. Tech., 1969-70; mem. sr. faculty Am. Film Inst., 1974-77; founder, tchr. Nina Foch Studio, Hollywood, Calif., 1973—; founder, actress Los Angeles Theatre Group, 1960-65; bd. dirs. Nat. Repertory Theatre, 1967-75. Motion picture appearances include Nine Girls, 1944, Return of the Vampire, 1944, Shadows in the Night, 1944, Cry of the Werewolf, 1944, Escape in the Fog, 1945, A Song to Remember, 1945, My Name Is Julia Ross, 1945, I Love a Mystery, 1945, Johnny O'Clock, 1947, The Guilt of Janet Ames, 1947, The Dark Past, 1948, The Undercover Man, 1949, Johnny Allegro, 1949, An American in Paris, 1951, Scaramouche, 1952, Young Man with Ideas, 1952, Sombrero, 1953, Fast Company, 1953, Executive Suite, 1954 (Oscar award nominee), Four Guns to the Border, 1954, You're Never Too Young, 1955, Illegal, 1955, The Ten Commandments, 1956, Three Brave Men, 1957, Cash McCall, 1959, Spartacus, 1960, Such Good Friends, 1971, Salty, 1973, Mahogany, 1976, Jennifer, 1978, Rich and Famous, 1981, Skin Deep, 1988, Sliver, 1993, Morning Glory, 1993, 'Til There Was You, 1996, Hush, 1998, Shadow of Doubt, 1998, How to Deal, 2003; appeared in Broadway plays including John Loves Mary, 1947, Twelfth Night, 1949, A Phoenix Too Frequent, 1950, King Lear, 1950, Second String, 1960; appeared with Am. Shakespeare Festival in Taming of the Shrew, Measure for Measure, 1956, San Francisco Ballet and Opera in The Seven Deadly Sins, 1966; also many regional theater appearances including Seattle Repertory Theatre (All Over, 1972 and The Seagull, 1973); actress on TV, 1947—, including Playhouse 90, Studio One, Pulitzer Playhouse, Playwrights 56, Producers Showcase, Lou Grant (Emmy nominee 1980), Mike Hammer; series star: Shadow Chasers, 1985, War and Remembrance, 1988, LA Law, 1990, Hunter, 1990, Dear John, 1990, 91, Tales of the City, 1993, Dharma and Greg, 1999, Just Shoot Me, 2000, recurring role Bull, 2000-01, State of Grace, 2003, When We Were Grown-ups, 2004, NCIs, 2005; many other series, network spls. and TV films; TV panelist and guest on The Dinah Shore Show, Merv Griffin Show, The Today Show, Dick Cavett, The Tonight Show; TV moderator: Let's Take Sides, 1957-59; assoc. dir. (film) The Diary of Anne Frank, 1959; dir. (nat. tour and on-Broadway) Tonight at 8:30, 1966-67, Family Blessings, 1997; assoc. producer re-opening of Ford's Theatre, Washington, 1968. Hon. chmn. Los Angeles chpt. Am. Cancer Soc., 1970. Recipient Film Daily award, 1949, 53. Mem. AAUP, Acad. Motion Picture Arts and Scis. (co-chair exec. com. fgn. film award, membership com., chair foreign lang. award com., 1998-99), Hollywood Acad. TV Arts and Scis. (bd. govs. 1976-77). Avocation: work. Office: PO Box 1884 Beverly Hills CA 90213-1884 Office Phone: 310-553-5805.

FOCHT, JOHN ARNOLD, JR., engineer; b. Rockwall, Tex., Aug. 31, 1923; s. John Arnold and Fay (Goss) F.; m. Edith Rials, Aug. 8, 1950; children: John Arnold III, Judith Lynn Schweitzer. BSCE, U. Tex., 1944; MSCE, Harvard U., 1946. Soils engr. U.S. Waterways Expt. Sta., Vicksburg, Miss., 1947-50, 52-53; sr. soils engr. McClelland Engrs., Inc., Houston, 1953-55, v.p. engring., 1955-72, exec. v.p., 1972-87; v.p. TERA, Inc., 1965-85; chmn. bd. Fugro-McClelland Inc., 1987-90; cons., 1991-99, Focht Consultants, Inc., 1999—2004. Contbr. articles to tech. jours. Chmn. ofcl. bd. Grace Methodist Ch., 1960-62; bd. dirs. N.W. YMCA, 1957-59; chmn. vis. com. dept. civil engring. U. Tex., Austin, 1974. Served to capt. AUS, 1944-46, 50-52. Recipient Disting. Engring. Grad. award, U. Tex., Austin, 1964, Tech. Pioneer for Found. Design, Offshore Energy Ctr., 2001. Fellow: ASCE (pres. Tex. sect. 1970—71, nat. dir. 1980—83, nat. pres. 1989—90, Thomas A. Middlebrooks award 1957, James Laurie prize 1959, Civil Engring. State of the Art award 1971, Thomas A. Middlebrooks award 1976, Civil Engring. State of the Art award 1979, Terzaghi lectr. 1993, William H. Wisely Am. Civil Engr. award 1999, GeoInst. Hero 2002, Tex. Sect. Lifetime Svc. award 2002); mem.: NSPE, NAE, Instn. Engrs. Ireland, Inst. Profl. Practice (dir. 1996—99), Houston Engring. and Sci. Soc. (treas., dir. 1973—76), Tex. Coun. Engring. Labs. (dir. 1972—75), Cons. Engrs. Coun. Tex. (dir. 1965—67), Am. Cons. Engrs. Coun., Tex. Soc. Profl. Engrs. (Engr. of Yr. award 1987), Tau Beta Pi, Chi Epsilon (Nat. Honor Mem. 2000). Methodist. Home: 12226 Perthshire Rd Houston TX 77024-4244

FOCHT, SANDRA JEAN, retired elementary school educator; b. Santa Monica, Calif., Aug. 1, 1944; d. George Allen and Pauline Estella De Bra; m. R. Duane Focht, Feb. 1, 1964; children: Jeremy D., Jennifer R. BS in Edn., Wright State Univ., 1969, MEd in Ednl. Media, 1981, cert. in Gifted Edn. 1-12, 1985. Cert. elem. tchr. Ohio, tchr. gifted Ohio. Tchr. Parkwood Elem., Beavercreek, Ohio, 1970—99, Ankeney Middle Sch., Beavercreek, 1999—2004; ret., 2004. Pres., dir. Beavercreek (Ohio) Cmty. Theatre, 1994—99; adv. Muse Machine, Dayton, Ohio, 1995—2004; founder Jr. Thespian Chpt. at Ankeney Middle Sch. Co-author: (textbook) Writing Step By Step, 1986. Recipient Golden Apple Achievement award, Ashland Oil, 1996; Jennings scholar, 1975. Mem.: NEA, Ednl. Theatre Assn., Ohio Edn. Assn., Nat. Coun. Tchrs. English, Phi Delta Kappa. Avocations: writing, directing plays, directing musicals, photography. Home: 224 Cleek Springs Ct Dayton OH 45440 Office Phone: 937-429-7567.

FOCHT, THEODORE HAROLD, lawyer, educator; Teaching assoc. Columbia U. Sch. Law, N.Y.C., 1959-60; atty. Office of Gen. Counsel SEC, Washington, 1960-61, legal asst. to Commr., Washington, 1961-63; mem. faculty U. Conn. Sch. Law, Hartford, 1963-71 (leave of absence, 1969-71); spl. counsel on securities legislation Interstate and Fgn. Commerce Com., U.S. Ho. of Reps., Washington, 1969-71; gen. counsel Securities Investor Protection Corp., Washington, 1971-94, pres., 1984-94; adj. prof. law American U. Sch. Law, Washington, 1979-84; mem. Fla. State Comptroller's Task Force on Regulatory DeCoupling, 1995. Home: 8436 Pinafore Dr New Port Richey FL 34653-6739

FOCKLER, HERBERT HILL, foundation executive; b. Summersville, W.Va., Feb. 18, 1922; s. William Okey and Annie Lee (Fitzwater) Fockler; m. Mary Hildegarde Ziegler, May 15, 1950; 1 child, Herbert. BA, W.Va. U., 1947, MA, 1948; cert., Oxford (Eng.) U., 1948, Harvard U., 1949; MS in Libr. Sci., Cath. U. Am., 1952. Adminstr. libr. Princeton (N.J.) U., 1952-54, Library of Congress, Washington, 1956-58; advisor White House Confs., Washington, 1959-60; exec. NIH, Bethesda, Md., 1961-69; chmn. Sci. and Tech. Coms., Washington, 1969-70; exec. dir. Sci. Founds., Washington, 1971-72; trustee, chmn. Am. Arts Internat. Found., Washington, pres., 1984—, also bd. dirs.; trustee Nat. Mus. of Health and Medicine Found., 1989—. Adv. Nat. Coun. for Sci. and Environment, 2000—; chmn., trustee World Tech. Found., Washington, 1988-89; bd. dirs. Nat. Info. Tech. Ctr.; advisor NSF, 1975, White House Conf. on Bus., 1975, 78, Montgomery Coll., Rockville, Md., 1978, World Bank, 1986, Winston Churchill Found., 1988, IMF, 1991, others; adv. coun. Coolfont Found., Berkeley Springs, W.Va., 1980-87; mem. Presdl. Rsch. Group; assoc. Woodrow Wilson Internat. Ctr., 1988—; mem. Bd. on Sci. Edn.; advisor Global Internet, 2000-01; bd. dirs. Calif. Ctr. for Strategic Studies, 2001—. Editor: Contemporary South, 1968, also conf. records and newsletters; contbr. articles to profl. jours. Adv. Stanford U., 1967-69, Georgetown U., 1975-85; trustee Threshold Environ. Found., Washington, 1969-75, Nat. Mus. Health and Medicine Found., 1989-90, adv. coun., 1991—; mem. pres.'s coun. Shenandoah Coll., Winchester, Va., 1982-87; mem. Found. Advancement Edn. in Scis., 1980—, Joint Bd. Edn. in Sci. and Engring., 1991—; bd. dirs. Nat. Mus. of Lang., 1999—, Global Children's Health Fund, 1999—, Nat. Fgn. Lang. Ctr., 2000—; chmn. Sustainable Value Found., 2003—. Staff sgt. U.S. Army, 1941-45. Mem. AAAS, Acad. Polit. Sci., Am. Polit. Sci. Assn., Washington Acad. Scis. (bd. dirs.), U.N. Assn., Smithsonian Assocs., Am. Assn. Mus., Air and Space Mus., Nat. Trust Hist. Preservation, Libr. Congress Assocs., Colonial Williamsburg Found., SAR, Fgn. Policy Inst., World Affairs Coun., Policy Studies Orgn., Found. for Advancement Edn. in Sci., Internet Soc., Smithsonian Assocs., Am. Film Inst., Harvard Club, Princeton Club, W.Va. Club, W.Va. Acad. Sci., Nat. Press Club. Home and Office: 10710 Lorain Ave Silver Spring MD 20901-1512

FODERARO, ANTHONY HAROLDE, nuclear engineering educator; b. Scranton, Pa., Apr. 3, 1926; s. Edward and Myrtha (Bachman) F.; m. Rita Lacey, May 4, 1953; children— Anthony, John, Diana. BS in Physics, U. Scranton, 1950; PhD in Physics, U. Pitts., 1955. Supervisory scientist Westinghouse Atomic Power Div., Pitts., 1954-56; sr. nuclear physicist Gen. Motors Research, Warren, Mich., 1956-60; assoc. prof. nuclear engring. Pa. State U., University Park, 1960-63, prof., 1963-88; prof. emeritus, 1989—. Cons. on radiation protection govt. and industry. Author: The Elements of Neutron Interaction Theory, 1971, The Photon Shielding Manual, 1976; co-author: The Reactor Shielding Design Manual, 1956, The Engineering Compendium on Radiation Shielding, 1968; contbr. articles to publs. in field. Served with U.S. Army, 1944-46. Fellow Am. Nuclear Soc. (chmn. radiation protection and shielding div. 1969-70); mem. Am. Phys. Soc., Am. Assn. Physics Tchrs. Home: 301 S Gill St State College PA 16801-3963 E-mail: tony@foderaro.com.

FODIMAN, AARON ROSEN, publishing executive; b. Stamford, Conn., Oct. 10, 1937; s. Yale J. and Thelma F. BS, Tulane U., 1958; LLB, NYU, 1960, MBA, 1961; grad., L'Academie de CuisineCanardier, Washington, 1977. Bar: N.Y. 1960, D.C. 1961, Va. 1965. With FTC, Washington, 1961-65; practiced in Arlington, Va., 1965-78; pres. Fast Food Operators, Inc., N.Y.C., 1978-84, Hampton Healthcare, 1984-91, Kapok Tree Restaurants, Tampa Bay Publs., 1986—. Author: Life is not an Illusion, it Just Looks That Way, 1998; pub., editor: Tampa Bay Mag.; TV host local sports show, Dine Line, Tampa Bay Mag. Bd. dirs. Tampa Players Inc., Washington Ballet, Manhattan Punch Line Theatre, Kent Jewish Cmty. Ctr., Mahaffey Theater Found., Outdoor Art Found., Clearwater Arts Found., pres., chmn., 2003; bd. advisors Fla. Orch.; pres. Dunedin Art Ctr., Bay Ballet Theatre; chmn. Pinellas County Arts Coun., Golda Meir Ctr., Bay Ballet Theatre, A Taste of Pinellas; cmty. advisor Clearwater Dunedin Jr. League; mem. adv. bd. Am. Film Inst.; chmn. Ford Presdl. Campaign, 1976; advisor Fed. Res. Bank Atlanta; participant Leadership Pinellas; participant, founder Leadership Tampa Bay, Nat. Conf. Christians and Jews; Pinellas County amb. to Ringling Mus. Art. Recipient Hyam Soloman Freedom award, 1974, Miniature Palette award Miniature Art Soc. of Fla., 1987, Order of Salvador medal Dali Mus., 1989, Lifetime Achievement award Internat. Restaurant and Hospitality Rating Bur., 2000, Friends of Arts Pinellas County award, Svc. to Mankind award Sertoma Club, Arts Patron award Tampa Bay Bus. Com. for the Arts, 2003, arts award Tampa Bay Com. for the Arts, 2003; knighted as Baron Order of St. John of Jerusalem, 1999. Mem. Pinellas County Restaurant Assn. (pres.), Tampa Bay Restaurant Assn. (pres.), Fla. Restaurant Assn. (bd. dirs.), Tampa Bay Bus. Com. Arts (Bus. in Arts award 2003), Tampa Bay Food and Wine Soc., Chaine des Rotisseurs (chpt. officer), Internat. Legal Frat., Phi Delta Phi, Barrister Inn Club (Washington, pres.), B'nai Brith (pres. Washington). Office Phone: 727-791-4800.

FODOR, IMOLA KATALIN, mathematician, researcher; b. Targu Mures, Romania, May 5, 1971; arrived in U.S., 1990; d. Ludovic Fodor and Katalin Maria Barbassy; BA, Rutgers U., 1994; MA, U. Calif., Berkeley, 1996, PhD, 1999. Statis. cons. Kwasha Lipton, Ft. Lee, N.J., 1994; sr. tech. assoc. AT&T Bell Labs., Murray Hill, N.J., 1994; statis. cons. U. Calif., Berkeley, 1995, 97, grad. student rschr., 1996-99, Livermore, 1997; postdoctoral rschr. Lawrence Livermore Nat. Lab., 1999-2000, computational mathematician, 2000—. Contbr. articles to profl. jours. Fellow, AT&T Bell Labs., 1994—99, Grad., NSF, 1994—97; scholar Rutgers Coll. Merit, Rutgers U., 1993. Mem.: AAAS, Inst. Math. Stats., Am. Statis. Assn., Nat. Ctr. Sci. Edn. Office: Ctr For Applied Sci Comptg 7000 East Ave Livermore CA 94550-9516 Home: 3001 Oakham DR San Ramon CA 94583-2533 Business E-Mail: fodor1@llnl.gov.

FODOR, MARIANA DUARTE, army officer, nurse, educator; b. NYC, Mar. 8, 1938; d. Rodulfo Sindulfo and Orosia Diaz; m. Joseph E. Fodor, Sept. 1, 1972. RN diploma, NYU-Bellevue Hosp., 1958; BA, Hunter Coll., 1972; MEd, NYU, 1975; PhD, 2004; Apptd. ARC Nurse, 1970; Commd. 1st lt. Nurse Corps, US Army, 1967, advanced through ranks to lt. col., 1983; nursing supr. Hosp. Spl. Surgery, NYC, 1966-67; active duty, Yokohama, Japan, 1967-69; tchr., nurse Dept. Def. Schs.-Pacific, Japan, 1969-72; tchr. practical nursing New Rochelle High Sch. NYC, 1972-74; bio-med. coordinator Lehman High Sch., NY Bd. Edn., NYC, 1974-81; pub. affairs officer 8th Med. Brigade, 1977-80; asst. chief nurse, tng. officer 344th Gen. Hosp., Ft. Totten, NY, 1981-85; bd. govs. 77th Army Res. Command, NYC, 1982-85. Writer health edn. and family life curriculum Dept. Def. Schs., Pacific area, Japan, 1971; contbr. artwork and photography to books; artist exhbns. in various NYC, Midwest, S.W., Israel locations, 1990-2003; Recipient Expert Field Med. badge, US Army, 1977, Commendation medal, 1979, Meritorious Svc. medal Dept. Army, Washington, 1982, Achievement medal, 1983; Cmty. Svc. award Staten Island Hosp., NYC, 1979; Tchr. of Yr. award Outstanding Secondary Educators Am., 1975, Disting. Svc. award NY State, 1995; 1st woman mil. marshall Vets. Meml. Day Parade, NYC, 1984. Mem. NY Acad. Sci. (life), Res. Officers Assn. (life, adv. coun.), Assn. Mil. Surgeons US (life, exec. coun.).

FODOR, PETER BELA, plastic surgeon; b. Cluj, Romania, 1942; MD, U. Wis. Med. Sch., 1966. Intern Parkland Meml. Hosp., Dallas, 1966—67; resident, gen. surgery Columbia-Presbyn. Med. Ctr., 1967—68; resident, plastic surgery St. Luke's Hosp., N.Y.C., 1974—76; plastic surgeon Century Aesthetics, L.A. Office: Century Aesthetics 2080 Century Park E Ste 710 Los Angeles CA 90067

FODOR, SUSANNA SERENA, lawyer; b. Tg-Mures, Romania, Apr. 24, 1950; came to U.S., 1963; d. Bela Akos and Rachel (Rafira) F.; 1 child, Brooke Alexandra Bodoki-Fodor. BS, U. Wis., Milw., 1969; JD, U. Wis., Madison, 1972. Bar: Wis. 1972, N.Y. 1974. In ho. counsel Wis. Dept. Devel. Natural Resources, Madison, 1972-73, U.S. EPA, N.Y.C., 1973-74, Urban Devel. Corp., N.Y.C., 1975-77; assoc. Schulte, Roth & Zabel, N.Y.C., 1977-79; ptnr. Weil, Gotshal & Manges, N.Y.C., 1979-85, Shea & Gould, N.Y.C., 1985-89, Jones Day, N.Y.C., 1989—. Editor chpt. to book; contbr. articles to profl. publs., chpt. to book. Mem. ABA (real property, probate and trust constrn. form com.), Am. Coll. Real Estate Lawyers, Profl. Women in Constrn., Real Estate Bd. N.Y. (owner labor coordinating com.), Am. Coll. Constrn. Lawyers, Am. Arbitration Assn. (large complex case panel), Comml. Real Estate Women N.Y. (editl. bd.), Urban Land Inst., CoreNet Global; CoreNet Learning Advisory Bd.; Wis. State Bar Assn., N.Y. State Bar Assn., Hungarian-Am. C. of C. of N.Y./N.J. Avocations: sports, art, languages. Home: 200 E End Ave Apt 14F New York NY 10128-7887 Business E-Mail: ssfodor@jonesday.com.

FODREA, CAROLYN WROBEL, educational researcher, publisher, consultant; b. Hammond, Ind., Feb. 1, 1943; d. Stanley Jacob and Margaret Caroline (Stupeck) Wrobel; m. Howard Frederick Fodrea, June 17, 1967 (div. Jan. 1987); children: Gregory Kirk, Lynn Renee. BA in Elem. Edn., Purdue U., 1966; MA in Reading and Lang. Devel., U. Chgo., 1973; postgrad., U. Colo., Denver, 1986—87. Cert. elem. tchr., Ind., Ill. Tchr. various schs., Ind., Colo., 1966-87; founder, supr., clinician Reading Clinic, Children's Hosp., Denver, 1969-73; pvt. practice Denver, 1973—87, Deerfield, Ill., 1973—; creator of pilot presch.-kindergarten lang. devel. program Gary, Ind. Diocese Schs., 1987—, therapist lang. and reading disabilities, 1987—; pres. Reading Rsch. Ctr., Arlington Heights, Ill., 2000—. Conducted Lang. Devel. Workshop, Gary, Ind. 1988; tchr. adult basic edn. Dawson Tech. Sch., 1990, Coll. Lake County, 1991, Prairie State Coll., 1991—, Chgo. City Colls., 1991, R.J. Daley Coll., 1991, Coll. DuPage, 1991—; condr. adult basic edn. workshops for Coll. of DuPage, R.J. Daley Coll., 1992, Ill. Lang. Devel. Literacy Program; tchr. Korean English Lang. Inst., Chgo., 1996, Lang. Devel. Program for Minorities, 2000; dir. pilot study Cabrini Green Tutoring Ctr., Chgo., 2000; presenter in field. Author: Language Development Program, 1985, Presch. Kindergarten Lang. Devel. Program, 1988, A Multi-Sensory Stimulation Program for the Premature Baby in Its Incubator to Reduce Medical Costs and Academic Failure, 1986, Predicting At-Risk Babies for First Grade Reading Failure Before Birth A 15 Year Study, A Language Development Program, Grades 1 to Adult, 1988, 92; editor, pub.: ESL For Native Spanish Speakers, 1996, ESL for Native Korean Speakers, 1996. Active Graland Country Day Sch., Denver, 1981-83, N.W. Ind. Children's Chorale, 1988—; Ill. state chair Babies and You com. March of Dimes, 1999—. Mem. NEA, Am. Ednl. Rsch. Assn., Internat. Reading Assn., Am. Coun. for Children with Learning Disabilities, Am. Acad. Environ. Medicine (chhmn. pub. rels., mktg. com., chmn. town meeting com. 2005), Assn. for Childhood Edn. Internat., Colo. Assn. for Edn. of Young Children, Infant Stimulation Edn. Assn., Art Inst. Chgo., U. Chgo. Alumni Club (Denver area ann. fund, Pres. fund com. 1988—, com. mem. Denver area chpt. 1974-87). Roman Catholic. Avocations: sports, health and nutrition, literary and cultural activities, sewing. Office Phone: 847-632-0622, 800-748-0222. Personal E-mail: cfodrea1@aol.com. Business E-Mail: cfodrea@readingresearch.com. *The ability to think, to read and to learn is dependent upon intact, internalized language system. It is this internalized language system that is dysfunctional in those who have not been successful students and who must have this language system rebuilt first if they are to become successful learners, productive workers and original thinkers capable of problem analysis and problem solutions.*

FOERST, JOHN GEORGE, JR., retired fundraising executive; b. Queens, NY, June 8, 1927; s. John George and Mary Elizabeth (McGinn) F.; m. Marion Theresa Cassidy, June 27, 1953; children: Gerard M., Kathryn J. BA, St. Johns U., Queens, 1950. Regional rep. Nat. Found. for Infantile Paralysis, NYC, 1950-52; campaign dir., v.p. Cmty. Counselling Svc., NYC, 1952-59, v.p., asst. to pres., 1965-69, pres., 1969-87, chmn., 1987-96, chmn. emeritus, 1997-2001; pres. John G. Foerst, Inc., NYC, 1959-65. Spl. advisor to chmn. and bd. dirs. Changing Our World, Inc., 2001—. Contbg. author: complete Guide to Corporate Fund Raising, 1982. Trustee Pope John Paul II Libr. and Cultural Ctr., Washington, 1998—, Telecare, Uniondale, NY; chmn. Am. Assn. Fund Raising Counsel, NYC, 1982; mem. Cardinal's Com. of Laity Roman Cath. Archdiocese NY, 1984—; bd. dirs. St. Francis Hosp., Roslyn, NY, 1972—2002, The Ctr. for Devel. Disabilities, Woodbury, NY, 1974—87, Nat. Ctr. for Disability Svcs. Inc., Albertson, NY, 1988—99, Cath. Health Sys. of L.I., 1998—99, Help for the Poor Found., 1998—99, Mid-Atlantic Hosp. Trust, Bermuda. Mem. Union League, Knights of Malta. Republican. Home: 77 Dover Rd Manhasset NY 11030-3717

FOERSTER, BERND, architecture educator; b. Danzig, Dec. 5, 1923; came to U.S., 1947, naturalized, 1954; s. Joseph and Martha (Brumm) F.; m. Enell Dowling, May 13, 1950; children: Kent, Mark (dec.). Student, Columbia U., 1948-49; BS in Architecture, U. Cin., 1954; MArch, Rensselaer Poly. Inst., 1957. Various positions Govt. The Netherlands, 1945-47; with various engrs. and architects offices, 1950-59; cons. Ch. bldgs., design cons., 1954—; instr. architecture U. Cin., 1954, Rensselaer Poly. Inst., Troy, N.Y., 1954-56, asst. prof., 1956-62, assoc. prof., 1962-65, prof., 1965-71; dean Kans. State U., Manhattan, 1971-84, prof., 1971—99; adjunct prof. Grad. Program in Hist. Preservation Goucher Coll., 1995—. Cons. archtl. and cmty. surveys N.Y. State Coun. Arts, 1962-71; chmn. Gov.'s Adv. Com. Hist. Preservation N.Y. State, 1968-71; cons. Albany Hist. Sites Commn., 1967-71, Independence (Mo.) Heritage Commn., 1975-77; leader U.S. del. Preservation Planning to China, 1982, USSR and Ea. Europe, 1989; leader faculty team Coll. Architecture and Design, Kans. State U. to Poland, The Czech and Slovak Republics, and Hungary, 1990; cons. selection of archs. and design cons. for Fed. projects U.S. GSA, 1994-96. Author: Man and Masonry, 1960, Pattern and Texture, 1961, Architecture Worth Saving in Rensselaer County, N.Y., 1965; (with others) Independence, Missouri, 1978, 2d printing, 1989; (films) Man and Masonry, 1961 (Am. Film Festival selection), What Do You Tear Down Next?, 1964, Earth and Fire, 1964, Assault on the Wynantskill, 1967; editorial adv. bd. Preservation Forum, 1987-93. Bd. dirs. Albany Inst. History and Art, 1967-71, Mohawk-Hudson Council on Ednl. TV, 1968-71, v.p., 1970-71; co-chmn. Conf. on Rensselaer County, 1966; pres. Rensselaer County Council for Arts, 1963-64, 66-67; trustee Olana Historic Site, 1969-71; pres. bd. trustees Riley County Hist. Mus., 1977; chmn. Manhattan Downtown Redevel. Adv. Bd., 1979-85, City Fountain Restoration Com., 1983-86; mem. coun. Drayton Hall, Charleston, S.C., 1985-93; mem. Hist. Dist. Rev. Bd. Manhattan, 1997-99; mem. Manhattan Hist. Resources Bd., 1999-2005, vice chmn., 1999-2001; mem. planning bd. Riley County, Kans., 1997-99; chair Road and Bridge Adv. Com. Riley County, 1997-98; chair steering com. Downtown Tomorrow, Manhattan, 1998-2000. Named Disting. prof. Assn. Collegiate Schs. Architecture, 1988; recipient Kans. Gov.'s award for historic preservation, 1995, James Marston Fitch Lifetime Achievement award Nat. Coun. for Preservation Edn., 2000, Disting. Svc. award Kansas State U., 2004, Lifetime Achievement award Kansas Preservation Alliance, 2004. Fellow AIA (com. hist. resources 1977-92, vice chmn. 1986, chmn. 1987, state preservation coordinator 1979-92); mem. AIA Kans. (sec. 1975, exec. com. 1975-80, pres. 1979), Nat. Trust Hist. Preservation (bd. advs. 1979-81, trustee 1981-90, trustee emeritus 1990—), AAUP (chpt. pres. Rensselaer Poly. Inst. 1963-64, Kans. State U. 1987-88, v.p. Kans. conf. 1988-90, pres. 1990-92), The Land Inst. (bd. dirs. 1976-87), Manhattan Arts Coun. (bd. dirs. 1973-78, pres. 1976-77), LWV of Manhattan-Riley County (2d v.p. 1988-91, pres.-elect 91-92, pres. 92-93), Kans. Preservation Alliance (bd. dirs. 1979-85, hon. trustee 1990—), Nat. Council Preservation Edn. (bd. dirs. 1980-93, vice-chmn. 1981-85), Nature Conservancy, Audubon Soc., Scarab, Tau Sigma Delta, Phi Kappa Phi. Lodges: Rotary (Paul Harris fellow). Home: 920 Ratone St Manhattan KS 66502-5136 *Some places are so important, so fragile, or so beautiful that we must leave them alone.*

FOERSTER, CONRAD LOUIS, project engineer; b. Balt., Jan. 19, 1938; s. George Leroy Sr. and Jane Ruth (Carson) F.; m. Tina M. Capone, Sept. 20, 1964; children: Christopher C., George A. AS in Engring. Sci., Nassau C.C., 1971; BS in Engring. Sci., L.I. U., 1975; postgrad., Poly. Inst., N.Y.C., 1978, U.S. Partical Accelerator Sch., 1992. Vacuum technician Veeco Instrument Corp., Plainview, N.Y., 1959-68; electronic technician Gen. Instrument Inc., Hicksville, N.Y., 1968, eqipment supr., 1973; mfg. engr. Deutsch Relays Inc., East Northport, N.Y., 1968-73, product engr., 1973-79; project engr. Brookhaven Nat. Lab., Upton, N.Y., 1979-86, vacuum group leader, 1986—. Contbr. articles to profl. jours. With USAF, 1955-59. Achievements include research in vacuum science. Office: Brookhaven Nat Lab Nsls Bldg 725C Upton NY 11973 Office Phone: 631-282-4754. E-mail: foerster@bnl.gov.

FOERSTER, PAUL A., secondary school educator, writer; b. Birmingham, England, June 4, 1935; s. Adolph W. and Gladys H. Foerster; m. Peggy M Foerster, Mar. 20, 1994; stepchildren: J Scott McCaskill, Cristen Lea McCaskill; m. Jo Ann Foerster, Feb. 2, 1957 (dec. May 1993); children: David Paul, Holly A Kramaley, Barbara Jill Clark. BS in chem. engring., U. Tex. at Austin, 1952—57; tchg. cert., Tex. A&M U., 1961; MA in math., U. Tex. at Austin, 1966—67; LHD (hon.), Austin Coll., 1985. Ranch hand (summers) Cibolo Ranch, Sutherland Springs, Tex., 1951—54; chem. engr. EI. du Pont, Victoria, Tex., 1956; engring. duty officer U.S. Naval Nuc. Propulsion, Washington, 1957—61; ednl. rschr. U.S. Weather Bur., San Antonio, 1962; chem. engr. Louis Keonig Rsch., San Antonio, 1969—70; math. tchr. Alamo Heights H.S., San Antonio, 1961—. Tech. adv. com. (steering com.) NCTM, 1984—86; local arrangements chmn. NCTM Ann. Meeting, 1985; program chmn. NCTM San Antonio Meeting, 1978, gen. chmn., 70, NCTM Cosponsored Meeting, 1966; spkr. in field, 1963—; mem. Tex. State Textbook Com., 1968—69; reader Coll. Bd. Advanced Placement Exams, 1969—77; mem. Coll. Bd. Math. Examining Com., 1969—75, Ann. H.S. Math. Exam. Com., 1987—92; local arrangements adv. NCTM Ann. Meeting, 2003. Co-author: (textbook) Algebra: The Language of Mathematics, 1977; author: Trigonometry: Functions and Applications, Algebra and Trigonometry: Functions and Applications, Algebra I: Expressions, Equations and Applications, Precalculus with Trigonometry: Concepts and Applications, Calculus: Concepts and Applications; contbr. articles. Lt., sr. grade USNR, 1957—61, Washington, DC. Recipient Presdl. award for excellence in math. tchg., 1983, Trinity U. prize for excellence in tchg., 1982. Avocations: gardening, reading, astronomy, photography, scuba diving. Home: 203 Lamont Ave San Antonio TX 78209 Office: Alamo Heights H S 6900 Broadway San Antonio TX 78209 Office Phone: 210-820-8850. Business E-Mail: foerster@ahist.net.

FOGARTIE, JAMES EUGENE, retired clergyman; b. Brookhaven, Miss., June 20, 1924; s. Arthur Finley and Eugenia Elizabeth (Vance) F.; m. Ruth Ann Douglass, Aug. 30, 1946 (dec. 1976); children: Ann Douglass, Elizabeth Vance, Arthur Ford, James Eugene, Jr.; m. Vivian M. Reid, Feb. 18, 1978. BA, U. Tex., 1945, MA, 1948; BD, Austin Presbyn. Theol. Sem., 1948; ThM, Union Theol. Sem., Richmond, Va., 1954; DD, Austin Coll., 1969; LHD, Presbyn. Coll., Clinton, S.C., 1989. Ordained to ministry Presbyn. Ch., 1948. Minister First Presbyn. Ch., Marianna, Ark., 1948-52, Ft. Smith, Ark., 1952-55, Myers Park Presbyn. Ch., Charlotte, N.C., 1955-74, First Presbyn. Ch., Spartanburg, S.C., 1974-90, pastor emeritus, 1991—; supply minister St. Andrews Presbyn. Ch., Wemblen, Eng., 1952. Trustee Ctr. of Theol. Inquiry, Princeton, 1986—; mem. instnl. rev. bd. Spartanburg Regional Med. Ctr., 1978—. Author: No Room, 1958, In Search of Christmas, 1959. Recipient Silver Beaver award Mecklenburg Coun. Boy Scouts, 1971, Disting. Alumni award Austin Presbyn. Theol. Seminary, 1990; named one of Outstanding Young Men of Am., 1953. Mem. Spectator Club (pres. Spartanburg chpt. 1990), Rotary. Home: 104 N Carleila Lake Dr Spartanburg SC 29307-2631

FOGARTY, CHARLES JOSEPH, lieutenant governor; b. Providence, Sept. 15, 1955; s. Charles Joseph and Martha Jane (Hague) F. BA, Providence Coll., 1977; MPA, U. R.I., 1980. Policy assoc. Office Gov., Providence, 1978-84; spl. asst. to commr. R.I. Dept. Edn., Providence, 1985; town councilman Glocester, R.I., 1985-91; sr. policy analyst Office Gen. Treas., Providence, 1985-88; dir. policy Office Lt. Gov., Providence, 1989-91; state senator R.I., Providence, 1991-99; majority whip R.I. Senate, 1993-95, pres. pro tem, 1995-99; lt. gov. State of R.I., 1999—. Chmn. Glocester Dem. Town Com., 1979-85, R.I. Longterm Care Coord. Coun., 1996—; del. Dem. Nat. Conv., N.Y.C., 1980, 96, 2000; bd. dirs. N.W. Cmty. and Nursing Health Svc., 1994-2001, R.I. chpt. ARC, 1994— Mem. Lions (pres. Glocester chpt. 1991—). Democrat. Roman Catholic. Home: 230 Paris Irons Rd Harmony RI 02829 Office: Rm 116 State House Providence RI 02903

FOGARTY, EDWARD MICHAEL, lawyer; b. Woonsocket, RI, Feb. 25, 1948; s. Raymond Henry and Mary (Hogan) F.; m. Gail Higgins, Jan. 8, 1977. BA, Providence Coll., 1969; JD, Georgetown U., 1972. Bar: R.I. 1972, D.C. 1973, U.S. Supreme Ct. 1977. Law clk. U.S. Dist. Ct. R.I., Providence, 1972-73; assoc. Wilkinson, Cragun & Barker, Washington, 1973-79, ptnr., 1979-82, Baenen, Timme, De Reitzes & Middleton, Washington, 1982-83; counsel Spriggs & Hollingsworth, Washington, 1983-98. Legal counsel to speaker R.I. Ho. of Reps., Providence, 1987-93; legal counsel to majority leader R.I. Senate, Providence, 1993-2003, 04—, legal counsel to senate pres., 2003-04; arbitrator R.I. Superior Ct., 1989—. Trustee Festival Ballet Providence, 1988—, pres., 1994—96. Mem.: ABA, Am. Arbitration Assn. (nat. panel of arbitrators 1985—96), D.C. Bar, R.I. Bar Assn. (ho. dels. 1992—94), Univ. Club Providence, Univ. Club Washington. Democrat. Roman Catholic. Home: 488 Lloyd Ave Providence RI 02906-4550 Office: 316 State House Providence RI 02903 Office Phone: 401-222-3310. Business E-Mail: efogarty@rilin.state.ri.us.

FOGARTY, ELIZABETH RUMMANS, retired librarian, researcher; b. Portsmouth, Ohio, Nov. 1, 1916; d. George Rummans and Mattie Belle (Shaver) Jordan; m. Joseph Christopher Fogarty, Oct. 6, 1945 (dec. Jan. 1977); children: Patricia C., Michelle., Josephine S. BA magna cum laude, Ohio Wesleyan U., 1938; MLS, U. Ill., 1939. Post libr. U.S. Army, Camp Atterbury, Ind., 1942-45; organizer of libr. Legis. Auditor's Calif. Capitol Office, Sacramento. 1952-53; med. rsch. libr. U.S. Army Med. Ctr., Ryukyu Islands, Japan, 1967-70, U.S. Army Hosp., Ft. Polk, La., 1970-72; libr. pub. svcs. McAllen Pub. Libr., Tex., 1974-76. Researcher for Calif. state legislators and physicians. Chmn. coun. on ministries, mem. adminstrv. bd. St. Mark United Meth. Ch., McAllen, 1975—; Germany country commr. North Atlantic Girl Scout Bd. Europe, 1961-63. Mem. AAUW (pres. McAllen br. 1977-81, bd. dir. internat. rels. Tex. state div. bd. 1981-84, cond. internat. rels. workshops at Tex. state and nat. convs. 1981—, Outstanding Woman of yr. award 1980), DAR (regent Sam Maverick chpt. 1983-85), Colonial Dames 17th Century (pres. Capt. Thomas Jefferson chpt. 1985—, Tex. state bd. 1985—, v.p. 1987—, Uni985—, v.p. 1987—), United Daus. Confederacy (treas. Palo Alto chpt. 1982-84, pres. 1990—, registarar 1987—), ALA, LWV, Mortar Board, U.S. Daus. 1812, The Jamestowne Soc., Nat. Soc. Daus. Am. Colonists, Nat. Soc. Colonial Dames (state pres. Tex. 1989—), Nat. Soc. Magna Charta Dames (pres. UDC Palo Alto chpt. 1990—), Nat. Soc. Colonial Dames XVII Century (Tex. state pres. 1989-91, libr. gen. 1991-93, 93-95, 95-97, v.p. gen., 1997-99, hon. v.p. life, 2001), UDC (chpt. pres. 1990—), New England Women, Dames of Ct. of Honor, Soc. of Ky. Pioneers, Colonial Order of the Crown, Ams. Royal Descent, Sons and Daughters of the Pilgrims, Phi Beta Kappa, Delta Delta Delta, Delta Sigma Rho. Methodist. Home: Cottage 610 1204 S Border Ave Weslaco TX 78596-7447 Personal E-mail: bttyfogerty@aol.com.

FOGARTY, ROBERT STEPHEN, historian, educator, editor; b. Bklyn., Aug. 30, 1938; s. Michael Joseph and Marguerita (Carmody) F. BS, Fordham U., 1960; PhD, U. Denver, 1968. Instr. Mich. State U., 1963-67; asst. prof. Antioch Coll., Yellow Springs, Ohio, 1968-73, chmn. humanities area, 1973-74, 78-79, assoc. prof., 1974-80, prof. history, 1980—, John Dewey prof. emeritus; prof. Advanced Internat. Studies, Ctr. for Chinese-Am. Johns Hopkins U., 1986-87; editor Antioch Rev., 1977—; dir. Associated Colls. Midwest/Gt. Lakes Coll. Assn., Program in Humanities, Newberry Library, 1978-79; cons. Nat. Endowment for Arts, 1975-81, U. Waterloo, Ont., Can., 1981. Vis. fellow NYU Inst. for Humanities, 1992—93; Darwin lectr. human biology Galton Inst., London, 1994. Author: Dictionary of American Communal and Utopian History, 1980, The Righteous Remnant-The House of David, 1981, All Things New: Communes and Utopian Movements, 1860-1914, 1990, Special Love/Special Sex, 1994, Desire and Duty at Oneida: Tirzah Miller's Intimate Memoir, 2000; editor Antioch Rev., 1977—; contbr.: American Encyclopeida of American Culture, 2001; contbr. essays to The Nation, TLS, Mo. Rev. Recipient Martha K. Cooper award for editl. achievement, 1981, Nora Magid Award for Editing PEN Am. Ctr., 2003; grantee Am. Philos. Soc., 1976, Am. Coun. Learned Socs.; fellow NEH, 1980, All Souls Coll., Oxford U., 1988, Lloyd Lewis fellow Newberry Libr., 1995, Galton Inst. fellow, 1995; Fulbright Disting. Lectr. to Korea, 2000, Gilder Lehrman fellow 2001, Mary Baker Eddy libr. fellow, 2004. Mem.: PEN/Am. Ctr., Orgn. Am. Historians, Nat. Hist. Communal Sites Assn. (exec. com. 1975—2002), Am. Studies Assn. (bibliography com. 1981—). Office: Antioch Rev Inc PO Box 148 Yellow Springs OH 45387-0148 Office Phone: 927-769-1365.

FOGARTY, THOMAS JAMES, surgery educator; b. Cin., Feb. 25, 1934; s. William Henry and Anna Isabella (Ruthemeyer) F.; m. Rosalee Mae Brennan, Aug. 28, 1965; children: Thomas James Jr., Heather Brennan, Patrick Erin, Jonathan David. BS in Biology, Xavier U., 1956; MD, U. Cin., 1960; D (hon.), Xavier U., 1987. Intern U. Oreg. Med. Sch., Portland, 1960-61, resident, 1962-65, instr. surgery, 1967-68; chief resident, instr. surgery divsn. cardiovascular surgery Stanford (Calif.) U. Med. Ctr., 1969-70, asst. prof. surgery, 1970-71, asst. clin. prof. surgery, 1971-73; cardiovascular surgeon pvt. practice, Stanford, 1973-78; pres. med. staff Stanford U. Med. Ctr., 1977-79; cardiovascular surgeon pvt. practice, Redwood City, Calif., 1978-93; dir. cardiovascular surgery Sequoia Hosp., Redwood City, Calif., 1980-93; clin. prof. surgery Stanford U. Med. Ctr., 1993—. Bd. dirs. Acorn Cardiovascular Inc., Satellite Dialysis Ctrs., Inc.; co-founder, bd. dirs. AneuRx, Inc., Biopsys Med., Inc., Cardiac Pathways, Inc., Emergency Med. Sys., Windy Hill Tech., Inc., Gen. Surg. Innovations, Inc., LocalMed, Inc., Vital Insite, Inc., Raytel Med. Corp., Cardiovascular Imaging Sys., Inc., Devices for Vascular Intervention, Inc., Hancock Labs., Imagyn Med., Inc., Physiometrix, Inc., Ventritex, Inc., Xenotech; mem. scientific adv. bd. Autogenics, BioLink Corp., Cardio Thoracic Sys., Inc., bd. dirs.; pres., founder Fogarty Engring., Inc.; co-founder, sr. ptnr. Three Arch Ptnrs., Baccitus Vascular, Novare Surg., Vascular Archs. Safety; founder, proprietor Thomas Fogarty Winery, 1981-. Portrait included in Bay Area Hon. Mus., 1998; contbr. articles to profl. jours.; patentee in field. Fellow U. Cin. Coll. Medicine, Good Samaritan Hosp., 1961-62, Nat. Heart Inst. Surgery br., Bethesda, Md., 1965-67, rsch. fellow divsn. cardiovascular surgery Stanford Med. Ctr., 1968-69; recipient AstroLobe award Roger Bacon High Sch., 1974, Disting. Alumnus award U. Cin. Med. Sch., 1989, Lifetime Achievement award Phoenix Hall of Fame, 1997, No. Calif. 1998 Entrepreneur of Yr. award Ernst & Young, 1998, Lemelson-MIT $500, 000 Prize invention and innovation, 2000, Assn. Advancement Med. Instrumentation's Found.'s Ann. Laufman-Greatbatch prize, 2000, Sci. Leadership award Nat. Breast Cancer Coalition, 2000, Internat. Soc. award Excellence in Endovascular Innovation Internat. Soc. Endovascular Specialists, 2001, Jacobson Innovation award Am. coll. Surgeons, 2001; named Inventor of Yr., San Francisco Patent and Trademark Assn., 1980; inducted into the Nat. Inventors Hall of Fame, 2001. Mem. AMA, ACS, Am. Assn. Thoracic Surgery, Am. Bd. Thoracic Surgery, Am. Coll. Physican Inventors, Am. Heart Assn. (grantee), Am. Inst. Med. and Biol. Engring., Assn. for Advancement Med. Instrumentation, Med. Device Mfrs. Assn., Am. Med. Polit. Action Com., Am. Surg. Assn., Internat. Soc. Specialists Surgery, Western Thoracic Surg. Soc., Calif. Med. Soc., Pacific Coast Surg. Assn., San Francisco Surg. Soc., San Mateo County Med. Assn., Santa Clara County Med. Assn. (Achievement award in medicine), Internat. Soc. Cardiovascular Surg. (N.Am. chpt.), Soc. Clin. Vascular Surgery, Soc. Vascular Tech., Soc. Thoracic Surgeons, Soc. Vascular Surgery (past pres. 1995), Copco Lake Sportsmen Assn., Santa Cruz Mountain Winegrowers Assn., South Skyline Assn., Sports Car Club Am., Rapley Trail Improvement Assn., Soc. Med. Friends of Wine. Republican. Achievements include invention of balloon embolectomy catheter. Avocations: hunting, fishing, pond gardening, woodworking, geneology. Office: 3274 Alpine Rd Portola Valley CA 94028 also: Thomas Fogarty Winery 3270 Alpine Rd Portola Valley CA 94028*

FOGARTY, TIMOTHY JOHN, musician, writer, small business owner; b. Scranton, Pa., Jan. 22, 1962; m. Rachel Fogarty; children: Taylor, William. AA in Humanities, County Coll. Morris, Randolph, N.J., 1982. Owner and instr. guitar, bass and banjo Mice Will Play, Hackettstown, NJ, 1979—; instr. guitar, bass and banjo Phils Music Maker, Studio 46, Keyboard World, Ledgewood, The Music Emporium, Sparta. Webmaster; musician; songwriter. Author: The Staffmaster, The Guitar Workout; composer: (songs) Teachers class band, King Autore; musician: The Cincinnati Rail Tie Music Co. Mem.: Country Music Assn. (life). Achievements include development of Staffmaster, transcripion tool for guitar, bass and piano. Office: Mice Will Play 55 Winchester Ave Hackettstown NJ 07840 Office Phone: 908-979-0231.

FOGED, LESLIE OWEN, mathematician, educator; b. Cheyenne, Wyo., Sept. 26, 1953; s. Leif Clifford and Darlene Ann (Lutz) F.; m. Robyn Rachel Gilliom, May 30, 1981 (div. 1984); 1 child, Leif Erik. BA in Math., Midland Luth. Coll., 1974; PhD in Math., Washington U., St. Louis, 1979. Asst., assoc. prof. U. Tex., El Paso, Tex., 1979—, chmn. dept. math., 1987-88. Dir. U. Tex. H.S. Math. Contest, 1990—. Contbr. articles to profl. jours. Recipient Master Tchr. award Midland Luth. Coll., 1991. Achievements include discovery of an internal characterization of topological spaces which are closed images of metric spaces; constrn. of a consistent example of a quotient space of a separable metric space which is not stratifiable; construction of open-compact image of metric space with no point-countable closed quasibase. Office: U Tex at El Paso Dept Math El Paso TX 79968-0001

FOGEL, BRUCE MARTIN, lawyer; b. Northampton, Mass., Jan. 31, 1949; s. David and Rita (August) F.; m. Pauline Goldwater, July 30, 1978; children: Evan, Alex. BA in Am. History, Columbia U., 1970; JD, Western New Eng. Coll., 1975; LLM in Taxation, Boston U., 1978. Bar: Mass. 1975, U.S. Dist. Ct. Mass. 1976, U.S. Tax Ct. 1976. Ptnr., officer Fogel & Fogel, P.C., Northampton, Mass., 1971-87; ptnr. Fogel, Fogel, Gerard & Ghazey, P.C., 1988—; trustee, mem. trust com. Northampton Inst. for Savs.; lectr. tax and bus. law and planning. Trustee, Inst. of Open Edn., Cambridge Coll., Mass., 1976-83; co-chmn. Hampshire Community United Way, Northampton, 1977; dir., treas. Hampshire Regional YMCA, Northampton, 1977-83; dir., mem. fin. com. Hampshire County chpt. ARC, 1974-84; mem. City of Northampton Solid Waste Mgmt. Task Force, 1980-86; mem. Citizen's Adv. Com., State Hosp. Reuse; mem. Northampton Housing Partnership, 1994-96; bd. dirs. Northampton Ctr. Children and Families, 1978-82. Mem. ABA, Mass. Bar Assn., Hampshire County Bar Assn., Greater Northampton C. of C. (dir. 1982-86). Jewish. Office: Fogel Fogel Gerard & Glacy 78 Main St Northampton MA 01060-3111

FOGEL, DANIEL MARK, academic administrator, language educator, writer; b. Columbus, Ohio, Jan. 21, 1948; s. Ephim and Charlotte Edith (Finkelstein) F.; m. Rachel Kahn, June 24, 1973; children: Nicholas Alden Kahn-Fogel, Rosemary Luttrell. BA in English magna cum laude, Cornell U., 1969, MFA in Creative Writing, 1974, PhD in English, 1976. Tchr. English East Lyme (Conn.) High Sch., 1969-71; asst. prof. English La. State U., Baton Rouge, 1976-80, assoc. prof. English, 1980-84, prof. English, 1984—2002, assoc. dean grad. sch., 1990-92, assoc. vice chancellor acad. affairs, dean grad. sch., 1992-97, exec. vice-chancellor and provost, 1997—2002, prof. emeritus, 2002—; pres. U. Vt., Burlington, 2002—. Tchr. poetry writing workshops, Baton Rouge, 1980-87; instr. creative writing and lit. Instituto Allende, San Miguel de Allende, Guanajuato, Mex., 1972; mem. adv. com. Publs. MLA, 1986-90. Author: Henry James and the Structure of the Romantic Imagination, 1981 (Pulitzer prize nomination), Daisy Miller: A Dark Comedy of Manners, 1990, Covert Relations: James Joyce, Virginia Woolf, and Henry James, 1990, A Companion to Henry James Studies, 1993; author: (with others) The Aspern Papers Souvenir Book, 1988, The World Book Encyclopedia, 1991; author (poetry): A Trial of Resilience, 1975; author foreword: The Henry James Encyclopedia, 1989; editor/co-editor, author introduction: American Letters and the Historical Consciousness, 1987, New Essays on the Portrait of a Lady, 1987; editor: The Princess Casamassima, The Tragic Muse, The Reverberator, 1989; editor, founder Henry James Rev., 1979-95; mem. editorial staff Epoch, 1974-76; poetry editor Epoch, 1974, Nat. Forum 1981-86; editorial cons. Nat. Forum, 1980-84; consulting editor UMI Rsch. Press, 1983-89; author articles in field; contbr. poems to anthologies and periodicals. NEH summer stipend, 1977, 87; grantee La. Endowment for Humanities, 1990, Manship rsch. grantee, 1991-92. Mem. MLA, Henry James Soc. (exec. dir. 1979-2000). Jewish. Office: U Vt Pres Office Room 350B Waterman Bldg 85 S Prospect St Burlington VT 05405-0160 Home: 235 Thayer Bay Rd Colchester VT 05446-6618 Office Phone: 802-656-7878. Business E-Mail: daniel.fogel@uvm.edu.

FOGEL, HENRY, orchestra administrator; b. NYC, Sept. 23, 1942; s. Julius and Dorothy (Levine) F.; m. Frances Sylvia Polner, June 12, 1945; children—Karl Franz, Holly Dana Student, Syracuse U., 1960—63; doctorate (hon.), Northwestern U., Roosevelt U., Columbia Coll., Chgo. Program dir., v.p. Sta. WONO, Syracuse, NY, 1963-78; orch. mgr. N.Y. Philharm., N.Y.C., 1978-81; exec. dir. Nat. Symphony Orch., Washington, 1981-85; pres. Chgo. Symphony Orch. Assn., 1985—2003; pres., CEO Am. Symphony Orch. League, N.Y.C., 2003—. Record reviewer Fanfare Mag., 1979—; contbr. to Contemporary Composers. Mem. music panel NEA, 1986-90; past pres. U. Ill. Arts Alliance, 1988-94. Mem. NARAS, Am. Symphony Orch. League (bd. dirs. 1988—), Assn. Recorded Sound Collections (record reviewer jour. 1978). Office: Am Symphony Orch League 33 W 60th St 5th Fl New York NY 10023 Business E-Mail: hfogel@symphony.org.

FOGEL, IRVING MARTIN, consulting engineer; b. Gloucester, Mass., Apr. 15, 1929; s. Jacob and Ethel (David) F.; children: Ethan, Ronit. BS, Ind. Inst. Tech., 1954, D of Engring. (hon.), 1982. Registered profl. engr., 20 states, Israel. Civil engr. Ill. Hwy. Dept., Peoria, 1954-55; field engr. Peter Kiewit Sons Co., East Gary, Ind., 1955, field engr., progress engr., cost engr. Ogdensburg, N.Y., 1955-56; supt. grading and paving Merritt, Chapman & Scott, Binghamton, N.Y., 1956; cost engr. Drake-Merritt, Goose Bay, Labrador, 1956-57; constrn. mgmt. engr. Mil. Estimating Corp., Madrid, Spain, also P.I., 1957-58; project mgr. Ministry of Def., State of Israel, 1958-59, Frederic R. Harris (Holland) N.V., The Hague, also Tehran, Iran, 1959-61, Solel Boneh & Assocs., Addis Ababa, Ethiopia, 1961-63; asst. to tech. dir. Frederic R. Harris, Madrid, 1963-64; chief engr. McKee-Berger-Mansueto, Inc., N.Y.C., 1964-65, v.p. constrn. mgmt., 1965-69; pres. Fogel & Assocs., Inc., N.Y.C., 1969—. Lectr. in field. Author guides and handbooks on constrn. bus., latest being Construction Owner's Handbook of Property Development, 1992; contbr. articles to profl. jours. Fellow ASCE (life); mem. NSPE (life), NY State Soc. Profl. Engrs. (bd. dir. N.Y.C. chpt.). Home: 404 E 79th St #28D New York NY 10021-1404 Office: 61 Broadway Ste 1605 New York NY 10006-2714 E-mail: fogeleng@pangulf.com.

FOGEL, JACQUELINE, artist; b. Bklyn., Oct. 13, 1928; d. Alexander and Rose Fogel; divorced; children: Sue Klapholz, Michael Klapholz. Studied, Phila. Coll. Art, 1948—51. Exhibitions include Newark Mus., N.J., 1961, Bklyn. Mus., 1968, Sculpture Ctr., N.Y.C., 1979, Queens Mus., N.Y., 1983, Bergen County Mus., N.J., 1987, 1988, Housatonic Mus. Art, Bridgeport, Conn., 1991, Nassau County Mus., Roslyn, N.Y., 1996—2002, 2003, 2004, 2005, Guild Hall, E. Hampton, N.Y., 1993—2003, 2005, Michael Ingbar Gallery, N.Y., 1998, Cowparade, 2000, Apple Fest, 2004, DOGNY, 2002, one-woman shows include Krasner Gallery, N.Y., 1965, 1966, Aberbach Fine Art, 1974, Nassau County Mus., Roslyn, N.Y., 2005, Represented in permanent collections Housatonic Mus. Art, Brideport, Conn., Chrysler Mus., Norfolk, Va. Home: 82-61 166th St Jamaica NY 11432 Office Phone: 718-380-3913.

FOGEL, JENNIFER LYNN, medical technician; b. L.A., Apr. 15, 1976; d. Kenneth L. and Marcia Fogel. BS in Zoology, U. Tex., 1998; postgrad., Calif. State U., Northridge. Tech. assoc. US Borax Inc., Valencia, Calif., 1999—. Spkr. in field. Contbr. rsch. papers to profl. jours. Mem. AAAS, Internat. Rsch. Group, Forest Products Soc., U.S. Olympic Assn. Avocations: running, travel, reading, playing piano, singing. Office: US Borax Inc 26877 Tourney Rd Valencia CA 91355-1847 Office Fax: 661-287-6014. E-mail: jennifer.fogel@borax.com.

FOGEL, J(OAN) CATHY, lawyer; b. Chgo., Mar. 18, 1943; d. Norman Jack and Esther Lois (Grobstein) Friedman; m. Jay Bernard Lichtenberg, June 29, 1968 (dec. Apr. 1981); 1 child, Ian Robert; m. Donald Benjamin Fogel, Sept. 27, 1987; children: Alexis Jill, D. Brandon. BS, U. Wis., 1964; JD, Cath. U., 1977. Bar: U.S. Ct.Appeals (D.C. cir.) 1977, D.C. 1978, U.S. Ct. Appeals (7th cir.) 1979, U.S. Ct.Appeals (2d cir.) 1979, U.S. Supreme Ct. 1981, U.S. Ct. Appeals (3d cir.) 1984. Research librarian Library Congress, Washington, 1964—66; legislative research specialist Am. Pub. Power Assn., Washington, 1966—71; assoc. Duncan, Miller & Pembroke, Washington, 1977—83, ptnr., 1983—88, Verner, Liipfert, Bernhard, McPherson and Hand, Washington, 1989—2001, Sullivan & Worcester, 2001—, Washington, 2001—. Spl. asst. atty. gen. State of N.D., 1979-86. Contbr. articles to profl. jours. Mem. ABA, Women's Bar Assn., D.C. Bar Assn., Fed. Energy Bar Assn. (chmn. fed. power act parts I & II 1985-86, vice-chmn. power mktg. agys. 1988-89, chmn. power mktg. agys. 1989-90). Democrat. Jewish. Avocations: oenophile, travel. Home: 3804 Woodbine St Chevy Chase MD 20815-4957 Office: Sullivan & Worcester 1666 K St NW Washington DC 20006

FOGEL, JOSHUA, psychologist, researcher; BA, Bklyn. Coll., 1993; MA, Yeshiva U., 2000, PhD, 2002. Intern Queen Elizabeth II Health Sci. Centre, Halifax, Canada, 2001—02; fellow Johns Hopkins U., Balt., 2002—. Contbr. chapters to books The Management of Stress and Anxiety in Medical Disorders, Handbook of Health Psychology, Encyclopedia of Primary Prevention. Recipient Dr. H. Ralph Philips Award in Clin. Hypnosis, Dalhousie U. Sch. of Medicine, 2002. Mem.: APA (Dissertation Rsch. award 2001). Office: Johns Hopkins Univ 624 N Broadway Ste 861 Baltimore MD 21205 E-mail: joshua18@att.net.

FOGEL, PAUL DAVID, lawyer; b. Santa Monica, Calif., Sept. 19, 1949; s. Phillip and Betty (Distler) Fogel; m. Yvette Chalom, Feb. 11, 1981; 1 child, Daniele. AB, U. Calif.-Berkeley, 1971; postgrad., U. Paris II, 1972-73; JD, UCLA, 1976. Bar: Calif. 1976, U.S. Dist. Ct. (ctrl. dist.) Calif. 1977, U.S. Dist. Ct. (no. dist.) Calif. 1987, U.S. Supreme Ct. 1990, U.S. Ct. Appeals (9th cir.) 1981. Grad. fellow Ctr. for Law in Pub. Interest, L.A., 1976-77; dep. state pub. def. State Pub. Defender, L.A., 1977-79; Fulbright fellow U. Paris II Law Sch., 1979-80; dep. state pub. def. State Pub. Def., San Francisco, 1980-82; sr. supervising atty. Calif. Supreme Ct., San Francisco, 1982-87; assoc. Hinton & Alfert, Walnut Creek, Calif., 1987-88, Crosby, Heafey, Roach & May, San Francisco, 1988-89, ptnr., 1990—2002, Reed Smith LLP, San Francisco, 2003—. Lectr. Am. law USIA, Washington, 1980, 87, 99; lectr. U. Calif. Berkeley Boalt Hall Sch. Law, 1995, practitioner-advisor, 1991-94,

96—. Fellow Am. Acad. Appellate Lawyers, Calif. Acad. Appellate Lawyers (sec., treas. 2003-04, 2d v.p. 2004—); mem. Calif. State Bar Assn. (chmn. appellate cts. com. 1990-91), Bar Assn. San Francisco (chair appellate practice sect. 1999-2000), 9th cir. rules com. 1999-, appellate rules task force 1998—, Calif. jud. coun., appellate adv. com. 2004—, Amnesty Internat. Office: Reed Smith LLP 2 Embarcadero Ctr Ste 2000 San Francisco CA 94111-4191 Office Phone: 415-543-8700. Business E-Mail: pfogel@reedsmith.com.

FOGEL, ROBERT WILLIAM, economist, educator, historian; b. NYC, July 1, 1926; s. Harry Gregory and Elizabeth (Mitnik) Fogel; m. Enid Cassandra Morgan, Apr. 2, 1949; children: Michael Paul, Steven Dennis. AB, Cornell U., 1948; AM, Columbia U., 1960; PhD, Johns Hopkins U., 1963; MA (hon.), U. Cambridge, Eng., 1975, Harvard U., 1976; DSc (hon.), U. Rochester, 1987, U. de Palermo, Argentina, 1994, Brigham Young U., 1995, SUNY, Binghamton, N.Y., 1999. Instr. Johns Hopkins U., 1958—59; asst. prof. U. Rochester, 1960—64; Ford Found. vis. rsch. prof. U. Chgo., 1963—64, asso. prof., 1964—65, prof. econs., 1965—69, prof. econs. and history, 1970—75; prof. econs. U. Rochester, 1968—71, prof. econs. and history, 1972—75; Taussig rsch. prof. Harvard U., Cambridge, Mass., 1973—74, Harold Hitchings Burbank prof. polit. economy, prof. history, 1975—81; Charles R. Walgreen Disting. Svc. prof. Am. institutions U. Chgo., 1981—. Pitt prof. Am. history and insts. U. Cambridge, 1975—76; chmn. com. math. and statis. methods in history Math. Social Sci. Bd., 1965—72; rsch. assoc. Nat. Bur. Econ. Rsch., 1978—, co-dir. Cohort Studies program, 1998—, dir. DAE program, 1978—91; dir. Ctr. for Population Econ., Chgo. Author: The Union Pacific Railroad: A Case in Premature Enterprise, 1960, Railroads and American Economic Growth: Essays in Econometric History, 1964, Ten Lectures on the New Economic History, 1977, Without Consent of Contract: The Rise and Fall of American Slavery, Vol. 1, 1989, The Fourth Great Awakening and the Future of Egalitarianism, 2000, The Slavery Debates, 1952-1990: A Retrospective, 2003, The Escape from Hunger and Premature Death 1700-2100: Europe, America, and the Third World, 2004; author: (with others) The Reinterpretation of American Economic History, 1971, Dimensions of Quantitative Research in History, 1972, Without Consent of Contract: The Rise and Fall of American Slavery, Vols. 2-4, 1992; author: (with S.L. Engerman) Time on the Cross: The Economics of American Negro Slavery, 1974; author: (with G.R. Elton) Which Road to the Past? Two Views of History, 1983. Co-recipient The Bancroft prize, 1975, Gustavus Myers prize, 1990, Nobel prize, Nobel Found., 1993; recipient Arthur H. Cole prize, 1968, Schumpter prize, 1971, Disting. Alumnus award, Johns Hopkins U., 2000; fellow, Gilman, 1957—60, Social Sci. Rsch. Coun., 1960, Ford Found. Faculty Rsch., 1970; grantee Faculty Rsch., 1966, NSF, 1967, 1970, 1972, 1975—76, 1978, 1992—96, Fulbright, 1968, NIH, 1991—. Fellow: AAAS, Royal Hist. Soc., Econometric Soc., Brit. Acad. (corr.); mem.: NAS, Am. Philos. Soc., Internat. Union for Sci. Study of Population, Population Assn. Am., Am. Acad. Arts and Scis., Agrl. History Soc., Social Sci. History Assn. (pres. 1980—81), Assn. Am. Historians, Am. Hist. Assn., Econ. History Soc., Econ. History Assn. (trustee 1972—81, pres. 1977—78), Royal Econ. Soc., Am. Econ. Soc. (pres. 1998), European Acad. Arts, Scis. and Humanities, Phi Beta Kappa. Office: U Chgo Grad Sch Bus Ctr for Population Econ 5807 S Woodlawn Ave Chicago IL 60637-1511 Office Phone: 773-702-7709.

FOGELMAN, ANN FLORENCE, nutrition consultant, educator, researcher; b. Reading, Pa., Oct. 12, 1924; d. George Franklin Fogelman and Ruth Amelia Swartley Fogelman. BS, U. Del., 1950; MPH, U. Calif., Berkeley, 1957. Registered dietitian Am. Dietetic Assn., lic. dietitian Tex. Cook Art Camp, Cragsmoor, NY, 1948; asst. dir. YWCA Camp Otonka, Dagsboro, Del., 1949; asst. dietitian Meml. Hosp., Wilmington, Del., 1950—51; dietetic intern Frances Stern Food Clinic, Boston, 1952; clinic and tchg. dietitian Vanderbilt U. Hosp., Nashville, 1953—56; nutritionist Charlotte (N.C.)-Mecklenburg Health Dept., 1957—60; nutrition cons. Md. State Dept. Health, Balt., 1960—63; nutritionist dept. ob-gyn. U. Tex. Med. Br., Galveston, 1963—91; ret. Dietary dir. Tex. Nutrition Survey, 1968—69; liaison Tex. Home Econs. Assn. Tex. Dietetic Assn. Exec. Bd., 1968—69; pres., various other offices and coms. Tex. State Nutrition Coun., 1976—78; Tex. del. Am. Home Econs. Assn. Nat. Conv., 1971, 73; rec. sec. Houston Area Home Econs. Assn., 1967—68; pres. South Tex. Dietetic Assn., 1969—70. Contbr. chapters to books, articles to profl. jours. Vol. Clear Lake Regional Med. Ctr., Webster, Tex., 1992—96, Meml. Hermann S.E. Hosp., Houston, 1994—, Vitas Healthcare, Friendswood, Tex., 1994—, Sr. Learning Ctr., Webster, 1997—; active Clear Lake Presbyn. Ch., 1992—, deacon, 1996, Stephen min., 2000. With WAVES, 1944—46. Named one of 10 Most Outstanding Students, Sch. Home Econs. U. Del., 1962. Mem.: Waves Nat. (life), Bay Area Writers League, U. Tex. Med. Br. Retirees, Sr. Friends (Clear Lake chpt.), The Women's Meml. (charter), Beta Sigma Phi (pres. Charlotte chpt. 1959—60, pres. Pasadena chpt. 1974—75, Dickinson chpt. Girl of Yr. 1966—67, Girl of Yr. 1974—75). Avocations: travel, dance, reading. E-mail: annbird@hotmail.com.

FOGELMAN, MARTIN LEE, information technology manager, educator; b. NYC, Dec. 6, 1949; s. Edward Allan and Doris Ginsburg Fogelman; m. Elyse Helene Faber, July 11, 1976; children: Sarah Ellen, David Jacob. BA, U. Buffalo, 1971; MS, SUNY, Albany, 1973, MBA, 1984, PhD, 1999. Coll. instr., program coord. Russell Sage Coll., Albany, NY, 1978—80; tech. specialist, program coord. SUNY, Albany, NY, 1981—85, sr. programmer/analyst and project leader, 1985—90, bus. sch. faculty mgmt. faculty, 1998—. With Bethlehem Vol. Ambulance Svc., Selkirk, NY, 1999. Recipient H. L. Cannon Meml. Award Outstanding Undergraduate Tchg., Sch. Bus., U. Albany, 1999—2000. Mem.: Acad. Mgmt. Avocations: bicycling, hiking, reading. Office: SUNY Albany 1400 Washington Ave Albany NY 12222 Office Phone: 518-442-5545.

FOGELMAN, MORRIS JOSEPH, physician; b. Chgo., Feb. 27, 1923; s. Joseph and Tillie (Schwartz) F.; children— Evan, Joe, Margo. BA, U. Ill., 1941; MD, 1944, MS, 1948. Diplomate: Am. Bd. Surgery. Intern Wayne County Gen. Hosp., Eloise, Mich., 1944-45; resident Parkland Hosp., Dallas, 1948-51; research fellow dept. clin. sci. U. Ill. Coll. Medicine, Chgo., 1947-48, asst. physiology, 1947-48; asst. in physiology and pharmacology Southwestern Med. Sch., Dallas, 1948-50, fellow in surgery, 1948-52, instr. surgery, 1952-53, asst. prof. surgery, 1953, assoc. prof. surgery, 1953, prof. surgery, 1954-57, clin. prof. surgery, 1957—; practice medicine, specializing in surgery Dallas, 1952—; sr. attending surgeon Parkland Meml. Hosp., Dallas, 1953; assoc. med. dir. Intracorp Corp., 1994—. Cons. surgeon Baylor Hosp., 1957, Parkland Meml. Hosp., 1952, Presbyn. Hosp., Dallas; pres. med. staff Presbyn. Hosp., U4Dallas, U71973, Morris J. Fogelman, M.D. & Assocs., Dallas, 82, Windows & Walls, 1983; cons. Blue Cross/Blue Shield Tex., 1991—; assoc. med. dir. Intracorp Corp., 1997—. Author: Fluid Balance; Contbr. articles to various publs. Served to capt., M.C. AUS, 1945-47. Fellow Am. Assn. Surgery of Trauma; mem. ACS, AAAS, AMA, Dallas County Med. Soc., Dallas Soc. Gen. Surgeons, N.Y. Acad. Sci., Tex. Med. Assn. Home and Office: 6921 Norway Pl Dallas TX 75230-4252 Office Phone: 214-363-4242. *Do not go thru life believing everyone must love you. People differ in many ways and if you are kind with their differences, the may learn to love you.*

FOGELNEST, ROBERT, lawyer; b. Phila., Aug. 29, 1946; s. Phillip Harold and Charlotte (Wolkov) F.; m. M.J. Wolf, Jan. 21, 1972 (div. 1980); 1 child, B. Jacob; m. Susan W. Van Dusen, Mar. 27, 1991. BA, Temple U., 1973; JD, Rutgers U., 1976. Bar: Pa. 1976, N.Y. 1987, U.S. Dist. Ct. (ea. dist.) Pa. 1976, U.S. Dist. Ct. (ea. and so. dists.) N.Y. 1987, U.S. Dist. Ct. (we. dist.) Pa. 1988, U.S. Tax Ct. 1984, U.S. Ct. Appeals (3d cir.) 1985. Asst. dist. atty. Phila., 1976-79; ptnr. Ellis, Fogelnest & Newman, P.C., Phila., 1979-85; pvt. practice, N.Y.C., 1985—; mem. bd. regents Nat. Criminal Def. Coll.; faculty mem. Gerry Spence's Trial Lawyers Coll. Editorial adviser Inside Drug Law, 1984-89. Fellow Am. Bd. Criminal Lawyers (gov.), Pa. Assn. Crimininal Def. Lawyers, N.Y. Assn. Criminal Def. Lawyers (dir.); mem. Nat. Assn. Criminal Def. Lawyers (pres. 1995-96). Office: 475 Park Ave S Ste 3300 New York NY 10016-6901 E-mail: fogelnest@aol.com.

FOGERTY, JOHN CAMERON, musician, composer; b. Berkeley, Calif., May 28, 1945; Singer, guitarist Creedence Clearwater Revival, 1968-72; solo performer, 1973—; albums include (with Creedence Clearwater Revival) Creedence Clearwater Revival, 1968, Bayou Country, 1969, Willy & the Poor Boys, 1969, Green River, 1969, Cosmo's Factory, 1970, Pendulum, 1970, Creedence Gold, 1972, Mardi Gras, 1972, More Creedence Gold, 1973, Live in Europe, 1973, Chronicle, Vol. 1, 1976, Vol. 2, 1986, Down on the Corner, 1976, Hot Stuff, 1977, Greatest Hits, 1979, Concert, 1980, Creedence Country, 1981, Rollin' on the River, 1988, Travelin' Band, 1990; (solo) Blue Ridge Rangers, 1973, John Fogerty, 1975, Hoodoo, 1976, Centerfield, 1985, Knockin' on Your Door, 1986, Eye of the Zombie, 1986, Blue Moon Swamp, 1997, Deja Vu All Over Again, 2004. Inducted to Rock and Roll Hall of Fame, 1993. Office: Warner Bros 3300 Warner Blvd Burbank CA 91505-4694

FOGG, BLAINE VILES, lawyer; b. Boston, Mar. 29, 1940; s. Sanford L. and Dorothy (Viles) F.; m. Diane Abitbol, June 22, 1964; children: William, Matthew, Katherine. AB cum laude, Williams Coll., 1962; JD cum laude, Harvard U., 1965. Bar: NY 1966. Assoc. Skadden, Arps, Slate, Meagher & Flom LLP, NYC, 1966-71, ptnr., of counsel, 1971—, sr. advisor, Continental Europe, chair, fin. oversight and audit com. Spkr. in the field. Co-author: a major treatise on the Hart-Scott-Rodino Antitrust Improvements Act; author: numerous articles. Trustee Mount Sinai Med. Ctr., Inc. Named "senior statesman", Chambers USA, America's Leading Lawyers for Business, 2004—05. Office: Skadden Arps Slate Meagher & Flom LLP Four Times Sq New York NY 10036 Address: Skadden Arps Slate Meagher & Flom LLP 68 rue du Faubourg Saint-Honoré 75008 Paris France Office Phone: 212-735-3900, 011.33.1.55.27.11.00. Office Fax: 011.33.1.55.27.11.99, 917-777-3900. Business E-Mail: bfogg@skadden.com.

FOGG, ERNEST LESLIE, minister, retired; b. Butte, Mont., June 4, 1920; s. Ernest L. Fogg Sr. and Gertrude G. (Waller) Fogg-Parker; m. Margaret E. Fogg, June 17, 1943 (dec. Oct. 1962); children: Judith E., Dennis M. (dec.), Stephen William; m. Carolee Little, Sept. 1, 1965; 1 stepchild, Stephen Babcock. BA, Trinity U., San Antonio, 1943; MDiv, McCormick Theol. Seminary, Chgo., 1946; DD (hon.), Mary Holmes Coll., 1981. Ordained to ministry Presbyn. Ch., 1946. Missionary Bd. of Fgn. Missions/Presbyn. U.S.A., Thailand, 1946-59; field exec. Nat. Coun. of Chs., Indonesia, 1959-65; exec. Commn. on Ecumenical Mission and Rels./Presbyn. U.S.A., N.Y.C., 1965-70, Bd. Nat. Missions/Presbyn. U.S.A., N.Y.C., 1970-72; dir., Fund for Indochina World Coun. Chs., Geneva, 1973-76; sr. minister Cen. Presbyn. Ch., Montclair, N.J., 1977-87. Chmn. Am. Leprosy Mission, 1979-86. Contbr. articles to profl. jours. Mem. World Affairs Coun., San Antonio. Mem. Rotary (pres. 1986-87). Democrat. Avocation: woodworking. Home: 4900 Lucina Ct Fort Myers FL 33908-1672 E-mail: cleef8745@aol.com.

FOGG, JANET, architectural firm executive; Prin. OZ Arch., Denver, mng. ptnr., CFO, dir. human resources Boulder (Colo.) Studio, bd. dirs. Chmn. Downtown Boulder (Colo.), Inc., bd. dirs. Office: OZ Architecture Inc 3012 Huron St Ste 100 Denver CO 80202

FOGG, JOSEPH GRAHAM, III, investment company executive; b. Cleve., Oct. 22, 1946; s. Joseph G. Fogg; m. Leslie Kirk Solbert, Jan. 23, 1971; children: Nathaniel, Elizabeth Piper, Whitney Solbert. BA, Yale U., 1968; MBA, Harvard Bus. Sch., 1970. Adv. dir. Morgan Stanley & Co., N.Y.C., 1970—; chmn., CEO Westbury Capital Ptnrs., LLP, Westbury, NY, 1991—. Bd. dirs. Maxspeed Corp., Sunnyvale, Calif., 407 ETR Ltd., Toronto, Can., Pardee Resources Inc., Phila., QPass Inc., Seattle, Kennexa Corp., Phila., Aurora Flight Svcs., Manassas, Va., Advanced Interactive Sys, Inc, Seattle, Crystek, Inc., Sterling, Va, Yale U. Art Gallery, Keewayden Found., Rutland, Vt., Empower America, Washington. Office: Westbury Capital Ptnrs 501 Goodlette Rd N Ste B-102 Naples FL 34102

FOGG, RICHARD LLOYD, food products company executive; b. Boston, Jan. 22, 1937; s. Lloyd Clark and Mildred Ann (Cass) F.; m. Carolyn Ann Kane, Feb. 12, 1966; children— Amanda C., Jennifer S., Timothy L. AB, Bowdoin Coll., Brunswick, Maine, 1959; MBA, Cornell U., 1961. With brand mgmt. dept. Procter & Gamble Co., Cin., 1961-66; dir. mktg. mgmt. Hunt-Wesson Foods, Fullerton, Calif., 1967-76; sr. v.p. Amfac Food Group, Portland, Oreg., 1977; pres. subs. Fisher Cheese Co., Wapakoneta, Ohio, 1978-83; group v.p., COO Land O'Lakes Dairy Foods, Mpls., 1983-93; pres., CEO Orval Kent Food Co., Wheeling, Ill., 1994-96; pvt. investor, 1997—. Mem. Am. Mktg. Assn. Office Fax: 707-939-7859. Personal E-mail: sonomafogg@aol.com.

FOGG, WILLIAM V., lawyer; b. NYC, Feb. 21, 1966; BA magna cum laude, Brown Univ., 1988; JD, Columbia Univ., 1991. Bar: NY 1992. Assoc. Cravath Swaine & Moore LLP, NYC, 1991—99, ptnr., corp., 1999—. Mng. editor Columbia Jour. of Law and Social Problems. Named a Stone Scholar. Mem.: ABA, Assn. of Bar of City of NY, NY Bar Assn., NY Lawyers for the Pub. Interest. Office: Cravath Swaine & Moore LLP Worldwide Plz 825 Eighth Ave New York NY 10019-7475 Office Phone: 212-474-1131. Office Fax: 212-474-3700. Business E-Mail: wfogg@cravath.com.

FOGGAN, LAURA ANNE, lawyer; b. Lake Forest, Ill., Sept. 21, 1958; d. John and Sherry Hope Foggan. BA, MSEd, U. Pa., 1980; JD, George Washington U., 1983. Bar: D.C. 1983, U.S. Supreme Ct. 1987. Assoc. Wald, Harkrader & Ross, Washington, 1983-85, Piper & Marbury, Washington, 1985-87; ptnr. Wiley, Rein & Fielding, Washington, 1988—. Bd. dirs. Ayuda, Washington, 1994—2000; Inter-Insured Arbitration Panel, CPR Inst. for Dispute Resolution. Contbr. articles to profl. jours. Named Vol. of Yr. Women's Legal Def. Fund, 1990, Top 100 Women Bus. Ins. Mag., 2000, Am. Leading Lawyers, Chambers USA; recipient Hugh Johnson, Jr. award, AYUDA, 1993, pro bono award DC Coalition Against Domestic Violence, 1988. Mem. ABA (mem. ins. coverage litigation com., subcom. chair), Women's Bar Assn., Def. Rsch. Inst. Office: Wiley Rein & Fielding 1776 K St NW Washington DC 20006

FOGIEL, MAX, publishing executive; b. Magdeburg, Germany, Aug. 29, 1929; came to U.S., 1940; s. Abram and Sara (Pergericht) F. BME, Cooper Union U., N.Y.C., 1952; MME, Poly. Inst., Bklyn., 1954; PhD in Elec. Engring., Tech. U., Munich, Germany, 1965. Bar: U.S. Patent Office, 1958; registered profl. engr., N.Y., N.J. Sr. engr. Ford Instrument, Long Island City, N.Y., 1952-56, Control Instrument, Bklyn., 1956-59; rsch. engr. Loral Electronics, Bronx, N.Y., 1959-61; project engr. RCA, N.Y.C., 1961-64; pres., CEO, Rsch. & Edn. Assn., Piscataway, NJ, 1964—2004, dir. engring. seminars, 1964-66. Instr. in elec. engring. N.J. Inst. Tech., 1965-66. Author: Microelectronics, 1968, 1973, Life Insurance, 1972, Beauty Care, 1993, AIDS and HIV, 1995, Handbook of Electrical Engineering, 1996, Handbook of Chemical Engineering, 1998, Handbook of Mechanical Engineering, 1998; editor: 41 Problem Solvers, 1973—, Calculus Textbook, 2002, series bus. and math. books, 1999; pub. H.S. and coll. study guides and handbooks in sci. and tech.; editor: Basic Electronics, 2003, (test preparation books for) No Child Left Behind series, 2003. Achievements include invention of in field. Avocation: painting. Home: 44 Maple Ct Highland Park NJ 08904-1922 Office Phone: 732-214-8892.

FOGLAND, DENNIS JOHAN, lawyer; b. North Platte, Nebr., June 1, 1951; s. Max N. and Fern P. (Forsberg) F. BA, U. Nebr., 1976; JD, U. Va., 1980. Bar: Nebr. 1980. Ptnr. Baird Holm Law Firm, Omaha, 1980—. With U.S. Army, 1972-73. Named One of Ten Outstanding Young Omahans, Omaha Jaycees, 1988. Mem. ABA, Nebr. Bar Assn., Omaha Bar Assn., Rotary. Lutheran. Office: Baird Holm Law Firm 1500 Woodmen Towers Omaha NE 68102

FOGLE, JAMES LEE, lawyer; b. Doniphan, Mo., June 6, 1950; s. Carter Lemuel and Leatha Sue (Logan) F.; m. Pattylynn Raymond, Sept. 18, 1982; children: Kirsten Nicole, Ryan Christopher. BA, Whitman Coll., 1972; JD, Duke U., 1975. Bar: Mo. 1975, Ill. 1976. Assoc. Coburn, Croft & Putzell, St. Louis, 1975-79; ptnr. Coburn & Croft, St. Louis, 1979-96, mng. ptnr., 1980-84, mem. mgmt. com., 1985-89; ptnr. Thompson Coburn, LLP, St. Louis, 1996—. Bd. dirs. Life Skills Found., pres. 1996-98; bd. dirs. Rainbow Village; adj. prof. Fontbonne Coll., St. Louis, 1991-2000. Alumni admissions rep. Whitman Coll., Walla Walla, Wash., 1980—; mem. planned giving coun. DePaul Health Ctr. Found. Nat. Merit scholar Whitman Coll., 1968. Mem. ABA, Estate Planning Coun., Mo. Bar Assn. (tax com.), Am. Health Lawyers Assn., St. Louis Health Lawyers Assn., Mo. Athletic Club, Racquet Club Ladue (bd. govs. 2001-2005), Masons, Order of Coif, Phi Beta Kappa. Republican. Baptist. Avocations: tennis, snow skiing, golf, collecting political memorabilia. Office: Thompson Coburn LLP Ste 3500 One USBank Plz Saint Louis MO 63101-1623 Office Phone: 314-552-6035. E-mail: jfogle@thompsoncoburn.com.

FOGLEMAN, GUY CARROLL, physicist, mathematician, educator; b. Lake Charles, La., Dec. 29, 1955; s. Louis Carroll and Peggy Joyce (Trahan) F.; m. Jenny S. Kishiyama, Mar. 14, 1993; children: Elyssa Mayumi, Myles Masaru. BS in Physics, La. State U., 1977; MS in Physics, Ind. U., 1979, MA in Math., 1981, PhD in Physics, 1982. Rsch. assoc. Tri Univ. Meson Facility U. B.C., Vancouver, Canada, 1982—84; assoc. prof. San Francisco State U., 1984—87, adj. prof., 1987—; project scientist RCA Govt. Svcs., Moffett Field, Calif., 1987—88; prin. investigator Search for Extraterrestrial Intelligence Inst., Mountain View, Calif., 1988—89; mgr. advanced programs life scis. divsn. NASA Hdqrs., Washington, 1990—93; acting chief environ. sys. and tech. br. Life and Biomed Scis. and Applications divsn. NASA Hdqrs., Washington, 1993—95; program exec. human exploration and devel. of space advanced human support techs. program Life Scis. divsn. NASA, Washington, 1996—2000; acting dir. bioastronautics rsch. divsn. NASA Hdqrs., Washington, 2000—03, dir. bioastronautics rsch. divsn., 2003—. Vis. physicist Stanford (Calif.) Linear Accelerator Ctr., 1984-86. Contbr. articles to sci. jours. Travel grantee NSF and NATO, 1980; rsch. grantee NASA, 1988, 89. Mem. AIAA (sr.), AAAS, Am. Phys. Soc., Prometheus Soc. (ombudsman 1998-99), Mega Soc., Sigma Xi (assoc.), Sigma Pi Sigma, Internat. Acad. Astronautics (corr. mem.). Achievements include research in physics of particles in microgravity, theoretical elementary particle physics, technologies for the collection of cosmic dust particles, the origins of life and the philosophy of mind. Office: NASA Hdqrs Code UB Washington DC 20546-0001 E-mail: guy.fogleman@nasa.gov.

FOGLEMAN, JULIAN BARTON, lawyer; b. Memphis, Apr. 17, 1920; s. John Franklin and Marie Julia (McAdams) F.; m. Melba Margaret Henderson, Aug. 11, 1950; children: Margaret Elisabeth Heath, Julian Barton, John Nelson, Jennifer Leigh Vaughan, Frances Lorie Irwin. BS, U. Ark., 1941, LL.B., 1943, JD, 1969. Bar: Ark. 1943. Practiced in Marion, 1946-54, West Memphis, 1954—; pvt. practice, 1946-52; assoc. Hale & Fogleman, 1952-66, ptnr., 1967-73, Hale, Fogleman & Rogers, 1974—2001, Fogleman & Rogers, 2002—. City atty., Marion, 1951-81, dep. pros. atty., 1957-64 Chmn. fin. dir. Crittenden dist. Chickasaw coun. Boy Scouts Am., 1969, mem. exec. bd. coun., 1970-71, 75-80; bd. dirs. Crittenden County Charities, 1994-97, v.p., 1995; bd. dirs. Ark. Good Rds. Transp. Coun., 1976-96; mem. Ark. Cmty. Based Rehab. Commn., 1978-86, Crittenden County Bd. Edn., 1987-92. With inf. AUS, 1943-45, ETO. Fellow Am. Bar Found., Ark. Bar. Found. (bd. dirs. 1989-92); mem. ABA, Ark. Bar Assn. (ho. of dels. 1972-75, 81-84, exec. council 1972-75, 81-84, outstanding lawyer citizen award 1995-96), N.E. Ark. Bar Assn. (past pres.), Crittenden County Bar Assn. (past pres.), Phi Alpha Delta, Sigma Chi. Methodist. Home: 84 Turner Ave Marion AR 72364-1932 Office: PO Box 1666 123 W Broadway West Memphis AR 72301 Office Phone: 870-735-1900.

FOGLEMAN, RONALD ROBERT, retired air force officer, consultant; b. Juniata County, Pa., Jan. 27, 1942; s. Harry R. and Sara (Landis) F.; m. M. Jane Lauver, June 22, 1963; children: Harry R., William E. BS, USAF Acad., 1963; MA, Duke U., 1971. Commd. 2d lt. USAF, 1963, advanced through grades to gen., 1992, fighter, mobility and command pilot; chief Tactical Forces Divsn., The Pentagon, Washington, 1979-81; vice comdr. 388th Tactical Fighter Wing, Hill AFB, Utah, 1981-82; dir. fighter ops. Hdqrs. Tactical Air Command, Langley AFB, Va., 1982-83; comdr. 56th Tactical Tng. Wing, MacDill AFB, Fla., 1983-84, 836th Air Divsn., Davis-Monthan AFB, Ariz., 1984-86; dep. dir. Programs and Procedure, Hdqrs. USAF, Washington, 1986-88, dir., 1988-90; comdr. 7th Air Force, 1990-92; comdr. in chief U.S. Transp. Command, 1992-94; comdr. Air Mobility Command, 1992-94; chief of staff USAF, Washington, 1994-97, ret. gen., 1997; chmn., CEO Durango Aerospace Inc. Bd. dirs. Mesa Airgroup, N.Am. Airlines, Mitre Corp., World Airways, Rolls-Royce N.Am.; mem. Def. Policy Bd., 2001-. Chmn. Falcon Found., Airlift/Tanker Assn.; bd. dirs. Ft. Lewis Coll. Found., Mitre Corp.; mem. NASA Shuttle Return to Flight Task Group; chmn. Vision 2050: An Integrated Transp. Sys., Nat. Rsch. Council. Mem. Air Force Assn., USAF Acad. Assn. Grads., Daedalians (flight capt. 1983-84, 89-90), Coun. Fgn. Rels. Republican. Methodist. Avocation: rugby. Home: 406 Snow Cap Ln Durango CO 81303-3636*

FOGLER, DAN, actor; b. Bklyn., Oct. 20, 1977; Grad., Boston U. Performer: (off-broadway plays) The Detective Sketches, The Voyage of the Carcass, Bridges and Harmonies, Joe Fearless, 2000, The 25th Annual Putnam County Spelling Bee, 2004, 2005 (Lucille Lortel award for Outstanding Featured Actor, 2005), (off-off broadway) Bobby Gould in Hell, 2004, C-R-E-P-E-S-C-U-L-E, 2004, (Broadway plays) Joe Fearless, 2000, The 25th Annual Putnam County Spelling Bee, 2005— (Drama League award nomination for Disting. Performance, 2005, Outer Critics Circle award for Outstanding Featured Actor in a Musical, 2005, Theatre World award, 2005, Tony award for Best Performance by a Featured Actor in a Musical, 2005); stand-up comic appeared in comedy clubs such as Caroline's Comedy Club, Gotham Comedy Club, Stand Up NY and NYCC; performer: (Nat. Tour) Scooby Doo/Stage Fright; actor: (films) Brooklyn Thrill Killers, 1999, Home Field Advantage, 2000, Bust a Move, 2000, Hyper, 2002. Address: c/o Circle in the Square Theatre 1633 Broadway New York NY 10036*

FOGLESONG, JAMES STATON (JIM), retired music company executive; b. Lundale, W. Va., July 1922; m. Toni Foglesong; 4 children. Grad., Eastman Sch. of Music, Rochester, NY. Joined Columbia Records, NYC, 1951; head Epic Records, NYC; exec. prodr. RCA Records, NYC, 1963—70; pres. ABC/Dot Records, Nashville, 1970—79, MCA Nashville, Nashville, 1979—84, Capitol Records, Nashville, 1984—89; now cons., independent prodr, Nashville; adj. prof. music, Blair Sch. of Music Vanderbilt Univ., Nashville, 1991—; dir., music bus. program. Trevecca Nazarene Univ. Chmn. of bd. Country Music Assn., 1976, 87, trustee. Achievements include being credited with furthering careers of Garth Brooks, Reba McEntire, George Strait, Oak Ridge Boys, Tanya Tucker, others. Office: Trustee Country Music Assn One Music Cir South Nashville TN 37203

FOGO, PETER C., social studies educator, writer, poet; b. Glendale, Calif., Nov. 27, 1946; s. Dominic Guy and Elizabeth Elaine (Komenich) Fogo; m. Sharon Lee Miller, June 15, 1968 (div. Apr. 1976); children: Credence Elizabeth, Renard Marie; m. Georgia Holliday, Dec. 5, 1981. BA, U. Nev., 1969; MA, No. Mich. U., 1972. Lectr. No. Mich. U., Marquette, 1971-72; tchr. social studies Channelview (Tex.) H.S., 1988—. Featured poet Houston Poetry Fest, S.W. Writers Inst., 1995. Author: (poetry) Single Again, 1980, A Language That Keeps Company with the Moon, 1992 (novels) Nightsong, 1998, Bitterroot, 2001. Mem. Green Party. Home: Box 7743 Pasadena TX 77508

FOHL, TIMOTHY, investment company executive; b. Pitts., Apr. 21, 1934; s. Edward Zinn and Dorothy (Umbenhauer) F.; m. Nancy Lee Hattox, Apr. 15, 1961; children: Nicholas, Jeffrey, Peter. AB, Dartmouth Coll., 1956; MS, MIT, 1959, PhD, 1963; postgrad. exec. devel. program, Whittemore Sch. Bus. and Econs., 1977. Rsch. scientist Itek Corp., Lexington, Mass., 1962-63, Mt. Auburn Rsch. Assos., Newton, Mass., 1963-68, prin. scientist, dir., 1968-72; with GTE Products Corp., Danvers, Mass., 1972—88, mgr. new product devel. lighting group, 1977-82, mgr. engring. devel., 1982-85, dir. engring. devel., 1985-88; scientist GTE Labs., Inc., Waltham, Mass., 1988-92; pres. Tech. Integration Group, Carlisle, Mass., 1992—; v.p. Light Time in Space,

Inc., 1992—; dir. chief sci. officer Qualume Corp., 2002—. Contbr. articles to profl. jours.; patentee in field. Pres., trustee Carlisle Conservation Found., 1972-79; v.p. Carlisle Trails Assn., 1975—; fin. chmn. Town Republican Com., 1980; dir., chief sci. officer Qualume Corp., 2002. Recipient Leslie H. Warner Tech. Achievement award, 1990. Mem. Mass. Bus. Roundtable. Home: 681 South St Carlisle MA 01741-1517 Office Phone: 978-371-0194. E-mail: tfohl@tigco.com.

FOHRER, ALAN J., utilities company executive; BS, MS, U. So. Calif.; MBA, Calif. State U., Los Angeles. V.p., treas., CFO Southern Calif. Edison (SCE), 1991—93; sr. v.p., treas., CFO Edison Internat., SCE, Rosemead, Calif., 1993; chmn., pres., CEO Edison Mission Energy, Irvine, Calif., 2000—02; CEO Southern Calif. Edison (SCE), 2002—. Office: So Calif Edison 2244 Walnut Grove Ave Rosemead CA 91770*

FOK, AGNES KWAN, retired cell biologist, educator; b. Hong Kong, China, Dec. 11, 1940; came to US, 1962; d. Sun and Yau (Ng) Kwan; m. Fok, June 8, 1965; children: Licie Chiu-Jane, Edna Chiu-Joan. BA in Chemistry, U. Great Falls, 1965; MS in Plant Nutrition and Biochemistry, Utah State U., 1966; PhD in Biochemistry, U. Tex., 1971. Asst. rsch. prof. pathology U. Hawaii, Honolulu, 1973-74, Ford Found. postdoctoral fellow, anatomy dept., 1975, asst. rsch. prof., 1975-82, assoc. rsch. prof., 1982—96, rsch. prof. Pacific Biomed. Rsch. Ctr., 1988-96, grad. faculty, dept. microbiology, 1977—2003, dir., 1994-96, dir., prof. biology program, 1996—2003, prof. emeritus, 2003—. Contbr. articles to profl. jours. Mem. Am. Soc. for Cell Biology, Soc. for Protozoologists, Sigma Xi (treas. Hawaii chpt. 1979-2002). Avocations: reading, gardening, hiking, sewing. Office: U Hawaii Biology Program Honolulu HI 96822 Business E-Mail: fok@hawaii.edu.

FOK, THOMAS DSO YUN, civil engineer; b. Canton, China, July 1, 1921; came to U.S., 1947, naturalized, 1956; s D. H. and C. (Tse) F.; m. Maria M.L. Liang, Sept. 18, 1949. B.Eng., Nat. Tung-Chi U., Szechuan, China, 1945; MS, U. Ill., 1948; MBA Dr. Nadler Money Marketeer scholar, NYU, 1950; PhD, Carnegie-Mellon U., 1956. Registered profl. engr., N.Y., Pa., Ohio, Ill., Ky., W.Va., Ind., Md., Fla. Structural designer Lummus Co., N.Y.C., 1951-53; design engr. Richardson, Gordon & Assocs., cons. engrs., Pitts., 1956-58; assoc. prof. engring. Youngstown U., Ohio, 1958-67, dir. computing ctr., 1963-67; ptnr. Cernica, Fok & Assocs., cons. engrs., Youngstown, Ohio, 1958-64; prin. Thomas Fok & Assocs., cons. engrs., Youngstown, Ohio, 1964-65; ptnr. Mosure-Fok & Syrakis Co., Ltd., cons. Engrs., Youngstown, Ohio, 1965-76; cons. engr. to Mahoning County Engr. Ohio, 1960-65; pres. Computing Systems & Tech., Youngstown, Ohio, 1967-72; chmn. Thomas Fok and Assocs., Ltd., cons. engrs., Youngstown, Ohio, 1977—. Contbr. articles to profl. jours. Trustee Pub. Libr. of Youngstown and Mahoning County, 1973—; trustee Youngstown State U., 1975-84, chmn., 1981-83; mem. Ohio State Bd. Registration for Profl. Engrs. and Surveyors, 1992-96. Recipient Walter E. and Caroline H. Watson Found. Disting. Prof.'s award Youngstown U., 1966, Outstanding Person award Mahoning Valley Tech. Socs. Council, 1987. Fellow ASCE; mem. Am. Concrete Inst., Internat. Assn. for Bridge and Structural Engring., Am. Soc. Engring. Edn., Nat. Soc. Profl. Engrs., AAAS, Soc. Am. Mil. Engrs., Ohio Acad. Sci., N.Y. Acad. Sci., Sigma Xi, Beta Gamma Sigma, Sigma Tau, Delta Pi Sigma Lodges: Rotary. Achievements include development of a design method by computer for a solid-ribbed tied, through arch Ft. Duquesne Bridge; development of Analysis of Continuous Truss by Digital Computer. Home: 325 S Canfield Niles Rd Youngstown OH 44515-4020 Office: 3896 Mahoning Ave Youngstown OH 44515-3022

FOLAND, KENNETH A., geological sciences educator; b. Frederick, Md., May 25, 1945; s. Austin Franklin and P. Lillian (Wachter) F.; m. Ellen Lee Spero, June 18, 1968. BS, Bucknell U., 1967; MSc, Brown U., 1969, PhD, 1972. Postdoctoral fellow U. Pa., Phila., 1972-73, from asst. prof. to assoc. prof., 1973-80; assoc. prof. Ohio State U., Columbus, 1980-87, prof. geological scis., 1987—. Cons. divsn. nuclear chemistry Lawrence Livermore Nat. Lab., 1982-86, adv. com. nuclear waste U.S. Nuclear Regulatory Commn., 1990-99; mem. indoor radon panel Am. Lung Assn. Ohio, mem. steering and rev. com. Columbus and Franklin County Radon Study, Columbus Health Dept. Assoc. editor Isotope Geosci., 1982-99, Jour. Geophys. Rsch., Solid Earth, 1992-98; adv. editor Jour. Geol. Soc.; reviewer rsch. papers, rsch. proposals; author, co-author numerous rsch. papers, abstracts, revs. Recipient numerous grants NSF, NIH, DAAD and NATO. Fellow Geol. Soc. Am.; mem. Am. Geophys. Union, Geochem. Soc., Sigma Xi. Home: 4090 Fenwick Rd Columbus OH 43220-4870 Office: Ohio State U 125 South Oval Mall 379 Mendenhall Lab Columbus OH 43210 E-mail: foland.1@osu.edu.

FOLBERG, HAROLD JAY, lawyer, educator, dean; b. East St. Louis, Ill., July 7, 1941; s. Louis and Matilda (Ross) F.; m. Diana L. Taylor, May 1, 1983; children: Lisa, Rachel, Ross. BA, San Francisco State U., 1963; JD, U. Calif., Berkeley, 1968. Bar: Oreg. 1968. Assoc. Rives & Schwab, Portland, Oreg., 1968-69; dir. Legal Aid Service, Portland, 1970-72; exec. dir. Assn. Family and Conciliation Cts., Portland, 1974-80; prof. law Lewis and Clark Law Sch., Portland, 1972-89; clin. asst. prof. child psychiatry U. Oreg. Med. Sch., 1976-89; judge pro-tem Oreg. Trial Cts., 1974-89; dean, prof. U. San Francisco Sch. Law, 1989-99, prof. law, 1999—. Chair jud. coun. Calif. Task Force on Alternative Dispute Resolution and the Jud. Sys., 1998-99, Calif. Blue Ribbon Panel Experts on Arbitration Ethics, 2001-2002, chair jud. coun.; Rockefeller Found. scholar in residence Bellagio, Italy, 1996; vis. prof. U. Wash. Sch. Law, 1985-86; mem. vis. faculty Nat. Jud. Coll., 1975-88; mem. Nat. Commn. on Accreditation for Marriage and Family Therapists, 1984-90; cons. Calif. Jud. Coun., U.S. Dist. Ct. (no. dist.) Calif., JAMS. Author: Joint Custody and Shared Parenting, 1984, 2d edit., 1991; (with Taylor) Mediation-A Comprehensive Guide to Resolving Conflicts without Litigation, 1984; (with Milne) Divorce Mediation, 1988; (with others) Divorce and Family Mediation: Models, Techniques and Applications, 2004, Resolving Disputes: Theory, Practice and Law, 2005; mem. editl. bd. Family Counts Rev., Jour. of Divorce, Conflict Resolution Quar.; contbr. articles to profl. jours. Bd. dirs. Internat. Bioethics Inst., 1989-95, Oreg. Dispute Resolution Adv. Coun., 1988-89. Recipient Bernard E. Witkin award, Jud. Coun. Calif., 2002. Mem. ABA (chmn. mediation and arbitration com. family law sect. 1980-82, chmn. ethics com. dispute resolution sect. 2002-04), Oreg. State Bar Assn. (chmn. family and juvenile law sect. 1979-80), Am. Bd. Trial Advs., Multnomah Bar Assn. (chmn. bd. dirs. legal aid svc. 1973-76), Assn. Family and Conciliation Cts. (pres. 1983-84), Assn. Marriage and Family Therapists (disting. mem.), Am. Assn. Law Schs. (chmn. alternative dispute resolution sect. 1988), Acad. Family Mediators (bd. dirs., pres. 1988), CPR Inst. (panel disting. mediators), World Assn. Law Profs. (sec.-gen. 1995-2000). Office: U San Francisco Sch Law 2130 Fulton St San Francisco CA 94117-1080 Business E-Mail: folbergj@usfca.edu.

FOLBRE, NANCY, economics professor; BA in Philosophy, U. Tex., 1971, MA in Lat. Am. Studies, 1973; PhD in Econs., U. Mass., 1979. Trainee Nat. Inst. Child Health Care and Devel. Population Rsch. Ctr. U. Tex., 1974-75; postdoct. rsch. fellow Econ. Growth Ctr. Yale U., New Haven, Conn., 1979-80; asst. prof. econs. Bowdoin Coll., 1980-83, New Sch. Social Rsch., N.Y.C., 1983-85; assoc. prof. econs. U. Mass., Amherst, 1984-91, prof. econs., 1991—. Cons. Maine Commn. for Women, 1981, Beijer Inst. Author: A Field Guide to the U.S. Economy, 1988, Who Pays for the Kids? Gender and the Structures of Constrint, 1994, The New Field Guide to the U.S. Economy, 1995, War on the Poor: A Defense Manual, 1996, De la différence des sexes en économie politique, edit. des femmes, 1997; editor: The Economics of the Family, 1996; co-editor: Issues in Contemporary Economics, vol. 4, 1991; mem. editl. bd.: Explrations in Economic History, 1995—); contbr. numerous articles to profl. jours., newspapers, chpts. to books. Co-chair rsch. network on families in the economy The MacArthur Found., 1997. Tchg., rsch. fellow French-Am. Found., 1995-96; MacArthur fellow John D. and Catherine T. MacArthur Found., 1998; faculty rsch. grantee U. Mass., 1987, Healey Pub. svc. Endowment grantee U. Mass., 1989, grantee NSF, 1989. Mem. Am. Econs. Assn. (presenter), Internat. Assn. Feminist Econs. (bd. dirs. 1992—, program chair Ctr. Popular Econs. 1979—, presenter, spkr.). Office: U Mass Dept Econs Amherst MA 01003 Fax: 413-545-2921. E-mail: folbre@econs.umass.edu.

FOLDEN, NORMAN C. (SKIP FOLDEN), information systems executive, consultant; b. San Francisco, July 28, 1933; BS in Math./English/Engring., U.S. Mil. Acad., 1956. With IBM, various locations, 1966-83, U.S. program mgr. I/S tech. Sommers, N.Y., 1983-86; owner Folden Mgmt. (Palladin Advocacy), 1986-91, Folden Mgmt., Las Vegas, 1991—. Author: Drug Criminalization: Organized Crime Cash Cow, Prime Cause of U.S. Victim Crime and Threat to National Sovereignty, 1996, Delegation of Legislative Authority, 1997, Payback to Lippo Group or Grand Coincidence at Grand Staircase, 1997, Kosovo Negotiations Provisions-Five by Five Plan, 1999, ICTY Charges and Submission, 1999, Matrix of Deception: The Iraq War and the Betrayal of American Values, 2005; contbr. poetry to anthologies. Mem. Assn. Grads. U.S. Mil. Acad., Little Big Horn Assocs., Calif. Scholarship Fedn., Team Marcus. Avocations: ancient history/teachings/exploration, organized crime and drug policy, antiquities, constitutional law. Home and Office: 4329 Silvercrest Ct North Las Vegas NV 89032-0116 Personal E-mail: sfolden@ix.netcom.com.

FOLDI, ANDREW HARRY, retired vocalist; b. Budapest, Hungary, July 20, 1926; arrived in U.S., 1939, naturalized, 1947; s. Alexis and Ann Foldi; children from previous marriage: David John, Nancy Susanne; m. Marta Justus. PhB, U. Chgo., 1945, MA, 1948; pvt. student singing and piano. Pvt. tchr. voice, 1949-61; cantor, mus. dir. Temple Isaiah Israel, Chgo., 1949-61, English-Speaking Jewish Community of Geneva, 1963-71; vis. prof. voice and music Cleve. Inst. Music, 1978-81; chmn. opera dept. Cleve. Inst. Mus., 1981-91; dir. Chgo. Lyric Opera Ctr. for Am. Artists, 1991-95; ret., 1995; mem. faculty U. Chgo., 1947-49, dept. adult edn., 1951-61; instr., dir. opera workshop DePaul U., 1949-57. Vis. instr. voice Augustana Coll., 1950-51; mem. faculty apprentice tng. program Santa Fe Opera, 1959, 64, 76, 77, also stage dir.; stage dir. Pa. Opera Festival, 1982, 83, Utah Opera, 1986, 88, 91, Wolf Trap Festival, 1987, Toledo Opera, 1987, 89, Atlanta Opera, 1989, Chgo. Opera Theater, 1990, Chgo. Lyric Opera Ctr., 1992. Author: recorded text An Introduction to Music, 1959; also criticism, program notes; contbr. articles to profl. publs.; Leading bass, Met. Opera, N.Y.C., La Scala, Milan, Vienna Staatsoper, Teatro San Carlo, Naples, Vienna Festival, Grand Theâtre, Geneva, Theâtre Royale de la Monnaie, Brussels, Teatro Regio, Torino, Am. Nat. Opera, Cin. Opera, Stadttheater, Zurich, Teatro Comunale, Genoa, Nederlandsche Opera, Amsterdam, San Francisco Opera Co., Lyric Opera Chgo., Santa Fe Opera, Sociedad Pro Arte Mus., Havana, Cuba; guest soloist, Vienna Festival, Bavarian State Radio, Munich, Concertgebouw Orch., Amsterdam, Orch. de la Suisse Romande, Geneva, Nat. Orch. Monte Carlo, Pitts. Symphony Orch., Clarion Concerts, N.Y., Gulbenkian Found., Lisbon, Concerti sinfonici, Genoa, Atlanta Symphony Orch., Aldeburgh, Lucerne, Lausanne, Ravinia, Glyndebourne, Florence Maggio Musicale festivals, Chgo. Symphony Orch., N.Y. Philharmonic Orch., Boston Symphony, Cleve. Orchestra, San Francisco Symphony, Little Orch. Soc., N.Y., Rochester, Kansas City (Mo.) philharmonic orchs., Radio Sottens, Geneva, Radio Beromunster, Zurich, Grant Park Concerts, Chgo., Indpls. Symphony Orch., Internat. Soc. Contemporary Music, also numerous recitals, radio and TV appearances, recordings for Columbia, Vanguard, Concert Hall, La Voix d'Eglise.

FOLDS, FRANK ELLIOTT, music educator; b. Atlanta, Ga., July 13, 1957; s. Charlie Clifford Folds and Martha Frances McKee; m. Cheri Lynn Jones, Mar. 31, 1964; children: Frank Elliott, Ansley Elizabeth, Emily Katherine, Abigail Katelyn. MusB, U. of Ga., 1975—79, MusM, 1980—82, Edn. Specialist in Music Edn., 1999—2002. T-6 Ga. Profl. Standards Commn., 2002. Band dir. Baldwin County Pub. Schools, Milledgeville, Ga., 1980—80, Jeff Davis Bd. of Edn., Hazlehurst, Ga., 1983—86, Camden County Pub. Schools, Woodbine, Ga., 1986—88, Clayton County Pub. Schools, Jonesboro, Ga., 1988—89, Camden County Bd. of Edn., Woodbine, Ga., 1989—95, Gwinnett County Pub. Schools, Lawrenceville, Ga., 1995—. Mem. bd. dirs. U. of Ga. Alumni Band, 1986—2001; treas. Tara Winds Scholarship Found., Jonesboro, Ga., 2003—; chmn. of band masters hall of fame Phi Beta Mu Hon. Band Masters Frat., Atlanta, 2002—. Contbr. book, Orch. dir. W. R. Cannon United Meth. Ch., Snellville, Ga., 2001, 2001; lead tchr. Gwinnett County Pub. Schools, Lawrenceville, Ga., 2002—04. Recipient Tchr. of the Yr., Camden County Bd. of Edn., 1992—93, Selected as featured performing group, Ga. Music Educators Assn., 1997. Mem.: Music Edn. Leadership Inst. at Ga. State U., U. of Ga. Ednl. Enhancement Fund, PA of Ga. Educators (assoc.), Ga. Music Educators Assn. (assoc.; state band divsn. chmn. 1997—99), Ga. Music Educators Assn. (assoc.; v.p. 1991—93), Phi Beta Mu Hon. Band Masters Frat. (assoc.; mem. at large of exec. com. 2001—03). Christian, Protestant, United Meth. Home: 565 Georgian Hills Dr Lawrenceville GA 30045 Office: Alton C Crews Middle Sch 1000 Old Snellville Highway Lawrenceville GA 30044 Office Phone: 770-982-6940. Home Fax: 770-982-6942; Office Fax: 770-982-6942. Personal E-mail: folder57@aol.com. E-mail: frank_folds@gwinnett.k12.ga.us.

FOLDVARY, FRED EMANUEL, economist, educator; b. Haifa, Israel, May 11, 1946; came to U.S., 1952; s. Otto and Tina (Klein) F.; m. Janet Waara. BA in Econs./Computer Sci., U. Calif., Berkeley, 1970; MA in Econs., George Mason U., 1990, PhD in Econs., 1992. Editor Topical Time mag., 1981-87; prof. U. Latvia, Riga, 1993, Latvian U. Agr., Jelgara, 1992-93; prof. econs. Mary Washington Coll., Fredericksburg, Va., 1994, Va. Poly. Inst. and State U., Blacksburg, 1994-95, Calif. State U., Hayward, 1995—98; lectr. econ. Santa Clara U., 1998—. Dir. Embarcadero Fed. Credit Union, San Francisco, 1979-81. Author: Soul of Liberty, 1980, Public Goods and Private Communities, 1994, Dictionary of Free MarketEconomics, 1998. Chmn. Libertarian party, Alameda County, Calif., 1981-82. Bradley fellow Ctr. for Study of Pub. Choice, George Mason U., 1989-91. Mem. Am. Econ. Assn., Congress Polit. Economists, Common Ground Va. Office: Dept Economics Santa Clara Univ 500 El Camino Real Santa Clara CA 95053 Office Phone: 408-554-6968. Office Fax: 408-554-2331. Business E-Mail: ffoldvary@scu.edu.

FOLDY, SETH LEONARD, physician, educator; b. Cleve., Sept. 3, 1955; s. Leslie Lawrance and Roma (Bisgyer) F; m. Joan Marie Bedinghaus, June 7, 1986; children: Benjamin, Eva. BA in Human Biology with distinction, Stanford U., 1977; MD, Case Western Res. U., 1982; MA in Pub. Health, Medical Coll. Wis., 2005. Dilomate Am. Bd. Family Practice, Nat. Bd. Med. Examiners. Intern in family practice Cleve. Met. Gen. Hosp., 1982-83, resident in family practice, 1983-85, chief resident in family practice, 1984-85; family physician Great Brook Valley Health Ctr., Worcester, Mass., 1985-87; med. dir. MetroHealth Family Practice, Cleve., 1987-94, dir. cmty. health svcs., 1994-96; med. dir. City of Milw. Health Dept., 1996-98, health commr., 1998—2004; STA fac. appointee Argonne Nat. Lab., Argonne, Ill., 2004—. Asst. prof. family medicine Case Western Res. U., Cleve., 1987-96; assoc. clin. prof. family and cmty. medicine Health Policy Inst. Preventive Medicine, Med. Coll. Wis., Milw., 1996—, clin. prof. health adminstrn. and informatics, U. Wis., 2001-. Asst. editor: Urban Family Practice: A Resource Monograph, 1994; editor (newsletter) Urban Health News, 1990-96. Trustee Friends Sch. in Cleve., 1972-74; nat. com. War Resisters League, N.Y.C., 1970-74; mem. Nat. Health Policy Leadership Coun., Washington, 1991-92, Ohio legis. adv. com. on environ. lead abatement, Columbus, 1994-95, Wis. Turning Point Transformation Team, 1998—, Wis. pub. health system terrorism and pub. health emergencies legis. coun. com., 2002; mem. info. coun. U.S. CDC, 2000—, steering com. Rand Inst. Summits on Info. Tech. Infrastructure for Bioterrorism, Operation Combined Assistance, US Navy Project Hope Tsunami Task Force, 2005; bd. dirs. eHealth Initiative & Health Initiative Found., 2002—, Greater Milw. Bus. Group on Health, Southeast Wis. Bioterrorism Preparedness Group, Inc. Recipient award for Excellence in Info. Tech., Nat. Assn. County and City Health Officers, 1999. Fellow Am. Acad. Family Physicians; mem. AMA, APHA (gov. coun. 1992-94, 96-98, Roemer prize for Creative Local Pub. Health Wk., Am. Pub. Health Assn., 2002), Nat. Assn. City and County Health Officers (various coms.), Pub. Health Leadership Soc., Wis. Med. Soc., Milw. Acad. Medicine (bd. dirs. 2003-), Milw. County Med. Soc. (chair pub. health com. 1996—, Cmty. Svc. award 1997), Phi Beta Kappa. Avocations: fishing, hiking, birding. Office: Health Evolution Cons 3061 N Marietta Ave Milwaukee WI 53211 Office Phone: 414-339-3865. Personal E-mail: sfoldy@sbcglobal.net.

FOLEY, ANN, broadcast executive; BA, Mount Holyoke Coll., 1976. Exec. v.p. programming Showtime Networks, Inc., N.Y.C., 1988—96, exec. V.P. east coast programming, 1996—. Mem.: FCC Oversight Monitoring Bd., TV Parental Guidelines Monitoring Bd. Office: Showtime Networks Inc 1633 Broadway Fl 17 New York NY 10019-6708

FOLEY, CHERYL M., electric power industry executive; V.p., gen. counsel PSI Energy, Inc., Ind., 1989-91; v.p., gen. counsel, corp. sec. PSI Energy, Inc. and PSI Resources Inc., Ind., 1991-94; v.p., sec., gen. counsel Cinergy Corp., Cin., 1994-99, v.p., sec., 1999—; pres. Cinergy Global Resources subs. Cinergy Corp., Cin. Office: Cinergy Corp 221 E 4th St # 30 Cincinnati OH 45202-4124

FOLEY, CHRISTOPHER P., lawyer; b. 1953; BS, US Naval Acad., 1975; JD, Georgetown U., 1983. Bar: DC 1983, US Ct. Appeals (Fed. Cir.) 1983, Va. 2003, registered: US Patent & Trademark Office. Ptnr., Trademark & Copyright Practice Group Finnegan, Henderson, Farabow, Garrett & Dunner LLP, firm mng. ptnr., chmn. mgmt. com., mng. ptnr. Reston Office. Mem.: Am. Intellectual Property Law Assn., ABA, Bar Assn. DC, DC Bar. Office: Finnegan Henderson Farabow Garrett & Dunner LLP Two Freedom Sq 11955 Freedom Dr Reston VA 20190-5675 Office Phone: 571-203-2700. Office Fax: 202-408-4400. Business E-Mail: christopher.foley@finnegan.com.

FOLEY, DANIEL RONALD, personnel director, lawyer; b. Chgo., Dec. 13, 1941; s. Daniel Edward and Louise Jean (Connolly) Foley; m. Mae Geraldine Muscarello, Jan. 30, 1965; children: Louise Ann, Sarah Elizabeth. AB in Psychology, Marquette U., 1965; JD, Depaul U., 1971. Bar: Ill. 1971, U.S. Dist. Ct. (no. dist.) Ill. 1971, U.S. Supreme Ct. 1975, Mich. 1989. Pers. recruiter Civil Svc. Commn. City of Chgo., 1965-66; pers. adminstr. Alberto Culver Co., Melrose Park, Ill., 1966-67; pers. dir. Litton Industries, Des Plaines, Ill., 1967-68; equal opportunity coord., mgr. labor rels. Canteen Corp., Chgo., 1968-71; mgr. labor rels. Internat. Telephone and Telegraph World Hdqs., N.Y.C., 1971-79, dir. employee rels., 1979-81, 1981-85; dir. employee rels., environ. health and safety, group v.p. human resources IBP, Dakota City, Nebr., 1985-88; v.p. adminstrn., gen. counsel Domino's Pizza Inc., Ann Arbor, Mich., 1988-93; pres. Exec. Bus. Ptnrs., Inc., 1993-94; v.p. human resources MascoTech, Inc., 1994-96, Masco Corp., Taylor, Mich., 1996—. Spkr. labor law and bus. seminars Wharton Sch., U. Pa., St. Mary's Coll., LEGATUS; faculty mem. Mich. U. Mem.: Knights of Holy Sepulchre, Knights of Malta. Roman Catholic. Avocation: photography. Home: 3399 Robinwood Dr Ann Arbor MI 48103-1748 E-mail: dcn@aol.com, daniel_foley@mascohq.com.

FOLEY, DAVID, television and film actor; b. Toronto, Jan. 4, 1963; m. Tabatha Southey, 1991 (div. 1997); children: Edmund, Basil; m. Crissy Guerrero, Aug. 1, 2002; 1 child, Alina. Appeared in films High Stakes, 1986, Three Men and a Baby, 1987, It's Pat, 1994, Hacks, 1997, (voice) A Bug's Life, 1998, The Wrong Guy (aslo writer), 1998, Monkey Bone, 1999, Blast from the Past, 1999, Dick, 1999, (voice) South Park, 1999, (voice) Toy Story 2, 1999, (voice) Cyber World, 2000, Monkeybone, 2001, On the Line, 2001, Stark Raving Mad, 2002, Fancy Dancing, 2002, Swindle, 2002, My Boss's Daughter, 2003, Employee of the Month, 2004, Intern Academy, 2004, Childstar, 2004, Sky High, 2005; appeared in TV series Kids in the Hall (also writer, dir.), 1988-1994, NewsRadio, 1995-99, (voice) Committed, 2001.*

FOLEY, DAVID EDWARD, retired bishop; b. Worcester, Mass., Feb. 3, 1930; Student, St. Charles Coll., Catonsville, Md., St. Mary's Sem., Balt. Ordained priest Archdiocese of Washington, DC, 1956; ordained bishop, 1986; Titular Bishop of Ottaba, 1986—94; Aux. Bishop of Richmond, 1986—94; Bishop of Birmingham, 1994—2005.*

FOLEY, ELLEN MADALINE, journalist; b. Chgo., Apr. 13, 1952; d. Thomas Jennings and Joan Ellen (Murphy) F.; m. Thomas Foley Mullaney, June 30, 1984; children: Kaitlin, Maura. BA in Polit. Sci., U. Wis., 1974, MA in Journalism, 1988. Mng. editor Menominee (Mich.) Herald Leader, 1976-78; copy editor The Milw.-Sentinel, 1978-79, The Detroit News, 1979-80; reporter, copy editor The Star-Tribune, Mpls., 1980-91, asst. features editor, food editor, 1991-93; features editor The Kansas City (Mo.) Star, 1993-96, asst. mng. editor/features, 1996—98; mng. editor The Phila. Daily News, Phila., 1998—2004; editor Wis. State Jour., Madison, 2004—. Mem. Jr. League of Mpls., 1980—, bd. dirs., 1989; founder Violence Against Women Coalition, Mpls., 1988-93. Recipient Minn. Page One award, 1987, Vol. of Distinction award Assn. Jr. Leagues Internat., 1996; named Pulitzer Prize juror, 2005. Mem. Am. Assn. Sun. & Feature Editors (bd. dirs., conf. host. 1996-98, bd. dirs. associated press mng. editors 2004—), Am. Soc. Newspaper Editors (bd. dirs. 2005) Avocations: reading, hiking, family adventures. Office: Wis State Jour 1901 Fish Hatchery Rd PO Box 8058 Madison WI 53708 Office Phone: 608-252-6104. Business E-Mail: efoley@madison.com.

FOLEY, ERIC ALAN, music educator; b. Columbia, Mo., July 10, 1961; s. William Daniel and Carol Ann (Robertson) Foley; m. Kathy Jean Hutcherson, July 28, 1984; children: Alan Franklin, Ryan Daniel. BS in Edn. with honors, U. Mo., 1984, MusM in Choral Conducting, 1996; postgrad., U. Kans., 2005—. Cert. tchr. Mo. Dir. choral activities Affton (Mo.) HS, 1987—89; dir. vocal music Benton County R-3 Schs., Cole Camp, Mo., 1989—90; minister of music Wesley United Meth. Ch., Sedalia, Mo., 1990—91, 1st Bapt. Ch., Harrisonville, Mo., 1992—97; dir. choral activities Oak Park HS, Kansas City, Mo., 1993—2004; minister of music Meadowbrook United Meth., Gladstone, Mo., 2004—. Chmn. fine arts dept. Oak Park HS, Kansas City, 1995—2003. Asst. scoutmaster Boy Scouts Am., Kansas City, 2000—; active Antioch Bible Bapt. Ch., Kansas City, 2000—. Recipient Sweepstakes award, All Star Music Festival, 2000; Vocal Music scholar, U. Mo., 1979—84, Friends of Music scholar, 1984—86. Mem.: Internat. Assn. Jazz Educators, Music Educator's Nat. Conf., Am. Choral Dirs. Assn. (coord. x.c. metro 9-10 honor choir 2000). Avocations: fishing, hunting, canoeing, camping, reading.

FOLEY, EUGENE ARTHUR, accountant, consultant; b. San Jose, Calif., May 6, 1953; s. Eugene Frank and Shirley Ann (Merrill) Foley; m. Elaine Sayre, July 9, 1995; children: Eugene Welles, Patrick Michael, Brian Ross. BSBA, U. Hartford, 1976; MS in Taxation, Golden Gate U., 1979; MDiv, Princeton Theol. Sem., 1994; M in Acctg., Rutgers U., 2000. CPA Calif., N.J., cert. mgmt. acct., info. sys. auditor, internal auditor, govt. fin. mgr.; computer profl., networking specialist, info. tech. profl. Acct. J. K. Lasser et al, San Jose, 1976-79; internal auditor Carter Hawley Hale, L.A., 1979-81; lectr., asst. prof. Calif. State U., Sacramento, 1979-84; owner, cons. E. A. Foley Accountancy, Sacramento, 1981-84; corp. audit mgr. Emhart Corp., Farmington, Conn., 1984-86; controller Powers Mfg. div. Emhart Corp., Elmira, NY, 1986-88; owner, cons. Foley Cos., Elmira, 1988-92; asst. prof. Rider U., Lawrenceville, NJ, 1992-94; asst. Christian edn. Cold Spring Presbyn. Ch., 1993-96; pastor Court House Presbyn. Ch., 1996-2000; tchr. Cape May County Tech. Sch., 1999-2000; pvt. practice Camden, 2000—; dir. fin. Parking Authority of City of Camden, 2003—04; adminstr., CFO Tuckerton Borough, NJ, 2004. Bus. mgr. Calif. Polit. Rev., 1987—; lectr. Rutgers U., 2001—. Sec.-treas., exec. dir. Elmira YMCA, 1986—87; treas. Supreme Ct. Project, Calif., 1985—86; v.p. fin. Sullivan Trail Coun. Boy Scouts Am., 1987, treas., 1988, dist. commr. George Washington Coun., 1992—94, dist. commr. So. N.J. Coun., 1994—96, dist. exec., 1996—99, mem. N.E. region religious com., 2001—, mem. N.E. region Sea Scout com., 2003—; treas. Calif. Pub. Policy Found., 1987—; commr. Learning Life/Venturing, 1999—2003; mem. Scoutreach com., Camden, 2000—05, co-chair, 2003; mcpl. auditor, contr. State of N.J., Camden, 2000—02; dir. fin. Parking Authority of City of Camden, 2003; mgr., CFO Lower Twp., NJ, 1994—97; ruling elder West Collingswood Presbyn. Ch., 2002—04. Recipient Whitney M. Young Jr. Svc. award, Boy Scouts Am., 1989; Baden-Powell fellow, World

Scout Found., 2002. Fellow: N.J. Soc. CPAs, AICPA Acad. Exempt Orgns.; mem.: AICPA, Nat. Assn. Comm. Sys. Engrs., Assn. Govt. Accts., Am. Numismatic Assn. (life), Info. Sys. Audit and Control Assn., Inst. Cert. Mgmt. Accts., Inst. Internal Auditors (cert.), Nat. Assn. Presbyn. Scouters (regional dir. 1995—), Am. First Day Cover Soc., Mensa, Am. Topical Assn. (life), Scottish Rite, Masons. Avocations: coin collecting/numismatics, genealogy. Mailing: PO Box 355 Tuckerton NJ 08087 E-mail: gfoley@snip.net.

FOLEY, GARY J., chemical engineer, researcher, computer scientist, federal agency administrator; b. Staten Is.n, N.Y., Mar. 20, 1943; m. Barbara Ickes, 1986; children: William, Karen, Kevin, Ryan, Courtney. BChE, Manhattan Coll., 1964; MS, U. Wis., 1965, PhD in Chem. Engring., 1968. Engr. Am. Oil Co., 1968-73, EPA, 1973-76, 79-86; dir. Nat. Exposure Rsch. Lab., 1987-93, 95—, acting asst. adminstr. R&D, 1993-94. Mem. AiChE. Achievements include rsch. in air pollution, acid rain, emissions, transport and fate, human and ecosystem exposure and earth observing systems, total quality mgmt. in rsch. orgns. Office Phone: 919-541-2106. Business E-Mail: foley.gary@epa.gov.

FOLEY, HARRIET ELIZABETH, retired school librarian; b. Franklin, Ohio, Aug. 11, 1935; d. Milo A. and Nora Lucile (Babb) Fealy; m. Thomas R. Foley, Nov. 22, 1969. BA in Edn., Coll. of Mt. St. Joseph, Cin., 1957; MS in Libr. Sci., U. Ky., 1961; postgrad., Kent State U., 1965. Cert. tchr. elem. edn., libr. sci., Ohio. Elem. tchr. Carlisle (Ohio) Schs., 1957-61, tchr. secondary French, 1961-63, sch. libr., 1961-82. Editor: Carlisle, the Jersey Settlement in Ohio, 1980,90, Franklin in the Great Miami Valley, 1982, 2d edit., 2004; co-author: Foleys from County Clare, Ireland, 1994; editor Heir Lines, 1986—. Trustee, sec. Carlisle Fed. Credit Union, 1962—; mem. Bicentennial Com., Franklin, 1996; mem. various coms. Otterbein-Lebanon Retirement Com., 1990-98. Named to Franklin H.S. Hall of Fame, 2003. Mem. ALA, DAR (local chptr. treas. 1988—), Ohio Assn. Sch. Librs. (sec./treas. 1970-75), Ohio Ednl. Libr./Media Assn., Ohio Ret. Tchrs. Assn. (life), Franklin Area Hist. Soc. (life, all offices, charter mem., editor newsletter 1986—, treas. 1999—), Warren County Geneal. Soc. (editor 1982—, treas. 1998—), Ohio Geneal. Soc., Plantagenet Soc., Magna Charta Dames, First Families Ohio, First Families Belmont County, First Families Clark County, Early Settlers of Warren County, Ohio. Republican. Roman Catholic. Avocations: genealogy, local history. Home: PO Box 345 Franklin OH 45005-0345 Personal E-mail: hfoley@siscom.net.

FOLEY, JACK (JOHN WAYNE HAROLD FOLEY), poet, writer, editor-in-chief; b. Neptune, N.J., Aug. 9, 1940; s. John Harold and Juana (Terio) F.; m. Adelle Joan Abramowitz, Dec. 21, 1961; 1 child, Sean Ezra. BA, Cornell U., 1963; MA, U. Calif., Berkeley, 1965. Exec. prodr.-in-charge poetry program Sta. KPFA-FM, Berkeley, 1988—; editor-in-chief Poetry USA, Oakland, Calif., 1990-95. Resident artist The Djerassi Program, 1994. Author: (poetry and prose) Letters/Lights-Words for Adelle, 1987, (poetry) Gershwin, 1991, Exiles, 1996, (prose) O Her Blackness Sparkles! The Life and Times of the Batman Art Gallery, San Francisco, 1960-1965, 1995, O Powerful Western Star, 2000, Foley's Books: California Rebels, Beats and Radicals, 2000, (poetry) Greatest Hits 1974-2003, 2004; editor, contbr. The Fallen Western Star Wars, 2001, (with Ivan Arquelles) New Poetry From California: Dead, Requiem, 1998, Advice to the Lovelorn, 1998, (translations from the French) Some Songs by Georges Brassens, 2001; contbr. (film jour.) Bright Lights; contbg. editor Poetry Flash, 1992—, performances of poetry with wife Adelle, 1985—, columnist Foley's books, The Alsop Rev., 1998—. Woodrow Wilson fellow U. Calif., 1963-65; Poetry grant Oakland Arts Coun., 1992-95. Mem. MLA, Poets and Writers, Nat. Poetry Assn. (sec. San Francisco 1989-95), PEN Oakland (program dir. 1990-97). Avocations: playing guitar, tap dancing, writing songs. Home and Office: 2569 Maxwell Ave Oakland CA 94601-5521 E-mail: JASFOLEY@aol.com.

FOLEY, JAMES DAVID, computer scientist, educator; b. Palmerton, Pa., July 20, 1942; s. Marvin Winfield and Stella Elizabeth (Ziegler) F.; m. Mary Louise Herrmann, Aug. 22, 1964; children: Heather, Jennifer. BSEE, Lehigh U., 1964; MSEE, U. Mich., 1965, PhD, 1969. Group mgr. Info. Control Systems, Ann Arbor, Mich., 1969-70; asst. prof. U. N.C., Chapel Hill, 1970-76; sr. systems analyst Bur. of Census, Washington, 1976-77; assoc. prof. George Washington U., Washington, 1977-81, prof., 1981-90, chmn. dept. elec. engring. and computer sci., 1988-90; prof. Ga. Inst. Tech., Atlanta, 1991—, assoc. dean coll. computing, 2001—03; dir. Graphics Visualization and Usability Ctr., Atlanta, 1991-96, Mitsubishi Electric Rsch. Lab. (MERL), Cambridge, Mass., 1996-97; exec. v.p. Mitsubishi Electric Info. Tech. Ctr. Am., Cambridge, 1996-97, chmn., CEO, 1998-99; exec. dir. Ga.'s Yamacraw Mission, 1999—2000. Pres. Computer Graphics Cons., Washington, 1979-96; mem. industry program adv. com. NAS, 1997-99. Author: (with others) Fundamentals of Computer Graphics, 1982, (with others) Computer Graphics: Principles and Practice, 1990, (with others) Introduction to Computer Graphics, 1993; co-author (graphics standard) Core System, 1977. Bd. dirs. Patriot Trails coun. Girl Scouts. U.S., 1998-99. Fellow: IEEE, Computing Rsch. Assn. (bd. dirs. 1996—, treas. 1998—2000, chmn. 2001—05), Assn. for Computing Machinery; mem.: Assn. for Computing Machinery/Computer-Human Interaction Acad. (Spl. Interest Group for Graphs Coons award 1997), Nat. Computer Graphics Assn. (bd. dirs. 1982—84), Spl. Interest Group for Graphics (vice chmn. 1973—75), Human Factors Soc. Avocations: skiing, sailing, model railroading. Office: Georgia Inst Tech College of Computing Atlanta GA 30332-0280 Home: 1588 Friar Tuck Rd Atlanta GA 30309 Business E-Mail: foley@cc.gatech.edu.

FOLEY, JANE DEBORAH, foundation executive; b. Chgo., May 30, 1952; d. Colin Gray Stevenson and Bette Jane (Cullenbine) Coleman; m. George Edward Foley, Jan. 29, 1972; children: Sy Curtis, Shelly. BA, Purdue U., 1973, MS, 1977, PhD, 1992. Cert. elem. adminstr., Ind., cert. elem. adminstrn. and supervision. Tchr. phys. edn. and health Lafayette (Ind.) Jefferson H.S., 1973-74; tchr. music and phys. edn. Valparaiso (Ind.) Cmty. Schs., 1974-79, tchr. elem. phys. edn., 1979-90; prin. South Ctrl. Elem. sch., Union Mills, Ind., 1990-93, Flint Lake Elem. Sch., Valparaiso, 1993-98; v.p. Milken Family Found., Santa Monica, Calif., 1998—2003, sr. v.p., 2003—. Mem. panel experts The Master Tchr., 1996—98, NEH; coord. Milken Nat. Educator Awards, Milken Scholars, Children of Willesden Ln; keynote spkr.; presenter state and nat. confs. Author: Technology Integration: A School Administrator's Guide, 1998, Success in Restructuring: A Road Map for Administrators, 1998, The Administrator's Technology Training Booklet, 1998; contbr. articles to profl. jours. and books. Mem. Valparaiso Sch. Sys. PTA, mem. exec. bd., 1993-98; bd. dirs. Hold Onto Your Music, Wings Inc. Recipient Hoosier Sch. award, 1992, Ind. 2000 Designation award 1994, Outstanding Dissertation award Internat. Soc. Ednl. Planning, 1993, Nat. Educator award, Milken Family Found., 1994, Ind. Bell Ringer award Ind. Dept. Edn., 1994, Ind. 4 Star Sch. award, 1995, 96, 97, 98, Internat. Tech. Edn. Assn. award, 1995, Cmty. Improvement award Valparaiso C. of C., 1994, NCREL Pathways to Improvement Pilot Site, 1995, Ind. Sch. Improvement award, Ind. Dept. Edn., 1998, others; Ind. 2000 Planning grantee, 1993, Milken Educator Tech. Project leader, 1997, other grants. Mem.: ASCD (assoc.), Valparaiso Tchrs. Assn. (treas. 1989—90), Phi Kappa Phi. Avocations: running, reading, writing, computers. Office: Milken Family Found 1250 4th St Santa Monica CA 90401-1350 Office Phone: 310-570-4782. Business E-Mail: jfoley@mff.org.

FOLEY, JOHN PATRICK, archbishop; b. Darby, Pa., Nov. 11, 1935; s. John Edward and Regina Beatrice (Vogt) Foley. BA summa cum laude, St. Josephs Coll., Phila., 1957; BA, St. Charles Borromeo Sem., Phila., 1958; PhL, U. St. Thomas Aquinas, Rome, 1964, PhD cum laude, 1965; MS magna cum laude, Columbia U., 1966; LHD (hon.), St. Joseph's U., Phila., 1985, Allentown (Pa.) Coll., 1990, Cath. U. Am., 1996, John Cabot U., 1998, St. John's U., 2001; DST (hon.), Assumption Coll., Worcester, Mass., 1997; D Journalism (hon.), Regis U., 1997. Ordained priest Roman Cath. Ch., 1962, archbishop 1984. Asst. pastor Sacred Heart Ch., Havertown, Pa., 1962—63; Rome corr. Cath. Standard & Times, Phila., 1963—65; asst. pastor St. John the Evangelist Ch., Phila., 1966; faculty Cardinal Dougherty H.S., Phila., 1966—67; assoc. prof. philosophy St. Charles Borromeo Sem., Phila., 1967—84; titular archbishop Neapolis in Proconsulari, 1984—. Vice-chmn. Pa. State Ethics Commn., 1979—84; apptd. pres. Pontifical Commn. for Social Comm., Vatican City, 1984; pres. Vatican TV Ctr., 1984—89; bd. govs. Internat. Eucharistic Congress, 1974—76; mem. Pontifical Coun. for Culture, 1993—, Commn. for L.Am., 1984—89; comm. com. U.S. Cath. Conf., 1979—82; news sec. gen. meetings Nat. Conf. Cath. Bishops, 1969—84. Author: Natural Law, Natural Right and the Warren Court, 1965; mem. editl. bd. Cath. Standard & Times, 1963, 1967—70; editor: Cath. Standard & Times, 1970—84. Regional bd. dirs. NCCJ, 1969—82. Decorated knight comdr. with grand cross Order the Holy Sepulchre, Order the No. Star (Sweden), comdr. with grand cross Order Bernardo O'Higgins (Chile); named hon. prelate, Pope Paul VI, 1976, Hon. chaplain with Grand Cross, Sovereign Mil. Order of Malta; recipient Sourin award, Cath. Philopatrian Lit. Inst., Phila., 1990, Pres.'s medal, Holy Family Coll., Phila., 1996, Shield of Loyola award, St. Joseph's U., Phila., 1997, Cath. Leadership award, Cath. Leadership Inst., Phila., 2001, Ignatian award, St. Joseph's Prep. Sch., Phila., 2003, Pres.'s award, Cath. Acad. Comm. Arts Profls., 2005. Mem.: Cath. Press Assn. (St. Francis de Sales award 1984), Am. Cath. Philos. Assn., Am. Cath. Hist. Soc. (Barry award 1997). Roman Catholic. Home: Villa Stritch Via della Nocetta 63 00164 Rome Italy Office: Pontifical Coun Social Comm 00120 Vatican City Italy Fax: 011-39-06-6988-5373. Office Phone: 011-39-06-698-83197. Business E-Mail: pccs@vatican.va. *The most important reality in life is the existence of God, His love for every person exemplified in our redemption by His Son, Jesus Christ, and our eternal destiny to live with Him forever in heaven.*

FOLEY, JOSEPH LAWRENCE, sales executive; b. Albuquerque, June 14, 1953; s. Joseph Bernard and Joan Marie (Johnston) F.; m. Michelle Troglia, Jan., 1992; children: Joseph Louis, Kyle Benjamin. BS in Polit. Sci. & Mktg., Niagara U., 1975. Asst. retail buyer Lord & Taylor, N.Y.C., 1975, E.J. Korvette Co., N.Y.C., 1976-78, retail buyer, 1978-80, retail mdse. mgr., 1980; import sales coord. Block Industries, N.Y.C., 1980-81; v.p. sales Sutton Shirt Co., N.Y.C., 1981-83; exec. v.p. V.I.P. Imports, N.Y.C., 1984-97; prin. Long-Term Care Cons. of Ill., Inc., 1998—. Mem.: Million Dollar Roundtable, Chi Are Racing Assn. Republican. Roman Catholic. Avocations: marathon running, baseball, tennis, skiing, golf. Home and Office: 225 Sunset Ridge Rd Willowbrook IL 60527-8406

FOLEY, JOSEPH PATRICK, public relations executive; b. June 5, 1949; married; two children. BA, Elon U., 1971; MA, Am. U., 1980. State heath and social worker Fla. Health Dept., 1971-74; legis. floor asst. U.S. Ho. Reps., Washington, 1974-80; dir. legis. affairs, program analyst, congrl. liaison officer Fed. Emergency Mgmt. Agy. & Selective Svc. System, 1980-86; pres., sr. assoc. Foley Govt. and Pub. Affairs Inc., Potomac, Md., 1986—. Adj. prof. Sch. of Govt., Am. U. Office: Foley Govt and Pub Affairs Inc PO Box 61303 Potomac MD 20859 Office Phone: 301-294-0937. Business E-Mail: info@foleycoinc.com.

FOLEY, KATHERINE ELIZABETH, librarian; b. Ludington, Mich., Feb. 13, 1946; d. James Horace and Mary Elizabeth (Parrott) Reynolds; m. Michael Glen Foley, June 1, 1968. BA, Whittier Coll., 1968; MLS, UCLA, 1971. Environ. engring. libr. Calif. Inst. Tech., Pasadena, 1971-75; sch. libr. Columbia (Mo.) Pub. Schs., 1976-78; reference libr. Mo. State Libr., Jefferson City, 1978-80; audio-visual libr. Richland (Wash.) Pub. Libr., 1980-84, libr. supr., 1984-90; dean libr. svcs. Columbia Basin Coll., Pasco, Wash., 1990—. Appointed mem. Wash. State Adv. Coun. on Librs., Olympia, 1989-90. Mem. ALA, Wash. Libr. Assn. (local arrangements co-chair 1990), Beta Phi Mu. Avocations: jogging, backpacking, flying, cross country skiing, hiking. Office: Columbia Basin Coll Libr 2600 N 20th Ave Pasco WA 99301-3379 Office Phone: 509-547-0511 ext 2294. Business E-Mail: kfoley@columbiabasin.edu.

FOLEY, L(EWIS) MICHAEL, real estate executive; b. Detroit, Nov. 30, 1938; s. Raymond B. and Mabel F.; m. Pamela Wagner, June 16, 1962; children: Michael D., Kimberly B., Robin E. BS in Sci. Engring., U. Mich., 1960; MBA in Fin. and Mktg., Harvard U., 1964. Lic. real estate broker. Pres. Econ. Devel. Corp., Detroit, 1969-71; v.p. Chrysler Realty Corp., Troy, Mich., 1972-77; exec. v.p. Bell and Howell Video Group, Chgo., 1977-79; v.p. fin., chief fin. officer Bell and Howell Corp., Chgo., 1979-80; sr. v.p. Homart Devel. Co., Chgo., 1981-84, exec. v.p., 1984-93; sr. exec. v.p. Coldwell Banker Real Estate Group Inc., Chgo., 1986-93; chmn., CEO Sears Savs. Bank, Chgo., 1989-93; sr. v.p., CFO Coldwell Banker Corp., 1995-96. Chmn. Borrowers Choice Corp., 1992-93; non exec. chmn. bd. BRE Properties, Inc. Author: Management of Racial Integration in Business, 1965. Former vestry, jr. warden St. James by the Sea Episcopal Ch. Mem. Internat. Coun. Shopping Ctrs. (former v.p., trustee), Sigma Alpha Epsilon. Episcopalian. Office: 5824 Camino de la Costa La Jolla CA 92037-6551 Office Phone: 858-459-3988. Business E-Mail: lfoley1@san.rr.com.

FOLEY, MARILYN LORNA, artist; b. Arlington, N.J., Aug. 30, 1929; d. Archibald and Mary Ellen (Hall) Lyon; m. William Edward Foley, June 19, 1954; children: Katherine Ann Hastings, William Edward III. BA, Wellesley Coll., 1950; postgrad., Rutgers U., 1950-52; postgrad studies Art Students' League, N.Y.C., 1953. Art instr. Wellesley (Mass.) Coll., 1953-54; chair artists com. Art Show: Bedford, 1985-92. One-woman shows include St. Mary's Gallery, N.Y.C., 1989, Northridge Art Gallery, Ridgefield, Conn., 1990, 1992, Kim Iocovozzi Gallery, Savannah, Ga., 1997—99, 2000—05, exhibited in group shows at St. Peter's Gallery, 1997—2005, Salmagundi Club, N.Y.C., 1986, Nat. Arts Club, 1988, Knickerbocker Artists 40th Ann., 1990, Newington-Cropsey Gallery, Hastings on Hudson, N.Y., 1997 (1st prize watercolor), Broome St. Gallery, N.Y.C., 1997 (2d prize watercolor), Copley Soc. Mem. Show, 1982 (Juror's Choice prize), Art Show, Bedford, N.Y., 1983—87 (Emille Baker award, 1993), Landings Art Assn. Ann. Exhibitions (Best of Show 1996-2000), Mo. Nat. Winston Churchill Meml., 2003, 2004, Gallery One, Nashville, 2005, 28th Ann. So. Watercolor Exhbn., 2005; author: The Artists Mag., 1998, Watercolor Basics, 2003. Named Wellesley scholar, 1950. Mem. Hudson Valley Art Assn., Landings Art Assn., Catharine Lorillard Wolfe Art Club, Natl. Watercolor Soc. (signature mem.), Hilton Head Art League. Republican. Episcopalian. Avocations: travel, designer of church needlework. Studio: Foley Watercolors 2 Scotch Bonnet Ct Savannah GA 31411-2859 Office Phone: 912-598-8314. E-mail: mlfoley@bellsouth.net.

FOLEY, MARK ADAM, congressman; b. Newton, Mass., Sept. 8, 1954; Student, Palm Beach C.C. Owner, mgr. The Lettuce Patch Restaurant, 1975-81; real estate broker, pres. Foley-Smith & Assocs., Inc., 1975-94; commr. City of Lake Worth, 1977-79, commr., vice mayor, 1982-84; state rep. dist. 85 Fla., 1991—93; state senator dist. 35 Fla., 1993—95; mem. U.S. Congress from 16th Fla. dist., 1995—; mem. ways and means com.; dep. majority whip. Republican. Office: 104 Cannon Ho Office Bldg Washington DC 20515-0916

FOLEY, MAURICE BRIAN, federal judge; b. Ill., 1960; BA, Swarthmore Coll., 1982; JD, U. Calif., Berkeley, 1985; LLM in Taxation, Georgetown U., 1988. With Office of Chief Counsel, IRS, Washington, 1985-88; tax counsel, majority staff Com. on Fin., U.S. Senate, Washington, 1988-93; dep. tax legis. counsel U.S. Dept. Treasury, Washington, 1993-95; judge U.S. Tax Ct., Washington, 1995—. Mem. State Bar Calif. Office: US Tax Ct 400 2D St NW Washington DC 20217-0001 Office Phone: 202-606-8800.

FOLEY, MICHAEL PATRICK, marketing professional educator; b. Bethesda, Md., May 15, 1952; s. Patrick Walter and Marguerite Augusta (Boyer) F.; m. Marykate Maag, Aug. 25, 1973; children: Joshua, Erin, Natalie. Student, U. Dayton, 1970-71; BS in Edn., Va. Tech., 1975, MS in Edn., 1979. Cert. mktg. educator. Mktg. educator Fauquier H.S., Warrenton, Va., 1975-78, Osbourn Park H.S., Manassas, Va., 1979—. Bd. trustees Va. DECA. Mem. Distributive Edn. Clubs Am. (officer, advisor, bd. trustees, Va. 2005—), Va. Assn. Mktg. Educators (Tchr. of Yr. nominee 1990), Va. Vocat. Assn., U.S. Golf Assn., Va. State Golf Assn., PGA Tour Ptnrs. Roman Catholic. Avocations: golf, reading, outdoor sports, Scrabble. Home: 8028 Gracie Dr Manassas VA 20112-3738 Office: Osbourn Park H S 8909 Euclid Ave Manassas VA 20111-2404 E-mail: foleymike70@hotmail.com.

FOLEY, PAUL E., political scientist, educator; b. Detroit, Dec. 5, 1963; s. John C. and Elizabeth Marie Foley; m. Kimberly Anne Schuerger, May 7, 1994; children: Kellen Richard children: McKenna Louise. BA in Polit. Sci., Oakland U., 1988; MA in Polit. Sci., Am. U., 1991. Asst. prof., dept. chair St. Mary's Coll., Orchard Lake, Mich., 1992—2000; adj. prof. Mott C.C., Flint, Mich., 2000—. Visibility coord. Friends of Bob Carr, Waterford, Mich., 1988, polit. cons., 94; legis. aide U.S. Ho. Rep., Washington, 1989; adj. prof. Oakland C.C., Waterford, Mich., 1999—, Macomb C.C., Clinton Twp., Mich., 2000—. Asst. bd. dird. MHSTeCA, Lansing, Mich., 2000—03. Recipient Regional Coach of Yr., Mich. High Sch. Tennis Coach's Assn., 1997, 1998, 1999, 2000 & 2001, Coach of Yr., MCTCA, 1997 & 1999, M.A.C., 1998-99 & 1999-2000. Mem.: NEA (assoc.), Mich. Edn. Assn. (assoc.), Am. Polit. Sci. Assn. (assoc.). Personal E-mail: p1k2foley@aol.com.

FOLEY, RALPH MORTON, lawyer; b. Martinsville, Ind., Mar. 23, 1940; s. Charles Henry and Beatrice Louise (Myren) Foley; m. Anne Palmer Hall, Aug. 25, 1962; children: David Ryan, Brian Charles, Peter Ralph. AB, Ind. U., Bloomington, 1962, JD, 1965. Bar: Ind. 1965, U.S. Dist. Ct. (so. dist.) Ind. 1965. Assoc. Foley, Foley & Peden, Martinsville, 1965—67, ptnr., 1967—75, sr. ptnr., 1975—; dep. pros. atty. Morgan County, Ind., 1970—71. Chmn. County Election Bd., 1967—79; bd. mgrs. YMCA, 1977—78. Mem.: Ind. Trial Lawyers Assn., Ind. State Bar Assn. (bd. mgrs. 1981—82), Morgan County Bar Assn. (pres. 1975), Kiwanis Club of Martinsville. Republican. Methodist. Home: 400 Byram Blvd Martinsville IN 46151-1322 Office: 60 E Morgan St Martinsville IN 46151-1517

FOLEY, RIDGWAY KNIGHT, JR., lawyer, writer; b. Portland, Oreg., Oct. 7, 1937; s. Ridgway Knight and Eunice Alberta (Ammer) F. BS magna cum laude, Lewis & Clark Coll., 1959; JD, U. Oreg., 1963. Bar: Oreg. 1963. Assoc. Mautz, Souther, Spaulding, Kinsey & Williamson, Portland, 1964-71; gen. ptnr. Schwabe, Williamson & Wyatt (and predecessor firms), Portland, 1972-84, sr. ptnr., 1985-92; ptnr., shareholder Foley & Duncan, P.C., Portland, 1993-96; of counsel Greene & Markley PC, Portland, 1997—, med. office mgr., 1999—2004. Com. mem. Multnomah Lawyer Com., 1964-68, 90-93, chair, 1992-93. Contbr. more than 100 articles, essays to profl. jours. Trustee Found. Econ. Edn., Inc., Irvington-on-Hudson, N.Y., 1974-91, 93-96; founding dir. Paulist Fathers Cath. Ctr., Portland, 1978-85. Mem. ABA, Oreg. State Bar, Multnomah County Bar (dir. 1993-97), Univ. Club (Portland), Mt. Hood Philos. Soc. (founding trustee, officer 1972-85), Lang Syne Soc., Order of Coif. Episcopalian. Avocations: writing, lecturing, genealogy, publishing, history. Office: Greene & Markley PC 1515 SW 5th Ave Ste 600 Portland OR 97201-5449 Office Phone: 503-295-2668.

FOLEY, SYLVESTER ROBERT, III, human resources specialist, retired military officer; BA, Marquette U., 1977; MA, Norwich U., 1995; exec. edn. program, Harvard U., 1995; MBA, Regis U., 2002. Various command & leadership assignments USMC, 1977—91, commdg. officer, recruiting sta. New Eng. Portsmouth, NH, 1991—94, nat. dir. Recruiters Sch. San Diego, 1994—97; N.E. staffing mgr. Raytheon Co., Tewksbury, Mass., 1998—2000, univ. rels. mgr. ea. region, 2000—. Adv. bd. mem. Mass. Rehab. Commn., Boston, 1997—2004. Lt. col. USMC, 1994—97. Decorated Legion of Merit Dept. of Def., Meritorious Svc. medal, Navy Commendation medal, Navy Achievement medal, Combat Action Ribbon; recipient Leadership award, Mass. Rehab. Commn., 2001, 2004, Multicultural Innovation award, Ea. Assn. Coll. and Employers, 2004. Mem.: VFW (life), Nat. Assn. Colls. and Employers, N.E. Human Resources Assn., Alpha Sigma Nu (life). Roman Catholic. Office: Raytheon Co 50 Apple Hill Dr MS: T3MF40 Tewksbury MA 01876

FOLEY, WILLIAM EDWARD, retired historian; b. Kansas City, Mo., Sept. 20, 1938; s. William Delbert and Lorene M. Foley; m. Martha A. Ellenburg, May 30, 1967; children: Laura Ann Sindhi, David Edward. BS in Edn., Ctrl. Mo. State U., 1960, MA in History, 1963; PhD in History, U. of Mo., 1967. Tchr. Consol. Sch. Dist. No. 2, Raytown, Mo., 1960—62; from asst. prof. to prof. emeritusof history Ctrl. Mo. State U., Warrensburg, Mo., 1966—2001, prof. emeritus of history, 2001—. Bd. dir. Friends of the Mo. State Archives; mem. Mo. Adv. Coun. on Hist. Preservation, 1991—, chmn., 1999—2001. Author: A History of Missouri, 1673-1820, 1971 (Merit award Am. Assn. for State and Local History), The Genesis of Missouri: From Wilderness Outpost to Statehood, 1989 (Best Book award Mo. Conf. on History, 1990), Wilderness Journey: The Life of William Clark, 2004; co-author: The First Chouteaus: River Barons of Early St. Louis, 1983, Missouri: Then and Now, 2001; editor: Mo. Biography Series, 1990—; co-editor: An Account of Upper Louisiana by Nicolas de Finiels, 1989, Dictionary of Missouri Biography, 1999; mem. editl. bd.: Mo. Hist. Rev., 1986—. Mem. Warrensburg R-6 Bd. of Edn., Warrensburg, 1977—83, pres., 1979—80; bd. of trustees Trails Regional Libr., Warrensburg, Mo., 2000—. Recipient Mo. Gov.'s award for Tchg. Excellence, Mo. Dept. of Higher Edn., 2000. Mem.: Johnson County Hist. Soc. (bd. dirs. 2001—, pres. 2002—), State Hist. Soc. Mo. (Disting. Svc. award 2002), Soc. for Historians of the Early Republic, Western History Assn., Orgn. of Am. Historians. Presbyterian. Home: 1408 Kensington Court Warrensburg MO 64093

FOLEY, WILLIAM PATRICK, II, title insurance company executive; b. Austin, Tex., Dec. 29, 1944; s. Robert P. Foley; m. Carol J. Johnson, Nov. 15 1969; children: Lindsay, Robert P. II, Countney Diane, William P. III. BS, U.S. Mil. Acad., 1967; MBA, Seattle U., 1970; JD, U. Wash., 1974. Assoc. Streich, Lang, Weeks, Cardon & French P.A., Phoenix, 1974-76; ptnr., pres., dir. Foley, Clark & Nye P.A., Phoenix, 1976-84; pres. chief exec. officer Land Resources Corp., Scottsdale. Ariz., 1983-84; chmn. bd., pres., CEO Fidelity Nat. Title Ins. Co., Irvine, Calif., 1981—; also bd. dirs. Fidelity Nat. Title Ins., Irvine, Calif.; chmn. Checkers Drive-In Restaurants, Inc., Clearwater, Fl. Chmn. bd., dir., pres., chief exec. officer Fidelity Nat. Fin., Inc., Fidelity Nat. Title Ins. Co. of Calif., Fidelity Nat. Title Ins. Co. of Tenn., Fidelity Nat. Title Ins. Co. of Tex., So. Title Holding Co., Pacific Western Aviation, Inc., Western Am. Exch. Corp., Western Pacific Property & Casualty Agy., Inc., Fidelity Appraisal Group, Inc., Folco Devel. Corp., Western Pacific Acquisitions, Inc., Bristol Investment Corp.; chmn. bd., dir. Western Fin. Trust Co., Rocky Mountain Aviation, Inc.; chmn. bd. dir., chief exec. officer Fidelity Nat. Title Agy., Inc. Fidelity Nat. Title Agy. of Maricopa County, Inc., Fidelity Nat. Title Agy. of Pinal County, Inc., Fidelity Nat. Title Co. of El Paso, Fidelity Nat. Title Co. of Oreg., Ramada Inn Old Town Mgmt., Inc.; numerous other chairmanships and directorships in fin. industry; founder & mng. ptnr. Foley Estates Vineyard & Winery of Calif.; founder & mng. ptnr. LinCourt Vineyards of Calif.; chmn. bd. CKE Restaurants Inc. Mem. Jacksonville C. of C., Fla.; del. Rep. Nat. Conv., 1996; adv. bd. mem. U. Wash. Sch. Law; trustee Found. Bd. U. Calif. Santa Barbara. Capt. USAF. Recipient Semper Fidelis award, Marine Corps Scholarship Found., 1997. Avocations: golf, chess, winemaking.*

FOLK, FRANK ANTON, surgeon, educator; b. Chgo., Dec. 15, 1925; s. Frank A. and Anna (Pilisauer) F.; m. Lorna C. Hill, June 18, 1949; children: Laura, Lawrence, Patricia, Elizabeth, Thomas, James, Mary, Tracy Ann, William. BS, Northwestern U., 1945; postgrad., U. Wis., 1945-46; MD, U. Ill., 1949. Diplomate Am. Bd. Surgery, Nat. Bd. Med. Examiners; lic. Ill., Wis. Rotating intern Cook County Hosp., Chgo., 1949-51; resident in gen. surgery Cook County/Columbus Hosp., Chgo., 1951, Cook County Hosp., Chgo., 1954-57, surgeon, 1958-69, dir. of surgery, 1969-72; mem. faculty Stritch Sch. Medicine Loyola U., Maywood, Ill., 1958—, prof. surgery Stritch Sch. Medicine, 1972-96; prof. emeritus, 1997—; rsch. fellow Hektoen Inst., Chgo., 1959-64; asst. chief surgery VA Hosp., Hines, Ill., 1967-75, chief surg. svc., 1995-96. Mem. editl. bd.: The Am. Surgeon, 1984-92; contbr. articles to med. jours. including Am. Jour. Physiology, Jour. Occupl. Medicine, Annals of Surgery, Archives of Surgery, Jour. Trauma, Surg. Clinics of N.Am. Unit pres., exec. bd. Am. Cancer Soc., Chgo., 1972-89; mem. pres.'s adv. com.

Benedictine U., Lisle, Ill., 1965-90. Lt. USN, 1951-53, Korea. Decorated Bronze Star, 1953. Fellow ACS (gov., chmn. gen. surgery Chgo. com. on trauma 1975-83, pres. met. chpt. 1977-78, mem. SESAP com. II and III, instr. ACS advanced trauma life support course 1980-87); mem. Am. Surg. Assn., Am. Assn. for Surgery of Trauma, Assn. Mil. Surgeons of U.S., Assn. for Acad. Surgery, Soc. for Surgery of Alimentary Tract, Assn. VA Surgeons, Internat. Soc. Digestive Surgry, Ctrl. Surg. Assn., Midwest Surg. Assn. (pres. 1974-75), Western Surg. Assn., Ill. Surg. Soc. (pres. 1971-72), Chgo. Surg. Soc. (pres. 1989-90), Inst. Medicine of Chgo. Roman Catholic. Avocations: medical history, civil war history, central american civilizations. Office: VA Hosp Surg Svc PO Box 5000 Hines IL 60141-1489 Office Phone: 708-202-2036. Office Fax: 708-202-2180. Personal E-mail: fafolk@aol.com.

FOLK, ROBERT LOUIS, geologist, educator; b. Cleve., Sept. 30, 1925; s. George Billmyer and Marjorie Marshall (Kinkead) F.; m. Marjorie Thomas, Sept. 7, 1946; children: Robert T., Jennifer Louise, Charles Marshall. BS, Pa. State Coll., 1946, MS, 1950, PhD, 1952. Research geologist Gulf Oil Co., Houston, 1951-52; mem. faculty U. Tex., Austin, 1952—, prof. geol. scis., 1960—, Dave Carlton prof. geol. scis., 1977-88. Vis. lectr. Australian Nat. U., Canberra, 1965, Tong-Ji U., Shanghai, China, 1980; vis. researcher Universita degli Studi, Milan, Italy, 1973 Author: Petrology of Sedimentary Rocks, 1980; contbr. articles to sci. publs. Neil Miner award Nat. Assn. Geology Tchrs., 1989, H.C. Sorby medal Internat. Assn. Sedimentologists, 1990. Fellow Geol. Soc. Am. (Penrose medal 2000); mem. Soc. Econ. Paleontologists and Mineralogists (hon., Twenhofel medal 1979). Methodist. Achievements include first discovery of mineralized nannobacteria on earth; the same-appearing organisms were discovered by NASA in Martian meteorite. Home: 1107 Bluebonnet Ln Austin TX 78704-2005 Office: U of Tex Dept Geol Scis Austin TX 78801 Office Phone: 512-471-5294. *My unique characteristic is that I run my life randomly. At home each day, I put all the things I have/want to do in a list. Then I roll dice to see which thing to do and do that immediately whether it be a painful or pleasureful choice. Since I adopted this method I get immeasurably more work done and much greater pleasure out of daily life. Try it.*

FOLK, THOMAS ROBERT, lawyer; b. Milford, N.J., Jan. 9, 1950; s. Conrad Frank and Isabella Ramsey (Sickels) F.; m. JoAnn Elizabeth Lo Pinto, June 21, 1975; children: Elizabeth Frances, Karina Marie. BS, U.S. Mil. Acad., 1972; JD, U. Va., 1978. Bar: Va. 1978, U.S. Ct. Mil. Appeals 1978, U.S. Ct. Appeals (4th cir.) 1978, U.S. Supreme Ct. 1983, U.S. Ct. Claims 1985, U.S. Ct. Appeals (9th and fed. cirs.) 1985, D.C. 1986., U.S. Dist. Ct. D.C. 1987, U.S. Dist. Ct. Md. 1987. Commd. 2d lt. U.S. Army, 1972, advanced to maj., 1983, resigned, 1986, asst. to gen. counsel Washington, 1980-82, atty. litigation, 1983-86; assoc. Hazel & Thomas, P.C., Fairfax, Va., 1986-88, owner, 1989-99; ptnr. Reed Smith LLP, Fairfax, 1999—. Contbr. articles to profl. jours. Mem. Com. Armed Svcs. and Vets. Affairs, 1985-88. Col. USAR, 1995, ret. Mem.: Fairfax Bar Assn. (bd. govs. 1993—97), Va. State Bar (bd. govs. constrn. and pub. contracts 1993—99), West Point Soc. D.C (bd. govs. 1993—99). Home: 4902 Asquith Ct Fairfax VA 22032-2102 Office Phone: 703-641-4294. Personal E-mail: tfolk1@cox.net. Business E-Mail: tfolk@reedsmith.com.

FOLKENBERG, LOIS WAXTER, principal, educator, psychologist; b. Balt., June 17, 1943; d. Frank Shelby and Ruth Virginia (Meyer) Waxter; m. Donald Louis Folkenberg, June 12, 1966; children: Todd Louis, Laura Michelle. BA in Psychology, Columbia Union Coll., 1965; MA in Counseling and Testing, Am. U., 1967. Counselor Montgomery Jr. Coll., Rockville, Md., 1966-67, U. Calif., Riverside, 1967-68; tchr. Maxwell Preparatory Sch., Nairobi, Kenya, 1969; sch. psychologist Spokane (Wash.) Valley Coop., 1979-81; tchr. Ctrl. Valley Sch. Dist., Spokane, 1982-83; prin., tchr. Duluth (Ga.) Jr. Acad., 1986-93, Frederick (Md.) Adventist Sch., 1993-95, Atholton Adventist Sch., Columbia, Md., 1995—. Bd. mem. Chesapeake Conf. Ednl. Initiative, Columbia, Chesapeake Conf. Bd. Edn., Columbia, Columbia Union Curriculu Com. Facilitator student projects Global Mission Seventh-Day Adventists, Silver Spring, Md., 1990—. Recipient Zapara Excellence in Tchg. award Office Edn., N.Am. Divsn. Seventh-Day Adventists, Silver Spring, 1991; named Tchr. of the Yr., North Ga. Tchrs.' Assn., Calhoun, 1989-90. Home: PO Box 380 Huddleston VA 24104-0380 Office: Atholton Adventist Sch 6520 Martin Rd Columbia MD 21044

FOLKENFLIK, MAX, lawyer; b. Phila., Sept. 9, 1948; s. Bernard Folkenflik and Florence (Rogosin) Field; m. Margaret A. McGerity, Apr., 3, 1971; children: Alexander, Andrew. BS, Cornell U., 1970; JD, Georgetown U., 1975. Bar: N.Y. 1976, U.S. Dist. Ct. (so. dist.) N.Y. 1976, (ea. dist.) N.Y. 1976, U.S. Tax Ct. 1977, U.S. Ct. Appeals (2d cir.) 1994, U.S. Ct. Appeals (3d cir.) 1997. Assoc. Kronish, Lieb, Shainswit, Weiner & Hellman, N.Y.C., 1975-79, Cravath, Swaine & Moore, N.Y.C., 1979-83; ptnr. Morrison, Paul & Beiley, N.Y.C., 1983-84, Morrison, Cohen & Singer, N.Y.C., 1984-85, Wistendahl & Folkenflik, N.Y.C., 1985-88, Folkenflik & McGerity, N.Y.C., 1988—. Mem. staff Georgetown U. Law Review, 1973-74, editor 1974-75. Mem. ABA, Assn. of Bar of City of N.Y. Democrat. Jewish. Avocation: photography, cooking. Home: 261 W 90th St New York NY 10024-1119 Office: Folkenflik & McGerity 1500 Broadway Fl 21 New York NY 10036-4052

FOLKER, CATHLEEN ANN, business educator; b. West Allis, Wis., May 14, 1956; d. Norman Ralph and Lucille Catherine F. BA in Liberal Arts, Ambassador Coll., 1978; postgrad., U. Wis., Milw., 1986-91; MSBA, Tex. Tech. U., 1995, PhD, 1999. Customer rels. supr. Univ. Acctg. Svc., Milw., 1979-80; mktg. analyst Payco Am. Corp., Brookfield, Wis., 1980; controller West Allis Curtain & Drapery, 1980-92; mgmt. cons., 1992-93; tchg. asst. Tex. Tech U., Lubbock, 1994-97; lectr. U. Wis., Whitewater, 1998-99, U. Nebr., Lincoln, 1999-2000; asst. prof. entrepreneurship U. St. Thomas, St. Paul, 2000—05; asst. prof. mgmt. U. Wis.-Parkside, Kenosha, 2005—. Freelance writer, Oconomowoc, Wis., 1989-93; tax preparer, 1991-93; grad. tchg. asst. U. Wis., Milw., 1989-90. Avocations: walking, reading, travel, singing, biking.

FOLKERTS, JEAN, journalism educator; b. Aug. 6, 1945; d. Leonard Folkerts and Betty Manahan; m. Leroy Towns, Aug. 11, 1984; children: Sean, Jenny. BA in Journalism cum laude, Kans. State U., 1967, MS in Journalism and Mass Comm., 1973; MPhil in Am. Studies, U. Kans., 1979, PhD in Am. Studies, 1981. Asst. prof. journalism U. Tex., Austin, 1982-85; assoc. prof., chmn. dept. comm. Mt. Vernon Coll., Washington, 1985-90; assoc. prof. journalism George Washington U., Washington, 1990-94, prof., chmn. dept. journalism, 1994, from acting dir. to prof., dir. Sch. Media and Pub. Affairs, 1995—2001, interim dean Columbian Coll. Arts & Scis., 2001—02, assoc. v.p. special acad. initiatives, 2003—. Cons. Food Lion Inc., 1997-98, Newseum, Freedom Forum Found., 1995, Nat. Bank Washington, 1988-89; writer Kans. State U. Counseling Ctr., 1967. Author: Media Voices: An Historical Perspective, 1992, Voices of A Nation: A History of Mass Media in the U.S., 1992, 4th edit., 2002, Media in Your Life: The Role of Mass Media In Society, 1998, 3d edit., 2003; editor Journalism and Mass Comm. Quar., 1992-2002. Grantee AT& T Corp, 1995, Ctr. for Washington Area Studies, 1992. Mem.: Orgn. of Am. Historians, Assn. for Schs. and Depts. of Journalism and Mass comm., Assn. for Edn. and Mass Comm., Phi Kappa Phi. Office: George Washington U Sch Media and Pub Affairs 801 22nd St NW Suite 412 Washington DC 20052 Business E-Mail: jfolk@gwu.edu.

FOLKMAN, DAVID H., retail, wholesale and consumer products consultant; b. Jackson, Mich., Nov. 6, 1934; s. Jerome D. and Bessie (Schomer) F.; m. Susan Kleppner, June 22, 1958; children: Louis, Sarah, Karen, Jeffrey. AB, Harvard U., 1957, MBA, 1960. Mdse. mgr. Foley's, Houston, 1957-69; v.p. dir. stores Famous-Barr, St. Louis, 1969-74; sr. v.p., gen. mdse. mgr. Macy's Calif., San Francisco, 1974-82; pres., chief exec. officer Emporium Capwell, San Francisco, 1982-87; gen. ptnr. U.S. Venture Ptnrs., Menlo Park, Calif., 1987-90; venture ptnr., 1991-93; pres., chief exec. officer Laurel Burch, Inc., San Francisco, 1990-91; retail investor, cons., 1991-93; CEO Esprit de Corp, San Francisco, 1993-95; prin., Regent Pacific Mgmt. Corp., San Francisco, 1995—. Instr. U. Houston, 1968-69, Wash. U., St. Louis, 1970-73; bd. dirs. Regent Pacific Mgmt. Corp., Shoe Pavilion, Inc. Mem. Harvard Club (N.Y.C.). Office: Regent Pacific Mgmt Corp 425 California St Ste 1310 San Francisco CA 94104 Office Phone: 415-391-8500. Business E-Mail: dfolkman@regent-pacific.com.

FOLKMAN, MOSES JUDAH, surgeon, educator; b. Cleve., Feb. 24, 1933; s. Jerome D. and Bessie Folkman. BA, Ohio State U., 1953; MD, Harvard U., 1957; DSc (hon.), Mt. Sinai Sch. Medicine, 1996, Northwestern U., 1998, Muhlenberg Coll., 1999, Albany Med. Coll., 1999, Thomas Jefferson U., 2001, U. Conn., 2002, Oberlin Coll., 2002, N.E. Ohio U., 2002, U. Mass., Dartmouth, 2003, Northeastern U., 2004, McGill U., 2004; MD (hon.), Uppsala U., Sweden, 1998, Göteborg U., 2000; LHD (hon.), U. Mass., Lowell, 1999; DHL (hon.), Salem (Mass.) State Coll., 2004. From intern to asst. resident in surgery Mass. Gen. Hosp., Boston, 1957—60, sr. asst. resident in surgery, 1962—64, chief resident, 1964—65; chief resident in pediat. surgery Phila. Children's Hosp., 1969; instr. surgery Harvard U. Med. Sch., 1965—66, assoc. in surgery, 1967, prof. surgery, 1967—, Julia Dyckman Andrus prof. pediat. surgery, 1968—, prof. anatomy and cellular biology, 1989—. Asst. surgeon Boston City Hosp., 1965—66; assoc. dir. Sears Surg. Lab., 1966—67; sr. surgeon Children's Hosp. Med. Ctr., Boston, 1968—, surgeon-in-chief, 1968—81; dir. Surg. Rsch. Labs., 1968—. Co-author of papers describing a new method of hepatectomy for liver cancer, author 389 original peer-reviewed papers and 106 book chapters and monographs. With M.C. USN, 1960—62. Recipient Career Devel. award, NIH, 1966, Lila Gruber award, Am. Acad. Dermatology, 1974, Ledlie prize, Harvard U., 1987, Gairdner Found. Internat. award, Toronto, Can., 1991, Christopher Columbus Commemorative Sci. medal, U.S. Congress/NIH, Wolf award, Wolf Found., Jerusalem, 1992, Lucian award, Royal Coll. Surgeons Can., 1993, Steiner award, Josef Steiner Found., Switzerland, 1994, Bristol-Myers Cancer Rsch. award, 1995, Ernst Schering award, Germany, 1996, Gen. Motors Cancer Rsch. award, 1997, Ernst Jung Found. award, Germany, 1997, Med. prize, Keio (Japan) U., 1998, Chiron award in medicine, Italy, 1999, award in life sci., Benjamin Franklin Inst., Phila., 2001, Prince of Asturias award, Spain, 2004, Henry Bigelow medal, Boston Surg. Soc., 2005, Grand Prix Scientifique, Inst. France, 2005, Scientific Achievement award, 2005. Fellow: ACS (Sheen award 1989), German Surg. Soc. (hon.), Royal Coll. Surgeons (Ireland) (hon.); mem.: NAS (mem. Inst. Medicine), Assn. Am. Physicians, Mass. Med. Soc., Am. Pediat. Surg. Assn. (pres. 2005—), Assn. Acad. Surgery, Am. Surg. Assn. (pres. 2005—), Am. Acad. Arts and Scis., Am. Philos. Soc. Achievements include development of the first atrio-ventricular implantable pacemaker. Office: Children's Hosp Karp Rsch Bldg Fl 12 One Blackfan Cir Boston MA 02115-5724

FOLLET, ROBERT EDWARD, music librarian; b. Syracuse, N.Y., Aug. 12, 1942; s. Robert Edward and Grace (Weymer) F.; m. Diane Weber, June 15, 1968 (div. Apr. 1997). MusB, Oberlin Coll., 1964; MusM, U. Ill., 1966; MLS, U. Tex., 1979. Asst. music libr. U. North Tex., Denton, 1980-89; music libr. Rice U., Houston, 1989-92; head music libr. U. Ariz., Tucson, 1992-95, Ariz. State U., Tempe, 1995—2002, Arthur Freidheim Libr., Peabody Conservatory, Balt., 2002—. Author: Albert Roussel: A Biobibliography, 1986; contbr. over 75 revs. to Am. Record Guide, L.Am. Music Rev. and Notes. Violist Tempe and Mesa Symphony Orch. Mem. Music Libr. Assn. (co-chmn. local arrangements for nat. meeting 1999-2002, chmn. Mountain Plains chpt. 1998-2000), Internat. Assn. Music Librs. (treas. U.S. br. 1991-98). Episcopalian. Avocations: reading, tennis. Address: 9455 Ashley Cir Owings Mills MD 21117 E-mail: violaman55@comcast.net.

FOLLETT, KENNETH MARTIN, author; b. Cardiff, Wales, June 5, 1949; s. Martin D. and Lavinia C. (Evans) F.; m. Mary Emma Ruth Elson, Jan. 5, 1968 (div. 1985); children: Emanuele, Marie-Claire; m. Barbara Broer, Nov. 8, 1985. BA, U. Coll., London, 1970. Reporter, music columnist South Wales Echo, 1970-73; reporter Evening News, London, 1973-74; editorial dir. Everest Books Ltd., London, 1974—76, dep. mng. dir., 1976-77. Pres. The Dyslexia Inst.; chair Nat. Year of Reading, 1998-99; mem. coun. Nat. Literary Trust; bd. dirs. Stevenage Leisure Ltd.; patron Stevenage Home-Start, 2000—; v.p. Stevenage Cmty. Trust, 2002—. Author: The Shakeout, 1975, The Bear Raid, 1976, Secret of Kellerman's Studio, 1976, Eye of the Needle, 1978, Triple, 1979, The Key to Rebecca, 1980, The Man from St. Petersburg, 1982, On Wings of Eagles, 1983, Lie Down with Lions, 1985, The Pillars of Earth, 1989, Night over Water, 1991, A Dangerous Fortune, 1993, Pillars of the Almighty, 1994, A Place Called Freedom, 1995, The Third Twin, 1996, The Hammer of Eden, 1998, Code to Zero, 2000, Jackdaws, 2001, Hornet Flight, 2002, Whiteout, 2004; (as Martin Martinsen) The Power Twins and the Worm Puzzle, 1976; (as Symon Myles) The Big Needle, 1974, The Big Black, 1974, The Big Hit, 1975; (as Bernard L. Ross) Amok: King of Legend, 1976, Capricorn One, 1978; (as Zachary Stone) The Modigliani Scandal, 1976, Paper Money, 1977; screenwriter: Fringe Banking, 1978, A Football Star, 1979, Lie Down with Lions, 1987. V.p. Stevenage Boro Football Club, 2000—; bd. govs. Roebuck Primary Sch. and Nursery, 1998—, chair govs., 2001—; mem. coun. Nat. Literacy Trust, 1996—; pres. The Dyslexia Inst., 1998—; chair Nat. Yr. of Reading, 1998—99; chair adv. com. Reading Is Fundamental U.K., 2003—; mem. Yr Academi Gymreig; bd. dirs. Nat. Acad. Writing, 2003—. Recipient Edgar award Mystery Writers Am., 1979, Corine award, Germany, 2003; fellow Univ. Coll., London, 1994. Fellow Royal Soc. Arts. Office: PO Box 4 Stevenage SG3 6UT England

FOLLETT, M. PAUL, genealogist, librarian; b. Oakland, Calif., Aug. 5, 1958; s. Marvin Dana Follett and Elizabeth Joan Nicholson; m. Joanne Rusk, Aug. 22, 1986; children: Spencer, Sarah, Cesilie. BA in History, Brigham Young U., 1985, MLS, 1989. Head genealogy dept. Lawton Pub. Libr., Okla., 1989—. Author: (bibliography) Printed Sources for Oklahoma Genealogical and Historical Research; genealogy columnist: Lawton Constn., 2005—. Unit commr. Boy Scouts, Lawton, 2003—, cubmaster, asst. cubmaster, 1993—98. Recipient Eagle Scout, Boy Scouts of Am., 1971. Mem.: Southwestern Okla. Hist. Soc. (v.p. 2003—), SW Okla. Geneal. Soc. (bd. mem. 1989—). Lds Ch. Achievements include development of Kiowa Comanche and Apache Family Research Collection; speaker at 1997 Federation of Genealogical Society Conference in Dallas; organizer 2004 Native Am. and Genealogy Conf. Avocations: genealogy, reading, music. Office: Lawton Public Library 110 SW Fourth St Lawton OK 73501 Office Phone: 580-581-3450 6. E-mail: pfollett@cityof.lawton.ok.us.

FOLLETT, ROBERT JOHN RICHARD, publisher; b. Oak Park, Ill., July 4, 1928; s. Dwight W. and Mildred (Johnson) F.; m. Nancy L. Crouthamel, Dec. 30, 1950; children: Brian L., Kathryn R., Jean A., Lisa W. AB, Brown U., 1950; postgrad., Columbia U., 1950-51. Editor Follett Pub. Co., Chgo., 1951-55, sales mgr., 1955-58, gen. mgr. ednl. divsn., developer first multiracial textbook program, first textbooks for disadvantaged, first beginning-to-read books, 1958-68, pres., 1968-78; chmn., dir. Follett Corp., 1979-94. Pres. Alpine Guild, Inc., 1977—; dir. Assn. Am. Pubs., 1972—79; chmn. Sch. Pubs., 1971—73; dir. Ednl. Sys. Corp.; mem. Ill. Gov.'s Commn. on Schs, 1972; pres. Alpine Rsch. Inst., Adv. Coun. on Edn. Stats., 1975—77; chmn. Book Distbn. Task Force of Book Industry, 1978—81; adv. coun. Krannert Sch. of Mgmt., 1988—93; pres. Soda Creek Open Space Assn. Inc., 1994—; dir. Continental Divide Land Trust, 1996—2002; chmn. Rocky Mountain Resource Ctr., Inc., 1997—2002; lectr. Denver U. Pub. Inst., 1997—; mem. adv. bd. Ctr. for Living Democracy, 1997—2000; mem. Consortium on Renewing Edn., 1997—2000; chmn. Open Space for Summit, 1999; pres. Snake River Comty. Assoc., 2001—, Continental Divide Land Trust, 2001—03. Author: Your Wonderful Body, 1961, What to Take Backpacking and Why, 1977, How to Keep Score in Business, 1978, The Financial Side of Book Publishing, 1982, rev. edit., 1988, Financial Feasibility in Book Publishing, 1988, rev. edit., 1996. Bd. dirs. Village Mgr. Assn., 1964-84, Cmty. Found. Oak Park and River Forest, 1959-86, Fund for Justice, 1974-77, For Character, 1983-93, Ctr. Book Rsch., 1985-88; trustee Inst. Ednl. Data Sys., 1965-; trustee, pres. Rotary Found., 2000-; elected mem. Rep. State Com. from 7th dist. Ill., 1982-90, vice chmn., 1986-90; chmn. Ill. Reps. Strategic Planning Com., 1986-87; Presdl. Elector, 1988; pres. Keystone Citizens League, 1997-; mem. Keystone Mountain Responsibility Team, 1998-2000; mem. adv. coun. Colo. Mountain Coll., 2003-; hon. co-chair Colo. Mountain Coll. Campaign, 1998-99; mem. Wildlife/Wetlands Citizens Adv. Group, 2001-02; mem. adv. com. Keystone Sci. Sch., 2003-. Served in AUS, 1951-53. Named one of Torchbearers, Olympics, 2004; recipient Citizen of Yr. award, Summit County, 1999, Philanthropist of Yr. award, 2003. Mem.: Soc. Midland Authors, Ill. C. of C. (chmn. edn. com. 1977—79), Am. Book Coun. (v.p. 1987—88), Rocky Mountain Book Pubs. Assn., Mid.-Am. Pubs. Assn. (mng. dir. 1987—88, dir. 1988—93), Chgo. Pubs. Assn. (pres. 1976—94), Rotary Club Summit County, River Forest Tennis Club, Sierra Club. Office: Alpine Guild Inc PO Box 4848 Dillon CO 80435-4848 Home: 0160 Kinnikinnik Rd Keystone CO Business E-Mail: bob@alpineguild.com.

FOLLETT, RONALD FRANCIS, soil scientist; b. Laramie, Wyo., June 26, 1939; s. Roy Lawrence and Frances (Hunter) F.; m. Dorothy Mae Spangle, Jan. 1, 1967; children: William, Jennifer, Michael. BS, Colo. State U., 1961, MS, 1963; PhD, Purdue U., 1966. Rsch. soil scientist Agrl. Rsch. Svc., USDA, Mandan, N.D., 1968-75, nat. rsch. program leader Beltsville (Md.) and Ft. Collins (Colo.), 1976-86, rsch. leader soil-plant-nutrient rsch. unit Ft. Collins, 1986—; postdoctoral rsch. U.S. Plant-Soil-Nutrition Lab., Ithaca, N.Y., 1975-76. Co-author: The Potential of U.S. Cropland to Sequester Carbon and Mitigate the Greenhouse Effect, 1998; editor: Soil Erosion & Crop Productivity, 1985, Soil Fertility and Organic Matter as Critical Components of Production Systems, 1987, Nitrogen Management and Ground Water Protection, 1989, Managing Nitrogen for Ground Water Quality and Farm Profitability, 1991, Soil Processes & The Carbon Cycle, 1997, Soil Properties & Their Management for Carbon Sequestration, 1997, The Potential of U.S. Grazing Lands to Sequester Carbon and Mitigate the Greenhouse Effect, 2000, Nitrogen in the Environment, Sources, Problems and Management, 2001, Agricultural Practices and Policies for Carbon Sequestration in Soil, 2002; guest editor spl. issue Jour. Containment Hydrol.; contbr. over 150 articles to profl. jours. Officer 1st Presbyn. Ch., Mandan, then Ft. Collins; adult leader local Boy Scouts Am., Beltsville, then Ft. Collins. Capt. arty., U.S. Army, 1966-68; maj. Res. Recipient Disting. Svc. award, USDA, 1984, 1992, Superior Svc. award, 2000, U.S. Presdl. Rank Meritorious Svc. award, 2004, cet. of merit, Agr. Rsch. Svc./USDA, 1990, 1996, 1999—2003, cert. of appreciation, Soil Conservation Svc./USDA, 1992. Fellow Soil Sci. Soc. Am. (divsn. chmn. bd. dirs. 1985-88), Am. Soc. Agronomy, Soil and Water Conservation Soc. Am.(Colo. chpt. Presdl. citation 2002) Avocations: working with youth, skiing, fishing, gardening, woodworking. Office: USDA Agrl Rsch Svc Soil-Plant-Nutrient Rsch Unit 2150 Centre Ave Bldg D Ste 100 Fort Collins CO 80526-8119 Office Phone: 970-492-7220. Business E-Mail: ronald.follett@ars.usda.gov.

FOLLICK, EDWIN DUANE, law educator, dean, chiropractor; b. Glendale, Calif., Feb. 4, 1935; s. Edwin Fulfford and Esther Agnes (Catherwood) Follick; m. Marilyn K. Sherk, Mar. 24, 1986. BA in Social sci., Calif. State U., LA, 1956, MA in Edn., 1961; MA in Social sci., Pepperdine U., 1957, MPA, 1977; PhD in Social sci., DTh, Sem. Free Prot. Episc. Ch., London, 1958; MS in LS, U. So. Calif., 1963, MEd in Instructional Materials, 1964, AdvMEd in Edn. Adminstrn., 1969; postgrad., Calif. Coll. Law, 1965; LLB, Blackstone Law Sch., 1966, JD, 1967; DC, Cleve. Chiropractic Coll., L.A., 1972; PhD in Eccles. Law, Academia Theatina, Pescara, 1978; MA in Orgnl. Mgmt., Antioch U., L.A., 1990. Tchr., libr. adminstr. L.A. City Schs., 1957-68; law libr. Glendale U. Coll. Law, 1968-69; coll. libr. Cleve. Chiropractic Coll., L.A., 1969-74, dir. edn. and admissions, 1974-84, prof. jurisprudence, 1975—2003, dean student affairs, 1976-92, coll. chaplain, 1985—2003, dean of edn., 1989—2003, rector, 2003—04, rector emeritus, 2004—; assoc. prof. Newport U., 1982; extern prof. St. Andrews Theol. Coll., London, 1961; dir. West Valley Chiropractic Health Ctr., 1972-2000, West Valley Chiropractic Consulting, 2001—04; cons. instnl. chaplain, 2004—; libr. dir. South Baylo U., 2004—, u. chaplain, 2004—; libr. dir. Calif. U. Mgmt. and Sci., 2004—. Adj. prof. law Calif. U. Mgmt. and Sci., 2004—, libr. dir., 2004—, univ. chaplain, 2004—. Contbr. articles to profl. jours. Chaplain's asst. U.S. Army, 1958—60. Decorated cavaliere Internat. Order Legion of Honor of Immaculata (Italy); Knight of Malta, Sovereign Order of St. John of Jerusalem; Knight Grand Prelate, comdr. with star, Order of Signum Fidei; comdr. chevalier Byzantine Imperial Order of Constantine the Gt.; comdr. ritter Order St. Gereon; chevalier Mil. and Hospitaller Order of St. Lazarus of Jerusalem (Malta), Chaplain to the Order of St. Stanislas; numerous others. Mem. ALA, NEA, Am. Assn. Sch. Librarians, L.A. Sch. Libr. Assn., Calif. Sch. Libr. Assn., Assn. Coll. and Rsch. Librarians, Am. Assn. Law Librarians, Am. Chiropractic Assn., Internat. Chiropractors Assn., Nat. Geog. Soc., Internat. Platform Assn., Phi Delta Kappa, Sigma Chi Psi, Delta Tau Alpha. Democrat. Episcopalian. Home: 6435 Jumilla Ave Woodland Hills CA 91367-2833 Office: 590 N Vermont Ave Los Angeles CA 90004-2115 also: 7022 Owensmouth Ave Canoga Park CA 91303-2005 Address: 1126 N Brookhurst St Anaheim CA 92801 Office Phone: 323-906-2114, 714-533-6077. Business E-Mail: edwin.follick@cleveland.edu, edfollick@southbaylo.edu.

FOLLIT, EVELYN V., retail executive; b. 1947; BA in Math., MBA in Fin. and Info. Sys.; degree in Exec. Planning and Tech., Cornell U., MIT. With Dunn & Bradstreet; v.p. ops. and engring. AC Nielson; from v.p. human capital to v.p., COO RadioShack Corp., Fort Worth, Tex., 1997—99, v.p., 1999—, COO, 1999—, sr. v.p. orgnl. enabling svcs., 2003—. Bd. dir. Catalina Mktg. Corp., chmn. audit com., mem. fin. com.; chmn. CIO Coun. Nat. Retail Fedn., 2000—; mem. adv. bd. Ctr. Values Based Leadership, 2002—. Bd. visitors Tex. Christian U., Fort Worth. Named one of Top 10 CIOs in Retailing, Retail Tech. Mag., 1999, Top 10 CIOs Across Am., Info. Week, 1999, 100 Premier IT Leaders in Country, Computerworld, 2001, 25 Most Influential People in Retail, Retail Info Sys. News, 2001, Pioneering Women in Tech., Am. Friends Jerusalem Coll. Tech., 2002; recipient Leadership and Innovation award, Exec. Tech. Mag./Compaq Computer, 2002. Office: RadioShack Corp 100 Throckmarton Ste 1900 Fort Worth TX 76102

FOLMER, JOAN E., accountant; b. Lancaster, Pa., Nov. 13, 1944; d. John H. and Jean M. (Hershey) Kraybill; m. Roy R. Folmer, Aug. 12, 1967. BS in Biology summa cum laude, Elizabethtown Coll., 1967, postgrad., 1976-78. Sci. instr. Sch. Nursing Lancaster (Pa.) Gen. Hosp., 1968-79; staff acct. Hershey (Pa.) Chocolate N.Am., 1979-81, fin. acct., 1981-85, sr. fin. acct., 1985-86, mgr. fixed asset acctg., 1986—97; mgr. capital acctg. The Hershey Co., 1997—. Mem. user adv. com. Dunn & Bradstreet Software, Atlanta, 1985-93. With Oakmont Condominium Assn. Bd., Hershey, 1989-2000. Mem. Inst. Mgmt. Accts. Avocations: golf, biking, travel, jazz and classical music, walking. Home: 1186 Draymore Ct Hummelstown PA 17036-9018 Office: The Hershey Co 100 Crystal A Dr Hershey PA 17033-0810 Office Phone: 717-534-4254.

FOLSE, HENRY JOSEPH, JR., education educator; b. New Orleans, La., May 2, 1945; s. Henry Joseph and Helen Cambias Folse; m. Joan Laura Jackson, Apr. 15, 1972; children: Henry Joseph III, Andre Jackson. BA, Harvard Coll., 1963—67; MA, Tulane U., 1967—69, PhD, 1969—72. Assoc. prof. Coll. of Charleston, Charleston, SC, 1975—80; prof. Loyola U. New Orleans, 1980—. Author: (academic book) The Philosophy of Niels Bohr (Macmillan Sci. Book Club Alt. monthly selection, 1985); editor: (collection of essays) Niels Bohr and Contemporary Philosophy; co-editor: (annotated collection of essays) Philosophical Writings of Niels Bohr Volume IV: Causality and Complementarity; contbr. articles to profl. jours. Fellowship for Younger Humanists, Nat. Endowment for the Humanities, 1973—74. Mem.: So. Soc. for Philosophy and Psychology, Metaphysical Soc. of Am., Am. Philos. Assn., Philosophy of Sci. Assn., Harvard Club of La. (sec.-treas., v.p. 1999—2003). Avocations: travel, photography, amateur astronomy. Home: 3627 Carondelet St New Orleans LA 70115 Office: Loyola University New Orleans 6363 St Charles Ave New Orleans LA 70118 Office Phone: 504-865-3940. Personal E-mail: folse@loyno.edu.

FOLSOM, BURTON WHITMORE, JR., education educator; b. Lincoln, Nebr., Nov. 14, 1947; s. Burton Whitmore and Margaret (Reese) F.; m. Anita Prince, Apr. 8, 1979; 1 child, Adam. BA, Ind. U., 1970; MA, U. Nebr., 1973; PhD, U. Pitts., 1976. Teaching asst. U. Nebr., Lincoln, 1970-72, U. Pitts., 1972-75; prof. Murray (Ky.) State U., 1976—94, Hillsdale Coll., Mich., 1999,

2003—. Author: Urban Capitalists, 1981, Entrepreneurs vs. the State, 1987, The Myth of the Robber Barons, 1991, Empire Builders, 1998, No More FreeMarkets, 1999; editor Continuity: A Jour. of History, 1988—. Republican.

FOLSOM, LOWELL EDWIN, language educator; b. Pitts., Sept. 30, 1947; s. Lowell Edwin and Helen Magdalene (Roeper) Folsom; m. Patricia Ann Jackson, Aug. 30, 1969; 1 child, Benjamin Bradford. BA, Ohio Wesleyan U., 1969; MA, U. Rochester, 1972, PhD, 1976. Chmn. English dept. Lancaster (Ohio) H.S., 1969-70, 71-72; instr. Eastman Sch. Music, Rochester, NY, 1974-75; vis. asst. prof. SUNY, Geneseo, 1975-76; asst. prof. U. Iowa, Iowa City, 1976-82, assoc. prof., 1982-87, prof., 1987—, chair English dept., 1991-95, F. Wendell Miller disting. prof., 1997—2002, Carver prof., 2002—. Cons. Am. Coll. Testing Co., Iowa City, 1980—, Nat. Assessment Ednl. Progress, Denver, 1980—84; dir. Walt Whitman Centennial Conf., Iowa City, 1992, Walt Whitman Conf., Beijing, 2000; Fulbright sr. prof. U. Dortmund, Germany, 1996. Author: Walt Whitman's Native Representations, 1994 (Choice Best Acad. Book, 1995), Re-Scripting Walt Whitman, 2005; editor: Walt Whitman: The Centennial Essays, 1994, Walt Whitman: The Measure of His Song, 1981 (Choice Best Acad. Book, 1982), rev. edit., 1998 (Ind. Publisher Book award, 1999), Walt Whitman and the World, 1995, (CD-ROM) Walt Whitman, 1997 (Choice Best Acad. Book, 1998), Walt Whitman Quar. Rev., 1983—, Whitman East and West, 2002; co-dir.: Walt Whitman Hypertext Archive, 1997—; editl. bd. Walt Whitman Encyclopedia, 1994—98, PMLA, 1999—2002, Profession, 2002—. Named Disting. Scholar, U. Rochester, 1995; recipient Rsch. award, NEH, 1991—94, Collaborative Rsch. award, 2000—04, Faculty Excellence award, Iowa Bd. Regents, 1996, U. Iowa Collegiate Tchg. award, 2003, Preservation award, 2004, Pres. and Provost award Tchg. Excellence, 2005. Mem.: MLA, Whitman Scholars Assn. (dir. 1992—), Am. Studies Assn., Am. Lit. Assn. Home: 739 Clark St Iowa City IA 52240-5640 Office: Univ Iowa Dept English 308 EPB Iowa City IA 52242 Business E-Mail: ed-folsom@uiowa.edu.

FOLTA, CARL D., communications executive; b. Holyoke, Mass., 1957; Attended, Boston U., 1980. Account supr. Ruder Finn; joined Paramount Comm., Inc., 1984, sr. dir., corp. comm., 1992—94; v.p. corp. relations Viacom, Inc., N.Y.C., 1994, sr. v.p., corp. relations, 1994—2005, exec. v.p., 2005—. Office: Viacom Inc 1515 Brdwy New York NY 10036

FOLTER, ROLAND, historian, rare book dealer, writer; b. Fulda, Germany, May 27, 1943; s. Heinz and Annemie (Bennewitz) F.; m. Siegrun Heinecke, Aug. 28, 1967 (dec. 1988); m. Mary Ann Kraus, Apr. 29, 1989; 1 child, Elizabeth. MA, Brown U., 1967, PhD, 1969. Rare books cataloger Yale U., New Haven, 1966-68; prof. U. Ill., Urbana, 1969-77; dir. H.P. Kraus Rare Books, N.Y.C., 1977—2003; ret., 2003. Jury Internat. League Antiquarian Booksellers Prize for Bibliography. Author: Deutsche Dichterbibliotheken, 1975, The Gutenberg Bible in the antiquarian book trade, 1999; co-author: Bibliography: Its History, 1984; contbr. to ency. and articles to profl. jours. Violinist Frankfurt Youth Symphony Orchestra, Germany, 1960—65. Fellow Brown U., 1968, Faculty fellow U. Ill., 1970-75. Fellow Pierpont Morgan Libr.; mem. Bibliog. Soc. Am. (coun. 1982-90), Bibliog. Soc. London, N.Y. Philharm. Soc., Assn. Internat. de Bibliophilie, Maximilian Gesellschaft, Gesellschaft der Bibliophilen, Antiquarian Booksellers Assn. Am., Old Book Table (pres. 1995-97), Yale Libr. Assocs. Avocations: violin, chamber music, book collecting, mountain climbing. Office: H P Kraus Rare Books PO Box 949 Larchmont NY 10538 E-mail: rolandfolter@hpkraus.com.

FOLTZ, RODGER LOWELL, chemistry professor; b. Milw., Feb. 10, 1934; s. Ross Milton and Ida Louise (Campbell) F.; m. Ruth Lynch Bilbe, June 9, 1956; children: Richard C., Camilla M. BS, MIT, 1956; PhD, U. Wis., 1961. Research chemist Battelle Meml. Inst., Columbus, Ohio, 1961-76, sr. research leader, 1976-79; adj. prof. pharmacy Ohio State U., 1972-76, adj. assoc. prof. pharmacology, 1976-79; assoc. dir. Center for Human Toxicology, U. Utah, Salt Lake City, 1979—; rsch. assoc. prof. dept. pharmacology and toxicology U. Utah, Salt Lake City, 1980-85, rsch. prof. pharmacology/toxicology dept., 1985—; pres. CHT, Inc., 1985-87; exec. v.p., lab. dir. N.W. Toxicology Inc., 1987-94; lab dir. Northwest Bioanalytical, 1994—99; tech. dir. Tandem Labs., 2000—. Contbr. articles to profl. jours.; editl. adv. bd. Biomed. Mass Spectrometry, 1979-87, 90-95. Pres. N.W. Area Human Relations Council, Columbus, 1968-70; deacon First Congregational Ch., 1971-75; trustee Denison U. Research Found., 1977-79. Mem. Am. Chem. Soc. (chmn.-elect Columbus chpt. 1978, award Columbus chpt. 1977), Am. Soc. Mass Spectrometry (chmn. nominating com. 1980, 82, bd. dirs. 1988-90), Calif. Assn. Toxicologists (bd. dirs. 1990-91, v.p. 1994, pres. 1995-96), Am. Acad. Forensic Scis. (Alexander O. Gettler award 2000), Am. Assn. Pharm. Scientists. Home: 2080 Belaire Dr Salt Lake City UT 84109-1409 also: Tandem Labs 1121 E 3900 S Salt Lake City UT 84124-1215 E-mail: rodgerf@aol.com.

FOMON, SAMUEL JOSEPH, pediatrician, educator; b. Chgo., Mar. 9, 1923; s. Samuel and Isabel (Sherman) F.; m. Betty Lorraine Freeman, Aug. 20, 1948 (div. Apr. 1978); children: Elizabeth Ann Fomon Seiberling, Kathleen Lenore Fomon Anderson, David Bruce, Christopher, Mary Susan Fomon; m. Louise G. Thomson, June 27, 1986. AB cum laude, Harvard U., 1945; MD, U. Pa., 1947; D (hons.), U. Catolica de Cordoba, Argentina, 1974. Diplomate Am. Bd. Pediatrics, Am. Bd. Nutrition. Intern Queen's Gen. Hosp., Jamaica, N.Y., 1947-48; resident Children's Hosp., Phila., 1948-50; research fellow Cin. Children's Hosp. Research Found., 1950-52; asst. prof. pediatrics U. Iowa, Iowa City, 1954-58, assoc. prof., 1958-61, prof., 1961-93, prof. emeritus, 1993—. Adj. prof. pediat. Baylor Med. Coll., Houston, 2002-05; rev. com. child health and human devel. program project NIH, 1966-69, nutrition study sect., 1978-81; select com. GRAS-Generally Recognized as Safe substances Life Sci. Rsch. Office, 1974-80; expert to working group on infant formula US Food and Agrl. Orgn. of UN and WHO, 2003. Author: Infant Nutrition, 1st edit., 1967, 2d edit., 1974, Nutrition of Normal Infants, 1993. Recipient Career Devel. award NIH, 1962-67, Rosen von Rosenstein award Swedish Pediatric Soc., 1975, McCollum award Am. Soc. Clin. Nutrition, 1979, F. Cuenca Villoro Found. award, Zaragosa, Spain, 1981, Commr.'s spl. citation FDA, 1984, Nutricia Found. award, Rotterdam, The Netherlands, 1991, Bristol-Myers Squibb/Mead Johnson award, 1992, Harry Schwachman award N.Am. Soc. Pediatric Gastroenterology and Nutrition, 1992, A.O. Atwater 2000 Lectureship, Spl. award L.Am. Nutrition Soc., 2000, 2003. Fellow AAAS; mem. Am. Inst. Nutrition (pres. 1989-90, fellow 1989, Conrad A. Elvehjem award 1990), Am. Acad. Pediatrics (chmn. com. nutrition 1960-63, Borden award 1956, Nutrition award 2004), Am. Soc. Clin. Nutrition (pres. 1981-82), Fedn. Am. Socs. Exptl. Biology, Midwest Soc. Pediat. Rsch. (pres. 1963-64, Founder's award 1986), Am. Dietetic Assn. (hon.), El Colegio de Pediat. de Jalisco (hon.). Personal E-mail: samfomon@aol.com.

FONACIER, LUZ SISON, physician; b. Manila, Aug. 2, 1952; d. Gregorio Sison and Luz Mendoza-Sison; m. Jose R. Fonacier; children: Jose Roberto, Frances. AB in Math., St. Theresa's Coll., 1973; MD cum laude, U. of the Philippines, 1978. Clin. instr. U. of the Philippines, 1982-84, N.Y. Hosp.-Cornell, N.Y.C., 1989—91; attending physician Nassau County Med. Ctr., East Meadow, N.Y., 1992, L.I. Jewish Med. Ctr., New Hyde Park, 1992-93; asst. prof. medicine SUNY, Stony Brook, 1993-2000, assoc. prof. clin. medicine, 2000—. Head sect. allergy Winthrop U. Hosp., Mineola, N.Y., 1992—, chmn. latex task force, 1997—. Contbr. articles to profl. jours. Recipient Presdl. award Asian Pacific Congress of Allergology and Immunology, 1998; fellow Charles Revson Found., 1990. Fellow ACP, Internat. Assn. Filipino Allergists and Immunologists (pres. 1999), Am. Coll. Allergy Asthma and Immunology, Am. Acad. Allergy Asthma and Immunology, Phi Kappa Phi. Office: Winthrop U Hosp 222 Station Plz N Mineola NY 11501-3808

FONCELLO, MARTIN JOHN, JR., municipal official; b. Bridgeport, Conn., Nov. 22, 1952; s. Martin John Sr. and Geraldine F.; m. Mary Ann Catherine Grandieri, 1974; 1 child, Martin John III. BS, Boston Coll., 1974, MBA, 1982. Cert. sch. bus. adminstr., Conn. Gen. mgr. Grand Mfg. Corp., Danbury, Conn., 1981-83; EDP auditor Aetna Life & Casualty, Hartford, Conn., 1983-87; EDP audit officer People's Bank, Bridgeport, 1987-90; pres. Candlewood Mktg. & Cons., 1983—; first selectman Brookfield, Conn., 1999—. Adj. prof. Western Conn. State U., Danbury, 1983—. Pres. Greenridge Tax Dist., Brookfield, Conn., 1986-2000; sec. Brookfield Econ. Devel. Commn., 1992-2000; mem. Housatonic Valley Econ. Devel. Partnership, 1997-2003; rec. sec. Brookfield Rep. Town Com. Capt. US Army, 1974-79, lt. col., battalion comdr. USAR. Mem. Res. Officers Assn. (life), Assn. Former Intelligence Officers, Mil. Intelligence Corps. Assn., First Corps of Cadets, Order Sons of Italy, Brookfield Rotary Club (pres. 1996-97, Paul Harris fellow Rotary Internat.), KC (3d degree). Republican. Roman Catholic. Avocations: military intelligence, coaching little league, scouting. Home: 11 Drover Rd Brookfield CT 06804-3508 E-mail: foncellom@compuserve.com.

FONDA, BRIDGET, actress; b. Los Angeles, Jan. 27, 1964; SAG; d. Peter and Susan Fonda.; m. Danny Elfman, 2003; 1 child, Oliver Henry Milton. Films: Aria, 1987, You Can't Hurry Love, 1988, Shag, 1988, Scandal, 1989, Strapless, 1989, Frankenstein Unbound, 1990, The Godfather, Part III, 1990, Doc Hollywood, 1991, Out of the Rain, (also known as Remains), 1991, Single White Female, 1992, Singles, 1992, Bodies Rest and Motion, 1993, Point of No Return, 1993, Little Buddha, 1994, It Could Happen To You, 1994, Camilla, 1994, The Road to Wellville, 1994, Rough Magic, 1995, Balto (voice), 1995, Grace of My Heart, 1996, City Hall, 1996, South of Heaven, West of Hell, 2000, Delivering Milo, 2001, The Whole Shebang, 2001, Kiss the Dragon, 2001; TV appearances: (series) 21 Jump Street, 1989, Jacob Have I Loved, WonderWorks episode, 1989, (made for cable movie) Leather Jackets, 1991, Jackie Brown, 1997, A Simple Plan, 1998, Finding Graceland, 1998, The Break Up, 1998, South of Heaven West of Hell, 1999, South From Hell's Kitchen, 1999, Monkey Bone, 1999, Lake Placid, 1999; (TV movies) In the Gloaming, 1997, After Amy, 2001, The Snow Queen, 2002; (TV series) The Chris Isaak Show, 2001.

FONDA, JANE, actress; b. NYC, Dec. 21, 1937; d. Henry and Frances (Seymour) F.; m. Roger Vadim Aug. 14, 1965, (div. Jan. 16, 1973); 1 child, Vanessa; m. Tom Hayden, Jan. 20, 1973 (div. 1990); children, Troy Garity, Mary Luana Williams; m. Ted Turner, Dec. 21, 1991 (div. May 22, 2001). Student, Vassar Coll. Appeared on Broadway stage in There Was a Little Girl, 1960, The Fun Couple, 1962; appeared in Actor's Studio prodn. Strange Interlude, 1963; appeared in films Tall Story, 1960, A Walk on the Wild Side, 1962, The Chapman Resort, 1962, Period of Adjustment, 1962, Sunday in New York, 1963, In the Cool of the Day, 1963, The Love Cage, 1963, La Ronde, 1964, Cat Ballou, 1965, The Chase, 1966, Any Wednesday, 1966, The Game Is Over, 1967, Hurry Sundown, 1967, Barefoot in the Park, 1967, Barbarella, 1968, Spirits of the Dead, 1969, They Shoot Horses, Don't They?, 1969, Klute, 1970 (Acad. award for Best Actress), All's Well, 1972, Steelyard Blues, 1973, A Doll's House, 1973, The Blue Bird, 1976, Fun with Dick and Jane, 1977, Julia, 1977, California Suite, 1978, Comes a Horseman, 1978, Electric Horseman, 1979, Nine to Five, 1980, On Golden Pond, 1981, Rollover, 1981, Agnes of God, 1985, The Morning After, 1986, Retour, 1987, Leonard Part 6, 1987, Old Gringo, 1988, Stanley and Iris, 1990, Monster-in-Law, 2005; actor, prodr., Coming Home, 1978 (Acad. award for Best Actress), The China Syndrome, 1979; (TV movies) A String of Beads, 1961, Lily: Sold Out, 1981, The Dollmaker(Emmy award for Best Actress), 1984; (TV miniseries) A Century of Women, 1994; author: Jane Fonda's Workout Book, 1981, Women Coming of Age, 1984, Jane Fonda's New Workout & Weight-Loss Program, 1986, Jane Fonda's New Pregnancy Workout & Total Birth Program, 1989, (autobiography) My Life So Far, 2005 (New York Times bestseller list); video: Jane Fonda Workout Video, 12 additional videos. Recipient Golden Apple prize for female star of yr. Hollywood Women's Press Club, 1977, Golden Globe award, 1978; rated no. 1 heroine of young Ams., U.S. News Roper Poll., 1985, 4th most admired woman in Am., Ladies Home Jour. Roper Poll, 1985. Office: Creative Artists Agy care Kim Hodgert 9830 Wilshire Blvd Beverly Hills CA 90212-1804*

FONDA, PETER, actor, director, producer; b. N.Y.C., Feb. 23, 1939; s. Henry and Frances (Seymour) F.; m. Susan Brewer (div. Apr. 1974); 2 children. Student, U. Omaha. Film appearances include Tammy and The Doctor, 1963, The Victors, 1963, Lilith, 1964, The Young Lovers, 1964, The Trip, 1967, The Wild Angels, 1966, The Last Movie, 1971, Two People, 1973, Dirty Mary, Crazy Harry, 1974, Race With The Devil, 1975, 92 in the Shade, 1975, Killer Force, 1975, Fighting Mad, 1976, Futureworld, 1976, Outlaw Blues, 1977, High Ballin', 1978, Wanda Nevada, 1979, Open Season, Smokey and the Bandit II, 1980, Split Image, 1982, Certain Fury, 1985, Dead Fall, 1993, Nadja, 1994, Love and a .45, 1994, Painted Hero, 1996, Grace of My Heart (voice), 1996, Escape From L.A., 1996, Idaho Transfer, Spasm, 1983, Fatal Mission, 1990, The Tempest, 1998, The Passion of Ayn Rand, 1999, The Limey, 1999, Keeping Time, 1999, South of Heaven, West of Hell, 2000, Thomas and the Magic Railroad, 2000, Second Skin, 2001, Wooly Boys, 2001, The Laramie Project, 2002, The Maldonado Miracle, 2003, Back When We Were Grown Ups (TV), 2004; dir., actor in The Hired Hand, 1971, Two People, 1973; writer, co-producer, actor movie Easy Rider, 1969; TV movie appearances include The Hostage Tower, 1980, A Reason To Live, Don't Look Back, 1996, Ulee's Gold, 1997(won Golden Globe Award, Best Actor), Me and Will, 1998, South of Heaven West of Hell, 1999, The Passion of Ayn Rand, 1999, The Limey, 1999, Keeping Time, 1999; author Don't Tell Dad, 1998.*

FONDAHL, JOHN WALKER, civil engineering educator; b. Washington, Nov. 4, 1924; s. John Edmund and Mary (DeCourcy) F.; m. Doris Jane Plishker, Mar. 2, 1946; children: Lauren Valerie, Gail Andrea, Meredith Victoria, Dorian Beth. BS, Thayer Sch. Engring., Dartmouth, 1947, MSCE, 1948. Instr., then asst. prof. U. Hawaii, 1948-51; constrn. engr. Winston Bros. Co., Mpls., 1951-52; project engr. Nimbus Dam and Powerplant project, Sacramento, 1952-55; mem. faculty Stanford U., 1955—, prof. civil engring., 1966-90, Charles H. Leavell prof. civil engring., 1977-90, prof. emeritus, 1990—. Author reports in field. Served with USMCR, 1943-46. Recipient Golden Beaver award Heavy Constrn. Industry, 1976 Fellow ASCE (Constrn. Mgmt. award 1977, Peurifoy Constrn. Rsch. award 1990), Project Mgmt. Inst. (hon. life, Fellow award 1981); mem. Nat. Acad. Engring., Nat. Acad. Constrn., Phi Beta Kappa. Achievements include patent in field. Home and Office: 12810 Viscaino Rd Los Altos Hills CA 94022-2520 E-mail: fondahlj@aol.com.

FONDAW, RONALD EDWARD, artist, educator; b. Paducah, Ky., Apr. 25, 1954; s. Lex Alan and Rose Mary (Holley) Kilgore; m. Lynn S. Shepard, Oct. 7, 1987; children: Andrea Rose, Wyler S. BFA, Memphis Coll. Art, 1976; MFA, U. Ill., 1978. Instr. Ohio U., Athens, 1978; assoc. prof. art U. Miami, Coral Gables, Fla., 1978-95, prof., 1997—; prof. art Washington U., St. Louis, 1995—. Lectr., presenter workshops Ohio State U., Chgo. Art Inst., Tokyo U. Fine Art, Chautauqua Sch. Art. Exhbns. nat. and internat.; several public art commissions. Ford Found. fellow, 1977, Fla. Arts Coun. fellow, 1981, Guggenheim fellow, 1985, Pollack/Krasner fellow, 1997-98; grantee NEA, 1988; Kransberg award St. Louis Art Mus., 1998. Office: Wash U 721 Kingsland Ave Saint Louis MO 63130-3107 Home: 2004 Stemler Rd Columbia IL 62236-2926 E-mail: refondaw@art.wustl.edu.

FONDURULIA, JULIE A., computer scientist; b. Gardner, Mass., Sept. 24, 1973; d. Michael and Janet L. Fondurulia. BS in Math., Worcester (Mass.) State Coll., 1996; MS in Applied Sci., Worcester (Mass.) Polytechnic Inst., 1999. Database mgr. Ctr. for Health Policy U. Mass. Med. Sch., Worcester, Mass., 1999—2001; sr. sys. programmer Mass. Exec. Office Health & Human Svcs. IT, Boston, 2001—. Mem.: Am. Math. Soc., Acad. Health Scis. Rsch. and Health Policy, Am. Statis. Assn. Avocations: needlepoint, reading, walking. Home: 186 Main St Westminster MA 01473-1531 Office: Exec Office Health & Human Services IT 222 Maple Ave Chang Bldg Shrewsbury MA 01545 E-mail: j.a.fondurulia@verizon.net.

FONER, ERIC, historian, educator; b. N.Y.C., Feb. 7, 1943; s. Jack D. and Liza F.; m. Lynn Garafola, May 1, 1980. BA, Columbia U., 1963, PhD, 1969; BA, Oxford (Eng.) U., 1965. Prof. history City Coll., CUNY, N.Y.C., 1973-82, Columbia U., N.Y.C., 1982—; Pitt prof. Am. history and instns. Cambridge (Eng.) U., 1980-81. Harmsworth prof. Am. history Oxford (Eng.) U., 1993-94. Author: Free Soil, Free Labor, Free Men, 1970, Tom Paine and Revolutionary America, 1976, Politics and Ideology in the Age of the Civil War, 1980, Nothing But Freedom, 1983, Reconstruction: America's Unfinished Revolution, 1988, Readers' Encyclopedia of American History, 1991, Freedom's Lawmakers, 1993, The Story of American Freedom, 1998, Who Owns History?, 2002, Give Me Liberty!: An American History, 2004, Voices of Freedom, 2004, Forever Free, 2005; editor: The New American History, 1990, The Reader's Companion to American History, 1991. Recipient Bancroft prize Columbia U., 1989, L.A. Times Book award, 1989, Parkman prize Soc. Am. Historians, 1989, Owsley prize So. Hist. Assn., 1989, Lit. Lion prize N.Y. Pub. Libr., 1994; named Scholar of Yr., N.Y. Coun. for the Humanities, 1995; fellow ACLS, 1972-73, NEH, 1983-84, Guggenheim fellow, 1974-76. Mem. Am. Hist. Assn. (pres. 2000), Orgn. Am. Historians (Avery O. Craven prize 1989, pres. 1993-94), Am. Antiquarian Soc., Am. Acad. Arts and Scis., British Acad. Home: 606 W 116th St New York NY 10027-7011 Office Phone: 212-854-5253. E-mail: ef17@columbia.edu.

FONER, NANCY, anthropologist, educator; d. Moe and Anne (Berman) F.; m. Peter Swerdloff; 1 child, Alexis. BA, Brandeis U., 1966; PhD, U. Chgo., 1971. Asst. prof. anthropology CUNY, York, 1970-73, SUNY, Purchase, 1973-77, assoc. prof., 1977-85, prof., 1985—. Author: Status & Power in Rural Jamaica, 1973, Jamaica Farewell, 1978, Ages in Conflict, 1984, New Immigrants in New York, 1987, revised edit., 2001, The Caregiving Dilemma, 1994, From Ellis Island to JFK, 2000, Immigration Research for a New Century, 2000, Islands in the City, 2001. Fellow Am. Anthrop. Assn. Office: SUNY Social Sci Divsn Purchase NY 10577 E-mail: nancy.foner@purchase.edu.

FONES, MONTY GARTH, secondary school educator; b. Dalhart, Tex., Dec. 5, 1932; s. Wilbur Leslie and Bernice Hazel (Wiley) F.; m. Nancy Jeanne Mills, Dec. 23, 1972. BS in Math., Panhandle State U., Goodwell, Okla., 1955; MA in Edn., San Diego State U., 1964. Tchr. math. Redwood High Sch., Visalia, Calif., 1960-61, Costa Mesa (Calif.) High Sch., 1961-63, Corona Del Mar High Sch., Newport Beach, Calif., 1963-66; tchr. math. and sci. Estancia High Sch., Costa Mesa, 1966-68; resource tchr. Space Sci. Learning Project, Costa Mesa, Newport Beach, 1968-72, Sanborn Instructional Media Ctr., Costa Mesa, 1972-74; alternative educator secondary math. and sci. Alternative Edn. Ctr., Costa Mesa, 1974-89; ret., 1989. Editor: Colonizing A Planet, 1968, Metric Guide Book, 1972-75; author: Model Rocket Guidebook, 1972; author, editor: Technology in Curriculum, 1989. Lt. (j.g.) USNR, 1956-59. Grantee Calif. Assn. for Educators in Media and Tech., 1974; recipient Beacon award NMEA, 1975, Newport Schs. Found., 1987-88, 88-89. Methodist. Achievements include development of Mobile Sci. Lab., recognized for innovative materials and approach by NASA, Nat. Aviation Adminstrn. and other endl. groups. Avocations: computers, photography, music. Home: 910 Powell Ct Costa Mesa CA 92626-2942 Personal E-mail: montyfones@comcast.net.

FONG, BERNARD W.D., physician, educator; b. Honolulu, May 18, 1926; s. Leonard K. and Francis C. Fong; m. Roberta Wat, Aug. 14, 1950; children: Phyllis K., Jeffrey S., Camille K., Allison K. BS, Bucknell U., 1948; MD, Jefferson Med. Coll., 1952. Diplomate Am. Bd. Internal Medicine. Intern Germantown Hosp., Phila., 1952-53, chief med. resident, 1953-55; teaching fellow cardiology Jefferson Med. Coll. Hosp., Phila., 1955-56; attending physician Queen's Med. Ctr., Honolulu, 1956—2002, St. Francis Hosp., Honolulu, 1956-89; clin. prof. medicine U. Hawaii, Honolulu, 1982—2004; med. dir. medicare part B Aetna Ins. Co., Hawaii, Guam, 1988-97, Transamerica Occidental Life Ins. Co., Hawaii and Guam, 1997-2000, Noridian Adminstrv. Svcs., Hawaii and Guam, 2000—04; ret., 2004. Adv. coun. Nat. Heart, Lung and Blood Inst., NIH, Bethesda, Md., 1976-80, chmn. 3d forum on cardiovascular risk factors, 1985; adv. com. cardiovascular risk factors in minorities NIH, 1976-89; pres. Triple C, 1996-2001. Pres. Hawaii Heart Assn., Honolulu, 1962-63; bd. dirs. Am. Heart. Assn., N.Y.C., 1963-66; pres. Chung Shan Assn., Honolulu, 1969-70, United Chinese Soc. Hawaii, Honolulu, 1973-74; 1st v.p. Wong Leong Doo Benevolent Soc., Honolulu, 1973-2003; 1st v.p. Ocean View Cemetery, Honolulu, 1973-2003; bd. dirs. Palola Home, 2004-. With USNR, 1944-46, PTO. Fellow ACP (bd. govs. 1972-76, inaugural laureate internal medicine Hawaii chpt. 1986), Am. Coll. Cardiology (bd. govs. 1992-96, chair 1995-96, trustee 1997-2002), Am. Coll. Chest Physicians, Am. Heart Assn; mem. Am. Soc. Internal Medicine (pres. Hawaii chpt. 1980-82). Republican. Roman Catholic. Home: 97 Dowsett Ave Honolulu HI 96817-1107 Personal E-mail: Bernardfong@msn.com.

FONG, CYNTHIA ANN, language educator; d. Wilkaan and Henryetta Fong. AB in English with distinction, Stanford U., 1978; MA in Tchg. English as 2d Lang., UCLA, 1982. Instr. ESL Chinese Am. Civic Assn., Boston, 1984—85, Boston U., 1984; prof. ESL Bunker Hill C.C., 1985—. Author interactive program for computerized writing instrn.; co-creator coll. concert series with pedagogical aims; developer ESL course to support a sociology class; creator interactive program for verb tense editing. Recipient Excellence in Tchg. award, Nat. Inst. for Staff and Orgnl. Devel. (NISOD), 2002. Mem.: Mass. Tchrs. of Spkrs. of Other Languages (MATSOL), Tchrs. of English to Spkrs. of Other Languages (TESOL), Lexington Sinfonietta, Chamber Music Am. Avocations: freelance classical pianist and violinist, avid chamber musician, swimmer. Office: Bunker Hill CC 250 Rutherford Ave Boston MA 02129-2925 Office Phone: 617-228-3318. Personal E-mail: cfon@earthlink.net. E-mail: cfong@bhcc.mass.edu.

FONG, KEVIN MURRAY, lawyer; b. San Francisco, Jan. 25, 1955; AB magna cum laude, Harvard U., 1976; JD cum laude, 1979. Bar: Calif. 1979. Law clk. Chief Judge Constance Baker Motley, U.S. Dist. Ct. (so. dist.) N.Y., NYC, 1979-80; ptnr. Pillsbury, Madison & Sutro LLP, San Francisco, 1980—2001, Pillsbury Winthrop LLP, San Francisco, 2001—05; ptnr. litigation practice, co-chmn. appellate practice, co-chmn. diversity com. Pillsbury Winthrop Shaw Pittman LLP, San Francisco, 2005—. Bd. dirs. Lawyers for One America. Editor-in-chief Law Rev. Harvard civil rights-civil liberties, 1979. Mem. ABA (mem. com. racial and ethnic diversity), Calif. Acad. Appellate Lawyers, Asian Am. Bar Assn. (pres. 1989), Asian Pacific Bar Calif. (pres. 1990), Bar Assn. San Francisco (bd. dirs. 1991-92), Legal Aid Soc. San Francisco (treas. 1995-97, mem. exec. com.). Democrat. Office: Pillsbury Winthrop Shaw Pittman LLP 50 Fremont St San Francisco CA 94105 Office Phone: 415-983-1270. Office Fax: 415-983-1200. Business E-Mail: kevin.fong@pillsburylaw.com.

FONG, NELSON S., secondary school educator; b. San Francisco, Aug. 23, 1950; m. Lorraine Hom, Aug. 15, 1973; children: Keith, Kevin. AA, City Coll. San Francisco, 1970; BA, U. Calif., Berkeley, 1972. Tchr. Livermore Valley Joint Unified Sch. Dist., Livermore, Calif., 1973—. Recipient Cert. of Honor, Westinghouse Found., 1991. Mem. Nat. Coun. Tchrs. Math., Calif. Tchrs. Assn., Livermore Edn. Assn., Am. Assn. Physics Tchrs. Avocations: stamp collecting/philately, computer simulations, baseball. Home: 1312 Kathy Ct Livermore CA 94550-3713 Office: Livermore HS 600 Maple St Livermore CA 94550-3298 Office Phone: 925-606-4812.

FONG, PETER C. K., lawyer, judge, legal company executive; b. Honolulu, Oct. 28, 1955; s. Arthur S.K. and Victoria K.Y. (Chun) F. BBA with honors, U. Hawaii, 1977; JD, Boston Coll., 1980. Bar: Hawaii 1980, U.S. Dist. Ct. Hawaii 1980, U.S. Ct. Appeals (9th cir.) 1980, U.S. Supreme Ct. 1983. Law clk. to presiding justice Supreme Ct. Hawaii, Honolulu, 1980-81; dep. pros. atty. Pros. Atty.'s Office, Honolulu, 1981-84; with Davis, Reid & Richards, Honolulu, 1984-89; chief legal counsel, chief clk. Senate jud. com. Hawaii State Legislature, 1989—; judge per diem Dist./Family Ct., Hawaii, 1989—; ptnr. Hong, Kwock & Fong, Honolulu, 1990-91, Fong & Fong, Honolulu, 1989—; pres., CEO, dir. Chun Kim Chow, Ltd., Honolulu, 1998—. Gen. legal counsel Hawaii Jr. C. of C., 1983-84; pres., bd. dirs. Legal Aid Soc. Hawaii,

1984-90; pres., 1986-87; arbitrator Hawaiian Cir. Ct., 1986—, Am. Arbitration Assn., 1989—; mediator Arbitration Forums, Inc., 1989—. Editorial staff Boston Coll. Internat. and Comp. Law Rev., 1978-80. Mem. City and County Honolulu Neighborhood Bd., 1981-83; campaign treas. for Hawaii state senator, 1981-89; mem. aux. admissions com. Boston Coll. Law Sch., 1982—, major gifts com. and sustaining membership fundraising drive com. YMCA, 1988; del. Gov.'s Congress on Hawaii's internat. role, 1988; del. Hawaii Jud. Forsight Congress, 1991; mem. hearings com. Hawaii State Atty.'s Disciplinary Bd., 1991—. Recipient Pres.'s award Hawaii Jr. C. of C., 1984; named one of ten Outstanding Persons of Hawaii, 1990, 92. Mem. ABA, ATLA, Hawaii State Bar Assn. (co-chmn. and vice-chmn., jud. salary com., mem. legis. com., coord. legis. resource bank, mem. task force on disciplinary counsel), Hawaii Developer's Coun., Am. Judicature Soc., Hawaii Supreme Ct. Hist. Soc., Hawaii Trial Judges Assn., Nat. Coun. Juvenile and Family Ct. Judges, Rsch. Bd. of Advisors, Nat. Assn. Dist. Attys., U.S. Supreme Ct. Hist. Soc., Mortar Bd., Tu Chiang Shen (past pres.), Waialae Country Club. Home: 5255 Makalena St Honolulu HI 96821-1808 Office: Fong & Fong Grosvener Ctr Makai Tower 733 Bishop St Ste 1550 Honolulu HI 96813-4003 Office Phone: 808-528-2889.

FONG, PHYLLIS KAMOI, federal agency administrator, lawyer; b. Phila., Pa., Oct. 16, 1953; d. Bernard W.D. and Roberta (Wat) F.; m. Paul E. Tellier, Nov. 25, 1978. BA in Asian Studies, Pomona Coll., 1975; JD, Vanderbilt U., 1978. Bar: Tenn. 1978, DC 1982. Atty. U.S. Commn. on Civil Rights, Washington, 1978-81; asst. gen. counsel Legal Svcs. Corp., Washington, 1981-83; assoc. counsel to the insp. gen. U.S. Small Bus. Admin., Washington, 1983-88, asst. insp. gen. for mgmt. and policy, 1988-94, asst. insp. gen. for mgmt. and legal counsel, 1994-99, insp. gen., 1999—2002, U.S. Dept. of Agriculture, Washington, 2002—. Mem. ABA, Tenn. Bar Assn., D.C. Bar Assn. Office: USDA Rm 117 W Jamie Whitten Bldg 1400 Independence Ave SW Washington DC 20250*

FONICELLO, NANCY ANN, conservator; b. Middletown, Conn., June 3, 1962; d. Thomas and Patricia Fonicello. BS in Chemistry, SUNY, Syracuse, 1984. Prof. artist, Livingston, Mont., 1982—98; conservator Ancient Airways Studio, Wilsall, Mont., 1998—. Founding advisor Material Culture of Prairie, Plains and Plateau Conf., Great Falls, Mont., 2000—04. Seminar instr. Lewis & Clark Interpretive Ctr., Great Falls, 2000, 2001. Fellow, Andrew W. Mellon Found., 2001, Smithsonian Instn., Nat. Mus. Am. Indian. Mem.: Am. Inst. Conservation Hist. and Artistic Works (assoc.). Avocation: classical piano. Office: Ancient Artways Studio 18 Becker Ln Wilsall MT 59086 Office Phone: 406-587-2067. Business E-Mail: porcupine@ancientartways.com.

FONKALSRUD, ERIC WALTER, pediatric surgeon, educator; b. Balt., Aug. 31, 1932; s. George and Ella (Fricke) F.; m. Margaret Ann Zimmermann, June 6, 1959; children: Eric Walter Jr., Margaret Lynn, David Loren, Robert Warren. BA, U. Wash., 1953; MD, Johns Hopkins U., 1957. Diplomate Am. Bd. Surgery, Am. Bd. Pediatric Surgery, Am. Bd. Thoracic Surgery. Intern Johns Hopkins Hosp., Balt., 1957-58, asst. resident, 1958-59, U. Calif. Med. Ctr., Los Angeles, 1959-62, chief resident surgery, 1962-63, asst. prof. surgery, chief pediatric surgery, 1965-68, assoc. prof., 1968-71, prof. LA, 1971—2001, emeritus prof., 2001—, vice chmn. dept. surgery, 1981-89; resident pediatric surgery Columbus (Ohio) Childrens Hosp. and Ohio State U., 1963-65; practice medicine specializing in pediatric surgery LA, 1965—. Mem. surg. study sect. NIH; James IV surg. traveller to, Gt. Britain, 1971 Mem. editl. bd. Jour. Surg. Rsch., Archives Surgery, Am. Jour. Surgery, Annals Surgery, Surgery, Current Problems in Surgery, Jour. Pediat. Surgery, World Jour. Surgery, Japanese Jour. Surgery, Turkish Jour. Pediat. Surgery, Med. Video Jour. Surgery; contbr. over 650 articles to profl. jours., chpts. to books; co-author: The Undescended Testis, 1981, Infections and Immunologic Disorders in Pediatric Surgery, 1993, Essentials of Pediatric Surgery, 1995, Gastroesophageal Reflux in Childhood; Current Problems in Surgery, 1996, Pediatric Surgery, 1998, Principles of Pediatric Surgery, 2003. Recipient Golden Apple award UCLA Sch. Medicine, 1968; John and Mary R. Markle scholar, 1963-68; named Tree Farmer of Yr. Western Wash., 1998; Johns Hopkins U. Soc. of Scholars, 2003; Profl. Achievement Award, UCLA Sch. of Medicine, 2003. Fellow ACS (surg. forum com., bd. govs. 1978-84, pres. So. Calif. chpt. 1995-96, Mead Johnson award 1963), Am. Acad. Pediat. (exec. bd., chmn. surg. sect. 1986-87, Salzberg award 2000), German Assn. for Surgery (hon.), Polish Assn. Pediat. Surgery (hon.), Japanese Pediat. Surgery Assn. (hon.), John Hopkins Soc. Scholars (hon.); mem. AMA, Am. Thoracic Surg. Assn., Am. Acad. Sci., Am. Assn. Acad. Surgery (pres. 1972), Soc. Univ. Surgeons (pres. 1976, sec. 1972-76), Calif. Med. Assn., Crohns and Celitis Found. of So. Calif. (Man of Yr. 1999), Internat. Surg. Group (treas. 1993-2003), Lilliputian Surg. Soc. (chmn. 1989), L.A. County Med. Assn., Am. Surg. Assn., Pan Pacific Surg. Assn., Pacific Coast Surg. Assn. (recorder 1979-85, pres. 1989), Am. Pediat. Surg. Assn. (bd. govs. 1975-78, pres. 1989), Pacific Assn. Pediat. Surgeons (pres. 1983-84, Coe medal 1998), S.W. Pediatric Soc., L.A. Pediat. Soc., Soc. for Clin. Surgery, Transplantation Soc., Pediat. Surgery Biology Club, Bay Surg. Soc., L.A. Surg. Soc. (sec. 1988-90, pres. 1991), Town Hall (L.A.), Pithotomy Club (pres. 1956-57), Sigma Xi, Alpha Omega Alpha. Methodist. Home: 428 24th St Santa Monica CA 90402-3102 Office: U Calif Med Ctr Dept Surgery Los Angeles CA 90095 Office Phone: 310-825-6712. E-mail: efonkalsrud@mednet.ucla.edu.

FONKEN, GERHARD JOSEPH, retired chemistry professor, retired academic administrator; b. Krefeld, Germany, Aug. 3, 1928; came to U.S., 1930, naturalized, 1935; s. Henry A. and Wilhelmina Katerina (von Eyser) F.; m. Carolyn Lee Stay, Dec. 20, 1952; children: David, Katherine, Steven, Karen, Eric. BS, U. Calif., Berkeley, 1954, PhD, 1957. Chemist Procter & Gamble Co., 1957-58; chemist Stanford (Calif.) Research Inst., 1958-59; instr. U. Tex., Austin, 1959-61, from asst. to assoc. prof., 1961-72, prof. chemistry, 1972-94, asso. provost, 1972-75, acting v.p. acad. affairs, 1975-76, exec. asst. to pres., 1976-79, v.p. research, 1979-80, v.p. acad. affairs and research, 1980-85, exec. v.p., provost, 1985-94; retired, 1994. Contbr. articles to chemistry jours. Served with U.S. Army, 1946-49, 50-51, Korea. Decorated Order of the Crown, Kingdom of Belgium; grantee NIH, 1961-64, Robert A. Welch Found., 1962-79. Mem. Am. Chem. Soc. Home: 6612 Lost Horizon Dr Austin TX 78759-6116 Business E-Mail: fonken@mail.utexas.edu.

FONS, MARGARET E., elementary school educator; d. James Louis and Nancy Ann Fons. BS in Recreation Adminstrn., U. Wis., LaCrosse, 1982; M of Ednl. Leadership, No. Ariz. U., 1992. Cert. tchr. Ariz. State U., 1986, English as 2d lang. tchr. Ariz. State U., 1992. Tchr. elem. sch. Maricopa Unified Sch. Dist., Ariz., 1986—92; tchr. 4th grade Mesa Unified Sch. Dist., 1992—. V.p., pres. elect, pres. Ariz. Ski Coun., Phoenix, 2003—05; pres. Scottsdale Sea & Ski Club, 1994—99; bd. mem. Far West Ski Assn. Named Woman of Yr., Far West Ski Assn., 1994; recipient, 2004; grantee, Salt River Project, 1996, Mesa Found., 1996. Mem.: ASCD (assoc.). Roman Catholic. Avocations: skiing, travel, golf, dance, gardening. Office: Mesa Unified Sch Dist 591 W Mesquite Chandler AZ 85225 Office Phone: 480-472-3600. Business E-Mail: mefons@mpsaz.org.

FONSECA, DANIEL J., engineering educator; b. San Jose, Feb. 18, 1969; s. Jose D. Fonseca and Lilia Alvarado; m. Lucia Torres-Ugarte, July 29, 1995; children: David, Daniel. BS in Indsl. Engring., U. Ala., 1992, MS in Indsl. Engring., 1994; MS in Engring. Sci., La. State U., 1997, PhD in Engring. Sci., 1998. Prof. engring. Monterrey Inst. Tech., Mexico City, 1994; sales mgr. Kimberly Clark, San Jose, 1994-95; asst. prof. U. Ala., Tuscaloosa, 1998-99; curricular dir. Monterrey Inst. Tech., Tampico, Mex., 1999-2000; asst. prof. U. Ala., Tuscaloosa, 2000—. Internat. cons. NASA, Inverlat, Cidsa, others, 1992—. Contbr. articles to profl. jours. Recipient H. Paul Hassel Jr. award U. Ala., 1993-94. Mem. Inst. Indsl. Engrs., Am. Soc. Engring. Edn., Mallet Assembly Hon. Soc., golden Rey Nat. Honor Soc., Alpha Pi Mu, Tau Beta Pi. Office: Dept Indsl Engring U Ala Tuscaloosa AL 35487 E-mail: dfonseca@roe.eng.ua.edu.

FONSECA, JOSEPH MOJICA, JR., political science professor; b. Seattle, Wash., Sept. 27, 1951; s. Joseph Mojica Fonseca Sr. and Maria Flores (Torres) Fonseca; m. Eva Rivas, Jan. 14, 1989; children: Monica, Frank Daniel, Jason, Nicole Jolene, Joseph Anthony, Jacob Matthew. AA, San Antonio (Tex.) Coll., 1979; BA in Polit. Sci. and Psychology, St. Mary's U., 1998, MA, 2002. Adminstrv. aide Senator Glenn H. Kothmann, San Antonio, 1982-89; tax and mortgage analyst Bexar County Tax Office, San Antonio, 1989-95; fed., state and county process server Daniel Rivans Jr. owner, San Antonio, 1995-97; fin. analyst CitiGroup Investment Svcs., San Antonio, 1998—2003; prof. Northwind Vista Coll., San Antonio, 2003—. Pres., SIMCONG leg St. Mary's U., San Antonio, 1996—97, chair coll. dems., 1995—97, 1st pres. Mem. Bexar County Dems., San Antonio, 1995—; rape crisis vol. Rape Crisis Ctr., Seattle, 1973—74; spousal abuse vol. Spousal Abuse Ctr., Phoenix, 1973—74. Decorated 3 Purple Hearts, Silver Star for valor, Congl. Medal of Honor presented by Pres. Richard M. Nixon. Mem.: K.C. (chancellor 1977—79), Acad. of Polit. Sci., Am. Legion, Rho Ki. Roman Catholic. Avocations: quarter horse racing, reading, football. Home: 2510 Village Pkwy San Antonio TX 78251-2539 Office: Northwest Vista Coll 3535 N Ellison Dr San Antonio TX 78251 Office Phone: 210-875-9301. E-mail: jaqijugi777@yahoo.com.

FONSECA, JULIO, retired secondary school educator; b. Portland, Maine, May 18, 1923; s. Julio Fonseca and Lelia Hale; m. Sara Fonseca, Dec. 12, 1953 (dec. Apr. 24, 1998). BA, NYU, 1951; MEd, U. Houston, 1959. Cert. tchr. Tex., Fla. Civil servant GS 7 Dept. Army, Tokyo, 1949—55, Bar le Duc, France, 1955—56; educator Houston Sch. Dist., 1957—69, Manatee County Sch. Dist., Bradenton, Fla., 1970—84. Chmn. supervisory com. Fed. Govt. Employees Credit Union, Houston, 1958—59. Author: (book) My Best to You, 1994, Bountiful Harvest, 1997, Addenda, 2000, Addenda Plus, 2002, The Blessed Pathway, 2004. Sgt. U.S. Army, 1942—45. Named Outstanding Educators in Am., Tomi Publs., 1977, 1978. Master: VFW (sr. vice comdr. post 7991 1990, chaplain post 7991 1994). Baptist. Avocations: teaching Sunday school, fishing, writing, reading. Home: PO Box 426 Dunnellon FL 34430

FONSECA, PETER, surgeon; b. New Bedford, Mass., Mar. 9, 1956; s. George and Isabel Fonseca; m. Mary M. Fonseca, Dec. 30, 1985; children: Lauren, Peter, Philip, Margaret, Mary, Elizabeth, John, Paul, Thomas, Matthew, Marian. BS, U. Mass., 1978; PhD, Purdue U., 1983; MD, St. Louis U., 1987. Diplomate Am. Bd. Thoracic Surgery, Am. Bd. Surgery. Resident surgeon Wright State U., Dayton, Ohio, 1987-92, Med. Coll. Wis., Milw., 1992-94; surgeon St. Louis, 1998—. Contbr. articles to profl. jours. Comdr., attending physician USN, 1994-98. Fellow ACS, Am. Coll. Chest Physicians, Soc. Thoracic Surgeons; mem. Phi Beta Kappa, Sigma Xi. Roman Catholic. Avocations: sailing, reading, model railroading. Office: 10004 Kennerly Rd Ste 345A Saint Louis MO 63128 Office Phone: 314-543-5252.

FONTAINE, JOHN C., foundation administrator, lawyer, former newspaper company executive; BA, U. Mich., 1953; LLB, Harvard U., 1956. Bar: NY 1957. Pres. Knight-Ridder, Inc., Miami, Fla.; ptnr. Hughes Hubbard & Reed LLP, NYC, 1997—. Bd. mem. Samuel H. Kress Found., 1975—, chmn., 1994—; mem. bd. trustees Nat. Gallery Art, Washington, DC, 1984—2000, 2002—; bd. mem. Jacob's Pillow Dance Festival, Nat. Exec. Svc. Corp. Office: Samuel H Kress Found 174 E 80th St New York NY 10021*

FONTAINE, KATHLEEN STUREY, policy analyst; b. Balt., Mar. 22, 1962; d. Peter Sturey and Geraldine Marie Teodori; m. Mark Roselius Fontaine, Dec. 21, 1997; children: Elissa Anne Pedelty, Andrew Dylan Pedelty, Scott Gerald Pedelty, Michelle Rossi, Matthew. BS in Physics with Astrophysics Option, N.Mex Inst. Mining and Tech., 1984; MA in Sci. Tech. and Pub. Policy, George Washington U., 2002. Master trainer AchieveGlobal, 1999, MBTI (Myers Briggs Type Indicator) qualified Ctr. for Applications of Psychol. Type, 1998. Human resources devel. specialist NASA GSFC (Goddard Space Flight Ctr.) Office Human Resources, Greenbelt, Md., 1998—2002; policy analyst NASA GSFC Global Change Data Ctr., Greenbelt, 2002—. Contbr. articles to profl. jours. Bd. dirs. Anne Arundel County Sch. Bd. Nominating Conv. Com., Annapolis, Md., 2001—; vol., leader Girl Scout Coun. of the Nation's Capitol, Bowie, Md., 1993—97; adult vol. Girl Scout Coun. Ctrl. Md., Annapolis, 1997—. Mem.: AGU, AIAA, Women in Aerospace. Democrat. Avocations: music, travel, cooking, sailing. Office: NASA Goddard Space Flight Center Code 902 Greenbelt MD 20771 Personal E-mail: ksfontaine@juno.com. Business E-Mail: kathy.fontaine@nasa.gov. E-mail: kathleen.s.fontaine@nasa.gov.

FONTAINE, SUE (JEANE FONTAINE), public relations professional; b. Rolfe, Iowa; d. Vernette M. and Dorothy (Messinger) Gaskins m. Henry A. Fontaine, Jr., July 1, 1948 (div. 1970); children: Eva Joel, Jeffrey David. BA in Journalism, U. Iowa, 1947; MLS, U. Mo., 1977. Radio and TV dir. Swigart Advt., Inc., New Orleans, 1948-54, 62-65; producer Sta. WDSU-TV, New Orleans, 1948-54; dir. pub. rels. La. State Libr., Baton Rouge, 1960-62, Tulsa City-County Libr., 1965-67, 70-76; spl. projects asst. U. Mo. Sch. Libr., Info. Sci., Columbia, 1976-77; pub. info. officer Wash. State Libr., Olympia, 1977-81; assoc. mgr. pub. rels. N.Y. Pub. Libr., N.Y.C., 1981-85; pub. rels./mktg. dir. Queens Borough Pub. Libr., Jamaica, N.Y., 1985-91; owner SF PR/Mktg., N.Y. and Fla., 1991—. Mktg., pub. rels. cons. to various libraries and comml. clients, 1960—. Editor: (with Susan Phelps) Communications for the Humanities, 1975; Public Relations: Tick/Click, 1975; Best of Library Literature, 1981; contbr. articles to profl. jours. Bd. mem. Friends St. Pete Beach Pub. Libr., 1999—. Recipient 5 John Cotton Dana Pub. Rels. awards, 1965-75; Coun. on Libr. Resources fellow, 1975-76. Mem. ALA (past sect. chmn., bd. dirs., com. chair 1990—), Pub. Rels. Soc. Am., Women In Comms. (past chpt. pres.), N.Y. Libr. Assn. (chmn. pub. rels. round table, viburnum pub. awareness grant project 1992-95), Iowa-Yucatan Ptnrs., Libr. Pub. Rels. Coun. (mem. exec. bd., past pres.), Alpha Xi Delta. Episcopalian. Home: 2612 Lakeside Ave Milford IA 51351-7231

FONTAINE, VALERIE ANNE, lawyer, consultant; b. Honolulu, May 17, 1955; d. Warren Tremlett Chaffey and Dorine Marks Foster. AB, UCLA, 1976; JD, Hastings Coll., 1979. Atty. O'Melveny & Myers, L.A., 1979—81; cons. Lee, Jackson & Bowe, Beverly Hills, Calif., 1981—83; v.p. Bench Ltd., L.A., 1983—88; ptnr. Seltzer Fontaine Beckwith, L.A., 1988—. Contbr. articles to profl. jours. and newspapers. 1st v.p., past pres., trustee Hastings 1066 Found. Mem. State Bar Calif., L.A. Bar Assn., Women Lawyers Assn. L.A. (bd. dirs., co-chair status of women lawyers com. 1989-92, co-chair legal edn. and spl. programs com., chair publ. com., co-chair mentoring and bus. devel. com., mem. adv. coun.), Hastings Alumni Assn. (bd. dirs. 1988—, pres. L.A. chpt. 1992-93), Phi Beta Kappa. Democrat. Jewish. Avocations: exercise, foreign cooking, reading, gardening. Office: Seltzer Fontaine Beckwith 2999 Overland Ave Ste 120 Los Angeles CA 90064-4243 Office Phone: 310-839-6000. Business E-Mail: vfontaine@sfbsearch.com.

FONTANA, MARIO H., nuclear engineer; b. West Springfield, Mass., Mar. 30, 1933; s. Remo and Sabina F.; m. Sue Janeway, Apr. 12, 1958; children: Richard, Edward. BS, U. Mass., 1955; MS, MIT, 1957; PhD, Purdue U., 1968. Registered engr., Tenn. Mem. rsch. staff Oak Ridge (Tenn.) Nat. Lab., 1957-63, 65-81, asst. dir. nuc. safety rsch., 1968-72, head advanced concepts devel. engring. tech. divsn., 1972-81, asst. to dir. engring. tech. divsn., 1990-92; group leader Advanced Concepts, 1993-94; instr. Purdue U., Oak Ridge, Tenn., 1964-65; dir. industry degraded core program Tech for Energy, Inc., Knoxville, Tenn., 1981-84; v.p. engring. Energex Oak Ridge, 1984-85; dir. nuclear safety tech. IT Corp. and Tenera, L.P., Knoxville, 1985-90; sr. scientist Avco Rsch. and Advanced Devel., Wilmington, Mass., 1963-64. Cons. AEC, Washington, 1972-73, Nuc. Regulatory Commn., Washington, 1979-81, 91—, U.S. Dept. Energy, Washington, 1986-89; rsch. prof. U. Tenn., 1995—; mem. Adv. Com. on Reactor Safeguards, 1995-99. Author more than 100 reports and articles. Fellow Am. Nuclear Soc. (chmn. nuclear reactor safety divsn. 1972-73, 94-95); mem. ASME, Rotary Internat., Sigma Xi, Tau Beta Pi. Achievements include patents for method of arc synthesis of uranium carbide from UF6 and Graphite, others.

FONTANA, ROBERT EDWARD, electrical engineer, educator, retired military officer; b. Bklyn., Nov. 26, 1915; s. Valentino and Secondina (Lesca) F.; m. Victoria E. Mauriello, Dec. 2, 1945; children: Robert Edward, Thomas Paul, Mary Joan. B Elec. Engring, NYU, 1939; MS, U. Ill., 1947, PhD, 1949. Commd. 2d lt. USAAF, 1942; advanced through grades to col. USAF, 1959, ret., 1969; research scientist Sandia Corp., 1949-54; spl. asst. nuclear devel. Hdqrs. USAF, 1954-58; head nuclear applications (Air R&D Command), 1958-61; dir. (Aerospace Rsch. Labs.), Wright-Patterson AFB, Ohio, 1961-66; chmn. dept. elec. engring. Air Force Inst. Tech., Wright-Patterson AFB, 1966-84, prof. emeritus, 1984—. Pres. Honors Seminars Met. Dayton, 1966-86. Decorated Legion of Merit with oak leaf cluster, Exceptional Civilian service award Dept. Air Force, 1985 Fellow IEEE (chmn. Dayton sect. 1971, editor edn. group newsletter 1970-81, meritorious service award 1983); mem. Am. Soc. Engring. Edn. (editor elec. engring. div. newsletter 1970-81, chmn. energy conversion com. 1978-80), Sigma Xi, Tau Beta Pi, Eta Kappa Nu. Home: 6534 Brook Lake Dr Dallas TX 75248-3915

FONTANA, THOMAS MICHAEL, television producer, scriptwriter; b. Buffalo, Sept. 12, 1951; s. Charles Louis and Marie Angelica (Internicola) Fontana. BA in Theater, State U. Coll., Buffalo, 1973; LittD (hon.), SUNY, 1997. Playwright in residence The Writers Theatre, N.Y.C., 1975-93; prodr., writer St. Elsewhere, NBC-TV, 1982-88; writer The Fourth Wiseman, MOW/ABC-TV, 1985; exec. prodr., writer Tattinger's NBC-TV, 1988-89, Nick and Hillary, 1989, Home Fires NBC-TV, 1991, Homicide: Life on the Street NBC-TV, 1993-99, Oz HBO-TV, 1997—2003, The Jury ABC-TV, 2004; exec. prodr., writer Strip Search MOW/HBO, 2004, Homicide: Life Everlasting, MOW, NBC-TV, 2000; writer, exec. prodr. The Beat, UPN, 2000, Judas, MOW/ABC, 2003—. Exec. prodr.: (TV films) The Press Secretary, PBS, 2001, Shot in the Heart, MOW, HBO, 2001, American Tragedy, CBS, 2000; contbr. articles to N.Y.Times, TV Guide, Esquire, TV special, A Tribute to Heroes. Named Amnesty Internat. Filmmaker of Yr., 2005; named to Buffalo Theatre Hall of Fame, 2003; recipient Peabody Award, 1983, 1993, 1996, 1998, Humanitas Prize, 1984, Emmy Award for St Elsewhere, 1985, 1987, Emmy Award for Homicide-Life in the Street, 1993, Christopher Award, Nat Asn Cath Broadcasters, 1986, Autism Award, Nat Asn Autistic Children, 1986, Maggie Award, Planned Parenthood Asn, 1986, Distinguished Alumnus Award, State Univ Col, Buffalo, 1987, Founder's Award, VQT, 1995, Best Drama Series Award, 1996, Best Drama Series and Program of the Yr Award, TV Critics Asn, 1996, 1997, 1998, Nancy Susan Reynolds Award, 1996, Marylander of the Yr Award, Baltimore Sun, 1996, Best Drama Series Oz, Cable Ace Award, 1997, Prix Poula Meillevre Series Oz, 1997, Literacy in Media award for Oz, 1999, Caths in the Media Award, 1999, Lifetime Achievement Award, Casting Soc Am, 2000, Evelyn Burkey Lifetime Achievement Award, WGA, 2000, Fortune Soc. Award for Oz, 2000, award, Media Action Network for Asian-Ams., 2002, Outstanding TV Writer's award, Austin Film Festival, 2003, Excellence award, Can. Film Ctr., 2002, 2003, Raven award, Mystery Writers Am., 2005, Lifetime Achievement award, Caucus of TV Writers, Prodrs. and Dirs., 2005. Mem.: Prodrs. Guild Am., Auths League Am, Writers Guild Am. East (Ann Award 1987, 1993, 1994), Dramatists Guild, West Side Rowing Club (Buffalo). Democrat. Roman Catholic. Office: Fatima Prodns 185 Broome St New York NY 10002 Office Phone: 212-206-3585. E-mail: tomfontana@aol.com.

FONTANA, VINCENT ROBERT, lawyer; b. Bklyn., Mar. 1, 1939; s. Joseph E. and Sadie (Guastella) F.; m. Joanne F. D'Antonio, Aug. 5, 1967; children: Joseph John, Anne Louise. BS in Actg., Holy Cross Coll., 1960; JD, Fordham U., 1964. Bar: N.Y. 1965, U.S. Ct. Appeals (2d cir.) 1967, U.S. Supreme Ct. 1974, U.S. Dist. Ct. (ea. so. and we. dists.) N.Y. 1981, U.S. Ct. Appeals (11th cir.), 1985, U.S. Ct. Appeals (9th cir.) 1987, U.S. Ct. Appeals (3d cir.) 1989. Assoc. Wilkie, Farr & Gallagher, N.Y.C., 1965-66, Mendes & Mount, N.Y.C., 1966-75, ptnr., 1975-77; assoc. Wilson, Elser, Moskowitz, Edelman & Dicker, N.Y.C., 1977-78, ptnr., 1979-2000; of counsel L'Abbate, Balkan, Colavita & Contini LLP, 2001—. Author: Municipal Liability: Law and Practice, 1990-00; contbr. articles to profl. jours. Pres. Bklyn. Assn. Brian Injured Children, 1974-77, N.Y. Assn. for Learning Disabled, 1977-79. Mem. ABA, N.Y. State Bar Assn., Internat. Mcpl. Lawyers Assn. Republican. Roman Catholic. Home: 133 Stewart Ave Garden City NY 11530 Office: Wilson Elser Moskowitz Edelman & Dicker 150 E 42d St New York NY 10017-5612

FONTANAROSA, PHIL BERNARD, emergency physician; b. Youngstown, Ohio, 1954; m. Kristine Fontanarosa, Aug. 1977; children: Jennifer, Joel, Beth, Julie. Youngstown State U., 1975; MD, Med. Coll. Ohio, 1978; postgrad., Kent St. U., 1992-93. Diplomate Am. Bd. Emergency Medicine. Intern Akron (Ohio) City Hosp., 1978-79, resident in emergency medicine, 1979-81; assoc. prof., rsch. dir. emergency medicine Northeastern Ohio Universities Coll. Medicine, 1983-93; adj. prof. medicine Northwestern Med. Sch., Chgo. Dep. editor, dir. editl. affairs Jour. AMA; editor-in-chief text: Physicians' Evaluation and Educational Review in Emergency Medicine, 1996, Alternative Medicine: An Objective Assessment, 2000. Mem. Am. Coll. Emergency Physicians. Office: AMA 515 N State St Chicago IL 60610-4325

FONTÉ, RICHARD W., university administrator; BS in Internat. Affairs, Georgetown U., 1967; M in Am. Dem. Theory, Ind. U., 1969; PhD in C.C. and Higher Edn. Fin., U. Mich., 1988. Asst. for workforce edn. to Gov. Edgar, Ill.; asst. to Gov. Edgar, workforce cons., 1970-77; v.p., interim pres. Triton Coll., Ill.; pres. South Suburban Coll., Ill., 1988, Austin (Tex.) C.C., 1997—2003; nat. dir. We the People, NEH, Washington, 2004—. Co-author: (books) Shaping the Community College Image, Strategic Marketing for Presidents; contbr. articles to profl. jours. Bd. dirs. numerous comty. orgns. including Ill. Philharm. Orch., Austin 2010, Tex. Edn. Agy. Task Force on Adult Edn. Accountability, State Theatre Bd., Capital Area Workforce Devel. Bd., Austin, Capital Area Tng. Found. Mem. Greater Austin C. of C. (bd. dirs.). Address: 5930 Middle Fiskville Rd Austin TX 78752-4341

FONTENOT, ANDREA DEAN, communications executive; b. Drumright, Okla., Mar. 14, 1944; d. Howard G. and Ruby Jewell (Harvison) Harris; m. Lloyd John Culver, Aug. 12, 1962 (widowed Feb. 1966); m. Ronald Ray Fontenot. BS in Speech and Broadcasting, McNeese State U., Lake Charles, 1978, MFA in Creative Writing, 1985; ABD in English, Tex. Tech. U., Lubbock, 1997, PhD in English, 1998. Cert. Distance Educator. Jr. acct. exec. Harris & Weinstein Ad Agy., Atlanta, 1973-75; grad. teaching asst. McNeese State U., Lake Charles, La., 1981-85, adjunct prof., 1985-89, Davis Monthan Air Force Base, Pima CC Tucson, 1989-90; grad. teaching asst. Tex. Tech. U., Lubbock, Tex., 1990-96; rsch. asst. Distance Edn. College Engring., Lubbock, Tex., 1996, sr. dir. engring. outreach and literacy, 2003—; mgr. dir. CLEAR project Southwestern Bell Comms. Found., Lubbock, Tex., 1997—. Adv. bd. Teaching Learning and Tech. Ctr., Lubbock, Tex., 1996-98; teaching on internet ind. cons. Lubbock, Tex., 1993—; rsch. asst. Internet Cons. SCATE, Lubbock, Tex., 1996-97; sr. dir. engring. outreach and lit., 2003. Author: (short story) Minotaur, 1985, Hayden's Ferry Review, 1986; contbr. articles to profl. jours. Mem. Rural Assistance Initiative Task Force, 1998—; mem. Collaborative Cmty. Network Task Force, 1998—, Ctr. for Partnerships in Sci. and Tech.; mem. Svc. Learning Adv. Coun.; mem. High Plains Rural Broadband Network. Recipient Paul Whitfield Horn scholarship, 1995, Outstanding Grad. Tchr., 1993, 95, McNeese Award in Fiction, 1984, 85, Outstanding Classroom Practices award Conf. Coll. Composition and Comm., 1998. Mem.: Am. Soc. Engring. Educators, Grad. English Soc., Soc. for Tech. Comm., South Ctrl. MLA, Nat. Coun. Tchrs. English, Alliance Minority Engrs., Tex. Learning Orgn., Assoc. Writing Program. Home: 5020 Kenosha Ave Apt A Lubbock TX 79413-3948 Office: Ctr for Engring Outreach COE Tex Tech Univ Lubbock TX 79409 Office Phone: 806-742-3451. Business E-Mail: dean.fontenot@ttu.edu.

FONTENOT, CHESTER J., humanities educator, minister; b. L.A., Calif., Feb. 5, 1950; s. Chester and Albertha Lee Fontenot; m. Olufunke Abimbola Bowen, July 2, 2002; children: Camara Olasani Bello, Jasmine Christina, Chester J. III. BA, Whittier Coll., Calif., 1975; PhD, U. Calif., Irvine, 1975. Ordained minister Am. Bapt. Conv., 1985. Asst. prof. of English U. of Nebr., Lincoln, 1975—77; asst. prof. of Africana studies Cornell U., Ithaca, NY,

1977—79; assoc. prof. of English U. of Ill. at Urbana-Champaign, Urbana, 1979—99; Benjamin Griffith prof. of English and dir., African Am. studies program Mercer U., Macon, Ga., 1999—. Disting. prof. of African and African Am. culture U. of Yaounde I, Yaounde, Cameroon, 2002; disting. vis. scholar of African Am. film Ind. U.-East, Richmond, Va., 1989—89; disting. vis. scholar of black theater Purdue U., West Lafayette, Ind., 1979—80; disting. vis. scholar of African Am. lit. Colgate U., Hamilton, NY, 1978; disting. vis. scholar of black theater SUNY at Binghampton, 1977; founding gen. editor book series Voices of the African Diaspora. Author: (literary criticism (book) Writing About Black Literature, (cultural criticism and theory) Frantz Fanon: Language Gone Astray in the Flesh; editor: (literary criticism and theory) Studies in Black American Literature: Black American Prose Theory, Studies in Black American Literature: Belief vs. Theory in Black American Literary Criticism; author: (cultural criticism) Black Identity: Reach Out Vol. X; editor: (cultural criticism and theory) W.E.B. Du Bois and Race: Essays on the Centennial Anniversary of the Publication of The Souls of Black Folk. Bd. dirs. ARC, Connersville, Ind., 1984—89; chair Cmty. Task Force on Gangs, Danville, Ill., 1992—94, Mayor's Cmty. Diversity Com., Macon; mem. Cmty. Devel. Corp., Danville, Ill., 1992—95. Named to, Outstanding Young Men of Am., 1977—85; recipient Universal award of Accomplishment, Am. Biog. Inst., 2001—; fellow Yale U. Summer Faculty fellow, Yale U., 1981, Maude Hammond Fling Disting. Faculty Rsch. fellow, U. Nebr.-Lincoln, 1977, Postdoctoral fellow, Sch. of Criticism and Theory, U. of Calif. Irvine, 1976; grantee Humanities Faculty Rsch. grantee, Cornell U., 1978, Am. Coun. of Learned Societies grantee, 1977. Mem.: MLA (founding chair divsn.black Am. lit. and culture), Coll. Lang. Assn. (life), Langston Hughes Soc. (life). D-Liberal. Christian. Avocations: travel, sports, music, reading. Office: Mercer University 1400 Coleman Ave Macon GA 31207 Office Phone: 478-301-2345. Home Fax: 478-301-2726; Office Fax: 478-301-2726. Personal E-mail: fontenotcj@cox.net. E-mail: fontenot_cj@mercer.edu.

FONTES, PATRICIA J., psychologist; b. Providence, Dec. 10, 1936; d. Manuel William and Sadie Elizabeth (Sousa Conceicao) F. BS in Edn., Boston U., 1957; MEd, Boston Coll., 1965, PhD, 1968. Tchr. Warwick (R.I.) pub. schs., 1957-59; religious sister/superior Sisters of Our Lady of Providence, 1959-65; asst. prof. U. R.I., Kingston, 1968-69; asst./assoc. prof. Salve Regina Coll., Newport, R.I., 1969-72; cons. psychologist Girl Scouts of R.I., Inc., Providence, 1972-73; research fellow Ednl. Research Ctr., St. Patrick's Coll., Dublin, 1973-88; cons. psychologist Girl Scouts R.I., Providence, 1989-92; prof. CEFOPE/IEC U. Minho, Braga, Portugal, 1992—2003; ret. Lectr. in field. Author: Equality in Primary Teaching 1985, As Crianças como Agentes de Mudança Ambiental, 1998, Os Alunos com Necessidades Educativas Especiais, 1998; contbr. articles to profl. jours. Boston U. scholar, 1953-57; Boston Coll. fellow, 1965-68; Inst. for Portuguese Lang. and Culture grantee, 1982. Mem. APA, Internat. Coun. Psychologists (sec.-gen. 1991-94). Roman Catholic. Avocations: biking, mountain walking, travel, gardening, reading, cooking. Personal E-mail: patfontes@netscape.com.

FONTES, PAULO A., surgeon, educator; b. Sao Paulo, Brazil, Jan. 20, 1962; came to U.S., 1991; s. Paulo B. and Mildred (Chaves) F.; m. Monica M. Mollerstrand, Sept. 9, 1991; children: Rafaella M., Karl Liam M. MD, Sao Paulo State U., 1985. Bd. cert. gen. surgery Brazilian Coll. Surgeons. Intern Sao Paulo State U. Sch. Medicine, Botucatu, Brazil, 1984-85; resident Prof. Edmundo Vasconcelos Hosp., Sao Paulo, 1986-88, mem. med. staff, 1990-91, supr. gen. surgery residents, 1990-91; rsch. fellow Sao Paulo Fed. U., 1990-91, U. Pitts. Med. Ctr., 1991-93, vis. asst. prof. surgery, 1993-96, clin. fellow, 1996-98, attending surgeon, asst. prof., 1998—, med. dir. Organ Referral Ctr., 2004—. Dir. S. & Am. divsn. U. Pitts. Med. Ctr. Overseas Inc., 1998—, co-dir. liver transplant program. Contbr. articles to profl. jours. Recipient Bradesco Found. prize, 1988, 89; scholar Sao Paulo State Govt., 1980-85. Fellow: ACS. Avocations: sailing, biking, working out, surfing. Home: 1244 Beechwood Blvd Pittsburgh PA 15206-4548 Office: U Pitts Med Ctr 725N MUH 3459 5th ave Pittsburgh PA 15213-3403 Office Phone: 412-692-4184. Office Fax: 412-692-4180.

FOOLADI, MIKE M., physician, educator; b. Zolghadar, Iran, Feb. 22, 1937; arrived in U.S., 1960; m. Marjan Fooladi, Aug. 28, 1974; children: Michael, Mark. BS, Baylor U., 1965; MS, Tex. So. U., 1968; PhD, U. So. Miss., 1979; MD, Juarez Med. Sch., 1982; MPH, U. So. Miss., 1997. Lic. Iran, Mex. Prof. chemistry Miss. C.C., Gulfport; prof. biotechnology U. Tehran, Iran; cons. to min. Ministry Agr., Tehran; cons. Shaheed Modaress, Tehran; pres. Fuladi Rsch. Ins., El Paso, Tex., 1985—2001; v.p. Alpina Lab, Bay Minette, Ala.; corp. rsch. dir. Vicksburg (Miss.) & Vertac. Pres. Coosa Chem. Co., Childensburg, Ala., 1978—80. Author: (book) Tal Viva 2021, 1998; contbr. articles to profl. jours. Mem.: AMA, Am. Chem. Soc. Achievements include patents in field. Avocations: walking, horseback riding, reading, writing. Home: 2100 Sunset Dr Hattiesburg MS 39402 Office: Miss Gulf Coast Cmty 2226 Switzer Rd Gulfport MS 39507

FOOTE, AVON EDWARD, web developer/producer, communications educator; b. Sept. 24, 1937; s. Avon Ruble and Lila Frances (Broughton) F.; m. Dorothy Veronica Gargis, Mar. 15, 1960; children: Anthony E., Kevin A., Michele. *Richard Foote, kinsman of half-brother Samuel and Samuel's son Topham of Windsor in Berkshire, settled in the 1680's in Virginia. The migration was documented in Chotankers: A Family History (Thornwood Publishers, 1982) and at Chotank.com. Family moves included: Cornwall; London; Chotank; Caswell County, North Carolina; Chester County, South Carolina; Lancaster County, South Carolina; Giles County, Tennessee; Tishomingo County, Mississippi, where Avon Ruble Foote and Lila Frances Broughton Foote resided on January 1, 2004. Chotankers reminds descendants, "To all those who came before; they make this book possible. To all those who follow; the possibility is all there."* Cert., NYU, 1961; BS, Florence State U., 1963; MS, U. So. Miss., 1968; PhD, Ohio State U., 1970. Announcer Sta. WJOI, Florence, Ala., 1958-60; prodn. mgr. Sta. WOWL-TV, Florence, 1960-64; advt. coord. Plough Inc., Memphis, 1964-66; faculty adviser Sta. WMSU, U. So. Miss., Hattiesburg, 1966-67; prodr.-dir. telecomm. Ohio State U., Columbus, 1967-69; assoc. prof. broadcasting U. Miss., Oxford, 1971-72; project dir. (part-time) Ohio Valley TV Sys., Columbus, 1972-74, Ohio State, 1972—74; faculty, coord. grad. studies Sch. Journalism/Mass Comm. U. Ga., Athens, 1974-80; prof. broadcasting U. North Ala., Florence, 1980—. Prof., London, 1990-91; awards judge Ohio State Awards, 1968-73; chmn. faculty screening com. Peabody Radio-TV Awards, 1976-79; jury chair NY Festivals Internat. TV awards, 2002-04; founder Worldwide Web pages including Worldserver, 1995, Web cons. chotank.com, flytheshoals.com, fasthealth.com; developer Gulf War Video Collection, 1992-2001, Libr. Am. Broadcasting, U. Md., College Park, 2002—; faculty Ohio State U., 1972-74; cons. in field. Editor: The Challenges of Educational Communications, 1970, CBS and Congress: The Selling of the Pentagon Papers, 1972, Nat. Assn. Ednl. Broadcasters Broadcasting Rev., 1969-73; author: (with Koenig and others) Broadcasting and Bargaining, 1970, Chotankers, 1982, online author: Burke's Peerage and Gentry, 2003; prodr. ednl. TV programs; editor ref. shelf materials Nat. Pub. Broadcasting Archives, U. Md., College Park, 2002; contbr. and author: www.burkespeerage.net; contbr. articles to profl. jours. Bd. dirs. Florence YMCA, 1982-86. Recipient Cmty. Svc. award Florence Civitan Club, 1990, 1st pl. award Corp. Video Profl. Competition Nat. Broadcasting Soc., 1991, regional 1st pl. award, Nat. 3d pl. award Coll. Emmy award Hollywood Acad. TV Arts and Scsi., 1984, Honorable Mention Comedy awards Nat. Broadcasting Soc., 1987; Industry Faculty Seminar fellow Internat. Radio-TV Soc., 1987, NDEA fellow, 1967, NATAS Meml. fellow, 1970. Mem.: BBC Networking Club, Radio TV News Dirs. Assn. Republican. Anglican. Home: 222 Shirley Dr Florence AL 35633-1434 Office: Comm Bldg PO Box 5158 Florence AL 35632-0001 Office Phone: 256-765-4489. Personal E-mail: chotank@aol.com.

FOOTE, EDWARD THADDEUS, II, academic administrator, lawyer; b. Milw., Dec. 15, 1937; s. William Hamilton and Julia Stevenson (Hardin) F.; m. Roberta Waugh Fulbright, Apr. 18, 1964; children: Julia, William, Thaddeus. BA, Yale U., 1959; LLB, Georgetown U., 1966; LLD (hon.), Washington U., St. Louis, 1981, Barry U., 1991; hon. degree, Tokai U., Tokyo, 1984; LLD (hon.), Barry U., 1991. Bar: Mo. 1966. Reporter Washington Star, 1963-64, Washington Daily News, 1964-65; exec. asst. to chmn. Pa. Ave. Commn., Washington, 1965-66; assoc. Bryan, Cave, McPheeters & McRoberts, St. Louis, 1966-70; vice chancellor, gen. counsel, sec. to bd. trustees Washington U., St. Louis, 1970-73, dean Sch. Law, 1973-80, spl. adv. to chancellor and bd. trustees, 1980-81; pres. U. Miami, Coral Gables, Fla., 1981—. Mem. exec. com., bd. dirs. Am. Coun. Edn., 1986-88; chmn. citizens com. for sch. desegregation, St. Louis, 1980; chmn. desegregation monitoring and adv. com., St. Louis, 1980-81. Author: An Educational Plan for Voluntary Cooperation Desegregation of School in the St. Louis Met. area, 1981 Mem. Coun. on Fgn. Rels.; founding pres. bd. New City Sch., St. Louis, 1967-73; mem. gov.'s task force on reorganization State of Mo., 1973-74, steering com., chmn. governance com. Mo. Gov.'s Conf. on Edn., UN Assn. Greater St. Louis chpt., 1977-79, adv. com. Naval War Coll., 1979-82, Fla. Coun. of 100, Southern Fla. Metro-Miami Action Plan, exec. com. Miami Citizens Against Crime; founding chmn. Miami Coalition for a Drug Free Community, 1988—. Recipient Order of Sun (Peru). Democrat. Office: U Miami PO Box 248006 Miami FL 33124-8006

FOOTE, EVELYN PATRICIA, retired military officer; b. Durham, N.C., May 19, 1930; d. Henry Alexander and Evelyn Sevena (Womack) Foote. BA summa cum laude, Wake Forest U., 1953, LLD (hon.), 1989; student, U.S. Army Command & Gen. Staff Coll., Leavenworth, Kans., 1971-72, U.S. Army War Coll., Carlisle, Pa., 1976-77; MS in Govt. and Pub. Affairs, Shippensburg State U., 1977; student, U. Va. Sch. Bus. Adminstrn., 1980. Commd. 1st lt. U.S. Army, 1960, advanced through grades to brig. gen., 1986, platoon officer WAC Ft. McClellan, Ala., 1960-61, selection officer 6th recruiting dist. Portland, Oreg., 1961-64; comdr. WAC Co. U.S. Army Engr. Brigade, Ft. Belvoir, Va., 1964-66; student Adj. Gen. Officer Advanced Course, Ft. Benjamin Harrison, Ind., 1966; exec. officer, chief adminstrv. div. pub. affairs office U.S. Army, Vietnam, 1967; exec. officer, office personnel ops. WAC, Washington, 1968-71, plans and programs officer OFC, dir., 1972-74; personnel mgmt. officer U.S. Army Forces Command, Ft. McPherson, Ga., 1974-76; comdr. 2d basic tng. bn. U.S. Army Tng. Brigade and Military Police Sch., Ft. McClellan, Ala., 1977-79; faculty mem. U.S. Army War Coll., 1979-82; student Fgn. Service Inst., Dept. of State, Washington, 1982-83; comdr. 42d Mil. Police Group, Mannheim, Fed. Republic of Germany, 1983-85; spl. asst. to comdg. gen. 32d Army Air Def. Command Hdqrs., Darmstadt, Fed. Republic of Germany, 1985-86; dep., insp. gen. for inspections Hdqrs. Dept. of the Army, Washington, 1986-88; dep. comdg. gen. Mil. Dist. Washington, comdr. Ft. Belvoir, Va., 1988-89; ret. U.S. Army, 1989, recalled to active duty Sr. Rev. Panel, 1996-97, ret., 1997. Lectr. various U.S. Army and civilian groups. Contbr. articles to mil. jours. and books. Mem. Am Battle Monuments Commn., 1994—2001; bd. visitors Wake Forest U., 1991—2003, chmn. bd. visitors, 2001—03; trustee Fund for Peace, 2002—; bd. dirs. U.S. Army Women's Mus. Found., 1995—. Decorated DSM, Legion of Merit with oak leaf clusters, German Cross of Svc. 1st class; named Spokesperson of the Yr., Dept. Army, 1997—98; named to Disting. Fellows Hall of Fame, U.S. Army War Coll., 1996, Regimental Hall of Fame, U.S. Army MP Corps, 1998; recipient Disting. Pub. Svc. award, Wake Forest U., 1987, DSM, Am. Battle Monuments Commn., 2001. Democrat. Lutheran. Avocations: music, reading, hiking.

FOOTE, HORTON, playwright, scriptwriter; b. Wharton, Tex., Mar. 14, 1916; s. Albert Horton and Hallie (Brooks) Foote; m. Lillian Vallish, June 4, 1945; children: Barbara Hallie, Albert Horton, Walter Vallish, Daisy Brooks. Student, Pasadena Playhouse Sch. Theatre, Calif., 1933-35, Tamara Daykarhanova Sch. Theatre, N.Y.C., 1937-39. Actor, N.Y.C., 1939-42; mgr. prodn. co. Productions Inc., Washington, 1942-45; vis. disting. dramatist Baylor U., 2002—. Tchr. playwriting. Author: (plays) The Chase, 1956, (screenplays) Storm Fear, 1956, To Kill a Mockingbird, 1962 (Academy award best screenplay, 1962, Writers Guild Am. award, 1962), Baby, The Rain Must Fall, 1965, Hurry Sundown, 1966, Tomorrow, 1971, Tender Mercies, 1983 (Academy award best screenplay, 1983), 1918, 1984, On Valentine's Day, 1985, The Trip to Bountiful, 1985 (Academy Award nomination best screenplay, 1985), Spring Moon, 1987, Convicts, 1991, Of Mice and Men, 1992, (plays) Texas Town, Out of My House, 1942, Only The Heart, 1944, Celebration, 1948, The Chase, 1952, The Trip to Bountiful, The Midnight Caller, 1953, A Young Lady of Property, 1954, The Traveling Lady, The Roads to Home, 1955, Harrison, Texas: Eight Television Plays, 1959, Tomorrow, 1960, Three Plays, Roots in a Parched Ground, 1962, Getting Frankie Married...and Afterward, 2002—, (musical adaption) Gone with the Wind, 1971, The Road to the Graveyard, 1985, Blind Date, 1986, Selected One Act Plays of Horton Foote, Habitation of Dragons, 1988, Dividing the Estate, 1989, Talking Pictures, 1990, Horton Foote: Four New Plays, 1994, The Young Man From Atlanta, 1994 (Pulitzer Prize for drama, 1995), Night Seasons, Laura Dennis, Talking Pictures, 1994, The Carpetbagger's Children, also (play series) The Orphans' Home Cycle, 2001, The Last of the Thorntons, 2002, (TV films) Only The Heart, 1947, Ludie Brooks, 1951, The Travelers, 1952, The Old Beginning, The Trip to Bountiful, Midnight Caller, John Turner Davis, Young Lady of Property, The Oil Well, Rocking Chair, Expectant Relations, Death of the Old Man, Tears of My Sister, 1953, The Shadow of Wilie Greer, The Dancers, 1954, The Roads to Home, 1955, Flight, 1956, Drugstore: Sunday Noon, 1956, Member of the Family, Traveling Lady, 1957, Old Man, 1959, Tomorrow, 1960, 1971, The Shape of the River, 1960, The Night of the Storm, 1961, Gambling Heart, 1964, The Displaced Person, 1977, Barn Burning, 1980, Keeping On, 1983, The Habitation of Dragons, 1992, Mr. and Mrs. Loving, 1996; dir.: When They Speak of Rita, 2000. Recipient Evelyn Burkey award Writer's Guild, 1989, Nat. medal of Arts, 2000.

FOOTE, JOHN HOLLAND, lawyer; b. Birmingham, Ala., Aug. 4, 1946; s. John Elbert and Wanda Delashaw (Holland) F.; m. Rosamond P. Tompkins, July 26, 1980; children: Nathaniel Lucas, Samuel Tompkins. ABin Govt., La. State U., 1968; JD, U. Va., 1974. Bar: Va. 1974, DC 1976, U.S. Dist. Ct. (ea. dist.) Va. 1977, U.S. Ct. Appeals (2d. cir. 1977, U.S. Supreme Ct. 1979, U.S. Ct. Appeals (4th cir.) 1982, U.S. Dist. Ct. (w. dist.) Va., 1994, U.S. Ct. Appeals (11th cir.) 1996. Policy analyst Office of Policy and Planning U.S. Dept. Justice, Washington, 1974-77; assoc. gen. counsel Pres. Ford's Viet Nam Era Clemency Program, Washington, 1975-76; trial atty. criminal divsn. U.S. Dept. Justice, 1974—77; from dep. county atty. to county atty. Prince William County, Manassas, Va., 1977-89; owner Hazel & Thomas, P.C., Manassas, 1989-99, also bd. dirs.; prin. Walsh, Colucci, Lubeley, Emrich & Terpak, P.C., 1999—. Chmn. Prince William-Manassas Regional Jail Bd., 1978-82; bd. dirs. Hist. Manassas, Inc., 1992-96, Project Mend-a-House, 1995-97. Lt. U.S. Army, 1968-71, Vietnam. Mem. Va. State Bar (5th dist. com. disciplinary sys. 1992-95, faculty professionalism 1992-95), Prince William County Bar Assn. (pres. 1987-88), Local Govt. Attys. of Va. (pres. 1987-88). Democrat. Methodist. Avocations: reading, bicycling, guitar. Home: 10542 Knollwood Dr Manassas VA 20111-2834 Office: Walsh Colucci Lubeley Emrich Terpak P C 4310 Prince William Pkwy Prince William VA 22192 Office Phone: 703-680-4664. E-mail: jfoote@pw.thelandlawyers.com.

FOOTE, JOHN JEFFREY, communications executive, consultant, manufacturing engineer; b. San Gabriel, Calif., May 5, 1962; s. Arleth John and Judith Ann Foote; m. Martha Liliana Monroy, May 8, 1999; m. Rebecca Joann Waymack, July 4, 1985 (div. July 2, 1996); m. Janice Lynn Mendoza, July 26, 1980 (div. Apr. 16, 1984); 1 child, Johnathan Allon. AS in Mfg. Engring., Rancho Santiago Coll., Santa Ana, Calif., 1993. Master of Communication Technology, Nat. Radio Examiners, Inc/Dallas, TX, 2004. Pvt. cons., Westminster, Calif., 2002; pres. and CEO RF Spectrum Sys., Las Vegas, 2004—. Contbr. articles to jours. and periodicals. Comm. officer Orange County Search and Rescue, Silverado, Calif., 1997—2002, USAF Aux. CAP, Costa Mesa, 2002, USCG liaison, 2002, comdr. Saddleback Composite squadron 68. Decorated Meritorious Svc. USAF Aux., Leadership award with Silver star, Garber award with Bronze Star; named Sr. Mem. of Yr. Group 7 Calif. Wing, 2004; recipient Comdr.'s commendation, 2002, 2003, 2004, Squadron 68 Sr. Mem. of Yr., 2003, Loening award, 2004. Master: Nat. Radio Examiners, Inc. (licentiate Master Comm. Tech. 2004). R-Consevative. Pentacostal. Achievements include invention of portable antenna. Avocations: weather spotter, amatuer radio, search and rescue, pilot. Home: 5832 Camphor Ave Westminster CA 92683 Office: RF Spectrum Systems Inc 5832 Camphor Ave Westminster CA 92683 Office Phone: 714-401-1548.

FOOTE, KAY REBBER, artist; b. Long Beach, Calif., Mar. 3, 1923; d. Leland Lester Rebber and Mary Alice Thomas; m. John Taintor Foote, Dec. 24, 1943; children: Carol Ann, John Taintor Jr., Ellen Jackson. BFA, U. So. Calif., Los Angeles, 1943; postgrad., Art Ctr. Coll., Los Angeles, 1943-45, Chouinard Art Inst., 1943-45. Co-owner Gallery Xyst, Laguna Beach, Calif., 1975-84. Juror Calif. State Fair, 1979, Laguna Hills Art Assn., 1980. Works exhibited Laguna Beach Art Mus., 1976-79, City of Newport Beach (Calif.) Ann. Juried Show, 1976-77, Dafca Show, Disney Studios, L.A., 1977, Laguna Beach Festival Art, 1976-98, Brea (Calif.) Mcpl. Art Gallery, 1987, Designs Recycled Gallery, Brea, 1984, San Bernardino County (Calif.) Mus. Art, 1983, Laguna Beach Art Mus. Invitational, 1983, Realism Exhbn. John Wayne Airport, 1991. Donated works to Laguna Beach Boys' Club, Our Lady of Angels, Junior League, Children's Home Soc. Recipient Past Pres. award Nat. Watercolor Soc., Los Angeles, 1987, Spl. award Laguna Beach Art Mus., 1983; named Best of Show Laguna Niguel Echoes & Visions, 1997. Signature mem. Nat. Watercolor Soc. (Past Pres. award 1987). Home: 74 Emerald Bay Laguna Beach CA 92651-1266 Office Phone: 949-497-1829. E-mail: footeloose@cox.net.

FOOTE, NATHAN MAXTED, retired physical science educator; b. Woodlawn, Pa., Oct. 8, 1913; s. Myron Tinkham and Ada May (Maxted) F.; m. Laura Belle Gruey, Sept. 5, 1936 (dec. June 2001); children: Jonathan W., L. Nadine, Frances C., Willard G. AB, DePauw U., 1935; MS, Purdue U., 1939. Jr. chemist U.S. FDA, Phila., 1939-40; Rsch. engr. RCA, Camden, N.J., 1940-49; rsch. scientist Colgate Palmolive, Jersey City, N.J., 1950-52; rheologist B.F. Goodrich Chem. Co., Avon Lake, Ohio, 1953-58; acting head, Dept. Physics Baldwin Wallace Coll., Berea, Ohio, 1958-60; vis. asst. prof. Physics Pa. State U., University Park, 1960-61, asst. prof. Physics, Behrend Coll. Erie, 1964-78, ret., 1979; assoc. prof. Phys. Sci. SUNY, Geneseo, 1961-64. Author: Industrial and Engineering Chemistry, 1944, Industrial and Engineering Chemistry, 1947. Del. Ohio Coun. Am. Bapt. Men, 1955-58. Mem.: AAAS, Am. Chem. Soc. (50 Yr. award 1993), Sigma Xi. Avocation: stratospheric chemical change. Home: Elyria United Methodist Village 807 W Ave Apt 5309 Elyria OH 44035-9204

FOOTE, PAUL SHELDON, business educator, administrator, consultant; b. Lansing, Mich., May 22, 1946; s. Harlon Sheldon and Frances Norene (Rotter) Foote; m. Badri Seddigheh Hosseinian, Oct. 25, 1968; children: David, Sheila. *Wife, Badri Seddigheh Hosseinian, BA, University of Shiraz, Iran, international banking training, Barclays Bank, London, England, 1967-68, manager, Bank Melli Iran, attended Harvard University Graduate School of Design, 1971-72. Son, David Reza Foote, attended University of California at Berkeley, CEO, FBM Software, Inc., privacy, security, and productivity software (ZeroSpyWare, ZeroAds, ZeroNetHistory, ZeroSpam). Daughter, Sheila Parisa Rossi, BS 1998, University of California, Berkeley, is wife of Stephen Edward Rossi, BA 1997, University of California, Berkeley, MBA 2003, Georgetown University, Vice President, Corporate Finance, Platinum Equity, and the mother of Iyla Parisa Rossi and Leily Sahar Rossi.* BBA, U. Mich., 1967; MBA, Harvard U., 1971, postgrad, 1971—72, New Eng. Sch. Law, 1971—72; PhD, Mich. State U., 1983. Advanced profl. cert. NYU, 1975. Br. mgr., divisional mgr. Citibank, NYC, 1972—74, Bombay, 1972—74, Beiru, Lebanon, 1972—74; mgr. planning and devel. Singer Co. Africa/Middle East, 1974—75; lectr. acctg. Mich. State U., Lansing, 1977; instr. U. Mich., Flint, 1978—79; asst. prof. U. Windsor, Canada, 1979—81, Oakland U., Rochester, Mich., 1982—83, NYU, 1983—87; assoc. prof. Saginaw Valley State U., University Center, Mich., 1981—82, Pepperdine U., Malibu, Calif., 1987—89; prof. dept. acctg. Coll. Bus. and Econs., Calif. State U., Fullerton, 1989—; prof. Sultan Qaboos U., Muscat, Oman, 1994—96. Lectr. Chapman U., 1998, vis. prof., 98, U. Wash., Seattle, 1999—2000; lectr. George L. Argyros Sch. Bus. and Econs., 2004—, U. Calif., Irvine, 2004; assoc. dean George L. Argyros Sch. Bus. and Econs., 2004—05; cons., spkr. in field. *International consultant on fraud auditing and forensic accounting, accounting information systems, forecasting, strategic planning. Conference, seminar, and workshop leader. Public speaker on business, Middle East, and political topics. Litigation support and expert witness experience. Radio talk-show host and guest.* Mem. editl. bd. Jour. Bus. Forecasting, 1983—; author: Corporate Profitability: Determinants and Forecasts; contbr. articles to jour. Lt. AUS, 1968—69, Vietnam. Loomis-Sayles fellow, Harvard U., Doctoral Consortium fellow, Haskins and Sells, 1977. Mem.: Inst. Bus. Forecasting, Am. Acctg. Assn. Achievements include research in biometrics, information security, and automatic identification using SAP R/3 and bioLock (realtime North America). Office: Calf State U Dept Acctg PO Box 6848 800 N State Coll Fullerton CA 92834-6848 Office Phone: 714-278-2682. Personal E-mail: pfoote@fullerton.edu. Business E-Mail: pfoote@mba1971.hbs.edu.

FOOTE, ROBERT HUTCHINSON, animal physiology educator; b. Gilead, Conn., Aug. 20, 1922; s. Robert E. and Annie (Hutchinson) F.; m. Ruth E. Parcells, Jan. 12, 1946 (dec. Jan. 1992); children: Robert W., Dale H.; m. Barbara J. Johnson, Sept. 25, 1993. BS, U. Conn., 1943; MS, Cornell U., 1947, PhD Animal Physiology/Biochem. Genetics, 1950. Grad. asst. Cornell U., Ithaca, N.Y., 1946-50, asst. prof. animal physiology, 1950-56, assoc. prof., 1956-63, prof., 1963-93, Jacob Gould Schurman chair, 1980-93; emeritus, 1993—. Mem. study sect. NIH, 1974-78; cons. Shell Oil, 1985-89, EPA, 1988-96; program mgr. USDA competitive grants, 1986-87. Author: Animal Reproduction, 1954, AI to Cloning, 1998; mem. editl. bds. 5 jours., 1958-96, Cloning, 1999-2002, Reproductive Physiology, 1992-99, Cryobiology, 1991-94; contbr. some 500 articles to profl. jours., chpts. to books. Chmn. trustees Congregation Ch., Ithaca, 1955-60. Served to capt. inf. U.S. Army 1943-46, ETO. Recipient Sci. medal N.Y. Farmers, 1969, Nat. Physiology and Endocrinology award Am. Soc. Animal Sci., 1970, Casida Physiology Reprodn. award, 1991, JSPS award, 1996, SUNY Chancellor award, 1980, Superior Svc. award USDA, 1988, Alumni Merit award U. Conn., 1996, CALS Alumni Outstanding Faculty award, 2003; named hon. prof. Beijing Agrl. U., 1995. Fellow: AAAS; mem.: Internat. Embryo Transfer Soc. (Pioneer Biotech. award 2002), Am. Soc. Theriogenology (editl. bd. 1976—89, Robert H. Foote Symposium in his honor 1992), Am. Soc. Andrology (editl. bd. 1982—88, Outstanding Andrologist 1984, Upjohn physiology award 1985), Nat. Assn. Animal Breeders (Physiology award 1970), Soc. Study Reprodn. (bd. dirs. 1976—78, pres. 1985, Hartman Lifetime Rsch. award 2000), Am. Dairy Sci. Assn., Gamma Sigma Delta, Phi Kappa Phi, Sigma Xi. Republican. Home: 474 Savage Farm Dr Ithaca NY 14850-6508 Office: Cornell U Dept Animal Sci 204 Morrison Hall Ithaca NY 14853-4801 Office Phone: 607-255-2866. Business E-Mail: rhf4@cornell.edu.

FOOTE, WARREN EDGAR, neuroscientist, psychologist, educator; b. Boston, Nov. 5, 1935; s. Warren Edgar and Edith Irene Foote; m. Cynthia Sue Hall, July 21, 1973; children: Pamela Fowler, Sarah Canby, Julia Landry, Christopher Warren. BA, Hamilton Coll., 1958; MA, Boston U., 1960; PhD, Tufts U., 1965. Rsch. assoc. Harvard U. Med. Sch., 1966—67, vis. asst. prof. psychology, 1970—73, asst. prof., 1974—83, assoc. prof., 1983—. USPHS postdoctoral fellow Yale U., 1967—69; rsch. scientist Norwich State Hosp., Conn., 1969—70; sr. Fulbright scholar Max-Planck Inst., Munich, 1973—74; assoc. pscyologist Mass. Gen. Hosp., Boston, 1974—, psychologist, 1984—95, sr. psychologist, 1995—; cons. Gen. Foods Corp., 1970—74, Neurotech Corp., 1987—88; advisor Wayland Pub. Sch. Found., 1982—. Contbr. articles and revs. to profl. jours. With M.C. U.S. Army, 1959—60. Recipient McCurdy prize, Mass. Soc. Rsch. in Psychiatry, 1962; fellow Sr. Fulbright fellow, 1973—74; grantee Nat. Inst. Neurol. Disease and Stroke grantee, 1974—77, NIMH grantee, 1970—73, Nat. Eye Inst. grantee, 1979—. Nat. Inst. Communicative Disorders and Stroke grantee, 1983—. Mem.:

AAAS, APA, Soc. Neurosci., N.Y. Acad. Sci., Harvard Club (Boston), Sigma Xi. Home: 5 Hilltop Park Wilbraham MA 01095-1753 Office: Mass Gen Hosp PO Box 70 Boston MA 02114 Office Phone: 617-726-3832. Business E-Mail: wfoote@partners.org.

FOOTE, WILLIAM CHAPIN, manufacturing executive; b. Milw., Mar. 15, 1951; s. Peter Chapin and Mary Jane (Manierre) F.; m. Kari H. Foote, July 27, 1969; children: Tracy, Leslie Suzanne. BA, Williams Coll., 1973; MBA, Harvard U., 1977. Asst. treas. Chase Manhattan Bank, N.Y.C., 1973-75; sr. engagement mgr. McKinsey & Co., Inc., Chgo., 1977-83; v.p. USG Corp., Chgo., 1984-94, pres., COO, 1994-99; pres. CEO L&W, USG Interiors Inc., 1994, chmn., pres., CEO, 1996-2000; now chmn. bd., pres., CEO USG Corp., Chgo., 1999—. Mem.: Economics Chgo.

FOOTMAN, GORDON ELLIOTT, educational administrator; b. L.A., Oct. 10, 1927; s. Arthur Leland and Meta Fay (Neal) F.; m. Virginia Rose Footman, Aug. 7, 1954; children: Virginia, Patricia, John. BA, Occidental Coll., 1951, MA, 1954; EdD, U. So. Calif., 1972. Tchr., Arcadia, Calif., 1952, Glendale, Calif., 1956; psychologist Burbank (Calif.) Schs., 1956-64, supr., 1964-70, dir. pupil pers. svcs., 1970-72; dir. divsn. ednl. support svcs. L.A. County Office Edn., Downey, Calif., 1972-91; cons. ednl. adminstrn., counseling and psychol. svcs., 1991—. Pres. Calif. Assn. Adult Devel. and Aging, 1994-95; lectr. ednl. psychology U. So. Calif., 1972-75, asst. prof. ednl. psychology, 1976-85. Pres. Coun. for Exceptional Children, 1969-70; pres. Burbank Coordinating Coun., 1969-70; mem. Burbank Family Svc. Bd., 1972-72. Served with AUS, 1945-47. Mem. ACA (senator 1983-86, gov. coun. 1989-93, exec. com. 1990-93, parliamentarian 1991-92, western region br. assembly publs. editor 1985-87, chair 1988-89, chair bylaws com. 1995-97), Am. Ednl. Rsch. Assn., Am. Assn. Humanistic Edn. and Devel. (bd. dirs., treas. 1996—), Calif. Assn. for Counseling & Devel. (pres. 1981-82, exec. coun. 1996—. bylaws chair 2000--), Calif. Assn. for Counseling and Devel. Found., Nat. Assn. Pupil Pers. Adminstrs., Calif. Assn. Pupil Pers. Adminstrs. (monograph editor 1977-80), Calif. Assn. Counselor Educators and Suprs. (trustee), Calif. Soc. Ednl. Program Auditors and Evaluators (sec. 1975-76, v.p. 1976-77, pres.), Calif. Assn. Measurement and Evaluation in Counseling and Devel. (sec. 1976, pres. 1979-80, 96-97, pres. 1997-98, cons. ednl. and pupil svcs. adminstrn. 1991—), Calif. Inst. Tech. Assocs., Assn. Humanistic Edn. and Devel. (bd. dirs. 1996-99, treas. 1996—, pres. 2000-2001. conv. coord. 1999--), Huntington Libr. Soc. Fellows, Phi Delta Kappa, Phi Beta Kappa, Phi Alpha Theta, Psi Chi. Republican. Presbyterian. Home and Office: 1259 Sherwood Rd San Marino CA 91108-1816

FOPMA, MARY LOUISE, music educator; b. Des Moines, Iowa, Feb. 23, 1956; d. Dick Gerrit; m. Alvin Lee Fopma; children: Jodi Marie, Amy Dawn, Jamie Lee, Amber Nicole. Para educator, Area Edn. Agy., 2002. Group underwriter Bankers Life, Des Moines, 1974—75; piano tchr. Self Employed, Grinnell, Iowa, 1985—93; vocal tchr. Sully Christian Sch., Sully, Iowa, 2000—05, Peoria Christian Sch., Peoria, Iowa, 2001—05. Organist, pianist Sully Christian Reformed Ch., Sully, Iowa, 1972—2000, music coord., praise team leader, 2004—05; dir. programs and fine arts Sully Christian Sch., 2000—05; organist Prairie City Reformed Ch. Coord. Angel Tree, Prison Fellowship, Sully, Iowa, 1990—2000. Mem.: Iowa Choral Dirs. Assn. Republican. Avocations: sewing, piano. Home: 4549 Hwy 146 Grinnell IA 50112 Office: Sully Christian Schs 12629 S 92nd Ave E Sully IA 50251 also: Peoria Christian Schs 110 Peoria W St Pella IA 50219

FORAN, DAVID JOHN, public relations consultant; b. Milw., July 15, 1937; BS in Journalism, Marquette U., 1959, postgrad., 1966-68. Reporter Cath. Herald Citizen, Milw., 1960, Milw. Jour., 1960-66; dir. news. bur. Marquette U., Milw., 1966-74, assoc. dir. pub. rels., 1974-81, exec. dir., 1981-92, instr. journalism, 1975-81; dir. pub. rels. and advt. Milw. Pub. TV, Milw., 1994-99; moderator TV program Sta. WTMJ, Milw., 1982-83. Past mem. bd. dirs. Wis. Heart Assn., past chmn. pub. rels. com.; past bd. mem. Walnut Improvement Coun.; past pres. Human Rels. Radio and TV Coun. of Milw., Milw. Pen and Mike Club. With U.S. Army, 1959, 61-62. Mem. Soc. Profl. Journalists-Sigma Delta Chi (past pres., chmn., dir. Milw. chpt.), Milw. Press Club, Milw. Broadcasters Club. Home: 209 W Lexington Blvd Glendale WI 53217-5017 E-mail: forand@execpc.com.

FORBES, ALFRED DEAN, religious studies researcher; b. Pomona, Calif., Mar. 2, 1941; s. Paul Edward and Lela Irene Forbes; m. Ellen Moss, May 8, 1971. BA in Physics, Harvard Coll., 1962; MDiv, Pacific Sch. Religion, 1969. With U.S. Peace Corps, Nigeria, 1962—64; prin. med. dept. scientist Hewlett-Packard Labs., Palo Alto, Calif., 1971—98; vis. scholar U. Calif., San Diego, 1999—2002. Vis. scholar Stanford (Calif.) U., 1986-89, U. Calif., Berkeley, 2003—; adj. prof. Jewish studies Pa. State U., 1998-2003; lectr. Assn. Internat. Bible et Informatique, 2000; charter mem. Bibl. Colloquium West, 2002—; adv. bd. Turgama, Leiden U. Author: (with F.I. Andersen) Spelling in the Hebrew Bible, 1986, The Vocabulary of the Old Testament, 1989; (with F.I. Andersen and D.N. Freedman) Studies in Hebrew and Aramaic Orthography, 1992; co-editor: Foundations for Syriac Lexicography, 2005, others; algorithms editor Jour. Clin. Monitoring and Computing, 1985-2001; contbr. articles to profl. jours. Trustee, v.p. Whitney Edn. Found., Los Altos, Calif., 1981—88. Mem. Soc. Bibl. Lit., IEEE (sr. mem.), Internat. Brotherhood of Magicians (Order of Merlin). Avocations: travel, magic. Home: 820 Loma Verde Ave Palo Alto CA 94303-4112 Personal E-mail: adforbes@ix.netcom.com.

FORBES, ALVIS R., orthopaedic surgeon; b. Yakima, Wash., Nov. 29, 1950; s. Carl Earl and Pearl Evelyn (Carter) F.; m. Barbara Ann Norris, Sept. 8, 1973; children: Amy, Colleen, Michelle, Ryan. BS in Food Sci. and Tech., Wash. State U., 1974; MD, U. Wash., 1978. Diplomate Am. Bd. Orthop. Surgery. Intern William Beumont Army Med. Ctr., El Paso, Tex., 1978-79; orthop. on-job-trainee U.S. Army, Frankfurt, Germany, 1979-81; orthop. resident Madigan Army Med. Ctr., Tacoma, 1981-85; chief orthop. surgery U.S. Army, Ft. Leavenworth, Kans., 1985-87; orthop. surgeon Lakeport, Calif., 1987-89, Orthopaedics of Jackson Hole, Wyo., 1989—2004, Orthop. Assocs., Jackson Hole, 2004—. Sports medicine fellow Jackson Orthopaedics, 1985. Lt. col. USAR, 1991, lt. col. Nat. Guard U.S. Army, 1991—. Fellow Am. Acad. Orthop. Surgeons. Avocations: water-skiing, skiing, softball. Home: 4600 Runway Rd Jackson WY 83001-9452 Office: Orthops Assocs and Spine Care PO Box 7375 Jackson WY 83002

FORBES, BRIAN L., lawyer; BA, Univ. Calif., Berkeley, 1970; JD, Univ. Calif., Hastings, 1974. Bar: Calif. 1974, Tex., US Dist. Ct. (so. dist. Calif.) 1974, US Dist. Ct. (no. dist. Calif.) 1989, US Ct. Appeals (9th cir.) 1990, US Tax Ct. 1989, US Supreme Ct. 1980. Gen. counsel Gray Cary & Freidenrich, 1999—2004; profl. responsibility ptnr. DLA Piper Rudnick Gray Cary, San Diego, 2005—. Mem.: Thurston Soc., Order of the Coif. Office: DLA Piper Rudnick Gray Cary Suite 1100 4365 Executive Dr San Diego CA 92121 Office Phone: 858-638-6842. Office Fax: 858-677-1401. Business E-Mail: brian.forbes@dlapiper.com.

FORBES, CHRISTOPHER (KIP FORBES), publisher; b. Morristown, N.J., Dec. 5, 1950; s. Malcolm Stevenson and Roberta Remsen (Laidlaw) F.; m. Baroness Astrid Cornelia Mathilde Von Heyl Zu Herrnsheim, Sept. 7, 1974; 1 child, Charlotte Adelaide Mathilde. BA in Art History magna cum laude, Princeton U., 1972; LHD (hon.), N.H. Coll., Manchester, 1986. Curator Forbes Mag. Collection, N.Y.C., 1970-80; ad salesman Forbes Mag., N.Y.C., 1972-76, assoc. pub., v.p., 1978-89, sec., 1981-92, vice-chmn., corp. sec., 1989—, also dir. Pub. Nineteenth Century, Phila., 1976-78. Author books and catalogues, including: Victorians in Togas, Paintings by Sir Lawrence Alma-tadem from the Collection of Allen Funt, 1973; the Royal Academy (1836-1901) Revisited, 1975; (with Margaret Kelly) War a la Mode: Meissonier Detaille, de Neuville, and Berne-Bellecour, 1975; (with Hermione Waterfield) Faberge: Imperial Eggs and Other Fantasies, 1978; (with Dr. Armand Hammer) Faberge Eggs, 1980, (with Susan Casteras) Victorian Childhood, 1986; editor: Masterpieces from the House of Faberge, 1984, (with Robyn Trommeur Brenner) Faberge, 2000. Active Cultural and Hist. Commn. Somerset County, N.J., 1984-96; bd. dirs. Newark Mus., Prince of Wales Found.; vice-chmn., bd. advisers Princeton U. Art Mus., N.J., Bklyn. Mus. Art, Victorian Soc.; nat. trustee Balt. Mus. Art; chmn. bd. trustees Am. Friends of the Louvre; formed Nat. Jewelry Inst. Decorated assoc. knight Venerable Order St. John Jerusalem. Mem. Grolier Club, Nat. Arts Club, Salmagundi Club, Century Club. Republican. Episcopalian. Office: Forbes Inc 60 5th Ave New York NY 10011-8882

FORBES, CYNTHIA ANN, music educator; b. Charlotte, N.C., Jan. 13, 1956; d. George Whitfield and Nancy Ann (Moore) Wentz; m. Robert Brad Forbes, Sept. 22, 1984; children: Robbie, Adam. Diploma in Music, Brevard Coll., 1976; BS in Secondary Edn. Vocal/Instrumental, Old Dominion, 1979; M in Curriculum and Instrn., George Washington U., 1995. Cert. tchr. Va. Choral dir. Landstown Mid. Sch., Virginia Beach, Va., 1987—2005, Cox H.S., Virginia Beach, 2005—. Choir dir., organist First Ch. God, Norfolk, Va., 1988—. Mem. PTA, Tarralton, Va., 1995—, Landstown, 1995—. Nominee Disney Tchr. of Yr., 2001, 2002; recipient Tchr. award, Target Stores, 1998. Mem.: Va. Music Educators Assn., Am. Choral Dirs. Assn., Music Educators Nat. Conf. Home: 8533 Halprin Dr Norfolk VA 23518 Office: Cox High School 2425 Shorehaven Dr Virginia Beach VA 23454

FORBES, DANIEL MERRILL, minister; b. Savannah, Ga., June 20, 1954; s. Marion and Mary Edna (Godbee) F.; m. Wanda Iris Rosa, Sept. 25, 1977; children: Daniel Felix, Amanda Iris. BA in Theology, So. Coll., Tenn., 1977; MA in Counselor Edn., U. South Fla., 1988, EdS, 1992; EdD in Counseling Psychology, Argosy U., 2004. Ordained to ministry 7th Day Adventist Ch., 1982; cert. cognitive behavior therapist, lic. mental health counselor, cert. Nat. Cert. Counselor, family life educator, family mediator Fla. Supreme Ct. Min. Fla. Conf. of Seventh-day Adventists, Orlando, 1977—. Cons. in field. Democrat. Seventh-day Adventist. Avocations: music, reading, nature, walking. Office: Univ Seventh Day Adventist Ch 9191 University Blvd Orlando FL 32817-1704 *Life, both temporal and eternal, is a gift of God to mankind. It is in our physical life that we are to prepare to partake of the eternal life. I think that the wise man, Solomon, said it best in Eccl. 12:13 when he wrote of the purpose of man's life and said, "Let us hear the conclusion of the whole matter: Fear God keep His commandments, for this is the whole duty of man."*.

FORBES, DAVID CRAIG, musician; b. Seattle, Feb. 12, 1938; s. Douglas James and Ruby A. (Niles) F.; m. Sylvia Sterling, Aug. 29, 1965 (div. Apr. 1973); 1 child, Angela Rose. Grad., USN Sch. Music, 1957; student, Western Wash. U., 1960-64. Prin. horn La Jolla (Calif.) Civic Orch., 1958-60, Seattle Worlds Fair Band, 1962, Seattle Opera Co., 1964—, Pacific Northwest Ballet, Seattle, 1964—; asst. prin. horn Seattle Symphony Orch., 1964—2003, ret., 2003; prin. horn Pacific Northwest Wagner Fest., Seattle, 1975—. Instr. horn Western Wash. State U., 1969-81, Cornish Inst., Seattle, 1964-78. Served with USN, 1956-60. Mem. NARAS, Internat. Horn Soc. Avocations: piano, golf, fishing. Home: 9050 15th Ave NW # 2 Seattle WA 98117-3429 E-mail: DavidForbes@webtv.net.

FORBES, DORSEY CONNORS, commentator, journalist; b. Chgo. d. William J. and Sarah (MacLain) C.; m. John E. Forbes; 1 dau., Stephanie. BA cum laude, U. Ill. Fl. reporter WGN-TV Rep. Nat. Conv., Chgo., Dem. Nat. Conv., L.A., 1960. Conducted: Personality Profiles, WGN-TV, Chgo., 1948-49, Dorsey Connors Show, WMAQ-TV, Chgo., 1949-58, 61-63, Armchair Travels, WMAQ-TV, 1952-55, Homeshow, NBC,1954-57, NBC Today Show, Dorsey Connors program, WGN, 1958-61, Tempo Nine, WGN-TV, 1961, Society in Chgo, WMAQ-TV, 1964; writer: column Hi! I'm Dorsey Connors, Chgo. Sun Times, 1965—; Author: Gadgets Galore, 1953, Save Time, Save Money, Save Yourself, 1972, Helpful Hints for Hurried Homemakers, 1988. Founder Ill. Epilepsy League; mem. woman's bd. Children's Home and Aid Soc., mem. women's bd. USO. Named one of Am.'s Outstanding Irish Am. Women, World of Hibernia mag., 1995. Mem. AFTRA, NATAS (Silver Cir. award 1995), SAG, Mus. Broadcast Comm. (founding mem.), Soc. Midland Authors, Chgo. Hist. Soc. (guild com., costume com.), Chi Omega. Roman Catholic. Office: Chgo Sun Times 401 N Wabash Ave Chicago IL 60611-5642

FORBES, EDWARD JOHN, III, retired developmental psychologist, educator; b. Syracuse, NY; s. Edward John Forbes Jr. and Helen Frances Forbes; m. Eileen Paula Kuehnel, June 8, 1963; children: Kirsten Heather, Kip Pieter, Michael Ian, Courtney Anne. BS in Microbiology, Syracuse U., 1963; MA in Psychology, W.Va. U., 1973. Penn State U. cert. in internat. distance edn. 1994. Rsch. asst. in med. microbiology SUNY Med. Ctr. Upstate, Syracuse, 1961; pharm. microbiologist Parke, Davis & Co., Detroit, 1963—69; rsch. asst. in psychology W.Va. U., Morgantown, 1969—74, instr. in psychology, 1970—74; asst. prof. psychology Mansfield U. Pa., 1974—80, Lock Haven U. of Pa., 1980—85, assoc. prof. psychology, 1985—, chmn. dept. psychology, 1985—89, pres. faculty assn., 1997—99, 2001—03, emeritus assoc. prof. psychology, 2003—. Trustee Ross Pub. Libr., Lock Haven, PR, 2005—. Trustee Ross Pub. Libr., Lock Haven, 2005—. Mem.: APA, Am. Psychol. Soc., Jean Piaget Soc., Soc. for Rsch. on Adolescents, Soc. for Rsch. in Child Devel., Phi Kappa Phi, Psi Chi. Democrat. Home: 219 W Water St Lock Haven PA 17745 Business E-Mail: tforbes@lhup.edu.

FORBES, GORDON MAXWELL, sportswriter, commentator; b. Bellport, N.Y., Feb. 6, 1930; s. Harlow Campbell and Grace Bain (DeVall) F.; m. June Lolita Cassidy, July 16, 1960 (dec. Jan. 1994); children— James Douglas, Christopher Bryan BA in English, Duke U., 1955. Sports writer Fla. Times Union, Jacksonville, 1957-62; pro-football writer Phila. Inquirer, 1962-82; pro-football editor USA Today, Rosslyn, Va., 1982—2002; sports commentator Home Box Office Cable TV, 1988, Sta. WIP Radio, Phila., 1992-95. Corr. Sports Illustrated, N.Y.C., 1963-89; selector Pro Football Hall of Fame, Canton, Ohio, 1975-87. Author: How to Win at the Trotters, 1966, Tales from the Eagles Sidelines, 2002; contbr. numerous articles to jours. and mags. Served to cpl. U.S. Army, 1952-54 Recipient Dick McCann award for outstanding pro football coverage, 1988; named to Suffolk County (N.Y.) Sports Hall of Fame, 2001. Mem. Duke U. Alumni Assn., Pro Football Writers of Am. Republican. Episcopalian. Avocations: jogging, tennis, weightlifting, thoroughbred horses (with Write Stuff Stable). Home and Office: USA Today 5 Summerlawn Dr Lakewood NJ 08701-7542 Office Phone: 732-477-4740. E-mail: gmforbes30@aol.com.

FORBES, JAMES RANDY, congressman; b. Chesapeake, Va., Feb. 17, 1952; BA, JD, U. Va. Mem. Va. Ho. Dels., 1990-98, Va. State Senate, 1998-2001, U.S. Congress from 4th Va. dist., 2001—; mem. armed forces com., sci. com.; mem. Judiciary Com. Chmn. Rep. Party Va. Republican. Baptist. Office: US Ho Reps 307 Cannon House Office Bldg Washington DC 20515 also: 524 Johnstown Rd Chesapeake VA 23322-5617*

FORBES, JOHN DOUGLAS, architectural and economic historian; b. San Francisco, Apr. 9, 1910; s. John Franklin and Portia (Ackerman) F.; m. Margaret Funkhouser, Feb. 4, 1937 (dec.); children: Pamela, Peter; m. Mary Elizabeth Lewis, July 26, 1980 and Dec. 24, 1999; 1 child, Michael. AB, U. Calif.-Berkeley, 1931; MA, Stanford U., 1932; A.M., Harvard U., 1936, PhD, 1937. Accountant J.F. Forbes & Co. (C.P.A.'s), San Francisco, 1937-38, 42-43; asst. to dir. fine arts, curator paintings San Francisco World's Fair, 1938-40; chmn. dept. fine arts U. Kansas City, Mo., 1940-42; faculty history Bennington Coll., 1943-46; assoc. editor Am. Enterprise Assn., 1944-46; assoc. prof. history and fine arts Wabash Coll., 1946-50, prof., 1950-54; prof. bus. history Darden Sch. U. Va., 1954-80; prof. emeritus U. Va., 1980—, lectr. art history sch. continuing edn., 1982—2003; adv. bd. Historic Am. Bldgs. Survey, 1974-78. Author: Israel Thorndike, 1953, Victorian Architect, 1953, Murder in Full View, 1968, Death Warmed Over, 1971, Stettinius, Sr., Portrait of a Morgan Partner, 1974, J.P. Morgan, Jr. (1867-1943), 1981, Death Among the Artists, 1993, I'd Be Tempted to Dip into Capitol First, 2004; editor: Jour. Soc. Archtl. Historians, 1953-58; adv. editor industry Ency. Britannica, 1956-58. 2d lt. AUS, 1942. Decorated officier Ordre des Palmes Académiques (France); cavaliere Ordine al Merito (Italy); named Hon. Alumnus Class of 1950, Assn. of Wabash Men, 1993. Mem. Am. Hist. Assn. (life), Coll. Art Assn. (life), Mystery Writers Am., Soc. Archtl. Historians (pres. 1962-64, life), Colonial Soc. Mass. (life), AIA (hon.), Audubon Soc., Wilderness Soc. (life), Sierra Club (life), Nature Conservancy (life), Mechanics Inst. (life), Victorian Soc. (life), Calif. Hist. Soc., Soc. Calif. Pioneers (life), Friends of Sea Otter (life), Tamalpais Conservation Club (life), Am. Kitefliers Assn. (life), Am. Soc. Dowsers (life), Save-the Redwoods League (life), Phi Beta Kappa. Clubs: Colonnade (Charlottesville) (life), Pacific-Union (San Francisco); Farmington Country (Charlottesville, life); Cambridge (Mass.) Boat. Home: PO Box 3607 Charlottesville VA 22903-0607 also: 1250 Jones St San Francisco CA 94109-4261

FORBES, JOHN EDWARD, financial consultant; b. Chgo., Sept. 18, 1925; s. Harry Charles and Jeanette Anne (Field) F.; m. Dorsey Connors, Aug. 10, 1961. Student, Rensselaer Poly. Inst., 1943-44, Franklin and Marshall Coll., Lancaster, Pa., 1943; BA, Monmouth Coll., 1949; postgrad., Northwestern U., 1949-50. Account exec. and commodity mgr. Merrill Lynch, Pierce, Fenner and Smith, Inc., Chgo., 1949-61; pres. San Jose Cigarette Co., Calif., 1958-68; account exec. Hornblower & Weeks, Hemphill, Noyes, Inc., Chgo., 1961-71, assoc. resident mgr., 1971-75, v.p., resident mgr., 1975-78; corp. v.p. Loeb, Rhoades, Hornblower & Co., Chgo., 1981—, Shearson Lehman Bros., Chgo., 1961—; sr. v.p. fin. cons. Smith Barney, Chgo., 1995—. Pres. 227 E. Delaware Corp, Chgo., 1980-86; bd. dirs. Trend Industries, Chgo. Lt. USN, 1943-46, PTO. Mem.: Econ., Chgo. Bond, Hundred Club of Cook County, Tavern (pres. 1981-82), Saddle and Cycle (bd. dirs. 1983-86), Soc. St. Andrew. Home: 227 E Delaware Pl Chicago IL 60611-7758 Office: Smith Barney Inc 10 S Wacker Dr Fl 2800 Chicago IL 60606-7438 Office Phone: 312-648-3476. E-mail: john.e.forbes@rssmb.com.

FORBES, KENNETH ALBERT FAUCHER, urologist, retired surgeon; b. Waterford, N.Y., Apr. 28, 1922; s. Joseph Frederick (dec.) and Adelle Frances (Robitaille) Faucher; adopted s. James Peter Forbes; m. Jeanne Ann Bonacci, June 18, 1947 (dec.); 1 child: Michael; m. Eileen Ruth Gibbons, Aug. 4, 1956; children: Diane, Kenneth E., Thomas, Maureen, Daniel. BS cum laude, U. Notre Dame, 1944; MD, St. Louis U., 1947. Diplomate Am. Bd. Urology. Intern St. Louis U. Hosp., 1947-48; resident in urol. surgery Barnes Hosp., VA Hosp., Washington U., St. Louis. U. schs. medicine, St. Louis, 1948-52; asst. chief urology Letterman Army Hosp., San Francisco, 1952-54; fellow West Roxbury (Harvard) VA Hosp., Boston, 1955; asst. chief urology VA Hosp., East Orange, N.J., 1955-58; practice medicine specializing in urology Green Bay, Wis., 1958-78, Long Beach, Calif., 1978-85; ret., 1999. Mem. cons. staff Fairview State Hosp. U. Calif. Med. Ctr., Irvine, VA Hosp., Long Beach; commr. State Med. Soc. Wisc., 1975—77, chmn. legal def. com., 1976—77; pres. Wis. Urological Soc., 1977—78; asst. clin. prof. surgery U. Calif., Irvine, 1978—85; cons. Vols. in Tech. Assistance, 1986—; locum tenens (cons. and surgery) 9 states, 1989—99. Contbr. articles to profl. jours. Served with USNR, 1944-46, ensign 1947-51; capt. U.S. Army, 1952-54. Named Outstanding Faculty Mem. by students, 1981. Fellow ACS, Royal Soc. Medicine (emeritus), Internat. Coll. Surgeons; mem. AMA, AAAS, Calif. Med. Assn., Am. Urol. Assn. (exec. com. North Ctrl. sect. 1972-75, Western sect. 1980—), N.Y. Acad. Scis., Surg. Alumni Assn. U. Calif.-Irvine, Justin J. Cordonnier Soc. Washington U., Urologists Corr. Club, Notre Dame Club (Man of Yr. award 1965), Union League Club of Chgo., Miles City Club (Mont.), Phi Beta Pi. Republican. Roman Catholic. Mailing: 2951 Sage Ridge Dr Reno NV 89509-7044 Personal E-mail: kff12jra@charter.net.

FORBES, KRISTIN J., federal official; BA summa cum laude, Williams Coll., 1992; PhD, MIT, 1998. With investment banking divsn. Morgan Stanley; policy rsch. dept. World Bank; economics group Fleet Fin. Insts.; Mistubishi devel. chair, assoc. prof. internat. mgmt. MIT, 2001—02; dep. asst. sec. quantitative policy analysis U.S. Treas., Washington; mem. Coun. Econ. Advisors, Washington, 2003—; faculty rsch. fellow Nat. Bur. Econ. Rsch. Vis. scholar U.S. Fed. Reserve Bd., Indian Coun. Rsch. on Internat. Econ. Rels. and Internat. Monetary Fund (ICRIER). Contbr. articles to profl. jours. Recipient Milken award Disting. Econ. Rsch., 2000. Office: 1800 G St NW Washington DC 20502*

FORBES, MICHAEL PATRICK, former congressman; b. Riverhead, N.Y., July 16, 1952; m. Barbara; children: Abigail, Theodore, Samuel, Maximilian. BA, SUNY Albany, 1983. Coord. various local, state and fed. polit. campaigns, 1979—89; exec. asst. to U.S. Senator Alfonse D'Amato, 1981-84; chief of staff to U.S. Rep. Connie Mack, 1985-87; owner pub. rels. small bus., 1985-89; regional adminstr. U.S. SBA, 1989-92; legis. dir., regional mgr. U.S. C. of C., 1993-94; mem. 104th-106th Congress from 1st N.Y. dist., 1995-2001; pres., CEO, PR/Strategies Internat., 2001—. Democrat.

FORBES, MORTON GERALD, lawyer; b. Atlanta, July 12, 1938; s. Arthur Mark and Mary Dean (Power) F.; m. Eunice Lee Haynsworth, Jan. 25, 1963; children: John, Ashley, Sarah. AB, Wofford Coll., 1962; JD, U. Ga., 1965. Bar: Ga. 1965, U.s. Dist. Ct. (mid. dist.) Ga. 1965, U.S. Dist. Ct. (so. dist.) Ga. 1968, U.S. Dist. Ct. (no. dist.) Ga. 1993, U.S. Ct. Appeals (5th cir.) 1974, U.S. Ct. Appeals (4th cir.) 1972, U.S. Ct. Appeals (11th cir.) 1981. Assoc. Pierce, Ranitz, Lee, Berry & Mahoney, 1967-70; ptnr. Pierce, Ranitz, Berry, Mahoney & Forbes, 1970-76, Pierce, Ranitz, Mahoney, Forbes & Coolidge, 1976-81; ptnr., sec. Ranitz, Mahoney, Forbes & Coolidge, P.C., 1981-91, Forbes & Bowman, Savannah, Ga., 1991—. Gen. counsel Ga. Fed. Young Rep. Clubs, 1971-72; guest lectr. dept. dental hygiene Armstrong State Coll., 1970-72. Mem. Savannah Port Authority (now Savannah Econ. Devel. Authority), 1973-2003, chmn., 1979-81; mem. Chatham County Devel. Authority, 1973-80; nat. com. Nat. Fedn. Young Reps., 1973; econ. adv. coun. Coastal Area Planning and Devel. Authority, 1980—; bd. dirs. Savannah Symphony Soc., 1971-75; Ga. del. to Japan/Southeast Trade Mission, Kyoto, Japan, 1983, S.E. Asia U.S.A./Japan Assn. meeting, Birmingham, Ala., 1984. With USN, 1965-67. Recipient Outstanding Service award, Savannah Port Authority, 1981. Mem. ABA, Internat. Assn. Def. Counsel, Fedn. Def. and Corp. Counsel, State Bar Ga., Ala. Def. Lawyer Assn. (hon.), Am. Judicature Soc., Nat. Assn. Bond Counsel, Ga. Def. Lawyers Assn. (v.p. 1987—, mem. exec. com. 1988, bd. dirs., exec. v.p. 1990-91, pres. 1991-92), Savannah Bar Assn. (exec. com. 1989-94, pres. 1992-93), Libel Def. Resource Ctr., Def. Rsch. Inst. (state chmn. 1992-99, bd. dirs. 1999-2002), Savannah Econ. Devel. Action Coun. (founding), Savannah Area Wofford Coll. Alumni Club (past pres.), Soc. of the Cincinnati (Va.), St. Andrews Soc. (bd. stewards), Soc. Colonial Wars, Sons of Revolution (sec. 1988-92), Chatham Club, Savannah Yacht Club, The Landings Club. Republican. Presbyterian. Office: Forbes & Bowman PO Box 13929 Savannah GA 31416-0929 Office Phone: 912-352-1190. Business E-Mail: salty@forbesbowman.com.

FORBES, PETER, architect; b. Berkeley, Calif., May 22, 1942; s. John Douglas and Margaret (Funkhouser) F.; m. Patricia Ann Marsh, Aug. 27, 1966 (div. 1982); children: Alexander John, Anne deMarken; m. Erica Longfellow deBerry, July 21, 1990; 1 child, Allegra Longfellow. BArch, U. Mich., 1966; MArch, Yale U., 1967; Dr. Engring. Tech. (hon.), Wentworth Inst. Tech., 1991. Registered architect, Mass., Va., Calif., Maine, R.I., N.Y., Mich., Conn., D.C.; cert. Nat. Council Archtl. Registration Bds. Project designer Skidmore, Owings & Merrill, Chgo., 1965-66; assoc. ptnr. PARD Team, Inc., Boston, 1967-71; pres. Forbes Hailey Jeas Erneman, Inc., Boston, 1972-80, Peter Forbes and Assoc., Inc., Boston, 1980-2000, Peter Forbes, FAIA Arch., Seal Harbor, Maine, 2000—. Mem. Commonwealth of Mass. Designer Selection Bd., 1986-89; mem. Spl. Commn. Concerning State and County Bldgs., 1978-81; bd. dirs. continuing edn. Boston Archtl. Ctr.; vis. critic U. Mich., 1980-82, Cath. U. Am., Rome, 1982; vis. lectr. Cath. U., Washington, 1997; lectr., vis. critic Va. Poly. Inst. and State U., 1989-92, 96, Columbia U., 1984; vis. critic N.C. State U., 1997; Thomas S. Monaghan Disting. vis. prof. U. Mich., 1987; vis. prof. Harvard U., 1989, 91, 94, G. Truman Ward vis. lectr. Va. Poly. Inst. and State U., 1996; vis. lectr. Lawrence Tech. U., 1996, Evergreen State Coll., 1996, U. B.C., 1996; guest lectr. Boston Mus. Fine Arts, 1997, Guido A. Binda vis. lectr. U. Mich., 1997, vis. prof. Wentworth Inst. of Tech., Gargonza, Italy, 2003 Author: Ten Houses: Peter Forbes and Associates, 1995; exhbns. include Cath. U. Am., 1982, 97, U. Mich., 1982, 87, 97, Va. Poly. Inst. and State U., 1983, Boston Athenaeum, 1986, Harvard U., 1986, Lawrence Tech. U., 1996; contbr. articles to profl. jours. Recipient

Record House award, 1983, 86, 87, 89, New Eng. Design awrd, 1986, 87, 89, 91, 94, 96, 97, 98, Archtl. Excellence award Am. Inst. Steel Constrn., 1987, Tucker award Bldg. Stone Inst., 1987, 90, Best and Brightest award, 1995, Honor award Am. Wood Inst., 1989, Nat. Housing Design award, 1990, Silver award Indsl. Designers Soc. Am., 1993, 94, Am. Arch. award Chgo. Athenaeum Mus. Arch. and Design, 1999. Fellow AIA (nat. jud. coun. 1987—, Nat. honor award 1986, 92, New Eng. regional coun./design award 1986, 87, 89, 91, 94, 96, 97, 98, Washington D.C. merit award 1994; Excellence in Arch. award Maine chpt. 1995), Boston Soc. Archs. (bd. dirs., commr. pub. affairs, chmn. ethics com., v.p., pres. 1988-89, Excellence in Arch. award 1988-89, 91-94, 98, Honor award 1995, 97, 98, Excellence in Housing design award 1996, 98); mem. Soc. Archtl. Historians (life), Century Club, Newport Reading Rm., Racquet and Tennis Club, Nat. Tennis Club, Yale Club, Boston Athenaeum. Home: Greenings Is Southwest Harbor ME 04679 also: Viale Giovanni Milton 65 50129 Florence Italy Office: 12 Main St Seal Harbor ME 04675 Office Phone: 207-276-0970. E-mail: pfamaine@adelphia.net, pfafirenze@dada.it.

FORBES, PETER EDWIN, sculptor; b. Detroit, Mich. s. Edwin Fisher Forbes and Grace Campbell Fisher; m. Leona Collins Forbes, July 1, 1961; 1 child, Wyndham Fisher. BS in design, U. Mich., 1961, MA in design, 1963. Art instr. Mich. State U., 1964, U. Ill., 1964—69, SUNY, 1974—86, Syracuse U., 1991—99; vis. artist Rochester Inst. of Tech., 1999—2000; art instr. Syracuse U., 2000—03. Tech. sculpture cons. Syracuse, 2003; freelance indsl. designer Syracuse area, 1980; resident artist Sculpture Space Inc., Utica, 2002. Sculpture, Norfolk Internat. Airport, 1995, Shaffer Art Bldg., Syracuse U., 1994, Downtown Syracuse area, 1992, exhibitions include 4th Biennale Internazionale dell'ArteContemporanea, Florence, Italy, 2003, multimedia presentation, Vienna, Austria, 2000, juried shows, Schweinfurth Meml. Art Ctr., NY, 2001, Meml. Art Gallery, Rochester, NY, 1999, Nexus Gallery, NYC, 1998, Paint Creek Ctr. for the Arts, Rochester, 1998, Zaner Gallery, 1985, juried show, Chelsea, N.Y., 2005 (winner Amsterdam Whitney Internat. Fine Arts Chelsea Global Showcase competition, 2005). Vol. art cons. and builder of displays Erie Canal Mus., Syracuse, 2003—04; mem. Outer Comstock Neighbor Assn., Syracuse, 1994—2005. Recipient Spl. Opportunity Stipend, NY Found for the Arts, 2002. Avocations: walking, jogging. Home: 336 Vincent St Syracuse NY 13210 Personal E-mail: forbes010@aol.com.

FORBES, RAMONA FRANCES BLUNT, music educator; b. Denver, Nov. 1, 1913; d. Lester Phelps Blunt and Hazel Margaret Forbes; m. Charles Sidney Forbes, Feb. 15, 1950 (dec. 1983); children: Douglas Paul, Ramona Margaret Forbes Mendoza. MusB, edn. cert., U. Colo. Music, art, sci. tchr. Campot Lamar H.S., Colo., 1934—38; music, art tchr. Endicott Coll., Mass., 1938—42; sec., head graphics Selective Svc. and Reconstruction Fin., U.S. Govt., 1942—47; head music dept. Sidwell Friends Sch., Washington, 1947—48, 1948—50; music tchr. Nat. Cathedral Sch. for Girls, Washington, 1954—55. Mem.: Washington Cathedral Choral Soc. (sec.-treas., head sect. leaders, Order of Merit). Republican. Episcopalian. Avocations: dance, sports, horseback riding.

FORBES, RICHARD MATHER, biochemistry professor; b. Wooster, Ohio, Jan. 8, 1916; s. Ernest Browning and Lydia Maria (Mather) F.; m. Mary Medlicott, Feb. 26, 1944; children: Sally Allen, Anne Mather, Stephen Harding. BS, Pa. State Coll., 1938, MS, 1939; PhD, Cornell U., 1942. Instr. biochemistry Wayne State U., 1942; research fellow Cornell U., Ithaca, N.Y., 1942-43; asst. prof. U. Ky., Lexington, 1946-49; assoc. prof. U. Ill., Champaign-Urbana, 1949-55, prof. nutritional biochemistry, 1955-85, emeritus prof., 1985—. Contbr. articles to profl. jours. Served to capt. U.S. Army, 1943-46. Recipient H. H. Mitchell award U. Ill., 1981 Fellow AAAS, Am. Inst. Nutrition (Borden award 1984); mem. Am. Soc. Animal Sci. (Gustav Bohstedt award 1968), Sigma Xi. Democrat. Mem. United Ch. of Christ. Clubs: Nat. Exchange, Izaak Walton League . Home: 101 W Windsor Rd Apt 2105 Urbana IL 61802-6663

FORBES, STEVE (MALCOLM STEVENSON FORBES JR.), publishing executive; b. Morristown, NJ, July 18, 1947; s. Malcolm Stevenson and Roberta Remsen (Laidlaw) Forbes; m. Sabina Beekman, June 19, 1971; children: Sabina, Roberta, Catherine, Moira, Elizabeth. BA in history, Princeton U., 1970; LHD (hon.), Lycoming Coll., Jacksonville U., Kean Coll., Seton Hill U.; LLD (hon.), Lock Haven U., Westminster Coll., Sacred Heart U., Centenary Coll., Iona Coll., Pepperdine U., Lehigh U., New Hampshire U., Siena Coll.; LittD (hon.), Spring Arbor U.; LLD (hon.), Caldwell Coll.; ScD (hon.), N.Y. Inst. Tech., Lynn U., U. Francisco Marroquin; D.P.S. (hon.), U. Rio Grande; PhD (hon.), Hillsdale Coll., UEES Universidad Espiritu Santo, Ecuador; DBA (hon.), Lincoln Coll., New Bulgarian Univ.; AA (hon.), Raritan Valley CC. With Forbes Inc., NYC, 1970—, pres., COO, 1980-90, dep. editor-in-chief, 1982-90, editor-in-chief, pres., CEO, 1990—. Author: The Moral Basis of A Free Society, 1999; co-author (filmscript): Some Call It Greed, 1977, A New Birth of Freedom, 1999; editor: Fact and Comment, 1974. Pres. Somerset County Park Commn., 1981—91; mem. Bd. for Internat. Broadcasting, 1983—93, chmn., 1985—93; trustee Brooks Sch., North Andover, Mass., 1978—97; pres., bd. trustees Freedom House, 1993—, Heritage Found., 2001—, Found. for the Def. Democracies, 2001—; bd. visitors Pepperdine U., 2002—; bd. trustees Princeton U., 1992—2002, pres., 1987—96; Ronald Reagan Presdl. Found., 1990; Rep. presdl. primary campaign candidate, 1995—96, 1999—2000; internat. adv. bd. Brit. Am. Bus. Coun., 2001—; pres. bd. trustees Brooks Sch., 1987—96; bd. overseers Meml. Sloan-Kettering Cancer Ctr., 1989—; chmn. bd. dirs. Empower Am., 1993—96, Ams. Soc., 1992—; bd. dirs Nat. Endowment for Democracy, 1994—98; bd. dirs. Nat. Taxpayers Union, 1997, Jackie Robinson Found., 1996—; mem. Coun. for Nat. Policy, 1998; bd. dirs. Abraham Lincoln Presdl. Libr., 2001—. Republican. Office: Forbes Inc 60 Fifth Ave New York NY 10011-8882 Office Phone: 212-620-2200. Office Fax: 212-620-2245. E-mail: sforbes@forbes.com.

FORBES, THEODORE MCCOY, JR., arbitrator, mediator, retired lawyer; b. Atlanta, Oct. 28, 1929; s. Theodore M. and Mary Beatrice (Christie) F.; m. Margaret Paty, Dec. 12, 1953; children: Theodore McCoy, Margaret Paty. BS in Chemistry, Ga. Inst. Tech., 1950; LLB, U. Va., 1953. Bar: Ga., 1952, D.C. 1973, U.S. Ct. Appeals (5th cir.) 1976, U.S. Ct. Appeals (11th cir.) 1981. Instr. Culver (Ind.) Summer Naval Sch., 1950; from assoc. to ptnr. Smith, Gambrell & Russell, and predecessor firms, Atlanta, 1953—58, ptnr., 1958-91; solo practice, 1992-95. Bd. dirs. Travelers Aid Soc., Atlanta, 1974-90, pres., 1975-76, 86-89; bd. dirs., corp. sec. Shepherd Spinal Ctr., Atlanta, 1975-95; bd. dirs. Ga. Fund for Edn., 1986-89. Lt. (j.g.) USNR, 1950-62. Fellow Ga. Bar Found.; mem. Atlanta Bar Assn., State Bar Ga. (emeritus), Ga. C. of C. (bd. dirs. 1986-95), Capital City Club (life). Avocations: golf, american history, fishing. Home: 2520 Peachtree Rd NW Apt 202 Atlanta GA 30305-3617

FORBES, TIMOTHY CARTER, publishing executive; b. Morristown, N.J., Oct. 5, 1953; s. Malcolm Stevenson and Roberta (Laidlaw) F.; m. Anne Shepard Harrison, Mar. 4, 1983. AB with honors, Brown U., 1976, LHD (hon.), 1996. Prodr. Seven Seas Cinema, N.Y.C., 1977-81; prodr., screenwriter N.Y.C., 1981-85; pres. Am. Heritage Mag., 1986—2000; v.p. Forbes Inc., N.Y.C., 1986—, COO, 1996, also chmn. bd. dirs. Dir., producer: (films) Some Call It Greed, 1977, Lost to the Revolution, 1979, Golden Age of Toy Boats, 1981, Happily Ever After?, 1992. Mem. bd. fellows Brown U., 2000—; bd. dirs. Margaret Thatcher Found., 1993—, Hist. House Trust N.Y.C., 1990—. Mem. Am. Antiquarian Soc. Office: Forbes Inc 60 5th Ave New York NY 10011-8882

FORBES-RICHARDSON, HELEN HILDA, state agency administrator; b. Detroit, July 26, 1950; d. Henry and Trunetta (Adams) Forbes; m. Leon Richardson (div.); 1 child, Leon Ronald Jr. BA in Edn. and Human Svcs., U. Detroit, 1972; MPA, Harvard U., 1989. Cert. tchr. Mich. Substitute tchr. Detroit Bd. Edn., 1972-75; assistance payment worker State Dept. Social Svcs., Detroit, 1975-79, supr. assistance payment, 1979-85, section mgr., 1985—; adminstrv. asst. to chief dep. dir. Wayne County Dept. Social Svcs., Detroit, 1989-90. Mem. case rev. com. Mich. Dept. Social Svcs. Gen. Assistance, 1985, 87, labor rels. subcom., quality initiative task force tng. com., 1985; co-chairperson quality initiative error reduction com. and conf. planning com.; mem. tng. com. quality initiative task force Mich. Dept. Social Svcs., 1984, client svc. subcom., 1989—, coord. employee recognition program, 1989-90, chmn. procedure com., Grand River Warren local office, 1990—, coord. state employee recognition program, Wayne County, 1980-90; chair security plan com. client info. system County of Wayne, 1989, mem. UAW Secondary Contract Negotiations Team, 1988; mem. conf. planning com. Mich. County Social Svcs. Assn., 1988; chairperson Grand River/Warren Procedures Com., 1990, employee recognition awards program level 1 Grand River/Warren Dept. Social Svcs., 1990; pres. Forbes-Richardson Ltd., 1990—, mgmt. cons., 1990; owner, editor Adams-Forbes Pub. Co., Detroit. Pub.: (poetry) I Am, 1997. Coordinator Social Svc. United Found. Dr., Lafayette local office 1985, Social Svc. Black United Fund Dr. 1987, speaker Nat. Polit. Congress Black Women, 1986; student project coord. Wayne County Community Coll., Wayne County Dept. Social Svcs., 1989; coord. scholarship project Mary Holmes Coll. Spirit of Detroit Leadership award, 1985. Mem. Am. Pub. Welfare Assn. (planning com. 1986), Am. Legion Aux. Avocations: reading, sewing, billiards.

FORBEY, JOHNATHAN DAVID, psychology professor; b. Evansville, Ind., May 25, 1972; s. David Forbey and Linda Ingram. BS in Psychology, Ind. U., 1994; MA in Clin. Psychology, Kent State U., Ohio, 1996; PhD in clin. Psychology, Kent State U., 2001. Post-doctoral rsch. assoc. Kent State U., Kent, Ohio, 2001—04; asst. prof. of clin. psychology Ball State U., Muncie, Ind., 2004—. Cons. editor Assessment, 2004—. Author: (test monograph) A Critical Item Set for the MMPI-A, Non-gendered Norms for the MMPI-2; contbr. articles to profl. jours., chapters to books. Mem.: APA, Soc. for Personality Assessment, Alpha Lambda Delta, Phi Eta Sigma, Golden Key, Phi Beta Kappa, Psi Chi. Office: Department of Psychological Science NQ 121 - Ball State University Muncie IN 47306 Office Phone: 765-285-3460.

FORCE, ROBERT, law educator; b. Phila., Aug. 11, 1934; s. Charles and Dora (Woloshin) F.; m. Ruth Morris, Aug. 18, 1962; children: Joshua Simon, Seth Daniel. BS, Temple U., 1955, LL.B., 1958; postgrad., U. Adelaide, 1958-59; LL.M., NYU, 1960. Bar: Pa. 1961. Law clk. to presiding justice Pa. Ct. Common Pleas., Phila., 1960-61, U.S. Dist. Ct., Phila., 1961-62; instr. Temple U., Phila., 1960-61; assoc. Kleinbard, Bell & Brecker, Phila., 1963-64; asst. prof. Ind. U. Law Sch., Indpls., 1964-67, assoc. prof., 1968; prof. Tulane U., New Orleans, 1969—, Thomas Pickles prof. law, 1979-89, Niels F. Johnsen prof. maritime law, 1989—, acting dean, 1977-78. Dir. emeritus Tulane Maritme Law Ctr. Co-author: Hall's Criminal Law, 1993, Admiralty and Maritime Law: Cases, Notes and Text, vols. 1 and 2, 1997, Marine Pollution: Conventions, Statutes, Cases and Text, 1998, (with M. Norris) The Law of Seamen, 5th edit., 2003, (with M. Norris) The Law of Maritime Personal Injuries, 2004, Admiralty and Maritime Law, 2005. Fulbright fellow, 1958-59 Mem. ABA, Beta Gamma Sigma, Omicron Delta Kappa Home: 1038 Eleonore St New Orleans LA 70115-4311 Office: 6329 Freret St Ste 255 New Orleans LA 70118-6231 Business E-Mail: rforce@law.tulane.edu.

FORCE, RONALD WAYNE, librarian; b. Sioux City, Iowa, Sept. 7, 1941; s. Robert N. and Madeline (Heine) F.; m. Jo Ellen Hitch, May 31, 1964; children: Emily, Alicia. BS, Iowa State U., 1963; MA, U. Minn., 1968; MS, Ohio State U., 1975. Asst. to head dept. librs. Ohio State U., Columbus, 1968-70, head engring. librs., 1970-72, head edn./psychology libr., 1972-79; asst. dir. pub. svcs. Wash. State U. Librs., Pullman, 1979-82; asst. sci. libr. U. Idaho Libr., Moscow, 1982-84, pub. svcs. libr., 1984-85, humanities libr., 1985-88, assoc. dean libr. svcs., 1988-91, dean libr. svcs., 1991—. Mem. adv. coun. Libr. Svcs. and Constrn. Act. Author: Guide to Literature on Biomedical Engineering, 1972; contbr. articles to profl. jours. Mem. Sacajawea Coun. Campfire Bd., 1980-85, mem. Pullman Dist. Campfire Com., fin. com., 1980-82, chair, 1983-84, treas., 1985, Sacajawea County Self-Study Com., 1986; mem. adv. bd. N.W. Net Info. Resources, 1994-95, 2000—; mem. Idaho Network Adv. Com., 1993-95; mem. LSCA Adv. Coun., 1989-95; mem. Libraries Linking Idaho Bd., 2000—. Mem. ALA, Idaho Libr. Assn. (2d v.p. 1997-98, 1st v.p. 1998-99, pres. 1999-2000). Home: 545 N Blaine St Moscow ID 83843-3626 Office Phone: 208-885-6534.

FORCHESKIE, CARL S., former apparel company executive; b. Shamokin, Pa., Feb. 3, 1927; s. John A. and Helen F.; m. Barbara Ann Pierz; children from previous marriage: Carl, Gail, Caroline Karen. BA, Pa. State U., 1951. Mgr. Coopers & Lybrand, 1951-62; cons. U.S. Dept. Treasury, 1962-63; chief fin. officer Loral Corp., 1963-69; exec. v.p. Salant Corp., N.Y.C., 1969-81, pres., chief exec. officer, 1981-85; ret., 1985. Mem. Planning Bd. Hastings-on-Hudson, N.Y. Served with AUS, 1945-46. Mem. AICPA, N.Y. State Soc. CPAs, Fin. Execs. Inst., Am. Apparel Mfrs. Assn., St. Andrews Golf Club, Union League, Paupack Hills Golf and Country Club. Roman Catholic. Home: 101 Beechwood Ln Greentown PA 18426-9052

FORD, ALMA REGINA, retired union official, educator; b. Owings, W.Va., Oct. 4, 1939; d. Charles Feathers and Pearl (Costello) Ford. AB, Fairmont State Coll., 1960; MA, W.Va. U., 1964, Ball State U., 1984; postgrad., Sorbonne. Cert. counselor. Tchr., Ohio, 1961—78, 1961—78, 1961—78, 1961—78, 1961—78, 1961—78, 1961—78; v.p., dep. rep. Dept. Def. Dependents Schs.-Europe; negotiator Overseas Fedn. Tchrs., 1978—80; tchr. Zweibrucken, Germany, 1980—, counselor, 1997; ret., 1999. Recipient Sustained Superior/Performance award, Dept. Army, 1972—76, Exceptional Performance award, 1984; NDEA fellow, 1968. Mem.: LWV, AARP, AAUW, Marion County Ret. Tchrs. Assn., W.Va. Sheriff's Assn., Overseas Fedn. Tchrs., Am. Fedn. Tchrs., Speech Assn. Am., Nat. Assn. Ret. People, Nat. Coun. Tchrs. English, Nat. Assn. Ret. Fed. Employees, Zweibrucken Alumnus Assn., Fairmont State Coll. Alumnus Assn., Ret. Eagles Club, W.Va. Travelers Club, Moose, Elks, Eagles Ladies Aux., Am. Legion Ladies Aux., VFW Ladies Aux., Alpha Psi Omega, Phi Delta Kappa. Home: 13 Eldora St Fairmont WV 26554-7967 Office Phone: 304-534-4091.

FORD, ANDREW THOMAS, academic administrator; b. Cambridge, Mass., May 22, 1944; s. Francis Lawler and Eleanor (Vahey) F.; m. Anne M. Monahan, July 2, 1966; 1 dau., Lauren Elizabeth. BA, Seton Hall U., 1966; MA, U. WIs., 1968; PhD, U. Wis., 1971. Asst. prof. history Stockton State Coll., Pomona, N.J., 1971-72, asst. to v.p. for acad. affairs, 1972-74; acting dir. Nat. Materials Devel. Ctr. for French and Portuquese, Bedford, N.H., 1976-77; acad. programs coordinator N.H. Coll. and Univ. Council, Manchester, 1975-78; v.p. acad. affairs R.I. Sch. Design, Providence, 1978-81; dean Allegheny Coll., Meadville, Pa., 1981-93, provost, 1983-93; pres. Wabash Coll., Crawfordsville, Ind., 1993—. Mem. adv. bd. Marine Bank, 1987-93; founding mem. Commonwealth Partnership. Author: (with R. Chait) Beyond Traditional Tenure, 1982; mem. editl. bd. Liberal Edn., 2000—. Bd. dirs. Vis. Nurse Assn., Providence, 1979-81, Allegheny Summer Music Festival, Meadville, 1981-89, Meadville Med. Ctr., 1985-87; bd. incorporators Spencer Hosp., 1981-85; mem. Nat. Com. on U.S.-China Rels., 1986—; trustee Higher Learning Commn. North Ctrl. Assn. Schs. and Colls., 2002—; dir. Crawfordsville Main St. Program, 2001—. Democrat. Home: 400 E Pike St Crawfordsville IN 47933-2520 Office: Wabash Coll Office of Pres Crawfordsville IN 47933 Office Phone: 765-361-6221. E-mail: forda@wabash.edu.

FORD, ANN K., lawyer; b. Cleve., July 12, 1954; BA, Georgetown Univ., 1976; JD, Duke Univ., 1980. Bar: DC 1981, NY 1987. Ptnr., nat. chair Trademark, Copyright and Media Practice Group DLA Piper Rudnick Gray Cary US LLP. Contbr. articles to profl. jours. Mem.: ABA, Internat. Trademark Assn. Office: DLA Piper Rudnick Gray Cary US LLP 1200 19th St NW Washington DC 20036-2412 Office Phone: 202-861-3920. Office Fax: 202-689-7540. Business E-Mail: ann.ford@dlapiper.com.

FORD, ANNA MARIA, language educator; b. Starachowice, Poland, Aug. 17, 1940; arrived in U.S., 1954; d. Antoni Niedzwiedzki and Wanda Gluszkiewicz; married; 1 child, Alexandra Joanna Paszowski. BA, Wayne State U., 1963, MA, 1970. Cert. secondary edn. tchr. French, Spanish, English Mich., SC, advanced placement French tchr. SC, tchr. adolescence young adulthood/English lang. arts. Tchr. French and Spanish Ford Mid. Sch., Highland Park, Mich., 1965-66; tchr. fgn. lang. dept. Highland Park Cmty. HS, 1966-97, head fgn. lang. dept., 1968-70, 73-78, lang. arts facilitator, 1991-94; owner, founder Horizons-Internat., Grosse Pointe Park, Mich., 1993-97; dist.-wide lang. cons./coord. Highland Park Pub. Schs., 1994-97; Spanish, French and English lang. tchr. Georgetown (S.C.) County Sch. Dist., 1997—. Ind. contractor, cons. Langs. and Svcs. Agy., 1993—; assessor, field study, tchr. performance lang. arts Nat. Bd. Profl. Tchg. Stds., Mich., 1994; scorer writing proficiency assessments Mich. Dept. Edn., 1994—97, trainer of tchrs., 1995, trainer of trainers, 1995—97, elem. and secondary content literacy com., 1995—; instrnl./profl. devel. task force Mid. Cities Assn., Lansing, Mich., 1995—97; mem. North Ctrl. Accreditation Evaluation Teams, 1970—97; cons. Coastal Area Writing Project, SC, 1998—; adept team evaluator, asst. tng. evaluator, SC, 1999—; advisor H.S. yearbook Polar Bear, 1985—86. Editor: (newsletter) Happenings, 1977—79, Mich. Writing Assessment News, 1994—97. Bd. dirs. Friends of Polish Art, Mich., 1995—97, French Inst. Mich., Southfield, 1985—97. Named Tchr. of Yr., Howard Adult Ctr., Georgetown, SC, 2005; recipient Big E award, Josten's Printing Divsn., 1986, cert. appreciation for participation in Classrooms of Tomorrow program, Mich. Gov., 1990. Mem.: AAUW, Alliance Francaise (Detroit/Grosse Pointe/Charleston), Alpha Mu Gamma. Roman Catholic. Avocations: travel, sailing, skiing, literature, music. Home: 38 Wexford Ln River Club Pawleys Island SC 29585-7614 Office: Horizons Internat 38 Wexford Ln Pawleys Island SC 29585-7614 Office Phone: 843-546-0219. Home Fax: 843-237-5352. Personal E-mail: anoushka@earthlink.net.

FORD, BARBARA JEAN, librarian, educator; b. Dixon, Ill., Dec. 5, 1946; BA magna cum laude with honors, Ill. Wesleyan U., 1968; MA in Internat. Rels., Tufts U., 1969; MS in Libr. Sci., U. Ill., 1973. Dir. Soybean Insect Rsch. Info. Ctr. Ill. Natural History Survey, Urbana, 1973-75; from asst. to assoc. prof. U. Ill., Chgo., 1975-84, asst. documents libr., 1975-79, documents libr., dept. head, 1979-84, acting audiovisual libr., 1983-84; asst. dir. pub. svcs. Trinity U., San Antonio, 1984-86, assoc. prof., assoc. dir., 1986-91, acting dir. librs., 1989, 91; prof., dir. univ. libr. svcs. Va. Commonwealth U., Richmond, 1991-98; asst. commr. Chgo. Pub. Libr., 1998—2002; dir., disting. prof. Mortenson Ctr. Internat. Libr. Programs, U. Ill., Urbana, 2003—. Women's re-entry adv. bd. U. Ill., Chgo., 1980-82, student affairs com., 1978-80, student admissions, records, coll. rels. com., 1981-84, univ. senate, 1976-78, 82-84, chancellor's libr. coun. svcs. com. 1984, campus lectrs. com. 1982-83; admissions interviewer for prospective students Trinity U., 1987-91, reader for internat. affairs theses, 1985-91, libr. self-study com., 1985-86, internat. affairs com., 1986-91, inter-Am. studies com., 1986-91, faculty senate, 1987-90; libr. working group U.S./Mex. Commn. Cultural Coop., 1990; presenter in field Contbr. articles to profl. jours. Bd. dirs. Friends of San Antonio Pub. Libr., 1989-91; adv. com. chair Office for Libr. Pers. Resources, 1994-95; steering com. Virtual Libr. Va., 1994-98, chair user svcs. com., 1995-96. Celia M. Howard fellow Tufts U., 1969; sr. fellow UCLA Grad. Sch. Libr. and Info. Sci., 1993. Mem. ALA (conf. program com. 1985-91, libr. edn. assembly 1983-84, membership com. 1978-79, status of women in librarianship com. 1983-85, exec bd., 1996-99, Lippincott Award Jury 1979-80, Shirley Olofson Meml. award 1977), ALA Coun. (at-large councilor 1985-89, chpt. councilor Ill. Libr. Assn. 1980-84, com. on coms. 1987-88, spl. coun. orientation com. 1982-83, ALA exec. bd., 1996-99, pres.- elect 1996-97, pres. 1997-98), Assn. Coll. and Rsch. Librs. (bd. dirs. 1989-92, pres.-elect 1989-90, pres. 1990-91, publs. com. 1990-91, conf. program planning 1990-91), Nat. Assn. State Univs. and Land Grant Colls. (commn. info. tech. 1992-94), Internat. Fedn. Libr. Assns. and Instns. (sec. ofcl. pubs. sect., gen. info. com. 1985 conf., moderator Latin Am. seminar on ofcl. pubs. 1991, univ. and other rsch. librs. sect. standing com. 1999—, governing bd. 2005—), Spl. Librs. Assn. (program com. 1976-77, 80-82, publicity com. 1977-79, chair 1978-79, chair spl. projects com. 1981-82, sec./treas. divsn. social sci. internat. affairs sect. 1984-86), Assn. Libr. Info. Sci. Edn. (chair local arrangements conf. planning com. 1988, 92), Ill. Libr. Assn. (chair election com. 1976-77, exec. bd. 1978-79, 80-84, bd. govt. documents round table 1976-79, chair 1978-79, long range planning com. 1980-84), Tex. Libr. Assn. (pubs. com. 1985-87, legis. com. 1986-87, judge best of exhibits award 1987, task force Amigos Fellowship 1990, del. conf. on librs. and info. svcs., 1991), Va. Libr. Assn. (ad hoc. com. distance learning 1992), Va. State Libr. and Archives (Va. libr. and info. svcs. task force 1991-93, steering com. Arbuthnot lecture 1992-93, coop. continuing edn. adv. com. 1992-94), VIVA (steering com. 1994-98), Chgo. Libr. Club (2d v.p. 1983-84), Richmond Acad. Libr. Consortium (v.p. 1991-92, pres. 1992-93), Beta Phi Mu, Phi Kappa Phi, Phi Alpha Theta, Kappa Delta Pi. Office Phone: 217-244-1898. E-mail: bjford@uiuc.edu.

FORD, BETTY ANN (ELIZABETH ANN FORD), former First Lady of the United States, health facility executive; b. Chicago, Apr. 8, 1918; d. William Stephenson and Hortence (Neahr) Bloomer; m. to William G. Warren (div. 1947); m. Gerald R. Ford (38th Pres. U.S.), Oct. 15, 1948; children: Michael Gerald, John Gardner, Steven Meigs, Susan Elizabeth. Studied, Bennington Sch. of Dance, 1936, 37; studied with Martha Graham, Graham Sch. of Dance, N.Y.C., 1937; LL.D. (hon.), U. Mich., 1976. Dancer Martha Graham Concert Group, N.Y.C., 1939-41; fashion dir. Herpolscheimer's Dept. Store, Grand Rapids, Mich., 1943-48; dance instr. Grand Rapids, 1932-48; First Lady of the United States, 1974—77. Co-founder Susan G. Komen Foundation, 1982; chmn., co-founder The Betty Ford Ctr., Rancho Mirage, Calif., 1982—. Author: autobiography The Times of My Life, 1978, Betty: A Glad Awakening, 1987. Bd. dirs. Nat. Arthritis Found. (hon.); trustee Martha Graham Dance Ctr., Eisenhower Med. Ctr., Rancho Mirage; hon. chmn. Palm Springs Desert Mus.; nat. trustee Nat. Symphony Orch.; bd. dirs. The Lambs, Libertyville, Ill. Named to Mich. Women's Hall of Fame, 1987; recipient Presidential Medal of Freedom, 1991, Congressional Gold Medal, 1999, Woodrow Wilson Pub. Svc. award, 2003. Republican. Episcopalian. Home: PO Box 1560 Rancho Mirage CA 92270 Office: Betty Ford Center 39000 Bob Hope Dr Rancho Mirage CA 92270

FORD, BURCH TRACY, headmaster; BA, Boston U.; MSW, Simmons Coll.; EdM, Harvard U. Former teacher and sch. counselor Groton Sch., 1978—88; former teacher & dean of students Milton Acad., 1988—93; head of sch. Miss Porter's Sch., Conn., 1993—. Former pres. Nat. Coalition of Girls Schools; former chair Commn. on Independent Schools, New England Assn. of Schools and Colleges; bd. mem. Nat. Assn. of Principals of Schools for Girls. Bd. mem. Chewonki Found., Nutmeg Big Brothers Big Sisters Found. Office: Miss Porter's Sch 60 Main St Farmington CT 06032*

FORD, CARL W., JR., consulting firm executive, former federal agency administrator; b. Hot Springs, Ark., 1943; married. BA in Asian Studies, Fla. State U., 1968, MA in East Asian Studies. China analyst CIA, 1974—78, congl. fgn. affairs fellow, 1978; legis. asst. for arms control and fgn. policy Office of Senator John Glenn; staff mem. Senate Com. on Fgn. Rels., 1979—81; fgn. policy and def. issues dir. Office of Senator John Glenn, 1981—84; fgn. policy and def. advisor John Glenn Presl. Campaign, 1984; nat. intelligence officer for East Asia CIA, 1985—91; prin. dep. asst. sec. of def. for internat. security affairs U.S. Dept. Def., 1989, acting asst. sec., 1991, dep. asst. sec. for Near East and South Asian affairs, 1991—93; ret. CIA, 1993; asst. sec. for intelligence & rsch. U.S. Dept. State, Washington, 2001—03; exec. v.p. Cassidy & Associates, Washington, 2003—. With U.S. Army, 1963—66, Vietnam, with U.S. Army, 1969—74. Office: Cassidy & Associates 700 13th St NW Ste 400 Washington DC 20005

FORD, CECILIA S., federal agency administrator; Grad., U. Va. Atty. Bus. and Adminstrv. Law Divsn. Health and Human Svcs. Office Gen. Counsel; air deartmental. appeals bd. U.S. Dept. Health and Human Svcs., Washington, 1999—, also bd. dirs. Office: US Dept Health and Human Svcs Departmental Appeals Bd 200 Independence Ave SW Rm 637-D Washington DC 20201

FORD, CHARLES NATHANIEL, otolaryngologist, educator; b. NYC, June 25, 1940; s. Charles Nathaniel and Marie (Casa) F.; children: C. David, Brian C.; m. Sharon L. James, Feb. 3, 1990; stepchildren: Scott James, Julie James. BA, SUNY, Binghamton, 1961; MD, U. Louisville, 1965. Intern and resident Henry Ford Hosp., Detroit, 1965-70, staff, 1970-71; with Gundersen Clinic, LaCrosse, Wis., 1973-81; chief otolaryngology Middleton VA Hosp., Madison, Wis., 1982-94; prof. otolaryngol. divsn. dept. surgery U. Wis., Madison, 1981-93, chmn. otolaryngol. divsn. dept. surgery, 1993—. Mem.-at-large med. bd. U. Wis. Ctr. for Health Scis., 1989-91, sec., 1992-93, v.p., 1994-95, pres. med. staff, chair med. bd. 1996-98; DeWeese lectr. U. Oreg., 1994; Manion Meml. lectr. Ind. U., 1995; Hough lectr. U. Okla., 1996; Sartian lectr. U. Tex., 1998; keynote lectr. Brit. Voice Assn., 2000, Voice Symposium Australia, 2002, G. Paul Moore lectr. Voice Found., Phila., 2003. Author, editor: Phonosurgery: Assessment and Surgical Management of Voice Disorders, 1991; mem. editl. bd.: Jour. Voice, Otolaryngol. Head and Neck Surgery, Laryngoscope, Microsurgery; author editor numerous sci. papers, chpts. and abstracts. Maj. USAF, 1971-73. Avalon Found. scholar, 1962-63; named to Best Drs. in Am., Woodward/White, Inc., 1991—. Fellow ACS, Am. Laryngol., Rhinol. and Otolog. Soc., Am. BronchoEsophagological Assn. (past pres.), Am. Laryngol. Assn., Am. Soc. for Head and Neck Surgery, Am. Acad. Otolaryngology, Head and Neck Surgery (honor award 1992); mem. AMA, Soc. Univ. Otolaryngologists-Head and Neck Surgeons (past pres.), Internat. Assn. Phonosurgeons, Am. Speech-Lang.-Hearing Assn. Democrat. Unitarian Universalist. Avocations: tennis, golf, theater, art, music. Office: U Wis Ctr Health Sci 600 Highland Ave Madison WI 53792-0001 Office Phone: 608-263-0192.

FORD, CHARLES REED, state legislator; b. Tulsa, Aug. 2, 1931; s. Juell Reed and Marzee (Lane) F.; m. Patricia Ann Ojers, 1951; children: Christopher Reed, Roger Howard, Karin Rebecca, Robyn Ann. Student, Okla. State U., 1949-51. Engr., aide U.S. Corps. Engrs., 1951-53; designer SunrayDX, 1953-55; asst. mktg. engr. Tidewater Oil Co., 1955-58; real estate investor Charles Ford Co., 1958—. Pres. Gothic Investments, Inc.,1963; mem. Okla. Ho. of Reps., 1967-81, minority floor leader, 1970-76, asst. minority leader, 1981; mem. Okla. Senate, 1981—, caucus chmn., 1982-83, caucus whip, 1984-86, asst. minority leader, 1987-88, minority leader, 1991-92; mem. Southwest region adv. com. Nat. Park Service, 1982-88. Trustee Tulsa Expn. and Fair Corp., 1955-67; vice chmn. Tulsa Met. Area Planning Commn., 1960-65; former officer Tulsa County Young Rep.; del. Rep. Nat. Conv., 1972, 84, 88; bd. govs. Spartan Sxh. Aeronautics, 1993—. Served with USNR, 1948-53. Named Legislator of Yr. Rep. Legis. Assoc., 1988, Outstanding Legis. Leader Nat. Conf. State Legislators, 1992. Mem. Jaycees (Okla. pres. 1959-60, U.S. v.p. 1960-61, internat. v.p. 1963, chmn. trustees War Meml. Fund 1963—), Nat. Petroleum Coun., Am. Inst. Architects (pres.'s award, 1998), Okla. Heritage (disting. svc. award, 1999, gov.'s Art award, 1999), Alpha Sigma Eta. Republican. Office: Okla Senate Rm 527A Oklahoma City OK 73105

FORD, CHARLES WILLARD, medical educator; b. Bloomsburg, Pa., Oct. 28, 1938; s. John Willard and Pauline Teresa Ford; m. Barbara Marie Hanawalt, June 6, 1959; children: Lane(dec.), Lori, Lanae, Lanette. BA, Taylor U., 1960; BS, Pa. State U., 1961, MEd, 1962; PhD, SUNY, Buffalo, 1970; postgrad., U. Mich., 1976—77. HS tchr., 1961-64; mem. faculty Erie CC, 1965-70; fgn. svc. officer Peace Corps, Ghana, 1970-72; various positions Sch. Health Related Professions, SUNY, Buffalo, 1972-75, 77-79, assoc. dean Sch. Health Related Professions, 1978—79; with Grand Rapids (Mich.) Med. Edn. Ctr., 1975-77; dean U. Health Scis./Chgo. Med. Sch., 1979—80; dean undergrad. colls. U. New Eng., Biddeford, Maine, 1982-84, pres., 1984-91, prof. health sci., 1983—. Active in accreditation and curriculum program develop in 40 states and 6 countries; vis. prof. Israel, Tel Aviv, Jerusalem, Haifa, spring, 1999—2004. Author (with M. K. Morgan): (book) Teaching in the Health Professions, Clinical Education for the Allied Health Professions; contbr. articles to profl jours. Pres. Maine Higher Edn. Coun., 1987—88, Maine Ind. Coll. Assn., 1988—89; bd. govs. Am. Assn. Coll. Osteo. Medicine, 1984—91. Recipient Study Exch., Rotary, Germany and Turkey, 1995. Mem.: NEA (life), Assn. Schs. Allied Health Profls. (life), Am. Assn. Higher Edn. (life). Office: U New Eng Biddeford ME 04005 Office Phone: 207-283-0171. Business E-Mail: cford@une.edu.

FORD, CHRISTOPHER ASHLEY, federal official, lawyer; s. Ashley Lloyd and Barbara Hill Ford; m. Jennifer Lynn Davis-Ford, June 27, 1992; 1 child, Stella-Grace Annabelle. AB summa cum laude, Harvard Coll., 1989; PhD, Oxford U., 1992; JD, Yale Law Sch., 1995. Bar: 4th Cir. Ct. Appeals 1996, Va. 1996, DC 1998, Ct. Veterans Appeals 1997. Assoc. Shea and Gardner, Washington, 1995—97; asst. counsel Pres. Intelligence Oversight Bd., Washington, 1996; counsel spl. investigation Senate Govtl. Affairs Com., Washington, 1997, chief investigative counsel, 1999; nat. security advisor for Senator Susan Collins, Washington, 1998; chief coun./staff dir. Permanent Subcommittee Investigations, Washington, 2000; minority counsel/gen. counsel Senate Select Com. Intelligence, Washington, 2001—03; prin. dep. asst. sec. US State Dept., Washington, 2003—.

FORD, CLARENCE QUENTIN, mechanical engineer, educator; b. Glenwood, N.Mex., Aug. 6, 1923; s. Clarence Noel and Elsie May (Jones) F.; m. Ruth Madge McKinney, June 11, 1950; children— Glenn Mac, Dabney Ann. BS, U.S. Mcht. Marine Acad., 1944; BS in Mech. Engring., N.Mex. State U., 1949; MS in Mech. Engring., U. Mo., 1950; PhD, Mich. State U., 1959. Registered profl. engr. Inst. U. Mo., 1949-50; instr. Wash. State U., 1950-53, asst. prof., 1953-56; instr. Mich. State U., 1956-59; prof. N.Mex. State U., Las Cruces, 1959-88, head dept. mech. engring., 1960-70, assoc. dean engring., 1974-80, 81-88, dean engring., 1980-81, prof. and assoc. dean emeritus, 1988—; prin. Ford & Assocs., 1964—. Mem. N.Mex. Bd. Registration Profl. Engrs. and Land Surveyors, 1978-88, chmn., 1980-81, 86-87, mem. emeritus, 1989—; mem. N.Mex. State Hwy. Commn., 1989-95, sec., 1991-95. Editor: Space Technology and Earth Problems, Vol. 23 Sci. and Tech. Series, 1969 Served to lt. USNR, 1942-46 Fellow AAAS; mem. ASME, Am. Soc. Engring. Edn., Nat. Coun. Examiners for Engring. and Surveying (v.p. 1986-88, Disting. Svc. award 1989, Disting. Svc. award with spl. commendation 1990), N.Mex. Soc. Profl. Engrs. (Outstanding Engr. 1964), Masons, York Rite, Kiwanis, Sigma Xi, Phi Kappa Phi, Pi Tau Sigma, Tau Beta Pi, Pi Mu Epsilon. Presbyterian. Home: 1985 Crescent Dr Las Cruces NM 88005-3300 Office Phone: 505-524-6753. E-mail: Chapache@aol.com.

FORD, DANIEL (DANIEL FRANCIS FORD), writer; b. Nov. 2, 1931; s. Patrick Joseph and Anne Theresa Ford; m. Sarah Lansing Paine; 1 child, Katharine Serena. BA, U. N.H., 1954; postgrad., U. Manchester, Eng., 1954-55. Reporter Overseas Weekly, Frankfurt, Germany, 1958; asst. editor N.H. Profiles mag., Portsmouth, 1959-60; publs. editor U. N.H., 1961-68; freelance writer Durham, N.H., 1969—. Corr. The Nation, South Vietnam, 1964; contbg. editor Air & Space/Smithsonian Mag., 1994—; pub. Warbird's Forum, 1997—. Author: Now Comes Theodora, 1965, Incident at Muc Wa (transl. in Dutch, filmed as Go Tell the Spartans), 1967, The High Country Illuminator, 1971, The Country Northward, 1976, Flying Tigers: Claire Chennault and the American Volunteer Group, 1991, Glen Edwards: The Diary of a Bomber Pilot, 1998, Remains, 2000, The Only War We've Got: Early Days in South Vietnam, 2001, Michael's War, 2003; editor: The Lady and the Tigers, 2002; contbr. Wall St. Jour., 2001—. With U.S. Army, 1956-57. Recipient award of excellence Aviation-Space Writers, 1992; Fulbright fellow U. Manchester, 1954-55, Verville fellow Nat. Air & Space Mus., 1989-90; Stern Found. Mag. Writers grantee, 1964; resident scholar U. N.H., 1996—. Mem. Authors guild, Met. Opera Guild, Phi Beta Kappa, Phi Kappa Phi. Office: 433 Bay Rd Durham NH 03824-3439

FORD, DEXTER, retired insurance company executive; b. Utica, N.Y., Nov. 18, 1917; s. David E. and Anna Mae (Dexter) F.; m. Jean Brand McGowan, Nov. 1, 1944; children: David K., Dexter T., Nancy E. BS, St. Lawrence U., 1939. With Aetna Life & Casualty Co., Hartford, Conn., 1946—, v.p. mktg., 1968-76, v.p. personal ins. dept., 1976-80. Chmn. bd. mgmt. YMCA, 1978-80. Served to lt. (s.g.) USNR, 1941-45. Recipient St. Lawrence U. Alumni citation, 1978 Mem. St. Lawrence U. Alumni Assn. (pres. 1974-75) Republican. Congregationalist (chmn. bd. trustees 1970). Home: Apt 213 156 Lawrence St Saratoga Springs NY 12866-1351

FORD, DONALD HERBERT, psychologist, educator; b. Sioux City, Iowa, Aug. 15, 1926; s. Herbert Owen and Esther (Sanow) F.; m. Carol Clark, May 30, 1948; children— Russell, Martin, Douglas, Cameron. BS, Kans. State U., 1948; MS, 1951; PhD, Pa. State U., 1955. Counselor Kans. State U., 1948-52; asst. prof. psychology Pa. State U., University Park, 1955-64, assoc. prof., 1964-67, assoc. prof. human devel., 1967-72, prof. human. devel., 1972—, prof. biobehavioral health, 1992—. Asst. dir. div. counseling, 1956-59, dir., 1959-67; dean Coll. Human Devel., 1967-77, head dept. Communications Disorders, 1988-89, head biobehavioral health, 1992. Author: Systems of Psychotherapy; A Comparative Study, 1963, Humans as Self-Constructing Living Systems, 1987, 2d edit., 1992, Developmental Systems Theory, 1992, Contemporary Models of Psychotherapy, 1998. Served with USAAF, 1944-45. Mem. AAAS, Am. Psychol. Assn., Am. Psychol. Soc., Ea. Psychol. Assn. Home: 130 Slab Cabin Rd State College PA 16801-6971 Office: Penn State U Coll Health & Human Devel University Park PA 16802 E-mail: dhf6@psu.edu. *My basic values are rooted in the "teaching by example" of my parents, serving the objectives of being of service to others as well as to self, utilizing a strong, caring family unit as the best cornerstone of psychological, social, and economic health. My basic professional goal is to help harness the fruits of technological advances, resulting from the intensive application of the principle of specialization, to the evolution of humanistic societies designed to serve people as open, living systems. This requires a new scientific model of Man as a coherent unit, enabling us to synthesize the fruits of analytical science and to put "Humpty Dumpty" back together again as a person with purposes and values as well as productive potential.*

FORD, EILEEN OTTE (MRS. GERARD W. FORD), modeling agency executive; b. N.Y.C., Mar. 25, 1922; d. Nathaniel and Loretta Marie (Laine) Otte; m. Gerard William Ford, Nov. 20, 1944; children: Margaret (Mrs. Robert Craft), Gerard William, M. Katie (Mrs. Andre Balazs), A. Lacey (Mrs. John Williams). BS, Barnard Coll., 1943. Stylist Elliot Clarke Studio, N.Y.C., 1943-44, William Becker Studio, 1945; copywriter Arnold Constable, N.Y.C., 1945-46; reporter Tobe Coburn, 1946; co-founder Ford Model Agy., N.Y.C., 1946—, now chmn. bd. Author: Eileen Ford's Model Beauty, Secrets of the Model's World, A More Beautiful You in 21 Days, Beauty Now and Forever, 1977. Bd. dirs. London Philharmonic, 1948— . Recipient Harpers Bazaar award for promotion internat. understanding., Woman of Yr. in Advt. award, 1983 Office: Ford Modeling Agy 142 Greene St New York NY 10012-3236

FORD, FAITH, actress; b. Alexandria, La., Sept. 14, 1964; d. Charles and Pat F., m. Robert Nottingham, 1989 (div. 1996); m. Campion Murphy, June 27, 1998. Actress: (films) You Talkin' to Me, 1987, For Goodness Sake, 1993, North, 1994, Sometimes They Come Back...For More, 1999, The Pacifier, 2005; (TV series) One Life to Live, 1983, Another World, 1983-84, Popcorn Kid, 1987, Murphy Brown, 1988-97 (Emmy nominee Supporting Actress - Comedy Series, 1989, 90, 91, 94), Maggie Winters, 1998, The Norm Show, 1999, Hope and Faith, 2003-; (TV films) If It's Tuesday, It Still Must Be Belgium, 1987, Poisoned by Love: The Kern County Murders, 1993, A Weekend in the Country, 1996, Night Visitors, 1996, Her Desperate Choice, 1996, Moms on Strike, 2002; TV appearances include Hardcastle & McCormick, 1985, Webster, 1986, Scarecrow and Mrs. King, 1986, Cagney & Lacey, 1986, Thirtysomething, 1987, 88, Murder She Wrote, 1990, The Hidden Room, 1993, (voice) Family Guy, 2000.*

FORD, FORD BARNEY, retired federal official; b. Norton, Va., Nov. 19, 1922; s. William Zachary and Annis Louvinia (Ford) Godbey; m. Norma Isabel Lentz, Jan. 16, 1945; children: Robert Barney, Jack T. (dec.). Student, Va. Mil. Inst., Lexington, 1942-43; BS, U. Calif., Berkeley, 1948; LLD (hon.), Huston Tillotson Coll., 1985. Registered indsl. and safety engr. Acting postmaster, Bishop, Calif., 1951-54; adminstrv. analyst Calif. Joint Legis. Budget Com., Sacramento, 1955-59; exec. dir. Calif. Senate Fact-Finding Com. on Natural Resources, Sacramento, 1959-67; dep. sec. Calif. Resources Agt., Sacramento, 1967-73; chmn. and mem. Calif. Occupl. Safety and Health Appeals Bd., Sacramento, 1973-78; v.p. Calif. Inst. Indsl. and Govtl. Rels., Sacramento, 1978-81; asst. sec. labor for mine safety and health US Dept. Labor, Arlington, Va., 1981-83, undersec. Washington, 1983-85, acting sec., 1984-85; chmn. Mine Safety and Health Rev. Commn., 1985-92; ret., 1992. Rsch. publs. on fire prevention, geothermal devel. East Wilmington oil field. With U.S. Army, 1943-46, ETO. Decorated Combat Infantryman badge. Mem. DAV, SAR, VFW (comdr. Bishop, Calif. 1948-50), Elks, Masons, Shriners. Methodist. Personal E-mail: fordbarneyford@cs.com.

FORD, GAIL, library administrator; b. Sacramento, Mar. 5, 1952; d. R. Eugene and Jeanne P. Ford; m. Clive Matson, Jan. 15, 1993; 1 child, Ezra John Matson-Ford. AB in Philosophy, Stanford U., 1973. Adminstrv. analyst U. Calif. Berkeley Libr., 1984—; pub. Broken Shadow Publs., Oakland, Calif., 1993—. Pub.: (book) Emptiness That Plays So Rough, 1995, Under a Gibbous Moon, 1996, Squish Boots, 2002. Home: 472 44th St Oakland CA 94609-2136

FORD, GEORGE BURT, retired lawyer; b. South Bend, Ind., Oct. 1, 1923; s. George W. and Florence (Burt) Ford; m. Charlotte Ann Kupferer, June 12, 1948; children: John, Victoria, George, Charlotte. BS in Engring. Law, Purdue U., 1946; LLB, Ind. U., 1949. Bar: Ind. 1949, US Dist. Ct. (no. dist.) Ind. 1949. Assoc. Jones, Obenchain & Butler, South Bend, 1949-52; ptnr. Jones, Obenchain, Ford, Pankow & Lewis, South Bend, 1953-93, of counsel, 1994—2003; ret., 2003. Co-author: (book) Forms for Indiana Corporations, 1967, 2d edit., 1977. With U.S. Army, 1943—45, ETO. Fellow: Am. Coll. Trust and Estate Counsel; mem.: ABA, St. Joseph County Bar Assn. (pres. 1976—77), Ind. Bar Assn., Phi Delta Phi, Phi Gamma Delta.

FORD, GERALD RUDOLPH, JR., 38th President of the United States; b. Omaha, July 14, 1913; s. Gerald R. and Dorothy (Gardner) F.; m. Elizabeth Bloomer, Oct. 15, 1948; children: Michael, John, Steven, Susan. AB, U. Mich., 1935; LL.B., Yale U., 1941; LL.D., Mich. State U., Albion Coll., Aquinas Coll., Spring Arbor Coll. Bar: Mich. 1941. Practiced law at, Grand Rapids, 1941-49; mem. law firm Buchen and Ford; mem. 81st-93d Congresses from 5th Mich. Dist., 1949-74, elected minority leader, 1965; v.p. served under Pres. Richard Nixon Washington, 1973-74; pres. U.S., 1974-77. Del. Interparliamentary Union, Warsaw, Poland, 1959, Belgium, 1961, Bilderberg Group Conf., 1962; mem. internat. adv. coun. Inst. Internat. Studies; bd. dir. Citigroup, Inc. Served as lt. comdr. USNR, 1942-46. Recipient Grand Rapids Jr. C. of C. Distinguished Service award, 1948; Distinguished Service Award as one of ten outstanding young men in U.S. by U.S. Jr. C. of C., 1950; Silver Anniversary All-Am. Sports Illustrated, 1959; Distinguished Congressional Service award Am. Polit. Sci. Assn., 1961, Medal of Freedom, 1999, Congressional Gold Medal, 1999, Profile in Courage award, 2001. Mem. Am., Mich. State, Grand Rapids bar assns., Delta Kappa Epsilon, Phi Delta Phi. Clubs: University (Kent County), Peninsular (Kent County). Lodges: Masons. Republican. Episcopalian. Office: PO Box 927 Rancho Mirage CA 92270-0927

FORD, GORDON BUELL, JR., literature educator, writer; b. Louisville, Sept. 22, 1937; s. Gordon Buell Sr. and Rubye (Allen) F. AB summa cum laude in Classics, Medieval Latin, and Sanskrit, Princeton U., 1959; AM in Classical Philology and Linguistics, Harvard U., 1962, PhD in Linguistics, Slavic and Baltic Langs. and Lits., 1965; postgrad., U. Oslo, 1962-64, U. Sofia, Bulgaria, 1963, U. Uppsala, Sweden, 1963-64, U. Stockholm, 1963-64, U. Madrid, 1963. CPA. Yeager, Ford, and Warren Found. Disting. prof. Indo-European, Classical, Slavic, and Baltic linguistics, Sanskrit, and Medieval Latin Northwestern U., Evanston, Ill., 1965—; Lybrand, Ross Bros., and Montgomery Found. Disting. prof. English and linguistics U. No. Iowa, Cedar Falls, 1972—; sr. exec. v.p. for real estate acctg. fin. mgmt., bd. dirs. The Southeastern Real Estate Co., Inc., Louisville, 1976-93; sr. exec. v.p. reimbursement and rates acctg. fin. mgmt., hosp. acctg. divsn. Humana Inc., The Hosp. Co., Louisville, 1976-93; ret., 1993; bd. dirs. Southeastern Investment Trust, Inc., Louisville, 1976-93; ret., 1993; rsch. prof. The Southeastern Investment Trust, Inc. Rsch. Found., Louisville, 1976—. Vis. prof. Medieval Latin, U. Chgo., 1966—; vis. prof. linguistics U. Chgo., Downtown Ctr., 1966—; prof. English evening divs. Northwestern U., Chgo., 1968-69, prof. anthropology, 1971-72. Author: The Ruodlieb: The First Medieval Epic of Chivalry from Eleventh-Century Germany, 1965, The Ruodlieb: Linguistic Introduction, Latin Text with a Critical Apparatus, and Glossary, 1966, The Ruodlieb: Facsimile Edition, 1965, 3d edit. 1968, Old Lithuanian Texts of the Sixteenth and Seventeenth Centuries with a Glossary, 1969, The Old Lithuanian Catechism of Baltramiejus Vilentas (1579): A Phonological, Morphological, and Syntactical Investigation, 1969, Isidore of Seville's History of the Goths, Vandals, and Suevi, 1966, 2d edit. 1970, The Letters of Saint Isidore of Seville, 1966, 2d edit. 1970, The Old Lithuanian Catechism of Martynas Mazvydas (1547), 1971, others; translator: A Concise Elementary Grammar of the Sanskrit Language with Exercises, Reading Selections, and a Glossary (Jan Gonda), 1966, The Comparative Method in Historical Linguistics (Antoine Meillet), 1967, A Sanskrit Grammar (Manfred Mayrhofer), 1972; contbr. numerous articles to many scholarly jours. Appointed to Hon. Order Ky. Cols. (life). Mem. Linguistic Soc. Am. (life, Sapir life patron), Internat. Linguistic Assn. (life), Societas Linguistica Europaea (charter, life), Am. Philol. Assn. (life), Classical Assn. of the Atlantic States (life), Classical Assn. of the Middle West and South (life), Classical Assn. of N.Eng. (life), Medieval Acad. of Am. (life), Renaissance Soc. of Am. (life), MLA (life), Am. Assn. Tchrs. Slavic and East European Langs. (life), Am. Assn. Advancement Slavic Studies (life), Am. Coun. Tchrs. Russian (life), Assn. for Advancement Baltic Studies (life), Inst. Lithuanian Studies (life), Tchrs. of English to Speakers of Other Langs. (charter, life), SAR (life), Princeton Club (N.Y.C., Chgo.), Princeton Alumni Assn. (Louisville), Harvard Club (N.Y.C., Chgo., Louisville, Lexington, Ky.), Pres.'s Soc. Bellarmine Coll. (life), Louisville Country Club, KC (life), Phi Beta Kappa (life). Baptist. Home: 3619 Brownsboro Road Louisville KY 40207-1863 also: PO Box 2693 Clarksville Br Jeffersonville IN 47131-2693

FORD, H. ROSS, III, real estate company executive; Interim dist. mgr. Grubb & Ellis Cos., N.Y.C., NY; v.p., dist. mgr. Axiom Real Estate Mgmt., Inc., 1993—; pres. TCN Worldwide, Plano, Tex. Office: TCN Worldwide Ste A 2419 Coit Rd Plano TX 75075

FORD, HAROLD EUGENE, consultant, former congressman; b. Memphis, Tenn., May 20, 1945; s. Newton J. and Vera (Davis) F.; m. Dorothy Bowles, Feb. 10, 1969; children: Harold, Newton Jake, Sir Isaac. BS, Tenn. State U., 1967; AA, John Gupton Coll., 1969; MBA, Howard U. Mem. Tenn. Ho. of Reps., 1970-74; mem. 94th-106th Congresses from 9th Tenn. dist., 1975—96, edn. and workforce com., govt. reform and oversight com.; consult., founder The Harold Ford Group, Memphis, 2001—. Ways and means com., subcom. on oversight, mem. subcom. human resources, Dem. whip representing Tenn., La., Miss. during 99th Congress. Bd. dirs. Met. Memphis YMCA affiliated with Alpha Phi Alpha frat.; nat. adv. bd. St. Jude Children's Research Hosp. Named Outstanding Young Man of Year Memphis Jaycees, 1976, Outstanding Young Man of Year Tenn. Jaycees, 1977, Child Advocate of Yr. Child Welfare League Am., 1987. Democrat. Office: The Harold Ford Group 6060 Poplar Ave #150 Memphis TN 38119-0917*

FORD, HAROLD EUGENE, JR., congressman, lawyer; b. Memphis, Tenn., May 11, 1970; s. Harold E. Ford. BA, U. Pa., 1992; JD in Am. History, U. Mich., 1996. Spl. asst. Econ. Devel. Adminstrn., 1993, Clinton & Gore Transition Team, 1992; mem. U.S. Ho. of Reps. from 9th Tenn. dist., 1997—. Aide Senate Budget Com.; mem. Blue Dog Coalition, Com. Edn. & Workforce, Com. Fin. Svcs. Democrat. Baptist. Office: US Ho Reps 325 Cannon Ho Office Bldg Washington DC 20515-4209 also: Dist Office 167 N Main St Ste 369 Memphis TN 38103*

FORD, HARRIET-LYNN, language educator; b. Wichita Falls, Tex., May 27, 1952; d. Wesley Craig and Alice Ann Stallcup; 1 child, Michael Adam Brown; m. John Ceburn Ford Jr., Aug. 20, 1983. BA in English Edn., Okla. Ctrl. State U., 1977, MA in English, 1979. Adj. instr. Pellissippi State Tech. C.C., Knoxville, Tenn., 1989-90, instr. to assoc. prof. English, 1990-99, interim dept. head acad. devel. divsn., 1994-95, program coord. for remedial and devel. English, 1995—. Co-editor, co-author: textbook Preparing for College Writing, 1996, editor, co-author:, 1997, 1999, 2001, 2004. Docent Knoxville Zoo, 1990-97. Mem. AAUP (chpt. pres.), AAUW, Nat. Coun. Tchrs. English. Avocations: reading, celtic music, golf, harp. Office: Pellissippi State Tech CC Hardin Valley Rd Knoxville TN 37933

FORD, HARRISON, actor; b. Chgo., July 13, 1942; m. Mary Marquardt, 1964 (div. 1979); children: Willard, Benjamin; m. Melissa Mathison, 1983 (div. 2004); children: Malcolm, Georgia. Ed., Ripon Coll. Appeared in motion pictures including: Dead Heat on a Merry-Go-Round, 1966, Luv, 1967, The Long Ride Home, 1967, Getting Straight, 1970, Zabriske Point, 1970, American Graffiti, 1973, The Conversation, 1974, Star Wars, 1977, Heroes, 1977, Force 10 From Navarone, 1978, Hanover Street, 1979,More American Graffiti, 1979, The Frisco Kid, 1979, Apocalypse Now, 1979, The Empire Strikes Back, 1980, Raiders of the Lost Ark, 1981, Blade Runner, 1982, Return of the Jedi, 1983, Indiana Jones and the Temple of Doom, 1984, Witness, 1985, Mosquito Coast, 1986, Frantic, 1988, Working Girl, 1988, Indiana Jones and the Last Crusade, 1989, Presumed Innocent, 1990, Regarding Henry, 1991, Patriot Games, 1992, The Fugitive, 1993, Clear and Present Danger, 1994, Sabrina, 1995, A Hundred and One Nights, 1995, Devil's Own, 1996, Air Force One, 1997, Six Days Seven Nights, 1998, Random Hearts, 1999, What Lies Beneath, 2000, K-19: The Widowmaker, 2002, Hollywood Homicide, 2003; appeared in TV movies The Intruders, 1970, Judgement: The Court-Martial of Lt. William Calley, 1975, James A. Michener's Dynasty, 1976, The Possessed, 1977; numerous TV appearances including Ironside, The Mod Squad, The F.B.I., My Friend Tony, Gunsmoke, Kung-Fu, The Virginian, Young Indiana Jones Chronicles.

FORD, IRENE ELAINE, pastor; b. West Union, W.Va., Oct. 6, 1927; d. Clurel Cecil Powell and Lillian Violet Gaskins; m. Claudius Arnold Ford, Jan. 24, 1946 (dec. Oct. 20, 1997); children: Richard Freeman, Michael Leroy. Student, Northern C.C., Weirton, W.Va., W.Va. Wesleyan Coll., 1984—87, Duke Divinity, 1984—89. Ordained deacon United Meth. Ch., 1992. Pastor Bristol Charge United Meth. Ch., Bristol, W.Va., 1983—89, pastor Christ-Owings Charge Shinnston, W.Va., 1989—94, assoc., 1992; pastor Graysville-Washington Lands United Meth. Ch., Moundsville, W.Va., 1994—96, Nessly Chapel United Meth. Ch., New Cumberland, W.Va., 1997—. Parish coord. United Meth. Ch., Bristol, W.Va., 1986—89, Shinnston, W.Va., 1989—94; pres., v.p. WHG dist. United Meth. Women, 1980; coun. mem. Race Track Chaplaincy Am./Mountaineer Race Track, 2005—. Pres. W.Va. Congress Parent Tchr. Orgn., 1975—77; sch. bd. mem. Hancock County, 1979—84. Mem.: W.Va. Ann. Conf. (assoc.; deacon). Methodist. Avocation: family activities.

FORD, JEREMIAH, III, architect; b. Phila., Apr. 22, 1932; s. Jeremiah II and Mary Sterling (Hewitt) F.; m. Judith Oakes Seidler, June 17, 1954 (div. 1973); children: Amanda Hewitt, Katherine Brewster; m. Elizabeth Dana Stewardson, Mar. 1, 1975; children: Elizabeth Connolly, Caroline Thornewill, Dana H. Stewardson. AB, Princeton U., 1954, MFA, 1959. Registered architect, N.J., Mass., Pa., Fla., Del. Designer Harrison and Abramovitz Architects, N.Y.C., 1960-61, Port of N.Y. Authority World Trade Ctr., N.Y.C., 1961-62; archtl. apprentice Kenneth Kassler Architect, Princeton, 1962-64; ptnr. Walker Sander Ford and Kerr Architects, Princeton, 1965-74, Short and Ford Architects, Princeton, 1974-93, Ford Farewell Mills and Gatsch Architects, Princeton, 1993—2004, Ford 3 Architects, Princeton, 2004—. Prin. works include Marriott Hotel and Conf. Ctr., Trenton, N.J. State House, Trenton, Summit (N.J.) City Hall, 1973, Morristown (N.J.) Libr., 1985, Princeton Cmty. Housing, 1982, Cranbury (N.J.) Sr. Housing, 1990, pvt. residences. Capt. USMC, 1954-57, Korea, Japan. Episcopalian. Avocations:

painting, gardening. Home: 820 Pretty Brook Rd Princeton NJ 08540-7532 Office: Ford 3 Architects 32 Nassau St Princeton NJ 08542 Office Phone: 609-924-0043. Personal E-mail: jerryfiii@aol.com. Business E-Mail: jerryf@Ford3.com.

FORD, JOE THOMAS, telephone company executive, former state senator; b. Conway, Ark., June 24, 1937; s. Arch W. and Ruby (Watson) F.; m. Jo Ellen Wilbourn, Aug. 9, 1959; children: Alison, Scott. BS, U. Ark., 1959. With Allied Telephone Co., Little Rock, 1959-83, v.p.-treas., 1963-77, pres., 1977-83, ALLTEL Corp., 1983-87, pres., chief exec. officer, 1987-91, chmn., pres., chief exec. officer, 1991-93, chmn., CEO, 1993—; now chmn. Alltel Corp., Little Rock, A.R. Mem. Ark. Senate, 1967-82; dir. Comml. Nat. Bank, 1970-85, Little Rock, Security Bank, Conway, Dial Corp., Textron Inc., EnPro Industries Inc. Recipient Disting. Alumni cert. U. Ark., 1987. Baptist. Home: 2100 Country Club Ln Little Rock AR 72207-2040 Office: Alltel Corp PO Box 2177 1 Allied Dr Little Rock AR 72203*

FORD, JOHN CHARLES, communications executive; b. Washington, Oct. 8, 1942; s. Edgar Martin and Mary (Crowley) F.; m. Sandra Sollod Poster, June 11, 1994. BA, U. Md., 1964, postgrad., 1964-65, NYU, 1966, N.Y. Inst. Fin., 1967-68, New Sch. for Social Rsch., 1969, Crowell-Collier Inst., 1969, Friesen-Kaye Inst., 1971, Sterling Inst., 1975, U. Wis., 1977, Colgate-Darden Sch. Bus., U. Va., 1978, Harvard Bus. Sch., 1982. TV prodn. asst. USIA, Washington, 1963-65; instr. U. Md., 1965; acct. exec. Ruder & Finn Inc., N.Y.C., 1965-66; asst. to exec. v.p., mgr. edn1. svcs. Am. Stock. Exch., N.Y.C., 1966-70; mgr. comm. and audio visual tng. Merrill Lynch, Pierce, Fenner & Smith Inc., N.Y.C., 1970-74; dir. edn. and tng. CBS Inc., 1974-77, dir. employee devel. and edn., 1977-79; pres. Travel U., v.p. Travel Network subs. ABC, N.Y.C., 1979-81; dir. human resources Home Box Office, Inc., 1981-84; comm. cons., pres. John C. Ford Assocs., 1984—. Mem. faculty N.Y. Inst. Fin., 1971-73, Katherine Gibbs Sch., 1972-74. Bd. dirs., treas. Archeus Found.; trustee U. Md. Found., 1984-89; mem. chancellors adv. coun. sys. U. Md., 1989-99; mem. U. Md. Pres.'s Club, bd. dirs., 1984—; chmn. Carnegie Hall concert U. Md. Piano Festival; bd. overseers Emerson Coll., Boston, 1978—; mem. bd. advisors corp. and cable comm. program Manhattan C.C., CUNY; bd. trustees Neumann Coll., Aston, Pa., 1993, vice chmn. bd. trustees, 1994-96, chmn., 1996-99, chmn. devel. com., 1999—; bd. dirs., v.p. 15 W 81st St. Tenants Corp., 1978-80, 1992-96, pres., 1979-81, treas. 1995-96; mem. Coun. of West Side Coops.; guest spkr. Iowa Assn. for Life Long Learning; established John Charles Ford Professorship and Scholarship in Dramatic Arts U. Md., 1990; mem. leadership coun., Clarice Smith Ctr. for Performing Arts, 2002—; founder John C. Ford Acad. Resource Ctr., Neumann Coll., 2003. Mem. NATAS (bd. govs. 1969-84, sec. 1971-74, trustee 1973-80), ASTD (award 1978-80), Fin. Industry Tng. Assn. (pres. 1969-71), AAUP, Nat. Comm. Assn., Eastern Comm. Assn. (area chmn. 1975), N.Y. State Comm. Assn. (spkr.), West 70th St. Assn., Fedn. West Side Block Assns., W. 82d St. Block Assn., Internat. Radio & TV Soc., Nat. Soc. Programmed Instrn., Wall Street Tng. Dirs.'s Assn., Presidents Assn. of Am. Mgmt. Assn. (seminar leader), Assn. Cath. Colls. and Univs. (seminar leader), U. Md. Alumni Assn. Greater N.Y. (dir. 1966-70), N.Y. Personnel Mgrs. Assns., Orgnl. Devel. Network, N.Y. Human Resource Planners, Internat. Coach Fed., Omicron Delta Kappa, Phi Delta Theta. Home and Office: 15 W 81st St New York NY 10024-6022 Personal E-mail: johncfordassoc@aol.com.

FORD, JOHN CHARLES, artist; b. Choudrant, La., Sept. 29, 1929; s. John Leon Ford and Jessie Faye Dugdale; m. Margaret Ann Preston, Sept. 1959 (div. Apr. 1964); 1 child, John Charles Jr. BFA, La. Poly. Inst., 1950; BDiv, Austin Pres. Theol. Sem., 1953; MFA, U. Oreg., 1960. One-man shows at Leicester Galleries, London, 1967, Otto Seligman Gallery, Seattle, 1962, 72, Francine Seders Gallery, Seattle, 1972, Avanti Gallery, N.Y., 1972, L.I. Painters Awards Exhbn., 1974, Country Art Gallery, Locust Valley, 1974, La. State U., Baton Rouge, 1974, Neuberger Mus., Purchase, N.Y., 1977, Sid Deutsch Art Gallery, N.Y., 1977, RR Gallery, N.Y., 1980, Jack Gallery, N.Y., 1982, Phillip Dash Gallery, N.Y., 1986, Ruston (La.) Art Assn., 1991, Shreveport (La.) Arts Coun., Centenary Gallery, Shreveport, 2001; two-man shows at Labette C.C., Parsons, Kans., 1998; represented in permanent collections at Solomon R. Guggenheim Mus., NYU, N.Y., Hirshhorn Mus. and Sculpture Garden, Washington, Corcoran Gallery of Art, Washington, Neuberger Mus., Purchase, N.Y., Herbert F. Johnson Mus., Ithaca, N.Y., Seattle Art Mus., Addison (Mass.) Gallery Am. Art, Nuffield Found., London, Birmingham (Ala.) Mus. Art, U. Oreg., Ark. Arts Ctr., Little Rock, Ea. Oreg. Coll., La Grande. Avocations: writing, gardening. Home: 1592 Highway 145 Choudrant LA 71227-3600

FORD, JOHN GILMORE, interior designer; s. John Gilmore and Marian Brunner (Mainhart) F.; m. Berthe Diana Hanover, Aug. 19, 1972. B.F.A., Md. Inst. Coll. Art. Founder, 1962; since pres. John Ford Assoc., Inc., Balt.; tchr. seminars Md. Inst. Coll. Art, Md.; lectr. Indo-Asian art Johns Hopkins U., Towson State Coll. Served with USCGR. Recipient citation of merit Md. Inst. Coll. Art, 1960 Fellow Am. Soc. Interior Designers (past nat. v.p., pres. Md. chpt.; Presdl. citation); mem. Internat. Chinese Snuff Bottle Soc. (pres., co-editor jour.), Asia Soc., Am. Soc. Appraisers (sr. mem.). Clubs: Masons (32 deg.). Office: 2601 N Charles St Baltimore MD 21218-4514 Home: 17 Roland Mews Baltimore MD 21210-1563

FORD, JUDITH ANN TUDOR, retired natural gas distribution company executive; b. Martinsville, Ind., May 11, 1935; d. Glenn Leyburn and Dorotha Mae (Parks) Tudor; m. Walter L. Ford, July 25, 1954 (dec. 1962); children: John Corbin, Christi Sue. Student, Wichita State U., 1953-55; student, U. Nev.-Las Vegas. Legal sec. S.W. Gas Corp., Las Vegas, 1963-69, asst. corp. sec., 1969-72, corp. sec., 1972-82, v.p., 1977-82, sr. v.p., 1982-88, also bd. dirs., dir. 7 subs. Bd. dirs. NBA Svcs., Nev., residence for handicapped, 1989-97, treas., 1990-91, chmn., 1994-97; trustee Nev. Sch. Arts, Las Vegas, 1979-90, chmn. bd. dirs., 1985-86; trustee Disciples Sem. Found., Claremont Sch. Theology and Pacific Sch. Religion, San Francisco, 1985-91, 92-98, 99-2005, vice chmn., 1993-94, chmn., 1994-98; mem . Ariz. Acad., Ariz. Town Halls, 1986-92. Mem. Am. Soc. Corp. Secs., Greater Las Vegas C. of C. (bd. dirs. 1979-85), Pacific Coast Gas Assn. (bd. dirs. 1984-88), Ariz. Bus. Women Owners (exec. com. 1985-88). Democrat. Mem. Christian Ch. (Disciples Of Christ).

FORD, KAREN ANN, elementary school educator; b. Paducah, Ky., Feb. 25, 1954; d. Isaac Eli and N. Ruth (Lyons) F. BS in Elem. Edn., David Lipscomb Coll., 1976. Cert. tchr. Tenn. Tchr. Jackson (Tenn.) Christian Sch., 1976-87, Nashville Christian Sch., 1987—. Avocations: reading, sewing, gardening. Office: Nashville Christian Sch 7555 Sawyer Brown Rd Nashville TN 37221-1210 Office Phone: 615-356-5600.

FORD, KENNETH M., computer scientist, educator; b. Hampton, Va. BS in mgmt., NH Coll., 1982; MS in computer sci., U. West Fla., 1984; PhD in computer sci., Tulane U., 1987. Founder, dir. Inst. Human and Machine Cognition U. West Fla., Pensacola, 1990—. Bd. dirs. Nat. Sci. Bd., itFlorida.com; assoc. dir. to dir. Ctr. Excellence and Info. Tech. Ames Rsch. Ctr., NASA, 1997—99; mem. bd. supervisors Fla. Space Authority; editor-in-chief AAAI/MIT Press; past pres. Fla. Artificial Intelligence Rsch. Soc. Author: over 100 sci. papers, Android Epistemology, 1995, Expertise in Context: Human and Machine, 1997, Knowledge Acquisition as Modeling, 1993; co-author (with Patrick J. Hayes): Advances in Human & Machine Cognition, 1999, On Computational Wings: Rethinking the Goals of Artificial Intelligence, 2003. Fellow: Am. Assn. Artificial Intelligence. Office: Inst for Human and Machine Cognition 40 S Alcaniz St Pensacola FL 32502 Office Phone: 850-202-4462. Office Fax: 850-202-4440.

FORD, KENNETH WILLIAM, physicist; b. West Palm Beach, Fla., May 1, 1926; s. Paul Hammond and Edith (Timblin) F.; m. Karin Stehnike, Aug. 27, 1953 (div. 1961); m. Joanne Baumunk, June 9, 1962; children: Paul T., Sarah E., Caroline A., Adam B., Jason L., Ian L.; 1 stepdau., Nina Tannenwald. Student, John Carroll U., 1945, U. Mich., 1945—46; AB, Harvard Coll., 1948; PhD, Princeton U., 1953. Rsch. asst. Los Alamos Sci. Lab., 1950-51; rsch. assoc. Princeton U., 1951-52; from rsch. assoc. to assoc. prof. Ind. U., 1953-58, asst. prof. physics, 1954-57; from assoc. prof. to prof. Brandeis U., 1958-64; prof. U. Calif., Irvine, 1964-70, chmn. dept. physics, 1964-68; prof. physics U. Mass., Boston, 1970-75; pres. N.Mex. Inst. Mining and Tech., Socorro, 1975-82; exec. v.p. U. Md., Adelphi, 1982-83; pres. Molecular Biophysics Tech. Inc., 1983-85; edn. officer Am. Phys. Soc., 1986-87; exec. dir. Am. Inst. Physics, 1987-93; tchr. Germantown Acad., 1995-98; sci. program dir. David and Lucile Packard Found., 1998-99; tchr. Germantown Friends Sch., 2000-2001. Mem. Commn. Coll. Physics, 1968—71; cons. in field. Author: The World of Elementary Particles, 1963, Basic Physics, 1968, Classical and Modern Physics, 3 vols., 1972-74; (with John Wheeler) Geons, Black Holes, and Quantum Foam: A Life in Physics, 1998, The Quantum World: Quantum Physics for Everyone, 2004; mem. editl. bd. Phys. Rev., 1960-62, The Physics Tchr., 2000—; contbr. articles to profl. jours. With USNR, 1944-46. Fulbright fellow Max Planck Inst., Germany, 1955-56, NSF sr. postdoctoral fellow Imperial Coll. London, 1961-62, MIT, 1962. Fellow AAAS (coun. del. physics electorate 1983-86), Am. Phys. Soc. (chmn. forum on physics and soc. 1981, councilor 1984-87, sec.-treas. forum on history of physics 2001-05); mem. Am. Assn. Physics Tchrs. (pres. 1972, Disting. Svc. citation 1976), Fedn. Am. Scientists E-mail: kwford@verizon.net.

FORD, LORETTA C., retired dean, educator, consultant, nurse; b. N.Y.C., Dec. 28, 1920; d. Joseph F. and Nellie A. (Williams) Pfingstel; m. William J. Ford, May 2, 1947; 1 child, Valerie. BSN, U. Colo., Boulder, 1949, MS, 1951, EdD, 1961; DSc (hon.), Ohio State Med. Coll., 1997; DSc (hon.), Simmons Coll., 1997, U. Colo., 1997; LLD (hon.), U. Md., 1990; DSc (hon.), U. Rochester, 2000; LHD (hon.), Binghamton U., 2001. RN N.J. Staff nurse New Brunswick Vis. Nurse Svc., 1941—42; supr., dir. Boulder County (Colo.) Health Dept., 1947—58; from asst. prof. to prof. U. Colo. Sch. Nursing, 1960—72; dean Sch. Nursing, DON, prof. U. Rochester, NY, 1972—86, acting dean Grad. Sch. Edn. and Human Devel., 1988—89; vis. prof. U. Fla., 1968, U. Wash., Seattle, 1974, St. Lukes Coll. Nursing, Tokyo, 1987. Mem. educators adv. panel GAO; dir. Security Trust Co., Rochester, Rochester Telephone Co.; internat. cons. in field. Contbr. chapters to books, articles to profl. jours. Mem. adv. com. Commonwealth Fund Exec. Nurse Fellowship PRogram; bd. dirs. Threshold Alt. Youth Svcs., Easter Seal Soc., ARC, Monroe Cmty. Hosp. With Nurse Corps USAF, 1942—46. Named Colo. Nurse of Yr., Colo. Nurses Assn., Alumni of Century, U. Colo. Sch. Nursing Alumni Assn., 1998; recipient N.Y. State Gov.'s award for women in sci., medicine and nursing, Modern Healthcare Hall of Fame award, Modern Health Care Jour., 1994, Lillian D. Wald Spirit of Nursing award, N.Y. Vis. Nurse Svc., 1994, Lifetime Achievement award, Nat. Conf. Nurse Practitioners, 1999, Trailblazer award, Am. Coll. Nurse Practitioners, 2003, Elizabeth Blackwell award, Hobart and William Smith Colls., 2003. Fellow: Nat. League Nursing (Linda Richards award), Am. Acad. Nursing (Living Legend award 1999); mem.: NAS Inst. Medicine (Gustav O. Leinhard award 1990), ANA, APHA (Ruth B. Freeman award), Am. Coll. Nurse Practitioners (Crystal Trailblazers award 2003), Am. Coll. Health Assn. (Boynton award), Sigma Theta Tau, Alpha Omega Alpha (hon.). Personal E-mail: lorettaford@cfl.rr.com.

FORD, LUCILLE GARBER, economist, educator; b. Ashland, Ohio, Dec. 31, 1921; d. Ora Myers and Edna Lucille (Armstrong) Garber; m. Laurence Wesley Ford, Sept. 1, 1946; children: Karen Elizabeth, JoAnn Christine. AA, Stephens Coll., 1942; BS in Commerce, Northwestern U., 1944, MBA, 1945; PhD in Econs., Case Western Res. U., 1967; PhD (hon.), Tarkio Coll., 1991, Ashland U., 1995. Cert. fin. planner. Instr. Allegheny Coll., Meadville, Pa., 1945-46, U. Ala., Tuscaloosa, 1946-47; personnel dir., asst. sec. A.L. Garber Co., Ashland, Ohio, 1947-67; prof. econs. Ashland U., 1967-95, chmn. dept. econs., 1970-75; dir. Gill Ctr. for Econ. Edn. Ashland Coll., 1975-86, v.p., dean Sch. Bus., Adminstrn. and Econs., 1980-86, v.p. acad. affairs, 1986-90, provost, 1990-92; exec. asst. to pres., 1993-95; pres. Ashland Comm. Found., 1995—. Bd. dirs. Peco II, Inc., Western Res. Econ. Devel. Coun., Ohio Coun. Econ. Edn.; lectr. in field; mem. govs. adv. com. on econ. devel. Author: University Economics-Guide for Education Majors, 1979, Economics: Learning and Instruction, 1981, 91; contbr. articles to profl. jours. Mem. Ohio Gov.'s Commn. on Ednl. Choice, 1992; candidate for lt. gov. of Ohio, 1978; trustee Stephens Coll., 1977-80, Ashland U., 1995—, North Cen. State Coll., 1998—; elder Presbyn. Ch.; bd. dirs. Presbyn. Found., 1982-88; chair, trustee Synod-Presbyn. Ch., 1994-2000; active ARC. Named to Ohio Women's Hall of Fame, 2001; recipient Outstanding Alumnus award, Stephens Coll., 1977, Outstanding Profl. award, Ashland U., 1971, 1975, Roman F. Warmke award, 1981, Women of Achievement award, 1998, Outstanding Fundraiser award, Assn. Fund Raising Profls., 2001, Spirit of Chamber award, Ashland Area C. of C., 2001, Disting. Ashland H.S. award, Ashland City Sch. Acad. Found., 2002, Gleanch Clayton award, Ashland U., 2003. Mem. Am. Econs. Assn., Nat. Indsl. Rsch. Soc., Am. Arbitration Assn. (profl. arbitrator), Assn. Pvt. Enterprise Edn. (pres. 1983-84), North Ctrl. Assn. Colls. and Schs. (commr.), Omicron Delta Epsilon, Alpha Delta Kappa. Republican. Office: Ashland Co Comm Found 300 College Ave Ashland OH 44805-3803 Office Phone: 419-281-4733. Business E-Mail: accf@hmltd.net.

FORD, MARK L., lawyer; b. Lexington, Ky., Nov. 7, 1960; s. Thomas Robert and Harriet (Lowrey) F.; m. Sue Thomas, May 17, 1986; children: Darian, Thomas, Caleb. BA, Ind. U., 1982; JD, U. Ky., 1985. Bar: Ky. 1985, U.S. Dist. Ct. (ea. dist.) Ky. 1987, U.S. Ct. Appeals (6th cir.) 1990, Ct. Vet. Appeals 1990, U.S. Supreme Ct. 1997. Rschr. Coun. State Govts., Lexington, 1984-85; assoc. Forester & Forester, Harlan, Ky., 1985-88; ptnr. Smith & Ford, Harlan, 1988-90; pvt. practice law Harlan, 1990—. Pres. Ea. Broadcasting Co., 1998— Author: Hey, It Could Happen, 1999; co-author: Emergency Management in the States, 1984. Mem. Harlan (Ky.) County Pub. Libr. Bd. Trustees, 1990-94, pres. 2001-. Mem. Harlan County Bar Assn. (treas. 1990-97). Office: 105 Central St Harlan KY 40831

FORD, MARK LEE, aerospace engineer, researcher, entrepreneur; b. Toronto, Ont., Can., Jan. 8, 1966; s. Jeffrey Theo Maurice and Elaine Joan Maude (de Lang) F. BSc, U. Toronto, 1989; MS, Boston U., 1993, PhD, 1996. Profl. engr. Grad. rsch. fellow Boston U., 1992-93, Am. Chem. Soc.-Petroleum Rsch. Fund fellow, 1993-96; U.S. Nat. Sci. Found. fellow Ministry Internat. Trade and Industry, Tsukuba, Ibaraki, Japan, 1996-98; strategy cons. Accenture (formerly Andersen Consulting), 2000—03; founder, pres. The Moneo Co., 1999—. Rsch. cons., sci. collaborator Mech. Engring. Lab., Tsukuba, 1994-98; investigator in field. Contbr. articles to profl. jours. and mags. Vol. Aijien Children's Home and Orphanage, Tsukuba, 1997—. Mem. AIAA, ASME, Am. Phys. Soc., Am. Astronautical Soc., Asiatic Soc. Japan (bd. dirs.), Am.-Japan Soc., Japan-Brit. Soc., Rotary Club (Roppongi Hills), Tau Beta Pi. Achievements include research and development of stratospheric airships as aerospace platforms; co-derivation of Ford-Nadim equation for thermocapillary migration of drops.

FORD, MARY (POLLY) WYLIE, retired physical education educator; b. Rock Hill, S.C., Oct. 20, 1927; d. William Calvin and Orene Poe Wylie; m. Jack Buening Ford, June 25, 1960 (dec. Aug. 25, 1992). BS cum laude, Winthrop U., 1948; MEd, U. Va., 1953; PhD, U. Iowa, 1957. Instr. Anderson (S.C.) Coll., 1948—50, Stratford Coll., Danville, Va., 1950—55; grad. asst. U. Iowa, Iowa City, 1955—57; asst. prof. Ea. Ill. U., Charleston, 1957—60; prof. dept. chair Winthrop U., Rock Hill, 1960—92; ret., 1992. Mem. phys. edn. textbook selection panel State Dept. Edn., Columbia, SC, 1995—95. Bd. dirs. Rock Hill YMCA, 1975—78; mem. adv. coun. home care Catawba Health Dist., Lancaster, SC, 1998—; adv. bd. Fewell Pk. Recreation Ctr., Rock Hill, 1998—2002; trustee Presbyn. Home S.C., Columbia, 2005—, Winthop U., Rock Hill, 2002—; profl. adv. com. Home Health, Inc., Rock Hill, 1995—. Named to First Class of Disting. Phys. Edn. Alumni, Winthrop U., 2000. Mem.: AAHPERD (bd. govs., pres. So. dist. 1986—89, Honor award So. Dist. 1975, Profl. Svc. award So. Dist. 1991), S.C. Assn. for Health, Phys. Edn., Recreation and Dance (pres. 1970—71, President's Honor award 1970, Pres. Svc. award 1993), So. Assn. Phys. Edn. Coll. Women (pres. 1984—86), Perihelion Club (pres. 1994—96), Phi Kappa Phi. Democrat. Presbyterian. Avocations: bridge, tennis, travel. Home: 335 Shurley St Rock Hill SC 29732 Personal E-mail: pford@cetlink.net.

FORD, PATRICK KILDEA, Celtic studies educator; b. Lansing, Mich., July 31, 1935; s. Oliver Patrick and Ina Mildred (Spence) F.; m. Carol Mae Larsen, June 20, 1959 (div. 1978); children: Anne Kristina, Paul Kildea, James Oliver; m. Chadine Pearl Bailie, Nov. 17, 1979. BA, Mich. State U., 1959; MA, Harvard U., 1966, PhD, 1969. Asst. prof. English Stanford U., 1968-70; asst. prof. Indo-European studies UCLA, 1970-71, asst. prof. English, 1971-74, assoc. prof., 1974-79, prof. English and Celtic studies, 1979-91, dir. Folklore and Mythology Ctr., 1979-84, chmn. Indo-European studies program, 1972-73, 74-75, 79-82, dir. writing programs, 1989-91; Margaret Brooks Robinson prof. Celtic Harvard U., Cambridge, Mass., 1991—; Wallace E. and Grace Connolly prof. Celtic Stanford U., 1986. Founder, pres. Ford & Bailie Pubs./Book Distbrs. Author: The Poetry of Llywarch Hen, 1974, The Mabinogi and Other Medieval Welsh Tales, 1977, Ystoria Taliesin, 1992, The Celtic Poets: Songs and Tales from Early Ireland and Wales, 1999, Math uab Mathonwy, 1999, Manawydan uab Llyr, 2000; editor, contbr.: Celtic Folklore and Christianity: Essays in Memory of William W. Heist, 1983; co-author: Sources and Analogues of Old English Poetry: Celtic and Germanic, 1984, The Irish Literary Tradition, 1992. With AUS, 1956-57. NEH fellow, 1972, UCLA fellow, 1973, Fulbright fellow, 1973-74; grantee Skaggs Found., 1981-83, Am. Council Learned Socs., 1985, NEH, 1986, 94, 96, 99, 2002; hon. fellow Ctr. for Advanced Welsh and Celtic Studies/U. Wales. Mem. MLA, Internat. Arthurian Soc. (pres. N.Am. br. 1981-83), Medieval Acad. Am., Celtic Studies Assn. N.Am. (v.p. 1984-86, pres. 1987-89). Modern Humanities Rsch. Assn. (pres. 2005). Office: Harvard U Dept Celtic Lang and Lit Barker Ctr 12 Quincy St Cambridge MA 02138-2030 Business E-Mail: pford@fas.harvard.edu.

FORD, PAUL B., lawyer; b. Augusta, Ga., Dec. 1, 1943; s. Paul Brendan Ford and Augustine Marie Roy; m. Nancy Young; children: Brendan, Ian, Hunter, Jade. BA magna cum laude, Boston Coll., 1965; JD, Duke U., 1968. Ptnr. Simpson Thacher & Bartlett LLP, NYC, 1976—. Contbr. articles to profl. jours. Active Nat. Com. on U.S. China Rels., N.Y.C., 1999—; chmn. U.S. Fgn. Policy Assn., N.Y.C., 1993—2000; dir. New Haven Symphony Orch., New Haven, 1992—. Mem.: ABA, Coun. Fgn. Rels., Japan Soc., Korea Soc., Inter Pacific Bar Assn., Internat. Bar Assn., Union Internat. des Avocats, Assn. Bar City of NY. Avocations: sailing, skiing. Office: Simpson Thacher & Bartlett LLP Rm 2109 425 Lexington Ave New York NY 10017 Business E-Mail: pford@stblaw.com.

FORD, PETER C., chemistry professor; b. Salinas, Calif., July 10, 1941; s. Clifford and Thelma (Martin) F.; children: Vincent, Jonathan; m. Mary E. Howe-Grant. BS with honors, Calif. Inst. Tech., 1962; MS, Yale U., 1963, PhD, 1966. Postdoctoral fellow Stanford U., 1966-67; asst. prof. chemistry U. Calif., Santa Barbara, 1967-72, assoc. prof. chemistry, 1972-77, prof. chemistry, 1977—. Grad. advisor dept. chemistry U. Calif., 1980-81, co-grad. advisor, 1985-92, 99—, chmn., 1994-96; vis. fellow Australian Nat. U., 1974; guest prof. H.C. Oersted Inst., Denmark, 1981; lectr. U. Berne, Switzerland, 1989, MITI-ASTI, Japan, 1990; guest investigator radiation biology br. Nat. Cancer Inst., 1994. Contbr. to profl. jours. Fellow NIH, 1963-66, NSF, 1966-67, Sterling fellow Yale U., 1963, sr. fellow Fulbright Found., 1974; Dreyfus Found. Tchr. scholar, 1971-76; recipient Alexander von Humboldt-Stiftung U.S. Sr. Scientist Rsch. award, 1992, Richard C. Tolman medal Am. Chem. Soc., 1993. Fellow: AAAS; mem.: Inter-Am. Photochem. Soc. (v.p. 2002—04, pres. 2004—). Achievements include research in the photochemical, photocatalytic and photophysical mechanisms of transition metal complexes and with homogeneous catalysis mechanisms as probed by modern kinetics techniques; the bioinorganic chemistry of metal nitrosyl complexes. Office: Univ of California Dept of Chemistry 552 University Rd Santa Barbara CA 93106-0001

FORD, RALPH A., lawyer, moving and relocation company executive; b. 1946; BA in Polit. Sci., Morgan State U., 1968; JD, Boston U. Sch. Law, 1971. Bar: Md. 1972, US Dist. Ct. Dist. Md. 1972. Assoc. Venable, Baetjer & Howard, 1971—73; atty. Dupont Co., 1973—77; group counsel Bell and Howell Co., 1977—81; mem. legal dept. GE, 1981—99; gen. counsel GE Indsl. Control Systems, 1992—99; sr. v.p., gen. counsel, sec. Sirva, Inc., Westmont, Ill., 1999—. Mem.: Am. Corp. Counsel Assn. Office: Sirva Inc 700 Oakmont Ln Westmont IL 60559*

FORD, RICHARD, writer; b. Jackson, Miss., Feb. 16, 1944; s. Parker Carrol and Edna (Akin) F.; m. Kristina Hensley, 1968. BA in English, Mich. State U., 1966; MFA, U. Calif., 1970. Author: (novels) A Piece of My Heart, 1976, The Ultimate Good Luck, 1981, The Sportswriter, 1986 (PEN/Faulkner citation for fiction 1986), Wildlife, 1990, Independence Day, 1995, Women with Men: Three Stories, 1997; author: (short stories) Rock Springs, 1987, A Multitude of Sins, 2002; author: (play) American Tropical, 1983, (screenplay) Bright Angel, 1991; editor: (with Shannon Ravenel) The Best American Short Stories, 1990, The Granta Book of the American Short Story, (with Michael Kreyling), Eudora Welty: Complete Novels, 1998, Eudora Welty: Stories, Essays, and Memoir (Eudora Welty), 1998, The Granta Book of the American Long Story, 1999; contbr. articles to popular publs. Recipient Pulitzer prize for fiction, 1996, PEN/Faulkner prize for fiction, 1996; Guggenheim fellow, 1977-98, Endowment for the Arts, 1979-80, 85-86. Mem. U. Mich. Soc. Fellows, Am. Acad. Arts and Letters. Home: PO Box 510 East Boothbay ME 04544-0510

FORD, RICHARD EDMOND, lawyer; b. Ronceverte, W.Va., May 3, 1927; s. Grady Williams and Hazel Loraine (Fry) F.; m. Sally Frances Alexander, June 14, 1952; children: Richard Edmond Jr., Sally Anne, Melinda J. Student, U. N.C., 1950; BS in Bus. Adminstrn., W.Va. U., 1951, LL.B., 1954. Bar: W.Va. 1954. Assoc. Holt & Haynes, Lewisburg, W.Va., 1954-55; ptnr. Haynes & Ford, Lewisburg, 1955-74, Haynes, Ford & Rowe, Lewisburg, 1975-96, The Ford Law Firm, Lewisburg, 1997—. Dir. W.Va. Power Co., First Nat. Bank Ronceverte, Greenbrier Cable Corp. Bd. dirs. W.Va. U. Found., Daywood Found., v.p., 1986—; bd. dirs. Faculty Merit Found. W.Va., W.Va. Legal Svcs. Plan, 1973—79; trustee Greenbrier Coll. for Women, 1960—73; mem. exec. bd. Buckskin Coun. Boy Scouts Am.; mem. adv. bd. Greenbrier C.C. Ctr.; mem. vis. com. Coll. Law W.Va. U., 1972—74; mem. W.Va. Legislature, 1961—64. Served as ensign U.S. Maritime Svc., 1945—47. Recipient Outstanding Alumnus award W.Va. U. Law Sch., 1980, W.Va. U., 88. Fellow Am. Bar Found., Am. Judicature Soc.; mem. ABA (ho. of dels. 1977-80), W.Va. Bar Assn. (v.p. 1965-66, 75-76, pres. 1978-79), Greenbrier County Bar Assn. (pres. 1964-66, 81-82), W.Va. Law Sch. Assn. (pres. 1966-67), Nat. Conf. Commrs. Uniform State Laws, Am. Coll. Real Estate Lawyers, W.Va. U. Alumni Assn. (pres. 1971), Phi Beta Kappa, Sigma Chi, Phi Delta Phi, Order of Vandalia. Clubs: Masons, KT, Shriners, Lewisburg Elks. Democrat. Methodist. Office: The Ford Law Firm 203 W Randolph St Lewisburg WV 24901-1023

FORD, RICHARD THOMPSON, law educator; b. 1966; AB in Polit. Sci., Stanford U., 1988; JD cum laude, Harvard U., 1991. Housing policy cons. City of Cambridge, Mass., 1990—91; litig. assoc. Morrison & Foerster, San Francisco, 1991—93; Reginald Lewis Fellow Harvard Law Sch., Cambridge, Mass., 1993—94; assoc. prof. law Stanford Law Sch., 1994—99, prof., 1999—, Justin M. Roach, Jr. faculty scholar, 2003—04, George E. Osborne prof. law, 2004—. Vis. prof. law Columbia Law Sch., NYC, 2000; commr. Housing Authority of the City and County of San Francisco, 1997—98. Office: Stanford Law Sch Crown Quadrangle 559 Nathan Abbott Way Stanford CA 94305-8610 Office Phone: 650-723-2796. Business E-Mail: rford@stanford.edu.*

FORD, ROBERT MACDONALD, III, architect, educator; b. Seattle, Apr. 4, 1934; s. Robert MacDonald Jr. and Nancy Elizabeth (McFate) F.; m. Ruth Evelyn Keene, 1957 (div. 1980); children: Karen, Judith, Robert IV; m. Martha Evelyn Cooper, Mar. 11, 1983 (div. 2000); m. Deborah Mahoney

Nettles, Feb. 28, 2003. BArch, U. Wash., Seattle, 1962; MArch, U. Ill., 1963. Registered architect, Miss. Asst. prof. architecture U. Ill., Urbana, 1963-66, Wash. State U., Pullman, 1966-69, assoc. prof. architecture, 1969-74, prof. architecture, 1974-75, Miss. State U., Starkville, 1975-96, prof. emeritus architecture, 1996—. Vis. prof. Oreg. Sch. Design, Portland, fall 1982, U. P.R., San Juan, spring 1990; pres. Ford & Assocs., Architects, Miss., 1975-92; pres. Architecture/South, Miss., Tenn., 1992-97, Ford Properties, 1997—; Miss. commr. Clan Donald, 2002—. Councilman City of Pullman, 1969-74. With U.S. Army, 1953-56. Fellow AIA (bd. dirs. Miss. 1987, 90, 98, 2000--, sec.-treas. 1988, v.p. 1989, pres.-elect 1991, pres. 1992, state design awards 1981, 82, 83, 88, 99, regional design awards 1981, 84, 85, 91, 92), Archtl. Found., Tau Sigma Delta. Democrat. Avocations: sailing, genealogy, travel. Home and Office: 308 Mangrove Palm St Starkville MS 39759 E-mail: robmford3@hotmail.com.

FORD, ROLLIN, retail executive; BS in Bus. Adminstrn. and Sys. Analysis, Taylor U. With Wal-Mart Stores, Inc., 1983—, with distbn. and logistics ops., v.p. splty. distbn./transp., 1996—98, v.p. distbn. ops., 1998—2000, sr. v.p. logistics, 2000—03, exec. v.p. logistics, 2003—. Bd. dirs. Thurgood Marshall Scholarship Found. Office: Wal-Mart Stores Inc 702 SW Eighth St Bentonville AR 72716*

FORD, SALLY J., physical education educator; b. Vincennes, Ind., July 2, 1950; d. Marion C. and Peggy A. (Clark) Ford; 1 child from previous marriage, Chanda D. BA, McKendree Coll., 1973; MS, Eastern Ill. U., 1980; PhD, So. Ill. U., 2000. Tchr., coach Effingham (Ill.) HS, 1974-80; head coach Bradley U., Peoria, Ill., 1980-83; exercise physiologist Curtiss Ave. Clinic, Sarasota, Fla., 1985-87; conditioning coord. Kansas City Royals, 1987-88; prof. Pima CC, Tucson, 1989—2001, Tusculum Coll., Greeneville, Tenn., 2001—04; speed devel. trainer pvt. practice, 2004—. With U.S. Men's Sprint Com., 1982—86, Competitive Edge, Calif., 1993—95. Named to Sports Hall of Fame, McKendree Coll., 1991. Mem.: Clinics Speed Devel., Athletic Congress, Nat. Strength and Conditioning Assn., N.Am. Soc. Sport Mgmt., Am. Alliance Health, Physical Edn., Recreation and Dance. Avocations: running, weightlifting. Office: 4529 Cinnamon Dr Sarasota FL 34238 Office Phone: 941-922-5157.

FORD, SCOTT T., telecommunications company executive; married; 3 children. B in Fin., U. Ark., Fayetteville, 1984. With Merrill Lynch Capital Markets, NY, Stephens Group Inc., Little Rock, 1986—96; exec. v.p. Alltel Corp., Little Rock, 1996, pres., 1997—, COO, 1998, CEO, 2002—, bd. dir., 1996—. Chmn. Cellular Telecommunications and Internet Assn. Mem. Little Rock Branch of the Fed. Reserve Bank of St. Louis. Office: Alltel Corp One Allied Dr Little Rock AR 72202*

FORD, STEVEN J., lawyer, manufacturing executive; b. Queens, N.Y., Sept. 20, 1959; s. Joseph and Helen Ford; m. Patricia A. Lynn, Mar. 28, 1987. BS, Villanova U., 1981; JD, St. John's U., 1985; LLM in Taxation, NYU, 1988. Bar: NY 1986. With Coopers & Lybrand, Cowan, Liebowitz & Latman, Bond, Schoeneck & King, Syracuse, NY; v.p. Carlisle Cos., Inc., Charlotte, NC, 1995—, sec., 1995—, gen. counsel, 1995—. Mem.: ABA, NY State Bar. Office: Carlisle Cos Inc 250 S Clinton St Ste 201 Syracuse NY 13202*

FORD, SUZANNE WHITTEN (SOOZI WHITTEN), minister; b. San Antonio, Aug. 3, 1956; d. Robert Greely Whitten and Maida Ray Emrick; m. Homer Clinton Ford; children: Ashley Elizabeth, Holly Suzanne. BA, Ottawa U., 1978; MDiv, Ctrl. Bapt. Theol. Sem., 1982. Ordained rev. Am. Baptist Chs. USA, 1982. Mem. faculty Sterling (Kans.) Coll., 1983—87; assoc., interim pastor 1st Bapt. Ch., Casper, Wyo., 1989—98; assoc. exec. min. Mid-Am. Bapt. Chs., Des Moines, 1999—. Contbr. articles to Bapt. Leader mag.; author: (curriculum) American Baptist Churches Uniform Lesson Series, Youth Leader Core American Baptist Churches, USA0, 1990, Change-God Changes My Life, 2001, Abundance, 2002, Synergy, 2000. Chaplain Wyo. Med. Ctr., Casper, 1994—98; pres. Am. Bapt. Chs. Rocky Mountains, Denver, 1998, v.p., 1996—97; bd. dirs., officer Adult Day Ctr., Casper, 1993—97. Mem.: AAUW, Min.'s Coun. Office: Mid-Am Bapt Chs 2400 86th St Ste 15 Des Moines IA 50322

FORD, THOMAS W., JR., lawyer; b. Austin, Tex., 1955; BA in Acctg., U. Tex., Austin, 1978; JD, U. Houston, 1981. Bar: Tex. 1981. Ptnr., tax dept. Andrews Kurth LLP, Houston. Mem.: Nat. Assn. Real Estate Investments Trusts, ABA, State Bar Tex., Houston Bar Assn., Houston Tax Roundtable, Phi Delta Phi, Beta Alpha Psi, Gamma Delta Sigma, Order of Barons. Office: Andrews Kurth LLP 600 Travis St Ste 4200 Houston TX 77002-3090 Office Phone: 713-220-4498. Office Fax: 713-238-4285. Business E-mail: tford@andrewskurth.com.

FORD, TOM, apparel designer, apparel executive; b. Austin, Tex., 1962; Postgrad., NYU, Parsons Sch. Design, N.Y., Paris. Sr. designer Cathy Hardwick, 1986—88; design dir. Perry Ellis Women's Am. Divsn., 1988—90; chief women's ready-to-wear designer Gucci, 1990—92, design dir., 1992—94, creative dir., 1994—2004, creative dir. Yves Saint Laurent Rive Gauche, YSL Beauté line, 2000—04; CEO, pres. Tom Ford Co., 2005—. Collaborator fragrance and beauty products line Tom Ford for Estee Lauder, 2005—. Named Internat. Designer of Yr., Coun. Fashion Designers Am., 1996, Womenswear Designer of Yr., 2001, Accessory Designer of Yr., 2002, Internat. Designer of Yr., Fashion Editor's Club of Japan, 1996, Best Designer of Yr., 2001, Internat. Man of Yr., British GQ, 2000, Best Fashion Designer, Time Mag., 2001, Designer of Yr., GQ Am., 2001, Future's Best New Designer, VH1/Vogue Fashion Awards, 1995, Menswear Designer of Yr., 1996, Womenswear Designer of Yr., 1996, 1999; recipient Style Icon award, Elle Style Awards, 1999, Commitment to Life award, AIDS Project, L.A., 1999, Designer of Yr. Yves Saint Laurent Rive Gauche, VH1/Vogue Fashion Awards, 2002, Superstar award, Fashion Group Internat. Night Stars, 2000. Office: Creative Artists Agency 9830 Wilshire Blvd Beverly Hills CA 90212*

FORD, VICKIE LOUISE ARP, lawyer; b. Cartersville, Ga., Jan. 8, 1956; d. Perry H. and Marjorie Woods Arp; m. William Geary Ford, Apr. 16, 1947. JD, John Marshall Law Sch., Atlanta, 1998. Bar: Ga. 1999, U.S. Ct. Appeals Ga. 2001, U.S. Dist. Ct. Ga. 2001. Owner Ford Law Firm, Cartersville, Georgia 30120, Ga., 1999—. Active Rep. Party, Cartersville, Atlanta, Ga. Recipient Wall of Tolerance, Rosa Parks, Morris Dees, 2002. Mem.: Phi Alpha Theta. Republican. Baptist. Avocations: reading, gardening. Office: Ford Law Firm 703 Joe Frank Harris Pkwy Cartersville GA 30120 E-mail: vickiefordlaw@aol.com.

FORD, VICTORIA, retired public relations executive, writer, oral historian; b. Carroll, Iowa, Nov. 1, 1946; d. Victor Sargent and Gertrude Francis (Headlee) F.; m. John K. Frans, July 4, 1965 (div. Aug. 1975); m. David W. Keller, May 2, 1981 (div. Nov. 1985); m. Jerry W. Lambert, Mar. 30, 1991 (div. Aug. 2002). AA, Iowa Lakes Community Coll., 1973; BA summa cum laude, Buena Vista Coll., 1974; MA in Journalism, U. Nev., Reno, 1988. Juvenile parole officer Iowa Dept. Social Services, Sioux City, 1974-78; staff reporter Feather Pub. Co., Quincy, Calif., 1978-80; tng. counselor CETA, Quincy, 1980; library pub. info. officer U. Nev., Reno, 1982-84; pub. relations exec. Brodeur/Martin Pub. Relations, Reno, 1984-87; pub. relations dir. Internat. Winter Spl. Olympics, Lake Tahoe (Calif.) and Reno, 1987-89; owner Ford Factor Pub. Rels. cons. firm, Reno, 1989—2002. Staff writer Publs. and Pub. Info. Office Truckee Meadows C.C., 2001—05; comm. specialist U. Nev. Coop. Ext., 2005—. Author: Making Their Mark: Reno-Sparks YWCA History, 1997; author: (with R.T. King and Ken Adams) War Stories, 1997; author: Jean Ford: A Nevada Woman Leads the Way (oral history), 1998, Silver Peak Oral History Project, 2001, Charlotte Hunter Arley, 2001, Never a Ghost Town: Silver Peak, Nevada, 2002, Cliff Young, Chief Justice, Nevada Supreme Court, 2002, Arthur Bernard, Nevada Mine Inspector and PrisonWarden, 2003, Victor Kral (oral history), 2004; contbr. articles to profl. jours. Mem. adv. bd. Reno Philharm., 1985-87, Reno-Sparks Conv. and Visitors Authority, 1985-91; bd. dirs. Truckee Meadows Habitat for Humanity, 1992-93, half-time exec. dir., 1994; mem. Gov.'s Com. on Fire Prevention, 1991-92; mem. U. Nev. Reno Oral History Program, 1994; bd. dirs. Nev. Women's Archives, 1996; state sec. and roll of honor Nev. Women's History Project, 1998, 2001, com. Nev. Writers Hall of Fame, 1993-96; bd. dirs. Friends of the U. Nev. at Reno Libr., 1995-98. Mem.: NOW, Women Writing the West, Assn. Personal Historians, S.W. Oral History Assn. (bd. dirs. 2000—02, State Hist. Rec. adv. bd. 2002—), Pub. Rels. Soc. Am. (charter v.p. Sierra Nev. chpt. 1986—87, pres. 1987—88), Sigma Delta Chi. Democrat. Home and Office: PO Box 33993 Reno NV 89533-3993 Office Phone: 775-784-7070.

FORD, VICTORIA, author, educator; b. South Bend, Ind., Dec. 29, 1952; d. G. Burt and Charlotte Ann (Kupferer) F. BA, Ohio Wesleyan U., 1975; MA, Ind. U., 1978. Design team mem. Morningside Acad., Seattle, 1995-99. Adj. faculty Seattle Ctrl. C.C., 1990-99, Antioch U., Seattle, 1995-99; instrl. design Headsprout, Seattle, 1999—. Author: Following the Swan, 1988, Rain Psalm, 1996.

FORD, WILLIAM CLAY, automotive executive, professional sports team executive; b. Detroit, Mar. 14, 1925; s. Edsel Bryant and Eleanor (Clay) F.; m. Martha Firestone, June 21, 1947; children: Martha, Sheila, William Clay, Elizabeth. BS, Yale U., 1949. Sales and advt. staff Ford Motor Co., 1949; indsl. relations, labor negotiations with UAW, 1949; quality control mgr. gas turbine engines Lincoln-Mercury Div., Dearborn, Mich., 1951, mgr. spl. product ops., 1952, v.p., 1953, gen. mgr. Continental Div., 1954, group v.p. Lincoln and Continental Divs, 1955, v.p. product design, 1956-80; dir., 1948—; vice chmn. bd., 1980-89; mem. fin. com. Ford Motor Co., 1987—, dir. emeritus; owner, chmn. Detroit (Mich.) Lions, Inc., 1964—. Mem. adv. coun. Tex. Heart Inst.; chmn. emeritus Edison Inst.; hon. life trustee Eisenhower Med. Ctr. Mem. Soc. Automotive Engrs. (asso.), Automobile Old Timers, Econ. Club Detroit, Masons, K.T., Phelps Assn., Psi Upsilon. Office: Ford Motor Co Design Ctr PO Box 6012 Dearborn MI 48121-6012 also: The Detroit Lions Inc 222 Republic Dr Allen Park MI 48101

FORD, WILLIAM CLAY, JR. (BILL FORD), automotive executive; b. Detroit, May 3, 1957; married. BA, Princeton U., 1979; MBA in Mgmt., MIT, 1984. Prodn. planning analyst, advisor vehicle devel. design ctr., mfg. engr. auto assembly divsn., mgr. Ford Motor Co., N.Y., 1979-82, mem. nat. bargaining team Ford/UAW labor talks, mktg. strategy analyst No. Am. Auto Opns., advt. specialist, 1982-83, internat. fin. specialist, mem. fin. staff, 1984-85, planning mgr. car prodn. devel., 1985-86, dir. com. vehicle mktg. Europe divsn., 1986-87, chmn., mng. dir. Switzerland divsn., 1987-89, mgr. heavy truck engr. and mfg. Ford Truck Opns., 1989-90, dir. bus. strategy Ford Auto Group, 1990-91, exec. dir. bus. strategy Ford Auto Group, 1991-92, gen. mgr. climate control divsn., 1992-94, v.p. com. Trucking Vehicle Ctr. Ford Auto Ops., 1994-95, chmn. fin. com., 1995—2001, chmn. bd., 1998—, CEO, 2001—. Vice chmn. Detroit Lions; mem. fin. com., properties com. NFL; bd. dir. eBay, Inc., 2005-. Chmn. bd. trustees Henry Ford Mus., Greenfield Village; trustee Henry Ford Health Sys., Detroit Renaissance; mem. World Econ. Forum's Global Leaders for Tomorrow. Alfred P. Sloan fellow MIT, 1983-84. Office: Ford Motor Co 1 American Rd Dearborn MI 48126-2798*

FORD, WILLIAM F., banker; b. Huntington, N.Y., Aug. 14, 1936; s. William Freithaler; m. Diane McDonald, June 11, 1960; children: Eric W., Kristin E. BA in Econs. summa cum laude, U. Tex., 1961; MA, U. Mich., 1962, PhD, 1966; DSc (hon.), Fla. Inst. Tech., 1981; grad. sr. exec. program, Stanford U., 1983. Part-time teaching asst. U. Mich., 1962-63, instr., 1965-66; economist Rand Corp., 1966, cons., 1967-68, 70-71; asst. prof. econs. U. Va., 1967-69; assoc. prof. Tex. Tech. U., Lubbock, 1969-70; prof. econs., dean Transylvania Coll., Lexington, Ky., 1970-71; exec. dir., chief economist rsch. and planning group Am. Bankers Assn., 1971-75; sr. v.p., chief economist Wells Fargo Bank, San Francisco, 1975-80; pres., chief exec. officer Fed. Res. Bank Atlanta, 1980-83; pres., chief operating officer First Nationwide Savs., 1983-85; pres., chief exec. officer Broadview Savs. Bank, Cleve., 1986-89; dean coll. bus. U. Denver, 1990-91; prof. and chair fin. Mid. Tenn. State U., Murfreesboro, 1992—. Mem. faculty Stonier Grad. Sch. Banking, 1976—80; mem. fed. open market com. Fed. Res. Sys., 1982—83; sr. econ. advisor TeleCheck Svcs. Inc., 1992—2001; spkr. in field. Author: Mexico's Foreign Trade and Economic Development, 1968; also over 100 articles, revs., TV script. Bd. vis. Berry Coll., 1984—89. With USN, 1954—57. Woodrow Wilson fellow, 1961; NDEA fellow, 1961-63; Ford Found. fgn. area fellow, Mex., 1964-65; Rotary fellow, Chile, 1970; co-winner Fred M. Taylor Prize U. Mich. Mem. Stanford Grad. Sch. Bus. Adminstrn. Alumni Assn. (bd. dirs. 1985-86), Am. Econ. Assn., Nat. Assn. for Bus. Econs. (bd. dirs. 2002-), U.S. C. of C. (bd. dirs. 1989-91, chmn. econ. policy com. 1990-93), Phi Beta Kappa. Methodist. Office: Mid Tenn State U Coll Bus PO Box 27 Murfreesboro TN 37133-0027 E-mail: swfford@mtsu.edu.

FORD, WILLIAM FRANCIS, retired bank holding company executive; b. Albany, NY, Mar. 11, 1925; s. Patrick J. and Ellen M. F.; m. Marcia J. Whalen, Jan. 7, 1956; children: William Francis, Michael P., Timothy K., Daniel J., Cathleen A. BA in Acctg. with honors, St. Michaels Coll., 1950. V.p. Equitable Credit Corp., Albany, 1950-60, Am. Fin. Systems Inc., Silver Spring, Md., 1960-65, Gen. Electric Credit Corp., Stamford, Conn., 1965-74; chmn., chief exec. officer Security Pacific Fin. Corp., San Diego, 1974-81; exec. v.p., adminstr. specialized fin. services group Security Pacific Corp., Los Angeles, 1981-84, vice chmn., 1984-91. Bd. dirs., vice chmn. Ford Fin. Svcs., 1991—. Served with USN, 1943-46. Mem. Am. Fin. Svcs. Assn. (chmn., dir. emeritus exec. com.) Clubs: Stone Ridge Country. Home: 741 Cypress Hills Dr Encinitas CA 92024-2376

FORDE-MAZRUI, KIM ABUBAKAR ALI, law educator; b. Kampala, Uganda, Nov. 21, 1968; s. Ali Al'Amin Mazrui and Molly Vickerman Walker; m. Kathleen Gayle Forde, June 30, 1990; 1 child, Will Nielsen. BA summa cum laude, U. Mich., 1990, JD magna cum laude, 1993. Bar: Mich. 1993, U.S. Dist. Ct. (ea. dist.) Mich. 1994, U.S. Ct. Appeals (6th cir.) 1994, D.C. 1996. Jud. clk. U.S. Ct. Appeals (6th cir.), Detroit, 1993—94; assoc. Law Firm of Sidley & Austin, Washington, 1994—96; asst. prof. law U. Va. Sch. Law, Charlottesville, 1996—97, assoc. prof. law, 1997—2001, prof. law, 2001—, Barron F. Black rsch. prof., 2002—04, Justice Thurgood Marshall rsch. prof., 2004—, dir. Ctr. for the Study of Race and Law, 2003—. Vis. prof. law U. Mich. Law Sch., Ann Arbor, 2003—04. Contbr. articles to profl. jours. Student-lawyer Family Law Project, Ann Arbor, Mich., 1990—91. Recipient Honors award, Recordings for the Blind, Inc., 1990, First Pl. ABA Regional Client Counseling Competition, ABA Law Student Divsn., 1992, Beverly Harmon Svc. to Black Law Student Assn. award, U. Va. Black Law Student Assn., 2002; James B. Angell scholar, U. Mich., 1989—90, Merit scholar, Am. Brotherhood of the Blind, 1990, Clarence Darrow scholar, U. Mich. Law Sch., 1990—93, Henry M. Bates Meml. scholar, 1993. Mem.: Assn. Am. Law Schs., Mid-Atlantic People of Color Legal Scholarship Conf., U. Mich. Lawyer's Club, Golden Key, Order of the Coif, Phi Beta Kappa. Office: Univ Va Sch Law 580 Massie Rd Charlottesville VA 22903-1789 Office Phone: 434-924-3299. Office Fax: 434-924-7536. Business E-mail: kimfm@virginia.edu.

FORDEMWALT, JAMES NEWTON, microelectronics engineering educator, consultant; b. Parsons, Kans., Oct. 18, 1932; s. Fred and Zenia (Chambers) F.; m. Suzan Lynn Hopkins, Aug. 26, 1958 (div. June 1961); m. Elizabeth Anna Hoare, Dec. 29, 1963; children: John William, James Frederick. BS, U. Ariz., 1955, MS, 1956; PhD, U. Iowa, 1960. Sr. engr. GE Co., Evandale, Ohio, 1959-60, U.S. Semcor, Inc., Phoenix, 1960-61; sect. mgr. Motorola Semiconductor Products Div., Phoenix, 1961-66; dept. mgr. Philco-Ford Microelectronics Div., Santa Clara, Calif., 1966-68; assoc. dir. R & D Am. Microsystems Inc., Santa Clara, 1968-71; assoc. rsch. prof. U. Utah, Salt Lake City, 1972-76; dir. microelectronics lab. U. Ariz., Tucson, 1976-87; assoc. prof., lab. mgr. Ariz. State U., Tempe, 1987—2001, prof. emeritus, 2001—, assoc. chair microelectronics, 1992—2001, asst. chair dept. electronic and computer tech., 1993—2001. Cons. Integrated Cirs. Engring., Scottsdale, Ariz., 1976—, Western Design Ctr., Mesa, Ariz., 1980—; mem. semiconductor com. United Techs. Corp., Hartford, Conn., 1978-87. Author: Silicon Wafer Processing Technology, 1979; editor: Integrated Circuits, 1965; contbr.: MOS Integrated Circuits, 1972. Mem. IEEE, Internat. Soc. for Hybrid Microelectronics (chpt. pres. 1982-83), Electrochem. Soc. Avocations: pilot, photographer. Home: 613 W Summit Pl Chandler AZ 85225-7798 E-mail: jfordemwalt@cox.net.

FORDEN, DIANE CLAIRE, magazine editor; b. N.Y.C., Apr. 6, 1951; d. Joseph Anthony and Helen (Nash) F. BA in English Edn. summa cum laude, Montclair (N.J.) State U., 1973. Fashion editor Seventeen Mag., N.Y.C., 1975-81; fashion and beauty dir. YM Mag., N.Y.C., 1981-85; fashion dir. Avon Fashions, N.Y.C., 1985-87, Prima Mag., N.Y.C., 1987-88; from fashion and beauty editor to editor in chief and v.p. Bridal Guide Mag., N.Y.C., 1989—. Author: How to Have an Elegant Wedding-Without Going Broke, 2002, How to Find the Perfect Wedding Dress, 2003, New Etiquette for Today's Bride, 2004. Mem. Am. Soc. Mag. Editors, Fashion Group Internat., N.Y. Women in Comms. Avocations: piano, biking, skiing, photography. Home: 10 River Rd Apt F Nutley NJ 07110-3459 Office: Bridal Guide Mag 3 E 54th St New York NY 10022-3108

FORDHAM, CHRISTOPHER COLUMBUS, III, dean, academic administrator, medical educator; b. Greensboro, NC, Nov. 28, 1926; s. Christopher Columbus and Frances Long (Clendenin) Fordham; m. Barbara Byrd, Aug. 16, 1947; children: Pamela Fordham Richey, Susan Fordham Crowell, Betsy Fordham Templeton. Student, U. NC, 1943—45, student, 1946—47, cert. in medicine, 1949; MD, Harvard U., 1951. Diplomate Am. Bd. Internal Medicine. Intern Georgetown U. Hosp., 1951—52; asst. resident Boston City Hosp., 1952—53; sr. asst. resident NC Meml. Hosp., Chapel Hill, 1953—54; fellow in medicine U. NC Sch. Medicine, 1954—55, instr. medicine, 1958—60, asst. prof., 1960—64, assoc. prof., asst. dean Sch. Medicine, 1964—68, prof., assoc. dean, 1968—69, prof. medicine, 1971—, vice chancellor for health affairs, 1977—80, chancellor, 1980—88, chancellor emeritus and prof. medicine, 1988—93, prof. medicine emeritus, 1993—, chancellor emeritus, dean emeritus, prof. medicine emeritus, 1993—; practice medicine, specializing in internal medicine Greensboro, 1957—58; prof. medicine, v.p. for medicine, dean Sch. Medicine, Med. Coll. Ga., Augusta, 1969—71; dean Sch. Medicine U. NC, 1971—79; acting asst. sec. for health Dept. HEW, Washington, 1977. Chair Gov.'s Com. on NC Awards, 1993—2000; chmn. NC Awards Com., 1993—2000; bd. dirs. Royal Soc. Med. Found., NYC, 1990—95. Officer USAF, 1955—57. Master: ACP; fellow: AAAS; mem.: AMA (Spl. award 1990), AAUP, Elisha Mitchell Sci. Soc., Inst. Medicine of NAS (coun. 1985—90), NY Acad. Scis., Am. Assn. Med. Coll. So. Regional Deans (chmn. 1972—73, 1975—75, chmn. nat. coun. deans 1977), Am. Assn. Med. Colls. (exec. coun. 1975—78, rep. liaison com. med. edn. 1977—79), Soc. Health and Human Values, Am. Fedn. Clin. Rsch., Am. Soc. Nephrology, So. Soc. Clin. Investigation, NC Med. Soc., Nat. Assn. State Univs. and Land Grant Colls. (chair coun. univ. governance 1990—91), Order Golden Fleece, Alpha Omega Alpha, Sigma Xi. Office: Univ NC Sch Medicine Campus Box 7000 Rm 130 MacNider Bldg Chapel Hill NC 27514

FORDIS, JEAN BURKE, lawyer; b. Ashiya AFB, Japan, Feb. 25, 1956; BA in Biology with distinction, Calif. State U., 1978; JD cum laude, Am. U., 1985. Bar: Md. 1985, US Ct. Appeals (Fed. Cir.) 1986, DC 1988, US Supreme Ct. 1993, Calif. 2005, registered: US Patent & Trademark Office. Law clk. to Hon. Philip Nichols Jr., Sr. Cir. Judge US Ct. Appeals (Fed. Cir.), 1985—86; biologist Nat. Inst. Health, Uniformed Services U. for Health Sci.; ptnr. Finnegan, Henderson, Farabow, Garret & Dunner LLP, Palo Alto, Calif., mng. ptnr. Pa. office. Mem. Am. U. Law Rev., 1983—85. Mem.: Md. Patent Law Assn. (sec. 1990—92, v.p. 1993—94, pres. 1995—97), Licensing Exec. Soc., Am. Intellectual Property Law Assn. (chmn. awards com. 1988—90), Phi Kappa Phi. Office: Finnegan Henderson Farabow Garrett & Dunner LLP 700 Hansen Way Stanford Rsch Park Palo Alto CA 94304-1016 Office Phone: 650-849-6600. Office Fax: 650-849-6666. Business E-mail: jean.fordis@finnegan.com.

FORD-REED, LILLIE MAE, geriatrics services professional; b. Near Blackville, S.C., Oct. 9, 1939; d. William Henry and Joanne Coleman Reed; m. Phinnize Ford; children: Monica D. Ford, Marie C. Ford, William H. Ford, Maude L. Ford, Phinnize E. Ford, Lee A. Ford, Merlinda Ford, Christopher E. Ford. A in Paralegal, Orangeburg Calhoun Tech. Coll., 2000. Pres. usher bd. Thankful Bapt. Missionary, Bamberg, SC; program chairperson Bapt. Usher Bd. Union, Bamberg; therapeutic asst. Northhampton Assocs., Orangeburg, SC, S.C. Mentor Network, Columbia; quality control insp. Allied Signal Aerospace Electronics, Orangeburg; vol. solicitor's office, victim witness sect. Helpline, Aiken, SC; vol. VITA Tax Svc.; pvt. caregiver Aiken, SC. Named to Wall of Tolerance So. Poverty Law Ctr., Mont.; recipient Honor award for Internship, Senator Strom Thurmon, 1984, Spl. Recognition award, Continental Challenge II Team, 2003, cert. of Appreciation, Girl Scouts U.S. Mem.: NAACP, Christian Burial Aid Assn. (pres. lodge #46), Smith-Hazel Phraise Modeling Team, Smith-Hazel Phraise Dance Group, Smith-Hazel Sr. Citizens Art and Crafts Club. Avocations: quilting, crafts, reading, sewing, dance.

FORDTRAN, JOHN SATTERFIELD, physician; b. San Antonio, Nov. 15, 1931; s. William M. and Josephine (Bell) F.; m. Jewel Evans, July 25, 1953; children: William, Bess, Josephine, Amy. Student, U. Tex., 1949-52; MD, Tulane U., 1956; DSc (hon.), Med. Coll. Wis., 1988; MD (hon.), Karl Franzens U., Graz, Austria, 1995. Internal medicine intern Parkland Meml. Hosp., Dallas, 1956-57, asst. resident internal medicine, 1957-58; research fellow gastroenterology Mass. Meml. Hosp., Boston, 1960-62; instr. internal medicine U. Tex. Southwestern Med. Sch., Dallas, 1962-63, asst. prof. internal medicine, 1963-67, assoc. prof. internal medicine, 1967-69, prof., 1969-79, chief sect. gastroenterology, 1963-79; chief dept. internal medicine Baylor U. Med. Center, Dallas, 1979-96; pres. Baylor Rsch. Inst., Baylor U. Med. Ctr., Dallas, 1991-2000. Mem. attending staff Parkland Meml. Hosp., Dallas, 1963-79; cons. gastroenterology Dallas VA Hosp., 1963-79. Contbr. articles to profl. jours.; editorial bd. Jour. Clin. Investigation, 1968-73; editor Gastroenterology, 1977-81; co-editor: Gastrointestinal Disease, 5th edit., 1993. Served with USPHS, 1958-60. Recipient King Faisal prize in medicine Saudi Arabia, 1984 Fellow Royal Coll. Physicians Eng.; mem. ACP, Am. Soc. Clin. Investigation (past pres.), Am. Gastroent. Assn. (Disting. Achievement award 1971, Kirsner prize 1990, Disting. Educator award 1991, Friedenwald medal 1993), Am. Gastroenterology Assn. (Lifetime Achievement in Digestive Sci. award, 1999). Home: 3508 Hanover St Dallas TX 75225-7434 Office: Baylor U Med Ctr 3500 Gaston Ave Dallas TX 75246-2096

FORDYCE, JAMES GEORGE, physician; b. Detroit, Jan. 9, 1945; s. James Alexander and Stella Marie (Pakron) F.; m. Kathleen Marie Ray, June 17, 1967; children: James A., Jonathan A., Jared A. BS, Mich. State U., 1966, DVM, 1968; MD, Wayne State U., 1974. Diplomate Am. Bd. Pediats., Am. Bd. Allergy and Immunology. Intern, resident Children's Hosp. Mich., Detroit, 1973-76; fellow allergy and clin. immunology Henry Ford Hosp., Detroit, 1976-78; physician Dearborn (Mich.) Allergy and Asthma Clinic, PC, 1978—. Cons. Metro Med. Group, Detroit, 1979-95. Author: Asthma in Clinical Pulmonary Medicine, 1992. Bd. trustees Oakwood Healthcare, Inc., 1996-2000. Fellow Am. Acad. Pediats., Am. Acad. Allergy, Asthma and Immunology, Am. Coll. Allergy, Asthma and Immunology; mem. Mich. Allergy and Asthma Soc. (pres. 1991-92). Avocations: fishing, flying, sailing. Office: Dearborn Allergy & Asthma Clinic PC 20200 Outer Dr Dearborn MI 48124-2634 Office Phone: 313-565-3565. Personal E-mail: jgfordyce@comcast.net.

FORDYCE, JAMES STUART, non-profit organization executive; b. London, Dec. 10, 1931; arrived in US, 1947, naturalized, 1994; s. James Wilfred and Doris Vera (McRae) F.; m. Beverly Ann Arnold, June 12, 1954; children: Cameron James, Jean Margaret. AB, Dartmouth Coll., 1953; PhD in Phys. Chemistry, MIT, 1959. Rsch. scientist Parma (Ohio) rsch. lab. Union Carbide Corp., 1959-66; rsch. scientist Lewis rsch. ctr. NASA, Cleve., 1966-68, head electrochemical fundamentals, 1968-73, mgr. environ. monitoring office, 1973-76, chief electrochemistry br., 1976-80, dep. chief space power tech. divsn., 1980-81, chief, 1981-84, dep. dir. aerospace tech., 1984-85, dir.,

1985-91, dep. ctr. dir., 1991-94; v.p., chief scientist Ohio Aerospace Inst., Cleve., 1995-2000, sr. cons., 2000—. Spl. lectr. Internat. Space U.; disting. space tech. lectr. Columbia U., 1988; bd. trustees Edison Polymer Innovation Corp., Akron, Ohio, 1991—. Author: (with others) Solar Power Satellites, 1993; contbr. articles to profl. jours. Mem. spl. com. Mus. Natural History, Cleve., 1991-96, 2000—02; active Leadership Cleve., 1992—93; internat. mem. program adv. bd. Ctr. for Rsch. in Earth and Space Tech., Toronto, 2001—; mem. Eng. adv. bd. Ohio U., Athens, 2002—. Fellow AIAA (assoc.); mem. AAAS, Am. Chem. Soc., Fedn. Am. Scientists, Electrochem. Soc. (lectr. 106th mtg. 1985), Sigma Xi, Phi Beta Kappa, Dartmouth Coll., Phi Beta Kappa. Democrat. Unitarian Universalist. Avocations: sailing, hiking, travel, music. Home: 21295 Cromwell Ave Fairview Park OH 44126-2714 Personal E-mail: stfordyce@cox.net.

FORE, HENRIETTA HOLSMAN, federal agency administrator; m. Richard L. Fore. AB, Wellesley Coll., 1970; MS, U. No. Colo., 1975. Pres. Stockton Wire Products, Burbank, Calif., 1977-89; chmn., pres. Pozacorp, Inc., 1981—89; asst. adminstr. for pvt. enterprise US Agy. for Internat. Devel., Washington, 1990-91, asst. adminstr. for Asia, 1991-93; dir. U.S. Mint US Dept Treasury, Washington, 2001—05; under sec. for mgmt. US Dept. State, Washington, 2005—. Chmn. US Asia Environ. Partnership, 1991—93. Mem. Com. of 200. Mem. Young Pres. Orgn. Office: US Dept State 2201 C St NW Rm 7207 Washington DC 20520

FOREHAND, JOSEPH W., finance company executive; b. Alexander City, Ala. m. Gayle Forehand; 2 children. BS in Indsl. Engring., Auburn U., 1971; MS in Indsl. Adminstrn., Purdue U., 1972. With Anderson Cons., 1972—, various positions with product group, regional dir. products industry, office mng. ptrn. Dallas, head Ams. products group, mng. ptrn. products Dallas and Paris, 1997-98, mng. ptnr. global comms. and high tech market unit; mng. ptrn., CEO Accenture(formerly Anderson), 2001—04; chmn. bd. dirs. Accenture, 2001—. Spkr. in field. Recipient Most Influential Cons., Consulting Mag., 2001, Morgan Stanley Leadership award, 2003. Office: Accenture 161 N Clark St Fl 11 Chicago IL 60601-3362

FOREMAN, ALFRED G., theologian, philosopher; b. Sulfur, La., Mar. 19, 1960; s. Grover Foreman and Stella Kibodeaux. BA, U. La., Lafayette, 1987; MA, Liberty U., 1991. Founder S. La. Weather Sta., Crowley, 1986—; pastor Ch. of God, Crowley, 1986—2002; with Imam Al-Ruh-Al-Amin Masjid, Crowley, 2003—. Lectr. Islamic Ctr., Lafayette, La., 1983-84, La. Philos. Inst. Humanities, Crowley, 1993-2004. Author: The Ecclesiastic Order: The Apology, 2002, The Christian and Islamic Thesis in History, 2002, Exposition of Islamic Knowledge: Incoherence of the Secularist, Book of Islamic Philosophy, Prophetic Wisdom and Directives; dir. South La. Weather Jour., 1986—. Mem. Internat. Palm Soc. (La. and Calif.) Ctr. for Islam and Sci. Home: 130 Palms Rd Crowley LA 70526-1907 Personal E-mail: faithandreason2005@yahoo.com.

FOREMAN, CAROL LEE TUCKER, consumer advocate; b. Little Rock, May 3, 1938; d. James Guy and Willie Maude (White) Tucker; m. Jay Howell Foreman, June 13, 1964; children: Guy Tucker, Rachel Marian. AA, William Woods Coll., 1958; AB, Washington U., 1960; postgrad., Am. U.; LLD (hon.), William Woods Coll., 1976. Rsch. asst. Com. Govt. Ops. U.S. Sen., 1961; assoc. Fed. Counsel Assocs., 1961-63; instr. Am. govt. William Woods Coll., Fulton, Mo., 1963-64; exec. asst. to Rep. James Roosevelt, 1964; dir. rsch. & publs. Dem. Nat. Com., 1965-66; Congl. liaison aide HUD, 1967-69; chief info. liaison Ctr. Family Planning Program Devel. Planned Parenthood-World Population, 1969-71; dir. policy coordination Commn. on Population and Am. Future, 1971-72; exec. dir. Citizens Com. on Population and Am. Future, 1972-73, Paul Douglas Consumer Rsch. Ctr., 1973-77, Consumer Fedn. Am., 1973-77; asst. sec. food and consumer svcs. Dept. Agriculture, Washington, 1977-81; dir. U.S. Commodity Credit Corp., 1977-81, U.S. Consumer Coop. Bank, 1977-81; pres. Foreman & Co., 1981-86, Foreman Heidepriem & Mager, 1986—99; disting. fellow, dir. The Food Policy Inst. Consumer Fedn. Am., 1999—. Mem. Pres.'s Commn. on White House Fellows, 1996—2001, Nat. Adv. Com. Meat and Poultry Inspection, 1997—2002, EU/US Consultative Forum Biotech., 2000, US Agriculture Policy Adv. Com. for Trade, 2002-; adv. com. Joint Inst. Food Safety and Applied Nutrition, 2000-05; mem. adv. com. on agrl. biotech. USDA, 2000—. Editor: Regulating for the Future, 1991. Exec. dir. Ctr. Women Policy Studies, 1983-84, mem. Interdeptl. Task Force on Women, 1973-74; bd. dirs. Consumer's Union, 1982-83, chmn., 1993—; bd. dirs. Food Rsch. & Action Ctr., 1983, Christianity and Crisis, 1990-92; vice chmn. Ctr. Nat. Policy, 1982-84, bd. dirs., 1981-99; trustee Washington U., St. Louis, 1987-95; bd. dirs. Bread for the World, 2000—. Recipient disting. alumni award Washington U., 1979, 2000. Mem. Women's Equity Action League (past pres. local chpt.), Nat. Policy Assn. (dir. 1985-97), Phi Beta Phi. Presbyterian. Office: Consumer Fedn Am 1424 16th St NW Ste 604 Washington DC 20036-2239 Home: 5600 Wisconsin Ave Ste 502 Chevy Chase MD 20815 Office Phone: 202-797-8551. Personal E-mail: tuckfore@aol.com.

FOREMAN, EDWARD RAWSON, retired lawyer; b. Atlanta, May 15, 1939; s. Robert Langdon and Mary (Shedden) F.; m. Margaret Reeves, Oct. 19, 1968; children: Margaret Langdon, Mary Rawson BA, Washington & Lee U., 1962; JD, Emory U., 1965. Bar: Ga. 1965. Assoc. Jones, Bird & Howell, Atlanta, 1965-70, ptnr., 1970-82, Alston & Bird, Atlanta, 1982-99; ret., 1999. Chmn. McAliley Endowment Trust, 1978—; lectr. Inst. for Continuing Legal Edn. in Ga., 1989; panelist, moderator Bus. Atlanta's Office Leasing and Tenant Opportunities in 1990s. Mem. editl. bd. Comml. Leasing Law and Strategy, 1996-98. Bd. dirs. Ansley Park Beautification Found., Atlanta, 1984-99, Midtown Alliance, Atlanta, 1988-96, sec., chmn. fundraising com., 1989-91, v.p., 1991, pres., 1992; trustee Paidela Sch. Endowment Fund, Atlanta, 1980-99, Woodruff Arts Ctr., Atlanta, 1985-90; chmn. Emory U. Law Fund, Atlanta, 1981; chmn. legal divsn. United Way Met. Atlanta, 1984; chmn. strategic planning com. High Mus. Art, 1986-95, chmn., bd. dirs. 1998—99, chmn. nominating com., 1993-95; vestryman, sr. warden St. Luke's Episc. Ch., 1975, 94, 2001, com. mem., 1975-90; pres. Atlanta Legal Aid Soc., 1975-76; comm. chair and pres. Atlanta Preservation Ctr., 1986-91; trustee Miss Hall's Sch., Pittsfield, Mass., 1990-2001. Recipient Cmty. Svc. award Martin Luther King Jr. Ctr. Nonviolent Social Change, 1980, Outstanding Svc. award Atlanta Preservation Ctr., Inc., 1983. Mem. ABA (mem. comml. leasing com. 1987-95), State Bar Ga. (chmn., panelist, moderator comml. leasing seminars 1979-86), Atlanta Bar Assn. (chmn., panelist, moderator leasing seminars 1979-86, chmn. hdqrs. search com. 1988-96), Lawyers Club Atlanta (chmn. long-range planning com. 1989-90), Atlanta Bar Found. (bd. dirs.), Old War Horse Lawyers Club, Nine O'Clocks Club (mem. centennial com. 1983), Highlands Country Club N.C. Democrat. Episcopalian. Personal E-mail: mccoy10@mindspring.com.

FOREMAN, EDWARD VAUGHT, voice educator, book publisher, writer, translator, composer, singer; b. Jacksonville, Ill., May 19, 1937; s. Orville Nicholas and Helen Louise Cleary Foreman; m. Judith Ann Bosserman, Oct. 19, 1960; children: Timothy Waite, Emily Susan Rosenmeier, Amy Elizabeth Simmer, Bridget Cathleen Blankenship. Student, Curtis Inst. Music, 1956—58; BA, Ill. Coll., 1960; MusM, U. Colo., 1965; D in Music Arts, U. Ill., 1969. Voice faculty U. Colo., Boulder, 1963—64, U. Ill., Urbana, 1966—68, U. Minn., Mpls., 1971—73; pub. Pro Musica Press, Mpls., 1967—; chair. voice faculty, founder opera theatre U. Wis., Milw., 1968—71; resident bass-baritone Ctr. Opera Co., Mpls., 1971—72; pvt. voice tchr., 1971—; bass-baritone soloist Desto/CRI Recs., 1971; soloist Third Ch. Christ, Scientist, 1987—. Author: (non-fiction book) Transformative Voice, Voice Without Technique, Authentic Singing, Being the History and Practice of the Art of Singing and Teaching, Baroque Singing; translator, pub. (non-fiction book) Practical Reflections on Figured Singing, Observations on Figured Singing, Grammar, or Rules for Singing Well, Late Renaissance Singing, composer, prodr., dir. (1 act opera) The Dalmatian of Faust, The Trojan Women; composer: (3 act opera) Macbeth, (choral music) Pax (Top Honors, 2002), numerous choral music pieces; composer, performer over 60 ch. vocal solos. Lt. (j.g.) USNR, 1960—63, Pacific Fleet. Unicum Pub. grant, Martha Baird Rockefeller Found., 1972, Book Pub. grant, Lila Wallace Found., 1972. Mem.: Am. Musicological Soc. Home and Office: Pro Musica Press 2501 Pleasant Ave Minneapolis MN 55404-4213 Office Phone: 612-872-8362. Personal E-mail: voyceking@iphouse.com.

FOREMAN, EDWIN FRANCIS, economist, real estate broker; b. Syracuse, N.Y., July 24, 1931; s. Herve Joseph and Ruth M. Foreman; m. Colleen Frances Tapp, July 7, 1962; children: Lisa C., Eric E. BAE in Econs. and Fgn. Trade, U. Fla., 1957; postgrad. in real estate, Fla. Internat. U., 1974-75. Owner, prin. Edwin F. Foreman, Mortgage Broker, Hollywood, Fla., 1974—; with Consol. Energy Corp., Hollywood, 1977—, pres., chmn. bd., 1977—; v.p. Ea. State Securities, Inc., 1977-92, J.S. Securities, 1994-97, Northridge Capital Corp., 1999—; owner, prin. Edwin F. Foreman, Real Estate Broker, 1978—. Pres., chmn. One-Fore-Devel., Inc., 1985, Three-Fore-Devel., Inc., 1985, L&E Comm. Inc., 1985; chmn., CEO Universal Traction, Hollywood, 1988—; gen. ptnr. Four-Fore Devel. Ltd., Five-Fore-Devel. Ltd., Six-Fore Devel., Ltd., 1987—, CCS Ventures, 1990—; mem. Funds Coordinating Group Internat., L.L.C., 1998—; econ. cons. Michael I. Warde de Colombia Ltd.; guest lectr. econs. Xavier U., Bogota, Colombia. Served with USAF, 1950-53. R.J. Reynolds fellow U. N.C., 1961; NSF fellow. Mem. Hollywood C. of C. (econ. devel. com.), Ft. Lauderdale World Trade Coun., Jockey Club (Miami), Grove Isle Club (Miami), Fisher Island Club. Democrat. Unitarian Universalist. Avocations: camping, fishing, bicycling, photography, travel. Office: PO Box 7570 Hollywood FL 33081

FOREMAN, GEORGE EDWARD, retired boxer, minister, boxing commentator; b. Marshall, Tex., Jan. 10, 1949; s. J. D. and Nancy Foreman; m. Mary Foreman, children: Michi, Freeda, Natalie, George Jr., George III, George IV, George V, George VI. Profl. boxer, 1969—77, 1987—97; minister, 1977—; founder, minister Ch. Lord Jesus Christ, Houston, 1984—; promoter The George Foreman Lean Mean Grilling Machine, 1995—, The George Foreman Signature Collection, 2004—; expert commentator HBO's World Championship Boxing; founder George Foreman Enterprises Inc., 2005. Author: (with Joel Engel) By George: the Autobiography of George Foreman, 1995, George Foreman's Knock-Out-The-Fat: Barbecue and Grilling Cookbook, 1996,(with Barbara Witt) George Foreman's Big Book of Grilling, Barbecue, and Rotisserie: More than 70 Recipes for Family and Friends, 2000, (with Linda Kulman) George Foreman's Guide to Life: How to Get up Off the Canvas When Life Knocks You Down, 2003, (with Kathryn Kellinger) George Foreman's Indoor Grilling Made Easy: More Than 100 Simple, Healthy Ways to Feed Family and Friends, 2004; film appearance: Lets Do It Again, 1975; TV series: George, 1993; TV appearances:The Six Million Dollar Man, 1975, Sanford and Son, 1976, Good Sports, 1990, Home Improvement, 1991, The Larry Sanders Show, 1992, King of the Hill (voice only); numerous TV commercials and endorsements. Founder George Foreman Cmty. Ctr., Houston. Named Boxer of the Year, World Boxing Assn., 1974, Male Athlete of Yr., AP, 1994; named to The US Olympic Hall of Fame, 1990, The World Boxing Hall of Fame, 2002, Internat. Boxing Hall of Fame, 2003. Achievements include winning a gold medal for boxing in the 1968 Olympic Games, Mexico City; Nat. AAU Heavyweight Chamipon, 1968, World Heavyweight Boxing Champion, 1973-74, 94-95; becoming the oldest Heavyweight Champion in boxing history (45 yrs. old).

FOREMAN, GREGORY C., music educator, musician; b. Springfield, Mo., Aug. 24, 1960; s. Arthur C. Foreman and J. Foreman Betty; m. Melodie E. Coker, June 2, 1984. MusB in Edn., Cert. of Piano Performance, Evangel U., Springfield, Mo., 1981; MA in Tchg., Webster U., Kansas City, Mo., 2000. Cert. Vocal and Instrumental Music, K-12 Mo., 1981. Lead elem. music tchr. R-7 Sch. Dist., Lee's Summit, Mo., 1982—. Web mgr. Highland Pk. Elem., Lee's Summit, 2002—05, profl. staff devel. affiliate, 2000—03, bus. partnership facilitator Partners in Edn., 2003—, children's choir dir., Independence, Mo. Author: (music teacher resource book) Making the Grade; soloist Liszt's Second Piano Concerto, Kansas City Symphony (Kans. City Symphony Honors Audition). Music dir. One Spirit United Meth. Ch., Kansas City, Mo., 1999—2004. Grantee, Lee's Summit Ednl. Found., 1998, Yamaha Music Corp., 1998. Mem.: Music Educato's Nat. Conf. (assoc.), Pi Kappa Lambda. Avocations: theatre organist, ragtime pianist. Home: 17800 Bolger Road Unit 106A Independence MO 64055 Office: Highland Park Elementary School 400 SE Millstone Avenue Lees Summit MO 64063 Office Phone: 816-986-2250. Office Fax: 816-986-2275. Personal E-mail: greg.foreman@comcast.net. E-mail: greg.foreman@leesummit.k12.mo.us.

FOREMAN, JAMES LOUIS, retired judge; b. Metropolis, Ill., May 12, 1927; s. James C. and Anna Elizabeth (Henne) F.; m. Mabel Inez Dunn, June 16, 1948; children: Beth Foreman Banks, Rhonda Foreman Wittig, Nanette Foreman Love. BS in Commerce and Law, U. Ill., 1950, JD, 1952. Bar: Ill. Ind. practice law, Metropolis, Ill.; ptnr. Chase and Foreman, Metropolis, until 1972; state's atty. State of Ill., Massac County, asst. atty. gen.; chief judge U.S. Dist. Ct. (so. dist.) Ill., Benton, 1979-92, sr. status, 1992—. Pres. Bd. of Edn., Metropolis. With USN, 1945-46. Mem. Ill. State Bar Assn., Metropolis C. of C. (past pres.). Republican. Home: 660 Whitney Dr Paducah KY 42001 Office: US Dist Ct 301 W Main St Benton IL 62812-1362

FOREMAN, JOHN DANIEL, financial executive; b. Wheeling, W.Va., Aug. 24, 1940; s. William Carroll and Mary Katheryn (Leese) F.; m. Helen Virginia Donato, Sept. 2, 1967; children: Sean, Christopher. BA, Wheeling (W.Va.) Coll., 1962; MA, W.Va. U., 1965. Banking officer Wheeling Dollar Bank, 1964-67; prof., dept. chair Seton Hill Coll., Greensburg, Pa., 1967-81; mem. faculty, adminstr. Westmoreland County Community Coll., Youngwood, Pa., 1971-81; dir. continuing edn. St. Vincent Coll., Latrobe, Pa., 1981-84, dean enrollment and planning, 1984-87; chief fin. officer The Eye and Ear Inst., Pitts., 1987-93. Pres. Aquillian Corp., Greensburg, Pa., 1981—. Contbr. articles to profl. jours. Treas. bd. dirs. Westmoreland Symphony Orch., Greensburg, 1989—; bd. dirs. SUC Small Bus. Devel. Ctr., Latrobe, 1983-90, Westmoreland Trust, 1992—. Mem. Pitts. Athletic Assn., Pitts. Club. Office: 419 College Ave Greensburg PA 15601-1526

FOREMAN, JOHN PATRICK, electrical engineer; b. Lake Charles, La., Aug. 16, 1954; s. John Calvin Foreman and Daisy Mae (Finley) Foreman Milsted; m. Nadine Rachelle Dudek, Nov. 10, 2001. BSEE, McNeese State U., 1976. Registered profl. engr., Tex., Calif., La., Oreg., Mass., Wash., Nev. Elec. engr. Fluor Engrs. & Contractors, Houston, 1977-83, Jacobs Engring. Group, Houston, 1983, Burgess & Niple, Ltd., Houston, 1984-86; project mgr. Turpin & Rattan Engring., San Diego, 1986-92, TH Rogers & Assocs., Oakland, Calif., 1993, Alfa Tech. Cons. Engrs., San Jose, Calif., 1994-99; assoc. TKG Cons. Engrs., San Diego, 2000—03, Bechard Long & Assocs., Inc., 2003—. Mem.: NSPE, IEEE, Tex. Soc. Profl. Engrs. Democrat. Roman Catholic. Avocations: darts, skiing, volleyball, softball, martial arts. Home: Apt A-10 12532 Oak Knoll Rd Poway CA 92064 Office: Bechard & Assocs 12127 Kirkham Rd Poway CA 92064 Personal E-mail: jp816foreman@aol.com. Business E-Mail: pforeman@bech.com.

FOREMAN, JOHN WILLIAM, pediatrician, educator; b. Washington, June 23, 1947; s. William Roy and Elizabeth Roberts (McLean) F.; m. Linda Poffenberger, May 27 1973; children: Matthew John, Jennifer Lynne. BS, Duke U., 1969; MD, U. Md., 1973. Diplomate Nat. Bd. Med. Examiners, Pa., Va., N.C., Am. Bd. Pediatrics, subbd. pediatric nephrology. Intern, resident Montreal (Que., Can.) Children's Hosp., 1973-75; asst. chief resident pediatrics Children's Hosp. Phila., 1975-76, fellow pediatric nephrology, 1976-79, staff physician, 1979-86; instr. pediatrics U. Pa. Sch. Medicine, Phila., 1976-79, clin. asst. prof., asst. prof., 1979-85, assoc. prof., 1985-86; assoc. prof. pediatrics Med. Coll. Va., Va. Commonwealth U., Richmond, 1986-90, prof., 1990-93; prof., chief divsn. pediatric nephrology Duke U. Med. Ctr., Durham, N.C., 1993—. Cons. WHO, 1984; chmn. med. adv. bd. Nat. Kidney Found. Va., 1989-92, mem. exec. com. pediatric urology and nephrology coun.; mem. pediatric delegation to Chinese Med. Assn. of People's Republic of China. Contbr. articles to profl. jours., chpts. to books. Bd. dirs. Transplant Found., Richmond, 1991. Daland fellow Am. Philos. Soc., Phila., 1980-81; grantee Am. Heart Assn., 1984-88, NIH, 1988-91. Fellow Am. Acad. Pediat.; mem. Soc. Pediatric Rsch., Am. Pediatric Soc., So. Soc. Pediatric Rsch. (councillor 1989-91), Internat. Pediatric Nephrology Soc. (councillor 1993-98), Am. Soc. Pediatric Nephrology (coun. mem. 2002--), Am. Soc. Nephrology, mem. exec. com. sect. on Nephrology Am. Acad. of Pediatrics. Avocations: reading, bicycling. Home: 9 Streamley Ct Durham NC 27705-5396 Office: Duke U Med Ctr PO Box 3959 Durham NC 27710-0001 Office Phone: 919-684-4246. Business E-Mail: forem001@mc.duke.edu.

FOREMAN, JUDY, journalist; b. Ft. Bragg, N.C., 1944; BA in Anthropology/Sociology, Wellesley Coll., 1966; MEd, Harvard U., 1970. City Hall reporter Lowell (Mass.) Sun, 1970-73; gen. assignment reporter Times, London, 1982-83; stringer Boston Globe, 1976-78, sci. and medicine reporter, 1983-95, columnist Health Sense, 1995—. Office: Boston Globe PO Box 2378 Boston MA 02107-2378 also: Boston Globe 135 Morrissey Blvd Boston MA 02125-3310

FOREMAN, LEE DAVID, lawyer; b. Tacoma, July 6, 1946; s. Lee Alfred and Shirley Alma (Stone) F.; m. Susan Lynn Hinke, Apr. 2, 1978; children: Seth Lee, Emily Park. AB with distinction, Stanford U., 1968, JD, 1972. Bar: Colo. 1972, U.S. Dist. Ct. Colo. 1972, U.S. Ct. Appeals (10th cir.) 1977. Dep. state pub. defender Colo. State Pub. Defender's Office, Denver, 1972-77; ptnr. Haddon, Morgan, Mueller, Jordan, Mackey & Foreman, P.C., Denver, 1978—. Fellow Am. Coll. Trial Lawyers; mem. ABA, Denver Bar Assn. (vol. lawyer of yr. 1988), Boulder Bar Assn., Colo. Bar Assn., Colo. Criminal Def. Bar (pres. 1981-82, bd. dirs. 1982—), Nat. Assn. Criminal Def. Lawyers. Democrat. Avocations: golf, trout fishing. E-mail: ldforeman@hmflaw.com.

FOREMAN, RICHARD, theater director, playwright; b. N.Y.C., June 10, 1937; s. Albert and Claire (Levine) F. BA, Brown U., 1959, ArtsD (hon.), 1993; MFA, Yale U., 1962. Artistic dir. Ontological-Hysteric Theater, N.Y.C., 1968—. Dir.-in-residence N.Y. Shakespeare Festival, N.Y.C., 1975-76; artistic dir. Theatre O.H., Paris, 1973-85. Dir. Broadway and off-Broadway plays including 3-Penny Opera, 1976; author, dir. Dr. Selavy's Magic Theater, 1972, Rhoda in Potatoland, 1976 (Obie award Village Voice 1976), Film Is Evil: Radio is Good, 1987 (Obie award Village Voice, 1987), Pearls for Pigs, 1997 (Obie award Village Voice, 1997), Benita Canova, 1998 (Obie award Village Voice, 1998); over 40 others; author: Unbalancing Acts, 1992 and others. Mem. panel theatre div. Nat. Endowment for Arts, Washington, 1976-79. Guggenheim fellow, 1972, Rockefeller fellow, 1974, Creative Artist's Pub. Svc. fellow, 1974, Creative Artist's Pub. Svc. fellow N.Y. State Arts Coun., 1971, MacArthur fellow, 1995-2000; recipient Lifetime Achievement award NEA, 1990, Am. Acad. Arts and Letters prize in lit., 1992, PEN/Laura Pels Master Am. Dramatist award, 2001; officer Order Arts and Letters, France, 2003. Mem. Dramatist's Guild, Soc. Stage Dirs., PEN. Jewish. Avocations: philosophy, psychoanalysis. Home and Office: 152 Wooster St New York NY 10012-5330 E-mail: mmeedwarda@earthlink.net.

FOREMAN, SPENCER, pulmonologist, hospital administrator, director; b. Phila., Nov. 10, 1935; s. Samuel and Freda F.; m. Sandra Lee Finkelstein, June 10, 1961; children: Corinne, Todd, Cheryl, Andrea. BS, Ursinus Coll., 1957; MD, U. Pa., 1961. Diplomate in internal medicine and pulmonary disease Am. Bd. Internal Medicine. Intern Henry Ford Hosp., Detroit, 1961-62; med. officer USPHS, San Pedro, Calif., 1962-63; resident in internal medicine USPHS Hosp., New Orleans, 1963-65; fellow in pulmonary diseases Tulane U., 1965-67; asst. chief dept. internal medicine USPHS Hosp., Balt., 1967-68, chief dept. internal medicine, 1968-73, hosp. dir., 1971-73; CEO Sinai Hosp., Balt., 1973-86; pres. Montefiore Med. Ctr., Bronx, N.Y., 1986—. Prof. medicine, prof. social medicine and epidemiology Albert Einstein Coll. Medicine, Bronx; mem. Accreditation Coun. on Med. Edn., 1981-87, ProPAC (Prospective Payment Assessment Commn.) 1996. Contbr. articles to med. jours. Commr. Md. Health Resources Commn., 1982-86, Liaison Com. for Med. Edn., 1989-91; bd. dirs. Am. Jewish Joint Distbn. Com., Inc., Ursinus Coll., Collegeville, Pa.; chmn. Biomed. Rsch. Alliance N.Y., 1998-2000, chmn., 2000-; vice chmn. Ursinus Coll., 2002-04, chmn., 2004-. Capt. USPHS, 1962-73. Fellow ACP, N.Y. Acad. Medicine; mem. Inst. Medicine Nat. Acad. Scis., Assn. Am. Med. Colls. (rep. assembly, chmn. 1986, adminstrv. bd. Coun. Tchg. Hosps., chmn.-elect assembly 1991-92, chmn. 1992-93), Am. Hosp. Assn. (bd. dirs. 1995-98), Health Forum (bd. dirs. 1998-99), Greater N.Y. Hosp. Assn. (bd. dirs., vice chmn., chmn.), League Vol. Hosps. (bd. dirs., sec.-treas., chmn.), Soc. Med. Adminstrs. (pres. 2000-02). Office: Montefiore Med Ctr 111 E 210th St Bronx NY 10467-2401 E-mail: sforeman@montefiore.org.

FOREMAN, TERESA, educational consultant, educator; d. E. T. and Elmer Mae McCrory; m. Larry Foreman, Dec. 10, 1977. BA in Elem. Edn., N.E. La. U., Monroe, 1970—74, MA in Elem. Edn., 1974—76, MA +30, 1976—79. Tchr. Ouachita Parish Sch. Bd., Monroe, La., 1974—79, 1982—89; br. mgr. First Mortgage Corp., Tuscaloosa, Ala., 1979—82; program coord., trainer La. State U., Baton Rouge, 1989—90; profl. accountability coord. La. Dept. Edn., Baton Rouge, 1990—99; accountability and testing mgr. Monroe City Sch. Bd., La., 1999—. Staff devel. cons. SchoolWorks, Monroe, La., 1989—. Media and mktg. Monroe City Sch. Bd., La., 2001; vice chair Workforce Investment Bd. Area 81, Monroe, La., 2002, bd. mem., 1999. Recipient Outstanding Young Educator, Monroe C. of C., 1987. Mem.: La. Sch. Supervisor's Assn., ASCD, Phi Delta Kappa. Avocations: travel, reading, music, the arts. Office: Monroe City Sch Bd 2101 Roselawn Ave Monroe LA 71201 Office Phone: 318-325-0601. E-mail: tforeman@monroe.k12.la.us.

FOREMAN, THOMAS ALEXANDER, dentist; b. Tionesta, Pa., Oct. 24, 1930; s. James Aura and May (Lanson) F.; m. Dorothy Jean Wolf, June 12, 1953; children: Bonnie Jean, Julie Marie, Mary Aleta, Lloyd George. Student, Grove City Coll., 1948-50; BS, Allegheny Coll., 1952; DDS cum laude, U. Pitts., 1957, DMD, 1970. Gen. practice dentistry, Clarion, Pa., 1961—. Active Clarion Hosp. Assn., 1965—; exec. bd. Colonel Drake coun. Boy Scouts Am., 1969-72, mem.-at-large French Creek coun., 1972-73, vice-chmn. Indian Trails dist., 1971-73; governing coun. Alpha Christian Acad. Sch., 1977-81. Capt. with Dental Corps USAF, 1957—61. Fellow, Pierre Fauchard Acad. Fellow Acad. Dentistry Internat., Am. Coll. Dentists, Internat. Coll. Dentists, Royal Soc. Health; mem. ADA, Pa. Dental Assn. (dir. 8th dist. 1964-87, 91—, pres. 1974-76, trustee 1987-91), Acad. Gen. Dentistry (master), AMA (affiliate), Clarion County Dental Soc. (pres. 1983-87), S.A.R. (pres. Capt. Samuel Brady chpt. 1970-71, 77-80), Soc. Mayflower Descs., Pilgrim Edward Doty Soc., Fedn. Dentaire Internat., Pa. Soc., Western Pa. Conservancy, Cook Forest Ctr. for Arts, Clarion County Hist. Soc., Mason (Shriner), Phi Beta Phi, Omicron Kappa Upsilon, Delta Sigma Delta, Theta Chi. Presbyn. (pres. bd. trustees 1966-67, supt. Sunday sch. 1966-67, chmn. endowment trust fund dirs. 1980-84, elder 2001—). Home: 147 S 7th Ave Clarion PA 16214-2006 Office: 832 E Main St Clarion PA 16214-1168

FOREMAN, WILLIAM ANTHONY, JR., systems administrator; Diploma, Desktop Specialist Profl. Career Devel. Inst., 1998; BS in Info. Tech. and Network Adminstrn., Computer Learning Ctrs. Inc., Madison Heights, Mich., 2001. MCSE Windows 2000 2001. Contract network adminstr. Ford Motor Co., Dearborn, Mich., 1995—97; contract network engr. Gen. Motors Corp., Romulus, 1997—98; dist. tech. support specialist HR Block Income Tax, Ann Arbor, 1998—2001; network adminstr. Johnson Controls, Plymouth, 2001—. Address: 33260 Creston St Westland MI 48186

FORER, ARTHUR H., biology professor, researcher, editor; b. Trenton, N.J., Dec. 17, 1935; arrived in Can., 1972; s. Bernard and Rose Ethel Forer; m. Alexandra Engberg Westengaard, Dec. 18, 1964; children— Michael, David. B.Sc., MIT, Cambridge, 1957; postgrad., U. Rochester, 1957-59, U. Wash.-Friday Harbor, summer 1959; PhD in Molecular Biology, Dartmouth Med. Sch., 1964. Postdoctoral fellow Am. Cancer Soc. Carlsberg Labs., Copenhagen, 1964-66; research asst. Cambridge U., Eng., 1966-67, Helen Hay Whitney Found. fellow, 1967-69, Duke U., Durham, N.C., 1969-70; lektor Odense U., Denmark, 1970-72; assoc. prof. biology York U., Toronto, Canada, 1972—75, prof. biology, 1975—2001, prof. emeritus, sr. scholar, 2001—. Mem. grant selection panel Natural Scis. and Engring. Rsch. Coun., 1976-78. Editor: Mitosis/Cytokinesis, 1981; mem. editorial bd. Jour. Cell

Sci., 1972-84, Can. Jour. Biochemistry and Cell Biology, 1982-93, Cell Biology Internat. Reports, 1984—; contbr. articles to profl. jours. Active Amnesty Internat., Ottawa, Ont., 1980—, Cmty. Theatre Orchs., Toronto, A Pack-O-Lips Now Saxophone Quartet, Toronto. Fellow Royal Soc. Can., Acad. Scis.; mem. AAAS, Am. Soc. Cell Biology, Stankel Ben Soc. (charter mem. 1960—), Tarragon Theatre, Shaw Festival (supporting). Avocations: music, gardening, bicycling, hiking. Home: 17 Michigan Dr Willowdale ON Canada M2M 3H9 Office: York U Biology Dept 4700 Keele St Downsview ON Canada M3J 1P3 Business E-Mail: aforer@yorku.ca.

FORESE, JAMES JOHN, business machine company executive; b. Coatesville, Pa., Dec. 31, 1935; s. Samuel and Edith (Mastrangelo) Forese; m. Florine Skutnik, June 27, 1959; children: Laura Lee, James Anthony, Diane Edith, John Thomas. BSEE, Rensselaer Polytech. Inst.; MBA, MIT. With IBM, Armonk, NY, 1959—95; exec. v.p., COO Alco Std., 1996; exec. v.p., pres. internat. ops. IKON Office Solutions, Inc., 1997—98, pres., CEO, 1998—2000, chmn., 2000—. Bd. dirs. NUI Corp., Am. Mgmt. Sys., IBM Latin Am., IBM Credit Corp., Lexmark Internat. Trustee Rensselear Polytech. Inst.; mem. CBA Found. adv. coun. Coll. Bus. Adminstrn.; mem. engring. found. adv. coun. Coll. Engring. U. Tex.-Austin. Office: IKON Office Solutions Inc 70 Valley Stream Pkwy Malvern PA 19355-1453

FOREST, EVA BROWN, nursing administrator, composer; b. Ontario, Va., July 7, 1941; d. William Butler and Ruth Pauline (Simpson) Brown; m. Willie J. Forest Jr., Sept. 16, 1961; children: Gerald, Darryl, Angela. AA, Bismarck (N.D.) State Coll., 1981; BSN, U. Mary, Bismarck, 1984. RN Colo. Charge nurse St. Alexius Med. Ctr., Bismarck, 1984—85, Cedars Health Care Ctr., Lakewood, Colo., 1989—90; staff devel. coord. Pk. Ave. Bapt. Home, Denver, 1990—91; supr., charge nurse Cedars Health Care Ctr., Lakewood, Colo., 1991—; charge nurse Villa Manor Health Ctr., Lakewood, Colo., 1991—93, Stovall Care Ctr., Denver, 1995—96, supr., 1997—98, supr., charge nurse, 1999—2003; nursing supr. Rose Ter. Care Ctr., Commerce City, Colo., 2003—. Songwriter, prodr., 1999; recorded (CD) God Has Begun a Good Work in Me, 1999. Vol. for cultural exch. lang., culture and fashions YWCA, Kano, Nigeria; vocalist gospel music workshop, ND; pianist adult and children's choir, ND; mem. MADD, Habitat for Humanity Internat., HALT, Vols. of Am. Mem. Nat. Multiple Sclerosis Soc., DAV Commdrs. Club, Vols. of Am. Office Phone: 303-716-9346. Personal E-mail: Webmaster@foresteb.net.

FORESTER, JEAN MARTHA BROUILLETTE, innkeeper, retired librarian, educator; b. Port Barre, La., Sept. 7, 1934; d. Joseph Walter and Thelma (Brown) Brouillette; m. James Lawrence Forester, June 2, 1957; children: Jean Martha, James Lawrence. BS La. State U., 1955; MA, George Peabody Coll. Tchrs., 1956. Libr. Howell Elem. Sch., Springhill, La., 1956—58; asst. post libr. Fort Chaffee, Ark., 1958; command libr. Orleans Area Command, U.S. Army, Orleans, France, 1958—59; acquisitions libr. Northwestern State U., Natchitoches, La., 1960; serials libr. La. State U., New Orleans, 1960—66, mem. faculty Eunice, 1966—85, asst. libr., 1972—85, assoc. libr., 1985—87, acting libr., 1987—88, dir. libr., 1988—89, libr. emeritus, 1989—, asst. prof., 1972—85, faculty senator, 1978—80, 1985—86, 1987—89; innkeeper Crown'n'Anchor Inn, Saco, Maine, 1989—. Co-author: Robertsons's Bill of Fare; contbr. articles to profl. jours. Active Eunice Assn. Retarded Children. Fellow Carnegie, 1955—56. Mem.: UDC, La. Libr. Assn. (sect. sec. 1971—72, coord. serials interest group 1984—85), Delta Kappa Gamma (chpt. parliamentarian 1972—74, rec. sec. 1984—86), Order Ea. Star, Phi Mu, Phi Gamma Mu, Alpha Beta Alpha. Democrat. Baptist.

FORESTER, JOHN GORDON, JR., lawyer; b. Wilkesboro, NC, Jan. 14, 1933; s. John Gordon and Mary Hope (Hendren) F.; m. Georgina Ramirez, June 26, 1957; children: John Gordon III, Robert Raoul, Georgina Yasué, Richard Alexander. BS, in Indsl. Rels., U. NC, 1955; LLB, George Washington U., 1962. Bar: DC 1962, Md. 1993. Internat. economist Dept. Commerce, 1958-62; confidential asst. to dep. asst. sec. commerce, 1962-63; law clk. US Dist. Judge L.P. Walsh, 1963-64; pvt. practice Washington, 1964-80; ptnr. Pohoryles & Greenstein, P.C., Washington, 1980-89, Greenstein Delorme & Luchs, P.C., Washington, 1989-95; pvt. practice, 1995—. Mem. Jud. Conf. DC Cir., 1981, 82, 92, adv. com. Civil Justice Reform Act, US Dist. Ct., 1991-93; pres. Lawyers Mut. Ins. Co. DC, 1990-92. Contbr. articles to profl. jours. Pres. Friendly Citizens Assn., 1963, Gonzaga Fathers Club, 1974-76; chmn. bd. dirs. Henson Valley Montessori Sch.; bd. dirs. Sursum Corda Neighborhood Ctr., 1975-77. Lt. comdr. USNR, 1955-58. Mem. ABA (mem. ho. dels. 2000-2002), DC Bar Assn. (pres. 2001-02), Md. Bar Assn., Coun. Ct. Excellence (chmn. ct. improvement com.), George Washington U. Law Alumni Assn. (pres. DC chpt. 1988-89), Counsellors (pres. 1984-85), Barrister Inn (pres. 1976-77), Order Golden Fleece, Kappa Alpha Order, Phi Delta Phi. Roman Catholic. Office: 1914 Sunderland Pl NW Washington DC 20036 Office Phone: 202-293-3353. Personal E-mail: jgfcadence@aol.com.

FORET, MICKEY PHILLIP, air transportation company executive; b. McComb, Miss., Oct. 23, 1945; s. Fadias Phillip and Christine (Brown) F.; m. Mary Ann Tramonte, Aug. 12, 1966; 1 child, Keri. BS in Fin., MBA in Fin., La. State U., 1971. Dir. credit/interim dir. internal audit Tex. (Houston) Internat. Airlines, 1975-77, dir. cash mgmt., 1977-78, asst. treas., 1978-81, v.p. fin. svcs., 1981-82; v.p., treas. Continental Airlines, L.A., 1982-84, v.p., chief fin. officer, 1984-86, also bd. dirs.; sr. v.p. fin. and internat. Eastern Airlines, Miami, Fla., 1987-88, v.p., chief fin. officer, 1986—, also bd. dirs.; sr. v.p. Tex. (Houston) Air Corp., 1988—; exec. v.p. fin. and planning Continental Airlines, Houston, 1988-89, pres., 1989-90; exec. v.p., CFO Northwest Airlines, 1992-96; pres. Atlas Air, Inc., 1996-1997; spec. projects offcr. Northwest Airlines, 1998—, CFO, exec. v.p., 1998—. Chmn. bd. dirs., chief exec. officer Chelsea Catering Co., Houston. Pres. Clear Wood Improvement Assn., Houston, 1975-78; coach Friendswood (Tex.) Girls Softball Team, 1981. Served with USAF, 1966-69, Vietnam. Mem. Phi Kappa Phi, Beta Gamma Sigma. Republican. Baptist. Avocations: boating, water-skiing, biking. Home: 7001 Valley View Rd Edina MN 55439-1652

FORGANG, DAVID M., curator; b. N.Y.C., Mar. 26, 1947; s. Joseph Hyman and Clarice (Ishbia) F.; m. Joyce Enid Blumenthal, June 15, 1968 (div. May 1979); children: Adam, Bradley. B in Anthropology, U. Ariz., 1968, M in Anthropology, 1971. Mus. curator So. Ariz. Group Nat. Pk. Svc., Phoenix, 1971-77, regional curator we. region San Francisco, 1977-82, curator Yosemite (Calif.) Mus., 1982—. Pres. Yosemite Renaissance Art Competition, 1983-94; dir. Yosemite Artist in Residence Program, 1985—. Mariposa County advisor El Portal (Calif.) Town Planning Adv. Bd., 1984-94. Recipient Unit Award citation US Dept. Interior, 1974. Democrat. Jewish. Avocations: fishing, canoeing, hunting, gardening. Office: Nat Pk Svc PO Box 577 Yosemite National Park CA 95389-0577

FORGER, ROBERT DURKIN, retired professional association administrator; b. Norwalk, Conn., May 24, 1928; s. Alois John and Elsie Marie (Durkin) F.; m. Eleanor Marie Goddard, May 14, 1951; children: Gary Robert, Jeffrey Alois. BS, Norwich U., Northfield, Vt., 1949; grad., U.S. Army Command and Gen. Staff Coll., 1970. Research and devel. engr., mgr. tech. publicity Dorr-Oliver Inc., Stamford, Conn., 1949-59; conf. mgr., pub., exec. dir. Soc. Plastics Engrs., Brookfield, Conn., 1959-93; ret., 1993. Chmn. Westport (Conn.) Pub. Housing Authority, 1959-64; treas. Plastics Edn. Found., 1971-75; bd. dirs. Norwich U. Alumni Assn., 1981-86, pres., 1984-86; trustee Norwich U., 1987-92, Nat. Plastics Mus., 1983-93; mem. plastics engring. curriculum adv. com. U. Mass., Lowell, 1974-93. Lt. col. USAR. Named Conn. Assn. Exec. of Yr., 1983, elected to Plastics Hall of Fame, 1996; named Disting. Alumnus, Norwich U., 1999. Mem. Soc. Plastics Engrs. (disting. mem. 1984, pres.'s cup, 1992), Am. Soc. Assn. Execs. (life), Coun. Engring. and Sci. Soc. Execs. (bd. dirs. 1983-85, sec. 1985-86, v.p. 1986-87, pres. 1987-88), Plastics Pioneers Assn. Home: 42 DeForest Rd Wilton CT 06897-1909

FORGET, MARK ALAN, educational consultant, educator; s. Timothy Paul and Marie Caroline Forget; m. Kim Elaine Weitz Forget, July 25, 2002; m. Karen Wilson Forget (div.); children: Jon Andre, Ian Andrew, Nathan Willis, Andrew Jeffrey. BA in Polit. Sci., U. Rochester, 1973, MA in Edn., 1974; PhD in Urban Sciences, Old Dominion U., 1999. Tchr., coach McQuaid HS, Rochester, NY, 1974—77, Hampton Roads Acad., Newport News, Va., 1977—78, Green Run HS, 1985—94; investment advisor Paine-Webber, Virginia Beach, 1978—84; tchr. Va. Beach Friends Sch., 1984—85; tchr., dir. Ocean Lakes HS, 1994—99; dir. reading staff devel. So. Regional Edn. Bd., Atlanta, 1999—2001; pres., dir. staff devel. Max Teaching, Inc., Findlay, Ohio, 2004—. Author: MAX Teaching with Reading and Writing, 2004; co-author: Reading for Success, 1996. Dir. youth coaching William & Mary Soccer Camp, Williamsburg, Va., 1986—94. Chief warrant officer U.S. Army, 1968—70. Decorated 2 Purple Hearts U.S. Army, Disting. Flying Cross, Bronze Star. Mem.: Findlay Country Club. Avocation: golf.

FORGEY, BENJAMIN FRANKLIN, architecture and art critic; b. Ashland, Ky., July 31, 1938; s. Chauncey Eaton F. and Joyce Evangeline (Shafer) Heinzen; m. Julie A. Savage, Sept. 1963 (div. 1967); 1 son, Benjamin Eric; m. 2d Gabriella A. von Joeden, Aug. 14, 1967; children: Elisa Gabriella, Martina Jane. BA, Princeton U., 1960. Reporter, editor, art critic Washington Star, 1964-81; architecture critic Washington Post, 1981—. Juror, profl. awards Am. Soc. Landscape Architects, 2003. Contbr. articles to Landscape Architecture mag. Served with USAR, 1961-67. Fulbright fellow, Japan, 1985-86. Mem.: Am. Inst. Architects (hon.). Home: 2856 28th St NW Washington DC 20008-4110 Office: Washington Post 1150 15th St NW Washington DC 20071-0002*

FORGIONE, DANA ANTHONY, accounting educator; BBA, U. Mass., 1975; MBA, 1977, MS in Acctg., 1980, PhD, 1987; Cert. in Christian Leadership with high honors, Heritage Bapt. Inst., 1979, Cert. in Ch. Ministries, 1983. CPA Md., Tex., Fla., CMA, cert. fraud examiner. Asst. prof. C.W. Post Ctr. Sch. Profl. Accountancy L.I. U., Greenvale, NY, 1981-83; asst. prof. Sch. Bus. We. New Eng. Coll., Springfield, Mass., 1983-87; asst. prof. Coll. Bus. Adminstrn., Grad. Sch. Bus. Tex. A&M U., College Station, 1987-93; assoc. prof. Merrick Sch. Bus. U. Balt., 1993-2000, prof., 2000-2001, dir. profl. MBA program Merrick Sch. Bus., 1993-2000, advisor MBA specialization in healthcare mgmt., 1993-2001; affilliate assoc. prof. Sch. Pharmacy U. Md., Balt., 1996-2000, affiliate prof., 2000-2001; dir., prof. Sch. Acctg. Fla. Internat. U., Miami, 2001—. Prin. Global Anti-Fraud Cons., Inc., Balt., 1998—2001; cons. U.S. Dept. Vets Affairs, 1997; cons in field. Author: Costly Reflections in a Midas Mirror, 1994, Costly Reflections in a Midas Mirror, 2d edit., 1999; co-author: Pet Polygon Mfg. Company Management Accounting Case, 1992, Pet Polygon Mfg. Company Management Accounting Case, 3d edit., Laser Logos, Inc., 1994, Laser Logos, Inc., 2d edit., 1997; editor: Rsch. in Healthcare Fin. Mgmt., 1994—2000, 2000—, chmn. editl. rev. bd. The White Paper, 1996—99, columnist Jour. Health Care Finance, reviewer Internat. Jour. Pub. Adminstrn., Govt. Accts. Jour., Govtl. and Non Profit Acctg., 1992—, mem. editl. bd. Today's CPA, 1992—93, Jour. Econs. and Fin., 1992—95, Pub. Budgeting, Acctg. and Fin. Mgmt., 1994—, Jour. Health Care Fin., 1996, Rsch. in Govt. and Nonprofit Acctg., 1996—, rev. Issues in Acctg. Edn., 1997—, mem. editl. bd., 1998—, Fin. Accountability and Mgmt., 1994—, assoc. editor N.Am., 1998—; contbr. articles to profl. jours.; rev.: Internat. Jour. Pub. Adminstrn., 2001—. Litig. support, expert testimony, cons. Tex. Atty. Gen., 1992—93. Symposium fellow Office for Govt. Acctg. Rsch. and Edn. U. Ill. Chgo., 1984; recipient Chancellor's Citation for Undergrad. Instrs., U. Mass., 1973, Hon. Mention Manuscript award Mass. Soc. CPAs, 1976, Outstanding Fac. Mem. award, Beta Alpha Psi (acctg. Hon. Fraternity), 1992, Incentive Grant for Tchg., Ctr. for Tchg. Excellence, Tex. A&M U., 1992, Curriculum Funds Development Awd., Merrick Sch. Bus., 1994, Manuscript award Nat. Assn. Accts., Black and Decker Rsch. Awd., Merrick Sch. Bus., U. Balt., 1995, 99, Top 10 List, Merrick Sch. of Bus., 1995, Diploma of Honor, U. San Marcos, Peru, 2004; named hon. prof. Ricardo Palma U., Peru, 2004—. Mem.: Inst. Pub. Sector Acctg. Rsch. U. Edinburgh (internat. assoc.), Assn. Cert. Fraud Examiners (bd. regents 1999—2000, regent emeritus 2001—), Internat. Soc. Rsch. in Healthcare Fin. Mgmt. (dir. 1994—, founder), Internat. Assn. Mgmt. (Internat. Regional Publ. award 1996, sr. editor jour. 1996—98, chmn. healthcare mgmt. divsn. 1997—98, Divsn. award 1998), Am. Acctg. Assn. (mem. exec. com. Mid-Atlantic region 1994—2001, pres. Mid-Atlantic region 1996—97, mem. nat. coun. 1996—97, sec., treas. govt. and nonprofit sect. 2003—04, pres.-elect govt. and nonprofit sect. 2004—). Baptist. Avocations: computers, biblical chronology, woodworking. Office: Fla Internat U Univ Park Miami FL 33199 Business E-Mail: forgione@fiu.edu.

FORKAN, PATRICIA ANN, foundation executive; b. N.Y.C., June 13, 1944; d. Robert James and Elaine May F. BA in Polit. Sci., Pa. State U., 1966; postgrad., Am. U., 1968-69. Manpower analyst Dept. Labor, Washington, 1967-69; nat. coord. Fund for Animals, N.Y.C., 1970-76; v.p. program and comms. Humane Soc. of U.S., Washington, 1976-86, sr. v.p., 1987-91, exec. v.p., 1992—. Weekly web-active commentator Soap Box, 1999—2004; bd. dirs. Solar Elec. Light Fund, 1990-2000; mem. U.S. del. Internat. Whaling Commn., 1978, 93, 94 Re-negotiation of Conv. for Regulation of Whaling, 1978, U.S. del. North Pacific Fur Seal Commn., 1985; mem. U.S. Public Adv. Com. to Law of the Sea, 1978-83; bd. dirs. Coun. for Ocean Law; advisor, contbr. weekly TV show Living with Animals, 1985-91; advisor Animal Polit. Action Com.; sr. v.p. Humane Soc. Internat., 1991-2004; pres. Humane Soc. Internat., 2004—, Global Alliance Humane and Sustainable Devel., 2004—; coun. woman Friendship Heights (Md.) Village, 1993-2001; pres. Nat. Assn. Humane and Environ. Edn., 1994—; pres. Worldwide Network (Women in Devel. and Environ.), 1998-2004; presdl. appointed mem. trade and environment policy adv. com. U.S. Trade Rep., 2000—. Contbr. articles to environ. and animal welfare publs.; co-host weekly radio show, 1986-87. Office: Humane Soc of US 2100 L St NW Washington DC 20037-1596

FORKER, OLAN DEAN, agricultural economics professor; b. Kendallville, Ind., Aug. 18, 1928; s. Fred Forrest and Mary May (Butler) F.; m. Kathleen Rose Buuck, Apr. 21, 1951; children: Michael, Brent, Susan. BS, Purdue U., 1950; MS, Mich. State U., 1958; PhD, U. Calif., Berkeley, 1962. Fieldman Halderman Farm Mgmt. Service, Wabash, Ind., 1954-58; extension economist U. Calif. at Berkeley, 1961-65; assoc. prof. Cornell U., Ithaca, N.Y., 1965-70, prof., 1971-95, prof. emeritus, 1995—; chmn. dept. agrl. econs., 1976-85; fellow U. Manchester, 1981-82; dir. Universal Foods Corp., Inc., Milw., 1974-96. Cons. AID, Turkey, 1970-71, Ford Found., 1978, Nat. Dairy Promotion and Rsch. Bd., 1984-88; Naumes Family vis. prof. Santa Clara U., 1985-86; adj. prof. U. Fla., 1988-89; dir. Tompkins Co. Nutrition for Elderly, Inc. Author: (with Ron Ward) Commodity Advertising: The Economics and Measurement of Generic Programs, 1993; contbr. articles to profl. jours. Officer, council mem. Trinity Luth. Ch., Ithaca, 1967-69, 72—; trustee Cornell U., 1984-88. Lt. col., ret., U.S. Army. Recipient award for profl. excellence for quality of discovery in pub. research Am. Agrl. Econs. Assn., 1975 Mem. Am. Agrl. Econs. Assn., Am. Agrl. Econs. Found. (pres. 1988-89), N.E. Agrl. and Resource Econs. Assn. (life, pres. 1991-92, Jour. award 1991, Disting. Mem. award 1994). Office: Cornell U 349 Warren Hall Ithaca NY 14853-7801 Home: 724 Bone Plain Rd Freeville NY 13068-9782 E-mail: okforker@earthlink.net.

FORLENZA, PHILIP RUSSELL, lawyer; b. N.Y.C., Feb. 24, 1942; s. Russell Joseph and Domenica Mae (Serio) F.; m. Kathleen Patricia Porr, Oct. 15, 1982; children: Meredith, Sean. BA, Wagner Coll., 1963; LLB, Fordham U., 1966. Bar: N.Y. 1967, U.S. Dist. Ct. (so. dist.) N.Y. 1970, U.S. Supreme Ct. 1976, U.S. Ct. Appeals (2d cir.) 1977. Assoc. Cahill Gordon Reindel, N.Y.C., 1966-71, Hawkins Delafield & Wood, N.Y.C., 1971-74, ptnr., 1974-87, Patterson Belknap Webb & Tyler, N.Y.C., 1987—. Office: Patterson Belknap et al 1133 Avenue Of The Americas New York NY 10036-6710

FORLINES, FRANKLIN LEROY, minister, educator; b. Winterville, N.C., Nov. 14, 1926; s. John Leroy and Leta Nanny (Manning) F.; m. Carolyn Le Fay Gilbert, Aug. 4, 1956; children: Jonathan Gilbert, James Franklin. BA, Freewill Bapt. Bible Coll., Nashville, 1952; MA, Winona Lake Sch. of Theology, Ind., 1959; BD, No. Bapt. Theol. Sem., Chgo., 1962; ThM, Chgo. Grad. Sch. of Theology, 1970. Ordained to ministry Free Will Bapt. Ch., 1951. Pastor 1st Free Will Bapt. Ch., Newport News, Va., 1952-53; mem. faculty Free Will Bapt. Bible Coll., 1953-59, 1962—, chmn. Bible dept., 1965—93, dean of men, 1953-59, 65-71, dean of students, 1971-74, prof. emeritus, 1999—. Guest lectr. Bapt. sems. and insts., Kiev and Odessa, Ukraine, 1996, Moscow, 1996, 2001, 04, Kazakhstan, 2003; chmn. theol. commn. Nat. Assn. Free Will Baptists, 1962—; condr. pastors' conf., India, 1999; spkr. in field. Author: Biblical Ethics, 1973, Biblical Systematics, 1975 (transl. into Russian and Spanish), Romans, The Randall House Bible Commentary, 1987, Quest for Truth, 2001; columnist Contact mag., 1970-80. Mem. Evang. Theol. Soc., Bible Sci. Assn. Nashville (v.p. 1988-96). Home: 3801 Rolland Rd Nashville TN 37205-2537 Office: Free Will Bapt Bible Coll 3606 W End Ave Nashville TN 37205-2403

FORMAN, ANNE, artist; b. N.Y.C., Sept. 22, 1925; m. Julius Goldin, Jan. 31, 1964; children: Alison, Richard; stepchildren: David, Roberta, Eric. Student, Pratt Inst., Bklyn., 1943—45, Art Student League, N.Y.C., 1945—46; BA, Adelphi U., 1954; MFA, Columbia U., 1961. Cert. art tchr., N.Y. Art cons. Wantagh (N.Y.) Pub. Schs., 1954-60; artist-in-residence Wantagh CAP & WPS, 1970-75; artistic dir. Wantagh Community Arts Prog., 1970—. Lectr., in-svc. tchr., workshops, L.I., 1955-57. Author booklets in field; contbr. articles to profl. jours. Grantee N.Y. State Coun. on Arts, 1970-75; recipient Paint award Nat. Arts Club., N.Y., 1965, Graphics award, Hofstra U., Hempstead, N.Y., 1958, 59, other painting honors, Am. Watercolor Soc., N.Y., 1960, 65, Glassboro (N.J.) State Coll., 1966. Mem. Nat. Mus. Women in Arts (charter mem., slides of work in archives), Delta Kappa Gamma, Alpha Phi. Unitarian-Universalist. Avocations: teaching, travel, reading. Home: 1580 Wantagh Ave Wantagh NY 11793-3902

FORMAN, BETH ROSALYNE, specialty food trade executive; b. N.Y.C., Oct. 15, 1949; d. Philip and Dorothy Lea (Vilensky) F. BA in English with honors, NYU, 1971; MA with honors, Columbia U., 1972; MBA in Fin., Rutgers U., 1980. Asst. to contr. Colin Hochstin Co., N.Y.C., 1971-78; instr. Columbia U., N.Y.C., 1974-76; adj. faculty Bergen Community Coll., Paramus, N.J., 1985-87; communications cons. B.R. Forman & Co., Paramus, 1981-87; proposal mgr. Ogden Svcs.Corp., N.Y.C., 1988-89; dir. tech. svcs. Ogden Entertainment Svcs., Rosemont, Ill., 1990-92, dir. mktg. comms. N.Y.C., 1993-96; dir. mktg. Euro-Am. Brands, LLC, Paramus, N.J., 1999—. Bd. dirs. new leadership div. United Jewish Community Bergen County, River Edge, N.J., 1981-87, chmn. fundraiser, 1983, chmn. edn. com., 1983-86, treas., 1984-86; mem. steering com. Viewpoints div. Am. Jewish Com., 1991-93. Pres.'s fellow Columbia U., 1973; recipient Masters award Ogden Svcs. Corp., 1994. Mem. NAFE, Women in Comm. (v.p. spl. programs 1992-93 Chgo. chpt., mem. career devel. com. 1994-95, mem. pub. rels. com. and Matrix awards fundraising com. 1995-96), Columbia U. Club of N.Y., Mensa. Democrat. Avocation: acting. Home: 421 Yuhas Dr Paramus NJ 07652-4125 Office: Euro-Am Brands LLC 15 Prospect St Paramus NJ 07652-2712

FORMAN, CHARLES WILLIAM, religious studies educator; b. Gwalior, India, Dec. 2, 1916; s. Henry and Sallie (Taylor) F.; m. Helen Janice Mitchell, Mar. 12, 1944; children: David, Sarah, Harriet. BA, MA, Ohio State U., 1938; PhD, U. Wis., 1941; BD, Union Theol. Sem., N.Y.C., 1944, STM, 1947. Ordained to ministry Presbyn. Ch., 1944. Prof. North India United Theol. Coll., Saharanpur, 1945-50; sec. program emphasis Nat. Coun. Chs., 1951-53; mem. faculty Divsn. Sch., Yale U., New Haven, 1953—; D. Willis James prof. missions Div. Sch., Yale U., New Haven, 1961-87, D. Willis James prof. missions emeritus, 1987—. Chmn. theol. edn. fund World Coun. chs., 1965-70, mem., 1970-77; mem. commn. ecumenical mission United Presbyn. Ch., 1962-71, chmn., 1965-71; chmn. Found. for Theol. Edn. in SE Asia, 1970-89, mem. 1966-69, 90—. Author: A Faith for the Nations, 1958, The Nation and the Kingdom, 1964, Christianity in the Non-Western World, 1967, The Island Churches of the South Pacific, 1982, The Voice of Many Waters, 1986. Mem. bd. edn., Bethany, Conn., 1957-66; bd. dirs. Community Action Agy., New Haven, 1978-81, Overseas Ministries Study Center, New Haven, 1979-2000. Home: 200 Leeder Hill Dr Hamden CT 06517-2726

FORMAN, DONALD T., biochemist, educator; b. NYC, Feb. 27, 1932; s. Jack and Fannie (Jaffee) F.; m. Florence Sporn, Aug. 22, 1953; children: Joan Diane, Steven Lawrence, Debra Helene. BS, Bklyn. Coll., 1953; MS, Wayne State U., 1957, PhD, 1959. Clin. biochemist Mercy Hosp. Med. Center, Chgo., 1959—63; dir. clin. biochemistry, asso. prof. biochemistry and pathology Evanston Hosp./Northwestern U. Med. Sch., Chgo., 1963—78; rsch. prof. U. Stockholm and Royal Postgrad. Med. Sch., London, 1975; prof. pathology and biochemistry U. N.C., Chapel Hill, NC, 1978—2002, dir. clin. chemistry, 1978—2002, prof. emeritus pathology and biochemistry, 2002. Cons. clin. chemist, industry and govt., 1965— Editor: Clinical Chemistry, 1976. Served with AUS, 1953-55. Recipient Chgo. Clin. Chemists award, 1974, Sunderman award as clin. scientist for 1986, Spl. Recognition award for clin. chemistry Am. Chem. Soc., 2000; Mich. Heart Assn. fellow, 1957-59 Mem. AAAS, AAUP, Assn. Clin. Scientists (pres. 1973-74), Am. Assn. Clin. Chemistry (dir., award for outstanding contbn. to animal clin. chemistry 1995), Sigma Xi, Phi Lambda Upsilon. Achievements include research on enzymology, inborn errors of metabolism, tumor-associated markers, atherosclerosis, human alcohol metabolism, clinical biochemistry and critical care chemistry. Home: 2559 Owens Ct Chapel Hill NC 27514-1737 Office: U NC Med Sch Dept Pathology Chapel Hill NC 27514 E-mail: dforman@nc.rr.com.

FORMAN, EDGAR ROSS, mechanical engineer; b. Camden, N.J., Oct. 5, 1923; s. Edgar Charles and Annie (Baragwanath) F.; m. Alma Kuppinger, Sept. 26, 1953; children: Bruce, Dianne. BSME, Drexel U., 1950, MBA, 1953. Registered profl. engr., Pa. Project engr. Penn Instrument div. Burgess Manning Co., Phila., 1950-55; application engr. Moore Products Co., Phila., 1955-59; chief instrument engr. Catalytic Co., Phila., 1959-67, mgr. mgmt. sys. dept., 1967-71; supervising instrument engr. United Engrs. & Constructors, Inc., Phila., 1971-78; mgr. instrument and controls dept. Day & Zimmermann, Inc., Phila., 1978—89; dir. Automation Tech., 1989-93; cons., 1993—2002. Guest lectr. U.S. Naval Acad., Sun Oil Co., U. Del. Contbr. articles to profl. jours. Past mem. Boy Scouts Am.; mem. pres. coun. Spring Garden Coll., 1979-83, chmn. indsl. adv. com., 1984-89; past pres. Erdenheim Civic Assn. Served with AUS, 1943-46. Fellow: Instrument Soc. Am. (Phila. sect. pres. 1960, v.p. dist 2 1982—84, chmn. food and pharm. divsn. 1986—87, nat. v.p. 1989—93, nat. honrs and awards com. 1993—96, China visitation team 1996, Engrs. Week liaison 1997—2001, founder Outstanding Tech. Achievement award 1998—2002, cert. instr. 1998—2002, rev. Power Industries Divsn. 2002—05, past chmn. edn. commn., Eckman award 1982, Man of Yr. 1987, Golden Achievement award 1989, Outstanding Svc. award 1990, Dist. 2 Svc. award 1999, Old Shoe award 2001); mem.: NSPE (pres. Valley Forge chpt. 1982—83, Engrs. Week coun. 1990—99, county Mathcounts coord. 1994—95, Man of Yr. award Del. Valley Engrs. 1990), ASME (life; past chmn. dynamic sys. and controls divsn., old guard com.), 94th Inf. Divsn. Assn. (pres. Del. Valley chpt. 2003—05), Ea. Star, Commandry, Shriners, York Rite, Masons, Scottish Rite, Pi Tau Sigma (pres.), Pi Nu Epsilon, Alpha Phi Omega (nat. pres.). Episcopalian.

FORMAN, HOWARD IRVING, lawyer, government agency administrator; b. Phila., Jan. 12, 1917; s. Jacob and Dora (Moses) F.; m. Ada Pressman, Aug. 2, 1938; children: Kenneth J., Harvey R. BS in Chemistry, St. Joseph's Coll., 1937; LLB, Temple U., 1944; MA, U. Pa., 1949, PhD, 1955. Bar: D.C. 1945, Pa. 1973. Rsch. chemist Frankford Arsenal, Dept. Army, Phila., 1940-44, patent atty., 1944-46, chief patents br., 1946-56; asst. dir. Pitman-Dunn Rsch. Labs., 1955-56; lectr. polit. sci. Temple U., 1956-63; from patent atty. to trademark and internat. corp. counsel Rohm and Haas Co., Phila., 1956-76; dep. asst. sec. U.S. Dept. Commerce, Washington, 1976-81; also dir. Office of Product Standards Policy; chmn. interagy. com. on standards policy Weiser, Stapler & Spivak, Phila., 1974-76; head. U.S. dels. to UN internat. confs., Geneva, 1976-81; sec., dir. Rohm & Haas Asia, Inc., 1973-76; v.p., gen. counsel, dir. Brilliant Internat., Inc., Bala-Cynwyd, Pa., 1974-83; sec., dir. Far East Chem. Services, Inc., Wilmington, Del., 1973-76, Rohm and Haas

GmbH, Zug, Switzerland, 1975-76; dir. U.S. Pharm. Corp., 1975-83; pvt. practice Phila., 1981—. Advisor to asst. sec. for econ. affairs relative to internat. intellectual property matters Dept. State, 1968-72; orginator Internat. Lab. Accreditation world-wide biennial confs. (ILAC), 1977—; chmn. ANSI accredited stds. com., Z21, on performance and installation gas burning appliances and accessories, 1981-97. Author: Inventions, Patents and Related Matters, 1957, Patents-Their Ownership and Administration by the U.S. Government, 1957; Editor: Patents, Research and Management, 1961, The Law of Chemical, Metallurgical and Pharmaceutical Patents, 1967; author plays: The Birth of the American Patent System, 1976, The Birth of the American Patent and Copyright Systems, 1990.; contbr. to publs. in field. Bd. dirs. Lower Moreland Twp. Sch. Bd., Montgomery County, Pa., 1969-75; bd. dirs. Eastern Montgomery County Vocat.-Tech. Sch., 1969-75, sec., 1970-75; bd. dirs. Warminster (Pa.) Gen. Hosp., 1983-91; emeritus dir. Allegheny United Hosps., Inc., 1991-94; life trustee Med. Coll. Pa. and Hahnemann U. Hosps., 1994-98. Recipient Robert J. Painter Meml. award Stds. Engring. Soc.-ASTM, 1978, Leo B. Moore award Stds. Engring. Soc., 1981. Fellow Am. Inst. Chemists; mem. ABA, FBA, AAAS, ASTM (hon. life, bd. dirs. 1985-87), Internat. Assn. Protection Indsl. Property, Am. Nat. Stds. Inst. (bd. dirs. 1977-80, Finegan Stds. medal 1996), Nat. Coun. Patent Law Assn. (chmn. 1967-68), Am. Chem. Soc., Sci. Rsch. Soc. Am., Am. Assn. Lab. Accreditation (dir. 1983-91), Am. Patent Law Assn. (bd. mgrs. 1970-73), Am. Coll. Legal Medicine, Phila. Bar Assn. (sec. 1973-74, com. on jurimetrics, tech. and patents, v.p. 1975), Phila. Patent Law Assn. (pres. 1964-66), Licensing Execs. Soc., Stds. Engring. Soc. (Robert J. Painter Meml. award 1978, Leo B. Moore award 1981), Franklin Inst. (vice chmn. Futures Ctr. campaign), Nat. Lawyers Club, Gas Appliance Mfrs. Assn. (meritorious svc. award 1996), Am. Soc. Gas Engrs. (hon.), Sigma Xi. Achievements include being the principal draftsman, prime mover in devel. original OMB Circular A-119 which established nat. policy calling for primary dependence of Fed. Govt. on private sector standards orgns. for devel. of standards required for procurement and regulatory purposes by govt. agencies. Home: 1033 Corn Crib Dr Huntingdon Valley PA 19006-3335 Office: Albidale-Windmill Circle PO Box 66 Huntingdon Valley PA 19006-0066 Fax: (215) 947-5036. *My life has been a slow-but-sure progression in which patience, diligence and determination, mixed with a readiness to adapt myself to each new circumstance, have enabled me to overcome numerous obstacles and forge a useful career and a happy life as a husband, father and grandfather that have been personally gratifying and rewarding. My creed consists of truth, simplicity, candor, tolerance, genuine humility and faith in God and my fellow men and women.*

FORMAN, J(OSEPH) CHARLES, chemical engineer, consultant, writer; b. Chgo., Dec. 22, 1931; s. Joseph O. and Marie (Smith) F.; m. Ursula Diane Weston, July 22, 1953; children: Stephen Charles, Diane Brigitte, Mary Erika. S.B., M.I.T., 1953; MS, Northwestern U., 1957, PhD, 1960. Registered profl. engr., Ill. Trainee chem. engring. Dow Chem. Co., Midland, Mich., 1953-54; from sr. chem. engr. to dir. mfg. ops. agrl. vet. div. Abbott Labs., North Chicago, Ill., 1956-77; assoc. exec. dir. Am. Inst. Chem. Engrs., N.Y.C., 1977-78; exec. dir., sec., pub. Am. Inst. Chem. Engrs. Jour., Internat. Chem. Engring., Biotech Progress, Plant/Ops. Progress, Energy Progress, Environ. Progress, 1978-87; pres. and prin. Forman Assocs. Cons. and Tech. Svcs., 1987—. Cons. in field, accreditation insp. chem. engring. curricula; mem. ednl. council MIT, 1961-74, 78-95; mem. chem. engring. consultor coun. Manhattan Coll., N.Y.C., 1985—. Mem. Lake Bluff (Ill.) Bd. Edn., 1967-73, pres., 1971-73; pres. Lake County (Ill.) Sch. Bd. Assn., 1969-71; mem. Lake Bluff Plan Commn., 1973-77, chmn., 1976-77; mem. Darien (Conn.) Pers. Adv. Commn., 1986-92, Darien Park and Recreation Commn., 1999-2005, Darien Sewer Commn., 2005—; dist. chmn. Boy Scouts Am., 1994-97. With USAF, 1954—56. Fellow Am. Inst. Chem. Engrs., AAAS; mem. Am. Chem. Soc., Am. Soc. Assn. Execs., Coun. Engring. and Sci. Soc. Execs. (dir. 1980-83, sec. 1983-84, v.p. 1984-85, pres. 1985-86), Nat. Eagle Scout Assn., Sigma Xi, Tau Beta Pi, Phi Lambda Upsilon, Alpha Tau Omega. Achievements include patents in field. Home and Office: 77 Stanton Rd Darien CT 06820-5128 Office Phone: 203-655-4189. E-mail: jcforman@alum.mit.edu.

FORMAN, LEONARD P., media company executive; b. N.Y.C., June 7, 1945; s. William and Jean (Feldman) F.; m. Barbara Rubin, June 2, 1968; children: Daniel, Matthew. BA in Econs., CUNY, 1967; PhD, NYU, 1975. Asst. prof. econs. Fordham U., N.Y.C., 1971-72; rsch. econs. Fed. Res. Bank, N.Y.C., 1973—74; dir. planning N.Y. Times Corp., N.Y.C., 1974-86; sr. v.p. ops. Telemundo, Inc., N.Y.C., 1986—89; pres., CEO Newspaper Advt. Bur., 1989—92; COO Newspaper Assn. Am., 1992—94; pres., CEO Nynex/Newsday electronic svc. joint venture, 1994—95; media cons., 1995—96; sr. vp. corp. devel. N.Y. Times Corp., N.Y.C., 1996-98; pres. and CEO N.Y. Times Mag. Group, 1998—2001; sr. v.p. The N.Y. Times Co., 2001, sr. v.p., CFO, 2002—04, exec. v.p., CFO, 2004—. Adj. asst. prof. Queens Coll. CUNY, 1972-75; assoc. prof. Pace U., 1975-77; lectr. Fordham U., 1977-80; adj. prof. Fordham U. Grad. Sch., 1972-73, Yale U., 1981, prin. researcher CEAR, N.Y.C., 1982—; chmn. telecommunications com. Am. Newspaper Pubs. Assn.; cons. Social Systems Inc., Chapel Hill, N.C., 1977-82. Editor Managerial and Decision Econs. jour., 1981-84; contbg. editor Managerial Planning jour.; contbr. articles to profl. jours. Named teaching fellow U. Mass., 1969-70; recipient research assistantship N.Y.U., 1972-73. Mem. Am. Econ. Assn., Managerial Econ. Assn., Econometric Soc., Nat. Assn. Bus. Economists, N.Am. Soc. Corp. Planning, Planning Execs. Inst., Ops. Research Soc., Inst. Mgmt. Sci., Omicron Delta Epsilon. Avocations: race car driving, reading, tennis. Home: Ridge Rd Glen Cove NY 11542 Office: NY Times Co 229 W 43rd St New York NY 10036-3959

FORMAN, MICHELE, secondary school educator; b. Biloxi, Miss., Apr. 7, 1946; m. Dick Forman; children: Elissa, Laura, Tim. BA in hist., Brandeis U., 1967; MA in tchg., U. Vt. Cert. Profl. Tchg. Standards Nat. Bd. Tchr. Middleburg (Vt.) Union HS, 1986—. Alcohol drug edn curriculum spec. Vt. Dept. Edn. Mem. Vt. State Dept. Edn., Task Force HS Reform; vol. Peace Corp., Nepal, 1960. Named Nat. Tchr. of Yr., 2001, Vt. State Tchr. of Yr., 2001; recipient mary K. Bonsteel Tachau Pre-Collegiate Tchg. award, 1999. Mem.: Academic Coun. The Coll. Bd., Hist. Soc. Studies Academic Adv. Com., Nat. Bd Profl. Tchg. Standards. Office: Middlebury Union HS Hist Social Studies Dept 73 Charles Ave Middlebury VT 05753

FORMAN, SANDRA H., theater educator; b. Charlotte, N.C., July 9, 1944; d. Willis Edward Hopper and Mary Harriet Blackwell; m. Richard Charles Forman, Apr. 16, 1967; children: Rhyan Danette, Anna Regan, Daniel Edward. BA, U. N.C. Greensboro, 1966, MFA, 1971. Instr. Guilford Coll., Greensboro, NC, 1969—72; lectr., asst. prof., assoc. prof. U. N.C. Greensboro, 1977—89; prof. Theatre No. Ky. U., Highland Heights, 1990—. Dir. Va. Shakespeare Festival, Williamsburg, 2002. Author: Your Voice and Articulation, 1984, Public Speaking: Today and Tomorrow, 1989, Only Mystery: Lorca's Poetry etc., 1992; actor: N.C. Shakespeare, 1988, Charlotte Repertory Theatre, 1992, Fox Rock Theatre Co., 2000; dir.: Diana Shakespeare Festival, 2002. Dist. pres.-Mid Atlantic Nat. Coun. Jewish Women, 1982—84. Mem.: Southeastern Theatre Conf. (auditions com.), Internat. Hemingway Soc. Office: No Ky Univ Theatre Dept Nunn Dr Highland Heights KY 41099 Office Phone: 859-572-6303. Business E-Mail: forman@nku.edu.

FORMENTI, SILVIA C., radiation oncologist; b. Italy; MD, Universita degli Studi di Milano, 1980. Cert. Radiation Oncology 1991. Intern San Carlo Borromeo Hosp., Milan, 1980—83; fellow, hematology, oncology USC Med. Sch., Los Angeles, 1984—85; resident, radiation oncology Nat. Cancer Inst., Milan, 1984—88; resident, radiation oncology USC Sch. Medicine, Los Angeles, 1985—90; assoc. prof. radiation oncology and medicine USC, Keck Sch. Medicine, 1990—2000; assoc. dir. clin. rsch., leader of breast cancer rsch. program NYU Cancer Inst., 2000—; Sandra and Edward H. Meyer chmn. NYU Sch. Medicine, Radiation Oncology Dept., 2000—. Office: NYU Med Ctr Dept Radiation Oncology 566 First Ave New York NY 10016-6402

FORMENTO, DANIEL, radio company executive, writer; b. Pitts., Aug. 11, 1954; s. Stephen P. and Betty Jean (McCorkle) F.; m. Alison Ashley, Oct. 7, 1995; children: Alexander Daniel, Natalie Annette. Grad. high sch., Mt. Lebanon, Pa. Program mgr. The Source/NBC Radio Network, N.Y.C., 1979-82; prin. Dan Formento Prodns., N.Y.C., 1982-84; pres. Radio Today Entertainment, N.Y.C., 1984—, West Hill Studios, N.J., 1993—. V.p., creative dir. ABC Radio Network, 1998. Author: Rock Chronicle, 1982; producer radio programs including Flashback, 1984, Rock Stars, 1985—, Walter Cronkite's 20th Century, 1988, Pop Quiz, 1992—; radio comml. Grog Shop, 1976 (Aftra award 1976); announcer radio feature Today in Rock History, 1979—; TV comml. Short Cuts, 1989—; producer radio feature One Minute With, 1976 (Golden Quill award 1976), Pop Quiz, 1992— (Internat. Radio Festival of N.Y. grand award 1992). Democrat. Avocations: swimming, tennis, audio enthusiast. Office: ABC Radio Network 444 Madison Ave New York NY 10022-6903

FORMENTO, DENNIS ANTHONY, education educator, writer; b. New Orleans, Oct. 8, 1954; s. Anthony John and Clare Azzalea Formento. BA, U. New Orleans, 1977; cert., Naropa Inst., 1984; MA, U. Colo., 1988. Instr. Delgado C.C., New Orleans, 1990—92, U. New Orleans, 1992, Xavier U., New Orleans, 1993, S.E. La. U., Hammond, 1993; dir. Writing Ctr., tchr. So. U. New Orleans, 1996—2005; publ. Surregegional Press, 1993—. Author: Ra Blues Are; editor: Mesechabe: Jour. Surregionalism, 1993—2000. Mem.: NAACP, Ctr. Gulf South History and Culture, Amnesty Internat. Home: 1640 5th St Slidell LA 70458

FORMO, BRENDA TERRELL, travel company executive; b. Greensboro, N.C., May 18, 1946; d. Walter C. Terrell and Eunice W. Kirkman; m. Robert A. Formo, Oct. 14, 1978; 1 child, Eric Victor. BSBA, East Carolina U., 1968; MA in Bus. Adminstrn., Webster U., 1977; postgrad., U. 1970, 72, 77, 84, 87; grad., Army War Coll., 1990. Commd. 2d lt. U.S. Army, 1969, advanced through grades to col., 1991, ret., 1993; acctg. instr. U.S. Army Fin. Sch., Ft. Harrison, Ind., 1969-71; women's officer recruiter U.S. Army Kansas City Recruiting Main Sta., 1971-73; recruiting ops. officer U.S. Army SW Recruiting Command, San Antonio, 1973-75; area comdr. U.S. Army San Antonio Dist. Recruiting Command, 1975-77; chief pay and examination divsn. U.S. Army Fin. and Acctg. Office, Yongsan, Korea, 1977-78; asst. chief acctg. U.S. Army Mil. Dist. Washington Fin. and Acctg. Office, 1978-80; banking officer U.S. Army Europe Office of the Dep. Chief of Staff for Resource Mgmt., 1980-84; fin. and acctg. officer Def. Nuclear Agy., 1984-87; investigator Office of Dept. of the Army Inspector Gen., 1987-91; chief programs and analysis divsn. Dept. Army Office of Dep. Chief of Staff for Logistics, 1991-93; fin. mgmt. cons., 1993-96; co-founder, pres. BRE Travel, 1996—. Active Guilford Coll. United Meth. Ch., Greensboro. Decorated Legion of Merit with oak leaf cluster (2 awards), Meritorious Svc. medal with 3 oak leaf clusters (4 awards), Army Commendation medal with 4 oak leaf clusters (5 awards). Mem. Assn. U.S. Army, Cardinal Golf and Country Club (Greensboro). Address: 4116 Obriant Pl Greensboro NC 27410-8372

FORMO, NANCYE GLYNN, music educator; b. Jacksonville, Fla., Jan. 21, 1947; d. Jon Warren and Bettye Glynn (White) Formo. BA in Music Edn. and Voice, Columbia (S.C.) Coll., 1969. Tchr. Forsyth County Schs., Winston-Salem, NC, 1969—99; ret., 1999. Pvt. music tchr., 1969—; part-time tchr. Forsyth County Schs., Winston-Salem, 1999—. Singer: Lake Junaluska (N.C.) Singers, 1968—78, The Revelation Singers, 1969—95. Singer Little Symphony Forsyth County, Winston-Salem, 1999—; handbell dir. Ardmore Unitec Meth. Ch., Winston-Salem, 1984—2005. Mem.: Music Educators Nat. Conf., Am. Assn. Ret. Persons. Home: 259 Joyce Dr Winston Salem NC 27107

FORNAGE, BRUNO DENIS, radiologist, educator; b. Reims, France, July 2, 1949; came to U.S., 1987; s. Louis and Genevieve (Mercier) F.; m. Brigitte Wittmer, Oct. 18, 1991; 1 child, Louis Bruno. MD, Med. Sch. Reims, 1974. Diplomate French Bd. Radiology, French Bd. Oncology. Resident in oncology Inst. Jean-Godinot Regional Cancer Ctr., Reims, 1974-76, resident in radiology, 1976-79, asst. dept. biophysics and nuc. medicine, 1976-82, dir. dept. radiology, 1982-87; assoc. prof. radiology U. Reims, 1986-87; assoc. prof. radiology, chief sect. ultrasound U. Tex. M.D. Anderson Cancer Ctr., Houston, 1987-2000, prof. radiology, 1990—, prof. surg. oncology, 1999—. Author 5 textbooks; editor 2 textbooks; mem. editl. bd. various jours.; editor-in-chief Jour. of Clin. Ultrasound, 1997—; reviewer jours.; contbr. chpts. to books, articles to profl. jours.; patentee in field. Fellow Am. Inst. Ultrasound in Medicine, Soc. Radiologists in Ultrasound, Soc. Breast Imaging; mem. Am. Roentgen Ray Soc., Radiol. Soc. N.Am., Am. Coll. Radiology, Am. Soc. Breast Disease, Internat. Skeletal Soc., numerous others. Office: U Tex MD Anderson Canc Ctr 1515 Holcombe Blvd Houston TX 77030-4009 Personal E-mail: fornage@swbell.net. Business E-Mail: bfornage@di.mdacc.tmc.edu.

FORNARA, CHARLES WILLIAM, historian, classicist, educator; b. N.Y.C., Nov. 19, 1935; s. Charles and Dorothy Mae (Stind) F.; 1 son, Charles William III. BA, Columbia U., 1956; MA, U. Chgo., 1958; PhD, UCLA, 1961. Instr. Ohio State U., Columbus, 1961-63; from asst. prof. to prof. classics and history Brown U., Providence, 1963—, David Benedict prof. classics, 1989—. Vis. prof. U. Tex., Austin, 1976; prof. Greek history Inst. Ancient History, Ann Arbor, Mich., summer 1977; vis. fellow Humanities Rsch. Ctr. Australian Nat. U., Canberra, spring 1983; lectr. Australian univs., 1983, English univs., 1987, U. Amsterdam, 1995. Author: Herodotus, An Interpretative Essay, 1971, The Athenian Board of Generals, 1971, Archaic Times to the End of the Peloponnesian War, 1977, 2d edit., 1983, The Nature of History in Ancient Greece and Rome, 1983, (with Loren Samons II) From Cleisthenes to Pericles, 1991 (commentary) Continuation of Felix Jacoby, Die Fragmente der griechischen Historiker III c, 1994; contbr. articles and revs. in field to profl. jours. John Simon Guggenheim fellow, 1988-89. Mem. Am. Philol. Assn., Soc. for Promotion Hellenic Studies. Clubs: Providence Art. Home: 527 Mooresfield Rd Saunderstown RI 02874-1208 Office: Brown Univ Dept Classics Providence RI 02912-0001 Office Phone: 401-863-2123.

FORNARI, VICTOR MASLIAH, psychiatrist; b. N.Y.C., June 20; s. Ermanno and Alice (Notrica) F.; m. Alice Johnson, Mar. 27, 1977; children: Eric, Amy, Marci. BS in Biology, Cornell U., 1974; MS in Human Nutrition, Columbia U., 1975; MD, SUNY-Downstate Med. Ctr., Bklyn., 1979. Diplomate Am. Bd. Psychiatry and Neurology, Am. Bd. Child and Adolescent Psychiatry and Neurology. Intern L.I. Coll. Hosp., Bklyn., 1979-80; resident in psychiatry Hosp. U. Pa., Phila., 1980-82; fellow in child and adolescent psychiatry L.I. Jewish Med. Ctr., New Hyde Park, N.Y., 1982-84; staff child psychiatrist Schneider's Children's Hosp./L.I. Jewish Med. Ctr., New Hyde Park, 1984-85; physician-in-charge Child Psychiatry Inpatient Unit/L.I. Jewish Med. Ctr., New Hyde Park, 1985-86; physician-in-charge, child psychiatry cons. liaison svc., eating disorders program North Shore-Cornell U. Hosp., Manhasset, N.Y., 1986-91, dir. tng./clin. svcs. div. child and adolescent psychiatry, 1991—. Assoc. prof. psychiatry, pediatrics, Cornell U. Med. Coll., N.Y.C., 1991—. Fellow Am. Psychiat. Assn., Am. Acad. Child and Adolescent Psychiatry; mem. Greater L.I. Psychiat. Soc. (pres.), Am. Assn. of Dirs. of Psychiat. Residen Tng., Soc. of Profs. of Child and Adolescent Psychiatry.

FORNARIS, CARL A., lawyer; b. Oct. 22, 1968; BS, Univ. Miami, 1990; JD, Cath. Univ. Am., 1993. Bar: Fla. 1993, DC 1995, US Ct. Appeals (DC cir.), US Dist. Ct. (DC dist.). Atty. Arnold & Porter, Washington; dir., head legal and compliance, Latin Am. Regional Off. Barclays Bank PLC and Barclays Capital; now shareholder, co-chair nat. fin. institutions internat. Greenberg Traurig LLP, Miami, Fla. Office: Greenberg Traurig LLP 1221 Brickell Ave Miami FL 33131 Office Phone: 305-579-0626. Office Fax: 305-579-0717. Business E-Mail: fornarisc@gtlaw.com.

FORNERIS, JEANNE M., lawyer; b. Duluth, Minn., May 23, 1953; d. John Domenic and Elva Lorraine (McDonald) F.; m. Michael Scott Margulies, Feb. 6, 1982. AB, Macalester Coll., 1975; JD, U. Minn., 1978. Bar: Minn. 1978. Assoc. Halverson, Waters, Bye, Downs & Maki, Ltd., Duluth, 1978-81, Briggs & Morgan, P.A., Mpls., St. Paul, 1981-83; ptnr. Hart & Bruner, P.A., Mpls., 1983-86; assoc. gen. counsel M.A. Mortenson Co., Mpls., 1986-90, v.p., gen. counsel, 1990-96; with Gen. Counsel, Ltd., Mpls., 1997-98; v.p., sr. counsel Medtronic, Inc., Mpls., 1999—. Instr. women's studies dept. U. Minn., Mpls., 1977-79. Author profl. edn. seminars; contbr. articles to profl. jours. Bd. dirs. Good Will Indusries Vocat. Enterprises, Inc., 1979-81; chmn. bd. trustees Duluth Bar Libr., 1981; mem. United Way Family and Individual Svcs. Task Force, Duluth, 1981. Nat. Merit Assn. scholar, 1971. Fellow Am. Coll. Constrn. Lawyers (bd. dirs.); mem. AMA, Am. Arbitration Assn. (mem. large complex case panel), Minn. State Bar Assn., Minn. Women Lawyers (bd. dirs.), U.S. Dist. Ct. Hist. Soc. (pres.). Democrat. Roman Catholic. Office: Medtronic Inc 7000 Central Ave NE Minneapolis MN 55432-3576 Office Phone: 736-514-3329.

FORNESS, STEVEN ROBERT, educational psychologist; b. Denver, May 13, 1939; s. Robert E. and Rejeana C. (Houck) F. BA in English, U. No. Colo., 1963, MA in Ednl. Psychology, 1964; EdD in Spl. Edn., UCLA, 1968. Tchr. Santa Maria (Calif.) H.S., 1964—66; counselor Sch. Edn. UCLA, 1966—68; spl. educator Neuropsychiat. Inst., 1968—2003, chief ednl. psychology child outpatient dept., 1970—2003, mem. mental retardation rsch. ctr., 1970—2003, prof. dept. psychiatry, 1972—2003, prin. inpatient sch., 1976—2003, dir. mental retardation and devel. disabilities tng. program, 1985—92, disting. prof. emeritus, 2003—. Grant rev. panelist U.S. Dept. Edn., 1974-2000; cons. Nat. Assn. Exceptional Children, Venezuela, 1974-2000; commn. ednl. psychology Calif. State Bd. Behavioral Scis. Examiners, 1977-99. Specialist in classroom observation tech. early identification of children with learning and behavior disorders; author publs. including (with Frank Hewett) Education of Exceptional Learners, 3d edit., 1984, (with K. Kavale) Science of Learning Disabilities, 1985, (with Kavale and Bender) Handbook of Learning Disabilities, vols. I, II and III, 1987, 88; (with K. Kavale) Nature of Learning Disabilities, 1995, Efficacy of Special Education, 1999, (with E. Sinclair) Learning Disabilites and Related Disorders, 2002; cons. editor various jours. Sr. scholar Shaklee Inst. on Spl. Edn., 1996-2001. Fulbright scholar Ministry of Edn., Portugal, 1976. Fellow Internat. Acad. Rsch. in Learning Disabilties, Am. Assn. Mental Retardation; mem. Tchr. Educators of Children with Behavior Disorders (pres. 1985-86), Coun. Children with Behavior Disorders (pres. 1987-88, Leadership award 1995), Am. Assn. Univ. Affiliated Programs in Developmental Disabilities (interdisciplinary coun. 1972-89), Internat. Coun. for Exceptional Children (del. Assembly 1988-91, Wallin award 1992, Excellence in Tchr. Edn. award 1995, honors com. 1999-2002), Acad. on Mental Retardation (exec. com. 1989-91), Nat. Mental Health and Spl. Edn. Coalition (co-chair of Definition Task Force 1987-2000), Am. Psychiat. Assn. (DSM IV subcom. on learning disorders 1988-94), Profl. Group for Attention and Related Disorders (com. profl. advisors 1990-91), Midwest Symposium on Behavioral Disorders (Leadership award 1993), Am. Acad. Child and Adolescent Psychiatry (co-chmn. practice parameters on learning disabilities 1996-98, Sidney Berman award on learning disorders 2000), Knights of Malta (Order of St. John 1994). Home: 11901 W Sunset Blvd Los Angeles CA 90049-4240 Office: UCLA Dept Psychiatry 760 Westwood Plz Los Angeles CA 90095-8353

FORNEY, G(EORGE) DAVID, JR., retired electronics executive; b. N.Y.C., Mar. 6, 1940; s. George David Forney and Priscilla (Brush) Forney McDonnell; m. Harriett A. Bascom, June 9, 1962 (div. 1989); children: Mark Hamilton, Priscilla Jean, William McDonnell. BS in Engring., Princeton U., 1961; MSc, MIT, 1963, ScD, 1965. Mem. tech. staff Codex Corp., Watertown, Mass., 1965-70, v.p. rsch. Newton, Mass., 1970-75, v.p. R&D, 1975-78, v.p. rsch. Mansfield, Mass., 1978-82, v.p. tech. and bus. dept., 1986-89; v.p., dir. tech. and planning Motorola Info. Sys. Group, Mansfield, 1982-86; v.p. tech. staff Motorola, Inc., Mansfield, 1980-99. Vis. scientist Stanford (Calif.) U., 1971—72, vis. prof., 1990, mem. adv. coun., 1990—94; mem. adv. coun. dept. elec. engring. Princeton (N.J.) U., 1977—99, Columbia U., N.Y.C., 1986—93, Harvard U., Cambridge, Mass., 1995—2003; adj. prof. MIT, Cambridge, 1980—82, Cambridge, 1996—. Author: Concatenated Codes, 1966; contbr. articles to profl. jours. Overseer Shady Hill Sch., Cambridge, 1980—86; bd. dirs. Am. Field Svc., N.Y.C., 1971—74, Aware, Inc., 1999—; trustee Lehman Inst., N.Y.C., 1973—80, Mt. Auburn Hosp., Cambridge, 1986—2004. Named to Mass. Telecom. Hall of Fame, 2001; recipient Christopher Columbus award in Internat. Comm., 1996; Marconi Internat. fellow, 1997. Fellow: IEEE (editor jour. 1970—73, Info. Theory Group award 1970, Browder J. Thompson prize paper award 1972, Centennial medal 1984, Donald G. Fink prize paper award 1990, Edison medal 1992, Shannon award 1995, Info. Theory Golden Jubilee award 1998), AAAS, Am. Acad. Arts and Scis.; mem.: NAS, NAE, IEEE Info. Theory Soc. (pres. 1992), Popov Soc. (Russia) (hon.). Achievements include patents in field. Home and Office: 1010 Memorial Dr Apt 3G Cambridge MA 02138-4853 Office Phone: 617-868-4855. Business E-Mail: forneyd@comcast.net.

FORNEY, LARRY J., chemical engineer, educator; b. Waterloo, Iowa, Nov. 1, 1944; s. Loren John and Ramona Leary F.; m. Paula Hickey, Aug. 3, 1974; 1 child, Megan Catlin. BS, Case Inst. Tech., 1966; MS, MIT, 1968, ME, 1969; PhD, Harvard U., 1974. Rsch. engr. Norton Rsch. Corp., Cambridge, Mass., 1968, Walden Rsch. div. Abcor, Inc., Cambridge, Mass., 1972-74; asst. prof. dept. civil engring. U. Ill., Urbana, 1974-79; assoc. prof. chem. engring. Ga. Inst. Tech., Atlanta, 1979—. Cons. Comml. Union Ins. Co., 1977, Lockheed Ga. Co., 1982-83, Sverdrup Tech. Inc., 1983-87, Dupont, 1989-91, Leeds & Northrup, 1991, Dow Corning Corp., 1994-96, Chem. Products Corp., 2004; phys. scientist USAF Rocket Propulsion Lab., Edward AFB, Calif., 1983. Contbr. articles to profl. jours. Active Clean Air Coun., Ga. Lung Assn., 1980-82. NIH fellow, 1968, SCEEE fellow, 1982, NASA fellow, 1988; NSF grantee, 1975-77, EPA grantee, 1976-78, U.S. Dept. Energy grantee, 1977-81, USAF grantee, 1983-84, 1989-95. Mem. Am. Inst. Chem. Engrs. (coordinator of sessions 1983, 88, 2000 ann. meetings), Harvard Soc. Engrs. and Scientists, North Am. Mixing Forum, Harvard Club, MIT Club. Achievements include patents pending for Taylor-Couette Flow: UV disinfection of fluids. Office: Ga Inst Tech Sch Chem Engring Atlanta GA 30332-0001 Office Phone: 404-894-2825. Personal E-mail: flll44@aol.com. Business E-Mail: larry.forney@chbe.gatech.edu.

FORNEY, RONALD DEAN, elementary school educator, counseling administrator; b. Kearney, Nebr., June 28, 1954; s. Carl Roger and Florence Alyce (Gordon) F. Student, Community Coll. Denver, 1972-73; BA in Liberal Arts, Loretto Heights Coll., Denver, 1975; AS in Devel. Psychology, Arapahoe Community Coll., Denver, 1977; MBA, Calif. State Coll., San Bernardino, 1992; MS in Ednl. Adminstrn., Nat. U., 1993. Cert. tchr., English tchr., Calif.; cert. ednl. therapist. Tchr. Lake Elsinore (Calif.) Sch. Dist., 1985-87, Banning (Calif.) Unified Sch. Dist., 1987—, master tchr., classroom mgmt.-assertive discipline cons., 1990—, asst. prin. Ctrl. Elem. Sch., 1996-98. Cons. visual and performing arts, motivation and self-esteem bldg; ednl. therapist in pvt. practice, 1998—. Recipient cert. in affective domain Lake Elsinore Sch. Dist., 1986, Outstanding Tchr. award Hemmerling Sch., Banning, 1989. Avocations: theater, reading, writing and reading haiku poetry.

FORNI, PATRICIA ROSE, nursing educator; b. St. Louis, Feb. 14, 1932; d. Harold and Glenda M. (Keay) Brown. BSN., Washington U., St. Louis, 1955, MS (USPHS trainee), 1957; PhD (USPHS fellow), St. Louis U., 1965; postgrad. (USPHS scholar), U. Minn., summers 1968, 70. Staff nurse McMillan EENT Hosp., St. Louis, summer 1955, Renard Psychiat. Hosp., St. Louis, part-time 1955-57; rsch. asst. Washington U. Sch. Nursing, St. Louis, 1957-59, rsch. assoc., 1959-61, asst. prof., 1964-66, assoc. dean in charge grad. edn., assoc. prof. gen. nursing sci., 1966-68; assoc. prof. pub. health nursing Wayne State U., Detroit, 1968-69; asst. dir. for manpower and edn. Ill. Regional Med. Program, Chgo., 1969-71; project dir. Midwest Continuing Profl. Edn. for Nurses, St. Louis U., 1971-75; dean, prof. nursing So. Ill. U., Edwardsville, 1975-88; dean Coll. Nursing U. Okla., Oklahoma City, 1988—2004, prof. Coll. Nursing, 1988—. Grant proposal reviewer Divsn. Nursing, USPHS, 1972-79, 88, 91, NSF, 1978, U.S. Dept. Edn., 1980; mem. Ill. Implementation Commn. on Nursing, 1975-77, Okla. State Health Plan Adv. Com., 1994—. Mem. peer rev. panel Nursing Outlook, 1987-91; mem. editl. bd. Health Care for Women Internat., 1984—, Jour. Profl. Nursing, 1988-90. Chairwoman articulation of nursing programs task force Okla. State

Regents for Higher Edn., 1990-91; bd. dirs. Greater St. Louis Health Sys. Agy., 1976-81, Adult Edn. Coun. Greater St. Louis, 1973-76, Edwardsville unit Am. Cancer Soc., 1981-88. Fellow WHO, Sweden, Finland, 1985. Mem. Nat. League for Nursing (accreditation site visitor 1979—, nominating com. Coun. Baccalaureate and Higher Degree Programs 1979-82, pub. policy and legis. com. 1981-85, bd. dirs. 1991-93, treas. 1991-93, mem. fin. com. 1991-95), Nat. League for Health Care (trustee 1991-93), Nat. League for Nursing Accrediting Commn. (peer review panel, baccalaureate and higher degree programs 1997-2000, commr. 2000-, chmn. 2001-), Am. Nurses Assn. (chmn. continuing edn. publs. com. 1975-76), Mo. Nurses Assn. (chmn. edn. com. 1973-77), Greater St. Louis Soc. Health Manpower Edn. and Tng. (chmn. legis. com. 1974-75), Midwest Alliance in Nursing (1st governing bd. 1979-80, 93-96, chmn. nominations com. 1980, 81, mem. fin. com. 1993-94, chair fin. com. 1994-96, treas. 1994-96, pres. 1998-2000), Am. Assn. Colls. Nursing (program com. 1978-82, mem.-at-large, bd. dirs. 1990-92, chair rsch. com. 1990-92), Ill. Coun. Deans/Dirs. Baccalaureate and Higher Degree Programs in Nursing (chmn. 1979-81), Am. Acad. Nursing (treas., chairwoman fin. com., mem. gov. coun. 1989-93, editor Newsletter 1982-87), Ill. Nurses Assn. (commn. on adminstrn. 1983-87, commn. on edn. 1987-89), Okla. Nurses Found. (pres. bd. trustees 1990-93), Sigma Theta Tau Internat. (charter mem. Epsilon Eta chpt. 1980). Office: U Okla Coll Nursing PO Box 26901 Oklahoma City OK 73190-0001

FORNOFF, FRANK J(UNIOR), retired chemistry educator, consultant; b. Mt. Carmel, Ill., Mar. 29, 1914; s. Frank and Ada (Arnold) F. AB, U. Ill., 1936; MS, Ohio State U., 1937, PhD, 1939. Asst. prof. Lehigh U., Bethlehem, Pa., 1942-44; chem. engr. Western Electric Co., N.Y.C., 1944-45; asst. prof. chemistry Lehigh U., 1945-47, assoc. prof., 1947-53, Kans. State U., Manhattan, 1953-56; lectr. Rutgers U., New Brunswick, N.J., 1956-84; sr. examiner Ednl. Testing Svc., Princeton, N.J., 1956-93, group head, 1956-83. Editor AP Chemistry newsletter, 1976-90; contbr. articles to profl. jours. Active Boy Scouts Am., Princeton, 1957-93. NRC fellow U. Calif., Berkeley, 1939-40; Procter and Gamble fellow Ohio State U., 1938-39. Mem. AAAS, Am. Chem. Soc. (chmn. local sect. assn. publs. 1960-70), Am. Soc. Engring. Edn., Nat. Sci. Tchrs. Assn., Nat. Council Measurements in Edn., N.J. Acad. Sci., N.Y. Acad. Sci. Methodist. Home: 110 E 7th St Mount Carmel IL 62863-2033

FORNSHELL, DAVE LEE, educational broadcasting executive; b. Bluffton, Ind., July 9, 1937; s. Harold Christman and Mary Ann Elizabeth (Fox) F.; 1 child, John David; m. Delphia Crum, May 18, 1991. BA, Ohio State U., 1959. Continuity dir. Sta. WTVN-TV, Columbus, Ohio, 1959-61; traffic dir., asst. program mgr. Sta. WOSU-TV, Columbus, 1961-69; ops. mgr. Md. Center for Pub. Broadcasting, Balt., 1969-70; exec. dir. Ohio Ednl. TV Network Commn., Columbus, 1970—; pres. Ohio Radio Reading Services; dir., mem. exec. com. Central Ednl. Network, 1972—, chmn. bd. dirs., 1986—. Mem. exec. com., chmn. Postsecondary Edn. Council of Central Ednl. Network; chmn. Higher Edn. Telecomm. Coun. of Ohio; mem. adv. com. Ohio State Awards. Pres. Landings Residents Assn., 1973; active March of Dimes, 4-H. Served with USAF, 1961-62. Recipient award Dayton Fedn. Women's Clubs, 1974, Civil Air Patrol, 1994. Mem. N.G. Assn., Ohio State U. Alumni Assn., Nat. Acad. TV Arts and Scis. (bd. govs. Columbus chpt. 1970—), Nat. Assn. Ednl. Broadcasters (chmn. state adminstrs. council), Broadcast Pioneers, Ohio State Awards Adv. Com., Health Scis. Communications Assn., Nat. Assn. TV Program Execs., Nat. Press Club, Am. Assn. Higher Edn., Alpha Epsilon Rho, Alpha Delta Sigma, Sigma Delta Chi. Clubs: University, Athletic (Columbus), Symposiarchs, Rotary. Home: 3388 Scioto Run Blvd Hilliard OH 43026-3002 Office: Ohio Ednl Broadcasting 2470 N Star Rd Columbus OH 43221-3405

FORONDA, BARBARA ELAINE, professional organizer, writer; d. Walter Alexander Conway and Myttie Louise Terry; m. Elmer Ganuelas Foronda, Sept. 15, 1974; children: Raenee Elaine, Nicole Michele; m. Charles Vernon Brollier, May 7, 1962 (div. May 10, 1972); children: Karen Alane Brollier, Vernon Alexander Brollier. BA in Economics, San Jose State U., 1983—90. Cert. Netware Adminstr., Novell, 1993; Tech. Comm. De Anza Coll., Calif., 2001. Project mgr. City of San Jose, 1989—90; acctg. Coopers & Lybrand, San Jose, 1996—96; proposal adminstr. ABB, Santa Clara, 1997—2001. Mem.: (NAPO) Nat. Assn. of Profl. Organizers (treasurer-elect 2003—03), (SSG) Seizure Support Group. Independent. Roman Catholic. Avocation: exercise. Office Phone: 408-249-1947.

FORREST, DANIEL STETSON, mathematics educator; b. NYC, Nov. 27, 1972; s. David Vickers and Lynne Stetson Forrest. BS in Math., Brown U., 1995; MS in Math., Purdue U., 1998. Tchr. asst. anthropolgy Purdue U., West Lafayette, Ind., 1998—2000; tchr. high sch. math. Thayer Acad., Braintree, Mass., 2000—. Recipient Vassar Book award, Rye High Sch., NY, 1991. Mem.: AAAS, Nat. Coun. Tchrs. Math., Math. Assn. Am. Avocations: Japanese culture, board games, reading.

FORREST, DAVID VICKERS, psychiatrist, educator; b. N.Y.C., July 8, 1938; s. Melbourne Arthur and Cleo Florence (Garello); m. Lynne Putnam Stetson; children: Daniel Stetson, Susannah Nissly. AB summa cum laude, Princeton U., 1960; MD, Columbia U., 1964, cert. in psychoanalysis, 1974. Cert. in psychiatry Am. Bd. Psychiatry and Neurology. Intern in medicine St. Luke's Hosp., N.Y.C., 1964-65; resident in psychiatry N.Y. State Psychiat. Inst., Columbia Presbyn. Med. Ctr., N.Y.C., 1965-68; chief psychiatric clinic 935th Med. Det. (KO) 93d Evacuation Hosp., Long Binh, Vietnam, 1968-69; chief psychiatric consultation Letterman Army Med. Ctr., San Francisco, 1969-70; pvt. practice psychiatry N.Y.C., 1970—; mem. psychiatry faculty Columbia U., N.Y.C., 1970—; dir. edn. ednl. rsch. dept. N.Y. State Psychiat. Inst., 1970-77; assoc. prof. clin. psychiatry Columbia U., Coll. Physicians and Surgeons, N.Y.C., 1984—, faculty psychoanalytic ctr., 1974—, consultation-liaison psychiatrist neurology (movement disorders), 1977—, clin. prof. of psychiatry N.Y.C., 2000—. Lectr. psychiatry U. Saigon Med. Sch., Vietnam, 1968-69; lectr. abnormal psychology Far East div. U. Md., Long Binh, Vietnam, 1969. Author: Selected American Expressions, 1974, 76, 82; co-author: Treating Schizophrenic Patients, 1983, (video cassette series) Electronic Textbook of Psychiatry, 1972-77; co-author, pub: The Ballet Company Game, 1973; founding editor, pub. Spring: The Jour. of the E. E. Cummings Soc., N.Y.C., 1980—; editor: Neural Net News, N.Y. State Psychiat. Inst., 1989-91; technical cons. Star Trek TV series, 1997—; contbr. articles to profl. jours., textbooks. Psychiat. cons. N.Y.C. Ballet Co., 1973; first aid instr. Boy Scouts Am., 1983—. Capt. USAF, 1968-70, Vietnam. Decorated Bronze Star; Gen. Motors nat. scholar. Fellow Am. Psychiat. Assn., Am. Coll. Psychiatrists, Am. Acad. Psychoanalysis (program chair), Am. Coll. Psychoanalysts (program chair 1987-89, bd. regents 1989-92, v.p. 1993, pres.-elect 1994, pres. 1995), Explorers Club; mem. Am. Acad. Neurology (assoc.), N.Y. Clin. Soc. (v.p. 1995, pres. 1996). Episcopalian. Avocations: invention, discovery, magic. Office: 133 E 73rd St Ste 211 New York NY 10021-3556 also: 155 W 68th St Apt 1219 New York NY 10023-5818 Office Phone: 212-988-4800.

FORREST, GAIL, human resources executive; b. McAllen, Tex., Apr. 18, 1955; d. Richard Baker Forrest and Diane Mattison; m. John A. Baker. BA, U. So. Calif., 1977; postgrad., George Washington U., 1978—82; MA, U. Md., 1987. Editl. asst. ABA, Washington, 1977-78; pers. asst. UNISYS Corp., McLean, Va., 1978-80, 1981-82, corp. dir. compensation and adminstrn., 1983-87, dir. pers., 1988-89, dir. human resources, 1989-90, dir. ops., 1991-94; dir. human resources Ameritech Corp., 1994-97; v.p. human resources Sears Corp., 1997—2002, Day & Zimmermann, 2003—. Cons. in field. Mem.: Soc. Human Resource Mgmt. Republican. Methodist. Home: 1241 Little Conestoga Rd Glenmoore PA 19343-1806 Office Phone: 215-299-8182. E-mail: glfrrst@aol.com.

FORREST, HERBERT EMERSON, lawyer; b. N.Y.C., Sept. 20, 1923; s. Jacob K. and Rose (Fried) F.; m. Marilyn Lefsky, Jan. 12, 1952; children: Glenn Clifford, Andrew Matthew. Student, CCNY, 1941, Ohio U., 1943-44; BA with distinction, George Washington U., 1948, JD with highest honors, 1952. Bar: Va. 1952, D.C. 1952, U.S. Supreme Ct. 1956, Md. 1959, U.S. Ct. Appeals (D.C. cir.) 1953, U.S. Ct. Appeals (1st cir.) 1992, U.S. Ct. Appeals (2d cir.) 1971, U.S. Ct. Appeals (3d cir.) 1957, U.S. Ct. Appeals (4th cir.) 1956, U.S. Ct. Appels (5th cir.) 1981, U.S. Ct. Appeals (7th cir.) 1996, U.S. Ct. Appeals (8th cir.) 1991, U.S. Ct. Appeals (9th cir.) 1994, U.S. Ct. Appeals (11th cir.) 1981. Plate printer Bur. Engraving and Printing, Washington, 1942-43, 1946-52; law clk. to chief judge Bolitha J. Laws U.S. Dist. Ct., Washington, 1952-55; pvt. practice Washington, 1952-87; with Welch & Morgan, 1955-65, Steptoe & Johnson, 1965-85, of counsel, 1986-87; trial atty. fed. programs br. civil divsn. U.S. Dept. Justice, Washington, 1987—; chmn. adv. bd. D.C. Criminal Justice Act, 1971-74; sec. com. admissions and grievances U.S. Ct. Appeals, D.C., 1973-79; title-1 audit hearing bd. U.S. Office Edn. HEW, 1976-79; edn. appeals bd. U.S. Dept. Edn., 1979-82. Mem. Lawyer's Support Com. for Visitors Service Ctr., 1975-87 Contbr. articles to profl. jours.; mem. editl. bd. Duke Law Jour, 1969-75. Pres. Whittier Woods PTA, 1970—71. With F.A., Signal Corps U.S. Army, 1943—46. Recipient Walsh award in Irish history, 1952, Goddard award in commerce, 1952. Fellow Am. Bar Found. (life), ABA (council 1972-75, 1981-84, budget officer 1985-88, vice chmn. task force on sect. devel. 1987-89, chmn. com. on agy. rule making 1968-72, 1976-81, chmn. membership com. 1984-85, editor ann. reports 1973-88, adminstrv. law sect., fellow adminstrv. law and regulatory practice, mem. comm. com. public utilities law sect., vice chmn. industry regulation com. 1985-86, chmn. comm. subcom. 1983-85, antitrust law sect., internat. law sect., sec. judicial adminstrn., sect. sci. and tech., comm. forum); mem. George Washington Law Assn., Am. Judicature Soc., Va. State Bar Assn., Fed. Bar Assn. (chmn. jud. rev. com. 1981-85, vice chmn. adminstrv. law sect. 1985-87), Fed. Comm. Bar Assn. (del. to ABA Ho. Dels. 1979-81, exec. com. 1967-71, 76-84, v.p. 1981-82, pres. 1982-83, chmn. telecomm. com. 1983-87), D.C. Bar Assn. (past sec., exec. com.), NAM, Nat. Conf. Bar Pres., Washington Council Lawyers, Legal Aid and Pub. Defender Assn., Am. Arbitration Assn. (comml. panel 1976-87), D.C. Unified Bar (bd. govs. 1976-79, chmn. com. on employment discrimination complaint service 1973-79, chmn. task force on services to public 1974-78, chmn. com. on appointment counsel in criminal cases 1978-88, co-chmn. com. on participation govt. employees in pro bono activities 1977-79), Broadcast Pioneers, Order of Coif, B'nai Brith, Phi Beta Kappa, Pi Gamma Mu., Artus, Phi Eta Sigma, Phi Delta Phi. Democrat. Home: 8706 Bellwood Rd Bethesda MD 20817-3033 Office: US Dept Justice 20 Massachusetts Ave NW Rm 7112 Washington DC 20530 Office Phone: 202-514-2809. Business E-Mail: herbert.forrest@usdoj.gov.

FORREST, KATHERINE B., lawyer; b. NYC, Feb. 13, 1964; BA with honors, Wesleyan Univ., 1986; JD, NYU, 1990. Bar: NY 1991. Summer assoc. Cravath Swaine & Moore LLP, NYC, 1989, assoc., 1990—98, ptnr., litig., 1998—. Mem.: NY State Bar Assn., Assn. of Bar of City of NY. Office: Cravath Swaine & Moore LLP Worldwide Plz 825 Eighth Ave New York NY 10019-7475 Office Phone: 212-474-1155. Office Fax: 212-474-3700. Business E-Mail: kforrest@cravath.com.

FORREST, KENNETH B., lawyer; b. Bklyn., N.Y., Jan. 16, 1952; BA magna cum laude, Bklyn. Coll., 1973; JD magna cum laude, SUNY, Buffalo, 1976. Bar: N.Y. 1977, US Dist. Ct. (so. & ea. N.Y.), US Ct. Appeals (2d, 9th & 11th cir.), US Supreme Ct. Ptnr. Wachtell, Lipton, Rosen & Katz, N.Y.C., 1982—, assigning ptnr. litigation dept. Editor (sr.): Buffalo Law Rev. Mem. Dean's Adv. Council SUNY Buffalo Law Sch. Mem.: ABA, Fed. Bar Council, N.Y. State Bar Assn., Assn. Bar City of N.Y. (mem. com. Fed. legislation & com. profl. responsibility). Office: Wachtell Lipton Rosen & Katz 51 W 52nd St New York NY 10019-6150 Office Phone: 212-403-1211. Office Fax: 212-403-2211. Business E-Mail: kbforrest@wlrk.com.

FORREST, PATRICIA ANNE, publishing executive, editor; b. Kingstree, S.C., July 16, 1935; d. John Symonds Hale and Clara Mae Smith; m. Richard Stockton Forrest, June 26, 1999; m. Dwight Ellsworth Whitton (div.); children: Laura Katherine, Robert Kennedy. BA, Agnes Scott Coll., 1955; MA, CUNY, 1969. Pub. New Plays Inc., Charlottesville, Va., 1962—, editor, 1962—. Lectr. in field. Author: Capture Them With Magic, 1982, Bringing the World Alive, 1996, (plays) The Little Mermaid, 1996. Bd. dirs. Internat. Assn. of Theatre for Children and Youth, 1981—87. Recipient Oustanding Svc. award, East Ctrl. Theatre Coop., 1996, Sace Spencer Lifetime Achievement award, 1997, award, Children's Theatre Found., 2004, Woodrow Wilson Centennial Celebration Commn. Plays winner, Hall Mirr. Fellow: Coll. Fellows Am. Theatre; mem.: Am. Alliance Theatre and Edn. (chmn. exhibits 1991). Democrat. Avocations: camping, water aerobics, snorkeling, cats. Office: New Plays Inc PO Box 5074 Charlottesville VA 22905

FORREST, SIDNEY, clarinetist, music educator; b. N.Y.C., Aug. 21, 1918; s. Paul and Esther Forrest; m. Faith Levine, Nov. 16, 1941; 1 child, Paula Forrest. Student, Juilliard Sch. Music, 1935—37; BA, U. Miami, Fla., 1939; MA, Columbia U., 1941; studied with Simeon Bellison, Otto Conrad, Alexander Williams. Prof. Peabody Conservatory of Music, Johns Hopkins U., Balt., 1946-85, prof. emeritus, 1985; dir. placement and career counseling Peabody, Balt., 1969-85. Clarinet soloist U.S. Marine Band and Symphony Orch., Washington, 1941-45; prin. clarinet Nat. Symphony, 1946-50; adj. prof. faculty Cath. U., 1954—; faculty Interlochen Ctr. for the Arts, Mich., 1959—, Am. U., 1961-81, Levine Sch. Music, Washington, 1980—; adjudicator Nat. Fulbright Commn., 1980-84, Que. Can. Nat. Conservatoire, 1969-84; former students mem. faculty major conservatories and univs. Editor and arranger clarinet solos including Entrance March of the Boyars: Halvorsen, Theme and Variations: Baermann Divertimento: Baermann, Nocturne No. 20: Chopin, Pastorale: Baermann, Twelve Fantasies for Solo Clarinet: Telemann, Variations on a Theme of Corelli: By Tartini, Four Hebraic Pictures (arranged by S. Bellison), Twelve Fantasies for Solo Saxophone: Telemann, Twelve Fantasies for Solo Oboe: Telemann, others; major full clarinet recitals include Carnegie Recital Hall, Bklyn. Mus., Nat. Art Gallery, Phillips Collection, Libr. Congress, others; solo clarinet recordings and recitals with Galimir Quarter, Erno Balogh, Bernard Greenhouse, Carlton Cooley, Leonid Hambro, others; recs. include (clarinet quintet) Mozart, (trio with viola and piano) Mozart, (trio with cello and piano) Brahms, (clarinet and piano) Hindemith Sonata, (with piano) Grand Duo Concertant, Variations op. 33: Von Weber; contbr. articles to profl. jours.; former students in major Am. and overseas opera and symphony orchs.; co-designer (with J. Hall) of Sidney Forrest Signature Clarinet Mouthpiece. Mem. Internat. Clarinet Assn., Music Tchrs. Nat. Assn. Avocations: photography, gardening, stamps, travel. Home: 9611 Kingston Rd Kensington MD 20895-3521 Office: Cath U Rome Sch Music Harewood Rd NW Washington DC 20064-0001

FORRESTER, ALFRED WHITFIELD, psychiatrist, educator; b. Springfield, Mass., May 15, 1953; s. Wallace Lomax and Alma Mae (Brooks) F. BA magna cum laude, Yale U., 1975; MD, Johns Hopkins U., 1979. Diplomate Nat. Bd. Med. Examiners, Am. Bd. Psychiatry and Neurology. Med. resident dept. medicine Mt. Auburn Hosp., Cambridge, Mass., 1979-82; psychiatry resident dept. psychiatry and behavioral scis. Johns Hopkins Med. Insts., Balt., 1982-85, research fellow, 1985-86, instr., 1986-93; clin. asst. prof. dept. psychiatry U. Md., Balt., 1987—; pvt. psychiat. practice, 1988—. Staff psychiatrist Cann Health Resources, Fallston, Md., 1987-88, The Sheppard and Enoch Pratt Hosp., 1988-97; dir. psychiat. svcs. Chase-Brexton Health Svcs., Balt., 1988-90, staff psychiatrist, 1985-2000; med. dir. Behavioral Sci. Assocs., Lutherville, Md., 1993-97, Nicotine Addiction Treatment Ctrs., Lutherville, 1997-2002; med. cons. Bon Secours Hosp., Balt., 1983-90; psychiat. cons. Shock-Trauma Ctr. U. Md. Hosp., 1987-90. Contbr. articles to profl. jours. Active Groton (Mass.) Sch. Bd. Govs., 1983-85, AIDS com., Med. and Chirurgical Faculty State of Md., 1988-91. Nat. Achievement scholar, 1971—75. Fellow APA; mem. AMA, ACP, Med. and Chirurgical Faculty State Md., Md. Psychiat. Soc., Md. Psychiat. Liaison Assn., Yale Alumni Assn. (fundraiser 1975-2003), Greater Balt. Bus. Profl. Assn., Mory's Assn. (New Haven), Yale Club (Md.), Johns Hopkins Club. Democrat. Episcopalian. Avocations: classical music, theater. Home: 115 Saint Dunstans Rd Baltimore MD 21212-3311 Office: 9515 Deereco Rd Ste 1001 Timonium MD 21093 Office Phone: 410-453-0901. Business E-Mail: a.w.forrester@att.net.

FORRESTER, ANN, nurse; AD in Nursing, Craven Community Coll., New Bern, N.C., 1977; LPN, Durham Tech. Inst., 1972. RN, N.C.; cert. by N.C. Eye and Tissue Bank for enucleation of donor eyes. Staff nurse ob-gyn., labor and delivery and nursery Carteret Gen. Hosp., Morehead City, N.C., 1977-78, head nurse, 1978-80; asst. dir. nursing, then dir. nursing Harborview Nursing Home, Morehead City, 1980-81; nursing supr. Calhoun County Med. Care Facility, Battle Creek, Mich., 1982-83; staff nurse, relief charge nurse med.-surg. unit Craven Regional Med. Ctr., New Bern, N.C., 1983-85, relief nursing supr., 1984-85, asst. dir. nursing, 1985-87; nursing supr. Britthaven Nursing Home, New Bern, N.C., 1987—; staff nurse in orthopedics Craven Regional Med. Ctr., 1987-88, asst. nurse mgr. orthopedics, 1988-94; nursing supr. Britthaven Nursing Home, New Bern, N.C., 1994-95, dir. nursing, 1995-97, 97-98; asst. dir. nursing Guardian Care of New Bern, N.C., 1998-99; dir. nursing New Bern Health Care Ctr. (formerly Guardian Health Care of New Bern), New Bern, N.C., 1999—; asst. dir. nursing Twin Rivers Nursing Ctr., New Bern, N.C. Mem. Internat. Platform Assn. Address: 30 Keith Cir New Bern NC 28562-6495

FORRESTER, JAY WRIGHT, management consultant, educator; b. Anselmo, Nebr., July 14, 1918; s. Marmaduke M. and Ethel Pearl (Wright) F.; m. Susan Swett, July 27, 1946; children: Judith, Nathan Blair, Ned Cromwell. B.Sc., U. Nebr., 1939, D.Eng. (hon.), 1954; M.Sc., MIT, 1945; D.Sc. (hon.), Boston U., 1969, Union Coll., 1973; D.Eng. (hon.), Newark Coll. Engring., 1971, U. Notre Dame, 1974; D.Polit. Sci. (hon.), U. Mannheim, 1979; LHD (hon.), SUNY, 1988; PhD (hon.), U. Bergen, Norway, 1990; Doctorate (hon.), U. de Sevilla, Spain, 1998. Instr., X-ray equipment rschr. MIT, Cambridge, 1939-40, co-founder Servomechanisms Lab., 1940, devel. electric and hydraulic servomechanisms for gun mounts and radar, 1940-44, asso. dir. servomechanisms lab., also supr. Whirlwind I digital computer devel., 1944-51, founder Digital Computer Lab., dir., 1951-56, div. head Lincoln Lab. for Air Def., 1951-56, prof. mgmt. Sloan Sch. Mgmt., 1956-72, Germeshausen prof., 1972-89, Germeshausen prof. emeritus, sr. lectr., 1989—. Former owner Forrester Cattle Ranch, Dunning, Nebr.; head System Dynamics Group, Sloan Sch., 1960-89. Lectures and tech. papers on digital computers and indsl. mgmt.; also dynamics indsl. and econ. behavior.; author: Industrial Dynamics, 1961, Principles of Systems, 1968, Urban Dynamics, 1969, World Dynamics, 1971, Collected Papers, 1975; patentee servomechanisms, digital info. storage, indsl. control. Recipient Inventor of Yr. award George Washington U., 1968, Valdemar Poulsen Gold medal Danish Acad. Tech. Scis., 1969, Outstanding Accomplishment award Systems, Man and Cybernetics Soc. of IEEE, 1972, Computer Pioneer award IEEE Computer Soc., 1982, Benjamin Franklin fellow Royal Soc. Arts, London, 1972, New Eng. award Engring. Socs. New Eng., 1973, Potts medal Franklin Inst., 1974; Harry Goode Meml. award Am. Fedn. Info. Processing Socs., 1977, Common Wealth award of Disting. Service, 1979, James R. Killain Jr. Faculty Achievement award MIT, 1987, Agricultura 2000 award, Italy, 1987, Info. Storage award IEEE Magnetics Soc., 1988, Lord Found. Leadership award, 1988, U.S. Nat. Medal of Tech., 1989, Pioneer award IEEE Aerospace & Electronic Systems Soc., 1990; named to Nat. Inventors Hall of Fame, 1979; Jay W. Forrester chair named in his honor, MIT. Fellow IEEE (medal of Honor 1972, Pioneer award 1990), Am. Acad. Arts and Scis., Acad. Mgmt.; mem. Nat. Acad. Engring., Inst. Mgmt. Scis., Soc. Mfg. Engrs. (hon.), Am. Phys. Soc., Assn. Computing Machinery, Eta Kappa Nu, Sigma Xi, Sigma Tau.

FORRESTER, PATRICIA TOBACCO, artist; b. Northampton, Mass., 1940; Student, Yale Summer Sch. Music and Art, 1961; BA, Smith Coll., 1962; BFA, Yale U., 1963, MFA, 1965. Resident Yaddo Found., 1979, 81, The MacDowell Colony Residency, 1980, Hand Hollow Found., 1981, San Francisco Mus. Art, 1967. One woman shows include Trutton Gallery, San Francisco, 1968, Capper's Gallery, San Francisco, 1970, William Sawyer Gallery, San Francisco, 1974, 81, 83, Smith Coll. Fine Arts Bldg., Northampton, 1975, M. H. de Young Meml. Mus., San Francisco, 1977, Kornblee Gallery, N.Y.C., 1978, 79, 81, 82, 83, Fendrick Gallery, Washington, 1978, 79, 81, 88, 90, Sebastian Moore Gallery, Denver, 1981, Contemporary Art Ctr., Honolulu, 1984, Frick Gallery, U. Pitts., 1984, 87, U. Conn., 1984, New Orleans Acad. Fine Arts, 1984, 91, Mattingly-Baker Gallery, Dallas, 1985, Fischbach Gallery, N.Y.C., 1987, 89, 90, 92, Reynolds/Minor Gallery, Richmond, Va., 1987, Braunstein/Quay Gallery, San Francisco, 1987, 89, 91, 94, 98, 2001, Gail Severn Gallery, Sun Valley, Idaho, 1988, Sierra Nevada Mus., Reno, 1988, N.Y. Stock Exch. Bldg., N.Y.C., 1989, Luria Gallery, Bay Harbor Island, Fla., 1990, Kalamazoo Inst. Arts, 1991, Stephen Scott Gallery, Balt., 1992, 97, Addison/Ripley Gallery, Washington, 1993, 96, 99, Gerald Peters Gallery, Santa Fe, 1994; exhibited in group shows Mattingly-Baker Gallery, Dallas, 1982, Springfield (Mo.) Art Mus., 1983, Pa. Acad. Fine Arts, Phila., 1983, Art Inst. Chgo., 1983, Corcoran Gallery, Washington, 1984, Bklyn. Mus., N.Y.C., 1985, William Sawyer Gallery, San Francisco, 1985, 88, Coll. of Mainland, Texas City, Tex., 1985, William's Coll. Art Ctr., Williamstown, Mass., 1985-86, Akron (Ohio) Art Mus., 1985-86, Madison (Wis.) Art Ctr., 1985-86, San Francisco Mus. Art, 1985-86, DeCordova and Dana Mus. Art, Lincoln, Mass., 1985-86, Archer M. Huntington Art Gallery U. Evanston, Ill., 1985-86, William's Coll. Art Ctr., Williamstown, Mass., 1985-86, Akron (Ohio) Art Mus., 1985-86, Madison (Wis.) Art Ctr., 1985-86, Metro. Mus., Miami, 1986, Springfield (Mo.) Art Mus., 1986, Art Mus. Santa Cruz County, 1987, The Sierra Nevada Mus. Art, Reno, Nev., 1988, William Sawyer Gallery, San Francisco, 1988, Kohler Arts Ctr., Sheboygan, Wis., 1988, Grand Ctrl. Art Galleries, N.Y.C., 1989, Fendrick Gallery, Washington, 1989, Gallery K., Washington, 1989, The Palmer Mus. Art, Pa., 1990, Steven Scott Gallery, Balt., 1990, Am. Acad. and Inst. Arts and Letters, N.Y.C., 1991, The Gallery at Bristol-Myers Squibb, Princeton, N.J., 1991, The Noves Mus., N.J., 1991, Ctr. Contemporary Arts, Miami, 1991, Nat. Mus. Women in the Arts, 1991-92, 2000, The Miyagi Mus. Art, Sendai, Japan, 1991-92, Sogo Mus. Art, Yokohama, Japan, 1991-92, Tokushima (Japan) Mod. Art Mus., 1991-92, Mus. Modern Art, Shiga, Japan, 1991-92, Kochi (Japan) Prefectural Mus. Folk Art, 1991-92; Kavesh Gallery, Ketchum, Idaho, 1993, Nat. Acad. Design, N.Y.C., 1993, Sewall Art Gallery Rice U., Houston, 1993, Gerald Peters Gallery, Santa Fe, N. Mex., 1993, Philbrook Mus., Davenport Mus., 2000, Meridian Internat. Ctr., Traveling to Vietnam, China, Singapore, Indonesia, 2000; represented in numerous pub. and pvt. permanent collections including The Achenbach Found., Art Inst. Chgo., Hawaii Arts Ctr., Indpls. Mus. Art., Meml. Art Gallery, Oakland Mus., N.Y. Pub. Lib., San Antonio Mus. Art, San Francisco Art Commn., Springfield Mus., The British Mus., The Brooklyn Mus., University Art Mus., Corcoran Gallery, Nat. Mus. Am. Art, Nat. Mus. for Women in the Arts; others. Guggenheim fellow in printmaking, 1967. Mem. Nat. Acad. Design, Phi Beta Kappa. Address: Addison Ripley Fine Art 1670 Wisconsin Ave NW Washington DC 20007*

FORRESTER, W. THOMAS, II, insurance company executive; With The Progressive Corp., Mayfield, Ohio, 1984—, treas., 1999—2001, CFO, 1999—, v.p., 2001—. Office: The Progressive Corp 6300 Wilson Mills Rd Mayfield OH 44143

FORRISTALL, GEORGE ZAPP, ocean engineer, consultant; b. NYC, June 30, 1944; s. George David and Dorothy Zapp Forristall; m. Mary Bremer; children: George Stewart, Anna Lisa Bremer. PhD, Rice U., Houston, 1970. Rsch. advisor Shell Internat. Exploration and Prodn., Rijswijk, Netherlands, 2001—04; treas., prin. Forristall Ocean Engring., Inc., Camden, Maine, 2004—. Contbr. over 70 articles to profl. jours. Recipient Offshore Mechanics and Arctic Engring. Conf. Industry Leadership award, ASME, 2004, Oceanography award, Soc. for Underwater Tech., 1996. Mem.: Am. Geophys. Union. Office: Forristall Ocean Engring Inc 101 Chestnut St Camden ME 04843 Office Phone: 207-236-7747. E-mail: george@forocean.com.

FORROW, BRIAN DEREK, lawyer; b. N.Y.C., Feb. 6, 1927; s. Frederick George and Doris (Williams) F.; m. Eleanor Reid, Mar. 8, 1952; children: Lisa Coggins, Brian Lachlan, Catherine Frances, Derek Skylstead. AB, Princeton U., 1947; JD, Harvard U., 1950. Bar: N.Y. 1950, Conn. 1967, U.S. Supreme Ct. 1954. From assoc. to ptnr. Cahill, Gordon, Sonnett, Reindel & Ohl (and predecessors), 1950-68; v.p., gen. counsel Allied Chem. Corp., 1968-85, dir., 1969-85; sr. v.p., gen. counsel Allied-Signal Inc., 1985-92; pvt. practice,

Greenwich, Conn., 1992—; of counsel Whitman Breed Abbott & Morgan, 1992-94. Bd. dirs. Union Tex. Petroleum, 1985-92. Contbr. articles to profl. publs. Mem. Greenwich Representative Town Meeting, 1993—; vestryman, former sr. warden, former diocesan rep., Episcopal Ch. Served to 1st lt. USAF, 1951-53. Mem. ABA, Am. Law Inst., Conn. Bar Assn., N.Y. State Bar Assn., Assn. Bar City of N.Y. (past chmn. com. corp. law depts.), Assn. Gen. Counsel, Am. Arbitration Assn. (bd. dirs. 1987-97), Corp. Bar Assn. Westchester-Fairfield (past pres., bd. dirs. 1986-91), Am. Corp. Counsel Assn. (bd. dirs. 1987-89), Assn. Corp. Counsel N.J. (past pres.), Indian Harbor Yacht Club (past bd. dirs.), Harvard Club N.Y., Ret. Men's Assn. Greenwich Conn. (officer, dir. 2003—). Republican. Home and Office: 704 Lake Ave Greenwich CT 06830-3361 Office Phone: 203-869-5441. E-mail: anchorforrow@aol.com.

FORRY, JOHN INGRAM, lawyer; b. Washington, Feb. 9, 1945; s. John Emerson and Marion Carlotta (MacArthur) Forry; m. Carol Ann Micken, Jan. 12, 1980; children: Alicia Ann, Camilla Lorraine. BA, Amherst Coll., 1966; JD, Harvard U., 1969. Bar: Calif. 1970, U.S. Supreme Ct. 1975, U.S. Tax Ct. 1977, DC 1998, N.Y. 1998. Founding ptnr. Forry Golbert Singer & Gelles, L.A., 1973-80; sr. ptnr. Morgan, Lewis & Bockius, L.A., 1980-97, McDermott, Will & Emery, N.Y.C., 1997-98, Ernst & Young LLP, N.Y.C., 1999—2003, Withers Bergman LLP, N.Y.C., 2004—05; prof. internat. fin. and taxation, 2005—. Co-author, editor: A Practical Guide to Foreign Investment in the United States, 1979, 3d edit., 1989, Joint Ventures in the United States, 1988, Differences in Tax Treatment of Foreign Investors, 1984, others; contbr. articles to profl. jours. Mem. adv. group to U.S. Commr. IRS, Washington, 1985—86; co-founder Fund in Philosophy and Sci., Amherst (Mass.) Coll., 1984—. Mem.: Internat. Fiscal Assn., Internat. Bar Assn. Republican. Roman Catholic. Avocations: philosophical implications of scientific developments, auto racing, mountain climbing, scuba diving. Office Phone: 212-848-9836. Business E-Mail: john.forry@withers.us.com.

FORRY, ROBERT H., lawyer; b. Indpls., Ind., 1947; BA magna cum laude, Emory Univ., Atlanta, 1969; JD, Univ. Va., 1972. Bar: Ga. 1972. Assoc. Troutman Sanders LLP, Atlanta, 1972—76, ptnr., energy, govtl. law, 1977—, and sect. chief, pub. law. Named a Super Lawyer, Atlanta Mag., 2004. Mem.: ABA, Fed. Energy Bar Assn., State Bar Ga. (past chmn., adminstrv. law sect.), Atlanta Bar Assn. Office: Troutman Sanders LLP 600 Peachtree St NE Ste 5200 Atlanta GA 30308-2216 Office Phone: 404-885-3142. Office Fax: 404-962-6559. Business E-Mail: robert.forry@troutmansanders.com.

FORRY, STEVEN, not-for-profit fundraiser; b. Bellflower, Calif., Aug. 30, 1952; s. Earl Forry and Darlys Gallagher; 1 child, Sarah Cathrine. BA French magna cum laude, BA English cum laude, U. Calif., Santa Barbara, 1978; MA English, Columbia U., 1984, PhD English, 1988. Dir. stewardship Columbia U., N.Y.C., 1987—89; sr. devel. officer Sharp Hosps. Found., San Diego, 1990—96; assoc. dir. devel. U. Calif., San Diego, 1996—99; dir. corp. rels. Orange County HS Arts, Santa Ana, Calif., 2000—01; dir. devel. Children's Hosp. of Orange County, 2001—. Author: (Critical Study) Hideous Progenies: Dramatizations of Frankenstein in the 19th Century, 1990, (screenplays) Squiggets, 2002. Recipient award for Best Essay on Theatre, Am. Theatre Assn., 1987, award for outstanding pub. speaking, Toastmasters Internat.; fellow, Columbia U., 1978—81, fellowship, 1982—83, English Dept. Tchg. fellowship, 1984—87; scholar Whiting scholar, 1984—86. Mem.: Assn. Fundraising Profls., Nat. Soc. Fund Raising Profl. (chair Fund Raising Day San Diego chpt. 1993, chair fund raising day San Diego chpt. 1995, Orange Co. Chpt. 2001—02), Orange County Triathlon Club. Avocations: jogging N.Y.C. and LA marathons, men's over thirty baseball, sailing, tennis. Address: 176 Mcknight Dr Laguna Beach CA 92651

FORSBERG, PETER, professional hockey player; b. Ornskoldsvik, Sweden, July 20, 1973; Profl. hockey player MODO Hockey Swedish League, 1990-94, Quebec Nordiques, Colo. Avalanche, 1994—2005, MoDo, Swedish Elite League, Sweden, 2004—05, Philadelphia Flyers, 2005—. Mem. Swedish Olympic Hockey Team, Lillehammer, Norway, 1994, Nagano, Japan, 98, Team Sweden, World Cup of Hockey, 1996, 2004. Named NHL First Team All-Star, 1998, 1999, 2003; named to NHL All-Rookie Team, 1995, NHL All-Star game, 1996, 1998, 1999, 2001, 2003; recipient Calder Trophy, 1995, Art Ross Trophy, 2003, Hart Memorial Trophy, 2003. Achievements include mem. Stanley Cup Champion Colorado Avalanche, 1996, 2001. Office: c/o Philadelphia Flyers 3601 S Broad St Philadelphia PA 19148

FORSBERG, SUZANNE, humanities educator, humanities speaker; b. Salt Lake City, May 16, 1940; d. J. Ernest and Maureen (Kendall) Forsberg; m. Raymond A. Joseph, Dec. 13, 1974; 1 child, André E.F. Joseph. MusB, U. Utah, 1962; MA, Harvard U, 1966; PhD, NYU, 1990. Instr. Brigham Young U, Provo, Utah, 1969—71; vis. instr. St. Francis Coll., Bklyn., 1975—76, adj. prof., 1976—91, prof., 1991—; instr. Newark Sch. of Arts, 1997—. Con. NYC Bd. of Ed., New York, NY, 1990; spkr. NY Coun. for the Humanities, New York, NY, 2003—05. Author: (articles) music ency. and jour., 2000—01. Participant in Franciscan leadership pilgrimage to Assisi St. Francis Pilgrimages, Assisi, Italy, 1999. Grantee fellowship, Woodrow Wilson/Harvard U, 1962—63, German Academic Exch./ Munich, Germany, 1971—72. Mem.: Am. Musicological Soc., Soc. for Eighteenth Century Music, Am. Bach Soc., Phi Beta Kappa. Achievements include discovery of The symphonic output of the Bavarian composer Joseph Anton Camerloher. Avocations: travel, art history. Home: 865 W End Ave Apt 8C New York NY 10025-8405 Office: St Francis College 180 Remsen St Brooklyn NY 11201 Business E-Mail: sforsberg@stfranciscollege.edu.

FORSEE, GARY D., telecommunications industry executive; b. Kansas City, Apr. 10, 1950; m. Sherry Forsee; children: Melanie, Kara. B in Engring., U. Mo. at Rolla, 1972. With Southwestern Bell Tele., 1972—80, AT&T, 1980—89; v.p., gen. mgr. govt. sys. divsn. Sprint Corp., 1989—91, pres.govt. sys., bus. svcs. group, 1991—93, sr. v.p. staff ops., long distance divsn., 1993—95, interim CEO, 1995, pres., COO long distance divsn., 1995—98, CEO, 2003—05, chmn. bd. dir., 2003—05; CEO, pres. Global One, Brussels, 1998—99; pres. Bell South Internat., 1999—2003; vice chmn. Bell South Corp., Atlanta, 1999—2003; pres., CEO Sprint Nextel Corp., 2005—. Bd. dirs. Goodyear Tire & Rubber Co., Sprint Corp., 2003—; appointed to Nat. Security Telecommunications Adv. Com., 2004. Vol. leader March of Dimes Birth Defects Found., 1988, bd. trustee, 1995, vice chair, 2000, chmn. nat. bd. trustees, 2001; chmn. March of Dimes WalkAmerica; adv. coun. sch. engring. U. Mo.-Rolla, bd. trustee; mem. Bus. Roundtable, Bus. Coun., Kansas City Civic Coun. Office: Sprint Nextel Corp 6200 Sprint Pkwy Overland Park KS 66251*

FORSHAY, STEVEN R., marketing professional, consultant; b. Knoxville, Tenn., Nov. 17, 1942; s. Raymond Leroy and Majorie Zoe Forshay; m. Judith Ann West, Sept. 7, 1963; children: Steven William, Ann Marie, Sarah Lewis. BS, U. Tenn., 1964; MBA, U. Tenn., Chattanooga, 1972. Mfg. engr. Am. Lava Corp., Chattanooga, 1967-75; indsl. ceramic sales staff 3M-Tech. Ceramics, Sunnyvale, Calif., 1976-78, mktg. mgr. St. Paul, 1979-89, bus. mgr. Dusseldorf, Germany, 1990-94; mktg. ops. staff 3M-New Products Dept., St. Paul, 1995—. Mktg. cons. in field. Chmn. staff parish Centennial United Meth., Roseville, Minn., 1988, chmn. long range planning, 1996. Capt. U.S. Army, 1964-66. Mem. Am. Ceramic Soc., Am. Soc. Metals, Am. Inst. Indsl. Engrs., Internat. Soc. Hybrid Microelectronics (com. chair 1976-78), Kiwanis Club Signal Mountain (pres. 1975-76). Avocation: international travel. Home: 19 Spring Farm Ln North Oaks MN 55127-2142

FORSHEE, GLADYS MARIE, insurance agent, writer; b. Loveland, Colo., July 1, 1942; d. Henry William Hansen and Bird Marie Smith; m. Larry Bill Forshee, Aug. 27, 1960 (widowed Dec. 1992). Score grad., Small Bus. Adminstrn., 2003. Cert. ins. agt. Customer svc. rep., acct. mgr. various ins. agys., Denver, 1970—2000; property and casualty divsn. agy. mgr., 2004—05; owner Superior Janitorial Svc., Colo., 1975—2000, A Appletree Pub., Superior, 1991—. Author, pub.: (history book) Where Memories Linger, 1994, (cookbook) A Superior Centennial, Culinary Fest Cookbook, 1996, also 11 researched, published and continous updated family histories. Asst. organizer Superior Hist. Soc., 1998; town clk., recorder Town of Superior, 1970—73; cmty. svc. dir. Colo. State Grange, Aurora, 1992—99, Boulder county dep., 1999—2001; rsch. asst. Nat. Archives, Lakewood, Colo.; asst. organizer Superior (Colo.) Vol. Fire Dept., 1972—81; mem., vol. Adams County Hist. Soc., Henderson, Colo., 1991—2005; mem., vol. citizens adv. com. Boulder County Recycling and Composting Authority, 2000—01; mem. com. Boulder County Hist. Preservation, 2002—04; mem. Boulder County Resource Conservation Adv. Bd., 2002—04, chair, 2003—04; mem. Adams County Centennial Roundtable, 2002; mem. scholarship Colo. Preservation Conf., 2004; citizen shareholder Colo. Dept. Transp. Environ. Impact statements for US36 corridor and northwest parkway corridor projects, 2004—05; donated plaque honoring coal miners killed in indsl. min-Superior, Boulder County, Colo., 1860-1946, 2004; citizen adv. Town of Superior, Colo., 2003—05; event coord. Christian Clown Posse, 2003. Mem.: Green Valley Grange. Achievements include organizing campaign for federal government legislation to create National Children's Day, 2005; organizing placement of sign on Boulder County, Colo. open space property regarding the Denver and interurban railroad electric trolley line from Denver to Boulder, 2005. Avocations: gardening, crocheting, camping, reading, playing the stock market. Home: 404 S 3d Ave Superior CO 80027

FORSHEY, MICHAEL S., lawyer; b. Akron, Ohio, May 30, 1956; BA, Univ. So. Fla., 1977; JD magna cum laude, Univ. Houston, 1981. Bar: Tex. 1981, US Dist. Ct. (no., so., ea. & we. dist.) Tex., US Ct. Appeals (5th cir.). Ptnr., Litigation & Dispute Resolution, Bus. Law practices Patton Boggs LLP, Dallas, co-chair wide pro bono com. Mem. Dallas Bar Pro Bono Activities Com. Contbr. articles to profl. jours. Mem.: Tex. Bar Assn., Dallas Bar Assn. (mem. Bus. Litigation & Sports & Entertainment Law sect., mem. pro bono activities com.), Order of the Barons. Office: Patton Boggs LLP Suite 3000 2001 Ross Ave Dallas TX 75201-8001 Office Phone: 214-758-3540. Office Fax: 214-758-1550. Business E-Mail: mforshey@pattonboggs.com.

FORSLUND, DAVID WALLACE, physicist; b. Ukiah, Calif., Feb. 18, 1944; s. Dero Bradford Forslund and Myrtle Ruth (Conner) Forsland Snyder; m. Jean Carolyn Monson, Aug. 17, 1968; children: Daniel, Luke. BS, U. Santa Clara, 1964; MA, Princeton U., 1967, PhD, 1969. Postdoctoral fellow Los Alamos Nat. Lab., 1967—71, mem. staff, 1971—77, assoc. group leader, 1977, alt. group leader, 1978—81, lab fellow, 1981—. Contbr. articles to profl. jours.; assoc. editor Physics of Fluids, 1983—85. Fellow: Am. Phys. Soc.; mem.: Los Alamos Nat. Lab. (sci. and engring. adv. coun. 1987—89, Disting. Performance award 1982). Presbyterian. Home: 309 Aragon Ave Los Alamos NM 87544-3504

FORSMAN, ALPHEUS EDWIN, retired lawyer; b. Montgomery, Ala., May 12, 1941; m. Greta Friedman, July 5, 1964; children: Ellen E., Jennifer Ann. BA with distinction, George Washington U., 1963, JD, 1967. Bar: Va. 1968, D.C. 1969, U.S. Supreme Ct. 1973, Mo. 1979. Trademark examiner U.S. Patent Office, Washington, 1967-69; atty. Marriott Corp., Washington, 1969-72; assoc. Roylance, Abrams, Berdo and Kaul, Washington, 1972-75, ptnr., 1975-78; trademark atty. Ralston Purina Co., St. Louis, 1978-81, trademark counsel, 1981-91, v.p., sr. trademark counsel, 1991-96; asst. v.p. Eveready Battery Co., Inc., St. Louis, 1986-98; asst. sec. Ralston Purina Co., St. Louis, 1999—2001, v.p., sr. counsel, 1996—2002; v.p. Eveready Battery Co., 1998-2000; v.p., sr. counsel Nestle Purina PetCare Co., 2001—02. Asst. sec. Continental Baking Co., 1990-95; adj. prof. law Washington U., 2000. Mem.: Bar Assn. Met. St. Louis. Home: 417 Glan Tai Dr Manchester MO 63011-4067 Personal E-mail: aforsman@att.net.

FORSON, NORMAN RAY, controller; b. Port Arthur, Tex., July 12, 1929; s. Hollis G. and Annie (Butler) F.; m. Nancy McAnelly, Dec. 6, 1952; children: James Hollis, Diana Nancy. BA, Baylor U., 1952; MBA, U. Houston, 1961. CPA, N.Y. Sales engr. Magcobar, New Orleans and Houston, 1956-57; buyer Transcontinental Gas Pipe Line, Houston, 1957-61; supr. Ernst & Young, Houston, 1961-65; sr. v.p., treas. Gulf & Western Inc., N.Y.C., 1965-83; sr. v.p., chief fin. officer Hi-Shear Industries, Inc., North Hills, N.Y., 1984-85, Jonathan Logan Inc., Teaneck, N.J., 1985-97; sr. v.p., comptroller United Mchts. & Mfgrs., Inc., Teaneck, 1987-97; cons., 1997—. Served to 1st lt. USAF, 1952-56. Home: 7315 Marigold Dr Irving TX 75063-5501

FORST, EDMUND CHARLES, JR., communications educator, administrator, consultant; b. Chgo., June 25, 1961; s. Edmund Sr. and Patricia Ann (Dopek) Forst; m. Kelly Lee Globke; children: Morgan Mae, Shannon Rose, Maximillian, Charles. BA, Ea. Ill. U., 1983, MA, 1984; EdD, W. Va. U., 1994. Leader, mem. staff Neighborhood Boys Club, Chgo., summer 1975-84; instr. in communication DePaul U., Chgo., 1988-93; instr. Waubonsee C.C., Sugar Grove, Ill., 1993-94, assoc. dean comms. and humanities, 1994-98; dean arts and scis. Triton Coll., River Grove, Ill., 1998—. Cons. comm. for Leon Spinks, 1990; pres.-elect Ill. Coun. CC Adminstrs., 2003—04, pres., 2004—05. Contbr. articles to profl. jours. Eucharist minister Our Lady of Mercy, Chgo., 1989-90; bd. dirs. Neighborhood Boys Club, Chgo., 1988-92,; bd. dirs. St. Leonard Sch., Berwyn, Ill., 2000-01, mem. parish coun., 2002-05, mem. fin. com., chair fundraising com., 2003-05. Mem. Aurora-Naperville Rotary, Forest Park C. of C. Republican. Roman Catholic. Avocations: sports, reading, collecting comic books, model railroads. Home: 6509 Sinclair Ave Berwyn IL 60402-3737 E-mail: eforst@triton.edu.

FORST, EDWARD C., investment company executive; With Goldman Sachs Group Inc., 1994—, co-head Global Credit Markets, fixed income, currency and commodities divsn., 2002—03, chief staff equities divsn., 2003—04, chief staff fixed income, currency, and commodities divsn., 2000—02, 2003—04, exec. v.p., chief adminstrv. officer, 2004—. Treas. Market Bond Assn., 2003—04, vice chmn., 2004—. Corp. mem. Woods Hole Oceanographic Instn., 2002—. Office: Goldman Sachs Group Inc 85 Broad St New York NY 10004

FORST, MARION FRANCIS, bishop; b. St. Louis, Sept. 3, 1910; s. Frank A. J. and Bertha T. (Gulath) F. Grad., Kenrick Sem., Webster Groves, Mo., 1934. Priest Roman Cath. Ch., 1934. Pastor St. Mary's Cathedral, Cape Girardeau, Mo., 1949—60; vicar gen. Diocese of Springfield-Cape Girardeau, 1956—60; bishop Dodge City, Kans., 1960—76; aux. bishop Archdiocese of Kansas City, Kans., 1976—86; ret., 1986. Kans. chaplain KC, 1964—. With Chaplains Corps USNR, WWII. Roman Catholic.

FORSTADT, JOSEPH LAWRENCE, lawyer; b. Bklyn., Feb. 21, 1940; BA, CCNY, 1961; LLB, NYU, 1964. Bar: N.Y. 1965, U.S. Supreme Ct. 1968. Spl. legal counsel to bd. justices Supreme Ct. N.Y. County, 1965-67; dep. commr. N.Y.C. Dept. Licenses, 1967-68, acting commr., 1968-69, N.Y.C. Dept. Consumer Affairs, 1969; asst. adminstr. Econ. Devel. Adminstrn., 1969; assoc. Stroock & Stroock & Lavan, N.Y.C., 1969-75, ptnr., 1976—. Lectr. trial practice N.Y. County Lawyers Assn., Practising Law Inst., 1993-94, Title Ins. Litig.; mem. N.Y.C. Rent Guidelines Bd., 1984-97; arbitrator U.S. Dist. Ct. (ea. dist.) N.Y.; spl. counsel Appellate Div. First Dept., Disciplinary Com.; mem. Housing Ct. Adv. Bd., 2001-02. Contbr. articles to profl. jours. Dist. campaign mgr. John V. Lindsay for Mayor of N.Y.C., 1965; campaign mgr. Congressman Theodore Kupferman, 1966; chmn. N.Y.C. Young People for Nixon, 1968, pres. N.Y. State Assn. Young Rep. Clubs, 1970-72; pres. N.Y. Young Rep. Club, 1969-71; vice-chmn. N.Y. Com. to Re-elect Pres. Nixon, 1972. Judge Jacob Markowitz scholar NYU Law Sch., N.Y.C., 1964; recipient Brotherhood award NCCJ, 1987. Mem. Fed. Bar Coun., Am. Judicature Soc., Am. Trial Lawyers Assn., Phi Alpha Delta. Office: Stroock & Stroock & Lavan 180 Maiden Ln Suite 32108 New York NY 10038-4937 Office Phone: 212-806-5662. Business E-Mail: jforstadt@stroock.com.

FORSTER, ARNOLD, lawyer, author; b. N.Y.C., June 25, 1912; s. Hyman Lawrence and Dorothy (Turits) Fastenberg; m. May Kasner, Sept. 29, 1940 (dec.); children: Stuart William (dec.), Janie Forster Berman. LLB, St. John's U., 1935. Bar: N.Y. 1935, U.S. Supreme Ct. 1949. Gen. practice law, 1935-40; dir. law dept. Anti-Defamation League of B'nai Brith, 1940-46; asso. dir. Anti-Defamation League of B'nai B'rith, 1946-78, gen. counsel, 1946—; of counsel Shea & Gould, N.Y.C., 1979-94, Baer Marks and Upham, N.Y.C., 1994—. Police justice N.Y. State, 1954-57 Author: Anti-Semitism in the United States, 1947, A Measure of Freedom, 1950, The Troublemakers, 1952, Cross-Currents, 1956, Some of My Best Friends, 1962, Danger on the Right, 1964, (with B.R. Epstein) Report on the Ku Klux Klan, 1965, Report on the John Birch Society, 1966, Radical Right: Report on the John Birch Society and Its Allies, 1967, Report From Israel, 1969, The New Anti-Semitism, 1974, Square One, 1988, Stubs-A Letter to His Children, 1994; author (TV/radio) Dateline Israel, 1967-83 Mem. bd. edn., New Rochelle, N.Y., 1962-66. Recipient Emmy award for film Avenue of the Just, 1980, Emmy award for film Zubin and the I.P.O., 1983 Home: 79 Wykagyl Ter New Rochelle NY 10804-3207 Office: Baer Marks and Upham 805 Third Ave New York NY 10022-7513 *In one's vintage years, it becomes unarguably clear that the only true satisfaction is in understanding that one's achievements, however small or large, made others happy and this earth a better place for living.*

FORSTER, BRUCE ALEXANDER, dean; b. Toronto, Ont., Can., Sept. 23, 1948; m. Margaret Jane Mackay, Dec. 28, 1968 (div. Dec. 1979); 1 child, Kelli Elissa; m. Valerie Dale Pendock, Dec. 8, 1979 (div. Oct. 2003); children: Jeremy Bruce, Jessica Dale. BA in Math., Econs., U. Guelph, Ont., 1970; PhD in Econs., Australian Nat. U., Canberra, 1974. From asst. prof. to prof. U. Guelph, 1973-87; vis. assoc. prof. econs. U. B.C., Vancouver, 1979; vis. assoc. fellow U. Wyo., 1979-80, vis. prof., 1983-84, 87, prof. econs., 1987-2000, dean Coll. Bus., 1991-2000; prof. econs. Ariz. State U. West, Phoenix, 2000—, dean Sch. Mgmt., 2000—04. Vis. prof. Profl. Tng. Ctr., Ministry of Econ. Affairs, Taiwan, 1990-2002; cons. in field; Jayes-Qantas vis. scholar U. Newcastle, Australia, 1983. Author: The Acid Rain Debate: Science and Special Interest in Policy Formation, 1993; co-author: Economics in Canadian Society, 1986; assoc. editor: Jour. Applied Bus. Rsch., 1987, mem. editl. adv. bd., 1987—; editl. coun.: Jour. Environ. Econs. and Mgmt., 1989, assoc. editor, 1989-91; contbr. articles to profl. jours. Trustee Wyo. Retirement Sys., 1995-2000, Laramie Sr. Housing, Inc., 1995-96; mem. City of Surprise Econ. Devel. Adv. Bd., 2002-04, Ariz. C. of C. Econ. Devel. com., 2002-04. Mem. Assn. to Advance Collegiate Schs. of Bus., Am. Econ. Assn., Assn. Environ. and Resource Economists, Mid-West Assn. Bus. Deans and Divsn. Heads (pres. 1995-96), Faculty Club U. Guelph (treas. 1981-82, v.p. 1982-83, 85-86, pres. 1986-87). Avocations: weightlifting, swimming, skiing, scuba diving. Office: Ariz State UWest Sch Mgmt Phoenix AZ 85069 Business E-Mail: Bruce.Forster@asu.edu.

FORSTER, CARL-PETER, automotive executive; b. London, May 9, 1954; B in Econs., Bonn U.; post grad in Aviation, Space Tech., Munich Tech. U. Cons. McKinsey & Co., Munich, 1982; dept. head, planning, logistics BMW, 1986, sys. project mgr., 1988, dept. head test pilot car mfg., 1990, overseer, 1993—96; mng. dir. BMW South Africa, 1996—99; overseer vehicle devel. projects BMW AG Mgmt. Bd., 1999—2000; v.p. GM Europe, 2001—04, pres., 2004—; chmn., mng. dir. GM Adam Opel AG, 2001—.

FORSTER, FRANCIS MICHAEL, neurologist, educator; b. Cin., Feb. 14, 1912; s. Michael Joseph and Louise Barbara (Schmid) F.; m. Helen Dorothy Kiley, June 15, 1937; children— Denis, Susan, Kathleen, Mark, Gabrielle. Student, Xavier U., Cin., 1930-32, LL.D., 1955; BS, U. Cin., 1935, B.M., 1936, MD, 1937; D.Sc. hon., Georgetown U., 1982. Diplomate: Am. Bd. Psychiatry and Neurology (dir.). Rotating intern Good Samaritan Hosp., Cin., 1936-37; house officer neurology and neurosurgery Boston City Hosp., 1937-38, resident neurology, 1939-40; fellow psychiatry Pa. Hosp., Phila., 1938-39; asst. neurology Harvard Med. Sch., 1939-40; Rockefeller Found. research fellow physiology Yale Sch. Medicine, 1940-41; instr. neurology Boston U. Sch. Medicine, 1941-43; asst. prof. neurology Jefferson Med. Sch., 1943-47, assoc. prof. neurology, 1947-50; prof. neurology, dir. dept. Georgetown U. Sch. Medicine, 1950-58, dean Sch. Medicine, 1953-58; prof., chmn. dept. neurology U. Wis. Sch. Medicine, 1958-78; emeritus, 1978—; dir. Epilepsy Center, VA Hosp., Madison, Wis., 1977-82. Cons. neurology. Author: Synopsis of Neurology, 1962, 66, 73, 78, Reflex Epilepsy, Behavioral Therapy and Conditional Reflexes, 1977; editor: Modern Therapy in Neurology, 1957, Evaluation of Drug Therapy, 1961. Mem. AMA (chmn. nervous and mental diseases sect. 1952-53), AAAS, D.C. Med. Soc. (chmn. sect. neurology and psychiatry 1955-56, pres. 1958), Am. Acad. Neurology (chmn. survey com. 1948-51, pres. 1957-59), Am. Neurol. Assn. (chmn. com. internat. collaboration 1954-55), Am. Epilepsy League (pres. 1951-52), Assn. Rsch. Nervous and Mental Diseases, Am. Physiol. Soc., Am. Assn. Electro-encephalographers, Med. Soc. Wis., Cosmos Club (Washington), Sigma Xi, Alpha Omega. Clubs: Cosmos (Washington). Home: 11200 Springfield Pike Apt H 215 Cincinnati OH 45246 Office: U Wis Med Sch 600 Dept Neurology Madison WI 53792-0001 Personal E-mail: fm-forster1@worldnet.att.net.

FORSTER, HARRIET HERTA, phycicist, educator; b. Vienna; d. Karl Samuel and Olga (Frankfurter) F.; m. Kurt Engelberg, Jan. 22, 1942 (div. 1952); m. George Frederick John Garlick, Jan. 6, 1977. Student, U. Vienna, 1936-38; MA, U. Calif., Berkeley, 1947, PhD, 1948. From instr. to prof. physics U. So. Calif., L.A., 1948-87, prof. emeritus, 1988—, chair dept. physics, 1962-64. Dep. chief investigator Nuclear Physics Lab., U. So. Calif. Contbr. articles to profl. jours. Founders fellow AAUW, 1956-57. Fellow Am. Phys. Soc.

FORSTER, MERLIN HENRY, foreign languages educator, writer, researcher; b. Delta, Utah, Feb. 24, 1928; s. Henry and Ila Almeda (Rawlinson) F.; m. Vilda Mae Naegle, Apr. 25, 1952; children: Celia Marlene, David Merlin, Angela, Daniel Conrad, Elena Marie. BA, Brigham Young U., 1956; MA, U. Ill., 1957, PhD, 1960. Instr. in Spanish U. Tex., Austin, 1960-61, asst. prof., 1961-62; asst. prof. Spanish and Portuguese U. Ill., Urbana, 1962-65, assoc. prof., 1965-69, prof., 1969-78, dir. Latin Am. studies, 1972-78; prof., chmn. dept. Spanish and Portuguese, U. Tex., Austin, 1978-87; disting. prof. Latin Am. lit. Brigham Young U., Provo, Utah, 1987-98, chmn. dept. Spanish and Portuguese, 1989-93, prof. emeritus, 1998—. Dir. summer seminars NEH, 1978, 89, 90, 93, 96, 98. Author: Los Contemporáneos, 1964, Fire and Ice, 1976, Historia de la poesía hispanoamericana, 1981, The Committed Word: Studies in Spanish American Poetry, 2002, Many Stages: Studies in Latin American Drama, 2004; editor: Index to Mexican Journals, 1966, Tradition and Renewal, 1975, De la Crónica a la Nueva Narrativa, 1986, Vanguardism in Latin American Literature: An Annotated Bibliographical Guide, 1990, La vanguardia literaria en México y la América Central, 2001. Rsch. grantee Social Sci. Rsch. Coun., Mexico City, 1965, Fulbright-Hays, Buenos Aires, 1971, NEH, Austin, 1986-87, Am. Coun. Learned Socs. and German Acad. Exch. Svc., 1993-94; fellow Ctr. for Advanced Study, Urbana, 1976-77. Mem. MLA, Latin Am. Studies Assn., Am. Assn. Tchrs. Spanish and Portuguese, Internat. Inst. Iberoam. Lit. (pres. 1981-83, 94-96). Mem. Lds Ch. Avocations: classical music, quartet singing, gardening, woodworking. Office: Brigham Young Univ Dept Spanish and Portuguese Provo UT 84602 E-mail: merlinforster@yahoo.com.

FORSTER, PETER C., construction executive; Degree in civil engring., Tex. A&M U., 1963. Pres., CEO Blount Bros. Corp; pres., COO George Hyman Constrn., 1987—96, CEO, 1989—96; chmn., CEO Clark Enterprises, Bethesda, Md., 1996—. Bd. dirs. City Ctr. Consortium. Mem.: Constrn. Industry Round Table (chmn., vice-chmn. 2000). Office: Clark Enterprises 7500 Old Georgetown Rd Bethesda MD 20814

FORSTER, SUSAN H., ophthalmologist, educator; b. Phila., Dec. 11, 1950; d. William and Gail Forster; children: Alison, Jessica, William, Benjamin. AB, Harvard U., 1972; MD, Columbia U., 1976. Cert. Am. Bd. Ophthalmology. Physician, chief of ophthalmology Yale Health Plan, New Haven, 1983—; assoc. prof. Yale U., New Haven, 1986—, dir. med. studies dept. ophthalmology and visual sci. Office: Yale Sch Medicine 330 Cedar St New Haven CT 06510 Office Phone: 203-785-2020. Business E-Mail: susan.forster@yale.edu.

FORSTER, WILLIAM HULL, management consultant; b. Shelby, Miss., June 24, 1939; s. William Oskar Hermann and Amy B. (Hull) F.; m. Francine O'Neill, June 1999; children: William Hull Jr., Robert Brown. BS in Chemistry, U. Ala., 1960; PhD in Nuclear Chemistry, U. Calif., 1965; grad., Air Force War Coll., Navy Test Pilot Sch. Entered U.S. Army, 1965, advanced through grades to lt. gen.; comdr. Battery C, 6/56th Arty., Vietnam, 1965-66, 173d Assault Helicopter Co., Vietnam, 1971-72, 10th Combat Aviation Bn., Ft. Lewis, Wash., 1976-78; detailed NASA Manned Spaceflight Ctr., Houston, 1973—75; chief aviation systems div. hdqrs. U.S. Army, Washington, 1981-82; project mgr. Army Helicopter Improvement Program, 1982-85; dep. comdg. gen. Army Aviation Systems Command, 1985-86; program mgr. Apache Advanced Attack Helicopter, 1986-87; program exec. officer Combat Aviation, 1987-88; dir. requirements hdqrs. U.S. Army, Washington, 1988-91; comdr. Army Operational Test and Evaluation Command, Alexandria, Va., 1991-92; dep. asst. sec. rsch., devel., and acquisition U.S. Army, Washington, 1992-95; ret., 1995; v.p. land combat systems Northrop G. Corp., 1996—2004; ret., 2004. Chmn. Nat. Acad. Sci. bd. Army Sci. and Tech., 1996—2001. Decorated D.F.C., D.S.M. with oak leaf cluster, Bronze Star with oak leaf cluster, Legion of Merit with oak leaf cluster, Air medal (15 awards). Fellow Am. Helicopter Soc. Internat. (chmn., bd. dirs. 2005); mem. Am. Phys. Soc., Russian Acad. Natural Sci., Army Aviation Assn., Nat. Aeronautic Assn. Presbyterian. Avocations: boating, automobile repair. Home: PO Box 106 Gibson Island MD 21056

FORSTING, SARA L., environmental epidemiologist; BS, U. Minn., 1999; MSPH, Emory U., Atlanta, 2001. Environ. epidemiologist DeKalb County Bd. Health, Decatur, Ga., 2001—. Office: DeKalb County Board Health 445 Winn Way Decatur GA 30030 Office Phone: 404-508-7986. E-mail: slforsting@gdph.state.ga.us.

FORSTMANN, THEODORE J., investment firm executive; b. Greenwich, Conn., 1940; 2 adopted children. Attended, Yale Univ., Columbia Univ., New York. Co-founder, ptnr. Forstmann Little & Co., N.Y.C., 1978—. Co-founder (with John Walton) Children's Scholarship Fund. Avocation: Brooklyn Dodgers. Office: Forstmann Little & Co 767 5th Ave Fl 44 New York NY 10153-0023

FORSTOT, STEPHAN LANCE, ophthalmologist; b. N.Y.C., Aug. 19, 1943; s. Shepard and Edith Forstot; m. Lynne Rochelle Bitton, June 15, 1945; children: Michele, Jordan. AB, Princeton U., 1965; MD, Johns Hopkins U., 1969. Diplomate Am. Bd. Ophthalmology. Ophthalmologist Corneal Cons. of Colo., Denver, 1982—, U. Colo. Sch. of Medicine, Denver, 1976-82, clin. prof., 1982—. Contbr. articles to profl. jours. Recipient Honor award Am. Acad. Ophthalmology, Sr. Honor award Am. Acad. Ophthalmology. Mem. Contact Lens Assn. of Ophthalmology (bd. dirs. 1985-87, 2004-), Internat. Soc. Refractive Surgery (bd. dirs. 1995-96). Avocation: tennis. Office: Corneal Cons Colo 8381 Southpark Ln Littleton CO 80120-4508 Office Phone: 303-730-0404. Personal E-mail: SL4STOT@aol.com.

FORSTROM, LEE ARTHUR, physician; b. Alpha, Minn., Oct. 4, 1936; s. Elmer Leroy and Ione Grace (Simpson) F.; m. Nancy Mulcahy, June 17, 1964; children: Michael, Jennifer, Kerstin, Eric. BA, U. Minn., 1957; MD, Yale U., 1962; PhD, Cambridge (Eng.) U., 1977. Diplomate Am. Bd. Internal Medicine, Am. Bd. Nuclear Medicine. Asst. prof. Simm Fraser U., Burnaby, Canada, 1965—66; resident U. Minn., Mpls., 1968-72, fellow in nuclear medicine, 1972-73; grad. rsch. asst. Cambridge (Eng.) U., 1974-75; asst. prof., physician U. Minn., Mpls., 1976-84; nuclear medicine cons., assoc. prof. Mayo Clin., Rochester, Minn., 1984—. Contbr. articles to profl. jours. including Jour. Nuclear Medicine, Radiology, among others. Pres. Am.-Swedish Inst. Ch., Mpls., 1978-80; bd. dirs. Luth. Ch. Good Shepherd, Mpls., 1980-82. Fellow Am. Scandinavian Found., 1959-60, NIH, 1975, HSF, 1963-65; grantee Am. Cancer Soc., 1958. Mem. AMA, Am. Coll. Nuclear Physicians, Soc. Nuclear Medicine, Brit. Soc. Philosophy Sci., European Assn. Nuclear Medicine, Am. Soc. Nuclear Cardiology. Lutheran. Avocations: music, photography, travel. Office: Mayo Clin 200 1st St NW Rochester MN 55901 Business E-Mail: lforstrom@mayo.edu.

FORSYTH, BARBARA JEAN, elementary reading specialist, writer, poet; b. Detroit, Nov. 20, 1946; d. Henry Gurney and Alice Elaine Shreve; m. Sid H. Forsyth, May 28, 1966.; children: Janelle Forsyth Bauer, Linette Forsyth McCash. BS in Edn., Taylor U., 1966; M in Edn., Calif. State U., L.A., 1980; adminstrv. credential, Calif. State U., Fullerton, 1997. Cert. tchr., reading specialist, Calif. Tchr. Rivera Elem. Sch., El Rancho Unified Sch. Dist., Pico Rivera, Calif., 1967-72; tchr. 3d and 4th grade LEP Class Hacienda La Puenta Unified Sch. Dist., Hacienda Hghts., Calif., 1979-80; reading specialist Monrovia Unified Sch. Dist., Monrovia, Calif., 1981-86, Alicia Cortez Elem. Sch., Chino, Calif., 1986—; cons. Houghton-Mifflin, San Jose, Calif., 1997—. Mentor Tchrs. of English Conf., San Diego, Calif., Calf. Reading Conf., Long Beach and Anaheim, Internat. Reading Assn., Albuquerque, N. Mex. Author: poetry, childrens' books; presenter How to Teach Reading using Readers' Theatre, 1996. Vol. Rep. campaign for state senate Chino, Calif., 1998. Recipient Editor's Choice award Nat. Libr. Poetry, Washington, 1997, 98, 99, 2000, 01. Fellow Internat. Soc. Poets; mem. ASCD, PTA, Internat. Reading Assn., Calif. Reading Assn., Foothill Reading Coun. Republican. Avocations: reading, writing plays, poetry, planning curriculum materials and weddings. Home: 3121 Genoa # G Ontario CA 91761 Office: Cortez Sch 12756 Carissa Ave Chino CA 91710-3701 E-mail: b4site@hotmail.com.

FORSYTH, BEN RALPH, retired academic administrator, medical educator; b. NYC, Mar. 8, 1934; s. Martin and Eva Forsyth; m. Elizabeth Held, Aug. 19, 1962; children: Jennifer, Beverly, Jonathan. Attended, Cornell U., 1950-53; MD, NYU, 1957. Diplomate Am. Bd. Internal Medicine. Intern, then resident Yale Hosp., New Haven, 1957-60; postdoctoral fellow Harvard U. Med. Shc., Boston, 1960-61; rsch. assoc. NIH, Bethesda, Md., 1963-66; assoc. prof. med. microbiology and prof. medicine U. Vt., Burlington, 1966—90, prof. emeritus medicine, 1990; sr. exec. asst. to pres. Ariz. State U., Tempe, 1990—2002, pres., 2002—, prof. health adminstrn. and policy, 1992—2002, prof. emeritus health mgmt. and policy, 2002—. Sr. cons. Univ. Health Ctr., Burlington, 1986-90; sr. adv. Ctr. Future Ariz., Phoenix, Ariz., 2003—. Contbr. articles to profl. jours. V.p., chmn. United Way Planning Com., Burlington, 1974—75, mem. ops. com., 1975—76, bd. dirs., officer, 1977—89; mem. New Eng. Bd. Higher Edn. Com., Burlington, 1985—89; chmn. U. Vt. China Project Adv. Bd., Burlington, 1989—90; trustee U. Vt., Burlington, 1996—2002. Lt. comdr. USN, 1962—63. Sinsheimer Found. faculty fellow, 1966-71. Fellow ACP, Infectious Diseases Soc. Am.; mem. Phi Beta Kappa, Alpha Omega Alpha. Avocations: hiking, gardening, travel. Personal E-mail: forsyth@asu.edu.

FORSYTH, ILENE HAERING, art historian; b. Detroit, Aug. 21, 1928; d. Austin Frederick and Eleanor Marie (Middleton) H.; m. George H. Forsyth, Jr., June 4, 1960. AB, U. Mich., 1950; AM (univ. fellow), Columbia U., 1955, PhD (Fulbright, AAUW, Fels Found. fellow), 1960. Lectr. Barnard Coll., 1955-58; instr. Columbia U., 1959-61; mem. faculty U. Mich., Ann Arbor, 1961—, prof. history of art, 1974-97, prof. emerita, 1998—, Arthur F. Thurnau prof., 1984—; vis. prof. Harvard U., 1980; Mellon vis. prof. U. Pitts., 1981; vis. prof. U. Calif., Berkeley, 1996. Mem. Nat. Com. History Art, 1975-97; bd. dirs. Internat. Ctr. Medieval Art, 1970-95, 2005-, v.p., 1981-85; mem. supervisory com. Woodrow Wilson Found., 1985-88; Rome prize juror Am. Acad. in Rome, 1986-88; bd. advisors Ctr. Advanced Study in the Visual Arts, Nat. Gallery Art, 1985-88; mem. vis. com. medieval dept. Met. Mus. Art, N.Y.C., 1990-95; Samuel H. Kress prof. Ctr. Advanced Study in the Visual Arts, Nat. Gallery Art, 1998-99, bd. advisors, 1999-2000, U. Mich. Mus. of Art, 2005- Author: The Throne of Wisdom, 1972 (Charles Rufus Morey Book award 1974), The Uses of Art: Medieval Metaphor in The Michigan Law Quadrangle, 1993 (Annie award for non-fiction 1994); co-editor: Current Studies on Cluny, 1988; contbr. articles to profl. jours. Rackham research grantee and fellow, 1965-66, 75-76; grantee Am. Council Learned Socs., 1972-73; mem. Inst. Advanced Study Princeton, 1977 Mem. Coll. Art Assn. (dir. 1980-84), Archaeol. Inst. Am., Medieval Acad. Am. (bd. advs. 1985-86, editorial bd. 1986-90), Medieval Club N.Y., Soc. francaise d'archéologie, Soc. Archtl. Historians, Acad. Arts, Scis. et Belles Lettres Dijon (France), Centre de recherches et d'études préromanes et romanes. Home: 5 Geddes Hts Ann Arbor MI 48104-1724 Office: U Mich Dept Art History Ann Arbor MI 48109

FORSYTH, RAYMOND ARTHUR, civil engineer, consultant; b. Reno, Mar. 13, 1928; s. Harold Raymond and Fay Exona (Highfill) F.; m. Mary Ellen Wagner, July 9, 1950; children: Lynne, Gail, Alison, Ellen; m. Adeline Skog, Nov. 15, 1996. BS, Calif. State U., San Jose, 1952; MCE, Auburn U., 1958. Jr. engr., asst. engr. Calif. Divsn. Hwys., San Francisco, 1952-54; assoc. engr., sr. supervising, prin. engr. Calif. Dept. Transp., Sacramento, 1961-83, chief geotech. br., 1972-79, chief soil mechanics and pavement br., 1979-83; chief Transp. Lab., Sacramento, 1983-89. Cons., lectr. in field; geotech. engr. cons., 1989—. Contbr. articles to profl. jours. Served with USAF, 1954-56. Fellow ASCE (pres. Sacramento sect., chmn. Calif. coun. 1980-81); mem. Transp. Rsch. Bd. (chmn. embankments and earth slopes com. 1976-82, chmn. soil mechanics sect. 1982-88, chmn. group 2 coun. 1988-91), ASTM. Home: 5017 Pasadena Ave Sacramento CA 95841-4149 Personal E-mail: slvrfox800@aol.com.

FORSYTH, STEPHEN A., lab administrator, venture capitalist; Prin. financier Accsys Chemicals PLC, Titan Wood Ltd., Medicsight PLC; chmn., founder The Internat. Cotton Co., 1998—; chmn. Medicsight, Inc., 2004—. Founding trustee Medicsight Found. Address: Medicsight Inc 46 Berkeley Sq London W1Y 7FF England

FORSYTHE, BETTY ANN, elementary school educator; d. Elza Elroy and LaVerne Dorothy Dudenbostel; children: Ashley, Michael. BS in Edn., So. Ill. U., 1977; degree in reading recovery, So. Ill. U., Edwardsville, 1997, title I reading cert., 2003. Tchr. 1st grade Coulterville (Ill.) Sch. Dist. #1, 1977—82; pvt. sec. Van Schaak Realty, Denver, 1982—84; tchr. reading recovery/power writing Marissa (Ill.) Sch. Dist. # 40, 1994—2004; title I reading tchr., math. tchr. Lebanon (Ill.) Sch. Dist. #9, 2005—. Tchr.'s aide Marissa Sch. Kindergarten, 1975; substitute tchr. Freeburg (Ill.) Schs., 1982—87, Marissa Sch., 1991—94, tutor, 1996. Sec. Marissa Booster Club, 2002, v.p., 2003. Mem.: Phi Lambda Theta, Phi Kappa Phi, Delta Kappa Gamma. Avocations: reading, writing, cake decorating, cooking, gardening. Office: Lebanon Sch Dist 9 102 Shuetz St Lebanon IL 62254

FORSYTHE, HENDERSON, retired actor; b. Macon, Mo., Sept. 11, 1917; s. Cecil Proctor and Mary Catherine (Henderson) F.; m. Dorothea Maria Carlson, May 26, 1942; children: Eric, Jason. Student, Culver-Stockton Coll., 1935-37; BA, State U. Iowa, 1939, M.F.A., 1940. Mem. faculty, dir. U. Iowa, summers 1953-55 Numerous appearances Broadway and off-Broadway plays, TV and film prodns., 1955—; sheriff in U.S. and London prodns. Best Little Whorehouse in Texas (Tony award); prin. role in TV series Eisenhower and Lutz, CBS, 1987-88, Nearly Departed, 1989; appeared in running role in daytime TV drama As the World Turns, 1960-91; prin. role in 110 in the Shade, N.Y.C. Opera, 1992; lead in Quarrel of Sparrows, 1993; TV comml./Col. Sanders for Kentucky Fried Chicken, 1994. Served with U.S. Army, 1941-46. Mem. Actors Equity Assn., AFTRA, Screen Actors Guild, ANTA. Presbyterian.

FORSYTHE, ROBERT ELLIOTT, economics professor; b. Pitts., Oct. 25, 1949; s. Robert Elliott and Dolores Jean (Davis) F.; m. Lynn Maureen Zollweg, June 17, 1970 (div. July 1978); m. Patricia Ann Hays, June 20, 1981; 1 child, Nathaniel Ryan. BS, Pa. State U., 1970; MS, Carnegie-Mellon U., Pitts., 1972, MS, 1974, PhD, 1975. Ops. rsch. analyst PPG Industries Inc., Pitts., 1970-72; instr. Carnegie-Mellon U., Pitts., 1974-75; asst. prof. Calif. Inst. Tech., Pasadena, 1975-81; assoc. prof. U. Iowa, Iowa City, 1981-86, prof. econ., 1986-90, chmn. dept. econ., 1990-94, sr. assoc. dean Coll. Bus., 1994—, Cedar Rapids Area Bus. Chair, 1992-2000, Leonard A. Hadley Chair in Leadership, 2000—. Founder Iowa Polit. Stock Market; pres. Iowa Market Systems, Inc., 1993-2000. Author: Forecasting Presidential Elections: Polls, Markets, Models; assoc. editor Jour. Econ. Behavior and Orgn., 1996-97, Jour. Exptl. Econs., 1997-2004. Recipient State of Iowa Regents award for faculty excellence, 2002; Univ. faculty scholar U. Iowa, 1985-88. Mem. Econometric Soc., Am. Econ. Assn., Econ. Sci. Assn. (sect. head 1989-92, pres.-elect 1992-93, pres. 1993-95). Congregationalist. Home: 1806 E Court St Iowa City IA 52245-4643 Office: U Iowa Tippie Coll Bus 108 Pappajohn Bus Bldg Iowa City IA 52242-1000 Office Phone: 319-335-0865. Business E-Mail: robert-forsythe@uiowa.edu.

FORSYTHE, THOMAS M., communications executive; b. Crookston, Minn., Feb. 6, 1958; s. Ernil L. and Malvina J. (Stahlback) F. BS magna cum laude, Moorhead State U., 1980. Comm. coord. Nat. Alliance Bus. of N.D., Fargo, 1981; dir. comm. divsn. N.D. Econ. Devel. Com., Bismarck, 1981—82; press sec. to Gov. Allen Olson, Bismarck, 1982—85; account exec. Flint Comm., Inc., Mpls., 1985; pres. Flint, Forsythe & Assocs., Mpls., 1985—91; dir. state govt. rels. General Mills, Inc., Mpls., 1991—, dir. corp. comm., v.p. corp. comm., 1994—. Campaign mgr. Lee A. Christoferson for U.S. Congress, Fargo, 1980; field dir. Mark Andrews for U.S. Senate, Fargo, 1980. With USMC, 1977. Mem. Internat. Assn. Bus. Communicators, Pub. Rels. Soc. Am. Republican. Lutheran. Office: General Mills One General Mills Blvd Minneapolis MN 55426

FORSYTHE-ADAMSON, VELMA BROWN, accountant, consultant, literature educator; b. California, Pa., Apr. 27, 1928; d. Ernest and Anne Leyland Brown; m. Forrest Evans Forsythe, Aug. 6, 1950 (dec. Oct. 1982); children: Leslie Ann, Lynn Allyson; m. Robert E.L. Adamson, June 22, 2002. BS in Bus. Edn., Ind. (Pa.) U., 1950; student various univs. and colls., Pa. and Wis., 1952-96. High sch. tchr. bus. edn., Pa. and Ohio, 1954-58; v.p., tax preparer Kincaid Tax Svc., Akron, Ohio, 1968-74; pub. acct. Pitts. and Akron, 1974-82; controller Holiday Inn, Dubois, Pa., 1982-86; asst. controller Radisson Hotel, Lexington, Ky., 1986-87; asst. to pres. Petrolec Inc.-Jadel Inc., Clearfield, Pa., 1987-88; acct., cons. Forsythe Bus. Svcs., Dubois, 1982—; tchr. ELI Ulaanbartar, Mongolia, 1999—. Vol. Internat. Exec. Svc. Corps., Egypt, Ghana, Slovak Republic, Stanford, Conn., 1992—; lay missionary fin. and edn. United Meth. Ch. Uganda, Mozambique, 1991—; missionary amb. to Indonesia, 1998; vol. exec. Citizens Democracy Corps, Republic of Georgia, spring, 2000, Russia, summer and fall, 2000; active Velma Scholarships, 85 children and adults, Uganda, 1992—. Mem. AAUW (program chair 1997-99, Woman of Yr. award 1998), Kappa Delta Pi, Delta Sigma Epsilon. Republican. Methodist. Avocations: travel, reading, hiking, canoeing. Home and Office: 717 Treasure Lk Du Bois PA 15801-9019 E-mail: vel4sythe@webtv.net.

FORT, ARTHUR TOMLINSON, III, obstetrician, educator; b. Lumpkin, Ga., Sept. 24, 1931; s. Thomas Morton and Gladys (Davis) F.; m. Jane Wilmer McClelland, June 15, 1957; children: Abby Lucinda, Arthur Tomlinson IV, Juliana Melody, Ernest Arlington, II. BBA, U. Ga., 1952; MD, U. Tenn., 1962. Diplomate: Am. Bd. Ob-Gyn, Am. Bd. Family Practice. Intern, then resident in ob-gyn U. Tenn.-City of Memphis Hosp., 1962-66; asst. prof. U. Tenn. Med. Sch., 1966-70; prof. ob-gyn, head dept. Sch. Medicine La. State U., Shreveport, 1970-73; prof. maternal-child health and family planning, head program family health Sch. Pub. Health Tulane U., 1973-74; practice medicine specializing in rural family medicine Vacharie, La., 1974-79; prof. ob-gyn and family medicine, head dept. family medicine and comprehensive care Sch. Medicine La. State U., Shreveport, 1980—. Author articles in field. Adv. bd. mem. State of La. Dept. Health and Human Resources, 1986-88. With USAF, 1952-57. Recipient Golden Apple Teaching award Student AMA, 1969, Golden Apple Teaching award Western Interstate Commn. on Higher Edn., 1973 Fellow Am. Coll. Ob-Gyn, Am. Acad. Family Practice; mem. AMA. Office: PO Box 33932 Shreveport LA 71130-3932

FORT, JEFFREY C., lawyer; b. Burlington, Iowa, Oct. 10, 1950; s. Lyman R. and Lucille (Gibb) F.; m. Diane Locandro; children: Christopher Glen, Elizabeth Anne. BA, Monmouth, 1972; JD, Northwestern U., 1975. Bar: Ill. 1975, U.S. Dist. Ct. (no. dist.) Ill. 1976, U.S. Ct. Appeals (7th cir.) 1977, U.S. Ct. Appeals (D.C. cir.) 1985, U.S. Supreme Ct. 1980. Law clk. to John M. Karns, Jr. Appellate Ct., Belleville, Ill., 1975-76; assoc. Martin Craig Chester, et al, Chgo., 1976-83, ptnr., 1983-88, Gardner Carton & Douglas, Chgo., 1988-90, Sonnenschein Nath & Rosenthal, Chgo., 1990—. Adj. prof. Northwestern U. Sch. Law, Chgo., 1990-92; bd. dirs. Delta Inst., 2000—; presenter in field. Author: Establishing an Effective Environmental Law Compliance Program, 1993—, Avoiding Liability for Hazardous Waste: RCRA CERCLA and Related Corporate law Issues, 2002, 05; editl. bd. Environmental Law for the Transactional Lawyer, 1991, rev. edit., 1994, 2001, Illinois Environmental Law, 1993, 2000; contbr. articles to profl. jours. Chair Lake Mich. States sect. Air and Waste Mgmt. Assn., Chgo., 1988-89, Am. Leading Bus. Lawyers, Ill. Environ., 2002-, Leading Lawyers in Ill. Environ. Law, 2002-; pres. Trevian Girls Softball Assn., 2004—; elder 1st Presbyn. Ch. Wilmette, Ill., 1990-93, 2001—04. Mem. ABA, Chgo. Bar Assn. (chair environ. law com. 1987-88), Met. Club. Office: Sonnenschein Nath & Rosenthal 8000 Sears Tower Chicago IL 60606 Office Phone: 312-876-2380. E-mail: jfort@sonnenschein.com.

FORT, RANDALL MARTIN, investment company executive, federal official; b. Richmond, Ind., July 4, 1956; Student, U. Cin., 1974-76; BA in Pub. Affairs with distinction, George Washington U., 1978. Various positions with rep. Willis D. Gradison Jr., Cin. and Washington, 1976-80; rsch. asst. office of hon. Roo Watanabe M.P., Tokyo, 1980-81; asst. dir., dep. exec. dir. Pres's. Fgn. Intelligence Adv. Bd., Washington, 1982-87; spl. asst. to sec. nat. security U.S. Dept. Treasury, Washington, 1987-89; dep. asst. sec. for functional analysis and rsch. U.S. Dept. State, Washington, 1989-93; dir. spl. projects TRW, Inc., Washington, 1993-96; v.p. Goldman Sachs, 1996—. Luce scholar Henry Luce Found., 1980. Mem. The Asia Soc., Phi Beta Kappa. Republican. Methodist. Office: Goldman Sachs 85 Broad St 6th Fl New York NY 10004

FORT, ROBERT BRADLEY, minister; b. Portsmouth, Va., Dec. 27, 1948; s. Richard Gould and Hazel Naomi (McBride) F.; m. Esther Faith Hardin, June 10, 1967; children: Yvonne René, Nathan Michael. Ordained to ministry United Evang. Ch., 1973. Evangelist United Evang. Chs., Monrovia, Calif., 1966, nat. youth dir., 1968-70, asst. to the pres., 1970-73, Calif. dist. supt., 1973-75; evangelist Assemblies of God, Springfield, Mo., 1976-78; sr. pastor Lynden (Wash.) Assembly of God, 1978-81, County Christian Ctr., Bellingham, Wash., 1981-87, First Assembly of God, Salinas, Calif., 1988—. Exec. dir. Life Mgmt. Sems., Salinas, 1989—; pres. Ft. Ministries, Salinas, 1967—; exec. v.p., chmn. bd., CEO United Evang. Chs., Hollister, Calif., 1996—; faculty NY Coll. Advanced Studies, 2002-05; plenary spkr. World Congress Evang. Chs., Nairobi, Kenya, Africa, 1993. Composer Love was the Color, 1980 (Grand prize Music City Songfest, Nashville, 1981); singer, musician 15 records. Chmn. resolutions com. NorCal/Nev. Dist. of the Assemblies of God, 1997-2000; mem. bd. adminstrn. Pentecostal/Charismatic Chs. N.Am., 2001—. Fellow: N.Am. Acad. Arts and Scis.; mem.: Am. Assn. Christian Counselors (charter mem.). Republican. Office: Fort Ministries PO Box 1000 San Juan Bautista CA 95045-1000 Business E-Mail: rbfort@uecol.org.

FORT, TOMLINSON, chemist, chemical engineering educator; b. Sumter, S.C., Apr. 16, 1932; s. Tomlinson and Madeline A. Kean (Scott) F.; m. Martha Kirby, Oct. 13, 1956; children: Tomlinson, III, Frances Clare; m. Nancy H. Blackwelder, Dec. 19, 1998. BS in Chemistry, U. Ga., 1952; MS, PhD in Phys. Chemistry, U. Tenn., 1957; A.E. and F.A.Q. Stephens postdoctoral fellow, U. Sydney, Australia, 1957-58; cert., Inst. Ednl. Mgmt., Harvard U., 1978. Instr. surface chemistry U. Sydney, 1957—58; rsch. chemist, then sr. rsch. chemist and project leader duPont Co., 1958—65; mem. faculty Case Western Res. U., 1965—73, prof. chem. engring., dir. surfaces research lab., 1971—73; prof. chem. engring. and chemistry, head dept. chem. engring. Carnegie-Mellon U., 1973—80, adj. prof., 1980—83; prof. chemistry and chem. engring., provost U. Mo., Rolla, 1980—82; v.p. acad. affairs Calif. Poly. State U., San Luis Obispo, 1982—83, provost, 1983—86, prof. chemistry and materials sci., 1986—89; Centennial prof. chem. engring., prof. materials sci. Vanderbilt U., Nashville, 1989—2002, Centennial prof. chem. engring. emeritus, 2002—, chair dept. chem. engring., 1989—96. Summer vis. prof. Nat. U. Mex., 1973, U. Copenhagen, 1978, 80; pres. Frances Fort Brown Realty Co., Chattanooga, 1970-94. Author papers on surface and colloid sci. Mem. AAAS, Am. Chem. Soc., Am. Inst. Chem. Engrs., Internat. Assn. of Colloid and Interface Scientists, KP, Sigma Xi, Phi Beta Delta, Gamma Sigma Epsilon, Alpha Chi Sigma, Sigma Chi. Home: 1015 Carlisle Ln Franklin TN 37064-4802 Office: Vanderbilt U Dept Chem Engring PO Box 1604 Station B Nashville TN 37235 Business E-Mail: tomlinson.fort@vanderbilt.edu.

FORTADO, MICHAEL GEORGE, lawyer; b. Wichita Falls, Tex., Oct. 29, 1943; s. Antonio and Flossie Juanita (Bowers) F.; m. Avis Ann Smith, Mar. 12, 1964; children: Michael Scott, Angela Avis, Shannon Michelle. BBA, Midwestern U., Wichita Falls, 1965; LLB, U. Tex., Austin, 1968. Bar: Tex. 1968. Assoc. atty. firm McClure & Sharpe, Houston, 1968-69; atty. Enserch Corp. (and predecessor), Dallas, 1969-71, corp. sec., asst. gen. counsel, 1971-88, v.p., corp. sec., asst. gen. counsel, 1988-96; sr. v.p., gen. counsel, corp. sec. Enserch Exploration, Inc., Dallas, 1996-97; v.p., gen. counsel, corp. sec. Trinity Industries, Inc., Dallas, 1997—. Mem. ABA, Am. Soc. Corp. Secs. (bd. dirs. 1980-83), State Bar Tex., Dallas Bar Assn., DAC Country Club, Kappa Alpha Order, Delta Sigma Pi, Phi Alpha Delta. Office: Trinity Industries Inc 2525 N Stemmons Fwy Ste 1000 Dallas TX 75207-2400 E-mail: mike.fortado@trin.net.

FORTE, CHRISTINA KIRBY, financial analyst; b. McKinney, Tex., Sept. 1, 1973; d. Karen D. Whittington; m. Michael E. Forte, Feb. 27, 1993; children: Joshua Michael, Noah Nathaniel. AA in Acctg., Collin County C.C., 1996; BS in Acctg., U. Tex., 2005. Engring. clk. Fisher Regulators, Divsn. Emerson, McKinney, Tex., 1995—97, accts. payable, 1997—99, payroll, 1999—2000, gen. acctg., 2000—02, sr. credit & collections analyst, 2002—04. Mentor, tutor Cmtys. in Schools, McKinney, 1998—2003. Mem.: Golden Key Internat. Honour Soc. (life scholar 2003), Beta Gamma Sigma (life). Avocations: writing, reading, cub scouts. Office: Fisher Regulators Divsn Emerson 310 East Univ Dr Mc Kinney TX 75070 Office Phone: 972-542-5512.

FORTE, MARY L., consumer products company executive; With Federated Dept. Stores, The May Dept. Stores Co., Inc., Macy's; v.p. Housewares Divsn. Rich's Dept. Store, 1989—91; sr. v.p. Bon Marchi Home Divsn. The Federated Dept. Store, 1991—94; sr. v.p. QVC Home Shopping Network, 1994; from pres. Gordon's to pres., CEO Zale Corp., Irving, Tex., 1994—2002, pres., 2002—, CEO, 2002—. Office: Zale Corp 901 W Walnut Hill Ln Irving TX 75038-1003

FORTENBAUGH, SAMUEL BYROD, III, lawyer; b. Phila., Nov. 6, 1933; s. Samuel Byrod Jr. and Katherine Francisca (Wall) F.; children: Samuel Byrod IV, Cristina Fortenbaugh Alemany, Katherine Fortenbaugh Silliman, Francesca Cowden, Harrison Selden; m. Sharon A. Swartz, Nov. 17, 2001. BA, Williams Coll., 1955; LLB, Harvard U., 1960. Bar: N.Y. 1961, U.S. Dist. Ct. (so. dist.) N.Y. 1961. Assoc. Kelley Drye & Warren, N.Y.C., 1960—69, ptnr., 1970—79, Morgan, Lewis & Bockius, 1980—2001, chmn., 1990—91, 1999, sr. counsel, 2001—02; pvt. practice, 2002—. Bd. dirs. Baldwin Tech. Co., Inc., Shelton, Conn., Security Capital Corp., Greenwich, Conn.; bd. dirs., sec. Furgueson Capital Mgmt. Inc., N.Y.C.; chmn. bd. dirs., sec. Wall Industries, Inc., Kannapolis, N.C.; chmn. bd. dirs. Knight Textile Corp, Saluda, S.C.; trustee Patroni Scholastici, New Brunswick, N.J., 1978—, sec. 1985—; lectr. profl. seminars. Contbr. articles to profl. jours. Mem. Assn. of Bar of City of N.Y. (mem. Young Lawyers com. 1962-65, corp. law com. 1976-79, com. on securities regulation 1982-85, chmn. com. on issue distbn. of securities 1984-85), Univ. Club (N.Y.C.), N.Y. Yacht Club, Indian Harbor Yacht Club (Greenwich, Conn.) (bd. dirs. 2000—, rear commodore 2003—), Phi Beta Kappa. Office Phone: 212-596-3379. Business E-Mail: sam@sfortenbaugh.com.

FORTENBERRY, DELORES B., dean; b. McComb, MS, Jan. 31, 1933; d. Isaac and Maude Elma (Carmel) Brown; m. John Prowell, Jan. 22, 1956 (div. 1960); children: Dennis A. Prowell, Stevie G. Prowell; m. Fred D. Fortenberry, Dec. 3, 1971. BS, Jackson State U., 1963; MA, Ball State U., 1974, EdD, 1988. Sci. & math. tchr. McComb (Ms.) Pub. Schs., 1962-65; sci. tchr. Chgo. Pub. Schs., 1965-68; sci., art tchr. E. Chgo. Pub. Sch., Ind., 1968-80; sci. tchr. Ball State U. Lab Sch., Muncie, IL, 1980-81; sci., math. tchr., gen. edn. E. Chgo. Pub. Sch., Ind., 1981-89, dean, 1989—. Pres. Dist. Sci. Fair com., McComb, Miss., 1964-65; nat. chairperson Pike County Agrl. H.S. Alumni, Chgo., 1991-2000, Pike County Agrl. H.S. scholarship fund; chmn. sci. com. Nat. Alliance Black Sch. Educators, Washington, Chgo. Alliance Black Sch. Educators, 1984-86. Fellow NSF, 1963-64, Ball State U., 1980-81; sabbatical leave E. Chgo. Pub. Sch., 1980-81. Mem. AAUW, Nat. Alliance Black Sch. Educators, Chgo. Alliance Black Sch. Educators (certificate 1986), Afro-Am. History Club (chairperson 1999-2000), Pike County Agrl. H.S. Alumni (nat. chairperson 1991-2000, recipient plaques 1992-94, 96-98), Am. Fedn. Tchrs., Nat. Sci. Tchrs. Assn., Hoosier Assn. Sci. Tchrs., Assn. Supervision and Curriculum Devel., Kappa Delta Pi, Gamma Phi Delta (basilieus, 1968-73), Phi Delta Kappa. Avocations: reading, travel, collecting recipes, collecting black history materials, sports. Home: 831 E 192nd St Glenwood IL 60425-2005 Office: Ctrl High Sch 1100 W Columbus Dr East Chicago IN 46312-2582

FORTENBERRY, JAMES DONALD, medical association administrator; b. Atlanta, Ga., Dec. 7, 1957; s. Robert Elwood and Florence Ford Fortenberry; m. Janet Hanner, June 1, 1980; children: Erin Elizabeth, Charles Benjamin, Sara Katherine. BA, U. NC, 1980; MD, Med. Coll. Ga., 1984. Pediat. Am. Bd. of Pediat., 1988, Pediat. Critical Care Am. Bd. of Pediat., 1992. Dir., dept. of medicine Children's Healthcare of Atlanta at Egleston, Atlanta, 2000—04, dir., critical care medicine, 2002—. Recipient Pediatric Sect. Rsch. award, Soc. of Critical Care Medicine; fellow, Am. Coll. of Critical Care Medicine, 2002. Fellow: Am. Acad. of Pediat. (critical care sect. program chair 2003—05), Am. Coll. of Critical Care Medicine. Achievements include research in Critical Care. Home: 2875 Thornbriar Rd Atlanta GA 30340 Office: Childrens Healthcare Atlanta 1405 Clifton Rd NE Atlanta GA 30322 Office Phone: 404-785-1600. Home Fax: 404-785-6233. Personal E-mail: james.fortenberry@choa.org.

FORTENBERRY, JEFF, congressman; b. Baton Rouge, La., Dec. 27, 1960; m. Celeste Fortenberry; 4 children. BA, La. State Univ.; MPP, Georgetown Univ.; M Theology, Franciscan Univ. Staff mem. U.S. Senate subcommittee on Intergovernmental Rels.; mem. City Council, Lincoln, Nebr., 1997—2001, U.S. Ho. Reps., 109th Congress, 1st Dist. Nebr., 2005—. Republican. Roman Catholic. Office: 1517 Longworth House Office Bldg Washington DC 20515-2701 Office Phone: 202-225-4806.*

FORTH, KEVIN BERNARD, beverage distributing industry consultant; b. Adams, Mass., Dec. 4, 1949; s. Michael Charles and Catherine Cecilia (McAndrews) F.; m. Alice Farnum (dec. 1994); children: Melissa, Brian; m. Deborah Newport. AB, Holy Cross Coll., 1971; MBA with distinction, NYU, 1973, Benjamin Levy fellow. Divsn. rep. Anheuser-Busch, Inc., Boston, 1973-74, dist. sales mgr. L.A., 1974-76, asst. to v.p. mktg. staff St. Louis, 1976-77; v.p. Straub Distbg. Co., Ltd., Orange, Calif., 1977-81, pres., 1981-93, chmn., CEO, 1986-93. Commr. Orange County Sheriff's Adv. Coun., 1988—; mem. adv. bd. Rancho Santiago C.C. Coll. Dist., 1978-80; exec. com., bd. dirs. Nat. Coun. on Alcoholism, 1980-83; mem. pres. coun. Holy Cross Coll., 1987-91; bd. dirs., pres. Calif. State Fullerton Titan Athletic Found., 1983-85, 89-90; mem. Calif. Beer Wholesalers Assn., dir., 1978-89, v.p., 1984, chmn., 1985; bd. dirs. Orange County Sports Hall of Fame, 1980-89, Children's Hosp. of Orange County Padrinos Found., 1983-85, Freedom Bowl, 1984-93 (founders award, 1993), v.p., 1984-85, pres., 1986, chmn., 1986-87, Orangewood Children's Found., 1988-93, St. Joseph's Hosp. Found., Anaheim Vis. and Conv. Bur., 1989-93, Wilcox Health Found., 2003-05; mem. Calif. Rep. State Ctrl. Com., 1988-93, Orange County Probation Dept. Cmty. Involvement Bd., 1992-93. Recipient Vol. of Yr. award, Calif. State U., Fullerton, Calif., 1990. Mem. Nat. Beer Wholesalers Assn. (bd. dirs. 1986-93, asst. sec. 1989-90, sec. 1989-91, vice-chmn. 1992, chmn. 1993; Lifetime Achievement Svc. award 2001), Holy Cross Alumni Assn., Sports Car Club Am. (Ariz. state champion 1982), Beta Gamma Sigma. Roman Catholic. Home and Office: 3636 Keoniana Rd Princeville HI 96722- Personal E-mail: kforth1204@aol.com.

FORTI, LENORE STEIMLE, business consultant; b. Houghton, Mich., Sept. 9, 1924; d. Russell Nicholas and Agnes (McCloskey) Steimle; m. Frank Forti, May 29, 1950 (dec.). BBA summa cum laude, Northwood U., 1973, Dr.Laws, 1969. Asst. corp. sec., purchasing agt. Fed. Life & Casualty Co., Detroit, 1942-53; supr. sectl. J.L. Hudson Co., Detroit, 1953-57, adminstrv. asst. to exec. v.p., 1957-86; instr. Wayne State U. and U. Mich. Adult Edn., Detroit, 1958-71; creator, dir. Seminars for Profl. People, 1971—. Co-author: The Professional Secretary; contbr. articles to profl. jours. Asst. br. dir. planning City of Detroit for Civil Def.; chmn. bd. trustees PSI Rsch. and Ednl. Found.; trustee PSI Retirement Home Complex, Albuquerque; elected dir. Property Owners and Residents Assn., Sun City West Mcpl. Govt., 1994—97; past pres. Women's Bd. Northwood U., Midland, Mich.; past pres. parish coun. Our Lady of Lourdes Ch., Sun City West, Ariz., 1988, pres. ladies guild, 1990, 1995; 1st v.p. Vol. Bur. of Sun Cities, 1989; pres. Sun City West Found., 2002—03; bd. dirs. Sun City West Cmty. Fund, 1998—99. Elected One of Detroit's Top Ten Working Women, 1969; elected to Exec. and Profl. Hall of Fame. Mem. Internat. Assn. Adminstrv. Profls. (internat. pres. 1967-69), Future Secs. Assn. (nat. coord.), Lioness Club (pres. 1991-92), Sun City West Singles Club (pres. 1988). Republican. Roman Catholic. Avocations: bridge, Mah Jongg, dance. Home and Office: 12613 W Seneca Dr Sun City West AZ 85375-4635

FORTI, WILLIAM BELL, manufacturing executive, management consultant; b. Washington, Dec. 6, 1941; s. Francis and Margaret Lee (Bell) F.; m. Martha Louise Goding; children: Scott, Jennifer, Meredith, Kimberly, Mark, Andrea. BS, U. Richmond, 1963, MComm., 1964. Fin. analyst SEC, Washington, 1964—66; economist Joint tax, House judiciary, Senate commerce coms. U.S. Congress, Washington, 1966—71; mgmt. positions in bus. planning and devel. Bendix Corp., Southfield, Mich., 1971—75, Internat. Paper Co., N.Y.C., 1975—78, Gen. Dynamics, St. Louis, 1978—92; founder, chmn. William Mark Corp., Claremont, Calif., 1992—. Patentee flying recreational products. Bd. visitors sch. ednl. studies Claremont Grad. U.; mem. World Affairs Coun., L.A., 2005; participant current strategy forum Naval War Coll., RI, 2005, nat. security forum Air War Coll., Maxwell AFB, Ala., 1997; trustee Naval War Coll. Found., 2001—; co-chmn. L.A. County Aerospace Task Force, L.A., 1992; chmn. internat. trade legislation working group Def. Planning Adv. Com. on Trade, 1986. Recipient Recognition of Dedicated Svc. County of L.A., 1992, Recognition of Contribution Naval War Coll. Found., 1997, Joint Civilian Orientation Conf., 1999. Mem.: Toy Industry Assn., Def. Orientation Conf. Assn. (bd. dirs. 1999—2001), Claremont C. of C., Naval War Coll. Found. (trustee 2001—), Radio Controlled Hobby Trade Assn., Kite Trade Assn., Rotary (dir. 2004), Claremont U. Club (asst. treas. 1994—). Republican. Avocations: travel, reading, hiking. Office: William Mark Corp 112 Harvard Ave Claremont CA 91711-4716

FORTIER, ALBERT MARK, JR., lawyer; b. Cambridge, Mass., July 22, 1936; s. Albert M. and Marie R. (Tagney) F.; m. Bente Mortensen, Nov. 10, 1964; children: John, Mark. AB, U. Chgo., 1955; LLB, Harvard U., 1958. Bar: Mass. 1958. Assoc. Richard S. Bowers, Boston, 1958-65; ptnr. Bowers, Fortier & Lakin, Boston, 1966-76, Rackemann, Sawyer & Brewster, Boston, 1976—. Contbr. articles to profl. jours. Mem. ABA, Am. Bar Found., Boston Bar Assn. (probate sect. former chair), Am. Coll. Trust and Estate Counsel (past state chair), Union Club (Boston, past bd. govs.). Home: 90 Craftsland Rd Chestnut Hill MA 02467-2632 Office: Rackemann Sawyer & Brewster One Financial Ctr Boston MA 02111 Office Phone: 617-542-2300. E-mail: amf@rackemann.com.

FORTIER, L. YVES, barrister; b. Quebec City, Que., Can., Sept. 11, 1935; s. Francois and Louise (Turgeon) F.; m. C. Carol Eaton, Sept. 26, 1959; children: Michel, Suzanne, Margot. BA summa cum laude, U. Montreal, 1955; BCL, McGill U., 1958; BLitt, Oxford U., 1960, LLD (hon.), 1989, LLD (hon.), 1992, LLD (hon.), 1993, LLD (hon.), 1999, LLD (hon.), 2004, LLD (hon.), 2005. Created Queen's counsel, 1976. Sr. ptnr., chmn. Ogilvy, Renault Advs., Barristers and Solicitors, Montreal, 1960—; Can. amb. to UN N.Y.C., 1988-92. Counsel Can. in Can.-USA, Gulf Maine Case in World Ct., 1984, Royal Commns., Commn. Inquiry War Criminals, Commn. Inquiry Lang. Air Tarffic Control, Commn. Inquiry R.C.M.P.; mem. Permanent Ct. Arbitration The Hague, 1984-1991; pres. London Ct. Internat. Arbitration, 1998-2001; chief negotiator Can.-France fishing dispute, 1987-89, Can.-U.S. Pacific Salmon Treaty dispute, 1993-98; Can.'s chief del. to 43d, 44th, 45th, 46th, sessions UN Gen. Assembly, Can. rep. UN Security Coun., 1989-90; v.p. UN 45th Gen. Assembly; gov. Hudson's Bay Co., Nortel Networks Corp.; bd. dirs. Royal Bank Can., Nova Chems. Corp.; chmn. bd. dirs. Alcan Inc. Bd. dirs. Can. Inst. Advanced Legal Studies, Internat. Peace Acad., UN Internat. Sch., Montreal Gen. Hosp. C.D. Howe Inst., Clin. Rsch. Inst., Can. Found. for AIDS Rsch.; trustee Internat. Acctg. Stds. Com. Decorated officer and companion Order of Can.; Rhodes scholar, 1960. Mem. ABA (hon.), Can. Bar Assn. (pres. 1982-83, founding dir. Law for Future Fund), Internat. Commn. Jurists (Can. sect.), Internat. Law Assn. (Can. br.), Am. Coll. Trial Lawyers (regent 1991-95), Internat. Assn. Permanent Reps. to UN (exec. bd.), Mount Royal Club (pres. 2002-03), Univ. Club, Montreal Indoor Tennis Club, Hermitage Country Club (pres. 1983-84), The Brook Club (N.Y.), The Toronto Club. Roman Catholic. Avocations: tennis, squash, skiing, golf. Home: 19 Rosemount Ave Westmount PQ H3Y 3G6 Canada Business E-Mail: yfortier@ogilvyrenaul.com.

FORTIER, MARDELLE LADONNA, language educator, writer; b. Brookings, S.D., Sept. 15, 1947; d. Leon Doneval and Edna Pearl (Rosenstock) Eide; m. Robert Frederic Fortier, July 27, 1974. BA, U. Minn., 1970; MA, U. Ill., 1971, PhD, 1978. Instr. Berlitz, Hinsdale, Ill., 1983-84, North Ctrl. Coll., Naperville, Ill., 1985; sr. lectr. Loyola U., Chgo., 1984-95; instr. Coll. DuPage, Glen Ellyn, Ill., 1985—; English instr. Benedictine U., Lisle, Ill., 1985, 95—. Cons. in field. Author: The Utopian Thought of St. Thomas More, 1994; author numerous poems, 9 short stories, book revs. Mem. Ill. State Poetry Soc., Poets and Patrons, Inc. (1st prize 1992, 2d prize 1995), Poets Club Chgo. Roman Catholic. Avocations: music, travel. Home: 5515 E Lake Dr Apt A Lisle IL 60532-2664 Office Phone: 630-829-6291.

FORTIN, JUDY, cable news anchor; BA in Govt. and French, Bowdoin Coll. Gen. assignment reporter various stas.; nat. corr. CNN Newsource, Atlanta, 1990; anchor CNN Airport Network, Atlanta; weekend anchor CNN Headline News, Atlanta. Recipient AP awards. Office: CNN Cable News Network 1 CNN Ctr NW Atlanta GA 30303-2762

FORTIN, RAYMOND D., lawyer; BA, U. Fla., 1974, JD, 1977. Bar: Ga. 1977. Pvt. practice, 1977-81; staff counsel The Citizens & So. Corp., 1981-89; mng. atty. SunTrust Banks, Inc., Atlanta, 1989-91, sr. v.p., 1991—. Office: SunTrust Banks Inc 303 Peachtree St NE Fl 30 Atlanta GA 30308-3201

FORTINO, ANDRES G., dean; arrived in U.S., 1961; s. Miguel Angel and Apolonia Fortino; m. Kathleen Fortino, June 6, 1970; 1 child, Hue Rhodes. BSEE, CCNY, 1970, MSEE, 1973; PhD, CUNY, 1976. Profl. engr., Mont. Asst. prof. Cooper Union, N.Y.C., 1979—80, Temple U., Phila., 1980—83; sr. lectr. Learning Tree Internat., L.A., 1983—97; assoc. dean George Mason U., Fairfax, Va., 1998—2004; dean Marist Coll., Poughkeepsie, NY, 2004—. With Ch. Universal, Gardiner, Mont., 1993—98. 2d lt. U.S. Army, 1970—71. Mem.: IEEE (sr.), TMEDA (pres.), Acad. Mgmt. Avocations: art, photography. Home: 75 Grist Mill Ln Pleasant Valley NY 12569 Office: Marist Coll 3399 North Rd Poughkeepsie NY 12601

FORTINO, JOEY, music educator, conductor; m. Renee Warney; 1 child, Jenna. MusB, San Jose State U., 1996. Band dir. Gilroy (Calif.) H.S., 1997—. Condr. South Valley Youth Orch. Office: Gilroy HS Band 750 West 10th St Gilroy CA 95020 Office Phone: 408-847-2424 2287. Personal E-mail: jfortino@gusd.k12.ca.us.

FORTNER, HUESTON GILMORE, lawyer, writer, composer; b. Tacoma, Nov. 1, 1959; s. Hueston Turner Jr. and Deborah Hewes (Berry) F. BS, Tulane U., 1981; JD, U. Miss., 1985. Bar: Miss. 1986, La. 1987, U.S. Dist. Ct. (no. and so. dists.) Miss. 1986, U.S. Dist. Ct. (ea., mid. and we. dists.) La. 1987, U.S. Ct. Appeals (5th cir.) 1986, bar: Calif. 1989, U.S. Dist. Ct. (cen. dist.) Calif. 1989, U.S. Dist. Ct. (so. dist.) Calif. 1999. Clk. Farrer and Co., London, Miss., 1985; assoc. Cliff Finch & Assocs., Batesville, Miss., 1986; pvt. practice New Orleans, 1987-88; atty. Parker, Milliken, Clark, O'Hara & Samuelian, L.A., 1989-90; pvt. prctice L.A., 1990—. Vis. lectr. Anhui U., Hefei, People's Rep. of China, Bejing Inst. of Petrochem. Tech., 1994; participanted in Leicester vs. Leicester Rugby Union, House of Lords, Eng., 1985; assisted Queen's Counsel in Yussuf Islam (Cat Stevens) vs. Bank of Westminster P.L.C. royalties litigation 1985, Newton vs. NBC, 1988; temporary judge L.A. County mcpl. Ct., 1991—; pres., CEO Orange Records, 1997—. Contbg. photographer Flix mag., 1993—; contbr. editor Rental, 1987-89. Recipient Space Devel. Strategies award NASA/U. Houston Advanced Rsch. Ctr., 1995; grantee NSF, 1976. Mem. Miss. Bar Assn., La. Bar Assn., State Bar Calif., Broadcast Music Internat., Phi Alpha Delta. Presbyterian. Avocations: music, film, scuba diving.

FORTNER, JOSEPH GERALD, surgeon, educator; b. Bedford, Ind., May 30, 1921; s. Everett Rex and Lula Alice (Robbins) F.; m. Roberta Olson, Nov. 4, 1948; children: Kathleen Alice Fortner, Joseph Jr. BS, U. Ill., 1944, MD, 1945; MSc in Immunology, Birmingham (Eng.) U., 1965. Diplomate: Am. Bd. Surgery. Intern St. Luke's Hosp., Chgo., 1945-46; resident in pathology Tulane U., New Orleans, 1948-49; surg. resident Bellevue Hosp., N.Y.C., 1949-51, Meml. Hosp., N.Y.C., 1951—54, clin. asst. surgeon, asst. to clin. dir., 1955-59, asst. attending surgeon, 1958-66, assoc. attending surgeon, 1966-69, attending surgeon, 1969-94, chief transplantation svc. and gastric and mixed tumor svc., 1970-78, chief surg. research service, 1978-91, assoc. chmn. for lab. affairs dept. surgery, 1978-84, chief div. surg. research, 1968-77; chief Gen. Motors Surg. Rsch. Lab., 1977-92; instr. surgery Sloan-Kettering Inst., N.Y.C., 1954-58, asst. prof. clin. surgery, 1958-64; clin. asst. prof. surgery Cornell U. Med. Coll., N.Y.C., 1964-70, assoc. prof. surgery, 1970-72, prof., 1972—. Contbr. articles to profl. jours.; editor Accomplishments in Cancer Research. Pres. Gen. Motors Cancer Rsch. Found., 1978-96, pres. emeritus, 1996—, trustee mem. awards assembly. With U.S. Army, 1946-48. Recipient Alfred P. Sloan award Sloan-Kettering Inst. Cancer Research, 1963 Fellow ACS, Royal Coll. Surgeons Edinburgh (hon.); mem. AAAS, Am. Assn. Cancer Research, Am. Gastroent. Assn., Am. Radium Soc., Am. Soc. Clin. Oncology, European Soc. Exptl. Surgery, Harvey Soc., Soc. Surg. Oncology, N.Y. County, N.Y. State med. socs., Am. Surg. Assn., N.Y. Surg. Soc., Soc. Univ. Surgeons, Hellenic Surg. Soc. (hon.), Chgo. Surg. Soc., Korean Surg. Soc., Am. Soc. Transplant Surgeons, Transplantation Soc., N.Y. Cancer Soc., Econ. Club of N.Y., Explorer Club N.Y., Met. Club N.Y., Madison Beach Club, Sigma Xi, Alpha Omega Alpha. Republican. Home: 131 E 66th St New York NY 10021-6129 Personal E-mail: jgfortnermd@cs.com.

FORTNER, NELL, professional athletics coach; b. Jackson, Miss. BS, U. Tex., 1982; MS, Stephen F. Austin U., 1987. Asst. coach women's basketball Stephen F. Austin U., Nacogdoches, Tex., 1986—90, Louisiana Tech U., 1991—95, USA Nat. Team, 1995—96; head coach women's basketball Purdue U., West Lafayette, Ind., 1996—97; head coach women's basketball, gen. mgr. Ind. Fever Women's Nat. Basketball Assn., Indpls., 1999—. Head coach women's basketball USA Basketball, 1997—2000, FIBA World Championship, 1998, R.William Jones Cup Tournament, Taiwan, 1998. Named Coach of Yr., Big Ten Conf., 1997, Nat. Coach of Yr., Basketball Times, 1997; recipient Gold medal, Olympic Games, 2000, FIBA World Championships, 1998, Olympic Games, 1996. Office: Indiana Fever 125 S Pennsylvania St Indianapolis IN 46204

FORTNOW, LANCE JEREMY, computer scientist, educator; b. N.Y.C., Aug. 15, 1963; s. Stanley and Linda Bartels; m. Marcy Appell Fortnow, Sept. 2, 1990; children: Annie, Molly. BA, Cornell U., 1985; PhD, MIT, 1999. Assoc. prof. U. Chgo. Dept. Computer Scientist, 1989-99; sr. rsch. scientist NEC Rsch. Inst., Princeton, N.J., 1999—. Presdl. faculty fellow NSF, 1992-97. Home: 12 Orly Ct Princeton Junction NJ 08550

FORTSON, BEN J., oil industry executive; m. Kay Kimbell Carter; children: Ben J. III, Lisa Burton, Karen Davis, Kimbell Wynne. Pres. Fortson Oil Co., Fort Worth, Tex.; v.p. & trustee Kimbell Art Found. & Museum, Fort Worth, Tex., 1975—. Trustee emeritus Tex. Christian Univ. Office: Fortson Oil Co Suite 3301 301 Commerce St Fort Worth TX 76102*

FORTSON, EDWARD NORVAL, physics educator; b. Atlanta, June 16, 1936; s. Charles Wellborn and Virginia (Norval) F.; m. Alix Madge Hawkins, Apr. 3, 1960; children— Edward Norval, Lucy Frear, Amy Lewis BS, Duke U., 1957; PhD, Harvard U., 1963. Research fellow U. Bonn., Federal Rep. Germany, 1965-66; research asst. prof. physics U. Wash., Seattle, 1963-65, asst. prof., 1966-69, assoc. prof., 1969-74, prof., 1974—. Fulbright travel grantee, 1965-66; Nat. Research Council fellow Oxford, Eng., 1977; Guggenheim fellow, 1980-81 Fellow AAAS, Am. Phys. Soc.; mem. NAS. Office: U Wash Dept Physics PO Box 351560 Seattle WA 98195-1560

FORTSON, JAMES LEON, JR., lawyer; b. Shreveport, La., May 5, 1949; s. James Leon and Hellon Mildred (Atkins) F.; children: Stephen Christopher, Travis Leon, Heather Helaine. BS, La. State U., 1971, JD, 1974. Bar: La. 1974, U.S. Dist. Ct. (we. dist.) La. 1974, U.S. Ct. Appeals (5th cir.) 1976. Pvt. practice, Shreveport, 1974—. Mem. La. Trial Lawyers Assn. (bd. govs. 1986-93, emeritus mem. bd. govs. 1993—), La. State Bar Assn. (mem. ho. of dels. 1990—, bd. cert. family law bd. legal specialization 1995—), La. Bd. Legal Specialization (family law adv. com.), N.W. La. Trial Lawyers Assn. (founding mem.), Lawyer-Pilots Bar Assn. Democrat. Avocation: pilot. Office: PO Box 7691 151 Freestate Blvd Shreveport LA 71107-6511

FORTSON, KAY KIMBELL CARTER, museum administrator; m. Ben J. Fortson; children: Ben J. III, Lisa Burton, Karen Davis, Kimbell Wynne. BA, Univ. Tex., 1956. Pres. & chmn. bd. trustees Kimbell Art Found. & Museum, Fort Worth, Tex., 1975—. Trustee Tex. Christian Univ.; honorary trustee Modern Art Mus., Fort Worth, Tex. Mailing: Kimbell Art Foundation Suite 2240 301 Commerce St Fort Worth TX 76102*

FORTUNA, WILLIAM FRANK, architectural engineer, architect; b. Paris, Ill., Apr. 3, 1948; s. William F. Sr. and Mary O. (Komatz) F. BArch, U. Ill., 1972, MS in Archtl. Engring., 1973. Lic. arch., Ill., Wis., Iowa, lic. structural engr., Ill., lic. profl. engr., Wis., lic. archtl. engr. specializing in crisis mgmt., Nat. Coun. Examiners for Engring. and Surveying, Nat. Coun. Archtl. Registration Bds. Designer Unteed Assocs. Ltd., Champaign, Ill., 1973-76; structural engr. Consoer Townsend, Chgo., 1976-79, Schmidt, Garden & Erikson, Chgo., 1979-83; sr. project structural engr. Skidmore Owings & Merrill, Chgo., 1983-87; pres. W.F. Fortuna Ltd., Archtl. Engring., Highland Park, Ill., 1987—. Project engr. World Trade Ctr., Cairo; structural engr. exhbn. ctr. McCormick Place Annex, Chgo., United Airlines terminal O'Hare Airport, Bishop's Gate, London; contract adminstr. One and Two Prudential Plaza, Chgo. (SEAOI Best Structure award and tallest concrete bldg. in the world). Active mem. Illinois Emergency Mgmt. Agency. Mem. AIA, NCARB, Structural Engrs. Assn. Ill., Nat. Coun. Examiners for Engring. and Surveying, Am. Concrete Inst., Am. Inst. Steel Constrn., Chgo. Hist. Soc., Nat. Trust His. Preservation. Home: WF Fortuna Ltd Archtl Engr 1420 Ridge Rd Highland Park IL 60035-2734 Office: Two Prudential Plz Chicago IL 60601 Office Phone: 847-579-8320. E-mail: bill42na@aol.com.

FORTUNATO, D'ANNA E., voice educator, mezzo soprano; b. Pitts., Feb. 21, 1945; d. Leonard Henry and Maxine Olein Fortunato; m. Marc Alan Widershien, June 16, 2001; stepchildren: Erik Widershien, Adam Widershien. MusB, New Eng. Conservatory, 1968, MusM, 1970. Voice prof. Long Sch. Music, Cambridge, Mass., 1977—, New Eng. Conservatory, Boston, 1990—. Vocal coach Bach Aria Group SUNY, Stony Brook, 1988—2000. Singer: NYC Opera, Merkin Hall, Carneige Hall, Emmanuel Music, Monadnock Music, Ky. Opera, Conn. Grand Opera, Opera San Jose, Rochester Opera, Fla. Grand Opera, Boston Lyric Opera, (30 CD's including) Amy Beach Songs, Victorian Baseball: Hurrah for our National Game, Deidamia, Jeanne d'arc au Bucher. Recipient 1st pl., Metro. Opera Regional Auditions, 1973, Alumni award, New Eng. Conservatory, 1986, Bucknell U., 1987, Jacobo Pehi award, New Eng. Opera Club, 1999. Mem.: Music Tchrs. Nat. Assn., Nat. Assn. Tchrs. Singing. Avocations: gardening, reading, hiking. Home: 33 Sycamore St Boston MA 02131 Office: New Eng Conservatory 290 Huntington Ave Boston MA 02115 Office Phone: 617-469-4880.

FORTUNATO, PAT DEAKIN, fine artist; b. Buffalo, Apr. 30, 1934; d. Edmund J. Deakin and Jane Wilson (Danahy) Ray; m. Thomas A. Fortunato, Apr. 7, 1956; children: Kathleen Yoder, Mark, Susan, Karen Voight, Steven, Thomas J. BS in Edn., State U., Buffalo, 1955. Elem. tchr. Buffalo Sch. System, 1955-57; substitute tchr. Williamsville (N.Y.) Schs., 1974-76; part-time workshop instr. Niagara C.C., Sanborn, N.Y., 1991-93. Workshop instr. 1990—, pvt. instr., Orchard Park, N.Y., 1992—. Exhibited at Albright-Knox Mems. Gallery, Buffalo, 1993, Burchfield-Penney Mus., Buffalo, 2004; travel exhibit Adirondacks Nat. Exhbn. of Am. Watercolors, 1999—, (award 2002); paintings included in several books. Liason Williamsville Sch. System, 1972-79. Recipient Award of Merit Nat. League of Am. Pen Women, 1988, Holbein award Batavia Internat. Exhibit, 1997. Mem. Midwest Watercolor Soc. (Award of Excellence 1987), Am. Watercolor Soc. (assoc.), Allied Artists of Am. (assoc.), Niagara Frontier Watercolor Soc. (editor 1983-87, chmn. 1988-94, Grumbacher Gold medal 1990, 2003), Buffalo Soc. of Artists (bd. dirs. 1994-95, 99—). Roman Catholic. Avocation: photography. Home and Office: 144 Lord Byron Ln Williamsville NY 14221-1998 E-mail: patfortunato@adelphia.net.

FORTUNE, JAMES MICHAEL, information technology manager; b. Providence, Sept. 6, 1947; s. Thomas Henry and Olive Elizabeth (Duby) F.; m. G. Suzanne Hein, July 14, 1973. Student, Pikes Peak Community Coll., Colorado Springs, Colo., 1981-83; BSBA, BS in Computer Info. Systems, Regis Coll., 1991. Owner Fortune Fin. Svcs., Colorado Springs, Colo., 1975-79; ptnr. Robert James and Assocs., Colorado Springs, 1979-81; pres. Fortune & Co., Colorado Springs, 1981-88; sr. v.p. mktg. and editorial Phoenix Communications Group, Ltd., Colorado Springs, 1985-95, also bd. dirs.; sr. network analyst Coastal States Mgmt. Corp., 1995-99; mgr. computer support Colo. Interstate Gas, 1999—. Bd. dirs. Interstate Gas Credit Union, 1998-99, N.Am. Internet, LLC; talk show host Sta. KRCC, fin. commentator Wall Street Report, Sta. KKHT, 1983-84. Editor Fortune newsletter, 1981-85, The Can. Market News, 1981-83; editor, pub. Penny Fortune newsletter, 1981-95, The Low Priced Investment newsletter, 1986-87, Women's Investment Newsletter, 1987-95; pub. Internal Revenue Strategies, 1990, Tax and Investment Planning Strategies for Medical Professionals, 1991; contbr. articles to profl. jours. Cons. Jr. Achievement bus. project, Colorado Springs, 1985, 97-2004. Sgt. U.S. Army, 1968-70, Vietnam. Mem. Direct Mktg. Assn., Elks. Avocations: fly fishing, skiing, hiking, backpacking. Office: PO Box 1087 2 North Nevada Ave Colorado Springs CO 80944

FORTUNE, JOHN B., medical educator; b. Indpls., Mar. 19, 1950; s. William Brooks and Joan Helen Fortune; m. Janellen Neely Fortune; children: Brooks, Neely. BA, Duke U., 1972, MD, 1975; DSc (hon.), Ind. Wesleyan U., 1999. Cert. MD. Asst. prof. surgery U. Calif., San Diego, 1982—84; assoc. prof. surgery Albany (NY) Med. Coll., 1984—94; prof. surgery U. Ariz., Tucson, 1994—2001, So. Ill. U., Springfield, 2002—04; prof. surgery, chief sect. trauma and critical care SUNY Upstate Med. U., Syracuse, 2004—.

Chief gen. surgery So. Ill. U., Springfield, 2002—04, residency dir., 2003—04. Contbr. articles various profl. jours. Dir. So. Ariz. Trauma Network, Tucson, 1994—2001. Fellow: ACS; mem.: Soc. Univ. Surgeons. Achievements include invention of Retrograde Intuhation Kit. Avocation: creative writing. Office: SUNY Upstate Dept Surgery 750 E Adams St Syracuse NY 13210 Office Phone: 315-464-4766. Business E-Mail: fortunej@upstate.edu.

FORTUNE, LARRY M., real estate broker; b. Fresno, Calif., Feb. 3, 1948; s. Donlad A. and Matheda B. Fortune; m. Jane B. Fortune, Apr. 26, 1980; children: Katherine, Patrick. BA, Stanford U., 1970; MBA, Trinity Coll. and U., 2002. Cert. Real Estate Broker Mgr. Realtors Nat. Mktg. Inst., Nat. Assn. Realtors, 1985, Residential Specialist Realtors Nat. Mktg. Inst., Nat. Assn. Realtors, 1986, Residential Broker Nat. Assn. Realtors, Arbitrator and Mediator Calif. Assn. Realtors, 1985, lic. in Real Estate Sales Calif., 1975, Broker 1978. Loan officer, asst. v.p. consumer and auto loan ctr. Bank. Calif., San Francisco, Sacramento, 1972—74; broker, owner Fortune Property Mgmt., Fresno, Calif., 1982—94, Fortune Assocs., Fresno, 1974—. Ct. receiver Fresno County Superior Ct.; trustee US Bankruptcy Ct., Ea. Dist. Calif.; real estate expert witness civil, criminal cts.; mediator in field; mem. BBB, 1982—, bd. dirs., 1995—98, chmn. membership devel. com., 1996—98; mem. Fresno Bus. Coun., 1999—, mem. pub. safety com., 2000—01; investor Econ. Devel. Corp. Serving Fresno County, 2002—, bd. dirs., 2004—, co-chmn. bus. pk. task force, 2004—; joint powers authority bd. dirs. Ctr. Advanced Rsch. and Tech., 2005—. Cub scout pack leader Boy Scouts Am., 1994—97, leadership mem., 1994—, asst. scout master, 1997—2002; mem. Fresno Athletic Hall of Fame, 1974—, bd. dirs., 1976—94, sec., 1980—90; mem. Fresno Multiple Listing Svc., 1975—99, bd. dirs., 1984—87, vice chmn., 1984, chmn., 1985; mem. Fig Garden Police Protection Dist., 1986—, bd. dirs., 2001—02, chmn., 2002—; mem. ctrl. area planning task force City of Fresno, 1986—87, chmn. redevelopment agy. project area com., 1998—, mem. mayor's task force Fresno empowerment zone, 2001; bd. dirs. Cmty. Housing Leadership Bd., 1987—90; pub. alt. local agy. formation commn. County of Fresno, 1990—96, pub. mem. local agy. formal commn., 1996—, chmn. local agy. formation commn., 2002—04, chmn. pub. safety citizens adv. com., 0203—2004, pub. mem. Indian gaming local cmty. benefit commn., 2004—; mem. cmty. rels. adv. com. Ctrl. Calif. Blood Ctr., 1991—96, bd. dirs., 2002—, mem. fin. com., 2002—, mem. exec. com., 2002—, sec., 2004—; mem. Tree Fresno, 1995—, treas., 2003—04, mem. projects com., 2003—, bd. dirs., 2003—05; mem. strategic planning com. facilities Fresno Unified Sch. Dist., 1999—2000; bd. dirs. Fresno Police Activities League, 2000—, mem. exec. com., 2001—, treas., 2001—; bd. dirs. Fresno County Workforce Investment Bd., 2001—, mem. info. tech. com., 2001—, chmn. info. tech. com., 2003—, mem. youth coun., 2002—, mem. exec. com., 2003—, vice chmn., 2004—, chmn., 2004—; mem. leadership coun. Regional Jobs Initiative, 2004—, chmn. infrastructure com., 2004—. Recipient Realtor of Yr., Fresno Assn. Realtors, 1987, Hon. Dir. Life, Calif. Assn. Realtors, 1991, Best Ednl. Program award, 1988. Mem.: Leadership Fresno Alumni Assn., Fresno City and County C. of C. (membership com. mem. 1976—80, Fresno beautiful com. mem. 2000—02, bd. dirs. FresPAC 2002—03), Stanford Alumni Assn. (life), Fresno Region Stanford Club (founding dir. 1979, bd. dirs. 1979—86, pres. 1984—85). Avocation: gardening. Office: Fortune Assocs 1195 W Shaw Ave Ste C Fresno CA 93711-3704

FORTUNE, ROBERT RUSSELL, financial consultant; b. Collingswood, N.J., Nov. 22, 1916; s. Colin C. and Minnie M. (Brown) F.; m. Christine E. Dent, Nov. 10, 1956. BS in Econs., U. Pa., 1940. CPA, Pa. With Haskins & Sells (C.P.A.s), 1940-42, 46-48; with Pa. Power & Light Co., Allentown, 1948-84, v.p. fin., 1966-75, exec. v.p. fin., dir., 1975-84. Chmn., CEO Assoc. Electric and Gas Ins. Svcs. Ltd., 1984-93, Chestnut St. Exch. Fund, chmn., 1994—. Tech. adv. com. on fin. FPC, 1974-75. Treas. Allentown Sch. Dist. Authority, 1963-85, Lehigh-Northampton Airport Authority, 1985-94. With USN, 1942-46. Mem. Fin. Execs. Inst., Am., Pa. insts. CPAs. Clubs: Lehigh Country. Republican. Home: 2920 Ritter Ln Allentown PA 18104-2823

FORTUÑO, LUIS, congressman; b. San Juan, PR, Oct. 31, 1960; m. Luce Fortuno. BS, Georgetown Univ.; JD, Univ. Va. Worked with New Progressive Party, PR; sr. advisor Pedro Rossello campaign, 1992, 1996; atty. private practice; sec. econ. devel. & commerce Commonwealth of PR, San Juan, 1994—97; resident commr. U.S. Ho. Reps., 109th Congress, PR at-large, 2005—, mem. ed. and workforce resources com., mem. transp. and infrastructure com. Republican. Roman Catholic. Office: US Ho of Reps 126 Cannon Ho Office Bldg Washington DC 20515-5401 also: Dist Office 250 Calle Fortaleza San Juan PR 00901 Office Phone: 202-225-2615.*

FORTUNO, VICTOR M., lawyer; b. N.Y.C., Jan. 24, 1952; s. Victor M. Fortuno and Ceda Aguayo; m. Vicki Ann Clark; children: Adam R., Victor III, Scott, Erica, Bryce. AB in Econs., Columbia U., 1974, JD, 1977. Bar: Pa. 1977, U.S. Dist. Ct. (ea. dist.) Pa. 1977, U.S. Ct. Appeals (3d cir.) 1977, U.S. Supreme Ct. 1980, U.S. Ct. Appeals (D.C. cir.) 1987, D.C. 1988, U.S. Dist. Ct. D.C. 1988, U.S. Ct. Appeals (4th cir.) 1988, U.S. Dist. Ct. Ariz. 1991. Staff atty. Cmty. Legal Svcs., Inc., Phila., 1977-78; asst. dist. atty. Office Dist. Atty., Phila., 1978-83; staff atty. Legal Svcs. Corp., Washington, 1983-85, acting dir. compliance divsn., 1985-86, asst. gen. counsel, 1986, sr. litigation counsel, 1986-88, acting gen. counsel, 1987, 91, dep. gen. counsel, 1988-91, gen. counsel, 1991—, corp. sec., 1995—, v.p. legal affairs, 1999—. Adj. faculty Grantham Coll. Engring., 2001-02. Bd. dirs. Middleford HOA, 2002-, Friends of Legal Svcs. Corp., 2001-04, Columbia Coll. Alumni Assn., 1981-83, Phila. Health Plan, 1980-83. Pulitzer Found. scholar, 1970-74, Assn. of Bar of City of N.Y. C. Bainbridge Smith scholar, 1974-77. Mem. ABA, D.C. Bar Assn., Fed. Small Agy. Coun. Home: 7479 Thorncliff Ln Springfield VA 22153-2153 Office: Legal Svcs Corp 3333 K St NW Washington DC 20007 Office Phone: 202-295-1620. Business E-Mail: vfortuno@lsc.gov.

FORZANI, RINALDO, III, lawyer; b. N.Y.C., Mar. 7, 1958; s. Rinaldo Jr. and Geraldine (Scarpinati) F.; m. Lorraine Susan Lionetti, July 3, 1982; 1 child, Benjamin Rinaldo. BA Politics wih honors, NYU, 1979; JD, Hofstra U., 1982. Bar: N.J. 1982, U.S. Dist. Ct. N.J. 1982. Assoc. Harry R. Howard, P.A., Florham Park, N.J., 1982-83, Howard and Gendel, Edqs., Paterson, N.J., 1984; ptnr. Harry R. Howard, P.A., Parsippany, N.J., 1985-91; prin. Rinaldo Forzani III, Esq., Bernardsville, N.J., 1991—. Mem. Morris County Bar Assn., Adams Village Condominium Assn. (treas. 1990-94, pres. 1995-98), Spring Ridge Condominium Assn. (v.p. 1990-97, pres. 1997-98). Avocations: skiing, hiking, tennis, jazz piano, reading. Home: 76 Commonwealth Dr Basking Ridge NJ 07920-3094 Office: Rinaldo Forzani III Esq 61 Claremont Rd Bernardsville NJ 07924-2232 E-mail: rforzani@hotmail.com.

FOSCARINIS, MARIA, lawyer; b. N.Y.C., Aug. 8, 1956; d. Nicolas and Rosa F. BA, Barnard Coll., 1977; MA, Columbia U., 1978, JD, 1981. Bar: N.Y. 1982, U.S. Dist. Ct. (so. and ea. dists.) N.Y. 1983, D.C. 1986, U.S. Dist. Ct. D.C., U.S. Ct. Appeals (D.C. cir.). Law clk. to judge U.S. Ct. Appeals (2d cir.), N.Y.C., 1981-82; assoc. Sullivan & Cromwell, N.Y.C., 1982-85; counsel Nat. Coalition for Homeless, Washington, 1985-89; founder and dir. Nat. Law Ctr. on Homelessness and Poverty, Washington, 1989—. Notes editor Columbia U. Law Rev., 1980-81. Harlan Fiske Stone scholar, 1978-79; John Dewey fellow. Mem. ABA (commr. homelessness and poverty, 1989-95, 2004—). Office: Nat Law Ctr Homelessness and Poverty 1411 K St NW Ste 1400 Washington DC 20005-3404 Home: 1752 Swann St NW Washington DC 20009-5535 Office Phone: 202-638-2535. Business E-Mail: foscarinis@nlchp.org.

FOSDICK, CORA PRIFOLD (CORA PRIFOLD BEEBE), management consultant; b. San Francisco, Nov. 3, 1937; d. George and Beatrice (Ehni) Prifold; m. Ronald Beebe, Jan., 1959 (div.); m. Donald James Fosdick, Oct. 12, 1997. Student, Hollins Coll., Va., 1955-57, Am. U., 1957-58; BA, U. Mich., 1959, MA, 1961; LHD (hon.), Southeastern U., 1993. Adminstrv. asst. Am. Polit. Sci. Assn., 1962-64; research assoc. Inst. Comparative Studies of Polit. Systems, Washington, 1963-65; program planning and evaluation specialist U.S. Office Edn., Washington, 1965-68, planning coordinator, 1968-73, dir. planning and budget div., 1973-80; prin. dep. asst. sec. for elem. and sec. edn. Dept. Edn., Washington, 1980-81; asst. sec. adminstrn. U.S. Treasury Dept., Washington, 1981-84; dir. office of policy, budget and program mgmt. OSWER, EPA, Washington, 1984-86; dir. office of planning, budget and evaluation Dept. Commerce, Washington, 1986-87; commerce & justice br. chief Office of Mgmt. and Budget, 1987-94, advisor to assoc. dir. gen. govt. and fin., 1994; exec. dir. adminstrn., chief fin. officer Office of Thrift Supervision, Washington, 1994-99; v.p. Jefferson Consulting Group, Washington, 1999—2002; ind. cons. Washington, 2002—. Mem. Washington Performing Arts Soc., 1983—, Coun. for Excellence in Govt. Recipient HEW Superior Svc. award, Presdl. Rank award, 1989; Inst. World Affairs fellow, 1956, Am. Edn. Abroad former fellow, 1960. Fellow: Nat. Acad. Pub. Adminstrn. (vice chair 2002—03, bd. dirs., chair audit com.); mem.: Nat. Press Club, Exec. Women in Govt. Program and Budget Analysis. Home: 1415 N Pegram St Alexandria VA 22304-1933 Personal E-mail: corabeebe@aol.com.

FOSHEE, DOUGLAS, gas industry executive; BBA, S.W. Tex. State U., 1982; MBA, Rice U., 1992; grad., So. Meth. U. Active comml. banking; various positions in fin. and new bus. ventures ARCO Internat. Oil and Gas Co.; COO, CEO Torch Energy Advisors, Inc., 1993—97; chmn., CEO, pres. Nuevo Energy Co.; CFO Halliburton, 2001, exec. v.p., COO, 2003; pres., CEO, dir. El Paso Corp., Houston, 2003—. Pres., bd. mem. Small Steps Nurturing Ctr.; bd. mem. Goodwill Industries, Houston, Tex. Bus. Hall of Fame Found.; mem. coun. of overseers Jones Grad. Sch. Adminstrn., Rice U. Mem.: Houston Prodrs. Forum, Ind. Petroleum Assn. Am. Office: El Paso Corp PO Box 2511 1001 Louisiana St Houston TX 77252-2511

FOSLER, GAIL D., economist, government official; b. Los Angeles Dec. 7, 1947; d. Richard E. and Helen Elizabeth (O'Gorman) Deschner. A.B. in Econs. U. So. Calif., 1969; M.B.A. in Fin., NYU, 1972. Research analyst Chgo. Dept. Human Resources, 1970-72; research assoc. I.C.F., Inc., 1972-74; asst. v.p., economist Manufacturers Hanover, 1974-78; chief economist Senate Budget Com., Washington, from 1981, dir. and chief economist, from 1986; now v.p., chief economist The Conf. Bd., Inc., N.Y.C. Office: The Conference Bd Inc 845 3rd Ave Fl 2 New York NY 10022-6600

FOSNOT, CATHERINE TWOMEY, education educator; b. Norwich, Conn., Aug. 22, 1947; d. Gerald Francis and Eileen (Rathbun) Twomey; m. John Douglas Fosnot, June 7, 1969 (div. 1982); children: Damien, Joshua. BS, U. Conn., 1969; MS, SUNY, Albany, 1976; EdD, U. Mass., 1983. Tchr. Roscoe (N.Y.) Cen., 1969-70, Harrison Elem., Hamilton, Ohio, 1970-71, Village South Elem., Centerville, 1973-73; tchr., administr. Albany (N.Y.) Area Open Sch., 1973-75; instr. dept. edn. Van den Berg Learning Ctr. SUNY, New Paltz, 1975-78; head tchr. dept. early childhood edn. univ. lab. day sch. U. Mass., Amherst, 1978-79, dir. student tng. sch. edn., 1979-83; asst. prof. dept. edn. So. Conn. State U., New Haven, 1983—. Cons. Summermath for Tchrs., 1986-92. Author: Enquiring Teachers, Enquiring Learners: A Constructivist Approach to Teaching; co-author: Reconstructing Mathematics Education; editor: The Constructivist, 1985—. Ednl. Communications and Tech./Eric Young Scholar, 1984. Mem. Assn. for Constructivist Teaching (pres. 1985-87), Assn. Ednl. Comms. and Tech. (reviewer 1987, bd. dirs. Rsch. and Theory Div., reviewer of Young Researcher award, 1986, 87). Home: Prentice Rd Worthington MA 01098-9587 Office: So Conn U Dept Edn 130 Davis St New Haven CT 06515-1611

FOSS, CLIVE FRANK WILSON, history professor; b. London, Aug. 30, 1939; came to U.S., 1945, naturalized, 1980; s. Victor Albert and Jeanne Francoise (Beurton) W. AB magna cum laude, Harvard U., 1961, MA, 1965, PhD, 1973. Instr. U. Mass., Boston, 1967-69, lectr., 1969-73, asst. prof., 1973-76, assoc. prof., 1976-80, prof. history, 1980—2002. Faculty Boston Coll., 1968-69; vis. prof. U. Lyon, France, 1977-79, U. South Africa, 1981, U. Calif., 1985, Harvard U., 1990-91, Georgetown U., 2001—; mem. Sardis Expdn., 1969-75, 79-83; dir. Medieval Castles Survey of Anatolia, 1982-85; assoc. Ephesus Excavations, 1973-74. Author: Byzantine and Turkish Sardis, 1976, Rome and Byzantium, 1977, Ephesus After Antiquity, 1979, Medieval Castles Survey I: Kutahya, 1985, II, Nicomedia, 1996, Byzantine Fortifications, 1986, History and Archaeology of Byzantine Asia Minor, 1990, Roman Historical Coins, 1991, Nicea, 1996, Cities, Fortresses and Villages of Byzantine Asia Minor, 1996, Juan and Eva Peron, 1999, Fidel Castro, 2000; contbr. articles to profl. jours. Norton fellow Am. Sch. Classical Studies, Athens, 1961-62; Am. Coun. Learned Socs. grantee, 1974, 80; Indo-U.S. fellow (CIES), 1983; CNRS rsch. assoc., Paris, 1983; NEH fellow, 1975-76; Guggenheim fellow, 1983-84; vis. fellow Dumbarton Oaks, 1973-74, 99-2000, All Souls Coll., Oxford U., 1983-84, Trinity Coll., Oxford U., 1997, 2005; fellow Inst. Advanced Studies, Hebrew U., Jerusalem, 1993. Fellow Soc. Antiquaries, Royal Numismatic Soc.; mem. Am. Philol. Assn., Am. Numismatic Soc., Brit. Inst. Archaeology of Ankara, Numismatic Soc. India, Harvard Club (N.Y.C.), Tavern Club (Boston), Cosmos Club (Washington), Phi Beta Kappa. Republican. Episcopalian. Office: Georgetown Univ Dept History Washington DC 20057 Home: 3536 T St Washington DC 20007-1818 Office Phone: 202-687-3264. E-mail: cff@georgetown.edu.

FOSS, DAVID HUGH, English educator; b. Kingston, Canada, Nov. 6, 1958; s. Donald Leslie and Margaret Jeannette Foss; m. Milagros Perez, May 5, 1997; children: Garrett Michael, Kacey Erin. Diploma in law and security adminstrn., Algonquin Coll. of Applied Arts and Tech., 1976—78; BA in english lang. and lit., Carleton U., 1981—89; MA in english lang. and lit., Queen's U., 1989—90; MA in edn., U. of the Incarnate Word, 1998—2002. Tchr. of english Incarnate Word H.S., San Antonio, 1997—98; English tchr. BrainPower Summer Sch., Incarnate Word H.S., San Antonio, 1998; acting chair, dept. of English Incarnate Word H.S., 1998—99, chair, dept. of English, 1999—2002; English tchr. Alamo Heights H.S., San Antonio, 2002—. Freelance editor, Kingston, Ontario, Canada, 1995—96; reading tutor Kazen Elem. Sch., Loredo, Tex., 1997; mem. grad. student soc. health plan sub-com. Queens U., 1995—96; sec./treas. Grad. English Soc., 1993—95; mem. at large Grad. English Soc., Queen's U., 1991—92. Vol. office worker Literacy Volunteers of Am., Laredo, Tex., 1997, vol. instr., 1997, sec. and mem. bd. dirs., 1997. Recipient Cert. of Commendation and Nominee for Sallie Mae First Class Tchr. award, Am. Assn. of Sch. Administrators and Sallie Mae, 1998, Educator of Distinction, Nat. Soc. of H.S. Scholars, 2004; Dean's fellowship, Queen's U., 1989, Queen's U. Grad. fellowship, 1990, 1991. Mem.: Nat. Edn. Assn., Tex. State Teachers Assn., ASCD, Nat. Coun. of Teachers of English. Anglican. Avocation: hockey. Home: 506 Stockton Dr San Antonio TX 78216-6438 Office: Alamo Heights HS 6900 Broadway San Antonio TX 78209 Office Phone: 210-820-8850. Personal E-mail: davidfoss@sbcglobal.net. E-mail: dfoss@ahisd.net.

FOSS, JOHN FRANK, mechanical engineering educator; b. Washington, Pa., Mar. 24, 1938; s. Maurice Felker and C. Catharine (Reynard) F.; m. Jacqueline Kay Voss, July 24, 1960; children: Judith Kathleen, Janette Diane. Student, Wilmington Coll., 1956—58; BS, Purdue U., 1961, MS, 0162, PhD, 1965. Mem. faculty Mich. State U., East Lansing, 1964—, assoc. prof. mech. engring., 1968-75, prof., 1975—; owner, pres. Digital Flow Techs., Inc., Mich., 1994—. Dir. fluid dynamics & hydraulics program NSF, 1998-2000; cons. McDonnel Douglas Helicopter Co., Ford Motor Co., Bd. Water and Light, Lansing, Tranter Corp., United Techs. Rsch. Ctr., East Hartford, Conn. Author: (with M.C. Potter) Fluid Mechanics, 1975; N.Am. editor Measurement Sci. and Tech., 1995-; assoc. editor AIAA Jour., 1982-85, ASME Jour. Fluids Engring., 1988-91. Mem. Oaks Recreation Program staff, 1976-78; moderator Edgewood United Ch., 1975-77. Sloan fellow John Hopkins U., Balt., 1970-71; Alexander von Humboldt fellow U. Karlsruhe, Fed. Republic Germany, 1978-79, U. Erlangen, Fed. Republic Germany, 1985-86, rsch. fellow U. Melbourne, Australia, 1995. Fellow ASME; mem. AIAA, AAAS, AAUP, Am. Soc. Engring. Edn., Am. Phys. Soc. (mem. exec. com. divsn. fluid dynamics 2003-), Soc. Scholars Johns Hopkins U., Sigma Xi, Tau Beta Pi, Pi Tau Sigma. Mem. United Ch. of Christ. Avocation: handball. Home: 2353 Sapphire Lane East Lansing MI 48823 Office: Mich State U Dept Mech Engring East Lansing MI 48824 Office Phone: 517-355-3337. Business E-Mail: foss@egr.msu.edu.

FOSS, KARL ROBERT, auditor; b. Aug. 26, 1938; s. Robert Henry and Ethel Caroline (Huston) Foss. Student, U. Wis., 1956-59, 62; BS, Madison Bus. Coll., 1961. Auditor Wis. Dept. Revenue, Madison, 1962-95; owner, mgr. LIST, Middleton, Wis., 1968-76. Pub.: Suppliers List, 1968, Suppliers List Directory, 1989. Bd. dirs. Middletown Hist. Soc., 1976—93, v.p., 1980; mem. legis. adv. Old Car Hobby, 1971—. Co-recipient Spl. Interest Autos Appreciation award, 1971. Mem.: Contemporary Hist. Vehicle Assn., Acctg. and Mgmt. Assn., Model T Ford Club Am., Vintage Chevrolet Club Am., Antique Automobile Club Am., Studebaker Drivers Club, Oldsmobile Club Am. (nat. bd. dirs. 1973—85, treas. 1981—85), Wis. Automobile Clubs Assn. Inc. (co-founder 1971, bd. dirs. 1971—, pres. 1972—74, 1977—78, 1980, 1986—87, v.p. 1975—76, 1979, 1985, 1995—). Home: PO Box 620021 Middleton WI 53562-0021

FOSS, LUKAS, composer, conductor, pianist; b. Berlin, Aug. 15, 1922; came to US from Paris, 1937, naturalized, 1942; s. Martin and Hilde (Schindler) F.; m. Cornelia Brendel, Sept. 1951; 2 children. Student, Paris Lycée Pasteur, 1932-37; grad., Curtis Inst. Music, 1940; spl. study, Yale U., 1940-41; pupil of, Paul Hindemith, Julius Herford, Serge Koussevitzky, Fritz Reiner, Isabelle Vengerova; hon. doctorate, Yale U., 1991; 15 other hon. doctorates. Pianist Boston Symphony Orch., Boston, 1944—50; prof. composition U. Calif., Los Angeles, 1953—62; music dir. Buffalo Philharmonic, 1963—71, Brooklyn Philharmonic, 1971—90; musical adviser Jerusalem Symphony, 1972—75; music dir. Milwaukee Symphony, 1982—86, condr. laureate, 1986—. Founder & condr. Improvisation Chamber Ensemble, 1957—62; composer-in-residence Harvard, Manhattan Sch. of Music, Carnegie Mellon U., Yale U.; guest conductor Boston Symphony, Chicago Symphony, Cleveland Orch., Los Angeles Philharmonic, NY Philharmonic, Phila. Symphony Orch., San Francisco Symphony, Berlin Philharmonic, Leningrad Symphony, London Symphony Orch., Santa Cecilia Orch., Tokyo Philharmonic. Former condr., music dir., Buffalo Philharmonic; music dir., condr., Bklyn. Philharmonic, 1971-90, condr. laureate, 1990—; music dir., condr. Milw. Symphony Orch., 1981-86, condr. laureate, 1986—; orchestral compositions performed by many major orch.; best known works include (opera) Griffelkin, Baroque Variations (orch.), Echoi (4 instruments), Time Cycle (songs with orch.), Renaissance concerto (flute and orch.); orch., chamber music, ballets, works commd. by, League of Composers, Nat. Endowment for Arts, NY Arts Coun., NBC opera on TV, Am. Choral Condrs. Assn., Ind. U., 1979 Olympics, Boston Symphony, Chgo. Symphony; (recipient NY Critic Circle citation for Prairie 1944, Soc. for Pub. Am. Music award for String Quartet in G 1948, Rome prize 1950, Horblit award for Piano concerto #2 1951, Naumburg Rec. award for Song of Songs 1957, Creative Music grant Inst. Arts and Letters 1957, NY Music Critics Circle award for Time-Cycle orch. songs 1961, for Echoi 1963, Ditson award for condr. who has done the most for Am. music 1973, NYC award for spl. contbn. to arts 1976, ASCAP award for adventurous programming 1979, CRI rec. award for Thirteen Ways of Looking at a Blackbird 1979). Guggenheim fellow, 1945; Creative arts award Brandeis U., 1983; Laurel leaf award Am. Composers Alliance, 1983; elected to Am. Acad. & Inst. of Arts & Letters, 1983; inductee Am. Classical Music Hall of Fame, 2002. Mem. Am. Acad. of Arts and Letters (Gold medal 2000).

FOSS, MICHELLE MICHOT, think-tank executive, economist; BS, Univ. La., Lafayette, 1976; MS, Colo. Sch. Mines, 1985; PhD with honors, Univ. Houston, 1995; postgraduate, Tex. A&M Univ., Rice Univ. Coord. Energy & Minerals Field Inst., Colo. Sch. Mines, 1982—85; sr. assoc. & dir. rsch. Rice Ctr., 1985—88; dir. rsch. Simmons & Co. Internat., 1988—89; exec. dir. Inst. Energy Law & Enterprise, Univ. Houston, 1991—. Ptnr. Harvest Gas Mgmt. LLC, Tex. Mem. bd. editors Internat. Jour. Regulation & Governance. Mem. vis. com. div. Economics & Business, Colo. Sch. Mines. Mem.: Women's Energy Network, Houston Geol. Soc., Assn. Internat. Petroleum Negotiators, Council on Fgn. Rels., U.S. Assn. Energy Economics (pres. 2001), Internat. Assn. Energy Economics (pres. 2003). Office: Institute for Energy Law & Enterprise University of Houston 100 Law Ctr Houston TX 77204-6060

FOSS, RICHARD JOHN, bishop; b. Wauwatosa, Wis., Dec. 27, 1944; s. Harlan Funston and Beatrice Naomi (Lindaas) F.; m. Nancy Elizabeth Martin, June 21, 1969; children: Susan, Naomi Foss Welsh, Elizabeth, Peter, Andrew. BA, St. Olaf Coll., 1966; MDiv, Luther Theol. Seminary, 1971; ThM, Luther N.W. Theol. Seminary, 1984. Ordained to ministry Luth. Ch., 1971. Pastor St. Andrews Ch. and Ch. of Christ the Redeemer, Mpls., 1971-77; assoc. pastor First Luth., Fargo, N.D., 1977-79; sr. pastor Prince of Peace Luth., Seattle, 1979-86, Trinity Luth., Moorhead, Minn., 1986-92; bishop Ea. N.D. Synod, Fargo, 1992—. Soloist F-M Opera Co., Fargo, 1979; coach St. James Girls' Basketball Team, Settle, 1982-84; vol. Wash. State Patrol Crisis Chaplaincy, Seattle, 1983-86; bd. dirs. Discovery, Inc., Mpls., 1972-77, Highline Boys' and Girls' Club, Burien, Wash., 1980-81, Luth. Compass Ctr., Seattle, 1983-86, v.p., 1985-86; mem. Master Chorale, 1987-99; bd. regents Concordia Coll., 1992—; bd. dirs. Daily Bread, 1991-2000, Luth. Social Svcs. of N.D., 1992—, Oak Grove Luth. H.S., 1990—, Luth. Resources Network, 1994-97, Healthy Congregations Adv. Bd., 1997—, chair 2004—, N.D. Conf. Chs., 1993—; mem. adv. bd. Thrivent Fin. for Luths., 2000—, Ctr. for Ethical Leadership, 2001-05; mem. United Way Cmty. Bd., 2001-02; bd. regents Luther Sem., 2002—. Lutheran. Avocations: golf, reading, travel, vocal performance. Home: 1510 2nd St S Moorhead MN 56560-4014 Office: Ea ND Synod 1703 32nd Ave S Fargo ND 58103-5936 Office Phone: 701-232-3381. E-mail: rick.foss@ecunet.org.

FOSS, ROBERT FLETCHER, lawyer; b. Portland, Maine, Nov. 21, 1952; s. Robert Macy Foss and Jane (Higgins) Hoy; m. Marlene Schuster, Aug. 21, 1976; children: Joel, Sean. JD, U. Honolulu, 1994. Bar: Calif. 1994, U.S. Dist. Ct. (ctrl. dist.) Calif. 1995, U.S. Dist. Ct. (no. dist.) Calif. 1996, U.S. Ct. Appeals (9th cir.) 1999. Paralegal Baum, Hedlund PC, L.A., 1986—94, atty., 1994—. Recipient Safety award, Nat. Air Disaster Found., 2002. Mem.: L.A. County Bar Assn., State Bar Calif. Avocation: skiing. Office: Baum Hedlund A Profl Corp 12100 Wilshire Blvd Ste 950 Los Angeles CA 90025-7107 Office Phone: 310-207-3233. Business E-Mail: rfoss@baumhedlundlaw.com.

FOSSATI, HUMBERTO MARIO, electrical engineer, researcher; b. Bryan, Tex., Nov. 16, 1965; s. Humberto and Nancy Miryam (Tejada) F. BS in Elec. Engring., Tex A&M U., 1987, MS, 1989; postgrad., Rice U. Staff engr. Space Sta., IBM, Houston, 1989—93; staff engr. LAMPS, IBM/Loral Fed. Systems, Owego, NY, 1993—95; with Compaq Computer Corp., Houston, 1995—2002, multimedia architect portable PC divsn., 1997—99, program mgr. advanced tech., 1999—2000; program mgr. microportable projects Access Bus. Group (ABG), Houston, 2000—02; solutions program mgr., personal workstas. Hewlett Packard Corp., Fort Collins, Colo., 2002—03, program mgr. Display Bus. unit Houston, 2003—. Rschr. Pleiades Rsch., 1989-96. Contbr. articles to profl. jours. Rice U. fellow, 1992; NSF grantee Tex. A&M U., 1987-89. Mem. IEEE, Sigma Xi. Republican. Roman Catholic. Avocations: collecting stamps, playing tennis, soccer, swimming. Home: 8206 Turnmill Ct Spring TX 77379 Office: 20555 SH 249 MS 070222 Houston TX 77070 E-mail: humberto.fossati@hp.com, fossati@highstream.net.

FOSSEL, ERIC THOR, medical biophysicist; b. Mpls., Dec. 11, 1941; s. Spencer M. and Jane (Nelson) F.; m. Anne H. Plant, June 14, 1964 (div. 1981);children: Karin, Lars; m. Jan McQuere McDonagh, Jan. 6, 1982; 1 child, Jonathan. MS in Chemistry, Yale U., 1966, MPhil, 1967; PhD in Chemistry, Harvard U., 1970, MTS, 2000. Assoc./biology, chemistry Harvard Coll., Cambridge, Mass., 1974-75; lectr. biophysics Harvard Med. Sch., Boston, 1975-76, asst. prof. biophysics, 1976-83, asst. prof. radiology, 1983-85, assoc. prof. radiology, 1985-95; dir. radiol. rsch. Beth Israel Hosp., Boston, 1987-95. Vis. scientist Francis Bitter Magnet Lab./MIT, 1976-83; cons. Inst. for Clin. Applications, Boston, 1990-93; pres. Strategic Sci. & Tech., Inc., 1995—. Contbr. articles to profl. jurs. Am. Heart Assn. established investigator, 1978-83. Mem. Am. Fedn. Clin. Rsch., Assn. of Univ. Radiologists, Soc. of Magnetic Resonance in Medicine (founding mem.), Biophys. Soc., Fellowship of Soc. St. John the Evangelist. Republican. Episcopalian.

Achievements include patents for NMR cancer blood test, major unique trans-dermal drug delivery system. Office: Strategic Sci & Tech Inc 58 Charles St Cambridge MA 02141 Office Phone: 617-299-4789. E-mail: efossel@strategicsci.com.

FOSSELLA, VITO JOHN, congressman; b. Staten Island, N.Y., Mar. 9, 1965; s. Vito John and Elizabeth Lucey Fossella; m. Mary Patricia Rowan, 1990. BS, U. Pa., 1987; JD, Fordham U., 1993. Mem. Cmty. Bd. 3, Staten Island, 1989-90; city councilman N.Y.C., 1994-97; U.S. Congressman 13th Dist. Staten Island, 1997—. Mem. commerce com., financial svcs. commn., telecomms. sub. com., capital mkts. subcom., environ. and hazardous materials subcom. U.S. Ho. of Reps. Mem.: Phi Sigma Epsilon. Republican. Roman Catholic. Address: 4434 Amboy Rd Fl 2 Staten Island NY 10312-3858 Office: US House of Representatives 1239 Longworth Washington DC 20515-0001*

FOSSETT, STEVEN, retired investor, adventurer; b. Calif., Apr. 22, 1944; Investor Lakota Trading, Inc., Marathon Securities, Inc. Bd. trustee Washington U. Named Rolex Yachtsman of Yr., US Sailing Assn., 2001; named an Disting. Eagle Scout, Boy Scouts of Am., 1998, Silver Buffalo, 1999; named one of Ballon and Airship Hall of Fame, FAI-CIA, 1997; named to Hall of Fame, Aviation Week and Space Technology, Laureate for Ops., 2003; recipient Victor award (Special), Victor Sports Awards, 1995, 1997, 2003, Prix De La Vauix, Fédération Aéronautique Internationale, 1995, 1997, 1998, 2002, Diplôme de Montgolfier, 1996, Gold Air Medal, 2002, Distinction in Exploration, Nat. Geographic Soc., 1998, Harmon Trophy, Nat. Aeronautic Assn., 1998, 2002, Prix de l'Aventure Sportive, Académie des Sports, France, 2002, Medaille de l'Aéronautique, Republique Francaise, 2003, Gold Medal, Royal Aero Club, UK, 2002, Grand Medaille de l'Aéro Club de France, 2003. Fellow: Royal Geographical Soc., Explorers Club (Explorers medal 2002); mem.: Academie Nationale de l'Air et de l'Elspace, Circumnavigators Club (hon. Magellan award 2003), Yacht Club de France (hon.), Nat. Yacht Club of Ireland (hon.), Aero Club de France (hon.), Adventurers Club (hon.). Holds current official World Records in five sports: Six Solo Round The World Attempts in Balloning (First to fly solo across the Pacific Ocean, flying from Seoul, South Korea, to Mendham, Saskatchewan, 1995, first to cross the African continent in a ballon, 1997, first to cross the European Continent in a Ballon, 1998, first to cross the South Atlantic and the Indian Oceans, 1998, first Solo Ballon Flight Round the World-Speed Record (nonstop) in the Bud Light Spirit of Freedom, June-July, 2002, 24 Hour Record (Speed), June-July, 2002); Two major Ballon Flights (with multi-persons); Thirteen Outright World Records in Sailing; Three Singlehanded Records in Sailing(Round the World, 58 days, 9 hours, 32 minutes, 45 seconds, 15.52 knots, 2004, TransAtlantic (NY to England) 4 dyas, 17 hours, 28 minutes, 6 seconds, 25.78 knots, 2001); Eight Race Records in Sailing (World's Fastest Yacht Race Record-Newport to Ensenada, 6 hours, 46 minutes, 40 seconds, 18.45 knots, 1998); One Solo Transatlantic Race in Sailing; Eleven Glider Records (with co-pilot Terry Delore); One Airship Speed Record (Absolute Airship Speed Record, Zeppelin NT, 2004); Three U.S. Transcontinental Records in Airplanes; Two Round the World Records in Medium Airplane-H Class; 6 other Airplane records; Two Cross Country Skiing records; piloted the Virgin Atlantic GlobalFlyer, first to fly solo, non-stop around the world without refueling, 2005; other sports adventures include: English Channel Swim (France to England), 1985, Leadville 100, 1991, Iditarod Dogsled Race, 1992, Ironman Triathalon (Hawaii), 1996, 24 Hours of Le Mans Sports Car Race, 1993 & 1996; donated the gondola of his ballon to the Smithsonian National Air and Space Museum in Washington, DC. Mailing: Marathon Racing Inc/ Steve Fossett Challanges Attn Brian Spaeth 401 South La Salle Ste 200 Chicago IL 60605*

FOSSUM, EUGENE ERIC, theater educator; b. Hollywood, Calif. s. Alvin Einar and Bernice Margret Fossum; m. Barbara Jan Erickson, Jan. 13, 1987. BA cum laude, St. Mary's Coll., L.A., 1999; MA Theater, Cinema, Calif. State U., San Bernardino, 2002. Actor NBC, LA, 1971—77, ABC, LA, 1977, contract actor N.Y.C., 1982—84, CBS, N.Y.C., 1984; adj. prof. Calif. State U., Pomona, 2000—02, San Bernardino, 2002—04, Mt. St. Mary Coll., L.A., 2004—. Author: (Book) Danny Daniels: A Life of Dance and Choreography. Home: 616 Masselin Ave Los Angeles CA 90036

FOSSUM, JERRY GEORGE, electrical engineering educator; b. Phoenix, July 18, 1943; s. George Clayton and Lillian Edith (McNeilis) F.; m. Mary Ellen; children: Kerry Ray, Kelly Lynn. AA, Phoenix Coll., 1963; BSEE, U. Ariz., 1966, MS, 1969, PhD, 1971. Mem. tech. staff Sandia Labs., Albuquerque, 1971-78; assoc. prof. elec. engring. U. Fla., Gainesville, 1978-80, prof., 1980—. Cons. Burr-Brown Rsch. Corp., Tucson, 1970-71, Jet Propulsion Lab., Pasadena, Calif., 1979, Harris Corp., Melbourne, Fla., 1984, Tex. Instruments, Inc., Dallas, 1988-89, 94-96, Ibis Tech. Corp., Danvers, Mass., 1995, Meta-Software, Campbell, Calif., 1995-96, Dynamics Rsch. Corp., San Diego, 1996-02; mem. adv. com. Semiconductor Rsch. Corp., 1991-95; mem. exec. com. IEEE SOI Conf., 1994-97. Contbr. articles to profl. jours.; assoc. editor: Solid-State Electronics, 1979—, IEEE Trans. Computer-Aided Design, 1988-91; patentee in field. Recipient Outstanding Rsch. award, Am. Soc. Engring. Edn., 1979. Fellow: IEEE (Best Paper award SOI Conf. 1992, J.J. Ebers award Electron Devices Soc. 2004). Office: U Fla Dept Elec and Computer Engr Gainesville FL 32611-6130 Office Phone: 352-392-4921. Business E-Mail: fossum@tec.ufl.edu.

FOSSUM, LOUIS ERIC, theater educator, writer; b. Hollywood, Calif. s. Alvin Einar and Bernice Margaret Fossum; m. Barbara Jane Erickson, Jan. 3, 1987. BA cum laude, Mt. St. Mary's Coll., 1999; MA Theater & Cinema, Calif. State U., 2002. Actor NBC TV Network, L.A., 1971—77, ABC TV Network, L.A., 1977—80, contract actor N.Y.C., 1982—84, CBS TV Network, N.Y.C., 1982—84; adj. prof. Calif. State U., Pomona, 2000—05, San Bernardino Valley Coll., 2002—04, Mt. St. Mary's Coll., L.A., 2004—. Author: (biography) Danny Daniels: A Life of Dance and Choreography. Mem.: United Tchrs. L.A. Home: 616 Masselin Ave #435 Los Angeles CA 90036 E-mail: lefossum@csu.pomona.edu.

FOSSUM, ROBERT MERLE, mathematician, educator; b. Northfield, Minn., May 1, 1938; s. Inge Martin and Tina Otelia (Gaudland) F.; m. Cynthia Carol Foss, Jan. 30, 1960 (div. 1979); children: Karen Jean, Kristin Ann; m. Barbara Joel Mason, Aug. 4, 1979 (div. 1993); children: Jonathan Robert, Erik Anton; m. Robin Karyl Goodman, Aug. 10, 1997. BA, St. Olaf Coll., 1959; MA, U. Mich., 1961, PhD, 1965. Instr. U. Ill., Urbana, 1964-66, asst. prof., 1966-68, assoc. prof., 1968-72, prof., 1972—, elect. and computer engring. Urbana, 2003—; prof. Beckman Inst., 2000. Lectr. Aarhus U., Denmark, 1971-73, Copenhagen U., Denmark, 1976-77; vis. prof. U. Paris VI, 1978-79, Oslo U., 1968-69. Contbr. articles to profl. jours. Bd. dirs. Planned Parenthood East Ctrl. Ill.; chmn. Campus Fund Drive, U. Ill. Recipient Disting. Alumni award Northfield H.S.; Fulbright fellow U. Oslo, 1967-68. Fellow: AAAS, Det Kongelig Norske Videnskabers Selskab (elected nat. sci. sect.); mem.: IEEE, Soc. Advancement Scandinavian Studies, European Math. Soc., Inst. Algebraic Meditation (sec.), Am. Math. Soc. (assoc. sec. cen. sect. 1983—87, sec. 1989—99), Soc. for Indsl. and Applied Math., Internat. Assn. Math. Physics, Assn. Computing Machinery, Nordmanns Forbundet, Heimskringla (Urbana), Sigma Pi Sigma, Sigma Xi, Phi Beta Kappa (pres. Ill. Gamma chpt.). Democrat. Lutheran. Office Phone: 217-244-3572. E-mail: rmfossum@uiuc.edu.

FOSSUO TALOM, PATRICK, research scientist; b. Yaounde, Cameroon, May 22, 1971; arrived in U.S., 1996; s. Lucien Fossuo Talom and Anne Marie Fonkwa Ngawa. B in Biology, Kean U., 2000; MBA in Pharm. studies, Fairleigh Dickinson, 2003. Analyst Aventis Pharms., Bridgewater, NJ, 1999—2001; assoc. scientist Johnson and Johnson, Raritan, NJ, 2001—. Mem.: Am. Assn. Pharm. Scientists (assoc.). Office: 1000 Rte 202 S Raritan NJ 08869

FOSTER, ALAN HERBERT, diversified financial services company executive, educator; b. Somerville, Mass., Nov. 7, 1925; s. Herbert and Margaret J. (Griffin) F.; m. Cynthia Ann Brooks, June 26, 1954; children— Mark Brooks, Andrew Herbert. BS, BA, Boston Coll., 1951; MBA, Harvard U., 1953. With Sylvania Electric Products, Inc., 1953-63; with Am. Motors Corp., 1963-77, corp. dir. financial planning and analysis, 1963-67, treas., 1967-68, v.p., treas., 1968-77; pres. A.H. Foster & Co. (Cons. in Corp. Fin.), Ann Arbor, Mich., 1977—, Fin. Risk Mgmt. Inc., Ann Arbor, 1983—, ret., 2002—. Adj. prof. corp. strategy and internat. bus. Grad. Sch. Bus., U. Mich. Author: Practical Business Management, 1962, Treasurer's Handbook; also articles. Served with USNR, 1945-46. Mem. Commanderie de Bordeaux, Fin. Execs. Inst. (pres. Detroit chpt. 1972-73), Baker Street Irregulars, Speckled Band Boston, Inst. Mgmt. Scis. (past nat. chmn. coll. planning), U. Mexico Club, Samuel Pepys Club, Harvard Club N.Y.C., Harvard Faculty Club. Home: 810 Earhart Rd Ann Arbor MI 48105-2711

FOSTER, B. JANE, artist; b. Boston, Apr. 8, 1960; d. Louis Irving and Pauline Malva (Seliger) Egelson; m. Fred Alfred Foster, July 31, 1993; children: Megan Isabella, Toby Mitchell. BFA, Alfred U., 1983. Prodn. potter Cottage Clayworks, Easthampton, Mass., 1983-84, White Dog Pottery, Easthampton, Mass., 1984-89; ceramic asst. Mara Superior, Hadley, Mass., 1986-94, 98—; ornament painter Tewksbury Ornaments, Greenfield, Mass., 1986-94; studio potter Brick House Pottery, Turners Falls, Mass., 1994—. Coun. mem. Gill-Montague (Mass.) Family Network, 1996-98, Peskeomskut Park Planning Com., Montague, 1997-98.

FOSTER, BARRY ALAN, cultural organization researcher, educator; b. Tacoma, Wash., Dec. 11, 1956; s. Glen H. Foster and Selma Landers; m. Sue Rose Foster, July 20, 1954; children: Nathan M., Zachary A., Kristen B. BA in Theology, Southeastern Coll., Lakeland, Fla., 1994; MBA in Managerial Leadership, City U., Renton, Wash., 1996; MA in Orgnl. Devel., The Fielding Inst., Santa Barbara, Calif., 1998, PhD in Human and Orgnl. Sys., 2000. Orgnl. culture change leader The Boeing Co., Seattle, 1999—. Author: (organizational change model) Essential Foundations of the Engaged Organization. Dir. Lemonaid Fund, Chgo., 1999—2002. Mem.: Am. Sociol. Assn. (assoc.; cert.). Achievements include research in barriers to servant leadership and large scale organizational culture change. Avocations: mountain biking, racquetball, flag football. Office: The Boeing Co PO Box 3707 MS 5F-98 Seattle WA 98124 Personal E-mail: barryfoster777@comcast.net. E-mail: barry.a.foster@boeing.com.

FOSTER, BAYARD EVERSON, writer; b. Knoxville, Aug. 11, 1934; s. Bayard Collis and Zella Mae (Price) Foster; m. Virginia May Hall, Dec. 24, 1964 (dec. May 1998); children: Karla June, Rex David, Ronald Elliott, Beatrice Irene, Richard Lawrence. BA, Tex. Tech. U., 1955. Commd. 2d lt. USAF, 1955, adv. through grades to maj., ret., 1980; equipment sel. specialist Saudi Arabian Airlines, Jeddah, 1980—84; maintenance data analyst Scitek, Inc., St. Louis, 1988—89; v.p. ops. Aviation Logistics Systems, 1989—90; tech. writer Am. Elecs. Labs., Bethalto, Ill., 1990—92. Author: Mission Iorg, 2000, Reap the Whirlwind, 2002. Founder Angel Flights Min., Troy, Mo., 1998. Methodist. Avocations: writing, photography, travel. Home: 5403 Everhart Rd Corpus Christi TX 78411 Office: Rancho Pacifico Properties 5403 Everhart Rd PMB B Corpus Christi TX 78411

FOSTER, BETTY LOUISE, educator; b. Lincoln, Nebr., Nov. 12, 1943; d. Burt Willis and Elizabeth Julia Hunt; m. Gary A. Foster; children: Ann Louise, Geofrey Algot; foster children: Matt Urbauer, Don Simmons, Ronda Real. BS in Elem. Edn., U. Nebr., 1965, postgrad. in Elem. Edn. Reading; postgrad. in Elem. Edn. and Reading, Kearney State Coll.; MA in Edn. Doane Coll., Crete, Nebr., 1994. Endorsement in teaching reading. Tchr. reading departmentalized grades 5-6 South Sioux City (Nebr.) Schs., 1967-69, supplemental reading tchr. Title I, 1970-71; supplemental reading tchr. Title I Grand Island (Nebr.) Schs., 1971-76; tchr. Jefferson Sch., Grand Island, 1976-2001; tech. tchr. Christ the King Sch., Omaha, 2001-, tech. tchr. St. Thomas More Sch., Omaha, 2005; adj. prof. Hamilton Coll., Council Bluffs, Iowa, 2005—. Contbr. articles to profl. jours. Organizer, tchr. Head Start in South Sioux City Community Center and Chs., 1968-69; active Girl Scouts U.S.A., 1970—, mentor for girls interested in art; v.p. Neighborhood Taskforce, Inc., 1980-82; pres. S. Locust/Barr Neighborhood Assn., 1980-81; mem. Mayor's Taskforce for Tornado Recovery, 1980-81; v.p. YWCA Grand Island, 1983; organizer Grand Island Women's Network, 1984; local rep., host family Grand Island Internat. Visitors Program, 1977-94, North Atlantic Cultural Exch. League, 1987-92; coach elem. level Olympics of the Mind, 1986-88, Oddyessy of the Mind, 1987-88; bd. dirs., dir. Aurora (Nebr.) Art Workshops, 1989-91; mem. amb. People to People Citizen Program, Japan, 1992, Grand Island Prarie Visions Team; chmn. Artel Show, Antiquariam Gallery, 1994-95. Mem. DAR (Major I Saddler La Belle Vue Cho 2004—), Nat., Nebr., Grand Island Edn. Assns. (chairwoman instrn. and career enhancement com. 1990-91), Internat. (sec. Central Council 1974—), Nebr., State reading assns., PTA of Children with Learning Disabilities (Jefferson Sch. chairwoman student assistance team 1989-92), AAUW (pres. Grand Island br. 1979-80, state v.p. 1981-82, state topic chmn. 1980-81), Nebr. Nebr. Ednl. Tech. Assn., Coalition of Women, LWV, Nat. Women's Cacus for Art (bd. dirs. 1995-2004), Nebr. Women's Cacus for Art (Nebr. state treas. 1995—), Artel Artist Networking Cmty, Assn. of Nebr. Art Clubs (chmn. state conv. 1987, sec. 1987—), Grand Island Art Club (pres. 1985-86), Grand Island Sketch Club, Meadows Cmty. Assn. (sec./treas. 2004—), Alpha Delta Kappa, Sigma Kappa. Developed self correcting games. Certified in elementary edn., kindergarten-8th grade, Nebr., Iowa; specialist in diagnosis and remediation of reading problems with learning disabilities problems, gifted children; trained to teach Jr. Great Books program, Productive Thinking Skills, Cooperative Learning, Quest-Skills for Growing K-5,trained discipline with a purpose. I'm Special 3-4; cert. foster home, Nebr. Home: 3515 S 48th Ave Omaha NE 68106 Office: St Thomas Moore Sch 3515 S 48th Ave Omaha NE 68106

FOSTER, B.J. See SHOEMAKER, BOBBY

FOSTER, BOBBY LEE, retired secondary school educator; b. Philadelphia, Miss., Nov. 2, 1938; s. Percy Lee and Emma (Campbell) F.; m. Frances Wilson, Mar. 11, 1971; children: Jamel, Natasha. BS, Rust Coll., Holly Springs, Miss., 1960; MEd, Miss. State U., 1976. Cert. tchr., Miss. Classroom tchr. social sci. and biology Kemper County High Sch., DeKalb, Miss., 1968—98; ret., 1998. Mem. Kemper Assn. Educators (pres.), Masons (worshipful master). Democrat. Methodist. Avocations: fishing, reading, gardening, hunting. Home: 227 Barrier Ave Philadelphia MS 39350-3132 Office Phone: 301-656-6354. Personal E-mail: fost3477@bellsouth.net.

FOSTER, BONNIE GAYLE, operating room nurse, real estate agent; b. Valentine, Nebr., Dec. 3, 1940; d. Isaac Robert and Helen Anita (Tucker) Bingham; m. Floyd E. Foster, July 4, 1973; m. Daniel A. Plummer, Aug. 8, 1963 (div. Oct. 1971). AA, RN, Oakland City Coll., 1963; BA in Sociology, U. Mo., Kansas City, 1975, M in Ednl. Adminstrn., 1978. RN Calif., Kans., Mo., cert. plastic surg. nursing. RN staff O.R. Herrick Hosp., Berkeley, Calif., 1963—64, Kaiser Hosp., Oakland, 1963—64; RN staff oper. room U. Kans. Med. Ctr., Kansas City, 1964—65; RN oper. room Rsch. Med. Ctr., Kansas City, Mo., 1965—78; RN, oper. room supr. Broadway Surg. Ctr., Kansas City, Mo., 1979—86; RN oper. room Menorah Med. Ctr., Kansas City, Mo., 1986—94, Sierra Surgi-Ctr., Walnut Creek, Calif., 1994—; realtor assoc. Pacific Real Estate Svcs., Pleasanton, Calif., 2003—; agt. Keller Williams Tri Valley. In svc. instr. Rsch. Hosp. and Med. Ctr., Kansas City, Mo., 1966—72, instr. CPR, 1976—88. Bus. assoc. Network Mktg.; chairperson fund raising program St. Paul's Episcopal Ch., Lee's Summit, Mo., 1976—94, chairperson bldg. expansion program, 1976—94, vestry mem., 1976—94; active St. Clare's Episcopal Ch., Pleasanton, 1994—. Mem.: Pleasanton North Rotary, Assn. Oper. Rm. Nurses (past pres. Greater Kansas City chpt., sec., chairperson Career Fair, co-chairperson Oper. Rm. Nurse of the Yr., panel moderator two-day inst., mem. several coms.). Republican. Episcopalian. Avocations: bicycling, hiking, golf, bridge, gardening. Home: 7567 Maywood Dr Pleasanton CA 94588 Office: Keller Williams Tri Valley Realty 5994 West Las Positas Blvd Ste 101 Pleasanton CA 94588 Office Phone: 925-462-3644. Business E-Mail: Bonnie@BonnieFoster.com.

FOSTER, BRUCE DUDLEY, minister; b. Gage, Okla., May 1, 1935; s. Ernest Edward and Ruth Anna (Berry) F.; m. Barbara Anne Walker; children: Teresa Lynn, Robyn Kathleen, Karen Leigh, Connie Ruth. BS in Biology, Pittsburg (Kans.) State U., 1958, MS in Edn., 1959; DD (hon.), Hyles-Anderson Coll., 1980. Cert. tchr., Kans., Colo., La.; ordained minister Bapt. Ch. Tchr. Thayer (Kans.) High Sch., 1958-59, New Castle (Colo.) High Sch., 1959-62, Mid-City Bapt. High Sch., New Orleans, 1962-63; athletic dir. Tenn. Temple U., Chattanooga, 1963-75; exec. v.p. Okla. Bapt. Coll., Oklahoma City, 1979-86; adminstr. College Heights Bapt. Acad., Farmington, N.Mex., 1986-92; pastor College Heights Bapt. Ch., Farmington, 1986-92, 2d Bapt. Ch., Festus, Mo., 1992—98, First Bapt. Ch., Gypsum, Colo., 2001—. Evangelist, conf. spkr., Christian author, speaker in field. Author: Creation Considered From a Biblical and a Scientific Viewpoint, 1970, The Home, 1976, The Doubt Problem, 1975, Let's Play Ball for Jesus Christ, 1978; writer weekly column Teen Talks, 1976-79. Pres. Twin City Christian Acad., Festus, 1992-98, Living Springs Camp, Festus, 1992-98. With U.S. Army, 1954-55. Mem. Phi Delta Kappa. Republican. Avocations: hunting, fishing. Home: PO Box 4076 Gypsum CO 81637 Office: 902 2d St Gypsum CO 81637 Office Phone: 970-524-7990. E-mail: brucedfoster@yahoo.com.

FOSTER, CARTER, curator; b. Atlanta; B in art history, U. Ga.; M in art history, Brown U., 1991. Intern Nat. Gallery Art, Washington; curatorial intern Phila. Mus. Art; print specialist, divsn. arts, prints, and photographs NY Pub. Libr.; staff mem. drawing dept. Cleveland Mus. Art, 1996—2004, chief drawing dept., 2002—04; curator, co-chair dept. prints and drawings LA County Mus. Art, 2004—05; curator of drawings Whitney Mus. Am. Art, NYC, 2005—. Office: Whitney Mus Am Art 945 Madison Ave New York NY 10021 Office Phone: 212-570-3651. Business E-Mail: feedback@whitney.org.

FOSTER, C(HARLES) ALLEN, lawyer; b. Aug. 26, 1941; s. Charles Shearer and Bessie Lea (Long) F.; m. Susan Coomes; children: Charles Shearer Sanders II, Susan Elizabeth Coomes, Charles Henry Edward. BA summa cum laude, Princeton U., 1963; BA in Jurisprudence 1st class honors, Oxford (Eng.) U., 1965, MA in Jurisprudence, 1971; JD magna cum laude, Harvard U., 1967. Bar: N.C. 1967, D.C. 1994, U.S. Dist. Ct. (mid. dist.) N.C. 1968, U.S. Dist. Ct. (we. dist.) N.C. 1968, U.S. Dist. Ct. (ea. dist.) N.C. 1968, U.S. Tax Ct. 1970, U.S. Ct. Appeals (4th cir.), U.S. Ct. Appeals (5th cir.) 1970, U.S. Ct. Appeals (11th cir.) 1991, U.S. Ct. Appeals (9th cir.) 2003, U.S. Ct. Appeals (10th cir.) 1993, U.S. Ct. Appeals (fed. cir.) 1995, U.S. Supreme Ct. 1971, U.S. Dist. Ct. D.C. 1985, U.S. Dist. Ct. (no. dist.) Tex. 1990, U.S. Dist. Ct. (so. dist.) Tex. 1991, U.S. Ct. Fed. Claims 1994. Assoc. McLendon, Brim, Brooks, Pierce & Daniels, Greensboro, N.C., 1967-72, ptnr., 1972-73; sec., dir., gen. counsel Spanco Industries, Inc., Greensboro and Sanford, N.C., 1973-75, Conestee, S.C., 1973-75; ptnr. Turner, Enochs, Foster, Sparrow & Burnley, Greensboro, 1975-81, Foster, Conner & Robson, 1983-88, Patton, Boggs LLP, 1988-99, Greenberg Traurig, Washington, 1999—. Sr. lectr. law Duke U., 1981-88; arbitrator Am. Arbitration Assn., mem. Nat. Acad. Arbitrators; pub. mem. N.C. Tax Rev. Bd., 1972-76; mem. N.C. Judicial Selection Study Commn., 1987-88; U.S. rep. Internat. Energy Agy. Dispute Resolution Ctr., Paris, 1984—; permanent panel arbitrator Martin Marietta and Atomic Trades and Labor Coun.; others. Author: Construction and Design Law, 1984—, Construction and Design Law Digest, 1981—, Law and Practice of Commercial Arbitration in North Carolina, 1984; contbr. articles to profl. jours. Co-founder, sec., bd. dirs. Greensboro Day Sch.; exec. com. Princeton U. Alumni Assn.; exec. com. Harvard Law Sch. Assn. N.C., 1970; Rep. candidate for atty.-gen. N.C., 1984; spl. counsel Rep. Nat. Com., 1989—; spl. litigation counsel N.C. Rep. Cen. Com., 1987—. Named one of top 20 trial lawyers in D.C., 2003. Mem. ABA (litigation sect., labor and employment discrimination law sect., forum com. on constrn. industry), Am. Law Inst., Am. Arbitration Assn. (bd. dirs. 1980-83, nat. panels labor, constrn., internat. comml. arbitrators 1975—, chmn. N.C. regional adv. coun. 1979-83), Am. Coll. Constrn. Arbitrators (pres. 1983-84), Princeton U. Alumni Assn. (pres. alumni coun., exec. com. 1978-79, pres. mid. N.C. chpt. 1968-80), Phi Beta Kappa, Cap and Gown Club. Home: 3846 Cathedral Ave NW Washington DC 20016 Office Phone: 202-331-3102. Business E-Mail: fostera@gtlaw.com.

FOSTER, CHARLES CARLTON, physicist; b. Jacksonville, Fla., Feb. 26, 1936; s. Charles Clarence and Dorcas Broward (Beckley) Drake; m. Carolynn J. Southmayd, June 6, 1958 (div. Mar. 1976); children: Sherry, Christopher, John; m. Dorothy Lee Mayberry, July 4, 1976; 1 child, Cynthia. BS in Physics with honors, Tulane U., 1957; PhD in Physics, Ind. U., 1967. Instr. Princeton (N.J.) U., 1967-70; asst. prof. physics U. Mo., St. Louis, 1970-74; staff physicist Ind. U., Bloomington, 1974—2001; pres. Foster Cons. Svcs., LLC, 2002—. Lt. USNR, 1957-59. Mem. IEEE, Am. Phys. Soc., Exch. Club. Office: Ind U 2401 Sampson Ln Bloomington IN 47408 Home: 3908 80th Ave W University Pl WA 98466-3234 E-mail: fosterchc@worldnet.att.net, foster@iucf.indiana.edu.

FOSTER, CHARLES CRAWFORD, lawyer, educator; b. Galveston, Tex., Aug. 1, 1941; s. Louie Brown and Helen (Hall) F.; m. Marta Brito, Sept. 7, 1967 (div. Apr. 1986); children: John, Ruth; m. Lily Chen, Jan. 7, 1989; children: Zachary, Anthony. AA, Del Mar Jr. Coll., 1961; BA, U. Tex., 1963, JD, 1967. Bar: Tex. 1967, N.Y. 1969. Assoc. Reid & Priest, N.Y.C., 1967-69, Butler & Binion, Houston, 1969-73; ptnr. Tindall & Foster, Houston, 1973—. Hon. consul gen. Kingdom of Thailand, 1996—; adj. prof. immigration law U. Houston, 1985-89; bd. dirs. Greater Houston Partnership, 1997-2003, chmn. econ. devel. adv. bd., 2000 World Trade Adv. Bd., 1997; chmn. Asia Soc.-Tex., bd. trustees, 1990—; bd. dirs. Houston World Affairs Coun., 1990; chmn. Inst. Internat. Edn., The Houston Club, 1999—, Houston Ballet Found., Houston Holocaust Mus.; mem. Mayoral Adv. Bd. for Internat. Affairs and Devel./Asia, 1999—2004; pres. Houston Forum, 2002-04; co-chmn. George Bush Monument Project, 2003-04. Contbr. articles to profl. jours. Chmn. immigration reform Gov.'s Task Force of Tex., 1984—87; mem. Bush-Cheney Transition Adv. Com., 2000—01. Admiral Texan Navy, 2003. Decorated knight comdr. 2d class Order of the Crown (Thailand), comdr. 3d class Exalted Order of White Elephant (Thailand); Rotary Internat. fellow U. Concepción, Chile, 1964; recipient Houston Internat. Svc. award Houston Jaycees, 1996, Disting. Friend of China award U.S. China Friendship Found., 2000; honoree Am. Immigration Law Found., 1998' commd. adm. Tex. Navy, Gov. Rick Perry, 2003. Mem. ABA (chmn. immigration com. internat. law and practice sect. 1982-90, chmn. coordinating com. on immigration and law 1987-89, fgn. rels. com. 2000—), Am. Immigration Lawyers Assn. (pres. 1981-82, Outstanding Svc. award 1985), Tex. Bar Assn. (chmn. com. law on immigration and nationality 1984-86), Tex. Bd. Legal Specialization (chmn. immigration adv. commn. 1979—), Houston Bar Assn., Asia Soc. (trustee 1992—, chmn. Houston Ctr. 1992—), Rotary, Houston Club (pres. 2001). Methodist. Avocations: mountain climbing, photography, travel. Home: 17 Courtlandt Pl Houston TX 77006-4013 Office: Tindall & Foster 2800 Chase Tower 600 Travis St Ste 2800 Houston TX 77002-3094 E-mail: cfoster@tindallfoster.com.

FOSTER, CHARLES H., real estate executive; With Lawyers Title, 1979-80, sr. v.p.-CFO, 1980-88, pres., 1988-90, CEO, 1990-91, LandAm. Fin. Group, Inc., 1991—2004, Chmn., 1991—. Mem. nat. adv. coun. Fannie Mae, 1999-2000; bd. dirs. Universal Corp., SunTrust Bank. Past chmn. Greater Richmond C. of C. Mem. Am. Land Title Assn. (pres.) Office: LandAm Fin Group Inc 101 Gateway Ctr Pky Richmond VA 23235

FOSTER, CHARLES HENRY WHEELWRIGHT, former foundation officer, consultant, author; b. Boston, Mar. 18, 1927; s. Reginald Candler and Frances Helen (Hoar) F.; m. Barbara Ann Duchaine, Sept 19, 1953; children: Frances H., Jonathan R., Susan C. BA, Harvard U., 1951; BSF, U. Mich., 1953, MS, 1956; PhD, Johns Hopkins U., 1969; DPA (hon.), Suffolk U., 1971; MA (hon.), Yale U., 1977. Exec. sec. Wildlife Conservation Inc., Boston,

1953-55; cons. Mass. Water Resources Commn., Boston, 1956-59; commr. Mass. Dept. Natural Resources, Boston, 1959-66; pres. Nature Conservancy, Washington, 1966-67; sr. staff mem. Conservation Found., Washington, 1967-68; chmn. bd. N.E. Natural Resources Ctr., Boston, 1969-70; sec. Mass. Exec. Office Environ. Affairs, Boston, 1971-75; sr. staff mem. A. D. Little, Inc., Cambridge, Mass., 1975-76; prof. environ. policy U. Mass., Amherst, 1975-76; dean Sch. Forestry and Environ. Studies Yale U., 1976-81; vis. scholar Stanford U., 1981-82; rsch. assoc. U. Calif., Santa Cruz, 1982; scholar in residence U. Va., 1983; pres. W. Alton Jones Found., Charlottesville, Va., 1983. Adj. prof. environ. studies Tufts U., 1984-85; vis. rsch. prof. Clark U., 1985-86; adj. rsch. fellow Harvard U., 1986—; vis. prof. environ. studies Brown U., 1987; cons., lectr. in field. Trustee of numerous natural resources and ednl. orgns. With U.S. Army, 1945-47. Bullard fellow Harvard U., 1969-70 Fellow AAAS; mem. Soc. Am. Foresters, Am. Water Resources Assn., Harvard Club (Boston). Office Phone: 617-495-1351. E-mail: charles_foster@harvard.edu.

FOSTER, CRAIG ALLEN, plastic surgeon; b. Mpls., Aug. 31, 1948; MD, U. Minn., 1974. Diplomate Am. Bd. Plastic Surgery, Am. Bd. Otolaryngology. Intern U. Minn., Mpls.; resident in gen. surgery U. Minn. Hosps., resident in otolaryngology; resident in plastic surgery NYU, N.Y.C.; pvt. practice plastic surgery N.Y.C.; plastic surgeon Manhattan EE Hosp., N.Y.C., N.Y. EE Infirmary, N.Y.C.; assoc. prof. N.Y. Med. Coll. Office: 850 Park Ave New York NY 10021-1845

FOSTER, DALE WARREN, political scientist, educator, management consultant, real estate broker, accountant; b. Bryan, Tex., Mar. 7, 1950; s. William Henry and Maysie Blanche (Hembree) F. BBA, Tex. A&M U., 1972, MA, 1979, Cert. in Profl. Teaching, 1987; BS, U. Houston, 1981, MEd, 1983; AAS, Houston C.C. Sys., 1982. Cert. in property mgmt. Dept. mgr. J.C. Penney Co., Bryan, 1973-74; shopper advt. mgr. Harte-Hanks Newspapers/Daily Eagle, Bryan, 1975-76; bus. mgr., contr. S.M. Hardee Enterprises, College Station, Tex., 1976-78; ops. mgr. Western Food Svcs., Inc., Pasadena, Tex., 1978-80; internal auditor Hermann Hosp., Houston, 1980-82; high sch. tchr. Cypress-Fairbanks Independent Sch. Dist., Houston, 1983-84; alternative sch. tchr. Alief Independent Sch. Dist., Houston, 1984-88; gov. prof. Houston C.C. System, 1980—, chmn. govt. dept. co-op program, 1992—; lead instr. Houston C.C. Sys., 1993—; supr. student tchr. U. Houston, 1989-90. Adj. instr. North Harris County Coll., Houston, 1983-96; fin. cons. Pro-Trac Econ. Planning Adv. Bd., Denver, 1985-86; Presdl. Scholars lectr. Minority Students Honors Program, Houston, 1986-89; coord. legis. practicum Harris County Congl. Internship Program, 1988—; exch. tchr., The Netherlands, 1992. Co-editor textbook supplement, curriculum guide, departmental political reader; author classroom instructional project. Mem. adv. com. Hermann Affiliated Fed. Credit Union, Houston, 1980-82; mem. fin. coun. Harris County Dem. Com., 1991-93; mem. dean's coun. U. Houston, 1992-96; trustee, treas. Wilmington-Barnard Found., 1992—. Named Tchr. of Yr., Cy.-Fair H.S., 1984, Alief Individualized Study Ctr., 1987, Master Tchr. Nat. Leadership Inst. U. Tex., Austin, 1991, host tchr. Washington Week Intern Program, 1995; recipient Adj. Teaching and Comty. Svc. award North Harris County Coll. Dist., 1990, Teaching Excellence medal Nat. Inst. Staff and Orgn. Devel., 1991, 98; Fulbright scholar, 1992, 98; Robert A. Taft fellow L.B.J. Sch. Pub. Affairs, 1995, Fulbright-Hays fellowship U.S. Dept. Edn., 1998. Fellow Am. Bd. Master Educators; mem. Tex. Jr. Coll. Tchrs. Assn., Tex. Coun. Social Studies, Inst. Mgmt. Accts., Am. Fin. Assn., Fulbright Assn., Houston C.C. Sys. Faculty Assn. (treas. 1997-2000, v.p. 2000-01, pres.-elect 2001-02, pres. 2002-03, Outstanding Tchr. award 1991, Tchr. of Yr. 1997), Phi Theta Kappa, Alpha Phi Omega, Kappa Delta Pi. Democrat. Baptist. Avocations: travel, reading, bowling, water sports, outdoor activities. Office: Houston C C NW 1010 W Sam Houston Pkwy N Houston TX 77043 E-mail: corps1972@yahoo.com.

FOSTER, DANIEL WILLETT, medical educator; b. Marlin, Tex., Mar. 4, 1930; married, 1955; 3 children. BA, Tex. Western Coll., 1951; MD, U. Tex., 1955. Intern internal medicine Parkland Meml. Hosp., 1955-56, asst. resident, 1956-58, chief resident, 1958-59; fellow biochemistry U. Tex. Southwestern Med. Sch., 1959-60; investigator Nat. Inst. Arthritis and Metabolic Disease, 1960-62; from asst. prof. to assoc. prof. U. Tex. Southwestern Med. Sch., 1962-69, prof. Dallas, 1969-86, Jan and Henri Bromberg prof., 1986-89, chmn. dept. internal medicine, 1988—2003, Donald W. Seldin Disting. chair, 1989—2003, John Denis McGarry Disting. chair, 2003—. Mem. metabolism study sect. NIH, 1968-70, chmn. sect., 1970-72, mem. NIDDK adv. coun., 1987-90, bd. sci. counselors Clin. Ctr., 1991-95, 98—; chief internal medicine Parkland Meml. Hosp. and Univ. Med. Ctr., Tex.; mem. Nat. Diabetes Adv. Bd., 1981-84; chair sci. adv. bd. Hartford Found.; cons. VA Hosp., Dallas, Presbyn. Hosp., Baylor U. Med. Ctr.; mem. sci. adv. bd. Merck, Inc., 1991-94; mem. sci. adv. coun. Abbott Labs., 1998—; mem. Pres.'s Coun. on Bioethics, 2002—. Assoc. editor: Jour. Clin. Investigation, 1972-77; editor: Diabetes, 1978-83. Master ACP; fellow AAAS, Am. Acad. of Arts and Scis.; mem. Assn. Profs. of Medicine (pres. 1997-98), Inst. Medicine-NAS, Am. Soc. Clin. Investigation, Am. Diabetes Assn. (Banting medal 1984, Joslin medal 1984, Upjohn award 1988), Am. Fedn. Clin. Rsch., Am. Soc. Biol. Chemists, Assn. Am. Physicians. Office: U Tex Health Sci Ctr Dept Internal Medicine Dallas TX 75235-9030*

FOSTER, DAVID LEE, lawyer; b. Des Moines, Dec. 13, 1933; s. Carl Dewitt and Dorothy Jo (Bell) F.; m. Marilyn Lee Bokemeier, Aug. 12, 1957 (div. June 1978); children: Gwendolyn Foster Reed, Cynthia Foster Curry, David Lee Jr.; m. Kathleen Carol Walsh, Mar. 24, 1979; 1 child, John Wickersham. Student, Simpson Coll., 1951-52; BA, U. Iowa, 1954, JD, 1957. Bar: Iowa 1957, N.Y. 1958, Ohio 1964, U.S. Supreme Ct. 1975. Assoc. Cravath, Swaine & Moore, N.Y.C., 1957-63; from assoc. to ptnr. Jones, Day, Cockley & Reavis, Cleve., 1963-72; ptnr., counsel Willkie Farr & Gallagher, N.Y.C., 1972—2004. Lectr. So. Meth. U., 1979-84, U. Pitts., 1984, Practicing Law Inst., N.Y.C., 1984-85; mem. adv. bd. Civil RICO Report LRP Publs., 1988—; bd. govs. N.Y. Ins. Exch., 1987-96. Contbr. chpts. to book, articles to legal jours. Mem., bd. trustees Cardigan Mountain Sch., 1995-2004, v.p., 2002-2003. Served with USNR, 1952-60. Fellow Am. Coll. Trial Lawyers, Internat. Acad. Trial Lawyers (bd. dirs. 1987-92); mem. Am. Counsel Assn. (pres. 1994-95, bd. dirs. 1992-98), River Club, Order of Coif, Phi Beta Kappa. Office Phone: 845-677-8189. Personal E-mail: qkwick@msn.com.

FOSTER, DAVID RAMSEY, soap company executive; b. London, May 24, 1920; (parents Am. citizens); s. Robert Bagley and Josephine (Ramsey) F.; m. Anne Firth, Aug. 2, 1957 (dec. June 1994); children: Sarah, Victoria; m. Alexandra Chang, May 24, 1996. Student in econs., Gonville and Caius Coll., Cambridge (Eng.) U., 1938. With Colgate-Palmolive Co. and affiliates, 1946-79; v.p., gen. mgr. Europe Colgate-Palmolive Internat., 1961-65, v.p., gen. mgr. household products divsn. parent co. N.Y.C., 1965-68, exec. v.p., 1968-70, pres., 1970-75, CEO, 1971-79, chmn., 1975-79. Author: Wings Over the Sea, 1990. Trustee Woman's Sport Found. Served to lt. comdr. Royal Naval Vol. Res., 1940-46. Decorated Disting. Svc. Order, D.S.C. with bar, Mentioned in Despatches (2); recipient Victor award City of Hope, 1974, Herbert Hoover Meml. award, 1976, Adam award, 1977, Harriman award Boys Club N.Y., 1977, Charter award St. Francis Coll., 1978, Walter Hagen award, 1978, Patty Berg award, 1986, Commr.'s award LPGA, 1995. Mem. Soc. Mayflower Descs., Hawks Club (Cambridge U.), Royal Ancient Golf Club (St. Andrews, Scotland), Royal Cinque Ports Golf Club (life), Sunningdale Golf Club, Sankaty Head Golf Club, Racquet and Tennis Club (N.Y.C.), Mission Hills Country Club, Bally Bunion Golf Club (life). Home: PO Box 2327 Vincentown NJ 08088-2327

FOSTER, DAVID SCOTT, lawyer; b. White Plains, N.Y., July 13, 1938; s. William James and Ruth Elizabeth (Seltzer) F.; m. Eleanore Stalker, Dec. 21, 1959; children: David Scott, Robert McEachron. BA in Physics, Amherst Coll., 1960; LLB, Harvard U., 1963. Bar: N.Y. 1963, D.C. 1977, Calif. 1978. Jud. law clk. U.S. Dist. Ct. (so. dist.) N.Y., 1963-64; assoc. Debevoise & Plimpton, N.Y.C., 1964-72; from counsel atty.-advisor to internat. tax counsel U.S. Treasury Dept., Washington, 1972-77; ptnr. Brobeck, Phleger & Harrison, San Francisco, 1978-90, Coudert Bros., San Francisco, 1990-91, Thelen, Reid & Priest LLP, San Francisco, 1991—. Mem. ABA, San Francisco Bar Assn., Internat. Fiscal Assn., Western Pension and Benefits Confs., St. Francis Yacht Club (San Francisco), Phi Beta Kappa, Sigma Xi. Presbyterian. Office: Thelen Reid & Priest LLP 101 2nd St Ste 1800 San Francisco CA 94105-3659 Office Phone: 415-369-7020. Business E-Mail: dsfoster@thelenreid.com.

FOSTER, DEBORAH SIMMONS, elementary school educator; b. Memphis, Nov. 1957; d. William Thomas Simmons and Maxie Lee (Broadway) Carter; m. Larry Allan Foster, June 5, 1983 (dec.); children: Ashley Nicole, Kelly Elizabeth, David William. BS in Elem. Edn., Spl. Edn., Memphis State U., 1980. Nat. Bd. cert. tchr., 2001. Tchr. Ednl. Svcs., Memphis, 1979-83; tchr. spl. edn. Southaven (Miss.) Jr. High/High Sch., 1981-83; tchr. spl. edn. learning disabled and regular edn. Whitesburg Mid. Sch., Huntsville (Ala.) City Schs., 1985—87, elem. tchr., 1987—. Mem., exec. bd., faculty rep. PTA, 1989—. Mem. NEA, Coun. for Exceptional Children, Nat. Assn. Acad. Suprs. and Prins., Ala. Edn. Assn., Huntsville Edn. Assn. Avocations: drawing, reading. Home: 1014 Riviera Ave SE Huntsville AL 35802-2647

FOSTER, DORIS REDMAN, retired foreign language educator; b. Butler, Pa., Mar. 3, 1937; d. Edward Gottlieb and Nellie Elizabeth (Mullin) Redman; m. John Kennedy Foster, Jr., June 11, 1960; children: John Kennedy III, Edward Allen. BA in German, Chatham Coll., 1959; MEd in Reading, U. Pa., Edinboro, 1978. Cert. tchr., Pa. Latin tchr. Northeastern Beaver County Schs., Ellwood City, Pa., 1959-60, Alexandria (Va.) Pub. Schs., 1960-62; edn. specialist with IRS, U.S. Govt., Washington, 1962-63; social studies tchr. Hampshire County Schs., Romney, W.Va., 1963-65; fgn. lang. tchr. Crawford Cen. Schs., Meadville, Pa., 1978—98, ret., 1998. Founder Women's Svcs., Inc., Meadville, 1977-80, 1st pres. 1978-80. Mem. AAUW, Am. Assn. Tchrs. of German (v.p. western Pa. chpt. 1987-89, pres. 1989-91), Am. Classical League, Am. Coun. on Teaching Fgn. Lang., Pa. Modern Lang. Tchrs., Meadville LWV (pres. 1972-73), Delta Kappa Gamma. Presbyterian. Home: 714 Alden St Meadville PA 16335-2351

FOSTER, DOROTHY D., music educator, composer, pre-school educator; d. Clarence H. DeMar and Margaret Lobdell Ilsley; m. Kenneth C. Foster (div.); children: Carol Homchick, William C. MusB in Composition, Boston U., 1952; postgrad., Peabody Conservatory, 1953; MA in Composition, Calif. State U., Fullerton, 1972; AA, Santa Ana Coll., 1995. Tchr. piano, organ, composition pvt. practice, Orange, Calif., 1970—2004; organist 1st Congrl. Ch., Buena Park, 1978—84; organist, dir. Placentia Meth. Ch., 1984—87, St. Wilfrids Episcopal Ch., Huntington Beach, 1987—89, St. Stephens Luth. Ch., Fullerton, 1989—99; organist 1st Ch. Christ, Orange, 1999—2005; tchr. piano, organ, composition pvt. practice, Cypress, 2005—. Composer: Two Psalms, Voice, Organ, 2004, Four Childrens Christmas Songs, 2004, Duets for Two Violins, 2004. Founder, dir. Orange County Children's Chorus, Placentia, 1980—85; helper girls club Hilltoppers, Tustin, 1965—70. Recipient 1st Pl. Composition Contest, Calif. Music Tchrs. Assn., 1969. Mem.: Am. Guild Organists, Mu Phi Epsilon. Avocations: gardening, interior decorating. Home and Studio: 14903 Cypress Waters Dr Cypress TX 77429

FOSTER, DUDLEY EDWARDS, JR., musician, educator; b. Orange, NJ, Oct. 5, 1935; s. Dudley Edwards and Margaret (DePoy) Foster. Student, Occidental Coll., 1953—56; AB, UCLA, 1957, MA, 1958; postgrad., U. So. Calif., 1961—73. Lectr. music. Immaculate Heart Coll., LA, 1960—63; dir. music Holy Faith Episcopal Ch., Inglewood, Calif., 1964—67; lectr. music Calif. State U., LA, 1968—71; assoc. prof. music LA Mission Coll., 1975—83, prof., 1983—, chmn. dept. music, 1977—. Mem. dist. acad. senate LA CC's, 1991—92; dir. music 1st Luth. Ch., LA, 1968—72. Organist, pianist, harpsichordist: numerous recital; composer: O Sacrum Convivium for Trumpet and Organ, 1973, Passacaglia for Brass Instruments, 1969, Introduction, Atroso & Fuque for Cello and Piano, 1974. Recipient Associated STudents Faculty award, 1988; fellow Trinity Coll. Music, London, 1960. Mem.: Mediaeval Acad. Am., LA Coll. Tchrs. Assn., Town Hall Calif., Acad. Senate, Nat. Assn. of Scholars, Am. Musicol. Soc., Am. Guild Organists. Republican. Angelican. Office: LA Mission Coll Dept Music 13356 Eldridge Ave Sylmar CA 91342-3200 E-mail: fostermusic@earlink.net, defoster@lamc.org.

FOSTER, EDWARD JOHN, engineer physicist; b. N.Y.C., Aug. 10, 1938; s. John Paul and Mildred Julia (Hassiak) F.; m. Sandra Thornton Christie (div. 1989); children: Sandra Foster Swindler, Mary Elizabeth Foster. BS in Physics cum laude, Fordham U., 1959; MS in Physics, Syracuse (N.Y.) U., 1965; MBA, Iona U., 1973. Mgr. magnetics dept. Shephard Industries, Inc., Nutley, N.J., 1960-61; founder, CEO S.E.D. Memories, Inc., Rutherford, N.J., 1961-63; br. mgr. rsch. CBS Labs., Stamford, Conn., 1963-73; v.p. tech. ByWord Corp., Armonk, N.Y., 1973-76; pres. Diversified Sci. Labs., Marco Island, Fla., 1976—. Cons. Electronics Industries Assn., Washington; dep. tech. advisor to U.S Nat. Com. Internat. Electrotech. Com. TC100, Geneva, Switzerland, 1982—. Author: Effects and Degrees of Error of Modulation-Demodulation, 1965; contbg. editor: Acquisition Reduction and Analysis of Acoustical Data, 1974; contbr. articles to profl. jours. Woodrow Wilson fellow, 1959, fellowship NSF, 1959-60. Fellow: Audio Engring. Soc. (v.p. ea. U.S./Can.); mem.: IEEE (sr.), Delta Mu Delta, Sigma Xi. Achievements include patents for Automatic Recording Level Control, Directional Microphone Arrays. Home and Office: 1952 San Marco Rd Marco Island FL 34145-6723 E-mail: DivSciLab@comcast.net.

FOSTER, EDWARD PAUL (TED FOSTER), process industries executive; b. Pawtucket, RI, Aug. 23, 1945; s. Edward Francis and Vivian Adrienne (Davagne) F.; m. Barbara Philomena Cook, Dec. 17, 1965 (div. Apr. 1978); children: Edward Robert, Gwendolyn Lucy; m. Johanna Helena Klaassen, June, 1985 (div. 1988). BSChemE with distinction, U. R.I., 1967; MSChemE, Worcester Poly. Inst., 1970; MBA, Lehigh U., 1981. Mfg. melting engr. Corning Glass Works, Central Falls, R.I., 1966-67; group leader rsch. and devel. The Babcock & Wilcox Co., Alliance, Ohio, 1968-71, mgr. tampella process Barberton, Ohio, 1972-74; from comml. devel. engr. to dir. bus. devel. in gases, metallurgy, coal, energy, chems. and polymers, and environ. areas Air Products and Chem., Inc., Allentown, Pa., 1974—. Cons. U.S. Army Natick (Mass.) Lab., 1966-67. Contbr. articles to profl. jours. Chmn. fin. Unitarian Ch., Bethleham, Pa., 1985, chmn. social, 1983-84. NDEA fellow HEW, 1967-69; ROTC scholar U.S. Army, 1965, Nat. Merit scholar, 1963. Mem. AIChE, Comml. Devel. Assn. (vice chmn. fall meeting 1996, nat. program chmn. 1997-99, bd. dirs.), Am. Chem. Soc., Comml. Devel. and Mktg. Assn. (bd. dirs. 2000—03), Gasification Tech. Coun. (bd. dirs., 2004-), Phi Kappa Phi, Tau Beta Pi, Theta Chi. Achievements include patents in field. Avocations: tennis, downhill skiing, sailing. Home: 6023 Fairway Ln Allentown PA 18106-9610 Office: Air Products and Chems 7201 Hamilton Blvd Allentown PA 18195-1526 Office Phone: 610-481-5307.

FOSTER, GARY, publishing executive, information technology executive; BA in Econs. and Internat. Studies, Am. U., 1977; MBA in Fin., U. Pa., 1984. With White House Comm. Agy., Washington, 1972—75; unit supr. budget rev. divsn. Exec. Office of the Pres., Office Mgmt. and Budget, Washington, 1978—81; various fin. and corp. devel. positions COMSAT Corp., Washington, 1983—89; region svc. mgr. GE Med. Sys., Milw., 1989—92, gen. mgr. svcs. mktg., 1992—97; pres. software, svcs. and corp. mktg. Foxboro (Mass.) Corp., 1997—98; pres., CEO PatientKeeper Inc. (formerly Virtmed Inc.), Brighton, Mass., 2000—02; pres., CEO global med. rsch. divsn. Wolters Kluwer Health, 2004—. Office: OVID Techs 20th Fl 333 Seventh Ave New York NY 10001

FOSTER, GEORGE MCCLELLAND, JR., anthropologist, educator; b. Sioux Falls, SD, Oct. 9, 1913; s. George McClelland and Mary (Slutz) F.; m. Mary Fraser LeCron, Jan. 6, 1938; children: Jeremy, Melissa Bowerman. BS, Northwestern U., 1935; PhD, U. Calif. at Berkeley, 1941; DHL (hon.), So. Meth. U., 1990. Instr. Syracuse U., 1941-42; lectr. UCLA, 1942-43; vis. prof. U. Calif.-Berkeley, 1953-55, prof. anthropology, 1955-79, prof. emeritus, 1979—, chmn. dept., 1958-61; acting dir. Mus. Anthropology, 1955—58; lectr. pub. health, 1955-64. Anthropologist Inst. Social Anthropology, Smithsonian Instn., 1943-52, dir., 1946-1952; field rsch. Calif. Indians, 1937, Spain, 1949-50, Mexico, 1940—2004; adviser AID, India-Pakistan, 1955, Afghanistan, 1957, Zambia, 1961, 62, Nepal, 1965, Indonesia, 1973-74, WHO, Sri Lanka, 1975, Malaysia, 1978, India, 1979, 80, 81, Manila, 1983; adviser UNICEF, Geneva, 1976 Author: Traditional Cultures and the Impact of Technological Change, 1962, Tzintzuntzan: Mexican Peasants in a Changing World, 1967, Applied Anthropology, 1969, (with B. Anderson) Medical Anthropology, 1978, Hippocrates' Latin American Legacy, 1993, others, also monographs and articles. Recipient Berkeley citation, 1979; Guggenheim fellow, 1949; fellow Center for Advanced Study in Behavioral Scis., 1969-70 Fellow Am. Anthrop. Assn. (pres. 1970, Disting. Service award 1980); mem. Southwestern Anthrop. Assn. (Disting. Research award 1981), Nat. Acad. Scis., Am. Acad. Arts and Scis., Soc. Applied Anthropology (Malinowski award 1982) Clubs: Cosmos (Washington). Home: 790 San Luis Rd Berkeley CA 94707-2030 E-mail: gmfoster@berkeley.edu.

FOSTER, HARRY ELLSWORTH, retired librarian; b. Jefferson City, Mo., Apr. 28, 1926; s. Harry Clarke and Anna A. (Frike) F.; m. Liliane Madeleine Lucie Greiner, Nov. 30, 1963. BA, Dartmouth Coll., 1950; MS in Libr. Sci., Columbia U., 1951. Cataloger Enoch Pratt Free Libr., Balt., 1951-53; head processing Md. State Dept. Edn., Balt., 1954-60; spl. asst. Va. Mus. Fine Arts, Richmond, Va., 1960-61; head libr., prof. Anne Arundel C.C., Arnold, Md., 1961-93; ret., 1993. Contbr. articles to profl. jours. Sec. Anne Arundel County Trust for Preservation, Annapolis, Md., 1975—. With USNR, 1944-47. Democrat. Presbyterian. Avocations: travel, photography, music, local history, architecture. Home: 1025 Omar Dr Crownsville MD 21032-1233 Address: 8 Rue Des Cesars 68180 Horbourg-Wihr France

FOSTER, HELEN R., language educator; b. Angleton, Tex., Oct. 19, 1950; d. C. Nolan and E. Lanore Ashley; m. Don L. Foster, Aug. 1, 1970; children: Thomas Blair, Mary Kathryn. BA, U. Tex., El Paso, Tex., 1990, MA, 1994; PhD, Purdue U., 2001. Ops. supr. Data Processing Divsn. Tex. Commerce Bank, Houston, 1975—84; adj. instr. U. Tex., El Paso, 1994—95; grad. instr. Purdue U., West Lafayette, Ind., 1995—97; vis. asst. prof. U. Tex., El Paso, 1998—99, asst. prof., 1999—. Instr. El Paso (Tex.) C.C., 1994; cons. Dept. Scis. U. Tex., 1994—95, instr., 1994; presenter in field; mem. various coms. U. Tex., 1997—. Contbr. articles to profl. jours. Mem.: AAUW, Internat. Reading Assn., Assn. Bus. Comm., Nat. Tchrs. Tech. Writing, Coll. Composition and Comm., Nat. Coun. Tchrs. English, Modern Lang. Assn., Coalition Women Scholars in History of Rhetoric and Composition, Sigma Tau Delta. Home: 6305 Los Altos Drive El Paso TX 79912 Office: U Tex English Dept 500 W University Ave El Paso TX 79968-8900

FOSTER, HOPE S., lawyer; b. 1948; BA, Wellesley Coll., 1970; JD with honors, George Washington U., 1973. Bar: DC 1973. Mem. Mintz Levin Cohn Ferris Glovsky & Popeo PC, Washington, co-mgr., Health Care Sect. Contbr. articles to profl. jour.; spkr. in field. Mem.: Am. Health Lawyers Assn., ABA (white collar crime com., health care com., antitrust com., health care fraud & abuse subcom.), DC Bar. Office: Mintz Levin Cohn Ferris Glovsky & Popeo PC 701 Pennsylvania Ave NW Washington DC 20004 Office Phone: 202-661-8758. Office Fax: 202-434-7400. Business E-Mail: hsfoster@mintz.com.

FOSTER, HUNTER, actor; b. June 25, 1969; m. Jennifer Cody. BFA in Theatre Studies, U. Mich., 1992. Actor: (nat. tour) Cats, 1992; (Broadway plays) Grease, 1994, King David, 1997, Les Miserables, 1998, Footloose, 1998, Urinetown, 2001 (nominee, Tony award), Little Shop of Horrors, 2003 (nominee, Tony award, best actor in a muscial, 2004), The Producers, 2004; (plays) Children of Eden, 1997, Martin Guerre, 1999, The Man in the White Suit, 2005; writer of libretto Summer of '42, 2002.

FOSTER, IAN TREMERE, computer scientist; b. Wellington, New Zealand, Jan. 1, 1959; arrived in US, 1989; s. Peter Kinnear and Eileen June (Gapes) F.; m. Angela Claire Smyth; children: Alexander Peter, Imogen Teresa. BSc with honors, U. Canterbury, Christchurch, New Zealand, 1979; diploma, PhD, Imperial Coll., London, 1988. Rsch. assoc., dept. computing Imperial Coll., London, 1985-88; asst. computer scientist Argonne Nat. Lab., Ill., 1989-93, scientist, 1993-96; assoc. prof. U. Chgo., 1996-2000; sr. scientist Argonne Nat. Lab., 1997-2000, assoc. div. dir., sr. scientist, head, Distributed Systems Lab Math. & Computer Sci. Argonne, Ill.; Arthur Holly Compton prof. computer sci. U. Chgo., 2000—. Software architect I-Way Experiment U. Chgo., 1995; co-founder Global Grid Forum; program chair High Performance Distributed Computing Conf., 1997, gen. chair, 2000, 01; program chair Frontiers of Massively Parallel Computation Conf., 1998; application evangelist chair Information Arch. Com. Conf., 2000; mem. SCxy Steering Com.; co-program chair HPC Asia, 2001; information arch. chair SC'2001, 2001; mem. World Tech. Network, 2003. Author: Strand: New Concepts in Parallel Programming, 1990, Systems Programming in Parallel Logic Languages, 1990, Designing and Building Parallel Programs, 1995, The Grid: Blueprint for a New Computing Infrastructure, 1999; contbr. to technical papers and reports; mem. editl. bd. IEEE Transactions on Parallel and Distributed Systems. Named Innovator of Yr., R&D Mag., 2003, Top 50 Agenda Setter, Silicon.com, 2003; named one of Ten Technologies that Will Change the World, MIT Tech. Review, 2003; recipient Tech. Innovation award, Brit. Computer Soc., 1989, Next Generation award, Global Info. Infrastructure, 1997, Gordon Bell award, 2001, Lovelace Medal, 2002, Most Promising New Technology award, R&D Mag., 2002, Fed. Lab. Consortium Tech. Transfer award, 2002, Ill. Innovation award, 2003, Innovator of Yr., InfoWorld, 2003. Fellow: British Computer Soc.; mem.: Assn. for Computing Machinery., AAAS. Achievements include co-design of Strand parallel programming language; contributions in algorithms and technologies for parallel computing; leadership in design of middleware for wide area computing; co-design of Globus network computing system. Address: U Chgo 1100 E 58th St Ryerson Hall Rm 155 Chicago IL 60637 Office Phone: 630-252-4619, 773-702-3487. Office Fax: 630-252-9556, 773-702-8487. Business E-Mail: foster@mcs.anl.gov, foster@cs.uchicago.edu.*

FOSTER, JAMES CALDWELL, dean, historian; b. Madison, Wis., Apr. 10, 1943; s. Mark A. and Ruth C. (Caldwell) Foster; m. Diane L. Mohn, Sept. 3, 1966 (dec. Sept. 2001); children: Jeffrey, Justin, Joshua; m. Mary Louise Pusch, June 25, 2004. BS, U. Wis., 1967; PhD, Cornell U., 1972. Assoc. dir. Wis. Humanities Commn., NEH, Madison, 1977-78; asst. prof. U. Alaska, College, 1971-74; dir. labor studies Ariz. State U., Tempe, 1974-81, Sch. for Workers, U. Wis., Madison, 1981-84; assoc. dean of campus Ohio State U., Newark, 1984-87; dean Coll. Arts, Scis. and Lit. U. Mich., Dearborn, 1987-92; dir. acad. affairs Pa. State U.-Fayette, Uniontown, 1993-95; v.p. acad. affairs Walsh U., Canton, Ohio, 1995-99, Mt. Senario Coll., Wis., 1999—2000, Mount Marty Coll., Yankton, SD, 2001—. Presenter North Ctrl. Assn. Coll. and Schs., 2005. Author: The Union Politic, 1975, American Labor in the Southwest, 1982; newspaper columnist, Kenosha (Wis.) Labor, 1981— (1st, 2d and 3d best story awards for column Lest We Forget, AFL-CIO 1984); commentator Wis. Pub. Radio, Madison, 1981-84. Exxon Edn. grantee, Tempe, 1976, Rockefeller Found. grantee, Tempe, 1977, German Marshall Fund grantee, Madison, 1981. Mem. Indsl. Rels. Rsch. Assn., Am. Arbitration Assn. Home: PO Box 509 Yankton SD 57078 Office: Mt Marty Coll 1105 W 8th St Yankton SD 57078 Office Phone: 605-668-1584. Personal E-mail: jcfosterml@earthlink.net. Business E-Mail: jfoster@mtmc.edu.

FOSTER, JAMES FRANKLIN, professional sports management executive; b. Iowa; s. M. (Egerer) F.; m. Susan Jane Salsi, July 19, 1976. BGS, U. Iowa, 1972; postgrad., U. Pa., 1982. Retail advt. specialist Maytag Co., Newton, Iowa, 1972-78; founder, gen. mgr. Iowa Nite Hawks AAA Pro Football Club, 1974-78; founder, dir. Am. Pro Football Tour of Europe, 1977, 79; promotion mgr. NFL Properties, Inc., N.Y.C., 1979-82; asst. gen. mgr. Ariz. Wranglers Pro Football Club, 1982-83; exec. v.p. Chgo. Blitz Pro Football Club, 1983-84; v.p. mktg. Chgo. Sting Indoor Soccer Promotions-Burke Promo Mktg. Inc., 1984—85; founder, pres. Arena Football, Chgo., 1985-90, commr., 1985-92, spl. cons., 1992-94; founder, mng. owner Iowa Barnstormers Arena Football, Des Moines, 1994—, Quad City Steamwheelers Arena

Football, Davenport, Iowa, 1999—. Co-founder Arena Football 2 League. Mem. Ill. Quad Cities Chamber, Davenport (Iowa) One Chamber; active YMCA. Recipient Golden Helmet Excellence award NFL Properties, Inc., 1981-82; named Minor Pro Football Exec. of Yr., Pro Football Weekly, 1976, No. States League Gen. Mgr. of Yr., AAA Football, 1976, Exec. of Yr., Arena Football League, 1995-96; named to Minor Pro Football Hall of Fame, 1982, one of Inaugural Class, Arena Football Hall of Fame, 1998. Mem. Iowa State Hist. Soc., Antique and Classic Boat Soc., Boat Owners Assn. U.S., U. Iowa Alumni Assn. (pres.'s club), Aircraft Owners and Pilots Assn., Nat. Iowa Varsity Lettermans Club, Iowa Assn. R.R. Passengers, Commn. Airforce (Iowa unit), U. Iowa Champions Ath. Club. Methodist. Achievements include patents for arena football game system. Home: 901 Mississippi Ave Davenport IA 52801-4418 Office: 200 W 3rd St Davenport IA 52801 Office Phone: 563-324-4888.

FOSTER, JAMES HENRY, advertising and public relations executive; b. Kansas City, Mo., May 14, 1933; s. Wendell F. and Lillian M. (East) F. BA, Drake U., 1955, postgrad., 1957. Reporter, editor Des Moines (Iowa) Register, 1951-61; pub. rels. and advt. exec. J. Walter Thompson Co., N.Y.C., 1961-73, 79-99, v.p., 1970-73; sr. v.p., gen. mgr. Brouillard Comm. divsn., N.Y.C., 1979-81, exec. v.p., gen. mgr., 1981-84, pres., CEO, 1984-94; chmn., CEO Brouillard Comm., 1994-97, chmn., 1997-99, chmn. emeritus, 1999—2003; v.p. pub. affairs Western Union Corp., Upper Saddle River, 1973-79; pres. Reputation Mgmt. Strategies, Durango, Colo., 1999—; bd. dirs. Music in the Mountains, Inc., Durango, 1999—, pres., 2000—03. Bd. dirs. Fort Lewis Coll. Found., 1999—, sec., 2005. Mem. Union League Club (N.Y.C.), Petroleum Club (Durango). Presbyterian. Office: Reputation Mgmt Strategies 1472 E Third Ave Durango CO 81301-5244

FOSTER, JAMES REUBEN, travel company executive; b. Chgo., May 28, 1930; s. Reuben Aaron and Marion (Philipson) F.; m. Claire Lynn Block, Aug. 16, 1953; children: Kim Petracca, Craig James, Kyle Foster Weinstein. BA, Trinity Coll., 1952; JD, Yale U., 1955. Bar: Ill. 1955, U.S. Ct. Claims 1955, U.S. Ct. Mil. Appeals 1956, U.S. Ct. Customs and Patent Appeals, 1956. Trial atty. U.S. Dept. of Justice, Washington, 1955—57; v.p. L.B. Foster Co., Pitts., 1957—82; pres. Fosco Fabricators, Chgo., 1961—64; v.p., sec. Foster Industries, Inc., Pitts., Pa., 1977—97; gen. ptnr. Real Estate Partnerships, 1975—93; v.p., sec. Fostin Securities, Inc., 1978—; pres., 1994—98; chmn. bd., chief exec. officer Travel Profls. Inc., 1984—; v.p. Foster Holdings Co., Pitts., 1998—2000; also bd. dirs. Fostin Mgmt. Co., Chgo. Sec. United Comms. Sys. Inc., Chgo., 1993—; bd. dirs. Foster Industries, Inc., Pitts., Fostin Capital Co., Pitts., L.B. Foster Co., Pitts., Travel Profls., Inc., Chgo., Pelouze Scale, Evanston, Ill., 1990-94, United Comm. Sys., Inc., Chgo., Fostin Securities, Inc., Fostin Mgmt. Inc.; chmn., pres. Foster Charitable Trust. Pres. Temple Jeremiah, Northfield, Ill., 1980-83; chmn. com. Chgo. Assn. Commerce and Industry, 1971-73; trustee, chmn. com. Lakeland Health Svcs./Highland Park Hosp., 1978-84, life trustee, 1985—; vice chmn., committeeman Lake County Reps. Ctrl. Com., Ill., 1964-74; bd. dirs., sec., treas. Groveland Health Svcs., Highland Park, 1982-90, sec., 1987-90; v.p. Am. Jewish Com., 1990-96, nat. coun., 1996—, exec. bd. Chgo. chpt. 1981—; mem., chmn., exec. bd. Am. Assocs. Ben Gurion U. of the Negev, 1991-95,2002; treas. collectors forum Mus. of Contemporary Art, Chgo., 1994-97. Mem. ABA, Am. Inst. Mgmt. (pres. coun.), Std. Club (bd. dirs. 1985-92), Northmoor Country Club. Republican. Jewish. Avocations: art collector, travel, golf, photography. Office: Travel Profls Inc 500 W Madison Ave Ste 411 Chicago IL 60611-4544 Office Phone: 312-681-2500 x23. Business E-Mail: jfoster@travpros.net.

FOSTER, JANE CALTON, elementary school educator; b. Portales, N.Mex., Mar. 20, 1953; d. George Charles and Clytie Lynn Calton; children: Jill, Jodie, Jana. BA, Ea. N.Mex. U., 1981, MA, 1985. Tchr. Muleshoe (Tex.) Ind. Sch. Dist., 1981—. Mem.: Nat. Assn. Bilingual Tchrs., Tex. Classroom Tchrs. Assn., Muleshoe Classroom Tchrs. Assn. Home: 1710 W Ave E Muleshoe TX 79347 Business E-Mail: jfoster@muleshoeisd.net.

FOSTER, JODIE (ALICIA CHRISTIAN FOSTER), actress, film director, film producer; b. L.A., Nov. 19, 1962; d. Lucius and Evelyn (Almond) F.; children: Charles, Kit BA in Lit. cum laude, Yale U., 1985. Acting debut in TV show Mayberry, R.F.D, 1969; numerous other TV appearances including My Three Sons, The Courtship of Eddie's Father, Gunsmoke, Bonanza, Paper Moon, 1974-75; TV spl. The Secret Life of T.K. Dearing, 1975; TV movies include Rookie of the Year, Smile, Jenny, You're Dead; motion picture appearances include Napoleon and Samantha, 1972, One Little Indian, 1973, Tom Sawyer, 1973, Alice Doesn't Live Here Anymore, 1974, Taxi Driver, 1976 (Acad. award nominee for Best Supporting Actress), Echoes of a Summer, 1976, Bugsy Malone, 1976, Freaky Friday, 1976, Moi, Fleur Bleue, 1977, Casotto, 1977, The Little Girl Who Lives Down the Lane, 1977, Candleshoe, 1977, Foxes, 1980, Carny, 1980, O'Hara's Wife, 1982, Hotel New Hampshire, 1984, The Blood of Others, 1984, Five Corners, 1987, Siesta, 1987, Stealing Home, 1988, The Accused, 1988 (Acad. award for Best Actress, 1989), Backtrack, 1989, The Silence of the Lambs, 1991 (Golden Globe award for Best Actress in Drama, 1992, Acad. award for Best Actress, 1992, BAFTA award for best actress, 1992), Shadows and Fog, 1992, Sommersby, 1993, Maverick, 1994, Contact, 1997, Anna and The King, 1999, Panic Room, 2002; dir., actress: Little Man Tate, 1991; prodr., actress: Mesmerized, 1986, Nell, 1994 (Acad. award nominee for Best Actress 1995), The Dangerous Lives of Altar Boys, 2002; dir., prodr. Home For the Holidays, 1995; exec. prodr. (Showtime) Babydance, 1998, Waking the Dead, 2000. Recipient Golden Globe award, 1989.

FOSTER, JOE B., oil company executive; b. Arp, Tex., July 25, 1934; s. William R. and Ruth D. (Knox) Foster; m. Harriet Foster; children: Warren, Ken, Jennifer. BS in Petroleum Engring., BBA, Tex. A&M U., 1957. Jr. petroleum engr. Tenneco Oil Co., Okla. City, 1957—59, petroleum engr. Lafayette, La., 1959—62, dist. engr., 1962—66, adminstrv. asst. to exec. com. Houston, 1966—68, chief econ. planning and analysis, 1968—70, mgr. exploration, 1970—72, v.p., 1972—74, sr. v.p., 1974—76, exec. v.p., 1976—78, pres. Tenneco Oil Exploration and Prodn., 1978—81; exec. v.p. Tenneco, Inc., Houston, 1981—89; chmn., CEO Newfield Exploration Co., Houston, 1989—2000; interim chmn., CEO Baker Hughes Inc., Houston, 2000. Bd. dirs. N.J. Resources, Meml. Hermann Hosp. Sys., McDermott Internat. Inc., Newfield Exploration, Valero Energy. Bd. dirs. Houston Mus. Natural Sci., YMCA of Greater Houston; chmn. Nat. Petroleum Coun., 1989—99. 2nd lt. U.S. Army, 1958. Mem.: All Am. Wildcatters Com., Ind. Petroleum Assn. Am., Soc. Petroleum Engrs., AIME, Royal Oaks Country Club. Methodist. Office: 10000 Memorial Dr Ste 520 Houston TX 77024-3411 E-mail: j64foster@aol.com.*

FOSTER, JOE C., JR., lawyer; b. Lansing, Mich., Feb. 5, 1925; s. Joe C. and Grace E. (McComb) F.; m. Janet C. Shanks, July 6, 1946; children: Cathy Foster Young, Susan Foster Ambrose, Thomas, John, Amy Foster Trenz. Student, Wabash (Ind.) Coll., 1943—44; JD, U. Mich., 1949. Bar: Mich. 1949, Fla. 1986. Assoc. Fraser, Trebilcock, Davis & Foster, and predecessors, Lansing, 1949-53, ptnr. and shareholder, 1954-2000; shareholder Foster Zack & Lowe, P.C., Okemos, Mich., 2001—. Co-author: Independent Probate Administration, 1980, 3d edit., 1995, Informal Estat Procs. in Mich., 2000, supplements, 2002, 03. Trustee, sec. Renaud Found., Lansing, 1960-87; bd. dirs., sec. Abrams Found., Lansing, 1960—; bd. dirs., officer ACTEC Found., L.A., 1983-87, 98-2004; trustee Jr. League Endowment Found., Lansing, 1984-90; trustee, chmn. Sparrow Hosp., Lansing, 1970-84; trustee, pres. Okemos Bd. Edn., 1962-66; bd. dirs., pres. county unit Am. Cancer Soc., 1950-60; bd. dirs., pres. Cmty. Nursing Bur., Lansing, 1956-57. Lt. USNR, 1943-46, PTO. Fellow Am. Coll. Trust and Estate Counsel (pres. 1985-86), Am. Coll. Tax Counsel, Am. Bar Found., Mich. Bar Found.; mem. ABA, Fla. Bar Assn., Mich. Bar Assn. (chmn. probate and estate planning sect. 1977-78), Internat. Acad. Estate and Trust Law (exec. coun. 1990-94), Joint Editl. Bd. for Uniform Probate Code, Rotary (bd. dirs. Lansing 1968-70), Phi Beta Kappa, Phi Gamma Delta. Avocations: sailing, running, tennis. Home: 1965 Yuma Trl Okemos MI 48864-2746 Office: Foster Zack and Lowe PC PO Box 27337 Lansing MI 48909-7337 E-mail: joe.foster@fosterzacklowe.com. *Honesty and kindness are two of our best precepts. They also are good business.*

FOSTER, JOHN BURT, JR., comparative literature educator and researcher; b. Chgo., Dec. 19, 1945; s. John Burt Foster and Jane Armour; m. Andrea Dimino, Mar. 28, 1970; 1 child, Sophia Maria Foster-Dimino. BA, Harvard Coll., 1963—67; PhD, Yale U., 1967—71. Asst. prof. English and comparative lit. Stanford U., Calif., 1972—81; Mellon faculty fellow in comparative lit. Harvard U., Cambridge, Mass., 1982—83; assoc. prof. English and European studies George Mason U., Fairfax, Va., 1983—92, prof. English and cultural studies, 1992—; vis. assoc. prof. comparative lit. NYU, 1986—87. Author: Heirs to Dionysus; A Nietzschean Current in Literary Modernism, 1981, Nabokov's Art of Memory and European Modernism, 1993; co-editor: Thresholds of Western Culture: Identity, Postcoloniality, Transnationalism, 2003; editor: The Comparatist, 1997—2004; contbr. articles to profl. jours. Fellow, Deutscher Akademischer Austauschdienst, 1971-1972, Am. Coun. Learned Studies, 1981—82; Fellowship Coll. Teachers, Nat. Endowment Humanities, 1987-1988, 1997—98. Mem.: MLA, Am. Assn. Advancement Slavic Studies, Internat. Assn. Philosophy and Lit. (conf. organizer 1995—96), So. Comparative Lit. Assn. (bd. mem. 1993—95, 2004—), Am. Comparative Lit. Assn. (bd. mem. 1998—99), Internat. Nabokov Soc. (pres. 1994—96). Unitarian Universalist. Avocations: swimming, travel, canoeing, nature walks. Home: 605 46th St Sarasota FL 34234 Office: MSN 3E4 (English) George Mason Univ 4400 University Dr Fairfax VA 22030-4444 Office Phone: 703-993-2774. Business E-Mail: jfoster@gmu.edu.

FOSTER, JOHN HORACE, consulting environmental engineer; b. Quincy, Mass., June 2, 1927; s. Horace Herbert and Alice Gertrude (Hatch) F.; m. Claire Alice Sabean, Aug. 31, 1952; children— Janet, Mark, David. BS, Tufts U., 1952; MS, Harvard U., 1953. Engr. Malcolm Pirnie Engrs., White Plains, N.Y., 1953-63; partner Malcolm Pirnie, Inc., 1963-70, pres., 1970-88, chmn. bd. dirs., 1988-95; chmn. emeritus, 1997—. Contbr. articles to profl. jours. Served with USN, 1945-47. Recipient Distinguished Service award Dept. Civil Engring. Tufts U., 1977 Mem. ASCE, Water Environment Fedn., Am. Water Works Assn., Am. Cons. Engrs. Coun. (v.p. 1989-91, pres. 1992-93), N.Y. Assn. Cons. Engrs. (v.p. 1987-92, Engr. of Yr. 1995). Clubs: Cedar Point Yacht (commodore 1975-76) Home: 53 Farrell Rd Weston CT 06883-2306 Office: Malcolm Pirnie Inc PO Box 751 104 Corporate Park Dr White Plains NY 10604-3335

FOSTER, JOHN ROBERT, lawyer; b. Long Beach, Calif., Feb. 13, 1940; s. Orlon c. and Catherine Rose Foster; m. Nancy Crandall, June 17, 1962; children: John Crandall, Christopher Peter, Blayney Robert, Courtland William. BA in History, San Jose State U., 1961; LLB, U. Calif., Berkeley, 1964. Bar: Calif. 1965, U.S. Dist. Ct. (no. dist.) Calif. 1965, U.S. Ct. Appeals (9th cir.) 1965; cert. specialist in probate, estate planning, and trust law. Dep. legis. counsel State of Calif., Sacramento, 1964-65; pres. Rusconi, Foster, Thomas & Wilson, APC, Morgan Hill, Calif., 1965—; asst. dist. atty. San Benito County, Hollister, Calif., 1967. Mem. Morgan Hill Unified Sch. Dist. Bd. Edn., 1967-74, 79-83, chmn. bd., 1969-71; councilman City of Morgan Hill, 1984-88, 97-98, mayor, 1984. Named Citizen of Yr., City of Morgan Hill. Mem. Calif. State Bar (past state bar exec. com. on estate planning, probate and trusts), Santa Clara County Bar Assn., Gilroy-Morgan Hill Bar Assn. (past pres.), Morgan Hill C. of C. (past pres.), Masons, Rotary (past pres. Morgan Hill). Republican. Methodist. Avocations: skiing, fly fishing, backpacking, camping. Home: 17630 Black Oak Ct Morgan Hill CA 95037-9442 Office: Rusconi Foster Thomas & Wilson 30 Keystone Ave Morgan Hill CA 95037-4325 Office Phone: 408-779-2106. E-mail: bob@rftw.com.

FOSTER, JOHN STUART, JR., physicist, former defense industry executive; b. New Haven, Sept. 18, 1922; s. John Stuart and Flora (Curtis) F.; m. Frances Schnell, Dec. 28, 1978; children: Susan, Bruce, Scott, John. BS, McGill U., 1948; PhD in Physics, U. Calif., Berkeley, 1952; DSc (hon.), U. Mon., 1979. Dir. Lawrence Livermore (Calif.) Lab., 1952-65; dir. def. rsch. and engring. Dept. Def., Washington, 1965-73; v.p. TRW Energy Systems Group, Redondo Beach, Calif., 1973-79; v.p. sci. and tech. TRW Inc., Cleve., 1979-88, also bd. dirs. Chmn. Def. Sci. Bd., 1989-93; chmn. GKN Aerospace Transparency Sys., Tech. Strategies & Alliances. Decorated knight comdr.'s cross, badge and star Order of Merit (Germany); comdr. Legion of Honor (France); recipient Ernst Orlando Lawrence Meml. award AEC, 1960, Disting. Pub. Svc. medal Dept. Def., 1969, 73, 93, Crowell medal, 1972, Enrico Fermi Award, U.S. Dept. of Energy, 1992, Eugene Fubini award, U.S. Dept. Def., 1998. Mem. NAE (Founders award 1989), AIAA, Am. Def. Preparedness Assn., Nat. Security Indsl. Assn. Office: Northrop Grumman 1 Space Park Bldg E1-5010 Redondo Beach CA 90278-1071

FOSTER, JOSEPH KEVIN, IV, entertainer, scribe; b. Waterbury, Conn., Feb. 29, 1960; s. Joseph Adrian and Stella Lucia (Vicedomini) F. Prin., owner JK Enterprises, Kaweah Commonwealth, Calif., 1978—. Author: Cycling Castro's Country: The Tour de Cuba, 2000, (screenplay) 9 Dragon, 1999; photography featured in Outside Mag., Bicycling Mag., various newspapers worldwide; actor (Broadway) Go Home, Spec 5, 1983-85, (Off Broadway) various, 1980-83, (TV) Kane and Abel, 1985, (film) Friday 13th, Part 2, 1980, Daniel, 1983; active W. Thomas Littleton's Southbury (Conn.) Playhouse, 1974-78, HB Studio, N.Y.C., 1981, Stella Adler, N.Y.C., 1981, The Am. Acad. Dramatic Arts, N.Y.C., 1980-81, The Actor's Studio, N.Y.C., 1981-85; actor, writer, prodr. Yesterday's Dreams, 2005. Recipient Guinness World Record award Guinness, London, 1989, Cyclist of Yr. award Cycling Industry Bicycling Mag., Emmaus, Pa., 1990. Mem. Internat. Press Assn., Highpointer's Club, Ch. at Kaweah. Office: JK Enterprises PO Box 72 Kaweah CA 93237 E-mail: captainamerica@kevin-foster.com.

FOSTER, JOY VIA, retired library media specialist; b. Besoco, W.Va., Aug. 11, 1935; d. George Edward and Burgia Stafford (Earls) Via; m. Paul Harris Foster, Jr., Dec. 8, 1956 (dec. Dec. 20, 1962); children: Elizabeth Lee, Michael Paul. BS, Radford Coll., 1971; MS, Radford U., 1979. Cert. libr. Va. Clk. Va. Tech. and State U., Blacksburg, 1955—57, Christiansburg Primary Sch., Va., 1971—72, libr., 1972—85, Auburn Mid. and H.S., Riner, Va., 1985—2000; ret., 2000. Meml. chmn. Am. Cancer Soc., Christiansburg, 1965—66; block worker, 1985—91; area chmn. Am. Heart Fund, Christiansburg, 1990—93; pres. Montgomery County Ret. Tchrs. Assn., 2002—04; trustee Montgomery-Floyd Regional Libr. Bd, 2003—. Mem.: Va. Ednl. Media Assn. (Meritorious Svc. award 1999). Presbyterian. Avocations: reading, bowling, flea marketing, antique collecting.

FOSTER, JUDITH CHRISTINE, lawyer, writer; b. Columbus, Ohio, Nov. 25, 1952; d. Paul Marvel and Jean Harper (Uhland) F.; m. Sabah Amin Wali, Dec. 28, 1973; children: Samed Michel, Russeen Paul. BS in Natural Sci. and BA in Linguistics, Pa. State U., 1973; JD, Coll. William & Mary, 1979. Bar: Va. 1979, U.S. Ct. Appeals (4th cir.) 1979, U.S. Ct. Appeals (9th cir.) 1996, U.S. Supreme Ct. 1984. Pvt. practice, Fairfax, Va., 1980-90, Encino, Calif., 1991—. Mem. counsel U.S. Justice Found., Escondido, Calif., 1982-90; judge Internat. Moot Ct. Competition Assn. of Student Internat. Law Soc., 1984, 86. Contbr. articles to newsletters. Del. Va. Reps., Fairfax, 1981, 85. Mem. Am. Immigration Lawyers Assn. (legis. com. 1985, D.C. chpt. 1980-90, L.A. chpt. 1992—). Business E-Mail: jfoster_attorney_at_law@yahoo.com.

FOSTER, KEN, writer, educator; b. Williamsport, Pa., Sept. 2, 1964; s. William Hepler and Gladys Marbeth Foster. BA, Lock Haven U., 1987; MEd, Northeastern U., 1989; MFA, Columbia U., 1996. Lit. curator The Drawing Ctr., N.Y.C.; curator KGB Bar Lit. Readings, 1994—98; instr. The New Sch. U.; vis. instr. Fla. State U., Tallahassee, 2002—. Author: The Kind I'm Likely to Get (NY Times Notable Book, 1999), The Dog Who Found Me, 2005; editor: (anthology) Dog Culture: Writers on the Character of Canines, (literary anthology) The KGB Bar Reader; cinematographer: (book revs. to NY Time, San Francisco Chronicle, others). Fellow, Yaddo, 1996, NY Found. Arts, 2000. Mem.: Nat. Book Critics Cir., Authors Guild. D-Liberal. Personal E-mail: krf7@columbia.edu.

FOSTER, KENNARD P., magistrate judge; b. 1944; Student, Purdue U., 1962-64; BS, Ball State U., 1966; JD, Ind. U., 1970. Bar: Ind. Spl. agt. FBI, 1970-71; atty. Jones, Foster & Loveall, 1971-76; asst. U.S. Atty., 1976-86; magistrate judge U.S. Dist. Ct. (so. dist.) Ind., Indpls., 1985—2002, recalled magistrate judge, 2002—. Mem. Fed. Bar Assn., Johnson County Bar Assn., Fed. Magistrate Judges Assn. Office: Birch Bayh Fed Bldg and US Courthouse Ste 255 Indianapolis IN 46204-1903

FOSTER, KENT B., information technology executive; b. 1944; BS in elec. engring., N.C. State U.; M in mgmt., U. S.C. Bd. dirs. GTE Corp., Irving, Calif., 1992—99, vice chmn. bd., 1993—99, pres., 1995—99; chmn., pres., CEO Ingram Micro Inc., Santa Ana, Calif., 2000—, officer, 2000—, dir., 2000—. Bd. mem. Campbell Soup Co., J.C. Penney Co., NY Life Ins. Co., Dallas Symphony Orch., Dallas Opera. Capt. USAF, 1966—70. Named Forbes' America's Most Powerful People. Office: Ingram Micro Inc 1600 E St Andrew Pl Santa Ana CA 92705-4931 Office Phone: 714-566-1000. Office Fax: 714-566-7900.

FOSTER, LESTER ANDERSON, JR., metal products executive; b. Apr. 4, 1929; s. Lester Anderson and Annie Lee (Swink) F.; m. Patricia White, July 9, 1955; children: Leslie Ann, Caroline Suzann, Lester Anderson, Samuel Timothy. Student, Elon Coll., 1947-50; BS, N.C. State U., 1952. With Bethlehem Steel Corp., Sparrows Point, Md., 1952-94, engr., 1956-57, med. foreman, 1957-59, asst. gen. foreman, 1959-61, asst. master mechanic, 1961-67, master mechanic, 1967-92; pres. L&M Cons. Steel Plant Facilities, Inc., 1992—. Pres. PTA, Sparrows Point, 1963—65; mem. exec. bd. nominating com. Balt. County Sch. Bd., 1964—65; dist. field svc. chmn. Boy Scouts Am., Balt., 1972—78, bicentennial show program chmn., 1976, dist. commr., 1979—83, dist. chmn., 1983—; pres. 7th Dist. Rep. Club, 1969—72; mem. Md. Rep. State Ctrl. Com., 1980—90. With U.S. Army, 1952—54, col. Md. Def. Force, 1995—. Recipient Silver Beaver award Boy Scouts Am., 1975, award of Merit, 1984. Mem. SAR (pres. Md. Soc. 1993, v.p. gen. Mid-Atlantic, Silver Good Citizenship medal, Meritorious medal, Patriot meda, Minuteman medal 1999), Am. Inst. Iron and Steel Engrs., Soc. Mfg. Engrs., Am. Mgmt. Assn., Soc. Advancement Mgmt., Nat. Football Found. and Hall of Fame, Sparrows Point Country Club, Sparrows Point Engrs. Clubs, Masons, Shriners, K.T. (Grand Comdr.). Lutheran. Home: 3006 Dunmore Rd Baltimore MD 21222-5131 Office Phone: 410-282-0758. Personal E-mail: lespatfoster@erols.com.

FOSTER, LINDA LEE, artist; b. Portland, Oreg. Student, Bellevue C.C., Foothills Coll., Wash. State U., Pratt Inst.; pvt. instrn. with numerous artists, including Joseph Bohler, Jackie Brooks, Jane Burnham, Ernie Young, others. Instr. adult watercolor classes Bellevue (Wash.) Parks Dept., Kirkland (Wash.) Arts Ctr. Watercolorist snow and water and floral still lifes, portraits, and abstract work; represented in numerous pvt., local, nat., and internat. collections. Recipient award Bellevue Sch. Dist. Staff Art Fair, 1990, Pacific Northwest Arts & Crafts Fair, 1990, 3rd Pl. award Sky Valley Artist's Guild, 1993, Merit award Parkland Gallery, 1993, Ilwaco Heritage Mus., 1993, Grand award Donald L. Johnson Meml. Art Competition, 1995, Best of Show award Women Painters Wash., 1996, awards several internat., nat. and western juried shows, including 1st place Eastside Jour. Newspaper/1997 Photo Contest, 1997, 3d place Greater Marysville Artists Guild, Seafirst Bank, Marysville, Wa., 1996, Best of Show Women Painters of Wash., Moss Bay Gallery, Kirkland, 1996, Grand award 9th Ann. Donald L. Johnson Meml. Art Competition, Seattle Telco Fed. Credit Union, Seattle, 1995, Hon. Mention award Puget Sound Area Exhbn., Frye Art Mus., Seattle, 1994, others; selected juried exhbns. include Women Artists of the West, San Juan Capistrano, Calif., 1997, 98, 99, 4th Internat. Juried Competition, Biloxi, Miss., 1997, Northwest Watercolor Soc. Invitational Exhibit, Goldendale, Wash., 1997, ann. show Women Artists of the West, Taos, N.Mex., 1995-98, Women Painters of Wash., Juried Kuwait Exhbn. Millennium Images, 1999, Ireland and Am., Washington, 1999, Clymer Mus., Ellensburg, Wash., 1999, Ariz. Aqueous VII, Tubac, Ariz., 1993, Fla. 19th ann. Watercolor Soc., Panama City, Fla., 1993, Ga. Watercolor Soc. ann., Stone Mtn., Ga., 1992, Pacific Northwest arts and crafts fair, Bellevue Art Mus., 1990, 1991, Aqueous Open 1989, Pitts. Watercolor Soc. 52d, LaFond Galleries, Pitts., Pa., 1989, 91, Open Painting Exhbn., Kimball Art Ctr., Park City, Ut., 1998, Klamath Juried Open, Klamath Art Gallery, Klamath Falls, Oreg., 1993, NE Watercolor Soc. (Signature mem.), 17th ann. nat. exhbn., Trotting Ho. Mus., Goshen, N.Y., 1993, Western Washington Watercolor Soc. Juried Competition, Richland, Wash., 1993, 94. Mem. Women Artists of the West (signature mem.), Northwest Watercolor Soc. (signature mem.), Women Painters of Wash. Home and Office: Phantom Lake Studio 16422 SE 17th St Bellevue WA 98008-5122 E-mail: lindaleefoster@msn.com.

FOSTER, LINDA TIMBERLAKE, state legislator; b. Portland, Maine, Feb. 8, 1943; m. Bernard Scott; 3 children. BS, U. Maine, 1965. Rep. Hillsborough Dist. 4 N.H. State Ho. of Reps., 1992—; policy leader Dem. Party, NH. Bd. dirs. Family Strength. Mem. N.H. Assn. Residential Care Homes (adv. bd.), So. N.H. Svcs. (exec. bd.), Phi Kappa Phi. Office: NH Ho of Reps Com on Fin State Capitol Concord NH 03301

FOSTER, MARGERY SOMERS, economics professor; b. Boston, Mar. 27, 1914; d. L. Brent and Grace F. (Butler) Foster. BA, Wellesley Coll., 1934; PhD, Radcliffe Coll., 1958; LittD, Russell Sage Coll., 1968. Asst. to actuary New Eng. Mut. Life Ins. Co., 1934—43; dep. comptroller, dir. devel. Wellesley Coll., 1946—54; lectr. econs. Harvard U. Sch. Bus. Adminstrn., 1956—58; lectr. econs., sec. coll. Mt. Holyoke Coll., 1958—64; prof. econs., dean coll. Hollins Coll., 1964—67, Douglass Coll. of Rutgers U., 1967—75; prof. econs. Rutgers U., 1975—80; prof. emeritus, 1980—; past dir. Prudential Ins. Co., NJ, 1973—85, Pub. Svc. Electric & Gas Co., NJ, 1973—85. Mem. commn. on tests coll. entrance exam bd., 1966—70, trustee, 1969—72; mem. commn. on instl. affairs Assn. Am. Colls., 1971—74; mem. Harvard U. overseer's vis. com. Warren Ctr. in Am. History, 1973—79; trustee Middle States Assn. Colls. and Schs., 1973—79, Island Inst., 1984—. Author: Out of Smalle Beginnings: An Economical History of Harvard College in the Puritan Period, 1962. Lt. Women's Res. USNR, 1943—46. Mem.: Econ. History Soc., Econ. History Assn., Am. Econ. Assn., Univ. Women's Club, Cosmopolitan, Appalachian Mountain. Achievements include research in American colonial economic history, history of education and public finance. Office: PO Box 60 Francestown NH 03043-0060 also: Great Diamond Island Portland ME 04104

FOSTER, MARK STEPHEN, lawyer; b. Edgerton, Mo., Feb. 6, 1948; s. George Elliott and Annabel Lee (Bradshaw) F.; m. Camille Pepper, June 27, 1970; children: Natalie Ashley, Stephanie Ann. BS, U. Mo., 1970; JD, Duke U., 1973. Bar: Mo. 1973, U.S. Ct. Mil. Appeals 1974, Hawaii 1975, U.S. Dist. Ct. Hawaii 1975, U.S. Dist. Ct. (we. dist.) Mo. 1977, U.S. Ct. Appeals (8th cir.) 1986, U.S. Supreme Ct. 1994. Assoc. Stinson, Mag & Fizzell, Kansas City, 1977-80, ptnr., 1980—2002, mng. ptnr., 1987-90, chmn. bd. dirs., 1998—2002; ptnr. Stinson Morrison Hecker LLP, Kansas City, 2002—, mng. ptnr., 2002—. Arbitration panelist Nat. Assn. Securities Dealers, N.Y.C., 1985—, Pvt. Adjudication Found., Durham, N.C., 1988—2000. Active Citizens Assn., Kansas City, 1982-92; pres. Spelman Med. Found., Smithville, Mo., 1984-88; bd. dirs. Alzheimers Assn. Metro. Kansas City, 1997—2004, 1st v.p., 1998, pres., 1999. Lt. comdr. USNR, ret. Mem. ABA, CCSA Kansas City (bd. dirs. 2001—), Hawaii Bar Assn., Mo. Bar Assn., Kansas City Met. Bar Assn., Am. Arbitration Assn. (panelist 1990—, large complex case adv. com. 1993—), Carriage Club (bd. dirs. 2000-04, 2d v.p. 2001, 1st v.p. 2002, pres. 2003), Lawyers Edn. Assistance Program (bd. dirs. 2000—, sec. 2004—), Masons. Home: 1035 W 65th St Kansas City MO 64113-1813 Office: Stinson Morrison Hecker LLP PO Box 419251 1201 Walnut St Ste 2800 Kansas City MO 64106-2117 Office Phone: 816-842-8600. Business E-Mail: mfoster@stinson.com.

FOSTER, MARY CHRISTINE, film producer, writer; b. L.A., Mar. 19, 1943; d. Ernest Albert and Mary Ada (Quilici) Foster; m. Paul Hunter, July 24, 1982. BA, Immaculate Heart Coll., L.A., 1967; M in TV News Documentary, UCLA, 1968. Dir. R & D Metromedia Producers Corp., L.A., 1968-71; dir. devel. and prodn. svcs. Wolper Prodns., L.A., 1971-76; mgr. film programs NBC-TV, Burbank, Calif., 1976-77; v.p. movies and mini series Columbia Pictures TV, Burbank, 1977-81, v.p. series programs, 1981; v.p. program devel. Group W. Prodns., L.A., 1981-87; agt. The Agency, L.A., 1988-90, Shapiro-Lichtman Agy., L.A., 1990-99; ind. prodr., 1999—. Lectr. in field. Creator (TV series) Sullivan, 1985, Auntie Mom, 1986; author: Immaculate Heart High School: A Herstory 1906-2006, 2005. Trustee Immaculate Heart H.S., L.A., 1980—; mem. exec. com. Humanitas Awards Human Family Inst., 1985—; mem. cmty. devel. com. Immaculate Heart Cmty., 2001—; mem. exec. com. L.A. Roman Cath. Archdiocesan Comm. Commn., L.A., 1986—90; bd. dirs., treas. Catholics in Media, 1992—2004; mem. vol. com., writer tour script, book, newsletter and website Cathedral of Our Lady of Angels, 2002—; chmn. pastoral coun. St. Francis of Assisi, 2003—05, chmn. stewardship com. and renovation com. Mem.: NATAS, Women in Film (bd. dirs. 1974—78). Democrat. Personal E-mail: fosterc@aol.com. *Fidelity to God's will yields life's greatest satisfaction. Love of family and community gives life fulfillment.*

FOSTER, MICHAEL KIRK, anthropologist, linguist; b. Athens, Greece, June 2, 1938; s. Andrew Brisbin and Barbara (Kirk) F.; m. Doris Elizabeth Wilkinson, Sept. 7, 1974; 1 child, Andrew Erskine. BA, Lawrence Coll., 1961; MAT, Harvard U., 1962; PhD, U. Pa., 1974. Instr. Ursinus Coll., Collegeville, Pa., 1964-66; ethnologist, curator Can. Mus. Civilization, Ottawa, Ont., Can., 1970-89; sessional lectr. Carleton U., Ottawa, 1975, 93; curator emeritus Can. Mus. Civilization, Ottawa, 1989—. Editor, co-editor 6 books; contbr. numerous articles on Iroquoian langs. and cultures to scholarly jours. and books. Grantee NSF, 1970-71, NEH, 1982-85, Am. Philos. Soc., 1990, 92, 97. Fellow Am. Anthrop. Assn.; mem. Can. Ethnology Soc., Soc. for Study of Indigenous Langs. of the Ams., Soc. for Linguistic Anthropology, Current Anthropology (assoc.). Home: 746 Pattrell Rd Norwich VT 05055-9479

FOSTER, MICHAEL WILLIAM, librarian; b. Astoria, Oreg., June 29, 1940; s. William Michael and Margaret Vivian (Carlson) F. BA in History, Willamette U., 1962; MA, U. Oreg., 1965; postgrad., So. Oreg. Coll., 1976. Tchr. Astoria High Sch., 1963-66, librarian, 1970-96; tchr. Am. Internat. Sch. of Kabul (Afghanistan), 1966-70. Bd. dirs. Astoria H.S. Scholarships, Inc., AG-BAG Internat. Ltd., Astoria Pacific Industries, Inc.; adv. bd. pacific region US Bank. Mem. Oreg. Arts Commn., Salem, 1983-91; commr. Oreg. Coun. Humanities, 1994—, chmn., 1995-97; commr. Oreg. Advs. for the Arts, 1994-97; bd. dirs. Am. Cancer Soc., Clatsop County, Oreg., 1980-87, Luth. Family Svcs., 1994-96, Oreg. Arts Advocates Found., 1994-98, Columbia Meml. Hosp. Found., 1992-2001, Edward Hall Scholarship Bd., bd. dirs. U. Oreg. Art Mus. Coun., 1991-, pres., 1993-95; bd. dirs., treas. Astoria Cmty. Concert Assn., 1964-88, pres., 1989-2004; bd. dirs., treas. Ed and Eda Ross Scholarship Trust; bd. dirs., pres. Clatsop CC Found., 1997-99, exec. dir., 1999-2003; mem. Oreg. Econ. Devel. Dept. Task Force, 1995-97; mem. adv. bd. Oreg. Symphony, 1992-97; bd. dirs. Columbia River Girl Scouts 1999-2004; coun. bd. Columbia River Girl Scouts, 1999-2004. Recipient Thanks Badge, Columbia River Girl Scouts, 2004. Mem. NEA, Oreg. Edn. Assn., Oreg. Edn. Media Assn., Clatsop County Hist. Soc. (bd. dirs., pres. 1983-87), Ft. Clatsop Hist. Assn. (treas. 1974-91, pres. 1991—, bd. dirs.), Astoria C. of C. (bd. dirs. 1982-88, George award 1985, pres. 1987), Lewis and Clark Trails Heritage Found., Rotary (pres. Astoria Club 1986), Astoria Golf and Country Club, Beta Theta Pi. Republican. Roman Catholic. Avocations: antique dealer, art collector, oil painter, golf, tennis. Home: 1636 Irving Ave Astoria OR 97103-3621

FOSTER, MILO GEORGE, manufacturing executive; b. San Diego, Aug. 2, 1957; s. Milo Hughes and Kathryn G. (Sevastos) F.; m. Barbara A. Vandenberg, Mar. 25, 1988; children: Kathleen Elaine, Anthony Hughes. BS, U. Mo., Rolla, 1979; MBA, Harvard U., 1983. Prodn. team mgr. Procter & Gamble, Cape Girardeau, Mo., 1979-81; strategic planner Hitchiner Mfg., Milford, N.H., 1982; tissue mfg. staff asst. Kimberly-Clark Corp., New Milford, Conn., 1983-84, tissue mfg. supt. Memphis, 1984-86, mgr. mfg. projects Neenah, Wis., 1986-87, feminine care plant mgr., 1987-89, dir. ops., feminine care, 1989-91, dir. feminine care expansion project, 1992-93, gen. mgr. family care Australia, 2000—; dir. World Support Group-Tissue, Neenah, 1993-94, v.p. ops. and engring., 1994—99. Avocations: skiing, cooking, singing, triathlons. Office: Kimberly-Clark 52 Alfred St Milsons Point NSW Australia Business E-Mail: mfoster@kcc.com.

FOSTER, NANCY HASTON, columnist, author; b. Austin, Tex., June 07; d. Arch B. and Verlea Haston; m. Joe D. Foster Jr. (div.). BJ, BA in Sociology, U. Tex. Writer, pub. rels. dept. Trinity U., San Antonio, Tex.; social worker pub. welfare dept. State of La., Lafayette; instr. sociology U. Tex., Austin; columnist San Antonio Light, 1982-83, San Antonio Express-News, 1989-90; freelance writer, 1977—. Author: San Antonio, A Texas Monthly Guidebook, 1983, rev. edit., 1989, 94, 98, San Antonio, Lone Star Guide, 1999, 2000, The Alamo and Other Texas Missions to Remember, 1984, Texas Missions, A Texas Monthly Guidebook, 1995, Texas Missions, Lone Star Guide, 1999; contbg. editor, writer: Texas, Fodor's Travel Guides, 1985, rev. edit., 1991, Fodor's American Cities, 1986, rev. edit., 1988, Texas, A Texas Monthly Guidebook, 1993, 98; contbr. articles to popular mags. Mem. Women in Comm., Phi Beta Kappa. Avocations: conversation, photography, collectibles. Home and Office: 201 Prinz Dr San Antonio TX 78213-1921

FOSTER, PAUL, playwright; b. Penn's Grove, N.J., Oct. 15, 1931; s. Elderidge M. and Mary (Manning) F. BA, Rutgers U., 1954; LLB, St. John's U., 1958. Pres. La Mama Theater Club, N.Y.C., 1962—; tchr. drama dept. NYU and U. Calif.-San Diego, 1983. Author: The Birthday Party Stories, 1962, Hurrah for the Bridge, 1963, The Recluse, 1964, Balls, 1964, Madonna In the Orchard, 1965, The Hessian Corporal, 1966, Tom Paine, 1967, Heimskringla, 1969, Satyricon, 1970, Elizabeth I, 1971, Silver Queen Saloon, 1972, Marcus Brutus, 1973-74, Murderers' Row, 1976, A Kiss is Just a Kiss, 1983, (stage trilogy) The Dark and Mr. Stone, 1985-87, (TV) The Tragedy of the Commons, 1979, The Vampyre and Dr. Frankenstein, 1980, Silver Saloon, 1992, (film) Andrew Mellon and the National Gallery of Art, 1980, Cop and the Anthem, 1982, Smile, 1983, Cinderella Story, 1984, (stage play based on Dickens) A Tale of Two Cities, 1988, Kisses, Bites and Scratches, 1990, Elizabeth Eins, 1992, Make Believe Musical Book and Lyrics, 1993, Murder in the Hollyhocks, 1995; translator: (Horvath) Back & Forth, Faith, Hope, Charity, 1983, Fritz Lang's M for stage, 1997, Masquerade, 1999-2000; contbr. e-zine opera revs. to Arts4All.com, 2000; The Lives of Artists, 12 minimovies for Discovery.com, 2004, song lyrics for musical Kisses, Bites and Scratches, 2004-05; donated collection of theatrical lit. to Rutgers U. Libr. Served to lt. (j.g.) USNR, 1955-57. Recipient Play award Irish Univs., 1967, 71, N.Y. Drama Critics award, 1968, Tony award nomination, 1973; Rockefeller Found. fellow, 1967-68; Creative Artists Pub. Service grantee, 1972; Nat. Endowment Creative Writing fellow, 1973; Guggenheim fellow, 1974. Mem. Eugene O'Neill Meml. Theater Found., New Dramatists, Dramatists Guild, Player's Club, Societe des Auteurs. Home: 115 Saint Marks Pl Staten Island NY 10301-1600 E-mail: caisby@aol.com, pfoster@virtualforum.com.

FOSTER, ROBERT CARMICHAEL, banker; b. Toledo, Ohio, Apr. 1, 1941; s. Robert Albert and Kate (Thompson) F.; m. Phyllis Lorainne Schmidt, Nov. 25, 1974; children: Brian Clinton, Suzanne Pamela, Robert Carmichael Jr. AB, Colo. Coll., 1963; MBA, U. Chgo., 1965; AMP, Harvard U., 1982. Analyst, programmer McDonnell-Douglas Corp., St.Louis, 1965-67; systems cons. Bristol-Myers Co., N.Y.C., 1967-70; comptroller Toledo Trust Co., 1970-73, sr. v.p., 1973-77, exec. v.p., 1977-87, also bd. dirs.; v.p. Trustcorp, Inc., 1975-86, exec. v.p., 1986-87; pres., dir. SeaGate Aviation Corp., Toledo, 1983-2000; pres., chief exec. officer, bd. dirs. West Mich. Nat. Bank & Trust, Frankfort, Mich., 1987—. Bd. dirs. Traverse Bay Econ. Devel. Corp., 1988—, exec. com. 1998—, treas. 2000-01, vice chmn. 2001—. Bd. dirs. Riverside Hosp., Toledo, 1978-85, Northcoast Health Sys., Inc., 1983-88, Lucas County Children Svcs., Toledo, 1981-85, Munson Healthcare Inc., 1990—, Traverse City, Mich.; trustee YMCA, Toledo, 1974-87; assoc. trustee Boys Club of Toledo, 1984-86, trustee, 1986-87; chmn. Lucas County U.s. Savs. Bond Program, Toledo, 1972-87; mem. planning commn. Crystal Lake Twp., 1988-97; sec.-treas. Paul Oliver Meml. Hosp., 1989-90, bd. dirs., pres., 1990-98; pres. Frankfort Indsl. Pk. Devel. Corp., 1989—; mem. Traverse Bay Cmty. Found., 1995-2000; chmn. Frankfort City-County Airport Authority, 1995—. Mem. Am. Inst. Banking, Bank Adminstrn. Inst., Toledo Area Govtl. Rsch. Assn. (pres., bd. dirs. 1974-79), Toledo C. of C. (aviation com.), Ottawa Skeet Club (treas.), Crystal Downs Country Club (treas. 1993-99), Rotary. Presbyterian. Avocations: flying, water and snow, hunting, tennis. Home: 70 Thomas Rd Frankfort MI 49635-9538

FOSTER, ROBERT FRANCIS, communications executive; b. Chgo., June 4, 1926; s. William John and Anna Alice (O'Farrell) F.; m. Mary D. Palella, May 4, 1963; children: Sean Terence, Nancy Marie, Patrick Daniel. Student, Cath. schs., Chgo. and Evanston, Ill. News and sports writer Sta. WGN, Chgo., 1943-55; with Chgo. Pub. Rels. Counselors, 1955-60, WGN Continental Broadcasting Co., Chgo., 1960-82, news bur. chief Springfield, Ill., 1961-63, Washington news bureau chief Washington, 1964-82; press sec. to Ill. Congressman Philip M. Crane, 1982-96; reporter and analyst at 10 nat. polit. convs. WGN-TV and WGN-Radio. Chgo. Stadium announcer Chgo. Blackhawks, 1955-64. Goalie 78th Divsn. ice hockey team, 1946. With AUS, 1944-46. Decorated Combat Inf. badge, Bronze Star. Recipient award best pub. service news Am. Coll. Radio Arts, Crafts and Scis., 1961. Mem. Radio-TV Corr. Assn. Washington (pres. 1976), Broadcast Pioneers, Radio TV News Dirs. Assn., Am. Legion, Chgo. Press Vets. Assn. Roman Catholic. Home: 5718 Marble Arch Way Alexandria VA 22315-4037

FOSTER, ROGER SHERMAN, JR., surgeon, educator, health facility administrator; b. Washington, Jan. 8, 1936; s. Roger Sherman and Genevieve Wakeman (Bartlett) F.; m. Joan Crile, June 25, 1960 (dec. Feb. 2000); children: Roger Sherman III, Charles Bartlett, Elizabeth Crile, Halle Crile Foster Moore; m. Baiba J. Grube, July 3, 2004. AB, Haverford Coll., 1957; MD, Case Western Res. U., 1961. Diplomate Am. Bd. Surgey, Nat. Bd. Med. Examiners; lic. Vt. Intern then resident in surgery Univ. Hosps., Cleve., 1961-66; research fellow Roswell Park Meml. Inst., Buffalo, 1966-68; asst. prof. surgery U. Vt., Burlington, 1970-73, assoc. prof. surgery, 1973-80, prof. surgery, 1980-92, dir. comprehensive cancer ctr., 1984-92; attending surgeon Med. Ctr. Hosp. of Vt., 1970-92; Wadley Glenn prof. surgery Emory U., Atlanta, 1992-99; chief surgical svcs. Crawford Long Hosp. of Emory U., 1992-99. Mem. cancer clin. investigation rev. com. NIH, 1987-92, chmn., 1991-92, chmn. various coms.; cons. Am. Internat. Health Alliance for Tblisi, Georgia Hosp., 1992-96. Assoc. editor: Clinical Surgery, 1987; co-editor: Essentials of Clinical Surgery, 1991; editor-in-chief: Breast Surgery: Index and Reviews, 1993-95; assoc. editor: Surgery: Problem-Solving Approach, 2d edit., 1995; co-editor: Q & A Review for Surgery, 1995; manuscript reviewer: Jour. AMA, Jour. Trauma, others; contbr. more than 100 articles to profl. jours. Trustee Univ. Health Ctr., Burlington, 1986-89; bd trustees, Vt. Ethics Network, 2001—. Served to maj. U.S. Army, 1968-69. Grantee NIH, 1971-92; summer rsch. fellow Josiah Macy Jr, Found., 1958-59. Fellow ACS (bd. regents 1991-2000, bd. govs. 1981-87, adv. coun. for gen. surgery 1989-92, 95-2000, sec./treas. Vt. chpt. 1979-80, v.p. 1980-81, pres. 1981-82), Am. Surg. Assn.; mem. AMA, AAAS, New Eng. Surg. Soc. (treas. 1986-89, exec. com. 1981-92, 2001-03, pres. 2001-02), Soc. Univ. Surgeons, So. Surg. Assn., Southeastern Surg. Congress, Soc. Surg. Oncology, Ea. Surg. Soc. (pres. 1994), Am. Endocrine Surg. Soc. (coun. 1992-95), Am. Soc. Clin. Oncology (pub. rels. 1989-91 and pub. issues coms. 1989-94), Transplantation Soc., New Eng. Cancer Soc. (treas. 1983-87, v.p. 1988-89, pres. 1989-90), Assn. Acad. Surgery, Newfoundland Club Am. (bd. dirs. 1976-78, 1st v.p. 1979), Nat. Surg. Adjuvant Breast Project, 1971-92 (exec. com. 1978-81). Avocations: white water canoeing, breeding newfoundland dogs, wilderness travel, chamber music. Home: 613 S Forty Dr Shelburne VT 05482-6492 E-mail: halirock@aol.com.

FOSTER, RON, agricultural products supplier, agricultural products executive; BS in Agr. Bus., Calif. Poly-San Luis Obispo Coll., 1981. Gen. mgr. McHenry Ave plant Foster Farms, Modesto, Calif., 1981—96, gen. mgr. Kans. Ave plant Fresno, Calif., 1981—96, pres. Livingston, Calif., 1996—, CEO, 1996—. Chmn. campaign com. Calif. Dairy Tech. Ctr.; mem. dean's adv. coun. U. Calif., Davis, Calif. Office: Foster Farms PO Box 457 Livingston CA 95334

FOSTER, ROSEMARY ALICE, lawyer, artist; b. Independence, Iowa, Oct. 2, 1944; d. James Charles Mooney and Hilda Marie Engelkes; m. Monty Foster, July 20, 1979 (dec. Jan. 17, 2000); 1 child, Daisy Ward. BA, Drake U., 1964; JD, George Washington U., 1967; MA in Psychology, U. Utah, 1973. Bar: D.C. 1968. Supr. neighborhood probation unit Second Dist. Juvenile Ct., Salt Lake City, 1968—73; legal cons. State of Idaho, Boise, Idaho, 1973—74; atty. Nat. Ctr. Law Handicapped, South Bend, Ind., 1974—75; adminstrv. law judge Wash. Office Adminstrv. Hearings, Olympia, Wash., 1976—2001; with STEPS Program Cmty. Mental Health, Homer, Alaska, 2001—02; hearing officer Workers Compensation Dept. Labor, Anchorage, 2002—. Exhibitions include Artist's Gallery, Olympia, Wash., 1995—97, Cuyamungue Stone Co., Homer, Alaska, 2003, Mystic Enterprises, 2003. Vol. Youth Ct., Olympia, 1998—2001; mem. Alaska Women's Polit. Caucus, Anchorage, 2003; bd. dir. South Peninsula Women's Svcs., Homer, Alaska, 2000—02. Recipient Svc. award, State of Wash., 2001. Mem.: LWV. Democrat. Roman Catholic. Office: 2440 E Tudor Rd Anchorage AK 99507

FOSTER, S. THOMAS, JR., quality management educator, consultant, writer, academic administrator; b. Waynesville, Mo., Sept. 24, 1957; s. Stephen T. Foster and Jeanne L. Berridge; m. Casie L. Foster, May 11, 1979; children: Kimberlee, Amie, Stephen, Daniel, Matthew. BS, Brigham Young U., 1984; MBA, U. Mo., 1988; PhD, U. Mo., Columbia, 1993. Analyst Shell Oil Co., Houston, 1984-88; grad. asst. U. Mo., Columbia, 1989-93; prin. Foster Mgmt. Cons., Boise and Kansas City, 1988—; prof. quality mgmt. Boise State U., 1993—. Vis. prof. Pa. State U., University Park, 1999—; founder www.frequality.org., 2000—. Author: Handbook on Quality, 1998, Managing Quality, 2001, 2003; mem. editl. bd. Jour. Operatio Mgmt., 1998—, Quality Mgmt. Jour., 1997—; contbr. articles to profl. jours. Mem. Decion Scis. Inst. (various coms.), Am. Soc. for Quality (bd. dirs. 1992—), Idaho Total Quality Inst. (bd. dirs. 1994-96), Acad. of Mgmt., Prodn. and Ops. Mgmt. Soc. (coms. 1992—), North Cen. Assn. Colls. and Univs. (adv. bd. 1998—), Am. Prodn. and Inventory Control Soc., Beta Gamma Sigma. Republican. Mem. Ch. Latter Day Sts. Avocations: skiing, guitar playing, spending time with family. Office: Boise State U No C 15 Boise ID 83725 Address: PO Box 805 Kuna ID 83634-0805 Office Phone: 208-426-4367.

FOSTER, SONJA MARGUERITE, musician, educator; d. Lyle P. and Ruth D. Foster; m. Frank Stephen Allen, Apr. 29, 1989. BMus in Violin Performance, Juilliard Sch., 1972. First violin Grant Pk. Symphony, Chgo., 1970—77; artist, tchr. Trinity Coll., Deerfield, Ill., 1972—78; violin faculty Wheaton (Ill.) Coll., 1975—83; instr. violin Studio for Gifted, Norcross, Ga., 1982—; artist, tchr. Emory U., Atlanta, 1985—92. Performer; tchr. master classes; presenter in field. Musician: (albums) Sacred Music for the Violin, 2003; author: Teaching Gifted Children, 2001. Mem. adv. bd. Gwinnett Philharm., Duluth, Ga., 1995—2001. Scholar Full scholar, Curtis Inst. Music, 1964—68, Meadowmount Sch. Music, 1965—68, The Juilliard Sch., 1968—72. Mem.: Atlanta Music Club, Am. String Tchrs. Assn., Music Tchrs. Nat. Assn. Republican. Achievements include research in stage fright and positive performing. Avocation: travel. Personal E-mail: sallen2000@comcast.net.

FOSTER, SUSAN STEPHAN, freelance artist, art educator; b. Chgo., May 5, 1950; d. William Alois and June Elizabeth (Ringquist) Stephan; m. David John Foster, Feb. 5, 1972; children: Andrea, Laura, Jamie. BA, Westminster Coll., New Wilmington, Pa., 1972. Founder, ptnr. Salem Crossroads Studies, Delmont, Pa., 1982-85; art instr. Idaho Falls (Idaho) Cmty. Edn., 1985-89; salesperson, framer Greensburg (Pa.) Art Supply, 1991—; art instr. Franklin Regional Adult Edn., Murrysville, Pa., 1990—. Co-op mem. Watercolors Gallery, Pitts., 1997—. Exhibited works in shows at Aqueous Open Internat., 1995, 97-99, 200-02, Pa. Watercolor Soc., 1995, 98, 2004, W.Va. Aqueous, 1999, 2004, Westmoreland Nats., 1995, 96, 98, 99, 2002, 03, Nat. Realism Show, 2000; solo show Hoyt Inst, 2003; contbr. Internat. Artist Mag. Recipient 1st place award Art Materials Assn. Conv., Toronto, 1996, Best of Show award Freeport Area Art Show, 1998, others. Mem. East Suburban Artists League (sec. 1984-86, treas. 1990-92, programs 1997-98, pres. 2002), Pitts. Watercolor Soc. (bd. dirs. 1992-94), Pa. Watercolor Soc. (signature mem.), Greensburg Art Club. Avocations: travel, antiques. Home: 4920 Simmons Cir Export PA 15632-9330

FOSTER, SUTTON, actress; b. Statesboro, Ga., Mar. 18, 1975; Postgrad., Carnegie Mellon U., Hunter Coll., N.Y.C. Actor: (Broadway musical) Grease, Annie, Scarlet Pimpernel, Les Misérables, Thoroughly Modern Millie (winner Tony award for Best Performance by a Leading Actress in a Musical, 2002), Little Women, 2004—05.

FOSTER, WALTER HERBERT, JR., real estate company executive; b. Belmont, Mass., Nov. 2, 1919; s. Walter Herbert and Gertrude (Sullivan) F.; m. Hazel Campbell, Aug. 7, 1942 (div. July 1979); children: Katherine D., Walter H. III, Stephen C., Banton T.; m. Nedra Ann Thompson, July 3, 1981; 1 child, Timothy John. Student, Harvard U., 1937-38; BS, U. Maine, 1947; grad. in real estate, Tri-State Inst., 1968-70. Cert. gen. appraiser, Maine. Owner, mgr. Foster Bros., Lyndeborough, N.H., 1947-56; ter. sales mgr. Beacon Milling Co., Oakland, Maine, 1956-64; v.p. Sherwood & Foster, Inc., Old Town, Maine, 1964-67; sales rep. Bangor (Maine) Real Estate, 1967-73; chief appraiser James W. Sewall Co., Old Town, 1970-73; mgr. J.F. Singleton Co., Bangor, 1973-80; pres. Coldwell Banker Am. Heritage, Bangor, 1980—. Dean Tri-State Inst., 1981; mem. Maine Real Estate Commn., 1987-93, chmn. 1991. Active Rep. Nat. Com., Washington, 1980; assessment bd. appeals Old Town, Maine, Holden Assessment Bd. of Appeals; bd. dirs. Penobscot Theatre, 1987-92, treas., 1989, mem. Maine State Bd. Property Rev., 1998—. Capt. USAF, 1941-46, USAFR ret., 1966. Mem. Nat. Assn. Realtors (bd. dirs. 1980-81), Maine Assn. Realtors (life, bd. dirs. 1976-80, pres. 1980, Realtor of Yr. 1984), Bangor Bd. Realtors (bd. dirs. 1973-74, pres. 1976, Realtor of Yr. 1976, 84), Maine Real Estate Commn. (chmn. 1991-92), Maine State Bd. Property Tax Review, Commn. to Study Real Estate Appraiser Cert. and Licensing, Nat. Assn. Rev. Appraisers, Am. Assn. Cert. Appraisers, Res. Officers Assn., Appraisal Inst. (assoc.), Nat. Assn. Ind. Fee Appraisers (sr.), Harvard Club of Ea. Maine (treas.), Rotary (bd. dirs. local club, Paul Harris fellow 2005), Am. Legion., Ret. Officers Assn., Mil. Officers Assn. Am. Episcopalian. Avocations: woodworking, gardening. Home: 68 Dole Hill Rd Holden ME 04429-9802 Office: Coldwell Banker Am Heritage 510 Broadway Bangor ME 04401-3468 Office Phone: 207-942-6773. Business E-Mail: cbah@midmaine.com.

FOSTER, WILLIAM EDWIN (BILL FOSTER), nonprofessional basketball coach; b. Ridley Park, Pa., Aug. 19, 1929; s. Howard M. and Viola Jane (Beaston) F.; m. Shirley Ann Junkin, June 17, 1957; children: Vicki R., Debra Jo, Julia Ann, Mary K. BS, Elizabethtown Coll., 1954; MEd, Temple U., 1957. Coach, tchr. Chichester (Pa.) High Sch., 1954-57, Abington (Pa.) High Sch., 1957-60; coach, instr. Bloomsburg (Pa.) State Coll., 1960-63; head basketball coach Rutgers U., New Brunswick, N.J., 1963-71, U. Utah, Salt Lake City, 1971-74; head basketball coach, asst. athletic dir. Duke U., Durham, N.C., 1974-80, U. S.C., Columbia, 1980-86; head basketball coach, interim athletic dir. Northwestern U., Evanston, Ill., 1986-93, athletic dir., 1993; assoc. commr. S.W. Conf., Dallas, 1993-96; cons. Com. of Big 12 Conf. for basketball, 1996-99; spl. asst. to the commr. Western Athletic Conf., 1999—. Chmn. of the bd. Naismith Meml. Basketball Hall of Fame, 1997-98, bd. trustees; pres. Nat. Sports Video Seminars. Served with USAF, 1951-52. Named Nat. Coach of Yr., Sporting News Playboy Mag., 1978, S.C. Coach of Yr., 1981, NIT Man of Yr., Met. Intercollegiage Basketball Assn., 2003, Nat. Invitation Tournament's Man of Yr., Met. Coaches Assn., 2003; named to Sports Hall Fame Elizabethtown Coll., Pa., Basketball Hall Fame Rutgers. U., Hall Fame Delaware County (Pa.), Hall Fame Interboro H.S, 2004, Glen-Nor H.S., 2004. Mem. Nat. Assn. Basketball Coaches (past pres., co-coach of yr. 1978), Met. Intercollegiate Basketball Assn. (elected 2003). Office: PO Box 5295 Galveston TX 77554-0295 Home: The Club of the Isle 3433 Cove View Blvd 1408 Galveston TX 77554 Office Phone: 409-996-4545. Personal E-mail: mfoster689@aol.com.

FOSTER, WILLIAM R., zoological park administrator; DVM. Dir., CEO Louiville (Ky.) Zool. Garden, Louisville, 1997—. Office: Louisville Zool Garden PO Box 37250 Louisville KY 40233-7250

FOSTER, WILLIAM SILAS, JR., retired minister; b. Kansas City, Mo., Nov. 5, 1939; s. William Silas and Edna LaResta (Scott) F.; m. Susan Jean Mannle, June 5, 1983; children Robert Light, Beth Light Sierra, Stacey Light; children from previous marriage, Beth Ann, Amy Lynne. BA, Mo. Valley Coll., 1962; MDiv, McCormick Sem., 1966. Ordained to ministry Presbyn. Ch. (USA), 1966. Asst. min. 1st Presbyn. Ch., Edwardsville, Ill., 1966-68; min. St. Paul's Presbyn. Ch., St. Louis, 1968-71, Moro (Ill.) Presbyn. Ch., 1971-83, 1st Presbyn. Ch., North Kansas City, Mo., 1983-84, Worland, Wyo., 1985—2004, ret., 2004—. Commr. to Gen. Assembly Presbyn. Ch. (U.S.A), Omaha, Balt., Albuquerque, 1973, 91, 95; stated clk. Presbytery Wyo., Casper, 1990-00, Com. of the Office of Gen. Assembly; instr. calligraphy Synod Sch., 1982-83; pres. Presbyn. Alcohol Info. Network, 1982-83, Ill. Impact Bd., 1983. Resource person 1980 Youth Triennium, Bloomington, Ind., 1980; bd. dirs. Edwardsville Sch. Bd., 1976-83, Mental Bd. Washakie County, 1989—2003, pres., 1999. Recipient M. Keith Upson award U.S. Jaycees, 1974; named Outstanding New Mem., Ill. Jaycees, 1972, Outstanding Mem., 1973. Home: 2505 Shelby Lane Ocean Springs MS 39564-0053 *In the 21st Century, we are called as Abraham to live on a wilderness frontier of life. This radically unique environment demands creative risks and personal ethical choices. Listening to one another's wilderness journeys, learning from each other and supporting others are the keys for genuine faith, hope and love in the future.*

FOTE, CHARLES T., computer company executive; BS, Ctrl. Conn. State Univ. V.p. ops. Farmington Trust; dir. spl. projects Am. Express (First Data) Corp., 1975—81, v.p. fin. & planning, 1981—85, exec. v.p., data svc. group, 1985—89, pres. IPS subsidiary, 1989—91; exec. v.p., payment & merchant svcs. First Data Corp., 1992—98, pres., COO, 1998—2002, pres., CEO, 2002—03, chmn., CEO, 2003—. Office: First Data Corp 6200 S Quebec St Englewood CO 80111*

FOTHERGILL, DAVID MARK, medical researcher; s. William Henry and Jennifer Peta Fothergill. BSc in Sports Sci. with honors, Liverpool (Eng.) John Moores U., 1985; MSc in Kinesiology, Simon Fraser U., Burnaby, B.C., Can., 1989; PhD, U. London, Royal Free Hosp. Sch. of Medicine, England, 1992. Cert. US Navy Diver (Diving Medical Officer) Naval Diving and Salvage Tng. Ctr., Panama City, FL, 2001, Qualified Nitrox Diver Internat. Assn. of Nitrox and Tech. Divers, FL, 2003, Advanced Undersea/hyperbaric Medical Team Training Hyperbarics Internat. Inc., Key Largo, FL, 2003. Nat. rsch. coun. fellow Naval Med. Rsch. Inst., Bethesda, Md., 1992—94; sr. scientist Naval Submarine Med. Rsch. Lab., Groton, 1997—, Naval Med. Rsch. Inst., Bethesda, Md., 1994—97, Rsch. Found., Ctr. for Rsch. and Edn. in Spl. Environments, Buffalo, 1994—. IRB co-chair Naval Submarine Med. Rsch. Lab., Groton, Conn., 1999—. Pres. Thames Regional Investment Club, Gales Ferry, Conn., 2001—. Scholar Grad. Rsch. fellowship, Simon Fraser U., 1986, 1987, 1988. Achievements include research in effects of CO2 and N2 partial pressures on cognitive and psychomotor performance in the hyperbaric environ., undersea biomedical rsch; utility of mechanical aids to reduce the physical demands of shipboard emergency damage-control tasks; diver respiratory responses to a tunable closed-circuit breathing apparatus; physiological and perceptual responses to hypercarbia during warm- and cold-water immersion; heart rate changes during exposure to low frequency underwater sound; towards exposure limits to low frequency underwater sound: methodological considerations for human testing; aerobic performance of Special Operations Forces personnel after a prolonged submarine deployment; recreational SCUBA divers' aversion to low frequency underwater sound; neoprene wetsuit hood affects low-frequency underwater hearing thresholds; dynamic and static strengths of the human in whole body exertions, internat. soc. of biomechanics newsletter; gender differences in emergency shipboard damage control task performance: human factors solutions; human strength capabilities during one-handed maximum voluntary exertions in the fore and aft plane; narcosis and exercise I: exercise tolerance while under the influence of inert gas narcosis; narcosis and exercise II: effects of inert gas narcosis on breathing and effort sensations during exercise with inspiratory resistive loading; hypercarbia recognition and thermal status of exercising divers exposed to cold water and elevated PICO2; effects of a prolonged submarine deployment on Special Operations Forces mission-related performance; field-based procedures for screening diver's air; submarine rescue system- hyperbaric oxygen treatment pack; recreational diver responses to 600—2500 Hz waterborne sound; psychological, physiological, and medical impact of the submarine environment on submariners with application to VIRGINIA class submarines; exercise aboard attack submarines: Rationale and new options; influence of handle designs and handle height on the strength of the horizontal pulling action; effects of nitrogen narcosis and hypercapnia on memory; protocol for the Omnidirectional Assessment of Manual Strength; sys. for the tri-axial measurement of manual strength; characteristics of maximal dynamic lifting on a hydrodynamometer; influence of task resistance on the characteristics of maximal one- and two-handed lifting exertions in men and women; effects of N2O narcosis on breathing and effort sensations during exercise and inspiratory resistive loading. Avocations: zymergy, skiing, bicycling, travel, swimming. Office: Naval Submarine Med Rsch Lab Box 900 Groton CT 06349-5900 Office Phone: 860-694-2536.

FOTHERGILL, WILLIAM COREY, counselor, consultant; b. Hartford, Conn., Jan. 14, 1966; s. Osiedell Allen. BA, Ctrl. Conn. State U., 1989; MA, L.I. U., 1992; postgrad., U. Conn., 2000—. Lic. profl. counselor, Conn. Tchr. Southend Cmty. Childcare, Hartford, 1986-88, Capitol Child Devel., Inc., Hartford, 1988-92; juvenile case mgr. Conn. Jr. Rep., Hartford, 1992-95; assoc. dir. Parisky Group Hartford Action Plan, 1995-96; clin. family social worker Town of Bloomfield, Conn., 1996-2000; counselor Ctrl. Conn. State U., New Britain, 1996—. Coach U.S. Track & Field, Inc., 1995—; trainer cons. Parisky Group: Hartford Action Plan, Inc., 1996—; therapeutic cons. South Windsor (Conn.) Pub. Sch., 2000—. Bd. dirs. Epesi Youth Achievement Program, Hartford, 1997—; justice of the peace City of Hartford, 1998—; dir. christian edn. St. James Bapt. Ch., New Britain, 1998—. Mem. AAUP, Amateur Athletic Union, Conn. Counseling Assn. Avocation: running. Office: 1615 Stanley St New Britain CT 06053-2439

FOTI, CHARLES C., JR., state attorney general; b. New Orleans, Nov. 30, 1937; s. Charles C. and Eleanore (Palmisano) F. Student, La. State U., New Orleans; JD, Loyola U., New Orleans. Bar: La., U.S. Dist. Ct. (ea. dist.) La., U.S. Ct. Appeals, U.S. Supreme Ct. Litigation atty. FHA, New Orleans; trial atty. Dist. Attys. Office, New Orleans, Legal Aide Bur., New Orleans; atty. New Orleans Police Dept.; head criminal div. City Attys. Office, New Orleans; criminal sheriff Orleans Parish, New Orleans, 1973—2004; attn. gen. state of La., 2004—. Judge ad hoc Mcpl. Ct. City New Orleans; chmn. La. Commn. on Peace Officers Standards and Tng.; chmn. Total Community Action; mem. adv. bd. Nat. Am. Bank, Internat. Trade Mart Br.; lectr. criminal justice Our Lady State U., La. State U.; mem. Gov.'s Prison Overcrowding Task Force; mem. adv. bd. Housing Authority New Orleans; mem. La. Commn. on Law Enforcement and Adminstrn. Criminal Justice; mem. exec. com. Mayor's Criminal Justice Coord. Coun., City New Orleans; bd. mem. Mayor's Interagy. Coun. Govt. chmn. United Way campaign; mem. Emergency Preparedness Adv. Com.; mem. adv. bd. 4-H Club; campaign dir. March of Dimes; mem. exec. bd. Times Picayune Doll and Toy Fund; mem. steering com. Barthelemy Campaign Fin. Com.; mem. adv. com. Health Promotion Continuing Edn. Grant; bd. trustees La. Children's Mus.; mem. community rels bd. New Orleans Job Corps Ctr.; co-chmn. Tulane's Athletic Devel. Com.; mem. adv. bd. Children's Crisis Mgmt. Program. With U.S. Army, 1955-58. Mem. ABA (nat. com. on prisons, pardons and paroles), Nat. Sheriff's Assn. (law and legis. com., detention and corrections com.), La. Sheriff's Assn. (mem. exec. bd., chmn. state supplemental pay com.), Am. Correctional Assn., Am. Correctional Food Svc. Assn., Am. Correctional Health Svcs. Assn., Am. Fedn. Police, Am. Pub. Works Assn., Am. Soc. Indsl. Security, Am. Soc. Personnel Adminstrn., Am. Trial Lawyers Assn., Correctional Edn. Assn., Internat. Assn. Chiefs Police, La. State Bar Assn. Democrat. Roman Catholic. Office: Office of the Attorney General 1885 North 3rd Street Baton Rouge LA 70802 also: PO Box 94095 Baton Rouge LA 70804-4095

FOTOPOULOS, JAMES, artist; b. Norridge, Ill., 1976; Guest lectr."Film One" production class U. Tex., Austin, 2001, 2003; guest lectr. NJ City U., 2003; founder Fantasma Inc., 1998. Dir.: (films) ZERO, 1997, Migrating Forms, 1999 (Best Feature Award, NY Underground Film Festival, 2000, Made in Chgo. Award, Chgo. Underground Film Festival, 2000), Back Against the Wall, 2000, Consumed, 2001 (Chgo. Underground Film Fund Grant, Chgo. Underground Film Festival, 2001), Christabel, 2001, The Lighthouse, 2004 (No Budget Award, Cinematexas Internat. Short Film & Video Festival, 2004), Spine Face, 2005; exhibitions include with Cory Arcangel Fotopoulos/Arcangel Part 5, NY Underground Film Festival, 2004, exhibitions include Whitney Biennial, Whitney Mus. Am. Art, 2004, and others. Office: Fantasma Inc 1400 West Devon 440 Chicago IL 60660 E-mail: info@jamesfotopoulos.com.

FOTSCH, GEORGE BERNARD, III, chemical addiction counselor; b. Abbeville, La., May 9, 1945; s. George Bernard Fotsch Jr. and Norma Jeanne Fotsch; m. Evelyn Colleen Hunziker, Oct. 17, 1971 (div. Dec. 1988); children: Sandra, George, Seth, Evelyn, Troy; m. Jamie Linn Harper, June 21; 1 child, Candice Nicole. Student, U. Md., 1962—64, U. S.W. La., 1967—68, Am. Petroleum Inst., Long Beach, Calif., 1974—75. Lic. chem. dependency counselor TCADA, 1998. Mgr. Hollywood Diamond Exch., Long Beach, Calif., 1969; regional mgr. LeeRoy Barrys Jewelers, Riverside, Calif., 1970; ops. mgr. Armstrong Petroleum, Newport Beach, Calif., 1971—72; gen. mgr. Burmah Phillips Petroleum, Huntington Beach, Calif., 1973—83; counselor-in-tng. VA Chem. Dependency Treatment, Canandeiqua, NY, 1983—86; chem. dependency counselor Tex. Alcoholism Found., Houston, 1987—92; clin. dir. Cenikor Found., Inc., Deer Park, Tex., 1993—2004; exec. dir. Multi Addiction Counseling, 2004—. Author: (book) Thee True Book, 2002. Avocations: astronomy, cosmology, physics. Home: 10026 Antrium Ln La Porte TX 77571 Office: George B Fotsch PO Box 1012 La Porte TX 77572 Office Phone: 832-414-7883.

FOTTLER, MYRON DAVID, health services educator; b. Boston, Sept. 5, 1939; s. Myron Dustin and Anna Eileen Fottler; m. Carol Ann Fottler, Aug. 11, 1972. BS, Northeastern U., 1962; MBA, Boston U., 1963; PhD, Columbia U., 1970. Asst. prof. SUNY, Buffalo, 1967—75; from assoc. prof. to prof. U. Ala., Tuscaloosa, 1976—83, prof., PhD program dir. Birmingham, 1983—99; prof., program dir. U. Ctrl. Fla., Orlando, 1999—. Cons. numerous legal firms and corps. Author 18 books; contbr. over 30 chpts. to books and over 100 articles to profl. jours. Recipient Hayhew award, Am. Coll. Health Care Execs., 1997, Outstanding Svc. award, Acad. Mgmt.-Healthcare Mgmt. Divsn., 1999, Faculty Pub. of Yr., Am. Acad. Med. Adminstrs., 2001. Episcopalian. Avocation: tennis. Office: Univ Ctrl Fla Coll Health and Pub Affairs 210A HPA2 Orlando FL 32816-0001 Office Phone: 407-823-5531. Business E-Mail: fottler@mail.ucf.edu.

FOUDREE, BRUCE WILLIAM, lawyer; b. Des Moines, Mar. 27, 1947; s. Shie and Dorothy F.;m. Suzanne J. F. Reade, May 31, 1986; children: Andrew A., Grant R., Zarina. BA, Drake U., 1969; student, U. Geneva, Switzerland, 1968, U. Vienna, Austria, 1968; JD, Drake U., 1972; LLM, U. Pa., 1975. Bar: Iowa 1972, U.S. Ct. Appeals (8th cir.) 1976, U.S. Supreme Ct. 1977, Ill. 1986. Asst. atty. gen. Iowa Dept. Justice, Des Moines, 1976-80; ins. commnr. Iowa Ins. Dept., Des Moines, 1980-86; of counsel Mitchell, Williams, Selig and Tucker, Little Rock, 1986-88; shareholder Keck, Mahin & Cate, Chgo., 1988-96; of counsel Lord, Bissell & Brook, Chgo., 1996—. Commr., chmn. Iowa Ins. Dept., 1980-86; commr. Iowa Health Data Commn., 1983-86, chmn. 1985. Assoc. editor Drake Law Rev., 1971-72; dir. Jour. Ins. Regulation, 1982-89. Mem. ABA (TIPS scope and correlation com. 1991-94, chmn. fin. svcs. com. 1990-91, professionalism com. 1994-96), Nat. Assn. Ins. Commrs. (chmn. 1984, pres. 1985), Ins. Regulatory Examiners Soc. Found. (bd. dirs. 1991—, chmn. 1999-2000), Iowa State Bar Assn., Life & Health Compliance Assn., Union League Club of Chgo. (chmn. ins. group 1989-92), The Chicago Lighthouse (bd. dirs. 1995—, sec. 1998, chmn. 2002-05). Avocations: travel, history, literature, music. Office: Lord Bissell & Brook 115 S La Salle St Fl 3600 Chicago IL 60603-3902 Office Phone: 312-443-1830. E-mail: bfoudree@lordbissell.com.

FOUDREE, CHARLES M., financial consultant; BS in acctg., Truman State U., 1966. CPA Kans., Mo. Mem. audit staff Peat, Marwick, Mitchell, and Co., Kans. City, Kans., 1966-72; CFO, bd. dir. Harmon Industries, Inc., Blue Springs, Mo., 1972-99. Bd. dir. OTR Express, Inc., Olathe, Kans., 1995—2001, Carondelet Health, Kansas City, Mo., Sceptor Industries, Mo., SLS Internat., Springfield. Past chmn. bd. assocs. St. Mary's Hosp., Blue Springs; bd. dir. treas. Harry S. Truman Libr. Inst.; treas., trustee St. Paul Sch. Theology, Kansas City, Mo.; chmn. St. Mary's Hosp. Found., 2003-2005; chmn. Truman State U. Found., 2003-05. Mem. AICPA, Mo. Soc. CPAs, Fin. Exec. Inst. (bd. dir., past pres. Kansas City chpt., nat. bd. dir. 199s5-98), Independence C. of C. (past dir., treas.); Rotary Club of Independence (bd. dir.), Blue Key, Sigma Tau Gamma. Home: 4124 N E Pembroke Ln Lees Summit MO 64064-1622 Office Phone: 816-591-5109. E-mail: cfoudree@aol.com.

FOUDY, JULIE MAURINE, retired professional soccer player, Olympic athlete; b. San Diego, Jan. 23, 1971; m. Ian Sawyers, July 1995. BSW in Biology, Stanford U., 1993. Mem. U.S. Women's Nat. Soccer Team, 1987—2004, capt., 1992—2004; profl. soccer player San Diego Spirit, 2001—03. Color commentator Men's World Cup, ESPN, 1998. Mem. Tyresco Football Club, Sweden, 1994; pres. Women's Sports Found. Named World Cup Champion, 1991, 1999; recipient Gold medal, Centennial Olympic Games, 1996, Athens Olympic Games, 2004, FIFA Fair Play award, 1997, Silver medal, Sydney Olympic Games, 2000, Bronze medal, World Cup, 2003. Achievements include mem. Bronze medal winning team World Championships, Sweden, 1995; CONCACAF, Montreal, 1994; voted #1 most powerful in sports, Sports Business Journal, 2004. Office: c/o US Soccer Fedn 1801 S Prairie Ave # 1811 Chicago IL 60616-1319

FOUGHT, LORIANNE, plant pathologist; b. Upper Darby, Pa., Oct. 5, 1962; d. Edwin Howard and Jeanette Marie Matthews; m. Daniel Lynn Fought, Jan. 22, 1990; children: Bethannie, Angelique, Daniel, Kaitlyn. BS, Pa. State U., 1985; MS, U. Ky., 1988, PhD, 1992; MBA, U. Kan., 1996. Rsch. aid Pa. State U., University Park, 1982-85; grad. rsch. asst. U. Ky., Lexington, 1985-91; chemist II Bayer Corp., Bayer Research Park, Kans., 1991-93; sci. and regulatory specialist Bayer Corp./Animal Health, Shawnee Mission, Kans., 1993-98; sr. field devel. rep. Bayer Corp. Crop Protection, Kansas City, Mo., 1998—2002; fungicide product devel. mgr. Bayer CropSci., Research Triangle Park, NC, 2002—. Contbr. articles to profl. jours. Tchr. So. Hills United Meth. Ch., Lexington, 1989-90; Bayer Corp. Cmty. amb. Sch.-to-Career Program. Dept. Plant Pathology fellow U. Ky., Lexington, 1985-91. Mem. Am. Phytopathol. Soc. (sec. grad. student com. 1990-91), Am. Chem. Soc., Gamma Sigma Delta. Republican. Achievements include research in metabolism of xenobiotics in plants and animals, compound isolated from cucumber tissues which induces systemic resistance to disease in cucumbers. Investigated metabolism of agricultural chemicals in plants and animals. Field research of crop protection products. Development of fungicides for argonomic crops. Office: PO Box 12014 Research Triangle Park NC 27709

FOUILLADE, JEAN-PAUL ERIC, management consultant; b. Neuilly-Sur-Seine, France, Aug. 7, 1950; arrived in U.S., 1989; s. Paul Henri and Andrèe Françoise Fouillade; m. Fabienne Patricia Ide, June 17, 1972 (div. June 1994); children: Jean-Sèbastien, Aurèlie, Lorraine; m. Katherine Ruth Hensel, Sept. 24, 1994 (div. Dec. 2001). MBA, Hautes Etudes Commerciales, HEC, Jouy-en-Josas, France, 1972. Asst. treas. Lesieur Group, Paris, 1972—74, UTA French Airlines, Paris, 1975-76, treas., 1977-80; dir. control Usinor Sacilor Group, Paris, 1981-89; sr. v.p. fin. and adminstrn. Francosteel Corp., NYC, 1990-96; pres. Whitridge Enterprises, Jersey City, 1997—2001. Prof. Inst. Formation Continue, Paris, 1978—79. Dir. Summit (NJ) Child Care Ctr., 1996-99; trustee Com. French Speaking Soc., 2000-03, French Am. Conservatory of Music, 2001-05. Mem.: Union pour un Mouvement Populaire. Union Pour La Democratie Francaise. Roman Catholic. Avocations: horseback riding, skiing, plane pilot. Home and Office: 69 Big Spring Rd Califon NJ 07830

FOUKE, JANIE M., academic administrator, educator; BS, St. Andrews Presbyn. Coll.; MS in Biomedical Math. and Engring., U. NC, Chapel Hill. Prof. Dept. Biomedical Engring. Case Western Reserve U., Cleve., 1981—99; div. dir. Div. of Bioengineering and Environ. Sys., NSF, Washington, DC; dean Coll. Engring. Mich. State U., 1999—2005; provost, sr. v.p. academic affairs U. Fla., Gainesville, 2005—. Adv. bd. mem. Engring. Directorate, NSF, Nat. Inst. of Bioimaging and Bioengineering, NIH. Author: Engineering Tomorrow, 2000 (Dexter Prize, Soc. for History of Tech.); contbr. articles to profl. jours. Fellow: AAAS, IEEE, Am. Inst. Med. and Biological Engring.; mem.: Biomedical Engring. Soc. Office: U Fla 235 Tigert Hall PO Box 113175 Gainesville FL 32611 Office Phone: 352-392-2404. Office Fax: 352-392-8735. E-mail: jfouke@aa.ufl.edu.*

FOULADVAND, HENGAMEH, artist; b. Tehran, Iran; naturalized U.S. citizen, 1974; d. Mansour and Mahin F.; m. Masoud B. Mansouri, Feb. 20, 1981; 1 child, Tia. BA, San Jose State U., 1976; M, Calif. State U., 1979. Exec. dir. Ctr. Iranian Modern Arts, 1998—. Art cons. T.H.E. Graphics & Design, 1990-96; graphic & prodn. cons. Metro Lables, 1994-96. Exhibited in solo and group shows including Columbia U., N.Y.C., 1989, L.I. U., 1989, 91, Strathmore Arts Ctr., Md., 1991, Port Washington Pub. Libr., 1991, Huntington Arts Coun., Hecksher Mus., 1993, 95, McArthur Airport Terminal Bldg., L.I., 1996-97, Columbia U., Hamilton Bldg., N.Y.C., 1997, Lindberg Gallery, N.Y.C., 1999, GORA Gallery, Montreal, 1999, La Maison Francaise, Columbia, 2000; represented in permanent collections Ency. Iranica Found., N.Y., Line & Tone Typographics, N.Y., numerous pvt. collections; mem. editl. bd.: Tavoos Art Quarterly, 1999--. Mem. N.Y. State Coun. Arts, N.Y. Found. Arts, Huntington Art League and Coun. Long Island. Home: 34 Lisa Dr Dix Hills NY 11746 E-mail: hengamehf@earthlink.net.

FOULKE, EDWIN GERHART, JR., lawyer; b. Perkasie, Pa., Oct. 30, 1952; s. Edwin G. and Mary Claire (Keller) F. BA, N.C. State U., 1974; JD, Loyola U., New Orleans, 1978; LLM, Georgetown U., 1993. Bar: S.C. 1979, U.S. Dist. Ct. S.C. 1979, U.S. Ct. Appeals (4th cir.) 1979, Ga. 1986, U.S. Ct. Appeals (11th cir.) 1986, D.C. 1989, U.S. Ct. Appeals (D.C. cir.) 1989, U.S. Supreme Ct. 1990, N.C. 1997. Assoc. Thompson, Mann & Hutson, Greenville, S.C., 1978-83, Rainey, Britton, Gibbes & Clarkson, Greenville, 1983-85; ptnr. Constangy, Brooks & Smith, Columbia, S.C., 1985-90; chmn. Occupational Safety and Health Rev. Commn., Washington, 1990-95; ptnr. Jackson Lewis, Greenville, S.C., 1995—. Instr. St. Mary's Dominican Coll., New Orleans, 1977-78. Field rep. Reagan/Bush Campaign, Columbia, 1980, S.C. state coord., 1984; sec., treas. Employment Labor Law Sect., Columbia, 1981-82. Mem. ABA, S.C. Bar Assn., Ga. Bar Assn., Greenville County Bar Assn. (chmn. pub. rels. com. 1984-85), SAR, Rotary. Roman Catholic. Avocations: swimming, tennis, skiing, golf. Office: Jackson Lewis LLP 55 Beattie Pl Ste 800 Greenville SC 29601-2168 Office Phone: 864-232-7000. E-mail: foulkee@jacksonlewis.com.

FOULKE, KEITH CHARLES, professional baseball player; b. Ellsworth AFB, S.D., Oct. 19, 1972; m. Mandy Foulke; 1 child. Student, Galveston Coll., Lewis-Clark State Coll. Pitcher San Francisco Giants, 1997, Chgo. White Sox, 1997—2002, Oakland A's, 2003, Boston Red Sox, 2004—. Named to, Am. League All-Star Team, 2003; recipient Am. League Rolaids Relief award, 2003. Achievements include led American League in Saves (43), 2003. Office: c/o Boston Red Sox 4 Yawkey Way Boston MA 02215-3496

FOULKROD, SARAH SUTHERLAND, librarian; b. Clintwood, Va., Aug. 26, 1949; d. Benjamin Fulton and Sarah Neal (Cothron) Sutherland; m. Charles Bruce Foulkrod, Aug. 4, 1973; 1 child, Charles Matthew. BA, U. Ky., 1971; MLS, U. Pitts., 1972. Reference libr. Wilmington (Del.) Inst. Libr., 1972-77, coordinator, acquisitions, 1974-77; libr. Solebury Sch., New Hope, Pa., 1993—. Trustee Free Libr. of Northampton Twp., Richboro, Pa., 1981-87; mem. Dist. Adv. Com. for Bucks County Librs., Doylestown, Pa., 1987-91; sec. Friends of the Libr., Richboro, 1989-92. Mem. AAUW, ALA, Am. Needlepoint Guild, Pa. Sch. Librarians Assn., Richard III Soc. Republican. Methodist. E-mail: sfoulk@solebury.com.

FOULSTON, NOLA TEDESCO, lawyer; b. Mt. Vernon, N.Y., Dec. 14, 1940; d. Dominick J. and Theresa M. (Pellino) Tedesco; m. Steven L. Foulston, Jan. 2, 1983; 1 child, Andrew. BA, Ft. Hays State U., 1972; postgrad., U. Kans., 1972-73; JD, Washburn U., 1976. Bar: Kans. 1977, U.S. Dist. Ct. Kans., U.S. Ct. Appeals (10th cir.). Asst. dist. atty. 18th Jud. Dist., Dist. Atty.'s Office, Wichita, Kans., 1977-81; assoc. Foulston, Siefkin, Powers & Eberhardt, Wichita, 1981-86; ptnr. Foulston & Foulston, Wichita, 1986-89; dist. atty. Office of Dist. Atty. Eigthteenth Jud. Dist. Sedgwick County Courthouse, Wichita, 1989—. Bd. dirs., legal counsel YWCA, Wichita, 1978-83, pres. 1980-81; active YWCA's Women's Crisis Ctr., Wichtia Area Sexual Assault Ctr.; bd. dirs. Exploited and Missing Children's Unit, Project Freedom, Community Corrections, County-Wide Substance Abuse Task Force, State of Kans. Law Enforcement Coordinating Com., Community Rels. Task Force, Inter-Agy. Truancy Adv. Com., Women's Rsch. Inst., Crime Stoppers of Wichita Adv. Bd.; apptd. by Gov. Hayden of Kans. to the Weigand Commn. on State Expenditures. Named one of Outstanding Young Women of Am., Outstanding Young Wichitan, Wichita Jaycees, 1990; recipient Alumni Achievement award Ft. Hays State U., 1992, Law Enforcement Commendation medal SAR, 1992. Mem. ABA, Kans. Bar Assn., Wichita Bar Assn. (Outstanding Atty. of Achievement 1992), Nat. County and Dist. Attys. Assn., Kansas County and Dist. Attys. Assn., Golden Key (hon.). Democrat. Roman Catholic. Office: 535 N Main Wichita KS 67203-3702

FOUND, SANDRA THRALL, mathematics educator, mathematics professor; b. New London, Conn., Feb. 15, 1967; d. Robert William and Ruth Augusta Thrall; m. Andrew Stephen Found, Aug. 29, 1992. BA, Mt. Holyoke Coll., 1989; MEd, U. Mass., 1990. Tchr. math. Brewster Acad., Wolfeboro, NH, 1990—96, Alton Ctrl. Sch., 1996—2001, Gilford Mid. Sch., 2001—02, Winnisquam Regional High Sch., Tilton, 2002—. Adj. prof. math. N.H. Tchg. Inst., Concord, 2000—. Mem.: N.H. Tchr. Math., Nat. Coun. Tchrs. Math. Avocations: golf, coaching. Home: 64 Siel Rd Pittsfield NH 03263 Office: Winnisquam Regional High Sch 435 W Main St Tilton NH 03276

FOUNTAIN, EDWIN BYRD, minister, librarian, poet; b. Manassas, Ga., Mar. 11, 1930; s. David Theodore and Laura Bertha (Phillips) F. BFA, U. Ga., 1951; BRE, ThB, Lexington Bapt. Coll., 1980, MRE, 1981, DD (hon.), 1990; MLS, U. Ky., 1984; PhD in Edn., Am. Bible Coll. and Seminary, 1998. Ordained to ministry Bapt. Ch., 1982. Pastor Riverview Bapt. Ch., Lexington, Ky., 1982-87; libr. asst. Lexington Bapt. Coll., 1980-81, tchr., libr., 1981-90; divisional chmn. libr. svcs. Tenn. Temple U., Chattanooga, 1990-91; librarian Statesboro (Ga.) Regional Libr., 1991-93. Author: The Sovereignty and Rightousness of God, 1997, Election and Redemption, 2000, (bibliography) Reformation in Italy and Southern France, 16th, 17th, 18th and 19th Centuries, 2000; compiler indexes for religious books: (by B.H. Carroll) An Interpretation of the English Bible, (by T.P. Simmons) A Systematick Study of Bible Doctrine, (with Jim Jeffries) A Student's Writers Guide, Fountains and Related Families, 2001, Hymn There Was a Night in Israel, 2002, (young adult novel) Whispers From the Past, 2004; contbr. articles to profl. publs., poetry to anthologies. U. Ky. fellow, 1990. Mem. ALA, SAG, SAR (local sec.), S.R., SCV, Christians Librs. Assn., Actors Equity Assn., Bulloch County Hist. Soc., Darlington County Hist. Commn., Lexington Bapt. Coll. Alumni Assn. (pres. 1982-87, 89-90), Armstrong State Coll. Alumni Assn., Beta Phi Mu. Home: 311 Jerriel St Cocoa FL 30474

FOUNTAIN, KAREN SCHUELER, retired physician; b. Aberdeen, SD, Oct. 14, 1947; BA, No. State Coll., Aberdeen, S.D., 1968; MD, U. Md., Balt., 1972. Diplomate Nat. Bd. Med. Examiners, Am. Bd. Radiology in Therapeutic Radiology. Intern Md. Gen. Hosp., Balt., 1972-73, resident in radiation oncology, 1973-74; fellow in radiation oncology Mayo Clinic, Rochester, Minn., 1974-76, cons. in oncology, 1976-81; clin. asst. prof. Columbia U., N.Y.C., 1981-83, residency program dir. dept. radiation oncology, 1981—93, clin. assoc. prof., 1983—2001, ret., 2004. Mem. med. bd. Presbyn. Hosp., N.Y.C., 1983-86; faculty coun. mem. Columbia U., 1982-89; del. N.Y. State Radiological Soc., N.Y.C., 1987—2004. Fellow Am. Coll. Radiology (councilor 1999—2004), Am. Radium Soc. (exec. com. 2004—), N.Y. Acad. Medicine; mem. Am. Soc. Therapeutic Radiology and Oncology, Radiol. Soc. N.Am., Am. Soc. Clin. Oncology, Am. Assn. for Women Radiologists (bd. dirs. 1995-96), N.Y. Roentgen Soc. (sect. chmn. 1989-90), N.Y. State Radiol. Soc. (bd. dirs. 1996-2002).

FOUNTAIN, KATHLEEN CARLISLE, librarian; b. Eugene, Oreg., Apr. 10, 1974; d. Paul Frederick and Cynthia Vivian Carlisle; m. Steven Michael Fountain, July 27, 1996. BA, Pacific Luth. U., 1996; MLS, U. Ill., 1997. Ref. libr. Creighton U., Omaha, 1997-99; ref., polit. sci. libr. Calif. State U., Chico, 1999—. Mem.: Assn. Coll. & Rsch. Librs. Office: Calif State U 215 Meriam Library Chico CA 95929-0295 Fax: 530-898-4443. E-mail: KFountain@csuchico.edu.

FOUNTAIN, ROBERT ROY, JR., retired engineering company executive, farmer, military officer; b. Norfolk, Va., Jan. 25, 1932; s. Robert Roy and Hilda (Burton) F.; m. Elizabeth Whitmarsh Bean, June 4, 1955; children: Robert, Dorothy, Sally, Edwin. Student, U. Rochester, 1950-51; BS Engring. with distinction, U.S. Naval Acad., 1955. Commd. ensign U.S. Navy, 1955, advanced through grades to rear adm., 1980; nuclear engr. serving in destroyers, cruisers, and nuclear submarines; comdg. officer U.S.S. Sea Devil, 1970-74; comdr. Submarine Devel. Squadron 12, New London, Conn., 1976-78; comdr. U.S. Naval Forces Marianas, comdr. U.S. Naval Base Guam comdr. in chief Pacific rep. Guam and Trust Ter. Pacific Islands, 1979-81; dep. chief Naval Sea Sys. Command, ASW and Undersea Warfare Sys., Navy Dept., Washington, 1981-85; ret., 1985; dir. Offshore Sys. Marine Sys. divsn. Honeywell, Seattle, 1986-88; v.p. Honeywell Advanced Marine Sys. Operation, Mpls., 1988, San Diego, 1989, Arlington, Va., 1990-91; dir. tech. plans & resources Alliant Techsystems Inc., Arlington, Va., 1991-92. Presdl. elector, 1996; chmn. Westmoreland County Rep. Com.; mem. Commn. on Va. Nat. Def. Indsl. Authority, 2005—. Decorated Legion of Merit (3), Def. Superior Service medal, Meritorious Service medal (2), Navy Commendation medal. Mem.: SAR, Assn. Preservation Va. Antiquities, Va. Small Grains Assn., No. Neck Hist. Soc. (pres.), Naval Submarine League, Mil. Officers Assn., Naval Acad. Alumni Assn., Am. Legion. Home: Stillwater 4750 Zacata Rd Montross VA 22520-3510

FOUNTAIN, RONALD GLENN, management consultant, corporate financial executive; b. Mason City, Wash., Feb. 12, 1939; s. Aldine Shirah and Ella Maude (Fordham) F.; m. Ethel Joan Hightower, Aug. 22, 1968; children: John Hightower, Dana Leigh. AS, Ga. Southwestern Coll., 1959; BS, Valdosta State U., 1965; MBA, Case Western Res. U., 1983, ExecDrMgmt, 1999. V.p. nat. accounts Ctrl. Bancshares, Birmingham, Ala., 1973-74; cash control mgr. White Consol., Cleve., 1974-76, asst. treas., 1976-79, treas., dir. investor rels., 1979-82, v.p., treas., 1982-83, v.p. fin., treas., 1983-86; pres. Dix & Eaton,

1986-88; v.p. fin., CFO M.A. Hanna Co., Cleve., 1988-93; mng. prin. The Commonwealth Group, Cleve., 1993-04; sr. exec. v.p. Roulston & Co., Cleve., 1994-96; adv. dir. InfoSource, Harris Co., 1995-98; ptnr. The Parkland Group, 1996—2003; pres., CEO United Truck Fin. & Mktg., 1998—2001; prof. mgmt. Walsh U., North Canton, Ohio, 2003—; prin. Capital Acceleration Ptnrs. LLC, 2003—. Adj. faculty Weatherhead Sch. Mgmt., exec. dir. profl. fellow program, 2000-02; bd. dirs. Dise & Co., Delta Sys. Inc., Ironrock Capital, GEI/VE. Trustee Notre Dame Coll., Cleve., 1984-90, Laurel Sch., 1986-90, Pub. Radio Sta. WCPN, 1990-93, MetroHealth Sys., Ctr. Families and Children; chmn. N.E. Hospice Study Com., 1989-93; bd. dirs. Jr. Achievement Cleve., 1982, Nat. Adoption Exch., Phila., 1983, Cleve. Edn. Fund, 1983-87. Mem.: Planning Forum (pres. 1992—94), Nat. Investor Rels. Inst. (pres. 1978—79), Assn. Corp. Growth, Fin. Execs. Inst. (membership chmn. 1983—84), Alumni Assn. Weatherhead Sch. Mgmt. (pres. 1985—88), Country Club, Union Club. Home: 2908 Paxton Rd Cleveland OH 44120-1824 Office Phone: 216-241-0500 x 32. E-mail: rgf2908@msn.com.

FOURAKER, MICHAEL DANA, zoological park administrator; s. Sarah Fouraker; m. Deborah Jean Olson, Dec. 4, 1998. Exec. dir. / ceo Ft. Worth Zool. Assn., Tex., 2001—. Nat. commn. advisor UNESCO, Washington, 2004—; bd. pres. Internat. Elephant Found., Azle, Tex., 1999—; founding bd. mem. Internat. Iguana Found., Ft. Worth, 2002—; bd. mem. Internat. Rhino Found., Ft. Worth, 1994—. Bd. mem. C. of C., Ft. Worth, 2005. Fellow: Am. Zoo and Aquarium Assn. Office: Fort Worth Zoological Park 1989 Colonial Parkway Fort Worth TX 76110 Office Phone: 817-759-7500.

FOUREMAN, NANCY LEE, artist; b. Greenville, Ohio, June 24, 1944; d. LaVern Columbus and Adonia Pauline (Lane) Foreman; m. Richard Allen Foureman, June 29, 1963; children: Stacy Lee, Steven Allen. Student, Ind. State U., 1962; BFA, Miami U. Ohio, Oxford, Ohio, 1963; postgrad., Eldison State Coll., Art Instrn. Schs., Mpls., 1966. Owner, mgr. Studio Gallery, Greenville, 1970—. Bd. dirs. Darke County Fair, Greenville; condr., judge freelance workshops and seminars; mgr. Hatfield's Color Shop, Rockport, Mass., 1988-89; dir., chmn. over 50 exhibits in midwest region; chmn. Nat. Wildlife Exhbn., Greenville Guild Regional Exhbn. One-woman shows include Riverbend Art Ctr., Dayton, Ohio, Ind. U., Middletown Fine Arts Ctr., Parma Art Ctr., Cleve., Indlps. State Mus., Garst Mus., Ohio, Cincinnati Mus. Natural History, Cleve. Mus. Natural History, Ohio State Mus., Richmond Art Mus., Ind.; exhibited in group shows at Am. Painters in Paris, Dayton Painters and Sculptors Exhbn., Hoosier Salon, Indpls., others; represented in permanent collections Cleve. Mus. Natural History, corp. collections. Trustee Darke County Ctr. for Arts, Darke County Ctr. for Arts, 1988—; cons. Greenville Sch. Bd., 1990—; bd. dirs. Greenville Guild and Theater, 1970-83, Greenville City Art Sch., 1977; chmn. bd. Greenville Art Gallery. Recipient Best of Show award Art Instrn. Schs., 1970, Garst Mus., 1983, Burkner Nat. Exhibit, Troy, Ohio, 1990, David Humphrey Miller award Wassenburg Art Ctr., May Van Landingham merit award Winchester Court House, Agnes T. Lontz merit award for watercolor, pastel award Lima Art Assn., watercolor award Middletown Fine Arts Ctr., Judges Choice award, Oil Painters Am., Chgo., 1992; Susan K. Black grantee. Mem. North Shore Arts Assn., Tri Arts (Dayton, Ohio), Greenville Art Guild (pres. 1975-93), Darke County Agrl. Soc. (bd. dirs., sec. 1977-93), Preble County Art Assn., Art Assn. Richmond (Ind.) (hon.), Dayton Painters and Sculptors, Master Works for Nature Artists, Western Ohio Watercolor Soc., Hoosier Salon, Ind. Plein Air Painters Assn. Avocations: swimming, grandchildren. Home: 6441 Daly Rd Greenville OH 45331-8402 Personal E-mail: rfoureman@skyenet.net.

FOURNARIS, THEODORE JAMES, lawyer; b. Lancaster, Pa., Apr. 27, 1946; s. James S. and Stella (Petrakis) Fournaris; children: Ana Nicole, Alexander. BA, Franklin and Marshall Coll., 1968; MA, Boston U., 1971; JD, U. Miami, 1973. Bar: Fla. 1974, U.S. Dist. Ct. (so. dist.) Fla. 1986. Staff atty. FPC, Washington, 1974; assoc. Friedman, Britton & Stettin, Miami, Fla., 1975-76; ptnr. Carey Dwyer Cole Selwood & Bernard, Miami, 1977-82; pvt. practice Fournaris & Sanet, P.A., Miami, 1982—. With U.S. Army Intelligence, 1968-71. Mem. ATLA, Am. Coll. Legal Medicine, Fla. Acad. Trial Lawyers. Avocations: boating, travel. Office: 145 Almeria Ave Coral Gables FL 33134-6008

FOURNET, LISA CLARK, music educator; d. William Spiva and Patsy Dunigan Clark; m. Dickens Quin Fournet, May 13, 2000. MusB, U. Miss., 1983; MusM Edn., Miss. State U., 1986. Choral music tchr. Ridgeland H.S., Miss., 2002—, Holmes C.C., Goodman, Miss., 2001—02; music tchr. Neshoba Ctrl. H.S., Philadelphia, Miss., 1995—2000; pvt. piano studio Louisville, Miss., 1986—95; organist/youth choir dir. First Presbyn. Ch., Louisville, 1987—95. Musician teacher. Life mem. Louisville Jr. Aux., Louisville, 1987—2003; regional dir. Miss. Jr. Miss Assn., Meridian, Miss., 1993—95; mem. Lydian Music Club, Philadelphia, Miss., 1995—2000. Recipient Miss Miss. Farm Bur., Miss. Farm Bur. Fedn., 1981. Mem.: Miss. Profl. Educators, Music Educators Nat. Conf., Am. Choral Directors Assn. Avocations: Nascar fan, travel, judging pageants.

FOURNIE, RAYMOND RICHARD, lawyer; b. Belleville, Ill., Jan. 3, 1951; s. Raymond Victor and Gladys M. (Muskopf) F.; m. Mary Lindeman, Sept. 2, 1978; children: Sarah Dozier, John David, Anne Gerard, David Raymond. BS, U. Ill., 1973; JD, St. Louis U., 1979. Bar: Mo. 1979, Ill. 1980. Assoc. Moser, Marsalek, et al., St. Louis, 1979-80, Brown, James & Rabbitt, P.C., St. Louis, 1981-82, Shepherd, Sandberg & Phoenix, P.C., St. Louis, 1982-86; shareholder Shepherd, Sandberg & Phoenix, St. Louis, 1986-88; ptnr. Armstrong Teasdale LLP, St. Louis, 1988—. U. Ill. fellow, 1974. Mem. Mo. Bar Assn., Ill. Bar Assn., St. Louis Bar Assn. (sec. trial sect.), Lawyers Assn. (v.p. 1987-88, pres. 1990-91), Actors Equity Assn. Roman Catholic. Avocations: professional singer and actor, baseball, golf. Home: 4 Ridgetop St Saint Louis MO 63117-1021 Office: Armstrong Teasdale LLP One Metropolitan Sq Ste 2600 Saint Louis MO 63102-2740

FOUSE, DAVID JESSE, corporate financial executive, architect, engineer; b. Little Rock, Ark., Dec. 14, 1960; s. Richard Paul and Alice Mae (Aguilera) F. BS in Meteorology, Tex. A&M U., 1983; BS in Computer Sci., U. Tex. at San Antonio, 1987; MS in Computer Sci., Tex. A&M U. at Commerce, 1992. Assoc. software engr. E-Sys. Greenville (Tex.) Divsn., 1988—90, software engr., 1990—92, sr. software engr., 1992—95, E-Sys. Garland (Tex.) Divsn., 1995—97; software engring. specialist Lockheed Martin Vought Sys., Grand Prairie, Tex., 1997—98; lead application developer Wyndham Internat., Dallas, 1998—2002; Java/J2EE devel. do IT solutions, Arlington, Tex., 2002—04; v.p. Citi Cards, Irving, Tex., 2004—. Asst. coach YMCA Youth Soccer, Greenville, 1994-95. Mem. KC. Roman Catholic. Avocations: running, weight tng, volley ball. Home: 1813 Kingsbrook Trl Fort Worth TX 76120 Office: Cit Cards 250 East Carpenter Freeway Irving TX 75062

FOUST, DIANE, music educator; b. Oxford, Miss., July 31, 1953; d. William Baxter and Lillie Overstreet Foust; m. James A. Nelson, Oct. 23, 1993. MusB in Vocal Performance, Millsaps Coll., 1975; MusM in Vocal Performance, So. Meth. U., 1978; EdD in Music Edn., U. Ill., 1993. Prof. music Viterbo U., La Crosse, Wis., 1985—. Mem.: Music Educators Nat. Conf., Am. Choral Dirs. Assn., Nat. Assn. Tchrs. Singing. Avocations: theater, golf, reading. Home: 2130 State St La Crosse WI 54601 Office: Viterbo U 900 Viterbo Dr La Crosse WI 54601 Office Phone: 608-796-3768.

FOUST, LAWRENCE L., lawyer; b. Houston, Apr. 22, 1953; s. William L. and Barbara J. Foust; m. Christine E. Wagener, Sept. 1, 1948. BA, Duke U., Durham, N.C., 1975; JD, U. of Va., 1978, LLM, 1980; MBA, U. of St. Thomas, Houston, 1996. Bar: Tex. 1980, Va. 1978; Master of Vessels USCG, 2004. Fellow U. of Va. Schs. of Medicine and Law, Charlottesville, 1978—80; atty. Wood, Lucksigner & Epstein, Houston, 1980—83; assoc. gen. counsel Sisters of Charity, Houston, 1983—95; shareholder Jenkens & Gilchrist, Houston, 1996—. Mem. audit com. UT Physicians, Houston, 2003—. Dir. Southampton Civic Assn., Houston, 2005, Houston Taping for the Blind Radio, Houston, 2004. Named Tex. Super Lawyer Health Law, Tex. Monthly Mag., 2003—04, Outstanding Physician Practice Atty., Beard Group, 2004. Mem.: Va. State Bar, Tex. State Bar, Houston Bar Assn., Am. Health Lawyers Assn. Lutheran. Avocations: sailing, travel. Home: 2240 Robinhood Houston TX 77005 Office: Jenkens & Gilchrist 1401 McKinney Ste 2600 Houston TX 77010 Office Phone: 713-951-3378. E-mail: lfoust@jenkens.com.

FOUST, ROBERT SCHMERTZ, legislative staff member; b. New Holland, Pa., Jan. 20, 1941; s. Wilson Arbogast and Elizabeth (Schmertz) F. BA in Polit. Sci., Upsala Coll., 1964; MA in Internat. Rels., Lehigh U., 1971. Asst. dir. admissions Upsala Coll., East Orange, N.J., 1965-69; legis. asst. Office of Senator Claiborne Pell, Washington, 1970-89; cons. Indochinese Cmty. Ctr., Washington, 1990-91; sr. policy adv. Office of Senator Kent Conrad, Washington, 1991—2005. Named Outstanding Young Men of Am., Jaycees, 1973; recipient U.S. Coast Guard commendation, U.S. Dept. Vets. Affairs commendation, Disabled Am. Vets. commendation, Career Resources Network Assn. commendation; grantee Nat. Assn. Federally Impacted Schs., Nat. Head Start Assn. Mem.: Asia Soc., The Army and Navy Club. Office: 530 Hart Senate Office Bldg Washington DC 20510-0001 E-mail: jurongsq@aol.com.

FOUT, MARY JANE, librarian, educator; b. East St. Louis, Oct. 26, 1937; d. William Pomeroy and Phebe Georgia (Anderson) Eaton; m. John Calvin Fout, Feb. 26, 1960 (div. May 1973); children: Justine Alyss, Elizabeth, John Eric. BA in German and History, U. Omaha, 1959, MA in History, 1963; M of Libr. and Info. Sci., U. Calif., Berkeley, 1977. Cert. tchr., Nebr., N.Y., Calif. Tchr. Indian Hills Jr. H.S., Omaha, 1959-60, Tech. Jr. High Sch., Omaha, 1962-64, Heidelberg Jr. H.S., Germany, 1964-65; archivist intern Social Welfare History Archives, U. Minn., Mpls., 1965-67; lectr. history U. Nebr., Omaha, 1967-68; interlibr. loan libr. Bard Coll., Annandale-on-Hudson, N.Y., 1971-73; career ctr./attendance clk. Armijo High Sch., Fairfield, Calif., 1974-76, career ctr./English Libr. libr., 1976-82, tchr. fgn. lang. and pub. svc., 1982-89, libr., 1989—. Summer youth employment tng. program counselor, summers 1980—. Contbg. author: Social Welfare History archives Collection, 1972. Mem. AAUW (past pres.), World Affairs Coun. No. Calif., Calif. Media Libr. Educators Assn. (charter), Am. Field Svc. (dist. rep., past pres. chpt., Pat Lawrence award 1990), Overseas Brats, Commonwealth Club, Alpha Xi Delta, Delta Kappa Gamma. Democrat. Avocations: reading murder mysteries, spectator sports, travel.

FOUTS, JAMES FREMONT, mining company executive; b. Port Arthur, Tex., June 3, 1918; s. Horace Arthur and Willie E. (Edwards) F.; m. Elizabeth Hanna Browne, June 19, 1948; children: Elizabeth, Donovan, Alan, James. BChemE, Tex. A&M U., 1940. Div. supt. Baroid divsn. N.L. Industries, U.S. Rocky Mountain area and Can., 1948-60; pres. Riley-Utah Co., Salt Lake City, 1960-67, Fremont Corp., Monroe, La., 1967—, Auric Metals Corp., Salt Lake City, 1972-2000. Bd. dirs. La Fonda Hotel, Santa Fe, High Plains Natural Gas Co., Canadian, Tex. Hon. asst. sec. of State of La. Served to lt. col. arty U.S. Army, 1942-46. Mem. Wyo. Geol. Assn. (v.p. 1958), Rocky Mountain Oil & Gas Assn. (bd. dirs. 1959), Res. Officers Assn. Wyo. (pres. 1948), Am. Assn. Petroleum Geologists, Internat. Geol. Assn., Mont. Geol. Assn., Ind. Petroleum Producers Assn. Clubs: Univ. Lodges: Elks. Republican. Episcopalian. Home: 4002 Bon Aire Dr Monroe LA 71203-3015 Office: Fremont Corp PO Box 7070 Monroe LA 71211-7070

FOWKE, BENJAMIN G.S., III, energy executive; BS in Fin. and Acctg. magna cum laude, Towson U. CPA 1982. Auditor KPMG; supr. internal audits Dart Group; mgr. fin. reporting DWG Corp.; various fin. positions FP&L Group; v.p. retail bus. unit New Century Energies; v.p., CFO Energy Markets; v.p., treas. Xcel Energy Inc., 2002, v.p., CFO, treas. Bd. mem. Milestone Growth Fund. Office: Xcel Energy Inc 800 Nicollet Mall Minneapolis MN 55402

FOWLE, BRUCE S., architect; m. Marcia Fowle; 3 children. BA in architecture, Syracuse U, School of Architecture, 1960. Assoc. Edward Larrabee Barnes, FAIA, 1970—77; co-founder, sr. principal Fox & Fowle Architects, P.C., 1978—. Co-founder Architects, Designers, and Planners for Social Responsibility, NYC, 1982; chmn. Syracuse U. School of Architecture Adv. Comm. Named Nat. Academician, Nat. Acad. of Design, 1994; named to Am. Institute of Architects College of Fellows, 1985; recipient George Arents Pioneer Medal, Syracuse U., 2001. Fellow: Institute for Urban Design; mem.: Am. Institute of Architects Design Comm. Office: Fox & Fowle 22 W 19th St New York NY 10011*

FOWLE, MARILYN M., academic administrator; d. Charles McCorkle and Marilyn Moore; m. Paul Fowle, 1986; children: Andrea, William. BA, U. Houston, Clear Lake, 1990; MBA, Rice U., 1994; EdD, U. Pa., 2005. Sr. budget analyst U. Houston, 1992—95, dir. operating budgets, 1995—96; assoc. v.p. adminstrn., asst. to CEO Tex. A&M. U., Galveston, 1996—2000, exec. asst. to CEO, 2000—02; v.p. bus. and adminstrn. Dakota State U., Madison, SD, 2002—. Bd. dirs. Jr. Achievement, Madison, SD, 2003—04; fin. subcom. Madison Ctrl. Sch. Dist., 2003—04; cowriter of grants. Office: Dakota State Univ 820 Washington Ave Madison SD 57042

FOWLER, ALAN BICKSLER, retired physicist; b. Denver, Oct. 15, 1928; s. Alan Bruce and Minnie Edna (Bicksler) F.; m. Kathleen Teresa Devlin, Sept. 4, 1950; children: Stephen B., Susan Fowler-Finn, Andrew A., Sarah A. BS, Rensselaer Poly. Inst., 1951, MS, 1952; PhD, Harvard U., 1958. Rsch. staff mem. Raytheon Mfg. Co., Rsch. Div., Waltham, Mass., 1953-56, IBM Rsch. Div., Yorktown Heights, N.Y., 1958-83; IBM fellow Yorktown Heights, N.Y., 1983-93; IBM fellow emeritus, 1993—. With U.S. Army, 1946-48, 1st lt. Signal Corps, 1952-53. Recipient John Price Wetherill medal Franklin Inst., 1981, Alexander von Humboldt Preistraeger, 1982, David Sarnoff medal IEEE, 1987, Buckley prize Am. Phys. Soc., 1988. Mem.: NAE, NAS, IEEE, Royal Soc. of London (fgn.), Am. Acad. Arts and Scis., Am. Phys. Soc. Office: IBM T J Watson Rsch Ctr PO Box 218 Yorktown Heights NY 10598-0218 Personal E-mail: alnfwl@aol.com.

FOWLER, ALYCE MILTON, health facility administrator; BSBA, Almeda Coll.; postgrad., Ea. Conn. State U. Regional supr., acting adminstr. Kaiser Permanente, 1980—85; dir. vol. svcs. Windham Hosp., 1985—88; pvt. practice, 1988—92; regional mgr. HealthNet Corp., Oakland, NJ, 1992—94; practices mgr. St. Francis Hosp. and Med. Ctr., Hartford, Conn., 1994—96; dir. physician practice mgmt., dir. med. practice ops., physician recruiter Englewood (NJ) Hosp. and Med. Ctr., 1996—97; cons. Primecare Health Ptnrs., NY, 1997; exec. adminstr. physician practice mgmt. Ctrl. Conn. Health Alliance, 1998—2000; exec. adminstr. Fairfield County Allergy, Asthma and Immunology Assoc., 2000—04, Ea. Conn. Cardiology Group, 2004—. Com. mem. J. Paul Getty Trust Preservation. Named Mgr. of Yr., HealthNet Corp., 1993—94; recipient Caregiver award, Conn. Hosp., 1986, Conn. Connie Regional award, Am. Cancer Soc., 1986—87, Merit award, EastConn, 1986—87. Mem.: Conn. Women in Health Care Mgmt., Conn. Med. Group Mgmt. Assn., Am. Coll. Med. Practice Execs., Med. Group Mgmt. Assn. (cert.). Avocations: pottery, art. Home: 408 Pilgrim Harbor Wallingford CT 06492

FOWLER, BETH, actress; b. Jersey City, Nov. 1, 1940; Actor: (Broadway plays) Gantry, 1970, A Little Night Music, 1974, 1600 Pennsylvania Avenue, 1976, Peter Pan, 1979—81, Baby, 1984, Take Me Along, 1985, Teddy & Alice, 1987—88, Sweeney Todd, 1989—90 (Tony nominee best actress musical, 1990), Beauty and the Beast, 1994 (LA Ovation award), Bells Are Ringing, 2001, The Boy From Oz, 2003 (Tony nominee best featured actress musical, 2004). Office: Imperial Theatre 249 W 45th St New York NY 10036

FOWLER, BRUCE ANDREW, toxicologist, researcher, public health service official; b. Seattle, Dec. 28, 1945; s. Andrew and Dolores Yvonne F.; children from previous marriage: Glenn Andrew, Randall Bruce. BS in Fisheries, U. Wash., 1968; PhD in Pathology, U. Oreg., 1972. From staff fellow to head metal toxicology Nat. Inst. Environ. Health Scis., Research Triangle Park, NC, 1972—86, head metal toxicology, 1986—87; dir. toxicology program U. Md., 1987—2001; sr. rsch. advisor Agy. for Toxic Substances and Disease Registry, Atlanta, 2002—03, asst. dir. for sci., divsn. toxicology, 2003—; scientist environ. health Sr. Biomed. Rsch. Svc. USPHS, 2003—. Prof. pathology U. Md. Med. Sch., 1987—2001, prof. epidemiology and toxicology, 2001—03, dir. lab. of cellular and molecular toxicology dept. of epidemiology and preventive medicine, 2001—03; dir. office collaborative studies on adaptive responses estuarine species U. Md., 1988—2001; Meyer Bodansky lectr. Dept. Pathology, U. Tex. Med. Br., Galveston; adj. assoc. prof. U. NC, NC; temporary adv. WHO; work group mem. Internat. Agy. Rsch. Against Cancer; mem., chmn. Sci. Com. on Toxicology of Metals; mem. Md. Gov.'s Coun. on Toxic Substances, 1988—93, chmn., 1990—93, Dahlem Workshop on Mechanisms of Cell Injury: Implications for Human Health, Berlin, 1985; mem. toxicology info. program com. on toxicology; chmn. com. on measuring lead in critical populations; mem. com. on women in sci. and engring., com. on biologic markers in urologic toxicology NAS/NRC, 1989—93, com. on evaluation on viability of augmenting potable water supplies with reclaimed water, 1996—97, subcom. on arsenic in drinking water, 1997—99; co-chmn. NY Acad. Scis. Conf. on Mechanisms of Chem.-Induced Porphyrinopathies, Rye, NY; Swedish Med. Rsch. Coun. vis. prof. Karolinska Inst., 1994—95; Colgate-Palmolive vis. prof. U. Wash., 1998—99; mem. Fulbright scholarship rev. com., Scandinavia, 1999—2001, chair, Scandinavia, 2000—01; mem. nat. metals assessment panel sci. adv. bd. U.S. EPA, 2002—03, mem. nat. metals risk assessment framework review panel sci. advisory bd., 2004—; mem. expert panel Ctr. Evaluation of Risks to Human Reproduction Nat. Toxicology Program, 2003—. Editor: Biological and Environmental Effects of Arsenic, 1983, Mechanisms of Cell Injury: Implications for Human Health; co-editor: Mechanisms of Chemical Induced Porphyrinopathies, Handbook on the Toxicology of Metals, 3d edit.; editl. bd. Chemico-Biol. Interactions, 1980-85, Environ. Health Perspectives, 1981-97, Toxicology and Applied Pharmacology, 1985-96, Jour. Toxicology and Environ. Health, 1986-97, Internat. Archives of Environ. Health, 1986—, Renal Failure, 1988—, Internat. Jour. Occupl. and Environ. Health, 1994-96, Jour. Biochem. and Molecular Toxicology, 2000—; contbr. articles to profl. jours., chpts. to books. Rsch. fellow Japanese Soc. Promotion of Sci., 1990; Fulbright scholar Karolinska Inst., 1994. Fellow Acad. Toxicol. Scis.; mem. AAAS (recruitment and screening panel ct. apptd. sci. experts project 2000—), Am. Inst. Biol. Scis., Am. Soc. Pharmacology and Exptl. Therapeutics, Soc. Toxicology (councilor mechanisms of toxicity sect., pres. metals splty. sect. 1996, councilor nat. capitol area regional chpt. 1994-95, v.p. in-vitro splty. sect. 2001-02, pres. in-vitro splty. sect. 2003-04, councilor, 2005-), Am. Coll. Toxicology (councilor 1995-98), Soc. Occupl. and Environ. Health (councilor 1988, v.p. 1993), Fulbright Assn., NY Acad. Sci., Internat. Commn. Occupl. Health (chmn. sci. com. toxicology of metals 1996-2002), Profl. Assn. Diving Instrs., Sigma Xi. Office: ATSDR MSF-32 1600 Clifton Rd NE Atlanta GA 30333 Office Phone: 770-488-7250. E-mail: drtox@earthlink.net, bxf9@cdc.gov.

FOWLER, CHARLES ALBERT, electronics engineer; b. Centralia, Ill., Dec. 17, 1920; s. Clarence J. and Bess (Maxwell) F.; m. Kathryn Elizabeth Grimes, Oct. 23, 1943; children: Patricia Ann Paul, Mary Catherine Leathem. BS in Engring. Physics, U. Ill., 1942. Mem. staff radiation lab. MIT, 1942-45; head radar systems dept. Airborne Instruments Lab., Deer Park, N.Y., 1946-66; dep. dir. (tactical warfare) def. research and engring. Dept. Def., 1966-70; v.p., mgr. equipment devel. labs. Raytheon Co., Sudbury, Mass., 1970-76; sr. v.p., gen. mgr. Bedford (Mass.) ops. Mitre Corp., 1976-85; pres C.A. Fowler Assocs., 1986—. Mem. sci. adv. com. Def. Intelligence Agy., 1971—2000, chmn. sci. adv. com., 1976—82; mem. Air Force Sci. Adv. Bd., 1971—77, Def. Sci. Bd., 1972—98, chmn., 1984—88, vice chmn., 1988—90. Contbr. articles in field. Mem. East Norwich Sch. Bd., 1955-61, East Norwich Library Bd., 1956-62. Fellow IEEE, AAAS, AIAA; mem. Nat. Acad. Engring. Office: 15 Woodberry Rd Sudbury MA 01776-2227 E-mail: bfowler@aol.com.

FOWLER, CHARLES ALLISON EUGENE, retired architect, civil engineer; b. Halifax, N.S., Can., Jan. 24, 1921; s. Charles Allison and Mildred (Crosby) Fowler; m. Dorothy Christine Graham, Aug. 30, 1947 (dec. Sept. 1998); children: Graham Allison, Beverly Anne; m. Ruby Joyce Crooks, Aug. 21, 2002. BSc, Dalhousie U., 1942; B in Engring., McGill U., 1944; BArch., U. Man., 1948; DEng (hon.), Tech. U. of Nova Scotia, 1975. With C.A. Fowler, Bauld & Mitchell, Ltd. (and predecessor firms), Halifax, 1946-80, sr. ptnr., 1950-70, pres., 1970-80, chmn., 1980-81; pres. C.A. Fowler & Co., 1950-70, 81-95; ret., 1995. Prin. works include Miners Mus., Glace Bay, N.S., Dalhousie U. Fine Arts Ctr., 1970, univ. ctr. Acadia U., Acad. Ctr. at Mt. St. Vincent U., Halifax Law Cts., Canadian Martyrs Ch., Can. Permanent Bldg. Hfx., Halifax Metro Ctr., Stadacona Hosp., Victoria Gen. Hosp., Centre 200, Sydney, N.S. Past chmn. bd. dirs. N.S. Coll. Art and Design. With Can. Army, 1943-46. Fellow AIA (hon.), Royal Archtl. Inst. Can. (pres. 1965), Can. Soc. for Civil Engring.; mem. Engring. Inst. Can. (life). Mem. United Ch. Home: 2 Hall's Rd Halifax NS Canada B3P 1P3

FOWLER, CONRAD MURPHREE, retired manufacturing company executive; b. Montevallo, Ala., Sept. 17, 1918; s. Luther J. and Elsie (Murphree) F.; m. Virginia Evelyn Mott, June 15, 1945; children: Conrad, Randolph. BS, U. Ala., 1941, JD, 1948. Bar. Ala. 1948. Practiced in, Columbiana, 1948-53; mem. firm Ellis and Fowler, 1948-53; dist. atty. 18th Jud. Circuit Ala., 1953-59; probate judge, chmn. Shelby County Commn. Shelby County Ct., Columbiana, 1959-77; v.p. pub. affairs West Point-Pepperell, Inc., 1977-89, ret., 1989. Mem. Presdl. Adv. Commn. on Intergovtl. Relations, 1970-77 Mem. Ala. Dem. Exec. Com., 1966-77; chmn. Ala. Constl. Commn., 1970-76; bd. dirs. Associated Industries Ala., 1979-87, Pub. Affairs Coun., 1979-89; v.p. Am. Lung Assn., 1980-82, pres., 1982-83; mem. coun. Nat. Mcpl. League, 1976-82; vice chmn. Pub. Affairs Coun., 1987-89; bd. dirs. Ga. Bus. Coun., 1987-89. Col. USMCR, 1941-78. Decorated Silver Star with gold star, Purple Heart (2); named to Ala. Acad. Honor, 1981; recipient William Crawford Gorgas award Ala. Med. Assn., 1985; Rotary Paul Harris fellow, 1997; Kiwanis George F. Hixson fellow, 1999. Mem.: West Ala. Ret. Officers Club (pres. 2000—01), Probate Judges Assn. Ala. (pres. 1968—69), Assn. County Commrs. Ala. (pres. 1970—71), Nat. Assn. Counties (pres. 1969—70), Murphree Geneal. Assn. (pres. 1990—91), U. Ala. Nat. Alumni Assn. (pres. 1969, Alumnus of Yr. 1992), Tuscaloosa Exch. Club. Home: 1605 Bellingrath Dr Tuscaloosa AL 35406-2020

FOWLER, DAVID COVINGTON, language educator; b. Louisville, Jan. 3, 1921; s. Earle Broadus and Susan Amelia (Covington) F.; m. Mary Gene Stith, Jan. 28, 1943; children: Sandra Fowler Berryman (dec.), Caroline F. Aaron. BA in English, U. Fla., 1942; MA in English, U. Chgo., 1947, PhD in English, 1949. Prof. English U. Wash., Seattle, 1952-92, prof. emeritus, 1992—. Author: The Bible in Early English Literature, 1976, The Bible in Middle English Literature, 1984, John Trevisa, 1993, The Life and Times of John Trevisa, 1995, The Governance of Kings and Princes: John Trevisa's Middle English Translation of the De Regimine Principum of Aegidius Romanus, 1997; contbr. articles to profl. jours. Lt. (s.g.) USNR, 1942-46. ACLS scholar U. Pa., 1951-52; Guggenheim fellow, 1962-63, 75-76. Mem. AAR/SBL N.W. (pres. 1974), Medieval Assn. of Pacific (pres. 1980-82), Modern Lang. Assn., UW Folklore Rsch. Group (chmn. 1981-87), Calif. Folklore Soc. Home: 6264 19th Ave NE Seattle WA 98115-6902 Office Phone: 206-543-2690.

FOWLER, DAVID LUCAS, corporate lawyer; b. Heidelberg, Germany, Sept. 26, 1952; s. James Daniel and Nannie Romay (Lucas) F.; m. Cynthia Lou Smith, Aug. 19, 1989. BS, U.S. Mil. Acad., 1974; JD, Georgetown U., 1981. Bar: N.J. 1982, Calif. 1990, U.S. Ct. Fed. Claims 1990, U.S. Dist. Ct. (cen. dist.) Calif. 1990. 2d lt. U.S. Army, 1974, advanced through grades to maj., infantry platoon leader Berlin, 1975-76, asst. protocol officer, 1976-77, aide-de-campe U.S. comdr., 1977—78; minority augmentation recruit officer U.S. Mil. Acad., 1978; chief adminstrv. law sect. U.S. Army Tng. Ctr., Ft. Dix, N.J., 1983-86; command judge advocate U.S. Army Field Sta., Sinop, Turkey, 1985-86; govt. contracts trial atty. U.S. Army Legal Svcs. Agy., Falls Church, Va., 1986-89; resigned U.S. Army, 1989; corp. staff counsel Hughes Aircraft Co., L.A., 1989-94, sr. sgt. counsel Electro-Optical Sys. El Segundo,

Calif., 1994-95, asst. gen. counsel Arlington, Va., 1996-97; v.p., dep. gen. counsel Raytheon Sys. Co., Arlington, 1998-99; v.p. legal Raytheon Washington Ops., 1999—; v.p., dep. gen. counsel Raytheon Co., Arlington, 2000—; v.p., gen. counsel, sec. Raytheon Internat. Inc., Arlington, 2000—. Mem. Army Sci. Bd., Bd. Contract Appeals Bar Assn. (bd. govs.). Avocations: reading, weightlifting, golf. Office: Raytheon Co 1100 Wilson Blvd Ste 2000 Arlington VA 22209-2297

FOWLER, DON WALL, lawyer; b. Apr. 19, 1944; s. Slayden Grimes and Dorothy Lavenia (Wall) Fowler; m. Ruthann Arneson, Sept. 16, 1968 (div.); 1 child; m. Deborah Dewar, Sept. 15, 1984 (dec. Feb. 1986); m. Marcia Petlin, Oct. 1, 1988 (div.). BA, Emory U., 1966; JD, U. Chgo., 1969. Bar: Ill. 1969, U.S. Dist. Ct. (no. dist.) Ill. 1969, U.S. Ct. Appeals (7th cir.) 1980. Assoc. Lord Bissell & Brook, Chgo., 1969—77, ptnr., 1977—. Mem.: Def. Rsch. Inst., Ill. Assn. Def. Trial Counsel, ABA, Ill. Bar Assn., Chgo. Bar Assn. Unitarian Universalist. Office: Lord Bissell & Brook 115 S La Salle St Chicago IL 60603-3902 Office Phone: 312-443-0237. Business E-Mail: dfowler@lordbissell.com.

FOWLER, FLORA DAUN, retired lawyer; b. Washington, Aug. 11, 1923; d. Herman Hartwell and Flora Elizabeth (Adams) Sanford; m. Kenneth Leo Fowler, Aug. 22, 1941; children: Kenneth Jr., Michael, Kathleen, Daun, Jonathan, Colin, Kevin, James, Shawn, Maureen, Wendelyn, Liam, Tobias, Melanie. Student, Wilson Tchrs. Coll., 1940-41; AA, U. Md., 1973; JD, U. Balt., 1976. Bar: Fla. 1977, U.S. Dist. Ct. (mid. dist.) Fla. 1979, U.S. Ct. Appeals (5th and 11th cirs.) 1981. Staff atty. Cen. Fla. Legal Services Inc., Daytona Beach, 1978-80, mng. atty., 1980-81; pvt. practice, Daytona Beach, 1981-93; ret., 2001. Past editor Seabrook Acres Citizens' League Newsletter; columnist Bowie Express & Community Times; contbr. poems to New Voices in American Poetry, 1974. V.p. Seabrook (Md.) Acres Citizens League, 1970; past v.p. Prince Georges County Civic Fedn., Md.; past unit chmn. League of Women Voters, Prince Georges County; past pres., v.p., publicity chmn. Lanham-Bowie Dem. Club, Seabrook. Recipient Evening Star Trophy award Prince Georges County Civic Fedn., 1969. Mem. Fla. S. Ct. Hist. Soc. Democrat. Roman Catholic. Avocations: swimming, creative writing, cursillo. Personal E-mail: daunfowler@msn.com.

FOWLER, FLOYD JACKSON, JR., researcher; b. Akron, Ohio, July 4, 1939; s. Floyd Jackson Fowler and Marion Vaughn Holoman; m. Julia Ann Chambliss, Nov. 19, 1977; m. Diane Davant West, Sept. 3, 1960 (div. June 1974); children: Alex J., Randolph W., Elizabeth D. BA, Wesleyan U., 1960; MA, U. Mich., 1962, PhD, 1966. Asst. dir. Cmty. Rsch. Project Combined Jewish Philanthropies, Boston, 1965—68; asst. dir. Survey Rsch. Program Joint Ctr. for Urban Studies MIT and Harvard U., Cambridge, Mass., 1968—71; sr. rsch. fellow Ctr. for Survey Rsch. U. Mass., Boston, 1971—. Pres. Found. for Informed Med. Decision Making, Boston, 2002—; rschr. Dartmouth Med. Sch., Hanover, NH, 1984—. Author: Improving Survey Questions, 1995, Survey Research Methods, 2002; co-author: Standardized Survey Interviewing, 1990, Survey Methodology, 2004; mem. editl. bd.: Pub. Opinion Quarterly, 2003—. Mem.: Am. Statis. Assn., Am. Assn. Pub. Opinion Rsch. Avocation: writing. Office: Center for Survey Research U Mass Boston 100 Morrissey Blvd Boston MA 02125

FOWLER, FRED J., energy executive; b. Braman, Okla., 1946; m. Jan Fowler; 3 children. B in Fin., Okla. State U., 1968. With Conoco, Inc., 1968—74; v.p. natural gas liquids supply Enterprise Products Co, 1974—76; sr. v.p. Gulf States Oil & Refining, 1976—78; pres. Wynn-Fowler Trading Co., 1978—85; from gen. mgr. to v.p., gen. mgr. Panhandle Trading Co., 1985—87; v.p. mktg., transp. and exch. Panhandle Ea. Pipe Line Co., 1987—88, Trunkline Gas Co., 1987—88, Panhandle Ea., Trunkline and Tex. Ea. Transmission Corp., 1989; pres. Trunkline, 1991; corp. v.p. mktg. PanEnergy, 1992—93, group v.p., 1996; pres. Tex. Ea., 1994—96; group pres. energy transmission Duke Energy, Charlotte, NC, 1997—2002, pres., COO, 2002—. Mem.: Interstate Natural Gas Assn. Am. (chmn. bd.). Office: Duke Energy Corp 526 S Church St Charlotte NC 28202-1803

FOWLER, H(ORATIO) SEYMOUR, retired science educator; b. Detroit, Mar. 1, 1919; s. Horatio Seymour and Bessie Liona (Ladd) F.; m. Kathleen M. Marshall, Nov. 21, 1945 (dec.); 1 dau., Kathleen Marie Fowler Barto. BS, Cornell U., 1941, MS, 1946, PhD, 1951. Tchr. sci. McLean (N.Y.) Central Sch., 1946-47, Dryden (N.Y.) Freeville Central Sch., 1947-49; asst. prof. sci. edn. So. Oreg. Coll., Ashland, 1951-52; asst. prof. biology U. No. Iowa, Cedar Falls; also dir. Iowa Tchrs. Conservation Camp, 1952-57; prof. edn., dir. Pa. Conservation Lab. for Tchrs., Pa. State U., University Park, 1957-83, chmn. sci. edn. faculty, 1969-83, coordinator div. acad. curriculum and instrn., 1974-76, prof. nature and sci. edn. emeritus, 1983—; dir. Pa. Gov.'s Sch. for Scis., 1978-79. Sci. advisor Nat. Jr. Sci. and Humanities Symposium, Program U.S. Army Research Office, Acad. Applied Sci., 1979—. Author: Secondary School Science Teaching Practices, 1964, Las Ciencias en la Esquelas Secundarias, 1968, Fieldbook of Natural History, 1974; contbr. articles to profl. jours. Served with 9th inf. div. AUS, 1942-45, ETO. Fulbright lectr. Korea, 1968-69; recipient citation Pa. Dept. Edn., 1970, 83, Centre County (Pa.) Conservation award, 1973, Faculty Service award Nat. Univ. Continuing Edn. Assn., 1983, citation Pa. Ho. of Reps., 1983, Service award U.S. Army Office of Research, 1983; Paul Harris fellow Rotary Club, 1983 Fellow AAAS, Iowa Acad. Sci., Explorers Club; mem. Am. Nature Study Soc. (pres. 1967), Nat. Assn. Biology Tchrs. (v.p. 1956, dir. region II 1971-74, hon. mem. 1974), Nat. Assn. Rsch. in Sci. Teaching, Nat. Sci. Tchrs. Assn. (Disting. Svc. citation 1976), Pa. Sci. Tchrs. Assn. (dir. 1971—, v.p. 1975, pres. 1976, meritorious svc. to sci. teaching citation 1975), Korean Sci. Tchrs. Assn., Royal Asiatic Soc., Masons, Shriners, Rotary (1st v.p. 1981, pres. 1982, gov. dist. 735 1988-89), Elks, Sigma Xi, Phi Kappa Phi, Phi Delta Kappa (chpt. v.p. 1973, pres. 1974-75, Leadership award 1983), Beta Beta Beta. Clubs: Masons, Shriners. Home: 12284 Kenwood Dr Petersburg PA 16669 Office: Pa State U Sci Edn Dept University Park PA 16802

FOWLER, JAMES D., JR., leadership executive; b. Washington, Apr. 24, 1944; s. James D. and Romay (Lucas) F.; m. Linda Marie Raiford, May 25, 1968; children— Scott, Kimberly Student, Howard U., Washington, 1962-63; BS, U.S. Mil. Acad., West Point, N.Y., 1967; MBA, Rochester Inst. Tech., 1975. With Xerox Corp., Rochester, N.Y., 1971-75; sr. cons. D.P. Parker & Assocs., Inc., Wellesley, Mass., 1975-76; mgr. staffing ITT World Hdqrs., N.Y.C., 1976-78; v.p. dir. of adminstrn. ITT Aetna, Denver, 1978; sr. v.p., dir. adminstrn. ITT Consumer Fin. Corp., Mpls., 1978-84, sr. v.p., dir. adminstrn. and mktg., 1984-87, exec. v.p., dir. adminstrn. and mktg., 1987-90, exec. v.p., dir. product mgmt., mktg. and adminstrn., 1990-92; exec. v.p., dir. of adminstrn., 1992-93; dir. govt. rels. ITT Washington Office, 1993-96; pres. Fowler & Assocs., 1996-97; exec. dir. Exec. Leadership Coun., 1997-99, pres., 1999-2000, ITT Industries, Inc., 2000—. Trustee U.S. Mil. Acad., West Point, N.Y., 1977-86, 87—; bd. dirs., chmn. ITT Ednl. Svcs., Inc.; bd. dirs. Duke Ellington Sch. Arts, 1993-2000, Suburban Hosp., Bethesda, Md., 1997-2000, Folger Shakespeare Libr., Washington; charter mem., bd. dirs. Exec. Leadership Coun., 1992-97. Capt. U.S. Army, 1967-71, Vietnam. Decorated Bronze Star with oak leaf cluster. Mem. Sigma Pi Phi. Office: ITT Industries Inc 4 West Red Oak Lane White Plains NY 10604 E-mail: james.fowler@itt.com.

FOWLER, JAY F., lawyer; JD, U. of Kans., 1980. Assoc. Foulston Siefkin LLP, Wichita, Kans., 1980—85, ptnr., 1985—. Fellow, Am. Coll. of Trial Lawyers, 2000. Office: Foulston Siefkin LLP 1551 N Waterfront Pl Ste 100 Wichita KS 67206-4466 Office Phone: 316-267-6371. Office Fax: 316-267-6345.

FOWLER, JOANNA S., chemist; b. Aug. 9, 1942; BA, U. South Fla., 1964; PhD in Chem., U. Colo., 1967. Sr. rsch. assoc. U. East Anglia, Norwich, England, 1968; rsch. assoc., med. dept. Brookhaven Nat. Lab., 1969—71, assoc. chemist, med. dept., scientist, 1974—76, chemist, chem. dept., 1976—88, sr. chemist, 1988, dir., Ctr. Translational Neuroimaging. Adj. prof. chem. dept. and biomedical engring. dept. Stony Brook U. Named Disting. Basic Scientist of Yr., Acad. Molecular Imaging, 2005; recipient Ernest Orlando Lawrence award, Dept. Energy, 1999, Alfred P. Wolf award, Soc. Nuclear Imaging in Drug Devel., 2000, Glen T. Seaborg award, nuclear and radiochemistry, Am. Chemical Soc., 2002. Mem. Soc. Nuclear Medicine, Am. Chem. Soc. (co-recipient Gustavus John Esselen Award for Chemistry in the Pub. Interest, northeastern sect., 1988, Francis P. Garvin & John M. Olin Medal, 1998), Nat. Acad. Sciences (mem. 2003). Office: Brookhaven Nat Lab Chem Dept Bldg 555A Upton NY 11973 Office Phone: 516-344-4365. E-mail: fowler@bnl.gov.*

FOWLER, JOHN DALE, JR., biotechnologist, consultant, investment banker; b. Norfolk, Va., May 15, 1957; s. John Dale and Margaret (Kimmel) F.; m. Corey Keane Phillips, Aug. 2, 1980; children: John Dale III, Douglas Houghton, Grace Phillips. BA, U. Va., 1979, MBA, JD, 1986. Asst. v.p. Jefferson Nat. Bank, Charlottesville, Va., 1979-82; fin. analyst Marine Midland Bank, N.Y.C., 1983; assoc. law Hawkins, Delafield & Wood, N.Y.C., 1984; assoc. Merrill Lynch Capital Markets, N.Y.C., 1985; v.p. Salomon Bros. Inc., N.Y.C., 1986-92; mng. dir. Wheat First Butcher & Singer Capital Markets, Richmond, Va., 1992; mng. dir. Health Care Group Salomon Bros. Inc., N.Y.C., 1992—98; mng. dir. J.P. Morgan, 1998—2001; pres. Large Scale Biology, 2001—03; mng. ptnr. Baycrest Capital LLC, 2003—; mng. dir. Bio-Strategic Dirs. LLC, 2004; vice chmn. Deutsche Bank Securities, Inc., N.Y.C., 2004—; bd. dirs. Beverly Enterprises Inc., 2002—. Mem. N.Y. Bar Assn. Office: 60 Wall St New York NY 10005 Office Phone: 212-250-3398. Personal E-mail: john_fowlerjr@yahoo.com.

FOWLER, JOHN M., finance company executive; b. Youngstown, Ohio, Apr. 12, 1949; s. William E. Jr and Jean L. (Moore) Fowler; m. Brooke McMurray, Oct. 1999; children: Evan, Ned 1 stepchild, Grey McMurray. BS, Yale U., 1971; JD, U. Pa., 1974. Bar: Pa 1974, US Dist Ct (ea dist) Pa 1974. Assoc. White and Williams, Phila., 1974-77; v.p., chief fin. officer Reading Co., Phila., 1977-81; gen. counsel U.S. Dept. Transp., Washington, 1981-83; exec. v.p., pres. Warner Amex Cable Comm., Inc., Blue Bell, Pa., 1983-86; pres., CEO Gulf Ins. Co., Dallas, 1986-94, chmn., 1991-94; exec. v.p., chief adminstrv. officer Primerica Co. (now Citigroup Inc.), N.Y.C., 1986-94; exec. v.p., CFO MoneyGram Payment Systems, Inc., 1996-98. Office: 149 E 73rd St New York NY 10021 Office Phone: 908-508-0092. Office Fax: 908-508-0093.

FOWLER, KAREN JOY, writer; b. Bloomington, Indiana; BA in Political Science, MA in Political Science, Berkeley U. Writer-in-residence Cleveland State U., 1990; instructor Clarion Writers Workshop, Mich. State U.; instructor & administrator Imagination Workshop, Cleveland State U.; instructor Stanford U., 1996—98. Published short stories & poetry in numerous magazines & journals including Asimov's, The Centennial Review, The California Quarterly, The Ohio Journal. Author: Peripheral Vision, 1990, Artificial Things, 1991, Letters from Home, 1991, Sarah Canary, 1998, The Sweetheart Season, 1998, Black Glass, 1999, Sister Noon, 2001, The Jane Austen Book Club, 2004, (short stories) Praxis, 1985, The Lake was Full of Artificial Things, 1985, War of the Roses, 1985, The Poplar Street Study, 1985, The Natives, 1985, Face Value, 1986, Wild Boys, 1986, The Dragon's Head, 1986, Contention, 1986, The Faithful Companion at Forty, 1987, Lily Red, 1988, Heartland, 1988, Duplicity, 1989, Game Night at the Fox and Goose, 1989, Faded Roses, 1989, Lieserl, 1990, The Dark, 1991, The Elizabeth Complex, 1996, Standing Room Only, 1997, Reefers, 1997. Recipient John W. Campbell award best new sci. fiction writer, 1987, Nebula nominee, 1987, 1990, 1991, 1992, 1997, 1998. Office: c/o Putnam Books 375 Hudson St New York NY 10014

FOWLER, MARILYN S. ATLAS, social worker; b. Portsmouth, Ohio, Apr. 20, 1954; d. Morton G. Atlas and Annadine K. Jaffee; m. John R. Fowler, Sept. 24, 1978 (div. Sept. 18, 1996); children: Gretchen R., Michelle J. BA in Psychology, U. Kans., 1976; MSSW, U. Wis., 1978. Diplomate Am. Psychotherapy Assn.; lic. ind. social worker S.C., cert. bd. cert. diplomate in clin. social work. Bd. cert. hypnotherapist Assocs. in Psychol. Medicine, St. Louis, 1984—87; psychotherapist Psychiat. Coverage, Ltd., St. Louis, 1987—89, Family Psychiat. Assocs., Myrtle Beach, SC, 1989—94; pres., psychotherapist Fowler Counseling Inc. dba Grand Strand Counseling Ctr., Myrtle Beach, 1990—. Recipient Undergrad. Rsch. award, NIMH; scholar. Mem.: NASW (diplomate in clin. social work), Nat. Guild Hypnotist, Am. Psychotherapy Assn., Optimist Club, Phi Beta Kappa. Jewish. Avocations: dance, camping, hiking, boating, swimming. Home: Unit 117D 424 D Garden Dr Myrtle Beach SC 29575 Office: 1700 A Oak St Myrtle Beach SC 29577

FOWLER, RAYMOND DALTON, psychologist, educator; b. Jasper, Ala., Dec. 22, 1950; s. Raymond Dalton and Willie (Sanders) F.; m. Nancy Allebach, Aug. 13, 1955 (dec.); children: Karen Sydney, Derek Tyson, Michael Allan; m. Sandra Mumford, May 5, 1984. Student, Vanderbilt U., 1948-50; BA, U. Ala., 1952, MA, 1953; PhD, Pa. State U., 1957. Diplomate in clin. psychology Am. Bd. Profl. Psychology; lic. psychologist, Ala. Rsch. asst. Psychoacoustics Lab., Pa. State U., University Park, 1953-54; fellow USPHS, 1954-56; asst. prof. psychology, asst. dir. Psychol. Clinic, U. Ala., Tuscaloosa, 1956-59, assoc. prof., dir. Psychol. Clinic Birmingham, 1959-65, prof., chmn. dept., 1965-83, prof. (on leave), 1983-86, prof. emeritus, 1986—; sr. cons. Psych. Sys. and Nat. Computer Sys., Balt. and Washington, 1983-86; prof. psychology, head dept. U. Tenn., Knoxville, 1986-89; exec. v.p., CEO APA, Washington, 1989—2002. Participant White House Conf. on Health, 1965, Nat. Conf. on Criminal Justice Stds. and Goals, 1973; mem. nat. adv. com. on alcoholism HEW, 1970-72, chmn. com. on rsch., 1970; mem. task panel on manpower and pers. President's Commn. on Mental Health, 1977-78; mem. Ala. Gov.'s Adv. Com. on Alcoholism and Drug Abuse, 1973-82; vice chmn. program com. N.Am. Congress on Alcohol and Drug Addiction, 1974; mem. sci. adv. com. Nat. Coun. on Alcoholism, 1974-78; mem. rsch. tng. rev. com. Nat. Inst. Alcohol Abuse and Alcoholism, 1975-78; dir. Ala. Prison Classification Project, 1976-77; chmn. So. Sch. Alcohol Studies, 1960-62; cons. Ala. Commn. on Alcoholism, 1958-70, VA, 1959-65, Estate of Howard R. Hughes, 1976-84; prin. cons. Roche Psychiat. Svc. Inst., Nutley, N.J., 1966-77, Med. Computer Svc., Basel, Switzerland, 1968-76, Med. Computer Svc., Hans Huber Verlag, Berne, Switzerland, 1976-89; cons. to adminstr. Law Enforcement Assistance Adminstrn., U.S. Dept. Justice, Washington, 1971-73; program cons. div. alcoholism Ala. Dept. Mental Health, 1973-75; sr. cons. Nat. Computer Sys., Mpls., 1983-89 Contbg. author: Assessment for Decision, 1987, Handbook of Psychological Assessment, 1990; editor Am. Psychologist, 1989-2002; contbr. articles and revs. to profl. jours. Vice pres. Ala. Coun. on Human Rels., 1965-68, Rehab. Rsch. Found., 1965-80; alumni fellow Pa. State U., 1988—; bd. dirs. Rosalynn Carter Inst. for Human Devel., 1988-98. Named Disting. Practitioner, Nat. Acad. Practice, 1986; recipient significant Minn. Multiphasic Personality Inventory contbn. award U. Minn., 1988; grantee Ala. Commn. on Alcoholism, 1962-63, 64-68, NIMH, 1963-64, Roche Psychiat. Svc. Inst., 1967-76, Ala. Dept. Mental Health, 1969-70, U.S. Dept. Justice, 1971-82, Ala. Bd. Corrections, 1972-73, Ala. Law Enforcement Planning Agy., 1972-74, Nat. Inst. Alcohol Abuse and Alcoholism, 1973-83. Fellow APA (pres. div. 13, 1978-79, coun. reps. 1965-68, 70-73, 75-78, bd. dirs. 1979—, treas. 1983-87, pres.-elect 1987-88, pres. 1988-89, presdl. citation 1990), Soc. for Personalaity Assessment; mem. AAUP (pres. U. Ala. chpt. 1969-70), Southeastern Psychol. Assn. (pres. 1971-72, dir. continuing edn. 1973-89, dist. speaker 1982, 87), Ala. Psychol. Assn. (pres. 1962, award for outstanding contbns. 1979), Alcohol and Drug Problems Assn. N.Am. (program chmn. 1974-76, bd. dirs. 1975-77), Internat. Coun. Psychologists (treas. 1994-2005), Sigma Xi (life), Psi Chi (nat. v.p. 1980-84, disting. speaker 1977, 88), Omicron Delta Kappa, Phi Kappa Phi. Democrat. Avocations: running, gardening, cooking. Home: 8276 Caminito Maritimo La Jolla CA 92037

FOWLER, RONALD JAMES, journalist; b. Orlando, Fla., Feb. 5, 1933; s. Clarence Benton and Bessie Florence Fowler; m. Betsy Helen McCall, Dec. 27, 1954; children: Betsy, Karen, James. B in Bus., U. Fla., 1955. Lic. fire and casualty agt. Fla.; cert. flight instr. FAA, ground instr. FAA. Ins. agt. Harry E. James, Inc., Jacksonville, Fla., 1955—60, R.J. Fowler Ins. Inc., Orlando, 1960—65; flight instr. Falcon Aviation, Orlando, 1966—83, Hangar One, Orlando, 1983—90; freelance aviation journalist Orlando, 1973—. Adj. prof. aviation Valencia C.C., Orlando, 1975—95; survey pilot Fla. Audubon Soc., Orlando, 1976—84. Author: Flying Precision Maneuvers, 1980, Preflight Planning, 1983, Making Perfect Landings, 1984, Making Perfect Takeoffs, 1991, Flying the Commercial Pilot Flight Test, 1994, Flying the Private Pilot Flight Test, 1997, Lessons from the Logbook, 2000; contbg. editor: Plane & Pilot Mag., 1996—; contbr. articles to profl. jours. Named Gold Seal Flight Instr., FAA, 1970—. Avocations: vintage airplanes, aviation history, music, art. Home: 3001 Sled Rd Christmas FL 32709

FOWLER, STEPHEN EUGENE, retired military officer, human resources executive; b. Pilot Point, Tex., Dec. 10, 1940; s. Stephen Lafette and Virginia (Whitten) F.; m. Patricia Ann Chichilla, July 16, 1966 (div. May 1982); children: Shannon Jean Imran, Brittany Michelle Inmon; m. Cristine Ann Buttafoco, May 25, 1985; 1 child, Beth Ann Skamser. BA, U. North Tex., 1966; MA, Ball State U., 1974. Commd. 2d lt. USAF, 1966, advanced through grades to lt. col., 1982; chief airman support assignment Hdqrs. USAF Europe, Ramstein AB, Fed. Republic of Germany, 1973-76; chief, sec. police, intelligence and OSI Air Force Mil. Personnel Ctr., Randolph AFB, Tex., 1976-79, chief Air Force Classification and Control Sect., 1979-81; comdr. 3537th Recruiting Squadron, Sumter, S.C., 1981-84; chief airman assignments Hdqrs. Strategic Air Command, Offutt AFB, Nebr., 1984-86; chief inspections and inquiries 55th Wing, Offutt AFB, Nebr., 1986-92; mgr. field and logistics hr. and team mem. rels. Pamida, Inc., Omaha, 1994—2001. Mem. Omaha Sister City Assn.; vol. tchr. non-profit agy.; mem. pvt. industry task force State of Nebr. Decorated Republic of Vietnam Cross of Gallantry; named Admiral (mythical) Nebr. Navy, Gov. Orr, State of Nebr. Mem. Pi Sigma Alpha. Republican. E-mail: sfowler@starstream.net.

FOWLER, SUSAN G., library and information specialist, artist; d. Wayne Fowler and Jo Anne Daily; m. Robert J. Grover, Aug. 5, 1995. BA in Psychology, U. Kans., Lawrence, 1981; MLS, Emporia State U., Kans., 1993. Info. mgmt. cons. SG Fowler & Assoc., Emporia, Kans., 1994—; artist Duck Creek Designs, Emporia, Kans., 2004—. Nat. faculty Emporia State U. Sch. of Libr. & Info. Mgmt., Emporia, Kans., 1996—. Author: Information Entrepreneurship: Information Services Based on the Information Lifecycle; contbr. chapters to books, articles to profl. jours. Com. mem. Emporia Diversity Coun., Kans., 2001—03, Emporia Main St. Bus. Enhancement, 2004—; mem. Kans. Children's Report Card Adv. Com., Topeka, 1997—2004; mem. and cons. Kans. FAS Prevention Com., Emporia, 2000—; precinct committeewoman precint 12 Dem. Party, 1996—98; chair staff parish rels. com. Grace United Meth. Ch., 2003—04, chair comms. ministry, 2003—04. Mem.: ALA, Kans. Libr. Assn. (chair ind. info. workers' roundtable 2001—03), Am. Assn. Law Librarians (pub. rels. com. 2005—), Sigma Delta Pi, Beta Phi Mu. Avocations: reading, gardening, knitting, home repair. Office: SG Fowler & Assoc PO Box 814 Emporia KS 66801 Office Phone: 620-342-4535.

FOWLER, THOMAS KENNETH, physicist; b. Thomaston, Ga., Mar. 27, 1931; s. Albert Grady and Susie (Glynn) F.; m. Carol Ellen Winter, Aug. 18, 1956; children: Kenneth, John, Ellen. BS in Engring, Vanderbilt U., 1953, MS in Physics, 1955; PhD in Physics, U. Wis., 1957. Staff physicist Oak Ridge Nat. Lab., 1957-65, group leader plasma theory, 1961-65; staff physicist Gen. Atomic Co., San Diego, 1965-67, head plasma physics divsn., 1967; group leader plasma theory Lawrence Livermore Lab., Livermore, Calif., 1967-69, div. leader, 1969-70, assoc. dir. magnetic fusion, 1970-87; prof., chmn. dept. nuclear engring. U. Calif., Berkeley, 1988-94, prof. emeritus, 1995—. Calif. Coun. Sci. Tech. fellow, 1997—. Fellow Am. Phys. Soc. (chmn. plasma physics div. 1970); mem. Nat. Acad. Scis., Sigma Xi, Sigma Nu. Home: 221 Grover Ln Walnut Creek CA 94596-6310 Office: U Calif Dept Nuclear Engring Berkeley CA 94720-1730 Business E-Mail: fowler@nuc.berkeley.edu.

FOWLER, VIRGINIA C., literature educator; b. Lexington, Ky., Mar. 29, 1948; d. Bill M. Fowler and Betty Wills Jacoby. BA in English, U. Ky., 1969; MA in English, U. Pitts., 1971, PhD in English, 1976. From asst. prof. English to prof. Va. Poly. Inst. and State U., Blacksburg, Va., 1977—96, Va. Poly. Inst., 1996—. Author: Henry James's American Girl, 1984, Nikki Giovanni, 1992, Gloria Nayler: In Search of Sanctuary, 1996. Fellow, Woodrow Wilson Found., 1969—70; grantee, NEH, 1990. Mem.: Phi Beta Kappa. Avocations: tennis, travel, book collecting. Home: 1000 Flint Drive Christiansburg VA 24073 Office: Dept English Virginia Tech Shanks Hall Blacksburg VA 24061-0112 E-mail: vfowler@vt.edu.

FOWLER, WAYNE LEWIS, SR., internist; b. Topeka, Kans., Jan. 5, 1923; s. Morrill George and Grace Anna (Carlson) F.; m. Violet June Ransom, Sept. 4, 1948; children: Wayne Jr., Deborah. BS, Washburn U., 1945; MD, U. Ind., 1947. Diplomate Am. Bd. Internal Medicine. Intern Kansas City (Mo.) Gen. Hosp., 1947-48, resident internal medicine, 1948-51; internist Galvin-Haughey Clinic, Concordia, Kans., 1953-95, NCK Med. Clinic, Concordia, Kans., 1995—. Past pres. med. staff St. Joseph Hosp., Concordia Kans. Capt. US Air Force, 1951-53, Fellow Am. Coll. Physicians (Laureate award Kans. chpt. 1994), Am. Coll. Chest Physicians; mem. AMA, Cl. County Med. Soc., Kans. Med. Soc., Am. Soc. Internal Medicine, Concordia Elks, Concordia Moose, Topeka Masonic Lodge # 17, Scottish Rite Bodies Topeka, ISIS Shrine alina. Republican. Episcopalian. Avocation: amateur radio. Home: 332 W 8th St Concordia KS 66901-3406 Office: NCK Med Inc 1010 3rd Ave Concordia KS 66901-4003

FOWLER, WESLEY CASWELL, JR., obstetrician, gynecologist; b. Dunn, N.C., Feb. 18, 1940; MD, U. N.C., 1966. Diplomate Am. Bd. Ob.-Gyn. Intern N.C. Meml. Hosp., Chapel Hill, 1967; resident N.C. Meml. Hosp, Chapel Hill, 1967-71; obstetrician-gynecologist U. N.C. Hosps., Chapel Hill, 1972—; prof., vice chmn. dept. ob.-gyn. U. N.C. Sch. of Medicine, Chapel Hill, 1972—. Mem. ACS, ACOG, Soc. Gynecologists and Obstetricians. Office: Univ NC Dept Ob-gyn CB #7570 - Macnider Chapel Hill NC 27599-0001 Office Phone: 919-966-1196.

FOWLER, WILLIAM RALPH, music educator; s. M. C. and Mary Virginia Fowler; m. Rita Jo Cook, Nov. 11, 1992; 1 child, Mary Katelyn. BA in Music Edn., Livingston U., 1972; MA, U. W.Ala., 1996, PhD in Edn. Adminstrn., 2004. Band dir. Northeast Lauderdale HS, Meridian, Miss., 1972—76, Pickens County HS, Reform, Ala., 1989—93, S. Lamar Sch., Millport, Ala., 1993—; profl. performer Artists Corp. Am., Milw., 1976—88. Mem.: Music Educators Nat. Conf., Ala. Bandmaster's Assn., Kappa Delta Pi. Democrat. Baptist. Avocation: gardening. Home: PO Box 309 433 Elizabeth St Millport AL 35576 Office: S Lamar Band 300 SLS Rd Millport AL 35576

FOWLER, WYCHE, JR., ambassador; b. Atlanta, Oct. 6, 1940; s. William Wyche and Emelyn (Barbre) F.; 1 dau., Katherine Wyche. BA, Davidson Coll., 1962; JD, Emory U., 1969. Bar: Ga. 1970. Chief asst. to Congressman Charles Weltner, 1965; mem. Atlanta Bd. Aldermen, 1969-73; pres. Atlanta City Council, 1973-77; mem. 95th-99th Congresses from 5th Ga. Dist., 1977-87; U.S. Senator from Ga., 1987-92; with Powell, Goldstein, Frazer & Murphy, Washington & Atlanta, 1993-95; pvt. practice law, 1996; U.S. amb., 1996—. Served in U.S. Army. Recipient Myrtle Wreath award, 1972, Congl. sunbelt coun. ann. award, 1981, Ga. Citizens Coalition on Hunger award, 1982; named Outstanding Young Man Atlanta Jaycees, 1972, Outstanding Young Man Ga. Jaycees, 1973 Mem. ABA, State Bar Ga., Phi Delta Theta. Democrat.

FOWLES, GEORGE RICHARD, physicist, researcher; b. Glenwood Springs, Colo., Apr. 2, 1928; s. Howard Payne and Phyllis Kathleen (Gibson) F.; m. Dorothy Ellen Evans, Oct. 8, 1954 (dec. Dec. 1987); children: John Reed Maxon, Louise, Kathleen, Jefferson; m. Colleen Elizabeth Murphy, Sept. 17, 1988; stepchildren: Karla Sanger, Joseph Sanger, Kristina Sanger. BS, Stanford U., 1952, MS, 1954, PhD, 1962. Geophysicist Phelps Dodge Corp., Douglas, Ariz., 1954-55; physicist SRI Internat., Menlo Park, Calif., 1955-62, group leader, 1962-66; assoc. prof. Wash. State U., Pullman,

1966-73, prof. physics, 1973-95, prof. emeritus physics, 1995—, chmn. dept., 1984-90. Vis. prof. Australian Nat. U., Canberra, 1983; cons. in field. Contbr. 50 sci. articles to physics jours. Served with USN, 1946-48. Fulbright rsch. fellow Nat. Edn. Found., U. Auckland, New Zealand, 1975. Fellow Am. Phys. Soc. Avocation: guitar making. Home: PO Box 327 Eastsound WA 98245-0327 E-mail: rfowles@rockisland.com.

FOWLKES, NANCY LANETTA PINKARD, social worker; d. Amos Malone and Nettie (Barnett) Pinkard; m. Vester Guy Fowlkes, June 4, 1955 (dec. 1965); 1 child, Wendy Denise. BA, Bennett Coll., 1946; MA, Syracuse U., 1952; MSW, Smith Coll., 1963; MPA, Pace U., 1982. Dir. publicity Bennett Coll., Greensboro, N.C., 1946-47, 49-50; asst. editor Va. Edn. Bull. ofcl. organ Va. State Tchrs. Assn., Richmond, 1950-52; asst. office mgr. Cmty. Svc. Soc., N.Y.C., 1952-55; social caseworker, asst. supr. Dept. Social Svcs. Westchester County, White Plains, N.Y., 1959-67, supr. adoption svcs., 1967-77, supr. adoption and foster care, 1977-89. Mem. adv. bd. White Plains Adult Edn. Sch. First v.p. Eastview Jr. H.S., 1970-71; area chmn. White Plains Cmty. Chest, 1964; sec. Mt. Vernon Concert Group, 1952-54; fund raising co-chmn. Urban League Guild of Westchester, 1967; pres. White Plains Interfaith Coun., 1972-74; pres. northeastern jurisdiction United Meth. Ch., 1988-92; chmn. adminstrv. bd. Meth. Ch., 1970-72, 82-83, vice chmn., 1978-80, vice chmn. trustees, 1973-77, treas., 1978-83; lay spkr., v.p. Met. dist. United Meth. Women, 1977-79, exec. bd. N.Y. conf.; N.Y. conf. rep. Upper Atlantic Regional Sch., 1981-83, mem. nominating com., 1982-83, trustee N.Y. conf., 1982-88, pres. N.Y. conf., 1983-87; bd. dirs. Global Ministries United Meth. Ch., 1988-96, women's divsn., 1988-96, v.p., chair sect. finance women's divsn., 1992-96, supt., 1997—, chair program divsn. N.Y. conf., 1989-93; v.p. superintendency commn. Met. North Dist., 1997—; chair Episcopal residence N.Y. Conf. Episcopacy Com., 1997—; mem. N.Y. Conf. Bd. Ordained Ministry, 2000—; chmn. Dist. Coun. on Ministry, 2002-05, lay leader 2005; bd. dirs. Family Svc. Westchester, Bethel Meth. Home, Ossining, N.Y., White Plains YWCA, 1985-93, Scarritt Bennett Ctr., Nashville, 1990-2000, Gum Moon Women's Residence, San Francisco, 1992-96, White Plains-Greenburg NAACP, 1993-98. Mem. NASW, Acad. Cert. Social Workers, Jack and Jill of Am. Inc. (chpt. pres. 1954-56, regional sec.-treas. 1967-71), Nat. Bus. and Profl. Women's Club (chpt. sec. 1954-56), Internat. Platform Assn., Theta Sigma Phi (sec.-treas.), Zeta Nu Omega, Alpha Kappa Alpha (pres. 1960-64, treas. 1975-78), Regency Bridge Club (pres. 1963-65). Home: 107 Valley Rd White Plains NY 10604-2316 E-mail: npfvalley@aol.com.

FOX, ANTHONY WILLIAM, pharmacologist; b. Cranham, Essex, Eng., June 11, 1956; s. William Gordon and Margaret Elaine Fox; m. Carola Gertrud Schropp. BS, U. London, 1977, MBBS, 1980, MD, 1988. Fellow Harvard Med. Sch., Boston, 1984-87; group leader Procter & Gamble, Norwich, N.Y., 1987-90; dir. Glaxo Inc., Research Triangle Park, N.C., 1990-94; v.p. Cypros Inc., Carlsbad, Calif., 1994—. Sci. adv. bd. mem. Anesta Inc., Salt Lake City, 1995—, Pozen Inc., Research Triangle Park, 1996—; cons. Glaxo-Wellcome Inc., Research Triangle Park, 1994—, Shook Hardy & Bacon, Kansas City, Mo., 1994—. Co-editor: Treating the Headache Patient, 1994; patentee in field; contbr. chpts. in books and articles to profl. jours. Fellow Rotary Internat., 1981-82, Ciba-Geigy, Boston, 1984-87; mem. faculty Pharm. Med. RCP Lond. Fellow Royal Soc. Medicine; mem. Am. Acad. Pharm. Physicians (charter), Faculty Pharm. Medicine (supr. 1994—), Worshipful Soc. Apothecaries (yeoman). Avocations: history of Essex, U.K., steam locomotive part-owner. Office: Cypros Pharm Corp 2714 Loker Ave W Carlsbad CA 92008-6603

FOX, ARTHUR CHARLES, cardiologist, educator; b. Newark, Sept. 16, 1926; s. Jacob and Mae (Bonda) F. Student, Harvard U., 1943-44; MD, NYU, 1948. Cert. Am. Bd. Internal Medicine, 1956, in internal medicine Am. Bd. Internal Medicine, 1974, in cardiovascular disease Am. Bd. Internal Medicine, 1975. Intern, asst. resident, chief resident medicine Bellevue Hosp., N.Y.C., 1948—52; from asst. to full prof. medicine NYU Sch. Medicine, N.Y.C., 1954—, chief cardiology sect., 1968—2001. Cons. Manhattan VA Hosp.; attending physician, NYU Hosp., Bellevue Hosp. Contbr. articles to profl. jours. 1st lt. to capt. USAF, 1952—54, prof. asst., 1953—54, Divsn. Med. Scis., Nat. Rsch. Coun. NIH fellow, 1954-56; grantee, 1956-80 Master ACP (gov. region 1981-86, Laureate award, NY Chpt.); fellow Am. Coll. Cardiology; mem. Am. Fedn. Clin. Research, NY Heart Assn. (pres. 1987-89), NY Cardiologic Soc. (pres. 1992-93), Alpha Omega Alpha, AAAS, Sigma Xi. Home: 330 E 33rd St Apt 20-L New York NY 10016-9466 Office: 550 1st Ave New York NY 10016-6402 Office Phone: 212-263-7229.

FOX, ARTHUR JOSEPH, JR., editor; b. Bklyn., Sept. 19, 1923; s. Arthur Joseph and Mary Loretta (Foley) F.; m. Ann Marie McElroy, Sept. 7, 1946; children: Jane Ann, John Arthur; m. Lorraine Cecelia Hodge, Sept. 10, 1993. BS in Civil Engring, Manhattan Coll., 1947, DSc (hon.), 1982. Structural designer Sanderson & Porter, N.Y.C., 1947-48; asst. editor Engring. News-Record, McGraw-Hill Publs., N.Y.C., 1948-54, asso. editor, 1954-58, sr. editor, 1956-57, sr. staff editor, 1957-60, mng. editor, 1960-64, editor-in-chief, 1964-88; mng. dir. Constrn. Industry Presidents Forum, Potomac, Md., 1989-97; exec. dir. Constrn. Industry Round Table, 1998. Mem. N.Y.C. Environ. Control Bd., 1974-77. Served with AUS, 1943-45. Decorated Bronze Star; recipient award of merit Am. Cons. Engrs. Council, 1975, medal of profl. excellence, 1985; recipient Met. Civil Engr. of Year award, 1975, We Dig America award Nat. Utility Contractors Assn., 1987, Golden Beaver svc. award, 1988; recipient Silver Shovel award Am. Subcontractors Assn., 1975, hon. mem. 1987, Carroll H. Dunn award Constrn. Industry Inst., 2000; elected to Nat. Acad. of Constructon, 2001; named hon. mem. AIA, 1986. Fellow ASCE (pres. 1975-76); mem. Am. Acad. Environ. Engrs. (past trustee), Engrs. Coun. for Profl. Devel. (dir. 1969-75), Nat. Constrn. Industry Coun. (exec. com. 1976-77, Saul Horowitz Career Achievement award 1987), N.Y. Bldg. Congress (bd. govs. 1969-73, 78-86), Engrs. Joint Coun. (dir. 1976-77, v.p. 1978-80), The Moles, Manhattan Coll. Alumni Soc. (past pres.), Chi Epsilon, Tau Beta Pi. Clubs: Congrl. Country. Home and Office: 10108 Garden Way Potomac MD 20854-3966 E-mail: coinrt@aol.com.

FOX, ARTURO ANGEL, Spanish language educator; b. Hoguín, Cuba, Aug. 2, 1935; came to U.S., 1962, naturalized, 1972; s. Arturo Roberto and Dulce Maria (Macle) F.; m. Rosa del Carmen Portilla, Jan 17, 1959 (dec. June 1998); children: Franz, Alexandra; m. Carol E. Fox, Dec. 8, 2003. B. Letters and Scis., Friends Sch., Holguin, Cuba, 1952; LL.D., U. Havana, 1960; MA in Spanish, U. Minn., 1968, PhD, 1971. Bar: Cuba 1960. Pvt. practice law, Holguín, 1960-62; instr. Spanish Luther Coll., Decorah, Iowa, 1963-66; asst. prof. Spanish Dickinson Coll., Carlisle, Pa., 1966-72, assoc. prof., 1972-79, prof., 1979-98, chmn. dept. modern langs., 1972-74, chmn. depts. Spanish and Italian, 1978-79, chmn. dept. Spanish, 1981-84, 90-93. Coord. Latin Am. Studies program, 1968-77; dir. Colombia Semester program Ctrl. Pa. Consortium, 1977-78, Dickinson in Spain, Malaga, 1985-86, 88-90, 93-95; apptd. William W. Edel prof. humanities; honorary chair, 1992. Author: three Spanish textbooks, (novel) Anecdotario del Comandante, 1976; (lit. criticism) El Edipo en Unamuno, 2001; contbr. articles in field to profl. publs. Ford grantee, 1969-70; Lilly and Mellon faculty devel. grantee, 1978, 79; recipient Christain R. and F. Lindback Found. Disting. Teaching award, 1981 Mem. Am. Assn. Tchrs. Spanish and Portuguese Office: Dickinson Coll Dept Spanish Carlisle PA 17013 Personal E-mail: foxar@aol.com.

FOX, AUDREY H., artist, educator; b. Phila., Sept. 14, 1954; d. Donald and Kay (Sklarz) F.; m. John Phillip Golden, Sept. 10, 1989. BFA, Tyler Sch. Art., 1976; postgrad., Barnes Found., 1976-80. Workshop coord., tchr. dept. urban outreach Phila. Mus. Art, 1972; coord., instr. art activities Lower Merion Twp. Dept. Recreation and Sch. Dist., 1972-74; designer murals (comml. and residential) Lower Merion Twp. Dept. Recreation, Lower Merion, 1978-79; designer murals, tchr. various programs Manayunk Ctr. for Arts, 1985-89; tchr. drawing and painting Notre Dame Acad., 1990; tchr. painting, sculpture printmaking, design and crafts, 1982—. Instr. semi-pvt. and pvt. art classes, 1982—85; lectr. in field. Exhibited in group shows at GK Collection, Phila., 1998—2002, Inprints Gallery, Berwyn, Pa., 1999—2000, Carol Schwartz Gallery, Chestnut Hill, Pa., 1999—, Art Effects Gallery, Merion, Pa., 1999—, Grecyn Gallery, Stamford, Conn., 2004, The Frederick Gallery Deal, N.J., 2005, prin. works include children's murals Children's Heart Hosp. Phila., 1976—77, glass painting Shippens Restaurant, 1978, mural Happy Hollow Recreation Ctr., 1983, mural Office of Dr. Marvin Krane, Phila., 1984, mural Phila. Mus. Art Cmty. Programs, Manayunk, Pa., 1985, painting Eastwick Med. Assocs., 1991, Represented in permanent collections. Recipient Best in Show award Nat. League Am. Pen Women, 1981, award of excellence Manhattan Arts Internat., 1994. Mem. Art Guild Delaware Valley (Merit award 1986, 92), Artists Equity (Phila. br., Art in Pub. Places award 1982), Women's Caucus for Art. Avocations: photography, crafts, dog showing and breeding, sports. Home: 631 Righters Mill Rd Narberth PA 19072-1426

FOX, BETH WHEELER, library director; b. Oklahoma City, May 4, 1945; d. Robert R. and Marjorie (Woodberry) Wheeler; m. Dennis Dean Fox, July 15, 1963; children: Rebecca, Julia, Bryce. BS in Libr. Sci./History cum laude, U. North Tex., 1967. Cataloger George Williams Coll., Downers Grove, Ill., 1967-68; br. libr. Libr., Ft. Benning, Ga., 1968-69; ref. libr. Palos Verdes (Calif.) Pub. Libr., 1969-72; libr. vol. Am. Luth. Sch. Libr., Burbank, Calif., 1979-81, Stevenson Elem. Sch. Libr., Burbank, 1981-82; libr. dir. Westbank Community Libr., Austin, Tex., 1983—. Mem. pub. libr. steering com. Tex. State Libr., 2002-03; presenter in field. Author: The Dynamic Community Library: Practical, Creative and Inexpensive Ideas of the Library Director, 1988, Behind the Scenes at the Dynamic Library: Simplifying Essential Operations, 1990. Bd. dirs. Westbank Community Bds. Recipient Hon. Svc. award Burbank Coun. PTA, 1981, Vol. of Yr. award, 1982. Mem. ALA (John Cotton Dana award 1986, 90), Tex. Libr. Assn. (co-founder small cmty. libr. round table 1986, program chmn. dist. III 1986, rep. state fin. rev. 1991, structure/orgn. coun. 1994, rsch. grant recipient 1987, pub. rels. com. 1995-98, scholarship com. 1995-98, Access Tex. com. 1996—, Cmty. Libr. of Yr. 1988, legis. com. 2000—, founder and chair dist. libr. discussion group 2000—, devel. pub. libr. task force, 2003, salary compensation task force 2003), Ctrl. Tex. Libr. Sys. (transitions com. 2004-05), Network for Smaller Librs. (founder 1985), Tex. Mcpl. Libr. Dirs. Assn., Settlement Club (vol. coord. book nook), Rotary (tchr. excellence com. 1997, program com. 1997-2000, bd. dirs. 2005—), Phi Alpha Theta. Avocations: genealogy, gardening, home repair, kayaking, sailing. Home: 1602 Ski Slope Dr Austin TX 78733

FOX, CAROL JEAN, librarian; b. LaSalle, Ill., May 9, 1942; d. Ralph Francis and Hazel Mabel Mindock;m. DeLon E. Fox, June 20, 1981; m. Curtis A. Wingerter, Feb. 20, 1965 (div. 1973); 1 child, Grechen Lynne Wingerter. BA, MacMurray Coll., 1964; MLS, U. R.I., 1968; postgrad., No. Ill. U., 1973-88, U. Ill., 1995—96. Libr. asst. Indpls. Pub. Libr., 1964-65; 6th grade tchr. Denby Park Day Sch., Norfolk, Va., 1965-66; children's librarian Newport (R.I.) Pub. Libr., 1966-69; sch. librarian Tiverton (R.I.) Pub. Schs., 1969-70; sch. libr. media specialist Rockford (Ill.) Pub. Schs., 1971-85; reading cons. Elgin (Ill.) Pub. Schs., 1986-88; sch. libr. media specialist Highland Park (Ill.) Sch. Dist. 108, 1988-89; youth svcs. cons. Ill. State Libr., Springfield, 1989-93; cons. No. Ill. Libr. System, Rockford, 1993—95; grant mgr., exec. dir. Sinn Valley Info. Network, 1995—96; libr. media specialist Mary Watts Elem. Sch., Naperville, Ill., 1996—2003, Montessori Magnet Sch., Rockford, Ill., 2003—. Adj. faculty Rockford (Ill.) Coll., 1976-88, Nat. Coll. Edn., Evanston, Ill., 1989; chair Rebecca Caudill Young Readers' Book Award Com. Co-author: Celebrate Literature, 1989; contbr. articles to profl. jours. Mem. ALA (mem. coun. 1992-4), ASCD, Ill. Sch. Libr. Media Assn. (bd. dirs., pres. 1995-96, Polestar award 1991), Am. Assn. Sch. Librs., Ill. Sch. Libr. Media Assn., Phi Delta Kappa.

FOX, CAROL TYLER, educational consultant; d. Marion Bean and Burnice Duell Tyler; m. Steven Fox, Aug. 17, 1969; children: Melissa Kathryn, Matthew Tyler. BA, SUNY Coll., Fredonia, 1969; MA, Case Western Res. U., 1970, PhD, 1972, JD, 2005. English tchr. Shaker Heights City Schs., Ohio, 1972—2002; tchr. cons. Ednl. Testing Svc., Princeton, NJ, 1992—, Coll. Bd., Evanston, Ill.; asst. examiner Internat. Baccalaureate Orgn., Cardiff, Wales, 1998—. Editor: Case Western Res. Law Rev. Avocations: ballroom dancing, gardening, bridge.

FOX, CHARLES DUNSMORE, IV, lawyer; b. Roanoke, Va., Jan. 12, 1953; s. Charles Dunsmore III and Preston (Wescoat) F.; m. Elizabeth McCabe, Dec. 16, 1989; children: Charles Dunsmore V, Edward Lee McCabe. AB, Princeton U., 1975; MA, Yale U., 1977; JD, U. Va., 1980. Bar: Va. 1980, Ill. 1980. Assoc. Schiff, Hardin & Waite, Chgo., 1980-86, ptnr., 1987—2005, McGuire Woods LLP, Charlottesville, Va., 2005—. Ptnr. chmn. Econs. of Practice of Trusts and Estates Mag., Atlanta, 1995-98; adj. prof. Northwestern U. Sch. Law, 1998—. Author: Estate Planning with Life Insurance, 1998, Estate Planning Strategies After Estate Tax Reform, 2001, Estate Planning Manual, 2002, Trust and Fiduciary Law Guide, 2004, Tax Law Guide, 2004; mem. editl. bd. Trusts and Estates Mag., 1997-2001, Trust and Investment Mag., 2001—, chair, 2003—. Active U. Va. Law Sch. Coun., Charlottesville, 1992-95, vice-chair nat. appeals, 1997-98, chair nat. appeals, 1998-2000; trustee Va. Law Sch. Found., 1998—, LaGrange Meml. Found., 1994-96, Episcopal H.S., Alexandria, Va., 1995-2001, chair capital campaign, 1998-2001; gen. counsel Cmty. Meml. Found., LaGrange, Ill., 1995—; co-chair planned giving task force Episcopal Diocese of Chgo., 2001—. Fellow Am. Coll. Trust and Estate Counsel (co-chair legal edn. com. 2002-05, asst. editor jour. 2004-05, editor 2005—); mem. ABA, Ill. State Bar Assn. Democrat. Episcopalian. Avocation: golf. Home: 506 Wellington Pl Charlottesville VA 22903 Office: McGuire Woods LLP Ste 300 Box 1288 310 Fourth St NE Charlottesville VA 22902-1288 Office Phone: 434-977-2500. Business E-Mail: cfcx@mcguirewoods.com. E-mail: skipfoxiv@earthlink.net.

FOX, CONNIE MARIE, artist; b. Fowler, Colo., Mar. 6, 1925; d. Hurley Wellington and Eva Katherine (Marty) F.; m. Blair Morton Boyd, April 14, 1954 (Oct. 1969); children: Megan Boyd, Brian Boyd. BFA, U. Colo., Boulder, 1947; MA, U. N.Mex., Albuquerque, 1954. Head art depts. Boulder H.S., U. Hill Jr. H.S., Boulder, 1947-48; tchr. U. N.Mex., Albuquerque, 1955-58, Albuquerque Modern Mus., 1956-58, Carnegie-Mellon U., Pitts., 1969-71, chmn. freshman curriculum com., 1970-71; tchr. New Experimental Coll., Thy, Denmark, 1971-72, Sweetwater Art Ctr., Sewickly, Pa., 1973-79, Southampton Coll., L.I. U., 1980-82; faculty mem. master workshop Southampton Coll., 1983-84; tchr. Art Barge, Napeague, N.Y., 1985-92; mem. painting faculty Vt. Studio Ctr., Johnson, 1990. Mem. bd. dirs., v.p. Pitts. Broadcasting Corp., 1974-76, Sweetwater Art Ctr., Sewickley, 1976-79, Anne Mackesey Dance Co., Sag Harbor, N.Y., 1986; mem. first com. Art in Public Places, East Hampton, 1987; curator (with Allan Frumkin) The New Frontier: Art From Western Queens, Queens Coun. on the Arts, 1987; master workshop Southampton Coll., L.I. U., 1988; lectr. Victor D'Amico Inst. Art, East Hampton, 1988, Mus. of Fine Art, U. N.Mex., Albuquerque, 1989, Weir Farm Heritage Trust, Wilton, Conn., 1992, Parrish Art Mus., 1993. Public collections include Albright-Knox Art Gallery, Buffalo, N.Y., Albuquerque Mus., Bklyn. Mus., Fayez-Sarofim, Inc., Houston, Greater Lafayette (Ind.) Mus. of Art, Greenville (N.C.) Mus. of Art, Guild Hall Mus., East Hampton, N.Y., Herbert F. Johnson Mus. of Art, Cornell U., Ithaca, N.Y., IND-COM, Pitts., Nat. Women's Mus., Washington D.C., New Sch. for Social Rsch., N.Y.C., Pacific Enterprises, First Interstate World Ctr., L.A., Parrish Mus., Southampton, N.Y., Roswell (N.Mex.) Mus. and Art Ctr., Santa Barbara (Calif.) Mus. of Art, Simpson, Thatcher and Bartlett, N.Y.C., U. N.Mex., Albuquerque, Weatherspoon Art Gallery, U. N.C., Greensboro, Xerox Corp., Stamford, Conn.; solo exhbns. include Elaine Benson Gallery, Bridgehampton, N.Y., 1981, Southampton Coll. Fine Arts Gallery, 1983, Peter S. Loonam Gallery, Bridgehampton, 1983, Il Punto Blu, Southampton, 1984, Ingber Gallery, N.Y.C., 1985, 86, 88, Vered Gallery, East Hampton, N.Y., 1985, 86, 88, 89, 90, East Hampton Ctr. for Contemporary Art, 1987, U. Mass., Amherst, 1989, Peconic Gallery, Suffolk Cmty. Coll., Riverhead, N.Y., 1991, Benton Gallery, Southampton, 1992, 93, Parrish Art Mus., Southampton, 1994, Weatherspoon Gallery, U. N.C. at Greensboro, 1994, Arlene Bujese Gallery, East Hampton, 1994, Ashawagh Hall, East Hampton, 1996, numerous others; Lorraine Kessler Gallery, Poughkeepsie, N.Y., 1992, Renee Fotouhi Fine Art, East Hampton, 1992, U. Art Gallery, Staller Ctr. for the Arts, SUNY, Stony Brook, 1994, Brenda Taylor Gallery, N.Y.C., 1996, Arlene Bujese Gallery, East Hampton, 1996, numerous others; contbr. numerous articles to profl. jours.; director, prodr. video interviews of artists, dealers and their galleries, 1982—. Recipient First award Southwest Biennial Mus. of N.Mex., Santa Fe, 1957, Purchase award Highlands U., 1959, First Purchase award Tri-State Exhibit, Amarillo, Tex., 1960, Circle Invitational Roswell Mus. of Art, 1960, Beatrice J. Ryan award San Francisco Mus. of Art, 1965, Joan Mitchell Found. award, 1995.

FOX, CONNIE STEITZ, freelance/self-employed writer, freelance/self-employed editor, graphics designer; b. Sanger, Calif., Oct. 25, 1946; d. Warren Chester and Viletta (Petersen) Steitz; m. Meredith George Fox, Sept. 27, 1969 (div. May 2003); children: Todd Christian Fox, Emily Kirsten Fox Samson. Student, Ariz. State U., 1964-66; Registered Dental Hygienist, U. Tex., Houston, 1969; cert. in tech. writing, desktop pub., Houston C.C., 1996; AAS in Tech. Comm. with high honors, Advanced Cert., 1999. Lic. dental hygienist, Tex., Ohio; lic. real estate sales, Tex. Dental hygienist Myers Thornton, DDS, Dallas, 1969-71, Rick Hammond DDS, Houston, 1980-83; owner, prin. Noteworthy Writing and Editing, Houston, 1987—. Contbr. Desktop Pub., Tex. Monthly, Wall St. Jour., corp. websites and publs., 1997—. Brownie leader Troop 5286, Houston, 1983-86; 1st soprano adult choir Kingsland Bapt. Ch., Katy, Tex., 1983-89, Tallowood Bapt. Ch., Houston, 1991-95; pres. Chronic Fatigue and Immune Dysfunction Support Group, Houston, 1989-90; ptnr. St. Jude's Children's Rsch. Hosp., Memphis, 1998—; charter mem. Rep. Nat. Com., Rep. Nat. Cmty. Victory Team, Rep. Party Tex. Profl. Digital Pubs. scholar, 1991. Mem. NAFE, Internat. Assn. Bus. Communicators, Robert Means Soc. U.S. Naval Academy, Nat. Women's History Mus. (charter mem., Wash. 2005), Phi Theta Kappa, Delta Delta Delta (mem. steering com. reunion, Tempe, Ariz. 2004). Republican. Avocations: travel, photography, gardening, investing. Office: PO Box 840648 Houston TX 77284-0648 E-mail: copyedit@wt.net.

FOX, DANIEL MICHAEL, foundation executive, writer; b. N.Y.C., Aug. 20, 1938; s. Alexander E. and Rose (Leitner) F.; m. Carol Anne Kemps, Sept. 8, 1963 (div. 1985); children: Aaron, Miriam, Joshua, Benjamin; m. Louise O. Vasvari, Dec. 26, 1988 (div. 2003). AB, Harvard U., 1959, AM, 1961, PhD, 1964. Instr. Harvard U., Cambridge, Mass., 1964-65, asst. prof., 1967-72; dir. field ops. Applachian Vols., Berea, Ky., 1965—66; assoc. dir. Commonwealth of Mass. Svc . Corps, 1965—67; prof., v.p. SUNY, Stony Brook, 1972-89. Assoc. dir. Nat. Ctr. for Health Svcs. Rsch., Rockville, Md., 1975-78; pres. Milbank Meml. Fund, N.Y.C., 1990—; cons. in field. Author: Engines of Culture, 1963, rev. edit., 1995, The Discovery of Abundance, 1967, electronic edit., 2002, Economists and Health Care, 1979, Health Policies, Health Politics, 1986, Photographing Medicine, 1988, AIDS: The Burdens of History, 1989, AIDS: The Making of a Chronic Disease, 1992, Power and Illness: The Failure and Future of American Health Policy, 1993, 2d edit., 1995. Bd. dirs. Village Care N.Y. Inc., vice chmn., 1996—; bd. dirs. Employee Benefit Rsch. Inst., treas., 2003—04; bd. dirs. ECRI, The Health Tech. Ctr., Am. for Better Care of the Dying, Global Enterprise for Water Tech., Health Quality Coun. Sask. Shaw traveling fellow Harvard U., 1959-60, Sheldon traveling fellow, 1962; also numerous grants. Mem.: APHA, N.Y. Acad. Medicine, Am. Assn. for the History of Medicine, Nat. Acad. Social Ins., Am. Hist. Assn. (Beveridge prize 1965), Coun. on Fgn. Rels., Inst. Medicine of NAS, Century Assn., Harvard Club of N.Y. Jewish. Office: Milbank Meml Fund 645 Madison Ave Fl 15 New York NY 10022-1010 Office Phone: 212-355-8400. Business E-Mail: dmfox@milbank.org.

FOX, DEBRA L., educational association administrator, business owner; m. Jules Rosen; children: Adam, Josh, Daniel, Rebecca. Reporter, anchor WTAE-TV, 1976—86; founder, owner, pres., CEO Fox Learning Systems Inc. (formerly Fox FarSight Prodn.), 1997—. Named One of Pa. Best 50 Women in Bus., 2004. Office: Fox Learning Systems Inc 401 Washington Ave Bridgeville PA 15017 Office Phone: 412-257-4989. Business E-Mail: debra@foxlearningsystems.com.

FOX, DIANE PORRETTA, nursing educator; d. Marvin and Mary Lou Porretta; m. Robert Curtis Fox, Nov. 7, 1975; children: Jesse Thomas Morgan, Patrick Robert. AS with honors, Washtenaw C.C., 1978; BA magna cum laude, Siena Heights Coll., 1989; BSN magna cum laude, U. Mich., 1997; MS in Nursing, Ea. Mich. U., 2003. Cert. tchg. healthcare sys., Ea. Mich. U., 2001; asthma educator Nat. Asthma Educator Certification Bd., 2003. Staff nurse, contingent ecmo nurse U. Mich. Hosp., Ann Arbor, 1990—; part-time faculty Monroe County C.C., 1990—2004; reg. respiratory therapist U. Mich., 1995—2000; staff nurse U. Mich.-Mich. Congenital Heart Ctr., 1997—99; asst. prof. nursing Sch. Nursing, Ea. Mich. U., Ypsilanti, 2004—. Dir. cardiopulmonary svcs. Saline Cmty. Hosp., Mich., 1988—95; adj. faculty Washtenaw C.C., Ann Arbor, 2000—04; presenter in field; ednl. leadership doctorate cohort Ea. Mich. U., 2005. Vol. Big Bros./Big Sisters, Adrian, Mich., 1997—2002. Named Outstanding Grad. Nursing Student, Ea. Mich. U., 2003; Joan Rodman Schrandt Nursing scholar, Saline Cmty. Hosp., 1995—97, Angell scholar, U. Mich., 1997. Mem.: AACN, Nat. Bd. Respiratory Care, Am. Assn. Respiratory Care, Transcultural Nursing Soc., Am. Assn. Adult and Continuing Edn., Stratford Shakespeare Soc., Golden Key Nat. Honor Soc., Sigma Theta Tau (assoc.; v.p. 2002—04, rsch. award 2003). Avocation: master gardener. Office: Ea Mich U 306 Marshall Ypsilanti MI 48197 Office Phone: 734-487-2154. Business E-Mail: dfox2@emich.edu.

FOX, DONALD THOMAS, lawyer; b. Council Bluffs, Iowa, June 12, 1929; s. Donald and Genevieve (Tinley) F.; m. Ana Clemencia Tercero-Graham; children: Mark, Matthew, Genevieve, Melissa. AB magna cum laude, Harvard U., 1951; LLB, N.Y. U., 1956; Brevet de Traduction et de Terminologie Juridiques, U. Paris, 1957, Diplome de Droit Comparé, 1961. Bar: N.Y. 1957, U.S. Ct. Claims 1960, U.S. Dist. Ct. (so. and ea. dists.) N.Y. 1960, U.S. Ct. Appeals (2nd cir.) 1960, D.C. 1968, U.S. Tax Ct. 1973. Instr. Inst. Comparative Law, NYU, 1957-59; assoc. Davis, Polk, Wardwell, Sunderland & Kiendl, N.Y.C., 1958-67; ptnr. Fox Horan & Camerini, LLP and predecessor firms, N.Y.C., 1968—. Bd. dirs. Washington Sq. Legal Svcs., Inc., N.Y.C., 1974-85, Uniroyal Goodrich Tire Co., 1990-96, Michelin Licensing Svcs. Inc., Globalstar do Brazil, 1995-99; mem. adv. com. on history and theory Harvard U. Grad. Sch. Design, 1990—95. Author: Conciliation of International Economic Disputes, 1964, Human Rights in Guatemala, 1979, Report on Contra Activity in Nicaragua, 1985, Violence in Colombia, 1989, Hungarian Constitutional Reform and the Rule of Law, 1993, Elections in Ethiopia, 1995, Elections in Nicaragua, 1996, 2000, Elections in Mexico, 1997, Lessons of the Colombian Constitutional Reform of 1991 (U.S. Inst. of Peace), 2002; editor: The Cambodian Incursion: Legal Issues, 1971; mem. panel advisors Jour. Internat. Law and Politics, 1968-99; contbr. articles to legal jours. Trustee Law Ctr. Found., N.Y.U., 1975-86, chmn. campaign fund, 1980; mem. Am. Soc., 1975—, pres.'s coun., 2005—; Coun. on Fgn. Rels., 1973—; Pres.'s assocs. Harvard U., 2000—. 1st lt. USAF, 1951-53. Named to Com. of Honor, Giulio Romano Exhbn., Mantova, Italy, 1989; Albert Gallatin fellow, 1978; Nat. scholar Harvard U., Root-Tilden scholar NYU, Fulbright scholar U. Paris. Fellow: Am. Bar Found. (life); mem.: The Century Assn. (chmn. wine com.), Humanitarian Found. for Nicaragua (exec. com. bd. dirs. 1991—96), NYU Alumni Fedn. (pres. 1983—85), NYU Law Alumni Assn. (pres. 1971—73), Assn. of Bar of City of N.Y. (chmn. com. lawyers role in search for peace 1969—71, chmn. com. profl. responsibility 1971—74, chmn. com. audit 1978—80, treas. 1982—84, chmn. fin. com. 1982—84), Am. Arbitration Assn. (panel arbitrators 1970—), Am. Assn. Internat. Commn. Jurists (exec. com., bd. dirs. 1970—, chmn. 1991—), Am. Law Inst. (sustaining life), Harvard Club of N.Y.C. Office: Fox Horan & Camerini LLP 825 3rd Ave New York NY 10022-7519 Fax: 212-269-2383. Office Phone: 212-480-4800. Business E-Mail: dtfox@foxlex.com.

FOX, DONNA M., dean, biology professor; d. Hatsuko Tanaka and John Forte; m. Alan I. Fox, June 12, 1976; children: Allison J., Kimberley A. MS, George Mason U., Fairfax, Va. Patent examiner US Patent and Trademark Office, Crystal City, Va., 1992—93; asst. dean George Mason U., 2000—, biology instr. Recipient Excellence in Tchg. award, George Mason U., 1998, U. Citizenship award, 2004. Mem.: Acad. Affairs Adminstrs. (assoc.; bd.

mem. 2004—05), Alpha Lambda Delta (hon. named Advisor of Yr. 2004), Alpha Epsilon Delta (hon.), Golden Key Internat. Honour Soc. (hon.). Office: George Mason Univ 4400 University Dr Fairfax VA 22030-4444 Business E-Mail: dfox1@gmu.edu.

FOX, EDWARD A., retired finance company executive; b. N.Y.C., July 17, 1936; s. Herman and Ruth Fox; children from previous marriage: Brian, Laura, Jacqueline. AB, Cornell U., 1958; MBA, NYU, 1975. Pres., CEO Student Loan Mktg. Assn., Washington, 1973-90; dean Amos Tuck Sch. Dartmouth Coll., Hanover, NH, 1990-94; chmn. SLM Corp. (Sallie Mae), Reston, Va., 1997—2005. Bd. dirs. Delphi Fin. Group, Inc., Greenwich Capital Holdings, Inc. Vice chmn. bd. dirs. Am. Ballet Theater.

FOX, EDWARD HANTON, lawyer; b. Oil City, Pa., June 3, 1945; s. Harry Hanton and Elizabeth Belle (Amsler) F.; children: Michael, Joseph, Katherine. AB, Cornell U., 1967, JD, 1971. Bar: N.Y. 1971, U.S. Dist. Ct. (we. and no. dists.) N.Y. 1971, U.S. Ct. Appeals (2d cir.) 1972, U.S. Supreme Ct. 1975. Staff atty. Monroe County Legal Assistance Corp., Rochester, N.Y., 1971-73; assoc. Harris, Beach & Wilcox, Rochester, N.Y., 1973-79, ptnr., 1980—. Counsel N.Y. Civil Liberties Union, 1972-83. Bd. dirs., Rochester Metnal Health Ctr., 1983-2001, Health Assn. Rochester and Monroe County, 1983—, Monroe County Legal Assistance Corp., 1993-2000, Rochester Health Care, 1993-96; pres. Park-Oxford Neighborhood Assn., 1977-83. Served with USAR, 1969-74. Recipient cert. of Appreciation, ACLU, 1982, Am. Arbitration Assn., 1984. Mem. Am. Bd. Trial Advocates, N.Y. Bar Assn., Monroe County Bar Assn. (trustee). Roman Catholic. Home: 10 Whitestone Ln Rochester NY 14618-4118 Office: Harris Beach Wilcox 130 Main St E Rochester NY 14604-1687

FOX, ELEANOR MAE COHEN, lawyer, educator, writer; b. Trenton, NJ, Jan. 18, 1936; d. Herman and Elizabeth (Stein) Cohen; children: Douglas Anthony, Margot Alison, Randall Matthew. BA, Vassar Coll., 1956; LLB, NYU, 1961. Bar: N.Y. 1961, U.S. Dist. Ct. N.Y. 1964, U.S. Supreme Ct. 1965. Ptnr. Simpson Thacher & Bartlett, 1970—76, of counsel, 1976—; prof. Law Sch. NYU, N.Y.C., 1976—, Walter J. Derenberg prof. trade regulation, 1999—. Mem. Pres. Carter's Nat. Commn. Rev. Antitrust Laws and Procedures, 1978-79; mem. adv. bd. Bur. Nat. Affairs Antitrust and Trade Regulation Reporter, 1977—; trustee NYU Law Ctr. Found., 1974-92; exec. com. Lawyers' Com. Civil Rights Under Law, 1988—, bd. dirs.; mem. Coun. Fgn. Rels., 1993—; mem. Pres. Clinton's internat. competition policy adv. com. to advise the U.S. Atty. Gen., 1997-2000; lectr. on antitrust law, European Union law, world competition, trade, and econ. devel. Author (with Byron E. Fox): Corporate Acquisitions and Mergers, 1968, 1970, 1973, 1981, 2005; author: (novel) W.L., Esquire, 1977; author: (with Lawrence A. Sullivan and Rudolph Peritz) Cases and Materials, U.S. Antitrust in Global Context, 2000; author: (with G. Bermann, R. Goebel, W. Davey) European Union Law, Cases and Materials, The Competition Law of the European Union--Cases and Materials, 2002; author: (with J. Fingleton, D. Neven, P. Seabright) Competition Policy and the Transformation of Central Europe, 1996; mem. editl. bd. NY Law Jour., 1976—99, Antitrust Bull., 1986—, Rev. Indsl. Orgn., 1990—2001, EEC Merger Control Reporter, 1992—, Gaceta Juridica de la CE y de la Competencia, 1992—2001, World Competition: Law and Economics Rev., 1999—, Inst. for Consumer Antitrust Studies, 2002—. Fellow Am. Bar Found., N.Y. Bar Found.; mem. ABA (chmn. merger com. antitrust sect. 1974-77, chmn. publs. com. 1977-78, chmn. Sherman Act com. 1978-79, coun. antitrust sect. 1979-83, 90-94, vice chmn. antitrust sect. 1992-94, chair NAFTA Task Force, 1993-99), N.Y. State Bar Assn. (chmn. antitrust sect. 1978-79, exec. com. antitrust sect. 1979-83), Fed. Bar Coun. (trustee 1974-76, v.p. 1976-78), Assn. of Bar of City of N.Y. (v.p. 1989-90, exec. com. 1977-81, chmn. trade regulation com. 1973-76, lawyer advt. com. 1976-77, chmn. com. on U.S. in global economy, 1991-94), Am. Law Inst., Assn. Am. Law Schs. (chmn. sect. antitrust and econ. regulation 1981-83), NYU Law Alumni Assn. (bd. dirs. 1974-79, 87-91), Am. Fgn. Law Assn. (v.p. 1979-82, 98-2001). Business E-Mail: eleanor.fox@nyu.edu.

FOX, FRANCIS HANEY, lawyer; b. Attleboro, Mass., May 28, 1933; s. Francis Joseph and Mary Frances (Brady) F.; m. Cynthia Ann Blundell, Dec. 27, 1959; children: Cynthia, Martin, Matthew, Kalarn. BS in Econs., Coll. Holy Cross, 1955; LLB, Harvard U., 1963. Bar: Mass. 1963, U.S. Ct. Appeals (1st cir.) 1963, U.S. Supreme Ct. 1977. Assoc. Bingham, Dana & Gould, Boston, 1963-70; ptnr. Bingham McCutchen LLP and predecessor firms, Boston, 1970—. Mem. adv. com. on civil rules Jud. Conf. of U.S., 1992-98. Capt. USNR, 1955—78. Fellow Am. Coll. Trial Lawyers; mem. Am. Law Inst. Home: 77 Cottage St Sharon MA 02067-2132 Office: Bingham McCutchen LLP 150 Federal St Boston MA 02110-1726 Office Phone: 617-951-8352. Business E-Mail: francis.fox@bingham.com.

FOX, FRANK G., librarian, writer; b. Lake Charles, La., Oct. 16, 1956; s. Hubert Jackson Fox and Mary Margaret Hebert. BS in Fin., McNeese State U., 1980; MS in Econs., La. State U., 1982, MS in Libr. Sci., 1985. Cert. journeyman wireman. Br. libr. Westwego, Jefferson Parish Libr., Metairie, La., 1986—87; asst. dir. St. Charles Parish Libr., Luling, La., 1987—89; info. broker Frankenstein's Fax, Harvey, La., 1990—94; sch. libr. Plaquemines Parish Sch. Bd., Belle Chasse, La., 1994—98; regional libr. FDIC, Memphis, 1998—2000; evening reference libr. S.W. Tex. State U., San Marcos, 2000—. Author: (book) Funky Butt Blues, 1996, Bizarre New Orleans, 1997 (River Rd. award, 1998), 19 1/2 Revelations, 2002, Jean Lafitte and the Big Ol' Whale, 2003 (Bank Street Best Children's Book of Yr.). Mem.: ALA, Internat. Brotherhood Elec. Workers, Assn. Ind. Info. Profls., Tex. Libr. Assn., Phi Kappa Phi. Democrat. Roman Catholic. Avocations: reading, writing, travel. Home: 421 W San Antonio St San Marcos TX 78666 Office: Tex State U Alkek Libr 601 University Dr San Marcos TX 78666 Personal E-mail: fgf01@yahoo.com. E-mail: ff10@txstate.edu.

FOX, GALEN W., state representative; b. Hilo, Feb. 24, 1943; children: Derek, MeiMei. BA, U. Redlands, 1965; MPA, Princeton U., 1967, PhD, 1978. Fgn. svc. officer U.S. Dept. of State, 1966—82; rsch. fellow East-West Ctr., Honolulu, 1982—84; exec. asst. Mayor of Honolulu, 1985—91; chief bus. devel. and mkrg. divsn. Hawaii Dept. of Econ. Devel., 1991—96; mem. Hawaii State Ho. of Reps., 1996—, Rep. whip, 1998—2000, Rep. leader, 2000—05. Chair Sec. of State's Open Forum, 1978—79; sec. Am. Fgn. Svc. Assn., 1979—81; chair, vice chair Neighborhood Bd. #3, 1989—96. Mem., treas. Oahu Pvt. Industry Coun., 1985—91; pres. Hawaii Cmty. Svcs. Coun., 1995—96; sec., treas. exec. com. East-West Ctr. Internat. Alumni, 1995—2000; mem. allocations com. Aloha United Way, 1996—; exec. bd. Ch. of the Crossroads, 2001—04. Mem.: Waikki Residents Assn., Waikki Improvement Assn. Republican. United Ch. Of Christ. Office: State Capitol Rm 318 415 S Beretania St Honolulu HI 96813 Office Phone: 808-586-8520. E-mail: repfox@capitol.hawaii.gov.

FOX, GARY DEVENOW, lawyer; b. Detroit, Sept. 8, 1951; s. Edward J. Fox. BA in Polit. Sci. and Drama, Drury Coll., 1973; JD, U. Fla., 1976. Bar: Fla. 1976, U.S. Dist. Ct. (so. and mid. dists.) Fla. 1977, U.S. Ct. Appeals (5th and 11th cirs.) 1977, U.S. Supreme Ct. 1981. From assoc. to ptnr. Frates, Floyd, Pearson, Stewart, Richman & Greer, Miami, 1976-84; ptnr. Stewart, Tilghman, Fox & Bianchi, PA, Miami, 1984—. Exec. editor U. Fla. Law Rev.; contbr. articles to profl. jours. Mem. ABA, Fla. Bar (cert. civil trial advocacy 1983, chmn. code and rules of evidence com. 1997—, civil procedure rules com., rules jud. adminstrn. com. 2003-), Fla. Bd. Bar Examiners, Dade County Bar Assn., Assn. Trial Lawyers Am. (substaining, lectr.), Acad. Fla. Trial Lawyers (diplomate, lectr.), Dade County Trial Lawyers Assn. (bd. dirs. 1986-89), Am. Bd. Trial Advocates (pres. Miami chpt. and Fla. fedn.), Nat. Coll. Advocacy Bd. Trustees, Assn. Trial Lawyers Am., Internat. Soc. Barristers, Bankers Club. Avocations: tennis, skiing. Office: 1 SE 3rd Ave Ste 3000 Miami FL 33131-1715 Business E-Mail: gfox@stfblaw.com.

FOX, GWEN, artist, educator; b. Jefferson City, Tenn., Jan. 25, 1943; d. Arthur Crowell and Margaret Fox; children: Mary, John. Student, Carson Newman Coll., Jefferson City, 1962-63, Fox Studio, 1998—, Taos Inst. Art, 2000. Tchr. art Belstead House, Ipswich, Eng., 1978-80, Barton Mills (Eng.) Edn., 1979-80, Bemis Art Ctr., Colorado Springs, Colo., 1992--94; tchr. art adult edn., Panama City, Fla., 1981-82; tchr. art Cheyenne Mountain Heritage Ctr., Colorado Springs, 1995—; tchr. Cottonwood Art Acad. One-woman shows, Honolulu, 1971, Mildenhall, Eng., 1977, Panama City, Fla., 1982, Monument, Colo., 1986, 87, Colorado Springs, Colo., 1995, 97; exhibited in group shows Poudre Valley Art League, 1993, N.W. Watercolor Soc., 1993, Fine Arts Ctr. and Taylor Mus., Colorado Springs, 1995 (MCI award 1995), Tex. Watercolor Soc., 1995, Colo. Watercolor Soc., 1995, U. Colo., 1997, Fine Arts Ctr. and Taylor Mus., Colo., 2000; represented in numerous pub. collections including Ctr. for Creative Leadership, ITT Industry Sys. Divsn., also numerous pvt. collections; represented in Flowers in Watercolor, 1996; included in Best of Watercolor Painting Color. Recipient Best of Show award Colorado Springs Nat., 1994, Golden award Rocky Mountain Nat., 1994, award Catherine Lorillard Wolfe, 1996. Mem. NOW, Colo. Watercolor Soc. (signature), Ala. Watercolor Soc., Pikes Peak Watercolor Soc. (pres. 1991-93). Avocations: gardening, reading, hiking. Home: 2017 Brookwood Dr Colorado Springs CO 80918-1135 Office Phone: 719-471-4909. E-mail: gwenfox@msn.com.

FOX, HAMILTON PHILLIPS, III, lawyer; b. Salisbury, Md., Sept. 18, 1945; s. Hamilton Phillips and Evelyn Louise (Jefferson) F.; m. Mary Shannon Lafans, Aug. 31, 1968 (dissolved); children: Gretchen Robinson, Hamilton Duke, Caleb Savage; m. Barbara Daniels Robinson, Dec. 13, 1986. BA with honors, U. Va., 1967; LLB, Yale U., 1970. Bar: Maine 1971, D.C. 1972, U.S. Dist. Ct. Md., U.S. Ct. Appeals (1st, 9th and D.C. cirs.), U.S. Supreme Ct. Law clk. to judge U.S. Ct. Appeals (1st cir.), Portland, Maine, 1970-71; law clk. to Hon. Stanley Reed and Lewis F. Powell Jr. U.S. Supreme Ct., Washington, 1971-72; asst. U.S. atty. U.S. Atty.'s Office, Washington, 1972-73, 74-77; asst. spl. prosecuter Watergate Prosecution Force, Washington, 1973-74; dep. chief organized crime sect. U.S. Dept. Justice, Washington, 1977-80; sole practice Washington, 1980-84; ptnr. Dewey, Ballantine, Bushby, Palmer & Wood, Washington, 1984-90; now ptnr. Sutherland, Asbill & Brennan, Washington. Lectr. law U. Va., Charlottesville, 1980-82; assoc. dep. counsel com. on standards of official conduct U.S. Ho. of Reps., 1983-84. Home: 729 Massachusetts Ave NE Washington DC 20002-6007 Office: Sutherland Asbill Brennan 1275 Pennsylvania Ave NW Ste 1 Washington DC 20004-2415

FOX, HAROLD EDWARD, obstetrician, researcher, gynecologist, educator; b. East Orange, N.J., Feb. 19, 1945; s. Willis Edward and Elizabeth (Strathearn) F.; m. Rhea Keller, June 18, 1966; children: Harold Hamilton, Andrhea Alicia. BA, U. Rochester, 1967, MS, MD with honors, 1972. Diplomate Am. Bd. Ob-Gyn., Am. Bd. Maternal-Fetal Medicine. Intern, resident Strong Meml. Hosp., Rochester, N.Y., 1972-75; dir. Regional Perinatal Program, Rochester, N.Y., 1975-79; dir. obstetrics and maternal fetal medicine U. Rochester, 1977-79; dir. maternal fetal medicine Columbia U., N.Y.C., 1979-95, dir. obstetrics, 1985-88, vice-chmn. ob-gyn., 1988-91, chmn. protem dept. ob-gyn., 1991-95; Oscar I. and Mildred S. Dodek prof., chmn. ob-gyn. George Washington U., Washington, 1995-96, exec. dir. Ctr. Excellence for Women's Health, 1995-96; ob-gyn. in-chief Johns Hopkins Medicine, Balt., 1996—, Dr. Dorothy Edwards prof. ob-gyn., 1996—, chair women's health ctr. oversight com., 1997—, chmn., dir. ob-gyn. Trustee Johns Hopkins Med. Svc. Corp., Johns Hopkins Home Care Group, 1996—, Kennedy Kreige Inst., 1996—2003; bd. dirs. JH Cmty. Physicians, JH Health Care; vice chair med. bd. Johns Hopkins Hosp., 1999-2002, chair med. bd., 2002-05, bd. dirs., 2002-05; mem. adv. bd. Johns Hopkins Medicine, bd. govs., chmn. govt. affairs com.; mem. Gov.'s Commn. on Infant Mortality, State of Md., 2000—; chmn. women and infant transmission study NIH, 1988-93; mem. pediat. com. AIDS clin. trials group, 1988-91; organizing mem. women's com.; mem. obstet. adv. com. N.Y.C. Dept. Health; bd. midwifery N.Y. State Edn. Dept., 1994-95; chmn. N.Y. Acad. Medicine Ob-gyn. sect., 1993-94; mem. Gov.'s Commn. on Infant Mortality, State Md., 1999—; co-chair innovations in patient care Editor Pediatric AIDS, 1991-95, Practical Revs. in Ob-Gyn., 2001—; contbr. articles to profl. jours. Grantee NIH, 1988-95, USPHS, 1991-95, March of Dimes. Fellow Soc. Gynecologic Investigation, Am. Coll. Ob-Gyn.; mem. Internat. AIDS Soc., Am. Gynecol. and Obstet. Soc., Am. Inst. Ultrasound in Medicine, Perinatal Rsch. Soc., Washington Acad. Medicine, Washington Gynecol. Soc., N.Y. Obstet. Soc., Med.Soc. State of Md. (chair maternal mortality com. 2003—), Alpha Omega Alpha, Phi Beta Delta. Avocations: boating, art, exercise. Home: PO Box 142 Gibson Island MD 21056-0142 Office: Johns Hopkins Medicine Dept Gyn-Ob 600 N Wolfe St Rm 264 Baltimore MD 21287-0005 Office Phone: 410-614-0178. Business E-Mail: hfox@jhmi.edu.

FOX, JACK JAY, chemist, educator; b. N.Y.C., Dec. 21, 1916; s. Samuel and Celia (Stern) F.; m. Ruth C. Inabu, June 13, 1939; children: Dolores M. Emspak, John Reed. AB, U. Colo., 1939, PhD, 1950. With Sloan-Kettering Inst. for Cancer Research, N.Y.C., 1952-88, mem. emeritus, 1988—; head Lab. Organic Chemistry, prof. biochemistry Cornell U. Grad. Sch. Med. Scis., N.Y.C., 1958—. Recipient Alfred P. Sloan award cancer rsch., 1956, C.S. Hudson award in carbohydrate chemistry Am. Chem. Soc., 1977, Pap award for sci. achievement, 1983, Norlin award U. Colo. Alumni Assn., 1984; NRC fellow, 1950-52; postdoctoral fellow Free U. Brussels, 1950-52; Damon Runyon Meml. Fund fellow, 1952-54. Mem. Am. Chem. Soc., Westchester Chem. Soc., Am. Soc. Biol. Chemists, Am. Assn. Cancer Rsch., Am. Soc. Antiviral Rsch., Sigma Xi. Achievements include research, numerous publs. on design, synthesis and structural elucidation of anticancer and antiviral agts., specific syntheses of compounds related to nucleic acid components, carbohydrate and heterocyclic chemistry. E-mail: jackfx252. Home: 110 S Henry St Apt 1511 Madison WI 53703-3168 Office: Meml Sloan-Kettering Cancer Ctr 1275 York Ave New York NY 10021-6094

FOX, JAMES CARROLL, federal judge; b. Atchison, Kans., Nov. 6, 1928; s. Jared Copeland and Ethel (Carroll) F.; m. Katharine deRosset Rhett, Dec. 30, 1950; children: James Carroll, Jr., Jane Fox Brown, Ruth Fox Jordan. BSBA, U. N.C., 1950, JD with honors, 1957. Bar: N.C. 1957. Law clk. U.S. Dist. Ct. (ea. dist.) N.C., Wilmington, 1957-58; assoc. Carter & Murchison, Wilmington, N.C., 1958-59; ptnr. Murchison, Fox & Newton, Wilmington, N.C., 1960-82; sr. fed. judge U.S. Dist. Ct. (ea. dist.) N.C., Wilmington, 1982—. Lectr. in field. Contbr. articles to profl. jours. Vestryman, St. James Episcopal Ch., 1973-75, 79-82. Mem. New Hanover County Bar Assn. (pres. 1967-68), Fifth Jud. Dist. Bar Assn. (sec. 1960-62). Office: US Dist Ct Alton Lennon Fed Bldg PO Box 2143 Wilmington NC 28402-2143

FOX, JAMES EDWARD, JR., federal agency administrator; b. Columbus, Ohio, Dec. 1, 1948; s. James Edward and Alice Jane (Andrix) F.; m. Julianne Feller, Sept. 12, 1970; children— Abigail, Katharine, James Edward BA, Ohio State U., 1972; MA, George Washington U., 1976. Research asst. U.S. Congress, Washington, 1973-74, legis. asst., 1974-75; minority cons. com. on fgn. affairs U.S. Ho. of Reps., Washington, 1975-83; dep. asst. sec. Dept. State, Washington, 1983-84, prin. dep. asst. sec., 1985; spl. asst. to Pres. White House, Washington, 1985-86; asst. sec. legis. affairs Dept. of State, Washington, 1986—89; asst. adminr. bur. for legis. and public affairs USAID, Washington, 2001—. Republican. Office: USAID Bur for Legis and Public Affairs RRB 1300 Pennsylvania Ave NW Washington DC 20523

FOX, JAMES MICHAEL, orthopedic surgeon; b. Milw., July 20, 1942; m. Ellen Fox. BS, U. Wis., 1964, MD, 1968. Diplomate Nat. Bd. Med. Examiners, Am. Bd. Orthop. Surgery. Intern Bronx (N.Y.) Mcpl. Hosp./Albert Einstein Coll. Medicine, 1968-69, surg. resident, 1969-70, orthop. surgery resident, 1970-72, chief resident orthop. surgery, 1972-73; asst. instr. orthop. surgery Albert Einstein Coll. Medicine, 1972-73; sports medicine fellow Nat. Athletic Health Inst., Inglewood, Calif., 1973-74, mem. med. adv. bd., 1974—; pvt. practice Sherman Oaks, Calif., 1976-81, So. Calif. Orthop. Inst., Van Nuys, Calif., 1981—. Mem. staff Centinela Valley Cmty. Hosp., Inglewood, 1973-74, Daniel Freeman Hosp., Inglewood, 1973-74, View Park Hosp., L.A., 1973-74, Keesler Med. Ctr., Keesler AFB, Miss., 1974-76, Encino (Calif.) Hosp., 1976-81, Sherman Oaks Cmty. Hosp., 1976-83, Valley Presbyn. Hosp., 1981—; med. cons. sports medicine video cassettes VCI-Nat. Athletic Health Inst., 1974-76; cons. cmty. outreach program on emergency treatment of athletic injuries Sherman Oaks Cmty. Hosp., 1978-80; cons., presenter in field; cons. Youth Soccer Mag.; med. dir. Ctr. for Disorders of Knee, Van Nuys; mem. Ctr. for Sports Medicine, Calif. State U., Northridge, 1990; med. examiner State of Calif. Dept. Indsl. Rels., 1993-95. Author: Save Your Knees; co-editor: Patello-Ferral Joint; mem. editl. bd. Jour. of Arthroscopy, 1989-93, video supplement, 1989, The Knee, 1994. Mem. Summer Olympics, 1984. Maj. Med. Corps USAF, 1974-76. Fellow ACS; mem. Am. Athletic Trainers Adv. Assn. and Cert. Bd. Inc. (mem. com.), Arthroscopy Assn. N.Am. (mem. rsch. com. 1986-89, bd. dirs. 1989-91, chmn. pub. rels. com. 1989, program chmn. 1993, sec. 1994-97), Calif. Med. Assn. Office: So Calif Orthop Inst 6815 Noble Ave Van Nuys CA 91405-3796 Office Phone: 818-901-6600. Business E-Mail: dfox@scoi.com.

FOX, JAN WOODWARD, lawyer; b. Dallas, Sept. 25, 1950; d. Jackson Spurgeon Woodward and Louie Woodward Henry; m. Robert Scott Ramsey Feb. 18, 1978 (div.); 1 child, Benjamin Ramsey. Student, U. Paris, 1970-71; BA cum laude, Harvard U., 1972; JD, U. Tex., 1975. Bar: Tex. 1975, U.S. Dist. Ct. (so., no., ea. dists.) Tex., U.S. Ct. Appeals (5th cir.), U.S. Supreme Ct.; bd. cert. civil trial and criminal law Tex. Bd. Legal Specialization. Assoc. Mitchell, George & Belt, Austin, Tex., 1975-76, Haynes & Fullenweider, Houston, 1976-80, shareholder, dir., 1980-89; pvt. practice Houston, 1989—. Contbr. articles to profl. jours. Mem. adv. com. Senate-House Select Com. Judiciary, 1983-84; dir. Homes St. Mark Adoption Agy., 1990-97, mem. planning com., 1991-93; chair Houston Trial Lawyers Found., 1993; bd. trustees Hockaday Sch., 1994-2000. Recipient Cmty. Svc. award Houston chpt. ACLU, 1997; named Super Lawyer Law & Politics, 2004, Tex. Monthly, 2005, Top Lawyer for the People Tex. Mag., 2005 Mem. ABA, ATLA (PAC trustee 1997-98), Nat. Coll. Criminal Def. Lawyers and Pub. Defenders, State Bar Tex. (mem. adminstrn. justice com. 1986-87, adminstrn. rules evidence com. 1985-87), Tex. Trial Lawyers Assn. (pres. 1996), Tex. Criminal Def. Lawyers Assn. Houston Bar Assn., Houston Trial Lawyers Assn. (pres. 1992). Home: 1757 Sunset Blvd Houston TX 77005-3356 Office: Lyric Ctr 440 Louisiana Ste 420 Houston TX 77002 Office Phone: 713-623-8600. E-mail: jwoodfox@ix.netcom.com, janfox@jwfplc.com.

FOX, JEAN MCGRIFF, writer; b. Norwood, Ohio, Jan. 25, 1917; d. Floyd and Ruth Worrall (Edwards) McGriff; m. Orville Taylor Fox, May 21, 1938 (dec. 1963); children: JoAnne, Susan Emily, John David. AB cum laude, Ind. U., 1937, MA in History, 1940; tchg. cert., Wayne U., 1957. Cert. tchr., Mich. Editor, pub. Southfield Sun, 1956-74; founder, editor, pub. Farmington Forum, 1967-74, Novi Sun-Forum, 1972-74. Author: The Windows of Old Mariners, 1974, 2nd edit., 1984, Farmington's Centennial Families, 1978, Watercolors of Lillian Drake Avery, 1985, Fred M. Warner, Three-Time Governor, 1986, More Than a Tavern: The 150 Years of Botsford Inn, 1986, The Underground Railroad, 1990; editor: The Natural History of Farmington, 1975, The Religious History of Farmington, 1976, Heritage Homes: If Walls Could Talk, 1980. Bd. mem. Mich. Ptnrs. of the Alliance, 1960-72; mem. Farmington Hills Hist. Commn., 1975-87, vice chair, 1980-85; sec. Farmington Hills Bd. Zoning Appeals, 1977-83, vice-chair, 1983-85, chmn., 1985-87; chmn. Farmington Hills Hist. Dist. Commn., 1980-87; mem. Oakland County Pks. and Recreation Commn., 1981-95, sec., 1982-84, vice chair, 1984-95; bd. mem. Oakland County Vol. Bur., 1983-90; city coun. mem. Farmington Hills City Coun., 1987-91; mayor City of Farmington Hills, 1990. Mem. Theta Alpha Phi, Theta Sigma Phi, Phi Beta Kappa, Alpha Lambda Delta, Kappa Kappa Gamma. Republican. Episcopalian. Avocations: genealogy, hiking, travel, writing. Home: 13511 Deakins Ln Darnestown MD 20874-3307

FOX, JOAN FRIEDLANDER, restaurant critic; b. Cin., Ohio, May 11, 1928; d. John Walter and Gladys Fleischmann (Onton) Friedlander; m. Frank Milford Fox, Jan. 3, 1979; children: Therese Steiner, Carl Steiner, Winthrop Wulsin. BA, Smith Coll., 1945—49. Restaurant critic Cin. Mag., Cin., 1975—2000. Author: The Best Man, 1990. Bd. mem. Provincetown Art Assn., Provincetown, Mass., 2000—05, The Ctr. for the Arts, 1990—2005; pres. Truro Ctr. for the Arts, 2000—02. Mem.: Cosmopolitan Club. Democrat. Home: 1071 Celestial St 2001 Cincinnati OH 45202 E-mail: foxyj@fuse.net.

FOX, JOHN, professional football coach; b. Virginia Beach, Va., Feb. 8, 1955; m. Robin Fox; children: Matthew, Mark, Cody, Halle. Student, Southwestern Coll., 1974—75; PhB, San Diego State; degree in sec. edn. tchg., 1977. Grad. asst. San Diego State, 1978; asst. coach U.S. Internat. U., 1979; sec. coach Boise State, 1980, Long Beach State, 1981, Utah, 1982, Kans., 1983, Iowa State, 1984, L.A. Express (USFL), 1985; defensive coord., sec. coach U. Pitts., 1986—88; sec. coach Pitts. Steelers, 1989—91; sec. coach San Diego Chargers, 1992—93; defensive coord. Oakland Raiders, 1994—95; cons. St. Louis Rams, 1996; defensive coord. N.Y. Giants, 1997—2001; head coach Carolina Panthers, 2002—. Named Asst. Coach of Yr., Pro Football Weekly. Office: Carolina Panthers 800 S Mint St Charlotte NC 28202

FOX, JOHN BAYLEY, JR., university dean; b. Cambridge, Mass., Nov. 6, 1936; s. John Bayley and Eunice (Jameson) F.; m. Julia Garrett, July 22, 1967; children— Sarah Cleveland, Thomas Bayley AB, Harvard U., 1959; BA, Oxford U., Eng., 1961, MA, 1962. Assoc. div. internat. fellowships Commonwealth Fund of N.Y., N.Y.C., 1963-67; dir. Office Career Services Harvard U., Cambridge, 1967-71, spl. asst., asst. dean of faculty, 1971-76, dean Harvard Coll., 1976-85, adminstrv. dean Grad. Sch. Arts and Scis., 1985-94, sec. Faculty Arts and Scis., sec. faculty coun., 1992—2005, sr. advisor to dean Faculty of Arts and Scis., 2005—. Unitarian. Home: 125 Prince St West Newton MA 02465-2603 Office: Harvard Univ Faculty Arts and Scis University Hall 401 Cambridge MA 02138-5722 Office Phone: 617-495-1522. Business E-Mail: John_Fox@harvard.edu.

FOX, JOHN DAVID, physics professor, physician; b. Huntington, W.Va., Dec. 8, 1929; s. David and Eleanor (Griffin) F.; children: Heidi Roberts Fox, Lise, Peter, Paul, Michelle Fox Lundy; m. Georgiana Fry Vines, Oct. 23, 1993. SB, MIT, 1951; Fulbright fellow, Rijksuniversiteit, Groningen, Netherlands, 1951-52; MS, U. Ill., 1954, PhD, 1960. Asst. physicist Brookhaven Nat. Lab., Upton, N.Y., 1956-59; asst. prof. physics Fla. State U., Tallahassee, 1959-63, asso. prof., 1963-65, prof., 1965-94, prof. emeritus, 1994—. Adj. prof. U. Tex., El Paso, 1996; guest scientist Max-Planck Inst. für Kernphysik, Heidelberg, Germany, 1968-69, Inst. für Kernphysik U. Köln, 1975; cons. physics divsn. Argonne Nat. Lab., 1982—; guest scientist Oak Ridge Nat. Lab., 1994—, program dir. nuclear physics NSF, 1990-92, 95-97; dir. Branchland Pipe & Supply Co., Huntington, W.Va., 1965-81; mem. MIT Ednl. Coun., 1981-90; cons. physics dept. U. Tenn., Knoxville, 1999—. Co-editor: Isobaric Spin in Nuclear Physics, 1966, Nuclear Analogue States, 1976; Contbr. articles to sci. jours. Mem. Leon County Dem. Com., 1970-74; mem. Dem. Nat. Com.; bd. dirs. LeMoyne Art Found., Tallahassee, 1971-73. NSF Grad. fellow, 1955-56; Sr. postdoctoral fellow, 1968-69; sr. U.S. scientist award Alexander von Humboldt-Stiftung, 1975 Fellow Am. Phys. Soc.; mem. AAAS, ACLU, Fedn. Am. Scientists.

FOX, JOHN JOSEPH, JR., historian, educator; b. Pittsfield, Mass., Dec. 20, 1931; s. John J. and Blanche Julia (Pellerin) F.; m. Marilyn Ann Volin, Feb. 23, 1957; 1 son, John Charles. BS, North Adams State Coll., 1959; MA in History, Lehigh U., 1964; postgrad., Boston U., 1968. Tchr. Pittsfield (Mass.) Pub. Sch. System, 1959-61; teaching asst. Lehigh U., Bethlehem, Pa., 1961-64; prof. dept. history Salem (Mass.) State Coll., 1964—98; ret. Pres. Oral History Research Assos.; cons. in oral, local history. Author: Oral History: Window to the Past, 1977, Parker Pride: Memories of Working Days At Parker Brothers, 1987; Window on the Past; A Guide to Oral History, 1980; Voices From the Past: Oral History in Massachusetts, in a Guide to the History of Massachusetts, 1988; Massachusetts and the Creation of the Federal Union in the Constitution and The States; Insuring the Future: The Holyoke Mutual Insurance Company in Salem, 1843-1993, 1993, Our Past Insures Our Future: The Lumber Insurance Companies, 1895-95; compiler of bibliography Up-Date in The Oral History, Rev., 1977; book review editor Oral History Rev., 1980-87; editor The England of Oral History Annual, The

New England Assn. Oral History Annual; mem. editorial bd. Jour. of Nursing History, 1985-89. Locus, 1987. Del. Democratic State Conv., Mass., 1970, 72; mem. Danvers Democratic Town Com., 1967-85; trustee Peabody Inst. Library, Danvers, Mass., 1976-84; mem. council Essex Inst., Salem, 1979-87. Served with inf. U.S. Army, 1952-54. Mem. Am. Hist. Assn., Orgn. Am. Historians, Supreme Ct. Judicial Ct. Hist. Soc. (adv. bd.), Social Sci. History Assn., Essex Inst. (council 1979-87), Oral History Assn. (exec. bd. 1984-87), New Eng. Assn. of Oral History (pres. 1974-77, exec. sec. 1985—, Harvey A. Kantor award 1982), Am. Soc. for Legal History. Democrat. Home: 134 Burley St Danvers MA 01923-2366

FOX, JOHN T., health facility administrator; b. Ont., Can. B in Econs. and History, Washington U., 1974; MBA in Fin., U. Cin., 1977. CPA. Dir. healthcare mergers and acquisitions, healthcare cons. Coopers and Lybrand; sr. v.p., CFO Scioto Valley Health Found. Inc., Portsmouth, Ohio; sr. v.p. Mercy Health Ctr., Ctrl. Iowa, 1985—87; v.p., CFO Johns Hopkins Hosp., Balt., 1987—89; exec. v.p. Clarian Health, Indpls., 1989—99; co-leader merger Meth. Health Sys. Clarian Health (formerly known as Ind. U. Med. Ctr. and Riley Children's Hosp.), 1995; pres., COO Emory Healthcare, Atlanta, 1999—2002, chmn. bd. dirs., dir. Woodruff Health Scis. Ctr. (WHSC), 1999, pres., CEO, 2002—. Mem.: Healthcare R & D Inst., Leadership Inst., Coll. Am. Healthcare Execs., Am. Assn. Health Plans. Office: Emory Healthcare 1440 Clifton Rd NE Atlanta GA 30322

FOX, KARL AUGUST, economist, educator, eco-behavioral scientist; b. Salt Lake City, July 14, 1917; s. Feramorz Young and Anna Teresa (Wilcken) Fox; m. Sylvia Olive Cate, July 29, 1940; children: Karl Richard, Karen Frances Anne. BA, U. Utah, 1937, MA, 1938; PhD, U. Calif., 1954. Economist USDA, 1942-54; head divsn. statis. and hist. rsch. Bur. Agrl. Econs., 1951-54; economist Coun. Econ. Advisers, Washington, 1954-55; head dept. econs. and sociology Iowa State U., Ames, 1955-66, head dept. econs., 1966-72, disting. prof. scis. and humanities, 1968-87, prof. emeritus, 1987—. Vis. prof. Harvard, 1960-61, U. Calif., Santa Barbara, 1971-72, 78, vis. scholar, Berkeley, 1972-73; William Evans vis. prof. U. Otago, N.Z., 1981; Bd. dirs. Social Sci. Rsch. Coun., 1963-67, mem. com. econ. stability, 1963-66, chmn. com. areas for social and econ. statistics, 1964-67; mem. Com. Reg. Accounts, 1963-68 Author: Econometric Analysis for Public Policy, 1958, (with M. Ezekiel) Methods of Correlation and Regression Analysis, 1959, (with others) The Theory of Quantitative Economic Policy, 1966, rev. edit., 1973, Intermediate Economic Statistics, 1968, rev. edit, (with T.K. Kaul), 1980, (with J. K. Sengupta) Economic Analysis and Operations Research, 1969, (with W.C. Merrill) Introduction to Economic Statistics, 1970, Social Indicators and Social Theory, 1974, Social System Accounts, 1985, The Eco-Behavioral Approach To Surveys and Social Accounts for Rural Communities, 1990, repub., 1994, Demand Analysis, Econometrics and Policy Models, 1992, Urban-Regional Economics, Social System Accounts and Eco-Behavioral Science, 1994; author-editor: Economic Analysis for Educational Planning, 1972; co-editor: Readings in the Economics of Agriculture, 1969, Economic Models, Estimation and Risk Programming (essays in honor of Gerhard Tintner), 1969, Systems Economics, 1987; contbr. articles to profl. jours. Recipient superior service medal USDA, 1948, award for outstanding pub. research Am. Agrl. Econs. Assn., 1952, 54, 57, for outstanding doctoral dissertation, 1953 Fellow Econometric Soc., Am. Statis. Assn. (Census Research fellow 1980-81), Am. Agrl. Econs. Assn. (v.p. 1955-56, award for publ. of enduring quality 1977), AAAS; mem. Am. Econs. Assn. (research and pubs. com. 1963-67), Regional Sci. Assn., Ops. Research Soc. Am., Am. Ednl. Research Assn., Phi Beta Kappa, Phi Kappa Phi. Home: 1801 20th St Apt J-31 Ames IA 50010-5166 Office: Iowa State U Econs Dept Ames IA 50011-0001 E-mail: ncfoxes@hotmail.com.

FOX, KELLY DIANE, financial advisor; b. Brockton, Mass., Sept. 9, 1959; d. James H. and Betty Jane (Calloway) F.; m. Alan David Goldberg, July 6, 1985; 1 child, Andrew Jason. BA, Allegheny Coll., 1980; postgrad. in Bus. Adminstrn., Suffolk U., 1983—84; student, Temple U., London, 1978, Syracuse U., 1979. Cert. fin. planner practitioner. Asst. mgr. Casual Male, Braintree, Mass., 1980, Hit or Miss, Braintree, 1981-82; merchandiser Foxmoor, West Bridgewater, Mass., 1982; distbr. Hill's Dept. Stores, Canton, Mass., 1982-85; asst. buyer BJ's Wholesale Club, Natick, Mass., 1985-92; advanced advisor team, personal fin. advisor Am. Express Fin. Advisors, 1993—. Am. Express Fin. Advisors Boston steering com., diversity chair 1995-96; mem. spkrs. bur. Women's Union, 1997-2001; contbr. ADVICE + program State Atty. Gen's. Office for Elder Affairs; guest lectr. MBA in a Day program Wheaton Coll.; mem. Mass. Dept. Edn. Gifted and Talented Adv. Cou., 1999-2002; founder Women's Resource Room, 1995-97; bd. dirs. New Hope, Inc., 1996-98; co-founder The Women's Connection, 2001-2002; founding bd. dirs., treas. Women at Work Mus., 2003—; founding bd. dirs. Young Women's Fin. Network, 2004. Contbr. columns in newspapers. Treas., bd. dirs. Attleboro Area Coun. Children, 1993—; bd. dirs. Attleboro Area Parents Anonymous, 1996, New Hope, 1996—98; cheerleading coach Avon High Sch., Mass., 1982—83; co-chair enrichment program Falls Elem. Sch., 1994—95, 1997—98; mem. John Woodcock Sch. Coun., 1993—94; vol. Foxborough Regional Charter Sch. SABIS. Recipient Woman of Achievement award, Attleboro Area Bus. and Profl. Women, 2003, Athena award, 2004. Methodist. Avocations: theater, travel, bell choir, art galleries. Office Phone: 508-695-2336. Business E-Mail: Kelly.D.Fox@AEXP.com.

FOX, KENNETH, physicist, educator, lawyer; b. Highland Park, Mich., Aug. 16, 1935; s. Abraham and Jennie (Krakowski) F.; m. Christina Diana Sabin, Aug. 15, 1982; children: Abram Jacob, Rachel Elizabeth, Matthew Tyler. BS, Wayne State U., 1957; MS, U. Mich., 1958, PhD, 1962; JD, U. Tenn., 1982. Bar: Tenn. 1983, D.C. 1985, Md. 1988. Prof. dept. physics Vanderbilt U., Nashville, 1964-65; prof. dept. physics and astronomy U. Tenn., Knoxville, 1965-85, 88-97; discipline scientist NASA Hdqrs., Washington, 1985-88; prof. sci. divsn. Anne Arundel C.C., Arnold, Md., 1997—2003. Vis. prof. dept. chemistry and biochemistry U. Md., Coll. Park, 1990-95; cons. Oak Ridge (Tenn.) Nat. Lab., 1965-67, Jet Propulsion Lab., Pasadena, Calif., 1969-71; mem. vis. staff Los Alamos Nat. Lab., 1975-77; sr. rsch. assoc. NAS, Washington, 1977-78. Contbr. articles to profl. jours.; editor sci. collections. Fellow Am. Phys. Soc., Explorers Club; mem. Tenn. Bar Assn., D.C. Bar Assn., Md. Bar Assn., Internat. Astron. Union, Phi Beta Kappa, Sigma Xi. Office: 14102 Guardian Ct Bowie MD 20715-1748 Office Phone: 301-809-6114. Business E-Mail: xofnek@aol.com.

FOX, LAWRENCE J., lawyer; b. Phila., July 17, 1943; s. William and Elainne B. Fox; m. Vicki Hessan (div.); children: Emily, Anthony. BA, U. Pa., 1965, LLB, 1968. Bar: Pa. 1968, NY 1970, US Dist. Ct. So. Dist. NY 1970, US Dist. Ct. Ea. Dist. Pa. 1972, US Ct. Appeals 3rd Cir. 1972, US Ct. Appeals 5th Cir. 1975, US Ct. Appeals 2nd Cir. 1978, US Supreme Ct. 1994. Law clk. to Justice Samuel J . Roberts Pa. Supreme Ct.; legal services lawyer Cmty. Action Legal Services, NYC; assoc. Drinker Biddle & Reath, Phila., 1972-76, ptnr., 1976—, former mng. ptnr. Lectr. in law U. Pa.; law firm rep. CPR Inst. for Dispute Resolution (formerly Ctr. for Pub. Resources), mem. disting. panel neutrals, mem. bd. editors Alternatives newsletter, mem. Commn. on Ethics and Standards of Dispute Resolution. Author: Legal Tender: A Lawyer's Guide to Professionalism Dilemmas, 1995; co-author (with Susan R. Martyn): Traversing the Ethical Minefield: Problems, Law, and Profl. Responsibility, 2004. Mem. bd. overseers U. Pa. Sch. Law, 1992—, nat. chmn. ann. giving, 1987-89; assoc. trustee U. Pa., 1992—; trustee Friends Select Sch., 1982-93, Beth Zion-Beth Israel Synagogue, 1988—; mem. bd. advisors United Way; active USCG Aux. Recipient Wachovia Fidelity Award, Phila. Bar Assn., 2004. Mem. ABA (former chair sect. litig.; mem. Standing Com. on Ethics and Profl. Responsibility 1990-97, chair 1996-97), Pa. Bar Assn., Am. Law Inst., Am. Coll. Trial Lawyers. Democrat. Avocations: sailing, writing. Office: Drinker Biddle & Reath 1345 Chestnut St Ste 1300 Philadelphia PA 19107-3496

FOX, LESLIE B., real estate company executive; MBA, JD, U. Denver. Exec. mgmt. positions NHP, Inc.; sr. mgmt. positions Asset, Investors Corp., Comml. Assets, Inc., 1993—96, pres., 1996—97; exec. v.p., COO, exec. v.p., investment mgmt. Lexford Residential Trust, 1997—99; pres., Lexford divsn. Equity Residential, Chgo., 1999—2001, exec. v.p., 0999—, chief info. officer, 2001—. Office: Equity Residential 2 N Riverside Plaza Chicago IL 60606

FOX, MARY ANN WILLIAMS, librarian; b. Savannah, Ga., Jan. 16, 1939; d. Alton F. and Arthur (Colquitt) Williams; m. William Francis Fox, Dec. 26, 1960 (div. 1984); children: Katherine Frances, William Francis Jr. BA, U. Ga., 1960; MLS, Rutgers U., 1984. Libr. Metuchen (N.J.) Pub. Libr., 1983-85, Mable Smith Douglas Libr. Rutgers U., New Brunswick, N.J., 1984, Firestone Libr. Princeton (N.J.) U., 1985, The Hun Sch. of Princeton, 1985—. Bd. dirs. Ctrl. Jersey Regional Libr. Coop., 1997-2005, Region 5 Libr. Coop., N.J., 1985-92. Trustee East Brunswick (N.J.) Pub. Libr., 1979-92; bd. dirs. Ctrl. Jersey YWCA, New Brunswick, 1985-88, Ctrl. Atlantic Conf. United Ch. of Christ, 1985-88. Mem. ALA, N.J. Libr. Assn., N.J. Ind. Sch. Assn. (chair libr. sect. 1988—), Edn. Media Assn. N.J. (bd. dirs. 1987-92), Librs. of Middlesex (pres.). Democrat. Mem. United Ch. of Christ. Home: 10 Redcoat Dr East Brunswick NJ 08816-2759 Office: Hun Sch Princeton 176 Edgerstone Rd Princeton NJ 08540 E-mail: mafox@hunschool.org.

FOX, MATTHEW IGNATIUS, publishing company executive; b. NYC, Apr. 10, 1934; s. Matthew I. and Lucille V. (Reilly) F.; children: Cathleen, Matthew, Patricia. AB, Rutgers U., 1956. Field rep. Prentice-Hall, Inc., N.Y.C., 1958-60, editor engring., 1960-67, exec. editor, asst. v.p., 1967-71, exec. editor, 1981-83, editor-in-chief, 1983-85, pub., 1985—; pres. Reston Pub. Co., Va., 1971-81. Cons. in pub., 1987—; bd. dirs. Fairmont Press, Atlanta. Dep. mayor, mayor, Rivervale (NJ), 1964-67, commr., Bergen County, NJ, 1966-70; del. Fairfax County (Va.) Dem. Com., 1976-81; leader City of Cape May Dem. Party. Mem. Rutgers U. Alumni Assn., Cape May Cottagers and Beach Club, Corinthian Yacht Club. Democrat. Roman Catholic. Home: 1103 Illinois Ave Cape May NJ 08204-2608

FOX, MAURICE SANFORD, retired molecular biologist, educator; b. N.Y.C., Oct. 11, 1924; s. Albert and Ray F.; m. Sally Cherniavsky, Apr. 1, 1955; children: Jonathan, Gregory, Michael. BS in Meteorology, U. Chgo., 1944, MS in Chemistry, PhD, U. Chgo., 1951; Docteur honoris causa, Université Paul Sabatier, Toulouse, France, 1994. Instr. U. Chgo., 1951-53; asst. Rockefeller Inst., 1953-55, asst. prof., 1955-58, assoc. prof., 1958-62, MIT, Cambridge, 1962-66, prof., 1966-79, Lester Wolfe prof. molecular biology, 1979-96, head dept. biology, 1985-89; ret., 1997. Mem. Radiation Effects Rsch. Found., Hiroshima, 1997—2000. Mem. Internat. Bioethics Com. UN Ednl., Sci. and Cultural Orgn., 1997-2003. Served with USAAF, 1943-46. USPHS fellow, 1952-53; Nuffield Rsch. fellow, 1957; Fogarty scholar, 1991. Fellow: AAAS; mem.: NAS, Am. Acad. Arts and Scis., Inst. Medicine. Office: MIT Dept Biology 77 Massachusetts Ave Cambridge MA 02139-4307 Office Phone: 617-253-4728. Business E-Mail: msfox@mit.edu.

FOX, MICHAEL DAVID, retired art educator; b. Dec. 29, 1937; s. Donald F. and Ethel (Allen) Sullivan; m. Carol Ann Hamptston, Nov. 5, 1967; 1 child, Kathryn Gabrielle. BS, SUNY, Buffalo, 1962, MS, 1969; cert. in sculpture, Bklyn. Mus. Sch., 1964. Tchr. art City Schs., Rochester, NY, 1962-63, 64-65; prof. art Morehead State U., Ky., 1965-67, SUNY, Oswego, 1967—2000; ret., 2000. Vis. artist univs. and art ctrs., United States, Canada; dir. Popular Image Gallery, Oswego, 1967—2004; spkr. in field; lectr. in field; judge local, state, regional and nat. exhibitions. Work featured on CBS-TV, 1976, 1978, 1980, also featured in N.Y. Times, Look, Evergreen Rev., Nat. Lampoon, Scanlon's Monthly, Cavalier, Sch. Arts, others, Represented in permanent collections, U.S., Can., Japan, Africa, Asia, Europe, S.Am.; reviewer textbooks; featured in texbook, Sculpture: Techniques, Form and Content, 1988, Beginning Sculpture, 2004, The Sculpture Reference, 2004. Recipient numerous awards for drawing, painting and sculpture, 1962—, Outstanding Tchg. award, Morehead State U., 1967, Chancellor's award for excellence in tchg., SUNY, 1981. Mem.: United Univ. Profs. (v.p., del). Home: 38 W End Ave Oswego NY 13126-1758 Office Phone: 315-591-3392. E-mail: cfox@oswego.edu.

FOX, MICHAEL J., actor; b. Vancouver, B.C., Can., June 9, 1961; s. Bill and Phyllis Fox; m. Tracy Pollan, July 16, 1988; 1 son, Sam Michael. Head Lottery Hill Entertainment, The Michael J. Fox Foundation for Parkinson's Rsch., 2000-. TV series include Leo and Me (CBC), 1976, Palmerstown USA, 1980, Family Ties, 1982-89 (Emmy award, 1986, 87, 88, Golden Globe best actor 1989), Spin City (also exec. prodr.), 1996-2000 (Emmy award best actor in comedy 2000, Golden Globe best actor 1998, 99, 2000), Scrubs, 2001; TV films include Letters From Frank, 1979, Poison Ivy, 1985, High School USA, 1985, I Am Your Child, 1997, Tales From the Crypt: The Trap (guest dir.), Don't Drink the Water, 1994; exec. prodr. TV series Anna Says, 1999, Otherwise Engaged, 2002; film appearances include Midnight Madness, 1980, Class of '84, 1981, Back to the Future, 1985, Teen Wolf, 1985, Light of Day, 1986, The Secret of My Success, 1987, Bright Lights, Big City, 1988, Casualties of War, 1989, Back to the Future, Part II, 1989, Back to the Future, Part III, 1990, The Hard Way, 1991, Doc Hollywood, 1991, (voice over) Homeward Bound: The Incredible Journey, 1993, Life with Mikey, 1993, For Love or Money, 1993, Where the Rivers Flow North, 1993, Greedy, 1994, Cold Blooded, 1995, Blue in the Face, 1995, The American President, 1995, Mars Attacks!, 1996, Homeward Bound II: Lost in San Francisco, 1996, The Frighteners, 1996, Stuart Little (voice), 1999, Atlantis: The Lost Empire (voice), 2001, Interstate 60, 2002, Stuart Little 2 (voice), 2002; author memoir Lucky Man, 2001. Office: Creative Artists Agy care Kevin Huvane 9830 Wilshire Blvd Beverly Hills CA 90212-1804 also: Michael J Fox Foundation for Parkinson's Research PO Box 4777 New York NY 10163

FOX, MICHAEL VASS, theology studies educator; b. Detroit, Dec. 9, 1940; s. Leonard W. and Mildred (Vass) F.; m. Jane Schulzinger, Sept. 4, 1961; children: Joshua, Ariel BA, U. Mich., 1962, MA, 1963; PhD, Hebrew U., Jerusalem, 1972. Ordained rabbi, 1968. Lectr. Haifa U., Israel, 1971-74, Hebrew U., Jerusalem, 1975-77; prof. Hebrew U. Wis., Madison, 1977—, chmn. dept., 1982-88, 92-99, Weinstein-Bascom prof. in Jewish studies, 1990—, Halls-Bascom prof., 1999—. Author: The Song of Songs and the Ancient Egyptian Love Songs, 1985, Shirey Dodim Mimitzrayim Ha'atiqa, 1985, Qohelet and his Contradictions, 1988, The Redaction of the Books of Esther, 1991, Character and Ideology in the Book of Esther, 1991, 2001, A Time to Tear Down and a Time to Build Up: A Rereading of Ecclesiastes, 1999; editor: Anchor Bible: Proverbs, vol. I, 2000, Ecclesiastes--JPS Commentary, 2004; contbr. articles to profl. jours. Named Vilas assoc., U. Wis., 1988—90; recipient Wahrburg prize, Hebrew U., 1971—72, Kellett Mid-Career award, U. Wis., 1999; fellow, Brit. Friends of Hebrew U., Liverpool, 1974—75, NEH, 1992, Nat. Humanities Ctr., 1999; Leverhulme fellow, U. Liverpool, Eng., 1974—75, Am. Coun. Learned Socs. fellow, 2001, Am. Acad. for Jewish Rsch. fellow. Mem. Soc. for Bibl. Lit. (editor SBL Dissertation Series 1994-99, editl. bd. Jour. Bibl. Lit. 1991-95; pres. midwest region 1998-2000), Nat. Assn. Profs. Hebrew (editor Hebrew Studies 1985-93, v.p. 2000-03, pres. 2003—). Home: 2815 Chamberlain Ave Madison WI 53705-3607 Office: U Wis Dept Hebrew 1220 Linden Dr Rm 1338 Madison WI 53706-1525 Office Phone: 608-238-5644.

FOX, MICHAEL WILSON, veterinarian, animal scientist; b. Bolton, Eng., Aug. 13, 1937; came to U.S., 1962; s. Geoffrey and Elizabeth (Wilson) F.; m. Deanna L. Krantz, May 1989; children by previous marriage: Michael Wilson, Camilla, Mara. B. in Vet. Medicine, Royal Vet. Coll., London, 1962; PhD, U. London, 1967, D.Sc., 1975. Postdoctoral fellow Jackson Lab., Bar Harbor, Maine, 1962-64; med. research assoc. State Research Hosp., Galesburg, Ill., 1964-67; assoc. prof. psychology Washington U., St. Louis, 1967-76; v.p. Humane Soc. U.S., Washington, 1986-98, sr. scholar bioethics, 1998—2002; chief cons./vet. India Project for Animals & Nature, 1996—. Author: syndicated newspaper column Ask Your Animal Doctor; author: Canine Behavior, 1965, Canine Pediatrics, 1966, Integrative Development of Brain and Behavior in the Dog, 1971, Behavior of Wolves, Dogs and Related Canids, 1971, Understanding Your Dog, 1972, Understanding your Cat, 1974, Concepts in Ethology: Animal and Human Behavior, 1974, Between Animal and Man: The Key to the Kingdom, 1976, The Dog, Domestication and Behavior, 1977, (juveniles) Wild Dogs Three, 1977, What Is Your Cat Saying?, 1978, The Wolf, 1973 (Christopher award), Vixie, The Story of a Fox, 1973, Sundance Coyote, 1974, Ramu and Chennai, 1975 (Sci. Tchrs. award); co-author: (juveniles) What is Your Dog Saying?, 1977, Dr. Fox's Fables, 1980, The Touchlings, 1981, Animals Have Rights Too, 1991, (adult) Understanding Your Pet, 1978, The Soul of the Wolf, 1980, One Earth One Mind, 1980, Returning to Eden: Animal Rights and Human Responsibility, 1980, How to be Your Pet's Best Friend, 1981, The Healing Touch, 1982, Love is a Happy Cat, 1982, Farm Animal Husbandry, Behavior and Veterinary Practice, 1983, The Whistling Hunters: Field Studies of the Asiatic Wild Dog (Cuon alpinus), 1984, The Animal Doctor's Answer Book, 1984, Laboratory Animal Care, Welfare and Experimental Variables, 1986, Agricide-The Hidden Crisis That Affects Us All, 1986, The New Animal Doctor's Answer Book, 1989, The New Eden, 1989, Superdog, 1990, Inhumane Society, The American Way of Animal Exploitation, 1990, You Can Save The Animals; 50 Things to Do Right Now, 1991, Supercat, 1991, Superpigs and Wondercorn: How the Brave New World of Biotechnology Will Affect Us All, 1992, The Boundless Circle: Caring for Creatures and Creation, 1996, Eating With Conscience: The Bioethics of Food, 1997, Beyond Evolution: The Genetically Altered Future of Plants, Animals, The Earth...and Humans, 1999, Bringing Life to Ethics: Global Bioethics for a Humane Society, 2001, The Healing Touch for Dogs, 2004, The Healing Touch for Cats, 2004, Killer Foods, 2004; editor: Abnormal Behavior in Animals, 1968, Readings in Ethology and Comparative Psychology, 1973, The Wild Canids, 1975, On the Fifth Day: Animal Rights and Human Ethics, 1978, Internat. Jour. for study of Animal Problems, Advances in Animal Welfare Sci. Mem.: AVMA, Brit. Vet. Assn. *My life was shaped in childhood by close contact with animals and nature. Empathy and concern for the well-being of non-human beings led to a veterinary degree and curiosity about their behavior and inner awareness to several years research. Most influential teacher: the wolf. My philosophy: reverence for all life; humankind as steward living in co-creative communion with nature and all.*

FOX, MITCHELL B., magazine publisher; married; 3 children. Degree, SUNY. Sr. v.p. sales and promotion Bergdorf Goodman; pub. Vanity Fair mag., N.Y.C., 1994—97, v.p., 1997—99; sr. v.p., corp. sales Conde Nast, 1999—2000, exec. v.p. sales and mktg., 2000—01; pres. The Golf Digest Cos., 2001—, CEO, 2001—. Office: Golf Digest Four Times Square New York NY 10036*

FOX, MURIEL, retired public relations executive; b. Newark, Feb. 3, 1928; d. M. Morris and Anne L. (Rubenstein) F.; m. Shepard G. Aronson, July 1, 1955 (dec. Nov. 10, 2003); children: Eric R., Lisa S. Student, Rollins Coll., 1944-46; BA summa cum laude, Barnard Coll., 1948. Art critic, bridal editor Miami (Fla.) News, 1946; reporter U.P.I., 1946-48; polit. speechwriter, publicist, 1949-50; from TV-radio writer to exec. v.p. Carl Byoir & Assos., N.Y.C., 1950-85; pres. subs. MediaCom Comm. Tng., 1975-85, By/Media Inc., 1981-85; sr. cons. Hill & Knowlton, Inc., 1986-90. Dir. Harleysville Ins. Co., Rorer Group Inc.; Co-chmn. Vice Presdl. Task Force on Women, 1968; mem. steering com. Women's Forum, 1974-79, pres., 1976-78; mem. Women's Econ. Adv. Com., N.Y.C., 1974-78; mem. nat. adv. com. Nat. Women's Polit. Caucus; nat. adv. bd. Women Today, Ethnic Woman Bd. dirs. N.Y. Diabetes Assn., 1956-66, Holy Land Conservation Fund, United Way of Tri-State, Internat. Rescue Com., 1977-84; v.p. Rockland Ctr. for the Arts, 1985-2004, pres., 2004—; pres. Hickory Hill Coop., Inc., 1995-99; chair bd. dirs. Vet. Feminists of Am., 1997—. Named one of 100 Top Corp. Women Bus. Week mag., 1976; recipient Matrix award Women in Communications, 1977, Bus. Leader of Year award ADA, 1979; Disting. Alumna award Barnard Coll., 1985, Eleanor Roosevelt Leadership award, 1985 Mem.: NOW (v.p. 1967—70, chmn. bd. 1971—73, chair nat. adv. com. 1973—74, bd. dirs. legal def. and edn. fund 1974—, v.p. fund 1977—78, pres. 1978—81, chair bd. 1981—92, hon. chair bd. 1993—, founder, Muriel Fox Comm. Leadership award 1991, Our Hero award 1995, Caroline Lexow Babcock award 1997), Am. Arbitration Assn. (bd. dirs. 1983—87), Am. Women in Radio and TV (bd. dirs. 1950—51, chair nat. publicity com. 1955—57, chair nat. pub. rels. com. 1957—59, Achievement award 1983), Vet. Feminists of Am. (chair bd. dirs. 2000—). Home and Office: 66 Hickory Hill Rd Tappan NY 10983-1804 Office Phone: 845-359-6075. Personal E-mail: mfox66@optonline.net. *As a business executive, a founder and leader of the modern women's movement, and a fulfilled wife and mother, I hope I have helped to prove that women can enjoy success at many levels-professionally, politically and personally-without being forced to sacrifice one aspect of life for another. I also hope I've helped make such multifaceted success more attainable for other women in the present and future.*

FOX, PATRICK JOHN, sociology educator; b. Ramey AFB, P.R., Sept. 25, 1953; s. Leon James and Frances Valeria Fox; m. Sabrina Watson, July 30, 1978. BS in Social Sci., MA in Edn., Calif. Poly. State U., 1976; MSW in Social Welfare, U. Calif., Berkeley, 1978; MA in Sociology, U. Calif., San Diego, 1977; CPhil in Sociology, U. Calif., San Francisco, 1984, PhD in Sociology, 1988. Pub. adminstrn. analyst Inst. Health & Aging U. Calif. Sch. Nursing, San Francisco, 1985-87, sr. pub. adminstn. analyst Inst. Health & Aging, 1987-89, prin. pub. adminstn. analyst Inst. Health & Aging, 1989-90, from asst. prof. to assoc. prof. sociology in residence, 1990—, assoc. dir. for rsch./strat. planning Inst. Health & Aging, 1996-99, assoc. dir. Ctr. Healthy & Active Aging/Inst. Health & Aging, 1999—, prof. sociology in residence dept. social/behavioral scis., 1999—, co-dir. Inst. Health & Aging, 1999—. Guest prof. Inst. for Population Studies, East China Normal U., Shanghai, 1997-2000; mem. Ctr. for Health and Cmty., U. Calif., San Francisco, 1996—; mini residency in geriatrics U. Calif. San Diego Med. Ctr., 1987; reviewer books and jours. for Scott, Foresman & Co., 1989—; Helen Nahm rsch. lectr. U. Calif., San Francisco; reviewer various panels and confs.; presenter in field. Reviewer: Social Science and Medicine, 1989—, The Gerontologist, 1989—, PharmacoEconomics, 1989—, Am. Jour. Preventive Medicine, 1989—, Am. Jour. Pub. Health, 1989—, Am. Jour. Managed Care, 1989—, Health Care for Women Internat., 1989—, Brain Research, 2002, Health Policy, 2002. Regents fellow U. Calif.-San Diego, 1981-82, Pew doctoral fellow U. Calif., San Francisco, 1985-87; Laura Hawkins scholar U. Calif., San Diego, 1981-82; Chancellor's Patent Fund grantee U. Calif., San Francisco, 1986. Mem. APHA, AAAS, Gerontol. Soc. Am., Am. Soc. on Aging, Assn. for Health Svcs. Rsch., Pi Gamma Mu. Avocations: music, swimming, film. Office: U Calif Ste 340 3333 California St San Francisco CA 94118

FOX, PAUL T., lawyer; b. N.Y.C., Jan. 17, 1953; BA, Northwestern U., 1975, JD cum laude, 1978. Bar: Ill. 1978, U.S. Dist. Ct. (no. dist. trial bar) Ill. 1979, U.S. Ct. Appeals (7th cir.) 1979, U.S. Supreme Ct. 1986, U.S. Ct. Appeals (fed. cir.) 1987, Wis. 1989. Co-mng. shareholder Greenberg Traurig LLP, Chgo. Faculty mem. Nat. Inst. for Trial Advocacy; adj. prof. Northwestern U. Sch. Law. Mem. ABA (mem. litigation sect.), State Bar Wis., Chgo. Bar Assn., Order of Coif. Office: Greenberg Traurig 77 W Wacker Drive Ste 2500 Chicago IL 60601 Office Phone: 312-456-8420. Business E-Mail: foxp@gtlaw.com.

FOX, PAULA (MRS. MARTIN GREENBERG), writer; b. N.Y.C., Apr. 22, 1923; d. Paul Hervey and Elsie (de Sola) F.; m. Richard Sigerson (div. 1954); children: Adam, Linda, Gabriel; m. Martin Greenberg, June 9, 1962. Student, Columbia U. Condr. writing Seminars U. Pa. Author: 22 children's books and 6 novels, including How Many Miles to Babylon, 1966, Portrait of Ivan, 1968, Blowfish Live in the Sea, 1970; (novels) Poor George, 1967, Desperate Characters, 1970, The Western Coast, 1972, The Slave Dancer, 1974 (John Newbery medal), The Widow's Children, 1976, The Little Swineherd and Other Tales, 1978, A Place Apart, 1983 (Am. Book award), A Servant's Tale, 1984, One-Eyed Cat, 1985 (Newbery honor book 1985), Maurice's Room, 1985, The Moonlight Man, 1986, The Stone-Faced Boy, 1987, The Village by the Sea, 1988, Lily and the Lost Boy, 1989, The God of Nightmares, 1990, Monkey Island, 1991, Amzat and His Brothers, 1993, Western Wind, 1993, The Eagle Kite, 1995, Radiance Descending, 1997, Borrowed Finery: A Memoir, 2000 (PEN/Martha Albrand award). Recipient Arts and Letters award Nat. Inst. Arts and Letters, 1972, Hans Christian Andersen medal,

1978, fiction citation Brandeis U., 1984, Empire State award for children's lit., 1994; Guggenheim fellow, 1972. Mem. Authors League, Am. Acad. Arts and Letters (recipient medal and cash award). Office: care Robert Lescher 47 E 19th St New York NY 10003-1323

FOX, PETER, soil scientist, educator; b. Chgo., Aug. 19, 1961; s. Rudolph and Alma Marie Fox; life ptnr. Melody Tulanian; children: Adam Jefferson, Jason Alexander. PhD, U. Ill., 1989. Dir. Nat. Ctr. Sustainable Water Supply, Tempe, Ariz., 1999—. Contbr. over 100 articles to profl. jours. Mem.: Ariz. Water Pollution Control Assn. (assoc.; dir. 1996—2005, faculty advisor 1996—2005, Quentin Mees Rsch. award 1991, 1994, 2002). Office: Arizona State University PO Box 5306 Tempe AZ 85287-5306 Office Phone: 480-965-1734. Office Fax: 480-965-0557.

FOX, RENÉE CLAIRE, sociology educator; b. N.Y.C., Feb. 15, 1928; d. Paul Fred and Henrietta (Gold) F. AB summa cum laude, Smith Coll., 1949, LHD, 1975; PhD, Harvard U., 1954; MA (hon.), U. Pa., 1971, U. Oxford, 1996; ScD (hon.), Med. Coll. Pa., 1974, St. Joseph's Coll., Phila., 1978; D (hon.), Katholieke U., Leuven, 1978; LHD (hon.), La Salle U., Phila., 1988; DSc (hon.), Hahnemann U., 1991, U. Nottingham, Eng., 2002. Rsch. asst. Bur. Applied Social Rsch., Columbia U., 1953-55, rsch. assoc., 1955-58; lectr. dept. sociology Barnard Coll., 1955-58, asst. prof., 1958-64, assoc. prof., 1964-66; lectr. sociology Harvard U., 1967-69; rsch. fellow Ctr. Internat. Affairs, 1967-68, rsch. assoc. program tech. and soc., 1968-71; prof. sociology, psychiatry and medicine U. Pa., Phila., 1969-98, Annenberg prof. social scis., 1978-98, chmn. dept. sociology, 1972-78, Annenberg prof. social scis. emerita, 1998—, sr. fellow Ctr. for Bioethics, 1999—, affiliated faculty Solomon Asch Ctr. for the Study of Ethnopolit. Conflict, 2001—. Rsch. assoc. Refugee Studies Centre, Queen Elizabeth House, U. Oxford, 1998—; sci. advisor Centre de Recherches Sociologiques, Kinshasa, Zaïre, 1963-67; vis. prof. sociology U. Officielle du Congo, Lubumbashi, 1965; vis. prof. Sir George Williams U., Montreal, summer 1968; Phi Beta Kappa vis. scholar, 1973-75; dir. humanities seminar med. practitioners NEH, 1975-76; maitre de cours U. Liège, Belgium, 1976-77; vis. prof. Katholieke U., Leuven, Belgium, 1976-77; Wm. Allen Neilson prof. Smith Coll., Mass., 1980; dir. d'Etudes Associè, Ecole des Hautes Etudes en Sciences Sociales, Paris, summer 1989; George Eastman vis. prof. Oxford U., 1996-97; vis. scholar Tokyo Med. and Dental U., 2001; mem. bd. clin. scholars program Robert Wood Johnson Found., 1974-80; mem. Pres.'s Commn. on Study of Ethical Problems in Medicine, Biomed. and Behavioral Rsch., 1979-81; dir. human qualities of medicine program James Picker Found., 1980-83; Fae Golden Kass lectr. Harvard U. Sch. Medicine and Radcliffe Coll., 1983, Kate Hurd Mead lectr. Med. Coll. Pa./Coll. Physicians Phila., 1990, Lori Ann Roscetti Meml. lectr. Rush-Presbyn.-St. Luke's Med. Ctr., Chgo., 1990; vis. scholar Women's Ctr., U. Mo., Kansas City, 1990, vis. scholar Case Western Res. Sch. of Med., 1992; opening address 13th Internat. Conf. on Social Scis. and Medicine, Hungary, 1994, vis. prof. U. Calif., San Francisco Sch. of Medicine, 1994; lectr. founds. of medicine Faculty of Medicine McGill U., Montreal, 1995; Supernumerary fellow Balliol Coll. Oxford U., 1996-97; WHR Rivers disting. lectr. dept. social medicine Harvard Med. Sch., 1998; assembly series lectr. Washington U., St. Louis, 1998; William J. Rashkind Meml. lectr, Am. Heart Assn., 1998, Salinger-Forlang lectr. U. Tex. Health Scis. Ctr. at San Antonio, 1999, Frances H. Schlitz lectr. U. Kans., Wichita, 2002; Stambaugh lectr. U. Louisville Sch. Medicine, 2004. Author: Experiment Perilous, 1959; author: (with Willy De Craemer) The Emerging Physician, 1968; author: (with Judith P. Swazey) The Courage to Fall, 1974, rev. edit., 1978, 2002; author: Essays in Medical Sociology, 1979, 2d edit., 1988, L'Incertitude Medicale, 1988, The Sociology of Medicine: A Participant Observer's View, 1989; author: (with Judith P. Swazey) Spare Parts: Organ Replacement in American Society, 1992; author: In the Belgian Château: The Spirit and Culture of European Society in an Age of Change, 1994, French lang. edit., 1997, Organ Transplantation: Meanings and Realities (edited with Stuart Youngner and Laurence O'Connell), 1996; author: (in Japanese) Looking Intimately at Bioethics: Fifty Years as a Medical Sociologist, 2003; editor (with Victor N. Lidz and Harold J. Bershalt): After Parsons: A Theory of Social Action for the Twenty-First Century, 2005; assoc. editor Am. Sociol. Rev., 1963—1196, Social Sci. and Medicine, Jour. Health and Social Behavior, 1985—87, Perspectives in Biology and Medicine, 1996—, mem. editl. com. Ann. Rev. Sociology, 1975—79, mem. editl. adv. bd. Tech. in Soc., Sci., 1982—83, mem. editl. bd. Bibliography of Bioethics, 1979—, Culture, Medicine and Psychiatry, 1980—86, Jour. of AMA, 1981—94, Am. Scholar, 1994—99, Current Revs. in Publs., 1994—, Am. Jour. Bioethics, 1999—, vice chair adv. bd. Am. Jour. Ethics and Medicine; contbr. articles to profl. jours.; A Festschrift published in her honor Society and Medicine: Essays in Honor of Renée Fox, 2003. Bd. dirs. Medicine in Pub. Interest, 1979-94; mem. tech. bd. Milbank Meml. Fund, 1979-85; mem. overseers com. to visit univ. health svcs. Harvard Coll., 1979-86; trustee Russell Sage Found., 1981-87; vice chmn. bd. dirs. Acadia Inst., 1990-97; mem. adv. com. Sch. Nursing LaSalle U., 1998—; mem. external bd. Ctr. for Bioethics, Columbia U., mem. advancement com. King Baudouin Found. U.S. Inc., 1998—, mem., sec. bd. dirs. Acadia Inst., 2002—; mem. info. sci. adv. coun. Innovia Found., Netherlands, 2002—; mem. external bd. Ctr. for Bioethics, Columbia U., 2002—; mem. Internat. and Sci. Adv. Coun., 2002—. Recipient E. Harris Harbison Gifted Tchg. award Danforth Found., 1970, Radcliffe Grad. Soc. medal, 1977, Lindback Found. award for tchg. U. Pa., 1989, Centennial medal Grad. Sch. Arts and Scis. Harvard U., 1993, Chevalier de l'Ordre de Leopold II (Belgium), 1995; Wilson Ctr., Smithsonian Instn. fellow, 1987-88, Guggenheim fellow, 1962, Sr. fellow Ctr. Bioethics U. Pa., 1999—, Andrew W. Mellon Emeritus fellowship, 2004-05; Fulbright Short-Term Sr. scholar to Australia, 1994; 1st W.H.R. Rivers Disting. lectr. Harvard Med. Sch., 1998. Fellow African Studies Assn., AAAS (dir. 1977-80, chmn. sect. K 1986-87), Am. Sociol. Assn. (coun. 1970-73, 79-81, v.p. 1980-81), Am. Acad. Arts and Scis. (co-chair Class III section I membership com., 1994-96), Inst. Medicine of NAS (coun. 1979-82), Inst. Soc., Ethics and Life Scis. (founder, gov.); mem. AAUP, AAUW, Assn. Am. Med. Colls., Social Sci. Rsch. Coun. (v.p., dir.), Ea. Sociol. Soc. (pres. 1976-77, Merit award 1993), N.Y. Acad. Scis., Soc. Sci. Study Religion, Inst. Intercultural Studies, 1969-93, (asst. sec. 1969-78, sec. 1978-81, 89-92, v.p. 1987-89), Am. Bd. Med. Specialists, Coll. of Physicians of Phila. (coun. 1993-98), Phi Beta Kappa (senate 1982-87, Ralph Waldo Emerson book award com. 1998-2001), Alpha Omega Alpha. Home: The Wellington 135 S 19th St #1104 Philadelphia PA 19103-4912 Business E-Mail: rcfox@ssc.upenn.edu.

FOX, RICHARD GABRIEL, anthropologist, educator; b. N.Y.C., Mar. 3, 1939; s. Joseph Fox and Elizabeth(Cetron) Swig; m. Judith Lynn Huff, Dec. 18, 1974; 1 child, Sarah. BA, Columbia U., 1960; MA, U. Mich., 1961, PhD, 1965. Asst. prof. Brandeis U., Waltham, Mass., 1965-68; assoc. prof. Duke U., Durham, N.C., 1968-74, prof. anthropology, 1974-93; prof. Washington U., St. Louis, 1993-99. Pres. Wenner-Gren Found. for Anthropological Rsch., 2000—; vis. scholar Sch. Am. Rsch., Santa Fe, 1987-88; mem. Inst. Advanced Study, Princeton, N.J., 1972-73. Author: Kin, Clan, Raja and Rule, 1972, Urban Anthropology, 1977, Lions of the Punjab, 1985, Gandhian Utopia, 1989. John Simon Guggenheim Found. fellow, N.Y.C., 1987-88; grantee NSF, NEH, NIH. Fellow Am. Anthropol. Assn. Office: Wenner-Gren Found 470 Park Ave South New York NY 10001-7708 E-mail: rfox@wennergren.org.

FOX, ROBERT WILLIAM, mechanical engineering educator; b. Montreal, Que., Can., July 1, 1934; s. Kenneth and Jessie (Glass) F.; m. Beryl Williams, Dec. 15, 1962; children— David, Lisa. BS in Mech. Engring, Rensselaer Poly. Inst., 1955; MS, U. Colo., 1957; PhD, Stanford U., 1961. Instr. mech. engring. U. Colo., Boulder, 1955-57; research asst. Stanford (Calif.) U., 1957-60; mem. faculty Purdue U., Lafayette, Ind., 1960-99, assoc. prof., 1963-66, prof., 1966-99, asst. head mech. engring., 1971-72, asst. dean engring. for instrn., 1972-76; acting head Purdue U. (Sch. Mech. Engring.), 1975-76, asso. head, 1976-98, chmn. univ. senate, 1971-72, prof. emeritus, 1999. Cons. Owens-Corning Fiberglass Co., Edn. Services Inc., Nelson Mfg. Co., Peoria, Ill., B. Offen Co., Chgo., Agard Co., Johns-Marsville Co., Richmond, Ind., Babcox & Wilcox, Alliance, Ohio. Named Standard Oil Outstanding Tchr. Purdue U., 1967; recipient Harry L. Solberg Outstanding Tchr. award, 1978, 83, Donald E. Marlowe awd., Am. Soc. for Engineering Education, 1992. Fellow ASME, Am. Soc. for Engring. Edn.; mem. Sigma Xi, Pi Tau Sigma, Tau beta Pi, Delta Tau Delta. Home: 3627 Chancellor Way Lafayette IN 47906-8809 Office: Purdue U Sch Mech Engring Lafayette IN 47907

FOX, RONALD ERNEST, psychologist; b. Conover, N.C., May 11, 1936; s. Fred Yount and Carolyn Victoria (Weeks) F.; m. Margaret Elizabeth Smith, Dec. 27, 1956; children: Kelley Victoria, Brett Anthony, Jonathan Eric. AB, U. N.C., 1958, MA, 1961, PhD, 1962. Diplomate Am. Bd. Profl. Psychology. Asst. prof. dept. psychiatry and psychology U. N.C., 1963-68; assoc. prof. dept. psychiatry and psychology Ohio State U., 1968-74, prof., 1974-77, coord. edn. and tng. dept. psychiatry, 1968-77, dir. Family Therapy Clinic, Med. Sch., 1970-77; dean Sch. Profl. Psychology, Wright State U., 1977-92; CEO Piedmont Care, Chapel Hill, NC, 1992-95; sr. ptnr. Norton, Fox and Assocs., Inc., Chapel Hill, N.C., Cin., 1993-97; exec. dir. The Cons. Group divsn. HRC, 1997—; chair of bd. Assn. Advancement of Psychology, 2002—. Author: (with others) Patients View Their Psychotherapy, 1968, (with others) Abnormal Psychology, 1972, (with Norton) The Change Equation: Capitalizing on Diversity for Effective Organizational Change, 1997; contbr. articles to sci. jours. Fellow APA (pres. 1994); mem. Ohio Psychol. Assn., N.C. Psychol. Assn., Nat. Acads. Practice. Home: 309 Brookside Dr Chapel Hill NC 27516-2905 Office: 100 Europa Dr Ste 260 Chapel Hill NC 27517-2394 Office Phone: 919-968-1614. E-mail: drronfox@nc.rr.com.

FOX, RONALD FORREST, physicist, educator; s. Sidney Walter and Raia (Joffe) F.; children: Daniel, Lara. BA, Reed Coll., 1964; PhD, Rockefeller U., 1969. Postdoctoral fellow Miller Inst., U. Calif., Berkeley, 1969-71; asst. prof. Ga. Inst. Tech., Atlanta, 1971-74, assoc. prof., 1974-79, prof., 1979—, Regents prof. physics, 1991—, asst. dir. Sch. Physics, 1982-84, assoc. dir. Sch. Physics, 1986-89, 97-99, acting chair, 1999-2000, chair, 2001—05. A.A. Knowlton lectr. Reed Coll., 1999. Author: Biological Energy Transduction, 1982, Energy and the Evolution of Life, 1988; contbr. over 100 articles to sci. jour., over 20 chpt. to books. Recipient W. Roane Beard Outstanding Tchr. award Ga. Inst. Tech., 1992, Sigma Xi Sustained Rsch. award Ga. Inst. Tech., 1997; fellow Alfred P. Sloan Found., 1974-78, Guggenheim fellow, 1985; grantee NSF, 1973-2003. Fellow Am. Phys. Soc.; mem. NY Acad. Sci. Avocations: racquetball, jazz piano. Office: Ga Inst Tech Dept Physics Atlanta GA 30332-0430 E-mail: ron.fox@physics.gatech.edu.

FOX, SAUL LOURIE, physician, researcher; b. Boston, July 5, 1906; s. Isadore H. and Bessie (Cohen) F.; m. Matilda R. Aronson Fox, Jan. 26, 1933 (widowed March 1975); children: Myra D., John O. AB cum laude, Harvard U., 1927, MD, 1931. Intern Sinai Hosp., Balt., 1931-32; asst. res., 1932-33; vol. fellow Johns Hopkins Hosp., Balt., 1933-34; intern Charles V. Chapin Hosp., Providence, 1934-35; physician in Internal Medicine Beverly Hills, Calif., 1935-77; attending physician Cedars Sinai Hosp., L.A., 1935-77; Harbor Gen. Hosp., Torrence, Calif., 1961-70; asst. clin. prof. UCLA Med. Sch., L.A., 1961-70. Contbr.: Textbook on Diseases of the Breast, 1950; contbr. articles to profl. jours. Capt. U.S. Med. Corps., 1944-46. Named Pres., 1968, Gov., 1969-71, Beverly Hills Med. Soc. Fellow ACP; mem. AMA, Am. Internal Medicine, Med. Bd. Med. Examiners, Nat. Bd. Med. Examiners, L.A. County Med. Assn., Phi Delta Epsilon Club. Home: 838 N Doheny Dr #506 West Hollywood CA 90069-4849

FOX, STACY L., lawyer; b. Ann Arbor, Mich., 1953; m. Michael Van Hemet; children: Kyle, Callan. BS with high distinction, U. Mich., 1974, JD, 1983. Assoc. Mintz, Levin, Cohn, Ferris, Glovskky & Popeo, P.C., Boston, 1983—88; gen. counsel Unisys Fin. Corp., 1988—89; group counsel automotive systems group and plastics tech. group Johnson Controls, Inc., 1989—93, group v.p., gen counsel automotive systems group, 1993—2000; sr. v.p. corp. transactions and legal affairs Visteon Corp., Dearborn, Mich., 2000—. Named one of 100 Leading Women in Automotive Industry, Automotive News, 2000. Office: Visteon Corp 1700 Rotunda Dr Dearborn MI 48120

FOX, STEVE, editor-in-chief; B in English, Yale U. Various editl. positions PC World mag., 1991—96, editor, 1998—99; editor-in-chief The Web Mag., 1996—98; editor in chief pcworld.com, 1999; editl. dir. CNET, 1999—2003; editor-in-chief InfoWorld Media Group, 2003—; mng. editor Omni mag.; with Popular Mechanics, IEEE. Spkr. in field. Office: 501 Second St San Francisco CA 94107

FOX, STUART IRA, physiologist; b. Bklyn., June 21, 1945; s. Sam and Bess F.; m. Ellen Diane Berley; 1 child, Laura Elizabeth. BA, UCLA, 1967; MA, Calif. State U., L.A., 1967; postgrad., U. Calif., Santa Barbara, 1969; PhD, U. So. Calif., 1978. Rsch. assoc. Children's Hosp., L.A., 1972; prof. physiology L.A. City Coll., 1972-85, Calif. State U., Northridge, 1979-84, Pierce Coll., 1986—. Cons. McGraw-Hill, 1976—. Author: Computer-Assisted Instruction in Human Physiology, 1979, Laboratory Guide to Human Physiology, 10th edit., 2003, Textbook of Human Physiology, 1986, 8th edit., 2003, Human Anatomy and Physiology, 1986, Perspectives on Human Biology, 1991, Laboratory Manual for Anatomy and Physiology, 1986;: 5th edit., 1999; co-author: Biology, 5th edit., 1999, Synopsis of Anatomy and Physiology, 1997. Mem. AAAS, Am. Physiol. Soc., Am. Anatomy & Physiology Soc., Sigma Xi. Home: 5556 Forest Cove Ln Agoura Hills CA 91301-4047 Office: Pierce Coll 6201 Winnetka Ave Woodland Hills CA 91371-0001 Office Phone: 818-710-2832. Business E-Mail: Foxsi@piercecollege.edu.

FOX, SUSAN FRANCES, mathematics professor, education educator; b. Gilmer, Tex., Aug. 12, 1948; d. Byron J. and Olga Patricia (Green) Smith; m. Al Fox, Nov. 20, 1970 (dec.); children: Michelle A., Amanda L. BS in Secondary Edn., Coll. of Artesia, 1971; MEd in Edn., Ea. N.Mex. U., 1985. Cert. instrnl. leader, secondary math. tchr. N.Mex. Math. tchr. Artesia (N.Mex) Pub. Schs., 1971-75; asst. prof. math./edn. Coll. S.W., Hobbs, N.Mex., 1989—. Adult mem. Girl Scouts U.S., Hobbs, 1993—94. Mem.: Delta Kappa Gamma (treas. 1994—96). Avocations: crafts, golf, bowling. Home: 905 W Lead Ave Hobbs NM 88240-2197 Office: Coll SW 6610 N Lovington Hwy Hobbs NM 88240-9120 E-mail: sfox@csw.edu.

FOX, SUZY, management consultant, educator; b. Chgo., June 8, 1950; d. Karl and Madlaine Fox; children: Jackie Menhart, Danny Menhart. BA in Psychology, Reed Coll., 1973; MMus in Applied Flute, Northwestern U., 1975; MBA, U. South Fla., 1993, MA, 1996, PhD in Indsl./Orgnl. Psychology, 1998. Programmer analyst Hertie GmbH, Frankfurt, Germany, 1981—84; sys. programmer, capacity and performance analyst First Fla. Bank, Tampa, 1984—91; instr. Psychology Dept. U. South Fla., Tampa, 1993—98, vis. asst. prof. Coll. Bus. Adminstrn., 1998—99; assoc. prof. Grad Sch. Bus. Loyola U., Chgo., 1999—2005, assoc. prof., 2005—. Co-founder Successful Women Worldwide Rsch. Group, Successful Women Inst. Contbr. articles to profl. jours. Mem.: Chgo. Indsl./Orgnl. Psychologists, Midwest Bus. Adminstrn. Assn., Soc. Human Resource Mgmt., Soc. Indsl./Orgnl. Psychology, Global Bus. and Tech. Assn., Acad. Mgmt. Jewish. Avocations: flute, piccolo, music. Office: Loyola Univ Chgo 820 N Michigan Ave Chicago IL 60611 Office Phone: 312-915-7518. Office Fax: 312-915-6231. Business E-Mail: sfox1@luc.edu.

FOX, SYLVAN, journalist, educator; b. Bklyn., June 2, 1928; s. Louis and Sophie (Shapiro) F.; m. Gloria R. Endleman, Sept. 8, 1948; 1 child, Erica. BA, Bklyn. Coll., 1951; MA, U. Calif., Berkeley, 1952. Reporter Little Falls (N.Y.) Evening Times, 1954, Schenectady (N.Y.) Union Star, 1954-55, Buffalo Evening News, 1955-59; successively rewriteman, asst. city editor, city editor N.Y. World Telegram and Sun, 1959-66; dep. police commr. for press relations City of N.Y., 1966-67; successively rewriteman, reporter, dep. met. editor, Saigon bur. chief N.Y. Times, N.Y.C., 1967-73; Nassau editor Newsday, L.I., N.Y., 1973-77, nat. editor, then asst. mng. editor nat. and fgn. news, 1977-79, editor editorial pages, 1979-88; travel columnist, 1994-95. Tchr. journalism NYU, 1965, L.I.U., 1967, Baylor U., Waco, 1985, 88; asst. prof. journalism NYU, 1989-90. Author: The Unanswered Questions About President Kennedy's Assassination, rev. edit., 1975. Recipient Pulitzer prize local reporting, 1963. Mem. Soc. of Silurians. Home: 401 E 65th St New York NY 10021-6943 E-mail: sylglo@aol.com.

FOX, THOMAS C., lawyer; b. McKees Rocks, Pa., June 1, 1941; BA in polit. sci., Muskingum Coll., New Concord, Ohio, 1963; LLB, George Washington U., 1966. Bar: Va. 1966, DC 1967. With Reed Smith LLP, 1970—, now ptnr. healthcare group & mem. exec. com.; spl. counsel Com. on Standards of Official Conduct Ho. of Reps., 1976, 1979. Trustee Muskingum Coll. Capt. U.S. Army, 1967—69. Mem.: Am. Health Lawyers Assn. Office: Reed Smith LLP 1301 K St NW Ste 1100 - East Tower Washington DC 20005 Office Phone: 202-414-9222. Office Fax: 202-414-9299. Business E-Mail: tfox@reedsmith.com.

FOX, THOMAS GEORGE, health science educator; b. N.Y.C., Sept. 15, 1942; s. Thomas Peter and Alice Cecilia (Ehler) F.; m. Mary Patricia Palmer, Aug. 29, 1980; children: Christopher Adam, Thomas Andrew, Stephen Baron. BA, Coll. N.J., 1964; MEd, U. Vt., 1966; PhD, U. Mich., 1972. Asst. to dean U. Mass., Amherst, 1966; dir. counseling and student svcs. U. Mich., Ann Arbor, 1966-68, sr. adminstrv. asst. Med. Ctr., 1968-69, adminstrv. assoc., 1969-71; asst. dean Robert Wood Johnson Med. Sch., Piscataway, N.J., 1972-77, assoc. dean, 1977-83; sr. v.p. Robert Wood Johnson U. Hosp., New Brunswick, N.J., 1983-86; exec. v.p. U. Health System of N.J., New Brunswick, 1986-90; prof., v.p. devel. and univ. rels. Oreg. Health Scis. U., Portland, 1990-94; CEO Univ. Found., 1990-94; pres., CEO, Liberty Sci. Ctr., Jersey City, 1994-96; CEO, Operation Smile, Norfolk, Va., 1996-2000; sr. v.p. advancement and sponsored programs Wheeling (W.Va.) Jesuit U., 2000—03; sr. v.p. advancement Fla. Inst. Tech., 2003—. Asst. prof. U. Medicine and Dentistry N.J., 1973-79, assoc. prof., 1979-83, clin. assoc. prof., 1983-90. Contbr. articles to profl. jours. Trustee Francis E. Parker Meml. Home, 1981-90, 96—. Fellow: Acad. Medicine N.J.; mem.: Coun. for Advancement and Support of Edn. (nstl.lead), Am. Coll. Healthcare Execs. (diplomate). Home: 895 Chatsworth Dr Melbourne FL 32940-2174 Office: Fla Inst Tech 328 W Hibiscus Blvd Melbourne FL 32901-2715 E-mail: tfox@fit.edu.

FOX, VICENTE (VICENTE FOX QUESADA), President of Mexico; b. Mexico City, July 2, 1942; s. Jose and Mercedes (Quesada) Fox; children: Ana Cristina, Vicente, Paulina, Rodrigo; m. Marta Sahagun Jiménez, July 2, 2001. Degree in bus. adminstrn., U. Iberoamericana, Mexico City, 1964; postgrad. Sch. Bus., Harvard U., 1974. Route supr. Coca Cola Export Co., Mexico, 1964-65, various mktg. positions, 1965-70, mktg. dir., 1970-75, pres., 1975-79, Grupo Fox, Lean, Mexico, 1980—; fed. congressman, 1988—91; gov. State of Guanajuato, 1995—99; pres. Republic of Mexico, 2000—. Pres. Patronato U. Iberoamericana, Patronato Casa Cuna Purigo Daniel A.C. Contbr. articles to profl. jours. Named Civic Man of Yr. Alianza Civica, 1991. Partido Accion Nacional. Roman Catholic. Avocations: sports, horses, reading, cultural activities. Office: Office of the President Puerti Col San Miguel 11850 Mexico City Mexico Office Phone: 5255 5091 1100 x1423. Business E-Mail: agutierrez@presidencia.gob.mx.

FOX, VIVICA, actress; Movies include Independence Day, 1996, Set It Off, 1996, Booty Call, 1997, Soul Food, 1997, Idle Hands, 1999, Teaching Mrs. Tingle, 1999, Little Secrets, 2001, Juwanna Mann, 2002, Boat Trip, 2002, Kill Bill: Vol. 1, 2003, Ride or Die, 2003, Motives, 2004, Ella Enchanted, 2004, Kill Bill: Vol. 2, 2004; (TV) Solomon, 1997, A Saintly Switch, 1999, City of Angels, 2000. Office: William Morris Agy 151 S El Camino Dr Beverly Hills CA 90212-2775

FOX, WAYNE C., stock exchange executive, corporate financial executive; BA, U. Waterloo, 1971; MBA, McMaster U., 1973; Advanced Management Program, Wharton School of Bus., 1992. With Can. Imperial Bank Commerce, head of world markets global capital markets activities, vice chmn. and chief risk officer, 1999—; chmn. Toronto Stock Exch., 2001—. Dir. Can. Imperial Bank Commerce ESC Advisors LLC, Can. Imperial Bank Commerce Investments Ltd., Can. Imperial Bank Commerce Mellon Global Securities Svcs. Co., Can. Imperial Bank Commerce Mellon Trust Co., Can. Imperial Bank Commerce Mortgages Inc., Can. Imperial Bank Commerce Offshore Banking Svcs. Corp., Barbados and Can. Imperial Bank Commerce Offshore Svcs. Inc., Can. Imperial Bank Commerce World Markets Inc. Bd. govs. McMaster U.; gov. emeritus Appleby Coll.; bd. dirs. and chmn. CanadaHelps.org Inc.; bd. dir. CIBC Charitable Found.; founder Wayne C. Fox Graduate Scholarship in Arts. Office: Toronto Stock Exch PO Box 450 3rd fl 130 King St W Toronto ON Canada M5X-1J2*

FOX, WAYNE CHARLES, music educator; b. Lebanon, Pa., Sept. 19, 1951; s. Wayne Charles and Jessie Holland Fox; m. Suzanne Jeanette Daubert, June 12, 1977; children: Lindsay Suzanne, Michael Wayne, Stephanie Alison. BS in music edn., Lebanon Valley Coll., 1973; MusM in jazz pedagogy, U. Miami, 1978. Cert. tchg. Pa. Music instr. Cornwall Lebanon Sch. Dist., Lebanon, Pa., 1974—; freelance musician Pa., 1969—. Co-leader Celebration, Pa., 1980—; chair music dept. Cornwall Lebanon Sch. Dis.t, Lebanon, Pa., 1984—; dir. Perseverance Band, Lebanon, 1979—; keyboard musician Hershey Theater, Hershey, Pa., 1994—; guest conductor PMEA Dist. 7 Youth Band Festival; grad asst. U. Miami, Miami, Fla.; dir. LVC Jazz Band, 1972—73; guest soloist Conestoga Valley Jazz Festival, Lancaster, Pa., 1991. Coun. pres. Zion Luth. Ch., Lebanon, Pa., 1997. Mem.: Am. Fed. of Musicians, Pi Kappa Lambda, Phi Beta Mu. Republican. Luth. Home: 1814 Martin Dr Lebanon PA 17046 Office: Cornwall Lebanon Sch Dist 105 E Evergreen Rd 17042 Office Phone: 717-273-4546. E-mail: wfox@clsd.k12.pa.us.

FOX, WILLIAM F., dean, law educator; BS, George Washington U., 1970; JD, Catholic U. Am. Sch. Law, 1972; LLM, Harvard Law Sch., 1974. Law clerk N.Mex Ct. Appeals, 1972—73; atty. vom Baur, Coburn, Simmons & Turtle, 1973—74; instr. Boston U. Law Sch., 1973—74; asst. prof. Indpls. Sch. Law, Indiana U., 1974—75; prof. Columbia Sch. Law, Cath. U. Am., 1975—, assoc. dean, 1975—78, dean, 2003—. Vis. prof. London Sch. Econs. and Polit. Sci., 1983—84; sr. assoc. mem. St. Anthony's Coll., Oxford U., 1983—84; vis. lectr. U. Dundee, Ctr. Petroleum & Mineral Law; mem. permanent faculty ALI-ABA prog. Author: Understanding Administrative Law, International Commercial Agreements, The Law of Veterans Benefits: Judicial Interpretation. Fulbright Scholar, Parahyangan Cath. U. Law Sch., Indonesia, 1993, Veterans Law Scholar, Paralyzed Veterans Am., 1994. Office: Columbus Sch Law Catholic U Am 3600 John McCormack Rd NE Washington DC 20064 E-mail: foxw@law.edu.

FOX, WILLIAM J., federal official, lawyer; b. Nebraska; m.; two children. BA in History, JD, Creighton U., Omaha. Atty., sr. counsel, then chief counsel Bureau of Alcohol, Tobacco and Firearms, 1988—2000; acting dep. asst. gen. counsel for enforcement US Dept. of Treas., 2000—01, principal asst. and sr. advisor to gen. counsel, 2001—03, acting dep. gen. counsel, 2002, assoc. dep. gen. counsel, 2002—03; dir. Financial Crimes Enforcement Network, 2003—. Recipient Meritorious Rank award, US Dept. of Treas. Office: Financial Crimes Enforcement Network US Dept of Treas 1500 Pennsylvania Ave NW Washington DC 20220*

FOX-CLARKSON, ANNE C., computer company executive; 1 child. BS in Edn., Bucknell U., 1967; MS in Reading, Syracuse U., 1973, PhD in Tchr. Edn., 1975. Cert. elem. tchr., adminstr., Idaho. Postdoctroal work in edn. adminstrn. U. Idaho; elem. sch. tchr.; prin., supt. pub. schs., 1978-84; assoc. prof. ednl. adminstrn. Gonzaga U., 1987-94; supt. pub. instrn. State of Idaho, 1995-98; v.p. ednl. markets Shop2gether.com, 2000; pres. Grant Writers, Inc., Boise, 2004—. Mem. State Bd. Edn., State Land Bd., State Libr. Bd., State Endowment Fund, State Investment Bd.; pres., co-founder Children's Village Homes for Abused Children; grant writer, mgmt. cons.; spkr. in field. Former pres. Idaho State Elem. Prin. Assn., Wash. State Univ. Profl. Adminstr. Assn. E-mail: Raand20@aol.com.

FOXE, MARYE ANNE, academic administrator; b. Canton, Ohio, Dec. 9, 1947; m. James K. Whitesell, 1990; stepchildren: Christopher Whitesell, Robert Whitesell; children: Robert Fox, Michael Fox, Matthew Fox. BS, Notre Dame Coll. of Ohio, 1969; MS, Cleve. State U., 1970; PhD, Dartmouth Coll., 1974; postgrad., U. Md., 1974-76; DSc (hon.), Notre Dame Coll., 1994, Cleve. State U., 1998; JD (hon.), Sandhills Cmty. Coll., 2000; degree (hon.), Universite Pierre et Marie Curie, 2001; LHD (hon.), Texas A&M, 2002; degree (hon.), Universidad Nacional de Educacion a Distancia, Madrid, 2003. Prof. chemistry U. Tex., Austin, 1976-91, Rowland Pettit Centennial prof., 1986-92, M. June and J. Virgil Waggoner regents chair chemistry, 1992-98, v.p. rsch., 1994-98; chancellor N.C. State U., Raleigh, 1998—2004, U. Calif. San Diego, 2004—. Mem. Nat. Sci. Bd., 1991-96, vice-chair, 1994-96; bd. dirs. Kenan Inst. Engring., Tech., and Sci., 1998—, Microelectric Ctr., NC, 1998—, mem. sci. adv. bd. Robert A. Welch Found., 1998—, David and Lucile Packard Found., 1998—; mem. Coun. on Competitiveness, 1999—; bd. trustees Nat. Inst. Statistical Sciences, 2000—; bd. dirs. Nat. Inst. Environment, 2001—, Boston Sci. Inc., 2001—, mem. President's Adv. Coun. of Advisors on Sci. and Tech., 2001—; bd. dirs. NC Bd. Sci. and Tech., 2002—, PPD Inc., 2002—, Red Hat Inc., 2002, Nat. Assn. State Universities and Land Grant Coll., 2003— Assoc. editor Jour. Am. Chem. Soc., 1986-94; mem. adv. bd. Jour. Organic Chemistry, Chem. Engring. News, Chem. Rev. Bd. trustees U. Notre Dame, 2002—; bd. dirs. N.C. Citizens for Bus. and Industry, 2003—. Recipient Agnes Faye Morgan Rsch. award Iota Sigma Pi, 1984, Arthur C. Cope scholar award Am. Chem. Soc., 1988; Garvan medal Am. Chem. Soc., 1988, Havinga medal Leiden U., 1991, Monie A. Ferst award, 1996; named to Hall of Excellence, Ohio Found. Ind. Colls., 1987, The Best of the New Generation, Esquire Mag., 1984; Alfred P. Sloan Rsch. fellow, 1980-82, Camille and Henry Dreyfus tchr. scholar, 1981-85. Fellow AAAS, Assn. Women in Sci.; mem. NAS (co-chair, Govt.-Univ.-Industry Rsch. Roundtable, 1999-), Am. Acad. Arts and Sci., Am. Philos. Soc., Sigma Xi (pres. 2001-02). Office: U Calif San Diego Chancellors Office 9500 Gilman Sr La Jolla CA 92093-0005*

FOXEN, LYNNE ANNE, management consultant; b. Teaneck, N.J., Mar. 8, 1950; d. Joseph Patrick and Yolanda A. (Franchini) F. BS, St. Peter's Coll., 1980. Asst. treas. arms div. Ashford Holding Corp., N.Y.C., 1975-77, fin. planning mgr. MIC div., 1977-82, asst. v.p., 1982-84; dir. Empire Blue Cross Blue Shield, N.Y.C., 1984-88; v.p. Am. Mgmt. Systems, Roseland, NJ, 1988—. Mem. Assn. Women in Prodn., NAFE. Home: 147 Magnolia Ave Tenafly NJ 07670-1831

FOXEN, RICHARD WILLIAM, manufacturing executive; b. N.Y.C., Nov. 12, 1927; s. William alyisus and Mae Dorothea (Scully) F.; m. Hilda Duran-Ballen, Feb. 11, 1956; children: Richard, Theresa, Thomas, Patricia, Anthony. B.M.E., Bklyn. Poly. Inst., 1950. V.p. corp. staffs Westinghouse Air Brake Co., Pitts., 1961-69; pres. European indsl. group Am. Std., Brussels, 1969-73; v.p. Europe bus. divsn. GE, Brussels, 1973-78; sr. v.p. Rockwell Internat., 1978-88. Adj. prof. bus. adminstrn. Carnegie Mellon U., U. Pitts.; chmn. Mercy Health Sys., Inc., Pitts.; bd. dirs. Cordis Corp. Bd. trustees N.Y. Poly. U.; bd. dirs. Mannesmann U.S. Adv. Conflict Resolution Ctr. Internat.; chmn. Mendelssohn Choir Pitts., Pressley-Ridge Schs., We. Pa. Family Ctr., Pitts. With U.S. Army, 1946-48. Mem. Pitts. Athletic Assn., Duquesne, Pitts. Athletic, Seabrook Is., Tau Beta Pi, Pi Tau Sigma. Roman Catholic. Home: 1292 Puritan Ave Birmingham MI 48009-4815

FOX-FREUND, BARBARA SUSAN, real estate company executive; b. Rocky Mount, N.C., Jan. 17, 1949; d. Albert Richard and Anita (Levinson) Fox; m. James Coleman Freund, Jan. 12, 1985. Student, Centenary Coll., 1968, Boston U., 1970. Real estate broker Whitbread-Nolan, Inc., N.Y.C., 1972-80; v.p. Stribling and Assocs., Ltd., N.Y.C., 1980-82; exec. v.p. Cross and Brown Residentials, Inc., N.Y.C., 1982-88; pres. Fox Residential Group, Inc., N.Y.C., 1988—. Bd. dirs. Riverside Symphony, N.Y.C., 1989-99, WOOF Animal Rescue, 2003—; bd. dirs., pres. 55 W. 73d St. Corp., N.Y.C., 1986-97; chmn. bd. Stray from the Heart, 2000-03; chmn. Woof Dog Rescue, Inc., 2003— Mem. Real Estate Bd. N.Y. (chmn. residential com. 1986-89, ethics com. 1989-92, bd. dirs. brokerage com. 1988-92, tchr. 1986—, chmn. inter-firm rels. com. 1991-93, bd. dirs. residential divsn. 1994-, bd. govs. 1994-99, chmn. interfirm forum 1995-99, residential ethics com. 1995-2002, co-chmn.; chmn. bd. dirs. brokerage com., 1999—. Republican. Jewish. Avocations: sculpture, tennis, skiing. Home: 55 W 73rd St New York NY 10023-3136 Office: Fox Residential Group Inc 1015 Madison Ave New York NY 10021-0261 Office Phone: 212-639-9711. E-mail: bfox@foxresidential.com.

FOX-GENOVESE, ELIZABETH ANN TERESA, humanities educator; b. Boston, May 28, 1941; d. Edward Whiting and Elizabeth Mary (Simon) Fox; m. Eugene Dominick Genovese, 1969. BA, Bryn Mawr Coll., 1963; MA, Harvard U., 1966, PhD, 1974; LittD (hon.), Millsaps Coll., 1992. Teaching fellow Harvard U., Cambridge, Mass., 1965-66, 1967-69; asst. prof. U. Rochester, N.Y., 1973-76, assoc. prof., 1976-80; prof. SUNY, Binghamton, 1980-86, Emory U., Atlanta, 1986—, Eleonore Raoul prof. of humanities, 1988—. Adj. prof. Auburn (Ala.) U., 1987; Eudora Welty prof. Millsaps Coll., 1990, Mem. Nat. Coun. Humanities, 2003-. Author: Origins of Physiocracy, 1976, (with others) Fruits of Merchant Capital, 1983, Within the Plantation Household, 1988, Feminism Without Illusions, 1991, Feminism Is Not the Story of My Life: How the Elite Women's Movement Has Lost Touch with the Real Concerns of Women, 1996, Women and the Future of the Family 2000; co-editor: Reconstructing History: The Emergence of a New Historical Society, 1999, (with others) The Mind of the Master Class: History and Faith in the Southern Slaveholders' World View, 2005, Marriage on Trial: The Future of an Endangered Institution, 2005; mem. editl. adv. bd. First Things; mem. editl. bd. Books and Culture; editor Jour. Hist. Soc., 1999—; contbr. numerous articles to profl. jours. Mem. acad. adv. bd. Inst. for Am. Values, 1994—; adv. bd. Campaign for the Am. Family, 1995—, Ind. Women's Forum, 1993—2000. Recipient Nat. Humanities Medal, 2003. Mem. LWV, MLA, Soc. Am. Historians, The Hist. Soc. (life, mem. bd. govs.), So. Hist. Assn. (life), So. Assn. for Women Historians (life), Am. Comparative Lit. Assn. (adv. bd. 1991-95), Orgn. Am. Historians (life, proglram com. 1991), Am. Studies Assn. (program com. 1987), Soc. for Study So. Lit. (exec. coun. 1990-93), South Atlantic MLA (chair women's studies network 1989-90), Social Sci. Hist. Assn. (exec. coun. 1986-88), Am. Hist. Assn., Am. Polit. Sci. Assn., Assn. of Lit. Scholars and Critics, Am. Acad. Liberal Edn. (bd. dirs.), Nat. Coun. on Hist. Standards (steering commn.), Hist. Soc. (life, mem. exec. com.), Atlanta Hist. Assn. (acad. adv. com.), Am. Antiquarian Soc., Nat. Alumni Forum (adv. bd.), Cosmos Club, Harvard Club of Boston, Harvard Club of NY. Roman Catholic. Avocations: family, films, fashion, reading, major league baseball. Home: 1487 Sheridan Walk NE Atlanta GA 30324-3253 Office: Emory U Dept History Atlanta GA 30322-0001 Office Phone: 404-727-4063.

FOXHOVEN, JERRY RAY, lawyer; b. Yankton, S.D., July 24, 1952; s. Elmer William and Ida Elizabeth (Lubbers) F.; m. Julie Ann Greco, Apr. 6, 1985; children: Anthony Michael, Peter Joseph. BS summa cum laude, Morningside Coll., 1974; JD, Drake U., 1977. Bar: Iowa 1977, U.S. Dist. Ct. (so. and no. dists.) Iowa 1977, U.S. Ct. Appeals (8th cir.) 1977, U.S. Supreme Ct. 1981, Nebr. 1985, U.S. Dist. Ct. Nebr. 1985, Wis. 1986. Assoc. Critelli & Pille, Des Moines, 1977-79, ptnr., 1979-82, Foxhoven & McCann, Des Moines, 1982-88, Peddicord, Wharton, Thune, Foxhoven & Spencer, P.C., 1988-91; pvt. practice, 1991-2000; adminstr. Child Advocacy Bd., Des Moines, 2000—; sr. fellow Ctr. Adoption Rsch., U. Mass., 2002—04. Instr. criminaljustice dept. Des Moines Area Community Coll., Ankeny, Iowa, 197 8-81, Am. Inst. Banking, 1982-85. Mem. steering con. Culver for U.S. Senate, Des Moines, 1980; chmn. Iowa State Foster Care Rev. Bd., 1986-99; bd. dirs., nat. pres. Nat. Assn. Foster Care Reviewers, 1988-01; mem. parish coun. Sacred Heart Roman Cath. Ch., West Des Moines, 1982. Recipient Angel in Adoption award, Congl. Adaption Coalition, 2004. Lodge: Masons (master 1990). Democrat. Home: 1608 NW 101st St Clive IA 50325-6716 Office: Lucas Bldg 321 E 12th St 4th Fl Des Moines IA 50319-0083 Office Phone: 515-242-6392. Personal E-mail: jfoxhoven@aol.com. Business E-Mail: jfoxhoven@dia.state.ia.us.

FOX-KEMPER, BAYLOR, oceanographer; s. Joseph Carter and Carol Spaulding Fox; m. Jordan St. John Kemper, June 20, 1998; 1 child, Miles Julian. BA in Physics, Reed Coll., 1996; MA in Physics, Brandeis U., 1998; PhD in Oceanography, MIT, 2003. Rsch. fellow Princeton U., NJ, 2003—04; rsch. scientist MIT, Cambridge, Mass., 2004—. Contbr. numerous articles to profl. jours.; author: (sail mag.) Weather and Sea Column. Nat. Def. Sci. and Engring. Grad. fellow, Dept. of Def., 1998—2001, Postdoctoral fellow, Nat. Oceanic and Atmospheric Adminstrn., 2003—05. Mem.: Am. Math. Soc., Am. Geophys. Union, Am. Meteorol. Soc., Phi Beta Kappa, Sigma Xi. Office: MIT 77 Mass Ave MIT RM 54-1410 Cambridge MA 02139 Business E-Mail: baylor@alum.mit.edu.

FOXMAN, ABRAHAM HENRY, advocacy organization administrator; b. Poland; came to U.S., 1950; s. Helen and Joseph F. BA in Polit. Sci., CCNY, 1962; postgrad., Jewish Theol. Sem., 1958-60, New Sch. Social Rsch., 1963-64; JD, NYU, 1965; LLD (hon.), Fla. Internat. U., 1992. Asst. dir. law dept. Anti-Defamation League of B'nai B'rith, N.Y.C., 1965-68, dir. Mid. Ea. affairs, 1968-73, nat. leadership dir., 1973-79, assoc. nat. dir., 1979-87, nat. dir., 1987—. Mem. Pres.'s U.S. Holocaust Meml. Coun., N.Y.C. Holocaust Meml. Commn. (adv. coun.), Am. Gathering, Jewish Holocaust Survivors. Office: Anti-Defamation League 823 United Nations Plz New York NY 10017-3518

FOXMAN, BRUCE MAYER, chemist, educator; b. Youngstown, Ohio, Mar. 12, 1942; s. Jerome Jay and Phyllis E. (Altshuler) Foxman; m. Carole J. Wittkopf, Sept. 14, 1968; children: Gregory Michael, Andrew Craig. BS with distinction, Iowa State U., 1964; PhD in Inorganic Chemistry, MIT, 1968. Rsch. fellow Australian Nat. U., Canberra, 1968-72; asst. prof. Brandeis U., Waltham, Mass., 1972-78, assoc. prof., 1978-85, prof., 1985—. Vis. prof. Thomas J. Watson Rsch. Ctr., IBM, Yorktown Heights, NY, 1975, Max-Planck-Inst. fuer Polymerforschung, Mainz, Germany, 1995—96; hon. prof. U. Birmingham, England, 2001; invited prof. U. Louis Pasteur, Strasbourg, France, 2002; cons. Polaroid Corp. Mem.: Coll. Bd. Advanced Placement Exam. Com. (chair chemistry 1993—96), Royal Soc. Chemistry, Materials Rsch. Soc., Am. Crystallographic Assn., Am. Chem. Soc., Sigma Xi, Phi Lambda Upsilon, Phi Kappa Phi. Home: 74 N Hill Ave Needham MA 02492-1223 Office: Brandeis Univ Dept Chemistry Waltham MA 02454-9110 Office Phone: 781-736-2532. Business E-Mail: foxman1@brandeis.edu.

FOX-WOLFGRAMM, SUSAN JO, business management educator; b. Denver, Mar. 14, 1961; d. Al and Angela Marlene (Allen) Fox; m. Dietrich George Wolfgramm, May 21, 1993. BS, U. Colo., 1983; MPA, Tex. Tech. U., 1984, PhD, 1991. Pers. asst. intern Tex. Dept. Human Resources, Lubbock, 1984; lectr. Tex. Tech. U., Lubbock, 1985-91; prof. San Francisco (Calif.) State U., 1991—. Senator Acad. Senate, San Francisco (Calif.) State U., 1993—. Coll. Bus. grantee San Francisco (Calif.) State U., 1992, 93; Samuel Moore Walton Free Enterprise fellow Students in Free Enterprise, Inc., 1992—; Price-Babson Coll. fellow Ctr. for Enterpreneurial Studies, Babson Coll., Mass., 1994. Mem. San Francisco State Univ. Women's Assn. (pres.), Commonwealth Club Calif., Beta Gamma Sigma. Avocations: scuba diving, mountain biking, piano, art, gardening. Office: San Francisco State Univ 1600 Holloway Ave San Francisco CA 94132-1722 E-mail: sfox@sfsu.edu.

FOXWORTH, JO, advertising agency executive; b. Tylertown, Miss. Grad. in Journalism, U. Mo. Exec. McCann-Erickson, Interpub. Group of Cos.; owner Jo Foxworth Inc., N.Y.C., 1968—. Author: Boss Lady, 1979, Wising Up, 1981, Boss Lady's Arrival and Survival Plan, 1986, The Bordello Cookbook, 1997, Murder Under Wraps, 2002. Named to AAF Hall of Fame, 1997. Office: 740 Broadway 8th Fl New York NY 10003-9518

FOXWORTH, JOHNNIE HUNTER, retired state agency administrator; b. Anderson, S.C., Feb. 13, 1921; d. John Ira and Bessie (Hatton) Hunter; m. Marvin Ardell, Sept. 21, 1941. Attended colls., univs., Atlanta, Bridgeport, Conn. Cashier examiner, office supr. Motor Vehicle Dept., State Conn., Bridgeport, 1957—72; br. office mgr. various locations in state, 1972—77; br. office dist. supr. Wethersfield, Conn., 1977—81; asst. dir., 1981—85; cons., tng. instr., 1985—88; ret. Writer: manual in field. Mem. Commrs. Affirmative Action Com., 1987. Recipient Profl. Achievement award, Bridgeport chpt. Nata. Bus. and Profl. Women, 1972, (2) Disting. Managerial Svc. award, State of Conn., Wethersfield, 1982, Woman of Yr. award, Nat. Coun. Negro Woman, Bridgeport, 1972. Mem.: The Links, Inc. (Waterbury) (pres. 1980—85), Les Treize (Bridgeport) (pres. 1966—68). Home: 496A Heritage Village Southbury CT 06488-1525

FOXWORTHY, JEFF, comedian, writer, actor; b. Atlanta, Ga., Sept. 6, 1958; m. Pamela Gregg Grethe, 1985; children: Jordan, Juliane. Grad., Ga. Inst. Tech., 1979. Computer engr. IBM, 1979-84; performing and rec. artist, comedian, writer, 1984—. Actor: (films) (voice) Racing Stripes, 2004; (TV series) The Jeff Foxworthy Show, 1995-97; (TV films) Banner Times, 1993, Blue Collar Comedy Tour Rides Again, 2004; actor, exec. prodr. (TV series) Blue Collar TV, 2004-; writer (TV films) Jeff Foxworthy: Totally Committed, 1998; author: You Might Be a Redneck If..., 1989, Hick Is Chic: A Guide to Etiquette for the Grossly Unsophisticated, 1990, Red Ain't Dead: 150 More Ways To Tell If You're a Redneck, 1991, Check your Neck: More of "You Might Be a Redneck If...," 1992, You're Not a Kid Anymore, 1993, (with Vic Henley) Games Rednecks Play, 1994, Redneck Classic: The Best of Jeff Foxworthy, 1995; albums include You Might Be a Redneck If..., 1994 (platinum cert.), Games Rednecks Play, 1995 (platinum cert.).*

FOXX, JAMIE, actor, comedian; b. Terrell, Tex., Dec. 13, 1967; s. Shaheed Abdulah and Louise Annette D.(div.); raised by great grandparents Mark and Ester Talley. Studied, U.S. Internat. U., San Diego; studied classical piano, Juliard Sch. Fine Arts. Stand-up comedian. Actor, dir., prodr., writer (TV series) The Jamie Foxx Show, 1996 (NAACP Image award for Outstanding Lead Actor in a Comedy Series, 1997), comedian, exec. prodr., writer (TV Spl.) Jamie Foxx: I Might Need Security, 2002; actor: (films) Toys, 1992, The Truth About Cats and Dogs, 1996, The Great White Hype, 1996, Booty Call, 1997, The Players Club, 1998, Held Up, 1999, Any Given Sunday, 1999, Bait, 2000, Date from Hell, 2001, Ali, 2001 (NAACP Image award for Outstanding Supporting Actor in a Motion Picture, 2002), Shade, 2003, Breakin' All the Rules, 2004, Collateral, 2004, Ray, 2004 (Named Best Actor Nat. Bd. Rev. Motion Pictures, 2004, Best Actor, Washington, DC Film Critics award, 2004, Best Actor, Boston Film Critics award, 2004, Golden Globe award for best actor musical or comedy, 2005, Screen Actors Guild Award, outstanding performance by male actor in leading role, 2005, Academy award for best actor in a leading role, 2005), Stealth, 2005; (TV films) Redemption: The Stan Tookie Williams Story, 2004; (TV series) In Living Color, 1991—94, (voice) C-Bear and Jamal, 1996; host MTV Video Music Awards, 2001, ESPY Awards, 2003. Named one of Time Mag. 100 Most Influential People, 2005. Office: The Gersh Agy 232 N Canon Dr Beverly Hills CA 90210*

FOXX, VIRGINIA ANN, congresswoman, small business owner; b. N.Y.C., June 29, 1943; m. Thomas A. Foxx, 1 child, 2 grandchildren. AB, U. N.C., Chapel Hill, 1968, MA in CT, 1972; EdD, U. N.C., Greensboro, 85. Pres., cons. Md. C.C.; owner, operator plant nursery, Banner Elk, N.C.; mem. N.C. Senate, Raleigh, 1995—2004, U.S. Ho. Reps., 109th Congress, 5th Dist. NC, 2005—. Mem. Watauga County Bd. Edn., 1976-88. Mem. Nat. Assn. Women Legislators, Am. Legis. Exch. Conf., NCCBI, N.C. Ctr. for Pub. Policy Rsch., N.C. Women's Forum. Republican. also: 11468 Hwy 105 Banner Elk NC 28604 Office: 503 Cannon House Office Bldg Washington DC 20515-3305 Office Phone: 202-225-2071.*

FOY, BETSY D., health facility administrator, educator; b. Milw., Apr. 5, 1953; d. Homer Charles Foy and Dorothy Louise Rohlfing; m. Mark T. Cockson, Sept. 2, 1978; children: Emily L. Cockson, Luke T. Cockson, Dylan J. Cockson. BA, St. Louis U., 1975; M in Health sci., Wash. U., St. Louis, 1996. Cert. Health Edn. Specialist Nat. Commn. for Health Edn. Credentialing, 1997; Qualified Profl. Mo. Dept. of Mental Health/Divsn. of Alcohol and Drug Abuse, 2001. Supr. social svc. worker Mo. Dept. of Social Svcs., St. Louis, 1975—90; child care specialist Mo. Dept. of Health, St. Louis, 1990—97; asst. dir. Wash. U. Student Health & Counseling Ctr., St. Louis, 1997—. Founder, chair St. Louis Higher Edn. Health & Wellness Collaborative. Author: (several articles) Jour. of Am. Coll. Health, (article) Health Promotion Practice Jour., Health Edn. and Behavior Jour.; cons. editor Jour. Am. Coll. Health, 2002—04. Parents adv. bd. Voluntary Interdistrict Coordinating Coun., St. Louis, 1995—99; fundraising Wash. U. Arts & Scis. Alumni Assn., St. Louis, 1998—2003; leader Girl Scouts of Am., St. Louis, 1992—94. Alcohol Prevention Grant, NCAA, 2002—05. Mem.: Soc. for Pub. Health Edn., Am. Coll. Health Assn. (alcohol & drug task force 1999—2005), Alpha Sigma Nu, Nat. Honor Soc. Achievements include development of WU Walks-Campus Walking Club. Avocations: walking, letter writing. Home: 7418 Hoover Saint Louis MO 63117 Office: Washington U Campus Box 1201 One Brookings Dr Saint Louis MO 63130 Office Phone: 314-935-7386. Personal E-mail: betsy_foy@wustl.edu.

FOY, CHARLES DALEY, retired soil scientist; b. Buena Vista, Ky., Aug. 19, 1923; s. Charles Clinton and Zylphia Gertrude (Binkley) F.; m. Doris Blanche Hornbaker, June 4, 1950; 1 child, David Alden. BS in Agriculture, U. Tenn., 1949; MS in Soil Sci., Purdue U., 1953, PhD in Soil Fertility, 1955. Tchr. Vets. Inst. on Farm Tng. Program, Connersville, Ind., 1949-51; rsch. fellow Purdue U., West Lafayette, Ind., 1951-55, asst. prof. agronomy, 1955-57; rsch. soil scientist, dept. agronomy USDA U. Ark., Fayetteville, 1957-61; rsch. soil scientist, climate stress lab. USDA Agrl. Rsch. Sta., Beltsville, Md., 1961-95; collaborator, 1995—. Cons. and lectr. in U.S. and abroad. Contbr. articles to profl. jours. With U.S. Army, 1943-46, PTO. Recipient Environ. Quality award Am. Soc. Hort. Sci., 1974, Cert. of Recognition for outstanding contbn. Orgn. Com. of IV Internat. Symposium on Plant-Soil Interactions at Low pH and Nat. Maize and Sorghum Rsch. Ctr., Belo Horizonte, Brazil, 1996; Purdue U. grad. rsch. fellow, 1953-55. Fellow Am. Soc. Agronomy, Soil Sci. Soc. Am., Crop Sci. Soc. Am. Personal E-mail: cdfoy@verizon.net.

FOY, JOHN N., real estate company executive; Exec. v.p. fin., sec. Lebovitz Family Shopping Ctr. Devel. Bus., 1968—70; with Shopping Ctr. Divsn. Arlen, 1970—78; assoc. Charles B. Lebovitz, 1978—85; chmn. bd. First Fidelity Savs. Bank, Crossville, Tenn., 1985—94; CFO CBL & Assocs. Properties, Inc., Chattanooga, 1993—, vice chmn. bd., treas., 1999—, mem. exec. com., bd. dirs. Mem. adv. bd. AmSouth Bank, Chattanooga; chmn. Chattanooga Airport Authority; dir. Chattanooga Neighborhood Enterprise. Mem.: Nat. Assn. Real Estate Investment Trusts (bd. govs.). Office: CBL Ctr Ste 500 2030 Hamilton Pl Blvd Chattanooga TN 37421-6000

FOY, KENNETH RAYMOND, music educator; b. Passaic, NJ, Jan. 14, 1953; s. Raymond Joseph and Jeanne Elizabeth Foy. BS in music edn., West Chest U., 1977; MusM, Manhattan Sch. Music, 1987; D of ednl. adminstrn., St. Peter's Coll., 2005—. Cert. Music Teacher K-12 NJ State Dept. Edn., 1977, Administrative Endorsement NJ State Dept. Edn., 2005. Dir. instrumental music Gloucester Twp. Schools, NJ, 1978—84, Old Tappan Schools, NY, 1986—91, Watchung Pub. Schools, 1998—. Pres. Gloucester Twp. Edn. Assn., 1982—84; chmn. Mid Atlantic State Philosophy Com., 1982—83. Co-creator music software, 2005, condr. Ctrl. Jersey Music Edn. Assn., 1984, 2003. Recipient NJ Governor's Tchr. Recognition award, NJ State Dept. Edn., 2000. Mem.: NJ Music Edn. Assn., Ctr. Jersey Music Edn. Assn. Home: 85 Clinton Ave Mt. Olive NJ 07828 Office: Valley View Sch 50 Valley View Rd Watchung NJ 07069

FOY, THOMAS PAUL, lawyer, retired state legislator, retired bank executive; b. Silver City, N.Mex., Oct. 19, 1914; s. Thomas J. and Mary V. Foy; m. Joan Carney, Nov. 17, 1948 (dec. June 1994); children: Celia, Thomas Paul Jr. (dec.), Muffet (Mary Ann), J. Carney, James B. BS in Commerce, Notre Dame U., 1938, JD, 1939; DHL (hon.), Western N.Mex U., 2004. Bar: N.Mex. 1946. Dist. atty. N.Mex. 6th Jud. Dist., Silver City, 1949-57; atty. Village of Bayard, N.Mex., 1954-68, Village of Ctrl., N.Mex., 1960-70; v.p., counsel, bd. dirs. Sunwest Bank, Silver City, 1946-84, chmn. bd. dirs., 1969-84, chmn. emeritus, 1984-97; state rep. Dist. 39 State of N.Mex., Grant-Hidalgo, 1971-98; chmn. jud. com. N.Mex. State Legis., Santa Fe, 1984-98; pres. Foy & Vesely and Foy, Foy & Castillo, Silver City, 1946-99, Foy Law Firm PC, 1999—. 1st lt. U.S. Army, 1941-46; prisoner of war, PTO, 1942-45. Decorated Bronze Star, Purple Heart, Asiatic-Pacific Ribbon with 3 oak leaf clusters; recipient Citizen of Yr. award Silver City-Grant County C. of C., 1965, Dedication to Advancement award Trial Lawyers Assn., 1993, N.Mex. Disting. Svc. medal, 1994. Mem. ABA, N.Mex. Bar Assn. (bar commr. 1967-85, v.p. N.Mex. bar commn. 1978-79, Disting. Svc. of Laws award 1987), Am. Judicature Soc., Bataan Vets. Orgn. (state comdr. 1965-66, 98-99, 2004—), KC (Grand Knight 1936-37), VFW (state comdr. 1959-60), Lions (dist. gov. 1956-57), Elks. Democrat. Roman Catholic. Avocations: football, baseball, travel, conventions. Office: Box 266 Bayard NM 88023-2660 Home: PO Box 266 Bayard NM 88023-0266 Office Phone: 505-537-3355.

FOY, WADE HAMPTON, retired research scientist; b. Richmond, Va., Jan. 26, 1925; s. Wade Hampton and Eliza Belle (Wilkinson) Foy; m. Raymonde van Laar, May 19, 1952; children: Virginia E. Foy Streeter, Wade Charles. BS, U.S. Naval Acad., 1946; BEE, N.C. State Coll., 1951; MSEE, MIT, 1955; D in Engring., Johns Hopkins U., 1962. Registered profl. engr., Calif. Sect. head math. Martin Co., Balt., 1956—62; engr. Stanford Rsch. Inst., Menlo Park, Calif., 1962—68; prin. scientist SRI Internat., Menlo Park, Calif., 1968—91; ret., 1991. Lectr. Drexel Inst. Tech., Balt., 1957—61; adj. lectr. Santa Clara (Calif.) U., 1963—2001. Contbr. articles to profl. jours. Ensign USN, 1946—48, lt. USNR, 1951—53. Mem.: IEEE, U.S. Naval Inst. Republican. Avocations: research, tennis, ship models. Home: 131 Callecita Los Gatos CA 95032 E-mail: wraymonde@aol.com.

FOYE, THOMAS HAROLD, lawyer; b. Rapid City, S.D., Nov. 23, 1930; s. Harold Herbert and Jean Winifred (McCormick) F.; m. Laurene Fowler, Aug. 7, 1972; children: David Snyder, Stewart Snyder BS in Commerce, Creighton U., 1952; LLB, Georgetown U., 1955. Bar: S.D. 1955, D.C. 1955, U.S. Supreme Ct. 1968. Trial atty. tax div. U.S. Dept. Justice, Washington, 1955-58; assoc. Bangs, McCullen, Butler, Foye & Simmons, predecessor firms, Rapid City, 1958-60, ptnr., 1960—. Lectr. in field Fellow Am. Coll. Trust and Estate Counsel, Am. Bar Found.; mem. ABA, State Bar S.D. (pres. 1982-83), Pennington County Bar Assn. (pres. 1962), Am. Coll. Real Estate Lawyers, Internat. Acad. Estate and Trust Law., Am. Coll. Tax Counsel. Clubs: Arrowhead Country (Rapid City). Democrat. Roman Catholic. Avocations: skiing, water-skiing, hiking. Office: Bangs McCullen Butler Foye & Simmons PO Box 2670 Rapid City SD 57709-2670 Office Phone: 605-343-1040. E-mail: tfoye@bangsmccullen.com.

FOYOUZI-YOUSSEFI, REYHANEH, pharmacologist; b. Tehran, Iran, Dec. 6, 1964; arrived in Switzerland, 1983. d. Amin and Seyedeh (Salimi-Eshkevari); m. Hamid R. Mostafavi, 2001; 1 child, Mahan Ali. Diploma of Asst. Pharmacist, Sch. Pharmacy, Geneva, Switzerland, 1988, Diploma of Pharmacy, 1991; PhD in Pharmacy, U. Geneva, Geneva, Switzerland, 1999. Pharmacist, Geneva, 1991—; sr. scientist Estee Lauder Cos., Inc., 2000—04. Contbr. articles to profl. jours.

FOYSTON, FREDERICK L. (RICK FOYSTON), literature and language educator, coach; b. Seattle, Oct. 28, 1945; s. Sidney C. and Marylin R. Foyston; m. Cherie L. Eacret; children: Trevor, Jacob, Heidi L. Nykaza, Heather L. Bryant, Haley A. Pozzi, Jershon C. BA in Edn., Western Wash. U., 1972; MEd, Lesley Coll., 1993; MA in Ednl. Adminstrn., Seattle Pacific U., 1995. Cert. prin. Wash. Shipping/receiving staff Tradewell Stores Inc., Kent, Wash., 1972—84; new constrn. sales mgr. Windermere Real Estate, Bellevue, Wash., 1984—86; English lang. arts instr. Kent Sch. Dist., 1987—. Athletic dir. Sequoia Mid. Sch., Kent, 1997—, curriculum devel./implementation staff, 1991—. Mem., tchr. LDS Ch., Kent, 1977—. Sgt. USAF, 1965—69. Mem.: Assn. Supervision and Curriculum Devel., Wash. Secondary Sch. Athletic Adminstrs. Assn. (assoc.). Achievements include development of Reality Edn.-Keys for Success curriculum; speed writing curriculum. Avocations: coaching, reading, outdoor activities, travel. Home: 23337 114th Pl SE Kent WA 98031 Personal E-mail: rfoyston@excite.com.

FRACIS, SOHRAB HOMI, writer, education educator; b. Bombay, Maharashtra, India, Aug. 19, 1958; s. Homi Burjorji and Dinsi Homi Fracis. MA in English (concentration in Creative Writing), U. North Fla., 1993; MCE, U. Del., 1983; B Tech. in civil engring., Indian Inst. Tech., Kharagpur, 1981. Adj. prof. U. North Fla., Jacksonville, 1993—2003; fiction and poetry editor State St. Rev., Jacksonville, 1994—2001; proofreader Kalliope, Jacksonville, 1998—2003. Vis. writer in residence Augsburg Coll., Mpls., 2004; final judge, presenter Page Edwards Short Fiction award Fla. First Coast Writers' Festival, 2004. Author: (story collection) Ticket to Minto: Stories of India and America (The Iowa Short Fiction Award, 2001). Fellow Individual Artist Fellowship in Lit., Fla. Dept. of State, Divsn. of Cultural Affairs (Judging Body: Fla. Arts Coun.), 1999-2000, Walter E. Dakin Fellowship in Fiction, Sewanee Writers' Conf., Tenn., 2002; scholar Key West Lit. Seminar Scholarship, Key West Lit. Seminar, Fla., 2004. Mem.: Authors Guild N.Y. Achievements include first Indian author to win the Iowa Short Fiction Award, judged by the Iowa Writers' Workshop, U. of Iowa. Home: 1134 Windy Willows Drive Jacksonville FL 32225 Personal E-mail: sfracis@hotmail.com.

FRACKMAN, NOEL, art critic; b. N.Y.C., May 27, 1930; d. Walter David and Celeste (Barman) Stern; m. Richard Benoit Frackman, July 2, 1950 (dec. Jan. 2, 2002); 1 child, Noel Dru Pyne. Student, Mt. Holyoke Coll., 1948—50; BA, Sarah Lawrence Coll., 1952, MA, 1953; postgrad., Columbia U., 1964—67; MA Inst. Fine Arts, NYU, 1976, PhD Inst. Fine Arts, 1987. Art critic Scarsdale (N.Y.) Inquirer, 1962—67, Patent Trader, Mt. Kiscoe, NY, 1962—71; assoc. Arts Mag., N.Y.C., 1968—92. Lectr. Aldrich Mus. Contemporary Art, Ridgefield, Conn., 1967—75, Gallery Passport Ltd., N.Y.C., 1968—96; curator edn. Storm King Art Ctr., Mountainville, NY, 1973—75; instr. continuing edn. divsn. SUNY, 1988—2002; contractual lectr. Met. Mus. Art, N.Y.C., 1994—95; adj. assoc. prof. humanities, 1997—2002. Contbr. articles and revs. to various mags., including Arts Mag., Harper's Bazaar, Feminist Art Jour., Art Voices. Bd. dirs. Friends of the Neuberger Mus. Art, 1994—. Scholar Sarah Williston scholar, 1948—50. Mem.: Coll. Art Assn., Art Table Inc., Internat. Assn. Art Critics.

FRACKMAN, RUSSELL JAY, lawyer; b. NYC, July 3, 1946; s. Sam and Doris (Wasserberg) F.; m. Myrna D. Morganstern, Aug. 3, 1980; children: Steven Howard, Abigail Zoe. BA in History, Northwestern U., 1967; JD cum laude, Columbia U., 1970. Bar: Calif. 1971, U.S. Dist. Ct. (ctrl., ea. and no. dists.) Calif., U.S. Ct. Appeals (2d and 9th cirs.), U.S. Supreme Ct. Assoc. Mitchell, Silberberg & Knupp LLP, LA, 1970-76, ptnr., 1976—, chmn. litigation dept., 1994-96. Lectr. on intellectual property and entertainment law various instns. including Practising Law Inst., L.A. Copyright Soc., Beverly Hills Bar Assn., U. So. Calif. Sch. Law, Am. Film Mktg. Assn., Calif. Copyright Conf. Bd. editors Columbia Law Rev., 1969-70; contbr. articles and revs. to legal jours. Co-chmn. internat. leadership devel. forum CARE, 1990; bd. trustees CARE Found., 1991—, Twitty, Milsap, Sterban Found., 1988-92. Mem. ABA (chmn. copyright subcom. litigation sect. 1990-93, lectr. various confs.), Am. Film Mktg. Assn. (mem. arbitration tribunal). Democrat. Jewish. Office: Mitchell Silberberg & Knupp LLP 11377 W Olympic Blvd Los Angeles CA 90064-1625 Office Phone: 310-312-3119.

FRADE, PETER DANIEL, chemist, educator, administrator; b. Highland Park, Mich., Sept. 3, 1946; s. Peter Nunes and Dorathea Grace (Gehrke) F.; m. Karen L. Kovich, Mar. 14, 1992. BS in Chemistry, Wayne State U., 1968, MS, 1971, PhD, 1978. Chemist Henry Ford Hosp., Detroit, 1968-75, analytical chemist, toxicologist dept. pathology, divsn. pharmacology and toxicology, 1975-86, sr. clin. lab. scientist dept. pathology divsn. clin. chemistry and pharmacology, 1987-96; assoc. prof. Eugene Applebaum Coll. of Pharmacy and Allied Health Sci. Wayne State U., Detroit, 1996—, interim chair dept. Mortuary Sci., 2000—03, chair, dept. Mortuary Sci., 2003—04, chair, dept. Fundamental and Applied Scis., 2004—. Rsch. assoc. in chemistry Wayne State U., Detroit, 1978—79; vis. scholar U. Mich., Ann Arbor, 1980—90; vis. scientist dept. hypertension rsch. Henry Ford Hosp., Detroit, 1986—88; adj. prof. Eugene Applebaum Coll. of Pharmacy and Health Scis. Wayne State U., 1991—96, dir. anat. pathologist assts. program, dir. mortuary sci. program, dir. mortuary sci. program. Contbr. sci. articles to profl. jours.; peer reviewer for profl. jours., 1988—; mem. editl. bd. Annals of Pharmacotherapy, 2003-. Mem. Rep. Presdl. Task Force, 1984-88; organist St. John's Episcopal Ch., Royal Oak, Mich., 1995-97. Recipient David F. Boltz Meml. award, Wayne State U., 1977, Teaching Excellence award. Fellow Am. Inst. Chemists, Nat. Acad. Clin. Biochemistry, Assn. Clin. Scientists; mem. Am. Coll. Forensic Examiners, Am. Chem. Soc., Am. Soc. Forensic Odontology, Am. Assn. Clin. Chemistry, Am. Guild Organists, Assn. Analytical Chemists, Mich. Inst. Chemists (treas. 1994—), N.Y. Acad. Scis., Am. Coll. Toxicology, Royal Soc. Chemistry (London), Titanic Hist. Soc., Virgil Fox Sox., Sigma Xi, Phi Lambda Upsilon, Alpha Chi Sigma. Episcopalian. Home: 20200 Orleans St Detroit MI 48203-1356 Office: Wayne State U 5439 Woodward Ave Detroit MI 48202-4009 Office Phone: 313-577-7874. Business E-Mail: ab8123@wayne.edu.

FRADKIN, DAVID MILTON, physicist, researcher; b. Los Angeles, Apr. 20, 1931; s. Aaron and Annie (Gordon) F.; m. Dorothea Edna Fairweather, Nov. 25, 1959; children: Lee, Mark, Steven. BS, U. Calif., Berkeley, 1954; PhD, Iowa State U., 1963. Exploitation engr. Shell Oil Co., Los Angeles, 1954-56; research assoc. Iowa State U. and Ames Lab., Ames, Iowa, 1963-64; NATO postdoctoral fellow U. Rome, 1964-65; asst. prof. physics Wayne State U., Detroit, 1965-69, assoc. prof., 1969-75, prof., 1975-94, chmn. dept. physics, 1981-91; prof. emeritus, 1994—. Del. Argonne (Ill.) Univs. Assn., 1981-83; vis. fellow U. Durham, Eng., 1991-92. Contbr. articles to profl. jours. Vice chmn. adv. bd. Detroit pub. schs., 1972-73; trustee Detroit Sci. Ctr., 1986-94. Recipient award Probus Club, 1973; sr. postdoctoral fellow U. Edinburgh, Scotland, 1977-78. Mem. Am. Phys. Soc., Sigma Xi. Avocations: tennis, fishing, golf, sailing.

FRADKIN, HILLEL GIDEON, foundation official, educator; b. Bklyn., Mar. 30, 1947; s. Abraham and Dorothy (Nacht) F.; m. Elizabeth B. Berns; children: Abigail Ruth, Rebecca Marion. BA, Cornell U., 1967; PhD, U. Chgo., 1978. Cons. Inst. Ednl. Affairs, N.Y.C., 1978-79; asst. prof. Columbia U., N.Y.C., 1979-86; program officer John M. Olin Found., N.Y.C., 1983-86; v.p. Lynda & Harry Bradley Found., Milw., 1986—. Vis. instr. Yale U., New Haven, Conn., 1977; vis. lectr. U. Chgo., 1987—; mem. nat. adv. bd. U.S. Dept. Edn., Washington, 1988—. Mem. Milw. Jewish Coun. Recipient Kaplun prize for Jewish Philosophy Hebrew U., Jerusalem, 1976. Mem. NEH, Nat. Humanities Coun., Am. Polit. Sci. Assn., Assn. Jewish Studies, Middle East Studies Assn., Am. Acad. Religion, Am. Oriental Soc., Univ. Club (Milw.).

FRADLEY, FREDERICK MACDONELL, retired architect; b. Bronxville, NY, July 31, 1924; s. Justis Frederick and Helen Josephine (Macdonell) F.; m. Dorothy Davis Richard, Aug. 7, 1948; children: Stephen Davis, Wendy Fradley Monroe. BS, Brown U., 1948; M.F.A. (Lowell M. Palmer fellow), Princeton, 1954. Office engr. Turner Constrn. Co., Phila., 1948-51; project arch. Vincent G. Kling, Phila., 1954-61; ptnr. Bower & Fradley Archs., Phila., 1961-78. Important works with Bower in Phila. area include 1500 Walnut St. Office Bldg., Internat. House Student Ctr., Wharton Grad. Ctr. (Vance Hall), Gallery at Market East, 1234 Market St. Office Bldg., Yarway Corp. Hdqs., SKF Industries Hdqrs., in Balt. the W.R. Grace Bldg. Served with USAAF, 1942-46, PTO. Mem. Phi Delta Theta. Home (Winter): 5000 4A Enighed # 332 St John VI 00830 Home (Summer): 20 McFarland Shore Rd New Harbor ME 04554-4827

FRADY, RITA R., music educator, information technology manager; d. Laurence Herbert and Evelyn T. Rice; m. Lamar K. Frady, Aug. 29, 1981; children: Leigha A., Keith B. MusB in Piano Performance, West Ga. Coll., 1980; M of Elem. Edn., Brenau U., 2005. Tchr. Cert. T-4 Ga., 1991. Music tchr. K-6 Cherokee County Bd. of Edn., Canton, Ga., 1991—. Intech redelivery Cherokee County Bd. of Edn., Canton, Ga., 2003—. Pres., v.p. Cherokee Basketball Boosters, Canton, Ga., 2000—02. Mem.: Music Educators Nat. Conf., Delta Kappa Gamma. Avocations: Tae Kwon Do, reading, travel. Home: PO Box 4925 Canton GA 30114-0246 Office: Hasty Elem Sch Canton GA 30114

FRAENKEL, GEORGE KESSLER, chemistry professor; b. Deal, NJ, July 27, 1921; s. Osmond Kessler and Helene (Esberg) F.; m. Johanna-Maria Herzog, June 30, 1951 (div. Aug. 1965); m. Elizabeth R. Rosen, Nov. 11, 1967 (div. Jan. 1990); m. Eva S. Cantwell, Feb. 3, 1990. BA, Harvard U., 1942; PhD, Cornell U., 1949. Research group leader National Def. Research Com., 1943-46; instr. chemistry Columbia U., N.Y.C., 1949-53, asst. prof., 1953-57, assoc. prof., 1957-61, prof., 1961-91, Eugene Higgins prof. Grad. Sch. Arts and Scis., 1986-91, prof. emeritus, 1992—, chmn. dept. chemistry, 1966-68, dean grad. sch. arts and scis., 1968-83, dean emeritus, 1983—, v.p. spl. projects, 1983-86. Mem. postdoctoral fellowship com. Nat. Acad. Sci.-NSF, 1964-65; chmn. Gordon Research Conf. Magnetic Resonance, 1967; mem. Arts Coll. adv. council Cornell U., 1964-74; mem., bd. dirs. Atran Found., N.Y.C., 1968—2005, com. on budget and fin., 1986—2005; treas. Atran Found., 1988—2005. Assoc. editor: Jour. Chem. Physics, 1962-64; Mem. adv. editorial bd.: Chemical Physics Letters, 1966-71; editorial bd.: Jour. Magnetic Resonance, 1969-70. Trustee Columbia U. Press, 1968-71, Walden Sch., N.Y.C., 1964-66. Recipient Army-Navy certificate of appreciation, 1948; Harold C. Urey award Phi Lambda Upsilon, 1972; decorated officer Ordre des Palmes Académiques. Fellow AAAS, Am. Phys. Soc., Am. Chem. Soc., Internat. Electron Spin Resonance Soc.; mem. Assn. Grad. Schs. (exec. com. 1976-80, v.p. 1977-78, pres. 1978-79, chmn. com. policies on grad. edn. 1969-71), Phi Beta Kappa, Sigma Xi, Phi Kappa Phi. Achievements include research in field of electron spin resonance with particular emphasis on the electron spin resonance of organic free radicals. Home: 520 W 114th St Apt 82 New York NY 10025-7852 E-mail: gkf520@cs.com.

FRAGALE, RICHARD P., academic administrator; BA, Muhlenberg Coll., 1958; MEd, Western Md. Coll., 1968; postgrad., U. South Calif. Supt. Cen. Union H.S. Dist., El Centro, Calif., 2000—, Trona (Calif.) Joint Unified Sch. Dist. Mem.: Small Sch. Dists. Assn. Calif. (treas. declining enrollment sch. dists. of Calif.), Am. Assn. Sch. Adminstrs. (pres. Imperial Valley chpt., region XVIII legis. com., Region XVIII Adminstr. of Yr. award 1992). Office: Cen Union H S Dist 351 Ross Ave El Centro CA 92243

FRAGASSI, RAYMOND G., corporate financial executive; Degree in Bus., Bucks County C.C., Newtown; degree in Fin., Pa. State U., Abingdon; graduate Cert. Program, Pa. State U. Cert. fire and allied lines, casualty and allied lines, lic. mutual and stock life ins. annuities Pa. Ins. Commn., accident and health ins. Pa. Ins. Commn.; cert. collector, supr., advanced collection expert, credit mgmt., credit assoc., assoc. credit exec., accts. receivable collection mgmt. Supr. and tng. coord. Allied Bond and Collection Agy., Trevose, Pa., 1983—91; sr. collections and compliance mgr. Penncro Assoc., Southampton, 1991—96; dir. and asst. v.p. portfolio risk GMAC Mortgage, Horsham, 1996—97; v.p. collections Mortgage Lenders Network USA, Middletown, Conn., 1997—99; v.p. receivable mgmt. outsourcing and receivable mgmt. svcs. Dun and Bradstreet, Bethlehem, Pa., 1999—2000; v.p. bus. planning, credit and collection Lenox Collections, Langhorne, 2000—04; COO FBCS, Inc., Phila, 2004—. Coach and com. mem. Northampton Coun. Rock Soccer Assn.; coach Coun. Rock Baseball Assn., Coun. Rock Soccer; CCD tchr. St. Bede's the Venerable Ch. Mem.: Nat. Assn. Life Underwriters, Mortgage Bankers Assn. Am., Manufactures Credit Coop., Gift Assn. Interchange, Direct Marketers Credit Assn., Internat. Credit Assn. (steering com.), Soc. Cert. Credit Execs., Am. Collectors Assn., Inc. (assoc.; legis. com.). Address: 2 Green Valley Dr Churchville PA 18966

FRAGER, ALBERT S., retired food products executive; b. Boston, Dec. 29, 1922; s. Oscar and Anna (Polterak) F.; m. Marion Nathan, June 15, 1950; children: Owen R., Bonnie L. Frager Franks, Laurie J. Burton, Sherri Frager Goodstein. Student, Amos Tuck Sch. Bus., Dartmouth Coll., 1943; BS in Bus. Adminstrn, Northeastern U., 1944. Internal revenue agt. IRS, 1945-56; v.p., controller Stop & Shop, Inc., Boston, 1956-67, treas., 1967-86, fin. v.p., 1969-79, sr. v.p., 1979-86. Past trustee South Palm Beach County Jewish Fedn.; bd. dirs. Donna Klein Jewish Acad.; mem. corp., past bd. overseers Northeastern U.; past pres. Jewish temple. With USNR, 1943-44. Mem. AICPA, Mass. Soc. CPAs. Home: 4740 S Ocean Blvd Apt 911 Highland Beach FL 33487-5354

FRAGNER, MATTHEW CHARLES, lawyer; b. NYC, Jan. 12, 1954; s. Berwyn N. and Marcia R. (Salkind) F.; m. Mariann Donahue, June 19, 1983; children: Rachel Jade, Jaron Roark, Bailyn Natalie, Talia Colby. BA, Yale U., 1975; JD, U. Calif., Berkeley, 1978. Bar: Calif. 1978, U.S. Tax Ct. 1979, U.S. Ct. Appeals (9th cret.) 1979. Atty. Thomas Shafran & Wasser, L.A., 1978-83; ptnr. Shafran & Fragner, L.A., 1984-87, Lane & Edson, L.A., 1987-88, Mayer Brown & Platt, L.A., 1989-92, Sonnenschein Nath & Rosenthal, L.A., 1992-2000; pres. Somnolence, Inc., L.A., 1989—96; gen. cousel, dir. investments Citadel Capital Mgmt. Corp., 2000—02; founder, chmn. Tools to Talent Non Profit Corp., 2001—; ptnr. Liner Yankelevitz Sunshine & Regenstreif, Santa Monica, Calif., 2002—03; prin. Fragner & Pace Law Corp., Los Angeles, 2003—05; ptnr. FSPW Law, LLP, L.A., 2005—. Lectr. U. So. Calif., 1994—99. Active Berkeley (Calif.) Law Found., 1978-83. Mem. Los Angeles County Bar Assn. (chair comml. devel. and leasing subsect.). Office: FSPW Law LLP 300 S Grand Ave 14th Fl Los Angeles CA 90071 Office Phone: 213-687-2320. Business E-Mail: mfragner@fspwlaw.com.

FRAGNUL, RITA MARIE, artist; b. N.Y.C., Feb. 23, 1922; d. Andrew and Josephine (Ferrari) Drago; m. Daniel F. Fragnul, Aug. 29, 1964. BA in Studio Art, U. Md., 1985, BA in Art History, 1986. Radio actor Sta. WEVD, N.Y.C., 1944-51, Sta. WAAT, Newark, 1944-51; Freelance photographer N.Y.C., 1953-58; freelance painter, 1959-64, Silver Spring, Md., 1968-90, Bethesda, Md., 1991—. Vol. staff congress U.S. House Reps., Washington, 1981-87. Mem. Nat. Mus. of Women in Arts. Democrat. Roman Catholic. Avocations: painting, history of art, opera, theater, photography. Home: 4400 E West Hwy Bethesda MD 20814-4524

FRAGOMENI, JAMES MARK, mechanical engineer, educator; b. Columbus, Ohio, Sept. 24, 1962; s. John and Kathleen Fragomeni. BS in Metall. Engring., U. Pitts., 1985; MS in Engring., Purdue U., West Lafayette, Indiana, 1988, PhD, 1994. Sumer rsch. intern Allegheny Ludlum Steel Corp. Rsch. Ctr., Brackenridge, Pa., 1984; mgmt. assoc. engr. US Steel Corp., Gary, Ind., 1985—86; asst. rschr. Dept. Defense Analysis Ctr., U. Purdue, West Lafayette, Ind., 1995; asst. prof. U. Ala., Tuscaloosa, 1995—97, Ohio U., Athens, 1997—2000; summer faculty fellow Wright Patterson AFB Materials and Mfg. Directorate, AFOSR, Dayton, 1998; asst. prof. U. Detroit Mercy, 2000—. Grad. rsch. asst. Purdue U., Engring. Rsch. Ctr., West Lafayette, Ind., 1986—94; summer faculty fellow NASA Marshall Space Flight Ctr., Huntsville, Ala., 1996, Huntsville, 97. Contbr. articles to profl. jours., scientific papers to sci. confs. Cmty. svc. vol., Portage, Ind., 1985—87. U. Pitts. Merit scholar, 1981-1985, Carpenter Tech. Corp. scholar, 1982. Mem.: Mich. Edn. Assn., Materials Soc. (corr.; mem. of Titanium com. 2000—04), Soc. Advancement Materials and Process Engring. (assoc.; faculty advisor student chpt. Ohio U. 1998—2000), Sigma Xi, Pi Tau Sigma (faculty advisor student chpt. U. Detroit Mercy 2002—04), Tau Beta Pi (inter-honorary coun. rep. student chpt. U.Pitts. 1983—85). Conservative. Roman Catholic. Achievements include research in Research On Aluminum-Lithium Alloys For Aerospace Applications. Avocations: travel, scuba diving, archery and rifle, physical fitness, tennis, skiing. Home: 25105 Biarritz Circle Oak Park MI 48237-4021 Office: Engineering & Science Consulting Service PO Box 1446 Royal Oak MI 48068-1446 Office Phone: 248-245-4843. Personal E-mail: jamesfrag@yahoo.com. E-mail: jamesmark88@yahoo.com.

FRAGOS, EMILY, poet, educator; b. Mt. Vernon, N.Y., May 11, 1949; d. Chris and Georgia Fragos. BA, Syracuse U., 1971; MA, La Sorbonne, Paris, 1975; MFA, Columbia U., 1996. Asst. prof. Fordham U., N.Y.C., 1996—, NYU, N.Y.C., 1996—, Coll. Mt. St. Vincent, N.Y.C., 1998—99, Columbia U., N.Y.C., 1999—. Author: (book of poetry) Little Savage, 2004; editor: (poetry anthology) The Great Cat, 2005; contbr. articles to lit. jours. and dance mags. Avocations: cello, piano. Office: Columbia U 612 Lewisohn Hall MC 4108 2970 Broadway New York NY 10027

FRAGUELA, JAMES, publishing executive; b. Bklyn. s. G. and Sophie (Vidal) F.; m. Susan Baron, Aug. 15, 1988; 1 child, Kate. BA in Bus. Adminstrn., Curry Coll. Sales rep. Woman's Day Mag., 1973-75; account mgr. Family Cir. Inc., 1975-81, assoc. Eastern mgr., 1981-82, Eastern advt. mgr., 1982-84, v.p., advt. dir., 1984-87; pub. Lear Pub., Inc., 1988-91; v.p., mktg. dir. Electronic Mktg. and Retail Comm., 1992-95; sr. v.p., pub. Globe Comm. Corp., N.Y.C., 1995-99; v.p., pub. Hachette Filipacchi Mags., N.Y.C., 2000—. Avocations: motorcycling, jogging, tennis. Home: 300 E 74th St New York NY 10021-3712

FRAHM, SHEILA, association executive, academic administrator, former government official; b. Colby, Kans., Mar. 22, 1945; m. Kenneth Frahm; children: Amy, Pam, Chrissie. BS, Ft. Hays State U., 1967. Mem. bd. edn. State of Kans., 1985-88; mem. Kans. Senate, Topeka, 1988-94, senate majority leader, 1993-94; lt. gov. State of Kans., 1995-96; mem. from Kans., U.S. Senate, Washington, 1996; exec. dir. Kans. Assn. C.C. Trustees, Topeka, 1996—. Mem. AAUW (Outstanding Br. Mem. 1985), Thomas County Day Care Assn., Shakespeare Fedn. Women's Clubs, Farm Bur., Kans. Corn Growers, Kans. Livestock Assn., Rotary (Paul Harris fellow 1988). Republican. Home: 410 N Grant Colby KS 67701-2036 Office: 700 SW Jackson St Ste 401 Topeka KS 66603-3757 Personal E-mail: sfrahm@colbyweb.com.

FRAIDEN, NORMAN ARTHUR, lawyer; b. N.Y.C., Mar. 2, 1943; s. Morris and Mollie (Tepper) F.; m. Arlene Joyce Zied, Dec. 24, 1967; children: David Alan, Mark Gerald. BA, Hunter Coll., 1964; LLB, Bklyn. Law Sch., 1967. Bar: N.Y. 1967, U.S. Dist. Ct. (so. dist.) N.Y. 1967. Ptnr. Blumenfeld and Fraiden, N.Y.C., 1970-95, Fraiden & Palen, 1996—. Corr. sec. Jewish Community Ctr. Men's Club, Harrison, N.Y., 1990—. Mem. ATLA, N.Y. State Trial Lawyers Assn., Bronx Bar Assn., N.Y. State Bar Assn. Avocations: tennis, chess, swimming, soccer. Office: Fraiden & Palen 327 E 149th St Bronx NY 10451-5685 Fax: 718-401-3328.

FRAIDIN, STEPHEN, lawyer; b. Boston, July 29, 1939; s. Morris and Freda (Rozeff) F.; m. Lori Kramer, Oct. 27, 2001; children from previous marriage: Matthew, Sam, Sarah AB, Tufts U., 1961; JD, Yale U., 1964. Bar: NY 1965. Assoc. Fried, Frank, Harris, Shriver & Jacobson, NYC, 1964—71, ptnr., 1971—2003, Kirkland & Ellis LLP, NYC, 2003—. Vis. lectr., Yale U. Law Sch., 1988—; men., Assn. Bar City NY (sec., Securities Regulation Com., 1971-74, chmn., Subcommittee on Tender Offers, 1987-88, 88-90, mem. securities regulation com. 2004-); Am. Bar Assn.(reporter, Com. on Fed. Regulation of Securities, Section on Corp., Banking, & Bus. Law, 1974-76, subcommittee mem., 1974-); mem. exec. com., Yale Law Sch. Assn., 1990-94; bd. overseers, Tufts U. Arts & Sciences, 1992-99, bd. dirs., Lawyers Divsn. of UJA-Fedn. NY, 1995-, chmn. 1995-97; bd. dirs. Coll. Summit 2004-. Contbr. numerous articles to profl. jours. Past chmn. N.Y. Lawyers Divsn. United Jewish Appeal Fedn. Recipient Judge Joseph M. Proskauer award, 2002. Mem.: ABA, Assn. of Bar of City of NY. Office: Kirkland & Ellis LLP Citigroup Ctr 153 E 53rd St New York NY 10022

FRAISTAT, NEIL RICHARD, English language educator; b. Bronx, N.Y., Apr. 19, 1952; s. Louis and Shirley (Putterman) F.; children: Shawn Cleveland, Ann Cleveland; m. Pamela Wessling. BA, U. Conn., 1974; MA, U. Pa., 1976, PhD, 1979. From asst. prof. to prof. English U. Md., College Park, 1979-91, prof. English, 1991—. Author: The Poem and the Book, 1985; editor: Poems in Their Place, 1986, The "Prometheus Unbound" Notebooks, 1991, The Complete Poetry of Percy Bysshe Shelley, 1999; (Website) Romantic Circles; mem. editl. bd.: Keats-Shelley Jour., 1996—, Studies in Romanticism, 1995—, Romanticism, 1993—, Romanticism on the Net, 1996—. Recipient Fredson Bowers Meml. prize for best essay on textual scholarship Soc. for Textual Scholarship, 1994, Disting. Scholar award, Keats-Shelley Assn., 2001; fellow for univ. tchrs. NEH, 1990, Am. Coun. Learned Socs. fellow, 1982, Huntington Libr. fellow, 1981. Home: 4202 Woodberry St Hyattsville MD 20782-1171 Office: U Md Dept English College Park MD 20742-0001

FRAKES, JAMES THOMAS, management consultant; b. Fayetteville, N.C., Aug. 27, 1967; s. James Wade and Judy Frakes; m. Susan Carol, Aug. 5, 1995; 1 child, Molly Susannah. BA, Ark. State U., 1990; MS, S.E. Mo. State U., 1992. Pub. affairs cons., Cape Girardeau, Mo., 1992-94; dir. Title III programs Dyersburg (Tenn.) State C.C., 1994-98, dir. Small Bus. Devel. Ctr., 1998—. Active March of Dimes, Am. Cancer Soc., United Way; vol. Nat. Marrow Donor Program; chmn. New Madrid County Ext. Coun. Recipient Vol. of Yr. Mo. Econ. Devel. Coun., 1999. Mem. Ark. State Alumni Assn. (pres.), Mo. Econ. Devel. Coun., Assn. Small Bus. Devel. Ctrs., Conservation Fedn. Mo., Tenn. Indsl. Devel. Coun., So. Econ. Devel. Coun., Nat. Assn. Title III Adminstrs., Tenn. Small Bus. Devel. Ctrs., County Ext. Coun. (chmn. 2000—), Kiwanis, Rotary, Jaycees (Portageville), Sigma Chi. Baptist. Avocations: camping, fishing, outdoor sports. Home: 2095 State Hwy EE Portageville MO 63873 Office: Tenn Small Bus Devel 1510 Lake Rd Dyersburg TN 38024 E-mail: jfrakes@dscc.cc.tn.us.

FRAKES, RODNEY VANCE, plant geneticist, educator; b. Ontario, Oreg., July 20, 1930; s. Wylie and Pearl (Richardson) F.; m. Ruby L. Morey, Nov. 27, 1952; children: Laura Ann, Cody Joe. BS, Oreg. State U., 1956, MS, 1957; PhD, Purdue U., 1960. Instr. dept. agronomy Purdue U., West Lafayette, Ind., 1959-60; asst. prof. dept. crop sci. Oreg. State U., Corvallis, 1960-64, assoc. prof., 1964-69, prof., 1969—, assoc. dean research, 1981-88, emeritus dean of rsch., prof. emeritus crop sci., 1989—. Author numerous papers and abstracts; contbr. to books in field Served with USCG, 1950-53 Named Man of Yr., Pacific Seedsmen's Assn., 1972; recipient Elizabeth P. Ritchie Disting. Prof. award Oreg. State U., 1980. Fellow Am. Soc. Agronomy, Crop Sci. Soc. Am.; mem. AAAS, Soc. Research Adminstrs., Nat. Council Univ. Research Adminstrs., Western Soc. Crop Sci. (pres. 1978), Model A Ford Club of Am., Model T Ford Club of Am., Rotary. Avocations: antique autos, American History, amateur radio. Home: 2625 NW Linnan Cir Corvallis OR 97330-1221 Office: Oreg State U Rsch Office Corvallis OR 97331

FRAKNOI, ANDREW, astronomy educator, astronomical society executive; b. Budapest, Hungary, Aug. 24, 1948; came to U.S., 1959; naturalized; s. Emery I. and Katherine H. (Schmidt) F.; m. Lola Goldstein, Aug. 16, 1992; 1 child, Alexander. BA in Astronomy, Harvard U., 1970; MA in Astrophysics, U. Calif.-Berkeley, 1972. Instr. astronomy and physics Cañada Coll., Redwood City, Calif., 1972-78; exec. dir. Astron. Soc. of Pacific, San Francisco, 1978-92; chmn. dept. astronomy Foothill Coll., Los Altos, Calif., 1992—. Prof. San Francisco State U., 1980-92; fellow Com. for Sci. Investigation of Claims of Paranormal, 1984—; bd. dirs. Search for Extra Terrestrial Intelligence Inst., Mountain View, Calif.,; host radio program Exploring the Universe Sta. KGO-FM, San Francisco, 1983-84. Author: Resource Book for the Teaching of Astronomy, 1978; (with others) Effective Astronomy Teaching and Student Reasoning Ability, 1978, Universe in the Classroom, 1985; (with T. Robertson) Instructor's Guide to the Universe, 1991, (with others) Exploration of the Universe, 1995; (with others) Voyages Through the Universe, 1997, Voyages to the Planets, 2000; editor: The Planets, 1985, Interdisciplinary Approaches to Astronomy, 1985, The Universe, 1987, The Universe at Your Fingertips Resource Notebook, 1995, Cosmos in the

Classroom, 2000, Voyages to the Stars and Galaxies, 3d edit., 2004; editor Mercury Mag., 1978-92, The Universe in the Classroom Newsletter, 1985-92, Astronomy Education Review, 2002—; assoc. editor: The Planetarian, 1986-88. Bd. dirs. Bay Area Skeptics, San Francisco, 1982-91. Recipient award of merit Astron. Assn. No. Calif., 1980, award Astron. League, 1993, Klumpke-Roberts award, 1994, Annenberg Found. prize in astronomy edn., 1994, Carl Sagan prize for sci. popularization, 2002; Asteroid 4859 named Asteroid Fraknoi, 1992. Fellow Calif. Acad. Scis.; mem. AAAS (astronomy sect. com. 1988-92), Am. Astron. Soc. (astronomy edn. adv. bd. 1988-2004), Astron. Soc. Pacific, Am. Assn. Physics Tchrs., Nat. Assn. Sci. Writers. Avocations: music, astronomy, science, literature. Office: Foothill Coll Dept Astronomy 12345 El Monte Rd Los Altos CA 94022-4504 E-mail: fraknoi@fhda.edu.

FRALEY, DONALD GREGORY, health facility administrator; b. Ironton, Ohio, June 7, 1954; s. Donald William and Josephine Lowe Fraley; m. Janet Lee Farley, Sept. 5, 1950; 1 child, Whitney Erin. B in criminal justice, Kennedy Western U., 2003, MBA, 2005. Trooper Ky. State Police, Boyd Co., Ky., 1983—89; security inspector Dept. Energy, Piketon, Ohio, 1989—93; owner, CEO DJW Enterprises, Russell, Ky., 1993—; asst. dir. Kings Daughters Hosp., Ashland, Ky., 2000—01; dir. King's Daughters Hosp., 2001—. Bd. mem. FIVCO Add Dist., Boyd County, Ky., 1999—, Boyd Greeup C. of C., Boyd, Ky., 2000—. Author: Can Hospital Owned Primary Care Clinics Turn a Profit?, 2005; contbr. articles various profl. jours. Councilman City of Russell, Russell, Ky., 1995—98, mayor, 1999—. Sgt. E-5 USAR, 1989—96. Decorated Airborn Wings U.S. Army, Army Achieve. medal U.S. Army, Sec. of Army; named Class Pres., Ky. State Police Acad., 1983; recipient Commanders award, Combat Med. Sch. Ft. Sam Houston, 1982, Honor Grad., Basic Tng., Ft. Jackson, SC, 1982, Honor Grad., Combat Engrs. Acad., Ft. Knox, 1986, U.S. Dept Energy Security Acad., 1989. Fellow: Am. Coll. Med. Practice Exec. Republican. Avocation: woodworking. Home: 40 Bittersweet Ct Flatwoods KY 41139 Office: Kings Daughters Med Ctr 2201 Lexington Ave Ashland KY 41101 Office Phone: 606-327-4670. E-mail: don.fraley@kdmc.net.

FRALEY, F. RONALD, lawyer; b. Steubenville, Ohio, Dec. 16, 1931; s. Floyd Emerson and Anna Margaret Fraley; m. Nancy Naylor, June 6, 1958; children: Ronald, Douglas, Gregory, Mitchell, Anne Marie. BA, Kenyon Coll., Gambier, Ohio, 1953; JD, U. Mich., 1958. Bar: Fla. 1958. Ptnr. Shackleford Farrior Stallings & Evans, Tampa, Fla., 1958-91; founder, ptnr. Fraley & Fraley, Tampa, 1991—. Sgt. USMC, 1953-55. Fellow Am. Coll. Trial Lawyers; mem. ATLA, Fla. Bar Assn., Acad. of Fla. Trial Lawyers, Univ. Club, Palma Ceia Golf and Country Club (bd. dirs. 1985), Commerce Club (pres. 1979). Avocations: golf, reading. Home: 1914 S Wykagyl St Tampa FL 33629 Office: Fraley and Fraley 501 E Kennedy Blvd #1200 Tampa FL 33602

FRALEY, ROBERT T., biotechnologist; b. Danville, Ill. m. Laura Fraley; children: Steven, Devin, Katherine. BS in Biology, U. Ill., 1974, PhD in Microbiology/Biochemistry, 1978; postgrad., Northwestern U., 1991. Post-doctoral fellow U. Calif., San Francisco, 1979—80; co-pres. agrl. sector Monsanto Co., St. Louis, 1980—2000, exec. v.p., chief tech. officer, 2000—. Contbr. articles to profl. jours. Named Man of the Year, Progressive Farming mag., 1995; recipient Nat. Medal Tech., 1998, Nat. Award for Agrl. Excellence in Sci., Nat. Agri-Marketing Assn., 1995, Kenneth A. Spencer award, 1995. Fellow: Am. Assn. for Advancement of Sci. Achievements include development of part of the team that developed the world's first practical system to introduce foreign genes into crop plants and development of insect-and-herbicide-resistant plants. Avocations: skiing, gardening, tennis. Office: Monsanto Co 800 N Lindbergh Blvd Saint Louis MO 63167-0001*

FRALINGER, JACK BRUCE, surgeon; b. Balt., Dec. 7, 1967; s. Jack Martin and Audrey Ann Fralinger; m. Ona Lynn Streitberger, Aug. 14, 1999; children: Bethany Cohnheim, Emma Cohnheim, Dandro George, Jackson William. BS in Zoology, BA in History, U. Nev., 1992; MD, U. Minn., 1996. Resident in surgery Swedish Med. Ctr., Seattle, 1996—99; physician Indian Health Svc., Neah Bay, Wash., 2001, N.E. Wash. Med. Group, Colville, Wash., 2001; resident in surgery Waterbury Surg. Residency, Conn., 2001—. Mem.: ACS, AMA, Assn. Am. Indian Physicians. Avocations: travel, cooking, hiking, hunting.

FRAM, FORD ERIC, music educator, assistant principal; b. Cleveland, Mar. 24, 1959; s. Forrest Fram Fram and Edwina Ann Ford; m. Janice Leigh Minerd, Nov. 15, 1997; children: Bradford Lee, Tyler Jacob. MusB in Music Edn., Grove City Coll., Pa., 1981; MA in Ednl. Adminstrn., Ursuline Coll., Pepper Pike, Ohio, 2003. Cert. tchg. music K-12 Ohio, Pa., adminstr. lic. Ohio, 2004. Music specialist Notre Dame Elem., Chardon, Ohio, 1984—2000, Mayfield Middle Sch., Ohio, 2000—01, Holy Name Elem. Sch., Cleveland, 2002—; music chmn. Benedictine HS, Cleveland, 2001—. Pres. Chagrin Valley Rotary, Rotary Internat., Chagrin Falls, Ohio, 1989, 1993. Mem.: Music Educator's Nat. Conf. Avocations: music, golf, photography, woodworking.

FRAME, ELISABETH JACKSON, librarian; d. Edwin Lafayette and Ruby Re Jackson; m. Edwin Alexander Frame, Feb. 20, 1982; children: Emilee Lauren, Elise Rachelle. BA with honors, U. Tex., 1977; MA with highest honors, St. Mary's U., 1984. Dir. presch. ministries Alamo City Christian Fellowship, San Antonio, 1988—98; tchr. English Alamo City Christian Acad., 1998—99, tchr. sci., 1999—2001; libr. San Antonio Christian Schs., 2000—. Adj. instr. U. Tex., San Antonio, 1987; cons. Gospel Light Pubs., Ventura, Calif., 1993—; online tutor AOL.com, San Antonio, 1998—2003; moderator Yahoo.com, 2005. Foster parent Buckner Bapt. Benevolences, San Antonio, 1985—88; tchr. Sunday sch. Wayside Chapel, 1999—. Republican. Baptist. Avocations: gardening, backgammon, reading. Office: San Antonio Christian Schs 19202 Redland Rd Bldg A San Antonio TX 78259 E-mail: fourefs@sbcglobal.net.

FRAME, NANCY DAVIS, lawyer; b. Brookings, S.D., Dec. 13, 1944; m. J. Davidson Frame, Mar. 28, 1970 (div. Oct. 1994); 1 child, Katherine Adele; m. Kelly C. Kammerer, Oct. 2, 1999. BS, S.D. State U., 1966; MA, Georgetown U., 1968, JD, 1976. Bar: D.C. 1976. Atty., advisor AID, Washington, 1976-81, asst. gen. counsel, 1981-86; dep. dir. Trade and Devel. Agy., Washington, 1986-99. Bd. dirs. Daktronics, Inc. Recipient Superior Honor award AID, 1984, Presdl. Meritorious Rank award, 1993, Disting. Alumnus award S.D. State U., 1998, Presdl. Disting. Rank award, 1998; Fulbright fellow, 1966, NDEA fellow, 1967. Address: Chemin de la Bernarde Route de Lorgues 83300 Draguignan France Personal E-mail: ndframe@hotmail.com.

FRAME, TED RONALD, lawyer; b. Milw., June 27, 1929; s. Morris and Jean (Lee) F.; m. Lois Elaine Pilgrim, Aug. 15, 1954; children: Kent, Lori, Nancy, Owen. Student, UCLA, 1946-49; AB, Stanford U., 1950; LLB, 1952. Bar: Calif. 1953. Gen. agri-bus. practice, Coalinga, Calif., 1953—; sr. pntr. Frame & Matsumoto and predecessor, Coalinga, 1965—. Trustee Baker Mus.; dir. West Hills Coll. Found. Mem. ABA, Calif. Bar Assn., Fresno County Bar Assn., Kings Co. Bar Assn., Am. Agrl. Law Assn., Coalinga C. of C. (past pres.), Masons, Shriners, Elks. Avocations: bicycling, hiking. Home: 1222 Nevada St Coalinga CA 93210-1239 Office: 201 Washington St Coalinga CA 93210-0895 Office Phone: 559-935-1552. Business E-Mail: lawfirm@lightspeed.net.

FRAMIL, ARMANDO RAMON, pharmaceutical executive; b. Aug. 12, 1948; came to U.S., 1960, naturalized, 1976; s. Armando and Maria Araceli (Fernandez) F.; m. Maria Del Carmen Rodriguez, May 12, 1977 (div. 2002); children: Carolynne, Carmen Victoria BA, Fla. Atlantic U., 1972; MEd, U. Miami, 1977. Counselor Office Youth Svcs. Fla. State Dept. Health and Rehab. Svcs., 1973-77; supr. City of Miami Police Dept., 1977-79, spl. projects mgr., 1979-80; sr. bus. developer internat. sect. City of Miami Dept. Trade and Commerce Devel., 1980-82; profl. rep. Merck, Sharp & Dohme divsn. Merck & Co., Inc., West Point, Pa., 1982-92, exec. rep., 1990-92, sr. hosp. rep., 1984—. Mgr. dist. sales Astra U.S.A. Inc., Westborough, Mass., 1992-95; sr. regional mktg. mgr. Simon & Schuster Tech. Group (a Viacom Co.), San Diego, 1995-98; pres., founder, dir. sales and mktg. A+ Techs. Corp., Miami, 1998-2000; sr. exec. clin. specialist Neuro Health Divsn., Glaxo-Smithkline, Inc., Rsch. Triangle Pk., 2000—. Assoc. inventor, patentee oscillating cutting mechanisms. Bd. dirs. Dade County Youth Adv. Bd., 1979-84; mem. Dade County Latin Substance Abuse Task Force, 1976, Drug Abuse Trust Fund, 1977-78; chmn., founder Coral Way Crime Prevention Subcouncil, 1988-91; vice-chmn. Miami Police Dept. Crime Prevention Coun., 1988-89, chmn., 1989-90; pres., founder Miami Rds. Neighborhood Civic Assn., 1986-2002; mem. Dade County Dem. Exec. Com., 1989-92; trustee Greater Miami C. of C., 1997, mem., 1999; trustee Miami-Dade One Comty. One Goal Edn. Com., 1997-2000, English Ctr. Edn. Excellence Coun., 1997-99; active Dade County Pub. Schs. Multilingual Task Force, 1997, Dade County One Comty. One Goal Edn. Com., 1997—. With USCG Aux., 1996—. Mem. Merck, Sharp & Dohme V.P.'s Club, Mary Brickell's Garden Club (founder, treas. 1990), Invest Learning Summit Club (100% Club 1997, Glayo Smith Kline Winner's Cir., 2002, 03). Home: 260 Woodcrest Rd Key Biscayne FL 33149-1320 Office: Glaxo Smith Kline Inc Neuro Health Divsn Research Triangle Park NC 27709 Personal E-mail: aframil@bellsouth.net.

FRAMME, LAWRENCE HENRY, III, political organization administrator, lawyer; b. Louisville, Oct. 8, 1949; s. Lawrence Henry and Margaret Gertrude (Hayes) F.; m. Frances Claire Schwacke, Dec. 27, 1969; children: Jessica Marie, Lawrence Henry IV, Benjamin Hayes. BA, Centre Coll., 1971; JD cum laude, Washington and Lee U., 1974. Bar: Va. 1974, U.S. Dist. Ct. Va., 1974, U.S. Ct. Appeals (4th cir.) 1974. Assoc. McGuire, Woods & Battle, Richmond, Va., 1974-81, Lacy & Baliles, Richmond, 1981-82; mem. firm, dir. Mezzullo, McCandlish & Framme, Richmond, 1982-90; sec. econ. devel. (gov's. cabinet) Commonwealth of Va., 1990-92; chmn. Virginians for Progress Found., 1992; v.p. LeClair, Ryan, Joynes, Epps & Framme, Richmond, 1992-95; prin. Framme Law Firm, 1995—; co-chmn. gov's. adv. coun. Workforce 2000, 1990-91. Chmn. Dem. Party Va., 1986-90, 2001-03. Va. State Bd. Cmty. Colls., mem. 1987-90, chmn. 1989-90; bd. visitors Va. Commonwealth U., 1992-96; mem. bd. dirs. Downtown YMCA, 1986-95, chmn. 1992-94; bd. dirs., sec. Va. Biotech. Rsch. Park Authority, 1991-92, 93-95, 2002-04, Va. Biotech. Rsch. Park Corp., 1994-2002, Leadership Metro Richmond, 1991-94; bd. dirs., legal advisor Richmond Urban League, 1985-86; mem. bd. dirs. Metro Richmond YMCA, 1995-2000. Recipient Legal award Housing Opportunities Made Equal, Richmond, 1983; named Alumni of Yr., Leadership Metro Richmond, 1990. Mem. ABA, VSB, Va. Bar Assn., Richmond Bar Assn., Omicron Delta Kappa. Roman Catholic. Office: Framme Law Firm PC 2812 Emerywood Pky Ste 220 Richmond VA 23294-3539 Home: 2420 Hanover Ave Richmond VA 23220 Business E-Mail: lframme@frammelaw.com.

FRAMPTON, PAUL HOWARD, physics researcher, educator; b. Kidderminster, Eng., Oct. 31, 1943; came to U.S., 1968; naturalized citizen, 1989; s. Harold Albert and Grace Elizabeth (Howard) Frampton; m. Anne-Marie Frampton, 1993. BA, U. Oxford, Eng., 1965, MA, DPhil, U. Oxford, Eng., 1968, DSc, 1984. Rsch. assoc. U. Chgo., 1968-70; fellow CERN, Geneva, 1970-72; vis. prof. Bielefeld (Germany) U., 1972, 99, Syracuse U., 1972-75; vis. assoc. prof. UCLA, 1975-77; vis. scholar Harvard U., Cambridge, Mass., 1978-81; from asst. prof. physics to prof. U. N.C., Chapel Hill, 1981-96; disting. prof. physics The Louis D. Rubin Jr., 1996—. Vis. prof. U. Tex., fall 1983, Boston U., 1986-87, U. d'Aix-Marseille, 1993, CERN, 1996, 98, 2000, 2003, Perimeter Inst., 2005; chmn. steering com. Workshops on Grand Unification, 1980-89; chmn. organizing com. 1st workshop U. N.H., 1980, 3d workshop, U. N.C., 1982, 10th and last workshop U. N.C., 1989; symposium chair 8th Internat. Symposium on Particles, Strings and Cosmology, U. N.C., 2001 Author: Dual Resonance Models, 1974, 2d edit., 1986, Gauge Field Theories, 1986, 2d edit., 2000, Festschrift: The Launching of La Belle Epoque of High Energy Physics and Cosmology, 2004; editor books in field; contbr. more than 350 articles to profl. jours., also chpts. to books. Gov.'s project dir. for supercollider in N.C., 1987. Fellow AAAS, Am. Phys. Soc., Brit. Inst. Physics. Achievements include research in high-energy theoretical physics including particle phenomenology, string theory and theoretical cosmology. Home: 101 Cedar Ridge Way Durham NC 27705 Office: U NC Dept Physics And Astromony Chapel Hill NC 27599-0001 Office Phone: 919-962-7207. Business E-Mail: frampton@physics.unc.edu.

FRAN, GRANDMA See BROWN, FRANCES

FRANCAVILLA, DONNA T., journalist; b. Camden, N.J., Dec. 4, 1960; d. Lelio and Aurora (DeVuono) Ciccotelli; m. Thomas Louis Francavilla, May 29, 1957; children: Michael, Lisa, Jessica, Gregory. BS, Emerson Coll., Boston, 1985. Talk show prodr. WWDB-FM Talkradio, Phila., 1980-81; desk asst., prodn. asst. KYW Newsradio 1060 AM, Phila., 1981-82; talk show prodr. WRKO-AM, Boston, 1982-85; news anchor radio network Internat. Media News, Washington, 1986-88; program dir., news dir. Westinghouse WPGC AM & FM, Washington, 1988-90; traffic reporter Metro Traffic Control, Phila., 1990-92; news anchor, all news radio WINZ-AM, Miami, 1993-94; news reporter NBC, WVTM-TV, Birmingham, Ala., 1996—99; radio corr. CBS Radio News, 1999—; freelance reporter/anchor Radio Ala., Alabaster; contbr. Westwood One's Am. in the Morning Program, 1999—; freelancer reporter, 2002—; freelance reporter Agy. France Presse, Washington, 2000—, CBS News Path, 2003—, Am. Urban Radio Networks, 2003—, Voice of Am. Owner Frankly Speaking Comm., LLC; participant RIAS German Journalist Exch. Program, 1999; freelance writer Birmingham Mag., 1999; news reporter APTV Ala. Pub. TV, Montgomery, 1999. Freelance wire svc. reporter Agy. French Press, 2000—. V.p. Greystone Ladies Club, Birmingham, 1995 Mem. Jefferson County Med. Alliance; public rels. dir., Jefferson County Med. Alliance. Roman Catholic. Avocations: exercising, dance, skiing, cooking, writing. Home: 5079 Greystone Way Birmingham AL 35242-6456 Office Phone: 205-243-1233. E-mail: franklyspeaking101@hotmail.com.

FRANCE, JOSEPH DAVID, financial analyst; b. Smithville, Mo., July 24, 1953; s. Raymond Hughes and Bonnie Lee (Cavin) F; m. Priscilla L. Gilbert; 1 child, Lucille Terrell. BS in Pharmacy, U. Kans., 1977, MBA, 1980. Chartered fin. analyst. Staff pharmacist U. Kans. Med. Ctr., Kansas City, 1977-80; securities analyst First Nat. Bank Chgo., 1980-82, Smith Barney, Harris Upham & Co., Inc., N.Y.C., 1982-86, mng. dir., 1986-93; 1st v.p. Merrill Lynch, N.Y.C., 1993-95; sr. v.p. Dillon, Read & Co., 1995-96; dir. CS First Boston, N.Y.C., 1996—2003; mng. dir. Banc Am. Securities, 2003—. Mem. Am. Soc. Health-Sys. Pharmacists, N.Y. Soc. Securities Analysts, Assn. for Investment Mgmt. and Rsch. Republican. Avocations: reading, writing. Office: Banc America Two International Pl 24th Fl Boston MA 02110 Office Phone: 617-856-8820.

FRANCE, NEWELL EDWIN, retired health facility administrator; b. Massillon, Ohio, Sept. 30, 1927; s. Lawrence Joel and Marcella Ruth (Nelson) F.; m. Eve Elisabeth Voluter, 1953; children: Philip J., Corinne E., Anne-Claire I., Stephen C., Louise A. BS, Northwestern U., 1953, MS in Hosp. Adminstrn, 1955. Adminstrv. resident Herrick Meml. Hosp., Berkeley, Calif., 1954-55; evening supt. Chgo. Wesley Meml. Hosp., 1955-56; asst. adminstr. St. Lukes Episcopal and Tex. Children's hosps., Houston, 1956-58, assoc. adminstr., 1958-64, adminstr., 1964-73, exec. dir., 1973-83; pres. emeritus Tampa Gen. Hosp., Fla., 1983-91, 91—; pres. Patrick Philbin & Assocs., Austin, 1993—; cons. Hok Architecture, 1995—. Assoc. adminstr. Tex. Heart Inst., Houston, 1958-64, adminstr., 1964-73, exec. dir., 1973-83; cons. adv. council HEW and NIH; staff cons. AID, 1969—; cons. program projects rev. com. Nat. Inst. Neurol. and Communicative Disorders and Stroke; mem. com. pediatrics NRC-Nat. Acad. Scis., 1975—; chmn. Greater Houston Hosp. Coun., Children's Hosps. Execs. Council, 1972-73; dir. Child Care Center, Tex. Med. Ctr., 1967—; adj. assoc. prof. Sch. Architecture, Rice U.; prof. health scis. Tex. Women's U. Bd. dirs. Met. Houston chpt. Nat. Found. March of Dimes, First City Bank Med. Center; trustee Pin Oaks Charity Horse Show Assn., Houston Bot. Soc.; mem. exec. bd. South Main Center Assn., Inc.; active Houston/Baku Sister City Assn. Served with USNR, 1946-48, 51-52. Fellow Am. Coll. Hosp. Adminstrs.; mem. Am. Hosp. Assn., Tex. Hosp. Assn. (chmn. coun. hosp. auxs. 1969-73, trustee 1972—, adviser, chmn. coun. on profl. svc. 1976—), Houston Area Hosp. Assn. (pres. 1968-69), Nat. Assn. Childrens Hosps. and Related Instns. (pres. 1969-70, conf. chmn. 1969, trustee 1971—, chmn. coun. past pres.'s 1973-74), Am. Assn. Hosp. Planning, Statutory Teaching Hosps. Coun. (Fla.) (chmn. 1988-91). Clubs: Rotary Internat; Doctors (Houston). Methodist. Home: 6609 Coolglen Dr Dallas TX 75248-2902

FRANCE, OLIN KENNETH, JR., psychologist; b. Miami Beach, Fla., Feb. 22, 1949; s. Olin Kenneth and Eva (Center) F.; m. Mary Duncan, Aug. 16, 1969; 1 child, Micah Duncan. BA, Wake Forest U., 1971; MS, Fla. State U., 1973, PhD, 1975. Lic. psychologist, Pa.; registrant Nat. Register of Health Svc. Providers in Psychology. Asst. prof. Francis Marion Coll., Florence, S.C., 1975-78; prof. Shippensburg (Pa.) U., 1978—; ind. practice of psychology SC, 1975—, 1975—. Coord. Pa. Summer Acad. Advancement Coll. Tchg., 1999-2005, Ann. Conf. Advancement Coll. Tchg. and Learning, Pa. State Sys. Higher Edn., 2001-03; tng. coord. Warm Line, Carlisle, Pa, 2004—. Author: Crisis Intervention, 1982, 4th edit., 2002, Body Conditioning, 1985, The Hospital Patient, 1987, Basic Psychological Skills, 1993, Helping Skills for Human Service Workers, 1995, 2d edit., 2006. Recipient Salute to Teaching, Shippensburg U. and the Pa. State Sys. of Higher Edn., 1990, Excellence Tchg. award Pa. Soc. Tchg. Scholars, 1999; named Vol. of Yr. New Hope Online, 2001. Mem. APA, Pa. Psychol. Assn., Am. Assn. Suicidology. Office: Shippensburg U Psychology Dept 1871 Old Main Dr Shippensburg PA 17257-2299

FRANCES, RICHARD JOSEPH, psychiatrist; b. N.Y.C., Mar. 3, 1946; s. Joseph and Julia (Levy) F.; 1 child, Jenny. BA, Columbia U., 1967; MD, NYU, 1971. Diplomate Am. Bd. Psychiatry and Neurology (added qualifications in addiction psychiatry, 1992). Resident and chief resident in psychiatry Albert Einstein Sch. Medicine, Bronx, N.Y., 1971-74, instr. in psychiatry, 1976; asst prof. New York Hosp., Cornell, White Plains, 1976-83; assoc. prof. psychiatry N.Y. Hosp., White Plains, 1983-86; prof. clin. psychiatry N.J. Med. Sch., Newark, 1986—; pvt. practice N.Y.C., 1976—; CEO, pres., med. dir. Silver Hill Hosp., New Canaan, Conn., 1997—. Vice chmn. residency tng., 1986-93, AIDS grant review com. Nat. Inst. Drug Abuse; vice chair Coun. on Addiction Psychiatry; dir. psychiatry Hackensack Med. Ctr., 1993-97; mem. faculty NYU, 1997—. Author: Concise Guide to Addiction Treatment, 1989; editor: Self Assessment in Psychiatry, 1986, Clinical Textbook of Addictive Disorders, 1991, 2d edit., 1998. Lt. comdr. USN, 1974-76. Fellow Am. Coll. Psychiatrists (Commr. 1998), Am. Psychiat. Assn. (chmn. com. on alcoholism 1990); mem. Am. Acad. Psychiatrists on Alcoholism and Addictions (founding pres. 1985), Am. Assn. Gen. Hosp. Psychiatrists, Coun. on Addiction Psychiatry, Am. Bd. Psychiatry and Neurology Addiction (psychiatry exam. com.) Home: 208 Valley Rd New Canaan CT 06840-3812 Office: 510 E 86th St Apt 1D New York NY 10028-7547 also: 200 E End Ave Apt 9B New York NY 10128-7891

FRANCESCONI, LEONARD G., JR., training services executive, retired military officer; At, So. Conn. State Coll. Cert. tng. mgr./dir. Langevin, 2005, surface warfare specialist USN, master tng. specialist USN. To rank of sr. chief petty offr. U.S. Navy, 1972—93; ret., 1993; sr. tng. cons. Acterna (formerly TTC), 1993—2002; bus. tng. mgr. Nextel Comm., 2002—. Decorated 3 Achievement medals USN. Address: 130 Pembroke Ln Falling Waters WV 25419

FRANCESCONI, LOUISE L., electronics executive; b. Calif., Mar. 1953; BA, Scripps Coll., 1975; MBA, UCLA, 1978. With Hughes Missile Systems Co., 1976—98, pres., 1996—98; sr. v.p., dep. gen. mgr. def. systems Raytheon Co., Tucson, 1998—99, v.p., gen. mgr. missile systems, 1999—2002, v.p., pres. missile systems, 2002—. Mem. Ariz. Gov.'s Coun. on Innovation and Tech., 2003—; nat. bd. advisors Eller Coll. Bus. and Pub. Adminstrn., U. Ariz.; bd. trustees Tucson Med. Ctr. Healthcare, Tucson Airport Authority.

FRANCH, RICHARD THOMAS, lawyer; b. Melrose Park, Ill., Sept. 23, 1942; s. Robert and Julia (Martino) Franch; m. Patricia Staufenberg, Apr. 18, 1971 (dec. Apr. 1994); children: Richard T. Jr., Katherine J.; m. Susan L. Rice, Sept. 1, 1995. BA cum laude, U. Notre Dame, 1964; JD, U. Chgo., 1967. Bar: Ill. 1967, U.S. Dist. Ct. (no. dist.) Ill. 1967, U.S. Ct. Appeals (7th cir.) 1971, U.S. Supreme Ct. 1980, U.S. Ct. Appeals (3d and 8th cirs.) 1981, U.S. Ct. Appeals (2d cir.) 1984, U.S. Dist. Ct. (no. dist.) Wis. 1989, U.S. Ct. Appeals (6th cir.) 1991, U.S. Tax Ct. 1994, U.S. Ct. Appeals (9th cir.) 1997, U.S. Ct. Appeals (4th cir.) 2003. Assoc. Jenner & Block, Chgo., 1967-68, 70-74, ptnr., 1975—. Former mem. Ill. Supreme Ct. Rules Com. Served to capt. U.S. Army, 1968—70. Decorated Bronze Star. Fellow: Am. Coll. Trial Lawyers; mem.: Am. Law Inst. Office: Jenner & Block Ste 4600 One IBM Plz Chicago IL 60611 Office Phone: 312-923-2965. Personal E-mail: dickfranch@aol.com. Business E-Mail: rfranch@jenner.com.

FRANCHINI, ROXANNE, bank executive; b. NYC, Mar. 20, 1951; d. Tullio and Jean (Brady) Franchini. Student, Emerson Coll., Ricker Coll., New Sch. Social Rsch. With Princess Marcella Borghese divsn. Revlon, NYC, 1972-73, TWA Airlines, 1973-74; asst. to pres. NY Shipping Assn., NYC, 1974-79; benefits mgr. Kidde, Inc., NYC, 1979-83; 2d v.p. pension trust fin. svcs. Chase Manhattan Bank, N.A., NYC, 1983-85, v.p. mgr. global securities, 1985-89; v.p., sales dir. global custody worldwide securities svcs. Citibank, NYC, 1989-91; v.p. Mellon Bank, Pitts., 1991—2001; 1st v.p. Mellon Fin. Corp., Pitts., 2002—05, Phila., 2005—. Chair fin. local fund raising campaigns. Mem.: So. Assn. Coll. and Univ. Bus. Offices, Ea. Assn. Coll. and Univ. Bus. Offices, Nat. Assn. Coll. and Univ. Bus. Offices. Home: 1415 Ocean Shore Blvd Ormond Beach FL 32176-3673 Office Phone: 215-553-4398.

FRANCIOSA, ANTHONY (ANTHONY PAPALEO), actor; b. NYC, Oct. 28, 1928; s. Anthony and Jean (Franciosa) Papaleo; m. Rita Thiel, 1970; children: Christopher, Marco, Nina. Ed. high sch., N.Y.C.; studied drama with Joseph Geiger; scholarship Dramatic Workshop, New Sch. Social Rsch.; studied Actor's Studio. Worked with drama groups including Off Broadway, Inc., N.Y. Repertory Theatre; internat. tour Grand Hotel, 1990-91, Love Letters, 1992-95; appeared in Broadway prodns. End as a Man, 1953, Wedding Breakfast, 1954-55, A Hatful of Rain, 1955 (Tony award nomination 1956, Daniel Blum's Theatre World award for best leading actor 1956, Acad. award nomination 1957); motion pictures include A Face in the Crowd, 1957, This Could Be the Night, 1957, Long Hot Summer, 1958, Naked Maja, 1959, Career, 1960 (Golden Globe award), Story on Page One, 1960, Go Naked in the World, 1960, Senilita, 1961, Period of Adjustment, 1962, Assault on a Queen, 1966, A Man Could Get Killed, 1966, The Swinger, 1966, Fathom, 1967, A Man Called Gannon, 1968, The Sweet Ride, 1968, In Enemy Country, 1968, Across 110th Street, 1972, Ghost in the Noonday Sun, 1973, The Drowning Pool, 1975, Firepower, 1979, The World is Full of Married Men, 1979, Death Wish II, 1982, Soot gli occhi dell'Assassino, 1982, Tenebrae, 1983, Avitami ai Sognare, 1984, La Cicala, 1985, Death House, 1988, La Morte e di Mona, 1990, Backstreet Dreams, 1990, Double Threat, 1992, City Hall, 1995; TV mini-series: Aspen, 1974, Wheels, 1975; movies for TV: Fame Is the Name of the Game, 1970, Earth II, 1971, The Deadly Hunt, 1974, Hide and Go Seek, 1975, The Catcher, 1976, This Is the Week That Was, 1977, Sideshow, 1979, The Black Widow, 1980, Matt Helm, 1982, Till Death Do Us Part, 1983, Stagecoach, 1987, Ghost Writer, 1990; star TV series Valentine's Day, 1964-65, The Name of the Game, 1968-72, Search, 1972-73, Matt Helm, 1975-76, Finder of Lost Loves, 1984-85; narrator A Lincoln Portrait with St. Louis Symphony Orch., 1971, conducted by Andre Previn. Recipient Count Volpe Di Misurata cup Venice Film Festival for Hatful of Rain, 1958, Critics Outer Circle award, 1956, Goledn Globe award for best motion picture actor in drama for film Career, World Foreign Press, 1960.

FRANCIOSA, JOSEPH ANTHONY, health care consultant; b. Easton, Pa., Apr. 24, 1936; s. Joseph and Letitia Beatrice (Cascioli) F.; m. Antonietta Battistoni, Feb. 8, 1964 (div. 1972); m. Barbara Ann Neilan, Aug. 3, 1973 (div. 1989); 1 child, Christopher David; m. Robin J. McGarry, Oct. 4, 1999. BA, U. Pa., 1958; MD, U. Rome, 1963. Diplomate Am. Bd. Internal Medicine; lic. in Pa., Md., Ark. Intern USPHS Hosp., S.I., N.Y., 1964-65; resident Washington Hosp. Ctr., 1967-69; cardiology fellow VA Hosp.-Georgetown U., Washington, 1969-71; chief ICU Va. Hosp., Washington, 1971-73; asst. prof. medicine Georgetown U. Med. Sch., 1971-73, assoc. dir. cardiovascular tng. program, 1974-75; dir. CCU Va. Hosp., Mpls., 1974-76; asst. prof. medicine U. Minn., Mpls., 1977-79; chief cardiology VA Hosp., Phila., 1979-82; assoc. prof. U. Pa., Phila., 1979-82. Adj. prof. 1987-98; adj. prof. medicine Mt. Sinai Med. Sch., N.Y.C., 1989—, Cornell U. Coll. Med., N.Y.C., 1999—; dir. cardiology div. U. Ark., Little Rock, 1982-86; prof., 1982-86; dir. cardio-renal drugs ICI Americas Inc., Wilmington, Del., 1986-88; v.p. R&D Zambon Corp., East Rutherford, N.J., 1988-90; exec. dir. med. affairs Ciba-Geigy Pharm., Summit, N.J., 1990-91; exec. dir. med. svcs. Ciba-Geigy, 1992-95; health care/pharm. cons., N.Y.C., 1995—. Contbr. numerous articles to med. jours. Mem. med. rsch. com. Am. Heart Assn., Mpls., 1976-79, Phila., 1981-82. Lt. comdr. US Pub. Health Svc., 1965—67. VA grantee, 1974-84, U. Ark. grantee, 1982-83, NIH grantee 1985-86. Fellow ACP, Am. Coll. Cardiology, Am. Coll. Chest Physicians (chmn. hypertension com. 1981-83, gov. Ark. 1984-86), Am. Heart Assn. (circulation coun. 1978—, coun. high blood pressure rsch. 1982—, clin. cardiology coun. 1984, bd. dirs. N.J. affiliate 1994-98); mem. Am. Soc. Clin. Pharmacology and Therapeutics (vice chmn. cardiopulmonary com. 1981-89), Assn. Univ. Cardiologists, Am. Acad. of Pharm. Physicians (charter mem. v.p. publs. com. 2002-2004), Heart Failure Soc. Am. Avocations: computers, physical fitness. Office Phone: 212-721-3030. E-mail: josephafranciosa@aol.com.

FRANCIS, BETTY J., minister; b. Manning, S.C., May 4, 1949; d. Myrtle Louise and James Francis; 1 child, Emily Robinson. M in Theological Studies, Evangel Ctr. Religious Studies, 1994, D in Ministry, 1996. Cert. christian counselor 2001. Employment counselor Broward Employment & Tng. Adminstrn., Ft. Lauderdale, Fla., 1976—95. Pastoral care counselor Atlantic Shores Hosp., Wackenhut Corp., Ft. Lauderdale, 1998—. Pres. Justice for All in Broward, Ft. Lauderdale, 2000—02; bd. dirs. Atlantic Shores Hosp., Wackenhut Corp., Ft. Lauderdale, 1998—2002; mem. ethics com. Florida Med. Ctr., Ft. Lauderdale, 1996—2002. Named Black Female Clergy of Yr., Am. Assn. Negro Bus. & Profl. Women, 1998. Mem.: Gospel Announcers Guild of the Gospel Music Workshop of Am. (v.p. South Fla. guild 2001—02), Am. Assn. Christian Counselors, Joint Coll. African-Am. Pentecostal Bishops' Congress. Pentecostal. Avocations: travel, movies, cooking, crafts. Office: Cathedral Of Praise Worship Ctr 4035 SW 18th St Hollywood FL 33023 Office Phone: 954-961-5962. Office Fax: 954-961-5514. E-mail: drfrancis@minister.com.

FRANCIS, CAROLYN RAE, music educator, musician, author, publisher; b. Seattle, July 25, 1940; d. James Douglas and Bessie Caroline (Smith) F.; m. Barclay Underwood Stuart, July 5, 1971. BA in Edn., U. Wash., 1962. Cert. tchr., Wash. Tchr. Highline Pub. Schs., Seattle, 1962-64; musician Olympic Hotel, Seattle, 1962-72; 1st violin Cascade Symphony Orch., 1965-78; tchr. Bellevue (Wash.) Pub. Schs., 1965-92; founder Innovative Learning Designs Strategies for Music Edn., Mercer Island, Wash., 1984-96. Profl. violinist for hotels, restaurants, TV, recs., mus. shows, 1962-85; violist Eastside Chamber Orch., 1984-86; pvt. tchr. string instruments, 1959-96; spkr., presenter in-svc. workshops, convs., music educators numerous cities, U.S., Can., London, 1984-96; adjudicator music festivals; instr. Music Instrument Digital Interface applications for educators, 1992-96, also related activities. Author-pub. Music Reading and Theory Skills (curriculum series), Levels 1, 2, 3, 4, 1984-2000; contbr. articles to profl. jours. Mem. Snohomish Indian Tribe. Bellevue Schs. Found. grantee, 1985-86, 86-87, 89-90; scholar U. Wash., 1959-62, We. Wash. State Coll., 1958-59; named Wash. All-State Orch., 1958. Mem. NEA, Am. String Tchrs. Assn. (regional mem. chmn. 1992-94), Music Educators Nat. Conf., Music Industry Coun., Nat. Sch. Orch. Assn. Avocations: hiking, travel, reading, sewing, sketching. Office: Innovative Learning Designs LLC 10900 NE 8th St Ste 900 Bellevue WA 98004-4448 E-mail: cfrancis@musicreading.com.

FRANCIS, CHARLES ANDREW, agronomy educator, consultant; b. Monterey, Calif, Apr. 12, 1940; s. James Frederick and G. Louise (Epperson) F.; m. Barbara Louise Hanson, June 23, 1962; children: Todd (dec.), Kevin, Andrea, Karen. BS, U. Calif., Davis, 1961; MS, Cornell U., 1967, PhD, 1970; DSc honoris causa, Helsinki U., 1999. Dir., maize breeder Internat. Ctr. for Tropical Agr., Cali, Colombia, 1970-72, dir., bean agronomist, 1973, dir. small farm systems, 1974-75, rsch. agronomist, 1976-77; prof. U. Nebr., Lincoln, 1977—, dir. Morocco project, 1982-84; dir. internat. program Rodale Inst., Emmaus, Pa., 1984-85. Agronomist US AID, Botswana, Liberia, Uganda, Malawi, Morocco, Senegal, Tanzania, 1978-94, World Bank, Colombia, So.Am., 1980; dir. Ctr. Sustainable Agr. Sys., 1990-2000; bd. dir., sec. The Land Inst., Salina, Kans., 1990—; cons. OTA, Rockefeller Found., FAO/UN, 1978—. Editor: Multiple Cropping Sys., 1986; co-editor: Sustainable Agr., 1990, Crop Improvement for Sustainable Sys., 1993; contbr. chpt. to books and numerous articles to profl. jour. Cubmaster Cub Scout Pack 20, Lincoln, 1978-81; mem. ch. bd. Unitarian Universalist Ch., Lincoln, 1987-89; bd. dirs., v.p. sch. bd. Colegio Bolivar, Cali, 1973-77. 1st lt. U.S. Army, 1961-63. Recipient Agr. Stewardship award, Sustainable Agr. Soc., 1997, 7th Generation Rsch. award, Ctr. for Rural Affairs and CSARE, 2000. Fellow Am. Soc. Agronomy (divsn. chair 1968-70, Robert E. Wagner award for Efficient Agr. 1992, fellow), Internat. Svc. in Agronomy, 2002, Crop Sci. Soc. Am., 1992; mem. Phi Kappa Phi, Phi Beta Delta, Gamma Sigma Delta, Alpha Zeta. Democrat. Avocations: bicycling, camping, jogging, reading, travel, organic. Office: U Nebr 225 Keim Hall Lincoln NE 68583-0910

FRANCIS, CHARLES GORDON, entrepreneur, writer; b. Murdo, S.D., July 31, 1924; s. John Russell and Constance Abby (Bottum) F.; m. Barbara Klipper Francis, June 15, 1949; children: Abby Constance, Paul Erwin. BA, UCLA, 1949. Reporter United Press, L.A., 1949-50; mem. pub. rels. staff Santa Barbara (Calif.) Coll., 1950-53, UCLA, 1953-57; comms. exec. IBM Corp., L.A., 1957-61, Armonk, N.Y., 1961-88; founder, owner IdeaBank, Inc., Rye, N.Y., 1988—. Contbr. articles to profl. publs. Pres. PTA, Chappaqua, N.Y., 1969. Staff sgt. U.S. Army, 1943-46. Mem. Assn. Nat. Advertisers (dir. 1982-88), Internat. Advt. Assn. (dir. 1982-88). Office: IdeaBank Inc 5025 Theall Rd Rye NY 10580 E-mail: francis@idea-bank.com.

FRANCIS, CHARLES K., medical educator; b. Newark, May 24, 1939; BA, Dartmouth Coll., 1961; MD, Jefferson Med. Coll., 1965. Med. intern Phila. Gen. Hosp., 1965—66; med. resident Boston City Hosp., Tufts U., 1969—70; clin. fellow cardiology Tufts Circulation Lab., 1970—71; clin. and rsch. fellow cardiology Mass. Gen. Hosp., 1971—72, sr. med. resident, 1972-73; chief cardiac catheterization lab. divsn. cardiology Martin Luther King Jr. Gen. Hosp., L.A., 1973—74, chief cardiology divsn., 1974—77; dir. cardiology divsn. Mt. Sinai Hosp., Hartford, Conn., 1977—80; assoc. dir. hypertension svc., assoc. prof. medicine, dir. cardiac catheterization lab. Yale Med. Sch., Hartford, Conn., 1980-87; dir. dept. medicine Harlem Hosp. Ctr., N.Y.C., 1987—98; prof. clin. medicine Columbia U. Coll. Physicians and Surgeons, 1987—98; pres. Charles R. Drew U. Med. and Sci., 1998—. Clin. instr. medicine Sch. Medicine Tufts U., 1970—71; tchg. fellow Harvard Med. Sch., 1971—72, clin. fellow, 1972—73; asst. prof. medicine Charles R. Drew Postgrad. Med. Sch. & Sch. Medicine U. Calif., 1973—75; asst. prof. medicine, dir. Burgdorf Hypertension Clin., Med. Sch. U. Conn., 1977—80; mem. cardiac adv. com. Nat. Heart, Lung & Blood Inst., NIH, 1977—79; asst. prof. medicine Sch. Medicine Yale U., 1980—81, assoc. prof., 1981—87; pres. Am. Coll. of Physicians, 2004—05. Fellow: ACP, Am. Coll. Cardiology; mem.: Assn. Black Cardiologists (chmn. bd. 1994—), Am. Heart Assn., Am. Fedn. Clin. Rsch., Inst. Medicine-NAS. Address: Charles Drew U Med & Sci 1621 E 120th St Los Angeles CA 90059-3025

FRANCIS, CLINTON WILLIAM, law educator; b. Wanganui, New Zealand, Aug. 29, 1951; s. Raymond and Jean (Dickie) F.; m. Steffani Weiss, May 29, 1982. LL.B. with honors, Victoria U., Wellington, New Zealand, 1973, LL.M. with honors, 1978; S.J.D., U. Va., 1982. Bar: New Zealand 1975. Jr. lectr. Victoria U. Law Sch., 1974-75; assoc. in law U. Calif., Berkeley, 1977-78; asst. prof. Northwestern U. Sch. Law, Chgo., 1978-82, assoc. prof., 1982-84, prof., 1984—. Contbr. articles to profl. jours. Victoria U. sr. scholar, 1974; DuPont fellow U. Va., 1975-77; Fulbright grantee, 1975-78; recipient Robert Childres award for teaching excellence Northwestern U., 1984; Walter Meyer Research grantee ABA, 1984. Home: 415 W Surf St Chicago IL 60657-6142 Office: Northwestern U Sch Law 357 E Chicago Ave Chicago IL 60611-3059 Office Phone: 312-503-6484. E-mail: cwfrancis@law.northwestern.edu.*

FRANCIS, CONNIE L., retired secondary education educator; b. Bellevue, Ohio, July 19, 1940; d. Edward and Viola (Kreh) Dick; divorced; children: Cynthia, Kelli, Scott. BS in Edn., Bowling Green State U., 1961; MS in Edn., Kearney State Coll., 1969; MA in Edn., U. Nebr., 1989. Tchr. Tiffin (Ohio) Pub. Schs., 1961-64, Old Fort (Ohio) Pub. Schs., 1964-65, Kearney Pub. Schs., 1965-97; lectr. U. Nebr., Kearney, 1985-2000. Judge speech & drama Nebr. Sch. Activities Assn., 1965—. Avocations: reading, writing, travel. Home: 9707 N 156th St Bennington NE 68007

FRANCIS, EDWARD D., architect; b. Cleve., Aug. 15, 1934; s. Michael and Anna (Buchinsky) F.; m. Betty-Lee Seydler, Aug. 25, 1956 (div. 1982); children— Tameron, Theron; m. Lynne Marie Merrill, Sept. 6, 1984. B.Arch, Miami U., 1957. Draftsman, designer David Maxfield, Oxford, Ohio, 1953-59; draftsman Austin Co., Cleve., summers 1954, 56; designer Meathe, Kessler & Assoc., Grosse Pointe, Mich., 1959-68; prin. William Kessler & Assoc., Detroit, 1968—, pres., 1985-95, Kessler Assoc. Inc., 1995-99; CEO Kessler/Francis/Cardoza Architects, 1999—2004; prin. Gunn Levine Archs., Detroit, 2004—. Mem. archtl. adv. com. Ferris State U., Big Rapids, Mich. Chmn. Franklin Village Hist. Commn., Mich., 1971-79; pres. Friends of Capitol, Lansing, 1984-85, State Hist. Preservation Rev. Bd., 1984-94. Fellow AIA (Gold medal Detroit and Mich. chpts.); mem. Frank Lloyd Wright Found., Frank Lloyd Wright Preservation Trust, Nat. Trust for Hist. Preservation, Mich. Hist. Preservation Network (Lifetime Achievement award 2001), Gabriel Richard Hist. Soc. (bd. dirs.). Office: Gunn Levine Archs 726 Lothrop Detroit MI 48202 Office Phone: 313-873-3868. Business E-Mail: edwardf@gunnlevine.com.

FRANCIS, JAMES CLARK, IV, federal judge; b. Tulsa, Okla., Oct. 3, 1952; s. James C. and F. Ruth Francis; m. Elizabeth Bradford, Aug. 19, 1978; children: Nathaniel, Jeremy. BA, Yale Coll., 1974, JD, 1978; M of Pub. Policy, Harvard U., 1978. Bar: NY 1979, US Dist. Ct. (so. dist.) NY 1979, US Dist. Ct. (ea. dist.) NY 1980, US Ct. Appeals (2nd cir.) 1980. Law clk. Hon. Robert L. Carter, NYC, 1978-79; staff atty. Legal Aid Soc., NYC, 1979-85; U.S. Magistrate judge U.S. Dist. Ct. (so. dist.) N.Y., NYC, 1985—; chief magistrate judge US Dist. Ct. (So. Dist.) NY, NYC, 1998—2000. Adj. prof. Fordham Law Sch., 2003—. Author: (chpts.) Moore's Federal Practice, 1997; curator exhibit Discreet Persons Learned in Law, 1995, Thou Shald Not Ration Justice, 2001. Mem. profl. adv. bd. Epilepsy Inst.,NYC; bd. dirs. Port Washington (NY) Soccer Club. Mem. NY State Bar Assn. (jud. com. 1989—), Assn. Bar of City of NY (fed. cts. com. 1995-98). Democrat. Avocations: travel, scuba, sports, coaching soccer. Office: Daniel P Moynihan US Courthouse Rm 1960 500 Pearl St New York NY 10007-1312

FRANCIS, JAMES DELBERT, oil industry executive; b. Orange, N.J., Jan. 8, 1947; s. Delbert Matthew and Margaret Janet F.; m. Shirley Ann Waters; children: Elizabeth M., John A., David S., Virginia a., Grace A., J. Thornley. BS in Commerce, U. Va., 1970; JD, U. Fla., 1973. Bar: Fla. 1973. Ptnr. Smith and Hulsey, Jacksonville, Fla., 1973-82; exec. v.p. Charter Oil Co., Fla., 1982-83, pres., 1983-86; chmn., CEO Ray Distbg. Co., 1987—; ptnr. First Coast Energy, LLP, 1997—. Bd. dirs. Petro Distbg., Inc. Bd. dirs., chmn. Children's Home Soc., Jacksonville, 1976-2003; elder St. Johns Presbyn. Ch., 1985—; pres. CHS Found., Inc., 2000-03; trustee Riverside Presbyn. Day Sch., 2001-02; bd. trustee The Bolles Sch., 2005-; bd. dirs. Seamark Ranch, Christian Healing Ministries, 2004-. Mem. ABA, Fla. Bar, Jacksonville Bar Assn., Fla. Yacht Club, River Club (Jacksonville), Timuquana Country Club. Republican. Home: 4284 Mcgirts Blvd Jacksonville FL 32210-4368 Address: First Coast Energy LLP 7014 A C Skinner Pkwy Ste 290 Jacksonville FL 32256-6940

FRANCIS, JAMES STEPHEN, JR., psychology professor, psychologist; b. Norwalk, Conn., Sept. 29, 1945; s. James Stephen and Elaine Fiske Francis; m. Sandra Maria Eisworth, Oct. 18, 1951; children: James Stephen III, Grover Magee. BA, U. Miami, 1969, MS, 1972, PhD, 1975. Instr. lab U. Miami, Coral Gables, 1970—75; rsch. assoc. Miami Heart Inst., Miami Beach, 1974—76, VA Hosp., Columbia, SC, 1976—77; asst. prof. U. Houston, 1977—80; prof. San Jacinto Coll., 1989—. Adj. asst. prof. Alvin Coll., Tex., 1980—89. Contbr. articles to profl. jours. Mem.: APA, Psi Beta (faculty advisor 1998—2005), Phi Delta Theta (pres. 1967—68). Democrat. Roman Catholic. Achievements include development of Internet Psychology Courses. Avocations: tennis, jogging, travel, teaching, reseach. Home: 2319 Colleen Dr Pearland TX 77581 Office: San Jacinto Coll 13735 Beamer Rd Houston TX 77089 Office Phone: 281-484-1900. Home Fax: 281-485-6993; Office Fax: 281-929-4693. Personal E-mail: jfphd@sbcglobal.net. Business E-Mail: james.francis@sjcd.edu.

FRANCIS, KAREN, painter, television producer; b. Memphis, Apr. 27, 1950; BA in Comm. Arts, Rhodes Coll., 1971; MA, U. Mo., 1973. Cert. tchr., Tenn. Secondary sch. tchr. Memphis City Schs., 1971-72; speech tchr. U. Ga., Athens, 1973-75; dir. computer systems installations Planning Rsch. Corp., McLean, Va., 1976-78; dir. account mgmt. TDX Systems, Cable & Wireless, Vienna, Va., 1978-80; cons. telecommunications MCI, Washington, 1985-87; producer Fairfax Cable Access, Merrifield, Va., 1991-96. Owner Art Promotions, McLean, 1989—. Exhibited paintings in numerous group and one-woman shows and in cyberspace including Mus. Contemporary Art, Washington, 1996, Arts Coun. Fairfax County, Va., 1999, many others; paintings numerous pvt. collections; author screenplay Sisters, 2003. Founder Non-Violence Award Program, 1998; bd mem., vol. several non profit cmty. orgns. Avocations: tennis, bridge, poetry, piano. Office: Art Promotions PO Box 3104 Mc Lean VA 22103-3104 Office Phone: 703-893-7482. E-mail: karen@artpro.com, karenartpro@aol.com.

FRANCIS, KEITH M., graphics designer, artist; b. New Bedford, Mass., May 29, 1965; s. Shelton J. and Madeleine E. Francis. BA, U. Mass., 1989. Graphic designer Purnell Co., Boston, 1991—96; sr. graphic designer Camp Dresser & McKee, Inc., Cambridge, 1996—98; prin. Francis Comm., Boston, 1998—. Commd. works, 2004 Dem. Nat. Conv. Poster (DNC Ofcl. Poster Artist, 2004), Leonard P. Zakim Poster (Leonard P. Zakim Bridge Ofcl. Poster, 2003), publ., (Graphis Poster Ann. 2004, 2004), meml., World Trade Center Meml. Competition (Recogniton award, 2003), exhibitions include Corporate Artist, DeCordova Mus., Space 200 Art Gallery, Firehouse Ctr. for the Arts. Graphic designer Dem. Nat. Com., Boston. Artists grantee, Mass., 1989. Mem.: Am. Inst. Graphic Arts (assoc.). Conservative. Achievements include patents for Electronic Book (US D445, 787S). Home: 183 North St Mattapoisett MA 02739 Office: Francis Comm 398 Columbus Ave #175 Boston MA 02115 Office Phone: 617-529-2958. Personal E-mail: kfrancis@franciscomm.com.

FRANCIS, MARION DAVID, consulting chemist; b. Campbell River, B.C., Can., May 9, 1923; arrived in U.S., 1949; s. George Henry and Marian (Flanagan) F.; m. Emily Liane Williams, Aug. 27, 1949 (dec. 1995); children: William Randall, Patricia Ann; m. Jacqueline S. Lohman, June 14, 1997. BA, U. B.C., Vancouver, 1946, MA, 1949; PhD, U. Iowa, 1953. Instr. U. B.C., Vancouver, Canada, 1946—49; chemist Can. Fishing Co., Vancouver, Canada, 1946; rsch. asst. U. Iowa, Iowa City, 1949—51; rsch. chemist Procter & Gamble Co., Cin., 1952—76, sr. scientist, 1976—85, Norwich Eaton Pharms., Inc., Norwich, NY, 1985-89; rsch. fellow Victor Mills Soc., Cin., 1990-93; cons. Cin., 1993—. Chmn. Gordon Rsch. Conf., N.H., 1968, 79, session chmn., 1985; panel mem. Internat. Conf. on Crystal Deposition and Dissolution in Tissues, Evion, France, 1985; session chmn. workshop, Sienna, Italy, 1992; co-chmn. Bisphosphonate Therapies for Osteoporosis: Today and Tomorrow Symposium, Davos, Switzerland, 1996, chmn. Internat. Conf. on Phosphorus Chemistry, Cin., 1998, others; session chmn. Internat. Congress on Arts and Comms., Lisbon, Portugal, 1999, Washington, 2000, Cambridge, Eng., 2001, Vancouver, B.C., 2002, Dublin, 2004, Honolulu, 2005; spkr. and lectr. in field Contbr. articles to sci. jours.; patentee in field. Dist. chmn. Cin. United Appeal, 1956-60. Recipient Profl. Accomplishment award Tech. and Sci. Socs. Cin., 1979, Tech. Innovation award Victor Mills Soc., 1990, Perkin medal Soc. of Chem. Industry, 1996, Disting. Alumnus Achievement award U. Iowa Carver Coll. Medicine, 2003; U.S. Pub. Health predoctoral fellow, 1951-52. Fellow AAAS, Am. Inst. Chemists; mem. Am. Soc. Bone and Mineral Rsch., Am. Chem. Soc. (program chmn. ctrl. regional meeting 1983, invited symposium spkr. nat. meeting 1987, 92, invited awards symposium spkr. 1994, Cin. Chemist of Yr. award 1977, Nat. Indsl. Chemist award 1994, Morley medal 1996, Heros of Chemistry award 2000), Am. Coll. Rheumatologists, Dance Club (pres. 1972-73), Wyo. (Ohio) Sunday Supper Club (pres. 1998-99, 2003-04). Republican. Roman Catholic. Home and Office: 23 Diplomat Dr Cincinnati OH 45215-2074 Office Phone: 513-772-3940. Personal E-mail: mfrancis3@cinci.rr.com.

FRANCIS, MARY FRANCES VAN DYKE, real estate executive, editor; b. Sedalia, Mo., Nov. 17, 1925; d. Frank B. and Mary Irene (Sims) Van Dyke; m. Harold E. Francis, Apr. 23, 1944 (div. 1980); children: David Eugene, Lois Irene Valero, Roland Wayne, Eric Brian. Student, Ctrl. Mo. State Coll. Tchr. grade sch. Pettis County, Mo., 1943-44; timekeeper Montgomery Ward & Co., Kansas City, Mo., 1944-45; instr. new operators Southwestern Bell Telephone Co., Independence, Mo., 1945-47; real estate salesman Russell Realtors, Independence, 1958-66; owner Mary Francis, Realtor, Independence, 1967—. Exec. sec., editor Ea. Jackson County Bd. Realtors, 1962-68; exec. asst., pub. rels. dir., editor Kansas City Realtor, 1968-71; mktg. asst. South Ctrl. region Chgo. Title Ins. Co., Kansas City, 1971-75; pres. Maranco, Inc., 1975-; v.p. Raintree Lake Realty, 1980-83. Contbr. articles to profl. jours. Cub Scout den mother Boy Scouts Am. Recipient Outstanding Svc. award Ea. Jackson County Bd. Realtors, 1964, Salesmanship award, 1965, CPW Real Estate Exch. award, Expo, 1983. Mem. Nat. Assn. Real Estate Bds. (charter pres. Greater Kansas City chpt., gov., pres. Mo. Women's Coun.), Mo. Real Estate Assn. (Spkrs. Bur.), Soroptimist (past pres.), Metro Kansas City Assn. Realtors (life), Mo. Assn. Realtors (life). Address: PO Box 1158 Independence MO 64051-0658

FRANCIS, MERRILL RICHARD, lawyer; b. Iowa City; children: Kerry L., David M., Robin A. BA magna cum laude, Pomona Coll., 1954; JD, Stanford U., 1959. Bar: Calif. 1960, Supreme Ct. 1970. Ptnr. Sheppard, Mullin, Richter & Hampton, L.A., 1959-00, of counsel, 2001—. Mem. Fellows of Contemporary Art, 1980—. Served to lt. (j.g.) U.S. Navy, 1954-56. Fellow Am. Bar Found., Am. Coll. Bankruptcy (chmn. 9th cir. admissions coun. 1992-95, bd. dirs. 1995—, chair bd. regents 1995-01); mem. ABA (bus. law sect., chmn. secured creditors com. 1981-85, chmn. bus. bankruptcy com. 1986-89, chmn. Task Force on Fed. Ct. Structure 1990-93, mem. Coun. Bus. Law sect. 1991-95, chmn. ad hoc com. on brown bag programs 1994-97, chmn. ad hoc com. bankruptcy ct. structure and insolvency process com. 2001-, sr. lawyers divsn., chmn. sr. housing and real estate practice com. 2001—), State Bar of Calif. (mem. debtor/creditor and bankruptcy com. of bus. law sect. 1978-79), L.A. County Bar Assn. (mem. real property sect., exec. com. 1970-80, mem. comml. law and bankruptcy sect., sect. chmn. 1976-77), Fin. Lawyers Conf. (bd. govs. 1970—, pres. 1972-73), La Canada-Flintridge C. of C. and Cmty. Assn. (pres. 1971-72), Order of the Coif, Jonathan Club, Phi Beta Kappa. Office: Sheppard Mullin Richter & Hampton 333 S Hope St Fl 48 Los Angeles CA 90071-1406 E-mail: mfrancis@smrh.com.

FRANCIS, NORMAN C., academic administrator; b. Lafayette, La., Mar. 20, 1931; s. Joseph Abel and Mabel F.; m. Blanche MacDonald, June 6, 1955; children: Michael, Timothy, David, Kathleen, Patrick, Christine. BA, Xavier U. of La., 1952; JD, Loyola U., New Orleans, 1955; EdD (hon.), Villanova U., 1969; LLD (hon.), Holy Cross Coll., 1969, Seton Hall U., 1969, St. Michael's Coll., 1972, Marquette U., 1977. Dean of men Xavier U. of La., New Orleans, 1957-63, dir. student pers. svcs., 1963-64, asst. to pres. for student affairs, 1964-65, asst. to pres. for devel., 1965-67, exec. v.p., from 1968, pres., 1968—. Trustee Coll. Entrance Exam. Bd., 1972-76, chmn., 1976-78. Commr. New Orleans Civil Svc. Commn., 1969-76; former pres. Urban league New Orleans; former chmn. New Orleans Aviation Bd.; mem. Pontifical Peace & Justice Commn., 1977. Office: Xavier U of La Office of President 1 Drexel Dt New Orleans LA 70125-1056*

FRANCIS, NORMAN CHARLES, physicist; b. Rochester, N.Y., Nov. 27, 1922; s. Morris Jacob and Jennie Pearl (Levy) F.; m. Beverly Ruth Cohen, May 31, 1947; children: Cynthia Lynn Gensheimer, Karen Ann Maher, Martha Joan Fischer. BA in Physics, U. Rochester, 1947, PhD in Physics, 1952. Rsch. asst. physics dept. Ind. U., Bloomington, 1952-55; rsch. scientist GE, Schenectady, NY, 1955-93, Lockheed Martin, Schenectady, NY, 1993—94. Adj. prof. Rensselaer Poly. Inst., Troy, N.Y., 1994—; guest scientist MIT, Cambridge, Mass., 1960-61 With USN, 1944-46. Fellow Am. Nuclear Soc. (chmn. reactor physics div. 1972, chmn. northeastern N.Y. sect. 1968); mem. Am. Phys. Soc. Democrat. Jewish. Home: 1323 Ruffner Rd Niskayuna NY 12309-2505 Office: Rensellaer Poly Inst Inst Mech Aeorspace and Nuc Troy NY 12180 Business E-Mail: francis@rpi.edu.

FRANCIS, PETER JAMES, physician, ophthalmologist; b. Walton, Surrey, United Kingdom, Aug. 7, 1968; s. Colin and Sylvia Francis; m. Beth Edmunds, Dec. 13, 1997; 1 child, William James. BSc with hon., U. Southampton, 1991; MD, U. Southampton Med. Sch., 1992; PhD, U. Coll. London, 2000. Fellowship Royal Coll. Ophthalmologists (London), 1996, cert. completion higher surg. tchg. Specialist Med. Tchg. Authority (UK), 2003, registered Specialist Register Gen. Med. Coun. (UK), 2003. House physician Southampton Hosp., England, 1992—93, sr. house physician, 1994—96, Walton Hosp. Neurosurgery, Liverpool, England, 1993—94, Taunton Somerset Hosp., England, 1994—94; specialist registrar King's Coll. Hosp., 1996—97, cons. sr. lectr., 2004—; specialist registrar Kent Canterbury Hosp., England, 1997—98, Moorfields Eye Hosp., London, 1998—2000, fellow, 2002—03; specialist registrar Sussex Eye Hosp., Brighton, 2000—01; specialist registrar and fellow St Thomas' Hosp., London, 2000—02; cons. sr. lectr. St Thomas Hosp., 2004—; fellow Casey Eye Inst., Portland, Oreg., 2003—04, asst. prof., 2005—; cons. sr. lectr. U. London, 2004. Grant bd. mem. Brit. Coun. Prevention Blindness, 2004—. Contbr. Trends in Genetics Jour., Nature Genetics Med. Jour., Human Molecular Genetics Jour., Am. Jour. Human Genetics;, author over 50 med. rsch. publ., over 80 rsch. presentations. Recipient Best Young Med. Rschr., BUPA Found., UK, 2003; grantee Project grant, Wellcome Trust, UK, 2000, Rsch. grant, Collins Med. Trust, USA, 2003, Brit. Eye Rsch. Found., UK, 2004, rsch. grant, Guide Dogs for the Blind Assn., UK, 2004; scholar Travelling scholarship, European Union, 2000, Travelling Scholarship, TFC Frost Charitable Trust, London, UK, 2001. Fellow: Royal Coll. Ophthalmologists (Fould's Trophy Best Ophthalmology Rsch. 2002, Traveling Scholarship 2001); mem.: Med. Soc. London. Achievements include patents for Human gene therapy advance, US Patent number: 60/539, 857; research in Understanding genetic causes of human cataract; First gene identified for age-related macular degeneration. Office: Casey Eye Inst 3375 SW Terwilliger Blvd Portland OR 97239 Office Phone: 503-494-7890.

FRANCIS, PHILIP HAMILTON, management consultant; b. San Diego, Apr. 13, 1938; s. William Samuel and Ruth Kathryn (Allison) F.; m. Regina Elizabeth Kirk, June 10, 1961 (div. May 1971); m. Diana Maria Villarreal, July 15, 1972; children: Philip Scott, Edward Philip, Mary Allison, Kenneth Joseph. BSME, Calif. Poly. State U., 1959; MSME, U. Iowa, 1960, PhD in Engrng. Mechanics, 1965; MBA in Mgmt., St. Mary's U., San Antonio,

1972. Registered profl. engr., Tex. With Douglas Aircraft Co., Santa Monica, Calif., 1960-62, S.W. Rsch. Inst., San Antonio, 1965-79; prof., chmn. dept. mech. and aerospace engring. Ill. Inst. Tech., Chgo., 1979-84; with Indsl. Tech. Inst., Ann Arbor, Mich., 1984-86; dir. advanced mfg. tech. Motorola Inc., Schaumburg, Ill., 1986-88; corp. v.p. Square D Co. (Schneider-N.Am.), Palatine, Ill., 1988-94; client ptnr. AT&T Solutions, AT&T, Chgo., 1995-96; mng. ptnr. Mascon Global, Ltd., Schaumburg, Ill., 1996—2002; pres. Group Francis, LLC, Georgetown, Tex., 2001—. Adj. prof. engring. Northwestern U., 2003—. Mem. various indsl. and acad. adv. bds. Recipient Gustas Larson award ASME and Pi Tau Sigma, 1978 Fellow ASME; mem. Soc. Mfg. Engrs., Sigma Xi, Tau Beta Pi, Pi Tau Sigma. Roman Catholic. Avocation: writing. Office Phone: 512-868-9568. Business E-Mail: phil@groupfrancis.com.

FRANCIS, PHILIP L., retail executive; Grad., U. Ill., Ind. U. Corp. v.p. wholesale Roundy's, Pewaukee, Wis.; sr. leadership positions Cardinal Health, Jewel Cos.; pres., COO Shaw's Supermkts., E. Bridgewater, Mass., 1991-98; pres., CEO PETsMART, Inc., Phoenix, 1998—, chmn. Mem. Greater Phoenix Leadership. Office: PetsMart 19601 N 27th Ave Phoenix AZ 85027*

FRANCIS, RON, professional hockey player; b. Sault Ste Marie, Ont., Can., Mar. 1, 1963; Center Hartford Whalers (now Carolina Hurricanes), 1981—91, Pitts. Penguins, 1991-98, Carolina Hurricanes, 1998—2004, Toronto Maple Leafs, 2004—. Player NHL All-Star game, 1983, 85, 90, 96. Recipient Frank J. Selke Trophy, 1995, Lady Byng Trophy, 1995, 1998, 2002, King Clancy Memorial Trophy, 2002, Stanley Cup Champion, 1991, 1992. Office: c/o Toronto Maple Leafs 40 Bay St, Ste 400 M5J 2X2 Toronto ON Canada

FRANCIS, SAMUEL TODD, columnist; b. Chattanooga, Apr. 29, 1947; s. Todd Ware and Julia (Ford) F. BA, Johns Hopkins U., 1969; MA, U. N.C., 1971, PhD, 1979. Policy analyst Heritage found., Washington, 1977-81; legis. asst. U.S. Senator John P. East, Washington, 1981-86; editl. writer Washington Times, 1986-87, dep. editl. page editor, 1987-91, acting editl. page editor, 1991, columnist, 1991-95; pres. Ctr. for Nat. Rsch., Alexandria, Va., 1995—. Author: Soviet Strategy of Terror, 1981, Power and History: The Political Thought of James Burnham, 1984, rev. edit., 1999, Beautiful Losers: Essays on the Failure of American Conservatism, 1994, Revolution from the Middle, 1997, America Extinguished, 2002; contbg. editor Chronicles: A Mag. of Am. Culture, Rockford, Ill., 1987-2003, polit. editor, 2003—; editor-in-chief Citizen's Informer; assoc. editor Occidental Quarterly, 2001. Nat. bd. dirs. Coun. of Conservative Citizens, 1995—. Recipient Disting. Editl. Writing award Am. Soc. Newspaper Editors, 1988, 89. Mem. The Phila. Soc. (bd. dirs. 1989-93), The John Randolph Club, Phi Kappa Psi. Office: PO Box 19627 Alexandria VA 22320-0627 Office Phone: 703-683-2372.

FRANCIS, STEVE, professional basketball player; Profl. basketball player Houston Rockets, 1999—2004, Orlando Magic, 2004—; owner We R One Clothing. Named to NBA All-Star Game, 2002—04. Office: c/o Orlando Magic 8701 Maitland Summit Blvd Orlando FL 32810

FRANCIS, THEO, reporter; BS in Journalism, Univ. Ill., Urbana-Champaign, 1994; MS in Journalism (with honors), Columbia Univ., NYC, 1997. Wash. bur. intern Chgo. Tribune, 1994—95; reporter-photog. Petersburg Pilot, Alaska, 1995—96; tech. prod. support asst. Publication Svcs. Inc, Champaign, Ill., 1996; mcpl. reporter Daily Record, Morris Co., NJ, 1997—98; bus. writer Ark Democrat-Gazette, Little Rock, 1998—2000; staff writer Wall St. Journal, Dallas, 2000, NYC, 2001—. Co-recipient George B. Polk award for econ. reporting, 2005; recipient First place, hist. features, Alaska Press Assn., 1995, First place, pub. svc. reporting, NJ Press Assn., 1998, First place, health-related topics, Ark. AP Mng. Editors Assn., 1998, First place, health-related topics; third place, bus. reporting; third place, svc. to freedom of info., 1999, Outstanding New Journalist award, Ark. Soc. of Prof. Journalists, 1998, Green Eyeshades awards, first place, bus. reporting, Atlanta Soc. Prof. Journalists, 1999. Office: Wall St Journal 200 Liberty St New York NY 10281*

FRANCIS, TIMOTHY DUANE, chiropractor; b. Chgo., Mar. 1, 1956; s. Joseph Duane and Barbara Jane (Sigwalt) F. Student, U. Nev., 1974—80, We. Nev. C.C., 1978; BS, L.A. Coll. Chiropractic, 1982, DC magna cum laude, 1984; postgrad., Clark County C.C., 1986—; MS in Bio/Nutrition, U. Bridgeport, 1990. Diplomate Internat. Coll. Applied Kinesiology, Am. Acad. Pain Mgmt., Am. Naturopathic Med. Bd.; cert. kinesiologist, applied kinesiology tchr.; lic. chiropractor, Calif., Nev. Instr. dept. recreation and phys. edn. U. Nev., Reno, 1976-80; from tchng. asst. to lead instr. dept. principles & practice L.A. Coll. Chiropractic, 1983-85; pvt. practice Las Vegas, 1985—. Asst. instr. Internat. Coll. Applied Kinesiology, 1990, chmn. exam review com., 1993, chmn. syllabus review com., 1994; adj. faculty The Union Inst. Coll. of Undergrad. Studies, 1993; joint study participant Nat. Olympic Tng. Ctr., Beijing, China, 1990. Mem. editl. rev. bd. Alternative Medicine Rev., 1996; contbr. articles to profl. jours. including Internat. Coll. Applied Kinesiology. Charles F. Cutts scholar, 1980. Fellow Internat. Acad. Clin. Acupuncture, British Inst. Homeopathy (homeopathy diploma 1993); mem. Am. Chiropractic Assn. (couns. on sports injuries, nutrition, roentgenology, technic, and mental health), Nev. State Chiropractic Assn., Nat. Strength and Conditioning Assn., Gonsted Clin. Studies Soc., Found. for Chiropractic Edn. and Rsch., Internat. Chiropractors Assn., Internat. Coll. Applied Kinesiology, Internat. Fedn. Practitioners Natural Therapeutics, Nat. Inst. Chiropractic Rsch., Nat. Strength and Conditioning Assn., Am. Naturopathic Med. Assn., Nat. Acad. Rsch. Biochemists, Phi Beta Kappa, Phi Kappa Phi (v.p. 1979-80, Scholar of the Yr. award, 1980), Delta Signa. Republican. Roman Catholic. Avocations: Karate, weightlifting. Home: 2620 Regatta Dr # 102Ste 100 Las Vegas NV 89128 Office Phone: 702-221-8870.

FRANCIS, WALTON JOSEPH, economist; b. Washington, July 19, 1942; s. Robert Joseph and Margaret Karen (Bittner) F.; m. Frances Leiko Enseki, June 9, 1969 (div. May 1988); children: Margaret Misao, Elizabeth Hanako; m. Sarah Willis Wilcox, Sept. 9, 1989. BA with highest distinction, Ind. U., 1963; MA, Yale U., 1964; MPA, Harvard U., 1971, M in Pub. Policy, 1972. Budget examiner Office Mgmt. and Budget, Washington, 1964-70; dir. policy analysis Office of Sec. HHS, Washington, 1972-97; economist, cons., 1997—. Author: CHECKBOOK'S Guide to Health Insurance Plans for Federal Employees, ann. edit., 1979—. Woodrow Wilson fellow, 1964. Mem. Phi Beta Kappa. Home and Office: 5700 Robeys Meadow Ln Fairfax VA 22030-5833 E-mail: waltonjf@aol.com.

FRANCIS, WARREN WILLIAM, retired surgeon, educator; b. NYC, Sept. 10, 1924; Grad., Princeton U., 1944; MD, Columbia U., 1948. Diplomate Am. Bd. Surgery. Intern Lenox Hill Hosp., N.Y.C., 1948-50; resident surgery R.I. Hosp., Providence, 1952-56, surgeon, 1956-97; surg. cons. Women & Infants Hosp., 1986-97; clin. assoc. prof. surgery Brown U., 1983-97, ret., 1997. Med. officer USNR, 1950-52. Fellow ACS; mem. EVS, New Eng. Surge. Soc., NESVS.

FRANCISCO, DORMAN EDWARD, language educator, writer; b. Chattanooga, Feb. 17, 1953; s. Dorman C. and Edna Lucille Francisco; m. Linda Kay Burton, Feb. 5, 1983; 1 child, Gabriel Edward. BA, U. Tenn., 1975, MA, 1980. Instr. English U. Tenn., Knoxville, 1980—90; assoc. prof. English Pellissippi State C.C., Knoxville, 1991—2003, writer-in-residence, 2003—. Author: (novels) The Dealmaker, 2003 (nominee for Pulitzer prize, 2003), Death, Child and Love, 2000 (nominee for Pulitzer prize, 2000), Life Boat; prin. editor The South in Perspective, 2001; co-author (with Michelle Brewer): Book Time for the Family. Co-sponsor Cath. Campus Orgn. of Pellissippi State C.C., 2002—; bd. dirs. World Citizenship Inst., Knoxville, 2002—, Inst. for Christian Spirituality, Knoxville, 2002—. Recipient Nat. Tchg. award, U. Tex.-NISOD, 1995, Excellence in Tchg. award, Pellissippi State C.C., 1995. Mem.: Tenn. Mountain Writers Orgn. (bd. dirs. 1990—96, 2004—). Roman Catholic. Home: 2221 Dawn's Pass Knoxville TN 37919 Office: Pellissippi State Cmty Coll Dept English Knoxville TN Office Phone: 865-694-6744.

FRANCISCO, EDITH GABA, medical/surgical nurse; b. Gattaran, Cagayan, The Philippines, Sept. 16, 1939; came to U.S., 1963; d. Leon and Maria (Manuel) Gaba; m. Pedro R. Francisco, June 27, 1965; children: Perry, Pierre, Eugene. BSN, Philippine Union Coll., 1961. RN, Calif., Ill., Pa. Staff nurse Children's Hosp. Phila., Michael Reese Hosp. & Med. Ctr., Chgo., U. Hosp., San Diego, Community Hosp. Chula Vista (Calif.), Paradise Valley Hosp., National City, Calif. Home: 1036 Dearborn Dr San Diego CA 92154-2156

FRANCISCO, GLEN LEIF, engineer, engineering executive; b. Little Falls, N.Y., Sept. 9, 1953; s. Lawrence Richard Francisco and Beatrice Wilson Love; m. Kimberly Ann Luebbert, Aug. 18, 1979 (div.); children: Melissa Jane, Grant Alan. BS in Aero./Astro Engring., Rensselaer Poly. Inst., 1975; MS in Aero./Astro Engring., MIT, 1977; MBA in Data Processing, Fla. Inst. Tech., 1984. Rsch. asst. MIT, Cambridge, 1975—77; guidance & control engr. MCDonnell Aircraft Co., St. Louis, 1977—80; sys. engr. Martin Marietta, Orlando, Fla., 1980—95; sys. engring. mgr. Tex. Instruments, Dallas, 1995—99; program mgr. Raytheon Comml. Infrared, Dallas, 1999—2004; bus./product devel. mgr. L-3 Comm. Infrared Products, Dallas, 2004—. Home: 424 Sloan Creek Pky Fairview TX 75069 Office: L3 Comm Infrared Products MS 37 13532 N Central Expy Dallas TX 75243 Office Phone: 972-528-1407. Business E-Mail: glen.francisco@L-3Com.com.

FRANCK, FREDERICK SIGFRED, artist, writer, oral surgeon; b. Maastricht, The Netherlands, Apr. 12, 1909; came to U.S., 1939, naturalized, 1945; s. Daniel and Helen (Foyer) F.; m. Claske Berndes Franck, July 15, 1960; 1 son, Lukas van Witsen Franck. Student, U. Amsterdam, 1926-31; Chirurgien Dentiste, Antwerp Dental Sch., 1935; LDS, Royal Coll. Surgeons, Edinburgh, Scotland, 1937; DMD, U. Pitts., 1942, DFA (hon.), 1963; ArtsD (hon.), Mt. St. Mary Coll., 1994. Practice dentistry, London, 1937-39; resident oral surgery U. Pitts., 1942-44; anaesthetist Elizabeth Steel Magee Hosp.; staff Children's Hosp., Pitts., 1942-44; service cons. Netherlands East Indies govt., 1944-46; dentist N.Y.C., 1946-66; vis. staff Albert Schweitzer Hosp., 1958-60. Chief mission Med. Internat. Coop., 1958; research fellow Nanzan U., Nagoya, 1981. Author: Open Wide, Please, 1957, Au Pays de Soleil, 1958, Days with Albert Schweitzer, A Lambarene Landscape, 1959, reissued 1992, (juvenile) My Friend in Africa, 1960, reissued 1995, African Sketchbook, 1961, My Eye is in Love, 1963 (Art Am. 50th Anniversary spl. citation 1963), Au Fil de L'Eau, 1964, Outsider in the Vatican, 1965, Met Het Oog Op Het Vatikaan, 1965, Au Pays Du Soleil, 1965, I Love Life, 1967, Exploding Church, 1968, Open Boek, 1967, Au Fil De L'Eau, 1968, Croquis Parisiens, 1969, Tutte le Strade portano a Roma, 1969, Le Paris de Simenon, 1969, Simenon's Paris, 1970, Tussen Broek en Brooklyn, 1971, The Zen of Seeing, 1973, Pilgrimage to Now/Here, 1973, (play) Inquest on a Crucifixion, 1975, An Encounter with Oomoto, 1975, The Book of Angelus Silesius, 1976, Zen and Zen Classics, 1977, EveryOne, The Timeless Myth of Everyman Reborn, 1978, The Awakened Eye, 1979, Art as a Way, A Return to the Spiritual Roots, 1981, The Buddha Eye, An Anthology of the Kyoto School, 1982, reissued, 2004, The Supreme Koan, Confessions of a Journey Inward, 1982, Messenger of the Heart, The Book of Angelus Silesius, 1982, 2005, De Zen van het Zien, 1983, 92, Echoes from the Bottomless Well, 1985, De Droomzolder--Oog in Oog met Venetie, 1985, Life Drawing Life, 1989, Little Compendium on that Which Matters, 1989, reissued 1993, 2004, To Be Human Against All Odds, 1991, reissued 1996, Zen Seeing, Zen Drawing: Meditation in Action, 1993, Fingers Pointing Toward the Sacred, 1994, The Tao of the Cross, 1996; co-author What Does It Mean to be Human?, 1998, 2000, Beyond Hiroshima, 1999, Watching the Vatican, 2000, Pacem In Terris A Love Story, 2000, Moments of Seeing, 2000, Seeing Venice: An Eye in Love, 2002, A Passion for Seeing, 2003, A Zen Book of Hours, 2003, What Matters, 2004, Ode to the Human Face, 2004, The Icon Reborn, 2005; contbg. editor Parabola Quar.; rsch. editor Nanzan Monograph Series; contbr. articles, drawings to various mags. and periodicals; one-man shows include Contemporary Arts Gallery, Lilienfield Galleries, Passedoit Gallery, Albert Landry Gallery, (all N.Y.C.), 1959-60, Saginaw (Mich.) Mus., Doll & Richards Gallery, Boston, Ringling Mus. Art, M.H. De Young Mus., San Francisco, Waddell Gallery, Far Gallery, both N.Y.C., Foster-White Gallery, Seattle, 1976, U. Puget Sound Gallery, Seattle, 1977, Thorpe Intermedia Gallery, N.Y.C., 1977, The InterFaith Ctr., N.Y.C., 2000, others; shows in Paris, Amsterdam, Geneva, London, Rotterdam, Brussels, Rome, Tokyo, Kyoto, 1971, U. Maine, 1970-72, Melbourne, Australia, 1972, Interchurch Ctr. Gallery, 1972, Greater Middletown Arts Coun., 1973, Far Gallery, 1973, Singer Meml. Mus., The Netherlands, 1986, Pa. State U., 1989, Cathedral of St. John the Divine, N.Y.C., 1993, Albert Schweitzer Ctr., Great Barrington, Mass., 1993, Quinnipiac Coll., Hamden, Conn., 1994, Amber Gallery, Leiden, The Netherlands, 1994, Van Rijn Gallery, Maastricht, The Netherlands, 1994, Oude Kerk, Amsterdam, The Netherlands, 1994, Paul Mellon Arts Ctr. Choate Rosemary Hall, Wallingford, Conn., 1996; touring exhbn. Drawings of Lambarene, Albert Schweitzer's Hospital in Action, 1995, 96, 97, 98, Cathedral of St. John the Divine, N.Y.C., Newark, 1996, Weimar Gallery, Germany, 1999, Vanderbilt Gallery U. Tenn., Interfaith Ctr., N.Y.C., 2000-2001, Rider U., Princeton, 2001, Albert Shahinian Fine Art and Poughkeepsie Art Mus. Galleries, 2003—, Yale Inst. Sacred Music, 2004, The Cathedral of St. John the Divine, 2005, The N.Y. Open Ctr., 2005; group shows include Met. Mus., Whitney Mus., Corcoran Biennale, Indpls. Mus., Mpls. Mus., Nanzan U. Mus., Nagoya, Japan, 1981; represented in permanent collections including M.H. De Young Mus., Fogg Art Mus., San Francisco Mus. U. Ill., Mus. Modern Art, The Vatican, Witherspoon Gallery, Raleigh, N.C., Tokyo Nat. Mus., Nat. Collection Fine Arts, Washington, Santa Barbara, Amsterdam, Eindhoven, Maastricht, N.Y. Pub. Libr., Seattle Mus., Dartmouth Coll., Cornell U., AschenbachFound., Ga. Mus., Whitney Mus., N.Y.U., State Capitol Mus., Wash., Fordham U. Lowenstein Gallery, Roanoke Mus. Fine Arts, Cathedral of St. John the Divine, N.Y.C., U. Nymegen, The Netherlands, U. Pa.,Kans. State U., New Harmony, Ind., Cath. Ctr., Stedelijk Mus., Bonnefanten Mus., Musées Nationaux Français, Nanzan U., Santa BarbaraMus., others; traveling exhbn. to 12 univs. and colls., 1970-72, to The Netherlands and Belgium, 1991, 92; drawing exhbn. Amber Gallery, Leiden, Holland, 1999; built Pacem in Terris Trans-religious Sanctuary, Warwick, N.Y., 1966; steel sculptures commd. Genesis Farm, N.J., 1990, Omega Inst., N.Y., 1991, Pa. State U., 1991, Ch. of Saviour, Washington, 1991, Wainwright House, Rye, N.Y., 1991, Fondacion Elpis, Buenos Aires, 1991, Cath. St. John the Divine, N.Y.C., Bucknell U., Peace Garden, Harrisburg, Pa., Hengelo, The Netherlands, 1993, Sarajevo, 1994, Belgium, 1995, Antwerp, 2003, New Cmty. Corp., Newark, 1995, Choate Rosemary Hall, Wallingford, Conn., 1995, Sequoia, Calif., 1995, Ittoen Found., Kyoto, Japan, 1997, Assisi, Italy, 1999, Dandelion Trust, England, Bosnia, Mt. Saviour, Elmira, NY, 2001, Gannon U., Erie, Pa., 2001, Pitts, 2002, Antwerp, Belgium, Buenos Aires, Devonshire, Eng., San Rafael, Calif., 2003, Megen, Netherlands, Yale U. Inst. for Sacred Music, 2005. Recipient award of Excellence, Chapmen U. and Albert Schweitzer Inst., 1995, purchase prize, U. Ill., Am. Inst. Arts Letters, Living Arts Found., 1st prize Garnegie Inst., prize, Musees Nationaux Francais, medal for drawings, Pope John XXIII, 1963, Revered Citizen award, Orange County, N.Y., 2000, Ruth Bayley Peace award, PeaceLinks, 2000, Disting Citizen award, Warwick, N.Y., 2000, Ut Diligatis Invicem award, Gannon U., 2001, World Citizen award, Nuclear Age Peace Found., Santa Barbara, Calif., 2001, Spirituality and Health award, 2001, Ressurection Cross, Antwerp, Belgium, Buenos Aires, Devonshire, Eng and San Rafael, Calif. Fellow Internat. Inst. Arts and Letters, Soc. for Arts, Religion and Contemporary Culture (dir.), Knighthood Order of Orange Nassau; mem. Artists Equity Assn. (hon. dir. N.Y.), P.E.N. Home: Pacem in Terris 96 Covered Bridge Rd Warwick NY 10990-2854 *I discovered that to defy the general trend towards specialization as a writer, painter, draughtsman, playwright, sculptor, does not mean "to spread oneself thin", is only seemingly a multiple commitment, and is in my case a single-minded obedience to what my very nature bids me to express in any medium I can handle.*

FRANCK, THOMAS MARTIN, law educator; b. Berlin, July 14, 1931; naturalized, 1977; s. Hugo and Ilse (Rosenthal) F. BA, U. B.C., 1952, LLB, 1953, LLD (hon.), 1995; LLM, Harvard U., 1954, SJD, 1956; DHL (hon.), Monterey Inst. Internat. Studies, 2003; LLD (hon.), U. Glasgow, 2004. Asst. prof. law U. Nebr., 1954-56; from assoc. prof. to prof. law NYU, 1960—2002, prof. law emeritus, 2002—, dir. Ctr. Internat. Studies, 1965—2002; judge ad hoc Internat. Ct. Justice, 2001—02. Acting dir. internat. law Carnegie Endowment Internat. Peace, 1973-75, dir., 1975-79; vis. prof. Stanford U., 1963, U. East Africa, 1964, 65, York U., 1972-73, 74-76, U. Calif., San Francisco, 2004; dir. rsch. UN Inst. Tng. and Rsch., 1980-82; cons. U.S. AID Dept. State, 1970-72, 85; constl. adviser govts. Tanganyika, 1963, Zanzibar, 1963, 64, Mauritius, 1965; mem. Sierra Leone Govt. Commn. Legal Edn., 1964, Nat. Liberal Adv. Coun. Can., 1952-53; lectr.in field; vis. fellow Trinity Coll., Cambridge, Eng., 1996-97. Author: Race and Nationalism, 1960, The United Nations in the Congo, 1963, East African Unity Through Law, 1965, Comparative Constitutional Process, 1968, The Structure of Impartiality, 1968, Why Federations Fail, 1968, A Free Trade Association, 1968, Word Politics, 1971, Secrecy and Foreign Policy, 1973, Resignation in Protest, 1975, Control of Sea Resources by Semi-Autonomous States, 1978, Foreign Policy by Congress, 1979, The Tethered Presidency, 1981, Human Rights in Third World Perspective, 1982, Nation Against Nation: What Happened to the U.N. Dream and What the U.S. Can Do About It, 1985, Judging the World Court, 1986, Foreign Relations and National Security Law, 1987, The Power of Legitimacy Among Nations, 1990, Political Questions/Judicial Answers, 1992, Fairness in the International Legal and Institutional System, 1993, Fairness In International Law and Institutions, 1995, The Empowered Self: Law and Society in the Age of Individualism, 1999, Recourse to Force: State Action Against Threats and Armed Attacks, 2002; co-author: U.S. Foreign Relations Law, vols. I-III, 1980-81, vols. IV & V, 1984, Foreign Relations and National Security Law, 2d edit., 1993; editor-in-chief Am. Jour. Internat. Law, 1984-93; editor: Delegating State Powers: The Effect of Treaty Regimes on Democracy and Sovereignty, 2000; co-editor: Internat. Law Decisions in Nat. Cts., 1996. Lt. Can. Army, 1953. Guggenheim fellow, 1973-74, 82-83. Mem. Inst. de Droit Internat., State Dept. Adv. Com. on Internat. Law, Can. Coun. Internat. Law, Assn. Am. Law Schs., Am. Soc. Internat. Law (pres. 1998-2000), Am. Acad. Arts and Scis., Internat. Law Assn. (v.p. U.S. br.), Coun. on Fgn. Rels. Home: 15 Charlton St New York NY 10014-4910 Office Phone: 212-998-6210.

FRANCK, WALTER ALFRED, rheumatologist, medical educator, health facility administrator; b. Shanghai, Sept. 2, 1941; s. August Albert and Hilda Sylvia (Vandamme) F.; m. Linda Ashley Callanen, June 6, 1964; children: Christopher, Patrick, Kevin, Natalee. BA, Yale U., 1960; MD, Columbia U., 1964. Intern U. Mich., Ann Arbor, 1964-65, resident in medicine, 1965-68; fellow in rheumatology Harvard U./Mass. Gen. Hosp., Boston, 1971-73; attending physician in medicine and rheumatology Mary Imogene Bassett Hosp., Cooperstown, N.Y., 1973—, chief of medicine, 1980—; prof. clin. medicine Columbia U., N.Y.C., 1981—, assoc. dean Bassett Healthcare-Coll. Physicians and Surgeons, 1998—. Adj. prof. clin. medicine Rochester (N.Y.) Sch. Medicine, Albany (N.Y.) Sch. Medicine, Hanover, N.Y., SUNY, Syracuse. Contbr. numerous articles to profl. pubs. Trustee, mem. fin. com. St. Mary's Ch., Cooperstown, 1991—. Maj. U.S. Army, 1968-71. Fellow ACP, Am. Coll. Rheumatology. Roman Catholic. Avocations: stamp collecting/philately, gardening, fishing, hiking. Home: 6 Lakeview Dr S Cooperstown NY 13326-3003 Office: Bassett Hosp 1 Atwell Rd Cooperstown NY 13326-1394 Office Phone: 607-547-3110. Business E-Mail: walter.franck@bassett.org.

FRANCKE, LINDA BIRD, journalist; b. NYC, Mar. 14, 1939; d. Samuel Curtis and Janet (King) Bird; m. G.D. Mackenzie, Jan. 12, 1961; 1 son, Andrew Mackenzie; m. Albert Francke III, Oct. 7, 1967; 2 daughters: Caitlin, Tapp. Student, Bradford Jr. Coll., 1958, New Sch. for Social Rsch., 1963—65. Copywriter Young & Rubicam, Inc., N.Y.C., 1960-63, Ogilvy & Mather, Inc., N.Y.C., 1965-67; contbg. editor N.Y. Mag., N.Y.C., 1968-72, 80—; gen. editor Newsweek Mag., N.Y.C., 1972-77; columnist N.Y. Times, 1977—; TV news commentator Spl. Edit., 1978-79. Dir. New Directions; juror Am. Book Awards, 1981; Co-chmn. Writer's Resource Center, Southampton, N.Y. Contbr. (works to anthologies including) The N.Y. Spy, 1967, The Power Game, 1970, Running Against the Machine, 1969, Women: A Book for Men, 1979, Hers: Through Women's Eyes, 1985, America Firsthand, Vol. II: From Reconstruction to the Present, 1994; author: The Ambivalence of Abortion, 1978, Growing Up Divorced, 1983, Ground Zero: The Gender Wars in the Military, 1997; collaborator: First Lady from Plains, 1984, Ferraro: My Story, 1985, A Woman of Egypt, 1987, Daughter of Destiny, 1989, Signature Life, 1998, Life So Far, 2000, On Faith, 2002, On The Road With Francis of Assisi, 2005. Mem. Women's Commn. for Refugee Women and Children, Internat. Rescue Com. Inc.; chmn. East End Choice; candidate N.Y. State Assembly, 2d Dist., 1990; del. to Dem. Nat. Conv., 1992; bd. dirs. Bridgehampton Child Care & Recreational Ctr., Inc., The Retreat. Recipient award Cannes Film Festival, 1969, Nat. Clarion award, 1994; finalist Helen Bernstein Book award Excellence in Journalism, 1998. Mem. Authors Guild, Women's Media Group N.Y.C., Eastville Hist. Soc., Women Mil. Aviators, Inc. E-mail: linda@hamptons.com.

FRANCKE, REND RAHIM, ambassador; b. Baghdad, Iraq, 1949; arrived in U.S., 1981, naturalized, 1987; d. Mahdi Rahim; m. Frederic B. Francke. MA in English, U. Cambridge; MA in French Lit., Sorbonne. Co-founder The Iraqi Found., Washington, 1991—2003, dir., 1991—2003; amb. Iraq Washington, 2003—. Co-author: The Arab Shi'a: Forgotten Muslims, 2000. Office: The Iraq Foundation 1012 14th St NW Ste 1110 Washington DC 20005 Home: 7017 Hector Rd Mc Lean VA 22101-2112

FRANCKE, UTA, medical geneticist, genetics researcher, educator; b. Wiesbaden, Germany, Sept. 9, 1942; arrived in U.S., 1969; d. Kurt and Gertrud Muller; m. Bertold Richard Francke, May 27, 1967 (div. 1982); m. Heinz Furthmayr, July 27, 1986. MD, U. Munich, Fed. Republic Germany, 1967; MS, Yale U., 1985. Diplomate Am. Bd. Pediatrics, Am. Bd. Med. Genetics (bd. dirs. 1981-84). Asst. prof. U. Calif., San Diego, 1973—78; assoc. prof. Yale U., New Haven, 1978—85, prof., 1985—88; prof. genetics Stanford (Calif.) U., 1989—. Investigator Howard Hughes Med. Inst., Stanford, 1989—2000, mem. sci. rev. bd., Bethesda, Md., 1986—88; mem. mammalian genetics study sect. NIH, Bethesda, 1990—94. Profl. advisor March of Dimes Birth Defects Found., White Plains, NY, 1990, Marfan Assn., Port Washington, NY, 1991. Mem.: Am. Soc. Human Genetics (pres. 1999, bd. dirs. Rockville, Md. chpt. 1981—84), Soc. for Inherited Metabolic Disorders, Soc. for Pediatric Rsch., Human Genome Orgn., Inst. Medicine of NAS (assoc.). Avocation: piloting. Office: Stanford U Med Sch Beckman Ctr Stanford CA 94305-5323 Office Phone: 650-725-8089. Business E-Mail: ufrancke@stanford.edu.

FRANCO, CARLO DIAZ, surgeon, anatomist, anesthesiologist; b. Valparaiso, Chile, Nov. 9, 1956; came to U.S., 1985; s. Ismael Segundo and Aida Rosa (Franco-Huerta) Diaz-Labarca; m. Jennifer Ann Leepard, Mar. 31, 1989 (div. May 1993). MD, U. Valparaiso, Chile, 1981. Instr. anatomy Sch. of Medicine Univ. Valparaiso, Chile, 1982; surgery resident U. Valparaiso, Chile, 1982-85; asst. prof. anatomy, surgery Univ. Valparaiso, Chile, 1983-89; vis. prof. anatomy Med. Coll. of Ohio, Toledo, 1985-86, 88-89; surgeon, pvt. practice Valparaiso U. Hosp., Chile, 1986-89; surgery resident Sinai Hosp., Detroit, 1990-91, anesthesiology resident, 1991-94; chmn. orthopedic anesthesia Cook County Hosp., Chgo., 1994—; assoc. prof. anesthesiology and anatomy Rush Med. Coll., Chgo., 2004—, assoc. prof. anatomy, 2004—. Contbr. articles to profl. jours. Grantee WHO, 1985-86, Ednl. Commn. for Foreign Med. Grads., 1988-89. Fellow AMA, Am. Soc. Anesthesiologists, Latin Am. Soc. Regional Anesthesia. Avocations: reading, writing, travel, tennis, ice skating. Home: 419 W Grand Ave # J Chicago IL 60610-4265 Office: Cook Co Hosp Dept Anesthesia 1901 W Harrison St Dept Chicago IL 60612-3785 Office Phone: 312-864-3217. Personal E-mail: carlofra@aol.com.

FRANCO, DON ALVADO, veterinarian; b. Port of Spain, Trinidad, Sept. 27, 1931; arrived in US, 1968; s. Errol George and Esme Rita Franco; m. Joyita Sabater Franco, May 21, 1960; children: Bruce Patrick, Miliza Jane, Audrey Ann. Diploma in agrl., U. Guelph, Canada, 1957; DVM, U. of Philippines, Quezon City, 1964; MPH, Emory U., 1985; diplomate (hon.), Am. Coll. of Vet. Preventative Medicine, 1982; fellow (hon.), Phila. Coll. of Vet. Pub. Health, Philippines, 1999. Inspector in charge U.S. Dept. of Agrl., Richmond,

Va., 1968—76, circuit supr. Montpelier, Vt., 1976—78, asst. regional dir. Atlanta, 1978—87, nat. coord. Wash., DC, 1987—90, dir., slaughter operations, 1990—92; v.p. Nat. Renderers Assn., Alexandria, Va., 1992—2002; pres. Animal Protein Products Industry, Alexandria, 1992—2002; adj. prof. Coll. of Vet. Medicine, Dept. Pathology and Parasitology, Tuskegee U., 1982—91; adj. asst. prof. Emory U. Dept. Cmty. Health, Sch. of Medicine, Atlanta, 1985—91; adj. prof. of medicine George Wash. U., Sch. of Medicine and Health Scis., Wash., 1993—; pvt. practice, 1964—68; ret., 2002. Pres. Ctr. for Biosecurity Food Safety and Pub. Health, Lake Worth, Fla., 2002—; invited spkr., Canada, Colombia, Mexico, Trinidad and Tobago, Argentina, Thailand, Philippines, Australia, Netherlands, Switzerland, South Africa, Honduras, Panama, Dominican Republic; scientific adv. World Health Organ. Cons. Pub. Health and Animal Transmissible Spongiform Encephalopathies, Risk and Rsch. Requirements, Geneva, 1999. Co-author: Food Animal Pathology and Meat Hygiene, 1991, Poultry Diseases and Meat Hygiene, 1996; co-editor: Animal Drugs and Human Health; editor: The Original Recyclers, 1996; author: Sanitation and Hygiene in the Production of Rendered Animal By-Products, 1997; contbr. chapters to books various profl. handbooks, articles various profl. jours. Mem. USA Delegation to the Codex Com., Nat. Scrapie/BSE Oversight Com.; bd. dirs. Food Recovery and Recycling Assn. of No. Am., 1999—; sec. Agrl. Foreign Animal and Poultry Diseases Nat. Adv. Com. Recipient Superior Svc. award for Notable Authorship, U.S. Dept. of Agrl., 1990; Honorary fellow, Philippine Soc. of Vet. Pub. Health, 1998. Mem.: Assn. Am. Feed Control Officials, Nat. Inst. for Animal Agrl. (bd. dirs. 1997—2000), Nat. Assn. Fed. Vets. (pres. 1979—80), Assn. Pub. Health Vets., Assn. Coll. of Vet. Preventive Medicine, U.S. Animal Health Assn., Am. Assn. Food Hygiene Vets., Am. Vet. Med. Assn. Cath. Home: 6430 Stonehurst Cir Lake Worth FL 33467

FRANCO, ELAINE ADELE, librarian; b. N.Y.C., Jan. 24, 1948; d. Alexander and Sarah Eleanor (Johnson) Franco; m. James Paul Webster, Dec. 29, 1982 (dec. Sept. 1993). BA magna cum laude, Hope Coll., Holland, Mich., 1969; MLS, U. Mich., 1975, MA, 1976. Cataloger U. Nebr.-Lincoln Librs., 1977-81, prin. cataloger, 1981-90, Shields Libr., U. Calif., Davis, 1990—. Bibliographer: MLA International Bibliography, 1979—, First Printings of American Authors, 1977-79; editor conf. procs. Recipient Disting. Svc award Nebr. Libr. Assn. Coll. and Univ. Sect. 1984. Mem. MLA, ALA (councilor-at-large 1987-91), Assn. Libr. Collections and Tech. Svcs. (chmn. coun. regional groups 2005—), Calif. Libr. Assn. (pres. access, collections and tech. svcs. sect. 1998-99), Calif. Acad. and Rsch. Librs., Beta Phi Mu. Office: U Calif Shields Libr 100 NW Quad Davis CA 95616-5292 Business E-Mail: eafranco@ucdavis.edu.

FRANCO, JAMES, actor; b. Palo Alto, Calif., Apr. 19, 1978; Owner Rabbit Bandini Productions. Actor: (TV series) Freaks and Geeks, 1999; (films) Never Been Kissed, 1999, Whatever It Takes, 2000, At Any Cost, 2000, If Tomorrow Comes, 2000, Some Body, 2001, James Dean, 2001, Mean People Suck, 2001, Blind Spot, 2001, Spider-Man, 2002, Deuces Wild, 2002, City by the Sea, 2002, Sonny, 2002, Mean People Suck, 2003, The Car Kid, 2003, Spider-Man 2, 2004, The Great Raid, 2005; exec. prodr., dir., writer: The Ape, 2004. Office: Miles Levy-James/Levy/Jacobson Mgmt 3500 W Olive Ave Ste 920 Burbank CA 91505

FRANCO, OMAR, government agency administrator; b. Miami, Fla., Oct. 11, 1965; s. Israel and Gloria (Santamaria) F.; m. Adria Elena Sierra, Aug. 16, 1997; children: Alyssa Nicole and Andrew Joseph (twins). AA, Miami-Dade C.C., 1985; BA in English and Bus., Fla. State U., 1988; postgrad., Fla. Internat. U., 2002—. Registered legis. lobbyist, Notary Pub. Dist. legis. asst. Rep. Art Simon, Miami, 1993-94; campaign mgr. Annie Betancourt Reelection Campaign, Miami, 1996; dist. legis. asst. Rep. Annie Betancourt, Miami, 1994-96; dist. sr. legis. asst. Sen. Mario Diaz-Balart, Miami, 1996-98; field office dir. Fla. Med. Assn., Tallahassee, 1998-99; dir. govt. rels. Sch. Medicine, U. Miami, 1999—2001, asst. v.p. govtl. rels., 2001—03; chief of staff Congressman Mario Diaz-Balart, 2003—. Pub. policy and advocacy com. U. Miami Mailman Ctr., 2000—02; mem. Miami-Dade Alliance for Aging, 2003. Mem. Leadership Miami; mem. Hispanic Leadership Tng. Program Cuban Am. Nat. Coun., 1996; mem. bd. dirs. Kendall Fedn. Homeowner's Assn., Miami, 1996—2000; v.p. Kendall Lakes Master Condominium Assn., Miami, 1998—2001; mem. steering com. Nat. Multiple Sclerosis Soc., Miami, 1998—99. Recipient Leadership award Nat. Multiple Sclerosis Soc., 1997. Mem. Am. Polit. Sci. Assn., Acad. Polit. Sci., Fla. Polit. Sci. Assn., Pi Sigma Alpha, Delta Sigma Pi, Sigma Phi Epsilon; Nat. Hispanic Working Group, Bush-Cheney 2004; House Adminstrv. Assistants/Chiefs of Staff Assn., 2004; One Thousand Great Americans, Internat. Biog. Ctr., 2004; participant, Miami-Dade Coll. Call Us Essential. Call Us the College initiative, 2003. Home: 12823 Dogwood Hills Lane Fairfax VA 22033 Office: 313 Cannon Bldg Washington DC 20515 Office Phone: 202-225-2778. E-mail: omar.franco@mail.house.gov.

FRANCO, ROBERT, economist; b. Cairo, Aug. 11, 1941; came to U.S., 1960; s. Edgard and Speranza Franco; m. Martine Pastor, June 9, 1978; children: Erik, Arnaud. BA, U. Calif., 1963, PhD, 1970; MA, San Diego State U., 1965. Economist Transp. Inst., Washington, 1970-72; mgr. CACI, Arlington, Va., 1972-74; asst. divsn. chief IMF, Washington, 1974-94, resident rep. Senegal, 1984-87; sr. country economist World Bank, Washington, 1994-96; resident rep. IMF, Harare, Zimbabwe, 1996-2000, Burkina Faso, 2001—. Cons. OECD, Paris, 1970-74; prof. U. Md., College Park, 1970-80. Mem. Am. Econ. Assn., AAUP, Omicron Delta Epsilon. Avocations: tennis, music, fishing, boating. Home: 3213 Duke St # 638 Alexandria VA 22314 Office: IMF C-200 700 19th St NW Washington DC 20431 E-mail: rfranco@imf.org.

FRANCO, VICTOR, theoretical physics educator; b. N.Y.C., Dec. 15, 1937; s. Isaac and Regina (Ferezy) F.; m. Jieying Zong, Sept. 12, 1983; children: Zachary M., Anna L., Eugene R. BS, NYU, 1958; MA, Harvard U., 1959, PhD, 1964. Research assoc. MIT, Cambridge, 1963-65, Los Alamos Sci. Lab., 1965-67, Lawrence Radiation Lab., Berkeley, Calif., 1967-69; assoc. prof. Bklyn. Coll., 1969-72, prof., 1973—. Guest sci. Internat. Centre for Theoretical Physics, Trieste, 1970, 75; vis. staff mem. Los Alamos Nat. Lab., 1969-75; vis. physicist Lawrence Berkeley Lab., 1974; fgn. collaborator Centre d'Etudes Nucleaires, Saclay, France, 1975-76, 86; vis. sci. U. Trondheim, Norway, 1980, U. Alta., Can., 1982, U. Karlsruhe, Germany, 1985; vis. scholar U. Wash., Seattle, 1980; sr. rsch. assoc. Harvard U. Cambridge, 1983-84; NAS exch. scholar Inst. High Energy Physics, Beijing, China, 1984; guest prof. New Sch. Social Rsch., N.Y.C., 1988, 89; cons. in the field 1973—. Contbr. numerous articles to sci. jours. Recipient various fellowships and research grants Fellow Am. Phys. Soc.; mem. Sigma Xi Office: Brooklyn College Physics Dept Brooklyn NY 11210 Office Phone: 718-951-5000 2856. E-mail: vfranco@brooklyn.cuny.edu.

FRANCOEUR, SHEILA T., state representative; b. Lowell, Mass., Feb. 18, 1938; m. Ronald Francoeur; two children. BA, Fla. State U., 1971. Banker, ret. 1993; ret., 1993; mem. dist. 15 N.H. Ho. of Reps., 1996—. Mem., chmn. econ. devel. com., City of Hampton; mem. vice-chmn. policy bldg. study com.; mem. mcpl. budget com.; spkr. Pro Tem, 2003-04. Bd. dirs. Leadership Seacoast; dir. Rockingham Econ. Development Corp.; chmn. Commerce Com., 2005. Mem. Rotary (v.p., bd. dirs.), AAUW (treas., bd. dirs.). Roman Catholic. Home: 88 Kings Hwy Hampton NH 03842-4317 Office: NH State Legis State House Concord NH 03301 E-mail: sheila.francouer@leg.state.nh.us.

FRANCOIS, FRANCIS BERNARD, retired professional society administrator, lawyer, transportation consultant; b. Barnum, Iowa, Jan. 21, 1934; s. Rudolph John and Irene Frances (McDonough) F.; m. Eileen M. Schmelzer, Feb. 6, 1960; children: Joseph, Marie, Michael, Monica, Susan. BS, Iowa State U.; LL.B., George Washington U. Bar: Md. 1960, U.S. Patent and Trademark Office. Chief judge Orphan's Ct. Prince George's County, Upper Marlboro, Md., 1962-66; commr. Prince George's County, Upper Marlboro, Md., 1966-71, councilman, 1971-80; exec. dir. Am. Assn. State Hwy. and Transp. Ofcls., Washington, 1980-99; retired; chmn. Md. Transp. Commn., 2002—03. Adv. com. Ctr. Transp. Studies, MIT, 1983-99; mem. adv. panel White House Intergovtl. Sci. and Engring. Tech., 1976-80; mem. Washington Suburban Transit Commn., 1978-80, chmn., 1979; dir. Washington Met. Area Transit Authority, 1978-80; exec. com. Transp. Rsch. Bd., 1980-99, Strategic Hwy. Rsch. Program, 1986-92; mem. permanent internat. commn. Permanent Internat. Assn. Rd. Congresses, 1990-99; bd. dirs. Internat. Rd. Fedn., 1991-99, Nat. Ctr. for Asphalt Tech., 1991-99, Intelligent Transp. Soc. Am., 1991—, chmn., 1992-93; chmn. Md. Transp. Commn., 2002-03, lectr. in field. Contbr. articles to profl. jours. Mem. adv. coun. Nat. Cmty. Energy Mgmt. Ctr., 1981-82; mem. local govt. energy policy adv. com. Dept. of Energy, 1979-80; vice chmn. Md. Potomac Water Authority, 1970-80; air quality control adv. coun. State of Md., 1975-80; chmn. Water Resources Planning Bd., 1975-77; mem. Gov.'s Interstate Water Quality Planning Com., 1973-74; v.p. Md. Com. for Fair Representation, 1962; counselor Washington Career Inst., 1963; bd. dirs. Bowie Jaycees, Bowie Fine Arts Soc., Bowie YMCA; trustee Md. Easter Seal Soc., Prince George's United Way, Md. Soc. Crippled Children and Adults. Recipient Cmty. Svc. award Nat. Capital chpt. ASCE, 1980, Cmty. Svc. award Bowie Jaycees, 1980, Cmty. Svc. award Cedar Heights Civic Assn., 1978, Profl. Achievement on Engring. award Iowa State U., 1984, W.N. Carey Jr. Disting. Svc. award Transp. Rsch. Bd., 1990; named Washingtonian of Yr. Washingtonian Mag., 1973; Theodore M. Matson Meml. award, Am. Assn. State Hwy. and Transp. Ofcls., Am. Rd. and Transp. Builders Assn., Fed. Hwy. Adminstrn., Am. Hwy. Users Alliance, Inst. Transp. Engrs., Matson Meml. Assocs., and Transp. Rsch. Bd., 1993; Pioneer award Conf. Minority Transp. Ofcls., 1995, Chi Epsilon, Nat. Civil Engring Honor Soc., 1995, Anson Marston Alumni medal for achievements in engring. Iowa State U., 2003. Mem. Nat. Assn. Counties (pres. 1979-80), Nat. Assn. Regional Coun. (pres. 1972-73), Washington Met. Coun. Govts. (dir. 1966-80, pres. 1971), Cmty. Assns. Inst. (dir. 1975-80, pres. 1979-80), K.C., Chi Epsilon. Democrat. Roman Catholic. Home and Office: 2512 Q St NW Washington DC 20007 E-mail: francis@francois.org.

FRANCOIS, WILLIAM ARMAND, lawyer; b. Chgo., May 31, 1942; s. George Albert and Evelyn Marie (Smith) F.; m. Barbara Ann Sala, Aug. 21, 1965; children: Nicole Suzanne, Robert William. BA, DePaul U., 1964, JD, 1967. Bar: Ill. 1967. Pvt. practice, Lyons, Ill., 1967-68; with Am. Nat. Can Group, Inc., Chgo., 1970, sec., 1974, v.p., 1978, sr. v.p., gen. counsel, sec., 1999-2000; dep. gen. counsel N.Am. Pechiney Group, 1996-99; pvt. practice Lake Forest, Ill., 2000—. Served to capt. U.S. Army, 1968—70. Mem. ABA, Ill. Bar Assn., Chgo. Bar Assn., Soc. Corp. Secs. and Governance Profls., Am. Corp. Counsel Assn. Office: 642 Balmoral Ct Lake Forest IL 60045-4842 Office Phone: 847-234-1702. E-mail: chgowaf@aol.com.

FRANCOMANO, CLAIR ANN, geneticist; BA, Yale U., 1976; MD, Johns Hopkins U. Sch. Medicine, 1980. Resident internal medicine Johns Hopkins U. Sch. of Medicine, Balt., 1980-82, fellow pediat. and med. genetics, 1982-84, asst. prof., 1984—92, assoc. prof., 1992—; chief molecular genetics br., clin. dir. Nat. Human Genome Rsch. Inst., 1994—2001, sr. investigator, chief human genetics and integrative medicine sect. genetics lab., 2001—. Clin. dir. Nat. Human Genome Rsch. Inst., Bethesda, Md., 1996—, chief med. genetics br., 1994-99; assoc. prof. dept. health policy and mgmt. Johns Hopkins U. Sch. of Hygiene and Pub. Health, Balt., 1996—. Achievements include research in genetic diseases of connective tissue and management of pain in those disorders. Office: Nat Human Genome Rsch Inst 10 Center Dr Msc 1852 Bldg 10 Bethesda MD 20892-1852 Fax: 301 496-7157. E-mail: francomanocl@grc.nia.nih.gov.

FRANCONA, TERRY JON, professional baseball manager; b. Aberdeen, S.D., Apr. 22, 1959; s. Tito F.; m. Jacque Lang, Jan. 9, 1982; children: Nick, Alyssa, Leah, Jamie. Student, U. Ariz. First baseman/outfielder maj. league baseball Montreal Expos, 1981—85, Chgo. Cubs, 1986, Cin. Reds, 1987, Cleve. Indians, 1988, Milw. Brewers, 1989—90; hitting instr. Sarasota, Gulf Coast Rookie League Chgo. White Sox orgn., 1991; mgr. S. Bend, 1992; coach Grand Canyon, Ariz. Fall League, 1992; mgr. Birmingham AA, 1993-95, Dominican Winter League, 1995-96, Phila. Phillies, 1996—2000; special asst., baseball ops. Cleve. Indians, 2001; bench coach Tex. Rangers, 2002, Oakland A's, 2003; mgr. Boston Red Sox, 2003—. Recipient So. League Title, 1993, Minor League Mgr. of Yr., So. League, 1993, Minor League Mgr. of Yr., Baseball Am., 1993; named Top Managerial Prospect among minor league mgrs. Baseball Am., 1994. Achievements include coach World Series Champion Boston Red Sox, 2004; coach Am. League All-Start Team, 2005. Avocation: golf. Mailing: c/o Boston Red Sox 4 Yawkey Way Boston MA 02215-3496 Fax: (215) 389-3050.*

FRANCUCH, PAUL CHARLES, broadcast journalist; b. Highland Park, Mich., June 26, 1950; s. Charles and Anna (Protasevich) F. BA, Wayne State U., 1972; MA, U. Mich., 1973. From midwest corr. to London bur. chief Voice of Am., Chgo., 1980—96, London bur. chief, 1996—99; sci. engring. editor U. Ill., Chgo., 2001—. Mem. Phi Beta Kappa. Avocations: bicycling, photography, amateur astronomy. Office: 601 S Morgan St MC 288 Chicago IL 60607-7113 Office Phone: 312-996-3457. E-mail: francuch@uic.edu.

FRANGOPOULOS, ZISSIMOS A., banker; b. Athens, Greece, Dec. 16, 1944; s. John and Thalia (Landi) F.; m. Ruth Snowdon Hoopes, Nov. 21, 1981. BA, Yale U., 1967; MBA, Columbia U., 1969. Lending officer Chem. Bank, N.Y.C., 1969-74, v.p. energy group London, 1974-79, sr. v.p. merchant banking N.Y.C., London, 1979-84; mng. dir., chief exec. officer Chem. Bank Internat. Ltd., London, 1981-84; sr. v.p., dir. for corp. fin. Chem. Banking Corp., N.Y.C., 1984-90, treas., 1990-92; sr. v.p., treas. Chem. Bank, N.Y.C., 1992-94; mng. dir. Chase Securities, Inc., N.Y.C., 1994-99; dir., treas. Cancer Care Connection, Inc., Newark, Del., 2000—01; exec. v.p., CFO, Christiana Bank & Trust Co., Wilmington, Del., 2001—02, pres., CEO, 2002—. Bd. dirs. Christiana Bank & Trust Co., Wilmington, Del. Home: 403 Spring Mill Rd Chadds Ford PA 19317 Office: PO Box 620 Mendenhall PA 19357 Business E-Mail: zissf@cbt-de.com.

FRANK, ALAN I W, manufacturing executive; b. Pitts., Mar. 6, 1932; s. Robert and Cecelia F.; children: Darcy Frank Mackay, Kimberly Frank Shaw. AB cum laude, Harvard U., 1954; LLB, Columbia U., 1960. Bar: NY 1961, Pa. 1982. Pres. Nat. Petroleum Corp., 1954-69; pres., chmn. bd. AIWF Corp., 1962—. Gen. chmn. $200 million campaign Pitts. area, Columbia U., N.Y.C., 1968-70, nat. devel. bd., 1974-84; mem. Rensselaer coun. Rensselaer Poly. Inst., 1974-83; com. mem., com. chmn. Harvard Coll., 1961-2000; trustee Pitts. History and Landmarks Found., 1996-2003. Patentee in field. Served with Counter Intelligence Corps, Spl. Agt. U.S. Army, 1955-57. Mem. N.Y. Bar, Pa. Bar, Mid Ocean Club (Bermuda). Address: 96 E Woodland Rd Pittsburgh PA 15232-2861

FRANK, AMÉLIE LORRAINE, marketing professional; b. L.A., Feb. 5, 1960; d. Lawrence Bruce and Phébé Exilda (Brodeur) Frank. BA in English, Creative Writing, U. Calif., Irvine, 1981. Letters editor Petersen Pub., West Hollywood, Calif., 1983—85; owner, writer Mysterious Affairs, Hollywood, 1984—88; script svcs. supr. Universal City (Calif.) Studios, 1985—86; mkt. rschr. Universal Pictures Mktg., Universal City, 1986—94; owner, pub. Sacred Beverage Press, Venice, Calif., 1994—; rsch. coord. Buena Vista Pictures Mktg., Burbank, Calif., 1994—2004; events coord. Red Hen Press, 2005—. Host poetry readings Hot House Cafe, North Hollywood, 1996—99, Exile Books & Music, 1999—2000; co-dir. Valley Contemporary Poets, 1999—2002; host Killer Poetry, 2000—01; co-webmaster Billybobapalooza Ofcl. Billy Bob Thornton website. Author: (poems) A Resilient Heart and Other Visceral Comforts, 1992, Flame and Loss of Breath, 1996, Doing Time on Planet Billy Bob, 2000; co-author: Drink Me, 1997, Bird Interpretations, 1998; editor: (book) God the Motion Picture, 1994; co-editor: Blue Satellite Jour., 1994—2000; performer spoken word (albums) The Essential Girl, 2001, Retro Hell music reviewer Ind. Revs. Site; CD, Michael Shipp Xcursion "The Adventures of Roosterboy". Facilitator buddy program AIDS Project, L.A., Hollywood, 1988—92; trustee Beyond Baroque, 1999—, artist, cmty. advisor coun., 1998—99; mem. med. staff Disney Disaster Preparedness, Burbank, 1994—. Named L.A. Newer Poet, Beyond Baroque in conjunction with L.A. Poetry Festival, 1999; recipient award for favorite new poetry book, Readership, NEXT Mag., 1996, Spirit of Venice award, 2003. Mem.: NOW, Poetry Soc. Am., Office Profl. Employees Internat. Union (newsletter editor 1991—94), PETA. Green Party. Avocations: reading, choral music, travel, films, working with animals. Office: The Sacred Beverage Press PO Box 10312 Burbank CA 91510-0312 Personal E-mail: poetamelie@aol.com.

FRANK, BARBARA BALIS, gastroenterologist, educator; b. Reading, Pa., Jan. 11, 1937; d. Irvin and Ruth Helen (Knoblauch) B.; m. Leonard Arnold Frank, Aug. 17, 1958; children: Michael Scott, Bradford Allan. BA magna cum laude, Smith Coll., 1958; MD, U. Pa., 1962. Diplomate Am. Bd. Internal Medicine and Gastroenterology. Intern and fellow in gastroenterology Hosp. U. Pa., Phila., 1962—64, instr. internal medicine, 1966—69; resident internal medicine Bryn Mawr (Pa.) Hosp., 1964-66; dir. divsn. gastroenterology Crozer-Chester Med. Ctr., Chester, 1968—89, attending gastroenterologist, 1968—94; clin. asst. prof. medicine Hahnemann U., Phila., 1973-75, clin. assoc. prof., 1975—85, clin. prof., 1985—. Cons. Sacred Heart Hosp., Chester, Pa., 1974-94; mem. sci. adv. com. Nat. Found. Ileitis and Colitis, Phila., 1980-85; mem. gastroenterology-urology devices panel, FDA, 1988-90, chmn., 1990-92, cons. 1993-94; mem. gastrointestinal drugs adv. com. FDA, 1995-99, cons., 2000—; mem. Physician Payment Rev. Commn., Consensus Panel for Evaluation and Mgmt. Svcs., 1990; rep. for gastroenterology carrier adv. com. Pa. Medicare, 1993-2005; v.p. N.Am. Congresso Panamericano de Endoscopia, 1993-95, 99-2001. Assoc. editor MKSAP in gastroenterology and hepatology 2; contbr. articles to profl. jours. Recipient History of Medicine prize U. Pa. Sch. Medicine, 1962, Legion of Honor award Chapel of Four Chaplains, Phila., 1978; rsch. grantee U. Pa., 1961-62. Fellow ACP, Coll. Physicians Phila., Am. Coll. Gastroenterology (ad hoc com. on women in gastroenterology 1989—, gov. ea. Pa. 1992-96, 2003—, regional councillor, bd. govs. 1994-96, chmn. com. for ICD-9-CM revision 1986-89, mem. govt. rels. com. 1987-88, sci. exhibits com. 1985-86, ann. sci. selection com. 1984-85, 90-91, nominating com. 1988-89, ednl. affairs com. 1992-2001); mem. Am. Soc. Gastrointestinal Endoscopy (councillor, governing bd. dirs. 1986-90, 92-94, pres. 1991-92, Disting. Educator award 2005), AMA, Am. Gastroenterol. Assn. (patient care com. 1986-88, tng. adn edn. com. 1989-90, abstract selection com. 199, nominating com. 1986-87, program evaluation com. 1981-85, mem. pub. policy com. 1992-93, mem. clin. svcs. task force 1994-95, chmn. nominating com. 1995-96, others, Disting. Educator award 2005) Am. Assn. Study Liver Disease, Am. Liver Found., Internat. Assn. for Study of the Liver, Pa. Med. Soc., Phila. GI Tng. Group (pres. 1987-93), Phila. Gastrointestinal Rsch. Forum, Delaware County Med. Soc., Delaware Valley Soc. Gastrointestinal Endoscopy (pres. 1984-86, councillor, governing bd. dirs. 1986-88), Pa. Soc. Gastroenterology councillor for Phila. 1982-84, 87-91, 2001—, governing bd. dirs.), Israel Med. Assn., Bockus Internat. Soc. of Gastroenterology (pres. elect 2005—), Alpha Omega Alpha, Sigma Xi, Alpha Phi, Kappa Psi, Phi Beta Kappa Del. Valley (gov. coun. 1991-93, 98— v.p. 1993-95, pres. 1995-97, 98—, gov. coun. 2000—). Democrat. Jewish. Avocations: sketching, dance. Office: Fl 5 MS 913 219 N Broad St Philadelphia PA 19107

FRANK, BARNEY, congressman; b. Bayonne, N.J., Mar. 31, 1940; s. Samuel and Elsie (Golush) F. AB, Harvard U., 1962, JD, 1977. Exec. asst. to mayor City of Boston, 1968-71; adminstrv. asst. to U.S. congressman, 1971-72; mem. Mass. Ho. of Reps., 1972-80, 97th-108th Congresses from 4th Dist. Mass., 1981—; lectr. Harvard U., JFK Sch. of Gov., 1978—80; mem. banking and fin. svcs. com., mem. judiciary com., homeland sec. com. Teaching fellow govt. Harvard U., 1963-67, asst. to dir. Inst. Politics John F. Kennedy Sch. Govt., 1966-67, fellow Inst. Politics, 1971. Pub.: numerous articles on politics and public affairs. Democrat. Office: US Ho of Reps 2252 Rayburn HOB Washington DC 20515-0001*

FRANK, CHARLES RAPHAEL, JR., financial consultant, director; b. Pitts, May 15, 1937; s. Charles Raphael and Lucille (Briscoe) M.; m. Susan Patricia Backman, Mar. 9, 1963 (div. June 1976); children: Elizabeth Grace, Stephen Raphael; m. Eleanor Sebastian, July 19, 1976; children: Paul Sebastian, Philip Sebastian; stepchildren: Joyce Oxman, Alan Oxman. BS in Math., Rensselaer Poly. Inst., 1959; MA in Econs., Princeton U., 1961, PhD in Econs., 1963. Sr. rsch. fellow East African Inst. Social Rsch. Makerere U. Coll., Kampala, Uganda, 1963-65; asst. prof. econ. Yale U., New Haven, 1965-67; assoc. prof. econ. and internat. affairs Princeton U., NJ, 1967-70, prof., 1970-74; assoc. dir. rsch. program econ. devel. Woodrow Wilson Sch., 1967-70, dir., 1970-74; sr. fellow Brookings Inst., 1972-74; mem. policy planning staff US Dept. State, 1974-77, dep. asst. sec. state for econ. and social affairs, 1977-78; v.p. Salomon Bros. Inc., 1978-87; pres. Frank & Co. Inc., 1987-88; v.p. project fin. GE Capital Corp., Stamford, Conn., 1988-97; 1st v.p. European Bank for Reconstruction and Devel., London, 1997-2001. Bd. dirs. Ctrl. and Eastern European Media Enterprises, Romanian Am. Enterprise Fund; ops. rsch. analyst US Steel, summers 1960, 61; cons. Govt. Uganda, 1964, UN Econ. Commn. for Asia and Far East, 1969, IBRD, 1969-72, Korea Devel. Inst., 1973-74, Mathematica, 1967-68, Nat. Conf. Bd., 1969-70, Nat. Bur. Econ. Rsch., 1970-75, Brookings Instn., 1969, Brit. Petroleum, 2001-02, LNH Group, 2002-03, Sabre Capital, 2003-05; mem. rsch. adv. com. AID, 1971-75, cons., Washington, 1966-68, Korea, 1971-73. Author: Prodn. Theory and Indivisible Commodities, 1969, The Sugar Industry in East Africa, 1965, (with Brian Van Arkadie) Econ. Accounting and Develop. Planning, 2d edit., 1969, Debt and the Terms of Aid, 1970, Stats. and Econometrics, 1971, Am. Jobs and Trade with the Develop. Countries, 1973, Fgn. Exchange Regimes and Econ. Develop., The Case of South Korea, 1975, Fgn. Trade and Domestic Adjustment, 1976, Income Distribution and Econ. Growth in the Less Developed Countries, 1977. Mem. Coun. Fgn. Rels.

FRANK, CURTIS W., chemical engineer, department chairman; PhD, U. Illinois, 1972. Chmn., Keck prof. of chemical engring. Stanford U., prof. chemistry, materials sci., engring. Principal investigator Nat. Sci. Found. Materials Rsch. Sci. & Engring. Ctr. on Polymer Interfaces and Macromolecular Assemblies. Author of numerous scientific articles in jours. including: Jour. of Adhesion, Jour. of Photochemistry & Photobiology Chemistry, Jour. of Am. Chemical Soc., Biophysical Jour., Jour. of Chemical Physics, Korea Polymer Jour. Recipient C.M.A. Stine award, Am. Inst. of Chemical Engineers. Fellow: Am. Physical Soc. Office: Stanford U Chemical Engring 381 N S Mall Stanford CA 94305-5025

FRANK, DENNIS, psychotherapist, educator; b. Cherry Point, N.C., Apr. 17, 1954; s. Charlotte Dotzauer and Robert Frank; children: Maximillian, Alexander. MS, U. Wis., Milw., 1997. Psychotherapist Ravenswood Clinic, Inc., Milw., 1997—2002; area supr. ATTIC Correctional Svcs. Inc., Milw., 1999—2001, also bd. dirs.; psychotherapist St. Mary's Hosp., 2001—; ad hoc prof. Concordia U. Grad Sch. Instr. Upper Iowa U., 2002—. Com. mem. The Benedict Ctr., Milw., 2000. Specialist Army, Germany, 1971-74. Mem. ACA, Am. Correctional Assn., Internat. Assn. of Addictions and Offender Counselors, Internat. Cmty. Corrections Assn. Office: Columbia St Mary's 2350 N Lake Dr Milwaukee WI 53211

FRANK, DIETER, retired chemicals executive; b. Erfurt, Thuringia, Germany, May 21, 1930; came to U.S., 1975; s. Karl Hermann and Luise (Metz) F.; m. Edith Anna Laufer, July 19, 1957; children: Martin, Susanne, Beate. DEng, Tech. U., Berlin, 1963. Rsch. chemist Glanzstoff A.G., Obernburg, Federal Republic of Germany, 1965-69, sect. head, 1969-71; assoc. dir. AKZO Corp. Rsch., Obernburg, Federal Republic of Germany, 1971-75; dir. rsch. ARMAK (AKZO), Chgo., 1975-76; v.p. rsch. AKZO Chems., Chgo., 1976-90, ret., 1990; tech. cons., 1991—96. Mem. indsl. adv. bd. U. Fla., Gainsville, 1987-90. Contbr. to Ullman Ency., 1985, 90, also articles on organic chemistry; patentee chemicals. County vice chmn. Social Dem. Party of Germany, Obernburg, 1968; pres. Soccer Club, Elsenfeld, Federal Republic of Germany, 1974, 75; chmn. bd. dirs. Fine Arts Found. Schleusingen, 2000-03. Recipient G.E. Meade award, Sugar Industry Technologists, 1986. Mem. AAAS, Indsl. Rsch. Inst. (rep. 1979-90, bd. editors 1981-83). Avocations: woodworking, jazz player. Home and Office: An der Hauptstr 93 98553 Schleusingen-Gethles Germany Personal E-mail: DFrankGeth@aol.com.

FRANK, EDGAR GERALD, retired finance company executive; b. Cin., May 15, 1931; s. Carl F. and Marcella M. F.; m. Joy Hueber, Oct. 30, 1954; children: Thomas, Phillip, Angela, Walter. BBA, U. Cin., 1955. Acct. Wm. S. Merrell Co., Cin., 1960-61; asst. sec. Emery Industries, Cin., 1961-66; fin. v.p. Samuel Moore & Co., Aurora, Ohio, 1966-79; v.p. fin. Telex Corp., Tulsa, 1979-88, ret., 1988. Served with USN, 1955-58. Mem. AICPA, Fin. Execs. Inst.

FRANK, EDWARD DAVID, II, history educator; b. Boston, June 7, 1951; s. Howard Alvin and Sally (Bernkopf) F.; m. Susan Gibson Lea, Dec. 13, 1997; children: William Howard Day, Edward Morgan Day; 1 stepchild: Eleanor Talbot West. JD, NYU, 1976; BA in History, Yale U., 1973; MA in Internat. Rels., U. Pa., 1984. Assoc. Sherman & Sterling, N.Y.C., 1976-79, Sullivan & Worcester, Boston, 1979-81; chief counsel Bur. Profl. and Occupl. Affairs Commonwealth of Pa., Harrisburg, Pa., 1982-83; internat. polit. risk cons. Bus. Environment Risk Info., Washington, 1985-86; history tchr. The Agnes Irwin Sch., Rosemont, Pa., 1985-97, chair history, 1997—. Spl. asst. to pres. Barnes Found., Merion, Penn., 1989-90. Bd. dir. Phila. Area Multicultural Resource Ctr., Bryn Mawr, Pa., 1990—; chair 25th Reunion of Yale Class of 1973, New Haven, Conn., 1993-98; trustee Lincoln U., 1985-91, Agnes Irwin Sch., Rosemont, 1992-95, pres. Cum Laude Soc., 1991- . Mem. Assn. Yale U. Alumni (bd. govs. 1972-73, sec. Class of 73, 1972-78). Home: 843 Parkes Run Ln Villanova PA 19085 Office: Agnes Irwin Sch Ithan Ave & Conestoga Rd Bryn Mawr PA 19010 Office Phone: 610-525-8400. E-mail: wigsfrank@aol.com.

FRANK, ELIZABETH, writer, educator; b. L.A., Sept. 14, 1945; d. Melvin G. and Anne R. Frank; 1 child, Anne Louise Buchwald. Student, Bennington Coll.; BA, U. Calif., Berkeley, 1967, MA, 1969, PhD, 1973. Prof. modern langs. and lit. Bard Coll., Annandale-on-Hudson, NY, 1982—, faculty Ctr. Curatorial Studies, Joseph E. Harry prof. modern langs. and lit. Author: Jackson Pollock, 1983, Louise Bogan: A Portrait, 1985 (Pulitzer prize for biography, 86), Esteban Vicente, 1995, Cheat and Charmer, 2004; contbr. articles to profl. jours. Fellow, Ford Found., 1967—72, Temple U., 1977, The Newbery Libr., 1977, Am. Coun. Learned Socs., 1977, NEH, 1978. Office: Joy Harris Lit Agy 156 5th Ave Ste 617 New York NY 10010-7002 also: Bard Coll Dept Lang & Lit Annandale On Hudson NY 12504

FRANK, ERICA, preventive medicine physician; b. Trenton, N.J., June 17, 1962; m. Randall White, 1990; 1 child, Ridge. MD, Mercer U., 1988. Intern Cleve. Clin., 1988-89; resident in preventive medicine Yale U., New Haven, 1989-90; rsch. fellow Stanford U., 1990—93; asst./assoc. prof. Sch. Medicine Emory U., Atlanta, 1993—. Co-editor-in-chief: Preventive Medicine, 1994—99. Recipient Clinician-Scientist award Am. Heart. Assn., 1995-96. Office: Emory U 69 Butler St SE Atlanta GA 30303-3033

FRANK, FREDERICK, investment banker; b. Salt Lake City, May 31, 1932; s. Simon and Suzanne (Seller) F.; m. Mary Ann Nahum (div. 1979); children: Jenny Ann, Laura Kim, Frederick S.; m. Mary Catherine Tanner. BA, Yale U., 1954; MBA, Stanford U., 1958. Chartered fin. analyst. Mng. dir. Smith Barney & Co., N.Y.C., 1958-69, Lehman Bros., N.Y.C., 1969-85, sr. mng. dir., 1985-95, vice chmn., 1995—. Bd. dirs. Pharm. Product Devel., Wilmington, NC, AXS, Berkeley, Calif., Diagnostic Products, L.A., Landec Corp., Bus. Engine Inc.; chmn. bd. dirs. Predic Pharms. Trustee Irvington Inst. of Immunological Rsch.; with Nat. Genetics Found., N.Y.C., 1985—; bd. dirs. Salk Inst., La Jolla, Calif.; trustee Hotchkiss Sch., Lakeville, Conn.; adv. dir. Yale U. Sch. Mgmt. With U.S. Army, 1954—56. Mem. Chartered Fin. Analysts, N.Y. Soc. Security Analysts. Avocations: skiing, tennis, running. Home: 109 E 91st St New York NY 10128-1601 Office: Lehman Bros 745 7th Ave New York NY 10019-0001 E-mail: ffrank@lehman.com.

FRANK, GEORGE ANDREW, lawyer; b. Budapest, Hungary, Apr. 6, 1938; arrived in U.S., 1957, naturalized, 1962; s. Alex and Ilona (Weiss) F.; m. Carole Shames, Feb. 14, 1979; children: Cheryl, Charles. BS in Chemisty, Colo. State U., 1960; PhD in Organic Chemistry, MIT, 1965; JD cum laude, Temple U., 1977. Bar: Pa. 1977, U.S. Dist. Ct. (ea. dist.) Pa. 1977, D.C. 1980, U.S. Ct. Appeals (fed. cir.) 1982, U.S. Supreme Ct. 1984. Sr. chemist Rohm & Haas Co., Phila., 1965-69; lab. head Borden Chem., Phila., 1969-73; sr. scientist Thiokol Corp., Trenton, N.J., 1973-74; counsel Du Pont Corp., Wilmington, Del., 1974-85, sr. counsel, 1986-92, corp. counsel, 1992-2001, intellectual property law group leader, 2000-2001; of counsel, chair licensing and tech. transfer practice group Drinker Biddle & Reath LLP, Philadelphia, 2001—. External adv. com. Colo. State U. Coll. Natural Scis., 1996—; mem. intellectual property adv. com. Pa. Bar Inst., 2002–. Contbr. articles to profl. jours; patentee in field. Recipient Merck award, Merck & Co., 1960; fellow, NIH, 1963—65; grantee Sun Oil Co. grantee, 1964. Mem. ABA (chair divsn. biotech. 1993-94, coun. 1994-98, chair chem. practice com. 1998-2000, chair divsn. biotech. and chem. practice 2000-02, chair divsn. profl. practice and sect. rels. 2002—04, chair lic. com. 2004-), Phila. Patent Lawyers Assn. (chair bioscis. com. 1983-87, bd. govs. 1987-92, pres. 1992-93), Am. Intellectual Property Law Assn. (chair task force 1986), Benjamin Franklin Am. Inn of Cts. (v.p. 1996-97, pres. 1997-98). Republican. Avocations: tennis, squash, travel, books, opera. Home: 520 Lindy Ln Bala Cynwyd PA 19004-1331 Office: Drinker Biddle & Reath LLP 1 Logan Square 18th & Cherry St Philadelphia PA 19103 Office Phone: 215-988-2822. Business E-Mail: frankga@dbr.com.

FRANK, GERALD WENDEL, advocate, journalist; b. Portland, Oreg., Sept. 21, 1923; s. Aaron and Ruth (Rosenfeld) Frank. Student, Stanford U., 1941-43, Loyola U., L.A., 1946-47; BA with honors, Cambridge U., 1948, MA, 1953; D Bus. Adminstrn. (hon.), Greenville (Ill.) Coll., 1971; LLD (hon.), Pacific U., 1983. Mgr. Meier & Frank Co., Salem, Oreg., 1955-65; v.p. Meier & Frank Co., Ltd., 1948-65; also bd. dirs.; pres. Gerry's Frankly Speaking, Salem, Oreg., 1996—; co-owner Gerry Frank's Konditorei, Inc., Salem, Oreg., 1982—. Commentator/reporter morning news shows Sta. KPTV, Portland, 1993—2001, Sta. KATU-AM, 2002—; mgmt. adv. bd. Acquitas Capital, 2003—; bd. dirs. AAA Oreg./Idaho. Author: Where to Find It, Buy It, Eat It in New York, 1980—, Joan and Gerry's Little Black Book of Shopping Secrets, 1991, Friday Surprise, 1995; sr. corr.: N.W. Reports, 1992—96. Active Found. Infantile Paralysis, Arthritis and Rheumatism Found., Nat. Coun., Boy Scouts Am., Travelers Aid Soc., Nat. Mcpl. League, Nat. Retail Merchants Assn., Am. Heart Soc., Portland C. of C., Salem Area C. of C.; active Sunshine divsn. Portland Police Res.; active Portland Area Coun., Cascade Area Coun., Cascade Area Pacific Coun., Portland Rose Festival Assn., Jr. Achievement, Salem Pub. Libr. Found., Portland United Fund, Marion-Polk Counties United Way, Salem Gen. Hosp., Citizens' Conf. for Govtl. Coop., Gov.'s Econ. Devel. Commn., Oreg. Retail Distbrs. Inst., Orge. Rsch. Assn., Salem 4-H Club, Willamette River Days, Salem YWCA, Grad. Inst. Sci. and Tech., Portland Met. Futures Unltd., Inc., Oreg. Coast Aquarium, 1990—, Oreg. Symphony Soc.; chair Oreg. State Police Found., 2002—; bd. trustees LWV; hon. chair Marion Polk Food Share Capital Campaign, 2003—; gen. chmn. Mark O. Hatfield for U.S. Sen., 1966, 1972, 1978, 1984, 1990; mgmt. com. U.S. Senate, 1978; chief of staff Sen. Mark O. Hatfield, 1973—92; active Culver Commn. on Reorgn. U.S. Senate, 1975—76; trustee Lorene Sails Higgins Charitable Trust, 1993—2000; exec. com. U.S. Com. for UNICEF, 1990—99; exec. com., Ray and Joan Kroc initiative com. Salvation Army, chair Krock initiative com., 2004—05; bd. trustees Willamette U.; active Marion-Salem Bldg. Study Com.; emeritus trustee Oreg. High Desert Mus.; exec. com. Salem Art Assn., Parry Ctr. Children, St. Vincent Hosp. and Med. Ctr., Oreg. Health Scis. U., OMSI, chair, dir., 1996—97; bd. dirs., exec. com. AAA Oreg./Idaho; bd. Oreg. Garden Found.; active Miss Oreg. Scholarship Program; chmn. Oreg. Tourism Commn., 1996—2001, Oreg. Ind. Coll. Found., 2000. Named Oreg. Premier Citizen, 2000; recipient numerous awards including Silver Beaver, Boy Scouts Am., 1963, Reginald H. Vincent trophy, United Good Neighbor of the Yr., 1980, Brotherhood Nat. Conf. Christians and Jews, Portland, 1984, Gov.'s Gold award, 2004; Tom Lawson McCall fellow, Pacific U., 1987. Mem.: Rotary (Paul Harris fellow 1986), Elks, Am. Legion. Avocations: travel, gourmet dining. Home: 3250 Crestview Dr S Salem OR 97302-5959 Office: Gerry's Frankly Speaking Inc 2601 25th St SE Ste 500 Salem OR 97302-1287 also: PO Box 2225 Salem OR 97308-2225 Office Phone: 503-585-8411. E-mail: gerry@teleport.com.

FRANK, HARVEY, lawyer, writer; b. N.Y.C., Aug. 24, 1930; s. Leon and Hannah (Lehr) F.; m. Judith Ellen Lewis, Nov. 29, 1959; 1 child, David . AB, NYU, 1951, LLM, 1961; JD, Harvard U., 1954. Bar: N.Y. 1954, Md. 1981, Ohio 1982. Ptnr. Hays Feuer Porter & Spanier, N.Y.C., 1963-69, Burns, Summit, Rovins & Feldesman, N.Y.C., 1970-74; prof. law Coll. William and Mary, Williamsburg, Va., 1974-80; adj. prof. Johns Hopkins U., Balt., 1981; ptnr. Benesch Friedlander, Coplan & Aronoff, Cleve., 1982-93; pvt. practice Law Offices Harvey Frank, Phila., 1993—. Sec. Banner Aerospace, 1990-93. Author: The ERC Closely Held Corporation Guide, 1981, 2d edit., 1984; contbr. articles to law jours. Mem. ABA, Am. Law Inst. Home and Office: Law Offices of Harvey Frank 1215A Waverly Walk Philadelphia PA 19147

FRANK, HOWARD, information technology executive; b. N.Y.C., June 4, 1941; s. Herman and Tina (Sander) F.; m. Jane Steinberg, Apr. 23, 1965; children: David, Laura, Erica. BSEE, U. Miami, 1962; MS, Northwesten U., 1964; PhD, Northwestern U., 1965. Asst. prof. U. Calif.-Berkeley, 1965-68, assoc. prof., 1969; exec. v.p. Network Analysis Corp., Glen Cove, N.Y., 1969, pres., 1970-81, Contel Info. Systems Inc., Great Neck, NY, 1982-85, Howard Frank Assocs., 1985—; chmn. Network Mgmt., Inc., 1987—91; dir. Def. Adv. Rsch. Project Agy.'s Info. Tech. Office; pres., CEO Contel Info. Sys. (sub. Contel Corp.); pres., CEO, founder Network Analysis Corp.; prof. mgmt. scis. Smith Sch., 1997—; dean Robert H. Smith Sch. Bus. U. Md., 1997—. Bd. dirs. Contel Corp.; vis. cons. Exec. Office Pres. U.S., 1968; founder, chmn., CEO Network Mgmt. Inc., Fairfax, Va., 1986-91; spkr. bus. and profl. meetings; adj. prof. decision scis. Wharton Sch.; assoc. prof. electrical engrng. and computer scis. U. (Berkeley) California. Author: Communications, Transmission and Transportation Networks, 1971; contbr. over 190 articles and chpts. in books on tech. and mgmt. of tech.; mem. 7 editl. bds. NASA fellow, 1963-65; Gen. Motors fellow, 1958-62 Fellow IEEE (Leonard G. Abraham 1969, Eric Sumner award 1999), SEI Ctr. Advanced Studies in Mgmt. (sr. fellow, mem. bd. dirs.); mem. AAAS, AACSB, Mid-Atlantic Assn. Colls. and Bus. Adminstrn. (pres), Ops. Research Soc., Ams. Internat. Acad. Mgmt. (vice chancellor), Carnegie Mellon's Heinz Sch. (mem. adv. bd.), Global Tech. and Mgmt. Consortium (mem. exec. com.), Macklin Inst. Mont. Coll. (bd. dirs.), Nat. Inst. Stds. and Tech.'s Advanced Tech. Program (fed. adv. com.), Nat. Acad. Engrng., N.Y. Acad. Scis. Office: Robert H Smith Sch Bus U Md 2410 Van Munching Hall College Park MD 20742-1815 Business E-Mail: hfrank@rhsmith.umd.edu.

FRANK, ISAIAH, economist, educator; b. N.Y.C., Nov. 7, 1917; s. Henry and Rose (Isserles) F.; m. Ruth Hershfield, Mar. 23, 1941; children: Robert E., Kenneth D. B in Social Sci., CCNY, 1936; MA in Econs., Columbia U., 1938, PhD in Econs., 1960. Rsch. assoc. in econs. Columbia U. Council for Research in Social Scis., 1936-39; tchg. fellow, instr. econs. Amherst Coll., 1939-41; Carnegie fellow Nat. Bur. Econ. Rsch., 1941-42; cons. WPB, 1942; sr. economist OSS, 1942-44; various positions U.S. Dept. State, 1945-63; dir. Office Internat. Trade, 1957-59, Office Internat. Financial and Devel. Affairs, 1961-62, dep. asst. sec. for econ. affairs, 1962-63; William L. Clayton prof. internat. econs. Sch. Advanced Internat. Studies, Johns Hopkins U., 1963—. Mem. Industry-Govt. Iron and Steel Mission to Europe, 1947; adviser U.S. del. Econ. Commn. for Europe, 1948; dep. dir. fgn. resources div. Pres.'s Materials Policy Commn., 1951-52; head U.S. del. Conf. on Dollar Liberalization, OEEC, Paris, 1955-56; chmn. U.S. del. GATT, Geneva, 1958; alt. U.S. rep. Fourth Meeting Devel. Assistance Group, London, 1961; chmn. U.S. del. to prep. com. UN Conf. Trade and Devel., Geneva, 1963—; U.S. rep. Spl. Trade Conf. OAS, Alta Gracia, Argentina, 1964; exec. dir. Pres.'s Commn. on Internat. Trade and Investment Policy, 1970-71; adv. com. UN Trade and Devel. Bd.; dir. internat. econ. studies Com. Econ. Devel.; mem. adv. council Inst. for Latin Am. Integration; mem. adv. com. Inst. Internat. Econs.; cons. World Bank; chmn. adv. com. on internat. investment State Dept.; mem. svcs. policy adv. com. U.S. Trade Rep.; mem. adv. com. on internat. econ. policy U.S. Dept. State. Author: The European Common Market: An Analysis of Commercial Policy, 1960, Foreign Enterprise in Developing Countries, 1980, Finance and Third-World Economic Growth, 1988, Breaking New Ground in U.S. Trade Policy, 1991, U.S. Trade Policy Beyond the Uruguay Round, 1994, U.S. Economic Policy Toward the Asia-Pacific Region, 1997; co-author, editor: The Japanese Economy in International Perspective, 1975; contbr. articles to profl. publs. 1st lt. AUS, 1944-45. Recipient Rockefeller Pub. Svc. award, 1959-60 Mem. Coun. Fgn. Rels., Am. Econ. Assn., Cosmos Club, Phi Beta Kappa. Home: 3102 Hawthorne St NW Washington DC 20008-3539 Office: Johns Hopkins U 1740 Massachusetts Ave NW Washington DC 20036-1903 Office Phone: 202-663-5685. Business E-Mail: ifrank@jhu.edu.

FRANK, JACOB, lawyer; b. Albany, Apr. 4, 1936; s. Isidore and Sara F.; m. Yoelith Frank, Aug. 26, 1936; children: Eytan, Michael, Adam, Orly. BEE, Rensselaer Poly. Inst., 1957; LLB, Am. U., 1963; postgrad., George Washington U. Coll. Law, 1964-67, NYU Law Sch., 1969-73. Bar: D.C. 1963, Mass. 1979, Va. 2001, U.S. Patent Office. Of counsel Alliance Law Group, Tysons Corner, Va., 2000—, Harrity & Snyder, Fairfax, Va. Home: 17040 Thousand Oaks Dr Haymarket VA 20169 Office Phone: 703-848-1720. Personal E-mail: jyfrank8@aol.com. Business E-Mail: jfrank@alliancelawgroup.com.

FRANK, JAMES S., automotive executive; b. Chicago, 1942; m. Karen Frank; 3 children. BS Phi Beta Kappa, Dartmouth Coll.; MBA, Stanford U. With ZF, Inc., Ill., 1965, Wheels, Inc., Des Plaines, Ill., 1965; pres. Four Wheels, Inc., Des Plaines, Ill., 1965; pres., CEO Frank Consol. Enterprises, Des Plaines, Ill., 1967—, Wheels (subs. Frank Consol. Enterprises), Des Plaines, Ill., 1974—. Trustee U. of Chgo., 1995. Pres. Michael Reese Med. Rsch. Inst. Coun. Jr. Bd.; bd. trustees U. Chgo. Hosps., U. Chgo.; bd. overseers Thayer Engring. Sch. Dartmouth Coll. Mem.: Am. Automobile Leasing Assn. (past pres. and chair, bd. dir., chair fed. gtax and legis. com., past chair industry com., dir. 2003—). Office: Frank Consol Enterprises 666 Garland Pl Des Plaines IL 60016-4725

FRANK, JAN L. H., education educator, consultant; b. Milw., May 2, 1955; d. Norman A. and Marilyn B. Hintz; m. Kerry D. Frank, Aug. 9, 1998. BA, Cardinal Stritch Coll., 1973—77; MS, U. of Wis.-Milw., 1979—83, PhD, 1984—90. Tchr., english dept. Milw. Luth. H.S., 1981—86; asst. prof. Concordia U. Wis., Mequon, Wis., 1986—90; prof. St. Cloud (Minn.) State U., 1990—. Contbr. articles, chapters to books. Mem.: Nat. Assn. for Multicultural Edn. Avocations: reading, movies, walking. Home: 650 Grove Ave Shoreview MN 55126 Office: St Cloud State University 720 Fourth Ave South Saint Cloud MN 56301 Office Phone: 320-308-4886. Business E-Mail: jlfrank@stcloudstate.edu.

FRANK, JEREMY D., computer scientist; b. Washington, Aug. 1, 1968; s. Steven B. and Katrin E. F.; m. Amy Lynn Schmieder, July 9, 2000. BA, Pomona Coll., 1990; PhD, U. Calif., Davis, 1997. Computer scientist Caelum Rsch. Corp., 1997—2001, QSS Group Inc., 2000—01, NASA Ames Rsch. Ctr., 2001—. Mem. Am. Assn. Artificial Intelligence, Am. Math. Soc. Avocations: cooking, literature, games of strategy. Home: 664 Vinemaple Ave Sunnyvale CA 94086-8455 Business E-Mail: frank@ptolemy.arc.nasa.gov.

FRANK, JOHN LEROY, lawyer, educator, federal official; b. Eau Claire, Wis., Mar. 13, 1952; s. George LeRoy and Frances Elaine (Torgerson) F. BS summa cum laude, U. Wis., Eau Claire, 1974; JD cum laude, U. Wis., Madison, 1977. Bar: Wis. 1977, U.S. Dist. Ct. (we. dist.) Wis. 1977, U.S. Supreme Ct. 1982. Instr. law U. Wis., Madison, 1976-77; assoc. Garvey, Anderson, Kelly & Ryberg, S.C., Eau Claire, 1977-81; legis. dir., counsel Congressman Steve Gunderson, Washington, 1981-85, chief of staff, counsel, 1985-89; staff coord. 92 Group, Washington, 1987-89; instr. Chippewa Valley Tech. Coll., 1989-93, 97—; dir. paralegal program, 1992—93, 1997—2001, 2003—04, chair dept. behavioral sci. & civic effectiveness, 2003—; pvt. law practice, 1990—93, 1997—; counsel, minority cons. House Subcommittee on Livestock, Washington, Wis., 1993-95; counsel Congressman Steve Gunderson, Washington, 1993-97; dep. minority counsel House Com. on Agr., Washington, 1993-95, dep. chief counsel, 1995-97; commr. W. Ctrl. Wis. Regional Planning Commn., Eau Claire, 1998—; vis. prof. U. of Wis. - Eau Claire, Wis., 2002—03. Pol. analyst, commentator WEAU-TV, Eau Claire, Wis., 1998—; mem. Bush-Cheney Transition Adv. Com., 2001. Mem.: Assn. Career and Tech. Edn. (mem. legis. com. 2003—, reorganization com. 2005—, Region III award of merit 2003), Wis. Bar Assn. (mem. paralegal task force 1998—2005), U. Wis. Alumni Assn. (outstanding sr. arts & scis. 1974, Disting. Achievement award 2001), Wis. Assn. for Career and Tech. Edn. (legis. com. chair 2000—01, bd. dirs. 2000—04, strategic planning com. chair 2001—02, pres. 2002—03, conf. com. chair 2003—04, nominations com. chair 2004—05, Hanbrescht award 2005), The Presto Found. (v.p. 1992—93, bd. dirs. 1992—93, 2000—, v.p. 2000—), Phi Gamma Delta (Durrance award 1978), Phi Delta Phi. Address: 2113 Meadow Ln Eau Claire WI 54701-7965

FRANK, JOHN V., foundation administrator; b. Cleve., Oct. 14, 1936; s. Paul A. and Frances (Halbert) Frank. Student, Babson Coll., 1956-57; BBA, U. Miami, Fla., 1960. Mgmt. trainee Nat. City Bank, Cleve., 1960-62; investment analyst First Nat. Bank, Akron, Ohio, 1962-70, asst. trust officer, 1970-73, trust officer, 1973-80, v.p., trust officer, 1980-81; pres. Summit Capital Mgmt. Co., Akron, 1982-99. Nat. coun. mem. Norman Rockwell Mus., 2002—04, trustee, 2004—; treas. Fairlawn Heights Assn., Inc., Akron, 1971—2002, trustee, 2004—; pres. Ohio Ballet, 1973—74; pres., trustee Burton D. Morgan Found., Akron, 1976—; trustee Howland Meml. Fund, Akron, 1974—, Akron Art Mus., 1976—83, pres., 1979—81; trustee Akron City Hosp. Found., 1980—83, 1992, Summa Health Sys. Found., 1992—, treas., chmn. fin. com., 2003—05; treas., chmn. Rectory Sch., 1999—, chmn. exec. com., 2001—04; active Akron Emergency Med. Adv. Bd., 1986—, Coun. Founds. Com. Legis. and Regulations, 1990—94, Akron Charter Rev. Commn., 1980, 2000, vice-chmn., 1990; bd. overseers Blossom Music Ctr., 1996—99; trustee Akron Rural Cemetery, 1994—, v.p., 1997—; pres., trustee Akron Civil War Meml. Soc., 1996—; found. pres. Friends of Glendale, 2003—; trustee Our Lady of Elms Sch., 2002, chair fin. com., treas., 2003; councilman City of Akron, 1978—98; 50th anniversary com. UN Grace Cathedral Ch., San Francisco, 1993—95, St. Paul's Episc. Ch.; nat. steering com. Coll. Wooster, 1992—96. 1st lt. USAR, 1963—69. Mem.: Cleve. Soc. Security Analysts, Hillsboro Club (Hillsboro Beach, Fla.), Portage Country Club. Republican. Episcopalian. Avocation: art collecting. Office: Burton D Morgan Found PO Box 1500 Akron OH 44309-1500 Office Phone: 330-258-6512.

FRANK, JOHN WILLIAM, management consultant; b. Kansas City, Mo., Nov. 30, 1939; Student, Iowa State U., Ames, 1957-59; BBA cum laude, State U. Iowa, Iowa City, 1961; MBA with distinction, Harvard U., 1965. Staff acct. Price Waterhouse, Chgo., 1961-64; security analyst Lehman Corp., N.Y.C., 1965-67; assoc. Arthur D. Little Inc., Cambridge, Mass., 1967-71; contr. Index Systems, Inc., Cambridge, 1972-73; assoc. Booz Allen & Hamilton, Inc., San Francisco, 1973-76, prin., 1976-78, N.Y.C., 1978-80; dir. Coopers & Lybrand, N.Y.C., 1981-83, ptrn., 1983-91, Li Pera Frank, Inc., N.Y.C., 1991-93; chief auditor Travelers Ins. Cos., Hartford, Conn., 1993-94, v.p. corp. sys., 1994; spl. projects mgr. Electronic Data Sys. Corp., Plano, Tex., 1994-96; chief info. officer The Hartford Steam Boiler Inspection & Ins. Co., 1996-2000, v.p. strategy and corp. devel., 2000—. Bd. dirs. Univec, Inc. Home: 74 Essex Rd Summit NJ 07901-2968 Office: The Hartford Steam Boiler Inspection & Insurance Co 1 State St PO Box 5024 Hartford CT 06102-5024

FRANK, JOSEPH ELIHU, lawyer; b. Burlington, Vt., Jan. 28, 1934; s. Max and Sara Ruth (Bramson) F.; m. Catherine Hartman Layne, Aug. 28, 1971; chldren: Sara Rebecca, Cheryl Elizabeth. AB, Harvard U., 1956, JD, 1959. Bar: Vt. 1960, U.S. Dist. Ct. Vt. 1960, U.S. Ct. Appeals (2d cir.) 1961. U.S. Supreme Ct. 1965. Law clk. to judge U.S. Dist. Ct. Vt., 1960; asst. U.S. atty. Dist. of Vt., 1961; sole practice Burlington, 1961-68; mem. Paul, Frank & Collins P.C., Burlington, 1968-96, of counsel, 1996—. Spl. counsel to Vt. Hwy. Bd., 1962-75, to Pub. Service Bd., 1965-69; chmn. adv. com. civil rules Vt. Supreme Ct., 1983-89. Alderman City of Burlington, 1971—73; trustee Med. Ctr. Hosp. of Vt., Burlington, 1977—86. Mem. ABA, Vt. Bar Assn. (pres. 1983-84), Chittenden County Bar Assn., Am. Judicature Soc. Home: 8 Bay Crest Dr South Burlington VT 05403-7713 Office: Paul Frank + Collins PC 1 Church St Burlington VT 05402-1307 Business E-Mail: jfrank@pfclaw.com.

FRANK, JOSHUA M., economist, think-tank executive; s. Lawrence and Dalia Frank; m. Pamela L Carlisle, Mar. 13, 1988. PhD Econ., Rensselaer Poly. Inst., Troy, N.Y., 2001. Mgr. strategic planning, fin. planning, & info systems Providian, San Francisco, 1992—97; exec. dir. FIREPAW, Albany, NY, 2001—. Cons. in field, 1983—2003. Author short stories; contbr. articles to profl. jor. Office: Firepaw 228 Main St #436 Williamstown NY 01267-2641 Personal E-mail: dogandponyshow@earthlink.net. Business E-Mail: firepaw@earthlink.net.

FRANK, JUDITH ANN (JANN FRANK), retired entrepreneur, small business owner; b. Fresno, Calif., Feb. 10, 1938; d. Walter R. Frank and Ethel Joan (Klomburg) Brinkerhoff; m. David Rogers, Oct. 1956 (div. June 1973). BA, Calif. State U., Fullerton, 1989, postgrad., 1990-91, Chapman U., 1991-93. Vault teller, new accounts, comml. Bank of Am., Fresno, 1956-64; new accounts and note teller Security First Nat. Bank, Fresno, 1965-68; br. bookkeeper, supr. Wells Fargo Bank, Santa Clara and San Jose, Calif., 1968-78; student asst. Fullerton Coll. Career Planning and Placement Ctr., 1982-83; founder, pres. Distant Drums Native Arts, 1994-97, Jann Frank Enterprises, Placentia, Calif., 1996-98; ret., 1997. Phys. and occupl. intern transitional tng. program for brain injured adults and impaired sr. citizens Rehab. Inst. So. Calif., Orange, 1978-80, vol., 1993; vol. St. Citizens Transp., Lunch and Counseling Program, Fullerton, 1981-82; vol. City Wide Disaster Drill, Whittier, Calif., 1987; vol. grad. Evolution of Psychotherapy Conf., Anaheim, Calif., 1990; bd. dirs. Native Am. Inst.; former amb. Placentia (Calif.) C. of C. Recipient Commendation for Vol. Svc. Orange County Coun. Women in C. of C., 1980, Woman of Distinction in Social Scis. award, 1984, Disting. Svc. award Rehab. Inst. So. Calif., Orange, 1993, Key award, 1997; tuition scholarship grantee Chapman U., Orange, 1991. Bd. dirs. Native Am. Inst., mem. Smithsonian Instn., Mus. Am. Indian, Am. Biog. Inst. Rsch. Assn. (lifetime dep. gov.), Order of Internat. Fellowship, Golden Key, Alpha Gamma Sigma, Libr. of Congress, The Internat. Govs. Club (Disting. Leadership award 1996, Internat. Cultural diploma of honor 1996, Twentieth Century Achievement award 1996, Woman of Yr. 1996, Millennium Hall of Fame 1997-98, Internat. Woman of Yr. 1997-98). Avocations: american indian and other cultural events, reading, travel, music, walking. Home: 835 S Brookhurst St Apt 333 Anaheim CA 92804-4328

FRANK, KERRY DEAN, psychology professor, consultant; b. Eunice, La., June 30, 1950; s. Letell and Wirvely Frank; m. Jan Louise Hintz, Aug. 9, 1998. BS, McNeese State U., 1972; MEd, U. Southwestern La., 1977; PhD, U. Minn., 1992. Cert. tchr., La., Minn.; cert. counselor and adminstr., La. Tchr. Maplewood (La.) Jr. H.S., 1972-73, Acadiana H.S., Lafayette, La., 1973-81; lectr., rsch. assoc. U. Minn., Mpls., 1981-89, tchr. asst. in stats. Humphrey Inst. Pub. Affairs, 1985-88; instr. psychology U. St. Thomas, St. Paul, 1989-92, asst. prof., 1992-2000, assoc. prof., 2000—. Counselor, advisor Black Learning Resource Ctr., U. Minn., 1987-88; cons. Mpls.-St. Paul Pub. Schs., 1989—; discussant Julian Parker Lecture Series, St. Paul, 1999—; reviewer Jour. Critical Inquiry, 1999—; presenter Internat. Soc. for Justice Rsch., Israel, 2000. Contbr. articles to profl. jours., including Procs. Nat. Assn. for Multicultural Edn. Cons., advisor gang resistance edn. and tng., St. Paul, 1993-95, Ramsey County Juvenile Ctr., St. Paul, 1998—; vol. Ctr. for Victims of Torture, St. Paul, 2000—. Mem. APA, NAACP, Am. Ednl. Rsch. Assn., Soc. for Psychol. Study Social Issues, Nat. Assn. for Multicultural Edn., Kappa Alpha Psi. Avocations: jogging, reading, playing chess, playing horns, travel. Home: 650 Grove Ave Saint Paul MN 55126 Office: U St Thomas 1000 LaSalle Ave Minneapolis MN 55403-2009 Office Phone: 651-962-4839. Business E-Mail: kdfrank@stthomas.edu.

FRANK, LAURA JEAN, computer scientist; b. New Rochelle, N.Y., May 21, 1945; d. James Florian and Erma (Guttag) F. BA, U. Vt., 1967; MBA, Iona Coll., New Rochelle, 1971; postgrad., China Inst., N.Y.C., Polytechnic Inst., White Plains, N.Y.; Assoc. Masters, George Washington U., 2001. Cert. project mgmt. profl. Project Mgmt. Inst., 2002, Project Mgmt. Inst. With Equitable Life Assurance Soc., N.Y.C., 1967-79, project leader, 1978-79; sr. planning specialist PHH Relocation, Wilton, Conn., 1979-80, project mgr., 1980-83, sys. mgr., 1983-88, mgr. office tech., 1988-91; founding prof. Homequity U., Wilton, Conn., 1985-91; sys. cons. LJF Assocs., Stamford, Conn., 1991-95; sys. mgr. Fiberlux, Purchase, NY, 1994-98; pjt mgr. Synapse Group, Stamford, 1998—. Bd. dirs. Tri-State Trainers. Editor and bd. dirs.: newspaper Stamford First Nighter; contbr. articles to profl. jours. Mem. Stamford Hist. Soc., Women in Mgmt., Friends of Stamford Symphony, Literacy Vols. of Am. Office: 4 High Ridge Park Stamford CT 06905-1325 E-mail: lfrank@synapsemail.com.

FRANK, LAWRENCE, professional basketball coach; m. Susan Frank; 2 children. BS in Edn., Ind. U., 1992; MS in Edn. Adminstrn., Marquette U. Mgr. Hoosiers Ind. U.; staff asst. U. Tenn., 1992, asst. coach, Vancouver Grizzlies, 1997—2000, N.J. Nets, East Rutherford, NJ, 2000—04, head coach, 2004—. Office: 390 Murray Hill Pkwy East Rutherford NJ 07073

FRANK, LAWRENCE JAMES, library director; b. Detroit, Oct. 9, 1943; s. George A. and Marjorie J. (McConkey) Frank; m. Bonnie L. Bonsky; children: Alyssa Ann, Nathan D. BA with honors, We. Mich. U., 1976, MA magna cum laude, 1977; AMLS, U. Mich., 1979; cert. pub. adm. advanced mgmt. program, Miami U., Oxford, Ohio, 1983; cert. edn., U. Wis., 1996. Exec. dir. Amos Meml. Pub. Libr., Sidney, Ohio, 1981—85, Boyd County Pub. Libr., Ashland, Ky., 1986—95, St. Clair County Libr., Port Huron, Mich., 1995—99, Onondaga County Pub. Libr., Syracuse, NY, 1999—2001, Hinsdale Pub. Libr., Ill., 2001—03, Knox County Libr., Knoxville, Tenn., 2003—. Cons./tchr., missionary The Lang. Inst., Japan Luth. Ch., Tokyo and Niigata, Japan, 1968—71; cons. in libr. design and orgn. Port Huron, 1996—98. Author: (novel) The Arius Scrolls, 2004, (anthology) Sensual Rhythms of Appalachia, 1985, numerous poems; contbr. articles to profl. jours. Bd. dirs. Ky. Coun. on Econ Edn., Ashland, 1986-95; mem. chronic disease steering com. U. Cin. Children's Hosp., Ashland, 1987-90. Named Boss of Yr., Jaycees, Ashland; U. Mich. scholar, Ann Arbor, 1978-79. Mem.: PLA, ACLU, ALA, ASPA. Avocations: writing, drawing, hiking, design, painting. Office Phone: 865-215-8703. E-mail: lawf1009@yahoo.com.

FRANK, LILLIAN GORMAN, human resources executive, management consultant; b. N.Y.C., July 4, 1953; d. Helmuth H. and Ida (Malitsch) Degen; m. Stephen E. Frank, Feb. 10, 2001. BA in Psychology, Lehman Coll., CUNY, 1975; MA in Indsl. Psychology, Case Western Res. U., 1978, PhD in indsl. Psychology, 1979; MBA in Corp. Fin., U. So. Calif., 1986. Econ. benefits asst. Girl Scouts U.S.A., N.Y.C., 1971—75; psychologist Pers. Rsch. Svcs., Cleve., 1975—79; cons. psychologist Pers. Rsch. & Devel. Corp., Cleve., 1977—78; mgr. pers. rsch. 1st Interstate Bank, L.A., 1979—82, v.p., mgr. human resource planning and devel., 1982—85; v.p., mgr. human resource planning and exec. devel. 1st Interstate Bancorp, L.A., 1985—86; exec. v.p., human resources dir. First Interstate Bank of Calif., 1986—90; exec. v.p. human resources First Interstate Bancorp, 1990—96; sr. v.p. human resources Edison Internat., Rosemead, Calif., 1996—2000; prin. Frank Insights, L.A., 2000—. Trustee Autry Mus. Western Heritage, 2001—05; bd. dirs. INROADS/So. Calif., 1986—2005, YMCA of Met. L.A., 2002—05. Mem. APA, Soc. for Psychologists in Mgmt. (bd. dirs. 1993-97), Orgn. for Women Execs., Soc. for Human Resources Mgmt. Home and Office: 5865 Strasbourg Ct Reno NV 89511 Business E-Mail: lillian@avantwireless.com.

FRANK, LLOYD, lawyer, director, retired chemicals executive; b. N.Y.C., Aug. 9, 1925; s. Herman and Selma (Lowenstein) F.; m. Beatrice Silverstein, Dec. 26, 1954; children: Margaret Lois, Frederick. BA, Oberlin Coll., 1947; JD, Cornell U., 1950. Bar: N.Y. 1950, U.S. Supreme Ct. 1973. Lawyer, N.Y.C., 1950—; sec., dir. Grow Group, Inc., N.Y.C., 1964-95; sr. ptnr., exec. com., chmn. corp. dept. Parker Chapin LLP, N.Y.C., 1985—2000; sr. ptnr. Jenkens Gilchrist Parker Chapin, LLP, N.Y.C., 2001—04, of counsel, 2004, Trautman Sanders, LLP, 2005—. Bd. dirs. Volt Info. Scis. Inc., (NYSE) N.Y.C., Madison Industries, Inc., N.Y.C., Dryclean, USA, Inc., Miami, Fla., AMEX, Pub. Art Fund, Inc., N.Y.C., Park Electrochem. Corp., (NYSE) Lake Success, N.Y., Internat. Longevity Ctr. U.S.A. Ltd., N.Y.C., Kulite Semicondr., Inc., Leonia, N.J.; sec. Esquire Radio & Electronics, Inc., Bklyn.; lectr. Am. Mgmt. Assn., 1967-77, Probe Internat., Inc., 1975-77, Corp. Seminars, Inc., 1968-71. Mem. ABA (com. negotiated acquisitions), Assn. Bar City of N.Y. (com. on internat. environ. law com. on product liability, com. on lawyers in transition, com. on securities law). Home: 25 Central Park W Apt 17Q New York NY 10023-7211 Office: Troutman Sanders LLP 405 Lexington Ave New York NY 10174-0002 Office Phone: 212-704-6187. Business E-Mail: Lloyd.frank@troutmansanders.com.

FRANK, MARTIN, physiologist, educator, medical association administrator; b. Chgo., Oct. 22, 1947; s. Edward D. and Ann (Horwitz) F.; m. Cheryl Lynn Motel, Aug. 19, 1970; children: Beth Susan, Eric Lawrence. AB (Evans scholar), U. Ill., 1969, MS, 1971, PhD, 1973. USPHS predoctoral research trainee U. Ill., 1971-73; research assoc. Mich. Cancer Found., Detroit, 1973-74; dept. pharmacology Mich. State U., 1974-75; assoc. prof. physiology George Washington U., 1980—. Exec. sec. physiology study sect. divsn. rsch. grants NIH, Bethesda, Md., 1978—85; exec. dir. Am. Physiol. Soc., Bethesda, 1985—; pres., treas., bd. dirs. Commn. on Profls. in Sci. and Tech., 1986—2000; mem. internat. adv. panel Galileo Found., 1990—93; mem. life scis. subcom. NASA Space Sci. and Applications Adv. Com., 1991—94. Editor Physiologist, 1985—; contbr. articles to profl. jours. Vice pres., bd. dirs. Bennington Community Assn., Gaithersburg, Md., 1976-78, 80-81, mem. Gaithersburg City Planning Commn., 1982-85. Recipient Disting. Alumni award dept. molecular and integrative physiology U. Ill., Urbana, 2001, Presdl. award 2003; grantee Nations' Capitol Affiliate Am. Heart Assn.,1975-78, NIH, NSF. Mem. AAAS, Am. Physiol. Soc., Am. Soc. Assn. Execs., Coalition Engring Scientific Soc. Execs. Office: Am Physiol Soc 9650 Rockville Pike Bethesda MD 20814-3998 Office Phone: 301-634-7118. E-mail: mfrank@the-aps.org.

FRANK, MAURICE JEROME, mathematics professor; b. Omaha, Dec. 20, 1942; s. Maurice Jerome and Helen (Beeson) F.; m. Patricia Grady, Aug. 23, 1970; children: Elizabeth, Theodore. SB in Math., U. Chgo., 1965; MS, Ill. Inst. Tech., 1969, PhD, 1972. Asst. prof. U. Mass., Amherst, 1972—73, Ill. Inst. Tech., Chgo., 1976—83, assoc. prof., 1983—93, prof. math., 1993—, chmn. dept. math., 1986—92; lectr. U. Wis., Milw., 1973—75. Contbr. articles to profl. jours. Mem. Am. Math. Soc., Math. Assn. Am. Office: Ill Inst Tech Applied Math Chicago IL 60616 Business E-Mail: frankm@iit.edu.

FRANK, MICHAEL M., physician; b. Bklyn., Feb. 28, 1937; s. Robert and Helen (Prakin) F.; m. Ruth Sybil Pudolsky, Nov. 5, 1961; children: Robert E., Abigail B., Brice S.H. AB, U. Wis., 1956; MD, Harvard U., 1960. Intern Boston City Hosp., 1960-61; resident in pediatrics Johns Hopkins Hosp., 1961-62, 64-65; vis. scientist Nat. Inst. Med. Research, London, 1965-66; with NIH, 1967-90; chief lab. of clin. investigation, clin. dir. Nat. Inst. Allergy and Infectious Diseases, Bethesda, Md., 1977-90; prof. Duke U. Med. Ctr., Durham, NC, 1990—, chmn.Ddept. Pediatrics, 1990—2004. Mem. ACP, Assn. Am. Physicians, Am. Soc. Clin. Investigation, Soc. Pediatric Rsch., Am. Pediatric Soc., Infectious Diseases Soc., Am. Acad. Allergy, Am. Acad. Pediatrics. Office: Duke U Med Ctr PO Box 3556 Durham NC 27710 Office Phone: 919-684-4626. Business E-Mail: frank007@mc.duke.edu.

FRANK, MICHAEL VICTOR, risk assessment engineer; b. NYC, Sept. 22, 1947; s. David and Bernice (Abrams) F.; m. Jane Griminger, Dec. 21, 1969; children: Jeffrey, Heidi, Heather. BS, UCLA, 1969, PhD, 1978; MS, Carnegie-Mellon U., 1972. Registered profl. engr., Calif.; cert. mgmt. cons., cert. hazard and operability study leader. Engr. Westinghouse Electric Corp., Pitts., 1970-72, So. Calif. Edison, LA, 1972-74; lectr. U. Calif., Santa Barbara, 1976-77; task leader Gen. Atomics, San Diego, 1977-81; sr. exec. engr. NUS Corp., San Diego, 1981-85; with Mgmt. Analysis Co., San Diego, 1985-86; sr. cons. PLG, Newport Beach, Calif., 1986-89; pres. Safety Factor Assocs., Inc., Encinitas, Calif., 1989—. Tech. dir. risk and reliability studies of NASA facilties, space and launch vehicles, internat. space sta., stratospheric obs. for infrared astronomy, space nuc. power systems and terrestrial nuc. facilities worldwide; NASA hdqrs., NASA Ames Rsch. Ctr.; lectr. on risk assessment at NASA ctrs.; probabilistic risk assessment cons. to U.S. Nuc. Regulatory Commn., Ctr. for Nuc. Waste Regulatory Analysis and Utility Co., qualified forensic cons. in product defects and hazards, fires and explosions, safety and reliability; engring. risk mgmt. cons. European Space Agy.; mem. tech. program com. probabilistic safety assessment and mgmt. confs. Contbr. more than 85 articles to Reliability Engring. and System Safety, Risk Analysis, Nuc. Engring. and Design, ASME, European Safety and Reliability Soc., Am. Nuc. Soc., others. Mem. AIAA, IEEE (past pres. San Diego chpt. Reliability Soc.), Soc. Risk Analysis, Inst. Mgmt. Cons. Avocations: family activities, running, skiing, hiking. Office: Ste 16 1410 Vanessa Cir Encinitas CA 92024-2440 Office Phone: 760-436-9132. Business E-Mail: riskexpert@ieee.org.

FRANK, PAULA FELDMAN, business executive; b. Tulsa; d. Maurice M. and Sarah (Bergman) Feldman; m. Gordon D. Frank, Dec. 15, 1955; children: Cynthia Jan, Margaret Jill. B.S., Northwestern U., 1954. Directed, wrote and appeared in TV films for Nat. Safety Coun., Chgo., 1954-55; appeared in TV comml s., 1955-56; asst. prodn. mgr. Kling Films, Chgo., 1956; pres. Gaston Ave. Optical Inc., ret. 1990; Dallas. Social chmn. Baylor Hosp. Vol. Corp., Dallas, 1962—; asst. dir. Des Plaines (Ill.) Theater Guild, 1956-57, Pearl Chappell Playhouse, Dallas, 1962-63, Dallas Theater Center, 1964. Mem. Hockaday Alumni Assn., Tau Gamma Epsilon, Phi Beta, Sigma Delta Tau. Home: 7123 Currin Dr Dallas TX 75230-3645

FRANK, PETER SOLOMON, art historian, curator, art critic; b. N.Y.C., July 3, 1950; s. Reuven and Bernice (Kaplow) F. BA in Art History, Columbia U., 1972, MA in Art History, 1974. Art critic SoHo Weekly News, N.Y.C., 1973-76; chief art critic Village Voice, N.Y.C., 1977-79; art critic, columnist L.A. Weekly, 1988—; critic Long Beach Press-Telegram, 1993-96; L.A. corr. Contemporanea, 1989-91; curatorial assoc. Ind. Curators Inc., N.Y.C. and Washington, 1974—; co-curator Documenta VI, Kassel, W. Ger., 1976-77; assoc. editor Nat. Arts Guide, Chgo., 1979-81, Art Express, N.Y.C., 1980-81; curator Exxon Nat. Exhbn. of Am. Artists, Guggenheim Mus., N.Y.C., 1980-81, Dokumenta, Kassel, Germany, 1981; art critic Diversion mag., 1983-90; former editor Visions Art Quarterly; columnist Angeleno mag. Mem. faculty New Sch. for Social Rsch., 1974, Pratt Inst., 1975-76, Columbia U. Sch. Arts, 1978, Claremont Grad. Sch., 1989, 92-94, 95-97, U. Calif., Irvine, 1988-90, Calif. State U., Fullerton, 1990-91, U. Calif., Santa Barbara, 1994, Tyler Sch. Art; Am. curatorial advisor Documenta 8, 1986-87; organizer numerous theme and survey shows; co-curator "On Ramps: Moments of Transition in California Art", Pasadena Mus., California Art and "Fluxus Film and Video", Museo Reina Sofia, Madrid. Author: The Travelogues, 1982, Something Else Press: An Annotated Bibliography, 1983; co-author: New, Used and Improved: Art in the '80s, 1987; assoc. editor Tracks mag., 1974-76; editor Re Dact, 1983-85, contbg. editor Art Economist, 1981-84; contbr. articles to art periodicals including ARTnews and Art on Paper; writer on intermedia and Fluxus artists, many catalogues to one person and group exhbns.; edited Ken Friedman:Events for Jaap Rietmann, Inc. Nat. Endowment for Arts art critics travel fellow, 1978; critics project fellow, 1981; Royal Norwegian Ministry of Fgn. Affairs Fluxus rsch. fellow, 1987. Mem. Internat. Assn. Art Critics (v.p.), Coll. Art Assn., Internationale Künstlers Gremium Home: PO Box 24a36 Los Angeles CA 90024-1036 Office: LA Weekly PO Box 4315 Los Angeles CA 90078*

FRANK, RICHARD ASHER, lawyer, health products executive; b. Omaha, Nov. 4, 1936; s. Alexander David and Sarah R. (Katz) F.; m. Susan Marie Kling; children: Brian, Hilary, Alexander, Nicholas. AB, Harvard U., 1958, JD, 1962. Bar: D.C. 1962, U.S. Supreme Ct. Asst. legal advisor U.S. State Dept., Washington, 1962-69; dir. Ctr. Law and Social Policy, Washington, 1970-77; adminstr. NOAA, Washington, 1977-81; ptnr. Wald, Harkrader, Ross, Washington, 1981-87; pres. Population Svcs. Internat., Washington, 1987—. Adj. prof. Georgetown Law Sch., 1988—. Editor: The Constitution and the Conduct of Foreign Policy, 1976; contbr. articles to profl. jours. 1st lt. U.S. Army, 1959—66. Mem.: Coun. Fgn. Rels. Avocations: sailing, tennis. Home: 3405 Lowell St NW Washington DC 20016-5024 Office: Population Svcs Internat 1120 19th St NW Washington DC 20036-3605 Office Phone: 202-785-0072. Business E-Mail: rfrank@psi.org.

FRANK, RICHARD CALHOUN, architect; b. Louisville, May 17, 1930; s. William George and Helen (Calhoun) F.; children: Richard, Scott, Elizabeth, William, Jennifer, Philip. BArch, U. Mich., 1953. Assoc. archtl. firms, Lansing, Mich., 1953-61; pres. Frank & Stein Assocs., Inc., Lansing, 1961-70; prin. Johnson, Johnson & Roy, Ann Arbor, 1971-75; pres. Preservation/Urban Design/Inc., Ann Arbor and Washington, 1975-84; pvt. practice Saline and Gregory, Mich., 1985—2004; pres. Frank, McCormick & Khalak, LLC, 2004—. Ind. contractor C.S. Mott Found., 1999-2000. Life trustee Hist. Soc. Mich. Fellow AIA (gold medal Mich. 1992); mem. Nat. Trust for Historic Preservation (trustee emeritus), Victorian Soc. Am. (v.p.). Home: 1408 Joliet Pl Detroit MI 48207 Office: 28 W Adams Detroit MI 48226 Office Phone: 313-234-8700. Personal E-mail: rcffaia@comcast.net. Business E-Mail: rcfrank@fmkdetroit.com.

FRANK, RICHARD G., healthcare educator; b. Boston, Apr. 27, 1952; BA in Econs., Bard Coll., 1974; PhD in Econs., Boston U., 1982. Prof. dept. health econs. Harvard Med. Sch., Boston, 1994-99, Margaret T. Morris prof. health econs., 1999—. Rsch. assoc. Nat. Bur. Econ. Rsch., Cambridge, Mass. and N.Y.C., 1987—. Office: Harvard Med Sch Dept Health Care Policy 180 Longwood Ave Boston MA 02115-5821

FRANK, RICHARD SANFORD, retired magazine editor; b. Paterson, N.J., July 28, 1931; s. David and Shirley (Dwoskin) F.; m. Margaret Schwartz, June 30, 1957 (dec. Apr. 2001); children: Daniel, Peter. BA, Syracuse U., 1953; MA, U. Chgo., 1956. Reporter Balt. Evening Sun, 1957-64, Phila. Bull., 1965-71; asst. to mayor City of Balt., 1964-65; reporter Nat. Jour., Washington, 1971-72, editor, 1972-76, editor-in-chief, 1976-97. Served with U.S. Army, 1953-55. Mem. Am. Soc. Mag. Editors Home: 5111 Wessling Ln Bethesda MD 20814-1232 E-mail: richard.s.frank@verizon.net.

FRANK, ROBERT ALLEN, media consultant; b. Albany, N.Y., Sept. 26, 1932; s. Edward and Marian (Kostelanetz) Frank; m. Cynthia Tull, Aug. 1984; children: David, Chelsea, Alison. BA, Colby Coll., 1954; MBA, Amos Tuck Sch. Bus. Adminstrn., Dartmouth Coll., 1958. Cost control adminstr. ABC-TV, N.Y.C., 1958-59; corp. auditor CBS, Inc., N.Y.C., 1959-60, TV sales svc. account exec., 1961, account exec. radio network sales, 1962-69; exec. v.p., co-founder SFM Media Corp., N.Y.C., 1969—, pres. Media Svc. div., 1981; pres., CEO, SFM Media LLC, N.Y.C., 1998-2000; vice-chmn. Media Planning Group USA, N.Y.C., 2001—02; pvt. cons., 2003—04. Bd. dirs. Judge Rotenberg Ednl. Ctr., 2004—. Radio-TV cons. Nat. Kidney Fund, 1974; trustee Nat. Child Labor Com., 1984—96, vice chmn., 1994—96; trustee Myasthenia Gravis Found., 1984—93; judge Rotenberg Edn. Ctr., 2004—; active radio TV for various polit. campaigns Robert Kennedy for Senator, 1964, Richard Nixon for Pres., 1972, Ford for Pres., 1976, Bush for Pres., 1980, Reagan for Pres., 1980, Du Pont for Pres., 1988; mem. leadership coun. Nat. Rep. Congl. Com., Rep. Nat. Com., Pres.'s Club, 1984—88; mem. Citizens Rep. Pres. Com., 1984—88; mem. inner cir. Rep. Nat. Senatorial Com., 1985—88; bd. dirs. Rotenberg Edn. Ctr., 2004—. Served to capt. USAF, 1954—56. Recipient Lifetime Achievement award, Media Week, 2001. Mem.: Internat. Radio-TV Soc., Amos Tuck Alumni Assn. N.Y. (pres. 1976—77, bd. dirs. 1979), Dartmouth Club (N.Y.C.), Pi Gamma Mu. Home: 35 Lounsbury Rd Ridgefield CT 06877-4710 Office: Conn Mktg One Grumman Hill Rd Wilton CT 06897

FRANK, ROBERT J., lawyer; b. NYC, July 27, 1924; BEE, Cornell U., 1949; MEE, Polytechnic Inst., NY, 1955; JD, Brooklyn Law Sch., 1959. Bar: NY 1960, US Dist. Ct., NY (So. & Ea. Dist.) 1968, Va. 1972, US Ct. of Customs and Patent Appeals 1974, DC 1978, US Dist. Ct., DC 1979, US Ct. of Appeals, Federal Circuit 1982, US Supreme Ct. 1984, US Ct. of Appeals, DC Circuit 1984, US Patent and Trademark Office. Engnr., 1954—; ptnr., technology div. Venable LLP, Washington. Mem.: IEEE, ABA, Am. Intellectual Property Law Assn., Va. State Bar Assn., DC Bar Assn. Office: Venable LLP 575 7th St NW Washington DC 20004 Office Phone: 202-344-4013. Office Fax: 202-344-8300. Business E-Mail: rjfrank@venable.com.

FRANK, ROBERT LOUIS, lawyer; b. Balt., Mar. 26, 1958; s. Louis Jr. and Beryl (Oppenheimer) F.; children: Robert Louis Jr., Michael David, Cameron Alexander, Victoria Rochelle. BSEE, Duke U., 1980; JD, U. Md., 1983. Bar: Md. 1983. Assoc. Belsky & Akman, Towson, Md., 1984-85; pvt. practice Reisterstown, Md., 1985; ptnr. Blitz Frank & Blitz, Owings Mills, Md., 1986-92, Needle, Montague & Frank, P.C., 1992-94; mem. Md. Ho. Dels., Annapolis, 1994-98; pvt. practice, 1994—98; pres. Liberty Showcase Theatre, 2004—. Vice-chair sci. and tech. subcom.; prof. Villa Julie Coll., 2005—. Pres. Pikesville (Md.) Recreation Parks Bd., 1988, Pikesville Baseball, 1984-86; pres. Reisterstown, Owings Mills C. of C., 1991; bd. dirs. Soldier's Delight Conservation, Inc. Mem. ABA, Md. State Bar Assn. (bd. govs. 1987-88, chmn. gen. practice sect. 1987-88), Balt. County Bar Assn., Balt. City Bar Assn., Psi Upsilon (scholarship 1978). Democrat. Home: 15 Sunnyking Dr Reisterstown MD 21136-6143

FRANK, ROBERT WORTH, JR., English language educator; b. Logansport, Ind., Apr. 8, 1914; s. Robert Worth and Grace Alice (Haun) F.; m. Gladys Martine Loeb, May 11, 1940 (dec. Mar. 1994); children: Thaisa, Elizabeth Ann. AB, Wabash (Ind.) Coll., 1934; MA, Columbia U., 1939; PhD, Yale U., 1948; DLitt in Humanities (hon.), Wabash Coll., 1997. Instr. English Lafayette Coll., Easton, Pa., 1937-39, U. Rochester (N.Y.), 1940-42, Princeton U., 1942-44, Northwestern U., 1944-48; asst. prof., then assoc. prof. Ill. Inst. Tech., 1948-58; prof. English Pa. State U., 1958-79, head dept., 1975-79, emeritus, 1979—; O'Connor prof. lit. Colgate U., 1980, 85. Charles Rahter Meml. lectr., Susquehanna U., 1977, 91. Author: Piers Plowman and the Scheme of Salvation, 2d edit, 1969, The Responsible Man: The Insights of the Humanities, rev. edit, 1965, The Critical Question, 1964, Chaucer and the Legend of Good Women, 1973; editor The Chaucer Rev., 1966—; mem. editorial bd. Revised Chaucer Analogues, 1988—. Fellow Am. Coun. Learned Socs., 1951-52, 60-61, Fund Advancement Edn., 1955-56, Guggenheim Found., 1970-71, assoc. fellow Clare Hall, Cambridge (Eng.) U., 1971, 76, vis. fellow, 1972-73. Mem. Mediaeval Acad. Am., MLA, New Chaucer Soc. (trustee 1980-84, pres. 1986-88). Clubs: Lit. (State College, Pa.). Democrat. Office: 116 Burrowes Pa State Univ University Park PA 16802 also: Chaucer Rev Pa State U Press Barbara Bldg 820 N University Dr Ste C University Park PA 16802-1012 E-mail: rwf4@psu.edu.

FRANK, ROBERTA, literature educator; b. N.Y.C., Nov. 9, 1941; d. Norman Berton and Doris F.; m. Walter André Goffart, Dec. 31, 1977. BA, NYU, 1962; MA, Harvard U., 1964, PhD, 1968. Asst. prof. U. Toronto, 1968-73, assoc. prof., 1973-78, prof. English, 1978-2000, Univ. prof., 1995-2000, dir. grad studies dept. English, 1980-85, dir. Ctr. for Medieval Studies, 1994-99; Douglas Tracy Smith prof. English Yale U., 2000—. Mem. bus. bd. U. Toronto Press. Author: Old Norse Court Poetry, 1978, also articles; co-editor: Computers and Old English Concordances, 1970, A Plan for the Dictionary of Old English, 1973; gen. editor: Toronto Old English Series, 1976-2003; publs. of Dictionary of Old English, 1984-2003. Recipient Guggenheim award, 1985, Bowdoin prize in humanities Harvard U., 1968. Fellow Medieval Acad. Am. (councillor 1981-84, Elliott prize 1972), Royal Soc. Can.; mem. MLA (mem. Old English exec. com. 1974-78, 95-99), Internat. Soc. Anglo-Saxonists (pres. 1985-87). Home: 171 Lowther Ave Toronto ON Canada M5R 1E6 Office: Yale U Dept English New Haven CT 06520-8302 Office Phone: 203-432-2238. Business E-Mail: roberta.frank@yale.edu.

FRANK, RONALD EDWARD, marketing educator; b. Chgo., Sept. 15, 1933; s. Raymond and Ethel (Lundquist) F.; m. Iris Donner, June 18, 1958; children: Linda, Lauren, Kimberly. BSBA, Northwestern U., 1955, MBA, 1957; PhD, U. Chgo., 1960. Instr. bus. statistics Northwestern U., Evanston, Ill., 1956-57; asst. prof. bus. adminstrn. Harvard U., Boston, 1960-63, Stanford U., 1963-65; assoc. prof. mktg. Wharton Sch., U. Pa., 1965-68, prof., 1968-84, chmn. dept. mktg., 1971-74, vice dean, dir. rsch. and PhD programs, 1974-76, assoc. dean, 1981-83; dean, prof. mktg. Krannert Grad. Sch. Mgmt., Purdue U., 1984-89; dean, Asa Griggs Candler prof. mktg. Goizueta Bus. Sch. Emory U., Atlanta, 1989-98, dean, Asa Griggs Candler prof. mktg. emeritus, 1998-99; mktg. cons., 1999—; pres. Singapore Mgmt. U., 2001—04. Bd. dirs. Lafayette (Ind.) Life Ins. Co., The MAC Group, Home Hosp., Lafayette; cornerstone rsch. cons. to industry; mem. strategic issues com. Am. Assembly Collegiate Schs. of Bus., 1988-92, chmn. audit com., 1993-94, mem. strategic planning and ops. com,. 1994-95; chmn. Orgn. for the Future Task Force, 1996-97; trustee U. Singapore, 2000-01; chmn. strategic issues adv. com. Singapore Mgmt. U., 2004—. Author: (with Massy and Kuehn) Quantitative Techniques in Marketing Analysis, 1962, (with Matthews, Buzzell and Levitt) Marketing: an Introductory Analysis, 1964, (with William Massy) Computer Programs for the Analysis of Consumer Panel Data, 1964, An Econometric Approach to a Marketing Decision Model, 1971, (with Paul Green) Manager's Guide to Marketing Research, 1967, Quantative Methods in Marketing, 1967, (with Massy and Lodahl) Purchasing Behavior and Personal Attributes, 1968, (with Massy and Wind) Market Segmentation, 1972, (with Marshall Greenberg) Audience Segmentation Analysis for Public Television Program Development, Evaluation and Promotion, 1976, The Public's Use of Television, 1980, Audiences for Public Television, 1982. Bd. dirs., fin. com. Home Hosp. of Lafayette, 1985-89; bd. dirs. The Washington Campus, 1984-89, 95-98. Recipient pub. TV rsch. grants John and Mary R. Markle Found., 1975-82. Mem. Am. Mktg. Assn. (dir. 1968-70, v.p. mktg. edn. 1972-73), Inst. Mgmt. Sci., Assn. Consumer Rsch. Office Phone: 404-321-6655. Business E-Mail: ref@bus.emory.edu.

FRANK, RONALD WILLIAM, lawyer; b. Greensburg, Pa., Mar. 11, 1947; s. William John and Louise (Mautino) F.; m. Marsha Ann Kolesar, Aug. 30, 1969. BSChemE, Carnegie Mellon U., 1969; JD, Duke U., 1972. Bar: Pa. 1972. Ptnr. Buchanan Ingersoll P.C., Pitts., 1972-93, Babst, Calland, Clements & Zomnir, P.C., Pitts., 1993-99, Reed Smith LLP, Pitts., 2000—. Sec. Akers Nat. Roll Co.; chmn. PaintStar Paintball LLC. Contbr. articles to profl. jours. Chmn. nat. fund raising com., Carnegie-Mellon U., Pitts., 1983-88, bd. advisors Sch. Engring. and Sci., Carnegie Mellon U.; mem. bd. visitors sch. law Duke U., Durham, N.C. Mem. ABA, Pa. Bar Assn. (chmn. Internat. and Comparative law sect. 1992—), Allegheny County Bar Assn., Internat. Bar Assn., Duquesne Club, Shannopin Country Club. Avocations: golf, skiing, computers, amateur radio. Home: 1675 Gloucester Ct Sewickley PA 15143-8518 Office: Reed Smith 435 6th Ave Pittsburgh PA 15219-1886 Office Phone: 412-288-4044. Personal E-mail: rwfrank@aol.com. Business E-Mail: rfrank@reedsmith.com.

FRANK, SCOTT M., mechanical engineer, consultant; s. Robert A. and Bernadette A. Frank; m. Amy S. Kohman, Oct. 5, 1991; 1 child, Hunter. BSME, U. Wis., 1989; degree in mech. design tech., Moraine Park Tech. Coll., 1996. Designer Busse, Inc., Randolph, Wis., 1989—95; mech. engr. Water Tech., Inc., Beaver Dam, 1995—98; engr., project mgr. Pro-Tech., Inc., Columbus, 1998—2000, Frank Designs LLC, Beaver Dam, 1996—. Pres. Fox Lake Hist. Soc., Wis., 2002—, 2d Wis. Vol. Inf. Assn. Co., 2001—; instr. Hunter Edn., Beaver Dam, 1991—. Avocations: Civil War reenactor, history, camping. Office: Frank Designs LLC W9041 Spruce Rd Beaver Dam WI 53916 Office Phone: 720-296-0254.

FRANK, STANLEY DONALD, publishing company executive; b. NYC, June 30, 1932; s. Arthur and Jessie (Schwartz) F.; m. Sheila Rose, Dec, 25, 1958; children: Bradley Scott, Tracy Lynne. BS, CCNY, 1953, MS, 1956; EdD, Columbia U., 1961. Counselor N.Y.C. Pub. Schs., 1955-61; dir. pupil pers. svcs. San Diego County Dept. Edn., 1959-61; dir. mktg. Sci. Rsch. Assocs. subs. IBM, Chgo., 1961-68, v.p. mktg. and ops., 1968-73; pres. Holt, Rinehart & Winston, Inc. subs. CBS, N.Y.C., 1974-77, CBS Ednl. Pub. Div., 1975-78; exec. v.p., chief oper. officer CBS Pub. Group, 1978-80, pres., 1980-84, Britannica Learning Corp., Chgo., 1985-90; exec. v.p. Ency. Britannica, Inc., 1985-93; pres. Comptons Multi Media Pub. Group, Inc., Chgo., 1991—; chmn. bd. dirs. Am. Learning Corp., 1985—; pres., CEO Ctr. for the Assessment of Human Potenial Inc., Boca Raton, Fla., 1994—; mng. ptnr. New Media Ventures, Boca Raton, 1995; pres. New Media Ptnrs., Inc., 1999—; chmn. Restorigen, Inc., 2001—. Bd. dirs. Childcraft Ednl. Corp., Designware, Inc.; cons. Morgan Stanley Capital Markets, 1996—; dir. Golbal Learning Systems.com, 2000—. Mem. Bd. Edn. Dist. 67, Niles, Ill., 1972-73; mem. council Rockefeller U. Served with AUS, 1953-55. Andrew Wellington Cordier fellow Columbia U. Sch. Internat. Affairs. Mem. Am. Psychol. Assn., Phi Delta Kappa. Personal E-mail: drsdf@aol.com.

FRANK, STEPHEN IRA, political science professor, department chairman; b. Seattle, Oct. 14, 1942; s. Nancy Ann (Schwartz) Frank; m. Barbara Ann Covey; 1 child, Thomas Aaron. BS in Edn., History and Polit. Sci., Ctrl. Mich. U., 1966, MA in Polit. Sci., 1969; PhD in Polit. Sci., Wash. State U., Pullman, 1976. Tchr. social sci. Clarkston HS, Mich., 1967-69; instr. in polit. sci. Gogebec Cmty. Coll., Ironwood, Mich., 1967-69, Lamar U., Beaumont, Tex., 1975-76; prof. polit. sci. N.E. La. U., Monroe, La., 1976-78, St. Cloud State U., Minn., 1978—, chair dept. polit. sci., 2001—03. Co-dir., founder St. Cloud State U. Survey. Author: We Shocked the World: A Case Study of Jesse Ventura's Election As Governor of Minnesota, 1999, 2d edit., 2001; contbr. articles to profl. jour., and chapters to books. Mem. Am. Polit. Sci. Assn., Minn. Polit. Sci. Assn. (bd. dirs., treas., pres. 2000-), Am. Assn. Pub. Opinion, Nat. Assn. Prelaw Advisors, Midwest Prelaw Advisors Assn. (bd. dirs. 1999-2002), St. Cloud State U. Faculty Assn. (pres. 1993-94), Phi Kappa Delta. Avocations: gardening, walking, reading. Office: St Cloud State U Dept Polit Sci 319 Brown Hall Saint Cloud MN 56301-4444 Office Phone: 320-308-4131. Business E-Mail: sfrank@stcloudstate.edu.

FRANK, STEVEN NEIL, chemist; b. Red Oak, Iowa, Feb. 15, 1947; s. Robert Joseph and Joyce (Erickson) F.; m. Carol Bert Femmer, Jan. 4, 1975. BS, Colo. State U., 1969; PhD, Calif. Inst. Tech., 1974. Sr. mem. tech. staff, solar energy project Tex. Instruments, Dallas, mgr. fuel cell devel., 1980-83, mgr. charge coupled imagers, 1983-86, mgr. wafer fabrication, focal plane array, 1986-88, mfg. mgr., focal plane array, 1988-90, mgr. focal plane array assembly and testing, 1990-91, mgr. uncooled IR imaging, 1990-99; chief engr. Raytheon Comml. Infared, Dallas, 1999—2002, chief tech. officer, 2002—04; v.p., chief tech. officer L-3 Comm. Infrared Products, 2004—. Presenter in field. Author: (with others) Laboratory Techniques in Electro-Analytical Chem, 1996; referee Jour. Applied Physics, 1977—, Jour. Phys. Chemistry, 1977—; contbr. articles to profl. jours. Robert A. Welch fellow U. Tex., 1974-77. Mem. AAAS, Am. Chem. Soc., Electrochem. Soc. Achievements include patents in field. Home: 471 Hackberry Dr Mc Kinney TX 75069-1569 Office Phone: 972-670-7408. E-mail: steven.frank@l-3com.com.

FRANK, STUART, cardiologist; b. N.Y.C., Dec. 25, 1934; s. Henry and Kitty (Sternberg) F.; m. Nanchen O'Brien, Aug. 1976 (div. Feb. 1980); children: Rachel Arthur, Sebastian Noah; m. Amber Barnhart, June 22, 1982; children: Amelia Elizabeth, Abigail Kitty, Jessica Cole. BS in Chemistry, MIT, 1956; MD, NYU, 1960. Diplomate Am. Bd. Internal Medicine, Am. Bd. Cardiovascular Disease. Intern and resident in internal medicine Yale U. New Haven Hosp., 1960-64; postdoctoral fellow Inst. Cardiology, London, 1964-65, Nat. Heart Inst., Bethesda, Md., 1965-67; chief cardiology Kaiser Permanente Med. Ctr., San Francisco, 1967-77; assoc. prof. dept. medicine So. Ill. U., Springfield, 1977-86, chief div. cardiology, 1977-90, asst. chmn. dept. medicine, 1981-88, prof. dept. medicine, 1986—, dean of students, 1990-95. Author: The People's Handbook of Medical Care, 1972; contbr. numerous articles to profl. jours. Recipient Nellie Westerman prize Am. Fedn. Clin. Research, 1986. Fellow ACP, Am. Coll. Cardiology, Am. Coll. Chest Physicians, Am. Heart Assn. (council clin. cardiology), Laennec Soc. Office: So Ill Univ Medicine Dept Cardiology PO Box 19636 Springfield IL 62794-9636 Office Phone: 217-545-0185.

FRANK, TARA ELIZABETH, academic administrator, dean; b. Norfolk, Va., July 30, 1974; d. William George and Marcia Elizabeth Frank, Rhonda Frank (Stepmother). BA in psychology, Shippensburg U., Shippensburg, PA, 1992—96; MS in counselling, Shippensburg U., Pa., 1997—99. Asst. dir., leadership and student involvement Rutgers Coll., New Brunswick, NJ, 1999—2002; assoc. dir., student activities Emory U., Atlanta, 2002—03; asst. dean, student activities Lehigh U., Bethlehem, Pa., 2003—. Mem.: Am. Coll. Pers. Assn. (assoc.). E-mail: tef2@lehigh.edu.

FRANK, THEODORE DAVID, lawyer; b. Bklyn., Apr. 1, 1941; s. Paul and Bessie Frank; m. Louise Quinby Gorrell, Oct. 19, 1969; children: Carolyn Quinby Judge, Rachel Jackson. BS in Math., Rensselaer Polytech. Inst., 1963; LLB, U. Tex., 1966; LLM, Harvard U., 1969. Bar: Tex. 1966, D.C. 1969, U.S. Ct. Appeals (1st cir. and 2d cir.) 1977, U.S. Ct. Appeals (5th and 9th cir.) 1980, U.S. Ct. Appeals (3rd cir. and 11th cir.) 1981, U.S. Ct. Appeals (D.C. cir.) 1970, U.S. Supreme Ct. 1978. Law clk. to Hon. Walter P. Gewin U.S. Cir. Ct., 5th cir., Tuscaloosa, Ala., 1966-67; faculty asst. for Ames Competition Harvard Law Sch., Cambridge, Mass., 1967-69; assoc. Arent, Fox, Kintner, Plotkin & Kahn, Washington, 1969-75, ptnr., 1976-97, Arnold & Porter LLP, Washington, 1997—. Hearing com. bd. profl. responsibility DC Bar, 1997-2003; co-chmn. Nat. Telecomms. Moot Ct. Com., 1999-2001. Chmn. zoning and tax coms. Springfield Civic Assn., Bethesda, Md., 1989—98. Mem. ABA, Fed. Comm. Bar Assn. (exec. com. 1996-98, co-chmn. profl. responsiblity com. 2001-03). Jewish. Avocations: woodworking, bike riding. Office: Arnold & Porter LLP 555 12th St NW Washington DC 20004-1206 Office Phone: 202-942-5790. Business E-Mail: theodore_frank@aporter.com.

FRANK, THOMAS, construction executive, management and design executive; b. Salt Lake City, Nov. 23, 1937; s. Simon and Suzanne (Seller) F. BFA, U. Utah, 1963. Lic. contractor Utah. Owner Thomas Frank Designers & Specifiers, Salt Lake City, 1962—; owner, pres. OmmiComputer West, Salt Lake City. Bd. dirs. Electronic Learning, Inc., Electronic Learning, Inc.; instr. design, textiles and drafting LDS Jr. Coll., Salt Lake City, 1963-86; lectr. on interior design for jr. and high schs. Bus. & Industry Coop. Edn. Program; profl. adviser interior design curriculum devel. program U. Utah; inter-profl. adv. coun. Utah State Bldg. Bd.; cons., lectr., presenter in field. Contbr. articles to profl. publs. Exec. v.p. Salt Lake Art Ctr., 1977-80; spl. advisor Children's Ctr.; co-chmn. spl. events Utah divsn. Am. Cancer Soc., 1978. Recipient awards U. Utah, 1962, Utah Designers Craftsman Guild, 1962, State Fair Fine Arts, 1962, Recognition award Gov. Mrs. Scott Matheson, 1980, Honor award Utah Soc. AIA, 1980. Fellow Am. Soc. Interior Designers (bd. dir. Intermountain chpt. 2004-05); mem. N.Am. Autocadd Users Group, Nat. Kitchen and Bath Assn. (pres. mountain states chpt. west 1991-92), Am. Soc. Interior Designers (nat. long-range planning com. 1985-87, nat. comms. area coord. 1985, nat. membership devel. com. 1986-87, nat. regional dir. 1991-92, nat. edn. com. 1981, nat. chmn. energy conservation 1980-82, nat. chpt. pres.' orientation task force 1980, nat. bd. dir. 1977-82, chmn. regional indsl. rels. 1977-78, numerous other offices, numerous awards), AID (sec. Utah 1969-71, bd. govs. 1970-74, Utah pres. 1973-75), Nat. Coun. Interior Design Quantification. Avocations: tennis, skiing, art collecting. Home: 2360 Oakhill Dr Salt Lake City UT 84121-1520 Office: Thomas Frank Designers 3369 Highland Dr Salt Lake City UT 84106-3356 Office Phone: 801-484-1021. E-mail: tfdesigns@att.net.

FRANK, WILLIAM EDWARD, JR., executive recruitment company executive; b. Pitts., Aug. 28, 1943; s. William Edward and Grace (Hankey) F.; m. Lesley Ann Austin, July 22, 1992; children: William John, Jorell. BS in English, Slippery Rock U., 1965. Corp. employment mgr. Wometco Enterprises, Inc., Miami, Fla., 1967-71; v.p. human resources ITT Cmty. Devel. Corp., Miami, 1971-79; ptnr. TASA, Inc., Coral Gables, Fla., 1979-80; pres., CEO The Curtiss Group, Inc., Boca Raton, Fla., 1980—. Bd. dirs. IIC Ptnrs.; mem. pres.'s adv. coun. Slippery Rock U. Mem. Boca Grove Country Club, Boca Raton Premier Club. Avocations: golf, boating, baseball. Home: 7859 Mandarin Dr Boca Raton FL 33433-7427 Office: The Curtiss Group No Trust Plz 301 Yamato Rd Ste 2112 Boca Raton FL 33431-4929

FRANK, WILLIAM FIELDING, computer company executive, consultant; b. NYC, Oct. 27, 1944; s. Karl Frederick and Margaret Ruth (Denisson) F.; m. Linda Carol Hainfield, Dec. 20, 1965 (div. 1972); children: Aaron, Tobin. BA, Middlebury Coll., 1966; MA, U. Chgo., 1969; PhD, U. Pa., 1976. Assoc. prof. Oreg. State U., Corvallis, 1969-79; mem. tech. staff Bell Labs., Whippany, N.J., 1979-81; pres. Enterprise Engring. Assts. Inc., Warren, Vt., 1982-99; founder, chief scientist Cmty. Integration Tech., Manchester by the Sea, Mass., 1999—; with XTG, 2005—. Assoc. prof. MIT, Cambridge, 1981-85; cons. Citibank, 1982—, AT&T, 1984, N.Y. Times, 1985, Bank of Am., 1985, State of Calif., 1986—, Digital Equipment Corp., 1987-89, Soviet Ministry of Trade, 1990, Bankers Trust, 1991, Fidelity Investments, 1993—, Reuters, 1996, Ameritech, 1996, NEC, 1998—, U.S. chief delegate Internat. Stnds. Orgn., 1999—; tech. adv. bd. LIMITrader, 2000—, Bank of N.Y., 2000—. Contbr. articles to profl. jours. Rsch. grantee NSF, 1971, 77, NEH, 1976, 81. Mem. Assn. for Computing Machinery, Computer Soc. IEEE. Republican. Congregationalist. Achievements include pioneering of object-oriented enterprise modelling, client role modelling and research in business rule driven software design. Home and Office: XTG 363 7th Ave 11th Fl New York NY 10001

FRANK, WILLIAM NELSON, lawyer, accountant; b. Cin., June 3, 1953; s. Nelson A. and Marion A. (Kirbert) F.; m. Brenda L. Norwood, Sept. 30, 1995. Student, Capital U., 1971-74; BS in Edn., Bowling Green State U., 1975; JD, U. Toledo, 1978; postgrad., U. Cin., 1980-82. Bar: Ohio, 1978, U.S. Dist. Ct., U.S. Tax Ct., U.S. Supreme Ct.; CPA, Ohio; cert. tchr., Ohio. Asst. city prosecutor City of Columbus, Ohio, 1978-80; asst. pub. defender Hamilton (Ohio) County, 1981-84; sole practice William N. Frank, Columbus, 1978-85; regional fin. mktg. mgr. Primerica Fin. Svcs., Columbus, 1984-90, Cin., 1990-92; atty., acct. Tyirin, Benvie & Co., Cin., 1990-92; atty. Hyatt Legal Svcs., Cin., 1992-93; pvt. practice Cin., 1993—; spl. counsel to Ohio Atty. Gen., 1996—. Auditor Phillip Willeke, Inc., Columbus, 1985-87; securities rep. 1st Am. Nat. Securities, Columbus, 1985-92; lectr. in law Hondros Career Ctr., 1993—, special council to the Ohio Attorney Gen., 1996—; regional dir. Excel Comm., 2000—. Mem. Hamilton County Rep. Club, Cin., 1981—. Named to Hon. Order Ky. Cols. Commonwealth of Ky., 1978. Mem. AICPA, Cin. Bar Assn., Ohio Soc. CPAs, Cheviot Masons (worshipful master, master 1999), Royal Order of Scotland, Knights Templar, Royal Arch Mason, Order of Eastern Star, Shriners, Cin. Hist. Soc. (tour dir.), Order of DeMolay (gov. 7th dist. Ohio coun., chevalier degree 1972, Legion of Honor 1994), Delta Tau Upsilon, Phi Alpha Delta. Republican. Mem. Ch. of Christ. Avocations: tennis, scottish bagpipe musician, martial arts. Home: 3260 Milverton Ct Cincinnati OH 45248-2857 Office: 3050 Harrison Ave Cincinnati OH 45211-5752 E-mail: wfrank@myexcel.com, wmfrank@zoomtown.com.

FRANK, WILLIAM P., lawyer; b. NYC, 1941; AB, Georgetown U., 1963; JD, Fordham U., 1966. Bar: NY 1967. Assoc. Skadden, Arps, Slate, Meagher & Flom LLP, NYC, head NYC office, 1992, nat. legal practice ptnr. for litigation, 1994—, serves on Policy Com. Exec. sec., planning and program com. Judicial Conference of the Court of Appeals for the Second Circuit, 1981—88; frequent panelist on seminars sponsored by Practising Law Institute, ABA, Glasser, ALI/ABA Law Journal Seminars-Press and NY Bar Assn. Bd. trustees Fordham U., 1988—; bd. dirs. Georgetown U., 1991—, bd. regents, 1988—94, bd. regents chmn., 1991—94; bd. dirs. Gregorian U. Found., 1994—. Mem.: ABA (chmn. class action and derivatives suits com. 1982—87, mem. class action improvements spl. com. 1982—87, mem. com. on jud. conf. 1988—92, mem. standing com. Judicial Selection, Tenure, Compensation 1993—95, chmn. com. 1995), Practicing Law Inst. (trustee 2002—), Fed. Bar. Coun. (mem. com. 2nd cir. Ct. of Appeals 1988—94, trustee 1989—99). Office: Skadden Arps Slate Meagher & Flom LLP 4 Times Sq Fl 24 New York NY 10036-6595 Office Phone: 212-735-2400. Office Fax: 917-777-2400. Business E-Mail: wfrank@skadden.com.

FRANKE, BRENT DOUGLAS, real estate/insurance executive; b. Milw., Feb. 13, 1949; s. Herbert Carl and Margaret A. (Custer) F. Assoc. Equitable/Stefaniak Realty, Brookfield, Wis., 1985-89, Prudential Life Ins. Co., 1989-90; agt. Nat. Guardian Life Ins. Co., Menomonee Falls, Wis., 1987-89. Owner Poplar Creek Enterprises Inc., 1989—, Opus IV Ltd., Brookfield, 1989— (formerly Poplar Creek Ltd.); State of Wis. regional mgr. Builder Profile Mag., 1991-94; illustrated parts list writer Briggs and Stratton Corp., Wauwatosa, Wis., 1994—. With USNR, 1970-76. Mem. Grad. Realtors Inst. Avocations: skiing, photography, reading, computers, home remodeling. Home and Office: 2126 N Wauwatosa Ave Wauwatosa WI 53213-1731 Office Phone: 414-259-5486. Personal E-mail: franke.brent@basco.com.

FRANKE, JACK EMIL, foreign language educator; b. Pine Bluff, Ark., July 8, 1965; s. Ernest Rudolph and Charlotte (Harris) F.; m. Lyudmila Veniaminovna Vagun, Aug. 30, 1996; 1 child, Maria. BA, U. Tex., 1987; MA, Monterey Inst. Internat. Studies, 1992; PhD, St. Petersburg (Russia) State U., 1995. Interpreter/at-sea rep. Marine Resource Corp., Seattle, 1988-90; tng. specialist-Russian Def. Lang. Inst., Monterey, Calif., 1990-94, prof. Russian, 2001—; computer-aided lang. instrn. dir. Dept. Fgn. Langs. George C. Marshall Ctr., Garmisch-Partenkirchen, Germany, 1994-97. Pres. Ganbaru Yudanshakai, Monterey, 1997—2001, Monterey, 2005—; chmn. acad. adv. coun. Def. Lang. Inst., 2002—04. Co-author: Russian Topical Reader, 1992; (CD-ROM) Basic Military Language Course-Russian, 1993, The Big Silver Book of Russian Verbs, 2004. Pres. acad. adv. coun. Def. Lang. Inst. Fgn. Lang. Ctr., 2002—04. With U.S. Army, 1983—85. Named Dinsting. Alumnus, U. Tex., 2005, Exemplary Educator, Smart Tech Corp., 2005; recipient Campus Tech. Innovator award, Syllabus Mag., 2005. Mem. DAV, Am. Legion, U.S. Judo Fedn., Computer-Aided Lang. Instrn. Consortium, Am. Coun. on Tchg. Fgn. Langs., Phi Sigma Iota. Republican. Russian Orthodox. Avocations: Judo, racquetball, travel. Home: 370 Clay St Apt 13 Monterey CA 93940-2254 Office: Def Lang Inst PO Box 5818 Monterey CA 93944-0818 Fax: (831) 373-2782. E-mail: drfranke@yahoo.com.

FRANKE, JOHN CHARLES, retired human resources executive; b. Rochester, Minn., June 21, 1937; s. John Paul and Sophie (Thorson) F.; m. Marlys Jean Nordin, Jun 4, 1960 (div. Dec. 1978); children: John Richard, Gregory Wayne; m. Lois Ann Monnin Jones, Dec. 22, 1979; step child, Timothy Jones. BBA, U. Minn., Mpls., 1959, MA in Indsl. Rels., 1968. Life cert. sr. profl. in human resources. Rsch. asst. U. Minn. Indsl. Rels. Ctr., Mpls., 1960-61; group pers. dir. Mead Johnson & Co., Evansville, Ind., 1961-69; dir. pers. Charles F. Kettering Found., Dayton, Ohio, 1969-72; v.p. pers. Assoc. Mortgage Cos., Inc., Washington, 1972-74; founder, prin. Johns Assocs., Inc., Fairfax, Va., 1974-77; div. dir. human rels. TRW Motor Div., Dayton, 1977-82; dir. human resources Miami Valley Pub. Co., Dayton, 1983-84; dir. pers. Sverdrup Tech., Inc., 1984-85; v.p., dir. human resources Sverdrup Corp., St. Louis, 1986-93; dir. human resources, svc. contracts divsn. Calspan Corp., Tullahoma, Tenn., 1993-96. Adj. prof. Wright State U., Dayton, 1982-83, vis. asst. prof., 1983-84; cons., adj. prof. U. Evansville, Ind., 1964-67; conf. speaker Profl. Svcs. Mgmt. Assn., Washington, 1986; seminar speaker Profl. Women in Architecture/Engring., Phoenix, 1988. Bd. dirs. Fairfax (Va.) Little League, 1975-76; v.p. exec. com. Fairfax Police Youth Club, Inc., 1974-77; bd. dirs. Inroads of St. Louis, Inc., 1988-93; mem. Tullahoma Regional Planning Commn. and Bd. Zoning Appeals, 1994-96. Named Disting. Alumnus, Tech. H.S., 2001. Mem. Soc. Human Resource Mgmt., Am. Mgmt. Assn., Human Resource Mgmt. Assn. Greater St. Louis (bd. dirs. 1990-93), Highland Rim Human Resource Mgmt. Assn. (treas. exec. com. 1985, pres. 1994, chair exec. com. 1994, exec. com. 1995), Tenn. State Coun., Soc. Human Resource Mgmt. (sec.-treas. 1995), St. Louis Area Health Care Buyers Coalition (adv. bd. 1992), Franklin/Coffee County Health Care Coalition (v.p. 1985), Imperial Lakes Condominium I Assn (pres. 2002, treas 2003), Master Assn. (sec./treas. 2001, v.p./sec. 2003), Condominium Assn., (v.p 2004, pres. 2005) Rotary, Lakewood Country Club. Republican. Avocations: photography, classic films, music, genealogy. E-mail: eknarf@webtv.net.

FRANKE, KATHERINE M., law educator; BA magna cum laude, Barnard Coll., 1981; JD, Northeastern U., 1986; LLM, Yale U., 1993, JSD, 1998. Supervising atty. NYC Commn. on Human Rights, 1987—90; exec. dir. Nat. Lawyers Guild, 1990—91; assoc. prof. law U. Ariz. Coll. Law, 1995—97, Fordham Law Sch., 1997—2000; prof. law Columbia U. Sch. Law, 2000—, co-dir. Ctr. for Study of Law & Culture. Founder, dir. AIDS and Employment Project, San Francisco, 1986—87. Mem.: Am. Soc. for Legal Hist., Soc. Am. Law Tchrs., Law and Soc. Assn., Ctr. for Non-Violent Edn. (mem. adv. coun.), Ctr. for Lesbian and Gay Studies (mem. adv. bd.). Office: Columbia Law Sch 435 W 116 St New York NY 10027 Office Phone: 212-854-0061. Office Fax: 212-854-7946. E-mail: kfranke@law.columbia.edu.

FRANKE, WILLIAM AUGUSTUS, manufacturing executive; b. Bryan, Tex., Apr. 15, 1937; s. Louis John and Frances (Hanna) F.; m. Carolyn Diane Franke; children: Catherine Anne, Paige Estelle, Brian Hanna, David Parker, Rebecca. BA, Stanford U., 1959, LLB, 1961. Bar: Wash. 1961. With MacGillivray, Jones, Clark & Schiffner, Spokane, 1962-69; ptnr. S.W. Forest Industries, Phoenix, 1970-86; CEO S.W. Forest Industries (merged with Stone Container Corp.), Phoenix, 1978—87; pres., owner Franke & Co., Inc., Phoenix, 1987—; chmn., CEO Am. West Holdings, Corp., Phoenix, 1992—2001; mng. ptnr. Newbridge L.Am., LLP, 1996—, Indigo Ptnrs. LLC, 2001—. Chmn. bd., CEO Am. West Airlines, Inc., Phoenix, 1994—2001; bd. dirs. Phelps Dodge Corp.; mng. ptnr. Newbridge Latin Am. LLP; pres., CEO Indigo Ptnrs. LLC; chmn. Tiger Airways PTE. Ltd., WIZZ Air, Hungary. Served to capt. U.S. Army, 1961-62. Mem. ABA, Wash. Bar Assn., Chief Execs. Orgn., Paradise Valley Country Club. Episcopalian. Office: 2525 E Camelback Rd Ste 800 Phoenix AZ 85016-4230

FRANKEL, ANDREW JOEL, management consultant, information scientist; b. N.Y.C., Oct. 7, 1945; s. Lazar Hirsch and Estelle Rose (Fuchs) F.; m. Marilyn Judith Marcus, Dec. 24, 1967; children: Jennifer Lauren, Jonathan Matthew. BSChemE, N.J. Inst. Tech., 1968; M of Engring., NYU, 1970; postgrad. in fin., U. Hartford, 1971-72. Cert.: CompTIA (A-plus cert.), Dell (DCSE). Physicist ABB Combustion Engring., Windsor, Conn., 1970-76, lead engr., 1976-77; nat. dir. non-proliferation programs Oak Ridge (Tenn.) Nat. Lab., 1977-78; mgr. mkt. intelligence dept. NAC Internat., Inc., Atlanta, 1978-80, gen. mgr., dir. Fuel-Trac divsn., 1980-86; mgr. mktg. info. systems Martin Marietta Energy Systems, Inc., Oak Ridge, 1986-89, mgr. info. resources, 1989-91; mgr. fin. and strategic planning Martin Marietta Utility Svcs., Inc., Oak Ridge, 1991-94; ops. cons. Lockheed Martin Utility Svcs. Inc., Bethesda, Md., 1994-97; sr. mgr. info. tech., bus. proc. re-engring Universal Scheduling Co., Bala Cynwyd, Pa., 1997-98; prin. AJF Consulting Solutions, Paducah, Ky., 1998-2000; interim v.p., dir. software devel. VR2Ltrade.net, Inc., Orlando, Fla., 2000; prin., indsl. cons. and sys. practice Am. Mgmt. Systems, Inc., Fairfax, Va., 2000—01; ind. cons. Orlando, 2001—. Contbr. articles to profl. jours. U.S. del. Internat. Nuc. Fuel Cycle Evaluation, Washington, 1977-78; nat. security cons. White House, Washington, 1977-78; nuc. safety advisor Conn. Gov.'s Office, Hartford, 1975-77. NSF fellow, 1968-70. Mem. Am. Nuc. Soc. (sec. Conn. chpt. 1976-77), Tau Beta Pi (v.p. N.Y.C. Met. chpt. 1969, pres. 1970), Omega Chi Epsilon. Republican. Methodist. Achievements include research in nuclear power, nuclear safety, nuclear arms control, nuclear non-proliferation, business process re-engineering and ERP software solutions; privatization of U.S. government uranium enrichment program. Office: 1963 Lake Shadow Way Suwanee GA 30024 Business E-Mail: afrankel@ajfconsulting.com.

FRANKEL, BRUCE WARREN, economist, educator; b. Bklyn. s. Milton David and Ceil Frankel; children: Mia, Amanda, Max. BA with hons., Rutgers U., 1968; MA in City Planning, U. Pa., 1970, PhD in Planning and Econs., 1974. Cert. environ. risk screener Nat. Assn. Environ. Risk Screeners, 1980, lic. profl. planner N.J., 1984, realtor N.J., 1988, cert. real estate appraiser N.J. State Bd. Real Estate Appraisers, 1992. Asst. prof. Rutger U., Camden, NJ, 1972—78; dir. Dept. Cmty. Devel., Camden, 1978—82; prin., owner Frankel Devel. Corp., Doylestown, Pa., 1982—2002, Ind. City Corp., Muncie, Ind., 2002—. Co-adj. prof. U. Pa., Phila., 1972—85; prof. Ball State U., Munci, 2002—; expert witness in field; planner FDG, Inc., 1983—; economist The Meyers Group, 2000—02; cons. in field. Co-author: Policy Cycle, 1978; contbr. articles to profl. jours. Recipient Lifetime Achievement award, Jewish Fedn., 1992; scholar, Rutgers U., 1968. Mem.: Nat. Assn. Environ. Risk Auditors, Men's Sr. Baseball League. Jewish. Avocations: skiing, horseback riding, hiking, kayaking. Office: Urban Planning Ball State Univ AB 327 Muncie IN 47306 Office Phone: 765-285-5869. Business E-Mail: bfrankel@bsu.edu.

FRANKEL, CRAIG M., lawyer; b. Atlanta, Aug. 16, 1961; s. Theodore Golden and Sidelle Simmons Frankel; m. Jana A. Eplan, Mar. 2, 1991. BA, U. N.C., 1983. Bar: Ga. 1986, Ga. Supreme Ct. 1986, Ga. Ct. Appeals 1986, U.S. Dist. Ct. (no. dist.) Ga. 1987, U.S. Ct. Appeals (11th cir.) 1987. Jud. clk. John C. Godbold, Chief Judge, U.S. Ct. Appeals (11th cir.), Montgomery, Ala., 1986—87; assoc. Long, Aldridge & Norman, Atlanta, 1987—93; lawyer Meadows, Ichter & Trigg, Atlanta, 1993—99, Frankel & Assocs., LLC, Atlanta, 1999—. Exec. editor Ga. Law Rev., Athens, 1985—86. Mem. Am. Jewish Com., Atlanta, 1990—2004; bd. of trustees Hillside Hosp., Atlanta, 1998—2004; violinist Atlanta Cmty. Symphony Orch., Atlanta, 1987—2004, Montgomery Symphony Orch., Montgomery, Ala., 1986—87; founding vol. Hands On Atlanta, Atlanta, 1988—2004; mem. Morningside-Lenox Neighborhood Assn., Atlanta, 1990—2004; bd. of trustees; bd. of edn.; v.p. Temple Sinai, Atlanta, 1988—2001. Recipient Order of the Grail Honor Soc., U. of NC, 1983; Bryant T. Castellow scholar, U. Ga. Sch. Law, 1983—86. Mem.: ATLA, ABA, Atlanta Bar Assn., Ga. Bar Assn., Phi Beta Kappa. Avocation: violin. Office: Frankel & Assocs LLC Ste 2840 75 Fourteenth St Atlanta GA 30309 Office Phone: 404-888-3741.

FRANKEL, ERNST GABRIEL, shipping and aviation business executive, educator; b. Beuthen, Germany, Oct. 17, 1923; came to U.S., 1959, naturalized, 1964. s. Siegfried Samuel and Martha (Blumenthal) F.; m. Inna Kordonsky, Sept. 9, 1990; 1 child, Michael. BS, London U., 1948; MS in Marine-Mech. Engring., MIT, 1960; MBA, Boston U., 1979, D of Bus. Adminstrn., 1986; PhD in Econs., U. Wales, 1985. Chief engr. ZimNav Co., Haifa, Israel, 1950-59; asst. prof. MIT, Cambridge, Mass., 1960-64, assoc. prof., 1964-65, mem. faculty, 1970—, prof. marine systems, 1970—, prof. mgmt. Sloan Sch., 1993—; chief divsn. operation analysis maritime adminstrn. Dept. of Commerce, 1965-66; tech. dir. Litton Industries, Beverly Hills, Calif., 1966-70. Pres. E.G. Frankel, Inc., Boston, 1969—; port, shipping and aviation advisor World Bank, 1982-89; sr. advisor on ports to sec. gen. Internat. Maritime Orgn., 1987-98; chmn. Am. Pres. Lines, Inc., 1997-2000; bd. dirs. Am. Eagle Tankers, 2003-, Am. Pres. Lines Inc., APL Inc., 1992-2002; mem. bd. advisors Panama Canal Authority; advisor Maritime Port Authority of Singapore, 1997-02. Author: Ocean Transportation, 1973, Regulation and Policies of American Shipping, 1982, Management and Operations of American Shipping, 1982, Systems Reliability and Risk Analysis, 1984, Port Planning and Development, 1986, The World Shipping Industry-Economic Transition, 1987, Project Management, 1989, Management of Technological Change, 1989, In Pursuit of Technological Excellence, 1993, Ocean Environmental Management, 1994, America's Institutional Dilemma, 1998, Managing Development, 2005. Served with Royal Navy, 1942-45. Recipient Gold medal Brit. Govt., 1956. Mem. Am. Soc. Civil Engrs., Soc. Naval Architects and Marine Engrs., Ops. Rsch. Am., The Inst. of Man Scis., Soc. Internat. Devel., Royal Inst. Naval Architects, Inst. Marine Engrs., Internat. Assn. Maritime Economists (pres. 2003—). Home: 283 Buckminster Rd Brookline MA 02445-5841 Office Phone: 617-253-6763. Business E-Mail: efrankel@mit.edu.

FRANKEL, FRANCINE RUTH, political science professor; b. N.Y.C., Aug. 31, 1935; d. William and Dora (Tuchschneider) Goldberg; m. Douglas Vernon Verney, Nov. 28, 1975; stepchildren: Andrew, Jonathan. BA, CCNY, 1956; MA, Johns Hopkins U., 1958; PhD, U. Chgo., 1965. Asst. prof. U. Pa., Phila., 1965-70, assoc. prof., 1970-79, prof., 1979—, prof. South Asian studies, 1978—, Madan Lal Sobt prof. study contemporary India, 2004—, founding dir. Ctr. Advanced Study of India, 1992—. Vis. fellow Ctr. of Internat. Studies, Princeton (N.J.) U., 1969-73; resident scholar Bellagio Study and Conf. Ctr., 1975; vis. mem. Inst. Advanced Study, 1976; mem.-at-large Commn. Internat. Rels., Nat. Acad. Scis., 1973-79; mem. del. South Asian specialists to China, 1986; founding mem., mem. governing coun. U. Pa. Inst. for Advanced Study of India, New Delhi, 1995—. Author: India's Political Economy, 1947-2004, 2005, The Gradual Revolution, 1978, Chinese edit., 1990, 2d edit., 2004, India's Green Revolution, 1971; editor, contbr. Dominance and State Power in Modern India, Decline of a Social Order, 2 vols., 1989-90, Bridging the Non-Proliferation Gap: India and the United States, 1995, Transforming India, Social and Political Dynamics of Democracy, 2000, The India-China Relationship: What the United States Needs to Know, 2004; contbr. articles on India's polit. economy to profl. jours. Grantee Am. Inst. Indian Studies, 1979-80, Smithsonian Instn., 1983-86, Social Sci. Rsch. Coun., 1989-91; Woodrow Wilson fellow, 1997-98. Mem. Am. Polit. Sci. Assn., Assn. Asian Studies, Coun. Fgn. Rels. Home: 104 Pine St Philadelphia PA 19106-4312 Office: Ctr Advanced Study of India 3600 Market St Philadelphia PA 19104 E-mail: ffrankel@sas.upenn.edu.

FRANKEL, JACK, pediatrician, allergist; b. NYC, Sept. 9, 1920; s. Max H. and Fanny F. Frankel; m. Irene J. Kittredge, Apr. 18, 1948; children: Barbara Meg, Judith Ann, Richard Harris, Carolyn, Joan Ellen. BS, Tulane U., 1941, MD, 1945. Diplomate Am. Bd. of Pediat. Intern Queens Gen. Hosp., Jamaica, N.Y., 1945-46; resident in pediat. and contagious diseases, 1948-50; pediatrician, allergist Manatee Family Physicians, Bradenton, Fla., 1993—; allergist, immunologist LIJ Hosp., New Hyde Park, 1974-77. Asst. prof. clin. pediatrics and allergy SUNY, Stony Brook, 1955-75, NYU, 1970-75; cons. Blake Meml. Hosp., Bradenton, Fla., 1970—, Manatee Meml. Hosp., Bradenton, 1977—. Capt. M.C. U.S. Army, 1946—48. Fellow Am. Acad. Pediat., Am. Coll. Allergy. Jewish. Avocations: tennis, jogging. Home: PO Box 8452 Longboat Key FL 34228-8452 Office Phone: 941-383-1569, 413-738-5127. Home Fax: 941-383-1087. Personal E-mail: jiflbk@aol.com.

FRANKEL, JAMES BURTON, retired lawyer; b. Chgo., Feb. 25, 1924; s. Louis and Thelma (Cohn) F.; m. Louise Untermyer, Jan. 22, 1956; children: Nina, Sara, Simon. Student, U. Chgo., 1940-42; BS, U.S. Naval Acad., 1945; LLB, Yale U., 1952; MPA, Harvard U., 1990. Bar: Calif. 1953. Mem. Steinhart, Goldberg, Feigenbaum & Ladar, San Francisco, 1954-72; of counsel Cooper, White & Cooper, San Francisco, 1972-97; ret., 2000. Sr. fellow, lectr. in law Yale U., 1971—72; lectr. Stanford U. Law Sch., 1973—75; vis. prof. U. Calif. Law Sch., 1975—76, lectr., 1992—2000, U. San Francisco Law Sch., 1994—2000; adj. asst. prof. Hastings Coll. Law, 1996—2000. Pres. Coun. Civic Unity of San Francisco Bay Area, 1964-66; chmn. San Francisco Citizens Charter Revision Com., 1968-70; mem. San Francisco Pub. Schs. Commn., 1975-76; trustee Natural Resources Def. Coun., 1972-77, 79-92, staff atty., 1977-79, hon. trustee, 1992—; chmn. San Francisco Citizens Energy Policy Adv. Com., 1981-82. Mem. ABA, Calif. Bar Assn.

FRANKEL, KENNETH M., lawyer; b. NYC, Apr. 22, 1948; BS, U. Pa., 1970; JD with honors, George Washington U., 1973. Bar: Va. 1973, DC 1981, lic.: US Supreme Ct. 1979, US Ct. Appeals (Fed. Cir.) 1982, US Dist. Ct. (Ea. Dist.) Va. 1995. Law clk. to Hon. George Willi US Ct. of Claims, 1973—74; trial atty. US Justice Dept, Antitrust Divsn.; ptnr. Finnegan, Henderson, Farabow, Garrett & Dunner LLP, Reston, Va., leader, Intellectual Property Specialties Practice Group, leader, Intellectual Property Specialties Sect. Bd. dir. DC Computer Law Forum, 1987—92, pres., 1988—89. Mem.: ABA (Litig. Sect., Antitrust Sect., Patent & Trademark & Copy Law Sect.), Va. State Bar, Am. Intellectual Property Law Assn. (chmn. antitrust law com. 2001—03). Office: Finnegan Henderson Farabow Garrett & Dunner LLP Two Freedom Sq 11955 Freedom Dr Reston VA 20190-5675 Office Phone: 571-203-2700. Office Fax: 202-408-4400. Business E-Mail: kenneth.frankel@finnegan.com.

FRANKEL, KENNETH MARK, thoracic surgeon; b. Bklyn., July 29, 1940; s. Clarence Bernard and Ruth (Rutes) F.; m. Felice Cala Oringel, Dec. 10, 1967; children: Matthew David, Michael Jacob. BA, Cornell U., 1961; MD, SUNY, Bkyln., 1965. Diplomate Am. Bd. Surgery, Am. Bd. Thoracic Surgery. Intern in surgery Yale New Haven Hosp., 1965-66; resident in surgery Kings County-SUNY Med. Ctr., Bklyn., 1966-67, 69-71, chief resident in gen. surgery, 1971—72, resident in thoracic surgery, 1972-73, chief resident thoracic and cardiovasc. surgery, 1973-74; sr. attending thoracic surgeon Mercy Hosp., Springfield, Mass., 1974—; attending thoracic surgeon Holyoke (Mass.) Hosp., 1974—2004; pvt. practice medicine specializing in thoracic surgery Springfield, 1974—; chief thoracic surgery Baystate Med. Ctr., Springfield, 1977—; clin. prof. cardiothoracic surgery Tufts U. Sch. Medicine, 1978—; dir. Baystate Thoracic Surgery Assocs., 2004—. Cons. Shriners Hosp. for Children, Mary Lane Hosp., Ware, Mass., 1997-2004; bd. dirs. Pioneer Health Care Inc., 1997—, sec. of bd., 1998-2001, v.p. of bd., 2001-04 Contbr. articles to profl. jours. Rep. to Blue Cross/Blue Shield Regional Health Care Improvement Coun., 1995-98. Capt. U.S. Army, 1967-69. Decorated Bronze Star, Gallantry Cross (Republic of Vietnam). Fellow ACS, Am. Coll. Chest Physicians; mem. AMA, ACLU, Soc. Thoracic Surgeons, Am. Thoracic Soc., New Eng. Cancer Soc., Springfield Acad. Medicine (past pres.), Mass. Med. Soc. (councilor 1981-83), Hampden Dist. Med. Soc. (exec. com. 1990-96), Physicians for Social Responsibility, Maimonides Med. Club (past pres.), Amnesty Internat., Internat. Physicians for Prevention Nuc. War, Union Concerned Scientists, Cornell Club Wester Mass., Porsche Club Am. Democrat. Jewish. Home: 202 Ellington Rd Longmeadow MA 01106-1510 Office: Baystate Med Ctr Office Bldg 2 Medical Center Dr Ste 304 Springfield MA 01107-1271 Office Phone: 413-794-8050. Personal E-mail: k.frankel@comcast.net.

FRANKEL, MARTIN RICHARD, statistician, educator, consultant; b. Washington, June 16, 1943; s. Lester R. and Vera B. Frankel; m. Jean L. Kaiser, Mar. 24, 1970; children: Jennifer, Margaux. BA, U. N.C., 1965; MA, U. Mich., 1967, PhD, 1971. Asst. prof. stats., assoc. prof. U. Chgo., 1971—76; prof. stats and computer info. sys. Baruch Coll. CUNY, 1977—, assoc. chair, 1995—. Tech. dir. Nat. Opinion Rsch. Ctr. U. Chgo., 1972—96; sr. statis. scientist Abt Assocs., Cambridge, Mass., 1996—; chmn. Quality Rsch. Coun. Nat. Rsch. Found., 1988—, cons. statis. methods and quality control, 1965—; mem. panel occupl. and health stats., com. nat. stats. Nat. Rsch. Coun. NAS, 1985—87. Author: Inference from Survey Samples: An Empirical Investigation, 1971; co-author: SEPP: Sampling Error Program Package, 1972, Total Survey Error: Applications to Improve Health Surveys, 1979; contbr. articles to profl. jours. Fellow: Internat. Statis. Inst., Royal Statis. Soc., Am. Statis. Assn. (chmn. census adv. com. 1981, chmn. sect. survey rsch. methods 1975—76, editl. bd. jour.); mem.: Market Rsch. Coun. (pres. 1995—96), Am. Assn. Pub. Opinion Rsch. (chmn. stds. com.). Home: 14 Patricia Ln Cos Cob CT 06807-1734 Office: Baruch Coll 17 Lexington Ave New York NY 10010-5518 Business E-Mail: martin_frankel@baruch.cuny.edu.

FRANKEL, MAX, retired journalist; b. Gera, Germany, Apr. 3, 1930; came to U.S., 1940, naturalized, 1948; s. Jacob A. and Mary (Katz) F.; m. Tobia Brown, June 19, 1956 (dec. Mar. 1987); children: David M., Margot S., Jonathan M.; m. Joyce Purnick, Dec. 11, 1988. AB, Columbia, 1952, MA in Polit. Sci, 1953. Mem. staff N.Y. Times, N.Y.C., 1952-94, chief Washington corr., 1968-73, Sunday editor, 1973-76, editl. pages editor, 1977-86, exec. editor, 1986-94; ret., 1995. Columnist N.Y. Times mag., 1995-2000. Served with AUS, 1953-55. Recipient Pulitzer prize for internat. reporting, 1973 Office: 15 West 67 St New York NY 10023-6226 E-mail: maxmaxnyt@yahoo.com.

FRANKEL, SHERMAN, physicist, educator; b. N.Y.C., Nov. 15, 1922; s. Harry and Rose F.; m. Ruzena Bajcsy, Oct. 22, 1981; 1 son by previous marriage, Walter. BA, Bklyn. Coll., 1943; MS, U. Ill., 1947, PhD, 1949. Mem. staff radiation lab. MIT, 1943-46; instr. U. Pa., Phila., 1950-52, asst. prof. physics, 1952-56, assoc. prof., 1956-60, prof., 1960—. Vis. scientist Niels Bohr Inst., Denmark, 1968, C.E.R.N. Geneva, 1975, C.E.N. de Saclay, France, 1979; guest fellow Stanford U. Ctr. for Internat. Security Arms Control, 1987; guest scholar Brookings Inst., 1987; Security Progrm sr. fellow MIT, 1998-2004; vis. prof. bioengring. U. Calif., Berkeley, 2002-04 Assoc. editor Rev. of Sci. Instruments, 1952-53. Guggenheim fellow, 1957, 79 Fellow Am. Phys. Soc.; mem. N.Y. Acad. Sci., Sigma Xi, Pi Mu Epsilon. Home: 2320 Delancey Pl Philadelphia PA 19103-6407 Office: U Pa Physics Dept 33d and Walnut Sts Philadelphia PA 19104 Office Phone: 215-898-8146. Business E-Mail: frankel@frankel.hep.upenn.edu, frankel@sas.upenn.edu.

FRANKEL, STUART, real estate company executive; m. Maxine Frankel; 2 children. BBA, U. Mich., 1961. Founder & CEO Stuart Frankel Devel. Co. Named one of Top 200 Collectors, ARTnews Mag., 2004; recipient Civic Leader Award art & culture, Mich. Gov., 2004. Mem.: Downtown Devel. Authority. Avocation: collector of modern & contemporary art, especially Latin Am., ceramics & sculpture. Office: Stuart Frankel Develop Inc 3221 West Big Beaver Rd Troy MI 48084*

FRANKEN, AL, comedian, writer, actor; b. N.Y.C., May 21, 1952; s. Joe and Phoebe Franken; m. Franni Bryson, 1975; 2 children. Grad., Harvard U., 1973. Stand-up comic, Mpls. Network commentator for presdl. campaigns Comedy Ctrl., 1992, fellow, Harvard U. Kennedy School of Government, Shorenstein Center on the Press, Politics, and Public Policy, 2003. Writer, actor (TV series) Saturday Night Live, NBC-TV, 1973—95 (Emmy awards (with others) best writing in comedy series, 1976, 1989), Lateline, 1998; author: I'm Good Enough, I'm Smart Enough, and Doggone It, People Like Me, 1992, Rush Limbaugh Is a Big Fat Idiot and Other Observations, 1996, Why Not Me? The Inside Story of the Making and Unmaking of the Franken Presidency, 1999, Oh, the Things I Know! A Guide to Success, or, Failing That, Happiness, 2002, Lies and the Lying Liars Who Tell Them: A Fair and Balanced Look at the Right, 2003; author, actor (screenplays) Stuart Saves His Family, 1995, co-author, exec. prodr. When a Man Loves a Woman, 1994; actor: (TV series) Clerks, 2000; host with Katherine Lanpher (radio) The O'Franken Factor, (now The Al Franken Show) Air America Radio, 2004—; featured: (TV films) The First Amendment Project: Fox vs. Franken, 2004. Emmy award (with others) for best writing in a comedy, The Paul Simon Special, 1977, Grammy award for best spoken comedy album, Rush Limbaugh Is a Big Fat Idiot, 1997. Democrat. Office: c/o Creative Artists Agy 9830 Wilshire Blvd Beverly Hills CA 90210*

FRANKEN, DARRELL, counselor, writer, publishing executive; b. Oskaloosa, Iowa, Oct. 28, 1930; s. Henry E. and Harriet J. (Dykshorn) F.; m. Marilyn (Tanis); children: Kent, Julie, Todd. BA, Ctrl. U. Iowa, 1952; MDiv, Western Theol. Sem., Holland, Mich., 1955; MA, U. Chgo., 1963; PhD, La Salle U., 1995. Pastor New Life Reformed Ch. (formerly Everglades Reformed Ch.), Grand Rapids, Mich.; missionary Bahrain Arabian Gulf; counselor Christian Counseling Svc., Holland, Mich.; pub. Wellness Publications. Author: Health Through Stress Reduction, 1985, Life Stress and Coping Strength Inventory, 1985, Psychological First Aid Kit, 1992, Character Education Psychology: Optimum Psycho-Social Lifeskills, 1996-2005, Mich. 13 Personality Profile (Core Values), 1990, Franken Transactional Analysis Profile, 1992, Lifeskills 101: Higher Core Values Winners Live By, Lifeskills 202: Skills for Optimum Personal Relations, Lifeskills 303: Optimum Lifeskills for Stress Management, Personal Strengths: Positive Psychology, 2003-05, Moving Up: Positive Psychology, 2004; founder of Lifeskills Trng. Ctrs. Inc. Fellow Am. Assn. Pastoral Counselors, Mich. Lic. Marriage and Family Counselors. Avocations: photography, auto restoration. Home: 930 S Shore Dr Holland MI 49423-4539 E-mail: dfranken@lifeskillstraining.org.

FRANKENBERGER, BERTRAM, JR., investor, consultant; b. New Haven, Jan. 24, 1933; s. Bertram and Thelma (Wisan) F.; m. Marjorie Green, Dec. 20, 1953 (dec. June 1997); children: Linda Sue Reason, Wendy Beth Goldstein; m. Harriet Feldman Newman, July 26, 1998. BS cum laude, U. Conn., 1954. CPA, Conn. Auditor Haskins & Sells, New Haven, 1956-61; ptnr. Weinstein & Timm CPAs, New Haven, 1961-70, Deloitte Haskins & Sells, New Haven, 1970-76; U.S. ptnr in charge mergers and acquisitions exec. office N.Y.C., 1976-85; dir. Sheffield Mgmt. Co., N.Y.C., 1985-99, Sheffield Investments, Inc., N.Y.C., 1985-96, Lafayette Am. Bank & Trust, Hamden, 1985-96. Treas. Human Rels. Area Files, New Haven, 1963-70, 86—, assoc. sec., 1985—; cons., New Haven, 1985-94, Boynton Beach, Fla., 1994—; chmn. bd. Chargar Corp., Hamden, Conn., 1980—, Graham-Worldtek Travel, New Haven, 1985-2001; lectr. in field. Contbr. articles to profl. publs., chpt. to book. Pres., dir. Camp Laurelwood, Madison, Conn., 1970-72; pres., trustee Congregation Mishkan Israel, Hamden, Conn., 1974-76; bd. trustees Union Am. Hebrew Congregations, N.Y.C., 1976-84; treas. Religion in Am. Life, N.Y.C., 1983-89, dir., 1983-94. Capt. USAF, 1954-56. Recipient Pres.'s award New Haven Jaycees, 1960; Pres.'s award Camp Laurelwood, 1969. Mem. AICPA, Conn. Soc. CPAs, Hunters Run Golf and Racquet Club (Boynton Beach), Okemo Valley Golf Club. Avocations: skiing, golf, tennis, stamp collecting/philately.

FRANKENHEIM, SAMUEL, retired lawyer; b. N.Y.C., Dec. 20, 1932; s. Samuel and Mary Emma (Ward) F.; m. Nina Barbara Mennerich, Sept. 2, 1960; children: Robert Mennerich, John Frederick. BA, Cornell U., 1954, LLB, 1959. Bar: N.Y. 1959, Mass. 1976. Law clk. N.Y. Ct. Appeals, 1959-61; assoc. Shearman & Sterling, attys., N.Y.C., 1961-68, ptnr., 1968-69; sr. v.p., dir. Damon Corp., Needham Heights, Mass., 1969-78; sr. v.p., gen. counsel mem. Office of Chmn. Gen. Cinema Corp., Chestnut Hill, Mass., 1979-92; counsel Ropes & Gray, Boston, 1992-2000. Mem. corp. Ptnrs. Healthcare Sys., Inc., 1999—2004. Bd. govs. Newell Health Care Sys., 1983—93; trustee Wang Ctr. for Performing Arts, Boston, 1987—97, Huntington Theatre Co., Boston, 1993—2002, overseer, 2002—04; chmn. bd. Internat. Alliance of First Night Celebrations, 1994—99, treas., 1999—2000; overseer Newton-Wellesley Hosp., Newton, Mass., 1973—85, pres., 1980—82; overseer Wang Ctr. for Performing Arts, Boston, 1985—87; assoc. First Night, Inc., 1988, chmn. bd., 1991—93. 1st lt. USAF, 1955—57. Mem. ABA. Home: 115 Shornecliffe Rd Newton MA 02458-2420 E-mail: sfrankenheim@msn.com.

FRANKENTHALER, HELEN, artist; b. N.Y.C., Dec. 12, 1928; d. Alfred and Martha (Lowenstein) F.; m. Robert Motherwell, Apr. 5, 1958 (div.); m. Stephen DuBrul, June 1994. BA, Bennington Coll., 1949; LHD (hon.), Skidmore Coll., 1969, Hofstra U., 1991; DFA (hon.), Smith Coll., 1973, Moore Coll. Art, 1974, Bard Coll., 1976, NYU, 1979; DFA, Phila. Coll. Art, 1980, Williams Coll., 1980; DFA (hon.), Marymount Manhattan Coll., 1989, Adelphi U., 1989, Washington U., St. Louis, 1989; DArt, Radcliffe Coll., 1978, Amherst Coll., 1979; DArt (hon.), Harvard U., 1980; DFA (hon.), Yale U., 1981, Brandeis U., 1982, U. Hartford, 1983, Syracuse U., 1985, Dartmouth Coll., 1994, Parsons Sch. Design, 1996, U. Pa., 1996, R.I. Sch. Design, 1996, Tufts U., 1998. Tchr., lectr. Yale U., 1966, 67, 70, Hunter Coll., 1970, Princeton U., 1971, Cooper Union, N.Y.C., 1972, Washington U. Sch. Fine Arts, 1972, Skidmore Coll., 1973, Swathmore Coll., 1974, Drew U., 1975, Harvard, 1976, Radcliffe Coll., 1976, Bard Coll., 1977, Detroit Inst. Arts, 1977, NYU, U. Pa., Sch. Visual Arts, Goucher Coll., Wash. U., Yale Grad. Sch., U. Ariz., 1978, Graphic Arts Council N.Y., 1979, Harvard U., 1980, Phila. Coll., 1980, Williams Coll., 1980, Yale U., 1981, Brandeis U., 1982, U. of Hartford, 1983, Syracuse U., 1985, Sante Fe Inst. Fine Arts, 1986, 90, 91; U.S. rep. Venice Biennale, 1966, lectr. in field. One-woman shows include, Tibor de Nagy Gallery, N.Y.C., 1951-58, Andre Emmerich Gallery, N.Y.C., 1959-73, 75, 77, 78, 79, 81, 82, 83, 84, 86, 87, 89, 90, 91, 92, 93, Jewish Mus., N.Y., 1960, Everett Ellin Gallery, Los Angeles, 1961, Galerie Lawrence, Paris, 1961, 63, Bennington Coll., 1962, 78, Galleria dell'Ariete, Milan, 1962, Kasmin Gallery, London, 1964, David Mirvish Gallery, Toronto, 1965, 71, 73, 75, Gertrude Kasle Gallery, Detroit, 1967, Nicholas Wilder Gallery, Los Angeles, 1967, Andre Emmerich Gallery, Zurich, 1974, 80, Swarthmore (Pa.) Coll., 1974, Solomon R. Guggenheim Mus., N.Y.C., 1975, Corcoran Gallery Art, Washington, 1975, Seattle Art Mus., 1975, Mus. Fine Arts, Houston, 1975, 85, 86, Ace Gallery, Vancouver, B.C., Can., 1975, Rosa Esman Gallery, N.Y.C., 1975, 83, 89, 3d Internat. Contemporary Art Fair, Paris, 1976, 81, retrospective Whitney Mus. Am. Art, 1969, Whitechapel Gallery, London, Eng., 1969, Kongress-Halle, Berlin, Kunstverein, Hannover, 1969, Heath Gallery, Atlanta, 1971, Galerie Godard Lefort, Montreal, 1971, Fendrick Gallery, Washington, 1972, 79, John Berggruen Gallery, San Francisco, 1972, 79, 82, Portland (Oreg.) Art Mus., 1972, Waddington Galleries II, London, 1973, 74, Janie C. Lee Gallery, Dallas, 1973, Houston, 1975, 76, 78, 80, 82, Met. Mus. Art, N.Y.C., 1973, Gallery Diane Gilson, Seattle, 1976, Greenberg Gallery, St. Louis, 1977, Galerie Wentzel, Hamburg, Germany, 1977, Jacksonville (Fla.) Art Mus., 1977-78, Knoedler Gallery, London, 1978, 81, 83, USIA exhbn., 1978-79, Atkins Mus. Fine Art, William Rockhill Nelson Gallery Art, Kansas City, Mo., 1978, 80, Saginaw Art Mus., Mich., 1980, Gimpel and Hanover and Andre Emerich Galleries, Zurich, 1980, Gallery Ulysses, Vienna, 1980, Knoedler Gallery, London, 1981, 83, Buschlen/Mowalt Fine Arts, Vancouver, 1989, Mus. Modern Art, N.Y.C., 1989, Douglas Drake Gallery, N.Y.C., 1989, Mizografia Gallery, L.A., 1989, Gerald Peters Gallery, Santa Fe, 1990, Kukje Gallery, Seoul, Korea, 1991, Assn. Am. Artists, N.Y.C., 1992, Knoedler & Co., N.Y.C., 1992, 94, 95, 96, 97, Nat. Gallery Art, Washington, 1993, San Diego Mus. Art, 1993, Mus. Fine Arts, Boston, 1994, Contemporary Arts Ctr., Cin., 1994, Meredith Long and Co., Houston, 1994, 95, 96, 97, Dennos Mus. Ctr. Northwestern Mich. Coll., Travers City, 1995, Tyler Graphics Ltd., Mt. Kisco, N.Y., 1995, Bobbie Greenfield Gallery, Santa Monica, Calif., 1995, Meyerovich Gallery, San Francisco, 1995, Greg Kucera Gallery, Seattle, 1995, Gallery One, Toronto, Canada, 1995, 97, Ace Contemporary Exhbns., L.A., 1996, Tasenda Gallery, L.A., 1997, Remba Gallery, West Hollywood, Calif., 1997, Thomas Segal Gallery, Balt., 1997, numerous others; exhibited in group shows including, Whitney Mus., 1958, 71, 75-79, 82, 89, Carnegie Internat., Pitts., 1955, 58, 61, 64, Columbus Gallery Fine Arts, 1960, Guggenheim Mus., 1961, 76, 80, 82, Seattle World's Fair, 1962, Art Inst. Chgo., 1963, 69, 72, 76, 77, 82, 83, San Francisco Mus. Art, 1963, 68, Krannert Mus., U. Ill., 1959, 63, 65, 67, 80, Washington Gallery Modern Art, 1963, Pa. Acad. Fine Arts, 1963, 68, 76, N.Y. World's Fair, 1964, Am. Fedn. Arts Circulating Exhbn., 1964, U. Austin Art Mus., 1964, Rose Art Mus. Circulating Exhbn., 1964, Detroit Inst. Arts, 1965, 67, 73, 77, U. Mich. Mus. Art, 1965, Md. Inst., 1966, Norfolk Mus. Arts and Scis., 1966, Venice Biennale, 1966, Smithsonian Instn., 1966, Expo '67, Montreal, 1967, Washington Gallery Modern Art, 1967, Ga. Mus. Art, Athens, 1967, U. Okla. Mus. Art, Norman, 1968, Philbrook Art Center, Tulsa, 1968, Cin. Mus., 1968, U. Calif. at San Diego, 1968, Mus. Modern Art, N.Y.C., 1969, 75, 76, 80, 82, Met. Mus., N.Y.C., 1969-70, 76, 79, 81, Va. Mus., Richmond, 1970, 74, 87, Balt. Mus. Art, 1970, 76, 89, Boston U., 1970, Boston Mus. Fine Arts, 1972, 82, 90, Des Moines Art Center, 1973, Mus. Fine Arts, Houston, 1974, 82, Smith Coll. Mus. Art, Northampton, Mass., 1974, El Instituto de Cultura Puertorriquena, San Juan, 1974, Basil (Switzerland) Art Fair, 1974, 76, Finch Coll. Mus. Art, N.Y.C., 1974, S.I. Mus., 1975, Denver Art Mus., 1975, Visual Arts Mus., N.Y.C., 1975, 76, Mus. Modern Art, Belgrade Yugoslavia, 1976, Chrysler Mus., Norfolk, Va., 1976, Everson Mus., Syaracuse, N.Y., Galleria d'Arts Moderna, Rome, 1976, Grey Art Gallery, N.Y.C., 1976-78, 81, Bklyn Mus., 1976-77, 82, Edmonton Art Gallery, Alta., Can., 1977, 78, Albright-Knox Mus., Buffalo, 1978, Fogg Art Mus., Harvard U., 1978, 83, Art Gallery Ont., 1979, Hirshorn Mus. and Sculpture Garden, Washington, 1980, Phoenix Art Mus., 1980, Nat. Gallery Art, Washington, 1981, Tate Gallery, London, 1981, Walker Art Ctr., Mpls., 1981, Milw. Art Mus., 1982, Mus. Fine Arts, Boston, 1982, Whitney Mus. Am. Art, N.Y., 1982, St. Louis Art Mus., 1982, High Mus. Art, Atlanta, 1989, Nelson-Atkins Mus. Art, Kansas City, Nat. Gallery Can., 1990, Williams Coll. Mus. Art, Williamstown, Mass., 1991, Aldrich Mus. Contemporary Art, Ridgefield, Conn., 1992, Mus. Modern Art, Mexico City, 1992, Yokohama Mus. Art, Japan, 1992, Marugame Inokuma-Genichiro Mus. Contemp. Art, 1992, Mus. Modern Art, Wakayama, 1992, Tokushima Modern Art Mus., Japan, 1992, Hokkaido Obihiro Mus. Art, 1993, Whitney Mus. Am. Art, Stamford, Conn., 1993, Gallery One, Toronto, Can., 1994; represented in permanent collections, Bklyn. Mus., Met. Mus. Art N.Y., Solomon R. Guggenheim Mus., NYU, Mus. Modern Art, Albright-Knox Art Gallery, Buffalo, Whitney Mus., N.Y.C., U. Mich., High Mus., Atlanta, Milw. Art Inst., Wadsworth Atheneum, Hartford, Newark Mus., Yale U. Art Gallery, U. Nebr. Art Gallery, Carnegie Inst., Pitts., Detroit Inst. Art, Balt. Mus. Art, Univ. Mus., Berkeley, Calif., Bennington (Vt.) Coll., Art Inst. Chgo., Cin. Art Mus., Cleve. Mus. Art, Columbus Gallery Fine Arts, Honolulu Acad. Arts, Contemporary Arts Assn., Houston, Pasadena Art Mus., William Rockhill Nelson Gallery Art, Kans. City, Kans., Kans. City Art Inst., Atkins Mus. Fine Arts, Kans. City, Kans., City Art Mus., St. Louis, Mus. Art, R.I. Sch. Design, Providence, San Francisco Mus. Art, Everson Mus., Syracuse, N.Y., Smithsonian Instn., Walker Art Inst., Mpls., Washington Gallery Modern Art, Wichita Art Mus., Brown Gallery Art, Nat. Gallery Victoria, Melbourne, Australia, Australian Nat. Gallery, Canberra, Victoria and Albert Mus., London, Eng., Tokyo Mus., Ulster Mus., Belfast, No. Ireland, Elvehjem Art Center, U. Wis., Israel Mus.-Instituto Nacional de Bellas Artes, Phila. Mus. Art, Phoenix Art Mus., Corcoran Gallery Art, Boston Mus. Fine Arts, Springfield (Mass.) Mus. Fine Arts, Witte Mus., San Antonio, Abbott Hall Art Gallery, Kendal, Eng., Mus. Contemporary Art, Nagaoka, Japan, Guggenheim Mus., N.Y.C., 1984, others; was subject of film Frankenthaler: Toward a New Climate, 1978. Trustee Bennington Coll., 1967— . Fellow Calhoun Coll., Yale U., 1968—; recipient 1st prize for painting Paris Biennale, 1959, Gold medal Pa. Acad. Fine Arts, 1968, Great Ladies award Fordham U., Thomas Moore Coll., 1969, Spirit of Achievement award Albert Einstein Coll. Medicine, 1970, Gold medal Commune of Catania, III Biennale della Grafica d'Arte, Florence, Italy, 1972, Garrett award 70th Am. Exhbn., Art Inst. Chgo., 1972, Creative Arts award Nat. Women's div. Am. Jewish Congress, 1974, Art and Humanities award Yale Women's Forum, 1976, Extraordinary Woman of Achievement award NCCJ, 1978, Alumni award Bennington Coll., 1979, N.Y.C. Mayor's award, 1986, Lifetime Achievement award Coll. Art Assn., 1994, Lotos medal of merit, 1994, Artist of Yr. award, 1995, Jerusalem prize, 1999, Lifetime Achievement award, 1999. Mem. NEA, Am. Acad. (vice-chancelor 1991), Am. Acad. Arts and Scis., Nat. Coun. Arts, Nat. Inst. Arts and Letters. Office: M Knoedler & Co Inc 19 E 70th St New York NY 10021-4907*

FRANKENTHALER, STAN, food service executive; Degree in English, U. Ga.; grad., Culinary Inst. Am. Poissioner Hotel Meridian, Boston; with Jasper's, sous chef, lead chef; with Hamersley's Bistro; owner Choice Catering Co.; co-owner, chef The Blue Room; owner, chef Salamander, Cambridge, Mass., 1994—. Developer Red Herring, Boston, 1997, Beehive, Boston, 1997; tchr. classes Boston U., Culinary Inst. Am., Williams-Sonoma, Cakebread Cellars, Bloomingdale's, New England Culinary Inst., Whole Foods, Hay Day, Salamander; invited cook James Beard House, N.Y.C., 1989—96; chosen by Julia Child to cook for Nat. Gov.'s Conf., 1994; host Hasty Pudding Award Luncheon, 1994—99; bd. overseers Chef's Collaborative 2000, 1st vice chair. Salamander featured in N.Y. Times, Washington Post, Esquire, Met. Home, Art Culinaire, Food and Wine, Food Arts, Harvard Mag., Bon Appetit, Gourmet, appeared WCVB-TV, 1997, TVFN, Food New Eng. on PBS. Active Share Our Strength, James Beard Found., AIDS Action, Cmty. Servings, The Greater Table, Rosie's Pl. Named Face to Watch and Best Caterer, Boston Mag., 1990, The Blue Room Best Restaurant, 1992, The Blue Room Best Restaurant in Am., Esquire, 1993, Salamander four-star restaurant in the making, Boston Globe, 1994, Rising Star Chef, Restaurant Hospitality Mag., 1995, The one not to miss, Travel and Leisure Mag., 1995, Salamander Most Creative Cuisine, The Tab, 1997, Salamander Am.'s Top Tables, Gourmet Mag., 1996—98, rep., Cascadian Farms, 1998; named one of Top Ten Restaurants in Boston, Zagat Survey, 1995, Best Restaurants in the Country, Gourmet, 1996; named to Celebrity Chef Series, Wild Harvest Markets, 1998; recipient Winner Best Chocolate Dessert, Boston Mag., 1991, Best Wine List short list category for Salamander, Restaurant Hospitality Mag., 1995, DiRONA award, 1997, four star rev., Microsoft's Sidewalk.com, 1998, Award of Excellence, Wine Spectator, 1998. Office: Salamander PO Box 470718 Brookline Village MA 02447-0718

FRANKFORT, LEW, consumer products company executive; BA, Hunter Coll.; MBA, Columbia Univ. Past commr. Agy. for Child Development, NYC; v.p. New Bus. Devel. Coach, 1979—85, pres., 1985—95, chmn. & CEO, 1995—. Office: Coach Inc 516 W 34th St New York NY 10001-1394*

FRANKFURT, HARRY GORDON, philosophy professor; b. May 29, 1929; m. Joan Gilbert; children: Jennifer, Katherine. BA, Johns Hopkins Univ., 1949, PhD, 1954. Asst. prof. Ohio State Univ., 1956—62; assoc. prof., philosophy SUNY, Binghamton, 1962—63; rsch. assoc. Rockefeller Univ., 1963—64, assoc. prof., philosophy, 1964—69, prof., 1969—76, chair, philosophy group, 1966—73; prof. Yale Univ., 1976—90, chair, philosophy dept., 1978—87; prof., philosophy Princeton Univ., 1990—2002, prof. emeritus, 2002—, Romanell-Phi Beta Kappa prof. philosophy, 1999—2000. Vis. prof. Univ. Calif., Riverside, 2000. Editor: Leibniz: A Collection of Critical Essays, 1972; author: (nonfiction) Demons, Dreamers & Madmen: The Defense of Reason in Descartes' Meditations, 1970, The Importance of What We Care About, 1988, Necessity, Volition & Love, 1999, On Bullshit, 2005 (Publishers Weekly Bestseller hardcover nonfiction list, 2005, No. 1 NY Times Bestseller list, 2005). With U.S. Army, 1954—56. Grantee Nat. Endowment for Humanities fellowship, Guggenheim fellowship. Fellow: AAAS. Office: 109 Marx Hall Princeton Univ Princeton NJ 08544 Office Phone: 609-258-4296. Business E-Mail: fraharg@princeton.edu.

FRANKINO, STEVEN P., law educator; b. 1936; AB, Cath. U. Am., 1959, JD, 1962. Bar: D.C. 1963, Nebr. 1977. Tchg. fellow Northwestern U. Sch. Law, Chgo.; asst. prof. Cath. U. Am., Washington, 1963-65, dean sch. law, gen. counsel, 1979-86; prof. law Villanova U., 1965-71; dean Creighton U. Sch. Law, Omaha, 1971-77; ptnr. Kutak, Rock & Huie, Omaha, 1977-79; dean Villanova (Pa.) U. Law Sch., 1987-97, prof. law, 1997—. Rsch. editor Cath. U. Law Jour. Mem. Am. Law Inst., Am. Bar Found., Pa. Bar Found., Knight of Malta, Order of Coif. Office: Villanova U Law Sch Garey Hall Villanova PA 19085 E-mail: frankino@law.villanova.edu.

FRANK-KAMENETSKII, MAXIM D., biomedical engineer; b. Nizhniy Novgorod, Russia, Aug. 7, 1941; came to U.S., 1993; s. David A. and Elena E. (Fridman) F.; m. Alla D. Voskoboinik, Jan. 7, 1961 (dec. 1985); 1 child, Michael. MS, Moscow Phys. & Tech. Inst., 1964, PhD, 1967; DSc, Inst. Chem. Physics Moscow, 1972. Jr. scientist Kurchatov Inst. Atomic Engery, Moscow, 1967-72, sr. scientist, 1972-78; head lab. Inst. Molecular Genetics, Moscow, 1979-89, head. dept., 1989-93; prof. Boston U., 1993—. Disting. vis.prof. U. Ala., Birmingham, 1989, Ohio State U., Columbus, 1991-92. Author: Unraveling DNA, 1993, 97. Avocation: tennis. Office: Boston U Dept Advanced Biotechnology 36 Cummington St Boston MA 02215-2427 Office Phone: 617-353-8498. Business E-Mail: mfk@bu.edu.

FRANKL, DANIEL RICHARD, physicist, researcher; b. N.Y.C., Sept. 6, 1922; s. William and Frances (Lerner) F.; m. Estelle Marder, Aug. 26, 1951; children— Joseph Frederick, Phyllis Gail. BSChemE, Cooper Union, 1943; PhD, Columbia, 1953. With U.S. Rubber Co., Detroit, 1943-50; with Gen. Telephone & Electronics Labs., Inc., Bayside, N.Y., 1953-63; vis. prof. phys. metallurgy U. Ill., Urbana; (on leave Gen. Telephone & Electronics Labs.), 1962-63; prof. physics Pa. State U., University Park, 1963-88, emeritus, 1988—. Vis. sr. research assoc. U. Sussex, 1969-70; vis. research physicist U. Calif., San Diego, 1978-79; vis. fellow Fitzwilliam Coll. U. Cambridge, 1986 Author: Electrical Properties of Semiconductor Surfaces, 1967; Electromagnetic Theory, 1986. Fellow Am. Phys. Soc. Research, publs. on internal friction, electroluminescence, surface properties of solids, thermal conduction, atomic beam scattering. Home: 438 Sierra Ln State College PA 16803-1409 Office: Pa State Univ Dept Physics University Park PA 16801

FRANKL, SPENCER NELSON, dentist, dean; b. Phila., Nov. 19, 1933; s. Louis and Vera F.; m. Rhoda Lee, June 12, 1955; children: Elizabeth Ann, Catherine Susan. D.D.S., Temple U., 1958; postgrad., Children's Hosp. D.C., 1958-59; MS, Tufts U., 1961. Asst. prof. dentistry Tufts U., 1961-64; asso. prof. Boston U., 1964-67, prof., 1967—, chmn. dept. dentistry, 1964-67, asst. dean, 1970-73, asso. dean, 1973—; dean Boston Univ. Sch. of Dental Medicine, 1977—; dep. dir. Boston U. Med. Ctr., 1980—. Chief pedodontics Boston U. Med. Center U. Hosp., 1964; head pediatric dentistry Beth Israel Hosp., 1964; chief dental service Joseph P. Kennedy Jr. Meml. Hosp., Brighton, Mass., 1968— Contbr. articles to profl. jours. Fellow Am. Coll. Dentists, Internat. Coll. Dentists, Am. Acad. Pediatric Dentistry; mem. APHA, ADA, Am. Soc. Dentistry for Children, Mass. Soc. Dentistry for Children (past pres.), Internat. Assn. for Dental Rsch., Am. Bd. Pedodontics (examiner). Office: 100 E Newton St G-317 Boston MA 02118-2308

FRANKL, WILLIAM STEWART, cardiologist, educator; b. Phila., July 15, 1928; s. Louis and Vera (Simkin) F.; m. Razelle Sherr, June 17, 1951; children: Victor S. (dec.), Brian A. BA in Biology, Temple U., 1951, MD, 1955, MS in Medicine, 1961. Diplomate Am. Bd. Internal Medicine, Am. Bd. Cardiovasc. Disease. Intern Buffalo Gen. Hosp., 1955—56; resident in medicine Temple U., Phila., 1956—57, 1959—61; faculty Temple U. Sch. Medicine, 1962—68, dir. EKG sect. dept. cardiology, 1966—68, dir. cardiac care unit, 1967—68; prof. medicine, dir. divsn. cardiology Med. Coll. Pa., Phila., 1970—79; prof. medicine, assoc. dir. cardiology divsn. Thomas Jefferson U., Phila., 1979—84; physician-in-chief Springfield Hosp., Mass., 1968—70; prof. medicine, co-dir. William Likoff Cardiovasc. Inst. Hahnemann U., Phila., 1984—86, dir. William Likoff Cardiovasc. Inst., dir. divsn. cardiology, 1986—92, Thomas J. Vischer Prof. medicine, chmn. dept. medicine, 1987—92; prof. medicine, dir. cardiovasc. regional programs Allegheny U. of Health Scis., 1992—98; dir. cardiovasc. regional programs Allegheny U. Hosps., 1992—98; v.p. cardiovasc. program devel. Allegheny U. Hosps. Sys., 1995—98; prof. medicine cardiology divsn. dept. medicine Temple U. Sch. Medicine, 1998—2000. Cons. cardiology Phila. Va Hosp., 1970-79; Fogarty Sr. Internat. fellow Cardiothoracic Inst., U. London, 1978-79; pres. Pa. affiliate Am. Heart Assn., 1985-86; clin. prof. of medicine, Temple U. Sch. of Medicine, 2000—. Contbr. articles to profl. jours. Capt. (M.C.) U.S. Army, 1957—59. Cardiovascular Rsch. fellow U. Pa., Phila., 1961-62; recipient Golden Apple award Temple U. Sch. Medicine, 1967; award Med. Coll. Pa., 1972; Lindback award for disting. teaching, 1975. Fellow ACP, Am. Coll. Cardiology (gov. Ea. Pa. 1986-89), Phila. Coll. Physicians, Am. Coll. Clin. Pharmacology (regent 1980-85, 93-98), Coun. Clin. Cardiology of Am. Heart Assn. (coun. on arteriosclerosis); mem. AAUP, AAAS, N.Y. Acad. Scis., Am. Fedn. Clin. Rsch., Assn. Am. Med. Colls., Am. Heart Assn. (bd. govs. S.E. Pa. chpt. 1972-84, pres. 1976, Pa. affiliate pres. 1984-85), Am. Soc. Clin. Pharmacology and Exptl. Therapeutics, Phila. County Med. Soc. (pres. 1993-94, 1st dist. trustee to Pa. Med. Soc. bd. trustees 1998-2001). Home and Office: 536 Moreno Rd Wynnewood PA 19096-1121 Office Phone: 610-649-5947. Personal E-mail: bfrankl@comcast.net. *The essence of humanity and being human is caring. When one cares, life takes on a new dimension and provides one the ability to transcend the thin veneer which separates human and animal.*

FRANKLE, DIANE HOLT, lawyer; BA, Coll. of Wooster, 1975; JD magna cum laude, Georgetown Univ., 1979. Bar: DC 1979, Md. 1980, Calif. 1985. Law clk. Judge R. Dorsey Watkins, US Dist Ct. (Md. Dist.), 1979—81; assoc. Ginsburg, Feldman & Bress, Washington, 1981—84; ptnr., co-chmn. Mergers & Acquisitions practice group DLA Piper Rudnick Gray Cary, Palo Alto, Calif. Faculty mem. ABA Nat. Inst., 1997—, Practising Law Inst., 1995—. Editor (in chief): Guide to Calif. Securities Law Practice, 2004; contbr. articles to profl. jours. Mem. adv. bd. Corp. Counsel Inst., Georgetown Univ., 2003—04; mem. Cmty. Working group, Opportunity Ctr., Palo Alto, Calif.; bd. mem. Silicon Valley Campaign for Legal Svc. Named a No. Calif. Super Lawyer, San Francisco mag., 2004. Mem.: ABA (co-chmn. Task Force on Pub. Co. Acquisitions 1995—), State Bar Calif., Phi Beta Kappa. Office: DLA Piper Rudnick Gray Cary 2000 University Ave Palo Alto CA 94303 Office Phone: 650-833-2026. Office Fax: 650-833-2001. Business E-Mail: diane.frankle@dlapiper.com.

FRANKLIN, ARETHA LOUISE, singer; b. Memphis, Mar. 25, 1942; d. Clarence L. and Barbara (Siggers) Franklin; m. Ted White, 1961 (div. 1969); children: Clarence, Edward, Kecalf, Teddy; m. Glynn Turman, Apr. 11, 1978 (div. 1984); 3 stepchildren. First record at age 12, rec. artist with Columbia Records, N.Y.C., 1961, then with Atlantic records, now with Arista Records; singer: (albums) Aretha, 1961, Electrifying, Tender Moving and Swinging, 1962, Laughing on the Outside, 1963, Unforgettable, Songs of Faith, Running Out of Fools, 1964, Yeah, 1965, Soul Sister, 1966, Queen of Soul, Take It Like You Give It, Lee Cross, Greatest Hits, I Never Loved a Man, Once in a Lifetime, Aretha Arrives, 1967, Lady Soul, Greatest Hits, Vol. 2, Best of Aretha Franklin, Live at Paris Olympia, Aretha Now, 1968, Soul 69, Today I Sing the Blues, Soft and Beautiful, Aretha Gold's, Satisfaction, I Say a Little Prayer, 1969, This Girl's in Love with You, Spirit in the Dark, Don't Play that Song, 1970, Live at the Fillmore West, Young Gifted and Black, Aretha's Greatest Hits, 1971, Amazing Grace, 1972, Hey Hey Now, Firest 12 Sides, 1973, Let Me Into Your Life, 1974, With Every Thing I Feel in Me, You, 1975, Sparkle, Ten Years of Gold, 1976, Sweet Passion, 1977, Almighty Fire, Star Collection, 1978, La Diva, 1979, Aretha, 1980, Who's Zoomin' Who, 1985, One Lord, One Faith, One Baptism, 1987, Aretha Sings the Blues, 1965, 85, Lady Soul, 1988, Through the Storm, 1989, What You See is What You Sweat, 1991, Jazz to Soul, 1992, Aretha After Hours, Chain of Fools, 1993, Unforgettable: A Tribute to Dinah Washington, 1995, Love Songs, 1997, The Delta Meets Detroit, A Rose Is Still A Rose, 1998, Amazing Grace, 1999, The Queen in Waiting: The Columbia Years 1960-1965, 2002, So Damn Happy, 2003; actress (films) Blues Brothers, 1980, Shindig! Presents Soul, Shindig! Presents Groovy Gals, 1991, History of Rock 'N' Roll, 1995, Blues Brothers 2000, 1998, (TV films) Bob Hope on Campus, 1975, Aretha Franklin: The Queen of Soul, 1988, (TV miniseries) Motown 40: The Music Is Forever, 1998; performer (Showtime prodn.): Aretha, 1986; performer: (concert tours) in U.S. and Europe; performer: at Pres. Carter's Inauguration, 1977, at Pres. Clinton's Inauguration, 1992. Named Top Female Vocalist, 1967, Number One Female Singer 16th Internat., Jazz Critics Poll, 1968, 9th greatest rock 'n' roll artist of all time, Rolling Stone mag.; named to Hollywood Walk of Fame, 1979, Rock and Roll Hall of Fame, 1987; recipient Grammy award for best female rhythm and blues vocal, 1967—74, 1981, 1985, 1987, for best rhythm and blues rec., 1988, for best soul gospel performance, 1972, for best rhythm and blues duo vocal (with George Michael), 1987, Am. Music award, 1984, Grammy Legend award, 1991, Kennedy Center Honor, 1994, 1994. Achievements include first woman admitted in Rock & Roll Hall of Fame. Office: care Arista Records c/o Gwen Quinn 6 W 57th St New York NY 10019-3901*

FRANKLIN, BARBARA HACKMAN, former government official; b. Lancaster, Pa., Mar. 19, 1940; d. Arthur A. and Mayme M. (Haller) Hackman; m. Wallace Barnes, 1986. BA with distinction, Pa. State U., 1962; MBA, Harvard U., 1964. Mgr. environ. analysis Singer Co., N.Y.C., 1964—68; asst. v.p. Citibank, N.Y.C., 1969—71; White House staff asst. to the Pres. for recruiting women to govt. Washington, 1971—73; commr. U.S. Consumer Product Safety Commn., Washington, 1973—79, vice chair, 1973—74, 1977—78; sr. fellow, dir. govt. and bus. program Wharton Sch. U. Pa., Phila., 1980—88; pres., CEO Franklin Assocs., Washington, 1984—92; U.S. sec. commerce Dept. Commerce, Washington, 1992—93; pres., CEO Barbara Franklin Enterprises, Washington, 1995—; commentator Nightly Bus. Report, 1997—. Mem. Pres.'s Adv. Com. for Trade Policy and Negotiations, 1982—86, 1991—92, chair task force on tax reform, 1985—86, mem. NAFTA task force, 1991—92; alt. Rep. and public del. 44th session UN Gen. Assembly, 1989—90; mem. cons. panel U.S. Comptroller Gen., 1984—92, 1994—98; bd. dirs. Aetna, Inc., Medimmune, Inc.; chmn. audit com. GenVec, Inc., 1995—; chair governance com. Dow Chem. Co., 1980—92, 1993—. Trustee Fin. Acctg. Found., Pa. State U., 1976—82; bd. regents U. Hartford, 1986—88; bd. advisors Harvard Bus. Sch., 1998—2003; co-chmn. nat. fin. com. George Bush for Pres., 1987—88, George W. Bush for Pres., 1999—2000. Named Dir. Yr., NACD, 2000, Outstanding Dir., Bd. Alert, 2003; named one of 50 Most Influential Corp. Dirs., Am. Mgmt. Assn., 1990; recipient Disting. Alumni award, Pa. State U., 1972, John J. McCloy award for audit excellence, 1992, Alumni Achievement award, Harvard Bus. Sch., 2004. Mem.: Fin. Acctg. Found., U.S. China Bus. Coun. (vice-chair), Nat. Com. U.S.-China Rels., Coun. Fgn. Rels. (Atlantic Coun. dir.), Nat. Assn. Corp. Dir. (Blue Ribbon Commn., CEO evaluation 1994, Blue Ribbon Commn., audit effectiveness 1999, co-chair Blue Ribbon Commn., exec. compensation 2003), Nat. Symphony Orch., Heritage Found. (chair Asian studies adv. coun.), Internat. Women's Forum (founding mem.), Econ. Club NY (chmn. bd. dirs. Atlantic coun.), Union League Club N.Y. Avocations: exercise, hiking, reading, painting. Office: 2600 Virginia Ave NW Ste 506 Washington DC 20037-1905 Office Phone: 202-337-9100.

FRANKLIN, BENJAMIN A., editor, reporter; b. N.Y.C., Nov. 12, 1927; s. Benjamin A. and Zilpha C. Franklin; m. Jane Burrage, June 10, 1950; children: Abigail, Elizabeth, Clare. BA, U. Pa., 1948; MS in Journalism, Columbia U., 1950. Reporter Evening Star, Washington, 1948—50, ABC Radio News, Washington, 1953—59, N.Y. Times, Washington, 1959—91, Nucleonics Week, Washington, 1991—93; editor Washington Spectator, 1993—. Lt. (j.g.) USCG, 1950—53, N. Atlantic. Recipient Weatherford award, Berea Coll., Ky., 1970, Disting. Svc. award, Soc. Profl. Journalists, 1973, Honors award, Environ. Policy Inst., Washington, 1974. Mem.: Washington Nat. Press Club. Democrat. Episcopalian. Home and Office: PO Box 90 11404 Rokeby Ave Garrett Park MD 20896 Office Phone: 301-933-0370. Personal E-mail: franklinben@mindspring.com.

FRANKLIN, BLAKE TIMOTHY, lawyer; b. San Mateo, Calif., Sept. 28, 1942; s. Harvey James and Marie Agnes (Leane) F. AB, Dartmouth Coll., 1963; JD, Harvard U., 1966. Bar: Calif. 1966, D.C. 1969, U.S. Supreme Ct. 1970, N.Y. 1976. AID contractor Peace Corps; vis. prof. comml. law U. Costa Rica, San Jose, 1966-68; assoc. Coudert Bros., Washington, 1969-74, ptnr. N.Y.C., 1975-83, Gibson Dunn & Crutcher, N.Y.C., 1983—. Bd. dirs. Union Theol. Sem., N.Y., 1996-2004, Nat. Law Ctr. for Inter-Am. Free Trade, Tucson, Bolivian-Am. C. of C., Andean Resources, S.A. Chancellor of vestry St. Michael's Ch., N.Y.C., 1987-93; trustee Aids Svc. Found. of Orange County, Calif., 1994-97; St. Hilda's and St. Hugh's Sch., N.Y.C., 1988-92; mem. bd. gov.'s USO, 1987-90. Mem. ABA, Inter-Am. Bar Assn., Am. Soc. Internat. Law, Assn. of Bar of City of N.Y. Episcopalian. Office: Gibson Dunn & Crutcher 200 Park Ave Fl 47 New York NY 10166-0193

FRANKLIN, BONNIE GAIL, actress; b. Santa Monica, Calif., Jan. 6, 1944; d. Samuel Benjamin and Claire (Hersch) F. BA, UCLA, 1966. Mem. regional theatres in, N.Y., Mass., Ohio, Maine, N.H., Conn., Pa., 1972-99. Stage appearances include Your Own Thing, San Francisco, L.A., N.Y.C., 1968, Dames At Sea, 1969, Applause, N.Y.C., 1970-72 (Aegis Theatre Club award 1970, Theatre Club award 1970, Outer Critics Circle award 1960-70, Tony nomination), Happy Birthday and Other Humiliations, N.Y., 1987, Frankie & Johnny in the Clair de Lune, 1988, Grace & Glorie, 1996; tv appearances include One Day At A Time, 1975-84. Mem. AFTRA, SAG, Actors Equity Assn., Dirs. Guild Am. Democrat. Jewish. Address: 15745 Royal Oak Rd Encino CA 91436-3907 *To avoid criticism: say nothing, do nothing, be nothing.*

FRANKLIN, BRUCE WALTER, lawyer; b. Ellendale, N.D., Feb. 26, 1936; s. Wallace Henry and Frances (Webb) F.; m. Kristy Ann Jones, Feb. 7, 1944; children: Kevin, Monica, Taylor. Student, U. Mich., 1954-56; LLB, Detroit Coll. Law, 1962. Bar: Mich. 1963. Sole practice, Troy, Mich., 1962-90; mng. ptnr. Franklin, Bigler, Berry & Johnston, P.C., Troy, Mich., 1991-98, Franklin & Davis, Troy, 1998—. Bd. dirs. First Union-Newnan Bank; pres., CEO Landward III Devel. Corp. (Arbor Springs Plantation). Past chmn. Mich. Young Reps., United Meth. Retirement Cmtys.; bd. dirs. Peachtree Hosp., Wesley Woods. Served with U.S. Army. Office: Landward III 215 Arbor Shores N Newnan GA 30265 E-mail: bwfranklin@yahoo.com.

FRANKLIN, CHARLES E., manufacturing executive; b. Birmingham, Ala., July 17, 1938; BS in Mech. Engring, Ga. Inst. Tech., 1961; MS in Aeromech. Engring., Air Force Inst. Tech., 1967. Ret. as lt. gen. USAF, 1996; v.p. Lockheed Martin, 1998—2002; sr. exec. Raytheon Co., Tewksbury, Mass., 1998—.

FRANKLIN, EDWARD WARD, international investment consultant, lawyer, actor; b. N.Y.C., Sept. 23, 1926; s. Albert Ward and Edith (Meyers) F.; m. Joan Rice, Aug. 25, 1956; children— Caroline, Melissa, Edward Ward. AB magna cum laude, Harvard U., 1947, LLB, 1950. Bar: N.Y. 1951. Assoc. Cadwalader, Wickersham & Taft, N.Y.C., 1950-56; gen. counsel N.Y. Air Brake Co., 1956-67, v.p. internat. and legal, 1962-67; v.p., gen. counsel Gen. Signal Corp., N.Y.C., 1967-80, sec., 1969-80, sr. v.p., 1980-83, vice chmn., 1983-85. Chmn. bd. Hamworthy Hydraulics, Ltd., Poole, Eng.; dir. Holborn Internat. Portfolio Mgrs., Ptnrs. Fund, Inc., Pacus Ventures Ltd., Chase NBW Bank. Life gov., trustee N.Y. Presbyn. Hosp., Trinity Episcopal Schs. Corp.; chmn. bd. trustees Gracie Square Hosp., N.Y.C. Mem. AEA, SAG, AFTRA, Assn. Bar City of N.Y., The Players, Knickerbocker Club, Harvard Club (N.Y.C.), Misquamicut Club (Watch Hill, R.I.), Phi Beta Kappa. Home and Office: 1185 Park Ave New York NY 10128-1308

FRANKLIN, GENE FARTHING, engineering educator, consultant; b. Banner Elk, N.C., July 25, 1927; s. Burnie D. and Delia (Farthing) F.; m. Gertrude Stritch, Jan. 1952; children: David M., Carole Lea. BSEE, Ga. Inst. Tech., 1950; MSEE, MIT, 1952; DEngSc, Columbia U., 1955. Asst. prof. Columbia U., N.Y.C., 1955-57; prof. elec. engring. Stanford (Calif.) U., 1957-95, prof. emeritus, 1995—. Cons. IBM, Rochester, Minn., 1982-94. Author: Sampled-Data Control, 1958, Digital Control, 1980, 3d edit., 1997, Feedback Control, 1986, 4th edit., 2001. With USN, 1945-47. Recipient Edn. award Am. Automatic Control Coun., 1985, Bellman Award, 2005. Fellow IEEE (life), Control Soc. of IEEE (Bode lectr. 1994). Democrat. Office: Stanford U Dept Elec Engring Stanford CA 94305 Business E-Mail: franklin@ee.stanford.edu.

FRANKLIN, G(EORGE) CHARLES, retired academic administrator; b. Normangee, Tex., Dec. 27, 1935; married; 3 children. BBA, Sam Houston State U., 1958, postgrad., 1958—. Chief acct., instr. acct. Sam Houston State U., Huntsville, Tex., 1959-62; asst. to dir. Commn. on Coord. Higher Edn. Fin. State of Ark., 1962-64; contr. Ark. State U., Jonesboro, 1964-65; v.p. for bus. affairs Midwestern U., Wichita Falls, Tex., 1965-69; bus. mgr. U. Tex., Austin, 1969-71, v.p. for fiscal affairs San Antonio, 1971-72, v.p. for adminstrn. and fin., Health Sci. Ctr. Houston, 1972-79, v.p. adminstrv. svcs. Austin, 1979-80, v.p. for bus. affairs, 1980-2000, sr. v.p., CFO, 2000—01; ret., 2001. 2d lt. U.S. Army, 1958—59. Mem. Nat. Assn. Coll. and Univ. Bus. Officers, So. Assn. Coll. and Univ. Bus. Officers, Tex. Assn. State Sr. Coll. and Univ. Bus. Officers (pres. 1988). Home: 24 Drifting Wind Run Austin TX 78738 Personal E-mail: g.c.franklin@austin.rr.com.

FRANKLIN, HAROLD LEROY, graphic artist, filmmaker; b. Mobile, Ala., Mar. 14, 1934; s. Harold Leroy and Julia (Nicholson) F.; m. Frances Sanders, Aug. 24, 1996; 1 child, Lavarr K. Zuber. Diploma, Phila. Coll. Art, 1958. Art dir. City of Phila., 1961-97; film prodr., dir. EKO Prodns., Phila., 1969—. Freelance artist Phila. Inquirer Sunday Mag., 1970, N.Y. Times Sunday Mag., Bus. Week Mag., 1971. Author: Which Way to Go, 1969, A Garden on Cement, 1971, Once Around the Track, 1974, A Trip Back to Elmwood, 1991; film prodr. The Classroom Channel, Lakewood, Colo., 1987-90, WHYY-TV, Channel 12, Phila., 1986, 92, The Black Filmmaker Found., 1987-88. Mem. Black Peoples' Unity Movement, Phila., 1968-71. With U.s. Army, 1958-60. Recipient Spl. Jury's prize Phila. Internat. Film Festival, 1986; Pa. Coun. Arts film fellow, 1992. Mem. Phila. Ind. Film/Video Assn. Democrat. Baptist. Avocations: writing, historical research, movies, plays, flea markets. Home: 1315 S 53rd St Philadelphia PA 19143-4901 Office: EKO Prodns PO Box 5492 Philadelphia PA 19143-0492 Fax: 215-727-4504.

FRANKLIN, J. RICHARD, principal; b. Milan, Mo., July 15, 1934; m. Joyce Ann Fishback; children: James, Elizabeth. BS, Truman State U., 1956; MA, U. Mo., 1963; postgrad., Ctrl. Mo. State U., 1972—. Prin. Ft. Osage High Sch., Independence, Mo. State rep. dist. 53 Mo. Ho. of Reps., mem. edn. com., retirement com., banking com.; chmn. budget com. Mem. State Hist. Soc. Mo. (pres.), Masons, Shriners. Address: 1829 S Aztec Avenue Independence MO 64057

FRANKLIN, JAMES BURKE, lawyer; b. Statesboro, Ga., Mar. 11, 1938; s. Sam J. and Eva Claire (Burke) Franklin; m. Fay Foy Smith, Mar. 20, 1976; children: Julie Foy, Rebecca Claire. BS, Ga. Inst. Tech.; JD, U. Ga. Bar: Ga., U.S. Dist. Ct. (so., mid., and no. dists.), U.S. Ct. Appeals (11th cir.). Ptnr. Allen, Edenfield, Brown & Franklin (formerly Allen & Edenfield), 1969—74; sr. ptnr. Franklin, Taulbee, Rushing, Snipes and Marsh, P.C., and predecessor firms, Statesboro, Ga., 1974—. Magistrate U.S. Dist. Ct. (so. dist.) Ga., 1979—81; chmn. Devel. Authority Bulloch County. Pres. Bulloch County (Ga.) C. of C. To lt. U.S. Army, 1964—66. Named Designated Ga. Super Lawyer, 2005; recipient Amicus Curiae Award, Ga. Supreme Ct., 2005, Disting. Svc. Scroll, U. Ga. Law Sch., 2005. Mem.: State Bar Ga. (bd. govs., pres. 2001—02), Rotary Club (Statesboro) (pres.). Methodist. Office: 12 Siebald St PO Box 327 Statesboro GA 30458 Office Phone: 912-764-9055.

FRANKLIN, JERRY FOREST, forest ecologist, educator; b. Waldport, Oreg., Oct. 27, 1936; m. Phyllis C.; children: James Lyman, Lewis Forest, Virginia Sandalee, Heather Ann. BS in Forest Mgmt., Oreg. State U., 1959, MS in Forest Mgmt. and Stats., 1961; PhD in Botany and Soils, Wash. State U., 1966; LLD (hon.), Simon Fraser U., Burnaby, BC, 2001. Rsch. forester USDA Forest Svc. Pacific N.W. Rsch. Sta., Corvallis, Oreg., 1959—75, chief plant ecologist, 1975—91; dir. Ecosystem Studies Program NSF, Washington, 1973-75; prof. dept. botany and plant pathology & dept. forest sciences Oreg. State U., Corvallis, 1975—92; prof. ecosystem analysis U. Wash., Seattle, 1986—; dir. Wind River Canopy Crane Rsch. Facility, 1993—. Contbr. articles to Landscape Ecology, BioSci., Forest Watch, Ecol. Applications, others. Named Conservationist of Yr., Pacific Rivers Coun., 1992; recipient Superior Svc. Award, USDA, 1970, 1986, Disting. Scientist Award, N.W. Sci. Assn., 1971, Arthur S. Flemming Award for outstanding young person in Fed. govt., 1972, Barrington Moore Award, Soc. Am. Foresters, 1986, Olaus & Margaret Murie Award, The Wilderness Soc., 1988, Howard Vollum Award, Reed Coll., Portland, 1992, George Melendez Wright Award for Excellence, George Wright Soc., 1992, Philip C. Hamm Award, Monsanto Agrl. Co. & U. Minn. Coll. Agrl., Food and Environ. Sciences, 1995, William B. Greeley Award, Am. Forests Assn., 1996, Heinz Award for the Environment, 2005; Charles Bullard Fellow for Forest Rsch., Harvard U., 1985—86. Fellow: AAAS; mem.: Internat. Assn. Landscape Ecology (Leadership in Action Award, US chpt. 2001), Soc. Conservation Biology (LaRoe Award 2004), Brit. Ecol. Soc., Am. Inst. Biol. Sciences, Ecol. Soc. Am. (pres. 1993—94). Office: U Wash Coll Forest Resources Campus Box 352100 Seattle WA 98195-2100 Office Phone: 206-543-2138. Office Fax: 206-543-7295. Business E-Mail: jff@u.washington.edu.*

FRANKLIN, JOEL NICHOLAS, mathematician, educator; b. Chgo., Apr. 4, 1930; m. Patricia Anne; 1 dau., Sarah Jane. BS, Stanford, 1950, PhD, 1953. Research asso. N.Y. U., 1953-55; asst. prof. math. U. Wash, 1955; mem. faculty Calif. Inst. Tech., 1957—, prof. applied sci., 1966-69, prof. applied math., 1969—. Author: Matrix Theory, 1968, Methods of Mathematical Economics, 1980, also articles. Mem. Am. Math. Soc., Soc. Indsl. and Applied Math., Phi Beta Kappa. Home: 1763 Alta Crest Dr Altadena CA 91001-2130 Office: Calif Inst Tech 217 50 Pasadena CA 91125-0001

FRANKLIN, JOHN HOPE, historian, educator, author; b. Rentiesville, Okla., Jan. 2, 1915; s. Buck Colbert and Mollie (Parker) Franklin; m. Aurelia E. Whittington, June 11, 1940; 1 child, John Whittington. AB, Fisk U., 1935; AM, Harvard, 1936, PhD, 1941; hon. degrees, Morgan State Coll., Va. State Coll., Lincoln (Pa.) U., Cambridge (Eng.) U., Drake U., Mich. State U., U. Ill. at Chgo., Carnegie-Mellon U., Columbia U., Columbia Coll., Chgo., Loyola

U., Bklyn. Coll., Bard Coll., Boston Coll., Brown U., Tuskegee Inst., Grand Valley Coll., Marquette U., Lincoln Coll., Ill., Princeton, Hamline U., Fisk U., R.I. Coll., Dickinson Coll., Howard U., U. Md., U. Notre Dame, Tulsa U., Morehouse Coll., Miami U., Johnson C. Smith U., Lake Forest Coll., Tougaloo Coll., Union Coll., Northwestern U., Whittier Coll., U. Mass., U. Mich., Seattle U., U. Toledo, Yale U., L.I. U., Catholic U. Am., Tulane U., Temple U., Kalamazoo Coll., Washington U., St. Louis, Trinity Coll. (Conn.), Ariz. State U., SUNY, Albany, No. Mich. U., U. Utah, Coll. New Rochelle, George Washington U., Governors State U., Harvard U., U. Pa., Ripon Coll., Atlanta U., Wayne State U., U. N.C.-Chapel Hill, Dillard U., Manhattan Coll., Roosevelt U., N.C. Central U., Ind. State U., St. Olaf Coll., Emory U., U. Miami, U. Conn., U. N.C.-Charlotte, Brandeis U., Wake Forest U., Wilkes Coll., Queen's Coll., N.Y., Wilmington Coll., Hope Coll., Bryant Coll., SUNY-Binghamton, Indiana U., N.C. Weslyan U., N.C. State U., So. Meth. U., Berea Coll., Grad Ctr. CUNY, Suffolk U., Washington Coll., Eckerd Coll., Rutgers U., U. N.C., Greensboro, St. Augustine Coll., U. Okla., Oreg. State U., Winston-Salem State U., Queens Coll., Charlotte, N.C., Ill. State U., Bates Coll., Williams Coll., U. of the South, U. N.C.-Wilmington, Am. U.; hon. degree, Furman U., Georgetown U., Tufts U., Elizabeth City State U., Shaw U., San Francisco U., Washington and Lee U., Columbia U., Chgo., Lincoln Meml. U., Elmira Coll., Lane Coll., Bethune-Cookman Coll., Amherst Coll., U. Cin., Dartmouth Coll., U. Ky., Duke U., San Francisco State U., York Coll., Northeastern U., Occidental Coll., U. Akron, U. Vermont, Bennett Coll., San Diego U., Pa. State U., Tex. A&M U., Pomona Coll., U. San Diego, U. Vt., U. Akron, U. N.C., Pembroke, S.C. State U., U. DC. Prof. history St. Augustine's Coll., 1936—37, N.C. Coll. at Durham, 1943—47, Howard U., 1947—56; chmn. dept. history Bklyn. Coll., 1956—64; prof. Am. history U. Chgo., 1964—82, chmn. dept. history, 1967—70, John Matthews Manly Distinguished Service prof., 1969—82; James B. Duke prof. history Duke U., 1982—85; prof. legal history Duke U. Law Sch., 1985-92. Pitt. prof. Am. history and instns. Cambridge U., 1962—63; vis. prof. Harvard U., U. Wis., Cornell U., Salzburg Seminar, U. Hawaii, U. Claif.; chmn. bd. fgn. scholarships, 1966—69, Nat. Coun. on Humanities, 1976—79; trustee Nat. Humanities Ctr., 1980—91, chmn. adv. bd. to pres.'s initiative on race, 1997—98; Fulbright prof., Australia, 1960; lectr. in field; chmn. adv. bd. Nat. Pk. Svc. Author: Free Negro in North Carolina, 1943, From Slavery to Freedom: A History of African Americans, 2000, Militant South, 1956, Reconstruction After the Civil War, 1961, The Emancipation Proclamation, 1963, A Southern Odyssey, 1976, Racial Equality in America, 1976, George Washington Williams, A Biography, 1985, Race and History, 1990; co-author: Land of the Free, 1966, Illustrated History of Black Americans, 1970, The Color Line: Legacy for the 21st Century, 1993; co-author: (with Loren Schweninger) Runaway Slaves: Rebels on the Plantation, 1999, In Search of the Promised Land: A Slave Family in the Old South, 2005; editor: Civil War Diary of James T. Ayers, 1947, A Fool's Errand by Albion Tourgee, 1961, Army Life in a Black Regiment by Thomas Higginson, 1962, Color and Race, 1968, Reminiscences of an Active Life by John R. Lynch, 1970; co-editor (with August Meier): Black Leaders in the Twentieth Century, 1982; co-editor: (with Abraham Eisenstadt) Harlan Davidson's American History Series; mem. editl. bd.: Am. Scholar, 1972—76, 1994—, My Life and An Era (with John W. Franklin), —. Trustee Chgo. Symphony, 1976—80, Fisk U., 1947—80; bd. dirs. Salzburg Seminar, Mus. Sci. and Industry, 1968—80, DuSable Mus., 1970—. Named to Okla. Hall of Fame, 1978, Okla. Historians Hall of Fame, 1996; recipient Cleanth Brooks medal, Fellowship So. Writers, 1989, Gold medal, Ency. Britannica, 1990, Caldwell medal, N.C. Coun. on Humanities, 1992, 1993, Charles Frankel medal, 1993, Spingarn medal, NAACP, 1995, Bruce Catton award, Soc. Am. Historians, 1994, award, Cosmos Club, 1994, Presdl. medal of Freedom, 1995, Peggy V. Helmerich Disting. Author award, 1997, Smithson Bicentennial medal, 1997, Lincoln prize, 2000, Harold Washington Lit. award, 2000, Gold medal award, Am. Acad. Arts and Letters, 2002, Disting. Author award, Bergen County, 2002, Arthur Schlesinger Lifetime History award, 2002; fellow Edward Austin fellow, 1937—39, Guggenheim fellow, 1950—51, 1973—74, Pres.'s fellow, Brown U., 1952—53, Ctr. for Advanced Study in Behavioral Sci., 1973—74, Sr. Mellon fellow. Fellow: Am. Acad. Arts and Scis.; mem.: AAUP, Am. Philos. Soc. (Jefferson medal 1993), Am. Studies Assn. (past pres.), Assn. for Study Negro Life and History, Orgn. Am. Historians (pres. 1974—75), So. Hist. Assn. (pres. 1970—71), Am. Hist. Assn. (pres. 1978—79), Phi Alpha Theta, Phi Beta Kappa (senate 1966—82, pres. 1973—76, Sidney Hook award 1994).

FRANKLIN, JON DANIEL, writer, journalist, educator; b. Enid, Okla., Jan. 12, 1942; s. Benjamin Max and Wilma Irene (Winburn) F.; m. Nancy Sue Creevan, Dec. 12, 1959 (div. 1976, dec. 1987); children: Teresa June, Catherine Cay; m. Lynn Irene Scheidhauer, May 20, 1988. BS with high honors, U. Md., 1970; LHD (hon.), U. Md., Balt. County, 1981, Coll. Notre Dame, Balt., 1982. With USN, 1959-67; reporter/editor Prince Georges (Md.) Post, 1967-70; sci. and feature writer Balt. Evening Sun, 1970-85; assoc. prof. U. Md. Coll. Journalism, 1985-88, prof., 1988-89; prof., chmn. dept. journalism Oreg. State U., Corvallis, 1989-91; prof. creative writing, dir. U. Oreg., Eugene, 1991-98; sci. writer, spl. assignments editor Raleigh News and Observer, Raleigh, N.C., 1998-2001; Philip Merrill prof. journalism U. Md., College Park, 2001—. Author: Shocktrauma, 1980, Not Quite a Miracle, 1983, Guinea Pig Doctors, 1984, Writing for Story, 1986, The Molecules of the Mind, 1987. pub.: *Bylines*, WriterL. Recipient James T. Grady medal Am. Chem. Soc., 1975, Pulitzer prize for feature writing, 1979, Pulitzer prize for explanatory journalism, 1985, Carringer award Nat. Mental Health Assn., 1984, Penney-Mo. Spl. award for health reporting, 1985; named to Newspaper Hall of Fame, Md.-Del.-D.C. Press Assn.,also Feature Writers Hall of Fame, 2002. Mem. Nat. Assn. Sci. Writers (bd. dirs.), Soc Profl. Journalists, Authors Guild. Home: PO Box 206 Sunderland MD 20689-0206

FRANKLIN, JUDE ERIC, electronics executive; b. St. Marys, Pa., Aug. 3, 1943; s. William Nelson and Elizabeth (Kronenwetter) F.; m. Mary Frances Bizot, Sept. 17, 1966; children: Pamela Mary, Erik Jude. BEE, Cath. U., 1965, MEE, 1968, PhDEE, 1980. Program mgr. Chesapeake Instrument Corp. (now divsn. of GE), Shadyside, Md., 1966-75; v.p. MAR, Inc., Rockville, Md., 1975-81; mgr. Navy Artifical Intelligence Ctr. Naval Rsch. Lab., Washington, 1981-85; sr. v.p. tech. div. Planning Rsch. Corp., McLean, Va., 1985-87, sr. v.p., 1987-92, chief tech. officer and v.p., 1991—. Bd. dirs. Am. Univ., Washington Juvenile Diabetes Found. Contbr. to Artifical Intelligence Ency., 1987; also articles to profl. jours. V.p. Prince Mont Swim League; vol. U.S. Swimming Referee and Starter; PRC team leader Juvenile Diabetes Found., 1995. Recipient Meritorious Svc. award Armed Forces Communications and Electronics Assn., 1988, Fed. "100" award Fed. Computer News, 1992, Best Paper of Yr. award Signal Mag., 1995. Fellow AIAA (assoc.), Washington Acad. Sci.; mem. IEEE (sr., guest editor Expert Mag., 1989), Kettering Civic Fedn. (pres. 1971-72), Sigma Xi. Democrat. Roman Catholic. Home: 7616 Carteret Rd Bethesda MD 20817-2021 Office: Ste 1700 1100 Wilson Blvd Arlington VA 22209 Personal E-mail: jude_e_franklin@raytheon.com.

FRANKLIN, JULIAN HAROLD, political science professor; b. N.Y.C., Mar. 26, 1925; s. Jerome A. and Molly (Seidenstein) F.; m. Paula Angle, Feb. 23, 1928. BA summa cum laude, Queens Coll., 1946; MA, Columbia U., 1950, PhD, 1960. Instr. Columbia U., N.Y.C., 1951-59, assoc. prof., 1962-68, prof., 1968-96, prof. emeritus, 1997—; vis. asst. prof. New Sch. for Social Rsch., N.Y.C., 1959-60; asst. prof. Princeton (N.J.) U., 1960-62. Acting chmn. summer session Columbia U., 1962—, dir. grad. studies polit. theory, 1968—, dept. rep., 1971-72, 86—, dept. del. com. on instruction faculty polit. sci., 1971-73, 81-82, chmn., 1973-74, co-founder, adj. chmn. sem. on polit. and social thought; mem. adv. coun. dept. politics Princeton U., 1973-76. Author: Jean Bodin and the Sixteenth Century Revolution in the Methodology of Law and History, 1963, Constitutionalism and Resistance in the Sixteenth Century, 1969, Jean Bodin and the Rise of Absolutist Theory, 1973, rev. edit. (in French), 1993, John Locke and the Theory of Sovereignty, 1978, Animal Rights and Moral Philosophy, 2005; editor and translator: Jean Bodin on Sovereignty, 1992; editl. cons. in polit. theory Polit. Theory, 1977-79; mem. editl. bd. Polit. Theory; contbr. articles to profl. jours. Served with USAF, 1943-46. Queens Coll. scholar, 1946, Social Sci. Rsch. Coun. fellow, 1950-51, William Bayard Cutting travelling fellow, 1950-51, NEH fellow, 1975-76, 89-90, Phi Beta Kappa fellow, 1990. Mem. Conf. for Study Polit. and Social Thought. Jewish. Office: Columbia U Dept Polit Sci 116th St And Broadway New York NY 10027

FRANKLIN, KENNETH RONALD, diversified financial services company executive, consultant; b. N.Y.C., June 6, 1932; s. Lawrence and Gladys (Siegel) Franklin; m. Harriet Faye Lewis, Dec. 27, 1960; children: Gregg E., Erica G. BS, Syracuse U., 1953, MBA, 1954. Cert. mgmt. cons. Instr. Harpur Coll. Syracuse U., Vestal, N.Y., 1956-57; sales rep. IBM, Pitts., 1957-64; br. mgr. ABS, Pitts., 1964-66; v.p. franchising Arby's Inc., Youngstown, Ohio, 1966-70; pres. Franchise Devel. Inc., Pitts., 1970—. With Spl. Svcs., 1954-56, ETO. Mem. Inst. Mgmt. Cons., Pitts. Athletic Assn., Concorcia Club, Westmoreland C.C. Avocations: tennis, reading, travel. Office: Franchise Devel Inc Hampshire Hall 4730 Centre Ave Pittsburgh PA 15213-1759 Office Phone: 412-687-8484. Personal E-mail: franchise-dev@earthlink.net.

FRANKLIN, LINDA ANN, education educator; b. St. Louis, Feb. 7, 1950; d. Lynn Harold and Laurel Inez Dittman; m. Densil Dean Staton, Feb. 28, 1971 (div. June 1981); 1 child, Rebecca Lynne Staton Deskins; m. Donald LeRoy Franklin, Dec. 30, 1981; children: Daniel Carl, Douglas Lynn. BS in Edn., Ctrl. Mo. State U., 1971; MS in Edn., William Woods U., 1998. Tchr. Hume (Mo.) R-8 Sch., 1972—74, Hale (Mo.) R-1 Sch., 1978—81, Tri-County R-7 Sch., Jamesport, Mo., 1981—82, North Ctrl. Mo. Coll., Trenton, 1989—2004; spl. edn. tchr. North Davies R-III, 2004—. Tax collector Jefferson Twp., Grundy County, Mo., 1990—99. Sponsor Psychology/Sociology Club, Trenton, 1992—93; tutor ARC, Trenton, 2003; cmty. leader Pleasant Ridge Boosters 4-H Club, Trenton, 1995. Mem.: Eastern Star. Baptist. Avocations: reading, crafts, gardening. Home: 676 SW 56th St Jamesport MO 64648 E-mail: franklin@grm.net.

FRANKLIN, LYNNE, corporate communications specialist, writer; b. St. Paul, Aug. 24, 1957; d. Lyle John Franklin and Lois Ann (Cain) Kindseth, Thomas John Kindseth (Stepfather); m. Lawrence Anton Pecorella, Sept. 12, 1989; 1 stepchild, Lauren Pecorella. BA in Psychology and English, Coll. St. Catherine, 1979; MA, Hamline U., 1989. Residential treatment counselor St. Joseph's Home, Mpls., 1979-80; staff writer Comml. West Mag., Mpls., 1980-81; acct. exec. Edwin Neuger & Assocs., Mpls., 1981-83, Hill and Knowlton, Mpls., 1983-84; mgr. pub. rels. Gelco Corp., Eden Prarie, Minn., 1984-86; dir. fin. rels. Dunstan & Assocs., Mpls., 1986; cons. MC Assocs., Chgo., 1986-87; v.p. Fin. Rels. Bd., Chgo., 1987—; prin. Wordsmith, Glenview, Ill., 1993—; trainer SkillPath Seminars, Mission, Kans., 2004—, 2004. Trustee Lawrence Hall Youth Svcs.; former pres., v.p., sec. Skokie Valley chpt. Bus. Networking Internat., 2003—05; judge achievement awards Internat. Assn. Bus. Comm., Mpls., 1986, Publicity Club Chgo., 1992—94; presenter in fin. rels., 1990; presenter ann. report seminar Nat. Investor Rels. Inst., Chgo., 1992; presenter investor rels. survey, 2003; mktg. presenter Nat. Assn. Profl. Organizers, Chgo., 2005, World WIT Nat. Conf., Lake Geneva, Wis., 2005. Author: (novels) Second Sight, 1989. Tchr. Great Books Program, St. Paul, 1976—79, Minn. Literacy Coun., 1985—87. Recipient Ann. Report Excellence award, Fin. World Mag., 1991—98, award, MerComm-ARC Competition, 1992—2003, Nat. Assn. Investors Corp., 1994—2003, Equities Mag., 1999—2002. Office: Wordsmith 2019 Glenview Rd Glenview IL 60025-2849 Office Phone: 847-729-5716. Business E-Mail: lynne@yourwordsmith.com.

FRANKLIN, MARC ADAM, law educator; b. Bklyn., Mar. 9, 1932; s. Louis A. and Rose (Rosenthal) Franklin; m. Ruth E. Korzenik, June 29, 1958 (dec. Dec. 2000); children: Jonathan, Alison. AB, Cornell U., 1953, LLB, 1956. Bar: N.Y. 1956. Assoc. Proskauer Rose Goetz & Mendelsohn, N.Y.C., 1956-57; law clk to Hon. Carroll C. Hincks, New Haven, 1957-58; prof. law Stanford U., Calif., 1962-76, Frederick I. Richman prof. law, 1976—2001, emeritus, 2001—; prof. law Columbia U., 1959-62; law clk to Earl Warren, U.S. Supreme Ct., Washington, 1958-59. Author: Biography of a Legal Dispute, 1968, Dynamics of American Law, 1968, Cases and Materials on Tort Law and Alternatives, 1971; co-author (with R.L. Rabin): Cases and Materials on Tort Law and Alternatives, 7th edit., 2001; author: Mass Media Law, 1977; co-author (with D.A. Anderson and L.C.B. Lidsky): Mass Media Law, 7th edit., 2005; author: The First Amendment and the Fourth Estate, 1977; co-author (with T.B. Carter and J.B. Wright): The First Amendment and the Fourth Estate, 9th edit., 2005; author: The First Amendment and the Fifth Estate, 1986; co-author (with T.B. Carter and J.B. Wright): The First Amendment and the Fifth Estate, 6th edit., 2003. Fellow Ctr. for Advanced Study in Behavioral Scis., 1968—69; scholar Fulbright, Victoria U., 1973. Home: 999 Green St # 2005 San Francisco CA 94133 Office: Stanford U Law Sch Nathan Abbott Way Stanford CA 94305 Business E-Mail: marcf@stanford.edu.

FRANKLIN, MARGERY BODANSKY, psychology professor, researcher; b. N.Y.C., Mar. 18, 1933; d. Oscar and Barbara (Biber) Bodansky; m. Raymond S. Franklin, Aug. 22, 1962; children— Kenneth, David AB, Swarthmore Coll., 1954; MA, Clark U., 1956, PhD, 1961. Instr. psychology Vassar Coll., Poughkeepsie, N.Y., 1960-62, asst. prof., 1962-64; research assoc. Bank St. Coll. Edn., N.Y.C., 1967-72; prof. Sarah Lawrence Coll., Bronxville, NY, 1965—2002. Dir. Child Devel. Inst. Sarah Lawrence Coll., 2003—. Co-editor: Developmental Processes: Heinz Werner's Selected Writings, 1978, Symbolic Functioning in Childhood, 1979, Child Language: A Reader, 1988, Development and the Arts: Critical Perspectives, 1994; contbr. articles to profl. jours., chpts. to books. Fellow Am. Psychol. Assn. (pres. psychology and arts divsn. 1990-91); mem. Soc. for Rsch. in Child Devel. Avocation: photography. Office Phone: 914-395-2630.

FRANKLIN, MARY ANN WHEELER, academic administrator, consultant; b. Boston; d. Arthur E. Wheeler Sr. and Madeline Ophelia (Hall) Wheeler-Brooks; m. Carl Matthew Franklin; 1 child, Evangeline Rachel Hall Franklin. BS, U. N.H., 1942; MEd, U. Buffalo, 1948; EdD, U. Md., 1982. Cert. tchr., N.Y., Ga. Instr. sci. edn. W.Va. State Coll., 1947; tchr. gen. sci. John Marshall Jr. High Sch., Bklyn., 1952-58, 59-60; assoc. prof. sci. Elizabeth City State Coll., 1960-67; asst. dean of the coll. Morgan State Coll., Balt., 1967-77; asst. dean Coll. Arts and Scis. Morgan State U., Balt., 1977-78, asst. v.p. acad. affairs, 1978-82; asst. prof. bus. Catonsville (Md.) Community Coll., 1982; asst. to dean evening and weekend coll. So. U. New Orleans, 1983-92. Cons. numerous locations including Herford County Tchrs., Murfreesboro, N.C., 1961, St. Catherine's Sch., Elizabeth City, N.C., 1962-64, St. Elizabeth Cath. Sch., Elizabeth City; cons., bd. dirs. Archbishop Keough H.S., Balt., 1970-80, Hampton (Va.) Inst., 1971, St. Paul Coll., 1972; presenter confs., seminars and workshops; spkr. in field. Editor Morgan State U. Acad. Affairs Newsletter, 1980-82; editor, pub. Morgan State U. Catalog, 1969-82, So. U. New Orleans Catalog, 1986-84, 89-92; author: The How and Why of Testing at Elizabeth City State College, 1962, Report on Princeton University Program for Physics Teachers in HBCU's, 1964, A Descriptive Report of Pre-College Study Booster Program, 1965, 66, Learning Summer Camp Code, National Library of Poetry, 1992, Interrogations of a Metropolis of the Day, Who Are We/Who We Are, 1994. Mem. cmty. higher edn. Citizens League, Balt., 1979-81; assoc. dir. youth camp NCCJ, 1974-75, bd. dirs., 1969-80; dir., originator Vestibule Program and Parents Workshop for New Citizens and Residents, SUNO Summer Learning Camp, 1984-95, Ctr. Women Against Crime Conf.; pres. Lake Willow Homeowners Assn., 1994-96. Fellow NSF, Harvard U., 1958-59, Carnegie-Ford-NSF, Princeton U., 1964; recipient Education award Am. Assn. of Coll. Tchrs. Edn., 1966. Mem. AAUW, Am. Mgmt. Assn., Nat. Coun. Negro Women, Am. Assn. Higher Edn., Am. Assn. Continuing Higher Edn., Nat. Assn. Trainers and Educators for Alcohol and Substance Abuse Counselors (bd. dirs.), La. Assn. Continuing Higher Edn., Md. Assn. Higher Edn., Urban League, Delta Sigma Theta, Phi Sigma, Pi Lambda Theta. Avocations: fine arts, portraits, pastels, listening to classical music and popular show tunes, swimming.

FRANKLIN, MARY ELENA, retired mathematician, retired computer specialist; b. Colorado Springs, Colo., Apr. 27, 1924; d. Thomas Tudor and Mary Isabel (McKenna) Davis; m. Robert Ayers Franklin, July 14, 1947; children: Maureen Rizzoli, Ronald, Timothy, Douglas, Mark, James, Lawrence. BS, U. N.Mex., 1944, MA, 1968. Mathematician Bur. of Ships, Washington, 1944-45, Navy Electronics Lab., San Diego, 1945-48, Lovelace Found. for Med. Edn. and Rsch., Albuquerque, 1960-63; computer specialist, applied mathematician USN Naval Weapons Evaluation Facility, Albuquerque, 1963-84; applied mathematician USAF Weapons Lab., Albuquerque, 1984-91. Lt. (j.g.) USN, 1944-47. Mem. N.Mex. Network for Women in Sci. and Engring. (bd. dirs. 1978-80), N.Mex. Acad. Sci. (life, sec. 1982-88), Sigma Alpha Iota. Avocation: world travel.

FRANKLIN, MICHAEL HAROLD, arbitrator, lawyer, consultant; b. Los Angeles, Dec. 25, 1923; m. Betty Chernow, 1989; children from previous marriage: Barbara, John, James, Robert. AB, UCLA, 1948; LL.B., U. So. Calif., 1951. Bar: Calif. 1951. Practiced in, Los Angeles, 1951-52; pvt. practice, 1951-52; atty. CBS, 1952-54, Paramount Pictures Corp., 1954-58; exec. dir. Writers Guild Am. West, Inc., 1958-78; nat. exec. dir. Dirs. Guild Am., Inc., 1978-88. Mem. Fed. Cable Adv. Commn. Served with C.E. AUS, 1942-46. Mem. Order of Coif.

FRANKLIN, PATT, artist, educator; b. N.J. s. Sigmund and Alice (Toner) Robbins; 1 child, Petra. BFA, Pratt Inst., 1962; MFA, Tulane U., 1970. Tchr. summer sch. Haystack Mountain, Deer Isle, Maine, 1976; summer sch. prof. Mass. Coll. Art, Boston, 1973; assoc. prof. U. So. Maine, Gorham, 1970-87, prof., 1988—; artist Varley & Stevens, Portsmouth, N.J., 1985. Illustrator, Chemstrand/Pratt Inst., 1962; artist in sculpture and clay (Silvermine 24th Ann. Mr. and Mrs. Fellar award 1973); artist drawings U. So. Maine, 1984; one-person shows include Wheelock Coll., Boston, 1984, Portland (Maine) State Co., 1986, Unity (Maine) Coll., 1989, Merrimack Coll., Andover, Mass., 1990, Rissho U., Tokyo, 1993; exhibited in group shows at Davis Gallery, Tucson, 1988, Hartell Gallery, Cornell U., Ithaca, N.Y., 1989, Ogunquit (Maine) Art Ctr., 1990, Frick Gallery, Belfast, Maine, 1991, U. N.H., Durham, 1991, Bowdoin Coll. Mus., Brunswick, Maine, 1992, O'Farrell Gallery, Brunswick, Ratliff Williams, Sedona, Ariz., 1993; pub. collectors include ITT, N.Y., Bowdoin Coll. Mus., Brunswick, Boston Libr. Print/Drawing Coll., Boston, Gillette Corp., Boston, Colby Coll. Mus., Waterville, Maine.

FRANKLIN, RICHARD MARK, lawyer; b. Chgo., Dec. 13, 1947; s. Henry W. and Gertrude (Gross) F.; m. Marguerite June Wesle, Sept. 2, 1973; children: Justin Wesley, Elizabeth Cecilia, Catherine Helena, Caroline Lucinda. BA, U. Wis., 1970; postgrad., U. Freiburg, Fed. Republic Germany, 1968-69; JD, Columbia U., 1973. Bar: Ill. 1973, U.S. Dist. Ct. (no. dist.) Ill. 1973, U.S. Ct. Appeals (7th cir.) 1973. Assoc. Baker & McKenzie, Chgo., 1973-79, Frankfurt, Fed. Republic Germany, 1979-80, ptnr. Chgo., 1980—. Mem. ABA, Ill. Bar Assn., Chgo. Bar Assn. Mem. United Ch. Christ. Avocations: music, literature, theater, outdoor activities. Home: 1161 Oakley Ave Winnetka IL 60093-1437 Office: Baker & McKenzie 1 Prudential Plz 130 E Randolph St Ste 3500 Chicago IL 60601-6342 Office Phone: 312-861-8860. E-mail: rmfwinn@aol.com, richard.m.franklin@bakenet.com.

FRANKLIN, ROBERT DRURY, oil industry executive, lawyer; b. Mead, Okla., June 6, 1935; s. Sam Wesley and Frankie Marjorie (Gooding) F.; m. Barbara Jean Bellis, May 30, 1958 (div. 1973); children: Philip Foster, Elizabeth Jean. BS in Petroleum Engring., U. Okla., 1957; JD, So. Methodist U., 1964. Registered profl. engr., Tex. Petroleum engr. Mobil Oil Corp., Denver City, Tex., 1957-59; prodn. mgr. Bayview Oil Corp., Dallas, 1959-65; sec., dir. Siboney Corp., Dallas, 1965-70; pres., dir. Northland Oils Ltd., Dallas, 1970-89, Costa Resources, Inc., Dallas, 1972—; v.p., dir. Internat. Oil & Gas Corp., Dallas, 1979-84; with Tex. Legal Svcs. Ctr. Mem. Rep. Eagles, Washington. Mem. State Bar Tex., Ind. Petroleum Assn. Am., Soc. Petroleum Engrs., Am. Petroleum Inst., Energy Club of Dallas, Mensa, Willow Bend Polo Club, Midland Country Club. Presbyterian. Avocations: polo, tennis, skiing. Office: 815 Brazos St Ste 1100 Austin TX 78701

FRANKLIN, ROBERT MCFARLAND, book publisher; b. Memphis, Mar. 13, 1943; s. Robert Dumont and Mary McFarland (Wilson) F.; m. Cheryl Jane Roberts, Jan. 18, 1975; children: Charles McRee, Nicholas Roberts, William Holliday. AB, Yale U., 1965. With Columbia U. Libr., N.Y.C., 1965-66; editor to exec. editor Scarecrow Press, Metuchen, N.J., 1969-79; pres., founder McFarland & Co., Inc., Publishers, Jefferson, N.C., 1979—. Pub. Jour. Info. Ethics, 1992—; contbr. articles to profl. jours. Dir., actor Ashe County Little Theatre, Jefferson, 1980—; libr. adv. bd. Appalachian State U., 1995—. With U.S. Army, 1966-68. Recipient Gov.'s Bus. award in arts and humanities, State of N.C., 1984, 87, 97, N.C. State Arts Coun. Outstanding Vol. award 1991, Ashe County Outstanding Vol. award, 2004. Mem. ALA (pub. com. 1984-88, coun. governing body 1988-2000, pay equity com. 1991-93, intellectual freedom com. 1994-96), Am. Soc. for Psychical Rsch. (dir. 1984-88). Avocations: chess, Go, European languages and cultures, acting, piano. Home: 338 Cut Laurel Gap Rd Creston NC 28615-9049 Office: McFarland & Co Inc Pubs Box 611 Jefferson NC 28640-0611 Office Phone: 336-246-4460. Business E-Mail: rfranklin@mcfarlandpub.com.

FRANKLIN, ROOSEVELT, minister; b. Chattanooga, Aug. 30, 1933; s. James R. and Cora Ann (Ponds) F.; m. Darnell Pinkston, Sept. 30, 1972; children: Sophia, Siemoran Dellazar. BS, Northeastern U., 1958; MA (hon.), Savannah State Coll., 1962; M. of Cybernetics, Grad. Sch. Wicca, St. Charles, Mo. Lic. metaphysician. Pastor Free For All Bapt. Ch., Greenwood, S.C., 1959-61; radio min. Spiritual Ch., Aiken, S.C., 1961-63; nat. lectr. United Coun. Spiritual Ch., Raleigh, N.C., 1963-66; min. Holy Trinity House of God, Macon, Ga., 1966—. Youth dir. Holy Trinity Ch., Macon, 1966-72, talent coord., 1966-73; dir. Spiritual Singers, 1966—; lectr. in field; world renown authority on witchcraft and transcendental meditation; expert in clairvoyance, spiritual meditation; supporter Macon County Little League Baseball; internat. tour Prosperity Way of Living Teachings. Editor: Prosperity Way of Living. Organizer voters registration, Macon, 1977; pub. relations vol. Nat. Dem. Party, Atlanta, 1984; bd. dirs. Retired Persons Assn., 1980—. Capt. U.S. Army, 1951-54, Korea. Named extrovert promoter Music Workshop, 1979; recipient Proclamation and Key to City, Roanoke, Va., 1977, Afro Am. Heritage award Afro Am. Heritage Mus., 1987, Golden Eagle award Macon Courier, 1988, Nat. Achievers award Nat. Black Secs. Assn., 1990, Ednl. award Ptnrs. Youth Club, 1991, Golden Eagle award 500 Black Men of Am. Club, 1992, Black Achievement award Nat. Negro Achievers Assn., 1993, Humanitarian award. Gov. of Ga., 1993, Nat. Rschrs. Occult award United Spiritual Coun. Chs., 1994, Hon. Citizens award, Tuskegee, Ala., 1994, Mahogany Triumph award Am. Black Affluent Assn. Am., 1995, Cert. Recognition City of Memphis, 1995, Concerned Citizens award People in Action Club, 1996, Good Samaritan award United Youth Fellowship Club, 1997, Model Citizen's award Office of the Gov. Ga., 1997, Registered Spiritual award, Registered Psychic award and Mystic award United Spiritual Coun. Assn., 1998, Self Awareness Lecture award, Howard U., 1998, Appreciation award for continuous contbns. UNCF, 1998, Commemorative award Ga. Farmer's Assn., 1998, Activist award Boys Clubs Am., 1998, Outstanding Activities award United Fraternities Am., 1998, Presdl. Acknowledgement, Nat. Assn. Disabled Persons, 1999, Dr. of Metaphysics award, Dr. of Biblical Counseling award and Dr. of Religion award, 1999, Outstanding Citizenship award, Pilot Club, 1999, Contemporary Spkr. award, Chgo., 2000, Lectr. of Yr. award Nat. Bible Soc., Silver Raven award, 2002, Ea. Mysteries award for excellence, 2002, Order of Nostradamus, Cert. Seminar of Appreciation, 2002, Spkr. of Yr. award Spiritism, 2002, others. Mem. NAACP (life), SCLC (life), Nat. Assn. Pastoral Counselors (career specialist advisor 2000, dir. conf. on prosperity), Ednl. Media Assn. (founder 2002, counseling tax force 2001, Pursuit of Excellence award 2002), Inner Circle Congl. Aides, C. of C., Ministers Alliance (v.p. 1966—, Citizens award 1979), Ga. Black Am. Pageant (coord. 1980—, Leadership award 1982), Direct Sellers League, Smooth Ashlar (dist. dep. 1970—), Rolls-Royce Club, Woodsmen of Am., Pioneer Club, Shriners (nat. amb.), Masons (33 deg., sovereign grand gen. inspector, Grand Orator 33 deg. Scottish Rite 2002), Optimists, Kiwanis, Civitan, Elks, Nat. Lodge (treas. 1987—), Potentate of the Rosicruscians, Sertoma, Lions, VFW (life), DAV (life), Am. Legion (life). Democrat. Avocations: martial arts, billiards. Office: Holy Trinity House of God 280 Straight St Macon GA 31204-6100

FRANKLIN, SAMUEL C, statistician, researcher; b. Kalamazoo, Mich., Jan. 4, 1979; s. Bonnie J. Galloway and Robert G. Robinson (Stepfather), Robert Ben Franklin. BSBA, Georgetown U., 2000; MA in Cognitive Studies, Columbia U., 2003. Grad. rschr. Columbia U. Tchrs. Coll., NYC, 2001—; stats. cons. NYC, 2004—05. Dir. Saturday enrichment program Columbia U., NYC, 2004—. Contbr. chapters to books. Mem.: Am. Psychol. Soc., Mensa, Kappa Delta Pi. Office Phone: 646-256-3557.

FRANKLIN, SHIRLEY CLARKE, mayor; b. Phila., May 10, 1945; d. Eugene Haywood Clarke and Ruth (Lyons) White; m. David McCoy Franklin, Feb. 5, 1972 (div. 1986); children: Kai Ayanna, Cabral Holsey, Kali Jamilla. BA, Howard U., 1968, LLD (hon.), 2002; MA, U. Pa., 1969. Contract compliance officer U.S. Dept. Labor, Washington, 1966-68; instr. social scis. Talledega (Ala.) Coll., 1969-71; from dir. to commr. Dept. Cultural Affairs, Atlanta, 1978-82; chief adminstrv. officer City of Atlanta, 1982-90, exec. officer for ops., 1990—2001; pvt. practice, 1997—; mayor, 2002—. Trustee Atlanta Symphony Orch., 1977-81, Atlanta Found., 1980—; mem. Ga. Council for the Arts, Atlanta, 1979-82, adv. bd. Ga. Women's Polit. Caucus, Atlanta, 1982-84; chmn. expansion arts panel Nat. Endowment for the Arts, Washington, 1980-82; bd. dirs. Nat. Urban Coalition, Washington, 1980-83; dep. campaign mgr. Young for Atlanta, 1981-82; sr. v.p. external rels. Atlanta Com. Olympic Games, 1991-97; majority ptnr. Urban Environ. Solutions, LLC, 1998-. Recipient Disting. Alumni award Nat. Assn. for Equal Opportunity Higher Edn., 1983, Leadership award Atlanta chpt. NAACP, 1987; named to Acad. Women Achievers YWCA Greater Atlanta, 1986. Mem. Nat. Forum Black Pub. Adminstrs. Clubs: Chautauqua Circle. Democrat. Avocations: gardening, travel, politics, fine arts. Office: City Hall 55 Trinity Ave SW Atlanta GA 30303-3520*

FRANKLIN, SHIRLEY MARIE, marketing consultant; b. Kansas City, Mo., Apr. 13, 1930; d. Eric E. and Marie M. (Kilpatrick) Snodgrass; div. 1967; 1 child, Scot Wesley. BA, State U. Iowa, 1952; MS, Simmons Coll., 1954; MA, Kans. U., 1974. Cert. tchr., Kans., Mass., N.J., Ariz., Calif. Tchr., adminstr. various schs., 1952-76; gifted student program designer Leavenworth County (Kans.) Pub. Schs., 1976-77; sales cons., mgr. Sealight Co., Inc., Kansas City, Mo., 1978-82; dir. chain sales Haagen Dazs Ice Cream Co., Teaneck, N.J., 1982-87; program dir. case space mgmt. Ice Cream Industry, 1986-88; prin. Shirley Franklin Consulting, Basehor, Kans., 1987—; U.S. brands dir. Mövenpick Co., Zurich, Switzerland, 1990—94; mktg. cons. Franklin & Assocs., 1994—. Speaker at dairy industry meetings, seminars. Contbr. articles to profl. jours. and mags. Nat. com. steering com. U.S. Congress Arts Caucus, Washington, 1983—89; foster parent World Vision, Pasadena, Calif., 1986—99; vol. ct. appointed spl. advocate for children in trouble Kans., 1994—97; steering com. Fred Harvey Mus., 2000—03, grant writer, Fred Harvey home restoration, 2000—03; apptd. City Planning Commn., 1996—99; project dir. St. Paul Episc. Ch., 1995—, mem. vestry, 2003—; ESL com. Leavenworth City Schs.; bd. dirs. Preservation Alliance Leavenworth, 2004. Recipient Excellence in Sales Promotions award Dairy and Food Industries Supply Assn. Mem. Internat. Ice Cream Assn. (mktg. coun. 1979—), Internat. Platform Spkrs. Assn., Alpha Delta Kappa, Delta Delta Delta. Republican. Episcopalian. Avocations: writing, walking, reading, travel, bridge. Home and Office: 910 Columbia Ave Leavenworth KS 66048-3133

FRANKLIN, TIMOTHY A., editor; m. Alison Franklin; 2 children. BJ and Polit. Sci., Ind. U., 1982. Reporter county govt. to assoc. mng. editor Chgo. Tribune, 1982—97; v.p., editor Ind. Star, 2000, Orlando Sentinel, 2000—04; editor, sr. v.p. Balt. Sun, 2004—. Nominee Pulitzer prize, series state's child welfare sys., 1986; named One of the Nation's Most Influential Bus. Journalists, TJFR mag.; recipient Barney Kilgore award, Soc. Profl. Journalists. Mem.: Am. Soc. Newspaper Editors (mem. leadership com.), Fla. Soc. Newspaper Editors (co-chmn. orgn.'s pub. access com.). Office: Balt Sun Tribune Co 501 N Calvert St Baltimore MD 21278

FRANKLIN, WARREN E., JR., information scientist, educator; s. Warren and Adrienne Franklin; m. Dianne L. Simon, Apr. 15, 2000; 1 child, Mary Ileene. AAS in Computer Sys. Tech., NYC Coll. Tech., Bklyn., 1992; BS in Computer Info. Sys. Analysis and Mgmt., CUNY, 1994. Cert. in Novell adminstrn., in Microsoft adminstrn., Dell sys. specialist; ordained interfaith min. Universal Life Ch., Bklyn., 2000. Higher edn. officer, network adminstr. CUNY, Bklyn., 1993—; adj. prof. computer sys. tech. NYC Coll. Tech., Bklyn., 1995—. Cons. Franklin Computer Cons., Bklyn., 1990—. Recipient cert. of excellence, NYC Coll. Tech., 1992, Svc. award, 2001, 2004. Roman Catholic. Avocations: electronic and computer security, space, model railroader, gadgeteer, military. Office: NYC Coll Tech 300 Jay Street Brooklyn NY 11201 Office Phone: 718-260-5610.

FRANKLIN, WILLIAM EMERY, international business educator; b. Sedalia, Mo., Apr. 6, 1933; s. Russell George and Edith Mae (Van Dyke) Franklin; m. Beverly Jean Feig, Mar. 25, 1933 (div. 1963); children: Stephen, Julia, Angela. BS in Bus., U. Mo., 1954; postgrad., Harvard U., 1982. With forestry ops. Weyerhaeuser Co., Longview, Wash., 1954; pres. Weyerhaeuser Far East Ltd., Hong Kong, 1980-96, Franklin Internat., Ltd., Seattle, 1996—. Chmn. Weyerhaeuser China Ltd.; pres. Weyerhaeuser Korea; mem. U.S.-Japan Bus. Coun., Pacific Basin Econ. Coun.; bd. dirs. NCR Japan Ltd.; mem. Eisenhower Fellowship Com., adv. com. on investment and devel. U.S. Dept. State; past chmn. forestry working group industry coop. program of UN-FAO, com. on internat. trade U.S. Dept. Commerce; adj. prof. U. Puget Sound, Am. Grad. Sch. Internat. Mgmt.; guest lectr. U. Internat. Bus. Econs., Beijing, Columbia U., Internat. U. of Japan, Seattle U. Trustee Pacific N.W. Ballet; chmn. Far East Coun. Friends of Scouting. Mem. Am. C. of C. in Japan (pres.), Yomiuri Internat. Econ. Soc. (bd. dirs.), Coun. Fgn. Rels., World Affairs Coun., U.S.-Asian Bus. Coun., Fgn. Corrs. Club, Tokyo Lawn Tennis Club, Tokyo Club. Avocations: tennis, music, sailing. E-mail: franklininternational@msn.com.

FRANKLIN-GRIFFIN, CATHY LOU HINSON, nursing educator; b. Newton, NC, Nov. 8, 1950; d. Willie A. and Evelyn Irene (Thornton) Hinson; 1 child, John Eric; m. Harry Griffin. ADN, Western Piedmont Comm. Coll., 1971; BSN, East Carolina U.; postgrad., Med. U. SC; MA, Appalachian State U., 1990; PhD, U. NC, Greensboro, 2004. RN, N.C., S.C., Ga., Ala., N.D., Calif., Va. Patient educator Wayne County Meml. Hosp., Goldsboro, N.C., developer cardiac rehab. & permanent pacemaker implantation programs, 1980-81; infection control nurse Charleston (S.C.) Meml. Hosp., 1981-83; instr. nursing United Health Careers, Inc., San Bernardino, Calif., 1986-88, Caldwell Community Coll., CCC & TI, Hudson, NC, 1988—91; rsch. coord. weekend/evening nursing program CCC and TI, Boone, N.C., 1991-93; dean nursing & allied health Rockingham C.C., Wentworth, N.C., 1993-2000; freelance contract nurse edn. Rowan-Cabarrus C.C., 2000—04; dir. program svcs. NCCCS, 2004—. Cons., contract grant writer, 2000—; spkr.'s bur. Rockingham C.C.; bd. dirs. Rockingham Mental Health Ctr., Free Clinic Reidsville; legis. chair NC ADN Coun., 1997-99, pres. NC Conference Dirs. ADN Programs, 1999-2000; nurse educator NC Bd. Nursing, 2000-02, bd. dirs.; dir. program svcs. NC CC Sys., 2004—; spkr. in field. Author (with others): Fundamentals of Nursing, Nursing the Whole Person; author: Survival Guide for Directors of Nursing Programs in Community Colleges in North Carolina, 2002; pub.: CCC & TI Skillbook, editorial cons. Lippincott-Mosby Nursing Texts, ind. contractor: NCCCS manual. Capt. fundraising for Civic Ctr.; mem. faculty dept. Chairs Inst. Named one of Outstanding Young Women of Am., 1987. Mem. ADN (pres., bd. dirs., chmn. legis. adv. coun., liaison N.C. PN educators), Phi Theta Kappa, Phi Kappa Phi, Sigma Theta Tau. Office Phone: 919-807-7118. Business E-Mail: griffin@nccs.cc.nc.us. E-mail: healthdean@aol.com.

FRANKOVIC, KATHLEEN ANN, journalist; b. Passaic, N.J., Jan. 31, 1947; d. Frank Joseph and Olga Szemancso F.; m. Hal Glatzer, Aug. 22, 1992. AB, Cornell U., 1968; student, Ohio U., 1969; PhD, Rutgers U., 1974. Asst. prof. in govt. Case Western Res. U., Cleve., 1973-74; asst. prof. in polit. sci. U. Vt., Burlington, 1974-77, dir. social sci. rsch. lab., 1975-77; mgr. surveys CBS News, N.Y.C., 1977-83, dir. surveys, prodr., 1983—. Vis. prof. Cornell U., Ithaca, NY, 1985; bd. mgrs. Voter News Svc., N.Y.C., 1997—2001; trustee Roper Ctr. U. Conn., Storrs, 1993—2002; trustee Nat. Coun. Pub. Polls, Washington, 1990—; mem. adv. bd. dirs. Gallup Rsch. Ctr. U. Nebr., Lincoln, 1999—2001; mem. adv. bd. dirs. Barnard-Columbia Ctr. Leadership in Urban Pub. Policy, N.Y.C., 1994—, Pub. Opinion Quarterly, Phila., 1995—99, Coun. Social Sci. Assns., Washington, 1999—2001; mem. nat. adv. com. Inst. Social Rsch. U. Mich., 2002—; mem. nat. adv. com. Survey Rsch. Inst. Cornell U. Co-author: The Election of 2000, 2001; contbr. articles to profl. jours., chpts. to books. Mem. Am. Assn. Pub. Opinion Rsch. (pres. 1992-93, award of outstanding achievement N.Y. chpt. 1999), World Assn. for Pub. Opinion Rsch. (pres. 2003-04), Am. Polit. Sci. Assn. (mem. exec. coun. 1988-90, Mary Lepper award Women's Caucus 1995), Market Rsch. Coun., Coffee Ho Office: CBS News 524 W 57th St New York NY 10019 Office Phone: 212-975-6615.

FRANKOWIAK, JAMES RAYMOND, public relations executive; b. Milw., Oct. 23, 1946; s. Raymond James and Stephanie Carlene (Sztorc) F.; m. Janice Lynn Kantorski, Aug. 24, 1968; children: Jennifer Anne, Jessica Lynn. BA, Marquette U., 1970. Asst. dir. alumni rels. Marquette U., Milw., 1970-72; publicist GE News Bur., Louisville, 1972-74; acct. exec. Pub. Comm. Inc., Chgo., 1974-76, acct. supr., 1976-78, v.p., 1978-80; with pub. affairs dept. GTE Data Svcs., Tampa, Fla., 1979-80; v.p. Pub. Comm. Inc., Tampa, 1980-83, exec. v.p., 1983-87, pres., 1987—. Bd. dirs. Salvation Army, Tampa, 1990—. Mem. PRSA (accredited, dist. chair, mem. nat. hons. and awards com.). Office: Pub Comm Inc 707 N Franklin St Tampa FL 33602-4419

FRANKS, CHARLES LESLIE, investments executive; b. Columbus, Miss., Jan. 21, 1934; s. Leslie J. and Almeda (Morris) F.; m. Cecile Alice Cronovich, Feb. 7, 1959; children— Carolyn Anne, Charles Christopher. BS summa cum laude, Miss. State U., 1956. Cert. internal auditor; C.P.A.; chartered bank auditor. Acct. Arthur Andersen & Co., Houston, 1959-61; mgr. internal audit dept. Bank of S.W., Houston, 1961-71; gen. auditor Southwest Bancshares, Inc., 1972-79; v.p., auditor Merc. Nat. Bank, Dallas, 1979-82, sr. v.p., auditor, 1982-86; sr. v.p., dir., internal auditor Bright Banc, Dallas, 1986-89, sr. v.p., chief fin. officer, 1989-90; pvt. practice investments, 1991—. Instr., speaker various Bank Adminstrn. Inst. seminars, meetings and convs. Served to capt. USAF, 1956-59. Mem. Tex. Soc. C.P.A.s (sec. Houston chpt. 1971-72), Bank Adminstrn. Inst. (v.p. Gulf Coast chpt. 1971-72, pres. 1973-74, dir. 1974-75, state dir. 1975-77, dir. Dallas chpt. 1980-84), Am. Inst. Banking, Inst. Internal Auditors (gov. 1973-78, pres. Houston chpt. 1974-75), Houston C. of C., Arnold Air Soc., Phi Eta Sigma, Chi Lambda Rho, Phi Kappa Phi, Alpha Kappa Psi. Roman Catholic. Home: 206 Brocket St Stafford TX 77477-4708

FRANKS, HERBERT HOOVER, lawyer; b. Joliet, Ill., Jan. 25, 1934; s. Carol and Lottie (Dermer) F.; m. Eileen Pepper, June 22, 1957; children: David, Jack, Eli. BS, Roosevelt U., 1954; postgrad., Am. U., 1960. Bar: Ill. 1961, U.S. Dist. Ct. (no. dist.) Ill. 1961, U.S. Supreme Ct. 1967. Ptnr. Franks, Gerkin & McKenna, 1985—. Mem. Ill. Cts. Commn., 2003—; chmn. State Bank Group, 1979—, First Nat. Bank, Marengo, Ill., 1976—84, mem. exec. com., 1976—, chmn., 1976—90. Bus. editor Am. U. Law Rev., 1959, 60. State pres. Young Dems. of Ill., 1970-72; trustee Hebrew Theol. Coll., Skokie, Ill., 1974—; trustee, sec. Forest Inst. Profl. Psychology, Springfield, Mo., 1979-91; chmn. Forest Hosp., Des Plaines, 1980-88. With U.S. Army, 1956-58. Mem.: Ill. Trial Lawyers (mng. bd. 1975—92, treas. 1985—87), Ill. State Bar Assn. (state pres. 2000—01), Shriners, Masons (33 deg.), Sigma Nu Phi (pres. 1980—82). Home: 19324 E Grant Hwy Marengo IL 60152-9438 Office: Franks Gerkin & McKenna 19333 E Grant Hwy Marengo IL 60152-8234 Office Phone: 815-923-2107. Personal E-mail: franklaw@mc.net. Business E-Mail: hfranks@fgmlaw.com.

FRANKS, HERSCHEL PICKENS, judge; b. Savannah, Tenn., May 28, 1930; s. Herschel R. Franks and Pickens Vada; m. Judy Black; 1 child, Ramona. Student, U. Tenn., U. Md.; JD, U. Tenn., Knoxville; grad., U. Nev. Bar: Tenn. 1959, US Supreme Ct. 1968. Claims atty. US Fidelity & Guaranty Co., Knoxville, Tenn., 1958; ptnr. Harris, Moon, Meacham & Franks, Chattanooga, 1959—70; chancellor 3d Chancery divsn. Hamilton County, 1970—78; judge Tenn. Ct. Appeals, 1978—, presiding judge, 2004—. Spl. justice Tenn. Supreme Ct., 1979, 1986—87, 2002—04; presiding judge Hamilton County Trial Cts., 1977—78; spl. judge Tenn. Ct. Criminal Appeals, 1990—92, commn. to study appellate cts., 1990—92. With N.G. USAF, 1949—50, with USAF, 1950—54. Mem.: ABA (Merit award), Inst. Jud. Adminstrn., Am. Judicature Soc., Chattanooga Bar Assn. (pres. 1968—69, Founds. of Freedom award 1986), Chattanooga Bar Found., Tenn. Bar Found., Tenn. Bar Assn. (Merit award 1968—69), Mountain City Club, City Farmers Club, Optimists (pres. 1965—66, Cmty. Svc. award 1971), Phi Alpha Delta. Mem. United Ch. Of Christ. Address: 540 Mccallie Ave Ste 562 Chattanooga TN 37402-2039 Office Phone: 423-634-6344.

FRANKS, JAMES R. (JAMIE), JR., lawyer, state legislator; b. Tupelo, Miss., Dec. 26, 1972; BA in Polit. sci., U. Miss.; JD. Mem. Miss. Ho. of Reps., 1996—, mem. conservation and water resrouces com., chmn. ways and means com., mem. pub. health and welfare com. Mem. Nat. Shoot to Retrieve Assn., Houston Birdhunters Club. Democrat. Mem. Ch. of God. Home: PO Box 182 Mooreville MS 38857-0182 Office: State Capitol Bldg PO Box 1018 Jackson MS 39215-1018

FRANKS, JOHN JULIAN, anesthesiologist, educator; b. Pueblo, Colo., Apr. 9, 1929; s. Frank Alec and Lila Ethelda (Ownbey) F.; m. Kathryne Jean Sammon, Dec. 27, 1951 (dec. May 1999); children: John Alec, William Thomas, Margaret Lila, Elizabeth Ellen; m. Mary Lou Hawkins Shattuck, Apr. 9, 2004. BA, U. Colo., 1951, MD, 1954. Assoc. dir., dir. clin. rsch. ctr. U. Colo., Denver, 1969-81; assoc. chief of staff rsch. Denver VA Hosp., 1969-82, chief hematology div., 1983; resident in anesthesiology Vanderbilt U. Hosp., Nashville, 1984-86; prof., dir. rsch. div. Vanderbilt U., Nashville, 1987-98, dir. div. organ transplant anesthesia, 1989-98, interim chmn. dept. anesthesiology, 1993-94, prof. emeritus, 1999—. Author chpts. in books; contbr. articles to Jour. Gen. Physiology, Jour. Clin. Investigation, New Eng. Jour. of Medicine, Anesthesiology and N.Y. Acad. Sci.; contbr. numerous articles to profl. jours. Col. USAF, 1955-63, 68-69. NIH grantee U. Colo., 1963-69, 64-82, Vanderbilt U., 1992-96, U.S. VA grantee Denver VA Hosp., 1969-83. Mem. Am. Soc. Anesthesiologists, Am. Physiol. Soc., Cen. Soc. Clin. Rsch., Internat. Soc. Thrombosis Haemostosis, Soc. Gen. Physiologists. Office: Vanderbilt U Med Ctr Nashville TN 37232-0001 E-mail: franksj1@vanderbilt.edu, franksjj@comcast.net.

FRANKS, JON MICHAEL, lawyer, mediator; b. Marshall, Tex., Sept. 26, 1941; s. Francis William and Clara Bell (Caldwell) F.; m. Sue Powers, May 23, 1987; children: Brian Alan, Michael Shawn. BA, Southwestern U., 1963; LLB, U. Tex., 1966. Bar. Tex. 1966, U.S. Dist. Ct. (no. dist.) Tex.; cert. family lawyer, Tex. Bd. of Legal Specialization. Lawyer Pettigrew and Buckley, Grand Prairie, Tex., 1966-67; pvt. practice Irving, Tex., 1967-68, 71-79, 88—; ptnr. Franks and Vice, Irving, 1968-71, Franks and Luce, Irving, 1979-88. Mem. child support and visitation guidelines com. Tex. Supreme Ct., Austin, 1989; mem. Southlake Ct. of Records Com., 1990—. Commr. Irving Planning and Zoning Bd., 1971-74; judge Mcpl. Ct., Irving, 1974-78, Southlake, Tex., 1978-88, Southlake City Coun., 1992—. Named Tex. Monthly Super Lawyer, 2003—; recipient various awards. Fellow Am. Acad. Matrimonial Lawyers; mem. ABA (family law sect.), Tex. Acad. Family Law Specialists (bd. dirs. 1988-90), North Tex. Assn. Family Law Specialists (pres. 1985-87), Tex. Bar Assn. (family law sect.), Dallas Bar Assn. (pres. family law sect. 1989), Tarrant County Family Law Assn., Am. Acad. Atty.-Mediators. Republican. Methodist. Avocations: gun collector, competition shooting. Office: 128 E Texas St Grapevine TX 76051-5307 Office Phone: 817-329-5573. E-mail: jonmfranks@aol.com.

FRANKS, LEWIS E., electrical and computer engineering educator, researcher; b. San Mateo, Calif., Nov. 8, 1931; s. Lloyd C. and Leora (Embree) F.; m. Mary B. Harris, June 21, 1954; children: Janet K., Jill M., Daniel J. BSEE, Oreg. State U., 1952; MSEE, Stanford U., 1953, PhD, 1957. Mem. tech. staff Bell Telephone Labs., Murray Hill, N.J., 1958-62, supr. North Andover, Mass., 1962-69; assoc. prof. U. Mass., Amherst, 1969-71, prof., 1971-96, chmn. dept elec. and computer engring., 1975-78, acting head dept. elec. and computer engring., 1991-93, prof. emeritus, 1996—. Author: Signal Theory, 1969; editor: Data Communication, 1974; contbr. over 60 articles to profl. jours. Hewlett-Packard fellow, Stanford U., 1952. Fellow IEEE; mem. NSF (program dir. networking and communications rsch., 1988-90). Office: Univ of Mass Dept of Elec & Computer Engring Amherst MA 01003 Personal E-mail: franks@ecs.umass.edu.

FRANKS, MARTIN DAVIS, broadcast executive; b. Michigan City, Ind., Sept. 27, 1950; s. R. Wendell and Alice (Barnard) F.; m. Mari J. Schleuning. BA in Politics, Princeton U., 1972. Staff asst. Dem. Senatorial Campaign Com., Washington, 1972-74; dep. chief staff U.S. Senator John Tunney, Washington and L.A., 1975-77; chief staff U.S. Senator Patrick Leahy, Washington, 1977-79; nat. rsch. and issues dir. Carter/Mondale Presdl. Com., Washington, 1979-80; exec. office of pres. The White House, Washington, 1980-81; exec. dir. Dem. Congl. Campaign Com., Washington, 1981-87; v.p. Charls Walker Assocs., Washington, 1987-88, CBS Inc., Washington, 1988-94; sr. v.p. CBS Corp., N.Y.C., 1994—2000; exec. v.p. CBS N.Y.C., 2000—. Office: CBS TB 51 W 52d St 19th Fl New York NY 10019

FRANKS, ROBERT D. (BOB FRANKS), former congressman; b. Hackensack, N.J., Sept. 21, 1951; s. Norman A. and June Evans F. BA, Depauw U., 1973; JD, So. Methodist U., 1976. Exec. dir. People for Bateman, 1977; cons. Jim Courter for Congress Com., 1978; v.p. Med Data Inc., 1978-80; co-owner County News, 1980-83; cons. Tom Kean for Gov. Com., 1981; mem. N.J. State Assembly from 22nd Dist., Trenton, 1979-93, 103d-106th Congresses from 7th N.J. Dist., 1993-2001; mem. budget com., mem. transp. and infrastructure com.; pres. Healthcare Institute of N.J. Bd. dirs. Intrenet.; mgmt. cons. in field; founder CREO; mem. Econ. Steering Com., 1980, Com. on Energy and Nat. Resources, 1981-83, Com. on State Govt., Civil Svc., Elections, Pensions and Vet. Affairs, 1981-85, N.J. State Pension Study Commn., 1982, Com. Revenue, Finance and Appropriations, 1984-93, State and Local Expenditure and Revenue Policy Commn., 1985-93, Waste Mgmt. Planning and Recycling Com., 1990-91; chmn. Task Force to Reform Congress Redistricting Process, 1982, N.J. Coalition for Regulatory Efficiency, 1985-93, Republican Policy Com., 1990-91, N.J. State Rep. Party, 1988-93; campaign mgr. Congressman Jim Courter, 1982, Congressman Dean Gallo, 1984; assembly liaison Rep. Majority. 1985. Bd. mgrs. Children's Specialized Hosp., Mountainside, N.J., 1980; mem. long range planning com. Overlook Hosp., Summit, N.J., 1982; mem. domestic task force Hands Across Am., 1986; mem. N.J. Jaycees. Named Legislator of Yr. Nat. Rep. Legislators Assn., 1986. Republican. Office: PO Box 813 Hillside NJ 07205-0813

FRANKS, RONALD DWYER, dean, psychiatrist, educator; b. Balt., Jan. 15, 1946; s. Wylie and H. Jeanette (Dwyer) F.; m. Vicky Ruth Vicklund; children: Aaron Matthew, Alexis Linda. Student, Albion Coll., 1964-67; MD with distinction, U. Mich., 1971. Intern Virginia Mason Hosp., Seattle, 1971-72; resident in psychiatry U. Colo. Med. Ctr., Denver, 1972-76; instr. psychiatry U. Colo. Sch. Medicine, Denver, 1976-77, asst. prof. psychiatry, 1977-83, assoc. prof., 1983-88, asst. dean student affairs, 1982-84, asst. dean student and curricular affairs, dir. inpatient svcs. dept. psychiatry, 1986-88; dean, prof. psychiatry U. Minn. Sch. Medicine, Duluth, 1988-97; v.p. health affairs, dean James H. Quillen Coll. Medicine, prof. psychiatry and behavioral scis. East Tenn. State U., Johnson City, 1997—. Bd. dirs. Bank of Tenn., 2004—; chmn. State Health Planning and Adv. Bd., Tenn. Contbr. numerous articles to profl. jours. Mem. AMA, So. Med. Assn., Tenn. Med. Assn., Am. Psychiat. Assn., Alpha Omega Alpha. Home: 3007 Moss Creek Dr Johnson City TN 37604-2203 Office: East Tenn State U James H Quillen Coll Med PO Box 70694 Johnson City TN 37614-1710

FRANKS, STEPHEN FIELD, retired judge; b. Biltmore, NC, June 12, 1930; s. Thomas Hendricks and Margaret (Field) Franks; m. Mary Elizabeth Volbeda, Apr. 28, 1962 (div. 2004); children: Stephen Bruce, Andrea Carol, Craig Thomas; m. Betty J. Causey, Nov. 21, 2004. BA, Duke U., 1952; LLB, JD, U. N.C., 1955. Bar: N.C. 1955, Calif. 1964, U.S. Supreme Ct. 1966. Dep. city atty. City Atty. Office, San Bernardino, Calif., 1964—66; counsel to mayor Mayor's Office, San Bernardino, 1966—69; legis. adv. County of San Bernardino, Sacramento, 1970—81; pvt. practice Hendersonville, NC, 1981—88; judge Dist. Ct. N.C., Hendersonville, 1988—2002; ret., 2002. Fed. aid coord. City of San Bernardino, 1966—69. Mem. San Juan Unified Sch. Dist., Sacramento, 1978—81, chmn., 1979; pres. County Bd. Edn., 1977—78; mem. Child Fatality Prevention Team, Hendersonville, NC, 2002; dir. Sacramento County Mental Health Assn., Sacramento, 1973—80, pres., 1978—79. Comdr. JAG USN, 1955—60. Fellow: ATLA; mem.: N.C. Bar Assn., Univ. Club, Elks, Rotary (bd. dirs.). Republican. Episcopalian. Avocation: hiking. Office: 514 5th Ave W Hendersonville NC 28739 Office Phone: 828-697-6238. Business E-Mail: sffranks@mchsi.com.

FRANKS, TOMMY RAY, retired military officer; b. Wynnewood, Okla., June 17, 1945; m. Cathryn Carley, Mar. 22, 1969; 1 child, Jacqueline Franks Matlock. BSBA, U. Tex., Arlington, 1971; MS in Pub. Adminstrn., Shippensburg U. Pa., 1985; grad., Armed Forces Staff Coll., U.S. Army War Coll. Commd. 2d lt. U.S. Army, 1967, advanced through grades to gen., 2000; comdr. 2d bn. 78th F.A. 1st Armored Divsn., Germany, 1981-84; dep. asst. chief staff G3 III Corps, Ft. Hood, Tex., 1985-86; comdr. div. arty. 1st Cav. Div., 1987-88, chief staff, 1988-89, asst. divsn. comdr. Operation Desert Shield-Storm, 1990-91; asst. comdt. U.S. Army F.A. Sch., Ft. Sill, Okla., 1991-92; dir. La. Maneuvers Task Force, Office Chief of Staff U.S. Army, Ft. Monroe, Va., 1992—94; asst. chief staff C3/J3/G3 UN and combined forces command U.S. Forces Korea, 8th U.S. Army, 1994—95; commdr. second infantry divsn., 1995-97; comdr. 3rd United States Army Ft. McPherson, Ga., 1997-2000; comdr. US Ctrl. Command, MacDill AFB, Fla., 2000—03; with Operation Enduring Freedom Afghanistan, 2001—02; with Operation Iraqi Freedom, 2003. Co-author (with Malcolm McConnell): (memoir) American Soldier, 2004 (Publishers Weekly Bestseller). Decorated Def. Disting. Svc. Medal, Disting. Svc. Medal with one oak leaf cluster, Legion of Merit with 3 oak leaf clusters, Bronze Star medal with V device and 4 oak leaf clusters, Purple Heart with 2 oak leaf clusters; named Knight Comdr. of the Brit. Empire, 2004, Presdl. Medal of Freedom, 2004. Office Phone: 813-839-8234. Business E-Mail: admin@tommyfranks.com.

FRANKS, TRENT, congressman; b. Uravan, Colo., June 19, 1957; m. Josephine Franks. Student, Ottawa U. Mem. Ariz. Ho. Reps., 1985—87, vice-chmn. commerce com., chmn. sub-com. on child protection and family preservation, mem. human resources com., mem. agr. com., mem. judiciary com.; head Ariz. Govs. Office for Children, 1987; exec. dir. Ariz. Family Rsch. Inst.; pres. Strategic Consulting and Liberty Petroleum Corp.; mem. U.S. Congress from 2nd Ariz. dist., 2003—. Pres. Children's Hope Scholarship Assn.; active North Phoenix Bapt. Ch. Republican. Office: 1237 Longworth House Office Bldg Washington DC 20515-0302 also: Ste 200 7121 W Bell Rd Glendale AZ 85308

FRANSE, R. NELSON, lawyer; b. Clovis, N.Mex, Feb. 5, 1961; s. Roy and Jerrie Lou Franse; m. M. Marie McCulloch; 1 child, Colson Brack. BS in U. Studies, U. N. Mex., 1984, JD, 1987. Bar: N. Mex. 1987, U.S. Dist. Ct., Dist. N. Mex. 1987, U.S. Ct. Appeals, tenth cir. 1987. Ptnr. Rodey, Dickason, Sloan, Akin & Robb PA, Albuquerque, leader profl. liability sect. Rep. to ABA, Law Student Div. U. N. Mex., 1985—87. Named one of best lawyers in Am., 2003—04. Mem.: Am. Bd. Liability Atty. (diplomat with spl. competence in area of legal profl. liability), Profl. Liability Underwriting Soc., State Bar N.Mex., ABA, Albuquerque Bar Assn. Baptist. Avocations: monday morning quarterbacking, Monday morning quarterbacking. Office: Rodey Dickason Sloan Akin & Robb PA 201 Third St NW Ste 2200 PO Box 1888 Albuquerque NM 87103 Office Phone: 505-765-5900. Business E-Mail: nfranse@rodey.com.

FRANSSEN, JOHN P., music educator; b. Lincoln, Nebr., Jan. 25, 1965; s. James Edward Franssen Sr., Magdalen Ann Franssen; 1 child, Alexis Marie. B in Music Edn., U. Nebr., 1989. Instr. Instrumental music Aquinas-St. Mary's Cath. Sch., David City, Nebr., 1989—94, Weeping Water Pub. Schs., Weeping Water, Nebr., 1994—97, Wilber-Clatoria Pub. Schs., Wilber, Nebr., 1999—2001, Hastings Cath. Schs., Hastings, Nebr., 2001—. Dir. band Am. Legion Boys/Girls State, Lincoln, 1987—. Mem.: KC (Grand Knight 1989—90), Nebr. State Bandmasters Assn. (Outstanding Young Band Dir. award 1995), Nebr. Music Educators Assn., Music Educators Nat. Conf. Democrat. Roman Catholic. Avocations: hunting, fishing, coaching, playing in dance bands. Home: 1122 E 5th St Hastings NE 68901 Office: Hastings Cath Schs 521 N Kansas Ave Hastings NE 68901

FRANTISKA, JOSEPH JOHN, JR., systems engineer, educator; b. Westfield, Mass., July 22, 1957; s. Joseph John and Madeline Francis Frantiska. BA in Math./Gen. Sci., Westfield State Coll., 1979; cert. in Software Engring., Northeastern U., 1986; MS in Computer Sci., Fitchburg State Coll., 1989, BS in Bus. Adminstrn., 1992; cert. in Artificial Intelligence, Northeastern U., 1990; EdD, U. Mass., 2001; MBA, Western New Eng. Coll., 1997. EMT Mass., 1982, CPR instr. Am. Heart Assn., 1996; lic. comml. pilot FAA, 1979. Mem. tech. staff MITRE Corp., Bedford, 1981—84, Calspan Corp., Lexington, 1984—85; software engr. Raytheon Co., Bedford, 1985—88; sys. engr. G.T.E., Needham, 1988—93, MITRE Corp., Bedford, 1993—95; database developer U. Mass., Amherst, 1995—97; course developer Progress Software, Bedford, 1997—99; sys. engr. / tech. writer Raytheon Co., 1999—2004; ind. rschr. and scholar, 2004—. Faculty cons. Ednl. Testing Svc., Princeton, NJ, 1994; textbook reviewer Jones and Bartlett, Sudbury, 2001—02; industry faculty mem. Northeastern U., Dedham, Mass., 1987—89, 1993; vis. lectr. Fitchburg State Coll., Mass., 1990—. Mem. editl. rev. bd. Assn. for Advancement of Computing in Edn. Jour. Computers in Math. and Sci. Tchg., 2004—. Mem.: IEEE, NEA (assoc.), ISTE (assoc.), Conn. Aviation Hist. Assn. (assoc.). Avocations: flying, sailing, golf, aviation history, emergency medical technology.

FRANTZ, ANDREW GIBSON, endocrinologist, educator, dean; b. N.Y.C., May 22, 1930; s. Angus Macdonald and Virginia (Kneeland) F. AB magna cum laude, Harvard U., 1951; MD, Columbia U., 1955. Intern Presbyn. Hosp., N.Y.C., 1955-56, resident in medicine, 1956-58; fellow in endocrinology Columbia U., N.Y.C., 1958-60, asst. prof. medicine, 1966-68, assoc. prof., 1968-73, prof., 1973—, chief divsn. endocrinology, 1971-87; chmn. admissions com., assoc. dean for admissions Columbia U. (Coll. Physicians and Surgeons), 1981—. Assoc. in medicine Harvard U., 1962-66; asst. in medicine Mass. Gen. Hosp., Boston, 1962-66; mem. staff Presbyn. Hosp., N.Y.C.; mem. med. adv. bd. Nat. Pituitary Agy., 1970-73; established investigator Am. Heart Assn., 1968-73 Contbr. articles on prolactin and other pituitary hormones and functions to med. and sci. jours.; mem. editorial bd.: Jour. Clin. Endocrinology and Metabolism, 1971-76; assoc. editor: Metabolism, 1969— . Served to lt. comdr. USNR, 1960-62. Recipient Silver Medal Coll. Physicians and Surgeons, Columbia U., 1981, Alumni Fedn. medal Columbia U., 1984, Disting. Tchr. award, Coll. Physicians and Surgeons, Columbia U., 1989. Mem. AAAS, Endocrine Soc., Assn. Am. Physicians, Am. Soc. Clin. Investigation, Internat. Soc. for Neuroendocrinology, Harvey Soc., Practitioners Soc. (pres. 1993-2000), Charaka Club, Am. Fedn. Med. Rsch., N.Y. Acad. Scis., N.Y. Acad. Medicine, Union Club, Century Assn. (N.Y.C.), P and S Alumni Assn. (pres. 1991-93), Alpha Omega Alpha. Episcopalian. Home: 1185 Park Ave New York NY 10128-1308 Office: 630 W 168th St New York NY 10032-3702 Office Phone: 212-305-3595. Business E-Mail: agf2@columbia.edu.

FRANTZ, DAVID JOSEPH, lawyer; b. Cleve., Nov. 13, 1948; s. Joseph Clarence and June Marie (Clancey) F.; m. Diahn Case, May 10, 1976; children: Dana, Christopher, Lauren. BSBA, Georgetown U., 1970, LLB, 1974. Bar: Va. 1974, D.C. 1975, U.S. Ct. Appeals (D.C. and 4th cirs.) 1975, U.S. Dist. Ct. Md. 1989, U.S. Supreme Ct. 1999. Assoc. Lamb, Eastman & Keats, Washington, 1974-79; pvt. practice Washington, 1979-82; ptnr. Menler & Lamb, Washington, 1982-85, Conlon, Frantz, Phelan & Pires, Washington, 1985—. Lectr. D.C. Bar Continuing Legal Edn. Program, Washington, 1985—. Mem. ABA (litigation sect.), Va. Trial Lawyers Assn., Order of Barristers. Office: Conlon Frantz Phelan & Pires 1818 N St NW Washington DC 20036-2406

FRANTZ, FRANCIS X., telecommunications industry executive, lawyer; BA with honors, U. Akron; JD, Ohio State U. Sch. Law. Ptnr. Thompson, Hine & Flory; sr. v.p. external affairs, gen. counsel ALLTEL Corp., Little Rock, 1990—, corp. sec., 1992—, exec. v.p. external affairs, 1998—. Office: ALLTEL Corp 1 Allied Dr Little Rock AR 72202-2099

FRANTZ, PHARES ALBERT, architect; b. New Orleans, Nov. 1, 1923; s. Roy Florestan and Marie Lucile (O'Kelley) F.; m. Elinor Mae(McCloskey), Feb. 20, 1954; children: Ninette Marie, Colleen Marie, Melinda Marie. BArch, Tulane U., La., 1950. Registered arch., La., Miss., Tenn. Draftsman Richard Koch Arch., New Orleans, 1950-52, arch., 1952-55; assoc. Richard Koch & Samuel Wilson Jr. Archs., New Orleans, 1955-72; ptnr. Koch and Wilson, Archs., P.C., New Orleans, 1986-96. Mem. Citizens Adv. com. Studying Revisions to City Zoning Ordinance, 1969; bd. dirs. Incarnate Word Parish Sch. Bd., 1971-80, pres., 1977-80; bd. dirs. France Amerique, 1981; pres. La. Polit. Com. Design Profls., 1984. Decorated Order of St. Louis Archdiocese of New Orleans. Mem. AIA (mem. hist. resources com. 1975-83, mem. New Orleans chpt. 1950—, pres. 1969, dir. 1970-71, state preservation coord. 1982), La. Inst. Bldg. Scis. (dir. 1980), La. Archs. Assn. (pres. 1980), Constrn. Specifications Inst. (pres. New Orleans chpt. 1960), Friends of Cabildo, La. Landmarks Soc., Sons of the Revolution, Nat. Trust, Mag. St., Round Table Club (v.p. 1992-93, pres. 1994-95), Delta Tau Delta. Republican. Roman Catholic. Home: 7525 Pearl St New Orleans LA 70118-3835

FRANTZ, RAY WILLIAM, JR., retired librarian; b. Princeton, Ky., Aug. 17, 1923; s. Ray William and Marjorie (Kevil) F.; m. Doris Methvin, Aug. 26, 1951; children: Katherine Kevil, Paul William. AB, U. Nebr., 1948; MLS, U. Ill., 1949, MA, 1951, PhD in English, 1955. Dir. libr. U. Richmond, Va., 1955-60; asst. dir. Ohio State U. Libr., Columbus, 1960-62; dir. libraries U. Wyo. Libr., 1962-67; libr. U. Va. Libr., Charlottesville, 1967-93. Chmn. bd. dirs. Southeastern Libr. Network, 1975-76; vice chmn., bd. dirs. 18th Century Short-Title Catalogue, N.Am., 1985—. With inf. AUS, 1943-46. Mem. ALA, Assn. Rsch. Librs. (pres. 1977-78), Assn. Southeastern Rsch. Librs. (chmn. 1975—), Bibliog. Soc. Am., Bibliog. Soc. U. Va. (sec.-treas. 1967—).

FRANTZ, ROBERT WESLEY, lawyer; b. Long Branch, N.J., Dec. 31, 1950; BS, Rutgers U., New Brunswick, N.J., 1973; JD, Rutgers U., Newark, 1977. Bar: N.J. 1977, U.S. Dist. Ct. N.J. 1977, U.S. Ct. Appeals (4th and 10th cirs.) 1978, U.S. Ct. Appeals (6th, 7th and 8th cirs.) 1979, D.C. 1980, U.S. Ct. Appeals (9th cir.) 1980, U.S. Dist. Ct. D.C. 1981. Trial atty. U.S. Dept. Justice, Washington, 1977-80; assoc. Hamel and Park, Washington, 1980-82; asst. gen. counsel Chem. Mfrs. Assn., Washington, 1982-85; counsel, environ. protection GE, Fairfield, Conn., 1985-88, Pittsfield, Mass., 1988-89; mgr. and counsel Environ. Remediation Program, Fairfield, Conn., 1989-95; mgr., sr. counsel Environ. Ops. Program, Fairfield, 1995-98; gen. mgr., counsel GE Engines Svcs., Cin., 1998—2003; v.p. environment, health and safety Tyco Internat., Princeton, NJ, 2003—. Mem. sci. adv. bd. subcom. on risk reduction options U.S. EPA, 1996—2003. Contbr. articles to profl. publs.; editorial bd. Rutgers Law Rev., 1976. Mem. Newtown (Conn.) Charter Revision Commn., 1986-87, Glendale Planning Commn., 2000—03. Mem. ABA (exec. editor Natural Resources and Environment 1986-93, coun. mem. sect. natural resources 1993-96). Avocations: sailing, golf, skiing, bicycling, woodworking. Office: Tyco Internat 9 Roszel Rd Princeton NJ 08540

FRANTZE, DAVID WAYNE, lawyer; b. Kansas City, Mo., Jan. 28, 1955; s. James W. and Margaret M. (Pursley) Frantze; m. Geri L. Sexton, July 28, 1979; children: Kevin, Lisa, Christopher, Timothy. BA, Avila U., 1976; JD, U. Mo., Kansas City, 1981. Ptnr. Stinson Morrison Hecker LLP, Kansas City, 2002—. Trustee Mid-Am. chpt. Leukemia and Lymphoma Soc., 1992—, chpt. pres., 1998—2000, nat. trustee, 2001—04, mem. exec. com., 2003—04, nat. bd. dirs., 2004—, vice chair, 2004—; trustee Victor and Caroline Schutte Found., 2000—, U. Mo.-Kansas City Law Found., 1996—2003, exec. com., 2000—03, treas., 2000—01; mem. Civic Coun. Kansas City, 1995—, urban core com., 1996—, bd. dirs., 2001—, Kansas City Spirit, Inc., 1986—88, pres., 1988, adv. coun., 1989—2004; bd. dirs. Kansas City Neighborhood Alliance, 1987—, chmn., 1994—96; mem. Greater Downtown Devel. Authority, 2002—05; bd. counselors Avila U., 1989—2002, trustee, 2002—; bd. dirs. Econ. Devel. Corp., Kansas City, Mo., 2003—, Truman Med. Ctr. Charitable Found., 2005—. Mem.: ABA, Am. Coll. Real Estate Lawyers, Lawyers Assn. Kansas City, Kansas City Met. Bar Assn. (chmn. real estate law com. 1992), Mo. Bar Assn. Roman Catholic. Home: 11812 Central St Kansas City MO 64114-5536 Office: Stinson Morrison Hecker LLP 1201 Walnut St Ste 2600 Kansas City MO 64106-2150 Office Phone: 816-691-3181. E-mail: dfrantze@stinsonmoheck.com.

FRANTZEN, ALLEN JOHN, English language educator; b. New Hampton, Iowa, Oct. 20, 1947; s. John Victor and Dorothy Mae (Birmingham) F. BA, Loras Coll., Dubuque, Iowa, 1969; MA, U. Va., 1973, PhD, 1976. Asst. prof. English Oberlin (Ohio) Coll., 1976-78, Loyola U., Chgo., 1976-82, assoc. prof., 1983-88, prof., 1988—. Author: Literature of Penance, 1983, King Alfred, 1986, Desire for Origins, 1990, Before the Closet: Same-Sex Love from "Beowulf" to "Angels in America", 1998, Bloody Good: Chivalry, Sacrifice, and The Great War, 2003; editor: Speaking Two Languages, 1991, Troilus and Criseyde: The Poem and the Frame, 1993, (with D. Moffatt) The Work of Work, 1994, (with J. Niles) Anglo-Saxonism and the Construction of Social Identity, 1997. Pres. Edgewater Cmty. Coun., Chgo., 1984-85. With U.S. Army, 1969-72, Korea. Named Alexander von Humboldt Found. grantee, 1979, NEH fellow, 1990-91, Guggenheim Found. fellow, 1994; recipient Tempo All-Professor Team, Humanities, Chicago Tribune, 1993. Office: Loyola U Lake Shore Campus Dept English 6525 N Sheridan Rd Dept English Chicago IL 60626-5344 E-mail: afrantz@luc.edu.

FRANTZEN, HENRY ARTHUR, retired investment company executive; b. Orange, N.J., Nov. 28, 1942; s. Henry and Natalie (Johnson) F.; m. Julie Louise Haverty, Aug. 14, 1965; children: John Blair, Jill Marie, Eric Patrick Student, Hamline U., 1960-62; BSBA, U. N.D., 1964. Sr. securities analyst Chem. Bank, 1968-71; adminstrv. asst. Coll. Retirement Equities Fund, 1971, asst. investment officer, 1972, investment officer, 1973, asst. v.p., 1974-76, 2d v.p., 1976, v.p., investment mgr., mem. investment com., 1976; sr. v.p., investment mgr. Tchrs. Ins. and Annuity of Am., N.Y.C., 1980-87, Coll. Retirement Equities Fund, N.Y.C., 1980-87; dir. SBC Portfolio Mgmt. Internat. Inc., Amsterdam, 1987-89; chmn., chief investment officer Yamaichi Capital Mgmt. Corp., 1987-89; pres. Yamaichi Funds Inc., 1987-89, chmn., 1988-89; exec. v.p., dir. equities Oppenheimer Mgmt. Corp., N.Y.C., 1989-91; CIO, exec. v.p. Federated Global Investment Mgmt., N.Y.C., 1995—2002. Mgr. Brown Bros Harriman & Co., 1992-95; mng. dir. Brown Bros. Harriman & Co. Investment Mgmt. Ltd., London, 1992-95; exec. v.p. Federated Global Investment Mgmt. Corp., 1995-2002; exec. v.p. Federated Investment Mgmt. Corp., 1995-2002; v.p. Federated Investors, 1995; chief investment officer Global Equities and Fixed Income; chmn. Frantzen Capital Mgmt., 2004—. Served to lt. USNR, 1964—68. Fellow Fin. Analysts Fedn.; mem. N.Y. Soc. Security Analysts, Naples Soc. Securities Analysts, Econs. Club (N.Y.C.), Sigma Nu, Alpha Kappa Psi. Republican. Avocations: sailing, golf, tennis, bodysurfing. Home: 669 Gulf Shore Blvd N Naples FL 34102 Office Phone: 813-223-6400. Personal E-mail: fjuliehawk@aol.com. Business E-Mail: hfrantzen@frantzencapital.com.

FRANTZIS, THEODOSIOS GEORGE, periodontist; b. Tampa, Fla., Oct. 13, 1941; s. George Theodosios and Zula (Pappas) F.; m. Carol Elaine Timm, Dec. 12, 1971; children: Franklyn Timothy, Hariklia Maria, Georganna Eleni. Student, U. Fla., 1959-60, Fla. state U., 1960-62; DDS, Emory U., 1966; MS in Dentistry, Mayo Grad Sch./U. Minn., 1971. Diplomate Am. Bd. Periodontology, lic. healthcare risk mgr. State Fla. Agy. for Health Care Adminstrn. Pvt. practice, Clearwater, Fla., 1971-78; asst. prof. periodontics Med. Coll. Va., Va. Commonwealth U., Richmond, 1978-80; pvt. practice Tampa, Fla., 1986—. Pres., CEO Mermaid Gifts, Inc., Tarpon Springs, 1985—; clin. asst. prof. U. N.C. Chapel Hill, 1985-86, U. Tex. Dental Br., Houston, 1981-82, U. Tex. Dental Br., San Antonio, 82-84; founding chmn. Leadership Pinellas, 1977, Dental Forum Clearwater, 1972-73; chmn. City of Tarpon Springs, Firefighters Pension Bd., 1989; apptd. mem. City of Tarpon Springs Health Facilities Authority Bd., 1995, apptd. mem. City of Tarpon Springs Planning and Zoning Bd., 2005. Author: Recognizing and Describing Gingival Changes in Chronic Inflammatory Periodontal Disease, 1979, Setting Up a Speaker's Bureau, 1977; co-editor: Strangers at Ithaca: Story of the Spongers of Tarpon Springs, 2001; contbr. articles to sci. publs. Mem. Sunday sch. tchg. staff St. Nicholas Greek Orthodox Cathedral, Tarpon Springs, 1995. Capt. U.S. Army, 1966-68, lt. col. USAF, 1980-85, 91, Persian Gulf War, USAFR, 1985-98, ret. Mayo Found. fellow, Mayo Clinic, 1968-71, Diabetes Vascular Rsch., 1968-70; A.D. Williams Rsch. grantee Med. Coll. Va., 1978-80. Mem. ADA, Am. Acad. Periodontology (continuing edn. com. 1981-82, pub. rels. com. 1982-85, constn. by-laws com. 1983-84, Rsch. award 1970), Fla. Dental Assn. (chmn. speakers bur. 1975-76), Fla. Soc. Periodontists (chmn. pub. rels. com. 1975-76), Fla. Soc. Healthcare Risk Mgmt., Fla. Hosp. Assn., West Coast Dental Assn. (chmn., founder speaker's bur. 1975-76, chmn. Ho. of Dels. 1976-77, chmn. coun. on publs. and pub. info. 1977), Mayo Grad. Sch. Medicine Alumni Assn., Dental Forum Milw. (hon. life), Richmond Dental Soc. (chmn. speaker's bur. 1979-80), Gulf Coast Dental Study Club (Pinellas/Pasco chpt.), West Pasco Dental Implant Study Club, Toastmasters (Speaker Yr. 1973, Toastmaster Yr. 1974), Alpha Epsilon Delta, Psi Omega. Republican. Greek Orthodox. Avocations: photography, bass fishing, jogging, walking, deep-sea fishing. Home: 1005 Rosetree Ln Tarpon Springs FL 34689-2854 Office: 612 S Lincoln Ave Clearwater FL 33756 Office Phone: 727-462-9007. E-mail: tgfdds@hotmail.com.

FRANZ, CRAIG JOSEPH, academic administrator, biology professor; b. Balt., Apr. 12, 1953; s. Harry Joseph and Vera Lee (Garrett) F. BA in Biology, Bucknell U., Lewisburg, Pa., 1975; MSc in Environ. Engring. & Sci., Drexel U., Phila., 1977; PhD in Biology, U. R.I., Kingston, 1988. Tchr. biology LaSalle Coll. High Sch., Phila., 1977-79; instr. biology St. John's Coll., Washington, 1980-84; teaching asst. U. R.I., Kingston, 1984-86; malacological researcher Estacion de Investigaciones, Margarita, Venezuela, 1986-87; univ. fellow U. R.I., Kingston, 1987-88; asst. prof. biology LaSalle U., Phila., 1988—94; exec. asst. to pres. and dean Sch. Math. and Scis. Saint Mary's U., Minn., 1994—97, pres., 2005—, Saint Mary's Coll., Calif., 1997—2004. Author: Invertebrate Zoological Investigations, 1988; co-author: The Cornerstone, 1989. Bd. mem. IRB, Einstein Med. Ctr., Phila., 1989—; bd. trustees Calvert Hall Coll., Balt., 1982-84. Univ. fellow U. R.I., Kingston, 1987. Mem. AAAS, Am. Soc. Zoologists, Am. Malacological Union, Delta Upsilon (bd. dirs. 1975, 1989—), Phi Kappa Phi, The Demosthenean Club (bd. dirs. 1987-89). Democrat. Roman Catholic. Achievements include discovery of new species of chiton, new genus of copepod. Office: Saint Mary's U 700 Terrace Heights Winona MN 55987-1399 E-mail: cfranz@stmarys-ca.edu.*

FRANZ, DARREN M., writer; b. Jamaica, NY, Nov. 20, 1966; s. James Robert Franz and Anna Katharine Fischer; m. Barbara Ann Secrist, Sept. 2, 1990; 1 child, Robert Matthew. Grad., Richmond Hill (NY) H.S., 1984. Guest author I-Con Convention, Stonybrook, NY. Author: Jack Frost, 2000; contbr. short story to lit. publ.; author: Ghost Train, 2004. Cpl. U.S. Army, 1988, 84. Recipient Best Short Story award, Writer's Forum, 2000, Top Internat. Horror Contest award for best short story, U.K. Rainfall Books, 2003. Mem.: Horror Writer's Assn. Avocations: reading, hobby kits, pool, hiking. Home: 733 Stowe Ave Baldwin NY 11510 E-mail: darfranz@earthlink.net.

FRANZ, DAVID ARTHUR, library director; b. Albany, N.Y., June 10, 1943; s. Norman Joseph and Mary Frances (Loux) F.; m. Clara Rose (Plumeri), Nov. 23, 1973; 1 child, Thomas. BA, SUNY, Albany, 1965, MA, 1966, MLS, 1974; PhD, U. N.Mex., 1973. Cert. pub. libr., secondary social studies tchr., N.Y. Reference libr. Vestal (N.Y.) Pub. Libr., 1974-86; dir. Ogdensburg (N.Y.) Pub. Libr., 1986—. Chmn. Lib. Comm. St. Lawrence County, 1997. 1st lt. U.S. Army, 1966-68. Mem. ALA, N.Y. Libr. Assn., North Country Pub. Libr. Dirs. Orgn. (pres. 1991-92, sec. 1993, 2004, 2005). Republican. Roman Catholic. Avocations: collecting rocks, minerals and stamps, coin shooting. Home: 815 Knox St Ogdensburg NY 13669-2725 Office: Ogdensburg Pub Libr 312 Washington St Ogdensburg NY 13669-1518 E-mail: franz@northnet.org.

FRANZ, DENNIS, actor; b. Chgo., Oct. 28, 1944; Stage appearances include: Bleacher Bums, 1978, Brothers, 1983; films include: The Fury, 1978, Remember My Name, 1978, Stony Island, 1978, A Wedding, 1978, A Perfect Couple, 1979, Dressed to Kill, 1980, Popeye, 1980, Blow Out, 1981, Psycho II, 1983, Body Double, 1984, A Fine Mess, 1986, The Package, 1989, Die-Hard 2, 1990, The Player, 1992, American Buffalo, 1996, City of Angels, 1998; TV appearances include: (series) Chicago Story, 1982, Hill Street Blues, (as "Bad Sal" Benedetto) 1982-83 (as Lieutenant Norman Buntz) 1987-88, Bay City Blues, 1983, Beverly Hills Buntz, 1987-88, Nasty Boys, 1990, NYPD Blue, 1993—2005 (Emmy award 1994) (movies) Deadly Messages, 1985, Kiss Shot, 1989, Moment of Truth: Caught in the Crossfire, 1994, Texas Justice, 1995, Buddy Fatso, 1998. Recipient Emmy awards, 1996, 97, 99, SAG awards, 1995, 97, Golden Globes, 1995, Q awards, 1994, 96-99, Star on Walk of Fame, 1999. Office: Paradigm Talent Agency 10100 Santa Monica Blvd Fl 25 Los Angeles CA 90067-4003

FRANZ, ELIZABETH, actress; b. Akron, Ohio, June 18, 1941; Actress with Broadway credits in: Death of a Salesman, The Cripple of Inishmaan, Brighton Beach Memoirs (Tony and Drama Desk nominations), Broadway Bound, Uncle Vanya, Getting Married, The Cemetery Club, The Octette Bridge Club, The Cherry Orchard, Mornings at Seven, 2002; off-Broadway credits include: Sister Mary Ignatius (Obie award, Drama Desk nomination), Minutes from the Blue Route, The Comedy of Errors; regional credits include: Eleanor of Aquataine in The Lion in Winter (Cleve.), Amanda in The Glass Menagerie, Dividing the Estate (Great Lakes), A View From the Bridge, Woman in Mind (Berkshire Theatre Festival), Dolly in The Matchmaker, Agnes of God, Hamlet, Buried Child, The Wicked Witch in The Wizard of Oz, Miss Haversham in Great Expectations, The Bird Sanctuary, 2005; appeared in numerous TV series and movies including: Roseanne, Sister, A Town's Revenge (Emmy nomination), Notes for My Daughter, Nothing Personal, Shameful Secrets, Face of a Stranger, Dottie, The Rise and Rise of Daniel Rocket, Love and Other Sorrows, A Girl Thing, Death of a Salesman (Emmy nomination, 2000), Gilmore Girls, 2001, Judging Amy, 2001; film credits include: Sabrina, 1995, The Substance of Fire, 1996, The Pallbearer, 1996, Thinner, 1996, Twisted, 1997, Jacknife, 1989, Secret of My Success, 1987, School Ties, 1992 Winner 1999 Tony award for featured actress in Death of a Salesman, also Drama Desk award, Outer Critics Circle award.*

FRANZ, FRANK ANDREW, academic administrator, physicist, educator; b. Phila., Sept. 16, 1937; s. Russell Ernest and Edna (Keller) F.; m. Judy Rosenbaum, July 11, 1959; 1 child, Eric Douglas. BS in Physics, Lafayette Coll., 1959; MS in Physics, U. Ill., 1961, PhD in Physics, 1964. Research assoc. U. Ill., Urbana, 1964-65; asst. prof. physics Ind. U., Bloomington, 1967-70, assoc. prof., 1970-74, prof., 1974-85, assoc. dean Coll. Arts and Scis., 1974-77, dean faculties, 1977-82; prof. physics, provost, v.p. academic affairs and research W.Va. U., Morgantown, 1985-91; prof. physics, pres. U. Ala., Huntsville, 1991—. Guest scientist Swiss Fed. Inst. Tech., Zurich, 1965-67, U. Munich, 1978. Contbr. articles to profl. jours. NSF fellow, 1965-67, Alfred P. Sloan fellow, 1968-70. Fellow AAAS, Am. Phys. Soc.; mem. AAUP (pres. Bloomington, Ind. chpt. 1972-73), Am. Assn. Physics Tchrs., Sigma Xi, Phi Kappa Phi. Avocation: tennis. Office: U Ala in Huntsville Office of the President Huntsville AL 35899-0001

FRANZ, HOLLY JO, lawyer; b. Mpls., July 2, 1957; d. Gerald A. and Delores E. (Dahle) F. BS, Mont. State U., 1983; JD, U. Mont., 1986. Bar: Mont., 1986, U.S. Dist. Ct., 1986. Ptnr. Gough, Shanahan, Johnson and Waterman, Helena, Mont., 1986—2004, Franz & Driscoll PLLP, 2004—. Pres. Mont. Water Resources Assn., Helena, 1999-2001. Author: Montana Law Journal, 1986; contbr. articles to profl. jours. Legis. Com. Women's Law Caucus, Missoula, Mont., pres. or bd. mem. The State Bar of Mont. (Women's Law Sect.), 1986—, treas. Mont. Women's Lobby, Helena, 1990-95. Recipient Award of Merit Mont. Legal Svcs., 1984, Belle Winestine award Mont. Women's Lobby, 1993. Mem. ABA, First Jud. Bar Assn. (pres. 1998—). Avocations: gardening, skiing, hiking, wildlife viewing, camping. Office: Franz & Driscoll PLLP PO Box 1155 Helena MT 59624 Office Phone: 406-442-0005. E-mail: hollyjo@franzdriscoll.com.

FRANZ, JENNIFER DANTON, public opinion and marketing researcher; b. Oakland, Calif., Oct. 31, 1949; d. Joseph Periam and Lois (King) Danton; m. William Edwin Behnk, July 30, 1978. BA, Antioch Coll. West, 1973; MA, Stanford U., 1974; PhD, U. Calif., Berkeley, 1991. Cert. Community Coll. Student Personnel Worker, Calif., Community Coll. Supr., Calif. Cons. Alum Rock Union Elem. Sch. Dist., San Jose, Calif., 1973-75; rsch. asst. Far West Lab. for Ednl. Rsch. and Devel., San Francisco, 1974-75; project dir. Hartnell Coll., Salinas, Calif., 1975-77; project dir. Chancellor's Office Calif. Community Colls., Sacramento, 1978-80; pres., owner J.D. Franz Rsch., Sacramento, 1981—. Topic expert Nat. Mktg. Summit, 1995; adj. asst. prof. Golden Gate U., 1982—; instr. mktg. cert. program U. Calif. at Davis Extension, 1990—; lectr. Calif. State U., Sacramento, 1995—; instr. U. Calif.-Berkeley Ext., 1997—. Contbr. numerous articles to profl. jours. Mem. small bus. adv. com. Calif. Senate, Sacramento, 1986-92; bd. dirs. Jr. Achievement Sacramento, 1989-91, Episc. Cmty. Svcs. Sacramento, 1991-92; bd. dirs. Sacramento (Calif.) Philharmonic Orch., 2002—, v.p., 2003—. Recipient various rsch., svc. awards. Mem. Am. Mktg. Assn., Am. Assn. Pub. Opinion Rsch. (bd. dirs. Pacific Coast chpt., 2002—, sec., 2003-04, treas, 2004—), Am. Ednl. Rsch. Assn. (editor 1984-86, mem. div. H evaluation steering com. 1984-85, polit. edn. spl. interest group, survey rsch. spl. interest group, judge div. H awards competition 1984, program reviewer 1982—), Mktg. Rsch. Assn., Sacramento Met. C. of C. (bd. dirs. 1990-93, state govt. affairs, local govt. affairs, pub. rels. coms. 1985—), Sacramento Valley Mktg. Assn. (bd. dirs. 1987-94, pres. 1993-94). Democrat. Episcopalian. Avocations: playing piano, swimming, reading, playing organ, tennis. Address: JD Franz Rsch 550 Bercut Dr Ste H Sacramento CA 95814 Office Phone: 916-440-8777. E-mail: jdfranz@jdfranz.com.

FRANZ, JOHN E., bio-organic chemist, researcher; b. Springfield, Ill., Dec. 21, 1929; m. Elinor Theilken, Aug. 18, 1951; children: Judith, Mary, John, Gary. BS, U. Ill., 1951; PhD, U. Minn., 1955. Sr. research chemist Monsanto Agrl. Co., St. Louis, 1955—60, research group leader, 1960—63, fellow, 1963—75, sr. fellow, 1975—80, disting. fellow, 1980—90; ret., 1991. Co-author: Glyphosate: A Unique Global Herbicide, 1997; inventor roundup herbicide, holder 840 U.S. and fgn. patents; contbr. 42 articles to sci. publs. Recipient Indsl. Rsch. Mag. award, 1977, Indsl. Rsch. Inst. Achievement award, Washington, 1985, J.F. Queeny award, Monsanto Co., 1981, Inventor of Yr. award, St. Louis Bar Assn., 1986, The Nat. Medal of Tech., Washington, 1987, Outstanding Achievement award, U. Minn., 1988, The Mo. award, Gov. of Mo., 1988. Mem.: Am. Chem. Soc. (Carother's award Del. sect. 1989, Perkin medal Am. sect. 1990).

FRANZ, JUDY R., physics professor; BA in Physics, Cornell U., 1959; MS in Physics, U. Ill., 1961, PhD in Physics, 1965. Rsch. physicist IBM Rsch. Lab., Zurich, Switzerland, 1965-67; asst. prof. dept. physics Ind. U., 1968-74, assoc. prof., 1974-79, prof., 1979-87; prof. dept. physics W.Va. U., 1987-91, U. Ala. Huntsville, 1991—; exec. officer Am. Phys. Soc., 1994—. Vis. prof. Tech. U. Munich, 1978-79, Cornell U., 1985-86, 88, 90; assoc. dean coll. arts and scis. Ind. U., 1980-82; mem. coun. on materials sci. Dept. of Energy, 1997-2002; mem. rev. com. for materials sci and tech. divsn. Los Alamos Nat. Lab., 1999-2002; sec. gen. Internat. Union Pure & Applied Physics, 2002—, assoc. sec. gen., 1999-2002; mem. U.S. Commn. for UNESCO, 2005—. Mem. editorial bd. Am. Jour. Physics, 1985-88; contbr. numerous articles to profl. jours. Mem. divsn. materials rsch. adv. com. NSF, 1986-89, mem. divsn. undergrad. edn. adv. com., 1991-93. Humboldt rsch. fellow Munich, 1978-79; recipient Distinguished Service Citation awd., Am. Assn. of Physics Teachers,

1993, Disting. Alumni award Coll. Eng., U. Ill., Urbana-Champaign, 1997. Fellow AAAS (coun. 1995-98), Am. Phys. Soc. (various coms. and offices, chair exec. com. divsn. condensed matter physics 1993-94), Assn. Women in Sci.; mem. Am. Assn. Physics Tchrs. (pres. 1990-91), Am. Inst. Physics (various coms., gov. bd. 1994—, exec. com. 1996-00), Coun. Sci. Soc. Pres. (exec. bd. 1990), Phi Beta Kappa, Sigma Xi (pres. local chpt. 1981-82). Avocations: tennis, reading. Business E-Mail: franz@aps.org.

FRANZ, TIMOTHY MARTIN, psychology professor; b. Pitts., 1964; BA, SUNY, Oneonta, 1982; MA, U. Buffalo, 1986—90; PhD, U. Ill., Chgo., 1993—97. Asst. prof. Ind. U., South Bend, 1997—2000, St. John Fisher Coll., Rochester, NY, 2000—04, assoc. prof., 2004—. Grantee, NIH/Nat. Libr. Medicine, 1997—2002. Fellow: Acad. Mgmt.; mem.: Soc. Personality and Social Psychology, Am. Psychol. Soc., Soc. for Indsl. and Orgnl. Psychology. Office: St John Fisher Coll 3690 East Ave Rochester NY 14618 Office Phone: 585-385-8170. Office Fax: 585-385-7311. E-mail: tfranz@sjfc.edu.

FRANZE, LAURA MARIE, lawyer; b. Pitts., Apr. 20, 1956; d. Catherine Franze; m. Kenneth Charles Morton, Aug.13, 1977; 1 child, Irena Everly Morton. BA summa cum laude, Thiel Coll., 1976; JD, Duke U. Law Sch., 1979. Bar: Ohio 1979, Tex. 1982, Ohio 1990, N.Mex. 1990, US Ct. Appeals (no., so. and we. dists.) Tex.; cert. labor and employment law Tex. Bd. Legal Specialization 1984. Atty. Smith & Schnacke, Dayton, Ohio, 1979-81, Gardere & Wynne, Dallas, 1981-93, McKenna & Cuneo, Dallas, 1993-95, Akin, Strauss, Hauer & Feld, Dallas, 1995—, now ptnr., chair labor and employment practice group and mem. mgmt. com. Counsel Coalition of Responsible Employers; commentator (TV show) Ask a Lawyer. Sr. editor Texas Employment Law (2 vol.), 1998. Vice chair legal/ethical task force Dallas AIDS Commn., 1988. Recipient 40 under 40 award Dallas Bus. Jour., 1993, Top Practitioner, Texas Lawyer 2001, One of Best Lawyers in Dallas, D Mag. 1997, 2001, One of Best Labor & Employment Lawyers, Corporate Counsel Mag. 2002. Fellow Tex. Bar Found. Dallas Bar Found.; mem. Dallas Bar Assn., ABA, Dallas Employment Law Sect. (coun., officer 1993—), Dallas Area Labor and Employment Law Group (pres. 1986-87), State Bar Tex. (advanced labor law com. 1993—). Office: Akin Gump Strauss Hauer & Feld LLP 1700 Pacific Ave Ste 4100 Dallas TX 75201-4675 Office Phone: 214-969-2779. Business E-Mail: lfranze@akingump.com.

FRANZEN, BYRON T. (JOHN FRANZEN), media specialist; b. Britton, SD, Apr. 16, 1946; s. Harold G. and Marian E. (Swenson) F. BA in English and Philosophy, Concordia Coll., 1968; MA in English, McGill U., Montreal, Oue., Can., 1971. Press sec. McGovern for Pres. Campaign, N.H., Ill. Oreg., N.Y., 1971-72; pub. rels. and press. sec. various orgns., Washington, Ala., N.Y., 1973-74; legis. aide Hon. Michael Harrington U.S. Ho. Reps., Washington, 1975-76; mgr. Panetta for Congress Campaign, Calif., 1976; chief staff Hon. Leon Panetta U.S. Ho. Reps., Washington, 1977-78; pres., prin. Franzen & Co., Washington, 1979—. Lectr. U.S. Info. Agy., various countries, 1988—. Designer Harriman Comm. Ctr., Nat. Dem. Hdqs., Washington, 1982-85; works represented in permanent collection Smithsonian Mus. Am. History. Founding chmn. R.A. Overbeck Capitol Hill History Project. Recipient Excellence award Internat. TV Assn., 1985, Silver award Houston Internat. Film Festival, 1987, Gold award, 1988, Nat. Telly award, 1987, 93, 98, 99, Nat. Silver Microphone award, 1987, 94, 97, 2001, Addy award, 1987, Vision award, 1992, 95, 2000. Mem. Am. Assn. Polit. Cons. (bd. dirs. 1991—2005, Pollie award 1986, 88, 94, 2000). Avocations: architectural design, art, antiques, community history. Office: Franzen & Co 610 C St NE Washington DC 20002-6002

FRANZEN, JANICE MARGUERITE GOSNELL, magazine editor; b. LaCrosse, Wis. d. Wray Towson and Anna Gosnell; m. Ralph Oscar Franzen, 1964. BS cum laude, Wis. State U., LaCrosse; MRE, No. Bapt. Theol. Sem. Dir. Christian Writers Inst., 1950—63, dir. studies, 1964-86; fiction editor Christian Life Mag., Wheaton, Ill., 1950-63, woman's editor, 1964-72, exec. editor, 1972-86; mem. editorial bd. Creation House, Wheaton, 1972-86. Speaker writers confs. Author: Christian Writers Handbook, 1960, 61, The Adventure of Interviewing, 1989; editor: Christian Author, 1949-54, Christian Writer and Editor, 1955-63; compiler, contbr.: The Successful Writers and Editors Guidebook, 1977; contbr. articles to various mags. Sec., bd. dirs. Christian Life Missions, Lake Mary, Fla., 1971-95; bd. dirs. Ralph O. Franzen Charitable Found., 1990—, Wesley Luehring Found., 2000—. Home: 140 Windsor Park Dr Apt E201 Carol Stream IL 60188-5314

FRANZEN, JONATHAN, writer; b. Western Springs, Ill., Aug. 17, 1959; s. Earl T. and Irene Franzen; m. Valerie Cornell, Oct. 2, 1982 (div.). BA, Swarthmore Coll., 1981. Rsch. asst. earth and planetary scis. Harvard U., 1983—87; contbg. writer New Yorker. Author: The Twenty-Seventh City, 1988 (Whiting Writers' award), Strong Motion, 1992, The Corrections, 2001 (Nat. Book award for fiction Nat. Book Found.), How To Be Alone: Essays, 2002. Recipient Am. Acad. Berlin prize, 2000; fellow, Guggenheim Found., 1996. Office: Farrar Straus and Giroux Publicity Dept 19 Union Square West New York NY 10003

FRANZEN, LARRY WILLIAM, aerospace electronics engineer; b. Joliet, Ill., Sept. 6, 1945; s. Elmer William and Evelyn M. (Leonard) F.; m. Pennie Ann Gardner, Aug. 10, 1968 (div. Aug. 1975). A in Applied Tech., DeVry Tech. Inst., 1966; BSEE, Marquette U., 1969. Assoc. engr. McDonnell Douglas Aerospace, St. Louis, 1969-70, engr., 1970-76, sr. engr. Langley AFB, Va., 1977-78, lead engr. Eglin AFB, Fla., 1978-93, sr. project engr., 1994—. Mem. Choctaw Multihull Assn., Ft. Walton Yacht Club, Emerald Coast Cyclist. Avocations: sailing, bicycling, skiing. Home: 1421 Bayshore Dr Niceville FL 32578-3401 Office: McDonnell Douglas Aerospace PO Box 1867 Eglin Afb FL 32542-0867

FRANZEN, ULRICH J., architect; b. Rhineland, Germany, Jan. 15, 1921; s. Erik and Elizabeth (Hellersberg) F.; m. Joan Cummings, May, 1942 (div. 1962); children— Peter, David, April; m. Josephine Laura Hughes, Sept. 2, 1980 BFA, Williams Coll., 1942, LHD (hon.), 1972; MArch, Harvard U., 1949. Designer I.M. Pei & Ptnrs., N.Y.C., 1950-55; head Ulrich Franzen & Assocs., N.Y.C., 1955—. Vis. critic, prof. Washington U., St. Louis, 1960-61, Yale U., New Haven, 1962-69, 79, 80, 81, Harvard U., Cambridge, Mass., 1961, Columbia U., N.Y.C., 1983, 84; chmn. Archtl. Bd. Rev., Rye, N.Y., 1960-62; mem. Cin. Archtl. Bd. Rev., 1964-66 Prin. works include Alley Theatre, 1968 (AIA honor 1970), Agronomy Bldg., 1970 (AIA honor 1971), Christensen Hall, 1970 (AIA honor 1972), Harlem Sch. of Arts, 1982, Hunter Coll. N.Y.C., 1983, Philip Morris World Hdqrs., 1984, Whitney Mus. Br., 1984, Champion Internat. World Hdqrs. with Whitney Mus. Br., 1985. With U.S. Army, 1943-45. Decorated Bronze Star, Croix de Guerre Avec Palme, Belgium; recipient Bruner prize Inst. Arts and Letters, N.Y.C. Fellow AIA (Thomas Jefferson award); mem. AIA (gold medal N.Y. chpt.), Archtl. League N.Y. (pres. 1968-70, bd. dirs. 1962—), N.Y.C. Landmarks Preservation Commn. (commr. 1992-96), Century Assn. Home: 27 Lamy Dr Santa Fe NM 87506-6907

FRANZEN, WOLFGANG, physicist, researcher; b. Duesseldorf, Rhineland, Fed. Republic Germany, Apr. 6, 1922; came to U.S., 1937; s. Erich and Elizabeth (Hellersberg) F.; m. Cola Mae Wakefield, June 1, 1943. BS, Haverford Coll., 1942; MA, Columbia U., 1944; PhD, U. Pa., 1949. Instr. Princeton (N.J.) U., 1949-53; asst. prof. U. Rochester, N.Y., 1953-56; exchange scholar U. Basel, Switzerland, 1954-55; sr. scientist Arthur D. Little, Inc., Cambridge, Mass., 1956-61; prof. Boston (Mass.) U., 1961-86, prof. emeritus, 1986—; rsch. physicist Army Rsch. Lab., Watertown, Mass., 1986-95. Pres. Phi Beta Kappa, Boston, 1976-79; chmn. Woodrow Wilson Fellowship, selection com., Boston, 1963-70. Contbr. over 80 articles to profl. jours. With U.S. Army, 1944. Named Mary Amanda Wood fellow, U. Pa., Phila., 1947-49, NATO Sr. fellow, U. Toulouse, France, 1970, Fulbright fellow, U. Colombia, Bogota, 1977. Fellow Am. Phys. Soc. Achievements include 4 patents. Office: Boston Univ Physics Dept 590 Commonwealth Ave Boston MA 02215-2521

FRANZKE, RICHARD ALBERT, lawyer; b. Lewistown, Mont., Mar. 7, 1935; s. Arthur A. and Senta (Clark) F.; divorced; children: Mark, Jean, Robert. BA in Polit. Sci., Willamette U., 1958, JD with honors, 1960. Bar: Oreg. 1960, U.S. Dist. Ct. Oreg., 1960, U.S. Supreme Ct., 1961. Ptnr. Stoel, Rives, Portland, 1960—. Bd. dirs., chmn. various coms. Assn. Gen. Contractors Am., Portland, 1972-79; mem. com. on legis. affairs Assn. Builders & Contractors, Portland, 1983—. Author: A Study of the Construct by Contract Issue, 1979. Mem. Gov.'s Task Force on Reform of Worker's Compensation, Salem, Oreg., 1980-81; atty. gen.'s com. on Pub. Contracting. Recipient SIR award Assn. Gen. Contractors, 1979, Nat. Winner Outstanding Oral Argument award U.S. Moot Ct., 1959. Mem. ABA (sect. pub. contract law), Oreg. Bar (law sch. liaison, com. on practice and procedure specialization), Multnomah County Bar Assn. Republican. Avocations: antique autos, antique furniture, boating. Home: 14980 SW 133rd Ave Tigard OR 97224-1646 Office: Stoel Rives 900 SW 5th Ave Ste 2300 Portland OR 97204-1229 E-mail: rafranzke@stoel.com.

FRANZONE, ERIC SCOTT, psychologist; b. Bklyn., Feb. 21, 1967; s. Robert Anthony and Barbara Adeline Franzone; m. Rosita Betancourt Franzone, Aug. 6, 1995; children: Sarah, Katherine, Hannah. BSc, Franciscan U. of Steubenville, 1989; MSc, St. John's U., 1994; PhD, Forkauf Grad. Sch. Psychology, 2001. Sch. psychologist NYC Bd. Edn., 1993—2005; mem. com. spl. edn. Port Jervis City Sch. Dist., 2001—04. Sch. psychologist Best Friends Preschool, Monticello, NY, 2004—05. Mem.: Nat. Assn. of Sch. Psychologists. Republican. Roman Catholic. Home: 376 Raymondskill Rd Milford PA 18337 Office: NYC Dept Edn 715 Ocean Terr Staten Island NY 10303

FRAPWELL, SHARON ANN, mathematics educator; b. Stamford, Conn. d. Thomas Malcolm Robertson and Nancy Ellen Hemingway; m. Robert T. Frapwell, May 28, 1977; children: Jennifer, Marianne. BS, Purdue U., 1977. Cert. tchr. Ga. Math. tchr. St. John Neumann Regional Cath. Sch., Lilburn, Ga., 1989—, curriculum coord., 2000—. Food donation coord. Quinn Ho., Lawrenceville, Ga., 1994—2004; treas. St. Pius X H.S. Mothers' Club, Atlanta, 2002. Mem.: ASCD, Nat. Coun. Tchrs. Math. Roman Catholic. Avocations: tennis, walking. Office: St John Neumann Regional Cath Sch 791 Tom Smith Rd Lilburn GA 30047 Office Phone: 770-381-0557. E-mail: sfrapwell@sjnrcs.org.

FRARY, CHARLES O., III, (CHUCK FRARY), venture capitalist; b. Chgo., Mar. 9, 1931; s. Charles Ossian Frary Jr. and Violet Brunner; m. Doris Lorraine Money, Apr. 18, 1953 (div. July 15, 1979); children: Charles, Lori, Lisa; m. Joyce Ellen McCulley, Apr. 23, 1983; children: Ashley, Kelley. Student, U. Miami, 1950, student, 1953, U. Calif., 1951—52. Cert. internat. financier. Buyer, merchandise mgr. Rich's, Burdines, H&S Pogue, Atlanta, Miami, Cin., 1954—62; founder, pres. Chuck Frary Interiors, Inc., Evansville, Ind., 1962—92; founder, chmn. Concept Devel. Assoc., Evansville, 1986—2005; founder, pres. Dealmaker Capital Corp., Evansville, 1993—2005; founder, chmn. Internat. Dealmaker Acad., 2005—. Editor: (newspaper) Clark Field News, 1951—54; columnist: Evansville Courier & Press, 1980; contbr. articles to newspapers;, author numerous poems. Chmn. tourism C. of C., Henderson, Ky., 1969; chmn. fundraising Am. Heart Assn., Evansville, 1971—73; pres. Evansville Civic Theatre, 1971—74; founder Riverview Art Gallery/Supper Club/Dinner Theatre. Tech. sgt. USAF, 1950—54. Named Ky. Col., Commonwealth Ky., 1970. Mem.: Internat. Dealmaker Acad. (founder 2005), Internat. Soc. Dealmakers, Internat. Soc. Financiers (bd. advisors 1994—2003, dir. policy 1995—2002, chmn. stds./ethics 1995—2003, founder, chmn. 2005—), Evansville C. of C., Better Bus. Bur., Arts and Edn. Coun., Downtown Evansville Inc, Venture Club Ind., Petroleum Club. Republican. Methodist. Avocation: golf. Home: PO Box 15245 Evansville IN 47716 Office: Concept Devel Assocs Inc PO Box 15245 Evansville IN 47716 Office Phone: 812-471-3334. Fax: 812-477-6499.

FRASCONI, ANTONIO, artist, educator; b. Buenos Aires, Apr. 28, 1919; came to U.S., 1945; s. Franco and Armida (Carbonai) F.; m. Leona Pierce, July 18, 1951; children: Pablo, Miquel. Student, Circulo Bellas Artes, Montevideo, Uruguay, 1944-46, New Sch. Social Rsch., 1947-48. Polit. cartoonist Marcha and La Linea Maginot, Montevideo, 1940; tchr. The New Sch., N.Y.C., 1951; prof. visual arts SUNY, Purchase, 1980. Author: 12 Fables of Aesop, 1954 (chosen 1 of 50 books of yr. Am. Inst. Graphic Arts 1954), See and Say, 1955, Frasconi Woodcuts, 1957, The House That Jack Built, 1958, Birds from My Homeland, 1958, The Face of Edgar Allen Poe, 1959, W. Whitman Portrait, 1960, Known Fables, 1964 (chosen 1 of 50 books of yr. Am. Inst. Graphic Arts), The Cantilever Rainbow, 1965 (chosen 1 of 50 books of yr. Am. Inst. Graphic Arts), Unstill Life, 1969, Overhead the Sun, 1969, Elijah the Slave, 1970, On the Slain Collegians, 1971, Frasconi Against the Grain, 1975; films include: The Neighboring Shore, 1960 (Grand Prix award Venice Film Festival 1960), Antonio Frasconi--Graphic Artist, 1975; one man shows include Montevideo, Mex., Bklyn Mus., Pasadena Art Inst., Pan Am. Union, Va. Mus. Fine Arts, Balt. Mus. Art, many others; exhibited in group shows at Ateneo Montevideo, 1939, AIAPE, Montevideo, 1944, Santa Barbara Mus. Art, Calif., 1946, Bklyn. Mus., 1946, Weyhe Gallery, N.Y.C., 1948, Cleve. Mus. Art, 1952, Smithsonian Inst. Traveling Exhbn. Svc., 1953, Balt. Mus. Art, 1963, Bklyn. Mus., 1964, 34th Biennale Internat. d'Arte, Venice, 1967, Cooper-Hewitt Mus., N.Y., 1980, Am. Inst. Graphic Arts, N.Y., 1980; represented in permanent collections including Mus. Modern Art, N.Y.C. Pub. Libr., Art Inst. Chgo., numerous others. Guggenheim fellow, 1952-53; Art Students League scholar, 1944-46, Yaddo scholar, 1952; grantee Xerox Corp., 1978, Tamarind Lithography, 1962; named Nat. Academician Nat. Acad. Design, 1969; recipient Grand Prix award Venice Film Festival, 1960, purchase prize Bklyn. Mus., 1946, U. Nebr., 1951, Erickson award Soc. Am. Graphic Arts, 1952, prize Pa. Acad. Fine Arts, Nat. Inst. Arts and Letters award, 1954, Joseph H. Hirshorn Found. prize Soc. Am. Graphic Artists, 1963, W.H. Walker prize Print Club Phila., 1964, prize 2nd Biennale d'Art Graphique, 1966, Salon Nat. de Bellas Artes, Grand Premio Exposition de la Habana, 1968, others.*

FRASE, LARRY LYNN, medical oncologist, medical association administrator; b. Austin, Tex., June 18, 1957; s. Leland Leo and Mary Dawn (Courtney) F.; m. Debra Lynn Kimble, May 26, 1979; children: Scott, Laura, Kevin. BS summa cum laude, Baylor U., 1979; MD, U. Tex. Southwestern, 1983. Diplomate in internal medicine and med. oncology Am. Bd. Internal Medicine. Chief med. resident, asst. instr. internal medicine U. Tex. Southwestern Med. Sch., Dallas, 1986-87; internist, v.p. Internal Medicine Assn. Longview, Tex., 1988-95; physician Tex. Oncology, P.A., 1997—. Chief of medicine Good Shepherd Med. Ctr., Longview, 1990—92, pres. med. staff, 1993—94. Contbr. articles to med. jours. Pres. Am. Heart Assn., Longview, 1992-93. Student rsch. fellow Am. Gastroenterol. Assn., 1981. Mem. ACP, Tex. Acad. Internal Medicine (bd. dirs. 1999—), Tex. Med. Assn., Am. Soc. Clin. Oncology, Am. Soc. Hematology, Phi Beta Kappa, Alpha Omega Alpha. Republican. Methodist. Avocations: tennis, computers, wine tasting. Home: 104 Deer Run Trail Longview TX 75605 Office: Longview Cancer Ctr 1300 N 4th St Longview TX 75601-5500 E-mail: larry.frase@usoncology.com.

FRASE, RICHARD STOCKWELL, law educator; b. Washington, June 19, 1945; BA, Haverford Coll., 1967; JD, U. Chgo., 1970. Bar: Ill. 1970, Minn. 1977. Law clk. to L. Swygert, Chief Judge U.S. Ct. Appeals 7th Cir., Chgo., 1970-71; assoc. atty. Sidley & Austin, Chgo., 1972-74; rsch. assoc. U. Chgo. Law Sch., 1974-77; assoc. prof. law U. Minn. Law Sch., Mpls., 1977-81, prof. law, 1981-91, Davis prof. law, 1988-89, Berger prof. law, 1991—. Reporter Speedy Trial Act Planning Group, U.S. Dist. Ct. (no. dist.) Ill., Chgo., 1975-80; adv. bd. Fed. Sentencing Reporter, 1994—. Co-author: (textook) Criminal Justice System, 1980, (practice treatise) Minnesota Misdemeanors, 1982, 3d edit., 1999; author: (practice treatise) Criminal Evidence, 1985; co-author: (fgn. code translation) French Code of Criminal Procedure, 1988; co-editor: Encyclopedia of Crime and Justice, 2d edit., 2001, Sentencing and Sanctions in Western Countries, 2001; mem. U. Chgo. Law Rev. Mem. Am. Law Inst., Phi Beta Kappa. Office: U Minn Law Sch 229 19th Ave S Minneapolis MN 55455-0400 E-mail: frase001@umn.edu.

FRASER, ARVONNE SKELTON, retired diplomat; b. Lamberton, Minn., Sept. 1, 1925; d. Orland D. and Phyllis (Du Frene) Skelton; m. Donald M. Fraser, June 30, 1950; children: Thomas Skelton, Mary MacKay, John Du Frene, Lois MacKay (dec.), Anne Tallman (dec.), Jean Skelton Fraser. BA, U. Minn., 1948; LLD (hon.), Macalester Coll., 1979. Staff asst. Office Congressman Donald M. Fraser, 1963-70, adminstrv. asst., campaign mgr., 1970-76; regional coord. Carter-Mondale Com., 1976; counsellor office presdl. pers. The White House, 1977; coord. office women in devel. U.S. Agy. Internat. Devel., Washington, 1977-81; dir. Minn. and Chgo. coms. peace petition dr. Albert Einstein Peace Prize Found., Chgo., 1981-82; co-dir. ctr. on women and pub. policy Hubert H. Humphrey Inst. Pub. Affairs, U. Minn., Mpls., 1982-94; head U.S. del. Commn. On The Status of Women, UN, 1993-94, U.S. rep., amb., 1994; co-founder, dir. Internat. Women's Rights Action Watch, 1985-93. Bd. dirs. Minn. DFL Edn. Found., Internat. Women's Yr. Conf., Mexico City, 1975, UN Commn. on Status of Women, 1974, 78, Internat. Bur. Edn. Conf., Geneva, 1977; cons. Kenya Women's Leadership Conf., 1984; organizer, chairperson Orgn. Econ. Coop. and Develp./Devel. Assistance com./Women in Devel. experts group for aid-donor nations, 1978-80; dir. Ford. Found. Women's Equity Action League Fund Intern Project and World Plan Project, treas. 1974-77, bd. dirs. 1970-77, 81-83, nat. pres. 1972-74, past legis. chairperson Washington office. Author: U.N. Decade for Women: Documents and Dialogue, 1987; (with others) Women in Washington: Advocates for Public Policy, 1983, Women, Politics and the United Nations, 1995; co-editor: Developing Power: How Women Transformed International Development, 2004. Trustee Macalester Coll., St. Paul, 1982-84; candidate Lt. Gov. Minn., 1986; pres. Friends of Mpls. Pub. Libr., 2002-04 Recipient Disting. Svc. award Women's Equity Action League, 1977, Superior Honor award U.S. Agy. Internat. Devel., 1981, Elizabeth Boyer award Women's Equity League, 1984, Leader of Leaders Outstanding Achievement award Mpls. YWCA, 1979, Resourceful Woman award Tides Found., 1992; sr. fellow Humphrey Inst. Pub. Affairs U. Minn., 1981-94, emeritus 1995; Prominent Women in Internat. Law award Am. Soc. of Internat. Law, 1995, Mpls. Internat. Citizen award, 1995. Home and Office: 821 7th St SE Minneapolis MN 55414-1331 Office Phone: 612-379-9451.

FRASER, BRENDAN, actor; b. Indpls., Dec. 3, 1968; m. Afton Smith, Sept. 27, 1998; children: Griffin Arthur, Holden Fletcher. BFA, Cornish Coll. Arts, Seattle. Actor: (films) Dogfight, 1991, Encino Man, 1992, School Ties, 1992, Twenty Bucks, 1993, Son in Law, 1993, Younger and Younger, 1993, With Honors, 1994, In the Army Now, 1994, Airheads, 1994, The Scout, 1994, The Passion of Darkly Noon, 1995, Balto (voice), 1995, Now and Then, 1995, Kids in the Hall: Brain Candy, 1996, Mrs. Winterbourne, 1996, Glory Daze, 1996, George of the Jungle, 1997, Still Breathing, 1998, Gods and Monsters, 1998, Sinbad: Beyond the Veil of Mists (voice), 1999, Ringside, 1999, Monkey Bone, 1999, Blast from the Past, 1999, The Mummy, 1999, Dudley Do-Right, 1999, Bedazzled, 2000, The Mummy Returns, 2001, The Quiet American, 2002, Looney Tunes: Back in Action, 2003, Revenge of the Mummy: The Ride, 2004, Crash, 2004. Office: William Morris Agy 151 El Camino Dr Beverly Hills CA 90212*

FRASER, CASSANDRA LYNNE, chemist, educator; b. Norfolk, Va., Nov. 11, 1962; d. John Robert and Norma Jean Fraser. BA, Kalamazoo Coll., 1984; ThM, Harvard Div. Sch., 1988; PhD, U. Chgo., 1993. Postdoctoral fellow Calif. Inst. Tech., Pasadena, Calif., 1993—95; asst. prof. chemistry U. Va., Charlottesville, Va., 1995—2001, assoc. prof. chemistry, 2001—05, cavaliers' disting. tchg. prof., 2004—, prof. chemistry, 2005—. Jefferson scholars found. grad. fellowship adv. com. Jefferson Scholars Found., Charlottesville, Va., 2002—; editl. adv. bd., macromolecules Am. Chem. Soc., 2003—; chem. sciences panelist NRC, Washington, 2003—; faculty arts, sciences steering com. U. Va., student mentor. Dir.:. Recipient Career Award, NSF, 1998, Young Investigator award, Dupont, 1999, Pres. Early Career Award for Scientists and Engineers (PECASE), White Ho., NSF, 1999, Non-tenured Faculty award, 3M Corp., 2001, Mead Hon. Faculty, U. Va Alumni Assn., 2002—03, women's leadership award, Lantern Soc. (U. Va.), 2004, Cavaliers' Disting. Tchg. Professorship, U. Va., 2004—06; fellow Rsch. Fellowship, Alfred P. Sloan Found., 1999; grantee Chemistry, Bioengineering Sciences sci. rsch. grants, NSF, 1995—, Chemistry rsch. grants, Petroleum Rsch. Fund, 2002—04. Mem.: NIH, Am. Chem. Soc., Nat. Acads. Scis., Engring. and Medicine (life), Phi Beta Kappa. Achievements include Co-designed and led Color across the spectrum, interdisciplinary course, program, U. Va; design of Careers & Society Forum, U. Va., exploring the societal implications of science and the many roles and venues in society where scientific knowledge and training is valuable; Designed and synthesized polymeric metal complexes, a new class of bio-inspired materials combining polymer and inorganic chemistry fields. Proposed unique capabilities expected for these materials. Avocations: reading, sports, hiking, writing. Office: Univ Va Chemistry Dept McCormick Rd PO Box 400319 Charlottesville VA 22904-4319 Office Phone: 434-924-7998. E-mail: fraser@virginia.edu.

FRASER, CATHERINE ANNE, Canadian chief justice; b. Campbellton, N.B., Can., Aug. 4, 1947; d. Antoine Albert and Anne (Slevinski) Elias; m. Richard C. Fraser, Aug. 17, 1968; children: Andrea, Jonathan. BA, U. Alta., Can., 1969, LLB, 1970; ML, U. London, 1972. Assoc., ptnr. Lucas, Bishop & Fraser, Edmonton, Canada, 1972-89; justice Ct. Queen's Bench Alta., Edmonton, 1989-91, Ct. Appeal Alta., Edmonton, 1991-92, chief justice Alta. and N.W. Ter., 1992—, chief justice Nunavut, 1999—. Dir. Can. Inst. Adminstrn. Justice, 1991-95. Recipient Tribute to Women award YWCA, 1987. Mem. Can. Bar Assn. Office: Ct Appeal Alta Law Courts Bldg Edmonton AB Canada T5J OR2

FRASER, CATRIONA TRAFFORD, art gallery director, photographer; b. Reading, Eng., Jan. 8, 1972; arrived in U.S., 1992; d. Nigel Trafford Fraser and Christine Ilsley; m. Florencio Lennox Campello, Jan. 7, 1995; 1 child, Callum Fraser-Sharp. Diploma, Plymouth Coll. Arts and Design, Devon, Eng., 1988—89; graduated, Wallingford Sch., Oxfordshire, England, 1988. Asst. photographer trainee Reading Evening Post, Reading, England, 1987; founder Cairn Photography, Fettercairn, Scotland, 1991; dir. Fraser Gallery, Washington, 1996—, Bethesda, Md., 2002—. Founder Secondsight, 2003—; dir. Bethesda Fine Arts Festival; chair Trawick Art Prize. Photographer Dunnottar Castle, 1992 (1st prize No. Va. Fine Arts Festival, 1995), Kinnaird Castle, 1992 (1st prize No. Va. Fine Arts Festival, 1994), Glamis Castle, 1992 (1st place 6th Ann. Roseville Photography Competition, Calif., 1993), Fleur No. II, 1992 (Best of Show 17th Ann. Internat. Photo Competition Ark., 1993); exhibitions include Nat. Art. Competition, 1996, Castlegait Gallery, Scotland, 1992, Sacramento Fine Arts Ctr., 1992, New Image Gallery, Va., 1992, Carnegie Mus., Pitts., 1992, St. Helena Art League, Calif., 1993, Brusque Mus., Santa Caterina Brazil, 1993, Art League Gallery, Va., 1994, 1995, Va. Commonwealth U., 1995, Eklektikos Gallery, Washington DC, 1996, Fraser Gallery, Washington DC, 1996, 1997, 1999, 2000, 2002, Infrared Gallery, Chgo., 1998, Bruce Gallery, Edinboro Coll., Pa., 2001, Am. Ctr. Physics, Md., 2004. Adv. panel Bethesda Art and Entertainment; adv. bd. Washington Sch. of Photography. Recipient Honor Award, 42d Ann. Boardwalk Internat. Arts Festival, 1998, Best of Show, Ann. Edzell Scottish Art Invitational, Paul Ostaseski Meml. Award, Roanoke Art Festival, 1998, Merit Award, Spring Stockley Gardens Art Festival, Va., 1995, 20th Ann. Princess Anne Art Show, Va., second place, 37th Ann. Northern Calif. Art Festival, 26th Ann. Otero Mus. Nat. Exhbn., Colo., Waynesboro Fall Arts Festival, Va., 1997, 1996, Bel Air Festival Arts, Md., 1994, Fall Stockley Gardens Art Festival, Va., 1995, Bellgrade Art Festival, Va., 1995, 1997, Judge's Award, 1994. Mem.: Art Dealers Assn. Greater Washington, Bethesda C. of C. Office: Fraser Gallery 7700 Wisconsin Ave Ste E Bethesda MD 20814 Office Phone: 202-298-6450. Office Fax: 202-298-6450. Business E-Mail: info@thefrasergallery.com.*

FRASER, DAVID CHARLES, investment banker; b. Phila., Aug. 2, 1942; s. Charles Walter and Althea Mary (Mathis) F.; m. Carole Ann Geren, June 16, 1962 (div. 1989); children: Mark Samuel, Steven David, Tanya, Adam Scott, Luke Wesley; m. Mary Kay Naumann, Nov. 18, 1993. BA, Taylor U., 1965. Pres. Am. Intertel Corp., Mt. Holly, N.J., 1969-74, Figure World, Inc., Moorestown, N.J., 1978-80; corp. fin. Herzog, Heine, Geduld, Inc., N.Y.C.,

1982-84; v.p. Goldman Sacks & Co., 1983-84; sr. v.p. Lord Securities Corp., N.Y.C., 1984—90; CEO Internat. Vehicle Care, Inc., Kansas City, 1997—. Dir. 28 fin. cos. managed by Lord Securities; pres., CEO Lord Capital Corp., 1989—; vice chmn. Tex. State Optical, 1990—94; chmn., CEO Providence Energy Co. Ltd., Houston, 1992—95, Covenant Capital Corp.lve a t, Colorado Springs, Colo., 1993—95; gen. ptnr. Ammex Captial Ptnrs., Ltd., Houston; chmn. Way Refining and Mktg., Inc., Houston, 1990—92; bd. dirs. Rio Grande Mining Co., Plainsboro, NJ. Mem. Taylor U. Alumni Assn. (pres. 1972-74). Republican. Avocations: tennis, golf, music. Home and Office: PO Box 3298 Olathe KS 66063-3298

FRASER, DAVID WILLIAM, epidemiologist; b. Abington, Pa., May 10, 1944; s. Grant Clippinger and Ella Finlaw (Ayars) F.; m. Barbara Josephine Gaines, June 25, 1966; children: Evan Grant, Leigh Robertson. BA, Haverford (Pa.) Coll., 1965, DSc (hon.), 1991; MD, Harvard U., 1969; ScD (hon.), Moravian Coll., 1987. Diplomate Am. Bd. Internal Medicine. Intern in internal medicine U. Pa. Hosp., Phila., 1969-70, resident, 1970-71, chief resident in internal medicine, 1973-74, fellow in infectious diseases, 1974-75; commd. officer USPHS, 1971-73, 75-82; chief spl. pathogens br., bacterial diseases divsn. Bur. Epidemiology, Ctr. Disease Control, USPHS, Atlanta, 1975-80, med. epidemiologist, asst. dir. bacterial diseases divsn., 1981-82; pres. Swarthmore (Pa.) Coll., 1982-91; head dept. social welfare Secretariat of His Highness Aga Khan, Gouvieux, France, 1991-95; cons. in internat. health and edn., 1996, 2000—; exec. dir. INCLEN, Inc., 1996-2000; rsch. assoc. Asian sect. U. Pa. Mus. Archaeology and Anthropology, 1999—; rsch. assoc. The Textile Mus., Washington, 2004—. Adj. prof. medicine U. Pa. Sch. Medicine, 1983-91, adj. prof. epidemiology, 1997—. Author: A Guide to Weft Twining and Related Structures with Interacting Wefts, 1989, (with Barbara G. Fraser) Mantles of Merit: Chin Textiles from Myanmar, India and Bangladesh, 2005; editl. bd. Annals of Internal Medicine, 1991-94; contbr. articles to profl. med. and textile jours. Bd. mgrs. Haverford Coll., 1980-83; bd. advisors Educators for Social Responsibility, 1986-91; chmn. bd. Consortium on Financing Higher Edn., 1986-87; trustee The Textile Mus., Washington, 1986-2003, v.p., 1990-91, 96, pres., 1997-2003; bd. dirs. Albert G. Oliver Found., 1985-91; sci. adv. bd. Ctr. for Infectious Diseases, 1989-91; mem. immunization practices adv. com. Ctrs. for Disease Control, 1988-92; mem. com. to visit med. sch. and sch. dental medicine Harvard U., 1988-94; costume and textile com. Phila. Mus. Art, 1988-91. Recipient Meritorious Svc. medal USPHS, 1978, John Scott award, 1986; Clementine Cope fellow Haverford Coll., 1965, Daland fellow Am. Philos. Soc., 1974. Fellow ACP (Richard and Hinda Rosenthal Found. award 1979), Infectious Diseases Soc. Am., Am. Coll. Epidemiology; mem. Am. Epidemiol. Soc., Aesculapian Club, Founders Club (Haverford Coll.). Home and Office: 907 N Pennsylvania Ave Yardley PA 19067-2023 Office Phone: 215-295-2016. E-mail: dwffraser@earthlink.net.

FRASER, DONALD C., engineering executive, educator; b. N.Y.C., Apr. 20, 1941; s. Donald Fraser and Anna Thurston; children: Lynn, Eric. S.B., MIT, Cambridge, 1962, MS, 1963, Sc.D., 1967. Tech. staff MIT Instrumentation Lab., Cambridge, Mass., 1967-69; divsn. leader C.S. Draper Lab., Inc., Cambridge, 1969-81, v.p. tech. ops., 1981-88, exec. v.p., 1988-90; dep. dir. operational test and evaluation Office Sec. Def., Washington, 1990-91; prin. deputy under sec. def. for acquisition Office Sec. of Def., Washington, 1991-93; vis. prof. Stanford U., Calif., 1970-71; lectr. MIT Aero/Astro Dept., Cambridge, 1972-91; founder, dir. Ctr. Photonics prof. engring. and physics Boston U., 1993—. Active Air Force Studies Bd. Com. Advanced Avionics, 1979-83; chmn. Air Force Studies Bd. Com. Fault Isolation, 1982-85; active USAF Aero Systems Divsn. Adv. Group, 1984-90; mem. NASA Adv. Coun. Space Systems and Tech. Adv. Com., 1982-91, U.S. Army Sci. Bd., 1987-90, NRC Aeronautics and Space Engring. Bd., 1995-2001; mem. adv. coun. NASA, 2002—; bd. dirs. DRS Techs., Aurora Flight Scis., Photo Secure, PhotoDetection Sys., Iprovica, Solx, Ctr. for Tech. Commercialization. Assoc. editor AIAA Jour. Spacecraft and Rockets, 1970-72, editor-in-chief, 1974-78; founder, editor-in-chief AIAA Jour. Guidance, Control and Dynamics, 1977-91. Recipient Def. Disting. Svc. medal, Navy League Roosevelt Gold Medal for Tech. Fellow AAAS, AIAA (bd. dirs. New Eng. sect. 1973-75, publs. com. 1973-74); mem. NAE, Tau Beta Pi, Sigma Xi, Sigma Gamma Tau. Avocations: flying, hiking, skiing, bicycling.

FRASER, DONALD MACKAY, retired mayor, retired congressman; b. Mpls., Feb. 20, 1924; s. Everett and Lois (MacKay) F.; m. Arvonne Skelton, June 30, 1950; children: Thomas Skelton, Mary MacKay, John DuFrene, Lois MacKay (dec.), Anne T. (dec.), Jean Skelton. BA cum laude, U. Minn., 1944, LLB, 1948. Bar: Minn. 1948. Ptnr. Lindquist, Fraser & Magnuson (and predecessors), 1948-62; Minn. State senator, 1954-62; sec. Senate Liberal Caucus, 1955-62; mem. 88th-95th Congresses from 5th Dist. Minn., mem. fgn. affairs com., chmn. subcom. on internat. orgn., mem. budget com.; mayor City of Mpls., 1980-93; mem. study and rev. com. Dem. Caucus; mem. Commn. on Role and Future Presdl. Primaries, 1976; adj. prof. law and pub. affairs U. Minn., Mpls. Vice chmn., dir. Mpls. Citizens Com. on Pub. Edn., 1950-54; Sec. Minn. del. Democratic Nat. Conv., 1960; chmn. Minn. Citizens for Kennedy, 1960; mem. platform com. Dem. Nat. Conv., 1964, mem. rules com., 1972, 76; vice chmn. Com. Dem. Selection Presdl. Nominees, 1968; chmn. Democratic Study Group Congress, 1969-71, Commn. on Party Structure and Del. Selection Dem. Party, 1971-72; 1st Am. co-chmn. Anglo-Am. Parliamentary Conf. on Africa, 1964; mem. U.S. del. 7th spl. session and 30th session UN Gen. Assembly, 1975; Congl. adviser to U.S. del. to UN Conf. on Disarmament, 1967-73, to U.S. del. to 3d Law of Sea Conf., 1972, to UN Commn. on Human Rights, 1974; cons. on families HUD, 1994. Chair health com. U.S. Conf. Mayors; bd. dirs. Mpls. United Way, 1986-93, Twin Cities Rise!, 1994—2002, Connect/U.S.-Russia, 1994—, Greater Mpls. Coun. Chs., 2000—03; co-chair Ctr. for Internat. Policy, 1976-94, Early Care and Edn. Fin. Commn., 1999-2002; co-founder, chair Dem. Farmer-Labor Edn. Found.; pres. S.E. Mpls. Coun. on Learning, 2003-; co-chair, bd. dirs. Ready 4K, 2001-; mem. Mpls. Charter Commn., 1997-2004; initiated numerous youth programs such as Transitional Work Internship Program, Youth Work Internship Program, Neighborhood Early Learning Ctrs., Youth Coordinating Bd., Youth Trust. Lt. (j.g.) USNR, 1944-46. Recipient 1st Minn. Internat. Human Rights award, 1985, Disting. Svc. award Mpls. United Way, 1992; fellow Kennedy Sch., spring 1994. Mem. Mpls. Fgn. Policy Assn. (pres. 1952-53), Citizens League Greater Mpls. (sec. 1951-54), Minn. Bar Assn., Hennepin County Bar Assn., Ams. for Dem. Action (nat. chmn. 1973-76), Dem. Conf. (nat. chmn. 1976-78), U. Minn. Law Alumni Assn. (dir. 1958-61), Univ. Dist. Improvement Assn. (pres. 1950-52), Nat. League of Cities (2d v.p. 1991, 1st v.p. 1992, pres. 1993), Minn. Advocates for Human Rights (co-founder, bd. dirs. 1983-92, 2000—), League of Minn. Cities (bd. dirs. 1991-93).—. Democrat. Personal E-mail: dfled@goldengate.net.

FRASER, KATHLEEN JOY, poet, creative writing professor; b. Tulsa, Mar. 22, 1935; d. James Ian and Marjorie Joy (Axtell) F.; m. Jack Marshall, July 10, 1960 (div. 1970); 1 child, David Ian; m. Arthur Kalmer Bierman, June 30, 1984 BA in English Lit., Occidental Coll., 1958; doctoral equivalency, San Francisco State U., 1976. Vis. prof. writing, lectr. in poetry The Writer's Workshop, U. Iowa, Iowa City, 1969-71; writer in residence Reed Coll., Portland, Oreg., 1971-72; dir. Poetry Center San Francisco State U., 1972-75, prof. creative writing, 1972-92. Founder-dir. Am. Poetry Archives, San Francisco, 1973-75; founder-editor How(ever), Jour. for poets/scholars interested in modernism and women's innovative writing, 1983-91. Author: (children's book) Stilts, Somersaults and Headstands, 1967; (poetry) What I Want (New and Selected Poems), 1974, New Shoes, 1978, Something (even human voices in the foreground) A Lake, 1984, Notes Preceding Trust, 1988, When New Time Folds Up, 1993, Il Cuore: The Heart, Selected Poems 1970-95, 1997, Translating the Unspeakable: Poetry and the Innovative Necessity, 2000, Discrete Categories Forced Into Coupling, 2004 Recipient Frank O'Hara Poetry prize, 1964; Nat. Endowment for Arts fellow, 1978, Guggenheim fellow, 1981.

FRASER, MALCOLM CAVANAGH, mayor; b. Englewood, N.J., Nov. 26, 1929; s. Stanley and Helen L. (Cavanagh) F.; m. Joan Marie Iversen, May 1, 1954; children: Gordon, David, Stephen, Janice, Bruce, Andrew. Mech. Engr., Stevens Inst. Tech., 1951, Alexander Hamilton Inst., 1958. Mktg. engr. Ingersoll-Rand Co., N.Y.C., 1951—60, internat. coord., 1960—66, mgr. govt. ops. Painted Post, NY, 1967—75, gen. mgr. European Ops. The Hague, Netherlands, 1975—80, gen. mgr. for oil industry Houston, 1980—82; internat. mgr. IR Compression Svcs., Houston, 1983—86; dispute resolution and corp./customer polit. coms. Dresser-Rand Co., Painted Post, 1981—90, mgr. gas engine product, 1986—90; ret., 1990. Mayor Borough Cape May Point, NJ, 1992—; mem. coastal area facilities and residential act com. N.J. Dept. Environ. Protection, 1998—2000, mem. SMART growth com., 2002—; mem. pub. works com. State of N.J., 2004—; del. N.J. Citizens Tax Assembly, 2003—04. Author: (book) The Charmed Circle, 1986. Pres. YMCA Men's Svc. Club, Westfield, N.J., 1967; residential co-chair United Fund, Westfield, 1967; treas. troop com. Boy Scouts Am., Corning, N.Y., 1968-72; ch. vestryman, Corning, 1971-74; bd. dir. YMCA, Corning, 1967-75, pres. 1970-73; mem. Am. Sch. Bd. The Hague, Netherlands, 1978-80; bd. dir. Taxpayers Assn., Cape May Point, 1988-92, pres. 1990-92; trustee Hist. St. Peters-by-the-Sea Ch., Cape May Point, 1990—. Cpl. U.S. Army, 1954-56 Recipient Excellence in Cmty. Svc. award DAR, Cape May County, 1997, Outstanding Leadership award N.J. Mayor's Assn., Dunellen, 1998, Lifetime Achievement award Cape May Point Taxpayers Assn., 2001; award established in his name N.J. Rural Water Assn., Tuckerton, N.J., 1999. Mem. ASME, N.J. Rural Water Assn. (pres. 1995-98, bd. dirs. 1994-2000), N.J. State League of Municipalities (bd. dirs., econ. devel. com. 2003-), Cape May County League of Municipalities (v.p., pres. 1996-98), N.J. Conf. Mayors (bd. dirs., legis. com. 2002-, v.p. 2005-) Episcopalian. Avocations: baseball, history. Home: PO Box 323 Cape May Point NJ 08212-0323 Office: Borough of Cape May Point PO Box 490 215 Lighthouse Ave Cape May Point NJ 08212 Office Phone: 609-884-2080. E-mail: joan.fraser/@verizon.net.

FRASER, PAMELA, artist; b. Smyrna, Tenn., 1965; BFA, Sch. Visual Arts, N.Y.C., 1988; MFA, UCLA, 1992. Prof. U. Tenn., Northwestern U.; asst. prof. art dept. Ohio State U., Columbus, 2001—. One-woman shows include Casey Kaplan, N.Y.C., 1998, 2000, exhibited in group shows at Lotus Motel, Inglewood, Calif., 1995, White Columns, N.Y.C., 1996, Exit Art, 1999, Elga Wimmer Gallery, 1999, Pudewil, Berlin, 2000, Wurtembergischer, Stuttgart, 2000, Dundee Ctr. of Contemporary Art, Scotland, 2000, others. Recipient Louis Comfort Tiffany award, 1997; Skowheghan Sch. Painting and Sculpture fellow, 1988. Office: Ohio State Univ Dept Art 146 Hopkins Hall 128 N Oval Mall Columbus OH 43210 Fax: 212-645-7335.

FRASER, ROBERT BURCHMORE, lawyer; b. Newton, Mass., Aug. 13, 1928; s. Alfred Alexander and Helen Louise (Comiskey) F.; m. Mary-Ann Jackson, Sept. 7, 1963; children: Melanie, Jennifer Amy, Matthew John. AB, Harvard U., 1949, LLB, 1952, LLM, 1955. Bar: Mass. Assoc. Goodwin Procter LLP, Boston, 1955-63, ptnr., 1964-97, chmn., 1984-97. Spl. advisor to Mayor of Boston and Boston Police Commr., 1997-2000; bd. dirs. Investors Fin. Svcs. and Investors Bank and Trust Co., 1996—. Mem. Mass. Gov.'s Jud. Nominating Commn., 1979-82; mem. adv. com. Mass. Commr. Revenue, 1979-82; chmn. adv. com. Mass. Housing Fin. Agy, 1979-83; chmn. Boston Pub. Health Commn., 1996-97; chmn. Vol. Lawyers for Arts of Mass., 1990-97; bd. dirs. Greater Boston YMCA, 1981-87, Greater Boston Arts Fund, 1987—, Boston Pvt. Industry Coun., 1988-99, Citywide Ednl. Coalition, 1988-2000, Boston Against Drugs, 1988-93, chmn. 1990-93, Boston Ptnrs. in Edn., 1989-99, Am. Student Assistance Corp., 1989-97, Greater Boston C. of C., 1993—, Jobs for Mass., 1993-98, Boston Pub. Libr. Found., 1992-2000, Boston Mgmt. Consortium, 1994-2001, NCCJ, 1994-2002, chmn. 1997-99, Mass. Bus. Alliance Edn., 1995—, Ctr. for Collaborative Edn., 1998-99, The Med. Found., 1995-99, MassInc., 1996—; trustee New Eng. Conservatory Music, 1982-2001, Boston Plan for Excellence in Pub. Schs., 1987-99, chmn., 1992-95, Boston Adult Literacy Fund, 1989-96; trustee Lesley Coll., 1992-96; overseer Boston Lyric Opera, 1994-99; chmn. Boston Music Edn. Collaborative, 1999-2001; chmn. Arts & Bus. Coun. Greater Boston, 2000—. Mem. ABA, Mass. Bar Assn., Boston Bar Assn., Harvard Mus. Assn. Harvard Club (Boston.). Home: 90 Allandale St Jamaica Plain MA 02130-3442 Office: Goodwin Procter Exchange Pl Boston MA 02109-2803 Office Phone: 617-570-1234. Personal E-mail: fraserrb@comcast.net.

FRASER, WILLIAM NEIL, retired federal agency administrator; b. Vancouver, B.C., Can., May 25, 1932; s. James Herbert and Katherine Baikie (Grieve) F.; m. Marie Helm, Dec. 19, 1986; children by previous marriage: Gordon, Alan, Katherine, Ian. Student, Banff Sch. Advanced Mgmt., 1967. Product mgr. Masonry, Deeks-McBride Ltd., Vancouver, 1952-68; gen. mgr. Masonry Contractors Assn. B.C., Vancouver, 1968-71; exec. dir. Can. Masonry Contractors Assn., Toronto, 1971-87; mem. Ont. Labour Rels. Bd., 1988-98, ret., 1999. With Can. Navy Res., 1953-57. Mem.: Royal Can. Mil. Inst., Inst. Assn. Execs. (past pres. Toronto chpt.), Capt. Olde 78th Fraser Highlanders, Monarchist League of Can., Royal Heraldry Soc. Can., St. Andrew's Soc. of Toronto, Clan Fraser Soc. Can. (chmn.), Scottish Studies Found. (patron, gov.), Heraldry Soc. of Scotland, Grant of Arms Can. Heraldic Authority, Clans and Scottish Socs. of Can. (past pres.). Home: 71 Charles St E Apt 1101 Toronto ON Canada M4Y 2T3 E-mail: neil.fraser@clanfraser.ca.

FRASIER, CLARK, business owner, chef; Owner import-export bus., San Francisco; advanced to chef torunant Stars, San Francisco; co-owner (with Mark Gaier) Arrows, Ogunquit, Maine, 1988—. Office: Arrows Berwick Rd Ogunquit ME 03907

FRASIER, RALPH KENNEDY, lawyer, bank executive; b. Winston-Salem, N.C., Sept. 16, 1938; s. LeRoy Benjamin and Kathryn O. (Kennedy) F.; m. Jeannine Quick, Aug. 1981; children: Karen D. Frasier Alston, Gail S. Frasier Cox, Ralph Kennedy Jr., Keith Lowery, Marie Kennedy, Rochelle Doar. BS, N.C. Cen. U., Durham, 1963, JD, 1965. Bar: N.C. 1965, Ohio 1976. With Wachovia Bank and Trust Co., N.A., Winston-Salem, NC, 1965—75, v.p., counsel, 1969-70; asst. counsel, v.p. parent co. Wachovia Corp., 1970-75; v.p., gen. counsel Huntington Nat. Bank, Columbus, Ohio, 1975-76, sr. v.p., 1976-83, sec., 1981-98, exec. v.p., 1983-98, cashier, 1983-98. V.p. Huntington Bancshares Inc., 1976-86, gen. counsel, 1976-98, sec., 1981-98; sec., dir. Huntington Mortgage Co., Huntington State Bank, Huntington Leasing Co., Huntington Bancshares Fin. Corp., Huntington Investment Mgmt. Co., Huntington Nat. Life Ins. Co., Huntington Co., 1976-88; v.p., asst. sec. Huntington Bank N.E. Ohio, 1982-84; asst. sec. Huntington Bancshares Ky., 1985-97; sec. Huntington Trust Co., N.A., 1987-97, Huntington Bancshares Ind., Inc., 1986-97, Huntington Fin. Services Co., 1987-98; dir. The Huntington Nat. Bank, Columbus, Ohio, 1998-2004; of counsel Porter Wright Morris & Arthur LLP, Columbus, 1998—; trustee OCLC Online Computer Libr. Ctr., Inc., Dublin, Ohio, 1999—, mem. fin. com., 2000-04, mem. audit com., 2000-04, chair 2002-04, exec. com., 2002—, pers. and compensation com., 2002-03; dir. ADATOM.COM, Inc., Milpitas, Calif., 1999-2001, mem. compensation com., 1999-2001, chair audit com., 1999-2001. Bd. dirs. Family Svcs. Winston-Salem, 1966-74, sec., 1966-71, 74, v.p., 1974; chmn. Winston-Salem Transit Authority, 1974-75; bd. dirs. Rsch. for Advancement of Personalities, 1968-71, Winston-Salem Citizens for Fair Housing, 1970-74, N.C. United Community Svcs., 1970-74; treas. Forsyth County (N.C.) Citizens Com. Adequate Justice Bldg., 1968; trustee Appalachian State U., Boone, N.C., 1973-83, endowment fund, 1973-83, Columbus Drug Edn. and Prevention Fund, Inc., 1989-92; trustee, vice chmn. employment and Edn. Commn. Franklin County, 1982-85; mem. Winston-Salem Forsyth County Sch. Bd. Adv. Coun., 1973-74, Atty. Gen's Ohio Task Force Minorities in Bus., 1977-78; bd. dirs. Inroads Columbus, Inc., 1986-95, Greater Columbus Arts Coun., 1986-94, Columbus Urban League Inc., 1987-94, vice chmn., 1990-94; trustee Riverside Meth. Hosp. Found., 1989-90, Grant Med. Ctr., 1990-95, Grant/Riverside Meth. Hosps., 1995-97; trustee Ohio Health Corp., 1997-2004, treas. fin./audit com., 2001, 04, chair fin./audit com., 2001-04, exec. com., 2002-04; dir. Cmty. Mutual Ins. Co., Cin., 1989-92, mem. audit com., 1989-92; trustee N.C. Ctrl. U., Durham, N.C., 1993-2001, vice-chmn., 1993-94, chmn. 1995, chair ednl. planning and acad. affairs com., 1995-98, audit, devel. and personnel coms., 1998-2001, chair audit com., 1999-2001; mem. Ohio Bd. Regents, 1987-96, vice-chmn., 1993-95, chmn., 1995-96; trustee Nat. Jud. Coll., Reno, Nevada, 1996-2002, fin. and audit com., 1997-2002 treas., chair, 1999-2002, Columbus Bar Found., 1998-2005 (fellows com. 1998—, grants com., 1998-2005); AEFC Pension Adminstrn. Com. defined benefit plan of the ABA, Am. Bar Endowment, Am. Bar Found., and Nat. Jud. Coll., Chgo, Ill., 1998-2002. With AUS, 1958-64. Fellow: Ohio State Bar Found. (disting. life fellow, Ritter award 2003); mem.: ABA, Columbus Bar Assn., Ohio Bar Assn., Nat. Bar Assn. Office: Porter Wright Morris & Arthur LLP 41 S High St Ste 3100 Columbus OH 43215-6194 Office Phone: 614-227-2125. Personal E-mail: rkfrasier@msn.com. Business E-Mail: rfrasier@porterwright.com.

FRASK, ROBIN ANN KOSTANESKY, secondary school educator; b. Hazleton, Pa., Apr. 27, 1971; d. John F. and Karen A. (Brandmier) Kostanesky; m. Randy Michael Frask, July 2, 1999; children: Gabrielle, Anthony. BS in Edn., Biology and Gen. Sci., Mansfield U., 1993; MEd, Wilkes U., 1999; postgrad., Lehigh U., 2005—. Cert. ESL specialist Pa., supr. curriculum and instrn. cert. Lehigh U. Substitute tchr. Weatherly (Pa.) Area Sch. Dist., 1994-96, Hazleton (Pa.) Area Sch. Dist., 1994-96, sci. tchr., 1996—2004, ESL tchr., 2004—. Mem. NEA, Pa. State Edn. Assn., Assn. Suprvn. & Curriculum Devel. Home: 4 High Meadow Dr Drums PA 18222 Personal E-mail: robinfrask@yahoo.com. Business E-Mail: fraskr@hasd.k12.pa.us.

FRASSINELLI, GUIDO JOSEPH, retired aerospace engineer; b. Summit Hill, Pa., Dec. 4, 1927; s. Joseph and Maria (Grosso) F.; m. Antoinette Pauline Clemente, Sept. 26, 1953; children: Lisa, Erica, Laura, Joanne, Mark. BS, MS, MIT, 1949; MBA, Harvard U., 1956. Treas. AviDyne Rsch., Inc., Burlington, Mass., 1958-64; asst. gen. mgr. Kaman AviDyne divsn. Kaman Scis., Burlington, 1964-66; asst. dir. strategic planning N. Am. ACFT OPNS, Rockwell Internat., L.A., 1966-69; from mgr. program planning to project mgr. advanced programs Rockwell Space Sys. Divsn., Downey, Calif., 1970-94; ret. Rockwell Space Systems Div., Downey, 1994. Mem. Town Hall of Calif., L.A., 1970—; treas. Ecology Devel. and Implementation Commitment Team Found., Huntington Beach, Calif., 1971-75; founding com. mem. St. John Fisher Parish Coun., Rancho Palos Verdes, Calif., 1978-85. Recipient Tech. Utilization award, NASA, 1971, Astronaut Personal Achievement award, 1985. Fellow AIAA (assoc.; tech. com. on econs. 1983-87, exec. com. L.A. sect. 1987-91, 94-98), Inst. for Advancement of Engring.; mem. Sigma Xi, Tau Beta Pi. Roman Catholic. Achievements include determination of aircraft damage limits and atomic-weapon-delivery capabilities of aircraft; development of cost models to account for advances in engineering state of art, of cost prioritization techniques for space shuttle improvements, of software to produce business plans. Home: 29521 Quailwood Dr Rancho Palos Verdes CA 90275

FRATANTONI, JOSEPH CHARLES, medical researcher, biotechnologist, hematologist; b. Bklyn., May 14, 1938; s. Joseph Edward and Providence Adeline (Bellante) F.; m. Pauline F. Jones, Jan. 30, 1965; children: David, Michael, Joan. BS in Chemistry egregia cum laude, Fordham Coll., 1959; MA in Chemistry, Harvard U., 1961; MD, Cornell U., 1965. Diplomate Am. Bd. Internal Medicine. Rsch. assoc. Sloan-Kettering Inst., N.Y.C., 1960-61; fellow dept. pharmacology Cornell U., 1961-64; intern, resident in medicine Cornell-N.Y. Hosp., 1965-67; staff assoc. Nat. Inst. Arthritis and Metabolic Diseases NIH, 1967-69; resident in medicine Cornell-N.Y. Hosp., 1969-70, fellow in hematology dept. medicine, 1970-71; instr. in medicine Cornell U., 1970-71; asst. prof. medicine, dir. Coagulation Lab. Georgetown U., 1971-72, from clin. asst. to assoc. prof. medicine and pharmacology, 1972-85; sr. staff physician hematology svc. Clin. Ctr. NIH, 1972-74; thrombosis program dir. Nat. Heart, Lung and Blood Inst., 1974-75, chief blood diseases br., 1975-77, chief blood resources br., 1977-78; chief lab. of cellular hematology Ctr. for Biologics Evaluation and Rsch., FDA, 1978-92; from assoc. prof. to clin. prof. medicine Uniformed Svcs. U., 1976-96; dir. divsn. hematology FDA, 1992-96; v.p. biologics C.L. McIntosh and Assocs., Rockville, Md., 1996-99; v.p. med. affairs, clin. devel. Max Cyte Inc., Gaithersburg, Md., 1999—. Presenter in field. Patentee in non-invasive optical assessment of platelet viability, measurement of platelet aggregation using a microplate reader; contbr. over 100 articles to profl. jours. Served to capt. USPHS, 1967-96, ret. Recipient Spl. Citation, FDA Commr., 1988, Citation, USPHS, 1989, Meritorious Svc. medal USPHS, 1991. Fellow ACP; mem. Internat. Soc. Cellular Therapy, Am. Soc. Hematology, Am. Assn. Blood Banks (Disting. Svc. award 1998). Achievements include rsch. in hemostasis, platelet function and blood substitutes. Home: 9412 Overlea Dr Rockville MD 20850-3735 Office: MaxCyte Inc 22 Firstfield Rd Ste 250 Gaithersburg MD 20878

FRATER, ROBERT WILLIAM MAYO, surgeon, educator; b. Cape Town, South Africa, Nov. 12, 1928; came to U.S., 1964, naturalized, 1974; s. Kenneth and Ethel (Barrow) F.; m. Elaine Glynn Nagle, Aug. 27, 1954; children: Hugh R., Dirk A., Phillipa. M.B., B.Chir. (Jagger Scholar, Medalist, Anatomy, Surgery, Pathology), U. Cape Town Med. Sch., 1952; MS in Surgery (Minn. Heart Assn. fellow), U. Minn., 1961. Intern medicine and surgery Groote Schuur Hosp., Cape Town, 1953; resident casualty officer Lewisham Hosp., London, 1955; fellow in gen. and thoracic surgery Mayo Clinic, Rochester, Minn., 1955-61; sr. lectr. cardiothoracic surgery U. Cape Town, 1962-64; asst. prof. surgery Albert Einstein Coll. Medicine, N.Y.C., 1964-68, assoc. prof., 1968-72, prof. surgery, 1972—, chief cardiothoracic surgery, 1968—, acting chmn. dept. surgery, 1971-75; mem. Albert Einstein Coll. Medicine (Senate Council), 1971-74; chief cardiothoracic surgery Montefiore Hosp. and Med. Center, 1975-92; mem. staff, exec. council Bronx Mcpl. Hosp. Center, Albert Einstein Coll. Hosp., 1969—; mem. staff Lawrence Hosp., Bronxville, N.Y.; pres. Glycar, Inc., Bronxville. Mem. organizing and sci. coms. Internat. Symposium on Cardiac Bioprosthesis, 1982, 95, 88, 91, 94, honored guest, 1985; pres. Glycar Inc.; med. dir. St. Jude Med. Inc., 2000—. Editor: Jour. Valvular Heart Disease, Replacement Cardiac Valves, New Horizons and the Future of Heart Valve Bioprostheses, 1994; mem. editl. bd. Cardiac Chronicle, Jour. Cardiac Surgery, 1987—. Mem. Concern for Dying Coun., 1982-88. Recipient award Noble Found., 1961, Bronx Coun. of the Arts Humanitarian award, 1989, Disting. Alumnus award Mayo Found, 2001; grantee NIH, 1965-70, 68-70, 74-78, 79-81, 82-84, Am. Heart Assn., 1966, 71. Fellow ACS, Royal Coll. Surgeons, Am. Coll. Cardiology, Am. Heart Assn. (exec. com. coun. on Cardiovascular Surgery 1979-84, program com. 1979-82); mem. Am. Assn. Thoracic Surgery, Soc. Thoracic Surgeons (postgrad. edn. com. 1978, chmn. postgrad. program 1981), N.Y. Soc. Thoracic Surgery (pres. 1978), N.Y. Surg. Soc. (mem. coun. 1975-80), Thoracic Surgery Dirs. Assn. (exec. coun. 1982-85), Assn. Acad. Surgeons, Soc. Cardiothoracic Surgeon Great Britain and Ireland (hon. guest and mem. 1989), Soc. Heart Valve Disease (founder, chmn. membership com. 2001-, honored guest biennial Vancouver meeting, 2005), Bronxville Field Club (squash capt., bd. govs. 1987-90, hon. lectr. 4th Biennial Mtg. 2005). Home: 17 Gladwin Pl Bronxville NY 10708-2201 Office: 1575 Blondell Ave Bronx NY 10461-2660 Personal E-mail: rwmfglycar@aol.com. *The good fortune to use both mind and hand in asking questions, finding answers and healing others.*

FRATESCHI, LAWRENCE JAN, economist, statistician, educator; b. Chgo., Oct. 7, 1952; s. Lawrence and Olga (Los) F. BS in Math. and Psychology, U. Ill., Chgo., 1975, MA in Econs., 1979, MS Pub. Health in Biostats. and Epidemiology, 1990, PhD in Econs., 1992. Teaching asst. dept. math, lectr. dept. info. and decision scis. U. Ill., Chgo., 1978-80, rsch. assoc. epidemiology and biostatistics Sch. Pub. Health, 1989-90; statistician Argonne (Ill.) Nat. Labs., 1980-81; asst. prof. econs. and stats. Coll. of DuPage, Glen Ellyn, Ill., 1981-86, assoc. prof., 1986-90, prof. econs., stats., 1990—; rsch. prof. epidemiology and biostats. Sch. Pub. Health U. Ill., Chgo., Ill., 1993—. Contbr. articles to profl. publs. Mem. Am. Econ. Assn., Am. Statis. Assn., Am. Pub. Health Assn., Soc. Epidemiologic Rsch., Midwest Econs. Assn., Ill. Econs. Assn., Ill. Pub. Health Assn., Phi Eta Sigma, Phi Kappa Phi, Delta Omega. Office: Coll of DuPage 425 22nd St Glen Ellyn IL 60137-6784 E-mail: fratesch@cdnet.cod.edu.

FRAUENHOFFER, ROSE MARIE, visual artist; b. Evanston, Ill., July 24, 1926; d. Edward John and Rose Louise (Pantle) Kossow; m. Harold Voight Frauenhoffer, Oct. 14, 1950. Lic. cosmetologist, Ill. Mgr., buyer Del-Mar, Evanston, 1948-52; asst. mgr., buyer House of Harold Salon, Evanston,

1952-2000; mgr. buyer House of Harold Gifts, Evanston, 1952—; mgr. House of Harold Gallery, Evanston, 1952-2000; asst. mgr., designer House of Harold Engraving, Evanston, 1952-2000; artist, designer House of Harold Studio, Evanston, 1999-2000; artist, dir. Peinture de la Monde Studio, Gallery divsn. House of Harold, Evanston, 2000—04; dir., visual artist Blue Door Art Gallery and Studio, 2004—. One-woman shows include Aurelia Gallery, Evanston, Garland Bldg. Gallery, Chgo., Bank of Lincolnwood, Levy Ctr. La-Petite Gallery, Loft Gallery, Skokie, Ill., Friends of the Wilmette Area Libr. Exhibit (Hon. Mention, 1992); group shows at Loft Gallery, John G. Blank Ctr. for Arts, Michigan City, Ind., Margaret Harwell Art Mus., Poplar Bluffs, Mo., Wilmette (Ill.) Pub. Libr.; Nappa valley Nat. Exhibit (Hon. Mention, 1992), Evanston Woman's Club Area Exhibit (Third Watercolor award, 1999), Margaret Marwell Art Mus. Nat. Small Painting Exhibit (Second Watercolor award, 2004); 200 miniature paintings in juried nat. and internat. exhbs.; others Alumnus, vol. Evanston Citizens Police Acad., 1997—; co-chair Skokie Centennial Art and Craft Fair, 1988. Award winner Nat. Art Juried Show, 2004. Mem. Skokie Art Guild (v.p. 1980-81, pres. 1981-82), Midwest Watercolor Soc., Nat. Mus. Women in the Arts, Ill. Arts Coun., Evanston Arts Coun., Chgo. Artists Coalition. Avocations: gardening, photography, sewing. Office Phone: 847-864-0791.

FRAULINO, PHILIP SAMUEL, telecommunications industry executive; b. Hartford, Conn., Apr. 10, 1952; BA, Upsala Coll., 1974; MA, Seton Hall U., 1977; MLS, CUNY, 1984. Sr. libr. asst. Commn. Blind and Visually Impaired N.J. Dept. Human Svcs., Newark, 1977—80; libr., libr. technician Nat. Oceanic and Atmospheric Adminstrn. U.S. Dept Commerce, Princeton, NJ, 1980—87; tech. info. specialist, telecommunication technician U.S. State Dept., Washington, 1987—. Chmn. Princeton (N.J.) Transp. Com., 1983—87. Recipient Franklin award, U.S. State Dept., 1999, 2000, Extra Mile award, 2001, 2003. Mem.: Am. Soc.Info. Sci. and Tech., Coll. English Assn., Nat. Assn. Rail Passengers. Home: 75 East Wayne Ave Apt 611 Silver Spring MD 20901 Office: US State Dept 2201 C St NW Washington DC 20520 E-mail: fraulinops@state.gov.

FRAUMENI, JOSEPH FRANCIS, JR., epidemiologist, research scientist, educator, military officer; b. Boston, Apr. 1, 1933; s. Joseph Francis and Pauline (Malta) Fraumeni; m. Patricia Welch D'Arcy, Apr. 23, 1977. AB, Harvard U., 1954; MD, Duke, 1958; ScM, Harvard U., 1965. Diplomate Am. Bd. Internal Medicine. Commd. lt. USPHS, 1962, advanced through grades to rear admiral (asst. surgeon gen.), 1997; med. intern, resident Johns Hopkins Hosp., Balt., 1958-60; med. resident, chief resident Meml. Sloan-Kettering Cancer Ctr., N.Y.C., 1960-62; staff assoc. Nat. Cancer Inst., Bethesda, Md., 1962-65, assoc. chief, 1966-75, chief environ. epidemiology br., 1975-82, dir. epidemiology & biostats. program, 1979-95, dir. epidemiology & genetics divsn., 1995—. Attending physician Clin. Ctr. NIH, Bethesda, Md., 1966—; adj. prof. epidemiology Uniformed Svcs. U., Bethesda, 1985—, Harvard U. Sch. Pub. Health, Boston, 1993—, George Washington U. Med. Ctr., 1997—. Mem. editl. bd.: more than a dozen med. and sci. jours.; contbr. chpts. to books, 750 articles to profl. jours. Recipient Disting. Svc. medal, USPHS, 1983, Gorgas medal, Assn. Mil. Surgeons U.S., 1989, W.W. Sutow award, U. Tex. M.D. Anderson Cancer Ctr., 1992, Disting. Alumnus award, Duke U. Med. Ctr., 1992, Alumni Award of Merit, Harvard Sch. Pub. Health, 1993, Wick Williams Meml. award, Fox Chase Cancer Ctr., 1993, Dir.'s award, NIH, 1994, Charles Mott prize, GM Cancer Rsch. Found., 1995, John Snow award, APHA, 1995, Selikoff award, Ramazzini Inst., 1996, Robert S. Gordon award, NIH, 1996, Dr. Nathan Davis award, AMA, 2002, Alton Ochsner award relating smoking and health, Am. Coll. Chest Physicians, 2002. Fellow: ACP (James D. Bruce Meml. award 1997), AAAS, Am. Coll. Preventive Medicine, Am. Coll. Epidemiology (bd. dirs. 1985—89, Abraham Lilienfeld award 1993, hon. fellow 1998); mem.: NAS, Assn. Am. Physicians, Am. Assn. Cancer Rsch. (bd. dirs. 1983—87, Am. Cancer Soc. award rsch. excellence epidemiology, prevention 1993), Am. Soc. Preventive Oncology (pres. 1981—83, Disting. Achievement award 1993), Inst. Medicine. Office: Nat Cancer Inst EPS/8070 Div Cancer Epidemology & Genetics Executive Plz S Rm 8070 Bethesda MD 20892-7242

FRAUNFELDER, FREDERICK THEODORE, ophthalmologist, educator; b. Pasadena, Calif., Aug. 16, 1934; s. Reinhart and Freida Fraunfelder; m. Yvonne Marie Halliday, June 21, 1959; children— Yvette Marie, Helene, Nina, Frederick, Nicholas. BS, U. Oreg., 1956, MD, 1960, postgrad. (NIH postdoctoral fellow), 1962. Diplomate Am. Bd. Ophthalmology (bd. dirs. 1982-90). Intern U. Chgo., 1961; resident U. Oreg. Med. Sch., 1964-66; NIH postdoctoral fellow Wilmer Eye Inst., Johns Hopkins U., 1967; chmn. dept. ophthalmology U. Ark. Health Scis. Ctr., 78-98, prof., 1978—; prof., chmn. dept. ophthalmology Oreg. Health Scis. U. Dir. Casey Eye Inst., 1992-98, Nat. Registry Drug-Induced Ocular Side Effects, 1976—; vis. prof. ophthalmology Moorfields Eye Hosp., London, 1974. Author: Drug-Induced Ocular Side Effects and Drug Interactions, 1976, 5th edit., 2001, Current Ocular Therapy, 1985, 5th edit., 2001, Recent Advances in Ophthalmology, 8th edit., 1985; assoc. editor: Jour. Toxicology: Cutaneous and Ocular, 1984-2002; mem. editl. bd. Am. Jour. Ophthalmology, 1982-92, Ophthalmic Forum, 1983-90, Ophthalmology, 1984-89; contbr. over 200 articles on ocular toxicology or ocular cancer to med. jours. Served with U.S. Army, 1962-64. FDA grantee, 1976-86; Nat. Eye Inst. grantee, 1970-87. Mem. AMA, ACS, Am. Acad. Ophthaolmology, Assn. Univ. Profs. in Ophthalmology (pres. 1976), Am. Ophthalmol. Soc., Am. Coll. Cryosurgery (pres. 1977), Assn. Research in Ophthalmology. Clubs: Lions, Elks. Home: 13 Cellini Ct Lake Oswego OR 97035-1307 Office: Casey Eye Inst 3375 SW Terwilliger Blvd Portland OR 97201-4197 Office Phone: 503-494-5686. Business E-Mail: fraunfel@ohsu.edu.

FRAUTSCHI, STEVEN CLARK, physicist, researcher; b. Madison, Wis., Dec. 6, 1933; s. Lowell Emil and Grace (Clark) F.; m. Mie Okamura, Feb. 16, 1967; children: Laura, Jennifer. BA, Harvard U., 1954; PhD, Stanford U., 1958. Rsch. fellow Kyoto (Japan) U., 1958-59, U. Calif.-Berkeley, 1959-61; mem. faculty Cornell U., 1961-62, Calif. Inst. Tech., Pasadena, 1962—, prof. theoretical physics, 1966—, exec. officer physics, 1988-97, master student houses, 1997—2002. Vis. prof. U. Paris, Orsay, 1977-78. Author: Regge Poles and S-Matrix Theory, 1963, The Mechanical Universe, 1986. Guggenheim fellow, 1971-72. Mem. Am. Phys. Soc. Achievements include research and publications on Regge poles, bootstrap theory, cosmology. Home: 1561 Crest Dr Altadena CA 91001-1838 Office: 1201 E California Blvd Pasadena CA 91125-0001

FRAUTSCHI, TIMOTHY CLARK, lawyer; b. Madison, Wis., Apr. 8, 1937; s. Lowell E. and Grace C. (Clark) F.; m. Pamela H. Hendricks, June 23, 1964; children: Schuyler, Jason; m. Susan B. Brumm, June 13, 1981; 1 child, Jacob. BA, U. Wis., 1959; LL.B., London Sch. Econs., U. Wis., 1963. Bar: Wis. 1963, U.S. Ct. Claims 1976, U.S. Tax Ct., 1976. Assoc. firm Foley & Lardner, Milw., 1963-70, ptnr., 1970—. Editor Wis. Law Rev. Co-founder Milw. Forum; pres. Lakeside Cmty. Coun., Present Music, Inc., 1991—98, Skylight Comic Opera, Ltd., 1980—85, Next Act Theatre, 2001—; bd. dirs. Am. Players Theater, Milw., Repertory Theater, Northcott Neighborhood House, United performing Arts Fund, Inc., Milw., Children's Svc. Soc., Wis. Theatre Tesseract; pres. Next Act Theatre, 1986—89, Watertower Landmark Trust, 1986—89; v.p. Frank Lloyd Wright Wis. Conservancy, 2001—; bd. dirs. St. Mary's Milw. Hosp. Found., pres., 2003—. Mem. Milw. Jr. Bar Assn. (pres. 1969-70), Milw. Bar Assn. (dir. 1971-74), Order of Coif, Phi Beta Kappa (pres. Milw. chpt. 1968-70), Phi Kappa Phi, Phi Eta Sigma Office: Foley & Lardner US Bank Ctr 777 E Wisconsin Ave Ste 3800 Milwaukee WI 53202-5367 Office Phone: 414-297-5737.

FRAWLEY, THOMAS FRANCIS, retired internist, medical educator; b. Rochester, N.Y., June 27, 1919; s. Thomas J. and Mary (Leddy) F.; m. Marigrace Cecelia Gould, Feb. 23, 1946; children: Thomas Joseph II, Colleen, Brian (dec.). AB, U. Rochester, 1941; MD, U. Buffalo, 1944. Diplomate Am. Bd. Internal Medicine, Am. Bd. Endocrinology and Metabolism. Intern St. Mary's Hosp., Rochester, 1944-45; resident Buffalo Gen. Hosp., 1945-48; research fellow Harvard Med. Sch., 1948-52; resident Peter Bent Brigham Hosp., Boston, 1948-52; chief endocrinology and metabolism Albany (N.Y.) Med. Sch., 1952-58, assoc. prof. medicine, 1952-58, prof. medicine, 1960-63; research assoc. NIH, 1958-60; prof. medicine St. Louis U. Sch. Medicine, 1963—77, chmn. dept. internal medicine, 1963-73, chmn. emeritus, 1977—; chmn. Office of Grad. Med. Edn., St. John's Mercy Med. Center, St. Louis, 1981-95; physician-in-chief St. Louis U. Hosp., 1963-73. Mem. drug efficacy study panel Nat. Acad. Scis., 1966-69; med. adv. com. Cath. Hosp. Assn., 1966-69; mem. sci. rev. com. NIH, 1970-74; commr. Joint Commn. Accreditation of Hosps., 1976—, mem. resident rev. com. Int. Medicine, 1980-82, 89-93. Author books in field.; contbr. articles to profl. jours. Served to lt., M.C. AUS, 1946-47; surgeon USPHS, 1958-60. Recipient Disting. Alumni award U. Buffalo Sch. Medicine, 1989, Health Care Ministry award Archdiocese St. Louis, 2002. Fellow ACP (gov. Mo. 1971-75, regent 1976—, pres. 1981, master 1982, Laureate award 1986, Stengel award 1993), Royal Coll. Physicians Ireland, Royal Soc. Medicine London; mem. Assn. Am. Physicians, Am. Fedn. Clin. Rsch., Endocrine Soc., Ctrl. Soc. Clin. Rsch., So. Soc. Clin. Investigation, Am. Thyroid Assn., Am. Diabetes Assn. (profl. edn. com. 1983), Am. Clin. and Climatol. Assn., St. Louis Med. Soc. (Schlueter award 1994, St. Louis Health award 2002), Sigma Xi, Alpha Omega Alpha.

FRAWLEY BAGLEY, ELIZABETH, government advisor, ambassador; b. Elmira, NY, July 13, 1952; m. Smith Bagley; 2 children. BA in French and Spanish cum laude, Regis Coll., 1974; JD in Internat. Law, Georgetown U., 1987. Staff Office Congl. Rels. Dept. State, spl. asst. to Amb. Sol Linowitz, congl. liaison Conf. on Security and Cooperation in Europe, amb. to Portugal Washington, 1993-97, US adv. commn. pub. diplomacy, 2001—. Adj. prof. law Georgetown U. Washington, 1992-94. Home: 1539 29th St NW Washington DC 20007-3061

FRAY, LIONEL LOUIS, management consultant; b. Paris, Jan. 17, 1935; came to U.S., 1942; s. Maurice and Esther Fray; m. Joanne Caroline Liberman, June 30, 1963; children: Sharon June, Elizabeth Ann. BS, MIT, 1957, MS, 1958; MBA, Harvard U., 1962. Co-founder U.S. Sonics, Inc., Cambridge, Mass., 1957-58; with Mitre Corp., Bedford, Mass., 1958-60, Mgmt. Systems Corp., 1962-64; v.p. Harbridge House, Boston, 1964-73, TBS Capital Corp., Lexington, Mass., 1973-86, Temple, Barker & Sloane, Lexington, Mass., 1973-86; pres. Lionel L. Fray Assocs., Inc., Lexington, Mass., 1986—. Bd. dirs. Am. Technion Soc.; pres., CEO, AOA Geophysics, Inc. AOA Geomarine Ops. LLC subs. Schlumberger, Inc., 2002—; co-founder, bd. dirs., Technion Inst. of Mgmt. Author: Handbook of Strategic Management, 1985, How to Develop the Strategic Plan, 1987; contbr. articles to profl. jours. Mem. Strategic Leadership Forum, Inst. Mgmt. Cons. Clubs: Harvard. Avocations: tennis, skiing, jazz violin, flying. Home: 2361A Massachusetts Ave Lexington MA 02421-6733 Office: Lionel L Fray Assoc Inc 1620 Mass Ave Lexington MA 02420-3831 Office Phone: 781-861-0222. Business E-Mail: lionel_fray@agoem.com.

FRAYN, MICHAEL, playwright; b. London, Sept. 8, 1933; s. Thomas Allen and Violet Alice (Lawson) Frayn; m. Gillian Palmer, Feb. 18, 1960 (div. 1989); 3 children; m. Claire Tomalin, June 1993. BA, Emmanuel Coll., Cambridge U., Eng., 1957. Gen. reporter Guardian, Manchester, Eng., 1957-59, columnist, 1959-62, Observer, London, 1962-68; contbr. weekly comedy series Beyond A Joke BBC, 1972. Author: (novels) The Tin Men, 1965 (Somerset Maugham award, 1966), The Russian Interpreter, 1966 (Hawthornden prize, 1967), Towards the End of the Morning (also published as Against Entropy), 1967, A Very Private Life, 1968, Sweet Dreams, 1973, The Trick of It, 1989, A Landing on the Sun, 1991 (Book of Yr., Sunday Express), Now You Know, 1993, Headlong, 1999, Spies, 2002 (Whitbread Novel award, 2002, Commonwealth Writers prize, 2003); author: (with David Burke) Celia's Secret: An Investigation, 2000; author: (plays) Zounds!, 1957, The Two of Us: Four One-Act Plays for Two Players, 1970, The Sandboy, 1971, Alphabetical Order, 1975 (Evening Standard Best Comedy of Yr. award, 1975), Donkeys' Years, 1976 (Soc. West End Best Comedy of Yr. award, 1976, Laurence Olivier award, best comedy, 1976), Clouds, 1976, Liberty Hall, 1977, Make or Break, 1980 (Evening Standard award, best comedy of yr., 1980), Balmoral, 1988, Look, Look, 1990, Jamie on a Flying Visit and Birthday, 1990, Listen to This: Twenty One Short Plays and Sketches, 1991, Here, 1993, Now You Know, 1995, Alarms and Excursions: Mores Plays Than One, 1998, (Broadway plays) Noises Off, 1983 (Evening Standard Best Comedy of Yr. award, 1982, Soc. West End Theatres Best Comedy of Yr. award, 1982), 2001, Benefactors, 1985 (Evening Standard Best Comedy of Yr. award, 1984, Soc. West End Theatres Best Comedy of Yr. award, 1984, Tony award nom., best play, 1984, Lawrence Olivier Best Play award, 1984, Plays and Players Best New Play award, 1986, NY Drama Critics' Cir. award, best play, 1986, BBC award, best new play, 1984), Wild Honey, 1986, Copenhagen, 2000 (Evening Standard award, best play of yr., 1998, Critics' Cir. award, best new play, 1998, Tony award, best play, 2000), Democracy, 2004, (opera libretto) La Belle Vivette, 1995, (documentary films, teleplays) One Pair of Eyes, 1968, Birthday, 1969, Lawrence Sterne Lived Here, 1973, Making Faces, 1975, Imagine a City Called Berlin, 1975, Vienna: The Mask of Gold, 1977, Three Streets in the Country, 1979, The Long Straight, 1980, Great Railway Journeys of the World, 1981, Jerusalem, 1984, Magic Lantern: Prague, 1993, (TV documentary) Budapest: Written in Water, 1996, (screenplays) Clockwise, 1986, First and Last, 1989 (Emmy award), Remember Me?, 1997; translator: (plays) The Cherry Orchard by Anton Chekhov, 1978, The Fruits of Enlightenment by Leo Tolstoy, 1979, Three Sisters by Anton Chekhov, 1983, Wild Honey by Anton Chekhov, 1984, The Seagull by Anton Chekhov, 1986, Uncle Vanya by Anton Chekhov, 1987, The Sneeze by Anton Chekhov, 1988, Exchange by Yuri Trifonov, 1990; author: The Day of the Dog (articles reprinted from The Guardian), 1962, The Book of the Fub (articles reprinted from The Guardian), 1963, On the Outskirts (articles reprinted from The Observer), 1964, A Bay At Gear Street, 1967, Constructions, 1974, The Original Michael Frayn: Satirical Essays, 1983, After the Beep: Studies in the Art of Communicating with Inanimate and Semi-animate Objects, 1995; editor: The Best of Beachcomber by John Bingham Morton, 1963; editor: (with Bamber Gascoigne) Timothy: The Drawings and Cartoons of Timothy Birdsall, 1964. Russian interpreter Brit. Army, 1952—54. Recipient Nat. Press Club Disting. Reporting award, Internat. Pub. Corp., 1970, Heywood Hill Literary Prize, 2002. Mem.: Royal Soc. Literature. Fluent in Russian. Office: Greene & Heaton 37 Goldhawk Rd London W12 8QQ England*

FRAZELLE, KENNETH, composer, educator; b. Jacksonville, Nc, Dec. 2, 1955; s. Kenneth and Olive Ann (Shaw) Frazelle; life ptnr. Rick Mashburn. MusB, The Juilliard Sch., N.Y., 1978. Composer N.C. Sch. Of The Arts, Winston-Salem, NC, 1987—. Composer in residence Santa Rosa Symphony, Calif., 1996—2000; vis. artist Am. Acad. in Rome, Italy; composer in residence Isabella Stewart Gardner Mus., Boston, 1997—98, LA Chamber Orch., Calif., 1998—2001; instr. of composition N.C. Sch. of the Arts, Winston-Salem, NC, 1987—. Composer: (dance score) Still/Here, (voice and piano) From the Song of Songs (Barlow Internat. Prize), Sunday at McDonald's, (violin and piano) Fiddler's Galaxy, (chamber orch./choral) The Motion of Stone, (chamber orch.) Concerto for Chamber Orchestra, (flute and piano) Blue Ridge Airs II, (voice and piano) Appalachian Songbook, (cello and piano) Goldberg Variations II Project, (string orch.) Elegy for Strings, (piano) Blue Ridge Airs I, (chamber) Sonata for Cello and Piano. Recipient Gretchaninoff Award, The Juilliard Sch., 1978, Joseph H. Bearns Prize, Columbia U., 1979, Goddard Lieberson Award for Outstanding Achievement in Composition, AAAL, 2000, Barlow Internat. Prize, Barlow Found., 2001; fellow Vis. Artist Fellowship, Am. Acad. in Rome, 1998; grantee Composition Fellowship, N.C. Arts Coun., 1989, 1997; scholar Scholarship, The Juilliard Sch., 1974-1978. Achievements include Works performed by such artists as: Yo-Yo Ma, Dawn Upshaw, Odetta, Bill T. Jones/Arnie Zane Dance Co., Jeffrey Kahane, Emmanuel Ax, LA Chamber Orch., Paula Robison, Israel Chamber Orch., others. Home: 155 Piedmont Ave Winston Salem NC 27101 Office: NC School of the Arts PO Box 12189 Winston Salem NC 27117-2189

FRAZER, DAVID HUGH, JR., allergist; b. Montgomery, Ala., Mar. 31, 1937; s. David H. and Sue Ray (Durrett) F.; m. Johnnie Bowie Swetenburg, July 5, 1941; children: David Hugh III, Bowie Swetenburg Frazer Campbell, Wills Findley. BS, Tulane U., 1958, MD, 1961. Private practice, Atlanta, 1966-67, Montgomery, 1967—. Bd. dirs. S. Ala. State Fair, Montgomery, Brantwood Children's Home, Montgomery Metro YMCA Bd. With USAF, 1962-64. Fellow Am. Coll. Allergy and Immunology; mem. Am. Acad. Allergy and Immunology, Montgomery Kiwanis Club (bd. dirs.). Republican. Presbyterian. Office: 1420 Narrow Lane Pky Montgomery AL 36111-2654

FRAZER, JENDAYI ELIZABETH, federal agency administrator, former ambassador; BA political sci., MA internat. policy/internat. devel., PhD political sci., Stanford U. Fellow Coun. Foreign Relations Internat. Affairs, 1998-99; asst. prof. pub. policy, John F. Kennedy Sch. Govt. Harvard U., 1999—2001; spl. asst. to the Pres. & sr. dir. for African affairs NSC, Washington, 2001—04; US amb to South Africa US Dept. State, Pretoria, 2004—05, asst. sec. for African Affairs Washington, 2005—. Vis. fellow Ctr. Internat. Security and Arms Control, Stanford U.; rsch. assoc. Inst. Devel. Studies, U. Nairobi, Kenya. Mem. Women in Internat. Soc. (exec. bd. 1998—). Office: US Dept State 2201 C St NW Rm 6234A Washington DC 20520*

FRAZER, JOHN HOWARD, tennis association executive, retired manufacturing executive; b. Cin., June 3, 1924; s. H. Howard and Amelia (Spieth) F.; m. Joann Elizabeth McEvoy, Nov. 3, 1956; children: John Howard Jr., Victoria F. Fuller. BA, U. Cin., 1948, JD, 1950. Bar: Ohio 1950. V.p. H. Howard Frazer Co., Cin., 1950-62, pres., 1962-76; treas., dir. Cin. Transit Co., 1957-73; dir. Am. Controlled Industries, Cin., 1973-86, pres., 1974-75, exec. v.p., 1975-86; dir. Vulcan Corp., Cin., 1960-91, pres., 1975-88; sec., dir. Valley Industries, 1973-86, Colorpac, Inc., 1973-86. Chmn. U.S. Open Tennis Championships, 1993-94. Chmn. men's com. Cin. Symphony Orch., 1971-73; pres. Cincinnatus Assn., 1969-70; chmn. Western Tennis Championships, Cin., 1970-73; dir. Internat. Tennis Hall of Fame, 1979-2002, hon. dir., 2002—, exec. com. 1985-2002, chmn. internat. coun. 1996—. Served with USAAF, 1942-45. Named to Greater Cin. Tennis Hall Fame, 2004; recipient Highest Effort award, Sigma Alpha Epsilon, 1995, Chmn.'s award, Internat. Tennis Hall of Fame, 2000, induction into USTA/Midwest Tennis Hall of Fame, 2001, Golden Achievement award, Tennis Hall of Fame, 2003. Mem. USTA (mem. exec. com. 1975—, chmn. sanction and schedule com. 1973-86, bd. dirs. 1986-96, v.p. 1986-88, sec. 1988-90, 1st v.p. 1990-92, pres. 1993-94, chmn. nat. men's ranking com. 1971-73, long-range planning com. 1981-87, internat. com. 1999—, hon. chair 2003—), Internat. Tennis Fedn. (del. 1991-96, mem. com. mgmt. 1993-97, v.p. 1995-97, hon. life counsellor 1997—, mem. vets. com. 1996-99, chmn. vets. com. 1996-97, mem. constl. com. 1997-2003, mem. PILA com. 2000--, Svc. to the Game award 1998), Lawn Tennis Clubs of USA, France, Mex., Am. Footwear Industries Assn. (dir.), Rubber Mfrs. Assn. (dir.), Shoe Last Mfrs. Assn. (pres. 1978-79), Univ. Club, Cin. C.C., Cin. Tennis Club, Quail Creek C.C., (Naples), Bay Colony Club (Naples), All-Eng. Lawn Tennis Club (Wimbledon), Royal Poinciana Golf Club (Naples). Home: 8171 Bay Colony Dr Apt 1701 Naples FL 34108-7566 Personal E-mail: joandbumpyfrazer@att.net.

FRAZER, ROBERT LEE, retired landscape architect; BS in Landscape Architecture, Tex. A&M U., 1948; MS in Agriculture, East Tex. State U., 1951. Registered landscape architect, Tex. Landscape architect, instr. vocat. horticulture San Antonio Sch. Dist., 1948-49; landscape architect, instr., head campus maintenance East Tex. State U., Commerce, 1949-54; dir. parks and recreation City of San Antonio, 1955-73; univ. landscape architect, prof. landscape architecture Tex. Tech. U., Lubbock, 1973-74; v.p., prin., dir. landscape architecture Groves Fernandez Frazer & Assocs., Inc., San Antonio, 1974-83, Fernandez Frazer White & Assocs., Inc., San Antonio, 1984-92, v.p. emeritus, 1992—. Adj. prof. U. Tex., Arlington, 1993. Contbr. articles to profl. jours. Recipient Robert H. Hugman award for devel. San Antonio River Walk, 1987, Disting. Svc. award San Antonio Conservation Soc., 1973. Fellow Am. Soc. Landscape Architects (Terry Hershey award for Excellence in Field of Recreation Parks or Tourism), Am. Inst. Park Execs., Am. Acad. for Park and Recreation Adminstrn., Tex. Recreation and Park Soc.; mem. S.W. Park and Recreation Tng. Inst. (past pres., co-organizer), Tex. Mcpl. Park and Recreation Assn. (past pres., organizer), Tex. Turfgrass Assn. (past pres., co-organizer), Nat. River Parks and Waterfront Assn. (past bd. dirs.), Nat. Recreation Assn. (past mem. nat. adv. com.). Office: Fernandez Frazer White & Assoc 11824 Radium St San Antonio TX 78216-2711 Personal E-mail: ffw@ffwinc.com.

FRAZIER, AMY, professional tennis player; b. St. Louis, Mo., Sept. 19, 1972; Prof. tennis player WTA Tour, 1990—. Mem. 1995 U.S. Fed. Cup Team. Named World Team Tennis MVP, 1995. Achievements include winner 7 career Singles Titles and 5 career Doubles Titles, WTA Tour; appeared in 18 consecutive U.S. Open Tournaments. Avocations: ceramics, painting, bicycling. Office: USTA 70 W Red Oak Ln White Plains NY 10604-3602

FRAZIER, ANTHANY VINCENT EARL, addictions, small business, and technology specialist; b. Chgo., May 16, 1951; s. Sidney S. and RoxieMaria (McNutt) F.; m. Ruth Mary Fairfax, Jan. 12, 1970; children: Annika S. Frazier Muhammad, Darrius R. BA, Chgo. State U., 1977; Cert., Congl. Rsch. Svc. Libr. of Congress, 1990; Cert. internat. trade exec. prog., U. Ill., Ill. World Trade Ctr., 1991; Cert. internat. trade prog., DePaul U., 1991; Cert. of Completion, Dartmouth Coll., 1992; MA, Govs. State U., 1993; Cert. law prog. cmty. developers and social workers, John Marshall Law Sch., 1996; Cert. of Completion, MIT, 1997. Cert. CPR specialist ARC, cert. profl. educator, Ill, Cert. of Completion, Mental Health: Alcoholism and Substance Abuse Counseling, Harold Washington Coll., Chgo., Ill., 2002. Exec. dir. South Shore Caucus Legis. and Cmty. Action., Chgo., 1979-81; grad. tchr. Govs. State U., Park Forest, Ill., 1982; adj. cmty. prof., grad. tchg. asst. Roosevelt U., Chgo., 1982; adminstrv. asst. Hon. Timothy C. Evans, Chief Judge, Cir. Ct. Cook COunty, former 4th Ward Alderman and Committeeman, Chgo., 1982-83; staff asst., legis. aide U.S. Senator Alan J. Dixon (Democrat-Ill.), Washington, 1983-86; fed. grants, contracts mgr. U.S. Rep. Charles A. Hayes (Democrat-Ill.), Chgo., 1987-92; congressional liason First Congressional District of Ill housing and small business task forces, 1987—92; social security ins. specialist, mem. Spkr.'s and Cmty. Outreach Bur. Social Security Adminstrn., Chgo., 1993—; vol. mgmt. cons., trainer AVEF Vol. Mgmt. Cons. and Trainer, Chgo., 1992—; aging specialist and mem. Ill. Coun. on Aging, Gubernatorial Reappointment by the Honorable George H. Ryan State of Ill., 2000—. Chmn. econ. devel. subcom. Cmty. Devel. Adv. Com., Richard M. Daley, Mayor, City of Chgo., 1987-93; mgmt. cons., trainer Minority Bus. Resource Adv. Com., NASA, Washington, 1992-96 (mem., chmn. technology-transfer rsch. and devel. and physically-disabled applications subcom., 1992-96); parlimentarian Black affairs adv. com. Soc. Security Adminstrn., 1993-1994; spkr. in field. Co-author: The Changing Economic Standing of Minorities in the Chicago Metropolitan Area, 1992, Chgo. Housing Authority Memorandum of Accord Legal Agreement, 1985-1986; Contbr. articles to profl. jours; television documentary, Second Summit for Fair Housing, 1987. Mem. affirmitive action com. Dem. Party Ill., Dem. Nat. Conv., 1992; vol. fundaiser, spkr. Combined Fed. Campaign, 1996, CARE, (ctrl. region), 1996—, Chgo. Fed. Exec. Bd., 1996, Internat. Svc. Agencies, 1999—; pres. Sunshine Club, Chgo., 1999—, Chgo. East Field Office, Social Security Adminstrn., 1999-2000. Recipient Certificate of Jury Svc. State of Ill., Circuit Court of Cook County, 1997, Meritorious Citation Combined Fed. Campaign Chgo. Fed. Exec. Bd., 1996, Small Business Advocacy award Grant Thornton, Inc., 1989, Homeless Network and Provider award Bur. of the Census U.S. Dept. of Commerce, 1989, Outstanding Achievement award for Vol. Svc. Soft Sheen Products, 1987, Cert. Appreciation Spl. Recognition for Outstanding Pub. Svc. U.S. Rep. Charles A. Hayes, 1993, NASA Minority Bus. Adv. Com., 1997, Pub. Employees Roundtable Pres.'s Intragency Coun. on Adminstrv. Mgmt., 2000; Named Perfect Resource Person Dearborn Homes Resident Mgmt. Corp. Chgo. Housing Authority, 1988, one of Outstanding Young Men of Am., 1990; Ill. Gen. Assembly scholar, Springfield, Ill., 1970; mem. nom. com. Outstanding Young Women of Am. award, 1997. Mem. Am. Fedn. Govt. Employees, Nat. Acad. Recording Arts and Scis., Latin Recording Acad., Hyde Park Coop. Soc., Lakefront Properties Housing Task Force, Acad. Country Music. Democrat. Baptist. Avocations:

music, outdoorsman, writing, volunteering, spiritual consultant. Home and Office: AVEF Vol Mgmt Cons and Trainers 5521 S Everett Ave Ste B Chicago IL 60637-1956 E-mail: avefraz@aol.com.

FRAZIER, CHARLES ROBINSON, writer; b. Asheville, N.C., Nov. 4, 1950; s. Charles O. and Betty Frazier; m. Katherine Frazier, 1976; 1 child, Annie. BA, U. N.C., 1973; student, Appalachian State U.; PhD, U. S.C., 1986. Co-author: Adventuring in the Andes: The Sierra Club Guide to Peru, Bolivia, the Amazon Basin, and the Galapagos, 1985; author: Cold Mountain, 1997 (Nat. Book award Nat. Book Found., 1997). Office: Amanda Urban Internat Creative Management Inc 40 West 57th St New York NY 10019

FRAZIER, DOUGLAS ALMEDA MCREE, volunteer, former energy facility analyst; b. Soddy, Tenn., Feb. 6, 1923; d. Clarence Douglas and Nannie (Eldridge) McRee; m. Earl Lee Frazier, Aug. 25, 1963. BA, U. Chattanooga, 1944, B of Music, 1949, MEd, 1958. Various positions TVA, Chattanooga, power supply analyst, 1945-87. Vol. for TVA retirees, Chattanooga Visitors Ctr., Chattanooga Health Coun.; mem. Adult Edn. Coun., Chattanooga Employees Recreation Assn., Sr. Neighbors Orch., Chattanooga, 1990—, v.p. Ret. Sr. Vol. Program; organist, pianist Soddy United Meth. Ch.; past sec. Soddy-Daisy H.S. Alumni Assn.; life mem. First Presbyn. Ch.resbyn. Ch. Grand Organist, O.E.S., Tennessee, 1999—; Listed in 1st Families Tenn., 1996. Mem. AAUW (life; past pres., Names Gift award 1965), AARP (past pres., Cmty. Citizen award), DAR, East Tenn. Hist. Soc., Chattanooga Engrs. Club (past. sec., v.p., pres., People-to-People award 1989), U. Chattanooga Alumni Coun., Soddy C. of C., Soddy Lioness Club, Order of Eastern Star (past matron, grand rep. 1965-67, grand rep. Tenn. 1996, 97, grand organist 1999), Soddy High Alumni Assn. (past sec., past pres.), Pilot Club of Chattanooga. Life-long mem. of the First Presbyterian Church of Soddy, Tennessee. Home: 11313 Hixson Pike Soddy Daisy TN 37379-6371 Address: PO Box 223 Soddy Daisy TN 37384-0223

FRAZIER, HENRY BOWEN, III, retired federal agency administrator; b. Bluefield, W.Va., Aug. 9, 1934; s. Henry Bowen and Margaret Beale (West) F.; m. Joan McIntosh, Dec. 30, 1959. BA with honors, U. Va., 1956; JD with honors, George Washington U., 1967; LLM in Labor Law, Georgetown U., 1969, MLT, 1985. Bar: Va. 1967, D.C. 1980, U.S. Supreme Ct. Pers. adminstr. Army Dept. Washington, 1959-63, spl. projects officer, 1963-67; dep. for civilian pers. policy and civil rights Office Sec. Army, 1967-70; chief program divsn. Fed. Labor Rels. Coun., Exec. Office Pres., 1970-71, dep. exec. dir., 1971-72, exec. dir., 1973-78; mem. Fed. Labor Rels. Authority, Washington, 1979-87, acting chmn., 1984-85; adminstrv. law judge EPA, Washington, 1987-89, chief adminstrv. law judge, 1990-94. Chmn. Employee Relations Commn., U.S. Fgn. Service, 1979-81; acting chmn. Fgn. Service Labor Relations Bd., 1984-85 With USAF, 1961-62. Mem. SAR, Fed. Adminstrv. Law Judges Conf., Jefferson Soc., U. Va. Alumni Assn. (nat. v.p. 1984-85, nat. pres. 1985-86, bd. mgrs. 1980-87), Va. Student Aid Found. (trustee 1990-97, v.p. 1995, pres. 1996), U. Va. Athletic Adv. Coun., Raven Soc., Order of Coif, Colonnade Club (bd. govs. 1997-2000), Glenmore Country Club, Duck Woods Country Club, First Flight Soc. (bd. dirs., 2002-, treas., 2003-), Phi Beta Kappa, Omicron Delta Kappa, Phi Kappa Psi.

FRAZIER, JO FRANCES, religious organization administrator, writer; b. Tulsa, Dec. 20, 1928; d. Joseph and Eva Mae Fulcher; m. Chester Jerome Frazier, July 19, 1950; children: David, Linda Frazier Parizo, Susan Frazier Kelly. Student, Duke U., 1946—49; BA, Tulsa U., 1950. Publicity chmn. Ventura (Calif.) County Mental Health Adv. Bd., 1978—81; adv. bd. mem. Charter Hosp. Bd. Trustees, Bakersfield, Calif., 1983—85, Desert Counseling Ctr., Bakersfield, 1983—85; founder, dir. Saints Alive Ministry, Bakersfield, 1995—. Lectr./spkr. in field. Prodr.: (films) Any One of Us, 1980, (video) Saints Alive Ministry, 1999; author: Second Chance, 1987, Saints for Today's Youth, Books 1, 2 and 3, 1995—2002, (children's book) Saint Thérèse of the Child Jesus, Joan of Arc, Francis of Assisi, Martin de Porres, Blessed Kateri Tekakwitha, others. Mem.: Audobon Soc., Nature Conservancy, World Wildlife Fund, Italian Cath. Fedn. (sec. 1984—86). Avocations: swimming, reading. Home and Office: Saints Alive Ministry 4707 Mount Hood Dr Bakersfield CA 93309 Office Phone: 661-398-8575.

FRAZIER, JOHN M., music educator, musician; s. George and Nancy Mae Herr Frazier; m. Ruth Elaine Sassaman Wright (div.); children: Madeleine Rose, John Thomas 1 stepchild, Griffin Wright. MusB, New Sch. Music, Phila., 1987; diploma, St. Louis Conservatory Music, 1988; MusM, Temple U., 1994. Cert. instructional music Pa. Clarinet, saxophone instr. Settlement Music Sch., Phila., 1989—96; instrumental music tchr. Instrumental Music Program, Wilmington, Del., 2001—04, Phila. Sch. Dist., 2004—. Prin. clarinetist Maddenfield (N.J.) Symphony, 1990—93; substitute clarinetist Harrisburg (Pa.) Symphony, 1995—99, Dela. Symphony, Wilmington, 1995—99; adj. prof. Temple U., Phila., 1999, Urinus Coll., 2000. Recipient Eagle Scout award, Boy Scouts Am. Mem.: Am. Fedn. Musicians. Democrat. Espiscopalian.

FRAZIER, KENNETH C., pharmaceutical executive, lawyer; b. Phila., Dec. 17, 1954; m. Andrea Frazier; 2 children. BA in Polit. Sci., Pa. State U., 1975; JD, Harvard U., 1978. Bar: Pa. 1978, U.S. Dist. Ct. (ea. dist.) Pa. 1978, U.S. Supreme Ct. 2002. Ptnr. dept. litigation Drinker Biddle & Reath, 1978—92; v.p., gen. counsel, sec. Astra Merck, 1992—94; v.p. pub. affairs Merck & Co., Inc., 1994—96, v.p. pub. affairs, asst. gen. counsel, 1997—98, v.p., dep. gen. counsel, 1999, sr. v.p., gen. counsel Whitehouse Sta., NJ, 1999—. Bd. dirs. Cornerstone Christian Acad., Legal Svcs. N.J.; chmn. Ethics Resource Ctr.; mem. adv. bd. Law and Econ. Ctr., U. Pa.; mem. adv. bd. Health Law and Policy Ctr., Seton Hall U.; mem. adv. bd. Rand Inst. for Civil Justice, CorporateProBono.Org; mem. Corp. Exec. Bd.'s Gen. Counsel Roundtable; mem. CLO Roundtable-U.S., Coun. on Fgn. Rels. Named to Am. Law Inst. Coun., 2003. Mem.: ABA, Am. Law Inst., Pa. Bar Assn. Office: Merck and Co Inc One Merck Dr Whitehouse Station NJ 08889-0100

FRAZIER, LEROY See DYYON, MARIO

FRAZIER, MARIE DUNN, speech professional, public relations executive, personnel director; b. Milton, Mass., Oct. 26, 1932; d. Lawrence Daniel and Margaret Ethel (Henry) D.; m. M. Timothy Sullivan, Apr. 17, 1960 (div. 1974); 1 child, M. Timothy Dunn Sullivan; m. John Robinson Frazier, Aug. 28, 1975. BA, Emerson Coll., 1954, MA, 1958. Cert. tchr., Mass. Mng. theater dir. Peabody Playhouse, Boston, 1955-60; dir. alumni rels. Emerson Coll., Boston, 1971-73; dir. activities, personal devel. faculty Katharine Gibbs, Boston, 1974-78; dir. rsch. and devel. Aquinas Coll., Milton, Mass., 1981-82; dir. cmty. rels. Bryman Sch., Brookline, Mass., 1981-84; resource developer Quincy (Mass.) Cmty. Action, 1987-89; adjunct faculty, lead program Eastern Nazarene Coll., Quincy, Mass., 1993-98. Adv. bd. Ctr. Lifelong Learning, Curry Coll., Milton, 1977; tng. in speech comm. for Digital Corp., Am. Sci. and Engring. Co., Gen. Time and Security Corp., Children's Hosp., Milton Savs. Bank; mem. speech comm. faculty Garland Jr. Coll., Boston, 1967-70, Aquinas Coll., Newton, Mass., 1991. Developed (seminar) Reflections on Tea, 1993. Bd. dirs. ACCLAIM Arts Group, Milton, 1989, D.W. Dunn Co., Jamaica Plain, Mass., 1962-65, Milton Hist. Soc., 1990-92, Coastline Coun. for Children, 1987; mem. bd. Mayor's Commn. for Women, Quincy, 1988-2003; ambassador South Shore C. of C., Quincy, 1990—. Mem. AAUP, Zeta Phi Eta. Home: 25 Whitelawn Ave Milton MA 02186-3514

FRAZIER, MARK WILLIAM, musician, educator; b. Bartlesville, Okla., Aug. 14, 1959; s. Robert William and Angelene Marie Frazier. MusB, Coll. Wooster, 1981; MusM, U. Iowa, 1990. Asst. musical dir. 1st Presbyn. Ch., Wooster, Ohio, 1981—83; dir. music ministries Chestnut St. United Meth. Ch., Lumberton, NC, 1985—87, 1997—, 2d Presbyn. Ch., Portsmouth, Ohio, 1990—91, Trinity Episcopal Ch., Arlington, Va., 1991—97; dir. music 1st Bapt. Ch., Marion, Iowa, 1988—90; instr. music appreciation U. N.C., Pembroke, NC, 2001—. Composer: Sonata for Spring, 1976, Jubilate Deo, 1980, Andante Cantable, 1982, (commd. work) The Weaver, 1985, The Great Commission, 1999. Accompanist to Ms. Kathleen Battle Solo County Pub. Schs. Program, Portsmouth, 1991; vol. Robeson County Ch. and Cmty. Ctr., Lumberton, 2000—02, 2004; bd. dirs., chair pers. Carolina Civic Ctr., Lumberton, 2002—04; v.p. Fellowship United Meths. Music and Worship Arts, NC, 2000—03. Mem.: Am. Guild Organists (dean Cape Fear chpt. 1998—99). Avocations: photography, web design, aural recording. Home: 809 Barker Ten Mile Rd Apt #6 Lumberton NC 28358 Office: Chestnut St United Meth Ch 2000 E 8th St Lumberton NC 28358

FRAZIER, MARY ANN, artist; b. Tulsa, Okla., Sept. 11, 1937; d. Dolphus Leonard and Elouise (Reedy) Cagle; m. Robert E. Frazier, May 14, 1954 (div. Mar. 1971); children: Robert E. Frazier, Jr. (dec.), Robbyne Elisa. Student, Tulsa C.C., 1990-92; studied with numerous artists, including, David Leffel, Ben Konis, Doug Dawson, William Herring, Mary Russell, Del Gish, others. Oil portrait David Moss, David L. Moss Correctional Ctr., Tulsa; permanent collections of portrait and other paintings in pub. and pvt. collections throughout the U.S. Home: 3338 E 27th Pl Tulsa OK 74114-5910 Office Phone: 918-742-5420.

FRAZIER, PAUL IGNATIUS, marketing professional; b. Mt. Vernon, N.Y., June 22, 1962; s. George James and Dolores Fox F.; m. Eileen Sophie Morris, Apr. 15, 1994 (div. Nov. 1998); m. Dorian Hughes, Dec. 4, 1999; 1 child, Justin James. BS in Econs., Strayer U., 1999. Specialist Merrill Lynch Mortgage Capital, N.Y.C., 1988-91; mktg. mgr. Reuters Am., Inc., N.Y.C., 1992-97; v.p. mktg. & bus. devel. Applix, Inc., Westboro, Mass., 1998-99; chief tech. officer Spatial Techs. Industry Assocs., Washington, 1998-2000; v.p. mktg. Infovista Corp., Columbia, Mo., 2000—. Dir. tech. com. GWB Network, Washington, 1999-2000. Inventor in field. Mem. Rep. Nat. Com., Washington, 1990—. Mem. SAR. Roman Catholic. Office: Infovista Corp 12950 Worldgate Dr 4th Fl Herndon VA 20170 E-mail: paul@intervaluary.com.

FRAZIER, RONALD F., museum administrator; b. Braintree, Mass. s. Bernard E and Lucille Frazier; m. Mary Small Frazier, June 29, 1968; children: R Forrest J II, Sarah Anne. AS with honors, Quincy Coll., 1973; BA, Del. State U. Gen. mgr. South Shore C. of C., 1973—83; CEO Builders Assn. of Greater Boston, 1982—90; cons. Frazier Cons., 1990—93; CEO Dedham Hist. Soc., 1993—. Contbr. articles to profl. jours. Town mtg. mem. Braintree Town, 1978—; chmn. Braintree Hist. Commn.; mem. Braintree Men's Club, 1975—, Friends of Thayer Pub. Libr., 1974—. AIC USAF, 1960—64, US, Europe, Vietnam. Recipient Gilbert L. Bean award, Braintree Hist. Soc., 1986; fellow, Mass. Hist. Soc., 2003. Mem.: Acadian Genealogy Exchange, Am. Legion, Acadian Cultural Soc. (life), Wedgwood Soc. of Boston (life; pres.). Independent. Roman Cath. Avocations: ceramics, genealogy, historic preservation. Office: Dedham Hist Soc P O Box 215 Dedham MA 02027 Business E-Mail: frazier@dedhamhistorical.org.

FRAZIER, SHERVERT HUGHES, JR., psychiatrist, educator; b. Shreveport, La., June 12, 1921; s. Shervert Hughes and Mary (Lowman) F.; m. Gloria Barger, July 20, 1947; children: Elise, Alan, Rosalie, Stephen. Student, Baylor U., 1936-39; BS, U. Ill., Chgo., 1941, MD, 1943; D.Sc. (hon.), U. Ill., 1986; MS in Psychiatry, U. Minn., 1957; cert. psychoanalytic medicine, Columbia Coll. Physicians and Surgeons, 1963; MA (hon.), Harvard U., 1972. Diplomate: Am. Bd. Psychiatry and Neurology (dir. 1965, pres. 1972), Am. Bd. Family Practice (by-laws com. 1979-80, exam. com. 1979-86, research and devel. com. 1979-80, chmn. patient mgmt. problem panel). Intern U. Ill. Research and Ednl. Hosp., 1943-44; fellow internal medicine Mayo Found., 1951-52, fellow psychiatry, asst. to staff, 1954-56; pvt. practice Harrisburg, Ill., 1946-50, 53; adminstr. Harrisburg Med. Found., 1948-51; cons. sect. psychiatry Mayo Clinic, St. Marys Hosp., also Meth. Hosp., Rochester, Minn., 1956-58; chief research scientist internal medicine N.Y. State Psychiat. Inst., 1958-61, dep. dir., 1968-72; asst. attending psychiatrist Presbyn. Hosp., N.Y.C., 1958-63; dir. inpatient cons. service in psychiatry, 1961-62; later attending psychiatrist; dir. Houston Psychiat. Inst., 1962-65; psychiatrist in chief Ben Taub Gen. Hosp., Houston, 1962-68; cons. VA Hosp., Houston, 1962-68; sr. attending psychiatrist Meth. Hosp., Houston, 1962-68; chief exec. officer, psychiatrist-in-chief McLean Hosp., Belmont, Mass., 1972-84; dir. NIMH Rockville, Md., 1984-86; gen. dir., psychiatrist-in-chief McLean Hosp., 1986-88; assoc. in psychiatry Columbia Coll. Phys. and Surg., Joske asst. prof. psychiatry, 1958-62, prof., 1968-72; prof. psychiatry, chmn. dept. Baylor U. Coll. Medicine, 1962-68; prof. psychiatry Harvard, Boston, 1972—. Cons. Rice U., 1963-68; commr. Mental Health and Mental Retardation for Tex., 1965-67; pres. VI World Congress Psychiatry; mem. vis. com. Yale U. Med. Sch., 1977-81 Contbr. numerous articles to profl. jours. Served as officer, M.C. USNR, 1944-46, PTO. Recipient disting. alumnus award Mayo Found., 1983; Menninger award ACP, 1986 Fellow N.Y. Acad. Medicine (chmn. Salmon lecture com., trustee, mem. coun. 1987—); mem. AMA (council continuing physician edn. 1976-81), Mass. Med. Assn., Middlesex County Med. Soc., Am. Coll. Psychiatrists (regent 1972, v.p. 1977-79, pres. 1979-81), Am. Psychiat. Assn. (chmn. program com. 1965-68, chmn. joint commn. pub. affairs, sec. 1983-85), World Psychiat. Assn. (v.p. 1977-84), Central Neuropsychiat. Assn., Assn. Research Nervous and Mental Disease (pres. 1972, chmn. bd. 1976-78), Boston Psychoanalytic Soc. and Inst., Sigma Xi, Alpha Omega Alpha. Home: PO Box 79215 Waverley MA 02479-0215 Office: 115 Mill St Belmont MA 02478-1041

FRAZIER, STEVEN CARL, lawyer; b. Kingsport, Tenn., Jan. 8, 1954; s. Carl Dexter and Jean (Winegar) F.; divorced; children: John Carl, Jacob Steven. BS, U. Tenn., 1976, JD, 1979. Bar: Tenn. 1980. Sole practice, Church Hill, Tenn., 1980-82; ptnr. Frazier & Faulk, Church Hill, 1982-83; appeals referee dept. employment sec. State of Tenn., Kingsport, 1983; sole practice Church Hill, Tenn., 1983—. Intern Senator Bill Brock, 1975; atty. City of Mt. Carmel, Tenn., 1986-88; chmn. Foster Care Rev. Bd., Rogersville, Tenn., 1981-85; city judge Town of Church Hill, 1988—. Parlimentarian Hawkins County Young Reps., Rogersville, 1986; deacon First Bapt. Ch., Church Hill. Named one of Outstanding Young Men Am., 1982, 84. Mem. ABA, Tenn. Bar Assn., Hawkins County Bar Assn., Kingsport Bar Assn., Church Hill Jaycees (pres. 1984-86), Gideons Internat., Tenn. Capital Club, Kiwanis (pres. 1983-84, 88-89, 96-97), East Hawkins C. of C. (sec. 1994-95). Baptist. Home and Office: PO Box 1208 Church Hill TN 37642-1208

FRAZIER, WALTER, JR., (CLYDE FRAZIER), radio announcer, television analyst, retired professional basketball player; b. Atlanta, Mar. 29, 1945; Student, So. Ill. U., 1963-67. Basketball player N.Y. Knicks, 1967-77, Cleve. Cavaliers, 1977-79; radio announcer, analyst Sta. WFAN, N.Y.C. Mem. All-NBA First Team, 1970, 72, 74-75, All-NBA Second Team, 1971-73, NBA All-Defensive First Team 1969-75, NBA All-Rookie Team, 1968, NBA All-Star MVP, 1975, NBA Championship Teams, 1970, 73; inducted into Naismith Meml. Basketball Hall of Fame, 1986. also: MSG Network c/o Broadcast Dir 2 Penn Plz New York NY 10121-0101

FRAZIER, WALTER RONALD, real estate investment company executive; b. Mar. 3, 1939; s. Walter and Gracie Neydene (Bowers) F.; m. Bertina Jan Simpson, May 10, 1963; children: Ronald Blake, Stephen Bertram. BSCE, BS in Archtl. Constrn., Tex. A&M U., 1962. Tech. dir. Marble Inst., Washington, 1965-68; dir. mktg. Yeonas Co., Vienna, Va., 1969-72; pres. McCarthy Co., Anaheim, Calif., 1972-76; chmn. Equity Programs Investment Corp., Falls Church, Va., 1980-85; pres., dir. Cmty. Constrn. Co., Falls Church, 1982-85; pres. Palestrina Corp., Falls Church, 1987-99; prin. The Williamson Group, 1999—. Bd. dirs. Annandale Jaycees, 1967-69, Annandale Nat. Little League, 1983-85. 1st lt. U.S. Army, 1963-65. Named as one of Outstanding Young Men of Am., U.S. Jaycees, 1973. Mem. Nat. Assn. Home Builders (bd. dirs. 1991-96), No. Va. Bldg. Industry Assn. (1st v.p., bd. dirs. 1991-95, pres. 1994), Prince William County C. of C. (pres. bd. dirs. 1989-92). Republican. Methodist. Avocations: golf, boating. Home: 4203 Elizabeth Ln Annandale VA 22003-3668 Office: The Williamson Group 1700 Rockville Pike Ste 440 Rockville MD 20852 Office Phone: 240-290-0800. Personal E-mail: ron.frazier@cox.net.

FRAZIER, WILLIAM SUMPTER, lawyer, pharmacist; b. Mexia, Tex., Aug. 8, 1941; s. William Sumpter and Johnnie Ione (Archer) F.; m. Carolyn Casey, July 26, 1946; children: Casey Rene, Kelley Shea. AA with honors, Navarro Jr. Coll.; BS in Pharmacy, U. Tex.; JD with honors, South Tex. Coll. Law. Bar: Tex. 1972, U.S. Dist. Ct. (so. dist.) Fla. 1982, U.S. Supreme Ct. 1973. Pharmacist Tidelands Hosp., Channelview, Tex., 1967-69; chief pharmacist San Jacinto Meth. Hosp., Baytown, Tex., 1969-71; sole practice law Houston, 1971—. Mem. ABA, Tex. Bar Assn., Tex. Pharm. Assn., Am. Pharm. Assn. Mem. Ch. of Christ. Home: 27127 Glencreek Dr Huffman TX 77336-3712 Office: PO Box 968 Huffman TX 77336

FRAZZETTA, THOMAS HENRY, evolutionary biologist, educator; b. Rochester, N.Y., May 13, 1934; s. Joseph H. and Louise V. (Cross) F. BS, Cornell U., 1957; PhD, U. Wash., 1964. Instr. in zoology U. Wash., Seattle, 1963-64; assoc. in herpetology Harvard U., Cambridge, Mass., 1964-65; asst. prof. U. Ill., Urbana, 1965-71, assoc. prof., 1971-76, prof. dept. ecology, ethology, evolution, 1976—. Author: Complex Adaptations in Evolving Populations, 1975; contbr. articles to jours. Active ACLU, World Wildlife Fedn., Planned Parenthood Fedn. Am., Zero Population Growth, Amnesty Internat. NIH postdoctoral fellow, 1964; NSF research grantee, 1969, 77, 86. Mem. AAAS, Am. Soc. Naturalists, Soc. Study of Evolution, Am. Soc. Ichthyologists and Herpetologists, Am. Elasmobranch Soc., Soc. for Integrative and Comparative Biology. Democrat. Office: Univ Ill Dept Animal Biology 515 Morrill Hall Urbana IL 61801 Office Phone: 217-333-4199. E-mail: tomfrazz@life.uiuc.edu.

FREAR, DAVID J., broadcast executive; b. 1957; MBA, U. Michigan. Various mgmt. positions Deloitte & Touche, Transway Internat.; investment banker Credit Suisse, Bear, Stearns & Co., Inc.; CFO Millicom Inc., 1990—93; senior v.p., CFO Orion Network Systems Inc. (acquired by Loral Space & Communications Ltd.), 1993—98; independent consultant telecomm., 1998—99; exec. v.p., CFO, dir. SAVVIS Communications, Mo., 1999—2003; exec. v.p., CFO Sirius Satellite Radio, NYC, 2003—. Office: SIRIUS Satellite Radio 1221 Ave of the Americas New York NY 10020

FREAS, GEORGE WILSON, II, computer scientist, consultant; b. Franklin, Ky., Oct. 27, 1955; s. George Wilson and Audrey Carolyn Freas; m. Cynthia Anne Fleming, Feb. 19, 1984 (div. Oct. 1990); 1 child, Alexander Morange. BS in Computer Sci., Western Ky. U., 1979; MS in Computer Sci., U. Ala., Huntsville, 1994. Pres. Synergistic Cons., Inc., Huntsville, 1991—; software cons. Bell South Telecom., Birmingham, Ala., 1995-98; software cons. Boeing Internat. Space Sta. Marshall Space Flight Ctr., Ala., 1999—. Adj. prof. Am. Coll. Computer and Info. Scis., Birmingham, Ala., 1997—; guitarist Joyful Creations, 1999—. Author: Canny Canon, 1990; author: (software) GEN7 Desktop, 1993, LALL-LL(1), 1992. Home: PO Box 2885 Huntsville AL 35804-2885 Office: Synergistic Consultants Inc PO Box 18888 Huntsville AL 35804-8888 E-mail: marquis@gen7.net.

FREAS, THOMAS A., music professor; s. R. Bruce and Audrey Freas. BFA, SUNY, Purchase, NY, 1989; MusM, Manhattan Sch. Music, NYC, 1991. Prof. trumpet Western Conn. State U., Danbury, 1993—2000, U. Bridgeport, Conn., 1995—; artistic dir., founder Fanfare Concerts, Ltd. Inc., Monroe, Conn., 1997—. CEO Champignon Internat., Sherman, Conn., 1997—. Musician (producer): (audio cd) Soaring; musician: Bach: The Brandenburg Concertos, Fireworks, Vivaldi Concerto for Two Trumpets. Grantee Conn. Commn. Culture and Tourism, 2003, 2004, Monetary, Parker Pub. Trust. Mem.: Chamber Music Am., Early Music Am. Office: Fanfare Concerts Ltd Inc PO Box 784 Monroe CT 06468 Office Phone: 203-733-9733. Office Fax: 203-459-4249. Business E-Mail: tfreas@fanfareconsort.com.

FREASIER, AILEEN W., special education educator; b. Edcouch, Tex., Nov. 12, 1924; d. James Ross and Ethel Inez (Riley) Wade; m. Ben F. Freasier (dec.), Mar. 9, 1944 (div.); children: Ben C., Doretha J. Christoph, Barbara F. McNally Protzman, Raymond E. (dec.), John F. BS HE, Tex. A and I Coll., 1944; MEd, La. Tech. U., 1966; postgrad. 90 hours, La. Tech. U. Tchr. Margaret Roane Day Care Ctr., Ruston, La., 1965-71; tchr. spl. edn. Lincoln Parish Schs., Ruston, 1971-81; individualized edn. program facilitator La. Tng. Inst. Monroe Spl. Sch. Dist. # 1, 1981-89; ednl. diagnostician LTI Monroe (La.) SSD # 1, 1985-95. R.S.V.P. vol. tutor, Lincoln Parish Detention Ctr., 1995—; citizen amb. People Conf. on Edn., Beijing, 1992, South Africa, 1995; presenter in field. Mem. editl. bd.: Jour. Correctional Edn., 1983—95, editor learning tech. sect.:, 1991—95; contbr. articles to ednl. publs. and profl. jours.; author: 5 comml. handwriting duplicating books. Treas. Ruston Mayor's Commn. on Women, 1996—. Named Spl. Sch. Dist. #1 Tchr. of Yr., 1988; recipient J.E. Wallace Wallin Educator of Handicapped award La. Fedn. CEC, 1994, Meritorious Svc. award La. Dept. Pub. Safety and Corrections, 1995, Pres.'s award La. CEC-Tech. and Media, 1997. Mem.: AAUW (state co-chair diversity task force 1993—94, state chmn. diversity com. 1994—2002, pres. North La. br. 1995—, state treas. 2001—03, La. Named Gift honoree AAUW Edn. Found. 1994), Lincoln Parish Ret. Tchrs. Assn. (yearbook editor 1996—, pres. 1998—2000), Internat. Correctional Edn. Assn. (spl. edn. spl. interest group, newsletter editor 1991—94, chmn. 1994—96, editl. bd. CEA Yearbook of Correctional Edn. 1998—), CEC-Tech. and Media (treas. La. divsn. 1993—96, 2001—, Pres.'s award 1997), Vet.'s Patients Com. (chmn. 2000—), Nat. Soc. DAR (Long Leaf Pine chpt., regent 1997—99, constitution week chmn. 2000—), Kappa Kappa Iota (Epsilon conclave pres. 1985—87, state pres. 1991—92, nat. scholarship com. 1995—97, nat. tech. com. 1997—99, chmn. nat. tech. com. 1999—2000, Epsilon conclave pres. 1999—2000, nat. profl. devel. com. 2001—03, v.p. 2003, nat. scholarship com. 2003—04, chmn. bylaws com. 2003—04, chmn. Eta state scholarship com. 2003—05, Loretta Doerr com. chmn. 2004—05, nat. scholarship com. 2004—05, chmn. Loretta Doerr Achievement com. 2004—05, Epsilon conclave pres. 2005—, Eta State Loretta Doerr award 1995), Phi Delta Kappa (newsletter editor 1989—93, past pres. chpt. 1994—96, newsletter editor 1997—98, treas. 2002—). Home: PO Box 1595 Ruston LA 71273-1595 E-mail: aileenwf@bayou.com.

FRÉCHET, JEAN MARIE JOSEPH, chemistry professor; b. Chalon, France, Aug. 18, 1944; came to U.S., 1967; children: Jacques Christopher, Marc Alexander. MSc, SUNY, Syracuse, 1969, PhD, 1971, Syracuse U., 1971; Doctorate (hon.), U. Lyon, 2002, U. Ottawa, 2004. Asst. prof. chemistry U. Ottawa, Canada, 1973-78, assoc. prof. chemistry, 1978-82, prof. chemistry, 1982-87; IBM prof. chemistry Cornell U., Ithaca, NY, 1987-95, P.J. Debye chair chemistry, 1996—98; prof. chemistry U. Calif., Berkeley, 1996—, H. Rapoport chair organic chemistry, 2003—; head materials synthesis Lawrence Berkeley Nat. Lab., 1999—. Vis. scientist IBM Rsch. Lab., San Jose, Calif., 1979, 83; vice dean grad. studies and rsch. U. Ottawa, 1983-87; cons. Xerox Corp., 1979-88, Allied Signal Corp., Morristown, 1986-93, Exxon Corp., Linden, NJ, 1988—, E.I. duPont de Nemours, Wilmington, 1990-93, Loctite, 1993—2002, Pharmacia, 1993-95, Miles, 1994-96, Rhone Poulenc, 1994-99, Pharmacopeia, 1995-2001, Bayer, 1996—, Symyx, 1996—2004, Kodak, 1997—, Unilever, 1997—, Xenoport, 2000—, 3M Corp., 1999-2002, ICI, 2002—; bd. dirs. Ont. Ctr. for Materials Rsch., Toronto, Dendritic Nanotechnologies, Inc. Contbr. numerous articles to profl. jours.; patentee in field. Recipient Internat. Union Pure and Applied Chemistry award, 1983, Polymer Soc. Japan, 1986, A.K. Doolittle award, 1986, Coop. Rsch. award Am. Chem. Soc., 1994, Applied Polymer Chem. award Am. Chem. Soc., 1996, 2000, Kosar Meml. award Soc. Imaging Sci. Tech., 1999, Salute to Excellence award Am. Chem. Soc., 2001; A.C. Cope scholar Am. Chem. Soc., 2001; numerous rsch. grants. Fellow AAAS; mem. NAS, NAE, Am. Acad. Arts and Scis. Avocation: oenophile. Office: U Calif 718 Latimer Hl Berkeley CA 94720-1460 Office Phone: 510-643-3077.

FRECHETTE, JOHN ROBERT, lawyer; b. Apr. 16, 1952; s. Leroy John and Martiena Marie (Weaver) Frechette. AB in Polit. Sci. magna cum laude, Ind. U., 1973, JD, 1975. Bar: Ind. 1975, U.S. Dist. Ct. (so. dist.) Ind. 1975, U.S. Dist. Ct. (no. dist.) Ind. 1976, U.S. Ct. Appeals (7th cir.) 1977, U.S. Supreme Ct. 1979. Mem.: City Bar Assn. (pres. 2005), Elkhart City Bar Assn., Ind. State Bar Assn., Masons. Democrat. Lutheran. Office: PO Box 366 Elkhart IN 46515-0366

FRÉCHETTE, LOUISE, international organization official; b. Montreal, Can., July 16, 1946; BA, Coll. Basile Moreau, 1966; licence es lettres degree in history, U. Montreal, 1970; postgrad. diploma in econ. studies, Coll. Europe, Bruges, Belgium, 1978; Doctorate (hon.), St. Mary's U., Halifax, 1993, Kyung Hee U., Seoul, U. Ottawa, U. Toronto, Laval U., Quebec. Mem. General Assembly, Canada, 1972; second sec. Canadian Embassy, Athens, 1972—75; with European Affairs Div., Dept. of External Affairs, Canada, 1975—77; first sec. Canadian Mission to the UN, Geneva, 1978—82; deputy dir. Trade Policy Div., Dept. of External Affairs, 1982—83; dir. European Summit Div., 1983—85; Can. amb. to Argentina, Uruguay, Paraguay, 1985—88; asst. dep. min. for L.Am. and Caribbean Dept. External Affairs and internat. trade, 1988—91; asst. dep. min. for econ. policy and trade competitiveness Ministry of Fgn. Affairs, 1991-92; permanent rep. of Canada UN, 1992—95; assoc. dep. min. Can. Dept. Fin., 1994-95; dep. minister def. Govt. of Can., 1995-98; dep. sec. gen. UN, 1998—. Chmn., Steering Com. on Reform and Mgmt. Policy UN; chmn., advisory bd. UN Fund for Internat. Partnerships (UNFIP). Named Office of the Order of Can., 1998; named one of most powerful women, Forbes mag., 2005.*

FRECHETTE, PETER LOREN, dental products executive; b. Janesville, Wis., Aug. 15, 1937; s. Francis Michael and Gladys Jean F.; m. Patricia Jean O'Brien, June 24, 1961; children: Kathleen and Kristen (twins). BS in Econs., U. Wis., 1960; MBA, Northwestern U., 1980. Pres. Sci. Products, McGaw Park, Ill., 1975-82; pres., CEO Patterson Dental Co., Mpls., 1982—. Served with U.S. Army, 1961-63. Mem. Am. Dental Trade Assn. Office: Patterson Dental Co 1031 Mendota Heights Rd Mendota Heights MN 55120-1401 Office Phone: 651-686-1700. E-mail: pete.frechette@pattersondental.com.

FRECKELTON, SONDRA, artist; b. Dearborn, Mich., June 23, 1936; d. William and Elizabeth (Zimmerman) F.; m. W.H. Jack Beal, Sept. 3, 1955. Student, Sch. Art Inst. Chgo., 1954—56, U. Chgo., 1954—56; LittD (hon.), Hollins Coll., 1994. Artist self-employed, 1958—. Tibor de Nagy Gallery, N.Y.C., 1953—64, B.C. Holland Gallery, Chgo., 1964—67, Lo Giudice Gallery, Chgo., 1968—71, Brooke Alexander Gallery, N.Y.C., 1975—85, 1991, Robert Schoelkopf Gallery, N.Y.C., 1986—91, Alice Simsar Gallery, Ann Arbor, Mich., 1987—, Maxwell Davidson Gallery, N.Y.C., 1991—98. Co-author: Dynamic Still-Lifes in Watercolor, 1983; one-person exhbns. include Robert Schoelkopf Gallery, 1986, 88, 90, John Berggruen Gallery, 1982, Brooke Alexander, Inc., 1976, 79, 80, 81, Fendrick Gallery, 1980, Allan Frumkin Gallery, Chgo., 1977, Lo Giudice Gallery, 1970, B.C. Holland Gallery, 1965, Tibor de Nagy Gallery, 1961, 63, Maxwell Davidson Gallery, 1994, Kalamazoo Inst. Arts, 1994, Huntington Mus., W.Va., 1998-99; group shows including Mt. Holyoke Coll., Yale U. Art Gallery, Art Mus. of Santa Barbara, Va. Mus. Fine Arts, 1987-88, Detroit Inst. Arts, 1991, Madison Art Ctr., Wis., 1998, Columbus Mus. Art, Ga., 1998, and others. Recipient Print award, Bradford Mus., 1979, Pollock-Krasner award, 2002; grantee, Grant Ingram-Merrill Found., 1960, Pollock-Krasner Found., 2002. Avocations: horticulture, gardening. Home and Office: HC64331 Epps Rd Oneonta NY 13820-6451

FRED, ROGERS MURRAY, III, veterinary oncologist; b. Leesburg, Va., July 22, 1955; s. Rogers Murray Jr. and Barbara Ann (Stewart) F.; m. Kimberly Edna Shepherd, Oct. 15, 1989; 1 child, Asa Hugh Shepherd. BS, Washington and Lee U., 1977; post grad., U. Ga., 1979-81; DVM, Va. Tech., 1985. Staff veterinarian Abbey Animal Hosp., Balt., 1986-89; resident in vet. oncology U. Pa., Phila., 1989-91; clin. oncologist, dept. head Red Bank Vet. Hosp. and Referral Svc., NJ, 1991—. Lectr. in vet. field. Co-author: Connective Tissues in Health and Disease, 1980; Globule Leukocyte Tumor in Cats: 6 Cases, 1993; Liposome-Encapsulated Doxorubicin (Doxil) and Doxorubicin in the Treatment of Vaccine-Associated Sarcoma in Cats, 2002. Bd. dir. Ebenezer Ch. and Cemetery Co., Bloomfield, Va., 1986—, Monmouth Hills N.J., Inc. Mem. SCV (camp comdr. 1988-90); Am. Vet. Med. Assn.; Vet. Cancer Soc.; N.J. Vet. Med. Assn.; Civil War Preservation Trust; Phi Kappa Phi; Phi Zeta. Republican. Episcopalian. Avocations: reading, walking, battlefield tours, birdwatching. Home: 15 Monmouth Hills Highlands NJ 07732 Office: Red Bank Vet Hosp 210 Newman Springs Rd Red Bank NJ 07701-1465 Office Phone: 732-747-3636.

FREDA, MICHAEL R., psychotherapist, educator; b. Vineland, NJ, Aug. 29, 1951; s. Rudolph A. and Gloria T. Freda; m. Karen S. Goodwill-Freda, July 13, 1994; children: Trudie L. Kibala, John E. Goodwill, Christopher M., Candace M. BSBA, U. Nev., 1986; AS, CZ Coll., Panama, 1976; MA, U. Nev., 1996, PhD, 2001. Lic. Marriage and Family Therapist MFT Examiners Bd., Nev., 1999, Lic. Alcohol and Drug Counselor Bur. of Alcohol and Drug Abuse, Nev., 2000, Lic. Sch. Psychologist Dept. of Edn., Nev., 2000. Clinic coord. U. Nev., Reno, 1994—99; pvt. practitioner Ridgeview Counseling Group, 1996—. Counseling educator U. Phoenix, Reno, 2001—. Bd. mem. Friends of Coll. Edn., Reno, 2001—. Staff sgt. U.S. Army, 1969—77, Vietnam, NJ, Panama Canal Zone. Decorated Several U.S. Army. Mem.: APA (assoc.), ACA (assoc.), 14th Eng. Bn. (CBT) Orgn., Reno Host Lions Club (1st v.p. 2004—05). Avocations: travel, woodworking, exercise, motorcycling. Office: Ridgeview Counseling Group 3650 Warren Way Reno NV 89509 Office Phone: 775-823-4099. Office Fax: 775-823-4099. Personal E-mail: freda@775.net. E-mail: michael.freda@sbcglobal.net.

FREDERICH-STUBBS, NANCY A., publishing executive; b. Champaign, Ill., Jan. 26, 1943; d. Walter E. Ivey and Betty Jane Bullock; m. Walter Stubbs, Nov. 24, 1999; children: Robert Walton Parke III, Jeffrey Scott Parke. Cert. Nat. Assn. Parliamentarians, 1995. Acctg. asst. Country Mut. Ins. Co., Bloomington, Ill., 1961—65; data processing mgr. Decker & Assocs., Bloomington, 1973—78; sales assoc. Coldwell Banker Real Estate, Bloomington, 1980—85; office mgr. Blair Clark Esq., St. Petersburg, Ill., 1985—89; v.p. Fla. Seacoast Realty, Inc., Madeira Beach, 1989—93; CEO Murmaid Pub., Largo, Fla., 2002—. Editor novels, chap books; contbr. articles to publs. Bd. mem. Planning Bd., Madeira Beach, 1987—89, Civil Svc. Commn., Madeira Beach, 1989—93; dir. Keep Pinellas County Beautiful, Fla., 1994—96; vol. Egmont Key Alliance, St. Petersburg, 1995—2003; fund raising Boys & Girls Clubs of the Suncoast, St. Petersburg, 1993—99; past pres. Women's Cahmber of Commerce of the Greater Gulf Beaches, Treasure Island, Fla., 1990—2005, Treasure Island (Fla.) Art Guild, 1989—95, Island Cmty. Theatre, St. Pete Beach, Fla., 1998—2005; mem. Pinellas Parliamentarians, Madeira Beach. Mem.: Travel Writers Internat. Network, Pinellas Authors and Writers Orgn. (assoc.), Fla. Writer's Assn. (assoc.), Nat. Assn. Photoshop Profls. (assoc.). Home: 14381 Mark Dr Largo FL 33774 Office Phone: 727-403-1551. Business E-Mail: murmaid@tampabay.rr.com.

FREDERICK, ALBERT R., JR., ophthalmologist, surgeon; b. St. Petersburg, Fla., May 17, 1935; s. Albert R. Frederick; m. Suzanne Margareta Westerberg, May 3, 1969. SB, U. Fla., 1957; MD, Harvard U., 1961. Diplomate Am. Bd. Ophthalmology. Intern Boston City Hosp. II & IV Med. Svcs., 1961; resident then fellow Mass. Eye & Ear Infirmary, Boston, 1962—65; ophthalmic surgeon Ophthalmic Consultants Boston. Capt. USAF, 1966—68. Mem.: Boston Harvard Club. Avocations: photography, hunting, beekeeping, scuba diving, coin collecting/numismatics. Office: Ophthalmic Cons Boston Ste 600 50 Staniford St Boston MA 02114 Office Phone: 617-367-4800. Business E-Mail: arfrederick@eyeboston.com.

FREDERICK, AMY L., science administrator; b. Flint, Mich., Oct. 13, 1972; BA, Cumberland U., Lebanon, Tenn., 1994; MA, Howard U., 1996, PhD, 2000. Tech. commercialization fellow NASA, Greenbelt, Md., 1995—99; program adminstr. Global Sci. and Tech., Inc., Greenbelt, 1999—2000; sr. staff Sci. Applications Internat. Corp., Vienna, Va., 2000—. Presenter in field. Author: The Election of Women and African-American to Congress; contbr. articles to profl. jours. Recipient NASA Goddard Space Flight Ctr. Group award, NASA, 1996; Hawthorne Dissertation fellow, Howard U., 1999, Cumberland U. scholar, 1992—94. Mem.: Phi Sigma Alpha. Office: Science Applicatios Internat Corp 8401 Corporate Dr Landover MD

FREDERICK, EDWARD CHARLES, university official; b. Mankato, Minn., Nov. 17, 1930; s. William H. and Wanda (MacNamara) F.; m. Shirley Lunkenheimer, Aug. 16, 1951; children: Bonita Frederick Treangen (dec.), Diane Frederick Fox, Donald, Kenneth, Karen Frederick Swenson. BS in Agrl. Edn, U. Minn., 1954, MS in Dairy Husbandry, 1955, PhD in Anatomy and Physiology, 1957. Animal scientist, instr. N.W. Sch. and Expt. Sta. U. Minn., Crookston, 1958-64, supt. So. Sch. and Expt. Sta. Waseca, 1964-69, provost Tech. Coll., 1969-85, chancellor Tech. Coll., 1985-90; sr. fellow Hubert H. Humphrey Inst. Pub. Affairs, 1990-91, U. Minn. Coll. of Agr., Food and Environ. Sci., 1991—. Mem. Tech. Agrl. Edn. Study Team to Morocco, 1977. Contbr. articles on dairy physiology, mgmt., agrl. edn. and adminstrn. to tech. jours. and popular publs. Bd. dirs. Bob Hodgson Student Loan Fund, 1971-90, Minn. Agrl. Interpretive Ctr., 1978—, chair, 1994—; bd. dirs. Minn. Agri-Growth Coun., 1980—, pres. 1992—; bd. dirs. Southeastern Minn. Initiative Fund, 1986-92, v.p., 1991-92; bd. dirs. Waseca area United Way, 1988-94, pres., 1992; bd. dirs. Minn. Agriculture in the Classroom, 1993-99, pres., 1995-96. Recipient Alumni award 4-H, 1972, Good Neighbor award, WCCO, 1990, Ed Frederick Day award State of Minn., 1990, Award of Merit Gamma Sigma Delta, 1994, Waseca Cmty. Svc. Above Self award, 2002, Minn. Rural Ptnrs. Lifetime Leadership award, 2002, So. Minn. Initiative Found. Ground Breaker award, 2002; named to Minn. FFA Hall of Fame, 2004; finalist So. Minn. Agrl. Amb. of Yr., 2004. Mem. Am. Dairy Assn., Am. Soc. Animal Prodn., AAAS, Nat. Assn. Colls. and Tchrs. Agr. (pres. 1976-77), Am. Assn. Community and Jr. Colls. (pres. Council of Two Yr. Colls. of Four Yr. Instns. 1988-90), Minn. FFA Alumni Assn. (pres. 1998-00), South Central Edn. Assn. (Disting. Service award 1971), Waseca Area C. of C. (dir. 1979), Phi Kappa Phi. Clubs: Foresters. Lodges: Rotary (gov. dist. 596 1982-83); K.C. Roman Catholic. Home: 39031 State Highway 13 Waseca MN 56093-4212 Office: U Minn Coll Agrl Food and Env Sci Waseca MN 56093 Office Phone: 507-835-3422. Business E-Mail: frede010@umn.edu.

FREDERICK, ELIZABETH ELEANOR TATUM, watercolor artist, retired educator; b. Clovis, N.Mex., Dec. 22, 1915; d. John Hardy Tatum and Bessie Elizabeth Weathers Tatum; m. George Achias Frederick, June 7, 1937 (dec. Apr. 1991); children: Ronald W., George Douglas, Barbara Elizabeth Frederick Ewing, John Lawrence. BS in Edn., U. N.Mex., 1937, MS, 1943; postgrad., Highland U., Las Vegas, N.Mex., 1944, Ea. N.Mex. U., 1944, 45. Tchr. Ctrl. H.S., Kirtland, N.Mex., 1936-37, Bellview (N.Mex.) H.S., 1940-42, Hot Springs (N.Mex.) Jr. H.S., 1943-45, 1951-53, Hot Springs (N.Mex.) H.S., 1954; ret., 1967. Exhibitions include Sierra Art Soc., N.Mex., Willamette Oaks Retirement Ctr., Eugene, Oreg., 1995, 2005, El Paso Mus. Art, N.Mex. Art League, N.Mex. Watercolor Soc., Albuquerque, Represented in permanent collections. Mem. Nat. League Am. Pen Women (pres. Rio Grande br. 1975-76), Sierra Art Soc. (pres. 1974-75, funding and program chmn. 1975-89), N.Mex. Watercolor Soc., Black Range Artists (sec.-treas. 1978-79). Republican. Avocations: sweepstakes, worldwide travel.

FREDERICK, JANE Y., architect; b. Tullahoma, Tenn., Sept. 12, 1959; d. James D. and Ann Lunsford Young; m. Michael D. Frederick, Aug. 13, 1983; children: Jana Gray, Jessica Todd. BArch, Auburn U., 1982. Registered Architect, SC, 1985, cert. Nat. Coun. of Archtl. Registration Bds., 1989. Prin. Jane Frederick Architects, Alexandria, Va., 1985—89, Frederick + Frederick Architects, Beaufort, SC, 1989—. Mem. S.C. Bd. Archtl. Examiners, Columbia, 1999—2004, chairperson, 2001—03; sec. Region 3 Nat. Coun. Archtl. Registration Bds., 2001—03, mem. archtl. registration exam. com., 2001—, vice chairperson Region 3, 2003—04, chair region 3, 2004—05. Mem. Ladys Island planning com. Beaufort County, SC, 1999—2005; Artscapade co-chair Beaufort Art Found./Beaufort County Sch. Dist., 1996; PTO v.p. Ladys Island Elem. Sch., Beaufort, 1993—94; Odyssey of the Mind coach Beaufort Humanities Sch., 1998—99; sr. troop leader Girl Scouts, Alexandria, Va., 1984—88, jr. troop leader Beaufort, 1994—98; chmn. Beaufort County Corridor Rev. Bd., 1995—2001; chair preservation com. Hist. Beaufort Found., 2002—04; mem. Leadership Beaufort Beaufort C. of C., 1991; mem. Leadership S.C. U. S.C., Columbia, 1998; mem. Lowcountry Habitat for Humanity, Beaufort, 1991—92; Dem. candidate 2nd Congl. Dist. of S.C., 1998—2000; chair Beaufort County Dem. Party, 2004—05; vestry, warden, bldg. and grounds com. chair St. Helena's Episcopal Ch., Beaufort, 1992—95; bd. dirs. Planned Parenthood of S.C., Columbia, 1999—2001; trustee Hist. Beaufort Found., Beaufort, SC, 1991—94. Named Woman of Distinction, Carolina Lowcountry Girl Scouts, 1998; recipient Home of Yr. award, Met. Home Mag., 1991, Cmty. Svc. Person of Yr., Beaufort C. of C., 1997, Best Exterior Renovation award, Main St. Beaufort, 2002; Liberty fellow, S.C., 2004. Mem.: AIA (Honor award 2004), Parris Island Master Swim Team. Avocations: swimming, reading, backpacking. Office: Frederick + Frederick Architects 38 Meridian Rd Beaufort SC 29907 Office Phone: 843-522-8422.

FREDERICK, JOHN, retired actor, writer; b. Norwalk-Ditto; *The corn grows tall in Iowa; so do its men. John Frederick (Stiffler), son of pioneering parents, Maude and Fred Stiffler, who settled via the covered wagon in the fertile, rolling hills of Norwalk. Sustaining a university football injury, followed by a four-year teaching stint, a Hollywood talent search took John to California where he married another newly arrived aspirant. Conflicting East/West Coast careers resulted in early divorce. Following 67 guest-starring TV roles and eight top film roles in Hollywood and Rome, Palm Springs mayor proclaimed, "John Frederick will receive his own celebrity star on our city's prestigious 'Walk of Stars.'" John Frederick appeared in eight major film roles and has worked for film director greats Fellini, Visconte, Leone, and De Sica. In 1986, Iowa's governor Branstad proclaimed a "John Frederick Day" at its town and country festival in Norwalk. The high school band played and marched in the parade. John was introduced, praised, and applauded when he presented the annual John Frederick Scholarship in the Performing Arts to a graduating senior ad infinitum. Following an illustrious career, John settled in the Palm Springs California desert where he tends his garden and trims his citrus trees; he is still active in local charities and lives the good life.* Author: (memoir) Name Droppings on Your Head; actor: (Broadway plays) Something for the Boys, Catherine Was Great, Miracle in the Mountain, First Ms. Fraser, Destry Rides Again, Stalag 17, Annie Get Your Gun, Where's Charles; actor, actor: (Broadway plays) Take Me Along, Agatha Christie's Ten Little Indians; guest starred over 65 TV series; actor: (TV series) My Three Sons, NBC, Bonanza, Naked City, Death Valley Days, Wagon Train, The Restless Gun, Tales of the Texas Rangers, Undercurrent, Adventures of Wild Bill Hickok, Frontier, The Jack Benny Program, Stories of the Century, Tales of Wells Fargo; (films, Sica) for Fellini, Visconte, Leone, De Sica, Cleopatra, 1963, (playing fictional Am. Cardinal Carlin); (films, starring Anthony Quinn) Shoes of the Fisherman, 1968; (films) Once Upon a Time in the West, 1968, Colpt rovente, 1969, La Caduta delgli dei, 1969, The Adventurers, 1970, Pussycat, Pussycat, I Love You, 1970, Jennifer on My Mind, 1971, Giu la testa, 1971, The Statue, 1971, Ten Commandments, Superman, Tarzan, (Pope Clemente VIII) Beatrice Cenci; contbr. articles to profl. jours. Active local charities. Avocation: gardening.

FREDERICK, JOHN HOWARD, academic administrator, chemist, educator; b. Ft. Benning, Ga., Jan. 19, 1958; s. John Howard and Marian Barbour Frederick; m. Mimi W. Yu, Dec. 18, 1992; children: Alice Marie, Peter Alexander. AB in Chemistry, Princeton (N.J.) U., 1980; AM in Chemistry, Harvard U., 1982, PhD in Chemistry, 1985. Postdoctoral rsch. assoc. Dept. Chemistry U. Washington, Seattle, 1985—88; prof. chemistry U. Nev., Reno, 1988—, chmn. Dept. Chemistry, 1999—2001, exec. v.p., 2001—, provost, 2001—. Treas. Telluride (Colo.) Sci. Rsch. Ctr., 1997—2004, pres., 2001—04; dir. Chem. Physics Program Dept. Chemistry U. Nev., 1990—2001. Contbr. over 48 articles to profl. jours. Bd. dir. Leadership Reno-Sparks, 2005—. Recipient Alan Bible Tchg. Excellence award, Coll. Arts and Scis. U. Nev., 1995, F. Donald Tibbits Disting. Tchr. award, U. Nev., 1996; fellow, NSF, 1981—84. Mem.: Am. Phys. Soc., Am. Chem. Soc. (sec. Sierr (Nev.) sect. 1990, program officer Sierr (Nev.) sect. 1991, chmn. Sierr (Nev.) sect. 1992—93). Avocations: travel, golf, reading. Office: University Nevada Office of Provost 005 Reno NV 89557

FREDERICK, PATRICK JAY, secondary school educator; s. Howard Weatherly and Nell Fowler Frederick. BFA, Abilene Christian U., 1986. Cert. secondary art specialist Tex., Maine. Tchr. Dallas Ind. Sch. Dist., 2000—. Mem.: NEA (assn. rep. 2002—, bd. dirs. 2002—04), Tex. State Tchrs. Assn. Personal E-mail: gtp4me@sbcglobal.net.

FREDERICK, PAULA J., lawyer; b. Riverside, Calif., Apr. 11, 1958; d. Henry Lewis and Hattie Maude (McCollom) F. BA, Duke U., 1979; JD, Vanderbilt U., 1982. Bar: Ga. 1982, U.S. Dist. Ct. (no. dist.) Ga. 1982. Staff atty. Atlanta Legal Aid Soc., 1982-86, mng. atty., 1986-88; asst. gen. counsel State Bar of Ga., Atlanta, 1988-92, dep. gen. counsel, 1992—. Bd. dir. Ga. Legal Svcs. Found. Mem. ABA (mem. standing com. on profl. discipline 1997-99, commr. Commn. on Opportunities for Minorities in the Profession 1994-96, mem. ho. of dels. 1993—, bd. gov. 2002-), Atlanta Bar Assn. (bd. dirs. 1994-96, pres. 1999-2000), Ga. Assn. Black Women Lawyers (pres. 1998), Ga. Assn. Women Attys. (Kathleen Kessler award 2002). Office: State Bar of Georgia Suite 100 104 Marietta St NW Atlanta GA 30303-2702 Office Phone: 404-527-8720.

FREDERICK, ROBERT ALLEN, history professor; b. Mishawaka, Ind., Feb. 3, 1928; s. Ralph Leon and Garnet Laree (Bowles) F.; m. Mary Billington Swartz, Nov. 23, 1950 (div. Sept. 1967); children: Julia Christian, John Billington, Peter Carey; m. Saradell Carolyn Ard, Sept. 9, 1969 (div. April 1983). BA, Hanover Coll., 1950; MS in Edn., Ind. U., 1951, PhD in History, 1960. Assoc. dean students Tex. Technol. Coll., Lubbock, 1951-53; instr. history U.S. Naval Acad. Prep Sch., 1953-56; grad. asst. history Ind. U., Bloomington, 1956-58, fellow dept. history, 1958-60; assoc. prof. history Alaska Meth. U., Anchorage, 1960-66, prof. history, chmn. dept., 1966-73; exec. dir. Alaska Hist. Commn., Anchorage, 1973-80; ind. rschr./writer Alaska Hist. Soc., Anchorage, 1980-85; editor Ind. German Heritage Soc., Indpls., 1986-88; Richard Lieber rschr. Brown County Hist. Soc., Nashville, Ind., 1988-93. Dir. Alaska humanities task force NEH, 1972-73. Editor/contbr. Frontier Alaska: Historical Opportunity, 1968, Writing Alaska's History: A Guide to Research, 1974; contbr., hist. photo editor Anchorage: Star of the North, 1982; author: Alaska's Quest for Statehood: 1867-1959, 1985, Passage to Community: Creating the State-Based Alaska Humanities Forum, 1973; editor: newsletter Ind. German Heritage Soc., 1986-89. Pres. Cook Inlet Hist. Soc., Anchorage, bd. dirs., 1963-66; pres. Alaska Hist. Soc., 1968-69, bd. dirs., 1967-74; mem. nat. archives adv. bd. Nat. Archives and Records Svcs., Regions IX and X, 1974-77; chmn. Nat. Trust for Hist. Preservation, 1975-77, bd. advisors, 1969-78, advisor emeritus, 1979—; dir. A Pioneer Family in Alaska (film) U. Alaska Found., Homer, 1982. Lt. USNR, 1953-56. Ind. Heritage Rsch. grantee Ind. Humanities Coun., 1987-91. Mem. Historic Landmarks Found. Ind., Sigma Chi (life). Democrat. Avocations: hiking in wilderness, visiting natural and historical sites. Home: 1950 S Dayton St #220N Denver CO 80247-3454 Office Phone: 303-755-5512.

FREDERICK, ROBERT GEORGE, lawyer; b. Evanston, Ill., Feb. 11, 1948; s. George D. and Lee (Miller) F.; m. Pamela Kaye Kline, June 13, 1970 (div. Sept. 1977); m. Ellen Marie Due, Oct. 25, 1980; children: Robert, Christina. BS, No. Ill. U., 1969; JD, U. Ill., 1972. Bar: Ill. 1972, U.S. Dist. Ct. (cen. dist.) Ill. 1974, U.S. Ct. Appeals (7th cir.) 1975, U.S. Supreme Ct. 1978. Asst. states atty. Champaign County, Urbana, Ill., 1972-75, pub. defender, 1975-79; commr. State Ill. Claims Ct., Springfield, 1984—; ptnr. Johnson, Frank & Frederick, Urbana, 1975—. Mem. ABA, Ill. State Bar Assn., Ill. Trial Lawyers Assn., Champaign County Bar Assn., Order of Coif. Republican. Methodist. Office: Johnson Frank Frederick & Walsh 129 W Main St Urbana IL 61801-2714

FREDERICK, THOMAS JAMES, lawyer; b. Grand Rapids, Mich., Oct. 6, 1956; s. Charles Murr and E. Marjorie (Loye) F. BA, Mich. State U., 1978; JD, U. Mich., 1984. Bar: Ill. 1984, U.S Dist. Ct. (no. dist.) Ill. 1984, U.S. Ct. Appeals (2d and 7th cir.) 1989, U.S. Supreme Ct., 1993. Assoc. to. ptnr. Winston & Strawn, Chgo., 1984—. Assoc. editor: Michigan Law Review, 1982—83; editor, 1983—84. Mem. ABA, Chgo. Bar Assn., Seventh Cir. Bar Assn., Order of Coif. Office: Winston & Strawn 35 W Wacker Dr Chicago IL 60601-9706 Office Phone: 312-558-5983. Office Fax: 312-558-5700. Business E-Mail: tfrederick@winston.com.

FREDERICK, VIRGINIA FIESTER, state legislator; b. Rock Island, Ill., Dec. 24, 1916; d. John Henry and Myrtle (Montgomery) Heise; m. C. Donnan Fiester (dec. 1975); children: Sheryl Fiester Ross, Alan R., James D.; m. Kenneth Jacob Frederick, 1978. BA, U. Iowa, 1938; postgrad., Lake Forest Coll., 1942-43, LLD, 1994, MLS, 1999. Freelance fashion designer, Lake Forest, Ill., 1952-78; pres. Mid Am. China Exch., Kenilworth, Ill., 1978-81; mem. Ill. Ho. of Reps., Springfield, 1979-95, asst. minority leader, 1990-95. Alderman first ward, Lake Forest, 1974-78; del. World Food Conf., Rome, 1974; subcom. pensions and employment Ill. Commn. on Status of Women, 1976-79; co-chair Conf. Women Legislators, 1982-85; bd. dirs. Lake Forest Coll., 1995-98, Lake Forest Symphony Guild, 1998—; city supr. City of Lake Forest, 1995-98. Named Chgo. Area Women of Achievement, Internat. Orgn. Women Execs., 1978; recipient Lottie Holman O'Neal award, 1980, Jane Addams award, 1982, Outstanding Legislator award Ill. Hosp. Assn., 1986, VFW Svc. award, 1988, Joyce Fitzgerald Meml. award, 1988, Susan B. Anthony Legislator of Yr. award, 1989, Delta Kappa Gamma award, 1991, Outstanding Legislator award, 1995, Svcs. for Srs. award, Ill. Dept. Aging, 1991, Ethics in Politics award, Rep. Womens's Club, 1992, Woman of Achievement award YWCA North Eastern Ill., 1994, Ill. Women in Govt. award, 1994, Lifetime Achievement award Equip for Equality, 1999. Mem. LWV (local pres. 1958-60, state dir. 1969-75, nat. com. 1975-76), AAUW (local pres. 1968-70, state pres. 1975-77, state dir. 1963-69, nat. com. 1967-69, Legislator of Yr. 1993), UN Assn. (bd. dirs.), Chgo. Assn. Commerce and Industry (bd. dirs.). Home: 1290 N Western Ave Lake Forest IL 60045-1258 E-mail: k13v16@aol.com.

FREDERICK-MAIRS, T(HYRA) JULIE, administrative health services official; b. Islip, N.Y., Jan. 4, 1941; d. Manuel and Thyra C. (Thorsen) Cajiao. BA, Adelphi U., 1961; MSW, U. So. Calif., 1972, MPA, 1991. Social worker L.A. County Dept. Social Svcs., 1966-67, social work supr., 1967-70, planning cons., 1972-76; dep. to supr. 4th dist. L.A. County, 1976-80; asst. dir. L.A. County Office Alcohol Programs, 1980-90; assoc. adminstr. ELACO Health Ctrs., 1990—2003; CEO East Country Health Ctrs.; health care process improvement and change mgmt. cons., 2003—. Fellow U. So. Calif., 1988-90. Author: (with others) Youth Program Planning, 1975. Trustee LEARNS, 1992; active L.A. Child Sexual Abuse Project, Commn. for Sexual Equality, L.A. Unified Sch. Dist., Harbor Policy Cmty. Adv. Coun., L.A.; mem. Perinatal Substance Abuse Coun. L.A.; mem. ops. com. Interagy. Coun. Child Abuse and Neglect; adv. com. UCLA Alcohol Rsch. Ctr. Mem. Los Amigos de la Humanidad, DHS Latino Mgrs., Alpha Epsilon Delta, Beta Beta Beta, Bus. and Profl. Women's Club, Soroptimists (pres. L.A. Club, dir. Found. of L.A. 1986-88).

FREDERICK-RECASCINO, CHRISTINA MARIE, psychologist, educator; b. Brockport, N.Y., Aug. 27, 1964; d. George E. and Ruth A. Frederick; m. Anthony Recascino, Aug. 14, 1999; 1 child, Anthony George. BA in Psychology, SUNY, Geneseo, N.Y., 1985; MS in Edn., U. Rochester, 1990, PhD in Edn. and Human Devel., 1991. Computer analyst U. Rochester, NY, 1988—93; asst. prof. So. Utah U., Cedar City, 1993—98, assoc. prof., 1998; asst. prof. U. Ctrl. Fla., Daytona Beach, 1998—2000; assoc. prof. Embry Riddle Aero. U., Daytona Beach, 2000—, asst. provost, rsch./grad. studies. Editor: Jour. Sport Behavior, 2001—03; co-author: Handbook of Self Determination Research, 2002; contbr. articles to profl. jours. Mem. Quality of Life Bd., Ormond Beach, Fla., 2001—; adv. bd. Samaritan Ministries, Flogler Beach, Fla., 2001—. Mem.: APA, Am. Inst. Aero. and Astronautics, Am. Psychol. Soc. Avocations: reading, antiques, home improvement, travel. Office: Embry Riddle Aeronautical Univ 600 Clyde Morris Blvd Daytona Beach FL 32114 Office Phone: 386-226-7037.

FREDERICKS, DALE EDWARD, communications company executive; b. Springfield, Ill., Mar. 12, 1943; m. Jean Schmidt, June 8, 1968; children: Michael J., Amy C. BS with honors, Bradley U., 1965; JD, U. Ill., 1968. Bar: D.C. 1969, Calif. 1971, U.S. Supreme Ct. 1978. Gen. counsel Summit Fidelity and Surety Co., Minneapolis, 1988-93, Hampton Ct. Holdings, Inc., San Francisco, 1989-93; ptnr. Sheppard, Mullin, Richter & Hampton, 1991-96, mng. ptnr. San Francisco office, 1993-95; CEO C5 Comm. LLC, Incline Village, Nev., 1999—. Pres. Sangamon Properties Co., Incline Village, Nev., Sangamon Devel. Co., Sangamon Energy Co., Lafayette, Calif. Capt. USMCR, 1968-72. Mem. ABA (antitrust law and litigation sects.), Calif. Bar Assn., San Francisco Bar Assn., Internat. Bar Assn., World Trace Club. Republican. Avocations: golf, real estate development.

FREDERICKS, JEANNE MARIA JUDSON, literary agent; b. Mineola, N.Y., Apr. 19, 1950; d. Howard William and Christina Hannah Judson; m. Wesley Charles Fredericks, Jr., May 19, 1973; children: Carolyn Anne, Wesley Charles III. BA, Mt. Holyoke Coll., 1972; MBA, NYU, 1979; publ. procedures course, Radcliffe Coll. Asst. to editl. dir., subs. rights dir. Basic Books, N.Y.C., 1972-74; asst. mng. editor Macmillan Publ. Co., N.Y.C., 1974-76, mng. editor, 1976-78, acquisitions editor, 1978-80; editl. dir. Ziff-Davis Books, N.Y.C., 1980-81; literary agent Susan P. Urstadt, Inc., New Canaan, Conn., 1990-96, acting dir., 1996-97; pres. Jeanne Fredericks Literary Agy., Inc., New Canaan, 1997—. Spkr. in field. Co-chair, co-founder Mothers' Group Congl. Ch., Wilton, Conn., 1984-87; bd. dirs. New Canaan H.S. Crew, 1999—2002, co-pres., 2002-03; trustee New Canaan Congregational Ch., 2001-2004, mem. social action com., 2004—. Mem. Assn. Authors' Reps., Authors Guild, Inc., Phi Beta Kappa. Republican. Congregationalist. Avocations: crew, tennis, gardening, reading. Office: Jeanne Fredericks Literary Agy Inc 221 Benedict Hill Rd New Canaan CT 06840-2913 Office Phone: 203-972-3011.

FREDERICKS, MARGARET MATTERSON, elementary school educator; b. Syracuse, N.Y., Nov. 9, 1930; d. Curtiss Dutton and Elizabeth Logan (Morrison) Matterson; m. Roland S. Fredericks, Sept. 1951; children: Margaret Jean, Elizabeth Clara. Degree, Syracuse U., 1952, Moray House, Edinburgh U., Scotland, 1966; M of Liberal Learning, Marietta Coll., 1984. Sch. savs. Amsterdam (N.Y.) Savs. Bank, 1967-70; 5th grade tchr. Amsterdam Pub. Schs., 1970; elem. edn. tchr. Marietta City Schs., 1971-98, ret., 1998; organizer, founder Marietta Boys and Girls Club of Washington County, 1998—. Course of study lang. arts. Marietta City Schs. Mem. Dems. for Ohio; elder Presbyn. Ch. Recipient Citizen of Yr., Civitan Club, 2002. Mem. AAUW, LVW, Ret. Tchrs. Ohio, Ret. Tchrs. Washington County, Marietta Natural History Soc., Betsey Mills Club (women's bd. dirs.), Washington County Hist. Soc., Antique Club, The Castle, Delta Kappa Gamma. Avocations: hiking, canoeing, reading, gardening. Home: 303 Ohio St Marietta OH 45750-3139

FREDERICKS, ROBERT JOSEPH, language company executive; b. NYC, Dec. 26, 1934; s. Harold D. and Mary E. (McCarthy) F.; m. Jeanette C. Kubin, July 7, 1984. BS in Chemistry, Villanova U., 1957; MS in Chemistry, St. Joseph's Coll., Phila., 1959; PhD in Chemistry, Lehigh U., 1965. Rsch. chemist GAF Corp., Easton, Pa., 1960—67; rsch. supr. Allied Chem. Corp., Morristown, NJ, 1968—72; mgr. analytical chemistry Ethicon, Inc., Somerville, NJ, 1972—74, dir. rsch. svcs., 1974—76, assoc. dir. rsch., 1976—78; v.p. R&D, bd. dirs. Surgikos, Piscataway, NJ, 1978—79, Johnson & Johnson Dental Products Co., East Windsor, NJ, 1980—82; sr. v.p., gen. mgr., COO Biosci. Med. Products, Somerville, 1982—85; pres. Allen Transl. Svc., Morristown, NJ, 1985—. Author: X-Ray Diffraction for the Industrial Chemist, 1971; contbr. articles to profl. jours. Pres. Morris County Hist. Soc., Morristown, 1982—86, trustee, 1975—93; pres. Washington Assn. N.J., Morristown, 1988—92, 1993—99, trustee, 1983—2002, Craftsman Farms Found., 1994; mem. adv. bd. New Philharm., NJ, 1992—99, trustee, 1994—98, 1st v.p., 1995—98; hon. historian Twp. of Morris, 1992—. Lt (j.g.) USN, 1958—60. Recipient Achievement award Washington Assn., 2000, Svc. award Assumption Coll. for Sisters, 2005 Mem.: AAAS, N.Y. Acad. Scis., Am. Chem. Soc., Am. Assn. Sovereign Mil. Order of Malta (N.J. state chmn. 2003—, chmn. Lourdes 2003 pilgrimage, N.J. Hospitaller, bd. councillors 2004), Rotary (bd. dirs. 1992—93), Morristown Club (bd. govs. 1996—, v.p. 1998, pres. 1999—2002), Morristown Field Club, Sigma Xi, Delta Epsilon Sigma. Republican. Roman Catholic. Avocations: tennis, gardening. Home: 16 Butterworth Dr Morristown NJ 07960-2625 Office Phone: 973-292-2737.

FREDERICKS, WARD ARTHUR, venture capitalist, consultant; b. Tarrytown, N.Y., Dec. 24, 1939; s. Arthur George and Evelyn (Smith) F.; m. Patricia A. Sexton, June 12, 1960; children: Corrine E., Lorrine L., Ward A. BS cum laude, Mich. State U., 1962, MBA, 1963, PhD. Assoc. dir. Technics Group, Grand Rapids, Mich., 1964-68; gen. mgr. logistics systems Massey-Ferguson, Inc., Toronto, Ont., Can., 1968-69, v.p. mgmt. svcs., comptr., 1969-73, sr. v.p. fin., dir. fin. Americas, 1975—; comptr. Massey-Ferguson Ltd., Toronto, Ont., Can., 1973-75; prin. W.B. Saunders & Co., Washington, 1962—64; sr. v.p. mktg. Massey.Ferguson, Inc., 1975-78, also pres., gen. mgr. tractor divsn., 1978-80; gen. mgr. Rockwell Graphic Sys., 1980-82; pres. Goss Co., Chgo.; v.p. ops. Rockwell Internat., Pitts., 1980-84; v.p. Fed. MOG, 1983-84; chmn. MIXTEC Group LLC, 1998—2002; also dir., chmn.; prin. Venture Assocs., 1993—. Dir. Polyfet RF, Inc., Venture Assocs., Badger Horthland, Inc., MST, Inc., Calif., Tech-Mark Group, Inc., Spectra Tech., Inc., Mixtec Group-Venture Capital, Inc., Unicorn Corp., Mixtec Food Group Calif., Mixtec Signal Tech., Harry Ferguson, Inc., M.F. Credit Corp., M.F. Credit Co. Can Ltd.; chmn. ProduceCareers.com., 2000-2002.; mem. bd. councillors Calif. State U., 2002. Author: (with Edward Smykay) Physical Distribution Management, 1974; author: Management Vision, 1988, Competitive Advantage in Technology Organizations, 1986, Competitive Advantage in Technology Firms, 1996; contbr. articles to profl. jours. Bd. dirs., mem. exec. com. Des Moines Symphony, 1975-79; pres. Conejo Symphony, 1988-90; pres. Westlake Village Cultural Found., 1991; mem. exec. com. Alliance for Arts; pres. Conejo Valley Indsl. Assn., 1990, 93; mem. Constn. Bicentennial Com., 1987-88, Ventura County Airport Commn., 1995-99, La Quinta Arts Found.; mem. World Affairs Coun. of the Desert, pres., 2002--; bd. dirs. Ventura County Bus. Incubator, 1996-99, Cochella Valley Cmty. Concerts Assn., 1992-95, coll. The Desert Found., 2003—, chmn. investment com., 2004; pres. Indian Wells Desert Symphony, 2002; v.p. Com. Leaders Club, 1988, pres., 1989-90, pres. Westlake Cultural Found., 1991; vice chair Alliance for the Arts; bd. regents Calif. Luth. U., 1990-99, chmn. acad. affairs, 1993-99, exec. com., 1992-99, chmn. acad. affairs, 1992-99, vice chmn., 1997-98; pres. Aviation C.C. of Calif., 2001; pres. coun. McCallun Theater, Palm Desert; mem. Pres.'s circle Coll. of the Desert, Palm Desert; mem. Rep. Ctrl. Com., State of Calif., 1993-98; bd. dirs. Indian Wells Desert Symphony, 2001-02; pres. World Affairs Coun. of the Desert, 2001—; bd. dirs. Coll. of Desert, 2003—, Boys and Girls Club Coachella Valley, 2003-; pres. Fredericks Found., 2002—; chmn. Westlake Village C. of C., 1990; nat. councillor World Affairs Coun., Washington, 2004—; bd. dirs. Coll. of the Desert Found., 2002—; chair investment com. COD Found., 2002—, exec. com., 2005-. Fellow Am. Transp. Assn.; mem. AAAS, IEEE, SAR, Am. Mktg. Assn., Nat. Coun. Phys. Distbn. Mgmt. (exec. com. 1974), Produce Mktg. Assn., United Fresh Fruit and Vegetable Assn., Internat. Fresh-Cut Produce Assn., Soc. Automotive Engrs., U.S. Strategic Inst., Tech. Execs. Forum (Tech. Corridor 100 award 1989), Internat. Food Mfg. Assn., Produce Mktg. Assn., Toronto Bd. Trade, English-Speaking Union (bd. dirs. 2004—), Westlake Village C. of C. (chmn. 1990), Old Crows, Assn. Advanced Tech. Edn., Air Force Assn., Aerospace Soc., Exptl. Aircraft Assn., Mil. Order World Wars, Conf. Air Force (Col.), Westlake Village C. of C. (chmn. bd. 1990-91), Cmty. Leaders Club, Pres.'s Club Mich. State U., Pres.'s Circle/Coll. of the Desert, English-Spkg. Union, Friends of Parliament, Old Bold Pilots Club, Indian Wells Country Club, Sherwood Country Club, St. Georges Club (U.K.), Aviation Country Club of Calif. (v.p. 1999, pres. 2000), Rotary (dir. 2003—), Flying Rotarians, World Affairs Coun., Beta Gamma Sigma. Lutheran. Home: 75375 Painted Desert Dr Indian Wells CA 92210 Office: 709 E Colorado Blvd Pasadena CA 91101

FREDERICKS, WESLEY CHARLES, JR., lawyer; b. N.Y.C., Mar. 31, 1948; s. Wesley Charles and Dionysia W. (Bitsanis) F.; m. Jeanne Maria Judson, May 19, 1973; children: Carolyn Anne, Wesley Charles III. BA, Johns Hopkins U., 1970; JD, Columbia U., 1973. Bar: N.Y. 1974, Conn. 1976, U.S. Supreme Ct. 1979. Assoc. Shearman & Sterling, N.Y.C., 1973-83; chmn. bd. Lotus Performance Cars, L.P., Norwood, N.J., 1983-87; group exec. cons. Group Lotus PLC, 1987; automotive industry cons., 1988-90; pres., CEO Mfrs. Products Co., 1990-94; counsel Gersten, Savage, Kaplowitz & Fredericks, LLP, N.Y.C., 1994, ptnr., 1995-98, Dorsey & Whitney LLP, N.Y.C., 1998—, dep. mng. ptnr., 2004—. Mem. Johns Hopkins U. Alumni Schs. Com. With USMC, 1968-69. Mem. ABA (chmn. bus. law sect. com. on internat. bus. law, 2004—, mem. com. on negotiated acquisitions 1997—), Weston Gun Club (Conn.), Mpls. Club, Preston Mountain Club. Republican. Congregationalist. Office: Dorsey & Whitney LLP 250 Park Ave New York NY 10177-0001

FREDERICKS, WILLIAM CURTIS, lawyer; b. Washington, July 3, 1961; s. J. Wayne and Anne Curtis Fredericks; m. Ivy Lindstrom, Jan. 21, 1995; children: Charlotte Lindstrom, Thomas Curtis. BA in Polit. Sci. with high honors, Swarthmore Coll., 1983; MLitt in Internat. Rels., Oxford (Eng.) U., 1988; JD, Columbia U., 1988. Bar: N.Y. 1990, U.S. Dist. Ct. (so. and ea. dists.) N.Y. 1990, U.S. Ct. Appeals (2d cir.) 1991, U.S. Ct. Appeals (10th cir.) 1997, U.S. Ct. Appeals (6th cir.) 1998, U.S. Dist. Ct. Colo. 1998, U.S. Ct. Appeals (3d cir.) 2001. Law clk. hon. Robert S. Gawthrop U.S. Dist. Ct. Pa., Phila., 1988—89; assoc. Simpson Thacher & Bartlett, NYC, 1989—93, Willkie Farr & Gallagher, NYC, 1993—97, Milberg Weiss Bershad & Schulman LLP, NYC, 1997—98, ptnr., 1999—. Articles editor Columbia Jour. Transnational Law, 1987-88. V.p. Swarthmore Coll. Alumni Assn., 1988-90. Mem. Assn. of the Bar of the City of N.Y. (chair com. on mil. affairs and justice 1997-99, mem. com. on fed. cts., 2004-). Democrat. Office: Milberg Weiss Bershad & Schulman LLP One Pennsylvania Plaza New York NY 10119-0165

FREDERICKSEN, DICK HARTMAN, retired computer programmer; b. Great Falls, Mont., Jan. 16, 1931; s. Frederick Hartman and Helen Dickinson Fredericksen; m. Ann Bancroft, July 30, 1960 (div. Oct. 1990); children: Diane, Judith, Alice, Victor. AB, U. Chgo., 1951, postgrad., 1951-60, MS, 1968. Systems engr. IBM Corp., Chgo., 1960-64, programmer Poughkeepsie, 1965-66, programmer T.J. Watson Rsch. Ctr. Yorktown Heights, N.Y., 1969-90; part-time programmer Nat. Optical Astronomy Observatories, Tucson, 1990-92, ret., 1992. Nat. chmn. Young Peoples Socialist League, 1951-53; active L5 Soc./Nat. Space Soc., NY, Ariz., 1976—. Mem. Sonoran Arthropod Studies Inst., Tucson Space Soc. (v.p. 2000, sec.-treas. 2001-03), Tucson Computer Soc. Avocations: web publishing, hiking, motorcycling, wildlife photography, commentary. Home: 7351 E Speedway Blvd Apt 11G Tucson AZ 85710-1513 Personal E-mail: dhfred@mindspring.com.

FREDERICKSEN, SCOTT L., lawyer; b. Williston, N.D., Sept. 20, 1952; s. Earl H. and Lillian H. Fredericksen; m. Dana Pugh, May 30, 1987; children: Jason, Anders, Erik. BA, U. N.D., 1974; JD, Boston U., 1977. Bar: Ill. 1977, U.S. Dist. Ct. (no. dist.) Ill. 1977, U.S. Ct. Appeals (7th cir.) 1978, U.S. Ct. Appeals (5th cir.) 1982, D.C. 1985, U.S. Ct. Appeals (D.C.) 1985, U.S. Ct. Appeals (4th cir.) 1989, Va. 1991, Wash. 1994, U.S. Dist. Ct. (we. dist.) Wash. 1994, U.S. Dist. Ct. (ea. dist.) Wash. 1998. Atty. Williams and Montgomery, Chgo., 1977-79, Freeman, Atkins & Coleman, Chgo., 1980-84; asst. U.S. atty. U.S. Atty.'s Office, D.C., Washington, 1984-89, U.S. Atty.'s Office, Ea. Dist. Va., Alexandria, 1989-91; assoc. ind. counsel Office of Ind. Counsel, Washington, 1991-94; ptnr. Stoel Rives LLP, Seattle, 1994—, chair L&E group. LMem. ABA (white collar crime, litigation and L&E sects.), AUSA (D.C. chpt.). Home: 9524 SE 68th St Mercer Island WA 98040-5119 Office: Stoel Rives LLP 600 University St Ste 3600 Seattle WA 98101-4109

FREDERICKSON, ARMAN FREDERICK, mining executive, petroleum engineer; b. Glenboro, Man., Can., May 5, 1918; came to U.S., 1923, naturalized, 1940; s. Albert F. and Ethel M. (Wilton) F.; m. Mary Maxine Stubblefield, Sept. 23, 1943; children: Mary Christene, Clover Diane, Penny Kathlene, Kimberly Mei, Sigrid, Janice BS in Mining Engring, U. Wash., 1940; MS in Metall. Engring, Mont. Sch. Mines, 1942; Sc.D. in Geology, Mass. Inst. Tech., 1947. Registered profl. engr., Tex., Colo., Nev., Mo.; cert. petroleum geologist. Mining engr., chief geologist Cornucopia Gold Mines, Oreg., 1939-40; instr. mineral dressing Mont. Sch. Mines, 1941-42; research asst. Mass. Inst. Tech., 1942-43; prof. geology and geol. engring. Washington U., St. Louis, 1947-56; organizer, supr. geol. research Standard (Amoco) Oil and Gas Co., Tulsa, 1955-60; prof. geology, chmn. dept. earth and planetary sci., dir. oceanography U. Pitts., 1960-65; sr. v.p., dir. research, mgr. petroleum prospecting and mineral programs in U.S., Middle East, Africa, Latin Am., 1965-71; pres., chief engr. Sorbotec, Inc., Houston, 1971-74; pres. Global Survey, 1972—. V.p. Samoco (Panama) Challenger Desert Oil Corp., 1977-81; cons. in mining and petroleum exploration, 1971—; v.p. SAMOCO, Del., 1977-81; v.p. ops. CHADOIL, 1978-81, Crown Gems, Inc., Thailand; pres. Global-Thai Exploration Corp., Thailand; organizer, past chmn. clay minerals com. Nat. Acad. Sci.-NRC; organizer, econ. analyst land and real estate projects, Calif.; negotiator oil, gemstone and mining programs, U.S., Africa, Thailand, Middle and Far East, Latin Am., exploration specialist. Author tech. papers in field, hist. novels; patentee fertilizer, oil and water pollution processes and products. Served with USNR, 1943-45. Fulbright prof. Norway, 1955. Fellow Geol. Soc. Am., Mineral Soc. Am.; mem. Am. Inst. Mining, Metall. and Petroleum Engrs., Am. Assn. Petroleum Geologists, Soc. Econ. Geologists, Geochem. Soc. Am., Underwater Soc. Am. Republican. Lutheran. numerous clubs. Home: 97 Mission Dr Petaluma CA 94952-5228 Office Phone: 707-658-0404.

FREDERICKSON, CHRISTOPHER JOHN, neuroscientist; b. Norman, Okla., Aug. 1, 1945; s. John Henry and Joan Munson Frederickson; m. Cathleen Jean McCartney, Apr. 30, 1995; 1 child, Isabel. AB magna cum laude, Harvard Coll., 1968; PhD, U. Chgo., 1972. Asst. prof. neurosci. Carnegie Mellon, Pitts., 1972-75, U. Tex. Dallas, Richardson, 1975-78, assoc. prof. neurosci., 1978-85, full prof. neurosci., 1985-99; CEO NeuroBio Tex, Little Elm, Tex., 1999—. Dir. biotech. MicroFab Tech., Inc., Plano, Tex., 1996—99, U. Tex. Med. Br., Galveston, 1999—2000; mem. adv. bd. Tex. A&M Biomed. Engring., College Station, 1998—99; inaugural chair NIH Zinc in Health/Zinc in the Brain/Metals in Medicine, 2002; spkr. in field. Editor: Zinc Neurobiology, 1985; contbr. articles to profl. jours.; patentee in field. Bd. mem. YMCA, Richardson, 1995. Small Bus. Innovation and Rsch. grantee NIH, Washington, 1998. Mem. Soc. for Neurosci., Soc. Photo-Optical Instrumentation Engrs., Am. Chemosensory Soc. Avocation: sailing. Office: NeuroBioTex 101 Christopher Columbus 14th Stus 14 Galveston TX 77550 E-mail: c.j.frederickson@neurobiotex.com.

FREDERICKSON, HORACE GEORGE, retired academic administrator, humanities educator; b. Twin Falls, Idaho, July 17, 1937; s. John C. and Zelpha (Richins) F.; m. Mary Williams, Mar. 14, 1958; children— Thomas, Christian, Lynne, David. BA, Brigham Young U., 1959; M.P.A., UCLA, 1961; PhD, U. So. Calif., 1967; LL.D. (hon.), Dongguk U., Korea. Intern Los Angeles County, 1960; research asst. Bur. Govtl. Research, U. Calif., Los Angeles, 1960-61; lectr. pub. adminstrn. U. So. Calif., 1962-64; lectr. govt. and politics U. Md., 1964-66; asst. prof. polit. sci. Maxwell Sch., Syracuse U., 1967-71; assoc. dir. Met. Studies Program, 1970-72, assoc. prof. polit. sci., 1971-72; fellow in higher edn. fin. adminstrn. U. N.C. System, 1972; chmn. Grad. Program, Sch. Pub. and Environ. Affairs, Ind. U., 1972-74, assoc. dean for policy and adminstrv. studies, 1973-74; dean Coll. Pub. and Community Services, prof. regional and community affairs U. Mo., Columbia, 1974-76; pres. Eastern Wash. U., Cheney, 1976-87; Edwin O. Stene Disting. prof. pub. adminstrn. U. Kans., Lawrence, 1987—; John G. Winont vis. prof. Am. Gov., fellow U. Oxford, 2003—. Author: New Public Administration, 1980, The Spirit of Public Administration, 1997; editor: Ethics and Public Administration, 1993, Public Policy and the Two States of Kansas, 1994, Ideal and Practice in Council-Manager Government, 2nd edit., 1994; editor in chief Jour. Pub. Adminstrn. Rsch. and Theory, 1991—. Haynes Found. fellow U. So. Calif., 1963-64 Mem. Am. Soc. Pub. Adminstrn. (pres.), Nat. Acad. Pub. Adminstrn. Home: 3420 Doral Ct Lawrence KS 66047-2131 Office: U Kans 1541 Lilac Ln #318 Lawrence KS 66044-3177

FREDERIKSEN, PATIENCE ANN, librarian; b. Warwick, R.I., Aug. 21, 1957; d. Robert Christian and Winifred Holmes (Valentine) F.; 1 child, Christian Lawrence Klint. BA in Creative Writing/History, Carnegie Mellon U., 1979; MLS, Syracuse U., 1986. Reference libr. Anchorage Mun. Librs., 1986-88; reference coord. Juneau (Alaska) Pub. Librs., 1988-89; documents libr. Alaska State Libr., Juneau, 1989, collection devel. libr., 1989-91, head govt. publs. sect., 1991-95, head govt. publs. and tech. svcs. sect., 1996—99; grants adminstr, regional libr. Talking Book Ctr. Alaska State Libr., 1999—. Steering com. Fed. State Coop. Sys. for Pub. Libr. Statistics, 2003—. Recipient Nat. Merit Scholarship, Carnegie-Mellon U., Pitts., 1975-79 Mem. Alaska Libr. Assn. (founder and chair Documents Roundtable, 1992-94, editor Newspoke 1994-97, chair Juneau chpt. 1995-98). Democrat. Avocations: quilting, genealogy, reading. Office: Alaska State Libr 344 W 3d Ave Ste 125 Anchorage AK 99501 Home: 7511 Huckleberry Cir Anchorage AK 99502-2880 Office Phone: 907-269-6566.

FREDMANN, MARTIN, ballet company executive, educator, choreographer; b. Balt., Feb. 3, 1943; s. Martin Joseph and Hilda Adele (Miller) Fredmann; m. Kaleriyam Fedicheva Fredmann (div. Jan. 2, 1973); m. Patricia Renzetti, June 12, 1980. Student, Nat. Ballet Sch., Washington, 1962-64, Vaganova Sch., Leningrad, 1972. Prin. dancer The Md. Ballet, Balt., 1961-64; dancer The Pa. Ballet, Phila., 1964-65, Ballet of the Met. Opera Co., N.Y.C., 1965-66; prin. dancer Dortmund (Fed. Republic Germany) Ballet, 1973-75, Scapino Ballet, Amsterdam, Holland, 1975-76; tchr. German Opera Ballet, West Berlin, Fed. Republic Germany, 1979, Netherlands Dance Theater, 1979, Royal Swedish Ballet, 1980, San Francisco Ballet, 1981; tchr., coach Australian Ballet, 1982; tchr. Tokyo City Ballet, Hong Kong Ballet, 1985, 86, 87, London Festival Ballet, 1981-83; dir. ballet Teatro Comunale, Florence, Italy, 1984-85; artistic dir. Tampa (Fla.) Ballet, 1984-90; artistic dir. in alliance with The Tampa Ballet Colo. Ballet, Denver, 1987-90, artistic dir., 1987—. Tchr. German Opera Ballet, 1982, Ballet Rambert, London, 1983, Bat Dor summer course, Israel, 1983, Cullberg Ballet, Sweden, 1983, Hong Kong Acad. For Performing Arts, 1985—89, 1991, Tokyo City Ballet, 1985—90, Ballet West, 1990, Nat. Ballet Korea, 1991, Dance Divsn. Tsoying High Sch., Kaohsiung, Taiwan, 1992; guest lectr., tchr. Cen. Ballet China, Beijing Dancing Acad., P.L.A. Arts Coll., Beijing, 1990; tchr. Legat Sch., 1978, examiner, 80; tchr. Eglevsky Sch., N.Y.C., 1980; asst. dir. ballet master Niavaron Cultural ctr., Tehran, Iran, 1978; tchr. Ballet Arts Sch. Carnegie Hall, N.Y.C., 1979—81; choreographer Estonia Nat. Theatre, Russia, 1991; dir. Marin Ballet., Calif., 1981. Choreographer Romeo and Juliet, 1983, Sachertorte, 1984, A Little Love, 1984, Ricordanza, 1986, Cinderella, 1986, Coppelia, 1987, The Nutcracker, 1987, Beauty and the Beast, 1988, Masquerade Suite, 1989, Silent Woods, 1989, The Last Songs, 1991, Centenial Suite, 1994. Recipient Recipient Mayor's award, Denver, 1996, Dance Mag. award, 1999, Bonfils-Stanton Found. award, 2000, Order of the Rising Sun, Gold Rays with Rosette, Govt of Japan, 2005. Mem.: Nat. Assn. Regional Ballet., Fla. State Dance Assn, Am. Guild Mus. Artists. Avocations: cooking, cook book collecting, travel, opera. Home: 836 E 17th Ave Apt 3A Denver CO 80218-1449 Office: Colo Ballet 1278 Lincoln St Denver CO 80203-2114 Office Phone: 303-837-8888 11.

FRED-MENSAH, BEN KWAME, international development educator, consultant; b. Accra, Ghana, Oct. 8, 1953; s. Frederick Kofi Mensah Gbotsyo and Rosina Adzoyo Atitoe; m. Josephine Afi Dzoku, May 22, 1963; children: Selorm, Akorfa. MPhil, Cambridge (Eng.) U.; PhD, Johns Hopkins U., 1999. Tchr., supt. Ghana Edn. Svc., 1973-86; cons. World Bank, Washington, 1991-96; asst. prof. govt. Hamilton Coll., Clinton, N.Y., 1998-2000, hon. vis. scholar Arthur Levitt Pub. Affairs Ctr., 2001—; dir. African Ctr. for Innovative Literacy and Learning, Washington, 2001—. Postdoctoral fellow, Brown U., Providence, 1996-98. Numerous publs. in field. Recipient numerous awards; Rockefeller Found. fellow, 1994. Mem. Fellow Cambridge Commonwealth Soc. at Cambridge in U.K. (life). Presbyterian. Avocation: observing nature.

FREDREGILL, ALAN, lawyer; b. Adel, Iowa, Mar. 19, 1948; BBA, U. Iowa, 1970; JD with honors, Drake U., 1974. Bar: Iowa 1975, Nebr. 1984. Atty. Heidman, Redmond, Fredregill, Patterson, Plaza, Dykstra & Prahl, LLP, Sioux City, Iowa. Mem.: Am. Mock Trial Assn. (Judges Hall of Fame 2002), Woodbury County Bar Assn., Internat. Assn. Arson Investigators, Iowa Acad. Trial Lawyers, Am. Coll. Trial Lawyers, Def. Rsch. Inst., Internat. Assn. Def. Counsel, Iowa Def. Counsel Assn. (bd. dirs. 1981—, pres. 1990—91), Iowa State Bar Assn. (unauthorized practice com. 1985—95, chmn. 1987—89, bd. govs. 1996—2003, pres. 2002—03), Nebr. State Bar Assn., Order of Coif, ABA (litigation sect.). Office: Heidman Redmond Fredregill et al PO Box 3086 701 Pierce St Ste 200 Sioux City IA 51102

FREDRICK, CHUCK, information technology executive; BS in Computer Sci., Embry Riddle Aeronautical U.; MBA with Mktg. Emphasis, U. Colo. Cert. Project Mgmt. Profl. Project Mgmt. Inst. Info. systems project engr. USAF, 1993—95, exec. officer devel. planning, 1995—97, project mgr. advanced space command and control applications, 1997—2000, capt., acquisition officer; info. tech. mgr. planning and requirements Nextel Comm., 2000—01, info. tech. mgr. call ctr. application svcs., 2001—02, sr. info. tech. mgr. call ctr. application, devel. and integration, 2002—03, sr. info. tech. mgr. program mgmt. and project execution, 2004—.

FREDRICK, LARITA DENISE, science educator; b. Springfield, Mo., Sept. 27, 1954; d. Ordra Paul Pippin and Bernice Orene Kirkey, Clarence William Kirkey, Jr. (Stepfather); m. Gail L. Fredrick, Nov. 13, 1987. BS in Secondary Edn., S.W. Mo. State U., 1983, MS in Secondary Edn., 1994. Cert. tchr. Dept. of Elem. and Secondary Edn., Mo., 1983. Tchr. sci. H.S. Springfield (Mo.) Pub. Schs., 1985—2001, curriculum coord. k-12 sci., 2001—. Adj. instr. Ozarks Tech. Coll., Springfield, 1994—2001, S.W. Mo. State U., 1996—2002, Drury U., Springfield, 2002—. Ex-officio mem. Springfield (Mo.) Pub. Schs. Found., 2002—05. Named Outstanding Young Alumni, S.W. Mo. State U., 2000; recipient Triple E Edn. award, 1998, Nat. Edn. award, Milken Family Found., 1999, Mo. Eddy award, Dept. Elem. and Secondary Edn., Mo., 2000. Mem.: NEA, Am. Soc. Curriculum Devel., Nat. Assn. Sci. Tchrs. Office: Springfield Public Schools 940 N Jefferson Springfield MO 65802 Office Phone: 417-523-5556. Personal E-mail: ldenisefredrick@sbcglobal.net.

FREDRICK, LAURENCE WILLIAM, astronomer, educator; b. Stroudsburg, Pa., Aug. 27, 1927; s. Ishmeal T. and Grace (Slider) F.; m. Frances I. Schwenk, Feb. 5, 1949; children— Laura Grace, Theodore David, Rebecca Lyn BA, Swarthmore Coll., 1952, MA, 1954; PhD, U. Pa., 1959. Research asst. Sproul Obs., Swarthmore, Pa., 1952-56; research assoc. Flower and Cook Obs., Malvern, Pa., 1957-59; astronomer Lowell Obs., Flagstaff, Ariz., 1959-63; mem. faculty U. Va., Charlottesville, 1963-95, prof. astronomy, 1965-95, rsch. prof., 1995—; prof. U. Vienna, Austria, 1972-73. Cons. in field; Fulbright-Hays exch. lectr., Austria, 1972-73; assoc. astronomer European So. Obs., Munich, Fed. Republic Germany, 1982-83; vis. fellow Australian Nat. U., Canberra, 1991-92. Co-author: Astronomy, 10th edit., 1976, Descriptive Astronomy, 1978, An Introduction to Astronomy, 9th edit., 1980 Served with USN, 1945-48 Named Alumnus of Yr., Milton Hershey Sch., 1961 Mem. Am. Astron. Soc. (sec. 1969-80), Internat. Astron. Union (sec. U.S. nat. com. 1970-80), Am. Inst. Physics (bd. govs. 1969-79), Univs. for Space Research Assn. (trustee), Royal Astron. Soc., Soc. Sci. Exploration (sec. 1981-2005), Sigma Xi Home: 2602 Bennington Rd Charlottesville VA 22901-2211 Office Phone: 434-924-4905.

FREDRICKSON, GEORGE MARSH, history professor; b. Bristol, Conn., July 16, 1934; s. George Fredrickson and Gertrude (Marsh) F.; m. Helene Osouf, Oct. 16, 1956; children: Anne, Laurel, Thomas, Caroline. AB, Harvard U., 1956, PhD, 1964. Instr. history Harvard U., Cambridge, Mass., 1963-66;

assoc. prof. history Northwestern U., Evanston, Ill., 1966-71, prof., 1971-84, William Smith Mason prof. Am. history, 1979-84; Edgar E. Robinson prof. U.S. history Stanford (Calif.) U., 1984—2002, prof. emeritus, 2002—. Fulbright prof. Moscow U., 1983, Harmsworth prof. Am. history Oxford U., 1988-89. Author: The Inner Civil War, 1965, 2d edit., 1993, The Black Image in the White Mind, 1971, 2d edit., 1987 (Anisfield-Wolf award 1972), White Supremacy, 1981 (Ralph Waldo Emerson award 1981, Merle Curti award, 1982, Pulitzer prize finalist 1982), The Arrogance of Race, 1988, Black Liberation, 1995, The Comparative Imagination, 1997, Racism: A Short History, 2002; co-author: America: Past and Present, 7th edit., 2004; editor: A Nation Divided, 1975; co-editor: Not Just Black and White, 2004. Served to lt. USN, 1957-60. Guggenheim fellow, 1967-68; NEH fellow, 1973-74; Ctr. for Advanced Studies in Behavioral Scis. fellow, 1977-78; NEH fellow, 1985-86; Ford sr. fellow DuBois Inst., Harvard U., 1993. Fellow Soc. Am. Historians, Am. Antiquarian Soc., Am. Acad. Arts and Scis.; mem. Am. Hist. Assn., Orgn. Am. Historians (pres. 1997-98), So. Hist. Assn. Home: 741 Esplanada Way Palo Alto CA 94305-1013 Office: Stanford Univ Dept History Stanford CA 94305 Business E-Mail: fredrick@stanford.edu.

FREDRICKSON, KAREN LORAINE, librarian; b. Kansas City, Mo., Sept. 27, 1952; d. Kenneth Eugene Kruse and Loraine Lulu (Neugebauer) Morse; m. Timothy Dean Cox, Sept. 1, 1973 (dec. Sept. 1984); m. David Dean Fredrickson, June 10, 1989; children: Jennifer, Rachel. BS, Cen. Mo. State U., 1974, MS, 1979. Cert. tchr. Kans., Mo. Tchr./libr. Lone Jack (Mo.) Schs., 1974-76; tchr. Clarksville-Montgomery County Schs., Tenn., 1977; tchr./libr. St John's Luth. Sch., Indpls., 1978-82; libr. media specialist Lawrence (Kans.) Public Schs., 1985—. Mem. Lawrence In-Svc. Coun., 1986-88. Recipient Kans. Ednl. Excellence Program award Southwestern Bell, Lawrence, 1991. Mem. ALA, Am. Assn. Sch. Libr., Kans. Assn. Sch. Libr. Luth. Avocations: sewing, crocheting. Office: Langston Hughes Sch 1101 George Williams Way Lawrence KS 66049 Office Phone: 785-832-5890 106. E-mail: klfredri@usd497.org.

FREDRICKSON, L(AWRENCE) THOMAS, composer; b. Kane, Pa., Sept. 5, 1928; s. Eric Lawrence Fredrickson and Esther Linnea (Skoog) Bussell; m. Betty Jean Blessing, July 30, 1950; children: Lawrence Alan, Linda Kay, Gail Diane. MusB, Ohio Wesleyan U., 1950; MusM, U. Ill., Urbana, 1952, MusD, 1960. Jazz musician, Ill., 1952—; composer, arranger Urbana, Ill., 1952—; instr. music U. Ill., Urbana/Champaign, 1952-60, asst. prof., 1960-63, assoc. prof., 1963-67, prof., 1967-93, prof. emeritus, 1993, dir. Sch. of Music, 1970-74. Composer: Brass Quintet, Impressions, Deja Vu, Music for the Double Bass Alone; commns. include works for orch., band, chamber music, solo works; performer double bass in chamber music and jazz groups, symphony orchs. Mem. ASCAP, Am. Fedn. of Musicians. Home: 1814 Robert Dr Champaign IL 61821-6031

FREDRIK, BURRY, theater producer, theater director; b. NYC, Aug. 9, 1925; d. Fredric Kreuger and Erna Anita (Burry) Gerber; m. Gerard E. Meunier, Dec. 27, 1945 (div. 1949). Grad., Sarah Lawrence Coll., 1947. Ind. theatrical dir., producer U.S. and abroad, 1955—; lit. mgr., dir. Boston Post Road Stage Co., 1988—92; artistic dir. Fairfield County Stage Co. (formerly Boston Post Road Stage), 1992—93. Prodr.: (Broadway plays) Too Good to be True, 1964—65 (nominated Tony award, 1965), Travesties, 1976 (Tony award, 1976), An Almost Perfect Person, 1977, The Night of the Tribades, 1978, To Grandmother's House We Go, 1981, The Royal Family, 1975—76 (Drama Desk award, 1976), (off-Broadway plays) Thieves Carnival, 1955 (Spl. Tony award, 1955), Exiles, 1956 (OBIE award, 1956), Buried Child (Pulitzer prize, 1980); dir.: (nat. tours) Misalliance, 1953, Milk and Honey, 1963, Dark at the Top of the Stairs, 1958, Dear Love, 1971, To Grandmother's House We Go, 1982, (off-Broadway prodns.) The Decameron, 1961, Catholic School Girls, 1981, (Broadway prodn.) Wild and Wonderful, 1972; prodr.: (off-Broadway) Pretzels, 1974; dir.: (plays, Sad Hotel) White Barn Theatre, 2001—; (plays, Swansong), 2002—. Chmn. Weston Commn. Arts, 1997—2000; mem. fin. commn., trustee Long Wharf Theatre, New Haven, 1998—. Recipient Disting. Adv. Arts award, State of Conn. Commn. Arts, 2001. Home and Office: 51 Hillside Rd N Weston CT 06883-1513 Office Phone: 203-227-9349. Office Fax: 203-222-9478.

FREDRIKSEN, JOHN CONRAD, historian, consultant; b. N. Kingston, R.I., Feb. 18, 1953; s. John Wilhelm Fredriksen and Erselia Borrelli. BA, UCLA, 1980, MA, 1984, U. Mich., 1989; PhD, Providence Coll., 1993. Cel painter Motion Picture Screen Cartoonists, Hollywood, Calif., 1977—87; historian self employed, 1993—. Grad. hist. asst. Providence Coll., 1990; grad. student fellow Can. Embassy, 1991. Author: (ref. books) American Military Leaders, 1999, Green Coats and Glory: The U.S. Regiment of Riflemen, 1808-1821, 1999. Vis. scholar Adv. Rsch. scholar, Eccles Libr., 2001. Mem.: Am. Hist. Assn., Phi Alpha Theta. Republican. Roman Catholic. Achievements include complied and published the first bibliography on the War of 1812; U.S. Mil. History 1783-1846; authority on War of 1812 printed and primary resources. Avocations: history, paleontology, dolphins, rock and roll music, animation. Home: 154 Carpenter Dr South Kingstown RI 02879-6355 Office Phone: 401-788-9016. Personal E-mail: jfreksen@sisna.com.

FREE, HELEN MURRAY, chemist, consultant; b. Pitts., Feb. 20, 1923; d. James Summerville and Daisy (Piper) Murray; m. Alfred H. Free, Oct. 18, 1947 (dec. May 2000); children: Eric, Penny, Kurt, Jake, Bonnie, Nina. BA in Chemistry, Coll. of Wooster, Ohio, 1944, DSc (hon.), 1992; MA in Clin. Lab. Mgmt., Ctrl. Mich. U., 1978, DSc (hon.), 1993. Cert. clin. chemist Nat. Registry Cert. Chemists. Chemist Miles Labs., Elkhart, Ind., 1944—78, dir. mktg. svcs. rsch. products divsn., 1978-82; chemist, mgr., cons. diabetes care divsn. Bayer HealthCare, Elkhart, 1982—. Mem. adj. faculty Ind. U., South Bend, 1975—96. Author (with others): (books) Urodynamics and Urinalysis in Clinical Laboratory Practice, 1972, 1976; contbr. articles to encys. and profl. jours. Bd. dirs. Nat. Inventors Hall of Fame Found.; women's chmn. Centennial of Elkhart, 1958; mem. adv. bd. Intellectual Property Sch. Law, Akron U.; indsl. adv. bd. chemistry/chem. engring. Tri-State U., Angola, Ind. Named Woman of Yr., YWCA, 1993, Kilby Found. laureate, 1996; named to Hall of Excellence, Ohio Found. Ind. Colls., 1992, Nat. Inventors Hall of Fame, 2000, Engring. and Sci. Hall of Fame, 1996; recipient Disting. Alumni award, Coll. of Wooster, 1980, award, Medi Econ. Press, 1986, Nat. Leadership award, Lab. Pub. Svc., 1994. Fellow: AAAS, Royal Soc. Chemistry, Am. Inst. Chemists (co-recipient Chgo. award 1967); mem.: Nat. Com. Clin. Lab. Stds. (bd. dirs.), Am. Soc. Clin. Lab. Sci. (chmn. assembly, Achievement award 1976), Soc. Chem. Industry (hon.), Assn. Clin. Scientists (diploma of honor 1992), Am. Assn. Clin. Chemistry (coun., bd. dirs., nat. membership com., nominating com. and pub. rels. com., coord. profl. affairs, pres.), Am. Chem. Soc. (pres. 1993, bd. dirs., chmn. Chemistry Week task force, bd. com. pub. affairs and pub. rels., chmn. women chemists com., internat. activities com., grants and awards com., prof. and mem. rels. com., nominating com., coun. policy pub. affairs and budget, councilor, chair Progress project, Garvan medal 1980, Svc. award local chpt. 1981, co-recipient Mosher award 1983, 1st recipient Helen M. Free Pub. Outreach award 1995, Helen M. Free award named in her honor 1995), Altrusa (pres. 1982—83, bd. dirs.), Sigma Delta Epsilon (hon.), Iota Sigma Pi (hon.). Presbyterian. Achievements include patents in field. Home: 3752 E Jackson Blvd Elkhart IN 46516-5205 Office: Bayer HealthCare Diabetes Care Divsn 1884 Miles Ave Elkhart IN 46514-2291 E-mail: Hmfree23@aol.com, helen.free.b@bayer.com.

FREE, MARY MOORE, biological and medical anthropologist; b. Paris, Tex., Mar. 6, 1933; d. Dudley Crawford and Margie Lou (Moore) Hubbard; m. Dwight Allen Free Jr., June 26, 1954 (dec.); children: Hardy (dec.), Dudley (dec.), Margery, Caroline. Student, Ward-Belmont Coll., 1951; BS, So. Meth. U., 1954, MLA, 1981, MA, 1987, PhD, 1989. Instr. So. Meth. U., Dallas, 1982-89, prof. continuing edn., 1989-90; prof. So. Meth. U., Dedman Coll., Dallas, 1990—; adj. asst. prof. dept. anthropology So. Meth. U., Dallas, 1990—. Prof. Richland C.C., Dallas, 1986; house anthropologist Baylor U. Med. Ctr., mem. adv. bd. Inst. for Study of Earth and Man, 1995, preceptor clin. edn. affiliation, 1990—, chair Class 1954 sustentation drive, organ/tissue transplantation task force, 1997; cardiothoracic transplantation team Baylor U. Med. Ctr., S.W. transplantation team Baylor U. Med. Ctr./U. Tex. Southwestern Med. Sch., 1990— (cardiothoracic transplantation award for excellence in svc., 1998); adv. bd. geriatrics Vis. Nurse Assn., Dallas, 1984-91; presenter in field anthropology, medicine, women's issues; bd. Dedman Coll. SMU Excellence in Sci. Lecture Series, Dallas Soc. SMU, Collegium de Vinci, SMU; contbr. AMA/JAMA protocol on authorship; spokesperson, adv. bd. Lisa Landry Childress Found. for Organ Donation Awareness. Author: The Private World of the Hermitage: Lifestyles of the Rich and Old in an Elite Retirement Home, 1995; contbr. numerous chpts. in sci. books, ednl. TV, and articles to Anthropology Newsletter, Am. Anthropologist, Am. Jour. Cardiology, Cahiers de Sociologie Economique et Culturelle-Ethnopsycholie, Jour. Heart Failure, Jour. Internat. Soc. Dermatology, Jour. Leadership Ctr., Baylor Health Care System, Jour. Lisa Landry Childrens Found.,; mem. editl. bd. Baylor U. Med. Ctr. Procs.; editor/contbr. Jour. Kimberly H. Courtwright and Joseph W. Summers Inst. of Metabolic Disease, BUMC, 1998; contbr. numerous articles to profl. jours. Bd. dirs. New Hearts and Lungs, Baylor Med. Ctr., 1994—, Lisa Landry Childress Found. for Organ Donor Awareness, Victims Outreach, 1997—, Isis Soc. and internat. issues com. Baylor U. Med. Ctr.; active various svc. and social orgns. Named one of Notable Women of Tex., 1984; recipient Outstanding Svc. Cardiothoracic Transplantation award Baylor U. Med. Ctr., 1998; provide Dr. Mary Moore Free Endowment for grad. study fieldwork in anthropology So. Meth. U. Fellow Am. Anthrop. Assn., Inst. for Study of Earth and Man; mem. AAAS, Internat. Soc. Heart Failure (sci. adv. bd.), Internat. Acad. Cardiology Inc. (internat. sci. adv. bd.), Internat. Congress Heart Disease (internat. sci. adv. bd.), Internat. Soc. Heart Disease (sci. adv. bd.), Soc. Heart Edn. (sci. adv. bd.), Dallas Women's Club, Dallas Petroleum Club, Brook Hollow Golf Club, Pi Beta Phi. Methodist. Achievements include development of position of house anthropologist in non-academic medical center, community medicine program; cross-cultural research on old age, women and cardiology. Home: 4356 Edmondson Ave Dallas TX 75205-2602 Office: Baylor U Med Ctr 3500 Gaston Ave Dallas TX 75246-2096

FREE, RHONA CAMPBELL, economics professor; BA, Sarah Lawrence Coll., 1978; MA in Econs., U. Notre Dame, 1980, PhD, 1983. Sr. tchg. fellow U. Notre Dame, 1981—83; asst. prof. Ea. Conn. State U., 1983—88, acting dept. chmn. Dept. Econs. and Mgmt. Sci., 1988, assoc. prof., 1988—93, prof., 1993—, dir. Ctr. Ednl. Excellence. Recipient Outstanding Master's Univ. and Coll. Prof. of Yr., Coun. for Advancement and Support of Edn. & Carnegie Found. for Advancement of Tchg., 2004. Office: Dept Econs Ea Conn State U Willimantic CT 06226 E-mail: free@easternct.edu.

FREEBORN, MICHAEL D., lawyer; b. Mpls., June 30, 1946; s. Andrew W. and Verena M. (Keller) F.; m. Nancie L. Siebel, Oct. 19, 1947; children: Christopher A., Nathan M., Joel C., Paul K. BS, USAF Acad., 1968; MBA, U. Chgo., 1975; JD, Ind. U., 1972. Bar: Ill. 1972, Ind. 1972, U.S. Ct. Appeals 3rd, 6th, 7th & D.C. cir., U.S. Supreme Ct. Assoc., ptnr. Rooks, Pitts & Poust, Chgo., 1972-83; ptnr. Freeborn & Peters, Chgo., 1983—. Writer, lectr. in field. Assoc. editor Ind. Law Rev., 1970-71. Vice chmn. Voices for Ill. Children, 1993—; bd. dirs. Constnl. Rights Found. Chgo., 1996—, Chgo. Youth Ctrs., 1998—; chmn. citizens adv. coun. Ill. Coastal Zone Mgmt. Program, Chgo., 1979. Capt. USAF, 1968—72. Recipient Founders Day award Ind. U. Law Sch., 1972. Mem. Ill. Bar Assn. (Assembly del.), Ind. Bar Assn., Union League, Legal (Chgo.). Lutheran. Avocations: scuba diving, coin collecting/numismatics, flying, racquetball. Office: Freeborn & Peters 311 S Wacker Dr Ste 3000 Chicago IL 60606-6679

FREEBORN, PHILIP, information technology executive; Dep. head, info. tech. UBS Warburg, London, mng. dir. info. tech., global head of info. tech. Stamford, Conn., 2003—. Mem. Fin. Services Roundtable. Named named one of top tech. innovators, Info. Week mag., 2004. Office: Global Head Info Tech UBS Warburg 677 Washington Blvd PO Box 300 Stamford CT 06912-0300

FREED, AMANDA LOUISE, Olympic athlete; b. Cypress, Calif., Dec. 26, 1979; d. Dave and Karen Freed. Degree in sociology, UCLA, 2002. Mem. USA Women's Softball Team, Athens Olympics, 2004. Named First Team All American, NFCA (Nat. Fastpitch Coach's Assn.), 1999, 2002. Achievements include mem. UCLA NCAA Championship Team, 1999; mem. USA Women's Softball Gold Medal Team, ISF World Championships, 2002, Athens Olympic games, 2004.

FREED, ARTHUR, civil engineer; b. Dec. 11, 1930; s. Harry and Mollie (Feinberg) Freed; m. Judith Lois Kaplan, July 31, 1960; children: Lisa Anne, Andrew Scott. BCE, CCNY, 1953. Registered profl. engr., NY. Jr. civil engr. Westchester County (NY) Dept. Pub. Works, 1953—58, asst. civil engr., 1958—60, sr. civil engr., 1960—62, traffic engr., 1962—79, dir. traffic engring. and hwy. safety, 1979—86, 1986—87, dep. commr. pub. works, chief of ops., 1987—91, exec. dir. Traffic Safety Bd., 1971—91; ret., 1991. Vis. lectr. U.S. Mil. Acad., West Point, NY; instr. FBI Command Sch.; lectr. in field. Contbr. articles to profl. jours.; currently exhibited in NYC museums and mus. ship models for NYPD, FDNY and USCG. Mem. NY State traffic engring. adv. com. to Dept. Motor Vehicles, 1959—68, Nat. Adv. Com. on Uniform Traffic Control Devices, 1972—79; chmn. Nat. Assn. Counties Del.; rep. Pres.' Com. on Traffic Safety; mem. Hwy. Rsch. Bd. Commn. on Motor Vehicle and Traffic Law, 1965—76; v.p. NY State Assn. Traffic Safety Bds., 1972—79, pres., 1979—81; mem. tech. transfer adv. com. Cornell U., Westchester C.C., 1971—91; mem. adv. bd. on tech. transfer Cornell U.; instr. NY State Police Acad.; mem. Gov.'s Youth Safety Com., Gov.'s Task Force on Alcohol and Hwy. Safety.; mem. traffic engring. adv. com. NY State Dept. Transp., 1978—; fundraiser N.Y. C. Police Mus.; bd. dirs. White Plains Beautification Found., 1986—2003. With U.S. Army, 1953—55. Recipient award of merit, State Traffic Safety Coun., 1964, Engr. of Yr. award, Internat. Inst. Transp., 1978, award for pub. svc., Nat. Hwy. Traffic Safety Adminstrn., 1985. Fellow: NSPE (hon.; pres.-coll. guidance com.); mem.: NAS, ASCE, Nat. Assn. County Info. Officers (award of excellence 1981), Nat. Hwy. Traffic Safety Adminstrn., Nat. Assn. Counties (chmn. traffic adv. com., County achievement award 1977, 1981, 1985, 1987, 1989), Physicians for Auto Safety, Am. Rd. and Transp. Builders Assn., Am. Pub. Works Assn., Hwy. Users Fedn., Greater NY Safety Coun., NY State Safety Coun., NY Soc. Profl. Engrs. (chmn. guidance com. Westchester county, state scholastic coord., Outstanding Engr. in Cmty. Svc. award 1982, Outstanding Engr. in Svc. to Profession award 1984, Engr. Yr. 1988), Inst. Transp. Engrs. (pres. NY-NJ 1965—66, chmn. student activities, Disting. Mem. 1991). Home: 6 Patricia Ln White Plains NY 10605-4009 Personal E-mail: afreedpe@verizon.net.

FREED, CHARLES, engineering consultant, researcher; b. Budapest, Hungary, Mar. 21, 1926; came to U.S., 1949; s. Erno and Ernestine (Duschnitz) F.; m. Florence Joan Wallach, Apr. 16, 1956; children: Lisa Ernestine, Josie Anne. BEE, NYU, 1952; SM, MIT, 1954, EE, 1958. Registered profl. engr., Mass. Rsch. asst. MIT, Cambridge, Mass., 1952-55, mem. staff, 1955-58; sr. engr., dept. head Raytheon, Waltham, Mass., 1958-62; mem. staff Lincoln Lab., Lexington, Mass., 1962-78, sr. staff mem., 1978-94, cons., 1994—. Lectr. dept. elec. engring. and computer sci. MIT, Cambridge, 1969-99. Contbr. over 60 articles to profl. jours. Fellow IEEE, Mil. Sensing Symposia; mem. Tau Beta Pi, Eta Kappa Nu, Sigma Xi. Achievements include patent in field. Home: 16 Browning Ln Lincoln MA 01773-3911 Office: MIT Lincoln Lab 244 Wood St Lexington MA 02421-6426

FREED, DANIEL JOSEF, law educator; b. New York, May 12, 1927; s. Jules L. and Sara (Lobel) F.; m. Judith Darrow, June 30, 1967; children: Peter Jacob, Emily Sara;children from previous marriage: Jonathan Michael, Amy. BS, Yale U., 1948, LLB, 1951; LLD (hon.), New England Coll., 1994. Bar: N.Y. 1952, D.C. 1953, U.S. Supreme Ct. 1955; Justice of the Peace, Guilford, Vt, 2005—. Atty.-investigator, preparedness subcom., com. on armed svcs., U.S. Senate, Washington, 1951-52; assoc. Ford, Bergson, Adams & Borkland, Washington, 1952-59; sr. trial atty. antitrust divsn. U.S. Dept. Justice, Washington, 1959-64, assoc. dir. office of criminal justice, 1964-66, acting dir., 1966-68, dir., 1968-69; prof. law and its adminstrn. Yale U., New Haven, 1969-75, clin. prof., 1975-94, clin. prof. emeritus, profl. lectr. in law, 1994—. Dir. clin. program law Yale U., 1969-72, dir. Daniel and Florence Guggenheim program in criminal justice, 1972-87, dir. criminal sentencing program, 1988-96. Co-author: (with Wald) Bail in the United States: 1964, publ.1964; co-editor (periodical) Fed. Sentencing Reporter, 1988—; contbr. articles to profl. jours. Trustee Vera Inst. Justice, NY, 1970—, Boston Grad. Sch. of Psychoanalysis, 2001—; pres. Yale Law Sch. Assn. Washington, 1968. With USN, 1945—46. Recipient Glenn R. Winters award Am. Judges Assn., 1992. Democrat. Jewish. Avocations: metal sculpture, swimming. Home: 53 Freed Rd Guilford VT 05301 Office: Yale Law Sch 127 Wall St PO Box 208215 New Haven CT 06520-8215 Office Phone: 203-432-4843. Business E-Mail: daniel.freed@yale.edu.

FREED, DAVID CLARK, artist; b. Toledo, May 23, 1936; s. J. Clark and Thelma F.; m. Mary Lichtenwald, Sept. 3, 1962; children— Aaron, Michael. BFA, Miami U., Oxford, Ohio, 1958; MFA, U. Iowa, 1962; postgrad., Royal Coll. Art, 1963-64. Instr. art Toledo Mus., 1964-66; prof. emeritus printmaking Va. Commonwealth U., Richmond, 1966—; instr. Central Sch. Art, London, 1969. One-man shows include Franz Bader Gallery, Washington, 1967, 70-71, 73, 76, 79, 82, Va. Mus. Fine Arts, 1977, Am. Cultural Ctr., Belgrade, 1982, Il Bisonte, Florence, Italy, 1989; retrospective exhbn. Anderson Gallery at Va. Commonwealth U., 2001; exhibited in group shows at World Print Show, San Francisco Mus. Modern Art, 35 Artists of the S.E., High Mus., Atlanta Art of Poetry, Nat. Coll. Fine Arts; represented in permanet collections Corcoran Gallery Washington, Mus. Modern Art, N.Y.C., Nat. Mus. Am. Art, Washington, Chgo. Art Inst., Victoria and Albert Mus., govt. collections of U.K., Yale U., U. of Va., N.Y. Pub. Libr.; artist books include (with Steven Lautermilch) What Light Guides This Hand—Poems by Izumi Shikibu; (with Charles Wright) 6 Poems, 1964, Yard Journal, 1985; (with Larry Levis) Elegy with a Thimbleful of Water, 1995; (with Philip Levine) An Ordinary Morning, 1995. Fulbright grant, 1963-64; Va. Mus. fellow, 1983-84, Nattie Marie Jones fellow creative work, 1983, Theresa Pollak award Home: 1825 W Grace St Richmond VA 23220-2104 Studio: 308 S Laurel St Richmond VA 23220-6231 Office Phone: 804-643-2731. E-mail: commenius@vcu.org.

FREED, DEBOW, academic administrator; b. Hendersonville, Tenn., Aug. 26, 1925; s. John Walter and Ella Lee (DeBow) F.; m. Catherine Carol Moore, Sept. 10, 1949; 1 child, Debow II. BS, U.S. Mil. Acad., 1946; grad., U.S. Inf. Sch., 1953, U.S. Army Command and Gen. Staff Coll., 1959; MS, U. Kans., 1961; PhD, U. N.Mex., 1966; grad., U.S. Air War Coll., 1966; LLD, Monmouth (Ill.) Coll., 1987; DLitt (hon.), Ohio No. U., 1999. Comdg. officer U.S. Army, 1946; comdr. 35th Inf. Japan, 1947-48; asst. to cmdr. 17th Airborne Div., 1948-49; comdr. 26th Inf., Federal Republic of Germany, 1949-51; asst. to chief U.S. Mission, Iran, and chief Middle Ea. Affairs, 1951-53; instr. The Inf. Sch., 1953-56; comdr. 32d Inf., Korea, 1956-57; instr. Command and Gen. Staff Coll., 1957-58; chief nuclear br. U.S. Atomic Energy Agy., 1961-65; chief plans divsn. US Army, Vietnam, 1966-67; prof. physics dept. U.S. Mil. Acad., 1967-69, ret., 1969; dean Mt. Union Coll., 1969-74; pres. Monmouth Coll., 1974-79, Ohio No. U., Ada, 1979—99, pres. emeritus, 1999—; pres. U. Findlay, 2003—. Chmn. Assoc. Colls. of Midwest, 1977-79, others. Author: Using Nuclear Capabilities, 1959, Pulsed Neutron Techniques, 1965; contbr. articles, revs. to profl. publs.; editor: Atomic Development Report, 1962-64. Bd. dirs. Presbyn. Coll. Union, 1974-79; trustee Ctr. Sci. and Industry, 1982—, Toledo Symphony, 1994—, Blanchard Valley Health Assn., 1999—, Blanchard Valley Health Found., 2000—; chmn., bd. trustees, COSI Endowment Found., 2001; v.p., dir. Buckeye coun. Boy Scouts Am., 1972-74, dir. Prairie coun., 1974-78. Decorated Bronze Star, (2) Legion of Merit, Legion of Honor Iran, Army Commendation medal, Air medal, Joint Svcs. Commendation medal, others; recipient various civic awards; Associated Western Univs. fellow, 1963-65; AEC fellow, 1963-65; Fgn. Policy Rsch. Inst. fellow, 1966; named Ohio Commodore, 1990. Mem. Assn. Meth. Colls. and Univs. (bd. dirs. 1979-99), Ohio Coll. Assn. (bd. dirs. 1980-84, 85-88, pres. 89-90), Ohio Found. Independent Colls. (bd. dirs. 1979-99), Am. Assn. Pres. of Colls. and Univs. (bd. dirs. 1988-99, treas. 1997-98, v.p 1998-99), Ohio Commodores, Sixma Xi, Phi Kappa Phi, Phi Eta Sigma, Delta Theta Phi, Omicron Delta Kappa. Home: 1115 N Main St Findlay OH 45840 Office: Office of Pres U Findlay Findlay OH 45840 Office Phone: 419-434-4510. Business E-Mail: freed@findlay.edu.

FREED, HERMINE, artist, educator; b. N.Y.C., May 29, 1940; d. Israel and Eleanor Herma (Schaap) Gerberg; m. Ned Benhalm, 1961 (div. 1965); m. James Ingo Freed, May 28, 1967; 1 child, Dara Michaella. Curator art rental Inst. Contemporary Art, Boston, 1963-65; instr. NYU Sch. Cont. Edn Art Collection, N.Y.C., 1965-67; asst. prof. Sch. Art Inst. Chgo., 1977; instr. Sch. Visual Arts, N.Y.C., 1973—. One-woman shows include De Saisset Art Mus., U. Santa Clara, Calif., Herbert Johnson Mus., Cornell U., Ithaca, N.Y., Ileana Sonanbend Gallery, N.Y.C., 1975, Everson Mus., Syracuse, N.Y., 1978, Columbia U. Coll. Architecture, 1979, Stefanotti Gallery, N.Y.C., 1981, So. Light Gallery, 1987, Amarillo (Tex.) Coll., 1987, Sherrat Gallery; group shows include Castelli Gallery, N.Y.C., 1973, 74, 78, Corcoran Gallery, Washington, 1975, 81, Whitney Mus., N.Y.C., 1975, 78, Art Gallery Ont., 1978, H. Johnson Mus., Cornell U., Ithaca, 1978, Pratt Manhattan Ctr., 1979, Mus. Modern Art travelling exhbn., 1980, 81, Aspen Ctr. Visual Arts, 1980, Mus. Folkwang, Essen, Germany, Am. Cultural Ctr. Exhbn., Paris, Weatherspoon Gallery, U. N.C., 1980, Stefanotti Gallery, N.Y.C., 1981, 82, S. Ohio Mus., 1981, Aldrich Mus., Ridgefield, Conn., 1982, Palais de Beaux Arts, Charleroi, Belgium, 1983, Taghinia-Milani Gallery, N.Y.C., 1983, Artists' Call, N.Y.C., 1984, Colby Coll., 1984, Artists Space, N.Y.C., 1985, Am. Film Inst., 1985, Bernice Steinbaum Gallery, 1985, Gallery Camino Real, Boca Raton, Fla., 1986, Mus. Modern Art, N.Y.C., 1986; represented in permanent collection Govt. austria, Hartwick Coll., Oneonta, N.Y., Otis Art Inst., La., U. Mass., Amherst, Guild Hall, East Hampton, N.Y., Calif. Inst. Arts, Valencia, Va. Commonwealth U.,De Saisset Art Mus., Santa Clara, Calif., U. N.C., Berlin Film Festival, Smith Coll., Northampton, Mass., Sch. Chgo. Art Inst., Anthology Film Archives, N.Y., Donnell Libr., N.Y., Grossmont Coll., El Cajon, Calif., U.Ga., Teheran Mus. Contemporary Art, Denver Art Mus., Queens U., Kingston, Can., Nat. Gallery Victoria, Melbourne, Australia, U. Ill., Chgo., Hamburger Kunsthaller, Hamburg, Germany, New Castle on Tyne, Poly. Inst., Eng., Inter Communications Agy., Washington, Stedlijk Mus., Amsterdamm Epiphany br. N.Y. Pub. Libr., N.Y.C.; also pvt. collections. Contbr. articles to profl. jours. Fellow NEA, 1974, Creative Artists Pub. Svc. Program, N.Y. State, 1978, Rockefeller Found., 1978; artist-in-residence N.Y. State Coun. on Arts WNET-TV Lab, 1974; grantee N.Y. State Coun. Arts, Air Gallery Project N.Y.C. Home: 60 Gramercy Park N New York NY 10010-5423

FREED, JACK HERSCHEL, chemist, educator; b. NYC, Apr. 19, 1938; s. Nathan and Pauline (Wolodarsky) F.; m. H. Renée Strauch, Mar. 25, 1961; children: Denise Elaine, Nadine Debra. BE, Yale U., 1958; MS, Columbia U., 1959, PhD, 1962. NSF fellow Cambridge U., 1962-63; asst. prof. chemistry Cornell U., 1963-67, asso. prof., 1967-73, prof., 1973—. Vis. prof. Tokyo U., 1969, Weizmann Inst. Sci., 1970, Aarhus U., 1974, U. Geneva, 1977, Delft U. of Tech., 1978, École Normale Supérieure, Paris, 1984—85, Hebrew U., Jerusalem, 1990, U. Padua, Italy, 1991, Yamagata U., 1998; fellow Inst. for Advanced Study, Hebrew U.; dir. Nat. Biomed. Ctr. for Advanced Electron Spin Resonance Techs., 2001—. Mem. edit. bd. Jour. Chem. Physics, 1976-78, Jour. Phys. Chemistry, 1979-83, 2004, Chem. Phys. Letters, 1988-90, Applied Magnetic Resonance, 1990—, Magnetic Resonance Rev., 1993—; contbr. articles to profl. jours. Recipient Buck-Whitney award Ea. N.Y. sect. Am. Chem. Soc., 1981, Gold medal Internat. Electron Spin Resonance Soc., 1994, Irving Langmuir prize Am. Phys. Soc., 1997, Internat. Zavoisky award Zavoisky Inst. Russian Acad. Scis., 1998; named Ramsay Meml. fellow, 1962-63, A.P. Sloan Found. fellow, 1966-68, sr. Weizmann fellow, 1970, Guggenheim fellow, 1984-85, Bruker lectr. Chem. Soc. U.K., 1990, MacDowell lectr. in chemical physics, U.B.C., 1997. Fellow Am. Phys. Soc., Am. Acad. Arts and Scis.; mem. Nat. Magnetic Resonance Soc. India (hon.). Jewish. Home: 108 Homestead Cir Ithaca NY 14850-6214 Office: Cornell U Dept Chemistry Baker Lab Ithaca NY 14853-1301 Office Phone: 607-255-3647. Business E-Mail: jhf@ccmr.cornell.edu.

FREED, JAMES INGO, architect; b. Essen, Germany, July 23, 1930; arrived in U.S., 1939, naturalized, 1948; s. Michael and Dora Freed; m. Hermine Gerberg, May 28, 1967; 1 child, Dara Michaella. BArch, Ill. Inst. Tech., 1953; DHL (hon.), Hebrew Union Coll.-Jewish Inst. Religion, 1995, N.J. Inst. Tech., 1995, Ill. Inst. Tech., 1998. Registered N.Y., D.C., Ill., Ohio, Nebr., Mo., Wis., Calif., Tex., Ark., Ariz., Minn., Colo., Va., N.J., Conn. Designer archtl. divsn. Webb & Knapp, Inc., 1950—55; practice architecture Danforth & Speyer, Chgo., 1951—52, Michael Reese Planning Assn., Chgo., 1952—53; designer Mies Van der Rohe, N.Y.C., 1955—56, I.M. Pei & Assocs., N.Y.C., 1955—66, I.M. Pei & Ptnrs., N.Y.C., 1966—80, ptnr., 1980—89, Pei Cobb Freed & Ptnrs., N.Y.C., 1989—. Prof. architecture, dean Coll. Architecture, Planning and Design Ill. Inst. Tech., 1975—78; adj. prof. architecture Columbia U., 1984; Eero Sarrinen prof. archtl. design Yale U., 1985; adj. instr. design Cooper Union, 1958—59, 1965—69; vis. critic Cornell U., 1963, 67, RISD, 1983; bd. mem. Creative Time, N.Y.C., 1974—84, Bright New City, Chgo., 1976—78; jury mem. Reynolds Award, 1975; mem. steering com. Coun. on Tall Bldgs. and Urban Habitat, 1982—; mem. Assn. Collegiate Schs. Arch. Jury, 1981, chmn., 82; critic, jury mem. various universities; lectr. in field. Prin. works include Gray Gallery, Chgo., 1976, Walter Kelly Gallery, 1977, Graham Found., 1978, Walker Art Ctr., Mpls., 1978—79, The New Sch., N.Y.C., 1982, U. Calif., Berkeley, 1982, Whitney Mus., N.Y.C., 1984, San Francisco Mus. Modern Art, 1985, Cleve. Ctr. for Contemporary Art, 1985, NAD, 1987, Am. Acad. and Inst. Arts and Letters, 1987, Ill. Inst. Tech. Exhbn., Chgo., 1988, N.Y. Architects, 1987—88, Chgo. Antheneum, 1993—94, Century Assn., N.Y.C., 1994, Kips Bay Plz. Apts., 1962 (City Club N.Y. Albert S. Bard award, 1965), NYU Towers, 1969 (Concrete Industry Bd. award, 1966, AIA Honor award, 1967, City Club N.Y. Albert S. Bard award, 1967), Univ. Plz. (AIA Honor award, 1967), 88 Pine St., NY Fin. Dist., N.Y.C., 1973 (R.S. Reynolds Meml. award, 1974, AIA Honor award, 1975), FAA Air Traffic Control Towers, various cities, 1965—72, Nat. Bank Commerce, Lincoln, Nebr., 1976 (Concrete Reinforcing Steel Inst. award, 1977), West Loop Plz., Houston, 1980, Gem City Savs. and Home Savs., Dayton, Ohio, 1981, 499 Park Ave, Manhattan, N.Y., 1981, Warwick Post Oak, Houston, 1982, Jacob K. Javits Conv. Ctr., N.Y.C., 1986, 1988 (AIA Honor award, 1988, Concrete Industry Bd. award of merit, 1988), Potomac Tower, Rosslyn, Va., 1990, First Bank Pl., Mpls., 1992, 1299 Pennsylvania Ave., Washington, 1993, LA Convention Ctr., 1993 (Art/LA Internat. Arts award for architecture, 1993), U.S. Holocaust Meml. Mus., Washington, 1993 (AIA Honor award, 1994), San Francisco Main Libr., 1996, Ronald Reagan Bldg. and Internat. Trade Ctr., Washington, 1998, The Washington House, Alumni Ctr. at Ball State U., 1998, Science and Engring. Quad at Stanford U., 1999, Roman L. Hruska U.S. Courthouse, Omaha, Nebr., 2000, Air Force Meml., Air Force Meml. Found., Arlington, Va., 2003, Broad Ctr. for the Biol. Sciences, Calif. Inst. Tech., numerous others; published (books and articles). Archtl. commr. Art Commn. of N.Y.C., 1983—91; archtl. commn. U. Washington, Seattle, 1984—91; bd. dirs. Creative Time, N.Y.C., 1974—84, Bright New City, Chgo., 1976—78, Art in Pub. Places, Chgo., 1976—78, 1980—; mem. N.Y. Mcpl. Arts Soc., 1983—, Syracuse U. Adv. Com., 1983—88, Archtl. Commn. U. Wash., Seattle, 1984—91; bd. dirs. Regional Plan Assn., NY, 1995—98, 1995—98, 1995—98; mem. steering com. Coun., on Tall Bldgs. and Urban Habitat; jury mem. Assn. Collegiate Schools Architecture, 1981, chmn., 1982. C.E. U.S. Army, 1953—55. Named one of "The Twelve Most Fascinating People of 1993", Barbara Walters Special, 1993; recipient R.S. Reynolds Meml. award, 1974, Poses Creative Arts award medal for arch., Brandeis U., 1981, Chgo. Arch. award, Ill. Coun. Am. Inst. Architects, 1985, Men of Industry award, Concrete Industry Bd. Inc., 1987, Sixth Ann. Jewish Cultural Achievement award, Nat. Found. for Jewish Culture, 1994, Internat. Arts award for Architecture, ART/LA, 1993, Tucker award, Bldg. Stone Inst., 1994, Nat. Arts medal, NEA, 1995, Outstanding Achievement in Design for the Govt. of the U.S., 1997, Award for Design Excellence, Presdl. Design Awards, 1997, Interfaith Lifetime Achievement award, Interfaith Com. Remembrance, 1998. Fellow: AIA (nat. com. on design 1972—73, vice chmn. nat. com. on design 1974, chmn. nat. com. on design 1975, Chgo. Architecture award Ill. Coun. 1985, medal of honor N.Y. chpt. 1987, Nat. Honor award 1988, 1st ann. Thomas Jefferson award for Pub. Architecture 1992, Nat. Honor award 1994, Presdl. Citation for Lifetime Achievement 1998, award of merit N.Y. state 1999), Am. Acad. Arts and Scis.; mem.: NEA (tilted arc adv. panel 1987), Am. Acad. Design, Mcpl. Art Soc. N.Y., Am. Acad. Arts and Letters (com. for prizes in arch. 2000, Arnold W. Brunner Meml. prize in Architecture 1987, Presdl. Design award 1997), Nat. Acad. Design (assoc.), N.Y. Mcpl. Arts Soc., N.Y. Soc. Architects (Lifetime Achievement award 1992, Architectural Achievement award 1994), Archtl League N.Y. Office: Pei Cobb Freed & Ptnrs 88 Pine St New York NY 10005 Office Phone: 212-751-3122. Office Fax: 212-872-5443. Business E-Mail: pcf@pcf-p.com.

FREED, JOEL M., lawyer; b. Oct. 28, 1943; BA, Lehigh Univ., 1965, BSME, 1966; JD, Georgetown Univ., 1970. Bar: Va. 1970, D.C. 1970. Ptnr., Intellectual Property & Tech. group Arnold & Porter, Washington. Instr., legal methods U.S. Patent & Trademark Office, 1980—90; adj. prof. Georgetown Univ. Law Ctr. Mem.: Pi Tau Sigma, Phi Delta Phi. Office: Arnold & Porter 555 Twelfth St NW Washington DC 20004-1206 Office Phone: 202-942-6602. Office Fax: 202-942-5999. Business E-Mail: joel.freed@aporter.com.

FREED, KARL FREDERICK, chemistry professor; b. Bklyn., Sept. 25, 1942; s. Nathan and Pauline Freed; m. Gina P. Goldstein, June 14, 1964; children: Nicole Yvette, Michele Suzanne. BS, Columbia U., 1963; A.M., Harvard U., 1965, PhD, 1967. NATO postdoctoral fellow U. Manchester (Eng.), 1967-68; asst. prof. U. Chgo., 1968-73, assoc. prof., 1973-76, prof. chemistry, 1976—, dir. James Frank Inst., 1983-86. Bd. dirs. Telluride Sci. Rsch. Ctr., 2003—. Author: Renormalization Group Theory of Macromolecules, 1987; editl. bd. Jour. Statis. Physics, 1976-78, Advances in Chem. Physics, 1985—, Computational Theoretical Polymer Sci., 1996—; adv. editor Chem. Physics, 1979-92, Chem. Revs., 1981-83, Internat. Jour. Quantum Chemistry, 1995-99; assoc. editor Jour. Chem. Physics, 1982-84; contbr. articles to profl. jours. Recipient Marlow medal Faraday div. Chem. Soc. London, 1973; recipient Pure Chemistry award Am. Chem. Soc., 1976; fellow Sloan Found., 1969-71; Guggenheim fellow, 1972-73; fellow Dreyfus Found., 1972-77 Fellow: Am. Phys. Soc.; mem.: Am. Chem. Soc., Royal Soc. Chemistry. Office: U Chgo 5640 S Ellis Ave Chicago IL 60637-1433 E-mail: k-freed@uchicago.edu.

FREED, MAYER GOODMAN, law educator; b. Phila., Oct. 26, 1945; s. Abraham H. and Fannie (Rothenberg) F.; m. Paulette Kleinhaus, Aug. 23, 1970; children: Daniel, Joshua. AB cum laude, Columbia Coll., 1967, JD, 1970. Bar: N.Y. 1971, Ill. 1975, U.S. Dist. Ct. (so. and ea. dists.) N.Y. 1972, U.S. Ct. Appeals (2d cir.) 1972, U.S. Supreme Ct. 1974. Assoc. Proskauer Rose Goetz & Mendelsohn, NYC, 1970-71; staff atty. Nat. Employment Law Project, NYC, 1971-73, sr. staff atty., 1973-74; asst. prof. law Northwestern U. Sch. Law, Chgo., 1974-77, assoc. prof., 1977-79, prof. law, 1979—, assoc. dean acad. affairs and curriculum, 1986—. Contbr. articles to legal publs.; bd. editors Columbia Law Rev., 1969-70. Bd. dirs. Legal Assistance Found. Chgo., 1980-82. Stone scholar, 1968-69. Mem. ABA. Office: Northwestern U Sch Law 357 E Chicago Ave Chicago IL 60611-3059 E-mail: mfreed@law.northwestern.edu.*

FREED, MELVYN NORRIS, retired higher education administrator and educator, writer; b. Kans. City, Mo., Apr. 30, 1937; s. Carl and Betty (Wachtel) F.; m. Janet Lea Triplitt, Dec. 26, 1971; children: David A., Edward L. BA in Econs. with distinction, U. Mo., Kansas City, 1959; MS in Edn., So. Ill. U., Carbondale, 1962, PhD in Higher Edn., 1965. Dir. instl. rsch. Ark. State U., Jonesboro, 1965-72, v.p. for adminstrn., 1972-76, Govs. State U., University Pk., Ill., 1977-82, univ. prof., rsch. assoc., 1982-87; writer, 1987—. Co-founder, past dir. measurement and rsch. So. Ctrl. Region Edn. Lab., Little Rock; past evaluator rsch. grants U.S. Office of Edn., Washington; sustaining life mem. Evans Scholars Found., Par Club, 2002—; co-founder U.S. River Acad. (chartered by Congress) in the late 1960s. Author: In Search of a Beginning: The Eastern Arkansas Scottish Rite Bodies, 1976; Co-author: The Educator's Desk Reference, 1989 (1 of 30 Best Reference Books 1989, Best Single Vol. Reference Book in Edn. 1989), 2d edit., 2002, Business Information Desk Reference, 1991, Patient's Desk Reference, 1994; contbr. articles to profl. jours.; editor: Handbook of Statistical Procedures and Their Computer Applications, 1991; tool inventor. Village trustee, Hazel Crest, Ill., 1997—2005; plan commr., 1988—97; adminstrv. asst. Congressman William Alexander, Washington, 1969; v.p., bd. dirs. Calumet Coun. Boy Scouts Am., Munster, Ind., 1978—95, 2001—; bd. dirs. Bremen H.S. Dist. 228 Ednl. Found., 1998—2004, pres., 2002—04. Recipient U.S. Congl. citation, Washington, 1971, Silver Beaver award Boy Scouts Am., 1976, Disting. Svcs. award Ark. State U., 1975, Nat. Endowment award; James E. West fellow Calumet Coun. Boy Scouts Am., 2002, Daniel Carter Beard Masonic Scouter award Boy Scouts Am., 2003. Mem. Masons (past master), Ill. Masonic Homes Endowment Commn., Scottish Rite (knight comdr. Ct. of Honor 1979), Alpha Epsilon Pi, Phi Kappa Phi, Omicron Delta Kappa. Home: 17023 Magnolia Dr Hazel Crest IL 60429-1020

FREED, RICHARD (DONALD), music critic; b. Chgo., Dec. 27, 1928; s. Abraham Jay and Ann (Bernstein) F.; m. Louise Sumiko Kono, Mar. 19, 1958; 1 child, Erica Lesley. PhB, U. Chgo., 1947. Staff music critic N.Y. Times, N.Y.C., 1965; asst. to dir. Eastman Sch. Music U. Rochester, N.Y., 1966-70; exec. dir. Music Critics Assn., Inc., Rockville, Md., 1974-90. Annotator, broadcast host St. Louis Symphony Orch., 1973-96; program annotator Phila. Orch., 1974-84; record critic Washington Post, 1976-84; annotator Nat. Symphony Orch., Washington, 1977—. Author: (with Peter Eliot Stone) Virtuosi, 1985 (Deems Taylor award 1986); contbg. editor Stereo Rev., 1973—99. Decorated knight 1st class Order of the Lion of Finland; recipient Deems Taylor award for concert notes, 1984, Grammy award, 1995. Democrat. Jewish. Avocations: hiking, puzzles. E-mail: priamclay@aol.com.

FREED, STANLEY ARTHUR, retired museum curator; b. Springfield, Ohio, Apr. 18, 1927; m. Ruth Shelley, Sept. 12, 1955. Ph.B., U. Chgo., 1949; BA, U. Calif. at Berkeley, 1951, PhD, 1957. Vis. asst. prof. anthropology U. N.C., 1959-60; mem. staff Am. Mus. Natural History, N.Y.C., 1960—, curator, chmn. dept. anthropology, 1969-76, curator, 1976-2000, retired, 2000. Adj. prof. Columbia U., 1992—; research fellow Am. Inst. Indian Studies, 1977-78 Served with AUS, 1945-46. Postdoctoral fellow Social Sci. Research Council, 1957; Postdoctoral fellow NSF, 1958 Mem. N.Y. Acad. Scis. (chmn. anthropology sect. 1974-75) Office: Am Mus Natural History Central Park W & 79th St New York NY 10024 E-mail: sfreed@amnh.org.

FREED, WALTER EVERETT, petroleum company executive, state representative; b. Providence, R.I., Aug. 13, 1951; s. Richard Anthony and Alice Marie (Livesey) F.; m. Margery Anne Tyler, Oct. 19, 1974; children: Jonathan, Meghan, Meredith. BA, Dartmouth Coll., 1974. V.p. Johnson's Fuel Svc. Inc., Manchester, Vt., 1979-85; pres. Apollo Industries, Inc. (formerly Johnson's Fuel Svc., Inc.), Manchester, Vt., 1985—; state rep. dist. 15 Vt.; spkr. of the House, 2001—. Elected chair, freshman Rep. caucus, 1993. State chmn. Vt. Rep. Party, Montpelier, 1988-91; state rep. Vt. Gen. Assembly, 1992, 94, 96, house minority whip, 1995, house minority leader, 1997; bd. dirs. Vermont C. of C., Southern Vermont Art Center, Long Trail Sch., Manchester Little League. Former chair, Dorset sch. bd.; former dir., Bennington-Rutland Supervisory Union. Former Rep. Nat. Conv. Del. 1992, 1996, 2000. Mem. Mcpl. Corp. Com. 1993-1994, local govt. & Rules Com., 1995-1996, Fish, Wildlife, and Water Resources Com., Rules & Joint Com. 1997-1998, local govt., Rules, and Joint Rules Com., 1999-2000. Avocations: sailing, flying, skiing, tennis. Office: Apollo Industries Inc 105 N End Dr North Clarendon VT 05759-9762 also: Office of the Speaker of the House Vermont State House Montpelier VT 05633-5201

FREEDBERG, A. STONE, physician; b. Salem, Mass., May 30, 1908; s. Hyman and Rachel Leah (Freedberg) F.; m. Beatrice Gordon, Aug. 29, 1935; children: Richard Gordon, Leonard Earl. AB, Harvard U., 1929; MD, U. Chgo. (Rush), 1935. Diplomate: Am. Bd. Internal Medicine (cardiology). Intern Mt. Sinai Hosp., Chgo., 1934-35, Mass. Meml. Hosp., Boston, summer 1935; resident Cook County Hosp., Chgo., 1935-36; house officer pathology R.I. Hosp., 1936-37; practice medicine, specializing in internal medicine Boston, 1946—. Asst. in medicine Beth Israel Hosp., 1938-40, jr. vis. physician, 1940-46, assoc. in med. research, 1940-50, assoc. vis. physician, 1946-48, vis. physician, 1949-63, assoc. dir. med. research, 1950-63, sr. Ziskind fellow, 1956, physician, 1964-84, acting physician-in-chief dept. medicine, 1973, dir. cardiology unit, 1964-69, bd. consultation, 1984-87, hon. bd. consultation, 1988—; research fellow medicine Med. Sch., Harvard U., 1941-42, asst. in medicine, 1942-46, instr. medicine, 1946-47, assoc. in medicine, 1947-50, asst. prof., 1950-57, assoc. prof., 1958-69, prof., 1969-74, prof. emeritus, 1974-, adminstrv. bd. faculty medicine, 1958-62; physician Harvard U. Health Svcs., 1974-2004, hon. physician emeritus, 2004—; cons., com. mem. med. div. Oak Ridge Inst. Nuclear Studies, 1955-56; spl. cons. metabolism study sect. USPHS, 1956-60; mem. sr. cons. staff Nuclear Medicine Inst., 1966-67 Mem. editorial bd.: Circulation, 1956-60, 62-67; contbr. articles profl. jours. Guggenheim fellow Oxford U., 1967-68 Fellow Am. Heart Assn. (bd. dirs.; mem. council clin. cardiology); mem. Mass. Heart Assn. (dir., past pres., com. chmn.), Am. Thyroid Assn. (v.p.), Mass., Charles River Dist. med. socs., Am. Soc. Clin. Investigation, Am. Physiol. Soc., Assn. Am. Physicians, New Eng. Cardiovascular Soc. (pres. 1971-72), Assn. Profs. Medicine. Home: 111 Perkins St Boston MA 02130-4313 Office: 275 Longwood Ave Boston MA 02115-5704 Office Phone: 617-432-1370. Personal E-mail: gordonbea@comcast.net.

FREEDBERG, DAVID ADRIAN, art educator, art historian; b. Capetown, South Africa, June 1, 1948; s. William and Eleonore (Kupfer) F.; children: Hannah, William. BA, Yale U., 1969; DPhil, Oxford U., 1973. Lectr. art Westfield Coll., U. London, 1973-76, Courtauld Inst. Art, U. London, 1976-84; prof. Barnard Coll., Columbia U., N.Y.C., 1984-86, Columbia U., 1986—, dir. Italian Acad. Advanced Studies in Am., 2000—. Slade prof. fine art U. Oxford, 1983-84; dir. Print Quar., London, 1983—; Andrew W. Mellon prof. Nat. Gallery Art, 1996-98. Author: Dutch Landscape Prints of the Seventeenth Century, 1980, Rubens: The Life of Christ After the Passion, 1984, Iconoclasts and Their Motives, 1985, Iconoclasm and Painting in the Revolt of the Netherlands, 1566-1609, 1988, The Prints of Pieter Bruegel the Elder, 1989, The Power of Images: Studies in the History and Theory of Response, 1989, Joseph Kosuth the Play of the Unmentionable, 1992, Peter Paul Rubens: Paintings and Oil Sketches, 1995, The Eye of the Lynx: Galileo, His Friends, and the Beginnings of Modern Natural History, 2002; author: (with E. Baldini) The Paper Museum of Cassiano dal Pozzo: Citrus Fruit, 1997; author: (with A. Scott) The Paper Museum of Cassiano dal Pazzo: Fossil Woods, 2000. Mem. Am. Acad. Arts and Scis., Am. Philos. Soc. Office: Columbia U Italian Acad Advanced Studes Am New York NY 10027

FREEDLENDER, SUSAN See HOMESTEAD, SUSAN

FREEDMAN, AARON DAVID, medicine and biochemistry educator, retired dean; b. Albany, N.Y., Jan. 4, 1922; s. Jacob Abraham and Pauline Rebecca (Hoffman) F.; m. Alice Maurer, Sept. 10, 1948, dec. 2001; children: Abigail, Jonathan, Jeremy; m. Virginia Weliky, Apr. 14, 2005. AB, Cornell U., 1942; MD, Albany Med. Coll., 1945; PhD, Columbia U., 1958; MA, U. Pa., 1972. Diplomate Am. Bd. Internal Medicine. Asst. prof. medicine and biochemistry Columbia U., N.Y.C., 1958-65; clin. prof. U. Kans., Kansas City, 1965-69, chmn. dept. medicine Menorah Med. Ctr., 1965-69; prof., assoc. dean U. Pa., Phila., 1969-75, exec. dir. Grad. Hosp., 1972-75; prof. medicine Med. Sch. CUNY, 1975—, acting dean, 1978-79, dep. dean acad. affairs, 1990-92. Examiner N.Y. State Bd. Med. Examiners, Albany, 1962-65; cons. Touro Coll., N.Y.C., 1980; career investigator N.Y. Pub. Health Rsch. Coun., 1963-65; dir. Danciger Med. Inst., Kansas City, Mo., 1966-69. Mem. Ardsley (N.Y.) Bd. of Edn., 1962-65. Libman Fund fellow, 1951-54, USPHS fellow, 1958-60. Mem. Am. Soc. for Cell Biology, Am. Soc. Biochemistry and Molecular Biology. Jewish. Office: CUNY Med Sch 138th St & Amsterdam Ave New York NY 10031 Office Phone: 212-650-7237. Business E-Mail: adf53@columbia.edu.

FREEDMAN, ALBERT Z., publishing company executive; b. Taunton, Mass. s. Frank and Bessie (Kanaber) F.; m. Esther Hilda Katz, Sept. 23, 1954 (dec.); children: Mara (dec.), Lisa Jolie Harris, Tani Josette Ruiz, Derek Justin; m. Nancy Lee Dworman, Aug. 17, 1984. Student, Boston U., 1945-46; BA, U. So. Calif., 1948; postgrad., Inst. Hautes Etudes Cinématagraphiques, Paris, 1949-50; PhD, Inst. for Advanced Study Human Sexuality, San Francisco, 1981. Radio writer, Los Angeles, N.Y.C., 1950-52; TV writer, producer WOR-TV, N.Y.C., 1952, NBC, CBS, 1952-58; playwright Mex., 1959-60; with KTLA, ABC-TV, L.A., 1961-64; free lance writer London, 1964-66; editor Forum, Jour. Human Rels., London, 1967-75, co-pub. N.Y.C., 1975-82; mng. dir. Penthouse Publs., London, 1970-75; v.p. Penthouse Internat., 1982—97; cons. Gen. Media, N.Y.C., 1997—2004. Prof. Inst. for Advanced Study of Human Sexuality, bd. dirs. Mem. Am. Coll. Sexologists (diplomate, commr., bd. dirs.), Soc. Sci. Study of Sex. Home: 11 Laderman Ln Greenbrae CA 94904-2482 Personal E-mail: azurof@comcast.net.

FREEDMAN, ALFRED MORDECAI, psychiatrist, educator; b. Albany, NY, Jan. 7, 1917; s. Jacob Abraham and Pauline Rebecca (Hoffman) F.; m. Marcia Irene Kohl, Mar. 24, 1943; children: Paul Harris, Daniel Sholom. AB, Cornell U., 1937; MD, U. Minn., 1941. Diplomate Am. Bd. Psychiatry and Neurology. Intern Harlem Hosp., N.Y.C., 1941-42; resident and fellow Bellevue Hosp., N.Y.C., 1948-51, sr. psychiatrist, 1951-54; asst. pediatrician Babies Hosp.-Columbia, N.Y.C., 1953-60; assoc. prof. psychiatry SUNY Downstate Med. Sch., Bklyn., 1955-60; prof., chmn. psychiatry N.Y. Med. Coll., Valhalla, 1960-89, chmn. and prof. psychiatry emeritus, 1989—. Vis. prof. Harvard Med. Sch., Boston, 1988-93; hon. prof. Hunan Med. U., China, 1993; dir. psychiatry Westchester Med. Ctr., Valhalla, 1979-89; cons. WHO, Geneva, 1984, 89—; Roche vis. prof., Australia and New Zealand, 1988; S.Y. Mak vis. prof. U. Hong Kong, 1989; mem. awards jury Anna Monika Stiftung, Dortmund, Germany, 1983-94; mem. Internat. Com. Prevention and Treatment of Depression, 1983-96; sec.-treas. Ctr. for Comprehensive Health Practice Svc., N.Y.C., 1990—adv. com. Memory Ctrs., Internat., 1997—. Sr. editor: (textbook) Comprehensive Psychiatry, 1967-80; sr. editor: Issues in Psychiatric Classification, 1986; editor-in-chief Polit. Psychology, 1981-90, Integrative Psychiatry, 1981-97; editor: Highlights of Modern Psychiatry, 2000; adv. bd. Philosophy, Psychiatry and Psychology Jour., 1990—; contbr. articles to profl. jours. Mem. N.Y. State Commn. to Evaluate Drug Laws, Albany, 1970-73; founding trustee Ctr. for Urban Edn., N.Y.C., 1965-70; dir. Upper Park Ave. Boys Club of Am., N.Y.C., 1970-80; NGO rep. UN for World Psychiat. Assn., 1985-90, NGO rep. UN for World Assn. Psychosocial Rehab., 1990—; trustee N.Y. Acad. Medicine; trustee Internat. Found. for Human Scis., Paris, 1987-97. Recipient Henry Wismer Miller award, Manhattan Soc. Mental Health, 1964, Terence Cardinal Cooke medal, N.Y. Med. Coll., 1985, Lapinlahti medal, U. Helsinki, 1990, Wyeth Ayerst award, World Psychiat. Assn., Athens, 1989, A.M. Freedman Ann. award, Internat. Soc. for Polit. Psychology, 1990, Tom Levin award for cmty. svc., Am. Assn. Psychosocial Rehab., 1999, Alice Fordyce award for pub. svc., 2004. Fellow: Acad. Medicine et Psychiatricae Found. (founding fellow, pres. 1990—), Am. Orthopsychiat. Assn. (dir. 1962—64), Am. Coll. Neuropsychopharmacology (pres. 1972—73, coun. global psychiatry 1999), Am. Psychiat. Assn. (pres. 1971—72, ethics appeals bd. 1993—99, disting.fellow 2000, ethics appeals bd. 2003—, coun. on global psychiatry 2004—, Rush medal 1974, ann. award, Spl. Presdl. commendation 1999), Am. Psychopathol. Assn. (pres. 1973—74, Hamilton medal 1972); mem.: Inst. Victims of Trauma (trustee 1992), Assn. Advancement of Philosophy and Psychiatry (founding exec. com. 1989—), Internat. Found. Mental Health and Neuroscis. (U.S. dir., v.p. 1996—2004), Nat. Com. on Confidentiality of Health Records (pres. 1976—95), N.Y. Psychiat. Soc. (pres. 1986—87). Avocations: music, travel, gardening, sailing. Home and Office: 1148 Fifth Ave New York NY 10128-0807 Office Phone: 212-348-8661. E-mail: alfredm@pipeline.com.

FREEDMAN, BART JOSEPH, lawyer; b. New Haven, Sept. 27, 1955; s. Lawrence Zelic and Dorothy (Robinson) F.; m. Esme Detweiler, Sept. 28, 1985; children: Luke Edward, Samuel Meade, Benjamin Zelic. BA, Carleton Coll., 1977; JD, U. Pa., 1982. Bar: Wash. 1984, U.S. Dist. Ct. (we. dist.) Wash. 1984, U.S. Ct. Appeals (9th cir.) 1985, U.S. Dist. Ct. (ea. dist.) Wash. 1988. Law clk. to chief justice Samuel Roberts Supreme Ct. Pa., Erie, 1982—83; asst. city solicitor City of Phila., 1984; assoc. Perkins Coie, Seattle, 1984—90; ptnr. Preston Gates & Ellis, Seattle, 1990—. Editor: Natural Resource Damages, 1993. Bd. dirs. Seattle Metrocenter YMCA, 1988-97, chmn. 1993-97, 2002—; bd. dirs. Leadership Tomorrow, 1996-97; chair Sierra Club Inner City Outings Program, Seattle, 1986-90; chmn. bd. advisors Earth Svc. Corps/YMCA, Seattle, 1990-97. Mem. ABA (com. on corp. counsel 1985-95), Wash. State Bar Assn., Seattle-King County Bar Assn. (participant neighborhood legal clinics 1985-94). Office: Preston Gates & Ellis 701 5th Ave Ste 5000 Seattle WA 98104-7078 Office Phone: 206-370-7655. E-mail: bartf@prestongates.com.

FREEDMAN, BERNARD BENJAMIN, lawyer; b. Buffalo, July 18, 1939; s. Isadore and Clare (Sugarman) F.; m. Lynda Lee Bargman, July 3, 1963; children: Amy, Andrew, Betsy. Student, U. Buffalo, 1957-60; JD, SUNY, Buffalo, 1964. Bar: N.Y. 1964, U.S. Dist. Ct. (we. dist.) N.Y. 1965, U.S. Supreme Ct. 1982. Assoc. Maidy, Donnelly & Manchester, Buffalo, 1964-65, Lesher, Howitt, Manchester & Jenkins, Buffalo, 1965-66, Lippes & Kaminsky, Buffalo, 1966-70; chief civil divsn. Legal Aid Bur. Inc., Buffalo, 1970-81; pvt. practice Kenmore, N.Y., 1970-82; hearing examiner Erie County Family Ct., Buffalo, 1982; ptnr. Norton Radin Hoover Freedman, Kenmore, 1982-96, sole proprietor, 1996—. Pres. Legal Aid Bur., Buffalo, Inc. Past mem. bd. editors Buffalo Law Rev. Past bd. dirs. Temple Shaarey Zedek; sec. bd. ethics Town of Amherst, N.Y. Mem. ABA, N.Y. State Bar Assn. (past mem. ho. of delegates), Erie County Bar Assn. (past bd. dirs., former pres.), SUNY at Buffalo Law Sch. Alumni Assn. (past mem. bd. dirs.), Greater Buffalo Track Club. Democrat. Jewish. Avocation: marathon runner. Home: 74 Heritage Rd W Buffalo NY 14221-2314 Office: Norton Radin Hoover Freedman 2858 Delaware Ave Buffalo NY 14217-2733

FREEDMAN, CHARLES, retired bank executive; b. Toronto, Ont., Can., Sept. 1, 1941; s. Nathan and Freda (Glicksman) F.; m. Aviva Kravetz, Aug. 21, 1966; children: Barry, Daniel. BComm., U. Toronto, 1963; BA (hon.), Oxford (Eng.) U., 1965; PhD, MIT, 1970. Asst. prof. U. Minn., Mpls., 1969-74; rsch. advisor Bank of Can., Ottawa, 1974-78, dep. chief, 1978-79, chief, 1979-84, advisor to gov., 1984-88, dep. gov., 1988—. ret. Author: Foreign Currency Business of Canadian Banks, 1974; contbr. 80 articles to profl. jours., conf. volumes. Gov.'s Gen. medal U. Toronto, 1963; Can. Coun. fellow, 1968. Mem. Am. Econs. Assn., Can. Econs. Assn. Jewish. Avocations: reading, travel, cross country skiing. E-mail: cfreedman@bank-banque-canada.ca.

FREEDMAN, DANIEL, computer scientist, educator; b. Mpls., June 4, 1971; s. Charles and Aviva Freedman; m. Catriella Masha Stein, May 27, 1995; children: Evyatar Binyamin, Kalanit Shoshana, Talya Tehilla. AB, Princeton U., 1993; PhD, Harvard U., 2000. Asst. prof. Rensselaer Poly. Inst., Troy, NY, 2000—. Recipient CAREER award, NSF, 2002—. Mem.: IEEE, Sigma Xi. Jewish. Achievements include research in Computer Vision, Computational Geometry, Medical Imaging. Office Phone: 518-276-4785.

FREEDMAN, DAVID AMIEL, statistics educator, consultant; b. Montreal, Que., Can., Mar. 5, 1938; came to U.S., 1958; s. Abraham and Goldie (Yelin) F.; children: Deborah, Joshua. B.Sc., McGill U., Montreal, 1958; MA, Princeton U., 1959, PhD, 1960. Prof. stats. U. Calif.-Berkeley, 1961—, Miller prof., 1991, chmn. dept. stats., 1981-86. Cons. Bank of Can., Ottawa, 1971-72, WHO, 1973, Carnegie Commn., 1976, Dept. Energy, 1978-87, Bur. Census, 1983, 98, Dept. Justice, 1984, 89-92, 96, 2002, Brobeck, Phleger & Harrison, 1985-89, Skadden Arps, 1986, 2002, County of Los Angeles, 1989, Fed. Jud. Ctr., 1993. Author: Markov Chains, 1971, Brownian Motion and

Diffusion, 1971, Approximating Countable Markov Chains, 1972, Mathematical Methods in Statistics, 1977, Statistics, 1978, 3d edit., 1997; contbr. numerous articles to profl. publs. Recipient John J. Carty award for Advancement of Sci., NAS, 2003; fellow, Can. Coun., 1960, Sloan Found., 1964. Mem.: Am. Acad. Scis. Home: 901 Alvarado Rd Berkeley CA 94705-1551 Office: U Calif-Berkeley Dept Stats Berkeley CA 94720-3860

FREEDMAN, DAVID NOEL, religious studies educator; b. NYC, May 12, 1922; s. David and Beatrice (Goodman) F.; m. Cornelia Anne Pryor, May 16, 1944; children: Meredith Anne, Nadezhda, David Micaiah, Jonathan Pryor. Student, CCNY, 1935-38; AB, UCLA, 1939; BTh, Princeton Theol. Sem., 1944; PhD, Johns Hopkins U., 1948; LittD, U. Pacific, 1973; ScD, Davis and Elkins Coll., 1974. Ordained to ministry Presbyn. Ch., 1944; supply pastor in Acme and Deming, Wash., 1944-45; tchg. fellow, then asst. instr. Johns Hopkins U., 1946-48; asst. prof., then prof. Hebrew and Old Testament lit. Western Theol. Sem., Pitts., 1948-60; prof. Pitts. Theol. Sem., 1960-61, James A. Kelso prof., 1961-64; prof. Old Testament San Francisco Theol. Sem., 1964-70, Gray prof. Hebrew exegesis, 1970-71, dean of faculty, 1966-70, acting dean of sem., 1970-71; prof. Old Testament Grad. Theol. Union, Berkeley, Calif., 1964-71; prof. dept. Nr. Ea. studies U. Mich., Ann Arbor, 1971-92, Thurnau prof. Bibl. studies, 1984-92, dir. program on studies in religion, 1971-91; prof., endowed chair in Hebrew Bibl. studies U. Calif., San Diego, 1987—, dir. religious studies program, 1989-97. Danforth vis. prof. Internat. Christian U., Tokyo, 1967; vis. prof. Hebrew U., Jerusalem, 1977, Macquarie U., N.S.W., Australia, 1980, U. Queensland (Australia), 1982, 84, U. Calif., San Diego, 1985-87; Green vis. prof. Tex. Christian U., Ft. Worth, 1981; dir. Albright Inst. Archeol. Rsch., 1969-70, dir., 1976-77; lectr. in field. Author: The Published Works of W.F. Albright, 1975, Pottery, Poetry and Prophecy, 1980, The Unity of the Hebrew Bible, 1991 (paperback edit., 1993), Divine Commitment and Human Obligation, 1997, Psalm 119, 1999, The Nine Commandments, 2000; co-author: (with J.D. Smart) God Has Spoken, 1949, (with F.M. Cross, Jr.) Early Hebrew Orthography, 1952, (with John M. Allegro) The People of the Dead Sea Scrolls, 1958, (with R.M. Grant) The Secret Sayings of Jesus, 1960, (with F.M. Cross, Jr.) Ancient Yahwistic Poetry, 1964, rev. edit., 1975, 97, (with M. Dothan) Ashdod I, 1967, (with L.G. Running) William F. Albright: Twentieth Century Genius, 1975, 2d edit., 1991, (with B. Mazar, G. Cornfeld) The Mountain of the Lord, 1975, (with W. Phillips) An Explorer's Life of Jesus, 1975, (with G. Cornfeld) Archaeology of the Bible: Book by Book, 1976, (with K.A. Mathews) The Paleo-Hebrew Leviticus Scroll, 1985, The Unity of the Hebrew Bible, 1991, (with D. Forbes and F. Andersen) Studies in Hebrew and Aramaic Orthography, 1992, (with Sara Mandell) The Relationship between Herodotus' History and Primary History, 1993; co-author, editor: (with F. Andersen) Anchor Bible Series Hosea, 1980, Anchor Bible Series Amos, 1989, Micah, 2000; editor: (with G.E. Wright) The Biblical Archaeologist, Reader I, 1961, (with E.F. Campbell, Jr.) The Biblical Archaeologist, Reader 2, 1964, Reader 3, 1970, Reader 4, 1983, (with W.F. Albright) The Anchor Bible, 1964—, including, Genesis, 1964, James, Peter and Jude, 1964, Jeremiah, 1965, Job, 1965, 2d edit., 1973, Proverbs and Ecclesiastes, 1965, I Chronicles, II Chronicles, Ezra-Nehemiah, 1965, Psalms I, 1966, John I, 1966, Acts of the Apostles, 1967, II Isaiah, 1968, Psalms II, 1968, John II, 1970, Psalms III, 1970, Esther, 1971, Matthew, 1971, Lamentations, 1972, 2d edit., 1992, To the Hebrews, 1972, Ephesians 1-3, 4-6, 1974, I and II Esdras, 1974, Judges, 1975, Revelation, 1975, Ruth, 1975, I Maccabees, 1976, I Corinthians, 1976, Additions, 1977, Song of Songs, 1977, Daniel, 1978, Wisdom of Solomon, 1979, I Samuel, 1980, Hosea, 1980, Luke I, 1981, Joshua, 1982, Epistles of John, 1983, II Maccabees, 1983, II Samuel, 1984, II Corinthians, 1984, Luke II, 1985, Judith, 1985, Mark, 1986, Haggai-Zechariah 1-8, 1987, Ecclesiasticus, 1987, 2 Kings, 1988, Amos, 1989, Titus, 1990, Jonah, 1990, Leviticus I, 1991, Deuteronomy I, 1991, Numbers 1-20, 1993, Romans, 1993, Jude and 2 Peter, 1993, Zechariah 9-14, 1993, Zephaniah, 1994, Colossians, 1995, Joel, 1995, James, 1995, Obadiah, 1996, Tobit, 1996, Ecclesiastes, 1997, Ezekiel 21-37, 1997, Galatians, 1997, Malachi, 1998, Acts of the Apostles, 1998, Exodus 1-18, 1999, Jeremiah 1-20, 1999, Mark 1-8, 2000, Numbers 21-36, 2000, 1 Peter, 2001, Isaiah 1-39, 2000, Thessalonians 1&2, 2000, Leviticus 17-22, 2000, Proverbs 1-9, 2000, Micah, 2000, Philemon, 2000, Timothy 1&2, 2001, Hebrews, 2001, Leviticus 23-27, 2001, Habakkuk, 2001, 1 Kings, 2001, Isaiah 40-55, 2002, Isaiah 56-66, 2003, Jeremiah 21-36, 2004, 1 Chronicles 1-9, 2004, 1 Chronicles 10-29, 2004, Jeremiah 37-52, 2004; editor Anchor Bible Ref. Libr., Jesus Within Judaism, 1988, Archaeology of the Land of the Bible, 1990, The Tree of Life, 1990, A Marginal Jew Vol. 1, 1991, The Pentateuch, 1991, The Rise of Jewish Nationalism, 1992, History and Prophecy, 1993, Jesus and the Dead Sea Scrolls, 1993, The Birth of the Messiah, 1993, The Death of the Messiah, 2 vols., 1994, Introduction to Rabbinical Literature, 1994, A Marginal Jew, vol. 2, 1994, vol. 3, 2001, The Scepter and the Star, 1995, The Gnostic Scriptures, 1995, Reclaiming The Dead Sea Scrolls, 1995, An Introduction to the New Testament, 1997, Education in Ancient Israel, 1998, Warrior, Dancer, Seductress, Queen, 1998, A History of the Synoptic Problem, 1999, Archaeology of the Land of the Bible, vol. 2, 2001, A Marginal Jew, vol. 3, 2001, Peoples of an Almighty God, 2002, Introduction to the Gospel of John, 2003, Life After Death, 2004; editor: Eerdmans Critical Commentary, 1 and 2 Timothy, 1999, The Psalms, 2003, Bible in its World Series:The Parables of Jesus, 2000, The Rivers of Paradise, 2000, David's Secret Demons, 2001, Music in Ancient Israel/Palestine, 2002, Injustice Made Legal: Deuteronomic Law and the Plight of Widows, Strangers, and Orphans in Ancient Israel, 2002, Piety and Politics, 2003, Familiar Stranger, 2004, Chieftains of the Highland Clans, 2005; (Biblical Resource Series) Studies in Ancient Yahwistic Poetry, 1975, 1995, Ancient Israel: Its Life and Institutions, 1961, 1997, The Use of the Tenses in Hebrew, 1874, 1998, Semitic Background of The New Testament, 1997, To Advance The Gospel, 1981, 1998, Memory and Manuscript, 1961, 1998, Between Athensand Jerusalem, 2000, Pharisees, Scribes, and Sadducees, 1988, 2001, Letters to the Seven Churches of Asia, 1986, 2001, The Faith of Jesus Christ, 1983, 2002, Till the Heart Sings, 2004, What Are the Gospels?, 2004, Psalms in Israel's Worship, 2004, He That Cometh, 2005,; (with J. Greenfield) New Directions in Biblical Archaeology, 1969; (with J.A. Baird) The Computer Bible, 1971, A Critical Concordance to the Synoptic Gospels, 1971, An Analytic Linguistic Concordance to the Book of Isaiah, 1971, I, II, III John: Forward and Reverse Concordance and Index, 1971, A Critical Concordance to Hosea, Amos, Micah, 1972, A Critical Concordance of Haggai, Zechariah, Malachi, 1973, A Critical Concordance to the Gospel of John, 1974, A Synoptic Concordance of Aramaic Inscriptions, 1975, A Linguistic Concordance of Ruth and Jonah, 1976, A Linguistic Concordance of Jeremiah, 1978, Syntactical and Critical Concordance of Jeremiah, 1978, Synoptic Abstract, 1978, I and II Corinthians, 1979, Zechariah, 1979, Galatians, 1980, Ephesians, 1981, Philippians, 1982, Colossians, 1983, Pastoral Epistles, 1984, 1 & 2 Thessalaians, 1985, Density Plots in Ezekiel, 1986, Exodus, 1987, Hebrews, 1988, Ruth, 1989, James, 1991, 1 & 2 Peter, 1991, 1, 2 & 3 John and Jude, 1991, Psalms, Job and Proverbs, 1992, Apocalypse, 1993, The Pentateuch, 1995, Aramaic Inscriptions, 1975, (with T. Kachel) Religion and the Academic Scene, 1975, Am. Schs. Oriental Research publs; co-editor: Scrolls from Qumran Cave I, 1972, Jesus: The Four Gospels, 1973, Palestine in Transition, 1983, The Bible and its Traditions, 1983, Pomegranates and Golden Bells, 1995; Reader's Digest editor: Atlas of the Bible, 1981, Family Guide to the Bible, 1984, Mysteries of the Bible, 1988, Who's Who in the Bible, 1994, The Bible Through the Ages, 1996, Complete Guide to the Bible, 1998; The Leningrad Codex, 1998, Untold Stories: The Bible and Ugaritic Studies in the Twentieth Century, 2001, Interpreting Discontinuity, 2004, On Human Nature, 2004; assoc. editor Jour. Bible Lit., 1952-54, editor, 1955-59; cons. editor Interpreter's Dictionary of the Bible, 1957-60, Theologisches Wörterbuch des Alten Testaments, 1970—, English Translation Theological Dictionary of the Old Testament, 1975—; editor in chief The Anchor Bible Dictionary, 6 vols., 1992, Eerdmans Dictionary of the Bible, 2000; co-editor (with W.H. Propp and Baruch Halpern) The Hebrew Bible and Its Interpreters, 1990; contbr. articles to profl. jours. Recipient prize in New Testament exegesis Princeton Theol. Sem., 1943, Carey-Thomas award for Anchor Bible, 1965, Layman's Nat. Bible Com. award, 1978, 3 awards for Anchor Bible Bibl. Archaeol. Soc., 1993; William H. Green fellow in Old Testament, 1944, William S. Rayner fellow Johns Hopkins U., 1946, 47, Guggenheim fellow, 1959, Am. Assn. Theol. Schs. fellow, 1963; Am. Coun. Learned Socs. grantee-in-aid, 1967, 76; named Disting. Faculty lectr. U. Calif., San Diego, 2002. Fellow U. Mich. Soc. Fellows (sr., chmn. 1980-82); mem. Soc. Bibl. Lit. (pres. 1975-76), Am. Oriental Soc., Am. Schs. Oriental Rsch. (v.p. 1970-82, editor bull. 1974-78, editor Bibl. Archeologist 1976-82, dir. publs. 1974-82), Archaeol. Inst. Am., Am. Acad. Religion, Bibl. Colloquium (sec.-treas. 1960-90), Bibl. Colloquium West (sec., treas. 2000—). Presbyterian. Office: U Calif San Diego Dept History 0104 9500 Gilman Dr La Jolla CA 92093-0104 Office Phone: 858-534-3542. Business E-Mail: dnfreedman@ucsd.edu.

FREEDMAN, ERIC, journalist, educator, writer; b. Brookline, Mass., Nov. 6, 1949; s. Morris and Charlotte (Nadler) Freedman; m. Mary Ann Sipher, May 24, 1974; children: Ian Sipher, Cara Sipher. BA, Cornell U., 1971; JD, NYU, 1975. Bar: N.Y. 1976, Mich. 1985. Congl. aide U.S. Rep. Charles Rangel, Washington and N.Y.C., 1971—76; reporter Knickerbocker News, Albany, NY, 1976—84, Detroit News, Lansing, Mich., 1984—95. Asst. prof. journalism Mich. State U., 1996—; Fulbright sr. lectr. Uzbekistan, 2002. Author: Pioneering Michigan, 1992, On the Water, Michigan, 1992, Michigan Free, 1993, Great Lakes, Great National Forests, 1995, How to Transfer to the College of Your Choice, 2002; co-author: What to Study, 1997; contbr. articles to profl. jours.; co-editor: John F. Kennedy in His Own Words, 2005. Recipient Merit citation, Am. Judicature Soc., Journalism awards, AP, Pulitzer Prize for beat reporting, 1994. Mem.: N.Y. State Bar Assn. (Journalism awards), State Bar Mich., Investigative Reporters and Editors (Journalism award), Am. Soc. Writers on Legal Subjects. Avocations: travel, writing. Home and Office: 2698 Linden Dr East Lansing MI 48823-3814 Office Phone: 517-355-4729. Business E-Mail: freedma5@msu.edu.

FREEDMAN, F. KENNETH, psychotherapist; b. Washington, July 12, 1942; s. Donald K. Freedman and Elinor B. Harvey; children: Paul LeBlanc Gerard Philippe, Joe Acevedo. MFA, Yale Sch. Drama, New Haven, Conn., 1967; MA, Prescott Coll., Ariz., 1998. Lic. profl. counselor Alaska, 1998. Psychotherapist F. Ken Freedman Counseling, Anchorage, 1997—. Gay activist. Office: F Ken Freedman Counseling Ste 20 650 W Internat Airport Rd Anchorage AK 99518-1121 Office Phone: 907-566-1708. Personal E-mail: fken@alaska.net.

FREEDMAN, GERALD M., lawyer; b. Hampton, Va., July 26, 1943; s. Henry and Arlene L.; m. Kristin King; 1 child, Eliza King. BA, Columbia U., 1964, JD, 1967. Bar: N.Y. 1968, U.S. Dist. Ct. (so. and ea. dists.) N.Y. 1970, U.S. Ct. Appeals (2d cir.) 1976. Adminstr. Columbia U., N.Y.C., 1967-69; assoc. Kelley, Drye & Warren, N.Y.C., 1969-71, Trubin Sillcocks Edelman & Knapp, N.Y.C., 1971-76, ptnr., 1976-84, Morgan, Lewis & Bockius, N.Y.C., 1984—. Ptnr. N.Y.C. Partnership, 2000—04. Contbr. articles to profl. jours. Mem.: ABA, Assn. of Bar of City of N.Y., Sharon Country Club, Univ. Club. Office: Morgan Lewis & Bockius 101 Park Ave Fl 44 New York NY 10178-0060 E-mail: gfreedman@morganlewis.com.

FREEDMAN, HARRY, composer; b. Lodz, Poland, Apr. 5, 1922; arrived in Can., 1925; s. Max and Rose (Nelken) F.; m. Mary Louise Morrison, Sept. 15, 1951; children: Karen Liese, Cynthia Jane, Lori Ann. Student, Winnipeg Sch. Art, 1936—40, Royal Conservatory Music, 1945—50. Musician Toronto Symphony, 1946—70; dir. Can. Music Centre. Composer: Tableau, 1952, Images, 1958, Tokaido: chorus and wind quintet, 1964, (orch.) Tangents, 1967, Tapestry, 1973, A Dance on the Earth, 1988, Town, 1981, Concerto for Orch., 1982, Third Symphony, 1983, Manipulating Mario, 2003, (ballets) Rose Latulippe, 1966, Romeo and Juliet, 1973, Oiseaux Exotiques, 1984, (soprano and flute) Toccata, 1968, Debussy orchestration Piano Preludes, 1971, (childrens choir) Keewaydin, 1971, Rhymes from the Nursery, 1986, Aqsaqniq, 2001, (violin and piano) Encounter, 1974, (clarinet) Lines, 1974, (narrator and chamber ensemble) The Explainer, 1976, (saxophone and orch.) Celebration, 1977, (choir) Green...Blue...White, 1978, Voices, 1999, Valleys, 2002, (Operas) Abracadabra, 1979, (chorus and orch.) Nocturne 3, 1980, (brass quintet and orch.) Royal Flush, 1980, (clarinet and string quartet) Chalumeau, 1981, (narrator and orch.) A Garland for Terry, 1985, (string orch.) Contrasts, The Web and the Wind, 1986, (music theater) Fragments of Alice, 1987, (concerto for percussion ensemble and orch.) Touchings, 1989, (marimba solo) Bones, 1989, (piano and choir) Songs from Shakespeare, 1990, (soprano and string quartet) Spirit Song, 1990, (22 solo strings) Indigo, 1994, (flute, viola and harp) Touchpoints, 1994, (soprano and lute) Bright Angels, 1995, (saxophone quartet) Saxtet, 1995, (bass clarinet and cello) Higher, 1996, (orchestra and 4 choirs) Borealis, 1997, (harp solo) Dances, 1997, (viola and orch.) Marigold, 1999, (16 solo strings) Graphic 9: for Harry Somers, 2000, (string quartet) Graphic 8, 2000, Phoenix, 2003, (symphonic) Duke, 2001, (flute) Romp and Reverie, 2002, (scores) Stratford Shakespeare Festival, films, stage, TV, (violin, cello and piano) A Gift for King Freddy, 2004, (flute, clarinet, violin, cello and piano) Graphic 10 (Matisse: Jazz), 2004; host: Music on a Sunday Afternoon, 1987. Served with RCAF, 1942-45. Decorated officer Order of Can.; Can. Coun. sr. arts grantee, 1960, 63, 73-74, 81, 97-98; recipient Can. film awards, 1970, Composer of Yr. award Can. Music Coun., 1979, Lynch-Staunton award Can. Coun., 1998; Tanglewood scholar, 1949, Royal Conservatory scholar, 1950. Mem. Can. League Composers (founding mem., pres. 1975-78). Address: 616 Avenue Rd Ste 503 Toronto ON Canada M4V 2K8 E-mail: freedman@nobelmed.com.

FREEDMAN, HELEN E., judge; b. NYC, Dec. 15, 1942; d. David Simeon and Frances (Fisher) Edelstein; m. Henry A. Freedman, June 7, 1964; children: Katherine Eleanor, Elizabeth Sarah. BA, Smith Coll., 1963; JD, NYU, 1967. Bar: N.Y. 1970, U.S. Dist. Ct. (so. and ea. dists.), U.S. Supreme Ct. 1979. Staff atty. office of gen. counsel Am. Arbitration Assn., N.Y.C., 1967-69; assoc. Hubbel, Cohen & Stiefel, N.Y.C., 1970-71, Shaw, Bernstein, Scheuer, Boyden & Sarnoff, N.Y.C., 1971-74; law sec. Civil Ct., N.Y.C., 1974-76; sr. atty. housing litigation bur. N.Y.C. Dept. Housing Preservation and Devel., 1976; supervising atty. Dist. Coun. 37 Legal Svcs. Plan, N.Y.C., 1976-78; judge Civil Ct., N.Y.C., 1979-88; acting justice Supreme Ct., N.Y.C., 1984-88, justice, 1989-95; apptd. to appellate term 1st dept. NY Supreme Ct., N.Y.C., 1995-99, apptd. to comml. divsn., 2000—, pres. judge mass tort litigation panel, 2002—. Co-chair State Judges Mass Tort Litigation Com.; mem. pattern jury instrns. com., Supreme Ct. Justices; adj. prof. N.Y. Law Sch., 1999, 2000, 03, 04; lectr. in field. Author: New York Objections, 1999, 6th revised edit., 2004; contbr. articles to profl. jours. Recipent Disting. Alumna award Smith Coll., 2000, Disting. Svc. award, Civil Ct. N.Y., 2004, Louis J. Capozzoli Gavel award N.Y. Ct. Lawyers Assn., 2005. Fellow Am. Bar Found., NY State Bar Found.; mem. ABA (chair small claims ct. com. 1986-89, bioethics com. nat. conf. spl. ct. judges, NY State Ct. del. to ann. meetings, nat. conf. spl. ct. judges, 1987-88, Spl. Cts. Conf. award 1987, 88, 93, Jud. Excellence award 1998), Nat. Assn. Women Judges, NY State Bar Assn. (del.), NY Fed. State Jud. Coun., NY Women's Bar Assn., NY State Assn. Women Judges (pres. 1995-97), Assn. of Bar of City of NY (com mem., chair com. med. malpractice, v.p. 1994-95), Judges and Lawyers Breast Cancer Alert (pres. 2001-03). Home: 150 W 96th St New York NY 10025-6469 Office: NY Supreme Ct 60 Centre New York NY 10007-1488 Office Phone: 646-836-3208.

FREEDMAN, JANET WHITTLE, retired academic administrator, writer; b. Balt., Oct. 23, 1945; d. Howard Marvin Whittle and Margaret Ethel Nash; m. Irving Freedman, Dec. 14, 1970; children: Jason Matthew, Jeannette Elizabeth. BFA, The Md. Inst., Balt., 1970; M.Liberal Arts, Johns Hopkins U., Balt., 1999. With Johns Hopkins U., Balt. Chair alumni adv. bd. Master of Liberal Arts Program, Johns Hopkins U., Balt., 2002—03. Author: (memoir and history) Kent Island:The Land That Once Was Eden. Mem.: Phi Delta Gamma (v.p.). Avocation: painting. Home: 1920 Greenhaven Dr Baltimore MD 21209 Personal E-mail: jfreed@baltimorefirst.com.

FREEDMAN, JAY WEIL, lawyer; b. Washington, May 19, 1942; s. Walter and Maxine (Weil) F.; m. Linda Newman, Aug. 7, 1966; children: Courteney, Spencer. BA, Williams Coll., 1964; JD, Yale U., 1967. Bar: D.C. 1968, U.S. Supreme Ct. 1973. Atty. office of gen. counsel FCC, 1967-68; assoc. Freedman, Levy, Kroll & Simonds, Washington, 1968-72, ptnr., 1972-2001, Foley & Lardner LLP, Washington, 2001—. Pres. Am. Jewish Com., Washington, 1987—89, Washington Hebrew Congregation, 1982—84; bd. dirs. Smithsonian Instn. Librs., 2001—, Georgetown Bus. Improvement Dist., 2002—, treas., 2004—; bd. dirs. Heifitz Internat. Music Inst., 2003—; bd. trustees The Kreeger Mus., 2002—. Mem. ABA, D.C. Bar Assn., Woodmont Country Club (pres. 1997-99), Yale Law Sch. Alumni Assn. (exec. com. 1999-2004, sec. 2003-04), Econ. Club, Phi Delta Phi. Office: Foley & Lardner 3000 K Street NW Ste 500 Washington DC 20007 Business E-Mail: jfreedman@foley.com.

FREEDMAN, JOEL F., lawyer; BA cum laude, Brandeis Univ., 1986; JD magna cum laude, Boston Univ., 1989. Bar: Mass. 1989. V.p. & gen. counsel Dial Call, 1994—96; ptnr. corp. dept. Ropes & Gray, Boston, 1996—, co-head venture capital & tech. practice group. Office: Ropes & Gray 1 International Pl Boston MA 02110-2624 Office Phone: 617-951-7309. Office Fax: 617-951-7050. Business E-Mail: joel.freedman@ropesgray.com.

FREEDMAN, JONATHAN BORWICK, journalist, writer, lecturer, educator; b. Rochester, N.Y., Apr. 11, 1950; s. Marshall Arthur and Betty (Borwick) F.; children: Madigan, Nicholas; m. Isabelle Rooney, 1999; children: Genevieve, Lincoln. AB in Lit. cum laude, Columbia Coll., N.Y.C., 1972. Reporter AP of Brazil, Sao Paulo and Rio de Janeiro, 1974-75; editorial writer The Tribune, San Diego, 1981-90; syndicated columnist Copley News Service, San Diego, 1987-89; free-lance opinion writer L.A. Times, 1990—; free-lance editorial writer N.Y. Times, 1990-91; dir. Hope Lit. Project, 1998—. Dist. vis. lectr. and adj. faculty San Diego State U., 1990—; mem. U.S.-Japan Journalists Exch. Program, Internat. Press Inst., 1985. Author, illustrator: The Man Who'd Bounce the World, 1979; author: The Editorials and Essays of Jonathan Freedman, 1988, Wall of Fame, 2000; contbg. author: Best Newspaper Writing, From Contemporary Culture, 1991, (nonfiction) From Cradle to Grave: The Human Face of Poverty in America, 1993; freelance columnist, 1979-81; dir. (TV documentary) Pedaling Hope, 1998; contbr. articles to N.Y. Times, Chgo. Tribune, San Francisco Examiner, Oakland Tribune, others. Moderator PBS, San Diego, 1988; bd. dirs. Schs. of the Future Commn., San Diego, 1987. Recipient Copley Ring of Truth award, 1983, Sigma Delta Chi award, 1983, San Diego Press Club award, 1984, Spl. citation Columbia Grad. Sch. Journalism, 1985, Disting. Writing award Am. Soc. Newspaper Editors, 1986, Pulitzer prize in Disting. Editorial Writing, 1987; Cornell Woolrich Writing fellow Columbia U., 1972, Eugene C. Pullian Editorial Writing fellow Sigma Delta Chi Found., 1986, Media fellow Hoover Instn., Stanford, Calif., 1991, Kaiser Media fellow, 1995, Peacemaker award San Diego Mediation Ctr., 1999, one of 45 Am. Heroes, Esquire mag., 1998. Mem. Soc. Profl. Journalists (Disting. Svc. award 1985, Casey medal for meritorious journalism 1994), Nat. Conf. Editl. Writers, Authors Guild, Phi Beta Kappa. Jewish. Avocations: skiing, tai chi. Office: 755 Genter St La Jolla CA 92037-5459

FREEDMAN, JUDITH GREENBERG, retired elementary school educator, state legislator; b. Bridgeport, Conn., Mar. 11, 1939; d. Samuel Howard and Dorothy (Hoffman) G.; m. Samuel Sumner, Dec. 24, 1964; 1 child, Martha Ann. Student, Boston U., 1957—58, U. Mich., 1958—59; BS, So. Conn. State U., 1961, MS, 1972. Tchr. Hollywood (Fla.) Pub. Schs., 1961-62, White Plains (N.Y.) Pub. Schs., 1962-64, Wilton (Conn.) Pub. Schs., 1964-66, Weston (Conn.) Pub. Schs., 1966-72, 1982-84, tutor, 1977-80; owner Judith's Fancy, Westport, Conn., 1984—; mem. Dist. 26 Conn. Senate, Hartford, 1987—. Ranking mem. human svcs. com. Conn. Senate, 1987—88, ins. com., 1987—94, ranking mem. appropriations com., 1989—94, chmn. program rev. and investigation, 1992—94, chmn. commn. on innovation and productivity, 1994—95, ranking mem. edn. com., 1995—96, dep. pres. pro tem, 1995—97, 1995—2000, chair edn. com., 1998—2000, asst. minority leader, 1998—2002, co-chair edn. sub. com. appropriations, 1998—, mem. legis. mgmt. com., 1998—, mem. appropriation com., 1998—, ranking mem. higher edn. com., 2002—04; mem. exec. com. ea. region Coun. State Govts., chair program rev. and investigation, 2000—, dep. minority leader, 2000—02; edn. commn. of the states Conn. steering com., 2000—; mem. exec. com. ERCCSG, 2004—. Pres., v.p. 4th Congl. Rep. Women's Assn., 1976-80; pres. Rep. Women of Westport, 1976-79; mem. Bd. Edn., Westport, 1983-87, 89—; treas. Conn. Order Women Legislators. Mem. Order of Women Legislators (treas.), Weston Kiwanis, Fairfield County Navy Leagues. Jewish. Avocations: reading, art, golf. Home: 17 Crawford Rd Westport CT 06880-1823 Office Phone: 860-240-8826. Business E-Mail: judith.g.freedman@po.state.ct.us.

FREEDMAN, LOUIS MARTIN, dentist; b. Newark, Mar. 19, 1947; s. Morris and Sylvia (Swimmer) F.; m. Elizabeth Norine Palmer, June 17, 1978; children: Steven, Julie, Brian. Student, Emory U., 1963—66, DDS, 1970. Dentist Freedman, Freedman & Weitman DDS, P.C., Atlanta, 1970—; clin. instr. Emory U. Dental Sch., Atlanta, 1970—77. Team dentist Atlanta Hawks Basketball Team, 1971—, Atlanta Flames Hockey Team, 1979-80, Atlanta Knights Hockey Team, 1992-96, Atlanta Fire Ants Roller Hockey Team, 1994-96. Mem. Exch. Club, Atlanta, 1970-73; mgr. Sandy Springs Youth Sports Little League Baseball, 1979-96; head coach Sandy Springs United Meth. Ch. basketball program, 1991-96. Mem. Acad. Osseointegration, Alpha Epsilon Delta, Omicron Kappa Upsilon. Jewish. Avocations: softball, little league managing, gardening, skiing, water-skiing, swimming. Office: Freedman Freedman & Weitman 3111 Piedmont Rd NE Atlanta GA 30305-2507 Office Phone: 404-261-5388.

FREEDMAN, MICHAEL HARTLEY, mathematician, educator; b. L.A., Apr. 21, 1951; s. Benedict and Nancy (Mars) Freedman; m. Leslie Blair Howland, Sept. 18, 1983; children: Hartley, Whitney, Jake; 1 child. PhD, Princeton U., 1973. Lectr. U. Calif., Berkeley, 1973—75; faculty mem. Inst. Advanced Study, Princeton, NJ, 1980—81, mem., 1975—76; asst. prof. U. Calif., San Diego, 1976—79, assoc. prof., 1979—80, prof., 1982—85, Charles Lee Powell chair math., 1985—; sr. rsch. scientist Microsoft Corp., 1997—. Author: Classification of Four Dimensional Spaces, 1982; author: (assoc. editor) Jour. Differntial Geometry, Math. Rsch. Letters and Topology, 1982—, Annals of Math., 1984—91, Jour. Am. Math. Soc., 1987—. Named Calif. Scientist of Yr., Calif. Mus. Assn., 1984; recipient Veblen prize, Am. Math. Soc., 1986, Fields medal, Internat. Congress of Mathematicians, 1986, Nat. medal of Sci., 1987, Humboldt Award, 1994; fellow MacArthur Found., 1984—89, Guggenheim, 1989, 1994. Mem.: NAS, N.Y. Acad. Scis., Am. Assn. Arts and Scis. Avocation: technical rock climber (soloed Northeast ridge Mt. Williamson winter 1970, Great Western boulder climbing champion 1979). Office: Microsoft Rsch One Microsoft Way Redmond WA 98052 also: Univ Calif San Diego Dept Math 0112 9500 Gilman Dr La Jolla CA 92093-0112 E-mail: mfreedman@ucsd.edu.

FREEDMAN, MICHAEL LEONARD, geriatrician, educator; b. Newark, Dec. 12, 1937; s. David Hyman and Alice Ella (Zwain) F.; m. Cora Ruth Singer, June 24, 1962; children: Lawrence Andrew, Deborah Lynn. AB with honors, Colgate U., 1959; MD cum laude, Tufts U., 1963. Diplomate Am. Bd. Internal Medicine, Am. Bd. Hematology, Am. Bd. Geriatric Medicine. Intern, then resident NYU/Bellevue Med. Ctrs., 1963-65, 68-69; rsch. assoc. lab physiology to staff investigator Nat. Cancer Inst., NIH, Bethesda, Md., 1965-68; asst. prof. NYU Med. Ctr., 1969-74, assoc. prof., 1974-77, prof., 1977—, firm chief, dir. geriatrics, 1979—; Diane and Arthur Belfer prof. geriatric medicine NYU, 1987—. Cons. CBS, Inc., Bristol Meyers Corp., Kimberly-Clark Corp., Pfizer Corp., Nutrasweet Corp., Citicorp. Editor: Hematology in the Elderly, 1985; contbr. over 185 articles to profl. jours. Lt. comdr. USPHS, 1965-68. NIH rsch. grantee, 1969—; recipient Wholeness of Life award Hosp. Chaplaincy, 1988; named one of the Heroes of Bellevue, 1987. Fellow ACP, Am. Geriatrics Soc. (com. chmn. 1985—), Am. Soc. Hematology, Gerontol. Soc. Am. (com. chmn. 1984—); mem. Am. Soc. Clin. Investigation, Am. Soc. Hematology, AAAS, Am. Fed. Aging Rsch. (founder, mem. nat. adv. coun.), Alpha Omega Alpha. Democrat. Jewish. Avocations: photography, travel, tennis. Office: NYU Med Ctr 550 1st Ave New York NY 10016-6402 Office Phone: 212-263-7043. Business E-Mail: freedm01@med.nyu.edu.

FREEDMAN, MONROE HENRY, law educator; b. Mt. Vernon, N.Y., Apr. 10, 1928; s. Chauncey and Dorothea (Kornblum) F.; m. Audrey Willock, Sept. 24, 1950 (dec. 1998); children: Alice Freedman Korngold, Sarah Freedman Izquierdo, Caleb (dec. 1998), Judah. AB cum laude, Harvard U., 1951, LLB, 1954, LLM, 1956. Bar: Mass. 1954, Pa. 1957, D.C. 1960, U.S. Dist. Ct. (ea. dist. N.Y.), U.S. Ct. Appeals (D.C. cir.) 1960, U.S. Supreme Ct. 1960, U.S. Ct. Appeals (2d cir.) 1968, N.Y. 1978, U.S. Ct. Appeals (9th cir.) 1982, U.S. Ct. Appeals (11th cir.) 1986, U.S. Ct. Appeals (Fed. cir.) 1987. Assoc. Wolf, Block, Schorr & Solis-Cohen, Phila., 1956-58; ptnr. Freedman & Temple, Washington, 1969-73; dir. Stern Community Law Firm, Washington, 1970-71; prof. law George Washington U., 1958-73; dean Hofstra Law Sch., Hempstead, N.Y., 1973-77, prof. law, 1973—, Howard Lichtenstein Disting. prof. legal ethics, 1989—2003; Drinko-Baker & Hostetler chair in law Cleve. State U., 1992; CFO Olive Tree Mktg. Internat., 1998—. Faculty asst. Harvard U. Law Sch., 1954-56, instr. trial advocacy and legal ethics, 1978—; lectr. on lawyers' ethics; exec. dir. U.S. Holocaust Meml. Coun., 1980-82, gen. counsel, 1982-83, sr. adviser to chmn., 1982-87; cons. U.S. Commn. on Civil Rights, 1960-64, Neighborhood Legal Services Program, 1970; legis. cons. to Senator John L. McClellan, 1959; spl. com. on courtroom conduct N.Y.C. Bar Assn., 1972; exec. dir. Criminal Trial Inst., 1965-66; expert witness on legal ethics state and fed. ct. proceedings, U.S. Senate and House Coms., U.S. Dept. Justice, FDIC; spl. investigator Rochester Inst. Tech., 1991; reporter Am. Lawyer's Code of Conduct, 1979-81; mem. Arbitration panel U.S. Dist. Ct. (ea. dist.) N.Y., 1986—; Inaugural Wickwire lectr. Dalhousie Law Sch., N.S., 1992; lectr. S.C. Bar Found., 1993, numerous profl. confs; adv. subgroup on ethics U.S. Dist. Ct. (ea. dist.) N.Y., 1994-96; mem. Nat. Com. Right to Counsel, 2002—. Author: Contracts, 1973, Lawyers' Ethics in an Adversary System, 1975 (ABA gavel award, cert. of merit 1976), Teacher's Manual Contracts, 1978, American Lawyer's Code of Conduct, 1981, Understanding Lawyers' Ethics, 1990, (with Abbe Smith) 4th edit., 2004, Group Defamation and Freedom of Speech—The Relationship Between Language and Violence, 1995; co-editor; columnist Cases and Controversies, Am. Lawyer Media, 1990-96, (with Supreme Ct. Justice Ruth Bader Ginsburg) Freedom, Life, & Death: Materials on Comparative Constitutional Law, 1997; mem. panel acad. contbrs. Black's Law Dictionary, 2002-2003; television appearances include Donohue, CNN Money Line, CBS 60 Minutes, CNN Late Edition, Court TV, C-SPAN, O'Reilly Factor, and others; contbr. articles to profl. jours. Recipient Martin Luther King Jr. Humanitarian award, 1987, The Lehman-LaGuardia Award for Civic Achievement, 1996. Fellow Am. Bar Found. (life); mem. ABA (ethics adv. to chair criminal justice sect. 1993-95, ethics and professional responsibility com. 2005—, Michael Franck award 1998), ACLU (nat. bd. dir. 1970-80, nat. adv. coun. 1980—, spl. litigation counsel 1971-73), Am. Law Inst. (consultative group on the law governing lawyers, 1990-99, consultative group on Uniform Comml. Code art. 2 1990-2002), Soc. Am. Law Tchrs. (mem. governing bd. 1974-79, exec. com. 1976-79, chmn. com. on profl. responsibility 1974-79, 87-90), ABA (vice chmn. ethical considerations com. criminal justice sect. 1989-90, ethics advisor to chmn. criminal justice sect., 1993-96), N.Y. State Bar Assn. (com. on legal edn. and admission to bar 1988-92, criminal justice sect. com. on profl. responsibility, 1990-92, award for Dedication to Scholarship and pub. svc. 1997), Assn. Bar City N.Y. (com. on profl. responsibility 1987-90, com. on profl. and jud. ethics 1991-92), Fed. Bar Assn. (chmn. com. on profl. disciplinary standards and procedures 1970-71), Am. Soc. Writers on Legal Subjects (mem. com. on constitution and bylaws 1999—), Am. Bd. Criminal Lawyers (hon.), Am. Jewish Congress (nat. governing coun. 1984-86), Am. Arbitration Assn. (arbitrator, nat. panel arbitrators 1964—, cert. svc. award 1986), Nat. Network on Right to Counsel (exec. bd., exec. com. 1986-90), Nat. Com. on the Right to Counsel, Nat. Prison Project (steering com. 1970-90), Nat. Assn. Criminal Def. Lawyers (vice chmn. ethics adv. com. 1991-93, co-chmn., 1994), Am. Bd. Criminal Lawyers (hon.). Democrat. Jewish. Address: The Wyndham West 804 111 Cherry Valley Ave Garden City NY 11530 Office Phone: 516-873-6622. Business E-Mail: lawmhf@hofstra.edu.

FREEDMAN, PAUL HARRIS, historian, educator; b. N.Y.C., Sept. 15, 1949; s. Alfred M. and Marcia (Kohl) F.; m. Bonnie Roe, Aug. 15, 1982. BA, U. Calif., Santa Cruz, 1971; PhD, U. Calif., Berkeley, 1978. Asst. prof. to prof. history Vanderbilt U., Nashville, 1979-97; prof. history Yale U., New Haven, 1997—2004, chair dept. history, 2004—. Author: The Diocese of Vic, 1983, The Origins of Peasant Servitude in Medieval Catalonia, 1992 (Premio del Rey prize 1992), Images of the Medieval Peasant, 1999, (Kayden prize 2000, Gründler prize 2001, Haskins prize, 2002). Fellow Medieval Acad. Am., Inst. Catalan Studies (corr.), Real Academia de Bnenas Letras (corr.). Office: Yale U Dept History P O Box 208324 New Haven CT 06520 Office Phone: 203-432-1364. Business E-Mail: paul.freedman@yale.edu.

FREEDMAN, PHILIP, internist, educator; b. London, June 25, 1926; came to U.S., 1963, naturalized, 1970; s. Myer and Mildred (Frankel) F.; m. Jean Kennis Cunningham, Dec. 21, 1954; children: Simon John, Marion Rose, Mark Alexander, Paul Daniel, Adam James. MB, BS with honors, Univ. Coll. Hosp. Med. Sch., London, 1948, MD, 1951. House surgeon Univ. Coll. Hosp., 1948, med. registrar, 1953-56, rsch. asst. professorial med. unit, 1956-57, Bilton Pollard fellow, 1957-59; sr. house physician Chase Farm Hosp., 1949; 1st asst. physician St. George's Hosp., London, 1959-60; cons. Woolwich Hosp. Group, London, Redhill Hosp. Group, Surrey, Eng., 1960-63; chief Chgo. Med. Sch. Divsn., Dept. Medicine Cook County Hosp., 1963-66; prof., chmn. dept. medicine Chgo. Med. Sch., 1967-74; dir. renal unit Cook County Hosp., Chgo., 1963-66; chmn. dept. medicine Mt. Sinai Hosp. Med. Ctr., Chgo., 1966-79; prof., sr. attending physician Rush Med. Coll., Rush-Presbyn.-St. Luke's Med. Ctr., Chgo., 1975-96; clin. prof. medicine U. Ill. Coll. Medicine, Urbana-Champaign, 1999—. Contbr. articles to profl. jours. With M.C. Brit. Army, 1951-53. Fellow ACP, Royal Coll. Physicians; mem. Ctrl. Soc. Clin. Investigation, Med. Rsch. Soc. London, Alpha Omega Alpha (faculty mem.). Home: 2304 Sandpoint Champaign IL 61822-9297 Business E-Mail: pfreedman@uiuc.edu.

FREEDMAN, ROBERT LOUIS, lawyer; b. Phila., Apr. 8, 1940; s. Abraham L. and Jane G. (Sunstein) F.; m. Diane Stoller, July 25, 1965; children: Elizabeth, Paul, Jonathan AB, Harvard U., 1962; MA in Econs., Columbia U., 1963, LLB, 1966. Bar: Pa. 1967. Law clk., 1966-68; assoc. Dechert Price & Rhoads, Phila., 1968-75, ptnr., 1975—; lectr. in law Temple U. Law Sch., 1969-74. Adj. prof. U. Pa. Law Sch., 1997—2001. Adv. com. on decedents' estates Pa. Joint State Govt. Commn.; chmn. bd. Fgn. Policy Rsch. Inst. Mem. Am. Law Inst., Am. Coll. Trust and Estate Counsel, Phila. Bar Assn. (chmn. sect. on probate and trust law 1983) Clubs: Germantown Cricket. Jewish. Office: Dechert LLP 4000 Bell Atlantic Tower 1717 Arch St Philadelphia PA 19103-2793 Office Phone: 215-994-2558. Business E-Mail: robert.freedman@dechert.com.

FREEDMAN, RONALD, sociology educator; b. Winnipeg, Man., Can., Aug. 8, 1917; came to U.S., 1924, naturalized, 1930. s. Isador and Ada (Greenstone) F.; m. Deborah Gail Selin, May 4, 1941 (dec. 2000); children: Joseph Selin, Jane Ilene (dec.). BA, U. Mich., 1939, MA, 1940; PhD, U. Chgo., 1947. Mem. faculty U. Mich., Ann Arbor, 1946—, prof. sociology, 1954—, Roderick D. McKenzie prof. sociology, 1979-87, now Roderick D. McKenzie disting. prof. emeritus; rsch. assoc. Survey Rsch. Ctr., 1954-70; dir. Population Studies Ctr., 1962-71. Co-dir. Taiwan Population Studies Ctr., 1962-64; cons. to Taiwan govt., 1962-88; mem. tech. adv. com. 1970 Census of Population, 1965, Pres.'s Adv. Com. on Population and Family Planning. Author: The Sociology of Human Fertility, 1960, (with others) Family Planning, Sterility and Population Growth, 1959, Principles of Sociology, 1952, Family Planning in Taiwan, 1969; also articles and monographs. With USAAF, 1942-45. Recipient award excellence on teaching U. Mich. Class of, 1952, Disting. Faculty Svc. award U. Mich., 1970, Taeuber award, 1981; Guggenheim fellow, 1957-58; Fulbright fellow, 1957-58; fellow Center for Advanced Study in Behavioral Scis., 1970; Lady Davis fellow and Einstein fellow Hebrew U., 1987 Fellow Am. Acad. Arts and Scis., U.S. Nat. Acad. Sci., Am. Statis. Assn.; mem. NAS, Population Assn. Am. (pres. 1964-65), Internat. Union Study Population (v.p. 1966-67), Am. Sociol. Assn., Sociol. Rsch. Assn., Phi Beta Kappa. Home: # 510 1200 Earhart Rd Ann Arbor MI 48105-2768

FREEDMAN, RUSSELL BRUCE, author; b. San Francisco, Oct. 11, 1929; s. Louis Nathan and Irene (Gordon) F. BA, U. Calif., Berkeley, 1951. Newsman AP, San Francisco, 1953-56; with dept. TV publicity J. Walter Thompson Co., N.Y.C., 1956-60; faculty New Sch. for Social Rsch., N.Y.C., 1969-86. Author: Teenagers Who Made History, 1961, Jules Verne: Portrait of a Prophet, 1963, 2000 Years of Space Travel, 1965, Thomas Alva Edison, 1966, Scouting with Baden-Powell, 1967, Animal Architects, 1971, The First Days of Life, 1974, Growing Up Wild, 1975, Animal Fathers, 1976, Animal Games, 1976, Hanging On: How Animals Carry Their Young, 1978, Getting Born, 1978, Tooth and Claw, 1980, They Lived with the Dinosaurs, 1980, Immigrant Kids, 1980, When Winter Comes, 1981, Farm Babies, 1981, Animal Superstars, 1982, Killer Fish, 1982, Killer Snakes, 1982, Can Bears Predict Earthquakes? Unsolved Mysteries of Animal Behavior, 1982, Dinosaurs and Their Young, 1983, Children of the Wild West, 1983 (Western Heritage Wrangler award, Outstanding Western Juvenile Book award 1984), Rattlesnakes, 1984, Cowboys of the Wild West, 1985, Sharks, 1985, Holiday House: The First Fifty Years, 1985, Indian Chiefs, 1987, Abraham Lincoln: A Photobiography, 1987 (John Newbery medal 1988, Jefferson Cup award 1988), Buffalo Hunt, 1988, Franklin Delano Roosevelt, 1990 (Orbis Pictus award 1991, Jefferson Cup award 1991), The Wright Brothers: How They Invented the Airplane, 1991 (Newbery Honor Book 1992, Jefferson cup award 1992, Golden Kite award 1991), An Indian Winter, 1992 (Western Heritage Wrangler award 1993), Eleanor Roosevelt: A Life of Discovery, 1993 (Newbery Honor Book 1994, Golden Kite award 1993, Boston Globe Horn Book award 1993), Kids at Work, 1994 (Golden Kite award 1994, Jane Addams Book award 1995), The Life and Death of Crazy Horse, 1996 (Spur award Best Western Juvenile Non-fiction 1996), Out of Darkness: The Story of Louis Braille, 1997, Martha Graham: A Dancer's Life, 1998 (Golden Kite award 1998), Babe Didrikson Zaharias: The Making of a Champion, 1999, Give Me Liberty! The Story of the Declaration of Independence, 2000, In the Days of the Vaqueros: America's First True Cowboys, 2001 (Spur award Best Western Juvenile non-fiction, 2002), Confucius: The Golden Rule, 2002, In Defense of Liberty: The Story of America's Bill of Rights, 2003, The Voice that Challenged a Nation: Marion Anderson and the Struggle for Equal Rights, 2004 (Newbery Honor Book, 2005, Robert F. Sibert Informative Book award, 2005); co-author: (with James E. Morris) How Animals Learn, 1969, Animal Instincts, 1970, The Brains of Animals and Man, 1972. With M.I., U.S. Army, 1951-53; Korea. Mem. PEN, Author's Guild.

FREEDMAN, SAMUEL ORKIN, university official; b. Montreal, Que., Can., May 8, 1928; s. Abraham Orkin and Elvira (Gottheil) F.; m. Norah Lee Maizel, Aug. 28, 1955; children: David Orkin, Daniel Ari, Abraham Edward, Elizabeth Vera. B.Sc., McGill U., Montreal, 1949, MD, C.M., 1953, D.Sc. (hon.), 1992. Intern Jewish Gen. Hosp., Montreal, 1953-54; resident in internal medicine and allergy Montreal Gen. Hosp., also Roosevelt Hosp., N.Y.C., 1954-59; mem. faculty McGill U. Med. Faculty, 1959—, prof. medicine, physiology, 1968-2000, prof. medicine, physiology emeritus, 2000—, dean, 1977-81, vice-prin. (acad.), 1981-91; sr. advisor Jewish Gen. Hosp., Montreal, 2000—. Vis. prof. U. London, Eng., 1973-74; dir. divsn. clin. immunology and allergy Montreal Gen. Hosp., 1967-77; bd. dirs. Nat. Cancer Inst. Can., 1979—; chmn. com. immunology and transplanatation Med. Rsch. Coun. Can., 1968-73, mem. program grants com., 1975-78. Editor: Clinical Immunology, 2d edit, 1976. Decorated Order of Can.; recipient Queen's Silver Jubilee medal, 1977; Gairdner Internat. award for outstanding med. rsch., 1978, Commemorative medal for the 125th Anniversary of the Confedn. of Can., 1992, prix Armand Frappier, 1998, prix de Que., 1998, Queen's Golden Jubilee medal, 2002, Order of Que., 2004. Fellow Royal Soc. Can., Royal Coll. Physicians and Surgeons Can., ACP, Am. Acad. Allergy; Mem. Internat. Assn. Allergology and Clin. Immunology (v.p. 1982-88); mem. Am. Soc. Clin. Investigation, Am. Assn. Immunology, Am. Thoracic Soc., Canadian Soc. Clin. Investigation. Clubs: Univ. (Montreal). Jewish. Achievements include co-discoverer of the CEA test for cancer. Home: 658 Murray Hill Ave Montreal PQ Canada H3Y 2W6 Office: Jewish Gen Hosp 3755 Cote Ste Catherine Rd Montreal PQ Canada H3T 1E2 Office Phone: 514-340-7571. Business E-Mail: sfreedma@ldi.jgh.mcgill.ca. E-mail: freedman@videotron.ca.

FREEDMAN, SANDRA WARSHAW, former mayor; b. Newark, Sept. 21, 1943; m. Michael J. Freedman; 3 children. BA in Govt., U. Miami, 1965. Mem. Tampa (Fla.) City Coun., 1974—, chmn., 1983-86; mayor City of Tampa, 1986-95. Author: Specialties of the House (Recipes for People on the Go!), 2002. Bd. dirs. Jewish Cmty. Ctr., Boys and Girls Clubs Greater Tampa, Hillsborough Coalition for Health, Tampa Cmty. Concert Assn., Hillsborough Edn. Found., Judeo Christian Clinic, NCCJ, Human Rights Task Force; mem. sports adv. bd. Hillsborough Community Coll., 1975-76; sec. Downtown Devel. Authority, 1977-78; bd. dirs., v.p. Fla. Gulf Coast Symphony, 1979-80; vice chmn. Met. Planning Orgn., 1981-82; corp. mem. Neighborhood Housing Service; bd. fellows U. Tampa; mem. steering com. Hillsborough County Council of Govt.'s Constituency for Children; mem. exec. bd. Tampa/Hillsborough Young Adult Forum; chmn. bd. trustees Berkeley Prep. Sch.; trustee Tampa Bay Performing Arts Ctr., Inc., Tampa Mus.; mem. ethics com. Meml. Hosp.; mem. Tampa Preservation, Inc., Tampa/Hillsborough County Youth Council, Davis Islands Civic Assn., Tampa Hist. Soc., Met. Ministries Adv. Bd., Rodeph Sholom Synagogue, Sword of Hope Guild of Am. Cancer Soc., Friends of Arts. Recipient Spessar L. Holland Meml. award Tampa Bay Com. for Good Govt., 1975-76, Human Rights award City of Tampa, 1980, award Soroptimist Internat. Tampa, 1981, Status of Women award Zonta of Tampa II, 1986, Woman of Achievement award Bus. & Profl. Women, Jewish Nat. Fund Tree of Life award, Disting. Citizen award U. South Fla., 1995, Nat. Conf. of Christian and Jews Humanitarian award, 1995; named to Fla. Home Builders Hall of Fame. Mem. Hillsborough County Bar Aux., Greater Tampa C. of C., C. of C. Com. of 100 (exec. com.), Fla. League of Cities (bd. dirs.), Tampa Urban League, Nat. Council Jewish Women, U. Miami Alumni Assn., Athena Soc., Hadassah. Office: 3435 Bayshore Blvd Apt 700 Tampa FL 33629-8827

FREEDMAN, SARAH WARSHAUER, education educator; b. Wiliming-ton, N.C., Feb. 23, 1946; d. Samuel Edward and Miriam Warshauer; m. S. Robert Freedman, Aug. 20, 1967; 1 child, Rachel Karen. BA in English, U. Pa., 1967; MA in English, U. Chgo., 1970; MA in Linguistics, Stanford U., 1976, PhD in Edn., 1977. Tchr. English Phila. Sch. Dist., 1967-68, Lower Merion H.S., 1968-69; instr. English U. N.C., Wilmington, 1970-71; instr. English and linguistics Stanford U., 1972-76; asst. and assoc. prof. English San Francisco State U., 1977-81; asst. prof. edn. U. Calif., Berkeley, 1981-83, assoc. prof. edn., 1983-89; dir. Nat. Ctr. for the Study of Writing and Literacy, 1985-96; prof. edn. U. Calif., 1989—. Resident Bellagio Conf. and Study Ctr., Rockefeller Found., 1997; mem. nat. task force Nat. Writing Project, 1998—. Author: Response to Student Writing, 1987, Exchanging Writing, Exchanging Cultures, Lessons in School Reform from the United States and Great Britain, 1994, (with E.R. Simons, J.S. Kalnin, A. Casareno and M-Class teams) Inside City Schools, Investigating Literacy in Multi-cultural Classrooms, 1999; editor: The Acquisition of Written Language: Response and Revision, 1985, (with A. Ball) Bakhtinian Perspectives on Language, Literacy, and Learning, 2004; contbr. chpts. to books and articles to profl. jours. Recipient Richard Meade award for Pub. Rsch. in Tchr. Edn. Nat. Coun. Tchrs. English, 1989, 94, Ed Fry book award, 1996, 2000, Multicultural Book award, Nat. Assn. Multicultural Edn., 2000; fellow Nat. Conf. on Rsch. in English, 1986, Ctr. Advanced Study Behavioral Scis., 1999-00; grantee Spencer Found. 1996-2003, Nat. Ctr. for Study of Writing and Literacy grantee Office Ednl. Rsch. and Improvement, 1985-95, Minority Undergrad. Rsch. Program U. Calif., 1988, 89, 92, 93, USIP, 2003-05, numerous other grants. Mem. Nat. Coun. Tchrs. English (standing com. on rsch. 1981-87, ex-officio 1987—, chair bd. trustees rsch. found. 1990-93, co-chair rsch. assembly 1999—, chmn. standing com. rsch. 2005), Am. Ednl. Rsch. Assn. (chair spl. interest group on rsch. in writing 1983-85, numerous other coms.) Office: U Calif Dept Edn Berkeley CA 94720-0001

FREEDMAN, STANLEY LEWIS, assistant principal; s. David and Diana Freedman; m. Phyllis Duchin, July 4, 1971; 1 child, Randi Beth. BA, Bethel Coll., 1965—69; MA, Newark State Coll., 1973—75. Language Arts NJ. State Dept. of Edn., 1970, Physical Education and Health NJ. State Dept. of Edn., 1970, Administration and Supervision NJ. State Dept. of Edn., 1975. Asst. prin. Rahway Bd. of Edn., 1998—, supr. of lang. arts, 1994—98, program dir. of sch. devel., 1993—94, dept. chmn., area supr., and acting asst. prin., 1977—93, tchr. of lang. arts and phys. edn., 1970—77. Secondary sch. validation team chmn. Mid. Atlantic States' Commn. on Secondary Schools, Phila., 2005—; validation team mem. Mid. Atlantic States Commn. on Secondary Schools, Phila., 1974—2004; mid. atlantic states co-internal coord. Rahway Pub. Schools, 2004—; mem. of statewide nj. mid. sch. peer leadership initiative adv. bd. NJ. State Dept. of Edn., 1993; pres., edn. assn. Rahway Pub. Schools, 1975—76. Dir.: (musical comedy) Funny Girl (First Pl. Winner of the Garden State Arts Ctr. Musical Comedy, 1972). Mem.: Rahway Edn. Assn. (licentiate; pres. 1975—76), ASCD (licentiate), NJ Principals and Supervisors Assn. (licentiate). Avocations: crossword puzzles, bridge, sports, weightlifting, dog grooming. Home: 2601 Taggert Dr Belle Mead NJ 08502-6418 Office: Rahway HS 1012 Madison Ave Rahway NJ 07065 Office Phone: 732-396-1080. Home Fax: 732-669-0626; Office Fax: 732-669-0626. Personal E-mail: freedmanstanley@hotmail.com. Business E-Mail: sfreedman@rahway.net.

FREEDMAN, STANLEY MARVIN, manufacturing executive; b. Frederick, Md., Aug. 26, 1923; s. Jacob Menaham and Ethel (Freiman) F.; m. Lynn Maureen Katchen, Apr. 24, 1957 (dec.); children: Rita, Lynn, Michael, Richard, Jon, Jack; m. Lottie Carnell, Dec. 31, 1994 (div.). Student, Georgetown U., 1944; AB in English, High Point Coll., 1946. Owner, operator retail bus., Bound Brook, N.J., 1949-63; dir. mktg. Franklin State Bank, Somerset, N.J., 1963-65; program dir. mktg. div. Am. Mgmt. Assn. N.Y.C., 1965-67; exec. dir. Internat. Bus. Forms Industries, Washington, 1967-69; dir. communications, dir. office machines group Bus. Equipment Mfrs. Assn., Washington, 1969-72; div. pres. Litton Industries, Hampton, Va., 1972-74, group v.p., paper, printing and forms group Virginia Beach, Va., 1974-86. Cons. bus. planning and devel; univ. lectr., 1986-91; dir. Somerset County Savs. & Loan; exec. in residence U. Wis. Grad. Sch. Bus., 1973; entrepreneur in residence U. of the Pacific, Stockton, Calif., 1996. Mem. Bound Brook Bd. Edn., 1955-63; trustee Raritan Valley Hosp., Somerset, N.J., 1960-62; chmn. Urban Devel., Bound Brook, N.J., 1963; mem. def. conversion team AID, Warsaw, Poland, 1995-96. Served with U.S. Army, 1943-46, PTO. Mem. Am. Mgmt. Assn. Home and Office: 7501 E Thompson Peak Pkwy Scottsdale AZ 85255 E-mail: stanrlmrjj@msn.net.

FREEDMAN, WENDY LAUREL, astronomer, educator; b. Toronto, Ont., Can., July 17, 1957; arrived in U.S., 1984; d. Harvey Bernard and Sonya Lynn Freedman; m. Barry F. Madore, June 23, 1985, two children. BSc, U. Toronto, 1979, PhD in astronomy and astrophysics, 1984. Fellow Carnegie Observatories, Pasadena, Calif., 1984-87, faculty, 1987—, Crawford H. Greenewalt chair dir., 2003—. Bd. dirs. Assn. Univs. for Rsch. in Astronomy, Inc., Washington; co-chair com. on astronomy and astrophysics NRC, 2002—. Named a Fellow of Am. Acad. of Arts and Scis., 2000; recipient Marc Aaronson Lectureship and prize, 1994, John P. McGovern award, 2000, Helen Sawyer Hogg award, 2000. Mem. Nat. Acad. Scis., Am. Astron. Soc., Can. Astron. Soc., Astron. Soc. of the Pacific, Am. Physical Soc., Member, Nat.Rsch. Coun. Bd. on Physics and Astronomy; exec. bd., Ctr. for Particle Astrophysics; NASA's scientific oversight com. planning the Next Generation Space Telescope. Achievements include first to being first woman to join Carnegie's permanent scientific staff, 1987. Office: Carnegie Observatories 813 Santa Barbara St Pasadena CA 91101-1292

FREEDSON, GRACE ELIZABETH, publishing executive; b. N.Y.C., July 17, 1951; d. Oscar and Anna (Selzer) Chandler; m. Mark D. Freedson, June 6, 1971; 1 child, Brett Heather. BA, Boston U., 1972. Asst. dir. publicity Stein & Day Pubs., N.Y.C., 1973-75; freelance publicist L.I., N.Y., 1975-83; dir. pub. rels. and acquisitions Barron's Ednl. Series, Hauppauge, N.Y., 1983-90, managing editor, dir. acquisitions, 1990—2000; owner Grace Freedson's Pub. Network, Woodbury, NY, 2000—. Avocations: skiing, tennis. Office: Grace Freedsons Pub Network Ste 406 20 Crossways Park North Woodbury NY 11797

FREEH, LOUIS JOSEPH, lawyer, former FBI director; b. Jersey City, N.J., Jan. 6, 1950; m. Marilyn Freeh; 6 children. AB, Rutgers U., 1971, JD, 1974; LLM in Criminal Law, NYU, 1984. Pvt. practice, 1974-75; spl. agt. FBI, NYC, 1975-80, spl. agt. supr., 1980-81, dir. Washington, 1993—2001; dep., assoc. U.S. Atty. Office, 1987-91; asst. U.S. atty. U.S. Dist. Ct. (so. dist.) N.Y., 1981-91, judge N.Y.C., 1991-93; vice chmn., gen. coun. MBNA Corp., Wilmington, Del., 2001—. Adj. assoc. prof. Fordham Law Sch., 1988-92, Widener Law Sch., 2003-04. 1st lt. JAGC USAR, 1985-91. Recipient Fed. Law Enforcement Officers award, 1989, Presdl. award, Disting. Svc. award Atty. Gen., 1987, 91. Mem. N.Y. County Lawyers Assn., Res. Officers Assn. U.S., Phi Beta Kappa. Office: MBNA 1100 N King St Wilmington DE 19884

FREEHILL, MAURICE F., retired educational psychology educator; b. Chgo., Nov. 29, 1915; s. Pat and Anna (Dillon) F.; m. Kay M. Cronan, Nov. 3, 1924; 1 child, Bernard J. B.Ed., U. Alta., Can., 1945; MA, Stanford U., 1947, Ed.D., 1948. Cert. tchr., Alta. Tchr., then prin., Alta., 1937-45; prof. ednl. psychology Western Wash. U., Bellingham, 1948-62, U. Wash., Seattle, 1962-86, prof. emeritus, 1986—. Author: Gifted Children, Their Psychology and Education, 1961, repub., 1982; editor: Disturbed and Troubled Children, 1973; contbr. numerous articles to profl. jours., chpts. to books. Ellwyn Morey fellow, Australia Fellow APA (diplomate). Home: 350 N 190th St # 509B Shoreline WA 98133-3856

FREEHLING, ALLEN ISAAC, rabbi; b. Chgo., Jan. 8, 1932; s. Jerome Edward and Marion Ruth (Wilson) F.; m. Lori Golden; children: Shira Susman, David Matthew, Jonathan Andrew. Student, U. Ala., 1949-51; AB, U. Miami, Fla., 1953; B of Hebrew Letters, Hebrew Union Coll., 1965, MA, 1967; PhD, Kensington U., 1977; DD (hon.), Hebrew Union Coll., 1992. Ordained rabbi, 1967. Asst. to pres. Stylaneze, Inc., 1953-54, Univ. Miami, 1954-56; exec. dir. Temple Israel, Miami, 1956-57; asst. to pres. Stevens Markets, Inc., 1957-59; acct. exec. Hank Meyer Assocs., 1959-60; exec. dir. Temple Emanu-El, Miami Beach, Fla., 1960-62; assoc. rabbi The Temple, Toledo, 1967-72; sr. rabbi Univ. Synagogue, L.A., 1972—2002, rabbi emeritus, 2002—; exec. dir. City L.A. Commn. on Human Rels., 2002—. Adj. prof. Loyola-Marymount U., St. Mary's Coll.; v.p. Westside Ecumenical Coun., 1979-81; v.p. Bd. Rabbis of So. Calif., 1981-85, pres., 1985-87; mem. com. on rabbinic growth Cen. Conf. Am. Rabbis; chair Regional Synagogue Coun., 1984-86; bd. dirs., mem. several coms. and commns. Jewish Fedn. Coun.; cons. social actions Union of Am. Hebrew Congregations, mem. nat. and Pacific-S.W. region coms. on AIDS; mem. Rabbinic Cabinet, United Jewish Appeal; bd. dirs. Israel Bonds Orgn., Nat. Jewish Fund; bd. govs. Synagogue Coun. Am.; bd. dirs., newsletter editor Am. Jewish Com. Guest columnist L.A. Herald Examiner (Silver Angel award Religion in Media, 1987, 88); guest religion progs. Sta. KCBS, KABC; radio/TV host Nat. Conf. Christians and Jews. Chaplain L.A. Police Dept., 1974-86; bd. dirs., mem. exec. com., chair com. on pub. policy, chair govt. affairs com. AIDS Project L.A.; founding chair, exec. com. chmn. AIDS Interfaith Coun. So. Calif.; adv. bd. L.A. AIDS Hospice Com., Westside Children's Mus., Interreligious Info. Ctr.; apptd. mem., founding chair L.A. County Commn. on AIDS, 1987-89, chair svcs. com., 1989-91, L.A. County Commn. on Mental Health, 1992-95; AIDS-related grants proposal rev. com. Robert Wood Johnson Found., AIDS Task Force of United Way; com. on ethics, medicine and humanity Santa Monica Hosp., L.A. County Commn. on Pub. Social Svcs., 1984-86, Gateways Hosp. bd dirs., 1992-95, Jewish Big Bros., 1994—; City of L.A. Task Force on Diversity of Families, Commn. to Draft Ethics Code for L.A.

City Govt.; mem. L.A. County Commn. on Juvenile Delinquency and Adult Crime, 1991—; bd. dirs. Jewish Homes for Aging of Greater L.A., NCCJ, 1989, exec. com., 2000—; chmn. com. on fed. legislation commn. on law and legislation L.A. Jewish Cmty. Rels. Com., trustee; chair Ctrl. Conf. Am. Rabbi's/Union Am. Hebrew Congregations com. on HIV AIDS, Progressive Religious Alliance, City of L.A. 1998; Vol. Restival adv. com. Internat. Conf. on Allocation of Health Resources, Washington, 1997, Vienna, 1999, Cairo, 2000; mem. exec. com., treas. sec., chair nominating com., bd. dirs. Heal the Bay; adv. com. Disability Rights Advocates; founding mem. Calif. Commn. Fair Adminstrn. Justice hon. bd. dirs. Jewish Fedn. Western Region. Recipient Bishop Daniel Corrigan commendation Episcopal Diocese, 1987, Humanitarian award NCCJ, 1988, Social Responsibility award L.A. Urban League, 1988, Nat. Friendship award Parents and Friends of Lesbians and Gays, 1989, AIDS Hospice Found. Gene La Pietra Leadership award, 1989, Cath. Archdiocese's Serra Tribute award, 1989, Univ. Synagogue's Avodah award for Cmty. Svc., 1990, Am. Jewish Congress Tzedek award for Cmty. Leadership and Svc., 1990, Crystal Achievement award AIDS Project L.A., 1996, Planned Parenthood Disting. Svc. award, 1996, Cmty. Leadership award Beth Chayim Chadashim Congregation. Mem. Am. Jewish Congress (pres. 1977-80, 82-84), Ams. for Dem. Action, Internat. Assn. Physicians in AIDS Care (chmn. bd. dirs.), AIDS Nat. Interfaith Network (bd. dirs.), Jr. C. of C. (chair internat. rels. com.), Sigma Alpha Mu, Omnicron Delta Kappa, Phi Mu Alpha. Jewish. Office: Human Rels Commn City of LA 200 N Spring St #1625 Los Angeles CA 90012 Office Phone: 213-978-1660. Business E-Mail: rabbiallenf@mailbox.lacity.org.

FREEHLING, DANIEL JOSEPH, dean, law educator; b. Montgomery, Ala., Nov. 13, 1950; s. Saul Irving and Grace L. BS, Huntingdon Coll., 1972; JD, U. Ala., 1975, MLS, 1977. Ref. libr., asst. to assoc. dean U. Ala. Sch. Law, Tuscaloosa, 1975-77; assoc. law libr. U. Md., Balt., 1977-79, Cornell U., Ithaca, N.Y., 1979-82; law libr. dir., assoc. prof. U. Maine, Portland, 1982-86; law libr. dir., assoc. prof. law Boston U., 1986-92, prof., 1992—, assoc. dean for adminstrn., 1993-97, assoc. dean for info. svcs., 1999—. Mem. steering com., law program com. Rsch. Librs. Group, 1989-91; treas. New Eng. Law Libr. Consortium, 1989-91; vice chair, chair-elect sect. on law librs. Assn. Am. Law Schs., 1990-91, chair, 1992. Mem.: ABA (accreditation com. 1995—2001, coun. sect. legal edn. and bar admission 2002—), Am. Assn. Law Librs. (chair acad. law librs. spl. interest sect. 1981—82, edn. com. 1982—83, membership com. 1983—84, program chair 1987—88, local arrangements co-chair 1992—93, chair mentoring and retention com. 1995—96). Home: 106 Washington St Topsfield MA 01983 Office: Boston U Law Sch Pappas Law Libr 765 Commonwealth Ave Boston MA 02215-1401 Office Phone: 617-353-2309.

FREEHLING, STANLEY MAXWELL, investment banker; b. Chgo., July 2, 1924; s. Julius and Juliette (Stricker) F.; m. Joan Steif, Jan. 26, 1947; children: Elizabeth, Robert Stanley, Margaret J. Student, U. Chgo., 1942-43, Ind. U., 1943-44, U. Stockholm, Sweden, 1946-47. With 1st Nat. Bank Chgo., 1947—52; ptnr. Freehling Bros., Chgo., 1948—, Freehling & Co., Chgo., 1960—87; spl. ltd. ptnr. Cowen & Co., 1987—2000; v.p. Lehman Bros., 2000—. Mem. Ill. Pub. Employees Pension Laws Commn., 1962-66; chmn. Ravinia Festival Assn., 1967-71; pres. men's coun. Art Inst. Chgo., 1962-65, trustee, 1970—, life trustee; trustee Glenwood (Ill.) Sch. for Boys, 1967-80, Lake Forest Coll., 1972-83, Shedd Aquarium, Cradle Soc.; life trustee U. Chgo.; hon. mem. The Court Theatre; chmn. bd. Ill. Arts Coun., 1971-72; bd. dirs. Northwestern Meml. Hosp., Chgo., Chgo. Pub. Libr. Found.; hon. chmn. bd. Goodman Theatre; chmn. Pub. Arts Adv. Com., 1978-90; mem. Pres.'s Com. on Arts and Humanities, Washington, 1984-88; bd. govs. Smart Mus. Art. Mem. Northwestern U. Assocs., Arts Club, Bond Club, Commercial Club (Chgo.), Lake Shore Country Club (Glencoe, Ill.), Old Elm Country Club (Highland Park, Ill.), Mid-Day. Clubs: Arts, Bond, Commercial (Chgo.); Lake Shore Country (Glencoe, Ill.); Mid-Day. Home: 121 Belle Ave Highland Park IL 60035-2503 Office: 190 S La Salle St Chicago IL 60603-3410

FREELAND, ALAN EDWARD, orthopedic surgery educator, physician; b. Youngstown, Ohio, July 30, 1939; s. Harold Edward and Esther Amelia (Hanley) F.; m. Janis Ann Foerschl, Oct. 11, 1969; children: Matthew, Jennifer, Rebecca, Michael. BA, Johns Hopkins U., 1961; MD, George Washington U., 1965. Cert. hand surgery Am. Bd. Orthopaedic Surgery. With Church Home and Hosp., Balt., 1965-66; resident Johns Hopkins Hosp., Balt., 1967-70, Letterman Army Med. Ctr., San Francisco, 1973-75; prof. dept. orthopaedic surgery U. Miss. Med. Ctr., Jackson, 1978—, dir. hand surgery fellowship program, 1991—, chief of staff, 1986-87, also bd. dirs. Rowland Med. Libr., 1996-98. Chief surgery Miss. Meth. Rehab. Ctr., Jackson, 1991-93, pres. elect med. staff, 1994, pres. med. staff, bd. dirs., 1995-97. Author: Stable Internal Fixation of the Hand and Wrist, 1986, The First Twenty-Five Years: History of the American Association for Hand Surgery, 1996, Hand Fractures: Repair, Reconstruction and Rehabilitation, 2000; mem. editl. bd. Orthopedics, Slack, Inc., 1986—, Jour. Orthop. Trauma, 1993—2002, Year Book of Hand Surgery, 1997, Trauma Update, Orthop., 1989—; sect. editor, sr. editor hand surgery: Jour. Orthop. Trauma, 1997—2002; bd. editors Microsurgery, 2001—, sect. editor Trauma Update, Orthop., 1989—, Hand Surgery, 1997—2002. Mem. Fire Protection Dist., Brandon, Miss., 1990-93; bd. dirs. Miss. Sports Hall of Fame, 2002—. Lt. col. U.S. Army, 1971-78. Fellow: Am Acad. Orthopaedic Surgeons; mem.: S.E. Hand Club (sec.-treas. 1998—2000, v.p. 2001, pres.-elect 2002, pres. 2003), Miss. State Orthopaedic Assn. (pres. Jackson chpt. 1985, pres. 1986), Internat. Fedn. Socs. for Surgery of Hand (chmn. bone and joint com. 1992—), Am. Assn. Hand Surgeons (parliamentarian 1994, exec. com., bd. dirs. 1994—, historian 1995, treas. 1996—98, historian 1999, v.p. 2000, pres.-elect 2001, pres. 2002), Am. Soc. Surgery of Hand (governing coun. 1989—92), Am. Orthopaedic Assn. Home: 303 Swallow Dr Brandon MS 39047-6454 Office: 2500 N State St Jackson MS 39216-4500 Office Phone: 601-815-1220. Business E-Mail: afreeland@orthopedics.umsmed.edu.

FREELAND, CHARLES HARRELL, literature educator; b. Los Angeles, 1965; s. Harrell Richard and Judith Ann Freeland; m. Marlene Paz Galupo (div.); 1 child, Isabel; m. Carly Michelle Wells, Aug. 11, 2001; 1 child, Olivia. BA in phil., Miami U., 1988; MFA in English, creative writing, U. Ark., 1993. Grad. asst. U. Ark., Fayettville, Ark., 1989—93; adj. prof. Sinclair Cmty. Coll., Dayton, Ohio, 1996—2001, asst. prof., 2000—05, assoc. prof., 2005—. Poetry editor Flights Literary Journal, Dayton, Ohio, 2001—. Contbr. articles various profl. jours.; author: (poetry) Salon Noir, 2005, The Idea of Two, 2005. Recipient 49th Parallel Poetry award, The Bellingham Review, 1989; Lily Peter fellowship, U. Ark., 1993. Mem.: Coll. English Assn., Nat. Coll. Tchrs. of English. Office: Sinclair Cmty Coll 444 W Third St Dayton OH 45402 Office Phone: 937-512-2589. E-mail: charles.freeland@sinclair.edu.

FREELAND, CLAIRE ANN BENNETT, psychologist; b. Washington, July 28, 1955; d. Lawrence H. and Devora M. (Spintman) Bennett; m. Howard S. Freeland, June 18, 1978; children: Rachel M., David S. BA, Johns Hopkins U., 1976; MA, Ind. U., 1978; PhD, U. Md., 1981. Lic. clin. psychologist. Instr. Sch. Medicine U. Md., Balt., 1981-84; psychologist Hearing and Speech Agy., Balt., 1981-88; pvt. practice in pediatric/child clin. psychology Balt., 1988—; cons. psychologist Union Meml. Hosp. Hearing and Speech Agy., 1988-99. Contbr. articles to profl. jours. Mem.: Am. Psychol. Assn. Office: 744 Dulaney Valley Rd Baltimore MD 21204-5132 Office Phone: 410-583-8335.

FREELAND, JOHN HALE, lawyer; b. Oxford, Miss., Dec. 20, 1956; s. Thomas Henry and Judith Lee (Hale) F.; m. Cynthia Rose Strobl, Mar. 21, 1987. BA, U. Miss., 1974, JD, 1986. Bar: Miss., U.S. Dist. Ct. (no. dist.) Miss. 1987. Law clk. Miss. Supreme Ct., Jackson, 1986-87, U.S. Dist. Ct. (no. dist.) Miss., Oxford, 1987-88; ptnr. Freeland & Freeland, Oxford, 1988-95; shareholder Markow, Walker & Reeves, P.A., Oxford, 1995—. Adj. prof. Law, U. Miss. Editor MS Lawyer, 1998-99). Elder, fin. sec., Sunday sch. tchr. 1st Presbyn. Ch., Oxford. Lt. USNR, 1979-83. Fellow: Miss. Bar Young Lawyers, Miss. Bar Found.; mem.: Miss. Bar Assn. (dir. young lawyers div. 1993—94, pres. young lawyers div. 1994—95, Outstanding Young Lawyer 1995—96), Rotary. Presbyterian. Avocations: sailing, gardening, hiking. E-mail: hale@mnrjxn.com.

FREELAND, JUDY CREECH, pre-school educator; d. Bobby and Louann Creech; m. Richard Allen Freeland, June 29, 1985; 1 child, Kevin Allen. BS, Winthrop U., Rock Hill, S.C., 1975; MEd, U. S.C., Columbia, 1978. Cert. tchr. S.C., 2001, Nat. Bd. Profl. Tchg. Stds. Kindergarten tchr. Greendale Elem. Sch., New Ellenton, SC, 1975—83, Denmark-Olar Elem. Sch., Denmark, 1983—85; tchr. grades 1 and 2 Kelly - Edwards Elem. Sch., Williston, 1985—88; tchr. grade 1 McCormick Elem. Sch., 1988—2005, pre-kindergarten tchr., 2005—. Bd. mem. First Steps, McCormick, SC, 2000—02. T-ball and soccer coach McCormick County Recreation, McCormick, SC, 2003—05; tchr. St. Paul United Meth. Ch., Plum Branch, 2000—05, bd. mem. Mem.: NEA (assoc.), S.C. Edn. Assn. (assoc.; newsletter editor 1999—2003, local pres. 1999—2003, Small Local Assn. Best Newsletter 2001). Methodist. Avocations: travel, camping, motorcycling, children's crafts. Office: McCormick Elem Sch 6977 Hwy 28 S Mc Cormick SC 29835 Office Phone: 864-443-2292. Office Fax: 864-443-2755. Business E-Mail: freelandj@mccormick.k12.sc.us.

FREELAND, PETE, aerospace transportation executive, consultant; b. Portland, Oreg., Nov. 29, 1965; s. Bill and Dori Freeland; m. Melissa Williams, Sept. 22, 2001; 1 child, Mitchell. BS in Aerospace Engring., U. So. Calif., 1988; MS in Aeronautics, Embry Riddle Aero. Univ., 1992; PhD in Engring. Mgmt., Lacrosse U., 2004. Lic. Pvt. Pilot FAA, 1987, cert. Navigator USAF, 1989, Scuba Divemaster Nat. Assn. Underwater Instrs., Fla., 2000. Customer support engr., pilot Flight Dynamics, Portland, Oreg., 1992—98; internat. space sta. and advanced vehicles engring. mgr. Boeing Human Spaceflight, Palmdale, Calif., 1998—2001; ctr. mgr., mech. integration and test Northrop Grumman Space Tech., Redondo Beach, Calif., 2001—04; sr. engring. mgr. Raytheon Space Systems, El Segundo, Calif., 2004—. V.p. Nat. Mgmt. Assn., Palmdale, Calif., 2000—01; chmn. Northrop Grumman Veterans Group, Redondo Beach, Calif., 2003—. Advisor, tchr. CAP, Lancaster, Calif., 1999—2001; mem. Nat. Ctr. for Men - Father's Rights, Portland, Oreg., 1994—99. Capt. USAF, 1988—92. Decorated Disting. Grad.-Top Gun USAF B-52 Crew Tng. Course; named Nat. Cadet of the Yr., CAP, 1984, Presdl. scholar, Pres. Ronald Reagan, 1984; recipient Silver Snoopy Award, NASA-Astronaut Office, Johnson Space Ctr., 2000; ROTC 4-Yr. scholarship, USAF, 1984. Mem.: AIAA (v.p. 2000—01). Achievements include development of Advanced Mfg & Test for Manned Spacecraft; Fluid dynamics experiment on space shuttle; Launch and support crew for STS-96; research in Flight test, team member on X-38 Crew Return Vehicle, support to Ansari X-Prize. Avocations: scuba diving, flying, international travel. Home: 15213 Cordary Ave Lawndale CA 90260 Office Phone: 310-616-7124. Personal E-mail: freeland1@acninc.net.

FREELAND, RICHARD ALAN, psychiatrist, medical educator; b. Hammond, Ind., Mar. 13, 1952; s. Wendell Stober and Dorothy Amanda Freeland; m. Carol Anne Underwood, Mar. 26, 1983. BS, MIT, 1974; MD, St. Louis U., 1978. Diplomate Am. Bd. of Psychiatry and Neurology, 1986. Staff psychiatrist Hawaii State Hosp., Kaneohe, 1983—85; assoc. physician Carle Clinic Assn., Urbana, Ill., 1985—89; staff psychiatrist Harding Hosp., Worthington, Ohio, 1989—2000; assoc. prof. of clin. psychiatry Ohio State U., Columbus, 2000—. Clin. instr. psychiatry U. Hawaii, Honolulu, 1983—85; clin. asst. prof. psychiatry Ohio State U., Columbus, 1990—96, clin. assoc. prof. psychiatry, 1996—2000; chief clin. officer Harding Hosp., Worthington, Ohio, 1998—2000; dir. clin. ops. Ohio State U., Columbus, 2000—; med. dir. for behavioral health Ohio State U. Managed Health Care Sys., Columbus, 2000—. Mem.: Ohio Psychiat. Assn., Psychiat. Soc. Ctrl. Ohio, Am. Psychiat. Assn. Avocations: sailing, gardening. Home: 844 Oxford St Worthington OH 43085-4136 Office: Ohio State Univ 1670 Upham Dr Ste130 Columbus OH 43210 E-mail: freeland-1@medctr.osu.edu.

FREELAND, RICHARD MIDDLETON, academic administrator, historian; b. Orange, NJ, May 13, 1941; s. Harry Middleton and Margaret Lyons (Child) F. BA in Am. Studies, Amherst Coll., 1963; PhD in Am. Civilization, U. Pa., 1968; DHL (hon.), Amherst Coll., 1998, Am. Coll. Greece, 2000. Asst. to pres. U. Mass., 1970, asst. to chancellor Boston, 1971-72, dir. Office of Ednl. Planning, asst. prof., 1972-74, dean Coll. Profl. Studies, 1974-79, assoc. prof., 1974-92, dean Coll. of Arts and Scis., 1982-92, prof. history, 1992; prof. history Grad. Sch. & Univ. Ctr. CUNY, 1992-96; vice chancellor for acad. affairs, pres. CUNY Rsch. Found., 1992-96; pres., prof. history Northeastern U., Boston, 1996—. Proposal reviewer NEH, Divsn. Rsch., 1989, Divsn. Edn. Programs, 1985, R.I. Bd. Higher Edn., 1987, Fund for the Improvement of Post Secondary Edn., 1988, Rockefeller Found., 1985, Am. Univ., 1988, 89, 90; cons. Am. Coun. Edn., 1994, U.S. Dept. Edn., 1989-90, 92; dir. Mass. Bus. Roundtable, Citizens Bank Mass., The Boston Globe, Boston Plan for Excellence, Assn. Ind. Colls. and Univs. Mass. Author: The Truman Doctrine and the Origins of McCarthyism, 1972, Academia's Golden Age, 1992; reader, reviewer numerous profl. jours. Recipient Rsch. grants Ford Found., 1979-80, NEH, 1980-81, Rockefeller Found., 1988. Office: Northeastern U 110 Churchill Hall 380 Huntington Ave Boston MA 02115-5000 E-mail: r.freeland@neu.edu.*

FREELS, JESSE SAUNDERS, JR., lawyer; b. Sherman, Tex., Feb. 8, 1943; s. Jesse Saunders Sr. and Margaret (Stout) F.; m. Valerie Wood, Jan. 16, 1971; children: J.S. "Trey" III, John Andrew. BA, BS, Howard Payne U., 1965; JD, St. Mary's U., San Antonio, 1969. Bar: Tex. 1969, U.S. Dist. Ct. (ea. and we. dists.) Tex. 1971. Asst. county atty. Grayson County, Sherman, 1969-71; ptnr. Doss, Thompson & Freels, Denison, Tex., 1971-78; judge Grayson County, Sherman, 1978-83; pres. Freels & Johnston, P.C., Sherman, 1983-2000; sole practice, 2000—. Bd. dirs. Am. Bank of Tex., Sherman, 1975—, Tex. Ctr. for the Judiciary, Austin, 1979-83. Mem. Tex. Bar Assn., Grayson County Bar Assn., Tex. Bar Found. (life), Masons (past master Lodge 403, Denison). Home: 109 Spring Valley Dr Denison TX 75020-3724 Office: 114 S Crockett St Sherman TX 75090-5906 Office Phone: 903-868-9449.

FREEMAN, ALGEANIA WARREN, academic administrator; b. Benson, N.C. m. Ernest Freeman; 1 child, Ernest III. BS in English, Fayetteville State U., 1970; MS in Speech Pathology and Audiology, So. Ill. U., 1972; PhD in Speech Comm., Ohio State U., 1977; postgrad., Harvard U., 1993, postgrad., 1998. Ordained min. African Meth. Episcopal Zion Ch. Instr. Norfolk State U., 1973, acting v.p. advancement, prof.; asst. v.p., dean Morgan State U.; with East Tenn. State U., Orange Coast Coll., N.C. A&T State U.; v.p. advancement and program devel. So. Calif. Coll.; prof. speech comm. Norfolk U.; pres. Livingstone Coll., Salisbury, NC. Internat. cons. W.K. Kellogg Found. in So. Africa; mem. Va. Task Force on Sci. and Tech., Va. Bd. Examiners for Audiology and Speech Pathology. Bd. dirs. Calif. Assn. Instrnl. Adminstrs., Found. for the Carolinas, Kids Voting of Va., Montebello Rehab. Hosp./U. Md. Hosp. Sys., Md. Easter Seals, Friends of the Norfolk Juvenile Ct., Girl Scouts Ea. Tenn.; pres. Nat. Soc. Allied Health; exec. dir. Nat. Black Assn. for Speech, Lang. and Hearing. Fellow, U.S. Pentagon in the Army Ctr. Mil. History, Washington, 1999—2000. Fellow: Am. Soc. Allied Health. Office: Livingstone Coll 701 W Monroe St Salisbury NC 28144 Office Phone: 704-216-6151. E-mail: tjohnson@livingstone.edu.

FREEMAN, ARTHUR J., physics educator; b. Lublin, Poland, Feb. 6, 1930; s. Louis and Pearl (Mandelbaum) F.; m. Rhea B. Landin, June 21, 1952 (div. 1990); children: Jonathan (dec.), Seth, Claudia, Sarah; m. Doris Caro, Mar. 1991. BS in Physics, Mass. Inst. Tech., 1952, PhD, 1956. Instr. Brandeis U., 1955-56; solid state physicist Army Materials Research Agy., Watertown, Mass., 1956-62; instr. Northeastern U., 1957-59; assoc. lab. dir., leader theory group Francis Bitter Nat. Magnet Lab., Mass. Inst. Tech., 1962-67; prof. physics Northwestern U., Evanston, Ill., 1967-83, Morrison prof. physics, 1983—, chmn. dept. physics, 1967-71. Cons. Argonne Nat. Lab., Los Alamos Nat. Lab. Editor: Hyperfine Interactions, 1967, The Actinides: Electronic and Related Properties, Handbook on the Physics and Chemistry of the Actinides, Internat. Jour. Magnetism, 1970-75, Jour. Magnetism and Magnetic Materials, 1975—; mem. editl. adv. bd. Computational Materials Sci., 1992, Jour. Computer-Aided Materials Design, 1993; contbr. numerous articles to tech. lit. Guggenheim fellow, 1970-71; Fulbright-Hays fellow, 1970-71; Alexander von Humboldt Stiftung fellow 1977-78; 1st recipient medal Materials Rsch. Soc., 1990, award in magnetism Internat. Union Pure and Applied Physics, 1991. Fellow Am. Phys. Soc.; fgn. mem. Acad. Natural Scis. Russia, Russian Acad. Scis., Polish Acad. Scis. Home: 2739 Ridge Ave Evanston IL 60201-1719 Office: Northwestern Univ Dept Of Physics Evanston IL 60208-0001

FREEMAN, ARTHUR MERRIMON, III, psychiatry educator, dean; b. Birmingham, Ala., Oct. 10, 1942; s. Arthur Merrimon II and Katherine (Lide) F.; m. Linda Poynter; children: Arthur M. IV, Katherin Leigh, Edward Todd. AB in Philosophy, Harvard U., 1963; MD, Vanderbilt U., 1967. Diplomate Am. Bd. Psychiatry and Neurology; lic. psychiatrist, Ala., N.C., La. Asst. prof. dept. psychiatry and behavioral scis. Stanford (Calif.) U., 1974-77; prof., vice chmn. dept. psychiatry U. Ala., Birmingham, 1977-90; med. dir. Appalachian Hall Hosp., Asheville, N.C., 1990-91; prof., chmn. dept. psychiatry La. State U. Med. Ctr., Shreveport, 1991—2003, dean, 1993-96; prof., chmn. dept. psychiatry Health Sci. Ctr. U. Tenn., Memphis, 2003—. Regional med. dir. divsn. mental health La. Dept. Health and Hosps., 1992-94. Author: Psychiatry for the Primary Care Physician, 1979. Bd. dirs. Vols. of Am., Shreveport, 1993-96, Shreveport Symphony, C. of C., 1993-96. Lt. comdr. M.C., USN, 1972-74. Nat. Merit scholar Harvard U., 1959-63; Biochemistry fellow Karolinska Inst., Stockholm, 1965, fellow in hepatic disease Royal Free Hosp., London, 1966, Disting. Paul Harris fellow Rotary Club. Fellow APA, Am. Coll. Psychiatrists (Laughlin fellow 1971), Acad. Psychosomatic Medicine, So. Psychiat. Assn.; mem. Am. Assn. Chmn. of Depts. of Psychiatry, Biomed. Rsch. Found. N.W. La. (bd. dirs. 1993-96), La. Psychiatry Med. Assn. (pres.-elect), Royal Coll. Psychiatrists, Collegium Internationale Neuropsychopharmacologia. Home: 5929 E Ridge Dr Shreveport LA 71106-2423 Office: La State U Med Ctr Dept Psychiatry 1501 Kings Hwy Shreveport LA 71103-4228

FREEMAN, BOB A., retired microbiology educator, retired dean; b. Eastland, Tex., May 7, 1926; s. Oswald Ledbetter and Osielee (Wilcox) F.; m. Rosemary David, June 4, 1960; children: Susan A., Robert D., Katherine E., Andrew W. BA, U. Tex., 1949, MA, 1950, PhD, 1954. Instr. biology Tex. A & M U., College Station, 1950-51; rsch. scientist I U. Tex., Austin, 1951-54; instr., asst. prof. U. Chgo., 1954-64; assoc. prof. U. Tenn., Memphis, 1964-66, prof., 1966-88, chmn. microbiology dept., 1970-83, vice chancellor, 1982-88, Disting. Svc. prof., 1988-96, interim dean Coll. Grad. Health Scis., 1993-96, dean, prof. emeritus, 1997—. Cons. WHO, Calcutta, India, 1968. Author: Burrows Textbook of Microbiology, 21st edit., 1979, 22d edit., 1984; mem. edit. bd. Jour. Dental Edn., 1980-83, U. Tenn. Press., 1983-2001; contbr. articles to profl. jours. Bd. dirs. Memphis Heart Gala, 1984-90. With USN, 1944-46, PTO. Grantee U.S. Army Rsch. and Devel. Command, USPHS, U.S. Dept. Agr. Mem. AAAS, Am. Soc. for Microbiology (br. councillor 1969-71), Imhotep Soc. (Memphis), Sigma Xi (chpt. pres. 1974-75). Republican. Methodist. Avocations: woodworking, outdoor activities. Home: 1319 E Crestwood Dr Memphis TN 38119-5000

FREEMAN, BRUCE GEORGE, fundraising consultant; b. Perth Amboy, N.J., Feb. 17, 1929; s. Benjamin George and Beatrice (Wright) F.; children: David B., Judith Ann, Mark D.; m. Marjorie V. Kler, Dec. 1983. BA, Rutgers U., 1952; MDiv, New Brunswick Theol. Sem., 1955; postgrad., Albany Med. Ctr., 1955-58, Andover Newton Theol. Ctr., 1955-58. Min. Presbyn. Ch., various locations, N.Y., 1955-64; asst. to pres. Buena Vista Coll., Storm Lake, Iowa, 1964-66; area dir. United Presbyn. Ch. U.S.A., 1966-67; campaign mgr. Marts & Lundy, N.Y.C., 1967-75, also bd. dirs., v.p., 1975-80, treas., 1980-82, founder electron. screening div. Lyndhurst, N.J., 1984, pres., 1982-91, chmn., CEO, 1991-94, ret., 1994; CEO B.G.F. Assocs., 1994—. Inventor Electric Screening. Trustee East Jersey Olde Towne, Inc., Piscataway, 1980—, Wilson Coll. Chambersburg, Pa., 1992-2000; trustee Makassed Found. Am., Rutgers U., 1994—; bd. dirs. Nat. Orgn. on Disability, Washington, 1990. Mem. Nassau Club (bd. dirs.), Raritan Valley Country Club. Republican. Avocations: sports, art. Home: 6 Mimosa Ct Princeton NJ 08540-9423

FREEMAN, CAROLYN RUTH, oncologist; b. Kettering, Eng., Jan. 2, 1950; emigrated to Can., 1974, naturalized, 78; d. Ivor Thomas and Winifred Mary (Scotney) F.; m. J.C. Negrete, July 25, 1981. Student, King's Coll. London U., 1967-69; MB, BS, Westminster Med. Sch. London U., 1972. Prof., chmn. dept. radiation oncology, faculty medicine McGill U., Montreal, 1979—; radiation oncologist-in-chief McGill U. Hosps., Montreal, 1979—. Contbr. articles to med. publs. Fellow Royal Coll. Physicians (Can.); mem. Can. Assn. Radiol. Oncologists (pres. 1991-93), Am. Soc. Therapeutic Radiology and Oncology. Home: 4270 deMaisonneuve W Montreal PQ Canada H3Z 1K6 Office: 1650 Cedar Ave Montreal PQ Canada H3G 1A4 Office Phone: 514-934-8040. Business E-Mail: carolyn.freeman@muhc.mcgill.ca.

FREEMAN, CATHERINE E., researcher; d. Robert Louis and Carol Ann Freeman. BS, Vanderbilt U., Nashville, 1993; MEd, U. Tex., Austin, 1996; PhD, Vanderbilt U., Nashville, 2000. Sr. rsch. analyst Ga. State U. Fiscal Rsch. Ctr., Atlanta, 2000—02; rsch. specialist US Dept. Edn., Washington, 2002—. Vol. In2Books, Washington, 2004, Wash. Scholarship Fund, Washington, 2004; bd. dirs. Aged Woman's Home of Georgetown, Washington, 2002—; v.p. Bullis Sch. Alumni Assn., Potomac, Md., 2004. Mem.: Am. Edn. Fin. Assn. (assoc.), Jr. League Wash. Office: US Dept Edn 1990 K St NW Washington DC 20006 Office Phone: 202-502-7336. Business E-Mail: catherine.freeman@ed.gov.

FREEMAN, CHARLES E., state supreme court justice; b. Richmond, Va., Dec. 12, 1933; m. Marylee Voelker; 1 child, Kevin. BA in Liberal Arts, Va. Union U., 1954; JD, John Marshall Law Sch., 1962, LLD (hon.), 1992. Bar: Ill. 1962. Pvt. practice, 1962—76; pvt. practice, Cook County, Chgo., 1962—76, asst. state's atty., 1964; asst. atty. Bd. Election Commrs., Chgo., 1964—65; mem. Ill. Indsl. Commn., Chgo., 1965—73, Ill. Commerce Commn., Chgo., 1973—76; judge law and chancery divsns. Cook County Cir. Ct., Chgo., 1976—86; judge Appellate Ct. Ill., 1986—90; justice Ill. Supreme Ct., 1990—, chief justice, 1997—2000. Recipient Cert. Achievement, Internat. Christian Fellowship Missions, Earl B. Dickerson award, Chgo. Bar Assn., Merit award, Habilitative Sys., Statesmanship award, Monarch Awards Found. of Alpha Kappa Alpha, Freedom award, John Marshall Law Sch. Mem.: ABA (task force opportunities minorities in jud. adminstrn. divsn., coms. opportunities minorities in profession, cert. Recognition), DuPage County Bar Assn., Cook County Bar Assn. (Kenneth E. Wilson award, Cert. Merit, Ida Platt award, Presdl. award, Jud. award), Ill. Judges' Assn., Ill. Jud. Coun. (Kenneth Wilson Meml. award, Meritorious Svc. award), Ill. State Bar Assn., Am. Judicature Soc., Am. Judges' Assn. Achievements include being first African-American to swear in a Mayor, City of Chicago, to serve on Illinois Supreme Court, 1990; being leader in case disposition by published opinion, 1988, 89.*

FREEMAN, CHARLES E., writer, musician; b. Darwin, Ill., June 11, 1942; s. Andrew Jackson and Evelyn Veleine Freeman; m. Janet Leigh Tryon, Apr. 10, 1976 (div. July 5, 1988); children: Scott Eric, Derek Charles; m. Dorothy Marie Babcock, Apr. 3, 1993. Student, Inst. for Children's Writing, Long Ridge Writer's Group. Author: (book) The Promised One, 2001. Ssgt. USAF, 1959—75. Republican. Baptist. Avocations: mountain dulcimer, mandolin. Home: 906 Pine Marshall IL 62441

FREEMAN, CHAS. W., JR., federal agency administrator, writer, ambassador; b. Washington, Mar. 2, 1943; divorced; 3 children; m. Margaret Van Wagenen Carpenter, 1993. BA, Yale U., 1963; JD, Harvard U., 1975. Joined Fgn. Svc., 1965, assigned to India and Taiwan; Am. interpreter for Pres. Nixon People's Republic of China, 1972; vis. fellow East Asian Legal Rsch. Ctr., Harvard U., 1974-75; dep. dir. for Taiwan affairs, dir. pub. programs, dir. plans and mgmt. U.S. Dept. State, Washington, 1975-78; dir. program coord.

and devel. USIA, Washington, 1978, acting U.S. coord. for refugee affairs; dir. China affairs U.S. Dept. State, 1979; dep. chief of mission Am. Embassy, Beijing, 1981, Bangkok, 1984; prin. dep. asst. sec. state for African affairs U.S. Dept. State, Washington, 1986; amb. to Saudi Arabia Riyadh, 1989-92; asst. sec. def. The Pentagon, Washington, 1993-94; dist. fellow U.S. Inst. of Peace, Washington, 1994-95; chmn. bd. Projects Internat. Inc., Washington, 1995—. Co-chmn. U. S. China Policy Found., 1996—; vice-chmn. Atlantic Coun., 1997; bd. visitors Def. Regional Ctrs., 1998—2001; mem. U.S. Nat. Security Study Group, 1999—2001; internat. adv. bd. China Nat. Offshore Oil Co., 2004—; pres. Mid. East Policy Coun.; bd. dirs. Inst. for Def. Analyses, World Affair Coun., Washington, Assn. for Diplomatic Studies and Tng., Pacific Pension Inst., Acad. Am. Diplomacy; mem. bd. overseers Roger Williams U.; mem. adv. bd. Stanley Found., 2005—. Author: The Diplomat's Dictionary, 1994, rev. edit., 1997, Arts of Power, 1997. Recipient Sec. Def. Meritorious Civilian Svc. award, 1991, Disting. Pub. Svc. awards, 1993-94, Sec. State Disting. Honor, 1991, Dir. Ctrl. Intelligence Shield Medallion award, 1991, First Class Order of Abd Al-Aziz award Saudi Arabian Govt., 1992. Mem.: Am. Acad. Diplomacy (bd. dirs.), Met. Club. Office: Projects Internat Inc 1800 K St NW Ste 1000 Washington DC 20006-2202 also: Mid East Policy Coun 1730 M St NW Ste 512 Washington DC 20036-4516 Home: 2500 Massachusetts Ave NW Washington DC 20008-2821 Office Phone: 202-333-1277. Business E-Mail: cfreeman@projectsinternational.com.

FREEMAN, CLARENCE CALVIN, retired diversified financial services company executive; b. Lancaster, Pa., July 2, 1923; s. Clarence Calvin and Margaret (Hollinger) F.; m. B. Virginia Miller, Aug. 26, 1944; children: Margaret Ann, Elizabeth Ann, Martha Suzanne. AB cum laude, Franklin and Marshall Coll., 1951. Asst. bookkeeper Battery & Brake Service Co., Lancaster, 1941-42; supr. inventory records and receiving Armstrong Cork Co., Lancaster, 1946-48; accountant Internat. Latex Corp., Dover, Del., 1951-52, Ebasco Services, Inc., Holtwood, Pa., 1952-53; office mgr., accountant A.O. Smith Corp., Leola, Pa., 1953-54; office mgr., plant accountant Sybron-Permutit divsn. Lancaster, 1954-57; divsn. controller BCA divsn. Fed. Mogul Corp., Lancaster, 1957-64, controller Southfield, Mich., 1964-74; v.p., controller Addressograph-Multigraph Corp., Cleve., 1974-78; adminstrv. v.p., controller Irvin Industries, Stamford, Conn., 1978-79; v.p. fin. Technical Tape Inc., New Rochelle, N.Y., 1979-80; v.p. fin., treas., dir. K-D Mfg. Co., Lancaster, 1980-83; CFO C-F Manbeck, Inc., 1984-86; exec. v.p. Sensenich Corp., Lancaster, 1986-90, also bd. dirs.; sr. v.p. fin., CFO Sensenich Propeller Co., Lancaster, 1991-94; ret. Owner acctg. svc., 1953-64, Dairy Queen, 1956-60; lectr. Franklin and Marshall Coll., 1957-58, adj. faculty, 1983-89; lectr. Wayne State Grad. Sch., 1966-67; guest speaker Nat. Assn. Accts. Mem. Oakland County Planning Commn., 1967-68; adviser Jr. Achievement, 1957-58. Served with AUS, 1943-46, PTO. Mem. Nat. Assn. Accountants, Fin. Execs. Inst., Phi Beta Kappa (v.p. Detroit), Pi Gamma Mu. Republican. Presbyterian (elder, deacon). Club: Conestoga Country. Lodges: Masons, Kiwanis, Elks. Home: Apt H2 1117 Wheatland Ave Lancaster PA 17603-2462 *To succeed in life, it is important to have faith and confidence in one's own capability but to rely on this alone is disastrous; a faith and belief in a supreme being (God) more powerful than any human being is necessary not only to sustain us in times of our own failure, but each and every day as we face life's challenges.*

FREEMAN, CORINNE, financial analyst, retired mayor; b. N.Y.C., Nov. 9, 1926; d. Bernard J. Hirschfeld and Sidonie (Daxe) Lichtenstein; m. Michael S. Freeman, Mar. 14, 1948; children: Michael L., Stephan J. Student, Adelphi Coll. Sch. Nursing, 1944—47. RN, N.Y., Mass. Nurse numerous hosps. in N.Y. and Mass., 1948-64; mayor St. Petersburg, Fla., 1977-85; mem. Pinellas County Sch. Bd., St. Petersburg, Fla., 1989-98, chmn., 1996-98; bd. trustees Palms of Pasadena Hosp., St. Petersburg, 1998—, dir., 1998—2004. Fin. advisor Prudential Securities, Wachovia Securities; bd. dirs. Creativity in Child Care. Chmn. Social Svc. Allocations Com., St. Petersburg, 1972-76, City Budget Rev. Com., 1973-76, Youth Svc. System, Pinellas County, 1975-76, West Coast Regional Water Supply Authority; past mem. community redevel. com. U.S. Conf. of Mayors; past pres. Fla. League Cities; past mem. Pinellas County Mayors Coun.; past mem. Nat. League of Cities Revenue and Fin. Task Force; pres. LWV, St. Petersburg, 1970-72, 75-76; trustee Fire Pension Bd., St. Petersburg, 1989-92, Bayfront Med. Ctr.; dir. Palms of Pasadena Hosp., 1999-2003; adv. com. Jr. League St. Petersburg, 1990-92. Recipient Disting. Alumni award Adelphi U. Mem. Fla. Nursing Assn. Mem.: Treasure Island Yacht and Tennis Club (bd. dirs. 2004—). Republican. Home: 2101 Pelham Rd N Saint Petersburg FL 33710-3659 Office: 5858 Central Ave Saint Petersburg FL 33707-1728 Office Phone: 727-384-2000. Business E-Mail: corinne_freeman@wachoviasec.com.

FREEMAN, DAVID FORGAN, retired foundation executive; b. Chgo., June 25, 1918; s. Halstead Gurnee and Marion Kerr (Forgan) Freeman; m. Hazel Simms Farr, Sept. 5, 1947 (dec. Dec. 2001); children: David Forgan, Sims, Marion, John, Francis. AB, Princeton U., 1940; LLB, Yale U., 1947. Bar: N.Y. 1948. Atty. Debevoise, Plimpton & McLean, N.Y.C., 1947-50; exec. assoc. Ford Found., 1950-52; sec. Fund for the Republic, N.Y.C., 1952-54, v.p., 1954-57; assoc. Rockefeller Bros. Fund, N.Y.C., 1957-67; pres. Council on Founds., N.Y.C., 1968-78; exec. dir., treas. Scherman Found., N.Y.C., 1979-93; pres. So. Edn. Found., Atlanta, 1965-79; bd. dirs. Fund for N.J., 1980-87; exec. sec. major awards program Gulf & Western Found., 1981-86. Author: The Handbook on Private Foundations, 1981, rev. edit., 1991. Mem. Rumson Bd. Edn., N.J., 1952-55; mem. Monmouth County Mental Health Bd., N.J., 1985-90; mem. com. on religion and race Presbyn. Ch., 1958-61. With USNR, 1940-45. Decorated Legion of Merit. Home: 6 Clay Ct Locust NJ 07760-2307

FREEMAN, DAVID JOHN, lawyer; b. N.Y.C., Aug. 9, 1948; s. John L. and Josephine F. (Wilding) F.; m. Ellen Gogolick, Dec. 29, 1974; children: Matthew, Julie. BA, Harvard U., 1970; JD, 1975. Bar: Mass. 1975, D.C. 1977, N.Y. 1982, U.S. Dist. Ct. D.C. 1981, N.Y. 1982, U.S. Dist. Ct. D.C. 1981, U.S. Dist. Ct. (so. and ea. dists.) N.Y. 1982, U.S. Ct. Appeals (D.C. cir.) 1979, U.S. Ct. Appeals (2nd cir.) 1982, U.S. Supreme Ct. 1988. Spl. asst. to U.S. Senator Frank E. Moss, 1970-72; trial atty. FTC, Washington, 1975-77; assoc. Ginsburg, Feldman & Bress, Washington, 1977-81, Holtzmann, Wise & Shepard, N.Y.C., 1981-84; ptnr., 1984-94; ptnr., chair environ. dept. Battle Fowler, 1994-2000; chair N.Y. environ. practice group Paul, Hastings, Janofsky & Walker, N.Y.C., 2000—. Spl. legal counsel N.Am. Environ. Affairs, UN Environ. Programme; co-chair emeritus ISO 14000 Legal Issues Forum, U.S. Tech. Com. to TC-207, Internat. Com. Standardization. Editor-in-chief: Jour. Environ Law Practice (West), 1998-2000. Mem. ABA (environment, energy and resources sect.), Assn. Bar City of N.Y., Harvard Law Sch. Assn., N.Y. State Bar Assn. (environ. law sect., co-chair hazardous waste/site remediation com., co-chair task force on brownfields/ superfund reform). Office: Paul Hastings Janofsky & Walker LLP 75 E 55th St New York NY 10022-3205 Office Phone: 212-318-6555. Business E-Mail: davidfreeman@paulhastings.com.

FREEMAN, DELMA C., JR., science association director; m. Diana Freeman. B in Aerospace Engring., U. Va., 1964. Joined NASA Langley Rsch. Ctr., 1960, asst. dir. aerothermodynamics br. Space Systems Divsn., 1983—86, head vehicle analysis br., 1986—91, asst. chief Space Systems Divsn., 1991—94, leader space transp. thrust Space and Atmospheric Scis. Program, 1994—96, dir. Aerospace Transp. Tech. Office, 1996—99, dep. dir., 2000—02, acting dir., 2002—03. Fellow: AIAA (Hampton Roads sect. chmn. 1992—93).

FREEMAN, DONNA COOK, small business owner; b. Waldron, Ark., Apr. 18, 1937; d. Oliver Raymond and Lura Edna (Doyel) Cook; m. Clarence Lee Freeman, Jan. 21, 1954; children: Scott, Kevin, Steven, Melissa, Melinda. Staff dept. aquaculture U. Calif. Bodega Marine Lab., 1976—77; real estate assoc., 1978—82; co-owner fishing vessel Noyo Belle, 1981—84; ptnr. Freeman's Union 76 Svc., Bodega Bay, 1983—93; designer Compass Rose Gardens, 1986—, owner, 1987—. Vice chmn. Shoreline Trust Ednl. Program Svcs., 1981—85; founding chmn. Bodega Bay Fisherman's Festival, 1973—74, 1983; chmn. Spud Point Adv. Bd., 1985—; grand juror Sonoma County, Calif., 1983—84; hon. dir. Sonoma County Fair, 1995—; dir. Bodega Bay Fire Protection Dist., 1987—; alt. mem. Dem. Ctrl. Com., 1982; mgr. polit. campaign, 1984; bd. dirs. Bodega Bay Area Rescue, 1973—74; mem. local bd. SSS, 1982—; bd. dirs. Sonoma County Fair, 1985—95, Coastal Fisheries Found., 1986—; mem. regional adv. bd. Sonoma County Libr. Commn., 2002—. Mem.: Bodega Bay Cmty. Assn., Bodega Bay C. of C. (pres. 1979—81, bd. dirs. 1982—86), Bodega Bay Fisherman's Auz., Bodega Bay Grange. Home: PO Box 1060 Bodega Bay CA 94923-1060 E-mail: donna@compassrosegardens.com.

FREEMAN, EDWARD CARL, JR., music minister; b. Roanoke, Va., Feb. 18, 1936; s. Edward Carl Freeman Sr. and Alberta Frances Fringer. Student, Peabody Conservatory, 1959, Johns Hopkins U., 1959—61; MusB, Peabody Conservatory, 1962. Organist, dir. U. Bapt. Ch., Balt., 1958—68; asst. organist, dir. Balt. Hebren Congregation, 1964—68; min. music River Rd. Ch., Richmond, Va., 1968—; faculty music Collegiate Sch. Girls, 1968—69, U. Richmond, 1970—73. Advisor, cons. to bd. trustees Peabody Conservatory, Balt., 1966—69, mem. alumni coun., 1983—85. Recipient Dirs. award, Peabody Inst. Johns Hopkins U., 1993, honor, Va. Gen. Assembly, 2003. Mem.: Am. Guild Organists (life). Avocations: reading, travel. Home: 2614 Southbay Dr Richmond VA 23233 Office: River Rd Ch 8000 River Rd Richmond VA 23229 Office Phone: 804-288-1131. E-mail: carlfreeman@rrcb.org.

FREEMAN, ERNEST ROBERT, engineering executive; b. Bklyn., Oct. 3, 1933; s. Nathan and Rose (Beginsky) F.; m. June Gladys Moser, June 6, 1954; children: Jesse David, Miriam Lisa, Sarah Ellen, Beth Bayla BSE.E., U. Miami, Coral Gables, Fla., 1955; M.E.A., George Washington U., 1966; Sc.D. (hon.), London Inst., 1977. Registered profl. engr., Md., NJ. Mem. tech. staff Bell Telephone Labs., Whippany, N.J., 1959-61; mgr. engrng. dept. IIT Research Inst., Annapolis, Md., 1961-68; dir. engring. dept. Vertex Corp., Kensington, Md., 1968-69; pres., chief exec. officer SFA Inc., Landover, Md., 1969-91, exec. advisor, 1991-98, pres., chmn., CEO Largo, Md., 1998—. Lectr. Am U. Ctr. for Tech. and Adminstrn.; dir. Data Range Ltd., High Wycombe, England; mem. engring. adv. bd. U. DC, Washington. Author: (with others) Electromagnetic Compatibility Design Guide, 1981; Interference Suppression Techniques for Antennas and Transmitters, 1982; contbg. editor Attorney's Guide to Engring., 1986; editor-in-chief IEEE NCAC Scanner, 1997-98. Trustee People to People Internat. Served with USAF, 1956—59. Recipient Bausch & Lomb award, 1951, Electro '76 Best Session award. Fellow: IEEE (life), VFW (life), Washington Acad. Sci. (life); mem.: Assn. Fed. Comm. Cons. Engrs. (life), Mensa. Avocations: scuba, flying, sailing. Home: 5357 Strathmore Ave Kensington MD 20895-1160 Office: SFA Inc Ste 405 2200 Defense Hwy Crofton MD 21114 Office Phone: 301-858-1230. Personal E-mail: erfreeman@earthlink.net. Business E-Mail: efreeman@sfa.com.

FREEMAN, FRANKLIN EDWARD, JR., government agency administrator; b. Dobson, N.C., May 5, 1945; s. Franklin Edward and Clara E. (Smith) F.; m. Margaret Carson McKnight, 1966 (div. 1974); children: Margaret Elizabeth, Nancy Lorrin; m. Katherine Lynn Lloyd, Aug. 12, 1978; children: Katherine Ann, Franklin Edward III, Alexander Lloyd, Mary Claire. BA, U. N.C., 1967, JD, 1970. Bar: N.C. 1970. Rsch. asst. Assoc. Justice Dan K. Moore, Raleigh, N.C., 1970-71; asst. dist. atty. 17th jud. dist. N.C. Ct. System, 1971-73; exec. sec. Jud. Coun., 1973-78; asst. dir. Adminstrv. Office of Cts., Raleigh, 1973-78, dir., 1981-93; dist. atty. 17th jud. dist. N.C. Ct. System, 1979-81; sec. N.C. Dept. Correction, Raleigh, 1993-97; chief staff Gov. James B. Hunt, Jr., 1997-99; assoc. justice N.C. Supreme Ct., 1999-2001; sr. asst. for govt. affairs Gov. of N.C., 2001—. Contbr. articles to profl. jours. Tchr. Sunday sch. Main Street United Meth. Ch., Reidsville, 1974-81, chmn. every mem. canvas, 1980, chmn. adminstrv. bd., 1981; mem. Hayes Barton Meth. Ch., Raleigh; pres. Raleigh Host Lions Club, 1994—95. Recipient Svc. award Conf. Superior Ct. Judges, Svc. award Conf. Dist. Ct. Judges, Svc. award N.C. Clks. Superior Ct. Assn., Svc. award N.C. Magistrates Assn. Mem. N.C. State Bar, N.C. Correctional Assn., Surry County Bar Assn., Rockingham County Bar Assn., 10th Dist. Bar Assn., 17th Dist. Bar Assn., State Correctional Adminstrs., Conf. State Ct. Adminstrs. (pres-elect 1992-93, bd. dirs. 1987-90, 94-95), Lions Club (pres. Raleigh Host club 1994), Delta Upsilon. Democrat. Avocations: horses, history, reading. Office: Gov's Office 20301 Mail Svc Ctr Raleigh NC 27699-0301

FREEMAN, FRED WESLEY, forester, educator; b. Logan, Ohio, Aug. 27, 1924; s. Harry and Ora May (Hicks) Freeman; m. Laura Alice Furgason, Oct. 17, 1986; children: Fred II, Cynthia Kogut, Carol Flegler; m. Jeanne Elizabeth Harbourt, July 12, 1946 (div. Nov. 30, 1973); stepchildren: Cheryl Vincent, Terry Furgason. BS, Mich. State U., 1949, MS, 1951, PhD, 1963. Registered forester Ohio, Mich. Soil scientist Bur. Reclamation, Bismarck, ND, 1950—51; forest ranger Ohio Divsn. Forestry, Rockbridge, 1951—53, forester Athens, 1953—55; horticulturist Hidden Lake Gardens Mich. State U., Tipton, 1955—61, dir. and asst. prof. Hidden Lake Gardens, 1961—68, dir. and assoc. prof. Hidden Lake Gardens, 1968—86, assoc. prof. emeritus E. Lansing. Trustee Mich. Horticulture Soc., Mich., 1967—71; dir. Am. Assn. Bot. Gardens and Arboretums, 1968—71; mem. Gov.'s Commn. Sch. Reorganization - Lenawee County, Mich., 1970. Editor: (jour.) Am. Assn. Bot. Gardens and Arboretums, 1965; contbr. articles to numerous mag. and newspaper articles. Treas. Tecumseh Sch. Bd., Mich., 1964—74. Sgt. airborne U.S. Army, 1943—46, S. Pacific. Fellow in horticulture, English Speaking Union, Brit. Isles & W. Europe, 1963, Complimentary fellow, Royal Horticulture Soc., London, 1976. Mem.: Am. Legion. Democrat. Avocations: reading, gardening, hunting, fishing, politics. Home: Heather Fields 180 Stoli Ct Onsted MI 49265

FREEMAN, GEORGE CLEMON, JR., lawyer; b. Birmingham, Ala., Jan. 3, 1929; s. George Clemon and Annie Laura (Gill) F.; m. Anne Colston Hobson, Dec. 6, 1958; children: Anne Colston McEvoy, George Clemon III, Joseph Reid Anderson. BA magna cum laude, Vanderbilt U., 1950; LLB, Yale U., 1956. Bar: Ala. 1956, Va. 1958, D.C. 1974. Law clk. to Justice Hugo L. Black U.S. Supreme Ct., 1956; assoc. Hunton & Williams, Richmond, Va., 1957-63, ptnr., 1963-95, sr. counsel, 1995—. Contbr. articles to profl. jours. Pres. Va. chpt. Nature Conservancy, 1962—63; counsel Va. Outdoors Recreation Study Com. Va. Legis., 1963—65; mem. sect. 301 Superfund Act Study Group Congl. Adv. Com., 1981—82; mem. Falls James Com., 1973—89; chmn. adv. coun. Energy Policy Studies Ctr. U. Va., 1981—85; chmn. legal adv. com. to Va. Commn. on Transp. in the 21st Century, 1986—87; mem. Va. Gov.'s Commn. to Study Historic Preservation, 1987—88, Va. Coun. on the Environment, 1989—91; chmn. Va. Bd. Hist. Resources, 1989—91; mem. The Atlantic Coun., 1986—95; bd. dirs. Nat. Mus. Am. History, 1997—2002; chmn. Richmond City Dem. Com., 1969—71. Lt (j.g.) USN, 1951—54. Ctr. for Pub. Resources fellow, 1990—. Fellow Am. Bar Found. (Va. state chmn. 1986-90); mem. ABA (chmn. standing com. on facilities of Law Libr. of Congress 1967-73, coordinating group on regulatory reform 1981-85, nominating com. 1984-87, chmn. civil justice coordinating com. 1990-92, sect. bus. law, sect. coun. 1976-79, chmn. ad hoc com. on Fed. Criminal Code 1979-81, chmn. program com. 1981-82, chmn. ad hoc com. on tort law reform 1986-87, sect. del. to ho. of dels. 1983-87, sec. 1987-88, vice-chmn. and ed. The Business Lawyer 1988-89, chmn.-elect 1989-90, chmn. 1990-91), Richmond Bar Assn., Va. Bar Assn., Am. Law Inst. (coun. 1980—, advisor to coun. on project on compensation and liability for product and process injuries 1986-91, advisor restatement law, THRD, torts apportionment 1993-97, advisor restatement law THRD torts gen. prins. 1997—), Am. Judicature Soc., Country Club of Va., Knickerbocker Club, Met. Club, Phi Beta Kappa, Phi Delta Phi, Omicron Delta Kappa, Alpha Tau Omega. Democrat. Episcopalian. Avocation: gardening. Office: Hunton & Williams 951 E Byrd St Richmond VA 23219-0005 Office Phone: 804-788-8365. Business E-Mail: gfreeman@hunton.com.

FREEMAN, GERALD RUSSELL, lawyer; b. Mpls., Feb. 14, 1928; s. Samuel W. Freeman and Mildred Lorraine (Linton) Wofford; m. Ann Leslie Alton; 1 child, Brady Michael; children by previous marriage: Gerald Russell, Jon L., Craig V., Pamela A., Kelley M. BA, U. Minn., 1952; BS in Law, William Mitchell Coll. Law, Mpls., 1958, JD, 1960. Bar: Minn. 1960. Sole practice, Mpls., 1960-67; ptnr. Collins, Freeman & Flakne, Mpls., 1967-73, Freeman, Gill, Keating & Ebersold, Mpls., 1973-86, Freeman, Alton, Dodd & Greer, Mpls., 1986-91, Freeman & Alton, Ltd., Mpls., 1991—. Lectr. Golden Valley Med. Ctr., Mpls., 1976-81; adj. prof. Hamline Law Sch., St. Paul, 1981; legal counsel, bd. dirs. Vinland Nature Ctr., Mpls., 1984-85. Mem. chm. dependency adv. com. United Hosp., St. Paul, 1988-94. With U.S. Army, 1946-48. Mem. ABA (com. on alcohol and drug abuse), Minn. Bar Assn. (bd. dir., 2000-04), Hennepin County Bar Assn., Am. Trial Lawyers Assn., Minn. Trial Lawyers Assn., Am. Judicature Soc., Am. Arbitration Assn. (nat. panel arbitrators), Minn. Bd. Profl. Responsibility, Minn. Hist. Soc., Douglas K. Amdahl Inn of Ct., Minn. Lawyers Concerned for Lawyers (bd. dirs. 1976—). Home: 2105 Xanthus Ln N Minneapolis MN 55447-2055 Office: 12450 Wayzata Blvd Ste 224 Minnetonka MN 55305-1927 Fax: 612-475-1214.

FREEMAN, GLENN, political organization worker, retired non-commissioned military officer; b. Fayetteville, NC, July 6, 1935; Student, Met. C.C., 1986—87. Enlisted USAF, 1955, advanced through grades to Chief Master Sgt., 1985, ret., 1985. Author: Good Racism-Bad Racism, 1999. Appt. to U.S. Commn. on Civil Rights, 2000—04; pres. Omaha chpt. Freedoms Found. at Valley Forge; appt. commr. State Equal Opportunity Commn., 1989; dir. Douglas County Atty.'s Victim-Witness Program; hosp. svc. coord. Disabled Am. Vets., 1991—97; sr. aide US Sen. Chuck Hagel; asst. chmn. Couglas County Rep. Party, Nebr. Rep. Party; chmn. outreach com. Nebr. Rep. Party. Decorated Bronze Star, two meritorious Svc. medals, four Air Force commendation medals.

FREEMAN, HARRY LYNWOOD, retired accountant; b. L.A., May 5, 1920; s. Edward Church and Mildred Eaton (Noyes) F.; m. Ruth Turner, Feb. 14, 1941; children: Tracy Ruth (Mrs. Richard W. Flatow), Martin Harry. BS, UCLA, 1942. CPA, Calif. With Price Waterhouse & Co., CPAs, 1942-56, ptnr. Mexico City, 1956-73, ptnr.-in-charge Middle Americas firm, 1973-80. Chmn. auditing com. Am. Brit. Cowdray Hosp., 1962-68; bd. dirs., treas. YMCA of Mexico, 1967-73; bd. dirs. Inst. Mexicano-Norteamericano de Relaciones Culturales, 1961-69, Eastridge Homeowners Assn., 2000—; trustee, v.p. Fallbrook Hosp. Found., 1987-90, pres., 1990-92; bd. dirs. Fallbrook Hosp. Dist., 1994-98, v.p., 1996-98. With AUS, 1944-46. Mem. AICPA, Calif. Soc. CPAs, Am. C. of C. Mex. (past pres.), Assn. Am. C. of C. in Latin Am. (past pres.), Aero Club of So. Calif., Book Club Calif. Home: 1002 Ridge Heights Dr Fallbrook CA 92028-3671

FREEMAN, HERBERT, computer engineering educator; b. Frankfurt, Germany, Dec. 13, 1925; came to U.S., 1938; s. Leo and Johanna (Friedmann) F.; m. Joan Sleppin, Nov. 25, 1955; children: Nancy, Susan, Robert. BSEE, Union Coll., 1946; MSEE, Columbia U., 1948, DEngSc, 1956. Registered profl. engr., N.Y. Project engr. Sperry Gyroscope Co., Great Neck, N.Y., 1948-53, section head, 1953-57, dept. head, 1957-60; assoc. prof. computer engring. NYU, 1960-64, prof., chmn., 1965-75; prof. Rensselaer Poly. Inst., Troy, N.Y., 1975-85; dir. Ctr. for Computer Aids for Indsl. Productivity Rutgers U., New Brunswick, N.J., 1985-90. Dir. Nat. Ctr. Geographic Info. and Analysis, 1988-93. Author: Discrete-Time Systems, 1965; co-editor: Map Data Processing, 1980, Software Engineering, 1981; editor: Introduction to Computer Graphics, 1981, Machine Vision for Three-Dimensional Scenes, 1990. NSF postdoctoral fellow, 1966, Guggenheim fellow, 1972; recipient Medaglia Teresiana award U. Pavia, Italy, 1996. Fellow IEEE (Computer Pioneer award 1999), Internat. Assn. for Pattern Recognition (treas. 1982-88, pres. 1978-80, K.S. Fu award 1994); mem. Computer Soc. of IEEE (chmn. Pattern Analysis and Machine Intelligence sect. 1976-78), Internat. Fedn. Info. Processing (program chmn. 1974, Silver Core award 1974), Assn. Computing Machinery, Pattern Recognition Soc. Avocations: stamp collecting/philately, swimming. Office Phone: 609-716-7552. Personal E-mail: hfreeman@comcast.net.

FREEMAN, J. P. LADYHAWK, vicar, underwater exploration, security and transportation executive, educator, fashion model, legislative advocate; b. Berkley, Calif., Feb. 21, 1951; d. Gilbert Richard Freeman (dec.) and P.M. (Ann) Raistrick; children: Jennifer Patricia (dec.), Schne F. (dec.). BA in English, Davis & Elkins Coll., W.Va., 1973; grad., USAF Air Weapons Controller Sch., Tyndall AFB, Fla., 1973, USAF Air Command and Staff Coll., 1982, U.S. Marine Corps Command and Staff Coll., 1982, Dept. Def. Computer Inst., 1984; M in Aviation M in Aviation Mgmt., postgrad., Embry-Riddle Aeronautical U., Daytona Beach, Fla., 1986; grad., USAF Air War Coll., Montgomery, Ala., 1988. Cert. EMT; ordained vicar Universal Ch., 2002. Mem. 56th spl. ops. rescue for Southeast Asia NKP Royal Thai Air Force Base, 1974, 75; chief wing radar standardization/evaluation RAF Alconbury, England, 1980-83; commdr. joint U.S. forces Operation Raleigh, 1986; support chief of staff Hdqs. NORAD, Colorado Springs, Colo., 1987-89; dep. base commdr. NATO Hdqs. Allied Forces No. Europe, Norway, 1989-91; chief airport mgmt. divsn. Whiteman AFB, Knob Noster, Mo., 1991-93; dir. spl. projects USAF Acad. Regional Hosp., Colorado Springs, 1993-94; systems performance specialist Colo. Sport & Spine Rehab., Colorado Springs, 1994-95; dir. FLEET Internat. Explorations and Svcs. Co., Colorado Springs, 1995-97; fashion model, 1996—2001; vicar, 2002—. Spl. adv. for anti and counter terrorist security design for 1994 Internat. Olympic Games, Oslo, Norway, 1989-91; designer Automated Provider Credentialing System USAF Acad. Regional Hosp., USAF Acad., Colo., 1993-94; spl. adv. comms. NATO German High Commd., 1977-80; paralyzed Vet. of Am., sr. legist. advocate. U.S. Congress for Colo., Mont. Ut. and Wyo., 2002-05; experience in 37 countries. Poet, poems included in numerous anthologies. Mem. bd. dirs. Johnson County (Mo.) United Way, 1991-93; surgery life support specialist ARC, USAF Acad. Regional Hosp., 1993-95; mem. nat. scholarship com. Red River Valley Fighter Pilots Assn., 1993-96; hosp. vol., med. technician, provider credentialing system designer, oral surgery life support system specialist. Recipient 53 awards and decorations including Defense Meritorious svc. medal with 1 oak leaf cluster, Meritorious Svc. medal with 2 oak leaf clusters, Joint Svc. Commendation medal with 1 oak leaf cluster, air force commendation medal, Armed Forces Expeditionary medal with 2 bronze stars, 2 Humanitarian Svc. medals, 2 Kuwait Liberation medals, 2 Southwest Asia medals; named Adminstrsn. Officer of Yr. USAF, 1986; named one of the six top Support Officers USAF, 1986-87; 1st woman named dir. Fleet Internat. Mem. VFW, DAV, Am. Legion, Air Force Assn., Soc. of Profl. Journalists, Assn. of Old Crows, Lambda Lambda Lambda, Alpha Phi Omega, Iota Beta Sigma. Mem. United Anglican Ch. Avocations: writing, skiing, horseback riding, painting, music. Home: 5913 Amber Station Ave Las Vegas NV 89131

FREEMAN, JAMES MICHAEL, musician, vocalist; b. Pittsburgh, Pa., Aug. 28, 1955; s. Alfred and Laura Bell Freeman. Ride operator RCS Amusement, Tempee, Ariz., 1994—96; gen. contractor Self Employed, Long Beach, 1990—94; singer Consol. Energy Band, Pittsburgh, 1973—76; lead singer The Marcels, Pittsburgh, 1979—84; warehouse worker Robinson's May Co., Westminster, 1997; janitor 24-Hour Fitness, Irvine, 1999; gen. contractor Dan Mathis Contracting, Westminster, 2000. Author: (children's book) Willow Brook Pond. Driver Seniors & Disabled, Santa Ana, Calif., 2002; benefit shows Live Performances, Orange County, Calif., 1990—2000. Mem.: S.A.G. Avocations: fishing, playing video games. Home: 3337 S Bristol #48 Santa Ana CA 92704

FREEMAN, JANET L., librarian; b. Winston-Salem, N.C., Nov. 5, 1946; d. Vernon Charles and Lula M. (McHan) F. BA, U. N.C., Greensboro, 1969; MLS, George Peabody Coll. Tchrs., 1971. Ref. libr. Ga. Southwestern Coll., Americus, 1971-73; tech. svcs. libr. Furman U., Greenville, S.C., 1973-75; dir. libr. svcs. Wingate (N.C.) Coll., 1975-84; coll. libr. Meredith Coll., Raleigh, N.C., 1984—. Mem. ALA, N.C. Libr. Assn. (bd. dirs. 1987-89, pres.-elect. 1989-91, pres. 1991-93), Southeastern Libr. Assn. Avocation: music. Home: 2800 Rue Sans Famille Raleigh NC 27607-3049 Office: Meredith Coll 3800 Hillsborough St Raleigh NC 27607-5237

FREEMAN, JOHN MARK, pediatric neurologist; b. Bklyn., Jan. 11, 1933; s. Leon Lucas and Florence (Kann) F.; m. Elaine Kaplan, Aug. 26, 1956; children: Andrew David, Jennifer Beth, Joshua Leon. BA, Amherst Coll., 1954; MD, Johns Hopkins U., 1958. Intern Harriet Lane Home, Johns Hopkins U., Balt., 1958-59, resident in pediatrics, 1959-61; fellow in neurology Columbia Presbyn. Hosp., N.Y.C., 1961-64; asst. prof. pediatrics and neurology Stanford (Calif.) U., 1966-69; asso. prof. neurology and pediatrics Johns Hopkins U., Balt., 1969-82, prof., 1982—, Lederer prof. pediatric epilepsy, 1991—2003; dir. pediatric neurology Johns Hopkins, Balt., 1969-90; dir. pediatric epilepsy ctr. Johns Hopkins U., Balt., 1973—2002, dir. birth defects treatment center, 1969-90. Pres. Epilepsy Assn. Md., 1977-82; mem. profl. adv. bd. Epilepsy Found. Am., 1975-82, sec., 1977, v.p., 1982—, hon. life dir., 1991—. Contbr. articles to profl. jours. Served with AUS, 1964-66. Named Physician of Yr., Gov.'s Com. on Employment Handicapped, 1979, Health Care Profl. of Yr., Gov.'s Com. on Employment of Persons with Disabilities, 1990; recipient Cmty. Leadership award, Epilepsy Assn. Md., 1991. Fellow: Am. Acad. Pediats. (chmn. neurology sect. 1978—80), Am. Acad. Neurology; mem.: Am. Neurol. Assn., Am. Epilepsy Soc. (Lennox award 1993, Penry award 2001), Am. Fedn. Clin. Rsch., Am. Pediat. Soc., Child Neurology Soc. (exec. com. 1979—81, Hower award 2004), Profs. of Child Neurology (pres. 1980—82). Home: 1026 Rolandvue Ave Baltimore MD 21204-6815 Office: John Hopkins Med Inst 600 N Wolfe St 2-147 Meyer Baltimore MD 21287-0005

FREEMAN, JOHN WHEELOCK, retired editor, writer; b. Bronx, N.Y., June 30, 1928; s. Edward Woolsey and Dorothy (Perkins) Freeman; m. Sally Bennett (dec.); children: Robin, Jill, Kevin; m. Donna Byars; 1 child, Eric. BA, Yale U., 1950. Assoc. editor Opera News Mag., N.Y.C., 1960—2000; ret., 2000. Author: Sports Cars, 2002, Metropolitan Opera Stories, 1984, 1997; co-author: Toscanini, 1987. Pres., sec., bd. dirs. Bronx Arts Ensemble, 1975—; chmn. bd. trustees Perkins Gardens, Bronx, 1990—. Decorated knight 1st class Order of Lion Govt. of Finland; recipient Eleanor Belmont medal, Met. Opera Guild, 1993. Avocations: music, writing, photography. Home and Office: 4970 Independence Ave Bronx NY 10471

FREEMAN, JOSEPH, automotive historian; b. Hartford, Conn. s. Harrison Growell and Pauline Smith Freeman; m. Cynthia Forbes Lyman Freeman, May 19, 1973. AB, Yale U., 1966; MEd, Harvard U., 1972, MPA, 1979. Vol. U.S. Peace Corps, 1966—69; program develop. Cmty. Awareness Inc., New Haven, 1969—72; assoc. dir. Divsn. of Alcoholism, Mass. Dept. Pub. Health, 1973—79; freelance writer, automotive historian self-employed, 1980—. Bd. pres. Larz Anderson Auto Mus., Brookline, Mass., 2000—, v.p., 1997—2000. Contbr. articles. Maitre Commanderie De Bordeaux, Boston, 1990—2003, nat. bd. mem., 1988—. Recipient Monterey Cup Phil Hill award, Monterey Historic Races, 2001, Hulman award, Pebble Beach Concourse, 2001. Mem.: Am. Hist. Soc. (bd.mem. 2000—), Soc. of Automotive Historians (pres. 2003—, v.p. 2001—03). Democrat. Episc. Avocations: automotive vintage racing, sailing, book collecting, golf. Home: 346 Lee St Brookline MA 02445 Office: Racemaker 121 Mount Vernon St Boston MA 02108 Business E-Mail: jfeeman@racemaker.com.

FREEMAN, KENNETH W., laboratory executive; BS, Bucknell U.; MBA, Harvard U. Various positions Corning Inc., Corning, NY, 1972—95, v.p., corp. controller, 1985—87, named sr. v.p., 1987, gen. mgr. sci. products divsn., 1989—90, pres., CEO Corning Asahi Video Products Co., 1990—93, exec. v.p., 1993—95, pres., CEO Corning Clin. Labs., 1995—97; CEO, chmn. Quest Diagnostics, Inc. (formerly Corning Clin. Labs.), Teterboro, NJ, 1997—2004, chmn., 2004—. Office: Quest Diagnostics 1 Malcolm Ave Teterboro NJ 07608

FREEMAN, KIMBRALY MARIE DANSBY, secondary school educator; b. Pomona, Calif., June 13, 1962; d. Kenneth Ebern Dansby and Paula Sue (Way) Freeman; m. Greg Freeman. AA, Daytona Beach Community Coll., 1983; BS, Miss. State U., 1986, MEd, 1990. Tchr. educationally handicapped N.E. Lauderdale Jr., Sr. High Sch., Lauderdale County Sch. System, Meridian, Miss. Adv. bd., coach Area 5 Special Olympics. Recipient fellowship and honor awards, Nat. Speech Orgn., Outstanding Service awards Miss. Am. Fedn. Tchrs., 1989, 90, Good Apple award Lauderdale County Sch. System, March 1990. Mem. Am. Fedn. Tchrs. (local treas. 1989, sec. 1990, 91), Phi Rho Pi.

FREEMAN, LANCE, education educator; BS, SUNY, Buffalo, N.Y., 1987; M City and Regional Planning, UNC-Chapel Hill, Chapel Hill, N.C., 1991; PhD, UNC-Chapel Hill, Chapel Hill, 1997. Asst. prof. U. Del., Newark, 1998—99, Columbia U., N.Y., 1999—. Rschr. Mathematica Policy Rsch., Washington, 1996—98. Urban Scholar, U.S. HUD, 2001-2002. Avocations: basketball, bicycling, reading, baking. Office: Columbia Univ 400 Avery Hall New York NY 10027 Business E-Mail: lf182@columbia.edu.

FREEMAN, LEE ALLEN, JR., lawyer; b. Chgo., July 31, 1940; s. Lee Allen and Brena (Dietz) F.; m. Glynna Gene Weger, June 8, 1968; children: Crispin McDougal, Clark Dietz, Cassidy Bree. AB magna cum laude, Harvard U., 1962, JD magna cum laude, 1965. Bar: Ill. 1966, D.C. 1966, Mont. 1986, U.S. Supreme Ct. 1969. Practiced in, Washington, 1965-68, Chgo., 1968—; law clk. to Justice Tom C. Clark, Washington, 1965-66; asst. U.S. atty., 1966-68; pres. Freeman, Freeman & Salzman, P.C., 1970—; spl. dep. atty. gen. Commonwealth of Pa., 1971—82; spl. asst. atty. gen. in Ill., Ind., W.Va., Mich., Colo., Tex.; spl. asst. corp. counsel City of Chgo., 1971-76. Pres. Chgo. Lyric Opera Guild; pres. Fine Arts Music Found.; dir. Chgo. Lyric Opera, 1995—, mem. exec. com.; mem. Middlebury Coll. Arts Coun. Named Outstanding Young Citizen Chgo. Jaycees, 1976 Mem.: ABA (coun. mem. antitrust sect. 1985—87), Am. Coll. Trial Lawyers, Chgo. Inn of Ct., Std. Club. Home: 232 E Walton St Chicago IL 60611-1507 also: 52 Little Mission Creek Livingston MT 59047 Office: 401 N Michigan Ave Chicago IL 60611-4255 Office Phone: 312-222-5127. Business E-Mail: lfreemanjr@ffspc.com.

FREEMAN, LEONARD MURRAY, radiologist, nuclear medicine physician, educator; b. N.Y.C., Apr. 20, 1937; s. Joseph and Tillie (Krutman) F.; m. Marlene Carolyn Held, Apr. 28, 1967; children: Eric Lawrence, David Robert, Joy Esther. BA, N.Y. U., 1957; MD, Chgo. Med. Sch., 1961. Diplomate: Am. Bd. Radiology, Am. Bd. Nuclear Medicine. Intern Beth Israel Hosp. and Med. Center, N.Y.C., 1961-62; resident in radiology Bronx Municipal Hosp. Center, 1962-65; mem. staff Albert Einstein Coll. Medicine, N.Y.C., 1965—; co-dir. div. nuclear medicine Jacobi Med. Ctr., N.Y.C., 1965-83; dir. nuclear medicine Montefiore Med. Center, N.Y.C., 1976—, attending radiologist, 1977—; cons. nuclear medicine USPHS Hosp., S.I., N.Y., 1967-82, St. Barnabas Hosp., Bronx, 1967—, Beth Israel Hosp. and Med. Center, 1974—, Maimonides Hosp. and Med. Center, 1974-99, Bklyn. VA Hosp., 1984—; asst. instr. radiology Albert Einstein Coll. Medicine, Bronx, 1964-65, instr., 1965-67, asst. prof., 1967-72, assoc. prof., 1972-77, prof., 1977—, prof. nuclear medicine, 1983—, vice chmn. dept. nuclear medicine, 1987—. Mem. adv. com. nuclear medicine program Brookhaven Nat. Labs., Upton, N.Y., 1972-82; examiner nuclear medicine Am. Bd. Radiology. Author: Clinical Scintillation Scanning, 1969, Clinical Scintillation Imaging, 1975, Freeman and Johnson's Clinical Radionuclide Imaging, 1984; co-editor Seminars in Nuclear Medicine, 1970—, Physicians Desk Reference for Radiology and Nuclear Medicine, 1971-80; reviewer Jour. Nuclear Medicine, 1972—; editor Nuclear Medicine Ann., 1980-2004, Current Concepts in Diagnostic Nuclear Medicine, 1983-87, Advances in Functional Neuroimaging, 1988-90; mem. editl. bd. European Jour. Nuclear Medicine, 1979—, Jour. Nuclear Medicine and Allied Scis., 1982-96, Nuclear Medicine Communications, 1986-2002, Quar. Jour. Nuclear Medicine, 1996—; contbr. numerous articles to jours., also book chpts. Fellow Am. Coll. Radiology, Am. Coll. Nuclear Physicians, N.Y. Acad. Medicine (chmn. sect. nuc. medicine 2000-02); mem. Soc. Nuclear Medicine (gov. local chpt. 1973—, nat. trustee 1973-77, nat. v.p. 1977-78, nat. pres. 1979-80, chmn. pub. rels. com. 1981-91, chmn. correlative imaging coun. 1982-84, chmn. awards com. 1983-86, Disting. Edn. award 1993, Berson-Yallow award Greater N.Y. chpt. 1997), Radiol. Soc. N.Am., Soc. Gastrointestinal Radiologists, N.Y. State Med. Soc., New York County Med. Soc., Pan Am. Med. Assn. (hon. life), European Assn. Nuclear Medicine, L.I. Soc. Nuclear Med. Technologists (hon. life), Alpha Omega Alpha (hon.). Home: 50 Sutton Pl S New York NY 10022-4167 Office: 111 E 210th St Bronx NY 10467-2401 Office Phone: 718-920-6060. Business E-Mail: lfreeman@montefiore.org.

FREEMAN, LESLIE GORDON, anthropologist, educator; b. Warsaw, N.Y., Sept. 9, 1935; s. Leslie Gordon and Theresa Rosalie (Stanbro) F.; m. Susan Tax, Mar. 20, 1964; 1 child, Sarah Elisabeth. AB, U. Chgo., 1954, AM, 1961, PhD, 1964. Asst. prof. anthropology Tulane U., 1964-65; asst. prof. U. Chgo., 1965-70, assoc. prof., 1970-76, prof., 1976-2000, prof. emeritus, 2000—; pres. Inst. Prehistoric Investigations, Chgo., 1983—2001. Rsch. assoc. Mont. State U., Bozeman, 1992—. Author (with J. Gonzalez): Cueva Morin, 2 vols., 1971, 1973, Vida y Muerte en Cueva Morin, 1978, Le Paleolithique Inferieur et Moyen en Espagne, 1998, La Grotte d'Altamira, 2001; editor: Views of the Past, 1978; editor: (with Sol Tax) Horizons of Anthropology, 1976; editor: (with others) Altamira Revisited, 1987, Beato de Liebana, 1995, Estudio del Manuscrito del Apocalipsis de San Juan, Beato de Liebana de San Miguel de Escalada, 2000; editor: Beato de Liebana: Obres Comletas y Complementarias, vol. I (2d edit.), vol. II, 2004. Corporator Internat. Inst. Spain. With U.S. Army, 1957-59. Recipient Silver Plaque Provincial Deputation of Santander, Spain, 1973 Fellow AAAS, Am. Anthropol. Assn., Royal Anthropol. Inst.; mem. Reial Academia Catalana de Belles Arts de Sant Jordi Barcelona (corr.), Reial Academia Catalana de Bones Lletres Barcelona (corr.), Chgo. Acad. Scis. (trustee, 2d v.p. 1981-83). Office: U Chgo Dept Anthropology Haskell Hall M-306 Chicago IL 60637 Home: PO Box 369 Whitehall MT 59759

FREEMAN, LESLIE JEAN, neuropsychologist, researcher; b. San Diego, Feb. 17, 1965; d. Richard Joseph and Jean Doris (Weber) Currier; m. Drue Scott Freeman, Sept. 6, 1986. BA, U. Calif., Irvine, 1989; MA in Clin. Psychology, Antioch U., L.A., 1992; postgrad., Calif. Sch. Profl. Psychology, Fresno, 1993-98. Marriage, family and child counselor intern So. Calif. Counseling Ctr., L.A., 1990-93; marriage, family, child counselor intern/psychology intern Bakersfield (Calif.) Med. Hosp., 1993-94; intern, resident in neuropsychology pvt. practice and Drs. Hosp., Modesto, Calif., 1994-97; resident in neuropsychology VA Med. Ctr., Cleve., 1997-98; resident, fellow in neuropsychology U. Rochester (N.Y.) Med. Ctr., 1998—. Guest lectr. in field. Contbr. articles to profl. jours. Mem. APA, Nat. Acad. Neuropsychology, Internat. Neuropsychol. Soc., Am. Neuropsychiat. Assn., Calif. Assn. Marriage and Family Therapy, Calif. Assn. Psychology Providers. Avocations: collecting first edition mystery novels, collecting original animation art and disneyana, cooking, skiing, photography. Office: U Rochester Rochester NY 14642-0001

FREEMAN, LISA MARIE YACONO, psychologist; BA, Johns Hopkins U., 1994; MA, U. N.C., 1997, PhD, 2000. Lic. psychologist Bd. of Examiners Psychologists/Md., 2002. Predoctoral intern VAMHCS, Perry Point, Md., 1999—2000; postdoctoral fellow Johns Hopkins U. Sch. Medicine, Balt., 2000—02; psychologist EHP Behavioral Svcs., Balt., 2003—; pvt. practice psychology Columbia/Ellicott City, Md., 2003—. Mem.: Md. Psychol. Assn. (mem. bd. profl. practice 2004—). Office: 5054 Dorsey Hall Dr # 105 Ellicott City MD 21042 Office Phone: 410-992-5078.

FREEMAN, LOUIS S., lawyer; b. Cin., Apr. 21, 1940; s. Emanuel and Sadye (Harris) F.; m. Diane Ruth Edson, Jan. 28, 1967; children: Matthew E., James H., Jill E. BBA, U. Cin., 1963; JD, Harvard U., 1966; LLM in Taxation, NYU, 1972. Bar: Ohio 1966, N.Y. 1968, Ill. 1975. CPA. Mem. staff Coopers & Lybrand, N.Y.C., 1966-68; assoc. Mudge, Rose, Guthrie & Alexander, N.Y.C., 1968-74, Sonnenschein Nath & Rosenthal, Chgo., 1974-76, ptnr., 1976-97, Skadden, Arps, Slate, Meagher & Flom, Chgo., 1997—. Adj. prof. of taxation Ill. Inst. Tech., Chgo.-Kent Coll. of Law Grads. Program in Taxation, 1985-89 Mem. bds. of contbg. editors Jour. Corp. Taxation, Jour. Real Estate Taxation, Jour. Taxation of Investments; bd. advisors the M&A Tax Report, Jour. Corp. Taxation; also author articles. Fellow Am. Coll. Tax Counsel; mem. ABA (tax sect. com. on corp. tax), Chgo. Bar Assn., (chmn. exec. com. of fed. tax com. 1986-87), N.Y. Sate Bar Assn. (tax sect. exec. com. 1990-92), Am. Law Inst. (tax adv. group subchpt. C. Fed. Income Tax Project), Met. Club of Chgo. Office: Skadden Arps Slate Meagher & Flom 333 W Wacker Dr Chicago IL 60606-1220 Office Phone: 312-407-0650. Business E-Mail: LFreeman@skadden.com.

FREEMAN, MILTON MALCOLM ROLAND, anthropology educator; b. London, Apr. 23, 1934; arrived in Can., 1958; s. Louis and Fay (Bomberg) F.; m. Mini Christina Aodla; children: Graham, Elaine, Malcolm. BS, Reading U., Eng., 1958; postgrad., U. Coll., London, 1962-64; PhD, McGill U., 1965. Research scientist No. Affairs Dept., Ottawa, Ont., Can., 1965-67; asst. prof. Meml. U., St. John's, Nfld., Can., 1967-71, assoc. prof., 1971-72; dir. Inuit Land Use Study, Hamilton, Ont., 1973-75; prof. anthropology McMaster U., Hamilton, 1976-81; Henry Marshall Tory prof. U. Alta., Edmonton, Canada, 1982-99, prof. emeritus, 1999—, adj. prof. East Asian studies, 1993—99. Adj. prof. environ. studies U. Waterloo, Ont., 1977-81; sr. sci. advisor Indian and No. Affairs, Ottawa, 1979-81; sr. rsch. scholar Can. Circumpolar Inst., U. Alta., 1990—; McLean prof. Trent U., Peterborough, Can., 1995; chmn. UNESCO-MAB No. Sci. Network, 1983-88. Author: People Pollution, 1974, Cultural Anthropology of Whaling, 1989, Recovering Rights, 1992, Inuit, Whaling, and Sustainability, 1998; editor: Inuit Land Use and Occupancy Report, 1976, Procs. Internat. Symposium on Renewable Resources and the Economy of the North, 1981, Japanese Small-type Coastal Whaling, 1988, Endangered Peoples of the Arctic, 2000; co-editor: Adaptive Management of Marine Resources in the Pacific, 1991, Elephants and Whales: Resources for Whom?, 1994, Conservation Hunting: People and Wildlife in Canada's North, 2005 Bd. dirs. Sci. Inst. N.W.T., 1985-87; chmn. adv. bd. Can. Circumpolar Inst., 1990-2001; chmn. Man-Environ. Commn., Internat. Union Anthrop. and Ethnol. Scis., 1977-82. Fellow: Soc. Applied Anthropology Can. (pres. 1984—85), Soc. Applied Anthropology, Arctic Inst. N.Am., Am. Anthropol. Assn. Home: 103-10520 80th Ave Edmonton AB Canada T6E 1V3 Office: U Alta Can Circumpolar Inst Edmonton AB Canada T6G 0H1 Office Phone: 780-492-4682. E-mail: milton.freeman@ualberta.ca.

FREEMAN, MORGAN, actor; b. Memphis, June 1, 1937; s. Grafton Curtis and Mayme Edna (Revere) F.; m. Jeanette Adair Bradshaw, Oct. 22, 1967 (div. 1979); m. Myrna Colley-Lee, June 16, 1984; children: Alphonse, Saifoulaye, Deena, Morgana. Student, L.A. City Coll. Actor: (stage prodns.) Niggerlover (debut), 1967, Hello Dolly (Broadway), 1967, Jungle of Cities, 1969, The Recruiting Officer, 1969, Scuba-Duba, 1969, Purlie (ANTA Theatre, N.Y.C.), 1970, Black Visions, 1972, Sisyphus and the Blue-Eyed Cyclops, 1975, Cockfight, 1977, Mighty Gents, 1978 (Clarence Derwent award, Drama Desk award, Tony award nomination), White Pelicans, 1978, Coriolanus, also Julius (N.Y. Shakespeare Festival), 1979, Mother Courage and Her Children, 1980, Othello, also All's Well That Ends Well (both Dallas Shakespeare Festival), 1982, Buck, 1983, Medea and the Doll, 1984, The Gospel at Colonus (Obie awards), (feature films) Who Says I Can't Ride a Rainbow, 1971, Brubaker, 1980, Eyewitness, 1980, Harry and Son, 1983, Teachers, 1984, Street Smart, 1987 (Acad. award nomination), Clean and Sober, 1988, Lean On Me, 1989, Johnny Handsome, 1989, Driving Miss Daisy (Golden Globe award, Acad. award nomination), 1989, Glory, 1989, The Bonfire of the Vanities, 1990, Robin Hood, 1991, Unforgiven, 1992, The Shawshank Redemption, 1994 (Acad. award nomination), Outbreak, 1995, Seven, 1995, Chain Reaction, 1996, Moll Flanders, 1996, Deep Impact 1997, Kiss The Girls, 1997, The Long Way Home, 1996, Hard Rain, 1998, Water Damage, 1999, Under Suspicion, 1999, Mutiny, 1999, Nurse Betty, 2000, Along Came a Spider, 2001, High Crimes, 2002, The Sum of All Fears, 2002, Levity, 2003, Dreamcatcher, 2003, Bruce Almighty, 2003, Million Dollar Baby, 2004 (Outstanding performance by male actor in supporting role, Screen Actors Guild award, 2005, Academy award for best actor in a supporting role, 2005), Unleashed, 2005, Batman Begins, 2005, (narrator) War of the Worlds, 2005, (narrator) March of the Penguins, 2005, An Unfinished Life, 2005; dir. Bopha!, 1993; regular cast (TV show) The Electric Company, 1971-77; TV films include: Hollow Image, 1979, Attica, 1980, The Marva Collins Story, 1981, The Atlanta Child Murders, 1985, Resting Place, 1986, Flight for Life, 1987, Clinton and Nadine, 1988, Mutiny, 1999. With USAF, 1955-59. Former mechanic USAF.*

FREEMAN, NEAL BLACKWELL, communications corporation executive; b. NYC, July 5, 1940; s. Malcolm T. and Virginia (Neal) F.; m. Jane Louise Metze, Mar. 19, 1966; children: Malcolm Trowbridge II, James Bragdon, Kathryn R. BA magna cum laude, Yale U., 1962. Asst. to pres. Washington Star Syndicate, 1965-66; assoc. producer TV show Firing Line, 1966-67; exec. editor King Features Syndicate, N.Y.C., 1968-73; v.p., editor King Features div. Hearst Corp., 1973-76; pres. Jefferson Communications, Inc., 1976-86; chmn. bd., chief exec. officer Blackwell Corp., 1982—; dir. Intelsat, Ltd. Exec. prodr. Pub. TV; bd. dirs. Comsat Corp., BTG, Inc., Nat. Rev., Denver Nuggets Profl. Basketball Club, Colo. Avalanche Profl. Hockey Club, GRC Internat.; bd. visitors Inst. on Polit. Journ alism, Georgetown U.; chmn. Washington Selection Panel Pres.'s Commn. on White House Fellows, 1998-2002, Found. Mgmt. Inst., 2000—; chmn. of agts. Yale Alumni Fund; bd. dirs. Corp. for Pub. Broadcasting, 1972-75; bd. dirs., vice-chmn. Ethics and Pub. Policy Ctr. Bd. dirs. Wolf Trap Found., 1984-90. Mem. Colony Found., Cosmos Club (Washington), Yale Club (N.Y.C.), York Country Club (Maine), Nat. Press Club, Sigma Delta Chi. Office: The Blackwell Corp PO Box 320 York ME 03909

FREEMAN, PATRICIA ELIZABETH, multi-media specialist, educational consultant; b. El Dorado, Ark., Nov. 30, 1924; d. Herbert A. and M. Elizabeth (Pryor) Harper; m. Jack Freeman, June 15, 1949; 3 children. BA, Centenary Coll., 1943; postgrad., Fine Arts Ctr., 1942—46, Art Students League, 1944—45; BSLS, La. State U., 1946; postgrad., Calif. State U., 1959—61, U. N.Mex., 1964—74; EdS, Vanderbilt U., 1975. Libr. U. Calif., Berkeley, 1946-47; libr. Albuquerque Pub. Schs., 1964-67, ind. sch. libr. media ctr. cons., 1967—. One-woman shows include La. State Exhibit Bldg., 1948; author: Pathfinder: An Operational Guide for the School Librarian, 1975, Southeast Heights Neighborhoods of Albuquerque, 1993; compiler, editor: Elizabeth Pryor Harper's Twenty-One Southern Families, 1985; editor: SEHNA Gazette, 1988—93. Mem. task force Goals for Dallas-Environ., 1977—82; pres. Friends Sch. Librs., Dallas, 1979—83; v.p., editor S.E. Heights Neighborhood Assn., 1988—93. With USAF, 1948—49. Named honoree, AAUW Ednl. Found., 1979, 1996; recipient Vol. award for Outstanding Svc., Dallas Ind. Sch. Dist., 1978; AAUW Pub. Svc. grantee, 1980. Mem.: LWV (sec. Dallas 1982—83, editor Albuquerque 1984—86, editor Albuquerque/Bernalillo County Voters' Guide 1986, 1988, editor N.Mex. 2004—), AAUW (bd. dirs. Dallas 1976—82, bd. dirs. Albuquerque 1983—85, dir. N.Mex. editor 1999—, bd. dirs. Albuquerque 2003—), ALA, N.Mex Symphony Guild, Nat. Trust Historic Preservation, Friends Pub. Libr., Colorado Springs Fine Arts Ctr., Alpha Xi Delta. Home: 612 Ridgecrest Dr SE Albuquerque NM 87108-3365

FREEMAN, PETER SUNDERLIN, textile executive; b. Bklyn., Apr. 23, 1944; s. Graydon Lavern and Ruth Crosby (Sunderlin) F.; m. Linda Raissa Blanco, Sept. 23, 1972; 1 child, Victoria Blanco. BS, Cornell U., 1966; MBA in Fin., Syracuse U., 1969; cert. acctg., NYU, 1979. CPA, Colo. New bus. devel. and product mgr. CBS Pub. Group, N.Y.C., 1970-73; sr. fin. analyst W.R. Grace Retail and Textiles, N.Y.C., 1973-75; dir. fin. analysis and reporting Grace Textiles, N.Y.C., 1975-79, divsn. controller, 1979—81; v.p. fin. Toyobo subs. Rosewood Fabrics, N.Y.C., 1981-85; v.p. fin. and adminstrn. Vitreous Internat. Trading Co., Inc., Great Neck, N.Y., 1986; corp. contr. Liberty Fabrics, Inc., NYC, 1986—92, cons., 1993; v.p., fin. sec. Charles Samelson, Inc., NYC, 1995—. Served with U.S. Army, 1968-70, Vietnam. Mem. AICPA, Colo. Soc. CPA's, Cornell U. Lambda Alumni (pres. 1985-89, bd. dirs. 1982-96), Am. Life Fedn. (bd. dirs. 1997—, sec-treas. 2000—). Presbyterian. Avocations: sports, gardening. Home: 280 1st Ave Apt 5B New York NY 10009-1836 Office: Charles Samelson Inc 102 Madison Ave New York NY 10016-7417

FREEMAN, RALPH CARTER, investment banker, management consultant; b. La Grange, Ga. s. Ralph Carter and Alice (Cordell) F.; m. Carole Stephens, July 31, 1957 (div. 1977); children: Carter III, Allyson (dec.), Stephens, LeAnna; m. Nancy Lynn Brown, Apr. 8, 1977. BBA, Emory U., 1959. CPA, Mont.; cert. mgmt. cons.; real estate broker, Calif. Acct. Pannell Kerr Forster, Atlanta, Honolulu, 1959—72, ptnr., 1967—72; with Freeman and Noll Accts. and Auditors, 1962—66; mgmt. cons. Touche Ross & Co., Honolulu, Am. Samoa, Asia, South Pacific, 1972-75; pres. FP Industries, Inc., Hawaii, Mont., Ga., 1975-85, Janas Consulting, Huntsville, Ala. and San Francisco, Calif., 1986—95; chmn. Janas Assoc., China Specialist Investment Banking, Pasadena, Calif., 1995—. Founder Peoples Bank, LaGrange, Ga., 1966; founding investor Bank of Newnan, Ga., 1988, Profl. Bus. Bank, Pasadena, Calif., 2001—. Contbr. articles to profl. jours. and nat. trade mags. Mem. Inst. Mgmt. Cons. (cert., bd. dirs., treas. 1999-2000), All Cities Resource Group, Calif. Capital Market Pl., Sigma Alpha Epsilon. Avocations: fishing, tennis, camping. Office Phone: 626-432-7000. Business E-Mail: rcf@janascorp.com.

FREEMAN, RICHARD MERRELL, retired lawyer; b. Crawfordsville, Ind., July 2, 1921; s. F. Rider and Ruth (Merrell) F.; m. Joanne Spears, Nov. 26, 1943; children: Randy, Mark, Candy, Marcia. AB, Wabash (Ind.) Coll., 1943; LLB, Columbia U., 1948. Bar: Tenn. 1948, Ill. 1957. Atty. TVA, Knoxville, 1948-57, dir., 1978-86; partner firm Belnap, Spencer, Hardy & Freeman, Chgo., 1957-67; v.p. law Chgo. & Northwestern Transp. Co., Chgo., 1967-78, also dir., voting trustee. Exec. com. Fla. West Coast Symphony; bd. dirs. TVA, 1978-86. With USNR, 1943-46. Mem.: Phi Beta Kappa. Democrat. Mem. Community Ch. Home: 775 Longboat Club Rd #303 Longboat Key FL 34228

FREEMAN, ROBERT SCHOFIELD, musicologist, educator; b. Rochester, N.Y., Aug. 26, 1935; s. Henry Schofield and Florence Margaret (Knope) F.; m. Carol Jean Morgan, Dec. 10, 1976; children: John Frederick, Elizabeth Poon, Scott Alan Henry. AB summa cum laude, Harvard U., 1957; MFA, Princeton U., 1960, PhD, 1967; MusD (hon.), Hamilton Coll., 1988. Instr., asst. prof. Princeton U., 1963-68; asst. prof., assoc. prof. MIT, 1968-73; dir., prof. musicology Eastman Sch. Music, U. Rochester, 1972-96; pres. New England Conservatory, Boston, 1996-99; dean, Effie Marie Cain regents chair in fine arts Coll. Fine Arts U. Tex., Austin, 1999—. Chmn. nat. adv. bd. Ctr. for Black Music Research, Chgo., 1985-90; cons. for various Am. U.; vis. assoc. prof. Harvard U., 1972. Author: Opera Without Drama, 1981; contbr. articles to profl. jours. Trustee Conductors' Guild, China. Found. for Edn. and Culture. Harvard Sheldon fellow, 1958, Woodrow Wilson Found. fellow, 1959, Martha Baird Rockefeller Fund fellow, 1963, Fulbright fellow, 1960-62; recipient Civic medal Rochester C. of C., 1982. Mem. Am. Musicol. Soc. (chair New Eng. chpt. 1970-72, coun. mem. 1973-76), Coll. Music Soc. (coun. mem. 1973-76), Neue Bach Gesellschaft (chmn. 1977-82), Nat. Assn. Schs. Music (grad. commn. 1981-85), Harvard Music Assn., Headliner's Club of Austin, Princeton Club of N.Y., U. Tex. Club. Avocations: baseball, reading, animal welfare. Office: Coll Fine Arts U Tex at Austin Austin TX 78712 Office Phone: 512-475-7035. Personal E-mail: RF3519@aol.com. Business E-Mail: rsfreeman@mail.utexas.edu.

FREEMAN, SARAH ELISABETH, poet, literature and language educator; b. Chgo., May 21, 1971; d. Leslie Gordon and Susan Tax Freeman; m. Anthony Howard Swofford (div.). BA, Reed Coll., Portland, Oreg., 1993; MFA, U. Iowa Writer's Workshop, Iowa City, 2000. Fin. coord., program asst. Alliance of Artists' Communities, Portland, Oreg., 1997—98; instr., poetry writing U. Iowa, Iowa City, 1998—2000; secondary sch. tchr., humanities, Spanish, writing Scattergood Friends Sch., West Br., Iowa, 2000—01; instr., creative writing Cedar Rapids Recreation Dept., Cedar Rapids, 2001; tchr. English and Spanish Ctrl. Cath. HS, Portland, Oreg., 2001—03; tchr. English La Salle HS, Milwaukie, Oreg., 2003—. Lang. cons./adult edn. Lang. Co., Portland, Oreg., 1997—98, Fgn. Exch., Inc., Portland, Oreg., 1997—98; item writer ACT, Iowa City, 2001; admissions panelist Caldera Residency Program, Portland, Oreg., 2002—03; submissions reader Tin House Mag.,

Portland, Oreg., 2002—03. Co-editor: Loophole Mag., 2005; contbr. poems to mags. and jours. Recipient Artist Residency, Caldera, 2002, 2003; grantee Artist Grant, Iowa Arts Coun., 2001. Home: 4166A NE Beaumont Portland OR 97212

FREEMAN, SCOTT M., lawyer; b. 1959; AB in Econ., Harvard Univ., 1981; JD magna cum laude, Univ. Pa., 1984. Bar: NY 1985. Ptnr. mergers and acquisitions and securities offerings Sidley Austin Brown and Wood LLP, NYC, and mem. exec. com. Mem. adv. com. Ontario Securities Commn., 1995—99. Exec. editor Univ. Pa. Law Rev., 1983—84; contbr. articles to profl. journals. Mem.: Order of Coif. Office: Sidley Austin Brown & Wood LLP 787 Seventh Ave New York NY 10019 Office Phone: 212-839-7358. Office Fax: 212-839-5599. Business E-Mail: sfreeman@sidley.com.

FREEMAN, SHAREE M., federal agency administrator; b. N.Y. BA, St. Lawrence U.; JD, Georgetown U. Law clk. Norma Holloway Johnson U.S. Dist. Ct. D.C., Washington; asst. dist. atty. Phila., 1982—84; atty., Solicitor Gen. office U.S. Dept. Interior, 1984—97, acting asst. Solicitor Gen. Indian Legal Activities; counsel U.S. Ho. of Reps. Internat. Rels. Com., 1997—2001; dir. Cmty. Rels. Svc., U.S. Dept. Justice, Washington, 2001—. Trustee St. Lawrence Univ., 2003—. Office: Community Relations Service Suite 6000 600 E St NW Washington DC 20530*

FREEMAN, SHARON ELIZABETH, psychiatric clinical nurse specialist; b. Toledo, Sept. 26, 1955; d. Constantine Vincent Morgillo and Mary Elizabeth Dubry; m. David A. Cole, Feb. 18, 1984 (div. Oct. 18, 1993); 1 child, Heather Cole; m. Arthur Freeman, Apr. 29, 1997; children: April Stark, Laura Stone, Rebecca, Aaron, Andrew. BSN, Purdue U., 1991; MA Psychology, Adler Sch. Profl. Psychology, 1993; MSN, postgrad., U. Pa., 2000—; PhD, Canterbury U., 2002. Cert. advanced practice RN-CNS, addictions counselor. Program dir. Charter Med. Corp., Ft. Wayne, Ind., 1988—94; psychiat. nurse clinician John M. Rathburn, MD, PC, Ft. Wayne, 1994—97; assoc. faculty Purdue U., Ft. Wayne, 1995—97; corp. nurse recruiter U. Pa. Health Sys., Phila., 1997—99; clin. program dir. U. Pa. Presbyn. Med. Ctr., Phila., 1999—; invited faculty U. Pa. Sch. Medicine, Phila., 2001. Pres. Adler Assn., Ft. Wayne, 1992—94; assoc. faculty Adler Sch. Profl. Psychiatry, Ft. Wayne, 1992—94. Peer reviewer: AACN-Clin. Issues Jour., 2000—. Mem.: Ind. Assn. Alcohol/Drug Counselors (bd. dirs. 1993—97), Pa. Assn. Alcohol/Drug Abuse Counselors (pres. 2000—03), Assn. for Addiction Profls. (pres. elect 2004—), Am. Psychiat. Nurses Assn., Sigma Theta Tau. Roman Catholic. Office: Ctr For Brief Therapy 10314 Dawsons Creek Blvd Ste J Fort Wayne IN 46825 Personal E-mail: MorgilloFreeman@aol.com.

FREEMAN, SIDNEY LEE, minister; b. Madison, Wis., Jan. 23, 1927; s. Jack and Gertrude (Kaifetz) F.; m. Evelyn Marie Gronberg, Feb. 3, 1950 (div. 1965); children: Lynn Claire, David Eugene, Michael John; m. Gaynell Bradley, Apr. 28, 1967. BS, U. Wis., 1947; MA, Bowling Green State U., 1949; PhD, Cornell U., 1951. Ordained to ministry Unitarian Universalist Assn., 1957. Min. Unitarian Ch. Charlotte, N.C., 1957-89, min. emeritus, 1989—. Instr. comm. arts Ctrl. Piedmont C.C., Charlotte, part-time 1987—; chaplain Cedar Spring Hosp., Pineville, N.C., part-time 1989-98; pres. So. Unitarian Coun., Atlanta, 1953, Thomas Jefferson Unitarian Dist., Charlotte, 1963-64; lectr. Albert Schweitzer Coll., Churwalden, Switzerland, summer 1959, Starr King Sch. for Ministry, Berkeley, Calif., summer 1965. Pres. Charlotte Mental Health Assn., 1978-80; chair consulting bd. Cedar Spring Hosp., Pineville, N.C., 1993-98. Recipient Disting. Svc. award Charlotte Mental Health Assn., 1983, Part-time Faculty Excellence award Ctrl. Piedmont C.C., 2005. Mem. Unitarian Universalist Mins. Assn. (past sec.), Charlotte Area Clergy Assn. (past com.). Home: 4500 Rockford Ct Charlotte NC 28209-2924 *I try to live by the truth that sets us free, the hope that never dies, and the love that casts out fear.*

FREEMAN, SUSAN TAX, anthropologist, educator, culinary historian; b. Chgo., May 24, 1938; d. Sol and Gertrude Tax.; m. Leslie G. Freeman, Jr., Mar. 20, 1964; 1 dau., Sarah Elisabeth. BA, U. Chgo., 1958; MA, Harvard U., 1959, PhD, 1965. Asst. prof. anthropology U. Ill., Chgo., 1965-70, assoc. prof., 1970-78, prof., 1978—, prof. emerita, 1999—, chmn., 1979-82. Rsch. assoc. dept. sociology and anthropology Mont. State U., Bozeman, 1992—; panelist NEH, Council for Internat. Exchange of Scholars; mem. anthropology screening com. Fulbright-Hays Research Awards, 1975-78; mem. ad hoc com. on research in Spain Spain-U.S.A. Friendship Agreement, various yrs., 1977-84; field researcher Mex., 1959, Spain, 1962—, Japan, 1983; instr. Radcliffe Coll. Seminars on Food in History and Culture, 1998. Author: Neighbors: The Social Contract in a Castilian Hamlet, 1970, The Pasiegos: Spaniards in No Man's Land, 1979; assoc. editor: Am. Anthropologist, 1971-73, Am. Ethnologist, 1974-76; editl. bd. Gastronomica, 2000—. Fellow Inst. for the Humanities, U. Ill. Chgo., 1987-88; Wenner-Gren Found. for Anthrop. Research grantee, 1966, 83; NIMH grantee, 1967, 68-71; NEH fellowships, 1978-79, 89-90. Fellow Am. Anthrop. Assn. (nominating com. 1981-82, Centennial Adv. Commn. 1999-2002), Royal Anthrop. Inst. Gt. Britain and Ireland; mem. Soc. for Anthropology of Europe (exec. com. 1987-88), Soc. Spanish and Portuguese Hist. Studies (exec. com. 1990-92), Coun. European Studies (steering com. 1980-83), Internat. Inst. Spain (corporator, bd. dirs. 1982-87, 2000-2003), Centro Estudios Sorianos (hon.), Assn. Anthropologia Castilla y Leon (hon.). Home: PO Box 369 Whitehall MT 59759 Office: U Ill Dept Anthro M/C 027 1007 W Harrison St Chicago IL 60607-7135 Office Phone: 312-413-3570.

FREEMAN, THEODORE MONROE, physician; b. Orlando, Fla., Jan. 3, 1955; s. Fred Monroe and Mary Ann (Ridgeway) F.; m. Karen Bonaccorso, Aug. 11, 1978; children: Kathryn Maria, Michelle Terese, Jeannine Nicole, Jason Monroe. BS in Chemistry, Duke U., 1977; MD, U. So. Fla., 1980. Diplomate Am. Bd. Internal Medicine, Am. Bd. Allergy and Immunology. Intern Jacksonville (Fla.) U. Hosp., 1980-81; commd. capt. USAF, 1981, advanced through grades to col., resident internal medicine Keesler AFB Biloxi, Miss., 1981-83, staff physician Dyess AFB Abilene, Tex., 1983-84, fellow allergy and immunology Wilford Hall Med. Ctr., Lackland AFB San Antonio, 1984-86, fellow diagnostic lab. immunology Mass. Gen. Hosp. Boston, 1986-87, staff allergist and immunology Wilford Hall Med. Ctr., 1987-89, chmn. dept. allergy and immunology, program dir., 1989—2001. Med. dir. transplants Wilford Hall Med. Ctr., 1989-2002. Contbr. articles to profl. jours. Fellow ACP, Am. Coll. Allergy and Immunology, Am. Acad. Allergy and Immunology; mem. AMA, Soc. Air Force Physicians. Roman Catholic. Office Phone: 210-614-3923. Personal E-mail: tfree95900@aol.com. Business E-Mail: docfreeman@sanantonioallergydoc.com.

FREEMAN, TOM M., lawyer; b. Wauwatosa, Wis., Oct. 5, 1952; s. Max and Betty J. (Zimmerman) F.; m. Judith Casper, June 23, 1974; children: Sarah Carolyn, Benjamin Robert. BA with honors, U. Wis., 1974; JD cum laude, Harvard U., 1977. Bar: Wis. 1977, Ill. 1978, Calif. 1980, U.S. Dist. Ct. (we. dist.) Wis. 1977, U.S. Ct. Appeals (7th cir.) 1978, U.S. Dist. Ct. (no. dist.) Calif. 1980, U.S. Ct. Appeals (9th cir.) 1982. Law clk. Wis. Supreme Ct., Madison, 1977-78; staff atty. U.S. Ct. Appeals (7th cir.), Chgo., 1978-80; assoc. Brobeck, Phleger, Harrison, LLP, San Francisco, 1980-85, ptnr., 1985—2003, Morgan, Lewis & Bockius LLP, 2003—. Republican. Jewish. Office: Morgan Lewis & Bockius LLP Spear St Tower 1 Market San Francisco CA 94105 Office Phone: 415-442-1128. E-mail: tfreeman@morganlewis.com.

FREEMARK, MICHAEL SCOTT, pediatric endocrinologist, educator; b. Phila., Dec. 10, 1950; s. Morton and Molly (Blumberg) F.; m. Anne R. Slifkin, May 8, 1979; children: Samara, Yonah. BA magna cum laude, Brandeis U., 1972; postgrad., Temple U., 1972-74; MD, Duke U., 1976. Diplomate Am. Bd. Pediatrics, subspecialty bds. pediatric endocrinology, Nat. Bd. Med. Examiners; lic. physician, N.C. From resident pediatrics to prof. Duke U. Med. Ctr., Durham, NC, 1976—2003, prof. pediats., 2003—, chief pediatric endocrine divsn., 1991—. Moderator Duke Disputation Forum, 2003—; med. dir. Pediatric Clinics, Harnett and Hoke Counties, NC, 1979-80; ad hoc reviewer human embryology and devel. study sect. NIH, 1989-90; dir. weekly endocrine and pediatric fellows rsch. seminars; lectr. in field. Mem. editl. bd.: Jour. Clin. Endocrinology and Metabolism, 1990—93, 2000—, Endocrinology, 1998—; contbr. numerous articles and abstracts to profl. jours. and chpts. to books. Bd. dirs. Durham Nursery Sch. Assn., 1983-88; chmn. People's Alliance Subcom. on Pub. Edn.; mem. Durham County Commn. Merger Issues Task Force, 1988-89; tchr. Triangle Children's Shule, Chapel Hill, N.C., Durham Co. Comm. Child Protection Team, 1994-96. Recipient NIH-Nat. Rsch. Svc. award, 1982-85, NIH Clin. Investigator award, 1985-88, Rsch. award March of Dimes, 1988-92, NIH Rsch. Career Devel. award, 1990—; March of Dimes-Basil O'Connor Starter grantee, 1985-87, Trent Found. grantee, 1984-85, NIH grantee, 1988—; USEPA fellow, 1972, USPHS fellow, 1974, 75, Fogarty fellow, Paris, 1993. Mem. Am. Fedn. Clin. Rsch., N.C. Med. Assn., Am. Acad. Pediatrics, Endocrine Soc., Lawson-Wilkins Pediatric Endocrine Soc. (chair program com. 1991-94, chair drug and therapeutics com. 1999—), Soc. for Pediatric Rsch. (coun. endocrinology, metabolism and nephrology 1991-94). Home: 1309 Oakland Ave Durham NC 27705-3243 Office: Duke Univ Med Ctr PO Box 3080 Durham NC 27710-0001 Office Phone: 919-681-1848. Business E-Mail: freem001@mc.duke.edu.

FREER, COBURN, language educator; b. New Orleans, Nov. 5, 1939; s. Wilbert Coburn and Lillian Jackson (Hicks) F.; m. Ramona Jean Salminen; children: Meagan, Elinor. BA, Lewis and Clark Coll., 1960; PhD, U. Washington, 1967. Instr. U. Ariz., Tucson, 1965-67; asst. prof to prof. U. Mont., Missoula, 1967-80; head dept. U. Ga., Athens, 1980-92, prof., 1980—. Author: Music for a King, 1972, The Poetics of Jacobean Drama, 1981; contbr. articles to profl. jours. Recipient Sr. Fulbright-Hays lectureship U. Oulu, Finland, 1971-72, NEH fellowship, London, 1974-75. Mem. MLA, Internat. Assn. Univ. Profs. English, Milton Soc., South Atlantic MLA, Southeast Renaissance Conf. Home: 400 Saint George Dr Athens GA 30606-3940 Office: Univ Ga Dept English Athens GA 30602

FREER, ROBERT ELLIOTT, JR., lawyer; b. Washington, Jan. 19, 1941; s. Robert E. and Alice (Barry) F.; m. Roberta Stapleton Renchard, Dec. 31, 1972; children: Kimberly Dunlap, R. Elliott III, Ashleigh Hamilton, Daniel Renchard. AB, Princeton U., 1963; JD, U. Va., 1966. Bar: Va. 1966, D.C. 1968, U.S. Supreme Ct. 1973. Trial atty. FTC, 1966-69, atty. advisor to chmn., asst. to gen. counsel, 1969—71; exec. asst. to gen. counsel U.S. Dept. Transp., Washington, 1971-74; Washington counsel Kimberly Clark Corp., 1974-83; staff v.p., 1975-80; corp. v.p., 1980-84; gen. counsel Roswell, Ga., 1983-84; pvt. practice Washington, 1984-2000; corp. cons., 2000—02; founder Free Enterprise Found., 2002—; spl. correspondent Charleston (S.C.) Mercury, 2005—. Mem. President's Commn. on White House Fellowships, 1985-93; pub. mem. Adminstrv. Conf. U.S., 1981-86; capt. land team President's Pvt. Sector Survey on Cost Control in Fedn. Govt., 1982-83; sec., gen. counsel U.S.-Cuba Bus. Coun., 1994-2000; visiting prof. Citadel Sch. Bus. Adminstrn., 2004-. Contbg. author, editor: Finding Our Roots/Facing Our Future: America in the 21st Century, 1997; contbr. articles to profl. jours. Founder, chmn. bd. trustees Washington Episc. Sch., 1986-94, chmn. emeritus, 1994—; chmn. bd. visitors Regent U. Sch. Law, 1995-2004; trustee Corcoran Gallery Art, 1986-93, asst. sec., chmn. bylaws com., 1990, sec., 1991; bd. trustees, pres. and CEO Free Enterprise Found., 2002—; chmn. Lawyers for the Republic, 1988-2005; asst. gen. counsel Rep. Nat. Conv., 1988, 92, 96; mem. Parents coun. Coll. Charleston, 1997, chmn., 2000-02. Mem. Rep. Nat. Lawyers Assn. (bd. govs. 1985-2000, gen. counsel 1985-89, vice chmn. 1988-89), Washington Met. Area Corp. Counsel Assn. (founder, pres. 1980-81, bd. dirs. 1980-84), Rotary Club Charleston. Office: Free Enterprise Found PO Box 21569 Charleston SC 29413 Business E-Mail: robert.freer@citadel.edu.

FREERS, STEVEN GEORGE, lawyer; b. Indpls., Jan. 8, 1949; s. Howard P. and Eleanor (Reeder) F.; m. Christine Helena Lamos, Sept. 5, 1970; 4 children. JD, Wayne State U., 1974. Bar: Mich. 1974. Ptnr. Binkowski & Freers, Warren, Mich., 1979-85. Mem. Elks (sec. bldg. corp.). Home: 32749 Rugby Dr Warren MI 48088-6941 Office: 31730 Hoover Rd Ste C Warren MI 48093-1700 Office Phone: 586-795-4150. E-mail: freerslaw@aol.com.

FREESE, ANDREW, neurosurgeon, educator; b. Boston, July 4, 1959; s. Ernst and Elisabeth (Bautz) F.; m. Marcia Geary, June 14, 1986; children: John Alexander, Elisabeth Marguerite, Ernst Timothy, Matthew Andrew. BA, Harvard U., 1981; MD, Harvard U., Boston, 1990; PhD, MIT, 1990. Lic. physican, Pa.; trauma cert. Rsch. assoc. NIH, Bethesda, Md., 1982-83; surg. intern U. Pa., Phila., 1990-91, neurosurgery resident, 1991-97, dir. Lab. Molecular Neurosurgery Grad. Hosp., 1994-97, mem. Inst. Human Gene Therapy, 1994—97; assoc. prof. neurosurgery, dir. neurosurgery rsch. Thomas Jefferson U., Phila., 1997—2003, vice chmn. neurosurgery, 2000—03, assoc. dir CNS Gene Therapy Ctr., 1998—2002; prof. Drexel U. Coll. Medicine, 2003—04; prof. of neurosurgery U. Minn., 2004—. Vis. scientist Wistar Inst., Phila., 1994-95; pres. Neurel, Inc., Boston, 1987-88, sci. dir., 1988-90; cons. Polykinetix, Inc., N.Y.C., 1993; exec. dir. Parkinson's Disease Gene Therapy Consortium; vice chmn. neurosurgery U. Minn., 2004-, dir. spine surgery, 2004-. Editor: Biotechnology Processing, 1988, Neurological Disorders: Novel Experimental and Therapeutic Approaches, 1992; editor spl. issue Exptl. Neurology, 1997; contbr. articles to profl. jours. Fellow Sigma Xi; mem. AMA, Internat. Brain Rsch. Orgn., Soc. Neurosci., Congress Neurol. Surgeons, Controlled Release Soc. Achievements include patents for controlling the release of drugs using drug delivery system for neurological disorders; one of the first viral vector systems to deliver genes into neurons; the demonstration of the precursor effect on brain kynurenines; gene therapy for Parkinson's disease, epilepsy, pituitary adenomas, neurogenetic disorders, and stroke. Home: 2914 Casco Poin Rd Wayzata MN 55391 Office: Dept Neurosurgery Univ of Minnesota 420 Delaware St SE Mayo Memorial Bldg Minneapolis MN 55455

FREESE, KATHERINE, physicist, researcher; b. Freiburg, Germany, Feb. 8, 1957; came to U.S., 1957; d. Ernst and Elisabeth Gertrude Maria (Bautz) F.; 1 child, Douglas Quincy Adams. BA, Princeton U., 1977; MA, Columbia U., 1981; PhD, U. Chgo., 1984. Postdoctoral fellow Harvard/Smithsonian Ctr. for Astrophysics, Cambridge, Mass., 1984-85, Inst. for Theoretical Physics, Santa Barbara, Calif., 1985-87, U. Calif., Berkeley, 1987-88; asst. prof. physics MIT, Cambridge, 1988-91; prof. physics U. Mich., Ann Arbor, 1991—. Gen. mem. Aspen Ctr. for Physics, 1991—; bd. dirs. Inst. for Theoretical Physics. Contbr. articles to profl. jours. William Rainey Harper fellow U. Chgo, 1982; Sloan Found. fellow, 1989; Presdl. Young Investigator NSF, 1990, rsch. grantee, 1991, 94; Presdl. fellow U. Calif., 1987. Mem. Am. Phys. Soc., Assn. for Women in Sci. Democrat. Avocations: water polo, swimming, skiing, tennis. Office: U Mich Dept Physics Ann Arbor MI 48109

FREESE, MELANIE LOUISE, librarian, educator; b. Mineola, N.Y., May 12, 1945; d. Walter Christian and Agnes Elizabeth (Jensen) F. BS in Elem. Edn., Hofstra U., 1967, MA in Elem. Edn., 1969; MLS, L.I. U., 1977. Cert. tchr., N.Y. Bibliographic searcher acquisitions dept. Adelphi U. Swirbul Libr., Garden City, NY, 1973—79, res. desk libr., 1979—83; catalog libr., assoc. prof. Hofstra U. Axinn Libr., Hempstead, NY, 1984—, asst. dean, chair libr. tech. svcs., 1998—2000, sr. cataloger, 2000—. Ch. librarian St. Peters Evang. Luth. Ch., Baldwin, N.Y., 1977—. Founder libr. Salvation Army Wayside Home and Sch. for Girls, Valley Stream, N.Y., 1993. Mem. ALA, Nassau County Libr. Assn. (corr. sec. acad. and spl. librs. divsn. 1986-88, v.p., pres.-elect 1989-90, pres. 1991), Bus. and Profl. Women's Club (pres. Nassau County chpt. 1990-92, 95-97, Woman of Yr. 1994). Republican. Avocations: needlecrafts, knitting, crocheting. Office: Hofstra U Axinn Library 1000 Fulton Ave Hempstead NY 11550-1030 Office Phone: 516-463-6423. Business E-Mail: melanie-l-free@hofstra.edu.

FREESE, RICH, marketing executive; m. Karen Kreiger. Sr. v.p. sales, mktg. Nat. Book Network; pres., CEO Motorbooks, St. Paul, 2001—03; pres. Publishers Group West, Berkeley, Calif., 2003—. Exec. com. The Quills. Office: Publishers Group West 1700 Fourth St Berkeley CA 94710 Office Phone: 510-528-1444, 800-788-3123. Office Fax: 510-528-3444. Business E-Mail: info@pgw.com.*

FREGETTO, EUGENE FLETCHER, finance educator; b. Milw., Oct. 18, 1947; s. Fletcher Eugene and Eva Mary F.; m. Judith Ann Shafel, Dec. 26, 1969; children: Katherine Ann, Julie Lynn. Student, Mich. State U., 1965-67; BA in Journalism, Marquette U., 1970; AS in Architecture and Structural Engring., Milw. Sch. Engring., 1972; MBA in Mktg., De Paul U., 1983; PhD in Pub. Policy Analysis, U. Ill., Chgo., 1997. Tech. writer Chemetron Corp., Chgo., 1972-73; specification engr. Chgo. Transit Authority, 1973-83, procurement engr., 1983-84, sr. procurement engr., 1984-88, supt. procurement engrs., 1988-89, sr. contract adminstr., 1990-97; lectr. mktg. U. Ill., Chgo., 1983—2004, clin. assoc. prof. mktg., 2005—. Lectr. in mgmt. De Paul U., Chgo., 1983-91, co-developer grad. entrepreneurship program, purchasing mgmt. program, De Paul U.; founder, pres. MidwestTechnology Access Group, Inc., 1992—; assoc. clin. prof. mktg. U. Ill., Chgo., 2005—. Contbr. articles profl. jours. Civil Svc. Commnr. City of Des Plaines, Ill., 1989—92. Athletic scholar Mich. State U., 1965; scholar Milw. Sch. Engring., 1970-72. Fellow U.S. Assn. for Small Bus. and Entrepreneurship (founding, v.p. fin. 1983-90); mem. Nat. Assn. Purchasing Mgmt. (cert.), Purchasing Mgrs. Assn. Chgo. (chmn. 1986-91), Ill. Assn. Pub. Procurement Officials. Avocations: photography, fishing, hunting, camping. Home: 800 Laurel Ave Des Plaines IL 60016-7121 Office: U Ill at Chgo Managerial Studies Dept (M/C 243) 601 S Morgan St Chicago IL 60607 Office Phone: 312-413-0446. Business E-Mail: fregetto@uic.edu, fregetto@mtag.org.

FREGO, GEORGIA KAYE, elementary school educator; b. Blytheville, Ark., May 16, 1956; d. George and Faye Siebert; m. James R. Frego, Oct. 2, 1987; children: Heather, Seth. EdB, Ark. State U., 1978. Tchr. Cedar Pk. Elem., Trumann, Ark., 1978—85, Valley View Elem., Jonesboro, Ark., 1985—88, Westside Elem., Jonesboro, 1989—. Office: Westside Elem Sch 1834 Hwy 91 W Jonesboro AR 72404-9285

FREHSE, BECKY ANN, artist, art educator; b. Harvard, Ill., Jan. 23, 1955; d. Gerald Donald and Sally Mareta (Stock) F.; m. Gregory Livingston Youtz, Nov. 28, 1987; children: Katherine Violet Youtz, Clara Jade Youtz. BFA, Ariz. State U., 1980; MFA, Ctrl. Wash. U., 1984. Artist in residence Wash. State Arts Commn., Olympia, Wash., 1984-85; lectr. and artist in residence Pacific Luth. U., Tacoma, 1986-94, dir. The Women's Ctr., 1992-95; art instr. Charles Wright Acad., Tacoma, 1995—2000; artist in residence Wash. State Arts Commn., Olympia, Wash., 2001—. Tchr., artist-mentor Arts Impact in Edn. Artist; exhibits nationally; affiliated with The Sandpiper Gallery, Tacoma, Wash. Vol. Peace Corps, Tunis, Tunisia, 1985-86. Grants Artists Program grantee Artist Trust, Seattle, 1995. Mem. AAUW, NOW, Womens Caucus for Art (del. and panelist at 4th U.N. Non-Govt. Orgn. Forum, Huairou, People's Rep. China, 1995). E-mail: Becky@tacoma.com.

FREI, BRENT R., computer software executive; BS in Engrg., Dartmouth Coll., Hanover, N.H., 1989; MS, Dartmouth Coll. Mech. engr. Motorola Corp., 1989-90; progammer analyst Microsoft Info. Tech. Group, 1991-94; dir. ONYX, 1994—, pres., sec., treas., 1995-98, pres., CEO, Chmn., 1998—.

FREI, EMIL, III, physician, medical researcher, medical educator; b. St. Louis, 1924; m. Elizabeth Smith (dec. Apr. 1986); children: Mary, Emil, Alice, Nancy, Judy; m. Adoria Smetana Brock, May 1987; stepchildren: Stephen, Francis, Peter, Vincent, John. MD, Yale U., 1948. Diplomate Am. Bd. Internal Medicine, Am. Bd. Med. Oncology. Intern St. Louis U. Hosp., 1948—49; resident in pathology Barnes Hosp., St. Louis, 1952—53; resident in internal medicine St. Louis U., 1953—54, VA Hosp., St. Louis, 1954—55; chief gen. medicine br. Nat. Cancer Inst., Bethesda, Md., 1955—65; head devel. therapeutics, assoc. dir. M.D. Anderson Hosp. and Tumor Inst., Houston, 1965—72; dir., physician-in-chief Children's Cancer Research Found. (now Dana-Farber Cancer Inst.), Boston, 1972—91; physician-in-chief emeritus Dana-Farber Cancer Inst., 1991—; prof. medicine Med. Sch. Harvard U., Boston, 1972—, Richard and Susan Smith prof. medicine, 1985, Richard and Susan Smith disting. prof. medicine, 1994—; nat. cons. in internal medicine-oncology USAF, 1968—72; mem. Eleanor Roosevelt internat. cancer fellowships com. Internat. Union Against Cancer, 1968—72; chmn. anti-neoplastic disease drug panel, drug efficacy study NAS, 1968—72; nat. cons. in internal medicine-oncology USAF. Mem. bd. sci. counselors Nat. Cancer Inst., 1986—90, mem. Presdl. Commn. for New Drugs for Cancer and AIDS, 1988—90; chmn. antitumor drug panel NAS, 1996. Lt. M.C. USNR, 1950—52. Recipient Lasker award, 1972, Lila W. Gruber award, 1979, Kettering prize, GM, 1983, Hamao Umezawa award, 1985, Armand Hammer Cancer Rsch. award, 1989, Disting. Alumnus award, NIH, 1990, Emil Frei III professorship in medicine, 1992, Morse award, 1996, Sidney Farber medal for contbns. to cancer rsch., 1998, 50th Anniversary Commemorative award, Leukemia Soc. Am., 1999, La Medaille de la Ville de Paris, 2000, Claude Jacquillat award, 2002, Pollin prize in pediatric rsch., 2003, Lifetime Achievement in Cancer Rsch., Am. Assn. Cancer Rsch., 2004. Fellow: ACP, Am. Acad. Arts and Scis.; mem.: AMA, Icon of Oncology (mem. 2003), Nat. Acad. Medicine, Inst. of Medicine, Assn. Am. Physicians, Am. Soc. Clin. Investigation, Am. Soc. Hematology, Am. Cancer Soc. (ann. Nat. award 1981), Am. Soc. Clin. Oncology (pres. 1968—69, Disting. Scientist award 1992), Am. Assn. for Cancer Rsch. (past pres., Lifetime Achievement in Cancer Rsch. award 2004). Office: Dana Farber Cancer Inst Physician in Chief emeritus D-1618 44 Binney St Boston MA 02115-6084

FREIBAUM, BERNARD, real estate development company executive; b. 1953; V.p. fin. Stein & Co., sr. v.p. fin., CFO, 1988-93; CFO, contr. Gen. Growth Properties, Inc., Des Moines, 1993—. Office: Gen Growth Properties Inc 110 N Wacker Dr Chicago IL 60606-1511

FREIBERG, ROBERT JERRY, engineering executive; b. Chgo., Mar. 26, 1939; s. Jerry and Mildred (Lukes) F.; m. Deanna Corrine Qualls, July 8, 1968; children: Joseph, Sean, Jamison. BS in Physics, Rensselear Poly. Inst., 1961; MS in Physics, U. Ill., 1963, PhD, 1966. Postgrad. rsch. assoc. U. Ill., Urbana, 1966-67; rsch. scientist Hughes Rsch. Labs., Malibu, Calif., 1967-69; group mgr. United Tech. Rsch. Labs., East Hartford, Conn., 1969-75; gen. mgr. United Tech. Optical Sys., West Palm Beach, Fla., 1975-79; bus. mgr. optics TRW, Redondo Beach, Calif., 1979-83; program dir. Baxter Healthcare, Inc., Irvine, Calif., 1983-86; dir. engring. and mfg. ops. Pfizer Laser Sys., Irvine, 1986-92; dir. engring. Lumonics, Inc., Camarillo, Calif., 1992-94; sr. v.p. engring. and program mgmt. View Engring., Inc., Simi Valley, Calif., 1994-97; v.p. engring. Indsl. Electronic Engrs. Inc., Van Nuys, Calif., 1997-2000; v.p. engr. Knowledge Universe, Inc., Los Gatos, Calif., 2000—05. Gen. ptnr., sr. tech. cons. Internat. Mktg. and Cons. Assocs., Kalispell, Mont., 1991—92; chmn. tech. adv. bd. Premier Laser Sys., Irvine, 2001—; bd. dirs. SurgiLight, Orlando, Fla.; presenter in field. Contbr. numerous articles to Procs. IEEE, Laser Focus, Applied Optics, IEEE Jour. Quantum Electronics, Jour. Applied Physics, Phys. Rev., Applied Physics Letters, Bull. Am. Phys. Soc. Asst. scoutmaster Boy Scouts Am., Mission Viejo, Calif., 1989-92, varsity scoutmaster, Newbury Park, Calif., 1994-96. Fellow NSF, 1962-66. Fellow Internat. Soc. for Optical Engring. (mem. membership com. 1994-99, chmn. 1994-96); mem. IEEE, Am. Electronics Assn., Optical Soc. Am., Am. Soc. for Laser Surgery and Medicine, Nat. Ctr. Mfg. Scis. (Strategic Initiative Group com. 1995-97), Soc. Info. Displays, Sigma Xi. Achievements include numerous patents for surgical lasers, endoscopic instrumentation, medical catheters, novel optical resonators, laser devices, and diagnostic instruments. Home: 112 River View Dr Kalispell MT 59901 Personal E-mail: rjfreiberg@netscape.net.

FREIBERG, STEVEN J., diversified financial services company executive; m. Neena Freiberg; 2 children. BS in Econs., MBA. Mgmt. assoc. card products divsn. Citigroup, 1980, mktg., bus. planning, mgmt. scis. and fin.

positions, 1980—85, CFO, 1985—87; founding dir., CFO, chief investment officer, nat. sales dir. Citicorp Investment Svcs., 1987—92, mem. corp.-wide task force, 1992—93; mgr. distbn. Consumer Bank, 1993—95; CEO Citicorp Investment Svcs., Citicorp Ins. Group, 1995—97; mgr. strategic bus. groups credit card divsn. Citigroup Inc., 1997—; chmn., CEO Citi Cards N.A. Bd. dirs. Citicorp Credit Svcs., Inc., Citicorp Investment Svcs., Citicorp Ins. Group, Citibank Trust N.A., Citibank FS.B, MasterCard, DMA, NYU Mgmt. Decision Lab. Office: Citigroup Inc 399 Park Ave New York NY 10043

FREIBERGER, WALTER FREDERICK, mathematics professor, actuarial science consultant; b. Vienna, Feb. 20, 1924; came to U.S., 1955, naturalized, 1962. s. Felix and Irene (Tagany) F.; m. Christine Mildred Holmberg, Oct. 6, 1956; children: Christopher Allan, Andrew James, Nils H. BA, U. Melbourne, 1947, MA, 1949; PhD, U. Cambridge, Eng., 1953. Rsch. officer Aero. Rsch. Lab. Australian Dept. Supply, 1947-49, sr. sci. rsch. officer, 1953-55; tutor U. Melbourne, 1947-49, 53-55; asst. prof. divsn. applied math. Brown U., 1956-58, assoc. prof., 1958-64, prof., 1964—2002; prof. applied math., prof. cmty. health Brown U. Med. Sch., 1994—2002; prof. emeritus applied math, comm. math Brown U., 2002—, dir. Computing Center, 1963-69, dir. Ctr. for Computer and Info. Scis., 1969-76, chmn. divsn. applied math., 1976-82, chmn. grad. com., 1985-88, assoc. chmn. divsn. applied math., 1988-91, chmn. univ. ctr. for statis. sci., 1991—2002; joint appointment Brown U. Med. Sch., 1994—2002. Fmr. lectr., cons. program in applied actuarial sci. Bryant Coll.; joint appointment as prof. cmty. health Sch. Medicine Brown U., 1994-2002; mem. fellowship selection panel NSF, Fulbright fellowship selection panel; mem. Rep. Nat. Com. Author: (with U. Grenander) A Short Course in Computational Probability and Statistics, 1971; editor: The International Dictionary of Applied Mathematics, 1960, (with others) Applications of Digital Computers, 1963, Advances in Computers, Volume 10, 1970, Statistical Computer Performance Evaluation, 1972; mng. editor: Quarterly of Applied Mathematics, 1965—; Contbr. numerous articles to profl. jours. Served with Australian Army, 1943-45. Fulbright fellow, 1955-56; Guggenheim fellow, 1962-63; grantee NSF Office Naval Rsch. NIH. Mem. Am. Math. Soc. (assoc. editor Math. Reviews 1957-62), Soc. for Indsl. and Applied Math., Am. Statis. Assn., Inst. Math. Stats., Assn. Computing Machinery, Bristol Yacht Club, Univ. Club. Republican. Episcopalian. Home: 24 Alumni Ave Providence RI 02906-2310 Office: Box F Brown U 182 George St Providence RI 02912-9056 Business E-Mail: Walter_Freiberger@Brown.edu.

FREIDBERG, STEPHEN ROY, neurosurgeon; b. Bklyn., Oct. 16, 1934; s. Leslie Max and Bess Bernblum; m. Helen Deorsay, May 1, 1964; children: Michael, Jonathan. AB, U. Pa., Phila., 1956; MD, Albert Einstein Coll., 1960. Intern U. Okla. Hosp., 1960-61; resident King's County Hosp., Bklyn., 1964-68; fellow Nat. Hosp. Queen's Sq., London, 1965; staff physician Lahey Clinic Med. Ctr., Burlington, Mass., 1969—, chmn. divsn. surgery, 1995—2003. Chmn. dept. neurosurgery Lahey Clinic Med. Ctr., Burlington, 1984-2005, bd. govs., 1978-2003. Contbr. articles to profl. jours. Capt. U.S. Army, 1962-64. Mem. Am. Assn. Neurol. Surgeons, Congress Neurol. Surgeons, New Eng. Neurosurg. Soc. (pres. 1981-83), Mass. Med. Soc. Jewish. Avocations: hiking, skiing. Office: Lahey Clinic Med Ctr 41 Mall Rd Burlington MA 01805-0002 Office Phone: 781-744-8643. Business E-Mail: stephen.r.freidberg@lahey.org.

FREIDEL, DAVID ALAN, archaeologist, anthropologist, educator; b. July 11, 1946; m. Carolyn Freidel; 2 children. BA, Harvard U., 1968, PhD, 1976. From adj. asst. prof. to prof. anthropology So. Meth. U., Dallas, 1974—, acting chair Anthropology Dept., 1999, Univ. Disting. prof. archaeology, 2003—; archeologist Selz Found. Yazuna Project, 1986—97; field rschr. Waká Archeol. Project, Peten, Guatemala, 2003—. Co-author: Cozumel: Late Maya Settlement Systems, 1984, A Forest of Kings, 1990 (Gambrinus Guiseppe Mazzotti Lit. Prize, 2001), Maya Cosmos: Three Thousand Years on the Sharman's Path, 1993; contbr. articles to profl. jours. Office: So Meth U 6425 Boaz Lane Dallas TX 75205 Office Phone: 214-768-2000. E-mail: dfreidel@mail.smu.edu.*

FREIDELL, HUGH VERNON, internist, nephrologist; b. Santa Barbara, Calif., June 21, 1923; s. Hugh Fredrick and Selina Maria (Saari) F.; m. Anna Mae Davis, Apr. 6, 1952; children: Kathy Ann Freidell Day, Susan Lee Freidell Mosby, Sharon Maria Freidell Paratte, Debra Mary Freidell Babai. MD, Baylor U., 1948. Diplomate in internal medicine and nephrology Am. Bd. Internal Medicine; diplomate Am. Bd. Forensic Examiners. Intern Highland-Alameda Hosp., Oakland, Calif., 1948-49; resident Santa Barbara (Calif.) Cottage-County Hosp., 1949-50, Univ. Hosp. of Nebr., Omaha, 1950-52; fellow artificial unit Cleve. Clinic, 1958; practiced medicine/nephrology Santa Barbara, 1954—97. Chmn. dept. internal medicine Santa Barbara Cottage Hosp., 1961-62, 87-88, med. dir. acute renal unit, 1959-85; co-med. dir. Santa Barbara Cmty. Dialysis Ctr., 1975-91. With U.S. Army, 1943-46, capt. M.C., USAF, 1952-54. Fellow ACP; mem. Calif. Med. Assn., Santa Barbara County Med. Soc. (pres. 1971), Aquatic Med. Soc., Am. Soc. Nephrology, Masons, Shriners. Republican. Presbyterian. Avocations: scuba diving, flying, horseback riding, fishing, water sports. Home: 1101-B Senda Verde Santa Barbara CA 93105

FREIDENREICH, HARRIET PASS, history educator; b. Ottawa, Ont., Can., Jan. 8, 1947; came to U.S., 1968; d. Henry and Malca Pearl (Freedman) Pass; m. Philip Freidenreich, Aug. 20, 1972; children: David, Aron. BA with honors, U. Toronto (Can.), 1968; MA, Columbia U., 1970, PhD, 1973. Prof. history Temple U., Phila., 1975—. Author: The Jews of Yugoslavia, 1979, Jewish Politics in Vienna, 1991, Female, Jewish, and Educated: The Lives of Central European University Women, 2002; contbr. articles to profl. jours. Bd. dirs. Phila. Jewish Archives, 1982-87, Abrams Hebrew Acad., Yardley, Pa., 1989-93; chpt. v.p. and pres. Na'amat USA, Trenton, N.J., 1982-88; chair Sem. Zionist Thought, Phila., 1985—1995; mem. Leo Baeck Inst., YIVO Inst., Jewish Rsch. Mem. Assn. for Jewish Studies (bd. dirs. 1982-84), Temple Assn. U. Profs. Business E-Mail: hfreiden@temple.edu.

FREIDHEIM, CYRUS F., JR., fruit company executive; b. Chgo., June 14, 1935; s. Cyrus F. and Eleanor Freidheim; m. Marguerite VandenBosch; children: Marguerite Lynn, Stephen Cyrus, Scott. BSChE, U. Notre Dame, 1957; MS in Indsl. Adminstrn., Carnegie Mellon U., 1963; Dr of Internat. Laws (hon.), Am. Grad. Sch. Internat. Mgmt., 1999. Plant mgr. Union Carbide Corp., Whiting, Ind., 1961; cons. Price Waterhouse, Chgo., 1962; fin. analyst Ford Motor Co., Dearborn, Mich., 1963-66; vice chmn. Booz, Allen & Hamilton, Chgo., 1966—2002; chmn. Chiquita Brands Internat., Inc., Cincinnati, 2002—04, CEO, 2002—04. Bd. dirs. HSBC Finance Corp., Inc., Allegheny Energy, Inc.; chmn. Old Harbour Partners & Co., Inc., North Palm Beach, Fla., 2004—. Author: The Trillion Dollar Enterprise, 1998. Trustee Thunderbird, The Garvin Sch. Internat. Mgmt.; dir. Chgo. Coun. Fgn. Rels., Techno Serve; trustee Rush U. Med. Ctr., 1981—; life trustee Chgo. Symphony Orch.; trustee Brookings Instn., 1998—. With USN, 1957-61. Mem. Coun. Fgn. Rels., Am.-China Soc. (bd. dirs.), Chgo. Club, Econ. Club, Comml. Club, Racquet Club, Stanwich Club, Old Elm Club, Lost Tree Club, The Bear's Club. Office: 11105 Old Harbour Rd North Palm Beach FL 33408 Business E-Mail: cfreidheim@tmo.blackberry.com.

FREIDHEIM, STEPHEN C., investment company executive; b. Detroit, July 8, 1964; s. Cyrus Foster Freidheim and Marguerite Vanden Bosche. BA in Econs., Yale U., 1986. V.p. Kidder, Peabody & Co., N.Y.C., 1986-90; sr. v.p. Nomura Securities, N.Y.C., 1990-93; ptnr., mng. dir. Bankers Trust Co., N.Y.C., 1993-99; co-sr. mng. mem. Och ziff Freidheim, N.Y.C., 1999—. Bd. dirs. Intira Corp. Mem. Coun. Fgn. Rels., Yale Alumni Assn., Yale Club, N.Y. Athletic Assn. Avocations: 17th century swords, marathons. Office: Och Ziff Freidheim 9 W 57th St New York NY 10019

FREIDINGER, ROGER MERLIN, chemist, researcher; b. Pekin, Ill., July 26, 1947; s. Merlin Paul and Emily Mary Freidinger; m. Carol Ann Dunkel, June 28, 1969; children: Kathryn Elaine, Elizabeth Emily. BS in Chemistry, U. Ill., 1969; PhD, MIT, 1975. Sr. rsch. chemist dept. medicinal chemistry Merck Rsch. Labs., West Point, Pa., 1975-80, rsch. fellow, 1980-82, sr. rsch. fellow, 1982-85, asst. dir., 1985-87, assoc. dir., 1987-89, sr. scientist, 1989-92, sr. dir., 1992-95, exec. dir., 1995—2005. Ad hoc reviewer NIH, mem. biorganic and natural products chemistry study sect., 1990—94; mem. grad. fellowship panel NSF, 1999—2001, 2005—. Editl. adv. bd.: Jour. Organic Chemistry, 1988—92; contbr. articles to profl. jours. With U.S. Army, 1970—72. Recipient Vincent duVigneaud award, Peptide Gordon Conf., 1986. Fellow: AAAS; mem.: ACS (Ralph Hirschmann award in peptide chemistry 2003), Am. Peptide Soc. (pres.-elect 2001—03, pres. 2003—05). Mem.United Ch.Of Christ. Achievements include patents in field. Avocations: gardening, travel. E-mail: rfreidinger@comcast.net.

FREIER, ELLIOT G., lawyer; b. Huntington, N.Y., Apr. 2, 1961; s. Walter and Sondra J. Freier; children: Matthew V., Aaron M. BA in Econs., U. Va., 1983; JD, Yale U., 1986. Bar: Calif. 1986. Assoc. Irell & Manella LLP, L.A., 1986—92, ptnr., 1993—. Adv. bd. The M&A Tax Report, 1992—96. Mem. editl. adv. bd.: Mergers and Acquisitions: The Monthly Tax Jour., 2000—03. Mem.: ABA (chmn. affiliated and related corps. com. 1996—97, tax sect.), Phi Beta Kappa. Avocations: tennis, alpine skiing. Office: Irell & Manella LLP Ste 900 1800 Avenue of The Stars Los Angeles CA 90067 E-mail: efreier@irell.com.

FREIHEIT, CLAYTON FREDRIC, zoo director; b. Buffalo, Jan. 29, 1938; s. Clayton John and Ruth (Miller) F. Student, U. Buffalo, 1960; DHL (hon.), U. Denver, 1996. Caretaker Living Mus., Buffalo Mus. Sci., 1955-60; curator Buffalo Zool. Gardens, 1960-70; dir. Denver Zool. Gardens, 1970—. Contbr. articles to profl. jours. Named Outstanding Citizen, Buffalo Evening News, 1967 Mem. Internat. Union Dirs. Zool. Gardens, Am. Assn. Zool. Pks. and Aquariums (pres. 1967-68 Outstanding Svc. award). Home: 3855 S Monaco Pky Denver CO 80237-1271 Office: Denver Zool Gardens City Park Denver CO 80205

FREILICH, GERALD, mathematics professor; b. Bklyn., Dec. 29, 1926; s. Aaron and Yetta (Seidman) F.; m. Marion B. Freudenberger, June 28, 1953; children: Sandra Lynn, David Ira. BS, CCNY, 1946; MSc, Brown U., 1947, PhD, 1949. Instr. Brown U., Providence, 1949-50; from instr. to prof. CCNY, N.Y.C., 1950-71; prof. Queens Coll. CUNY, Flushing, 1971—. Vis. assoc. prof. Conn. Wesleyan U., summers 1962-65; chmn. math. dept. CCNY, 1966-70. Co-author: Calculus: A Short Course With Applications, 1985. With USNR, 1945. Brown U. fellow, 1946-49. Mem. Am. Math. Soc., Math. Assn. Am. (bd. govs. 1969-72), Phi Beta Kappa, Sigma Xi. Home: 1619 E 21st St Brooklyn NY 11210-5037

FREILICH, JOAN SHERMAN, utilities executive; b. Albany, NY, Nov. 3, 1941; d. Julius and Bess (Bergner) Sherman; m. Sanford J. Freilich, Jan. 24, 1965. AB in French magna cum laude, Barnard Coll., 1963; MA in French, Columbia U., 1964, PhD in French, 1971, MBA in Fin., 1980. Instr. CCNY, Columbia U., NYC, 1965-75; tchr. Walden Sch., NYC, 1970-74; asst. to dean Coll. of New Rochelle, NY, 1974-75, dir. admissions, 1975-78; sr. acct. Consol. Edison Co. NY, NYC, 1978-81, mgr. acctg. rsch., 1981-82, contr. power generation, 1982-86, gen. mgr. power generation, 1986-89, exec. asst. to pres., 1989, asst. v.p. corp. planning, 1989-90, v.p. corp. planning, 1990-92, v.p., contr., chief acctg. officer, 1992-96, sr. v.p., CFO, 1996-98, exec. v.p., CFO, 1998—2005, vice chmn., 2005—; also bd. dirs. Consol. Edison, Inc. and Consol. Edison of NY, Inc., NYC, 1997—2005. Author: Paul Claudel's "Le Soulier de satin": A Stylistic, Structuralist and Psychoanalytic Interpretation, 1973; assoc. editor Claudel Studies, 1973-78; contbr. articles to profl. jours. Trustee Citizens Budget Commn.; vice chmn. bd. trustees Coll. New Rochelle; mem. president's coun. The Cooper Union. Publ. grantee Humanities Rsch. Coun. Can., 1972; Pres.'s fellow Columbia U., 1964, Henry Todd fellow, 1967; recipient scholarship NY State Bd. Regents, 1959, Nat. Merit Found., 1959, Columbia U., 1965; Civic Spirit Award, Women's City Club of NY, 1999. Mem.: NY State Women in Comms. and Energy (steering com.), YWCA Acad. of Women Achievers, Phi Beta Kappa, Beta Gamma Sigma. Office: Consolidated Edison Co NY 4 Irving Pl New York NY 10003-3598

FREILICHER, JANE, artist; b. NYC, Nov. 29, 1924; d. Martin and Bertha (Niederhoffer); m. Joseph Hazan, Feb. 17, 1957; 1 dau., Elizabeth. AB, Bklyn. Coll., 1947; postgrad., Hans Hoffman Sch. Fine Arts, 1947; MA, Columbia U., 1948. Vis. lectr., critic art schs., colls. One-woman shows include Tibor de Nagy, 1952-68, 98, 2000, 02, 04, 05, John Bernard Myers Gallery, 1971, Fischbach Gallery, 1975, 77, 79-80, 83, 85, 88, 90, 92, 95, Utah Mus. Fine Arts, 1979, Lafayette Coll., 1981, Kansas City Art Inst., 1983, David Heath Gallery, Atlanta, 1990, Reynolds Gallery, Richmond, Va., 1993, Nat. Acad., 2002; group exhbns. include Met. Mus. Art, 1979-80, Denver Art Mus., 1979, Pa. Acad., 1981, Am. Acad. and Inst. of Arts and Letters, 1981, 84-85, Bklyn. Mus. 1984, Yale U., 1986, Tibor de Nagy Gallery, 1992, Whitney Mus., 1955, 72, 95, Whitney Mus., Stamford, Conn., 1999, Artists Eye NAD, 2002, Women of Acad. NAD, 2003; curator Nat. Acad., 2002; represented in permanent collections Met. Mus. Art, Hirschorn Mus., Bklyn. Mus., NYU, Rose Art Mus., Whitney Mus., Cleve. Mus. Art, San Francisco Mus. Art, others; travelling retrospective in Currier Gallery Art, Parrish Mus., Contemporary Arts Mus., McNay Mus., 1986-87; illustrator Turandot and Other Poems, 1953, Paris Review, 1965, Descriptions of a Masque, 1998. Recipient Eloise Spaeth award Guild Hall Mus., East Hampton, N.Y., 1991, Lifetime Achievement award Guild Hall Mus., 1996; AAUW fellow, 1974; Nat. Endowment Arts grantee, 1976; Benjamin West Clinedinst Meml. medal Artists' Fellowship, 1997. Mem. NAD (academician) (Saltus Gold medal 1987, Benjamin Altman landscape prize 1995, Edwin Palmer prize 2003), Am. Acad. Arts and Letters (Gold medal 2005).

FREILICHER, MORTON, lawyer, educator; b. NYC, June 23, 1931; s. Morris and Gertrude D. (Pedowitz) F.; m. Yseult A. Snepvangers, Dec. 3, 1972. BA, Columbia Coll., N.Y.C., 1953, JD, 1956. Bar: N.Y. 1957. Assoc. Hartman & Craven, NYC, 1956-60, Phillips, Nizer LLP, NYC, 1960-67, ptnr., 1967-94, counsel, 1995—. Adj. prof. Law Sch. Fordham U., N.Y.C., 1982-92. Author: Estate Planning Handbook, 1970; editor-in-chief Jour. of Estate and Tax Planning for the Elderly and Disabled, 1986-91. Chmn. trusts and estates lawyers divsn. UJA Fedn., 1985; dir. The Edouard Found., 1996—. Harlan Fiske Stone scholar Columbia Law Sch., 1956. Fellow Am. Coll. Trusts and Estates Counsel; mem. ABA, N.Y. State Bar Assn., N.Y.C. Bar Assn. Avocations: hiking, exercise, reading. Home: 200 E 57th St New York NY 10022 Office: Phillips Nizer et al 666 5th Ave New York NY 10103-0001

FREILING, MARIANNE, principal; b. Gmunden, Austria, Apr. 18, 1952; arrived in U.S., 1955; d. Peter and Maria Glatt; m. Phillip Freiling, Aug. 14, 1976; children: Paul, Tristan, Erika. BA summa cum laude, St. Louis U., 1974, MA, 2000. Cert. prin. Tchr. Hillsboro (Mo.) R-3 Schs., 1974—77, Columbia (Mo.) Cath. Sch., 1977—79, Columbia Pub. Schs., 1979—81, St. Simon the Apostle Sch., St. Louis, 1981—95; asst. prin. St. Francis of Assisi Sch., St. Louis, 1995—96; prin. St. Simon the Apostle Sch., St. Louis, 1996—. Kindergarten dir. German Cultural Soc., St. Louis, 1995—99. Recipient Svc. award, German Cultural Soc., 1999. Mem.: Internat. Reading Assn. (bd. dirs. 1996—98), St. Elizabeth Acad. (bd. dirs.), Mo. Nonpub. Sch. Accreditation Assn. (bd. dirs.), Phi Beta Kappa. Roman Catholic. Home: 5916 San Simeon Saint Louis MO 63128 Office: St Simon the Apostle Sch 11019 Mueller Rd Saint Louis MO 63123 Office Phone: 314-842-0181. E-mail: mfreiling@stsimonschool.org.

FREIMAN, ALVIN HENRY, cardiologist, educator; b. N.Y.C., Jan. 26, 1927; s. Maurice and Beatrice (Freeman) Freiman; m. Nadine Roehr, June 12, 1959; children: Audrey L., Gail L., Marshall A. BA, N.Y. U., 1947, MD, 1953; MS, U. Ill., 1949. Diplomate Am. Bd. Internal Medicine. Intern Montefiore Hosp., N.Y.C., 1953—54; resident in medicine and cardiology Beth Israel Hosp., Boston, 1954—56; fellow in cardiology Meml. Hosp., N.Y.C., 1956—58; individual practive medicine specializing in internal medicine and cardiology N.Y.C., 1954—. Attending staff cardiology Meml. Sloan-Kettering Cancer Ctr., N.Y.C., 1971—, dir. clin. info. ctr., 1974—; attending physician Sloan-Kettering Inst., N.Y.C., 1995; prof. medicine Cornell U. Med. Coll., N.Y.C., 1995—; adj. prof. medicine and neurosciences Rockefeller U., N.Y.C. Contbr. articles to profl. jours. With USNR, 1945—46. Mem.: AAAS, ACP, Internat. Coll. Angiology, N.Y. Acad. Scis., Am. Heart Assn., Am. Coll. Angiology, Am. Coll. Chest Physicians, Am. Coll. Cardiology, Nat. Cancer Inst., Sigma Xi, Alpha Omega Alpha. Home: 74 Homestead Rd Tenafly NJ 07670-1109 Office: 178 E End Ave New York NY 10128-7762

FREIMARK, ROBERT (BOB FREIMARK), artist; b. Doster, Mich., Jan. 27, 1922; s. Alvin O. and Nora (Shinaver) F.; m. Mary Carvin (dec.); 1 son, Matisse Jon; m. Lillian Tihlarik; 1 child, Christine Gay. B.E., U. Toledo, 1950; M.F.A., Cranbrook Acad. Art, 1951. Prof. art emeritus San Jose State U., 1964-86; W.I.C.H.E. prof. Soledad State Prison, 1967; prof. emeritus of art San Jose State U., 1986—. Established artist in residence program Yosemite Nat. Park,1984-85, Fire Clay and Tile, Aromas, Calif., 1998; artist in residence Museo Regla, Cuba, 2000, Ferencsik Janos Zeneskola, L. Balaton, Hungary, 2002; panelist SECOLAS S.E. conf. Latin Am. Studies, Vera Cruz, Mex. Guest artist Harvard U., 1972-73; first Am. to make tapestries in Art Protis technique at Atelier Vlnena, Brno, Czechoslovakia.; contbr. to profl. publs.; Numerous solo shows including, Minn. Inst. Arts, Toledo Mus. Art, Salpeter Gallery, Morris Gallery, N.Y.C., Des Moines Art Ctr., Santa Barbara Mus., Moravska Mus., Czechoslovakia, Brunel U., London, Amerika Haus, Munich, Stuttgart, Regensburg, Joslyn Ctr. for Arts, Torrance, Calif, Stanford U., San Jose (Calif.) Mus. Art, Triton Mus., Santa Clara, Calif., Guatemalteco, Guatemala City, Dum Umeni Brno, CSFR, Strahov Closter, Prague, 1990, Walter Bischoff Gallery, Stuttgart, 1990, Kunstler aus den USA, Kunsthaus Ostbayern and Amerika Haus, Stuttgart, 1991, Max Planck Inst., Munich, The Gag Theatre, Prague, 1992, Haus Wiegand, Munich, 1993, San Jose State U., 1964, 1967-68, 1981, 1994, Viva!, Tokyo, 1994, Gallery Q, Sacramento, 1997, Parish Gallery, Wash. D.C., 1997, 2002, Barton Gallery, Sacramento, 1997, 2002, 03; Galeria Galiano Havana, 1998, Galerie Weber, Viechtach, Germany, 1998, Point Gall., Brno, Czech Rep., 1998, Galerie Divadlo, Uherske Hradiste, C.R., 1998, Marco Polo Galleries, Carmel, Calif., 2001, Colton Hall Mus., Monterey, Calif., 2002, Hart Galleries, Palm Desert, Calif., 2003, Morgan Hill Cmty. Cultural Ctr., 2004; exhibited in group shows, Art Inst. Chgo., 1952, Pa. Acad. Fine Arts, 1953 (Lambert Fund prize), Detroit Inst. Arts, 1956, Mich. State U., 1956 (Purchase award), N.A.D., 1956, Boston Print Symposium, 1997, Internat. Print Exhibition Portland (Oreg.) Art Mus., 1997 (Purchase award), Honolulu Acad. Art, 1998, Internat. Graphic Triennial, Krakow, Poland, 1998, Internat. Small Engraving Salon, Florean Mus., Romania, Art Expo, N.Y.C., 2000, Internat. Woodprint Assn., Kyoto, Japan, 1999, Bklyn. Mus., Mus. Modern Art (Purchase award), Michael Stone Collection, D.C., Contempo Collection, Tokyo, Havana Bienale, 2000, others, L.A., Boston, San Francisco, Omaha, Oklahoma City, Des Moines, Dallas, Phoenix, San Jose, Havana, Tokyo, Manila, Rio de Janeiro, Mexico City, Sao Paulo, Brasilia, Buenos Aires, Prague, exhbn. 50 States toured, European Mus., 1970-71, represented in collections, Pa. Acad. Fine Art, Boston Mus. Fine Arts, Fogg Mus., Butler Inst. Am. Art, Ford Motor Co., South Bend Art Assn., Joslyn Art Mus., Seattle Art Mus., Ga. Mus., Huntington Gallery, Des Moines Art Center, Smithsonian Instn., Libr. Congress, L.A. County Art Inst., Brit. Mus., Nat. Gallery, Prague, Birmingham (Eng.) Mus., Moravske Mus., Brno, Czechoslovakia, Bibliotheque Nationale, Paris, Harn Mus., Gainsville, Fla., Portland Mus. Art (complete prints), Nat. Mus., Washington, Natl. Mus. of Cuba, La Habana, Nat. Mus. Costa Rica, San Jose, Nat. Mus. Egypt, Cairo, Mus. de Arte Contemporaneo, Bahia Blanca, Mus. Genaro Perez, Cordoba, Mus. de Bellas Artes, Cordoba, Argentina, Mus. Guayasamin, Quito, Ecuador, Mus. Nacional, Panama City, Panama, others; numerous tapestries in pub. and pvt. collections, created tapestry representing U.S. for Olympic Games, Moscow, 1980; prodr. film El Día Tarasco, 1982; prodr. video documentary: Arte Cubano (Contemporary Art and Culture in Cuba, 1999, 2000, 1st award, San Francisco Throwback Film Festival, Los Desaparecidos--The Disappeared Ones, 2003 (Freedom award Dahlonega Film Festival, also Best Documentary Short and Best of Show, Accolade Competition, Best Documentary Spl. Gold statuette, World Fest, Houston, 20 Internat. Festivals); guest artist Joslyn Meml. Mus., 1961, instr. painting and drawing, Ohio U., 1955-59, artist in residence, Des Moines Art Center, 1959-63, dir., Crystal Lake Art Center, Frankfort, Mich., (1955-57), guest lectr., one man show, Columbia U., 1963, solo exhibit, Northamerican Cultural Inst., Mexico City, 1963; guest artist Riverside Art Ctr., 1964, Agora Vienna, Austria, 1994, Museo Guayasamin, Quito, Ecuador, 2002; curated exhibit Stuttgart, 1993; founder Bob & Lil Freimark Collection Portland Art Mus.; artist in residence MuseoRegla, Cuba, 2002, Lake Balaton, Hungary, 2002; Am. corollary to Dakar Bienale, 5 works, Senegal, 2002, Art Workshop, Dakar, others; contbr. to craft and fibre publs. Served with USNR, 1939-46. Coxwain USN, 1939—46, Pacific. Recipient 2d award for oil Northwest Territorial exhibit, 1954, Roulet medal Toledo Mus. Art, 1957, 1st award Print Exhbn., 1958, purchase award Midwest Biennial and Northwest Printmakers, Jurors award Berkeley Art Ctr, 1996; Calif. State Coll. Sys. spl. creative leave edit. serigraphs; elected to New Talent in U.S.A., 1957; Ohio U. rsch. grantee, 1958-59, Ford Found. grantee, 1965; Western Interstate Commn. for Higher Edn. grantee, 1967, San Jose State Coll. Found. grantee, 1966, 67, 68, 69, 70, 71, 85; designated ofcl. U.S. Bicentennial Exhbn. Amerika Hausen, Fed. Republic Germany, 1976; donated Bob & Lil Freimark Collection, Mexican Arts & Crafts, Gavilan Coll., Gilroy, Calif., 1996; represented by Parish Gallery, Washington, Triad Gallery, Seal Rock, Oreg., Haus Wiegand, Munich, Art Foundry Gallery, Sacramento, Greg Barlon Gallery, Sacramento, Hart Gallery, Chgo., Palm Desert and Carmel, Calif. Independent. Achievements include being subject of TV interview, 1993. Home: 539A Dougherty Ave Morgan Hill CA 95037-9241 Office: Grass Valley Studios Morgan Hill CA 95037 Personal E-mail: bfreimar@pacbell.net.

FREIRE, JOSE A., physicist, writer; b. Cienfuegos, Cuba, Apr. 18, 1925; arrived in U.S., 1968; s. Jose M. Freire and Maria C. Valle; m. Maria C. Paula Freire, Dec. 16, 1950; children: Maria C., Jose L., Jose A. BS, Mercy Coll.; D in Physics and Chemistry, Havana (Cuba) U. Author: Application of the Mathematical, 1989, 1993, Experiment of Michelson-Morley and the Original Formula, 1994, Ether's Effect in Particles and Waves, 1997, Unification of Ether, Gravity and Electromagnetism, 1999, Gravitational Wave and Time, 2001. Mem.: Am. Assn. Physics Tchrs., Am. Legion (supporter). Republican. Roman Catholic. Home: 2356 SW 140 Pl Miami FL 33175

FREIREICH, EMIL J., hematologist, educator; b. Chgo., Mar. 16, 1927; s. David and Mary (Klein) F.; m. Haroldine Lee Cunningham, Mar. 13, 1953; children: Debra Ann, David Alan, Lindsay Gail, Thomas Jon. BS, U. Ill., 1947, MD with honors, 1949, D.Sc. (hon.), 1982. Diplomate Am. Bd. Internal Medicine. Intern Cook County (Ill.) Hosp., Chgo., 1949-50; resident in internal medicine Presbyn. Hosp., Chgo., 1950-53; rsch. assoc. in hematology Mass. Meml. Hosp., Boston, 1953-55; sr. investigator, head Leukemia Svc. USPHS, Nat. Cancer Inst., Bethesda, Md., 1955-65; prof. medicine U. Tex. System Cancer Ctr., Houston, 1965—, chief rsch. in hematology, 1965-85, head dept. devel. therapeutics, 1972-83, chmn. dept. hematology, 1983-85, dir. Adult Leukemia Rsch. Program, 1985—; prof. medicine U. Tex. Health Sci. Ctr. (Sch. Medicine), 1973—, chief divsn. oncology, 1973-81; mem. faculty Grad. Sch. Med., Health Scis. Ctr., 1965—, dir. Spl. Medical Edn. Programs, 2000—. Mem. rev. com. drug. devel. div. cancer treatment NIH, 1975-80; Ruth Harriet Ainsworth chair in devel. therapeutics, 1980—; spl. asst. dir. NCI, 1990-91. Assoc. editor Cancer, 1976—, Cancer Research, 1977-86; mem. editorial bd. Oncology News, 1975-90, Cancer Treatment Reports, 1976-80, Leukemia Research, 1976-87, Med. and Pediatric Oncology, 1974—, Leukemia 1987—; contbr. numerous articles on research in hematology and oncology to profl. jours. Recipient Albert Lasker Med. rsch. award, 1972, Charles F. Kettering prize Gen. Motors Cancer Rsch. Found., 1983, Outstanding Investigator award Nat. Cancer Inst., NIH, 1985-92, Alumnus award NIH, 1990; named Alumnus of Yr., U. Ill. Alumni Assn., 1974, Alumni Achievement award, 2000, Pollin prize Columbia U., 2003. Fellow ACP, AAAS; mem. Internat. Soc. Hematology, Am. Soc. Hematology, Am. Fedn. Clin. Research, Am. Soc. Clin. Pharmacology and Therapeutics, Am. Soc. Clin. Oncology (David A. Karnofsky award 1976, pres. 1980-81), Am. Soc. Clin. Investigators, Am. Assn. Cancer Research, Leukemia Soc. Am. (pres. Gulf Coast chpt. 1968-70, trustee 1968-70, Robert Roesler

DeVilliers award 1979, grant rev. subcom. 1986-89), Tex. Med. Assn., AMA (editorial bd. jour. 1973-83), Assn. Am. Physicians, Alpha Omega Alpha. Achievements include research in therapy of human acute leukemia and leukocyte physiology. Co-developer of combination chemotherapy and the cureative therapy for childhood acute lymphoblastic leukemia. Developed the first successful platelet replacement therapy. Inventor of continuous-flow cell separator. Home: 810 Monte Cello St Houston TX 77024-4515 Office: M D Anderson Cancer Ctr 1515 Holcombe Blvd Houston TX 77030-4009 Office Phone: 713-792-2660. E-mail: efreirei@mdanderson.org. *The search for eternal physical and mental health has been at the forefront of man's striving to understand and to control his destiny. The opportunity to investigate, to discover and to apply new remedies for major human illness is a rare privilege, one of man's highest callings.*

FREISCHLAG, JULIE ANN, surgeon; b. 1955; m. Phillip Roethle; 1 child, Taylor stepchildren: Paul, Matthew. BS, U. Ill., 1976; MD, Rush U., 1980. Asst. prof. in residence dept. surgery UCSD Med. Ctr., San Diego, 1987—89, UCLA Med. Ctr., L.A., 1989—92; chief vascular surgery sect. Wadsworth VA Med. Ctr., L.A., 1989—92, Zablocki VA Med. Ctr., Milw., 1992—96, chief surgery, 1996—98; assoc. prof. surgery, vice-chair sect. vascular surgery Med. Coll. Wis., Milw., 1997—98, prof. surgery, vice-chair sect. vascular surgery, 1997—98; prof. and chief vascular surgery UCLA Med. Ctr., 1998—2003; prof. and chief. divsn. vascular surgery David Geffen Sch. Medicine UCLA, L.A., 1998—2003, dir. Gonda (Goldschmied) Vascular Ctr., 1998—2003; head dept. surgery Johns Hopkins U.; surgeon in chief Hopkins Hosp., dir. surgery, 2003—. Named William Stewart Halsted Prof., 2003; recipient Outstanding Achievement award, Dept. Veterans, 1993. Fellow: ACS; mem.: Assn. Surg. Edn., Assn. VA Surgeons, Assn. Academic Surgery, Soc. Clin. Vascular Surgery, Peripheral Vascular Surgery Soc., Assn. Women Surgeons, Am. Assn. Vascular Surgery, Soc. Vascular Surgery, Soc. Univ. Surgeons, Ctrl. Surg. Assn. Achievements include first woman to be named surgeon in chief of The Johns Hopkins Hospital and Director of the Department of Surgery. Office: Dept Surgery Richard Staf Ross Rsch Bldg 720 Rutland Ave Rm 759 Baltimore MD 21205-2196

FREISHTAT, HARVEY W., lawyer; b. Balt., Dec. 28, 1946; AB cum laude, Princeton U., 1968; JD, Harvard U., 1972. Bar: Mass. 1972. Chmn. McDermott, Will & Emery LLP, Boston. Achievements include founding ptnr. McDermott Will & Emery LLP Boston office. Office: McDermott Will & Emery 28 State St Ste 33 Boston MA 02109-1775 Office Phone: 617-535-4050. Office Fax: 617-535-3800. Business E-Mail: hfreishtat@mwe.com.

FREITAG, CAROL WILMA, political scientist; d. Lowell William and Lois Marie (Robertson) Petersen; m. Henry Wesley Freitag, 1961 (dec. Nov. 1985); children: Bonita, Henry. Diploma in Dental Hygiene, Northwestern U., 1959; BA, Purdue U., Hammond, Ind., 1988. Registered dental hygienist, Ill. Pvt. practice dental hygiene Henry W. Freitag, D.D.S., Homewood, Ill., 1959-85; mem. group practice Chgo., 1970; faculty, interim dir. dental hygiene Prairie State Coll., Chgo. Heights, Ill., 1971-72; pvt. practice James J. Kreuz, D.D.S., Homewood, 1985-90. Contbr. articles to profl. jour. Chair US Constn. Bicentennial Commn., Village of Matteson, Ill., 1986-89; pres. Matteson Hist. Soc., 1987-89; panel spkr. South Suburban Heritage Assn., Homewood, 1990. Calumet rep. Bicentennial Com. Purdue U., 1988; vis. com. Northwestern Dental Sch., 1997-98; mem. centennial celebration com. Bloom Twp. HS, 2000; mem. Hist. Columbia Found. 2003—. Recipient Key to City, Village of Matteson, 1990, Svc. award Northwestern U., 1980, Good Neighbor award Village of Matteson, 1989, Outstanding Alumni 1950's Decade award Bloom Twp. H.S., 2000. Mem. Am. Dental Hygienists' Assn. (chair Ann. Session Program 1975), Ill. Dental Hygienists Assn. (pres. 1968-69, bd. dirs., Merit award 1979), G.V. Black Soc. (leader, pres. 1997-2001), Evelyn E. Maas Soc. (pres. 1989-90, bd. dirs., Merit award 1993), Northwestern Dental Sch. Alumni Assn. (bd. dirs. 1969-2001, pres. 1977-78, v.p. 1976-77, 90-93), Acad. Polit. Sci., Sigma Phi Alpha, Alpha Chi. Avocation: travel. Home: 117 Oak Trace Ct Chapin SC 29036

FREITAG, FREDERICK GERALD, osteopathic physician; b. Milw., Feb. 12, 1952; s. Frederick August and Shirley June (Siewert) F.; m. Lynn Nadene Stegner, Sept. 10, 1977; children: Crescentia Adella, Abigail Amadea, Genevieve Angelica. BS in Biochemistry, U. Wis., 1974; DO, Chgo. Coll. Osteo. Medicine, 1979. Cert. in headache mgmt. Intern Brentwood Hosp., Warrensville Heights, Ohio, 1979-80, resident in family practice, 1980-81; dir., physician Twinsburg (Ohio) Family Clinic, 1981-83; assoc. prof. family medicine Coll. Osteo. Medicine, Ohio U., Warrensville Heights, 1982-83; staff Diamond Headache Clinic, Chgo., 1983-86, assoc. dir., 1986—; attending staff Louis A. Weiss Meml. Hosp., Chgo., 1983-93; attending staff Columbus Hosp., 1993—2000, St. Joseph's Hosp., 2000—; clin. assoc. prof. family medicine Chgo. Med. Sch. Rosalind Franklin U. Health and Sci., 1999—. Clin. assoc. family medicine Midwestern U./Chgo. Coll. Osteo. Medicine, 1999—; mem. Janssen Rsch. Coun.; sec. Diamond Headache Rsch. and Edn. Found.; vis. lectr. dept. family medicine Chgo. Coll. Osteo. Medicine, 1984-99; clin. assoc. dept. medicine Pritzker Sch. Medicine U. Chgo., 1989-93; mem. editl. bd. Headache Quar., 1991-2003; chmn. instnl. rev. bd. Louis A. Weiss Meml. Hosp., 1991-93; mem. migraine adv. coun. Abbott, 1995-2003, mem. primary care adv. coun., 1997—; mem. adv. group Glaxo Wellcome, 1996-2005; mem. migraine adv. coun. Zeneca, 1996—; mem. U.S Headache Consortium guidelines project; bd. dirs. Nat. Bd. for Cert. in Headache Mgmt., 2000—, sec.-treas., 2000-2002, v.p., 2002—; mem. Allergan Botox Internat. Adv. Com., 2002—; co-chair Primary Care Migraine Partnership, 2002—; mem. Ortho-McNeil headache specialists adv. bd., 2003—. Coord. editor Headache Quar.; mem. editl. bd. Headache and Pain, 2003—; contbr. articles to profl. jours., chpts. to books. Bd. dirs. Nat. Headache Found., liaison standards of care com. to Am. Acad. Neurology. Fellow Am. Assn. for Study of Headache; mem. AMA, Am. Coll. Gen. Practioners in Osteo. Medicine, Am. Osteo. Assn. (chair headache coun. 2000—), Am. Soc. Clin. Pharmacology and Therapeutics (vice chmn. headache sect. 1995-96), Ill. Assn. Osteo. Physicians and Surgeons, Ill. Med. Soc., Internat. Assn. Study Pain, Am. Pain Soc., Am. Headache Soc. (chair primary care spl. interest sect. 1999-2004, mem. ethics com. 2002-04, mem. edn. com. 2002-04, co-chair PCMP), Nat. Headache Found., Chgo. Med. Soc. (spkrs. bur.), German Wine Soc. (past pres. Chgo. chpt.), U. Wis. Alumni Assn. Lutheran. Avocations: german oenophile, gardening, model railroading, home carpentry. Home: 931 Clinton Pl River Forest IL 60305-1503 Office: The Diamond Headache Clinic 467 W Deming Pl Ste 500 Chicago IL 60614-1726 Office Phone: 773-388-6383. Personal E-mail: dhcdoc@aol.com.

FREITAG, TERI LEE, secondary educator; b. Vancouver, Wash., Feb. 23, 1954; d. LeRoy C. and Mildred J. (Gasser) T.; m. K. Gordon Scott, Dec. 23, 1972 (div. Dec. 1990); children: Ian G., Simon G.; m. Steve R. Freitag, Dec. 14, 1991. BA in Edn., U. Oreg., 1976; MEdn, Portland State U., 1986. Tchr. Fairview Tng. Ctr., Salem, Oreg., 1976-83, Beaverton (Oreg.) Pub. Schs., 1983-91, Bend (Oreg.) LaPine Pub. Schs., 1991—. Cons. Alternative Edn., Bend, 1992—. Bd. dirs. Oreg. Spl. Olympics, Portland, 1986-90, Oreg. Spl. Olympics, Eugene, 1973-79; head ski coach Washington County Spl. Olympics, Beaverton, 1983-91. Named Tchr. of Yr. Assn. for Retarded Citizens, 1986, Master Tchr. Oreg. Pub. Broadcasting, 1993-95. Mem. NEA. Avocations: outdoor sports, freestyle cross-country skiing, alpine skiing, bike touring, hiking. Office: Mt View High Sch 520 NW Wall St Bend OR 97701-2608

FREITAG, WOLFGANG MARTIN, retired librarian, educator; b. Berlin, Oct. 27, 1924; came to U.S. 1955, naturalized, 1961; s. Georg and Anne Marie (Friess) F.; m. Doris Christiane Pfeil, Oct. 25, 1952; children— Thomas Martin, Tilman George Dr. Phil., U. Freiburg, W. Ger., 1949; postgrad., Harvard U., 1951-52; MS in Library Sci., Simmons Coll., Boston, 1956. Reference libr., program dir. U.S. Info. Ctr., Frankfurt, Germany, 1950-53; editor Droemer-Knaur Publ., Munich, 1953-55; cataloger Harvard Coll. Library, Cambridge, Mass., 1955-60; head librarian Gordon McKay Library, Harvard U., 1960-62; chief undergrad. library planning Stanford U., Calif., 1962-64; librarian Fine Arts Library Fogg Art Mus., Harvard U., 1964-91, sr. lectr. bibliography and art historiography, 1967-91; lectr. libr. sci. Simmons Coll., Boston, 1991-92; ret. Libr. cons. J.P. Getty Trust, L.A., 1982-83, U. Pitts, 1983, The Frick Collection, N.Y. 1984, Inst. Fine Arts, NYU, 1987; mem. vis. com. Met. Mus. Art, 1972-92; bd. vis. Sch. Info. Studies, Syracuse U., 1981-85, SUNY, Stony Brook, 1986, NYU Inst. Fine Arts, 1987. Editor: Artist Resource Manuals, Art Books: Monographs on Artists, 1985, 2d edit., 1997; cons. to pubs.; contbr. articles to profl. jours. Fulbright fellow, 1951, 68, Council Library Resources fellow, 1975. Mem. Art Libraries Soc. N.Am. (pres. 1980), Coll. Art Assn., Internat. Fedn. Library Assns. (exec. com. art librs. sect. 1985-93), Goethe Soc. New Eng., Boston Soc. Printers. Avocation: autograph collecting. Home: 43 Fair Oaks Dr Lexington MA 02421-6931 E-mail: wolfgangfreitag@lycos.com.

FREITAS, ROBERT ARCHIBALD, JR., periodical editor and publisher; b. Camden, Maine, Dec. 6, 1952; s. Robert Archibald and Barbara Lee (Smith) G.; m. Nancy Ann Farrell, Aug. 10, 1974. BS in Physics, BS in Psychology, Harvey Mudd Coll., 1974; JD, U. Santa Clara, 1979. Dir. Space Initiative Lobbying for Space, Santa Clara, Calif., 1977-82; space automation study editor, Ames Rsch. Ctr. NASA/Am. Soc. Engring. Edn., Moffett Field, Calif., 1980-81, computer sci. study editor, Goddard Space Flight Ctr. Balt., 1981-82, autonomy and human element in space study editor Ames Rsch. Ctr. Moffett Field, 1983-84; editor, pub. Value Forecaster, Pilot Hill, Calif., 1988—. Author: Lobbying for Space, 1978; contbr. articles to profl. publs. Recipient Best Fact Article award Analog Sci. Fact/Sci. Fiction, 1981. Mem. AAAS, Internat. Inst. Forecasters, World Future Soc., Nat. Space Soc. (life). Republican. Office: PO Box 605 Pilot Hill CA 95664-0605

FREIZER, LOUIS A., radio producer; b. N.Y.C., Oct. 10, 1931; s. Morris and Celia (Lassersohn) F.; m. Michèle Suzanne Orban, July 6, 1968; children: Sabine, Eric. BS, U. Wis., 1953; postgrad., U. Heidelberg, Germany, 1956; MA, Columbia U., 1964, postgrad., 1966—. Corr. UPI, Madison, Wis., 1953-54; desk asst. CBS News, N.Y.C., 1956-59, newswriter, 1959-60, Sta. WCBS, N.Y.C., 1960-62, news editor, 1963-68, sr. news prodr., 1968-73, sr. exec. news prodr., 1973—. Adj. prof. comm. Fordham U.; lectr., cons. journalism and internat. rels. Prodr.: (pub. affairs series) Let's Find Out, 1966, International Briefing series, 1968-72. Served to 1st lt. U.S. Army, 1954-56; capt. USAR. Recipient Am. Legion medal; Radio Journalism award AMA, Radio Journalism award Nat. Headliners Club, Radio Journalism Nat. award for Outstanding Newscast UPI, 1st place award for Best Regularly Scheduled Local News Program N.Y. State AP Broadcasters Assn., spl. mention for Best One Day News Effort N.Y. State AP Broadcasters Assn., Bene Merenti medal Fordham U.; winner German Study Program for U.S. Journalists sponsored by Radio in the Am. Sect. of Berlin Commn. and the Radio and TV News Dirs. Found.; fellow CBS News Found. Mem. Am. Polit. Sci. Assn., Acad. Polit. Sci., Am. Acad. Polit. and Social Scis., Radio-TV News Dirs. Assn., Broadcast Pioneers, Sigma Delta Chi. Home: 1619 3rd Ave New York NY 10128-3459 Office: Sta WCBS 51 W 52nd St New York NY 10019-6119 Address: c/o Ordan 142A Ave Louise Brussels Belgium Personal E-mail: Freizerl@aol.com.

FRELICK, ROBERT WESTCOTT, physician, consultant; b. Potsdam, NY, Feb. 27, 1920; s. H. Victor and Ruth (Scott) F.; m. Jane Hayden, Jan. 22, 1944; children: Susan, Alcy, Sally, William, Scott. AB, Union Coll., 1941; MD, Yale U., 1944. Diplomate Am. Bd. Internal Medicine, Am. Bd. Medical Onocology, Am. Bd. Nuclear Medicine. Intern New Haven Hosp., 1944—45; resident Meml. Hosp., Wilmington, Del., 1947—49, Meml. Hosp. Ctr., N.Y.C., 1949—50; pvt. practice Wilmington, 1950—82; program dir. Nat. Cancer Inst., Bethesda, Md., 1982—87; cons. Del. Divsn. Pub. Health, Wilmington, 1987—96; med. dir. South Jersey Cancer Ctr., 1995—97, cons., 1998—. Chief medicine Wilmington Med. Ctr., Del., 1965-72. Contbr. to profl. jours. Bd. CARE coun. bd. alumni, N.Y.C. then Atlanta, 1980-97; pres. Assn. Cmty. Cancer Ctrs., Rockville, Md., 1979-80. Capt. (Med. Svc. Corps.) U.S. Army, 1944-47. Recipient Disting. Svc. award Del. Med. Soc., 1977, Outstanding Svc. to Cmty. award Assn. Cmty. Cancer Ctrs., 1987, St. George's medal Am. Cancer Soc., 1990. Fellow ACP (laureate, gov.); mem. AMA, APHA, ACS (surveyor hosp. cancer programs 1988-97), Med. Soc. Del. (chair com. ethics, pres. 1980-81), Soc. Surg. Oncology, Am. Soc. Internal Medicine, Am. Soc. Clin. Oncology, Am. Sch. Health Assns. Home: 1018 Overbrook Rd Wilmington DE 19807-2236 Office Phone: 302-655-3460. Personal E-mail: rfrelick@comcast.net.

FRELING, RICHARD ALAN, lawyer; b. NYC, June 21, 1932; s. Jack C. and Natalie Freling; m. Sandra Satrapa; children: Richard, Alexandra; children from previous marriage: Darryl, Robert, Dana. BBA in acctg. with honors, U. Tex., Austin, 1953, JD with honors, 1956. Bar: Tex. 1956, US Dist. Ct. No. Dist. Tex. 1959, US Ct. Appeals 5th Cir. 1961, US Supreme Ct. 1962. Mem. Jenkins & Gilchrist, Dallas; ptnr. Johnson & Wortley, Dallas; sr. ptnr. Hopkins & Sutter, Dallas, 1995—96; of counsel Jones, Day, Reavis & Pogue (now Jones Day), Dallas, 1996—. Mem. exec. adv. committees U. Calif. Securities Regulation Inst., 1973—; adv. bd. BNA/Tax Mgmt., 1976—. Editor-in-chief Tex. Law Rev., 1955-56; contbr. articles to legal jours. Rsch. fellow Southwestern Legal Found. (now The Ctr. for Am. and Internat. Law), 1970—, chmn. Inst. on Oil and Gas Taxation, 1965—68, chmn. taxation divsn., 1968—71, trustee, 1983—, founder, former chair Symposium on Securities Regulation; bd. dirs. Dallas Symphony Assn., 1984—, v.p. ops., 1988—90, pres., 1990—92, chmn., 1992—94, chmn. emeritus, 1994—; trustee Colo. Outward Bound Sch., 1982—, mem. exec. com., 1986—92; gov., mem. exec. com. S.W. Outward Bound Sch., 1972—82, vice chmn., 1980—82; dir. The Greenhill Sch., 1972—80, mem. exec. com., 1972—75; trustee St. Mark's Sch. of Tex., 1971—78, mem. exec. com., 1972—75; trustee Retina Found. of S.W., 1975—90, Pine Manor Coll., Chesnut Hill, Mass., 1982—85, Aperture Found., 1984—90; bd. dirs. Friends of Dallas Pub. Libr., 1982—87, Isthmus Inst., Dallas, 1983—89; mem. governance com. Ctr. for Performing Arts, Dallas; pres. Sun & Star 1996, Dallas, 1992—96. Recipient Faculty Award, U. Tex. Sch. Law, 1981. Fellow Am. Coll. Tax Counsel, Tex. Bar Found.; mem. Am. Law Inst. (cons. fed. income tax project 1976—), ABA (chmn. com. corp. stockholder relationships 1979-81, coun. taxation sect. 1981-84), Tex. Bar Assn., Dallas Bar Assn., Tex. Law Rev. Publications Inc., U. Tex. Sch. Law Alumni Assn. Office: Jones Day 2727 N Harwood St Dallas TX 75201

FRELINGHUYSEN, RODNEY P., congressman; b. NYC, Apr. 29, 1946; m. Virginia Frelinghuysen; children: Louisine, Sarah. State and fed. aid coord., adminstrv. asst. Morris County, 1972; mem. Morris County Bd. of Chosen Freeholders, 1974-83, dir., 1980, mem. welfare and mental health bds., human svcs. and pvt. industry couns., mem. freeholder fin. com.; mem. N.J. Gen. Assembly, 1983-94, chmn. assembly appropriations com., 1988-89, 92-94; mem. U.S. Congress from 11th N.J. Dist., 1995—; mem. appropriations com. With 93d Engr. Bn. U.S. Army, 1969-71, Vietnam. Named Legis. of Yr. N.J. Assn. of Mental Health Agencies, Legis. of Yr. N.J. Assn. of Retarded Citizens. Mem. Am. Legion, VFW (Legis. of Yr.). Republican. Office: US House Reps 2442 Rayburn Ho Office Bldg Washington DC 20515-3011*

FRELOW, ROBERT DEAN, retired school system administrator, writer; b. Seminole, Okla., Aug. 1, 1932; s. Jasper Wallace and Florine (Hamilton) Frelow; m. Maxine Camille Gibbs Badgett, Dec. 25, 1952 (div. May 1983); m. Rena Hersh, Sept. 8, 1983; children: Robert Jr., Frederick, Michael. BA, San Francisco State U., 1954, MA, 1960; PhD, U. Calif., Berkeley, 1970. Cert. tchr. Calif., N.Y., adminstr. Calif., N.Y. Tchr. Oakland Unified Schs., Calif., 1960—66, Berkeley Unified Schs., Calif., 1966—67, asst. to supt., 1967—70; asst. supt. Greenburgh Schs., Hartsdale, NY, 1970—75, supt. schs., 1975—90. Adj. prof. Columbia U., N.Y.C., 1970—73, Pace U., N.Y.C., 1974—90; coord. sch. desegregation Berkeley Schs., 1967—70; cons. sch. desegregation, 1966—90; cons. Wise Svcs., White Plains, NY, 1990—. Author: The Berkeley Plan for Desegregation, 1968; co-author (editor): I Am a Blade of Grass., 1989; author: (novels) Blood Runs Deep, 2002; contbr. articles to profl. jours. Bd. dirs. Westchester Arts Coun., White Plains, NY, 1990, Westchester Cable Commn., White PlainsWhite Plains, 1990, Calif. Synod, Presbyn. Ch., 1966, Hartsdale Kiwanis, 2003. Capt. USAF, 1954—64. Recipient Citizen of the Yr. award, Kappa Alpha Psi, 1978, 1984, Exec. Leadership award, Bus. Careers Club, Hartsdale, 1991, Dedication, Dr. Robert D. Frelow Cultural Ctr., Hartsdale, 1991, honors, Greensburgh Ctrl. Seven Ednl. Found., 2005; grantee Urban Studies grantee, U. Calif.-Berkeley, 1969. Fellow: Rotary of Am. (bd. dirs., Paul Harris award 1991); mem.: U. Calif. Alumni Assn. Democrat. Presbyterian. Avocations: writing, reading, travel, photography, theater. Home: 17 Tara Dr Pomona NY 10970 Personal E-mail: rdf66@aol.com.

FRELS, KELLY, lawyer; b. Lolita, Tex., Dec. 28, 1943; s. Leon A. and Aileen K. Frels; m. Carmela Madden, Sept. 10, 1970; children: Jonathan, Catherine. BS in Edn., S.W. Tex. State U., San Marcos, 1966; JD, U. Tex., 1970. Bar: Tex., U.S. Dist. Ct. (so., no., we. and ea. dists.), U.S. Ct. Appeals (5th and 11th cirs.), U.S. Supreme Ct. Atty. Bracewell & Giuliani LLP (formerly Bracewell & Patterson), Houston, 1976—, mng. ptnr., 1995—2001, mng. ptnr. Houston office, 2001—03. Mem. bd. experts Lawyers Alert, 1984-95; mem. adv. bd. Edn. Law Reporter, 1981-88; contbr. numerous articles to profl. jours. Bd. dirs., mem. exec. com. Greater Houston Partnership, 1998-2003, chair govt. rels. com., 1998-99, chair environ. adv. com., 2000-2001, chair clean air task force, 2002-2003, chair quality of life com., 2002, chair flood task force, 2003, bd. mem. emeritus, 2004. Mem. ABA, Houston Bar Assn. (bd. dirs. 1988-96, 97-98, treas. 1990, 2d v.p. 1991, 1st v.p. 1992, pres. 1994), State Bar Tex. (bd. dirs. 1995-98, chmn. sch. law sect. 1977-78, chair long range planning com. 1997-98, co-chair legal svcs. for the poor task force 1996-97, chair lawyer referral com. 1998-2001, vice chair nominating com. 1997-98, chair ann. meeting com. 2002-03, pres.-elect 2003-04, pres. 2004-05), Tex. State U. Alumni Assn. (pres. 1973), Houston Club (pres. 1999-2000). Roman Catholic. Home: 5607 Bordley Dr Houston TX 77056-2329 Office: Bracewell & Giuliani 711 Louisiana St Ste 2300 Houston TX 77002-2770 Business E-Mail: kelly.frels@bracewellgiuliani.com.

FREMON, RICHARD C., retired infosystems specialist; b. St. Louis, May 28, 1918; s. Richard Horatio and Hazel Pauline (Rhea) F.; m. Virginia Isabelle Moore, Sept. 7, 1940; children: Carolyn E. Fremon Maycher, Richard L., James N., Nancy I. Brown. AB, Columbia U., 1939, BEE, 1940, MEE, 1944. With personnel Bell Telephones, N.Y.C., 1941-54; dir. salary adminstrn. Murray Hill, N.J., 1954-73; dir. adminstrv. systems, 1973-81; dir. computer ctr. Centenary Coll., Hackettstown, N.J., 1981-89. Contbr. chpt. to book in field. Trustee Sea Cliff Sch. Bd., N.Y., 1950-52; past chmn. Engring. Manpower Commn., N.Y.C., 1965. Mem.: Inst. Indsl. Engrs (sr.). Democrat. Presbyterian. Home: 32 Barn Owl Dr Hackettstown NJ 07840-3205 Personal E-mail: RCFremon@msn.com.

FRENCH, ANTHONY PHILIP, physicist, educator; b. Brighton, Eng., Nov. 19, 1920; came to U.S., 1955; s. Sydney James and Elizabeth Margaret (Hart) French; m. Naomi Mary Livesay, Oct. 6, 1945 (dec. 2001); m. Dorothy Ada Jensen, Apr. 30, 2002; children: Martin Charles, Gillian Ruth. BA with honors, Cambridge (Eng.) U., 1942, MA, 1946, PhD, 1948; ScD (hon.), Allegheny Coll., 1989. Mem. atomic bomb projects Tube Alloys and Manhattan Project, 1942-46; scientific officer Atomic Energy Rsch. Establishment U.K., 1946—48; demonstrator, lectr. physics Cambridge U., 1948-55; fellow Pembroke Coll., 1950-55; prof. physics U. S.C., 1955-63, chmn. dept., 1956-62; vis. prof. MIT, 1962-64, prof., 1964-91, prof. emeritus, 1991—; vis. fellow Pembroke Coll., Cambridge, 1975. Chmn. Internat. Commn. on Physics Edn., 1975-81. Author: Principles of Modern Physics, 1958, Special Relativity, 1968, Newtonian Mechanics, 1971, Vibrations and Waves, 1971, (with Edwin F. Taylor) Introduction to Quantum Physics, 1978, (with M.G. Ebison) Introduction to Classical Mechanics, 1986; editor: Einstein: A Centenary Volume, 1979, Physics in a Technological World, 1988; co-editor: Niels Bohr: A Centenary Volume, 1985, Physics History from AAPT Jours. II, 1995; contbr. articles to profl. jours. Recipient Univ. medal Charles U., Prague, 1980, Bragg medal Inst. Physics, U.K., 1988, Oersted medal Am. Assn. Physics Tchrs., 1989. Fellow Am. Phys. Soc.; mem. Am. Assn. Physics Tchrs. (pres. 1985-86, Oersted medal 1989, Melba Newell Phillips award 1993), Sigma Xi, Sigma Pi Sigma. Office: Mass Inst Tech Rm NE 25-4090 Cambridge MA 02139 Business E-Mail: apfrench@mit.edu.

FRENCH, BRENT ARTHUR, research scientist, engineering educator; b. Urbana, Ill., Dec. 18, 1956; s. Wilbur Lile and Yvonne (Henry) F.; m. Eileen Denney. PhD in Biochemistry, La. State U., 1987. Postdoct. fellow Baylor Coll. Medicine, Houston, 1987-91, asst. prof. medicine, 1991-95, U. Louisville (Ky.), 1995-98; assoc. prof. biomed. engring. U. Va., Charlotteville, 1998—. Mem. rsch. and rev. com. AHA, Dallas, 1995, Chgo., 1997. Pub. Health Svc. grantee NIH, 1997; recipient Established Investigator award AHA Nat. Ctr., 1997. Office: U Va Dept Biomed Engring PO Box 377 Charlottesville VA 22908-0001

FRENCH, CAROL ANN, reference librarian; b. Marion, Ohio, Feb. 13, 1944; d. Louis and Ruth Adeline (Dewiel) F.; m. Dennis LeRoy Furniss, Mar. 29, 1959; m. Raymond Swearingen, Sept. 11, 1962; children: Rick Furniss, Ron Furniss, Tammy Radabaugh, Toni Swearingen De Osegueda. Assoc. in Liberal Arts, Broward Community Coll., Pembroke Pines, Fla., 1984; BFA, Fla. Atlantic U., 1989; MLS, U. So. Fla. Br. mgr. Hallandale Beach Br. Libr., Broward County Librs. Artist: (pastel drawings) Inside Out, 1989 (hon. mention award 1989). Mem. Am. Libr. Assn., Broward County Libr. Assn. Avocations: reading, fishing, travel. Office: 300 S Federal Hwy Hallandale FL 33009 Office Phone: 954-457-1750. Business E-Mail: cfrench@browardlibrary.org.

FRENCH, CHRISTOPHER CHARLES, artist, writer; b. St. Louis, Aug. 5, 1957; s. Charles Berry French and Elizabeth Anne Pax; m. Terrie Frances Sultan, June 1, 1988. BA, U. Calif., Davis, 1980. Exec. dir. Wash. Project Arts, 1995—96; commentator Around Town, Wash. Ednl. Television Assn., Wash., 1997—2000; prof. Md. Inst. Coll. Art, Balt., 1999—2000; corr. Glasstire.com, Houston, 2001—, Flash Art, Milan, 2002—; prof. Glassell Sch. Art, Houston, 2002—. Mem. bd. Diverse Works, Houston, 2002—; mem. com. Mus. Fine Arts Houston Film Com., 2004—. Exhibitions include Bill Maynes Gallery, N.Y., 2000, Devin Borden Hiram Butler Gallery, Houston, 2005, survey exhbn., Galveston Art Ctr., 2003; editor: Facing History: The Black Image in American Art 1710-1940, 1990. Mem. co. N.Am. tour Royal Lichtenstein 1/4! Ring Circus, 1980—81. Fellow, Nat. Endowment Arts, Wash., 1993, Joan Mitchell Found., NY, 1999, Cultural Arts Coun., Houston, Harris County, 2003. Mem.: Internat. Art Critics Assn. E-mail: christopherfrench@mac.com.

FRENCH, CLARENCE LEVI, JR., retired shipbuilding company executive; b. New Haven, Oct. 13, 1925; s. Clarence L. Sr. and Eleanor (Curry) F.; m. Jean Sprague, June 29, 1946; children: Craig Thomas, Brian Keith, Alan Scott. BS in Naval Sci., Tufts U., 1945, BSME, 1947; ScD (hon.), Webb Inst., 1992. Registered profl. engr., Calif. Foundry engr. Bethlehem Steel Corp., 1947-56; staff engr., asst. supt. Kaiser Steel Corp., 1956-64; supervisory engr. Bechtel Corp., 1964-67; with Nat. Steel & Shipbldg. Co., San Diego, 1967-86, exec. v.p., gen. mgr., to 1977, pres., chief operating officer, 1977-84, chmn., chief exec. officer, 1984-86, outside dir., 1989-98. Past mem. maritime transp. rsch. bd. NRC. Bd. dirs. United Way, San Diego, YMCA, San Diego; past chmn., bd. dirs. Pres. Roundtable; chmn. emeritus bd. trustees Webb Inst. Lt. USN, 1943-53. Fellow Soc. Naval Architects and Marine Engrs. (hon., past pres.), Shipbuilders Council Am. (past chmn. exec. com.), ASTM, Am. Bur. Shipping; mem. Am. Soc. Naval Engrs., U.S. Naval Inst., Navy League U.S., Propeller Club U.S.

FRENCH, DAVID D., communications executive; BSEE, U. Rochester. In mgmt. pos. Tex. Instruments, Fairchild Semiconductor; v.p., gen. mgr. Analog Devices; pres., CEO Cirrus Logic, Austin, Tex., 1998—. Bd. dirs. Fabless Semiconductor Assn., Austin Idea Network. Office: Cirrus Logic 2901 Via Fortuna Austin TX 78746-7574

FRENCH, DORRIS TOWERS BRYAN, volunteer; b. Kissimmee, Fla., May 15, 1926; m. Lawrence Cornwell French, Sept. 7, 1947; children: Layne Bryan, Leyland Bradley. Student, Art Inst., Costa Rica, 1940-42; BFA, Tulane U., 1946; student, U. Mex., 1943-44. Fabric designer Wembley Co., 1945-46; designer silver and jewelry New Orleans, 1945-47; head art dept. pvt. sch., 1947. Columnist From the Mayor's Desk; editor pub. Paw Prints, 1981-93. Founder, v.p. Peoples Animal Welfare Soc., 1977-96; past art dir., coord. internat. gladiola show Garden Club, Binghamton. Mem. AAUW, Zeta Tau Alpha. Avocations: animal welfare, writing, art. Home: 3510 Aransas St Corpus Christi TX 78411-1302

FRENCH, ELIZABETH IRENE, biology professor, musician; b. Knoxville, Tenn., Sept. 20, 1938; d. Junius Butler and Irene Rankin (Johnston) F. MusB, U. Tenn., 1959, MS, 1962; PhD, U. Miss., 1973. Tchr. music Kingsport (Tenn.) Symphony Assn., 1962-64, Birmingham (Ala.) Schs., 1964-66; NASA trainee in biology U. Miss., Oxford, 1969-73; asst. prof. Mobile (Ala.) Coll. (name now U. Mobile), 1973-83, assoc. prof., 1983-94, prof., 1994—. Orch. contractor Am. Fedn. Musicians, 1983—; 1st violin Kingsport Symphony Orch., 1962-64, Birmingham Symphony Orch., 1964-66, Knoxville Symphony Orch., 1955-62, 66-68, Memphis Symphony Orch., 1970-73, Mobile Symphony Orch., 1974—, Pensacola Symphony Orch., Gulf Coast Symphony Orch., Mobile Symphony Players Com., 2001—; concertmaster Riviera Symphony Orch. and Chorus, Ala., 2005—. Violin recitalist Ala. Artists Series, 1978-81, Fairhope (Ala.) Concert Series, 1998. Mem. project Choctaw Nat. Wildlife Refuge, 1997-98. Named Career Woman of Yr., Gayfer's, Inc., 1985. Mem. Assn. Southeastern Biologists, Human Anatomy and Physiology Soc. (nat. com. to construct standardized test on anatomy and physiology), Wilderness Soc., Ala. Acad. Scis. (presenter 1996), Ala. Ornithol. Soc., Mobile Bay Audubon Soc. (bd. dirs. 1997—), Am. Fedn. Musicians, Ala. Fedn. Music Clubs (chmn. composition contest 1986-90, historian 1991-94), Schumann Music Club (pres. 1977-79, 85-87, 94-97, 2000-03, adv. bd. 2005—). Republican. Roman Catholic. Avocations: camping, photography, birdwatching. Home: 36 Ridgeview Dr Chickasaw AL 36611-1317 Office: U Mobile PO Box 13220 Mobile AL 36663-0220

FRENCH, HAROLD STANLEY, food company executive; b. Bklyn., Oct. 2, 1921; s. Morris and Fay (Kaufman) F.; m. Claire E. Weingart, Oct. 3, 1943 (dec. Mar. 1983); children: Madelaine Diane, Janet Gail. BA, L.I. U., 1942; postgrad., NYU, 1950, Columbia U., 1960, New Sch. U., 1970-71; PhD in Philosophy, Am. Coll., 1998. Asst. buyer R.H. Macy Co., N.Y.C., 1949-52; group mgr. Abraham & Straus Co., Hempstead, N.Y., 1952-54; mdse. mgr. Popular Club Plan, Passaic, N.J., 1954-60, Nat. Silver Co., N.Y.C., 1964-69; mktg. dir. Waverly Products Co., Phila., 1970-74; pres. Pet Food Industries, Inc., N.Y.C., 1974—, Harold French & Co., Inc., N.Y.C., 1974—, African Fruit Co. Inc., 1993—, Harold French Engring. Corp., 1993—. Pres. King Agro-Indsl. Corp., 1986, Globe King Agro-Indsl. Co. Ltd., Nigeria, 1988—; trade agt. to Nigerian Govt., 1992—, also builder workers' housing, supplier of housing materials; founder, pres. The People Speak mag., 1995; founder, pres., pub. New Century Pub. Co. Inc., 1998. Author: Dating and Mating for Women Over 50, Over 60, Over 70, 1999, You Can be a Hero, For Men Over 50, Over 60, Over 70, 1999. Chmn., pres. The Nigeria Fund, Inc., 1989—; contbg. patron N.Y. Met. Opera, N.Y.C. Ballet; home builder for Nigerian Govt. Workers. With mil. intelligence, U.S. Army, 1943-45. Decorated Bronze Star.

FRENCH, HENRY PIERSON, JR., retired historian, educator; b. Rochester, NY, Nov. 21, 1934; s. Henry Pierson and Genevieve Lynn (Johnson) F.; m. Beverly Anne Bauernschmidt, Aug. 22, 1959; children: Henry Pierson III, Donna Lynn (dec.), William Dean, Susan Gayle, John Douglas. AB, U. Del., 1960; MA, U. Rochester, 1961, MA in Edn., 1962, EdD, 1968. Tchr. Pittsford Ctrl. H.S., NY, 1962—66; field svc. assoc. U. Rochester, NY, 1962—66, assoc. lectr., 1967—68, vis. asst. prof. Coll. Edn. and East Asian Ctr., 1968—69, asst. prof. edn., 1969—70, assoc. prof. Ctr. Spl. Degree Programs, 1970—72, lectr. East Asian studies, 1972—74, sr. lectr., 1974—95; prof. history and polit. sci. SUNY, Monroe C.C., Rochester, 1964—2005; ret., 2005. Adj. asst. prof. history SUNY-Monroe C.C., 1964-67, asst. prof. history, 1967-70, assoc. prof., 1970-74, prof., 1974-2005, chief marshall, commencement, 2005, prof. emeritus history, 2005—, chmn. dept. history and polit. sci., 1979-85, chmn. retention, tenure and promotion com., 1985-2005, sabbatical leave, 1986, chair history and polit. sci. cluster in dept. anthropology, history, polit. sci. and sociology, 2001-04, coord. history and polit. sci. in dept. anthropology, history, polit. sci., sociology, 2001-04; moderator, host Disciplines Within the Social Scis. series, 1968; moderator, permanent panelist Fgn. Policy Assn. and Rochester Assn. for UN Great Decisions, 1973, 77, 78 series Channel 21 Ednl. TV, Rochester; cons., panelist Great Decisions TV series, 1982, 84; vis. prof. history, 1988-89; prof. Canisius Coll., 1968, 69, 71, 73, 89, Dunlop Tire Corp. Japan Inst. faculty, 1989, Rochester Inst. Tech., 1969-70, spring 1977, 98, SUNY, Brockport, 1971; adj. mentor SUNY-Empire State Coll., 1976, 88-89, 1997; co-dir., adminstr. NDEA insts., 1965-69; bd. dirs. Rochester Assn. UN, 1972-83, 85-91, chmn. policy com., 1972-74, v.p., 1975-77, pres., 1977-78, chmn. bd., 1978-79, chmn. nominating com., 1983-84; panelist Internat. Assn. Historians Asia, 1986, 1991, chair, 1994, Bangkok, 1996; presenter in field. Contbr. articles to profl. jours. Vestryman St. Thomas Episcopal Ch., Rochester, 1965-68, Christ Episc. Ch., Pittsford, 1976-79, jr. warden, 1979-80, sr. warden, 1980-81, chmn. rector selection com., 1982; del. to diocesan Conv., 1989-91, 94-97; 1st provisional lay dep. 1991; lay dep., 1994, 97; mem. commn. on Ordained Ministry, Episc. Diocese of Rochester, 1987-94, chmn., 1992-94; advisor Shanghai-Rochester Bishops' Visitation in U.S. and China, 1989-90, co-leader lay del. to Shanghai and China Christian Couns., China, 1992, 94, 97; coord. visit of Bishop Shen Yifan and Hong Luming to Rochester, Nov. 1-8, 1993; trustee Reynolds Libr. Bd., 1991—, pres. 2005—, Mendon Pub. Libr., 1996-97, Rochester Pub. Libr., 1992-2003, v.p., 1996-98, pres., 1998-2000; trustee Friends of Rochester Pub. Libr., 1983-2003, v.p., 1986-88, pres., 1988-91; trustee Rochester Regional Libr. Coun., 1998—; chmn. Rochester Lit. award to James Baldwin, 1986; active Edn. Adv. Bd., 1988-2005, Preferred Care HMO, 1988-2005, NY State Citizens' Com. for the Bicentennial of the French Revolution, 1988-90; Damon Benefactor Monroe Cmty. Coll. Found., 2003. Programs and Comparative Studies grantee, 1970; recipient SUNY Chancellor's medal for philanthropy for establishing endowed chair Henry Pierson French Sr. chair in bus. adminstrn./econs. at Monroe C.C. Rochester, 1999, establish scholarship fund in polit. sci. in the name of Henry Pierson French, III at Monroe C.C. Rochester, 2002; established endowed award in name of Henry Pierson French, Jr., Monroe C.C., Rochester, N.Y., 2005. Mem. Assn. Asian Studies, Mid. Atlantic and New Eng. Conf. for Can. Studies, Torch (bd. dirs. Rochester chpt. 1973-76, 97-2005, pres. 1974-75, Silver Torch award Internat. Assn. 2001), Brighton Schs. Alumni Assn. (co-chair 1999—), Univ. Club (v.p. 1975-76, sec. 1988-90, pres.-elect 1991-92, pres. 1992-93), Genesee Valley Club, Twenty Club, Delta Tau Delta. Episcopalian. Home: 78 Smith Rd Pittsford NY 14534-9727 Personal E-mail: hpfrench@rochestr.rr.com.

FRENCH, JOHN, III, lawyer, director; b. Boston, July 12, 1932; s. John and Rhoda (Walker) F.; m. Leslie Ten Eyck, Jan. 11, 1957 (div. 1961); children: John B., Lawrence C.; m. Anne Hubbell, Jan. 9, 1965 (div. 1983); children: Daniel J., Susanna H.; m. Marina Kellen, Nov. 21, 1987. BA, Dartmouth Coll., 1955; JD, Harvard U., 1958. Bar: NY 1959, D.C. 1988. Assoc. Milbank, Tweed, Hadley & McCloy, N.Y.C., 1961-68, Satterlee & Stephens, N.Y.C., 1968-73; asst. gen. counsel Continental Group, Inc., Stamford, Conn., 1973-81; v.p., gen. counsel, sec. Peabody Internat. Corp., Stamford, Conn., 1981-82; ptnr. Appleton, Rice & Perrin, N.Y.C., 1982-84, Beveridge and Diamond, N.Y.C., 1985-93, counsel, 1993-99; chmn. Tudor Assocs., LLC, N.Y.C., 1999—. Lectr. Practising Law Inst., 1979-83, Am. Law Inst., 1978; bd. dirs. Resorts Mgmt., Inc., Tudor Assocs., LLC, NYC, NY Philharmonic Soc., Salzburg Festival Soc., Inc. Contbr. articles to profl. jours. Trustee Hudson River Found., YMCA-YWCA Camping Svcs. Greater NY, Inc.; bd. dirs. Third St. Music Sch. Settlement House, Inc., NYC, Internat. House, Inc., NYC, Met. Opera Club, Young Concert Artists, Inc., 33 E. 70th St. Corp., Teatro alla Scala Found., Salzburg Festival Soc.; active Westchester County Planning Bd., 1974-85, NY State Environ. Bd., 1976-88. Capt. JAGC, USAF, 1958-61. Mem.: VFW, ABA, Am. Soc. Corp. Secs., Environ. Law Inst., Assn. of Bar City of N.Y. (lectr.), N.Y. State Bar Assn. (lectr.), Mayflower Descendants., Met. Opera Soc., Century Assn., Am. Legion, The Pilgrims, Knickerbocker Club, Harvard Club, River Club. Republican. Office: Tudor Assocs LLC 33 E 70th St New York NY 10021-4941 Office Phone: 212-585-3123. Personal E-mail: tudor33@aol.com, tudorassoc@aol.com.

FRENCH, JOHN DWYER, lawyer; b. Berkeley, Calif., June 26, 1933; s. Horton Irving and Gertrude Margery (Ritzen) F.; m. Annette Richard, 1955; m. Berna Jo Mahling, 1986. BA summa cum laude, U. Minn., 1955; postgrad, Oxford U., Eng., 1955-56; LLB magna cum laude, Harvard U., 1960. Bar: D.C. 1960, Minn. 1963. Law clk. Justice Felix Frankfurter, U.S. Supreme Ct., 1960-61; legal asst. to commr. FTC, 1961-62; assoc. Ropes & Gray, Boston, 1962-63, Faegre & Benson, Mpls., 1963-66, ptnr., 1967-75, mng. ptnr., 1975-94, chmn. mgmt. com., 1989-94. Mem. adj. faculty Law Sch. U. Minn., 1965-70, mem. search com. for dean of Coll. of Liberal Arts, 1996; mem. exec. com. Lawyers Com. for Civil Rights Under Law, 1978—; co-chmn. U.S. Dist. Judge Nominating Commn., 1979; vice chmn. adv. com., mem. dir. search com., chmn. devel. office search com. Hubert Humphrey Inst., 1979-87. Contbr. numerous articles and revs. to legal jours. Chmn. or co-chmn. Minn. State Dem. Farm Labor Party Conv., 1970-90, 94, chmn. Mondale Vol. Com., 1972, treas., 1974; assoc. chmn. Minn. Dem.-Farmer-Labor Party, 1985-86; mem. Dem. Nat. Com., 1985-86; mem. Dem. Nat. Conv., 1976, 78, 80, 84, 88; trustee Twin Cities Public TV, Inc., 1980-86, mem. overseers com. to visit Harvard U. Law Sch., 1970-75, 77-82; chmn. Minn. steering com. Dukakis for Pres., 1987-88; mem. Sec. of State's Commn. on Electoral Reform, Minn., 1994; mem. Mayor's Commn. on Regulatory Reform, Mpls., 1995. With U.S. Army, 1955-56. Rotary Found. fellow, 1955-56 Mem. ABA (editorial bd. jour. 1976-79, commn. to study fed. trade 1969—), Minn. Bar Assn., Hennepin County Bar Assn., Jud. Coun. Minn., Lawyers Alliance for Nuclear Arms Control (nat. bd. dirs. 1982-84), U. Minn. Alumni Assn. (exec. com. 1985-87, v.p. 1989-91, pres. 1991-92, Vol. of Yr. award 1988), Phi Beta Kappa. Episcopalian. Office: Faegre & Benson 2200 Wells Fargo Ctr 90 S 7th St Ste 2200 Minneapolis MN 55402-3901

FRENCH, JOSEPH JORDAN, JR., lawyer; b. Shreveport, La., Jan. 3, 1931; s. Joseph Jordan and Minnie Graham (Tomlinson) F.; m. Carol Jean Wesner, Dec. 22, 1954; children: Mary French Breckeen, Joseph Jordan III, Elizabeth French Pospick, Charles Robert. BS, Washington & Lee U., 1950; LLB, U. Tex., 1956. Bar: Tex. 1956, U.S. Dist. Ct. (no. dist.) Tex. 1956, U.S. Ct. Appeals (5th cir.), U.S. Tax Ct. Staff acct. W.O. Ligon & Co., Dallas, 1950-51; assoc. Thompson & Knight, Dallas, 1956-59; ptnr., shareholder Locke Purnell Rain Harrell, Dallas, 1959-93; prin. Joe French & Assocs., P.C., Dallas, 1993—. Sec. Trinity Industries, Inc., Dallas, 1969-97, Halter Marine Group Inc., 1996-97. 2nd lt. USAF, 1951-53. Home: 4440 Fairfax Ave Dallas TX 75205-3028 Office: Joe French & Assocs PC 5485 Beltline Rd Ste 150 Dallas TX 75254 Office Phone: 214-363-9800. Business E-Mail: jfrench@joefrench.com.

FRENCH, JUDSON CULL, federal official; b. Washington, Sept. 30, 1922; s. Morrison Brady and Ethel (Haviland) Cull French; m. Julia A. McAllister, Aug. 1, 1951; 1 child, Judson Cull. BS cum laude, Am. U., 1943; MS, Harvard U., 1949, postgrad. at bus. sch., 1968; postgrad., Johns Hopkins U., 1943-44, George Washington U., 1944-45, MIT, 1951. Instr. physics Johns Hopkins U., Balt., 1943-44, George Washington U., Washington, 1944-47; sec., dir. Home Title Ins. Co., Washington, 1956-71; with Nat. Bur. Standards (now Nat. Inst. Standards and Tech.), Commerce Dept., Washington, 1948—, asst. chief electron devices sect., 1964-68, chief electron devices sect., 1968-73, chief electronic tech. div., 1973-78, dir. Ctr. for Electronics and Elec. Engring., 1978-91; dir. Electronics and Elec. Engring. Lab., Nat. Inst. Standards and Tech., Gaithersburg, Md., 1991-99, dir. emeritus Electronics and Elec. Engring. Lab., 1999—. Guest rschr., 2000-; pvt. cons., 2000; mem. policy bd. Optoelectronic Computing Sys. Ctr. U. Colo., 1992—; bd. dirs. Nat. Electronics Mfg. Intitiative, Inc., 1998-99; co-chmn. jt. mgmt. com., U.S.-Japan Jt. Optoelectronics Project, 1992-2002; founder NBS/NIST semicondr. metrology program, 1955. Contbr. articles to profl. jours. Recipient Silver medal for meritorious svc. Commerce Dept., 1964, Gold medal for exceptional svc., 1978, Edward Bennett Rosa award Nat. Bur. Standards, 1971, presdl. rank of Meritorious Exec., Sr. Exec. Svc., 1980, Disting. Exec., 1984, 93; Judson C. French award established in his honor Nat. Inst. Stds. and Tech., 1999. Fellow IEEE; mem. Am. Phys. Soc., Nat. Acad. Engring., Sigma Pi Sigma, Pi Delta Epsilon, Alpha Kappa Pi. Office: Nat Inst Standards and Tech Metrology Bldg Rm B358 Electronics Electrical Engr Lab Gaithersburg MD 20899

FRENCH, KENNETH RONALD, finance educator; b. Franklin, N.H., Mar. 10, 1954; s. Vernon Cecil and Barbara Jean (Craig) F.; m. Vickie Anne Welch, Sept. 18, 1976; children: Robert Timothy, Laura Nancy, Elizabeth Anne. BSME, Lehigh U., 1975; MBA, U. Rochester, 1978, MS in Fin., 1981, PhD in Fin., 1983. Machine design engr. Eastman Kodak, Rochester, N.Y., 1975-77; rsch. fellow Found. for Rsch. in Econs. and Edn., UCLA, 1982-83; asst. prof. Grad. Sch. Bus., U. Chgo., 1983-85, assoc. prof., 1985-87, prof., 1987-89, Chgo. Mercantile Exch. prof., 1989-91, Leo Melamed prof., 1991-94; Edwin J. Beinecke prof. Yale Sch. Mgmt., New Haven, 1994-98, mng. dir. Intenat. Ctr. Fin., 1994-98; NTU prof. fin. Sloan Sch. Mgmt., MIT, Cambridge, Mass., 1998—2001; Heidt prof. fin. Tuck Sch. Bus., Dartmouth, Hanover, NH, 2001—. Rsch. assoc. Nat. Bur. Econ. Rsch., Cambridge, Mass., 1989—; dir. Ctr. for Rsch. in Security Prices, Chgo., 1990-94. Contbr. numerous articles to profl. jours. Batterymarch Investment fellow, 1986; Sloan Found. grantee, 1989. Home: 85 Trescott Rd Etna NH 03750-4505 Office: Tuck Sch Bus Dartmouth 100 Tuck Hall Hanover NH 03755-9000

FRENCH, LAURENCE ARMAND, social sciences educator; b. Manchester, NH, Mar. 24, 1941; s. Gerald Everett and Juliette Teresa (Boucher) F.; m. Nancy Picthall, Feb. 13, 1971. BA cum laude, U. N.H., 1968, MA, 1970, PhD, 1975; postdoctorate, SUNY, Albany, 1978; PhD, U. Nebr., 1981; MA, Western N.M. U., 1994. Diplomate Am. Bd. Forensic Medicine, Am. Bd. Forensic Examiners, Am. Bd. Psychol. Specialties in Forensic Psychology & Neuropsychology, Am. Coll. Advanced Practice Psychologists; lic. psychologist, Ariz. Instr. U. So. Maine, Portland and Gorham, 1971-72; asst. prof. Western Carolina U., Cullowhee, N.C., 1972-77, U. Nebr., Lincoln, 1977-80; psychologist I N.H. Hosp., Concord, 1980-81; psychologist II Laconia (N.H.) State Sch., 1981-88; sr. psychologist N.H. Divsn. for Children & Youth Svcs., Concord, 1988-89; prof., chair dept. social scis. Western N.Mex. U., Silver City, 1989—2003, prof. emeritus of psychology, 2003—; sr. rsch. assoc. justiceworks U. NH Inst. for Policy and Social Sci. Rsch., 2002—; prof., head dept. psychology Coll. Juvenile Justice and Psychology, Prairie View A&M U., 2003—04. Profl. adv. bd. Internat. Coll. Prescribing Psychologists; cons. N.C. Dept. Mental Health, 1972—77, Cherokee (N.C.) Indian Mental Health Program, 1974—77, Nebr. Indian Commn., Lincoln, 1977—80; cons. alcohol program Lincoln Indian Ctr., 1977—80; adj. assoc. prof. U. So. Maine, 1980—84; faculty adviser Psi Chi Nat. Honor Soc. in psychology Western N.Mex. U., 1995—2003; mem. Psi Chi Rocky Mountain Regional Steering Com., 2001—02; faculty adviser Psi Chi Nat. Honor Soc. in psychology Prairie View A&M U., 2003—. Author: The Selective Process of Criminal Justice, 1976; author: (with Richard Crowe) Wee Wish Tree: Special Qualla Cherokee Issue, 1976; author: (with Hornbuckle) Cherokee Perspective, 1981; author: (with Letman et al.) Contemporary Issues in Corrections, 1981; author: Indians and Criminal Justice, 1982, Psychocultural Change and the American Indian, 1987, The Winds of Injustice, 1994, Counseling American Indians, 1997, The Qualla Cherokee Surviving in Two Worlds, 1998, Addictions and Native Americans, 2000, Native American Justice, 2003; author: (with Manzanarez) NAFTA & Neocolonialism, 2004; spl. issue editor Quar. Jour. Ideology, Vol. II, 1987, mem. editl. bd. Jour. Police and Criminal Psychology; contbr. articles to profl. jours. Commr. Pilsbury Lake Village Dist., Webster, N.H., 1985-90. With USMC, 1959-63, Badge of Honor, Republic of China, 1998. Recipient Hon. medal Rep. China, 1998, Nat. Int. Drug Abuse 1st Leadership in Rsch. award, 1999, Lifetime Achievement award N.Mex. Assn. for Addiction Profls., 2004; Dissertation Yr. fellow U. N.H. 1971-72, Nebr. U. System grad. faculty fellow, 1978. Fellow: APA, Am. Coll. Forensic Examiners (diplomate), Soc. Psychol. Study Social Issues, Prescribing Psychologists Register (diplomate); mem.: VFW (life), N.Mex. Alcohol and Drug Abuse Counselors Assn. (Educator of Yr. 1997), Am. Soc. Criminology (life), Nat. Assn. Alcohol and Drug Abuse Counselors (clin. issue com. 1996—98, nat. chmn.), Internat. Coll. Prescribing Psychologists Inc. (profl. adv. bd.), Nat. Assn. Sch. Psychologists, 3rd Marine Divsn. Assn. (life), Psi Chi (steering com. Rocky Mountain region 1999—2003, Regional Faculty Advisor award 2002—03), Phi Delta Kappa (treas. Rocky Mountain region 1990—91, pres. 1991—92). E-mail: Laurence_French@unh.edu, frogwnmu@yahoo.com.

FRENCH, LENNY SUE, elementary school educator; b. Norwich, NY, Aug. 15, 1967; d. Leonard Albert and Bette Lou Mayne; m. Matthew Scott French; 1 child, Lane Matthew; 1 child, Ethan Michael. MusB, Crane Sch. Music, 1989; MSc in edn., State U. of NY Coll. at Potsdam, 1993. Vocal, music and drama tchr. Salmon River Ctrl. Sch., Ft. Covington, NY, 1989—99, Graham Mid. Sch., 1999—2003; math and sci. educator Mendenhall Mid. Sch., Greensboro, NC, 2003—. Diversity trainer Alamance County Schools, Burlington, NC, 2000—03, suicide intervention counselor, 2000—03. Musician Wendover Hills Wesleyan Ch., Greensboro, NC, 2000—01; canoeing/kayaking instr. Red Cross, 1986—94. Recipient Gold award, Girl Scout, 1985, Nat. Vocal Music award, Sherburne-Earlville Ctrl. Sch., 1985. Mem.: NY State Music Sch. Assn., NC Assn. of Music Educators, NC Assn. of Educators, Sigma Alpha Iota. Avocations: swimming, scrapbooks, gardening. Office: Mendenhall Mid Sch Willoughby Blvd Greensboro NC 27408

FRENCH, MARILYN, writer, critic, historian; b. N.Y.C., Nov. 21, 1929; d. E. Charles and Isabel (Hazz) Edwards; m. Robert M. French, Jr., June 4, 1950 (div. 1967); children: Jamie, Robert. BA, Hofstra Coll., 1951, MA, 1964; PhD, Harvard U., 1972. Secretarial, clerical worker, 1946-53; lectr. Hofstra Coll., 1964-68; asst. prof. Holy Cross Coll., Worcester, Mass., 1972-76; Mellon fellow Harvard U., 1976-77; writer, lectr., 1967—. Author: (criticism) The Book as World: James Joyce's Ulysses, 1976, Shakespeare's Division of Experience, 1981, The Women's Room, 1977, The Bleeding Heart, 1980, Beyond Power: On Women, Men and Morals, 1986, Her Mother's Daughter, 1987, The War Against Women, 1992, Our Father: A Novel, 1994, My Summer with George, 1996, A Season in Hell, 1998, From Eve To Dawn: A History of Women, Vol. I-III, 2002—03, (introductions) Summer and The House of Mirth, 1981, Her Mothers, 1985, A Weave of Women, 1985. Mem. Phi Beta Kappa. E-mail: mfrench187@aol.com.

FRENCH, MARY B., editor, photographer, poet, retired literature educator; b. Dallas, July 21, 1942; d. Harry Blake and Mary Virginia (Jones) F.; m. Richard Edelin Crouch, Feb. 6, 1965; children: John, Virginia. BA, Coll. William and Mary, 1965; MA, U. Va., 1966. Columnist, reporter Va. Gazette, Williamsburg, 1961-65; mng. editor William and Mary Rev., Williamsburg, 1963-64; asst. editor Microfilm Publ., U. Va., Charlottesville, 1966-67; lectr. Am. lit. and women in lit. U. Va., Falls Church, 1968-99. Instr. English, No. Va. C.C., Annandale, 1968-69; instr. English composition George Washington U., Washington, 1970; cons. in lit. humanities project Arlington County Libr., 1976. Author: The State Slate: A Guide to Legislative Procedures and Lawmakers, 1977; compiler: Women in Literature: A Bibliography, 1973; editor (with J.L. Anderson) Microfilm Edition of the Papers of R.M.T. Hunter, 1817-1887, 1966; editor Spokeswoman Mag., 1979-82, Washington Women's Rep. Newsletter, 1979-82; mng. editor Women's News Svc., 1979-82; assoc. editor Career Opportunities News, 1983-96; mng. editor Army Mag., 1984-93, editor, 1993-2002, editor in chief, 2002—; contbr. poetry to several anthologies. Com. on Status of Women, Arlington, Va., 1976, steering com. Coalition on Optimum Growth, 1970-73. Mem. MLA, AAUW (chmn. women's studies, dir. Arlington br. 1974-76, assoc. editor Grad. Women mag. 1982, mng. editor publ. 1983), the Am. News Women's Club, the Acad. of Am. Poets, the Lyon Village Citizens Assoc., Hillsboro Cmty. Assn., English-Speaking Union, Jane Austen Soc., US Congress Periodical Press Corrs.'s Assn., Nat. Trust Hist. Preservation, Preservation Soc. Loudoun County, Old House Group Loudoun County, Soc. Profl. Journalists, Am. Soc. Mag. Editors, Va. Hist. Soc., Land Trust of Va., The Nature Conservancy, Appalachian Trail Conf., Photo Commn. of the Nat. Press Club, (hon.) 101st Airborne Divsn. U.S. Army. Episcopalian. Address: 2624 N 18th St Arlington VA 22201-4049 Office: 2425 Wilson Blvd Arlington VA 22201-3326 Address: 14076 Mountain Rd Purcellville VA 20132 Office Phone: 703-907-2620. E-mail: mfrench@ausa.org.

FRENCH, MICHAEL BRUCE, marketing executive; b. Arlington, Va., Sept. 18, 1954; s. Orville Sidney and Doris (Goldberg) F.; m. Robin Ann Abenstein, Oct. 15, 1978; children: Brian Michael, Matthew Jeffrey, Sean Thornton. BA, Princeton U., 1976; M in Mgmt., Northwestern U., 1978. Brand asst., asst. brand mgr. Procter & Gamble Co., Cin., 1978—80, brand mgr., 1981—84; mktg. dir. Coca-Cola Bottling Mideast Inc. subs. P&G, Lexington, Ky., 1984—85; v.p. mktg. Coca-Cola Bottling Mideast, Inc., Lexington, 1985—87; brand mgr. Coca-Cola USA, Atlanta, 1987—89; mktg. mgr. chain accounts Coca-Cola Fountain, Atlanta, 1989, dir. channel mktg., 1989—93, dir. product definition and devel., 1993, asst. v.p. mktg. ops., 1993—94, v.p. mktg., 1994—95; dir. edn. mktg. Coca-Cola USA, Atlanta, 1995—97, dir. consumer occasions mktg., non-retail, 1997—99; dir. Coca-Cola Connection, 1999—2000; sr. cons. Monitor Co., Cambridge, Mass., 2000—02; v.p., mktg. insights Brown-Forman Corp., 2003—. Mem. Rep. Party of Ga., Atlanta, 1984-99; mem. baseball steering com. U. Ky., Lexington, 1986-87; fundraising chmn. Jr. Achievement of the Bluegrass, Lexington, 1986-87; chmn. pub. awareness subcom. Gov.'s Anti-Substance Abuse Commn., Frankfort, Ky., 1986-87; divsn. coord. Coca-Cola United Way Campaign, 1996; mem. Louisville Fund for Arts, 2003—. Named to Hon. Order of Ky. Cols., 1986. Mem. Princeton Club of Ky. Avocations: golf, youth baseball and football, reading, family. Office: Brown Forman 850 Dixie Hwy Louisville KY 40210 Home: 316 Longview Park Pl Louisville KY 40245 Office Phone: 502-774-7554. E-mail: frenchmike@msn.com, mike_french@b-f.com.

FRENCH, MICHAEL FRANCIS, medical educator; b. La Crosse, Wis., July 25, 1948; s. Albert Frank Jr. and Kathryn Patricia (MacKoske) F.; m. Janet Alan Streeter Head, Nov. 26, 1991. BS in Edn., U. Wis., 1972. Cert. emergency med. technician. Tng. coord. emergency med. svcs. Wis. Dept. Health and Social Svcs., Madison, 1975-80, tng. dir. emergency med. svcs., 1980-84, chief emergency med. svcs., 1984-90; co-dir. Area Health Edn. Ctrs. office Kirksville (Mo.) Coll. Osteo. Medicine, 1990—, adj. instr. family medicine and cmty. health, 1990—. Emergency med. svcs. cons., Kirksville, 1984—; founding mem. Continuing Edn. Coordinating Bd. for Emergency Med. Svcs., Inc., Kirksville, 1992. Author: (tng. curriculum) EMS Instructor Training Course-U.S. Dept. Transportation, 1985; editor newsletter, editor-in-chief publs. Nat. Assn. Emergency Med. Technicians, 1983-91; author book chpts. V.p., pres. bd. dirs. Adair County Ret. Sr. Vol. Program, Kirksville, 1992-95; com. chair, bd. dirs. Mo. Rural Opportunities Coun., 2000—. Recipient Lunda Trauma award Am. Trauma Soc., 1982, Svc. awards Nat. Coun. State EMS Tng. Coords., 1982, 83, A. Roger Fox Founders award Nat. Assn. Emergency Med. Technicians, 1989, others. Mem. ASTM, ASCD, ASTD, APHA, Nat. Rural Health Assn. (rural health policy bd. 1998—, gov. affairs com. 2000—, sec. 2005—, trustee 2005—), Mo. Rural Health Assn. (bd. dirs. 1995-96, 99—, pres.-elect 1996-97, pres. 1997-99, exec. com. 1999—), Mo. PEW Health Professions Partnership (chair exec. com. 1994-95), Mo. Pub. Health Assn. (awards chair 1996), Wis. Emergency Med. Tech. Assn., Am. Coll. Healthcare Execs. (assoc.), Nat. Orgn. Area Health Edn. Ctr. Program Dirs. (nominations com. 1996), Mensa Avocations: bicycling, reading, computer games. Office: KCOM AHEC Program 800 W Jefferson St Kirksville MO 63501-1443

FRENCH, PATSY, property manager, state representative; b. Randolph, Vt., Aug. 22, 1949; m. Patrick French; 2 children. BS in Edn., U. Vt., 1972. Owner, mgr. rental property; rep. Vt. State Ho. Reps., 2003—. Democrat. Home: 886 Harlow Hill Randolph VT 05060

FRENCH, RICHARD VAUGHN, federal agency administrator; b. Beckley, W.Va., Feb. 8, 1966; s. Zina Harold and Betty Jo (Hutchison) F.; m. Jamie Lyn Hart, Oct. 12, 1996. BA in Polit. Sci., W.Va. U., 1988, MPA, 1989. Staff asst. Rep. Nick J. Rahall II, Washington, 1990; labor rels. specialist U.S. Dept. Labor, Washington, 1990-95, program mgmt. specialist, 1995-97, program analyst, 1997-98, spl. asst. to asst. sec., 1998—. Spl. asst. Corp. Nat. Svc., Washington, Phila., 1997. Mem. Am. Soc. Pub. Adminstn., W.Va. Soc. Washington (1st v.p. 1997—). Office: US Dept Labor Rm S-2203 200 Constitution Ave NW Washington DC 20210-0001

FRENCH, RODERICK STUART, university chancellor; b. LaGrande, Oreg., Apr. 5, 1931; s. Stuart Gautier and Laura A. (Richards) F.; m. Evelyn Fagg, 1955 (div. 1964); children: Roderick Stuart, Jr., Sarah Suzanne; m. Sally Stedman, May 8, 1965. AB, Kenyon Coll., 1954; MDiv, Episcopal Div. Sch., 1957; STM, Union Theol. Sem., 1965; PhD, George Washington U., 1971. Dir. youth dept. World Coun. Chs., Geneva, 1959-64; freelance writer Balt., Washington, 1964-67; spl. asst. office pub. affairs Peace Corps., Washington, 1967-68; assoc. dir. office exptl. programs George Washington U., Washington, 1969-78, dir., 1978-84, v.p. acad. affairs, 1984-95, dir. univ. seminars program, 1995-97; chancellor Am. U. of Sharjah, United Arab Emirates, 1998—2002, dir. Washington office, trustee, 2002—. Editor: What is Humanistic Education?, 1973, An Independent University in a Free Society, 1988; co-editor: The Public Humanities, 1984; gen. editor monograph series GW Washington Studies, 10 vols., 1974-82; contbr. articles to profl. jours. Chmn. D.C. Humanities Coun., 1979-81; v.p. Nat. Humanities Alliance, 1986-88, pres. 1988-92, exec. com., 1988-94; bd. dirs. Nat. Fed. State Humanities Councils, Washington, 1983-86, Potomac River Basin Consortium, Washington, 1981-85; bd. mgrs. Columbia Hist. Soc., Washington, 1980-84; trustee, 1st v.p. Ctr. for Advanced Study of the Americas, 1984-87, pres. 1987-88; trustee Nat. Cultural Alliance, 1990-92. Recipient Citation for Outstanding Contbn. to Cultural Life in Washington, Washington Rev., 1979, D.C. Pub. Humanities award, 1988; named Hon. Citizen, Winnipeg, Man., Can., 1961. Mem. Am. Soc. Environ. History (v.p. 1977-81), Cosmos Club, Phi Beta Kappa. Democrat. Home: 2801 New Mexico Ave NW Apt 1124 Washington DC 20007-3912 Office: Am Univ Sharjah Washington Office 3201 New Mexico Ave NW Washington DC 20016 Office Phone: 202-885-1796. Business E-Mail: rfrench@american.edu.

FRENCH, STEPHANIE TAYLOR, corporate philanthropist; b. Newark; d. William Taylor and Connie V. French; m. Amory Houghton III, Sept. 8, 1979 (div.); children: Christina French Houghton, Amory Taylor Houghton. BA, Wellesley Coll., 1972; MBA, Harvard U., 1978. Freelance on-air performer, prodr. San Francisco and Oakland radio and cable TV stas., 1973-76; dir. European Gallery, San Francisco, 1974-75; acct. exec. Young & Rubican, NYC, 1978-79; acct. supr. Rives Smith Baldwin & Carlberg, Houston, 1980-81; mgr. cultural affairs and spl. programs Philip Morris Cos. Inc., NYC, 1981-86, dir. cultural and contbns. programs, 1986-90, v.p. corp. contbn. and cultural programs bds., 1990—2001; pvt. practice NYC, 2001—05; sr. v.p. US Trust Co., 2005—. Bd. dirs. New Mus. Contemporary Art, Mus. Arts and Design, Parsons Dance Co., Miller Theatre Columbia U., PERFORMA, Works and Process, Shen Wei Dance, Harkness Ctr. for Dance Injuries, Bus. Com. of the Met. Mus. Art, Arts and Edn. Adv. Coun. for Harvard Grad. Sch. Edn., Ballet Tech, Career Transitions for Dancers; bd. adv. com. Bill T. Jones/Arnie Zane Co.; dance com. Juillard Sch.; apptd. mem. Gov. of NY to Empire State Arts Commn., Mayor of NYC to the NYC Econ. Devel. Corp. Mem. Harvard Bus. Sch. Network of Women Alums, Wellesley Club.

FRENCH, TARENCE WADE, SR., minister; b. Indpls., Oct. 18, 1971; s. James Wayne French and Michelle Dianne Blackwell; m. Donna Marie Young, Apr. 15, 2001; children: Destini Marie Young, Tessa Iman, Alexa Seymone, Tarence Wanyai French, Jr. PhD, St. Luke Evang. Sch. of Bibl. Studies, Atlanta, 2003; ThD, United Theol. Sem., Ashland. Ind., 2004; cert. of Bibl. Mental Health, Master's Grad. Sch. of Continuing Studies, Evansville, Ind., 2003; DMin (hon.), So. Ind. Bible Coll. & Sem., Clarksville, 2004; DDIV (hon.), Mt. Carmel Inst. of Bibl. Studies, L.A., 2003, The Interfaith Sch. of Theology, London, 2003, Trinitarian Ministries Sch. of Theology, Hot Springs, Ark., 2002. Cert. tchr. Nat. Assn. of Pvt. Theol. Instns., 2004. Ceo Urban Harvest Ministries, Inc., Indpls., 1998—; founding pastor Divine Revelations Christian Ctr., Inc., Indpls., 2002—; pres. Urban Harvest Bible Inst., Indpls., 2002—; instr. Crossroads Bible Inst., Grandeville, Mich., 2002—. Mem. Mt. Carmel Inst. of Bibl. Studies, L.A., 2003; bishop elect Grace Valley Theol. Sem., Lubbock, Tex., 2004. Named Ky. Col., Gov. Paul E. Patton, 2003; recipient Name was placed on the Wall of Tolerance, Nat. Campaign for Tolerance, 2002. Mem.: Nat. Assn. Pvt. Theol. Instns. Office: Divine Revelations Christian Center Inc 2035 E 46th St Indianapolis IN 46205 Office Phone: 317-202-9313. Office Fax: 317-202-9506. E-mail: drtwfrench@yahoo.com.

FRENCH, WILLIAM HAROLD, retired newspaper editor; b. London, Ont., Can., Mar. 21, 1926; s. Harold Edward and Isabel (Brash) F.; m. Margaret Jean Rollo, June 23, 1951; children— Jane, Mark, Paul, Susan. BA, U. Western Ont., 1948; Nieman fellow, Harvard, 1954-55; DLitt (hon.), U. Western Ont., 1991. With The Globe and Mail, Toronto, Ont., Can., 1948-90, lit. editor, 1960-90; instr. journalism Ryerson Poly. Inst., 1955-88; asso. fellow York U., 1969-77; broadcaster Canadian Broadcasting Corp., 1964-90, ret., 1990. Cons. Can. Council, 1969— Author: A Most Unlikely Village, 1960. Recipient President's medal U. Western Ont., 1966; Nat. Newspaper award for critical writing, 1978, 79 Home: 78 N Hills Terr Don Mills ON Canada M3C 1M6

FRENIER, DIANE M., lawyer; b. Burlington, Vt., June 8, 1957; BS in mgmt. magna cum laude, Rutgers U., 1982, JD, 1986. Bar: NJ 1986. Assoc. Smith, Stratton, Wise, Heher & Brennan, Princeton, NJ, 1986—91, ptnr., 1993—2000; assoc. Hannoch Weisman, Roseland, NJ, 1991—93; ptnr. Reed Smith LLP, Princeton, NJ, 2000—, mem. exec. com. Mem.: NJ State Bar Assn., ABA (mem. bus. law sect.). Office: Reed Smith LLP Princeton Forrestal Village 136 Main St, Ste 250 Princeton NJ 08540 Office Phone: 609-514-5999. Office Fax: 609-951-0824. Business E-Mail: dfrenier@reedsmith.com.

FRENK, JULIO JOSE, secretary of health for Mexico, health systems researcher, consultant; b. Mexico City, Mex., Dec. 20, 1953; s. Silvestre and Alicia (Mora) Frenk; m. Josefina Quezada (div. 1955); children: Esteban Frenk Quezada, Emilio Jose Frenk Quezada; m. Felicia Marie Knaul, Nov. 11, 1995; 1 child, Hannah Sofia Frenk Knaul. MD, Nat. U. Mex., 1979; MPH, U. Mich., Ann Arbor, 1981, MA, 1982, PhD, 1983. Asst. prof. Sch. Pub. Health U. Mich., Ann Arbor, 1982—84; founding dir. Ctr. for Publ. Health Rsch. Min. Health, Mexico, 1984—87; founding dir. gen. Nat. Inst. Pub. Health, Cuernavaca, Mexico, 1987—92; vis. prof. Ctr. for Population and Devel. Studies Harvard U., Cambridge, 1992—93; dir. Project of Health and Economy Mexican Health Found., Mexico, 1993—94; exec. v.p., dir. Mexican Health Found., Mexico, 1995—98; exec. dir. evidence info. policy World Health Orgn., Geneva, 1998—; sec. of health Govt. of Mexico, 2000—. Adj. prof. doctoral program Nat. Inst. Pub. Health, Cuernavaca, 1994—; part time adv. World Bank, Washington, 1995—96; regional editor for L.Am. and Caribbean Health Policy Jour., Leuven, Belgium, 1993—, mem., 1987—. Author 8 books, 1976, 1978, 1988, 1992, 1993, 1994; contbr. chapters to books; editor 7 books, 1985, 1990, 1991, 1995, 1997; contbr. articles to profl. jours. Mem. adv. group on reconstrn. of health svcs., Mexico City, 1985—86; mem. Adv. Scientific Coun. Sci. Mus. Nat. U. Mex., Mexico City, 1995—. Named Nat. Rschr., Nat. Rschrs. Sys., Mex., 1984—; recipient Cecilio A. Robelo award for scientific rsch., State Govt. Morelos, Mex., Cuernavaca, 1993. Mem.: APHA, Inst. Medicine NAS, Nat. Acad. Medicine. Avocations: classical music, opera, kaleidoscopes. Home: Jazmin 62 Col Tetelpan 01700 Mexico City Mexico Office: Lieja Num 7 Colonia Juarez-10 PISO 06696 Mexico

FRENKEL, DOUGLAS N., law educator; b. 1947; BA, U. Pa., 1968, JD, 1972. Bar: Pa. 1972. Law clk. to Hon. Theodore O. Spaulding Superior Ct., Pa., 1972-73; from staff atty. to mng. atty. Community Legal Svcs., Phila., 1973-78; lectr., clin. supr. U. Pa., Phila., 1978-80, clin. dir., lectr., 1980-85, prof. law, dir. clin. programs, 1985—. Faculty coord. task force on alternate dispute resolutions Am. Arbitration Assn. Office: U Pa Law Sch 3400 Chestnut St Philadelphia PA 19104-6204 Office Phone: 215-898-4628. Office Fax: 215-573-2025. E-mail: dfrenkel@law.upenn.edu.*

FRENKEL, EUGENE PHILLIP, physician; b. Detroit, Aug. 27, 1929; s. David Eugene and Eva (Antin) Frenkel; m. Rhoda Beth Smilay, Dec. 21, 1958; children: Lisa Michelle, Peter Alan. BS, Wayne State U., 1949; MD, U. Mich., 1953. Diplomate Am. Bd. Internal Medicine (bd. govs. 1980-87, chmn. subspecialty com. hematology 1980-85), Am. Bd. Hematology, Am. Bd. Med. Oncology. Intern Wayne County Gen. Hosp., Eloise, Mich., 1953-54; resident in internal medicine Boston City Hosp., 1954-55; resident in internal medicine, then instr. U. Mich. Med. Center, 1957-62; mem. faculty U. Tex. Southwestern Med. Ctr., Dallas, 1962—, prof. internal medicine and radiology, 1969—, chief divsn. hematology-oncology, 1962-91, Patsy R. and Raymond D. Nasher Disting. chair in cancer rsch., 1990—, A. Kenneth Pye prof. in cancer rsch., 1994—; chief nuclear medicine, cons. hematology-oncology VA Med. Center, Dallas, 1962-80; Sydney and J.L. Huffines, Jr. disting. chair U. Tex. Southwestern Med. Ctr., 1998—, Elaine Dewey Sammons Disting. chair cancer rsch. in honor of Eugene P. Frenkel, MD, 2003—. Cons. com. evaluation rsch. hematology, nutrtion Nat. Inst. Arthritis and Metabolic Diseases, 1979—82; active Am. Joint Commn. Cancer, 1986—95; interim dir. divsn. hematology-oncology VA Med. Ctr., Dallas, 1995—97. Contbr. rsch. papers in field. Officer M.C. USAF, 1955—57. Named Elaine Dewey Sammons Disting. chair in cancer rsch., Honor of Eugene P. Frenkel, 2003—. Fellow: ACP (coun. subspecialty secs. 1992—), Internat. Soc. Hematology; mem.: Internat. Assn. Study Lung Cancer, Internat. Soc. Hematology (councillor 1992—97), Am. Fedn. Clin. Rsch., Soc. Nuc. Medicine, Am. Urol. Assn., So. Soc. Clin. Investigation, Am. Soc. Clin. Investigation, Am. Soc. Biol. Chemists, Am. Assn. Cancer Edn., Am. Assn. Cancer Rsch., Assn. Am. Physicians, Am. Cancer Soc. (pres. Dallas unit 1970—71, mem. sci. adv. com. clin. investigations II-chemotherapy and hematolog 1978—82, mem. nat. clin. fellowship com. 1978—87, dir. Tex. divsn. 1978—, Emma Freeman prof. 1981—91, mem. internat. rsch. grants com. 1988—90, mem. sci. adv. coun. 1991—97), Am. Soc. Clin. Oncology (chmn. membership com. 1982—85), Am. Soc. Hematology (treas. 1976—84), Alpha Omega Alpha. Office: U Tex Southwestern Med Ctr Dallas TX 75390-8852 Office Phone: 214-648-4180.

FRENKEL, JACOB AHARON, insurance company executive; b. Tel-Aviv, Israel, Feb. 8, 1943; came to U.S., 1967; s. Kalman H. and Lea (Zwibaum) F.; m. Niza Yair, Sept. 3, 1968; children: Orli-Miriam, Tahl-Ida. BA in Econs. and Polit. Sci, Hebrew U., Jerusalem, 1966, postgrad. (fellow), 1966-67; MA (fellow), U. Chgo., 1969, PhD in Econs. (Lilly Honor fellow), 1970. Mem. faculty Grad. Sch. Bus., U. Chgo., 1973-87, David Rockefeller prof. internat. econs., 1982-87; econ. counsellor, dir. research IMF, 1987-91; mem. faculty Tel Aviv U., 1991-96, Weisfeld prof. econs. of peace and internat. rels., 1994-96; gov. bank of Israel, Jerusalem, 1991-99; chmn. sovereign advisory group Merrill Lynch, London, 2000—04; chmn. Merrill Lynch Internat. Inc., 2000—04; vice chmn. Amer. Internat. Group, 2004—, chmn., global econ. strategies group, 2004—. Mem. G-7 Coun., adv. com. of Inst. for Internat. Econs.; mem. group of 30, disting. mem. adv. com. Korea Inst. for Global Econs.; chmn. bd. govs. Inter-Am. Devel. Bank, 1995-96; co-chmn. Israeli del. to multilateral peace talks on regional econ. devels., 1991—. Author numerous books on internat. and macro econs.; editor Jour. Polit. Economy, 1973-87; contbr. numerous articles to profl. jours. Decorated gran cruz Orden de Mayo al Merito (Argentina); recipient Czech Karel Englis prize in econs. Fellow Econometric Soc.; mem. Am. Acad. Arts and Scis. (fgn. hon.), Japan Soc. Monetary Econs. (hon.), Israel Assn. Grads. in Social Scis. and Humanities (hon. pres.). Office: Amer Internat Group 70 Pine St New York NY 10270

FRENKEL, STEVEN I., lawyer; b. Jan. 1, 1964; s. Michael and Barbara Frenkel; m. Lynne M. Price, Aug. 4, 1991; children: Jared Lawrence, Andrew Ross. BA with honors, Yeshiva U., 1986; JD, Columbia U., 1989. Bar: Conn. 1990, U.S. Dist. Ct. Conn. 1990, U.S. Dist. Ct. (so. and ea. dists.) N.Y. 1991. Ptnr. Cummings & Lockwood, Stamford, Conn., 1999—. Mem.: ORI, Defense Rsch. Inst., Stamford Bar Assn., Conn. Bar Assn. Home: 38 Revonah Cir Stamford CT 06905-4028 Office: Cummings and Lockwood PO Box 120 4 Stamford Plz Stamford CT 06904 Office Phone: 203-351-4206. Business E-Mail: SFrenk@cl-law.com.

FRENKIEL, RICHARD HENRY, retired systems engineer, consultant; b. NYC, Mar. 4, 1943; s. Lucjan and Stephanie (Komorowska) Frenkiel; m. Annamae Mary Rollason, Dec. 28, 1963; children: Scott Thomas, Kathleen Ann. BSME, Tufts U., 1963; MS in Engring. Mechanics, Rutgers U., 1965. Tech. staff Bell Labs., Holmdel, NJ, 1963—71, supr., 1973—77, dept. head, 1977—88, R & D dir., 1988—93, ret., 1993. Vis. prof. Rutgers U., dir. strategic planning WINLAB, 1994—. Com. mem. Manalapan Twp., NJ, 1995—99, dep. mayor, 1995, mayor, 1999. Named N.J. Inventor of Yr., 1995; named to Hall Fame, Consumer Electronics Assn., 2004; recipient Achievement award, Indsl. Rsch. Inst., 1992, Nat. medal, Tech. U.S. Dept. of Commerce, 1994; fellow, Bell Labs., 1990. Fellow: IEEE (spkr. Outstanding Lecture Tour 1975—76, Alexander Graham Bell medal 1987); mem.: Nat. Acad. Engring. Republican. Achievements include design of first cellular telephone system in U.S; cordless telephone products; invention of Metroliner Radiotelephone System; cell splitting method; patents in field. Office: Rutgers WINLAB 73 Brett Rd Piscataway NJ 08854-8060 Business E-Mail: frenkiel@winlab.rutgers.edu.

FRENKIL, STEVEN DAVID, lawyer; b. Balt., Jan. 18, 1954; s. Erwin Barry and Harriet Frenkil; m. Nancy Ellen Miller, June 25, 1978; children: Janet Lynn, David Richard, Eric Stuart. BA with distinction, George Wash. U., 1974; JD with honors, U. Md. Sch. Law, 1977. Bar: Md. 1977, D.C. 1978. Summer assoc. Steptoe & Johnson, Washington, 1975—75, Semmes, Bowen & Semmes, Balt., 1976—76, assoc., 1977—85, ptnr., 1985—92; prin. Miles & Stockbridge P.C., 1992—. Mem. section coun. Sect. on Labor and Employment Law, Md. State Bar Assn., Md., 1997—, section coun.; mem. Howard County Human Resources Soc., Columbia, Md., 2004—, bd. dirs.; spkr. in field. Co-author: (law book) Maryland Cases on Discrimination, (book) Know Your Legal Rights - A Basic Guide to Laws Affecting the Elderly; co-editor: (law book) Digest of Maryland Cases on Discrimination. Mem. President's Adv. Coun., Villa Julie Coll., Stevenson, Md., 2000—05, Devel. Com., Friends Sch., Balt., 2003—05, Governor's Adv. Com. Liability, Annapolis, Md., 1981—83; mem. pers. com. Balt. Hebrew Congregation, Balt., 2000—01; bd. dirs. Ctr. Stage Theatre, 1989—94; mem. bd. legislative chair Howard County Human Resources Soc., Columbia; pres. Am. Jewish Com., 1985—87; bd. dirs. Friends Sch. Balt., 1980—87; mem. Balt. Jewish Coun., 1990—92, 1987—92. Mem.: ABA (sect. labor and employment law 1980—), Soc. Human Resource Mgmt., Md. State Bar Assn. (bd. dirs. 1997—2005, sect. labor and employment law), Howard County Human Resources Soc. (mem. of bd. and legislative chair 2004—05), Nat. Assn. of Coll. and U. Attorneys (assoc.), Omicron Delta Kappa, Phi Beta Kappa, Sigma Phi Epsilon (hon.). Jewish. Avocations: golf, theater, art, tennis. Home: 4 Hurlingham Ct Baltimore MD 21208 Office: Miles & Stockbridge PC 10 Light St Baltimore MD 21202 Office Phone: 410-727-6464. Office Fax: 410-385-3700. E-mail: sfrenkil@milesstockbridge.com.

FRENTHEWAY, JOHN E., lawyer; b. Cheyenne, Wyo., Apr. 6, 1949; s. Charles Jake and Gladys (Lauver) F.; m. Erma Kay Pace, Aug. 15, 1970; children: Marcus John, Jarad Scott, Rebecca Kay, Seth Paul, Joshua Elias, Zachary Jason. BS in Animal Sci., U. Wyo., 1973, BS in Edn., 1976, JD, 1981. Bar: Wyo. U.S. Dist. Ct. Wyo. Sci. tchr. Laramie County Sch. Dist. # 1, Cheyenne, 1976-77; assoc. Graves, Hacker and Phalen, Cheyenne, 1981-83; asst. state pub. defender State Pub. Defenders Office Wyo., Cheyenne, 1982—; guardian ad litem Juvenile Ct. First Jud. Dist. Ct. Wyo., Cheyenne, 1982—; pvt. practice Cheyenne, 1983—. Wrestling coach Laramie County Sch. Dist. # 1, 1976-77; apptd. mem. Wyo. Juvenile Commn., Cheyenne, 1991-95, Wyo. Juvenile Adv. Coun., 1997—, Fed. Juvenile Advisor Coun., 2004—; adj. instr. Laramie County CC., 2003—; lectr. U. Wyo. Criminal Justice Dept.; mem. fed. juvenile adv. voun., 2003—. Host: Child At Risk series, 2002—; (radio talk show) John Frentheway Show. V.p., coach Cheyenne Soccer Assn., 1982-93; unit commr. Boy Scouts Am., Cheyenne, 1984-86, roundtable commr., 1984-88. Mem. Wyo. Bar Assn. (Pres. Select award 1998), Laramie County Bar Assn. (cert. exemplary svc. 1998). Home: 1878 Horse Creek Rd Cheyenne WY 82009 Office: PO Box 181 Cheyenne WY 82003-0181 Office Phone: 307-632-2979. E-mail: jnfrentheway@juno.com.

FRENZEL, FRANCES JOHNSON, nurse, educator, real estate broker, poet; b. Bedford, Va., Feb. 2, 1911; d. J. James and Willie Calpernia (Markham) Johnson; m. Paul H. Frenzel, Dec. 21, 1933 (dec. 1990); children: Virginia Lee Frenzel Lawrence, Helen Marie Frenzel LaGourgue. RN, Wash. Adventist Hosp., Takoma Park, Md., 1932; BS, Columbia Union Coll., 1933; real estate license, Glendale (Calif.) C.C., 1968. Cert. real estate broker. RN supr. Glendale (Calif.) Adventist Med. Ctr., 1933-34; instr. various flower show schs., Nat. Coun. State Garden Clubs, U.S. & Mex., 1951-98; flower design instr. Edinburg (Tex.) Coll., 1953. Founder, chmn. World Flower Festival L.A. Garden Club and Greater L.A. Dist. Calif. Garden Clubs, Inc., 1962-98; lectr. in many states including Hawaii. Author: Arrangements on Parade, 1950; contbr. poems to books and nat. and state mags.; contbr. photographs of flower arrangements to profl. jours. Mem. City of Glendale Beautification adv. council, 1974—, L.A. County Med. Auxiliary Glendale, 1956—, pres., 1968—69; founder The Golden Garden Angel fund, 1998; election precinct officer L.A. County, Glendale, 1956—2000. Recipient numerous Garden Club awards, 1962—, Editor's Choice award, 1999, Lifetime Beautification Achievement award, City of Glendale and Com. for a Clean and Beautiful Glendale, 2001, various other awards from organizations and Los Angeles County; named Guardian Angel, Staff Golden Gardens Mag., 2001; grantee Proton Treatment Ctr., Loma Linda (Calif.) Med. Ctr. Mem.: Internat. Soc. Poetry, L.A. County Med. Assn. Alliance (pres. Dist. IV 1968—69), L.A. Garden Club (pres. 1960—62), Judges Coun. Orange County, Judges Coun. So. Calif. (chmn. 1978—80), Internat. Soc. Poets, Ikebana Internat. (L.A. chpt.), Greater L.A. Dist. Calif. Gardens Club (dir. 1962—64), Nat. Coun. State Garden Clubs Inc. (life), Calif. Garden Clubs Inc. (life; pub. rels. chmn. 1999—, founder golden gardens angel fund for bd. 1999—, bd. dirs., Woman of Yr. 2002). Avocations: flower arranging, gardening, gourmet cooking, interior decorating. Home: 31423 S Coast Hwy Laguna Beach CA 92651-6998

FRERICHS, ERNEST SUNLEY, religious studies educator; b. S.I., Apr. 30, 1925; s. Ernest V. and Eva (Sunley) F.; m. Sarah Hazel (Cutts), Aug. 20, 1949; children: John Allen (dec.), David Sunley, Elizabeth Ann. BA, Brown U., 1948; MA, Harvard U., 1949; STB, Boston U., 1952, PhD, 1957; LHD (hon.), Hebrew Union Coll., 1992. Mem. faculty Brown U., Providence, 1953—, prof. religious studies, 1966-95, chmn. dept., 1964-70, asst. dean., 1958-59, dean grad. sch., 1976-82, program dir. in Judaic studies, 1982-95, prof. religious and Judaic studies emeritus, 1995—; exec. dir. Dorot Found., Providence, 1995—2003, pres., 2003—. Mem. Grad. and Profl. Sch. Fin. Aid Coun., 1978-82; mem. Grad. Record Exam. Bd., 1980-82; mem. com. on testing coun. Grad. Sch., 1980-82; mem. N.Am. com. Mellon Fellowship Program, 1982-92; chmn. coun. Grad. Studies in Religion, 1989-93. Region I and II selection com. Woodrow Wilson Found., 1959-69; trustee Am. Sch. Oriental Rsch., 1976-82, 93—, v.p., 1993-96; trustee Hiatt Inst., Brandeis U., 1979-82, Roger Williams Hosp., Providence, 1981-97, Palestine Endowment Fund Israel, Inc., 1999—, Albright Inst. Archeol. Rsch., Jerusalem, 1974—, pres., 1976-82; bd. dirs. Assn. Jewish Studies, 1990-98, Jewish Chautauqua Soc., 2002; acad. adv. coun. Ctr. for Jewish History, 2004—. With inf., AUS, 1943-46, ETO. Decorated Combat Infantryman's badge; recipient Disting. Alumnus Award Boston U., 1994; Beebe fellow Boston U., 1952-53; Lilly postdoctoral fellow Heidelberg U., 1962-63. Mem. Soc. Bibl. Lit. (exec. com. New Eng. coun. 1977-82); Am. Acad. Religion (pres. New Eng. 1970-71); Phi Beta Kappa (sec. Brown U. chpt. 1964-68, pres. 1975-77). Home: 229 Medway St Apt 209 Providence RI 02906 Office: Dorot Found 439 Benefit St Providence RI 02903-2934 E-mail: ernief@dorot.org.

FRERICHS, HERBERT DONALD, JR., lawyer; b. Bklyn., Aug. 17, 1957; s. Herbert Donald and Carol Ann (Gabrielsen) F.; m. Mary Elizabeth Cannon, Feb. 23, 1991; children: Mary Katherine, Colleen Ann. BS in Econ., U.S. Naval Acad., 1980; M in Marine Affairs, U. R.I., 1985; JD, U. Md., 1988. Assoc. Miles & Stockbridge, Balt., 1988-91, UNC Inc., Annapolis, Md., 1991; ptnr.-in-charge Downtown Balt. off. DLA Piper Rudnick Gray Cary, Balt. Lt. USN, 1980-85. Mem. ABA, Md. Bar Assn., Am. Corp. Counsel Bar Assn. Republican. Lutheran. Office: DLA Piper Rudnick Gray Cary Ste 1950 111 S Calvert St Baltimore MD 21202-6174 Office Phone: 410-580-3000. Office Fax: 410-580-3665. Business E-Mail: herbert.frerichs@piperrudnick.com.

FRESE, EDWARD SCHEER, JR., (TED FRESE), information technology executive, consultant; b. N.Y.C., Oct. 17, 1944; s. Edward Scheer and Sylvana (Cerutti) F.; stepson Mary Margaret (Richardson) F.; m. Christine Ann Robinson, Oct. 27, 1979; 1 child, Edward Robinson. AB in Latin, Hamilton Coll., 1966; postgrad., NYU, 1970-72. Programmer trainee Mfr.'s Hanover Trust Co., N.Y.C., 1969-70, systems analyst, 1970-75, officer, 1975-81; project mgr. Macmillan, Inc., N.Y.C., 1981-84; dir. fin. systems Maxwell Macmillan Inc., N.Y.C., 1984-89, dir. corp. info. systems, 1989-90; prin. Bremen Assocs., Inc., N.Y.C., 1991-97; v.p. Year 2000 Cahners Bus. Info., 1997-98; v.p. Bremen Assocs., Inc., N.Y.C., 1998—. Mem. Soc. Info. Mgmt., U. Club Republican. Episcopalian. Avocations: writing, swimming, sailing, music. Home: 79 North Ave Westport CT 06880-2722 Office Phone: 203-222-0264. E-mail: bremenai@aol.com.

FRESHWATER, MICHAEL FELIX, plastic surgeon, educator; b. NYC, Feb. 4, 1948; s. Jack and Rhonda Freshwater. BS magna cum laude, Bklyn. Coll., 1968; MD, Yale U., 1972. Diplomate Nat. Bd. Med. Examiners, Am. Bd. Plastic Surgery. Asst. resident in surgery Yale New Haven Hosp., 1972-74; fellow in plastic surgery Med. Sch. Johns Hopkins U., Balt., 1974-77; resident, then chief resident in plastic surgery Jackson Meml. Hosp., 1977-78; Kleinert fellow hand and microsurgery Jewish Hosp., Louisville, 1979; pvt. practice medicine specializing in plastic/hand surgery Miami, Fla., 1979—; pres., dir. Miami Inst. Hand and Microsurgery, 1980—; dir. hand and microsurgery Cedars Med. Ctr., 1985—, chief surgery, 1988-90. Vol. assoc. prof. plastic surgery U. Miami Sch. medicine, 1979—; vol. faculty mem. Barry U. Sch. Podiatric Medicine and Surgery, 1989—; vis. prof. Javeriana U., Bogota, 1983—85, Centro Medico de los Andes, 1983—86; cons. Fla. Children's Med. Svc., Tallahassee, 1979—, Fla. Elks Crippled Children Soc., Orlando, 1983—, Fla. Dept. Profl. Regulation, Tallahassee, 1984—95, League Against Cancer, 1983—, Scientists Inst. Pub. Info., 1985—, USCG, Miami Beach, 1992—. Editor: U. Miami Plastic Surgery News, 2004—; mem. bd. reviewers: Plastic and Reconstructive Surgery, 1976—; contbr. chapters to books, articles to profl. jours. Trustee Yale U. Med. Libr., New Haven, 1972—77, 2000—, D. R. Millard Found., 1987—; bd. dirs. V. and A. Gildred Found., 1980—86, Yale Sch. Medicine Fund, 1991—97, Campaign for Stuyvesant, 2003—; mem. nat. campaign com. Yale Sch. Medicine, 1993—97; mem. Fla. Bar Grievance Com., 1998—2001. Recipient Letter Commendation, Gov. Bob Graham, 1984; fellow Weinberger, NIH, 1974—76; scholar Jonas Salk, CUNY, 1968—72. Fellow: Internat. Coll. Surgeons; mem.: AAUP, AMA (Physicians Recognition award 1976, 1979, 1982, 1985, 1988, 1990, 1993, 1996, 1999, 2001), Miami Assn. for Surgery of Hand (dir. 1991—), Am. Soc. Peripheral Nerve, Miami Soc. Plastic Surgeons (sec.-treas. 1987—88, v.p. 1988—89, pres. 1989—90), Royal Soc. Medicine, Internat. Soc. Reconstructive Microsurgery, Am. Soc. Reconstructive Microsurgery, Am. Burn Assn., Am. Assn. Hand Surgery, Assn. Yale

Alumni in Medicine (bd. dirs. 1998—2000), Grove Isle Club (Miami), Yale Club (Miami, N.Y.), Phi Beta Kappa. Avocation: skiing. Office: 1 Datran Ctr Ste 502 Miami FL 33156-7814 Office Phone: 305-670-9988. E-mail: mff@miamihandsurgery.com.

FRESNE, JEANNETTE, music educator, researcher; b. Tex. d. Calvin and Virginia Fresne. MusB, U. Tex., 1989; MusM, Tex. State U., 1997; D of Musical Arts, Ariz. State U., 2004. Cert. tchr. music grades K-12 Tex. Clin. instr. U. N.C., Chapel Hill, 2001—02; tchr. music Northside Ind. Sch. Dist., San Antonio, 1992—96; asst. prof. U. South Ala., Mobile, 2002—. Dir. Arts Edn., Mobile, 2004—. Music specialist Ala. Course of Study Com., Montgomery, 2005; mem. bd. Ala. Inst. Edn. Arts, 2005. Grantee, Ala. Commn. Higher Edn. and No Child Left Behind, 2004—05, 2005—; scholar, U. Tex., Austin, 1983, Nat. Piano Guild Auditions, 1984, Mex.-Am. Bus. and Profl. Women's Club, 1984—88; Kodály scholar, Tex. State U., 1998, Regents Grad. Acad. scholar, Ariz. State U., 1999—2000, Dean's Coun. scholar, 2000—01. Office: U South Ala Music Dept 307 University Blvd North Mobile AL 36688-0002 Office Phone: 251-460-6697.

FRESTEDT, JOY LOUISE, research scientist, science administrator; b. Oak Park, Ill., Jan. 31, 1959; d. James Albert Machnicki and Wanda Louise (McConnaughhay) Katzman; m. Robert LeVance Frestedt, Aug. 8, 1987; 1 child, Megan Marie. BA in Biology, Knox Coll., 1980; PhD in Pathobiology, U. Minn., 1996. Rsch. asst. Knox Coll., 1978-80; cytogeneticist Ill. Masonic Med. Ctr., Chgo., 1980-81; med. tech., asst. scientist, rsch. scientist, lab. dir. U. Minn., Mpls., 1981-89, 91-96; cancer rsch. scientist III, lab. dir. Roswell Park Cancer Inst., Buffalo, 1989-90; rsch. scientist, lab. dir. Mpls. Children's Med. Ctr., 1990-91; grad. fellow, safety expert, sr. scientist Sci. Mus. Minn., St. Paul, 1993—2001; rsch. scientist St. Jude Med. Inc., St. Paul, 1996-97. Adj. faculty Mpls. Cmty. Tech. Coll., 1996-99, North Hennepin C.C., 1997-98, Anoka Ramsey C.C., 1997-98, Rasmussen Bus. Coll., 1998-99, Medtronic/Mpls. Cmty. Tech. Coll., 1998, Normandale C.C., 1999; mgr. Busulfex Clin. Devel. Orphan Med., Inc., 1999-2000; med. info. scientist AstraZeneca Pharm., 2000—01; ops. mgr. clin. trials svc. Mayo Clinic, 2001-03; contract compliance auditor, 3M, 2002; mgr. regional clin. affairs Ortho Biotech Products, LP, 2002-2004; exec. dirs rsch. Minn. Applied Rsch. Ctr., 2004—; adj. faculty Coll. of St. Catherine, 2005—. Co-author: Writing About Science, 1997, Considering Graduate School in the Sciences, 1999; contbr. articles to profl. jours. and books. Mem.: Soc. Clin. Rsch. Profls., Am. Soc. Clin. Oncologists, Am. Assn. Pharm. Scientists (reviewer JWMISE), Assn. Clin. Rsch. Profls. (CEH coord.), Grad. Women in Sci. (pres. 1996—97, bd. dirs. 1999—2003, chair bd. dirs. 2002—03), Assn. Women in Sci., Sigma Xi. Avocations: softball, camping. Home: 2708 Vernon Ave S Saint Louis Park MN 55416-1838 Office Phone: 952-974-4370. Business E-Mail: frest001@umn.edu.

FRESTON, THOMAS E., broadcast executive; b. N.Y.C., Nov. 22, 1945; s. Thomas E. and Winifred (Geng) F.; m. Margaret Badali, Oct. 18, 1980; 1 child, Andrew. BA, St. Michaels Coll., 1967; MBA, NYU, 1969. Dir. mktg.-MTV MTV Networks, N.Y.C., 1980-81, dir. mktg.- The Movie Channel, 1982-83; v.p. mktg.-MTV MTV Networks Inc., N.Y.C., 1983-84, v.p. mktg., 1984-85, sr. v.p./gen. mgr. affiliate sales, mktg., 1985, sr. v.p./gen. mgr. MTV, VH-1, 1985-86, pres. entertainment, 1986-87, pres., CEO, 1987-89; chmn., CEO MTV Networks, N.Y.C., 1989—2004; co-pres., co-COO Viacom Inc., N.Y.C., 2004—. Bd. dirs. Cable Advt. Bur., N.Y.C., 1987—, MTV Europe, London, 1986—, Rock 'n Roll Hall of Fame, N.Y.C., 1986—. Mem. Smithsonian com. Music in Am., 1987—. Named one of 50 Most Powerful People in Hollywood, Premiere mag., 2005. Mem. Cable TV Adminstrn. & Mktg. Assn., Nat. Acad. Cable Programming. Avocations: photography, travel, antique rugs. Office: Viacom Inc 1515 Broadway New York NY 10036*

FRETER, MARK ALLEN, marketing and public relations executive, consultant; b. Chgo., Oct. 31, 1947; s. John Maher and Christopher Patricia (Allen) F. BA, U. Calif., Santa Barbara, 1969; MBA, U. Calif., Berkeley, 1971. Regional dir. HBO Svcs., Inc., L.A. and Denver, 1979-84; v.p. affiliate rels. X-Press Info. Svcs., Denver, 1984-85; v.p. mktg. Telecrafter Corp., Denver, 1985-86; mktg. dir. Computer Svcs. Corp., Boulder, Colo., 1986-87; prin., v.p. pub. rels. svcs. MultiMedia, Inc., Denver, 1987-88; dir. documentation and corp. comm., product specialist, op. cons. Data Select Systems Inc., Woodland Hills, Calif., 1988-91; pres., CEO The Aspen Group Ltd., Valencia, Calif., 1988—; mgr. mktg. comm. WorldCom, San Antonio, 1991-96; sr. mgr. product devel. GCI, Inc., Anchorage, 1996-97; sr. product mgr. Qwest Comms., San Antonio, 1997-98; sr. product mgr. mgmt. Earthlink Network, Inc., Pasadena, Calif., 1998-99; sr. product mgr. value added internet svcs., e-commerce Broadwing Comms., Austin, Tex., 1999-2000; group mktg. mgr. e-bus. svcs. Verizon Comms., Irving, Tex., 2000—. Lectr. Internat. Coun. Shopping Ctrs., N.Y.C., 1977; conf. planner ICSC-West, San Francisco, 1978-79; tng. program devel. HBO, N.Y.C., 1982. Youth coach South Suburban YMCA, Littleton, Colo., 1984-86. Recipient First Pl. cert. for Retail Ad Campaign San Diego Advt. Assn., 1980. Mem. Calif. Cable TV Assn., No. Calif. Promotion Mgrs. Assn. (v.p. 1977-78), So. Calif. Promotion Mgrs. Assn. (sec., treas. 1976-77). Democrat. Mem. Soc. Friends. Avocations: skiing, ice hockey, reading, coaching youth sports.

FRETWELL, ELBERT K., JR., retired university chancellor, consultant; b. N.Y.C., Oct. 29, 1923; s. Elbert Kirtley and Jean (Hosford) F.; m. Dorrie Shearer, Aug. 25, 1951; children: Barbara Alice (Mrs. Peter Cooke), Margaret Jean (Mrs. John C. Cross), James Leonard, Katharine Louise (Mrs. Robert Saul). AB with distinction, Wesleyan U., Middletown, Conn., 1944; MA in Tchg., Harvard U., 1948; PhD, Columbia U., 1953; hon. doctorate, Tech. U. Wroclaw, Poland, 1976; LL.D. (hon.), Wesleyan U., 1981; D in Pub. Svc. (hon.), U. N.C., Charlotte, 1998. Stringer AP, 1942-44; staff writer ARC, 1944-45; vice consul Am. embassy, Prague, Czech Republic, 1945-47; tchr. Brookline (Mass.) Pub. Schs., 1948, Evanston (Ill.) Twp. High Sch. and Community Coll., 1948-50; adminstrv. sec. John Hay Fellowships, John Hay Whitney Found., 1951-53; asst. prof., asst. to dean Tchrs. Coll., Columbia U., 1953-56, assoc. prof., 1956; asst. commr. for higher edn. N.Y. State Dept. Edn., 1956-64; summer faculty U. Calif. at Berkeley, 1964; dean acad. devel. CUNY, N.Y.C., 1964-67; pres. SUNY Coll. at Buffalo, 1967-78; chancellor U. N.C., Charlotte, 1979-89, chancellor emeritus, 1989—; sr. assoc. MDC Inc., 1989-91; interim pres. U. Mass. 5 Campus Sys., 1991-92. Interim pres. U. North Fla., 1998; mem. comm. higher instns. Mid. States Assn. of Schs. and Colls., 1965-71, pres., chmn., 1973-74; trustee Carnegie Found. for Advancement Tchg., chmn., 1975-77; mem. Carnegie Coun. on Policy Studies in Higher Edn., 1973-79; bd. dirs. N.C. Transp. Mus. Found., 1996—; trustee Wesleyan U., 1967-70, Nichols Sch., Buffalo, 1969-78, Canisius Coll., 1969-76, Peace Coll., 1997-2003; exec. dir. com. on edn. N.Y. State Constl. Conv., 1967; mem. N.C. Med. Bd., 2001—. Decorated Order of Cultural Merit Poland; recipient Disting. Alumnus award Wesleyan U., 1974, Tchrs. Coll., Columbia U., 1983, Boy Scouts Am. Silver Beaver award. Mem. Am. Assn. State Colls. and Univs. (pres. 1978-79), Am. Assn. for Higher Edn. (pres. 1964-65), Am. Coun. Edn. (chmn. 1980-81), N.C. Assn. Colls. and Univs. (pres. 1985-86), Nat. Rlwy. Hist. Soc., Adirondack Mountain Club, Rotary (pres. Charlotte 1994-95). Home: 3738 Cypress Club Dr Apt D411 Charlotte NC 28210-2492 Office: U NC-Charlotte 9201 University City Blvd Charlotte NC 28223-0002 Office Phone: 704-687-2484.

FRETZ, DEBORAH MCDERMOTT, oil industry executive; m. Philip Fretz; two children. BS in Biology and Chemistry, Butler U., 1970; MBA, Temple U., 1977. Virologist Merck, Sharp & Dohme; fin. analyst Sun Co., Inc., 1977—, mgr. fin. analysis group, 1985-88, dir. wholesale fuels mktg., 1988-89, gen. mgr. fuels, 1989; pres. Sun Pipe Line Co. and Marine Terminals Sunoco, Inc., 1991—; sr. v.p. logistics Sunoco., Inc., 1994—2000; sr. v.p. lubricants Sunoco, Inc., 1997—2000, sr. v.p. MidContinent Refining, Mktg. and Logistics, 2000; pres., COO Sunoco Logistics Ptnrs., LP, 2001. Dir. GATX Corp., Cooper Tire and Rubber Co. Office: Sunoco Logistics Ptnrs LP Ten Penn Ctr 1801 Market St Ste Sl Philadelphia PA 19103-1699

FREUD, JOHN SIGMUND, lawyer; b. Johnstown, Pa., Dec. 11, 1956; s. Fred and Betty (Kapuloff) F.; m. Deborah Elizabeth O'Connor, May 25, 1986; children: Jessica Shaye, Alyxandra Jacqueline. Student, Harvard U., 1975; BA magna cum laude, Brandeis U., 1978; JD, U. Miami (Fla.), 1981. Bar: Fla. 1981, Mass. 1982, U.S. Dist. Ct. (so., no. and mid. dists.) Fla. 1982, U.S. Ct. Appeals (5th and 11th cirs.) 1982, U.S. Supreme Ct. 1985. Assoc. Braod and Cassel, Bay Harbor Islands, Fla., 1980-82; assoc. Guren, Merritt, Udell, Sogg & Cohen, Miami, Fla., 1982-84, Blank, Rome, Comisky & McCauley, Miami, 1984-86; ptnr. Levine, Geiger, Kuperstein & Freud P.A., Miami, 1986-90; pvt. practice Miami, 1990—. Recipient Antitrust Book award U. Miami Sch. Law. Mem. ABA, Am. Arbitration Assn., Fla. Bar Assn., Dade County Bar Assn. (young lawyers sect.), Mass. Bar Assn., Greater Miami C. of C. Democrat. Jewish. Avocations: tennis, basketball. Address: John Freud PA 999 Brickell Ave Ste 1000 Miami FL 33131-3044

FREUD, LUCIAN MICHAEL, painter; b. Berlin, Dec. 8, 1922; s. Ernst and Lucie F.; m. Kathleen Garman Epstein, 1948 (dissolved 1952); 2 children; m. Caroline Maureen Blackwood (dissolved 1957). Ed., Cen. Sch. Arts and Crafts, London, 1938-39, East Anglian Sch. Painting and Drawing. Tchr. Slade Sch. Art, 1948-58; vis. asst. Norwich Sch. Art, 1964-65. Exhibited in one-man shows at Lefevre Gallery, 1944, Nishimura Gallery, Tokyo, 1979, Thomas Agnew & Sons, 1983, Hirshhorn Mus. and Sculpture Garden Smithsonian Instn., Washington, 1987, Mus. Nat. d'Art Moderne, Paris, 1987-88, Hayward Gallery, London, 1988, Neue Nat. Gallery, Berlin, 1988, Scottish Nat. Gallery Modern Art, Edinburgh, Eng., 1988, The Fruitmarket Gallery, Edinburgh, 1988, Berggruen Gallery, Paris, 1990, Saatchi Collection, London, 1990, Nishimura Gallery, Tokyo, 1991, Thomas Gibson Fine Art Ltd., London, 1991, Palazzo Ruspoli, Rome, 1991, Castello Sforzesca, Milan, 1991-92, Tate Gallery, Liverpool, 1992, Queen's Gallery Buckingham Palace, 2002-03; numerous others; represented in pub. collections Tate Gallery, Nat. Portrait Gallery, Arts Coun. of Gt. Britian, Brit. Coun., Brit. Mus., Fitzwilliam Mus., Cambridge, Nat. Mus. Wales, Cardiff, Scottish Nat. Gallery Modern Art, Edinburgh, Hartlepool Art Gallery, Walker Art Gallery, Liverpool, Liverpool U., City Art Gallery, Whitworth Gallery, Art Gallery South Australia, Mus. Western Australia, Beaverbrook Art Gallery, N.B., Can., Centre Georges Pompidou, Paris, Bibliotheque Nationale, Paris, Victoria and Albert Mus., Sigmund Freud Mus., London, Centro Cultural Arte Contemporaneo, Mexico City, Nat. Gallery, Capetown, Republic South Africa, Art Inst. Chgo., Mus. Modern Art, NYC, Met. Mus. Art, Carnegie Inst., Pitts., Hirshhorn Mus., Washington, numerous others. With Brit. Navy, 1942. Named Companion of Honour, 1983; recipient Order of Merit, 1993. Mem. Am. Acad. and Inst. Arts and Letters (hon.), Am. Acad. Arts and Sciences (hon. fgn.) Address: care James Kirkman 46 Brompton Sq London SW3 2AF England

FREUD, NICHOLAS S., lawyer; b. N.Y.C., Feb. 6, 1942; s. Frederick and Fredericka (von Rothenburg) F.; m. Elsa Doskow, July 23, 1966; 1 child, Christopher. AB, Yale U., 1963, JD, 1966. Bar: N.Y. 1968, Calif. 1970, U.S. Tax Ct. 1973. Ptnr. Chickering & Gregory, San Francisco, 1978-85, Russin & Vecchi, San Francisco, 1986-93, Jeffer, Mangels, Butler & Marmaro, LLP, San Francisco, 1993—. Mem. joint adv. bd. Calif. Continuing Edn. of Bar, chair taxation subcom. 1987-87; mem. fgn. income adv. bd. Tax Management Internat. Jour., mem. bd. advs. The Jour. of Internat. Taxation; mem. adv. bd. NYU Inst. on Fed. Taxation; academician Internat. Acad. Estate and Tax Law; mem. tax commn., Union Internat. des Avocats. Author: (with Charles G. Stephenson and K. Bruce Friedman) International Estate Planning, rev. edit., 1997; contbr. articles to profl. jours. Fellow Am. Coll. of Tax Counsel; mem. ABA (tax sect. vice chair adminstrn. 2000-02, coun. dir. 1995-97, chair com. on U.S. activities of foreigners and tax treaties 1989-91, vice chair 1987-89, chair subcom. on tax treaties 1981-87), Calif. State Bar Assn. (taxation sect. exec. com. 1981-85, vice chair 1982-83, chair 1983-84, vice chair income tax com. 1981-82, chair 1982-83, vice chair personal income tax subcom. 1979-80, chair 1980-81, co-chair fgn. tax subcom. 1978-79, cert. specialist in taxation law), N.Y. State Bar Assn. (taxation sect., mem. com. on U.S. activities of fgn. taxpayers and fgn. activities of U.S. taxpayers), Bar Assn. of San Francisco, Bar Assn. of City of N.Y., San Francisco Tax Club (pres. 1988), San Francisco Internat. Tax Group. Office: Jeffer Mangels Butler & Marmaro LLP 5th Fl Two Embarcadero Ctr San Francisco CA 94111-3824 Office Phone: 415-398-8080. Business E-Mail: nsf@jmbm.com.

FREUDENHEIM, MILTON B., journalist; b. New Rochelle, N.Y., Mar. 4, 1927; s. Milton Benjamin and Lenore Patricia (Kroh) F.; m. Elizabeth Ege, Mar. 7, 1952 (dec. Dec. 30, 1996); children: Jo Louise, Susan Patricia, John Milton Otto, Tom Henry; m. Grace Glueck, Oct. 20, 2000. AB, U. Mich., 1948. Reporter Louisville (Ky.) Courier-Jour., 1948-49; reporter Akron (Ohio) Beacon Jour., 1949-52, Washington corr., 1953-56; UN corr. Chgo. Daily News, 1956-66, nat. and fgn. editor, 1966-69, Paris corr., 1969-77; dir. public affairs for Region V HEW, Chgo., 1978-79; copy editor, writer N.Y. Times Week in Rev., 1979—88; bus. and health reporter NY Times, 1998—. Adv. U.S. del. UNESCO Gen. Conf., 1978; Pres. UN Corrs. Assn., 1966, Anglo-Am. Press Assn., Paris, 1975 Mem. Phi Beta Kappa, Sigma Delta Chi. Home: 91 Central Park W New York NY 10023-4600 Office: NY Times 229 W 43rd St New York NY 10036-3959

FREUDENTHAL, DAVID D., governor; b. Thermopolis, Wyo., Oct. 12, 1950; m. Nancy Freudenthal; children: Don, Hillary, Bret, Katrina. BA, Amherst Coll., 1973; JD, U. Wyo. Coll. Law, 1980. Economist Wyo. Dept. Econ. Planning & Devel., 1973—75; state planning coord. State of Wyo., 1975—77; pvt. law practice, 1980—93; U.S. atty. for Wyo. U.S. Dept. Justice, Cheyenne, 1994—2001; gov. State of Wyo., Cheyenne, 2003—. Chmn. Wyo. State Demo. Ctrl. Com., 1981—85; mem. Wyo. Futures Project, 1984—87, Econ. Devel. & Stabilization Bd., 1985—89, Edn. Policy Implementation Coun., 1989—90, Gov. Substance Abuse and Violent crime Adv. Bd., 1994—2001. Office: Office of the Gov State Capitol Bldg Rm 124 Cheyenne WY 82002*

FREUDENTHAL, ERNEST GUENTER, technology and business educator; b. Mannheim, Germany, July 22, 1920; came to the U.S., 1937; s. Leopold and Selma (Rosenthal) F.; m. Stephanie Karlsruher, Dec. 26, 1948; children: Pamela Hausman, Joan Fraifeld. BA in Econs., Vanderbilt U., 1948, MA in Econs., 1971. Employee Werthan Industries, Nashville, 1942-44, 46-48, middle mgmt. staff, 1948-69, v.p. mfg., 1969-71, sr. v.p., 1971-90. Adj. assoc. prof. bus., tech., pub. policy, indsl. mktg. Vanderbilt U., Nashville, 1971—. Co-editor: The Holocaust and other Genocide, 2002. Mem. Com. on Employment Projections of the Bus. Rsch. Adv. Coun., Washington, 1997—, Holocaust Edn. Colloquium, 1999—2000; Mem. Bus. Res. Adv. Coun. to the Bur. Labor Statis., Washington, 1981—; chmn. Metro Social Svcs. Commn., Nashville, 1989—2001; commr., treas. Tenn. Holocaust Commn., Inc., 1998—; pres. Jewish Cmty. Ctr., Nashville, 1965—67; trustee Tenn. Hist. Soc., 2000—; bd. dirs. Goodwill Industries of Nashville and Middle Tenn. Staff sgt. U.S. Army, 1944—46, PTO. Recipient Sage award Coun. on Aging, Nashville, 1995. Mem. Jewish Fedn. Nashville (pres. 1974-76), The Temple (pres. 1986-88), Vanderbilt Inst. Pub. Policy Studies, Univ. Club, Phi Beta Kappa. Avocation: hiking. Home: 4406 Sunnybrook Dr Nashville TN 37205-3860 Office: PO Box 1518 Nashville TN 37202-1518

FREUDENTHAL, STEVEN FRANKLIN, lawyer, political organization worker; b. Thermopolis, Wyo., June 8, 1949; s. Lewis Franklin and Lucille Iola (Love) F.; m. Janet Mae Mansfield, Aug. 30, 1969 (div. Sept. 1996); children: Lynn Marie, Kristen Lee; m. Barbara A. Crofts, Jan. 1, 1998; stepchildren: Shane C., Jeanne N. BA, Trinity Coll., Hartford, Conn., 1971; JD, Vanderbilt U., 1975. Bar: Wyo. 1975, U.S. Supreme Ct. 1981. Tax acct. Conn. Gen. Life Ins. Co., Hartford, Conn., 1971-72; asst. atty. gen. Wyo. Cheyenne, 1975-77; atty. gen. Wyo., 1981-82; state planning coordinator Office Gov. Wyo., Cheyenne, 1977-78; dep. under sec. Dept. Interior, Washington, 1978-79, exec. asst. to sec., 1979-80; ptnr Sherman & Howard, Cheyenne, Wyo., 1980-81; ptnr. Freudenthal, Salzburg & Bonds, Cheyenne, 1983—; mem. Wyo. Ho. Reps., 1987-91. Trustee United Med. Ctr., 1990-97, pres., 1993-96; bd. dirs. Cheyenne LEADS, 1990-93; chmn. Wyo. Dem. Party, 1999-2001. Office: 123 E 17th St Cheyenne WY 82003-0387 Office Phone: 307-634-2240. Business E-Mail: steve@wyolaw.com.

FREUND, CYNTHIA M., dean; BSN, Marquette U., 1963; MSN, U. N.C., 1973, FNP, 1974; PhD in Bus. and Health Adminstrn., U. Ala., 1981. Staff nurse McHenry (Ill.) Hosp., 1963, 64-65, VA Hosp., Wood, Wis., 1963-64; instr. Milw. County Instns., Wauwatosa, Wis., 1965-68, supr. Milw. County Rehab. and Chronic Disease Hosp., 1968-70; instr. Sch. Nursing U. Wis., Milw., 1972-73; dir. FNP program Area L Health Edn. Ctr., Tarboro, N.C., 1973-74; asst. prof., assoc. dir. FNP program U. N.C., Chapel Hill, 1974-78, assoc. prof., chair social and adminstrv. sys. dept., 1984-92, dean, prof. nursing, 1992-99, prof. nursing, dean emeritus, 1999—; asst. prof. U. Pa., Phila., 1981-84, sr. rsch. assoc. Leonard Davis Inst. Health Econs., 1981-84, dir. MSN nursing adminstrn. program, PhD in nursing/MBA joint degree, 1981-84. Mem. Gov. Advocacy Com. for Children and Youth State of Wis., 1973; bd. dirs. N.C. Ctr. for Child and Family Health, 1996, N.C. Inst. Medicine, 1996—; mem. N.C. Med. Data Base Commn., N.C. Gen. Assembly, 1985-89; mem. nursing adv. panel P.E.W. Health Professions Commn., 1991-92; mem. nat. adv. com. for project future requirements for nurse practitioners and nurse midwives Dept. Health and Human Svcs., 1993-94, mem. joint adv. com. to project future requirements for primary care physicians, and others, Bur. Health Professions, 1994-95; cons., presenter in field. Author: (with D. del Bueno) Power and Politics in Nursing Administration, 1986 (Am. Jour Nursing Book of Yr. 1986), Nursing: A Kaleidoscopic View, 1991 (Am. Jour. Nursing Book of Yr. 1991); author chpts. to books; mem. editl. bd. Nursing Econs., 1982-84, manuscript reviewer, 1982—; manuscript reviewer Jour. Profl. Nursing, 1984—, Health Svc. Rsch., 1984—, Planning for Higher Edn., 1986; contbr. articles to profl. jours. Bd. dirs. N.C. Ctr. Child and Family Health, 1996, N.C. Inst. Medicine, 1996—. Pub. Health Svc. Doctoral fellow Nat. Ctr. for Health Svcs. Rsch., 1980-81, Rsch. fellow Nat. Health Care Mgmt. Ctr., 1980-81; recipient Profl. Svc. Alumni award Marquette U., 1992. Fellow Am. Acad. Nursing; mem. ANA (vice-chair coun. FNP and clinicians 1977-78, cert. adult nurse practitioner 1977, Jessie M. Scott award 1990), Nat. League Nursing, Acad. Mgmt., Am. Orgn. Nurse Execs., Am. Hosp. Assn. Office: U NC Sch Nursing Cb 7460 Carrington Hl Chapel Hill NC 27599-0001

FREUND, DEBORAH A., academic administrator; AB, Washington U., 1973; MPH, MA in Applied Econs., U. Mich., 1975, PhD in Econs., 1980. Rsch. asst. Washington U. Sch. Medicine, 1971—73; intern to dep. commr. for med. assistance N.Y. State Dept. Social Svcs., 1974; program asst. The Robert Wood Johnson Found., 1975—76; rsch. assoc. U. Mich., Mich., 1976—77; IPA Nat. Ctr. for Health Svcs. Rsch., Dept. Health and Human Svcs., 1977—79; core faculty mem. U. N.C., Chapel Hill, 1979—88, asst. prof., assoc. prof., 1979—88, dir. doctoral program, 1987—88; chair Sch. Pub. and Environ. Affairs Ind. U., 1987—88, dir. The Bowen Rsch. Ctr., 1989—99, assoc. dean for acad. affairs Bloomington, 1992—94, vice chancellor acad. affairs, 1994—99; prof. Syracuse (N.Y.) U., 1999—, vice chancellor, provost for acad. affairs, 1999—. Adj. asst. prof. Duke U., 1979—84; adj. prof. Ind. U., 1988—94, U. N.C., Chapel Hill, 1988—, SUNY, 2002—. Mem. editl. bd.: PharmacoEconomics, 1993—, Health Econs., 1994—2003, Med. Care Rsch. and Rev., 1994—2003; contbr. chapters to books, articles to profl. jours. Recipient Jay S. Drotman Meml. award, 1981, The Elvehjam Meml. medal, 1990, Kershaw Rsch. award, 1991; fellow, Kellogg Found. Nat. Leadership, 1986—89. Fellow: Nat. Acad. Social Ins.; mem.: N.Y. Acad. Medicine. Home: 5213 Silver Fox Dr Jamesville NY 13078 Office: Ctr for Policy Rsch 426 Eggers Hall Syracuse Univ Syracuse NY 13244-1020

FREUND, ECKHARD, electrical engineering educator; b. Düsseldorf, Germany, Feb. 28, 1940; s. Karl and Margret (Meya) F.; m. Brigitte Keudel; children: Viviane, Ariane. Diploma in engring., Tech. Sch. Darmstadt, Fed. Republic Germany, 1965; D Engring., Tech. U. Berlin, 1968. Scientist U. Raumfahrt, Oberpfaffenhofen, Fed. Republic Germany, 1965-70; guest prof. aero. engring. U. So. Calif., L.A., 1972-76, 83; guest scientist European Space Ops. Ctr., Darmstadt, Fed. Republic Germany, 1970-71; sci. coord. Fraunhofer Inst., Karlsruhe, Fed. Republic Germany, 1976-78; prof. dept. elec. engring. Fernuniversität, Hagen, Fed. Republic Germany, 1978-84; prof. dept. elec. engring., dir. Inst. Robotics Rsch. U. Dortmund, Fed. Republic Germany, 1985—. Sci. adviser Jet Propulsion Lab., NASA, Pasadena, Calif., 1983. Author: Time Variable Multivariable Systems, 1971, Sgtate Space Control, I/II, 1986, 87, Mobile Robots and Multi-Robot Systems, 1993; contbr. some 350 articles on robotics and automation to tech. publs. Office: Inst Robotics Rsch Dortmund Otto Hahn Strasse 8 D 44221 Dortmund Germany Office Phone: 0049(0)2304/44447.

FREUND, EMMA FRANCES, technologist; b. 1922; d. Walter R. and Mabel W. (Loveland) Ervin; m. Frederic Reinert Freund, March 4, 1953; children: Frances, Daphne, Fern, Frederic. BS, Wilson Tchrs. Coll., Washington, 1944; MS in Biology, Cath. U., Washington, 1953; MEd in Adult Edn., Va. Commonwealth U., 1988. Tchr. math and sci. DC Sch. Sys., Washington, 1944-45; technician in parasitology lab. U.S. Dept. Agr., Beltsville, Md., 1945-48; histologic technician dept. pathology Georgetown U. Med. Sch., Washington, 1948-49; clin. lab. technician Kent and Queen Anne's County Gen. Hosp., Chestertown, Md., 1949-51; histotechnologist Med. Coll. Va. Hosp., Richmond, 1951—. Cons. profl. meetings and workshops; exam. coun. Nat. Credentialing. Agy. Med. Lab. Pers. Co-author: (mini-course) Instrumentation in Cytology and Histology, 1985; editor Histo-Scope Newsletter. Asst. den leader Robert E. Lee coun. Boy Scouts Am., 1967-68, den leader, 1968-70. Mem. AAAS, NAFE, AAUW, APS, Am. Mgmt. Assn., Am. Soc. Clin. Lab. Sci. (rep. to sci. assembly histology sect. 1977-78, chmn. 1983-85, 89-96), Va. Soc. Med. Tech. (Richmond chpt. corr. sec. 1977-78, bd. dirs. 1981-82, pres. 1984-85), Va. Soc. Histotech. (pres. 1994-96), Nat. Credentialing Agy. (clin. lab. specialist in histotech., clin. lab. supr. clin. lab. dir.), NY Acad. Scis., Am. Assn. Clin. Chemistry (assoc.), Am. Soc. Clin. Pathology (assoc., cert. histology technician), Nat. Geog. Soc., Va. Govtl. Employees Assn., Nat. Soc. Histotech. (by-laws com. 1981—, C.E.U. com. 1981—, program com. regional meeting 1984, 85, 87, 97, 2000, chmn. regional meeting 1987, program chmn. state meeting 1998-99, Conv. scholarship award 1997, Clin. Chemists' Recognition award 1995, 98, 2002, 04), Am. Mus. Natural History, Smithsonian Inst., Am. Mgmt. Assn., Am. Chem. Soc., Am. Soc. Quality, Clin. Lab. Mgmt. Assn., Van Slyke Soc., Soc. Human Resource Mgmt., Nat. Soc. Hist. Preservation, Math. Assn. Am., Sigma Xi, Phi Beta Rho, Kappa Delta Pi, Phi Lambda Theta. Home: 1315 Asbury Rd Richmond VA 23229-5305

FREUND, FRED A., retired lawyer; b. N.Y.C., June 18, 1928; s. Sidney J. and Cora (Strasser) F.; m. Rosalie Sampo, Nov. 18, 1975 (div. Apr. 1983); m. Patricia A. Gardner, Mar. 13, 1957 (div. Jan. 1967); children: Gregory G., K. Bailey AB, Columbia U., 1948, JD, 1949. Bar: N.Y. 1949, U.S. Supreme Ct. 1968. Law clk. to chief judge U.S. Dist. Ct. So. Dist. N.Y., N.Y.C., 1949-51; assoc. Kaye, Scholer, Fierman, Hays & Handler, N.Y.C., 1953-58, ptnr., 1959-93, ret., 1993. Served to 1st lt. USAF, 1951-53. Mem. ABA, Assn. Bar City N.Y., Phi Beta Kappa Achievements include donation of the Freund Collection of Chinese/Japanese wood carvings to the Spurlock Museum, University of Illinois, Urbana-Champaign. Home: 1085 Park Ave Apt 4C New York NY 10128-1179 *Balancing the quest for excellence with humility and humor.*

FREUND, FREDRIC S., real estate broker, real estate manager; b. Denver, Sept. 23, 1930; AB, Brown U., 1952. Sr. v.p. Hanford, Freund & Co., San Francisco, 1956—. Past adv. dir. Western Investment Real Estate Trust; bd. dirs. Berkeley Antibody Co.; instr. real estate mgmt. U. Calif. Ext.; guest lectr. Stanford U. Sch. Bus. Adminstrn. Commr. Calif. Senate Adv. Commn. on Cost Control in State Govt.; chair code adv. com. Bldg. Inspection Dept., San Francisco. Mem. Am. Soc. Real Estate Counselors (CRE, pres. no. Calif. 1987-88), San Francisco Assn. Realtors (pres. 1974-75, Realtor of Yr. 1975), Bldg. Owners & Mgrs. Assn. San Francisco, Realtors Nat. Mktg. Inst.

(CCIM), Inst. Real Estate Mgmt. (CPM). Office: Hanford Freund & Co 47 Kearny St Ste 300 San Francisco CA 94108-5582 Home: 112 Alta St San Francisco CA 94133 Fax: 415-296-0725. Office Phone: 415-981-5780. E-mail: ffreund@hanfordfreund.com.

FREUND, LAMBERT BEN, engineering educator, researcher, consultant; b. McHenry, Ill., Nov. 23, 1942; s. Bernard and Anita (Schaeffer) F.; m. Colleen Jean Hehl, Aug. 21, 1965; children: Jonathan Ben, Jeffrey Alan, Stephen Neil. BS, U. Ill., 1964, MS, 1965; PhD, Northwestern U., 1967. Postdoctoral fellow Brown U., Providence, 1967-69, asst. prof., 1969-73, assoc. prof., 1973-75, prof. engring., 1975—, Henry Ledyard Goddard prof., 1988—, chmn. div., 1979-83. Vis. prof. Stanford (Calif.) U., 1974-75, 95; cons. Aberdeen Proving Ground, U.S. Steel Corp.; vis. scholar Harvard U., 1983-84; mem.-at-large U.S. Nat. Com. for Theoretical and Applied Mechancis, NRC, 1985-97; mem. IUTAM Gen. Assembly, 1987—, treas., 1996-2004; Russell Severance Springer prof. U. Calif., Berkeley, 1995; cons. Advanced Rsch. Projects Agy. Def. Scis. Rsch. Coun.; disting. vis. scientist Jet Propulsion Lab NASA, 1994—. Author: Dynamic Fracture Mechanics, 1990, Thin Film Materials, 2004; editor in chief: ASME Jour. Applied Mechanics, 1983-88, editor Cambridge monographs on Mechanics and Applied Mathematics, 1989-2004, Jour. Mechanics and Physics of Solids, 1992-2004; assoc. editor Proc Royal Soc., 2004—, Proc Nat. Acad. Sci., 2005—; mem. editorial adv. bd. Acta Mechanica Sinica, 1990-2001; contbr. articles to tech. jours. NSF trainee, 1964-67; grantee NSF, Office Naval Rsch., Army Rsch. Office, Nat. Bur. Stads., Air Force Office Sci. Rsch., Dept. Energy; recipient Alumni Honor award Coll. Engring., U. Ill., 1996. Fellow ASME (Henry Hess award 1974, mem. applied mechanics divsn. exec. com. 1989-94, S.P. Timoshenko medal 2003), Am. Acad. Mechanics, Am. Acad. Arts and Scis., Soc. Engring. Sci. (William Prager medal 2000); mem. NAS, NAE, ASTM (George R. Irwin medal 1987). Home: 4 Connor Ln Barrington RI 02806-2750 Office: Brown U Dept Engngring Box D Providence RI 02912

FREUND, ROBERT MICHAEL, management science educator; b. N.Y.C., Nov. 3, 1953; s. Richard Louis and Esta (Neiman) F. BA, Princeton U., 1975; MS, Stanford U., 1979, PhD with distinction, 1980. Asst. analyst BDM Corp., Vienna, Va., 1975-77; cons. assoc. ICF, Inc., Washington, 1980-83; prof. MIT, Cambridge, Mass., 1983—. Assoc. editor Mgmt. Sci. Jour., 1985—; co-editor Math. Programming Jour. Mem. Inst. Ops. Rsch. and Mgmt. Sci., Math. Programming Soc., Soc. Indsl. and Applied Math., Am. Math. Soc. Democrat. Avocation: bicycling. Office: MIT 50 Memorial Dr Cambridge MA 02142-1347

FREVERT, JAMES WILMOT, retired financial planner, investment advisor; b. Richland Twp., Iowa, Dec. 19, 1922; s. Wesley Clarence and Grace Lotta (Maw) F.; m. Jean Emily Sunderlin, Feb. 12, 1949; children: Douglas James, Thomas Jeffrey, Kimberly Ann. BS in Gen. Engring., MIT, 1948. Prodn. mgr. Air Reduction Chem. Co., Calvert City, Ky., 1955-61; plant mgr. Air Products & Chems., West Palm Beach, Fla., 1961-62; pres. Young World HWD, Ft. Lauderdale, Fla., 1962-66; v.p. Shareholders Mgmt. Co., L.A., 1966-73, Thomson McKinnon Secs., North Palm Beach, Fla., 1973-89, Raymond James & Assoc., West Palm Beach, Fla., 1989-91; ret. Founder, past pres. MIT Club Palm Beach County, dir., 1976—; ednl. council mem. 1977-81. Served to 1st lt. USAF, 1943-46. Mem. Palm Beach Pundits, Circumnavigators Club. Republican. Presbyterian. Home: 883 Country Club Dr North Palm Beach FL 33408

FREY, ANDREW LEWIS, lawyer; b. N.Y.C., Aug. 11, 1938; s. Daniel B. and Ruth J. Frey; children: Matthew S., Alexandra S. BA with high honors, Swarthmore Coll., 1959; LLB, Columbia U., 1962. Bar: N.Y. 1962, D.C. 1966, U.S. Supreme Ct. 1972. Law clk. to judge U.S. Ct. Appeals (D.C. cir.), 1962—63; spl. counsel to Gov. U.S. V.I., 1963-65; assoc. Koteen & Burt, Washington, 1965-70; ptnr. Dutton, Gwirtzman, Zumas, Wise & Frey, Washington, 1970-72; dep. solicitor gen. Office U.S. Solicitor Gen., Washington, 1972-86; ptnr. Mayer Brown Rowe & Maw, N.Y.C., 1986—. Notes editor Columbia Law Rev., 1961—62. Recipient John Marshall award Dept. Justice, 1975, Disting. Svc. award Atty. Gen., 1980, Presdl. award for Meritorious Svc., 1985. Mem. Am. Law Inst., Am. Acad. Appellate Lawyers, Phi Beta Kappa. Office: Mayer Brown Rowe & Maw 1675 Broadway Fl 19 New York NY 10019-5820 Office Phone: 212-506-2635. E-mail: afrey@mayerbrownrowe.com.

FREY, CHARLES FREDERICK, surgeon, educator; b. N.Y.C., Nov. 15, 1929; s. Charles N. and Julia (Leary) F.; m. Jane Louise Tower, July 20, 1957; children: Jane Elizabeth, Susan Ann, Charles Frederick, Robert Tower, Nancy Louise. BA, Amherst Coll., 1951; MD, Cornell U., 1955. Diplomate Am. Bd. Surgery. Intern Cornell Med. Ctr., N.Y.C., 1955-56, asst. resident, 1956-57, 59-61, 1st asst. resident, 1962, chief resident, 1963; instr. surgery U. Mich., Ann Arbor, 1964-65, asst. prof. surgery, 1965-68, assoc. prof., 1968-72, prof., 1972-76, U. Calif., Davis, 1976—, vice. chmn. dept. surgery, 1976-81, exec. vice-chmn. dept., 1981-95, emeritus prof. surgery, vice chmn. dept. surgery, 1998—; mem. staff VA Hosp., Martinez, Calif., chief surg. service, 1976-80; attending surgeon Sutter Hosps., Sacramento. Surg. cons. U. Mich., 1966-76, VA, 1971—, Highway Safety Research Inst., 1973-76. Assoc. editor, mem. editorial bd. The Pancreas, Internat. Jour. of Pancreatology; mem. editorial bd. Western Jour. Medicine, Jour. Gastrointestinal Surgery; contbr. numerous articles to profl. jours. Served to capt. USAF, 1957-59. Fellow ACS (chief regional com. on trauma 1976-89, disaster preparedness com. 1978—, med. motion picutres com. 1981-91, allied health com. 1981-82, program com. No. Calif. chpt., 1981—, credentials com. No. Calif. chpt. 1982—, mem. bd. govs. 1989-94, gov. 1988-94, adv. com. on ambulatory surgery, chmn. ambulatory surg. care com. 1990-94, pres. No. Calif. chpt. 1995-96), Am. Assn. Surgery Trauma; mem. AMA, Calif. Med. Assn., El Dorado-Scarmento Med. Soc., Am. Fedn. Clin. Rsch., Am. Assn. Automotive Medicine (bd. dirs. 1970-74), Internat. Assn. Accident and Traffic Medicine, Am. Trauma Soc. (founding, standards devel. com. 1978—, v.p. Calif. divsn. 1979—, bd. dirs. 1980—), Calif. Trauma Soc. (trustee 1977—), Nat. Trauma Com. of ACS (chmn. membership com. 1980-84, exec. com. 1981-85), Assn. Acad. Surgery, Am. Surg. Assn., Brazilian Surg. Soc., Western Surg. Assn., Ctrl. Surg. Assn. (membership com. 1971-73), Pacific Coast Surg. Assn., Sacramento Surg. Soc. (pres. 1994), Assn. VA Surgeons (publs., program coms. 1981—), Soc. Univ. Surgeons, Soc. Surgery Alimentary Tract (constn. and by-laws com. 1969—, chmn. 1972-76, v.p. 1995-96), Internat. Assn. Pancreatology (mem. editl. bd. 1986, steering com.), Internat. Biliary Assn., Am. Gastroenterology Assn., Pancreas Club (chmn. 1975-96). E-mail: cffreymd@pacbell.net.

FREY, DANIEL D., engineering educator, researcher; BS in Aeronautical Engring., Rensselaer Polytech. Inst., 1987; MS in Mech. Engring., U. Colo., 1993; PhD in Mech. Engring., Mass. Inst. Tech., 1997. Asst. prof. mech. engring. and engring. systems Mass. Inst. Tech., Cambridge, Mass., 1998—; with faculty Olin Coll., 2000—02. Decorated Joint Svc. Commendation Medal U.S. So. command USN; recipient R&D 100 award, R&D Mag., 1997; Hughes doctoral fellow, 1995—97. Mem.: AIAA, ASME, Am. Statistical Assn., Am. Soc. Engring. Edn. Achievements include research in system design methods including robust design, design of experiments, probability, manufacturing, and computational geometry. Office: Mass Inst Tech 77 Massachusetts Ave Bldg 3-449D Cambridge MA 02139-4307 Office Phone: 617-324-6133. Business E-Mail: danfrey@mit.edu.

FREY, DONALD NELSON, industrial engineer, educator, retired manufacturing executive; b. St. Louis, Mar. 13, 1923; m. Helen-Kay Eberley, Feb. 14, 2003; children: Donald Nelson, Judith Kingsley(dec.), Margaret Bente, Catherine, Christopher, Elizabeth. Student, Mich. State Coll., 1940—42; BS, U. Mich., 1947, MS, 1949, PhD, 1950, DSc (hon.), 1965; DSc, U. Mo., Rolla, 1966. Instr. metall. engring. U. Mich., 1949—50, asst. prof. chem. and metall. engring., 1950—51; rsch. engr. Babcock & Wilcox Tube Co., Beaver Falls, Pa., 1951; various rsch. positions Ford Motor Co. (Ford div.), 1951—57, various engring. positions, 1958—61, product planning mgr., 1961—62, asst. gen. mgr., 1962—65, gen. mgr. original Mustang auto, 1965—68, co. v.p. for product devel., 1965—67; pres. Gen. Cable Corp., N.Y.C., 1968—71, Bell & Howell Co., Chgo., 1973—81, chmn., CEO, 1971—88, also bd. dirs.; prof. of indsl. engring. and mgmt. sci. Northwestern U., Evanston, Ill., 1988—. Mem. exec. bd. World Bank, Washington; bd. dirs. Cin. Milacron, Clark Equipment Co., Packer Engring., My Own Meals, Hyatt Corp., Springs Industries, Quintar, 20th Century Fox Corp.; co-chair Japan study multinats. NRC, 1992—94; surveyor World Bank, Poland, 1990. Co-chmn. Gov.'s Commn. of Sci. and Industry, Ill., 1988—; exec. bd. mem. World Bank, 2003. With U.S. Army, 1942—46. Named Young Engr. of Yr., Engring. Soc. Detroit, 1953, Outstanding Alumni, U. Mich. Coll. Engring., 1957, Outstanding Young Man of the Yr., Detroit Jr. Bd. of Commerce, 1958, Man of the Yr., Weizmann Inst., 1988; recipient Nat. medal for tech., 1990; Inaugural fellow, INFORMS, 2002. Fellow: INFORMS, AAAS; mem.: ASME, Coun. on Fgn. Rels., Detroit Engring. Soc. (pres., bd. dirs. 1962—65), Soc. Automotive Engrs. (vice chmn. Detroit 1958, Russell Springer award 1956), Nat. Acad. Engring. (mem. coun. 1972), Am. Soc. Metals, Am. Inst. Mining and Metall. Engrs. (chmn. Detroit chpt. 1954, chmn., editor Nat. Symposium on Sheet Steels 1956), Econ. Club, Saddle and Cycle Club, Chgo. Club, Hundred Club Cook County, Chgo. Commonwealth Club, Phi Delta Theta, Tau Beta Pi, Phi Kappa Phi, Sigma Xi. Achievements include established Margaret and Muir Frey Prize for innovation in engring., Northwestern Univ., 2002; Clara McKitrick Prize for Design in engring., Northwestern Univ., 2004. Home: 2758 Sheridan Rd Evanston IL 60201-1728 Office: Northwestern U 2145 Sheridan Rd Rm M237 Evanston IL 60208-0834 Office Phone: 847-491-3326. E-mail: d-frey@northwestern.edu.*

FREY, FRANCIS M., finance educator; s. William J. and Helen M. Frey; m. Marcy H. Schnitzer, Oct. 25, 1997. PhD, Va. Tech, Blacksburg. Cert. in Mediation and Conflict Resolution Cmty. Mediation Ctr., 1998. Assoc. prof., mgmt. U. Va.'s Coll. at Wise, 1997—. Dir., Napoleon Hill scholars program U. Va.'s Coll. at Wise, 1998—. Scholar, Mary Reynold's Babcock Found., 2002. Mem.: Acad. Mgmt.

FREY, FRANZISKA S., printmaker, educator; arrived in US, 1994; d. Roland Max and Edith Maria (Vogt) Frey; m. Jean-Pierre Van De Capelle, June 27, 2000. MS, U. Zurich, Switzerland, 1988; PhD in natural scis., Fed. Inst. of Tech. Zurich, Switzerland, 1994. Rsch. scientist IPI/RIT, Rochester, NY, 1994—2001; prof. Sch. of Print Media, Rochester, 2001—. Mem.: Soc. of Imaging Sci of Tech. (v.p. 2004—). Office: Sch of Print Media 69 Lorg Meml Dr Rochester NY 14623 Office Phone: 585-475-2712. E-mail: fsfpph@rit.edu.

FREY, FREDERICK AUGUST, geochemistry researcher, educator; b. Milw., Apr. 1, 1938; s. Frederick August and Evelyn Dorothy (Lange) F.; m. Julie Ann Golden; 1 child, Oren. BSCE, U. Wis., 1960, PhD in Chemistry, 1967. Prof. dept. earth, atmospheric and planetary scis. MIT, Cambridge, 1966—, Francqui Found. prof. Belgium, 1996-97. Lectr. in field. Assoc. editor: Geochimica et Cosmochimica Acta; contbr. more than 195 articles to profl. jours. Fellow Geochem. Soc., European Assn. Geochemist; mem. Geol. Soc. Am., European Union Geoscis., Am. Geophys. Union (pres. VGP sect. 2000-2002, VGP Bowen award 1986). Office: MIT Dept Earth Atmos & Plan Sci 54 # 1226 Cambridge MA 02139

FREY, GLENN, songwriter, vocalist, guitarist; b. Detroit, Nov. 6, 1948; Former band mem. The Mushrooms, Four of Us, The Subterraneans, Heavy Metal Kids; founding mem., guitarist, keyboardist, vocalist The Eagles, 1971—; co-founder Mission Records. Performed with Bo Diddly and Linda Ronstadt, songs include Take it Easy, solo artist (albums) No Fun Aloud, 1982, The Allnighter, 1984, Soul Searchin', 1988, Strange Weather, 1992, Glen Frey Live, 1993, Solo Collection, 1995; composer (theme song): (TV series) Miami Vice, Body by Jake, 1988; TV appearance Wiseguy, 1988; actor: (TV series) South of Sunset, 1993; (films) Jerry Maguire, 1996; musician: (albums) (with Eagles) Eagles, 1972, Desperado, 1973, On the Border, 1974, One of These Nights, 1975, Hotel California, 1976 (Grammy award for album of yr., 1977), The Long Run, 1979. Co-recipient Grammy award for Lyin' Eyes 1975, for New Kid in Town 1977; named (with Eagles) to Rock and Roll Hall of Fame, 1998.*

FREY, HARLEY HARRISON, JR., retired anesthesiologist; b. Toledo, Feb. 22, 1920; s. Harley Harrison and Mina Rosina (Wiedemann) F.; m. Jane Luceia Murray, Aug. 28, 1944 (dec. 1964); children: Richard E., Martha J., Thomas C.; m. Emma Jean Hamilton, Apr. 15, 1966; 1 stepchild, Rick A. Gregory. BS, U. Toledo, 1942; MD, U. Cin., 1945. Diplomate Am. Bd. Anesthesiology. Intern Akron City Hosp., Ohio, 1946—47; fellow anesthesia U. Minn., Mpls., 1950; hon. mem. staff St. Elizabeth Hosp. Med. Ctr., Lafayette, Ind., 1950—, Lafayette Home Hosp., 1950—; ret. Bd. dirs. Lafayette Symphony Orch., 1952-54; counselor, committeeman Lafayette coun. Boy Scouts Am., 1955-63; ruling elder Presbyn. Ch., 1964-67, active deacon, 1991-94; bd. dirs. Lafayette Citizens Band, 1997-2000. Capt. U.S. Army, 1947—49. Fellow Am. Coll. Anesthesiology; mem. Am. Soc. Anesthesiology (bd. dirs. 1965-74), Ind. Soc. Anesthesiology (pres., bd. dirs. 1961-74, Disting Svc. award 1992), Ind. State Med. Soc. (Cert. Distinction 1995), Tippecanoe County Med. soc. (pres. 1961), Rotary (bd. dirs. 1992-95) Lafayette Country Club (bd. dirs. 1963-65). Avocations: music, painting. Home: 1700 Lindberg Rd Apt 321 West Lafayette IN 47906-7323 E-mail: hemfrey@tcconnections.com. *Personal philosophy: My philosophy of life is simple, whatever talent or wisdom I may have has been given to me by God as a gift. In any task I undertake, this gift should be used to the best of my ability, be fair, build goodwill, better friendships, exhibit truth and benefit all concerned.*

FREY, JOANNE ALICE TUPPER, art educator; b. Wakefield, Mass., Jan. 16, 1931; d. Arthur Andrew Tupper, Elva June Goddard, Joanne Alice Tupper; m. John Oscar Frey, June 14, 1953 (dec. Oct. 2000); children: David J., Donald A., Dale R., Alexandria Brennan. Grad. honors, Vesper George Sch. Art, Boston, 1951; student art history, NTL Art Gallery, London, 1979. Tchr. art Wishing Well Cards, Everett, Mass., 1951—54, Sarrin Studio, Wakefield, Mass., 1960—96; tchr. art oil, acrylic, and watercolor Wakefield H.S., Wakefield, 1997—. Antique and current doll authority; lectr. in field. Asst. resident dir. Boit Home for Women, Wakefield, Mass., 1996—; bd. dirs. The Hartshorne House. Mem.: Collie Fancier League of N.E., The Kosmos Club (decorator 1997—). Republican. Congregationalist. Avocations: painting, reading, walking, gardening, art history. Home: 701 Haverhill St Reading MA 01867

FREY, JOHN WARD, landscape architect; s. Philip Rockel and Sarah Helen (Dempwolf) F.; m. Wilma Emma Weggel, Feb. 11, 1961; children: Holly Frances, Allison Margaret, Frederika Elizabeth, Marietta Isabel. BA in Math., Coll. of Wooster, 1952; MLA, Harvard U., 1955. Urban designer The Architects Collaborative, 1955; assoc., designer Sasaki (Walker) Assocs., Inc., 1957-62; ptnr. Mason and Frey, Landscape Architects, 1963—. Registered landscape architect N.Y., Conn., Mass. Prin. works include Arlington (Mass.) Bicentennial Park, 1975, S.W. Corridor Park, Sect. III, Jamaica Plain, Boston, 1988, State U. Agricultural and Tech. Coll., Farmingdale, N.Y., 1963-71, State U. Coll., Geneseo, N.Y., 1963-73, Fulton Montgomery C.C., Johnstown, N.Y., 1967-70, Burlington (Mass.) High Sch., 1968-74, Wellesley Coll. Sci. Ctr., 1973, Lexington Ctr. Mall, 1967, Murray Hill, Manchester, 1973, Polaroid Corp., Waltham, Mass., 1970, Sandoz Pharm., East Hanover, N.J., 1964, 73, others incl. indsl., comml. office bldgs., land devel. and pvt. res. Adv. com. to planning bd. Lexington Design, 1973-76; mem. Revere Beach Design Rev. Bd., 1976-78, Lexington Tree Com., 1990—, Lexington Minuteman Commuter Bikeway Com., 1993-95, Mass. Recreational Trails Adv. Com., 1993—; chmn. Design Adv. Com., Lexington, 1988—. Recipient Boston Soc. of Architects award 1973, "A" Citation, Mass. Audubon Soc., 1968, Indsl. Plant Beautification award Govs. Conf. on Natural Beauty, 1967, NEA Presdl. Design award Fed. Design Achievement award, 1988. Fellow Am. Soc. of Landscape Architects (Merit award 1973, trustee Boston chpt. 1980-83); mem. BSLA (treas. 1966-67, program com. 1966-67, com. landscape architectural registration in Mass. 1966-67, pub. svc. com. 1963-71, examining bd. 1971-75, others) Charles River Watershed Assn., Appalachian Mountain Club, Appalachian Trail Conf., The Nature Conservancy, Mass. Audubon Soc., Rails to Trails Conservancy. Avocations: gardening, bicycling, hiking, canoeing, jogging. Home: 1133 Massachusetts Ave Lexington MA 02420-3818 Office: Mason & Frey Landscape Architects 1133 Massachusetts Ave Lexington MA 02420-3818 E-mail: jwfrey2@aol.com.

FREY, JULIA BLOCH, language educator, art historian, educator; b. Louisville, July 25, 1943; d. Oscar Edgeworth and Jean Goldthwaite (Russell) Bloch; m. Roger G. Frey, Dec. 27, 1968 (div. Mar. 1976); m. Ronald Sukenick, Mar. 9, 1992. BA, Antioch Coll., 1966; MA, U. Tex., 1968; MPhil, Yale U., 1970, PhD, 1977. Instr. Brown U., Providence, 1972-73; chargée de cours U. Paris, 1974-75; lectr. Yale U., New Haven, 1975-76; prof. Inst. Internat. Comparative Law, U. San Diego, Paris, 1979-89, adminstrv. dir., 1989; prof. French, art history U. Colo., Boulder, 1976—2001, prof. emeritus, 2002—, dir. undergrad. studies, 1985-95, assoc. chmn. for grad. studies, 1996-97, 98-99, chmn., 1999. Guest prof. Sarah Lawrence Coll., Bronxville, N.Y., 1983; curator Toulouse-Lautrec Met. Mus. Art Denver Art Mus., 1999, Toulouse-Lautrec, Museo Vittoriano, Rome, 2003-04. Author: Toulouse-Lautrec, a life, 1994, Toulouse-Lautrec l'homme qui aimait les femmes, 1996; editor: Gustave Flaubert's La Lutte du Sacerdoce et de L'Empire (1837), 1981; contbr. articles and monographs to profl. publs., chpts. to books; translator: René. Recipient Conn. Grad. Study award, 1970-73; grantee NDEA, 1967, Brown U. Research and Travel, 1973, Boulder Arts Com., 1979, 80, Ctr. for Applied Humanities, 1985, S.W. Inst. for Research on Women, 1985-86, NEH, 1986; fellow NDEA, 1966-68, Yale U., 1968-72, Gilbert Chinard, Inst. Français de Washington, 1977, Big 12 2000, Humanities Rsch. Ctr., Australian Nat. U., 2000; Pen Ctr. USA West Lit. award for non-fiction, 1995; Finalist Nat. Book Critics Cir. award for Biography, 1994. Mem. MLA, PEN U.S.A., Coll. Art Assn., Yale Club. Unitarian Universalist. Home: 355 8th Ave Apt 20B New York NY 10001 E-mail: julia.frey@aya.yale.edu.

FREY, LORYN ELIZABETH, music educator, singer; d. W. Kirk and Edith Ditmer Frey. MusB, Baldwin-Wallace Coll., 1973; MusM, U. Cin., 1975; D in Musical Arts, La. State U., 1990. Prof., vocal coord., dir. opera dept. music La. Coll., Pineville, 1975—. Pres. So. La. chpt. Nat. Assn. Tchrs. Singing, 1993—95. Singer: (Operas) La Boheme, The Merry Wives of Windsor, The Marriage of Figaro, La Traviata, Albert Herring, (operetta) Die Fledermaus; dir.: (Operas) Il Campanello, Dido and Aeneas, The Bartered Bride, La Serva Padrona, Amahl and The Night Visitors, Trial by Jury, Cosi fan Tutte; dir., singer: Hansel and Gretel; Gianni Schicchi; The Impessario; The Old Maid and the Thief. Adv. bd. mem., chmn. Salvation Army, Alexandria, La., 1995—2005. Mem.: Coll. Music Soc., Nat. Assn. Tchrs. Singing. Baptist. Office: Louisiana Coll Dept Music College Station Pineville LA 71359 Office Phone: 318-487-7511.

FREY, LOUIS, JR., lawyer, federal official; b. Jan. 11, 1934; m. Marcia Turner, 1956; children: Julie, Lynne, Louis III, Lauren, Christine. BA cum laude, Colgate U., 1955; JD, U. Mich., 1961; JD (hon.), Rollins Coll., 1977; DSc (hon.), Jones Univ., 1978; LLD (hon.), Rollins Coll., 2005. Bar: Fla. 1961, U.S. Supreme Ct. 1969. Asst. county solictor Orange County, Fla., 1961-63; gen. counsel Fla. State Turnpike Authority, 1966-67; congressman U.S. Ho. of Reps., 1969-79, Rep. leader, 1973-76, mem. interstate and fgn. commerce com., sci. and tech. com., select com. on narcotics, sub-com. on communications, sub-com. on energy research; ptnr. Lowndes, Drosdick, Doster, Kantor & Reed, P.A., Orlando, Fla., 1987—; commr. Dept. of Lottery State of Fla., 1987-88; founder Lou Frey Inst. Politics and Govt., U. Ctrl. Fla., 2002—. Del. or alternate del. to most Rep. Conv., 1968—; Rep. State Chmn. Pres. Ford, 1976—; nat. co-chmn., former mem. Congress for Reagan, 1980; nat. fin. com. Bush, 1988—92; mem. state fin. com. President Bush, 2000, 04; counsellor to sec. HUD, 2001; alumni bd. trustees Colgate U., 1973—75; leader Former Mems. of Congress Delegations to numerous countriew; ofcl. observer Ukraine Election, 2004. Contbr. weekly column to Fla. newspapers; author, editor: Inside The House Former Members Reveal How the House Works, 2001 co-anchor: Fla. Roundtable Radio Show; commentator pub. radio and TV. Chmn. Fla. Fedn. of Young Reps., 1965-66; treas. Rep. Party Fla., mem. state exec. com., 1966-67; past chmn., mem. exec. com. Fla. Coun. on Econ. Edn., 1991—; chmn. Former Mems. Congress, 1992-94, bd. dirs., 1992—; candidate Fla. Gov., 1978-86, U.S. Senate, 1980. Served with USN, 1955-58, capt. Res. ret. Recipient Watchdog of Treasury award, 1970, 72, 74, 76, 78, Guardian of Small Bus. award, Disting. Service award Ams. for Constitutional Action, Man of Yr. award Fla. Assn. Broadcasters, 1977, Masada award, 1977, Hope for Congress, Life Mag., 1975; elected to Sr. Citizen's Hall of Fame; named As one of 200 Rising Leaders in the U.S., Time Mags., 1974. Mem. Order of the Coif, Phi Gamma Delta, Phi Delta Phi. Lutheran. Home: 139 Genius Dr Winter Park FL 32789-5103 Office: Lowndes Drosdick Doster Kantor & Reed PA 215 N Eola Dr PO Box 2809 Orlando FL 32801-2095 Office Phone: 407-843-4600. Business E-Mail: lou.frey@lowndes-law.com.

FREY, LYNN MARIE, music educator; d. Carl Glenwood and Eloise Eleanor Marckel; m. Neal Edward Frey (div.); children: Jeffrey, Matthew. BM, Kent State U., Ohio, 1980; MM Akron U., Ohio, 1995. Organist St. Michael's, Powey, Calif., 1980—83; dir. music, choir master St. Joseph, Canton, Ohio, 1983—2005. Accompanist Glen Oak HS Band, Canton, Ohio. Mem.: Am. Guild of English Handbell Ringers (dist. leader), Nat. Pastoral Musicians, Am. Guild of Organists (dean Canton, Ohio br.). Office Phone: 330-836-2233. Personal E-mail: Lorgnst7@aol.com.

FREY, MARTIN ALAN, lawyer, educator; b. Rochester, NY, Feb. 26, 1939; s. Morrey and Betty (Weinstein) F.; m. Phyllis Sue Hurley, Apr. 19, 1966; 1 child, David Andrew. BS in Mech. Engring., Northwestern U., 1962; JD, Washington U., St. Louis, 1965; LLM, George Washington U., 1966. Bar: Mo. 1965, Okla. 1976, U.S. Dist. Ct. (no. dist.) Okla. 1983. Asst. prof. law Drake U., Des Moines, 1966-67; prof. law Tex. Tech. U., Lubbock, 1967-76, U. Tulsa, 1976—2001, assoc. dean, 1981-84, prof. emeritus, 2001—. Vis. prof. law U. Maine, Portland, 1974—75, Washington U., St. Louis, 1986—87, U. Ala., Tuscaloosa, 2003, Wake Forest U., 2005, Stetson U., 2005—06; adj. settlement judge US Dist Ct. and US Bankruptcy Ct. (no. dist.) Okla., 1988—; reporter adv. group Civil Justice Reform Act, U.S. Dist. Ct. (no. dist) Okla., 1991—97; dir. Ctr. Dispute Resolution U. Tulsa Coll. Law, 1994—2000. Author: Alternative Methods of Dispute Resolution, 2003; co-author (with T. Bitting): An Introduction to Contracts, 1988; co-author: (with T. Bitting and P.H. Frey) 3d edit., 2000; co-author: (with McConnico and P.H. Frey) An Introduction to Bankruptcy Law, 1990; co-author: (with T. Bitting and P.H. Frey) 2nd edit., 1993; co-author: (with McConnico and P.H. Frey) 3rd. edit., 1997; co-author: (with T. Bitting and P.H. Frey) study guide, 1994; co-author: West's Bankruptcy Practice Systems, 1991; co-author: (with P.H. Frey) Essentials of Contract Law, 2000; co-author: (with B. Bucholtz and M. Tatum) The Little Black Book: A Do-It Yourself Guide For Law Student Competitions, 2001; co-author: (with P.H. Frey and Sidney K. Swinson) An Introduction to Bankruptcy Law, 4th edit., 2005; founder, advisor: Tex. Tech. Law Rev., 1967—71; contbr. articles to profl. jours. Mem.: ABA (accreditation site evaluation teams 1978—2000), Am. Inns of Ct. (master emeritus Johnson/Sontag chpt.). Democrat. Jewish. Home: 9035 S Maplewood Ave Tulsa OK 74137-3040 Personal E-mail: martin_a_frey@yahoo.com.

FREY, PAUL HOWARD, chemical engineer, engineering consultants company executive; b. Gilman, Ill., Feb. 12, 1922; s. Carl Fredrick and Doretta Mary (Koritz) F.; m. Patricia Anne Leonard, Oct. 6, 1942; children: Paul H. Jr, Elizabeth Ann. BSChE, U. Ill., 1943. Registered profl. engr., Ill. Tech. advisor Manhatten Dist. (Atom Bomb Project) Union Carbide Corp., Tonawanda, N.Y., 1943-46, rsch. and devel. engr., 1946-49; project engr. Union Carbide Corp, Chgo., 1960-80, engring. mgr., 1980-86; plant engr. U.S. Reduction Co., East Chicago, Ind., 1949-54; project and sales engr. Sunbeam Corp., Chgo., 1954-58; plant mgr. Detinning Corp., Chgo., 1958-60; owner Freytone Co. Cons. Engrs., Spooner, Wis., 1986—. Inventor/patentee in field. Leader Citizens for Improved Edn., LaGrange, Ill., 1967-69; mem. vestry St. Alban's Episc. Ch., 1993—. Mem. AIChE, Lions (Lion Tamer officer Spooner chpt., 1992—), Jaycees (Key award Hammond, Ind. 1951), Waukegan Yacht Club (bd. dirs. to commodore 1976-82), No. Ill.

Venture Assn. (various officers to commodore 1974-78). Avocations: sailboat racing, long-distance sailing. Home and Office: N5683 Tanglewood Dr Spooner WI 54801-8480 E-mail: topfrey@centurytel.net.

FREY, STUART MACKLIN, automobile manufacturing company executive; b. Peoria, Ill., Feb. 13, 1925; s. Muir Luken and Margaret Bryden (Nelson) F.; m. Lillian Maxine Paxton, 1951; children: Mellissa June, Muir Paxton. BS in Mech. Engring, U. Mich., 1949; SM in Indsl. Mgmt, MIT, 1961. With Budd Co., 1949-53; with Ford Motor Co., 1953—, chief car research engr. Dearborn, Mich., 1974-75, chief vehicle engr., 1975-80, v.p. car engring., 1980-83, v.p. car product devel., 1983-87, v.p. engring. and mfg. staff, 1987-88, v.p. tech. affairs, 1988-90; with TRW, 1990—; v.p. auto tech. affairs, 1990-94. Contbr. articles to profl. jours. Served as officer AUS, 1943-46, 51-52. Sloan fellow, 1960-61 Fellow Soc. Automotive Engrs., Engring. Soc. Detroit; mem. Am. Soc. Body Engrs., Tau Beta Pi, Pi Tau Sigma. Home: 1035 Heather Way Bay City MI 48708 *The key ingredient that has contributed most importantly to my success has been the understanding and employment of the principles of employee involvement and participative management.*

FREY, SUSAN M., information specialist; d. Anthony T. and Martha M. Frey. BA, SUNY-Stony Brook, 1983; MS, L.I. U., 1986; MLS, Ind. U., 2002. Info. svcs. libr. Ind. U.-Purdue U., Ft. Wayne, 1991—99; asst. libr. dir. Ind. Inst. Tech., Ft. Wayne, 2000—01; info. specialist DePuy Orthopaedics, Warsaw, Ind., 2001—. Adj. lectr. Ind. U.-Purdue U., 2002; presenter in field. Contbr. articles to profl. jours. Mem.: ALA, Am. Soc. Info. Sci. and Tech., Assn. Computing Machinery (pres. 1997—98). Office: Ind State U Terre Haute IN 47809 Office Fax: 574-371-4984. Business E-Mail: sfrey@indstate.edu.

FREY, WILLIAM H., demographer, educator; b. Allentown, Pa., June 21, 1947; s. Elwood H. and Loretta C. Frey. BS, Ursinus Coll., 1969; PhD, Brown U., 1974. Sociology lectr. Rutgers U., New Brunswick, N.J., 1973-74; rsch. assoc. Ctr. for Studies in Demography and Ecology U. Wash., Seattle, 1974-75; project dir., assoc. Ctr. for Demography and Ecology U. Wis., Madison, 1975-81; rsch. prof. Population Studies Ctr. U. Mich., Ann Arbor, 1981—98, 2000—; prof. sociology SUNY, Albany, 1998-2001; sr. fellow Milken Inst., Santa Monica, Calif., 1998—. Vis. rsch. scholar Internat. Inst. Applied Sys. Analysis, Laxenburg, Austria, 1980-81; vis. fellow The Brookings Inst., Washington, D.C., 2003—; Andrew W. Mellon vis. scholar Popular Ref. Bur., Washington, 1988-89; cons. U.S. Census Bur., Population Divsn., Washington, 2000-; dir. ednl. devel. Pub. Data Queries, Inc., Ann Arbor, Mich., 1998-; pres. Frey-First Demographic Networks Inc., Ann Arbor, 1999-. Author: America by the Numbers: A Fieldguide to the U.S. Population, 2001, Regional and Population Growth and Decline in the U.S., 1988; contbr. articles to profl. jours. including Am. Sociol. Rev., Population and Devel. Rev., among others. Grantee Population Ref. Bus., 1998—, Nat. Inst. Aging, 1994-2000, Nat. Inst. child Health and Human Devel. Ctr. for Population Rsch., 1982-87, 1994-2000, NSF, 1996-2001, Russell Sage Found., 1992-93, Child Trends, Inc., 1995, others; vis. fellow Brookings Inst., 2003—. Fellow Urban Land Inst.; mem. Am. Sociol. Assn. (chair com. on nat. statistics 1997-99), Population Assn. Am. (com. on population statistics 1995-2001), Internat. Union for the Sci. Study Population. Avocations: bicycling, hiking, website creation. Office: The Univ Michigan 426 Thompson St Ann Arbor MI 48104-2321 Fax: 888-257-7244. Office Phone: 888-257-7244. Business E-Mail: billf@umich.edu. E-mail: bill.frey@usa.net.

FREY, WILLIAM RAYBURN, healthcare educator, consultant; b. Springfield, Tenn., July 20, 1948; s. Rayburn and Elma Faye (Nunley) F.; m. Carol Jackson, Jan. 2, 1971. BS in Occupational Therapy, U. Ill., Chgo., 1971; MEd, Ga. State U., 1973; MHA, Washington U., St. Louis, 1976; PhD, Ohio State U., 1987. Registered occupational therapist. Asst. prof. U. Ill., Chgo., 1974; hosp. adminstr. The Toledo Hosp., 1975-81; instr. Ohio State U., Columbus, 1981-85; hosp. adminstr. Nat. Med. Enterprises, York, Pa., 1985-87; assoc. prof. Slippery Rock (Pa.) U., 1987-88; prof. Coll. St. Francis, Joliet, Ill., 1988-92, St. Mary's Coll., Moraga, Calif., 1992—2003; dean U. Tenn., Memphis, 2003—. Cons. Commn. on Accreditation of Rehab. Facilities, Samuel Merritt Coll., Nat. Med. Enterprises. Author: Cross National Perspective on Health Care Reform, 1995, A Binational Study of the Role of Information-Technology in National Healthcare Systems, 2001; (jours.) Health Care Mgmt. Rev., Archives of Phys. Medicine and Rehab., Jour. of Head Trauma Rehab., Jour. of Allied Health. Juror Acad. Med. Films; bd. dirs. Easter Seals Rehab., Quincy Found. for Med. Rsch., 1997—; pres. Child Abuse Prevention, hon. adv. bd., 1982. Capt. U.S. Army, 1971-73. Fellow Am. Coll. Healthcare Execs.; mem. Am. Hosp. Assn., Am. Occupational Therapy Assn., Assn. Univ. Programs Health Adminstrn. Avocations: acting, musical comedy. Office: U Tenn Health Sci Ctr 930 Madison Ave Ste 601 Memphis TN 38163

FREYD, JENNIFER JOY, psychology professor; b. Providence, Oct. 16, 1957; d. Peter John and Pamela (Parker) F.; m. John Q. Johnson, June 9, 1984; children: Theodore, Philip, Alexandra. BA in Anthropology magna cum laude, U. Pa., 1979; PhD in Psychology, Stanford U., 1983. Asst. prof. psychology Cornell U., 1983-87, mem. faculty coun. of reps., 1986-87; assoc. prof. psychology U. Oreg., Eugene, 1987-92, prof., 1992—, mem. dean's adv. com., 1990-91, 92-93, mem. exec. com. Ctr. for the Study of Women in Soc., 1991-93, mem. child care com., 1987-89, 90-91, dir. undergrad. studies dept. psychology, 2004—. Elected mem. faculty coun. of reps. Cornell U., 1986-87; mem. dean's adv. com. U. Oreg., 1990—, exec. com. Ctr. for Rsch. Study of Women in Soc., 1991-92, Inst. of Cognitive and Decision Scis., 1991-94; mem. instl. rev. bd. U. Oreg., 2002—. Author: Betrayal Trauma: The Logic of Forgetting Childhood Abuse, 1996 (Disting. Publ. award Assn. of Women in Psychology 1997, Pierre Janet award Internat. Soc. for Study Dissociation 1997), Spanish edit., 2003; co-editor: (with A.P. De Prince) Trauma and Cognitive Science: A Meeting of Minds, Science, and Human Experience, 2001; mem. editl. bd. Jour. Exptl. Psychology: Learning, Memory, and Cognition, 1989-91, Gestalt Theory, 1985—, Jour. of Aggression, Maltreatment, and Trauma, 1997—, Jour. of Psychopathology and Behavioral Assessment, 2001-2003, Jour. Trauma Practice, 2003—, Jour. of Trauma and Dissociation, 1999-2005, assoc. editor, 2004, editor, 2005—; guest reviewer Am. Jour. Psychology, Am. Psychologist, others; contbr. articles to profl. jours. Recipient Grad. fellowship NSF, 1979-82, Univ. fellowship Stanford U., 1982-83, Presdl. Young Investigator award NSF, 1985-90, IBM Faculty Devel. award, 1985-87, fellowship Ctr. for Advanced Study in the Behavioral Scis., 1989-90, John Simon Meml. fellowship Guggenheim Found., 1989-90, Rsch. Scientist Devel. award NIMH, 1989-94, Pierre Janet award Internat. Soc. for the Study of Dissociation, 1997; other rsch. funding. Fellow AAAS, APA (liaison divsn. 35 to sci. directorate 1998—), Am. Psychol. Soc.; mem. Psychonomic Soc., Internat. Soc. for the Study of Traumatic Stress, Sigma Xi. Office: U Oreg 1227 Dept Psychology Eugene OR 97403-1227

FREYD, WILLIAM PATTINSON, not-for-profit fundraiser, director; b. Chgo., Apr. 1, 1933; s. Paul Robert Freyd and Pauline Margaret (Pattinson) Gardiner; m. Diane Marie Carlson, May 19, 1984. BS in Fgn. Svc., Georgetown U., 1960. Field rep. Georgetown U., Washington, 1965-67; campaign dir. Tamblyn and Brown, N.Y.C., 1967-70; dir. devel. St. George's Ch., N.Y.C., 1971; assoc. Browning Assocs., Newark, 1972-73; regional v.p. C.W. Shaver Co., N.Y.C., 1973-74; founder IDC, Henderson, Nev., 1974—. Prodr.: A Chorus Line, 2005. Bd. dirs. Nev. Symphony Orch., 1994-99, NJ Symphony Orch., 1991-94, Las Vegas Philharm., 2004, Nev. Opera Theater, 2004; apptd. Nev. Charitable Solicitation Task Force, 1994, pres.'s circle adv. coun. U.S. Naval Acad., 2003. Mem. SAG, Assn. Fundraising Profls. (nat. treas. 1980-81, pres. N.Y. chpt. 1974-76, cert. 1982), Am. Assn. Fund Raising Counsel (sec. 1984-86, designated Sage 2000), World Fund Raising Coun. (bd. dirs. 1995-99, treas. 1998-99), Georgetown U. (regional club coun.), N.Y. Yacht Club, Union League Club N.Y., Masons, Nassau Club, Circumnavigators Club. Achievements include invention of Phone Mail program. Office: IDC IDC Ctr 2500 Paseo Verde Pky Henderson NV 89074 Personal E-mail: wfreyd@aol.com. E-mail: wfreyd@goidc.com.

FREYER, DANA HARTMAN, lawyer; b. Pitts., Apr. 17, 1944; m. Bruce M. Freyer, Dec. 21, 1969. Student, L' Institut De Hautes Etudes Internationales, Geneva, 1963-64; BA, Conn. Coll., 1965; postgrad., Columbia U., 1968, JD, 1971. Bar: NY 1972, Ill. 1974, US Dist. Ct. (no. dist.) Ill. 1974, US Ct. Appeals (7th cir.) 1976, US Supreme Ct. 1977, US Dist. Ct. (so. dist.) NY 1978, US Dist. Ct. (ea. dist.) NY 1981, US Ct. Appeals (2d cir.) 1982. Staff atty. Legal Aid Soc. Westchester County, Mt. Vernon, NY, 1971-72; assoc. Friedman & Koven, Chgo., 1973-77, Skadden, Arps, Slate, Meagher & Flom, LLP, NYC, 1977-88; spl. counsel Skadden, Arps, Slate, Meagher & Flom, NYC, 1988-93, ptnr., arbitration and alternative dispute resolution, 1994—, mem. internat. arbitration group, head corp. compliance practice. Pres. Westchester Legal Services, Inc., White Plains, NY, 1985-87, bd. dirs., 1978-98; US Coun. for Internat. Bus. Arbitration Com.; adv. bd. World Arbitration and Mediation Report; mem. Coun. on Fgn. Rels.; lectr. in the field; leader in dispute resolution, Practical Law Company's Global Counsel Dispute Resolution Handbook, 2003-04. Contbr. articles to profl. publs.; author and co-author (articles in profl. jours. and publs.), mem. adv. bd. Bur. of Nat. Affairs' Alternative Dispute Resolution Report, 1987—90, Am. Arbitration Assn. Dispute Resolution Jour., 1996—, World Arbitration and Mediation Report, 1990—. Bd. legal advisors Legal Momentum, 2002—. Named one of World's Leading Expert in Commercial Arbitration, Euromoney, 50 Top Women Litigators in Am., Nat. Law Jour. Fellow Chartered Inst. Arbitrators; mem. ABA, Bar Assn. of City of NY, Internat. Bar Assn., adv. and spl. coms. on Alternative Dispute Resolution, Internat. Bar Assn.; co-chair and co-founder, Global Partnership for Afghanistan, 2002-; arbitrator, mem. corp. coun. com. and law com., Am. Arbitration Assn. Office: Skadden Arps Slate Meagher & Flom LLP 4 Times Sq New York NY 10036 Office Phone: 212-735-2506. Office Fax: 917-777-2506. Business E-Mail: dfreyer@skadden.com.

FREYER, DAVID ROBERT, pediatrician, educator; b. Elgin, Ill., Mar. 31, 1958; BA, DePauw U., 1978; DO, Des Moines U., 1981. Instr. dept pediats. Rush Med. Coll., Chgo., 1984—85; fellow in pediat. hematology, oncology U. Mich. Med. Sch., Ann Arbor, 1985—88; asst. prof. pediats. Wayne State U. Sch. Medicine, Detroit, 1988—90; mem. divsn pediat. hematology/oncology Children's Hosp. Mich., Wayne State U., Detroit, 1988—90; asst. prof. pediats. Mich. State U. Coll. Human Medicine, East Lansing, 1991—97, assoc. prof. pediats., 1997—; attending physician divsn. pediat. hematology/oncology and blood and bone marrow transplantation DeVos Children's Hosp., Grand Rapids, Mich., 1990—. Prin. investigator for children's oncology group activities DeVos Children's Hosp., Grand Rapids, 1991—, dir. after-care and transition program for childhood cancer survivors, 1992—; mem. multiple clin. study coms. Children's Oncology Group, Arcadia, Calif., 1990—, chair CCOP subcom. cancer control com., 2000—, mem. multiple adminstrv., other sci. coms., 2000—, chair survivor transition task force of adolescent/young adult com., 2002—; exec. bd. mem. Grand Rapids Clin. Oncology Program, 1999—; reviewer multiple med. jours. Author: (ednl. handbook) Patient-Family Educational Handbook for Newly-diagnosed Children and Adolescents with Cancer; contbr. articles, revs., and abstracts to profl. jours., chapters to books. Mem. Heritage Hill Assn., Grand Rapids, 1998—2001; pres. City High/Mid. Sch. Parent-Teacher-Student Assn., Grand Rapids, 2002—04. Edward Rector Found. acad. scholar, DePauw U., 1975—78. Fellow: Am. Acad. Pediats.; mem.: Histiocyte Soc., Am. Soc. Hematology, Am. Soc. Clin. Oncology, Am. Soc. Pediat. Hematology/Oncology, Sierra Club, Wilderness Soc., Phi Beta Kappa. Achievements include research in childhood clinical cancer. Avocations: wilderness canoeing and camping, civic affairs. Office: DeVos Children's Hosp Mailcode 85 100 Michigan NE Grand Rapids MI 49503 Office Phone: 616-391-2086. Office Fax: 616-391-9430. E-mail: david.freyer@spectrum-health.org.

FREYER, TONY ALLAN, historian, educator; b. Indpls., Dec. 28, 1947; s. Robert Albert Freyer and Ida Marie Hadley; m. Marjorie Faller, Aug. 12, 1976; 1 child, Allan. AB hist., San Diego State Univ., San Diego, Calif., 1970; MA hist., Ind. Univ., Bloomington, Ind., 1972, PhD hist., 1975. Lectr. in law Ind. Univ. Sch. of Law, Bloomington, Ind., 1974—75; asst. to assoc. prof. hist. Univ. Ark., Little Rock, 1976—81; asst. to full prof. hist. & law Univ. Ala., Tuscaloosa, Ala., 1981—90, Univ. rsch. prof. hist. & law, 1990—. Vis. prof. econ. hist London Sch. of Econ., London, 1986; vis. prof. constl. hist. Univ. Calif., L.A., 1987; bus. hist. rev. editl. bd. Harvard Bus. Sch., Boston, 1985—. Author: Producers Versus Capitalists Rights: Constitutional Conflict in Antebellum America, 1994, Regulating Big Business: Antitrust in Great Britian and America, 1880 to 1990, 1992, Hugo L. Black and the Dilemma of American Liberalism, 1990, The Little Rock Crisis, 1984, Harmony & Dissonance: The Swift & Erie Cases in American Federalism, 1981, Forums of Order: The Federal Courts and Business in American History, 1979; co-author (with Timothy Dixon): Democracy and Judicial Independence: Federal Courts in Alabama, 1820-1994, 1995; editor: Defending Constitutional Rights: Frank M. Johnson, 2001; contbr. chapters to books, articles to encyclopedias, to profl. jour.; rev. (70 books to profl. jour.). PFC USMC Res., 1970—72. Recipient Burnam Disting. Faculty award, Univ. Ala., 1991, Martin Luther King. Jr. Lectr., Vanderbilt Univ., 1991, Abe Fellow-Japan, Ctr. for Global Partnership, 1995—96; grantee Nat. Endowment for the Humanities, Summer Stipends, 1978, 1985, Rsch. Grants Com., Univ. Ala., 1983, 1985, Jud. Conf. of the U.S., Com. on the Bicentennial of the Constn. Summer Rsch. Grant, 1991, Ark. Endowment for the Humanities Rsch. Grants, 1978, 1980, 1981; Earhart Found. Fellowships, 1982, 1985, 1994—95, 2002—03, postdoctral fellow, Project '87, 1980, Hagley Mus. and Libr. Fellowship, 1979—80, Newcomer Fellowship, Harvard Bus. Sch., 1975—76, Charles Warren Fellowship, Harvard U., 1981—82, Fulbright Sr. Scholar award, U.K., 1986, Australia, 1993, Fulbright Disting. Chair Am. Studies, Warsaw Univ., Poland, 2000. Mem.: Ogrn. of Am. Hist., Am. Soc. for Legal Hist., Am. Hist. Assn., Phi Beta Kappa. Independent. Christian Sci. Avocations: travel, reading, execrise. Office: Univ Ala Sch Law Box 870382 Tuscaloosa AL 35487 Office Phone: 205-348-1116. Business E-Mail: tfreyer@law.ua.edu.

FREYERMUTH, CLIFFORD L., structural engineering consultant; BS in Civil Engring., State U. Iowa, 1956, MS in Structural Engring., 1958. Registered structural engr., Ariz. Consulting engr. structural design Ned L. Ashton, 1955-57; grad. teaching asst. structural mechanics State U. Iowa, 1957-58; with bridge divsn. Ariz. State Hwy. Dept., 1958-64; with Portland Cement Assn., Chgo., Skokie, Ill., 1964-71; dir. post-tensioning divsn. Prestessed Concrete Inst., 1971-76; mgr. Post-Tensioning Inst., 1976-88; pres. Clifford L. Freyermuth, Inc., 1988—. Mem. cable-stayed bridges com. Post-Tensioning Inst., editor various publs.; prin. investigator Nat. Coop. Hwy Rsch. Project, Washington, 1988. Contbr. articles to profl. jours. Recipient Martin P. Korn award Prestressed Concrete Inst., 1969, George C. Zollman award Precast/Prestressed Concrete Inst., 1999. Fellow Am. Concrete Inst. (prestressed concrete com., standard bldg. code com., bd. dirs. 1991—, Henry C. Turner medal 1992, Arthur R. Anderson award 2004); mem. ASCE (prestressed concrete com.), Internat. Assn. Bridge and Structural Engrs., Structural Engrs. Assn. Ariz., Chi Epsilon. Office: Clifford L Freyermuth Inc 9201 N 25th Ave Ste 150B Phoenix AZ 85021-2721 Personal E-mail: asbi@earthlink.net.

FREYERMUTH, VIRGINIA KAREN, art educator; BFA cum laude, Boston U., 1973, MFA, 1975; edn. cert., Suffolk U., 1975; PhD in Interdisciplinary Studies, Art Edn., Union Inst. and U., 2003. Cert. art tchr., Mass. Grad. asst. Boston U., Mass., 1973-75; art tchr. Quincy Pub. Sch., Mass., 1975-76, Plymouth Pub. Sch., Mass., 1976-78, 83-85; painting tchr. Brockton Fuller Mus. Art, Mass., 1978-79; art coord. grades K-12 Duxbury Pub. Sch., Mass., 1985-99; vis. lectr. art edn. U. Mass., Dartmouth, Mass., 1999—2004; pres. Virginia K. Freyermuth, Inc., Carver, Mass., 2004—. Art reviewer Patriot Ledger, Quincy, 1975-85; dir. Freyermuth Fine Arts Ctr., Plymouth, 1990-94; mem. adv. coun. Mass. Field Ctr. Tchg. & Learning, 1993-96; tchr. in electronic residence MCET, Cambridge, 1993-95; instr. art Massasoit C.C., Brockton, 1991-92; dir. Helen Bumpus Gallery, Inc., Duxbury, 1992-94; forum tchr. Goals 2000 U.S. Dept. Edn., 1994—, internat. space camp, 1994; master tchr. Connecting Oceans Acad., ECHO Project, New Bedford, Mass, 2004— Columnist Learning for Life, 1994. Mem. commn. on common core of learning Mass. Dept. Edn., 1993-94; bd. dirs. Mass. Alliance for Arts Edn., 1994-95. Named Mass. Tchr. of Yr., Mass. Dept. Edn., 1994, Nat. Outstanding Visual Art Tchr., Walt Disney and McDonald's, 1995, 1995-96 Profiled in Disney Channel. Mem. Mass. Art Edn. Assn., Nat. Art Edn. Assn., Tchr. Leadership Acad. Mass. (bd. dirs., founding fellow), Lucretia Crocker Acad. of Tchg. Fellows (bd. dirs.). Personal E-mail: virginiafreyermuth@yahoo.com.

FREYMAN, THOMAS C., pharmaceutical executive; b. Evanston, Ill., Sept. 8, 1954; B in Accountancy, U. Ill.; M in Mgmt., Northwestern U. CPA. Formerly acct. Ernst & Whinney, Chgo.; with Abbott Labs., Abbott Park, Ill., 1979—, fin. dir. European distbn. ctr. Netherlands, 1984—87, divsn. contr. corp. materials mgmt., 1987—88, treas. internat. divsn., 1988—91, v.p., treas., 1991—99, v.p., contr. hosp. products divsn., 1999—2001, sr. v.p. fin., CFO, 2001—. Bd. dirs. Vista Health, Chgo. Bot. Garden. Mem.: Econ. Club Chgo. Office: Abbott Labs 100 Abbott Park Rd Abbott Park IL 60064-6400

FREYMANN, JOHN GORDON, physician, educator; b. Omaha, Apr. 9, 1922; s. John Joseph and Marion (Wicks) F.; m. Ruth Ellen King, Dec. 16, 1950; children: Amanda, Martha, Sarah, Vance. BS, Yale U., 1944; MD, Harvard U., 1946; DSc, U. Nebr., 1982. Diplomate Am. Bd. Internal Medicine and Oncology. Asst. in medicine Mass. Gen. Hosp., Boston, 1954-59; dir. med. edn. Meml. Hosp., Worcester, Mass., 1959-65; gen dir. Boston Hosp. for Women, 1965-69; dir. edn. Hartford (Conn.) Hosp., 1969-75; pres. Nat. Fund for Med. Edn., Hartford, 1975-87; prof. dept. family medicine Sch. of Medicine U. Conn., Farmington, 1987—. Pres. Ednl. Commn. for Fgn. Med. Grads., Phila., 1968-77; cons. div. manpower intelligence HEW, Washington, 1973-75; advisor nat. health ins. House Ways & Means Com., U.S. Congress, Washington, 1975. Author: American Health Care System, 1974 (Welch award 1975); author chpts. in books; contbr. numerous articles to profl. jours. Mem. Wayland (Mass.) Bd. of Health, 1957-69; treas. Farmington Land Trust Inc., 1978-94. Lt. USPHS, 1947-49, ETO. Commonwealth Fund grantee, 1970; recipient Welch Meml. award Nat. Assn. Blue Shield Plans, 1975, John E. Leonard award Assn. for Hosp. Med. Edn., 1981. Fellow ACP; mem. AMA (adv. com. grad. med. edn. 1969-75), Soc. Med. Adminstrs. (pres. 1980-81), Am. Assn. for History of Medicine, Alpha Omega Alpha, Phi Beta Kappa. Avocations: travel, genealogy, skiing. Home: 2 Catalpa Ct Avon CT 06001-4510

FREYRE, ANGELA MARIANA, lawyer; b. Havana, Cuba, Sept. 18, 1954; BA, Wellesley Coll., 1976; D.E.J.G. Mention Assez Bien, Univ. Paris, France, 1978; JD, LLM, Georgetown Univ., 1980. Bar: NY 1984. Ptnr. prin. Latin Am. practice Coudert Bros. LLP, NYC. Trustee NY Studio Sch. Drawing, Painting & Sculpture, 1984—, LongHouse Reserve Ltd., 2000—; mem. City of NY Conflicts of Interest Bd. Fulbright scholar. Mem.: Assn. Bar City of NY. Office: Coudert Bros LLP 1114 Ave of the Americas New York NY 10036 Office Phone: 212-626-4487. Office Fax: 212-626-4120. Business E-Mail: freyrea@coudert.com.

FREYRE, FABIO, publishing executive; married; 2 children. BA, Hamilton Coll., 1983. Assoc. pub., advtsg. sales dir. Sports Illustrated Time Inc., New York, 1996-99, pub. Sports Illustrated mag., 1999—2003, group v.p., corp. sales & mktg., 2003—. Office: Time Inc 1271 Ave of the Americas New York NY 10020-1393*

FREYTAG, DONALD ASHE, management consultant; b. Chgo., Apr. 17, 1937; s. Elmer Walter and Mary Louise (Mayo) F.; m. Elizabeth Ritchie Robertson, Dec. 19, 1964; children: Donald C., Gavin K., Alexander M. BA, Yale U., 1959; MBA, Harvard U., 1963. Pres. Mgmts. West, LaJolla, Calif., 1963-65; mktg. asst. Norton Simon, Inc., Fullerton, Calif., 1965-67; product mgr. Warner-Lambert, Inc., Morristown, N.J., 1967-70; group mgr. mktg.-planning dir. advt. Pepsi-Cola Co., Purchase, N.Y., 1970-72; from v.p. mktg. to exec. v.p. Beverage Mgmt., Inc., Columbus, Ohio, 1972-76, pres., 1976-79, vice-chmn., 1979-80; pres. Freytag Mgmt. Co., Columbus, 1980-82, 84—, G.D. Ritzy's, Inc., Columbus, 1982-84. Bd. dirs. Antolino & Assoc., Atlas-Butler, Barney Corp., Century Resources, Contract Sweepers, Contrack Corp., Inc., Columbus Showcase Co., Columbus Paper and Copy Supply Co., Eastway Supplies, Inc., Greencrest Mktg., Ohio Full Ct. Press, Inc., Reitter Stucco, Inc., Profitworks Ltd., Paul Werth & Assoc., Coughlin Automotive Group, Newark, Hugo Bosca Co., Springfield, Ohio, Fenton Art Glass Co., Inc., Williamstown, W.Va., Scioto Properties, LLC, Columbus; ctrl. region dir. Ohio Com. for Employer Support of the Guard and Res., 1992—95. Pres. Cen. Ohio Ctr. for Econ. Edn., 1978-80, 81-87; bd. dirs. Columbus Acad., 1982-84. Capt. U.S. Army, 1959-61. Recipient Roman F. Warmke award, Ohio Coun. on Econ. Edn., 1991. Mem. Nat. Assn. Corp. Dirs., HBS Club Columbus, Yale Club. Avocations: bicycling, scuba diving, golf, reading. Office: 7955 Riverside Dr Dublin OH 43016-8234

FREYTAG, RICHARD ARTHUR, banker; b. Chgo., Oct. 26, 1933; s. Elmer Walter and Mary Louise (Mayo) F.; m. Pamela Burge, Feb. 11, 1989; children: Richard Christopher Hughes Freytag, Bliss Louise Mayo Smith. AB, Trinity Coll., Hartford, Conn., 1955; MBA, Harvard U., 1961; MS, MIT, 1971. Map salesman Rand McNally & Co., Chgo., 1955-56; internat. salesman Diversey Corp., Chgo., 1959-60; with Citibank, Japan, Taiwan, Korea, 1962-70, v.p., sr. credit officer, 1971-73, sr. officer Hong Kong, China, Vietnam, 1973—76, investor rels. and problem loan recovery mgmt. N.Y.C., 1977-84; pres. Citicorp Holdings, Inc., Citibank Overseas Investment Corp., 1984-96, vice chmn., dir., 1996-98; pres., CEO Citicorp Banking Corp., New Castle, Del., 1984-96, vice-chmn., dir., 1996-98; pres. Citibank Del., 1989-96, vice-chmn., dir., 1996-98. Vice-chmn. Far East Bank, Ltd., Hong Kong, 1973-76, sr. ptnr. Washington Capital Ptnrs., 1999-2002; bd. dirs. Citicorp Capital Investors Europe Ltd., The Thomas Group, Inc., Irving, Tex.; mem. Expanded Sr. Panel on N.E. Asian Ltd. Nuclear Arms Agreement, 1992—. Trustee Med. Ctr. of Del.; bd. visitors Nat. Def. U., 1988-93, 2002—; chmn. Nat. Def. U. Found., 1993-99, chmn. emeritus, 1999—; mem. Gov.'s Coun. on Banking, 1994-97. 1st lt. USAF, 1956-59, maj. gen. USAFR, 1986-93, fighter pilot operational in F-100 "supersabre", 1956-59. Decorated Air Force DSM, 1993, Medal for Disting. Pub. Svc. Dept. Def., 2000; recipient Brooks prize MIT, 1971; Alfred Sloan fellow The Nat. City Found., N.Y.C., 1969. Mem. Nat. Air Force Salute Found. (pres. 1988-90, chmn. 1990-92), Air Force Assn. (Iron Gate chpt. pres. 1988-90, chmn. 1990-92, Ira Eaker fellow 1991, Medal of Merit 1990, Exceptional Svc. award 1989), Coun. on Fgn. Rels., Falcon Found. (trustee), Del. Bankers Assn. (dir., pres. 1992-97), Del. Bus. Roundtable (vice chmn. 1994-96). Episcopalian. Office: PO Box 921 Montchanin DE 19710-0921

FREYTAG, SHARON NELSON, lawyer; b. May 11, 1943; d. John Seldon and Ruth Marie (Herbel) Nelson; children: Kurt David, Hillary Lee. BS with highest distinction, U. Kans., Lawrence, 1965; MA, U. Mich., 1966; JD cum laude, So. Meth. U., 1981. Bar: Tex. 1981, U.S. Dist. Ct. (no. dist.) Tex. 1981, U.S. Ct. Appeals (5th cir.) 1982, U.S. Supreme Ct. 1993, U.S. Dist. Ct. (so. dist.) Tex. 2001, U.S. Ct. Appeals (8th cir.) 2001, U.S. Ct. Appeals (fed. cir.) 2002. Tchr. English, Gaithersburg (Md.) H.S., 1966—70; instr. English, Eastfield Coll., 1974-78; law clk. U.S. Dist. Ct. (no. dist.) Tex., 1981-82, U.S. Ct. Appeals (5th cir.), 1982; ptnr., chmn. appellate practice sect. Haynes and Boone, Dallas, 1983—. Vis. prof. law So. Meth. U., 1985-86. Editor-in-chief Southwestern Law Jour., 1980-81; contbr. articles to profl. jours. Bd. dirs. Ctr. for Brain Health; dir. devel. bd. U. Tex. at Dallas. Named Tex. SuperLawyer, 2003, 2004; named one of 50 Women Tex. Super Lawyers, 2003, 2004, Best Lawyers in Am., 2005—; recipient John Marshall Constl. Law award, Baird Cmty. Spirit award, 1995; Woodrow Wilson fellow. Mem. ABA (mem. exec. com. coun. appellate lawyers, mem. exec. com. and long range planning com., chmn. program com., chmn. task force appellate advocacy), Fed. Bar Assn. (co-chmn. appellate practice and adv. sect. 1990-91), State Bar Tex. (bd. dirs., exec. com. 1997-2001, appellate coun. 1995-98), Dallas Bar Assn. (appellate section), Higginbotham Inn of Ct. (former barrister), Order of Coif, Phi Beta Kappa. Lutheran. Office: Haynes & Boone 901 Main Ste 3100 Dallas TX 75202 Office Phone: 214-651-5586. Business E-Mail: sharon.freytag@haynesboone.com.

FRI, ROBERT WHEELER, retired museum director; b. Kansas City, Kans., Nov. 16, 1935; s. Homer O. and Cora Ruth (Wheeler) F.; m. Jean Landon, Jan. 16, 1965; children— Perry, Sean, Kirk. BA, Rice U., 1957; MBA, Harvard U., 1959. Assoc. McKinsey & Co., Washington, 1963-68, prin., 1968-71, 73-75; dep. adminstr. EPA, Washington, 1971-73, acting adminstr., 1973; dep. adminstr. ERDA, Washington, 1975-77, acting adminstr., 1977; head U.S. del. to IAEA, Washington, 1977; pres. Energy Transition Corp., 1978-86, Resources for the Future, 1986-95; dir. Nat. Mus. Natural History, 1996-2001. Bd. dirs. Am. Electric Power Co., Sci. Svc., Inc., Electric Power Rsch. Inst.; mem. Nat. Petroleum Coun. Lt. USNR, 1959-62. Baker scholar. Mem. Phi Beta Kappa, Sigma Xi. Republican. Presbyterian.

FRIAS, JAIME LUIS, retired pediatrician, retired educator; b. Concepcion, Chile, Mar. 20, 1933; came to U.S., 1970; s. Luis Humberto and Olga Ana (Fernandez) F.; m. Jacqueline May Steel, Apr. 8, 1961; children: Jaime Arturo, Juan Pablo, Patricio Andres, Maria Josefina. MD, U. Chile, 1959. Diplomate Am. Bd. Pediatrics, Am. Bd. Human Genetics. Intern Hospital Regional, Concepcion, 1958-59; resident in pediatrics Calvo Mackenna Hosp., Santiago, Chile, 1960-62; clin. genetics and dysmorphology fellow U. Wis., Madison, 1965-66, U. Wash., Seattle, 1966-67; asst. prof. pediatrics U. Concepcion, 1967-69, U. Fla. Coll. Medicine, Gainesville, 1970-74, assoc. prof., 1974-77, prof., 1977-86, chief divsn. genetics, 1977-86, chmn. med. sch. admissions com., 1983-86; prof., chmn. dept. pediatrics U. Nebr. Med. Ctr., 1986—91; prof. pediatrics U. South Fla. Coll. Medicine, Tampa, 1991—2004, chmn. dept. pediatrics, 1991-99, dir. Birth Defects Ctr., 1999—2004, emeritus prof., 2004—; vis. scientist Nat. Ctr. for Birth Defects and Devel. Disabilities, CDC, Atlanta, 2004—. Chmn. Com. for Protection of Human Subjects, 1975-78; chmn. Fla. Com. on Prevention Devel. Disabilities, 1979-82, chmn. infant hearing screening adv. coun., 1982-86; cons. Spanish Collaborative Project on Congenital Malformation, Madrid, 1983—. Contbr. chpts. to books, articles to profl. jours. Trustee All Children's Hosp., 1991-99, Ronald McDonald Charities Tampa Bay, 1999-2001; exec. com. Assn. Med. Sch. Pediat. Dept. Chmn., 1993-96; steering com. Nat. Folic Acid Coun., 1999-2003. Named Tchr. of Yr., U. Fla. Coll. Medicine, 1978-79, Lewis A. Barness Endowed Chair Pediatrics, 1994-99. Mem. ACP (affiliate; W.K. Kellogg fellow 1965-67), Am. Acad. Pediatrics (com. genetics 1995-2002), Am. Pediatric Soc., Am. Soc. Human Genetics, Assn. Clin. Scientists, Smoke Rise Golf and Country Club. Democrat. Roman Catholic. Office: MS E-86 1600 Clifton Rd Atlanta GA 30333 E-mail: jfrias@hsc.usf.edu.

FRIAS, PATRICIO A., physician; s. Jaime L. and Jacqueline M. Frias; m. Anjie Troia; children: Nicholas A., Thomas P., James J. BA, Creighton U., Omaha, 1987—89; MD, U. Nebr. Coll. Medicine, Omaha, 1989—93. Diplomate Am. Bd. Pediat., 1996, Am. Bd. Pediat., Sub-Bd. Pediat. Cardiology, 2000. Pediatric resident Duke U. Sch. Medicine, Durham, NC, 1993—96; pediatric cardiology fellow Vanderbilt U. Sch. Medicine, Nashville, 1996—2000; asst. prof. pediat., pediat. cardiology Children's Healthcare Atlanta, Emory U. Sch. Medicine, Atlanta, 2000—. Vice chief, dept. medicine Children's Healthcare Atlanta at Egleston, Atlanta, 2005—. Mem.: Am. Coll. Physician Execs., Am. Coll. Cardiology, Heart Rhythm Soc., Am. Acad. Pediat. Roman Catholic. Office: Sibley Heart Ctr Cardiology 52 Executive Park S Ste 5200 Atlanta GA 30329 Office Phone: 404-256-2593.

FRIBERG, GEORGE JOSEPH, electronics company executive, entrepreneur; m. Mary Seymour; children: Fane George, Felicia Lynn Friberg Clark. BSME, U. N.Mex., 1962, MBA, 1982, postgrad. Sales engr. Honeywell, L.A., 1962-64; liaison engr. ACF Industries, Albuquerque, 1964-66; quality assurance mgr. data sys. divsn. Gulton Industries Inc., Albuquerque, 1966-72, mgr. mfg. Femco divsn. Irwin (Pa.), High Point (N.C.), 1972-77, v.p. mfg. data sys. divsn. Albuquerque, 1977-86; pres., CEO Tetra Corp., Albuquerque, 1986-92, also bd. dirs.; pres., CEO Laguna Industries Inc., Albuquerque, 1992-96; sr. dir. Tech. Ventures Corp., Albuquerque, 1996—. Adj. prof. U. N.Mex. Mgmt. Tech., 1998—, Dept. Mech. Engring., 2003-04; bd. dirs. Noonday, Inc. Mem. editl. bd. N.Mex. Bus. Jour., 1995-97. Mem. N.Mex. R&D Gross Receipts Task Force, 1988-89; mem. Econ. Forum of Albuquerque; bd. dirs. Technet, 1983-97, pres., 1983-84, 88-89; bd. dirs. Lovelace Insts., 1988-99, U. N.Mex. R.O. Anderson Bus. Sch. Found., 1988-92, N.Mex. Bus. Innovation Ctr., 1986-92, U. N.Mex. Found., 1999—, N.Mex. Golden Apple Found., 1998—, pres., 2003—04; mem. coun. trustees Lovelace Respiratory Rsch. Insts., 1999-, chmn, 2004-; bd. dirs. N.Mex. Natural History Mus. Found., 1999-2005, sec. 2002—, N.Mex. First, 2001—05, United Way, N.Mex., 2001-02; grad. Leadership N.Mex., 1998; mem. mech. engring. adv. coun. U. N.Mex., 1999—. Inducted Anderson Sch. of Bus. Hall of Fame, 1996, U. N.Mex. Athletic Hall of Honor, 2003; recipient Zia award U. N.Mex., 1998, Regents medal U. N.Mex., 1998, Lockheed Martin Nova award, 1998, Albuquerque High Harrington award, 2000; named to All-Time Football Team Albuquerque HS, 2001, Albuquerque HS Hall of Fame, 2004. Mem. Albuquerque C. of C. (bd. dirs. 1985—, polit. action com. 1983-84, chair Buy N.Mex. chpt. 1986-87, vice chmn. econ. affairs planning coun. 1987—, chmn. bd. 1990-91), N.Mex. Alumni Lettermen's Club, U. N.Mex. Alumni Assn. (bd. dirs. 1995-2001, pres.-elect 1997, pres. 1997-98, chair legis. com. 2000-). Home: 13234 Sunset Canyon Dr NE Albuquerque NM 87111-4220 Office Phone: 505-843-4286. Business E-Mail: george.j.friberg@lmco.com.

FRIBOURGH, JAMES HENRY, retired university administrator; b. Sioux City, Iowa, June 10, 1926; s. Johan Gunder and Edith Katherine (James) F.; m. Cairdenia Minge, Jan. 29, 1955; children: Cynthia Kaye, Rebecca Jo, Abbie Lynn. Student, Morningside Coll., 1944-47; BA, MA, U. Iowa, 1949, PhD, 1957; LHD (hon.), DHL (hon.), Morningside Coll., 1989. Instr. Little Rock Jr. Coll., 1949—56; assoc. prof. biology Little Rock U., 1957—60, prof., chmn. life scis. divsn., 1960—69; vice chancellor U. Ark., Little Rock, 1969—72, interim chancellor, 1972—73, exec. vice chancellor acad. affairs, 1973—82, interim chancellor, exec. vice chancellor acad. affairs, 1982, provost, exec. vice chancellor, 1983—, disting. prof., 1984—94, disting. prof. emeritus, 1994—. Cons. in field; assoc. Marine Biol. Lab., Woods Hole, Mass. Contbr. articles to profl. jours. Mem. Ark. Gov.'s Com. on Sci. and Tech., 1969-71; bd. dirs., mem. nat. adv. bd. Nat. Back Found., 1979; vice chmn. NCCJ, 1981-82; div. rep. United Way of Pulaski County, 1980-82; bd. dirs. Ark. Dance Theatre, Little Rock, 1980-82; vestryman Good Shepherd Episcopal Ch.; del. Episcopal Diocese of Ark.; fellow Ark. Mus. Sci. and History, 1987. Fribourgh Hall named in his honor, U. Ark., Little Rock, 1994; NSF fellow History of Sci. Inst., 1959-60. Fellow AAAS, Coll. Preceptors (London), Am. Inst. Fishery Rsch. Biologists, Ark. Mus. Sci. and History; mem. Am. Fisheries Soc. (chmn. com. on internationalism cert. fisheries scientist), AAUP (pres. Ark. conf.), Electron Microscopy Soc. Am., Am. Soc. Swedish Engrs. (corr. mem.), Ark. Acad. Sci. (pres. 1966), Ark. Dean's Assn. (pres. 1982), Am. Assn. State Colls. and Univs., Am. Swedish Inst., Swedish Club (Chgo.), Rotary (Paul Harris fellow), Vasa Order Am. Lodge, Sigma Xi, Phi Kappa Phi. Clubs: Swedish, Vasa Order Am. Lodges: Rotary (Paul Harris fellow). Democrat. Office: U Ark 33rd and University Ave Little Rock AR 72204 Office Phone: 501-569-3207. Business E-Mail: jhfribourgh@ualr.edu.

FRICK, BENJAMIN CHARLES, lawyer; b. Overbrook, Pa., Feb. 23, 1960; s. Sidney Wanning and Marie Pauline Frick; m. Stephanie Ann Sears, June 1, 1991; children: Sarah Marie, Anna Elizabeth, Charles Andrew. BA, Cornell U., 1982; JD, U. Richmond, 1985; LLM in Taxation, Villanova U., 1994. Bar: Pa. 1985. Clk. to Hon. John B. Hannum US dist. ct., 1984; trust officer Provident Nat. Bank, Phila., 1985-89; sole practice Bryn Mawr, Pa., 1989—. Deacon, elder, treas. Ardmore (Pa.) Presbyn. Ch.; bd. dirs. Civil War and Underground R.R. Mus. Phila., 2004—. Mem.: S.R. (bd. dirs. Pa. Soc. 1987—2003, sec. 1991—95, treas. 1995—97, v.p. 1997—2003), ABA, Phila. Bar Assn., Pa. Bar Assn., Mil. Order Loyal Legion US (sec. 1993—95, v.p. 1995—97, comdr. 1997—99, judge adv.-in-chief 1997—2001, nat. v.p. 2001—), St. Andrew's Soc. Phila., Soc. Colonial Wars (bd. dirs. Pa. chpt. 1999—, sec. 2004—), Soc. Mayflower Descs., Colonial Soc. Pa. (treas. 2000—03, v.p. 2003—), The Union League, The Phila. Club, Athenaeum Phila., Alpha Delta Phi, Phi Alpha Delta. Republican. Presbyterian. Office: Bldg 1 Ste 303 919 Conestoga Rd Bryn Mawr PA 19010-1352

FRICK, DAVID RHOADS, lawyer, retired insurance company executive; b. Ft. Wayne, Ind., June 28, 1944; s. Walter Henry and Margery Ellen (Rhoads) F.; m. Ann Gray Shane, June 19, 1965; children: Thomas Rhoads, Amy Gray. BA magna cum laude, Ind. U., 1966; JD cum laude, Harvard U., 1969; HHD, Butler U., 1987, U. Indpls., 1997. Bar: Ill. 1969, D.C. 1971, U.S. Ct. Appeals (D.C. cir.) 1971, Ind. 1972, U.S. Supreme Ct. 1976. Assoc. Mayer, Brown & Platt, Chgo., 1969-72, Baker & Daniels, Indpls., 1972-76; dep. mayor City of Indpls., 1977-82; ptnr. Baker & Daniels, Indpls., 1982—95; exec. v.p., chief legal & adminstrv. officer Anthem Inc. (now WellPoint Inc.), Indpls., 1995—2005. Bd. dirs. Artistic Media Ptnrs., Inc., Indpls., 1987—, Associated Ins. Cos., Inc., 1992—, Nat. Bank Indpls., 1993—. Bd. dirs., exec. com. 500 Festival Assocs., 1983-86, Commn. for Downtown, 1977-89, Greater Indpls. Progress Com., 1982-89, Indpls. Econ. Devel. Corp., 1984; bd. dirs. Ind. U. Coll. Arts and Scis. 1974-77, Pres. 1976, Indpls. Ctr. Advanced Rsch., Inc., 1987-90, Ind. Sports Corp., 1979-91, Indpls. Conv. and Visitors Assn., 1982-2000; mem. Ind. Gen. Assembly Local Govt. Study Com., 1978-81, State Ind. Commn. Enterprising Zones, 1981-82; trustee Eiteljorg Mus., 1988-91; chmn., trustee Brebeuf Prep. Sch., 1986-92, U. Indpls., 1990—98; treas., bd. mgrs. Marion County Capital Improvement Bd., 1982-92; adv. bd. Ind. U., 1986—, Purdue U., 1986—; chmn. Ind. Organizing Com. NCAA Final Four, 1987—; trustee, exec. com. Christian Theol. Sem., 1984-95. Recipient Sagamore of the Wabash award Gov. Ind., 1979-80, C.L. Whistler award Greater Indpls. Progress Com., 1984, L.A. Conrad award Ind. Soc. Assn. Exec., 1990, Pres. Medal Brebeuf Prep. Sch., 1992, Michael A. Carroll Award for Cmty. Involvement, Indpls. Bus. Jour., 1996. Mem. Indpls. C. of C. (bd. dirs. 1987—, exec. com. 1987—). Republican. Methodist. Avocations: jogging, hiking, reading.

FRICK, IVAN EUGENE, retired academic administrator, educational consultant; b. New Providence, Pa., May 19, 1928; s. Charles George and Lillie Jane (Miller) F.; m. Ruth Hudson, July 16, 1950; children: David Alan, Daniel Eugene, Susan Marie. AB, Findlay (Ohio) Coll., 1949; B.D., Lancaster Theol. Sem., 1952; S.T.M., Oberlin Coll., 1955; PhD, Columbia U., 1959; L.H.D. (hon.), Findlay Coll., 1976. Mem. faculty Findlay Coll., 1953-71, asst. to pres., 1963-64, pres., 1964-71, Elmhurst (Ill.) Coll., 1971-94, pres. emeritus, 1994—; cons. Ivan E. Frick, Cons. in Higher Edn., Willow Street, Pa., 1994—. Vice chmn. Fedn. Ind. Ill. Colls. and Univs., 1979-81, chmn., 1983-85; pres., chmn. exec. com. Associated. Colls. of Ill., 1991-93; chmn. West Suburban Regional Acad. Consortium, 1991-92. Mem. Am. Coun. on Edn. Commn. on Govtl. Rels., 1986-89; bd. dirs. United Cmty. Fund Findlay, 1965-71, Lizzadro Mus. Lapidary Art, Elmhurst, Elmhurst YMCA, 1971-84; mem. found. bd. Ray Graham Assn. for People With Disabilities, 1995-2000; chmn. non-pub. adv. com. Ill. Bd. Higher Edn., 1990-94. Danforth Found. fellow, 1959, Paul Harris fellow, 1988; recipient Disting. Alumnus award Findlay Coll., 1964, Outstanding Young Man award U.S. Jr. C. of C., 1964 Mem. Econ. Club Chgo. Business E-Mail: i.frick@elmhurst.edu. *Mentors have played a significant role in my life; these mentors have been teachers, older friends, father figures and administrative colleagues. They have supported, challenged and stimulated me and sometimes they have presented an opposite view or role model against which I have reacted. In all, they have helped me immeasurably.*

FRICK, JAMES CARLTON, physician assistant, director; b. Toledo, Ohio, June 13, 1947; s. Carlton Walter and Margaret Ann Frick; m. Madelyn Wyman, Aug. 27, 1977; children: Jamie, Paul, Cathryn. BS, Mercy Coll., 1976; MS, Kennedy Western Coll., 2000. Cert. physician asst. Clin. physician asst., Detroit, 1977—; dir. physician assts. Harper Hosp., Detroit, 1982; dir. multidisciplinary cancer program Detroit Med. Ctr., 1987; program dir. Wayne State U., 2000, dir. postgrad. program, 2004—. Mem. Nat. TV Curriculum Consortium, San Diego, 2005—. Contbr. articles to profl. jours.; author seminar in field. Pres. Mich. Physician Asst. Found., 2001—03, trustee, 2000—. Recipient Tchg. Excellence award, Coll. Pharmacy and Health Sci., Detroit, 2002; grantee, Rotary Internat., 2002; scholar, Fulbright Found., Washington, 2003. Mem.: Mich. Acad. Physician Assts., Am. Acad. Physician Assts. Avocations: photography, travel. Home: 1729 Roslyn Rd Grosse Pointe Woods MI 48236 Office: Wayne State U 259 Mack Ave Detroit MI 48201 Office Phone: 313-577-3954.

FRICK, OSCAR LIONEL, pediatrician, educator; b. N.Y.C., Mar. 12, 1923; s. Oscar and Elizabeth (Ringger) F.; m. Mary Hubbard, Sept. 2, 1954. AB, Cornell U., 1944, MD, 1946; M.Med. Sci., U. Pa., 1960; PhD, Stanford U., 1964. Diplomate: Am. Bd. Allergy and Immunology (chmn. 1967-72). Intern Babies Hosp., Columbia Coll. Physicians and Surgeons, N.Y.C., 1946-47; resident Children's Hosp., Buffalo, 1950-51; pvt. practice medicine specializing in pediatrics Huntington, N.Y., 1951-58; fellow in allergy and immunology Royal Victoria Hosp., Montreal, Que., Can., 1958-59; fellow in allergy U. Calif.-San Francisco, 1959-60, asst. prof. pediatrics, 1964-67, assoc. prof., 1967-72, prof., 1972—, dir. allergy tng. program, 1964—; fellow immunology Inst. d'Immunobiologie, Hosp. Broussais, Paris, France, 1960-62. Contbr. articles papers to profl. pubs. Served with M.C., USNR, 1947-49. Mem. Am. Assn. Immunologists, Am. Acad. Pediatrics (chmn. allergy sect. 1971-72, Bret Ratner award 1982), Am. Acad. Allergy (exec. com. 1972—, pres. 1977-78), Internat. Assn. Allergology and Clin. Immunology (exec. com. 1970-73, sec. gen. 1985—), Am. Pediatric Soc. Clubs: Masons. Home: 370 Parnassus Ave San Francisco CA 94117-3609

FRICKE, MARTIN PAUL, science company executive; b. Franklin, Pa., May 18, 1937; s. Frank Albert and Pauline Jane (Wentz) F.; m. Barbara Ann Blanton, Jan. 3, 1959. BS, Drexel U., Phila., 1961; MS, U. Minn., 1964, PhD, 1967. Program mgr., group leader Gen. Atomics, San Diego, 1968-73; program mgr., divsn. mgr. Sci. Applications Internat. Corp., La Jolla, Calif., 1973-77, v.p., 1977-80, corp. v.p., 1980-84; sr. v.p. Systems Group, The Titan Corp., San Diego, Calif., 1984-87, exec. v.p. Techs Group, 1987-89, sr. v.p. corp. ops., 1989-93; program adminstr. San Diego Supercomputer Ctr., 1995-97; ind. cons., 1997—. Mem. cross sect. evaluation working group, Upton, L.I., N.Y., 1970-73, U.S. Nuclear Data Com., Washington, 1970-73. Contbr. articles to profl. jours. Recipient postdoctoral fellowship U. Mich., Ann Arbor, 1967-68, scholarship Pa. Indsl. Chem. Co., 1956-60; grad. fellow Oak Ridge (Tenn.) Assoc. Univs., 1964-67. Fellow Am. Phys. Soc. (panel on pub. affairs 1982-84); mem. Phi Kappa Phi. Roman Catholic. Achievements include first measurements and theoretical analysis of certain polarization phenomena in nucleon-nucleus inelastic scattering. Home and Office: 14929 Caminito Ladera Del Mar CA 92014 Personal E-mail: mfricke@adelphia.net.

FRICKE, RICHARD JOHN, lawyer; b. Ithaca, NY, Apr. 17, 1945; s. Richard I. and Jeanne L. (Hines) F.; m. Carol A. Borelli, June 17, 1967 (div. 1990); children: Laura, Richard, Amanda; m. Penny Yrizarry, Dec. 29, 1990 (div. 1999); children: Stephanie, Matthew, Tyler. BA, Cornell U., 1967, JD, 1970. Bar: Conn. 1970. Assoc. Gregory & Adams, Wilton, Conn., 1970—73; ptnr. Crehan & Fricke, Ridgefield, Conn., 1973—90; gen. counsel Connex Internat. Inc.; corp. counsel, pres. Safe Alternatives Corp. of Am., Inc.; pres., gen. counsel, dir. T.F.I. Industries, Inc.; gen. counsel, dir. Gold Mustache Pub. Corp., Inc.; sec., dir. DXTC.COM, Inc.; dir. Village Bank & Trust Co.; town atty. Town of Ridgefield, 1973—81. Bd. dirs. Gold Mustache Pub. Corp., Inc.; mem. Closing Mgmt. Svcs. LLC. Co-patentee low reactive pressure foam, polyurethane foam for cellulostic products. Bd. dirs. Ridgefield Community Ctr., Ridgefield Montessori, Ridgefield Community Kindergarten; founder, pres. Ridgefield Lacross League; constable Town of Wilton, Conn.; mem. Conn. Bar Commn. on Women, 1976. Mem. ABA, Conn. Bar Assn., Danbury Bar Assn. Democrat. Roman Catholic. Address: 35 Old Ridgefield Rd Wilton CT 06897 Office Phone: 203-834-2105. Office Fax: 203-834-2140. Personal E-mail: rickfricke@aol.com.

FRICKLAS, MICHAEL DAVID, lawyer, broadcast executive; b. Somerville, NJ, Jan. 9, 1960; s. Richard L. and Anita (Alper) F.; children: Shanna E., Jaimee G., Gabriella S., Genevieve H.; m. Donna J. Astion, Jan. 14, 1996. BSEE, U. Colo., 1981; JD magna cum laude, Boston U., 1984. Bar: Calif. 1987, Colo. 1990, N.Y. 1993. Assoc. Ware & Freidenrich, Palo Alto, Calif., 1984-87, Shearman & Sterling, NY, San Francisco, 1987-90; v.p., gen. counsel Minorco (USA) Inc., Denver, 1990-93; sr. v.p., dep. gen. counsel, mem. ops. com. Viacom, Inc., NYC, 1993-98, sr. v.p., gen. counsel, sec., 1998-2000, exec. v.p., gen. counsel, sec., 2000—. Bd. dirs. Nat. Chamber Litigation Ctr. Trustee Jazz at Lincoln Ctr., 1995—, Am. Jewish Com., N.Y. chpt., 1998—; mem. bd. vis. Boston U. Sch. Law, 1997; bd. mem. Nat. Chamber Legal Ctr., Legal Aid Soc. NY Mem. ABA (exec. com. of gen. counsel com.), Assn. Gen. Counsel, Assn. Bar City NY(chair gen. counsel com.). Office: Viacom Inc 1515 Broadway New York NY 10036-8901

FRIDAY, ELBERT WALTER, JR., federal agency administrator, meteorologist; b. DeQueen, Ark., July 13, 1939; s. Elbert Walter and Mary Elizabeth (Ward) F.; m. Karen Ann Hauschild, Nov. 14, 1959; children: Kristine Ann, Kelly Sue. BS in Engring. Physics, U. Okla., Norman, 1961, MS in Meteorology, 1967, PhD in Meteorology, 1969. Commd. 2d lt. USAF, 1961, advanced through grades to col., weather officer, 1961-81, dir. environ. and life scis., Dept. Def., 1978-81, ret., 1981; dep. dir. Nat. Weather Svc., Silver Spring, Md., 1981-87, dir., 1987-97; asst. adminstr. Office Oceanic and Atmospheric Rsch., Silver Spring, 1997-98; dir. NAS, 1998—2002, mem. bd. atmosphere in scis. and climate, 2002—; Weather News prof. applied meteorology U. Okla., 2002—. Mem. com. on low level wind shear NAS, Washington, 1985-86; U.S. permanent rep. to UN World Meteorol. Orgn., 1988-98, mem. exec. coun., 1988-98; adj. prof. U. Okla., 1998; bd. dirs. Atmospheric Sci. and Climate, NRC, NAS, 1998-2002. Contbr. articles to prof. jours. Elder Calvary Christian Ch., Burke, Va., 1985-89, 2002—, trustee, 1989-93, chmn. bd., 1998-2002. Decorated Bronze Star; recipient Superior Svc. medal Dept. Def., 1981, Presdl. Rank award, 1988, Disting. Achievement award U. Okla., 1992, Fed. Exec. of Yr. award Fed. Exec. Inst. Alumni Assn., 1993. Fellow Am. Meteorol. Soc. (councilor 1988-90, pres. 2003, Cleve. Abbe award 1997); mem. AAAS, Nat. Weather Assn., Sigma Xi.

FRIDAY, FRANKIE SUE, learning support teacher; b. Waynesburg, Pa., Jan. 13, 1953; d. Lloyd and Marthanne (Wunder) Conner; m. Norman E. Friday, May 18, 1974; children: Jeremiah, Josh, Jessie. BS, Clarion U., 1974; MS, Gannon U., 1992. Cert. tchr., Pa. Individualized edn. program trainer Beaver Valley Intermediate Unit, Aliquippa, Pa., 1976-82; tchr. Riverside Beaver County Schs., Ellwood City, Pa., 1982—. Sponsor Christmas Caring Dr., Riverside Mid. Sch.; jr. class sponsor Riverside H.S., 1994—95. Recipient Gift of Time Tribute, Am. Family Inst., 1990; nominated Annie Sullivan award, 1991. Mem.: Pa. State Edn. Assn. (exec. bd.), Holy Redeemer Parish. Avocations: needlecrafts, gardening, stained glass windows. Office: Riverside Mid Sch 302 Country Club Dr Ellwood City PA 16117-9340

FRIDAY, GILBERT ANTHONY, JR., pediatrician; b. Pitts., Apr. 16, 1930; s. Gilbert Anthony and Susan Dorothy (Kumer) F.; m. Christina Cecilia McShane, Sept. 12, 1959; children: Martin, Peter, Martha, Timothy, Amy, Anne, Robert. BS, Bucknell U., 1952; MD, Temple U., 1956. Diplomate Nat. Bd. Med. Examiners. Rotating intern Phila. Gen. Hosp., 1956-57; pediatric resident Children's Hosp. of Phila., 1960-62, Children's Hosp. of Pitts., 1962-63, asst. med. dir. ops., 1963-66, preceptorship in allergy/immunology, 1962-67; clin. instr. to asst. prof. U. Pitts., 1963-87, clin. assoc. prof., 1987, prof. pediatrics, 1987—2001, clin. prof., 2001—. Chmn. bd. dirs. Pa. Blue Shield, Camp Hill, 1992-96. Contbr. articles to profl. jours., chpts. to books. Lt. comdr. USN MC, 1956-66. Wyeth Pediatric scholar. Fellow Am. Coll. Allergy, Asthma, and Immunology, Am. Acad. Allery, Asthma, and Immunology, Am. Acad. Pediats.; mem. AMA, Allegheny County Med. Soc. (pres. 1987), Pa. Med. Soc., Pa. Allergy Soc. (pres. 1975), Alpha Omega Alpha. Republican. Roman Catholic. Avocations: boating, fishing. Home: 1901 Highgate Rd Pittsburgh PA 15241-2210 Office: Allergy and Immunology Assocs 180 Fort Couch Rd Pittsburgh PA 15241-8811 Office Phone: 412-833-8811. Personal E-mail: friday1901@aol.com.

FRIDAY, KATHERINE ORWOLL, artist; b. Granite Falls, Minn., Dec. 3, 1917; d. Melvin Sylvester and Anna Elizabeth (Hustvedt) Orwoll; m. Erling Bjarne Struxness, May 8, 1943 (div. 1961); children: John Eric, Mimi Ann McNicholas, Mari Struxness; m. George Edward Friday, Apr. 12, 1969 (dec. Jan. 1997). Student, U. Minn., 1935-36, 40-41, Frederick Mizen Sch. of Art, Chgo., 1941. Designer, illustrator Josten's, Owatonna, Minn., 1936-39, 42-43; layout artist Tempo Inc., Chgo., 1941-42, Vogue-wright Studios, Chgo., 1943-44; layout, illustration Allan D Parson Advt. Agy., Chgo., 1945, Ad-Art, Wichita, Kans., 1952-54, 63; indsl. designer Harold W. Darr Assoc., Mpls., 1959-61; layout, illustration Lydiard Assoc., Mpls., 1961—62; owner Skyline Studio, Mpls., 1962—66; layout, illustration Comm. Cons., Wilmington, Del., 1971; freelance illustration, med. illustration dept. pathology U. Chgo., Chgo., 1946-48; freelance illustrator Hutchinson, Kans., 1948—52, 1954—58; art dir. SPF Adv., Intermedia, Mpls., 1966-69, Arne Westerman Adv., Portland, Oreg., 1970-71, Battle Advt., Wyncote, Pa., 1971-72; creative dir., owner A'La Carte Advt./Art, Bellevue, Wash., 1973-77; graphic illustration Courseware, Moffat Field, Mountain View, Calif., 1978, Quantic, Los Altos, Calif., 1979—; ret., 1982; represented by Portland Art Mus. Rental Gallery. Curator, judge internat. miniature art exhibit Festival of the Arts, Lake Oswego, Oreg., 2002. Exhibitions include Westminster Gallery, London, 1995, Hobart, Tasmania, 2000. Recipient Best of Show award, Internat. Miniature Art Show, Kirkland, Wash., 1997, 4th pl., 1999, 3d pl., 2001. Mem.: N.W. Artists' Support Group, Oreg. Soc. Artists and Local Colour, Main St. Art. Soc. (Best of show, 1st pl. and 2d pl. awards 2002, Best of Show, 1st pl. oil, 1st pl. watercolor 2003, Best of Show, 3d pl. 2004, Merit award, 1st and 2d pl. awards, Best of Show, 1st pl. portrait, 1st place floral 2005), Painters Showcase (Grand award 1999, Judges Choice award 2000—02), Oreg. Colored Pencil Soc. (2d pl. N.W. Regional show 2000—02), Watercolor Soc. Oreg. (Achievement award 1998, 2002), Cider Painters of Am. (award of excellence 1992—94, 1st pl. in floral 1993, still life award 1995, portrait award 1995, award of excellence 1997, portrait award 1998, Pres. award 1999, award of excellence 2001, Pres. award 2002, signature mem.), Ga. Miniature Artists Soc. (2d pl. and 3d pl. 1990, 1st pl. 1991, 1994, Merit award 1997), Miniature Art Soc. Fla. (1st pl. 1989—90, 2d pl. 1994—95, 1st pl. 1997—98, 2d pl. 1999, 1st pl. 2002—03), Miniature Artists of Am. (hon. signature), Colored Pencil Soc. Am., N.W. Watercolor Soc. (assoc.), Miniature Painters, Sculptors, Gravers Soc. (assoc. 3d pl. 1990, 1st pl. 1996, 1st of show 1998, 2d and 3d pl. 1999, Grumbacher award, 2d pl. 2001, Best of Show award). Avocations: painting, drawing, reading, music.

FRIDLEY, ROBERT BRUCE, agricultural engineer, educator; b. Burns, Oreg., June 6, 1934; s. Gerald Wayne and Gladys Winona (Smith) Fridley; m. Jean Marie Griggs, June 12, 1955; children: James Lee, Michael Wayne, Kenneth Jon. BSME, U. Calif., Berkeley, 1956; MS in Agrl. Engring., U. Calif., Davis, 1960; PhD in Agrl. Engring., Mich. State U., East Lansing, 1973; D (hon.), U. Poly., Madrid, 1988. Asst. specialist U. Calif., Davis, 1956-60, prof. agrl. engring., 1961-78, 1985—94, prof. emeritus, 1994—, acting assoc. dean engring., 1972, chmn. dept. agrl. engring., 1974-76, dir. aquaculture and fisheries program, 1985-89, exec. assoc. dean agrl. and environ. scis., 1989-94; dept. mgr. R & D Weyerhaeuser Co., Tacoma, 1977-85. Vis. prof. Mich. State U., East Lansing, 1970—71; NATO vis. prof. U. Bologna, 1975; bd. agrl. and natural resources NRC, 2000—02. Co-author: (book) Principles and Practices for Harvesting and Handling Fruits and Nuts, 1973; contbr. articles to profl. jours. Recipient Charles G. Woodbury award, Am. Soc. Hort. Sci., 1966, Alumni citation, Calif. Aggie Alumni Assn., 1990. Fellow: Am. Soc. Agrl. Engrs. (v.p. Found. 1989—93, pres. Found. 1993—96, pres. 1997—98, Young Rschrs. award 1971, Concept of the Yr. award 1976, Outstanding Paper award 1966, 1968, 1969, 1976, 1986, Disting. Svc. award 1988, 1997, 1999); mem.: NAE. Achievements include patents in field. Personal E-mail: rbfridley@ucdavis.edu.

FRIDOVICH, IRWIN, biochemistry professor; b. N.Y.C., Aug. 2, 1929; s. Louis and Sylvia (Appelbaum) F.; m. Mollie Finkel; children: Sharon E., Judith L. BS, CCNY, 1951; postgrad., Cornell U. Med. Coll., 1951-52; PhD, Duke U., 1955; hon. doctorate, U. Rene Descartes, Paris, 1980. Instr. biochemistry Duke U., Durham, N.C., 1956-58, assoc., 1958—; vis. research assoc. Harvard U., Cambridge, Mass., 1961-62; asst. prof. biochemistry Duke U., 1961-66, assoc. prof., 1966-71, prof., 1971—, James B. Duke prof., 1976—, emeritus, 1996—. Mem. study sect. Am. Cancer Soc., mem. adv. com. biochemistry and chem. carcinogenesis Mem. editorial bd. Jour. Biol.

Chemistry, Biochemica Biophysica Acta, Archives of Biochemistry and Biophysics, Biochem. Jour., Bioinorganic Chemistry, Biochemistry, Biochem. Pharmacology, Analytical Biochemistry; contbr. articles to sci. jours. Recipient Founders' award Chem. Industry Inst. Toxicology, 1980, Sr. Passano award Passano Found., 1987, Herty award Ga. sect. Am. Chem. Soc., 1980, Research Career Devel. award NIH, 1959-69, Cressy A. Morrison award N.Y. Acad. Sci., 1984, Townsend Harris medal City U. N.Y., 1990; co-recipient Cresson medal, Franklin Inst., 1997, City of Medicine award, Durham, N.C., 1998, Anlyan Lifetime Achievement award Duke Med. Ctr., 1998. Mem. NAS, Am. Acad. Arts and Scis., Am. Soc. Biol. Chemists (pres. 1982), N.C. Acad. Scis., Oxygen Soc. (pres. 1990), Soc. for Free Radical Rsch. Internat., (pres. 1992), Phi Beta Kappa, Sigma Xi Home: 3517 Courtland Dr Durham NC 27707-5134 Office: Duke U Med Center PO Box 3711 Durham NC 27710-0001 Office Phone: 919-689-5122. E-mail: fridovich@biochem.duke.edu.

FRIDSON, MARTIN STEVEN, finance company executive; b. Highland Park, Mich., Sept. 4, 1952; s. Harry Yale and Mariann (Rodd) F.; m. Elaine Rochelle Sisman, June 14, 1981; children: Arielle Amanda, Daniel Wolfe. BA cum laude in History, Harvard U., 1974; MBA, Harvard U., Boston, 1976. CFA. Trader Mitchell, Hutchins Inc., N.Y.C., 1976-77; asst. v.p. Scandinavian Securities Corp., N.Y.C., 1977-79; v.p. Paine Webber Jackson & Curtis, Inc., N.Y.C., 1980-81, Salomon Bros., Inc., N.Y.C., 1981-84; prin. Morgan Stanley & Co., Inc., N.Y.C., 1984-89; mng. dir. Merrill Lynch & Co., Inc., N.Y.C., 1989—2002; CEO FridsonVision LLC, N.Y.C., 2002—. Cons. bd. govs. Fed. Res.; mem. Harvard Com. on Univ. Resources, 2002—. Author: High Yield Bonds, 1989, Financial Statement Analysis, 1991, Investment Illusions, 1993, It Was a Very Good Year, 1998, How to Be a Billionaire, 2000; co-editor, The Yearbook of Fixed Income Investing, 1996, editor, Extraordinary Popular Delusions and the Madness of Crowds and Confusion de Confusiones, 1996; contbr. articles to profl. jours.; author light verse pub. in Playbill, N.Y. Times, Wall St. Jour., Graham and Dodd Scroll for Excellence in Financial Writing, 1994; mem. editl. bd. Fin. Analysts Jour., 1989—, CFA Digest, 1991—, Fin. Mgmt., 1993-99, Jour. Fin. Statement Analysis, 1995-98. Participation chmn. Harvard Coll. Fund, Class of 1974, 1991—, mem. spl. gifts com., 1992—; trustee The Intersch. Orch. of N.Y., N.Y.C., 1992—; v.p. Jane St. Block Assn., N.Y.C., 1979; bd. dirs. Candlewood Landing Condominium Assn., 1991—; adv. coun. Salomon Ctr., NYU, 1991-97; mem. exec. com. wall st. divsn. United Jewish Appeal Fedn., 2000—. Mem. Fixed Income Analysts Soc. (pres. 1984-85, named to Hall of Fame 2000), Harvard Bus. Sch. Club (v.p. 1983-84), N.Y. Soc. Security Analysts (bd. dirs. 2001-03, Vol.-of-Yr. award 1991-92), Fin. Mgmt. Assn. (practitioner dir. 1994-96, Outstanding Fin. Exec. award 2002), Inst. Chartered Fin. Analysts (trustee 1997-98), Assn. for Investment Mgmt. and Rsch. (bd. govs. 1997-2001), Harvard Club of N.Y., New Milford Racquet and Swim Club. Democrat. Jewish. Avocations: tennis, theater, opera. Home: 440 W End Ave Apt 10A New York NY 10024-5358 Office: FridsonVision LLC 54 W 21st St Ste 1007 New York NY 10010 Office Phone: 917-403-9194. Business E-Mail: martin_fridson_ab74@post.harvard.edu.

FRIEBERT, ROBERT HOWARD, lawyer; b. Milw., Aug. 24, 1938; s. Lewis and Erna F.; m. Susan Frances Sweed, Aug. 11, 1968; children: Jonathan, Ellen, Leslie. BBA, LLB, U. Wis., 1962. Bar: Wis. 1962, U.S. Dist. Ct. (we. dist.) Wis. 1962, U.S. Ct. Appeals (7th cir.) 1964, U.S. Supreme Ct. 1967, U.S. Dist. Ct. (ea. dist.) Wis. 1968, U.S. Ct. Appeals (9th cir.) 1977, U.S. Ct. Appeals (D.C. cir.) 1998. Asst. U.S. atty. U.S. Justice Dept., Madison, Wis., 1962-64; assoc. LaFollette, Sinykin, Doyle & Abrahamson, Madison, Wis., 1964-66; state pub. defender Wis. Supreme Ct., Madison, 1966-68; assoc. Shellow, Shellow & Coffey, Milw., 1968-71; ptnr. Friebert, Finerty & St. John, Milw., 1971—. Treas. campaign fund Wis. Gov. Pat Lucey, 1971; co-chmn. Pres. Carter Re-election Campaign, Wis., 1980, Gary Hart Campaign for Pres., Wis., 1984; chmn. Al Gore Campaign for Pres., Wis., 1988; trustee Med. Coll. Wis., 1993—. Recipient Human Rels. award, Am. Jewish Com., Milw., 1996. Fellow Am Acad. Appellate Lawyers; mem. Wis. Bar Assn. Office: Friebert Finerty & St John 330 E Kilbourn Ave Ste 1250 Milwaukee WI 53202-3158 E-mail: rhf@ffsj.com.

FRIED, BARBARA H., law educator; b. 1951; BA in English & Am. Lit., magna cum laude, Harvard U., 1977, MA in English & Am. Lit., 1980, JD cum laude, 1983. Bar: NY 1984. Law clk. to Hon. J. Edward Lumbard US Ct. Appeals 2nd Cir., 1983—84; assoc. tax dept. Paul Weiss Rifkind Wharton & Garrison, NYC, 1984—87; asst. prof. Stanford Law Sch., 1987—91, assoc. prof., 1991—93, prof. law, 1993—, Deanne Johnson faculty scholar, 1993—2003, William W. and Gertrude H. Saunders prof. law, 2003—. Vis. prof. NYU Law Sch., 1998—99, 2000. Author: The Progressive Assault on Laissez Faire: Robert Hale and the First Law and Economics Movement, 1998. Recipient John Bingham Hurlbut Award for Excellence in Teaching, Stanford Law Sch., 1991, 2000. Office: Stanford Law Sch Crown Quadrangle 559 Nathan Abbott Way Stanford CA 94305-8610 Office Phone: 650-723-2499. Business E-Mail: bfried@stanford.edu.*

FRIED, BELLE WARSHAVSKY, education educator; b. N.Y.C., Apr. 14, 1917; d. Maurice and Sarah (Brown) Bennett; m. Henry Warshavsky, Feb. 22, 1941 (dec.); children Barry Alyn, Beth, Benes; m. Joseph Fried, Jan. 13, 1986. BBA, St. Johns U., 1940; MSEd, Hofstra U., 1957; postgrad., NYU, 1962, profl. diploma in reading, 1965; PhD, Walden U., 1975; postgrad., C.W. Post U., 1994. Cert. gerontologist. Pvt. sec. real estate div. Home Owners Loan Corp., N.Y.C., 1935-39; pers. interviewer N.Y. State Arsenal, Bklyn., 1940-41; brokerage agt. Mut. Trust Life Ins. Co., N.Y.C., 1950-55; instr. Cen. Sch. Dist. No. 4, Plainview, N.Y., 1955-60, cons. in reading, 1961-85, dir. summer reading program, 1962-85. Instr. Kindergarten Workshops, 1961-63, Hofstra U. Reading Clinic, 1965-66; adj. instr. Queensboro C.C., 1970-79, asst. prof. 1994—, adj. prof., 1994—. Contbg. author: The Non-graded Primary—A Case History, 1986. Vice chmn. Nassau County Rep. Com., 1981; vice chmn. Rep. Com. Town of North Hempstead, 1983—; exec. leader Great Neck North Rep. Com.; mem. presdl. Task Force; leader Girl Scouts U.S.A., 1940-42; instr. 1st aid course for adults CD, 1941; aid welfare commr. Saddle Rock Civic Assn., 1962-80; rep. Long Term Care Ins. Mem. NEA, Nat. Soc. Study Edn., N.Y. State Tchrs. Assn., Nassau County Tchrs. Assn., Classroom Tchrs. Assn. (v.p., sec. 1958-60), Great Neck Edn. Assn. Nassau County, Internat. Reading Assn., Internat. Platform Assn., Sigma Tau Delta, Phi Delta Kappa. Address: 35 Cooper Dr Great Neck NY 11023-1908 also: 4302 Martinique Cir Coconut Creek FL 33066-1482

FRIED, BERNARD, parasitologist, biology educator; b. N.Y.C., Aug. 17, 1933; s. Harry and Anna (Bergstein) F.; m. Janet Avery, Aug. 25, 1959 (div.); 1 child, Neil; m. Grace Jean Evans, Jan. 31, 1969; 1 stepchild, David. AB, NYU, 1954; MS, U. N.H., 1956; PhD, U. Conn., 1961. NIH postdoctoral fellow parasitology Emory U., Atlanta, 1961-63; asst. prof. Lafayette Coll., Easton, Pa., 1963-69, assoc. prof., 1969-75, Kreider prof. biology, 1975-2000, Kreider prof. emeritus, 2000—. Cons. thin-layer chromatography Ctr. Profl. Advancement, East Brunswick, N.J., Kontes Glassware, Vineland, N.J. Author: Thin Layer Chromatography, 1982, 4th edit., 1999, Handbook of Thin Layer Chromatography, 3d edit., 2003, Practical Thin Layer Chromatography--A Multidisciplinary Approach, 1996, Advances in Trematode Biology, 1997, Echinostomes as Experimental Models for Biological Research, 2000; mem. editl. jour. Helminthology; contbr. more than 500 articles to profl. jours. Grantee NIH, NSF Rsch. Corp., Wellcome Trust Fund. Mem. Am. Soc. Parasitologists (exec. coun.), Am. Micros. Soc., Helminthol. Soc. Washington, Pa. Acad. Sci. (pres. 1972-73), Internat. Soc. Chem. Ecology. Office: Lafayette Coll High St Easton PA 18042

FRIED, BRUCE MERLIN, lawyer; b. Coral Gables, Fla., Sept. 10, 1949; BA, U. Fla., 1971, JD, 1974. Bar: Fla. 1975, DC 1981. With Fla. Legal Services, 1975-81, Nat. Sr. Citizens Law Ctr., 1981-86; exec. dir. Nat. Health Care Campaign, 1986-90; exec. v.p. The Wexler Group, 1990-94; chief coord. Clinton/Gore Campaign's Health Care Adv. Group, 1992; v.p. fed. affairs FHP Internat. Corp., 1994-95; dir. Ctr. for Health Plans and Providers, Health Care Financing Adminstrn. US Dept. Health and Human Services, Balt., 1995—98; ptnr. Shaw Pittman, Washington, 1998—2003, Sonnenschein Nath & Rosenthal, Washington, 2003—. Mem. global adv. bd. GE Med. Systems Info. Technologies; counsel Am. Acad. Ophthalmology, Calif. Assn. Physician Groups. Nat. adv. com. Berman Bioethics Inst. Johns Hopkins U.; chair adv. com. Dept. Health Policy George Washington U. Office: Sonnenschein Nath & Rosenthal Ste 600, E Tower 1301 K St NW Washington DC 20005 Office Phone: 202-408-9159. Office Fax: 202-408-6399. Business E-Mail: bfried@sonnenschein.com.*

FRIED, BURTON THEODORE, lawyer; b. N.Y.C., Feb. 26, 1940; s. Meyer S. and Minnie (Grossberg) F.; m. Gail K. Morgenstern, July 25, 1964; children: Marsha, Howard, Shari. BS, NYU, 1961; LL.B., Bklyn. Law Sch., 1964. Bar: N.Y. 1964, U.S. Dist. Ct. (ea. and so. dists.) N.Y. 1971. Assoc. atty. H. Bermack, N.Y.C., 1964-66, I. Towbis, N.Y.C., 1966-68; gen. counsel Medispas, Inc., N.Y.C., 1968-72; real estate counsel Michael Industries, Inc., N.Y.C., 1972-74, exec. v.p., gen. counsel and sec., 1974-86, The LVI Group, Inc., N.Y.C., 1982-85, vice chmn., gen. counsel, dir., 1985-91; pres. The LVI Group Inc., N.Y.C., 1991-93; pres., CEO LVI Svcs. Inc., N.Y.C., 1986—; chmn. LVI Holding Corp., N.Y.C., 1993—. Trustee Optometric Ctr. N.Y., 1993-99. Vice chmn. sch. bd. Forest Hills Jewish Ctr. Religious Sch., N.Y., 1983-84, chmn. sch. bd., 1984-85, trustee, 1985-88. Mem.: K.P. (Chancellor comdr. 1972-73). Office: LVI Svcs Inc 80 Broad St New York NY 10004

FRIED, CHARLES, law educator; b. Prague, Czechoslovakia, Apr. 15, 1935; arrived in US, 1941, naturalized, 1948; s. Anthony and Marta (Winterstein) F.; m. Anne Sumerscale, June 13, 1959; children: Gregory, Antonia. AB, Princeton U., 1956; BA, Oxford (Eng.) U., 1958, MA, 1961; LLB, Columbia U., 1960; LLD (hon.), New Eng. Sch. of Law, 1987, Pepperdine U., 1994, Suffolk U., 1996. Bar: D.C. 1961, Mass. 1966. Law clk. to Hon. John M. Harlan U.S. Supreme Ct., Washington, 1960; from asst. prof. to prof. law Harvard U., Cambridge, Mass., 1961-85, Carter prof. gen. jurisprudence, 1981-85, 89-95, Carter prof. emeritus, disting. lectr. Law Sch., 1995-99, Beneficial prof. law, 1999—; assoc. justice Supreme Jud. Ct. Mass., Boston, 1995-99. Spl. cons. Treasury Dept., 1961—62; cons. White House Office Policy Devel., Washington, 1982, Dept. Transp., Washington, 1981—82, Dept. Justice, 1983; solicitor gen. U.S., 1985—89. Author: An Anatomy of Values, 1970, Medical Experimentation: Personal Integrity and Social Policy, 1974, Right and Wrong, 1978, Contract as Promise: A Theory of Contractual Obligation, 1981, Order and Law: Arguing the Reagan Revolution, 1991, (with David Rosenberg) Making Tort Law: What Should Be Done and Who Should Do It, 2003, Saying What The Law Is: The Constitution in The Supreme Court, 2004; contbr. legal and philos. jours. Guggenheim fellow, 1971—72. Fellow Am. Acad. Arts and Scis.; mem. Inst. Medicine, Am. Law Inst., Mass. Hist. Soc., Phi Beta Kappa. Office Phone: 617-495-4636. Business E-Mail: fried@law.harvard.edu.

FRIED, DANIEL, federal agency administrator, former ambassador; b. Sept. 19, 1952; m. Olga Karpiw; children: Hannah, Sophie. BA in History magna cum laude, Cornell U., 1974; MA, Columbia U., 1977. Fgn. svc. officer, 1977—2000; jr. officer East-West Trade office Econ. Bus. Bur. State Dept., 1977-79; with Consulate Gen. Office, Leningrad, 1980-81; polit. officer U.S. Embassy, Belgrade, 1982-85; reg. affairs officer Soviet Desk State Dept., Washington, 1985-87; Polish desk officer US Dept. State, Washington, 1987-89, polit. counselor Warsaw, 1990-93; dir. European affairs NSC, Washington, 1993-95, spl. asst. to pres., sr. dir. ctrl. and Ea. Europe, 1995—; amb. to Poland US Dept. State, Warsaw, 1997—2000, prin. dep. spl. advisor to the Sec. of State for the new ind. states, 2000—01; spl. asst. to Pres. The White House, Washington, 2001—; sr. dir. European and Eurasian affairs Nat. Security Coun., 2001—05; asst. sec European & Eurasian Affairs US Dept. State, Washington, 2005—. Office: US Dept State Harry S Truman Bldg 2201 C St NW Rm 6226 Washington DC 20520

FRIED, DONALD DAVID, lawyer; b. NYC, Feb. 28, 1936; s. Fred and Sylvia (Falk) F.; m. Joan Hilbert, Sept. 15, 1963; children: Neil, Derek. BA, CCNY, 1956; JD, Harvard U., 1959. Bar: NY 1959. Assoc. Conboy, Hewitt, O'Brien & Boardman, N.Y.C., 1960-68, ptnr., 1968-86, Hunton & Williams, N.Y.C., 1986-88, 92-96; sr. counsel, 1996—; v.p., sec., assoc. gen. counsel Philip Morris Cos., Inc., N.Y.C., 1988-91. Home: 37 W 12th St New York NY 10011-8502 Office: Hunton & Williams 200 Park Ave New York NY 10166-0091 Office Phone: 212-309-1038. Business E-Mail: dfried@hunton.com.

FRIED, ELAINE JUNE, insurance company executive; b. L.A., Oct. 19, 1943; m. Howard I. Fried, Aug. 7, 1966; children: Donnoven Michael, Randall Jay. Grad., Pasadena (Calif.) H.S.; various coll. courses. Agt., office mgr. Howard I. Fried Agy., Alhambra, Calif., 1975—. V.p. Sea Hill, Inc., Pasadena, 1973-95; spkr. on psycho-social aspects of diabetes, insurance, diabetes, ins. medicine. Contbr. articles to profl. jours. Publicity chmn., unit telephone chmn. San Gabriel Valley unit Am. Diabetes Assn., past chmn., vol. lobbyist, mem. patient edn. com. region II Calif. chpt., 1998; past publicity chmn. San Gabriel Valley region Women's Am. Orgn. for Rehab. Tng. (ORT); chmn. spl. events publicity, Temple Beth Torah Sisterhood, Alhambra, membership chmn., 1991-92, v.p. membership, 1991-93; former mem. bd. dirs., pub. rels. com., pers. com. Vis. Nurses Assn., Pasadena and San Gabriel Valley; chmn. outside Sisterhood publicity Congregation Shaarei Torah, 1993-2003, pub. rels. chmn., 1993-2003, membership v.p., 1999-2002, mem. mktg. com., 2001-2003; mem. ways and means com. Congregation Shaarei Torah, 2003—; organizer monthly diabetes support groups. Recipient Vol. award So. Calif. affiliate Am. Diabetes Assn., 1974-77, 25 Yr. Vol. Svc. award, 1996, cert. of appreciation, 1987; co-recipient Ner Tamid Temple Beth Torah. Mem. ORT, Hadassah Home: 404 N Hidalgo Ave Alhambra CA 91801-2640 Personal E-mail: howie1818@aol.com.

FRIED, FLOYD ALAN, urologist; b. Bklyn, NY, Mar. 23, 1936; s. Herbert and Ann Fried; m. Ellen S Fried, July 1, 1962; children: Deborah, Daniel. BS, Bklyn. Coll, 1953—57; MD, U. Chgo., 1957—61. Surgical intern NY Hosp. Coun., 1961—62; jr. resident surgery U. Chgo., 1962—63, rsch. resident in urology, 1963—64, resident in urology, 1964—65, sr. resident in urology, 1965—66, chief resident in urology, 1965—66, asst. prof., 1967—70; assoc. prof. chief urology UNC, 1970—74, prof. surgery, 1974—93, 1993—99. Mem. editl. bd. Jour. of Urology. Major USAR, 1968—78, NC. Recipient Disting. Svc. award, U. Chgo., 1996. Mem.: Am. Coll. Surgeons.

FRIED, JEFFREY MICHAEL, health care administrator; b. Kansas City, Mo., Apr. 9, 1953; s. Harvey J. and SuEllen (Weissman) F.; m. Rosalyn Sue Matz. Student, Drake U., 1971-73; BGS, U. Kans., 1975; MHA, Washington U., St. Louis, 1979. Adminstrv. asst. Rsch. Med. Ctr., Kansas City, Mo., 1979-80; asst. to pres. Rsch. Health Svcs., Kansas City, 1980-81; asst. v.p. Sinai Hosp. Balt., 1981-83, Lancaster (Pa.) Gen. Hosp., 1983-85; v.p., chief oper. officer Lancaster (Pa.) Gen. Svcs. Corp., 1985-86, pres., 1986-88; sr. v.p. Lancaster Gen. Hosp., 1989-91, chief operating officer, 1992-94; pres., CEO Beebe Med. Ctr., Lewes, Del., 1994—. Pres., bd. dirs. Lancaster Med. Equipment, Barge Ganse Vena Care; sec., bd. dirs. Preferred Health Care, Lancaster; bd. dirs. Lancaster Diagnostic Imaging, Inc., Del. Nat. Bank; v.p., bd. dirs., pres. Welsh Mountain Med. and Dental Ctr., Lancaster, 1989-94; mng. ptnr. Rohrerstown Imaging Assocs., Lancaster, 1986-94; part-time mem. faculty dept. health adminstrn. and devel. Pa. State U., 1988-94, Coll. of St. Francis, 1988-94; mem. bus. adv. coun. Goodwill Industries, 1989-94; asst. prof. Lebanon Valley Coll., 1994—; mem. MBA program adv. bd. Wilmington Coll., 1996—; adj. faculty Wilmington Coll. Grad. Bus. Program, 1996—. Mem. Leadership Lancaster, 1987-88; pres. bd. dirs. Welsh Mt. Med. and Dental Ctr., 1989-94; pres. bd. dirs. Lancaster chpt. Nat. Commn. for Prevention of Child Abuse, 1986-89; treas., bd. dirs. Lancaster Jewish Fedn., 1986-89; bd. dirs. Lancaster Jewish Cmty. Ctr., 1989-94, DE Nat. Bank, 2002—, chmn. audit com., 2005—; bd. dirs. Temple Shaarai Shomayim, Clinic for Spl. Children, 1991-94, Pa. Acad. Music, 1994-96, Del. Hospice, 1996-99, Rehoboth Art League, 1996-2000, Lewes C. of C., 1999—, Dewey Beach Lions Club, 2001—, Slam Dunk to the Beach, 2001—, Am. Heart Assn., 2005—. Fellow: Am. Coll. Healthcare Execs. (com. on ethics 1991—93, credentials com. 1995—98); mem.: Am. Hosp. Assn. (ho. of dels. 1998—2000), Assn. Del. Hosps. (bd. dirs. 1995—), Lancaster County Bus. Group on Health (legis. com. 1992—94), Ctrl. Pa. Health Care Adminstrs., Young Pres. Orgn., World Pres. Orgn., Lewes C. of C. (v.p. 2001—03, pres. 2003—), Dewey Beach Lions Club. Jewish. Avocations: tennis, jogging, cooking, reading. Home: 17 Patriots Way Rehoboth Beach DE 19971-1057 Office: Beebe Med Ctr 424 Savannah Rd Lewes DE 19958-1490 Office Phone: 302-645-3537. Business E-Mail: jfried@bbmc.org.

FRIED, JOHN H., chemist; b. Leipzig, Germany, Oct. 7, 1929; s. Abraham and Frieda F.; m. Heléne Gellen, June 26, 1955; children: David, Linda, Deborah. AB, Cornell U., 1951, PhD, 1955. Steroid chemist, research assoc. Merck and Co., Rahway, N.J., 1956-64; with Syntex Research, Palo Alto, Calif., 1964-92, dir. inst. organic chemistry, 1967-74, exec. v.p., 1974-76, pres., 1976-92; sr. v.p. Syntex Corp., 1981-86, vice chmn., 1986-92; dir. Corvas Internat., Inc., 1992-99, chmn., 1997-99. Chmn. Alexion Pharms., Inc., 1992-2002; pres. Fried & Co., Inc., 1992—. Mem. Am. Chem. Soc. Office: 20 Faxon Forest Atherton CA 94027-4067

FRIED, JUNE A., artist; b. N.Y.C., July 21, 1923; d. David and Anna G. Aibel; m. Bernard Fried, June 20, 1943; children: Mark Lewis, Paula Fried-Woolman. Student, Am. Sch. Design, 1939-40, Pratt Inst., 1940-43. Art tchr. after sch. program N.Y.C. Sch., Bensonhurst Jewish Cmty. Ctr., 1943-45; set designer, art tchr. Jed Mack Camp, Great Barrington, Mass., 1956-57; cultural art dir. BBN Jewish Cmty. Ctr., Brookline, Mass., 1957-67, YMHA Miami, Fla., 1967-75; real estate broker Miami, 1975-88. 1st v.p. Miami Watercolor Soc., 1989-91, pres., 1991-93. Exhibited in group shows Miami Watercolor Soc., Am. Artist Profl. League, Poinciana Show, Mus. Sci. Shows; represented in pvt. collections. Vol. Sr. Life Ctr., Miami, 1989-2001, Cong. Bet Breira, Miami, 1996-2001. Mem. Fla. Profl. Artist Guild (pres. 1999-2001). Home: 10260 SW 92 Terr Miami FL 33176

FRIED, RICHARD L., lawyer; b. NYC, June 5, 1958; BS, Cornell Univ., 1980; JD cum laude, NYU, 1983. Bar: NY 1984. Co-adminstrv. ptnr., structured fin. practice area Stroock & Stroock & Lavan LLP, NYC. Frequent lectr. in field. Mem.: Order of Coif. Office: Stroock & Stroock & Lavan LLP 180 Maiden Ln New York NY 10038-4982 Office Phone: 212-806-6047. Office Fax: 212-806-6006. Business E-Mail: rfried@stroock.com.

FRIED, SAMUEL P., lawyer; b. Bklyn., Aug. 16, 1951; s. Zoltan and Helen (Katina) F.; m. Gigi Panush, Dec. 27, 1981; children: Eva M., Orly Z., Jacob J., Molly R., Susanna R. AB, Washington U., St. Louis, 1971; JD, Boston U., 1974, LLM, 1997. Bar: Mass. 1974, Ill. 1983, Mich. 1989; ordained rabbi, 1971. Assoc. Warner & Stackpole, Boston, 1974-77; staff atty. The Bendix Corp., Southfield, Mich., 1977-79, sr. atty., 1979-80, asst. treas., 1980-81; v.p., corp. counsel Clevite Industries, Inc., Glenview, Ill., 1981-83, v.p., sec., gen. counsel, 1983-87; v.p., sec. gen. counsel Exide Corp., Troy, Mich., 1987-91; v.p., gen. counsel The Limited Inc., 1991-99, sr. v.p., gen. counsel, sec., 1999—. Editor: Psychosurgery, 1974. Mem. ABA, Am. Corp. Counsel Assn., Mich. Gen. Counsels Assn., Phi Beta Kappa. Jewish. Avocations: music, reading. Office: The Limited Inc PO Box 16000 3 Limited Pkwy Columbus OH 43230-1467

FRIED, VANCE HOYT, finance educator; b. Mangum, Okla., Apr. 17, 1952; s. David Daniel and Elsie Elizabeth (Moreau) F.; m. Nancy Jane Petree, oct. 3, 1982; children: Regan, David. BS in Fin., Okla. State U., 1973, postgrad., 1986-87; JD, U. Mich., 1976. Atty., Stillwater, Okla., 1976-79, Wheatley & Fried, Stillwater, 1979-81; v.p., dir. and founding shareholder Red Eagle Exploration, Oklahoma City, 1981-84; v.p., corp. fin. Houchin, Adamson & Co., Oklahoma City, 1984-86; asst. to prof. Okla. State U., Stillwater, 1987—, dir. Entrepreneurship Ctr., 1994-99, 2004—. Fin. and strategic cons. Vance H. Fried, Ltd., Stillwater, 1987—; mem. applied sci. and tech. com. Okla. Futures, Oklahoma City, 1996. Editl. bd.: Entrepreneurship Theory and Practice, Waco, Tex., 1991-2004, Jour. Pvt. Equity, NY, 2002—; contbr. articles to academic and profl. jours. Sec., dir. Sheltered Workshop, Stillwater, Okla., 1996-99. Grantee Coleman Found., Chgo., 1998, Okla. Capital Investments Bd., 1988, 91, 98. Mem. Acad. mgmt., Okla. Investment Forum, Okla. Venture Forum (edn. com. 1991-98), Okla. Acad. (task force chair 1994). Republican. Achievements include rsch. on venture capital industry, mgmt. of venture capital-backed companies and corp. goverance; design of university-based programs to promote technol. entrepreneurship. Office: Okla State U Spears Sch Bus Stillwater OK 74078-0001 E-mail: vhfried@okstate.edu.

FRIEDAN, BETTY, writer, advocate; b. Peoria, Ill., Feb. 4, 1921; d. Harry and Miriam (Horwitz) Goldstein; m. Carl Friedan, June 1947 (div. May 1969); children: Daniel, Jonathan, Emily. AB summa cum laude, Smith Coll., 1942, LHD (hon.), 1975, SUNY, Stony Brook, 1985, Cooper Union, 1987; Doctorate (hon.), Columbia U., 1994. Rsch. fellow U. Calif., Berkeley, 1943; lectr. feminism univs., women's groups, bus. and profl. groups in US and Europe; co-founder NOW, 1966, 1st pres., 1966-70, chairwoman adv. com., 1970-72, mem. bd. dirs. legal def. and edn. fund; founding mem. Nat. Women's Polit. Caucas, 1971; organizer Internat. Feminist Congress, 1973, First Women's Bank, 1973, Econ. Think Tank for Women, 1974; co-founder Nat. Abortion Rights Action League (NARAL), v.p., 1970-73. Disting. vis. prof. sch. journalism and studies of women and men in soc., U. So. Calif., 1987; vis. prof. sociology Temple U., 1972, Queens Coll., 1975; vis. lectr. Calhoun Coll., fellow Yale U., 1974; lectr. New Sch. Social Research, NYC, 1971; sr. research assoc. Ctr. Social Scis., Columbia U., NYC, 1979-81; bd. dirs. NOW Legal Defense and Education fund; co-chmn. Nat. Comms. Women's Equality; del. White House Conf. on Family, 1980; del. UN Decade for Women Confs. in Mexico City, Copenhagen, Nairobi; mem. LORAN Commn. Harvard Community Health Plan; vis. scholar U. South Fla., Sarasota, 1985; Disting. vis. prof. Sch. Journalism and Social Work Sch. U. So. Calif., Cornell U., Sch. Industrial and Labor Rels, Ithaca, NY, 1998—; dir. New Paradigm Program, Inst. for Women and Work, 1998-. Author: The Feminine Mystique, 1963, It Changed My Life: Writings on the Women's Movement, 1976, The Second Stage, 1981, The Fountain of Age, 1993, Beyond Gender: The New Politics of Family and Work, 1998, Life So Far, 2000; mem. editl. bd. Present Tense mag.; contbg. editor McCall's mag., 1971-74; contbr. Atlantic Monthly; contbr. articles to NY Times, Cosmopolitan, Saturday Rev., Family Circle, Good Housekeeping, McCall's, Newsweek, The New Republic, The New Yorker, Harpar's Mag., American Behavioral Scientist, Social Policy, and others; papers being collected by Schlesinger Libr. Harvard U. Mem. exec. com. Am. Jewish Congress, co-chair nat. commn. women's equality, 1984-85; mem. nat. bd. Girl Scouts USA, 1976-82; mem. NY County Democratic Com. Recipient Humanist of Yr. award, 1974, Eleanor Roosevelt Leadership award, 1989; Inst. Politics fellow Kennedy Sch. Govt., Harvard U., 1982, rsch. fellow Ctr. Population Studies, Harvard U., 1982-83, Chubb fellow Yale U., 1985, Andrus Ctr. Gerontology fellow U. So. Calif., 1986, guest scholar Woodrow Wilson Ctr. for Internat. Scholars, 1995-96, disting. vis. prof. George Mason U., 1995, Mt. Vernon Coll., 1996; Ford Found. grantee, 1998. Mem. AFTRA, PEN, Author's Guild, Women's Ink, Women's Forum, Mag. Writers, Am. Soc. Journalists and Authors (1st recipient Mort Weisinger award for outstanding mag. journalism 1979, Author of Yr. 1982), Assn. Humanistic Psychology, Am. Sociology Assn., Gerontol. Soc. Am., Cosmos Club, Nat. Press Club, Phi Beta Kappa. Office: Cornell U 411 ILR Extension Bldg Ithaca NY 14853-3901*

FRIEDBERG, AARON LOUIS, political science professor; b. Pitts., Apr. 16, 1956; s. Simeon Adlow and Joan Libby (Brest) F.; m. Adrienne Louise Sirken, June 19, 1988; children: Eli, Gideon. BA, Harvard U., 1978, MA, PhD, Harvard U., 1986. Asst. prof. polit. sci. Princeton (N.J.) U., 1987-93, assoc. prof. polit. sci., 1993-99, prof. polit. sci., 1999—; dep. asst. for nat. security affairs Office of the Vice Pres., Washington, 2003—05. Author: The Weary Titan, 1988 (Edward Furniss award, Mershon Ctr., Ohio U., 1989), In the Shadow of the Garrison State; contbr. articles to pofl. jours. Fellow Ctr. for Internat. Affairs, Harvard U. 1987, Woodrow Wilson Ctr., Smithsonian Inst.,

1989, Norwegian Nobel Inst., 1998; recipient Helen Dwight Reid award Am. Polit. Sci. Assn., 1986. Mem. Coun. Fgn. Rels. Office: Princeton U Woodrow Wilson Sch 185 Prospect Ave Princeton NJ 08540 Home: 5230 Elliott Rd Bethesda MD 20816-2909

FRIEDBERG, BARRY SEWELL, investment banker; b. Atlantic City, Jan. 4, 1941; s. Herbert and Mildred (Salit) F.; m. Charlotte A. Moss, Oct. 10, 1985; children: Benjamin, James. BA, Princeton U., 1962. Trainee Chem. Bank, N.Y.C., 1963-64; with A.G. Becker, N.Y.C., 1964-84, mgr. mergers and acquisitions dept., 1980-83, mng. dir., 1974-84, mgr. investment banking div., 1984; mng. dir. Merrill Lynch & Co., N.Y.C., 1984—; mgr. investment banking div. Merrill Lynch Pierce Fenner & Smith Inc., N.Y.C., 1985-93, chmn. investment banking divsn., 1993—2003; exec. v.p., mem. exec. com. Merrill Lynch & Co., Inc., 1990—2003; pres. FriedbergMilstein, 2003—. Bd. dirs. N.Y.C. Ballet Co., 1988—96, 1997—, chmn., 2003—; bd. dirs. Boys Harbor, Inc., Lincoln Ctr. Performing Arts, 2003—, American Hosp. Paris Found. Mem. Princeton Club, Econs. Club. Office: FriedbergMilstein 6 E 43d St New York NY 10017 Office Phone: 212-406-6701. E-mail: bfriedberg@friedbergmilstein.com.

FRIEDBERG, MAURICE, retired Russian literature educator; b. Rzeszow, Poland, Dec. 3, 1929; came to U.S., 1948, naturalized, 1954; s. Isaac and Ida (Jam) F.; m. Barbara Bisguier, Mar. 18, 1956; children— Rachel Miriam, Edna Sarah. BS, Bklyn. Coll., 1951; A.M., Columbia U., 1953, PhD, 1958; certificate, Russian Inst., 1953. Lectr. Russian Bklyn. Coll., 1952, Middlebury Coll., 1960-61; assoc. Russian Rsch. Ctr., Harvard U., 1953, Hunter Coll., N.Y.C., 1955-65; prof. Slavic langs. and lits. Ind. U., 1966-75; dir. Russian and East European Inst., Ind. U, 1967-71; prof. Russian lit. U. Ill., Urbana-Champaign, 1975-2000, head dept. Slavic langs. and lit., 1975-95, 98-2000, dir. Russian and East European Ctr., 1995-98, Ctr. for Advanced Study prof., 1995-2000, prof. emeritus, 2000—. Vis. asst.prof. Russian lit. Columbia U., 1961-62; lectr. Russian lit. NYU, 1965; Fulbright vis. prof. Russian lit. Hebrew U., Jerusalem, 1965-66; dir. d'etudes invitè École des Hautes Études en Sciences Sociales, Paris, 1985; guest scholar Hoover Instn. Stanford U., 1986; fellow Inst. Advanced Study Hebrew U., Jerusalem, 1986-87; cons. Russian lit. and Soviet affairs to pub. radio; mem. acad. coun. Kennan Inst. Advanced Russian Studies, 1985-89; former bd. dirs., mem. selection com. Internat. Rsch. and Exchanges Bd.; juror Nat. Book Award, 1973; sr. univ. scholar U. Ill., 1987—; dir. Russian and East European Ctr., 1996-98. Author: Russian Classics in Soviet Jackets, 1962, The Party and the Poet in the USSR, 1963, A Bilingual Edition of Russian Short Stories, Vol. I, 1964, Vol. II, 1965, The Jew in Post-Stalin Soviet Literature, 1970 (also Portuguese edit), A Decade of Euphoria: Western Literature in Post-Stalin Russia, 1977, Russian Culture in the 1980's, 1985, How Things Were Done In Odessa, 1991, Literary Translation in Russia, 1997; editor: (Leon Trotsky author) The Young Lenin, 1972, The Red Pencil: Artists, Scholars and Censors in the USSR, 1989; deptl. editor: Ency. Judaica, 16 vols, 1971-72, Soviet Society Under Gorbachev, 1987; contbr. to scholarly jours. and popular mags. Guggenheim fellow, 1971, 81-82; fellow Ctr. for Advanced Study, 1981, 90, NEH fellow, 1990-91. Mem. Polish Inst. Arts and Scis. in Am. (corr.), Am. Assn. Advancement Slavic Studies (dir.), Am. Assn. Tchrs. Slavic Langs., Russian Acad. of the Humanities. Jewish. Home: 2406 N Nottingham Ct Champaign IL 61821-7017

FRIEDEBERG, PEDRO, painter, sculptor, designer; b. Florence, Italy, Jan. 11, 1937; s. Erwin and Gerda (Landsberg) F. Architecture degree, U. Iberomaericana, Mexico City, 1962. Exhibited in numerous one man exhbns. including Byron Gallery, N.Y.C., 1964, 66, 67, Souza Gallery, Mexico City, 1962, 64, 66, 68, Misrachi Gallery, Mexico City, 1970, 72, 74, Galerie Pecanins, Barcelona, 1976, Ft. Worth Art Ctr., 1979, Harcourts Gallery, San Francisco, 1980, Needleman Gallery, Chgo., 1981, Llewellyn Gallery, New Orleans, 1985, Museo de Arte Moderno Mex., 1986, Vorpal Gallery, N.Y.C., Museo Biblioteca Pape, Monclova, Mex., 1989, Galeria de Arte Mexicano, Mexico City, 1990; exhibited in numerous group shows including Biennale of São Paulo, 1964, Biennale of Paris, 1964, Labyrinthe, Berlin, 1968, Mus. of Modern Art, Toronto, Ottawa and Montreal, 1973-75, Biennales of San Juan, P.R., 1977-79, Bienal Coltejer, Medellin, Colombia, 1978, Llewellyn Gallery, New Orleans, 1989, Microbienal, Mexico City, Vorpal Gallery, N.Y.C., 1987, Museo de Arte Moderno, Mexico City, 1988, Hokin Galleries, Fla., 1988, 92, R.E.F. Studios, Houston; respresented in numerous mus. in Am., Europe, Argentina, Israel, including Musée Des Arts Decoratifs Du Louvre, Paris, Mus. Contemporary Art, New Orleans, Worcester (Mass.) Art Mus., Brandeis U., Washington and Lee U., Toronto Sci. Mus., Mus. Contemporary Art of Jerusalem and Tel Aviv, Mus. Modern Art of Mexico City, Mus. Modern Art, Bagdad, Iraq, Buenos Aires Mus. Modern Art, Casa de las Americas, Havana, Cuba, Nat. Rsch. Libr., Ottawa, Libr. of Congress, Washington, Museo Marco, Monterrey, Mex., others; Art editor: Mexico This Month, 1960-64; subject of book: Pedro Friedeberg (Ida Rodriguez), 1972, Pedro Friedeberg (A. Neuvillate). Recipient 1st prize Biennale of Córdoba, Argentina, 1967; 2d prize Exposición Solar, Mex., 1968; 1st prize Biennale of San Juan, P.R., 1979; 2d prize Triennale of Buenos Aires, 1979 Mem. Foro de Arte Contemporáneo, Accademia Italia delle Arti e del Lavoro, Gallery La Chinche Mexico City (dir.). Home: Recreo 48 San Miguel Allende 37700 Guanajuato Mexico Office: Apartado Postal 6-613 06600 Mexico City Mexico

FRIEDEL, JACQUES, retired physics professor; b. Paris, Feb. 11, 1921; s. Edmond and Jeanne (Bersier) F.; m. Mary Horder, June 2, 1952; children: Jean, Paul. Degree in engring., Ecole Polytechnique, Paris, 1946; post grad., Ecole des Mines, 1948; doctorate, U. Paris., 1954; PhD in Physics., U. Bristol, Eng., 1952; doctorat (hon.), Ecole Polytechnique, Lausanne, Bristol U., Geneva U., Zagreb U., Cambridge U. Engr. Ecole des Mines, Paris, 1948-56; prof. physics U. Paris, 1956-89, ret., 1989. Pres. Cons. Scientifique France Telecom Paris, 1991-98, Obs. Nat. la Lectr., 1994-2001; pres. Comite Consultatif de la Rechereche Scientifique et Technique, 1979-81. Author: Dislocations, 1956, 64, Graine de Mandarin, 1994; contbr. articles to profl. jours. With French Cavalry, 1944. Decorated grand officer Legion of Honor, comdr. Order Nat. Merit; recipient Gold medals CNRS, Ste. Française Metallurgie Paris, Acta Metallurgica, prize Holweck French Soc. Physics and Inst. of Physics, Dannie Heineman prize Acad. Göttingen, von Hippel and Italgas awards. Mem. Acad. des Scis. (past pres.), Swedish Royal Acad. Scis. (hon.), Royal Soc. London (hon.), Am. Acad. Arts and Scis. (hon.), Leopoldina (hon.), Inst. Physics London (hon.), Am. Phys. Soc. (hon.), Nat. Acad. Sci. (hon.), Royal Belgian Acad. Sci. (hon.), Brazilian Acad. Sci. (hons.), European Phys. Soc. (past pres.), Max Planck Gesellschaft (hon.). Avocation: gardening. Home: 2 rue Jean-Francois Gerbillon 75006 Paris France Office: Physique des Solides U Paris Sud 91405 Orsay France

FRIEDEL, MICHAEL GERALD, investment company executive; b. Des Moines, Feb. 28, 1948; s. Lawrence Joseph and Norma Jean (Morrissey) F.; m. Janice Ann Nahra, June 2, 1973 (div.); children: Matthew Nahra, Patrick Joseph. Student, U. Iowa, 1967-69; BA, Parsons Coll., 1971; MS, Coll. for Fin. Planning, 1995. Cert. fin. planner. Asst. sec.-treas. Citizens Fed. Savs. and Loan, Davenport, Iowa, 1972-75; account exec. Merrill Lynch, Davenport, 1975-79; fin. svcs. rep. E.F. Hutton, Bettendorf, Iowa, 1979-81; br. mgr. Fin. Planners Equity Corp., Bettendorf, 1982-84; br. mgr., registered prin. Titan Capital Corp. (now Tital Value Equities Group, Inc.), Bettendorf, 1984—95. Mem. adj. faculty Coll. for Fin. Planning, Denver, 1980-85, adv. com., 1984. Named to Hon. Order of Ky. Cols. Mem. Internat. Assn. Fin. Planning (bd. dirs. 1985-88), Internat. Assn. Registered Fin. Planners (bd. dirs. 1985-88), Bettendorf C. of C. (bd. dirs. 1985-88, elected trailblazer), Am. Philatelic Soc., Bermuda Collectors Soc., Moose, Davenport Club, Elks, Sons of Union Vets. of Civil War (Iowa dept. comdr. 1994-95), Theta Chi Funds for Leadership and Edn., Inc. (internat. adv. coun. 1991, bd. dirs., treas., 1991-96, regional counselor 1984-91, Alumni award 1986), Alpha Phi Omega. Republican. Roman Catholic. Avocations: genealogy, travel. Home: 6808 Forest Ct Windsor Heights IA 50311-1535

FRIEDEL, ROBERT OLIVER, physician; b. Corona, N.Y., Aug. 4, 1936; s. August W. and Denise G. (D'Aoust) F.; m. Susanne Weber, June 30, 1961; children: Christine, Scott, Karin, Linda. BS, Duke U., 1958, MD, 1964. Diplomate: Am. Bd. Psychiatry and Neurology. Intern Duke U. Med. Ctr., Durham, N.C., 1964-65, resident in psychiatry, 1967-70, asst. prof. psychiatry and pharmacology dept. psychiatry, 1970-73, assoc. prof. psychiatry and asst. prof. pharmacology, 1973-74; assoc. prof. psychiatry and pharmacology U. Wash. Sch. Medicine, Seattle, 1974-77, dir. div. psychopharmacology, 1974-77, vice chmn., dir. clin. services dept. psychiatry and behavioral scis., 1975-77; prof., chmn. dept. psychiatry Med. Coll. Va.-Va. Commonwealth U., Richmond, 1977-84; prof., chmn. dept. psychiatry, exec. dir. Mental Health Rsch. Inst. U. Mich., Ann Arbor, 1984-85; v.p. psychiat. medicine and rsch. Charter Med. Corp., Macon, Ga., 1985-90, psychiatrist in chief, 1987-90, sr. v.p. clin. svcs. and rsch., 1990, physician in chief, 1990, also bd. dirs.; prof., chmn. dept. psychiatry U. Ala., Birmingham, 1992-2001; disting. clin. prof., dept. psychiatry Va. Commonwealth U., Richmond, 2001—. Mem. sci. adv. bd. Nat. Edn. Alliance for Borderline Personality Disorder. Author: Borderline Personality Disorder Demystified, 2004, (with others) Behavioral Science: A Selective View, 1972; editor (with L.R. Baxter) Current Psychiatric Diagnosis and Treatment, 1999, (with D. Evans) Current Psychiatry Reports and Current Psychosis and Therapeutic Reports; mem. editl. bd. Jour. Clin. Psychopharmacology, Hosp. and Cmty. Psychiatry, 1986-92; contbr. book chpts. and articles. Bd. dirs. Nat. Mental Health Assn., 1987-92. Served to lt. comdr. USPHS, 1965-67. Fellow Am. Psychiat. Assn. (disting. life); mem. AMA, Am. Coll. Psychiatrists, Soc. Biol. Psychiatry, Med. Soc. Va., Am. Coll. Neuropsychopharmacology (life), Alpha Omega Alpha. Home: 13722 Hickory Nut Point Midlothian VA 23112 Office Phone: 804-744-5261. E-mail: rofriedel@aol.com.

FRIEDEN, B. ROY, mathematician, physicist; s. Max and Ida Frieden; m. Sarah Fay Ebner, Aug. 16, 1981; children: Mark E., Amy Beth Holler, Miriam L. Ph D, U. Rochester, 1966. Cons., cancer modelling, Tucson, 2000—; prof. optical scis. U. Ariz., Tucson, 1966—. Cons. in environ. modelling EPA, Cin., 2000—; mem. com. on devel. 2d generation space telescope NASA, Greenbelt, Md., 2001—. Author: (book) Science from Fisher Information, 2004, Probability, Statistical Optics and Data Testing, 2001; editor: The Computer in Optical Research, 1980. Fellow: Optical Soc. Am. (assoc. editor 1980—84). Achievements include discovery of in situ breast cancer growth law (2003); invention of laser beam shaping (1965); three dimensional imaging theory (1967); maximum entropy image processing (1971); discovery of Fisher information as foundation of science (1988—). Avocation: cello. Office: Optical Sciences U of Ariz Tucson AZ 85721 E-mail: roy.frieden@optics.arizona.edu.

FRIEDEN, CARL, biochemist, educator; b. New Rochelle, N.Y., Dec. 31, 1928; s. Alexander and Evelyn (Gutman) F.; m. Sari Ann Schneider, Dec. 20, 1953; children: Amy, Eric, Karen. BA, Carleton Coll., 1951; PhD, U. Wis., 1955. Mem. faculty biochemistry and molecular biophysics Washington U., St. Louis, 1957—, prof. biol. chemistry, 1963—, interim dept. head, 1986—89, 1996—2000, Alumni Endowed prof., 1994-2000, dir. med. scientist tng. program, 1986-91, Wittcoff prof., head, 2000—. Mem. NIH study sect., biochemistry, 1969-74, cellular molecular basis of disease, 1992-96. Mem. editorial bd.: Jour. Biol. Chemistry, 1963-68, 75-80, Archives Biochemistry and Biophysics, 1973-79, Biochemistry, 1975—. Protein Sci., 1992-96. Fellow AAAS, Am. Acad. Arts and Scis.; mem. Nat. Acad. Sci., Am. Soc. Biochemistry and Molecular Biology, Am. Chem. Soc. (St. Louis award 1976), Am. Soc. Cell Biology, Biophys. Soc., Protein Soc., Sigma Xi. Research, publs. on mechanism of enzyme action including correlation of protein structure to catalytic function, protein folding, devel., application of kinetic theory with respect to enzymes; properties of actin. Home: 7452 Wellington Way Saint Louis MO 63105-2926 E-mail: frieden@biochem.wustl.edu.

FRIEDEN, CLIFFORD E., lawyer; b. LA, Mar. 8, 1949; s. Sidney S. and Norma (Stern) F.; m. Dinah S. Baumring, June 20, 1971; children: Jamie, Kari, Curtis. BA, UCLA, 1971; JD, U. Calif., Berkeley, 1974. Bar: Calif. 1974, U.S. Dist. Ct. (so. dist.) Calif. 1974, U.S. Dist. Ct. (cen. dist.) Calif. 1977. Ptnr. Rutan & Tucker, Costa Mesa, Calif., 1974—. Mem. Orange County chpt. ARC, 1995-2001. Mem. Orange County Bar Assn. (del. state conv. 1983-95, chair judiciary com. 1987-88, bd. dirs. 1989-91), Order of Coif, Phi Beta Kappa. Avocations: sports, jogging. Office: Rutan & Tucker PO Box 1950 611 Anton Blvd Ste 1400 Costa Mesa CA 92626-1931 Office Phone: 714-641-3420. Business E-Mail: cfrieden@rutan.com.

FRIEDEN, FAITH JOY, obstetrician; b. N.Y.C., Sept. 15, 1960; MD, Mt. Sinai Sch. Medicine, 1984. Diplomate Am. Bd. Ob-Gyn., Am. Bd. Maternal and Fetal Medicine. Resident in ob-gyn. Beth Israel Med. Ctr., N.Y.C., 1984—88, attending physician, 1990—93; fellow in maternal fetal medicine Bellevue Hosp./NYU, N.Y.C., 1988—90; perinatology dir. maternal-fetal medicine Englewood (N.J.) Hosp. and Med. Ctr., 1993—, chief ob-gyn., 2001—. Mem. faculty Mt. Sinai Sch. Medicine, N.Y.C., 1991—. Named one of Top Drs. in N.Y. Metro Area, Castle Connolly, Top Drs. 2003, N.J. Monthly Mag. Office: Englewood Hosp and Med Ctr 350 Engle St Englewood NJ 07631 Office Phone: 201-894-3669.

FRIEDENBERG, DANIEL MEYER, investor, writer; b. Mt. Vernon, N.Y., Feb. 24, 1923; s. Samuel and Rose Abravanel (Klein) F.; m. Maria del Carmen Joy, May 1, 1956 (div. June 1964); children: Samuel Clark, Danielle Joy; m. June Meredith Daniels, Apr. 12, 1965 (div. May 1986); children: Jay Daniels, Bertrand Russell. BS, U. Pa., 1943. With John-Platt Enterprises, Inc., N.Y.C., 1947—, pres., 1957—. Curator coins and medals Jewish Mus., N.Y.C., 1960-83, emeritus, 1983—; guest lectr. Columbia U., N.Y.C., Yale U., New Haven, Swarthmore Coll., Hebrew U., Jerusalem. Author: Great Jewish Portraits in Metal, 1963, Jewish Medals from the Renaissance to the Fall of Napoleon, 1970, Jewish Mint Masters & Medalists, 1976, Medieval Jewish Seals from Europe, 1987, Life, Liberty and the Pursuit of Land, 1992, Sold to the Highest Bidder: The Presidency from Dwight D. Eisenhower to George W. Bush, 2002; contbr. articles to profl. jours. Exec. dir. N.Y. County Liberal Party, 1945; sec. Young Dems., N.Y.C., 1952. Served with AUS, 1943-44. Recipient spl. achievement award Loeb Mag., 1962, Loeb Newspaper, 1965, Heath Lit. award for disting. numismatic achievement, 1969, Nat. Jewish Book award, 1988, 3d prize Nat. Libr. Poetry, 1997. Fellow Am. Numismatic Soc. (life); mem. Am. Numismatic Assn. Office: 55 Central Park W New York NY 10023-6003 Home: PO Box 767 Greenwich CT 06836-0767

FRIEDENBERG, MIKE, publishing executive; MBA, U. Del. Mem. sales staff Cardinal Bus. Media; pub. Internetwork Mag., Midrange Sys., DEC Profl., ENT Mag.; from dist. mgr. to pub. Info. Week, Manhasset, NY, 1996—2000, pub., 2000—05; v.p. Camp Media LLC, Manhasset, 2000—05, sr. v.p strategic customer develop.; pres. & CEO CXO Media, Inc (subs. Internat. Data Group), Mass., 2005—. Office: CXO Media Inc 492 Old Connecticut Path Framingham MA 01701-9208 Office Phone: 508-935-4101. Office Fax: 508-872-0618.*

FRIEDENBERG, RICHARD MYRON, radiologist, educator, physician; b. N.Y.C., May 6, 1926; s. Charles and Dorothy (Steg) F.; m. Gloria Geshwind, Jan. 22, 1950; children: Lisa, Peter, Amy. AB, Columbia, 1946; MD, L.I. Coll. Medicine, 1949. Diplomate: Am. Bd. Radiology. Intern in medicine Maimonides Hosp., Bklyn., 1949-50; resident in radiology Bellevue Hosp., N.Y.C., 1950-51, Nat. Cancer fellow, 1951-52; fellow radiology Columbia-Presbyn. Hosp., 1952-53; cons. radiologist 3d Air Force, London, Eng., 1953-55; asst. prof. radiology Albert Einstein Coll. Medicine, 1955-66, assoc. clin. prof. radiology, 1966-68; dir., chmn. dept. radiology Bronx Lebanon Hosp. Center, 1957-68; prof., chmn. dept. radiology N.Y. Med. Coll., 1968-80; prof., chmn. dept. radiol. scis. U. Calif., Irvine, 1980—92, emeritus prof. radiol. scis., 1992—. Dir. radiology Flower Fifth Ave. Hosp., Met. Hosp. Ctr., Bird S. Coler Hosp., N.Y.C., Westchester County Med. Ctr., 1968—80. Author: (with Charles Ney) Radiographic Atlas of the Genitourinary System, 1966, 2d edit., 1981; Contbr. (with Charles Ney) articles to profl. jours. Fellow Am. Coll. Radiology, N.Y. Acad. Medicine; mem. Assn. Univ. Radiologists, Radiol. Soc. N.Am., Am. Roentgen Ray Soc., N.Y. Acad. Scis., Assn. Am. Med. Colls., AMA, Soc. Chairmen Acad. Radiology Depts. (past pres.), N.Y. Roentgen Soc. (past pres.), Orange CTY Radiology Soc. (past pres.). Home: 18961 Castlegate Ln Santa Ana CA 92705-2801 Office: U Calif Dept Radiology Irvine CA 92697-0001 Office Phone: 714-456-5303. Business E-Mail: rmfriede@uci.edu.

FRIEDER, GIDEON, computer scientist, educator; b. Zvolen, Czechoslovakia, Sept. 30, 1937; arrived in US, 1975; m. Dalia Bogler, Apr. 3, 1960; children— Ophir, Tally, Gony B.Sc., Israel Inst. Tech., Haifa, Israel, 1959, M.Sc., 1961, D.Sc., 1967. Staff mem. Israel Dept. Def. Research and Devel., Haifa, Israel, 1959-68, dir. computer sci., 1968-70; staff mem. IBM Sci. Ctr., Haifa, Israel, 1973-75; assoc. prof., then prof., chmn. SUNY, Buffalo, 1975-81; prof., chmn. dept. elec. engring. and computer sci. U. Mich., Ann Arbor, 1981-86; dean sch. computer info. science Syracuse (N.Y.) U., 1987-92; dean Sch. Engring. and Applied Sci., A. James Clark prof. George Washington U., 1992-97, A. James Clark chair, prof. engring., applied scis., 1997—. Cons. various industries; chief architect computers Nanodata Corp., Buffalo, 1976-80; expert witness patent and copyright cases; lectr. Contbr. articles to profl. jours.; patentee in field of computers, memory and orgn. Mem. Assn. Computing Machinery, IEEE Computer Soc. Office: 8012 Matterhorn Ct Potomac MD 20854-4058 Office Phone: 202-994-8884. Business E-Mail: gfrieder@gwu.edu.

FRIEDER, SAMUEL P., venture capitalist; AB, Harvard Coll. Sr. real estate analyst Mfr. Hanover Trust Co.; sr. assoc. capital funding group Security Pacific Bus. Credit, 1988—89; joined Kohlberg & Co., 1989, prin., 1995. Bd. dirs. Allied Aerospace Engring., Inc., Applied Graphics Tech., Inc., CUSA Busways, LLC, Holley Performance Products, Inc., Innotek, Inc., Katy Industries, Inc., Nancy's Specialty Foods, Inc., Nevamar Co., LLC, Orion Food Sys. LLC, Redaelli Tecna, S.p.A., Simplicity Mfg., Inc., KTTI Holding Co., Inc., Tinnerman Palnut Engring. Products LLC; mem. mgmt. com. Katonah Capital LLC. Office: Kohlberg & Co 111 Radio Cir Mount Kisco NY 10549 Office Phone: 914-241-7430. Office Fax: 914-241-7476.

FRIEDHEIM, JAN V., education administrator; b. Corpus Christi, Tex., Oct. 20, 1935; d. Roy Lee Conyers and Bertha Victoria (Ostrom) Hamm; m. John R. Eisenhour, Nov. 22, 1962 (div. 1983); m. Stephen B. Friedheim, Sept. 1, 1984; children: Neenah, Stephen II, Robert. BS, U. Tex., 1957; PhD (hon.), Constantinian U., Malta, 1994. Chmn. bd. Exec. Secretarial Sch., Dallas, 1960—2001; ptnr. Edn. Sys. and Solutions, 2001—. Vice-chmn. Tex. Vocat-.Adv. Bd., Austin, 1979-86; mem. adv. com. Dept. Edn., Washington, 1980-84; commr. So. Assn. Colls. and Schs. Commn. on Occupl. Edn. Instns., 1994-97; adv. com. State Postsecondary Rev. Entity, 1994; bd. dirs. Tex. Assn. Pvt. Schs., Career Coll. and Schs. of Tex.; commr. Coun. on Occupl. Edn., 1995-2001. Bd. dirs. Career Colls. and Schs. of Tex., 1995—. Named Disting. Evaluator, Accrediting Coun. Ind. Coll. Schs., 1999. Mem. Career Coll. Assn. (bd. dirs. 1999—), Assn. Ind. Colls. and Schs. (chmn. bd. dirs. 1980-81, commn. 1978-79, commr. 1974-79, Disting. Mem. 1974, 81, Mem. of Yr. 1979), Southwestern Assn. Pvt. Schs. (pres. 1982), Metroplex Assn. Pvt. Schs. (pres. 1989-90, 92-93), So. Assn. Colls. and Schs. (trustee 1981-85, commn. on occupational edn. instns. 1994-97), Tex. Assn. Pvt. Schs. (bd. dirs. 1992—), Career Colls. and Schs. Tex. (bd. dirs. 1995—, chmn.-elect 1998, chmn. 1999). Home: 6450 Patrick Dr Dallas TX 75214-2444 Office Phone: 214-662-5403. Personal E-mail: jfriedheim@aol.com.

FRIEDHEIM, JERRY WARDEN, museum director, consultant; b. Joplin, Mo., Oct. 7, 1934; s. Volmer Havens and Billie Alice (Warden) F.; m. Shirley Margarette Beavers, Oct. 17, 1956 (dec. Sept. 15, 2003); children: Daniel Volmer, Cynthia Diane, Thomas Eric; m. Jacqueline Wade Grant, April 24, 2004. BJ, U. Mo., 1956, AM, 1962. Reporter, editor, editorial writer Neosho (Mo.) Daily News, Joplin (Mo.) Globe, Columbia Missourian, 1956-61; instr. journalism U. Mo., Columbia, 1961-62; aide to Congressman Durward Hall from Mo., Washington, 1962-63; legis. asst., pres. sec., exec. asst. to U.S. Senator John Tower from Tex., Washington, 1963-69; dep. asst. Sec. Def. for Pub. Affairs, U.S. Dept. Def., Washington, 1969-72; asst. Sec. Def. for Pub. Affairs, Washington, 1973-74; v.p. pub. and govt. affairs AMTRAK, 1974-75; exec. v.p., gen. mgr. Am. Newspaper Pubs. Assn. and ANPA Found., Washington, 1975-87, pres., 1987-91; pub. Presstime mag., 1980-90; v.p. pub. affairs The Freedom Forum, Arlington, Va., 1991-95; exec. dir. The Freedom Forum Newseum, 1991-93; dep. dir. The Newseum, Arlington, Va., 1995-97, mem. adv. com., 1998—. Bd. dirs. World Press Freedom Com; past chmn. Nat. Press Found. Author: Where are the Voters, 1968. Capt. AUS, 1956-58. Congl. fellow Am. Polit. Sci. Assn.; recipient Disting. Svc. medal Dept. Def., 1972, 74. Home: 46865 Grissom St Sterling VA 20165-3575 Personal E-mail: friedheim1@msn.com.

FRIEDHEIM, STEPHEN BAILEY, educational consultant; b. Joplin, Mo., Nov. 13, 1934; s. Robert Wray and Virginia Grace (Bailey) F.; m. Jan V. Eisenhour, Sept. 1, 1984; children; Neenah Marie, Stephen Bailey II, Robert William. BA, U. Ark., 1956; DBA (hon.), Johnson and Wales U., Providence, 1978; DAM (hon.), Ctrl. New Eng. Coll., Worcester, Mass., 1984. Announcer Sta. KBRS, Springdale, Ark., 1956-57; newsman Sta. KFSB, Joplin, 1957; dir. pub. rels. Am. Pers. and Guidance Assn., Washington, 1961-66; exec. v.p. Am. Soc. Med. Tech., Houston, 1966-76; pres. Assn. Ind. Colls. and Schs., Washington, 1976-84; sr. v.p. Campbell Comm., Bethesda, Md., Dallas, 1984-90, King Edn. Svcs., 1984-89; pres. ESS Coll. Bus. (formerly Exec. Secretarial Sch.), Dallas, 1984-2001; prin. Edn. Solutions for Students LLC, 1991—2001; founder Edn. Systems & Solutions, LLC, 2001—. Cons. Profl. Scs., Internat., 1980-82, South-Western Pub. Co., 1984-88, Career Com Corp., 1984-91, Richard D. Irwin, Inc., Paradigm Pub., 1999, Masters Inst., 1997, Johnson & Wales U., 2002—, Coll. Am., 2002—, Coll. Am., 2002—, KD Studio Actors Conservatory, 2002-05, Vatterott Colls., 2003—; task force on transfer credit Coun. on Postsecondary Accreditation, 1977-78; mem. Nat. Task Force on Image of the Sec., 1980-97; pres. Am. Edn. Alliance, 1988-90; founder, mng. dir. EdVerify, 1998-2000. Editor: The Lead Generation, 1984—90, Tex. Times, 1994—2004. Bd. dirs. St. Aidan's Sch., Alexandria, Va., 1979-82, Trinity River Arts Ctr., 2002—; trustee Dollars for Scholars, 1982-84; vestry man Ascension Ch., Houston, 1973-76, sr. warden, 1976; narrator Minn. Symphony Orch., 1972; founding mem. local county workforce devel. bd. Dallas County, 1996-2001, chmn., vice-chmn., bd. dirs., 1999, chmn., 2000; bd. dirs., exec. com. Tex. Discovery Gardens, 2000-01; vice-chmn. Workforce Leadership Tex., 2000-01. With U.S. Army, 1957-61. Recipient Freedoms Found. award, 1960, 62, Broadcasting award Am. Legion Aux., 1963. Fellow Australasian Coll. Bio-med. Scientists; mem. Am. Soc. Assn. Execs. (cert.), Nat. Assn. Trade and Tech. Schs. (Outstanding Svc. award 1984), Assn. Ind. Colls. and Schs. (Disting. Svc. award 1991), Washington Soc. Assn. Execs., Work Force Commn. Creative Svc. (1st pl. award 1990, 91), Southwestern Assn. Ind. Colls. and Schs. (bd. dirs. 1985-92, pres. 1989-91), Met. Assn. Career Schs. (bd. dirs. 1985-86, pres. 1999), Assn. Ind. Colls. and Schs. (treas. 1985-89, bd. dirs. 1985-91, chmn. bd. 1990-91), Career Coll. Assn. (bd. dirs. 1991-9, 1st chmn. bd. 1991-94, past chmn. bd. 1994-95), Nat. Ct. Reporters Assn. (strategic alliance com. for edn. 1994-95), Nat. Alliance of Bus. (bus. adv. com. 1994-2000, S.W. regional bd. dirs. 1996-98), Career Tng. Found. (bd. dirs. 1992-95, trustee 1995—2000), Am. Assn. Higher Edn., Am. Vocat. Assn., Nat. Bus. Edn. Assn., Nat. Assn. Workforce Bds. (bd. dirs. 2000-01), Am. Vocat. Assn., Nat. Assn. Execs., Nat. Assn. Concerned Vets., Career Coll. Assn., Career Colls. and Schs. of Tex. (bd. dirs. 2000-04), U.S. C. of C. (edn., employment and tng. com. 1980-92, adv. bd. 1991-95), Ctr. Workforce Preparation and Quality Edn. Home: 6450 Patrick Dr Dallas TX 75214-2444 Office Phone: 214-827-5403. E-mail: sfriedheim@aol.com.

FRIEDL, RICK, lawyer, retired academic administrator; b. Berwyn, Ill., Aug. 31, 1947; s. Raymond J. and Ione L. (Anderson) F.; m. Dawn Friedl; children: Richard, Angela, Ryan, Ariana. BA, Calif. State U., Northridge, 1969; MA, UCLA, 1976, postgrad., 1984; JD, Western State U., 1987. Bar: Calif. 1988, U.S. Dist. Ct. (ctrl. dist.) Calif. 1992. Dept. mgr. Calif. Dept. Indsl. Rels., 1973-78; mem. faculty dept. polit. sci. U. So. Calif., 1978-80; pres. Pacific Coll. Law, 1981-86; staff counsel state fund Calif., 1988-89; prin. Law Offices of Rick Friedl, 1989—. Author: The Political Economy of Cuban Dependency, 1982; tech. editor Glendale Law Rev., 1984; contbr. articles to profl. jours. Calif. State Grad. fellow, 1970-72. Mem. ABA, Calif. State Bar Assn., Los Angeles County Bar Assn., Am. Polit. Sci. Assn., Latin Am. Studies Assn., Acad. Polit. Sci., Pacific Coast Coun. Latin Am. Studies, Calif. Trial Lawyers Assn. Home: PO Box 2095 California City CA 93504-0095 E-mail: rick@aroya.com.

FRIEDLAND, BERNARD, engineer, educator; b. Bklyn., May 25, 1930; s. Irving and Beckie (Kissen) F.; m. Zita Isa Silverman, Aug. 16, 1959; children: Barbara, Irene, Shelly. AB, Columbia U., 1952, BSEE, 1953, MSEE, 1954, PhD, 1957. Registered profl. engr., Calif. Instr. Columbia U., N.Y.C., 1953-57, asst. prof., 1957-61; head control lab. Melpar, Inc., Watertown, Mass., 1961-62; prin. scientist Kearfott Guidance and Navigation Corp. (formerly The Singer Co.), Little Falls, N.J., 1962-90; disting. prof. N.J. Inst. Tech., Newark, 1990—. Adj. prof. Columbia U., 1965-72, NYU, 1970-73, Poly. U. (formerly Poly. Inst. N.Y.) Bklyn., 1974-90; Lady Davis vis. prof. Technion (Israel Inst. Tech.), 1996-97. Author: Control System Design, 1986, Advanced Control System Design, 1996; co-author: Principles of Linear Networks, 1961, Linear Systems, 1965; contbr. more than 90 articles to profl. jours. Chmn. The Hilary Sch., Newark, 1965. Named to Bklyn. Tech. H.S. Hall of Fame, 1998. Fellow ASME (various offices, Oldenburger medal 1982), IEEE (disting. mem., various offices, recipient 3d millennium medal), AIAA (assoc.; assoc. editor jour.). Democrat. Jewish. Avocations: skiing, swimming, tennis, reading, sculpture. Office: NJ Inst Tech Dept Elec and Computer Engring Newark NJ 07102 Business E-Mail: bf@njit.edu.

FRIEDLAND, ELLEN BETH, lawyer; b. Forest Hills, N.Y., Mar. 7, 1958; d. Samuel J. and Judith (Galker) F.; children: Janel Sara, Jared, Gabriel; m. Curtis W. Fissel II, July 2, 2000. BA cum laude, Brandeis U., 1980; JD cum laude, Yeshiva U., 1983. Bar: Mass. 1985, N.Y. 1986, U.S. Dist. Ct. (so. dist.) N.Y. 1986, U.S. Dist. Ct. (ea. dist.) N.Y. 1986, N.J. 1989, U.S. Supreme Ct. 1991. Law clk. to judge U.S. Dist. Ct. (so. dist.) N.Y., N.Y.C., 1983-86; ptnr. Berkowitz & Friedland, N.Y.C., 1986-89; pvt. practice Upper Montclair, NJ; prodr., writer for video prodn. cos. JEM/GLO, Voices and Visions Prodns. Ltd. Cons. to N.J. Commn. on Legal and Ethical Problems in Delivery of Health Care, Princeton, 1988-91. Editor: Women's Annotated Legal Bibliography, 1983; mem. law rev. Yeshiva U., 1981-82; polit. corr. N.J. Jewish News, 1994-2001. Mem. polit. subcom. Nat. Abortion Rights Action League, 1989. Recipient Samuel L. Belkin Svc. award and scholar award Yeshiva U., 1983, Democrat. Jewish. Avocations: family activities, swimming, running, hiking, philosophy, writing. Office: Voices and Visions Prodns Ltd PO Box 43127 Upper Montclair NJ 07043

FRIEDLAND, LILLI, psychologist; b. Bad Gastein, Austria, Feb. 24, 1947; came to U.S., 1950, naturalized, 1956; d. Joseph and Marie (Bjerkenhejm) Rebhun; m. David Lee Friedland, Feb. 22, 1969; children: Jered, Elana, Ari, Micah. BA, U. Oreg., 1966; PhD, U. So. Calif., 1975. Diplomate Am. Bd Profl. Psychology. Rsch. asst. Rsch. Svc. Bur., L.A., 1968-70; cons. to Coun. Jewish Fedn., N.Y.C., 1969-70; research analyst L.A. Mental Health Dept., 1970-73; chief planning div. Office of Alcohol Abuse and Alcoholism, L.A. County, 1973-74, chief program and system evaluation, 1973-74; chief drug abuse planning L.A. County Dept. Health Svcs., 1973-76; dir. family devel. program Suicide Prevention Center, L.A., 1975-77; pres. Friedland Psychol. Assos., Inc., L.A., 1975—; cons. to pvt. secondary schs., Calif., 1973—; condr. workshops. Chairperson Devel. Disabilities Area Bd., Calif., 1977-79, Program Planning and Evaluation Com. Area Bd., 1975-77; mem. exec. com., cmty. svc. com., leadership devel. com., mem. program planning and budgeting com. Jewish Fedn. Coun., 1981—. Recipient certs. of appreciation Bd. Suprs. L.A. County, 1980, L.A. County Narcotics and Dangerous Drugs Commn., 1975; named one of Women Yr. Cetury City C. of C., 1988. Mem. APA (dir. 1986—, pres. pub. info. com., pres. media psychology divsn.), Bd. Psychology State Calif., Calif. State Psychol. Assn. chairperson div. VI media psychology, chairperson pub. info. com. 1985-87), L.A. County Psychol. Assn. (pres. 1985, bd. dirs. 1986—), L.A. County Clin. Psychol. Assn. (dir. 1980—), Assn. for Media Psychology (sec.), Women in Bus., Women's Referral Svc., Hadassah. Republican. Jewish. Home: 1216 Daniels Ave Los Angeles CA 90035-1104 Office: 2080 Century Park E Ste 1403 Los Angeles CA 90067-2017

FRIEDLAND, MICHAEL LAWRENCE, medical educator; b. Aug. 30, 1942; BS, Bklyn. Coll., 1963; MD, SUNY, Bklyn., 1967. Asst. prof. medicine, dir. hematology/oncology Brown U./Miriam Hosp., Providence, 1973-81; assoc. prof. medicine Med. Coll. Pa., 1981-82; prof. clin. medicine, sr. assoc. dean clin. affairs N.Y. Med. Coll., 1982-87, chmn. dept. medicine, prof. clin. medicine, 1987-92; dean Binghamton Clin. Campus SUNY, Syracuse, 1992-97; v.p.affiliated programs SUNY Health Sci. Ctr., Syracuse, 1993-95; interim exec. v.p. for acad. affairs/dean medicine Tex. A&M U. Sys. Health Sci. Ctr., College Station, Tex., 1997-99; dean of medicine U. Mo. Kansas City, 1999—2001; dean Eastern divsn. W.Va. U. Health Scis Ctr., Martinsburg, 2001—04; sr. assoc. dean for biomedical sci. Fla. Atlantic Univ., Boca Raton, 2004—. Mem. Medicare Coverage Adv. Com. Co-author: (abstract) IME 21st Ann. Session, 1996, (sect. of book) The Chemotherapy Source Book, 1996; contbr. over 50 articles to profl. jours. Bd. dirs. Brazos Valley chpt. Am. Lung Assn., Bryan, Tex., 1998. Mem. AMA (governing coun. sect. on med. schs., chair sect. on med. schs. 2002-), Mo. State Med. Assn. (coun. on med. edn.). Office: Florida Atlantic Univ Biomed Sci 777 Glades Road PO Box 3091 Boca Raton FL 33431-0991 Office Phone: 561-297-0113. Business E-Mail: michael.friedland@fax.edu.

FRIEDLANDER, CHARLES DOUGLAS (CHUCK FRIEDLANDER), aerospace scientist, consultant; b. N.Y.C., Oct. 5, 1928; s. Murray L. and Jeane (Sottosanti) F.; m. Diane Mary Hutchins, May 12, 1951; children: Karen Diane, Lauren Patrice, Joan Elyse. BS, U.S. Mil. Acad. West Point, 1950; exec. mgmt. program, NASA, 1965; grad., Command and Staff Coll. Ext. USAF, 1965, Air War Coll. Ext. USAF, 1966. Commd. 2d lt. U.S. Army, 1950, advanced 1st lt., officer inf., 1950-51, UN Forces Trieste Trieste, Italy, 1953—54, resigned, 1954; chief astronaut support office NASA, Cape Canaveral, Fla., 1963-67; space cons. CBS News, Cape Canaveral, Fla., 1967-69; exec. asst. The White House, Nat. Aeronautics and Space Coun., Washington, 1969—72. V.p. bd. dirs. Internat. Aerospace Hall of Fame, San Diego; space program cons., various cos., Boca Raton, Fla., 1967-69; mem. staff First Postwar Fgn. Ministers Conf., Berlin, 1954; radio/TV cons. space program. Author: Buying & Selling Land for Profit, 1961, Last Man at Hungnam Beach, 1952. V.p. West Point Soc., Cape Canaveral, Fla., 1964. Served to lt. col. USAFR, maj. USAR. Decorated Bronze Star V, Combat Inf. badge; co-recipient Emmy award CBS TV Apollo Moon Landing, 1960; recipient medal of honor N.Y.C., 1951. Mem. Explorer's Club, West Point Soc., Chosin Few Survivors Korea, NASA Alumni League, Nat. Space Soc, Missile Space and Range Pioneers. Avocations: fishing, travel.

FRIEDLANDER, D. GILBERT, retired lawyer; b. Hazleton, Pa., Sept. 10, 1946; BA in history, U. Tex., 1968, JD, 1971. Bar: Tex. 1972, N.Y. 1973. Sr. shareholder, bd. dirs. Johnson & Gibbs, 1973-91; v.p., gen. counsel EDS, Plano, Tex., 1991—96, sr. v.p., gen. counsel, 1996—2003, exec. v.p., gen. counsel, 2003—04; ret., 2004. Bd. dirs. Dallas Jewish Coalition for Homeless, Temple Emanu-El. Mem. ABA, N.Y. State Bar Assn., State Bar Tex. (corp. com., corp. banking and bus. law sect. 1980—, chmn. com. for rev. corp. tax law 1983-85), Dallas Bar Assn., Dallas Assn. Young Lawyers.

FRIEDLANDER, EDWARD JAY, journalist, educator; b. Portland, Maine, Apr. 24, 1945; s. Otto and Marguerite Evelyn (Smith) Friedlander; m. Roberta Kay Burford, July 12, 1975; 1 child, Erika Anne. BS, U. Wyo., 1967; MA, U. Denver, 1970; EdD, U. No. Colo., 1973. Reporter Denver Post, 1967-68, USIA, Washington, 1968-69; publicist Universal Pictures, N.Y.C., 1969-70; mag. editor Daily Times-Call, Longmont, Colo., 1970-71; media coord. Centaurus HS, Lafayette, Colo., 1972-73; asst. prof. mass communication Ctrl. Mo. State U., Warrensburg, 1973-75; from asst. prof. to assoc. prof. dept. journalism U. Ark., Little Rock, 1975—81, prof., 1981-95, chairperson dept. journalism, 1988-95; dir., prof. U. South Fla. Sch. Mass Comm., Tampa, 1995—. Cons. Bur. Indian Affairs, Washington, 1979, Ark. Press Assn., Little Rock, 1980—85; cons., editor FCC, Washington, 1979—81; adminstr. Waldo Proffitt award, 1998—. Author: (book) Excellence in Reporting, 1987, Feature Writing for Newspapers and Magazines, 1988, Feature Writing for Newspapers and Magazines, 5th edit., 2004, Modern Mass Media, 1990, Modern Mass Media, 2d rev. edit., 1994, Medios de Comunicación Social, 1992. German Acad. Exch. Svc. fellow, Bonn, 1982, European Acad. fellow, Berlin, 1984. Mem.: Soc. Profl. Journalists (officer exec. bd. Ark. profl. chpt. 1986—89, v.p. 1989—91, pres. 1991—92, officer exec. bd. Ark. profl. chpt. 1992—94), Assn. Schs. Journalism and Mass Comm. (exec. com. 1997—2000, 2003—04), Assn. Edn. Journalism and Mass Comm., Kappa Tau Alpha. Office: U South Fla Sch Mass Comms CIS # 1040 4202 E Fowler Ave Tampa FL 33620-7800

FRIEDLANDER, EDWARD ROBERT, pathologist; b. Evanston, Ill., Jan. 9, 1952; s. Robert and Joanne (Hiscox) F. AB, Brown U., 1973; MD, Northwestern U., Chgo., 1977. Diplomate Am. Bd. Pathology. Pathologist, Kansas City, 1988—; chmn. dept. pathology Univ. of Health Scis. Lectr. in field; operator free disease info. svcs. online. Author: (booklets) Christian Perspectives on Evolution, 1985, William Blake's Visions, 1986. Foster parent Juvenile Corrections, Johnson City, Tenn., 1984-85; bd. dirs. Tenn. Assn. Vols. Criminal Justice, 1983-86; prison vol. Yoke Fellow, Winston Salem, 1982-83. Fellow Coll. Am. Pathologists, Am. Soc. Clin. Pathologists, Lambda Chi Alpha. Home: 7909 Tauromee Ave Kansas City KS 66112-2639 Office: 1750 Independence Ave Kansas City MO 64106-1453

FRIEDLANDER, ERIC MARK, mathematics educator; b. Santurce, P.R., Jan. 7, 1944; s. Edward Jay and Helena Friedlander; m. Susan Poate. BA, Swarthmore Coll., 1965; PhD, MIT, 1970. Chair dept. math. Northwestern U., Evanston, Ill., 1999—, prof. math. dept. math., 1980—, assoc. dean sci., 1995—98. Author: (rsch. monograph) Cycles, transfers, and motivic homology theories, 2000, Filtrations on the homology of algebraic varieties, 1994, Etale homotopy of simplicial schemes, 1982; contbr. numerous jour. articles. Named Henry S. Noyes Prof. Math., Northwestern U., 1999—, invited address Internat. Congress of Mathematicians, Internat. Math. Union, 1998; recipient Humboldt Sr. Scientist Rsch. award, Humboldt Found., 1996—97. Mem.: Am. Acad. of Arts and Scis., Am. Math. Soc. (bd. trustees 2000—, 2002, Plenary lectr. U.S.-Mex. internat. meeting 2001). Office: Northwestern U 2033 Sheridan Rd Evanston IL 60208 Business E-Mail: eric@math.northwestern.edu.

FRIEDLANDER, GERHART, nuclear chemist; b. Munich, July 28, 1916; came to U.S., 1936, naturalized, 1943; s. Max O. and Bella (Forchheimer) F.; m. Gertrude Maas, Feb. 6, 1941 (dec. 1966); children: Ruth Ann F. Huart, Joan Claire F. Hurley; m. Barbara Strongin, 1983. BS, U. Calif., Berkeley, 1939, PhD, 1942; D (hon.), Clark U., 1991, U. Mainz, Germany, 1992. Instr. U. Idaho, Moscow, 1942-43; staff Los Alamos Sci. Lab., 1943-46; research assoc. Gen. Electric Co. Research Lab., Schenectady, 1946-48; vis. lectr. Washington U., St. Louis, 1948; chemist Brookhaven Nat. Lab., Upton, N.Y., 1948-52, sr. chemist, 1952-81, 89-91, cons., 1981-89, 91-93, chmn. chemistry dept., 1968-77. Chmn. Gordon Rsch. Conf. on Nuclear Chemistry, 1954. Author: (with J.W. Kennedy) Introduction to Radiochemistry, 1949, Nuclear and Radiochemistry, 1955, (with J.M. Miller), 1964, (with E.S. Macias), 1981; editor-in-chief Sci. Spectra, 1993-2000; editor Radiochimica Acta, 1972-73; assoc. editor Ann. Rev. Nuc. Sci., 1958-67; contbr. articles to profl. jours. Recipient Alexander von Humboldt award Institut für Kernchemie, Mainz, Fed. Republic of Germany, 1978-79, 87, 92, 93. Fellow AAAS; mem. Hungarian Acad. Scis. (hon.), Nat. Acad. Sci., Am. Acad. Arts and Scis., Am. Chem. Soc. (chmn. divsn. nuclear chemistry and tech. 1967, award for nuclear applications in chemistry 1967). Achievements include research in chemical effects of nuclear transformations, properties of radioactive isotopes, mechanisms of nuclear reactions, especially those induced by protons of very high energies; solar neutrino detection; cluster impact phenomena. Home: 22 St Charles Pl South Setauket NY 11720 E-mail: gfriedlander@msn.com.

FRIEDLANDER, JOHN BENJAMIN, mathematician, educator; b. Toronto, Canada, Oct. 4, 1941; s. Daniel Theodore and Beatrice Adele (Axler) Friedlander; m. Cherryl Lynne Thompson, Sept. 1, 1974; children: Jonathan, Diana, Amanda, Keith. BSc, U. Toronto, 1965; MA, U. Waterloo, Ont., Can., 1966; PhD, Pa. State U., 1972. Asst. to A. Selberg, Inst. Advanced Study, Princeton, NJ, 1972-73, mem. Sch. Math, 1973-74, 83-84, 95-96, 99-2000, 2004; lectr., dept. math MIT, Cambridge, 1974-76; vis. prof. Scuola Normale Superiore, Pisa, Italy, 1976-77; from asst. prof. to assoc. prof. U. Toronto, 1977—82, prof. math, 1982—, chair dept. math., 1987-91; lectr. U. Ill., Urbana, 1979-80; rsch. prof. Math Sci. Rsch. Inst., Berkeley, Calif., 1991-92. Mem. grant selection com. Nat. Scis. and Engring. Rsch. Coun. Can., 1991—94; lectr. ICM, 1994; mem. sci. adv. bd. Banff Internat. Rsch. Sta., 2003—, Field Inst. Rsch. Math. Sci., 1996—2000; math. convenor Royal Soc. Can., 1990—93; mem. gen. assembly Internat. Math. Union, 1994; lectr. in field. Contbr. articles to profl. jours. Recipient CRM Fields prize, 2002; Acad. Sci. fellow, Royal Soc. Can., 1988—, Killam Rsch. fellow, 2003—05. Mem.: Can. Math. Soc. (Jeffery-Williams prize lectr. 1999), Am. Math. Soc. Avocations: bridge, chess, sailing, barbecue. Home: 22 Stonemanse Ct Scarborough ON Canada M1G 3V3 Office: U Toronto Dept Math Toronto ON Canada M5S 3G3 also: Scarborough Coll Computer and Math Sci Scarborough ON Canada M1C 1A4 Office Phone: 416-978-4208. Office Fax: 416-978-4107. Business E-Mail: frdlndr@math.toronto.edu.

FRIEDLANDER, MICHAEL WULF, physicist, researcher; b. Cape Town, South Africa, Nov. 15, 1928; came to U.S., 1956; m. Jessica R. Friedlander; 2 children. BS in Physics, U. Cape Town, 1948, MS with 1st class honors, 1950; PhD in Physics, U. Bristol (Eng.), 1955. Jr. lectr. U. Cape Town, 1950-52; rsch. assoc. U. Bristol, 1954-56; asst. prof. physics Washington U., St. Louis, 1956-61, assoc. prof., 1961-67, prof., 1967—. Author: The Conduct of Science, 1972, Astronomy: From Stonehenge to Quasars, 1985, Cosmic Rays, 1989, At the Fringes of Science, 1995, A Thin Cosmic Rain, 2000; contbr. articles to Ency. Brit. and profl. jours. Guggenheim Found. fellow, vis. prof. Imperial Coll., London, 1962-63. Mem. AAUP (2d v.p. 1978-80, mem. nat. coun. 1975-78, 86-89), AAAS, Am. Phys. Soc., Am. Astron. Soc., History of Sci. Soc. Achievements include research in elementary particles, cosmic rays, infrared astronomy, and gamma ray astronomy. Office: Washington U Dept Physics One Brookings Dr Saint Louis MO 63130

FRIEDLANDER, SHELDON KAY, chemical engineering professor; b. NYC, Nov. 17, 1927; s. Irving and Rose (Katzewitz) F.; m. Marjorie Ellen Robbins, Apr. 16, 1934; children: Eva Kay, Amelie Elise, Antonia Zoe, Josiah. BS, Columbia U., 1949; SM, MIT, 1951; PhD, U. Ill., 1954. Asst. prof. chem. engring. Columbia U., NYC, 1954-57, Johns Hopkins U., Balt., 1957-59, assoc. prof. chem. engring., 1959-62, prof. chem. engring., 1962-64; prof. chem. engring., environ. health engring. Calif. Inst. Tech., Pasadena, 1964-78; prof. chem. engring. UCLA, 1978—, Parsons prof., 1982—, chmn. dept. chem. engring., 1984-88, chmn. steering com. Ctr. for Clean Tech., 1989-92. Chmn. EPA Clean Air Sci. Adv. Com., 1978-82. Author: Smoke, Dust, and Haze: Fundamentals of Aerosol Dynamics, 2nd edit., 2000. Served with U.S. Army, 1946-47. Recipient Sr. Humboldt prize Fed. Republic of Germany, 1985, Internat. prize Am. Assn. for Aerosol Rsch./Gesellschaft für Aerosolforschung/Japan Assn. for Aerosol Sci. and Tech., Fuchs Meml. award, 1990, Christian Junge award European Aerosol Assn., 2000, Aurel Stodola medal Swiss Fed. Inst. Tech., Zurich, 2004; Fulbright scholar, 1960-61; Guggenheim fellow, 1969-70. Mem.: AIChE (Colburn award 1959, Alpha Chi Sigma award 1974, Walker award 1979, Lawrence K. Cecil award in environ. chem. engring. 1995, Particle Tech. Forum Lifetime Achievement award 2001), NAE, Am. Assn. for Aerosol Rsch. (pres. 1984—86), Office: UCLA Dept Chem Engring 5531 Boelter Hall Los Angeles CA 90095-0001 Office Phone: 310-825-2206. Business E-Mail: skf@ucla.edu.

FRIEDLI, HELEN RUSSELL, lawyer; b. Indpls., July 8, 1956; d. William F. and Helen F. Russell; m. E. Kipp Friedli, May 19. BS, Purdue U., 1977; JD, Ind. U., 1980. Bar: Ill. 1980. Ptnr., mem. firm exec. mgmt. com. McDermott Will & Emery, Chgo., 1980—. ABA. Office: McDermott Will & Emery LLP 227 W Monroe St Ste 4700 Chicago IL 60606-5096 Office Phone: 312-984-7563. Office Fax: 312-984-7700. Business E-Mail: hfriedli@mwe.com.

FRIEDMAN, ALAN HERBERT, ophthalmologist; b. N.Y.C., 1937; m. Sandra Yasser, 1960; children: David, Jonathan, Lisa, Jennifer. BA in Chemistry with honors, Cornell U., 1959; MD, NYU, 1963. Diplomate Am. Bd. Ophthalmology (assoc. examiner). Intern in medicine Bellevue Hosp., N.Y.C., 1963-64; resident in ophthalmology NYU Med. Ctr., 1966-69, fellow ophthalmic pathology, 1969-70; rsch. fellow histochemistry Royal Postgrad. Med. Sch., London, 1972; practice medicine specializing in ophthalmology N.Y.C., 1970—; attending ophthalmologist and pathologist Mt. Sinai Hosp.; attending ophthalmologist Beth Israel Med. Ctr.; clin. prof. ophthalmology and pathology, dir. eye path. lab. Mt. Sinai Sch. Medicine. Cons. in field. Contbr. numerous articles to profl. publs. With M.C. USAR, 1964-66. Recipient Summer fellow NIH, 1960, 62-63). Fellow ACS, Royal Coll. Ophthalmologists London, Am. Acad. Ophthalmology (Sr. Honor award 1991), N.Y. Acad. Medicine, N.Y. Acad. Scis., Royal Soc. Medicine; mem. AMA, Am. Ophthal. Soc., French Ophthalmology, Am. Assn. Ophthalmic Pathologists (pres. 1992-94), N.Y. County Med. Soc., Med. Soc. State N.Y., Verhoeff Soc., Eastern Ophthalmic Pathology Soc., Pan Am. Assn. Ophthalmology. Address: Mt Sinai Sch Medicine Box 1183 1 Gustave L Levy Pl New York NY 10029-6500 also: 888 Park Ave New York NY 10021-0235

FRIEDMAN, ALAN HOWARD, writer, educator; b. N.Y.C., Jan. 4, 1928; s. Harry Morris and Mina F.; m. Lenore Ann Helman Friedman, Aug. 1, 1950 (div. July 15, 1967); 1 child, Gregory Lawrence Friedman; m. Kate Miller Gilbert Friedman, Oct. 30, 1977; 1 child, Alexander Nicholas Friedman. BA magna cum laude, Harvard Coll., Cambridge, Mass., 1949; MA, Columbia U., N.Y.C., 1950; PhD, U. Calif. Berkeley, 1964. Asst. prof. Columbia U., N.Y.C., 1965-67; assoc. prof. Swarthmore (Pa.) Coll., 1967-70; vis. assoc. prof. Queens Coll., CUNY, 1973-75; prof. U. Ill. at Chgo., 1978-99. Exec. bd. mem. Am. Pen Midwest, Chgo., 1985-89. Author: Hermaphrodeity, 1972, The Turn of the Novel, 1966, (book reviews) N.Y. Times Book Review, 1972-91, contbr. chpts. to books; author of short stories, poems and articles. Nominee Nat. Book award, 1973; recipient D.H. Lawrence fellowship, 1974, award, Nat. Endowment in the Arts, 1975, PEN Syndicated Fiction Project, 1987, Ill. Arts Coun., 1992, Grand prize, Nat. Libr. Poetry, 1998, Best Actor award, ACT, 2001. Home: 3530 Monte Real Escondido CA 92029-7910

FRIEDMAN, ALAN ROY, lawyer; b. N.Y.C., Mar. 18, 1953; s. Oscar B. and Helen (Rosenkrantz) F.; m. Maya Memling, Sept. 3, 1978; 1 child, Charles. AB, Hamilton Coll., 1973; JD, Yale U., 1976. Law clk. to Hon. M. Joseph Blumenfeld U.S. Dist. Ct., Hartford, 1976-77; assoc. Kramer Levin Naftalis & Frankel LLP, N.Y.C., 1977-84, ptnr., 1984—. Office: Kramer Levin Naftalis & Frankel LLP 1177 Ave of the Americas New York NY 10036 Office Phone: 212-715-9100. E-mail: afriedman@kramerlevin.com.

FRIEDMAN, ALAN WARREN, humanities educator; b. Bklyn., June 8, 1939; s. Leon and Anne (Markowitz) F.; m. Elizabeth Butler Cullingford, Nov. 22, 1985; children: Eric Lawrence, Scot Bradley, Lorraine Eve, Daniel Butler. Student, U. Edinburgh, Scotland, 1960-61; BA, Queens Coll., 1961; MA, NYU, 1962; PhD, U. Rochester, 1966. Grad. teaching asst. U. Rochester, 1963-64; from instr. English to prof. U. Tex., Austin, 1964—, dir. honors program, 1972-76, chmn. faculty senate, 1987-89, endowed prof., 2001—. Sr. Fulbright prof. U. Lancaster, Eng., 1977-78, Univ. Coll., Galway, Ireland, 1995; exch. prof. Universite Paul Valery, Montpellier, France, 1985, U. Paris, Sorbonne, 2000. Author: Lawrence Durrell and the Alexandria Quartet, 1970, Multivalence: The Moral Quality of Form in the Modern Novel, 1978, William Faulkner, 1984, Fictional Death and the Modernist Enterprise, 1995, Beckett in Black and Red: The Translations for Nancy Cunard's "Negro", 2000; editor books; contbr. essays and revs. to profl. jours. Chair Dem. Precinct Com.; del. state convs.; founder, 1st pres. Neighborhood Assn., Austin, 1973-74; bd. dirs. Peace Edn. Ctr., Hillel Found., Austin Hospice, Frontline Theatre Co. Recipient Fulbright Rsch. award, 1984—85, 1995, Travel award, France, 1990; fellow, NEH, 1970—71. Mem. MLA (del. assembly 1977-79, 82-84, 94-96, exec. com. divsn. on 20th century English lit. 1992-96), AAUP (pres. U. Tex. chpt. 1979-84, nat. coun. 1989-92, nat. exec. com. 1991-92, chair com. governance 1992-95), Tex. Higher Edn. Coord. Bd. (chair faculty adv. com. 1992-95), Tex. Assn. Coll. Tchrs., Nat. Collegiate Honors Coun., Fulbright Alumni Assn. (pres. ctrl. Tex. chpt.), Omicron Delta Kappa. Democrat. Jewish. Office: Univ Tex Dept English 1 Univ Sta B5000 Austin TX 78712 Office Phone: 512-471-4991. Business E-Mail: friedman@uts.cc.utexas.edu.

FRIEDMAN, ALVIN EDWARD, brokerage house executive; b. N.Y.C., Aug. 8, 1919; s. Harry and Frances (Levin) F.; m. Pesselle Rothenberg, Feb. 2, 1943; children: Jeffrey F., Joan M. BBA, CCNY, 1942; MBA, NYU, 1949. Ptnr. Kuhn Loeb & Co., N.Y.C., 1951-78; sr. mng. dir. Lehmann Bros. Kuhn Loeb, N.Y.C., 1978-84; dir. Dillon Read & Co., N.Y.C., 1984-86, sr. advisor, 1986—. Bd. dirs. Dreyfus Corp., Avnet, Inc. Pres. Hebrew Arts Sch., N.Y. Served to 1st lt. USAAF, 1943-46, PTO. Home: 101 Del Pond Dr Canton MA 02021-2753 Office: Dillon Read & Co 535 Madison Ave New York NY 10022-4212

FRIEDMAN, ANDREW MITCHELL, director housing and neighborhood preservation; b. N.Y.C., Jan. 29, 1950; BA, Antioch U., 1972; MS, U. Wis., 1984. Asst. dir. ARC, Green Bay, Wis., 1982-86; analyst City of Virginia Beach, Va., 1986-89, housing devel. adminstr., 1989-93, dir. housing and neighborhood preservation, 1993—. Mem. allocations com. United Way of South Hampton Roads, Norfolk; past pres. Va. Assn. Housing and Cmty. Devel. Ofcls. Office: City of Virginia Beach Mcpl Ctr Bldg 18A Virginia Beach VA 23456 Office Phone: 757-426-5752. E-mail: afriedma@vbgov.com.

FRIEDMAN, ARTHUR DANIEL, electrical engineer, computer scientist, educator, investment company executive; b. Bronx, NY, Apr. 24, 1940; s. Henry and Yetta Friedman; m. Barbara Allyn Bernstein, Mar. 31, 1968; children: Michael Kenneth, Steven David. BA, Columbia U., 1961, BS, 1962, MEE, 1963, PhD, 1965. Tech. staff Bell Labs., Murray Hill, N.J., 1965-72; assoc. prof. elec. engring. and computer sci. U. So. Calif., L.A., 1972-77; prof. George Washington U., Washington, 1977-97, dept. chmn., 1980-84, prof. emeritus, 1997—. Vis. prof. U. Calif., San Diego, 1999, 2002-04, mem. Chancellor's Assocs., 1999-2004; chmn. bd., co-founder W.H. Freeman & Co. (formerly Computer Sci. Press), Rockville, Md., 1974-88, co-editor-in-chief, 1988-89; co-founder, pres. investment mgmt. co. ABF Enterprises, 1988—, Friedman Family Found. Inc., ABF Capital Mgmt.; founder, pres. Market Mavens, 1998-2001; gen. ptnr. Potomac Ptnrs. LP, 1991; mem. Aztec Venture Networks, 2000-01, Tech Coast Angels, 1999-2001; mem. TIE 2002-03; mem. adv. com. on elec. engring. San Diego State U., 2003—, mem. adv. com. dept. elec. engring., mem. adv. bd. Entrepreneurial Soc. Author: (with Premanchandra Menon) Fault Detection in Digital Circuits, 1971, Theory and Design of Switching Circuits, 1975, Russian trans., Logical Design of Digital Systems, 1975 (translated into Russian), Fundamentals of Logic Design and Switching Theory, 1986; (with Melvin Breuer) Diagnosis of Digital Systems, 1976; (with Miron Abramovici and Melvin Breuer) Digital System Testing and Testable Design, 1990, 2d edit., 1995. Judge San Diego (Calif.) Sci. and Engring. Fair San Diego State U., judge venture challenge competition, 2002—04; pres. Friedman Family Found. Fellow IEEE; mem. Market Mavens. Avocations: reading, swimming, travel, writing. Home: 4969 Beauchamp Court San Diego CA 92130-2742

FRIEDMAN, AVNER, mathematician, educator; b. Petah-Tikva, Israel, Nov. 19, 1932; arrived in U.S., 1956; s. Moshe and Hanna (Rosenthal) Friedman; m. Lillia Lynn, June 7, 1959; children: Alissa, Joel, Naomi, Tamara. MSc, Hebrew U., Jerusalem, 1954, PhD, 1956. Prof. math. Northwestern U., Evanston, Ill., 1962—85; prof. Purdue U., West Lafayette, Ind., 1985—87, dir. Ctr. Applied Math., 1985—87; prof. math., dir. Inst. Math. and Its Applications U. Minn., Mpls., 1987-97, dir. Minn. Ctr. for Indsl. Math., 1994—2002; prof. Ohio State U., Columbus, 2002—; dir. Math. Bioscis.

Inst., 2002—. Author: (book) Generalized Functions and Partial Differential Equations, 1963, Partial Differential Equations of Parabolic Type, 1964, Partial Differential Equations, 1969, Foundations of Modern Analysis, 1970, Advanced Calculus, 1971, Differential Games, 1971, Stochastic Differential Equations and Applications, Vol. 1, 1975, Vol. 2, 1976, Variational Principle's and Free Boundary Problems, 1983, Mathematics in Industrial Problems, 10 vols., 1988—98; author: (with D.S. Ross) Mathematical Models in Photographic Science, 2001; contbr. articles to profl. jours. Recipient Creativity award, NSF, 1983—85, 1990—92; fellow, Sloan Found., 1962—65, Guggenheim, 1966—67. Mem.: NAS, AAAS, Soc. Indsl. Applied Math. (pres. 1993, 1994, chair bd. math. scis. 1994—97), Am. Math. Soc. Office: Ohio State U Math Dept 231 18th Ave Columbus OH 43210 Office Phone: 614-292-5296. Business E-Mail: afriedman@mbi.osu.edu.

FRIEDMAN, BARRY, law educator; b. 1958; BA, U. Chgo., 1978; JD, Georgetown U., 1982. Bar: DC 1983, Tenn. 1991. Law clk. to Hon. Phyllis A. Kravitch US Ct. Appeals 11th Cir., Savannah, Ga., 1982—83; assoc. Davis, Polk & Wardwell, Washington, 1984—86; asst. prof. Vanderbilt U. Law Sch., 1986—89, assoc. prof., 1989—91, prof., 1991—2000; prof. law NYU Sch. Law, 2000—, Jacob D. Fuchsberg prof. law. Vis. prof. law U. Ala., 1983—84, NYU Sch. Law, 1998—2000; adj. prof. Georgetown U., 1984—86. Office: NYU Sch Law Vanderbilt Hall Rm 317 40 Washington Sq S New York NY 10012-1099 Office Phone: 212-998-6293. E-mail: barry.friedman@nyu.edu.

FRIEDMAN, BART, lawyer; b. NYC, Dec. 5, 1944; s. Philip and Florence (Beckerman) F.; m. Wendy Alpern Stein, Jan. 11, 1986; children: Benjamin Alpern, Jacob Stein. AB, L.I. U., 1966; JD, Harvard U., 1969. Bar: N.Y. 1970, Mass. 1972. Rsch. fellow Harvard U. Bus. Sch., Cambridge, Mass., 1969-70; assoc. Cahill, Gordon & Reindel LLP, N.Y.C., 1970-72, 77-80, ptnr., 1980—; spl. counsel SEC, Washington, 1974-75, asst. dir., 1975-77. Bd. dirs. Calif. Inst. for the Arts, Sanford Bernstein Mutual Funds. Mem. Ind. Task Force on Post-Conflict Iraq, 2003—; vis. com. Harvard U. Grad. Sch. Edn., 1995—2001, com. on univ. resources, 1996—; trustee Juilliard Sch., 1988—2001, vice chmn., 1994—2001; coun. fgn. rels. Brookings Inst., 1995—, trustee, 1997—, chmn. N.Y. adv. com., 1997—2001, joint task force on resources for fgn. affairs, ind. task force on non-lethal weapons; del. NATO Hdqrs. and Field, 1998, 2003, del. to Libya, 2005; adv. bd. Remarque Inst. NYU, 1997—2002, Internat. Inst. for Strategic Studies, 2000—; bd. dirs. Lincoln Ctr. for Performing Arts, 2002—, trustee, mem. exec. com., 2002—; coun. fgn. rels. Bretton Woods Com., 2003—, Econ. Club; mem. oversight com. Milton Acad. Mountain Sch., 2004—. Mem. Assn. Bar City of N.Y., Coun. Fgn. Rels., Explorers Club, The River Club, Links Club, The Tuxedo Club, Century Assn., The Met. Club (Washington). Office: Cahill Gordon & Reindel LLP 80 Pine St Fl 17 New York NY 10005-1790 Office Phone: 212-701-3304. E-mail: bfriedman@cahill.com.

FRIEDMAN, BARTON ROBERT, language educator; b. Bklyn., Feb. 5, 1935; s. Abraham Isaac and Mazie Diana (Cooper) F.; m. Sheila Lynn Siegel, June 22, 1958; children— Arnold, Jonathan, Daniel, Esther. BA, Cornell U., 1956, PhD (univ. dissertation fellow), 1964; MA, U. Conn., 1958. Instr. Bowdoin Coll., Brunswick, Maine, 1961-63; from instr. to prof. English lit. U. Wis., Madison, 1963-78; prof. English lit. Cleve. State U., 1978-97, chmn. dept. English, 1978-87, prof. emeritus, 1997—. Visitor Psychoanalytic Inst. Cleve. Author: Adventures in the Deeps of the Mind: The Cuchulain Cycle of W.B. Yeats, 1977, You Can't Tell the Players, 1979, Fabricating History: English Writers on the French Revolution, 1988 (Nancy Dasher award for best scholarly book by mem. Coll. English Assn. Ohio 1989); mem. editl. bd. Irish Renaissance Ann., 1980-84, Lit. Monographs, 1970-76. Recipient William Kiekhofer Teaching Excellence award U. Wis., 1967, Disting. Scholar award Cleve. State U., 1990. Mem. MLA, Am. Com. Irish Studies, Coll. English Assn. Ohio (bd. govs. 1980-81), Soc. Lit. and Sci. (bibliographer Bibliography of Lit. and Sci. in Configurations 1996-98), Phi Kappa Phi. Jewish. Home: 2916 E Overlook Rd Cleveland OH 44118-2434 Office: Cleve State Univ Dept English Cleveland OH 44115 Personal E-mail: sheilaf@stratos.net.

FRIEDMAN, BENJAMIN MORTON, economics professor; b. Louisville, Aug. 5, 1944; s. Norbert and Eva (Lipsky) Friedman; m. Barbara Allan Cook, Dec. 17, 1972; children: John Norton, Jeffrey Allan. AB summa cum laude, Harvard U., 1966, AM, 1969, PhD, 1971; MSc King's Coll., Cambridge U., 1970. Economist Morgan Stanley & Co., N.Y.C., 1971-72; asst. prof. econs. Harvard U., Cambridge, Mass., 1972-76, assoc. prof., 1976-80, prof., 1980-89, William Joseph Maier prof. polit. economy, 1989—, chmn. dept. of econs., 1991-94. Dir. fin. markets and monetary econs. Nat. Bur. Econ. Rsch., Cambridge, 1977—93; bd. dirs. Pvt. Export Funding Corp., Ency. Brit., Inc. Author: Economic Stabilization Policy, 1975, Monetary Policy in the United States, 1981, Day of Reckoning, 1988, The Moral Consequences of Economic Growth, 2005; co-author: Does Debt Management Matter?, 1992; editor: New Challenges to the Role of Profits, 1978, The Changing Roles of Debt and Equity in Financing U.S. Capital Formation, 1982, Corporate Capital Structures in the United States, 1985, Financing Corporate Capital Formation, 1986, Handbook on Monetary Economics, 1990; assoc. editor: Jour. Monetary Econs., 1977—95. Trustee Coll. Retirement Equities Fund, N.Y.C., 1978—82, Standish Mellon Investment, 1989—; dir. Am. Friends Cambridge U., 1994—2000. Marshall scholar, Cambridge U., 1966—68, Soc. Fellows Jr. fellow, Harvard U., 1968—71. Mem.: Am. Econ. Assn., Brookings Panel Econ. Activity, Coun. Fgn. Rels., Harvard Club (N.Y.C.). Home: 74 Sparks St Cambridge MA 02138-2238 Office: Harvard U 127 Littauer Center Cambridge MA 02138

FRIEDMAN, BERNARD ALVIN, federal judge; b. Detroit, Sept. 23, 1943; s. David and Rae (Garber) F.; m. Rozanne Golston, Aug. 16, 1970; children: Matthew, Megan. Student, Detroit Inst. Tech., 1962-65; JD, Detroit Coll. Law, 1968. Bar: Mich. 1968, Fla. 1968, US Dist. Ct. (ea. dist.) Mich. 1968, US Ct. Mil. Appeals 1972. Asst. prosecutor Wayne County, Detroit, 1968-71; ptnr. Harrison & Friedman, Southfield, Mich., 1971-78, Lippitt, Harrison, Friedman & Whitefield, Southfield, 1978-82; judge Mich. Dist. Ct. 48th dist., Bloomfield Hills, 1982-88, US Dist. Ct. (ea. dist.) Mich., Detroit, 1988—, chief judge, 2005—. Lt. US Army, 1967-74. Recipient Disting. Service award Oakland County Bar Assn., 1986. Mem.: Oakland County Bar Assn., Mich. Bar Assn. Avocation: running. Office: US Dist Ct US Courthouse Rm 238 231 W Lafayette Blvd Detroit MI 48226-2700

FRIEDMAN, B(ERNARD) H(ARPER), writer; b. N.Y.C., July 27, 1926; s. Leonard and Madeline Friedman; m. Abby Noselson, Mar. 6, 1948; children: Jackson, Daisy. BA, Cornell U., 1948. With Cross & Brown Co., 1949-50; v.p., dir. Uris Bldgs. Corp., N.Y.C., 1950-63; lectr. creative writing Cornell U., 1966-67; staff cons., dir. Fine Arts Work Ctr., Provincetown, Mass., 1968-82. Mem. adv. coun. Cornell U. Coll. Arts and Scis., 1968—83, Herbert F. Johnson Mus., 1972—87. Author: (novels) Circles, 1962, (reprinted as I Need to Love), 1963, Yarborough, 1964, Whispers, 1972, Museum, 1974, Almost A Life, 1975, The Polygamist, 1981, (short stories) Coming Close, 1982, Between the Flags, 1990, Swimming Laps, 1999, (biographies) Jackson Pollock: Energy Made Visible, 1972; author: (with Flora Miller Biddle) Gertrude Vanderbilt Whitney, 1978; author: (plays) In Search of Luigi Pirandello, 1983, (revised as My Small Self), 1998, The Critic, 1986, Beauty Business, 1987, Heart of a Boy, 1993, Married Moments, 1999, Eros and Psyche, 2000; author: (with M. Benderoth) (screenplays) Heart of a Boy, 1997; editor: School of New York, 1959, Give My Regards to Eighth Street: Collected Writings of Morton Feldman, 2001; mem. adv. bd. Cornell Rev., 1977—79; contbr. articles to mags., anthologies and reference vols. Trustee Am. Fedn. Arts, 1958—64, Whitney Mus. Am. Art, 1961—, Broida Mus., 1983—86. With USNR, 1944—46. Recipient awards for short stories including Nelson Algren award, 1983; fellow, Camargo Found., 1991. Mem.: PEN, Dramatists Guild, Authors Guild, Century Assn. (N.Y.C.). Home: 439 E 51st St New York NY 10022-6473 Office Phone: 212-755-5723. E-mail: abob439@aol.com.

FRIEDMAN, CHARLES B., lawyer; b. N.Y.C., Apr. 5, 1960; m. Dena Ellen Friedman; 1 child, Emily Beth. BA, U. Rochester, 1982; JD, Columbia U., 1985. Bar: N.Y. 1986. Assoc. Olwine, Connelly, Chase, O'Donnell & Weyher, N.Y.C., 1985-91, Dechert Price & Rhoads, N.Y.C., 1991-92, Zimet, Haines, Friedman & Kaplan, N.Y.C., 1992-94, ptnr., 1994-98, Morrison & Foerster LLP, N.Y.C., 1998—2003, Duval & Stachenfeld LLP, N.Y.C., 2003—. Home: 85 Green Way Dr Irvington NY 10533-1844 Office: 300 E 42d St New York NY 10017 Office Phone: 212-692-5520.

FRIEDMAN, D. DINA, writer, educator; b. Tacoma Park, Md., June 13, 1957; d. Stanley David and Susan Loeserman Friedman; m. Shel Horowitz, Oct. 9, 1983; children: Alana Horowitz Friedman, Rafael Horowitz Friedman. BA in English, Cornell U., 1978; MSW, U. Conn., 1987. Co-dir. Accurate Writing & More, Northampton, Mass., 1987—; instr. Mt. Holyoke Coll., South Hadley, Mass., 1997—2002; instr. sch. mgmt. U. Mass., Amherst, 2000—. Writing workshop leader Amherst Writers and Artists, 1987—99; tchr. pub. speaking U. Mass., 1987—89. Co-founder Save the Mountain, Hadley, Mass., 1999—. Recipient Pallas award, Athena Press, 1988, Reed Smith prize, Amelia Mag., 1989. Mailing: 16 Barstow Lane Hadley MA 01035

FRIEDMAN, DANIEL MORTIMER, federal judge; b. NYC, Feb. 8, 1916; s. Henry Michael F. and Julia Freedman Friedman; m. Leah Lipson, Jan. 16, 1955 (dec. Dec. 1969); m. Elizabeth Ellis, Oct. 19, 1975 (dec. June 2002). AB, Columbia U., 1937, LLB, 1940. Bar: N.Y. 1941. Practice law, N.Y.C., 1940—42; with SEC, Washington, 1942—51, Justice Dept., Washington, 1951—59, asst. to solicitor gen., 1959—62, 2d asst. to solicitor gen., 1962—68, 1st dep. solicitor gen., 1968—78; chief judge Ct. Claims and U.S. Ct. Appeals, Washington, 1978—89, sr. judge, 1989—. With U.S. Army, 1942—46. Recipient Exceptional Svc. award, Atty. Gen., 1969. Office: US Ct Appeals Federal Circuit 717 Madison Pl NW Washington DC 20439-0002

FRIEDMAN, DENNIS J., lawyer; b. Sept. 28, 1944; BS, U. Pa., 1966; JD, Georgetown U., 1969. Bar: NY 1970. Mem. Morrison & Foerster, NYC; now ptnr. corp. transactions practice group Gibson Dunn & Crutcher LLP, NYC. Articles editor: Georgetown Law Rev., 1968-69. Office: Gibson Dunn & Crutcher 47th Fl 200 Park Ave New York NY 10166-0193 Office Phone: 212-468-8000, 212-351-3900. Office Fax: 212-351-6201. Business E-Mail: dfriedman@gibsondunn.com.

FRIEDMAN, DONALD M., writer, lawyer; b. Newark, June 25, 1943; s. Bert Friedman and Sylvia Worth; children: Jeffrey, Samantha. AB in English, Washington U., St. Louis, 1965; JD, Rutgers U., Camden, 1969; LLM, NYU, 1973. Bar: N.J. 1969, N.Y. 1981. Assoc. Shapira, Steiner & Walder Esqs., Newark, 1969—71; trial atty. N.J. Office of Pub. Defender, Essex County, 1971—72; gen. counsel, dep. dir. High Impact Anti-Crime Program, Newark, 1972—73; assoc. Gruen, Sorkow & Sorkow, Hackensack, NJ, 1973—74; ptnr. Friedman, Carney & Wilson Esqs., Newark, 1974—84; counsel to Essex County Exec. Newark, 1978; solo practice West Orange, NJ, 1984—2000. Mem. adj. faculty Rutgers U., Newark, 1976. Author: The Hand Before the Eye, 2000 (1st Series award for novel Mid List Press, 2000); contbr. short stories to jours. Bd. dirs. Ct. Apptd. Spl. Advocates, Essex County, 1998—99, The New Philharm. Orch., Morristown, NJ, 1998—2000. Office Phone: 973-669-0055.

FRIEDMAN, EDWARD ALAN, finance educator; b. Bayonne, N.J., Sept. 29, 1935; s. Philip Arthur and Esther (Weinstein) F.; m. Arline Joan Lederman, Jan. 13, 1963; children: Millard Timur, Philip Kerim BS, MIT, 1957; postgrad., Stanford U., 1957-58; PhD, Columbia U., 1963; M of Engring. (hon.), Stevens Inst. Tech., 1984. Asst. prof., assoc. prof. physics Stevens Inst. Tech., Hoboken, N.J., 1963-69, dean of coll., 1973-83, v.p. acad. affairs, 1983-85, prof. mgmt., 1980—, chmn. computer planning com., 1982, dir. Ctr. for Improved Engring. and Sci. Edn., 1988—; pres. Global Informatics Inc., 1991—. Vis. prof. Kabul U., 1965-67, dir. engring. coll. devel. program, Afghanistan, 1970-73; cons. Hudson Inst., 1962-63, Doubleday Book Co., 1969, Stevens Acad. Computing, 1985-87; chmn. Civic Affairs Com., Hoboken, 1968-69; vice chmn. bd. edn. Am. Internat. Sch. of Kabul, 1971-72; chmn. bd. dirs. N.Y. Scientists Com. for Pub. Info., 1977-78; chmn. Coun. for Understanding of Tech. in Human Affairs, 1979-82; sr. v.p. Afghanistan Relief Com., 1980—; mem. N.J. Commn. on Grad. Tchr. Edn., 1982-83; mem. vis. panel on measurement and tech. Ednl. Testing Svc., 1983-92; mem. R & D com. Coll. Bd., 1987-90; project mgr. for com. for econ. devel. on policy paper for tech. strategy to improve maths. and sci. edn. in Am. grades K-12, 1995, dir. NSF project to enhance maths. and sci. edn. in schs. throughout N.J. through classroom use of Internet, 1994—; frequent lectr. and cons. on applications of info. tech. Creator (television show) NJ Knowledge Net; co-founder, co-editor: Machine-Mediated Learning Jour., 1983— Trustee Hudson Higher Edn. Consortium, 1974; bd. dirs. Assn. Ind. Colls. and Univs. N.J., 1978-82. Recipient (with R.D. Andrews) Ottens Rsch. award Stevens Inst. Tech., 1970, 1st Class Edn. medal Govt. Afghanistan, 1973, award on impact of tech. on soc. Alfred P. Sloan Found., 1986, Albert Einstein Edn. award State N.J., 1992; Fulbright fellow, 1992. Mem. AAAS, N.Y. Acad. Scis., Am. Phys. Soc., Am. Assn. Engring. Edn., Computer Soc. Home: 901 Hudson St Hoboken NJ 07030-5100 Office: Stevens Inst Tech Castle Point Hoboken NJ 07030

FRIEDMAN, EDWARD DAVID, lawyer, arbitrator; b. Chgo. s. Jacob C. and Bessie (Levison) F.; m. Mary Louise Melia, Nov. 1, 1947 (dec. Feb. 1997); children: Michael, Daniel, Mary Eleanor, Elizabeth; m. Carol Green, Nov. 26, 1999. AB with honors, U. Chgo., 1935, JD cum laude, 1937. Bar: Ill. 1937, U.S. Ct. Appeals 1950, D.C. 1969, U.S. Supreme Ct. 1969. Law clk. to fed. master in chancery, Chgo., 1937-38; assoc. Rosenberg, Toomin & Stein, Chgo., 1938-39; gen. counsel staff SEC, 1939-42; chief counsel OPA, 1942-43; spl. asst. to dep. solicitor and solicitor Dept. Labor, Washington, 1943-48, dep. solicitor of labor, 1965-68, acting solicitor of labor, 1969; ptnr. Bernstein, Alper, Schoene & Friedman, Washington, 1969-75, Highsaw, Mahoney & Friedman, Washington, 1975-80, Friedman & Wirtz, 1980-90; chief law officer 5th regional office, also asst. gen. counsel NLRB, 1948-60; labor counsel to Senator John F. Kennedy, 1960-61, Senator Wayne Morse, 1961-65, U.S. Senate Labor and Pub. Welfare Com., 1961-65; counsel to majority and minority floor mgrs. Senators Clark and Case on Title VII of Civil Rights Bill, 1964; spl. asst. sec. labor fgn. farm labor program, 1965; counsel compaign conduct adminstrv. com. United Steelworkers Am., 1980-89. U.S. del. to OECD, Paris, 1968. Mem. editl. bd. U. Chgo. Law Rev, 1936-37. Mem. town coun., Garrett Park, Md., 1954-58, mayor, 1960-66; mem. Truro (Mass.)Zoning Bd. Appeals, 1999—. U. Chgo. James Nelson Raymond fellow, 1937. Mem. ABA, D.C. Bar Assn., Fed. Bar Assn., Order of Coif, U. Chgo. Alumni Club. Home: 24 Gospel Path PO Box 1123 Truro MA 02666-1123 Personal E-mail: edf1937@cox.net.

FRIEDMAN, EDWARD H., language educator; b. Richmond, Va., Jan. 19, 1948; s. Joseph H. and Sara Sherman Friedman; m. Susan Krug Friedman, May 19, 1974. BA, U. Va., 1970; MA, Johns Hopkins U., Balt., 1971; PhD, Johns Hopkins U., 1974. Asst. prof. Spanish Kalamazoo Coll., 1974—77, Ariz. State U., Tempe, 1977—79, assoc. prof. Spanish, 1979—86, prof. Spanish, 1986—89; prof. Spanish and comparative lit. Ind. U., Bloomington, 1989—2000, Vanderbilt U., Nashville, 2000—. Editor: Bull. of the Comediantes, 1999—. Fellow, Nat. Humanities Ctr., Rsch. Triangle Park, N.C., 1998—99; grantee Rsch. and Lectr. grantee, Fulbright Found., Lisbon, Portugal, 1996, NEH, 1981, 1989, 1993. Mem.: Cervantes Soc. Am. (pres. 2000—). Office: Vanderbilt Univ Dept Spanish/Portuguese VU Sta B351617 Nashville TN 37235-1617

FRIEDMAN, ELI A., nephrologist, educator; b. N.Y.C., Apr. 9, 1933; s. Israel and Ida (Gutman) F.; widowed; children: Amy Louise, Rebecca Alicia, Sara Jo. BS, Bklyn. Coll., 1953; MD, SUNY Downstate Med. Center, 1957; DSc (hon.), Maduri Kamaraj U., India, 1985, L.I. U., 1991. Intern in medicine Harvard Med. Sch., 1957-58; resident in medicine Peter Bent Brigham Hosp., Boston, 1960-61; Am. Heart Assn. rsch. fellow Harvard U., 1958-60; mem. faculty, chief divsn. renal disease Downstate Med. Ctr., Bklyn., 1963—; prof. Health Sci. Ctr. SUNY, Bklyn., 1972—, Disting. Tchg. prof., 1992—, dep. chair dept. medicine, 2003—, chair instnl. rev. bd., 2002—. Bd. dirs. Am. Bur. Med. Aid to China, 1979—, Cleve. Found., 1979—, Bklyn. Neprhology Found., 1978—; Kasperzak lectr. Cleve. Clinic, 1998; Alpha Omega Alpha lectr. SUNY Health Sci. Ctr., Bklyn., 1999; Conrad Pirani lectr. Columbia Coll. Physician and Surgeons, 2000; Helen and Payne Whitney lectr. N. Shore Univ. Hosp., 2001; excellence in dialysis participant, Karachi, Pakistan, 00; mem. faculty masters in nephrology U. Naples, Italy, 2001; rsch. grants coun. reviewer Nat. Natural Sci. Found. of China, 2001; George E. Schreiner lectr. Canisus Coll., Buffalo, 2003; vis. prof. Vanderbilt U., 2002. Author: Acute Renal Failure, 1973, Strategy in Renal Failure, 1978, Diabetic Renal-retinal Syndrome, 1980, Diabetic Renal-retinal Syndrome 3 Therapy, 1986, Diabetic Nephropathy, 1986, Diabetic Renal-retinal Syndrome 4: Management Strategy, 1987; editor: Journal of Diabetic Complications, 1986—. Mem. adv. bd. Nat. Kidney Found. Singapore, 1999. Lt. comdr. USPHS, 1961-63. Named one of Best Drs. in N.Y., N.Y. Mag., 2000, 2001, 2002, 2004, Am.'s Top Drs., 2001, 2002, Best Doctors in Am., 2003; recipient Hoenig award, Nat. Kidney Found., 1986, Silver medal, U. Bologna, 1988, Disting. Svc. to Black Kidney patients award, Howard U., 1989, Physicians award, Am. Assn. Kidney Patients, 1989, Alumni medal, SUNY Downstate Med. Coll., William Dock Master Tchr. award, Alumni Assn. SUNY Health Scis. Ctr., 1992, Recognition award, N.Y. Regional Transplant Program, 1994, Nat. Torchbearer award, Am. Kidney Fund, 1995, Excellence medal, 1996, award, Juvenile Diabetes Found., Bklyn., 1995, Medal of Excellence award, 1996, Torchbearer award, Organ Transplantation and Kidney Disease, 1998, Internat. Torchbearer award, India, 1998, Samuel L. Kountz award, Howard U., 1999, Peter Lundin award, Am. Assn. Kidney Patients, 2001, alumni award in nephrology, Downstate Med. Ctr., 2002, Excellence in Postgrad. Tchg., 2002, Lifetime Achievement award, Internat. Soc. Hemodialysis, 2005; grantee, NIH, Am. Kidney Fund, N.Y. State Kidney Disease Inst., USPHS, N.Y. Kidney Found. Fellow Explorers Club (1st prize photo competition 1995), Royal Coll. Physicians (hon.); mem. ACP (Master 1996), Am. Soc. Nephrology, Internat. Soc. Nephrology, Am. Soc. Artificial Internal Organs (pres. 1987—, editor Transactions 1985—), Am. Soc. Immunology, Transplantation Soc., Assn. Am. Physicians, Internat. Soc. Artificial Organs (pres. 1986), Italian Soc. Nephrology (hon.), Royal Soc. Medicine Belgium (corrs. mem.), German Soc. Clin. Nephrology (hon., Nils Alwall medal 2003), Internat. Soc. Geriatric Nephrology (pres. 2005). Home: 1049 E 17th St Brooklyn NY 11230-4412 Office: 450 Clarkson Ave Brooklyn NY 11203-2056 Office Phone: 718-270-1584. Personal E-mail: elifriedmn@aol.com. *Achievement is as much a function of unswerving persistence, which is a learned behavior pattern, as it is of intellectual endowment, over which we have no control. Effective individuals, though often very bright, have learned to stick with it even after initial or repetitive failure. All of us lose some or even most of the time indicating the need to extract maximal joy from our wins no matter how infrequent the event.*

FRIEDMAN, FRANCES, public relations executive; b. NYC, Apr. 8, 1928; d. Aaron and Bertha (Itzkowitz) Fallick; m. Clifford Jerome Friedman, June 17, 1950; children— Kenneth Lee, Jeffrey Bennett. BBA, CCNY, 1948. Dir. pub. rels. Melia Internat., Madrid, N.Y.C., 1971-73; sr. v.p. Lobsenz-Stevens, N.Y.C., 1973-75; exec. v.p. Howard Rubenstein Assocs., N.Y.C., 1975-83; pres., prin. Frances Friedman Assocs., N.Y.C., 1983-84; pres., chmn. bd. dirs. GCI Group Inc., N.Y.C., 1984-91, pub. rels. and editl. cons., 1991-93; mng. dir. L.V. Power & Assoc., Inc., 1993-97; pub. rels. cons. N.Y.C., 1997—. Media cons. White Ho. on Women's Issues, 1995; participant in Vital Voices Confs., Hillary Clinton's program for women in emerging democracies, 1996; feature writer Kenttribune.com, 2003—. Bd. dirs. United Nations Assn. (NW Ct. chpt.), 2003, Morris-Jumel Mansion, 1999-2001, Contemporary Guidance Svcs, 1999, 2001, City Coll. Fund, N.Y.C., 1970-79; mem. adv. bd. League for Parent Edn., N.Y.C., 1961-65; editor South Shore Democratic Newsletter, North Bellmore, N.Y., 1958-61, press sec. N.Y. State Assembly candidate, 1965, N.Y. State Congl. candidate, 1968; officer Manhasset Dem. Club, N.Y., 1965-69; mem. adv. com. N.Y.C. Coun. candidate, 1985. U. New Haven Bartels fellow, 1993. Mem. Pub. Rels. Soc. Am., Women in Comm. (Matrix award for pub. rels. 1989), The Counselors Acad., Pride and Alarm, City Club N.Y. Democrat. Jewish. Home: 30 Appalachian Rd Kent CT 06757-1009 Personal E-mail: ffried2078@aol.com.

FRIEDMAN, GARY DAVID, epidemiologist; b. Cleve., Mar. 8, 1934; s. Howard N. and Cema C. F.; m. Ruth Helen Schleien, June 22, 1958; children: Emily, Justin, Richard. Student, Antioch Coll., 1951-53; BS in Biol. Sci., U. Chgo., 1956, MD with honors, 1959; MS in Biostats., Harvard Sch. Pub. Health, 1965. Diplomate Am. Bd. Internal Medicine. Intern, resident Harvard Med. Svcs., Boston City Hosp., 1959-61; 2d yr. resident Univ. Hosps. Cleve., 1961-62; med. officer heart disease epidemiology study Nat. Heart Inst., Framingham, Mass., 1962-66; chief epidemiology unit, field and tng. sta., heart disease ctrl. program USPHS, San Francisco, 1966-68; sr. epidemiologist divsn. rsch. Kaiser Permanente Med. Care Program, Oakland, Calif., 1968-76, asst. dir. epidemiology and biostats., 1976-91, dir., 1991-98, sr. investigator, 1998-99, adj. investigator, 1999—; cons. prof. Dept. Health Rsch. and Policy Stanford U. Sch. Medicine, 1998—. Rsch. fellow, then rsch. assoc. preventive medicine Harvard Med. Sch., 1962-66; lectr. dept. biomed. and environ. health scis., sch. pub. health U. Calif. Berkeley, 1968-95; lectr. epidemiology and biostats. U. Calif. Sch. Medicine, San Francisco, 1980-2000, asst. clin. prof. 1967-75, assoc. clin. prof., 1975-92 depts. medicine and family and cmty. medicine; US-USSR working group sudden cardiac death NHLBI, 1975-82, com. on epidemiology and veterans follow-up studies Nat. Rsch. Coun., 1980-85, subcom. on twins, 1980-94, epidemiology and disease ctrl. study sect. NIH, 1982-86, US Preventive Svcs. Task Force, 1984-88, scientific rev. panel on toxic air contaminants State of Calif., 1988—, adv. com. Merck Found./Soc. Epidemiol. Rsch., Clin. Epidemiology Fellowships, 1990-94; sr. advisor expert panel on preventive svcs. USPHS, 1991-96. Author: Primer of Epidemiology, 1974, 5th edit. 2004; assoc. editor, then editor Am. Jour. Epidemiology, 1988-96, 99—; mem. editl. bd. HMO Practice, 1991-98, Jour. Med. Screening, 1997—; contbr. over 280 articles to profl. jours., chpts. to books; composer: Autumn for oboe and piano (First prize Composers Today Competition Music Tchrs. Assn. Calif. 1999), Fugue for Four Winds (Second prize Music Tchrs. Assn. Calif. 2000). Oboist San Francisco Civic Symphony, 1990—, Symphony Parnassus, 1994-2004, Bohemian Club Band, 1994—, Coll. Marin Orch., 2004—; bd. dirs. Chamber Musicians No. Calif., Oakland, 1991-98. Sr. surgeon USPHS, 1962-68. Recipient Roche award for Outstanding Performance as Med. Student; Merit grantee Nat. Cancer Inst., 1987, Outstanding Investigator grantee, 1989, 94; named to Disting. Alumni Hall of Fame Cleve. Heights High Sch., 1991. Fellow Am. Heart Assn. (chmn. com. on criteria and methods 1969-71, chmn. program com. 1973-76, coun. epidemiol.), Am. Coll. Physicians; mem. APHA, Am. Epidemiol. Soc. (mem. com. 1982-86, pres. 1999-2000), Am. Soc. Preventive Oncology, Internat. Epidemiol. Assn., Soc. Epidemiologic Rsch. (exec. com. 1998-2001), Med. Biol. Alumni Assn. U. Chgo. (Disting. Svc. award 2000), Phi Beta Kappa, Alpha Omega Alpha, Delta Omega. Achievements include research on cancer, cardiovascular disease, gallbladder disease, effects of smoking, alcohol and medicinal drugs, evaluation of health screening tests. Office: Stanford U Sch Medicine Dept Health Rsch and Policy Redwood Bldg Rm T210 Stanford CA 94305-5405 E-mail: gdf@stanford.edu.

FRIEDMAN, GEORGE, lawyer; b. Bronx, NY, Apr. 18, 1934; m. Vivian Friedman; children: Anthony, Paul. BA, U. Vt., 1956; LLB, NYU, 1959. Bar: NY 1960, US Dist. Ct. So. & Ea. Districts NY 1960. Assoc. Kronish & Lieb, 1959—64; gen. practitioner pvt. practice, 1964—94; mem. NY State Assembly, 1977—94; justice NY State Supreme Court 12th Jud. Dist., 1995—2002; ptnr. Wilson, Elser, Moskowitz, Edelman & Dicker LLP, NYC. Bronx Dem. County Leader, 1986—94; mem. Dem. Nat. Com., 1988—94; commr. NY State Commn. of Investigation, 2002—; mem. Commn. to Promote Pub. Confidence in Jud. Elections, 2003—04. Mem.: Assn. Supreme Ct. Justices of the City of NY, NY State Assn. Supreme Ct. Justices. Office: Wilson Elser

Moskowtiz Edelman & Dicker LLP 23rd Fl 150 E 42nd St New York NY 10017-5639 Office Phone: 212-490-3000 ext. 2666. Office Fax: 212-490-3038. Business E-Mail: friedmang@wemed.com.

FRIEDMAN, GEORGE JERRY, aerospace engineer, engineering executive; b. N.Y.C., Mar. 22, 1928; s. Sander and Ruth (Oberlander) F.; m. Ruthanne Goldstein, Sept. 7, 1953; children— Sanford, Gary, David BS, U. Calif.-Berkeley, 1949; MS, UCLA, 1956, PhD, 1967. Registered profl. mech. engr., controls engr., Calif. Mech. engring. assoc. Dept. Water and Power, Los Angeles, 1949-56; devel. engr. Servo Mechanisms, Hawthorne, Calif., 1956-60; v.p. Northrop Corp., Los Angeles, 1960-94; exec. v.p., rsch. dir. Space Studies Inst., Princeton, N.J., 1994—. Mem. indsl. adv. group NATO, Brussels, 1977-78; guest lectr. UCLA, 1983—, Calif. State U., Northridge, 1983—, dir. trust fund, 1984-89; cons. to sci. adv. bd. USAF, Washington, 1985—, bd. govs. Aerospace and Elec. Sys. Soc., L.A., 1985—, v.p. publs., 1999-2001; adj. prof. U. So. Calif., L.A., 1994—; pres. Internat. Coun. on Sys. Engring., 1994, fellow 1998. Contbr. articles to profl. jours. Served as pfc. U.S. Army, 1950-52 Recipient Engring. Excellence award San Fernando Valley Engring. Council, 1983 Fellow IEEE (Baker award 1970), AIAA (assoc.; chmn. planetary def. subcom. 1995-97); mem. Am. Def. Preparedness Assn. (exec. com., preparedness award 1985). Democrat. Jewish. Home and Office: 5084 Gloria Ave Encino CA 91436-1529 E-mail: gfriedma@usc.edu.

FRIEDMAN, GERALD MANFRED, geologist, educator; b. Berlin, July 23, 1921; came to US, 1946, naturalized, 1950; s. Martin and Frieda (Cohn) F.; m. Sue Tyler Theilheimer, June 27, 1948; children: Judith Fay Friedman Rosen, Sharon Mira Friedman Azaria, Devorah Paula Friedman Zweibach, Eva Jane Friedman Scholle, Wendy Tamar Friedman Spanier. BSc, U. London, 1945, DSc, 1977; MA, Columbia U., 1950, PhD, 1952; DSc (hon.), U. Heidelberg, Fed. Republic Germany, 1986. Agrl. laborer, England, 1938-39; baker, 1940-42; internee Brit. Army, 1940; lectr. Chelsea Coll., London, 1944-45; analytical chemist J. Lyons & Co., 1945—46, E.R. Squibb & Sons (now Bristol Myers-Squibb), New Brunswick, 1946—49; asst. geology Columbia U., 1950; temp. geologist NY State Geol. Survey, 1950; from instr. to asst. prof. geology U. Cin., 1950-54; cons. geologist Sault Ste. Marie, Ont., Can., 1954-56; from sr. rsch. scientist to supr. sedimentary geology rsch. Pan Am. Petroleum Corp. (now BP), 1956-64; Fulbright vis. prof. geology Hebrew U., Jerusalem, 1964; prof. geology Rensselaer Poly. Inst., 1964-84, prof. emeritus, 1984—; prof. geology Bklyn. Coll., 1984—88, Disting. prof. geology, 1988—2004, Disting. prof. geology emeritus, 2004, grad. dep., 2000—02; prof. earth and environ. sci. Grad. Sch. CUNY, 1984—88, disting. prof. earth and environ. sci., 1988—2004, disting. prof. emeritus, 2004—, dep. exec. officer, 1992-94; pres. Gerry Exploration Inc., 1982-88. Rsch. sci. Hudson Labs., Columbia, 1965-69, rsch. assoc. dept. geology Lamont Geol. Obs., 1968-73; vis. prof. U. Heidelberg, 1967; cons. sci. Inst. Petroleum Rsch. and Geophysics, Israel, 1967-71; lectr. Oil & Gas Cons. Internat., 1968-98; pres. Northeastern Sci. Found. Inc., 1979—; vis. scientist Geol. Survey of Israel, 1970-73, 78; mem. Com. Sci. Soc. Pres., 1974-76; Gerald M. Friedman fellow Inst. Earth Sci., Hebrew U., Israel, 1990—; vis. prof. Martin-Luther-Univ., Halle-Wittenberg, Germany, 1998. Co-author: Principles of Sedimentology (Outstanding Acad. Books, Choice, 1978/79), 1978, Exploration for Carbonate Petroleum Reservoirs, 1982, Exercises in Sedimentology, 1982, Principles of Sedimentary Deposits: Stratigraphy and Sedimentology, 1992; pub. Northeastern Environ. Sci., 1982-90; editor: Jour. Sedimentary Petrology (now Jour. Sedimentary Rsch.), 1964-70 (Best Paper award 1961, hon. mention 1964, 66, Twenhofel medal 1997), Northeastern Geology (now Northeastern Geology and Environ. Sci.), 1979—, Earth Sci. History, 1982-93, Carbonates and Evaporites, 1986—, 10th Internat. Congress on Sedimentology, 1978, Oil Industry History, 1999-2003; sect. co-editor: Chem. Abstracts (Mineral. and Geol. Chemistry), 1962-69, abstractor, 1952-69; editl. bd. Jour. Geol. Edn., 1951-55, Sedimentary Rsch., 1967-95, Israel Jour. Earth Sci., 1971-76, Coral Reef Newsletter, 1973-75, Jour. Geology, 1977—, GeoJour., 1977-83, Facies, 1987—2004; mng. editor Sedimentology for Earth Sci. Revs., 1992-2005; contbg. co-editor: Carbonate Sedimentology in Central Europe, 1968, Hypersaline Ecosystems: The Gavish Sabkha, 1985, editor, contbr.: Depositional Environments in Carbonate Rocks, 1969; co-editor: Modern Carbonate Environments, 1983, Lecture Notes in Earth Sci., 1985—; founding editor: Earth Sci. History, 1982, hon. life mem.; contbr. articles to profl. jour.; patentee in field Phys. edn. com., judo instr. Tulsa YMCA, 1958-64, chmn. awards com., 1962-64; adviser, instr. Judo Club, Rensselaer Poly. Inst., 1964-84; bd. dir. Troy Jewish Cmty. Coun., 1966-72, 74-77; v.p. Temple Beth El, 1986-89, pres., 1989-91, bd. dir., 1965-76; bd. dir. Leo Baeck Inst., NYC, 1986—; v.p., chmn. pub. com. Drake Well Found., 1998-2003, v.p., 2002—. Recipient award for devoted svc. Tulsa YMCA, 1963, Hon. West Virginian award, 1998, Hollis D. Hedberg award in energy Inst. for the Study Earth and Man, So. Meth. U., 2004, Disting. Svc. award SEPM, 2004; named hon. alumnus dept. geology Bklyn. Coll., 1989; grantee Office Naval Rsch., AEC, Dept. Energy, Petroleum Rsch. Fund, NY Gas Assn., NY State Energy Rsch. and Devel. Authority. Fellow: AAAS (councillor 1979—80, soc. rep. geology/geography sect. 1989—97), Soc. Econ. Geologists, N.Y. Acad. Sci. (vice chair geol. sci. sect. 1993—94, chmn. 1994—96, vice chair geol. sci. sect. 1996—97, chmn. 1997—2001), Geol. Assn. Can., Geol. Soc. London (life, chartered geologist, hon. fellow 1996), Mineral Soc. Am. (mem. nominating com. fellows 1967—69, mem. awards com. 1977—78), Mineral Soc. Gt. Brit. (abstractor mineralogical abstracts 1963—64), Geol. Soc. Am. (sr. chmn. sect. program com. 1969, candidate sect. chmn. 1969, publ. com. 1980—82, chmn. overseas pub. rels. com. internat. divsn. 1996—97, vice chair history geology divsn. 1997—99, chair 1999—2000, mem. awards nom. com. sedimentary geol. divsn. 1999—2000, chair history geology awards com. 2000—01, Mary Rabbit History Geology award 2005); mem.: Kodokan, Cin. Mineral Soc. (v.p. program chmn. 1953—54), N.Y. State Mus.-N.Y. State Geol. Survey (James Hall medal 1997), N.Y. State Geol. Assn. (pres. 1978—79, bd. dir. 1979—84), Geosci. Info. Soc. (mem. membership com. 1983—85, ad hoc com. to devel. criteria for reviewing geosci. jour. 1985—86), Assn. Earth Sci. Editors (v.p. 1970—71, pres. 1971—72, host 1991, Outstanding Editorial Pub. Contributions Award 1993), Nat. Assn. Geosci. Tchr. (nat. treas. 1951—55, subscription and circulation mgr. 1951—55, chmn. organizing and nominating com. establish east-ctrl.sect. 1952—53, assoc. editor Jour. of Geosci. Edn. 1953—55, pres. Okla 1962—63, pres. Ea. sect. 1983—84, Disting. Svc. Award 2001), Geol. Vereinigung, Deutsche Geol. Gesellschaft, Soc. Venezolana Historia Geociencias (intenat. corr. mem.), Indian Assn. Sedimentologists (mem. governing coun. 1978—82), Serbian Yugoslavian Geol. Soc. (hon. 1998), Geol. Soc. Israel (hon. 1992), Internat. Assn. Sedimentologists (nat. corr. USA 1971—73, v.p. 1971—75, pres. 1975—78, program com. Internat. Sedimentological Congress 1978, excursion com. Internat. Sedimentological Congress 1982, hon. mem. 1986), Geologists' Assn. (life), Am. Geol. Inst. (governing bd. 1971—72, 1974—75, Legendary Geoscientists award Sedimentology 2005), New Eng. Intercollegiate Geol. Conf. (convenor, editor 1979), Capital Dist. Geologists Assn. (chmn. program 1966—73), Hudson-Mohawk Profl. Geologists Assn. (bd. dir. 1995—2001, program com. 1996—97, chmn. program com. 1997—2001), History of the Earth Sci. Soc. (hon.; co-founder 1981), So. Venezolana Historia Geociencias (corr.; internat. corr. mem.), Paleontol. Soc., Soc. for Sedimentary Geology (sect. pres. pro tem 1966—67, chmn. Shepard award selection com. 1966—67, sect. pres. 1967—68, pres. 1974—75, Best Paper award Gulf Coast sect. 1974, Disting. Svc. award 2004), Am. Assn. Petroleum Geologists (chmn. carbonate rock com. 1965—69, mem. rsch. com. 1965—71, lectr. continuing edn. program 1967—88, chmn. Persian Gulf liaison com. 1968—70, marine geology com. 1970—74, Disting. lectr. 1972—73, adv. coun. 1974—75, disting. lectr. com. 1975—78, rsch. com. 1976—82, ho. of dels. 1977—80, Eastern Section sect. sec. 1979—80, sect. treas. 1980—81, alt. del. 1980—83, sect. v.p. 1981—82, sect. pres 1982—83, mem. vis. geologists program com. 1982—85, membership com. 1982—87, div. profl. affairs rep. from Eastern sect. 1983—84, hon. mem. Eastern sect. 1984, com. on convs. 1984—85, nat. v.p. 1984—85, ho. of dels. 1984—87, mem. select com. on future petroleum geologist 1985—86, chmn. sect. awards com. 1989—92, nat. hon. mem. 1990, ho. of dels. 1991—93, alt. del. 1993—98, sect. chmn. tech. program com. 1994—95, vice chair standing com. hist. petroleum geology 1997—2000, chair 2000—01, ho. of dels. 2002—05, cand. for chmn. ho. of dels. 2004, John T. Galey Meml. Award medal 1993, sect. cert. of merit 1995, Disting. Educator award 1996, Nat. Disting. Svc. award 1998, Sidney Powers Meml. award 2000, Divsn. Environ. Scis. Tchg. award 2001, award for excellence and dedication in tchg. environ. geology 2001), Am. Chem. Soc. (group leader 1962—63), Am. Inst. Profl. Geologists (cert.), Russian Acad. Nat. Sci. US sect. (Kapitsa Gold medal of honor 1996), Empire State Judo Assn., Okla. Judo Fedn. (pres 1959—60, v.p. 1961—64), U.S. Judo Fedn. (San Dan, cert. judo tchr.), Amateur Athletic Union (judo com. 1963, Okla.), Honorable Ky. Cols., Explorers Club NY, Sigma Xi, Sigma Gamma Epsilon (nat. pres. 1982—86). Home: 32 24th St Troy NY 12180-1915

FRIEDMAN, GREG STUART, investment company executive, lawyer, investment advisor; b. Washington, Oct. 3, 1951; s. Adolph Aaron and Florence (Haves) F.; children: Justin, Samantha, Brandon; m. Susan Hope Movshow, Feb. 9, 1996. Student, Emory U., 1969-71; BA in Urban Studies with honors, Washington U., St. Louis, 1972; JD, Boston U., 1976; postgrad., U. Md. Bus. Sch., 1981-84. Bar: Md. 1976, D.C. 1977, U.S. Dist. Ct. Md., U.S. Dist. Ct. D.C., U.S. Ct. Appeals (4th cir.), U.S. Supreme Ct. Assoc. Meisnere & Mika, P.C., Washington, 1976-79; counsel, asst. corp. sec. Nat. Corp. for Housing Partnerships, Washington, 1979-80; sr. assoc. Mahn Franklin & Goldenberg PC, Washington, 1982-85; prin. Deso & Greenberg, P.C., Washington, 1988-90; pvt. practice, Washington, 1980—82, 1985—88, Rockville, Md., 1990—; pres. Entity Mgmt. LLC, 1998—. Mem. D.C. LLC Legis. Adv. Panel, 1997. Trustee Hebrew Free Loan Assn. D.C., Rockville, 1993—; mem. alumni admission program Washington U., 1996—. Mem. Tax Mgmt. Real Estate Study Group. Democrat. Jewish. Avocations: skiing, watersports, investment matters. Home: 6216 Mazwood Rd Rockville MD 20852-3528 Office: Entity Mgmt LLC 109 N Adams St Rockville MD 20850 Office Phone: 301-340-0430. Personal E-mail: friedman.g@gmail.com.

FRIEDMAN, GREGORY H., energy administrator; BBA, Temple U.; MBA, Fairleigh Dickinson U. Sr. auditor U.S. Army Audit Agy., 1968-74; dep. dir. Office of Contingency Planning, FEA, Washington, 1974-80, assoc. dir. Gasoline Rationing Implementation Office, 1980-82; with Office of Insp. Gen. Dept. of Energy, Washington, 1982—, dep. asst. insp. gen. for audit ops., 1985-94, dep. insp. gen. for audit svcs., 1994-97, prin. dep. insp. gen., 1997-98, acting insp. gen., 1998, insp. gen., 1998—. Guest lectr. audit matters and govtl. affairs Princeton U., George Washington U. Office: Dept of Energy Insp Gen 1000 Independence Ave SW Washington DC 20585-0002

FRIEDMAN, HAROLD EDWARD, lawyer; b. Cleve., Apr. 7, 1934; s. Joseph and Mary (Schreibman) F.; m. Nancy Schweid, Aug. 20, 1961; children: Deborah, Jay, Susan. BS, Ohio State U., 1956; LL.B., Case Western Res U., 1959. Bar: Ohio 1960. Practiced in, Cleve., since 1960; ptnr. Simon, Haiman, Gutfeld, Friedman & Jacobs, 1967-80, Ulmer & Berne, 1981—; chair real property practice group. Sec., trustee Harry K. and Emma R. Fox Charitable Found.; pres. Jewish Vocat. Svcs., Cleve.; pres. Internat. Assn. Jewish Vocat. Svcs.; pres. Cleve. Hillel Found.; vice chmn. endowment fund Jewish Cmty. Fedn. Cleve., bd. dirs.; pres. Metro Health Found.; bd. dirs. Bur. Jewish Edn., Jewish Convalescence and Rehab. Ctr., Big Bros. Greater Cleve., Jewish Cmty. Fedn. Cleve., Jewish Family Svc. Assn., YES, Inc., Bellefaire/Jewish Children's Bur. Recipient Kane Leadership award Jewish Community Fedn. Cleve., 1974 Mem. ABA, Ohio Bar Assn., Cleve. Bar Assn., Oakwood Country Club. Home: 23149 Laureldale Rd Cleveland OH 44122-2101 Office: 900 Bond Ct Bldg Cleveland OH 44114 Office Phone: 216-931-6130. Personal E-mail: hedwfried@aol.com. Business E-Mail: hfriedman@ulmer.com.

FRIEDMAN, HARVEY MICHAEL, infectious diseases educator; b. Montreal, May 29, 1944; came to U.S., 1971; s. Sidney and Sybil (Garfinkle) F.; m. Cynthia Diane Mickey, Apr. 12, 1980; children: Lisa, Steven, Julie. BS, McGill U., 1965, MD, 1969. Cert. in internal medicine 1975, in infectious diseases 1976. Intern, resident Jewish Gen. Hosp., Montreal, 1969-71; fellow in virology Wistar Inst., Phila., 1971-73; fellow in infectious disease U. Pa. Hosp., Phila., 1973-75; asst. prof., assoc. prof. Med. Sch. U. Pa., Phila., 1975-91, prof. Med. Sch., 1991—. Med. dir. Clin. Virology Lab. Children's Hosp., Phila., 1975—96; chief infectious diseases U. Pa., 1990—. Contbr. numerous papers and book chpts. Grantee NIH, Found., 1978—. Fellow: Infectious Disease Soc. Am.; mem.: AAAS, Am. Clin. and Climatological Assn., Assn. Am. Physicians, Am. Soc. Clin. Investigation. Achievements include description of novel mechanisms used by herpes simplex virus glycoproteins that favor virus escape from immune attack. Office: U Pa Med Sch 502 Johnson Pavilion Philadelphia PA 19104-6073 Business E-Mail: hfriedma@mail.med.upenn.edu.

FRIEDMAN, HERBERT A., rabbi, educator, not-for-profit fundraiser; b. New Haven, Sept. 25, 1918; s. Israel and Rae (Aaronson) F.; children from previous marriage: Judith Rae, Daniel Stephen, Joan Michal; m. Francine Bensley, June 28, 1963; children: David Herbert, Charles Edward. BA, Yale U., 1938; MHL, Jewish Inst. Religion, 1943; DD (hon.), Hebrew Union Coll., 1969; PhD (hon.), Tel Aviv Univ., 2002. Ordained rabbi, 1943. Rabbi Temple Emanuel, Denver, 1943-52, Milw., 1952-55; exec. chmn. Nat. United Jewish Appeal, N.Y.C., 1955-75; pres. Am. Friends of Tel Aviv U., N.Y.C., 1982-85, Wexner Heritage Found., 1985-95, founding pres. emeritus, 1995—. Author: Collected Speeches, 1971, Roots of the Future, 1999. Chaplain (capt.) U.S. Army, 1944—47, ETO. Mem. Central Conf. Am. Rabbis, Yale Club (N.Y.C.). Home: 500 E 77th St Apt 2519 New York NY 10162-0008 Office: Wexner Heritage Found 551 Madison Ave New York NY 10022-3212

FRIEDMAN, IRA HUGH, surgeon; b. N.Y.C., July 17, 1933; s. Leonard Seymour and Ruth (Binder) F.; m. Erika Berger, Oct. 22, 1961; children: Richard Lawrence, Joanne Beth BA, NYU, 1953, MD, 1957. Diplomate Am. Bd. Surgery, Nat. Bd. Med. Examiners. Intern, resident in surgery Beth Isreal Med. Ctr., N.Y.C., 1957-59, 61-63; surg. resident Bellevue Hosp., N.Y.C., 1959-60; practice medicine specializing in surgery N.Y.C., 1963—. Attending surgeon Beth Israel Med. Ctr., pres. med. bd., 1981-82; assoc. clin. prof. surgery Albert Einstein Coll. Medicine; med. adv. to N.Y.C. dir. SSS, 1968. Contbr. articles to profl. jours. Bd. dirs. Union Orthodox Jewish Congregations Am., Am. Com. for Shaare Zedek Hosp. of Jerusalem, Yeshiva Sha-alvim, Israel; pres. P'Tach; co-chmn. bd. dirs. Yeshiva Chofetz Chaim, N.Y.C. Recipient Koach award Israel Bond Orgn., 1977; N.Y. Heart Assn. fellow, 1960-61 Fellow ACS (elected gov. 1996), Am. Coll. Gastroenterology, Am. Soc. Colon and Rectal Surgeons, Royal Soc. Medicine; mem. AMA, N.Y. Acad. Medicine, N.Y. Surg. Soc., Soc. Surgery of Alimentary Tract, Soc. Am. Gastrointestinal Endoscopic Surgeons, Am. Gastroent. Assn., Am. Soc. Gen. Surgeons, Am. Hernia Soc., Am. Soc. Breast Surgeons, N.Y. Gastroent. Assn., N.Y. Cancer Soc., N.Y. Soc. Colon and Rectal Surgeons, Collegium Internationale Chirugiae Digestive, N.Y. State Med. Assn., N.Y. County Med. Assn. Home: 1175 Park Ave New York NY 10128-1211

FRIEDMAN, J. ROGER, publisher; b. N.Y.C., Oct. 26, 1933; s. Arnold Darcy and Judith (Scheinberg) F.; m. Patricia Mosle, Dec. 1, 1962; children: Amanda, Randall. BA in English, Williams Coll., 1955. Salesman Chain Store Age, Drug Editions, N.Y.C., 1957-61; founder, sales mgr. Discount Store News, N.Y.C., 1961-63, publ. dir., 1963-65; v.p. sales Lebhar-Friedman, Inc., N.Y.C., 1965-68, exec. v.p., 1968-70, pres., 1970—; sec. Chain Store Guide, N.Y.C., 1970—, Dowden Health Media, Inc. Bd. dirs. Upper Pecos Assn., N.Mex., 1971, Brush Ranch Sch., N. Mex., 1974, pres., 1997—; bd. dirs. Students in Free Enterprise, 1977—, Am. Bus. Press, 1994—, Freedom Communications, 2000—; trustee, chmn. Bus. Press Ednl. Found., McElvain Oil & Gas Co.; hon. trustee Temple Rodeph Shalom, N.Y.C., 1987. Mem. Lotos (pres. 1983-87), Williams (N.Y.C.) (pres. 1991-95, hon. bd. mem.). Office: Lebhar-Friedman Inc 425 Park Ave Ste 501 New York NY 10022-3549

FRIEDMAN, JAMES DENNIS, lawyer; b. Dubuque, Iowa, Jan. 11, 1947; s. Elmer J. and Rosemary Catherine (Stillmunks) F.; m. Kathleen Marie Maersch, Aug. 16, 1969; children: Scott, Ryan, Andrea, Sean. AB in Polit. Sci., Marquette U., 1969; JD, U. Notre Dame, 1972. Bar: Wis. 1972, U.S. Ct. Appeals (D.C. cir.) 1973, U.S. Ct. Appeals (7th cir.) 1976, U.S. Supreme Ct. 1978, U.S. Ct. Appeals (6th cir.) 1989, Ill. 1996, U.S. Tax Ct. 1997. Pvt. practice, Milw., 1972—81; ptnr. Quarles & Brady, LLP, Milw., 1981—. Presenter in field; mem. legis. coun. spl. study com. on regulation of fin. instns. State of Wis., 1986-87; bd. dirs. Concours Motors, Inc., Wis. Equal Justice Fund, Inc., pres.-elect, 2005; mem. Wis. Dept. Fin. Instns. task force on fin. competitiveness 2005, State of Wis., 2000; mem., vice chair State of Wis. Supreme Ct., Office of Lawyer Regulation Preliminary Rev. Com., 2000-; mem. Gov.'s Adv. Coun. on Jud. Selection of the State of Wis., Ozaukee County, 2002. Mng. editor: Notre Dame Law Rev., 1971—72; contbr. articles to profl. jours. Alderman 4th and 7th dists. Mequon, Wis., 1979-85, pres. common coun., 1980-82, bd. ethics 1996-98, 2000—, chair blue ribbon visioning com. 1998-99; bd. dirs. Weyenrg, Pub. Libr. Found. Inc., 1983—, pres., 1984—; bd. dirs. Ptnrs. Advancing Values in Edn. Inc., 1987—, Wis. Law Found., 1998—; bd. visitors Marquette U. Ctr. for Study of Entrepreneurship, Milw., 1987-95; bd. dirs. Ozaukee Family Svcs., 1983-99, sec., 1993-98; bd. dirs. Notre Dame Club of Milw., 1984-88, sec., 1978, v.p., 1986-88; bd. dirs. Marquette Club of Milw., 1987-88; chair attys. unit United Way Fund Dr. Greater Milw., 1987; mem. St. James Ch., Mequon. Named Outstanding Sr., Coll. of Liberal Arts, Marquette U., 1969. Fellow Wis. Law Found., Am. Bar Found.; mem. ABA (banking law com. sect. bus. law); State Bar Wis. (chair bd. govs. 1999-2000, chair exec. com. 1999-2000, fin. com. 1997-98, strategic planning task force 1997-98, mem. leadership devel. com. 2004-, bd. govs. 1996-2000, exec. com. 1998-2000, internat. transactions sect. bd. dirs. 1984-99, sec. and chair-elect 1988-89, chair 1989-90, del. to ABA Ho. of Dels. 1980-82, standing com. on adminstrn. justice and judiciary 1979-81, legal edn. and bar admissions com. 1984-89, com. on minority lawyers 1992-99, chmn. 1997-1999, bd. dirs. young lawyers divsn. 1978-82, chmn. bar admission stds. and requirements com. 1979, So. Regional chair capital fund campaign 1998-99), Milw. Bar Assn., Wis. Acad. Trial Lawyers (bd. dirs. 1980-82), Wis. Bankers Assn., Milw. Country Club. Roman Catholic. Avocations: tennis, golf. Office: Quarles & Brady LLP 411 E Wisconsin Ave Ste 2040 Milwaukee WI 53202-4497 Office Phone: 414-277-5735. Personal E-mail: jdf@quarles.com.

FRIEDMAN, JAMES MOSS, lawyer; b. Cleve., Aug. 1, 1941; s. Senor I. and Rose L. (Moskowitz) F.; m. Ruth E. Aidlin, Aug. 2, 1964; children: Laura M., Seth M. AB, Dartmouth Coll., 1963; JD, Harvard U., 1966. Bar: Ohio 1966, U.S. Ct. Appeals (6th cir.) 1966, U.S. Dist. Ct. (no. dist.) Ohio 1967. Law clk. U.S. Ct. Appeals, 6th Cir., 1966-67; assoc. Gottfried, Ginsberg, Guren & Merritt, Cleve., 1967-71; chief staff Ohio Gov. John J. Gilligan, Columbus, 1971-72; ptnr. Guren, Merritt, Feibel, Sogg & Cohen, Cleve., 1972-84, Benesch, Friedlander, Coplan & Aronoff, Cleve., 1984—. Chmn. Ohio Civil Rights Commn., 1972-74; dir. Overseas Pvt. Investment Corp., Washington, 1978-82; spl. counsel Ohio Atty. Gen., Cleve., 1983-94. Co-author: The Silent Alliance, 1984. Mem. Am. Jewish Com., 1981—; vice chmn. nat. fin. coun. Dem. Nat. Com., 1975—85; pres. Fedn. for Cmty. Planning, Cleve., 1989—92; bd. dirs. United Way Svcs., Cleve., 1989—92, Cuyahoga C.C. Found., 1989—95, Citizens League Greater Cleve., 1989—95, v.p., 1993—95; pres. Fairmount Temple, 1993—96; pres. Cleve. chpt. Am. Jewish Com., 1991—93; mem. nat. bd. trustees Union for Reform Judaism, 1991—, mem. exec. com., 1997—. Jewish. Office: Benesch Friedlander 2300 BP Town Bldg 200 Public Sq Ste 2300 Cleveland OH 44114-2378

FRIEDMAN, JAMES WINSTEIN, economist, educator; b. Cleve., Sept. 25, 1936; s. Theodore and Gertrude (Winstein) F.; m. Marcia Sherman, Aug. 11, 1957; children: Nancy Elizabeth, Robert U. Student, MIT, 1954-56; BA, U. Mich., 1959; MA, Yale U., 1960, PhD, 1963; doctorate (hon.), U. Paris, 2004. Instr., then asst. prof. econs. Yale U., 1963-68; assoc. prof. U. Rochester (N.Y.), 1968-72, prof. econs., 1972-83; prof. Va. Poly Inst., Blacksburg, 1983-85; Kenan prof. U. N.C., Chapel Hill, 1985-2001, Kenan prof. emeritus, 2001—. Mem. rsch. staff Cowles Found., 1963-68, asst. dir., 1964-66; vis. prof. U. Bielefeld, Fed. Republic Germany, 1976, 87-88, Hebrew U., Jerusalem, 1979, Cath. U. Louvain, Belgium, 1987, 91, 99, U. Paris, 1991, 93, 2000, U. Alicante, Spain, 1992, U. Kobe, Japan, 1994. Author: Oligopoly and the Theory of Games, 1977, The Theory of Oligopoly, 1983, Game Theory with Applications to Economics, 1986, 2d edit., 1990; co-author: An Experiment in Noncooperative Oligopoly, 1979; editor: Problems of Coordination in Economic Activity, 1994; assoc. editor Japanese Econ. Rev., 1994—, Regional Sci. and Urban Econs., 1997-2005, Games and Econ. Behavior, 1998—; contbr. articles to profl. jours. Fellow Econometric Soc. (assoc. editor jour. 1975-81), Game Theory Soc. Avocations: cooking, reading.

FRIEDMAN, JANE, publishing executive; BA in English, NYU, 1967. Joined Random House, 1968, with publicity dept., exec. v.p. Knopf Pub. Group, pub. Vintage Books, founder, pres. Random House Audio, exec. v.p. Random House Inc., mem. exec. com.; pres., CEO HarperCollins, NYC, 1997—. Co-chair pub. divsn., vice chair entertainment, media and comms. divsn. UJA; mem. Am. adv. com. Jerusalem Internat. Book Fair; chmn. bd. dirs., adv. com. Assn. Am. Pubs.; bd. dirs. Poets and Writers; adv. com. Literacy Ptnrs., Yale U. Press. Named Person of Yr., LMP, 1999; named one of 200 Women Legends, Leaders and Trailblazers, Vanity Fair, 1998, N.Y.'s 100 Most Influential Women in Bus., Crain's N.Y. Bus., 1999, Am.'s 100 Most Important Women, Ladies Home Jour., 1999, 101 Most Important People in Entertainment, Entertainment Weekly, 1999—2002; recipient Matrix award, Women Who Change the World, 2001. Office: HarperCollins 10 E 53rd St New York NY 10022-5299

FRIEDMAN, JEFFREY J., lawyer; b. Perth Amboy, NJ, Aug. 14, 1956; BA, Franklin & Marshall Coll., 1978; JD cum laude, Villanova U., 1981. Bar: NY 1982, NJ 1982, US Ct. Appeals, 2nd and 3rd Cir., US Dist. Ct., NJ, US Dist. Ct., Ea. Dist. Mich., US Dist. Ct., Ea. and So Dist. NY, US Supreme Ct. Ptnr., mem. Bankruptcy, Reorganization and Creditors' Rights Practice Katten Muchin Zavis Rosenman, NYC. Mem.: ABA, Assn. Bar of City NY, NY State Bar Assn. Office: Katten Muchin Zavis Rosenman 575 Madison Ave New York NY 10022 Office Phone: 212-940-7035. Office Fax: 212-940-7109. E-mail: jeff.friedman@kmzr.com.

FRIEDMAN, JEFFREY ROBERT, psychiatrist, educator; b. Mpls., May 26, 1956; s. Harry Samuel and Gertrude (Rotenberg) F.; m. Laura Jean Weisblatt, July 14, 1985; children: Gabrielle Eve, Daniel Adam. BA, Yale U., 1978; MD, U. Chgo., 1982. Diplomate Am. Bd. Psychiatry and Neurology. Intern in medicine Mt. Auburn Hosp., Cambridge, Mass., 1982-83; intern in neurology Mass. Gen. Hosp., Boston, 1982-83; resident in psychiatry McLean Hosp., Belmont, Mass., 1983-86, asst. psychiatrist, 1986-88, asst. clin. psychiatrist, 1988—; instr. psychiatry Harvard U. Med. Sch., Boston, 1986-88, clin. instr., 1988—99, asst. clin. prof. psychiatry, 2000—, psychiatrist Harvard Community Health Plan, 1988-96; assoc. residency dir. Harvard Longwood Psychiatry Residency, Boston, 1995-99; psychiatrist Harvard Pilgrim Health Care, Boston, 1996-97, Harvard Vanguard Med. Assoc., Boston, 1997—2000. Candidate Boston Psychoanalytic Soc. and Inst., 1986-97; grad. analyst Boston Psychoanalytic Soc. and Inst. Recipient Paul Howard award McLean Hosp., 1986; Group for Advancement Psychiatry Ginsburg fellow, 1984-86. Mem. Am. Psychiat. Assn., Boston Psychoanalytic Soc. and Inst., Am. Bd. Geriatric Psychiatry, Am. Bd. Forensic Psychiatry, Am. Psychoanlytic Assn., Am. Acad. Psychiatry and Law. Avocations: tennis, cross country skiing. Office: 875 Massachusetts Ave Ste 51 Cambridge MA 02139-3015

FRIEDMAN, JEROME ISAAC, physics professor, researcher; b. Chgo., Mar. 28, 1930; married, 1956; 4 children. AB, U. Chgo., 1950, MS, 1953, PhD in Physics, 1956. Research assoc. in physics U. Chgo., 1956—57; research assoc. in physics Stanford U., Calif., 1957—60; from asst. prof. to assoc. prof. MIT, Cambridge, 1960—67, prof. physics, 1967—, dir. lab. nuclear sci., 1980—83, head dept. physics, 1983—88, William A. Collidge prof., 1988—90, inst. prof., 1990—. Recipient Nobel prize in Physics, 1990. Fellow: AAAS, Am. Phys. Soc. (co-recipient W.H.K. Panofsky prize 1989); mem.: NAS, Am. Acad. Arts and Scis. Achievements include first to conduct investigations concerning deep inelastic scattering of electrons on protons and bound neutrons, which have been of essential importance for the development of quark model in particle physics. Office: MIT Room 24-512/Dept Physics 77 Massachusetts Ave Cambridge MA 02139-4307*

FRIEDMAN, JOAN M., accountant, educator; b. N.Y.C., Nov. 30, 1949; d. Alvin E. and Pesselle Gail (Rothenberg) F.; m. Charles E. Blair III, Sept. 20, 1992. AB magna cum laude, Harvard U., 1971; MA, Courtauld Inst., U. London, 1973; MS with honors, Columbia U., 1974; MAS, U. Ill., 1993. CPA, Ill. Asst. research librarian Beinecke Library, New Haven, Conn., 1974-75; asst. research librarian Yale Ctr. for Brit. Art, New Haven, Conn., 1975-76, curator of rare books, 1976-90; computer cons., teaching asst. dept. accountancy U. Ill., Champaign, 1990-95; vis. asst. prof. acctg. Ill. Wesleyan U., Bloomington, Ill., 1995-99, asst. prof. acctg., 1999—. Cons. Johns Hopkins U., Balt., 1983; tchr. Sch. Library Service Columbia U., 1983-88, Sysop WordPerfect Users Forum on CompuServe, 1987-2000, Sysop, Tapcis Forum on CompuServe, 1988-95. Author: Color Printing in England, 1978; contbr. articles in field Recipient student achievement award Fedn. Schs. Accountancy, 1993; Nat. Merit scholar Harvard U., 1967; Moss Accountancy fellow U. Ill. 1990. Mem. ALA (chmn. rare books and manuscripts sect. 1982-83), Bibliog. Soc. Am. (coun. 1982-86, sec. 1986-88), Am. Printing History Assn., Phi Beta Kappa, Beta Phi Mu. Clubs: Grolier (N.Y.C.); Elizabethan (New Haven). Jewish. Avocations: microcomputers, bicycling. Office: Ill Wesleyan U Divsn Bus & Econs PO Box 2900 Bloomington IL 61702-2900 E-mail: jfriedma@iwu.edu.

FRIEDMAN, JOEL WILLIAM, law educator; b. Mar. 16, 1951; s. Max Aaron and Muriel (Yudien) F.; m. Vivian Stoleru, Apr. 5, 1987; children: Alexa Erica, Chloe Gabriella, Max Aaron. BS, Cornell U., 1972; JD, Yale U., 1975. Bar: Calif. 1975, U.S. Dist. Ct. (cen. dist.) Calif. 1975. Asst. prof. Tulane U., New Orleans, 1976-79, assoc. prof., 1979-82, prof. law, 1982—, C.J. Morrow prof. law, 1985-86, Jack M. Gordon prof. procedural law and jurisdiction, 2002—, dir. tech., 1996—, dir. ITESM PhD program, 2000—. Vis. prof. law U. Tel Aviv, Israel, 1983, U. Tex. Law Sch., 1985-86, Chuo Law Sch., Tokyo, 1988, Hebrew U. Jerusalem Law Sch., 1990; lectr. Fed. Jud. Ctr., Washington, 1987—; cons. La. Ho. of Reps., Baton Rouge, 1982-85; spl. master Pasadena Ind. Sch. Dist., Houston, 1987-93. Editor: Cases and Materials on Law of Employment Discrimination, 1983, 5th edit., 2001, The Law of Civil Procedure: Cases and Materials, 2002; contbr. articles to law revs. Pres., bd. dirs. Woldenberg Village, Inc., 1995-97; pres., bd. dirs., Jewish Fedn. Greater New Orleans, 2001—03. Recipient Felix Frankfurter Faculty award for disting. tchg. Tulane Law Sch., 1989; Fulbright scholar, Israel, 1990. Mem. Am. Assn. Law Schs. (chair sect. on employment discrimination law 1987-88), Am. Law Inst., B'nai B'rith Hillel Found. (pres. New Orleans 1987-91), Internat. Assn. of Jewish Lawyers and Jurists La. Br. (pres. 1994-95). Democrat. Avocations: running, squash, scuba diving, skiing. Home: 1230 State St New Orleans LA 70118-6027 Office: Tulane Law Sch 6329 Freret St New Orleans LA 70118-6231 Office Phone: 504-865-5985. Business E-Mail: jfriedman@law.tulane.edu.

FRIEDMAN, JOHN LEE, physician, consultant; b. Cin., Aug. 23, 1930; s. Leo Samuel and Janet (Meiss) F.; m. Carolyn Jacobson, Aug 15, 1954; children: Lisa K., Daniel H., Ellen C. BA, U. Mich., 1952; MD, U. Cin., 1956. Cert. Am. Bd. Internal Medicine, subspecialty bd. in pulmonary disease. Intern Cin. Gen. Hosp., 1956-57; resident internal medicine U. Iowa Hosps., Iow City, 1957-59; fellow pulmonary disease Gen. Hosp., Cin., 1961-62; asst. prof. internal medicine U. Cin, 1962-68; pvt. practice specializing in pulmonary medicine Cin., 1962-68, Phoenix, 1968—; dir. dept. medicine Synergos Neurol. Ctr., Phoenix, 1987—. Cons. pulmonary diseases VA Hosp., Phoenix, 1969—; tech. advisor to attys., 1982-97; attending physician, pulmonary disease cons. St. Vincent de Paul Free Med. and Dental Clinic, Phoenix. Contbr. papers to profl. jours. V.p., program chmn. Phoenix Chamber Music Soc., 1982-90, pres. Phoenix Chamber Music Soc., 1989-90; bd. dirs. Phoenix Symphony Assn., 1975-78; founding mem. Phoenix Symphony Coun., 1971-82. Capt. U.S. Army, 1959-61. Named Fellow Pulmonary Diseases, U. Cin. Hosps., 1961-62. Fellow Am. Coll. Physicians, Am. Coll. Chest Physicians (pres. Ohio chapt. 1967-8); mem. Ariz Thoracic Soc. (pres. 1973-74). Avocations: music, history, hiking, travel. Home: 135 E Winter Dr Phoenix AZ 85020-4067

FRIEDMAN, JOHN MAXWELL, JR., lawyer; b. N.Y.C., Oct. 31, 1944; s. John M. and Jane (Blum) F.; m. Laurie Suzanne Nevin, July 8, 1973 (div. 1988); children: David, Michael; m. Judith Zuckerman, Mar. 5, 1989; 1 child, Julia. AB, Princeton U., 1966; MA, U. Sussex, Brighton, Eng., 1967; JD, U. Chgo., 1970. Bar: N.Y. 1971, U.S. Ct. Appeals (2d cir.) 1971, U.S. Dist. Ct. (so. and ea. dist.) N.Y. 1972, U.S. Supreme Ct. 1974. Assoc. Dewey Ballantine, N.Y.C., 1970-78, ptnr., 1978-96. Home: 80 Rocky Mountain Rd Roxbury CT 06783-1623

FRIEDMAN, K. BRUCE, lawyer; b. Buffalo, Jan. 1, 1929; s. Bennett and Florence Ruth (Israel) Friedman; m. Lois G. Rosoff, June 15, 1986. AB, Harvard U., 1950; LLB, Yale U., 1953. Bar: N.Y. 1955, DC 1956, Calif. 1958. Atty. CAB, Washington, 1955—57; pvt. practice San Francisco, 1958—; mem. Zang, Friedman & Damir, 1969—78, Cotton, Seligman & Ray, 1978—79, Friedman, McCubbin, Spalding, Bilter, Roosevelt, & Montgomery, San Francisco, 1980—. Pres. Econ. Roundtable San Francisco, 1964; lectr. law U. Calif., Berkley, 1966—76. Trustee World Affairs Coun. No. Calif., San Francisco, 1970—76; pres. San Francisco Estate Planning Coun., 1973—74; bd. dirs. Am. Coll. Trust and Estate Counsel Found., 2000—; bd. dirs. San Francisco chpt. Am. Jewish Com., 1960—76; regional dir. No. Calif. Assn. Harvard Alumni, 1981—84. With U.S. Army, 1953—55. Fellow: Am. Bar Found., Am. Coll. Trust and Estate Counsel; mem.: ABA, U. Calif. San Francisco Found., San Francisco Com. Fgn. Rels., Am. Law Inst., Internat. Acad. Estate and Trust Law (treas. 1996—), San Francisco Bar Assn., State Bar Calif., Harvard Club San Francisco (pres. 1976—78), Commonwealth Club Calif., Calif. Tennis Club, Univ. Club, Rotary. Jewish. Office: Friedman McCubbin Spalding Bilter Roosevelt & Montgomery 425 California St Ste 2500 San Francisco CA 94104-2207 Business E-Mail: kbrucefriedman@fimlaw.com.

FRIEDMAN, KINKY (RICHARD FRIEDMAN), writer, musician; b. Chgo., Nov. 1944; s. Tom and Min Friedman. Grad., Univ. Tex., Austin. Vol. Peace Corps, Borneo, 1967; songwriter, 1964—; novelist, 1986—; columnist Tex. Monthly Mag., 2001—; independent candidate, gov. State of Tex., 2005. Performer (with Texas Jewboys Band): (albums) Sold American, 1973, Kinky Friedman, 1974; performer: (solo) Live from the Lone Star Cafe, 1982, Under the Double Ego, 1983, Old Testaments and New Revelations, 1992, Lasso from El Paso, 1993, From One Good American to Another, 1995, Pearls in the Snow, 1998, Classic Snatches from Europe, 2000; author: Greenwich Killing Time, 1986, A Case of Lone Star, 1987, When the Cat's Away, 1988, Frequent Flyer, 1989, Musical Chairs, 1991, Elvis, Jesus and Coca-Cola, 1993, Armadillos and Old Lace, 1994, Roadkill, 1997, Blast from the Past, 1998, Spanking Watson, 1999, The Mile High Club, 2000, Kinky Friedman's Guide to Texas Etiquette, 2001, Meanwhile, Back at the Ranch, 2002, Kill Two Birds and Get Stoned, 2003, The Great Psychedelic Armadillo Picnic, 2004, Prisoner of Vandam Street, 2004, 'Scuse Me While I Whip This Out: Reflections on Country Singers, Presidents and Other Troublemakers, 2004, Ten Little New Yorkers, 2005. Jewish. Office: 2100 Northland Dr Austin TX 78756 Address: c/o David Vigliano Assoc Ste 809 584 Broadway New York NY 10012 E-mail: kfcs@kinkyfriedman.com.*

FRIEDMAN, LAWRENCE M., law educator; b. Chgo., Apr. 2, 1930; s. I. M. and Ethel (Shapiro) F.; m. Leah Feigenbaum, Mar. 27, 1955; children: Jane, Amy. AB, U. Chgo., 1948, JD, 1951, LLM, 1953; LLD (hon.), U. Puget Sound, 1977, CUNY, 1989, U. Lund, Sweden, 1993, John Marshall Law Sch., 1995, U. Macerata, Italy, 1998. Mem. faculty St. Louis U., 1957-61, U. Wis., 1961-68; prof. law Stanford U., 1968—, Marion Rice Kirkwood prof., 1976—; David Stouffer Meml. lectr. Rutgers U. Law Sch., 1969; Sibley lectr. U. Ga. Law Sch., 1976; Wayne Morse lectr. U. Oreg., 1985; Childress meml. lectr. St. Louis U., 1987. Jefferson Meml. lectr. U. Calif., 1994; Higgins vis. prof. Lewis and Clark U., 1998; Tucker lectr. Washington and Lee U., 2000, Charter lectr. U. Ga, 2004; Johnson lectr. Vanderbilt U., 2005. Author: Contract Law in America, 1965, Government and Slum Housing, 1968, A History of American Law, 1973, 3d edit., 2005, The Legal System: A Social Science Perspective, 1975, Law and Society: An Introduction, 1977, American Law, 1984, Total Justice, 1985, Your Time Will Come, 1985, The Republic of Choice, 1990, Crime and Punishment in American History, 1993, The Horizontal Society, 1999, Law in America: A Short History, 2002, American Law in The 20th Century, 2002, Private Lives: Families, Individuals, and The Law, 2004; author: (with Robert V. Percival) The Roots of Justice, 1981; co-editor (with Stewart Macaulay): Law and the Behavioral Sciences, 1969, 2d edit., 1977; co-editor: (with Stewart Macaulay and John Stookey) Law and Society: Readings on the Social Study of Law, 1995; co-editor: (with Harry N. Scheiber) American Law and the Constitutional Order, 1978; co-editor: Legal Culture and the Legal Profession, 1996; co-editor: (with George Fisher) The Crime Conundrum, 1997; co-editor: (with Rogelio Prerz-Perdomo) Legal Culture in the Age of Globalization: Latin America and Mediterranean Europe, 2003; contbr. articles to profl. jours. Served with U.S. Army, 1953-54. Recipient Triennial award Order of Coif, 1976, Willard Hurst prize, 1982, Harry Kalven prize, 1992, Silver Gavel award ABA, 1994, Rsch. award Am. Bar. Found., 2000-01; Ctr. for Advanced Study in Behavioral Sci. fellow, 1974-75, Inst. Advanced Study fellow, Berlin, 1985. Mem. Law and Soc. Assn. (pres. 1979-81), Am. Acad. Arts and Scis., Am. Soc. for Legal History (v.p. 1987-89, pres. 1990-91), Soc. Am. Historians, Rsch. Com. Sociology of Law (hon. life, pres. 2003—). Home: 724 Frenchmans Rd Palo Alto CA 94305-1005 Office: Stanford U Law Sch Nathan Abbott Way Stanford CA 94305-9991 Business E-Mail: lmf@stanford.edu.

FRIEDMAN, LAWRENCE MILTON, lawyer; b. Chgo., Apr. 2, 1945; s. Armin C. and Mildred Friedman; m. Linda M. Friedman, June 25, 1967; children: Benjamin J., David K. BA, U. Ill., 1966; JD, Ohio State U., 1969. Bar: Ill. 1970, U.S. Tax Ct. 1970; CPA, Md., Ill. Ptnr. Coopers & Lybrand, Chgo., 1969-85, Lord, Bissell & Brook LLP, Chgo., 1985—. Adj. prof. law IIT Chgo. Kent Coll. Law, Chgo., 1990-2000; mem. adv. bd. Hartford Inst. Ins. Tax, 1995-2000; spkr. on mergers, aquisitions, fin. svcs. industries, and taxation. Mem. adv. bd. Ins. Tax Rev., 1987—; contbr. articles to law jours. Sec.-treas., dir. North Shore Performing Arts Ctr. Found. in Skokie, Ill., 1993-97; vice chmn., dir. Jewish Fedn. Met. Chgo., 1992-99. Mem. ABA, Chgo. Fed. Tax Forum. Office: Lord Bissell & Brook LLP 115 S La Salle St Ste 3200 Chicago IL 60603-3902 Office Phone: 312-443-1835.

FRIEDMAN, LOUIS FRANK, lawyer; b. Balt., May 26, 1941; s. Dave Sylvan and Miriam (Sugarman) F.; m. Phyllis Cole, Dec. 25, 1968; 1 son, Samuel. BS, U. Md., 1963, JD, 1965; LL.M. in Taxation, Georgetown U., 1968. Bar: Md. 1965. Since practiced in, Balt.; ptnr. firm Friedman & Friedman, 1965—. Prof. taxation U. Balt. Sch. Bus., 1975-88. Pres. 9400 Ocean Hwy. Condominium, Ocean City, Md., 1976; chmn. young lawyers div. Asso. Jewish Charities, 1975-76; bd. dirs. Carson Scholars Fund, Siani Hosp., Balt., Life Bridge Health. Mem. Md. Bar Assn. (tax counsel 1977-79), Order of Coif, Phi Alpha Delta. Lodges: Masons (tax counsel Masonic Charities Md. Inc. 1987—), Amicable. Jewish. Home: 19 Hambleton Ct Baltimore MD 21208-3333 Office: Merc Bank Bldg 409 Washington Ave Baltimore MD 21204-4920

FRIEDMAN, MARCIA L., photographer, writer, artist; b. Madison, Wis., Sept. 13, 1942; d. Stanleigh and Eleanor Friedman. BA, U. Wis., Madison, WI, 1964. Legal sec. Melvin Belli, San Francisco, 1965—65; flight attendant World Airways, Oakland, Calif., 1965—67; ground hostess TWA, Tel Aviv, 1967—69; mgr. Roland Agy., Los Angeles, Calif., 1970—72; owner, mgr. M. Friedman Agy., Los Angeles, Calif., 1972—76; fashion designer/owner Le Bag Swimwear, Los Angeles, Calif., 1976—83; design educator Otis Parsons Sch. Design, Los Angeles, Calif., 1979; free lance writer various, Los Angeles, Calif., 1982—90; cons. Adrienne Vitiadini, N.Y.C., 1985; writer The Jewish Press, New York, NY, 1999—; owner Marcia Friedman Gallery, Madison, Wis., 2004—. Photographer (book) Cuba: The Special Period; exhibitions include Biennale Internat. Dell Firte Contemporanca, Florence, Italy. Fundraising dir. Friends Jerusalem Coll., Los Angeles, Calif., 1989; tribute jour. chmn. Pacific Jewish Ctr., Los Angeles, Calif., 1987. Mem.: Mensa. Jewish. Avocations: reading non-fiction, animal interaction.

FRIEDMAN, MARIA ANDRE, public relations executive; b. Jackson, Mich., June 12, 1950; m. Stanley N. Friedman; children: Alexandra, Adam. BA cum laude, U. Md., 1972, MA, 1979; DBA, Nova U., 1993. Writer U.S. Bur. Mines, Washington, 1973-78; head writer Nat. Ctr. Health Svc. Rsch./Healthcare Tech. DHHS, Rockville, Md., 1978-85; chief publs. and info. br. Agy. for Healthcare Policy and Rsch., 1986-89; dir. office pub. affairs Healthcare Fin. Adminstrn., Washington, 1990—, acting assoc. adminstr. for comm., 1992-93, sr. rsch. advisor Balt., 1994-95, dir. disemination staff ORB, 1995-96, sr. advisor for ins. reform, 1997-99, Y2K outreach coord. for medicaid program, 1999—. Mem. Assn. Health Svcs. Rsch., Acad. of Mgmt. Office: Health Care Fin Adminstrn 7500 Security Blvd Baltimore MD 21244-1849 Home: 12535 Heurich Rd Silver Spring MD 20902-1441

FRIEDMAN, MARTIN, museum director, arts adviser; b. Pitts., Sept. 23, 1925; s. Israel and Etta (Louik) F.; m. Mildred Shenberg, Sept. 3, 1949; children: Lise, Ceil, Zoe. Student, U. Pa., 1943-45; BA, U. Wash., 1947; MA, UCLA, 1949; postgrad., Columbia, 1956-57, U. Minn., 1958-60, LHD (hon.), 1990, Bates Coll., 1983; DFA (hon.), Macalester Coll., 1983; LHD (hon.), Md. Inst., 1983; DFA (hon.), Hamline U., 1987, Phila. Coll. of Art and Design, 1989. Instr. art, curriculum cons. L.A. City Schs., 1949-56; instr. art U. Calif. Extension, L.A., 1950-51; fellow Bklyn. Mus., 1956-57; grantee Belgian-Am. Ednl. Found., Brussels, 1957-58; fellow Am. art U. Minn., 1959-60; curator Walker Art Center, Mpls., 1958-60, dir., 1961-90, dir. emeritus, 1990—: Mem. mus. adv. com. NEA, 1973-78, adv. coun. internat. exhbns., 1987-91, Nat. Coun. Arts, 1978-84, Smithsonian Coun., 1988-93; adv. Am. Ctr. Paris, 1990-92, Fed. Art Com. Internat. Exhbns., 1987-91; adviser art program Hall Family Found., Kansas City, 1991—, Nat. Gallery Art, Washington, 1991-92, Nelson Atkins Mus. Art, Kansas City, Mo., 1991—, contemporary art Va. Mus. Fine Arts, Richmond, 1992-93; guest curator Landscape as Metaphor exhbn. Denver Art Mus., 1992-94, Columbus Mus. Art, 1992-94; Am. fine arts commr. São Paulo Bienal, 1963; mem. Nat. Collection Fine Arts Commn., Washington, Commn. on Founds. and Pvt. Philanthropy; hon. mem. commn. Nat. Mus. Am. Art, Washington; mem. adv. bd. on environ. planning Bur. Reclamation, Washington, 1965-69; art adv. com. Japan House Gallery, N.Y.C., 1999-2000; adviser Ind. Curators, Inc., N.Y. Author numerous catalogues on internat. contemporary art, also books, articles; dir. numerous mus. exhbns. Trustee Spring Hill Found., Minn., 1970—81, Am. Fedn. Arts, 1972—85, Socrates Sculpture Pk., NY, 2000—02; mem. Internat. Mus. Com., Washington, 1976—78; mem. vis. com. J. Paul Getty Mus., Malibu, Calif., 1990—95. Ford Found. fellow, 1961-62; artist fellow Aspen Inst. Humanistic Studies, 1980, Intellectual Interchange fellow, Tokyo, 1982, Japan Found. fellow, 1991; Asian Cultural Coun. grantee, 1995; recipient Disting. Svc. award Mid-Am. Coll. Art Assn., 1987, Nat. Medal of Arts, White House, 1990, Lifetime Achievement award Internat. Sculpture Ctr., 1999; decorated officer Arts et Lettres (France); honoree DIA Ctr. for the Arts, 1997. Mem. Coll. Art Assn., Assn. Art Mus. Dirs. (pres. 1978-79, trustee 1979-81, citation for disting. svc. 1990). E-mail: mlfnyc@mindspring.com.*

FRIEDMAN, MARTIN BURTON, retired chemical company executive; b. N.Y.C., June 21, 1927; s. William L. and Ella (Holstein) F.; m. Rita Fleischman, Mar. 19, 1950; children— Jay Edward, Ellen Jane. Student, Mt. St. Mary's Coll., 1943-44, Cornell U., 1944-45; BA, Pa. State U., 1949; PhD, Wiltshire U., 2003. Mgr. advt. and promotion chems. group Sun Chem. Corp., N.Y.C., 1949-54; mgr. advt. and promotion textile chems. dept. Am. Cyanamid Co., N.Y.C., 1954-58, mgr. advt. and promotion, organic chems. div., 1958-60, gen. merchandising mgr., mgr. fibers div., 1961-64, dir. sales, 1964-65, dir. mktg., 1965-69, asst. gen. mgr. fibers div., 1969-72; v.p. IRC Fibers Co. (subs.), 1969-72; exec. v.p. Formica Corp., Cin., 1972-73, pres., 1973-80; pres. fibers div. Am. Cyanamid, 1980-84, corp. v.p., 1984-90. Chmn. bd. 4th Dist. Fed. Res. Bank, Cin.; adj. prof. Ramapo Coll., 1990-98; chmn. Mgmt. Decision Lab., NYU Grad. Sch. Bus., 1990-98. Author: The Leadership Myth; contbr. articles to textile and tech. publs. Served with USNR, 1945-46. Mem. Am. Chem. Soc., Am. Assn. Textile Chemists and Colorists. Clubs: Chemists (N.Y.C.). Home: 777 Butternut Dr Franklin Lakes NJ 07417-2281 Personal E-mail: friedmanm@prodigy.net. *Integrity should permeate every discussion of every facet of leadership. Integrity is the basic quality to be sought in consideration of any person's qualifications for assuming a position of trust and responsibility.*

FRIEDMAN, MERTON HIRSCH, retired psychologist, educator; b. Boston, Apr. 12, 1925; s. Isadore and Frances (Ponack) F.; m. Judith Lee Freeman, Nov. 27, 1955; 1 child, Eric Lund. BS, Coll. William and Mary, 1945; MA, U. Pa., 1947; PhD, U. Ill., 1952. Lic. psychologist, N.J., Mass. Psychology intern Conn. Valley Hosp., Middletown, 1947—48; postdoctoral intern Dept. VA Mental Health Clinic, Phila., 1952—53; staff psychologist Dept. VA Med. Ctr., Boston, 1953—59, chief psychology svc. Providence, 1959—62; chief psychologist Cmty. Mental Health Ctr., Brookline, Mass., 1962—64; dir. clin. svcs. Jewish Vocat. Svc., Milw., 1966—67; clin. assoc. prof. psychiatry U. Medicine and Dentistry N.J., 1968—92; chief psychology svc. Dept. VA Med. Ctr., East Orange, NJ, 1967—96; ret., 1996. Vis. lectr. Fulbright program Lund U., Sweden, 1964-66. Contbr. articles to profl. jours. USPHS Rsch. fellow, NIMH, U. Ill., 1951—52. Fellow Am. Orthopsychiat. Assn.; mem. APA, Mass. Psychol. Assn., N.J. Psychol. Assn., Sigma Xi (U. Ill. chpt.). Democrat. Jewish. Avocations: piano, hiking, stamp collecting/philately, classical music. Home: 79 Falcon Rd Livingston NJ 07039-4414

FRIEDMAN, MILDRED, architectural and design educator, curator, educator; b. L.A., July 25, 1929; d. Nathaniel and Hortense (Weinsveig) Shenberg; m. Martin Friedman; children: Lise, Ceil, Zoe. BA, UCLA, 1951, MA, 1952; DFA (hon.), Mpls. Coll. Art, 1984; DFA, Hamlin U., 1987. Instr. design L.A. City Coll., 1952-54; archtl. designer Cerny Assocs., Mpls., 1957-69; design curator Walker Art Ctr., Mpls., 1970-90; freelance cons. N.Y.C., 1990—. Mem. arch. and design panel Nat. Endowment Arts, 1975—78, mem. policy panel design arts, 1979—82, mem. presdl. design awards jury, 1991; mem. vis. com. Sch. Arch. and Planning MIT, 1985—88; mem. vis. com. Grad. Sch. Design Harvard U., 1994—; bd. dirs. Internat. Design Conf., Aspen, 1989—91, Chgo. Inst. Arch. and Urbanism, 1990—93, Nat. Inst. Archtl. Edn., 1993—; mem. deisgn jury Am. Acad. Rome, 1991; gueest instr. UCLA, 1992; mem. jury to select architect for Whitehall Ferry Terminal, N.Y.C., 1992; vis. instr. Harvard U., 1993; cons. Battery Park City Authority, N.Y.C.; guest curator Bklyn. Mus., 1992—2002; guest curator for Frank Gehry retrospective exhbn. Solomon R. Guggenheim Mus., N.Y.C., 2001; guest curator for Vital Forms exhbn. Bklyn. Mus. Art, 2001—02. Author, editor: Gehry Talks, 1999; editor Design Quar., 1970-91, numerous catalogues; participating author for catalogue on the work of Jack Lenor Larson, Mus. Arts & Design, 2004. Recipient Outstanding Achievement award YWCA, 1984, Outstanding Svc. award U. Minn., 1991; fellow Intellectual Interchange program Japan Soc., 1982, Chrysler Design award, 2002; grantee Nat. Endowment Arts, 1992-93, Graham Found. for Advanced Studies in Fine Arts, 1997; recipient Graham Found grant for Design Quar. Anthology. Mem. AIA (hon., nat. awards jury 1981, 87, bd. dirs. Minn. chpt. 1984-86, Inst. Honors 1994).

FRIEDMAN, MILTON, retired economist; b. Bklyn., July 31, 1912; s. Jeno Saul and Sarah Ethel (Landau) Friedman; m. Rose Director, June 25, 1938; children: Janet, David. AB, Rutgers U., 1932, LLD (hon.), 1968; AM, U. Chgo., 1933; PhD, Columbia U., 1946; LLD (hon.), St. Paul's (Rikkyo) U., 1963; LLD (hon.), Loyola U., 1971; LLD (hon.), U. N.H., 1975; LLD (hon.), Harvard U., 1979, Brigham Young U., 1980; LLD (hon.), Dartmouth Coll., 1980, Gonzaga U., 1981; DSc (hon.), Rochester U., 1971; LHD (hon.), Rockford Coll., 1969, Roosevelt U., 1975, Hebrew Union Coll., L.A., 1981, Jacksonville U., 1993; LittD (hon.), Bethany Coll., 1971; PhD (hon.), Hebrew U., Jerusalem, 1977; DCS (hon.), Francisco Marroquín U., Guatemala, 1978; D honoris causa (hon.), Econ. U. Prague, 1997. Assoc. economist Nat. Resources Com., Washington, 1935—37; mem. rsch. staff Nat. Bur. Econ. Rsch., N.Y.C., 1937—45, 1948—81; vis. prof. econs. U. Wis., Madison, 1940—41; prin. economist, tax research div. U.S. Treasury Dept., Washington, 1941—43; assoc. dir. research, statis. research group, War Research div. Columbia U., N.Y.C., 1943—45; assoc. prof. econs. and statistics U. Minn., Mpls., 1945—46; assoc. prof. econs. U. Chgo., 1946—48, prof. econs., 1948—62, Paul Snowden Russell disting. service prof. econs., 1962—82, prof. emeritus, 1983—; Fulbright lectr. Cambridge U., 1953—54; vis. Wesley Clair Mitchell research prof. econs. Columbia U., N.Y.C., 1964—65; fellow Ctr. for Advanced Study in Behavioral Sci., 1957—58; sr. rsch. fellow Hoover Inst., Stanford U., 1977—. Mem. Pres.'s Commn. All-Vol. Army, 1969—70, Pres.'s Commn. on White House Fellows, 1971—74, Pres.'s Econ. Policy Adv. Bd., 1981—88; vis. scholar Fed. Res. Bank, San Francisco, 1977. Author (with Carl Shoup and Ruth P. Mack): Taxing to Prevent Inflation, 1943; author: (with Simon S. Kuznets) Income from Independent Professional Practice, 1946; author: (with Harold A. Freeman, Frederic Mosteller, W. Allen Wallis) Sampling Inspection, 1948; author: Essays in Positive Economics, 1953, A Theory of the Consumption Function, 1957, A Program for Monetary Stability, 1960, Price Theory: A Provisional Text, 1962; author: (with Rose D. Friedman) Capitalism and Freedom, 1962; author: (with Anna J. Schwartz) A Monetary History of the United States, 1867-1960, 1963; author: Inflation: Causes and Consequences, 1963; author: (with Robert Roosa) The Balance of Payments: Free vs. Fixed Exchange Rates, 1967; author: Dollars and Deficits, 1968, The Optimum Quantity of Money and Other Essays, 1969; author: (with Walter W. Heller) Monetary vs. Fiscal Policy, 1969; author: (with Schwartz) Monetary Statistics of the United States, 1970; author: A Theoretical Framework for Monetary Analysis, 1972; author: (with Wilbur J. Cohen) Social Security, 1972; author: An Economist's Protest, 1972; author: (with Robert J. Gordon et al) Milton Friedman's Monetary Framework, 1974; author: There's No Such Thing as a Free Lunch, 1975, Price Theory, 1976, Tax Limitation, Inflation and the Role of Government, 1978; author: (with R.D. Friedman) Free to Choose, 1980; author: (with Schwartz) Monetary Trends in the U.S. and the United Kingdom, 1982; author: Bright Promises, Dismal Performance, 1983; author: (with R.D. Friedman) Tyranny of the Status Quo, 1984; author: Monetarist Economics, 1991, Money Mischief, 1992; author: (with Thomas S. Szasz) Friedman & Szasz on Drugs: Essays on the Free Market and Prohibition, 1992; author: (with R.D. Friedman) Two Lucky People: Memoirs, 1998; editor: Studies in the Quantity Theory of Money, 1956; bd. editors: Am. Econ. Rev., 1951—53, Econometrica, 1957—69, adv. bd.: Jour. Money, Credit and Banking, 1968—94, columnist: Newsweek Mag., 1966—84, contbg. editor:, 1971—84; contbr. articles to profl. jours. Chmn. bd. dirs. Milton and Rose D. Friedman Found.; mem. adv. bd. Calif. Parents for Ednl. Choice, 1999—. Decorated Grand Cordon of the 1st Class Order of the Sacred Treasure Japan; named Chicagoan of Yr., Chgo. Press Club, 1972, Educator of Yr., Chgo. Jewish United Fund, 1973; recipient Nobel prize in econs., 1976, Pvt. Enterprise Exemplar medal, Freedoms Found., 1978, Presdl. medal of Freedom, 1988, Nat. Medal of Sci., 1988, Prize in Moral-Cultural Affairs, Instn. World Capitalism, 1993, Earl M. Combs Jr. award, Chgo. Bd. Trade Ednl. Rsch. Found., 1991, Source award for lifetime achievement, The Primary Source, Tufts U., 1997, Robert Maynard Hutchins History Maker award for distinction in edn., Chgo. Hist. Soc., 1997, Templeton Honor Rolls Lifetime Achievement award, 1997, Goldwater award, 1997, James U. Blanchard III Freedom award, Jefferson Fin., 2001, Abraham Lincoln award, Am. Hungarian Found., 2002, Statesmanship award, Claremont Inst., 2002. Fellow: Econometric Soc., Am. Statis. Assn., Inst. Math. Stats.; mem.: NAS, Mont Pelerin Soc. (bd. dirs. 1958—61, pres. 1970—72), Am. Philos. Soc., Royal Econ. Soc., Western Econ. Assn. (pres. 1984—85), Am. Enterprise Inst. (adv. bd. 1956—79), Am. Econ. Assn. (exec. com. 1955—57, pres. 1967, John Bates Clark medal 1951), Quadrangle Club. Office: Hoover Instn 434 Galvez Mall Stanford CA 94305-6010 Office Phone: 650-723-0580. Business E-Mail: friedman@hoover.stanford.edu.

FRIEDMAN, MORTON LEE, lawyer; b. Aberdeen, S.D., Aug. 4, 1932; s. Philip and Rebecca (Feinstein) F.; m. Marcine Lichter, Dec. 20, 1955; children— Mark, Philip, Jeffrey. Student, U. Mich., 1950-53; AB, Stanford U., 1954, LL.B., 1956. Bar: Calif. bar 1956. Mem. firm Kimble, Thomas, Snell, Jamison & Russell, Fresno, 1957, Busick & Busick, Sacramento, 1957-59; sr. ptnr. firm Friedman, Collard & Poswall (name now Friedman, Collard & Panneton), Sacramento, 1959—. Lectr. various law schs. and seminars; mem. Calif. Bd. Continuing Edn. Pres. Mosaic Law Congregation, 1977-80, 97-99; v.p. Sacramento Jewish Fedn., 1980-82; chmn. Sacramento campaign United Jewish Appeal, 1981; bd. dirs., former nat. v.p. Am. Israel Pub. Affairs Com.; mem. bd. Calif. State U. Inst., 1995-99; bd. dirs. Nat. Bd. AntiDefamation League. 1st lt. USAF, 1956. Recipient Sacramento Businessman of Yr. award Sacramento Met. C. of C., 1991, Best Lawyers in Am. award, Outstanding Philanthropists award Nat. Soc. Fund Raising Execs., 1999; Fulbright candidate Stanford Law Sch., 1956. Fellow Am. Coll. Trial Lawyers; mem. ABA, ATLA, Calif. Bar Assn., Sacramento County Bar Assn. (pres. 1976, Lawyer of Yr. 1999), Calif. Trial Lawyers Assn. (v.p. 1973-75), Capitol City Lawyers Club (past pres.), Am. Bd. Trial Advocates (adv., pres. 1977, Calif. Trial Lawyer of Yr. 1988, SCALE award 2002), West Sacramento C. of C. (dir.), Order of Coif. Democrat. Home: 1620 McClaren Dr Carmichael CA 95608-5936 Office: Friedman Collard & Panneton 7750 College Town Dr Ste 300 Sacramento CA 95826-2386 Office Phone: 916-381-9011.

FRIEDMAN, MYLES IVAN, education educator; b. Chgo., Apr. 5, 1924; s. Max Edward and Ethel (Goldman) F.; m. Betty Ann McDowell, July 4, 1978; children: Gregg Alan, Myles Ivan Jr. MA, U. Chgo., 1957, PhD, 1959. Real estate, home builder, 1946-58; asst. prof. edn. Northwestern U., 1958-60, assoc. prof., 1960-64; chaired prof. edn. U. S.C., 1964—99; vis. prof. U. Calif., Berkeley, summer 1968. Cons. in field; dir. Head Start Evaluation and Rsch. Ctr.; dir. rsch. Regional Edn. Lab., Carolinas and Va.; pres. Inst. for Evidence-Based Decision-Making in Edn., 1995—. Author: Rational Behavior, 1975, Teaching Reading and Thinking Skills, 1979; sr. author: Improving Teacher Education, 1979, Human Nature and Predictability, 1981, Teaching Higher Order Thinking Skills to Gifted Students, 1983, The Psychology of Human Control, 1991, Taking Control: Vitalizing Education, 1993, Improving the Quality of Life, 1997, Handbook on Effective Instructional Strategies, 1998, Ensuring Student Success, 2000, Educators' Handbook on Effective Testing, 2003, No School Left Behind, 2005; contbr. articles to profl. jours. Served with USAAF, 1942-46. Mem. APA. Home: 1709 Seay Ct Columbia SC 29206-3117

FRIEDMAN, PAMELA RUTH LESSING, financial consultant, writer; d. Fred William and Helen D. Lessing; children: Elizabeth Lessing, Paul Lessing. BA, U. Rochester, 1972; MSLS, U. N.C., Chapel Hill, 1974. Dep. libr. Am. Soc. Internat. Law, Washington, 1974-76; with edn. dept. Nat. Air and Space Mus., Smithsonian Inst., Washington, 1976-84; ind. cons. fin. and art Boulder, Colo., 1984—; pub. C.S.B. Co., Boulder, 1989—. Lectr. in fields, 1989—; cons. Denver Art Mus., 1989-91, Asian Art Coordinating Coun., Denver, 1990—; pres. Kylin Resources, Boulder, Colo., 1995—; race ofcl., U.S. Ski Assn., 1998—; v.p. Linking Human Sys. (LINC), Boulder, 1997—. Author: (reference book) Chinese Snuff Bottles, 1990, The First Week with My New P.C.: A Very Basic Guide for Mature Adults and Everyone Who Wants to Get Connected, 2000, The First Week with My New iMac: A Very Basic Guide for Mature Adults and Everyoneho Wants to Get Connected, 2001, The First Week with My New Digital Organizer: A Very Basic Guide to Palm OS Personal Digital Assistants, 2002, The First Week with My New Digital Camera, 2003; editor: (reference book) Flight Service Directory, 1975. Rep. S.E.V.A.B., Smithsonian Instn., 1979-81, mem. exec. bd. docent coun. Nat. Air and Space Mus., 1977-81; mem. trustee coun. U. Rochester, N.Y., 1992-98, mem. vis. com. coll. of arts and scis. U. Rochester, 1994—; bd. dirs., mem. exec. com. bd., treas. Colo. Music Festival, Boulder, 1983-89; mem. exec. bd. Women's Incentive Fund Colo. U., Boulder, 1988-91; rep. Leadership Boulder, 1986-87; v.p. bd. dirs. Lessing Found., N.Y., 1988—; mem. exec. bd. Interfaith Coun., Boulder, 1987-90; dir. exec. bd. LINC Found., 2002—, Vail Film Festival, 2002—; life mem. RAF Mus., 1977—. Recipient Internat. Gold Test Pin award Swiss Skiing Fedn., St. Moritz, 1975. Mem. Internat. Chinese Snuff Bottle Soc., Army and Navy Club (Washington), Beach Point Club (Mamaroneck, N.Y.), Game Creek Club (Vail, Colo., adv. bd. 2001—). Avocations: private aviation, amateur radio, skiing, sailing, scuba diving, collecting.

FRIEDMAN, PAUL JAY, retired radiologist; b. N.Y.C., Jan. 20, 1937; s. Louis Alexander and Rose (Solomon) Friedman; m. Elisabeth Clare Richardson, June 18, 1960; children: Elizabeth Ruth Coley, Deborah Anne Yeager, Matthew Alexander Xu-Friedman, Rachel Clare Lentz. BS, U. Wis., 1955; postgrad., Oxford (Eng.) U., 1957-58; MD, Yale U., 1960. Diplomate Am. Bd Radiology. Intern Einstein Med. Sch., N.Y.C., 1960-61; resident in radiology Columbia-Presbyn. Hosp., N.Y.C., 1961-64; from asst. prof. to assoc. prof. U. Calif. San Diego Med. Sch., 1968-75, prof. radiology, 1975-2001, prof. emeritus, 2001—, from assoc. dean to dean acad. affairs, 1982-95. Cons. VA Hosp., 1971—2001; vis. scholar Inst. Med./NAS, AAMC, 1988—89; mem. adv. com. rsch. integrity HHS, 1991—93; cons. 26th, 27th, and 28th edit. Stedman's Med. Dictionary; specialist in chest radiology rsch. ethics, acad. pers. issues; bd. dirs. Am. Coun. Edn., 1996—97. Mem. editl. bd. Investigative Radiology, 1976—87, Am. Jour. Roentgenology, 1986—88; contbr. articles to profl. jours. Bd. dirs. La Jolla Symphony Assn., 1987—92. Lt. cmdr. MC USNR, 1964—66. Markle scholar acad. medicine, 1969—74, Picker Found. Advanced Acad. fellow and scholar, 1966—69. Fellow: Am. Coll. Radiology, Am. Coll. Chest Physicians; mem.: AAUP, Nat. Conf. Lawyers and Scientists (co-chair 2005—), Roentgen Ray Soc. (emeritus), Radiol. Soc. N.Am. (emeritus), Soc. Computer Applications Radiology, Assn. Univ. Radiologists (rep. to coun. acad. socs. Assn. Am. Med. Colls. 1985—97), Internat. Soc. Magnetic Resonance Medicine, Assn. Am. Med. Colls. (disting. svc. mem.), Flieschner Soc. (pres. 1994—95), Phi Beta Kappa, Alpha Omega Alpha. Avocations: choral singing, computers, gardening. Home: 5644 Soledad Rd La Jolla CA 92037-7048 Office: U Calif Sch Medicine Dept Radiology 200 W Arbor Dr San Diego CA 92103-8756 Business E-Mail: pfriedman@ucsd.edu.

FRIEDMAN, PAUL RICHARD, lawyer; b. Washington, Mar. 25, 1944; s. Herbert and Gertrude (Miller) F.; m. Ronna Lee Beck; children: Mali, Luke, Jed. BA, Princeton U., 1965; MA, Trinity Coll., Cambridge U., Eng., 1967; JD, Yale U., 1970; postgrad., Balt./D.C. Inst. Psychoanalysis, 1971—78. Bar: D.C. 1972, U.S. Ct. Appeals (D.C. cir.) 1972, U.S. Ct. Appeals (3d cir.) 1984, U.S. Ct. Appeals (4th cir.) 1979, U.S Supreme Ct. 1975. Law clk. to Hon. J. Skelly Wright U.S. Ct. Appeals (D.C. cir.), Washington, 1970-71; fellow Ctr. for Law and Social Policy, Washington, 1971-72; dir. Mental Health Law Project (now Bazelon Ctr.), Washington, 1972-81; mng. ptnr. Ennis, Friedman, Bersoff and Ewing, Washington, 1981-88; pvt. practice Washington, 1988—93, 1996—; dep. assoc. atty. gen. Dept. of Justice, Washington, 1993-96; of counsel Shea and Gardner, 2002—04, Goodwin Procter LLP, 2004—. Ct.-apptd. mediator and early neutral evaluator, 1988-89; chmn. Practicing Law Inst. Nat. Seminars on Legal Rights of Mentally Disabled Persons, 1979-80; coord. task panel on legal and ethical issues Pres.'s Commn. on Mental Health, 1977-78; mem. adv. com. on procedures U.S. Ct. Appeals (D.C. cir.) 1977-78; mem. steering com. Ctr. for Y2K & Soc., 1998-2000. Author: The Rights of Mentally Retarded Persons - An American Civil Liberties Handbook, 1976; editor: Legal Rights of Mentally Disabled Persons, 3 vols., 1979; note and comment editor Yale Law Jour., 1969-70, bd. editors 1967-69; contbr. articles to profl. publs. Trustee The Green Door, 1977-83. Nat. Merit scholar, Univ. scholar; Woodrow Wilson fellow, Keasbey fellow. Mem. ABA (mem. comm. on mentally disabled 1981-82), D.C. Bar, Am. Psychoanalytic Assn. (affiliate), Phi Beta Kappa. Avocations: tennis and other racquet sports, computers, photography. Office Phone: 202-346-4305. E-mail: pfriedman@goodwinprocter.com.

FRIEDMAN, PAULA KONOWITCH, dentist, academic administrator; b. Wildwood, N.J., June 22, 1948; d. Howard N. and Beatrice E. (Gibbs) Konowitch; m. Emanuel Friedman, Aug. 27, 1972; children: Daniel, Eric, Jeff. BS, U. Mass., 1970; DDS, Columbia U., 1974; MSD, Boston U., 1988, MPH, 1999. Attending dentist Beth Israel Med. Ctr., N.Y.C., 1975-78, Beth Israel Hosp., Boston, 1978-82; dir. DAU and TEAM program Boston U. Sch. of Dental Medicine, 1980-82, dir. divsn. of Oral Diagnosis and Radiology, 1982-87, asst. dean for adminstrn., 1987-91. Coord. GP residency Boston U. Sch. of Dental Medicine, 1980-82; assoc. dean adminstrn., 1991—; chair peer rev. panel HHS, BHPr, 1999-; acad. coord. Health Professions Edn. Program, 1998. Chair Coun. of Faculties Am. Assn., Dental Schs. Washington, 1997, adminstrv. bd. Cmty. and Preventative Dentistry, 1990-94. Recipient Disting. Alumni award Columbia U. Sch. of Dental and Oral Surgery, 1986. Fellow Am. Coll. Dentists, Internat. Coll. of Dentists; mem. ADA, Fisher Hill Assn. (bd. dirs. 1995—), Gerontol. Soc. of Am. (oral health v.p. 1994-97), Am. Assn. of Women Dentists, Am. Dental Edn. Assn. (pres. 2003-04, bd. dirs. 2002-), Phi Kappa Phi. Office: Boston U Sch of Dental Medicine 715 Albany St B308 Boston MA 02118-2308 Office Phone: 617-638-4741. Fax: 617-638-4729. E-mail: pkf@bu.edu.

FRIEDMAN, PAULINE POPLIN, civic worker, consultant; b. Scranton, Pa., Apr. 2, 1930; d. Harry and Lillian (Kushner) Poplin; m. Sidney Friedman, Aug. 3, 1952; children: Anne Friedman Glauber, Robert. BS, Pa. State U., 1952. Cons. AID, Washington, 1993—. Trustee Temple Israel, 1985-87, Jewish Cmty. Ctr., 1992—; mem. coun. King's Coll., 1992—; pres. Home Health Svcs.-vis. Nurse Assn., Kingston, Pa., 1987-88, Coun. Family Agys., Harrisburg, Pa., 1987-88, Family Svc. Wyoming Valley, Wilkes-Barre, 1988-90; mentor Leadership Wilkes-Barre; mem. pres.' coun. Wilkes U., 1991—, King's Coll.; v.p. United Way, Interfaith Coun. Wyoming Valley; bd. dirs. Ethics Inst. N.E. Pa., Dallas, 1994—, St. Vincent De Paul Soup Kitchen, Prevent Child Abuse Pa.; bd. alumni coun. Pa. State U.; mem. Jewish Cmty. Bd. Wyoming Valley; chairwoman United Jewish Campaign, Wyoming Valley, 1998-99; chair Speak-Out Day U.S.A., Luzerne County, First Cantorial Concert for Wilkes Barre, Scranton and Northeat Pa. Recipient Humanitarian award Interfaith Coun. Wyoming Valley, 1989, Phillip Mitchell Cmty. Svc. award Pa. State U., 1990, Woman of Yr. award Family Svc. Wyoming Valley, 1993, Pathfinders award Luzerne County Women's Conf., 1995, Disting. Svc. award B'nai Brith, 1996, Svc. award to Women, N.E. Pa. Boy Scouts Coun. Avocations: golf, tennis, travel. Home: 796 Milford Dr Kingston PA 18704-5308

FRIEDMAN, PENNY, lawyer; b. Cleve., Dec. 24, 1951; d. Harold Emanuel and Ruth (Resnick) F.; children: Rachel, Leah. AB in Econs. with high honors, U. Mich., 1973, JD cum laude, 1977. Bar: Ohio 1977. Atty. Taft, Stettinius & Hollister, Cin., 1977-80; v.p. property devel. Gt. Am. Broadcasting Co. (formerly Taft Broadcasting Co.), Cin., 1980-88; real estate portfolio mgr. Bartlett & Co., Cin., 1988-98; pres. BeneFactors, LLC, 1998—. Mem. Cin. Downtown Progress Com., 1991—95, mem. exec. com., 1993—95; v.p. Cin. chpt. Am. Jewish Com., 1992—96, pres., 1996—98, mem. exec. com., 1990—; v.p. Leadership Cin. Alumni Assn., 1987—89; chmn. Family Svc. Cin. Area, 1991—92, pres., 1988—90, 1985—88, trustee, 1979—93, trustee emeritus, 1993—; vice-chmn. Cin. Devel. Fund, 1989—95; vice chmn. Devel. Corp. Cin., 1990—92, trustee, 1989—92, Cin. Arts Assn., 1992—, mem. exec. com., 1994—; trustee Downtown Cin., Inc., 1998—2004, Cin. Psychoanalytic Inst., 1994—2002, The Wellness Cmty., 1999—2002; vice chair, trustee Knoledgeworks Found., 1999—2002, v.p., treas., 2002—; trustee Found. Family Svc., 2000—, v.p., 2002—05, pres., 2005—; trustee Greater Cin. Arts and Edn. Ctr., 1999—, mem. exec. com., 2005—; trustee Project Grad. Cin., 2003—; bd. dirs. Cin. Ctr. for Devel. Disorders, 1979—85, Seven Hills Neighborhood Houses, 1981—86. Mem. Cin. Bar Assn., Phi Beta Kappa. Office: BeneFactors LLC 312 Walnut St Ste 3560 Cincinnati OH 45202-4026 E-mail: benefactors@fuse.net, psoul@aol.com.

FRIEDMAN, RACHELLE, music retail executive; b. Israel; m. Joseph Friedman; children: Jason, Daryn. Grad., Poly. Inst. of Brooklyn. Co-founder, co-CEO J & R Music World, N.Y.C., 1971—, J & R Computer World, N.Y.C., 1990—. Adv. bd. Dealerscope mag. Trustee Poly. U. N.Y. (bd. dirs. Y.E.S. Ctr. Promise Fund); bd. dirs. Heritage Trails., Alliance Downtown N.Y.; Grammy Awards host com. Mem. Nat. Assn. Record Merchandisers (mem. bd. dirs., chmn., 1998-99). Avocations: travel, boating, working out, reading. Office: J & R Music World 23 Park Row New York NY 10038-2397

FRIEDMAN, RICHARD DAVID, law educator; b. 1951; BA, Harvard U., 1973, JD, 1976; PhD, Christ Ch. U., Oxford Eng., 1979. Bar: N.Y. 1977, D.C. 1978, Mich. 1989. Law clk. to Hon. Irving R. Kaufman US Ct. Appeals (2d cir.), NYC, 1978-79; assoc. litigation dept. Paul, Weiss, Rifkind, Wharton & Garrison, NYC, 1979-82; asst. prof. Yeshiva U., 1982-85, assoc. prof., 1985-87, prof. law, 1987-88, U. Mich., Ann Arbor, 1988—, Ralph W. Aigler Prof. Law. Vis. prof. U. Mich., 1987-88. Named Disting. Young Writer Nat. Soc. Arts & Letters, 1978. Mem. Phi Beta Kappa. Office: U Mich Law Sch 731 Legal Rsch 625 S State St Ann Arbor MI 48109-1215 Office Phone: 734-747-1078. Fax: 734-764-8309.*

FRIEDMAN, RICHARD EVERETT, librarian; b. Cleve., Nov. 24, 1942; s. Harry Martin and Miriam (Zavelson) F. BS, Columbia U., 1966, MA, 1968; MLS, Kent (Ohio) State U., 1984. Asst. curator Met. Mus. Art, N.Y.C., 1968-72; curator Phillips Collection, Washington, 1972-75; pres. Fine Arts Appraisal, Inc., Cleve., 1975-85; collection mgr. U. Akron, Ohio, 1984-86; head librarian Auburn (Ala.) U. Architecture Library, 1986-89; pres. Fine Art Appraisals, Akron, Ohio, 1989—. Assoc. prof. Cath. U., Washington, 1973-75. Author: (book) Hundertwasser, 1975. Trustee Cleve. Modern Dance Assn., 1979-83; life fellow Met. Mus. Art; life. mem. Cleve. Mus. Art. Served to cpl. U.S. Army, 1960-63. Fellow Soc. Archtl. Historians; mem. Assn. Coll. and Research Libraries, Art Libraries Soc./N.Am. (v.p. Ohio chpt. 1985-86, devel. com. 1987—), Irish Georgian Hist. Soc., St. Juan de Luz Club (France), Columbia U. Club, Walden Golf and Tennis Club (Aurora, Ohio). Clubs: Walden Golf and Tennis (Aurora, Ohio). Home: Champs Fleuris Boul D'Augusta 64200 Biarritz France Home and Office: 666 N Howard St Apt 501 Akron OH 44310-2959

FRIEDMAN, RICHARD NATHAN, lawyer; b. Phila., June 13, 1941; s. Martin Harry Friedman and Caroline (Fruchtman) Shaines; m. Nini A. Friedman; 1 child, Melissa Danielle. BA, U. Miami, 1962, JD, 1965; LLM in Taxation, Georgetown U., 1967. Bar: Fla. 1965. Staff atty. SEC, Washington, 1965—66; pvt. practice Washington, 1966—67, Miami, Fla., 1968—; CEO All-State Sports Agts., Inc., 1996—99; player agt. NBPA, 1996—99; spl. asst. village atty. Village of Pinecrest, Fla., 2001. Adj. prof. U. Miami, 1972-76; arbitrator N.Y. Stock Exch., 1973—, AAA, 1988-2000, AMEX, NASD, 1988—; founder, pres. All-Star Music Corp., 1996—. Columnist Cmty. Newspapers, Miami, 1989—; featured performer motion picture Lenny 1974, other TV and theatrical films; rec. artist, The Singing Attorney, For Love of Country, 1996, All My Love, 2001; author numerous pub. poems. Founder, pres. Am. Stockholders Assn., Inc., 1971-74, Stop Transit-Over People, Inc., 1975-87; chmn. Sales Taxes Oppressing People, Fla., 1987—; mem. endowment com. U. Miami, 1970—; mem. Soc. Univ. Founders, U. Miami, 1980-; co-chmn. sports com. Fla. Bar, 1997-99. Recipient Merit cert. Dade County Bar Assn., 1972-73; numerous certs. of appreciation Rotary Internat., Kiwanis and other svc. orgns., 1970—; Richard N. Friedman Week held in his honor City of Homestead, Fla., Apr. 1978; named Hon. Citizen State of Tenn., 1970, Citizen of Day Dade County (Fla.), Radio Sta. WINZ, 1980; recipient Leaders award Sunrise Cmty., 1986. Mem. NARAS, Unified Bar D.C. Office Phone: 305-666-2747. Personal E-mail: busorgs@aol.com.

FRIEDMAN, ROBERT BARRY, neurosurgeon; b. Bklyn., Dec. 28, 1953; s. Roy and Bernice (Berger) Friedman. BA, SUNY, Stony Brook, 1975; MD, SUNY Health Sci. Ctr., Bklyn., 1980. Diplomate Am. Bd. Neurol. Surgery. Gen. med. officer Indian Health Svc. USPHS, Sacaton, Ariz., 1981—82; neurosurgeon USAF, Wright Patterson AFB, Ohio, 1989—91, South Broward Neurosurg. Assn., Pembroke Pines, Fla., 1991—95, Cleve. Clinic Fla., Ft. Lauderdale, 1995—97, Spectrum Neurosurg. Specialists, Marietta, Ga., 1997—98, Henry Neurosurg. Specialists, P.C., Stockbridge, Ga., 1998—. Med. staff fellow NIH, Bethesda, Md., 1986—88. Contbr. articles to profl. jours. Maj. USAF, 1988—91. Recipient Neuroscience award, U. Pitts., 1989. Fellow: ACS; mem.: AMA, Fla. Med. Assn., So. Med. Assn., Congress Neurol. Surgeons, Am. Assn. Neurol. Surgeons. Libertarian. Avocations: private pilot, computers, photography. Home: 602 Redbud Ln Stockbridge GA 30281 Office: c/o Henry Neurosurg Specialists PC 297 Country Club Dr Stockbridge GA 30281-7350 Office Phone: 770-506-3303. Personal E-mail: robert3018@msn.com.

FRIEDMAN, ROBERT LAURENCE, investment company executive; b. Mt. Vernon, NY, Mar. 19, 1943; s. Alvin S. and Frances (Feinsod) F.; m. Barbara Lander, Dec. 25, 1964; children: Lisa, Andrew. AB, Columbia Coll., 1964; JD, U. Pa., 1967. Bar: NY 1968. Assoc. Simpson, Thacher & Bartlett, NYC, 1967—74, ptnr., 1974—99; sr. mng. dir. The Blackstone Group LP, NYC, 1999—2002, sr. mng. dir., chief adminstrv. officer, chief legal officer, 2003—. Bd. dir. Axis Capital Holdings, Houghton Mifflin Holdings, Northwest Airlines, TRW Automotive Holdings Corp. Office: The Blackstone Group LP 345 Park Ave Fl 31 New York NY 10154-0004

FRIEDMAN, ROBERT LEE, film company executive; s. Edward A. and Claire (Seidenberg) F.; m. Marlene Saltz; children: Marc, Lisa. Sales Universal Pictures, N.Y.C., 1948-52, 54-59; exec. v.p., distbn. & mktg. United Artists Corp., N.Y.C., 1959-79; pres., distbn. Columbia Pictures, Burbank, Calif., 1979-82; pres. AMC Entertainment Internat., L.A., 1984-92, pres. motion picture group, 1992-99; pres. RLF Entertainment, Beverly Hills, Calif., 1999—; CEO, pres. Stereo Vision Entertainment, Beverly Hills, 2000—. Radio announcer The Bob Friedman Hour, 1952-54; cons. RLF Prodns., Beverly Hills, Calif., 1982-84; sr. entertainment advisor, cons. Chanin Capital Ptnrs.; mem. bd. advisors Smart Video Tech. Exec. prodr., appeared in film 9 Deaths of the Ninja, 1984; appeared in film Stardust Memories, 1980; prodr. film Girls Gone Wild. Bd. dirs., chmn. Entertainment Industry com. Century City C. of C., L.A., 1988—; chmn. Will Rogers Hosp., 1980-81, also bd. dirs.; bd. dirs. Dare Am.; mem. vision fund The Lighthouse for the Blind. With U.S. Army, 1952—54. Named Man of Yr. N.Y. State Nat. Assn. Theatre Owners, 1981, Va., Md., Washington D.C. Assn. Theatre Owners, 1980. Mem. Acad. Motion Picture Arts & Scis. (bd. dirs. endowment fund, 1979—), Variety Club Am. (L.A.), Motion Picture Pioneers Am., Motion Picture Assocs. Found. (pres. 1970-73), L.A.-Century City C. of C. (Citizen of Yr., 1994) Avocations: going to movies, playing tennis, exercising, photography, spending time with my wife and grandchildren. Office: RLF Entertainment 2216 Summitridge Dr Beverly Hills CA 90210-1526 Office Phone: 310-550-7760. Personal E-mail: rlfblz@aol.com.

FRIEDMAN, ROBERT SIDNEY, political science professor; b. Balt., Mar. 1, 1927; s. Harry N. and Eva (Cohen) F.; m. Renee Cohen, Aug. 11, 1953 (dec. Oct. 4, 2002); children: Helene, David. BA, Johns Hopkins U., 1948; MA, U. Ill., 1950, PhD, 1953. Rsch. asst. Bur. Govt. Rsch., Md., 1953-55; instr. govt. and politics U. Md., 1955-56; from instr. to assoc. prof. govt. La. State U., 1956-61; rsch. assoc. Inst. Pub. Adminstrn., U. Mich., 1961-67, acting dir., 1967-68; assoc. prof. polit. sci. U. Mich., 1961-66, prof., 1966-68; prof., head dept. polit. sci. Pa. State U., 1968-78; dir. Center for Study Sci. Policy, Inst. for Policy Research and Evaluation, 1978-88, dir. policy analysis program, 1991-94; prof. emeritus, 1994—. Cons. in field. Co-author: Local Government in Maryland, 1955, Government in Metropolitan New Orleans, 1959, Political Leadership and the School Desegration Crisis in New Orleans, 1963; author: The Michigan Constitutional Convention and Administrative Organization: A Case Study in the Politics of Constitution-Making, 1971; contbg. author: Politics in the American States, 1965, 5th edit., 1990; contbr. articles to profl. jours. Bd. dirs. Pa. Civil Liberties Union, 1969-72; mem. State College (Pa.) Zoning Hearing Bd., 1976-79; chmn. study com. State College Mcpl. Govt., 1991-93; active State College Planning Commn., 1996-99; safety adv. bd. Three Mile Island-2 Cleanup, 1981-89; Pa. bd. Common Cause, 1998—; pres. Friends of Schlow Meml. Libr., 1999-2002, trustee, 2002—. With AUS, 1945-46. Recipient McKay Donkin award for disting. svc., 1980. Mem. Am. Polit. Sci. Assn. Home: 205 Horizon Dr State College PA 16801-8615 E-mail: rsf3@psu.edu.

FRIEDMAN, RODGER, antiquarian bookseller, consultant; b. Detroit, Nov. 10, 1951; s. Stanley B. and Miriam Elizabeth (Levin) F.; m. Kiki Nelson, July 1, 1983. BA, Kalamazoo Coll., 1973; MA, U. N.Mex., Albuquerque, 1979, CUNY, 1987, PhD, 1989; MLS, Pratt Inst., 1996. Libr. Century Assn., N.Y.C., 1982—88, Union League Club, N.Y.C., 1989—96. Mem. editl. bd. Ballet Rev., 1983-96; translator: Posthumous People by Massimo Cacciari, 1996; Quar. catalogue of rare books; contbr. articles to profl. jours. Recipient Frederick II medal U. Naples, 1991. Mem. Antiquarian Booksellers Assn. Am., Assn. Internat. Studi di Lingua Letteratura Italiana, Internat. Assn. for Neo-Latin Studies, The Sterling Forest Partnership. Home: 1 Mystic Cir Tuxedo Park NY 10987-5027 E-mail: rf@rarebookstudio.com.

FRIEDMAN, RONALD M., plastic surgeon; b. L.A., Aug. 18, 1966; s. Albert and Linda Friedman; m. Jin Oh Friedman, Sept. 1993; children: Andrew, Rachel. BS, Northwestern U., 1987, MD, 1989. Cert. Am. Bd. Plastic Surgeons, 1997. Intern U. Tex. Southwestern Med. Ctr., Dallas, 1989—92, resident, 1992—94; chief plastic surgery Parkland Meml. Hosp., 1995—96; plastic surgeon pvt. practice, Plano, 1996—. Composer: (songs) America; contbr. articles to profl. jours. Fellow, Loma Linda U. Med. Ctr., Calif., 1994—95. Fellow: Am. Coll. Surgeons; mem.: AMA, Dallas County Med. Soc., Tex. Soc. Plastic Surgeons, Tex. Med. Assn., Am. Soc. Aesthetic Plastic Surgery (com. mem. 1996—2001), Am. soc. Plastic Surgeons (instructional course com. 2000—03), Alpha Omega Alpha. Avocations: music, woodworking, marble sculpting, piano. Office: 6124 W Parker Rd Ste 23 Plano TX 75093 Office Phone: 469-467-0100.

FRIEDMAN, ROSELYN L., lawyer, mediator; b. Cleve., Dec. 9, 1942; d. Charles and Lillian Edith (Zalzneck) Friedman. BS, U. Pitts., 1964; MA, Case Western Res. U., 1967; JD cum laude, Loyola U., Chgo., 1977. Bar: Ill. 1977, U.S. Dist. Ct. (no. dist.) Ill. 1977. Mem. legal dept. No. Trust Co., Chgo., 1977-79; assoc. Rudnick & Wolfe, Chgo., 1979-84, ptnr., 1984-95, Sachnoff & Weaver, Ltd., Chgo., 1995—, ptnr., chmn. dept. estates and trusts, 2002—05. Mem. Loyola U., Chgo. law rev.; mem. profl. adv. com. Chgo. Jewish Fedn., chmn., 1999-2001; mem. profl. adv. com. Chgo. Cmty. Trust, 2001-. Trustee Jewish Women's Found., 1997—2001; mediator Ctr. for Conflict Resolution, 2000—. Fellow Am. Coll. Trust and Estate Counsel; mem. ABA, Am. Jewish Congress (gov. coun. Midwest region 1995-97), Chgo. Bar Assn. (cert. appreciation continuing legal edn. program 1984, chmn. trust law com. 1989-90), Chgo. Estate Planning Coun. (program com. 1992-94, 98-2000, membership com. 1997-98, bd. dirs. 2001-2003), spkr. Ill. Inst. CLE, Chgo. Fin. Exch. (bd. dirs. 1995-97, sec. 1996-97). Office: Sachnoff & Weaver Ltd 10 S Wacker Dr Ste 4000 Chicago IL 60606-7075 Office Phone: 312-207-6531. E-mail: rfriedman@sachnoff.com.

FRIEDMAN, S. LILA, librarian; b. Bklyn., Sept. 25, 1926; d. Ephraim Eliezer and Naomi (Weisdorff) Ritter; m. S. Lester Friedman, Jan. 25, 1946; children— Matthew, Joel, Amy. B.A., Bklyn. Coll., 1948; M.L.S., L.I. U., 1975. Cert. library media specialist, secondary sch. tchr. library, N.Y. Librarian, Hunter Coll. High Sch., N.Y.C., 1973-74, Hawthorne (N.Y.) Cedar Knolls Sch., 1976, Samuel Tilden High Sch., Bklyn., 1978-79, Bellerose Jewish Ctr., Floral Park, N.Y., 1980—, dir. library, 1980—; librarian Katharine Gibbs Sch., Huntington, N.Y., 1984— . Area chmn. Queens United Cerebral Palsy, 1969, 71. Recipient 25th Anniversary award State of Israel Bonds, 1975, Youth Services award B'nai B'rith, 1983. Mem. ALA, Assn. Jewish Libraries, L.I. Assn. Jewish Libraries (charter mem.), Am. Assn. Sch. Librarians. Jewish. Home: 80 49 252d St Bellerose NY 11426 Office: Bellerose Jewish Ctr 25404 Union Tpke Floral Park NY 11004-1293

FRIEDMAN, SAMUEL SELIG, lawyer; b. NYC, July 25, 1935; s. Nathan and Anne M. (Sobel) F.; m. Maxine E. Goldfarb, Jan. 7, 1961; 1 child, Alison J. BS, MIT, 1956; MBA, U. Pa., 1959; LLB, Columbia U., 1965. Bar: NY 1965, US Dist. Ct. (so. and ea. dists.) NY 1967, US Supreme Ct. 1984. Assoc. Lord, Day & Lord, NYC, 1965-72; ptnr., mem. exec. com. Lord Day & Lord, Barrett Smith and predecessor firm, NYC, 1972-94; ptnr. Morgan, Lewis &

Bockius LLP, NYC, 1994—2004. Vice chmn., dir., mem. exec. com. Times Square Bus. Improvement Dist., 1992-95. 1st lt. US Army, 1959-62. Mem. ABA, NY State Bar Assn., Assn. Bar City NY, MIT Club NY, Penn Club, Phi Delta Phi. Avocations: travel, wine, sports. Office: 400 West End Ave New York NY 10024-5751 Office Phone: 212-724-7859.

FRIEDMAN, SHELLY ARNOLD, cosmetic surgeon; b. Providence, Jan. 1, 1949; s. Saul and Estelle (Moverman) F.; m. Andrea Leslie Falchook, Aug. 30, 1975; children: Bethany Erin, Kimberly Rebecca, Brent David, Jennifer Ashley. BA, Providence Coll., 1971; DO, Mich. State U., 1982. Diplomate Nat. Bd. Med. Examiners, Am. Bd. Dermatology. Intern Pontiac (Mich.) Hosp., 1982-83, resident in dermatology, 1983-86; assoc. clin. prof. dept. internal medicine Mich. State U., 1984—89, adj. clin. prof., 1989—; med. dir. Inst. Cosmetic Dermatology, Scottsdale, Ariz., 1986—. Pres. Am. Bd. Hair Restoration Surgery. Contbr. articles to profl. jours. Mem. B'nai B'rith Men's Coun., 1973, Jewish Welfare Fund, 1973. Am. Physicians fellow for medicine, 1982. Mem. AMA, Am. Osteo. Assn., Am. Assn. Cosmetic Surgeons, Am. Acad. Cosmetic Surgery, Internat. Soc. Dermatologic Surgery, Internat. Acad. Cosmetic Surgery, Am. Acad. Dermatology, Am. Soc. Dermatologic Surgery, Frat. Order Police, Sigma Sigma Phi. Jewish. Avocations: Karate, horseback riding. Office: Scottsdale Inst Cosmetic Dermatology 5828 N 7th St Phoenix AZ 85014 Office Phone: 480-970-0300. Personal E-mail: haredoc@aol.com.

FRIEDMAN, SOFIA, social sciences educator, nutritionist, educator; b. San Carlos, Uruguay, Oct. 7, 1940; arrived in USA, 1988; d. Israel Iser and Szajndla Lea (Lebensohn) Friedman; m. Salomao Nejman, Dec. 26, 1959 (div. June 10, 1980); children: Helena (Nejman) Bardusco, Regina Nejman, Susana Nejman. BS nutrition, Univ. Rio De Janeiro, Rio de Janeiro, Brazil, 1979; MA social comm., Fed. Univ. of Rio de Janeiro, Rio de Janeiro, Brazil, 1987; MA polit. sci., City Univ. of Rio de Janeiro, New York, NY, 1995; PhD internat. studies, Fairfax Univ., London, Eng., 2000. Cert. Yoga Instr. Vayuananda Yoga Ctr./ Rio de Janeiro, Brazil, 1974, Internat. Sivananda Yoga Vedanta Ctr./Paradise Is., Bahamas, 1983. Asst. prof. Univ. of Rio de Janeiro, Rio de Janeiro, 1980—88; adj. instr. Hudson County Cmty. Coll., Jersey City, NJ, 1995—97, Stevens Inst. of Tech., Hoboken, NJ, 1997, La Guardia Cmty. Coll., NY, NY, 1995—2000. Founder, owner Redefining Life After Fifty ednl. seminars, Hoboken, 1997—. Author: (MA thesis dissertation) Food Scarcity and Abundance: Analysis of a Food Sys. in Natividade, Rio de Janeiro, 1987, The Emergence of a Condition of Food Insecurity in Brazil During the 1964-1985 Military Regime and the Rise of Civil Soc., 1995, (book) Brazil 1960-1990: Structures of Power and Processes of Change, 2003. Democrat. Jewish. Home and Office: 159 14th St Apt 5 Hoboken NJ 07030 Office Phone: 201-792-3815. E-mail: sfriedman@aol.com.

FRIEDMAN, STEPHEN, former federal official; m. Barbara Friedman. BA, Cornell U.; JD, Columbia U. With Goldman Sachs & Co., 1966—94, ptnr., 1973—92, co-chmn. N.Y.C., 1990—92, chmn., sr. ptnr., 1992—94; sr. prin. Marsh & McLennan Capital, Inc., 1998—2002; asst. to the Pres. for econ. policy The White House, Washington, 2002—04; dir. The Nat. Econ. Coun., Washington, 2002—04. Mem. Fgn. Intelligence Advisory Bd., 1993—95; chmn. emeritus bd. trustees Columbia U.; chmn. fin. com. Memorial Sloan-Kettering Cancer Ctr.; chmn. exec. com. Brookings Instn.; mem. bd. dirs. The Goldman Sachs Group In.; former mem. bd. dirs. Wal-Mart Stores Inc., Fannie Mae.

FRIEDMAN, STEPHEN J, lawyer; b. Mar. 19, 1938; s. A.E. Robert and Janice Clara (Miller) F.; m. Fredrica L. Schwab, June 25, 1961; children: Vanessa V., Alexander S. AB magna cum laude, Princeton U., 1959; LLB magna cum laude, Harvard U., 1962. Bar: N.Y. 1962, D.C. 1982. Law clk. to justice William J. Brennan Jr. U.S. Supreme Ct., 1963-64; spl. asst. to maritime adminstr. Maritime Adminstrn., Dept. Commerce, 1964-65; assoc. Debevoise & Plimpton, NYC, 1965-70, ptnr., 1970—77, 1981—86, 1993—2004; dep. asst. sec. for capital markets policy Dept. Treasury, Washington, 1977-79; commr. SEC, 1980-81; exec. v.p., gen. counsel E.F. Hutton Group Inc., NYC, 1986-88, Equitable Life Assurance Soc., NYC, 1988-93; dean Sch. Law, Pace U., 2004—. Lectr. law Columbia U., N.Y.C., 1974—77, 1982—85. Author: An Affair With Freedom, the Opinions and Speeches of William J. Brennan, Jr., 1967; contbr. articles on legal and policy aspects of fin. inst. to profl. jours. Active Coun. on Fgn. Rels.; trustee, chmn. emeritus Am. Ballet Theatre, N.Y.C.; pres., trustee Practising Law Inst.; mem. bd. govs. NASD, 1991-94, Chgo. Bd. Options Exch., 1982-88; pres. Practicing Law Inst.; chmn. Asian U. for Women Support Found. With USAR, 1962-68. Mem. ABA, Assn. of Bar of the City of N.Y. (chmn. com. on securities regulation), Univ. Club. Office: Pace U Sch of Law 78 N Broadway White Plains NY 10603 Office Phone: 914-422-4407. Business E-Mail: sfriedman@law.pace.edu.

FRIEDMAN, STEVEN ARTHUR, lawyer, internist; b. Detroit, 1940; m. Gail Kropnick, 1965; children: Douglas David, Craig Edward Arthur, Stacey Ruth Anne. MD, Jefferson, 1966; JD, Widener, 1995, LLM, 1999. Cert. Bd. Internal Medicine. Pvt. practice physician atty., Havertown, Pa., 1995—. Contbr. articles to profl. jours. Office: 850 West Chester Pike Havertown PA 19083 Office Phone: 610-789-0568.

FRIEDMAN, SUE TYLER, technical publications executive; b. Nürnberg, Germany, Feb. 28, 1925; came to U.S., 1938; d. William and Ann (Federlein) Tyler (Theilheimer); m. Gerald Manfred Friedman, June 27, 1948; children: Judith Fay Friedman Rosen, Sharon Mira Friedman Azaria, Devora Paula Friedman Zweibach, Eva Jane Friedman Scholle, Wendy Tamar Friedman Spanier. Student, Beth Israel Sch. Nursing, 1941—43. Exec. dir. Ventures and Publs. Gerald M. Friedman, 1964—90; owner Tyler Publs., Watervliet and Troy, NY, 1979—86; treas., dir. Northeastern Sci. Found., Inc., Troy, 1979—; treas. Gerry Exploration, Inc., Troy, 1982—88; office mgr. Rensselaer Ctr. Applied Geology, Troy, 1983—. Pres. Pioneer Women/Na'amat, Tulsa, 1961-64, treas., Jerusalem, Israel, 1964, pres., Albany, N.Y., 1968-70; bd. dirs. Temple Beth-El, 1965—, dir. Hebrew Sch., 1965-80; mem. social program com. Internat. Sedimentological. Congress, 1979. Named Hon. Alumna, Dept. Geology, Bklyn. Coll. at CUNY, 1989; Sue Tyler Friedman medal for distinction in history of geology created in her honor Geol. Soc. London, 1988; recipient Disting. Svc. award Temple Beth-El, 1991, Scroll of Honor, State of Israel Bonds, 1981. Mem. Geology Alumni Assn. (hon.). Avocation: world travel. Office: Northeastern Sci Found Inc Rensselaer Ctr Applied Geology PO Box 746 Troy NY 12181-0746 Personal E-mail: gmfriedman@nycap.rr.com.

FRIEDMAN, SYDNEY M., anatomist, educator, medical researcher; b. Montreal, Que., Can., Feb. 17, 1916; s. Jacob and Minnie (Signer) F.; m. Constance Livingstone, Sept. 23, 1940. B.Sc., McGill U., Montreal, Can., 1938, MD, C.M., 1940, M.Sc., 1941, PhD, 1946. Med. licentiate, Que. Teaching fellow anatomy McGill U., Montreal, Que., Can., 1940-42, asst. prof. anatomy, 1944-48, assoc. prof. anatomy, 1948-50; prof., head dept. anatomy U. B.C., Vancouver, Can., 1950-81, prof. anatomy, 1981-85, prof. emeritus, 1985—. Mem. panel on shock Def. Research Bd., Ottawa, Can., 1955-57; sci. subcom. Can. Heart Found., 1962-66, Am. Heart Assn., 1966-68, B.C. Heart Found., Vancouver, founding mem. Author: Visual Anatomy, 1950, 2d edit., 1970; contbr. more than 200 articles to profl. publs. Served as flight lt. RCAF, 1943-44. Recipient Premier award for rsch. in aging CIBA Found., 1955, Outstanding Svc. award Heart Found. Can., 1981, Disting. Achievement award Can. Hypertension Soc., 1987; Commemorative medal 125th Anniversary Can. Confedn.; Pfizer travel fellow Clin. Rsch. Inst., Montreal, 1971. Fellow AAAS, Royal Soc. Can., Coun. High Blood Pressure Rsch.; mem. Am. Anatomical Assn. (exec. com. 1970-74), Can. Assn. Anatomists (pres. 1965-66, J.C.B. Grant award 1982), Internat. Soc. Hypertension, Am. Physiol. Soc., Royal Vancouver Yacht Club, Vancouver Club, Alpha Omega Alpha. Avocation: painting. Home: 4916 Chancellor Blvd Vancouver BC Canada V6T 1E1

FRIEDMAN, THOMAS LOREN, foreign correspondent, writer; b. Mpls., July 20, 1953; s. Harold Abraham and Margaret (Phillips) F.; m. Ann Louise Bucksbaum, Nov. 23, 1978, 2 children. BA, Brandeis U., 1975; M.Phil., St. Anthony's Coll., Oxford U., 1978. Staff corr. UPI, London, 1978-79, Middle East corr. Beirut, 1979-81; reporter Bus. Day. sect. N.Y. Times, N.Y.C., 1981-82, Beirut bur. chief, 1982-84, Jerusalem bur. chief, 1984-89, chief diplomatic corr. Washington, 1989—, fgn. affairs columnist, 1995—. Author: From Beirut to Jerusalem, 1989 (Nat Book Award, 1989), The Lexus and the Olive Branch, 2000 (Overseas Press Club award, 2000), Longitudes and Attitudes: The World in the Age of Terrorism, 2002, The World Is Flat: A Brief History of the Twenty-First Century, 2005 (NY Times Bestseller list, 2005, Publishers Weekly Bestseller list, 2005). Recipient Pulitzer prize, 1983, 1988, George Polk award L.I. U., 1982, Livingston award Livingston Found., 1983, Overseas Press Club award, 1980, Robert D. Heinl Jr. Meml. award Marine Corps History, 1985, Page 1 award N.Y. Newspaper Guild, 1984. Jewish. Office: NY Times 1627 I St NW Washington DC 20006*

FRIEDMAN, TULLY MICHAEL, corporate financial executive; b. Chgo., Jan. 9, 1942; s. Louis P. and Dorothy G. Friedman; m. Elise Woolsey Dorsey; children: Albert Evans Walker (dec.), Abigail Fay, Alexander Louis, Allegra Woolsey. AB, Stanford U., 1962; JD, Harvard U., 1965. Bar: Calif. 1965, Ill. 1967. With Charles Percy for Senator Com., Chgo., 1966; assoc. Sidley & Austin, Chgo., 1967-70; corp. fin. assoc. Salomon Bros., N.Y.C., 1970-71, v.p., dir. West Coast corp. fin. San Francisco, 1972-79, gen. ptnr., 1979-81, mng. dir., 1981-84; founding ptnr. Hellman & Friedman, San Francisco, 1984-97; chmn., CEO Friedman, Fleischer & Lowe, LLC, San Francisco, 1997—. Bd. dirs. The Clorox Co., Mattel, Inc., Tempurpedic Internat., Inc., Archimedes Tech. Group, CapitalSource Holdings LLC. Trustee, treas. Am. Enterprise Inst., 1988—; dir. Telluride Found., 2001-. Office: One Maritime Pla Ste 1000 San Francisco CA 94111-3413 Office Phone: 415-402-2100. E-mail: tfriedman@fflpartners.com.

FRIEDMAN, WALKER C., lawyer; b. Ft. Worth, Sept. 24, 1952; s. Bayard H. and Cornelia (Cheney) Friedman; m. Joan Elizabeth Pearson; children: Dillon, Chase, Paige. BA, U. Tex., 1974; JD, So. Meth. U., 1977. Bar: Tex. 1977, US Dist. Ct. No. Dist. Tex., US Ct. Appeals 5th Cir. Assoc., then shareholder Law, Snakard & Gambill, Ft. Worth, 1977-93; shareholder Friedman, Suder & Cooke (formerly Friedman, Young & Suder), Ft. Worth, 1993—. Chmn. exec. com. Ft. Worth Transp. Authority, 1993-99; trustee Mary Potishman Lard Trust; bd. trustees Amon Carter Mus. Mem. ABA, Tex. Bar Assn., Tarrant County Bar Assn., Tarrant County Civil Trial Lawyers Assn. (pres. 1990), Tex. Bar Found., Tarrant County Bar Found., Ft. Worth Inn of Ct., Exch. Club, Ft. Worth Club. Office: Friedman Suder & Cooke Tindall Sq Warehouse No 1 Ste 200 604 E 4th St Fort Worth TX 76102 Office Phone: 817-334-0400. Office Fax: 817-334-0401.*

FRIEDMAN, WILBUR HARVEY, lawyer; b. N.Y.C., May 2, 1907; s. Isador Peter and Zara (Sloat) F.; m. Frances Margolis, May 21, 1943. AB, Columbia U., 1927, LLB, 1930. Bar: N.Y. 1931. Law sec. U.S. Supreme Ct. Justice Harlan F. Stone, 1930-31; staff atty. Office of U.S. Solicitor Gen., 1931-32; mem. firm Proskauer Rose Goetz & Mendelsohn (now Proskauer Rose LLP), N.Y.C., 1932-40; ptnr. Proskauer, Rose, Goetz, & Mendelsohn, N.Y.C., 1940—. Lectr. Inst. on Fed. Taxation, NYU, 1943-65, lectr. Sch. Gen. Edn., 1955-60; bd. dirs., sec. Lawrence M. Gelb Found.; bd. dirs. Cancer Rsch. Inst., 1983-99; chmn. exec. com. bd. visitors Law Sch., Columbia U., 1977-91. Contbr. articles to profl. jours. Chmn. bd. overseers Edith C. Blum Art Inst. at Bard Coll., 1985-93; mem. Rockefeller U. Coun., 1986—; mem. med. ctr. adv. bd. N.Y. Hosp.-Cornell Med. Ctr., 1986—. Mem. ABA (mem. ho. dels. 1978-87), N.Y. State Bar Assn. (mem. exec. com. sect. taxation 1968-76), Assn. of Bar of City of N.Y. (chmn. com. on mgmt. and operation of profl. practice 1981-85), N.Y. County Lawyers Assn. (pres. 1975-77, mem. exec. com. 1977-79, chmn. com. on taxation 1948-54, chmn. com. on group ins. 1960-74, chmn. spl. com. on consumer agreements 1977-83), Lotos Club, Princeton U. Club, Phi Beta Kappa, Phi Beta Kappa Assocs., Tau Delta Phi. Home: 1016 5th Ave Apt 2D New York NY 10028-0132 Office: Proskauer Rose LLP 1585 Broadway Rm 2016 New York NY 10036-8299 E-mail: wfriedman@proskauer.com.

FRIEDMANN, E(MERICH) IMRE, biologist, educator; b. Budapest, Hungary, Dec. 20, 1921; arrived in U.S., 1965; s. Hugo and Gisella (Singer) Friedmann; m. Roseli Ocampo, July 22, 1974; 1 child, Daphna. Student Sch. Agriculture, Hungary, 1943, student Sch. Agriculture, 1944, student U. Debrecen, 1948; PhD in Botany, Zoology, U. Vienna, 1951. Instr., lectr. Hebrew U., Jerusalem, 1952-66; assoc. prof. Queens U., Kingston, Canada, 1967-68, Fla. State U., Tallahassee, 1968-76, prof., 1976—2001, Robert Lawton Disting. prof., 1991—2001, dir. Polar Desert Rsch. Ctr., 1985—2001; sr. NRC rsch. fellow NASA Ames Rsch. Ctr., Moffett Field, Calif., 2001—. Concurrent prof. Nanjing U., People's Republic of China, 1987—; vis. prof. Fla. State U., Tallahassee, 1966-67, U. Vienna, 1975; disting. sr. vis. scientist Jet Propulsion Lab., 1999-2000. Editor Antarctic Microbiology, 1993; contbr. articles to profl. jours. Recipient Congl. Antarctic Svc. medal NSF, 1979, Alexander von Humboldt award, 1987, resolution of commendation Gov. of Fla., 1978, Bergey's medal Bergey's Manual Trust, 2001. Fellow: AAAS, Am. Acad. Microbiology, Am. Soc. Microbiology (Procter and Gamble award in environ. microbiology 1998), Royal Microsci. Soc., Linnean Soc. London, Exploreres Club; mem.: Internat. Soc. Study of Origins of Life, Soc. Phycol. France, Hungarian Algological Soc. (hon.), Internat. Phycol. Soc., Am. Phycol. Soc. (award of Excellence 2002), Indian Phycol. Soc., Brit. Phycol. Soc., Hungarian Acad. Scis. (fgn.). Jewish. Achievements include co-discovery of micro-organisms (cryptoendolithic lichens) living in Antarctic rocks, 1976; discovery of fossil bacteria in the Martian meteorite ALH 84001, 2001. Office: Space Sci Divsn 245-3 NASA Ames Rsch Ctr Moffett Field CA 94035 Home: 225 4th Ave Apt B-503 Kirkland WA 98033 E-mail: ifriedmann@mail.arc.nasa.gov.

FRIEDMANN, PATRICIA ANN, writer; b. New Orleans, La., Oct. 29, 1946; d. Werner and Marjorie Sybil (Cahn) F.; m. Robert E. Skinner, Mar. 17, 1979 (div. Nov. 1996); children: Esme Friedmann, Werner Friedmann II; m. Edward G. Muchmore, Nov. 11, 1999. AB, Smith Coll., 1968; MEd, Temple Univ., 1970; ABD, Univ. Denver, 1975. Fiction workshop facilitator, New Orleans, 1994—99; writer-in-residence Tulane U., 2001; reviewer Publishers Weekly, Brightleaf, Times-Picayune, 1993—99; spkr. in field. Author: Too Smart to Be Rich, 1988, The Exact Image of Mother, 1991, Eleanor Rushing, 1999 (Barnes & Noble Discover Great Writers selection, Borders Original Voices selection), Odds, 2000, Secondhand Smoke, 2002 (Book Sense 76 selection), (play) The Accidental Jew as part of Native Tongues, 1994, Lovely Rita as part of Native Tongues, 2000; contbg. author: The New Great American Writers Cookbook, 2003, Christmas Stories from Louisiana, 2003; author short stories. Mem. Authors Guild. Home: 8330 Sycamore Pl New Orleans LA 70118-2941 E-mail: afreelunch@aol.com.

FRIEDMANN, PAUL, surgeon, educator, research and development company executive; b. Vienna, Dec. 2, 1933; immigrated, 1938; naturalized, 1944. s. Erich and Rochelle (Behar) F.; m. Janee Armstrong, Apr. 24, 1962; children: Pamela, Cynthia. BA, U. Pa., 1955; MD, Harvard U., 1959; MBA, U. Mass., 2000. Diplomate, Am. Bd. Surgery (Vascular Surgery). Chmn. dept. surgery Baystate Med. Ctr., Springfield, Mass., 1971-98, sr. v.p. acad. affairs, 1996—2005; prof. surgery Sch. Medicine Tufts U., Boston, 1985—; exec. dir. Pioneer Valley Life Scis. Rsch. Inst., Springfield, 2005—. Prof. of surgery, Tufts U. Sch. Medicine, Boston, 1985—, chmn. ad interim dept. surgery, 1996-2001; mem. residency rev. com., 1985-91, chmn., 1989-91; chmn. RRC Coun., Accreditation Coun. for Grad. Med. Edn., 1989-91, mem., 1994-2000. Contbr. articles to profl. jours. Pres. Springfield Symphony Orch., 1999—2001, bd. chmn., 2001—03. Capt. USAF, 1961—63. Fellow ACS (bd. govs. 1978-84, 94—, vice chmn., 1998-99, pres. Mass. chpt. 1987, exec. com. bd. govs. 1996-99, adv. coun. for gen. surgery 1996-2003, chmn. 2001-03); mem. Am. Surg. Assn., Assn. Program Dirs. in Surgery (sec. 1985-87, pres. 1987-89), Coun. Med. Specialty Socs. (bd. dirs., sec. 1995-96, pres. elect 1996-97, pres. 1997-98), New Eng. Soc. Vascular Surgery (recorder 1989-90, pres.-elect 1990-91, pres. 1991-92), New Eng. Surg. Soc. (treas. 1991-95, pres.-elect 1995-96, pres. 1996-97), Accreditation Coun. for Grad. Med. Edn. (exec. com. 1995—, chmn. designate 1997-98, chmn. 1998-2000, John C. Gienapp award Contbns. Grad. Med. Edn. 2003). Office: Baystate Med Ctr 759 Chestnut St Springfield MA 01199-1001 Personal E-mail: p.friedmann@comcast.net.

FRIEDMANN, PERETZ PETER, aerospace engineer, educator; arrived in U.S., 1969, naturalized, 1977; s. Mauritius and Elisabeth Friedmann; m. Esther Sarfati. DSc, MIT, 1972. Research asst. dept. aeronautics and astronautics MIT, Cambridge, 1969-72; asst. prof. mech. and aerospace engrng. dept. UCLA, 1972-77, assoc. prof., 1977-80, prof., 1980-98, chmn. dept. mech. and aerospace engrng. Los Angeles, 1988-91; François-Xavier Bagnoud prof. aerospace engrng. dept. U. Mich., Ann Arbor, 1999—. Editor in chief Vertica-Internat. Jour. Rotocraft and Powered Lift Aircraft, 1980-90; contbr. numerous articles to profl. jours. Grantee NASA, Air Force Office Sci. Rsch., U.S. Army Rsch. Office, NSF. Fellow AIAA (recipient Structures, Structural Dynamics and Materials award 1996, Structures, Structural Dynamics and Materials Lectr. award 97), Am. Helicopter Soc.; mem. ASME (Structures and Materials award 1984, Spirit of St. Louis medal, 2003, ASME/Boeing Structures and Materials award 2004), Sigma Xi. Jewish. Office: U Mich Aerospace Engring Dept 3001 FXB Bldg Ann Arbor MI 48109-2140 Business E-Mail: peretzf@umich.edu.

FRIEDMANN, THEODORE, physician; b. Vienna, June 16, 1935; s. Eric and Rochelle (Behar) Friedmann; m. Ingrid Anna Stromberg, Jan. 3, 1965; children: Eric, Carl. BA, U. Pa., 1956, MD, 1960, MA, 1994. Diplomate Nat. Bd. Med. Examiners. Staff scientist NIH, Bethesda, Md., 1965-68; from asst. to full prof. pediatrics U. Calif. San Diego, La Jolla, 1970—, prof. pediatrics, dir. gene therapy, bd. dirs. Newton Abraham vis. prof., fellow Lincoln Coll., U. Oxford, England, 1994; mem. Congrl. Biomed. Ethics Adv. Com., U.S. Congress, Washington, 1988—92, Exptl. Virology Study Sect./NIH, 1986—90; Muriel Jeannette Whitehill chair biomed. ethics U. Calif., San Diego, 1989—; mem. com. on human cloning State of Calif., 2000—; mem. com. on medicine, health & rsch. IOC, World Anti Doping Agy., 2000—; mem. Recombinant DNA Adv. Bd./NIH, 1998—, chmn., 2002—. Author: (monograph) Gene Therapy: Fact and Fiction, 1993; editor: (book series) Molecular Genetic Medicine, 1989—; patentee in gene therapy. Recipient H.C. Jacobeaus prize, Nordic Rsch. Com., Sweden, 1995, Cross of Honor for Sci. and the Arts, Austria, 1996. Mem.: AAAS (chmn. adv. com. germ line gene therapy 1995—), NIH (chmn. DNA adv. com. 2001—). Avocation: music. Office: Univ Calif San Diego CMG Rm 122 9500 Gilman Dr La Jolla CA 92093-0634 E-mail: tfriedmann@ucsd.edu.

FRIEDRICH, CHARLES WILLIAM, industrial relations specialist; b. Elgin, Ill., Aug. 30, 1943; s. Charles Kenneth and Veronica Elizabeth (Sharpe) F.; m. Janet Lee West, June 20, 1970; children: Joan Elizabeth, Charles Kenneth II. Student, Loras Coll., 1961-63; BA, Parsons Coll., 1967. Salesman Bendix Corp., South Bend, Ind., 1967; safety dir., asst. pers. mgr. Nat. Castings divsn. Midland Ross, Cicero, Ill., 1968-69; pers. mgr. Continental Tube Co. divsn. Hofmann Industries, Bellwood, Ill., 1969, asst. mgr. indsl. rels., 1971-73, Midwest dir. indsl. rels. parent co., 1971-73; dir. indsl. rels., gen. mgr. Lemont (Ill.) Shipbldg. and Repair Co., 1973-75; indsl. rels. exec. Modern Mgmt. Methods, Inc., Deerfield, Ill., 1975-77; pres. Std. Cons. Svcs. Co., Inc., Hinsdale, Ill., 1977-88; chmn. bd. dirs., pres. B.I. Industries, Inc., Blue Island, Ill., 1986—2002, Brulé Pollution Control Co., Blue Island, 1986—2002, Radiant Products Co., Blue Island, 1986—2002. Past Ill. Pres., Burr Ridge (Ill.) Park Dist. Bd.; scoutmaster Boy Scouts Am., 1982-88; past treas. Palisades Sch. Dist. Mem. Packard Automobile Classics Club (pres. 1996—), Classic Car Club Am., Antique Automobile Club Am., Kiwanis, KC (former grand knight, trustee Mayslake coun.), Alpha Phi Omega. Home: 10 S 431 Glenn Dr Burr Ridge IL 60527-6859 Office: 8412 Wilmette Ave Darien IL 60561 E-mail: brulecee@aol.com.

FRIEDRICH, LAWRENCE VINCENT, research scientist; b. Madison, Wis., Aug. 12, 1960; s. Richard Paul and Alice Ann Friedrich; m. Sara Frances Seay, Mar. 11, 1995; children: Samuel Lawrence, Lance Andrew. BS in Pharmacy, U. Wis., 1984; PharmD, Med. U. S.C., 1987. Registered pharmacist Wis., 1985, S.C., 1992. Rsch. fellow infectious diseases Med. U. S.C., Charleston, 1988—91, rsch. assoc., 1991—92, rsch. faculty, 1994—99; asst. prof. U. South Ala., Mobile, 1992—94, Auburn U., Mobile, 1992—94; sr. med. sci. mgr. Bristol Myers Squibb, Charleston, 1999—2004; clin. sci. liaison Cubist Pharmaceuticals, Charleston, 2004—. Advisor Nat. Com. for Clin. Lab. Standards Subcommittee on Antimicrobial Susceptibility Testing, 2003—; presenter in field. Contbr. articles to profl. jours. Recipient Most Valuable Performer award, Bristol Myers Squibb, 2000, Gold Std. award, 2001, Vision Leadership award, 2003. Mem.: Soc. for Infectious Diseases Pharmacists (chair membership com. 1993—94), Am. Soc. for Microbiology, Am. Coll. Clin. Pharmacy. Office: Cubist Pharmaceuticals 804 Prince Ferry Ln Mount Pleasant SC 29464 Office Phone: 843-881-0191. Home Fax: 843-971-0426; Office Fax: 843-971-0426.

FRIEDRICH, PAUL, anthropologist, linguist, poet; b. Cambridge, Mass., Oct. 22, 1927; s. Carl Joachim and Lenore Louise (Pelham) F.; m. Lore Bucher, Jan. 6, 1950 (div. Jan. 1966); children: Maria Elizabeth, Susan Guadalupe, Peter Roland; m. Margaret Hardin, Feb. 26, 1966 (div. June 1974); m. Deborah Joanna Gordon, Aug. 9, 1975 (div. Nov. 1996); children: Katherine Ann, Joan Lenore; m. Domnica Radulescu, Nov. 10, 1996 (div. Jan. 2004); 1 child, Nicholas. BA, Harvard Coll., 1950; MA, Harvard U., 1951; PhD, Yale U., 1957. Instr. U. Conn., Storrs, 1956-57; asst. prof. Harvard U., Cambridge, Mass., 1957-58; jr. linguistic scholar Deccan Coll., Poona, India, 1958-59; asst. prof. anthropology U. Pa., Phila., 1959-62; assoc. prof. anthropology U. Chgo., 1962-67, prof. anthropology, linguistics and soc. thought, 1967-96, prof. emeritus (active), 1996—. Vis. prof. linguistics Georgetown U., winter, 1998-2001, U. Va., 2002. Author: Proto-Indo-European Trees, 1970, Agrarian Revolt in a Mexican Village, 1970, The Meaning of Aphrodite, 1978, Bastard Moons, 1979, Language, Context and Imagination, 1979, The Language Parallax, 1986, The Princes of Naranja, 1987; co-editor: Russia and Eurasia-China, 1994, Music in Russian Poetry, 1998. Served to pfc. U.S. Army, 1946-47, Germany. Grantee Wenner-Gren Found., 1955; grantee NIMH, summers 1961-62; fellow Social Sci. Rsch. Coun., 1966-67; Guggenheim fellow, 1982-83 Mem.: Am. Acad. Arts and Scis., Linguistic Soc. Am. (chmn. program com. 1972, chmn. nominating com. 1975, mem. exec. com. 1981—83). Home: 5500 S South Shore Dr Apt 1609 Chicago IL 60637-1986 Office: U Chgo Dept Anthropology 1126 E 59th St Chicago IL 60637-1580

FRIEDRICHS, EDWARD CHARLES, architect; BA, Stanford U., 1965; MArch, U. Pa., 1968. Lic. architect Calif., Nev., Utah, Hawaii, N.Y., N.J., Ind. Architect M. Arthur Gensler Jr. & Assocs., San Francisco, 1969—, dir. projects, 1973-76, mng. prin. L.A., 1976-95; pres. Gensler, San Francisco, 1995—, CEO, 2000—, also bd. dirs., mem. mgmt. com. Mem. exec. bd. San Francisco Bay Area Coun., Boy Scouts Am. Fellow AIA, Internat. Interior Design Assn.; mem. Nat. Coun. Archtl. Registration Bds., Urban Land Inst. Office: Gensler 2 Harrison Street Ste 400 San Francisco CA 94105

FRIEL, BRIAN (BERNARD PATRICK FRIEL), author; b. Omagh, County Tyrone, No. Ireland, Jan. 9, 1929; s. Patrick and Christina (MacLoone) F.; m. Anne Morrison, Dec. 27, 1955; children: Paddy, Mary, Judy, Sally, David. Student, St. Columb's Coll., 1941-46; BA, St. Patrick's Coll., Maynooth, Ireland, 1948; postgrad., St. Joseph's Tchrs. Tng. Coll., Belfast, Ireland, 1949-50; Litt.D. (hon.), Dominican Coll., Chgo., Nat. U. Ireland, New U. Ulster, Trinity Coll., Dublin, Ireland, Georgetown U. Tchr. various schs., Derry City, No. Ireland, 1950-60; freelance writer, 1960—; with Tyrone Guthrie Theatre, 1963; co-founder Field Day Theatre Co., Derry, No. Ireland, 1980. Author: (short stories) A Saucer of Larks, 1964, The Gold in the Sea, 1966, The Diviner: Brian Friel's Best Short Stories, 1983, (plays) This Doubtful Paradise, 1960, The Enemy Within, 1962, The Blind Mice, 1963, Philadelphia, Here I Come!, 1964, The Loves of Cass McGuire, 1966, Lovers, 1967, Crystal and Fox, 1968, The Mundy Scheme, 1969, The Gentle Island, 1971, The Freedom of the City, 1972, Volunteers, 1975, Living Quarters,

1977, Faith Healer, 1979, Aristocrats, 1979 (London Evening Standard Best Play award 1988, Best Fgn. Play award N.Y. Drama Critics Circle 1989), Translations, 1980 (Christopher Ewart-Biggs Meml. prize Brit. Theatre Assn. 1981, Plays and Players Best New Play award 1981), American Welcome, 1980, The Communication Cord, 1982, Making History, 1988, Dancing at Lughnasa, 1990 (Tony Best Play award 1992), Wonderful Tennessee, 1993, Molly Sweeney, 1994, Give Me Your Answer, Do!, 1997, The Yalta Game, 2001, Two Plays After, 2002; (translator) Three Sisters (Anton Chekhov), 1981, Uncle Vanya, 1998, Two Plays After, 2002, Performances, 2003; translator: Fathers and Sons (Ivan Turgenev), The Home Place, 2005; (screenplay) Philadelphia, Here I Come!, 1970; (version) A Month in the Country, Performances, 2003; editor: The Last of the Name; contbr. short stories to New Yorker. Mem. Irish Senate, 1987. Recipient Macauley fellow Irish Arts Coun., 1963; hon. fellow U. Coll., Dublin. Fellow Royal Soc. Literature; mem. Nat. Assn. Irish Artists, Am. Acad. Arts and Letters. Office: Drumaweir House Greencastle Donegal Ireland

FRIEL, DANIEL DENWOOD, SR., manufacturing executive; b. Queenstown, Md., Aug. 11, 1920; s. Samuel Edward Whiting and Martha Washington (Reynolds) F.; m. Helen June Hennessy, May 1, 1943; children: Barbara Friel Holme, Martha Friel Wilson, Patricia, Daniel D. Jr. BChemE, Johns Hopkins U., 1942. Supr. optical instruments Manhattan Project, U. Chgo., 1943-45; dir. applied physics E.I. du Pont, Wilmington, Del., 1945-61, mgr. investments, 1961-69, dir. electronic products, 1974-77, dir. instrument products, 1977-82; pres. Holotron Corp., Wilmington, 1969-71; pres., chmn. Edgecraft Corp., Wilmington, 1983-91, chmn. bd., chief exec. officer Avondale, Pa., 1991—. Chmn. Mt. Cuba Astron. Obs., Wilmington, 1960—. Co-author: Process Instruments and Control, 1960; contbr. articles to profl. jours. Trustee Tatnall Sch., Wilmington, 1967-74. Mem. Phys. Soc. Am., Optical Soc. Am., Instrument Soc. Am., Ams. for Competitive Enterprise System (bd. dirs.), Tau Beta Pi. Achievements include patents for radiation measurement, instruments, and household appliances; invention of radiation detection and analysis devices. Office: Edgecraft Corp 825 Southwood Rd Avondale PA 19311-9765

FRIELING, GERALD HARVEY, JR., specialty steel company executive; b. Kansas City, Mo., Apr. 29, 1930; s. Gerald Harvey and Mary Ann (Coons) F.; m. Joan Lee Bigham, June 14, 1952; children: John, Robert, Nancy. BS in Mech. Engring., U. Kans., 1951. Application engr. Westinghouse Elec. Corp., Pitts., 1951-53; mfg. mgr. Madison-Faessler Tool Co., Moberly, Mo., 1956-60; gen. mgr. wire and tubing Tex. Instruments Inc., Attleboro, Mass., 1960-69; v.p. Air Products & Chems. Co., Allentown, Pa., 1969-79; pres., chief exec. officer, chmn. bd. Nat. Standard Co., Niles, Mich., 1979-89, retired. CEO Tokheim Corp., 1990—91, chmn. bd., 1990—96, vice chmn., 1997—2000; bd. dirs., lead dir. Superior Metal Products; bd. dirs. Mossberg Printing Co., CTS; pres. Frieling & Assocs.; instr. Brown U., 1965—68; adj. prof. U. Notre Dame, Mendoza Sch. Bus., 1990—; mem. adv. bd. U. Kans. Sch. Engring., 1983—96. Author; patentee in field. Served to lt. USNR, 1953-56, Korea. Recipient Wire Assn. medal, 1966, Disting. Engring. Service award U. Kans., 1986. Mem.: Union League (Chgo.), Signal Point Country, Summit. Presbyterian. E-mail: nordict6@aol.com.

FRIEND, DAVID LEE, lawyer; b. Houston, May 23, 1951; s. Leonard Nathan and Sharlee Baruch (Freedman) F.; m. Deborah S. Grubb, July 17, 1982; children: Nathan Douglas, Matthew Joseph, Kara Elisabeth. BA with honors, U. Tex., 1973, JD, 1976. Bar: Tex. 1976, Wash. 1977, U.S. Dist. Ct. (we. and ea. dists.) Wash. Law clk to justice King County Superior Ct., Seattle, 1976-77; assoc. Garvey, Schubert, Adams & Barer, Seattle and Washington, 1977-83; ptnr. Weinrich, Gilmore & Adoph, Seattle, 1983-85, Franco, Asia, Bensussen & Coe, Seattle, Tapei, Hong Kong, Tokyo, Vancouver, B.C., 1985-96; pvt. practice Seattle, 1996—; pres. Puget Sound Dispatch LLC. Pres. MGER LLC, Pyget Sound Dispatch LLC, 1996—; chmn. Global Uniform Co., 2003—. Pres. U.S. Assn. Blind Athletes, Seattle region, 1979-81; organizer North End Jewish Cmty. Ctr., Seattle, 1984-87; v.p. Broadview Cmty. Coun., 1988-90; soccer coach Wash. State Youth Soccer Assn. Mem. ABA, Wash. State Bar Assn., Tex. Bar Assn., Wash. State Trial Lawyers Assn., Seattle C. of C. (chmn. internat. trade com. 1984-87), Green Lake C. of C. (v.p. 1996-98, pres. 1998-99), Rotary (sec., chmn. cmty. svcs. com., vocat. svcs. com., youth com., pres.). Avocations: soccer referee, travel. Home: 611 N 137th St Seattle WA 98133-7414 Office: 6850 E Green Lake Way N Ste 201 Seattle WA 98115-5412

FRIEND, DONALD AGAR, geomorphology educator, geographer; b. San Francisco, June 26, 1960; s. Edward Armand Friend and Nancy Jaicks Alexander; m. Lisa Mitchell, Mar. 19, 1994; children: Scanlon Parker, Reilly Rose. BS in Conservation of Natural Resources, U. Calif., Berkeley, 1984; MA in Geography, U. Colo., 1988; PhD in Geography, Ariz. State U., 1997. Instr. Colo. Outward Bound Sch., Denver, 1987-94; dir. earth scis. program, tchg. scholar fellow Minn. State U., Mankato, 1997—, asst. prof. geography, 1997-2001, assoc. prof. geography, 2001—, chair dept. geography, 2005—. U.S. rep. Internat. Commn. on Diversity in Mountain Sys. Internat. Geog. Union, Rome, 2000—; adv. bd. Mountain Studies Inst., Silverton, Colo., 2002—; sr. instr. Mountain Inst., Washington, 2002—; mem. adv. bd. for phys. geography and earth scis. McGraw-Hill Pubs., 2002—. Mem. editl. bd.: Mountain Sci., 2005—, guest editor: Geog. Rev., 2002; contbr. articles to profl. jours. Preparing Tomorrow's Tchrs. to Use Tech. grantee, U.S. Dept. Edn., 1999—2000, Fulbright Sr. scholar, Germany, 2004—05. Fellow Am. Geog. Soc.; mem. Internat. Mountain Soc., Internat. Permafrost Assn., Assn. Am. Geographers (founder, adv. bd. 1998-2004, chair mountain geography specialty group 1998-2001, J. Warren Nystrom award 1999, Internat. Geog. Congress Jr. scholar 2000), Gamma Theta Upsilon. Avocations: mountain climbing, running, travel. Office: Dept Geography Minn State Univ Mankato MN 56001 Office Phone: 507-389-2618. Office Fax: 507-389-2980. Business E-Mail: donald.friend@mnsu.edu.

FRIEND, EDWARD MALCOLM, III, lawyer, educator; b. Birmingham, Ala., Oct. 12, 1946; s. Edward M. Jr. and Hermione Frances (Curjel) F. BA in History, U. Ala., 1968, JD, 1971. Bar: Ala. 1971. Shareholder Sirote and Permutt, P.C., Birmingham, 1971—, pres., 1991-93. Chmn. So. Inst. Health Law, 1985-87, Birmingham Area C. of C., 1990-91; chmn. dist. bd. dirs. Colonial Bank Ala., Birmingham, 1985-2000; vice chair Colonial Bank Ctrl. Dist., 2000—; exec. residence, prof. U. Ala., Birmingham, 1994—, chmn. adv. bd. Sch. Bus., 2003—. Chmn. Birmingham Area chpt. ARC, 1987-88; chmn. bd. NCCJ, 1983, nat. bd., 1981-88; pres. coun. U. Ala., Birmingham, 1980-94, Birmingham Jewish Fedn., 1984-89, United Way Ctrl. Ala., 1984-99, chmn., 1993-94, gen. campaign chmn., 1989; bd. dirs. Childrens Hosp. Ala., 1986-2005; exec. com. Ala. Symphony Assn., 1980-82, bd. dirs., 1982-85, Birmingham Festival Arts, 1978-88, pres., 1984-85, chmn., 1985-86; mem. nat. leadership coun. United Way Am.; pres. Big Bros./Big Sisters Greater Birmingham, 1980, chmn., 1981-83; trustee St. Vincent's Hosp., 1982-86, v.p., 1984-86, Ala. Sch. Fine Arts Found., 1985-91; trustee Cmty. Found. of Greater Birmingham, 2002-04; chmn. Leadership Ala., 1993; bd. dirs. Boy Scouts Am., 1996-2005. Recipient Brotherhood award Nat. Conf. Christians and Jews, 1987; named to Ala. Acad. of Honor; named Lawyer of Yr., Birmingham Legal Secretarial Assn., 1976, Outstanding Alumnus, U. Ala. Sch. Law, 1984, Hon. Oustanding Alumnus, Sch. Bus., U. Ala., 2005. Mem. Nat. Health Lawyers Assn. (bd. dirs. 1992-95), Farrah Law Soc. (chmn. 1982-84), (hon.) U. Ala. Alumnus. Office: Sirote and Permutt PC 2311 Highland Ave South Birmingham AL 35205-4004 Office Phone: 205-930-5116. Business E-Mail: efriend@sirote.com.

FRIEND, HAROLD CHARLES, neurologist; b. Chgo., Nov. 28, 1946; s. Leonard Nathan and Sharlee (Friedman) F.; m. Karenanne; children: Reed, Chad. BA, U. Tex., 1968, MD, 1972. Diplomate Am. Bd. Neurology. Resident Upstate Med. Ctr., Syracuse, NY, 1972-73, Albert Einstein Coll. Medicine, Bronx, NY, 1973-75; mem. staff Boca Raton Cmty. Hosp., Fla., 1975—; pres. Neurosci. Ctr., Boca Raton, Fla., 1984—; rsch. prof. dept. brain sci. Fla. Atlantic U., Boca Raton, 2002—05, co-chair neurosci. and neurobehavior, 2004—, clin. prof. biomed. scis., 2004—. Spl. expert witness Fla. Agy. for Health Care Adminstrn.; expert med. advisor divsn. workers compensation Fla. Dept. Labor and Employment Security, 1994-2003; pres. Puget Sound Yellow Taxi, Inc., 1994-95. Author: Territorial Marking, 1968, Bell's Palsy, 1975, Transient Global Amnesia, 1977. Exec. bd., v.p. Gulfstream coun. Boy Scouts Am., 1988—93, pres. coun., 1993—95, area I v.p., 1990—92, area IV v.p., 1993—95, area IV pres., 1995—98, so. region exec. bd., 1993—, internat. scouting com., 1998—, chmn. direct svc. com., 1999—2004, nat. adv. coun., 2000—; treas. Interam. Scout Found., 2001—03, pres., 2003—05; bd. dirs. Raton Children's Mus., 1989—92; exec. bd. Palm Beach County agy. rels. com. United Way, 1992—95, allocation com., 1990—92. Recipient Order of Arrow Vigil Honor award Boy Scouts Am., 1983, Dist. Merit award, 1987, Silver Beaver award, 1990, Disting. Commr. award, 1991, Disting. Eagle Scout, 1997, Silver Antelope award, 1997; James West fellow, 1993, 1910 Soc., 1998, Baden Powell fellow, 2000. Fellow: Am. Acad. Neurology; mem.: Fla. Med. Assn., Fla. Soc. Neurology, NY Acad. Sci. (life), So. Clin. Neurol. Soc., Am. Soc. Neuroimaging (cert.), Internat. Fellowship Scouting Rotarians (N.Am. sect. chmn. 1995—96, internat. sec. 1996—98, internat. vice chair 1998—99, internat. chair 1999—2002, internat. commr. 2002—05, Silver Wheel award 2002), Rotary Internat. Fellowship Running and Fitness Rotarians (internat. chmn. 1992—98, internat. treas. 1998—99, internat. sec. 1999—2001, internat. chair 2003—05), Boca Raton Road Runners Club (pres. 1992—93), Sierra Club (life), Rotary (bd. dir., pres. Boca Raton Club dist. world fellowship chmn. 1992—94, dist. found. chmn. 1994, gov.'s rep. 1994—95, chmn. dist. conf. 1995, gov.'s rep. 1996—97, dist. gov. 1998—99, chmn. coll. gov. 1999—2000, zone coord. Children at Risk 2000—01, cmty. svc. task force 2001—02, fellowship com. RI chpt. 2004—05, Dist. Found. Svc. award 1992, Pres. Salute Commendation 1993, featured on cover of The Rotarian 2003, Paul Harris fellow), Phi Beta Kappa, Alpha Phi Omega, Theta Xi, Phi Kappa Phi. Avocation: marathons. Office: 1500 NW 10th Ave Ste 105 Boca Raton FL 33486-1344

FRIEND, HELEN MARGARET, chemist; b. Lyndon, Ohio, Jan. 30, 1931; d. Maurice Chapman and Margaret (Beath) Mossbarger; m. William Warren Friend, Oct. 9, 1982. BA in Chemistry, Coll. of Wooster, 1953. Rsch. chemist Union Carbide Co., Cleve., 1953-56, asst. patent coord. battery products div., 1956-59, patent coord., 1959-86, Eveready Battery Co., Westlake, Ohio, 1986-90, tech. patent assoc., 1990-95; ret., 1995. Mng. editor JEC Press-Internat. Battery Materials Assn., Cleve., 1978-97. Mng. editor Progress in Batteries and Battery Materials, 1978-98, JEC Battery Newsletter, 1987-98, ITE Battery Newsletter; tech. editor Electrochem. Soc. Japan, U.S. br., 1975-96; editor-in-chief Tech. English divsn. Internat. Tech. Exch. Soc., 1998—. Mem. Am. Chem. Soc., Electrochem. Soc., Phi Beta Kappa. Presbyterian. Avocations: little theater, reading, choral singing. Home: 576 Buckeye Dr Sheffield Lake OH 44054-1615

FRIEND, PATRICIA A., trade association administrator; b. Aug. 28, 1946; Student, Northeastern State Coll. Flight attendant United Airlines, 1966—. Mem. Dept. Transp. Rapid Response Team for Aircraft Security, 2001—. Mem.: Am. Fed. Labor Unions-Congress Indsl. Orgns., Assn. Flight Attendants (head United Coun. 8/ORD Chgo. local 1980—82, internat. pres. 1995—, v.p.). Mailing: 5th Fl 1275 K St NW Washington DC 20005

FRIEND, STEPHEN H., biotechnology company executive; BA Philosophy, MD, PhD Biochemistry, Ind. U. Faculty Mass. Gen. Hosp., Boston, 1990—95, Harvard Med. Sch., Cambridge, Mass., 1987—95; co-founder, co-dir. Seattle Project Fred Hutchinson Cancer Rsch. Ctr., 1995—2000, vis. scientist, then head dept. molecular pharmacology, 1994—2000; pres. Inpharmatics, Kirkland, Wash., 1996—. Office: 401 Terry Ave N Seattle WA 98109-5234

FRIEND, THEODORE WOOD, III, foundation executive, historian, writer; b. Pitts., Aug. 27, 1931; s. Theodore Wood and Jessica (Holton) F.; m. Elizabeth Groesbeck Pierson, Feb. 20, 1960 (dec.); children: Theodore Porter, Pierson, Elizabeth Robinson. BA, Williams Coll., 1953, LLD (hon.), 1978; PhD, Yale U., 1958. Mem. faculty SUNY, Buffalo, 1959-73, prof. history, 1966-73; pres. Swarthmore (Pa.) Coll., 1973-82; trustee Eisenhower Exchange Fellowships Inc., 1982—, pres., 1984-96. C.V. Starr disting. vis. prof. S.E. Asia studies Johns Hopkins U. Sch. Advanced Internat. Studies, 2004; bd. dirs. Metanexus Inst. on Religion and Sci. Author: Between Two Empires, The Ordeal of the Philippines, 1929-46, 65 (Bancroft prize in history 1966), The Blue Eyed Enemy: Japan Against the West in Java and Luzon, 1942-45, 88, Indonesian Destinies, 2003; (novel) Family Laundry, 1986. Dir. Phila. Savings Fund Soc., 1975-90; mem. Truman Scholarships Selection Panel, Pa., N.J., Del., 1993—, chmn., 1997—; mem. bd. advisors U.S.-Indonesia Soc., 2000—; mem. adv. com. Sabre Found., 2005—. Fulbright grantee, Philippines, 1957-59; Rockefeller Found. internat. rels. fellow, 1961-62; Nat. Def. Fgn. Lang. postdoctoral fellow, 1966-67; Guggenheim fellow, Indonesia, Philippines, Japan, 1967-68; fellow Woodrow Wilson Internat. Ctr., 1983-84, Bellagio Ctr. for Artists and Scholars fellow, 1988; recipient Dwight D. Eisenhower medal, 1997. Mem. Coun. on Fgn. Rels., Am. Hist. Assn., Soc. Historians Am. Fgn. Rels., Asia Soc., Phila. Com. on Fgn. Rels. (chmn. 1985-2000), Fgn. Policy Rsch. Inst. (sr. fellow), Phila. Club, Franklin Inn Club, Phi Beta Kappa. Presbyterian. Achievements include being a nationally ranked sr. squash player, 1983-93, 97—. Home: 264 S Radnor Chester Rd Villanova PA 19085-1306

FRIEND, WILLIAM BENEDICT, bishop; b. Miami, Oct. 22, 1931; s. William Eugene and Elizabeth F. Student, U. Miami, 1949—52; cert. in philosophy, St. Mary's Coll., St. Mary, Ky., 1955; cert. of ordination, Mt. St. Mary's Sem., Emmittsburg, Md., 1959; MA in Edn., Cath. U. Am., 1965; LLD, St. Leo Coll., 1986. Ordained priest Roman Cath. Ch., 1959. Parish priest, educator, counselor, adminstr., 1959—68; ednl. rsch. adminstr. U. Notre Dame, Ind., 1968—71; vicar for edn., supt. schs. Diocese of Mobile, Ala., 1971—76, chancellor adminstrn., vicar for edn., 1976—79; aux. bishop Diocese of Alexandria-Shreveport, La., 1979—83, diocesan bishop, 1983—86; first bishop Shreveport, La., 1986—. Chmn. campaign for human devel. Nat. Conf. Cath. Bishops, 1982—85; mem. sci. and human values com. Commn. of Bishops and Scholars, 1983—86, chmn., 1986—92, cons., 1993—, sec., 2000—04; mem. Pontifical Coun. for Culture. Editor handbooks and study guides for Cath. edn; editor: (with Ford and Daues) Evangelizing the Cultures in A.D. 2000, 1990; co-editor (with J. Anderson): The Culture of Bible Belt Catholics, 1995; contbr. articles on Cath. edn., Cath. ch. leadership and mgmt., theol. reflections to profl. publs. Bd. dirs., v.p. S.E. Regional Hispanic Ctr., Miami, 1986—; trustee Notre Dame Sem., 1976—, St. Joseph Coll. Sem., New Orleans, 1979—; bd. councillors Shreveport Cmty. Renewal; chmn. bd. Ctr. for Applied Rsch. in the Apostolate, 1997—2004; mem. adv. bd. The John J. Reilly Ctr. Sci., Tech. and Values U. Notre Dame; bd. dirs. La. Interchurch Conf. Decorated Order of Fleur de Lis K.C., knight comdr. with star Knights of Holy Sepulchre of Jerusalem; recipient Presdl. award, Nat. Cath. Ednl. Assn., 1978, O'Neil D'Amour award, Nat. Assn. Bds. Edn., 1982, NCCJ Brotherhood and Humanitarian award, 1987, Human Rels. Coun. award, 2000, Harry Blake award, 2004. Mem.: AAAS, World Futures Soc., N.Y. Acad. Scis., Cath. Acad. Sci. USA, Am. Acad. Religion, KC (former state chaplain La. coun.). Roman Catholic. Avocations: hiking, art, music, reading. Office: Diocese of Shreveport Catholic Ctr 3500 Fairfield Ave Shreveport LA 71104-4108

FRIENDLY, ED, television producer; b. NYC, Apr. 8, 1922; s. Edwin S. and Henrietta (Steinmeier) F.; m. Natalie Coulson Brooks, Jan. 31, 1952 (dec. May 9, 2002); children: Brooke Friendly, Edwin S. III; m. Paula Reddish Zinnemann, Nov. 27, 2003. *Mr. Friendly has two grandchildren, Kate Friendly-Jones and Rebecca Isabel Friendly. Wife, Paula Reddish Zinnemann, graduated Marjorie Webster Jr. College in 1955 and University of West Los Angeles School of Law in 1983. She was the 1984 President of Beverly Hills Board of Realtors. She is a former member of the County of Los Angeles Assessment Appeals Board and the City of Los Angeles Rent Adjustment Commission. She was Commissioner of the Department of Real Estate for the State of California from 1999-2003. In 2001, she received the Israel Cancer Research Fund "Women of Action Award". She is the 2005/2006 Chair of the Real Property Section of the Los Angeles County Bar Association.* Grad., Manlius Sch., 1941. Radio exec., dir. BBD&O, N.Y.C., 1946-49; sales exec. ABC-TV, N.Y.C., 1949-53; ind. producer and packager N.Y.C., 1953-56; producer, program exec. CBS-TV, N.Y.C., 1956-59; v.p. spl. programs NBC-TV, N.Y.C., 1959-67; pres., founding mem. Ed Friendly Prodns., Los Angeles, 1967—. Co-chmn. steering com. Caucus for Producers, Writers and Dirs. Exec. prodr.: (TV series) Laugh-In, (miniseries) Little House on the Prairie, 2005; prodr.: (films) Peter Lundy and the Medicine Hat Stallion (Emmy nomination), Young Pioneers, (miniseries) Backstairs at the White House (11 Emmy nominations), (motion pictures and TV spls.); exec. prodr./prodr. Barbara Cartland's The Flame is Love, 2005. Served to capt., U.S. Army, 1942-45, PTO. Recipient Spl. award Internat. Film and TV Festival N.Y., 1967; Emmy award for Laugh-In, 1968; Producer of Yr. award Producers Guild of Am., 1968; Golden Globe award Hollywood Fgn. Press, 1968; Gold medal of honor Internat. Radio and TV Soc., 1970; Christopher award for motion picture, 1975; Western Heritage award Nat. Cowboy Hall of Fame and Western Heritage Center, for Little House on the Prairie, 1975, for Peter Lundy and the Medicine Hat Stallion, 1978; Scout awards for best weekly series and show of yr. for Laugh-In, 1969 Mem. Calif. Horsemen's Benevolent and Protective Assn. (pres. 1994, former mem. bd. dirs.), Thoroughbred Owners Calif. (founder, pres., chmn. 1993-96, chmn. 1996-97, bd. dirs. 1993-2000), Nat. Thoroughbred Assn. (vice chmn., bd. dirs. 1996-98, founding mem.), Nat. Thoroughbred Racing Assn. (bd. dirs. 1997-99).

FRIER, BRUCE WOODWARD, law educator; b. Chgo., Aug. 31, 1943; s. Bill Edward and Jane Davies Frier. BA, Trinity Coll., 1964; PhD, Princeton U., 1970. Lectr. Bryn Mawr Coll., Pa., 1968—69; prof. classics and law U. Mich., Ann Arbor, 1969—, Henry King Ransom Prof. Law, Frank O. Copley Collegiate Prof. Classics and Roman Law, interim chair Dept. Classical Studies, 2001—02. Author: Landlords and Tenants in Imperial Rome, 1980 (Goodwin award of merit Am. Philological Assn., 1983), The Rise of the Roman Jurists, 1985, The Demography of Roman Egypt, 1994. Guggenheim fellow 1984-85; fellow Nat. Endowment for the Humanities, 1992-93. Fellow: Am. Acad. of Arts and Scis.; mem.: Am. Philol. Assn., Am. Soc. for Legal Hist. Avocations: bird watching, popular music, movies. Office: U Mich Law Sch 435 Hutchins Hall 625 S State St Ann Arbor MI 48109-1215 Office Phone: 734-936-3022. Office Fax: 734-763-9375. E-mail: bwfrier@umich.edu.

FRIES, ARTHUR LAWRENCE, life and health insurance broker, disability claim consultant; b. Bklyn., Aug. 21, 1937; s. Jack Edwin and Sophia (Kabat) F.; m. Cindy Ann Blum, Mar. 27, 1960; children: Stacey Jill, Todd Steven. AB, Nichols Coll., 1956; BS, Syracuse U., 1958. Registered health underwriter; diplomate Acad. Cert. Cons. and Experts. Various positions ins. sales and adminstrn. various firms, N.Y.C., 1962-72; life and health ins. agt. Washington Nat. Ins. Co., Los Angeles, 1973-85; pvt. practice, N.Y.C., Los Angeles and Northridge, Calif., 1962-72, Northridge, 1982-95, Newport Beach, Calif., 1996—. Blood chmn. Washington Nat. Ins. Co., 1976-79; spkr., lectr., cons. on individual disability income ins. claims; cons., expert witness and negotiator for non-can disability ins. claims. Contbr. articles to profl. jours. Chmn. memberships Vista Del Mar Men's Assn. for Orphaned Children, 1975. Recipient Nat. Sales Achievement award L.A. Gen. Agts. and Mgrs. Assn., 1965-94, Health Ins. Quality award, 1965-92, 93, Agt. of Yr. award 1976, 78, Nat. Quality award, 1980-91, Disting. Svc. award D.I.T.C. Rsch. Seminar, 1994. Fellow Am. Coll. Forensic Examiners, Inst. for Forensic Experts, Nat. Forensic Ctr., Nat. Assn. Life Underwriters (blood chmn. 1976-79, spkr. ann. conv. 1988, 90, 93 million dollar roundtable), Nat. Assn. Health Underwriters (life leading prodrs. roundtable), Calif. Assn. Life Underwriters, Calif. Assn. Health Underwriters (charter), San Fernando Valley Life Underwriters Assn., Orange County Assn. Ins. and Fin. Advisors, Orange County Assn. Health Underwriters, Forensic Cons. Assn. of Orange County, L.A. Assn. Health Underwriters (conf. spkr., spkrs. chmn. 1983-84, program chmn. 1984, bd. dirs., membership chmn. 1987-88), Am. Diabetic Assn., Am. Bd. Disability Analysts. Republican. Home and Office: 225 Via San Remo Newport Beach CA 92663-5511 Office Phone: 949-673-7190. Personal E-mail: friesart@hotmail.com.

FRIES, HELEN SERGEANT HAYNES, civic leader; d. Harwood Syme and Alice (Hobson) Haynes; m. Stuart G. Fries, May 5, 1938. Student, Coll. William and Mary, 1935-38. Mem. nat. nurses aid com. ARC, 1958-59; dir. ARC Aero Club, Eng., 1943-44; supr. ARC Clubmobile, Europe, 1944-46; mem. women's com. Nat. Symphony Orch., Washington, 1959—, chmn. residential and fund dr. for apts., 1959; bd. dirs. Madison Country Rep. Club, 1969-70; mem. nat. coun. Women's Nat. Rep. Club N.Y., 1963—, chmn. hospitality com., 1963-65; bd. dirs. League Rep. Women, 1952-61; patron mem., vol. docent Huntsville Mus. Art, Huntsville Lit. Assn.; vol. docent Weeen House, Twickenham Hist. Preservation Dist. Assn., Inc., Huntsville; mem. The Garden Guild, Huntsville, The Collectors Guild Constn. Hall Village, Huntsville, Hist. Huntsville Found., Huntsville Mus. Art., Corcoran Art Gallery. Recipient cert. of merit 84th Divsn., U.S. Army, 1945. Mem.: DAR, Assn. Preservation Va. Antiquities, Turkish-Am. Assn., English Speaking Union, Greensboro Soc. Preservation, Nat. Trust Hist. Preservation, Va., Nat., Valley Forge (Pa.), Eastern Shore Va., Nat. Soc. Colonial Dames Am., Daus. Am. Colonists, Huntsville-Madison County hist. socs., Friends of Ala. Archives, Nat. Soc. Lit. and Arts, Va. Hist. Soc., Cmty. Ballet Assn. Inc. (life bd. dirs.), Bot. Garden Club, Heritage Club, Redstone Yacht Club, Garden Club, Army-Navy Country Club, Capitol Hill Club, Washington Club, Army-Navy Club. Address: 6200 Oregon Ave NW Apt 480 Washington DC 20015-1549

FRIES, JAMES FRANKLIN, internal medicine educator; b. Normal, Ill., Aug. 25, 1938; s. Albert Charles and Orpha (Hair) F.; m. Sarah Elizabeth Tilton, Aug. 27, 1960; children: Elizabeth Ann, Gregory James. AB, Stanford U., 1960; MD, Johns Hopkins U., 1964. Diplmate Am. Bd. Internal Medicine. Intern Johns Hopkins Hosp., Balt., 1964-65, resident in medicine, 1965-66, fellow connective tissue disease divsn., 1966-68; resident in medicine Stanford (Calif.) U. Sch. Medicine, 1968-69, instr. in medicine, 1969-71, asst. prof. medicine, 1971-77, assoc. prof. medicine, 1978-93, prof. medicine, 1993—. Dir. Arthritis, Rheumatism, Aging Med. Info. Sys., Stanford, 1975—; chmn. bd. dirs. Healthtrac Found., Menlo Park, Calif.; chmn. Healthtrac, Inc., 1984-2001; exec. com. The Health Project, 1992—. Author: Take Care of Yourself, 1975, 2004, Prognosis, 1981, Living Well, 1997, 1999, Taking Care of Your Child, 2005, The Arthritis Helpbook, 2005, Arthritis, 1999; mem. editl. bd. Jour. Rheumatology, Jour. Clin. Rheumatology. Named Best Med. Specialist in U.S., Town and Country mag., 1984, Best Dr. in U.S., Good Housekeeping mag., 1991, Rsch. Hero, Arthritis Found., 2001; named one of Best Drs. in Am., Woodward-White, 1995; recipient C. Everett Koop Nat. Health award, 1994. Master Am. Coll. Rheumatology (Clin. Rsch. award 2005); fellow ACP, Am. Coll. Med. Info Avocations: skiing, running, expedition mountain climbing. Home: 135 Farm Rd Woodside CA 94062-1210 Office: Stanford U Sch Medicine 1000 Welch Rd Ste 203 Palo Alto CA 94304-1808 E-mail: jff@stanford.edu.

FRIES, THOMAS ANTHONY, music educator; b. Cleve., Feb. 20, 1954; s. Barney Frank and Jarmila Marie (Jilek) Fries; m. Ellen Gaynell Winters, May 19, 1990; 1 child, Timothy Carl. MusB in Percussion Performance, Baldwin-Wallace Coll., 1976; MusM in Percussion Performance, Kent State U., 1982. Percussion instr., asst. dir. Koch Sch. Music/Cleve. Music Sch. Settlement, Rocky River, Ohio, 1973—89; part-time music instr. Hiram (Ohio) Coll., 1978—2000, Cuyahoga C.C. Western Campus, Parma, Ohio, 1980—88, Mount Union Coll., Alliance, Ohio, 1989—95; part-time percussion instr. Cleve. State U., 1992—2001, U. Akron, Ohio, 1993—94; adj. music instr. Coll. Wooster, Ohio, 1991—. Percussionist N.Y. Met. Opera, Cleve. Orch., Cleve. Ballet, Cleve. Opera, Cleve. Chamber Symphony, Great Lakes Theatre Festival, Am. Ballet Theatre, Miami City Ballet, Ohio Boy Choir, Lyric Opera, many others; leader Tom Fries Band. Founder, dir., performer: CD Mellow Blend, 2004, performer numerous CD recordings. Grad. assistantship, Kent State U., 1976—77. Mem.: Music Talent Cleve. (bd. mem., pres.), Am. Fedn. Musicians, Ohio Music Edn. Assn. (adjudicator musical events 1987—), Music Educators Nat. Conf. (clinician, lectr., performer 1977,

1994). Avocations: travel, scuba diving, photography, international wine judge. Office: Coll of Wooster Scheide Music Ctr University and Beall Sts Wooster OH 44691 Office Phone: 330-287-3000 2852. E-mail: tafries@core.com.

FRIESE, GEORGE RALPH, retail executive; b. Chgo., Feb. 15, 1936; s. George R. and Marie D. (Pilz) F.; m. Patricia J. Brown, Aug. 24, 1957; children: Christine Carol, Kurt Michael. BA, Monmouth Coll., 1956; JD, Chgo. Kent Coll. Law, 1960. Bar: Ill. 1961, U.S. Dist. Ct. Ill. (no. dist.) 1961, U.S. Supreme Ct. 1965. Asst. gen. counsel, v.p. Banner Mut. Ins. Cos., Chgo., 1959-63; ptnr. Madsen & Friese, Park Ridge, Ill., 1963-68; corp. counsel, sec. SCOA Industries, Inc., Columbus, Ohio, 1968-71, v.p. legal, sec., 1971-81, pres., 1981-85; vice chmn., dir. Hills Dept. Stores Inc., Canton, Mass., 1986—95. Propr. Portsmouth (N.H.) Athenaeum, 1993—. Bd. dirs. Columbus Symphony Orch., Greater Columbus Art Coun.; chmn., trustee New Eng. Red Cross; trustee Boy Scouts Am., Columbus, 1981-86, Boston Lyric Opera, 1988-95, Strawbery Banke Mus., 1994—, treas., 1996-98; mem., trustee Greater Piscataqua Cmty. Found., 1995—, vice chmn., 1998-2000, chmn., 2000, City of Portsmouth Cultural Commn., 2004- Mem. ABA, Ill. Bar Assn., Columbus Athletic Club, Lotus Club (N.Y.), Tau Kappa Epsilon, Phi Delta Phi. Unitarian Universalist. Home and Office: PO Box 690 New Castle NH 03854-0690

FRIESE, ROBERT CHARLES, lawyer; b. Chgo., Apr. 29, 1943; s. Earl Matthew and Laura Barbara (Mayer) F.; m. Chandra Ullom; children: Matthew Robert, Mark Earl, Laura Moore. AB in Internat. Rels., Stanford U., 1964; JD, Northwestern U., 1970. Bar: Calif. 1972. Dir. Tutor Applied Linguistics Ctr., Geneva, 1964-66; atty. Bronson, Bronson & McKinnon, San Francisco, 1970-71, SEC, San Francisco, 1971-75; ptnr. Shartsis, Friese & Ginsburg, San Francisco, 1975—. Pres., bd. dirs. Custom Diversification Fund Mgmt., Inc., 1993—; dir.-co-founder Internat. Plant Rsch. Inst., Inc., San Carlos, Calif., 1978-86 Chmn. bd. suprs. Task Force on Noise Control, 1972-78; chmn. San Franciscans for Cleaner City, 1977; exec. dir. Nob Hill Neighbors, 1972-81; bd. dirs. Nob Hill Assn., 1976-78, Palace Fine Arts, 1992-94, San Francisco Beautiful, 1986—, pres., 1988-2000; chmn. Citizens Adv. Com. for Embarcadero Project, 1991-98; mem. major gifts com. Stanford U.; bd. dirs. Presidio Heights Neighborhood Assn., 1993—, pres., 1996-98; bd. dirs. Inst. of Range and the American Mustang, 1990—. Mem. ABA (co-chmn. enforcement subcom., litigation sect.), Assn. Bus. Trial Lawyers (bd. dirs.), Calif. Bar Assn., Bar Assn. San Francisco (bd. dirs. 1982-85, chmn. bus. litigation com. 1978-79, chmn. state ct. civil litigation com. 1983-90, new courthouse com. 1993-95), Assn. SEC Alumni (bd. dirs. 1995—, pres. 2005—), Lawyers Club of San Francisco, Mensa, Calif. Hist. Soc., Commonwealth Club, Swiss-Am. Friendship League (chmn. 1971-79). Office: Shartsis Friese & Ginsburg 1 Maritime Plz Fl 18 San Francisco CA 94111-3404 Office Phone: 415-421-6500. Business E-Mail: rcf@sfglaw.com.

FRIESECKE, RAYMOND FRANCIS, health company executive; b. Mar. 12, 1937; s. Bernhard P. K. and Josephine (De Tomi) F. BS in Chemistry, Boston Coll., 1959; MSCE, MIT, 1961. Product specialist Dewey & Almy Chem. divsn. W. R. Grace & Co., Inc., Cambridge, Mass., 1963-66; market planning specialist USM Corp., Boston, 1966-71; mgmt. cons. Boston, 1971-74; dir. planning and devel. Schweitzer divsn. Kimberly-Clark Corp., Lee, Mass., 1974-78; v.p. corp. planning Butler Automatic, Inc., Canton, Mass., 1978-80; pres. Butler-Europe Inc., Greenwich and Munich, Conn., Germany, 1980; v.p. mktg. and planning Butler Greenwich Inc., 1980-81; pres. Strategic Mgmt. Assocs., San Rafael, Calif., 1981-96; chmn. Beyond Health Corp., 1994—, Health-E-America Found., 2000—. Bd. dirs. Better Physiology, Ltd., 2000-05; corp. clk., v.p. Bldg. R&D, Inc., Cambridge, 1966-68. Host, prodr. The Ounce of Prevention Show, Sta. KEST, San Francisco, 1994—98, Sta. KBZS, 1998—2001, Stas. WRPT and WSRO, 1999—2001; host, prodr. KYCY, 2001—05; host, prodr. KRLA, KSBN, KFNX, 2003—; author: Management by Relative Product Quality, 1982, The New Way to Manage, 1983, Never Be Sick Again, 2002; pub.: Beyond Health News, 1995—; contbr. articles to profl. jours. State chmn. Citizens for Fair Taxation, 1972-73; state co-chmn. Mass. Young Reps., 1967-69; chmn. Ward 7 Rep. Com., Cambridge, 1968-70; vice-chmn. Cambridge Rep. City Com., 1966-68; bd. dirs. Kentfield Rehab. Hosp. Found., 1986-88, chmn., 1988-91; Rep. candidate Mass. Ho. of Reps., 1964, 66; pres. Marin Rep. Coun., 1986-91; chmn. Calif. Acad., 1986-88; sec. Navy League Marin Coun., 1984-91, v.p., 1994-2000; bd. dirs. The Marin Ballet, 1996-98; bd. dirs. Insts. for Behavioral Physiology, Seattle, 1999-2000. 1st lt. U.S. Army, 1961-63. Mem. NRA, Nat. Health Fedn., Am. Chem. Soc., Physicians Com. for Responsible Medicine, Marin Philos. Soc. (v.p. 1991-92), Ctr. for Sci. in Pub. Interest, Health Medicine Forum, Assn. of Am. Physicians and Surgeons, Orthomolecular Health Medicine Soc., The World Affairs Coun., Am. Holistic Health Assn. Office: 777 Grand Ave Ste 205 San Rafael CA 94901-3509

FRIESEN, DAVID DOUGLAS, musician, music educator, composer; b. Tacoma, Wash., May 6, 1942; s. Benjamin Wilfred and Clara Friesen; m. Kirsten Pedersen, May 16, 1964; children: David, Scott Benjamin, Tobin, Jenelle Dunkin. Panelist Nat. Endowment For The Arts, Washington, 1983—; dir. music clinic/workshops Thomastik-Infeld, Vienna, 1997—. Musician: (book) Departure; musician: (composer) (short film score) Creation (Acad. Award nominee, 1988); musician: (book) Years Through Time, (record) Through The Listening Glass (Voted in L.A. Times as one of the 10 best jazz records of the decade, 1981), (CD) Four to Go (One of the 5 best jazz recordings for 1996 Jazz Times Mag., 1996), The Name of a Woman (One of the 5 best jazz recordings for 2002 Jazz Times Mag., 2002), (performance) Solo Bass Concert (Most outstanding jazz artist Monterey Jazz Festival 1977, 1977), (short film score) To Try Again And Succeed (Acad. Award nominee, 1981). Nominee Best Jazz Bassist, Am. Jazz Awards, 1997; named, Down Beat Jazz Mag., 1979; named one of Ten Most Outstanding Jazz Artists, Swing Jour. Jazz Mag. (Japan), 1980; Jazz Performance grant, Nat. Endowment For the Arts, 1984, 1988, 1992. Mem.: Musicians Union. Achievements include design of Helped design original instrument.Hemage Bass. Small bass with a stand. Played same manner as acoustic bass but, much smaller fingerboard scale. Cherry wood body, ebony fingerboard, maple neck; Recorded 70 records/CD's as a leader/co-leader, over 150 recordings as a sideman; Toured as a leader throughout the United States playing concerts and over 20 other countries in the world; One of the pioneers of Solo Bass Concerts since 1972; Over 300 original compositions recorded. Avocations: wine collector, fishing, walking, films, travel. Office: Color Pool Music 1005 NE 78th Ave Portland OR 97213 Office Phone: 503-330-5999. Home Fax: 503-254-3510; Office Fax: 503-254-3510. Personal E-mail: cpm@davidfriesen.net.

FRIESEN, RONALD LEE, economics professor; b. Inman, Kans., Mar. 2, 1939; s. J.D. and Hilda Marie (Neufeld) F.; m. Phyllis Ruth Sawatzky, June 2, 1961; children: Janine Renee, Jon Alan, Julie Dyan. BA, Bethel Coll., 1961; MA in Econs., U. Kans., 1962; PhD in Econs., Columbia U., 1973. Tchr. Alliance Secondary Sch., Dodoma, Tanzania, 1962-65; prof. econs. Bluffton U., Ohio, 1969—2005, prof. emeritus, 2005. Past faculty chmn., past chmn. econ., bus. adminstrn. and acctg. dept. Bluffton U.; cons. in field. Contbr. book reviews and articles to profl. jours. and collected vols. Recipient Rsch. and Lectr., C. Henry Smith Trust, 1981-82; scholar faculty U. Kans., Lawrence, 1961-62, faculty fellow Columbia U., N.Y.C., 1965-69; Albert Schweitzer Chair fellow, N.Y.C., 1969. Mem. Am. Econs. Assn., African Studies Assn., Ohio Assn. Economists and Polit. Scientists, Economists for Peace and Security Avocations: tennis, stamp collecting/philately, coin collecting/numismatics, antique collecting. Office Phone: 419-358-1064. Business E-Mail: friesenr@bluffton.edu.

FRIESEN, STEVEN KENT, museum director; b. Lawrence, Kans., May 13, 1953; s. Orlando and Barbara Friesen; m. Monta Lee Dakin, Mar. 23, 1997; children: James Owens, Elizabeth. BA, Bethel Coll., 1975; MA, SUNY, Oneonta, 1977. Dir. Kauffman Mus., North Newton, Kans., 1976—77, Ctr. Disarmament Edn., Baton Rouge, 1982—84, 1719 Hans Herr Aouse, Lancaster, Pa., 1985—90, Molly Brown House Mus., Denver, 1993, Buffalo Bill Mus. and Grave, Denver, 1995—; mus. instr. Littleton (Colo.) His. Mus., 1978—82; supt. City of Greeley (Colo.) Mus., 1991—93. Prin. Friesen Cons., Denver, 1984—2004. Author: A Modest Mennonite Home, 1990; contbr. articles to profl. publs. Bd. dirs. Mennonite Urban Ministries, Denver, 2002—04. Mem.: Colo. and Wyo. Assn. Mus. (bd. dirs. 2004—), Mountain Plains Mus. Assn. (bd. dirs. 1999—2001). Avocations: hiking, skiing, cooking. Office: Buffalo Bill Mus and Grave 987 1/2 Lookout Mountain Rd Golden CO 80401 Business E-Mail: buffalobillmuseum@ci.denver.co.us.

FRIESON, RONALD E., telecommunications industry executive; B of Fin., U. Tenn.; MBA, Ga. State U. With TechSouth pub. Bellsouth Corp., 1985—89, ops. mgr. advt. & pub. group, 1989—95, v.p. advt. & pub., 1995—99, v.p., gen. mgr. consumer svcs., 1999—2000, v.p., gen. mgr. new product implementation comsumer svcs., 2000—01, v.p., chief diversity officer, 2001—02, v.p. transition and strategy Atlanta, 2002—. Bd. dirs. Summerbridge Atlanta, Greenforest Christian Acad., Ctrl. Atlanta Hospitality Childcare, Rape and Sexual Abuse Ctr. Tenn. Mem.: 100 Black Men (bd. dirs., mem. fundraising com., publicity chmn.).

FRIESTEDT, AMÉDÉE CHABRISSON, engineering company executive; b. Washington, Aug. 9, 1949; d. Wallace Eugene Danforth and Dorothy Anne (Ball) F. BA in Psychology, George Washington U., 1973; postgrad., Howard U., 1974-79; MS in Physiology and Biophysics, Georgetown U., 1988; postgrad., Walden U., 1993-99, U. Fairfax. Fin. records rep. George Washington U. Hosp., Washington, 1977-84; tech. writer, programmer Computer Scis. Corp., Fairfax, Va., 1984-87; sr. sys. analyst Network Mgmt., Inc., Fairfax, 1987-90; project sys. requirements analyst Unisys Corp., McLean, Va., 1990-92; lead sys. analyst Martin Marietta Tech. Svcs., Lockheed Martin, Inc., Bethesda, Md., 1992-98; sr. mem. SRA Internat., Inc., Bethesda, 1998—2001; tech. mgr., info. assurance analyst Bioinformatics Solutions, 2001—04; dir. KOG Exec. Group, 2004—; pres. Bitsyzygy Group, 2004—. Dir. computer ops. dept. physiology and biophysics Georgetown U., Washington, 1986-89; presenter in field. Editor: The Nurture of the Small, 1993, For Every Child, (newsletter) Every Child By Two. Mem. U.S.-China Capital Cities Friendship Coun., Inc., 1985; v.p. D.C. Head Injury Found., 1988-89; career mentor, peer counselor, pro bono computer cons. Epilepsy Found. for Nat. Capital Area, 1997. Recipient cert. of appreciation and letter of commendation Office of Personnel Mgmt., EPA, 1987, letter of commendation Gen. Svcs. Adminstrn., 1988, Office Rsch. and Devel., EPA, 1995, Nat. Human Genome Rsch. Inst., NIH, 1999. Mem. AAAS, NAFE, AAUW, Nat. Fedn. Bus. and Profl. Women (rec. sec. 1984-89), Women's Caucus for Art (pub. rels., newsletter editor, membership com., bd. dirs. Art for the Poeple, Living Labyrinths for Peace). Avocations: music, art, photography, poetry, philanthropy. Office Phone: 202-369-5786. Personal E-mail: amiefrie@yahoo.com.

FRIGARD, MONIQUE DENISE, journalist; d. Louis Theodore and Miriam Claudia Frigard. AA, Laney Coll., 1997; BA, San Francisco State U., 2001. Cmty. editor, author newsmakers and youth spotlight columns focusing on local citizens Las Vegas Rev.-Jour., 2003—. Guest reader to second graders Crestwood-Edison Elem. Sch. Editor: Laney Tower Newspaper; designer: newspaper layout (1st place on-the-spot layout for a tabloid newspaper, Journalism Assn. Cmty. Colls., 1995). Recipient Humanitarian award, Nev. Reading Week, cert. appreciation, 2004. Liberal. Avocations: reading, writing, gardening, movies, swimming. Office: Las Vegas Review Jour 1111 W Bonanza Rd Las Vegas NV 89125 Office Fax: 702-383-4676. Business E-Mail: mfrigard@reviewjournal.com.

FRIGO, JAMES PETER PAUL, industrial hardware company executive; b. Iron Mountain, Mich., Jan. 11, 1942; s. Louis and Giustina (Carollo) F.; m. Patricia Mary Nellen, June 21, 1969; children: Christine, Catherine, P.J. Ortiz, Pamela Aks, Steven, Sandy. BBA, U. Miami, 1966. Sales rep. Great Dane Trailers, Miami, 1966—67, Foster Inc., Miami, 1968, Lawson Products Inc., Miami, 1968—; pres. Jim Frigo Inc., Miami, 1972—. Asst. scoutmaster Troop 314 Boy Scouts Am. Mem.: KC. Republican. Roman Catholic. Office: Jim Frigo Inc 7420 SW 175th St Miami FL 33157-6313 Office Phone: 305-235-4121. Personal E-mail: jimfrigo@aol.com.

FRIGOLETTO, FREDRIC DAVID, JR., physician; b. Fitchburg, Mass., Feb. 20, 1933; s. Fredric David and Alba (Merlino) F.; m. Martha McKay, June 4, 1966; children: Susan, Laurie Anne. AB, Brown U., 1954; MA, Boston U., 1955, MD, 1962. Diplomate Nat. Bd. Med. Examiners, Am. Bd. Ob-Gyn. Intern in surgery Boston City Hosp., 1962-63, jr. asst. resident in surgery, 1963-64; resident in ob-gyn Boston Hosp. for Women, 1964-67, med. dir. ambulatory svcs., 1969-72, dir. ednl. svcs., 1973-80, dir. obstetrics, 1974-80; chief maternal-fetal medicine Brigham and Women's Hosp., Boston, 1980-89, med. dir. obstetrics, 1985-89, dir. antenatal diagnostic ctr., 1985-93, chief obstetrics, vice chmn. dept. obstetrics, 1989-93; chief Vincent Meml. Obstetrics divsn. Mass. Gen. Hosp., Boston, 1993—. William Lambert Richardson prof. obstetrics Harvard Med. Sch., 1986-93, Charles Montraville Green and Robert Montraville Green prof. ob-gyn., 1993—. Contbr. over 100 articles to profl. jours., chpts. 2 books; editor 2 books. Recipient award NIH. Fellow ACOG (chmn. com. on obstetrics 1982-85, chmn. com. on profl. stds. 1991—. pres.-elect 1995, pres. 1996); mem. Soc. Perinatal Obstetricians, Am. Gynecol. and Obstet. Soc., Am. Gynecologic Club. Office: Massachusetts Gen Hosp Dept Ob/Gyn 32 Fruit St Boston MA 02114-2620

FRIIS, ROBERT HAROLD, epidemiologist, health science educator; b. San Jose, Calif., July 15, 1941; s. Harold Hector and Florence Marie (Brant) F.; m. Carol Ann Speer, Oct. 28, 1966; children: Michelle Alanna, Erik Adler. BA, U. Calif., Berkeley, 1964; MA, Columbia U., NYC, 1966, PhD, 1969. Postdoctoral fellow U. Mich., Ann Arbor, 1969-71; asst. prof. Sch. Pub. Health Columbia U., 1971-74, Albert Einstein Coll. Medicine, Bronx, NY, 1974-76; assoc. prof. CUNY, Bklyn. Coll., 1976-78; dir. field epidemiology Orange County Pub. Health, Santa Ana, Calif., 1978-79; assoc. clin. prof. U. Calif., Irvine, 1979-93; prof., chairperson dept. health sci. Calif. State U., Long Beach, 1988—, now mem. acad. senate. Vis. rschr. Karolinska Inst., Stockholm, 1993; dir. Joint Studies Inst. Calif. State U. and Va. Med. Ctr., Long Beach, 1995—; adv. bd. Ctr. for Health Care Innovation Calif. State U., Long Beach; guest scientist Max Planck Inst. Psychiatry, Munich, 2001; vis. prof. clin. psychology and psychotherapy unit Dresden (Germany) Tech. U., 2001; bd. dirs. Long Beach Global Health Initiative, Long Beach Tobacco Edn. Program, Calif. Health Interview Survey, 2004; clin. prof. dept. cmty. and environ. medicine U. Calif., Irvine, 2003; mem. steering com. Ctr. for Internat. Trade and Transp., 2004; cons. in field. Sr. author: Epidemiology Public Health Practice, 1996, 3d edit. 2004; co-author: Introductory Biostatistics for the Health Sciences, 2003; contbr. articles to profl. jours. Faculty mentor Ptnrs. for Success, Long Beach, 1992-97. Grantee, U. Calif., Irvine, 1995, Mexus com. U. Calif., 1988, U. Calif. systemwide, 1988, U. Calif. Tobacco Related Disease Rsch. Program, 1998, 2003, Metrans Trans. Ctr., 2005. Fellow Royal Inst. Pub. Health; mem. APHA, Am. Statis. Assn. (So. Calif. sect.), Soc. Epidemiol. Rsch., Am. Assn. Health Edn.(life mem.), U. Calif. Berkley Alumni Assn., So. Calif. Pub. Health Assn. (bd. dir., pres.-elect 2005), adv. bd. Calif. Eta Sigma Gamma. Democrat. Avocations: reading, travel, coin collecting/numismatics, computers, gardening. Office: Calif State Univ Long Beach Dept Health Science 1250 N Bellflower Blvd Long Beach CA 90840-0006 Office Phone: 562-985-1537. Business E-Mail: rfriis@csulb.edu.

FRIIS-HANSEN, DANA, museum director; b. 1961; BA in Art History, Carleton Coll., 1983. Asst. curator and then curator List Visual Arts Ctr., MIT, Cambridge, Mass., 1985—91; assoc. curator Nanjo and Assocs. pvt. curatorial svc., Tokyo, 1991—95; sr. curator Contemporary Arts Mus., Houston, 1995—99; chief curator Austin (Tex.) Mus. Art, 1999—, interim exec. dir., 2001—02, exec. dir., 2002—. Panelist Pew Fellowships in the Arts, 2002; co-curator TransCulture, Venice Biennale, 1995. Author: Abastract Painting Once Removed, 1998; co-author: Cai Guo-Qiang, 2002, Takashi Murakami, 2000, The History of Japanese Photography, 2003, Terry Allen: Dugout, 2005. Helena Rubenstein fellow, Whitney Mus. Am. Art Ind. Study Program. Office: Austin Mus of Art 823 Congress St Austin TX 78701

FRIMMER, PAUL NORMAN, lawyer; b. N.Y.C., June 8, 1945; s. William and Irene (Alper) F.; m. Carol S. Zucker, June 9, 1968; children: Tracey, Scott. BS, Queens Coll., N.Y.C., 1966; JD cum laude, Fordham U., 1969. Bar: N.Y. 1969, Calif. 1971. Assoc. Stroock and Stroock, and Lavan, N.Y.C., 1969-71; ptnr. Irell and Manella, L.A., 1971—. Panelist Calif. Continuing Edn. of Bar, 1972, co-chmn. various sects. 73, 75, 76, 80, 86; instr. advanced profl. program U. So. Calif., 1977-80; lectr. 6th and 14th Insts. Estate Planning U. Miami Law Ctr., 1972, 80, Practicing Law Inst.-ABA programs, 1973-91, 31st Inst. Fed. Taxation U. So. Calif., 1979, other bar assn. groups on estate planning, probate, taxation, charitable giving and community property. Contbr. numerous articles to profl. jours. Nat. trustee, asst. sec. Leukemia Soc. Am., Inc., 1976-86, 91—, trustee, chmn. planned giving com. L.A. chpt., chpt. pres., 1973-86; trustee L.A. Children's Mus., 1982-86. Fellow Am. Coll. Trust and Estate Counsel, Internat. Acad. Probate and Trust Law; mem. ABA (real property, probate and trust law sect. com. charitable giving, trusts and founds., chmn. disclaimer task force), Calif. Bar Assn. Avocations: tennis, skiing. Office: Irell & Manella 1800 Avenue Of The Stars Los Angeles CA 90067-4276

FRINK, DWIGHT DAVID, management educator; b. F.E. Warren AFB, Wyo., Aug. 29, 1953; s. Emory Burdette and Mary Louise Frink; m. Nancy Katharine Wood, Apr. 2, 1977; children: Regan Elisabeth, Abigail Olivia, David Bradley, Ethan Clinton. BS in Mgmt., U. South Ala., 1990; AM in Labor and Indsl. Rels., U. Ill., 1992, PhD in Labor and Indsl. Rels., 1994. Estimator, project mgr. All Am. Roofing, Chickasaw, Ala., 1987—91; grad. asst. U. Ill., Champaign, 1991—94; vis. asst. prof. mgmt. U. Okla., Norman, 1994—95; asst. prof. mgmt. U. Miss., University, 1995—2000, assoc. prof. mgmt., 2000—, area coord. mgmt., 2000—02, chair dept. mgmt., 2002—. Author: Toward a Theory of Accountability, 1998; editor: Accountability in Organizations, 2004. Emergency med. responder; elder Oasis Ch., Oxford, Miss., 2002—. Named Self chair of free enterprise, PMB and William KMG Self Found., Marks, Miss., 2001; Jacob Javits fellow, U.S. Dept. Edn., 1990—94. Mem.: APA, Acad. Mgmt. Avocation: Christian writing. Office: Sch Bus U Miss 238 Holman Hall University MS 38677

FRISBEE, DON CALVIN, retired utilities executive; b. San Francisco, Dec. 13, 1923; s. Ira Nobles and Helen (Sheets) F.; m. Emilie Ford, Feb. 5, 1947; children: Ann, Robert, Peter, Dean. BA, Pomona Coll., 1947; MBA, Harvard U., 1949. Sr. investment analyst, asst. cashier investment analysis dept. 1st Interstate Bank Oreg., N.A., Portland, 1949-52; treas. PacifiCorp, Portland, 1958-60, then v.p., exec. v.p., pres., 1966-73, chief exec. officer, 1973-89, chmn., 1973-94; chmn. emeritus PacifiCorp., Portland, 1994-97. Bd. dirs. Wells Fargo Bank. Trustee Reed Coll.; former trustee Safari Game Search Found., High Desert Mus.; mem. cabinet Columbia Pacific coun. Boy Scouts Am.; founder Oreg. chpt. Am. Leadership Forum. 1st lt. AUS, 1943-46. Mem. Arlington Club, Univ. Club Multnomah Athletic Club, City Club. Fax: 503-224-4545.

FRISBIE, CURTIS LYNN, JR., lawyer; b. Greenville, Miss., Sept. 13, 1943; s. Curtis Lynn and Edith L. (Brantley) F.; m. Gena F. Johnson, May 30, 1965; children: Curtis L. III, Mark A. BSBA, U. Ala., 1966; JD, St. Mary's U., San Antonio, 1971. Bar: Tex. 1971; U.S. Dist. Ct. (no. dist.) Ga. 1974, U.S. Dist. Ct. (no. dist.) Tex. 1978, U.S. Dist. Ct. (we. dist.) Tex. 1985, U.S. Dist. Ct. (ea. and so. dists.) Tex. 1986, U.S. Dist. Ct. (ea. dist.) Wis. 1986; U.S. Tax Ct. 1986; U.S. Ct. Appeals (5th cir.) 1975, U.S. Ct. Appeals (10th cir.) 1982, U.S. Ct. Appeals (8th cir.) 1987; U.S. Supreme Ct. 1977. Trial atty. Antitrust divsn. U.S. Dept. Justice, Atlanta, 1971-73; assoc. King & Spalding, Atlanta, 1974-77; ptnr. Gardere Wynne Sewell LLP (formerly Gardere & Wynne LLP), Dallas, 1978—. Assoc. editor St. Mary's Law Jour., 1970-71. Bd. dirs. Tex. Hist. Found., 2002—. Capt. USMC, 1966-69, Vietnam. Named Tex. Superlawyers in Antitrust, Tex. Monthly, 2003, 2003, 2004, 2005; named one of Best Lawyers in Dallas, D Mag., 2003, 2004, 2005; named to Am.'s Leading Bus. Lawyers in Antitrust, Chambers & Ptnrs., 2004, 2005. Fellow Tex. Bar Found. (life), Dallas Bar Assn. (life); mem. ABA (antitrust and bus. law sect.), Tex. Bar Assn. (antitrust sect., mem. coun. 1995—, vice chair, chair elect 2000-01, chair 2001-02), Dallas Bar Assn. (pres. antitrust and trade regulation sect. 1993), Coll. State Bar Tex., Phi Alpha Delta. Avocations: scuba diving, fishing, hunting. Home: 5605 Palomar Ln Dallas TX 75229-6417 Office: Gardere Wynne Sewell LLP Thanksgiving Tower 1601 Elm St Ste 3000 Dallas TX 75201-4761 Office Phone: 214-999-4757. Business E-Mail: cfrisbie@gardere.com.

FRISBIE, JAMES HOWARD, retired internist; b. Lexington, Ky., Sept. 21, 1935; s. Howard I. Frisbie and Pauline Lucetta Clarkson; m. Judith Moore, Feb. 22, 1964; children: Carl Daniel, Margo Palombi. BA, Emory U., 1957, MD, 1961. Diplomate Am. Bd. Internal Medicine, Am. Bd. Phys. Medicine and Rehab. Resident in psychiatry Washington U., St. Louis, 1962—64, 1969—70, fellow in cardiology, 1968—69; resident in medicine Med. Coll. of Wis., Milw., 1964—66; staff physician Marshfield (Wis.) Clinic, 1970—71; postdoctoral fellow U. Conn., Farmington, 1971—72; staff physician VA Med. Ctr., West Roxbury, Mass., 1973—2001, ednl. cons., 2001—. Contbr. articles to profl. jours. Capt. U.S. Army, 1966—68, Vietnam. Mem.: Am. Paraplegia Soc., Internat. Soc. Paraplegia. Achievements include discovery of value of colostomy on the quality of life for spinal cord injured persons. Avocations: tennis, walking, boating. Home: 259 Hillcrest Rd Needham MA 02492 Office: Department of Veterans Affairs Hospital 1400 VFW Pkwy West Roxbury MA 02132 Office Phone: 617-323-7700 6575. Office Fax: 617-363-5553. Personal E-mail: jfrisbie@comcast.net. E-mail: james.frisbie2@med.va.gov.

FRISBY, HERBERT RUSSELL, lawyer; b. Balt., Dec. 28, 1950; m. June J. Frisby; children: Herbert R. III, James T. BA in Polit. Sci./Internat. Rels., Swarthmore Coll., 1972; JD, Yale U., 1975. Bar: Md. 1975, D.C. 1979. Asst. gen. counsel Md. Atty. Gen.'s Office, Balt., 1978-79; atty.-advisor FCC, Washington, 1979-80, legal asst., 1980-83; sr. atty. Weil, Gotshal & Manges, Washington, 1983-86; prin. Melnicove, Kaufman, Weiner & Smouse, PA, Washington, 1986-89; ptnr. Venable, Baetjer & Howard, Balt., 1989-95; chmn. Md. Pub. Svc. Commn., Balt., 1995-98; pres. Competitive Telecomm. Assn., Washington, 1998—2004; CEO CompTel/ASCENT Alliance (merged with Assoc. Communications Enterprises), 2004—05; interim CEO CompTel/ALTS, Washington, 2005; ptnr. Kirkpatrick & Lockhart Nicholson Graham, 2005—. Mem. NARUC Comms. Com., Washington, 1995-98. Bd. dirs. United Way of Ctrl. Md., Balt., 1989-97; v.p. Balt. Mus. Art, 1993-95. Recipient Charles Hamilton Houston award Minority Bus. Enterprise Legal Def. and Edn. Fund, 1989, Disting. Alumnus award Fund for Ednl. Excellence, 1991; named to Balt. City Coll. Hall of Fame, 1989. Fellow Md. Bar Found.; mem. ABA (budget officer adminstrv. law sect. 1995-98). Office: Kirkpatrick & Lockhart Nicholson Graham 1800 Massachusetts Ave NW Washington DC 20036 Office Phone: 202-778-9415. Business E-Mail: rfrisby@klng.com.

FRISBY, JAMES CURTIS, retired agricultural engineering educator; b. Bethany, Mo., Oct. 22, 1930; s. Jackson Carey and Gladys (Selby) F.; m. Hazel M. Kallenbach, Dec. 20, 1969. BS in Edn., U. Mo., 1952, BSAE, 1956; MS, Iowa State U., 1963, PhD, 1965. Registered profl. engr., Mo. Classroom instr., tech. writer, market analyst Caterpillar Tractor Co., Peoria, Ill., 1956-60; acting mgr. farm services dept. Iowa State U., Ames, 1961-63, instr., 1963-65; asst. prof. agrl. engring. U. Mo., Columbia, 1966-69, assoc. prof., 1969-74, prof., 1974-96, chmn. agrl. engring., 1989-94; prof. emeritus, 1996—; ret. Served to 1st lt. U.S. Army, 1952-54. Recipient award of merit Gamma Sigma Delta, 1976; recipient cert. of appreciation U. Mo. Coll. Engring., 1983, 87. Mem.: NSPE, Am. Soc. Agrl. Engrs. (Mem. of Yr. Mo. sect. 1995, Spl. Svc. award MidCtrl. Conf. 1996), Nat. Assn. Colls. and Tchrs. Agr. (Tchg. award of merit 1994), Am. Soc. Engring. Edn., Am. Soc. Agrl. Engrs. (chmn. mid-ctrl. region 1982—83, dir. mid-ctrl. region 1984—86), Mo. Soc. Profl. Engrs. (pres. ctrl. chpt. 1995—96), Kiwanis Internat. Mem. Ch. of Christ. Home: 1805 Bluff Pointe Dr Columbia MO 65201-6287 E-mail: jfrisby@coin.org.

FRISCH, HARRY LLOYD, chemist, educator; b. Vienna, Nov. 13, 1928; s. Jacob J. and Clara F. (Spondre) F.; children— Benjamin, Michael. BA, Williams Coll., 1947; PhD, Poly. Inst. Bklyn., 1952. Research asso. physics Syracuse U., 1952-54; instr. U. So. Calif., 1954-55, asst. prof., 1955-56; mem. tech. staff Bell Telephone Labs., Inc., Murray Hill, N.J., 1956-67; prof. chemistry SUNY, Albany, 1967-78, disting. prof. chemistry, 1978—. Assoc. dean Coll. Arts and Sci., 1969-71; vis. assoc. prof. physics Yeshiva U., 1963-65, Inst. Study Metals, U. Chgo., 1960; asst. to dean Belfer Grad. Sch. Yeshiva U., 1963-65; cons. in field. Editor: (with J. Lebowitz) The Equilibrium Theory of Classical Fluids, 1964, (with Z. Salsburg) Simple Dense Fluids, 1968; assoc. editor: Jour. Chem. Physics, 1964-66, Jour. Statis. Physics, 1970-75; mem. editorial bd.: Jour. Phys. Chemistry, 1976-80, Jour. Polymer Sci. (Physics edit.), 1976—, Jour. Membrane Sci, 1976-80, Jour. Colloid and Interface Sci., 1978-81, Jour. Adhesion, 1970-75; contbr. articles to profl. jours. NSF grantee, 1968—; recipient Sr. U.S. Scientist Humboldt award, 1987-89. Fellow Am. Phys. Soc.; mem. Am. Chem. Soc. (G.S. Whitby award rubber div. 1995, Joel Henry Hildebrand Award in the Theoretical & Experminetal Chemistry of Liquids, 2000), Cosmos Club, Williams Club, Sigma Xi. Democrat. Jewish. Office: Dept of Chemistry SUNYA 1400 Washington Ave Albany NY 12222-0100 Office Phone: 518-442-2586. Business E-Mail: hlf04@albany.edu.

FRISCH, IVAN THOMAS, computer and communications company executive; b. Budapest, Hungary, Sept. 21, 1937; came to U.S., 1939, naturalized, 1941; s. Laszlo and Rose (Balog) F.; m. Vivian Scelzo, June 6, 1962; children: Brian, Bruce. BS, MS, Columbia U., 1958, PhD, 1962. Asst. prof. elec. engring. and computer sci. U. Calif., Berkeley, 1962-65, assoc. prof., 1965-69; Ford Found. resident engring. practice Bell Labs., Holmdel, N.J., 1965-66; founding mem. Network Analysis Corp., Great Neck, N.Y., 1969—, sr. v.p., 1971—, gen. mgr., 1978-85; v.p. Contel Bus. Networks, 1985-87; dir. Ctr. on Advanced Tech. in Telecommunications, prof. Poly. U., Bklyn., 1987—; provost Polytech. U., 1992—. Adj. prof. computer sci. SUNY, Stony Brook, 1975—, Columbia U., N.Y.C., 1977—; cons. in field. Author: (with Howard Frank) Communication, Transmission and Transportation Networks, 1971; Founding editor-in-chief: Networks, 1971—; contbr. articles to profl. publs. Guggenheim fellow, 1969 Fellow IEEE (Eric E. Sumner award 1999, 3d Millenium award 2000); mem. N.Y. Acad. Scis., Cable TV Assn. Am., Nat. Acad. Engring., Phi Beta Kappa, Tau Beta Pi, Eta Kappa Nu. Office: Poly U Six Metrotech Ctr Rm JB-555 Brooklyn NY 11201-2907

FRISCH, JOSEPH, mechanical engineer, educator, consultant; b. Vienna, Apr. 21, 1921; came to U.S., 1940, naturalized, 1946; s. Abraham and Rachel (Lieberman) F.; m. Joan S. Frisch, May 26, 1962; children— Nora Theresa, Erich Martin, Jonathan David BSME, Duke U., 1946; MS, U. Calif., 1950. Registered profl. engr., Calif. Mem. faculty U. Calif.-Berkeley, 1947—, asst. prof. mech. engring., 1951-57, assoc. prof. mech. engring., 1957—, prof. mech. engring., 1963—, asst. dir. Inst. Engring. Rsch., 1961-63, chmn. div. mech. design, 1966-70, assoc. dean, 1972-75. Cons. to indsl. and govtl. labs. Contbr. articles to profl. jours. Fellow ASME (life); mem. Phi Beta Kappa, Sigma Xi, Tau Beta Pi, Pi Tau Sigma Clubs: U. Calif.-Berkeley Faculty. Office: U Calif Dept Mech Engring Berkeley CA 94720-1740 Office Phone: 510-642-3740. Business E-Mail: frisch@berkeley.edu.

FRISCH, PAUL ANDREW, librarian; b. Madison, Wis., Oct. 23, 1950; s. Arthur Joseph and Ruth Beverly (Myers) F.; m. Claudia Anna Maria Hirsch, Aug. 1, 1990. BA History, UCLA, 1975, MA History, 1977, MLS, 1986, PhD History, 1992. Social scis. libr. Trinity Univ., San Antonio, 1986-88; head ref. dept., libr. Southwest Mo. State U., Springfield, 1988-92; head of ref. dept., libr. U. Ill., Chgo., 1992-95; head libr. Washington & Jefferson Coll., Washington, Pa., 1995-2000; dir. Old Westbury Libr. SUNY, Old Westbury, NY, 2000—01; dean libr. Our Lady of the Lake, San Antonio, 2001—03, assoc. provost libr. instructional and tech. svcs., 2003—. Contbr. articles to profl. jours. Treas., trustee Citizens Libr., Washington, Pa., 1995-2000; mem. Friends of San Antonio Pub. Libr. Summer rsch. grantee S.W. Mo. State U., 1990. Mem.: Educause. Office: Lake U San Antonio TX 78207-4689

FRISCH, ROSE EPSTEIN, population sciences researcher; b. N.Y.C., July 7, 1918; m. David H. Frisch; children: Henry J., Ruth Frisch Dealy. BA, Smith Coll., 1939; MA, Columbia U., 1940; PhD, U. Wis., 1943. Assoc. prof. population scis. Harvard U., Cambridge, Mass., 1984-92, assoc. prof. emerita, 1992—2005, prof., 2005—. Author: (book) Female Fertility and the Body Fat Connection, 2002, paperback edit., 2004; contbr. articles to profl. jours. John Simon Guggenheim Meml. fellow, 1975-76; recipient Disting. Prof. Emeritus award, Harvard Sch. Pub. Health. Fellow Am. Acad. Arts and Scis.; mem. AAAS, Endocrine Soc. Am., Population Soc. Am., Sigma Xi (nat. lectr. 1989-90). Office: Harvard U Ctr Population Studies 9 Bow St Cambridge MA 02138-5103 Office Phone: 617-495-3013.

FRISCHHERTZ, LLOYD NICHOLAS, lawyer; b. New Orleans, July 8, 1948; s. Llyod Nicholas and Yvonne (Dupas) F.; m. Marcelle Livaudais, Aug. 18, 1972; children: Marc, Brad. BA, Loyola U., New Orleans, 1970, JD, 1973. Bar: La. 1973, U.S. Dist. Ct. (ea. dist.) La. 1973, U.S. Ct. Appeals (5th cir.) 1973, U.S. Supreme Ct. 1991. Assoc. Seelig & Cosse, New Orleans, 1973-77; ptnr. Frischhertz & Assocs., New Orleans, 1977—. Mem. ABA, Am. Trial Lawyers Assn., La. Trial Lawyers Assn., Loyola Law Alumni Assn. (pres. 1981-82). Democrat. Roman Catholic. Office: Frischhertz & Assocs LLC 1130 Saint Charles Ave New Orleans LA 70130-4332 E-mail: lnfrisch@aol.com.

FRISCHLING, CARL, lawyer; b. N.Y.C., Feb. 21, 1937; s. Irving and Anna (Klein) F.; m. Adele Frischling, June 21, 1959; children: William, James, Edward. BA, Columbia U., 1958, JD, 1962, MBA, 1963. Bar: N.Y. 1963, U.S. Dist. Ct. N.Y. 1968. Atty. Am. Stock Exchange, N.Y.C., 1963-65; asst. to chmn. Investors Funding, N.Y.C., 1965-67; exec. v.p. and gen. counsel Am. Gen. Capital Mgmt., N.Y.C., 1968-76; ptnr. Alexander Green, N.Y.C., 1976-79; sr. ptnr. Spengler Carlson Gubar Brodsky Frischling, N.Y.C., 1979-92; ptnr. Reid & Priest, N.Y.C., 1992-94, Kramer Levin, N.Y.C., 1994—. Bd. dirs. AIM Mut. Funds, Houston, Cortland Funds. Office: Kramer Levin 1177 6th Ave New York NY 10036

FRISCHWASSER, HEINZ FELIX See RA'ANAN, URI

FRISCO, LOUIS JOSEPH, retired electronics executive, electrical engineer; b. Patchogue, N.Y., Aug. 21, 1923; s. Anthony Michael and Rose Katherine (Lotito) F.; m. Verona May Kindig, Aug. 20, 1950; children: Richard Samuel (dec.), Charles Francis. BSEE, Johns Hopkins U., 1949, MSEE, 1952. Dielectrics lab. dir. Johns Hopkins U., Balt., 1950-64; dielectrics program mgr. GE, Schenectady, N.Y., 1964-65; various tech. and ops. mgmt. positions Raychem Corp., Menlo Park, Calif., 1965-79, dir. corp. product rev., 1979-83, gen. mgr. Wire and Cable div., 1983-89, tech. dir. Electronics Sector, 1989-90. Chmn. Conf. on Elec. Insulation, NAS/NRC, 1963-65; U.S. del. tech. com. TC-15 Internat. Electrotech. Commn., 1963-65, 79-82. Editor Digest of Lit. on Dielectrics, NAS/NRC, 1959, 60.; contbr. numerous articles to profl. jours. Fellow IEEE; mem. ASTM, Electrochem. Soc. (chmn. insulation div. 1957-59, bd. dirs. 1957-59, insulation div. editor jour. 1961-64), Tau Beta Pi, Sigma Xi. Roman Catholic.

FRISELL-SCHRÖDER, SONJA BETTIE, theater producer, theater director; b. Richmond, Surrey, Eng., Aug. 5, 1937; d. Bertel and Helena Margaret (Smith) Frisell; m. Rolf Peter Schröder, Feb. 3, 1976. Licentiate, Guildhall Sch. Music and Drama, London, 1958. Asst. dir. Arena Opera, Verona, Italy, summers 1962-65; from asst. dir. to head of regie and prodn. La Scala Opera Co., Milan, Italy, 1964-79; free-lance producer U.S.A., Can., Argentina, Brazil, Italy, France, Austria, Eng. Producer Ballo in Maschera, Paris Opera, 1981, Andrea Chenier, Miami, 1982, Marriage of Figaro, San Francisco, 1982, Khovanscina, San Francisco, 1984, Agrippina, Venice, 1985, Carmen, Teatro Colon, Buenos Aires, 1985, Salome, Seattle, 1986, Aida, Rio de Janeiro, 1986, Ballo, San Francisco, 1986, Ballo, Phila. (with Pavarotti), 1986, Magic Flute, Edmonton, Winnipeg, 1986, Trovatore, Chgo., 1987, Don Carlos, Tulsa, 1987, Marriage of Figaro, Treviso, 1987, Rigoletto, Seattle, 1988, Otello, Barcelona, 1988, Maometto II, San Francisco, 1988, Aida Met. N.Y., 1988, Ballo, Bologna, 1989, Forza del Destino, Washington, 1989, Don Carlos, Chgo., 1989, Daughter of the Regiment, Calgary, Can., 1990, Otello, P.R., 1990, Don Carlos, L.A., 1990, Siege of Calais, Donizetti Festival Bergamo, 1990, Magic Flute, Washington, 1990, Don Giovanni, Cape Town, South Africa, 1991, Don Carlos, Washington, 1991, Forza, San Francisco, 1992, Otello, Washington, 1992, Ballo, Chgo., 1992, Rigoletto, Goteborg, 1993, Trovatore, Chgo., 1993, Lucia diLammermoor, Calgary, 1994, Eugene Onegin, Calgary, 1996, Don Carlos, Chgo., 1996, La Gioconda, Milan, 1997, Elena di Feltre, Wexford, 1997, Magic Flute, Washington, 1998, Turandot, Seville, 1998, Turandot Trieste, Cagliari, Santander, Cordoba, 1999, Eugene Onegin, Tucson, Otello, Washington, 2000, Don Carlos, Washington, Carmen, Iceland, La Traviata, Rio de Janeiro, 2001, Salome, Tucson, Phoenix, 2003, Turandot, Helsinki, 2004. Arts scholar Can. Arts Coun., 1960. Mem. Am. Guild Mus. Artists. Avocations: archaeology, walking, dogs, gardening. Office: care CAMI 165 W 57th St New York NY 10019-2201 E-mail: frisellschroeder@hotmail.com.

FRISHMAN, WILLIAM HOWARD, cardiology educator, cardiovascular pharmacologist, gerontologist; b. N.Y.C., Nov. 9, 1946; s. Aaron and Frances (Fishel) F.; m. Esther Rose Sandowsky, Mar. 11, 1971; children: Sheryl Renée, Amy Helene, Michael Aaron. BA, MD, Boston U., 1969. Diplomate Am. Bd. Internal Medicine, Am. Bd. Cardiovascular Medicine, Am. Bd. Critical Care Medicine, Am. Bd. Clin. Pharmacology, Am. Bd. Geriatrics, Am. Bd. Med. Mgmt. Intern Montefiore Hosp., Bronx, NY, 1969—70, resident in medicine, 1970—71, Bronx Mcpl. and Einstein Hosps., 1971—72; fellow in cardiology N.Y. Hosp.-Cornell U. Med. Coll., N.Y.C., 1972—74, instr., 1974—76; dir. noninvasive cardiac labs. Einstein Hosp. and Montefiore Hosp., 1976—80, dir. cardiology svc., 1980—82, chief medicine, 1982—91; prof. medicine and epidemiology, assoc. chmn. dept. medicine Albert Einstein Coll. Medicine Yeshiva U., Bronx, 1991—97; prof. medicine and pharmacology, chmn. dept. medicine N.Y. Med. Coll., Valhalla, 1997—; chief of medicine Westchester Med. Ctr., Valhalla, NY, 1997—. Expert cons. cardiorenal divsn. FDA, Bethesda, Md., 1987—; panel mem. U.S. Pharmacopeial Conv., Rockville, Md., 1990—. Author: (med. book) Clinical Pharmacology of the Beta Blocking Drugs, 1980, 2nd edit., 1984, Management of Lipid Disorders, 1992; co-author: Calcium Channel Antagonists in Cardiovascular Disease, 1984, Therapy of Angina Pectoris, 1986, Current Cardiovascular Drugs, 1994, 4th edit., 2005, Beta-3 Adrenergic Agonism, 1995, Cardiovascular Pharmacotherapeutics, 1997, 2nd edit., 2003, Manual of Cardiovascular Pharmacotherapeutics, 1998, 2nd edit., 2004, Complementary and Integrative Therapies for Cardiovascular Disease, 2005; editor: Year Book of Medicine: Heart Disease, 1998—2003, Cardiology in Rev., Am. Jour. Medicine supplement; contbr. chapters to books and articles to profl. jours. Mem. fiscal affairs com. Village of Scarsdale, N.Y., 1991—. Lt. col. M.C., U.S. Army, 1969-90. Named to Boston Collegium of Disting. Alumni, Boston U., 1988, Disting. Alumnus sch. medicine, 1994; teaching scholar Am. Heart Assn., 1979-82; preventive cardiology acad. award Nat. Heart, Lung and Blood Inst., 1980-85; recipient Disting. Tchr. award AAMC-AOA, 1997, Med. Humanism award AAMC, 2001. Master: ACP; fellow: Am. Coll. Chest Physicians, Am. Coll. Cardiology (bd. govs. 1987—91, pres. N.Y. State chpt. 1991); mem.: N.Y. Cardiology Soc. (pres. 1996—97), Assn. Profs. Medicine, Am. Soc. for Clin. Rsch., Am. Soc. for Clin. Pharmacology and Therapeutics (McKeen Cattell award 1990), Scarsdale Town and Village Club, Alpha Omega Alpha (regional councilor, bd. dirs.). Jewish. Avocations: reading, family sports. Home: 7 White Birch Ln Scarsdale NY 10583-7634 Office: Munger Pavilion NY Med Coll Valhalla NY 10595 Office Phone: 914-594-4383.

FRISINA, ROBERT DANA, neuroscientist, educator; b. Evanston, Ill., Sept. 11, 1955; s. Robert and Louise (Boaz) Frisina; m. Susan Taylor Frisina, July 31, 1982; children: Laurin Taylor, Taylor Robert. AB in Exptl. Psychology summa cum laude, Hamilton Coll., 1977; PhD in Neurosci., Syracuse U., 1983. Rsch. asst. Hamilton Coll., Clinton, NY, 1977; Root fellow in sci. Inst. Sensory Rsch., Syracuse (NY) U., 1977-78, NSF grad. fellow, 1978-81, grad. rsch. assoc., 1981-83; NIH rsch. fellow Ctr. Brain Rsch. U. Rochester, 1983-85; asst. prof. physiology and otolaryngology U. Rochester, 1985-91, assoc. prof. surgery, neurobiology and anatomy, 1991-99, prof. surgery, neurobiology, anatomy, and biomed. engring., 1999—, dir. rsch. otolaryngology, 1988-92, assoc. chmn. otolaryngology, 1992—; v.p. and founder Auditory Sys. Technologies, Inc., Pittsford, 1989-98. Charter mem. adv. bd. Internat. Ctr. Hearing, Speech Rsch., 1988—2002, assoc. dir., 2002—; chmn. study sect. NIH, 2000—02; adj. assoc. prof. comm. sci. Nat. Tech. Inst. Deaf, Rochester, NY, 1993—2004, prof. comm. scis., 2004—; adj. prof. comm. scis. U. Buffalo, 1998—; disting. rsch. prof. Rochester (N.Y.) Inst. Tech., 2003—. Dir. vols. Hamilton Coll. Aspect Marcy Psychiat. Ctr., NY, 1974—77. Recipient 1st award in Communicative Disorders, NIH, 1988—94. Fellow: Acoustical Soc. Am. (assoc. editor jour. 1996—99), Am. Acad. Otolaryngology, Head, Neck Surgery; mem.: Acoustical Soc. Found. (charter, bd. dir. 1996—, gen. sec., chief fin. officer 1998—2005), Am. Speech, Hearing, Lang. Assn., Soc. Neurosci., Assn. Rsch. Otolaryngology, Psi Chi, Sigma Xi, Phi Beta Kappa. Roman Cath. Achievements include patents for for a noise suppression electronic circuit for enhancing speech in the presence of background noise; a hearing aid circuit which can be custom fit to a patients's hearing loss using laser trimming. Office: U Rochester Med Ctr Otolaryngology Divsn Rochester NY 14642-8629 Office Phone: 585-275-8130. Business E-Mail: rdf@q.ent.rochester.edu.

FRISON, RICK, agricultural company executive; b. Worland, Wyo., Aug. 22, 1949; s. David T. and Maureen M. (Nelson) F.; m. Nadine M. Van Overbeke; children: Cara M., Jennifer M. BS, Mont. State U., 1977. Salesman ConAgra Mont., Inc., Great Falls, 1977-81, mktg. mgr., 1981-83; div. mgr. ConAgra Fertilizer Co., Billings, Mont., 1983-86, div. mgr. no. region Knoxville, Tenn., 1986-89, v.p., gen. mgr. no. region, 1989-91, retail v.p., 1991-92, pres. Pekin, Ill., 1994—, Cropmate Co., Pekin, 1992—, United Agri Products, Greeley, Colo., 1993—. Mem. editl. adv. bd. Dealer Progress mag., Ballwin, Mo., 1992—; field editor Crop Protection mag., Eugene, Oreg., 1992—. Mem. Fertilizer Inst. (retail coun. 1992—). Office: Cropmate Co 3860 N Main St #A East Peoria IL 61611-5512

FRISSORA, MARK P., automotive parts manufacturing company executive; BA, Ohio State U.; postgrad., U. Pa., Thunderbird Internat. Sch. Mgmt. With lighting bus. group GE, 1977-87; various mgmt. positions Philips Lighting co., 1987-91; v.p. N.Am. mktg., sales and distbn. Aeroquip-Vickers Corp., 1991-96; v.p. original equipment sales and engring. Walker Mfg., 1996; sr. v.p., gen. mgr. original equipment bus.-program mgmt. Tenneco Automotive, Lake Forest, Ill., 1996-99, pres., CEO, 1999—, chmn., 2000—. Mem. The Bus. Roundtable; supplier's adv. coun. Nissan Motor Co.; automotive bd. gov. World Econ. Forum; bd. dir. NCR Corp., FMC Corp. Mem.: Motor & Equipment Mfr. Assn. (bd. dir.), Automotive Original Equipment Mfr. Assn., Soc. Automotive Engrs. Office: Tenneco Automotive 500 N Field Dr Lake Forest IL 60045-2595*

FRIST, BILL (WILLIAM HARRISON FRIST), senator, thoracic surgeon; b. Nashville, Feb. 22, 1952; m. Karyn McLaughlin Frist; children: Harrison, Jonathan, Bryan. AB in health care policy, Princeton U. Woodrow Wilson Sch. Pub. and Internat. Affairs, 1974; MD, Harvard U., 1978. Resident Mass. Gen. Hosp. Stanford U., 1978-83, rsch. fellow in surgery, 1983—84; chief registrar CT Surgery Southampton Gen. Hosp., Eng., 1983; chief resident CT Surgery Mass. Gen. Hosp. Stanford U., 1984-85; chief resident CT Surgery, sr. fellow cardiac transplant svc. Stanford U. Med. Ctr., 1985-86; founder, surgeon Vanderbilt Transplant Med. Ctr., 1986—, asst. prof. surgery, 1986-93, dir. heart and lung transplantation, 1986-93; founder, surgical dir. Vanderbilt Multi-Organ Transplant Ctr., 1989-93; senator from Tenn. U.S. Senate, 1995—, majority leader, 2003—. Mem. U.S. Senate coms. budget, commerce, sci. & transp., fgn. rels., health, edn., labor & pensions, Nat. Bipartisan Comm. on Future of Medicaire, 1998-99; vice chair Alliance for Health Reform, 1995; Chmn. Tenn. Medicaid Task Force, 1992-93; bd. dirs. Sergeant York Historical Assn., YMCA Found. Met. Nasville; bd. regents Smithsonian Inst.; bd. trustees Princeton U. Author: Transplant: A Heart Surgeon's Account of the Life-and-death Dramas of the New Medicine, 1989, When Every Moment Counts: What You Need to Know About Bio-terrorism from the Senate's Only Doctor, 2002; author: (with J. Lee Annis) Tennessee Senators, 1911-2001: Portraits of Leadership in a Century of Change, 1999; author: (with Shirley Wilson) Good People Beget Good People: A Genealogy of the Frist Family, 2003; editor (with J. Harold Helderman): Grand Rounds in Transplantation, 1995. Chmn. Nat. Rep. Senatorial com., 2001-03. Named one of most influential people, TIME mag., 2005; recipient Taxpayer's Hero award, Coun. for Citizens Against Govt. Waste, 1997, Taxpayer's Friend award, Nat. Taxpayer's Union, 1998, Champion of Sci. award, Sci. Coalition, 1999, Hero of the Taxpayer, Americans for Tax Reform, 2000, Disting. Bd. Dir. award, Healthcare Fin. Mgmt. Assn., 2002, Nat. Leadership award, The Nat. Ctr. for Leadership, 2002, Excellence in Immunization award, Nat. Partnership for Immunization, 2002, Congl. Champion award, YMCA, 2003, IRI Freedom award, Internat. Rep. Inst., 2003, James Madison award, Am. Whig-Cliosophic Soc., 2003, Woodrow Wilson award, Princeton U., 2003, Lifetime Achievement award, Nat. Minority Health Month, 2003. Mem. Alpha Omega Alpha, Am. Coll. Chest Physicians, Am. Coll. Surgeons, Am. & Tenn. Med. Assns., Am. Soc. Transplant Surgeons, Assn. Acad. Surgery, Internat. Soc. Heart & Lung Transplantation, Middle Tenn. Heart Assn., Soc. Thoracic Surgeons, So. Thoracic Surgical Assn., Tenn. Transplant Soc., United Way De Tocqueville Soc. Republican. Presbyn. Office: US Senate 509 Hart Senate Office Bldg Washington DC 20251 Office Phone: 202-224-3344. Office Fax: 202-228-1268. E-mail: senator_frist@frist.senate.gov.*

FRISTACKY, NORBERT, computer engineering educator, researcher; b. Puchov, Czechoslovakia, Nov. 8, 1931; s. Eduard and Anna (Janasova) F.; m. Hilda Matejcikova, Feb. 21, 1937; 1 child, Tomas. Dipl.-Ing., Slovak Tech. U., Bratislava, Czechoslovakia, 1954, PhD, 1964. Asst. prof. Slovak Tech. U., 1955-62, 63-70, assoc. prof., 1971-85, full prof., 1985—, head dept. computer engring., 1978-90, mem. sci. coun., 1988-92. Rschr. Krizik Rsch. Inst., Prague, Czechoslovakia, 1962; vis. lectr. Salford (Eng.) U., 1970-71; vis. prof. Tech. U., Dresden, Germany, 1986; mem. supervisory com. R&D Inst., VUVT Engring., Zilina, Czechoslovakia, 1990-91. Author: Programmable Logic Controllers, 1981 (Czechoslovakia Tech. Nat. Soc. prize 1981), Logic Circuits, 1986, 90 (Slovak Lit. Fund prize 1986), Digital Computers (Slovak Lit Fund prize, 1994), 1993; editor Elec. Engring. Jour., 1991-2002; mem. editl. bd. Jour. Computing and Informatics, 1981—. Rector Slovak Tech. U., 1990-91. Mem.: IEEE (chmn. Slovak com., Computer Soc. IEEE award Computer Pioneer 1996), Slovak Acad. Soc., Internat. Fedn. Info. Processing (Slovak nat. com., tech. com., working group), Slovak Informatics Soc., Czechoslovak Elec. Engring. Soc. (chmn. spl. interest group in informatics sci. and engring. 1977—92), Slovak Soc. Cybernetics and Informatics (v.p. 1991), Slovak Acad. Scis. (sci. com. electronics and cybernetics 1988—96), Am. Czechoslovak Soc. (hon.). Home: JC Hronskeho 14 Bratislava Slovakia Office: Slovenska Tech U Ilkovicova 3 81219 Bratislava Slovakia E-mail: fristacky@fiit.stuba.sk.

FRISTOE, MACALYNE, speech pathology/audiology services professional, psychologist, educator, writer; b. Nashville, Mar. 14, 1931; d. George Miller and Brownie Appleton Watkins; m. James Houston Fristoe, June 4, 1953 (div. Nov. 1964); children: James Houston Jr., Andrew McLean; m. John Leiper Freeman, Jr., Jan. 20, 1966 (div. Oct. 1973). BA cum laude, Vanderbilt U., 1953, MS, 1960, PhD, 1972. Lic. speech pathologist, Ind. Health Prof. Bur. Speech clinician East Tenn. Hearing & Speech Ctr., Knoxville, Tenn., 1953—54; speech clinician, speech pathologist Bill Wilkerson Hearing & Speech Ctr., Nashville, 1955—60, asst. dir. speech clinic, 1964—67; instr. speech pathology Sch. Medicine Vanderbilt U., Nashville, 1960, 1964—67, instr. psychology, 1971—72, asst. prof., 1972—74; dir. lang. intervention study project Ctr. Devel. & Learning Disorders Med. Ctr., U. Ala., Birmingham, 1974—76; asst. prof. to assoc. prof. dept. biocomm. U. Ala., Birmingham, 1974—76; dir. speech clinic Purdue U., West Lafayette, Ind., 1976—79, assoc. prof. to prof. dept. audiology & speech scis., 1976—96, dir. grad. programs dept. audiology and speech scis., 1986—90, 1992—96, assoc. dept. head audiology and speech scis., 1993—96, assoc. prof. to prof. dept psychol. scis., 1982—96, prof. emerita, 1996—. Speech clinician Nashville-Davidson County Schs., Nashville, 1955—57; cons. Vanderbilt Hosp., 1957—60, L.B. Wallace Devel. Ctr., Decatur, Ala., 1974—78; rsch. NIH-NIAMDD kidney disease contract Vanderbilt Med. Ctr., 1971—74; mem. adv. bd. Ind. Resource Ctr. for Autism, Ind. U., Bloomington, 1986—94, Steer Speech and Hearing Clinics, Purdue U., 2000—02; reviewer NIH, Bethesda, Md., 1990—96; sci. reviewer Nat. Inst. Neurological and Commn. Disorders and Stroke, NIH, Nat. Inst. Child Health and Human Devel., Nat. Inst. Deafness and Commn. Disorders, Sensory Disorders and Lang. Study sect. NIH, NSF, March of Dimes, Purdue U.; spkr. in field. Assoc. editor Jour. Childhood Comm. Disorders, 1975-78, reviewer, 1978-82; mem. pub. bd. CEC Divsn. Children with Comm. Disorders, 1977-79; editl. cons. Jour. Speech and Hearing Disorders, 1977-79, 1982—, Mental Retardation, 1977-80, Augmentative and Alternative Comm.; cons. editor Am. Jour. Mental Deficiency, 1979-83; reviewer Jour. Applied Rsch. in Mental Retardation; contbr. numerous articles to profl. jours.; co-author, developer: Filmstrip Articulation Test, 1966, Goldman-Fristoe Test of Articulation, 1969, Goldman-Fristoe-Woodcock Test of Auditory Discrimination, 1970, Goldman-Fristoe-Woodcock Auditory Skills Test Battery, 1975, Goldman-Fristoe Test of Articulation 2, 2000; author: Language Intervention Systems for the Retarded, 1975; editor: (book) Four Language Intervention Systems, 1977. Recipient Women in Rsch. award Kennedy Inst. Johns Hopkins U., Balt., 1976; scholar Vanderbilt U., 1952-53; fellow Nat. Def. Edn. Act., 1969; traineeship U. Miami, 1956, Columbia U., 1966, Vanderbilt U., 1969-70, 1970-71. Fellow APA, Am. Speech Lang. Hearing Assn. (cert. clin. competence in speech pathology), Am. Assn. Mental Retardation (v.p. comm. disorders 1985-86, pres. comm. disorders divsn. 1986-87); mem. Nat. Coun. Comm. Disorders (rep.), Phi Beta Kappa, Sigma Xi.

FRISWOLD, FRED RAVNDAL, manufacturing executive; b. Mpls., Jan. 21, 1937; s. Ingolf Oliver and Derrice Ernestine (Anderson) F.; m. C. Marie Martin, Sept. 14, 1957; children— Cynthia, Steven, Barry, Michelle (dec.), Benjamin. BBA with distinction in Fin, U. Minn., 1958. Chartered fin. analyst. With J.M. Dain & Co. (now Dain, Rauscher, Inc.), Mpls., 1958—; exec. v.p. Dain, Bosworth, Inc., 1976-82, pres., CEO, 1982-90, cons., 1990-92; CEO Tonka Equipment Co., Plymouth, Minn., 1992—. Chmn. bd. U. Gateway Corp., UMF Investment Advisors; mem. bd. advisors Otologics L.L.C. Bd. dirs. Met. Mpls. YMCA; trustee U. Minn. Found.; treas. Mpls. Rotary Found. Mem. Twin City Soc. Security Analysts, Wildwood Lodge, Mpls. Rotary (pres. 1997-98). Methodist. Office: Tonka Equipment Co 13305 Water Tower Cir Plymouth MN 55441-3803 Home: 5925 Tamarac Ave Edina MN 55436

FRITCH, JOHN WILLIAM, library and information scientist, educator; b. Indpls., Feb. 27, 1963; s. John Martin and Frances Antoinette Fritch. BA, Purdue U., 1987; MLS, Ind. U., 1995. Asst. prof. libr. sci. Purdue U., West Lafayette, Ind., 1998—2004, assoc. prof. libr. sci., 2004—. Tech. plan cons. Johnson County Pub. Libr., Franklin, Ind., 1997. Contbr. Libraries to the People: Histories of Library Outreach, 2003; author: web-based ednl. material; contbr. articles to profl jours., chpts. to books. Mem.: ALA, Beta Phi Mu (sec. chpt. 2000—04). Home: 3850 N State Rd 341 Attica IN 47918 Office: Purdue Univ Librs UGRL 504 W State St Lafayette IN 47907-2058 Office Phone: 765-494-6735. Business E-Mail: jfritch@purdue.edu.

FRITSCH, EDWARD, real estate company executive; BS in Bus. Adminstrn., U. N.C. Cert. property mgr. Inst. Real Estate Mgmt. Ptnr. SNL Fin. LLC; pres. Highwoods Properties, Inc., Raleigh, NC, COO. Bd. dir. Highwoods Properties, Inc. Office: Highwoods Properties Inc 3100 Smoketree Ct Ste 600 Raleigh NC 27604

FRITSCHE, CLAUDIA, diplomat, ambassador; Personal sec. Liechtenstein Head Gov., 1970-74, Dep. Head Gov., Liechtenstein, 1974-78; diplomatic collaborator Office of Fgn. Affairs, Liechtenstein, 1978-90; dep. Permanent Rep. to Coun. of Europe, Strasbourg, France, 1983-90; first sec. Liechtenstein Embassy, Berne, Switzerland, 1987-89, first sec., chargée d'affaires Vienna,

1989; permanent rep. of Liechtenstein UN, N.Y.C., 1990—2002; Liechtenstein amb. to U.S. Washington, 2002—. Head Liechtenstein Nat. Com. on Equality between Women and Men, 1987-90; sec. Liechtenstein parliamentary del. to the Coun. of Europe, parliamentary del. to the European Free Trade Assn. Office: Embassy of Liechtenstein 888 17th St NW Ste 1250 Washington DC 20006

FRITTON, KARL ANDREW, lawyer; b. Olean, NY, Mar. 29, 1955; s. William John and Margaret (O'Brian) Fritton.; m. Christine Evelyn Councill, June 9, 1984; children: Katherine Evelyn, Jessica Claire, Rebecca Lee. BS in economics, SUNY, Albany, 1977; JD, Rutgers U., 1980. Bar: Pa., 1981, NY, 1981, US Supreme Ct., 1985, State & Fed. courts of Pa. & NY. Assoc. Bond, Schoeneck & King, Syracuse, NY, 1980-81, Obermayer, Rebmann, Maxwell & Hippel, Phila., 1981-84, Sprecher, Felix, Visco, Hutchinson & Young, Phila., 1984-86, ptnr., 1987-91, Montgomery, McCracken, Walker & Rhoads, Phila., 1991-96, Reed Smith LLP (formerly Reed, Smith, Shaw & McLay LLP), Phila., 1996—, also practice group leader intellectual property group. Labor counsel Office of Atty. Gen., Pa. Contbr. articles to profl. jours. Active Phila. Vol. Lawyers for Arts, 1981—, bd. dirs. Mem ABA (labor law sect.). Democrat. Roman Catholic. Office: Reed Smith LLP 2500 One Liberty Pl 1650 Market St Philadelphia PA 19103 Office Phone: 215-241-7956. Office Fax: 215-895-1420. Business E-Mail: kfritton@reedsmith.com.*

FRITTS, EDWARD O., broadcast executive; b. Cape Girardeau, Mo., Feb. 21, 1941; m. Martha Dale; children: Kimberley, Timothy, Jennifer. Grad., U. Miss. Pres. Nat. Assn. Broadcasters, Washington, 1982—. Past chmn. joint bd. Nat. Assn. Broadcasters; vice chair U.S. State Dept. Internat. Media Fund. Cons. U.S. C. of C. Assns. Com.; chair media adv. com. U.S. Bicentennial Commn.; vice chmn. White House Pvt. Sector Initiatives Bd., 1985—88; mem. individual investors adv. com. N.Y. Stock Exch.; active Nat. Mus. Women in the Arts; dir. advt. coun., former trustee Mus. TV and Radio; active Wolf Trap Found., Arlington Hosp. Found.; bd. dirs. Nat. Commn. Against Drunk Driving, Partnership for a Drug-Free Am., Ctrs. for Disease Control's Bus. Responds to AIDS program. Recipient Silver Mike award, U. Miss. Mem.: Sigma Alpha Epsilon (Highest Effort award). Avocation: golf. Office: Nat Assn Broadcasters 1771 N St NW Ste 200 Washington DC 20036-2812

FRITTS, HAROLD CLARK, forester, educator; b. Rochester, N.Y., Dec. 17, 1928; s. Edwin Coulthard and Ava Lee (Washburn) F.; m. Barbara Smith, June 11, 1955 (dec.); children: Marcia L., Paul T.; m. Miriam Colson, July 19, 1982. AB, Oberlin Coll., 1951; MS, Ohio State U., 1953, PhD in Botany, 1956. Asst. prof. botany Eastern Ill. U., Charleston, 1956-60; asst. prof. dendrochronology U. Ariz., Tucson, 1960-64, assoc., 1964-69, prof., 1969-92, emeritus, 1992—; adj. prof. in rsch. Desert Rsch. Inst., U. Nev. Vis. scientist CSIRO forest products divsn., Melbourne, Australia, 1996; owner Dendro-Power, Tucson, 1992—; dir., founder Internat. Tree-Ring Data Bank, 1975-90; NSF faculty, mem. Task Group 3 adv. com. on paleoclimatology, Climate Dynamics Program, 1978-79; lectr. NATO Advanced Study Inst. on Climatic Variability, Sicily, 1980; vis. dir. U. Wyo. Summer Sci. Camp, summer 1956; mem. U. Ariz. del. to People's Republic of China, 1976; participant Nat. Def. U., 1978-79; mem. organizing group internat. conf. on dendroclimatology, Eng., 1980. Author: Tree Rings and Climate, 1976, reprinted 2001, Reconstructing Large-Scale Climate Patterns from Tree-Ring Data, 1991; mem. editorial adv. bd. Quaternary Rsch., 1977-82; contbr. articles to profl. jours. Mem. local sch. bd., 1971-72. Recipient Dendrochronologial award of Appreciation Sci. Cmty., Lund, Sweden, 1990, award for appreciation and recognition of outstanding contbns. to dendroclimatology Tree Rings and Climate-Sharpening the Focus, Tucson, 2004; Grad. fellow Ohio State U., 1954-56, NSF fellow Oreg. Inst. Marine Biology, summer 1957, Guggenheim fellow, 1968-69; grantee NSF 1971-87, U. Calif. Lawrence Livermore Lab., 1978-79, State of Calif., 1979-80, 85-86. Fellow: AAAS; mem.: Am. Meteorol. Soc. (Outstanding Achievement in Bioclimatology award 1982), Am. Inst. Biol. Scis., Ecol. Soc. Am. (editl. bd. 1964—66, chmn. paleoecology sect. 1984, coun. rep.), Am. Assn. Quaternary Environment (coun. 1978—82, adv. com. paleoclimatology), Tree-Ring Soc. (exec. com. 2000—01, mem.-at-large exec. bd.). Avocation: photography. Home: 5703 N Lady Ln Tucson AZ 85704-3905 Office Phone: 520-887-7291. Business E-Mail: hfritts@ltrr.arizona.edu.

FRITTS, HARRY WASHINGTON, JR., internist, educator; b. Rockwood, Tenn., Oct. 4, 1921; s. Harry Washington and Hyder (Smith) F.; m. Helen Dyer Goodwin, Aug. 25, 1949; children: John Goodwin, Benjamin Carroll, Patricia Louise. Student, Vanderbilt U., 1941; BS, Mass. Inst. Tech., 1943; MD, Boston U., 1951. Diplomate: Am. Bd. Internal Medicine (mem.). Mem. research staff MIT, 1946-47; intern, then resident Univ. Hosp., Boston, 1951-53; vis. fellow Columbia Coll. Physicians and Surgeons, 1953-56, mem. faculty, 1956-73, prof. medicine, 1967-73, Dickinson W. Richards prof. medicine, 1972-73; prof., chmn. dept. medicine Sch. Medicine, State U. N.Y. at Stony Brook, 1973-87, Edmund D. Pellegrino prof. medicine, 1986-87. William Harris vis. prof. Nat. Med. Sch. Taiwan, 1987-88; vis. physician Bellevue Hosp., 1957-68, Presbyn. Hosp., N.Y.C., 1961-73; vis. physician, cons. Manhattan VA Hosp., 1957-68; vis. prof. U. London, 1982; bd. dirs., adv. council research N.Y. Heart Assn.; mem. sci. council Parker Francis Found.; mem. physiology study sect., mem. cardiovascular tng. com. USPHS; mem. council Nat. Heart, Lung and Blood Inst. Author: On Leading a Clinical Department, 1997; assoc. editor: Jour. Clin. Investigation; mem. editl. bd.: Am. Rev. Respiratory Diseases; contbr. articles to profl. jours. Served to lt. (j.g.) USNR, 1943-46. Guggenheim fellow, 1959-60 Fellow ACP; mem. Am. Physiol. Soc., Am. Soc. Clin. Investigation, Assn. Am. Physicians, Am. Clin. and Climatol. Soc., Alpha Omega Alpha. Home: 79 Bevin Rd Northport NY 11768-1133 Office: SUNY at Stony Brook Dept Medicine Stony Brook NY 11794-0001 E-mail: hwfritts@aol.com.

FRITZ, EDWARD LANE, dentist; b. Evansville, Ind., Dec. 15, 1932; s. Edward E. and Virginia B. (Lane) F.; m. Bettye J. Samples, July 31, 1954; children: Mary Ann, Sarah Jane. AB, Ind. U., 1954, DDS, 1957; BS, U. Evansville, 1975, MBA, 1978. Pvt. practice dentistry, Evansville, 1959-99; ret.; pres., chmn. bd. Health Resources, Inc., 1986-99, chmn. bd., 1986—. Corp. bd. dirs. Va. Corp., Evansville, 1962-72, Dynatron, Inc., 1980-87; bd. dir. S.W. Ind. Oral Health Found. Editor: The Bulletin of the Am. Assn. of Dental Examiners, 1981-85. Capt. U.S. Army, 1957-59. Named Disting. Alumnus Ind. U. Sch. Dentistry, 1991. Fellow Am. Coll. Dentists (ethics achievement award 2004), Acad. Gen. Dentistry, Acad. Dentistry Internat., Internat. Coll. Dentists; mem. ADA (continuing edn. com. 1981-83, cons./evaluator 1980), Ind. Dental Assn. (trustee 1983-91, Disting. Svc. award 1996), Vanderburgh County Dental Soc. (pres. 1967, various offices), First Dist. Dental Soc. (pres. 1976-77, various offices), Am. Assn. Dental Examiners (pres. 1989, various offices), Ind. Bd. Dental Examiners (pres. 1982-83, sec. 1980-82), Acad. Operative Dentistry, Internat./Am. Assn. Dental Rsch., Am. Assn. Dental Editors, Acad. Gen. Dentistry, Pierre Fauchard Acad., Sagamores of the Wabash, Ky. Col., Phi Kappa Phi. Home: 12200 Edgewater Dr Evansville IN 47720-8169 E-mail: ebfritz@evansville.net.

FRITZ, HENRY EUGENE, historian, educator; b. Garrison, Kans., June 20, 1927; s. Frank Alfred and Esther (Anderson) Fritz; m. Dolores Ileen Moeller, Sept. 3, 1950; children: Esther Anne, Malin Eugenia, Marie Louise. BS, Bradley U., 1950, MA, 1952; PhD of History, U. Minn., 1957. Instr. history U. Wis. Milw., 1956—58; asst. prof. St. Olaf Coll., Northfield, Minn., 1958—62, assoc. prof., 1962—68, prof. Am. History, 1968, chmn. history dept., 1969—84. Founder, dir. Am. Minorities Studies St. Olaf Coll., Northfield, 1970—72; faculty fellow Newberry Libr., Chgo., 1968—69; expert witness on Indian rights to mineral and timber lands U.S. Dept. Justice. Author: The Movement for Indian Assimilation, 1860-1890, 1963; contbr. articles to profl. jours. With AUS, 1945—46, ETO. Louis and Maude Hill fellow, Hill Found. St. Paul, 1965. Mem.: We. History Assn. (hon.; chmn. local arrangements 24th ann. meeting 1984, chmn. local arrangements 37th ann. meeting 1997, awards of merit com. 1981—84, Award of Merit 1997), Orgn. Am. Historians (life), Kiwanis. Republican. Lutheran. Avocations: farming, horses, beef cattle, horticulture. Home: 805 W 4th St Red Wing MN 55066-2417 Personal E-mail: fritzh@redwing.net.

FRITZ, HERMANN MARC, civil engineer, educator; b. Zurich, Switzerland, May 20, 1972; PhD, Swiss Fed. Inst. Tech., 2002. Asst. prof. Ga. Tech, Savannah, 2003—. Achievements include research in Tsunami Scientist. Home: 528 Price St Savannah GA 31401 Office: Georgia Tech 210 Technology Cir Savannah GA 31407 Office Phone: 912-966-7947. Personal E-mail: hermitz72@hotmail.com. E-mail: hermann.fritz@gtsav.gatech.edu.

FRITZ, JAMES SHERWOOD, chemist, educator; b. Decatur, Ill., July 20, 1924; s. William Lawrence and Leora Mae (Troster) F.; m. Helen Joan Houck, Apr. 26, 1949 (dec. Oct. 1987); children— Barbara Lisa, Julie Ann, Laurel Joan, Margaret Ellen; m. Miriam Simons Reeves, July 15, 1989. BS, James Millikin U., 1945; MS, U. Ill., 1946, PhD, 1948. Asst. prof. chemistry Wayne State U., Detroit, 1948-51; asst. prof. Iowa State U., Ames, 1951-55, assoc. prof., 1955-60, prof., 1960-90, disting. prof., 1990—. Author: Acid Base Titrations in Nonaqueous Solvents, 1973, An Analytical Solid-Phase Extraction, 1999; co-author: Quantitative Analytical Chemistry, Ion Chromatography, 1982, 3d edit., 2000, Solid Phase Extraction, 1999; contbr. articles to profl. jours. Recipient Minn. Chromatography Forum award, 1987, Dal Nogare award in chromatography, 1991. Mem. Am. Chem. Soc. (award in chromatography 1976, award in analytical chemistry 1985) Methodist. Avocations: tennis, collecting wall hangings. Office: Iowa State U 322 Wilhelm Ames IA 50011-0001 Office Phone: 515-294-5987. E-mail: kniss@ameslab.gov.

FRITZ, JEAN GUTTERY, writer; b. Hankow, People's Republic China, Nov. 16, 1915; d. Arthur Minton and Myrtle (Chaney) Guttery; m. Michael Fritz, Nov. 1, 1941; children: David, Andrea. BA, Wheaton Coll., Norton, Mass., 1937, LittD (hon.), 1987, Washington and Jefferson Coll., 1982. Rsch. asst. Dobbs Ferry (N.Y.) Libr., 1937—41, children's libr., 1955—57; founder, instr. Jean Fritz Writers' Workshops, Katonah, NY, 1962—70; tchr. Bd. Co-operative Ednl. Svc., Westchester County, NY, 1971—73; faculty mem. Appalachian State U., Boone, NC, 1980—82. Author: Fish Head, 1954, The Late Spring, 1957, The Animals of Doctor Schweitzer, 1958, The Cabin Faced West, 1958, How to Read a Rabbit, 1958, Brady, 1960, I, Adam, 1963, Magic to Burn, 1964, Early Thunder, 1967, George Washington's Breakfast, 1969, Cast for a Revolution, 1972, And Then What Happened, Paul Revere?, 1973, Why Don't You Get a Horse, Sam Adams?, 1974, Where Was Patrick Henry on the 29th of May?, 1975, Who's that Stepping on Plymouth Rock?, 1975, Will You Sign Here, John Hancock?, 1976, The Secret Diary of Jeb and Abigail, 1976, What's the Big Idea, Ben Franklin?, 1976, Can't You Make Them Behave, King George?, 1977, Brendon the Navigator, 1979, Stonewall, 1979, Where Do You Think You're Going, Christopher Columbus?, 1980, The Man Who Loved Books, 1981, Traitor: The Case of Benedict Arnold, 1981, The Good Giants and the Bad Pukwudgies, 1981, Homesick: My Own Story, 1982 (Am. Book award 1983, Child Study Book award 1983, Honor Book, Newberry Medal Book 1983), China Homecoming, 1985, The Double Life of Pocahontas, 1983 (Boston Globe/Horn Book award 1984), Make Way for Sam Houston, 1986 (Western Writers award 1987), Shh! We're Writing the Constitution, 1987, China's Long March, 1988, The Great Little Madison, 1989, Bully for You, Teddy Roosevelt!, 1991, Around the World in 100 Years, 1994, Harriet Beecher Stowe and the Beecher Preachers, 1994, You Want Women to Vote, Lizzie Stanton?, 1995, Why Not, Lafayette?, 1999, Leonardo's Horse, 2001, The Lost Colony of Roanoke, 2002. Recipient Christopher award Cath. Library Assn., 1982, Regina Medal Cath. Library Assn., 1985, Laura Ingalls Wilder award ALA, 1986, Nat. Humanities medal, 2003. Home: 50 Bellewood Ave Dobbs Ferry NY 10522-2302

FRITZ, KRISTINE RAE, retired secondary school educator; b. Monroe, Wis. BS in Phys. Edn., U. Wis., LaCrosse, 1970; MS in Phys. Edn., U. N.C., Greensboro, 1978. Softball and fencing program coord. Mequon (Wis.) Recreation Dept., 1970; phys. edn., health and English tchr. Horace Jr. H.S., 1970—81; phys. edn. and health tchr. Sheboygan (Wis.) South H.S., 1982—2004; emeritus tchr. Sheboygan Early Learning Ctr., 2004—05; basketball and volleyball coach, 1972—89; girls track coach, 1972—2004; active early childhood phys. activity pilot program SASD. Mem. dist. wide curriculum and evaluation coms., 1978—2004; mem. sch. effectiveness team, 1991—94; sch. evaluation consortium evaluator, 1988—93; inbound/outbound coach Sport for Understanding, 1991—96. Contbr. articles to profl. jours. Active Sheboygan (Wis.) Spkrs. Bur., 1987—95, Women Reaching Women. Recipient Nat. H.S. Coaches award for girls track, 1987, Womans Sports Advocates of Wis. Lifetime award, 2003. Mem.: AAHPERD (chair 2004, Midwest dist. Tchr. of Yr. 1995, Pathfinder award 1997, chair 2003—04), NEA, Sheboygan Edn. Assn., Wis. Assn. Health, Phys. Edn., Recreation and Dance (life; pres.-elect 1998—99, pres. 1999—2000, Phys. Edn. Tchr. Yr. 1993). Home: 1841 N 26th St Sheboygan WI 53081-2008

FRITZ, NANCY H., educational researcher, administrator; b. Greenfield, Mass., Nov. 21, 1944; d. Gerard Martin and Helen (Cassidy) F. BA in English, Western New Eng. Coll., 1970; EdM in Psychology and Edn., Smith Coll., Northampton, Mass., 1982. Cert. tchr., Mass., N.Y., Vt. Title I reading recovery tchr., dir., Amherst, Mass.; ret. Lectr. in field. Contbr. articles to profl. jours. Recipient Eckel Human Rels. Cup, WRA Highest Achievement award. Mem. NEA, AAUW, Internat. Reading Assn., Nat. Coun. Tchrs. English, Nat. Coun. Tchrs. Math., Mass. Reading Assn. Home: The Deerfield Commons South Deerfield MA 01373-9620

FRITZ, RENE EUGENE, JR., manufacturing executive; b. Prineville, Oreg., Feb. 24, 1943; s. Rene and Ruth Pauline (Munson) F.; m. Sharyn Ann Fife, June 27, 1964; children: Rene Scott, Lanz Eugene, Shay Steven, Case McGarrett. BS in Bus. Adminstrn., Oreg. State U., 1965. Sales mgr. Renal Corp., Albany, Oreg., 1965-66, Albany Machine and Supply, 1965-66; pres. Albany Internat. Industries Inc., 1966-85, Wood Yield Tech. Corp., 1972-85, Albany Internat. DISC, 1972-85, Automation Controls Internat. Inc., 1975-85; co-founder, chmn. Albany Titanium Inc., 1981-89; prin. Torwest Capital, 1989; founder, pres. WY Tech. Corp., 1984-89, R. Fritz & Assocs., 1987-89. Pres. Chief Execs. Forum, 1989—, Fritz Grup, Inc., 1989—; fin. planner, investment banker M&A, Vancouver, Wash., 1991—; chmn. Stormwater Treatment LLC, CSF Treatment Sys., NTP, Wilsonville, Oreg., 1999—, Dentamax, Inc., Vancouver, 1999—, Human Capital Oreg./Wash., Vancouver, 1999—, MindNautilus, Inc., Portland, 2000—; bd. dirs. Max-Viz, Inc., 2002—04. Patentee computer controlled machinery. Pres. Oreg. World Trade Coun., 1982—; trustee U.S. Naval Acad. Found., Annapolis, Md., 1988—2004. Mem. Oreg. State Alumni, Forest Products Rsch. Soc., Young Pres. Orgn., Rotary, Elks. Presbyterian.

FRITZ, ROGER JAY, management consultant; b. Browntown, Wis., July 18, 1928; s. Delmar M. and Ruth M. (Sandley) F.; m. Kathryn Louise Goddard, Oct. 13, 1951; children: Nancy Goddard, Susan Marie. BA in Polit. Sci, Monmouth (Ill.) Coll., 1950; MS in Speech, U. Wis., 1952, PhD in Ednl. Counseling, 1956. Asst. dean men, asst. prof. Purdue U., 1953-56; mgr. pub. relations Cummins Engine Co.; also sec. Cummins Engine Found., 1956-59; sec. John Deere Found.; also mem. pub. relations staff Deere & Co., 1959-65, dir. mgmt. devel. and personnel research; also dir. John Deere Found., 1965-69; pres. Willamette U., 1969-72, Orgn. Devel. Cons., Naperville, Ill., 1972—. Bd. dirs. Intelligent Electronics, Inc., List Processing Co., Todays Computers Bus. Ctrs., Entre Computer Ctrs., Inc., Natural Golf, Inc., Quote Me, Optionize, Envisionworks, Inc. Author: A Handbook for Resident Counselors, 1952, The Argumentation of William Jennings Bryan and Clarence Darrow in the Tennesee Evolution Trial, 1952, How Freshmen Change, 1956, The Power of Professional Purpose, 1974, MBO Goes to College, 1975, Practical Management by Objectives, 1976, What Managers Need to Know-A Practical Guide for Management Development, 1978, Performance Based Management, 1980, Productivity and Results, 1981, People Compatibility System, 1983, Rate Yourself as a Manager, 1985, You're in Charge, 1986, Personal Performance Contracts: The Key to Job Success, 1986, Nobody Gets Rich Working for Somebody Else, 1987, Rate Your Executive Potential, 1987, The Inside Advantage, 1987, If They Can-You Can, 1988, Be Your Own Boss, 1988, Managing a Successful Team, 1989, Management Ideas That Work, 1989, Developing A Positive Attitude, 1990, The Entrepreneurial Family, 1991, Think Like a Manager, 1991, How to Export, 1992, How to Get Rich Working for Yourself, 1992, Sleep Disorders-America's Hidden Nightmare, 1993, The Sales Manager's High Performance Guide, 1993, How to Manage Your Boss, 1994, A Team of Eagles, 1994, The Small Business Troubleshooter, 1995, The Field Guide for Boss Types...And How to Deal With Them, 1996, An Idea-A-Day For Promotable People, 1996, Crime Crisis: Bold New Ideas to Fit Punishment with Crimes, 1997, Wars of Succession, 1997, One Step Ahead: The Unused Keys to Success, 1998, Bounce Back and Win, 1999, Fast Track-How to Gain Momentum and Keep It, 1999, Attitude Makes The Difference, 2000, Beyond Commitment: The Skills All Leaders Need, 2000, Family Ties and Business Binds, 2000, Magnet People: Their Secrets and How To Learn From Them, 2001, Little Things-Big Results, 2002, How To Make Your Boss Your Ally and Advocate, 2002, Building Your Legacy--One Decision at a Time, 2002, 100 Ways to Bring Out Your Best, 2003, After You-Can Humble People Prevail?, 2004, Sharpen Your Competitive Edge, 2004, Nothing Ventured, Nothing Gained, 2005, Who Cares--Are You a Giver, Taker or Watcher, 2005; also articles, papers; columnist Entrepreneur mag., New Bus. Opportunity mag., 1989, Benefits and Compensation Solutions Mag., Bus. Start Ups Mag., Bus. Ledger, 2004; mgmt. editor Communication Briefings Newsletter, 1989. Mem. com. preparation coll. tchrs. Ill. Bd. Higher Edn., 1965-67, mem. com. med. edn., 1967-68; edn. com. N.A.M., 1967-69; mem. Iowa-Ill. Indsl. Devel. Group, 1964-69; coun. contbr. Nat. Indsl. Conf. Bd., 1960-65, council devel., edn. and tng., 1966-69; adv. com. solicitations Nat. Better Bus. Bur., 1964-69; v.p. Oreg. Ind. Colls. Assn., 1969-72; mem. Pres. Johnson's Citizens Adv. Bd. on Youth Opportunity, 1968-69, Gov.'s Personnel Grievance Panel, Ill., 1974-77; trustee Monmouth Coll., 1957-79, chmn., 1961-69; trustee Oreg. Colls. Found., 1969-72, Ind. Coll. Funds Am., N.Y.C., 1972, Internat. Coll. Commerce and Econs., Tokyo, 1970-72, U. Chgo. Cancer Research Found., 1973-78. Recipient Achievement award, Monmouth Coll., 2002. Mem. Phi Eta Sigma, Omicron Delta Kappa, Tau Kappa Epsilon, Phi Alpha Theta, Sigma Tau Delta, Pi Kappa Delta. Clubs: Naperville (Ill.) Country. Republican. Methodist. Home: 1113 N Loomis St Naperville IL 60563-2745 Office: 1240 Iroquois Dr Naperville IL 60563-8536 Fax: 630-420-7835. Office Phone: 630-420-7673. Personal E-mail: rfritz3800@aol.com.

FRITZ, ROSANN, customer service administrator; b. Chgo., Mar. 9, 1958; d. Edward Walter and Rose Margaret (Cavlovic) Fritz. BA, DePaul U., 1984, postgrad., 1984—85. Cert. secondary tchr. Ill. Asst. editor Am. Dietetic Assn., Chgo., 1986; copy editor Desta Comm., Chgo., 1987—88; prodn. mgr. Maclean Hunter Pub., Chgo., 1988—91, Talcott Pub., Chgo., 1993; splty. mgr. PetSmart, Chgo., 1996—2003; sr. customer cons. FedEx Kinko's, Lansing, Ill., 2004—. Vol. South Suburban Cage Bird Club, Lansing, 1999—2004; vol. docent Ernest Hemingway Fedn., Oak Park, Ill., 2003—04, Chgo. Hist. Soc., 2004. Democrat. Unitarian. Avocations: bird clubs, reading, music. Office: FedEx Kinkos 16701 Torrence Lansing IL 60438 Office Phone: 708-889-1388.

FRITZ, STEVEN L., physicist; b. Kans. City, Mo., Aug. 10, 1944; s. John Henry and Barbara Jean Fritz; m. Carmen Ann Fiorella, June 15, 1968; children: John Eric, Stephanie Kristen Savolaine, Melissa Ann Manthorne. BS in physics, U. of Md., 1967; PhD, U. of Kans., 1979. Asst. prof. So. Ill. U., Springfield, Ill., 1976—77, U. of Kans., 1977—86; assoc. prof. U. of Md., 1986—2000, dir., tech. devel., 1995—97, assoc. v.p., 1997—2000; dir. tech. transfer Md. TEDCO, 2000—. SBIR rev. NIH, Washington DC, 1983—2002; bd. mem. DeJarnette Rsch. Systems, Towson, Md., 1999—. Coord. marriage prep. St. John the Evangelist, Columbia, Md., 2001—; pres. Johnson County Bd. of Cath. Schools, Kans., 1986—88. Comdr. USNR, 1967—94, USA. Recipient DAAD Rsch. visit, German Acad. Exch. Svc., 1997. Mem.: Assn. of U. Tech. Managers. Avocation: aviation. Office: Maryland TEDCO 5575 Sterrett Pl Ste 240 Columbia MD 21044 Business E-Mail: sfrtiz@marylandtedco.org.

FRITZ, THOMAS VINCENT, lawyer; b. Pitts., July 6, 1934; s. Zeno and Mary M. (Briley) F.; m. Barbara L. Jacob, Jan. 31, 1959; children: William T., James Z., Juliann W. BBA in Acctg. cum laude, U. Pitts., 1960; JD, Duquesne U., 1964; LLM, NYU, 1966; Advanced Mgmt. Program, Harvard Bus. Sch., 1975. Bar: Pa. 1964, U.S. Supreme Ct. 1969; CPA, Pa. 1962. Ptnr. Ernst & Young (formerly Arthur Young & Co.), Pitts., N.Y.C., Washington, 1970, regional mng. ptnr., vice chmn., 1977-89, vice chmn., 1989-92; pres., CEO, bd. dirs. Pvt. Sector Coun., Inc., Washington, 1992-2000; pres. Thomas V. Fritz & Assocs., Washington, 2000—. Adj. prof. Sch. Law Duquesne U., Pitts., 1966-79; adv. dirs. Pvt. Sector Coun., Washington, 1983-2004; bd. dirs. Innovative Sys., Inc.; chmn. Alliance for Free Enterprise, Washington, 1987-89. Editor Duquesne U. Law Rev., 1963-64. Active Century Club, Duquesne U.; bd. dirs. Evermay Comty. Assn., pres., 1994-96; bd. dirs. McLean Citizens Assn., 1994-97; co-chmn. U. Pitts. Katz Campaign 3d Century, 1988-91. With U.S. Army, 1955—57, with USAR, 1957—63. Recipient Gorley award, 1964, Disting. Alumni award U. Pitts., 1981, Advancement Info. Tech. award, 1988, Federal 100 Info. Tech. award, 1997. Mem. AICPA, ACBA, Pa. Inst. CPAs, Duquesne Club, Met. Club, Rolling Rock Club, Avenel Club, Beta Gamma Sigma, Beta Alpha Psi. Office: 6303 Long Meadow Rd Mc Lean VA 22101-2314

FRITZE, ROGER LAURENCE, security consultant; b. N.Y.C., Apr. 17, 1946; s. Paul Victor and Agnes Cathrine (Joly) F.; m. Joyce Elaine Graves, July 31, 1971; children: Kimberly, Kandice. BS in Adminstrv. Justice, Am. U., 1970; MBA, Miami (Fla.) U., 1983. Detective Met. Police Dept., Washington, 1968-73; spl. agt. Fla. Dept. of Law Dept., Miami, 1973-75; security mgmt. Fla. Power & Light Co., Miami, 1975-96; dir. investigations Exec. Office of Gov. Fla., Miami, 1998-99; dir. security Miami Jewish Home Hosp., 1999—. Pvt. cons., Miami, 1983; mem. Miami-Dade Pvt. Security Adv. Bd., 1990. Pres. Citizens Crime Commn. Miami, 1983, Passageway, Inc., Miami, 1989—; chmn. Law Edn. Goal and Learning, Miami, 1985, Crimestoppers of Dade County, Miami, 1989-93; v.p. devel. Youth Crime Watch Am., 1999; bd. dirs. Citizens Crime Watch Miami-Dade County. Sgt. U.S. Army, 1964-68. Recipient Chmn.'s award Citizens Crime Commn., 1982. Mem. Am. Soc. for Indsl. Security (svc. chmn. 1980-81, 93-94), Internat. Assn. Narcotic Investigators, Internat. Assn. Credit Card Investigators, Hurricanes. Roman Catholic. Avocations: running, fishing, reading, golf. Home: 8900 SW 192nd Dr Miami FL 33157-8828 Office: Miami Jewish Home Hosp 5200 NE 2d Ave Miami FL 33137 E-mail: RLF999@attglobal.net, RFritze@mjhha.org.

FRITZE, STEVEN L., service industry executive; B, MBA, U. Minn. Exec. v.p., CFO Ecolab, St. Paul. Office: Ecolab 370 Wabasha St N Saint Paul MN 55102 Business E-Mail: steve.fritze@ecolab.com.

FRITZKY, EDWARD V., biotechnology company executive; BA, Dusquesne U.; graduate Advanced Exec. Program, N.W. U., 1988. V.p. mktg. U.S. Searle Can., Inc.; pres. & gen. mgr. Searle Can., Inc. & Lorax Pharmaceuticals; v.p. Lederle Lab., pres.; CEO Immunex Corp., Seattle, 1994—. Bd. dir. Fred Hutchinson Cancer Rsch. Ctr., SonoSite, Inc., Geron Corp.; adv. bd. U. Wash. Bus. Sch.; bd. dir. Pacific Sci. Ctr.; chmn. Tech. Alliance. Adv. bd. U. Wash. Bus. Sch.; bd. dirs. Pacific Sci. Ctr.; chmn. The Tech. Alliance. Named Disting. Alumnus, Duquesne U.

FRITZSCHE, DAVID J., business educator; b. Woodstock, Ill., May 6, 1940; s. Melvin L. and Ireta Rae (Goble) Fritzsche; m. Nancy J. Olson, Sept. 5, 1965; children: Sonja R., Tanya J. BS, U. Ill., 1965, MS, 1968; DBA, Ind. U., 1972. Asst. and assoc. prof. mktg. Rochester Inst. Tech., NY, 1971—77; assoc. prof. mktg. Ill. State U., Bloomington, 1977—82; prof. mktg., chmn. managerial scis. dept. U. Nev., Reno, 1982—85; prof. bus. adminstrn. U. Portland, 1985—91; vis. prof. mgmt. and orgn. U. Washington, 1991—92; vis. prof. Fla. Internat. U., Miami, 1992—94. Contbr. articles to profl. jours.;, co-author two mgmt. simulations. Served to capt. U.S. Army, 1969—71. Mem.: Soc. for Bus. Ethics, Internat. Assn. Bus. and Soc., Assn.

for Bus. Simulation and Experiential Learning (pres. 1984—85), Am. Inst. for Decision Scis., Am. Mktg. Assn., Acad. Mgmt. (pres. Rochester chpt. 1976—77). Home: 133 Conestoga Rd Malvern PA 19355-1650

FRITZSCHE, HELLMUT, physics professor; b. Berlin, Feb. 20, 1927; came to U.S., 1952; s. Carl Hellmut and Anna (Jordan) F.; m. Sybille Charlotte Lauffer, July 5, 1952; children: Peter Andreas, Thomas Alexander, Susanne Charlotte, Katharina Sabine. Diploma in Physics, U. Göttingen, Fed. Republic Germany, 1952; PhD in Physics, Purdue U., 1954, DSc (hon.), 1988. Instr. physics Purdue U., Lafayette, Ind., 1954-55, asst. prof., 1955-56, U. Chgo., 1957-61, assoc. prof., 1961-63, prof., 1963-96, dir. Materials Rsch. Lab., 1973-77, chmn. dept., 1977-86, Louis Block prof. physics, 1989-96. V.p. Energy Conversion Devices, Inc., Rochester Hills, Mich.; bd. dirs. United Solar Systems Corp.; mem. adv. com. Ency. Britannica, 1969—96. Editor: 13 sci. books; assoc. editor Jour. Applied Physics, 1975-80; regional editor Jour. Non-Crystalline Solids, 1987-96; contbr. 280 articles to profl. jours.; patentee in field. Named hon. prof. Shanghai Inst. Ceramics, 1985, Nanjing U., 1987, Beijing U. Astronautics, 1988. Fellow AAAS, Am. Physical Soc. (Oliver Buckley Condensed Matter Physics prize 1989), N.Y. Acad. Scis. (chmn. divsn. condensed matter physics 1979-80). Avocations: the violin, sailing, skiing. Home: 3140 E Camino Juan Paisano Tucson AZ 85718-4206 Office: Energy Conversion Devices Inc 2956 Waterview Dr Rochester Hills MI 48309 Personal E-mail: hellmutf@aol.com.

FRITZSCHE, R(OBERT) WAYNE, research and development company executive; b. Woodbury, N.J., Jan. 8, 1949; s. Robert Edward and Mae Frances (Geiger) Fritzsche; m. Laurie Ann Owen, 2000 (dec.); children from previous marriage: Allison Anne, Benjamin Robert, Heather Leigh, Kelsey Marie. BA, Rowan U., 1971; MBA, U. San Diego, 1979. Sales rep. Warner Lambert, Morristown, N.J., 1972-74; group product mgr. Hoechst, San Diego, 1974-79; strategic planning Johnson & Johnson, Raritan, N.J., 1978-79; v.p. Cytogen, Princeton, N.J., 1979-80; sr. analyst Channing Weinberg, Inc., N.Y.C., 1980-81; founder, chmn. Fritzsche Pambianchi & Assocs., Inc., Somerville, NJ, 1981—91; founder Fritzsche & Assocs., Tampa, Fla., 1991—. Founder Immune Response Co., San Diego, 1987—, Cortex Pharm., Irvine, Calif., 1988—90, Med. Bus. Pub. Corp., Sommerville; bd. dirs. Hesed Biomed, Houston, Biokeys, San Diego, OccuLogix, Tampa, OPEXA Pharms.; pres. Organ Savers Inc., 2002—. Mem.: Am. Assn. Clin. Chemists, Am. Chem. Soc., N.Y. Acad. Sci. Republican. Avocations: piano, running. Office: 18925 Saint Laurent Dr Lutz FL 33558-2808 E-mail: wayneF2000@mindspring.com.

FRIZELL, DAVID J., lawyer; b. National Park, N.J., Sept. 13, 1948; s. Robert E. and Kathleen S. (Ford) F.; m. Aurelia M. Wright, Aug. 5, 1989; children: Brigid, St. John, Catherine. AB, Rutgers U., 1970, JD (with honors), 1973. Bar: N.J. 1973, U.S. Dist. Ct. N.J. 1973, U.S. Supreme Ct. 1986. Counsel Levin Affiliates, Plainfield, N.J., 1975-77; ptnr. Frizell & Pozycki, Metuchen, 1977-93, Frizell & Samuels, 1993—. Mem. N.J. Legislature Adv. Com. Land Use Law Revisions, 1979-86; lectr. Inst. for CLE, 1983—; pres. Frizell Real Estate Devel. Group, 1994—. Author: New Jersey Land Use Law, 2000; contbr. articles to profl. jours.; editor Land Use Law Newsletter, 1983-92; mem. editl. bd. Housing N.J. Mag., 1990-96. Bd. dirs. First Concern, Inc., 1998—. Mem. ABA, N.J. State Bar Assn. (dir., chmn. land use sect. 1983, dir. 1984-96, Outstanding Svc. award 1983), Metuchen C. of C. Democrat. Avocations: sailing, hiking. Office: PO Box 474 Metuchen NJ 08840-0474 E-mail: david.frizell@verizon.net.

FROBERG, BRENT MALCOLM, classics educator; b. Balt., Apr. 8, 1943; s. Lawrence Oscar and Ruth Louise (Lindner) F.; m. M. Gail Galloway, Feb. 27, 1970. BA, Ind. U., 1964, MA, 1965; PhD, Ohio State U., 1972. Instr. U. Tenn., Knoxville, 1968-69; asst. prof. U. S.D., Vermillion, 1970-74, assoc. prof., 1974-96. Vis. lectr. Baylor U., Waco, Tex., 2001—; cons. Medusa Nat. Mythology Exam, Nat. Greek Exam. Editor: (newsletter) Nuntius, 1978-96; writer Nat. Greek Exam., ATTIC, Level I, 1998-2000. Pres. Friends of the Libr., Vermillion, 1995-97, sec., 1997-99 Mem. Am. Philol. Assn. (award for excellence in tchg. 1994), Am. Classical League, Vergilian Soc. (membership chmn. 1990-94), Classical Assn. Mid. West & South (Ovatio award 1985, chair Manson Stewart scholarship com. 1998), Eta Sigma Phi (exec. sec. 1978-96, hon. life trustee). Avocations: crossword puzzles, travel. E-mail: Brent_Froberg@baylor.edu.

FROEBE, GERALD ALLEN, lawyer; b. The Dalles, Oreg., Feb. 16, 1935; s. Earl Wayne and Ethelene Alvina (Ogle) F.; m. Olivia Ann Tharaldson, Aug. 31, 1958; children: Dana Lynn, Heidi Ann. BBA, U. Oreg., 1956, LLB, 1961; LLM, NYU, 1962. Bar: N.Y. 1962, Oreg. 1962, U.S. Dist. Ct. Oreg. 1962. Auditor Arthur Andersen & Co., Seattle, 1956-58; lawyer, ptnr. Miller, Nash, Wiener, Hager & Carlsen, Portland, Oreg., 1962—99. Editor-in-chief Oreg. Law Rev., Eugene, 1960-61. Republican. Christian. Avocations: hiking, travel. Home: 1109 SW Ardmore Ave Portland OR 97205-1004 Office: 1109 SW Ardmore Ave Portland OR 97205

FROEBER, SARAH MARJORIE, actress, playwright, educator; b. Hollis, Okla., Dec. 15, 1946; d. Robert Jones and Marjorie Husband F.; m. John Peter Nussbaumer (div.); 1 child, Eric Robert Nussbaumer; m. Jeffrey Charles Lambdin, June 27, 1987 (div.) BA, Duke U., 1968; MA, Columbia U., 1969. Psychometrist Child Devel. Rsch. Project, N.Y.C., 1969-71; evaluator street acad. program N.Y. Urban League, N.Y.C., 1971-72; rsch. asst. Program Rsch. Media Assocs., N.Y.C., 1972-73, City Coll. N.Y., N.Y.C., 1973-74; instr. and dir. day care ctr. Vance-Granville C.C., Henderson, N.C., 1977-81; dir. day care ctr. Frank Porter Graham Child Devel. Ctr., Chapel Hill, N.C., 1981-84. Artistic dir., playwright Jelly Ednl. Theater, Carrboro, N.C., 1996-2000; playwright, dir. Scroggs Elem. Sch., Chapel Hill, N.C., 2000, McDougle Elem. Sch., Chapel Hill, 2000; instr. drama program Duke U., Durham, N.C., 1995—2001; psychology instr. Coll. of the Albemarle, Manteo, 2002-03. Actor regional stage cos., film, radio, and audiotape, 1985—2001; author (play for children) Samuel and the Wishards, 1996, Melvin the Pelican, 1997, The Prince Who Was Afraid of Peanut Butter, 1997, The Great Nut Hunt, 1998, Wheelchair Dancer, 1999, Spiders on Strike, 2000, Getting Help, 2000, Dolphins and Grolphins and the Keys to Success, 2000, Lovely, Lovely, Lily Pad, 2000, The Absolute Complete Definite Explanation of What Happened to the Lost Colony, 2001, Blackheards Blunder, 2002, Pelican and Pelican, 2003. Mem. SAG, Actors Equity Assn. Avocations: yoga, dance, cross country skiing, singing. Home: 3211 Gait Way Chapel Hill NC 27516-7607 E-mail: froeber@mindspring.com.

FROEHLE, BRYAN THOMAS, sociologist, director; b. Cin., Dec. 13, 1964; s. Andrew Lee and Kathleen Prendergast Froehle; m. Mary Christman, June 7, 1986; 1 child, Thomas Francis. BS in Fgn. Svc., Georgetown U., 1986; MA in Sociology, U. Mich., 1989, PhD in Sociology, 1993. Lectr. U. Mich., Ann Arbor, Mich., 1987—89; vis. prof. U. Cath. Andrés Bello, Caracas, Venezuela, 1990—91; rsch. assoc. Centro de Investigación, Caracas, 1990—91; asst. prof. U. SC, Spartanburg, 1992—95; sr. rsch. assoc. Ctr. Applied Rsch. in the Apostolate Georgetown U., Washington, 1995—98, exec. dir. Ctr. for Applied Rsch. in the Apostolate, 1998—2003; dir. Siena Ctr., Dominican U., River Forest, Ill., 2005—, assoc. prof. sociology, 2005—. Rsch. assoc. prof. Georgetown U., 1998—; bd. dirs. Loyola Press, Chgo., Nat. Ctr. for Study of Ch. Mgmt. Author: A Century and A Half, 1982, Catholicism USA, 2000, Global Catholicism, 2003; contbr. articles to profl. jours. Grantee, NSF, 1989, Calvin Inst., 2005. Mem.: Am. Assn. Pub. Opinion Rsch., Am. Sociol. Assn., Assn. Sociology of Religion (program chmn. 1998—99). Avocations: travel, reading. Office: 7200 W Division St River Forest IL 60305 Office Phone: 708-714-9111. E-mail: froehleb@dom.edu.

FROEHLICH, FRITZ EDGAR, communications educator, telecommunications scientist; b. Worms am Rhine, Hesse, Germany, Nov. 12, 1925; arrived in U.S., 1938; s. Julius and Ida (Heilborn) Froehlich; m. Eileen Karch, Dec. 25, 1949; children: Laurence Alan, Georgine K. Froehlich Scharff, Philip Marc. BS in Physics magna cum laude, Syracuse U., 1950, MS in Physics, 1952, PhD in Physics, 1955. Rsch. asst. Syracuse (N.Y.) U., 1950-54; asst. instr. Utica (N.Y.) Coll., 1952-54; with AT&T Bell Labs., 1954-87, tech. staff Whippany, NJ, 1954-56, supr. data transmission divsn. Murray Hill, NJ, 1956-63, head data theory dept. Holmdel, NJ, 1963—68, head telecom. and data sys. dept., 1968—83; head univ. rels. AT&T Info. Sys. and Comm., Lincroft, NJ, 1983—87; prof. telecom. U. Pitts., 1987—2002. Mem. adv. bd. Ctr. Info. and Comm. Scis. Ball State U., Muncie, Ind., 1987—93; nat. telecom. adv. coun. U. Pitts., 1992—95. Editor-in-chief: Ency. Telecom., 1988—2000, sr. editor: IEEE Trans. Comm., 1988—94; contbr. articles to profl. jours. Trustee Congl. B'nai Israel, Rumson, NJ, 1970—84, v.p. congregation, 1974—76; bd. dirs. Isles of Tamarac Homeowners Assn., 1992—2001, pres., 2001—02. With U.S. Army, 1944—46. Named Ann. Fritz Froehlich award in his honor, U. Pitts. Sch. Info. Sci., 1992—; recipient Hon. Alumnus award, Pitts. U., 1992. Fellow: IEEE (life; mem. data com., trans. sys. com. 1960—95, chmn. N.J. Coast sect. 1970, chmn. comms. terminal com. 1981—84, mem. multimedia, svcs. and terminals com. 1981—89, mem. awards bd. 1992—95), Comm. Soc. IEEE; mem.: Jewish War Vets. (vice comdr. Post 519 2005—), Phi Beta Kappa, Pi Mu Epsilon, Sigma Xi Sigma (pres. Syracuse U. chpt. 1949). Achievements include patents in field; development of first telephone data set and modem. Home: 10621 NW 71 Ct Tamarac FL 33321-2215 Office: 743 Slis Bldg 135 N Bellefield Ave Pittsburgh PA 15213-2609 E-mail: fefroehlich@att.net.

FROEHLICH, HAROLD VERNON, judge, retired congressman; b. Appleton, Wis., May 12, 1932; s. Vernon W. and Lillian F.; m. Sharon F. Ross, Nov. 20, 1970; children: Jeffrey Scott, Michael Ross. BBA, U. Wis., 1959, LLB, 1962. Bar: Wis. 1962. Staff acct. Ruschlien & Stortreon, CPAs, Madison, Wis., 1958-62; practiced in Appleton, 1962-81; judge Circuit Ct., 1981—; dep. chief judge 8th Jud. Dist. Wis., 1983-85, spl. dep. chief judge, 1985-88, chief judge, 1988-94; sec. Wis. Judicial Conf., 1991-97; mem. Wis. Ho. of Reps., 1963-73, speaker, 1967-71, minority floor leader, 1971-73; mem. 93d Congress from 8th Dist., Wis.; v.p. Black Creek Improvement Corp., 1967—2003, Outagamie County Family Ct. Commn., 1975-78. Chmn. Com. Chief Judges, 1992—94; chief adminstrn. judge Outagamie County, 1983—88, 1994—. Rep. precinct committeeman 19th ward, Appleton, 1956-62; chmn. Outagamie County Rep. Statutory Com., 1958-62; sec. Assembly Rep. Caucus, 1965-66; bd. regents Fox Valley Luth. H.S., Appleton, 1990-93; bd. dirs. Fox Valley Luth. H.S. Found., 1967—, v.p., 2002—. With USN, 1951-55. Mem. ABA, Am. Judges Assn. (bd. govs. 1997-99, asst. treas. 1998-99, treas. 1999—), Wis. Bar Assn., Outagamie County Bar Assns., Wis. Assn. Trial Judges (pres. 1991-2000), Am. Legion, VFW (judge adv. 1963-75, 82-99), Assn. Trial Judges in Wis. (sec. 1984-91, pres. 1991-00), Midwest Coun. State Govts. (vice chmn. 1968-69, chmn. 1969-70), Coun. State Govts. (nat. exec. com. 1970-72), Phi Alpha Delta. Office: 410 S Walnut St Appleton WI 54911-5920 Office Phone: 920-832-5602. Business E-Mail: harold.froehlich@wicourts.gov.

FROELICH, BEVERLY LORRAINE, foundation administrator; b. Vancouver, B.C., Can., Oct. 23, 1948; arrived in U.S., 1968; d. Kenneth Martin and Ethel Pulham; m. Eugene Leonard Froelich, Dec. 26, 1971; children: Craig, Grant. Cert. in fundraising, U. So. Calif., 1986; profl. designation in pub. rels., UCLA, 1987. Cert. in fundraising exec. Contract analyst Universal Studios, Calif., 1968-71; exec. dir. Olive View UCLA Med. Ctr. Found., Sylmar, 1987—. Pres. Beverly Froelich Pub. Rels., Sherman Oaks, Calif., 1988—90; prin. Tracy Susman & Co., Sherman Oaks, 1986—88. Co-author: (programs) Overcoming Chronic Arthritis Pain, 1989. Contbg. writer hosp. earthquake preparedness guidelines Hosp. Coun. So. Calif., 1991; founder San Fernando Valley br. Arthritis Found., Encino, 1983, pres., 1983—87, mem. mktg. com. Recipient Nat. Vol. Svc. award, Arthritis Found., 1991, Marilyn Magaram award for Cmty. Svc., 1997. Mem.: Assn. Fundraising Profls. (pres. San Fernando Valley chpt., Fundraising Profl. of Yr. 2000), Valley Industry and Commerce Assn. (bd. dirs. health care com.), UCLA Alumni Assn. Avocations: hockey, music. Office: Olive View Med Ctr Found Cottage J2 14445 Olive View Dr Sylmar CA 91342-1437 Office Phone: 818-364-3686. E-mail: ovinfo@earthlink.net.

FROEMMING, HERBERT DEAN, retired retail executive; b. Alexandria, Minn., Aug. 19, 1936; s. Herbert Edward and Bertha Anna (Hink) F.; m. Mary Louise Gapinski, Sept. 2, 1961; children— Mark, Traci, Scott. BBA, U. Minn., 1959; MBA, U. Mo. CPA, Minn. Fin. exec. The Kroger Co., various locations, 1960-69; exec. v.p. E.F. MacDonald Shopping Bag, L.A., 1969-73; also dir.; v.p., treas., dir. Western Auto Supply Co., Kansas City, Mo., 1973-78; sr. corp. v.p., controller Gamble-Skogmo Co., Mpls., 1978-80; exec. v.p. Red Owl Food Stores, Inc., 1980-84; v.p. Sullivan Assocs., Inc., 1985-88; sr. v.p.-adminstr., chief fin. officer Braun's Fashions Inc., Plymouth, Minn., 1989-94, pres., COO, 1994-97, vice chmn., 1997-98; chmn., CEO Millennium Plastics Tech., LLC, El Paso, Tex., 1999-2000. Served with AUS, 1955-57. Home: 104 Coventry Ln Edina MN 55435-5634

FROETSCHER, JANET, social services administrator; m. Roy Froetscher; 2 children. Bachelor's Degree, U. Va., 1981; M in Mgmt., Northwestern U., 1983. Leveraged buyout specialist First Chgo. Corp.; v.p. corp. fin. Bankers Trust Co., N.Y.C.; founding mng. ptnr. Exec. Options; exec. dir. Fin. Rsch. and Adv. Com. Civic Com. of the Comml. Club Chgo., 1992—99; sr. v.p. seminars Aspen Inst., 1999—2000, exec. v.p., 2000—01, COO, 2001—02; pres., CEO United Way Chgo., 2003, United Way Met. Chgo., 2003—. Named mem. Coun. of 100, Northwestern U., mem., The Chgo. Network; named one of Chgo. Most Influential Women, Crain's Chgo. Bus., 1996, 40 under 40, 1997; Henry Crown fellow, Aspen Inst., 1998. Office: United Way Met Chgo 560 W Lake Chicago IL 60661

FROHBIETER-MUELLER, JO, writer, artist, biologist, musician; b. Evansville, Ind., June 5, 1934; d. Edwin Henry and Sudie (Wilson) Frohbieter; m. Wayne Paul Mueller, June 9, 1957; children: Janet, D. Tom. BA in Biology, Evansville Coll., 1956; MA, Ind. U., 1962. Rsch. biologist NASA, Bloomington, Ind., 1956-62, Am. Cancer Soc., Evansville, 1961-72; writer Evansville, 1973—. Small bus. cons., Evansville; columnist Income Opportunities, N.Y.C., 1990-94, Small Bus. Opportunities, N.Y.C., 1989-93; spkr. in field. Author: Growing and Cooking Mushrooms, 1974, Practical Stained Glass, 1982, Your Home Business Can Make Dollars and Sense, 1990, Stay Home and Mind Your Own Business, 1988; Writing: Getting Into Print, 1994, Moonlighting, 1997; contbr. articles to profl. jours. ARSAF grantee; recipient numerous art awards. Mem. Acad. Arts and Scis., Ind. Acad. Scis., Ohio Valley Writers Guild. Avocations: flute, harp. Home: 2357 Trail Dr Evansville IN 47711-4015 E-mail: jofromueller@sprynet.com.

FROHLICH, EDWARD DAVID, medical educator; b. N.Y.C., Sept. 10, 1931; s. William and May (Zneimer) F.; m. Sherry Linda Fine, Nov. 1, 1959; children: Marjorie, Bruce, Lara. BA, Washington and Jefferson Coll., 1952; MD, U. Md., 1956; MS, Northwestern U., 1963; DSc (hon.), U. Buenos Aires, 2001. Diplomate Am. Bd. Internal Medicine. Intern, resident D.C. Gen. Hosp., 1956-58; resident Georgetown U. Hosp., Washington, 1958—60; clin. investigator VA Rsch. Hosp., Chgo., 1962-64; assoc. in medicine Northwestern U., 1963-64; staff mem. rsch. divsn. Cleve. Clinic, 1964-69; prof. medicine, physiology and biophysics U. Okla., Oklahoma City, 1969-76, George Lynn Cross rsch. prof., 1975-76; prof. medicine and physiology La. State U., 1976—; clin. prof. medicine, adj. prof. pharmacology Tulane U., 1976—; mem. staff, v.p. edn. and rsch. Alton Ochsner Med. Found., 1976—86, v.p. acad. affairs, 1986—89, disting. scientist, 1986—. Cons. in field. Editor: Pathophysiology-Altered Regulatory Mechanisms in Disease, 1972, 1976, 1984, Rypins' Medical Licensure Examinations, 13th - 18th edits., 1981—2001, Rypins' Intensive Revs., 13 vols., 1996, Take Heart, 1990, Hypertension: Evaluation and Treatment, 1998; editor-in-chief: Jour. Lab. and Clin. Medicine, 1973—76, Hypertension, 1994—2002; mem. editl. bd. (jours.) Am. Jour. Cardiology, 1982—91, Circulation, 1978—91, Archives of Internal Medicine, 1978—88, Modern Medicine, 1980—2000, Jour. Hypertension, 1994—2003; assoc. editor: Am. Jour. Physiology, Heart Circulation; contbr. chapters to books, articles to profl. jours. Capt. U.S. Army, 1960-62. Recipient Honors Achievement award, Angiology Rsch. Found., 1964, Ann. award, So. Med. Assn., 1971, Janice M. Pfeffer Disting. Lectureship, Internat. Soc. Heart Rsch., 2005; rsch. fellow, Georgetown U. Hosp., 1958—59. Master: ACP (laureate 1996); fellow: AAAS, Coun. High Blood Pressure Rsch. (exec. com. 1972—75, 1981—85, vice chmn. 1986—88, chmn. 1989—91), Am. Coll. Cardiology (gov. La. chpt. 1988—91, bd. trustees La. chpt. 1991—92, 1996—2000, Disting. Scientist award 2005), Royal Coll. Physicians and Surgeons Glasgow (hon.); mem.: Polish Acad. Arts Sci. (faculty medicine), Columbian Soc. Cardiology, Peruvian Soc. Cardiology, Assn. Am. Physicians, Am. Soc. Clin. Investigations, So. Soc. Clin. Rsch., Ctrl. Soc. Clin. Rsch., Am. Soc. Nephrology, Am. Physiol. Soc., Am. Soc. Clin. Pharmacology and Therapeutics (past pres.), Am. Soc. Pharmacology and Exptl. Therapeutics, Am. Soc. Clin. Investigation, Soc. Geriat. Cardiology (pres. 2000—01), Inter-Am. Soc. Hypertension (Lifetime Achievement award 1999), Am. Heart Assn. (dir. La. chpt. 1979—83, chmn. Coun. High Blood Pressure Rsch. 1988—91, award of merit 1986, Lifetime Achievement award 1994, Okamoto Internat. award 1994), Internat. Soc. Hypertension (sci. coun. 1974—84, treas. 1980—82, v.p. 1982—84, Astra award 2000), Alpha Kappa Alpha, Phi Sigma, Chi Epsilon Mu. Office: Ochsner Clinic Found 1516 Jefferson Hwy New Orleans LA 70121-2429 Office Phone: 504-842-3700. Business E-Mail: efrohlich@ochsner.org.

FROHMAN, LARRY PHILIP, neuro-ophthalmologist; b. N.Y.C., July 14, 1955; s. Peter and Arlene Joan (Horowitz) F.; m. Judith Anne Levy, July 9, 1978; children: Daniel, Charles. BA in Biology, Swarthmore Coll., 1976; MD, U. Pa., 1980. Intern Presbyn.-U. Pa. Med. Ctr., Phila., 1980-1; resident in ophthalmology NYU-Bellevue, 1981-84; fellow in neuro-ophthalmology NYU-Bellevue and N.Y. Eye and Ear Infirmary, 1984-85; assoc. prof. ophthalmology and neurology N.J. Med. Sch., 1992—, vice chair ophthalmolgoy, 1992—, chief neuro-ophthalmology, 1992—. Hunter GruBB scholar, 1976-80. Mem. AMA, Am. Acad. Ophthalmology (Secretariat award 2002, 2004, Sr. Honor award 2003), N.Am. Neuro-Ophthalmology Soc. (pres.2004-), Sigma Xi. Avocations: cooking, photography, mineral and tie collecting. Office Phone: 973-972-2025. E-mail: LPF2584@aol.com.

FROHNMAYER, DAVID BRADEN, academic administrator; b. Medford, Oreg., July 9, 1940; s. Otto J. and MarAbel (Braden) F.; m. Lynn Diane Johnson, Dec. 30, 1970; children: Kirsten (dec.), Mark, Kathryn (dec.), Jonathan, Amy. AB magna cum laude, Harvard U., 1962; BA, Oxford (Eng.) U., 1964, MA (Rhodes scholar), 1971; JD, U. Calif., Berkeley, 1967; LLD (hon.), Willamette U., 1988; D Pub. Svc. (hon.), U. Portland, 1989. Bar: Calif. 1967, U.S. Dist. Ct. (no. dist.) Calif. 1967, Oreg. 1971, U.S. Dist. Ct. Oreg. 1971, U.S. Supreme Ct. 1981. Assoc. Pillsbury, Madison & Sutro, San Francisco, 1967-69; asst. to sec. Dept. HEW, 1969-70; prof. law U. Oreg., 1971-81, spl. asst. to univ. pres., 1971-79; atty. gen. State of Oreg., 1981-91; dean Sch. Law U. Oreg., 1992-94, pres., 1994—. Chmn. Conf. Western Attys. Gen., 1985-86; chmn. Am. Coun. Edn. Govtl. Rels. commn, 1996-98; bd. dirs. Umpqua Holding Co. Mem. Oreg. Ho. of Reps, 1975-81; mem. coun. pub. reps. NIH, 1999-2000; bd. dirs. Fred Hutchinson Cancer Rsch. Ctr., 1994-2000, Nat. Marrow Donor Program, 1987-99, Fanconi Anemia Rsch. Fund, Inc., Ford Family Found., 2004—; active Oreg. Progress Bd., 1991-2004. Recipient awards Weaver Constl. Law Essay competition Am. Bar Found., 1972, 74, Advocacy award Research!Am., 1999, Albert B. Sabin Heroes of Sci. award Ams. for Med. Progress Ednl. Found., 2000, Learned Hand award Am. Jewish Com., 2004; Rhodes scholar, 1962. Fellow Am. Acad. Arts and Scis.; mem. ABA (Ross essay winner 1980), Oreg. Bar Assn., Calif. Bar Assn., Nat. Assn. Attys. Gen. (pres. 1987, Wyman award 1987), Round Table Eugene, Order of Coif, Phi Beta Kappa, Rotary. Republican. Presbyterian. Home: 2315 McMorran St Eugene OR 97403-1750 Office: U Oreg Johnson Hall Office Pres Eugene OR 97403 Office Phone: 541-346-3036. Business E-Mail: pres@uoregon.edu.

FROHNMAYER, JOHN EDWARD, lawyer, writer; b. Medford, Oreg., June 1, 1942; s. Otto J. and Marabel (Braden) F.; m. Leah Thorpe, June 10, 1967; children: Jason Otto, Jonathan Aaron. BA in Am. History, Stanford U., 1964; MA in Christian Ethics, U. Chgo., 1969; JD, U. Oreg., 1972. Bar: Oreg. 1972, Mont. 1995. Assoc. Johnson, Harrang & Mercer, Eugene, Oreg., 1972-75; ptnr. Tonkon, Torp, Galen, Marmaduke & Booth, Portland, Oreg., 1975-89; 5th chmn. Nat. Endowment for the Arts, Washington, 1989-92; writer, lectr. on art, ethics and politics, 1992—; pvt. practice, 1972-89, Bozeman, Mont., 1995—. Mem. Oreg. Arts Commn., 1978-85, chmn., 1980-84; bd. dirs. Internat. Sculpture Symposium, eugene, 1974; chmn. screening com. Oreg. State Capitol Bldg., 1977; affiliate prof. liberal arts Oreg. STate U., 2004—. Author: Leaving Town Alive, 1993, Out of Tune: Listening to The First Amendment, 1994; editor-in-chief Oreg. Law Rev., 1971-72; singer; appeared in recital, oratorio, mus. comedy and various other mus. prodns. Trustee Holladay Park Pla.; founding mem. chamber choir Novum Cantorum; bd. dirs. Chamber Music Northwest, Western States Arts Found.; mem. Nat. Endowment for the Arts Opera-Mus. Theater, 1982, 83. With USN, 1966-69. Sr. fellow Freedom Forum, 1993; recipient People for the Am. Way Ann. 1st Amendment award, 1992, Oreg. Gov. Arts award, 1993, Intellectual Freedom award Mont. Libr. Assn., 1997, Citation of Merit, Mu Phi Epsilon, 1998. Fellow Am. Leadership Forum; mem. ABA (com. comml. transactions litigation), Oreg. State Bar Assn. (chmn. bar com. domestic law 1975-76, procedure and practice com. 1984-85), Multnomah County Bar Assn., City Club Portland (bd. dirs.), Sta. L. Rowing Club (sec.), Order of the Coif (legal hon. 1972). Home and Office: 1356 SW Timain St Corvallis OR 97333 E-mail: frohn@comcast.net.

FROHOCK, FRED MANUEL, political science professor; b. Perry, Fla., Feb. 7, 1937; s. Fred Clifton and Marie Antonia (Domenech) F.; m. Val Jean Derrick, Sept. 7, 1963; children— Katherine Renee, Christina Marie BA, U. Fla., 1960, MA, 1961; PhD, U. N.C., 1966. Asst. prof. polit. sci. Syracuse U., N.Y., 1965-68, assoc. prof., 1968-74, prof., 1974—, chmn. dept. polit. sci., 1985-89, prof. Florence program, 1969-70, prof., chmn. Madrid program, 1972-74, prof., chmn. London Politics Seminar, 1984—; prof., chmn. dept. polit. sci. U. Miami, 2005—. Author: Nature of Political Inquiry, 1967, Normative Political Theory, 1974, Public Policy, 1979, Abortion: A Case Study in Law and Morals, 1983, Special Care: Medical Decisions at the Beginning of Life, 1986, Rational Association, 1987, Healing Powers, 1992, Public Reason: Mediated Authority in the Liberal State, 1999, Lives of the Psychics: The Shared Worlds of Science and Mysticism, 2000; contbr. numerous articles to profl. jours. Social Sci. Research Council fellow, 1964-65, 67-68; NEH summer fellow, 1988. Democrat. Roman Catholic. Avocations: golf, watching baseball. Home: 516 Savona Ave Coral Gables FL 33146 Office: U miami Polit Sci Dept Coral Gables FL 33124 Office Phone: 315-284-8362. Business E-Mail: ffrohock@maxwell.syr.edu.

FROLIK, LAWRENCE ANTON, law educator, lawyer, consultant; b. Lincoln, Nebr., Jan. 10, 1944; s. Elvin F. and Rita K. (Haley) F.; m. Ellen M. Doyle, Sept. 25, 1973; children: Winnefred, Cornelius. BA with distinction, U. Nebr., 1966; JD cum laude, Harvard U., 1969, LLM cum laude, 1972. Asst. prof. U. Pitts., 1975-78, assoc. prof., 1978-81, prof., 1981—. Bd. dirs. Kendal Corp. Author: Loss and Damage, 1987, Fed. Tax Aspects of Injury, 1993; co-author: Pa. Elder Law Manual, 1988, Advising the Elderly and Disabled Client, 1991, Elderly and the Law: Cases and Materials, 1991, 3d edit., 2004, Elder Law in a Nutshell, 1995;: 3d edit., 2003, Aging and the Law: An Interdisciplinary Reader, 1999, Law of Employer Pension and Welfare Benefits, 2004. Exec. com. Gruter Inst. Law and Behavioral Rsch., Pa. AARP exec. coun., 2002—, Pa. Coun. on Aging, 2003—. Capt. U.S. Army, 1969-71. Capt. U.S. Army, 1969—71. Fellow Am. Bar Found., Am. Coll. Trust and Estate Counsel; mem. Phi Beta Kappa. Home: 4345 Schenley Farms Ter Pittsburgh PA 15213-1206 Office: U Pitts Sch Law 3900 Forbes Ave. Pittsburgh PA 15260 Office Phone: 412-648-1363. Business E-Mail: frolik@law.pitt.edu.

FROMAN, SANDRA SUE, lobbyist, lawyer; b. San Francisco, June 15, 1949; d. Jay and Beatrice Froman. AB with honors, Stanford U., 1971; JD, Harvard U., 1974. Bar: Calif. 1974, U.S. Dist. Ct. (cen. dist.) Calif. 1974, U.S. Dist. Ct. (so. dist.) Calif. 1976, U.S. Dist. Ct. (no. dist.) Calif., U.S. Ct. Claims 1979, U.S. Tax Ct. 1984, Ariz. 1985, U.S. Dist. Ct. Ariz. 1985, U.S. Ct. Appeals (9th cir.) 1986, U.S. Supreme Ct. 1986. Assoc. Loeb & Loeb, L.A., 1974-80, ptnr., 1981-84; assoc. Bilby & Schoenhair, P.C., Tucson, 1985, shareholder, 1986-89; ptnr. Snell & Wilmer, Tucson, 1989-99. Vis. asst. prof. law U. Santa Clara, Calif., 1983-85; mem. Pima County Commn. on Trial Ct. Appointments, 1996-98. Trustee NRA Civil Rights Def. Fund, 1992-98, NRA Found., pres. 1997-2000; bd. dirs., 1st v.p. NRA, 1992-2005, pres. 2005-. Mem. Ariz. Bar Found. (pres. 1996—), Nat. 4-H Shooting Sports Found. (pres. 2002-04), Wildlife for Tomorrow Found. (pres. 1999—). Office: Ste 140 200 W Magee Rd Tucson AZ 85704-6492 Address: NRA 11250 Waples Mill Rd Fairfax VA 22030

FROMAN, VERONICA ZASADNI, career officer; BA in Polit. Sci., Seton Hill Coll.; grad., Armed Forces Staff Coll. Commd. U.S. Navy, 1970; advanced through grades to rear admiral, 1995; Naval Air Sta., Milton, Fla., 1970-72; Navy Recruiting Area Four, Columbus, Ohio, 1972-79; exec. officer Personnel Support Activity, Pearl Harbor, Hawaii, 1979-81; with Manpower Planner Joint Staff, 1983-86; commanding officer Personnel Support Activity, Pearl Harbor, 1986-90; Naval Edn. Tng. Support Ctr. Pacific, San Diego, 1981-83; exec. officer Naval Sta., Norfolk, Va., 1986-90; head edn. tng. staff placement Bur. Naval Personnel, Washington, 1990, also head gen. unrestricted line assignment br., 1990-93; commanding officer Naval Sta., Charleston, S.C., 1993-95; dir. manpower personnel Joint Staff, 1995-97; commander Naval Base, San Diego, 1997-2000; dir. FIMD USN, Arlington, Va., 2000—. Decorated Def. Disting. Svc. medal, Legion of Merit; named San Diego Press Club Headliner, 1998, San Diego Soroptomists' Woman of Accomplishment, 1998, Adv. of Yr., Nat. Assn. Women Bus. Owners, 1998. Office: Naval Sea Systems Command SE#1100 1333 Issac Hull Ave Washington DC 20376-1100

FROMBOLUTI, SIDEO, artist; b. Hershey, Pa., Oct. 3, 1920; s. Omero and Marina (Formiconi) F.; m. Nora Speyer. BFA, MFA, Tyler Coll. Fine Art. One-man shows include 37 exhibitions in U.S. and 6 in Europe; represented in permanent collections in 8 museums.*

FROMER, KEVIN, federal agency administrator; BA. Staff asst. Office of Rep. Harold Rogers Ho. of Reps., Washington, 1982—85, legis. dir., 1985—88, chief of staff, 1993—2002; asst. to ranking minority mem. com. on appropriations, commerce, justice, state judiciary subcom. Ho. of Reps., Washington, 1988—92, asst. to spkr. for policy, budget and appropriations office of spkr., 2002—05, asst. sec. treasury for legis. affairs, 2005—. Office: US Dept Treasury 1500 Pennsylvania Ave NW Rm 3134 Washington DC 20220 Office Phone: 202-622-1900. Office Fax: 202-622-0534.*

FROMKIN, AVA LYNDA, management consultant, healthcare risk management services; b. Toronto, Ont., Can., May 3, 1946; d. Joseph and Sara Ann (Hurovitz) F.; came to U.S., 1948, naturalized, 1953; BSN, U. Miami, 1969, cert. adminstrv. scis., 1975, MBA, cert. health adminstrn., 1983. Diplomate Am. Bd. Risk Mgmt. of Healthcare; lic. risk mgr. Nurse, Mt. Sinai Med. Ctr., Miami Beach, Fla., 1970-71, 73-76; dir. surg. svcs. Cedars of Lebanon Health Care Ctr., Miami, 1976-82; adj. prof. intraoperative nursing program Miami (Fla.)-Dade C.C., 1982-83; prin. A. Lynda Fromkin, Inc., Miami, Fla., 1982-94. Mem. ANA, Fla. Nurses Assn., Am. Soc. Post Anesthesia Nurses, Assn. Oper. Rm. Nurses (dir. Miami chpt. 1979-80), F.H.A. Soc. Healthcare Risk Mgmt., Alzheimer's Care Com. Notables, U. Miami Pres. Circle. Home: 555 NE 34th St Apt 2306 Miami FL 33137-4059

FROMLET, K. HUBERT, banking economist; b. Stuttgart, Germany, May 22, 1947; arrived in Sweden, 1975; s. Kurt and Marianne (Schnitzler) F.; m. Cristina Lindqvist, June 1, 1979; children: Camilla, Pia. Diploma in bus., U. Würzburg, Fed. Republic Germany, 1971, D. in Polit. Sci., 1975. Rschr. Saab-Scania, Södertälje, Sweden, 1975-81, Swedish Coop. Banks, Stockholm, 1981-83, chief economist, 1983-84, Swed Bank, Stockholm, 1984—; prof. internat. econs. Blekinge Inst. Tech., 2001—. Vis. prof. Baltic Sch. Bus., Sweden, 2001—; lectr. various univs. Author: Das schwedische Bankensystem, 1975; contbr. articles to profl. jours. Avocations: sports, art.

FROMM, ANNETTE BACOLA, historic site manager; b. Pitts., July 13, 1950; d. Marvin M. and Mollie B. Fromm; m. Danny B. Kolker, May 22; 1 child, Miriam. BA in African Studies, Kent (Ohio) U., 1973; MA in Folklore, Ind. U., 1977; student in Philos. Studies, U. Ioannina, Greece, 1983—84; PhD in Folklore, Ind. U., 1992. Collections asst. The Children's Mus., Indpls., 1977; curator, rsch. supr. Greater Cleve. (Ohio) Ehtnographic Mus., 1977—79, acting dir., curator, 1979—80; reference asst. Lilly Libr. Ind. U., 1984—85; exec. dir. The Fenster Mus. Jewish Art, Tulsa, 1985—89; sr. fellow Dept. Anthrop. U. Tulsa, Tulsa, Okla., 1987—95; dir. project Restoration Creek Coun. Ho., Okmulgee, Okla., 1992—94; sr. program devel. specialist Okla. Mus. Natural History U. Okla., Norman, Okla., 1995—98; dir. edn. and pub. programs Sanford L. Ziff Jewish Mus. Fla., Miami Beach, Fla., 1999—2001; vis. assoc. prof. Dept. Judaic and Holocaust Studies Fla. Atlantic U., Boca Raton, Fla., 2001—02; mgr. grants The Art Mus. Fla. Internat. U., Miami, Fla., 2002—03; mgr. The Deering Estate at Cutler, Miami, 2003—. Cons. in field; mem. editl. com. Sephardic and Greek Holocaust Libr., 2002—; various positions Inst. Mus. and Libr. Svcs., 1993—; adv. bd. Fla. Folklore Soc., 2000—. Editor: The Jour. Chickasaw History, 1995—2000, Jewish Folklore and Ethnology Rev., 1988—2000, Newsletter, 1981; author: African Art, Family Guide, 2003; co-author: Jewish Mothers Tell Their Stories, Acts of Love and Courage, 2000; contbr. chapters to books, articles to profl. jours. Merm. Fla. Folklife Coun., 2005—. Fellow, Meml. Found. Jewish Culture, 1983—84, The Grad. Sch. Ind. U., 1985; grantee, Grad. Sch. Ind. U., 1988; scholar, Broome and Allen Scholarship Fund, 1981—82; Humanist fellow, The Sephardic Jews Fla., 2002, Fulbright-Hays grantee, 1983—84. Mem.: Fla. Folklore Soc., Am. Folklore Soc., Fla. Assn. Mus., Am. Assn. State and Local History, Am. Assn. Mus., Internat. Coun. Museology, Internat. Com. Mus. Ethnography (exec. bd. 1986—92, 1995—2001, chmn. statutes com. 1994—95, sec. 2004—), Internat. Coun. Mus. Office: The Deering Estate Cutler 16701 SW 72d St Miami FL 33150 Office Phone: 305-235-1668 258. E-mail: AnnetteFromm@hotmail.com.

FROMM, ERWIN FREDERICK, retired insurance company executive; b. Kalamazoo, Oct. 24, 1933; s. Erwin Carl and Charlotte Elizabeth (Wilson) F. Student, U. Mich., 1951-52, Flint Jr. Coll., 1952-53; BA, Kalamazoo Coll., 1959; postgrad., Ill. State U., 1970-72. CPCU, CLU; cert. nursing home adminstr. Underwriter State Farm Ins., 1959-72; cons. Met. Property & Liability Ins. Co., Warwick, R.I., 1972-73, dir. underwriting and policyholders svcs., 1973, asst. v.p., 1973-74, v.p., 1974—. Sr. v.p. Royal Ins. Co., Charlotte, N.C., 1979-90; ret., 1990; nursing home exec. Royal Crest Health Care Ctr., Inc., 1990-92; pres. Royal Monarch Cons., Inc., 1990—; past chmn. All Industry Ins. Com. for Arson Control; chmn. Nat. Coun. on Compensation Ins.; past chmn. Comml. Lines Com. Ins. Svc. Office; past mem. adv. com. underwriting program Ins. Inst. Am.; cert. long term care ombudsman, 1998—. Past mem. adv. coun. Bus. Sch., U. R.I.; past bd. dirs. Charlotte Symphony; bd. dirs. N.C. Ins. Edn.; mem. Calif. Sr. Legisature, 2000—, mem. adv. coun. on aging; bd. dirs. Calif. Found. on Aging; bd. dirs. Compulsive Gambling Inst. Mem. CPCU Assn. (Calif. chpt.), CLU Assn. (Calif. chpt.), Masons, Shriners. Lutheran. Home and Office: 73 Colgate Drive Rancho Mirage CA 92270 E-mail: pssstca@aol.com.

FROMM, HANS, gastroenterologist, educator, medical researcher; b. Hagenow, Germany, Aug. 1, 1939; s. Johannes C. and Irene (Biermann) F.; m. Sharon A. Kleiv, June 8, 1968; children: H. Chris, Martin T. MD, Albert Ludwig U., Freiburg, Fed. Republic Germany, 1964. Intern Meml. Hosp., Worcester, Mass., 1966-67; resident Lemuel Shattuck Hosp., Boston, 1967-68, Albany Med. Ctr., 1968-70; fellow Mayo Clinic, Rochester, Minn., 1970-71; resident/fellow Medizinische Hochschule Hannover, Germany, 1971-74; asst. prof. medicine U. Pitts., 1975-80, assoc. prof. medicine, 1980-84, prof. medicine, 1984, George Washington U., Washington, 1984-99; dir. divsn. gastroenterology and nutrition George Washington Med. Ctr., Washington, 1984-99; prof. medicine Dartmouth Med. Sch., 1999—; dir. Dartmouth-Hitchcock Hepatopancreaticobiliary Disease Ctr., Lebanon, NH, 1999—. Mem. numerous grant rev. coms. including NIH, Merit Rev. Bd., Gastroenterology Med. Rsch. Svc. VA, Washington, 1984—87. Mem. editl. bd.: Hepatogastroenterology, 1981—88, mem. editl. bd.: Hepatology, 1985, 1991—2001; contbr. articles to profl. jours., chapters to books. Mem.: Orgn. Mondiale de Gastro-Enterologie/World Orgn. Gastroenterology (vice chmn. interamerican edn. com. 1998—2001), Am. Assn. Study of Liver Diseases (chmn. pubs. com. 1988—90, mem. com. on admissions 2002—), Am. Gastroent. Assn. (chmn. com. on admissions 1990—91, chmn. internat. liaison com. 1995—98, chmn. biliary disorders sect. 1997—99), Am. Soc. Clin. Investigation. Lutheran. Office: Dartmouth Hitchcock Med Ctr Sect Gastroenterology & Hepatology 1 Medical Center Dr Lebanon NH 03756-0002 Office Phone: 603-650-8343. E-mail: Hans.Fromm@Hitchcock.org.

FROMM, JEFFERY BERNARD, lawyer; b. Washington, Oct. 9, 1947; s. Seymour Morris and Frances Sylvia (Goldstein) F.; m. Mary Ellen Sommer, Sept. 11, 1971; children: Aaron M., David P. BS in Elec. Engring., BA in Physics, U. Pa., 1970; JD magna cum laude, Widener U., 1981. Bar: Pa. 1982, Calif. 1982, U.S. Ct. Appeals (9th and fed. cirs.) 1982, Colo. 1988. Patent atty. Hewlett-Packard Co., Palo Alto, Calif., 1981-83, sr. patent atty., 1983-85, mng. patent counsel Andover, Mass., 1985-87, sr. mng. counsel intellectual property Ft. Collins, Colo., 1987—2002; pvt. intellectual property legal practice, 2002—03; atty. Drinker, Biddle and Reath LLP, 2003—. Asst. scoutmaster Boy Scouts Am., Ft. Collins, 1988-96; asst. coach-umpire Little League, Andover and San Jose, Calif., 1983-87. Mem. IEEE, ABA, Am. Intellectual Property Law Assn., Pa. Bar Assn., Calif. Bar Assn., Colo. Bar Assn., Phi Delta Phi. Avocations: skiing, golf. Office: PO Box 7399 PMB 332 Breckenridge CO 80424-7399 Office Phone: 215-988-2717. Business E-Mail: jeff.fromm@dbr.com.

FROMM, JOSEPH, retired editor, financial consultant; b. South Bend, Ind., Jan. 6, 1920; s. Michael M. and Ethel (Mentzel) F.; divorced; children: Margot, Lisa; 1 stepchild, Erik. Student, U. Chgo., 1937-38, Northwestern U., 1938-39. Reporter S. Bend Tribune, 1935-37, Southtown Economist, Chgo., 1937-39; writer UP, Chgo., 1939-40; radio news bur. chief AP, Chgo., 1940-42; mng. editor air edit. Chgo. Sun, 1942; fgn. corr. U.S. News and World Report, 1946-74, dep. editor Washington, 1974-79, asst. editor, 1979-85, contbg. editor, 1985-88. Cons. to think tanks, U.S. Dept. Def., Nat. Security Coun., CIA, Joint Warfare Analysis Ctr.; lectr. on strategy and internat. rels.; mem. tech. adv. com. Ctr. Naval Analysis. Served with Brit. Army, 1943—44, commd. capt. Indian Army, 1945, discharged U.S. Army, 2002. Decorated Order Brit. Empire. Fellow Johns Hopkins Fgn. Policy Inst., Internat. Inst. Strategic Studies (founding mem. 1958, mem. governing coun. 1975-92); mem. Washington Inst. Fgn. Affairs, Coun. on Fgn. Rels., Midatlantic Club, Fgn. Corr. Club Japan (pres. 1950), Assn. Am. Corrs. in London (pres. 1967), Fgn. Press Assn. London (dir. 1972-74), Arms Control Assn., Cosmos Club Washington. Personal E-mail: joefromm@aol.com.

FROMM, PETER FRANCIS, author; b. Sept. 29, 1958; BS in Wildlife Biology, U. Mont., 1981. Author: The Tall Uncut, 1992, Indian Creek Chronicles, 1993, Monkey Tag, 1994, King of the Mountain, 1994, Dry Rain, 1997, Blood Knot, 1998, Night Swimming, 1999, How All This Started, 2000, As Cool As I Am, 2004. Recipient Pacific N.W. Bookseller awards, 1994, 98, 2001, 04, Pushcart Prize nominations, 1997, 98, Western Pub. Maggie award for Best Fiction, 2005. Personal E-mail: petefromm@msn.com.

FROMM, RONALD A., apparel executive; m. Cheryl Fromm; children: Dawn, Dana. BS in Acctg., MBA, U. Wis. Former v.p. Heath Corp.; dir. fin. Famous Footwear divsn. Brown Group, Madison, Wis., 1986-88, v.p., 1988-90, v.p., CFO, 1990-92, exec. v.p., then pres. Brown Shoe Co. divsn., 1992-99, pres., CEO, chmn. bd. dirs. St. Louis, 1999—. Bd. dirs. Footwear Distributors and Retailers of Am., Fashion Footwear Assn. N.Y., Two/Ten Footwear Industry charitable found. Office: Brown Shoe 8300 Maryland Ave Saint Louis MO 63105*

FROMMER, LAWRENCE JULIAN, retired travel company executive; b. Trenton, NJ, Sept. 8, 1917; s. Samuel Alexander Frommer and Fannie Cohen; m. Yolande Irene Foisy, Aug. 22, 1975. BA in Journalism, Ind. U., 1939, MS in Bus. Adminstrn., 1942. Cert. travel counselor. Writer Radio Sta. WOWO, Ft. Wayne, Ind., 1943—44, Radio Sta. WKRC, Cin., 1944—45, Radio Sta. WOL, Washington, 1945—53; travel agy. exec. Frommer Travel Svc., Washington, 1958—91; travel writer Washingtonian Mag., 1969—82, Asta Agy. Mgmt., N.Y.C., Washington, 1973—95; travel and restaurant writer Crystal City Mag., Arlington, Va., 1990—2004. Travel agy. adv. bd. State Maine, Augusta, 1980, Am. Express, NYC, 1983—90, Access Am., NYC, 1985—88; radio host Travel Talk, Wash., 1970—84. Contbr. articles to profl. jours. Pres. Louis D. Brandeis Zionist Dist., Washington, 1958—59, Skal Club Travel Execs., Washington, 1975—76; trustee Inst. Cert. Travel Agts., Wellesly, Mass., 1968—90; vol. Animal Welfare League Alexandria, Alexandria Symphony Orch., Va., US Holocaust Mus., Alexandria Homeless Shelter. Named Travel Agt. of Yr., Am. Soc. Travel Agts., Washington, 1985. Fellow: Louis D. Brandeis Zionist Dist. (life; pres.), Skal Club Washington (pres.). Avocations: music, theater, sports, volunteer work. Home: Apt 505 5902 Mount Eagle Dr Alexandria VA 22303-2516 E-mail: yonlarry@erols.com.

FROMMER, WILLIAM S., lawyer; b. Bklyn., Sept. 27, 1942; s. Herbert S. and Molly S. Frommer; m. Karen Beagle, July 31, 1966; 1 child, Hillary. BEE, Cornell U., 1965; JD, Am. U., 1969. Bar: NY 1970, U.S. Patent Office 1970, U.S. Ct. Customs and Patent Appeals 1975, U.S. Ct. Appeals (fed. cir.) 1982, U.S. Supreme Ct. 1985. Assoc. Marn & Jangarathis, NYC, 1969—73, Curtis, Morris & Safford, P.C., NYC, 1973—76, ptnr., 1976—97; founding ptnr. Frommer, Lawrence & Haug, NYC, 1997—. Lectr. NY Intellectual Propery Law Assn. Mem. Am. U. Law Rev., 1967—69; contbr. articles to profl. jours. Mem.: ABA, Internat. Bar Assn., Internat. Patent and Trade Assn., NY State Bar Assn., NY Patent Law Assn. Office: 745 5th Ave New York NY 10151-0099 Office Phone: 212-588-0800.

FRONE, MICHAEL R., psychologist, researcher; s. S. Henry and MaryAnn Frone; m. Joan Stockman. BA, SUNY at Buffalo, 1981, PhD, 1991. Pers. rsch. analyst IBM, North Tarrytown, NY, 1985; rsch. assoc. prof. dept. psychology SUNY at Buffalo, 1991—, sr. rsch. scientist Rsch. Inst. on Addictions, 1986—. Associate editor (journal) Journal of Occupational Health Psychology; author (editor): Psychology of Workplace Safety; contbr. articles numerous articles to profl. jours., chapters to books. Named Top 100 Fed. Grantees, SUNY at Buffalo, 2002; grantee, NIH: Nat. Inst. on Alcohol Abuse and Alcoholism grantee, 2000—04, Scientist Devel. award, NIH: Nat. Inst. on Alcohol Abuse and Alcoholism, 1994—2000; scholar Pre-doctoral Rsch. traineeship, SUNY at Buffalo and NIH: Nat. Inst. of Mental Health, 1981—84. Mem.: So. Mgmt. Assn., Soc. for Personality and Social Psychology, Soc. for Indsl. and Orgnl. Psychology, APA, Acad. of Mgmt. Achievements include research in developing a conceptual model of the work-family interface in 1992 and expanded it in 1997. This research has been highly cited and has influenced research on work-family conflict and facilitation; development of a model of employee substance use and productivity. Avocation: scuba diving. Office: SUNY-Buffalo 1021 Main St Buffalo NY 14203 Office Phone: 716-887-2519.

FRONTANI, MICHAEL ROY, communications educator; b. Inglewood, Calif., Jan. 14, 1962; s. Roy Francis and Thelma Imperiale Frontani; m. Stephanie Lyn Bettinger (div.); 1 child, Dante Alan; m. Heidi Glaesel Frontani, May 9, 2003. BA, Ohio State U., 1986; MA in Critical Studies, U. So. Calif., 1995; MA in History, Ohio State U., 1993; PhD, Ohio U., 1998. Assoc. prof. Sch. Comms. Elon (N.C.) U., 1999—. Mentor Periclean Scholars Class 2008 Elon (N.C.) U., 2005—. Contbr. articles to profl. jours. Fellow, Ohio State U., 1989—93. Mem.: Am. Journalism Historians Assn., Am. Italian Hist. Assn., Am. Culture Popular Culture Assn. Democrat. Roman Catholic. Avocations: writing, composing music. Office: School Comms Elon Univ CB 2850 Elon NC 27244 Office Phone: 336-278-5664.

FRONTZ, HOWARD CLINTON, III, music educator; b. Lancaster, Pa., Feb. 19, 1954; s. Howard Clinton II and Mary Ann Frontz; m. Debra Ellen Penrod, July 23, 1988; children: Amber, Lisa, Laura. BS in Edn., Auburn U., 1976, M in Edn., 1977. Band dir. Monroe Acad., Forsyth, Ga., 1977—81, Macon County H.S., Montezuma, Ga., 1981—2002, Schley County H.S., Ellaville, Ga., 2002—. Min. of music First Bapt. Ch., Montezuma, 1997—. Mem.: Profl. Assn. Ga. Educators, Music Educators Nat. Conf., Ga. Music Educators Assn., Macon County Hist. Soc. Avocations: golf, coaching baseball. Home: 406 Overlook Dr Montezuma GA 31063-1070 Office: Schley County HS 2131 Hwy 19 S Ellaville GA 31806 Office Phone: 229-937-0560. E-mail: frontz@alltel.net.

FRONTZ, LESLIE KAY, art educator; b. Cleve., Aug. 23, 1950; d. James W. and Mary K. Robinson; m. Harold Oliver Frontz, Jan. 28, 1972. BA cum laude, Muskingum Coll., 1972; MEd, Va. Poly. Inst. State U., 1976; BS summa cum laude, So. Oreg. State U., 1981; MFA, U. N.C., Greensboro, 1986. Studio artist Frontz Studio, Lexington, NC, 1986—; instr. art SW Elem. Sch., 1997—2003; adj. faculty art Davidson County CC, 1995—96; instr. art Wash. State CC, Marietta, Ohio, 1991—92; adj. faculty art history Front Range CC, Ft. Collins, Colo., 1989—90; instr. painting U. N.C., Greensboro, 1986—86. Mem., bd. of directors Ohio Watercolor Soc., Ohio, 1993—94. Exhibitions include Salem Coll. Fine Arts Ctr., Winston-Salem, N.C., 2003, Fountainside Gallery, Wilmington, N.C., 2003, Southern Watercolor Soc., Panama City, Fla., 2005, Soc. Women Artists, London, 2005, prin. works include Great Falls Tavern, Represented in permanent collections Smithsonian Inst., Washington; contbr. articles to profl. jours. Vol. asst. exhbns. . Loveland Mus. and Gallery, Colo., 1988—90, Davidson County Hist. Mus., Lexington, NC, 2003; mem. exec. bd. Lexington Herb Guild, NC, 1996—. Recipient Best of Show, Comer Mus. Art, Ala., 1995, Mason award, Batavia Nat. Exhbn., N.Y., 1993, Excellence award, Ohio Watercolor Soc., 1992, Best of Show, Nat. Art Mart, Colo., 1990; Holderness fellow, U. N.C. at Geensboro, 1986, profiled in, U.S. Art, 1989. Mem.: Soc. Women Artists, So. Watercolor Soc., Associated Artists of Winston-Salem. Presbyterian. Avocations: genealogical and historical research, gardening, travel. Office: Frontz Studio 296 Peace Haven Dr Lexington NC 27292 Office Phone: 336-357-5974. Business E-Mail: info@frontzstudio.com.

FROOM, DAVID, composer, music educator; b. Calif., 1951; Student, U. Calif., Berkeley, U. So. Calif., Columbia U.; studies with, Chen Wen-chung, Mario Davidovsky, Alexander Goehr, William Kraft. Tchr. Baruch Coll., U. Utah, Peabody Conservatory; prof. music St. Mary's Coll., Md., 1989—. Bd. dirs. N.Y. New Music Ensemble. Composer: music performed by numerous ensembles. Recipient commn., Fromm and Koussevitsky Found., Friedheim Awards 1st Prize, Kennedy Ctr., 3 Individual Artist award, State of Md.; Charles Ives scholar, fellow, John Simon Guggenheim Meml. Found., 2003, Tanglewood Music Festival, Wellesley Composers Conf., MacDowell Colony, grant, NEA, Fulbright grant, Cambridge U. Mem.: League of Composers/ISCM (mem. nat. adv. bd.). Office: St Mary's Coll Md 18952 E Fisher Rd Saint Marys City MD 20686-3001

FROOMAN, THOMAS E., lawyer; b. 1967; m. Susan Frooman; 2 children. BSBA, Citadel, 1989; JD, Salmon P. Chase Coll. of Law, 1994. Atty. Keating, Muething & Klekamp, Cincinnati, 1997—2001; v.p., gen. counsel, sec. Cintas Corp., 2001—. Office: Cintas Corp PO Box 625737 6800 Cintas Blvd Cincinnati OH 45262-5737

FROSH, BRIAN ESTEN, lawyer, state senator; b. Washington, Oct. 8, 1946; s. Stanley Benjamin and Judith Lee (Wirkman) F.; m. Marcy Masters, Nov. 19, 1984; children: Elena, Alexandra. Student, U. Stockholm, 1966-67; BA, Wesleyan U., 1968; JD, Columbia U., 1971. Legis. asst. Sen. Harrison Williams U.S. Senate, Washington, 1972-76; ptnr. Kass, Skalet & Frosh, Washington, 1976-79, Bingaman, Davenport & Lovejoy, Santa Fe, 1979-81; pvt. practice Bethesda, Md., 1981—96; ptnr. Karp, Frosh, Lapidus, Wigodsky and Norwind, Washington, 1996—; del. Md. Gen. Assembly, Annapolis, 1987-95, chmn. Montgomery County House del., 1991-93; state senator Md. State Senate, 1995—, dep. majority leader, 2001—02, chmn. jud. procs. com., 2003—; mem. gov.'s task force on energy Md. Gen. Assembly, Annapolis, 1989-94; chmn. environ. subcom. Econ. and Environ. Affairs Com., 1995—2002; mem. Chesapeake Bay Commn., 1995—; chmn. Chesapeake Bay Commn., 2001. Legis. acts include Md. Recycling Act, Newspaper Recycling Act, Oil Spills Bill, Bay Protection and Oil Exploration, also others; bd. dirs. State Nat. Bank Md. Bd. dirs. Hebrew Home Greater Washington, 1986-95, Jewish Cmty. Ctr. Greater Washington, 1983-89; mem. Montgomery County Charter Rev. Commn., 1983-86; nat. adv. commn. SBA, 1981-82. Recipient cert. of merit Montgomery County Common Cause Md., 1991, Clean Air award Sierra Club, 1991, Conservationist of Yr. award, 1989, Lawmaker of Yr. award Am. Lung Assn. Md., 1991, Outstanding Svc. award Am. Heart Assn. Md., John Kabler award Md. League Conservation Voters, 2003. Mem. Md. State Bar Assn. (Leadership and Outstanding Svc. award 2001), Wesleyan U. Alumni Assn. (exec. com. 1986-89). Address: Miller Senate Office Bldg 2E Annapolis MD 21401 Office: Ste 800W 7315 Wisconsin Ave Bethesda MD 20814-3217 Office Phone: 301-652-2888. E-mail: brian_frosh@senate.state.md.us.

FROSS, ROGER RAYMOND, lawyer; b. Rockford, Ill., Mar. 8, 1940; s. Hollis H. and Dorothy (George) F.; m. Madelon R. Rose, Feb. 14, 1970; 1 child, Oliver. AB, DePauw U., 1962; JD, U. Chgo., 1965. Bar: Ill. 1965. Assoc. Norman and Billick, Chgo., 1965-70; ptnr. Lord, Bissell & Brook, Chgo., 1970—, mng. ptnr., 1982-87. Bd. dirs. Hyde Park Bank and Trust Co., Chgo., 1975—; pres. Hyde-Park-Kenwood Devel. Corp., 1998—. Bd. dirs. Hyde Park Neighborhood Club, Chgo., 1970—, pres. 1972-73; bd. dirs., mem. exec. com. South East Chgo. Commn., 1978—; mem. Community Conservation Council, Chgo., 1980-99; bd. dirs., sec. Chgo. Metro History Fair, 1991—; bd. dirs. The Joyce Found., 1991—, Lab. Sch. U. Chgo., 1991-94, Citizens Com. of the Juvenile Ct., 1973-96. Rector schlor DePauw U., Greencastle, Ind., 1958-62. Mem. ABA, Ill. Bar Assn., Chgo. Bar Assn. (chmn. com. juvenile delinquents 1972). Office: Lord Bissell & Brook Harris Bank Bldg 115 S La Salle St Ste 3500 Chicago IL 60603-3801

FROST, A. CORWIN, architect, consultant; b. Bronxville, N.Y., Nov. 18, 1934; s. Frederick George Jr. and Gwendolyn Belle (Corwin) F.; m. Rosalie Randolph Halsey, Sept. 26, 1959; children: Frederick Halsey, Anne Randolph. AB, Princeton U., 1956; BS, R.I. Sch. Design, 1959. Registered architect, N.Y., other states. Designer, draftsman Harrison & Abramovitz, N.Y.C., 1959-60; project architect Frederick G. Frost Jr. and Assocs., N.Y.C., 1960-63, assoc., 1963-68; ptnr. Frost Assocs., N.Y.C., 1968-78; assoc. dir. archtl. and engring. services CBS Inc., N.Y.C., 1978-80, dir. planning and design, 1980-86, dir. facilities engring., 1986-88; prin. Frost Assocs. Cons., Bronxville, N.Y., 1988—; dep. dir. dept. design, cons. and mgmt. CUNY, 1992-95; cons. Newark Pub. Schs., 1995—. Chmn. Bronxville Planning Bd., 1990-2004; trustee Coun. for Arts in Westchester, White Plains, N.Y., 1972-81 (pres. 1974-75), R.I. Sch. Design, 1989-99, 2000—, Westchester County Hist. Soc., 1998—2004; trustee, mem. exec. com. Westchester Preservation League, 1989-98; mem. Bronxville Adult Sch., 1982-88, Bronxville Planning Commn., 1977-80. Mem. AIA (exec. com. N.Y. chpt. 1974-76, ethics com. 1978-80, corp. architects com. 1980-82, fin. com. 1981-87), Princeton Club, Bronxville Field Club (pres. 1992-96). Home and Office: Frost Assoc Cons 11 Sunset Ave Bronxville NY 10708-2208 E-mail: fiberarch@earthlink.net.

FROST, CAREN JEAN, education educator; b. San Francisco, Calif., Nov. 24, 1961; d. Douglas Lee and Janice Wilcox Frost; m. Hassan Bourija, June 25, 1994; 1 child, Sabrine Mariem Bourija. BA, U. Utah, 1979—82; MPH, Columbia U., 1986—88; PhD in anthropology, U. Utah, 1988—95. Ethics & Protection of Human Subjects Nat. Cancer Inst., 2005, U. of Miami Collaborative Tng. Initiative, 2005. Dir., bur. of services rev. Utah Dept. of Human Services, 1997—98; dir. of strategic improvements Utah Divsn. of Child and Family Services, 1998—2001; rsch. asst. prof. Coll. of Social Work, U. Utah, 2001—. Contbr. articles to profl. jours. Grants chair Salt Lake Affiliate, Susan G. Komen Found., 2005. Faculty fellow for Short Ethics Courses, U. of Utah, 2004—05, Faculty fellow for U. Exch. Program, 2004.

Fellow: Soc. for Applied Anthroplogy (life); mem.: Utah Pub. Health Assn., Soc. for Med. Anthropology, Am. Anthrop. Assn. Office: Univ of Utah 395 S 1500 E room 111 Salt Lake City UT 84112 Office Phone: 801-581-5287. Personal E-mail: caren.frost@socwk.utah.edu.

FROST, CHARLES ESTES, JR., lawyer; b. Houston, Aug. 17, 1950; s. Charles Estes and Lucille Fourmey (DeGravelles) F. BS, U.S. Mil. Acad., 1972; MBA, Armstrong State Coll., 1979; JD, U. Tex., 1981. Bar: Tex. 1982, U.S. Dist. Ct. (no., ea. and so. dists.) Tex., 5th circuit ct. appeals. Commd. 2d lt. U.S. Army, 1972, advanced through grades to capt., 1979; resigned from active duty, 1979; assoc. Strasburger & Price, Dallas, 1982-84, Chamberlain, Hrdlicka et al, Houston, 1985-88; shareholder Chamberlain Hrdlicka et al, Houston, 1989—. Mem. bd. advocates U. Tex. Law Sch. Note editor: Tex. Law Rev., U. Tex. Law Sch.1981-82. Mem. ethics com. Haris County Rep. Party, 2000. Lt. col. USAR, 1979-98. Mem. Am. Arbitration Assn. (comml. arbitrator), Houston Bar Assn. (dir. litigation sect. 2000-02). Avocations: running, church. Office: Chamberlain Hrdlicka et al 1200 Smith St Ste 1400 Houston TX 77002-4401 Office Phone: 713-654-9674.

FROST, DAVID, retired biology professor, medical editor, consultant; b. Bklyn., Dec. 19, 1925; s. Charles and Regina (Sad) Feivlowitz; m. Ruthann Steinberg, Dec. 24, 1946; children: Michael Joseph, Jane Alice. BS, CCNY, 1945, MED, 1949; MS, NYU, 1952, PhD, 1960. Instr. in biology CCNY, 1946-49; instr. in sci. Rhodes Sch., N.Y.C., 1949-52; asst. prof. biology Rutgers U., Newark, 1952-59, adj. prof. biology New Brunswick, 1960-78; sci. editor Squibb Inst. for Med. Rsch., Princeton, 1959-75; pvt. practice Plainfield, NJ, 1975—2002, Olmstedville, NY, 1975—2002; ret., 2002. Pres. N.J. SANE, 1964-65; co-chmn. Plainfield Joint Def. Com., 1970-85; newsletter editor Cen. Jersey/Masaya, Nicaragua Friendship Cities Project, 1985-97. Mem. Coun. Sci. Editors (pres. 1982-83), Schroon Lake Assn. (v.p., 1980—, pres. 1997—). Office: 1229 E 7th St Plainfield NJ 07062-1907 Home: 1637 Hoffman Rd Olmstedville NY 12857-2436

FROST, EDMUND BOWEN, lawyer; b. Pueblo, Colo., Dec. 5, 1942; s. Hildreth and Doris (Bowen) F.; m. Molly Spitzer, 1966; children: Julia A., Elizabeth E., Edmund N., Luette S. BA, Dartmouth Coll., 1964; JD magna cum laude, U. Mich., 1967. Bar: Colo. 1967, D.C. 1970, U.S. Supreme Ct. 1980. Assoc. Steptoe & Johnson, Washington, 1969-75; chief legal advisor to commr. ICC, Washington, 1975-76; asst. dir. for gen. litigation Bur. Competition, FTC, Washington, 1976-77; v.p., gen. counsel Chem. Mfrs. Assn., Washington, 1978-82; ptnr. Kirland & Ellis, Washington, 1982-88, Davis, Graham & Stubbs, Washington, 1988-94; sr. v.p. and gen. counsel Clean Sites, Inc., Alexandria, Va., 1994-99; shareholder, dir. Leonard Frost Levin Van Court & Marsh, PC, 1998—; bd. dirs., chmn., bd. environ., health and safety com. Philip Svcs. Co., 2000—03; gen. ptnr. Frost Bros., LLLP, 2004—. Contbr. articles to profl. jours. Participant pub. policy dialogs on environ. issues Keystone (Colo.) Ctr., 1980—; guest artisan Washington Nat. Cathedral, 1997—; co-pres., bd. dirs., exec. com. Cmty. Coun. for the Homeless at Friendship Place, DC; pres., bd. dirs. Vincent Palumbo Ctr. for Stonecarving and Indsl. Arts, Inc., 2001-. Capt. U.S. Army, 1967-69. Recipient Benjamin E. Cooper award for exceptional vol. leadership, Cmty. Coun. for the Homeless at Friendship Place, DC. Mem. Cosmos Club Washington. Avocations: sculpture and stone carving, skiing, mountain climbing, tuba and euphonium. Home: 3309 35th St NW Washington DC 20016-3141 Office Phone: 202-223-2500. Business E-Mail: ebfrost@leonardfrost.com.

FROST, ELIZABETH ANN MCARTHUR, physician; b. Glasgow, Scotland, Oct. 29, 1938; came to U.S., 1963; d. Robert Thomas and Annie M. (Ross) F.; m. Wallace Capobianco, Sept. 4, 1965 (dec. May 1988); children: Garrett, Ross, Christopher, Neil. MBChB, U. Glasgow, 1961. Diplomate Am. Bd. Anesthesiology, Royal Coll. Ob-Gyn., London. Intern in surgery Royal Infirmary, Glasgow, 1961-62; intern in medicine Victoria Infirmary, Glasgow, 1962; intern in obstetrics Royal Maternity Hosp., Glasgow, 1962-63; resident in internal medicine Englewood (N.J.) Hosp., 1963-64; resident in anesthesiology N.Y. Hosp., N.Y.C., 1964-66; instr. in anesthesiology Albert Einstein Coll. Medicine, Bronx, NY, 1966-68, asst. prof. to assoc. prof., 1968-81, prof. anesthesiology, 1981-91, mem. dept. history of medicine, 1973-91; prof. dept. anesthesiology N.Y. Med. Coll., Valhalla, 1992-99; clin. prof. dept. anesthesiology Mt. Sinai Med. Ctr., N.Y.C., 2000—; attending anesthesiology VA Bronx, 2000—04. Book reviewer New Eng. Jour. of Medicine, 1983—; editor Preanesthetic Assessment, Anesthesiology News, 1984—, Gen. Surgery News, 1991; author/contbr. books; contbr. articles to profl. jours. Mem. N.Y. State Soc. Anesthesiologists, Am. Soc. of Anesthesiologists, Assn. of Univ. Anesthesiologists, Soc. of Neurosurg. Anesthesia and Neurologic Supportive Care, Am. Assn. of Neurol. Surgeons, Anesthesia History Assn. Home: 2 Pondview West Purchase NY 10577 Office Phone: 212-241-7467. Personal E-mail: elzfrost@aol.com.

FROST, ELIZABETH DIANE, academic administrator; d. George Edward and Emily Marcella Higgins, Tebra Ester Higgins (Stepmother); m. Michael Adrian Frost, June 20, 1997; 1 child, Alexander Jonathan. BA, Notre Dame Coll. Md., Balt., 1997; MEd, No. Ariz. U., Flagstaff, 2002. Resident dir. Coll. of Notre Dame of Md., Baltimore, Md., 1997—99; resident dir., counselor, leadership coord. Embry-Riddle Aero. U., Prescott, Ariz., 2000—03; asst. dir. of residence life Frostburg State U., Md., 2003—04; coord. for residence life Ariz. Western Coll., Ariz., 2004—. Recipient Roy McDonald Leadership Award, McDonald Corp., 1993, Outstanding Club Advisor, Embry-Riddle Aero. U., 2001, Regina Russo Hammel '41 Outstanding Recent Grad. Award, Coll. of Notre Dame of Md., 2004. Fellow: RAAZ (chair 2002—03); mem.: Am. Coll. Pers. Assn., Eta Sigma Pi. Avocations: travel, scuba diving, scrapbooks. Office Phone: 928-344-7582.

FROST, ELLEN ELIZABETH, psychologist; b. N.Y.C. d. John Joseph and Josephine Mary (Cornell) F.; m. Jerry Melnick, Jan. 8, 1982; children: Mariel Frost, Matt James. BA magna cum laude, St. John's U., 1969; MA, Fordham U., 1971, PhD, 1982; candidate NYU Postdoctoral Program for Psychotherapy and Psychoanalysis, 1982—84. Cert. Eye Movement Desensitization Reprocessing tng., 2000. Clin. psychology intern Columbia-Presbyn. Psychiat. Inst., N.Y.C., 1972-73; asst. team leader staff psychologist Bensonhurst inpatient unit South Beach Psychiat. Ctr., Bklyn., 1973-75, sr. psychologist, Bensonhurst outpatient dept., 1975-81, assoc. psychologist, supr., 1982-89; dir. Phobia Svc., 1982-89; pvt. practice, 1983—; clin. supr. New Hope Guild, Bklyn., 1983—2000. Faculty L.I. Inst. Mental Health, 1990-97, supr., 1993-97. N.Y. State regents fellow, 1969-72; USPHS fellow, 1969-72. Mem. Am. Psychol. Assn., EMDR Internat. Assoc., Sigma Xi. Office: 200 E 33rd St Apt 25J New York NY 10016-4831 Office Phone: 212-725-0543. Office Fax: 212-725-0543. Personal E-mail: efrostphd@aol.com.

FROST, ELLEN LOUISE, political economist; b. Boston, Apr. 26, 1945; d. Horace Wier and Mildred (Kip) F.; m. William F. Pedersen, Jr., Feb. 2, 1974; 1 son by previous marriage, Jai Kumar Ojha; children: Mark Francis Pedersen, Claire Ellen Pedersen. BA magna cum laude, Radcliffe Coll., 1966; MA, Fletcher Sch. Law and Diplomacy, 1967; PhD, Harvard U., 1972. Teaching fellow, instr. Harvard U., Wellesley Coll., 1969-71; legis. asst. Office of Senator Alan Cranston, Washington, 1972-74; fgn. affairs officer Dept. Treasury, Washington, 1974-77; dep. dir. Office of Internat. Trade Policy and Negotiations, 1977; dep. asst. sec. of def. for internat. econ. and tech. affairs Dept. Def., Washington, 1977-81; dir. govt. programs Westinghouse Electric Corp., Washington, 1981-88; corp. dir., internat. affairs United Techs. Corp., Washington, 1988-91; sr. fellow Inst. for Internat. Econs., Washington, 1992-93, 95-98, vis. fellow; counselor to U.S. Trade Rep., Washington, 1993-95. Author: For Richer, For Poorer: The New U.S.-Japan Relationship, 1987, Transatlantic Trade: A Strategic Agenda, 1997; co-editor: The Global Century, 2001. Trustee Aspen Inst. Berlin, 1990—92. NSF trainee, 1967—69. Mem. Internat. Inst. Strategic Studies, Coun. Fgn. Rels., Phi Beta Kappa.

FROST, EVERETT LLOYD, academic administrator, anthropologist; b. Salt Lake City, Oct. 17, 1942; s. Henry Hoag Jr. and Ruth Salome (Smith) F.; m. Janet Owens, Mar. 26, 1967; children: Noreen Karyn, Joyce Lida. BA in Anthropology, U. Utah, 1965; PhD in Anthropology, U. Oreg., 1970. Field rschr. in cultural anthropology, Taveuni, Fiji, 1968-69; asst. prof. in anthropology Ea. N.Mex. U., Portales, 1970-74, assoc. prof., 1974-76, asst. dean Coll. Liberal Arts and Scis., 1976-78, dean acad. affairs and grad. studies, 1978-80, v.p. for planning and analysis, dean rsch., 1980-91, dean grad. studies, 1983-88, pres., 1991-2001, pres. emeritus, prof. anthropology emeritus, 2001—. Cons., evaluator N. Ctrl. Assn. Accreditation Agy. for Higher Edn., 1989-93—, mem. rev. bd., 1993-95—; commr., past pres. Western Interstate Commn. for Higher Edn., 1993-; pres. Lone Star Athletic Conf. Pres.'s Commn., 1992-93. Chmn. N.Mex. Humanities Coun., 1980-88; mem. N.Mex. Gov.'s Commn. on Higher Edn., 1983-86; mem. exec. bd. N.Mex. First, 1987-92, chmn. rsch. com., 1989-91, exec. bd. emeritus, 1992-; bd. dirs. Roosevelt Gen. Hosp., Portales, 1989-92; pres. bd. dirs. San Juan County Mus. Assn., Farmington, 1979-82; vice chair Portales Pub. Schs. Facilities Com., 1990-91. NDEA fellow, 1969-70; grantee NEW, 1979-80, NSF, 1968-69, Fiji Forbes, Ltd., 1975-76, others. Fellow Am. Anthropol. Assn., Am. Assn. Higher Edn., Soc. Coll. and Univ. Planning, Assn. Social Anthropologists Oceania, Anthrop. Soc. Wash., Sch. Am. Rsch., Western Assn. Grad. Deans, Current Anthropology (assoc.) Polynesian Soc., Phi Kappa Phi. Office Phone: 505-562-2883. Business E-Mail: everett.frost@enmu.edu.

FROST, HELEN MARIE, writer; b. Brookings, SD, Mar. 4, 1949; d. Reuben Bernhard and Jean Elizabeth (Timmons) F.; m. Chad Lawrence Thompson, July 23, 1983; 1 child, Glen Andrew Thompson; 1 stepchild, Lloyd Samuel Thompson. BS, Syracuse U., 1971; MAT, Ind. U., 1994. Cert. in elem. edn., Alaska, Ind., Mass. Tchr. Kilquhanity House Sch., Castle Douglas, Scotland, 1976-78; prin., tchr. Telida (Alaska) Sch., 1981-84; tchr. White Cliff Sch., Ketchikan, Alaska, 1990-91; tchr. English, dir. Writing Ctr. Ind. U./Purdue U., Ft. Wayne, 1996-97. Cons. numerous schs. and orgns., 1990—; mem. Lane Literary Guild, Eugene, Oreg., 1986-89, pres. 1988-89. Poetry tchr. program for at-risk youth Ft. Wayne Dance Collective, 1995—. Mem. Soc. Children's Book Writers and Illustrators, Tchrs. and Writers Collaborative, Poetry Soc. Am. (Robert Winner award 1992, Mary Carolyn Davies award 1993), Acad. Am. poets, Writers Ctr. Indpls. Avocations: crosscountry skiing, gardening, raising and releasing monarch butterflies. Home and Office: 6108 Old Brook Dr Fort Wayne IN 46835-2438 Office Phone: 260-485-1785. E-mail: helenfrost@comcast.net.

FROST, JAMES ARTHUR, former university president; b. Manchester, England, May 15, 1918; arrived in U.S., 1926, naturalized, 1942; s. Harry Arthur and Janet (Wilson) F.; m. Elsie Mae Lorenz, Sept. 14, 1942 (dec.); children: Roger Arthur (dec.), Janet Linda Frost Naleski, Elise Anita Frost Alair. BA, Columbia U., 1940, MA, 1941, PhD, 1949; LLD, So. Conn. State U., 1993. Tchr. Am. history Nutley (NJ) H.S., 1946-47; instr. SUNY Coll.-Oneonta, 1947-49, asst. to pres., 1949-52, dean, 1952-64; assoc. provost acad. planning Ctrl. Adminstrn., SUNY, 1964-65, exec. dean for four yr. colls., 1965-68, vice chancellor for univ. colls., 1968-72; exec. dir. Conn. State Colls., 1972-83; pres. Conn. State U., 1983-85, pres. emeritus, 1985—; instr. Am. history Columbia U., summers, 1947-48; Smith-Mundt prof. Am. history U. Ceylon, 1959-60. Mem. com. on rsch. and devel. Coll. Entrance Exam. Bd., 1973-76; mem. adv. bd. Conn. Rev., 1972-76; mem. commn. on higher edn. Mid. States Assn. Colls. and Secondary Schs., 1966-72; mem. Nat. Coun. Heads of Systems of Pub. Higher Edn., 1976-85, pres., 1979-80, now hon. mem. Author: Life on the Upper Susquehanna, 1783-1860, 1951; (with David M. Ellis, Harold Syrett, Harry J. Carman) A Short History of New York State, 1957, 2d edit., 1967; (with David M. Ellis and William B. Fink) New York: The Empire State, 1961, 5th edit., 1980; (with R.A. Brown, D.M. Ellis, William B. Fink) A History of the United States: The Evolution of a Free People, 1967, 2d edit., 1969, The Establishment of the Connecticut State University, 1965-85; Notes and Reminiscences, 1991, The Country Club of Farmington, Connecticut, 1892-1995, 1996; mem. editl. bd. SUNY Press, 1964-72; contbr. articles on history and edn. to mags. Trustee Conn. State U. Found., Inc., 1984—, bd. dirs., 1983—, treas., 1986—95, pres., 1995—98, treas., 1998—2003, chmn. investment com., 1995—2003; trustee Robinson Sch., Hartford, 1973—77; sponsor Soc. Columbia Scholars, 1997—. Maj. U.S. Army, 1941—46, lt. col. USAFR. Rockefeller grantee, 1959. Fellow NY State Hist. Assn.; mem. Country Club of Farmington, Conn. Congregationalist. Home: 17 Neal Dr Simsbury CT 06070-2801 Office: Conn State U 39 Woodland St Hartford CT 06105-2337

FROST, JEROME KENNETH, lawyer; b. July 4, 1939; s. Carl Kenneth and Madeline May (Michel) F.; m. Carol Ann Brown, May 16, 1967; children: Arthur, Carl, Anya, Jonah, Jerome. BA, Siena Coll., 1962; JD, Boston Coll., 1965. Bar: N.Y. 1965, U.S. Dist. Ct. (no. dist.) N.Y. 1965, U.S. Ct. Appeals (2d cir.) 1982. Assoc. Wagar, Taylor, Howd & Brearton, Troy, N.Y., 1965-66; ptnr. Lee, LeForestier & Frost, Troy, N.Y., 1967-75; sole practice Troy, N.Y., 1976—. Asst. corp. counsel City of Troy, 1970-73, Rensselaer County Pub. Defender, 1995—. Editor Boston Coll. Law Rev., 1965. Player, agt. Lansingburgh Little League, 1982-87. Named one of, Best Lawyers in Am., 2001—02, 2003—; Presdl. scholar, Boston Coll., 1965. Mem. Rensselaer County Bar Assn., Order of Coif, Alpha Sigma Nu, Delta Epsilon Sigma, Alpha Kappa Alpha, Alpha Mu Gamma. Roman Catholic. Avocation: French language. Home: 20 Deepkill Ln Troy NY 12182-9738 Office: 105 Jordan Rd Troy NY 12180-8376 Office Phone: 518-283-3000. E-mail: jfrost@frostfirm.com.

FROST, JERRY WILLIAM, retired religion and history educator, retired library administrator, research scholar; b. Muncie, Ind., Mar. 17, 1940; s. J. Thomas and Margaret Esther (Meredith) F.; m. Susan Vanderlyn Kohler; 1 son, James. BA, DePauw U., Greencastle, Ind., 1962; postgrad., Yale Div. Sch., 1962-63; MA, U. Wis.-Madison, 1965, PhD, 1968. Instr. Vassar Coll., 1967-68, asst. prof. history, 1968-73; assoc. prof. religion Swarthmore Coll., 1973—, prof. religion, 1980—, Howard M. and Charles F. Jenkins prof. of Quaker history and rsch., 1981—2002, sr. rsch. scholar, 2003—05, 2005—. Author: The Quaker Family in Colonial America, 1973, Connecticut Education in Revolutionary Era, 1974, A Perfect Freedom: Religious Liberty in Pennsylvania, 1990, A History of Christian, Jewish, Muslim, Hindu, and Buddhist Perspectives on War and Peace, 2004; co-author: The Quakers, 1988, Christianity: A Social and Cultural History, 1998; editor: The Keithian Controversy in Early Pennsylvania, 1980, Quaker Origins of Antislavery, 1981, Records and Recollections of James Jenkins, 1984, Seeking the Light: Essays in Quaker History, 1987; editor Pa. Mag. of History and Biography, 1981-86; contbr. articles to profl. publs. Bd. dirs. Friends Hist. Assn., 1973—. John Carter Brown Libr. fellow, 1970, Eugene M. Lang fellow, 1980-81, 97, Phila. Ctr. fellow, 1986; U.S. Inst. of Peace grantee, 1992. Mem. Soc. Of Friends. Address: Swarthmore Coll Friends Hist Libr Swarthmore PA 19081

FROST, JOHN ELLIOTT, minerals company executive; b. Winchester, Mass., May 20, 1924; s. Elliott Putnam and Hazel Lavera (Carley) F.; m. Carolyn Catlin, July 12, 1945 (div. 1969); children: John Crocker, Jeffrey Putnam, Teresa Baird, Virginia Nicholl; m. Martha Hicks, June 6, 1969 (div. 1984); m. Catherine Kearns, July 27, 1985 (dec. Jan. 1997); m. Betty Nelson, Sept. 12, 1997. BS, Stanford U., 1949, MS, 1950, PhD, 1965. Geologist Asarco, Salt Lake City, 1951-54; chief geologist, surface mines supt., gen. mgr. Philippine Iron Mines Inc., Larap, Camarines Norte, 1954-60; chief geologist Duval Corp. (Pennzoil Corp.), Tucson, 1961-67; minerals exploration mgr. Exxon Corp., Houston, 1967-71; divsn. minerals mgr. Esso Eastern Inc., 1971-80; sr. v.p. div. Exxon Minerals Co., Houston, 1980-86; pres. Exxon Minerals Internat., Houston, 1980-86, Frost Minerals Internat., Houston, 1986—; v.p. Kalahari Resources, 1996—. Bd. dirs. UnitedEngring. Trustees, NYC, chmn. real estate com., 1986—89, v.p., 1989—91, pres., 1991—93. Mem. adv. bd. Earth Scis., Stanford (Calif.) U., 1983-85; pres. SEG Found., 1984, bd. dirs., 1981-84, 94-98. Served to 1st lt. USAAF, 1943-45, PTO. Fellow Geol. Soc. Am., Soc. Econ. Geologists (pres. 1989-90, councilor 1982-84, program com., chmn. nominating com. 1982); mem. AIME (chmn. edn. com. Soc. Mining Engrs. 1971, Am. Inst. Profl. Geologists; Charles F. Rand medal 1984, Disting. Mem. award 1984, Disting. Svc. award 1991, named to Legion of Honor 2001), Australian Inst. Mining and Metallurgy, Am. Inst. Profl. Geologists, Sigma Xi. Republican. Presbyterian. Home and Office: 602 Sandy Port St Houston TX 77079-2419 Fax: 281-496-3638. Personal E-mail: frost-min@msn.com.

FROST, MARK, director, producer, writer; b. NYC, Nov. 25, 1953; Studied acting, directing and playwriting, Carnegie Tech., Pitts. Television writer Universal Pictures; lit. assoc. Guthrie Theater, Mpls.; playwright-in-residence Midwestern Playwright's Lab. Writer: (TV series) The Six Million Dollar Man, 1974-78, (films) Scared Stiff, 1986, Fantastic Four, 2005; writer, dir: (TV series) Hill Street Blues, 1981-87 (Writers Guild award, Emmy nomination), On the Air, 1992, Storyville, 1992; writer, assoc. prodr.: (films) The Believers, 1987; writer, exec. prodr.: (films) The Repair Shop, 1998, (TV series) Buddy Faro, 1998; exec. prodr.: (films) Hugh Hefner: Once Upon a Time, 1992, (TV series) All Souls, 2001; prodr.: (TV series) American Chronicles, 1990; creator (with David Lynch, TV series) Twin Peaks (Peabody award, 2 Emmy nominations); author: (plays) The Nuclear Family, Heart Trouble, (novels): The List of Seven (Edgar award nominee 1995, Nat. Bestseller 1995), The Six Messiahs, 1995.*

FROST, MARTIN, III, (JONAS MARTIN FROST III), former congressman; b. Glendale, Calif., Jan. 1, 1942; s. Jack and Doris (Marwil) Frost; m. Kathy George Frost; children: Alanna, Mariel, Camille. BA in History, BA in Journalism, U. Mo., 1964; JD, Georgetown U., 1970. Bar: Tex. 1970. Law clk. to Hon. Sarah T. Hughes U.S. Dist. Ct. (No. dist.) Tex., Dallas, 1970-71; legal commentator Sta. KERA-TV, Dallas, 1971-72; assoc. Carrington, Coleman, Sloman & Blumenthal, Dallas, 1972—73; ptnr. Barber & Frost, Dallas, 1974—77; atty. Law Office of Martin Frost, Dallas, 1977—78; mem. 96th-108th Congresses from 24th Tex. dist., Washington, 1979—2005, Select Com. on Homeland Security. Del. Dem. Commn. on Congl. Mailing Stds. Nat. Conv., 1976, 84, 88, 92, 96; coord. North Tex. Carter-Mondale Campaign, 1976; chmn. Dem. Caucus 1999-2003; Tex. del. chmn. Dem. Nat. Conv., mem. rules com.; del. Dem. Nat. Conv., 2000. USAR, 1966—72. Democrat.

FROST, MOLLY SPITZER, Chinese culture educator; b. Washington, Nov. 30, 1944; d. John Brumback and Lucy Ohlinger Spitzer; m. Edmund Bowen Frost, June 18, 1966; children: Julia, Elizabeth, Edmund, Luette. BA in English, Wellesley Coll., 1966; PhD in Chinese Linguistics, Georgetown U., 1982. Rsch. assoc., grant proposal writer George Washington U., 1975-93, asst. adj. prof., 1989-90, 93—. Trustee Cleveland Park Club, Washington, 1980-84, 93-99; trustee, sec. Internat. Student House, Washington, 1991—; trustee, pres. Parents Assn. Maret Sch., 1985-87; bd. dirs. Nat. Child Rsch. Ctr., 1982-84. Avocations: aerobics, swimming, travel. Home: 3309 35th St NW Washington DC 20016-3141 Office: East Asian Langs Dept Rome Hall 462 George Washington U Washington DC 20052-0001 E-mail: msf@gwu.edu.

FROST, ORCUTT WILLIAM, historian, educator; b. Cloquet, Minn., June 3, 1926; s. Orcutt William and Agnes Harriet Frost; m. Mary Denison Bills, June 22, 1954; children: Carol, William, Susan, Robert. BA co-salutatorian, U. Ill., Champaign-Urbana, 1949, MA, 1950, PhD, 1954. Assoc. prof. Willamette U., Salem, Oreg., 1954—63; prof. English Alaska Meth. U., Anchorage, 1963—76; prof. humanities Alaska Pacific U., Anchorage, 1977—91, prof. emeritus, 1991. Acad. dean Alaska Meth. U., Anchorage, 1963—71, 1975—76; exchange prof. Nagoya Gakuin U., Nagoya, Japan, 1969—70; mem. bd. dirs. Alaska Humanities Forum, Anchorage, 1978—84; dir. Bering-Chirikov Conf. Alaska Pacific U., Anchorage, 1991. Author: (Book) Joaquin Miller, 1967, Bering: The Russian Discovery of America, 2003; editor (and co-translator): G. W. Steller Journal of Voyage with Bering, 1988 (Alaskan Historian of Yr., 1989); author: (book) Young Hearn, 1958, Children of the Levee, 1957. V.p. Anchorage Native Welcome Ctr., Alaska, 1964—66; pres. Coun. of Chs., Salem, Oreg., 1958—60; bd. dirs. Alaska Lung Assn., Anchorage, 1975—76. Sgt. U.S. Army, 1944—46, Philippines, Japan. Mem.: Soc. for the History of Discoveries, Phi Beta Kappa. Presbyterian. Achievements include research in the history of Russian America, 1741-1867. Avocation: tennis. Home: 1130 Skyline Dr Medford OR 97504-8586

FROST, PATRICK JOSEPH, musician, studio recording engineer; b. Topeka, Nov. 10, 1956; s. James D. and Roberta Ann Frost; m. Maritza DelCarmen Argibay, Dec. 19, 1982; children: Maxwell, Maria. MusB, Capital U., 1978; MusM, U. Miami, 1981. Musician USAF, Dayton, Ohio, 1984—88; pvt. practice Dayton, 1988—91, Orlando, Fla., 1991—. With USAF, 1984—88, Ohio. Democrat. Roman Catholic. Home: 2613 Shinoak Dr Orlando FL 32837 Personal E-mail: pfrost1@cfl.rr.com.

FROST, PHILIP M., lawyer; b. Pontiac, Mich., Apr. 15, 1948; BA in History, Yale U., 1970; JD magna cum laude, U. Mich., 1973. Bar: Mich. 1973, US Ct. Appeals (6th cir.) 1979. Law clerk to Hon. Philip Pratt US Dist. Ct. (ea. dist.) Mich., 1973-74; assoc. Dickinson, Wright, Moon, Van Dusen & Freeman, Detroit, 1974—81, ptnr., 1981—96; clin. asst. prof. U. Mich. Law Sch., Ann Arbor, 1996—, assoc. dir. Legal Practice Prog. Contbr. articles to law jours. Mem. ABA (sects. litigation and antitrust), Fed. Bar Assn., State Bar Mich. (antitrust, franchising and trade regulation sect., mem. coun. 1987-93, chmn. 1991-92, corp. and fin. sect.), Order of Coif. Office: U Mich Law Sch 414 Hutchins Hall 625 S State St Ann Arbor MI 48109 Office Phone: 734-764-9327, 734-763-9375. E-mail: pmfrost@umich.edu.*

FROST, PHILLIP, pharmaceutical executive, dermatologist; MD, Albert Einstein Coll., Bronx, NY, 1961. Former chmn. dept. of dermatology Mt. Sinai Med. Center, Miami, Fla., 1972—90; chmn. Key Pharms., Miami, Fla., 1972—86; pres. Ivax Corp., 1991—95, founder, chmn., CEO Miami, Fla., 1987—. Chmn. bd. dirs. IVAX Diagnostics, Inc.; bd. dirs. Northrop Grumman Corp (aerospace), Continucare Corp. (healthcare), Ladenburg Thalmann Fin. Svcs., inc. (securities brokerage); bd. governors Am. Stock Exchange. Chmn. bd. of trustees U. of Miami. Office: Ivax Corp 4400 Biscayne Blvd Miami FL 33137-3212*

FROST, RICK, manufacturing executive; BS Indsl. Forest Mgmt., La. State Univ.; MBA, Northwestern State Univ., La. With SD Warren Co.; chmn., CEO Louisiana-Pacific, 2004. Office: Louisiana-Pacific Corp Ste 2000 414 Union St Nashville TN 37219

FROST, ROBERT EDWIN, chemistry professor; b. Gowanda, N.Y., Feb. 1, 1932; s. Sidney Mauthe and Mary Theresa (Bollinger) F.; m. Janice Ruth Young, May 31, 1958; children— Elizabeth Ann, Nancy Lynn, Barbara Jean. BS, Allegheny Coll., 1953; A.M., Harvard, 1955, PhD, 1957. Research chemist B.F. Goodrich Research Center, Brecksville, Ohio, 1957-61; assoc. prof. SUNY at Albany, 1961-64, prof. chemistry, 1964-95, prof. emeritus, 1995. Kettering vis. lectr. U. Ill., Urbana, 1965-66 Mem. Am. Chem. Soc., Phi Beta Kappa, Sigma Xi. Home: 329 W Highland Dr Schenectady NY 12303-5751

FROST, S. DAVID, retired naval officer; b. Southard, Okla., Apr. 21, 1930; s. Chester William and Martha Leah (Weber) F.; m. Dolores Marie Radja, Oct. 17, 1953; children: Kathleen D., David J., Karen T., Mary C. BS, U.S. Naval Acad., 1953; MBA, Stanford U., 1961; student, Naval War Coll., 1964-65. Commd. officer USN, 1953, advanced through grades to rear adm., 1977; jr. officer USS Henrico, 1953-55; with Navy Fin. Center, Cleve., 1956-58; supply officer USS Rankin, 1958-59; asst. planning officer Navy Ordnance Supply Office, Mechanicsburg, Pa., 1961- 64; with Navy Fleet Material Support Office, 1965-68; supply officer USS America, 1968-70; exec. asst. asst. sec. def. (comptroller) Washington, 1970-74; exec. officer Naval Supply Center, Norfolk, Va., 1974-75; comdg. officer Navy Supply Corps Sch., Athens, Ga., 1975-77; dep. comdr. plans, policy and systems devel. Navy Dept., Washington, 1977-78; dep. comptroller of the Navy, 1978-80, 81-83; comptroller, 1980-81; staff dir. for mgmt. Bd. Govs. FRS, 1983-99; ret., 1999.

Pres. Civic League, Virginia Beach, Va., 1969; bd. dirs. N.E. Ga. coun. Boy Scouts Am., 1976-77; bd. dirs. Brent Soc., 1986-92, pres., 1990-91; pres. Oakton Optimist Club, 1986-87, 92-93. Decorated Disting. Service Medal, Legion Merit, Vietnamese Gallantry cross. Mem.: Athens C. of C., Optimists Club, Knights of Malta, Rotary, Phi Delta Theta. Roman Catholic. Home: 10870 Meadow Pond Ln Oakton VA 22124-1446 *My life, both personal and professional, has been guided by allegiance to three primary areas: family, Christian faith, and the nation.*

FROST, SUSAN BETH, producer; b. South Kingston, R.I., Nov. 1, 1955; d. Cyril E. and Martha (Smith) F.; m. Daniel Francis Renn III, Feb. 16, 1991; 1 child, Martha Hope Renn. B in Theater, Smith Coll., 1977. Freelance theatrical mgr., N.Y.C., 1977-84; assoc. prodr. Goodspeed Opera House, East Haddam, Conn., 1985—2005. Chair panel NEA/New Am. Works, Washington, 1991-93; awards panelist Loewe Award/New Dramatists, N.Y.C., 1994, 95; mem. com. Smith Coll./Theatre Alumni, N.Y.C., 1985—, Alliance Music Theatre, N.Y.C., 1991—. Office: Goodspeed Opera House PO Box A East Haddam CT 06423-0281

FROST, WILLIAM LEE, foundation executive; b. Larchmont, N.Y., Nov. 5, 1926; s. Charles and Eva (Rodman) F.; m. Judith Spivak, Oct. 18, 1952 (dec. 1961); children— Rebecca, Hannah; m. Susan Lasersohn, June 16, 1966; children—Abigail, Robert BA, Harvard U., 1947, M.P.A., 1958; LL.B., Yale U., 1951. Assoc. Sherman & Goldring, N.Y.C., 1951-52; fgn. svc. officer Dept. State, Washington, 1952-59; pvt. practice law N.Y.C., 1959—. Exec. Lucius N. Littauer Found., N.Y.C., 1978—, pres., 1985— Contbr. articles to profl. publs. Mem. Pub. Health Coun. State of N.Y., 1975-96; trustee Collegiate Sch., N.Y.C., 1980-94, Radcliffe Coll., Cambridge, Mass., 1985-89, the Brearley Sch., N.Y.C., 1977-80; chmn. bd. dirs. Jewish Telegraphic Agy., N.Y.C., 1989-93, N.Y. Heart Assn., 1985-87; chair N.Y. State Archives Partnership Trust, 1994-97, Yale Law Sch. Fund, 1994-98. With USN, 1945-46, PTO. Hon. curator of Judaica, Harvard Coll. Libr., 1985-96. Mem. Assn. of Bar of City of N.Y., N.Y. County Bar Assn., N.Y. State Bar Assn., Harvard Alumni Assn. (bd. dirs. 1985), Harvard Club, Yale Club. Avocation: walking. Office: Lucius N Littauer Found 60 E 42nd St Ste 4600 New York NY 10165-2999

FROSTIC, FREDERICK LEE, strategic planning and defense policy consultant; b. Detroit; s. Frederick Ralph and Harriet Julia (Stroh) F.; children by previous marriage: Melinda Ann, Frederick Hollis; m. Dianne Kathleen Hughes, May 24, 2003. BS, USAF Acad., 1963; MS in Engring., U. Mich., 1971. Comml. pilot. Fighter pilot USAF, 1963-89, asst. prof. engring. sci., 1971-74, vice comdr. 50th Tactical Fighter Wing Hahn Air Base, Germany, 1984-87, comdr. Northeast Air Def. Sector Griffiss AFB, N.Y., 1987-89; sr. engr., assoc. programming dir. RAND, Santa Monica, Calif., 1989-94; dept. asst. sec. def. Dept. Def., Washington, 1994-97; prin. Booz, Allen & Hamilton, Inc., McLean, Va., 1997—. Mem. Long Range Airpower Panel, 1998—. Author: The New Calculus, 1994. Named Outstanding Young Man Am., 1970. Democrat. Presbyterian. Avocations: sports, reading. Home: 1357 Heritage Oak Way Reston VA 20194 Office: Allen & Hamilton Inc 8283 Greensboro Dr Mc Lean VA 22102-3802 E-mail: frostic_fred@bah.com.

FROSTICK, ROBERT MAURICE, secondary school educator; b. Charleston, W.Va., Aug. 31, 1954; s. Frederick Charles and Florence (Barber) F. BS, W.Va. U., 1977; MA, W.Va. U. Grad. Studies, 1989. Cert. permanent profl. 5-12 tchr., W.Va. Tchr. Gauley Bridge (W.Va.) Mid. Sch., 1977-84, Geary Sch., Left Hand, W.Va., 1986, Marmet (W.Va.) Jr. H.S., 1988-90; sci. dir. Sunrise Mus., Charleston, 1984-86; tchr. Horace Mann Jr. H.S., Charleston, 1990-97, John Adams Jr. H.S., Charleston, 1997—2002, George Washington H.S., 2002—. Instr. sci. W.Va. State Coll., Institute, 1984—, W.Va. Grad. Coll., Institute, 1990—, W.Va. Inst. Tech., Montgomery, 1992—; trainer AIMS Found., Fresno, Calif., 1990—, project wild, 1990—, Bell Atlantic World Sch., 1994—, steering com. project WET, 1995—; curriculum developer W.Va. Dept. Edn., Charleston, 1982, mem. videotape materials selection com., 1990; curriculum developer Roane County Bd. Edn., Spencer, W.Va., 1987; mem. W.Va. Commn. for Porfl. Tchg. Stds., 1997—, W.Va. Licensure Appeals panel, 1997-2002, W.Va. State Sci. Textbook Selection com., 1999, tchr. adv. bd. PBS, 1999-2000, tchr. adv. panel Life Quest, 2005. Bd. dir. Cave Conservancy of Vas., 1984-86. Recipient Gov.'s Cmty. Svc. award State of W.Va., 1982, Presdl. Conservation Edn. award, 1982, 83, award of honor Presdl. awards for excellence in math. and sci. tchg., 1993, Outstanding Young Educator Jaycees, 1994, First award BEAMS Acad., 1994, Golden Apple Achiever award Ashland Oil, 1995, Rising Star award STARS Tech. Competition, 1997, N.E. Region winner Tech. and Learning Tchr. of Yr., 1997, Svc. Recognition award PBS, 2000; named Tech. and Learning Tchr. of Yr., 1996, 97; Christa McAuliffe fellow, 1993. Mem. NSTA, Geol. Soc. Am. (award of excellence 1993), Nat. Speleological Soc., Nat. Assn. Earth Sci. Tchrs., W.Va. Sci. Tchrs. Assn., Kanawha Valley Astron. Soc. Avocations: exploring caves, photography, computers, astronomy. Home: PO Box 6885 Charleston WV 25362-0885 Office Phone: 304-348-7729. E-mail: bfrostic@access.k12.wv.us.

FROST-KNAPPMAN, (LINDA) ELIZABETH, publishing executive, editor, writer; b. Washington, Oct. 1, 1943; d. Edward Laurie and Lorena (Ameter) Frost; m. Edward William Knappman, Nov. 6, 1965; 1 child, Amanda. BA, George Washington U., 1965; postgrad., U. Wis., 1966, NYU, 1966. Editor Natural History Press, N.Y.C., 1967-69, William Collins and Sons, London, 1970-71; sr. editor Doubleday and Co., N.Y.C., 1972-80, William Morrow and Co., Inc., N.Y.C., 1980-82; founder, pres. New Eng. Pub. Assocs. Inc., Chester, Conn., 1982—. Lectr. New Eng. colls. and univs. Author: The World Almanac of Presidential Quotations, 1993, The ABC-CLIO Companion to Women's Progress in America, 1994 (Outstanding Acad. Book-Reference of Yr. award ALA), The Quotable Lawyer, 1986, 1998, Women Suffrage in America: An Eyewitness History, 1992, Courtroom Dramas, 3 vols., 1997; gen. editor: (CD-ROM) American Journey: Women in America, 1994, Women's Rights on Trial, 1998. Mem. Assn. Authors Reps., Authors Guild. Avocations: knitting, tennis, travel, reading, piano. Office: New Eng Pub Assocs Inc PO Box 5 Chester CT 06412-0005 Office Phone: 860-345-7323. E-mail: elizabeth@nepa.com.

FROT-COUTAZ, CECILE, television producer; b. Chambery, France, Apr. 18, 1966; m. M. Eliot Charles, Dec. 29, 2001; 1 child, Amelie. BA in Bus., ESSEC, 1988; MBA, INSEAD, 1994. Assoc. Mercer Mgmt. Consulting, London, 1988—93; exec. corp. strategy Pearson TV, London, 1994—98, dep. chief exec. officer So. Europe, mng. dir. France Paris, 1998—2000, head digital media, 2000—01; exec. v.p. comml. and ops. FremantleMedia N.Am., LA, 2001—02, COO, Santa Monica, Calif., 2002—, exec. prodr. Am. Idol, 2002—. Office: Fremantle Media Productions North America Inc 2700 Colorado Ave Ste 450 Santa Monica CA 90404

FROTHINGHAM, THOMAS ELIOT, pediatrician; b. Boston, June 21, 1926; s. Channing and Clara Morgan (Rotch) F.; m. Phyllis Mary Steiner, June 12, 1954 (div. 1983); children: Phyllis Eliot, Thomas Dean, Benjamin Rotch, David Griffith; m. Barbara Mathis, Dec. 28, 1987 (div. 2002). Student, Harvard U., 1944-46, MD, 1951. Intern Bellevue Hosp., N.Y.C., 1951-52; resident, rsch. fellow in infectious diseases Children's Hosp., Boston, 1955-59; asst. prof. epidemiology Tulane U. Med. Sch., 1959—60; assoc. mem. Pub. Health Rsch. Inst., City of N.Y., 1960-61; asst. prof., then assoc. prof. tropical pub. health Sch. Pub. Health Harvard U., 1961-69; pediatrician Corvallis (Oreg.) Clinic, 1969-73; prof. pediat., family and cmty. medicine Duke U. Med. Ctr., 1973-94, prof. emeritus, 1994—. Contbr. articles to profl. jours. Co-founder Ctr. for Child and Family Health, N.C., 1996—. With USNR, 1944-46, 52-55. Mem. Am. Soc. Tropical Medicine and Hygiene, Am. Acad. Pediatrics. Office: Ctr for Child and Family Health Ste 100 3518 Westgate Dr Durham NC 27707 Personal E-mail: tefro@mindspring.com.

FROULA, BARBARA SUE, artist, architect; b. Hot Springs, Ark., Nov. 30, 1955; d. James C. and Helen B. F.; m. Timothy W. Adams, Sept. 3, 1983. BArch, Auburn U., 1978. Cert. Royal Danish Acad. Fine Arts, Copenhagen, 1976-77; registered architect, Colo. Instr. Auburn (Ala.) U., 1978-79; architect Baer & Hickman, Denver, 1979-80; project adminstr. bldgs. divsn. Colo. Dept. Adminstrn., Denver, 1981; owner Barbara Froula Studio Gallery, Denver. One-woman shows include Trinity Place, 1983, Women's Bank, Denver, 1983, Boetcher Concert Hall, Denver, 1983, 84, Denver Ctr. Cinema, 1984, Savageau Gallery, Denver, 1988; group shows include Driscol Gallery, Denver, 1984, 85, Foothills Art Ctr., Golden, Colo., 1984, 85, Royce Galleries, Denver, 1984, 85, Temple Ctr., Denver, 1985, Art by Architects, 1981, 82, Cogswell Gallery, Vail, Colo., 1987, 88, Rocky Mt. Nat. Watermedia Exhibn., 2003; author: (with Engelken and Huth) Undiscovered Denver Dining, 1982; illustrator: Beyond Undiscovered Dining, 1983, Prague-Between History and Dreams, 2004; (posters) Historic Denver Dining, 1983, 84, 85 (award Honor 1985), Temple Ctr., 1985, The Mayan, 1985, An Afternoon in the City, 1985, Westin Hotel, Tabor Ctr., 1985, Historic Boulder, 1985, Westin La Paloma, Tucson, 1986, Rotary Club Golden, 1986, A Visit to 17th Ave., 1986, A Visit to San Rafael, 1988, Denver's Larimer Sq., 1989, San Francisco: Cityscape, Chinatown, The Marina, 1988; (bookcover) Denver: The City Beautiful, 1987, How to Unscramble Your Nest Egg, Hilltop Heritage, Country Club Heritage Co-sponsor, instr. Hmong Refugee Program, Denver, 1980. Recipient Best of Show award Denver Symphony Guild, 1983; scholar Rotary Internat. Found., 1976. Mem. Foothills Art Ctr., AIA (medal award 1978, juror's award 1982), Colo. Lawyers Arts (poster composite award 1983), Denver Art Mus., Hist. Denver, Inc., Nat. Trust Hist. Preservation, Colo. Hist. Soc., Friends of Mayan. Democrat. Roman Catholic. Studio: 186 S Pennsylvania St Denver CO 80209

FROULA, JAMES DEWAYNE, honor society administrator; b. Oak Park, Ill., May 17, 1945; s. James Clarence and Helen Barbara (Tanana) F.; m. Barbara Jean Leftwich, June 8, 1968; children: James Matthew, Anna Katherine. BSME, U. Tenn., 1967, MS, 1968. Lic. profl. engr., Tenn. Engr. IBM Corp., Lexington, Ky., 1970-74, engring. mgr. Boulder, Colo., 1974-82; exec. dir., sec.-treas., editor Tau Beta Pi, Knoxville, Tenn., 1982—; pres. Assn. Coll. Honor Socs., 1991-93. Editor: The Bent of Tau Beta Pi, 1982—; patentee magnetic brush roll. 1st lt. U.S. Army, 1968-70, Vietnam. Decorated Bronze Star; fellow NSF, 1967-68. Mem. ASME, NSPE (bd. dirs. Knoxville chpt. 1988-94, Outstanding Engr. 1994), Coun. Engring. and Sci. Soc. Execs., Tenn. Soc. Profl. Engrs. (chair divsn. profl. engrs. in edn. practice 1993-96), Am. Assn. Engring. Socs. (awards com. 1997-2000). Roman Catholic. Avocations: mountain climbing, hiking. Office: Tau Beta Pi PO Box 2697 Knoxville TN 37901-2697

FROW, RICHARD G., retired librarian; b. Miami, Fla., May 7, 1932; s. Franklin John Frow and Edith M. Pearce. AB in French, magna cum laude, U. Miami, 1954; MA in Libr. Sci., Fla. State U., 1961. Cert. libr. and tchr. social studies Fla. Tchr., libr. Dade County Pub. Schs., Miami, 1957—58; head libr. Miami Jackson H.S., 1958—64; summer intern libr. econs., divsn. NY Pub. Libr, NYC, 1962; asst. editor Pub. Affairs Info. Svc. Bull., N.Y.C., 1964—77; libr. planning dept. Metro-Dade County, Miami, 1978—79; head ref. libr. urban affairs sect. Miami-Dade Pub. Libr. Sys., 1979—92; ret., 1992. Editor: Urban Affairs Newsletter, 1979—92. Mem.: Am. Horticultural Soc., Am. Assn. Individual Investors, Nat. Audubon Soc., Am. Orchid Soc., Nat. Trust for Hist. Preservation, Phi Eta Sigma, Pi Delta Phi, Kappa Delta Pi, Beta Phi Mu, Phi Kappa Phi. Democrat. Baptist. Avocations: gardening, reading, music, studying foreign languages. Home: 406 SE 28 Ave Ocala FL 34471

FROWNER, BYRON, electrical engineer, researcher; s. Benjamin Franklin and Mary Magdalene Frowner; children: Blair, Ian, Sydny, Emanuel. BS in Elec. Engring., CUNY, 1959. Gen. engr. U.S. Navy, Bklyn., 1959—69; asst. elec. engr. N.Y.C. Transit Authority, Bklyn., 1970—78, Dept. Environ. Protection, N.Y.C., 1980—84; sr. project mgr. Health & Hosps. Corp., N.Y.C., 1985—91; sr. constrn. engr. N.Y. Power Authority, White Plains, 1994—2002; ret. Author: Special Relativity: Einstein's Error, 1994. Mem.: AAAS, N.Y. Acad. Scis. Avocations: history, sports. Personal E-mail: bfrowner@aol.com.

FRUCHER, MEYER S. (SANDY FRUCHER), stock exchange executive; BS in govt., Columbia U.; MPA, John F. Kennedy Sch. Govt., Harvard U. Chief labor negotiator State of N.Y., 1978—83; pres. and CEO Battery Park Authority, N.Y.C., 1984—88; exec. v.p. devel. Olympia and York (now World Fin. Properties, Inc.), 1988—96; chmn., CEO Phila. Stock Exch., 1998—. Mgmt. cons. Chmn. bd. Mass. Mus. Contemporary Art. Office: Phila Stock Exch 1900 Market St Philadelphia PA 19103*

FRUCHTER, ROSALIE KLAUSNER, retired elementary school educator; b. Bklyn., May 1, 1940; d. Marcus and Sarah (Twersky) Klausner; m. Marvin Fruchter, Aug. 15, 1970; children: Marcus, Alexander. BA, Bklyn. Coll., 1960; MA, Nat. Louis U., Evanston, Ill., 1988; postgrad., U. Chgo., 1962-65, Northeastern Ill. U., 1997—. Cert. Irlen Syndrome scotopic sensitivity syndrome screener 2001. Tchr. William H. Ray Sch./Chgo. Bd. Edn., 1961—2003; lead tchr. primary lang. arts structured curriculum project Chgo. Bd. Edn., 1997—2003; tchr. reading resource Dixon Elem. Sch., 1999—2003; ret.; pvt. reading tutor, 2004—. Cons. math project U. Chgo., 1985—87; presenter in field. Contbr. to math book: One Minute Math, 1990, (Chgo. pub. schs. writing program) Read Write Well, Lesson Resource Book, 1998, Handbook of Kids Primary Assessment Tools, 1998. Bd. dirs. Jewish Community Ctr. of Hyde Park, Chgo., 1978-84, Congregation KAM Isaiah Israel, Chgo., 1984-91, 93—; co-founder Nurit chpt. Hadassah, Hyde Park, 1980; mem. Hyde Park Neighborhood Club, Chgo., 1975—; mem. adv. bd. Humana Michael Reese Hyde Park HMO. Recipient Kate Maremont award Chgo. PTA, 1980, award Chgo. Found. for Edn., 1994; Chgo. Found. for Edn. grantee, 1990, 92, 93, 94, Oppenheimer grantee, 1991. Mem. ASCD, Nat. Coun. Tchrs. Math., Nat. Coun. Tchrs. English, Acad. Econ. Edn., Ill. Sci. Tchrs. Found., Chgo. Area Reading Assn. (bd. dirs. 1997—, treas. 1998—, pres.-elect 1999-2000, pres. 2000-01, past pres. 2001-02, mem. co-chair 2002-03), Chgo. Tchrs. Union, Internat. Reading Assn., Ill. Resource Coun., Pi Lambda Theta. Democrat. Avocations: embroidery, art, cross country skiing, walking, reading, history, drama, judaica. Home: 5434 S Hyde Park Blvd Chicago IL 60615-5802 Office Phone: 773-684-2488. E-mail: rfruchter@sbcglobal.net.

FRUCHTMAN, STEVEN MARTIN, physician; b. N.Y.C., Apr. 7, 1951; s. Harry and Anna F.; m. Miriam Baker, Aug. 18, 1985; 1 child, Genna BA, Cornell U., 1973; MD, N.Y. Med. Coll., 1977. Intern, then resident Downstate Med. Ctr., Bklyn., 1977-81; dir. sickle cell program Mt. Sinai Hosp., N.Y.C., 1986-90, assoc. prof. medicine, 1986—, dir. bone marrow transplantation, 1990—; dir hematology Tibotec, Bridgewater, NJ, 2004—. Author: Polychythemia Vera, 1991. Mem. ACP, Am. Coll. Hematology. Avocation: sports. Home: 449 A Ridge Rd Englewood NJ 07631-1120 Office: Tibotec 430 W Hwy 22 E Bridgewater NJ 08807 Office Phone: 908-541-4332. Personal E-mail: fruchs@optonline.net.

FRUDAKIS, ANTHONY PARKER, sculptor, educator; b. Bellow Falls, VT, July 30, 1953; s. Evangelos and Virginia Frudakis. Student, Duke U., 1972—73; cert. of completion, Pa. Acad. Fine Arts, 1976; MFA, U. Pa., 1992. Tchr. Fashion Inst. NY, NYC, 1982, Atlantic CC, Mays Landing, NJ, 1990—91; assoc. prof. Hillsdale Coll., Mich., 1991—; owner Frudakis Studio, 1976—. Tchr. Frudakis Acad. Fine Arts, Phila., 1976, Frudakis Studio, 1976—, Fashion Inst. Tech., N.Y.C., 1982, Atlantic C.C., Mays Landing, N.J., 1990-91; assoc. prof. Hillsdale (Mich.) Coll., 1991—. One-person shows include Ocean City (N.J.) Cultural Ctr., 1992, Sturgis (Mich.) Civic Ctr., 1992, Hillsdale Coll, 1999, Flatlanders Blissfield, Mich., 2004; exhibited in group shows NAD, N.Y.C., 1988, 91, 2003, Allied Artists Am., N.Y.C., 1982, Renaissance Gallery, Phila., 1988, Gloucester County Coll., Deptford, N.J., 1989, Grand Cen. Art Gallery, N.Y.C., 1990, 92, Toledo (Ohio) Art Mus., 1994, Nat. Scultpure Soc. N.Y., N.Y.C., 1997, Hillsdale Coll., 1997, 2001; represented in permanent collections Brookgreen (S.C.) Gardens Mus.; commd. Atlantic County Libr., Hammanton, N.J., 1983, Bally's Hotel, Atlantic City, N.J., 1986, Cape May Ct. House, N.J., 1989, Athens Sq., N.Y.C., 1993, Hillsdale Coll., 1992, 95 (Bronze award), St. Catherine's, Concord, Mich., 1996, St. Anthony's, Hillsdale, 1996, Adrian, Mich., 1998, St. Mary's Cathedral, Saginaw, Mich., 1999, East Lansing, Mich., 2000; featured in publs. including Masters of American Sculpture, N.Y. Art Review, Sculpture. Recipient Stewardson prize Pa. Acad. Fine Arts, 1974, 1st prize for sculpture N.J. State Juried Art Show, 1979, M.B. Hexter award Allied Artists of Am., 1982, L. Miselman prize Nat. Sculpture Soc., 1986, Gloria medal, 1983, Gold medal, 1982, Lantz award, 1978, Best Portrait award, 1977, Daniel Chester French award; Dolfinger MacMahon tuition scholar Pa. Acad. Fine Arts, 1973; NSS tuition scholar Pa. Acad. Fine Arts, 1974; Harold Bache Found. traveling grantee, 1975. Fellow NAD (Artist Fund prize 1991), Nat. Sculpture Soc. Office: Hillsdale College 33 East College Hillsdale MI 49242 Studio: 115 Cold Spring Cir Hillsdale MI 49242-1540 Office Phone: 517-437-7571. E-mail: tony.frudakis@ac.hillsdale.edu, tonyfrudakis@comcast.net.

FRUDAKIS, EVANGELOS WILLIAM, sculptor; b. Rains, Utah, May 13, 1921; s. William and Christina (Legerakis) F.; children— Anthony, Jennifer; m. Gerd Hesness, 1982 Student, Greenwich Work Shop, N.Y.C., 1935-39, Beaux Arts Inst. Design, 1940-41, Pa. Acad. Fine Arts, 1941-42, 45-49, Am. Acad. in Rome, 1950-52. Founder, instr. Frudakis Acad. Fine Arts, Phila., 1976-90. One-man shows include Atlantic City Art Center, 1956, 61, Woodmere Art Gallery, 1957, 62, Phila. Art Alliance, 1958, Pa. Acad. Fine Arts, 1962, Briarcliff Coll. Mus. Art, 1975, numerous group shows, 1940—, including, Pa. Acad. Fine Arts anns., N.A.D. anns., Am. Acad. in Rome, Audubon Artists, Phila. Mus. Art, Allied Artists Am., Nat. Arts Club, Pennsylvania Treasures show, Gov.'s Mansion, 1982; represented in permanent collections Pa. Acad. Fine Arts, Lehigh Valley Art Alliance, Woodmere Art Gallery, also pvt. collections; tchr., demonstrator sculpture, Nat. Acad. Design, N.Y.C., 1969-76, sculptor John F. Kennedy meml. monument Atlantic City Conv. Hall, 1964, Statesmen in Medicine Awards; portrait works Brian Brewer Blades, 1969, Melvin R. Laird, 1970, Barnes Woodhall, 1971, Aharon Katzir and Ephraim Katzir for Weizmann Inst., Israel, 1978, Dr. William Feinbloom, Pa. Coll. Optometry, 1989, Stephen E. Hyde, Trump Castle, Atlantic City, 1990; coins and medals Ted Shawn and Ruth St. Denis medal, Jacobs Pillow, Mass., Gemini Space Flights Nat. Commemorative Soc, 1966, Dacron medallion, Dupont, Wilmington, Del., Capt. James Cook medal, Hawaii Festival, Dolly Madison coin, medal Société Commemorative de Femmes Celebres, 1967, Joseph Brant coin, Internat. Fraternal Commemorat Soc., 1968, Paul Lawrence Dunbar medal, Am. Negro Commemorative Soc., 1969, St. Damasus I medal, Cath. Commemorative Soc., Life of Christ series 12 coin medals, 1968-70, Alfred the Great medal, Britannia Commemorative Soc., 1970, Prince of Peace medal, Cath. Commemorative Soc., Scapular medal, Cath. Art Guild, 1970, St. John the 4th Apostle 12 Apostle series, Cath. Commemorative Medal Soc., 1970, John Quincy Adams and Lillian Wald medals, Hall of Fame for Great Ams., 1971, Brian Brewer Blades award medal Statesmen in Medicine, 1970, Richardson Dilworth Meml. Plaque, Phila., 1978, Deng Xioping Portrait Medal, 1979, Fishing Bear fountain, Phila. Zool. Gardens., The Signer, Independence Nat. Hist. Park, Phila., 1982, Naiad Fountain, Phila. Civic Ctr., 1982, Statue of Liberty Greek Relief, Ellis Island, 1986; Welcome Fountain, The Ritten House, Phila., 1989, The Minute Man, Nat. Guard Bld., Washington, 1991, 9' Minute Man, Nat. Guard Readiness Ctr., Arlington, Va., 1995, Reaching Fountain, Brookgreen Gardens, S.C., 1997; mem. coins and medals Art Commn., Atlantic City, Served with AUS, World War II, ETO. Decorated Bronze Battle Star (3); recipient 2 1st prizes Greenwich Work Shop 1939, Beaux Art Inst. 1941, 1st Julian B. Slevin prize Pa. Acad. Fine Arts 1941, Stimson prize 1947, Stewardson prize 1947, Cresson European scholarship 1947, spl. citation achievement 1948, 1st hon. mention fellowship 1948, Fellowship gold medal 1949, 55, 56, Henry Scheidt Meml. scholarship 1949, 1st hon. mention Prix de Rome 1942, Prix de Rome 1950, 51, Helen Foster Barnett prize N.A.D. 1948, Thomas R. Proctor prize 1957, Eben Demarest Trust Fund prize 1949, Louis Comfort Tiffany scholarship 1949, Sculpture House award Allied Artists Am. 1959, best portrait sculpture award Nat. Sculpture Soc.-Nat. Art Club 1961, John Gregory award Nat. Sculpture Soc. 1963, Nat. Fountain Competition award Little Rock 1965, Elizabeth N. Watrous gold medal N.A.D., N.Y.C. 1968, Dessie Greer prize N.A.D., N.Y.C. 1970, Artists Fund prize 1975, 77, 90, Therese and Edwin H. Richards prize Nat. Sculpture Soc., N.Y. 1972, Gold medal 1972, Francis Keally prize 1974, Herbert Adams Meml. medal 1976), N.S.S. Meiselman prize, 1981; gold medal NAD, 1984 N.A. Fellow Pa. Acad. Fine Arts, Am. Acad. in Rome, Nat. Sculpture Soc. (council), founding mem. Acad. Scis. Phila.; mem. Allied Artists Am.; hon. men. Am. Inst. Commemorative Art. Address: 312 Valley Dr Kerrville TX 78028-3910 Personal E-mail: gareth@ktc.com.

FRUDAKIS, ZENOS ANTONIOS, sculptor, artist; b. San Francisco, July 7, 1951; s. Vasili and Kassiani (Alexis) F. Student, Pa. Acad. Fine Arts, Phila., 1973-76; BFA, U. Pa., 1982, MFA, 1983. Co-adj. prof. sculpture and drawing Rutgers U., 1984-85, 1993. Guest lectr. anatomy and sculpture Med. Coll. Pa., Phila., 1986-87; invited artist Utsukushi-Ga-Hara Open Air Mus., Japan, 1990. Exhibitions include Nat. Sculpture Soc., 1979—97, Allied Artists Am., N.Y.C., 1980—81, NAD, 1980, 1984, 1986, 1990, 1997, Pa. Acad. Fine Arts, 1981, Inst. Contemporary Art, Phila., 1981—83, Rutgers U., 1984—86; sculptor (numerous commd. works including) Air Force Meml., Arlington, Va., Richard Tufts Payne Stewart, Pinehurst, N.C., Frank Rizzo, Richardson Dilworth, Phila., Freedom, GSK, 16th Vine Sts, Phila., Ga. Gov. Ellis Arnall, Atlanta, Elephant Fountain, Burlington, N.J., 1993, Mike Schmidt, Steve Carlton, Richie Ashburn, Robin Roberts for Citizens Bank Pk. Recipient Hakone award, Rodin Grand prize Hakone Open Air Mus., Japan, 1990; inducted into Bobby Jones and Arnold Palmer, Ga. Golf Hall of Fame; devel. grantee Nat. Endowment for Arts, 1985, USIA travelling grantee, 1988-89. Fellow Nat. Sculpture Soc. (bd. dirs. 1988—, Art-in-Architecture award 1990, editor pro-tem Nat. Sculpture Rev. 1991-2002); mem. NAD (acad.), Academia Internat. per L'Unita della Cultura (Rome, academician), Lotos Club.

FRUE, WILLIAM CALHOUN, lawyer; b. Pontiac, Mich., Dec. 29, 1934; s. William Calhoun and Evelyn Laura Frue; m. Eloise Saunders, June 22, 1956 (div. Dec. 1989); m. Jane Torres Fletcher, Dec. 30, 1989; children: William C. III, John C., Michael C., Victoria. BA, Washington & Lee U., 1956; LLB, U. N.C., 1960. Bar: N.C. 1960, U.S. Dist. Ct. (we. dist.) N.C. 1961, U.S. Tax Ct. 1968, U.S. Ct. Appeals (4th cir.) 1988. Rsch. asst. Inst. of Govt., Chapel Hill, N.C., 1958-60; assoc. Wright & Shuford, Asheville, N.C., 1961-69; ptnr. Shuford, Frue & Sluder, Asheville, 1969-72, Shuford, Frue & Best, Asheville, 1973-84, The Frue Law Firm, Asheville, 1984—. Editor Popular Govt. mag., 1958-60. Chmn. Asheville Police Retirement Fund, 1973-83, Morehead Scholarship Selectincom., 1965-90, Asheville Planning and Zoning Commn., 1982-92. Mem. N.C. Bar Assn., Buncombe County Bar Assn., (sec., v.p. 1978-92), Trout Unl d. (N.C. coun. 1965). Democrat. Episcopalian. Avocations: fishing, camping. Office: PO Box 7627 Asheville NC 28802-7627 Office Phone: 828-258-0570.

FRUEHWALD, KRISTIN G., lawyer; b. Sidney, Nebr., May 15, 1946; d. Chris U. and Mary E. (Boles) Bitner; m. Michael R. Fruehwald, Feb. 23, 1980; children: Laurel Elizabeth, Amy Marie. BS with highest distinction in History, U. Nebr., 1968; JD summa cum laude, Ind. U., 1975. Bar: Ind. 1975, U.S. Dist. Ct. (so. dist.) Ind. 1975. Assoc. Barnes & Thornburg, Indpls., 1975-81, ptnr., 1982—. Spkr. in field. Contbr. articles to profl. jours. Trustee The Orchard Sch., 1993—99, chmn., 1997—98, bd. govs., 2005—; bd. dirs. Indpls. Parks Found., 1995—2000, Arts Ind., 1994—98, Ind. Continuing Legal Edn. Forum, 1993—2001, pres., 2000—01; bd. dirs. James Whitcomb Riley Meml. Assn., 1995—, treas., 2000—; bd. dirs. Planned Giving Group Ind., Fedn. Cmty. Defenders, Inc., 1993—99, pres., 1999—2001; bd. dirs . Ind. affiliate Am. Heart Assn., 1977—81, vice chmn. Marion County chpt., 1981; bd. trustees Ctrl. Ind. Land Trust, 2005—. Fellow: ABA (chmn. distributable net income subcom 1985—91, mem. real property, probate and trust sect.), Ind. State Bar Assn. (chmn. probate, trust and real property sects. 1987—88, mem. ho. of dels. 1987—, bd. mgrs. 1989—90, treas. 1996—97, chair ho. of dels. 1998—99, pres. 2001—02, mem. sect. taxation), Ind. Bar Found. (bd. dirs. 2003—, bd. govs. 2004—), Am. Coll. Trust and Estate Counsel (chmn. Ind. state laws com. 1992—95); mem.: Indpls. (Ind.) Bar Found. (bd. dirs. 1992—, chmn. 1997—99), Ind. Code Study Commn., Internat. Assn. Fin. Planners, Indpls. Estate Planning Coun., Indpls. Bar Assn.

(chmn. estate planning and adminstrn. sect. 1982—83, chmn. long range fin. planning com. 1988—89, pres. 1993). Office: Barnes & Thornburg 11 S Meridian St Indianapolis IN 46204-3535 Office Phone: 317-231-7245. Business E-Mail: kris.fruewald@btlaw.com.

FRUG, GERALD E., law educator; b. 1939; AB, U. Calif.-Berkeley, 1960; JD, Harvard U., 1963. Bar: Calif. 1964, N.Y. 1969. Frank Knox fellow London Sch. Econs., 1963-64; law clk. to chief justice Supreme Ct. Calif., 1964-65; assoc. Heller, Ehrman, White & McAuliffe, San Francisco, 1965-66; spl. asst. to chmn. EEOC, 1966-69; assoc. Cravath, Swaine & Moore, N.Y.C., 1969-70; gen. counsel Health Services Adminstrn., N.Y.C., 1970-72, 1st dep. adminstr., 1972-73, adminstr., 1973-74; assoc. prof. U. Pa. Law Sch., Phila., 1974-78, prof., 1978-81, Harvard U. Law Sch., 1981-94, Samuel R. Rosenthal prof. law, 1994-2000, Louis D. Brandeis prof., 2000—. Mem. Phi Beta Kappa. Office: Law Sch Harvard U Cambridge MA 02138

FRÜHBECK DE BURGOS, RAFAEL, conductor; b. Burgos, Spain, Sept. 15, 1933; s. Guillermo and Estefania (Ochs) Frühbeck de Burgos; m. Maria Carmen Martinez, Dec. 21, 1959; children: Rafael, Gema. Attended, Bilbao Conservatory, Madrid Conservatory, HS for Music, Munich; student, U. Munich, Richard Strauss Price, 1958, U. Madrid; D (hon.), U. Navarra, Pamplona, Spain, 1994, U. Burgos, 1998. Chief condr. Mcpl. Orch., Bilbao, Spain, 1958—62, Nat. Orch., Madrid, 1962—78, gen. music dir. Dusseldorf Symphony, Germany, 1966—71, music dir. Montreal Symphony, Can., 1974—76, Vienna Symphony, Austria, 1991—96, Deutsche Oper, Berlin, 1992—97, Rundfunk Symphony Orch. Berlin, 1994—2000, RAI Nat. Symphony Orch., Turin, Italy, 2001—, chief condr. Dresden Philharm. Orch., Germany, 2004—, prin. guest condr. Nat. Symphony, Washington, 1980—90, Yomiuri Nippon Symphony Orch., Tokyo, 1980—90, Dresden Philharm. Orch., 2003—04, hon. condr. Yomiuri Nippon Symphony Orch., Tokyo, 1991, Nat. Orch., Madrid, 1998. Decorated Encomienda Orden de Alfonso X El Sabio (Spain), Gran Cruz Orden del Merito Civil (Spain); recipient Prize of Musical Interpretation, Larios CEOE, Madrid, 1992, Ehrenmedaille in Gold, Burgermeister, Vienna, 1995, State of Vienna, Austria, 2000, Gold medal to the Civil Merit of Austria, 1996, Gold medal, Internat. Gustav Mahler Soc., Vienna, 1996, Fundacion Guerrero prize of Spanish Music, Madrid, 1996, Big Cross to the Civil Merit, Republic of Germany, Berlin, 2001, Gold medal to the Labour Merit, Madrid, 2004. Mem.: Real Acad. de Bellas Artes de San Fernando (Madrid). Office: care Musiespaña José Marañón 10 E-28010 Madrid Spain also: CAMI Columbia Artists Mgmt Inc 165 W 57th St New York NY 10019-2276 also: care Harold Holt Ltd 122 Wigmore St London W1H ODJ England

FRUITMAN, FREDERICK HOWARD, investment banker; b. Toronto, Oct. 8, 1950; s. Herbert Lance and Libby (Kamin) Fruitman; m. Marlin Sue Potash, Nov. 21, 1981 (div. Dec. 1996); children: Laura, Hilary; m. Susan Beth Levinsohn, Apr. 19, 1998; 1 child, Charles. SB, MIT, 1972; BA, Oxford (Eng.) U., 1974, MA, 1981; LLB, U. Toronto, 1976; MBA, Harvard U., 1981. Assoc. Davies, Ward & Beck, Toronto, 1976-77, Merrill Lynch White Weld Capital Markets Group, N.Y.C., 1978-79; cons. Bain & Co., Boston, 1981-82; v.p. Investors in Industry Corp., Boston, 1982-84; assoc. E.M. Warburg, Pincus & Co. Inc., N.Y.C., 1984-86; sr. v.p. The Stuart James Co. Inc., N.Y.C., 1986-89; mng. dir. Loeb Ptnrs. Corp., N.Y.C., 1990—. Mem. Law Soc. Upper Can., Can. Soc. of N.Y., Harvard Club (N.Y.C), Tuxedo Club. Office: Loeb Ptnrs Corp 61 Broadway New York NY 10006-2701

FRUMER, RICHARD J., lawyer; b. Phila., Feb. 2, 1966; s. Marshall and Hilda F. BA in Sociology, Pa. State U., 1988; JD, Villanova U., 1991. Pvt. practice, Wayne, Pa., 1993—. Office: 733 Old Lancaster Rd Bryn Mawr PA 19010

FRUMKIN, HOWARD, public health physician, epidemiologist; b. Poughkeepsie, N.Y., Oct. 14, 1955; s. Barnett A. and Eileen (Brooks) F.; m. Beryl Ann Cowan, June 8, 1986; children: Gabriel, Amara. AB, Brown U., 1977; MD, U. Pa., 1982; MPH, Harvard U., 1982, DrPH, 1993. Diplomate Am. Bd. Internal Medicine, Am. Bd. Preventive Medicine. Asst. prof. medicine U. Pa., Phila., 1988-90; chmn. environ. and occupational health Emory Sch. Pub. Health, Atlanta, 1990—2005; dir. CDC Nat. Ctr. Environ. Health/Agy. Toxic Substance Disease Registry, 2005—. Mem. Inst. Medicine Roundtable on Environ. Health, 2001—. Author: Urban Sprawl and Public Health, 2004, Environmental Health: From Global to Local, 2005; mem. editl. bd. Am. Jour. Indsl. Medicine, 1990—, Internat. Jour. Occupl. and Environ. Health, 1994—, Environ. Health Perspectives, 2003, Am. Jour. Preventive Medicine, 2003— Fellow ACP, Am. Coll. Occupl. and Environ. Medicine; mem. APHA (governing coun. 1993-96, chmn. sci. bd. 1997-99), Assn. Occupation and Environ. Clinics (exec. bd. 1991-97, pres. 1995-96), Soc. Occupl. and Environ. Health (exec. bd. 1992-04), Physicians for Social Responsability (exec. bd. 1995-2005) Home: 1770 E Clifton Rd NE Atlanta GA 30307-1252 Office: 1600 Clifton Rd MS E-28 Atlanta GA 30333

FRUMKIN, JOSEPH B., lawyer; b. Phila., May 5, 1958; s. Abe H. and Ceal S. (Brogan) F.; m. Debra A. Mayer, Aug. 13, 1982; 1 child, Alexandra. AB, Georgetown U., 1980; JD magna cum laude, U. Pa., 1985. Bar: NY 1986. Exec. asst. Sen. John Heinz, Washington, 1980-82; assoc. Sullivan & Cromwell, N.Y.C., 1985-89; investment banker Merrill Lynch & Co., N.Y.C., 1990; assoc. Sullivan & Cromwell, N.Y.C., 1991-93, ptnr., 1994—. Office: Sullivan & Cromwell 125 Broad St New York NY 10004-2498 Office Phone: 212-558-4101. Office Fax: 212-558-3588.

FRUMKIN, SIMON, political organization worker, writer; b. Kaunas, Lithuania, Nov. 5, 1930; came to U.S., 1949; s. Nicholas and Zila (Oster) F.; m. Rhoda Hirsch, June 1953 (div. 1978); children: Michael Alan, Larry Martin; m. Kathy Elizabeth Hoopes, June 22, 1981 (dec. 1994); m. Ella Zousman, Dec. 11, 1995. BA, NYU, 1953; MA in History, Calif. State U., Northridge, 1964. Pres., chief exec. officer Universal Drapery Fabrics, Inc., Los Angeles, 1953-87; chmn. Southern Calif. Council for Soviet Jews, Studio City, 1969—. Lectr. Simon Wiesenthal Ctr. for Holocaust Studies, Los Angeles, 1980—; chmn. Union of Councils for Soviet Jews, 1972-73. Columnist Heritage, numerous other So. Calif. newspapers, 1980—; corr. to columnist Panorama, U.S.A. Russian Lang., 1985—; contbr. articles to newspapers. Pres. Media Analysis Found., Los Angeles, 1988; chmn. Ams. for Peace and Justice, 1972-74; mem. Pres.' Senatorial Inner Circle, U.S. Senatorial Club. Honored by Calif. Govt., Los Angeles City Council, Los Angeles Office of City Atty., numerous Jewish orgns. Mem. Assn. Soviet Jewish Emigre's (pres. 1987—), Zionist Orgn. Am., Am. Israel Polit. Action Com., Russian Republican Club, Mensa. Avocations: writing, photography, skiing, exercise. Home and Office: 3755 Goodland Ave Studio City CA 91604-2313 Office Phone: 818-769-8862. E-mail: esfrumkin@adelphia.net.

FRUSH, CURTIS JAMES, lawyer; b. Trinidad, Colo., Sept. 12, 1950; s. Curtis Bain and Gevenie (Briscoe) F. BA in History, U. Denver, 1972; JD, Columbia U., 1975. Bar: Wash. 1975. Assoc. White & Case, N.Y.C., 1974-76, Riddell Williams, Seattle, 1976-80; asst. U.S. atty. Dept. Justice, Seattle, 1980-85; of counsel Schweppe Krug, Seattle, 1989-90; ptnr. Helsell Fetterman, Seattle, 1990-96, Gordon, Thomas, Honeywell, Malanca Peterson & Daheim PLLC, Seattle, 1996—. Am. Alpine Club (past pres.) Avocations: climbing, politics. Office: Cable Langenbach Kinerk & Bauer LLP 1000 2d Ave # 3500 Seattle WA 98104 Office Phone: 206-292-8800.

FRUTCHEY, SCOTT ALLEN, director; b. Lancaster, Pa., May 4, 1958; s. Clayton Allen and Edna Bishop Frutchey; m. Liese Weber Frutchey, Aug. 8, 1987. BS in Music Edn., Millersville U., 1980. Tchr. vocal music, chmn. Loch Raven High Sch., Towson, Md., 1981—92; assoc. dir. music Towson Presbyn. Ch., 1981—83; dir. choir, organist Gatch Meml. Meth. Ch., Balt., 1993—2000; tchr. vocal music, chmn. Dulaney High Sch., Timonium, 1992—. Performer, music dir. local cmty. and dinner theaters, Balt., 1985—; music dir. Babcock Presbyn. Ch., 2000—. Music merit badge advisor Boy Scouts Am., Cockeyville, Md., 2004—. Mem.: Contemporary A Capella Soc. Am., Music Educators Nat. Conf., Am. Choir Dirs. Assn. Republican. Home: 8527 Rhuddlan Rd Baltimore MD 21236 Office: Dulaney High Sch 255 Padonia Rd Timonium MD 21093

FRY, ALBERT JOSEPH, chemistry professor; b. Phila., May 12, 1937; s. Russell Mayne and Margaret (McCann) F.; m. Melissa Grant Betton, July 30, 1966; children: Anne Margaret, Peter, Jonathan. BS, U. Mich., 1958; PhD, U. Wis., 1963; MA, Wesleyan U., 1978. Postdoctoral fellow Calif. Inst. Tech., Pasadena, 1963-64, Wesleyan U., Middletown, Conn., 1964-65, asst. prof., 1965-72, assoc. prof., 1972-77, prof. chemistry, 1977—, E.B. Nye prof. chemistry, 1993—. Author: Synthetic Organic Electrochemistry, 1972, 2d edit., 1989; editor: Topics in Organic Electrochemistry, 1986, New Directions in Organic Electrochemistry, 2000; contbr. articles to profl. jours. Fellow Chem. Soc. London; mem. Am. Chem. Soc., Conn. Acad. Sci. and Engring., Electrochem. Soc., Internat. Soc. Electrochemistry, Sigma Xi, Alpha Chi Sigma, Phi Lambda Upsilon Roman Catholic. Home: 116 Maple Shade Rd Middletown CT 06457-5188 Office: Wesleyan Univ Dept Chemistry Middletown CT 06459-0001 Office Phone: 860-685-2622. Business E-Mail: afry@wesleyan.edu.

FRY, CHARLES GEORGE, theologian, educator; b. Piqua, Ohio, Aug. 15, 1936; s. Sylvan Jack and Lena Freda (Ehle) F. BA, Capital U., 1958; MA, Ohio State U., 1961, PhD, 1965; BD, Evang. Luth. Theol. Sem., 1962, MDiv, 1977; DMin, Winebrenner Theol. Sem., 1978; DD, Cranmer Sem., 2001; M of Sacred Theology, Holy Trinity Coll. and Sem., 2002, M of Religious Edn., 2003, D of Religious Edn., 2004. Ordained to ministry Luth. Ch. USA, 1963; diplomate Am. Psychotherapy Assn.; designated master therapist, 2005. Pastor St. Mark's Luth. Ch. and Martin Luther Luth. Ch., Columbus, Ohio, 1961-62, 63-66; instr. Wittenberg U., 1962-63, 71-72, Capital U., 1963-75, asst. prof. history and religion, 1966-69, assoc. prof., 1969-75; theologian-in-residence North Cmty. Luth. Ch., Columbus, 1971-73; assoc. prof. hist. theology, dir. missions edn. Concordia Theol. Sem., Ft. Wayne, Ind., 1975-84; sr. minister First Congl. Ch., Detroit, 1984-85; Protestant chaplain St. Francis Coll., Fort Wayne, 1982-92; prof. philosophy and theology Luth. Coll. of Health Professions, Ft. Wayne, 1992-98, U. St. Francis, Ft. Wayne, 1998-99, Winebrenner Theol. Sem., U. Findlay, Ohio, 1999—. Interim min. Arbor Grove Congl. Ch., Jackson, Mich., 1980, hon. min. emeritus 1996, First Presbyn. Ch., Huntington, Ind., 1988-89, St. Luke's Luth. Ch., Ft. Wayne, 1989-90, Mt. Pleasant Luth. Ch., 1990-91, St. Mark's Luth. Ch., 1990-91, Mt. Zion Luth. Ch., Ft. Wayne, 1991-93; interim min. Cmty. Christian Ch., New Carlisle, Ind., 1993-94, First Luth. Ch., Stryker, Ohio, 1994-95, Zion Luth. Ch., West Jefferson, Ohio, 1994-97, 98-2000, Agape Congl. Ch., Bowling Green, Ohio, 1997-98; interim min. Fairfield Parish, Lancaster, Ohio, 2000—; vis. prof. Damavand Coll., Tehran, 1973-74, Ref. Bible Coll., 1975-80, Concordia Luth. Sem. at Brock U., 1977, 79, Grad. Sch. Christian Ministry, Huntington (Ind.) Coll., 1986-89, Wheaton Coll., 1987-88; vis. scholar Al Ain U., United Arab Emirates, 1987; theologian-in-residence, tchg. theologian Queentown Luth. Ch., Singapore, 1991, 99-2000, 02; adj. faculty history Ind. U./Purdue U., Ft. Wayne, 1982-98, Winebrenner Theol. Sem., Findlay, Ohio, 1992, 99-, Holy Trinity Coll. and Sem., 1999—, Tung Ling Bible Coll., Singapore, 2000, 02, North Tenn. Bible Inst., 1998—; pastor-in-residence Wittenberg U., Springfield, Ohio, 1992, Deaconess Cmty. Evang. Luth. Ch. Am., Phila., 1993. Author books including Age of Lutheran Orthodoxy, 1979, Lutheranism in America, 1979, Islam, 1980, 2d edit. 1982, The Way, The Truth, The Life, 1982, Great Asian Religions, 1984, Francis: A Call to Conversion, 1988, Brit. edit., 1990, The Middle East: A History, 1988, Congregationalists and Evolution: Asa Gray and Louis Agassiz, 1989, Pioneering a Theology of Evolution: Washington Gladden and Pierre Teilhard de Chardin, 1989, Avicenna's Philosophy of Education: An Introduction, 1990, Explorations in Protestant Theology, 1992, Life's Little Lessons, 1997, Kant's Three Questions, 1997, Four Little Words, 1997, Goethe: Life and Truth, 2001, Washington Gladden as a Preacher of the Social Gospel, 1882-1918, 2003, Berthold von Schenk, 2003, Mattias Loy, 2005, Teaching the Bible in Tehran, 2005, others; co-prodr. Global Perspectives, IPFW-TV, Ft. Wayne, 1987-97. Bd. dirs. Luth. Liturgical Renewal, 1983-90, 94-2000, pres., 1999-2000; v.p. Internat. Luth. Fellowship, 1995-98, pres., 1998-2001, 2003-2004, presiding bishop, 2004-; consecrated bishop, so. region Internat. Luth. Fellowship, 1996; assoc. St. Augustine's Fellowship, 1996—; bd. dirs. Zwemer Inst., Ft. Wayne, Ind., 1997-2003. Recipient Praestantia award Capital U., 1970, Concordia Hist. Inst. citation, 1977, Archbishop Robert Leighton award Nat. Anglican Ch., 1997, Hancock County Ohio award for tchg. excellence, 2004; Regional Coun. for Internat. Edn. rsch. grantee, 1969; Joseph J. Malone postdoctoral fellow Egypt, 1986, Malone postdoctoral fellow, United Arab Emirates, 1987; named Ky. Col., 1999. Fellow Brit. Interplanetary Soc., Coll. Pastoral Counseling (diplomate), Am. Assn. Integrated Medicine (diplomate, bd. coll. pastoral counseling 2001-), Oxford Soc. Scholars; mem. Am. Hist. Assn., Am. Acad. Religion, Mid. East Inst. Gen. Soc. War of 1812 (compatriot 1994—, chaplain Ohio chpt. 1996—, chaplain gen. 2001-, pres., 2005—), German Soc. Md., Mil. and Hospitaller Order of St. Lazarus of Jerusalem (chaplain 2000—), Phi Alpha Theta. Democrat. Home: 158 W Union St Circleville OH 43113-1965 Office: 950 N Main St Findlay OH 45840-4416 Office Phone: 419-434-4200.

FRY, CLARENCE HERBERT, retired retail executive; b. Pottstown, Pa., June 27, 1926; s. Clarence H. and Rosa B. (Savage) F.; m. Barbara Ruth McGuire, Aug. 28, 1950; children: James Nathan, David Andrew, Joel Timothy, Ann Elizabeth. BS magna cum laude, Syracuse U., 1950. CPA, Pa. Accountant Peat, Marwick, Mitchell & Co., Phila., 1950-56, supr., 1956-60, mgr., 1960-69; controller Acme Markets, Inc. (now Am. Stores Co.), Phila., 1969-73; chief acctg. officer Am. Stores Group Services, Inc., Phila., 1974-78, contr., 1974-75, v.p., 1975-78; v.p., contr. Am. Stores Co., Wilmington, Del., 1979—80, Acme Markets, Inc. subs. Am. Stores Co., Phila., 1980-83, sr. v.p., treas., contr., 1983-87; sr. v.p. fin. Am. Superstores Inc. subs. Am. Stores Co., Wilmington, 1987-89; ret., 1990. Mem. food merchandisers LIFO adv. com. Food Mktg. Inst., 1975-82. Author: Easttown: Old in History, Young in Spirit, 1704-2004, 2004. Mem. Easttown Twp. Tricentennial Com., 2001—04; bd. dirs. Tredyffrin Historic Preservation Trust, 2003—. With 69th Inf. Div. AUS, 1944-46. Mem. AICPA, Pa. Inst. CPAs, Chester County Hist. Soc., Tredyffrin-Easttown History Club (pres. 1992-95, editor quar. 1996-2003). Presbyterian. Avocations: historical research, motorsports. Home: 519 Daventry Rd Berwyn PA 19312-1740

FRY, DONALD EDMUND, surgeon; b. Marion, Ohio, Aug. 16, 1946; s. Harold H. and Mary Ellen (Young) F.; m. Rosemary V. Jollis, Sept. 7, 1968; children: Angela Rae, Jonathan Matthew. BSc cum laude, Ohio State U., 1968, MD, 1972. Diplomate Am. Bd. Surgery. Intern Parkland Meml. Hosp., Dallas, 1972-73; resident in gen. surgery Affiliated Hosp., Louisville, 1973-77; instr. surgery U. Louisville Sch. Medicine, 1977-78, asst. prof. surgery, 1978-81, assoc. prof. surgery, 1981-82; staff surgeon VA Med. Ctr., Louisville, 1977-82; dir. Price Inst. Surg. Rsch., Louisville, 1980-82; prof. surgery Sch. Medicine Case Western Res. U., Cleve., 1982-87; chief surg. svc. VA Med. Ctr., Cleve., 1982-87; staff surgeon trauma svc. Met. Gen. Hosp., Cleve., 1985-87; prof., chmn. dept. surgery U. N.Mex. Sch. of Medicine, Albuquerque, 1987—; chief of surgery U. N.Mex. Hosp., Albuquerque, 1987—. Bd. dirs. U. N.Mex. Found.; bd. dirs. U. Physician Assocs., 1988—, sec., 1989-91, pres., 1991—, chmn. bd., 1991—; Howard Gans lectr. Mt. Sinai Med. Ctr., Cleve., 1983, Alpha Omega Alpha lectr. U. Louisville, 1984, Lunda vis. prof. trauma Med. Coll. Wis., Milw., 1989, Thomas G. Orr Meml. lectr. S.W. Surg. Congress, Scottsdale, Ariz., 1992, William Beaumont Meml. lectr. State Med. Soc. Wis., LaCrosse, 1993, E. L. Young Endowed lectr. Faulkner Hosp., Boston, 1993. Author: Surgical Infection-Discussions in Surgical Management, 1982, Reoperative Surgery of the Abdomen, 1986, Reoperative Abdominal Surgery, 1991, Multiple Organ Failure: Pathogenesis and Management, 1992, Peritonitis, 1993; author med. movies, computer programs and over 70 chpts. to books; mem. editorial bd. Circulatory Shock, 1983—, Archives of Surgery, 1985-87, Jour. Surg. Rsch., 1986-92, Surgery Report, 1988-90, Perspectives in Gen. Surgery, 1989—, Am. Jour. Surgery, 1991—, Advances in Therapy, 1992—, Surg. Infections: Index and Revs., 1993; contbr. articles, abstracts to profl. jours. Am. Cancer Soc. clin. fellow, 1976-77; grantee VA, 1977-80, 80-82, 82-86, 87-89, Ohio chpt., Am. Heart Assn., 1984-85, Hoffman-LaRoche, 1989-90, Merck Sharpe and Dohme, 1989-90, Roerig-Pfizer, 1989-93, 90-92, 91—, Glaxo, 1990-92, Upjohn, 1990-91, Ortho, 1990, Wyeth-Ayerst, 1991-92, Bristol-Myers Squibb, 1992—, Fujisawa, 1992-93, Pfizer, 1993—, Lederle, 1993—, Smithkline Beecham, 1993—; recipient Resident Essay award Soc. VA Surgeons, 1976, Charles M. Edelen Publ. award, 1977. Fellow Infectious Diseases Soc. Am.; mem. Albuquerque Acad. Surgery (program chmn. 1988-92, v.p. 1992-93, pres.-elect 1993-94), Am. Assn. Surgery of Trauma (program com. 1986-89), Am. Coll. Physician Execs., ACS (com. pre- and post-operative care 1985—, gov.'s subcom. AIDS 1991—, com. operating room environ. 1994—), AMA, Am. Surg. Assn., Am. Trauma Soc., Assn. Acad. Surgery (coun. mem. 1978-80, issues com. 1980-82, nominating com. 1982-83), Assn. VA Surgeons (program com. 1982-83, trauma com. 1982-87, chmn. coun. chiefs 1983-85, exec. com. 1983—, recorder 1984-87, sec. 1985-86, pubs. com. 1985-87, v.p. 1986-87, pres.- elect 1987-88, pres. 1988-89), Ctrl. Surg. Assn. (program com. 1986-89), Greater Albuquerque Med. Assn., Cleve. Surg. Soc. (chmn. resident rsch. forum 1984-87, exec. com. 1984-87), Hiram C. Polk., Jr. Surg. Soc. (sec.-treas. 1982-84, pres. 1984-85), N.Mex Trauma Soc. (bd. dirs. 1993—), Surg. Infection Soc. (sci. studies com. 1985-87, fellowship com. 1988-91, councillor 1993—), Shock Soc. (pubs. com. chmn. 1985-89, program chmn. 1988-89, pres. 1994—), U. N.Mex. Found. (bd. dirs. 1992—), U. N.Mex. Physicians Assocs. (bd. dirs. 1988—, sec. 1989-91, pres. 1991—, bd. chmn. 1991—). Home: 6017 Persimmon Ct NE Albuquerque NM 87111-6257 Office: Univ of New Mexico 2211 Lomas Blvd NE Albuquerque NM 87106-2745 Home: 11600 Academy Rd NE #3211 Albuquerque NM 87111 Business E-Mail: dfry@salud.unm.edu.

FRY, DONALD LEWIS, physiologist, educator; b. Des Moines, Dec. 29, 1924; s. Clair V. and Maudie (Long) F.; children: Donald Stewart, Ronald Sinclair, Heather Elise, Laurel Virginia. MD, Harvard U., 1949. Rsch. fellow Univ Minn Hosp., Mpls., 1952-53; sr. asst. surgeon gen. NIH, Bethesda, Md., 1953-56, surgeon, 1956-57, sr. surgeon, 1957-61, med. dir., 1961-80; prof. Ohio State U., Columbus, 1980—2004, prof. emeritus, 2004. Contbr. numerous articles and papers on physiology and biophysics of pulmonary mechanics, blood vascular interface, transvascular mass transport and the genesis of atherosclerosis to profl. jours., books. Mem. AAAS, Am. Physiol. Soc., Am. Soc. Clin. Investigation, Biophys. Soc., European Acad. Scis. Mailing: PO Box 340187 Columbus OH 43234-0187 Business E-Mail: fry.1@osu.edu.

FRY, DONALD OWEN, broadcasting company executive; b. Headlee, Ind., Mar. 5, 1921; s. George Mason and Nima E. (Ulrey) F.; m. Phyllis Amy McMillan, Feb. 2, 1947. BS, Calif. Coll. Commerce, 1953. Chief acct. Philco Dist., Inc., Los Angeles, 1953-58, Pacific Ocean Park (Calif.), 1958-59; controller Eleven-Ten Broadcasting, Pasadena, Calif., 1959-63, Los Angeles Standard, 1963-69; treas. Oak Knoll Broadcasting Corp., Pasadena, from 1969, v.p., gen. mgr., 1976-82, pres., chmn. bd., from 1982, dir., from 1974. Trustee, pres., chmn. bd. Broadcast Found. of Calif., Pasadena. Served with U.S. Army, 1940-45. Decorated Bronze star (2). Mem.: Masons, Scottish Rite, Shriners. Home: Lafayette, Ind. Died June 20, 2005.

FRY, ELIZABETH H. W., lawyer; b. Willimantic, Conn., Mar. 31, 1951; AB, Yale U., 1973; JD cum laude, Fordham U., 1978. Bar: Conn. 1978, N.Y. 1979. Ptnr., co-leader Individual Client Svc. practice Pillsbury Winthrop Shaw Pittman, N.Y.C. Assoc. editor Fordham Law Review, 1977-78. Mem.: NY State Bar Assn., Assn. Bar City of NY. Office: Pillsbury Winthrop Shaw Pittman 1540 Broadway New York NY 10036 Office Phone: 212-858-1520. Office Fax: 212-858-1500. Business E-Mail: elizabeth.fry@pillsburylaw.com.

FRY, HEDY, member of parliament; 3 children. MD, Royal Coll. Surgeons, Dublin, Ireland, 1968. Pvt. practice; mem., sec. of state (multiculturalism) (status of women) Can. Parliament/Vancouver Ctr., Ottawa, 1996—2002; chair B.C. Caucus, 2002—; mem. spl. com. on non-med. use of drugs, mem. standing com. on health, standing com. on justice and human rights Can. Parliament, Ottawa, Canada, 2002. Dr. Hirsh Rosenfeld Disting. Lectr. in family medicine McGill U., 1994; featured on Doctor-Doctor, CBC TV series, 1985-89. Mem. editl. bd. Med. Post. Mem. com. Royal Commn. on Reproductive Technologies.dn. Learning for Living Adv. Bd.; mem. Mayor's Spl. Com. on Urban Natives; bd. dirs. St. George's sch., 1989-91; adv. bd. B.C. Physicians Against Nuclear War; co-chair Liberal Party Health and Social Issues sect., Aylmer Conf., 1992, mem. Leader's Nat. Task Force on Women, 1992-93; parliamentary sec. Min. of Health, 1993-96, mem. task force on reform of social security sys., 1994, standing com. on health, 1994, subcom. on AIDS, mem. caucus com. on social policy. Recipient Cmty. Svc. award Commonwealth Caribbean Club, 1991, Black Achievement award, 1994, Congress of Black Women award, 1994. Mem. B.C. Fedn. Med. Women (pres. 1977), Vancouver Women's Network, Vancouver Med. Assn. (pres. 1988-89), B.C. Med. Assn. (pres. 1990-91, chief negotiator 1991-93), Can. Med. Assn. (chair obstetrics task force 1986-87, chair multiculturalism com. 1992-93), Coun. of Healthcare and Promotion (B.C. rep. 1984-92). Avocations: travel, gardening, reading.

FRY, JOHN, magazine editor; b. Montreal, Jan. 22, 1930; s. J. Stevenson and Beatrice (Pratt) F.; m. Marlies Stillinger, Feb. 19, 1965; children— Leslie, William, Nicole. Student, Lower Can. Coll., Montreal, 1936-47; BA, McGill U., 1951. Writer Forster McGuire & Co. Ltd., Montreal, 1951-57; assoc. editor to mng. editor Am. Metal Market, 1957-63; editor-in-chief Ski mag., N.Y.C., 1964-74, editl. dir., 1975-79, Ski Bus., 1964-79, 92—, Golf mag., 1968-71, 77-79, Outdoor Life, 1975-79, Cross Country Ski mag., 1975—; dir. publs. devel. Times Mirror Mags., 1979-83; editl. and publs. cons., 1983—; founding editor Snow Country mag., 1987-98; editor for new mag. devel. N.Y. Times mag. group, N.Y.C., 1995-97. Mem. World Cup com. Internat. Ski Fedn., 1970-75. Author: (with Phil and Steve Mahre) No Hill Too Fast, 1985. Bd. dirs. Beaver Dam Sanctuary, Chawkers Found. (Canada). Recipient Lifetime Achievement award Internat. Skiing History Assn., 1996; named to U.S. Nat. Ski Hall of Fame, 1995. Mem.: Internat. Skiing History Assn. (bd. dirs. 1995—, pres. 2001—04), Overseas Press Club of Am. Achievements include being the founder of the National Standard Ski Race and the Nations Cup of Alpine Skiing. Office: 23 E Lake Dr Katonah NY 10536-3501 E-mail: snowfry@worldnet.att.net.

FRY, JOHN ANDERSON, academic administrator; m. Cara Fry; children: Mia, Nathaniel, Phoebe. BA in Am. Civilization, Lafayette Coll., 1982; MBA, NYU, 1986; postgrad., U. Pa. Staff acct. Peat, Marwick, Mitchell & co., N.Y.C., 1982—84; adj. instr. NYU Stern Sch. Bus., 1985, Hunter Coll. CUNY, 1990; cons. KPMG Peat Marwick, N.Y.C., 1984—86, sr. cons., 1986—88, mgr., 1988—89, sr. mgr., 1989—91; mng. assoc. Coopers & Lybrand, N.Y.C., 1991—93, ptnr., 1993, ptnr.-in-charge, 1994—95; exec. v.p. U. Pa., Phila., 1995—2002; pres. Franklin & Marshall Coll., Lancaster, Pa., 2002—. Sr. fellow Inst. for Rsch. on Higher Edn. U. Pa.; pres., CEO Penn to Bus.; bd. dirs. Sovereign Bancorp, Ban Franklin Tech. Ptnrs.; trustee Del. Investments; mem., pres. coun. NCAA Divsn. III. Bd. dirs., mem. exec. com. Phila. Indsl. Devel. Corp.; trustee Morris Arboretum; bd. dirs., vice chmn. Univ. City Sci. Ctr.; founding mem., chmn. bd. dirs. Univ. City Dist.; trustee Pa. Acad. Fine Arts, Lafayette Coll.; bd. dirs., exec. com. Greater Phila. C. of C.; bd. trustee Fulton Opera House; chmn. James St. Improvement Dist.; bd. dirs. Greater Phila. Tourism and Mktg. Corp.; bd. dir. Lancaster Alliance, Lancaster Gen. Hosp., Lancaster County Conv. Ctr.; bd. trustee Lancaster Country Day Sch. Office: Office of the Pres Franklin & Marshall Coll Lancaster PA 17604

FRY, LOUIS EDWIN, JR., architect; b. Prairie View, Tex., Sept. 11, 1928; s. Louis Edwin and Obelia (Swearingen) F.; m. Genelle Wiley, Nov. 7, 1955; children— Jo Nisa, Louis Edwin, Vicki-Lynn, A'lexa AB, Howard U., 1949; B.Arch., Harvard U., 1953, M.Arch., 1954, M.Arch. in Urban Design, 1962. Registered profl. architect, D.C., Va., Md., N.J. Arch. McGowan & Johnson, Washington, 1955-59, Fry & Welch Assoc. PC, Washington, 1959—. Vis. critic Harvard U., Cambridge, Mass., 1970-74; bd. dirs. Mid Atlantic NCARB, Washington, 1979-81; pres. D.C. Arch. Registration Bd., 1979-84; mem. Redevel. Land Agy., 1978—; mem. design com. Harvard U., 1980—, vis. mem. Grad. Sch. Design Mem. Shepherd Park Community Assn., Washington, Georgia Ave. Profl. and Civic Assn., Washington Fulbright fellow, Holland, 1954-55 Fellow AIA; mem. Nat. Orgn. for Minority Architects, Omega Psi Phi Democrat. Avocation: breeding salt-water fish. Office: Fry and Welch Assocs PC 7100 Alaska Ave NW Washington DC 20012-1544 Personal E-mail: fryandwelch@yahoo.com.

FRY, MALCOLM CRAIG, retired clergyman; b. Detroit, June 6, 1928; s. Dwight Malcolm and Adrienne (Craig) F.; m. Myrtle Mae Downing, June 5, 1948 (dec.); children: Pamela Mae, Malcolm Craig Jr., Rebecca Fry Gwartney, Matthew Dwight. Student, Bible Bapt. Sem., 1950; Th.B., Am. Div. Sch., Chgo., 1959; student, McNeese State Coll., Lake Charles, La., 1958-61; BS, Austin Peay State Coll., 1962; M.Ed., U. Ariz., 1969; D. Laws and Letters (hon.), Clarksville Sch. Theology, 1974; D.Ministry, Luther Rice Sem., 1978. Ordained to ministry Free Will Bapt. Ch., 1955. Asst. jewelery store mgr. Sonne Bros., Norwich, N.Y., 1948-50; pastor in Lake Charles, La., 1955-58, 59-61, Bryan, Tex., 1958-59, Ashland City, Tenn., 1961-62; asst. pastor in Royal Oak, Mich., 1962-64; pastor First Free Will Bapt. Ch., Tucson, 1964-71; dir. curriculum and rsch. Bd. Ch. Tng. Svc. Nat. Assn. Free Will Baptists, Nashville, 1971-72; gen. dir., treas. Bd. Ch. Tng. Svc., 1972-78; dir. Nat. Youth Conf., 1972-83, asst. dir. Bd. Sunday Sch. and Ch. Tng., 1978-83; pastor Unity Free Will Bapt. Ch., Smithfield, N.C., 1983-89, Goodlettsville Free Will Bapt. Ch., Goodlettsville, Tenn., 1991-96; asst. dir. Randall House Publs., 1989—96; ret., 1996. Program writer, teen tng. mgr. Nat. Assn. Free Will Bapts., 1963-78, clk., 1965-67, chmn. stewardship commn., 1962-67, editor in chief bd. Sunday Sch. and Ch. Tng., 1989-95. Author: Total Involvement, 1964, Why Worry?, 1967, Precepts for Practice, 1971, Discipling and Developing, 1971, The Teacher-in-Training, 1972, Contemporary Topical Studies, 1973, rev. edit., 1991, The Ministry of Music, 1974, Balancing Christian Education, 1977, Leader's Guide Discipling and Developing, 1979, Leader's Guide the Ministry of Ushering, 1980. Served with AUS, 1946-48; with USAF, 1951-57, Korea. Mem. Evang. Philos. Soc., Kiwanis, Civitan, Phi Delta Kappa.

FRY, MICHAEL GRAHAM, historian, educator; b. Brierley, Eng., Nov. 5, 1934; s. Cyril Victor and Margaret Mary (Copley) F.; m. Anna Maria Fulgoni; children: Michael Gareth, Gabrielle, Margaret Louise. B.Sc. in Econs. with honors, U. London, 1956, PhD, 1963. Dir. Norman Paterson Sch. Internat. Affairs, Carleton U., Ottawa, Ont., 1973-77; dean, prof. internat. relations Grad. Sch. Internat. Studies, U. Denver, 1978-81; dir., prof. Sch. Internat. Relations, U. So. Calif., Los Angeles, 1981—. Vis. prof. Middle East Center, U. Utah, 1979, U. Leningrad, 1976 Author: Illusions of Security: North Atlantic Diplomacy, 1918-1922, 1972, Freedom and Change, 1975, Lloyd George and Foreign Policy, Vol. I, The Education of a Statesman, 1890-1916, 1977, Despatches from Damascus, 1933-39, 1986, History and International Studies, 1987, History, The White House and the Kremlin: Statesmen as Historians, 1991, Power, Personalities and Policies, 1992, The North Pacific Triangle: Canada Japan and the U.S. at Century's End, 1998, Guide to International Relations and Diplomacy, 2002. NATO rsch. fellow, 1970-71, rsch. fellow Annenberg Program, Washington, 1986-87; grantee Can. Coun. Fellow: Royal Hist. Soc. Roman Catholic. Home: 1358 Cassins St Carlsbad CA 92009-4856 Office: U So Calif Sch Internat Rels Los Angeles CA 90084-0001

FRY, MORTON HARRISON, II, lawyer; b. N.Y.C., May 15, 1946; s. George Thomas Clark and Louise Magdalen (Cronin) Fry; m. Patricia Laylin Coffin, May 29, 1971. AB, Princeton U., 1968; JD, Yale U., 1971. Bar: N.Y. 1973, U.S. Ct. Mil. Appeals 1973, U.S. Dist. Ct. (so. and ea. dists.) N.Y. 1975, U.S. Ct. Appeals (2d cir.) 1975. Assoc. Cravath, Swaine & Moore, N.Y.C., 1971-72, 75-79; dep. gen. counsel Columbia Pictures Industries, Inc., N.Y.C., 1979-81; v.p., gen. counsel Warner Home Video Inc., N.Y.C., 1982-83; exec.v.p. Warner Electronic Home Svcs., N.Y.C., 1983-84; sr. counsel corp. and new techs. Warner Comms. Inc., N.Y.C., 1984-85; pres., CEO, bd. dirs. The Congress Video Group, Inc., 1985-87; pres., cons. Fry Assocs., 1987-89; ptnr. Marshall, Morris, Bomser & Fry, N.Y.C., 1990-94, Rubin, Bailin, Ortoli, Mayer, Baker & Fry, N.Y.C., 1995-2000; of counsel Stairs, Dillenbeck & Finley, N.Y.C., 2000—. Active Dem. Nat. Fin. Com. Capt. USMC, 1966—75. Democrat. Congregationalist. Home: 235 E 18th St New York NY 10003 Office Phone: 212-697-2700. Personal E-mail: frylaw@mindspring.com.

FRY, RICHARD E., architectural firm executive; BArch, U. Mich. Registered arch. Mich., Minn., Colo.; cert. Nat. Coun. Archtl. Registered Bds. Pres., prin.-in-charge Fry & Ptnrs. Archs., Inc., Aspen, Col. and Ann Arbor, Mich., 1970—. Adj. prof. U. Mich. Coll. Archtl. and Urban Planning; archtl. instr. Washtenaw C.C.; rep. Mich. archs. Nat. AIA Bd., Washington. Prin. works include U. Mich. Vis. Ctr., No. Brewery Office Bldg., Ann Arbor, Mich. League-U. Mich., Ann Arbor Art Assn., U. Mich. Dental Sch. Sindecuse Mus., We. Mich. U. Bookstore, Burns Park Elem. Sch., Ann Arbor Ctrl. Fire Sta., Heydon Wash. St. Properties, Ann Arbor, pvt. residences, others. Past mem. Ann Arbor Planning Commn.; bd. dirs. Bldg. Bd. Appeals; mem. art acquisition com. Washtenaw C.C. Fellow AIA (pres. Mich. chpt., chmn. design awards & recognition com. Mich. chpt., chmn. design retreat com. Mich. chpt., chmn. mid-summer conf. Mich. chpt., regional dir. Mich. chpt., pres. Huron Valley chpt.). Office: Fry & Partners Architects 193 Hiscock St Ann Arbor MI 48109-9216

FRY, RONALD SYLVAN, music educator, director; b. Charleston, S.C., Apr. 2, 1948; s. Philip Henry and Effie Evelyn Fry; m. Cheryl Anne LeHeup, Aug. 23, 1975; 1 child, Loren Matthew. AA, The Coll. of Orlando, 1970; BA, U. South Fla., 1972; MA in Tchg., Rollins Coll., 1981. Cert. profl. tchr. State of Fla., 1973. Instr. adult basic edn. Osceola County Dist. Schs., Kissimmee, Fla., 1985—87, music edn. tchr., 1987—91, choral dir., 1987—91; music edn. tchr. Pasco County Dist. Schs., Land-O-Lakes, Fla., 1991—, choral dir., 1991—, Fox Hollow Elem. Sch., Port Richey, Fla., 1998—, music edn. tchr. Substitute tchr. Osceola County Dist. Schs., 1973—76; pvt. music instr., Port Richey, Fla., 1974—, St. Cloud, Fla., 1974—91; substitute tchr. Osceola County Dist. Schs., 1986—87; condr. and dir. Osceola (Fla.) Civic Orch., Kissimmee, 1975—78; mem. dist. level instrument com. Pasco County Dist. Schs., 1994—95; chmn. open house com. Hudson (Fla.) Elem. Sch., 1993—94; mem. sch. discipline com. Hudson (Fla.) Elem. Sch., 1997—98, Fox Hollow Elem. Sch., Port Richey, 1999—2000; mem. sch. safety com. Hudson (Fla.) Elem. Sch., 1994—96, Fox Hollow Elem. Sch., 2001—02, mem. sch. environ. com., 2001—02, mentor tchr., 2004—; mem. youth motivational program Osceola County Dist. Schs., 1989—90; mem. sch. leadership coun. Hudson (Fla.) Elem. Sch., 1993—94, 1996—97. Musician: George Grey Combo, 1970—85. Mem.: Kappa Delta Pi, Phi Mu Alpha (chpt. v.p. 1971—72). Republican. Avocations: reading, walking, history, movies, travel. Home: 8822 Forest Lake Drive Port Richey FL 34668-5819 Office: Fox Hollow Elementary 8309 Fox Hollow Drive Port Richey FL 34668 Office Phone: 727-774-7616. E-mail: rfry@pasco.k12.fl.us.

FRY, VIRGINIA MILNE, artist, poet; b. Mpls., June 14, 1929; d. Stewart James and Cora Woodward Milne; m. Donald Lewis Fry, Sept. 13, 1947 (div. Feb. 0, 1992); children: Donald Stewart, Ronald Sinclair, Heather Fry Raymond, Laurel Fry Erickson. MA, Am. U., Washington, DC, 1980; Grad. in Tech. Illustration, Columbia Tech. Inst., Arlington, Va., 1969. Tech. illustrator Dames & Moore Environ. Engring. Cons., Bethesda, Md., 1973—. Author: (book of poems and prints) Things Done Alone, (book of poetry) Best Poems of 1988; Exhibited in group shows at The Ohio State Fair Profl. Divsn., The West Annapolis Gallery, Annapolis, Md., St. John's Coll., The Columbus (Ohio) Mus. Art, The Copley Soc., Boston, The Columbus (Ohio) Art League Exhbns., The Columbus (Ohio) Cultural Art Ctr., one-woman shows include The Zanesville (Ohio) Art Ctr., Mount Carmel Hosp. East, Columbus, Ohio, Capital U., Franklin U., The Canal House Gallery, Washington, D.C., The Cosmos Club, Washington, The Online Computerized Libr. Ctr., Dublin, Ohio. Leader Girl Scouts Am., Bethesda, Md., 1962—63; rec. studio narrator Md. Libr. Blind, Balt., 1992—2003; ICU vol. Ohio State U. Hosp., Columbus, 1980—85; vol. Shelter Homeless, Annapolis, Md., 2001—02; pres. Ohio State U. Women's Club Poetry Group, Columbus, 1985—92. Recipient 3d Pl. award, Internat. Libr. of Poetry. Mem.: Acad. of Am. Poets, Annapolis Chorale, The Annapolis Kiwanis Club (pres. 1997—98, Disting. 1998). Presbyterian. Avocations: chorale soprano, tutoring, art judge. Home: 129 Bay Shore Avenue Annapolis MD 21403 Personal E-mail: gfkitty@aol.com.

FRY, W. LOGAN, artist; b. Columbus, Ohio, Sept. 5, 1944; s. Walter Logan and Frieda Mae Fry; m. Joanne Fry, Mar. 29, 1969. BA, Oberlin Coll., 1967; JD, Case Western Res. U., 1970. Bar: Ohio 1970. Law intern City of Cleve., 1968—69; trial atty. Antitrust divsn. U.S. Dept. Justice, 1970—73; counsel Goodyear Tire & Rubber Co., 1973—76, Goodyear Atomic Corp., 1976—79; pvt. practice, 1979—87; ret., 1987. Weaver, artist, 1987—; founder, dir. Digital Mus. Modern Art. Represented in permanent collections Cleve. Art Mus., Mpls. Inst. Arts, Smithsonian Am. Art Mus., San Francisco Mus. Fine Arts, Flaten Art Mus., St. Olaf Coll. Office: Digital Mus Modern Art PO Box 249 Richfield OH 44286 E-mail: director@dmoma.org.

FRY, WILLIAM N., IV, textiles executive; b. 1959; Dir. Dixie Group, Inc., 1988—, exec. v.p., COO, pres., CEO, 1998—. Office: Dixie Group Inc 1100 S Watkins St Chattanooga TN 37404-4615

FRYBURGER, VERNON RAY, JR., advertising executive, finance educator; b. Cin., June 9, 1918; s. Vernon Ray and Florence Rose (Steding) F.; m. Marjorie Anne Clarke, June 19, 1948; 1 dau., Candace. BS in Bus. Adminstrn., Miami U., Oxford, Ohio, 1939; PhD in Econs., U. Ill., 1950. Salesman U.S. Printing & Lithograph Co., 1940-41; instr. mktg. Miami U., 1941-43; assoc. rsch. dir. Nat. Assn. Broadcasters, 1946; asst. prof. journalism U. Ill., 1947-53; faculty Northwestern U., 1953-86, prof. advt. and mktg., chmn. dept. advt., 1959-84, ednl. dir. Inst. Advanced Advt. Studies, 1963-85, prof. emeritus, 1986—; nat. assoc. dean Am. Acad. Advt., 1964-65, nat. dean, 1965-66, chmn. bd.; cons. to bus., 1954—; adviser Advt. Ednl. Found., 1972-84. Vis. prof. U. Hawaii, 1965; cons. advt. U.S. Army, 1983-91. Author: (with C.H. Sandage and K. Rotzoll) Advertising Theory and Practice, 12th edit., 1989, (with Boyd and Westfall) Cases in Advertising Management, 1964; editor: (with C.H. Sandage) The Role of Advertising, 1960. Bd. dirs. Lake Forest Library. Served to lt., submarines USNR, 1943-46, PTO. Mem. Am. Mktg. Assn., Internat. Advt. Assn., Assn. Edn. Journalism, Beta Gamma Sigma, Kappa Tau Alpha, Delta Tau Delta, Delta Sigma Pi, Artus. Presbyterian. Home: 1921 Shore Acres Dr Lake Bluff IL 60044-1342

FRYDRYK, KARL ALLEN, financial executive; b. Sept. 8, 1954; m. Nancy J. Frydryk, May 5, 1984; 3 children. BS, Miami U., Oxford, Ohio, 1976. CPA, Ohio. Mgr. Touche Ross & Co., Dayton, Ohio, 1976-84; v.p. fin., sec., dir. Nord Resources Corp., Dayton, 1984—. Mem. AICPA, Ohio Soc. CPAs, Optimist Internat. (pres. Centerville 1994). Office: Genesis Worldwide Inc 130 Main St Callery PA 16024

FRYE, CLAYTON WESLEY, JR., finance company executive; b. L.A., May 18, 1930; s. Clayton Wesley Sr. and Mary Virginia (Briggs) F.; m. Dorothy Rumsfeld, Jan. 14, 1957; children: Carolyn Frye Halloran (dec.), Diane Frye Tanner. AB, Stanford U., 1953, MBA, 1959. Pres. Sutter Hill Devel. Co., Palo Alto, Calif., 1962-69; gen. ptnr. Johnson & Frye Investment Co., San Antonio, 1970-73; sr. assoc. Laurance S. Rockefeller, N.Y.C., 1973—. Ptnr. Rockefeller & Assocs. Realty, L.P., San Francisco, 1990-99, Pacific Property Svcs., San Francisco, 1984-98; bd. dirs. Col. Williamsburg (Va.) Co., Woodstock Resort Corp., Vt., chmn.; dir. Tejon Ranch Co., L.A., 1975-98, Rockefeller Ctr. Inc., 1976-81, Times Mirror Co., L.A., 1988-2000, King Ranch, Inc., Tex., 1996-2000. Trustee Hist. Hudson Valley, Tarrytown, N.Y.; trustee, chmn. Jackson Hole Preserve, Inc., Woodstock Found., White House Hist. Assn., bd. dirs.; vice-chmn., former trustee South St. Seaport Mus., N.Y.C.; vice-chmn., bd. dirs. Rockresorts, Inc., N.Y.C., 1973-87; bd. overseers Hoover Inst., 2004— Office: 30 Rockefeller Plz Rm 5600 New York NY 10112-0002

FRYE, DELLA MAE, portrait artist; b. Roanoke, Va., Feb. 16, 1926; d. Henry Vetchel and Helen Lavinia Theradosia (Eardley) Pearcy; m. James Frederick Frye, Nov. 1, 1944 (dec.) May 5, 2004; children: Linda Jeanne Frye, James Marvin, David Scott. Student, Hope Coll., 1968, Grand Valley State Coll., 1969-71. Asst. med. records librarian Bapt. Hosp., Little Rock, 1944; receptionist, sec. Stephens Coll., Columbia, Mo., 1945-46; art tchr. Jenison (Mich.) Christian Sch., 1965-67, pvt. classes, 1964-74; realtor, 1978-80; with Diversified Fin., 1979-82; portrait artist, 1967—. Cons. World Traders, Grand Rapids, Mich., 1986—. Author various poems; exhbns. include Salon Des Nations (cert. honor), 1984, Ann Arbor (Mich.) Art Guild, Kalamazoo Artists, Internat. Art Gallery, Hawaii, La Mandragore Gallery Internationale D'Art Contemporain, songwriter: (album) I Love America, 2000-2002 Pres. mother's club Jenison Christian Sch., 1965-66; treas. Band Boosters, Jenison, 1966. Recipient awards for nat. contests in portrait painting. Republican. Baptist. Avocations: songwriting, swimming. Home: 7677 Steele Ave Jenison MI 49428 also: 8901 SE 120th Pl Belleview FL 34420

FRYE, HENRY E., retired state supreme court chief justice; b. Ellerbe, N.C., Aug. 1, 1932; s. Walter A. and Pearl Alma (Motley) F.; m. Edith Shirley Taylor, Aug. 25, 1956; children: Henry Eric, Harlan Elbert. BS in Biol. Scis., A & T U., N.C., 1953; JD with honors, U. N.C., 1959. Bar: N.C. 1959. Asst. U.S. atty. (middle dist.), N.C., 1963-65; prof. law N.C. Central U., Durham, 1965-67; practice law Greensboro, N.C., 1967-83; rep. N.C. Gen. Assembly, 1969-80, N.C. Senate, 1980-82; assoc. justice N.C. Supreme Ct., Raleigh, 1983-99, chief justice, 1999—2001; of counsel Brooks, Pierce, McLendon, Humphrey & Leonard, LLP, Greensboro, NC, 2001—. Organizer, pres. Greensboro Nat. Bank, 1971-80. Deacon Providence Baptist Ch. Capt. USAF, 1953-55. Mem. ABA, N.C. Bar Assn., Greensboro Bar Assn., Nat. Bar Assn., Am. Judicature Soc. (chair bd. dirs. 1995-97), Kappa Alpha Psi. Office: Brooks Pierce McLendon humphrey & Leonard LLP 2000 Renaissance Plaza 230 N Elm St PO Box 26000 Greensboro NC 27420-1841 Office Phone: 336-373-8850. Business E-Mail: hfrye@brookspierce.com.

FRYE, JAY W., music educator; b. Monongahela, Pa., Apr. 19, 1951; s. Wilbur E. and Martha B. Frye; m. Esta Mae Henson, Nov. 6, 1976. MusB, W.Va. U., Morgantown, 1973. Cert. music edn. k-12 W. Va. Band and choir dir. Meadow Bridge H.S., Meadow Bridge, W.Va., 1973—76; stage band dir. Greenbrier West H.S., Charmco, 1978—89, asst. band dir. and choir dir., 1978—89; band and choir dir. Rainelle Jr. H.S., Rainelle, 1990—99; band dir. Western Greenbrier Jr. H.S., Crawley, 2000—. Adj. instr. tuba Glenville State Coll., W.Va., 1998—2000; prin. bass W. Va. Opera Theatre, Charleston, 1975—77, W. Va. Jazz Orch.; prin. tuba Greenbrier River Brass, Lewisburg, Shenandoah Symphony Orch., Lexington, Va.; participant Greenbrier County Faculty Recitals, Monongahela Cmty. Band, Monongahela, Pa.; clinician music edn. tuba and bass; guest condr. and adjudicator. Mem. Western Greenbrier Jr. H.S. Local Sch. Improvement Coun., Rainelle Jr. H.S. Local Sch. Improvement Coun. Recipient citation of Excellence, Nat. Band Dirs. Assn., Divsn. I ratings, W. Va. Band Adjudications. Mem.: W. Va. Edn. Assn., W. Va. Band Masters Assn., W. Va. Music Educators Assn., Am. Fedn. Musicians local 674. Avocations: fly fishing, saltwater fishing. Office: W Greenbrier Jr HS HC40 Box 14 Crawley WV 24931-8830 Home: PO Box 276 Meadow Bridge WV 25976

FRYE, LATOYA AISHA HORTENSE, newswriter; d. Lester Alton and Pansy Moraine (Williams) Frye. AS in Bus. Adminstrn., Piedmont Va. C.C., Charlottesville, Va., 1999; BS in Mktg., Va. Commonwealth U., 2000. Resident asst. Va. Commonwealth U., Richmond, 1998—2000; intern personal banker Bank of Am., Richmond, 1999; intern computer instr. Collis-Warner Found., Alexandria, 2000; mgmt. assoc. Wachovia Bank, Charlottesville, 2001—03, br. mgr., 2003—04; corresp. Charlottesville/Albernarle Tribune, 2004—. Vol. Salvation Army, Charlottesville, Va., 2002—. Mem.: Am. Mktg. Assn., Inroads/Richmond Inc. (Outstanding Acad. Achievement award 1999—2000), Golden Key, Phi Kappa Phi. Avocations: aerobics, rollerblading, tennis. Office: Charlottesville Albernarle Tribune 250 W Main St Ste 402 Charlottesville VA 22902

FRYE, RICHARD ARTHUR, judge; b. Akron, Ohio, Sept. 3, 1948; s. Virgil Arthur and Margaret (Mullen) F.; children: Kathleen, Emily, Abigail. BA, Wittenberg U., 1970; JD, Ohio State U., 1973. Bar: Ohio 1973, U.S. Dist. Ct. (so. dist.) Ohio 1974, U.S. Ct. Appeals (6th cir.) 1978, U.S. Supreme Ct. 1980, U.S. Ct. Appeals (fed. cir.) 1987, U.S. Ct. Appeals (9th cir.) 1998, U.S. Dist. Ct. (no. dist.) Ohio, 2003. Ptnr. Chester, Willcox & Saxbe LLP, Columbus, 1996—2005; judge Franklin County Ct. Common Pleas, 2005—. Co-author: Ohio Eminent Domain Practice, 1977, Personal Injury Litigation in Ohio, 1985. Bd. dirs. Am. Heart Assn., Franklin County, Ohio, 1985-87, J. Ashburn Youth Ctr., 1996-2000; bd. dirs. Legal Aid Soc. Columbus, 1996-2004, pres., 2003-2004; chmn. adv. com. on local rules U.S. Dist. Ct. for So. Dist. Ohio, 1990-2004; chmn. com. to rev. reporting of opinions Supreme Ct. of Ohio, 2000-03; life mem. 6th Circuit. Jud. Conf. Fellow Am. Coll. Trial Lawyers, Columbus Bar Found., Ohio State Bar Found.; mem. Fed. Bar Assn. (pres. Columbus chpt. 1991), Am. Bd. Trial Advocates. Methodist. Office: Common Pleas Ct 369 S High Street Court Rm 8A Columbus OH 43215 Office Phone: 614-462-6281, 614-462-6281. Business E-Mail: Richard_Frye@fccourts.org.

FRYE, ROLAND MUSHAT, JR., lawyer; b. Princeton, N.J., Feb. 8, 1950; s. Roland Mushat and Jean (Steiner) F.; m. Susan Marie Pettey, Jan. 23, 1988. AB cum laude, Princeton U., 1972; JD, Cornell U., 1975. Bar: Pa. 1975, D.C. 1978, U.S. Ct. Appeals (D.C. cir.) 1991, U.S. Supreme Ct. 1991. Litigation assoc. White and Williams, Phila., 1975-77; litigation atty. U.S. Dept. Energy, Washington, 1977-79, asst. solicitor, 1979-80; presiding officer Fed. Energy Regulatory Commn., Washington, 1980-83, chief presiding officer, 1983-85, supervisory atty., 1985-88, adv. atty., 1988-91; energy atty. Pepper, Hamilton & Scheetz, Washington, 1991-92; sr. atty. Office Commn. Appellate Adjudication U.S. Nuclear Regulatory Commn., Washington, 1992—. Mediator Ctr. for Cmty. Justice, D.C. Superior Ct., 1984-86. Editor Cornell Law Rev., 1974-75; mem. editl. bd. Sidwell Friends Sch. Alumni Mag., 1994-2003; contbr. articles to profl. jours. Mem. schs. and ann. giving coms. Princeton U., Washington and Phila., 1978-91; arbitrator Better Bus. Bur. Greater Washington, 1983-86, Phila. Ct. Common Pleas, 1975-77; mem. Sidwell Friends Sch. Parents Assn., treas. 2001-03. Capt. USAR. Recipient Outstanding Young Man Am. award U.S. Jaycees, 1979, Meritorious Svc. award U.S. NRC, 2004. Mem. ABA, D.C. Bar Assn. (fee arbitration panel 1983-89, com. on alt. dispute resolution 1983-87), Fed. Bar Assn., Fed. Energy Bar Assn. (adminstrv. practice com. 1991-92), Sidwell Friends Sch. Alumni Assn. (exec. com. 1985-93, 94-2003, v.p. 1987-89, pres. 1989-93, Newmyer award), Soc. Cin., Mayflower Soc., St. Andrews Soc., Prettyman-Leventhal Am. Inn of Ct. (barrister 1989-92, master 1992-99, exec. com. 1992-99, program chmn. 1993-95, counsellor 1995-96, pres.-elect 1996-97, pres. 1997-98, nat. mem. 1999—), Cosmos Club. Presbyterian. Avocations: trout fishing, singing, travel. Home: 220 N Royal St Alexandria VA 22314-3329 Office: US Nuclear Regulatory Commn 11555 Rockville Pike Rockville MD 20852-2739 Office Phone: 301-415-3505. E-mail: rmf@nrc.gov.

FRYE, WILBUR WAYNE, retired soil science educator, researcher, administrator; b. Finger, Tenn., Aug. 6, 1933; s. Alfred D. and Lela E. (Rouse) F.; m. Martha Hoskins, Apr. 20, 1957; children: Thomas W., John D. BS, U. Tenn., 1961, MS, 1964; PhD, Va. Tech, 1969. Cert. profl. soil scientist, cert. crop advisor. Air traffic controller FAA, Memphis, 1957-58; instr. Tenn. Tech. U., Cookeville, 1963-74; asst. prof. U. Ky., Lexington, 1975-78, assoc. prof., 1978-84, prof., 1984-2000, prof. emeritus, 2000—; exec. dir. Office Consumer and Environ. Protection, Ky. Dept. Agr. Contbr. numerous articles to profl. jours. and chpts. to books; editor books. Chmn. troop commn. Boy Scouts Am., Lexington, 1976-81; chmn. adminstrv. bd. First United Meth. Ch., Lexington, 1977-79; lay del. to Ky. Conf. United Meth. Ch., 1994-96. Recipient Sci. Faculty Fellowship award NSF, 1967, Master Tchr. award Gamma Sigma Delta, 1978, Great Tchr. award U. Ky. Alumni Assn., 1980, Pres.'s Citation Soil & Water Conservation Soc., 1976, 78; named Danforth Assoc., 1981. Fellow Soil and Water Conservation Soc. (bd. dirs. 1975-79), Soil Sci. Soc. Am. (bd. dirs. 1989-90, assoc. editor Jour. 1990-93, Soil Sci. Edn. award 1995), Am. Soc. Agronomy (Agronomic Resident Edn. award 1995); life mem. Coun. for Agrl. Sci. and Tech. (life, bd. dirs. 1991-99), Assn. Am. Feed Control Ofcls. (life, bd. dirs. 1995-97), Assn. Am. Plant Food Control Ofcls. (life), Lexington Lions Club Melvin Jones Fellow (chmn. program com. 2002-2004, Member of Yr. award, 2004). Methodist. Office: Ky Dept Agr 107 Corporate Dr Frankfort KY 40601 Office Phone: 502-573-0282. Business E-Mail: wilbur.frye@ky.gov. E-mail: wilburfrye@cs.com.

FRYE, WILLIAM EMERSON, physicist, engineer; b. Detroit, June 20, 1917; s. Nels and Lillie (Hagman) F.; m. Elizabeth K. Sayler, June 13, 1942 (dec. 1990); children: Ann, James. AA, Danville (Ill.) Jr. Coll., 1935; AB, U. Ill., 1937, MS, 1938; PhD, U. Chgo., 1941. Group leader, then asst. sect. head Naval Rsch. Lab., Washington, 1942-46; group leader N.Am. Aviation, Inc., L.A., 1946-48; staff mem. Rand Corp., Santa Monica, Calif., 1948-56; dept. mgr. Lockheed Missiles and Space Co., Palo Alto, Calif., 1956-59, consulting scientist, 1959-68, staff scientist, 1968—. Rsch. adv. com. NASA, Washington, 1960-64; lectr. in engring. UCLA, 1948-56; lectr. in elec. engring. Stanford (Calif.) U., 1960, 62, 64, 68. Editor: Impact of Space Exploration on Society, 1965. Calendar editor Coun. for Arts, Palo Alto, 1964-68. Recipient Meritorious Civilian Svc. award Naval Rsch. Lab., 1947. Assoc. fellow AIAA; mem. Am. Astronautical Soc. (bd. dirs. 1960-64), Am. Phys. Soc., Sigma Xi, Phi Beta Kappa. Democrat. Unitarian Universalist. Achievements include patents in RF Switch, in Pulse Generator Circuit. Home: 536 Lincoln Ave Palo Alto CA 94301-3232 E-mail: williamefrye@yahoo.com.

FRYE-MOQUIN, MARSHA MARIE, social worker; b. Tecumseh, Mich., Aug. 1, 1950; d. Jesse Roberts Gray and Evelyn Marie Binns Wade; children: Dawn M. Savidge, James M. Savidge Jr., David R. Frye. AS, Monroe County CC, Monroe, Mich., 1976; ADN, U. Vt., 1988; BA in Sociology, North Adams (Mass.) State Coll, 1992; MSW, SUNY, Albany, 1994; cert. in case mgmt., New Eng. Healthcare Assembly, 1997, Commn. Case Mgmt. Certification, 2004. Cert. clin. hypnotherapist; social worker Mass., lic. ind. cert. social worker Mass.; cert. case mgmt. Commn. for Care Mgr. Cert. Sales clk./cashier Woolworth's Dept. Store, Burlington, Vt.; clk., typist New Eng. Tel., Burlington, 1978-80; unit sec. Prince Georges Hosp., Cheverly, Md., 1969-72, Fairfax Hosp., Falls Church, Va., 1972-73; nurses aide Burlington Convalescent Ctr., 1976-77; EEG technician Med. Ctr. Vt., Burlington, 1980-88; lab. technician U. Vt., Burlington, 1987-88; staff nurse Berkshire Med. Ctr., Pittsfield, Mass., 1988-90, charge nurse, 1989-90; intern Women's Svcs. Ctr./Battered Women's Shelter, Pittsfield, Mass., 1991, No. Berkshire Health and Human Svcs. Coalition, North Adams, 1992, Hillcrest Ednl. Ctr., Lenox, Mass., 1992-93, Dept. Vet. Affairs Med. Ctr., Northampton, Mass., 1993-94; med. social worker Fairview Hosp., Great Barrington, Mass., 1994—, dir. mgmt., social svcs., patient adv., 1995—; nurse, med. social worker Vis. Nurses Assn. No. Berkshire, Williamstown, Mass., 1991-95. Faculty Mildred Elley Sch., Inc., 2001—02. Former mem. adv. bd. United Cerebral Palsy Assn. Berkshire County, Inc. Recipient Clin. Excellence award, Vt. State Nurses Assn., cert. of honor for vol. svc., Women's Svc. Ctr., 1991, cert. of appreciation, No. Berkshire Health and Human Svcs. Coalition, 1991, cert. in case mgmt., Commn. Case Mgmt., 2004. Mem.: NASW, New Eng. Sociol. Assn., Kiwanis, Alpha Chi. Avocations: concerts, theater, movies. Home: 10 Williams Ln Apt 4 Great Barrington MA 01230 Office Phone: 413-528-0790 ext 3036. Business E-Mail: mmoquin@bhs1.org.

FRYER, APPLETON, sales executive, diplomat; b. Buffalo, Feb. 25, 1927; s. Livingston and Catherine (Appleton) F.; m. Angeline Dudley Kenefick, May 16, 1953; children: Appleton, Daniel Kenefick, Robert Livingston, Catherine Appleton. AB cum laude, Princeton U., 1950. Head interpreter Hewitt-Robins, Inc., Buffalo, 1950—51; with advt. dept. Buffalo Evening News, 1953—55; field rep., advt. Ketchum, MacLeod & Grove, Inc., 1955—56; pres. Duo-Fast of We. N.Y., Inc., Buffalo, 1956—84; pub. Buffalo Bus. Jour., 1984—86; travel cons. Pieper Travel Bur., 1990; hon. consul gen. Japan, Buffalo, 1979—2002. Task force Inner Harbor Erie Canal, Buffalo, 2000—; co-chmn. Erie County Bi-centennial Commn., 1976. Dep. sheriff Erie County, NY, 1954-68; adv. bd. Children's Hosp. Buffalo; mem. Cmty. Welfare Coun. Buffalo and Erie county; co-chmn. corp. divsn. Episcopal Charities, 1988, chmn. devel. com., 1989; mem. bd. Erie County Sesquicentennial Commn., 1970-71, 74-76, chmn. devel. com., 1988-89; adv. City Buffalo Environ. Mgmt. Commn., 1973-75; trustee Theodore Roosevelt Inaugural Nat. Hist. Site Found., 1969-87; bd. dirs. Zool. Soc. Buffalo, 1972-78, Buffalo Fine Arts Acad., Albright-Knox Art Gallery, 1973-76; chmn. Buffalo-Kanazawa Sister Cities Com., 1978-79; pres. Arboretum Met. Buffalo, 1977-78; mem. Pan Am. Centennial com., 1998-2002; bd. dirs. Maud Gordon Holmes Arboretum, 1974-88, pres., 1976-78; mem. Buffalo Landmark and Preservation Bd., 1978-87, Erie County Preservation Adv. Bd., 1978-82; mem. coun. Charles Burchfield Ctr., 1974-92, Ctrl. Erie deanery Diocese We. N.Y., 1970, Young Life on Niagra Frontier, 1971-72; mem. Erie Canal Heritage Corridor Com., 2001—; chmn. planning com. Venture in Mission, 1979, campaign exec. com., 1979-80; chmn. N.Y. State sect. ann. giving Princeton U., 1979-82, We. N.Y. ann. giving regional com., 1978-79, nat. ann. giving com.; exec. dir. Landmark Soc. Niagara Frontier, 1998-2004, pres., 2005—; adv. bd. Erie County Cultural Resources, 1986-92, Concerned Ecumenical Ministry (West Side), 1986-98; chmn. devel. com. Crane Cutting Ctr., 1987-90; comdr. Lorenzo Burrows post Am. Legion, 1988-89; mem. N.Y. State com. Bicentennial French Revolution, 1988-90; historian We. N. Commandery Naval Order U.S., 1991-99, vice comdr., 1999-2001, comdr., 2001—; patients' rep. Buffalo Gen. Hosp., 1996—; mem. New Millennium Group We. N.Y., 2000—, Martin House Restoration Corp., 1999—; Eucharistic min. Diocese We. NY, 2004—. With USNR, 1945-46, to 1st lt. AUS, 1951-52. Recipient Key to City of Buffalo, Mayor Anthony Masiello, 1996, Long and Dedicated Svc. award, Buffalo-Kanazawa Sister City Com., 1997, Order of the Sacred Treasure, Gold Ray with ribbon, Govt. of Japan, 2002. Mem.: SAR (Buffalo chpt. v.p. 1993—94, pres. 1995—96), Buffalo Soc. Natural Scis., Am. Assn. Mus. (trustee 1978—81), Bi-Nat. Bridge Task Force (Peace Bridge), Order Colonial Lords of Manors, Landmark Soc. Niagara Frontier (pres. 1969—73, 2004—, Outstanding award 1979, Landmarker award 2000, Appleton Fryer Founder award 2003), Holland Soc. N.Y. (pres. Niagra Frontier br. 1969—79), Soc. Mayflower Descendants (regent Buffalo colony 1961—65), Niagra Frontier Indsl. Distbrs. Assn., Mil. Order Fgn. Wars U.S., Navy League U.S., Buffalo Area C. of C. (Buffalo Beautiful com.), Soc. Colonial Wars, Buffalo and Erie County Hist. Soc. (bd. mgrs. 1969—2005, v.p. 1977—82, pres. 1982—84), Old Ft. Niagara Assn. (dir. 1980—90), Princeton U. Alumni Assn. (chmn. schs. com. We. N.Y. area 1974—77), Canal Soc. N.Y. State, Scriptores, Porcupine Club (gov. 1969—73), U. Cottage Club, Nassau Club, Saturn Club (vice dean 1963, 1986, dean 1990), Princeton Club of We. NY (pres. 1960), Princeton Club NY, Rotary (internat. svc. com. 1978—90, bd. dirs. 1983—86), Masons. Episcolpalian (warden, lic. lay reader, Eucharistic min.). Home: 85 Windsor Ave Buffalo NY 14209-1018

FRYER, MINOT PACKER, surgeon; b. Willimantic, Conn., Mar. 16, 1915; s. Minot Samuel and Mary (Packer) F.; children: Edwin Samuel, Minot Packer; m. Luise R. Whiting, 1973. AB, Brown U., 1936; MD, Johns Hopkins U., 1940; D.Sc. (hon.), Brown U., 1971. Diplomate: Am. Bd. Surgery, Am. Bd. Plastic Surgery (mem. 1962-68, sec.-treas. 1963-67, vice chmn. 1967-68, sr. examiner 1977—). Intern Johns Hopkins Hosp., 1940-41; resident Barnes Hosp., St. Louis, 1941-44, fellow in plastic surgery, 1946-48, asst. surgeon, 1948-67; assoc. prof. clin. surgery Washington U. Med. Sch., St. Louis, 1957-67, prof. clin. surgery, 1967—; assoc. prof. clin. maxilo-facial surgery Washington U. Dental Sch. (Dental Sch.), 1957-67, prof. clin. maxilo-facial surgery, 1967—. Surgeon emeritus St. Louis Children's Hosp.; assoc. surgeon emeritus Barnes Hosp.; hon. staff DePaul Hosp., 1948—, chief surgery, 1962-64 Author: (with J. Brown) Surgery of Face, Mouth and Jaws, 1954, Postmortem Homografs, 1960; Cons. editor: Surgery, Gynecology and Obstetrics, 1960-65; Contbr. articles to sci. jours. Served to lt., M.C. USNR, 1944-46. Fellow A.C.S. (past chmn. council plastic surgery), Am. Assn. Surgery Trauma; mem. AMA, Am. Surg. Assn., St. Louis Med. Soc., Assn. Mil. Surgeons, Am. Soc. Plastic and Reconstructive Surgery, Am. Assn. Plastic Surgeons (pres. 1967-68), Central Surg. Assn., Soc. Head and Neck Surgeons, Western Surg. Assn., Halsted Soc. Home: PO Box 3907 Evansville IN 47737-3907

FRYER, THOMAS WAITT, JR., writer; b. Martinsville, Va., Oct. 6, 1936; s. Thomas Waitt and Wilma Pauline (Harp) F.; m. Mary Margaret Allshouse, Jan. 5, 1980; children— Laura Elizabeth, Matthew Thomas, John Anderson. AA, Mars Hill Coll., 1956; BA, Wayland Coll., 1958; MA (Ford Found. fellow), Vanderbilt U., 1959; PhD (Kellogg Found. fellow), U. Calif., Berkeley, 1968. Instr. in English Daytona Beach Jr. Coll., 1959-61; assoc. dean instrn. Chabot Coll., 1965-67; v.p., chief campus adminstr. Miami-Dade Community Coll., 1967-73; chancellor Peralta Colls., 1973-78; chancellor, dist. supt. Foothill-De Anza Community Coll. Dist., 1978-92; vice chmn. bd. dirs. Am. Council on Edn., 1979-80. Vis. prof. U. Calif. at Berkeley, 1988-92; pres. Fla. Assn. Community Colls., 1971-73. Chmn. WASC Accred Com. for Community and Jr. Colls., 1984-86; pres. chief exec. officers Calif. Community Colls., 1986-87; trustee, bd. chair Fla. C.C. Jacksonville, 1999-2003. Recipient Communication and Leadership award Toastermasters Internat., 1977, selected a Young Leader of Acad., 1978; named one of Most Effective Coll. Pres. in Nation Exxon Edn. Found., 1986, one of 50 best community coll. CEO's by U. Tex., Austin, 1988. Mem. Nat. Soc. Study Edn., Am. Assn. Higher Edn. (dir. 1975-78), Assn. for Study of Higher Edn., Phi Delta Kappa. Clubs: Commonwealth of Calif., Rotary. Office Phone: 925-947-5878. E-mail: tomfryer@juno.com.

FRYER, WILLIAM NEAL, retired psychologist; b. Cin., Mar. 10, 1922; s. Roy Charles and Alice (Carson) F.; m. Dorothy Elizabeth McClain, May 11, 1942; children: Bonnie Jean, Debra Lynn. BA, Harding Coll., 1948; MA, Columbia U., 1953, EdD, 1965. Aircraft painter Aero. Corp. Am., Cin., 1937-39; salesman Sears, Roebuck & Co., Covington, Ky., 1940-41; min. Bklyn. Ch. of Christ, 1948-56; asst. prof. psychology Abilene (Tex.) Christian Coll., 1956-65, assoc. prof., 1965-68, part-time tchr. psychology, 1968-70; chief psychologist Abilene State Sch., 1968-85. Author: (with Orval Filbeck, Max Leach) College, Classroom, Campus and You, 1959. Mem. Mayor's Com. on Mental Retardation, Abilene, 1964-65; past mem. exec. com., profl. adviser Abilene Suicide Prevention Svc.; bd. dirs., past mem. profl. adv. com. Abilene Assn. Mental Health, pres. 1958-59; past bd. dirs. Tex. Assn. Mental Health; vol. Christ's Prison Fellowship, 1989—. Capt. USAAF, 1941-46. Mem. Am., Southwestern, Tex., Abilene (pres. 1978-79) psychol. assns., AAAS, N.Y. Acad. Sci., Am. Assn. Mental Deficiency, Abilene Writers Guild (pres. 1990-91, 91-92), Kiwanis, Phi Delta Kappa, Kappa Delta Pi. Mem. Ch. of Christ. Home: 4149 Forrest Hill Rd Apt 5102 Abilene TX 79606-5495

FRYKENBERG, ROBERT ERIC, historian, educator; b. India, June 8, 1930; s. Carl Eric and Doris Marie (Skoglund) F.; m. Carol Addington, July 1, 1952; children: Ann Denise Lewis, Brian Robert, Craig Michael. BA, Bethel Coll., Minn., 1951; MA, U. Minn., 1953; MDiv, Bethel Theol. Sem., 1955; PhD, London U., 1961. Rsch. asst. U. Calif., Berkeley, 1955-57; instr. Oakland (Calif.) Jr. Coll., 1957-58; Ford and Carnegie rsch. and tchg. fellow U. Chgo., 1961-62; mem. faculty U. Wis., Madison, 1962—97, prof. history and S. Asian studies, 1971-97, emeritus prof. history and S. Asian studies, 1997—, chmn. dept., dir. Ctr. S. Asian Studies, 1970-73. Vis. prof. U. Hawaii, summer 1968; Radhakrishnan Meml. lectr. Oxford U., 1998; dir. Pew India Rsch. Advancement Projects, 1994-01. Author: Guntur District, 1788-1848: A History of Local Influence and Central Authority in South India, 1965, History and Belief: The Foundations of Historical Understanding, 1996; editor: Land Control and Social Structure in Indian History, 1969, 77, Land Tenure and Peasant in South Asia: An Anthology of Recent Research, 1977, Studies of South India, 1985, Delhi Through the Ages, 1986, 93, Christians and Missionaries in India: Cross-Cultural Communication since 1500, 2003, Tirunelveli's Evangelical Christians: Two Centuries of Family Traditions, 2003, Pandita Ramabai's America, 2003; co-editor: Studies in the History of Christian Missions series, 1997—, Christians, Cultural Interactions, and India's Religious Traditions, 2002; contbr. articles to revs. and profl. publs. Trustee Am. Inst. Indian Studies, 1971-81; dir. summer seminar NEH, 1976. Rockefeller fellow U. London, 1958-61; rsch. fellow Am. Coun. Learned Socs.-Social Sci. Rsch. Coun. 1962-63, 67, 73-74, 83-84, 88-89, Guggenheim fellow, 1968-69, HEW Fulbright Hays sr. fellow, 1965-66, NEH fellow, 1975, fellow Wis. Inst. Rsch. Humanities, 1975, Wilson Ctr., 1986, 91-92, Pew Rsch. fellow, 1997. Fellow Royal Hist. Soc., Royal Asiatic Soc.; mem. Internat. Conf. and Seminars, Soc. S. Indian Studies (pres. 1968-70, 82-84), Am. Hist. Assn. (pres. Conf. Faith and History 1970-72), Assn. Asian Studies, Inst. Hist. Studies India, Inst. Asian Studies India, Assn. S. Asian Studies Australia, Inst. Advanced Christian Studies (dir. 1979-83, 87-91, 98-2002, pres. 1981-83) Office: Univ Wis Humanities Bldg 455 N Park St Madison WI 53706 E-mail: refryken@wisc.edu.

FRYMER, MURRY, writer, film critic, theater critic; b. Toronto, Ont., Can., Apr. 24, 1934; came to U.S., 1945; s. Dave and Sylvia (Spinrod) F.; m. Barbara Lois Grown, Sept. 4, 1966; children: Paul, Benjamin, Carrie. BA, U. Mich., 1956; student, Columbia U., 1958; MA, NYU, 1964. Editor Town Crier, Westport, Conn., 1962-63, Tribune, Levittown, N.Y., 1963-64; viewpoints editor, critic Newsday, L.I., N.Y., 1964-72; asst. mng. editor Rochester Democrat & Chronicle, N.Y., 1972-75; Sunday and feature editor Cleve. Plain Dealer, 1975-77; editor Sunday Mag. Boston Herald Am., 1977-79; film and TV critic San Jose Mercury News, Calif., 1979-83, theater critic, 1983—, columnist, 1983—, San Jose Mag., 2000—. Instr. San Jose State U., Cleve. State U., judge Emmy awards NATAS, 1968; co-founder, sr. writer TheColumnists.com.; staff mem. Pulitzer Prize, 1990. Author: They are Coming for My Mattress, 1999; author, dir. musical revue Four by Night, N.Y.C., 1963; author (play) Danse Marriage, 1955 (Hopwood prize 1955); author, dir. 6th U.S. Army show A Dozen and One, 1958. Served with U.S. Army, 1956-58. Recipient Best Columnist/Critic award Calif. Publishers Assn., 1993; named Best Columnist, Peninsula Calif. Press Club, 1993. E-mail: mfrymer@yahoo.com.

FRYT, MONTE STANISLAUS, petroleum company executive, speaker, advisor; b. Jackson, Mich., Aug. 3, 1949; s. Marion S. and Dorothy A. (Fischman) F.; m. Pollyanna Hayes, May 26, 1990. BS in Aerospace Engring., U. Colo., Boulder, 1971; MBA in Mgmt., U. Colo., Denver, 1988. Field engr. Schlumberger Well Svcs., Bakersfield, Calif., 1971-75, computer R & D engr. Houston, 1975-77, account devel. engr. L.A., 1977-78, dist. mgr. Abilene, Tex., 1978-80, Williston, N.D., 1980-81; v.p. ops. Logmate Svcs. Inc., Calgary, Alta., Can., 1981-84; pres. Fryt Petroleum Inc., Denver, 1984-91; mgr. petrophysics Am. Hunter Exploration, Ltd., Denver, 1991-92; prin. Reservoir Evaluations Group, Denver, 1992-99; ptnr., mgr. Monteray Energy LLC, Denver, 1994-98; mgr. tech. Anschutz Exploration Corp., 1995—2003; cons. Worldwide Petroleum Engring & Geol., 2003—04; dir. tech. Direct Detection Experts (DDX) Corp., Denver, 2004—. Mem. Colo. Rep. Com., 1990—, Rep. Nat. Com., Colo. Rep. Leadership Program, 1992-93; mem. exec. com. Colo. Rep. Bus. Coalition, 1993-2002, vice-chmn., 1996-97, chmn., 1997-99. Mem. Am. Assn. Petroleum Geologists, Soc. Petroleum Engrs., Rocky Mountain Assn. Geologists, Elks, Rockies Venture Club, Independence Inst. Roman Catholic. Avocations: mountain climbing, skiing, running, cultural and political reading, Tae Kwon Do. Home and Office: 7400 S Curtice Ct Littleton CO 80120-3951 E-mail: sillymoon@comcast.net.

FRYWALD, J. ERIK, agricultural products executive; b. July 29, 1959; m. Mary Lou Frywald; 3 children. BSChemE, U. Del., 1981; postgrad., Harvard U., 1998. V.p., gen. mgr. Solae LLC; leader Zytel DuPont, prodn. supr. Nylon Intermediates, leader Engring. Polymers, v.p. e-commerce and bus. devel., head global sales and mktg. Engring. Polymers, v.p. corp. plans and bus. devel., v.p., gen. mgr. Qualicon, v.p., gen. mgr. LiquiBox, v.p., gen. mgr. Food Industry Solutions; group v.p. Agr. and Nutrition, Dupont, Wilmington, Del., 2003—; prodn. engr. DuPont, Wilmington, Del., 1981—. Office: Dupont Dupont Bldg 1007 Market St Wilmington DE 19898

FRYXELL, DAVID ALLEN, publishing executive; b. Sioux Falls, S.D., Mar. 8, 1956; s. Donald Raymond and Lucy (Dickinson) F.; m. Lisa Duaine Forman, June 16, 1978; 1 child, Courtney Elizabeth. BA, Augustana Coll., 1978. Assoc.-sr. editor TWA Ambassador, St. Paul, 1978-80, mng. editor, 1980-81; sr. editor Horizon, Tuscaloosa, Ala., 1981-82; circuit writer Telegraph Herald, Dubuque, Iowa, 1982-85; contbg. editor Horizon mag., 1982-85; dir. publs., exec. editor Pitt mag. U. Pitts., 1985-90; editl. dir. Quad/Creative Group Milwaukee Mag., 1991-92; exec. features editor, dir. new ventures St. Paul Pioneer Press, 1992-95, sr. editor technology and new ventures, 1995-96; sr. editor bus. and tech., 1996; exec. producer Twin Cities Sidewalk Microsoft Corp., 1996-98; mag. editl. dir. F & W Publs., Cin., 1998—2001, editor-in-chief, 2001—03; editor and pub. Desert Exposure, 2003—; pres. Continental Divide Pub. LLC, 2005—. Chief judge mags. Golden Quill awards, Pitts., 1980; nonfiction columnist Writer's Digest, 1994—; faculty Maui Writers Conf., 2000—. Author: Double-Parked on Main Street, 1988, How to Write Fast While Writing Well, 1992, Elements of Article Writing: Structure and Flow, 1996, Write Faster, Write Better, 2004; editor: Family Tree Mag., 2000-03, Comair Navigator Mag., 2001-02, Tufts University Guide to Healthy Living, 2004—; mng. editor Tufts Health and Nutrition Letter, 2004—; contbr. articles to mags. including Travel & Leisure, Playboy, Passages, AAA World, Savvy, Online Access, Diversion, Easy Living, Readers Digest, Link Up, others. Chief writer Anderson for Pres. Com., Minn., 1978. Mem. Iowa Newspaper Assn. (2d award master columnist 1983, 2d award best feature writing 1983, 2d award best series 1983), Chgo. Art Dirs. Club (Merit award for editing 1981), Coll. and Univ. Pub. Relations Assn. of Pa., Council for Advancement and Support of Edn. (Periodicals Improvement award 1987, 90, 91, Top Ten Mag. award 1990, 91, Articles of Yr. award 1990, Periodical Spl. Issues award 1991, Instl. Rels. Publs. award 1991, Periodical Resource Mgmt. award, 1990, 91), Augustana Coll. Fellows, Augustana Alumni Assn. (Decades of Leadership award 1978), Blue Key, Internat. Assn. Bus. Communicators (Golden Triangle award 1987, 89, best spl. publ. award 1988), Women in Communications (Matrix award 1990, hon. mention 1990, 91), City and Regional Mag. Assn. (Gen. Excellence award 1992, Spl. Sect. award 1992, Commentary award 1992, Investigative Writing award 1992), Mo. Lifestyle Awards (2d Gen. Excellence award 1994, 95). Democrat. Unitarian Universalist. Office: PO Box 191 Silver City NM 88062 Office Phone: 505-538-4374. Business E-Mail: editor@desertexposure.com.

FRYXELL, GRETA ALBRECHT, marine botany educator, oceanographer; b. Princeton, Ill., Nov. 21, 1926; d. Arthur Joseph and Esther (Andreen) Albrecht; m. Paul A. Fryxell, Aug. 23, 1947; children: Karl Joseph, Joan Esther, Glen Edward. BA, Augustana Coll., 1948; MEd, Tex. A&M U., 1969, PhD, 1975. Tchr. math and sci. jr. high schs., Iowa, 1948-52; research asst. Tex. A&M U., College Station, 1968-71, research scientist, 1971-80, asst. prof. oceanography, 1980-83, assoc. prof., 1983-86, prof., 1986-94, prof. emeritus, 1994—; adj. prof. botany U. Tex., Austin, 1993—. Vis. scientist U. Oslo, 1971; chmn. adv. commn. Provasoli-Guillard Ctr. for Culture Marine Phytoplankton, Bigelow Lab, Maine, 1985-87; hon. curator N.Y. Bot. Garden, 1992—; courtesy prof. U. Oreg., 1994—; sr. rsch. scientist U. Tex. Marine Sci. Inst., 1996—. Editor: Survival Strategies of the Algae, 1983; contbr. articles to profl. jours. Recipient Outstanding Woman award Brazos County, College Station, 1979, Outstanding Achievement award Augustana Coll., Rock Island, Ill., 1980; Faculty Disting. Achievement award in rsch. Tex. A&M U., 1991, Geoscis. and Earth Resources Adv. Coun. medal, 1993; grantee NSF. Fellow: AAAS; mem.: ACLU, Oceanographic Soc., Tex. Assn. Coll. Tchrs., Internat. Diatom Soc. (coun. 1986—92), Am. Soc. Plant Taxonomists, Internat. Phycol. Soc., Brit. Phycol. Soc., Phycol. Soc. Am. (editl. bd. 1976—79, 1982—85, chair Prescott award com. 1991, award of Excellence in Phycology 1996). Democrat. Unitarian-Universalist. Office: U Tex Sch Biol Scis Sect Integrative Biology Austin TX 78712 Mailing: 650 Harrison Ave Claremont CA 91711

FRYZ, BETTY FARINA, secondary school educator; b. Pitts., Mar. 29, 1930; d. Frank Joseph and Theresa (Pagliaro) Farina; m. Joseph Michael Fryz Sr., Aug. 6, 1955; children: Joseph Michael Jr., Deborah Lynn. BS in Music Edn., Ind. U., 1951; postgrad., Carnegie-Mellon U., 1953. Tchr. music elem. sch., jr. and sr. high schs. Moon Area Sch. Dist., Coraopolis, Pa., 1951-93, choral dir., tchr. piano, 1987—, head humanities dept., 1987—; pvt. piano tchr., 1994—. Pvt. practice piano tchr., Pa., 1960-80; cons. music Prentice-Hall, Pa., 1971-73; chmn. jr. high music curriculum com. Dist. 1, Pa., 1984-86. Mem. Mid. States Evaluating Com.; bd. dirs. Am. Youth Symphony and Chorus; Pa. State Rep. for Retired Music Tchrs., 1997—; choir dir. St. Margaret Mary Ch., 1999—. Named one of Outstanding Secondary Educators of Am., 1974. Mem. NEA, AAUW, Music Educators Nat. Conf. (chairperson 1987—), Pa. Music Educators Assn. (Citation of Excellence award 1989; rep. ret. music tchrs. 1997), Pi Kappa Sigma (pres. 1949-51). Roman Catholic. Avocations: tennis, golf. Office: Moon Area Sch Dist 1407 Beers School Rd Coraopolis PA 15108-2597

FTHENAKIS, EMANUEL JOHN, air transportation executive; b. Greece, Jan. 30, 1928; came to U.S., 1952, naturalized, 1956; s. John and Evanthia (Magoulakis) F.; m. Hermione Jane Coates, 1972; children: John, Basil. Diploma mech. and elec. engring., Tech. U. Athens, 1951; MS in Elec. Engring., Columbia U., 1954; postgrad., U. Pa., 1961-62. Mem. tech. staff Bell Tel. Labs., 1952-57; dir. engring. missile and space div. G.E., Phila., 1957-61; v.p., gen. mgr. space and re-entry div. Philco-Ford Co., Palo Alto, Calif., 1961-69; pres. ITT Aerospace Co., L.A., 1969-70; chmn. Am. Satellite Corp., Germantown, Md., 1971-85; v.p. Fairchild Industries, Germantown, 1971-80, sr. v.p., 1980-84, exec. v.p., 1984, pres., chief exec. officer Chantilly, Va., 1985-86, chmn., chief exec. officer, 1986-91; pres., COO Fairchild Corp., Chantilly, 1990-91, also bd. dirs.; chmn., chief exec. officer CEF Corp., Potomac, Md., 1991—. Adj. prof. U. Md., 1981-84; mem. Pres.'s Nat. Security Telecomms. Adv. Coun., 1982-91; chmn., CEO, Olympic Airways, 1993. Author: A Manual of Satellite Communications, 1984; patentee in field. Mem. bd. visitors Coll. Engring., U. Md., 1980—2005; bd. dirs. U. Md. Found., 1989—; bd. dirs. Challenger Ctr. for Space Sci. and Edn., 1988-96, chmn. bd., 1994-96; trustee Univs. Rsch. Assn., Inc., 1990—. Named Man of Yr., Electronic & Aerospace Systems Conf., 1982 Fellow IEEE; mem. AIAA (assoc.), The George Town Club. Greek Orthodox. Office: CEF Corp PO Box 59708 Rockville MD 20859-9708 Personal E-mail: efthe@aol.com.

FTHENAKIS, VASILIS, chemical engineer, consultant, educator; b. Chania, Crete, Greece, July 21, 1951; arrived in US, 1976, naturalized, 1986; s. Menelaos and Antonia Korkidis; m. Christina Georgakopoulos, Feb. 6, 1982; children: Antonia, Menelaos. Diploma in Chemistry, U. Athens, 1975; MS in Chem. Engring., Columbia U., 1978; PhD in Fluid Dynamics & Atmospheric Sci., NYU, 1991. Rsch. analyst Columbia U., N.Y.C., project engr.; sr. chem. engr. Brookhaven Nat. Lab., Upton, N.Y., 1980—. Cons. Exxon Mobil, Dow Chemical, 3M Corp., Amoco Oil, others; founder EnviroConsultants Inc., Upton, NY, 1991; chmn. confs.; adj. prof. environ. engring., chem. engring. CCNY, 1992-96, Columbia U., 1993—; expert witness on chem. process safety and environ. cases, 1997—; cons. in field. Author: Prevention and Control of Accidental Releases of Hazardous Gases, 1993; editor Fossil Energy and the Environ. newsletter, 1991-93; mem. editl. bd. Progress in Photovoltaics, 1996-, Jour. Loss Prevention, 1998-; contbr. over 200 articles to profl. jours., chpts. to books. Recipient Sci. Excellence award, EENS, 2002. Fellow AIChE, Internat. Energy Found.; mem. Ctr. Chem. Process Safety (panel experts), Semiconductor Safety Assn, Am. Meteorol. Soc., Am. Chem. Soc. Home: 9 Lucille Ln Dix Hills NY 11746-5848 Office: Brookhaven Nat Lab Environ Scis Dept Ctr Bldg 830 Upton NY 11973 Office Phone: 631-344-2830. E-mail: vmf@bnl.gov.

FTIZGERALD, JOAN V., artist; b. Batavia, N.Y., Jan. 24, 1930; d. Russell Edward Voyer and Marian Ruth Voyer Montague; children: Remy C. Orffeo, Jerome P. Orffeo, Andres Orffeo. BS in Art Edn., Buffalo State Coll., 1963, MS in Art Edn., 1968. Tchr. art Hamburg Ctrl. Schs., NY, 1964—85; asst. prof. Erie C.C., Buffalo, 1985—92, acting asst. acad. dean, 1989—90, instr. fine arts, 1992—98. Author: (children's book) The Magic Lunch Box, 2003, Not Another Christmas!, 2004, poems; paintings in more than 75 exhbns., (9 awards). Co-chair Environ. Conservation Commn., Hamburg, 1990—92; mem. People for Parks, 2001—05. Mem.: Western N.Y. Artists Group (bd. dirs. 2000—05), Buffalo Soc. Artists (pres. 1980).

FU, CARY T., electronics executive; MS accounting, U. of Houston. CPA. Controller Intermedics, 1983—86; asst. sec. Benchmark Electronics, 1988—90, sec., 1990—96, treas., 1986—96, bd. dir., 1986—88, 1990—, exec. v.p, Financial Administration, 1990—92, exec. v.p., 1990—2001, pres., COO, 2001—04, pres., CEO, 2004—. Office: c/o Benchmark Electronics 3000 Technology Dr Angleton TX 77515*

FU, DEXUE, medical researcher; s. Yushan Fu and Guoying Zhu; m. Jie Zhu, Jan. 28, 1991; children: Chengrui, May. PhD, Gunma (Japan) U., 1998. Lic. physician China, 1998. Rsch. scientist Uniformed Sci. U., Bethesda, Md., 2000—02, Johns Hopkins U., Balt., 2002—. Fellow, Japanese Govt., 1998—2000. Mem.: ASM (corr.). Achievements include first to made breakthrough on cancer study. Home: 49 Jones Valley Circle Baltimore MD 21209 Office: Johns Hopkins University 1650 Orleans Street Baltimore MD Office Phone: 410-502-7208. Personal E-mail: dfu@jhmi.edu. E-mail: dfu1@jhmi.edu.

FU, HUAXIANG, science educator; b. Linchuan, Jiangxi, China, July 19, 1969; arrived in U.S., 1995; s. Jufu Fu and Guajin Wang; m. Kun Jin; 1 child, Le J. BS, U. Sci. and Tech. China, Hefei, 1988; MS, Fudan U., Shanghai, 1991, PhD, 1994. Postdoctoral rschr. Nat. Renewable Energy Lab., Golden, Colo., 1995—98; rsch. assoc. Carnegie Inst. Washington, 1998—2000; mem. faculty Rutgers U., Camden, NJ, 2000—02, U. Ark., Fayetteville, 2002—. Contbr. articles to profl. jours. Mem.: Am. Phys. Soc. Achievements include development of ferroelectric material sciences; research in nanoscience and nanotechnology; first to organic-inorganic hybrid semiconductors. Avocations: exercise, sports. Office: U Ark Dept Physics 226 Physics Bldg Fayetteville AR 72701 Business E-Mail: hfu@uark.edu.

FU, I-PING PHYLLIS, language educator, researcher; b. Taiwan, Apr. 29, 1963; d. Chan Lu and I-Feng Fu; m. Szetsen Steven Lee, Nov. 18, 1993 (div. Mar. 15, 2000); children: Shannon Lee, Serena Lee. BA, U. Calif., Berkeley, 1986; MPA, U. Wash., 1990; PhD, Va. Tech, 2005. Cert. Chinese instr. Union Chinese Sch., N.J., 1995, Effective Chinese lang. tchr. III Chinese Am. Cultural Assn. Edn. Rsch. Ctr., N.J., 1996, English lang. instr. Nat. Taiwan Normal U., 1999, Tchr. Chinese as Second Lang. Nat. Taiwan U., 2001. Mem. faculty Radford U., Va., 2000—; Chinese lang. instr. Va. Tech, Blacksburg, 2000—, asst. to chair, 2002—03; Chinese lang. and cultural instr. Chinese Sch. of VPI, Blacksburg, Va., 2002—. Lang. cons. State and City Courts, Roanoke, Va., 2000—, Pulaski Furniture Corp., Va., 2003—. Fellow Assn. for Internat. and Mgmt., Grad. Sch. of Pub. Policy, U.C. Berkeley, 1995, John F. Kennedy Sch. of Govt., Harvard U., 1986, Grad. Sch. of Pub. Affairs, U. of Wash., 1987—88; grantee Rsch. Grant, Sapinia Culture and Edn. Found., 2002. Mem.: Tchr. Devel. Spl. Interest Group, Va. Tchrs. of English to Speakers of other Lang., Chinese Lang. Tchrs. Assn., Chinese Lang. Assn. of Secondary-Elem. Sch., Am. Coun. for Tchrs. of Fgn. Lang. (assoc.). Home: PO Box 602 Christiansburg VA 24068 Personal E-mail: ifu@vt.edu.

FU, LEE-LUENG, oceanographer; b. Taipei, Republic of China, Oct. 10, 1950; s. Yi-Chin and Er-Lan (Chen) F.; m. Cecilia C. Liu, Mar. 26, 1977; 1 child, Christine. BS, Nat. Taiwan U., Taipei, 1972; PhD, MIT, 1980. Postdoctoral assoc. MIT, Cambridge, Mass., 1980; mem. tech. staff Jet Propulsion Lab., Pasadena, Calif., 1981-85, tech. group supr., Topex/Poseidon, 1986-93, project scientist, 1988—, lead scientist/ocean scis., 1994, sr. rsch. scientist, 1994. Chmn. Jason sci. working team NASA, Washington, 1988—; vis. prof. Ocean U. Qingdao, China, 2002. Contbr. articles to profl. publs. Recipient Laurels award Aviation Week and Space Tech., 1993, CNES medal French Space Agy., 1994, Exceptional Scientific Achievement medal NASA, 1996, Outstanding Leadership Medal, 2004. Fellow: Am. Meteorol. Soc. (Editor's award 2005, Verner E. Suomi award 2002), Am. Geophys. Union; mem.: Oceanography Soc. Office: Jet Propulsion Lab MS 300-323 4800 Oak Grove Dr Pasadena CA 91109-8001 Business E-Mail: llf@pacific.jpl.nasa.gov.

FU, MICHAEL C., management science educator; s. Yuen-Sun and Ruth H. Fu; m. Fan Chen, June 24, 1989; children: Lara, David. SB, SM, MIT, 1985; MS, PhD, Harvard U., 1989. Prof. U. Md., College Park, 1989—. Author: Conditional Monte Carlo: Gradient Estimation and Optimization Applications, 1997. Recipient Ops. Rsch. Divsn. award Inst. for Indsl. Engr., 1999, Best Paper award, 1998; Outstanding Systems Engring. Faculty award Inst. for Systems Rsch., 2002; Distinguished Scholar-Tchr. U. of Md., 2004-2005. Mem. Inst. Ops. Rsch. and Mgmt. Sci. (Outstanding Pub. award 1998). Office: U Md Van Munching Hall College Park MD 20742-1815

FU, PAUL SHAN, law librarian, consultant; b. Shien-Yang, Liao-Ning, China, Sept. 7, 1932; came to U.S., 1961; s. Mu-Shia and Shih-Wei (Chang) F.; m. Doris S. Ku, Jan. 15, 1963; children: Eugene Y., Vincent Y. LLB, Soochow U., 1960; MCL, U. Ill., 1962; MSLS, Villanova U., 1968. Asst. libr., law lectr. Detroit Coll. of Law, 1968-69; law libr., asst. prof. law Ohio No. U., Ada, 1969-71, law libr., assoc. prof. law, 1971-72; law libr. Supreme Ct. of Ohio, Columbus, 1972—; pres. Asian-Am. Law Librs. Caucus, 1994. Dir. Nat. Conf. on State Ct. Librs., Columbus, 1993; cons. Supreme Ct. of Ill. Law Libr., Springfield, 1988, N.H. State Law Libr., Concord, 1987; judge West Pub. Excellence in Law Librarianship Awards Com., 1996. Author: Law Library Handbook of Ohio Supreme Court, 1974; columnist Ohio Lawyer, 1988—; contbr. articles to profl. jours. Recipient Award of Merit Columbus Bar Assn., 1996; U. Ill. fellow, 1961-62. Mem. ALA, Am. Assn. Law Librs. (sec. 1989-93, chair state, ct., and county law librs. sect. 1977-78), Am. Soc. Internat. Law, Univ. Club, Kiwanis (Columbus). Avocations: piano, painting, fiction, tennis. Home: 940 Evening St Worthington OH 43085-3051 Office: Ohio State Supreme Ct Law Libr 30 E Broad St Fl 4 Columbus OH 43215-3414

FU, QIANJIE, research scientist; b. Dongyang, Zhejiang, China; s. Xiaosong Wang; married; 1 child, William. BS, U. Sci. Tech. China, Hefei, 1991; MS, U. Sci. Tech. China, 1994; PhD, U. So. Calif., 1997. Rsch. assoc. House Ear Inst., L.A., 1996-98, scientist I LA, 1998—2001, scientist II, 2001—. Tchg. asst. U. So. Calif., L.A., 1994-95. Contbr. articles to profl. jours. NIH grantee, 1998-2001, 2001-2006. Mem. IEEE, Acoustical Soc. Am., Assn. Rsch. Otolaryngology. Office: House Ear Inst 2100 W Third St Los Angeles CA 90057

FU, SHOUCHENG JOSEPH, biomedicine educator; b. Beijing, Mar. 19, 1924; s. W.C. Joseph and W.C. (Tsai) F.; m. Susan B. Guthrie, June 21, 1951; children: Robert W.G., Joseph H.G., James B.G. BS, MS, Cath. U., Beijing, 1944; PhD, Johns Hopkins U., 1949. Postdoctoral fellow Nat. Insts. Health, Bethesda, Md., 1949—51, scientist, 1951—55; Gustav Bissing fellow Johns Hopkins U. at Univ. Coll. London, 1955—56; chief enzyme and bioorganic chemistry lab. Children's Cancer Rsch Found (now Dana Farber Cancer Inst.), 1956—65; rsch. assoc. Harvard U. Med. Sch., Boston, 1956—65; prof., chmn. bd. chemistry Chinese U., Hong Kong, 1966—70, dean sci. faculty, 1967—69; vis. prof. Coll. Physicians and Surgeons Columbia U., N.Y.C., 1970—71; prof. biochemistry and molecular biology U. Medicine and Dentistry of N.J., Newark, 1971—2003, prof. emeritus, 2003—, asst. dean, 1974—77; acting dean Grad. Sch. Biomed. Scis., 1977—78, prof. ophthalmology, 1989—2003, prof. emeritus, 2003—. Founder, pres. CMDNJ Credit Union (now North Jersey Fed. Credit Union), 1974-75. Contbr. articles to profl. jours. Capt. USPHS, 1959—. Named Hon. Disting. Prof. and Acad. Advisor Inner Mongolia Med. U., Huthot, Peoples Republic of China, 1988—. Fellow AAAS, Royal Soc. Chemistry (U.K.); mem. Royal Hong Kong Jockey Club, Am. Club Hong Kong, Sigma Xi (Newark chpt. pres. 1976-80, sec. 1974-76, 81-82). Home: 693 Prospect St Maplewood NJ 07040-3105 Office: U Medicine and Dentistry NJ Med Sch Med Sci Bldg 185 S Orange Ave Newark NJ 07103-2757 Office Phone: 973-972-4514. E-mail: fujo@umdnj.edu.

FUCCI, JOSEPH LEONARD, editor, college librarian; b. Mt. Vernon, N.Y., Jan. 31, 1950; s. Joseph Vito and Roselyn (Pecoraro) F.; m. Adrianne Darway, Aug. 7, 1977. AA, Bronx C.C., 1971; BA in English Lit., Herbert H. Lehman Coll., 1972; MLS, Columbia U., 1974; BArch, Pratt Inst., 1985. Head serials dept. Sarah Lawrence Coll. Library, Bronxville, N.Y., 1974-76; head circulation dept., Westchester Med. Ctr. Library, N.Y. Med. Coll., Valhalla, N.Y., 1976-77; head periodicals dept. Orange County Community Coll. Library, Middletown, N.Y., 1977-82; owner Archtl. Editing, Graphics & Info. Services, Middletown, 1982-90; asst. prof. of reader svcs. Sullivan County C.C., 1990-94, head reader svcs., 1992-94; prin., architect Aegis Design, Middletown, 1990—; asst. prof. bibliographic instrn. Westchester C.C., 1994-96. Home improvement consulting editor, Creative Homeowner Press, Upper Saddle River, N.J., 1998-2000; architect Sullivan Co. Dept. Pub. Works, 2001-02; mem. curriculum com. Orange County C.C., 1978-81, mem. acad. affairs bd., 1978-81, chair Info. Lit. and Bibliographic Instrn. Com. Sullivan County C.C., 1993-94; mem. environ. com. Westchester C.C., 1994-96. Editor: Architecture: Classified Bibliography, 1980, 3d. rev. ed., 1982, Quick Guide to Siding, 1999, Adding Value to Your Home, 1999, Home Wiring: Basic & Advanced Projects, 2000. Mem. St. John's Luth. Ch. coun., 2002—. Regents scholar, N.Y. State, 1968-72, Myra E. Sayer Meml. scholar in English, CUNY, 1970; recipient commencement scholarship awards in French, English, CUNY, 1971, cert. of merit in archtl. tech., SUNY, 1982. Mem. AIA (Westchester/Mid-Hudson chpt., mem. interprofl. com. for environ. design 1988-92), SUNY L.A., 1994-96. Lutheran. Avocations: reading, writing, design, environmentalism, mountain hiking. Home and Office: 38 Roosevelt Ave Middletown NY 10940-4635 Office Phone: 845-343-0963. E-mail: aegisdesign@citilink.net.

FUCHS, ALFRED HERMAN, psychologist, educator; b. Englewood, NJ, Nov. 29, 1932; s. Herman and Wilhemine Katharine (Dieling) F.; m. Phyllis Elizabeth Rocke, Aug. 27, 1955; children: Christopher Frederick, Jeffrey Alfred, Lisa Marie, Eric William. AB, Rutgers U., 1954; MA, Ohio U., 1958; PhD, Ohio State U., 1960. Psychologist, scientist Gen. Dynamics/Electric Boat Co., 1961-62; asst. prof. psychology Bowdoin Coll., Brunswick, Maine, 1962-66, assoc. prof., 1966-72, prof., 1972-98, prof. emeritus, 1998—, chmn. dept., 1965-75, 94-97, dean faculty, 1975-91. Summer research participant NSF, 1963, 64 Contbr. articles to profl. jours. NSF grantee, 1963-64, 64-65 Fellow APA (pres.-elect divsn. 26 1997-98, pres. 1998-99); mem. History of Sci. Soc., Internat. Soc. History Behavioral Scis., Sigma Xi. Democrat. Home: 5 Longfellow Ave Brunswick ME 04011-2535 Office: Bowdoin Coll Dept Psychology 6900 College Station Brunswick ME 04011

FUCHS, ANNE SUTHERLAND, magazine publisher; b. Volta Redonda, Brazil, Apr. 19, 1947; d. Paul Warner and Evelyn Coffman; m. James E. Fuchs, Feb. 6, 1982 Student, U. Paris at Sorbonne, 1967-68, Western Coll. for Women, 1966-67; BA, NYU, 1969. Registered architect. V.p., pub. Woman's Day Spl. Interest Mags.-CBS Mags., N.Y.C., 1980-82, Cuisine Mag., CBS Mags., N.Y.C., 1982-84; v.p., pub. Woman's Day mag. DCI Comm., Inc., N.Y.C., 1985-88; sr. v.p., pub. ELLE mag., N.Y.C., 1988-90, Vogue, N.Y.C., 1991—94; group pub. dir., sr. v.p. Harper's Bazaar/Hearst Mag., N.Y.C., 1994—2001; global CEO, chmn., mgmt. bd. Phillips, dePUry & Luxembourg, 2001—02; exec. v.p. LVMH Group, 2002; cons., 2003—. Chmn. mag. and print com. U.S. Info. Agy., 1989—. Author: (other) The Modular Pattern, 1945, British Prefabricated School Construction, 1962; other, Sch. Constrn. Systems Devel., 1964; contbr. numerous articles to profl.jours; other, De Laveaga Elem. Sch., Santa Cruz, Calif., 1966, Silvercreek High Sch., San Jose, Calif., 1969, Canady Hall Harvard U., 1974, Aaron Davis Hall, CCNY, 1978. Chmn. women's bd. Madison Sq. Boys and Girls Club, N.Y.C.; mem. Com. 200, USIA; bd. dirs. N.Y.C. Partnership, N.Y.C. Partnership Found. Recipient Innovation in Bldg. award, Am. Builder, 1965, Services to Building Industry award, Engring. News Record, 1966, Gov.'s Design award, State of Calif., 1966, Quarter Century award, Bldg. Rsch. Adv. Coun., 1977, named Constrn. Man of Yr., Engring. News Record, 1968; fellow Fulbright fellow, England, 1955—56. Mem. Fin. Women's Assn. N.Y., N.Y. Jr. League, Advt. Women of N.Y., Women in Communications, Women's Forum, Com. of 200, Fin. Women's Assn. N.Y. Clubs: Economic (N.Y.C.). E-mail: afuchs@hearst.com.

FUCHS, ELAINE V., molecular biologist, educator; b. Hinsdale, Ill., May 5, 1950; d. Louis H. and Viola L. (Lueck) F.; m. David T. Hansen, Sept. 10, 1988. BS in Chemistry with honors, U. Ill., Urbana, 1972; PhD in Biochemistry, Princeton U., 1977; Dsc (hon.), Mt. Sinai U., 2003. Postdoctoral fellow dept. biology MIT, 1977-80; from asst. prof. to prof. U. Chgo., 1980—89, prof. Dept. Molecular Genetics and Cell Biology, 1989—2002; prof. mammalian cell biology and devel. Rockefeller U., N.Y., NY, 2002—. Assoc. editor Jour. Cell Biology, 1993—; contr. numerous articles to profl. jours. Recipient R.R. Benesely award Am. Assn. Anatomists, 1988, Searle Scholar award Chgo. Cmty. Trust, 1981-84, Presdl. Young Investigator award NSF, 1984-89, NIH Merit award, 1993, 98, Wm. Montagna award Soc. Investigative Dermatology, 1995, Keith Porter Lecture award Am. Soc. Cell Biology, 1996, Sr. Woman Achievement award, 1997, Cartwright award 2001, Richard Lounsbery award, 2001, Novartis award, 2003, Dickson prize, 2004. Fellow Am. Acad. Arts and Scis., Am. Assn. Microbiology; mem. NAS, Am.Soc. Cell Biology (past pres.), Harvey Soc., N.Y. Acad. Sci., Phi Beta Kappa. Office: Rockefeller U Lab Mammalian Cell Biology and Devel 1230 York Ave Box 300 New York NY 10021

FUCHS, ELINOR, theater critic, playwright; b. Cleve., Jan. 23, 1933; d. Joseph Fuchs and Lillian Kessler; m. Michael Oakes Finkelstein, May 3, 1962 (div. 1984); children: Claire Oakes Finkelstein, Katherine Eban Finkelstein. BA summa cum laude, Radcliffe Coll., 1955; MA, Hunter Coll., 1975; M.Phil., CUNY Grad. Ctr., 1976. Research dir. Sextant Prodns.-ABC, N.Y.C., 1960-61; producer-writer Channel 13/WNET, N.Y.C., 1962-63; adj. lectr. SUNY-Stony Brook, 1975, 82; lit. mgr.-dramaturg Chelsea Theater Ctr., N.Y.C., 1978-79; staff theater critic Soho News, N.Y.C., 1979-82; contbg. critic Village Voice, N.Y.C., 1982—; dramaturg Women's Interart Theatre, N.Y.C., 1984-85; cons. Nat. Endowment for Arts, Washington, 1982-83; mem. Plays-in-Process selection com. Theatre Communications Group, N.Y.C., 1983-84; vis. prof. NYU, 1990, Emory U., 1987, sr. lectr., 1988—. Author play/book: (with Joyce Antler) Year One of the Empire (produced Odyssey Theatre, L.A. 1980, Drama-Logue Critic's award in playwriting 1980), 1973; contbr. numerous articles to periodicals, including Am. Theatre, Comparative Drama, Modern Drama, Theatre Communications, Vogue, Drama Rev., Performing Arts Jour.; co-editor spl. issues on Am. Theatre Alternatives théâ trales, Brussels, Nos. 9 and 10; editor: Plays of the Holocaust, an International Anthology, 1987; author: (with others) Apocalypse Culture, 1987, Strindberg's Dramaturgy, 1988, Sacred Theatre, 1989, From World to Image: The New Theatre in Germany and the United States, 1991, Making an Exit: A Mother-Daughter Drama with Alzheimer's, Machine Tools and Laughter, 2005; contbg. editor Am. Theatre, 1990—. V.p. Performing Artists for Nuclear Disarmament, N.Y.C., 1983-84; mem. Ad Hoc Com. for Peace, 1991. Scholar Swedish Inst., Stockholm, 1981; fellow MacDowell Colony, Peterborough, N.H., 1982; Rockefeller fellow, 1984-85; fellow Bunting Inst., Radcliffe Coll., 1985-86. Mem. Assn. Theater in Higher Edn., Women and Theatre Program, Modern Lang. Assn., Phi Beta Kappa. Democrat.

FUCHS, JEROME HERBERT, management consultant; b. N.Y.C., Jan. 7, 1922; s. Berthold and Fannie (Neuschotz) F.; m. Eleanor May DeRoo, May 26, 1945; children: Jerome S. Taylor, Susan Fuchs Decker, Sandra Fuchs Lombino. BS in Mktg. with honors, Syracuse U., 1950, MBA, 1951. Systems and methods analyst Carrier Corp., 1951-52; supr. systems and methods Lukens Steel, Coatesville, Pa., 1952-54; mgr. systems and methods PennWalt Co., Phila., 1955-57, mgr. systems and methods and office svcs. Amax, Inc., Greenwich, Conn., 1958-60; exec. asst. to pres. Rockbestos Wire & Cable Co., 1960-61; v.p. mfg. United Aircraft Products, Dayton, Ohio, 1970-71; exec. v.p. Bus. Supplies Corp. Am., N.Y.C., 1972; sr. ptnr. Fuchs Assocs., East Meadow, N.Y., 1960—2001; indsl. rsch. asst., Syracuse (N.Y.) U., 1949-51; adj. prof. Syracuse U., 1950-52, John Hopkins U., Balt., 1953-54, Drexel, Phila., 1955-57, Queens Coll., N.Y.C., 1963-65, SUNY, Stony Brook, 1987-91, Hofstra U., 1988—. Author: Making the Most of Management Consulting Services, 1975; Managment Consultants in Action, 1975; Computerized Cost Control Systems, 1976; Computerized Inventory Control Systems, 1977; Administering the Quality Control Function, 1979, The Prentice-Hall Illustrated Handbook of Advanced Manufacturing Methods, 1988. Served as 2nd lt. AC, U.S. Army, 1943-46. Mem. Soc. Profl. Mgmt. Cons. (charter, pres. 1977-79), Inst. Mgmt. Cons. (cert., founding mem.), Sigma Iota Epsilon. Home and Office: 1612 Salisbury Park Dr East Meadow NY 11554-5522 Office Phone: 516-542-0266.

FUCHS, LAWRENCE HOWARD, federal official, educator; b. N.Y.C., Jan. 29, 1927; s. Alfred F. and Frances S. (Scheiber) F.; m. Betty Corcoran Sept. 12, 1970; 1 adopted child, Carole Hooven; stepchildren: Michael Hooven, Fred Hooven, John Hooven; children by previous marriage: Janet Pearl, Frances Sarah, Naomi Ruth. BA, N.Y. U., 1950; PhD, Harvard U., 1955; DHL (hon.), Brandeis U., 2002. Tchg. fellow Harvard U., Cambridge, Mass., 1950-51; mem. faculty Brandeis U., Waltham, Mass., 1952—2002, chmn. dept. politics, 1959-60, dean faculty, 1960-61, prof. Am. civilization and politics, chmn. dept. Am. studies, 1970-86. On leave as dir. Peace Corps, Philippines, 1961-63; exec. dir. U.S. Select Commn. on Immigration and Refugee Policy, 1979-81; vice chmn. U.S. Commn. on Immigration Reform, 1992-97; part-time radio-TV news commentator for stas. WCRB and WGBH, Boston, 1951-59. Author: The Political Behavior of American Jews, 1955, Hawaii Pono: A Political and Ethnic History, 1961, John F. Kennedy and American Catholicism, 1967, Those Peculiar Americans: Peace Corps and American National Character, 1967, American Ethnic Politics, 1968, Family Matters, 1972, The American Kaleidoscope: Race, Ethnicity and the Civic Culture, 1990, Beyond Patriarchy: Jewish Fathers and Families, 2000. Former mem. nat. adv. bd. commn. law and social action Am. Jewish Congress; former mem. nat. adv. coun. Mexican Am. Legal Def. and Edn. Fund; Mass. Congress Racial Equality; mem. exec. coun. Am. Jewish Hist. Soc.; former vice chmn. Facing History & Ourselves; 1st chmn. Commonwealth Svc. Corps Commn.; former chmn. exec. com. sch. and soc. program Edn. Devel. Ctr., Inc.; founding pres. Self-Devel. Group, Inc. Served with USNR, 1945-47. Recipient Decade Humanity award Facing History and Ourselves, John Carroll Centennial award, John Hope Franklin award, 1991, Theodore Saloutos award, 1991, Carey McWilliams award, 1992; Woodrow Wilson fellow; grantee Social Scis. Rsch. Coun., East-West Ctr., Rockefeller Found., Ford Found., Exxon Found., Jaffe Found., Sloan Found. Mem. Phi Beta Kappa. Home: 202 Del Pond Drive Canton MA 02021

FUCHS, NANCY E., lawyer; BA summa cum laude, U. Pa., 1978; JD, NYU, 1981. Bar: NY 1981. Ptnr. corp. and fin. dept. Kaye Scholer LLP, NYC. Office: Kaye Scholer LLP 425 Park Ave New York NY 10022 Office Phone: 212-836-8565. E-mail: nfuchs@kayescholer.com.

FUCHS, OLIVIA ANNE MORRIS, lawyer; b. Louisville, Ky., May 2, 1949; d. H.H. Morris Jr. and Betty Jean Wills Saltkill; m. Robert Edward Fuchs, Dec. 27, 1969. BA, U. Louisville, 1977; JD cum laude, 1980. Bar: Ky. 1980, Ind. 1987, U.S. Dist. Ct. (we. dist.) Ky. 1985, U.S. Tax. Ct. 1987. Assoc. Brown, Todd & Heyburn, Louisville, 1981-87; mem. Conliffe, Sandmann & Sullivan PLLC, Louisville, 1987-97; pvt. practice Louisville, 1997—. Notes editor Jour. Family Law, 1979-80. Vol. advocate R.A.P.E. Relief Ctr. YWCA, Louisville, 1981—87. Mem. ABA, Ind. Bar Assn., Ky. Bar Assn., Louisville Bar Assn. (probate sect. chmn. 1990, profl. responsibility com., com. chmn. 1988), U. Louisville Law Alumni Coun. (bd. dirs., pres. 1997-98), Exec. Club Louisville (pres. 1996-97), Jefferson Club, Citizens for Better Judges, Phi Alpha Delta. Democrat. Presbyterian. Office: Ky Home Life Bldg 239 S 5th St Ste 1700 Louisville KY 40202-3248 Office Phone: 502-587-7700.

FUCHS, OWEN GEORGE, chemist; b. Austin, Tex., June 22, 1951; s. Emil George and Hazel June (Johnson) F.; children from previous marriage: Ginny Lynn, William Oberholz, Owen George; m. Caroline S. Crook, Dec. 15, 1990; children: Evan Ashbey, Lindsey Nicole, Allison Mae. AA, Lee Jr. Coll., 1970, AS, 1973; BS, U. Houston, 1972. Chemist, Merichem Co., Houston, 1972-73; lab. mgr. Superintendence Co., Inc., Houston, 1973-78; dir. labs. and hydrocarbon research Chas. Martin Internat., Pasadena, Tex., 1978-79; pres., chief exec. officer Alpha-Omega Labs., Inc., Houston, Tex., 1979-88; bd. dirs. A.O.L. Inc., Houston, 1988—; pres., chief exec. officer Owen G. Fuchs & Assocs., Houston, 1988—, Texas City Testing Inc., 1989—, Environ. Testing Enterprises, Inc., 1991—, La. Testing Labs., Inc., 1992—. Mem. ASTM, NRA, Am. Chem. Soc. Home: PO Box 613 Highlands TX 77562-0613 Office: PO Box 3921 Texas City TX 77592-3921

FUCHS, ROLAND JOHN, geography educator, academic administrator; b. Yonkers, NY, Jan. 15, 1933; s. Alois L. and Elizabeth (Weigand) F.; m. Gaynell Ruth McAuliffe, June 15, 1957; children: Peter K., Christopher K., Andrew K. BA, Columbia U., 1954, postgrad., 1956—57, Moscow State U., 1960—61; MA, Clark U., 1957, PhD, 1959, DSc (hon.), 1995. Asst. prof. to prof. emeritus U. Hawaii, Honolulu, 1958—, chmn. dept. geography, 1964-86, asst. dean to assoc. dean Coll. Arts and Scis., 1965-67, dir. Asian Studies Lang. and Area Ctr., 1965-67, adj. rsch. assoc. East West Ctr., 1980—, spl. asst. to pres., 1986; vice rector UN U., Tokyo, 1987-94; dir. Internat. Start Secretariat, 1994—. Vis. prof. Clark U., 1963-64, Nat. Taiwan U., 1974; mem. bd. internat. orgns. and programs NAS, 1976-81, chmn., 1980-81, mem. bd. sci. and tech. in devel., 1980-85; mem. U.S. Nat. Commn. for Pacific Basin Econ. Coop., 1985-87; sr. advisor UN U., 1986. Author, editor: Geographical Perspectives on the Soviet Union, 1974, Theoretical Problems of Geography, 1977, Population Distribution Policies in Development Planning, 1981, Urbanization and Urban Policies in the Pacific-Asia Region, 1987, Megacities: The Challenge of the Urban Future, 1994, Global-Regional Linkages in the Earth System, 2002; asst. editor Econ. Geography, 1963-64; mem. editl. adv. com. Soviet Geography: Rev. and Translation, 1966-85, Geoforum, 1988-96, African Urban Quar., 1987, Global Environ. Change, 1990-2000, Asian Geographer, 1991-98. Ford Found. fellow, 1956-57; Fulbright Rsch. scholar, 1966-67. Mem. Assn. Am. Geographers, Am. Geophys. Union, Internat. Geog. Union (v.p. 1980-84, 1st v.p. 1984-88, pres. 1988-92, past pres. 1992-96), Assn. Am. Geographers (Hon. award 1982), Am. Assn. Advancement of Slavic Studies (bd. dirs. 1976-81), Pacific Sci. Assn. (mem. coun. 1978—, mem. exec. com. 1986-99, sec. gen-treas. 1991-99), Acad. Europaea (elected fgn. mem.). Home: 1200 N Nash St Arlington VA 22209-3616 Office Phone: 202-462-2213. Business E-Mail: rfuchs@agu.org.

FUCHS, VICTOR ROBERT, economist, educator; b. New York, Jan. 31, 1924; s. Alfred and Frances Sarah (Scheiber) Fuchs; m. Beverly (Beck), Aug. 29, 1948; children: Nancy, Frederic, Paula, Kenneth. BS, N.Y. Univ., 1947; MA, Columbia Univ., 1951, PhD, 1955. Internat. fur broker, 1946—50; lectr. Columbia Univ., N.Y.C., 1953—54, instr., 1954—55, asst. prof. econ., 1955—59; assoc. prof. econ. N.Y. Univ., N.Y.C., 1959—60; program assoc. Ford Found. Program in econ., devel., and adminstrn., 1960—62; mem. sr. rsch staff Nat. Bur. Econ. Rsch., 1962—; prof. econ. Grad. Ctr. City Univ. of N.Y., N.Y.C., 1968—74; prof. cmty. medicine Mt. Sinai Sch. Medicine, 1968-74; v.p. rsch. Nat. Bur. Econ. Rsch., 1968—78; prof. econ. Stanford U., Stanford Med. Sch., 1974—95; Henry J. Kaiser Jr. prof. Stanford U., Stanford Med. Sch., 1988—95, prof. emeritus, 1995—. Author: The Economics of the Fur Industry, 1957; co-author (with Aaron Warner): Concepts and Cases in Econ. Analysis, 1958; author: Changes in the Location of Mfg. in the U.S. Since 1929, 1962, The Svc. Economy, 1968, Prodn. and Productivity in the Svc. Industries, 1969, Policy Issues and Rsch. Opportunities in Indsl. Orgn., 1972, Essays on the Economics of Health and Med. Care, 1972, Who Shall Live? Health, Economics, and Social Choice, 1975; co-author (with Joseph Newhouse): The Economics of Physician and Patient Behavior, 1978; author: Economic Aspects of Health, 1982, How We Live, 1983, The Health Economy, 1986, Women's Quest for Econ. Equality, 1988, The Future of Health Policy, 1993, Individual and Social Responsibility: Child Care Edn., Med. Care, and Long-term Care in Am., 1996, Who Shall Live? Health, Economics and Social Choice, expanded edit., 1998; contbr. articles to profl. jour. Served in USAF, 1943—46. Fellow: Am. Econ. Assn. (disting., pres. 1995), Am. Acad. Arts and Sci.; mem.: Am. Philos. Soc. (John R. Commons award), Am. Inst. Medicine of NAS, Beta Gamma Sigma, Sigma Xi. Home: 796 Cedro Way Stanford CA 94305-1032 Office: NBER 30 Alta Rd Stanford CA 94305-8006 Office Phone: 650-326-7639.

FUCHS, W. KENT, engineering educator; b. Elk City, Okla., Nov. 3, 1954; BS, Duke U., 1977; MDiv, Trinity Evang. Div. Sch., 1984; PhD, U. Ill., 1985. Asst. prof. U. Ill., Urbana, 1985-89, assoc. prof., 1989-93, prof., 1993-96; Disting. prof., head Sch. Elec. and Computer Engring., Purdue U., West Lafayette, Ind., 1996—2002; dean engring. Cornell U., Ithaca, NY, 2002—. Contbr. numerous articles to profl. jours. Scholar, U. Ill., 1991. Fellow IEEE, Assn. for Computing Machinery. Office: Cornell U Coll Engring 242 Carpenter Hall Ithaca NY 14853-2201 Office Phone: 607-255-9679. E-mail: engineering_dean@cornell.edu.

FUDA, SIRI NARAYAN K.K. (ELAINE T. BARBER), director; b. Albany, N.Y., June 13, 1941; d. Adam Henry and Anna Mae Farrell Barber; m. Michael G. Fuda, Nov. 23, 1962; children: Meredith-Anne Costello, Melanie Elsie Henderson, Michelle Germanne Fuda. BA in English with honors, SUNY, Albany, 1963, MA in English Lang. and Lit., 1965; postgrad., SUNY, Buffalo, 1967; MS in Exceptional Edn., Buffalo State Coll., 1982. Tchr. Albany Pub. Sch. Sys., 1964-67, curriculum developer, 1966-67; tchr. Buffalo Pub. Schs., 1981-99; dir. Ctr. for Healthy, Happy, Holistic Living, Buffalo, 1987—. Adj. prof. Buffalo State Coll., 1993—; edn. cons. just buffalo lit. ctr., 1990-99; yoga tchr. Women's Wellness Ctr. Western N.Y., 1999—, others; cons. SUNY, Buffalo, 1999; coord. Buffalo State Coll./Buffalo Pub. Schs. coop. program, 1993-99; writer-in-residence Khalsa Women's Tng. Camp, Espinola, N.Mex., 1993-94, just buffalo lit. ctr., 1994; developer, instr. Creative Writing Workshops, Buffalo, Santa Fe; reader Erie and Niagara County Writers Assn.; presenter workshops on yoga for personal stress reduction, expectant mothers and infants, and as metatherapy for emotionally disturbed students. Contbg. editor to lit. anthology Life Junkies: On Our Own, 1990; author: (poetry collections) Unconditional Love: The Sapphire Poems, 1992, Dancing with the Guru, 1994.; contbr. articles to profl. jours., poetry to Buffalo News, others. Founding mem. Lexington Real Foods Co-op, Buffalo, 1971; bd. dirs. Elmwood Ave. Bus. Assn., Buffalo, 1980-83; founder Children's Rm. Co-op Day Care Ctr., Buffalo, 1972-73. Recipient Labor in Lt. award AFL-CIO, Buffalo, 1995; grantee Arts Coun., Buffalo and Erie County, 1990. Mem. Buffalo Tchrs. Fedn. (coun. of dels. 1984-91), just buffalo lit. ctr., Internat. Kundalini Yoga Tchrs. Assn. Democrat. Sikh. Avocation: gardening. Home: 460 Ashland Ave Buffalo NY 14222-1502 Office: Ctr for Healthy Happy Holistic Living 460 Ashland Ave Buffalo NY 14222-1502 E-mail: SiriNarayan@aol.com.

FUDGE, ANN MARIE, advertising executive; b. Washington, Apr. 23, 1951; d. Malcolm R. and Bettye (Lewis) Brown; m. Richard E. Fudge, Feb. 27, 1971; children: Richard Jr., Kevin. BA, Simmons Coll., 1973; MBA, Harvard U., 1977; DHL (hon.), Adelphi U., 1995, Howard U., 1998, Simmons Coll., 1998, Marymount Coll., 1999. Manpower specialist GE, Bridgeport, Conn., 1973-75; mktg. asst. Gen. Mills, Mpls., 1977-78, asst. product mgr., 1978-80, product mgr., 1980-83, mktg. dir., 1983-86; assoc. dir., strategic planning Gen. Foods, White Plains, NY, 1986-87, mktg. dir., 1987-89, v.p. mktg. and devel., 1989-91, exec. v.p., gen. mgr., 1991-94; exec. v.p. Kraft Foods, 1994-97; pres. Maxwell House Coffee Co., White Plains, NY, 1994-97, Maxwell House Coffee and Post Cereal, Tarrytown, NY, 1997—2001; chmn., CEO Young & Rubicam, Inc., NYC, 2003—05, Y&R Brands, NYC, 2003—. Bd. dirs. GE, Marriott Internat.; trustee Am. Grad. Sch. Internat. Mgmt., Brookings Instn. Bd. dirs. Women's Econ. Devel. Corp., St. Paul, 1984-86; chair allocations panel United Way, Mpls., 1983-86; vol. Big Sisters/Big Bros., Fairfield County, Conn., 1988-90; bd. govs. Boys and Girls Clubs Am. Recipient Leadership award YWCA, Mpls., 1980, Black Achievers award Harlem YMCA, 1988, Candace award Nat. Coalition of 100 Black Women, 1991-92, Corp. Women's Network award, 1994, She Knows Where She's Going award Girls, Inc., 1994, Alumni Achievement award Harvard Bus. Sch., 1998; named Woman of Yr., Glamour Mag., 1995, Ad Woman of Yr., Advt. Women of N.Y., 1995, Sara Lee Frontrunner award, 1999, one of 50 Most Powerful Women in Am. Bus., Fortune mag. Mem. Exec. Leadership Coun. (pres. 1994-96, Achievement award 2000), Com. of 200, NY Women's Forum, Coun. on Fgn. Rels. Office: Y&R Advt 285 Madison Ave New York NY 10017-6486*

FUENTEALBA, VICTOR WILLIAM, professional society administrator; b. Balt., Sept. 1, 1922; s. Manuel Lagos and Antonia (Lengler) F.; m. Viola J. Henderson, Jan. 26, 1952; children: Victoria, Mary Lee, Donna Jean, Patricia. Student, Loyola Coll., 1946—47; JD, U. Md., 1950. Bar: Md. 1950, U.S. Supreme Ct. 1950. V.p. Musicians Union Met. Balt., 1951-53, sec., treas., 1953-58, pres., 1958-78; mem. internat. exec. bd. Am. Fedn. Musicians, N.Y.C., 1967-70, v.p., 1970-78, pres., 1978-87, pres. emeritus, 1987—. Bd. dirs. Hearing and Speech Agy., Balt., 1973-78; mem. Pres.' Com. on Employment of Handicapped; adv. coun. Ctr. Labor and Indsl. Rels. of N.Y. Inst. Tech., Assn. Concert Bands, Van Cliburn Internat. Piano Competition; chmn. bd. Nat. Music Coun.; v.p. Muscular Dystrophy Assn.; adv. bd. Music Industry Educators Assn.; judge Adv. Gen. Vets. Fgn. Wars of U.S., 2001-02. Served with inf. U.S. Army, WW II. Decorated Purple Heart. Mem. Md. State Bar Assn., Delta Theta Phi. Democrat. Roman Catholic. Home: 4501 Arabia Ave Baltimore MD 21214-3306 Office: 805 Court Sq Bldg 200 E Lexington St Baltimore MD 21202-3530 Office Phone: 410-539-5115. E-mail: VictorLagos@aol.com.

FUENTES, CARLOS, writer, retired ambassador; b. Mexico City, Nov. 11, 1928; s. Rafael Fuentes Boettiger and Berta Macías Rivas; m. Rita Macedo, 1959 (div. 1969); 1 dau., Cecilia; m. Sylvia Lemus, 1973; children: Carlos, Natasha Ed., U. Mex., Institut des Hautes Etudes Internationales, Geneva; hon. degrees, Columbia Coll., Chgo. State U., Cambridge U., Essex U., Harvard U., Dartmouth Coll., Bard Coll., New Sch., Georgetown U., Washington U., St. Louis, Brown U., Berlin U., UCLA. Mem. Mexican del. ILO, Geneva, 1950-52; asst. chief press sect. Mexican Ministry Fgn. Affairs, 1954; asst. dir. cultural dissemination U. Mex., 1955-56; head dept. cultural rels. Mexican Ministry Fgn. Affairs, 1957-59; fellow Woodrow Wilson Internat. Ctr. for Scholars, Washington, 1974; Mexican ambassador to France, 1975-77; prof. English and romance langs. U. Pa., 1978-83; prof. comparative lit. Harvard U., 1984-86, Robert F. Kennedy prof., 1987-89; prof.-at-large Brown U., Providence, 1995—; asst. chief Madrid U, Spain, Salamanca U, Spain, Veracmz U, Mexico, Puebla U, Spain. Norman Maccoll lectr. Cambridge U., 1977, Simon Bolivar prof., 1986-87; Virgina Gildersleeve prof. Barnard Coll., 1977; Henry L. Tinker lectr. Columbia U., 1978; pres. Modern Humanities Rsch. Assn., 1989—; founder Iberoamerican Forum, 2000—. Author: Los días enmascarados, 1954, La región más transparente, 1958 (pub. as Where the Air Is Clear, 1960), Las buenas conciencias, 1959 (pub. as The Good Conscience, 1961), Aura, 1962, La muerte del Artemio Cruz, 1962 (pub. as The Death of Artemio Cruz, 1964), The Argument of Latin America: Words for North Americans, 1963, Cantar de ciegos, 1964, Zona sagrada, 1967 (pub. as Holy Places, 1972), Cambio de piel, 1967 (pub. as A Change of Skin, 1968; Biblioteca Breve prize Barcelona 1967), Paris: la revolución de mayo, 1968, La nueva novela hispanoamericana, 1969, Cumpleaños, 1969, El mundo de Jose Luis Cuevas, 1969, Casa con dos puertas, 1970, Tiempo mexicano, 1971, Cuerpos y ofrendas, 1972, Chac Mool y otros cuentos, 1973, Terra Nostra, 1975 (Rómulo Gallegos prize Venezuela 1977), Cervantes: o, La crítica de la lectura, 1976 (pub. as Don Quixote: or, The Critique of Reading, 1976), La cabeza de la hidra, 1978 (pub. as The Hydra Head, 1978), Una familia lejana, 1980 (pub. as Distant Relations, 1982), Agua quemada, 1981 (pub. as Burnt Water, 1981), High Noon in Latin America, 1983, 84, El gringo viejo, 1985 (pub. as The Old Gringo, 1986; LA Times Book award nomination 1986, Rubén Darío prize 1988, Italo-Latino Americano Instituto prize 1988), Latin America: At War with the Past, 1985, Cristóbal Nonato, 1987 (pub. as Christopher Unborn, 1989), Gabriel García Marquez and the Invention of America, 1987, Myself with Others: Selected Essays, 1988, Constancia, y otras novelas para vírgenes, 1989 (pub. as Constancia and Other Stories for Virgins, 1990), La campaña, 1990 (pub. as The Campaign, 1991), Valiente Mundo Nuevo, 1991, The Buried Mirror: Reflections on Spain and on the New World, 1992, Witnesses of Time, 1992, Return to Mexico: Journeys Beyond the Mask, 1992, El Naranjo, 1993 (pub. as The Orange Tree, 1993), Geografia de la Novela, 1993, Diana the Goddess Who Hunts Alone, 1995, The Crystal Frontier, 1995, La Edad del Tiempo, 1994—, A New Time for Mexico, 1994, Por un Progreso Incluyente, 1997, Retratos en el Tiempo, 1998, (with Carlos Fuentes Lenuns) Los Anos con Laura Díaz, 1999 (pub. as The Years with Laura Díaz, 2002); Inez, 2000, Los cinco soles de Mexico, 2001, La silla del áquila (pub. as The Eagle's Throne, 2005), 2003, Inquieta Compañía, 2004, Viendo Visiones, 2004; (plays) Todos los gatos son pardos, 1970, El tuerto es rey, 1970, Los reinos originarios, 1971, Orquídeas a la luz de la luna, 1982 (pub. as Orchids in the Moonlight, 1982; Mexican Nat. award for lit. 1984); screenwriter: (films) Pedro Paramo, 1966, Tiempo de morir, 1966, Los Caifanes, 1967, (TV series) The Buried Mirror, 1991; contbr. to mag. and newspapers including Los Angeles Times, NY Times, Newsweek; editor: Revista Mexicana de Literatura, 1954-58, El Espectador, 1959-61, Siempre, 1960—, Política, 1960— Trustee NY Pub. Libr.; mem. Mexican Nat. Commn. Human Rights, 1991—; pres. Iberoamerican Inst., Berlin, 2004; bd. dirs. Alfonso Reyes Chair, 1998. Recipient Centro Mexicano de Escritores fellowship, 1956-57, Xavier Villaurrutia prize (Mex.), 1975, Alfonso Reyes prize (Mex.), 1979, Miguel de Cervantes Lit. prize Spanish Ministry of Culture, 1987, Medal of Honor for Lit., Nat. Arts Club, NYC, 1988, Rector's medal U. Chile, 1991, Casita Maria medal, 1991, UCLA medal, 1993, Order of Merit (Chile), 1992, French Legion of Honor, 1992, Menèndez Pelayo Internat. award U. Santander, 1992, Picasso medal UNESCO, 1994, Principe de Asturias prize, 1994, Premio Grinzane-Cavour, 1994; named hon. citizen Santiago de Chile, 1993, Buenos Aires, 1993, Veracruz, 1993, Order of the So. Cross award Brazil, 1997, French Order of Merit, 1998, Latin Civilization prize French and Brazilian Acad., 1999, Mexican Senate award, 2000, Delaware Commonwealth award, 2002, Pablo Neruda Centennial medal (Chile), 2004, Galileo prize Florence, 2005, Arzobispo San Clemento prize Coll. Students, Santiago de Compostela, Spain, 2005, Blue Metropolis prize Montreal, 2005. Mem. Am. Acad. and Inst. Arts and Letters, Nat. Coll. Mex., Inst. Nat. Strategy (bd. dir.). Achievements include founder (with Gabriel García Márquez) Julio Cortázar chair University of Guadalajara, Mexico; founder Alfonso Reyes chair ITM, Monterrey, Mexico.

FUENTES, JULIO M., federal judge; b. Humacao, PR, 1946; BA, So. Ill. U., 1971; MA, NYU, 1972; JD, SUNY, Buffalo, 1975; MA, Rutgers U., 1993. Private practice, Newark, 1975—81; judge Newark Mcpl. Ct., NJ, 1979—87, NJ Superior Ct., 1987—2000, U.S. Ct. Appeals 3rd Cir., 2000—. Mem. ABA; Essex County Bar Assn.; Nat. Hispanic Bar Assn.; NJ Bar Assn.; NJ Hispanic Bar Assn. 1st lt. U.S. Army, 1966—69 USAR, 1969—72. Office: US Ct Appeals 3rdCir M L King Jr Fed Bldg & Cthse 50 Walnut St Rm 5032 Newark NJ 07102*

FUENTES, JUNE TORETTA, language educator; d. Anthony James and Fortuna Katherine (Bianco) Toretta; m. Antonio Fuentes, Dec. 20, 1974; 1 child, Noelle Marie. BA, Coll. of New Rochelle, N.Y., 1963; MA, Fordham U., Bronx, N.Y., 1969; PhD, U. Tex., Austin, 1988. Lic. tchr. Kans. Elem. tchr. Blessed Sacrament Sch., New Rochelle, NY, 1963—68; separate acct. cons. Equitable Life Assurance Soc., N.Y.C., 1969—74; Jr. H.S. tchr. St. Mary's Cathedral Sch., Austin, Tex., 1975—76; media cons. and ESL instr. U. Tex. and St. Edward's U., Austin, 1976—83; instr. English U. Tex. and Austin Cmty. Coll., 1980—88; prof. English and ESL Ind. U. and Purdue U., Ft. Wayne, 1988—91; prof. English Western State Coll., Gunnison, Colo., 1991—94; dir. ESL Bethany Coll., Lindsborg, Kans., 1994—96; instr. ESL Salina Unified Sch. Dist. 305, Salina, 1996—2004; prof. ESL Kans. Wesleyan U., Salina, 2005—. Editl. writer Ft. Wayne Cardiology, Ind., 1989; editl. adv. bd. Collegiate Press, Ft. Wayne, 1990; mem tactic team Gunnison (Colo.) Watershed Sch. Dist., 1993—94. Author: Maria's Secret, 1992; contbr. articles to profl. publs.;, author poetry. Pub. rels. chair AAUW Art in the Pk., Gunnison, Colo., 1992; pres. AAUW (Gunnison chpt.), 1992—94; bd. dir. Rotary Internat., Lindsborg, Kans., 1995—96; docent Raymer Soc., 1996—2002. Recipient Ursula Laurus citation, Coll. New Rochelle, 2005; grantee U. Tex. Intensive English Program Mini-Grant, 1979, IPFW Faculty Summer Grant, 1990, Western State Coll. Mini-Grant, 1993, Bethany Burmeister Grant, 1995, Salina Edn. Found., 2003. Mem.: TESOL (Kans. chpt), Phi Kappa Phi, Kappa Delta Pi, Pi Lambda Theta. Avocations: poetry, children's stories, water color, reading detective fiction.

FUENTES, MARTHA AYERS, playwright; b. Ashland, Ala., Dec. 21, 1923; d. William Herny and Elizabeth (Dye) Ayers; m. Manuel Solomon Fuentes, Apr. 11, 1943. BA in English, U. South Fla., 1969. Lectr., instr. workshops on drama, writing for TV. Author: The Rebel, 1970, Mama Don't Make Me Go To College, My Head Hurts, 1963, Two Characters in Search of An Agreement, 1970, A Cherry Blossom for Miss Chrysanthemum; contbr. articles to local, regional and nat. newspapers, feature artcles to nat. mags.; author TV plays and feature articles for children and young adults. Mem. Nat. Rep. Senatorial Com., Rep. Pres. Task Force, Rep. Nat. Com., Rep. Party, Fla. Recipient George Sergel drama award U. Chgo., 1969. Mem. AAUW, NAFE, S.E. Playwrights Project, The Alliance of Resident Theatres, Stageworks, Authors Guild, Dramatists Guild, Romance Writers Am., Southeastern Writers Assn., Fla. Studio Theatre, United Daus. Confederacy. Roman Catholic. Avocations: reading, animal rights, environmental protection, theater, travel. Home and Office: 102 3rd St Belleair Beach FL 33786-3211 Personal E-mail: belfuentes@aol.com.

FUENTEZ, TANIA MICHELE, journalist; b. Manhattan, Nov. 21, 1966; d. C. Pedro Alvarez Carr and E. Kay (Samuels) Queally. BA in Comm. and Rhetorical Studies, Marquette U., 1991; MA in Mass Media Comm., U. Akron, 1996. Asst. rschr. V.I. Legislature, St. Thomas, 1991; reporter V.I. Daily News, St. Thomas, 1993-95; instr. news writing U. Akron, Ohio, 1995-96; copy editor The Akron Beacon Jour., 1997-2000; newswoman AP, Atlanta, 2000—03, nat. desk editor NYC, 2003—. Adv. bd. diversity com. V.I. Daily News, 1993-95. Contbr. articles to profl. jours. Bd. dirs. U.S. V.I. League of Women Voters, 1994-95; mem. Am. Cancer Soc., 1993-95, mem. St. Thomas Arts Coun., 1992-95. Recipient Cmty. Svc. award Pan African Support Group, 1995; scholar John S. Knight Meml. Fund, 1996, U. Akron, 1995-96. Mem. Soc. Profl. Journalists, Nat. Assn. Hispanic Journalists, Nat. Assn. Black Journalists, Comm. Workers Am.-AFL-CIO, News Media Guild, Local 31222. Roman Catholic. Avocations: writing, travel, photography, hiking, cooking. Office: The AP 450 W 33d St New York NY 10001 E-mail: tfuentez@ap.org.

FUERST, ANDREA SUE, secondary school educator; b. Detroit, Oct. 19, 1969; d. Charles and Eleanor Carbary; m. Tom Fuerst, Sept. 9, 1999; 1 child, Sarah. BS in Edn., Miami U., Oxford, Ohio, 1991. Cert. tchr. Ohio. Tchr. Middletown (Ohio) City Schs., 1991—2002, Butler Tech. Lakota Freshman Sch., West Chester, Ohio, 2002—. Bd. dirs. Ohio Career Based Intervention Career Connections, Columbus. Nominee David Thiel Humanitarian award, Lakota Local Schs., 2002, Career Educator of the Year award, Butler County Career Educators, 2003. Mem.: NEA, Internat. Reading Assn., Assn. Career and Tech. Edn. Avocations: travel, music. Office Phone: 513-682-4235 23126. E-mail: fuersta@butlertech.org.

FUERST, KATHRYN L, writer, registrar; b. N.Y. d. Thomas E and Mary A Fuerst. BA, Dickinson Coll., Carlisle, Pa., 2000; MA, Rosemont Coll., Pa., 2004. Corps mem. CityYear Phila., Phila., 2000—01; admissions asst. Eastern U., St Davids, Pa., 2001—02, adj. faculty, 2005—, asst. registrar, 2002—. Bd. dirs. Zatae Longsdorff Ctr. for Women, Carlisle, Pa., 1997—2000; editl. cons., Bryn Mawr, Pa., 2003—. Contbr. articles and short stories to profl. jours. Vol. swim instr. asst. YMCA, Webster, NY, 1997—2000. Office: Eastern University 1300 Eagle Rd Saint Davids PA 19087

FUERSTENAU, DOUGLAS WINSTON, mineral engineering educator; b. Hazel, S.D., Dec. 6, 1928; s. Erwin Arnold and Hazel Pauline (Karlerud) Fuerstenau; m. Margaret Ann Pellett, Aug. 29, 1953; children: Linda(dec.), Lucy, Sarah, Stephen. BS, S.D. Sch. Mines and Tech., 1949; MS, Mont. Sch. Mines, 1950; ScD, MIT, 1953; Mineral Engr., Mont. Coll. Mineral Sci. and Tech., 1968; doctorate (hon.), U. Liege, Belgium, 1989; DTech (hon.), Lulea U. Tech., Sweden, 2001. Asst. prof. mineral engring. MIT, 1953-56; sect. leader, metals research lab. Union Carbide Metals Co., Niagara Falls, N.Y., 1956-58; mgr. mineral engring. lab Kaiser Aluminum & Chem. Corp., Permanente, Calif., 1958-59; assoc. prof. metallurgy U. Calif., Berkeley, 1959-62, prof. metallurgy, 1962-86, P. Malozemoff prof. of mineral engring., 1987-93, prof. grad. sch., 1994—, Miller rsch. prof., 1969-70, chmn. dept. materials sci. and mineral engring., 1970-78; hon. prof. Huainan Inst. Tech., 2000—. Mem. Nat. Mineral Bd., 1975—78; Am. rep. Internat. Mineral Processing Congress Com., 1978—97. Editor: Froth Flotation-50th Anniversary Vol., 1962; co-editor-in-chief: Internat. Jour. Mineral Processing, 1974—98, hon. editor-in-chief:, 1998—; contbr. articles to profl. jours. Named Douglas W. Fuerstenau professorship at S.D. Sch. of Mines and Tech., 1998; named to S.D. Hall of Fame, 2005; recipient Alexander von Humboldt Sr. Am. Scientist award, Germany, 1984, Frank F. Aplan award, Engring. Found., 1990, Lifetime Achievement award, Internat. Mineral Processing Congress, 1995; fellow Rsch., Japan Soc. Promotion Sci., 1993. Fellow: Indian Nat. Acad. Engring. (fgn.), Australian Acad. Tech. Scis. and Engring. (fgn.); mem.: AIChE, NAE, Russian Fedn. Acad. Natural Scis. (fgn. mem.), Am. Chem. Soc., Soc. Mining Engrs. (bd. dirs. 1968—71, Disting. mem.), Am. Inst. Mining and Metall. Engrs. (chmn. mineral processing divsn. 1967, Robert Lansing Hardy gold medal 1957, Rossiter W. Raymond award 1961, Robert H. Richards award 1975, Antoine M. Gaudin award 1978, Mineral Industry Edn. award 1983, Henry Krumb disting. lectr. 1989, hon. 1989), Theta Tau, Sigma Xi. Congregationalist. Home: 1440 Le Roy Ave Berkeley CA 94708-1912 Office Phone: 510-642-3826. Business E-Mail: dwfuerst@berkeley.edu.

FUERSTENAU, M(AURICE) C(LARK), metallurgical engineer; b. Watertown, SD, June 6, 1933; m. 1953; 4 children. BS, S.D. Sch. Mines & Tech., 1955; MS, MIT, 1957, ScD in Metallurgy, 1961. Rsch. engr. N. Mex. Bur Mines, Socorro, 1961—63; from asst. prof. to assoc. prof. Colo. Sch. Mines, 1963-68; from assoc. prof. to prof. U. Utah, 1968-70; prof., dept. head S.D. Sch. Mines & Tech., 1970-87, interim v.p., 1987-88, acting head mech. engring., 1994-96; prof. U. Nev., Reno, 1988—2005, prof. emeritus, 2005—. Contbr. articles to profl. jours. Recipient Frank F. Aplan award, United Engring. Found., 2000. Mem. Nat. Acad Engrs., Am. Inst. Mining (v.p. 1983, Robert H. Richards award 1982, Mineral Industry Edn. award 1989), Soc. Mining Engrs. (pres. 1982, Arthur F. Taggart award 1978, Antoine M. Gaudin award 1979). Office: Univ Nevada Dept Chem & Metall Engring Reno NV 89557-0001 Office Phone: 775-784-4310. Business E-Mail: mcf@unr.edu.

FUERSTNER, FIONA MARGARET ANNE, ballet company executive, educator; b. Rio de Janeiro, Apr. 24, 1936; d. Paul G. and Agnes Ethel (Stothard) F.; m. Dane LaFontsee, June 7, 1969 (div. 1992); 1 child, Liana Marie. Studied with San Francisco Ballet, Royal Ballet (London), Ballet Rambert (London) Ballet Theatre Sch. (N.Y.C.), Sch. Am. Ballet (N.Y.C.). With corps de ballet San Francisco Ballet, 1952-55, soloist, 1955-58, prin. dancer, 1958-62; toured with Walter Terry's Am. Dances, 1962-63; prin. dancer Les Grands Ballets Can., Montreal, 1963-64, Am. Choreographer's Co. of N.Y., 1964, Pa. Ballet, 1965—74, ballet mistress, instr. co. class, apprentice class, 1974-77, ballet mistress, instr. co. class, 1977—86; ballet mistress Nashville Ballet, 1986-87, ballet mistress, asst. to artistic dir., 1987-91; ballet mistress Milw. Ballet, 1990-95, asst. to artistic dir. ballet mistress, 1995—2003. Guest dancer Ballet Concerto, Miami, 1967, 68, Erie Civic Ballet, 1969; guest instr. Marsha Woody Dance Acad., Beaumont, Tex., 1974, U. Louisville, 1977-78, co. class San Francisco Ballet, 1985, Tenn. Assn. Dance Nashville Conf., 1988, So. Regional Workshop Chgo., Nat. Assn. Dance Masters in Nashville, 1989, BalletMet, 1991, Memphis Classical Ballet, 1992, 97, 99, Nashville Ballet, 1992; guest ballet mistress BalletMet, 1993; faculty tchr. Sch. of Pa. Ballet, 1977-78, 78-86; organized concert group, ballet mistress, dancer Pa. Ballet, 1971; mem. dance panel Nat. Found. Advancement in the Arts, 1995-98; master tchr. South Eastern Regional Ballet Assn. Festival, 1998, Nat. Found. for Advancement in the Arts, 1999, 2001, 2005; guest tchr. Ind. U. Ballet Dept., 2000, Western Mich. U., 2002, DanceWorks Studio 1661, Milw., Wis., 2005, Dancenter North, Libertyville, Ill., 2005; master tchr. USDAN Ctr. for the Creative and Performing Arts, Wheatley Heights, NY, 2004—; vis. asst. prof. dance Wright State U., 2004; dance panelist Midwest Regional, Nat. Found. for Advancement in the Arts, 2001, 2002. Staged Allegro Brillante, Sch. Pa. Ballet Student Showcase, 1986, Nashville Ballet, 1988, Madrigalesco, Pacific NW Ballet, 1981, (parts) Nutcracker, Nashville Ballet, 1989, Carmina Burana (Butler), Milw. Ballet, 1989, Scotch Symphony, Pa. Ballet, 1993, Carmina Burana, Alberta Ballet, 1993, Concerto Barocco, Ballet Omaha, 1994, Ballet Met, 1995, Serenade, Milw. Ballet Sch., 1994, 95, 96, Serenade, Milw. Ballet, 1998-99, Serenade, Western Mich. U., 1999-2000, Concerto Barocco, The Four Temperaments for Milw. Ballet, 1999-2000, Allegro Brillante for Milw. Ballet, 2000-01, (excerpts) Who Cares?, Western Mich. U., 2003, Serenade, Wright State U., 2004. Office Phone: 414-254-4086. E-mail: fionafio@earthlink.net.

FUERTH, GLENN J., lawyer; b. NYC, Jan. 11, 1953; BA, George Washington U., 1975; JD, Fordham U., 1978. Bar: NY 1979, US Dist. Ct. So. Dist. NY, US Dist. Ct. Ea. Dist. NY, US Ct. Appeals 2nd Cir., US Ct. Appeals 3rd Cir. Ptnr. Wilson, Elser, Moskowitz, Edelman & Dicker LLP, NYC. Mem.: Assn. Trial Lawyers of Am., NY State Bar Assn. (trial law sect., ins. sect.). Office: Wilson Elser Moskowitz Edelman & Dicker LLP 23rd Fl 150 E 42nd St New York NY 10017-5639 Office Phone: 212-490-3000 ext. 2369. Office Fax: 212-490-3038. Business E-Mail: fuerthg@wemed.com.

FUESS, BILLINGS SIBLEY, JR., advertising executive; b. N.Y.C., Mar. 11, 1928; s. Billings Sibley and Lucile (McNeill) F.; m. Doris Vannoy, July 19, 1952; children: Billings Sibley III, Doris Jr., Frederick, Lucile. AB in Journalism, U. N.C., 1949. Analyst Gallup & Robinson, Princeton, N.J., 1952-53; writer Kenyon & Eckhardt, N.Y.C., 1953-59, Batten, Barton, Durstine & Osborn, N.Y.C., 1959-65; creative dir. Ogilvy & Mather, N.Y.C., 1965-89; pres. Billings S. Fuess Advt., Summit, N.J., 1989—. Mem. selection com. N.C. Advt. Hall of Fame award. Author, editor: How to Use the Power of the Printed Word, 1985. Mem. N.Y. Philharmonic Vol. Coun., 1976—. Stephen E. Kelly award Mag. Pubs. Assn., N.Y.C., 1983, Recipient Grand award Internat. Film and Television Festival N.Y., 1984, Gold award Art Dirs. Club N.J., numerous top industry awards; elected to N.C. Advt. Hall of Fame, U. N.C., Chapel Hill, 1995. Mem.: Art Dirs. Club NJ (treas. 1997—2004). Home: 19 Highland Dr Summit NJ 07901-3108

FUESSEL, SUSAN GERHARTER, parochial elementary educator; b. St. Joseph, Mo., Feb. 17, 1947; d. Erwin P. and Shirley A. (Barrows) Gerharter; m. Odis E. Fuessel, Aug. 3, 1973; children; Joel Dan, Jason Stan. AA, Concordia Coll., 1967; BA, Concordia Tchrs. Coll., 1970. Tchr. 1st and 2d grade Trinity Luth. Sch., Springfield, Ill.; thcr. kindergarten and 1st grade Eola (Tex.) Ind. Sch. Dist.; tchr. Trinity Luth. Sch., San Angelo, Tex. Cons. ednl. svcs., Tex. Scholarship James Phillips Williams Found. Home: 8925 Fm 765 San Angelo TX 76905-7514

FUGATE, EDWARD, minister; b. Springfield, Ohio, Aug. 22, 1956; s. Claude and Arminda (Noble) F.; m. Adina Sue Campbell, Oct. 6, 1979; children: Malinda Renee, Rebecca Ellen. BA, Berea Coll., 1978; MDiv, United Theol. Seminary, 1986. Ordained to ministry Meth. Ch. as deacon, 1984, as elder 1988. Sales agt. Commonwealth Ins. Co., Springfield, Ohio, 1979-80, sales mgr. Piqua, Ohio, 1980-82; pastor New Paris (Ohio) United Meth. Ch., 1982-86, Seaman (Ohio) United Meth. Ch., 1986-87, Piketon-Jasper United Meth. Ch., Piketon, Ohio, 1987-89, Ft. Jefferson United Meth. Ch., Greenville, Ohio, 1989-96. Field assoc. United Theol. Sem., 1991-96. Vol. chaplain Reid Meml. Hosp., Richmond, Ind., 1982-83, Pike Community Hosp., Waverly, Ohio, 1987-89; camping coord. United Meth. Ch., Portsmouth Dist., 1988-89. Named an Outstanding Young Man of Am. 1985, 86. Mem. Kiwanis (bd. dirs. New Paris 1983-85, com. chmn. 1984-86), Lions. Home and Office: North Dover United Meth Ch 11080 State Route 108 Wauseon OH 43567-9514 *"The secret to joy is love. The secret to love is that it is a gift not an investment. To love is to give without hope of return. To give so freely is to know joy". John 15:9-12.*

FUGATE-WILCOX, TERY, artist; b. Kalamazoo; Represented in permanent collections Solomon R. Guggenheim Mus., N.Y.C., Australia Nat. Gallery, Canberra, Mus. Modern Art, N.Y.C., Western Mich. U., J. Hood Wright Park, N.Y.C., J. Patrick Lannan Found. Mus., Palm Beach, Fla., Nat. Shopping Ctrs., Harrisburg, Pa., Prudential Ins. Co., Newark, Damson Oil Co., N.Y.C., N.Y.C. Dept. Parks and Recreations, Princess Gloria von Thurn and Taxis, Regensburg, Germany; sculpture located 7th Ave and Waverly, N.Y.C., City Wall, Lafayette, Houston, N.Y.C., Holland Tunnel Entrance, N.Y.C., 40-ft. sculpture Riverside Dr. and Jay Hoodwright Park, N.Y.C., 30-ft. self-watering sculpture The Prudential Gateway 4, Newark. Named laureate Nat. Endowment for Arts. *Actual art includes in its statement the long-suppressed dimension of time, in the context of the naturally occurring changes that are part of the life of any material and make it part of the life of the work of art incorporating that material.*

FUGAZY, WILLIAM DENIS, transportation company executive; Grad., Fordham U., Cornell U., Columbia U. Midshipmen's Sch. Chmn. Fugazy Franchise Internat. Corp., N.Y.C., 1947—. Founder, master-host All-Am. Collegiate Golf Found., chmn. ann. tournament A Day with the All-Ams., Palm Springs, Calif.; founder John V. Mara Meml. Fund for Cancer Rsch. St. Vincent's Hosp., N.Y.C., Cath. Youth Orgn. Summer Camps Program, Silver Shield Found. Scholarship Fund; chmn. Nat. Ethnic Coalition Orgns., N.Y. Yankee Homecoming Dinner, N.Y. Giants Football Luncheon, N.Y. Statue of Liberty Centennial Commn., Ellis Island Medals of Honor Selection Com.; pres. Coalition Italo-Am. Assns.; active Columbus Citizens Com.; apptd. to Westway Commn., Nat. Svcs. Bd. City of N.Y., Mayor's Immigration Coalition, 1997, Westway Commn., Nat Svcs. Bd.; bd. dirs., mem. exec. com. Police Athletic League, Cath. Youth Assn.; bd. instrnl. TV Archdiocese of N.Y.; chmn. The Forum Club, N.Y. State Trooper Found., N.Y. Statue of Liberty Centennial Commn.; named hon. fire commr., N.Y.C.; vice-chmn. U.S. Holocaust Meml. Coun.; hon. chmn. Dr. Martin Luther King Jr. Nat. Holiday Celebration Ambassadorial Reception and Program. Lt. Comdr. USN Seals, WWII. Decorated knight Equestrian Order Holy Sepulchre, Knight of the Grand Cross; recipient Meritorious award Pres. of Italy; co-recipient Congl. Gold Medal of Honor U.S. Congress, Gold medal Armenian Ch. U.S., 1986, Honor medal; named Sportsman of Yr. Cath. Youth Orgn. of Archdiocese N.Y., N.Y. Athletic Club, B'nai B'rith, 1983, Man of Yr. ITV-TV of Archdiocese N.Y., N.Y.C. Police Dept., 1984, Westchester County, 1985, Archbishop of N.Y., 1986, Angel Guardians, 1988, Italian Welfare League, N.Y. Baseball Fedn., St. Jude's Children's Rsch. Hosp., Distinguished Citizen of Yr., N.Y. Conf. Italian-Am. Legislators, 1992, New Yorker of Yr. award Bowling Green Assn., 1993; recipient Congl. Ellis Island Medal of Honor, B'nai B'rith Sportsman of Yr. Citizen's award N.Y. State Br. Sons of Italy, 1983, Man of Yr. award Angel Guardians, 1988, Most Outstanding Role Model award Italian Am. Student Assn., 1989, Humanitarian award Coun. for Unity, N.Y. Industry award St. Mary's Hosp. for Children, 1990, Lifeline award Cooley's Anemia Found., 1991, Edward Corsi award LaGuardia Meml. House, 1992, Tree of Life award Jewish Nat. Fund, 1993, Donald C. Platten award We Care About N.Y., 1994, Humanitarian medal of honor Tara Cir., Inc., 1995; honored Italian Am. Club of No. Westchester, 1988, Cerebral Palsy of Westchester, 1988, Grand Lodge of State of N.Y., 1988, Columbian Lawyers Assn. Nassau County, 1989, Columbus Day Soc. of Harrison (Grand Master Parade), 1989, Ancient Order of Hibernians, 1995, Cath. Mus. Am., 1995, Order of Sons of Italy in Am., 1997, Am. Inst. Stress, 1997; others. Mem. Sons of Italy (co-recipient Citizen's award N.Y. State br. 1983), Coalition of Italo-Am. Assn., Golf Coaches Assn. Am. (hon.), The Forum Club (founder). Office: Fugazy Internat 555 Madison Ave New York NY 10022-3301

FUGGI, GRETCHEN MILLER, education educator; b. Westerly, R.I., Aug. 26, 1938; d. John Louis and Harriet (Scheid) M.; m. William Joseph Fuggi, Aug. 15, 1960; children: Gretchen, Juliann, John, Kristen. BS, So. Conn. State U., 1960, MS, 1969, 6th yr. diploma, 1991, 6th yr. Ednl. Leadership diploma, 1994. Reading cons. Washington Magnet Sch., West Haven, Conn., 1974—; adj. prof. So. Conn. State U., New Haven, 1988—. Pres. Cath. Charity League of Greater New Haven, 1989-90; bd. dirs. New Haven Symphony Aux., 1992—. Named Tchr. of Yr., West Haven Fedn. Tchrs., 1998-99. Mem. AAUP, Internat. Reading Assn., Conn. Reading Assn.,

Stonington Hist. Soc. of Conn., Delta Kappa Gamma Soc. Internat., Grad. Club New Haven. Roman Catholic. Home: 19 Westview Rd North Haven CT 06473-2013 E-mail: Fuggi@Juno.com.

FUHR, EDWARD JOSEPH, lawyer; b. N.Y.C., Mar. 8, 1962; s. Joseph Ernest and Erika Joan Fuhr; m. Joy Isabel Cummings, Nov. 6, 1993; children: Anna Isabel, Laura Isabel, Sarah Isabel. BA, U. Va., 1984; JD, U. Chgo., 1987. Jud. clk. hon. Boyce F. Martin Jr. U.S. Ct. Appeals 6th Cir., Louisville, Ky., 1987-88; atty.-advisor Office Legal Counsel, Dept. Justice, Washington, 1988-89; ptnr. Hunton & Williams, Richmond, Va., 1990—. Adj. prof. U. Richmond T.C. Williams Law Sch., 1995. Chmn. Henrico County Rep. Com., Richmond, 1992-98, Charitable Gaming Commn., Va., 1995-2000; vol. atty. for battered women Women's Shelter Project, Richmond, 1995-96; counsel inagural com. Gov.-elect James S. Gilmore III, Richmond. Named one of Top 40 Under 40, Inside Bus., Richmond, 1997. Mem. ABA, Va. Bar Assn., Richmond Bar Assn. Office: Hunton & Williams 951 E Byrd St Richmond VA 23219-4074 Fax: 804-788-8218. E-mail: efuhr@hunton.com.

FUHR, GRANT, professional hockey player; b. Spruce Grove, Alta., Canada, Sept. 28, 1962; m. Candice Fuhr, July 28, 1995; children: Kendyl, R. J., Rochelle, Janine. Goalie Edmonton Oilers, 1981-91, Toronto Maple Leafs, 1991-93, Buffalo Sabers, 1993—95, Los Angeles Kings, 1994—95, St. Louis Blues, 1996-99, Calgary Flames, 1999—2000; goalie coach Phoenix Coyotes, 2004—. Mem. Stanley Cup Championship Team, 1984, 85, 87, 88, 90; player All-Star Game, 1982, 1984—86, 1988—89. Named All-Star MVP, 1986; named to NHL First All-Star Tem, 1988; recipient Vezina Trophy (top NHL Goaltender), 1988, William Jennings Trophy, 1994. Achievements include inducted into the Hockey Hall of Fame, 2003. Office: c/o Phoenix Coyotes 9375 E Bell RD Scottsdale AZ 85260

FUHRMAN, SUSAN H, dean, education educator; BA in history with highest honors, Northwestern U., 1965, MA in history, 1966; PhD in polit. sci. and edn., Columbia U., 1977. Prof. of edn. policy Eagleton Inst. of Polit. at Rutgers U., 1989—95; prof., dept. of pub. policy Edward J. Bloustein Sch. of Planning and Pub. Policy, Rutgers U., 1994—95; dean grad sch. edn. U. Penn, 1995—, George & Diane Weiss prof. edn. Bd. mem. Carnegie Found. for the Advancement of Tchg.; founder and chmn. Consortium for Policy Rsch. in Edn. (CPRE), 1985—; mem. of coun. Corp. and Sch. Partnerships of the Coca-Cola Found.; former co-chair Nat. Adv. Panel for the Third Internat. Math and Sci. Study. Editor: From the Capitol to the Classroom: Standards-Based Reform in the States, One Hundredth Yearbook of the National Society for the Study of Education, 2001, Designing Coherent Education Policy: Improving the System, 1993; co-editor (with Jennifer O'Day): Rewards and Reform: Creating Educational Incentives that Work, 1996; co-editor: (with Melissa Carr) Making Money Matter: Equity and Adequacy in Education Finance, 1999. Achievements include research in state education reform, state local relationships, state differential treatment of districts, federalism in education, incentives and systemic reform, legislatures and education policy. Office: U Penn Grad Sch Edn 3700 Walnut St Philadelphia PA 19104*

FUJIMARA, MAKOTA, painter; b. Boston, 1960; BA cum laude, Bucknell U., 1983; MFA, Toyko Nat. U. of Fine Arts and Music, 1989. Mem. Nat. Coun. on Arts, Nat. Endowment for Arts, 2003—. Exhibitions include Contemporary Nihonga Exhbit, Comtemporary Mus. Toyko, 1998, One Hundred Years of Nihonga, Toyko Nat. Univ of Fine Arts and Music Mus., 2000, Like a Prayer, Tryon Ctr. Visual Arts, 2003, Considering Peace, Sato Mus., 2003, one-man shows include Gravity and Grace, Bellas Artes, 2002, Columbines, Gallery at Matsuya Ginza, 2002, Four Quartets, Kristen Frederickson Contemporary, 2003, Golden Pines, Dillon Gallery, 2003, The Still Point, Takashimaya Gallery, 2003—04, exhibited in group shows at Art as Prayer, Cooper Union Gallery, 2001, TriBeCa Temporary Exhibits, 2001, WATERwalks, Ise Cultural Found., 2002, The Return of Beauty, Kristen Frederickson Gallery, 2002, The WRONG Exhbit, Birmingham, England, 2003, Represented in permanent collections Contemporary Mus. Tokyo, Nerima Mus. Art, Oxford House, Sato Mus., St. Louis Art Mus., Tamaya Collection, Toyko Nat. U. of Fine Arts and Music, Yamaguchi Prefecture Mus. Office: Nat Endowment for Arts 1100 Pennsylvania Ave, NW Washington DC 20506 Office Phone: 202-682-5400. E-mail: fujimura@jamny.org.*

FUJIMOTO, JAMES G., electrical engineering educator; b. Chgo., Sept. 28, 1957; s. Harold H. and Jane S. (Sakoda) F.; m. Carla Helen Millhauser. BSEE, MIT, 1979, MSEE, 1981, PhD, 1985. Asst. prof. MIT, Cambridge, 1985-88, assoc. prof., 1988-94; prof., 1994—. Vis. lectr. Harvard Med. Sch., Boston, 1987-91; cons. MIT Lincoln Lab., Lexington, Mass., 1985-96; adj. prof. ophthalmology Tufts U., 1994—. Recipient Presdl. Young Investigator award NSF, 1986, William Baker award NAS, 1990, Award for Initiatives in Rsch., NAS, 1990; traveling lectr. award Lasers and Electro-Optics Soc., 1990. Fellow IEEE; mem. NAE, AAAS, Optical Soc. Am., Am. Phys. Soc. Office: MIT Bldg 36-361 Dept Elec Engring-Comp Sci Cambridge MA 02139

FUJIMOTO, JUNICHIRO, pathologist; b. Osaka, Japan, May 25, 1951; MD in Medicine, Gifu (Japan) U., 1977; PhD in Medicine, Sapporo U., Hokkaido, Japan, 1984. Sr. investigator dept. pathology Nat. Children's Med. Rsch. Ctr., Tokyo, 1985-89, dir. dept. pathology, 1989—2002; dir. dept. devel. biology Nat. Rsch. Inst. Child Health Devel., 2002—. Avocation: driving. Office: Nat Rsch Inst Child Health Devel 3-35-31 Taishido Setagaya Tokyo 154-8567 Japan Fax: 81-3-3487-9669. E-mail: jfujimoto@nch.go.jp.

FUJIMURA, MAKOTO, artist; b. Dec. 30, 1960; BA, Bucknell U., 1983; MFA, Tokyo Nat. U. of Fine Arts, 1990. Exhibitions include Sato Mus., Tokyo, 1997, 99-2000, Tamaya Gallery, Tokyo, 1988-97, Dillon Gallery, N.Y., 1995-2000, Sen Gallery, Tokyo, 1999-2000; represented in permanent collections St. Louis Mus. Art, Tokyo Contemporary Mus. Art Mem. Nat. Coun. on the Arts; founder, dir. Internat. Arts Movement. Office: 69 Murray St Apt 2F New York NY 10007-2137

FUJINAMI, ROBERT SHIN, neurology educator; b. Salt Lake City, Dec. 8, 1949; BA, U. Utah, 1972; PhD, Northwestern U., Chgo., 1977. Instr. microbiology and immunology Northwestern U., Chgo., 1973-76; rsch. fellow immunopathology Scripps Clinic and Rsch. Found., La Jolla, Calif., 1977-80, rsch. assoc. immunopathology, 1980-81, asst. mem., asst. prof. dept. immunology, 1981-85, vis. investigator dept. immunology, 1985-89; vis. investigator dept. neuropharmacology divsn. virology Scripps Rsch. Inst. (formerly Scripps Clinic and Rsch. Found.), La Jolla, 1989-90; rsch. immunopathologist dept. pathology U. Calif., San Diego, 1980-82, assoc. prof. pathology, 1985-90; prof. neurology U. Utah, Salt Lake City, 1990—, adj. prof. dept. pathology divsn. cell biology and immunology, 1991—. Mem. Weber immunology adv. com., dept. pathology U. Utah, Salt Lake City, 1991—, mem. neurosci. steering com., 1992-96, mem. biosafety com., 1992-96, chmn., 1994-96, chmn. safety com., dept. neurology, 1993—, chmn. promotion, retention and tenure com., 1993-96, mem. univ. promotions and tenure adv. com., 1995-98, chair oversight com. Fluorescence Activated Cell Sorter (FACS) Sch. Medicine, 1996-99, mem. univ. rsch. com., 1999—2004, disting. rsch. award subcom., 1999—2001, senate task force on RPT procedures, 1999—2000, adv. com. core facilities Huntsman Cancer Inst., 1999—2000, dir. grad. studies pathology PhD program, 1999—2002, chmn. tenured faculty rev. com., dept. neurology, 1999—2000. Contbr. chpts. to books, 130 articles to profl. jours. Recipient New Investigator award NIH, 1981-83; NIH scholar, 1989-96. Fellow AAAS; mem. Nat. Multiple Sclerosis Soc. (bd. dirs. Utah chpt. 1992-99—, Hary M. Weaver Neurosci. award 1982-86). Office: U Utah Dept Neurology 30 N 1900 E 3R330 SOM Salt Lake City UT 84132-0001 Office Phone: 801-585-3305. Business E-Mail: Robert.Fujimami@hsc.utah.edu.

FUJINO, MICHIMASA, aeronautical engineer; s. Michio and Kuniko Fujino; m. Yukiko Fujino, July 14, 1986. BS, Tokyo U., 1984. Chief engr. Honda R&D Americas, Inc., Greensboro, NC, 1995—98, chief project engr., 1998—2005, v.p., 2005—. Mem.: AIAA. Achievements include leading the design and development of the HondaJet, which is the world's most fuel-efficient business jet. Office: Honda R&D Americas Inc 6423B Bryan Blvd Greensboro NC 27409 Office Phone: 336-662-0849. Office Fax: 336-662-0852. Business E-Mail: mfujino@oh.hra.com.

FUJIOKA, JO ANN OTA, educational administrator, consultant; b. Bellflower, Calif., Apr. 30, 1939; d. Richard Masayoshi and Lillian Chiyono (Ihara) Ota; m. Arthur Fujioka, Feb. 19, 1961; 1 child, Dana Kay. BSN, U. Colo., 1961, MSN, 1970; PhD, Colo. State U., 1987. RN; cert. adminstr., supt., spl. edn. dir., sch. nurse, vocat. edn. adminstr., instr. Nurse pub. health, psychiat. Denver Gen. Hosp., Denver Vis. Nurse Svc., 1961-71; sch. nurse Jefferson County Sch. Dist., Golden, Colo., 1971-76, mgr. program, supr. sch. health program, 1976-79, mgr. spl. edn. and related svcs., adminstr. elem. bldg., 1979-95; cons. Fujioka Cons., Denver, 1995—. Cons. Ctrl. Kans. Bd. Coop. Ednl. Svcs., Salina, 1992, Denver Children's Home, 1996, Colo. Assn. of Family and Children's Agencies, 1997, Colo. Mediation Project, 1998. Contbr. articles to profl. jours. Vice chmn. bd. dirs. Creative Exch., 1997—99, chmn. bd. dirs., 1999—2001, mem. adv. bd., 2002—03; mem. edn. adv. com. PBS, 2001—; mem. Cross Cultural Dialogue, 2001—; hon. bd. dirs. Colo. Women's Hall of Fame, 2002—. Mem.: AAUW, NOW, Jefferson County Adminstrs. Assn., Colo. Sch. Health Coun. (pres. 1978—80), U. Colo. Health Scis. Ctr. Srs. Assn. (chpt. pres. 1992—94, Internat. Dist. IV project grant dir. 1993, fall conf. chair 1993—2005, Internat. Dist. IV project grant dir. 1999, internat. coord. for ethical leadership project 2000—, bd. dirs. 2000—), Am. Assn. Sch. Execs., Alliance Profl. Cons. (exec. bd.), Japanese Am. Nat. Mus., Phi Delta Kappa (internat. del. 1993, area coord. 1996—2001, internat. v.p. bd. dirs. 2001—03, dist. IV project grant dir. 2003, internat. pres. elect 2003—05, internat. pres. 2005—, internat. centennial com. 2005, Douglas County Chpt. award 1999, Denver U. Chpt. Svc. award 1999, Jefferson County Chpt. Svc. award 2001, Jefferson County Chpt. Leadership award 2003, George H. Reavis Assoc. 2003, dist. IV project grant dir. 2003, mem. centennial com. 2005—). Democrat. Buddhist. Avocations: crossword puzzles, jigsaw puzzles, crocheting, tai chi, reading. Home and Office: 540 S Forest St #K Denver CO 80246-8164 Office Phone: 303-377-6641. E-mail: fujicons@aol.com.*

FUJITA, JAMES HIROSHI, history educator; b. Honolulu, July 24, 1958; s. George Hideo and Teruko (Miyano) F. BA, U. Hawaii, 1980, MA, 1983. Grad. asst. U. Hawaii at Manoa, Honolulu, 1980-85, lectr. history, 1986—, Kapiolani C.C., Honolulu, 1987-97; adj. staff Hawaii Pacific U., Honolulu, 1998—. Lectr. Elderhostel Program, Honolulu, 1992, Leeward C.C., 1997—; adj. staff Chaminade U., Honolulu, 1998—. Mem. NEA, World History Assn., U. Hawaii Profl. Assembly, Phi Alpha Theta. Office: Hawaii Pacific U 1188 Fort Street Mall Honolulu HI 96813-2713

FUJITSUBO, LANI CHARLENE, psychology educator; b. L.A., June 21, 1954; d. WIlliam Sadao and Sylvia Toshiko Fujitsubo. BA, SCC, Costa Mesa, Calif., 1980; MA, U.S. Internat. Univ., San Diego, 1988, PhD, 1991. Lic. psychologist, Oreg., Alaska. Psychology intern Children's Hosp., Orange, Calif., 1990-91; prof., psychologist U. Alaska, Fairbanks, 1991-93; prof. So. Oreg. Univ., Ashland, 1993—, dir. testing, 1994—, chmn. Dept. Psychology, 2004—. Pvt. practice, Ashland, 1993—; cons., 1991—. Bd. dirs. Girl Scout Coun., Winema, Oreg. Mem. Am. Psychol. Assn., Western Psychol. Assn., Oreg. Psychol. Assn., Assn. Women in Psychology. Democrat. Avocations: stained glass, piano, travel. Office: So Oreg U 1250 Siskiyou Blvd Ashland OR 97520-5010 Office Phone: 541-552-6940.

FUJIWARA, CHRIS, writer; Bassist Cul de Sac, Cambridge, Mass., 1992—97; contbg. editor Hermenaut, Jamaica Plain, 1997—. Vis. prof. film studies program Yale U., New Haven, 2001; adj. prof. dept. visual and media arts Emerson Coll., Boston, 2001—. Author: Jacques Tourneur: The Cinema of Nightfall; contbr. articles to profl. jours. Mem.: AAUP, Boston Soc. Film Critics. Home: 88 Boston St Somerville MA 02143 Personal E-mail: chris.fujiwara@verizon.net.

FUJIWARA, HIDEJI, chemist, researcher; b. Tamano, Okayama, Japan, Nov. 19, 1943; s. Motoyoshi and Sumiko Fujiwara; m. Mieko Ogawa, Apr. 29, 1978; children: Kenichiro, Mikiko Kay. BS, Sci. U. Tokyo, 1967; MS, Stevens Inst. Tech., 1969, PhD, 1974. Postdoctoral fellow Stevens Inst. Tech., 1974-75, rsch. scientist, 1975-77; rschr. Exxon br. Tao Nenryo Kogyo KK, Saitam, Japan, 1962-67; sr. rsch. chemist (specialist) Monsanto Co., St. Louis, 1977-87, assoc., full sci. fellow, 1987-2000; sci. fellow Pharmacia Co., Chesterfield, Mo., 2000—. Contbr. articles to sci. jours., includinfg Jour. Agrl. Food Chemistry, Chem. and Engring. News. Trustee Bethany Bapt. Ch., 1990—. Schering postdoctoral fellow Stevens Inst. Tech., 1975-76. Em. Am. Chem. Soc., Am. Soc. for Mass Spectrometry, N.Y. Acad. Scis., St. Louis Japan Soc., Toastmasters (treas. Life Scis. chpt. 1999-2000), Sigma Xi. Office: Pharmacia Co 700 Chesterfield Pky Chesterfield MO 63017 Fax: 636-737-7099. E-mail: hideji.fujiwara@pharmacia.com.

FUKASAWA, KENJI, medical researcher; s. Fukuyo and Isamu Fukasawa. PhD, Columbia U., New York City, 1987—91. Rsch. scientist Nat. Cancer Inst., Frederick, Md., 1991—97; assoc. prof. U. Cin. Coll. Medicine, 2004—. Fellow, Nat. Cancer Inst., 2001—02;, Ruth Lyon Cancer Rsch. Found., 1998—2004. Office: U Cin 3125 Eden Ave PO Box 670521 Cincinnati OH 45267-0521 E-mail: kenji.fukasawa@uc.edu.

FUKATSU, TANEFUSA, retired classicist, educator; b. Toyota, Aichi, Japan, Apr. 23, 1923; s. Kingo and Shizu (Noba) F.; m. Michiko Kato, Jan. 17, 1954 (dec. 1981); children: Tomonao, Arikata. BA, Tokyo U., 1951. Tchr. Chinese classics Musashi High Sch., Tokyo, 1957-89; asst. prof. Chinese classics Musashi U., Tokyo, 1971-74, prof. Chinese classics, 1974-85; retired, 1989—. Lectr. Chinese classics Nisho-Gakusha U., Tokyo, 1967-93, guest prof., 1993—. Author: Juzi Tongbian Jingdianshiwen, 1978, Lunyu Xidu, 1990, Laozi Xidu, 1994, Thought and Life of the Ancient Chinese-Mirror-, 1996, Japanese Culture and Chinese Culture-White Chrysanthemum and Yellow Chrysanthemum, 1997, Studies on the Latent Thought in Chinese Characters and Poetry, 1997, Chinese Thought and Culture, 1998, Studies of the Book of Laozi, 1999, Thought and Life of the Ancient Chinese-Cock-, 1999, Thought and Life of the Ancient Chinese—The Source and Course of the Thought of "The Book of Laozi", 2000. Mem. Nippon-Chugoku-Gakkai, Shibunkai (dir. 1990-93, councilor 1993—). Home: 86-1-501 Konya-Cho Saiwai-Ku Kawasaki-Shi Kanagawa 212-0026 Japan

FUKETA, TOYOJIRO, physicist; b. Japan, Feb. 10, 1930; s. Tatsukichi and Fuji (Tsukamoto) Koga; m. Sumiko Fuketa, Oct. 26, 1955; children: Toyoshi, Sachi. BS, Osaka U., Japan, 1953, MS, 1955, DS, 1961. Rsch. physicist Japan Atomic Energy Rsch. Inst., Tokai-Mura, Tokyo, Japan, 1957-93, exec. dir. Tokyo, 1987-88, v.p., 1989-93; vis. scientist Oak Ridge (Tenn.) Nat. Lab., 1962-63; rsch. assoc. Rensselaer Polytech. Inst., Troy, N.Y., 1963-64; pres. Nuclear Energy Data Ctr., Tokai-Mura, 1993-95, Rsch. Orgn. Info. Sci. & Tech., Tokai-Mura, 1995-97; chmn. Inst. Environ. Sci., Rokkasho-Mura, Aomori-Ken, 1997-2000; pres. Japan Marine Sci. Found., Tokyo, 2000—. Named Hon. Citizen State Of Tenn., 1962, City of Knoxville, 1991. Mem. Atomic Energy Soc. Japan (v.p. 1992-94). Home: 1-19-5 Shoan Suginami-Ku Tokyo 167-0054 Japan E-mail: fwkd6357@mb.infoweb.ne.jp.

FUKS, BORIS BORISOVICH, immunologist, researcher; b. Tomsk, Russia, Oct. 18, 1926; came to U.S., 1996; s. Boris Ilyich and Zinaida Lvovna Fuks; m. Irina Vitalyevna Konstantinova, Sept. 9, 1949 (dec. Aug. 1998); 1 child, Alexandr Borisovich Konstantinov; m. Susanna E. Staroselsky. MD, Med. Inst., Novosibirsk, Russia, 1948; PhD, Med. Inst., Tomsk, 1951, DSc, 1960. Asst. for chair of pathology Inst. Postgrad. Tng., Novokuznetsk, Russia, 1951-53; head of lab. of cytochemistry Rsch. Inst. Traumatology and Orthopaedics, Novosibirsk, 1953-58; head of lab. of histochemistry Inst. Exptl. Biology/Medicine Siberian br. USSR Acad. Sci., Academishen Town, 1958-63; prof. for chair med. biology Siberian U., Novosibirsk, 1960-63; head dept. exptl. biology Inst. Cytology and Genetics Siberian br. USSR Acad. Sci., Novosibirsk, 1962-64; head lab. of cellular immunology and biotech. Rsch. Inst. Human Morphology, Russian Acad. Med. Sci., Moscow, 1964-96; v.p. N-DIA, Inc., Plainsboro, N.J., 1991—; pres. Calif. Rsch. LLC, Mountain View, Calif., 1996-98. Author: (books) The Immune System in Space and Other Extreme Conditions, 1991, Glycoconjugates as Modifiers of Antitumor Immunity, 1991; contbr. articles and monographs to profl. jours.; patentee in field. Named Honored Scientist of Russia, Pres. of Russia, 1994. Mem. Nat. Soc. Immunologists (head immunol. br., mem. presidium). Achievements include research in reduction of human T-cells and NK activity and alteration of lymphokine production in outer space; phenomenon of tumor cell toxicity for lymphocytes and NK; conception: escape of tumor cells out of immune control. Home: Apt 335 1 Kulas Ln Parlin NJ 08859 E-mail: foux2000@aol.com.

FUKS, ZVI Y., medical educator; b. Tel Aviv, Apr. 7, 1936; came to U.S, 1984; married; children: Yaron, Tamar. MD, Hebrew U., Jerusalem, 1960. Am. Bd. Radiology-Radiation Therapy. Intern Hadassah U. Hosp., Jerusalem, Israel, 1961; resident in radiation therapy and med. oncology Hadassah Hosp., Tel Aviv U. Sch. Medicine, Israel, 1964-69; asst. prof. radiology Stanford (Calif.) U., 1969-76; prof., head radiation oncology Hadassah U. Hosp., Jerusalem, 1976-78, prof., chmn. dept. radiation oncology, 1978-84; chmn. dept. radiation oncology Meml. Sloan-Kettering Cancer Ctr., N.Y.C., 1984-98, dep. physician in chief for planning, 1998—, acting dir. clin. rsch. tng. office, 2000—. Mem. Am. Coll. Radiology, Am. Soc. Clin. Oncology, Am. Soc. Therapeutic Radiologists, European Soc. Therapeutic Radiol. Oncologists, Nat. Rsch. Coun., Calif. Med. Assn., European Cancer Assn., N.Y. Cancer Soc., N.Y. Roetgen Soc., Radiation Rsch. Soc. Office: Meml Sloan-Kettering Ctr 1275 York Ave New York NY 10021-6094

FUKUI, HATSUAKI, retired electrical engineer, art historian; b. Yokohama, Japan, Dec. 14, 1927; came to U.S., 1962, naturalized, 1973; s. Ushinosuke and Yoshi (Saito) F.; m. Atsuko Inamoto, Apr. 1, 1954 (dec. 1973); children: Mayumi, Naoki; m. Kiku Kato, Dec. 12, 1975. Diploma, Miyakojima Tech. Coll. (now Osaka City U.), 1949; BS, Sci. U. Tokyo; D.Eng., Osaka U., 1961. Rsch. assoc. Osaka City U., 1949-54; engr. Shimada Phys. and Chem. Indsl. Co., Tokyo, 1954-55; sr. engr. to mgr. semi-condr. divsn. Sony Corp. (formerly Tokyo Tsushin Kogyo KK), Tokyo, 1955-61; mgr. engring. div. Sony Corp., 1961-62; mem. tech. staff Bell Telephone Labs., Murray Hill, N.J., 1962-69, supr., 1969-73; v.p. Sony Corp. Am., N.Y.C., 1973; asst. to chmn. Sony Corp., Tokyo, 1973; staff mem. Bell Labs., Murray Hill, N.J., 1973-81, supr., 1981-83, Lucent Techs. (formerly AT&T Bell Labs.), 1984-89. Lectr. Tokyo Met. U. (part-time), 1962 Author: Esaki Diodes, 1963, Solid-State FM Receivers, 1968; contbr. to: Semiconductors Handbook, 1963, GaAs FET Principles and Technologies, 1982; editor: Low-Noise Microwave Transistors and Amplifiers, 1981; contbr. articles to profl. jours.; patentee in field. Fellow IEEE (life; standardization com. 1976-82, edit. bd. IEEE Transactions on Microwave Theory and Techniques 1980-90, com. on U.S. competitiveness 1988-90); mem. Inst. Electronics, Info. and Comm. Engrs. Japan (Inada award 1959), IEEE Comms. Soc., IEEE Electron Devices Soc., IEEE Lasers and Electro-Optics Soc., IEEE Microwave Theory and Techniques Soc. (Microwave prize 1980, Pioneer award 1990), Electromagnetics Acad., Japan Soc. Applied Physics, Inst. TV Engrs. Japan (tech. steering com. 1973-74), Medieval Acad. Am., Assn. Art History, Am. Assn. Museums, Gakushikai, Internat. House Japan. Home: 53 Drum Hill Dr Summit NJ 07901-3141 also: 1-21-16-802 Nakane Meguro Tokyo 152-0031 Japan Personal E-mail: hfukui@ieee.org.

FUKUI, YOSHIO, biology professor; b. Shinagawa, Tokyo, Japan, Jan. 4, 1942; came to U.S., 1985; s. Shizuo and Momoko Fukui; m. Yumiko Fukui, Mar. 12, 1978; children: Ibuki, Maya. BA, Internat. Christian U., 1966; MS, Osaka (Japan) U., 1969, PhD, 1972. Rsch. assoc. prof. Osaka U., 1972-74, asst. prof., 1974-77; rsch. assoc. Princeton (N.J.) U., 1977-78; assoc. prof. Osaka U., 1978-85; vis. assoc. prof. Northwestern U., Chgo., 1985-89, assoc. prof. cell, molecular, structural biology (tenured), 1989—, courtesy prof. mech. engr. Evanston, 2005. Prof. cell molecular biology, Yamada exch. scientist Yamada Sci. Found., Osaka, 1978; Yoshida exch. visitor Yoshida Chem. Found., Tokyo, 1983. Contbr. articles to profl. jours. including Nature, Proc. Nat. Acad. Sci. Jour. Cell Biology, Internat. Rev. Cytology, others. Recipient Matsunaga Rsch. award Matsunaga Meml. Found., Tokyo, 1976; rsch. grantee NIH, 1988—. Mem. Cooperation of Marine Biol. Lab. (Woods Hole, Mass.), Am. Soc. for Cell Biology, Soc. Advancement of Sci., N.Y. Acad. Scis. (elected), Japan Soc. for Cell Biologist (Tokyo). Office: Northwestern Med Sch 303 E Chicago Ave Chicago IL 60611-3008

FUKUMOTO, LESLIE SATSUKI, lawyer; b. L.A., Mar. 10, 1955; parents: Robert Fukumoto and Florence Teruko Kodama Kuroda. BA, U. Hawaii, 1977; JD, William S. Richard Sch. Law, 1980. Bar: Hawaii 1980, U.S. Dist. Ct. Hawaii 1980, U.S. Ct. Appeals (9th cir.) 1981. Dep. pub. defender State of Hawaii, Honolulu, 1980-81; assoc. Pyun, Kim & Okimoto, 1981-83; ptnr. Pyun, Okimoto & Fukumoto, 1983-84; sole practice, 1984-85; ptnr. Fukumoto & Wong, 1985-93, Tanaka & Fukumoto, 1993-94; prin. Fukumoto Law Corp., 1994—. Bd. dirs. Ichiryo Enterprises, Inc., Honolulu. Assoc. editor U. Hawaii Law Rev., 1979-80. Mem. ATLA, Honolulu Club. Office: 841 Bishop St Ste 1711 Honolulu HI 96813-3924 Office Phone: 808-537-4541. E-mail: fukulaw@mail.com.

FUKUSHIMA, BARBARA NAOMI, financial advisor; b. Honolulu, Apr. 5, 1948; d. Harry Kazuo and Misayo (Kawasaki) Murakoshi; m. Dennis Hiroshi (div. 2001); 1 child, Dennis Hiroshi Jr. BA with high honors, U. Hawaii, 1970; postgrad., Oreg. State U., 1971, 73, U. Oreg., 1972. Intern Coopers & Lybrand, Honolulu, 1974; auditor Haskins & Sells, Kahului, Hawaii, 1974-77; pres. Book Doors, Inc., Pukalani, Hawaii, 1977-97, Barbara N. Fukushima CPA, Inc., Wailuku, Hawaii, 1979-86, sec. treas. Target Pest Control, Inc., 1979-96; internal auditor, acct. Maui Land & Pineapple Co., Inc., Kahului, Hawaii, 1977-80; auditor Hyatt Regency, Maui, Hawaii, 1980-81; ptnr. D & B Internat., Pukalani, Hawaii, 1980-91; instr. Maui C.C., 1982-85; fin. advisor Merrill Lynch, Pierce, Fenner & Smith, Inc., 1986—. Recipient Phi Beta Kappa Book award, 1969. Mem.: AICPA, Hawaii Soc. CPAs, C. of C. of Hawaii, Phi Beta Kappa. Christian. Home: 1088 Bishop St Apt 1117 Honolulu HI 96813-3134 Office: 1001 Bishop St PH Honolulu HI 96813-3429 E-mail: barbnf@yahoo.com.

FUKUSHIMA, KIYOHIKO, economist; b. Nishinomiya, Hyogoken, Japan, Dec. 6, 1944; s. Tohta and Yasuko Fukushima; m. Chizuko Yamauchi, Nov. 2, 1970; children: Izumi, Nobuhiko. BA in Econs., Hitotsubashi U., Tokyo, 1967, MA, 1969. Econ. corr. Mainichi Shinbun, Tokyo, 1969-77; sr. economist Nomura Rsch. Inst., Tokyo, 1978-80; guest scholar Brookings Instn., Washington, 1980-81; sr. economist Nomura Rsch. Inst., N.Y.C., 1981-83, gen. mgr. Washington, 1983-86, dep. dir. econ. rsch. Tokyo, 1986-89, dir. policy rsch. dept., 1989-92, gen. mgr., sr. economist, 1992-94, chief economist, 1996—, chief economist Tokyo hdqrs., 2002—04; pres. Nomura Rsch. Inst. Europe, Ltd., 1999—2002; profl. lectr. sch. advanced internat. studies Johns Hopkins U., Washington, 1994-96; prof. Rikkyo U., Japan, 2005—. Vis. fellow Princeton (N.J.) U., 1976-77. Author: Regionalism and Foreign Direct Investment, 1993, The Age of the Pacific, 1994. Recipient Takahashi Kamekichi award Toyo Keizai Pubs., Inc., 1984, Okita Saburo award Econ. Planning Agy., 1995. Mem. Inst. Internat. Strategic Studies (Japan com. 1992—), Policy Rsch. Com. Avocations: athletics, jogging, movies. Home: 5 20 Higashi 4 Chome Kunitachi shi Tokyo 186-0002 Japan

FUKUTA, NORIHIKO, professor in meteorology, researcher; b. Tokoname, Aichi-ken, Japan, May 11, 1931; came to U.S., 1966; s. Teizo and Haru (Takeuchi) F.; m. Yoko Kuriyama, Mar. 3, 1966. BS, Nogoya (Japan) U., 1954, MS, 1956, PhD, 1959. Lab. dirs. Meteorology Research, Inc., Pasadena, Calif., 1966-68; lab. Head U. Denver, 1968-75, prof., 1968-75, adj. prof., 1976-77, div. head, 1968-77; prof. U. Utah, Salt Lake City, 1977—; dir. atmospheric physics lab. U. Utah Research Inst., 1986-88. Sr. academician NOAA, 1984-85; guest prof. U. Vienna, 1991. Recipient Huffsmith award U. Denver, 1971, Sesquicentennial medal Leningrad U., 1980. Mem. Am. Meteorol. Soc. (assoc. editor Jour. Atmos. Scis. 1976-83, Jour. Applied Meteorology 1972-79, Editor's award 1974), Japanese Meteorol. Soc. (assoc.

editor Atmospheric Rsch. 1992—, guest editor 1993), Am. Geophys. Union, Am. Phys. Soc., Am. Chem. Soc., Sigma Xi. Office: Dept Meteorology U Utah 819 Wbb Salt Lake City UT 84112 Office Phone: 801-581-8987. E-mail: nfukuta@met.utah.edu.

FULCHER, HUGH DRUMMOND, author; b. Lynchburg, Va., Feb. 4, 1945; s. Lewis Page and Frances Louise (Drummond) F.; m. Cheryl Brenn Phelps, July 29, 1972 (div. July 1990); children: Keston Hugh, Kara Brenn. BS in Physics, Math., Va. Poly. Inst. and State U., 1967, MS in Nuclear Engring., 1970. Lic. nuclear reactor operator, Md. Physics instr. Va. Poly. Inst. and State U., Danville, 1968-69, Danville C.C., 1969-71; nuclear engr. supr. Babcock & Wilcox Inc., Lynchburg, 1971-82; nuclear engr. Energy Inc., Richmond, Va., 1982-85; computer engr. Ariz. Pub. Svcs., Phoenix, 1985-90; nuclear engr. Scientech, Inc., Rockville, Md., 1990-91; writer H.D. Fulcher Pubs., Inc., Lynchburg, 1992—. Cons. engr. Fla. Power and Light, Miami, 1985, Westinghouse Svannah River, Aiken, S.C., 1991-92. Author: Emotional Mind Modeling (A Possible Cure for Manic-Depression and A Metaphysical Study of God and His Creation), 1995. Argonne Nat. Lab. Grad. Engring. scholar, 1969. Methodist. Avocations: tennis, pool. Home: 1450 Hawkins Mill Rd Lynchburg VA 24503-4952 Office: H D Fulcher Publishers Inc 1450 Hawkins Mill Rd Lynchburg VA 24503-4952

FULCO, ARMAND JOHN, biochemist; b. L.A., Apr. 3, 1932; s. Herman J. and Clelia Marie (DeFeo) F.; m. Virginia Loy Hungerford, June 18, 1955 (div. July 1985); children: William James, Lisa Marie, Linda Susan, Suzanne Yvonne; m. Doris V.N. Goodman, Nov. 29, 1987. BS in Chemistry, UCLA, 1957, PhD in Physiol. Chemistry, 1960. NIH postdoctoral fellow Lipid Labs. UCLA, 1960-61; NIH research fellow dept. chemistry Harvard U., Cambridge, Mass., 1961-63; biochemist, prin. investigator Lab. Nuclear Medicine and Radiation Biology, UCLA, 1963-80; asst. prof. dept. biol. chemistry David Geffen Sch. Medicine, UCLA, 1965-70, assoc. prof., 1970-76, prof., 1976—2003, prof. emeritus recalled, 2003, prin. investigator lab. biomed. and environ. scis., 1981-93; prin. investigator lab. structural biology/molecular med. UCLA-Dept. of Energy, 1993-95. Cons. biochemist VA, Los Angeles, 1968-79; mem. UCLA Molecular Biology Inst., 1991—; co-dir. Lipid-Hormone Core Lab., UCLA, 1989-96; mem. Jonsson Comprehensive Cancer Ctr. UCLA, 1994—. Author: (with J.F. Mead) The Unsaturated and Polyunsaturated Fatty Acids in Health and Disease, 1976; contbr. over 90 articles to sci. jours. Served with U.S. Army, 1952-54. Mem. AAAS, Am. Chem. Soc., Am. Soc. Biol. Chemistry and Molecular Biology, Am. Soc. Microbiology, Internat. Soc. for Study of Xenobiotics, Harvard Chemists Assn., Sigma Xi. Office: UCLA David Geffen Sch Medicine Dept Biol Chemistry PO Box 951737 Los Angeles CA 90095-1737 Office Phone: 310-825-8750. Office Fax: 310-206-5272. Business E-Mail: fulco@mednet.ucla.edu.

FULCO, PAULA, artist; b. Hartford, Conn., May 22, 1966; d. Paul Anthony and Jane Buell (Emerson) F. BFA, Syracuse U., 1989. Portrait artist, Syracuse, NY, 1985—, Kingdom Portraits, 2002—; cartoonist The Daily Orange, Syracuse, 1985-87; freelance illustrator, 1993-97. Author and illustrator: Kingdom Kartoons: The Jesus Story, 1995. Avocations: running, reading. Home and Office: PO Box 56 Camillus NY 13031 E-mail: kingdomportraits@yahoo.com.

FULD, FRED, III, computer consultant, financial planner; b. San Pedro, Calif., July 31, 1952; s. Fred Jr. and Gloria Mary F.; m. Sharon Elizabeth Fuld; 1 child, Fred IV. BA in Bus., BA in Econs., Rockford Coll., 1974; postgrad., Heriot-Watt U., Berkeley/Edenburgh. Cert. tchr. credential, Calif.; Registered Investment Advisor, SEC, 1981. Investment mgr. San Diego Securities, 1974-78; market maker Pacific Stock Exch., San Francisco, 1978-79; v.p. CGR Conss., San Francisco, 1979-83; pvt. practice fin., computer cons. Concord, Calif., 1983—; exec. prodr. Mt DTV Ednl. TV series. Adj. prof. dept. computer information systems, sch. bus., Calif. State U., Hayward, 1997—; computer mgr. Calif. State U., Hayward, 1999—. Author: (software) Personal Financial Planning, 1984, (software) Asset Allocation, 1986, (software) Business Valuation, 1986; author: Stock Market Secrets, 1985, 101 Most Asked Questions about the MAC, 1992. Mem. Mensa Soc. (life), The Magic Castle (life). Avocations: swimming, jogging, collecting antique stock certificates. Office: 3043 Clayton Rd Concord CA 94519-2730

FULD, RICHARD SEVERIN, JR., investment banking executive; b. NYC, Apr. 26, 1946; s. Richard Severin and Elizabeth (Schwab) F.; m. Kathleen Ann Bailey, Sept. 24, 1978; children: Jacqueline, Christine, Richard S. III. BS, U. Colo., 1969; MBA, NYU, 1973. Mng. dir. Lehman Bros., NYC, 1969-84; vice chmn. Shearson Lehman (merger Shearson and Lehman Bros.), NYC, 1984-90; pres., co-CEO Shearson Lehman Bros. Inc., NYC, 1990—93; pres., CEO Lehman Bros. Holdings, NYC, 1993—94, chmn. bd., CEO, 1994—. Mem. PSA Govt. and Fed. Agy. Securities Com.; dir. Fed. Reserve Bank of NY; mem. exec. com. Partnership for NYC, Bus. Roundtable and Bus. Coun. Trustee Mt. Sinai Med. Ctr., NYC; former chmn. Mt. Sinai Children's Ctr. Found., mem. exec. com.; bd. dirs. Ronald McDonald House; bd. trustees Middlebury Coll. Mem.: bd. dirs. Middlebury coll. Avocations: squash, photography. Office: Lehman Brothers Holdings Inc 745 Seventh Ave, 30 Fl New York NY 10019*

FULDA, MICHAEL, political scientist, educator, space policy researcher; b. Liverpool, Eng., Apr. 21, 1939; came to U.S., 1962, naturalized, 1966; s. Boris and Catherine (Von Dehn) F.; m. Rosa Bongiorno, July 19, 1970; children: Robert, George. Student, Polytechnique, Grenoble, France, 1956-57, Tech. U., West Berlin, Germany, 1957-58, Karl Eberhardt U., Tubingen, Germany, 1963-66; MA, Am. U., 1968, PhD in Internat. Studies, 1970. Ballroom dance coor., 2001—; prof. polit. sci. Fairmont State U., W.Va., 1971—. Vis. prof. Bauman Moscow State Tech. U., 2002; internat. rels. specialist NASA, Washington, 1979. Author: Oil and International Relations, 1979; (with others) United States Space Policy, 1985; contbr. articles to profl. jours. Bd. dirs. Fairmont Chamber Music Soc., 1983—; W.Va. state com. chmn., dir. space policy Nat. Unity Campaign for John Anderson, 1980; mem. nat. adv. com. John Glenn Presdl. Com., 1984, space policy group Dukakis/Bentsen Com., 1988; dist. advancement com. Boy Scouts Am.; active psychol. ops. Vets. Assn. With U.S. Army, 1962-66. Fellow NASA Marshall Ctr., Huntsville, Ala., 1977, Langley Ctr., Hampton, Va., 1976, Woodrow Wilson Found., 1969-70; grantee Humanities Found. W.Va., 1978-80, NASA W.Va. Space Grant Consortium, 1991-2004; named del. to Aerospace States Assn. by Gov. of W.Va., 2001 Fellow AIAA (assoc.), Brit. Interplanetary Soc.; mem. Am. Astronautical Soc., Nat. Space Soc. (dir. 1991-93, 2002-04), German Assn. for Luft and Raumfamrt, Soc. Espacial Mexicana, Nat. Space Club, Assn. Argentina Tech. Space, Inst. for Social Sci. Study of Space (pres. 1988—), Fairmont Elks Lodge (edn. com.). Avocations: physical fitness, weightlifting, tango, ballroom dancing. Home: 2 Briarwood Terr Fairmont WV 26554-1331 Office Phone: 304-367-4674. Business E-Mail: mfulda@fairmontstate.edu.

FULGHUM, ROBERT L., author, lecturer; b. Waco, Tex., June 4, 1937; s. Lee and Eula (Howard) F.; m. Marcia McClellan, 1957 (div. 1973); children: Christian, Hunter, Molly; m. Lynn Edwards, 1976. Attended, Univ. Colo.; grad., Baylor Bapt. Univ., 1957, Starr King Sch. for the Ministry, Berkeley, Calif. Ordained to ministry Unitarian Ch., 1961. Part time min., Bellingham, Wash., from 1961, Edmonds Unitarian Ch., Seattle, Wash., 1966-85, min. emeritus, 1985—; instr. art Lakeside Sch., Seattle, Wash., 1971-88; author and lecturer. Author: All I Really Need to Know I Learned in Kindergarten: Uncommon Thoughts on Common Things, 1988, It Was on Fire When I Lay Down on It, 1989, Uh Oh: Some Observations from Both Sides of the Refrigerator Door, 1991, Maybe (Maybe Not): Second Thoughts on a Secret Life, 1993, From Beginning to End: The Rituals of Our Lives, 1995, True Love, 1997. Office: c/o Random House Inc 299 Park Ave New York NY 10171

FULGINITI, TODD E., music educator; b. Lancaster, Pa., July 5, 1969; s. Ronald Eugene and Brenda Joy Fulginiti; m. Tammy Sue Lynes, June 29, 1991; children: Bailey Clarke, Ally Noelle. BS in Edn., Millersville U., 1991. Cert. tchr. Pa. Tchr. music Hampfield Sch. Dist., Landisville, Pa., 1992—93, Warwick Sch. Dist., Lititz, 1995—. Composer, arranger various sch. and profl. music groups, Lititz, 1991—, Lancaster, 1991—. Composer (arranger): Fanfare for A Brave Occasion, 1998; Holiday Horns, 2004. Mem. Greenpeace, 1990—98. Mem.: NEA, Am. Fedn. Musicians (nominations bd. 1991—), Warwick Edn. Assn. Avocations: bicycling, travel, video games. Home: 131 S Spruce St Lititz PA 17543

FULK, ROSCOE NEAL, retired accountant; b. Lebo, Kans., June 23, 1916; s. Roscoe Lloyd and Maude (Calvert) F.; m. Marie Therese Rabbitt, June 15, 1946; children: Thomas, Janet, David, Robert, Kenneth, Howard. BS, U. Ill., 1940. With Ernst & Ernst, C.P.A.s, Chgo., 1940-76, partner, 1957-76; mem. Ill. Bd. Examiners in Accountancy, 1976-79. Treas. Exec. Svc. Corps., Chgo., 1978-91, also bd. dirs. Treas. Winnetka (Ill.) Caucus Com., 1956, vice chmn., 1962; chmn. accountants group United Republican Fund Ill., 1958, Met. Crusade of Mercy, 1970; pres. Civic Fedn. Chgo., 1968-70; pres. New Trier Twp. Citizens League, 1961-65; mem. Gov.'s Adv. Council, 1969-73; mem. adv. com. to Coll. Commerce and Bus. Administrn., U. Ill., 1970-76; pres., dir. Juvenile Protective Assn., 1970-73; v.p., bd. govs. Chgo. Met. Housing and Planning Council, 1970-75; chmn. Winnetka Zoning Bd. Appeals, 1968-71; mem. Parking Adv. Council Chgo., 1970-74; mem. grand council Am. Indian Center, 1973-76; chmn. pres.'s council bus. assos. Elmhurst Coll., 1969-70; bd. dirs. U. Ill. Found., 1973-79, State Equity Council, 1969-72; pres. United Charities Chgo., 1973-75; v.p. Catholic Charities Chgo., 1973-75, Met. Easter Seal Soc. Chgo., 1973-77; pres.' council U. Chgo., 1973-76; bd. dirs. St. Francis Hosp., Evanston, Ill., 1978-87; trustee, treas. Chgo. Orchestral Assn., 1977-80. Served to lt. USNR, 1942-46. Mem. Am. Inst. C.P.A.s (mem. council 1968-72), Ill. Soc. C.P.A.s (dir. 1963-64, pres. 1969-70), Chgo. Assn. Commerce and Industry (dir. 1975-77) Clubs: Sunset Ridge Country (Winnetka) (dir. 1961-65), Paradise Valley Country (Phoenix). Home: 6829 N 3rd Pl Phoenix AZ 85012-1008

FULKER, EDMUND NORMAN, management consultant; b. Pittsfield, Mass., June 14, 1927; s. Herbert Ernest Creal Fulker and Albina Archambault; m. Jeanette Ruth Fletcher, July 31, 1948; children: Pamela J. Fulker Leonard, Glen Herbert. BS, Purdue U., 1951, MS in Psychology, 1952; EdD in Adult Edn., Am. U., 1970. Lic. psychologist, D.C. Instr. Purdue U., Indpls., 1952-54; tng. officer USAF Hdqrs., Pentagon, Washington, 1954-57, Hdqrs. USDA, Washington, 1957-59; asst. dir. USDA Grad. Sch., Washington, 1959-80, dir., 1980-85; cons. The World Bank, Washington, 1987-99. Adj. faculty Am. U., Washington, George Washington U., Ctrl. Mich. U., Nat. Cheng Chi U., Taiwan; pres. Washington chpt. ASPA, 1977-78, nat. coun. mem., 1979-81. Contbr. articles to profl. jours. Mgmt. cons. U. Mich., Taipei, Taiwan, 1963, Ford Found., New Delhi, India, Nepal, 1970-71, Ohio State U., Ankara, Turkey, 1993, Egypt Gen. Petroleum Co., Cairo, 1996-99. With USNR, 1945-47. Recipient Outstanding Pub. Adminstr. award ASPA, Washington, 1984. Mem. ASTD (pres. chpt. 1964-65, Outstanding Trainer award 1963), Royal Palm Yacht Club (Ft. Myers, Fla.). Avocations: boating, golf, travel. Home: 15240 Sam Snead Ln Fort Myers FL 33917-3260 Personal E-mail: edfulker@aol.com.

FULKERSON, WILLIAM, health facility executive, pulmonologist; b. Charlotte, NC, Sept. 8, 1951; Grad., U. N.C., Chapel Hill, 1973; MD, U. N.C., 1977; grad., Duke U. Intern Vanderbilt U. Hosp., Nashville, 1977—78, resident internal medicine, 1978—81, fellow pulmonary disease, 1981—83; asst. prof. medicine Duke U. Sch. Medicine, 1983—90, assoc. prof., 1990—95, prof., 1995—, vice chmn. dept. medicine, 1997—98, chief pulmonary and critical care medicine, 1997—99, exec. med. officer Private Diagnostic Clinic PLLC, 1997—99; chief med. officer Duke U. Hosp., 2000—, CEO, 2002—. Contbr. articles to profl. jours., chapters to books. Fellow: Soc. Critical Care Medicine, Am. Coll. Chest Physicians; mem.: Am. Thoracic Soc., ACP. Office: Duke Univ 14209 Hosp S Box 3708 Med Ctr Durham NC 27710

FULKERSON, WILLIAM MEASEY, JR., college president; b. Moberly, Mo., Oct. 18, 1940; s. William Measey and Edna Frances (Pendleton) F.; m. Grace Carolyn Wisdom, May 26, 1962; children: Carl Franklin, Carolyn Sue. BA, William Jewell Coll., 1962; MA, Temple U., 1964; PhD, Mich. State U., 1969. Asst. to assoc. prof. Calif. State U., Fresno, 1981—; asst. to pres. Calif. State U.-Fresno, 1971-73; assoc. exec. dir. Am. Assn. State Colls., Washington, 1973-77; acad. v.p. Phillips U., Enid, Okla., 1977-81; pres. Adams State Coll., Alamosa, Colo., 1981-94, State Colls. in Colo., 1994—. Interim pres. Met. State Coll., Denver, 1987-88, Western State Coll., 1996. Author: Planning for Financial Exigency, 1973; contbr. articles to profl. jours. Commr. North Ctrl. Assn., Chgo., 1980—; bd. dirs. Acad. Collective Bargaining Info. Svc., Washington, 1976, Office for Advancement Pub. Negro Colls., Atlanta, 1973-77, Colo. Endowment for Humanities, 1988-2000, pres., 1998-99. Named Disting. Alumni William Jewell Coll., 1982, Outstanding Alumnus Mich. State U. Coll. Comm., Arts & Scis., 1987. Mem. Am. Assn. State Colls. and Univs. (parliamentarian, bd. dirs. 1992-94), Am. Coun. on Edn. (bd. dirs.), Assn. Pub. Coll.s and Univs. Pres.s (pres. 1994-95), Nat. Assn. Sys. Heads, Alamosa C. of C. (dir., pres. 1984 Citizen Yr. award), Rotary. Office: State Colleges in Colorado Ste 1200 1380 Lawrence St Denver CO 80204-2059

FULKS, ROBERT GRADY, computer company executive; b. Kansas City, Apr. 8, 1936; s. Hilburne Grady and Dora Elouise (Johnson) Fulks; children: Stephanie, Scott Grady. BSEE, MIT, 1958, MSEE, 1959. Engr., chief engr., v.p. engring and product mktg. GenRad, Inc. (formerly Gen. Radio Co.), Concord, Mass., 1959—73; pres. Micro Sys., Inc., 1973—75, Omnicomp, Inc., Phoenix, 1975—80; gen. mgr. advanced tech. divsn. GenRad, Inc. (formerly Omnicomp, Inc.), Phoenix, 1980—86, v.p. parent co.; v.p. engring. Telesis Sys. Corp., Chelmsford, Mass., 1986—87; v.p., gen. mgr. PCB CAD divsn. Valid Logic Sys., 1987—89, group v.p. product divsn., 1989—91; v.p. Cadence Design Sys., Chelmsford, 1992—. Bd. dirs. Cirrus Sigma Ltd., Fareham, England, Texcon Corp., Phoenix, Custon Data Mgmt., Inc., Phoenix, Markwood, Inc., Phoenix, Office Tech. Ltd., Boston. Contbr. articles to profl. jours. Mem.: IEEE, Assn. Computing Machinery, Concord C. of C. (former bd. dirs., chmn. fin. com.), Sigma Xi. Achievements include patents in field. Office: 270 Billerica Rd Chelmsford MA 01824-4140

FULL, ROBERT WITMER, lawyer; b. Parkersburg, W.Va., Aug. 8, 1949; s. Donald Davis and Mary Alberta (Witmer) F.; m. Sharon Lynn Barcic, June 21, 1975; children: Robbie, Amy, Ryan, Eric. BA, W.Va. U., 1971, JD, 1974. Bar: W.Va. 1974, U.S. Dist. Ct. (so. dist.) W.Va. 1974, U.S. Ct. Appeals (4th cir.) 1990. Asst. prosecuting atty. Wood County Prosecutor's Office, Parkersburg, 1974-76; assoc. Ronning & Brown, Parkersburg, 1974-77, Ronning, Wilson & Brown, Parkersburg, 1982-84; ptnr. Ronning, Brown & Full, Parkersburg, 1977-82; assoc. Goodwin & Goodwin, Parkersburg, 1984-87, ptnr., 1988—. Asst. city atty. City of Parkersburg, 1978-79. Bd. dirs. Mid Ohio Valley United Way, campaign chmn., 1999, bd. chmn. 2000—. Mem. ABA, Wood County Bar Assn. (pres. 1983-84), W.Va. State Bar Assn., W.Va., W.Va. Bar Assn., Mid-Ohio Valley C. of C., Rotary (pres. 1993-94), ELks, Sigma Chi. Republican. Roman Catholic. Home: Lakeview Estates 824 Lakeview Dr Apt 306-c Parkersburg WV 26104-1649 Office: Goodwin & Goodwin Towne Square 201 3rd St Parkersburg WV 26101-5355

FULL, SUSAN GAYLE, librarian, educator; b. Springfield, Ill., Aug. 6, 1961; d. Everett Austin and Susie Abigail (Smith) Moss; m. Donald Raymond Full, Nov. 28, 1987. BS in Edn., Western Ill. U., 1983; MS in Libr. and Info. Sci., U. Ill., 1995. Cert. tchr. grades K-9 Ill., 1983. Elem. tchr. PORTA Sch. Dist., Petersburg, Ill., 1986—88; libr. asst. Robert Morris Coll., Springfield, Ill., 1989—94; asst. to dean academic affairs Springfield Coll., 2001—03, dir. libr. svcs., 1994—2005. Sec.-treas. Sangamon Valley Academic Libr. Consortium, Springfield, 1997—2000; treas. Capital Area Consortium, Springfield, 2003—05; mem. reciprocal borrowing task force Rolling Prairie Libr. Sys., Decatur, Ill., 1997—98, mem. adv. bd., 1998—2000, bd. mem. governing bd., 1998—2002. Associational ch. libr. dir. Capital City Bapt. Assn., Springfield, 1989—; ch. media libr. specialist Ill. Bapt. State Assn., Springfield, 1999—; mem. Athens (Ill.) Libr. Bd., 1984—87. Mem.: Ch. and Synagogue Libr. Assn., Evang. Ch. Libr. Assn., Assn. Christian Librs. (co-chair conf. planning team 2003—04), Health Sci. Librs. Ill., Beta Phi Mu. Baptist. Avocations: reading, piano, embroidery, genealogy, crocheting. Home: 22081 Montgomery Ave Greenview IL 62642 Personal E-mail: sfull@abelink.com.

FULLAM, JOHN P., federal judge; b. Gardenville, Pa., Dec. 10, 1921; s. Thomas L. and Mary Nolan F.; m. Alice Hilliar Freiheit, Apr. 15, 1950; children: Nancy, Sally, Thomas, Jeffrey. BS, Villanova U., 1942; JD, Harvard U., 1948. Atty., Bristol, Pa., 1948-60; judge Pa. Ct. Common Pleas, 7th Jud. Dist., 1960-66, U.S. Dist. Ct. (ea. dist.) Pa., Phila., 1966—, chief judge, 1986-90; now sr. judge. Lectr. in law U. Pa. Law Sch., Phila., Temple U. Law Sch., Phila.; mem. adv. com. Codes of Conduct of Jud. Conf. U.S., mem. adminstrn. magistrates sys., mem. com. to rev. jud. coun. disciplinary and disability orders. Democratic candidate for U.S. Congress, 1954, 56 Mem. Am. Law Inst., Pa. Bar Assn., Bucks County Bar Assn., Phila. Bar Assn. Office: 15614 US Courthouse Ind Mall W 601 Market St Philadelphia PA 19106-1713 Office Phone: 215-597-0436.

FULLARD, HENRIETTA, minister; d. Henry Graham and Janie Lillie Scott; children: Adrienne Yolanda Small, John Harold. BS, S.C. State U., Orangeburg, 1964; MA, Columbia U., 1972; MDiv, New Brunswick (N.J.) Theol. Sem., 1992; EdD, DD, Faith Coll., Mobile, Ala., 1994. Cert. sch. adminstrn. St. John's U., 1982. Endocrinology rschr. Interfaith Hosp. (formerly Bklyn. Jewish Hosp.), Bklyn., 1964—65; tchr. Andrew Jackson H.S., Cambria Heights, NY, 1965—90, asst. prin. sci. Cambria Heights, NY, 1990—94; prin. Math., Sci. Rsch. And Tech. Magnet H.S., Cambria Heights, 1994—99; pastor Bethel AME Ch., Arverne, 1995—2004; presiding elder numerous chs. African Meth. Episcopal Ch., Phila., 2004—. CEO Bethel Arverne Cmty. Devel. Corp., Arverne, 1999—; founder, job-trainer, developer Bethel Home Health Aide Program. Advisor Arverne Civic Assn., 2000—; mem. Cmty. Planning Bd. 14, Arverne, 1998—; v.p. Rockaway/Inwood Ministerial Coalition, Far Rockaway, NY, 1999—; mem. AME Ch. Ministerial Alliance, N.Y.C., 1995—, Habitat For Humanity, Jamaica, NY, 2000—; pres. S.E. Queens Clergy For Cmty. Empowerment, Inc., Jamaica, NY, 1999—; sec. adv. bd. York Coll., Jamaica, 1998—; adv. bd. St. John's Episcopal Hosp., Far Rockaway, 1999—. Recipient Congl. Record Award Of The 107Th Session, U.S. Ho. of Reps., 2002, Women Of The Millennium award, Nat. Coun. Of Negro Women, 2000, citation, N.Y. State Assembly, 1998, Nassau County, N.Y., 2000, Svc. To Women award, Ladies Of Distinction, Inc., 2002. Democrat. Avocation: travel. Personal E-mail: hefullard@aol.com.

FULLENWEIDER, DONN CHARLES, lawyer; b. Milw., Jan. 25, 1935; s. Russell Charles and Anne Mae (Murphy) F.; m. Wendy Lattimer; 1 child, Keith Rabon. BS, U. Houston, 1957, JD, 1958. Bar: Tex. bar 1958; Cert. in family law and civil trials Tex. Bd. Legal Specialization. Assoc. Fred Parks, Houston, 1958-65; partner Haynes & Fullenweider, Houston, 1965-89; pvt. practice, Houston, 1989-93; ptnr. Fullenweider and Wardell L.L.P., 1993-97, The Fullenweider Firm, 1997—. Adj. assoc. prof. law U. Houston Bates Coll. Law, 1972-74 Mem. 43d Joint Civilian Orientation Conf., 1973; mem. Tex. Bd. Legal Specialization, 1977-98. Recipient Emison award Tex. Acad. Family Specialists, 1993. Fellow Am. Bar Found., Houston Bar Found., Tex. Bar Found. (dir. 1973-76), Am. Acad. Matrimonial Lawyers (pres. Tex. chpt. 1979-81, bd. dirs. 1981-84, treas. 1985-88, pres.-elect 1988-89, pres. 1990-91); mem. ABA, Am. Bd. Trial Advoacy (advocate), Houston Bar Assn. (treas. 1961-62, 2d v.p. 1962-63, dir. 1971, 73, 1st v.p. 1970-73, Outstanding Svc. award 1974), Am. Coll. Family Trial Lawyers (diplomate 1994—), State Bar Tex. (dir. 1973-76, chmn. bd. 1975-76, exec. com. 1976-77, chmn. litigation sect. 1979-81), Am. Trial Lawyers Assn., Houston Trial Lawyers Assn. (v.p. 1971), Def. Orientation Conf. Assn., Houston C. of C., River Oaks Country Club, Sigma Chi, Phi Delta Phi. Home: 5555 Del Monte Dr Apt 2402 Houston TX 77056 Office: 4265 San Felipe St Ste 1400 Houston TX 77027-2999 Office Phone: 713-624-4100.

FULLER, ANGELA M., secondary school educator, assistant principal; b. Rochester, N.Y., Jan. 17, 1956; d. Mary K.; 1 child, Shannon Mary. AA, Finger Lakes C.C., 1992, AS, 1998; BA, St. John Fisher U., 1994, MS in Edn., 2003. Tchr. chemistry Victor (N.Y.) H.S., Greece Arcadia H.S., Rochester, NY; asst. prin. Greece Athena H.S., Rochester. Tchr. Johns Hopkins C.C., Albany, NY. Recipient Presdl. Leadership award, St. John Fisher Sch., 2003. Home: 163 South Main St Apt 1 Fairport NY 14450

FULLER, ANNE ELIZABETH HAVENS, English language and literature educator, consultant; b. Pomona, Calif., Jan. 20, 1932; d. Paul Swain and Lorraine Elizabeth (Hamilton) Havens; m. Martin Emil Fuller, II, June 17, 1961; children: Katharine Hamilton, Peter David Takashi. AB, Mount Holyoke Coll., 1953; BA (Fulbright scholar), Somerville Coll., Oxford U., 1955, MA, 1959; PhD (Univ. fellow), Yale U., 1958. Instr. English, Mount Holyoke Coll., 1957-59; instr. Pomona Coll., 1959-61; asst. prof. U. Fla., Gainesville, 1961-63; lectr. U. Denver, 1964-68, 71-73; assoc. prof., chmn. center for lang. and lit. Prescott (Ariz.) Coll., 1968-70; tchr. Colo. Rocky Mountain Sch., 1970-71; dean of faculty Scripps Coll., Claremont, Calif., 1973-80, prof. English, 1973-80; spl. asst. to pres., sec. to corp. Claremont U. Center, 1981-83; v.p. for acad. affairs Austin Coll., Sherman, Tex., 1982-84, faculty mem., 1984-96. Mem. SW dist. Rhodes Scholar Selection Com., 1975-83 Bd. dirs. Am. Council on Edn., 1979-81. Mem. Assn. Am. Colls. (dir. 1977-81, chmn. 1980-81), Am. Conf. Acad. Deans (dir. 1976-79), Commn. on Women in Higher Edn., Am. Assn. Higher Edn., Modern Lang. Assn. Am. Democrat. Episcopalian. Home: 11304 Pinos Altos Ave NE Albuquerque NM 87111-5701 E-mail: ahnefu@nmia.com.

FULLER, BETTY STAMPS, music educator; b. Prentiss, Miss., Feb. 19, 1938; d. Henry Buford and Genevieve (Bozeman) Stamps; m. Allan Riggs Fuller, Dec. 19, 1957 (dec. May 1987); children: Melodie, Valerie. Attended, Miss. Coll., 1958; BA, McNeese State U., 1983; post grad., Loyola U., 1985. Music tchr. Bearss Acad., Jackson, Miss., 1969—73, Episcopal Day Sch., Lake Charles, La., 1975—85, Our Lady's Sch., Sulpher, 1985—. Mentor tchr. Alliance for Cath. Edn., Notre Dame U., Notre Dame, Ind., 2000—01. Coord. youth orch. Miss. Coll., Clinton, Miss., 1967—72; bd. mem. Lake Charles (La.) Symphony Orch., 1975—77. Named Citizen of the Day, KLOU Radio Station, Lake Charles, 1975, Tchr. of Yr., KC Coun., 1994; Fine Arts grant, La. Divsn. of Arts, 1994—95, Arts and Humanities Coun. SW La., 1996. Mem.: Nat. Cath. Edn. Assn. Episcopalian. Avocations: production of musical plays, visual arts, historical preservation, environmental activities. Home: 2715 Roxton St Sulphur LA 70663

FULLER, BONNIE, editor; b. Canada; m. Michael Fuller; 4 children. BA in History, U. of Toronto, 1977. Fashion reporter Toronto Star, 1978; sportswear editor Women's Wear Daily; editor-in-chief Flare mag., Canada, 1982, YM, NYC, 1989—94; founding editor Marie Claire, 1994—96; dep. editor Cosmopolitan, 1996—97; editor-in-chief Cosmopolitan Hearst Mags., N.Y.C., 1997—98; editor-in-chief Glamour, Conde Nast, 1998—2001; editor US Weekly, 2002—03; exec. v.p. Am. Media Inc., Boca Raton, Fla., 2003—, chief editl. dir., 2003—. Author: From Geek to Oh My Goodness, 2003. Recipient Spotlight award, Amnesty Internat., 2000.*

FULLER, CAROL S., theater educator, writer; b. Dallas, Jan. 14, 1952; d. William Stokes Jr. and Mary Nell Shelton; m. Jon R. Fuller, Sept. 1, 1974; children: Meghan, Patrick. M in secondary edn., speech, theatre, English, U. of West Ga., 1982. Lang. arts educator Lithia Springs (Ga.) HS, 1980—84; prof. lang. arts, bus. comm. Chattahoochee Tech. Coll., Dallas, 1996—97; theatre arts educator South Cobb HS, Austell, Ga., 1997—. Author: short stories, poetry, 1994. Mem.: Theatre Comm. Group, Nat. Assn. Educators, Nat. Assn. Theatre Educators, The Alliance Theatre Inst. for Educators, Alpha Delta Kappa for Women in Education. Methodist. Avocations: reading, writing, theater, music. Home: 2434 Alexander Lake Dr Marietta GA 30064 Office: South Cobb HS 1920 Clay Rd Austell GA 30106 Home Fax: 770-528-0353. Personal E-mail: cwrite@bellsouth.net.

FULLER, CASSANDRA MILLER, applications specialist; b. Norwalk, Conn., Dec. 10, 1965; d. George Louis and Bernice (Simmons) Miller; m. David Norman Fuller, Dec. 24, 1988; 1 child, Jessica Ashley. BS, S.C. State Coll., 1987; MBA, U. Bridgeport, 1995. Interior decorator's apprentice Marty Rae Interiors, Orangeburg, S.C., 1984-85; asst. mgr. Dairy Queen, Orangeburg, S.C., 1986-87; day mgr. The Bedford, Stamford, Conn., 1987-88; dept. mgr. Burlington Coat Factory Warehouse, Danbury, Conn.; asst. mgr. Kidstuff, Inc., Orange, Conn., 1989-92; Postage By Phone customer assistance specialist Pitney Bowes, Stamford, Conn., 1992-95, programmer analyst, 1996-98; applications specialist GE Capital Vendor Fin. Svcs., Danbury, Conn., 1998—. Cons. Orangeburg Metro Transit 1987. Mem. Nat. Assn. Negro Bus. and Profl. Women's Clubs Inc., Nat. Black MBA Assn., NAFE, African Am. Forum, Kappa Omicron Phi. Democrat. Baptist. Office: GE Capital Corp Vendor Fin Svcs 10 Riverview Dr Danbury CT 06810-6268

FULLER, DAVID OTIS, JR., lawyer; b. Grand Rapids, Mich., May 28, 1939; s. David Otis and Virginia Chapin (Emery) F.; m. Isabelle Patrice Gigout, July 5, 1968; children: Thomas Andrew, Christian Scott, Pierre Emery, Margaret Isabelle. BA, Wheaton Coll., 1961; JD, Harvard U., 1964; postgrad., George Washington U., 1963, U. Paris, 1966. Bar: Mich., 1964, N.Y., 1967, U.S. Supreme Ct., 1968. Law clk. U.S. Ho. of Reps. Judiciary Com., 1963; assoc. Amberg, Law & Fallon, Grand Rapids, 1964-65; asst. dist. atty. N.Y. County, 1966-72, law sec. to justice, 1972-73; corp. atty. Pan Am. World Airways, Inc., 1973-74; dep. gen. counsel Reader's Digest Assn., Inc., 1974-84; pvt. practice N.Y.C., 1984-87; ptnr. Baker, Nelson & Williams, N.Y.C., 1987-94, Bosworth, Gray & Fuller, Bronxville, N.Y., 1994—; justice Tuckahoe Village, N.Y., 1986—. Lectr. Am. Bar Assn., Practicing Law Inst., Bronx C.C. Editor: Harvard Jour. on Legislation, 1962-64; contbr. articles to profl. jours. Warden Episc. Ch., 1991-97. Mem.: ABA, Fed. Bar Coun., Westchester County Magistrates Assn. (pres. 1993—94), Westchester County Bar Assn., NY State Magistrates Assn. (v.p. 2002—), Am. Arbitration Assn. (arbitrator 1983—96), Assn. Bar City NY (comms. law com. 1984—87), NY State Bar Assn. (chmn. privacy com. 1982—84), Bras Coupé Fishing Club, Harvard Club (N.Y.C.). Republican. Avocations: fishing, skiing, coins, racquet sports, French. Office: Bosworth Gray & Fuller 116 Kraft Ave Bronxville NY 10708-3810 Office Phone: 914-337-3626. E-mail: dofjr@aol.com.

FULLER, EDWIN DANIEL, hotel executive; b. Richmond, Va., Mar. 15, 1945; s. Ben Swint and Evelyn (Beal) F. Student, Wake Forest U., 1965; BSBA, Boston U., 1968; postgrad., Harvard Sch. Bus., 1987. Security officer Pinkerton Inc., Boston, 1965-68; sales dir. Twin Bridges Marriott Hotel, Arlington, Va., 1972-73; nat. sales mgr. Marriott Hotels & Resorts, NYC, 1973-76, dir. nat. and internat. Marriott sales Washington, 1976-78, v.p. Marriott Hotels mktg., 1978-82, gen. mgr. Hempstead, NY, 1982-83, Marriott Copley Pl., Boston, 1983-85; v.p. ops. Midwest region Marriott Corp., Rosemont, Ill., 1985-89, v.p. ops. Western and Pacific regions Santa Ana, Calif., 1989-90; sr. v.p., mng. dir. Marriott Hotels & Resorts-Internat., Washington, 1990-93; exec. v.p., mng. dir. internat. lodging Marriott Lodging Internat., Washington, 1994-97, pres., mng. dir., 1997—. Chmn. bd. dir. SNR Reservation Sys., Zurich, Switzerland, 1979-81; bd. dirs. Boston U. Hotel Sch., 1984—, Barnby Books, Barnaby Books, Honolulu, 1997—; treas. MEI Pacific Honolulu, 1985—, chmn. Pres. Boston U. Gen. Alumni Assn., 1993-1996, v.p., 1990-93; v.p. Boston U. Sch. Mgmt. Alumni Bd., 1985—; mem. adv. bd. Boston U. Hospitality Mgmt. Sch., 1985—; trustee Boston U., mem. exec. com. bd. trustees, 1994—,dir., Prince of Whales Hotel Environ. Orgn., 1995-pres., dir. Internat. bd. of United Way. Capt. U.S. Army, 1968-72, Vietnam. Decorated Bronze Star, Army Commendation medal. Mem. Boston U. Alumni Coun. (v.p.), Harvard Sch. Bus. Advanced Mgmt. Program (fund agt.), Sigma Alpha Epsilon, Delta Sigma Pi. Republican. Avocations: real estate, travel, golf, history. Home: 25362 Derbyhill Dr Laguna Hills CA 92653 Office: Marriott Hotels & Resorts 1 Marriott Dr Washington DC 20058-0001 Office Phone: 301-380-8990. Business E-Mail: ed.fuller@marriott.com.

FULLER, GLENN R., park ranger; b. Van Nuys, Calif., Sept. 1, 1946; s. Earl D. and Virginia (Allen) F. Masters, Calif. State U., Sacramento, 1972. Park ranger Grand Canyon (Ariz.) Nat. Park, 1975-80, Cape Cod Nat. Park, Wellfleet, Mass., 1980-81, Rocky Mountain Nat. Park, Estes Park, Colo., 1981-82, Golden Gate NRA, San Francisco, 1982-83; park supt. Muia Woods Nat. Monument, Mill Valley, Calif., 1983—; supt. Eugene O'Neill Nat. Hist. Site, Danville, CA. Sgt. U.S. Army, 1970-68. Mem. Friends of the River, Assn. Nat. Park Rangers.

FULLER, JACK WILLIAM, writer, retired publishing executive; b. Chgo., Oct. 12, 1946; s. Ernest Brady and Dorothy Voss (Tegge) Fuller; m. Debra Moskovits; children: Timothy, Katherine. BS, Northwestern U., 1968; JD, Yale U., 1973. Bar: Ill. 1974. Reporter Chgo. Tribune, 1973—75, Washington corr., 1977—78, editl. writer, 1978—79, dep. editl. page editor, 1979—82, editl. page editor, 1982—87, exec. editor, 1987—89, v.p. and editor, 1989—93, pres., CEO, 1993—97, pub., 1994—97; pres. Tribune Pub. Co., 1997—2004; dir. Torstar Corp., 2004—. Spl. asst. to atty. gen. U.S. Dept. Justice, Washington, 1975—77. Author: Convergence, 1982 (Cliff Dwellers award, 1983), Fragments, 1984 (Friends of Am. Writers award, 1985), Mass, 1985, Our Fathers' Shadows, 1987, Legends' End, 1990, News Values, 1996, The Best of Jackson Payne, 2000. Mem. Pulitzer Prize Bd., 1991—2000; trustee U. Chgo., Field Mus.; dir. MacArthur Found. With U.S. Army, 1969—70, Vietnam corr., Pacific Stars and Stripes. Recipient Gavel award, ABA, 1979, Pulitzer prize for editl. writing, 1986. Fellow: Am. Acad. Arts and Scis.; mem.: Inter-Am. Press Assn. (pres. 2003—04), Inter-Am. Dialogue. Office: Tribune Co 435 N Michigan Ave Chicago IL 60611-4066

FULLER, JAMES CHESTER EEDY, retired chemical company executive; b. Toronto, June 5, 1927; came to U.S., 1968; s. James Clifford and Marion Winifred (Eedy) F.; m. Doris Shirley Johnson, June 16, 1951 (dec. June 1992); children— Hilary, John; m. Shirley Patricia Honeyman, Feb. 8, 1993. BSA., U. Toronto, 1948; MBA, U. Western Ont., 1955. Sales and mktg. ofcl. Uniroyal Chem. Co., Man. and Ont., Can., 1948-53, 55-64; with Akzo Chemicals and affiliates, 1964-90; gen. mgr. Armour Indsl. Chems., Toronto, 1964-68, nat. sales mgr., asst. to pres., internat. dir. Chgo., 1968-70; mng. dir. Armour-Hess Ltd., Harrogate, Yorkshire, Eng., 1970-73; exec. v.p. Akzo Chemie Am., Chgo., 1973-74, pres., 1975-87; exec. v.p. Akzo Chemicals B.V., Amersfoort, The Netherlands, 1988-90. Mem. Chem. Inst. Can. Home: 403-2605 Windsor Rd Victoria BC V8S 5H9 Canada E-mail: jfuller@vicsurf.com.

FULLER, JAMES WILLIAM, financial planner; b. Rochester, Ind., Apr. 3, 1940; s. Raymond S. and Mildred (Osteimeier) F.; children: Kristen Anne, Glen William. AA, San Bernardino (Calif.) Valley Coll., 1960; BS, San Jose (Calif.) State U., 1962; MBA, Calif. State U., 1967. V.p. Dean Witter, San Francisco, 1967-71, Shields & Co., San Francisco, 1971-74; dir. fin. programs SRI Internat., Menlo Park, Calif., 1974-77; sr. v.p. N.Y. Stock Exch., N.Y.C., 1977-81, Charles Schwab & Co., San Francisco, 1981-85; pres. Bull & Bear Corp., N.Y.C., 1985-87; dir. Bridge Info. Systems, San Fransico, 1987—. Bd. dirs. Action Trac Inc., L.A., Current Techs. Inc., Vancouver, B.C., Environ. Scis. Inc., San Diego; chmn. bd. dirs. Pacific Rsch. Inst., 1992—; vice chmn. San Francisco Rep. Party, Calif. State Rep. Party. Dir. Securities Industry Protection Corp., Washington, 1981-87, Global Econ. Action Inst., N.Y.C., 1989—; trustee U. Calif., Santa Cruz. Lt. USN, 1963-66. Mem. The Family Club (San Francisco), Olympic Club (San Francisco), Jonathon Club (L.A.), Univ. Club (N.Y.C.), The Lincoln Club (San Francisco), Polit. Com. for Econ. Growth, Internat. Platform Assn., Newcomer Soc., World Affairs Coun., Coun. on Formulations (San Francisco com.), Commonwealth Club. Republican. Presbyterian. Avocations: tennis, politics, public affairs. Home: 2584 Filbert St San Francisco CA 94123-3318 Office Phone: 415-922-2500. E-mail: jamesfuller1@gmail.com.

FULLER, JANICE MARIE, secondary school educator; b. Flagler, Colo., Feb. 7, 1948; d. William Harrison and Ruth Elsie (Jensen) Martin; m. William Edward Fuller, Sept. 16, 1966; children: James Edward, David William, John Justin. A.Gen. Studies, Pikes Peak C.C., Colorado Springs, Colo., 1982; BS in Biology, Met. State Coll., Denver, 1986. Gen. office mgr. Schmidt Environ. Enterprises, Commerce City, Colo., 1972-77; v.p., sec. Fuller Constrn., Inc., Larkspur, Colo., 1993—; tchr. math. and sci. Douglas County Schs., Castle Rock, Colo., 1988-92; tchr. sci. Christ the King Sch., Denver, 1992-96; tchr. biology Ellicott Jr.- Sr. High Sch., Calhan, Colo., 1996—. Tutor math./sci.; coach track, gymnastics, volleyball Castle Rock Jr. H.S., 1990-92; nominated 1st U.S./Russia Joint Conf. on Edn. in Moscow, U. Iowa Citizen Ambassador Program, 1994; mem. dist. accountability com. Ellicott Sch. Dist., 1996—. Mem. dist. accountability commn. Douglas County Sch. Dist., Castle Rock, 1987-91, dist. comm. com., 1990. Mem. ASCD, NAFE, AAUW, Nat. Assn. Student Activity Advisors, Nat. Sci. Tchrs. Assn., Met. State Coll. Alumni Assn. Avocations: cooking, sewing, country living. Office: Ellicott Jr-Sr H S 375 S Ellicott Hwy Calhan CO 80808-8963

FULLER, JEAN, school system administrator; AA, Bakersfield Cmty. Coll.; BA, Calif. State U., Fresno, 1972; MPA, Calif. State U., LA, 1982; PhD in Ednl. Policy and Orgnl. Studies, U. Calif., Santa Barbara, 1989. Cert. tchr. comm., English, Soc. Sci. Calif. State U., 1972. Elem. and secondary tchr., 1972—80; elem. and mid. sch. prin. Westside Union Sch. Dist, Calif., 1980—83, cons. 803 computer, 1987; elem. prin. and dir. of tech. svcs. Keppel Union Sch. Dist, 1983—88, dir. state and fed. projects, spl. edn. and pers., 1988, asst. supt., 1988—90, supt., 1990—99, Bakersfield City Sch. Dist, 1999—. Attendee U. So. Calif. Supt. Symposium, LA, 1991, Harvard Grad. Sch. of Edn. Supt. Seminars, Cambridge, Mass., 1998, Cambridge, 99; mem. Kern County Supt.'s Adv. Bd., 1999—. Mem. Jim Burke Ednl. Found., Vision 2020 Ednl. Com.; Mayor's Youth Devel. Coun.; mem. Kern County Network Children Bd.; bd. dir. Boys and Girls Club, 2002—, mem. mktg. com., 2002—. Recipient Calif. Supt. of Yr., Am. Assn. of Sch. Adminstrs., 1995, Nat. Leadership Learning award, 1998. Mem.: Am. Assn. of Sch. Adminstrs. Office: Bakersfield City Sch Dist 1300 Baker St Bakersfield CA 93305

FULLER, JOHN WILLIAMS, economics professor; b. Phoenix, Nov. 8, 1940; s. John W. and Myrtle Arabella (Parr) F.; m. Annette Cunkle, June 16, 1962 (dec. 1977); m. Kathy J. Fait, Feb. 17, 1980; children: Helen, Douglas, Andrew, Elizabeth. AB, San Diego State U., 1962; PhD, Wash. State U., 1968. Chief econ. analysis Wis. Dept. Transp., Madison, 1968-74, dir. environ. and policy analysis, 1974-76; hwy. commr. State 0f Wis., 1976-77; deputy exec dir. Nat. Transp. Policy Study Commn., Washington, 1977-79; prof. econs., urban and regional planning and geography U. Iowa, Iowa City, 1979—, chair grad. program in urban and regional planning, 1996-99; cons. Bur. Transp. Stats., Washington, 1993—2001. Cons. Fed. Hwy. Adminstrn., Washington, 1980-82, legis. coun. Iowa Gen. Assembly, Des Moines, 1980-91; dir. Legis. Extended Assistance Group, Iowa City, 1979-2001. Contbr. articles to profl. jours. Mem., vice chair Johnson County Broadband Telecom. Commn., 1982-88; chmn. Zoning Bd. Adjustment, Johnson County, 1987-92; mem. West Branch Zoning Bd. of Adjustment, 1993-2003, West Branch Hist. Preservation Commn., 2002-, sec. 2005; trustee West Branch Libr., 1995-2001, pres. 1997-2001. Recipient Fulbright award, Venezuela, 1985. Mem. Transp. Rsch. Bd., Am. Assn. RR Supts., Am. Soc. Transp. and Logistics, Assn. Am. Geographers, Nat. Assn. Environ. Profls., Am. Econ. Assn., Am. Planning Assn., Transp. Rsch. Forum, Am. Inst. Cert. Planners. Congregationalist. Office: U Iowa 344 Jessup Hall Iowa City IA 52242-1316 Business E-Mail: john-w-fuller@uiowa.edu.

FULLER, JONATHAN, geologist; b. Columbus, Ohio, 1949; s. J. O. and M. C. Fuller. Ba in Geology, Hope Coll., 1971; postgrad., U. Wis., Milw., 1974; MS in Geology, Western Mich. U., 1978. Lab. asst. Fairleigh Dickenson U., St. Croix, 1973—74, tchg. rsch. asst., 1975; tchg. asst. Western Mich. U., Kalamazoo, 1975—77, field asst., 1976; geologist III Ohio Dept. Natural Resources Divsn. Geol. Survey, Sandusky, 1978—2002, geologist IV, 2002—. Contbr. articles to profl. publs.; author: USGS Open File Report, 1996, abstracts, reports, guidebooks in field; editor: Guidebook to the Geology and Ecology of Some Marine and Terrestrial Environments., 1974. Mem. Cmty. Theatre., Sandusky, 1974, pres., 1981, trustee, 1982—2000; mem. Internat. Torch, Sandusky, 1990—; active Harlequins Cmty. Theater, Sandusky; mem. Sandusky Bay Area Food Coop.; trustee Unitarian Universalist Fellowship, Sandusky, 1985—88. Mem.: Marine Tech. Soc., Soc. Sedimentary Geology, Ohio Acad. Sci., Internat. Assn. Gt. Lakes Rsch., Commn. Coastal Environment, Am. Shore and Beach Preservation Assn., Firelands Torch Club. Home: 36 Cincinnati Ave Huron OH 44839 Office: Ohio Geol Survey 1634 Sycamore Ln Sandusky OH

FULLER, KATHRYN SCOTT, former environmental services administrator; b. N.Y.C., July 8, 1946; d. Delbert Orison and Carol Scott (Gilbert) F.; m. Stephen Paul Doyle, May 29, 1977; children: Sarah Elizabeth Taylor, Michael Stephen Doyle, Matthew Scott Doyle. BA English, Am. Lit., Brown U., 1968, LHD (hon.), 1992; JD with honors, U. Tex., 1976; postgrad., U. Md., 1980-82; DSci. (hon.), Wheaton Coll., 1990; LLD (hon.), Knox Coll., 1992. Bar: Tex. 1977, D.C. 1979. Rsch. asst. Yale U., New Haven, 1968-69, Am. Chem. Soc., 1970-71, Harvard U. Mus. Comparative Zoology, Cambridge, Mass., 1971-73; law clerk Dewey, Ballantine, Bushby, Palmer & Wood and Vinson & Elkins, N.Y.C., Houston, 1974-76, U.S. Dist. Ct. (so. dist.), Tex., 1976-77; atty., advisor Office Legal Counsel Dept. Justice, Washington, 1977-79, atty. Wildlife and Marine Resources sect., 1979-80, chief Wildlife and Marine Resources sect., 1981-82; exec. v.p., dir. Traffic USA, pub. policy, gen. counsel World Wildlife Fund, Washington, 1982-89, pres., CEO, 1989—2005. Contbr. articles to profl. jours.; bd. dirs. Alcoa Inc., 2002—, Student Conservation Assn., Fondo Mexicano para la Conservacion de la Naturaleza; mem. World Bank Adv. Com. on Sustainable Devel. Bd. trustees Ford Found., Brown U. Recipient William Rogers Outstanding Grad. award Brown U., 1990, UN Environment Programme Global 500 award, 1990; Named outstanding woman law student Tex. scholar, 1975. Mem. State Tex. Bar, D.C. Bar, Coun. Fgn. Rels., Zonta Internat. (hon.). Avocations: squash, trekking, scuba diving, gardening, fishing.*

FULLER, KATHY J., special education educator, consultant, researcher; b. Lamar, Colo., Oct. 24, 1957; d. Alfred L. and Leona M. Fuller; 1 child, Samantha Devon Blake. MA, Calif. State U. Northridge, 1993; PhD in Psychol. Studies of Edn., UCLA, 2004. Prof. UCLA ext., 1999—, Pacific Oaks Coll., Pasadena, Calif., 2002—; cons. L.A. County of Edn., 2002—. Tchr. Pasadena Unified Sch. Dist., Calif., 1992—94; tchr., full inclusion specialist LA Unified Sch. Dist., 1994—2000; prof. Calif. State U., L.A., 1999—2002, adj. prof., 1997—; presenter in field; owner Teacher Talk, 2003—. Musician: (singer) New Life - Kora Music for the 21st Century (Prince Diabate CD); poet (poem) Helpless Hoping (Editor's Choice award); contbr. articles to profl. jours.; contbg. author: Rescued Tails, 2005. Pet therapist Love on 4 Paws, L.A., 2002; edn. dir. Beagles & Buddies, Orange County Cavy Haven. Recipient 1st place Edn. award, 2001, 2d place Behavioral/Social Scis. award, 2002; grantee Nat. Rsch. grant, Nat. Assn. Alternative Cert., 1999—. Mem.: Am. Ednl. Rsch. Assn., Coun. for Exceptional Children (assoc.), Phi Lambda Theta. Achievements include design of Fuller-Blake Academic Inventory. Home: 790 Monterey Rd South Pasadena CA 91030 Office Phone: 626-685-2532. Personal E-mail: kfullerbla@aol.com.

FULLER, KEVIN RICE, lawyer; b. Santa Ana, Calif., Nov. 16, 1958; s. Kenneth D. and Judith (Rice) F.; m. Sharla S. Neill, Nov. 10, 2002; children: Hudson McGregor Fuller, Cody N. Fuller, Casey John Fuller. BS in Econs., Tex. A&M U., 1981; JD, Baylor U., 1984. Bar: Tex. 1984. Ptnr. Koons, Fuller & Vandeneykel, Dallas, 1984—. Contbr. articles to profl. jours. Bd. dirs. Dallas Child Guidance Clinic, 1990-96. Mem. Dallas Bar Assn. (chair family law sect. 1987). Avocation: horses. Office: Koons Fuller & Vandeneykel 2311 Cedar Springs Rd Ste 300 Dallas TX 75201-1899

FULLER, LAWRENCE ARTHUR, lawyer; b. Miami Beach, Fla., Mar. 8, 1949; s. Bernard Charles and Ruth (Katz) F.; m. Hope Kourland, May 26, 1974; children: Allison, Andrew. BS, Boston U., 1971; JD, U. Miami, 1974. Bar: Fla. 1974, Ohio, NY, DC, U.S. Dist. Ct. (so. and no. dists.) Fla. 1975, U.S. Dist. Ct. (mid. dist.) Fla. 1985, U.S. Ct. Appeals (5th cir.) 1978, U.S. Ct. Appeals (11th cir.) 1981. Law clk. Fla. Supreme Ct., Tallahassee, 1974-75; mem. Stephens, Thornton, Magill & Sevier, Miami, 1975-76; ptnr. Fuller, Feingold & Mallah, Miami Beach, 1976-90, Fuller, Mallah & Assocs., Miami Beach, 1990-2000, Fuller, Fuller & Assoc., Miami Beach, 2001—. Mem. Miami Beach Budget Adv. Bd., 1980—85, Miami Beach Youth Adv. Bd., 1985—91; mem. com. City of Miami Beach Young Profls.; mem. Miami Beach Tourist and Conv. Ctr. Expansion Authority, 1995, Dade County Equal Opportunity Bd., Miami Beach Bd. Adjustment, 1999—2000; mem. adv. bd. Miami Beach Hosp., 2001—. Mem.: ATLA, Am. Arbitration Assn. (arbitrator), Acad. Fla. Trial Lawyers, Dade County Bar Assn., Miami Beach Bar Assn. (bd. dirs. 1984—90), Miami Beach C. of C., Kiwanis (pres. 1999—2000). Avocations: golf, boating, water-skiing. Home: 925 N Shore Dr Miami Beach FL 33141-2439 Fax: (305) 534-9894. Office Phone: 305-891-5199. E-mail: lfuller@fullerfuller.com.

FULLER, MARNEY CECELIA, painter, graphics designer; b. Covina, Calif., Oct. 12, 1960; d. Andrew Julian Fuller and Shirlie Roberta Foster; m. Andrew Scott Mazo, May 23, 1997; 1 child, Chase Maxon Mazo. MFA, Pratt Inst., 1986; BA, Western Wash. U., 1982. Artist, Bklyn., 1977—. Tchg. asst. Pratt Inst., Bklyn., 1985—86; artist lectr. 92 St. Y, N.Y.C., 2002; artist Centrum Artist Colony, Port Townsend, Wash., 1977—78. One-woman shows include Clark Gallery, Lincoln, Mass., Wolffer Estate, Sagaponack, NY, Pratt Inst., Bklyn., domogallery, Summit, N.J., 2004, exhibited in group shows at AMMO Exhbn. Space, Bklyn., Pratt Inst., Western Wash. U., Bellingham, Viking Union Gallery, Cornish Sch. Art, Seattle (3rd Pl., 1978), Clark Gallery, Lincoln, Mass., Gale Gates, Bklyn., Dumbo Art Center Inaugural Show, 8th Floor Gallery, N.Y.C., La Mama La Galleria, Domo Gallery, Summit, NJ, 2004, Hidden Treasures Group Show, Art Gotham Gallery, NYC, 2005. Grantee, Change Inc., 2002. Mem.: Dumbo Art Ctr. Office: Artist Studio 68 Jay Street Brooklyn NY 11201

FULLER, MARTHA M., poet; Author: Tattle Tales, 1997, Days Gone By, 1997 (Editor's Choice award Nat. Libr. Congress), Sounds of Poetry, 1998, After Thoughts, 2002, among others. Recipient numerous awards. Mem. Poetry Hall of Fame, Internat. Soc. Poets. Home: 34 Worthington Dr Apt 202 Westbrook CT 06498-1994 E-mail: quidfit@snet.net.

FULLER, MAXINE COMPTON, retired secondary school educator; b. Tiny, Va., Aug. 23, 1921; d. Perry and Lillie (Sutherland) Compton; m. David Thompson Fuller Jr., 1946 (dec. Mar. 1975); children: Davine Miller, Patricia Machen, Shirley Allen, Dorothy Brunson, David Thompson III BS, Longwood Coll., 1943; MA, U. Ala., 1966; AA in Edn., U. Ala., Birmingham, 1980. Receptionist Goodyear Tire and Rubber Co., Richmond, Va., 1943, office mgr. trainee Selma, Ala., 1943-44; office mgr. Goodyear Service, Bessemer, Ala., 1944-46; sec., ops. mgr. Birmingham So. Coll., 1966; tchr. Manpower-Bessemer State Tech. Coll., 1966-68, McAdory H.S., 1968-71; bus. edn. coord. Hueytown (Ala.) H.S., 1971-88; ret. Hueytown H.S., 1988. Vis. com. mem. So. Assn. Secondary Schs. and Colls., 1980, 84. Sunday sch. tchr. Pleasant Ridge Bapt. Ch., Hueytown, 1962-88, pers. com., 1980-83; mem. Hueytown High PTA, 1986-87; liaison officer Adopt-A-Sch. program Hueytown High/Lloyd Noland Hosp., 1987-88; chmn. bus. edn. dept. Hueytown H.S., 1971-88. Mem. NEA, Nat. Ret. Tchrs. Assn., Ala. Edn. Retirees Assn, Bibb County Edn. Retirees Assn (sec. 2000—), former mem. Echo Study Club (pres. 1987-88, sec. 1991-92), former mem. Culture Club of Hueytown (pres. 1994-96), Longwood Coll. Alumni Assn., former mem., Alpha Delta Kappa (corr. sec. XI chpt. 1982-84), Delta Kappa Gamma (treas. Gamma Lambda chpt. 1976-80). Baptist.

FULLER, MELVIN STUART, botany educator; b. Livermore Falls, Maine, May 5, 1931; s. George Raymond and Hilda Gordon (Pike) F.; m. Barbara Paul Newman, Apr. 2, 1955; children: Erica Ann, Scott Eliot, Amy Elizabeth. BS, U. Maine, 1953; MS, U. Nebr., 1955; PhD, U. Calif., 1959; Master's ad eundum, Brown U., 1963. Instr. Brown U., 1959, asst. prof., 1960-63, assoc. prof., 1963-64; asst. prof. U. Calif., 1964-65, assoc. prof., 1965-68; prof. botany U. Ga., 1968—, head dept., 1968-73, 86-89, univ. prof., 1990—; vis. agrl. rsch. biologist Sandoz Ltd., Basel, Switzerland, 1983; vis. rsch. prof. U. Uppsala, Sweden, 1985, 86; adj. prof. botany U. Maine, 1992—; emeritus univ. prof. and emeritus prof. botany U. Ga., 1995—. Mem. editorial bd. for publs. in biology McGraw Hill; sec. 2d Internat. Mycol. Congress; organizer Fifth Internat. Fungus Spore Meeting, 1991. Author: The Science of Botany, 1962, Lower Fungi in the Laboratory, 1978, Zoosporic Fungi in Teach. and Research, 1987. Bd. dirs. DaPonte String Quartet, 2002—. Fellow British Mycological Soc.; mem. Bot. Soc. Am., Mycol. Soc. Am. (counselor 1966-68, 70-72, pres. 1975, Disting. Mycologist Award, 1992), Soc. Study of Growth and Devel., Am. Phythopath. Soc., Gulf of Maine Found. (pres. 1997-99). Achievements include research on growth and development of aquatic fungi, ultrastructure, mechanism of action of fungicides. Home: 48 Water St Damariscotta ME 04543 E-mail: msfuller@adelphia.net.

FULLER, MICHAEL B., communications executive; BS in Engring., U.S. Mil. Acad., West Point, N.Y.; MBA, U. Kans., Lawrence. Fin. analyst, corp. staff United Telecommunicatoin, 1974, various ops., mktg. and strategic planning pos., asst. v.p.-planning for telephone ops., 1981—83, various key mgmt. pos. in long-distance bus., 1983—88, v.p.-planning, ISACOMM, 1983—84, sr. v.p.-adminstrn. and plannig for US Telecom, 1985—86; pres. Southeast divsn. US Sprint, Atlanta, 1986—87, sr. v.p.-planning devel. and internat. svcs., 1987—88, exec. v.p.-staff, 1988—89; pres., United Telephone of the Northwest, Local Telecomm. Divsn. Sprint Corp., 1989—96, pres. and COO, Local Telecomm. Divsn., 1996—. Office: 6200 Sprint Pkwy Overland Park KS 66251*

FULLER, MILLARD DEAN, foundation administrator, lawyer; b. Lanett, Ala., Jan. 3, 1935; s. Render and Estin (Cook) F.; m. Linda Caldwell; children: Christopher, Kimberly, Faith, Georgia. BS in Econs., Auburn U., 1957; LLB, U. Ala., 1960; LHD (hon.), Ea. Coll., Pa., 1985, Ottawa U., 1987, Susquehanna U., 1989; D Pub. Svcs. (hon.), DePauw U., 1988; HHD (hon.), Coll. of Wooster, 1989, Wake Forest U., 1990, Mercer U., 1990, Westminster Coll., 1990, Whitworth Coll., 1990, Dallas Bapt. U., 1994, Lynchburg Coll., 1992, North Park Coll., 1992, Tech. U. Nova Scotia, 1992, U. North Ala., 1994, Providence Coll., 1994, Presbyn. Coll., Clinton, S.C., 1995, Bluffton Coll., 1995, Elon Coll., 1995, Nova Southeastern U., 1996; HHD (hon.), U. Ala., 2004. Bar: Ala. 1960, Ga. 1972. Co-founder Fuller and Dees Mktg. Group, Inc., Montgomery, Ala., 1960, pres., 1960-65; ptnr. Fuller and Dees (law firm), Montgomery, 1960-65; devel. dir. Tougaloo (Miss.) Coll., 1966-68; dir. Koinonia Ptnrs., Inc. (developer various bus. ops. for Koinonia Christian community), Americus, Ga., 1968-72; dir. devel. Ch. of Christ, Zaire, Equator region Africa, 1973-76, initiator housing project for low-income families, Mbandaka, Zaire Equator region Africa; founder Habitat Humanity Internat., Inc., Americus, 1976—2005; founder, pres. The Fuller Ctr. Housing, Inc., 2005—. Author: Bokotola, 1977, Love in the Mortar Joints, 1980, No More Shacks!, 1986, The Excitement is Building, 1990, Theology of the Hammer, 1994, A Simple, Decent Place to Live, 1995, More than Houses, 2000, Building Materials for Life, 2002. Adv. com. Albert Schweitzer Fellowship of Am., 1992. Lt. U.S. Army, 1960. Recipient Outstanding Achievement award Coun. State Housing Agys., 1986, Clarence Jordan Exemplary Chistiran Svc. award So. Bapt. Theol. Sem., 1986, Dr. Marting Luther King, Jr. Humanitarian award, 1987, Disting. chrisitan Svc. in Social Welfare award N.Am. Assn. christians in Social Work, 1988, Internat. Humanity Svc. award Am. Overseas Assn. ARC, 1989, Pub. Svc. Achievement award Common Cause, 1989, M. Justin Herman Meml. award Nat. Assn. Housing and Devel. Ofcls., 1989, The Temple award for Creative Altruism, 1990, Joseph C. Wilson award Rochester Assn. for the UN, 1990, Amicus Certus award Luth. Social Svcs. Ill., Martin Luther Jr. Humanitarian award Ga. State Holiday Commn., 1992, Profl. Achievement award Partnership Affordable Housing, 1993, Harry S. Truman Pub. Svc. award City of

Independence, 1994, The McConnell award Truett-McConnell Coll., Ga., 1995, Faithful Servant award Nat. Assn. of Evangelicals, 1996, Spirit of Ga. award, 1996; named Builder of Yr. Profl. Bldr. mag., 1995, Nat. Housing Hall of Fame, 1996, Presdl. Medal of Freedom, 1996, Jefferson award 1999. Mem. Ala. Bar Assn., Ga. Bar Assn. Baptist. Avocations: reading, walking. Office Phone: 229-924-2900. Business E-Mail: fuller35@hotmail.com.

FULLER, NORINE LEAS, lobbyist, educational administrator; b. L.A., Dec. 31, 1952; BA in Sociology, UCLA, 1975. Exec. dir. student fin. svcs. Fashion Inst. Design and Merchandising, Washington, 1977—; sr. cons. Gray and Co., Washington, 1982-84; creator, exec. prodr. EBN Edn. Bus. News, Arlington, Va., 1998—. Mem. bd. Nat. Adv. Com. on Accreditation and Instnl. Eligibility, Washington, 1986, 88; cons. Office of First Lady, New Orleans, 1984, Dallas, 1988, Rep. Nat. Convs.; negotiator negotiated rule-making com. U.S. Dept. Edn., Washington, 1993. Prodr., writer videos Credit for my Vette, 1985 (1st place pub. rels. award Assn. Ind. Colls., 1986, College Costs with Rep. Buck McKeon (R-CA) and Sen. Jim Jeffords (D-VT), 1997; dir., writer counseling video and handbook Default Detours, 1987. Chmn. Rep. Women's Fed. Forum, Washington, 1992. Fax: 202-295-5070. E-mail: nfuller@fidm.com.

FULLER, PERRY LUCIAN, lawyer; b. Central City, Nebr., Oct. 26, 1922; s. Perry L. and Ruth (Howorth) F.; m. Alice Moorman, Mar. 6, 1948; 1 child, Leslie Ann Fuller. Student, U. Chgo. Law Sch., 1946-47; AB, U. Nebr., 1947, JD, 1949. Bar: Ill. 1950, U.S. Supreme Ct. Mem. staff Chgo. Crime Commn., 1949; sr. ptnr. Hinshaw & Culbertson and predeccessors, Chgo., 1956—. Lectr. in law U. Chgo., 1970-76, mem. vis. com., 1991-93. Vice chmn. exec. com. Law in Am. Soc. Found., 1966, chmn., 1967—69, pres., 1969—95; chmn. Cook County CSC, 1967—69; mem. Ill. Law Enforcement Commn., 1971—72; v.p. Fed. Defender, Inc., 1964; trustee Village of Winnetka, 1992—96; bd. dir. Winnetka Cmty. Chest, Ill., 1966—69, Ill. Humane Soc., 1978—, pres., 1986. 1st lt. USMC, 1942—46, Capt. USMC, 1952—53. Decorated Air medal. Fellow Am. Coll. Trial Lawyers (state chmn. 1972-74), Am. Bar Found., Ill. Bar Found.; mem. ABA (chmn. pub. relations com. 1968-69, gavel awards com. 1974-77, chmn. 1976-78), Ill, Fed., 7th Cir. Chgo. (bd. mgrs. 1967-69) bar assns., Am. Law Inst., Am. Judicature Soc., Internat. Assn. Def. Counsel (chmn. Continuing Legal Edn. bd. 1982-86, exec. com. 1983-86), Soc. Trial Lawyers Ill. (bd. dirs. 1967-68, 73-74, sec. 1975-76, pres. 1977-78), Def. Rsch. Inst. (chmn. insts. com. 1986-90), Scribes, Legal Club, Law Club (pres. 1987-88). Republican. Home: 1093 Fisher Ln Winnetka IL 60093-1503 Office: Hinshaw & Culbertson 222 N La Salle St Ste 300 Chicago IL 60601-1081 Office Phone: 847-441-6068. Personal E-mail: peelegs@aol.com.

FULLER, REGINALD HORACE, clergyman, biblical studies educator; b. Horsham, Eng., Mar. 24, 1915; came to U.S., 1955, naturalized, 1995; s. Horace and Cora L. (Heath) F.; m. Ilse Barda, June 17, 1942; children: Caroline Fuller Sloat, Rosemary Fuller Bazuzi (dec.), Sarah. BA with 1st class honours in Classics and Theology, Cambridge U., 1937, MA, 1942; STD, Gen. Theol. Sem., N.Y.C., 1960, Phila. Div. Sch., 1962; DD, Seabury-Western Theol. Sem., Evanston, Ill., 1983; DHL, Nashotah House, Wis., 1993; DD, U. of the South, 1995. Ordained to ministry Ch. of Eng. as deacon, 1940, priest, 1941. Curate, Bakewell, Eng., 1940-43, Ashbourne-w-Mapleton, Eng., 1943-46, Edgbaston, Birmingham, Eng., 1946-50; lectr. theology Queen's Coll., Birmingham, 1946-50; recognized lectr. theology U. Birmingham, 1946—50; prof. theology St. David's Coll., Lampeter, Wales, 1950-55; exam. chaplain to Bishop of Monmouth, 1950-55; prof. N.T. lit. and langs. Seabury-Western Theol. Sem., Evanston, Ill, 1955-66; Baldwin prof. sacred lit. (N.T.) Union Theol. Sem., N.Y.C., 1966-72; adj. prof. Columbia U., 1966-72; Molly Laird Downs prof. N.T. Va. Theol. Sem., 1972-85; prof. emeritus, 1985—; canon theologian of Brit. Honduras; also Bishop's commissary for U.S.A., 1968-72. Vis. prof. Grad. Theol. Union, Berkeley, 1975, Union Theol. Sem., Richmond, Va., 1985, Episcopal Sem. S.W., Austin, Tex., 1986, Nashotah House, 1986, 91, 93, 98, 2000, 02, vis.prof., 04; vis. prof. Coll. Emmanuel and St. Chad, Saskatoon, Sask., Canada, 1978, Saskatoon, 88, St. Mark's Coll. Ministry, Canberra, Australia, 1987, Wesley Theol. Sem., Washington, 1990; adj. prof. Va. Theol. Sem., 1994—2002; mem. study commn. World Coun. Chs., 1957—61; mem. Episcopal-Luth. Conversations, 1969—72, 1977—80, Anglican-Luth. Conversations, 1970—72, Luth.-Cath. Dialogue (U.S.) Task Force, 1971—73. Author (with R. Hanson): The Church of Rome, A Dissuasive, 1948, The Mission and Achievement of Jesus, 1954; author: (with G. Ernest Wright) The Book of the Acts of God, 1957; author: What is Liturgical Preaching?, 1957, Luke's Witness to Jesus Christ, 1958, The New Testament in Current Study, 1962, Interpreting the Miracles, 1963, The Foundations of New Testament Christology, 1965, 2002, A Critical Introduction to the New Testament, 1966; author: (with B. Rice) Christianity and Affluence, 1966; author: Lent with the Liturgy, 1969, The Formation of the Resurrection Narratives, 1971, Preaching the Lectionary, 1974, The Use of the Bible in Preaching, 1981; author: (with Pheme Perkins) Who is This Christ?, 1983; author: He That Cometh, 1990, Christ and Christianity, 1994; contbr. to books, encys.; translator (D. Bonhoeffer): The Cost of Discipleship, 1948; translator: (by D. Bohnoeffer) Letters and Papers from Prison, 1953; translator: (H.W. Bartsch, editor) Kerygma and Myth I, 1953; translator: (R. Bultmann) Primitive Christianity, 1956; translator: (J. Jeremias) Uniknown Sayings of Jesus, 1957; translator: (W. von Loewenich) Modern Catholicism, 1959; translator: Kerygma and Myth II, 1962; translator: (H. Flender) St. Luke Theologian of Redemptive History, 1967; translator: (J. Moltmann and J. Weissbach) Two Studies in the Theology of Bonhoeffer, 1967; translator: (A. Schweitzer) Reverence for Life, 1969; translator: (T. Rendtorff) Church and Theology, 1971; translator: (G. Bornkamm) The New Testament, A Guide to Its Writings, 1973; translator: (E. Schweizer) The Holy Spirit, 1980; translator: (R. Schnackenburg) The Johannine Epistles, 1992; subject of book: Christ and His Communities: Essays in Honor of Reginald H. Fuller, 1990. Named Hon. Canon., St. Paul's Cathedral, Burlington, Vt., 1988; recipient Schofield prize and Crosse studentship, 1938, Ecumenism award, Washington Consortium, 2001; fellow, Am. Assn. Theol. Schs., 1961—62. Mem. Studiorum Novi Testamenti Societas (pres. 1983-84, editorial com. 1978-81), Chgo. Soc. Bibl. Research, Soc. Bibl. Lit. (com. hon. membership 1978-81) Home: Westminster Canterbury House 1600 Westbrook Ave Apt 320 Richmond VA 23227-3328

FULLER, RENEE NUNI, psychologist, educational publisher; b. Mannheim, Germany, Apr. 14, 1929; arrived in U.S., 1938; d. Eric Woldemar and Fridel Gronau (Henning) Stoetzner; widowed. Student, Swarthmore (Pa.) Coll., 1947—49; BA, Hunter Coll., 1951; MA, Columbia U., 1953; PhD, NYU, 1963. Rsch. scientist Letchworth Village NY State Dept. Mental Hygiene, Thiells, 1961—67; project dir. S.I. (NY) Soc. Mental Health, 1967—68; chief psychol. svcs. Rosewood Hosp. Ctr., Owings Mills, Md., 1968-75; pres. Ball-Stick-Bird Publs. Inc., Williamstown, Mass., 1975—. Author: In Search of the IQ Correlation, 1977, (reading series) Ball-Stick-Bird; contbr. articles to profl. jours. Recipient Disting. Achievement award, Fairleigh-Dickinson U., N.J., 1979. Fellow Am. Psychol. Soc.; mem. APA, Soc. for Rsch. in Child Devel. Office: Ball Stick Bird Publs Inc PO Box 429 Williamstown MA 01267 Business E-Mail: info@ballstickbird.com.

FULLER, RICHARD KENNETH, retired alcohol/drug abuse services professional; b. Chgo., Apr. 2, 1935; s. Marc Cornelius and Edna Jane (Gibson) F.; m. Kathleen Julia Brain, Oct. 22, 1960; children: Julia, Douglas. BA, Monmouth Coll., 1957; MD, Western Res. U., 1962; MS, Case Western Res. U., 1971. From staff physician to asst. chief GI sect. VA Hosp., Cleve., 1971-90; dir. divsn. of clin. and prevention rsch. Nat. Inst. on Alcohol Abuse and Alcoholism, Rockville, Md., 1990—2003; ret., 2003. Asst. prof., assoc. prof. medicine Case-Western Res. U., Cleve., 1974-90, asst. prof. biometry, 1972-90. Contbr. chpts. in books and articles to profl. jours. Capt. USAF, 1964-66.

FULLER, ROBERT FERREY, lawyer, investor; b. St. Paul, Aug. 11, 1929; s. Robert Garfield and Gwendolen (Ferrey) F.; m. Marcelle McIntosh, June 6, 1953 (div. 1984); children: Julie, Gordon McIntosh; m. Sheila Nolan Mensing, May 25, 1985; stepchildren: Andrew Mensing, Allison Mensing. AB magna cum laude, Harvard, 1950, JD, 1953. Bar: N.Y. 1956, Conn. 1988, U.S. Dist. Ct. (so. and ea. dists.) N.Y. 1960, U.S. Ct. Appeals (D.C. cir.) 1988, U.S. Ct. Internat. Trade 1988. Assoc. Patterson, Belknap & Webb, N.Y.C., 1955-66; sec., gen. counsel Reuben H. Donnelley Corp., N.Y.C., 1966-68; mng. dir. R.H. Donnelley Internat. Ltd., London, Eng., 1970-73; asst. sec., internat. counsel Am. Can Co., Greenwich, Conn., 1973-86; asst. sec., asst. gen. counsel Am. Can Co. (name changed to Am. Can Packaging Inc. 1986), Greenwich, Conn., 1986-87; ptnr. Bentley, Mosher & Babson, Stamford and Greenwich, Conn., 1987-89, of counsel, 1990-92. Underwriting mem. Lloyd's, 1977-97. Active Rep. Town Meeting, Greenwich, 1986-96. Served to lt. (j.g.) USCGR, 1953-55; lt. comdr. Res. ret. Mem. Camp Fire Club Am., Harvard Club N.Y.C., Greenwich Country Club, Loxahatchee Club. Republican. Presbyterian. Avocations: golf, shotgun sports, reading, genealogy. E-mail: higun1@aol.com.

FULLER, ROBERT KENNETH, architect, urban designer; b. Denver, Oct. 6, 1942; s. Kenneth Roller and Gertrude Ailene (Heid) F.; m. Virginia Louise Elkin, Aug. 23, 1969; children: Kimberly Kirsten, Kelsey Christa. BArch, U. Colo., 1967; MArch and Urban Design, Washington U., St. Louis, 1974. Registered profl. arch., Colo. Archtl. designer Fuller & Fuller, Denver, Marvin Hatami Assocs., 1968-69; architect, planner Urban Research and Design Ctr., St. Louis, 1970-72; urban designer Victor Gruen & Assocs., 1973-75; prin. Fuller & Fuller Assocs., Denver, 1975—. Past pres. Denver East Ctrl. Civic Assn., Country Club Hist. Dist.; bd. dirs. Cherry Creek Steering Com., Cherry Creek Found.; pres. Horizon Adventures, Inc.; permanent sec.-treas. Archtl. Edn. Found., AIA Colo. Sgt. USMCR, 1964-70. Mem.: AIA (past pres. Denver chpt.), Rocky Mountain Vintage Racing Assn., Colo. Arlberg Club (past pres.), Delta Phi Delta, Phi Gamma Delta. Home: 2244 E 4th Ave Denver CO 80206-4107 Office: 3320 E 2nd Ave Denver CO 80206-5302 Office Phone: 303-333-3320.

FULLER, SAMUEL ASHBY, retired lawyer, mining executive; b. Indpls., Sept. 2, 1924; s. John L.H. and Mary (Ashby) F.; m. Betty Winn Hamilton, June 10, 1948; children— Mary Cheryl Fuller Hargrove, Karen E. Fuller Wolfe, Deborah R. BS in Gen. Engring, U. Cin., 1946, JD, 1947; cert. fin. planner, Coll. for Fin. Planning, 1989. Bar: Ohio 1948, Ind. 1951, Fla. 1984. Cleve. claims rep. Mfrs. and Mchts. Indemnity Co., 1947-48; claims supr. Indemnity Ins. Co. N.Am., 1948-50; with firm Stewart, Irwin, Gilliom, Fuller & Meyer (formerly Murray, Mannon, Fairchild & Stewart), Indpls., 1950-85, Lewis Kappes Fuller & Eads (name changed to Lewis & Kappes), Indpls., 1985-89, 1990—2000; pres., dir. Irsugo Consol. Mines, Ltd., 1953-80; ret., 2000. Dir. Ind. Pub. Health Found., Inc., 1972-84; staff instr. Purdue U. Life Ins. and Mktg. Inst., 1954-61; instr. Am. Coll. Life Underwriters, Indpls., 1964-74; mem. Ind. State Bd. Law Examiners, 1984-96, treas. 1987-88. Bd. dirs. Southwest Social Centre, Inc., 1965-70; pres., dir. Westminster Village North, Inc., 1981-89. Fellow: Am. Coll. Trust and Estate Counsel, Indpls. Bar Found.; mem.: Fla. Bar, 7th Cir. Bar Assn., Ind. State Bar Assn. (bd. mgrs. 1986—88), Lincoln Hills Golf Club, Sun City Ctr. Golf and Racquet Club, Masons, Beta Theta Pi. Republican. Roman Catholic. E-mail: samuel105@peoplepc.com.

FULLER, S(HERI) MARCE, energy executive; BSEE, U. Ala.; MS in Power System Engring., Union Coll. Student engr. Ala. Power (subs. The So. Co.), 1980-83; engr. power system engring. dept. GE, 1983-85; electric system planning engr. Ala. Power (subs. The So. Co.), 1985-87; sr. fin. analyst corp. finance So. Co. Svcs., 1987-89, prin. strategic planning, asst. to pres., 1989-91; bus. devel. mgr. So. Electric (subs. The So. Co.), 1991; v.p. domestic bus. devel. So. Electric, 1994-96, sr. v.p. domestic ops., 1996; pres., CEO Mirant Corp., Atlanta, 1999—. Bd. dirs. Curtiss-Wright Corp., Earthlink; chairperson electricity adv. bd. U.S. Dept. Energy; mem. bd. councilors The Carter Ctr.; mem. Pres. Internat. Bd. Advisors, Philippines. Trustee Atlanta Internat. Sch. Office: Mirant 1155 Perimeter Ctr W Atlanta GA 36338

FULLER, THEODORE, retired insurance executive; b. Yonkers, N.Y., Dec. 7, 1918; s. Clarence Wendel and Mary Edgar (Denniston) F. AB cum laude, Princeton U., 1941; LLB, Columbia U., 1948. Bar: N.Y. 1948. With Savs. Bank Life Ins. Fund, N.Y.C., 1948-83, exec. v.p., 1964-65, pres., 1965-83. Former mem. N.Y. State Adv. Bd. Life Ins.; cons. Nat. Exec. Svc. Corps, Svc. Corps Retired Execs. Tax counselor Am. Assn. Ret. Persons. Comdr. USNR, World War II, Korea. Mem. Assn. of Bar of City of N.Y., Princeton Club, Univ. Glee Club, Indian Harbor Yacht Club, Retired Men's Assn. (former pres.), Ea. Packard Club, Antique Automobile Club Am., Classic Car Club Am. (former bd. dirs.), Rolls Royce Owners Club, Pierce Arrow Club, Sound Investments Club. Home: 3 Mercia Ln Greenwich CT 06830-7068

FULLER, TIMOTHY RICHARD, college administrator; b. Syracuse, N.Y., May 20, 1957; s. Richard Harlow and Lillian Edith (Petzinger) F.; m. Carol Jay Zimmerman, Sept. 22, 1979; children: Rebecca, Daniel, Jonathan. BA, Houghton Coll., 1979; MBA, SUNY, Buffalo, 1989. Loan adjuster Merchants Nat. Bank, Syracuse, 1979-80; admissions counselor Houghton (N.Y.) Coll., 1980-83, asst. dir. admissions, 1983-86, dir. admissions and retention, 1986-91, exec. dir. alumni and admissions, 1991-94, v.p. alumni and admissions, 1994—96, v.p. external affairs, 1996—98, v.p. enrollment mgmt., 1998—. Cons. Ont. Bible Coll., Toronto, Can., 1990, Ind. Wesleyan U., Marion, 1988-89, Huntington (Ind.) Coll., 1989, 92-94, Cen. Wesleyan Coll., 1988, Prairie Bible Inst., 1992. Editor: Becoming an Admissions Professional, 1989, 90, 91. Mem. Nat. Assn. Christian Coll. Admissions Pers. (v.p. 1983-85, pres. 1985-88, Admissions Officer of Yr. 1990). Republican. Wesleyan. Avocation: personal computer. Office: Houghton Coll 1 Willard Ave Houghton NY 14744

FULLER, VINCENT J., lawyer; b. Ossining, N.Y., June 21, 1931; BA, Williams Coll., 1952; LLB, Georgetown U., 1956, LLD, 1988. Bar: D.C. 1956, N.Y. 1957, U.S. Dist. Ct. (so. dist.) N.Y. 1964, U.S. Ct. Appeals D.C. 1956, U.S. Ct. Appeals (2d cir.) 1965, U.S. Ct. Appeals (5th cir.) 1967, U.S. Ct. Appeals (6th cir.) 1969, U.S. Ct. Appeals (7th cir.) 1977, U.S. Supreme Ct. 1962. With Williams & Connolly, 1956—, ptnr. Washington. With USN, 1952—54. Fellow Am. Coll Trial Lawyers; mem. ABA, DC Bar Assn., NY State Bar Assn., The Barristers, Am. Bd. Criminal Lawyers. Avocation: history. Office: Williams & Connolly 725 12th St NW Washington DC 20005-5901 E-mail: vinful81@msn.com.

FULLER, WAYNE ARTHUR, statistics educator; b. Corning, Iowa, June 15, 1931; s. Loren Boyd and Eva Gladys (Darrah) F.; m. Evelyn Rose Steinford, Dec. 22, 1956; children: Douglas W., Bret E. BS, Iowa State U., 1955, MS, 1957, PhD, 1959. Asst. prof. Iowa State U., Ames, 1959-62, assoc. prof., 1962-66, prof., 1966-83, disting. prof. stats., 1983—2001, disting. prof. emeritus, 2001—. Cons. Doane Mktg. Rsch., Inc., St. Louis. Author: Introduction to Statistical Time Series, 1976, 2nd ed. 1996, Measurement Error Models, 1987; also articles. Served as cpl. U.S. Army, 1952-54 Fellow Am. Statis. Assn. (v.p. 1991-93), Inst. Math Stats., Econometric Soc.; mem. Internat. Statis. Inst., Royal Statis. Soc. Home: 3013 Briggs Cir Ames IA 50010-4705 Office: Iowa State U Statis Lab 221 Snedecor Hall Ames IA 50010 Office Phone: 515-294-9773. Business E-Mail: waf@iastate.edu.

FULLER, WILLIAM SIDNEY, lawyer; b. Auburn, Ala., Aug. 9, 1931; s. William Melton and Ernestine (Torbert) F.; m. Joyce Jeffrey, Nov. 5, 1953; children: Jeffrey Melton, Barbara Rush. BS, Auburn U., 1953; LLB, U. Ala., 1956, JD, 1969. Bar: Ala. 1956. Student asst. to dean U. Ala. Law Sch., 1954—55; law clk. to U.S. dist. judge, Montgomery, Ala., 1956—57; practice law Andalusla, 1957—; former city atty. City of Andalusia. Dir., sec. Covington County Bank; lectr. Southeastern Trial Inst.; mem. grievance com. Ala. State Bar, 1968-71, mem. bd. commrs., 1979-81; mem. law and contemporary affairs adv. council Auburn U. Author: Personal Injury Treatises. Mem. ABA, Ala., Covington County bar assns., Am. Trial Lawyers Assn., Am. Bd. Trial Advocates, Ala. Plaintiff Lawyers Assn., Ala. Trial Lawyers Assn. (pres. 1968), Phi Delta Phi, Kappa Alpha, Alpha Phi Omega. Presbyterian (elder, trustee, past chmn. bd. deacons Sunday sch. tchr.). Club: Andalusia (dir., pres. 1972), Topsl Beach and Racket (Destin, Fla.). Home: 100 S Ridge Rd Andalusia AL 36421-4214 Office: 28 S Court Sq Andalusia AL 36420-3918

FULLER, WRENDA SUE, music and secondary school educator; b. Aberdeen, S.D., Oct. 21, 1947; d. LeRoy William and Annette Karlene (Robinette) Herther; m. Larry Fray Fuller, Aug. 22, 1970; 1 child, Heather Sue. BA in Music, History, Dakota Wesleyan U., 1969; MA in Govt., U. Va., 1970. Sr. state human resources planner Commonwealth of Va., Richmond, 1970-73; cons. Social Security Adminstrn., S.W. Va., 1973-74; educator Russell County Sch. Bd., Lebanon, Va., 1974—2004; staff accompanist choir S.W. Va. C.C., 2004—; dir., founder Summer Music, Art, Drama Camp, 2005; accompanist SVCC Cmty. Choir, 2004—. Mem. faculty Va. Gov.'s Sch., 2000; founder/artistic dir. S.W. Va. Children's Choir, 2003—; founder S.W. Va. Music, Art, Drama Summer Camp, 2005; accompanist SWVA Cmty. Choir, 2004—. Author: (directory) Listing and Evaluation of Available Human Services in Russell County, 1975; also articles. Mem. Health Svcs. Adv. Bd., S.W. Va., 1982-84; pres. Lebanon Women's Club, 1982-84; minister of music, Lebanon Meml. United Meth. Ch., 1982—; sponsor Boy Scouts Bloomington, Ind. (nat. winner mock trial), 1994, 96-98, 2000—, Nat. Hist. Day, College Park, Md., 1994—. Named Outstanding Young Educator Jaycees, 1980, Econs. fellow U. Va., Charlottesville, 1988, Robert Cross History award, 1998, Gov.'s Coun. for the Arts award, 2000, UFW Citizenship award, 1998, Alumni Edn. award Dakota Wesleyan U., 2001. Mem. NEA, Music Educators Nat. Conf. (chmn. dist. VII, Va., 1989-91, 95—), Am. Choral Dirs. Assn. Avocations: reading, directing musicals, piano. Home: RR 4 Box 81 Lebanon VA 24266-9734 Business E-Mail: wsfull@naxs.com.

FULLERTON, GAIL JACKSON, retired academic administrator; m. Stanley James Fullerton, Mar. 27, 1967; children by previous marriage— Gregory Snell Putney, Cynde Putney Mitchell. BA, U. Nebr., 1949, MA, 1950; PhD, U. Oreg., 1954. Lectr. sociology Drake U., Des Moines, 1955-57; asst. prof. sociology Fla. State U., Tallahassee, 1957-60, San Jose (Calif.) State U., 1963-67, assoc. prof., 1968-71, prof., 1972-91, dean grad. studies and rsch., 1972-76, exec. v.p. univ., 1976-78, pres., 1978-91; ret., 1991. Bd. dirs. Assoc. Western Univs., Inc., 1980-91; mem. sr. accrediting commn. Western Assn. Schs. and Colls., 1982-88, chmn., 1985-86; mem. Pres.'s Commn. NCAA, 1986-91; bd. dirs. Am. Coll. Assn., 1991. Author: Survival in Marriage, 2d edit, 1977, (with Snell Putney) Normal Neurosis: The Adjusted American, 2d edit, 1966. Carnegie fellow, 1950-51, 52-53; Doherty Found. fellow, 1951-52. Mem. Phi Beta Kappa, Chi Omega. *Our lives are the summations of the choices we make, one at a time, by intention or by default. I have tried to choose by deliberate and rational intent, so that even when the choice proves wrong, it is clear to me that I am responsible for myself.*

FULLERTON, JANE WYATT, artist; b. Oklahoma City, June 6, 1932; d. Cecil Claude and María Adelina (Baizan) Wyatt; m. Charles Michael Fullerton, Dec. 27, 1954; children: Stephanie Malia, Christopher Damien, Amy Juliet. BFA, U. Okla., 1954; postgrad., U. Tex., El Paso, 1955-56, U. Hawaii, Hilo, 1970's, U. N.Mex., 1970's. Geophys. draftsman Carter Oil Co., Oklahoma City, 1954; engring. draftsman Dept. of the Interior BLM, Socorro, N.Mex., 1961-64; freelance artist, 1952—; factotum The Studio Showplace, Socorro, 1982—. Exhibited in group shows at Women Artists of the Big Island, U. Hawaii, Hilo, 1982, Centennial Exhibit, N.Mex. Tech., Socorro, 1988, Women's Stories, N.Mex. State U., Las Cruces, 1994, Masks, Albuquerque, 1994. Recipient Purchase 1 Painting, Honolulu Advertiser Collection, 1981, Aquisition award State of Hawaii SFCA, 1984, Purchase 3 Paintings, N.Mex. Pub. Art for N.Mex. Tech. Libr., 1991. Mem. AAUW, N.Mex. Watercolor Soc., Hawaii Watercolor Soc. (signature mem.), Socorro Art League, Socorro Garden Club (sec. 1991). Avocations: travel, geology, local history, swimming, bird watching. Studio: The Studio Showplace Val Verde Hotel 203 Manzanares Ave E Socorro NM 87801-5023

FULLERTON, JEAN LEAH, retired language educator, researcher, census researcher; b. Johnstown, Pa., Aug. 5, 1929; d. Elmer M. and Elizabeth (Schultz) Daily; m. Bernell Houston Fullerton, Nov. 8, 1952; children: Kenneth Leon, Michele Marie Kelley, Brian Hugh, Madeline Elizabeth McMahon. *Husband, Bernell Fullerton, is a member of the Distinguished Flying Cross Society and a lifetime member of the Hump Club, having served in World War II. Parents, Elmer and Elizabeth Daily, owned several hotels in Ebensburg, Pennsylvania, which was managed by Jean's mother from 1934 to 1961. At the same time, her father was founder and president of the Middle Atlantic and Pennsylvania Minor Baseball Leagues. During their existence from 1925 to 1952, they sent over 500 players to the major leagues.* BA, Seton Hill U., Greensburg, Pa., 1951; MS, Towson State U., 1980. Cert. English Tchr. Md., Master's Equivalency Cert. Tchr. English Balt. County Sch. Sys., Towson, Md., 1967—89; interviewer/rschr. Census Bur. US Dept. Commerce, Phila., 1990—. Author poetry. Vol. Rep. Party, Towson, 1960—82. Roman Catholic. Avocation: genealogy. Home: 185 Sandyhook Road Ocean Pnes MD 21811 Personal E-mail: bfullerton@mchsl.com.

FULLERTON, R. DONALD, banker; b. June 7, 1931; married. BA, U. Toronto, 1953. With Can. Bank of Commerce, Vancouver, 1953—, exec. v.p., chief gen. mgr., 1973, dir. of bank, 1974—, pres., COO, 1976, chmn., CEO, 1984, ret. chmn., CEO, 1992, chmn. exec. com., 1992-99, ret. dir., 2004. Bd. dirs. George Weston Ltd., Asia Satellite Telecomms. Holding, Ltd., Husky Energy, Ptnr. Comm. Co. Ltd. Avocations: skiing, golf. Office: CIBC Commerce Ct W Toronto ON Canada M5L 1A2 E-mail: rd.fullerton@cibc.com.

FULLERTON, ROSEMARY, accountant, educator; d. Millward and Joye Robinson; m. Herb Fullerton, July 16, 1994; children: Shane Daniels, Danette Daniels, Nathan Daniels, Dustin Daniels(dec.). BA in English, Brigham Young U., 1970; BSc in Acctg., Utah State U., 1985, MA in Acctg., 1989; PhD, U. Utah, 1998. CPA Utah, 1984. Cpa Davis & Bott, CPA's, Brigham City, Utah, 1983—89; vis. prof. of acctg. McGill U., Montreal, Canada, 1997—98; assoc. prof. acctg. Utah State U., Logan, Utah, 1999—. Examiner Shingo Prize, Logan, 1998—. Recipient Top Utah State U. Grad. award, Fedn. Schs. Accountancy, 1990, Shingo Prize for Excellence in Rsch., 2004. Mem.: Inst. of Mgmt. Accountants, AICPA, Am. Acctg. Assn., Utah Assn. CPA's (pres. Cache Valley chpt. 1990—91, Outstanding Student award 1990). Office: Utah State University School of Accountancy Logan UT 84322-3540 Office Phone: 435-797-2332. Business E-Mail: rosemary.fullerton@usu.edu.

FULLERTON, THOMAS MANKIN, JR., economist; b. Ft. Worth, Aug. 31, 1959; s. Thomas Mankin and Katherine Jane (Copeland) F.; m. Lourdes Licon; children: Kristy, Steven, Brett. BBA, U. Tex., El Paso, 1981; MS, Iowa Stata U., 1984; MA, U. Penn., 1988; PhD, U. Fla., 1996. Assoc. economist El Paso (Tex.) Electric Co., El Paso, 1981-83; economist Exec. Office of the Gov., Boise, Idaho, 1984-87; internat. economist Wharton Econometrics, The WEFA Group, Bala Cynwyd, Pa., 1988-91; sr. economist U. Fla., Gainesville, 1991-96; rsch. assoc. U. Fla. Ctr. for Latin Am. Studies, Gainesville, 1991-96; assoc. prof. U. Tex. El Paso, 1996—, coord. border region modeling project, 1996—. Alternate, Nat. Gov.'s Assn. Energy Com., Boise, 1985-86; Idaho state expert, Wharton Econometrics Regional Network, Boise, 1986-87; Idaho coord., Fed. Program Population Estimates, Boise, 1985-87; broadcaster, Radio YSKL, San Salvador, El Salvador, 1976-77. Sponsor Save the children, Bogota, Colombia, 1985—; commr. U. Tex. Student Election Bd., El Paso, 1978-79, mortar bd. U. Tex., El Paso, 1981. Dean's fellow, Wharton Sch., 1987-88. Mem. Nat. Assn. Bus. Economists (policy panel 1989—, forecast panel 1984-88), Rio Grande Econs. Assn., Wharton Alumni Assn., Beta Gamma Sigma, Phi Kappa Phi, Alpha Chi. Presbyterian. Office: U Tex Dept Econs And Fin El Paso TX 79968-0543 E-mail: tomf@utep.edu.

FULLING, SHARON S., college nursing program director; RN, St. Mary's Hosp. Sch. Nursing, Evansville, Ind., 1959; BSN, U. Evansville, 1978, MSN, 1981. Asst. dean, Dir. Nursing Mississippi County C.C., Blytheville, Ark., 1981—, mem. profl. standards com. Chmn. by-laws com. Ark. Nursing Rsch.

Consortium, Coun. of Nurse Adminstrns. of Nursing Edn. in Ark.; mem., past recorder for Coun. of Deans and Dirs. for RN Edn. of Ark. State Bd. Nursing, past chmn. ADN coun.; presenter health care career symposiums. Mem. adv. bd. Mississippi County Dept. Pub. Health. Mem. ANA, Ark. Nursing Assn., Ark. Leagoe for Nursing Assn., Ark. State Nursing Assn., Ark. Nurses Assn., Ark. Orgn. for Advancement of Assoc. Degree Nursing, Sigma Theta Tau. Office: Miss County CC PO Box 1109 Blytheville AR 72316-1109

FULLMAN, ROBERT LOUIS, metallurgy consultant; b. Sewickley, Pa., Sept. 13, 1922; m. Doris Hite; children: Janice, Grant. BEng, Yale U., 1943, DEng in Metallurgy, 1950. Instr. metallurgy New Haven YMCA Jr. Coll., 1947-48; rsch. assoc. GE, 1948-55, mgr. materials and processes studies, 1955-59, mgr. metal studies, 1960-63, mgr. fuel cell studies, 1964-65, mgr. properties br., 1965-68, mgr. planning & resources, material sci. & engring., 1969-72, metallurgist R & D Ctr., 1972-83; cons., 1983—. Vis. lectr. Rensselaer Polytech. Inst., 1951-56, adj. prof., 1956-65; sec.-treas. bd. govs. Acta Metallurgica, 1965-96, treas., 1997-2000. Recipient J. Herbert Holloman award Acta Metallurgica, 1995. Fellow Am. Soc. Metals (Geisler Meml. award 1955), Am. Inst. Mining, Metallurgy & Petroleum Engrs. Achievements include research on deformation of metals; interfacial energies in solids; crystal growth; origin of microstructures; recrystallization and grain growth; relationships between microsctructure and properties of metals. Home: 1710 Jamaica Way Apt 206 Punta Gorda FL 33950-5175 E-mail: rlfullman@aol.com.

FULLMER, DANIEL WARREN, former psychologist, educator; b. Spoon River, Ill., Dec. 12, 1922; s. Daniel Floyd and Sarah Louisa (Essex) F.; m. Janet Satomi Saito, June 1980; children: Daniel William, Mark Warren. BS, Western Ill. U., 1947, MS, 1952; PhD, U. Denver, 1955. Post-doctoral intern psychiat. div. U. Oreg. Med. Sch., 1958-61; mem. faculty U. Oreg., 1955-66; prof. psychology Oreg. System of Higher Edn., 1958-66; faculty Coll. Edn. U. Hawaii, Honolulu, 1966-95, retired, 1995, prof. emeritus, 1974—; pvt. practice psychol. counseling. Cons. psychologist Grambling State U., 1960-81; founder Free-Family Counseling Ctrs., Portland, Oreg., 1959-66, Honolulu, 1966-74; co-founder Child and Family Counseling Ctr., Waianae, Oahu, Hawaii, Kilohana United Meth. Ch., Oahu, 1992, v.p., sec., 1992; pres. Human Resources Devel. Ctr., Inc., 1974—; chmn. Hawaii State Bd. to License Psychologists, 1973-78. Author: Counseling: Group Theory & System, 2d. edit., 1978, The Family Therapy Dictionary Text, 1991, MANABU, Diagnosis and Treatment of a Japanese Boy with a Visual Anomaly, 1991; co-author: Principles of Guidance, 2d. edit., 1977; author (counselor/cons. training manuals) Counseling: Content and Process, 1964, Family Consultation Therapy, 1968, The School Counselor-Consultant, 1972, Family Therapy as the Rites of Passage, 1998; editor: Bulletin, Oreg. Coop Testing Service, 1955-57, Hawaii P&G Jour., 1970-76; assoc. editor: Educational Perspectives, U. Hawaii Coll. Edn. Served with USNR, 1944-46. Recipient Francis E. Clark award Hawaii Pers. Guidance Assn., 1972, Thomas Jefferson award for Outstanding Pub. Svc., 1993; named Hall of Fame Grambling State U., 1987. Mem. Am. Psychol. Assn., Am. Counseling Assn. (Nancy C. Wimmer award 1963), Masons. Methodist. Office: 1750 Kalakaua Ave Apt 809 Honolulu HI 96826-3725 Office Phone: 808-942-2072. *I grew up along Spoon River. The people of Spoon River had a principle of life: Improve on what you are. The purpose is to be able to help others help themselves. From here, it is like stepping into a river of life; the deeper you got, the stronger the current. Then, suddenly, here you are nearing the delta. Just ahead lies a beautiful ocean.*

FULMER, DANIEL A., music educator, composer; b. Apr. 4, 1964; s. James B. and Martha G. Fulmer; m. Sharee Fulmer, July 20; children: Maeghan, Micah. B.Music Theory, Stetson U., DeLand, Fla., 1991; M.Music Composition, Fla. State U., 1994; DMA, U. Miami, 1998. Tchg. asst. adj. U. Miami, Coral Gables, Fla., 1994—97; asst. prof. Trinity Bible Coll., Ellendale, ND, 1997—98; adj. interim prof. music composition Middle Tenn. State U., Murfreesboro, 1998; adj. prof. music Volunteer State C., Gullatin, Tenn., 1999—2000; asst. prof. music Southwestern U., Waxahachie, Tex., 2000—. Composer: (classical concert music) A Mortuis Excitare Et Obviam Domino in Aera (Symphony No. 4), 2002, (for band) March to Babylon, 2002, (concert music) Quintet for Bassoon and Strings, 2000, Symphony No. 2, 1997, (for soprano and 13 instruments) Set Me as a Seal, 1995, (for soprano, mixed chorus and eighteen instruments) Lamentum, 1994, (for large orch.) Lacrymosa, 1991, (for orch.) Symphony No. 3, numerous others. Recipient ASCAP-Raymond Hubbell Music scholar, 1996; grantee U. Miami grantee, 1997. Mem.: ASCAP (award for composition 1997—2002), Pi Kappa Lambda.

FULMER, DOUGLAS ALAN, political scientist, consultant, journalist; b. Akron, Ohio, June 12, 1959; s. Gordon Lozier and Marjorie Helen (Glandorf) F.; m. Alice Marie Fry, Aug. 16, 1980 (div. Aug. 16, 1982). BA, Mt. Union Coll., Alliance, Ohio, 1981; MA, Syracuse U., 1982. Dir. state and local affairs Coalition for Scenic Beauty, Washington, 1987-89; internat. field coord. Nat. Space Soc., Washington, 1989-91; exec. dir. Com. To Preserve Assateague Island, Towson, Md., 1991; sr. assoc. Phil Noble and Assocs., Towson, 1991-92; pres. Douglas Fulmer and Assocs., Hermitage, Tenn., 1993—; freelance journalist Hermitage, Tenn., 1990—. Contbr. articles to periodicals, newspapers, mags., and Web sites. Vol. numerous polit. campaigns, 1972-80; mem. campaign staff numerous polit. campaigns, 1982-86; field rep. Am. Fedn. State, County and Mcpl. Employees, Indpls., 1986; campaign cons. Md. State Tchrs. Assn., Annapolis, Md., 1986; field rep. Am. Fedn. State, Jersey City, 1985; dir. del. selection George McGovern for Pres., Washington, 1984; field dir. Lane Evans for Congress, Rock Island, Ill., 1984; field coord. Elain Lytel for Congress, Syracuse, 1982. Home: 4100 Central Pike # 1420 Hermitage TN 37076 Office: 51 Fawn Creek Pass Nashville TN 37214-4502 E-mail: Dougfulmer@bellsouth.net.

FULMER, HUGH SCOTT, physician, educator; b. Syracuse, N.Y., June 18, 1928; s. Herbert C. and Emily (Price) F.; m. Zola M. Jones, July 12, 1952; children: James, Kim, Scott. AB, Syracuse U., 1948; MD, SUNY-Syracuse, 1951; M.P.H., Harvard U., 1961. Intern R.I. Hosp., 1951-52; resident internal medicine SUNY-Syracuse, 1954-57; fellow pulmonary medicine SUNY, Syracuse, 1957-58; asst. dir., rsch. assoc. Navajo-Cornell Field Health Research Project, 1958-60; instr. pub. health and preventive medicine Cornell U. Coll. Medicine, 1958-60; asst. prof. community medicine U. Ky. Coll. Medicine, 1960-64, assoc. prof., 1964-66, prof., 1966-68, dir. sr. med. student internat. cross-cultural program, 1964-68, dir. preventive medicine residency program, 1964-68; tech. cons. health Peace Corps, Malaysia, 1968-69; prof., chmn. dept. community and family medicine U. Mass. Med. Sch., 1969-77, asso. dean for clin. edn. and primary care, 1975-79, chief sect. gen. medicine, dept. medicine, 1978-83; dir. ambulatory and community svcs. Carney Hosp., Boston, 1983-88, dir. community-oriented primary care program, 1988-93, dir. preventive medicine residency, 1988-93; exec. dir. Ctr. for Cmty. Responsive Care, Boston, 1992—2000, dir. preventive medicine residency & COPC fellowship program, 1992—2002. Adj. prof. socio-med. scis., cmty. medicine and pub. health Boston U. Sch. Medicine and Pub. Health, 1983-96; clin. prof. family medicine Medicine State U. NY at Syracuse, 2005-. Served with M.C., USAF, 1952-54. Mem. AMA, APHA, Mass. Med. Soc., Assn. Tchrs. Preventive Medicine (past pres., Outstanding Tchr. award 1993), Am. Assn. Pub. Health Physician, Am. Coll. Preventive Medicine (bd. regents 1988-94). Achievements include research on community responsive care. Home: 61 Cherlyn Dr Northborough MA 01532-1135 Business E-Mail: hsfulmer@massmed.org.

FULMER, MICHAEL CLIFFORD, food company administrator; b. Cin., May 8, 1954; s. William George and Mirella Martha (Kloeker) F. BBA, U. Cin., 1980. Aux. police City of Norwood, Ohio, 1977-79, councilman, 1980-85, 92-93, 96—; asst. dock supr. Lee Way Motor Freight, Inc., Cin., 1981; supr. Serv-A-Portion div. Di Giorgio Corp., Cin., 1981-85, shift mgr., 1986-88; prodn. supt. Borden, Cin., 1988-91; prodn. adminstrn. Pierre Frozen Foods, 1992—. Lector St. Matthew Ch., Norwood, 1978-94; precinct exec. Norwood Centennial Com., 1987-88, 90—; pres. St. Matthew Parish Coun., Norwood, 1979-80; precinct exec., 1990—; chmn. fin. City of Norwood, 1982-83. Named Sailor of Yr. USN, 1976. Mem. Nat. Audubon Soc., Lighthouse Preservation Soc., Wilderness Soc., Sierra Club, U. Cin. Bus. Tribunal (pres. 1979-80, award 1980), Kiwanis (bd. dirs. 1991-92). Roman Catholic. Avocations: photography, jogging, gardening, reading, hiking. Home: 3737 Hazel Ave Cincinnati OH 45212-3823 Office: Pierre Frozen Foods 9990 Princeton Rd Cincinnati OH 45246

FULMER, PHILLIP, university football coach; b. Winchester, Tenn., Sept. 1, 1950; m. Vicky Morey; children: Phillip Jr., Courtney, Brittany, Allison. BA, U. Tenn., 1972. Offensive line coach Wichita (Kans.) State U., 1974, 77-78, linebacker coach, 1975-76; asst. football coach Vanderbilt U., Nashville, 1979; grad. asst. U. Tenn., Nashville, 1972, defensive coord. freshman team, 1973, asst. coach, 1980-91, head coach, 1992—. Head coach East-West Shrine Game, 1998; coach Fla. Citrus Bowl, 1993, Orange Bowl, 1997. Led U. Tenn. Vols. to Southeastern Conf. championship, 1997; named, Nat. and SEC Coach of Year, 1998; recipient, Brotherhood/Sisterhood award from Nat. Conf.for Cmty. and Justice, 2000, State Farm Eddie Robinson Coach of Distinction award, 2000. Mem. Am. Football Coaches Assn. (trustee 1996—, mem. Hall of Fame com., I-A coaches legis. issues com., Kodak Region 2 Coach of Yr. award 1993). Office: Head Football Coach Univ Tenn PO Box 15016 Knoxville TN 37901-5016

FULMER, VINCENT ANTHONY, retired college president; b. Alliance, Ohio, Oct. 23, 1927; s. Anthony and Catherine (Long) F.; m. Mary Alma Pineau, Dec. 27, 1950; children: Kevan, Kristine, David, Amy, Charles, Alma Leigh. AB cum laude, Miami U., Oxford, Ohio, 1949; postgrad., Harvard U., 1950; S.M., MIT, 1963; LL.D., Suffolk U., 1971; D.Sc., Fla. Inst. Tech., 1982; Ed.D., Hawthorne Coll., 1988. Mem. staff MIT, 1951-86, exec. asst. office chmn., 1960-63, v.p., 1963-73, sec. inst., 1963-85; v.p. adminstrn. William Underwood Co., 1973-75; sec. MIT Corp., 1979—85; v.p., dir. Video Optics Corp., Waltham, Mass., 1985-86; pres. Hawthorne Coll., Antrim, N.H., 1986-88, pres. emeritus, 1988—. Bd. dirs. Barbour Stockwell, Inc., Control Air, Inc., Fiberspar Corp.; instr. econs. Williams Coll., 1952. Contbr. chapters to books and mags. Bd. dirs. Planning Office for Urban Affairs, Archdiocese of Boston, 1968-93; trustee Suffolk U., 1972—, chmn., 1976-81; trustee Hawthorne Coll., 1982-92, chmn., 1985-92; corporator New Eng. Coll. Optometry, 1985-87, trustee, 1987-93; bd. dirs. Sml. Bus. High Tech. Inst., Washington, 1982—; mem. exec. com. MIT Enterprise Forum, 1978—, vice-chmn. 1992-93; chmn. Tech. Capital Network, 1990-95, chmn. emeritus, 2005—. With USNR, 1944-46. Mem. Am. Econ. Assn., AAAS, Ops. Rsch. Soc. Am., Inst. Mgmt. Scis., Phi Beta Kappa, Sigma Chi, Omicron Delta Kappa. Home and Office: 26 Kimball Rd Arlington MA 02474-1206 Office Phone: 781-646-8670. *While individuals may address themselves exclusively to high personal attainments within the existing framework of our institutions, or devote prodigious efforts to improve or restructure those institutions, in the end it is our lifetime example that counts more heavily than all else.*

FULOP, LASZLO G., architect; arrived in U.S., 1957; s. Pal Fulop Fülöp and Mária-Irma Rózsa; m. Sue Ellen Wilson, Feb. 10, 1962 (div. Nov. 1985); children: Angela, Paul, Zsuzsa; m. Agnes Maria Sylvester, Dec. 30, 1988. Student, U. Vienna; BArch, U. Minn., 1963. Registered architect, Minn., Wis. NCARB draftsman and designer Horty, Elving & Assocs., Mpls., 1963—66; designer, project mgr., and assoc. Baker Assocs., Inc., Mpls., 1966—70; mgr. design and planning Minn. State U. Sys., St. Paul, 1970—75; dir. planning U. Minn., Mpls., 1975—83; dir. planning and constrn. U. Wis., Madison, 1983—89; pres. L.G. Fulop Archs. and Planners, Mpls., 1991—. Adj. instr. N. Hennepin C.C., Brooklyn Park, Minn., 1969—76; mem. long range regional river devel. and acquisition com. City of Mpls., 1976—77; coord. joint pub. works com. Madison City-U. Wis.-Madison, 1984—89, mem. ad-hoc S. Campus planning com., 1987—89, mem. liaison com., 1988—89; ex officio mem. campus planning com. U. Wis.-Madison, 1983—90; mem. Univ. Hill Farms Archtl. Control Com., 1983—90, Univ. Rsch. Pk. Design Rev. Bd., 1983—90. Co-author: The Hurricanes are Coming, 1996, author short stories, poems; contbr. articles to profl. jours. Mem. Town Planning Commn., Baytown, Minn., 1975—83; vol. host. Spl. Olympics, Mpls., 1991; apptd. mem. Convocation Ctr. Com., 1986—88; mem. Nat. Trust for Hist. Preservation; pres. Minn.-Hungarians, 1976—78, mem. cultural exhibit com., 1990—2005, sec., 1991—2005; chair pub. rels. com. cultural exhibit com., 1996—2005; pres. Communion Hungarian Friends, 1999—2002; mem. exec. com. Hungarian Am. Coalition, Washington, 1996—, bd. dirs., 1996—2004. With forced mil. labor div., 1954—55, Communist Hungary. Mem.: Soc. Coll. and Univ. Planning, Minn. Half-Arabian Horse Assn. (bd. dirs. 1980—81, pres. 1981—83, regional del. IAHA nat. conv. 1983, 1985). Independent. Avocations: writing, history, tennis, stamp collecting/philately. Office: LG Fulop Architects and Planners 6650 Vernon Ave S Minneapolis MN 55436 Office Phone: 952-930-0043. Business E-Mail: laszlofulop@mn.rr.com.

FULTON, AMY LOU, realtor, artist; b. Edmonds, Wash., July 19, 1969; d. James Edward Palm and Charlee Theresa Pond; m. David Dean Fulton, June 29, 1991; 1 child, Kent Alex. Student, Rockwell Inst., 2004; student in Fashion Merchandising, Shoreline C.C., 1988; student in Acctg., Edmonds (Wash.) C.C., 1990; degree as Dental Asst., Harcourt Learning, Scranton, Pa., 2002. Cert. dental asst. Scranton, PA, 2002; fashion merchandising Shoreline C.C., 1990, lic. realtor Calif. Dept. Real Estate, 2004. Title clk. Barrier Jaguar-Porsche-Audi, Bellevue, Wash., 1998—2000; realtor Coldwell Banker-Dunnigan Co, Elk Grove, Calif., 2004—. Pvt. artist and designer; illustrator Bedrock Pub. Co. Author: Mischievous Guido, 2003. Preschool Bible class tchr. North Seattle Ch. of Christ, 1991—2004; tchr. children's bible class Folsom (Calif.) Point Ch. Christ, Folsom, Calif., 2005—. Grantee, Pell Grant, 1987. Mem.: Nat. Assn. Realtors, Calif. Assn. Realtors, Sacramento Assn. Realtors (hon.). Republican. Avocations: painting, horseback riding, skiing, travel, gardening. Office: Coldwell Banker - The Dunnigan Company 9165 Elk Grove-Florin Rd Elk Grove CA 95758 Office Phone: 916-714-2400. Office Fax: 916-714-2424. Personal E-mail: amyfulton1@aol.com.

FULTON, DANIEL S., corporate real estate executive; BA in Econs., Miami U., Ohio, 1970; MBA, U. Wash., 1976; grad. exec. program, Stanford U., 2001. Former officer USN Supply Corps; mem. investment evaluation dept. Weyerhaeuser Co., 1976—78; planning mgr. Weyerhaeuser Real Estate Co., 1978—79; investment mgr. Weyerhaeuser Venture Co., 1978—87; CEO Cornerstone Columbia Devel. Co., 1987—88; pres., CEO Weyerhaeuser Realty Investors, 1988—98, Weyerhaeuser Venture Co., 1998—2001. Former officer USN Supply Corps; mem. investment evaluation dept. Weyerhaeuser Co., mem. sr. mgmt. team, 2003—; planning mgr. Weyerhaeuser Real Estate Co., 1978—79, pres., CEO, 2001—; investment mgr. Weyerhaeuser Venture Co., 1979—87, pres., CEO, 1998—2001; CEO Cornerstone Columbia Devel. Co., 1987—88; pres., CEO Weyerhaeuser Realty Investors, 1988—98. Bd. dirs. United Way of King County; mem. adv. bd. U. Wash. Bus. Sch.; bd. govs. Lambda Alpha Internat. Land Econs. Soc., High Prodn. Homebuilder Coun. of Nat. Assn. Homebuilders. Office: Weyerhaeuser Co 33663 Weyerhaeuser Way S Federal Way WA 98063-9777

FULTON, JUDITH P., management consultant; b. Princeton, N.J., Oct. 30, 1955; m. Mark P. Howard; children: David I. Fulton-Howard, Brian E. Fulton-Howard. BA in Computer Sci., Harvard U., 1978, MBA, 1983. Software devel. engr. Hewlett-Packard Co., 1978—81; dir. external sourcing, dir. strategic planning, bus. analysis mgr., mgr. mktg., MIS mgr. Bristol-Myers Squibb Co., 1983—90; mgr. flexible benefits bus. unit, mktg. mgr. Blue Cross & Blue Shield Md., 1990—94; dir. physician billing ops., dir. planning and bus. devel. HealthCare Automation Inc., 1995—97; CEO, treas. NovoVasc In., 1997—99; mgmt. cons. Eager St. Group, 1999—; CEO Cornerstone Mgmt., 2000—. Mentor Dingman Ctr. for Entrepreneurship, Smith Sch. Bus., U. Md., College Park, 1999—; mem. bd. trustees, sec., v.p. bd., mem. exec. com., chair com. on trustees, mem. mktg. and devel. coms., co-chair ann. fund raising Norbel Sch., 1995—; mem. bd. mgrs., chair program and membership com., chair ann. support campaign gen. teams Towson YMCA, 1993—96; adviser to pres., bd. Bright Vision Therapeutic Riding, 2000—. Recipient one of Md.'s Top 100 Women, Daily Record, 1998. Office: 1903 Indian Head Rd Baltimore MD 21204

FULTON, KENNETH RAY, professional association administrator; b. Cleve., Dec. 22, 1948; BS in Social Scis., U. Md., 1973; MS in Mgmt., Am. U., 1977. Mem. staff Nat. Acad. Scis., Washington, 1971-80, dir. membership, 1980-84, spl. asst. to pres., 1984-93; exec. dir. Acad. Scis., Washington, 1993—. Mgr. membership and program activities Nat. Acad. Scis.; organizer numerous sci. confs. and symposia, art exhibitions and cultural programs; mem. U.S. delegation to Codex Alimentarius Commn. UN, 1977-80. Publisher Proceedings of the Nat. Acad. Scis. With U.S. Navy. Mem. AAAS, Internat. Coun. for Sci. (com. on dissemination of sci. info.), Am. Soc. Assn. Execs., Soc. Scholarly Publishers. Office: Nat Acad Scis 500 Fifth St NW Washington DC 20001 Business E-Mail: kfulton@nas.edu.

FULTON, NORMAN ROBERT, credit manager; b. LA, Dec. 16, 1935; s. Robert John and Fritzi Marie (Wacker) F.; m. Nancy Butler, July 6, 1966; children: Robert B., Patricia M., Frank F., Mary Jane. AA, Santa Monica Coll., 1958; BS, U. So. Calif., 1960. Asst. v.p. Raphael Glass Co., L.A., 1960-65; credit adminstr. Zellerbach Paper Co., L.A., 1966-68; gen. credit mgr. Carrier Transicold Co., Montebello, Calif., 1968-70, Virco Mfg. Co., L.A., 1970-72, Superscope, Inc., Chatsworth, Calif., 1972-79; asst. v.p. credit and adminstrn. Inkel Corp., Carson, Calif., 1980-82; corp. credit mgr. Gen. Consumer Electronics, Santa Monica, Calif., 1982-83; br. credit mgr. Sharp Electronics Corp., Carson, Calif., 1983-96; credit mgr. Rocheux Internat., Inc., Carson, 1997-99; with Barron Chestney, Internat., 2000—. With AUS, 1955-57. Fellow Nat. Inst. Credit (cert. credit exec.). Home: 12635 Hidalgo St Desert Hot Springs CA 92240

FULTON, ROBERT LESTER, sociology educator; b. Toronto, Ont., Can., Nov. 30, 1926; s. Edgar John and Mary Grace (Ouderkirk) F.; m. Patricia Alma Brown, July 29, 1948 (div.); children: David, Richard; m. Julie Ann Rockman, June 13, 1964; 1 son, Regan. AB cum laude, U. Ill., 1951; MA, U. Toronto, 1953; PhD, Wayne State U., 1959. Instr. U. Wis., 1957-58; asst. prof. sociology Calif. State U., L.A., 1958-65, prof. sociology, 1965-66, U. Minn., Mpls., 1966-97; dir. Ctr. for Death Edn. and Rsch., 1969-97. Vis. prof. U. Minn., 1963-65, U. Osmania, India, 1967, St. Christopher's Hospice, London, 1975, Radium Hemmet, Stockholm, 1975, U. Calif.-Irvine, 1975, U. Calif.-San Diego, 1978, 79, U. Calif.-San Francisco, 1986, U. Vt., 1983, 84, 86, 88, 89, 92, St. Luke's Coll., Tokyo, 1985, U. Cape Town, 1993, Rikkyo U., Tokyo, 1993, Nankai U., Tianjin, China, 1995. Author: Death and Identity, 1965, 3rd rev. edit., 1993; Education and Social Crisis, 1967, Death, Grief and Bereavement: Bibliography 1845-1975, 1977, Death and Dying: Challenge and Change, 1978; assoc. editor Omega, 1970-73. With Royal Can. Navy, 1944. Fellow Am. Sociol. Assn.; mem. Internat. Workgroup on Death, Dying and Bereavement, Société de Thanatologie de la Langue Française. Home: 139 Nina St Saint Paul MN 55102-2129 Office Phone: 651-292-0716. E-mail: fult001@umn.edu.

FULTON, THOMAS, theoretical physicist, educator; b. Budapest, Hungary, Nov. 19, 1927; came to U.S., 1941; s. Michael and Irene (Weisz) F.; m. Babette Pilzer, June 14, 1952; children: Ruth Carol, Judith Pamela. BA, Harvard U., 1950, MA, 1951, PhD, 1954. Prof. emeritus Johns Hopkins U., Balt., 2000—; Frank B. Jewett Found. postdoctoral fellow Inst. Advanced Studies, Princeton, N.J., 1954-55; NSF postdoctoral fellow Princeton, N.J., 1955-56; from asst. prof. to assoc. prof. physics Johns Hopkins U., Balt., 1956-64, prof., 1964-2000. Rsch. cons. and vis. scientist numerous orgns., 1954—. Author: (with others) Resonances in Strong Interaction Physics, 1963; assoc. editor Jour. Math. Physics, 1968-71; contbr. over 100 articles to profl. jours. Bd. dirs. Shriver Hall Concert Series, Balt., 1981-91. With U.S. Army, 1946-47. John Simon Guggenheim Found. fellow, U. Vienna, 1964-65, Fulbright sr. rsch. fellow, 1964-65; prin. investigator rsch. grantee NSF, Johns Hopkins U., 1960-92. Fellow Am. Phys. Soc.; mem. Archeol. Inst. Am., Sigma Xi. Home: 5600 Roxbury Pl Baltimore MD 21209-4502 Office: Johns Hopkins U Dept Physics And Astro Baltimore MD 21218 Office Phone: 410-516-7363.

FULTON, WILLIAM, mathematics professor; b. Aug. 29, 1939; BA, Brown U., 1961; PhD, Princeton U., 1966. Instr. Princeton (N.J.) U., 1965-66; from instr. to asst. prof. Brandeis U., 1966-69; assoc. prof. Brown U., 1970-75, prof., 1975-87, U. Chgo., 1987-98, Charles L. Hutchinson Disting. Svc. prof., 1995-98; Keeler prof. math. U. Mich., Ann Arbor, 1998—. Vis. asst. prof. Princeton U., 1969-70; vis. prof. U. Genoa, 1969, Aarhus U., 1976-77, Orsay, 1987; vis. mem. Inst. des Hautes Etudes Scis., 1981, Inst. Advanced Study, 1981-82, 94, Math. Scis. Rsch. Inst., 1992-93, Ctr. Advanced Study, Oslo, 1994; Erlander prof. Mittag-Leffler Inst., 1996-97; lectr. in field. Author: Intersection Theory, 1984, Introduction to Intersection Theory in Algebraic Geometry, 1984, Introduction to Toric Varieties, 1993, Algebraic Topology, 1995, Young Tableaux, 1997; (with R. MacPherson) A Categorical Framework for the Study of Singular Spaces, 1981; (wih S. Lang) Riemann-Roch Algebra, 1985, (with J. Harris) Representation Theory; a first course, 1991; (with S. Bloch and I. Dolgachev, editors) Proceedings of the US-USSR Symposium in Algebraic Geometry, Univ. of Chicago, June-July, 1989, 1991; assoc. editor Duke Math. Jour., 1984-93, Jour. Algebraic Geometry, 1992-93; editor Jour. Am. Math. Soc., 1993-99, mng. editor, 1995-98; mem. editl. bd. Cambridge Studies in Advanced Math., 1994—, Chgo. Lectures in Math., 1994-98. Grantee NSF, 1976—, Sloan Found., 1981-82; Guggenheim fellow, 1980-81; named Erlander prof. Swedish Sci. Found., 1996-97. Mem.: NAS, AAAS, Royal Swedish Acad. Sci. Office: U Mich 530 Ch St Ann Arbor MI 48109-1043

FULTON-QUINDOZA, DEBRA ANN, emergency nurse practitioner; b. Anne Arundel, Md., Dec. 16, 1961; d. William D. and Patricia A. (Rensel) Fulton; m. Stephen S. Quindoza, Nov. 17, 1997 (div. Aug. 2005); children: William Benjamin Quindoza, Allison Marie Quindoza 1 stepchild, Costas Quindoza. BSN, U. Tex., Galveston, 1983, MSN, 1986; postgrad., U. North Fla., 2003. Cert. advanced RN practitioner Fla., profl. nurse practitioner, profl. coder AAPC. Clin. nurse specialist Arnold Palmer Hosp. for Childen and Women, Orlando, Fla., 1989-90; pediatric and internal medicine nurse practitioner Office Dr. Shirley Nagel, Mt. Dora, Fla., 1990-91; project leader in med. policy-med. rev. Medicare Fla., Jacksonville, Fla., 1991-93, sr. healthcare data analyst dept. benefits/program integrity divsn., 1998—2000, mgr., 2000—03; med. cons., outreach educator, project mgr. Medicare Fraud Br., Jacksonville, 1993-98; advanced RN practitioner part time Dr. Perry G. Carlos, 1995-2000; urgent care nurse practitioner Solantic, Jacksonville, 2003—. Adj. instr. Coll. Continuing Edn. U. N. Fla., 2001—03; med. cons. in field. Office: Solantic 12303 San Jose Blvd Jacksonville FL 32223 Home: 4090 Hodges Blvd 612 Jacksonville FL 32224 Office Phone: 904-514-1416. Business E-Mail: dqnp@earthlink.net. E-mail: dgnp@earthlink.net.

FULTON ROSS, GALE, artist, actor; b. Medford, Mass., July 28, 1947; d. Herman Fulton Jr. and Henrietta Kelly, Joseph, Barksdale, Jr.; m. Craig Ross Sr., Dec. 18, 1964 (div. Aug. 7, 1977); 1 child, Craig Jr. Ross. Studied with artist Melvin Johnson, Instr. Melvin George Sch. Art, Boston, 1965—76; studied with artist Cleveland Bellow, Oakland, Ca. of the DeYoung Mus., 1976—81; studied with artist Pierre Parsus, France, 1993; studied, Berlin, 1996, studied, 2005. Trustee Nat. Urban League, N.Y.C., 1976—78; local/state judge Miss Am. Pageant, 2000—. Paintings/traveling exhibition, Billie (Nat. Coalition of 100 Black Woman Artistic Achievement Award, 1995); actor(role of Hazel): (film) Blue Hill Avenue, (role of Tituba): The Crucible; exhibitions include Earth N' Arts Gallery, Oakland, 1971—76, Black Expo, San Francisco, 1972, Oakland Mus., 1971, The Gallery, LA, 1978, Brockman Gallery, 1984, Calif. African Mus., 1986, Cousen Rose Gallery, Boston, 1987—89, Phila. AA Hist. Cultural Mus., 1995, US Dept. Health and Human Svcs., Wash., 1996, Pa. State U., 1996, Chuck Levitan Gallery, NYC, 1996, Tampa City Ctr., Francecsca Anderson Gallery, Lexington, Mass., Sarasota Ctr. for Visual Arts, 1997, SoBo Fine Art, Tulsa, 1999, Gallery Bershad, Boston, 1999, Artjaz Gallery, Phila., 1999, various others, one-woman shows include Nat. Coun. Chs. Hdqs., NYC, 1991, Castillion Fine Art, 1991, Zora Neal Hurston Mus., 1994, Monique Knowlton Gallery, NYC, 1994, Don Roll Gallery, Sarasota, 1995, African Am. Mus., Tampa, 1995, Represented in permanent collections Am. Mus. African Am. Artists, Ca. Mus. African Am. Art, Forbes Gallery, NYC, The Arthur Ashe Found.,

Thurgood Marshall Estate, NC U., Women's Mus Ar., Wash., commissioned works include, Archbishop Desmond Tutu, Nat. Orgn. Black Law Enforcement Officers, Congressman Ronald Dellums, Ambassador Bradlet Holmes, Gov. Michael Dukakis, Mayor Andrew Young, J. Bruce Llewellyn, Jackie Robinson for Mrs. Rachel Robinson, Dr. Arthur Logan for Marian Logan, Byard Rustin, Gov. L. Douglas Wilder, Pres. Coun. Chs. R. William David, Law office of Rosen & Shapiro, Sarasota, Law office of Shaffer Zapson, NYC, San Francisco Gen. Hosp., Singer Whitney Houston, 100 Black Women, Boston, Dr. Lorna Thomas, Former mayor of Detroit, Dennis Archer. Activie artistic development study program, Berlin; founder, pres. Fulton Ross Fund For Visual Artists, Inc., Sarasota, Fla., 1998. Recipient Atlanta Life Painters award, 1990, Artistic Achievement award, Nat. Coalition 100 Black Women, 1995, Humanitarian award, West Coast Ctr. Human Devel., 1996, Arts and Humanity award, Nat. Coalition of 100 Black Women; fellow, LaNapoule Found., 1990—92; grantee Merit Purpose award, Pollock-Krasner Found., 1993. Home: PO Box 15022 Sarasota FL 34239 Office Phone: 944-955-9881. Personal E-mail: fultonross@fultonross.com.

FULTZ, PHILIP NATHANIEL, management analyst; b. N.Y.C., Jan. 29, 1943; s. Otis and Sara Love (Gibbs) F.; m. Anita Neu, Nov. 8, 1998. AA in Bus., Coll. of the Desert, 1980; BA in Mgmt., U. Redlands, 1980, MA in Mgmt., 1982. Enlisted USMC, 1967, advanced through grades to capt., 1972, served in various locations, 1964-78, resigned commn., 1978; CETA coord. County of San Bernardino, Yucca Valley, Calif., 1978-85; mgmt. analyst Advanced Technology, Inc., Twentynine Palms, Calif., 1985-88; spl. transit analyst Omintrans, San Bernardino, Calif., 1988-89; tech. analyst Atlantic Rsch. Corp. (formerly Calculon Corp.), Twentynine Palms, Calif., 1988—; mgmt. analyst Marine Corps Base, Twentynine Palms, Calif., 1991—. Adj. asst. prof. mgmt. Chapman U., Orange, Calif., 1992—. Founding dir. Unity Home Battered Women's Shelter, Joshua Tree, Calif., 1982, Morongo Basin Adult Literacy; bd. dirs. Twentynine Palms Water Dist., 1991-95; bd. trustess Copper Mountain C.C., 1999, 2003. Mem. Rotary (sec. Joshua Tree chpt. 1983-85). Republican. Home: 73477 Desert Trail Dr Twentynine Palms CA 92277-2218 Office: Morale Walfare & Recreation Marine Corps Base Twentynine Palms CA 92277-2302 Office Phone: 760-830-6371. Personal E-mail: 4anita_phil2@verizon.net.

FULWEILER, HOWARD WELLS, language professional; b. Media, Pa., Aug. 26, 1932; s. Howard Wells and Mary Louise (Boyles) F.; m. Sally Starr Nichols, Dec. 28, 1953; children— Peter, John, Mary, Ann. Grad., Kent Sch., 1950; BA, U. S.D., 1954, MA, 1957; PhD, U. N.C., 1960. Teaching fellow U. S.D., 1956-57; teaching fellow U. N.C., 1957-59, 59-60; asst. prof. U. Mo. at Columbia, 1960-64, assoc. prof., 1964-70, prof. English, 1970—2000, chmn. dept., 1967-71, prof. emeritus, 2000—. Author: Letters from the Darkling Plain, 1972, Here a Captive Heart Busted, 1993; contbr. articles to profl. jours. Served to lt. AUS, 1954-56. Mem. Modern Lang. Assn. Am., Midwest Modern Lang. Assn., AAUP. Democrat. Episcopalian. Home: 601 S Greenwood Ave Columbia MO 65203-2768 E-mail: EulweilerH@missouri.edu.

FULWILER, ROBERT NEAL, oil industry executive; b. Belton, Tex., Nov. 5, 1937; s. Charles Calvin and Luella (Smith) F.; m. Sylvia Jean Marshall, Dec. 26, 1959; 1 child, Roger Neal. AA, Temple Jr. Coll., 1959; BBA, U. Tex., 1961. Statis. asst. Tex. Eastern Transmission Corp., Houston, 1961-62; adminstrv. asst. subs. LaGloria Oil & Gas, Houston, 1969-76, v.p., 1976; exec. v.p. La Jet, Inc., Houston, 1976-81, pres., 1981-82; chmn. bd. dirs. EnJet Inc., 1982-88; chief exec. officer Trend Energy, Houston, 1989—. Bd. dirs. BFC Assocs., Inc. Author: Competition and Growth in American Energy Markets, 1947-1985, 1968. Mem. Aspen Found., Colo. Mem. Knights of Momus., The Aspen Inst. (assoc.), Houston Mus. Fine Arts. Republican. Mem. Ch. of Christ. Office: Trend Energy 5100 Westheimer Rd Ste 200 Houston TX 77056-5597 Personal E-mail: trendenergy@sbcglobal.net.

FUNARI, ROBERT GLENN, health care services executive; b. Pitts., Sept. 20, 1947; s. Mario Ronald and Virginia Alice Funari; m. Marilyn Romcea, July 18, 1970; children: Carla Marie, Michael Anthony. BSME, Cornell U., 1969; MBA, Harvard U., 1975. Dir. distbn. Baxter Internat., Deerfield, Ill., 1977-79, v.p. materials mgmt., 1979-83; pres. Medcom, Inc., Garden Grove, Calif., 1983-86, Paramax Sys. Baxter Internat., Irvine, Calif., 1986-89; corp. v.p. and pres. Pharmaseal divsn. Baxter Internat., Valencia, Calif., 1989-93; exec. v.p., COO Syncor Internat., Woodland Hills, Calif., 1993-96, pres., CEO, 1996—2002; CEO Crescent Healthcare, 2004—. Bd. dirs. Bay Cities Nat. Bank, Redondo Beach, Calif., Cmty. First Group, English, Ind., Pope and Talbot Inc., First Consulting Group; chmn. exec. coun. Adaptive Bus. Leaders, Newport Beach, Calif., 1998-99; mem. Rand Health Bd. of Advisors. Baker scholar, 1975. Mem.: Ctr. for Corp. Innovation. Home: 25615 Melbourne Ct Calabasas CA 91302-3165 Office: 26500 W Agoura Rd Ste 102-581 Calabasas CA 91302

FUNCHION, MICHAEL F., historian, educator; b. N.Y.C., Oct. 4, 1943; s. Richard Funchion and Mary Lynch; m. Margaret Claire Bullers, July 25, 1976; children: John, Maura. BA, Iona Coll., New Rochelle, N.Y., 1966; MA, Loyola U., Chgo., 1968, PhD, 1973. Asst. prof. history S.D. State U., Brookings, 1973—76, assoc. prof. history, 1976—83, prof. history, 1983—. Author: Chicago's Irish Nationalists, 1976; editor: Irish American Voluntary Organizations, 1983; co-author: The Irish in Chicago, 1987. Mem.: Immigration History Soc., Am. Conf. Irish Studies, Orgn. Am. Historians. Democrat. Roman Catholic. Home: 1424 Wisconsin St Brookings SD 57006 Office: S D State U Box 504 Brookings SD 57007 Office Phone: 605-688-4908. Business E-Mail: Michael.Funchion@sdstate.edu.

FUNDERBURG, JAN, telecommunications industry executive; Numerous positions including operator svcs., human resources, network ops., sales, mktg. Bellsouth Corp., v.p. customer svcs., 1997—2002, pres. interconnection svcs. Atlatna, 2002—. Active Am. Cancer Soc., Woodruff Arts, Jr. Acheivement, United Way; bd. dirs. ARC Disaster Svcs. Divsn. Recipient Oustanding Woman Achievement award, YWCA, 1997, Person Yr. award, Ga. Interconnection Assn., 1988. Office: Bellsouth Corp 1155 Peachtree St NE Atlanta GA 30309-3610

FUNDERBURK, DAVID BRITTON, retired congressman, ambassador, consultant; b. Langley Field, Va., Apr. 28, 1944; married; 2 children. BA, Wake Forest Coll., 1966; MA, Wake Forest U., 1967; PhD, U. S.C., 1974. Instr. Wingate (NC) Coll., 1967—69; U. SC, Columbia, 1969—70; assoc. prof. history Hardin-Simmons U., Abilene, Tex., 1972—78; prof. history Campbell U., Buies Creek, NC, 1978—81, 1985—86; U.S. amb. to Romania Bucharest, 1981—85; cons. U.S. Dept. Edn., 1987—88; mem. Nat. Edn. Com. on Internat. Ednl. Programs, 1987—90, 104th Congress from 2nd N.C. dist., Washington, 1994—96. Candidate for U.S. Senate from N.C., 1986; exec. dir. Conservatives for Freedom Polit. Action Com., 1988-94; chmn. Internat. Romanian Relief Fund, 1990-94; mem. U.S. Congress, 1994-96; hon. consul gen. Albania for N.C. Republican. Office: 130 Canter Ln Pinehurst NC 28374 E-mail: ambromdf@aol.com.

FUNDERBURK, RAYMOND, judge; b. Phila., Mar. 2, 1944; s. Walter and Inez (Prince) F. AA, Olive-Harvey Coll., 1972; BA, U. Ill., 1974; MPA, Roosevelt U., 1975; JD, U. Ill., 1978. Bar: Ill. 1979, U.S. Dist. Ct. (no. dist.) Ill. 1979, U.S. Ct. Appeals (7th and fed. cirs.) 1983, U.S. Supreme Ct. 1983. Staff atty. Cook County Legal Assistance, Harvey, Ill., 1978-80, mng. atty., 1980-82; assoc. O. Kenneth Thomas Ltd., Harvey, 1982-83, Jones, Ware & Grenard, Chgo., 1983-88, Earl L. Neal and Assocs., Chgo., 1988-93; judge Cir. Ct. of Cook County, Chgo., Ill., 1993—. Bd. dirs. Cook County Legal Assistance Found., Oak Park, Ill., chmn. 1985-87; active legal adv. bd. Thornton Community Coll., South Holland, Ill., 1982—, Aunt Martha's Service, Park Forest, Ill., 1981-83. Chmn. Zoning Bd. of Appeals, Park Forest, 1988-99, Housing Bd. of Appeals, Park Forest, 1988-99, Equal Employment Opportunity Bd., Park Forest, 1988-99, Housing Rev. Bd., Park Forest, 1988-99; bd. dirs. Park Forest Pub. Library, 1982. Served with U.S. Army, 1965-67. Recipient Cert. of Appreciation Aunt Martha's Youth Svc., 1980, Thornton C.C., 1985, Wendell Phillips H.S., 1985, South Suburban YMCA, 1986, 1987, City Ptnr. award U. Ill. Chgo., 1995; named Disting. Grad., U. Ill. Coll. of Law, 1998-99, Olive-Harvey Jr. Coll., 2001. Mem. ABA, Chgo. Bar Assn., Cook County Bar Assn., Ill. Jud. Coun., Ill. Judges Assn., Phi Alpha Delta, Alpha Phi Alpha. Democrat. Avocations: running, chess, tennis. Office: Cir Ct of Cook County Ill Rm 2600 Richard J Daley Ctr Dearborn & Randolph Sts Chicago IL 60602

FUNDORA, THOMAS, art director, artist; b. Havana, Cuba, Mar. 7, 1935; came to U.S., 1960; s. Evangelio and Juana Evangelina (Rodriguez) F.; m. Marlene Delgado, Feb. 10, 1954 (div. June 1957). Degree in art journalism, Candler Coll., 1953; degree in modern art and restoration, Escola Arte Bologna, Italy, 1961; student, Escuela San Alejandro, Havana, 1950. Dir. gen., dir. exhbns. Fundora Gallery, Miami, Fla. Pres., bd. dirs. Song Festival, N.Y.C., Internat. Song Festival, Trujillo, Internat. Song Festival, Chiclayo, Festival of Song, Buenos Aires, Internat. Song Festival, Viña del Mar, Miami, others; former sr. v.p. Record World, Internat. Music Rev. mag.; pub., editor USA 23 Millones, Miami. Author: Union Panamericana, Washington, 1959, Galeria Duneen Graham, NYC, 1959, Condon Relley Gallery, NY, 1959, Muestra Arquitectonica Neocolonial Colegio de Arquitectos, Havana, 1959, Emociones, 1963 (award 1964), Lo Mejor de Mi Vida, 1984, Inquietudes, 1988 (award 1990), Tu y Ellos, 1989; exhbns. include Lyceum de La Havana, 1949, Asociacion de Reporters, Havana, 1954, Galeria Gratacielo, Milan, 1961, Galeria del Canale, Venice, Los Grandes de Am., Hotel Woodstock, NY, 1964, Mamma Leones Art Show, NY, 1965 (Internat. Grand prize 1966), Glovier Club, NY, 1965, Hotel Turistas, Trujillo, Peru, 1965, IRT Art Exhibit, Bklyn., 1966 (medalla de plata), Internat. Exhibition Friends of P.R., NYC, 1967, Bienal de Sao Paulo, 1967, Roland de Aenlle Gallery, NY, 1967, Cayre Art Exhibit, 1968, Inst. Arte Latino, Washington, 1968, Inst. P.R., NY, 1969, Internat. Art Gallery, Miami, 1989, Strokes and Motion of Light and Matter, Miami, 1989-90, Martin's Art Gallery, Coral Gables, Fla., 1990, Catalina Art Gallery, Kendall, Fla., 1996, 98, Domingo Padron Art Gallery, Coral Gables, 1997, Frame USA Gallery, Kendall, 1997, Izzo's Artery Gallery, Chgo., 1998, 2001, Ocean Reef Art League, Key Largo, Fla., Estefan Enterprises, Inc., Bongos Cuban Cafe, Miami, 2002, One Ear Soc. Coconut Grove Gallery, 2003, Radisson Mart Plaza Hoter, 2004. Named Artist of the Yr. Carteles Mag., 1967. Mem. Assn. Painters N.Y. (pres. 1969-73), Assn. Latin Am. Painters N.Y., Cir. Painters Miami, Monroe Coun. Arts (mem. adv. bd.), Fla. Artists Registry.com Republican. Avocations: fishing, boating, travel. Studio: 205 Camelot Dr Tavernier FL 33070-2805 Office Phone: 305-852-1516. E-mail: thomasfund@aol.com.

FUNG, FREDERICK HO, physician; b. Hong Hong, June 22, 1951; came to U.S., 1968; s. Kwai-Kuen and Yuk-Ping (Chan) F.; m. Rita Apachee, Oct. 16, 1977; children: Naomi, Adrienne, Christopher. BA, NYU, 1973, MD, 1977. Diplomate Am. Bd. Internal Medicine. Resident Long Beach (Calif.) VA Hosp., 1977-80; ptnr. Vellayan & Fung P.S.C., S. Williamson, Ky., 1980-83; staff physician, asst. med. dir. MacGregor Med. Assn., Houston, 1983—2002. Active staff Meth. Hosp., 1995-02. Contbr. article to European Jour. of Pharmacology, 1977. Mem. Am. Coll. Physician Execs., Tex. Med. Soc., Travis County Med. Soc., Phi BEta Kappa. Avocations: portrait painting, violin, photography. Office: Austin Diag Clin 12221 N Mopac Expy Austin TX 78758 Office Phone: 512-901-4009. Personal E-mail: ffung0510@hotmail.com. Business E-Mail: ffung@adclinic.com.

FUNG, JOHN JULIAN, transplant surgeon, immunologist; b. Bethlehem, Pa., July 9, 1956; s. Sui-An and Shu-Nung (Wu) F.; m. Beth Ann Loftus, 1986; children: Justin, Lauren, Brendan, Shannon. BS, Johns Hopkins U., 1975; PhD, U. Chgo., 1980, MD, 1982. Diplomate Am. Bd. Surgery. Gen. surg. resident U. Rochester, N.Y., 1982-84; chief resident, transplant fellow U. Pitts., 1984-86; chief resident U. Rochester, 1986-88, dir. histocompatibility, 1987-88; from instr. surgery to prof. U. Pitts., 1989—99, prof. surgery, 1999—2004; chmn. Dept. Gen. Surgery Cleve. (Ohio) Clinic, 2004—. Mem. sci. adv. bd. Astella Healthcare Bd. dirs. Family House, Pitts., 1993-2004, Nat. Kidney Found., 1994—2004, Lt. col. USAR, 1987-2003, Desert Storm. Recipient Sci. Rsch. award Ortho Biotech, 1988, Outstanding Abstract award Transplant Soc., 1990, Nat. Kidney Found. award, 1994, Vectors Man of Yr. in Sci., 1997, award Am. Liver Found., 1997. Fellow ACS; mem. AMA, Am. Soc. Transplant Surgeons, Am. Assn. Study Liver Diseases, Internat. Soc. Liver Transplantation (councilor 1993, pres. 1997-99), Am. Surgical Assn. Presbyterian. Achievements include use of OKT3 with Cyclosporine in treatment of rejection; use of FK506 in organ transplantation; clinical attempts at baboon to human transplantation. Home: 65 Winding River Trail Chagrin Falls OH 44022 Office: Dept Gen Surgery Cleveland Clin Found 9500 Euclid Ave A80 Cleveland OH 44195 Office Phone: 216-444-3776. Business E-Mail: fungj@ccf.org.

FUNG, PAUL, JR., cartoonist, illustrator; b. Seattle, Mar. 9, 1923; s. Paul Fung and Mabel Seung; m. Carol Lorraine M. Fung; children: Lorraine Mae Gardephe, Paul Randall. BA, Pratt Inst., Bklyn., 1946. Artist Richard & Gunther Advt. Agy., N.Y.C., 1947-48; artist, prodn. mgr. Dowd, Redfield, Johnstone Advt. Agy., N.Y.C., 1947-48; prodn. mgr. Theatre Arts Mag., N.Y.C., 1947-49; cartoonist King Features Syndicate, N.Y.C., 1949-79, Pines Pub. Co., N.Y.C., 1948-49, Charlton Pub. Co., Derby, Conn., 1960-78, Western Printing & Pub. Co., N.Y.C., 1968-72. Writer, illustrator more than 492 Blondie and Hong Kong Phooey comic books, illustrator (prin. works) Blondie, Bulwinkle and Rocky, George of the Jungle, Hong Kong Phooey; exhibitions include Libr. Congress, Washington, Smithsonian Inst., Mus. Modern Art, N.Y.C., N.Y.C. Libr., Internat. Mus. Cartoon, Boca Raton, Fla., Cartoon Art Mus., Chgo., San Francisco, Orlando, Fla., Ohio State U. Art Libr. With USAF, 1941—46. Recipient medal, ASPCA, 1934. Mem.: Nat. Cartoonist Soc. (Best Comic Book Cartoonist of the Yr. 1964, Best Comic Book Humorist 1980), Masons (freelance artist 1969—), Lions (dir. Greenwich N.Y. chpt. 1968—2000, 30 Yr. award 1999). Republican. Episcopalian. Avocations: cooking, gardening, hunting, fishing, swimming. Home: 227 Langley Hill Rd Greenwich NY 12834 Office Phone: 518-695-7591.

FUNG, YUAN-CHENG BERTRAM, bioengineering educator, writer; b. Yuhong, Changchow, Kiangsu, China, Sept. 15, 1919; arrived in U.S., 1945, naturalized, 1957; s. Chung-Kwang and Lien (Hu) F.; m. Luna Hsien-Shih Yu, Dec. 22, 1949; children: Conrad Antung, Brenda Pingsi. BS, Nat. Ctrl. U., Chungking, China, 1941, MS, 1943, DSc (hon.), 2002; PhD, Calif. Inst. Tech., 1948; DSc (hon.), Hong Kong U. Sci. and Tech., 1992, Drexel U., 2001, Sichuan U., 2002, Nat. Cheng Kung U., 2003, Northwestern U., 2004. Rsch. fellow Bur. Aero. Rsch. China, 1943-45; rsch. asst., then rsch. fellow Calif. Inst. Tech., 1946-51, mem. faculty, 1951-66, prof. aerospace, 1959-66; prof. bioengring. and applied mechanics U. Calif., San Diego, 1966—2000, prof. emeritus bioengring., 2000—. Cons. aerospace indsl. firms, 1949—; hon. prof. 15 univs., China; hon. chair World Coun. Biomechanics, 1998. Author: The Theory of Aeroelasticity, 1955, 69, 93, Foundations of Solid Mechanics, 1965, A First Course in Continuum Mechanics, 1969, 77, 93, Biomechanics, 1972, Biomechanics: Mechanical Properties of Living Tissues, 1980, 1993, Biodynamics: Circulation, 1984, Biomechanics: Circulation, 1996, Biomechanics: Motion, Flow, Stress and Growth, 1990, Selected Works on Biomechanics and Aeroelasticity by Y.C. Fung, 1997, Classical and Computational Solid Mechanics, 2001, Introduction to Bioengineering, 2001; also papers; editor Jour. Biorheology, Jour. Biomech. Engring. Hon. bd. trustees Chongqing U.; hon. chair, bd. trustees Nanjing U., China. Recipient Achievement award Chinese Inst. Engrs., 1965, 68, 93, Lifetime Achievement award of Asian Ams. in Engring., 2004; Landis award Microcirculatory Soc., 1975, Poiseuille medal Internat. Soc. Biorheology, 1986, Engr. of Yr. award San Diego Engring. Soc., 1986, von Karman medal ASCE, 1976, ALZA award Biomed. Engring. Soc., 1989, Borelli award Am. Soc. Biomechanics, 1992; Guggenheim fellow, 1958-59, Founders award, NAE U.S., 1998, U.S. Nat. Medal of Sci., 2000. Fellow AIAA, ASME (hon., Lissner award 1978, Centennial medal 1978, Worcester Reed Warner medal 1984, Timoshenko medal 1991, Melville medal 1994); mem. Japan Soc. Mech. Engrs. (Bioengring. award 1995), NAS, NAE, Inst. Medicine, Soc. Engring. Sci., Microcirculatory Soc., Am. Physiol. Soc., Nat. Heart Assn., Acad. Sinica, Chinese Acad. Scis. (fgn. mem.), Basic Sci. Coun., Sigma Xi. Home: 2660 Greentree Ln La Jolla CA 92037-1148 Office: U Calif Dept Bioengring 9500 Gilman Dr La Jolla CA 92093-0412

FUNG-CHEN-PEN, EMMA TALAUNA SOLAITA, librarian, program director; b. Pago Pago, Am. Samoa, Sept. 4, 1951; d. Talauna and Ema (Tauoa) S.; m. Su'a oelu T. Fung-Chen-Pen, Nov 1, 1971; children: John Kevin, Juliet Ruth, Jacqueline Josie, Jennifer Lorna, Jonathan Emosi. AA Gen. Edn., Am. Samoa C. C., 1973, AS Libr. Studies, 1974; BA, Brigham Young U., Honolulu, 1977; MS in Librarianship, U. Hawaii, 1979. Libr. clerk Libr. Svcs., Pago Pago, 1971-74, libr. technician, 1974-76, libr. II, 1976-79, program dir., 1980—. Sec. Seventh Day Adventist Leone (Am. Samoa) Ch., 1990-94; dir. Seventh Day Adventist Leone Pathfinder, 1993—; pres. Parent-Tchr. Assn.-Sch., 2000-; active SDA Sch. Bd., 1991-98, mem. exec. bd. Samoa Mission, 1999-; mem. libr. bd. Feleti Barstow Pub., 2000-; mem. Samoa bd. dirs., coun. Read to Me, 1998-; mem. TV ministry bd. Leone SDA Ch., 1999-. Avocations: volleyball, reading, walking. Home: PO Box 1952 Pago Pago AS 96799-1952 Office: Am Samoa-Office of Lib Svcs PO Box 1329 Pago Pago AS 96799-1329

FUNK, ALICE MARIE, elementary school educator; b. Harrisburg, Pa., Aug. 25, 1947; d. Whalen Frank Seagrist and Mildred Elsie Phillips Seagrist; m. Charles Edward Funk Jr., Aug. 10, 1968; children: Clinton Eric, Celene Erika. BS, Shippensburg U., 1968, MEd, 1971; posgrad., Millersville U., 2005—. Tchr. Ctrl. Dauphin Sch. Dist., Harrisburg, Pa., 1968—71, Messiah Luth. Ch., Halifax, 1979—80, Halifa Area Sch. Dist., 1980—. Mem. social studies task force Halifax Area Sch. Dist., 1990—. Mem. No. Dauphin County Arts Alliance, Harrisburg, 1995—; mem. libr. bd. Dauphin County Libr. Sys., 1985—, pres., 1988—89; mem. Halifax Area Garden Club, 1995—, Halifax Hist. Soc., 1985—, Ladies Aux. VFW, 1995—, Ned Smith Sci. and Nature Ctr., 2000—, Cmtys. That Care, 2000—. Mem.: NEA, Pa. State Edn. Assn. (bldg. rep. 1996—). Office: Halifax Area Elem Sch 3940 Peters Mountain Rd Halifax PA 17032-9505 Home: 1556 Armstrong Valley Rd Halifax PA 17032

FUNK, CARLA JEAN, library association director; b. Wheeling, W.Va., Sept. 21, 1946; d. David H. and Jean (Duffy) Belt. BA in Psychology, Northwestern U., 1968; MLS, Ind. U., 1973; MBA, U. Chgo., 1985. Libr. adult svcs. Northbrook (Ill.) Pub. Libr., 1973-77; dir. Warren-Newport Pub. Libr. Dist., Gurnee, Ill., 1977-80; cons. Suburban Libr. Sys., Burr Ridge, Ill., 1980-83; dir. automation and tech. svcs., med. student svcs. AMA, Chgo., 1983-92; exec. dir. Med. Libr. Assn., Chgo., 1992—. Adj. faculty Dominican U., 1986—2000. Contbr. articles to profl. jours. Mem. Internat. Fedn. Libr. Assns. and Insts. (treas., mgmt. libr. assn. sec.), Am. Soc. Assn. Execs. (cert. assn. exec.), Assn. Forum of Chicagoland, Beta Phi Mu, Phi Delta Zeta. Office: 65 E Wacker Pl Ste 1900 Chicago IL 60601-7246 Business E-Mail: funk@mlahq.org.

FUNK, CYRIL REED, JR., agronomist, educator; b. Richmond, Utah, Sept. 20, 1928; s. Cyril Reed and Hazel Marie (Jensen) F.; m. Donna Gwen Buttars, Feb. 2, 1951; children: Bonnie Arlene, David Christopher, Carol Jean. BS (Scholarship A 1955), Utah State U., 1952, MS, 1955; PhD, Rutgers U., 1961; DAgr (hon.), Utah State U., 1994. Mem. faculty Rutgers U., New Brunswick, NJ, 1956—, rsch. prof. turfgrass breeding plant biology and pathology dept., 1969—, also instr. grad. faculty. Author, patentee in field. Served to 1st lt. AUS, 1952-54. Recipient Green Sect. award U.S. Golf Assn., 1980, Achievement award Lawn Inst., 1977; named to Hall of Disting. Alumni, Rutgers U. Fellow Crop Sci. Soc. Am., Am. Soc. Agronomy (research award N.E. sect. 1979); mem. AAAS (fellow 1992), Am. Sod Producers Assn. (hon.), Golf Course Supts. Assn. (hon. mem.; Disting. Service award 1979), Internat. Turfgrass Soc., N.J. Turfgrass Assn. (Achievement award 1976, Hall of Fame award 1984), N.J. Golf Course Supts. Assn. (hon.), N.J. Acad. Scis., Sigma Xi, Phi Kappa Phi, Acad. Scis. Uzbekistan (hon.), Acad. Agrl. Scis. Kyrgyzstan (hon.). Mem. Lds Ch. Achievements include developing numerous turfgrasses. Home: 4 Delaware Dr East Brunswick NJ 08816-3255 Office: Rutgers U Cook Coll New Brunswick NJ 08901 Personal E-mail: reedonna1@comcast.net.

FUNK, DAVID ALBERT, retired law educator; b. Wooster, Ohio, Apr. 22, 1927; s. Daniel Coyle and Elizabeth Mary (Reese) F.; children— Beverly Joan, Susan Elizabeth, John Ross, Carolyn Louise; m. Sandra Nadine Henselmeier, Oct. 2, 1976 Student, U. Mo., 1945—46, Harvard Coll., 1946; BA in Econs., Coll. of Wooster, 1949; MA, Ohio State U., 1968; JD, Case Western Res. U., 1951, LLM, 1972, Columbia U., 1973. Bar: Ohio 1951, U.S. Dist. Ct. (no. dist.) Ohio 1962, U.S. Tax Ct. 1963, U.S. Ct. Appeals (6th cir.) 1970, U.S. Supreme Ct. 1971. Ptnr. Funk, Funk & Eberhart, Wooster, Ohio, 1951-72; assoc. prof. law Ind. U. Sch. Law, Indpls., 1973-76, prof., 1976-97, prof. emeritus, 1997—. Vis. lectr. Coll. of Wooster, 1962-63; dir. Juridical Sci. Inst., Indpls., 1982—. Author: Oriental Jurisprudence, 1974, Group Dynamic Law, 1982; (with others) Rechtsgeschichte und Rechtssoziologie, 1985, Group Dynamic Law: Exposition and Practice, 1988; contbr. articles to profl. jours. Chmn. bd. trustees Wayne County Law Library Assn., 1956-71; mem. Permanent Jud. Commn., Synod of Ohio, United Presbyn. Ch. in the U.S., 1968. Served to seaman 1st class USNR, 1945-46 Harlan Fiske Stone fellow Columbia U., 1973; recipient Am. Jurisprudence award in Comparative Law, Case Western Res. U., 1970 Mem. Assn. Am. Law Schs. (sec. comparative law sect. 1977-79, chmn. law and religion sect. 1977-81, sec.-treas. law and social sci. sect. 1983-86), Pi Sigma Alpha. Republican. Home: 6208 N Delaware St Indianapolis IN 46220-1824

FUNK, JAMES WILLIAM, JR., insurance agency administrator, business owner; b. Vincennes, Ind., May 31, 1947; s. James William and Elizabeth (Bauer) F.; m. Janis Burrell, Aug. 11, 1973; children: Christopher James, Kelly Elizabeth. BA, Butler U., Indpls., 1969. Cert. ins. counselor, 1991, cert. profl. ins. agt., 1999; chartered property casuality underwriter, 2002. Mem. campaign staff U.S. Senator Birch Bayh, Indpls., 1968; bus. cons. Dun & Bradstreet, Inc., Indpls., 1969-71; dir. ops. Terry Properties, Inc., Springfield, Ill., 1971-72; pers. mgr. Am. Underwriters, Inc., Indpls., 1972-73, adminstrv. asst. to pres., 1973-75, asst. sec., 1975-78, v.p. pub. rels., 1978-79; adminstrv. mgr. Affiliated Agys., Inc., Indpls., 1979-93; ind. agt., v.p., sec. Ctrl. Ins. Assocs., Inc., 1993-98, pres., 1999—. Owner Bauer Bros. Exploration Co.; lectr., instr. A.D. Banker Co., 1997-2001 Sec., treas. Ctrl. North Civic Assn., Indpls., 1976, pres. 1977-78; bd. dirs. Ind. Amateur Baseball Assn., 1993—, sec. 1999; active Bishop Chatard H.S. PTO, 1995-97, pres. 1997—; bd. dirs. Clearwater Cove Homeowners Assn., 1999-2000, pres., 2000. Mem. Ind. Soc. Chgo., Profl. Ins. Agts Ind. (v.p. 1984-85, pres. 1986-87, chmn. legis. com., treas. polit. action com., bd. dirs. 1982-88, 99—, pres.-elect 2002, pres. 2003, 04, agt. of yr. 1990, 2005, v.p. 2001—, apptd. by gov. to Ind. ins. continuing edn. com., 2003-2005), Preussian Benefit Soc., Heimaths Benefit Soc., Butler Univ. Pres.'s Club, K.C. Roman Catholic. Home: 6491 N Sherman Dr Indianapolis IN 46220 Office: 8900 Keystone Crossing Ste 450 Indianapolis IN 46240 Personal E-mail: jwfunkjr@aol.com.

FUNK, SHERMAN MAXWELL, former government official, writer, consultant; b. N.Y.C., Nov. 13, 1925; s. Bernard and Dorothy (Arkin) F.; m. Elaine Myrl Bayer, Mar. 6, 1953 (dec. 1977); children: Katherine Sara, Bernard Eugene; m. Sylvia Grunbaum Straka, June 3, 1978; children Eric, Marc, Paul. AB, Harvard U., 1950; postgrad., Columbia U., 1956, U. Ariz., 1958. Salesman, sales exec. Bernard Funk Co., N.Y.C., 1950-54; history tchr. Catskill (N.Y.) High Sch., 1954-57; polit. sci. teaching asst. U. Ariz., Tucson, 1957-58; mgmt. intern USAF Hdqrs., Washington, 1958, war planning officer, mgmt. analyst, 1958-63, chief Air Force Mgmt. Improvement Programs Office, 1963-67, chief Air Force Cost Reduction Office, 1967-70; successively asst. dir. adminstrn. and program devel., dir. rsch. and program devel., asst. dir. planning and evaluation Office Minority Bus. Enterprise, Dept. Commerce, 1970-79; spl. asst. for small bus. Dept. Energy, 1979-81; insp. gen. Dept. Commerce, 1981-87, Dept. State, 1987-94, adviser to fgn. govts. on anti-corruption efforts, 1994—; vice chmn. Pres.'s Coun. on Integrity and Efficiency, 1989-90. TV commentator. Contbr. articles to profl. jours., major newspapers. Mem. Bowie City Council, (Md.), 1963-65, chmn. human relations com., 1964-65, chmn. charter rev. com., 1968; pres. Bethesda Jewish Congregation, 1986. Served with inf. AUS, 1943-46. Decorated Purple Heart; recipient Presdl. Unit Citation, spl. award Sec. Air Force, 1968, prizes Washington-Md.-Del Press Assn., 1970, 71, 73, 75, Silver medal Commerce Dept., 1972, Disting. honor award State Dept., 1992. Mem. Fed. Investigators Assn. Mailing: 2982 Salem Dr Ann Arbor MI 48103-6811 E-mail: smfunk@comcast.net. *My years in government were marked by paradox: I worked with some extraordinarily able people and with important and challenging programs. Yet I increasingly came to doubt the ability of these and other federal programs to solve many national ills. Too many of them are subverted externally by political pork and internally by waste, fraud and don't-rock-the boat thinking. As an Inspector General, under three pres., I tried to fight such abuse, and to help change the poor image of federal service-both appointive and career-which scares off exactly the kind of bright and aggressive talent needed in government. As a private citzen now, free of the constraints levied on appointees, I shall continue this fight with redoubled vigor.*

FUNK, VICKI JANE, librarian; b. Frankfurt am Main, Hesse, Federal Republic of Germany, Apr. 7, 1951; d. George N. and Maymie Lou Funk; m. David Robert Koble, July 11, 1986. BS, Ind. State U., 1971; MLS, Okla. U., 1975; cert. in comparative libraries, Oxford U., Eng., Summer 1978; cert. in Scottish lit., St. Andrews U., Scotland, Summer 1985. Elem. open concept team tchr. Plainfield (Ind.) Pub. Schs., 1971-72; media specialist, tchr. elem. schs. Enid (Okla.) Pub. Schs., 1972-73, librarian, 1973-74; libr. media specialist Bartlesville (Okla.) Sr. H.S., 1975-96. Chmn. library evaluation teams North Cen. Assn., Okla., 1982-86; pres. V.I.E.W. adv. bd. Okla. State Dept. Vocat. Edn., 1980-81; tchr. pub. library continuing adult edn. program, Bartlesville, 1986. Storyteller Ednl. TV Bartlesville Cable, 1975-77, Oral Children's Program Pub. Library, 1985-86; book reviewer Okla. State Dept. Libraries "Gushers and Dusters", 1986-87; mem. book rev. selection com. Bartlesville Pub. Library. V.P. Friends of the Pub. Library, Bartlesville, 1986. Recipient Outstanding Svc. award Okla. Dept. Vocat. Edn., 1981; Emiline Libr. scholar Ind. State U., 1970; Innovative Edn. grantee Bartlesville Pub. Edn. Found., 1990, 91. Mem. NEA, AAUW (edn. officer 1980-81), Okla. Edn. Assn., Bartlesville Edn. Assn., Bartlesville Art Assn., Okla. Libr. Assn., Kappa Kappa Iota (v.p. 1990-91, secd. 1996-98). Democrat. Presbyterian. Avocations: bridge, travel, skiing, acting, painting.

FUNK, WILLIAM HENRY, retired environmental engineering educator; b. Ephraim, Utah, June 10, 1933; s. William George and Henrietta (Hackwell) F.; m. Ruth Sherry Mellor, Sept. 19, 1964 (dec.); 1 dau., Cynthia Lynn; m. Lynn Bridget Robson, Mar. 30, 1996. BS in Biol. Sci, U. Utah, 1955, MS in Zoology, 1963, PhD in Limnology, 1966. Tchr. sci., math. Salt Lake City Schs., 1957-60; research asst. U. Utah, Salt Lake City, 1961-63; head sci. dept. N.W. Jr. High Sch., Salt Lake City, 1961-63; mem. faculty Wash. State U., Pullman, 1966-99, assoc. prof. environ. engring., 1971-75, prof., 1975-99, chmn. environ. sci./regional planning program, 1979-81; dir. Environ. Research Center, 1980-83, State of Wash. Water Research Ctr., 1981-99; ret., 1999. Cons. U.S. Army C.E., Walla Walla, Wash., 1970—74, Harstad Engrs., Seattle, 1971—72, Boise Cascade Corp., Seattle, 1971—72, Wash. Dept. Ecology, Olympia, 1971—72, ORB Corp., Renton, Wash., 1972—73, U.S. Civil Svc., Seattle, Chgo., 1972—74; mem. High Level Nuclear Waste Bd., Wash., 1986—89, Wash. 2010 Com., 1989, Pure Water 2000 Steering Com., 1990; co-dir. Inst. Resource Mgmt.; co-founder Terrene Inst., Washington, 1991, pres., 1993—2002. Author publs. on water pollution control and lake restoration. Served to capt. USNR, 1955-88. Grantee NSF Summer Inst., 1961, U.S. Army C.E., 1970-74, 94-96, 97-98, Office Water Resources Rsch., 1971-72, 73-76, EPA, 1980-83, 93-94, 95-96, U.S. Geol. Survey, 1983-94, 95-96, 97-98, 99-00, Nat. Parks Svc., 1985-87, Colville Confederated Tribes, 1990-92, Nez Pierce Tribe, 1992-95, Wash. Conservation Commn., 1992-95, Clearwater Co., 1992-93, Idaho Dept. Environ. Quality, 1995-96, U.S. Bur. Reclamation, 1995-98; USPHS fellow, 1963; recipient Pres.'s Disting. Faculty award Wash. State U., 1984. Mem. Naval Res. Officers Assn. (chpt. pres. 1969), Res Officers Assn. (U.S. Naval Acad. info. officer 1973-76), N.Am. Lake Mgmt. Soc. (pres. 1984-85, Secchi Disk award 1988), Pacific N.W. Pollution Control Assn. (editor 1969-77, pres.-elect 1982-83, pres. 1983-84), Water Pollution Control Fedn. (Arthur S. Bedell award Pacific N.W. assn. 1976, nat. bd. dirs. 1978-81, bd. dirs. Rsch. Found. 1990-92), Nat. Assn. Water Inst. Dirs. (chair 1985-87, bd. dirs. univ. council on water resources 1986-89), Wash. Lakes Protection Assn. (co-founder 1986, Friend of Lakes award 1999), Am. Water Resources Assn. (v.p. Wash. sect. 1988), Am. Soc. Limnology and Oceanography, Am. Micros. Soc., N.W. Sci. Assn., North Am. Lake Mgmt. Soc. (co-founder 1972), Sigma Xi, Phi Sigma. Home: 202 W 200 S Manti UT 84642-1309 Personal E-mail: wfwhf@mail.manti.com.

FUNSETH, ROBERT LLOYD ERIC MARTIN, political scientist, consultant, retired diplomat, foundation administrator; b. International Falls, Minn., May 10, 1926; s. Martin Emmanuel and Agnes Evangeline (Guibault) F.; m. Marilyn Ann Schuelke, Mar. 23, 1957; 1 child, Eric Christian. BA, Hobart Coll., 1948, postgrad., 1950-51, Cornell U., 1950, 51, Sch. Advanced Internat. Studies, Johns Hopkins U., 1951-52; MS, George Washington U., 1969; LL.D, Hobart and William Smith Colls., 1978. Editor Coachella Desert Barnacle, (Calif.), 1948; mng. editor Anaheim Gazette, (Calif.), 1948-50; corr. AP, 1950; resident tutor Hobart Coll., 1950-51; info. officer U.S. Mut. Security Agy., 1952-53; editor USIA, 1953-54; joined U.S. Fgn. Service, 1954; advanced to rank of minister-counselor Career Sr. Fgn. Service; vice consul Tehran, Tabriz, Azerbaijan and Kurdistan, Iran, 1954-56; 3d sec. Am. embassy, Beirut, 1957-59; UN polit. affairs officer Dept. State, 1959-61; Am. consul (Bordeaux), France, 1961-64; Portuguese desk officer Dept. State, Washington, 1964-66; mem. U.S. del. 20th UN Gen. Assembly, 1965; dep. dir. Iberian affairs Dept. State, 1966-68; assigned to Nat. War Coll., 1968-69; dir. mgmt. U.S. diplomatic and consular posts Dept. State, Mex. and Central Am., 1969-70, coordinator Cuban affairs, 1970-72, sr. fgn. service insp., 1972-73; counselor Am. embassy, Ottawa, Ont., Can., 1973-74; dep. dept. spokesman and dir. office of press relations Dept. State, Washington, 1974-75, dept. spokesman and spl. asst. to sec. of state for press relations, 1975-77, dir. office No. European affairs, 1977-82, dep. asst. sec. for refugee resettlement, 1982-83, sr. dep. asst. sec. Bur. Refugee Programs, 1983-91, cons., 1991—; trustee, pres. Diplomatic and Consular Officers Ret.-Bacon House Found., Washington. Detailed to U.S. Falkland Island Peace Mission to London and Buenos Aires, 1982; vis. disting. alumni scholar in residence Hobart and William Smith Colls., 1978, Nat. Cathedral Assn.; vis. fellow Woodrow Wilson Found., Princeton, NJ; lectr. Am. studies U. Tabriz, 1955-56; mem. numerous U.S. Delegations, 1976-89 including NATO Ministerial Meetings in Ottawa, Brussels, Oslo, U.S. China Consultations, Beijing, former Pres. Ford's 1975 visit to Philippines, OECD, Paris, SALT, Moscow, U.S.-So. Africa Initiative, Nairobi, Dar es Salam, Lusaka, Kinshasa, Monrovia, Dakar, UN Trade and Devel. Conf., Kenya, OAS Ministerial Meeting, Santiago, Chile, 1976 econ. summit former Pres. Ford Puerto Rico, 1st U.S. South African Ministerial meeting, Grafenau, Germany, U.S.-Iran Joint Commn., Tehran, U.S. Bilateral Consultations with Afghanistan and Pakistan, 1976 Inauguration Mexican Pres. Lopez-Portillo; head U.S. dels. U.S.-Vietnamese Refugee Consultations, Geneva, Switzerland, 1982-90; head U.S. del., U.S.-Vietnamese negotiations, Resettlement Vietnamese Polit. Prisoners, Hanoi, Vietnam, 1988, 89, 2d internat. conf. Indochinese Refugees, Geneva, 1989. U.S. observer Internat. Cath. Migration Commn. Conf., Vatican City, 1990; bd. dirs. Episcopal Ch. Presiding Bishop's Fund for World Relief; mem. peace commn. Episcopal Diocese of Washington. Lt. (j.g.) USNR, 1943—46, PTO. Recipient Outstanding Service commendation Am. Forces Spl. Command, Middle East, 1958, Disting. and Superior Honor Group awards Dept. State, 1959, 61, 70, Superior Honor award Dept. State, 1977, Sesquicentennial award Hobart Coll., 1972, Presdl. honor awards Sr. Fgn. Svc., 1986, 88, 91, Disting. Honor award Dept. State, 1989, Resolutions of Commendation Calif. State Senate, 1989, 91, Wilbur Carr disting. svc. award Dept. State, 1991, medal of excellence Hobart Coll. Alumni Assn., 1997, Hero of the Vietnamese Polit. Prisoners award Fedn. U.S. Assns. Vietnamese Polit. Prisoners, 1999, Disting. Svc. award, 2005, Mil. Order of Caraboo Disting. Svc. award, 2005 Mem.: Johns Hopkins Alumni Assn. (exec. coun. 1968—70), Diplomatic and Consular Officers Ret. (bd. govs. 1999—, v.p. 2001—03, pres. 2003—, sec., pres. Dacor-Bacon House Found.), Assn. Diplomatic Studies, Am. Fgn. Svc. Assn., Journalism Soc. (hon.), Mil. Order of Carabao, Nat. War Coll. Alumni Assn., Sch. Advanced Studies Alumni Assn. (mem. adv. coun. 1969, 1970, pres.), Hobart Coll. Alumni Assn. (medal of excellence 1997), George Washington U. Alumni Assn., Ebenezer Sch. Alumni Assn., West Seneca (N.Y.) Hist. Soc., Am. Fgn. Svc. Club, Phi Delta, Phi Sigma Kappa. Office Phone: 202-682-0500 x10. Personal E-mail: dacor@dacorbacon.org.

FUQUA, CHARLES JOHN, classicist, educator; b. Paris, Oct. 5, 1935; s. John Howe and Gillian Elynor (Quennell) F.; m. Mary Louise Morse, Aug. 26, 1961; children— Andrew Morse, David Reed, Gillian Quennell. BA magna cum laude, Princeton, 1957; MA, Cornell U., 1962, PhD, 1964. Instr. classics Dartmouth Coll., Hanover, NH, 1964, asst. prof., 1965-66; assoc. prof. classics, chmn. dept. classics Williams Coll., Williamstown, Mass., 1966-72, Garfield prof. ancient langs., chmn. dept. classics, 1972-86; ret., 2003. Mem. adv. council Am. Acad. in Rome, 1966, chmn. exec. com., 74. Served to lt. (j.g.) USNR, 1957-60. Mem.: Vergilian Soc., Classical Assn. Mass., Classical Assn. New Eng., Am. Philol. Assn., Phi Beta Kappa, Phi Kappa Phi. Home: 96 Grandview Dr Williamstown MA 01267-2528 Personal E-mail: charles.fuqua@verizon.net.

FUQUA, JOHN BROOKS, retired consumer products and services company executive; b. Prince Edward County, Va., June 26, 1918; s. J.B. Elam and Ruth F.; m. Dorothy Chapman, Feb. 10, 1945; 1 son, John Rex. Grad. high sch., Prospect, Va.; LLD (hon.), Hampden-Sydney Coll., 1972, Duke U., 1973, Fla. Meml. Coll., 1982, Oglethorpe U., 1986; LHD (hon.), Queens Coll., 1987, Longwood Coll., 1990; LLD (hon.), U. Tulsa, 1991, Mercer U., 1991; DHL (hon.), Queens Coll., Charlotte, 1995; D in Adminstrn. (hon.), Cumberland Coll., 1995. Chmn. Fuqua Industries, Inc., Atlanta, 1965-89. Mem. adv. bd. Norfolk So. Corp.; established Ctr. for USSR Mgr. Devel., tng. program for top Soviet mgrs. at Fuqua Sch. Bus. Duke U., 1990. Author: Fuqua-A Memoir, 2002. Mem. Augusta Aviation Commn., 1945-67; past mem., fin. chmn. Augusta Hosp. Authority; past mem. Ga. Sci. and Tech. Commn.; mem. Ga. Ho. of Reps., 1957-62, chmn. House Banking Com., 1959-63; mem. Ga. Senate, 1963-65, chmn. Senate Banking and Fin. Com., Dem. Party and Exec. Com. Ga., 1962-66; bd. visitors Emory U., 1970-76; former mem. adv. council Ga. State U.; former trustee Ga. State U. Found.; trustee Duke U., 1974-87; trustee Hampden-Sydney Coll., 1976-91; bd. dirs. Horatio Alger Assn. Disting. Americans; bd. dirs. Lyndon B. Johnson Found; bd. visitors Fuqua Sch. Bus., Duke U.; past dir. Atlanta C. of C.; donor $10 million to found Fuqua Sch. Bus., Duke U., 1980, $5.5 million to build the Dorothy Chapman Fuqua Conservatory, Atlanta Bot. Gardens, 1989, $10 million to establish Fuqua Sch., Va., 1993, $3 million to establish the Fuqua Heart Ctr. of Atlanta at Piedmont Hosp., 1995, $1.5 million to Atlanta Com. for Spl. Games, 1996, $4 million to Jr. Achievment Internat., 2001, $1 million to PACE Acad., Atlanta, 2002, $1 million to The Wesley Woods Found., 2002, $1 million to The Nuc. Threat Initiative, 2002; established Fuqua Internat. Christian Comm., Crystal Cathedral, 1991, Fuqua Orchid Ctr. for Conservation and Edn., 1997, Fuqua Ctr. Late-Life Depression at Wesley Woods Geriatric Ctr., 1997, J.B. Fuqua chair pub. speaking, Pace Acad., 1999. Recipient Horatio Alger award, 1984, award U. Pa. Wharton Grad. Sch. Bus., 1985, Disting. Entrepreneurship award, 1985, Free Enterprise medal Entrepreneur of Yr. Shenandoah Coll., 1991, Pinnacle award Sales and Mktg. Execs. Internat. Acad. Achievement, 1993, Fellow of the Coll. award Capitol Coll., 1994, Shining Light award Atlanta Gas Light & WSB, 2000, Disting. Georgian award Augusta State U., 2002, Philanthropist of the Yr. award Bus. to Bus. Mag., 2003; named Boss of Yr. Augusta Jaycees, 1960, Broadcaster-Citizen of Yr. Ga. Assn. Broadcasters, 1963, Broadcast Pioneer of Yr., 1979, Outstanding Bus. Leader Northwood Inst., 1986, Mktg. Statesman Sales and Mktg. Execs. Internat., 1986, Bus. Statesman Harvard Bus. Sch. Club Met. Atlanta, 1987, Georgian of Yr., 1989, Philanthropist of Yr. Ga. chpt. Nat. Soc. Fund Raising Execs., 1989, Philanthropist of Yr. Nat. Assn. Fund Raising Execs., 1993, Entrepreneur of Yr. Stanford Bus. Sch. Alumni Assn., 1992; The Fuqua Heart Ctr. of Atlanta at Piedmont Hosp. named in his honor; inducted into J. Mack Robinson Coll. of Bus. Hall of Fame, Ga. State U., 2001, Atlanta Bus. Hall of Fame, Jr. Achievement Ga., 2002, Bus. Hall of Fame, Jr. Achievement Nat., 2002. Mem.: Chief Exec. Orgn. Home: 3574 Tuxedo Rd NW Atlanta GA 30305-1049 Office: The Fuqua Cos 1201 W Peachtree St NW Ste 5000 Atlanta GA 30309-3467

FURASH, EDWARD ELLIOTT, investment company executive, banker, educator, writer, theater producer; b. Boston, Oct. 31, 1934; s. Moses Harry Furash and Sara (Jacobs) Dorfman; m. Elizabeth Louise Wilson, Jan. 2, 1959; children: Jennifer Lee, Jonathan Wilson, James Shortlidge. AB magna cum laude, Harvard Coll., 1956; MBA, U. Pa., 1958; postgrad., Harvard Bus. Sch., Boston, 1959-67. Rsch. asst. Harvard Grad. Sch. Bus., Boston, 1958-59; asst. editor Harvard Bus. Review, Boston, 1959-62; instr. bus. adminstrn. Harvard Grad. Sch. Bus., Boston, 1961-62; sec. com. on space Am. Acad. Arts & Scis., Boston, 1962-64; sr. staff assoc., bus. mgr. Arthur D. Little, Inc., Cambridge, Mass., 1964-67; v.p. mktg. Nat. Shawmut Bank Boston, 1967-72, sr. v.p. mktg., 1972-74; sr. v.p. corp. planning Shawmut Corp. Boston, 1972-78; mng. dir. Golembe Assocs., Washington, 1978-80; chmn. Furash & Co., Washington, 1980-98; vice chmn. dir. Headway Corp. Resources, Inc., N.Y.C., 1995-98; CEO Furash Holdings, Washington, 1994-2000; chmn. Monument Fin. Group, Alexandria, Va., 1999—, Effinity Fin. Corp., Alexandria, 1999—2003, Treasury Bank, 2000—03. Bd. dirs. Inova Alexandria Hosp. Found., Metrostage, Pa. Bus. Bank, City First Bank, Washington, Online Resources; interviewed on TV ABC, CBS, CNBC, PBS; lectr. Williams Sch. of Banking, 1974—78, Am. Inst. Banking, 1968—98, Stonier Sch. Banking, 1994, 95. Gen. editor: Technology Space & Soc.; contbr. (newspapers, mags.) including Wall St. Jour., Bus. Week, Bankers Mag., Am. Banker, RMA Jour. Credit and Risk Mgmt., and many others; contbr. to profl. jours. Chmn. appropriations com. Town of Lexington, Mass., 1967-78; participant Lexington Town Meetings, 1969-78; trustee The Carroll Sch., Lincoln, Mass., 1976—. Shell Oil Found. fellow U. Pa., 1957-58. Mem. Am. Assn. Bank Dirs. (bd. dirs. 1998—), Cosmos Club, City Club Washington, Harvard Club, Nat. Press Club, Harvard Club of Boston, Belle Haven Country Club, The Penn Club, Beta Gamma Sigma. Republican. Office: Monument Fin Group 400 Madison St Alexandria VA 22314-1437 Office Phone: 703-549-4569. E-mail: efurash@aol.com.

FURBUSH, DAVID MALCOLM, lawyer; b. Palo Alto, Calif., Mar. 25, 1954; s. Malcolm Harvey and Margaret (McKittrick) F. BA, Harvard U., 1975, JD, 1978. Bar: Calif. 1978, U.S. Dist. Ct. (no. dist.) Calif. 1978, U.S. Ct. Appeals (9th cir.) 1987, U.S. Supreme Ct. 1990. Assoc. Chickering & Gregory, San Francisco, 1978-81, Brobeck, Phleger & Harrison, San Francisco, 1981-85, ptnr. Palo Alto, Calif., 1985—. Office: Brobeck Phleger & Harrison 2000 University Ave East Palo Alto CA 94303

FURCHES, W. RALPH, JR., writer; s. W R and Ethel Alexander Furches; m. Alicia Furches, Dec. 7, 1950; children: Paulo, Melanie, Amanda, Monica, Alicia-Michelle, Raul-Antonio. AA, Chipola Jr. Coll., Mariannna, Fla., 1970. Prof. Pontifical Cath. U. of Peru, Lima, Peru, 1971—73, Peruian-Am.Cultural Inst., Lima, Peru, 1971—74; mgr. Asheville, NC, 1975—. Author: (book of short stories) Reminiscent Pendezvous, (3 novellas) Gemstones, (short stories, novellas) Journeys to the far places, From the Quill. Home: 15 Lance Rd Candler NC 28715 Personal E-mail: avespirit@juno.com.

FURCHGOTT, ROBERT FRANCIS, pharmacologist, educator; b. Charleston, S.C., June 4, 1916; married, 1941; 3 children. BS, U. N.C., 1937; PhD in Biochemistry, Northwestern U., 1940; DM (hon.), Autonomous U. Madrid, 1984, U. Lund, 1984; DSc (hon.), U. N.C., 1989, U. Ghent, 1995; degree (hon.), Mt. Sinai Med. Sch., 1995, Ohio State U., 1996, Med. U. S.C., 1997, Med. Coll. Ohio, 1997, Northwestern U., 1998, U. Coll., London, 1998, Washington U., 2001, Charles U., Prague, 2003. Rsch. fellow medicine Med. Coll. Cornell U., 1940—43, rsch. assoc., 1943—47, instr. physiology, 1943—48, asst. prof. med. biochemistry, 1947—49; from asst. prof. to assoc. prof. pharmacology Med. Sch. Wash. U., 1949—56; chmn. dept. pharmacology SUNY Coll. Med. (now SUNY Health Sci. Ctr.), Bklyn., 1956—82; prof. dept. pharmacology SUNY Health Sci. Ctr., Bklyn., 1956—88, Disting. prof., 1988—89, disting. emeritus prof. pharmacology, 1990—. Mem. pharmacol. tng. com. USPHS, 1961—64, mem. pharmacotoxicol. rev. com., 1965—68; Commonwealth fellow, 1962—63; vis. prof. U. Geneva, 1962—63, U. Calif., San Diego, 1971—72, Med. U. S.C., 1980, UCLA, 1980; adj. prof. pharmacology, Sch. Medicine U. Miami, 1988—2001; disting. vis. prof. Med. Univ. South Carolina, 2001. Recipient rsch. achievement award, Am. Heart Assn., 1990, Bristol-Myers Squibb award for achievement in cardiovasc. rsch., 1991, Gairdner Found. Internat. award, 1991, medal, N.Y. Acad. Medicine, 1992, Roussel Uclaf prize for rsch. in cell communication and signalling, 1993, Wellcome Gold medal, Brit. Pharmacology Soc., 1995, ASPET award for exptl. therapeutics, 1996, Gregory Pincus award for rsch., 1996, Albert Lasker award for basic med. rsch., Lasker Found., 1996, Lucian award, 1997, Nobel prize for Medicine, 1998. Mem.: NAS, AAAS, Harvey Soc., Am. Soc. Pharmacology and Exptl. Therapeutics (pres. 1971—72, Goodman and Gilman award 1984), Am. Soc. Biochemistry, Am. Chem. Soc., Am. Acad. Arts and Scis., Polish Physiol. Soc. (hon.), Sigma Xi. Office: SUNY Health Sci Ctr Dept of Pharmacology 450 Clarkson Ave Box 29 Brooklyn NY 11203-2056

FURCHTGOTT-ROTH, HAROLD WILKES, economist, consultant; b. Knoxville, Tenn., Dec. 13, 1956; s. Ernest and Mary A. (Wilkes) Furchtgott; m. Diana Elizabeth Roth, June 21, 1983; children: Leon Adam, Francesca Cecily, Jeremy Bernard, Godfrey Eugene, Theodore Raphael, Richard Abraham. SB, MIT, 1978; PhD, Stanford U., 1986. Rsch. fellow Brookings Instn., Washington, 1983-84; rsch. analyst Ctr. for Naval Analyses, Alexandria, Va., 1984-88; sr. economist Economists Inc., Washington, 1988-95; chief economist U.S. House Commerce Com., 1995-97; mem. FCC, 1997—2001; vis. fellow Am. Enterprise Inst., 2001—03; pres. Furchtgott-Roth Econ. Enterprises, 2003—. Mem. Am. Econ. Assn., Econometric Soc. Home: 2705 Daniel Rd Chevy Chase MD 20815 Office: 1200 New Hampshire Ave Washington DC 20036 Business E-Mail: hfr@furchgott-roth.com.

FURCO, ANDREW, secondary school educator; b. Bklyn., Apr. 17, 1961; s. Geiuseppe and Marianna (Sarcona) F. BA, UCLA, 1984, MA, 1986; postgrad., Columbia U. Cert. clear teaching, Calif., severely handicapped, Calif. Intern Devereux Found., Goleta, Calif.; tchr., dept. chair Mountain View Sch. Dist., El Monte, Calif. Recipient Raymond Moremen Choral Conducting award, 1984; named Outstanding Achievement in Music Teaching, 1988, Tchr. of Yr., 1989. Mem. NEA, Assn. for Supervision and Curriculum Devel., So. Calif. Band and Orch. Assn. Home: 4345 Mont Eagle Pl Los Angeles CA 90041-3414

FURCON, JOHN EDWARD, management and organizational consultant; b. Mar. 17, 1942; s. John F. and Lottie F.; children: Juliana, Annalisa, Diana BA, DePaul U., 1963, MA, 1965; MBA, U. Chgo., 1970. With Human Resources Ctr. Chgo. U., 1963-81, project dir., 1966-70, rsch. psychologist, divsn. dir., 1970-81; with orgn. change practice Harbridge House, Inc., Northbrook, Ill., 1981—93, v.p., 1987-93; ptnr. human resource adv. group Coopers & Lybrand, 1993-98; ptnr. Global Human Resource Solutions Pricewaterhouse-Coopers LLP, 1998—2001, prin., 2001—; regional practice leader, human resource mgmt. cons. Buck Cons., Chgo., 2002—. Faculty Traffic Inst., Northwestern U., 1969-84, DePaul U. Sch. for New Learning, 1974-82, Ctr. Pub. Safety Northwestern U., 2004—; cons., lectr. in field. Contbr. articles to profl. jours. Active parents bd. Marquette U., 1988-89. Served to lt. AUS, 1963-65. Mem. Soc. Indsl. and Orgnl. Psychology, Indsl. Psychology Assn. Chgo. (chmn. 1973-75), Internat. Assn. Chiefs of Police, Chgo. Coun. Fgn. Rels., World Future Soc., Human Resource Mgmt. Assn. Chgo. Office: Buck Consultants One N Dearborn St Chicago IL 60602 Office Phone: 312-846-3650. Business E-Mail: john.furcon@buckconsultants.com.

FUREY, ROGER P., lawyer; b. Washington, DC, May 30, 1954; BS, George Mason U., 1979; JD, U. Va., 1983. Bar: DC 1983, Va. 1984, US Dist. Ct., Ea. Dist. Va., US Dist. Ct., DC, US Dist. Ct., Md., US Ct. Appeals, 4th, 6th, 9th and DC Cirs., US Ct. Appeals, Fed. Cir., Va. Supreme Ct. Ptnr. Katten Muchin Zavis Rosenman, Washington, DC. Mem.: Va. Bar Assn., Internat. Trademark Assn., Internat. C. of C., DC Bar Assn. Office: Katten Muchin Zavis Rosenman East Lobby, Ste 700 1025 Thomas Jefferson St, NW Washington DC 20007 Office Phone: 202-625-3630. Office Fax: 202-339-8268. E-mail: roger.furey@kmzr.com.

FURGASON, ROBERT ROY, retired academic administrator, engineering educator; b. Spokane, Wash., Aug. 2, 1935; s. Roy Elliott and Margaret (O'Halloran) F.; m. Gloria L. Althouse, June 14, 1964; children: Steven Scott, Brian Alan. BSChemE, U. Idaho, 1956, MSCE, 1958; PhD in Chem. Engring., Northwestern U., 1961; postdoctoral, U. Wis., 1961. Registered profl. engr., Idaho. Design engr. Phillips Petroleum Co., Bartlesville, Okla., 1956; rsch. engr. Martin Marietta Co., Denver, 1958; instr. chem. engring. U. Idaho, Moscow, 1957-59, asst. prof., 1961-63, assoc. prof., 1963-67, acting head dept. chem. engring., 1964-65, chmn. dept. chem. engring., 1965-74, prof., 1967-84, dean Coll. Engring., 1974-78, v.p. acad. affairs and rsch., 1978-84; prof., vice chancellor acad. affairs U. Nebr., Lincoln, 1984-90; prof., pres. Tex A&M U.-Corpus Christi, 1990—2004; dir. Harte Rsch. Inst. TAMU CC, 2005—. NSF advisor scientists and engrs. in econ. devel. program Escuela Politecnica Nacional, Quito, Ecuador, 1973-74, 76; proposal reviewer NSF, 1965-84; program reviewer Clearwater Econ. Devel. Assn., 1978-84; mem. long-range planning commn. Idaho State Bd. Edn., 1978-80, Gov.'s Com. Faculty Salary Equity, 1980, State of Idaho Energy Policy Bd., 1980-84, adv. com. Northwest Power Policy Coun., 1982-84, engring. accreditation commn. Accreditation Bd. Engring. and Tech., 1981-96, exec. bd., 1984-89, vice chmn., 1985-87, chmn., 1988-89, bd. dirs., 1989-95, fellow, 1990, pres., 1993-94; bd. dirs. Hanover Cos.; bd. dirs. Am. Bank. Bd. of trustees, Driscoll Hospital Founnd., 2002— . Contbr. articles to profl. jours. Chmn. Idaho-Ecuador Ptnrs. of Ams., 1975-77; commr. Moscow Parks and Recreation Commn., 1977-81; mem. charter revision comm. City of Lincoln, 1989-90; chair Nebr. Energy Mgmt. Plan Adv. Com., 1989-90; mem. chem. engring. vis. com. Colo. Sch. Mines, 1989-99; exec. adv. bd. Coastal Bend United Way, 1991-93; bd. dirs. S.W. Moscow Cmty. Assn., 1977-84, Am. Festival Ballet, 1978-80, Lincoln Cancer Ctr., 1988-90, Tex. Econ. Edn. Commn., 1991-2001, Ada Wilson Children's Rehab. Ctr., 1993-96, Tex. State Aquarium, 1994—; adv. bd. Sta. KEDT-TV, Sta. KEDT-FM. Recipient Pub. Svc. award Idaho State Libr. Assn., 1978, Phillip Carrol Nat. award Soc. Advanced Mgmt., 1996, Grinter award Accreditation Bd. Engring. and Tech., 1996, Baldwin award Corpus Christi C. of C., 2000, Humanitarian award, NCCJ, 2002; named Citizen of Yr. Kappa Sigma, 1980, Newsmaker of the Yr., Corpus Christi Caller-Times, 1997, Newsmaker of the Decade, 2000; CASE Chief Exec. Leadership award, 2001; Walter P. Murphy fellow. Fellow AIChE (chmn. nat. tech. sessions 1967, sec. dept. heads forum 1971-72, chmn. 1981, nat. vis. lectr. 1977-79, edn. and accreditation com. 1981-92, chair 1989-91, accreditation visitation group 1977—); mem. Am. Soc. Engring. Edn. (Pacific Northwest coord. effective tchg. 1962-64, bd. dirs. chem. engring. divsn. 1974-77, Centennial medal 1993), Idaho Soc. Profl. Engrs. (No. Idaho chpt. pres. 1970, state pres. 1980, Idaho's Young Engr. of Yr. 1967), Northwest Coll. and Univ. Assn. Scis. (exec. com. bd. dirs. 1976-80, 81-84, chmn. bd. dirs. 1979-80), Corpus Christi C. of C. (bd. dirs. 1990-94), Crucible Club, Wranglers Club, Lions (program chmn., corr. sec., bd. dirs.), Rotary, Sigma Xi, Phi Kappa Phi, Phi Eta Sigma, Sigma Tau. Avocations: piloting, skiing, camping, woodworking. Home: 1334 Sandpiper Dr Corpus Christi TX 78412-3818 Office: Tex A&M U Harte Rsch Inst 6300 Ocean Dr Corpus Christi TX 78412-5503 E-mail: robert.furgason@tamucc.edu.

FURGESON, WILLIAM ROYAL, federal judge; b. Lubbock, Tex., Dec. 9, 1941; s. W. Royal and Mary Alyene (Hardwick) F.; m. Marion McElroy, Aug. 15, 1964 (div.); m. Juli Ann Bernat, July 29, 1973 (div.); children: Kelly Lynn, Houston, Joshua, Seth, Jill; m. Marcellene Malouf, July 5, 2003. BA in English, Tex. Tech Coll., 1964; JD with honors, U. Tex., 1967. Bar: Tex. 1969, U.S. Dist. Ct. (we. dist.) Tex. 1971, U.S. Ct. Appeals (5th cir.) 1974, U.S.

Supreme Ct. 1976. Law clk. to presiding judge U.S. Dist. Ct. for No. Dist. Tex., 1969-70; ptnr. Kemp, Smith, Duncan & Hammond, El Paso, Tex., 1970-94; judge U.S. Dist. Ct. (we. dist.) Tex., Midland/Odessa, 1994—2003, San Antonio, 2003—. Gen. campaign chmn. El Paso United Way, 1979, 1st v.p., 1980, pres., 1981; mem. Jewish Fedn., El Paso, 1980-86; trustee Baylor U. Coll. Dentistry, 1982-86; chmn. YWCA Capital Devel. Campaign, 1986-87. Served to capt. U.S. Army, 1967-69 Decorated Bronze Star; recipient Service award Social Workers of El Paso, 1982, Faculty award U. Tex. Law Sch., 1983, Dean Leon Green award Tex. Law Review, 2001, Jurist of Yr., Tex. ABOTA, 2004. Mem. El Paso Bar Assn. (pres. 1982-83, Outstanding Young Lawyer award 1972), Am. Law Inst., U. Tex. Law Sch. Assn. (pres. 1978), U. Tex. Law Rev. Assn. (pres. 1982-83), El Paso Legal Assistance Soc. (bd. dirs. 1972-78), NCCJ (chmn. El Paso region 1980), ABA, Fed. Bar Assn. (pres. West Tex. chpt. 1987), Am. Law Inst., Tex. Bar Assn. (sec., treas., chair anti-trust and trade regulation sect. 1985-86), Am. Bar Found., Tex. Bar Found. Democrat. Jewish. Office: US Dist Ct 655 E Durango San Antonio TX 78206

FURGURSON, ERNEST BAKER, JR., (PAT FURGURSON), writer; b. Danville, Va., Aug. 29, 1929; s. Ernest Baker and Passie Durham (Ferguson) F.; m. Mary Louise Stallings (div.); children— Ernest Baker III, Elisabeth Glyn; m. Cassie Woodward Thompson, Apr. 21, 1973. Student, Averett Coll., 1948-50; AB, Columbia, 1952, MS, 1953. Reporter Danville Comml. Appeal, Sta. WDVA, 1948-51; with Roanoke (Va.) World-News, 1952, Richmond (Va.) News Leader, 1955-56; reporter, Washington corr. Balt. Sun, 1956-61, chief Moscow bur., 1961-64, White House corr., nat. polit. corr., Saigon corr., nat. affairs columnist, 1964-92, chief Washington bur., 1975-87, assoc. editor, 1987-92; syndicated by L.A. Times Syndicate, 1970-90. Author: Westmoreland: The Inevitable General, 1968, Hard Right: The Rise of Jesse Helms, 1986, Chancellorsville 1963: The Souls of the Brave, 1992, Ashes of Glory: Richmond at War, 1996, Not War But Murder: Cold Harbor 1864, 2000, Freedom Rising: Washington in the Civil War, 2004; contbg. editor Washingtonian mag., 1973-83, Mid-Atlantic Country mag., 1983-96. 1st lt. USMC, 1953-55. Mem. Gridiron Club, Cosmos Club. Home: 4812 Tilden St NW Washington DC 20016-2330

FURINO, ANTONIO, economist, educator; b. Rome; JD, U. Rome, 1955; MA, U. Houston, 1965, PhD, 1972. Asst. prof. to assoc. prof. econs. St. Edwards U., Austin, Tex., 1967—70; dir. regional analysis Alamo Area Coun. Govts., San Antonio, 1970—73; prof. econs. U. Tex., San Antonio, 1973—90, dir. Ctr. for Studies in Bus., Econs. and Human Resources, 1973—79, dir. human resource mgmt. and devel. program, 1979—82; sr. ptnr., dir. Devel. Through Applied Sci., San Antonio, 1972—; prof. econs. U. Tex. Health Sci. Ctr., San Antonio, 1985—, dir. Ctr. for Health Econs. and Policy, 1987—, dir. Regional Ctr. for Health Workforce Studies at Ctr. for Health Econs. and Policy, 2001—; sr. rsch. fellow U. Tex. IC 2 Inst., Austin, 1986—. Cons. in field. Home: 16114 Robinwood Ln San Antonio TX 78248-1744 E-mail: furino@uthscsa.edu.

FURLANE, MARK ELLIOTT, lawyer; b. Joliet, Ill., Aug. 2, 1949; s. Francis Emilio and Tosca (Cipriani) F.; m. Susan M. Keegan, July 4, 1987; children: Gahan Patricia, Michael Keegan. BA magna cum laude, Ctrl. Coll., 1971; JD with honors, George Washington U., 1974; MBA in Finance Specialization, U. Chgo., 1982. Bar: Ill. 1974, U.S. Dist. Ct. (no. dist.) Ill. 1979, U.S. Ct. Appeals (5th, 6th, 7th, 9th and 11th cirs.), U.S. Ct. Mil. Appeals, U.S. Supreme Ct. 2001. Ptnr. Gardner Carton & Douglas, Chgo., 1979—. Bd. mem. Ctr. for Disability and Elder Law, 2000—, Abraham Lincoln Local Sch. Coun., Chgo. Boy Choir; bd. dirs. Friends of Lincoln. Capt. USMCR. Mem. FBA (labor and employment com. 1996—, trustee 1999—), Chgo. Bar Assn. (chmn. labor and employment com. 1994-95), GSB Chgo. Club. Democrat. Roman Catholic. Office: Gardner Carton & Douglas 191 N Wacker Dr Chicago IL 60606-1698 Office Phone: 312-569-1332. Business E-Mail: mfurlane@gcd.com.

FURLAUD, RICHARD MORTIMER, pharmaceutical company executive; b. N.Y.C., Apr. 15, 1923; s. Maxime Hubert and Eleanor (Mortimer) F.; children: Richard Mortimer, Eleanor Jay, Elizabeth Tamsin; m. Isabel Phelps Furlaud. Student, Institut Sillig, Villars, Switzerland; AB, Princeton U., 1944; LLB, Harvard U., 1947. Bar: N.Y. 1949. Assoc. Root, Ballantine, Harlan, Bushby & Palmer, 1947-51; with legal dept. Olin Mathieson Chem. Corp., 1955-56, asst. to exec. v.p. for finance, 1956-57, asst. pres., 1957-59, v.p., 1959-64, gen. counsel, 1957-60, gen. mgr., v.p. internat. div., 1960-64, exec. v.p., 1964-66, now dir., 1964-94; pres., dir. E. R. Squibb & Sons, Inc., 1966-68; pres., chief exec., dir. Squibb Beech-Nut, Inc. (renamed Squibb Corp. 1971), Princeton, N.J., 1968-74; chmn., chief exec., dir. Squibb Corp. (merged with Bristol-Myers Co.), N.Y.C., 1974-89; pres., bd. dirs. Bristol-Myers Co. (renamed Bristol-Myers Squibb Co.), N.Y.C., 1989-91. Mem. profl. staff Ho. of Reps. Com. Ways and Means, 1954; chmn. Rockefeller U. Coun.; trustee John M. Olin Found. 1st lt. JAGC U.S. Army, 1951-53. Mem. Assn. Bar City of N.Y., Coun. on Fgn. Rels., River Club. Home: 745 HiMount Rd Palm Beach FL 33480 Office: 8th Fl West 777 S Flagler Dr West Palm Beach FL 33401 Office Phone: 561-515-6016. Personal E-mail: ternaboutx@aol.com.

FURLONG, CHARLES RICHARD, broadcasting executive; b. Glen Ridge, N.J., Mar. 12, 1950; s. Robert Gordon and Mary Frances (Johnson) F.; m. Silvia Maria Martinez, Jan. 12, 1949; children: Lisa Davis, Emily Cochran, Audrey Frances. Cert., St. Andrews (Scotland) U., 1972; AB in English, Fordham Coll., 1973; postgrad., Columbia U., 1976—. Promotion coordinator ABC-TV Network, N.Y.C., 1973-76, copywriter, 1976-78, sr. copywriter, 1978-79; editor Info. Services Group W, Westinghouse Broadcasting Co., N.Y.C., 1979-82, mgr. Info Services Group W, 1982-83, dir. Editorial Services Group W, 1983-84, dir. Communications Group W Radio, 1984-87; v.p. Communications Group W Radio, N.Y.C., 1987—; communications dir. Westinghouse Broadcasting Co., N.Y.C., 1987—; pres., mng. dir. INTERMEDIA ARTS, 1992—. Speechwriter Washington Cable Club, 1987, Radio Bur. Can., 1987; exec. producer Radio Mercury Awards with Dick Clark, 1992-96, Super Bowl Saturday Night with Ray Charles, 1993; bd. dirs Radio Creative Fund, N.Y.C. Marathon, 1992—; fellowship chair Nat. Assn. Coll. Broadcasters/Mercury Awards Scholarship, 1996. Exec. producer: (radio documentary) The Dream Forever, 1987 (Gold medal Internat. Radio Festival N.Y.). Liasion Martin Luther King, Jr. Fed. Holiday Commn., Washington, 1986; bd. dirs. ARC, Montclair, N.J., 1979. Mem. Internat. Radio and TV Soc. (mem. steering com. industry faculty conf.), Radio Advt. Bur. Pub. Relations (mem. adv. bd.). Republican. Roman Catholic.

FURLONG, GEORGE MORGAN, JR., museum program director, retired military officer; b. Muskogee, Okla., Nov. 23, 1931; s. George M. and Anna (Moore) F.; m. Ryland Hagood Blakey, June 5, 1956; children: Morgan, William. BS in Naval Sci., U.S. Naval Acad., 1956; BS in Aero. Engring., U.S. Naval Postgrad. Sch., 1963. Commd. ensign U.S. Navy, 1956, advanced through grades to rear adm. (upper half), 1981; F-14 program mgr. Comdr. Naval Air Forces, U.S. Pacific Fleet, 1973-74; wing comdr. Attack Carrier Air Wing 14, USS Enterprise, 1974-75; comdg. officer USS Ponchatoula, Pearl Harbor, Hawaii, 1975-76, USS Independence, Norfolk, Va., 1977-78; chief of staff U.S. Sixth Fleet, Gaeta, Italy, 1978-80; dir. Air Warfare Systems Analysis Staff, Office Chief of Naval Ops., Washington, 1980-81; comdr. Fighter Airborne Early Warning Wing. U.S. Pacific Fleet, Naval Air Sta., Miramar, San Diego, 1981-83; dep. chief Naval Edn. and Tng., Pensacola, Fla., 1983-85; ret., 1986; exec. v.p. Naval Aviation Mus. Found., Pensacola, 1986-96; dir. devel. Bapt. Health Care Found., Pensacola, 1997—2001; cons. Naval Aviation Mus. Found., 2001—. Deocorated Legion of Merit with gold star; recipient John Paul Jones award Nat. Navy League Assn., 1971 Office: Naval Aviation Mus Found Inc 1750 Radford Blvd Ste B Pensacola FL 32508- Office Phone: 850-436-4948. Personal E-mail: skipone@aol.com.

FURLOTTI, ALEXANDER AMATO, real estate development company executive; b. Milan, Apr. 21, 1948; came to U.S., 1957; s. Amato and Polonia Concepcion (Lopez) F.; m. Nancy Elizabeth Swift, June 27, 1976; children: Michael Alexander, Patrick Swift, Allison Nicole. BA in Econs., U. Calif. Berkeley, Berkeley, 1970; JD, UCLA, 1973. Bar: Calif. 1973, U.S. Dist. Ct. (9th cir.) 1973. Assoc. Alexander, Inman, Kravetz & Tanzer, Beverly Hills, Calif., 1973-77, ptnr., 1978-80, Kravetz & Furlotti, Century City, Calif., 1981-83; pres. Quorum Properties, L.A., 1984—. Trustee Harvard-Westlake Sch., L.A., 1989-97, Yosemite Nat. Inst., San Francisco, 1990-92. Recipient Grand award Pacific Coast Bldrs. Conf., 1993, 98, Golden Nugget award, 1993, 98, Grand award Nat. Assn. Home Builders, 1993, Platinum award, 1997, Best Attached Housing award, 1998, Residential Project of Yr., 1998; finalist Pillars of Industy award Nat. Assn. Homebuilders, 2004 Mem. Am. Bar Assn., Urban Land Inst., The Beach Club, Calif. Club. Republican. Episcopalian.

FURLOW, MACK VERNON, JR., retired treasurer, financial analyst; b. Summit, Miss., Aug. 20, 1931; s. Mack Vernon and Trudie Dena (Ratcliff) F.; m. Barbara Elaine Rolfs, Mar. 20, 1954 (div. Dec. 1985); children— David Wayne, Kevin Rolfs. BS, La. State U., 1953; grad., advanced mgmt. program Harvard, 1968. Financial and systems analyst Humble Oil & Refining Co., Baton Rouge, 1957-61; asst. controller Skyland Internat. Corp., Chattanooga, 1961-65; v.p., corp. controller Blount, Inc., Montgomery, Ala., 1965-71; pres. Pipeco Steel Co., Inc., Wilmington, Del., 1971-73; v.p. fin., treas. Huber, Hunt & Nichols, Inc., Indpls., 1973-96, dir., 1977-96. Asst. treas. 54th Advanced Mgmt. Program class Harvard Bus. Sch., 1968— Served to 1st lt. AUS, 1953-57. Mem. La. State U. Alumni Assn. (mem. adv. com. Montgomery chpt. 1967-71), Nat. Assn. Accts. (nat. bd. dirs. 1976-78), Fin. Execs. Inst. (nat. bd. dirs. 1994-97). Republican. Lutheran. Home: 9337 Spring Forest Dr Indianapolis IN 46260-1269 *The creation of a management climate or environment which causes people to want to excel and perform to their fullest capabilities is a far superior approach than is a management style which causes people to perform because they are constantly afraid of the consequences of failing to perform.*

FURLOW, WILLIAM LAWRENCE, retired financial consultant; b. Castroville, Tex., July 19, 1944; s. William Elmer and Mary Ellen (Griffin) F.; m. Patricia Mary Nevins, July 20, 1974; 1 child, Christopher Randolf. Student, U. Ky., 1962-64, Santa Monica City Coll., Calif., 1966, La. Poly., 1972. Shipping clk. Coastal Dynamics Corp., Venice, Calif., 1964; sr. PC clk. Vol-Shan Mfg. Co., Culver City, Calif., 1965-68; materials coord. Hughes Aircraft, Culver City, 1969-70; PC clk. Everest & Jennings Inc., L.A., 1970-72; supr. Audio Magnetics Corp., Compton, Calif., 1973-74, Am. Safety Corp., Pacoima, Calif., 1975-76; agent Combined Ins. Co. Am., Virginia Beach, Va., 1977; buyer Perma-Bilt Industries, Torrance, Calif., 1978-80; gen. mgr. Cweco, Gardena, Calif., 1980-83, Saferail Inc., Gardena, 1980-83; PC mgr. DB Products Inc., Pasadena, Calif., 1984-92; CFO Bulltek Ltd., Running Sprints, Calif., 1996—2005, ret., 2005. Cons. in field, Ocean Springs, Miss., 2000-05; affiliate Maple Leaf Meds, Kirkland, Wash., 2003-05; owner websites. Author poems. Enumerator U.S. Census Bur., Gulfport, Miss., 2000. Pfc USAR, 1963—69. Mem. Am. Legion, Internat. Soc. Photographers, Internat. Soc. Poets, Hist. Ocean Springs Assn. Republican. Methodist. Avocations: coin collecting/numismatics, stamp collecting/philately, writing, photography. Home: 1408 Churchill Dr Ocean Springs MS 39564 Office Phone: 228-365-8341. Personal E-mail: furlow_nevins@msn.com.

FURMAN, ANTHONY MICHAEL, public relations executive; b. L.A., Nov. 5, 1934; s. LeRoy S. and Geraldine P. Furman; m. Betty Gayle Morgan, Nov. 1, 1970; 1 child, Michael Jason. BA, Bethany Coll., W.Va., 1957; post grad., Columbia U., 1957—58. Asst. account exec. Jules Beitler, Pub. Rels., Newark, 1958; account exec. . Barber & Baar Pub. Rels. Corp., N.Y.C., 1959—60; account exec. and media dir. Sydney S. Baron & Co., Inc., 1961—66; pres. Anthony M. Furman, Inc., 1966—81; v.p. and mng. dir. sports devel. divsn. Hill & Knowlton, Inc., 1981—85; pres. Dorf and Stanton Sports Mktg., 1985—86, Anthony M. Furman, Inc., 1986—. Adj. prof. L.I. U., 1986—91; guest lectr. NYU, 1989, adj. prof., 1992—2004; bd. dir. FKP Assoc., Lake Placid, NY. Prodr.: (films) Floating Free, 1977 (Acad. award nominee, 1978). With MC U.S. Army, 1957—58. Recipient Outstanding Alumnus award, Bethany Coll., 1987. Mem.: Pub. Rels. Soc. Am. Democrat. Jewish. Office: Ste 1501 250 W 57th St New York NY 10107 Office Phone: 212-956-5666. Business E-Mail: tony@furmansports.com.

FURMAN, HOWARD, arbitrator, lawyer, mediator; b. Newark, Nov. 30, 1938; s. Emanuel and Lilyan (Feldman) F.; m. Elaine Sheitleman, June 12, 1960 (div. 1982); children: Deborah Toby, Naomi N'chama, David Seth; m. Janice Wheeler, Jan. 14, 1984. BA in Econs., Rutgers U., 1966; JD cum laude, Birmingham Sch. Law, 1985. Bar: Ala. 1985, U.S. Dist. Ct. (no. dist.) Ala. 1986, U.S. Dist. Ct. (so. dist.) Ala. 1996. Designer/draftsman ITT, Nutley, NJ, 1957-61; pers. mgr. Computer Products Inc., Belmar, NJ, 1962-64, Arde Engring. Co., Newark, 1964-66; econs. instr. Rutgers U., New Brunswick, NJ, 1966-74; dir. indsl. rels. Harvard Ind. Frequency Engring. Labs. Divsn., Farmingdale, NJ, 1966-74; commr. Fed. Mediation and Conciliation Svc., Birmingham, Ala., 1974-96; pvt. practice Birmingham, 1985—. Instr. bus. law Jefferson State C.C., 1989-95; instr. human resources mgmt. Nova U., 1993; prof. personal property, adminstrv. law, sales and alternative dispute resolution Birmingham Sch. Law, 1993—. Pres. Ocean Twp. (NJ) Police Res., 1968. Recipient ofcl. commendation Fed. Mediation and Conciliation Svc., 1979, 81-82, 88. Mem. ABA, Ala. Bar Assn., Birmingham Bar Assn., Soc. Profls. in Dispute Resolution, Fed. Soc. Labor Rels. Profls., Indsl. Rels. Rsch. Assn., Sigma Delta Kappa. Jewish. Office Phone: 205-853-8204. Personal E-mail: hfesq@bellsouth.net.

FURMAN, L. ROBERT, principal, music educator; b. Washington, Pa., Mar. 12, 1972; s. Robert Louis and Rosalie Furman; m. Tiffeni Sue Patrick, Dec. 26, 1999; 1 child, Robert Lucas. BS in Music Edn., W.Va. U., 1995; MS in Ednl. Adminstrn., Duquesne U., 2000, postgrad., 2003—. Cert. tchr. music edn. k-12 W.Va. Dept. Edn., 1995, Pa. Dept. Edn., 1995, edn. aminstrn. K-12 Duquesne U., Pa. Dir. H.S. band Owings Mills H.S., Balt., 1995—97, Elizabeth Forward Sch. Dist., Pa., 1997—2000, Joshua Sch. Dist., Tex., 2000—01; mid. sch. music tchr. Pitts. Pub. Schs., 2001—03; asst. prin. Gateway Sch. Dist., Monroeville, Pa., 2003—. Instr. percussion Baltimore Ravens Marching Band, 1995—97; dir. Western Pa. Honors Band/Pa. Music Educators Assn., Pitts., 1997—2000, dir. European tour, 1998—99. Recording, Teachable Moment, 2005. Recipient Charles Gray award Music Edn., Civic Light Orch., 2002; Music scholarship, Pa. State U., 1990. Mem.: Percussive Arts Soc., Pa. Mid. Sch. Assn., Pa. Music Educators Assn., Phi Mu Alpha Sinfonia, Kappa Delta Rho. Roman Cathloic. Avocations: recording music, photography, videography, hunting, boating. Home: 174 Sylvania Dr Pittsburgh PA 15236 Office: Gateway Sch Dist 9000 Gateway Campus Blvd Monroeville PA 15146 Home Fax: 724-745-6457; Office Fax: 412-373-5885. E-mail: rfurman@gatewayk12.org.

FURMAN, MARK EVAN, neuroscientist; b. Bronx, N.Y., Mar. 14, 1962; s. Edward and Charlotte F.; m. Beth Ann Schad, Aug. 9, 1987; children: Lauren Ashley, Jonathan Cyle. BA in Behavioral Scis./Psychology, Coll. of S.I., 1984. Cert. practitioner of neuro-linguistic programming. Dir. edn. and rsch. Assoc. Schs. Music, Inc., Cooper City, Fla., 1988-97; spkr., author, human performance cons., 1990—; founder, exec. dir. Furman Rsch. Assocs., Boca Raton, Fla., 1987—; dir. edn. and rsch. The Keys to Success, Inc., Coral Springs, Fla., 1992—2000, Ozone Park, NY, 1992—2000; human performance cons. Interactive Response Techs., 2001—04; dir. behavioral scis. Burton Tng. Group, Inc., 2004—. Lectr. in field of neurosci.; founder, exec. dir. Furman Rsch. Assocs.; designer comm. program Jewish Ednl. Found. of Am., theoretical tng. model Syntonics Ednls., Switzerland; cons. Keys to Success Music Sch., N.Y., Century 21, Fla.; founder Internat. Soc. for Edn. Neurosci.; developer Intelligent Learning Systems, Neuroprint, Human Performance Modeling & Engineering; numerous others application models. Author: Mind in Motion, The Human Performance Technology for the Next Millenum, 1996; author: Jour. for the Soc. of Neuro-Linguistic Programming, 1995-2002, The Neurophysics of Human Behavior: Explorations at the Interface of Brain, Mind, Behavior and Information, 1999; contbg. author: Energy Psychology in Psychotherapy, 2002; contbr. articles to profl. jours. Mem.: APA (affiliate, divsn. 48, divsn. peace psychology), AAAS, Soc. for Study of Peace, Conflict and Violence, Internat. Soc. for Cognitive Neurophysics (founder). Achievements include developing intelligent learning systems (ILS); currently pioneering coordinated research and development efforts in the field of education neuroscience, studying the neurophysics of human information processing and its application to the field of human education, psychotherapy, marketing, crisis negotiation and the management sciences; advanced standard theory: Pattern-Entropy dynamics of matter and energy interaction; formerly established the interdisciplinary branch of science known as cognitive neurophysics. Home: 9559 Trivolo Pl Boca Raton FL 33434-2057 Office: Furman Rsch 9559 Trivolo Pl Boca Raton FL 33434

FURMAN, ROY LANCE, investment banker, theater producer; b. NYC, Apr. 19, 1939; s. Joseph M. and Frances L. (Kurlander) F.; m. Frieda Anne Bueler, Nov. 7, 1965; children: Jill Tracy, Stephanie Gail. AB, Bklyn. Coll., 1960; LL.B., Harvard U., 1963. Atty. Western Electric Co., N.Y.C., 1964-67; v.p. Continental Tel. Supply Co., N.Y.C., 1967-68; with Seiden & de Cuevas, Inc., N.Y.C., 1968-73, pres., 1972-73; co-founder, pres. Furman Selz LLC, N.Y.C., 1973-98, also bd. dirs., 1973-98; chmn., CEO Livent Inc., N.Y.C., 1998-99; vice chmn. Furman Selz LLC, N.Y.C., 1997-99, ING Barings, N.Y.C., 1999—2001, Jefferies and Co., N.Y.C., 2001—; chmn. Jefferies Capital Mgmt., N.Y.C., 2001—. Former nat. fin. chmn. Dem. Nat. Com.; past chmn. splty. firms adv. com. N.Y. Stock Exch.; bd. dirs. Westfield Group, Broadway TV Network. Chmn. emeritus Film Soc. of Lincoln Ctr.; v.p. N.Y.C. Opera; vice chmn. Lincoln Ctr. for Performing Arts; past nat. chmn. Harvard Law Sch. Fund; chmn. Bklyn. Coll. Found., 2001-; exec. com. dean's adv. bd. Harvard Law Sch. Mem.: East Hampton Golf Club, Palm Beach Country Club (Fla.), Harmonie Club (NYC). Office: Jefferies and Co 520 Madison Ave New York NY 10022

FURMAN, SEYMOUR, surgeon; b. Bronx, N.Y., July 12, 1931; s. Joseph and Bertha Kellert Furman; m. Evelyn Mae Katz, June 1, 1957 (dec. Sept. 9, 2002); children: Bruce, Gary, Neil. Degree, NYU, 1951; MD, SUNY, Bklyn., 1955, DSc (hon.), 2001. Diplomate Am. Bd. Surgery, Am. Bd. Thoracic Surgery. Intern Montefiore Hosp., Bronx, 1955—56, surg. resident, 1956—60, attending surgeon, 1963—; thoracic surg. resident Baylor U. Affiliated Hosps., Houston, 1962—63; attending surgeon Jack D. Weiler Hosp., Bronx, 1963—; attending cardiologist Montefiore Med. Ctr., Bronx, 1994—. Presenter in field; founder NASPExAM; founder, editor Heartweb, Pacing and Clin. Electrophysiology, Electricity and the Heart website; vis. prof. Ben Gurion U., Israel, 1992; disting. vis. scholar The Bakken Mus., Mpls., 2004. Author (with D.J.W. Escher): Principles and Techniques of Cardiac Pacing, 1970, Cardiac Pacing and Pacemakers: Medcom Famous Teachings in Modern Medicine, 1973, Modern Cardiac Pacing-A Clinical Overview, 1975; author: (with M. Schaldach) Advances in Pacemaker Technology, 1975; author: (with D.J.W. Escher) Cardiac Pacing and Pacemakers: Part I: Fundamenals: Medcome Famous Teachings Modern Medicine, 2d edit., 1982; author: Cardiac Pacing and Pacemakers: Part II: Dual Chamber Pacing: Medcom Famous Teachings in Modern Medicine 2d edit., 1983; author: (with D.L. Hayes and D.R. Holmes) A Practice of Cardiac Pacing, 1986, 2d edit., 1989, 3d edit., 1993; author: Procs. of IX World Symposium on Cardiac Pacing and Electrophysiology, 1991; contbr. articles to profl. jours., chpts. to books. Lt. comdr. USNR, 1960—62. Recipient Disting. Svc. award, Inter-Soc. Commn. for Heart Disease Resources, 1971, Pioneer in Cardiac Pacing award, Cardiostim '88, Monte Carlo, Monaco, Disting. Alumnus award, Montefiore Staff and Alumni Assn., 1990, Disting. Scientist award, Am. Coll. Cardiology, 1996, award for contbns. to cardiac pacing, Europace '97, Plate of Merit, Citta di Ferrara and Arcispedale "S. Anna" di Ferrara, Italy, 1997. Fellow: Israel Heart Soc. (hon.); mem.: Argentinian Soc. Elec. Stimulation (hon., corr.), Heart Rhythm Soc., N.Am. Soc. Pacing and Electrophysiology (pres. 1981—82, founder, founder oral history program, Disting. Svc. award 1989, Disting. Achievement award 1996, Heart Rhythm Soc. Founders award 2004), Internat. Cardiac Pacing and Electrophysiology Soc. (founder), Internat. Cardiac Pacing Soc. (founder), Latin Am. Soc. Pacing (hon.), Brazilian Soc. Cardiac Pacing (hon.), Brit. Cardiac Soc. (hon.), Argentine Soc. Cardiac Stimulation (hon.), Chilean Cardiol. Soc. (hon.). Achievements include development of transvenous cardiac pacing; demonstration of prolonged patient survival with transvenous cardiac pacing; development of strength duration curve of human cardiac stimulation; relation of electrode size to stimulation threshold; development of transtelephone pacemaker monitoring; design of pacemaker management of Bradycardia Tachycardia Syndrome; development of three position pacemaker code; database and statistical definition of pulse generator and lead quality; delineation of dual chamber pacemaker mediated tachycardia; development of oral history of cardiac pacing, implantable cardiac defibrillation and clinical cardiac eletrophysiology. Office: Montefiore Med Ctr 111 E 210th St Bronx NY 10467-2109

FURMAN-MARKOWITZ, JOANNA FLORENCE, dance educator; b. Balt., Md., Sept. 28, 1952; d. Henry John Furman and Irene Anna Russ; m. Jack Saul Markowitz, May 3, 1986; children: Jesse Michael, Jacob Alexander. BS in Clin. Psychology, Towson U., 1975. Dancer Linda Kohl & Dancers, N.Y.C., 1984—86, Theatre Dance Ensemble, N.Y.C., 1980—86; adminstrv. asst. Dance Theater Workshop, N.Y.C., 1980—86; dir., choreographer Little Feet Dance Co., Monroe, NY, 1992—; dance instr. Bklyn. Coll., 1980—87; dance prof. Orange County C.C., Middletown, NY, 1986—2004; owner, dir. Orange County Sch. Dance, Monroe, 1992—. Choreographer (modern dance) Graphic Illusion, 2000, For One, 1977. Named Advisor of Yr., Orange County C.C., 1989; recipient Appreciation award. Roman Catholic. Avocations: gardening, reading, music. Office: Orange County Sch Dance 16 Lake St Monroe NY 10950 Office Phone: 845-782-2482. E-mail: schoolofdance@yahoo.com.

FURNAD, V. ROBERT (BOB FURNAD), television news executive; BA in Radio/TV, American U. Fl. dir., film editor, assoc. dir., prodr. Sta. WMAL-TV, Washington; with ABC News, 1964-68, 69-83; from polit. news dir. to exec. v.p. and sr. exec. prodr. CNN, 1983—, now pres. Headline News network, 1997—. Recipient George Foster Peabody award, Acad. for cable Excellence GoldenACE, Emmy award, Overseas Press Club award, Alfred I. duPont award.

FURNAS, BARNABY, painter; b. 1973; BFA, Sch. Visual Arts, NY, 1995; MFA, Columbia U., 2000. One-man shows include, Marianne Boesky Gallery, NY, 2002, 2003, Modern Art Inc., London, 2004, exhibited in group shows at Urban Romantics, Lombard Fried Gallery,NY, 1999, All Terrain, Friedrich Petzel Gallery, NY, 1999, @, P.P.O.W. Gallery, NY, 2000, Project Room, Artists Space, NY, 2000, Collectors's Choice, Exit Art, NY, 2000, All. Am., Bellwether, Bklyn., 2001, The Fourth Ann. Altoids Curiously Strong Collection, LA Contemporary Exhbn., 2002, Officina Americana, Galleria d'Arte Moderna, Bologna, Italy, 2002, Drawings, Metro Pictures, 2003, Transnational Monster League, Derek Eller Gallery, NY, 2003, Funny Papers: Cartoons & Contemporary Drawing, Daniel Weinberg Gallery, LA, 2003, War (What Is It Good For?), Mus. Contemporary Art, Chgo., 2003, Go Johnny Go, Kunsthalle Wien, Austria, 2003, Watercolor Worlds, Dorsky Gallery, Long Island City, 2004, Whitney Biennial, Whitney Mus. Am. Art, 2004, 179 Ann.: Invitational Exhbn. Contemporary Art, Nat. Acad. Design, NY, 2004, Seeing Other People, Marianne Boesky Gallery, 2004. Mailing: c/o Marianne Boesky Gallery 535 West 22nd St New York NY 10011*

FURNAS, DAVID WILLIAM, plastic surgeon, educator; b. Caldwell, Idaho, Apr. 1, 1931; s. John Doan and Esther Bradbury (Hare) F.; m. Mary Lou Heatherly, Feb. 11, 1956; children: Heather Jean, Brent David, Craig Jonathan. AB, U. Calif.-Berkeley, 1952, MS, 1957, MD, 1955. Diplomate Am. Bd. Plastic Surgery, Royal Coll. Surgeons. Intern U. Calif. Hosp., San Francisco, 1955-56, asst. resident in surgery, 1956-57; asst. resident in psychiatry, NIMH fellow Langley Porter Neuropsychiat. Inst. U. Calif., San Francisco, 1959-60; resident in gen. surgery Gorgas Hosp., Panama Canal Zone, 1960-61; asst. resident in plastic surgery N.Y. Hosp., Cornell Med. Center, N.Y.C., 1961-62; chief resident in plastic surgery Cornell U. Svc., VA Hosp., Bronx, N.Y., 1962-63; registrar Royal Infirmary and Affiliated Hosps., Glasgow, Scotland, 1963-64; assoc. in hand surgery U. Iowa, 1964-68, sr. resident, faculty assoc. in surgery, 1964-65, asst. prof. surgery, 1966-68, assoc. prof., 1968-69; assoc. prof. surgery, chief div. plastic surgery U. Calif., Irvine, 1969-74, prof., chief div. plastic surgery, 1974-80, clin. prof., chief div. plastic surgery, 1980-99, clin. prof. plastic surgery, 1999—2002, emeritus prof. plastic surgery, 2002—. Surgeon East Africa Flying Drs. Svc., African Med. and Rsch. Found., Nairobi, Kenya, 1972-73; plastic surgeon S.S. Hope, Nicaragua, 1966, Sri Lanka, 1968; mem. Balakbayan med. mission Mindanao and Sulu, The Philippines, 1980-82; overseas vis. prof. plastic surgery Ednl. Found., 1994; Godrej vis. prof. Assn. Plastic Surgeons of India, 2000; keynote spkr. Pan African Assn. Plastic Surgeons, 2000; dir. Am. Bd. Plastic Surgeons, 1979-85; trustee Royal Coll. Surgeons Found., 1995-2002. Contbr. chpts. to textbooks, articles to profl. jours.; author, editor 5 textbooks; mem. editl. bd. Jour. Hand Surgery, Annals of Plastic Surgery, Jour. Craniofacial Surgery; reviewer Plastic and Reconstructive Surgery. Expedition leader Flag 171 Skull Surgeons of the Kisii Tribe Explorer's Club, Kenya, expedition leader Flag 44 Skull Surgeons of the Marakwet Tribe, 1987; bd. govs. Bowers Mus. Cultural Art, 2000—02. Capt. M.C. USAF, 1957—59, col. M.C. USAR, 1989—92. Recipient Golden Apple award U. Calif.-Irvine Sch. Medicine, 1980, Kaiser-Permanente award U. Calif.-Irvine Sch. Medicine, 1981, Humanitarian Svc. award Black Med. Students, U. Calif. Irvine, 1987, Sr. Rsch. award (Basic Sci.) Plastic Surgery Ednl. Found., 1987, Cert. of Spl. Recognition, U.S. Congress, 1998; named Orange County Press Club Headliner of Yr., 1982, Physician of the Year, Orange County Med. Assn., 1998. Fellow ACS, Royal Coll. Surgeons Can., Royal Soc. Medicine, Explorers Club (chmn. So. Calif. chpt. 2001-02), Royal Geog. Soc.; mem. AMA (Disting. Svc. award 2002), Calif. Med. Assn., Orange County Med. Assn. (Physician of Yr. 1998), Am. Soc. Plastic Surgery (bd. dirs. 1970-73), Am. Soc. Reconstructive Microsurgery, Soc. Head and Neck Surgery, Am. Cleft Palate Assn., Am. Soc. Surgery of Hand, Soc. Univ. Surgeons, Am. Assn. Plastic Surgeons (trustee 1983-86, treas. 1988-91, v.p. 1993-94, pres.-elect 1994, pres. 1995, Godrej vis. prof. 2000), British Assn. Plastic Surgeons (hon.), Am. Soc. Craniofacial Surgery, Am. Soc. Aesthetic Plastic Surgery, Am. Soc. Maxillofacial Surgeons, Assn. Acad. Chairmen Plastic Surgery (bd. dirs. 1986-89), Assn. Surgeons East Africa, Assn. Plastic and Reconstructive Surgeons So. Africa (hon.), Pacific Coast Surg. Assn., Internat. Soc. Aesthetic Plastic Surgery, Internat. Soc. Reconstructive Microsurgery, Internat. Soc. Craniomaxillofacial Surgery, Pan African Assn. Neurol. Sci., African Med. and Rsch. Found. (bd. dirs. U.S.A. 1987-2002, team leader Reconstruct! mission for victims of Am. Embassy bombing, Nairobi, Kenya, 1999), Muthaiga Club, Ctr. Club, Club 33, Univ. Club, Phi Beta Kappa, Alpha Omega Alpha. Personal E-mail: daktari1@cox.net. *A crisis, at the outset, usually augurs nothing but ill. In the long run, however, my crises have more often than not marked a new course for my life, which is more fulfilling, and more exciting than anything in the past. Yes, a bit of good luck is needed, but the special feature of a crisis is that you are suddenly cut off from past patterns, habits, and interdependencies. Along with the distress and pain is freedom! Freedom to build again, with a new foundation and modern structure, using wisdom you didn't have the last time you built.*

FURNAS, HOWARD EARL, recreational facility executive, retired federal official; b. Battle Creek, Mich., Jan. 29, 1919; s. Howard Earl and Dorothy Anna (Collings) F.; m. Gail Abbott, May 14, 1942; children: Howard Earl III, Paul Abbott, Christopher Collings. AB, Hillsdale (Mich.) Coll., 1940; postgrad., Harvard U., 1945-47. Joined Fgn. Svc. Dept. State, 1947; assigned to embassy, Paris, 1948—49; asst. to spl. asst. to sec. state for intelligence, 1949-52, 54-57; assigned to U.S. mission to NATO, Paris, 1952-54; mem. policy planning staff, also alternate Dept. State rep. to plannning bd. NSC, 1957-61; dep. spl. asst. to sec. state for atomic energy and outer space, 1961-62; dept. exec. sec. Dept. State, 1962-63; del. 2d Nat. Conf. Peaceful Uses Space, Seattle, 1962; dep. spl. asst. to sec. state for multilateral force negotiations, 1963-64; spl. asst. to sec. state, 1964-65; mem. VIII sr. seminar in fgn. policy, 1965-66; assigned Office Undersec. State Polit. Affairs, 1966-69; spl. asst. to dir. ACDA, 1969-71, spl. adviser to chmn. gen. adv. com. on arms control and disarmament, 1969-71; prof. internat. rels. Windham Coll., Putney, Vt., 1971-76, also trustee; pres. Unipro Tennis Svcs., Howard Furnas Assocs., Windsor, Vt., 1974—, Chuckle Hill, Ltd., 1975-76. Pres. The Vermont Group, Internat. Cons., 1989-90. Contbr. articles to profl. jours. and newspaper columns. Bd. dirs. Montgomery County (Md.) Scholarship Fund, 1954-60; trustee Woodstock (Vt.) Country Sch., 1973-75; vestryman St. James Ch., Woodstock, Vt.; justice of peace West Windsor, Vt., 1986-95, U.S. joint chief of staff, Washington, DC, 1945. Maj. USAAF, 1942-45, ETO. Recipient Alumni Achievement award Hillsdale Coll., 1957. Mem. Kenwood Golf and Country Club (Washington), Woodstock Country Club, Twin States Valley Club, The Round Table, Delta Tau Delta. Episcopalian. Home and Office: 3850 Galleria Woods Dr Apt 335 Birmingham AL 35244 E-mail: bluestar@vermontel.com.

FURR, QUINT EUGENE, marketing executive; b. Concord, N.C., Sept. 21, 1921; s. Walter Luther and Mary (Barnhardt) F.; m. Helen Wilson, Dec. 30, 1961; children: Tiffany Grantham, Quentin, Robert; stepchildren: Pamela Erickson, Erik Erickson. Grad. Belmont Abbey Coll., BA, U. N.C., Chapel Hill, 1943, postgrad. Law Sch., 1946-47. Promotion rep. Sears, Roebuck & Co., Atlanta and Greensboro, N.C., 1947-49; nat. advt. and sales promotion mgr. Western Auto Supply Co., Kansas City, Mo., 1949-61; regional mgr. J.F. Pritchard Co., Charlotte, N.C., 1961-63; gen. mgr. Hogan Rose Advt., High Point, N.C., 1963-65; regional mgr. Top Value Enterprises, Washington, 1965-67; v.p. corp. mktg. Textilease Corp., Beltsville, Md., 1967-85; v.p. sales and mktg. Am. Directory Service Agy., Bethesda, Md., 1985-88; Marketing Consultant, 1988—. Lt. USNR, World War II, Korea. Recipient Mktg. award Textile Leasing Industry, 1970-74. Mem. Sales and Mktg. Execs. Internat., Inst. Indsl. Laundries (past chmn. mktg. com.), Am. Legion, VFW, Pi Kappa Alpha. Roman Catholic. Club: AD (Washington). Lodges: Moose, Elks. Home and Office: 32 Obsidian Dr Chambersburg PA 17201-8207

FURRER, JOHN RUDOLF, retired manufacturing executive; b. Milw., Dec. 2, 1927; s. Rudolph and Leona (Peters) Furrer; m. Annie Louise Waldo, Apr. 24, 1954; children: Blake Waldo, Kimberly Louise. BA in Econs., Harvard Coll., 1946—49. Spl. rep. ACF Industries, Madrid, 1949-51, dir. product devel. N.Y.C., 1954-59; asst. supr. thermonuclear devel. and test Los Alamos, 1952-53; dir. machinery, systems group, central engring. labs. FMC Corp., San Jose, Calif., 1959-68, gen. mgr. engineered systems div., 1968-70, v.p. in charge planning dept., ctrl. engring. labs. and engineered sys. divsn. Chgo., 1970-71, v.p. material handling group, 1971-77, v.p. corp. devel., 1977-88, sr. v.p., 1988-90; ret., 1990. Chmn. San Jose Chpt., Children's Home Soc. Calif., 1964—66; trustee Ravinia Festival, 1986—90, Grand Teton Music Festival, 2002—. With USN, 1945—46, with V-5 pilot tng. program, 1945—46. Mem.: ASME, Coun. Planning Execs. (chmn. conf. bd. 1986—87). Republican. Episcopalian. Achievements include patents in field. Avocations: boating, skiing, photography, genealogy, music. Home: PO Box 10849 Jackson WY 83002-0849 also: 203 Spinnaker Dr Vero Beach FL 32963-2953 Personal E-mail: jrfurrer@aol.com.

FURRY, BENJAMIN K., chemist; b. Wadsworth, Ohio, Nov. 21, 1923; s. James Lewis Furry and Vita (Garn) Betz; m. Eleanor G. Coffman, Sept. 10, 1945; children: Eric, Kay, Gordon. BS, Muskingum Coll., 1944; student, Akron (Ohio) U., 1944-45. With Firestone, Akron, 1944-45, Seiberling Latex, New Bremen, Ohio, 1945-74, Goodrich, Avon Lake, Ohio, 1967; v.p. MCM-G.D. Searle, El Reno, Okla., 1974-79, Akron Catheter, Chippewa Lake, 1979-83; cons. Oak Rubber Cons., Ravenna, Ohio, 1983-88, Internat. Exec. Svc. Corp., Stamford, Conn., 1988—. Home and Office: 751 West St Wadsworth OH 44281-1676

FURSE, ELIZABETH, former congresswoman, small business owner; b. Nairobi, Kenya, 1936; came to U.S., 1958, naturalized, 1972; children: Amanda Briggs, John Briggs; m. John Platt. BA, Evergreen State Coll., 1974; postgrad., U. Wash., Northwestern U., Lewis and Clark Coll. Dir. Western Wash. Indian program Am. Friends Svc. Com, 1975-77; coord. Restoration program for Native Am. Tribes Oreg. Legal Svc., 1980-86; co-owner Helvetia Vineyards, Hillsboro, Oreg.; mem. 103rd-105th Congresses from 1st Oreg. dist., 1993-98, mem. commerce com. Exec. dir. Inst. for Tribal Govt., Portland State U. Co-founder Oreg. Peace Inst., 1985. Address: 22485 NW Yungen Rd Hillsboro OR 97124-8146 also: Inst Tribal Govt PO Box 751 Portland OR 97207*

FURST, ALEX JULIAN, thoracic and cardiovascular surgeon; b. Augusta, Ga., Aug. 21, 1938; m. George Alex and Ann (Segall) F.; m. Elayne Kobrin, Aug. 11, 1962; children: James Andrew, Jeffrey Michael, Joseph Robert. Student, U. Fla., 1963; MD, U. Miami, 1967. Intern U. Miami Hosp., 1967-68, resident, 1968-72, clin. instr. dept. surgery, 1974-91; chief resident in thoracic and cardiovascular surgery Emory U. Hosp., Atlanta, 1972-73, sr. surg. registrar of thoracic unit, 1972-73, Hosp. for Sick Children, London, 1973-74; practice medicine specializing in thoracic and cardiovascular surgery Miami, Fla.; clin. assoc. prof. surgery and cardiology, chief surg. svc. Miami VA Med. Ctr., 1991—, clin. prof., surgery and medicine, chief of surgery; chief surgeon West Palm Beach Med. Ctr., Va., 2000—02. Chief thoracic surgery, pres. med. staff Mercy Hosp.; mem. staff Bapt. Hosp., South Miami Hosp., Doctor's Hosp. (all Miami), North Ridge Gen. Hosp., Ft. Lauderdale; program dir. cardiothoracic surgery U. Miami Sch. of Medicine, 1998-2000. Fellow ACS, Am. Coll. Cardiology, Am. Coll. Chest Physicians; mem. Dade County Med. Assn., Fla. Med. Assn., Heart Assn. Greater Miami, Soc. Thoracic Surgeons, So. Thoracic Surg. Assn. Home: 8802 Arvida Dr Miami FL 33156-2302

FURST, ARTHUR, toxicologist, educator; b. Mpls., Dec. 25, 1914; s. Samuel and Doris (Kolochinsky) F.; m. Florence Wolovitch, May 24, 1940; children: Carolyn, Adrianne, David Michael, Timothy Daniel. AA, L.A. City Coll., 1935; AB, UCLA, 1937, AM, 1940; PhD, Stanford U., 1948; ScD, U. San Francisco, 1983. Mem. faculty, dept. chemistry San Francisco City Coll., 1940-47; asst. prof. chemistry U. San Francisco, 1947-49, assoc. prof. chemistry, 1949-52; assoc. prof. medicinal chemistry Stanford Sch. Medicine, 1952-57, prof., 1957-61; with U. Calif. War Tng., 1943-45, San Francisco State Coll., 1945; rsch. assoc. Mt. Zion Hosp., 1952-82; clin. prof. pathology Columbia Coll. Physicians and Surgeons, 1969-70; dir. Inst. Chem. Biology; prof. chemistry U. San Francisco, 1961-80, prof. emeritus, 1980—, dean grad. div., 1976-79. Vis. fellow Battelle Seattle Research Center, 1974; Michael vis. prof. Weizmann Inst. Sci., Israel, 1982; cons. toxicology, 1980—; cons. on cancer WHO; mem. com., bd. mineral resources NRC; emeritus mem. scientific advisory bd. Golden Neo Life Diamite Internat., Fremont, Calif. Author: Toxicologist as Expert Witness, 1997, 151 Myths in Everyday Science, 2004; contbr. over 300 articles to profl. and ednl. jours. Recipient Klaus Schwartz Commemorative medal Internat. Toxological Congress, Tokyo, 1986, Profl. Achievement award UCLA Alumni Assn., 1992, Henry Hall Clay award U. San Francisco, 1977; ann. lectureship named in his honor Stanford U. Health Libr. Fellow Acad. Toxicological Scis. (diplomate), AAAS, Am. Coll. Nutrition, Am. Coll. Toxicology (nat. sec., pres. 1985, Lifetime Contbn. award 2001), N.Y. Acad. Scis., Am. Inst. Chemists; mem. Am. Soc. Pharmacology and Exptl. Therapeutics, Am. Chem. Soc., Am. Assn. Cancer Rsch., Soc. Toxicology (Lifetime Achievement award 2004), Sigma Xi, Phi Lambda Upsilon. Achievements include research activities on organic synthesis, chemotherapy cancer, carcinogenesis of metals and hydrocarbons. Home: 23500 Cristo Rey Dr Unit 211D Cupertino CA 95014-6524 Office: U San Francisco Inst Chem Biology San Francisco CA 94117-1080 Home Fax: 650-967-4488. Personal E-mail: artfurst@aol.com.

FURST, HENRY FAIRCHILD, lawyer; b. Newark, May 30, 1951; s. William and Barbara (Horowitz) F. AB, Princeton U., 1974; JD, Rutgers U., 1977. Bar: N.J. 1977, U.S. Dist. Ct. N.J. 1977, U.S. Ct. Appeals (3d. cir.) 1979, U.S. Ct. Appeals (2d and D.C. cirs.) 1980, U.S. Supreme Ct. 1980. Ptnr. Brown, Brown & Furst, Newark, 1977-85; pvt. practice West Orange, N.J., 1985—, Newark, 1990—; ptnr. Furst & Menendez, Union City, N.J., 1992-93; sole practice Union City, N.J., 1993-94. Editoral chief Rutgers Jour. of Computers and the Law, 1976-77. Asst. to gov., State of N.J., Trenton, 1974. Mem. ABA, Essex County Bar Assn., Am. Trial Lawyers Assn., N.J. Bar Assn., Assn. Criminal Def. Attys. N.J. (trustee 1987-93), N.J. State Bar Assn. (trustee criminal law sect. 1988—, chair 1990-91). Avocation: golf. Office: 80 Main St West Orange NJ 07052-4938

FURST, WARREN ARTHUR, retired electronics company executive; b. Chgo., May 2, 1924; s. Joseph and Elizabeth (Pratscher) Furst; m. Billie L. Arvidson, Dec. 1, 1951; children: Ronald, Jeanette, Shirley, Mary, Kathryn. BS, Ill. Inst. Tech., 1944; JD, John Marshall Law Sch., 1950; MBA, U. Chgo., 1962. Mgr. indsl. rels. Am.-Marietta/Martin Marietta, Chgo., 1952—65; v.p. Wedron Silica Sand Co., Chgo., 1965—68; mgr. indsl. rels. MSL Industries, Chgo., 1968; v.p. indsl. rels. Consol. Packaging Corp., Chgo., 1969; v.p., sec. Katy Industries, Inc., Elgin, Ill., 1970—93; ret., 1993. Lt. (j.g.) USNR, 1943—46. Mem.: Ill. Bar Assn. Republican. Presbyterian. Home: 277 Otis Rd Barrington IL 60010-5123

FURSTE, WESLEY LEONARD, II, surgeon, educator; b. Cin., Apr. 19, 1915; s. Wesley Leonard and Alma (Deckebach) F.; m. Leone James, Mar. 28, 1942; children: Nancy Dianne, Susan Deanne, Wesley Leonard III. AB cum laude (Julius Dexter scholar 1933-34); Harvard Club scholar 1934-35), Harvard U., 1937, MD in Anatomy, 1941. Diplomate: Am. Bd. Surgery. Intern Ohio State U. Hosp., Columbus, 1941-42; fellow surgery U. Cin., 1945-46; asst. surg. resident Cin. Gen. Hosp., 1946-49; sr. asst. surg. resident Ohio State U. Hosps., 1949-50, chief surg. resident, 1950-51; limited practice medicine specializing in surgery Columbus, 1951—; instr. Ohio State U., 1951-54, clin. asst. prof. surgery, 1954-66, clin. assoc. prof., 1966-74, clin. prof. surgery, 1974-85, clin. prof. emeritus, 1985—. Mem. surg. staff Mt. Carmel Med. Center, chmn. dept. surgery, 1981-85, dir. surgery program, 1981-82; mem. surg. staff Children's, Grant Med. Ctr., Univ., Riverside, Meth. Hosps., St. Anthony Med. Ctr., Park Med. Ctr. (all Columbus); surg. cons. Dayton (Ohio) VA Hosp., Columbus State Sch., Ohio State Penitentiary, Mercy Hosp., Benjamin Franklin Hosp., Columbus, Columbus Cmty. Hosp.; regional adv. com. nat. blood program ARC, 1951-68, chmn., 1958-68; invited participant 2d Internat. Conf. on Tetanus, WHO, Bern, Switzerland, 1966, 3d, São, Paulo, Brazil, 1970, 4th, Dakar, Sénégal, 1975, 5th, Ronneby Brunn, Sweden, 1978, 6th, Lyon, France, 1981, 7th, Copanello, Italy, 1984, 8th, Leningrad, USSR, 1987, 9th, Granada, Spain, 1991; invited rapporteur 4th Internat. Conf. on Tetanus, Dakar, Sénégal, 1975; mem. med. adv. com. Medic Alert Found. Internat., 1971-73, 76-80, bd. dirs., 1973-76; Douglas lectr. Med. Coll. of Ohio, Toledo; founder Digestive Disease Found; lectr. U.S. Army M.C. on WWII Chinese activities during 1943-46; invited orator for new citizens at naturalization ceremonies U.S. Dist. Ct. (so. dist.) Ohio. Prime author: Tétanos; Tetanus: A Team Disease; contbg. author: Advances in Military Medicine, 1948, Management of the Injured Patient, Immediate Care of the Acutely Ill and Injured, 1978, Anaerobic Infections, 1989, Procs. of Internat. Tetans Confs. in Switzerland, Brazil, Sweden, Sénégal, France, Italy, USSR, Current Therapy in Emergency Medicine, Surgical Infectious Diseases (3 edits.), Currenty Emergency Therapy, Surgical Infections, Current Diagnosis (multiple edits.), Current Therapy (multiple edits.), Surgical Infections, 5 Minute Clinical Consult, 8 edits. (4 and 5 CD-Rom, Internet), Medical Microbiology and Infectious Diseases, editor Surgical Monthly Review; contbr. articles to profl. jours. Mem. Ohio Motor Vehicle Med. Rev. Bd., 1965-67, Pres. Club, Ohio State Univ.; bd. dirs. Am. Cancer Soc. Franklin County, pres., 1964-66; adv. coun. Upper Arlington Sr. Ctr., 2000. Served to maj., M.C. AUS, 1942-46, CBI, 1951-53. Recipient China Liberation medal, 2 commendations for surg. service in China U.S. Army; cert. of merit Am. Cancer Soc.; award for outstanding achievement in field clostridial infection dept. surgery Ohio State U. Coll. Medicine, 1984, Outstanding Service award, 1985; award for outstanding and dedicated service Mt. Carmel Med. Ctr., 1985; award for over 25 yrs. service St. Anthony Med. Ctr., U.S.A. Nat. Softball Squash Champion for age group, (1975—), Houston, 1992, (1980—), Denver, 96. Mem. AMA, AAAS, APHA, Cen. Surg. Assn., Surgical Infection Soc., Internat. Biliary Assn., Shock Soc., Soc. Am. Gastrointestinal Endoscopic Surgeons (com. on stds. of practice, resident and fellow edn., com. legis. review), Soc. Surgery of Alimentary Tract, A.C.S. (gov.-at-large, chmn. Ohio com. trauma; nat. subcom. prophylaxis against tetanus in wound mgmt., Ohio chapter Disting. Service award 1987; regional credentials com.), Am. Assn. Surgery of Trauma, Internat. Fedn. of Surg. Colls., Ohio Surg. Assn., Columbus Surg. Assn. (hon. mem.; pres. 1983), Am. Trauma Soc. (founding mem., dir.), Ohio Med. Assn., Acad. Medicine Columbus and Franklin County (Award of Merit for 17 yrs. service, chmn. blood transfusion com., 50 Year Svc. award), Acad. Medicine Cin., Am. Med. Writers Assn., Grad. Surg. Soc. U. Cin., Robert M. Zollinger Surg. Ohio State U. Surg. Soc., Mont Reid Grad. Surg. Soc., Am. Geriatrics Soc., N.Y. Acad. Scis., Assn. Program Dirs. in Surgery, Assn. Physicians State of Ohio, Collegium Internationale Chirurgiae Digestivae, Assn. Am. Med. Colls., Internat. Soc. Colon and Rectal Surgeons, Soc. Internat. de Chirurgie, Am. Assn. Sr. Physicians, Société Internationale sur le Tëtanos, Am. Physicians Art Assn., Am. Assn. Retired Persons (bd. dirs. Franklin County Unit), China-Burma-India Vets., Assn. Columbus Basha (vice comdr. 1992-93, comdr. 1993-94, V-J Day coord., surgeon gen. 1994—), Am. Legion NW Post # 443, Am. Med. Golfing Assn., Internat. Brotherhood Magicians, Soc. Am. Magicians, N.Y. Cen. System Hist. Soc., U.S. Squash Racquets Assn. (mem. ranking com., med. adv. com., Nat. Softball Champion, 1992, 1996), Am. Platform Tennis Assn., Columbus Squash Racquets Assn. (bd. dirs.), VFW of U.S. (lectr.), Pres.'s Club (Ohio State U.). Presbyterian. Home and Office: 697 Garrett Dr Columbus OH 43214-2913 Fax: 614-457-5119. E-mail: wfursteii@aol.com.

FURTADO, BEVERLY ANN, financial aid administrator; b. Bellville, Ill., Feb. 2, 1951; d. George C. and Bertha D. Carroll; m. James R. Furtado, July 18, 1970; children: Jeffrey, Cynthia. AS in Criminal Justice, Fisher Coll., Boston, 1994; BA in Liberal Studies, Western New Eng. Coll., 1998. Fin. aid counselor Fisher Coll., Boston, 1999; career cons. Job Tng. and Edn. Corp., Hyannis, Mass., 1998—2000; fin. aid assoc. Labouré Coll., Boston, 2000—01; fin. aid specialist Quincy Coll., Mass., 2001—; assoc. fin. aid dir. Quincy, Mass. Avocations: reading, quilting, sewing. Home: 781 Cotuit Rd Mashpee MA 02649 Office: Quincy Coll 34 Coddington St Quincy MA 02169

FURTADO, NELLY KIM, vocalist; b. Victoria, B.C., Can., Dec. 2, 1978; Singer: (albums) Whoa Nelly!, 2000 (Grammy award for Best Female Pop Performance, 2002), Folklore, 2003; background vocals: albums Phrenology (The Roots), 2002, vocals: albums Bunkka (Oakenfold), 2002.

FURTERER, SANDRA LEE, management educator, department chairman; d. Melvin Lewis and Joan Dorothy Brumback; m. Daniel Frederick Furterer, Sept. 3, 1988; children: Kelly Lynn, Erik Daniel, Zachary Louis. BS in Indsl. and Sys. Engring., Ohio State U., 1983, MS, 1985; MBA, Xavier U., 1990; PhD of Indsl. Engring., U. Ctrl. Fla., 2004. Cert. Six Sigma Black Belt, Am. Soc. for Quality Control, 2004, Quality Engr., Am. Soc. for Quality Control, 1991, Am. Soc. for Prodn. and Inventory Control, 1990. Mfg. mgmt. trainee Cooper Industries, Springfield, Ohio, 1985—87; computer sys. analyst Computer Scis. Corp., Cin., 1987—90; mfg. mgmt. sr. cons. Coopers & Lybrand, Cin., 1990—92; mgr. indsl. engring. Mead Data Ctrl., Miamisburg, Ohio, 1992—93; mgr. sys. and process consulting Ernst & Young LLP, Columbus, Ohio, 1996—97; mgr. and lead sys. analyst AT&T, Cin., 1997—2000; mgmt. consulting mgr. BKD Olive LLP, Cin., 2000—02; grad. tchg. asst. Indsl. Engring. and Mgmt. Sys. Dept. U. Ctrl. Fla., Orlando, 2002—04, asst. dept. chair Indsl. Engring. and Mgmt. Sys. Dept., 2004—. Dir. EMG Consulting, Orlando, 2002—, DEB Ventures, Inc., Margate, Fla., 2005. Recipient Appreciation Pin, Girl Scouts USA, 2002, Award for Excellence in Grad. Student Tchg., U. Ctrl. Fla., 2004; Merit Scholarship Indsl. Engring. and Mgmt. Sys. Dept., 2002—03. Mem.: Am. Soc. for Engring. Mgmt., Am. Soc. for Engring. Edn., Inst. Indsl. Engrs., Am. Soc. for Quality Control (chair elect and student chpt. advisor 2004—05), Alpha Pi Mu (hon.). Achievements include Dissertation research developed a framework for implementing Lean Six Sigma to improve the productivity and quality of transaction-based processes. Office: Univf Ctrl Florida 4000 Central Florida Blvd Orlando FL 32816 Office Phone: 407-823-2204.

FURTH, FREDERICK PAUL, lawyer; b. West Harvey, Ill., Apr. 12, 1934; s. Fred P. and Mamie (Stelmach) F.; children: Darby, Ben Anthony, Megan Louise; m. Peggy Wollerman, July 19, 1986. Student, Drake U., 1952-53; BA, U. Mich., 1956, JD, 1959; postgrad., U. Berlin, 1959, U. Munich, Fed. Republic Germany, 1960. Bar: Mich. 1959, N.Y. 1961, D.C. 1965, U.S. Supreme Ct. 1965, Calif. 1966. Assoc. Cahill, Gordon, Reindel & Ohl, N.Y.C., 1960-64; with Kellogg Co., Battle Creek, Mich., 1964-65; assoc. Joseph L. Alioto, San Francisco, 1965-66; sr. ptnr. The Furth Firm LLP, San Francisco, 1966—. Bd. dirs. Robert Half Internat.; chmn., propr. Chalk Hill Winery. Trustee, chmn. bd. Furth Family Found., San Francisco; bd. dirs. Franklin and Eleanor Roosevelt Inst., 1996—, The Ctr. for Democracy, Washington; chmn. Internat. Jud. Conf., Strasbourg, France, 1992-. Mem. ABA, Internat. Bar Assn., N.Y. Bar Assn., San Francisco Bar Assn., State Bar Calif., Assn. of Bar of City of N.Y., St. Francis Yacht Club, Olympic Club. Office: Furth Firm LLP 225 Bush St 15th Flr San Francisco CA 94104 E-mail: fpfurth@aol.com.

FURTH, JOHN JACOB, molecular biologist, educator, pathologist; b. Phila., Jan. 25, 1929; s. Jacob and Olga (Berthauer) F.; m. Mary Autry, June 24, 1959; children: Karen, Susan, Robin. BA, Cornell U., 1950; student, Yale Law Sch., 1950-51; MD, Duke U., 1958; MA, U. Pa., 1972. Intern Bellevue Hosp., N.Y.C., 1958-59; resident in pathology NYU Sch. Medicine, N.Y.C., 1959-60, postdoctoral fellow dept. microbiology, 1960-62; mem. faculty dept. pathology U. Pa. Med. Sch., Phila., 1962—, prof., 1978—2001, emeritus prof., 2001—. Contbr. articles to profl. jours. Bd. dirs., chmn. hist. sites com. Darby Creek Valley Assn., 1984-96, 1st v.p. 1997—; bd. dirs., founder Friends of the Swedish Cabin (constructed circa 1654), Upper Darby, Pa., 1987, pres. 2002—03; bd. dirs. Fair Housing Coun. of Suburban Phila., 1995-97, 2d dist. leader Upper Darby Democratic Party, 1994—2002, chmn., 2002—; candidate for Congress, 7th Dist. Pa. 2d lt. Q.M.C., U.S. Army, 1951-53. Recipient Hoffman LaRoche award, 1958; Eleanor Roosevelt fellow, 1977-78. Mem. AAAS, Am. Soc. Biol. Chemists and Molecular Biologists, Am. Assn. Cancer Rsch., Am. Assn. Pathologists. Democrat. Mem. Soc. Of Friends. Achievements include codiscovery of RNA polymerase. Home: 43 Roselawn Ave Lansdowne PA 19050-2317 Office: U Pa Sch Medicine Dept Pathology and Lab Med Philadelphia PA 19104-6082 E-mail: jjfurth@mail.med.upenn.edu.

FURTH, KAREN J., artist; BA in Am. History, U, Pa., 1983; MA in Photography, NYU, 1988. Photographer Smithsonian Instn., 1989—94; freelance photographer, 1994—; tchr., cons. Ctr. Urban Cmty. Svcs. The Times Sq., 1994—2002; tchr. Internat. Ctr. Photography at The Point, N.Y.C., 1998—; adj. tchr. photography Eugene Lang Coll. New Sch. Social Rsch., 1999—2005. Artist-in-residence Creative Ctr. N.Y.C. Hosp., 2003—. One-woman shows include 494 Gallery, N.Y.C., 1991, 1992, 1994, Eugene Lang Coll. New Sch. for Social Rsch., 1999—2005, Pulse Art Gallery, 1997, exhibited in group shows at 494 Gallery, 1991, 1992, Synchronicity Space, 1995, Sullivan County Mus., 1995, Pulse Art Gallery, 1996, Golin/Harris, 1998, 2002, at A.I.R., 2004, others, curatorial projects include, The Times Sq. Photography Project, Met. Transp. Authority, 1999; presenter in field; contbr. articles to profl. jours.; Represented in permanent collections J.P. Morgan, Mt. Sinai Hosp., others. Recipient Gilbert Graphic Paper award, 1993; fellow Open Soc. Inst. Individual Project fellow, Soros Found., 1997; scholar Faculty scholar, U. Pa., 1979—83; Internat. Outreach grante, 1993—94. Personal E-mail: kfurth@rcn.com.

FURTH, YVONNE, advertising executive; BS in Mktg., postgrad., Georgetown U., DePaul U. Asst. account exec. Draft Worldwide, 1981—88, gen. mgr., 1988—92, pres. of Chicago office, 1992—96, pres. & COO US operations, 1996—2001, pres., COO Chgo., 2002—. Mem.: Chgo. Assn. Direct Mktg., Direct Mktg. Assn. Office: Draft Chicago 633 N St Clair St Chicago IL 60611

FURTWANGLER, VIRGINIA WALSH (ANN COPELAND), fiction writer; b. Hartford, Conn., Dec. 16, 1932; d. William and Agnes (Bresnahan) Walsh; m. Albert Joseph Furtwangler, Aug. 17, 1968; children: Thomas, Andrew. BA, Coll. New Rochelle, 1954; MA, Cath. U. Am., 1959; PhD,

Cornell U., 1970; LLD (hon.), U. New Brunswick, 1997. Instr. Coll. New Rochelle, N.Y., 1963-66; asst. prof. English Ind. U. Northwest, Gary, 1970-71, Mt. Allison U., Sackville, N.B., Canada, 1976-77; vis. prof. English Linfield Coll., McMinnville, Oreg., 1980-81; vis. fiction writer U. Idaho, Moscow, 1986-87; writer in residence Bemidji State U., 1987, Wichita State U., 1988, Mt. Allison U., 1990-91; Hallie Ford chair English Willamette U., Salem, Oreg., 1996-99. Author (under pseudonym Ann Copeland): At Peace, 1978, The Back Room, 1979, Earthen Vessels, 1984, The Golden Thread, 1989, Strange Bodies on a Stranger Shore, 1994, Season of Apples, 1996, The ABCs of Writing Fiction, 1996. Recipient Can. Coun. awards, 1980, 88, Ingram Merrill award, 1990; Writing fellow NEA, 1978, 94. Roman Catholic. Avocations: piano, ballroom dancing. Home: 235 Oak Way NE Salem OR 97301-4333 E-mail: vfurtwan@willamette.edu.

FURUBOTN, EIRIK GRUNDTVIG, economics professor; b. N.Y.C., Apr. 18, 1923; s. Konrad Martin and Caroline (Grundtvig) F.; m. Florence Birkby Duckworth; children— Karin Florence, Erik Grundtvig, Kristian George BA, Brown U., 1948; MA, Columbia U., 1950, PhD, 1959. Instr. Wesleyan U., Middletown, Conn., 1953-55; asst. prof. Lafayette Coll., Easton, Pa., 1958-60; assoc. prof. Emory U., Atlanta, 1960-63; prof. SUNY, Binghamton, 1963-67, Tex. A&M U., College Station, 1967-82; James L. West prof. econs. U. Tex., Arlington, 1982-96; rsch. fellow pvt. enterprise rsch. ctr. Tex. A&M U., College Station, 1996—. Com. mem. Tex. A&M Univ. Press, College Station, 1974-82; co-dir. Ctr. for Study of New Instl. Econs., U. Saarland, W.Ger., 1986—; mem. bd. advs. Utrecht Sch. Econs., Utrecht U., Netherlands, 2002. Co-author: (with R. Richter) Neue Institutionen Okonomik, 1996, The Evolution of Modern Demand Theory, 1972; co-editor: The Economics of Property Rights, 1974, The New Institutional Economics: An Assessment, 1991, Institution and Economic Theory, 1997, also Russian and Chinese transls.; mem. editl. bd. Applied Econs., London, 1971-72; mem. bd. editors So. Econ. Jour., 1979-81, Zeitschrift für die gesamte Staatswissenschaft, 1984—; contbr. articles to profl. jours. Trustee Allen Acad., Bryan, Tex., 1974-76; mem. adv. coun. Polit. Economy Rsch. Ctr., Bozeman, Mont., 1984-92; mem. nat. adv. bd. Nat. Ctr. for Privatization, Wichita, Kans., 1985-95. Cpl. U.S. Army, 1942-46, ETO. Francis Wayland scholar Brown U., 1948; named Honorarprofessor für Volkswirtschaftslehre U. Saarland, Fed. Republic of Germany. Mem. Am. Econ. Assn., So. Econ. Assn. (exec. com. 1975-77), Phi Beta Kappa, Omicron Delta Epsilon, Beta Gamma Sigma, Omega Rho. Republican. Episcopalian. Avocations: antiques, travel. Home: 750 N Rosemary Dr Bryan TX 77802-4307 Office: Tex A&M U Pvt Enterprise Rsch Ctr PO Box 3327 College Station TX 77841-3327 Business E-Mail: perc@tamu.edu.

FURUMOTO, DAVID JOHN, theater educator; s. Howard Hosaku and Viola Gilbertine Furumoto. BA in Theatre, U. Hawaii, 1978, MFA, 1982. Actor, dir., playwright Honolulu Tcht. Youth, 1984—90, various theatres, San Francisco, 1990—95, L.A., 1995—2000; asst. prof. drama and theatre U. Wis., Madison, 2000—. Bd. dirs. ASSITES/USA. Author: (plays) The Pocket Kabuki, 1986, Wondrous Tales of Old Japan, 1998. Scholar, Crown Prince Akihito, Tokyo, 1982. Mem.: Screen Actors Guild, Actors Equity Assn. Avocations: classical Japanese dance, Scottish pipes. Office: U Wis 6010 Vilas Hall 821 Univ Ave Madison WI 53706 Office Phone: 608-265-2723. E-mail: furumoto@wisc.edu.

FURUYA, KATRYN N., pediatrician, educator; arrived in U.S., 2002; d. Hironori and Grace T. Furuya; m. Michel M. Polanchet. MD, U. Toronto, Can., 1985; undergrad., McMaster U., Hamilton, Ont., Can. Cert. pediatrics Royal Coll. Physicians and Surgeons Can., 1989, pediatric gastroenterology Royal Coll. Physicians and Surgeons Can., 1992, Am. Bd. Pediat., 1992. Intern Hosp. for Sick Children, U. Toronto, resident, fellow; asst. prof. pediat. LeBonheur Children's Hosp., U. Tenn., Memphis, 1993—94, Hosp. for Sick Children, U. Toronto, 1994—2002; med. dir. pediat. liver transplant program, assoc. prof. pediat. U. NC, Chapel Hill, 2002—04; assoc. prof. pediat. divsn. pediat. gastroenterology Pa. State Hershey Med Ctr., Hershey, 2004—. Contbr. articles to profl. jours. Recipient Aaron Rappaport Prize in Basic Sci., U. Toronto, 1996. Mem.: Am. Gastroent. Assn., North Am. Soc. for Pediatric Gastroenterology, Hepatology and Nutrition (Clin. Sci. Young Investigator award 1997), Am. Assn. for the Study of Liver Disease (Am. Liver Found. fellow rsch. prize 1992). Achievements include research in Biliary atresia, PABA as a new test of liver function. Office: Pa State Hershey Med Ctr Divsn Pediat Gastroenterology 500 University Dr PO Box 850 MC H085 Hershey PA 17033 Office Phone: 717-531-5901.

FURYK, JAMES MICHAEL, professional golfer; b. West Chester, Pa., May 12, 1970; m. Tabitha Furyk; children: Caleigh Lynn, Tanner James. Grad. in Gen. Bus., U. Ariz., 1992. Profl. golfer PGA, 1992—. Mem. Ryder Cup team, 1997, 99, 2002, 04, Presidents Cup team, 1998, 2000, 03, World Cup team, 2003. Winner Nike Miss. Gulf Coast Classic, 1993, Las Vegas Internat., 1995, United Airlines Hawaiian Open, 1996, Argentine Open, 1997, Las Vegas Invitational, 1998, Fred Meyer Challenge, 1998, Doral-Ryder Open, 2000, Mercedes Championship, 2000, Memorial Tournament, 2002, U.S. Open Championship, 2003, Buick Open, 2003, Western Open, 2005; 2d pl. Meml. Tournament, 1997, The Tour Championship, 1997. Avocation: sports. Office: c/o PGA America Box 109601 100 Ave of Champions Palm Beach Gardens FL 33410

FUSARELLI, BONNIE CAROL, education educator, consultant; b. Houston, Tex., Apr. 12, 1968; d. William Osband and Catherine Ann Edwards; m. Lance Darin Fusarelli, July 5, 2003; 1 child, Drew Austin. BA in govt., U. Tex. at Austin, 1989; MA in ednl. leadership, U. Tex. at San Antonio, 1998; PhD in ednl. adminstrn., Pa. State U., 2001. Tchr. Lago Vista Ind. Sch. Dist., 1992—93, Anderson H.S., Austin, Tex., 1993—96, Boerne H.S., Tex., 1996—98; rsch. asst. Pa. State U., 1998—2001; asst. prof. U. Ky., 2001—03, NC State U., 2003—. Recipient Drexel award, Pa. State U., 2000, C.M. Branch Endowment for Teaching Excellence award, 1997; Rsch. and Profl. Develop. grant, NC State U., 2004—05, grant, US Dept Edn., 2002, Fgn. Travel grant, U. Ky., 2002, 2003, Lavanda P. Muller Grad. fellowship, Pa. State U., 2000—01, Graham fellowship, 1998—99. Mem.: Phi Lamda Theta. Office: NC State U 608 Poe Hall, Campus Box 7801 Raleigh NC 27695 Office Phone: 919-515-6359. Business E-Mail: bonnie_fusarelli@ncsu.edu.

FUSARO, RAMON MICHAEL, dermatologist, preventive medicine physician, researcher; b. Bklyn., Mar. 6, 1927; s. Angelo and Ida (Pucci) F.; m. Lavonne Johnsen, Nov. 6, 1971; children: Lisa Ann, Toni Ann; stepsons: Jeff, Scott. BA, U. Minn., 1949, BS, 1951, MD, 1953, MS, 1958, PhD, 1965. Diplomate Am. Bd. Dermatology. Intern Mpls. Gen. Hosp., 1953-54, resident in dermatology, 1954—57; from instr. to assoc. prof. U. Minn., 1957-70, dir. outpatient dermatology clinic, 1962-70; prof., chmn. dept. dermatology U. Nebr. Med. Center, Omaha, 1970-82; prof. dermatology sect. dept. internal medicine U. Nebr. Med. Ctr., Omaha, 1982-91, acting chief sect. dermatology, 1991-94; prof., chmn. dept. dermatology Creighton U., Omaha, 1975-87; prof. dermatology dept. internal medicine Creighton U. Sch. Medicine, Omaha, 1983-89; prof. Creighton U., Omaha, 1989—; dir. dermatology residency program Creighton/Nebr. Univs. Health Found., 1975-83; prof. dept. pub. health and preventive medicine Hereditary Cancer Inst., Creighton U., 1984—. Contbr. chapters to books, articles to profl. jours. With USN, 1944-46. Mem. Am. Acad. Dermatology, Sigma Xi. Home: 908 Beaver Lake Blvd Plattsmouth NE 68048-4500 Office: 984360 Nebr Med Ctr Omaha NE 68198-4360 also: Creighton U Med Sch Criss III Dept Prev Med 2500 California Plz Omaha NE 68178-0403 Office Phone: 402-559-4399. Personal E-mail: rfusaro@unmc.edu. Business E-Mail: rmfusaro@Creighton.edu.

FUSCO, ANDREW G., lawyer; b. Punxsutawney, Pa., Jan. 11, 1948; s. Albert G. and Virginia N. (Whitesell) F.; m. Deborah K. Lucas; children: Matthew, Geoffrey, David. BS in Bus. Adminstrn. and Fin., W.Va. U., 1970, JD, 1973. Bar: W.Va. 1973, US Ct. Appeals (4th cir.) 1974, US Supreme Ct. 1977, US Ct. Appeals (fed. cir.) 1985, US Tax Ct. 1995, US Ct. Appeals (9th cir.), 2003. Pvt. practice, Morgantown, W.Va., 1973-85; prin. Fusco & Newbraugh, L.C., Morgantown, 1985-98, The Fusco Legal Group, L.C., Morgantown, 1998-2001; mem. Eckert Seamans Cherin & Mellott, LLC, 2001—. Pros. atty. Monongalia County, W.Va., 1977—81; instr. Coll. Bus. and Econs., Law Ctr., W.Va. U., 1975—76, W.Va. U. Sch. Journalism, 1997—2003. Author: Antitrust Law (West Virginia Practice Handbook), 1991; editor, contbg. author: Twenty Feet From Glory (John R. Goodwin), 1970, Business Law (John R. Goodwin), 1972, Beyond Baker Street (Michael Harrison), 1976. Bd. dirs. W.Va. Career Colls., 1971-76; profl. adv. bd. Childbirth and Parent Edn. Assn., 1975-82, Rape and Domestic Violence Info. Ctr., 1977-81; mem. W.Va. Sec. State's Tribunal on Election Reform, 1977-81; chmn. Monongalia County Drug Edn. Task Force, 1978-80; bd. advisors Nat. Smokers Alliance, 1998-99; vis. com. W.Va. U. Coll. Law, 2000-03. Recipient Am. Jurisprudence award Bancroft-Whitney Publ. Co., 1971; named Outstanding Young Man of Morgantown, 1979. Mem. ABA (Civil RICO com., antitrust law sect.), Monongalia County Bar Assn., Am. Judicature Soc., W.Va. Bar Assn., Baker St. Irregulars of NY, Sherlock Holmes Soc. London, Bootmakers of Toronto, Nat. Dist. Attys. Assn., Sons of Italy, W.Va. Law Sch. Assn., Monongalia Arts Ctr. (pres., treas., vice-chmn., trustee). Democrat. Roman Catholic. Home: 2054 Iron Bridge Cir Morgantown WV 26508 Office: Eckert Seamans Cherin & Mellott 2400 Cranberry Sq Morgantown WV 26508-9209 Office Phone: 304-594-1000. Office Fax: 304-594-1181. Business E-Mail: afusco@eckertseamans.com.

FUSCO, AURILLA MARIE, director; d. Delmar A. and Catherine F. (Bryan) Thibodeau; m. John A. Fusco (div.); 1 child, Craig L. Jr. BS in Paralegal/Govt. Bus., U. Md., 1986; MPA, Troy State U., 1990; postgrad., Concord Sch. Law. Staff asst. to Sen. George J. Mitchell U.S. Senate, Washington, 1981—85, staff asst. to Sen. Albert Gore, Jr. Nashville, 1985—86, staff asst, office mgr. subcom. on children, families, drugs and alcoholism, 1987; program analyst, adminstrv. officer Dept. of Army, Germany, 1987—91; dir. child care River Valley Child Devel., Huntington, W.Va., 1992—97; exec. dir. Child Advocates of Blair County, Altoona, Pa., 1998—2001; regional mr. capital gifts Bucknell U., Lewisburg, Pa., 2001—04; dir. devel. Main Campus Librs. Georgetown U., Washington, 2004—. Presenter Nat. Assn. for Edn. of Young Children; cons. W.Va. Welfare Reform Coalition, 1996—98; exec. dir. nonprofit R&D Gamday, LLC, Altoona, Pa., 2000—. Co-chair Children's Issues Advocates, W.Va., 1997—98; pres. Jr. League, Huntington, 1997—98; sustainer adviser Jr. League Williamsport, 2003—04; mem. devel. com. Heurich House Found.; mem. parents com. Bishop Ireton H.S. Hockey Team. Mem.: Sunrise Rotary. Office: Lavinger Libr Georgetown U 37th and O St NW Washington DC 20057-1174

FUSCO, JANET ELLEN, secondary school educator; b. Newark, N.J., June 22, 1951; d. Joseph John and Angelina (Russomanno) F. BA, Bloomfield (N.J.) Coll., 1973; MA in Teaching, Fairleigh Dickinson U., 1979. Cert. tchr., N.J. Contract analyst Blue Cross of N.J., Newark, 1973-78; tchr. St. Vicnent Acad., Newark, 1978-79, Queen of Peace High Sch., North Arlington, N.J., 1979—. Recipient Archdiocese of Newark Tchr. Recognition award, 1992. Office: Queen of Peace High Sch 191 Rutherford Pl North Arlington NJ 07031-6091

FUSCO, RICHARD, English literature educator; b. Phila., Apr. 27, 1952; BA, U. Pa., 1973, MA, 1974, U. Miss., 1982; PhD, Duke U., 1990. Instr. English St. Joseph's U., Phila., 1988-91, asst. prof. English, 1997—2003, assoc. prof. English, 2003—. Author: Maupassant and the American Short Story: The Influence of Form at the Turn of the Century, 1994, (pamphlet) Fin de millénaire: Poe's Legacy for the Detective Story, 1993; contbr. articles to profl. jours. Served as intelligence officer U.S. Navy, 1975-79. Mem. MLA. Home: 2237 S 23rd St Philadelphia PA 19145-3321 Office: Dept English St Joseph's U 5600 City Ave Philadelphia PA 19131-1308 Office Phone: 610-660-1887. Business E-Mail: fusco@sju.edu.

FUSELIER, HAROLD ANTHONY, JR., urologist, director, educator; b. Abbeville, La., Dec. 1, 1942; s. Harold Anthony and May Elizabeth (Fowler) F.; m. Ann Valentino, May 17, 1968; children: Harold Anthony III, F. Scott, J. Prentice, Mims Michael. BS, La. State U., Baton Rouge, 1964; MD, La. State U., New Orleans, 1967. Diplomate Am. Bd. Urology. Internship Charity Hosp., New Orleans, 1967-68; residency urology Alton Ochsner Medical Found., 1970-74; mem. dept. urology Ochsner Clinic Found., New Orleans, 1974—, chmn. dept. urology, 1989—2002; med. dir. surgery Ochsner Found. Hosp., New Orleans, 1990—; clin. prof. urology Tulane U. Med. Ctr., New Orleans, 1988—, La. State U. Med. Ctr., New Orleans, 1990—. Program dir. La. State U./Ochsner Urology Tng. Program, 1991—. Contbr. articles to profl. jours. Capt. USAF, 1968-70. Fellow ACS; mem. Am. Urol. Assn., Soc. Internat. d'Urologie, Soc. for Study of Impotence, Soc. Univ. Urologists. Roman Catholic. Avocations: golf, hunting, fishing. Office: Ochsner Clinic 1514 Jefferson Hwy New Orleans LA 70121-2483 Office Phone: 504-842-4084. E-mail: hfuselier@ochsner.org.

FUSELIER, LOUIS ALFRED, lawyer; b. New Orleans, Mar. 26, 1932; s. Robert Howe and Monica (Hanemann) F.; m. Eveline Gasquet Fenner, Dec. 27, 1956; children: Louis Alfred, Henri de la Claire, Elizabeth Fenner. BS, La. State U., 1953; LL.B., Tulane U., 1959. Bar: La. 1959, Miss. 1964, U.S. Supreme Ct. 1965. Trial atty. NLRB, New Orleans, 1959-62; pres., ptnr. Fuselier, Hector, Robertson & Ott and successor firms, 1969-94; v.p., ptnr. Young, Williams, Henderson & Fuselier, P.A., Jackson, Miss., 1994—. Capt. USAF, 1953-56. Fellow Am. Acad. Hosp. Attys., Am. Coll. Labor and Employment Lawyers, The Am. Employment Law Coun., Am. Law Inst.; mem. ABA (practice and procedure com. of labor law sect.), La. Bar Assn. (past chmn. labor law sect.), Miss. Bar Assn., Hinds County Bar Assn., Miss. Bar Found., Miss. Def. Lawyers, Miss. Wildlife Fedn. (pres. 1975-76), Newcomen Soc., Soc. Human Resource Mgmt. (accredited pers. diplomate), Miss. Econ. Coun. (dir. 1996-97), Miss. Mfrs. Assn., Boston Club (New Orleans), Country Club of Jackson, Univ. Club (Jackson), Rotary (Paul Harris fellow). Home: 3804 Old Canton Rd Jackson MS 39216-3521 E-mail: lfuselier@ywhf.com, lfusel@aol.com.

FUSFELD, DANIEL ROLAND, economist; b. Washington, May 23, 1922; s. Irving Sidney and Cecile (Leban) F.; m. Harriet Miller, Aug. 30, 1947; children: Robert, Sarah, Yaakov Sadeh. BA, George Washington U., 1941; MA, Columbia U., 1947, PhD, 1953. Instr. Hofstra Coll., Hempstead, N.Y., 1947-53, asst. prof., 1953-56, Mich. State U., East Lansing, 1956-60; assoc. prof. U. Mich., Ann Arbor, 1960-64, prof., 1964-87, prof. emeritus, 1987—. Lectr. USAF Inst. Tech., Dayton, Ohio, 1958-59; vis. assoc. prof. Columbia U., N.Y.C., 1960; bd. dirs. Spectrum Human Svcs., 1992-98, Avalon Housing, Inc. Author: Economic Thought of Franklin D. Roosevelt, 1956, The Age of the Economist, 1966, 9th edit. 2001, Economics, 1972, The Basic Economics of the Urban-Racial Crisis, 1973, Rise and Repression of Radical Labor, 1877-1918, 1985; co-author: The Political Economy of the Urban Ghetto, 1984; co-editor: The Soviet Economy, 1962; also articles. With U.S. Army, 1943—46. Mem. Am. Econ. Assn., Assn. for Evolutionary Econs. (v.p. 1970, pres. 1971), Internat. Network for Econ. Method (chmn. 1989-92), Hist. Econ. Soc. Home: Apt 324 4001 Glacier Hills Dr Ann Arbor MI 48105 Office: U Mich Dept Econs Ann Arbor MI 48109 E-mail: hadafusf@yahoo.com.

FUSFELD, HERBERT IRVING, research management and public policy executive; b. Bklyn., Feb. 13, 1921; s. Harry and Fanny (Stitch) F.; m. Ruth Lachman, July 11, 1943; children: Alan Roy, Warren Edward. BA, Bklyn. Coll., 1941; MA, U. Pa., 1945, PhD, 1950. Rsch. physicist, head physics, math. divsn. Frankford Arsenal, Phila., 1941-53; sr. physicist Am. Machinery & Foundry Co., Stamford, Conn., 1953-55; dir. Ctrl. Rsch. Lab., 1955-59, dir. rsch., 1959-63, Kennecott Copper Corp., N.Y.C., 1963-78; dir. Ctr. for Sci. and Tech. Policy NYU, 1978-86; dir. Ctr. for Sci. and Tech. Policy Lally Sch. Mgmt. Rensselaer Poly. Inst., Troy, NY, 1986-90; chmn., adv. bd., prof. Lally Sch. of Mgmt., Troy, NY, 1990—95; chmn. Fusfeld Group Inc., 1991—. Dir. Hazeltine Corp., 1976-88, Electronics Assocs. Inc., 1984-90; vis. lectr. physics of metals Grad. Sch. U. Pa., 1952-53; chmn. Internat. Temperature Symposium, 1954; mem. numerical data adv. bd. NRC, 1970-75; mem. Nat. Materials Adv. Bd., 1975-79; adv. group on transnat. enterprises U.S. Dept. State, 1975, expert cons., 1976-80; chmn. adv. com. Inst. Materials Rsch., Nat. Bur Standards, 1976-78; mem. expert group tech. and econ. growth OECD, 1976-80; adv. coun. NSF, 1977-80; mem. adv. com. corp. assocs. Am. Chem. Soc.; mem. U.S.-USSR Joint Commn. on S&T Cooperation. Author: The Technical Enterprise, 1986, Industry's Future: Changing Patterns of Industrial Research, 1994; bd. editors Rsch. Mgmt.; contbr. articles in field to profl. jours. Mem. sci. adv. bd. Found. of San Paolo Bank, 1988-92. Fellow AAAS; mem. Indsl. Rsch. Inst. (dir., pres. 1973-74, chmn. fed. sci. and tech. com. 1974-76), Am. Phys. Soc., Am. Ordnance Assn., Am. Inst. Physics (governing bd.), Am. Inst. Mining and Metall. Engrs., Am. Mgmt. Assn. (trustee, v.p. R & D coun.), Sky Club (N.Y.C.). Home: 45 Mohawk Trl Stamford CT 06903-1608 Office: Lally Sch Mgmt Rensselaer Poly Instit Troy NY 12180 Office Phone: 203-968-0079. E-mail: hifusfeld@snet.net.

FUSILLO, ALICE ELBERT, retired sociologist, sculptor; b. Balt., Dec. 13, 1922; d. Francis Wilson and Alice Margaret (Jones) Zeigler; m. Matthew Henry Fusillo, Sept. 13, 1947 (dec. Aug. 3, 1980); children: Lawrence Joseph, Lisa Ann, Jessica Jean, Susan Frances. BS, U. Md., 1948, MA, 1966. Pub. health analyst NIH, Bethesda, Md., 1968—74; statistician Bur. Census, SESA, Suitland, Md., 1974; consumer sci. specialist FDA, Washington, 1974—79; statistician Dept. Health and Human Svcs., Washington, 1979—88; sculptor Washington, 1988—. Contbr. articles to profl. jours.; exhibitions include Carego Foxley Leach Gallery, Washington, D.C., 1991, Whitehall Gallery, Corcoran, Washington, 1990, Washington Square Sculpture Show, 2003. Recipient Mary Lay Sculpture award, Corcoran Sch. Art, 1986, Visual Art award, Capitol Hill Art League, 2002. Mem.: AAUW, Goodwill Industries, Washington Sculptors Soc., Internat. Sculpture Ctr., The Art League (Best in Show 1988), Sierra Club. Achievements include patents for Dying Swan sculpture. Avocations: landscape and portrait painting, ballroom dancing. Home: Apt N604 560 N St SW Washington DC 20024-4617

FUSNER, HENRY S., musician, educator; b. Parkersburg, W. Va., June 16, 1923; s. Ebert P. Fusner and Caroline Hettinger. BS, Juilliard Sch., 1944, MS, 1945; D of Sacred Music, Union Theol. Sem., 1951. Music theory instr. Juilliard Sch., NYC, 1944—49; head organ dept. Cleve. Inst. Music, 1956—70; head music theory dept. Blair Sch., Vanderbilt U., Nashville, 1971—88; organist, choir master Emmanuel Baptist Ch., Bklyn., 1943—56, Ch. of Covenant, Cleve., 1956—71, 1st Presbyn. Ch., Nashville, 1970—89. Mem.: Am. Guild Organists (assoc.). Home: 500 Elmington Ave #309 Nashville TN 37205

FUSSELL, DAVID DEAN, lawyer; b. Atlanta, June 19, 1956; s. Cosby Corneilous and Ruth Louise (Fountain) F.; m. Jill Watkins, Sept. 25, 1993; 1 child, David Austin. BS, Fla. State U., 1979, JD, 1984. Bar: Fla. 1984. With Leon County Sheriff's Dept., Tallahassee, Fla., 1978-84, investigator anti-drug unit, 1980, supr. spl. investigation drug unit and task force, 1981-84; counsel Fla. Game and Fresh Water Fish Commn., Tallahassee, 1984-86, insp. maj. bur. aviation, investigation and comm., 1985-86; asst. pub. defender 9th Jud. Cir. of Fla., 1987-90; capital trial atty., 1988-90; assoc. Law Office Mark L. Horwitz, Orlando, Fla., 1991-94; ptnr. Horwitz & Fussell, Orlando, Fla., 1994—. Mem. Nat. Assn. Criminal Def. Lawyers (govt. misconduct com. 1989-90, mem. state and fed. forfeiture task force 1992-94, bd. dirs. 1996—, co-chair coun. of affiliates 1997), Fla. Assn. Criminal Def. Lawyers (bd. dirs. 1995—, co-chair legis. com. 1997—), Ctrl. Fla. Criminal Def. Attys. Assn. (chmn. lawyers assistance strike force 1992-94, chmn. com. bylawaws 1993—, v.p. 1993-94, bd. dirs. 1992-93, pres.-elect 1994-95, pres. 1995-96), Orange County Bar Assn., Orlando Touchdown Club (bd. dirs. 1995—, pres.-elect 1998-99). Office: 17 E Pine St Orlando FL 32801-2607

FUSSELL, KEITH BAUGUS, minister; b. Dickson, Tenn., Apr. 23, 1961; s. Herman Clyde Jr. and Carey Alberta (Baugus) F.; m. Kimberly Diane McDowell, June 29, 1985; children: Joshua Keith, Joanna Hillary, Joel McDowell. BA, David Lipscomb U., 1983; MA in Religion, Harding U., 1990. Lic. profl. counselor, Tenn.; cert. Nat. Bd. for Cert. Counselors. Assoc. minister Sunset Ch. of Christ, Miami, Fla., 1983-87; minister Kiski Valley Ch. of Christ, Apollo, Pa., 1987-88; asst. campus minister Highland St. Ch. of Christ, Memphis, 1989-90; lead geriatric counselor N.E. Mental Health Ctr., Memphis, 1990-92; family life minister Sycamore View Ch. of Christ, Memphis, 1993—. Mem. Am. Assn. Christian Counselors, Am. Assn. Marriage and Family Therapy (assoc.), Psi Chi. Office: Sycamore View Ch of Christ 1910 Sycamore View Rd Memphis TN 38134-6634 E-mail: Kfussell@sycamoreview.org.

FUSSELL, PAUL, writer, literature educator; b. Pasadena, Calif., Mar. 22, 1924; s. Paul and Wilhma Wilson (Sill) F.; m. Betty Ellen Harper, June 17, 1949 (div. 1987); children: Rosalind, Samuel; m. Harriette Rhawn Behringer, Apr. 11, 1987. BA, Pomona (Calif.) Coll., 1947, LittD (hon.), 1981; MA, Harvard U., 1949, PhD, 1952; MA (hon.), U. Pa., 1983; LittD (hon.), Monmouth (NJ) U., 1985. Instr. English Conn. Coll., 1951-55; mem. faculty Rutgers U., 1955—, John DeWitt prof. English lit., 1976-83; Donald T. Regan prof. English lit. U. Pa., Phila., 1983-94, prof. emeritus, 1994—. Cons. editor Random House, 1963-64; lectr. Am. univs., 1965—; vis. prof. Kings Coll., London, 1990-92. Author: The Rhetorical World of Augustan Humanism, 1965, Poetic Meter and Poetic Form, 1965, rev., 1979, Samuel Johnson and The Life of Writing, 1971, The Great War and Modern Memory (Nat. Book Critics Circle award 1975, Nat. Book award 1976), Abroad: British Literary Traveling Between the Wars, 1980, The Boy Scout Handbook & Other Observations, 1982, Class: A Guide through the American Status System, 1983, Thank God for the Atom Bomb & Other Essays, 1988, Wartime: Understanding and Behavior in the Second World War, 1989; BAD: or The Dumbing of America, 1991, The Anti-Egoist: Kingsley Amis, Man of Letters, 1994, Doing Battle: The Making of a Skeptic, 1996, Uniforms: Why We Are What We Wear, 2002, The Boys Crusade, 2003; contbg. editor Harper's, 1979-83, The New Republic, 1979-85. Served with AUS, 1943-46. Decorated Purple Heart, Bronze Star; recipient James D. Phelan award Phelan Found., 1964; Lindback Found. award, 1971; Ralph Waldo Emerson award Phi Beta Kappa, 1976; sr. fellow NEH, 1973-74; Guggenheim fellow, 1977-78; Rockefeller Found. fellow, 1983-84 Fellow Royal Soc. Lit., Soc. Am. Historians; mem. MLA, Acad. Lit. Studies. Home: 2020 Walnut St 4H Philadelphia PA 19103-5635

FUSTÉ, JOSÉ ANTONIO, federal judge; b. San Juan, Puerto Rico, Nov. 3, 1943; BBA, U. P.R., San Juan, 1965, LLB cum laude, 1968. Ptnr. Jimenez & Fuste, Hato Rey, P.R., 1968-85; judge US Dist. Ct. P.R., San Juan, 1985—, chief judge. Prof. U. P.R., 1975—85, 1996—2002. Office: US Courthouse CH-133 150 Ave Carlos Chardon San Juan PR 00918-1758 Office Phone: 787-772-3120.

FUSTER, JAIME B., state supreme court justice; b. Guayama, PR, Jan. 12, 1941; s. Jaime L. and Maria Luisa (Berlingeri) Fuster; m. Mary Jo Fuster, Dec. 19, 1966; children: Maria Luisa, Jaime. BA, Notre Dame U., 1962; JD, U. P.R., 1965; LLM, Columbia U., 1966; SJD, Harvard U., 1974; LLD (hon.), Temple U., 1985. Bar: P.R. 1966. Prof. law U. PR, 1966—73, 1978—80; dean Law Sch. U. PR, 1974—78; project dir. Study on Legal Profession of P.R. Ctr. Social Rsch., 1970—73; ednl. cons. Office of Cts. Adminstrn. Govt. of PR, 1978—80; dep. asst. atty. gen. U.S. Dept. Justice, Washington, 1980—81; pres. Cath. U. PR, 1981—84; mem. Congress from PR, Washington, 1984—92; resident commr. Commonwealth of PR, 1984—92; assoc. justice PR Supreme Ct., 1992—. Cons., lectr. in field. Author: Political and Civil Rights in Puerto Rico, 1968, The Duties of Citizens, 1973, The Lawyers of Puerto Rico: A Sociological Study, 1974, Law and Problems of Elderly People, 1978; editor-in-chief: U. P.R. Law Rev., 1964—65; contbr. chapters to books, articles to profl. jours. Named One of Outstanding Young Men of Am., U.S. Jr. C. of C., 1978. Mem.: Interam. Bar Found. (bd. dirs. 1975—79), Assn. Am. Colls. (adv. bd. 1980—84). Democrat. Roman Catholic. Avocation: tennis. Office: PO Box 2392 San Juan PR 00902-2392 Office Phone: 787-723-0856. Business E-Mail: jaimefb@tribunales.gobierno.pr.

FUSTER, VALENTIN, cardiologist, educator; b. Barcelona, Jan. 20, 1943; s. Joaquin and Pilar Fuster; m. Angela-Maria Guals, Sept. 3, 1968; children: Pablo, Silvia. Baccaluarate, Colegio Jesuitas, Barcelona, 1961; MD, Barcelona U., 1967. Diplomate Am. Bd. Internal Medicine (mem. com. subsplty. bd. cardiovas. disease), Am. Bd. Cardiology. Intern Hosp. Clinico, Barcelona, 1967-68; rsch. fellow U. Edinburgh, Scotland, 1968-71; fellow in medicine and cardiovasc. diseases Mayo Grad. Sch. Medicine, Rochester, Minn., 1971-74; asst. prof. medicine Mayo Med. Sch., Rochester, 1974-77, assoc. prof. medicine, 1978-81, assoc. prof. pediat., 1980—, prof. medicine and cardiovasc. diseases, 1981-82. Arthur A. and Hilda M. Master prof. medicine Mt. Sinai Sch. Medicine, N.Y.C., 1982-91, chief divsn. cardiology, 1982-91; head cardiology unit Mass. Gen. Hosp., 1991-93; Mallinckrodt prof. medicine Harvard Med. Sch., Boston, 1991-93; dir. Cardiovasc. Inst. Mt. Sinai Med. Ctr., N.Y.C., 1993—; mem. cardiology adv. com. NIH; mem. com. Am. Bd. Cardiology; hon. lectr. numerous orgns.; mem. adv. coun. Nat. Heart, Lung and Blood Insts., 1997, strategic planning com. Stanley J. Sanroff Endowment for Cardiovasc. Sci., 2002-04; editor-in-chief Nature Jour. on Cardiovasc. Medicine, 2004-. Mem. editl. bd. Am. Jour. Cardiology, 1982, Arteriosclerosis, 1982, Jour. The Am. Coll. Cardiology, 1987, Circulation, 1988, consulting editor, 1992, circulation rsch. consulting editor, 1997; contbr. over 400 articles to profl. jours. Recipient 30 rsch. and tchg. awards including Gruntzig award European Soc. Cardiology, 1992, Disting. Sci. award Am. Coll. Cardiology, 1993, Disting. Conner Lectr. award Am. Heart Assn., 1993, Principe de Asturias award for sci. and tech. Found. Principe de Asturias, Oviedo, Spain, Principe de Asturias award for sci. and tech. U. Asturias in conjunction with Royal Family of Spain, 1996, Andreas Gruntzig award Internat. Soc. Interventionalists, 2002; named Disting. Scientist, AHA/ASA, 2003. Fellow Am. Coll. Cardiology (chair tng. dirs. com. 1997, Disting. Bishop Lectr. award 1994, Disting. Svc. award 2000, chair cardiology tng. and workforce com., 2000-03), Royal Coll. Physicians; mem. Am. Heart Assn. (chmn. pub. com., bd. dirs. 1994, pres.-elect 1997, pres. 1998—99, Disting. Achievement award 1997, Herrick award, 2001), Am. Soc. Clin. Investigations, Assn. Am. Physicians, European Soc. Clin. Investigation, Brit. Cardiac Soc. (corr.), European Soc. Cardiology (U.S. bd. dirs. and Industry), World Heart Fedn. (pres-elect 2003-04). Office: Mt Sinai Med Ctr 1 Gustave L Levy Pl # 1030 New York NY 10029-6500

FUSTERO, ROBERT RAYMOND, retired political organization worker; b. Atlantic City, N.J., June 29, 1951; s. Jose M. and Genevieve (Solanas) Fustero. BA, Am. U., 1976. Clk. Giant Food Inc, Landover, Md., 1973—2001; dir. Jose&Genevieve Fustero Instn., Silver Spring, Md., 2001—03, ret., 2003—, lectr., 2001—. Gubernatorial candidate Dem. Party, Md., 2002. Mem.: Americana Finnmark Assn. (treas. 2003, v.p. 1998—2000, pres. 2000—02), Montgomery Citizens Safer Md. (assoc.). Conservative. Avocations: writing, lectures, consultations. Office: Jose&Genevieve Fustero Institution 2005 Coleridge Dr Silver Spring MD 20902 Office Phone: 301-585-1034. Personal E-mail: rfustero@aol.com.

FUTAMI, NORMAN AKIO, lawyer; b. Hermosa Beach, Calif., Jan. 5, 1960; arrived in Japan, 1993; s. Akimasa and Reiko (Nobe) F.; m. Jean Kiyoko Kashiwabara, July 11, 1987; 1 child, Gregory Minoru. BA, Yale U., New Haven, Conn., 1981; JD, Harvard U., Cambridge, Mass., 1984. Bar: Calif. 1984, Japan 1993. Assoc. Paul, Hastings, Janofsky & Walker LLP, L.A., 1984-92, ptnr. Tokyo, 1988—90, 1993—95, L.A., 1990—93, 1995—, vice chmn. mgmt.-L.A. Office. Office: Paul Hastings Janofsky & Walker LLP 515 S Flower St Los Angeles CA 90071-2228 Office Phone: 213-683-6321. Office Fax: 213-627-0705. Business E-Mail: normanfutami@paulhastings.com.

FUTCH, DOROTHY HELEN, librarian, paralegal; b. Alachua, Fla., Aug. 17, 1931; d. David Malcolm and Burdine (Slaughter) Futch. BA, Fla. State U., 1951; MS, Simmons Coll., 1960; cert. paralegal, City Coll. San Francisco, 1980. Cataloger Oakland (Calif.) Pub. Libr., 1961—76; file supr. Orrick, Herrington & Sutcliffe, San Francisco, 1977—80; probate paralegal R.E. Neuman Probate Referee, San Francisco, 1982—89; database mgr. Natkin, Weisbach, Higginbothan, San Francisco, 1990—93; adminstr. Cool Shades Internat., San Francisco, 1995—. Editor: (newsletter) Oak Leaves, 1969—76; translator: Astucia, 1995—2000; author: Hippie Generations, 2004. Pres. Oakland Pub. Libr. Staff Assn., 1973; active Rep. Nat. Com., 2003—. Lewis State Tchrs. scholar, State of Fla., Tallahassee, 1948—51. Mem.: Luis Inclan Soc. (pres. 2003—), Gamma Phi Beta. Republican. Baptist. Home: Apt 212 631 O'Farrell San Francisco CA 94109 Personal E-mail: dorfu@earthlink.net.

FUTRELL, ALVIN, director; BSE in Phys. Edn., MSE in Phys. Edn., Henderson State U.; EdS in Ednl. Adminstrn., Ark. State U.; EdD in Secondary Edn., Ball State U., 1987. Prof. dept. secondary edn. Henderson State U., Arkadelphia, Ark., 1975—88, dir. tchr. admissions and field experiences, 1988—99, asst. to pres. for diversity, 1999—. Mem.: S.W. Ednl. Lab. (bd. mem. 2003—). Office: Henderson State Univ WO 311 1100 Henderson St Arkadelphia AR 71999-0001

FUTRELL, ELIZABETH J., lawyer; b. Augsberg, Germany, Aug. 31, 1956; d. Richard L. and Alma L. Jones; m. John M. futrell, Dec. 12, 1981; 1 child, Richard L.J. BA in History with high honors, U. Tenn., 1978; JD with honors, U. Miss., 1981. Assoc. Jones Walker Waechter Poitevent Carrère & Denègre, New Orleans, 1981-85, ptnr., 1985—. Contbr. numerous articles to profl. jours. Pres. New Orleans Outreach Inc., 1995-96, bd. dirs. Fellow Am. Coll. Bankruptcy; mem. Am. Bankruptcy Inst. Office: Jones Walker 49th Fl New Orleans LA 70170 E-mail: efutrell@joneswalker.com.

FUTRELL, JEAN H., research scientist, administrator, educator; b. Grant Parish, La., Oct. 20, 1933; s. Homer E. and Ellen Catherine (Padgett) Futrell; m. Earlene Welch, June 3, 1955 (div. Oct. 1976); children: Craig Forrest, Alison Renee; m. Nancy Nielson Futrell, Oct. 30, 1976 (div. Nov. 1987); m. Anne Krohn Graham, June 26, 1988. BSChemE, La. Tech. U., 1955; PhD in Chemistry, U. Calif., Berkeley, 1958. Rsch. scientist Exxon Rsch. Labs., Baytown, Tex., 1958-59; sect. chief high energy chemistry Aeropace Rsch. Labs., Dayton, Ohio, 1961-66; assoc. prof. of chemistry U. Utah, Salt Lake City, 1966-67, prof. chemistry, 1967-86; chair chemistry and biochemistry U. Del., Newark, 1986-97, Willis F. Harrington prof., 1989-99, Willis F. Harrington prof. emeritus, 1999—; dir. W.H. Wiley Environ. Molecular Scis. Lab., U.S. Dept. Energy, Richland, Wash., 1999—2002, sr. Battelle fellow, chief sci. officer, 2002—. Adj. prof. U. Utah, 1999—, Wash. State U., 1999—, U. Idaho, 2000—, U. Ariz., 2002—; bd. visitors Wash. State U., 1999—; mem. math and phys. sci. adv. bd. NSF, 2002—. Alexander Von Humboldt fellow Hahn-Meitner Inst., Berlin, 1984-85, Fullbright fellow U. Innsbruck, Austria, 1978-79; numerous grants NSF, NIH, DOE, Petroleum Rsch. Fund of the Am. Chem. Soc., Air Force Office of Scientific Rsch., EPA, Fellow AAAS, Am. Phys. Soc.; mem. NAS (math. and phys. scis. adv. com.), NSF (adv. com. on environ. rsch. and edn.), Nat. Rsch. Coun., Nat. Magnet Lab. (adv. com.), Chem. Scis. Roundtable (governing bd. of coun. for chem. rsch. 1995-2000, exec. com. 1995-2000, chair govt. rels. com. 1994-97, program chair 1998, chair 1999), Am. Soc. for Mass Spectrometry (founding mem. 1967, pres. 1976-78), Am. Chem. Soc., Am. Inst. of Physics, Indian Soc. for Mass Spectrometry, Hungarian Soc. for Mass Spectrometry, Internat. Soc. Mass. Spectrometry, Sigma Xi, Tau Beta Pi. Home: 2802 Appaloosa Way Richland WA 99352-9646 Office: Pacific NW Nat Lab Office of Dir Richland WA 99352 Office Phone: 509-372-4140. E-mail: jean.futrell@pnl.gov.

FUTRELL, JOHN WILLIAM, environmental agency executive, lawyer; b. Alexandria, La., July 6, 1935; s. J.W. and Sarah Ruth (Hitesman) F.; m. Iva Macdonald, Aug. 13, 1966; children: Sarah, Daniel. BA, Tulane U., 1957; postgrad., Free U. Berlin, 1958; LLB, Columbia U., 1965. Bar: La. 1966. Atty. Lemle & Kelleher, New Orleans, 1966-71; prof. law U. Ala., 1971-74, U. Ga., 1974-80; pres. Environ. Law Inst., Washington, 1980—2003, Sustainable Devel. Law Assocs., Arlington, Va., 2003—. Lectr. USIA, Japan and India, 1978, Austria, 1979, Sweden, Germany, U.K. and Ireland, 1980, Argentina, 1988, Brazil, 1991, 92, 2004, Mex., 1992, Germany and Chile, 1993, India, 1997, 2000; Woodrow Wilson fellow Smithsonian Instn., Washington, 1978-80. Co-author: Sustainable Environmental Law, 1993. Del. UN Conf. on Water, 1977, White House Conf. Inflation, 1974. Capt. USMC, 1957-62. Recipient Chair's award, Natural Resources Coun. Am., 2005; scholar, Fulbright, 1958. Mem.: ABA (Disting. Achievement award 2004), Am. Law Inst., Sierra Club (nat. bd. dirs. 1971—81, pres. 1977—78, hon. v.p. 2002—), Cosmos Club, Marines' Meml. Club, Phi Beta Kappa, Order of Coif. Office: Sustainable Devel Law Assocs 4600 7th St N Arlington VA 22203 Office Phone: 703-522-0247. Personal E-mail: futrellfam@aol.com.

FUTRELL, STEPHAN RAY, lawyer; b. Rockingham, N.C., Jan. 1, 1956; s. Wilton Ray and Bettie Ann (Horton) F. BA, Wake Forest U., 1978; JD, Georgetown U., 1981. Bar: N.C. 1981, U.S. Dist. Ct. (mid. dist.) N.C. 1981, U.S. Dist. Ct. (we. dist.) N.C. Assoc. Womble Carlyle Sandridge & Rice, Winston-Salem, N.C., 1981-83, Allman Spry Humphreys & Armentrout, Winston-Salem, N.C., 1984-85; ptnr. Kitchin Neal Webb Webb & Futrell, PA, Rockingham, 1985—; atty. City of Hamlet, N.C., 1997—; county atty. Richmond County, N.C., 1999—. Pres. Richmond County Young Democrats, Rockingham, 1987-88; mem. Rockingham Civitans, 1986-89, sec. 1987-89; dir. Richmond County Arts Coun., 1995—, v.p., 1996-98, pres., 1998-2000. Mem. ABA, N.C. Def. Lawyers Assn., N.C. Bar Assn., Richmond County Bar Assn. Democrat. Home: 701 Hillcrest Dr Rockingham NC 28379-2561 Office: Kitchin Neal Webb Webb & Futrell PA PO Box 1657 Rockingham NC 28380 E-mail: sr_futrell@etinternet.net.

FUTROVSKY, CHERYL JEAN, foundation administrator, performing company executive; b. Santa Paula, Calif., Oct. 31, 1946; d. Ralph Vernon and Mary Ermadee Mashburn; m. John Henry Ablard, Aug. 26, 1965 (div. Sept. 30, 1991); children: James Vernon Ablard, Tracie Jean Grant; m. Steven Henry Futrovsky, Jan. 22, 2000. Student, Ventura Jr. Coll., 1964—65, Ottawa U., 1965—66, U. Md., Eng., 1976—77, Mont. Coll., 1987—88. Cert. Notary Pub., Md., 1991-. Mgr. purchasing Choice Hotels Internat., Silver Spring, Md., 1978—83; mgr. office Audy Group, Inc., Silver Spring, 1985—91, Eric B. Cohen, P.C., Rockville, Md., 1992—93; events mgr., devel. assoc. Jewish Found. Group Homes, Inc., Rockville, 1993—. Bd. dirs. devel. com. Jewish Found. Group Homes, Inc., Rockville, 2001—, com. employee recognition, 2002—; cons. events Cmty. Svs. Autistic Adults and Children, Rockville, 2001—. Author, editor: newsletter Audy Group, 1987—91, Home Notes, 2001—02. Troop leader Boy Scouts Am., England, 1975—77, mem. coun. Silver Spring, 1978—82; leader troop Girl Scouts Am., Silver Spring, 1978—83; organizer Desert Storm Benefit, Silver Spring, 1991; vol. United Jewish Fedn. Greater Wash., Rockville, 1993—; coord. United Way/CFC, Rockville, 2001—; mem. campaign staff Joel Chasnoff County Coun., Silver Spring, 1982, Isiah Leggett County Coun., Silver Spring, 1983; vol. Homeless Shelter Christ Congl. Ch., Silver Spring, 1981—83, Helping Hand, Silver Spring, 1985—87; facilitator Coop. Edn. Programs Mont. County Pub. Schs., Silver Spring, 1986—88; vol., tech. crew Burtonsville Cmty. Theatre, Md., 1988—89; creator, facilitator comparative religions Christ Congl., Silver Spring, 1981—82, developer lead travel program, 1983—85, creator, leader jr. ch., 1985—87; pres. Protestant Women Chapel, Germany, 1974—75. Recipient Cert. of Honor, European Congress Am. Parents and Tchrs., Frankfurt, Germany, 1975, Award of Excellence, Award of Excellence, Manor Care, Inc., Silver Spring, 1983. Mem.: Assn. Fundraising Profls. Democrat. Congregationalist. Avocations: golf, reading, travel, knitting. Office: Jewish Found Group Homes 6010 Executive Blvd #800 Rockville MD 20852-3814 Business E-Mail: cfutrovsky@jfgh.org.

FUTTER, ELLEN VICTORIA, museum administrator; b. NYC, Sept. 21, 1949; d. Victor and Joan Babette (Feinberg) F.; children— Anne Victoria, Elizabeth Jane. Student, U. Wis., 1967-69; AB magna cum laude, Barnard Coll., 1971; JD, Columbia U., 1974, LLD (hon.), 1984, Hamilton Coll., 1985, NY Law Sch.; DHL (hon.), Amherst Coll., Hofstra U., 1994, CCNY, 1996, LI City Coll., 1995; DHL (hon.), Yale U., 2000; DL, Columbia U.; degree (hon.), Stadmore Coll., 2003, Williams Coll., 2004, Skidmore Coll., 2005. Bar: N.Y. 1975. Assoc. Milbank, Tweed, Hadley & McCloy, N.Y.C., 1974-80; acting pres. Barnard Coll., N.Y.C., 1980-81, pres., 1981-93, Am. Mus. Natural History, N.Y.C, 1993—. Bd. dirs. Bristol Myers Squibb, Am. Internat. Group, JP Morgan Chase, Consol. Edison of N.Y., Overseer Meml. Sloan Kettering Cancer Ctr., N.Y.; trustee Am. Mus. Natural History. Recipient L. Sachar award Brandeis U., Elizabeth Cutter Morrow, Distinction medal Barnard Coll., Excellence medal Columbia U., Gold medal award Nat. Inst. Social Scis., Legacy Conservation award Theodore Roosevelt Sanctuary, Visionary award New Vision in Pub. Sch. Mem. ABA, Am. Acad. Arts and Scis., N.Y. State Bar Assn., Assn. Bar City N.Y., Nat. Inst. Social Scis., Coun. Fgn. Rels., Cosmopolitan Club, Century Club, Phi Beta Kappa. Office: Am Mus Natural History Central Park West at 79th New York NY 10024

FUTTER, JOAN BABETTE, former school librarian; b. N.Y.C., Nov. 15, 1921; d. Samuel S. and Helen (Mosher) Feinberg; m. Victor Futter, Jan. 26, 1943; children: Jeffrey Leesam, Ellen Victoria, Deborah Gail Futter Cohan. AB, NYU, 1941; MS, L.I. U., 1966. Sch. libr. Carrie Palmer Weber Jr. High Sch., Port Washington, NY, 1966—91. Bd. dir. Port Washington Edn. Assn., Port Washington, NY. Mem. LWV, AAUW, L.I. Sch. Media Assn., Port Washington Edn. Found. (bd. dirs.), C.W. Post Libr. Assn., Cold Spring Harbor Beach Club, Manhasset Bay Yacht Club. Home: 61 Canary Crescent Manhasset NY 11030-4022

FUTTER, VICTOR, retired lawyer; b. N.Y.C., Jan. 22, 1919; s. Leon Nathan and Merle Caroline (Allison) F.; m. Joan Babette Feinberg, Jan. 26, 1943; children: Jeffrey Leesam, Ellen Victoria Futter, Deborah Gail Futter Cohan. AB in Govt. and English, Columbia U., 1939, JD, 1942. Bar: N.Y. 1942, U.S. Supreme Ct. 1948. Assoc. Sullivan & Cromwell, 1946-52; with Allied Corp. (now Honeywell Internat.), Morristown, N.J., 1952-84, assoc. gen. counsel, 1976-78, v.p., sec., 1978-84; dir. Allied Chem. Nuclear Products, 1977-84; gen. counsel, sec. to bd. trustees Fairleigh Dickinson U., 1984-85, ret. Spl. prof. law Hofstra Law Sch., 1976-78, 88-89, 94-2004, spl. cons. to the dean, 1997-2004; lectr., seminar on corp. in modern soc. Columbia U. Law Sch., 1986-98. Editor: Columbia Law Rev.; editor-in-chief: Nonprofit Governance and Management, 2002, Resource Guide for Nonprofits, 2004; contbr. articles to profl. jours. Trustee, dep. mayor Village of Flower Hill, N.Y., 1974-76; mem. senate Columbia U., 1969-75; chmn. bd. Columbia Coll. Fund, 1970-72; pres. parents and friends com. Mt. Holyoke Coll., 1978-80; pres. Flower Hill Assn., 1968-70; bd. dirs. N.Y. Young Dems., 1948-52, Nat. Exec. Svc. Corps, 1997-2003, Soc. Columbia Grads., 1998-2003; co-chmn. fund drive Port Washington Cmty. Chest, 1965-66, bd. dirs., 1965-75; mem. coun. overseers C.W. Post, 1984-85; bd. dirs. Acad. Polit. Sci., 1986-94; bd. dirs. Greenwich House, 1985-2004, vice chair, 1999-2004, dir. emeritus, 2004—; bd. dirs. Nat. Assn. Local Arts Agys.-Arts for Am., 1989-91, Am. Soc. Corp. Secs., 1987-90, pres. N.Y. chpt., 1983-84; chmn. Com. on Nonprofits, 1992-97; bd. dirs. Justice Resource Ctr., 1992-97; chair ad hoc Lunch Group for Nonprofits, 1993-2004. Maj. AUS. Recipient Alumni medal Columbia U., 1970, Disting. Svc. award Am. Soc. Corp. Secs., 1994; James Kent scholar. Fellow Am. Bar Found.; mem. ABA (coun. sr. lawyers divsn. 1989-97, chair 1995-96, chair Editl. Bd. Experience, 1989-95, liaison to ABA CEELI program 1990-99, sec. on bus. law, corp. laws com., com. on non-profit corps., com. on corp. govs., sect. on internat. law and practice 1990-2004, bd. govs., program and planning com. 1999-2002, ad hoc com. model profit act 2002-04), Assn. of Bar of City of N.Y. (com. on internat. human rights 1983-85, com. on 2d century 1985-89, sr. lawyers com. 1989-2002, chair 1992-95, nonprofit com. 1995-96, Disting. Svc. award Individual Mentor Program 1995), Am. Law Inst. (consultative group for restatement of law governing lawyers 1987-98, consultative group for prins. of non profit orgns. 2002—), Nat. Assn. Corp. Dirs. (pres. N.Y. chpt. 1988-89), Nat. Assn. Coll. Univ. Attys. (sec. on personal rels., tenure and retirement programs 1984-86), Am. Judicature Soc., N.Y. Lawyers Alliance for World Security, Columbia Coll. Alumni Assn. (pres. 1972-74, Pres.'s Cup award 1999), The Supreme Ct. Hist. Soc., Playwrights First, U.S. Lawn Tennis Assn., Am. Philatelic Soc., Univ. Club (coun. 1996-99, chair spl. events com. 1993-2000, chair club activities com. 1996-99), Manhasset Bay Yacht Club, Cold Spring Harbor Beach Club, Village Club of Sands Point (golf com. 1999-2000), Phi Beta Kappa. Personal E-mail: vandjfut@optonline.net.

FUZEK, BETTYE LYNN, secondary school educator; b. Knoxville, Tenn., Oct. 24, 1924; d. Wallace Paul and Bess (Wallace) Bean; m. John F. Fuzek, May 31, 1943; children: Mary Ann, Mark Lynn, Martha Elizabeth. Student, U. Tenn., 1944-45, East Tenn. State U., 1959-64; BS, Milligan Coll., 1966; postgrad. summers, various schs., 1966—. Sci. tchr. Dobyns-Bennett High Sch., Kingsport, Tenn., 1969-72; subs. tchr. Sullivan County High Schs., Kingsport, 1973-86; violin tchr. Symphony Assn. of Kingsport Talent Edn. Prog., 1973-80, Kingsport Suzuki Assn., 1980-90; pvt. tchr. violin, 1990—. Violinist Kingsport Symphony Orch., 1980-85. Tchr. Literacy Coun. Kingsport, Inc., 1990—. Mem DAR. Presbyterian. Avocations: rose gardening, ballroom dancing, square and round dancing, clothes modeling. Home: 4603 Mitchell Rd Kingsport TN 37664-2125

FUZEK, JOHN FRANK, chemical consultant; b. Knoxville, Tenn., Dec. 21, 1921; s. John and Maria (Pucher) F.; m. Bettye Lynn Bean, May 31, 1943; children: Mary Ann, Mark Lynn, Martha Elizabeth. BS in Chem. Engring., U. Tenn., 1943, MS in Phys. Chemistry, 1945, PhD in Phys. Chemistry, 1947; post PhD fellow, Office Naval Rsch., 1947-48. Chemist Hercules Powder Co., Wilmington, Del., 1943-44; research chemist N. Am. Rayon Corp., Elizabethton, Tenn., 1948-55; head research physics dept. Beaunit Fibers, Elizabethton, 1955-66; sr. research chemist Tenn. Eastman Co., Kingsport, 1966-70; research assoc. chemicals div. Eastman Kodak Co., Kingsport, 1970-86; cons. Kingsport, from 1986. Author: (with others) (chpt.) Clothing Comfort, 1977, Water in Polymers, 1980; contbr. articles in Jour. Am. Chem. Soc., I&EC Product R&D, ASTM Standard News; patents dyeable polypropylene fibers, process for spinning viscose, silk-like polyester fiber, silk-like textile fiber; contbr. articles to profl. jours. Recipient Sci. Research award Oak Ridge (Tenn.) Inst. of Nuclear Studies, 1950. Fellow AAAS, ASTM (vice chmn. com. D-13 on textiles 1984-90, Cert. of Appreciation 1983, Merit award 1990), Am. Inst. Chemists (pres. Tenn. chpt. 1971-72); mem. Am. Chem. Soc. (nat. councilor 1964-66, chmn. N.E. Tenn. chpt. 1957-58, nat. alt. councilor 1978-80, Speaker of Yr. 1979), Fiber Soc. (Lectr. of Yr. 1980-81), Coblentz Soc., Am. Crystallographic Assn., Am. Assn. Textile Chemists and Colorists, Sigma Xi. Republican. Presbyterian. Avocations: solar eclipse chasing, ballroom dancing, photography. Home: Kingsport, Tenn. Died June 23, 2005.

FUZESI, STEPHEN, JR., lawyer, communications executive; b. Budapest, Hungary, Aug. 3, 1948; naturalized, US, 1963; s. Stephen Sr and Marta Fuzesi; m. Nancy J Steinhardt, Apr. 5, 1975; children: Stephen Joseph, Timothy Roger. AB, Princeton U., 1970; JD, U. Pa., 1974. Bar: NY 1975, DC 1982. Atty. Davis, Polk & Wardwell, N.Y.C., 1974-82; ptnr./of counsel Reid & Riege, PC, Hartford, Conn., 1982-83; 1st. sr. v.p., gen. counsel and sec. Am. Savings Bank, FSB, N.Y.C., 1984-87; sr. v.p., gen. counsel, sec. Stamford Capital Group, Inc., 1987-90; of counsel White & Case, N.Y.C., 1990-94; v.p., sec., chief counsel Newsweek, N.Y.C., 1994—. Contbr. articles to profl jours, newspapers. Mem. Coun. Fgn. Rels., 1976—81, Am. Coun. Germany, 1977—80, Greenwich Bd. Edn., 1987—91, Greenwich Dem. Town Com., 1985—94; candidate 36th dist. Conn. State Senate, 1986; trustee Greenwich Round Hill Cmty. Ch., 2003—; bd. dirs. Greenwich Soccer Assn., 1989—94, Media Law Resource Ctr., 2004—. Recipient Keedy Law Rev. award, U. Pa. Law Sch., 1974. Mem.: Mag. Pubs. Assn. (legal affairs comt 1994—, chmn bus affairs subcommittee 1995—99), Assn. Bar City N.Y. (comt int human rights 1979—81, banking law comt 1987—90, com. on comm. and media law 1995—99, 2002—). Office: Newsweek 251 W 57th St New York NY 10019-1802

FYE, W. BRUCE, III, cardiologist; b. Meadville, Pa., Sept. 25, 1946; s. W. Bruce Jr. and Anne Elizabeth (Schreck) F.; m. Lois Eileen Baker, May 10, 1969; children: Katherine Anne, Elizabeth Jane. AB, Johns Hopkins U., 1968, MD, 1972, MA in Med. History, 1978. Diplomate Am. Bd. Internal Medicine, Am. Bd. Cardiovascular Diseases. Intern N.Y. Hosp.—Cornell Med. Ctr., N.Y.C., 1972-73, asst. resident, 1973-74, sr. asst. resident, 1974-75, fellow cardiology, 1975; fellow in cardiology Johns Hopkins U. Sch. Medicine, Balt., 1975-77, postdoctoral fellow in med. history, 1976-78, instr. in medicine, 1977-78; dir. cardiographics lab. Marshfield (Wis.) Clinic, 1978-99, chmn. dept. cardiology, 1981-99, dir. noninvasive cardiology, 1999; assoc. prof. medicine Med. Coll. Wis., Milw., 1988-99; prof. medicine and history medicine Mayo Clin. Coll. of Medicine, Rochester, Minn., 2000—. Vice chief of staff St. Joseph's Hosp., Marshfield, 1989-99, exec. com., bd. dirs., 1994-97; clin. prof. medicine, adj. prof. history medicine U. Wis., Madison, 1990—; sr. assoc. cons. Mayo Clinic, Rochester, 2000, cons., 2001—. Author: The Development of American Physiology, 1987; editor: William Osler's Collected Papers on the Cardiovascular System, 1985, Classic Papers on Coronary Thrombosis and Myocardial Infarction, 1991; editor-in-chief: Classics of Cardiology Library, 1985—; author: American Cardiology; The History of a Specialty and Its College, 1996; mem. editl. bd. Marshfield Med. Bull., 1985-95, Am. Jour. Cardiology, 1990—, Clin. Cardiology, 1994—; co-editor (with J. Willis Hurst, Richard Conti, W. Bruce Fye): Profiles in Cardiology, 2003. Named to Soc. Scholars, Johns Hopkins U., 2005. Fellow Am. Coll. Cardiology (chmn. libr. com. 1991, historian 1991—, gov. Wis. chpt. 1993-96, steering com. bd. govs., 1994—, nominating com., 1994-96, chair govt. rels. com. 1996-99, trustee 1997—, v.p. 1999—, pres. 2002—); mem. Am. Assn. for History of Medicine (program chair 1987), State Med. Soc. Wis. (alt. del. 1990-94), Am. Hist. Assn., Am. Osler Soc. (pres. 1988-89), Am. Heart Assn. (exec. com. coun. on clin. cardiology 1991-97, chmn. membership com. coun. on clin. cardiology 1994-97, chair credentials com. coun. on clin. cardiology 1994-97), Inst. for Study of Cardiovasc. Medicine (bd. dirs. 1994—), Found. for Advances in Medicine and Sci., Phi Beta Kappa, Alpha Omega Alpha, Grolier Club. Presbyterian. Avocation: collecting and selling antiquarian medical books. Home: 1533 Seasons Ln SW Rochester MN 55902 Office: Mayo Clinic Coll of Medicine 200 1st St SW Rochester MN 55905-0002 Office Phone: 507-266-4130. Business E-Mail: fye.bruce@mayo.edu.

FYFE, WILLIAM SEFTON, geochemist, educator; b. New Zealand, June 4, 1927; s. Colin Alexander and Isabella Fyfe; m. Patricia Walker, Feb. 27, 1981; children: Christopher, Catherine, Stefan. BSc, U. Otago, New Zealand, 1948, MS, 1949, PhD, 1952; DSc (hon.), Meml. U., Lisbon, Portugal, 1989, 90, Lakehead U., 1992, Guelph U., 1994, St. Mary's U., Otago, New Zealand, 1994, Otago U., New Zealand, 1995, U. Western Ont., 1995. Prof. chemistry in, N.Z., 1955-58; prof. geology U. Calif., Berkeley, 1958-66; research prof. Manchester U. and Imperial Coll., London, 1966-72; chmn. dept. geology Western Ont. U., 1972-84, prof. dept. geology, 1984-92, prof. emeritus dept. earth sci., 1992—, dean faculty sci., 1986-90. Decorated companion Order of Can.; Commemorative medal (New Zealand), Commemorative medal (Canada); recipient Logan medal Geol. Assn. Can., Arthur Holmes medal European Union of Geoscis., Can. Gold medal for Sci. and Engring., 1991; Guggenheim fellow, 1964, 83; named hon. prof. U. Beijing. Fellow Geol. Soc. London (hon.; Wollaston medal 2000), Royal Soc. London, Geol. Soc. Am. (hon. life, Day medal), Mineral Soc. Am. (Roebling medal); mem. AAAS (chmn. geology geography sect. 2000—), Internat. Union Geoscis. (pres. 1992-96, Grand Cross Ordem Nacional do Merito Cientifico, Brazil, 1996), Nat. Sci. and Engring. Rsch. Coun. Can., Royal Soc. Can., Acad. Sci. Brazil, Brit. Chem. Soc., Russian Acad. Sci., Indian Acad. Sci., Chinese Acad. Sci. Home: 1197 Richmond London ON Canada N6A 3L3 Office: U Western Ont Dept Earth Scis London ON Canada N6A 5B7 Fax: 519-661-2179. E-mail: pjfyfe@uwo.ca.

FYFFE, RICHARD COLEMAN, school librarian; b. Asheville, N.C., June 15, 1956; s. William and Alice Queen Fyffe. BA, U. Conn., 1979; MS, Simmons Coll., Boston, 1984; MA, U. Conn., 1998. Asst. cataloguer N.Am. imprints program Am. Antiquarian Soc., Worcester, Mass., 1982—83, cataloguer N.Am. imprints program, 1984—84, sr. catalogue cataloguer of Am. children's books, 1984—86; dir. libr. Essex Inst., Salem, Mass., 1986—2000; curator lit. and cultural archives U. Conn. Librs., Storrs, 1990—91, humanities bibliographer, 1992—96, head collections svcs., 1996—2000; asst. dean for scholarly comm. U. Kans. Librs., Lawrence, 2000—. Treas., bd. dirs. BioOne; dir.-at-large ESIG (EPSCoR Sci. Info. Group). Author: (bibliography) Essex Institute Historical Collections; contbr. articles to profl. jours. Recipient Excellence in Consortial Leadership award, Thomson-ISI, 2003; Sr.

fellow and Vis. scholar, UCLA Grad. Sch. of Edn. and Info. Studies, 1999. Mem.: ALA, Soc. Scholarly Pub., Soc. Philosophy & Tech., Assn. Libr. Collections and Tech. Svcs., Assn. Coll. and Rsch. Librs., Beta Phi Mu, Phi Beta Kappa. Office: Univ Kans 351 Watson Libr 1425 Jayhawk Blvd Lawrence KS 66045 Office Phone: 785-864-4611. Office Fax: 785-864-5311. Business E-Mail: rfyffe@ku.edu.

FYLE, CLIFFORD NELSON, publishing executive, educator; b. Freetown, Sierra Leone, Mar. 29, 1933; arrived in U.S., 1998; s. Benoni Owen and Gwendoline Winifred Fyle; m. Rachel Omodele Davies (dec.); children: Clifford, Desmond, Rachel; m. Rose Marie Momoh Nelson-Fyle, June 19, 1983; children: Amie, Yatta, Norma, Sombo. BA in Langs. and Math., Fourah Bay Coll., Freetown, 1953, grad. in edn., 1954; MA in Edn., U. Durham, Eng., 1958; BA in English, U. Durham, 1960; grad. in ednl. materials, Ind. U., 1962; higher diploma in linguistics, U. Leeds, Eng., 1966; postgrad., UCLA, 1966—67. Sr. tchr. English Meth. Boys H.S., Freetown, 1954—55, 1960—62; edn. officer, sch. inspector Ministry of Edn., Freetown, 1962—64; sr. lectr. lang. arts, linguistics U. Sierra Leone, Freetown, 1964—76, dean faculty art, prof. English and linguistics, 1976—78; specialist in African langs. UNESCO, Paris, 1978—90, chief literacy and basic edn. for Africa, 1990—93, world coord. mother tongue langs., 1988—93; dir. ednl. langs. program Govt. Sierra Leone, Freetown, 1993—95; founder, mng. dir. Lekon Pub., Freetown, 1995—, Lekon New Dimensions Pub., Yonkers, NY, 2000—. Team mem. nat. edn. survey Sierra Leone UNESCO, Paris, 1992, 93; cons. in reading U. Leeds, 1965; organizer 6th ann. congress West African Linguistic Soc., Freetown, Sierra Leone, 1970; cons. UN, N.Y.C., 1998—2001; exch. prof. Ford Found., 1977; mem. exec. bd. Sci. Edn. Program for Africa, Sierra Leone, 1965—69; mem. West African Exams. Coun., Accra, Ghana, 1967—74. Author: Nat. Anthem of Sierra Leone, 1961, Books for Developing Countries, 1965, African Community Languages and their Use in Literacy and Education: A Regional Survey, 1985, International Language Charter of the Organization of African Unity, 1996, (fiction) Blood Brothers, 1998 (nominee Internat. IMPAC Libr. award), The Alpha, 2004, The Conquest of Freedom, 3 vols., 2004, These Old Colonial Hills, 2004; author, linguist (with Eldred Jones): A Krio-English Dictionary, 1980; co-editor: Sierra Leone Jour. Edn., 1961—73; contbr. articles to profl. jours. Mem. exec. coun. Rural Devel. Tech. Transfer Network, Sierra Leone; pres. UN Students Orgn., Sierra Leone, 1952—54. Mem.: Royal Commonwealth Soc., Pubs. Mktg. Assn., African Studies Assn., Sierra Leone Assn. for Tchg. of English (pres. 1970—77), West African Linguistic Soc., Internat. Assn. Rsch. in Mother Tongue Edn. (v.p. 1990—). Achievements include introduction of scientific grammar, word description and dictionary arrangement, all hailed as "blazing a worldwide trail" in modern linguistic study and lexicography. Avocations: music, writing for children, cooking. Home: 38 Centre St Yonkers NY 10701 Office: Lekon New Dimensions Pub PO Box 504 38 Centre St Yonkers NY 10702 Office Phone: 914-965-5181. Fax: 914-965-8291. E-mail: cliffordfy@msn.com.

FYLER, CARL JOHN, dentist; b. Spearville, Kans., May 14, 1921; s. John Henry and Helen Elsie (Parthie) F.; m. Marguerite E. Burris, Feb. 14, 1946. DDS, U. Mo., Kansas City, 1950. Practice dentistry, Topeka, Kans., 1950-92; ret., 1992. Author: Staying Alive. Served to maj. USAF, 1942-46, ETO. Decorated Disting. Flying Cross, Silver star. Mem. ADA (life), Kans. Dental Assn., Shawnee County Dental Assn., Internat. Fedn. Dentists, Am. Ex-Prisoners of War (nat. dir. 1974-85, nat. jr. vice comdr. 1984-85), Kans. Ex-Prisoners of War (Gov.'s adv. com. 1978-86), 303d H.B.G. Assn. (pres. 1987-89), Eighth Air Force Hist. Soc. (bd. dirs. 1989-92, heavy bomb group), Mil. Order of World Wars (pres. Topeka chpt. 1996—), Distinguished Flying Cross Soc., Am. Legion, D.A.V., Am. Vets. Republican. Presbyterian. Avocations: flying, lapidary, rock hunting. Home: 300 SW Yorkshire Rd Topeka KS 66606-2260

FYLER, JOHN MORGAN, language educator; b. Chgo., Sept. 17, 1943; s. Earl Harris and Harriet (Morgan) F.; m. Julia Ann Genster, Aug. 5, 1978; children: Amanda, Lucy. AB, Dartmouth Coll., 1965; MA, U. Calif., Berkeley, 1967, PhD, 1972. Asst. prof. Tufts U., Medford, Mass., 1972-78, assoc. prof., 1978-88, prof., 1988—. Author: Chaucer and Ovid, 1979; contbg. editor: Riverside Chaucer, 1986. ACLS fellow, 1975-76, Guggenheim fellow, 1982-83, Camargo Found. fellow, 2002; fellow Clare Hall, U. Cambridge, 2003. Home: 126 Central St Concord MA 01742-2911 Office: Dept English Tufts U Medford MA 02155 Office Phone: 617-627-2379. E-mail: john.fyler@tufts.edu.

GAAL, JOHN, lawyer; b. Flushing, N.Y., Oct. 10, 1952; s. Stephen Alfred and Marjorie (Lappin) G.; m. Barbara Jeanne Zacher, Aug. 5, 1973; children: Bryan A., Adam C., Benjamin Z. BA cum laude, U. Notre Dame, 1974, JD magna cum laude, 1977. Bar: N.Y. 1978, U.S. Ct. Appeals (D.C. cir.) 1978, U.S. Dist. Ct. (no. dist.) N.Y. 1979, U.S. Supreme Ct. 1986. Law clk. to judge U.S. Ct. Appeals (D.C. cir.), Washington, 1977-78; assoc. Bond, Schoeneck & King, Syracuse, N.Y., 1978-85, ptnr., 1986—. Bd. dirs. Legal Svcs. of Ctrl. N.Y., Syracuse, 1981-87, 94-2000, pres. 1999-2000—; adj. prof. Sch. of Mgmt., Syracuse U., 1989-92, Coll. of Law, 2001. Editor: Senior Citizens Handbook, 1988; contbg. author: Public Sector Labor and Employment Law, 1988; mem. editl. bd. Jour. Coll. and Univ. Law, 1998—, co-chair, 2000-02; columnist The Bus. Jour., 1998-2000; mem. bd. advs. N.Y. Employment Law Practice Newsletter, 2001-04; contbr. articles to profl. publs. Bd. dirs. Transitional Living Svcs., 2001—, Dunbar Assn., Crouse Health Hosp. Found. Fellow Am. Bar Found., Am. Coll. Labor and Employment Lawyers; mem. ABA (labor and employment law sect.), N.Y. State Bar Assn. (exec. com. labor and employment law sect., chair young lawyer sect. 1989-90, spl. com. on AIDS and the law 1988, spl. com. on mandatory pro bono svc. 1989, ho. of dels. 1987-89, 90-91, co-chair com. ethics 1999—). Democrat. Roman Catholic. Home: 8006 Austrian Pine Cir Manlius NY 13104- Office: Bond Schoeneck & King 1 Lincoln Ctr Fl 18 Syracuse NY 13202-1324 Office Phone: 315-218-8288. Business E-Mail: jgaal@bsk.com.

GAAL, PETER, electrical engineer, researcher; b. Oroszlany, Hungary, 1966; arrived in U.S., 1993; m. Farideh Khaleghi, 2003; 1 child, Daniel. BS in elec. engring., Tech. U. Budapest, Hungary, 1985—90; MS in elec. engring., U. So. Calif., LA, 1993—94; PhD in elec. engring., U. So. Calif., 1995—99. Rsch. asst. Ctrl. Rsch. Inst. Physics, Budapest, Hungary, 1990—93; systems engr. QUALCOMM, Inc., San Diego, 1999—. Office: QUALCOMM Inc 5775 Morehouse Dr San Diego CA 92121 Business E-Mail: pgaal@qualcomm.com.

GAAR, MARILYN AUDREY WIEGRAFFE, political scientist, educator, property manager; b. St. Louis, Sept. 22, 1946; d. Arthur and Marjorie Estelle (Miller) W.; m. Norman E. Gaar, Apr. 12, 1986. AB, Ind. U., 1968, MA, 1970, MS, 1973. Mem. faculty Stephens Coll., Columbia, Mo., 1971—73, Johnson County CC, Overland Park, Kans., 1973—; vis. scholar Moscow (Russia) Symphony Orch., 2003. Interviewer fellowship candidates Fulbright Hayes Tchr. Exch., Kansas City, Mo., 1982—92; mem. state selection com. Congress Bundestag Youth Exch. Program, Kans., 1985; pres. faculty del. Kans. Assn. CCs, 1984—85; gov.'s appointee, admissions interviewer, mem. selection panel Sch. Medicine U. Kans., 1991—95, mem. admissions criteria and admissions process rev. com., 1992. Author: (book) Profile of Kansas Government, 1990; contbg. editor: (instr.'s manual) Am. Democracy (Thomas Patterson). Pres. LWV Johnson County, 1987—89, prodr. candidates forum, mem. governing bd., 1993—95; mem. Johnson County Elder Net Coalition, 1988; mem. governing bd. Johnson County Mental Health Ctr., 1981—86, chmn., 1985—86; vol., translator Russian Refugee Resettlement Program of Jewish Family and Children Svcs., Kansas City, 1979—81; treas. Heart of Am., Japan Am. Soc., 1979; hon. dir. Rockhurst Coll., Kansas City; sec. Ctrl. Slavic Conf., 2000—05; alt. mem. Rep. State Com., Kans., 1984—86; chmn. Rep. City Com., Shawnee, Kans., 1982—86; program chmn. Kans. Fedn. Rep. Women, 1984—87; bd. dirs. Substance Abuse Ctr., Johnson County, 1983—85, Huntington Farms Homes Assn., Leawood, Kans., 1984—87, Internat. Rels. Coun., Kansas City, 2001—04. Fellow Univ., NEH, 1990; grantee Fulbright Hayes, Japan, 1975, The Netherlands, 1982, Europaische Akademie, West Berlin, 1984, 1992, 1997, Scholars in Residence, Johnson County C.C., 1998, 1999, 2001, 2003, Sr. Scholar award, 2003—05. Mem.: Ctrl. Assn. Russian Tchrs. Am. (bd. dirs. 2003—04), Soc. Fellows, Assn. Russian and Am. Historians (sec. 1998—99), Internat. Rels. Coun. Kansas City (exec. com. 2001—03, governing bd. 2001—04, bd. dir. 2001—), Kans. Polit. Sci. Assn., C.C. Humanities Assn., Russian and Am. Internat. Studies Assn. (sec. 1999—), People to People, Nelson-Atkins Mus. Arts, Phi Beta Kappa, Dobro Slovo Nat. Slavic Honor Soc., Phi Sigma Alpha. Episcopalian. Avocations: piano, gardening. Office: Johnson County C C 12345 College Blvd Shawnee Mission KS 66210-1283

GAAR, NORMAN EDWARD, lawyer, former state senator; b. Kansas City, Mo., Sept. 29, 1929; s. William Edward and Lola Eugene (McKain) G.; children: Anne, James, William, John; m. Marilyn A. Wiegraffe, Apr. 12, 1986. Student, Baker U., 1947-49; AB, U. Mich., 1955, JD, 1956. Bar: Mo. 1957, Kans. 1962, U.S. Supreme Ct. 1969. Assoc. Stinson, Mag, Thomson, McEvers & Fizzell, Kansas City, 1956-59; ptnr. Stinson, Mag & Fizzell, Kansas City, 1959-79; mng. ptnr. Gaar & Bell, Kansas City, St. Louis, Overland Park, Wichita, Kans., 1979-87; ptnr. Burke, Williams, Sorensen & Gaar, Overland Park, Kans., L.A., Camarillo, Fresno, Costa Mesa, Calif., 1987-96; shareholder McDowell, Rice, Smith & Gaar, Overland Park, 1996—2004; ptnr. Gaar Buxbaum & Roth, Overland Park, 2005—. Mem. Kans. Senate, 1965-84, majority leader, 1976-80; faculty N.Y. Practising Law Inst., 1969-74; adv. dir. Panel Pubs., Inc., N.Y.C.; chmn. Lone Summit Bank, Lake Lotawana, Mo., 2004—. Mcpl. judge City of Westwood, Kans., 1959-63, mayor, 1963-65. With USN, 1949-53. Decorated Air medal (2); named State of Kans. Disting. Citizen, 1962. Fellow Am. coll. Bd. Coun.; mem. ABA, Kans. Bar Assn., Mo. Bar Assn., Am. Radio Relay League, Nat. Assn. Bond Lawyers, Calif. Assn. Bond Lawyers (charter), Russian-Am. Internat. Studies Assn. (dir. 2000--), Flying Midshipmen Assn., Assn. Naval Aviators, Tailhook Assn., Antique Airplane Assn., Exptl. Aircraft Assn. (dir. Kans. City chptr.), People to People. Republican. Episcopalian. Office: 7101 College Blvd Ste 250 40 Executive Hills Overland Park KS 66210-1891 Home: 11126 Brookwood Ave Leawood KS 66211-3092 Office Phone: 913-338-2150. Business E-Mail: ngaar@gbrattorneys.com. E-mail: ngaar@earthlink.net.

GAASTERLAND, DOUGLAS E., physician, ophthalmologist; married. MD, John Hopkins U., Balt., 1961—65. Cert. in Ophthalmology Am. Bd. of Ophthalmology, 1971. Sr. staff ophthalmologist, dir. glaucoma and laser svc. Nat. Eye Inst., NIH, Bethesda, Md., 1970—84; prof., ophthalmology Georgetown U., Washington, 1984—92; ophthalmologist, glaucoma sub-splty. UOCW, Chevy Chase, Md., 1992—; clin. prof., ophthalmology Georgetown U., Sch. of Medicine, Washington, 1992—, George Wash. U., Sch. of Medicine, Washington, 1996—. Dir. Advanced Glaucoma Intervention Study; ocular hypertension treatment study Wash. Clin. Ctr. Author of over one hundred twenty five articles and book chapters. Fellow: Am. Acad. Ophthalmology; mem.: Am. Ophthal. Soc. Achievements include patents for G-probe for laser treatment of glaucoma; laser delivery sys. for operating microscopes. Office: Univ Ophthal Consultants of Washington 2 Wisconsin Cir Chevy Chase MD 20815 Office Phone: 301-215-7100. Business E-Mail: degaasterland@uocw.com.

GABA, BARBARA BLASSINGAME, educational psychologist; b. N.Y.C., May 29, 1947; d. Samuel Timothy and Johnnie Mae (Thomas) Blassingame; m. Peter A. Gaba, May 24, 1946; children: Lanre, Ayorkor. BA, SUNY-Stonybrook, 1969; MEd, Rutgers U., 1972; PhD, Bayero U., Kano, Nigeria, 1986. Psychol. cons. N.Y. Human Resources Adminstrn., N.Y.C., 1971-74; asst. higher edn. officer Hunter Coll. of CUNY, 1974-76; lectr. Bayero U., Kano, Nigeria, 1976-85; protocol asst. to U.S. ambassador Am. Embassy, Lagos, Nigeria, 1986-87; assoc. dir. N.J. Dept. Higher Edn., Trenton, 1988-94; asst. to v.p. for acad. and student affairs Camden County Coll., Blackwood, N.J., 1994—. Contbr. articles to profl. jours. Mem. Am. Cmty. Liaison Network, Lagos, 1986-87; trustee Margaret E. Meggan Libr. Washington Twp., 1992—, Washington Twp. Edn. Found., 1996—. Mem. Am. Assn. for Higher Edn., Nat. Assn. Women in Edn., N.J. Libr. Trustee Assn. Avocations: gardening, personal computer. Office: Camden County Coll Acad and Student Affairs PO Box 200 Blackwood NJ 08012-0200

GABARRA, CARIN LESLIE, professional soccer player, professional soccer coach; b. East Orange, N.J., Jan. 9, 1965; m. Jim Gabarra. Degree in bus. mgmt., U. Calif., Santa Barbara, 1987. Mem. U.S. Nat. Women's Soccer Team, 1987—96; head coach, women's soccer Westmont Coll., 1987—88; assist. coach, women's Soccer Harvard U., Boston, 1988—93; head coach, women's soccer Navy, 1993—. Mem. U.S. Olympic World Festival team, 1986—89; mem. women's soccer U.S. Naval Acad., 1993. Named U.S. Soccer's Female Athlete of Yr., 1987, 1992; named to, U. Calif.-Santa Barbara Athletic Hall of Fame; recipient Golden Ball, FIFA Women's World Championship, China, 1991, gold medal, Atlanta Summer Olympic Games, 1996. Achievements include ranked as 3d-leading goal scorer in U.S. women's history; mem. CONCACAF Championship team, 1993, 94. Office: c/o US Soccer Fedn 1801 S Prairie Ave # 1811 Chicago IL 60616-1319*

GABAY, DONALD, lawyer; b. Bklyn., Apr. 1935; s. Harry I. and Rachel Gabay. BBA, CCNY, 1956; LLB, Bklyn. Law Sch., 1961. Bar: N.Y. 1962. Pvt. practice law, N.Y.C., 1962-75; chief counsel N.Y. State Assembly Com. on Ins., Albany, 1975-78; 1st dep. supt. N.Y. State Ins. Dept., N.Y.C., 1978-84; ptnr. Stroock & Stroock & Lavan, LLP, N.Y.C., 1984—. Pres. Ins. Fedn. N.Y., 1994-98, 99-2005, chmn. With U.S. Army, 1956—58. Named Ins. Man of Yr., Ind. Ins. Brokers Assn., 1973; recipient Pub. Svc. award Bklyn. Ins. Brokers Assn., 1977, ann. achievement award Coun. Ins. Brokers, 1981, Outstanding Achievement award CCNY Alumni Assn., 1981, Pub. Svc. award Ind. Ins. Agts. Assn., 1984, Torch of Liberty award ins. divsn. Anti-Defamation League, 1984. Office: Stroock Stroock & Lavan LLP 180 Maiden Ln New York NY 10038-4925 Office Phone: 212-806-5541. Business E-Mail: dgabay@stroock.com.

GABAY, ELEONORA V., mechanical engineer, educator; b. Leningrad, Russia, Apr. 20, 1938; arrived in US, 1991; d. Victor N. and Antonina V. Gabay; m. Natan A. Kogan, May 27, 1961; 1 child, Leon N. Kogan. BSME, U. Cinema Engring., St. Petersburg, 1959, MSME with honors, 1961. Author: (tchrs.' tool) FeedBack Cards (Diploma of All-Union contest on instrnl. tools, 1986), (instrnl. tool) Hands-on COLORIDE workbooks, 1999. Coord. Russian Leadership Com., Edison, NJ, 2001—03. Achievements include patents for Workbook with movable colored tabs. Home: 1412 Stone Ridge Cir Helmetta NJ 08828 Office Phone: 732-605-0956. Personal E-mail: nevka@comcast.net.

GABBARD, DOUGLAS, II, (JAMES GABBARD), judge; b. Lindsay, Okla., Mar. 27, 1952; s. James Douglas and Mona Dean (Dodd) G.; m. Connie Sue Mace, Dec. 30, 1977 (div. Feb. 1979); m. Robyn Marie Kohlhaas, June 18, 1981 (div. Aug. 2003); children: Resa Marie, David Ryan, James Douglas III, Michael Drew. BS, Okla. U., 1974, JD, 1977; grad., Nat. Jud. Coll., 1987, U. Kans. Law Orgnl. Econs., 1997. Bar: Okla. 1978. Ptnr. Stubblefeild & Gabbard, Atoka, Okla., 1978; sole practice Atoka, 1979; asst. dist. atty. State of Okla., Atoka, 1979-82, 1st asst. dist. atty. Atoka, Durant and Coalgate, 1982-85; dist. judge 25th Jud. Dist. State of Okla., Atoka and Coalgate, 1985—; presiding judge South East Adminstrn. Dist., Okla., 1992—, State Ct. Tax Review, Okla., 1992—. Presiding judge of emergency panel of State Ct. Criminal Appeals, State Ct. on Judiciary Trial divsn., 1997-04, vice-presiding judge 2003-04, appellate divsn. 2005—; mem. Supreme Ct. Com. on Civil Jury Instructions, 2002—; dir. Okla. Trial Judges Assn., 1996-; mcpl. judge City of Atoka, 1978-79; chmn. Chickasaw Nation Ethics Commn., 2003—; nominated to Okla. State Supreme Ct. by State Judicial Nominating Com., 2004. Mem. Bryan County/Durant Arbitration Com., 1984; negotiator Bryan Meml. Hosp. Bd., Durant, 1984-85. Nominated to Okla. Supreme Ct., State Jud. Nominating Commn., 2004. Mem. Okla. Bar Assn. (legal ethics com. 1988-90, jud. adminstrv. com. 1988-90, resolutions com., 1998, long range planning com., bench and bar com. 1999), Okla. Jud. Conf., Am. Judges Assn., Masons. Democrat. Methodist. Avocations: painting, carpentry, reading. Home: 125 E 3rd St Atoka OK 74525 Office: County Ct House Atoka OK 74525 Office Phone: 580-889-2423. E-mail: doug.gabbard@oscn.net.

GABBARD, GLEN OWENS, psychiatrist, psychotherapist; b. Charleston, Ill., Aug. 8, 1949; s. Earnest Glendon and Lucina Mildred (Paquet) G.; children: Matthew, Abigail, Amanda, Allison; m. Joyce Eileen Davidson, June 14, 1985. BS, Eastern Ill. U., 1972; MD, Rush Med. Coll., 1975; degree in psychoanalytic tng., Topeka Inst. for Psychoanalysis, 1984. Diplomate Am. Bd. Psychiatry and Neurology. Resident in psychiatry Menninger Sch. Psychiatry, Topeka, 1975-78, mem. faculty, 1978—; staff psychiatrist C.F. Menninger Hosp., Topeka, 1978-83, sect. chief, 1984-89. Med. dir., 1989-94; tng. analyst Topeka Inst. for Psychoanalysis, 1989-2001, dir., 1996-2001; v.p. for adult svcs. Menninger Clinic, 1991-94; clin. prof. psychiatry U. Kans. Med. Sch., 1991-2001; Callaway Disting. prof. Menninger Clinic and Karl Menninger Sch. Psychiatry, 1994-2001; prof. psychiatry Baylor Coll. Medicine, 2001—, Brown Found. chair psychoanalysis, 2003—. Author: With the Eyes of the Mind, 1984, Psychiatry and the Cinema, 1987, 2d edit., 1999, Medical Marriages, 1988, Sexual Exploitation in Professional Relationships, 1989, Psychodynamic Psychiatry in Clinical Practice, 1990, Portuguese transl., 1992, Italian transl., 1992, 2d edit., 1994, Korean transl., 1996, Japanese transl., 1997, 4th edit., 2005, Treatments of Psychiatric Disorders: the DSM-IV Edition, 1995; meml. editl. bd. Am. Jour. Psychiatry, Am. Psychiat. Press; joint editor-in-chief Internat. Jour. Psychoanalysis; contbr. articles to profl. jours. V.p. Topeka Civic Theatre, 1981-82, pres. 1982-83, bd. dirs. 1981-83. Named one of Outstanding Young Men in Am. U.S. Jaycees, 1984. Mem. AAAS, Am. Psychoanalytic Assn. (assoc. editor jour., mem. editl. bd.), Am. Psychiat. Assn. (Falk fellow 1976, Edward A. Strecker award 1994, Disting. Psychiatrist lectr. 1995, C. Charles Burlingame award 1997, Mary S. Sigourney award 2000, Disting. Svc. award 2002, Adolf Meyer award 2004), Sch. Psychotherapy Rsch., Menninger Sch. Psychiatry Alumni Assn. (pres. 1982-83), Alpha Omega Alpha. Avocations: theater, music. Home: 1290 Jimmy Phillips Blvd Angleton TX 77515 Office: Dept Psychiatry Baylor Coll Medicine One Baylor Plz MS 350 Houston TX 77030 Office Phone: 713-798-6397. Business E-Mail: ggabbard@bcm.tmc.edu.

GABBARD, LUCINA PAQUET, retired literature educator, actress; b. New Orleans, Jan. 16, 1922; d. Algernon Wernet and Cordelia Owens Paquet; m. Earnest Glendon Gabbard, Jan. 29, 1942; children: Krin Ernest, Glen Owens. *Husband, E. Glendon, served approximately 25 years as chairman of the theatre arts department at Eastern Illinois University. His production of Sam Shepard's Seduced was presented at the Kennedy Center in Washington, DC, winner of a National College theater festival in the 1970s. Son, Krin, is a professor of comparative literature at SUNY in Stony Brook, NY. He is the author of four books, three of which highlight his major scholarship, Jazz in American films. Son, Glen O., is a psychiatrist and psychoanalyst as The Baylor College of Medicine in Houston. He has authored 5 books on varying aspects of psychiatry, including a two volume textbook.* BA, La. State U., 1942; MA, U. Iowa, 1947; PhD, U. Ill., 1974; LittD (hon.), Ea. Ill. U., 1994. From instr. to prof. English Ea. Ill. U., Charleston, 1950—84. Author: The Dream Structure of Pinter's Plays, 1972, The Stoppard Plays, 1982; contbr. articles to profl. jours.; actor: (plays) Grapes of Wrath, The Gift, Divided States, Buckets o' Beckett: End Game, A Summer Remembered, Steel Magnolias, Driving Miss Daisy, Close of Play, Another Part of the Forest, The Octette Bridge Club, The Government Inspector; (films) Children on their Birthdays, The Third Rail, Novocaine, Redemption, Everything He Touched, My Best Friend's Wedding, Groundhog Day, Prelude to a Kiss, The Wendell Baker Story, Sin City; (TV series) Early Edition, Cupid, Turks, Missing Persons, The Untouchables, America's Most Wanted, Grapes of Wrath; also numerous commls., indsl. films. Mem.: AFTRA, SAG, Actors Equity Assn., Phi Kappa Phi, Delta Delta Delta. Home: 777 N Post Oak Rd # 1703 Houston TX 77024

GABBE, STEVEN GLENN, dean, educator, obstetrician, gynecologist; b. Newark, Dec. 1, 1944; s. Charles Paul and Marcia May Gabbe; m. Jessica Gabbe, June 26, 1966 (div. 1980); children: Amanda, Daniel; m. Patricia Temple, July 26, 1981. BA, Princeton U., 1965; MD, Cornell U., 1969; MA (hon.), U. Pa., 1983. Diplomate Am. Bd. Ob-Gyn (examiner 1980—2001), Am. Bd. Maternal-Fetal Medicine (examiner 1979-2001). Intern in medicine N.Y. Hosp., N.Y.C., 1969-70; rsch. fellow reproductive medicine Boston Hosp. for Women, 1970-71, resident in ob-gyn, 1972-74; rsch. fellow in biol. chemistry Harvard Med. Sch., Boston, 1970-71, clin. fellow ob-gyn., 1972-74; asst. prof. ob-gyn U. So. Calif., L.A., 1975-77; assoc. prof. U. Colo. Sch. Medicine, Denver, 1977-78; assoc. prof. ob-gyn. and pediatrics U. Pa. Sch. Medicine, Phila., 1978-87, prof. radiology, 1987; mem. staff Hosp. of U. Pa., Phila., 1978-87, dir. Jerrold R. Golding divsn. fetal medicine, 1978-87, mem. med. bd. and numerous coms., 1984-87; prof. U. Pa. Sch. Nursing, Phila., 1982-87; prof., chmn. dept. ob-gyn Ohio State U. Coll. Medicine, Columbus, 1987-96; prof., chmn. dept. ob/gyn. U. Wash. Sch. Medicine, Seattle, 1996—2001; dir. Jerrold R. Golding divsn. fetal medicine Hosp. of U. Pa., Phila., 1978-87, mem. med. bd. and numerous coms., 1984-87; dean Sch. of Medicine Vanderbilt U., Nashville, 2001—. Vis. prof. ob-gyn King's Coll. Hosp., London, 1985-86; dir. maternal and infant care program Phila. Dept. Health, Disease Prevention and Health Promotion, 1982-87; mem. maternal and infant care adv. coun. Dept. Pub. Health, Phila., 1983-87; mem. subcom. on pregnancy and weight gain NRC, NAS, 1981; mem. internat. sci. bd. Reproductive Toxicology Ctr., 1984—; bd. dirs., med. adv. bd. Diabetes Treatment Ctrs. Am., 1984, others; mem. Coun. Univ Chairs of Ob-Gyn., 1996—; chair Maternal Fetal Medicine Rsch. Network Nat. Inst. Child and Human Devel. Author: Clinical Obstetrics and Gynecology: Diabetes and Pregnancy, 1985, Clinical Obstetrics and Gynecology: Obstetric Ultrasound Update, 1988; (with J.R. Niebyl and J.L. Simpson) Obstetrics: Normal and Problem Pregnancies, 1986, 4th edit., 2002; contbr. numerous articles to profl. jours. and chpts. to books; editor in chief Am. Jour. Perinatology, 1983—87; mem. numerous editl. bds. Mem. Pa. Diabetes Task Force, 1981-87, Ohio Diabetes Task Force, 1987—; bd. dirs. UNITE, Jeanes Hosp., 1980-87. Recipient Sr. Resident's award for Excellence in Tng., L.A. County Women's Hosp., 1976, Disting. Tchr. award from Graduating Class, U. Wash., 1999; grantee Juvenile Diabetes Found., 1981, HHS, 1984, 1985, Diabetes Treatment Ctrs. Am., 1986. Fellow Am. Coll. Obstetricians and Gynecologists (mem. PROLOG self assessment program task force 1981-82, chmn. 1986, mem. PROLOG subcom. 1986—); mem. Am. Gynecol. and Obstet. Soc., Am. Inst. Ultrasound in Medicine, Perinatal Rsch. Soc., Soc. Gynecologic Investigation, Soc. Perinatal Obstetricians (v.p. 1986, pres. 1987-88, bd. dirs. 1983-88, chmn. credentials, constn. and by-laws com. 1983-87), Am. Diabetes Assn. (mem. nat. rsch. bd. 1981-83, chmn. coun. on diabetes in pregnancy 1985, com. on food and nutrition 1976-80), Juvenile Diabetes Found. (mem. med. sci. rev. com., med. sci. adv. bd. 1981-83), Phila. Neonatal Soc., Obstet. Soc. Phila. (program chmn. 1986-87), Phila. Perinatal Soc. (pres. 1982-84), Columbus Ob-Gyn Soc., Pa. Diabetes Acad. (acad. steering com. 1986—, editorial rev. com. 1986—), Union League (Phila.), Phi Beta Kappa, Alpha Omega Alpha. Avocations: sports, running. Office: Vanderbilt U Sch Medicine 21st Ave South at Garland Ave Nashville TN 37232 E-mail: steven.gabbe@mcmail.vanderbilt.edu.

GABBERT, JANICE JEAN, history, literature and language educator; b. Cleve., May 31, 1940; d. Jack Sylvester and Anna (Keba) Gerbec; m. Richard David Gabbert, Apr. 30, 1960 (div. 1980). Cert., Ins. Inst. Am., 1959; BA summa cum laude, Wright State U., 1970; MA, U. Cin., 1972, PhD, 1982. Sec. Great Am. Ins. Co., N.Y.C., 1958-59; ins. underwriter Hartford Ins. Group, Oklahoma City, 1962-64; office mgr. WNUE Radio, Ft. Walton Beach, Fla., 1965-66; computer libr. USAF, Eglin AFB, Fla., 1966-68; from instr. to prof. Wright State U., Dayton, Ohio, 1978—2003, chmn. Dept. Classics, 1986—2003, prof. emeritus, 2004—. Mng. com. Am. Sch. Classical Studies, Athens, Greece, 1988—; com. mem. Ohio Classical Conf., 1979-87, 1997-2002; bd. dirs. Midwest Space Devel. Conf., Columbus, Ohio, 1988-91. Author: Classics Compendium, 1991; mem. community bd. contbrs. Dayton Daily News, 1987; contbr. articles to profl. jours. Founding mem., steering com. Wright State U. Friends Libr., 1978-79; active Dayton Internat. Airshow,

1978—, Heritage Found., 1983—, High Frontier, 1983—. With USAF, 1959-60. Fellow Intercollegiate Studies Inst., 1971-72; grantee Ohio Humanities Coun., 1987. Mem. Am. Classical League, Am. Mil. Inst., Internat. Plutarch Soc., U.S. Naval Inst., Am. Philol. Assn., Classical Assn. the Middle West and South, Friends Ancient History, Assn. Ancient History. Republican. Avocations: community booster, science fiction, jazz. Office: Wright State U Dept Classics Dayton OH 45435

GABBOUR, ISKANDAR, city and regional planning educator; b. Mansura, Egypt, Feb. 6, 1929; s. Iskandar Gabbour and Mathilde Louli; m. Amy Surur, Feb. 4, 1956; children: May, Tamer, Rami. B.Arch. with honors, Cairo U., 1953; M.Arch., M.C.P., U. Pa., 1963, PhD, 1967. Arch., chief designer Devel. & Popular Housing Co., Cairo, 1954-61; rschr. assoc. U. Pa., Phila., 1966-67; prof. city and regional planning U. Montreal, Que., Can., 1967-97, vice dean acad. affairs, faculty environ. design, 1993—97, hon. prof., 1997—, interim chmn. dept. landscape architecture, 2000—02. Cons. UN Ctr. for Human Settlements, Nairobi, Kenya, 1985; vol. advisor Tech. Studies and Devel. Office, Abidjan, Ivory Coast, 1998. Contbr. numerous articles to profl. jours. Mem. Am. Planning Assn. (charter), Am. Inst. Cert. Planners (charter), Can. Inst. Planners, Royal Archtl. Inst. Can., Assn. Collegiate Schs. Planning, Order Urbanists of Que. Home: 5510 Ashdale Ave Montreal PQ Canada H4W 3G4 Fax: (514) 484-8245. E-mail: iskandar.gabbour@umontreal.ca.

GABEL, CONNIE, chemist, educator; b. Green Bank, W.Va. d. William Ashby and Marie Lowry; m. Richard Gabel; children: Greg, Keith, Debbie. BS in Chemistry magna cum laude, James Madison U.; MA in Ednl. Adminstrn. summa cum laude, U. Colo., 1984, PhD in Ednl. Leadership and Innovation, 2001. Tchg. asst. U. Wis., Madison, 1969-70, specialist endocrinology, 1970-71; tchr. Dept. Def. Schs., Tokyo, 1972-74, Poudre R-1 Schs., Ft. Collins, Colo., 1975-78, Boulder (Colo.) Valley Schs., 1985-87, 96-98, intern asst. prin., 1984-85; intern supt. Jefferson County Schs., Golden, Colo., 1992; tchr. Mapleton Pub. Schs., Thornton, Colo., 1992-95; internat. studies Egyptian program Regis U., Denver, 1994; instr. chemistry Colo. Sch. Mines, 1995-98; dean students Horizon HS, Thornton, Colo., 1995-96; project 2061 coord. dept. chemistry/edn. U. Colo., Denver, 1998-2000; instr. St. Mary's Acad., Englewood, Colo., 2000—03, Met. State Coll. Tchr. Edn. and Chemistry, Denver, 2004—. Cons. sch. fin. Colo. Dept. Edn., Denver, 1984; rschr. AMC Cancer Rsch. Ctr., Denver, 1993, Colo. U. Med. Ctr., Denver, 1994; display tech. Boulder-Chemistry Rsch., 1995. Charter mem., pres. Friends Louisville (Colo.) Libr., 1985—; charter mem. Nat. Women's History Mus.; charter mem., pres., v.p. Coal Creek Rep. Women, Louisville, 1987—; sec., mem. Boulder County Reps., 1988—98, precinct chair; mem. Nat. Rep. Women, Washington, 1987—; sec. Dist. 17 Colo. Senate, Dist. 13 Colo. Ho., 1993—2002; mem. Colo. Fedn. Rep. Women, 1987—, Colo. Rep. Ctrl. Com. Mem.: AAUW, AAAS, ASCD, NY Acad. Sci., Math., Engring. and Sci. Achievement (dir., advisor 1992—97, mem. state level adv. bd. 1992—96), Colo. Chemistry Tchrs. Assn., Colo.-Wyo. Acad. Sci., Colo. Assn. Sci. Tchrs., Nat. Soc. Study Edn., Nat. Assn. Rsch. Sci. Tchg., Am. Chem. Soc., Nat. Assn. Sci. Tchrs., Am. Ednl. Rsch. Assn., Phi Delta Kappa. Avocations: reading, hiking, gardening. Business E-Mail: cgabel@mscd.edu.

GABEL, EMMA MARGARET, retired librarian; b. Perkasie, Pa., Aug. 10, 1928; d. William U. and Mary Amanda (Kramer) G. BS in Edn., Kutztown U., 1950; MS Libr. Sci., Syracuse U., 1957. Libr. Morrisville (Pa.) High Sch., 1950-52; asst. libr. Susquehanna U., Selinsgrove, Pa., 1952-56, Indiana U. of Pa., 1956-66; head cataloger, asst. to dir. of libr. High Libr., Elizabethtown (Pa.) Coll., 1966-94; ret., 1994. Mem. Elizabethtown Hist. Soc., 1980—, Dem. Party Orgn., Elizabethtown. Mem. ALA, Pa. Libr. Assn., Pa. Citizens for Better Librs., Delta Kappa Gamma Soc. Internat. 9state pres. Alpha Alpha state 1987-89). Lutheran. Avocations: reading, gardening, knitting, travel.

GABEL, GEORGE DESAUSSURE, JR., lawyer; b. Jacksonville, Fla., Feb. 14, 1940; s. George DeSaussure and Juanita (Brittain) G.; m. Judith Kay Adams, July 21, 1962; children: Laura Gabel Hartman, Meredith Gabel Harris. AB, Davidson Coll., 1961; JD, U. Fla., 1964. Bar: Fla. 1964, D.C. 1972. With Toole, Taylor, Moseley, Gabel & Milton, Jacksonville, 1966—74, Gabel & Hair (formerly Wahl & Gabel), Jacksonville, 1974—98; ptnr., mem. dirs. com. Holland & Knight, Jacksonville, 1998—2001, exec. ptnr., 2002—. Mem. Fla. Jud. Nominating Commn., 4th cir., 1982-86.; delegate to the Comit-é Maritime Internat. Conferences in Sydney, Australia, Antwerp, Belgium, and Singapore; mem. exec. coun., World Affairs Coun., 2001-. Pres. Willing Hands, Inc., 1971-72; chmn. N.E. Fla. March of Dimes, 1974-75; mem. budget com. United Way, 1972-74, chmn. rev. com., 1976; bd. dirs. Ctrl. and So. brs. YMCA, 1973-79, Camp Immokalee, 1982-86; elder Riverside Presbyn. Ch., 1970-77, 80-86, 90-92, 97-2003, clk. session, 1975-76, 85-86, trustee, 1988-91; pres. Riverside Presbyn. Day Sch., 1977-79; chmn. Nat. Eagle Scout Assn., 1974-75; pres. Boy Scouts Am., North Fla. Coun. 1993-96, silver Beaver award, 1978; trustee Davidson Coll., 1984-95; Norwegian Consul for N.E. Fla., 1989-2002; pres. Jacksonville Consular Corps, 1992-93, 1996-2002; mem. nat. adv. bd. Tulane Admiralty Law Inst., 2001—. Capt. U.S. Army, 1964-66. Named Internat. Person of Yr., Jacksonville Regional C. of C., 2002. Fellow Am. Coll. Trial Lawyers, Am. Bar Found.; mem. ABA (chmn. admiralty and maritime law com., 1980-81. chmn. media law and defamation torts com. 1988-89. tort and ins. practice sect.), Am. Counsel Assn. (bd. dirs. 1980-82, pres. 1992-93), Maritime Law Assn. U.S. (bd. dirs. 1994-97), Assn. Average Adjusters (U.S.) (overseas subscriber-London), Fla. Bar (chmn. grievance com. 1973-75, chmn. admiralty law com. 1978-89, chmn. media and comms. law com. 1990-91), Southeastern Admiralty law Inst. (bd. govs. 1973-75), Duval County Legal Aid Assn. (bd. dirs. 1971-74, 81-84), Am. Inn of Ct. (master of bench, sec.-treas. 1990-95), Rotary of Jacksonville (bd. dirs. 1982-84, 88-89, pres. 87-88), World Affairs Coun. of Jacksonville (exec. com. 2001—), Jacksonville Regional C. of C. (bd. dirs. 2005—, internat. chair), DC Bar, Chester Bedell Inn of Ct. (master of bench), U.S. Dist. Ct. for Middle Dist. Fla. (fed. rules adv. com., 1993-96), Libel Def. Resource Ctr. (mem. def. counsel sect.). Democrat. Office: Holland & Knight LLP 50 N Laura St Ste 3900 Jacksonville FL 32202-3622 Office Phone: 904-353-2000, 904-798-7360. E-mail: ggabel@hklaw.com.

GABEL, KATHERINE, retired academic administrator, director; b. Rochester, N.Y., Apr. 9, 1938; d. M. Wren and Esther (Conger) G.; m. Seth Devore Strickland, June 24, 1961 (div. 1965). AB, Smith Coll., Northampton, Mass., 1959; MSW, Simmons Coll., 1961; PhD, Syracuse U., 1967; JD, Union U., 1970; bus. program, Stanford U., 1984. Psychol. social worker Cen. Island Mental Health Ctr., Uniondale, N.Y., 1961-62; psychol. social worker, supt. Ga. State Tng. Sch. for Girls, Atlanta, 1962-64; cons. N.Y. State Crime Control Coun., Albany, 1968-70; faculty Ariz. State U., Tempe, 1972-76; supt. Ariz. Dept. of Corrections, Phoenix, 1970-76; dean, prof. Smith Coll., 1976-85; pres. Pacific Oaks Coll. and Children's Sch., Pasadena, Calif., 1985-98; western region v.p. Casey Family Program, Pasadena, 1998—2001; cons. svcs., 2001—. Advisor, del. UN, Geneva, 1977; mem. So. Calif. Youth Authority, 1986-91. Editor: Master Teacher and Supervisor in Clinical Social Work, 1982; author report Legal Issues of Female Inmates, 1981, model for rsch. Diversion program Female Inmates, 1984, Children of Incarcerated Parents, 1995. Vice chair United Way, Northampton, 1982-83; chair Mayor's Task Force, Northampton, 1981. Mem. Nat. Assn. Social Work, Acad. Cert. Social Workers, Nat. Assn. Edn. Young Children, Western Assn. Schs. and Colls., Pasadena C. of C., Athenaeum, Pasadena Rotary Club. Democrat. Presbyterian. Avocation: collecting south west Indian art, aviary. Office Phone: 213-382-7600. Personal E-mail: gabelk@prodigy.net.

GABEL, RONALD GLEN, telecommunications executive; b. Allentown, Pa., Nov. 22, 1937; s. Glen Harry and Mary (Oberlin) G.; m. Claire A. Hollern (div.); children: Debra K., Jeffrey A., Stacy L.; m. Elaine M. Petro, Sept. 29, 1988. Student, Pa. State U., 1957-58. Cert. elec. and electronic mfg. engr. Design draftsman Mack Trucks Inc., Allentown, 1958-62, Bell Telephone Labs., Allentown, 1962-66; indsl. engr. Western Electric, Allentown, 1966-84; sr. engr. AT&T, Allentown, 1984-95, Lucent Technologies, Allentown, 1995-97. Cons. expert Man at Arms Mag.; gen. chmn. Engrs.' Week Joint Planning Coun., Lehigh Valley, 1981; cost reduction coord. Western Elec. Allentown Works, 1982-86; Western Electric Speakers Bureau, 1972-83; adminstr. Tel. Pioneers Am., Allentown, 1987-94. Co-author: Work Simplification by Motion Economy Handbook, 1982; coord. Western Elec. Allentown Works Indsl. Engring. newsletter, 1973-85. Advisor Lehigh County Dept. Human Svcs., 1989—93; solicitor United Way, 1974, 1982, 1989, 1990; dir. Lehigh County Hist. Soc., 1999—2000; v.p. Jacobsburg Hist. Soc., 1999—2000, pres., 2000—01; dir. Lehigh County Mus. Commn., 1977—81; sec. devel. and prodn. com. Lehigh County Bicentennial Commn., 1977; pres. Indian Guides Allentown YMCA, 1972, v.p., 1971; treas. Jacobsburg Hist. Soc., 2003—; sec. ch. coun. St. James Luth. Ch., 1964—67; advisor St. James Luther League, 1964—67. Mem.: Am. Inst. Indsl. Engrs. (pres. 1976—77, editor nat. mfg. sys. divsn. newsletter 1979—80, dir. Lehigh Valley chpt. 1983, Outstanding Svc. award 1978, 5 nat. awards for profl. soc. newsletters 1971—75), Internat. Inst. Indsl. Engrs., Ky. Rifle Found. (pres. 2001—03), Forks of Del. Weapons Assn., Tex. Gun Collectors Assn., Pa. Antique Gun Collectors Assn. (bd. dirs. 1996—97, v.p. 1998—99, sec./treas. 1999—, editor Bugle newsletter 2001—), Ducks Unltd., Am. Soc. Arms Collectors (bd. dirs. 1988—91, v.p. 1991—94, pres. 1994—95), Ky. Rifle Assn. (newsletter editor 1974—), NRA (life), U.S. Power Squadrons (dist. lt. D-5 1991—95), Delhigh Power Squadron (comdr. 1990—91, pres. past comdr. club 2000—01), Nat. Soc. Pershing Rifles, Pa. Antiques Appraisers Assn., Ky. Rifle Assn. (pres. 1972—73), Mercedes Benz Club (v.p. N.E. Pa. sect. 2002—03), Shriners, Knights Templar, Upper Lehigh Lions (pres. 1987—2003, treas. 1998—), Rajh Temple, Internat. Order DeMolay. Republican. Avocation: antique firearms. E-mail: rggabel@fast.net.

GABELLI, MARIO J., diversified financial services company executive; 4 children. Grad. summa cum laude, Fordham U., 1965; MBA, Columbia U., 1967. Founder Gabelli Funds LLC, 1977—; chmn., CEO, chief investment officer Gabelli Asset Mgmt. Inc., 1999—; CEO, chmn. Lynch Corp., 1986—2001, vice chmn., 2001—; chmn. Lynch Interactive Corp., 1999—2002, CEO, dir., 1999—. Gov. Am. Stock Exchange. Trustee Winston Churchill Found.; mem., bd. overseers Columbia U. Grad Sch. Bus.; bd. trustees Fairfield U., Roger Williams U.; bd. dirs. Bruce Mus.; trustee E.L. Wiegand Found., Reno; chmn., patron's com. Immaculate Conception Sch., Bronx, NY. Recipient Columbus Citizens Found. Award, 1994, Ellis Island Medal of Hon. for Bus. Leaders, 1996, Cavaliere, Italian Legions of Merit. Office: Gabelli Funds Inc One Corporate Center Rye NY 10580-1430*

GABELNICK, HELENE S., education educator; m. Stephen D Gabelnick, 1965; children: Elliot J, Aaron M. BS in chemistry, U. of Mich., 1960—64; PhD, U. of Calif., 1964—68. Prof. Harold Wash. Coll., Chgo., 1982—. Mem.: AAAS (assoc.), Phi Beta Kappa. Office: Harold Washington Coll 30 E Lake St Chicago IL 60601 Office Phone: 312-553-5794. E-mail: hgabelnick@ccc.edu.

GABELNICK, HENRY LEWIS, medical research administrator; b. Boston, May 10, 1940; s. Murray and Lillian G.; m. Faith Schectman, June 17, 1962; children: Deborah Anne, Tamar Miriam; m. Judith Andai, Mar. 15, 2003. BS, MIT, 1961, MS, 1962; PhD, Princeton U., 1966. Sr. chem. engr. Monsanto Co., Springfield, Mass., 1966-68; biomed. engr. NIH, Bethesda, Md., 1968-1986; dir. extramural rsch. CONRAD Program Ea. Va. Med. Sch., Arlington, 1986-89, dep. dir. CONRAD Program, 1989-90, dir. CONRAD Program, 1990—. Tech. expert UN Devel. Program, Haifa, Israel, 1973; tech. advisor WHO, Geneva, 1977—; pres. Reprodn. Rsch. Inst., 1997—2001; mem. FIGO Adv. Panel on Contraception, 1998—; mem. adv. coun. dept. chem. engring. Princeton U., 2004—; bd. dirs. Alliance for Microbicide Devel.; founding bd. mem., sec. Internat. Partnership for Microbicides. Editor: Rheology of Biological Systems, 1973, Drug Delivery Systems, 1976, Heterosexual Transmission of AIDS, 1990, Barrier Contraceptives, 1993, Biology, Pharmacology, and Clinical Applications of Androgens, 1996. Fellow Textile Resch. Inst.; mem. APHA, N.Y. Acad. Scis., Am. Chem. Soc., Controlled Release Soc., Soc. for Reproductive Care (bd. dirs. 2000—, v.p. 2001-02, pres. 2002—), Assn. Reproductive Health Profls., Indian Soc. fr Study of Reprodn. and Fertility (life), Global Health Coun., Cosmos Club, Sigma Xi. Avocation: nature photography. Home: 6315 Swords Way Bethesda MD 20817 Business E-Mail: hgabelnick@conrad.org. E-mail: hgabelnick@alum.mit.edu.

GABER, ROBERT, psychologist; b. N.Y.C., Nov. 5, 1923; s. William and Freda (Harris) Gaber; m. Heidi Walters, Apr. 3, 1967 (div. Jan. 5, 1976); 1 child, Nathan. BA, NYU, 1949, MA, 1951; PhD, Columbia Pacific U., San Rafael, Calif., 1982. Psychotherapist Nat. Hosp. Speech Disorders, N.Y.C., 1954-57; psychologist Indsl. Home for the Blind, N.Y.C., 1957-58; sch. psychologist Roosevelt Sch., Stamford, Conn., 1958-60; sr. clin. psychologist N.Y. State Dept. Mental Hygiene, Thiells, 1960-64; staff psychologist N.Y. Med. Coll., N.Y.C., 1965-66; cons. psychologist Salvation Army, Phila., 1971-72; psychologist Md. Dept. Mental Hygiene, 1975-76, Dept. Corrections, Balt., 1979-80; CEO Axxiom De-Stress Ctrs., Balt., 1980—; dir. Ctr. Stress Rsch., Norristown, Pa., 1994—. Dir. mental health, nursery divsn. Dept. Welfare, N.Y.C., 1953—56; cons. Gov., Pa. Dept. Corrections, 1971, Family Crisis Ctr. Balt., 1973—74. Author: (book) The Experience of Enlightenment, 1980, Federal Prisoners' Attitudes Toward Crime and Confinement, 1982, Personality Traits and Behaviorisms of a Well-Adjusted Person, 1993, What Kind of Person is the Drug Addict?, 1996, The Psychodynamics of Self-Hypnosis, 1998, The SEEP Factors in Crime, 1999, (booklet) Comprehensive Therapy Questionnaire, 1978; contbr. articles to profl. jours. With USAF, 1942—46, PTO. Mem.: APA. Democrat. Avocations: golf, horseback riding, skiing, water-skiing, tennis. also: Ctr for Stress Rsch 11 W Lafayette St Norristown PA 19401-4709 Office Phone: 610-239-7777. Personal E-mail: robegab7@cs.com.

GABERINO, JOHN ANTHONY, JR., lawyer; b. Tulsa, Aug. 6, 1941; s. John A Sr and Elizabeth (McCafferty) Gaberino; m. Marjory Ann Diamond, Aug. 21, 1965; children: Christina M, Megan E, Courtney L, John A III, Kathleen A. AB cum laude, Georgetown U., 1963, JD, 1966. Bar: Okla 1966, US Dist Ct (no & we dists) Okla, US Ct Appeals (10th cir) 1968, US Tax Ct 1968, US Supreme Ct 1994. Assoc. Huffman, Arrington & Kihle, Tulsa, 1968-75; ptnr. Arrington, Kihle, Gaberino & Dunn, Tulsa, 1975-87, also bd. dirs., 1987-97; sr. v.p., gen. counsel ONEOK, Inc., 1998—. Counsel, bd dirs St Francis Health Sys, Inc, Tulsa, Okla., 1989—97. Chmn. Law Ctr. Alumni Bd. Georgetown U., 1990—92, bd. govs., 1990—2004, chair, 2000—02, bd. dirs., 2000—02; pres. Georgetown U. Club Okla; past chmn. Georgetown U. AAP Okla.; bd. regents Georgetown U., 2002—04; past chmn. Christ the King Bd. Edn.; past pres. bd. trustees Monte Cassino Sch.; past chmn. bd. trustees Monte Cassino Sch. Endowment Fund; bd. dirs. W.K. Warren Found, Tulsa Pub. Schs. Found., Tulsa Area United Way, 2000—, campaign chmn., vice chmn., 2005—; chmn. bd. dirs. Operation Aware Inc, 1991; bd. dirs. The Salvation Army-Tulsa Region, 2002—04. Capt U.S. Army, 1966—68. Recipient John Carroll Medal, Georgetown Univ, 1993. Mem.: NCCJ (bd dirs Tulsa chpt, pres 1993—95, Ann. Dinner honoree 2003), Okla. Fellows of the Am. Bar Found. (chair 2000—01), Tulsa County Bar Found (bd dirs 1993—99, pres 1994), Tulsa Bar Asn (secy 1988, chmn construction and bylaws comt, bd dirs 1989, 1991—94, pres 1993), Okla Bar Asn (mem bd govs 1990—92, 1995, vpres 1995, mem bd govs 1997—99, pres 1998), Metropolitan Tulsa CofC (bd dirs 1996—, chair 2001), Southern Hills Country Club (mem bd govs 1990—95, 1st vpres 1991—93, pres 1994), Knights Holy Sepulchre (chair Tulsa Diocese rev. bd. 2002—, hon soc Cath ch), Phi Beta Kappa. Republican. Roman Catholic. Avocations: golf, tennis. Office: ONEOK Inc 100 W 5th St Tulsa OK 74103-4240 Office Phone: 918-588-7906.

GABERMAN, HARRY, retired lawyer; b. Springfield, Mass., May 6, 1913; s. Nathan and Elizabeth (Binder) G.; m. Ingeborg Luise Gruda, Sept. 24, 1953; children: Claudia, Natalie Razzook, Victor Lucius. JD, George Washington U., 1941; LLM, Cath. U. Am., 1954. Bar: D.C. 1942. Priorities analyst War Prodn. Bd., 1942, asst. indsl. and indsl. analyst, 1943-45; asst. chief industry control sect., legal and intercorp. rels. analyst U.S. Mil. Govt. and U.S. High Commn. for Germany, Berlin, Frankfurt, Bonn; atty.-investigator, atty-advisor; indsl. specialist, bus. economist U.S. Mil. Govt. and U.S. High Commn. for Germany, Berlin, Frankfurt, Bonn, 1945—53; asst. legal advisor, attache, dep. U.S. agt. Italian-U.S. Conciliation Commn., Am. Embassy, Rome, 1953; pvt. practice Washington, 1953-55; intelligence analyst Army Transp. Intelligence Agy., Gravelly Point, Va., 1955-56; supervisory atty.-advisor, atty.-advisor Air Force Sys. Command, Andrews AFB, Md., 1956-75; ret. Asst. to U.S. mem. Four-power liquidation of German War Potential Com., Berlin, 1946; chief deconcentration br. U.S. High Commn., Frankfurt, 1949; acting dep. U.S. mem. law com. Allied Kommandatura, Berlin, 1951; U.S. mem. 3-power Film Reorgn. Com., Bonn, 1949-50. Contbr. articles to profl. jours. Recipient Profl. Achievement award George Washington U. Law Assn., 1983. Mem. Fed. Bar Assn. (dep. coun. and com. coord. 1982, coun. and com. coord. 14 substantive law couns. containing 83 constituent coms. 1983, chmn. coun. on govt. contracts 1970-75, 80-81, chmn. internat. procurement com. 1977-79, dep. chmn. sect. on internat. law and its newsletter editor 1984-97, dep. chmn. sect. on internat. law and its newsletter contbg. editor 1998-99, found. advisor 1996-2000; numerous Disting. Svc. and other awards), D.C. Bar Assn. (chmn. govt. contracts com. 1964-66), Diplomatic and Consular Officers Ret. (charter mem., DACOR House), Am. Fgn. Svcs. Assn., Air Force Assn. Avocations: walking, reading, listening to classic and semi-classic music.

GABIL, DIANE RAPSON, retired educator; b. Jan. 1, 1947; m. Michael Gabil, 1978. BS, Cen. Mich. U., 1969, MA, 1971, Edn. Specialist degree, 1989. Tchr. spl. edn. Bangor Twp. Schs., Bay City, Mich., 1969-2001. Dir. handicapped children summer day camp, 1980—; dir. handicapped teenager summer day camp, 1999—; ind. facilitator, 2003—. Mem. Ams. Disabilities Act Com., Bay County, Mich., 1999—; vol. Thumb Octagon Barn, Gagetown, Mich., Santa Ho., Bay City, Mich. Mem.: Red Hot Soc. (Queen Mother), Phi Delta Kappa. Episcopalian. Avocations: antiques, crafts, gardening, golf, walking. Home: 1031 N Jones Rd Essexville MI 48732-9692 E-mail: drapson@mas.com.

GABINET, SARAH JOAN, lawyer; b. Salem, Oreg., Dec. 19, 1953; d. Leon and Laille Gabinet; m. John M. Siegel, Jan. 5, 1986; 1 child, Nathan. BA, Oberlin Coll., 1975; MS, Ind. U., 1977; JD, Case Western Res. U., 1982. Bar: Ohio 1982, U.S. Dist. Ct. (no. dist.) Ohio, U.S. Ct. Appeals (6th cir.). Judicial clk. Ohio Ct. Appeals (8th dist.), Cleve., 1982-83; ptnr. Kohrman, Jackson & Krantz PLL, Cleve., 1983—. Author: (book chpt.) Civil Discovery Practice, 1995. Mem. bd. trustees Temple Tifereth Israel, Cleve., 1995—. Mem. Ohio State Bar Assn., Cleve. Bar Assn. Avocations: golf, ice hockey. Office: Kohrman Jackson & Krantz 1375 E 9th St Cleveland OH 44114-1724

GABLE, CARL IRWIN, management consultant, writer, investor, lawyer; b. Charleston, SC, Aug. 7, 1939; s. Carl Irwin and Charlotte Belle (Kersey) G.; m. Sarah Alice Bogle, June 6, 1964; children: Ashley Grinnell, Carl Irwin III, James Kersey. BA, Harvard U., 1961; JD, Harvard, 1964. Bar: Ga. 1964, D.C. 1976. Assoc. Kilpatrick & Cody, Atlanta, 1964-70, ptnr., 1970-84; pres. Interface Inc., Atlanta, 1984-85; vice chmn. Intermet Corp., Atlanta, 1985-90, also bd. dirs.; of counsel Booth, Owens & Jospin, 1992—96, Troutman Sanders L.L.P., Atlanta, 1996-98. Pres. Boglewood Corp., Kiev, Ukraine, 1993-96; bd. dirs. Interface, Inc. Contbr. articles to profl. jours.; author: Murano Magic, 2004; co-author (Sarah B. Gable): Palladian Days, 2005. Bd. dirs. Atlanta Coun. Internat. Visitors, Inc., 1987-93, Atlanta Opera, Inc., 1980-2002, Michael Carlos Mus. Emory U., 1994-2003; bd. dirs. Spoleto Festival USA, Inc., 1993-99, treas., 1993-95; founder, chmn. Atlanta Opera Endowment, Inc., 1986-2000. Fellow Am. Coll. Investment Counsel; mem. ABA., Capital City Club. Achievements include invention of interlocking modular carpet. Avocation: italian studies.

GABLE, EDWARD BRENNAN, JR., lawyer; b. Shamokin, Pa., Mar. 15, 1929; s. Edward Brennan and Kathleen (Welsh) G. B.S., Villanova U., 1953; J.D., Georgetown U., 1957; m. Judy Lipshy July 17, 1981; children by previous marriage: Karen Lynn, Kimberly Ann, Katherine Rebel; stepchildren: Steven H., Karen Sue, Scott Michael. Bar: D.C. 1957, U.S. Dist. Ct. D.C. 1957, U.S. Ct. Appeals (D.C. cir.) 1957, U.S. Ct. Customs and Patent Appeals, 1959, U.S. Customs Ct., 1961, U.S. Ct. Mil. Appeals, 1966, U.S. Supreme Ct., 1967, U.S. Ct. Appeals (fed. cir.) 1982. With U.S. Customs Svc., Treasury Dept., Washington, 1958-88, chief documentation br., 1965-66, chief carrier rulings br., 1966-76, chief penalties br., 1976-78, spl. asst. to asst. commr. Office of Regulations and Rulings, 1978-82, dir. carriers, drawback and bonds div., 1983-88, legal cons. in martime law, Washington, 1988—; pres. Griffin Unit Owners' Assn., 1999—; dir. Foggy Bottom Assn., 1992—; mem. U.S. del. Intergovtl. Maritime Cons. Orgn., London, 1972-75, U.S. rep., inter-sessional meeting, Hamburg, Fed. Republic Germany, 1973. Pres., Customs Fed. Credit Union, 1967-69. Recipient Superior Performance award Treasury Dept., 1962, commendation letter from asst. sec. treasury, 1964, Customs Outstanding Performance award, 1983, Customs Cash Performance award, 1984, 85. Mem. Customs Lawyers Assn. (pres. 1965-66), Fed. Bar Assn., Propeller Club U.S., United Seamen's Svc. (council of trustees 1986-88), Nat. Lawyers Club, Elks, Delta Pi Epsilon, Delta Theta Phi. Roman Catholic. Home and Office: 955 26th St NW Washington DC 20037-2009 E-mail: edwardbgable@aol.com.

GABLE, JOHN ALLEN, historian, educator; b. Rockford, Ill., Nov. 14, 1943; s. Allen Herman and Mary Jane (Kirkpatrick) G. AB, Kenyon Coll., 1965; PhD in History, Brown U., 1972. Asst. prof. history Briarcliff Coll., Briarcliff Manor, N.Y., 1974-77; exec. dir. Theodore Roosevelt Assn., Oyster Bay, N.Y., 1974—; adj. assoc. prof. C.W. Post L.I. U., Greenvale, N.Y., 1977-89; adj. prof. New Coll. Hofstra U., Hempstead, N.Y., 1989—. Editor, founder Theodore Roosevelt Assn. Jour., 1975—; author, editor 6 books in field; contbr. articles to profl. jours. Vestry Christ Ch., Oyster Bay, 1979-2002. Mem. Orgn. Am. Historians. Episcopalian. Home: 64T Glen Keith Rd Glen Cove NY 11542-3515 Office: Theodore Roosevelt Assn PO Box 719 Oyster Bay NY 11771-0719 Office Phone: 516-921-6319. E-mail: tra_gable@sprynet.com.

GABLE, KAREN ELAINE, health science educator; b. Des Moines, Nov. 12, 1939; d. John E. and Mabel I. (Davis) Clay; m. Robert W. Gable, Jr., Feb. 4, 1961; children: Susan Kay, Barbara Lynne, R. J. Kent. AS, 1969; BS in Edn., Ind. U., Indpls., 1976, MS in Edn., 1979, EdD, 1985. Registered dental hygienist Ind. U., cert. dental asst. Ind. U. From clin. instr. dental hygiene program Sch. Dentistry to assoc. prof. Ind. U., Indpls., 1976—94, assoc. prof. Sch. Health and Rehab. Scis., 1994—, program dir., 1994—, chair dept. health sci., 2002—. Contbr. articles to profl. jours. Recipient Disting. Dental Hygiene Alumna award, Ind. U. Sch. Dentistry. Mem.: ACTE/Health Occupations Edn. (mem. policy bd. 2002—), Ind. Career and Tech. Edn. Assn. (Outstanding Svc. awards), Ind. Dental Hygienists Assn. (sec.), Ind. Health Careers Assn. (pres.-elect, pres.), Health Occupations, Supvs. and Tchr. Educators Coun. (treas., pres.), Sigma Phi Alpha. Office Phone: 317-278-1353. Business E-Mail: kgable@iupui.edu.

GABLE, ROBERT ELLEDY, real estate investment company executive; b. N.Y.C., Feb. 20, 1934; s. Gilbert E. and Paulina (Stearns) G.; m. Emily Brinton Thompson, July 5, 1958; children: James, Elizabeth, John. BS, Stanford U., 1956. Asst. to pres. The Stearns Co. Ltd. (formerly Stearns Coal & Lumber Co. Inc.), Lexington, KY, 1958-60, sec., 1960-70, treas., 1961-62, v.p., 1962-70, chmn. bd., 1970—, pres., dir., 1975-78. Past chmn. bd., dir. Ky. & Tenn. Railway, Stearns, Ky., Lexington; past chmn. bd. Lumber King Inc., Stearns; past dir., audit com. Kuhn's Big K Stores Corp., Nashville, 1979-81; dir. emeritus Blue Cross and Blue Shield Ky.; past dir. Bank of McCreary County. Bd. dirs. Lexington Conv. and Tourist Bur., 1982—85; pres. Frazier Rehab. Found., Inc., Louisville, 1982—84, Headley-Whitney Mus., Lexington, 1985—90; pres., CEO Kentuckians for Fair Redistricting, Inc., 2001—03; chmn. Ky. Arts Coun., 2004—; Rep. candidate for U.S. Senate from Ky., 1972; Ky. co-chmn. Fin. Com. for Re-election of Pres., 1972; mem. Rep. Nat. Com., 1986—94, mem. budget com., 1989, Rep. Nat. Fin. Com., 1971—76; rep. state fin. chmn., 1973—75, 1986; mem. Ky. Rep. Ctrl. Com., 1974—94, 2004—05; state chmn. Rep. Party Ky., 1986—94; Rep. nominee for gov. Ky., 1975, 1995; mem. nat. leadership coun. Rep. Exch. Satellite Network, Nashville, 1993—95; former mem. missions bd. Episcopal Diocese of Lexington; mem. bd. founders Nat. Coun. Econ. Edn. (formerly Joint

Coun. Econ. Edn.), N.Y.C., 1982—; mem. Nat. Com. for Performing Arts, John F. Kennedy Ctr. for Performing Arts, Washington, 1993—2004, pres., CEO, 1993—97; commr. Ky. Dept. Parks, 1967—70; mem. pub. lands com. Interstate Oil Compact Commn., 1968—70; mem. adv. com. Ky. Ednl. TV, 1971—75; former mem. Breaks Interstate Park Commn.; past pres., past dir. McCreary County Indsl. Devel. Corp.; former trustee Stearns Recreational Assn., Inc.; mem. S.E. regional adv. com. Nat. Pk. Svc., 1973—78, sec., 1977—78; former bd. dirs. Ky. Mountain Laurel Festival Assn., v.p., 1974—75; mem. McCreary County Air Bd., 1967—81; mem. adv. bd. U. Ky. for Somerset Cmty. Coll., 1965—73; rep. state fin. chmn., 1973—75; trustee George Peabody Coll. for Tchrs., Nashville, 1970—79, mem. exec. com., 1976—79, chmn. bd., 1979; former trustee Capital Day Sch., Frankfort, Ky.; bd. dirs., past chmn., past pres., founder Ky. Coun. on Econ. Edn., Inc.; trustee Ky. State U. Found., 1979—82, Vanderbilt U., Nashville, 1979—87, former mem. budget com.; past mem. bd. dirs. Ky. Better Roads Coun., Inc., vice chmn., 1976—79; bd. trustees Epworth Assembly, Ludington, Mich., 1995—2001, treas., 1995—2000, pres., 2000—01; founding bd. Lexington Fund for the Arts, 1984—86; mem. So. Assn. of Rep. State Chmn., 1987—94; apptd. Pres. Adv. Com. Arts, 1992—93; bd. dirs., treas., exec. com. Ky. Ctr. for the Arts, 2004—. Served to lt. (j.g.) USNR, 1956—58. Named Ky. Col., Mr. Coal of Ky., 1970. Mem. Ky. Coal Assn. (dir. 1972-86, exec. com. 1974-78, sec. 1979-86), Ky. C. of C. (regional v.p., 1971-72, 76-80, exec. com. 1971-72, 76-80, dir. 1971-80, fin. com. 1978-79), Lexington C. of C. (dir. 1982, 84-87), Frankfort Country Club, Keeneland Club, Lafayette Club, Thoroughbred Club, Lexington Club, Bluegrass Auto Club (former bd. dirs.), Pendennis Club, River Valley Club, Capitol Hill Club, Coral Beach Club, Tau Beta Pi, Alpha Kappa Lambda (past chpt. pres.). Home: 1715 Stonehaven Dr Frankfort KY 40601-8624 Office: 200 W Vine St Ste 600 Lexington KY 40507-1616

GABLE, ROBERT S., psychology educator; b. Canton, Ohio, Mar. 21, 1934; s. Harry C. and Mary (Blackburn) Schwitzgebel. EdD, Harvard U., 1964; PhD, Brandeis U., 1964; LLD (hon.), San Fernando Valley Coll. Law, 1982. Asst. prof. psychology UCLA, 1964-70; assoc. prof. Claremont (Calif.) Grad. Sch., 1970-86, prof., 1986—. Bd. dirs. Human Interaction Rsch. Inst., L.A., 1987-92; CEO Life Sci. Rsch. Group, Inc., Claremont, 1975—; mem. rev. panel NSF 1979. Co-author: Law and Psychological Practice, 1980, (text) Computer Aptitude and Literacy, 1984; contbr. articles to profl. publs. Grantee NIMH, 1970, 74-77, John Randolf & Dora Haynes Found., 1990. Mem. APA, Am. Psychology-Law Soc. Achievements include patent for radio controlled audio-resonators. Office: Claremont Grad Sch Psychology Dept Claremont CA 91711

GABLER, ELIZABETH, film company executive; m. Lee Gabler. Agent motion picture literary dept. ICM; creative exec. Columbia Pictures; v.p. prodn. United Artists; with 20th Century Fox, Beverly Hills, Calif., 1988—, exec. v.p. prodn.; pres. Fox 2000 Pictures, 1999—. Mem. adv. bd. Ctr. Film, TV and New Media U. Calif., Santa Barbara. Named one of 100 Most Powerful Women in Entertainment, Hollywood Reporter, 2004. Office: 20th Century Fox PO Box 900 Beverly Hills CA 90213-0900

GABLIK, SUZI, art educator, writer; b. N.Y.C., Sept. 26, 1934; d. Anthony Julius and Geraldine (Schwartz) G. BA, Hunter Coll., 1955. Vis. prof. art Sydney Coll. Arts, 1980, U. of the South, Sewanee, Tenn., 1982, 84, U. Calif., Santa Barbara, 1985, 86, 88, Va. Commonwealth U., Richmond, 1987, Va. Tech., Blacksburg, 1990, U. Colo., Boulder, 1990. Endowed lectr. U. Victoria, B.C., 1983, Colo. Coll., 1983, U. Santa Barbara, 1985, Va. Tech., 1989. Author: Magritte, 1979, Has Modernism Failed?, 1984, The Reenchantment of Art, 1991, Conversations Before the End of Time, 1995, Living the Magical Life, 2002. Recipient Lifetime Achievement award, Women's Caucus for Art, 2003. Home: 3271 Deer Run Rd Blacksburg VA 24060-9075 E-mail: suzi@swva.net.

GABOR, FRANK, insurance company executive; b. Apr. 15, 1918; Pres. Gabor & Co., Inc., 1948-83, Anglo-Am. Agrl. Underwriters, Inc., Havana, Cuba, 1950-52; v.p., dir. Wilson Nat. Life, 1957-73; pres. Fla. Assn. Health Underwriters, 1960-66, Variable Income Planning Co., 1966, Bent Tree Farm, Inc., 1971—. Dir., mem. exec. com. Stanwood Corp., Charlotte, NC, 1975—89; pres. Gabor Reins. Mgmt Corp, 1975—93; pres. Ins. Svc. Agy. Inc; chmn. Gabor Agy. Inc., 1983—2000; underwriting mgr., cons. Life Disability, Property & Casualty Ins Cos. Home: 600 Biltmore Way Coral Gables FL 33134-7541 Office: 7270 NW 12th St Ste 130 Miami FL 33126-1928 E-mail: fgabor@gaborinsurance.com.

GABOR-HOTCHKISS, MAGDA, research scientist, librarian; b. Paris, Mar. 21, 1934; arrived in U.S., 1967; d. Andor and Olga (Halpern) Gabor; m. Rollin D. Hotchkiss, May 21, 1967 (dec. Dec. 2004). D of Natural Scis. summa cum laude, Eotvos Lorand Sci. U., 1963. Intern Plant Physiology Humboldt U., Berlin, 1957—58; rsch. asst., rsch. assoc. Inst. Genetics Hungarian Acad. Scis., Budapest, 1959—67; rsch. assoc. Rockefeller U., N.Y.C., 1967—82; asst., assoc. libr. Hancock Shaker Village Mus., Pittsfield, Mass., 1985—94, coord. libr. collections, 1995—99, vol. libr., archivist, 2000—. Postdoctoral Bacterial Genetics, Animal Viruses Cold Spring Harbor Lab. of Quantitative Biology, NY, 1965; guest investigator Rockefeller U., N.Y.C., 1964—66; mem. adv. bd. We. Mass. Libr. Assn., Hadley, 1996—97; adj. asst. prof. biology SUNY, Albany, NY, 1982—2002, multilingual contbg. indexer for film/lit. index, Film and TV Document Ctr., 1985—94. Author, compiler: Guide to Hancock Shaker Village Library Collections, 2001—03, annotator, editor: The Shaker Image, 1994; contbr. chpts. to sci. books, articles to sci. jours. Vol. libr. Berkshire Mus., Pittsfield, 1998—; tutor ESL Lit. Vols. Am., Pittsfield, 2001—. Mem.: N.Y. Acad. Scis., Genetics Soc. Am., Sigma Xi. Achievements include discovery of entry of various forms of purified DNAs into bacterial cells of pneumococcus progresses in a linear fashion; recombination patterns of induced bacterial diploids (via protoplast fusion in Bacillus subtilis) follow the classical mechanism found in eucaryotic cells. Avocations: reading, photography, yoga, languages.

GABOVITCH, STEVEN ALAN, lawyer, accountant; b. Newton, Mass., Feb. 7, 1953; s. William and Annette (Richman) G.; m. Rhonda Merle Kitover, Aug. 6, 1978; childre: Daniel J., Lindsey D. BS in Acctg., Boston Coll., 1975, JD, 1978; LLM in Taxation, Boston U., 1982. Bar: Mass. 1978, R.I. 1979, U.S. Dist. Ct. R.I. 1979, U.S. Tax Ct. 1980, U.S. Ct. Appeals (1st cir.) 1980, U.S. Dist. Ct. Mass. 1981, U.S. Ct. Appeals (fed. cir.) 1982, U.S. Supreme Ct. 1983; CPA, Mass. Tax specialist Peat, Marwick, Mitchell & Co., Providence, 1978-80; prin. William Gabovitch & Co., Boston, 1980-97; pvt. practice Stoughton, Mass., 1998—. Lectr. on bankruptcy taxation. Contbr. articles to profl. jours. Mem.: Boston Bar Assn., Mass. Bar Assn., R.I. Bar Assn., Nat. Soc. Tax Profls., Beta Gamma Sigma. Office: 378 Page St 3 Deerfield Corp Ctr Stoughton MA 02072 E-mail: steve@gabovitch.com.

GABOW, PATRICIA ANNE, internist, health facility executive; b. Starke, Fla., Jan. 8, 1944; m. Harold N. Gabow, June 21, 1971; children: Tenaya Louise, Aaron Patrick. BA in Biology, Seton Hill Coll., 1965; MD, U. Pa. Sch. Medicine, 1969. Diplomate Am. Bd. Internal Medicine, Am. Bd. Nephrology, Nat. Bd. Med. Examiners; lic. Colo. Internship in medicine Hosp. of U. of Pa., 1969-70; residency in internal medicine Harbor Gen. Hosp., 1970-71; renal fellowship San Francisco Gen. Hosp. and Hosp. of U. Pa., 1971-72, 72-73; instr. medicine divsn. renal diseases, asst. prof. U. Colo. Health Scis. Ctr., 1973-74, 74-79, assoc. prof. medicine divsn. renal diseases, prof., 1979-87; chief renal disease, clin. dir. dept. medicine Denver Gen. Hosp., 1973-81, 76-81, dir. med. svcs., 1981-91; CEO, med. dir. Denver Health and Hosps., 1992—. Intensive care com. Denver Gen. Hosp., 1976-81, med. records com., 1979-80, ind. rev. com., 1978-81, continuing med. edn. com., 1981-83, animal care com., 1979-83; student adv. com. U. Colo. Health Scis. Ctr., 1982-87, faculty senate, 1985, 86, internship adv. com., 1977-92; exec. com. Denver Gen. Hosp., 1981—, chmn. health resources com., 1988-90, chmn. pathology search com., 1989, chmn. faculty practice plan steering com., 1990-92. Mem. editorial bd. EMERGINDEX, 1983-93, Am. Jour. of Kidney Disease, 1984-96, Western Jour. of Medicine, 1987-98, Annals of Internal Medicine, 1988-91, Jour. of the Am. Soc. of Nephrology, 1990-97; contbr. numerous articles, revs. and editorials to profl. publs., chpts. to books. Mem. Mayor's Safe City Task Force, 1993; mem. sci. adv. bd. Polycystic Kidney Rsch. Found., 1984-96, chmn., 1991; mem. sci. adv. bd. Nat. Kidney Found., 1991-94; mem. Nat. Pub. Health and Hosps. Inst. Bd., 1993-2001, 03—. Recipient Sullivan award for Highest Acad. Average in Graduating Class, Seton Hill Coll., 1965, Pa. State Senatorial scholarship, 1961-65, Kaiser Permanente award for Excellence in Tchg., 1976, Ann. award to Outstanding Woman Physician, 1982, Kaiser Permanente Nominee for Excellence in Tchg. award, 1983, Seton Hill Coll. Disting. Alumna Leadership award, 1990, Florence Rena Sabin award U. Colo., 2000, Nathan Davis award AMA, 2000, Good Housekeeping Women in Govt. award, 2002; named one of The Best Doctors in Am., 1994-95, 2002; grantee Bonfils Found., 1985-86, NIH, 1985-90, 91-96, 96-2000, W.K. Kellogg Found., 1997—, AHRQ, 2000-03; named to Colo. Women's Hall of Fame, 2004. Mem. Denver Med. Soc., Colo. Med. Soc., Am. Fedn. Clin. Rsch., Am. Physiol. Soc., Polycystic Kidney Disease Rsch. Found. (sci. advisor 1984-96), Western Assn. Physicians, Nat. Kidney Found. (sci. adv. bd. 1987-91), Women's Forum of Colo., Inc., Assn. Am. Physicians. Roman Catholic. Office: Denver Health 660 Bannock St Denver CO 80204-4506 Address: Denver Health 777 Bannock St Denver CO 80204

GABRIEL, EBERHARD JOHN, lawyer, bank executive; b. Bucharest, Romania, Mar. 22, 1942; arrived in U.S., 1952, naturalized, 1955; s. William and Margaret (Eberhart) Krzyzewski; m. Janice Josephine Jedrzejewski, Aug. 21, 1965; children: John, Stephanie, Christopher. BA in English, St. Joseph's Coll. of Ind., 1963; JD, Georgetown U., 1966. Bar: Md. 1966, U.S. Supreme Ct. 1972, Minn. 1993. Staff atty. Fgn. Claims Settlement Commn., Washington, 1966-68; sr. v.p., gen. counsel Govt. Employees Fin. Corp., Denver, 1968-87; pres., CEO MNC Am. Indsl. Banks, Denver, 1987-89; v.p., asst. gen. counsel and compliance officer ITT Consumer Fin. Corp., Mpls., 1989-94; pvt. practice Mpls., 1994-95; coun. Comml. Credit Co., Balt., 1995-99; sr. v.p., gen. counsel Citibank USA, Wilmington, Del., 1995—2002; assoc. gen. counsel Citi Fin., Balt., 2002—04; v.p., gen. counsel Citicorp Trust Bank, Denton, Tex., 2004—. Fellow St. Joseph's Coll.; sec., treas. Indsl. Bank Savs. Guaranty Corp., Colo., 1973—83, pres., Colo., 1983—87; lectr. advanced mgmt. program Am. Fin. Svcs. Assn., 1974—81, 1985, 87, mem. law com., 1978—89, bd. dirs., 1988—89. Bd. dirs. Jeffco/Lakewood (Colo.) C. of C., 1974—80, 1982—86, chmn., 1984—85; mem. Jefferson County DA Adult Diversion Coun., 1985—89; mem. adv. coun. Colo. Office Regulatory Reform, Colo. Dept. Regulatory Agys., 1984—89; chmn. Lakewood on Parade, 1980; vice chmn. fin. divsn. United Way Metro Denver, 1982; trustee Lakewood Polit. Action com., 1978—89, chmn., 1986—87. Mem.: ABA, Am. Corp. Counsel Assn., Phi Alpha Delta. Roman Catholic. Office: Citicorp Trust Bank 9113 Gardenia Dr Denton TX 76207 Office Phone: 972-652-7170. Personal E-mail: gabelex@aol.com. Business E-Mail: eberhard.j.gabriel@citigroup.com.

GABRIEL, JEANETTE HANISEE, curator, art historian; b. Long Beach, Calif., Jan. 12, 1940; d. William Edward and Lorena (Mansell) Lester; m. Robert Maxwell Hanisee, Sept. 28, 1973 (div. 1986); children: Robb Andrew Hanisee, Michele Alpoente Hanisee, Leigh Mathilde Hanisee, Caleb Joseph Hanisee, Patricia Lorena Hanisee, Molly Beverly Hanisee; m. Angelo Julius Gabriel, Oct. 1, 1992. BS, MS, Calif. State U., Northridge, 1978; MA, U. Calif., Santa Barbara, 1988. Instr. Ventura (Calif.) Coll., 1979-81; dir., founder Adoptions Unltd., Ontario, Calif., 1981-83; curator L.A. County Mus. Art, 1988-92, Gilbert Collection, London, 1994—2002; dir. art collections Gilbert Found., LA, 2001—02; pvt. practice, 2003—. Author: The Gilbert Collection Micromosaics, 2000, The Gilbert Collection Hardstones; co-author: By Judgement of the Eye: The Varya and Hans Cohn Collection at the Los Angeles County Museum of Art, 1991, The World of Jade, 1992; contbr. articles to profl. jours. Mem. Internat. Churchill Soc., The Churchill Ctr. (founding mem., Clementine Churchill assoc. 1998), Reform Club London. Avocations: antiques, writing. Office: Gilbert Found 9454 Wilshire Blvd # 700 Beverly Hills CA 90212 also: 1309 Stonewood Ct San Pedro CA 90732 Personal E-mail: jeanettegabriel@aol.com.

GABRIEL, MARTIN GEORGE, engineering consultant; b. Chgo., Sept. 21, 1926; M. Marie T. DeBlasio, June 25, 1949; children: Martin, James, Kathleen, Jeanne, Mary. BSME, Ill. Inst. Tech., 1947; MS in Engring. Mechanics, U. Mich., 1955. Engr. Borg Warner Corp., Chgo., 1947-50; rsch. engr. Ford Motor Co. Rsch. Lab., Dearborn, Mich., 1950-52; supr. automatic transmissions Ford Motor Co., Livonia, Mich., 1952-75; reliability engr., supr. Ford Car product Devel., Livonia, Mich., 1975-91; sr. reliability engr. Ford Powertrain Ops., Dearborn, 1991-95; ret., 1995; pres. Martin G. Gabriel and Assocs., Inc., Bloomfield Hills, MI, 1995—. Instr. automotive dynamics Oakland U., Rochester, Mich., 1965-68. Author: Innovations in Automotive Transmission Engineering, 2004; contbr. articles pub. to profl. jours. Past pres. Cath. Youth Orgn., Detroit, 1992-93; bd. dirs. Detroit Area Coun. Boy Scouts. Am., 1969—; past coun. pres. St Owens Parish. Recipient Outstanding Engr. award Profl. Engrs. Industry, Mich., 1988, Pres.'s citation Ill. Inst. Tech., 1992, Silver Beaver award, 1979. Fellow MSPE (Engr. of Yr. 1994); mem. ASME (life), Soc. Automotive Engrs. (life, elected bd. dirs. 1996-99, chmn. engring. meetings bd. 1994-95, Forest McFarland award 1986), Mich. Soc. Profl. Engrs. (pres. 1991-92), Sokol Detroit, Sr. Men's Club of Birmingham. Roman Catholic. Achievements include patents in field. Avocations: violin, portrait painting, golf, small fruit orchard. Home: 4396 Geislers Ct Bloomfield MI 48301 Personal E-mail: Hornblwr1@aol.com.

GABRIEL, MICHAEL, psychology professor; b. Phila., May 5, 1940; s. Michael and Josephine (Alesio) G.; m. Linda Prinz, June, 1967 (div.); 1 child, Joseph Michael; m. Sonda S. Walsh, 1984. AB in Psychology, St. Joseph's Coll., 1962; MA, U. Wis., 1965, PhD, 1967. Asst. prof. Pomona Coll., Claremont, Calif., 1967—70; staff psychologist Pacific State Hosp., Pomona, Calif., 1968-70; NIMH sr. postdoctoral fellow U. Calif.-Irvine, 1970-72; asst. prof. U. Tex.-Austin, 1973-77, assoc. prof., 1977-82; prof. psychology U. Ill., Urbana, 1982—2004, appointee Ctr. for Advanced Study, 1990-91, prof. emeritus dept. psychology and Beckman Inst., 2004. Area chmn. Biol. Psychology Program, U. Tex., Austin, 1979-82; mem. rev. panel in behavioral and neural scis. NSF, 1988-91, prin. investigator database system for neuronal pattern analysis project, 1992—, ad hoc mem. biopsychology rev. panel, 1997-98; faculty Beckman Inst., U. Ill., Urbana, 1989—; chmn. Neuronal Pattern Analysis Group, Beckman Inst., mem. neuroinformatics rev. panel, NIH, 2000-. Co-editor: (with J. Moore) Learning and Computational Neuroscience: Foundations of Adaptive Networks, 1989, (with B. Vogt) Neurobiology of Cingulate Cortex and Limbic Thalamus, 1993; mem. editl. bd. Neural Plasticity, Neurobiology of Learning and Memory. Grantee NIMH, 1978-88, 98—, NIH, 1988—, Air Force Office Sci. Rsch., 1988-91, NSF, 1992—, NIDA, 1996-2001. Fellow Am. Psychol. Soc., Internat. Behavioral Neurosci. Soc.; mem. Sigma Chi. Office: Beckman Inst Univ Ill Urbana IL 61801-2325 E-mail: michaelgabriel@bellsouth.net.

GABRIEL, MORDECAI LIONEL, biologist, educator; b. N.Y.C., Mar. 18, 1918; s. Joseph and Bertha (Fram) G.; m. Elinor Rosenstein, Nov. 11, 1945; children— Alisa, Jessica. AB, Yeshiva U., 1938; MA, Columbia, 1938, PhD, 1944. Instr. genetics U. Conn., 1943-45; mem. faculty Bklyn. Coll., 1945—, prof. biology, 1963—, chmn. dept., 1965-71; dean Bklyn. Coll. (Sch. Sci.), 1971-76, acting v.p. for acad. affairs, 1981-82; assoc. provost Bklyn. Coll., 1982-88, assoc. provost emeritus, 1988—. Vis. prof. Columbia, 1956; Fulbright lectr., vis. prof. U. Tel Aviv, 1959-60; mem. Marine Biol. Lab., Woods Hole, Mass., 1950— Author: (with S. Fogel) Great Experiments in Biology, 1956. Ford Found. faculty fellow, 1955-56 Fellow AAAS; mem. Am. Soc. Zoologists, Am. Assn. Anatomists, N.Y. Acad. Scis., Soc. Study Evolution, Vertebrate Paleont. Soc., AAUP (pres. Bklyn. Coll. chpt. 1964-66), Phi Beta Kappa, Sigma Xi. Home: 120 Old Mill Rd Great Neck NY 11023-1936 Office: Brooklyn Coll Brooklyn NY 11210

GABRIEL, PETER PAUL, business educator; b. Halle, Germany, July 11, 1929; s. Paul and Eva Wernecke G.; m. Linea Elizabeth Larson, Sept. 9, 1950; children: Paul Lawrence, John Peter, Kathryn Anne, Christina Eva. MBA, Harvard U., 1962, DBA, 1965. Various adminstrv. positions, Germany, France, S. Am., 1948-60; assoc. McKinsey & Co., N.Y.C., 1966-69, ptnr., 1969-73; prof. of mgmt. dean Sch. of Mgmt. Boston U., 1972-76; prof. bus. adminstrn. U. Ulm, Germany, 1989-92. Contbr. articles and essays to publs. in field of internat. bus. and investment Recipient G.M. Loeb award for Disting. Writing in Bus. and Fin., U. Conn., 1967, Horace G. Crockett award McKinsey & Co., N.Y., 1966. Home: 240 Beldingville Rd Ashfield MA 01330

GABRIEL, RICHARD WEISNER, lawyer; b. Greensboro, N.C., Nov. 2, 1949; s. George Deeb and Lillian (Weisner) G.; m. Elizabeth Diane Burton, June 23, 1979; children: Margaret Elizabeth, Richard Weisner Jr. AB, Duke U., 1971; MBA, U. N.C., Greensboro, 1977; JD, Wake Forest U., 1975. Bar: N.C. 1975, U.S. Supreme Ct. 1978, U.S. Tax Ct. 1981, U.S. Dist. Ct. (mid. dist.) N.C. 1975. Pvt. practice, Greensboro, 1975-77; mng. ptnr. Gabriel, Berry & Weston LLP, Greensboro, 1978—. Vis. lectr. Guilford Coll., Greensboro, 1977-81; counsel Internat. Home Furnishings Reps. Assn., High Point, N.C., 1988—. Co-author: (manuals) Proving Damages in North Carolina, 1989, Trial Advocacy in North Carolina, 1990, Trying the Automobile Injury Case in North Carolina, 1992, 93, 95, Counseling the Small Business Client in North Carolina, 1996, Negotiating and Drafting Acquisition Agreements in North Carolina, 1999; contbg. author Contact Mag., 1988—; editor-in-chief Wake Forest Jurist, 1975. With N.C. Army N.G., 1971-77. Recipient award for exemplary svc. Upjohn Health Care Svcs., 1988, Presdl. Citation, IHFRA, 1991. Office: Gabriel Berry & Weston LLP 214 Commerce Pl Greensboro NC 27401-2427

GABRIEL, RONALD SAMUEL, child neurologist; b. Monterey, Calif., Mar. 19, 1937; s. Philip Louis and Theresa Shaheen Gabriel; children: Philip Louis III, Paula Shaheen, Matthew William. BA with honors, Yale U., 1959; MD, Boston U., 1963. Diplomate Am. Bd. Psychiatry and Neurology (examiner 1978-88), Am. Bd. Pediatrics. Intern, resident in pediatrics Los Angeles County Gen. Hosp., 1963-66; fellow in neurology and pediatric neurology UCLA med. ctr., 1966-68, 70-71; head physician, cons. Calif. Children's Svcs., 1970—; clin. prof. neurology/pediatrics UCLA Sch. Medicine, 1971—, dir. pediat. neurology/outpatient, 1971-76. Cons. Regional Ctr.-Calif., 1971—; vis. prof. Prince of Wales, Royal Children's Hosp., Sydney and Melbourne, Australia, 1978; mem. expert panel L.A. Superior Ct., 1992—; founding and mng. gen. ptnr. Med. Imaging of So. Calif., L.A., 1980-94; mng. dir. GFA Cattle and Farm Co. Author: The 410 Shotgun, 2000, Diary of a Mountain Hunter, 2000; contbr.: Textbook of Child Neurology, 1974, 4 edits., 1990, Difficult Diagnoses in Pediatrics, 1990, Founders of Child Neurology, 1990. Mng. dir. GFF Natural History Mus. Maj. U.S. Army, 1968-70. Spl. fellow Nat. Inst. Neurol. Disease/Stroke, 1966-68, 70-71. Fellow Am. Acad. Pediatrics, Am. Acad. Neurology; mem. Calif. Med. Assn. (mem. sci. adv. panel 1987-94, chmn. sci. adv. com. 1989-90). Roman Catholic. Avocations: writing, mountain climbing, hunting. Office: Neurology-Pediat Neurology Assocs 2080 Century Park E Ste 203 Los Angeles CA 90067-2005 Fax: (310) 277-9285.

GABRIELE, CHARLES, composer, educator; b. N.Y.C., May 31, 1921; s. Benedict and Rose Tese Gabriele; m. Dina Kurochkin; 1 child, Joanna (dec.). BA, NYU, 1943, MA, 1944; PhD, Marshall Grad. Sch., Jersey City, N.J., 1948; D Music (hon.), Coll. Music, Rome, 1981. Tchr. Rice HS, N.Y.C., 1945—46; instr. St. Peters Coll., Jersey City, 1946—48; assoc. prof. Monmouth Coll., Highland Park, NJ, 1948—50; prof. Rutgers U., New Brunswick, NJ, 1950—57; pub. affairs officer U.S. Dept. Def., Washington, 1960—77; composer Comet Press, Bowie, Md., 1978—93; composer in residence U.S. Naval Acad. Band, Annapolis, Md., 1976—81, Venice Concert Band, Venice, Fla., 1994—. Composer: Christopher Columbus March, 1976 (medal, 1977), Clarinet Concertino, 1992 (plaque, 1992), Lilia Craige Overture, 1995 (trophy, 1996). Lt. USN, 1957—60. Recipient Knighthood in Order of Merit award, Rep. Italy, 1979, honor, U.S. Congress, 1980, 1991, namesake for Gabriele Pavilion, Daytona Beach Coll., 1992. Mem.: Am. Assn. Composers Authors. Democrat. Roman Catholic. Avocation: model railroading. Home: 864 Connemara Cir Venice FL 34292-2260

GABRIELSON, CHARLES, publishing executive; Various mgt. pos. Gannett Co., Inc., 1971—84; formerly advert. dir. Bambergers Co., NY; mkt. sales dir. Advert. Age, 1986—89; exec. V.P., USA Weekend Gannett Co., Inc., 1989—96, pub. USA Weekend, 1996—. Office: Gannett Co Inc 535 Madison Ave Fl 21 New York NY 10022-4212*

GABRILOVE, JACQUES LESTER, physician; b. NYC, Sept. 21, 1917; s. Benjamin and Pauline (Levine) G.; m. Hilda R. Weiss, May 19, 1946; children: Sandra Leslie Saltzman, Janice Lynn Gabrilove Dirzulaitis. BS magna cum laude, CCNY, 1936; MD Alpha Omega Alpha prize, NYU, 1940. Diplomate Am. Bd. Internal Medicine. Intern Mt. Sinai Hosp., N.Y.C., 1940-41, rotating intern, 1941-43, vol. radiology, 1943, resident medicine, 1943-44, Blumenthal fellow medicine, 1946-48, research asst. medicine, 1949-51, asst. attending physician, 1952-60, assoc. attending physician, 1960-68, attending physician, 1969—. Clin. prof. medicine Mt. Sinai Sch. Medicine, 1969-82, chief endocrine clinic, 1969-92, Baumritter prof., 1982-90, Baumritter prof. emeritus, 1990—, prof., 1995—, cting dir. divsn. endocrinology, 1985, assoc. dir. divsn., 1986—, dir. endocrine fellowship program, 1986—; Libman fellow in medicine Yale U., 1945; clin. asst. prof. SUNY Coll. Medicine, N.Y.C., 1957-59, clin. assoc. prof., 1959-66, clin. prof., 1966-69, professorial lectr., 1969—; cons. endocrinology VA Hosp., East Orange, N.J., 1958-66, Elizabeth A. Horton Hosp., Middletown, N.Y., 1961—, VA Hosp., Bronx, N.Y., 1969—, Norwalk (Conn.) Hosp., 1974—, Elmhurst (N.Y.) City Hosp., St. Francis Hosp., Port Jervis, N.Y.; mem. panel on metabolic and rheumatoid diseases U.S. Pharmacopeia, 1956; mem. spl. com. on rsch. tng. grants in diabetes, endocrinology and metabolism NIH, 1976-79, mem. com. on diabetes rsch. and tng. ctrs., 1977-79; Saltzman lectr. Mt. Sinai Hosp., Cleve., 1974; cons. Jour. Urology, 1984-89. Mem. editl. bd. Mt. Sinai Jour.; contbr. chpts. to books, articles to profl. jours. Trustee, v.p. area Jewish synagogue. Recipient Globus prize Mt. Sinai Jour., Townsend Harris medal CCNY Alumni Assn., 1998; J. Lester Gabrilove award established in his honor, 1988; named to Hall of Fame Alumni Assn. Townsend Harris H.S. Fellow ACP, Am. Coll. Endocrinology (Disting. Clin. Endocrinologist award 1996, Festschrift in his honor on 80th birthday), N.Y. Acad. Medicine, Phi Beta Kappa; mem. AMA, AAAS, Am. Assn. Clin. Endocrinologists (Disting. Clin. Endocrinologist award 1996), Am. Diabetes Assn., Harvey Soc., Endocrine Soc., Royal Soc. Medicine, Pan Am. Med. Assn. (v.p. N.Am. endocrinology), Peruvian Endocrine Soc. (hon.), N.Y. Acad. Scis., N.Y. County Med. Soc., N.Y. Diabetes Assn., Mt. Sinai Alumni Assn. (pres. 1970, Jacobi medallion 1973), Lotos Club (bd. dirs.), Alpha Omega Alpha. Achievements include research in delineaton of hyperfunctioning and hypofunctioning endocrine disorders of the adrenal cortex and gonads; mechanism of gynecomastia; medical treatment of thyrotoxicosis; med. treatment of benign prostatic hyperplasia; pathogenesis of the polycystic ovary syndrome. Home: 25 E 86th St New York NY 10028-0553 Office Phone: 212-241-5907. Business E-Mail: lester.gabrilove@mssm.edu.

GABRIS, GEORGE STEVEN, sculptor, welder; b. N.Y.C., Jan. 2, 1953; s. Stephen John and Kveta (Rybička) G.; m. Stephanie Anne Mazanek, Dec. 30, 1989. Cert. in Welding, Albuquerque Tech. Vocat. Inst., 1979. Tchr. art, recreation instr. N.Y.C. Housing Authority, 1975-76; artist, 1977; prodn. welder Environ. Bldg. Products, Albuquerque, 1979-81, H&L Iron Works, Albuquerque, 1982, Hemisphere Steel Co., Bklyn., 1984-85; test welder R&D Eutectic Corp. of Eutectic and Castolin Inc. Internat., Flushing, N.Y., 1985-88; car maintainer in train overhaul shop N.Y.C. Transit Authority, 1988—. One-man shows include N.Y.C.T., Bklyn., 2004; Group exhbns. include Lever House, N.Y.C., 1964, 75, A.S.A. Gallery, Albuquerque, 1981, 82, Gelabert Studios, N.Y.C., 1992, Abney Gallery, N.Y.C., 1992, Crossland Svs. Bank, L.I. and Manhattan, N.Y., 1993, Limner Gallery, N.Y.C., 1993, 94, Westbeth Gallery, N.Y.C., 1974, 94, 97, Art Initiatives, N.Y.C., 1996, Broome St. Gallery, N.Y.C., 1996, Stephen Gang Gallery, N.Y.C., 1997, (website) Internat. Artists Interface, 1996-, Americas Towers Lobby, 1998-99, N.Y.C.T. Employees Gallery, Bklyn., 2005; represented in numerous pvt. collections; published in Creative INsight, 2000. Vol. dept. social and cmty. svcs. N.Y.C.

Housing Authority, 1974, 75; youth project coord. Visions/Urban Youth Project, N.Y.C., 1976. Recipient Critics' Pix award Manhattan Arts Internat. Mag., 1994, Showcase award, 1996, award of excellence, 1998, 99, 2000; 1st prize Internat. Art League, 1998. Mem. Nat. Sculpture Soc., Am. Welding Soc. (cert.), Orgn. Ind. Artists, Transit Workers Union (local 100), N.Y. Artists Equity Assn., Inc., Artists Talk on Art. Democrat. Avocations: art collector, bread baker, gourmet cook, exotic birds. Home: 440 E 8th St #2 Brooklyn NY 11218 E-mail: gssculp@aol.com.

GACH, JAY ANTHONY, composer; b. NYC, Mar. 9, 1955; s. Morris Gach and Phyllis Schilleci-Gach; m. Ellen Carroll Zaehringer, Nov. 19, 1982; children: Lee Anthony, Lauren Emmy. MusM, Hartt Coll. Music, 1982; PhD, SUNY, Stony Brook, 1982; diploma of fellowship, London Coll. Music, 1993. Rsch. assistantship SUNY, Tubingen, Germany, 1981—82; fellow music composition Am. Acad., Rome, 1983—84; freelance composer NYC, 1985—89, London, 1990—99, NYC, 2000—. Rec. sec. L.I. Composers Alliance; guest instr. London Coll. Music, 1993—95. Composer: (music for chamber orchestra) I Venti d'Estate (IL Ponentino) (St. Paul Chamber Orch. Am. Composers Competition Winner, 1985), (music for large orchestra) Chants for Orchestra (Frederick P. Rose Bklyn Philharm. 1st Prize, 1988), (music for chamber ensemble) Idle Hands are the Devil's Workshop (Howard B. Auchincloss Prize Soc. for New Music, 2005). Recipient NY Found. for the Arts Music Composition award, NY Found. Arts, 1985, Std. awards, ASCAP, 1998—2005, composition prize, Fromm Found., Harvard U., 1992, Music Composition prize for Emmy, Delta Omicron; fellow, Am. Acad. in Rome, 1983—84; grantee Meet The Composer, Am. Music Ctr., 1988/89/90/02/05, 1989, 1990, 2002, 2005. Mem.: Soc. Promotion New Music England, Coll. Music Soc., Am. Music Ctr. Achievements include Commission: Childrens Aid Society Chorus, USA 2005; Saxtet Publications Composition Competition, England 2004; Commission: Society for the Promotion of New Music/Huddersfield Music Festival, UK 1998; Commission: Haydn Chamber Orch of London, UK 1997; Commission: Islington International Festival, UK 1995; Commission: Third British Contemporary Piano Competition, UK 1994; Commission: The National Italian Youth Orch., Italy 1993. Home: 324 West Penn St Long Beach NY 11561 Home Fax: 516-889-5454. Personal E-mail: jayanthonygach1@aol.com.

GADAL, LOUIS STEPHEN, artist; b. L.A., Apr. 10, 1936; s. Louis A. and Lois Anna (Northup) G.; m. Lynn M. Gary, May 15, 1966; children: Eric Spencer, Stephanie Jenet. Cert., Chouinard Art Inst., L.A., 1959; postgrad., Otis Art Inst., L.A., 1962-63. Painter Walt Disney, Anaheim, Calif., 1960; freelance illustrator Louis Gadal Illustration, L.A., 1959-62; illustrator QA Archtl. Illustration, L.A., 1962-68, Carlos Diniz Assocs., L.A., 1968-70; drawing instr. Calif. Inst. Arts, Valencia, Calif., 1980-88, Otis Parsons Art Inst., L.A., 1988-90; illustrator Louis Gadal/Archtl. Illustrator, L.A. and Santa Monica, 1970—2001. Contbr. Landscapes in Watercolor, 2002. 1st sgt. USNG, 1954-62. Recipient Cert. of Excellence San Bernardino Mus., Redlands, Calif., 1980, 2d Prize Sea Heritage Marine Art, Glen Oaks, N.Y., 1990, Liquitex Watercolor award Pa. Watercolor Soc., Mechanicsburg, Pa., 1990, Bronze Maritime Merit award Nat. Park Acad. of Arts, Jackson Hole, Wyo., 1992, Philip D'Huc Dressler Meml. award Pa. Watercolor Soc., Somerset, Pa., 1993, Combined Donors award Nat. Watercolor Soc., 1994, Dagmar Tribble award, Am. Watercolor Soc., 1995, Maritime Merit award Arts for the Parks 10th annual top 100, 1996, Region One Silver medal Arts for the Parks 12th annual top 100, 1998, Newington award Am. Artist Profl. League, 2000, Purchase award Arts for the Parks, Yellowstone Nat. Pk., 2001; included in traveling exhbn. Am. Watercolor Soc. 126th Internat. Exhibit, 1993, Nat. Watercolor Soc. 74th annual Exhibit, 1994, Am. Watercolor Soc. 128th Internat. Exhibit, 1995; contbr. to publs. including Best of Watercolor 2, Best of Watercolor Painting Light & Shadow. Mem. Niagara Frontier Watercolor Soc., Pa. Watercolor Soc., Watercolor West Soc., Nat. Watercolor Soc., Am. Soc. Marine Artist, Northwest Watercolor Soc., Phila. Watercolor Soc., Am. Watercolor Soc. Republican. Roman Catholic. Avocations: printmaking, archaeology, history, poetry, writing. Home: 3648 Coolidge Ave Los Angeles CA 90066-3310 E-mail: lgadal@earthlink.net.

GADBERRY, VICKI LYNN HIMES, librarian; b. Frederick, Md., Jan. 3, 1950; d. Guilford Swisher and Eloise Alberta (Twentey) Himes; m. Eric Brett Gadberry, Aug. 15, 1971. BS, U. Md., 1971; MLS, U. S.C., 1974; postgrad., Penland Sch. Crafts, 1989, 96, Sul Ross State U., 1997-98. Cert. media coord. N.C. Dept. Pub. Instrn. Media coord. N.C. Pub. Schs., Fayetteville, 1976-78, Hendersonville, 1980-85, Asheville, 1985-88; pub. svcs. coord. Mars Hill (N.C.) Coll., 1990-92, reference svcs. libr., 1992-97; asst. exec. dir., adminstrn. Fort Davis (Tex.) C. of C., 1998—; owner Off The Wall Photos & Art, 2001—. On-site dir. Children's Art in the Mountains Program, Marshall, N.C., summer 1992, tchr. fiber art, summer 1990; artist-in-residence Mountain Arts Program, Waynesville, N.C., 1990. Project designer book: Molas!, 1998; contbr. articles, revs., index to profl. publs. Mem. planning com. Beacon Handloom Weaving Show, Asheville, N.C., 1988, 90-92, chair, 1989; bd. dirs. Children's Art in the Mountains Program, Marshall, N.C., 1991-93. Mem. Handweaver's Guild Am. (orgnl. C.O.E. Weaving com. co-chair 1992-94), Grant County Fiber Guild, Mogollon Rim Fiber Guild (sec.). Avocations: weaving, photography. Home: PO Box 393 Fort Davis TX 79734-0393 also: 18 Gulch Ln Silver City NM 88061 E-mail: gadberry@gilanet.com.

GADDES, RICHARD, opera company director; b. Wallsend, Northumberland, Eng., May 23, 1942; s. Thomas and Emilie Jane (Rickard) G. L.T.C.L. in piano, L.T.C.L. for sch. music; G.T.C.L., Trinity Coll. Music, London, 1964; D. Mus. Arts (hon.), St. Louis Conservatory, 1983; D.F.A. (hon.), U. Mo.-St. Louis, 1984; D.Arts (hon.), Webster U., 1986. Founder, mgr. Wigmore Hall Lunchtime Concerts, 1965; dir. Christopher Hunt and Richard Gaddes Artists Mgmt., London, 1965-66; bookings mgr. Artists Internat. Mgmt., London, 1967-69; artistic adminstr. Santa Fe Opera, 1969—75, assoc. gen. dir., 1995—2000, gen. dir., 2000—, Opera Theatre of St. Louis, 1975-85, bd. dirs., 1985—. Bd. dirs. Grand Ctr., Inc., 1988—, pres., 1988-95; bd. dirs. William Matheus Sullivan Found. Mem. bd. advisors Royal Oak Found. Recipient Lamplighter award, 1982, Mo. Arts award, 1983, St. Louis award, 1983, Human Relations award Jewish-Am. Com., St. Louis, 1985, Nat. Inst. for Music Theatre award, 1986, Cultural Achievement award Young Audiences, 1987. Office: Santa Fe Opera PO Box 2408 Santa Fe NM 87504-2408

GADDIS, ANNE L, elementary school educator; d. Frank and Ann Ola Gaddis; children: Stephanie Alicia Montague-Smith, Ananias Marcellous Montague, II. BA in Early Childhood Edn., Roosevelt U., Chgo., 1978, MA in Early Childhood/Spl. Edn., 1981; MA in Adminstrn. and Supervision, Chgo. State U., 1995. General Administrative State Tchr. Certification Bd/IL, 1996, Standard Early Childhood Teaching State Tchr. Certification Bd/IL, 1988, Standard Elementary Teaching State Tchr. Certification Bd/IL, 1996, Illinois Administrators' Academy Ill. State Bd. of Edn./IL, 2002. Tchr. asst. Chgo. Pub. Schs., 1969—77, head tchr., 1979—; receptionist, console operator Coll. Bus. Roosevelt U., Chgo., 1977—78, grad asst., resource curriculum coord., Coll. Edn., 1979—81; tchr., asst. dir. Jackson Day Care/After Sch. Program, Chgo., 1977—78; supervising head start tchr. dept. spl. programs Chgo. Archdiocese, 1978—79; tchr., asst. dir. Mike and Julie's Ednl. Ctr., Chgo., 1980—81; program planner, reading-math coord., tchr. Project Edn. Plus/Cabrini-Green, Chgo., 1980—82. Consulting, mentor tchr. Chgo. Pub. Schs., 1998—2005. Mem.: Nat. Assn. for Edn. of Young Children, Chgo. Metro Assn. for Edn. of Young Children, Assn. for Supervision andCurriculum Devel. Baptist. Avocations: travel, reading, dance. Office: Chgo Pub Schs 125 S Clark St Chicago IL 60603 Home Fax: 773-568-4369. Personal E-mail: sapphyre01@sbcglobal.net.

GADDIS, CHARLES RONNIE, music educator; b. Franklyn County, Ga., Nov. 10, 1951; s. Wilson Edgar and Ruth Lee Gaddis; m. Shelia Dianne Parker, June 7, 1980; children: Julie Anne, Melody Anne. BS in Music Edn., Jacksonville State U., 1973; MusM, U. Tenn., 1983. Band dir. West Side H.S., Rocky Face, Ga., 1973—75; dir. bands, chmn. dept. fine arts SE Whitfield H.S., Dalton, Ga., 1975—2002; dir. bands Weaver (Ala.) Jr. and Sr H.S., 2002—05, Model High Sch., Rome, Ga., 2005—. Min. music First Bapt. Ch., Tunnel Hill, Ga., 1973—76, Antioch Bapt. Ch., Dalton, Ga., 1976—77, Calvary Bapt. Ch., Dalton, Ga., 1982—85, Ctr. Point Bapt. Ch., Dalton, Ga., 1985—93, First Evangelistic Ch., Dalton, Ga., 1985—85, Pine Grove Bapt. Ch., Dalton, Ga., 1996—97; music dir. Pleasant Grove Meth. Ch., Dalton, Ga., 1981—82. Deacon First Bapt. Ch., Tunnel Hill, Ga. Recipient Star Tchr. award, Whitfield County Sch. Sys., 1980. Home: 1937 Sourwood Dr Dalton GA 30720-4971 Office Phone: 706-236-1895. Office Fax: 706-802-6750. Personal E-mail: crgaddis@charter.net. E-mail: rgaddis@flaydbee.net.

GADDIS, JOHN LEWIS, history professor; b. Cotulla, Tex., Apr. 2, 1941; m. Toni Dorfman. BA, U. Tex., 1963, MA, 1965, PhD, 1968. Asst. prof. Ind. U. S.E., Jeffersonville, 1968-69; asst. prof. history Ohio U., Athens, 1969-71, assoc. prof., 1971-76, prof., 1976-83, disting. prof. history, 1983-97, dir. Contemporary History Inst., 1987-93; Robert Lovett prof. history Yale U., New Haven, 1997—. Vis. prof. Naval War Coll., 1975-77; Bicentennial prof. Am. history, U. Helsinki, 1980-81; vis. prof. politics Princeton U., 1987; Harmsworth prof. Am. History Oxford U., 1992-93, Eastman prof., 2000-01. Author: The United States and the Origins of the Cold War, 1941-47, 1972, Russia, the Soviet Union, and the United States: An Interpretive History, 1978, 2d edit., 1990, Strategies of Containment: A Critical Appraisal of Postwar American National Security Policy, 1982, 2d edit., 2005, The Long Peace: Inquiries into the History of the Cold War, 1987, The United States and the End of the Cold War, 1992, We Now Know: Rethinking Cold War History, 1997; The Landscape of History: How Historians Map the Past, 2002, Surprise, Security, and the American Experience, 2004. Fellow Woodrow Wilson Ctr., 1995-96; recipient Bancroft prize, 1973, Stuart L. Bernath prize, 1973, Nat. Hist. Soc. prize, 1973. Mem. Am. Hist. Assn., Orgn. Am. Historians, Soc. for Historians of Am. Fgn. Rels., Coun. on Fgn. Rels.

GADDIS, JOHN ROBERT, music educator; b. Greenville, Ky., Nov. 14, 1949; s. Millard and Dorothy Louise (Lovell) G.; m. Anna Jeanne Berry, Dec. 17, 1971; children: John Mark, Charles Nathan, Jessica Dawn. BMus, Western Ky. U., 1972, MA in Edn., 1981; EdD, U. Ky., 1992. Choral and band dir. Elizabethtown (Ky.) High Sch., 1972—73; band and choral dir. Ctrl. City (Ky.) H.S., 1973—77; band dir. Franklin (Ky.)-Simpson H.S., 1977-79; asst. band dir. Western Ky. U., Bowling Green, Ky., 1981-82; prof. music, dean Sch. Music Campbellsville (Ky.) U., 1982—. Pres. Ky. Music Educators Assn. Adjudicator for band festivals and contests, guest conductor for honors bands and choirs, tuba soloist; youth choir dir. Forest Park Bapt. Ch., Bowling Green, 1970-71; min. of music Mill Creek Bapt. Ch., Radcliff, Ky., 1973, Calvary Bapt. Ch., Franklin, Ky., 1979-82, First Bapt. Ch., Albany, Ky., 1987-88, Lebanon Bapt. Ch., 1990-. Mem. Nat. Assn. for Coll. Wind and Percussion Instrs., Music Educators Nat. Conf., Soc. for Music Tchr. Edn. (state chmn. 1991-), Ky. Music Educators Assn. (bd. dirs. 1989-), Ky. Coalition for Music Edn. (bd. dirs. 1992-). Republican. Baptist. Avocations: golf, fishing, camping. Home: 109 Canterbury Way Campbellsville KY 42718-9546 Office: Campbellsville Univ One University Dr Campbellsville KY 42718

GADDIS ROSE, MARILYN, literature educator, translator; b. Fayette, Mo., Apr. 2, 1930; d. Merrill Elmer and Florence Georgia (Lyon) Gaddis; m. James Leo Rose, Dec. 23, 1956 (div. 1966); m. Stephen David Ross, Nov. 16, 1968; 1 child, David Gaddis Ross. BA, Central Meth. Coll., 1952; MA, U. S.C., Columbia, 1954-55; PhD, U. Mo., 1958; LHD, Ctrl. Meth. Coll., 1987. Instr. Stephens Coll., Columbia, Mo., 1958-68; assoc. prof. Ind. U., Bloomington, 1968; prof. comparative lit. SUNY, Binghamton, 1968—, disting. svc. prof., 1991—, dir. translation program, 1973—2002. Translator: (book) Axel, 1970, 1986, Eve of the Future Eden, 1981, Lui: A View of Him, 1986, Adrienne Mesurat, 1991, Volupté, The Sensual Man, 1995, Translation Horizon, 1996, Translation and Literary Criticism, 1998, Beyond the Western Tradition, 2000; editor, contbr.: book Translation Spectrum, 1981; editor: Translation Perspectives; contbr. articles to profl. jours. Fulbright fellow, U. Lyon, France, 1953—54, Humanities Rsch. Centre Sr. fellow, Australian Nat. U., 1977. Mem.: MLA (del. assembly 1974—78, pres. N.E. sect. 1975—76, del. assembly 1984—87, exec. coun. 2004—), Am. Translators Assn. (bd. dirs. 1986—88, mng. editor series 1986—96, endowed lectr. 1998—, Spl. Svc. award 1983, 1995, Alexander Gode award 1988), Am. Lit. Translators (sec.-treas. 1981—83), PEN N.Y. Home: Apt 204 5 Riverside Dr Binghamton NY 13905-4644 Office Phone: 607-777-6726. Personal E-mail: mgrose@binghamton.edu.

GADDY, JAMES LEOMA, chemical engineer, educator; b. Jacksonville, Fla., Aug. 16, 1932; s. Leoma Ithama and Mary Elizabeth (Edwards) Gaddy; m. Betty Maricella, Sept. 7, 1952; children: James, Teresa. BSChemE, La. Poly. U., 1955; MSChemE, U. Ark., 1968; PhDChemE, U. Tenn., 1972. Registered prof engr, Ark. Process engr. Ethyl Corp., Baton Rouge, 1955-60; project mgr., engrng. supr. Ark.-La. Gas, Shreveport, La., 1960-66; assoc. prof. chem engrng. U. Mo., Rolla, 1972-79, prof., dir. rsch. ctr., 1979-80; prof., head chem. engrng. U. Ark., Fayetteville, 1980-88, disting. prof., 1988-91, emeritus disting. prof., 1991—. Pres Bioengineering Resources, Fayetteville, 1984—; consult to 15 orgns; teacher numerous short courses in chemical eng for indust; adminr research contracts various cos; vis. prof. Swiss Fed. Inst. Tech. Zurich, 1978. Mem ed bd: Biomass and Biofuels, Chemical Eng R&D; contbr. to numerous presentations and publs. Mem.: AAAS, AIChE (mem speakers bur), Am Soc Eng Educ, Am Chemical Soc, Omega Chi Epsilon, Alpha Chi Sigma, Tau Beta Pi (Eminent Eng 1976). Baptist. Home: 2207 Tall Oaks Dr Fayetteville AR 72703-6126 Office: Bioengring Resources 1650 Emmaus Rd Fayetteville AR 72701-7283 Office Phone: 479-521-4544. E-mail: jlgaddy@aol.com.

GADE, MARVIN FRANCIS, retired paper company executive; b. Clinton, Iowa, Nov. 10, 1924; s. Bernhardt Henry and Anna Mae (Jessen) G.; m. Lorraine F. McDonald, Dec. 2, 1944 (dec.); children: Michael David, Patricia Ann Gade Conn, Steven Dennis, Laura Jean Gade Quattlebaum, Mary Kay Gade Brock, Karen Lynn Gade Murphy, Jeffrey Scott; m. Carmell M. Clayton, July 16, 1994. BS in Engring., U. Iowa, 1952; postgrad. exec. program, UCLA, 1960-61. Process instrumentation engr. Standards Brands Co., Clinton, 1946-50; with Kimberly-Clark Corp. (hdqrs.), Neenah, Wis., 1952-88, sr. v.p., group exec., 1974-77, exec. v.p. Coosa Pines, Ala., 1977-88; also dir. Kimberly-Clark Corp.; pres. Kimberly Clark Health Care, Paper and Spltys. Cos., 1981-88, vice chmn. bd., 1983-88. Dir. First Bank of Childersburg, Ala. Bd. dirs. Calif. Water Quality Control Bd., 1964-67, S.C. Tech. Edn. Bd., 1968-70; bd. dirs., sec. Children's Harbor, Alexander City, Ala.; chmn. bd. adv. com. St. Jude's Hosp., Fullerton, Calif., 1962-67; trustee Fulton County Ga. Hosp. Authority, Northside Hosp., Oglethorpe U., Atlanta, Wesley Woods Hosp., Atlanta, Woodruff Art Alliance; bd. visitors Emory U., Atlanta. Served as aviator USNR, 1943-46. Home: The Brittany # 705 4021 Gulf Shore Blvd N Naples FL 34103-2232 *In my lifetime of managing operations and administration I never met a "small" person - just small jobs.*

GADEN, ELMER LEWIS, retired engineering educator; b. Bklyn., Sept. 26, 1923; s. Elmer Lewis and Gertrude Estelle (McClellan) G.; m. Jennifer Marie Soley, Mar. 28, 1964; children: David Andrew, Paul Alexander; 1 dau. by previous marriage, Barbara Joan. BS, Columbia U., 1944, MS, 1947, PhD, 1949; DEngring (hon.), Rensselaer Poly., 1987. Rsch. engr. Pfizer Inc., 1948-49; mem. faculty Columbia, 1949-74, prof. chem. engring., 1958-74, chmn. dept., 1960-69, 71-74; dean Coll. Engring. Math. and Bus. Adminstrn., U. Vt., Burlington, 1975-79; Wills Johnson prof. chem. engring. U. Va., Charlottesville, 1979—94, prof. emeritus, 1994—, chmn. dept., 1985—88. Editor: Biotech. and Bioengring. jour., 1959-83. Served with USNR, 1943-46. Mem.: AIChE, NAE, Am. Chem. Soc. Home: 3400 Rodman Dr Charlottesville VA 22901-9450 Office: U Va Dept Chemical Engineer Charlottesville VA 22903 E-mail: jasp@cstone.net.

GADIESH, ORIT, management consulting executive; b. Haifa, Israel, Jan. 31; BA in psychology summa cum laude, Hebrew U., Israel, 1973; MBA, Harvard Bus. Sch., 1977. With Israeli Army; asst. prof. Hebrew U., Israel; with Bain & Co., Boston, 1977—, head Boston office, 1991—93, chmn., 1993—. Bd. dir. Peres Inst. for Peace, Israel. Named one of 100 Most Powerful Women in World, Forbes mag., 2005. Mem.: Coun. Fgn. Rels. Office: Bain & Co Two Copley Pl 131 Dartmouth St Boston MA 02116*

GADOMSKI, ROBERT EUGENE, consulting executive, retired gas industry executive; b. Chgo., Mar. 24, 1947; s. Chester and Adeline (Carpinelli) G.; m. Susan Freed, Aug. 12, 1972; children: Stephen, Andrew, Elizabeth. BS, Purdue U., 1969, MS in Indsl. Adminstrn., 1970, D of Engring. (hon.), 2001, PhD (hon.), 2001; grad. advanced mgmt. program, Harvard U., fall 1990. Bus. mgr. indsl. chems. div. Air Products and Chems., Inc., Allentown, Pa., 1974-77, gen. sales mgr. indsl. chems. div., 1977-78, asst. gen. mgr. indsl. chems. div., 1978-81, mgr. chems. group mfg. div., 1981-83, gen. mgr. chems. group mfg. div., 1983-84, v.p., gen. mgr. chems. group mfg. div., 1984-86, v.p., gen. mgr. indsl. chems. div., 1986-88, v.p., gen. mgr. process systems group, 1988-90, mgmt. com., 1988—96, group v.p. process systems group, 1990-92, group v.p. chems. group, 1992-96, exec. v.p., mem. corp. exec. com., 1996—2004, exec. v.p. chems., Asia and Latin Am., 1998-99, exec. v.p. gases and equipment, 1999—2004; mng. dir. Napowan Assocs., LLC Bus. Consulting, 2004—. Bd. dirs. Reeb Millwork, Quality Distbn., Inc. Chmn. March of Dimes Walkathon, Allentown, 1985; v.p. Minsi Trails coun. Boy Scouts Am., 1998—99, 2002—03; bd. dirs. South Whitehall Planning Commn., Allentown, 1984—89, Lehigh Valley United Way, Allentown, 1991—94, 1999—2000, Kemerer Mus. Decorative Arts, 1991—94, St. Luke's Hosp., Bethelehem, Pa., 1994—99, Hist. Bethlehem Partnership, 1993—2002, Phila. Acad. Scis., 1999—2002, Nat. Assn. Mfg., 1999—2000. Named Disting. Alumnus, Krannert Sch. Mgmt., Purdue U., 1988, Sch. Engring., 1992. Mem. AIChE; mem. Nat. Petroleum Refiners Assn. (bd. dirs. 1986-93), Internat. Oxygen Mfrs. Assn. (bd. dirs. 2000-03), Mfrs. Alliance/MAPI (trustee 2000-03), Pa. Bus. Roundtable (exec. com. 2001-03). Roman Catholic. Avocations: golf, fine dining. Office Phone: 610-745-0659. Business E-Mail: gadomsre@cs.com.

GADON, STEVEN FRANKLIN, lawyer; b. Roxbury, Mass., Oct. 27, 1931; s. Sydney A. and Sarah G. (Feinstein) G.; m. Barbara Kaminsky, Sept. 5, 1954; children: Richard, Susan, Amy, Beth. BS, U. Pa., 1954; LLB, Temple U., 1959; LLM, NYU, 1964. Bar: Pa. 1963; CPA, Pa. Acct. Main, Lafrentz & Co., Phila., 1956-62; ptnr. MacCoy, Evans & Lewis, Phila., 1962-66, Meltzer & Schiffrin, Phila., 1966-76, Spector, Gadon & Rosen, Phila., 1976—. Sec., bd. dirs. Simkins Industries, Inc., New Haven. Mem. Am. Assn. Attys.-CPA's, AICPA, Pa. Inst. CPA's. Jewish. Avocations: running, opera. Home: Grays Lane House 500 100 Grays Ln Haverford PA 19041-1727 Office: Spector Gadon & Rosen 1635 Market St Fl 7 Philadelphia PA 19103-2217

GADSBY, ROBIN EDWARD, chemical company executive; b. St. Leonards on Sea, Eng., Mar. 22, 1939; arrived in U.S., 1977, naturalized, 1988; s. John Ernest and Emily Louisa (Burt) G.; m. Olwyn Diane Bowen, Aug. 5, 1961 (div. 1981); children: Tricia Clare, Tracey Carolyn; m. Margaret Alice Fuessel, Dec. 29, 1983 (div. Dec. 15, 2004) MA in Natural Scis., Cambridge U., Eng., 1960, MEng, 1961; MBA, U. Chgo., 1982. CFA. Chem. engr. ICI Billingham (Eng.) div., 1961-62, corp. planner, 1962-65; plant mgr. ICI PLC Agrl. div., Heysham, Eng., 1965-67, chem. engring. mgr. Billingham, 1967-70, process tech. mgr., 1970-76, research group mgr., 1976-77; pres. Katalco Corp., Oak Brook, Ill., 1978-83; gen. mgr. Rubicon Chems. Inc., Wilmington, Del., 1984-86; pres. polyurethanes group div. ICI Ams., Inc., Wilmington, 1986-90, pres. chems. and polymers group, 1990-97. Bd. dirs. Ricerca LLC, Concord, Ohio. Mem. AIChE, Am. Chemical Soc., CFA Inst., Inst. Chem. Engrs. (U.K. editl. bd. 1976-77), Internat. Isocynates Inst. (pres. 1990-91), N.Y. Acad. Scis., Fin. Analysts Soc. Phila., Lely Resort and Country Club, (Fla.), Beta Gamma Sigma. Home and Office: PO Box 630 West Chester PA 19381-0630 Office Fax: 610-399-9551.

GADSDEN, JAMES IRVIN, ambassador; b. Charleston, S.C., Mar. 12, 1948; BA cum laude, Harvard U., 1970; MA in East Asian Studies, Stanford U., 1972; postgrad., Princeton U., 1984. Various positions to counselor for econ. affairs U.S. Embassy, Paris, 1989—93, dep. chief of mission Budapest, 1994—97; dep. asst. sec. of state for European Affairs U.S. Dept. of State, 1997—2001; spl. negotiator for agrl. biotechnology Bur. for Econ. and Bus. Affairs, Washington, 2001—01; U.S. amb. to Iceland, 2002—. Office: Am Embassy Reykjavik PSC 1003 Box 40 FPO AE 09728 E-mail: gadsdenji@state.gov.

GADUS, GAYLE ANN, performing arts association administrator; b. Columbus, Ohio, Aug. 14, 1950; d. Louis C and Jeanann Studer; m. Ronald G Gadus; children: Alicia M Gadus Thompson, Lauren E. BS, Bowling Green State U., 1968—72; MA, No. Ariz. U., 1988—90, Ednl. Adminstrn., 1990—92. Spanish tchr. & dept. chair Bedford City Schools, Ohio, 1972—76; admin. asst. coll. of educ. Bowling Green State U., 1976—78; spanish tchr. & dept. chair Xavier Coll. Prep., Phoenix, 1980—84, Thunderbird H.S., Phoenix, 1984—98; fine arts & fgn. lang. curr. coord. Glendale Union H.S. Dist., Glendale, Ariz., 1990—. Ednl. cons. Glendale OBI Team, Ariz., 1989—92, Pearson Edn., Chgo., 1998—2004. Fine arts advocacy Ariz. Alliance for the Arts, 2002—04. Recipient Outstanding THS Teacher of Year, 1988, Outstanding Young Women of Am., 1978, Ariz. Music Edn. Assn. Achievement award, Visual Arts Assessment Program, Golden Bell award, 2004. Mem.: Ariz. Fgn. Lang. Assn. (assoc.). Avocations: theater, music, dance. Office Phone: 623-435-6695.

GADUS, PEG, religious organization administrator, director; d. Frank O'Brien and Katherine Alexander; children: Thomas J., Timothy J., Katherine M., Kevin M. BS in Edn., Calumet Coll., 1976; cert., Liturgical Inst., St. Anselmo, Rome, Italy, 1999. Cert. lay minister Archdiocese Chgo., 1996, bereavement minister Cath. Cemeteries, 2001. Tchr. elem. sch. Joliet (Ill.) Diocese, 1955—57, Rockford (Ill.) Diocese, 1957—59, Archdiocese Chgo., 1959—2003, dir. religious edn., 1992—, pastoral assoc., 1994—. With mktg. St. Florian Sch., Chgo., 2003—05. Office: St. Florian 13145 Houston Ave Chicago IL 60633

GAEBEL, PAUL RALPH, secondary school educator; b. McKeesport, Pa., Nov. 28, 1952; s. Ralph Walter and Audrey Louise Gaebel; m. Deborah Ann Reed, Apr. 8, 1978; children: Alyssa Helen, Andrew Paul. BS, Lock Haven U., 1974. Social Science Commonwealth of Pa., 1974, Safety Education - Driver Education Commonwealth of Pa., 1976. Tchr. social studies Bellefonte Area Sch. Dist., Pa., 1974—, chmn. social studies dept., 1998—. Tchr. driver edn. Bellefonte Area Sch. Dist., 1999—. Mem. parks and recreation com. Spring Twp., Bellefonte, 1998—2000; com. chmn. Cub Scouts Pack 352, Hublersburg, 1994—97; little league baseball asst. coach Marion Walker, 1995—98; day of caring participant The United Way, State College, 1993—2004. Mem.: NEA (assoc.), Pa. Assn. Safety Edn. (assoc.), Pa. State Edn. Assn. (assoc.). Achievements include Completed the Harrisburg Marathon, 1985; Completed the Pittsburgh Marathon, 1993; Completed the Marine Corps Marathon, 1993 and 1995. Avocations: family activities, travel, fitness, cars. Home: 1782 Airport Rd Bellefonte PA 16823 Office: Bellefonte Area Sch Dist 318 North Allegheny St Bellefonte PA 16823 Office Phone: 814-355-4814.

GAEDE, JAMES ERNEST, physician, medical educator; b. Calgary, Alta., Can., July 2, 1953; s. John Ernest and Florence Eleanor (Hilmer) G.; married, Dec. 23, 1994; children: Graham, Jason, Nikki, Mary Frances, Sydney, Camille. BA, Augustana Coll., 1975, MA, 1976; MD, U. S.D., 1980. Diplomate Am. Bd. Family Practice. Staff physician Queen of Peace, Mitchell, SD, 1983—2001, chief of staff, 1988, med. dir., 1988-89, St. Joe's Med. Assn., Howard, SD, 1988—2000, Women's Health Clinic, Mitchell, SD, 1983—2000; assoc. prof. U. S.D. Sch. Medicine; med. dir. Desert Regional Med. Ctr., Palm Springs, Calif., 2001—, Tenet Home Health, 2005. Presenter U.S. Senate, Washington, 1991; med. dir. Cave South Home Health, 2005, Sleep Disorders of Palm Springs, 2005 Contbr. articles to profl. jours. Bd. dirs. Dakota Weslayan U., Mitchell, 1986-89, Dakota Mental Health, Mitchell, 1988-90; mem. Commn. 2000 S.D., Sioux Falls, 1988-00; pub. health officer City of Mitchell, 1983-01. Named one of Top 100 Family

Physicians in U.S., Consumer Rsch. Coun., Washington, Top 70 Drs. in 35 Specialties, Caste Connolly Med. Ltd. Fellow Am. Acad. Family Practice (Active Tchrs. award 1984—); mem. AMA, Calif. Acad. Family Practice, S.D. Assn. Family Practice, S.D. State Med. Assn. (del. 1983-2000, sec. 1998-99, v.p. 1999, pres. 2000), Calif. State Med. Assn., Mitchell C. of C., Mayo Alumni Assn., Doctors Mayo Soc. Avocations: sailing, music, auto restoration. Home: 2525 N Farrell Dr Palm Springs CA 92262-2601 Office: 555 Tachevah Ste 2E-101 Palm Springs CA 92262

GAENG, PAUL AMI, foreign language educator; b. Budapest, Hungary, Aug. 17, 1924; arrived in U.S., 1948, naturalized, 1955; s. Hans Peter and Therese (Brule) G.; m. Joan Elisabeth Gallagher, Apr. 6, 1967. Grad., U. Geneva, 1948; MA, Columbia U., 1950, PhD (Woodbridge hon. fellow), 1965. Fgn. editorial asst. McGraw Hill Book Co., N.Y.C., 1951-54; translator-interpreter Guaranty Trust, N.Y.C., 1954-56; fgn. lang. tchr. Montclair (N.J.) Acad., 1957-63; asst., assoc. then full prof., chmn. dept. fgn. langs. Montclair State Coll., Upper Montclair, N.J., 1964-69; assoc. prof. Romance philology U. Va., Charlottesville, 1969-72; head dept. Romance lang. and lit. U. Cin., 1972-76; head dept. French, U. Ill., Urbana, 1976-88, assoc. Ctr. for Advanced Studies, spring 1983, head dept. French, 1988-95, prof. emeritus French and linguistics, 1995—. Vis. lectr. Hofstra Coll., Hempstead, N.Y., 1963, Queens Coll., N.Y.C., 1966, Columbia U., 1967-69 Author: Introduction to the Principles of Language, 1971, An Inquiry into Local Variations in Vulgar Latin, 1968, Studies in Honor of Mario Pei, 1972, A Study of Nominal Inflection in Latin Incriptions, 1977, (with Mario Pei) The Story of Latin and the Romance Languages, 1976, Collapse and Reorganization of the Latin Nominal Flection as Reflected in Epigraphic Sources, 1984, Le monde de l'entreprise française, 1989, 3rd edit., 1993, 4th rev. edit., 2001, Visage économique de la France contemporaine, 1992 Decorated officier Ordre des Palmes Académiques. Home: 1735 Palo Alto Ave Lady Lake FL 32159-9195 E-mail: pgaeng@aol.com.

GAENGLER, PETER WOLFGANG, dentist, researcher; b. Meissen, Saxony, Germany, Oct. 30, 1941; s. Wolfgang Ernst-Otto and Dorothea Friedericke (Moebius) G.; m. Sabine Gertrud Ahlborn, Nov. 6, 1970; children: Felix Peter, Beate Petra. Stomatology Diploma, Faculty of Dental Medicine, Leningrad, Russia, 1965; DrMedDent, Sch. Dental Medicine, Dresden, Germany, 1967, PhD, 1974; DHC (hon.), Semmelweis U., Budapest, 2004. Diplomate in dentistry. Dentistry Community Hosp., Wittenberg, Germany, 1965-66; asst. prof. Sch. Dental Medicine, Dresden, 1966-75, prof., chmn. Erfurt, Germany, 1975-92; dean Faculty of Dental Medicine, Witten/Herdecke, Germany, 1992—; bd. dirs. U. Witten/Herdecke, 1995—2002, mem. exec. bd., 2002—. Mem. FDI/WHO Joint Working Group 1/10, Geneva, 1979; v.p. for rsch. U. Witten/Herdecke, 2003—. Author: Lehrbuch der Konservierenden Zahnheilkunde, 4th edit., 2005; editor Medizin aktuell, 1975-90; mem. editl. bd. European Jour. Dental Edn., 2000—, Jour. Oral Rehab., 2001— Recipient Humboldt medal Ministry Higher Edn., Berlin, 1978; grantee in field. Mem.: Internat. Assn. for Dental Rsch. (mem. publs. com., com. on membership and recruitment 1989—93), Assn. Dental Edn. Europe (exec. com. 1997—2001), Assn. Stomatology (v.p. 1988—90, Philip-Pfaff medal 1988), Assn. Conservative Dentistry (pres. 1978—87), Hungarian Assn. Dentistry (hon. Semmelweis medal 1993), Polish Assn. Dentistry (hon.). Avocations: literature, sailing, skiing. Home: Waldweg 9 D-58313 Herdecke Germany Office: U Witten/Herdecke Faculty Dental Medicine D-58448 Witten Germany E-mail: peter.gaengler@uni-wh.de.

GAENSLER, BRYAN MALCOLM, astronomer, educator; b. Sydney, Australia; s. Frank R. and Isobel E. Gaensler; m. Laura E. Bugg, 2002; 1 child, Fineas Charles Bugg. BS with honors, U. Sydney, 1994, PhD, 1998. Clay postdoctoral fellow Smithsonian Astrophysy. Obs., Cambridge, Mass., 2001—02; asst. prof. astronomy Harvard U., Cambridge, 2002—; postdoctoral fellow MIT, Cambridge, 1998—2001. Recipient Young Australian of the Yr., Nat. Australia Day Coun., 1999. Mem.: Internat. Astronomy Union, Astronomy Soc. Australia, Am. Astronomy Soc. Achievements include research in Neutron stars, interstellar magnetism, supernova explosions. Avocations: cricket, baseball, squash, rugby. Office: Harvard Univ 60 Garden Street MS 6 Cambridge MA 02138 Office Phone: 617-496-7854. E-mail: bgaensler@cfa.harvard.edu.

GAER, MICHAEL IRA, financial planner; b. Englewood, NJ, Sept. 27, 1968; s. Arthur and Linda Gaer; m. Jayne A Macognone, Mar. 30, 2001; children: Joseph Vincent, Brandon Logan. BBA, U. of Miami, 1986—90. Cert. CFP Bd. of Standards, Inc., 2003. Pres. Gaer Fin. Group, Inc., Rochelle Park, NJ, 1998—. Honoray chmn. nat. Rep. Congl. Com. Bus. Adv. Coun., Washington, 2001. Mem.: Fin. Planning Assn. Office: Gaer Financial Group Inc 5 West Passaic St Rochelle Park NJ 07662 Office Phone: 201-291-2337.

GAERTNER, DONELL JOHN, retired library director; b. St. Louis, Sept. 30, 1932; s. Elmer Henry and Norine Helen (Colomb) G.; m. Darlene Oberbeck, Mar. 17, 1956; children: Karen Elaine, Keith Alan. AB in Econs., Washington U., 1954; M.L.S., U. Ill., 1955. Adminstrv. asst. St. Louis County Library, 1957-64, asst. dir., 1964-68, dir., 1968-97; ret., 1997. Past pres. bd. dirs. Emmaus Homes Inc. (for adult mentally retarded). Served to 1st lt. U.S. Army, 1955—57. Mem.: ALA, Spl. Libr. Assn., Mo. Libr. Assn. (past pres.), Order Eastern Star, Masons, Omicron Delta Gamma, Phi Beta Mu. United Ch. Of Christ. E-mail: dgaertner@charter.net.

GAFFIKIN, LYNNE, epidemiologist, researcher; b. Toronto, Can., July 15, 1953; arrived in U.S., 1963; d. James Brian and Marjorie Gaffikin; m. Paul David Blumenthal, July 10, 1984; 1 child, Joshua Blumenthal. BA, U. Calif., Berkeley, 1977; MPH, UCLA, 1980; DPH, U. Ill., Chgo., 1988. Epidemiologist Columbia U., Niamey, Niger, 1986—88; health info. sys. advisor Tulane U., Nairobi, Kenya, 1988—90; dir. Rsch. and Evaluation Office JHPIEGO, Balt., 1991—96; pres. Earth, Inc., Balt., 1996—; sci. dir. CECAP/JHPIEGO, Balt., 1999—. Assoc. Bloomberg Sch. Pub. Health, Johns Hopkins U., Balt., 1994—; rsch. advisor Tulane U., Peru, 1996—99, Brazil, 1996—99; health, population environ. fellow Pub. Health Inst., Madagascar, 2004—. Contbr. articles to profl. jours. Mem.: APHA, Internat. Primatology Soc., Global Health Coun., Internat. Soc. for Ecosystem Health, Delta Omega, Alpha Lambda Delta, Phi Beta Kappa. Avocations: hiking, cross country skiing, bicycling, birdwatching, conservation.

GAFFIN, DAVID MORRIS, meteorologist, researcher; b. Fayetteville, Tenn., May 16, 1968; s. Morris Chadwick and Marilyn Hallberg Gaffin. BA, U. Tenn., 1990; MS, Tex. A&M U., 1993. Meteorologist intern Nat. Weather Svc., Memphis, 1994—98, gen. forecaster Morristown, Tenn., 1998—2001, sr. forecaster, 2002—. Tchg. asst. Tex. A&M U., College Station, 1991—92, asst. to state climatologist, 1992—93. Contbr. articles to profl. jours. Trail guide Sommers Canoe Base Boy Scouts Am., Ely, Minn., 1986, aquatics camp couselor Wichita Falls, Tex., 1987—91; cir. giving leader United Way, Morristown, 1999—; rsch. ptnr. Am. Diabetes Assn., Washington, 2004—. Recipient Eagle Scout, Boy Scouts Am., 1983; Band scholar, U. Tenn., 1986—90. Mem.: Nat. Weather Assn., Am. Meteorology Soc. (v.p. Smoky Mountain chpt. 2003—). Avocations: golf, tennis, music, canoeing, hiking. Personal E-mail: david_gaiffin@yahoo.com.

GAFFNEY, DONALD LEE, lawyer; b. Phoenix, July 7, 1952; s. Leroy H. and Myriam (Brazeal) G.; m. Debby Dunn, May 31, 1974; children: Brian, Colin, Caitlin. BA, Austin Coll., 1974; JD, U. Tex., 1977. Bar: Ariz. 1979, U.S. Ct. Appeals (9th cir.) 1979, U.S. Ct. Appeals (10th cir.) 1984, U.S. Supreme Ct. 1984. Ptnr. Streich & Lang, Phoenix, 1977-89, Snell & Wilmer, Phoenix, 1988—. Adj. prof. Ariz. State U. Law Sch., Tempe, 1983-84; dean's council U. Tex. Law Sch., atty. rep. 9th Cir. Ct. Appeals Judicial Conf. Co-author: Bankruptcy, 1987; note comment and book review editor: Tex. Law Review 1976-77; contbr. to profl. jours. Mem. Gov.'s Task Force Ctrl. Ariz. Project, 1993. Austin scholar. Mem. ABA, Am. Arbitration Assn. (com. panel), Comml. Law League of Am. (bankruptcy com. 1980-84), State Bar Ariz. (chmn. bankruptcy sect., 1982-84, com. on bankruptcy rules 1979-81, uniform comml. code com. 1980—), Phi Delta Phi. Democrat. Roman Catholic. Office: Snell & Wilmer 1 Arizona Ctr Phoenix AZ 85004-0001

GAFFNEY, EDWARD MCGLYNN, law educator, dean; b. San Francisco, Aug. 18, 1941; s. Edward McGlynn and Mary Catherine (Wright) G.; m. Jane Ann Mullen, Feb. 1972 (div. Feb. 1982); children: Margaret Mairead, Elizabeth Atkins; m. A'ine O'Healy, May 29, 1982; children: Deirdre, Miriam. BA, St. Patrick's Coll., 1963; STL, Gregorian U., Rome, 1967; JD, MA in History, Cath. U., 1975; LLM, Harvard U., 1976. Bar: Calif. 1990, U.S. Ct. Appeals (D.C. cir.) 1975, U.S. Ct. Appeals (7th cir.) 1980, U.S. Ct. Appeals (5th and 11th cirs.) 1981, U.S. Ct. Appeals (9th cir.) 1983, U.S. Ct. Appeals (2d cir.) 1985, U.S. Dist. Ct. (ctrl. dist.) Calif. 1990, U.S. Dist. Ct. (so. dist.) Ind. 1992, U.S. Supreme Ct. 1980. Assoc. dir. Nat. Conf. Cath. Bishops Ecumenical and Interreligious Com., Washington, 1970-72; atty. advisor Office of Atty Gen. U.S. Dept. of Justice, Washington, 1976-77; assoc. dir. Ctr. for Constitutional Studies, Notre Dame, Ind., 1977-81, dir., 1981-83; Bradley prof. constitutional law Loyola Law Sch., L.A., 1983-85, assoc. prof., 1985-89; scholar in residence Stanford Law Sch., Palo Alto, Calif., 1989-90; dean and prof. law Valparaiso (Ind.) U. Sch. of Law, 1990-97; scholar-in-residence Pepperdine U. Sch. of Law, Malibu, Calif., 1997-98; prof. law Valparaiso U. Sch. of Law, Ill., 1998—. Mem. bd. editors Jour. Law and Religion, St. Paul, 1980—; ednl. cons. Williamsburg Ctr. Found., Washington, 1987-89; bd. dirs. Ctr. for Constitutional Studies, Waco, Tex., 1990—, Christian Legal Soc., Annandale, Va., 1992-98, Ind. Bar Found., Ind. Continuing Legal Forum; dir. of content Nat. Constn. Ctr., Phila., 2000-01. Author: Government and Campus, 1980, State and Campus, 1982, Ascending Liability in Religious and Non-Profit Organizations, 1983, Church and Campus, 1989; co-author: (with John. T. Noonan, Jr.) Religious Freedom, 2001; editor: Public Schools and the Private Good, 1981. Recipient Champion of Justice award Am. Forum for Jewish-Christian Cooperation, Washington, 1981. Fellow Ctr. for Ch.-State Studies, Internat. Acad. for Freedom of Religion and Belief; mem. ABA, Am. Law Inst., Assn. Am. Law Schs. (chmn. sect. on law and religion, sect. on law and edn. 1981-83). Democrat. Roman Catholic. Office: Valparaiso U Sch of Law Wesemann Hall Valparaiso IN 46383

GAFFNEY, ELIZABETH MALLORY, editor, writer, literature educator, translator; b. NYC, Dec. 22, 1966; d. Richard Waring and Ann Walker Gaffney; m. Alexis David Boro, July 15, 1995. BA, Vassar Coll., 1988; MFA, Bklyn. Coll., 1997. Mem. editl. staff The Paris Rev., N.Y.C., 1988—93, mng. editor, 1993—95, editor-at-large, 1995—2004, adv. editor, 2004—05. Writing tchr. NYU, N.Y.C., 1997—. Translator: The Arbogast Case, 2003, The Pollen Room, 1998, Invisible Woman, 2000, author short stories, (novels) Metropolis, 2005. Resident/fellow, MacDowell Colony, Peterborough, N.H., 1996, 1997, Blue Mountain (N.Y.) Ctr., 1999, Yaddo, Saratoga Springs, N.Y., 2000, 2001, 2004. Mem.: PEN, Phi Beta Kappa. Democrat. Avocations: hiking, kayaking, bicycling, camping. Office: The Paris Rev 541 E 72 St New York NY 10021

GAFFNEY, JOHN T., lawyer; b. Poughkeepsie, NY, May 10, 1960; BA, George Washington Univ., 1982; MBA, JD, NYU, 1986. Bar: NY 1987. Assoc. Cravath Swaine & Moore LLP, NYC, 1986—93, ptnr., corp., 1993—. Mem.: NY State Bar Assn., Assn. of Bar of City of NY. Office: Cravath Swaine & Moore LLP Worldwide Plz 825 Eighth Ave New York NY 10019-7475 Office Phone: 212-474-1122. Office Fax: 212-474-3700. Business E-Mail: jgaffney@cravath.com.

GAFFNEY, JOSEPH M., lawyer; b. 1944; BCS in Acctg., Seattle Univ., 1967; JD, Univ. Calif., 1972; LLM in Tax., NYU, 1975. Bar: Wash. 1972. Atty., tax, bus., estate planning Dorsey & Whitney LLP, 2000—03, ptnr.-in-charge, Seattle, tax, estate planning group Seattle, 2003—, mem., mgmt. com.; and officer & dir. Dorsey & Whitney Trust Co. Bd. trustees Seattle Univ., Wash. Edn. Found., Wash. Assn. Ind. Coll. & Univ., Nesholm Family Found., 1989—. Bd. trustees Arts Fund, Seattle; adv. bd. ElderHealth Northwest. Named a Super Lawyer, Wash. Law & Politics; recipient Disting. Alumni award, Seattle Univ., 1991. Fellow: Am. Coll. Trust & Estate Counsel; mem.: King Co. Bar Assn., Wash. State Bar Assn., Seattle Estate Planning Coun., Order of Coif. Office: Dorsey & Whitney LLP Ste 3400 US Bank Ctr 1420 Fifth Ave Seattle WA 98101-4010 Office Phone: 206-903-5448. Office Fax: 206-903-8820. Business E-Mail: gaffney.joe@dorsey.com.

GAFFNEY, KATHLEEN MARY, writer, videographer; b. Queens, N.Y., Aug. 22, 1959; d. Joseph Frances and Margaret Ann (Denza) G. B in Comm. magna cum laude, Adelphi U., 1981. Videographer Town of Hempstead (N.Y.) Cablevision Long Island, 1983-94. Lectr., guest spkr. Adult Learning Inst., Columbia-Greene Coll., Hudson, N.Y., 1995; televised guest lectr. Columbia-Greene Coll. at Mid-Hudson Cablevision, Catskill, N.Y., 1995; videographer and editor monthly program Cablevision of L.I.; instr., lectr. broadcast/prodn. videography classes on L.I. Prodn. asst. (pub. svc. announcement) U.S. Pres. Coun. on Phys. Fitness, 1982; videographer, editor (pub. svc. announcement) Hempstead L.I. Animal Shelter, 1985; contbr. articles to profl. jours., newspapers and mags. Active Town of Cairo (N.Y.) Task Force, 1993—. Mem. Wallace Nutting Collector's Club. Democrat. Roman Catholic. Avocations: writing children's books, screen and tele-play writing, cartoon illustrating, antique collecting. Home: 4 Holzmann Ext Acra NY 12405 E-mail: kathy@mhonline.net.

GAFFNEY, MARK HOWARD, writer; b. Okla. City, Okla., Apr. 23, 1948; BS in physical sci., Colo. State U., 1978. Author: Dimona: The Third Temple? The Story Behind The Vanunu Revelation, 1989, The First Tree of the Day, 2002, Gnostic Secrets of the Naassenes, 2004. Recipient Boy Scout Eagle Scout award, Altare Dei award. Personal E-mail: mhgaffney@sbcglobal.net.

GAFFNEY, MARK WILLIAM, lawyer; b. Spokane, Wash., July 3, 1951; s. William Joseph and Anne Veronica (McGovern) G.; m. Jean Elizabeth O'Leary, Oct. 8, 1988. BA, U. Notre Dame, 1973; JD, George Washington U., 1976. Bar: Wash. 1976, N.Y. 1982, D.C. 1984, Conn. 1984. Law clk. antitrust divsn. U.S. Dept. Justice, Washington, 1974-76; trial atty. N.Y.C., 1976-81; assoc. Solin & Breindel, P.C., N.Y.C., 1982-83; ptnr. Chapman, Moran & Gaffney, Stamford, Conn., 1984-85; of counsel Kaplan & Kilsheimer, N.Y.C., 1985-93; corp. counsel Sta. WLNY-TV, Inc., Melville, N.Y., 1993-95; atty. Bellavia Gentile & Assocs. LLP, Mineola, NY, 2004—. Recipient Spl. Achievement award U.S. Dept. Justice, 1978, 79. Mem. ABA, Assn. of Bar of City of N.Y., Conn. Bar Assn., N.Y. Athletic Club. Republican. Roman Catholic. Home: 1395 Roosevelt Ave Pelham NY 10803-3605 Office: Bellavia Gentile Assocs LLP 200 Old Country Rd Mineola NY 11501 Office Phone: 516-873-3000. Personal E-mail: markgaffney@verizon.net. Business E-Mail: mgaffney@bellavialaw.com.

GAFFNEY, PATRICIA MOUNTS, principal; d. James and Virginia Eon Mounts; m. Michael J. Gaffney; children: Sean, Damien. BA, Rutgers U., 1973, MA, 1976; EdM, Houston Bapt. U., 1988; EdD, U. Houston, 1998. Tchr. Montgomery Twp. Schs., Skillman, NJ, 1973—76, Anne Arundel County Pub. Schs., Annapolis, Md., 1976—77, The Calverton Sch., Huntingtown, Md., 1977—81, Alief Ind. Sch. Dist., Houston, 1981—91; asst. prin. Pasadena (Tex.) Ind. Sch. Dist., 1991—99; edn. specialist Region IV Edn. Svc. Ctr., Houston, 1999—2001; prin. Ft. Worth Ind. Sch. Dist., 2001—04. Mem. goal setting, tchr. adv. and career ladder selection coms. Alief Ind. Sch. Dist., 1988—91; mem. Leadership Acad. Pasadena Ind. Sch. Dist., 1995—99; mem. HIPPA, spl. edn. adv. coms. Ft. Worth Ind. Sch. Dist., 2002—04; ednl. cons., 2004—. Vol. Am. Field Svc., Houston, 2000—01, U. Dallas, Irving, Tex., 2001—05, Allied Cmtys. of Tarrant, Ft. Worth, 2002—05. Mem.: ASCD, Tex. Assn. Sch. Adminstrs., Am. Ednl. Rsch. Assn., Kappa Delta Pi, Phi Delta Kappa.

GAFFNEY, PAUL GOLDEN, II, academic administrator, retired military officer; b. Attleboro, Mass., May 30, 1946; s. Paul G. and Elfrieda L. (Piepenstock) G.; m. Linda L. Myers; 1 child, Crista L. BS, U.S. Naval Acad., 1968; MS in Engring., Cath. U. Am., 1969; grad. with highest distinction, Naval War Coll., Newport, R.I., 1979; MBA, Jacksonville U., 1986, LHD (hon.), 2002, U. S.C.; doctorate (hon.), Jacksonville U., 2002, U. S.C., 2002, Catholic U. of Am., 2003. Commd. ensign USN, 1968, advanced through grades to vice adm., 1994, ops. officer USS Whipporwill Sasebo, Japan, 1969-71, advisor Vietnamese Combat Hydrog. Survey Team Vietnam, 1971-72, ocean svcs. officer Fleet Weather Cen. Rota, Spain, 1972-75, exec. asst. Office of Oceanographer Alexandria, Va., 1975-78, rsch. fellow Naval War Coll Ctr. Advanced Rsch. Newport, R.I., 1978-78, comdg. officer Oceanographic Unit 4 Indonesia, 1979-80, dir. Arctic and Earth Scis. Rsch. Office Naval Rsch. Arlington, VA, 1980-81; mil. asst. internat. security affairs to Asst. Sec. Def. Washington, 1981-83; comdg. office Oceanography Command Facility USN, Jacksonville, Fla., 1983-86, dir. resources Office of Oceanographer Washington, 1986-89, asst. chief, Office Chief of Naval Rsch. Arlington, Va., 1989-91, comdg. officer Naval Rsch. Lab. Washington, 1991-94, commdr. Naval Meteorology and Oceanography Command Stennis Space Ctr., Miss., 1994-97, chief naval rsch. and naval test/evaluation/tech. requirements for the Navy Staff, dep. comdt. USMC for sci. and tech. Arlington, Va., 1996-2000; pres. Nat. Def. U., Washington, 2000—03; commr. U.S. Commn. Ocean Policy, 2000—; pres. Monmouth U., West Long Branch, NJ, 2003—. Bd. dirs. Ocean Design Inc., Diversified Offshore Drilling Inc.; grad. rsch. asst. Cath. U. Am., Washington, 1968—. Mem. policy com. Jour. Def. Rsch., 1989-91. Acad. adv. bd. NATO Def. Coll., Rome, 2001—04, U.S. Inst. of Peace, 2000—03; bd. dirs. Marymount U., 2000—03, Fla. State U. Rsch. Found., Jacksonville U., 2002—03, Jacksonville (Fla.) U., 2002—03. Decorated DSM, Legion of Merit with three gold stars, Bronze Star with V; recipient Middendorf prize Naval War Coll., 1979. Fellow Am. Meteorol. Soc., Explorer's Club; mem. Naval Acad. Alumni Assn., Sigma Xi. Roman Catholic. Avocations: running, track and field and cross country announcing and officiating. Office: Office of the Pres Monmouth U 400 Cedar Ave West Long Branch NJ 07764-1898 Business E-Mail: president@monmouth.edu.

GAFFNEY, ROBERT BRIAN, psychiatrist; b. Tupper Lake, N.Y., July 21, 1970; s. James and Barbara Gaffney; m. Andrea Julia Gemperle, Sept. 20, 1997; children: Noah, Kate. BA, U. Colo., 1993, MD, 1999. Diplomate Am. Bd. Psychiatry and Neurology. Resident U. Calif., Davis, 1999—2002, chief resident, 2002—03; pvt. pratctice Olympic Valley, Calif., 2003—. Author: Squallywood, A Guide to Square Valley's Most Exposed Lines, 2002. Mem.: Am. Group Psychotherapy Assn., Am. Psychiatric Assn., Phi Beta Kappa. Avocations: skiing, surfing, hiking. Office: 1604 Christy Hill Rd Olympic Valley CA 96146

GAFFNEY, THOMAS, retired banker; b. San Francisco, Sept. 22, 1915; s. John and Hannah (Doherty) G.; m. Claire Bastian, Dec. 15, 1945; children: Bruce Edward, Bryan Keith. Cert., Am. Inst. Banking, 1940. Bank insp. Bank of Am., 1935-50; asst. cashier First Nat. Trust and Savs. Assn., Santa Barbara, Calif., 1950-51; asst. cashier, asst sec. Oakland Central Bank, Calif., 1951-53; chief insp. Transamerica Corp., San Francisco, 1953-55; v.p., auditor First Western Bank, San Francisco, 1955-61; v.p. New First Western Bank, Los Angeles, 1961-74; v.p. and auditor Lloyds Bank Calif., Los Angeles, 1974-80; ret., 1980. Pres. Golden Gate chpt. Bank Adminstrn Inst., San Francisco, 1961, nat. bd. dirs., 1965-67, gen. chmn. conv., L.A., 1967, speaker bank convs., nationwide; chmn. crime deterrant com. Calif. Bankers Assn., 1977-79; banking cons., 1980—. Mem. Ad Hoc Com. City of L.A. to study and recommend controls on all city depts., 1977—. Mem.: Elks (bd. dir. Locker Room 67 club San Francisco 1960). Personal E-mail: ewolfram@cox.net.

GAFFNEY, THOMAS EDWARD, physician; b. East St. Louis, Ill., Nov. 5, 1930; s. John V. and Leola (Heisner) G.; m. Edith Ann Heitholt, June 12, 1954; children— John, David, Michael. AB, U. Mo., 1951, MS, 1953; MD, U. Cin., 1957. Intern Harvard Med. Service of Boston City Hosp., 1957-58; resident medicine Mass. Gen. Hosp., 1958-59; instr. pharmacology, asst. medicine U. Cin., 1959-60; clin. assoc. Nat. Heart Inst., 1960-62; assoc. prof. pharmacology U. Cin., 1962-67, asst. prof. medicine, 1962, dir. div. clin. pharmacology, 1962-72, prof. pharmacology, 1967-72, prof. medicine, 1969-72; prof., chmn. dept. pharmacology, prof. medicine Med. U. S.C., 1972-90, disting. prof., 1986-90; vis. scientist Merck Sharp & Dohme Rsch. Labs., Rahway, NJ, 1989-93; vol. clinician Buncombe County Health Ctr., 1998—2004; clin. prof. medicine U. S.C. Sch. Medicine, Columbia, 2004—. Mem. cardiovascular panel NAS Drug Efficacy Study, 1967-70; mem. pharmacology and exptl. therapeutics study sect. Nat. Heart Inst., 1967-69; mem. med. adv. bd. Coun. High Blood Pressure Rsch., 1969—; mem. Coun. on Basic Scis. of Am. Heart Assn., 1969—, mem. cardiovascular A study sect., 1972; mem. program rev. com. pharmacology and toxicology Nat. Inst. Gen. Med. Scis., 1971-75, chmn. 1973-75; mem. tech. adv. bd. S.C. Rsch. Authority, 1986-89. Mem. editorial bd. Jour. Pharmacology and Exptl. Therapeutics, 1965-77, Ann. Rev. Pharmacology and Toxicology, 1986-91. Served with USPHS, 1960-62. Recipient research career devel. award Nat. Heart Inst., 1962, 67, 72; Myrtle Wreath award for research Hadassah, 1980; NIH sr. rsch. fellow, 1989. Mem. Am. Fedn. Clin. Rsch., Am. Soc. Pharmacology and Exptl. Therapeutics, Ctrl. Soc. Clin. Rsch., Am. Soc. Clin. Investigation, Alpha Omega Alpha. Home: 348 Sugar Hollow Rd Fairview NC 28730-9560 Personal E-mail: tegaff@worldnet.att.net.

GAFFNEY, THOMAS FRANCIS, private investor; b. Rockford, Ill., Aug. 29, 1945; s. Francis William and Catherine Zeta (Haeberle) G.; m. Donna Lee Gottfried, Apr. 17, 1971; 1 child, Cory. BA, Brown U., 1967; MBA, U. Chgo., 1969. CPA Ill. Fin. cons. Duff and Phelps, Inc., Chgo., 1969-70; dir. adminstrn. Masury-Columbia Co. subs. Alberto-Culver Co., Melrose Park, Ill., 1970-75; exec. v.p., dir. Guardian Industries Corp., Northville, Mich., 1975-87; chmn. bd. The Oxford Investment Group, Bloomfield Hills, Mich., 1985-90; chmn. bd., CEO Automotive Plastic Techs., Inc., Sterling Heights, Mich., 1990-92; chmn. Ashland Products, Inc., Chgo., 1992-95; mng. dir. Raymond James Captial, Inc., St. Petersburg, Fla., 1997—2002. Bd. dirs. Amerus Decorated chevalier de L'Orde Grand Ducal de le Couronne de Chene (Luxembourg). Mem.: AICPA. Home: 2091 Oceanview Dr Tierra Verde FL 33715-2512 Office Phone: 727-866-8729. Personal E-mail: gaffneyd@aol.com. Business E-Mail: tom@andersongroup.biz.

GAGARIN, MICHAEL, literature educator; BA, Stanford U., 1963; MA, Harvard U., 1965; PhD, Yale U., 1968. Instr. then asst. prof. classics Yale U., 1968—73; prof. classics U. Tex., Austin, 1973—, from asst. to prof. classics, 1973—, James R. Dougherty, Jr. Centennial prof. classics, 1997—. Mem.: Am. Philological Assn. (pres. 2002—03). Office: Dept of Classics C3400 Univ Texas at Austin Austin TX 78712-0308

GAGE, ANASTASIA JESSICA, healthcare educator, researcher; arrived in US, 1986; d. Samuel David and Augusta Jestina Gage; m. Dominique Armand Meekers, May 27, 1994; children: Namdi Victor Brandon, M'Bilia Martha Meekers. BA in Geography with honors, U. Sierra Leone, 1982; PhD, U. Pa., 1990. Vis. rsch. assoc. Population Coun., N.Y., 1990—91; assoc. population affairs officer UN, N.Y., 1991—92; analyst Macro Internat., Inc., Calverton, Md., 1993—95; asst. prof. Pa. State U., State College, Pa., 1996—97; sr. tech. advisor Pub. Health Inst., Washington, 1997—2000; tech. officer performance and results monitoring Acad. Ednl. Devel., Washington, 2000—01; assoc. prof. Tulane U., New Orleans, 2001—. Cons. UN Children's Fund, Niamey, Niger, 2003—03, AED & UNFPA/Niger, Washington, 2001—01; mem. adv. panel protecting the next generation Alan Guttmacher Inst., N.Y., 2002—; mem. panel transitions to adulthood in developing countries NRC, Washington, 2001—02, mem. working group social dynamics adolescent fertility, 1990—92; bd. dirs. African Population and Health Rsch. Ctr., Nairobi, Kenya. Contbr. articles to profl. jours. Recipient Outstanding Achievement and Commitment to Excellence award, Tulane U. Health Sciences Ctr., 2003, 2004; fellow, UN Fund for Population Activities, 1982—86, Rockefeller Found., 1986—89, Population Coun., 1989—90; grantee, Spencer Found., 1996—97, U. N.C., 2003—, Compton Found., 2004—. Mem.: APHA,

Internat. Union Sci. Study of Population (mem. com. reproductive health 1995—99), Population Assn. Am. Home: 5633 Durham Drive New Orleans LA 70131 Office Phone: 504-988-3647. Office Fax: 504-988-3653. Personal E-mail: agage11961@aol.com.

GAGE, BEAU, artist; b. Rye, N.Y., Dec. 3, 1945; d. John Alden and Frances (Johnston) G.; m. Glenn A. Ousterhout, May 24,1980. BA, St. John's Coll., Santa Fe and Annapolis, Md., 1971; student, Internat. Ctr. Photography, N.Y.C., 1981-82, 82-83, Art Students League N.Y., 1983-87, The Sculpture Ctr. Sch., N.Y.C., 1985-87, Nat. Acad. Design, 1988-89. Staff asst. to the pres. The White House, Washington, 1972-73; key accounts mgr. Sterling Drug, Inc., Montvale, N.J., 1975-79. Works exhibited at Internat. Ctr. Photography, 1981-83, Art Students League, 1984-87, The Sculpture Ctr., 1985-87, Westbeth Gallery, N.Y.C., 1984, 86, Sotheby's Auction House, 1990, others; permanent pub. sculpture Jacksonville (Fla.) Jaguars, Inc.; permanent exhbn. Jacksonville Mus. Sci. & History. Supporter, guild mem. Martha Graham Dance Co., N.Y.C., 1989—; canopy assoc. Rainforest Alliance, 2000—; mem. adv. bd. Buglisi/Foreman Dance Co., N.Y.C., 2001—; leader Perlman Music Program, N.Y.C., 2001—. Fellow Mus. Modern Art; mem. Met. Mus. Art, Internat. Ctr. Photography, Orgn. Ind. Artists, The Nature Conservancy, Mass. Soc. Mayflower Descendants, Poets House (N.Y.C.). Avocations: astronomy, sailing, yoga. Home: 320 E 46th St Apt 34E New York NY 10017-3039 Personal E-mail: beau7gage@aol.com.

GAGE, EDWIN C., III, (SKIP GAGE), travel and marketing services executive; b. Evanston, Ill., Nov. 1, 1940; s. Edwin Cutting and Margaret (Stackhouse) G.; m. Barbara Ann Carlson, June 26, 1965; children— Geoff, Scott, Christine, Richard BS in Bus. Adminstrn., Northwestern U., 1963, MS in Journalism, 1965. Account exec. Foote, Cone and Belding, 1965-68, dir. mktg. devel. & rsch., 1968-70; v.p. direct mktg. Carlson Mktg. Group of Carlson Cos., Mpls., 1970-75, exec. v.p., 1975-77, pres., 1977-83, also bd. dirs.; exec. v.p., COO Carlson Cos. Inc., Mpls., 1983, pres., CEO, 1984-89, pres., chief exec. officer, 1989-91; now chmn., CEO Gage Marketing Group, Mpls. Bd. dirs. Gage Mktg. Group, Carlson Holdings Inc., Carlson Real Estate, Carlson Real Estate Co., Inc., Supervalu Stores Inc., Fingerhut Cos., Kellogg adv. bd. Northwestern U., Minn. Coun. Quality, Mpls. Inst. Arts. Lt. USN. Mem. Young Pres. Orgn., Minn. Execs. Orgn. Avocations: music folk and popular, tennis, golf, hunting, fishing. Office: Gage Marketing Group 10000 Highway 55 Ste 100 Minneapolis MN 55441-6365

GAGE, FRED H., neuroscientist, medical educator; PhD, Johns Hopkins U., Balt. Assoc. prof. dept. histology U. Lund, Sweden; prof. dept. neurosci. U. Calif., San Diego; prof. biology Salk Inst. for Biol. Studies, San Diego, 1995—. Contbr. articles to profl. jours., over 235 articles to profl. jours. Recipient Merit award, NIH, Decade of the Brain medal, Neurosci. award, Pew Found., Neurosci. Rsch. award, Bristol-Meyers Squibb, 1987, IPSEN prize in neuronal plasticity, 1990, Charles A. Dana award, 1993, Christopher Reeves medal, 1997, Max Planck Rsch. prize, 1999, Pasarow Found. award, 1999, award for med. rsch., MetLife, 2002, Klaus Joachim Zulch prize, Max Planck Soc., 2003; fellow predoctoral fellow, NIMH. Fellow: Am. Acad. Arts & Sci., Nat. Acad. Sci., Inst. Med.; mem.: Soc. for Neuroscience (pres. 2001), Inst. of Medicine of NAS. Achievements include first successful strategies to stimulate recovery of function following brain and spinal cord injuries. Office: The Salk Inst for Biol Studies PO Box 85800 San Diego CA 92186-5800*

GAGE, FRED KELTON, lawyer; b. Mpls., June 20, 1925; s. Fred K. and Vivian L. G.; m. Dorothy Ann, Sept. 7, 1974; children: Deborah, Penelope, Amy, Lawrence. BS, U. Minn., 1948, LLB, 1950. Bar: Minn. 1950. Assoc. Wilson, Blethen & Ogle, Mankato, 1950-55; ptnr. Blethen, Gage, Krause, Blethen, Corcoran, Berkland & Peterson and predecessor firms, Mankato, 1955-90, of counsel, 1991—. Mem. State Bd. Profl. Responsibility, Minn. Supreme Ct., 1974-82, mem. legal svcs. adv. com., 1996—. Mem. Mankato Sch. Bd., 1957-66, Minn. State Coll. Bd., 1960-64; mem. Minn. Senate from 11th Legis. Dist., 1966-72; Mem. Minn. Sports Facilities Commn., 1976-84. Served with USN, 1943-46. Named Mankato Outstanding Young Man of Yr., 1956, Outstanding Man of Minn., Mankato Jr. C. of C., 1958 Fellow Am. Bar Found.; mem. ABA (assembly del. 1980-86), Minn. Bar Assn. (chmn. tax sect. 1956-58, pres. 1977-78), Order of Coif. Methodist. Office: Blethen Gage & Krause PO Box 3049 127 S 2nd St Mankato MN 56001-3658 E-mail: kgage@bglow.com.

GAGE, GASTON HEMPHILL, lawyer; b. Charlotte, N.C., June 16, 1930; s. Lucius Gaston and Margaret (White) G.; m. Jane Basinger, July 11, 1959; children: Gaston Hemphill Jr., John Robert, Stephen Matheson. BA, Duke U., 1953; LLB, U. N.C., 1958. Bar: N.C. 1958, U.S. Ct. Appeals (4th cir.) 1964, U.S. Ct. Appeals (7th and fed. cirs.) 1983, U.S. Supreme Ct. 1965, U.S. Ct. Fed. Claims. Ptnr. Grier, Parker, Poe, Thompson, Bernstein, Gage & Preston, Charlotte, 1964-84, Parker, Poe, Thompson, Bernstein, Gage & Preston, Charlotte, 1984-90, Parker, Poe, Adams & Bernstein, Charlotte, 1990—. Dir. Elon Homes for Children, Elon Coll., N.C., 1986—, vice chair, 1995-96, chair, 1996-97; pres. Boys Town of N.C., Charlotte, 1974-78, A.G. Jr. High PTA, Charlotte, 1974-75, Mecklenburg Kiwanis, Charlotte, 1968; sec., ofcl. bd. Myers Park United Meth. Ch., Charlotte, 1970-72; trustee Oak Ridge Mil. Acad., 2001—. Mem. ABA, N.C. Bar Assn., N.C. State Bar Assn., Mecklenburg County Bar Assn., Kiwanis (lt. gov. Carolinas dist. 1995-96). Methodist. Home: 324 Lockley Dr Charlotte NC 28207-2330 Office: Parker Poe Adams & Bernstein 401 S Tryon St Ste 3000 Charlotte NC 28202

GAGE, GEORGE HENRY, retired high technology company executive; b. Rochester, N.Y., Oct. 1, 1924; s. George Henry and Ethel (Morley) G.; m. Frances Irvine, Dec. 21, 1946; children: Betsey Gage La Breche, James George, Nancy Gage Mandeville. BSEE, Rensselaer Poly. Inst., 1948. Application engr. GE, Owensboro, Ky., 1948-56, comml. engr. Syracuse, N.Y., 1957-58; mgr. product planning CBS Electronics, Danvers, Mass., 1959-61; dir. planning EG&G, Inc., Bedford, Mass., 1962-75, v.p. Wellesley, Mass., 1975-83, sr. v.p., 1983-86; dir. Adams Russell Co., Inc., Waltham, Mass., 1979-89; gov. Newell Health Corp., Newton-Wellesley Hosp., 1979-87; ret. Contbg. author: Industrial Electronics Handbook, 1957, Implementation of Strategic Planning, 1982. Staff sgt. U.S. Army, 1943-46, PTO. Mem. Sigma Xi (assoc.), Tau Beta Pi, Eta Kappa Nu. Avocations: computer simulations, reading, walking. Home: 23 Fiddlers Green Lansing NY 14882-8877

GAGE, JOHN, labor union administrator; b. 1946; m. Patti McGowan. Grad., Wheeling Jesuit U., 1968. Profl. baseball player Balt. Orioles, 1968—69; with Liberty Mut. Ins. Co.; disability examiner Social Security Adminstrn., 1974—82; pres. Am. Fedn. Govt. Employees, Balt., 1985—2003, nat. pres. Washington, 2003—. Office: Am Fedn Govt Employees 80 F St NW Washington DC 20001

GAGE, NATHANIEL LEES, psychologist, educator; b. Union City, N.J., Aug. 1, 1917; s. Hyman and Rose (Lees) Gewirtz; m. Margaret Elizabeth Burrows, June 27, 1942; children: Elizabeth, Thomas Burrows, Sarah, Anne. Student, CCNY, 1934—36; AB magna cum laude, U. Minn., 1938; PhD, Purdue U., 1947, LittD (hon.), 1978; PhD (hon.), U. Liège, 2001. Asst. prof. div. ednl. reference Purdue U., 1947-48; prof. edn. U. Ill., Urbana, 1948-62; mem. Air Univ. Far East Rsch. Group for Human Resources, 1950—51; prof. edn. and psychology Stanford U., 1962-87, Margaret Jacks prof. edn., 1981-87, prof. emeritus, 1987—. Sachs vis. prof. Tchrs. Coll., Columbia U., 1977; lectr. U. Hamburg, 1978, Taipei, 1989, Madrid, 1992, U. Ill., 1994, numerous others; vis. fellow Brasenose Coll., Oxford U., 1983; vis. prof. NYU, 1959, Harvard U., 1984, SUNY, Albany, 1988; mem. rsch. adv. com. Am. Coun. Edn., 1967-73, chmn., 1972-73; mem. Nat. Adv. Com. on Edn. Labs, 1966-69; cons. Internat. Inst. Ednl. Planning, Paris, 1973-74; chmn. exec. bd. Stanford Ctr. Rsch. and Devel. in Tchg., 1968-76, founding co-dir., 1965-68; also dir. program on teaching effectiveness Ctr. for Ednl. Rsch., Stanford, 1972-83; vis. scholar, chmn. planning conf. on studies in teaching Nat. Inst. Edn., 1974; chmn. project coun. internat. classroom environ. study Internat. Assn. for Evaluation of Ednl. Achievement, 1979-81; Fulbright lectr., Brazil, 1985; mem. final selection com. Spencer Found. Dissertation Yr. Fellowships, 1987, 88; participant U. S. Dept. Edn. Conf. on School-Linked Comprehensive Svcs. for Children and Families, 1994. Author: Teacher Effectiveness and Teacher Education, 1972, Scientific Basis of the Art of Teaching, 1978, Hard Gains in the Soft Sciences: The Case of Pedagogy, 1985; co-author: Educational Measurement and Evaluation, 1943, 2d edit., 1955, A Practical Introduction to Measurement and Evaluation, 1960, 2d edit., 1965, Educational Psychology, 1975, 6th edit., 1998; editor: Handbook of Research on Teaching, 1963, Mandated Evaluation of Educators, 1973, Psychology of Teaching Methods, 1976; founding editor Teaching and Teacher Education: An Internat. Jour. Rsch. and Studies, 1983-86; co-editor: Readings in the Social Psychology of Education, 1963; cons. editor Jour. Ednl. Psychology, numerous other jours. Served with USAAF, 1943-45. Recipient Creative Leadership award NYU Sch. Edn., 1980, Outstanding Writing award Am. Assn. Colls. Tchr. Edn., 1986, Disting. Alumnus award Purdue U., 1994, Rsch. and Dissemination Program award Am. Fedn. Tchrs., 2000; fellow Ctr. for Advanced Study in Behavioral Scis., 1965-66, 87-88, USPHS, 1965-66, Guggenheim fellow, 1976-77. Fellow APA (pres. divsn. ednl. psychology 1961-62, Thorndike award 1986), Am. Psychol. Soc. (charter fellow); mem. Am. Ednl. Rsch. Assn. (pres. 1963-64, Disting. Contbns. award 1988), Nat. Soc. Study Edn. (bd. dirs. 1970-80, chmn. 1972, 74, 78), Nat. Acad. Edn., Fulbright Assn., Phi Beta Kappa, Sigma Xi, Phi Delta Kappa (award for meritorious contbns. to edn. 1981). Home: 85 Peter Coutts Cir Stanford CA 94305-2512 Office Phone: 650-725-7387. Business E-Mail: nlgage@stanford.edu.

GAGE, PATRICK (LEONARD PATRICK GAGE), biotechnologist, pharmaceutical consultant; b. Endicott, N.Y., May 4, 1942; s. Leonard Augustine and Mary Margaret (O'Brien) G.; m. Nancy Virginia Graffius, Aug. 7, 1965 (div. Mar. 1985); children: Darren, Cynthia; m. Evelyn Anne Devine, June 29, 1985; children: Christopher, Devin. BS, MIT, 1964; PhD, U. Chgo., 1969. NIH postdoctoral fellow Carnegie Inst., Washington, 1969-71; mem. dept. cell biology Roche Inst. Molecular Biology, 1971-80, dir. dept. molecular genetics Nutley, N.J., 1981-83, v.p. biol. R & D, 1983-84; v.p. exploratory rsch. Hoffmann-La Roche Inc., Nutley, N.J., 1984-89; exec. v.p. Genetics Inst., Inc., Cambridge, Mass., 1989-93, COO, 1993-97, pres., 1997-98, Wyeth Rsch., Collegeville, Pa., 1998—2002; sr. v.p. sci. and tech. Wyeth, 2001—02. Chmn. Dublin Molecular Medicine Ctr., 2002—04, Compound Therapeutics, 2003—05, Acceleron Pharma, 2004—; mem. sci. adv. bd. Perkin Elmer Inc., Functional Genetics; life sci. adv. bd. Warburg Pincus; bd. dirs. Biotech. Inst., Neose Technologies, Inc., Protein Design Labs, Inc., Serono S.A., Compound Therapeutics, Immune Control, In.c; adv. Flagship Venture, Cambridge. Bd. dirs. Phila. Orch. Avocations: skiing, golf. Office Phone: 617-460-4020. Personal E-mail: patrickgage@comcast.net.

GAGE, ROBERT CLIFFORD, minister; b. Beverly, Mass., Nov. 20, 1941; s. George V. and Elizabeth B. (May) Gage; m. Mary Neefe, June 17, 1961; children: Joanna, Jonathan, Judith, Joshua, Joy. Student, Tenn. Temple U., 1961-62; BA, Phila. Coll. of Bible, 1964; postgrad., Ea. Bapt. Theol. Sem., 1966-67, New Sch. Soc. Rsch., 1975-76; D in Religion, Newport U., 1983. Ordained to ministry Gen. Assn. Regular Bapt. Chs., 1964. Pastor Whitehall Bapt. Ch., Phila., 1964-65, Glencroft Bapt. Ch., Glenolden, Pa., 1966-68, 1st Bapt. Ch., Newfield, NJ, 1969-70, Hackensack, 1971-79, Wealthy St. Bapt. Ch., Grand Rapids, Mich., 1979-88; evangelist, 1988-91; pastor Haven Bapt. Ch., Winter Haven, Fla., 1991-2000; adminstr. Haven Christian Acad., Winter Haven, Fla., 1996-2000; pastor 1st Bapt. Ch., N.Y.C., 2000—. Radio min., 1988; dir. Sword and Shield Ministries/Rivendel Pastor's Retreat, Deposit, NY, 2003—. Author: The Birthmarks of the Christian Life, 1976, Our Life in Christ, 1978, The Pastor's Counseling Workbook, 1983, The Pre-Marriage Counseling Workbook, 1984, Discipleship Evangelism, 1985, Cultivating Spiritual Fruit, 1986, Basic Discipleship, 1987, Why Me, Lord, 1988, The Unveiling, 1990; editor: Sword and Shield, 1969—; columnist: Pers. Pub. Clinic, Winter Haven News Chief, 1991—2004; contbr. sermons to ch. publs., articles to profl. jours. Mem.: Christian Writers League (founder 1996), Internat. Freelance Photographer Orgn. (life). Home: 4 Main St Deposit NY 13754 Office: 265 West 79th St New York NY 10024 Office Phone: 212-724-5600. E-mail: drbobgncy@yahoo.com. *Lord Jesus Christ, the work is Thine, not ours but Thine alone, and prospered by thy power Divine, can never be overthrown.*

GAGGINI, JOHN EDMUND, lawyer; b. Chgo., Dec. 17, 1949; BA cum laude, Knox Coll., 1971; MS, Ohio U., 1972, JD magna cum laude, 1975; LLM, NYU, 1976. Bar: Ill. 1975, D.C. 1977; CPA, Ill. Law clk. to Hon. Shiro Kashiwa U.S. Ct. Claims, 1976-77; ptnr. McDermott, Will & Emery, Chgo. Adj. prof. law Chgo.-Kent Coll. Law, 1987—. Mem. ABA, Ill. State Bar Assn., Chgo. Bar Assn. (chmn. state and local tax com. 1986-87), Phi Kappa Phi, Phi Beta Kappa, Beta Alpha Psi, Phi Gamma Mu, Phi Alpha Delta. Office: McDermott Will & Emery 227 W Monroe St Ste 4700 Chicago IL 60606-5096

GAGGIOLI, RICHARD ARNOLD, mechanical engineering educator; b. Highwood, Ill., Dec. 3, 1934; s. Gustavo and Constantina Lucille (Mordini) G.; m. Anita Catherine Sage, Nov. 9, 1957; children: Catherine Anne, Michael James, Daniel Richard, Edward Thomas, Mary Esther. BME, Northwestern U., 1957, MS (NSF fellow), 1958; PhD (Gen. Electric, NSF fellow), U. Wis., 1961. Registered profl. engr., Wis., 1965. Coop. student engr. Abbott Labs. (pharms.), North Chicago, Ill., 1954-58; asst. prof. mech. engring. U. Wis., Madison, 1962-66, assoc. prof., 1966-69; prof., chmn. dept. mech. engring. Marquette U., Milw., 1969-72, prof., 1969—81, 1990—2001, rsch. prof., 2002—; dean engring. and architecture Cath. U. Am., Washington, 1981-84; prof. mech. engring. U. Mass., Lowell, 1985-89. Mem. U.S. Army Math. Rsch. Ctr., Madison, 1964-66; NSF-Soc. Indsl. and Applied Math. vis. lectr., 1969-72, engring. cons., 1970—. Author: (with E.F. Obert) Thermodynamics, 1963; editor: Thermodynamics-Second Law Analysis, Vol. 1, 1980, Vol. 2, 1983, Analysis of Energy Systems, 1985, Computer-Aided Engineering of Energy Systems, 1986; (with M.J. Moran) Analysis and Design of Advanced Energy Systems: Fundamentals, 1987; (with G. Tsatsaronis) Fundamentals of Thermodynamics and Energy Analysis, 1990; (with G.M. Reistad) Thermodynamics and Energy Systems: Fundamentals, 1991, (with R.F. Boehm et al.) Thermodynamics and the Design of Energy Systems, 1992; hon. editor Internat. Jour. Applied Thermodynamics, 1998-2004; contbr. articles to profl. jours. Chmn. bd. trustees Montrose Sch., Westwood, Mass., 1987-89. Recipient Emil H. Steiger Meml. Tchg. award U. Wis., 1965, Pere Marquette award Marquette U., 1976, Best Paper award Am. Chem. Soc. Chem. Tech. jour. 1977; NSF postdoctoral fellow chem. engring. U. Wis., 1961-62; vis. fellow Battelle Meml. Inst., 1968-69; invited lectr., Rome, 1987, 95, Shanghai, 1986, Dalian, 1986, Beijing 1986, 89, 97, Abu Dhabi, 1988, Zaragoza 1993, Florence, 1989, 2003, Athens, 1991, Istanbul, 1995, Bucharest, 1997, Nancy, 1997, Krakow, 1994, 98, Tokyo, 1999, others. Fellow ASME (life; James Harry Potter gold medal 1988, advanced energy sys. divsn. best paper award 1991, E.F. Obert best paper award 2000); mem. AIChE, Summit Edn. Assn. (sec., trustee 1993—), Sigma Xi, Pi Tau Sigma, Tau Beta Pi. Roman Catholic. Office: Marquette U Dept Mech Engring Milwaukee WI 53201-1881 Home: W2202 Wilmers Grove Rd East Troy WI 53120 Office Phone: 414-430-5240. Business E-Mail: richard.gaggioli@marquette.edu.

GAGIN, LAWRENCE VINCENT, ceramics engineer, consultant; b. Sterling, Ill., Oct. 19, 1918; s. Charles Francis and Lillian Ella Gagin; m. Marion Winifred Buffinger, May 28, 1942; children: Jean, Paula, Lawrence, Mary, James. BS in Engring., U. Ill., 1942. Registered profl. ceremic engr., Nat. Inst. Ceramic Engring. Rsch. engr. Libbey Glass Co., Toledo, 1946—48; asst. dir. glass tech. Kimble Glass Co., Toledo, 1948—54; chief ceramic engr. Glass Fibers, Inc., Toledo, 1954—58; mgr. rsch. Johns-Manville Fiber Glass, Toledo, 1958—76, Denver, 1976—82; tech. cons. in field, 1982—. Instr. chem. engring. night sch. U. Toledo, 1950—52; ASTM E-38 Resource Recovery Glass, 1978—82; vis. scientist Elem. and HS, 1989—98. Contbr. articles to profl. publs. Vol. exec. Internat. Exec. Svc. Corp., Bangkok, 1989; chmn. planning and zoning Town of Columbine Valley, Colo., 1979—84; scoring observer Internat. Golf Tournament, 1986—2002. Capt. Corps Engrs. U.S. Army, 1942—46, ETO. Fellow: Am. Ceramic Soc.; mem.: Nat. Inst. Ceramic Engrs., ASTM (mem. mortars for masonry com. 1974—82, mem. glass and glass products coms. 1970—82), Columbine Country Club. Republican. Roman Catholic. Achievements include development of Dyna Quartz pure silica fiber insulation for Boeing Dyna-Soar, first vehicle designed to return from space; patents for low lead television glass; low viscosity glass for glass fibers; superior durability, easily fiberized glass; high temperature glass for fibers; fiber die pad for extruding hot metals; fluroine free glass for fiber glass insulations; alkali resistant glass for reinforcing cement; low viscosity glass for air attenuating glass fibers. Avocations: golf, woodworking, photography. Home: 18 Wedge Way Columbine Valley CO 80123

GAGLIANO, GINA SAPONARA, art educator; b. Metairie, La., May 15, 1973; d. Victor Joseph and Marilyn Clements Saponara; m. Tommy Christopher Gagliano, June 14, 1996; children: Victoria Angela, Isabella Katerina. BA, La. State U., Baton Rouge, 1995. Art tchr. St. Charles Parish Pub. Schools, Luling, La., 1996—2000; fine arts dept. chair Archbishop Chapelle H.S., Metairie, La., 2000—. Portraits, faux finishes and murals. Mem.: Nat. Art Edn. Assn. (assoc.). R-Consevative. Catholic. Office: Archbishop Chapelle High School 8800 Veterans Blvd Metairie LA 70003 Office Phone: 504-467-3105.

GAGLIARDI, RAYMOND ALFRED, physician; b. New Haven, Nov. 20, 1922; s. Carl Albert and Carmela (Esposito) G.; m. Patricia DeTuncq, Apr. 6, 1946; children: Laura E. Quigley, John Bell. BS, Yale U., 1943, MD, 1945. Pvt. practice radiology, Pontiac, Mich., 1951-92; chmn. dept. radiology St. Joseph Mercy Hosp., Pontiac, 1976-91, chmn. emeritus, 1991—. Clin. faculty radiology Wayne Univ. Sch. of Medicine, 1951—92. Author: The Golf Story: An Anecdotal History of Golf, 1999, Reflections and Recollections, 2000; editor-in-chief History of the Radiological Sciences, 1995; contbr. articles to profl. jours. Capt. U.S. Army, 1946-48; PTO. Fellow Am. Coll Radiology; mem. Am. Roentgen Ray Soc. (pres. 1987-88, Gold Medal award 1989, Hartman medal 1995, Centennial lectr. 2000), Mich. Radiol. Soc. (pres. 1972), Mich. Med. Soc. (Disting. Svc. award 1988), Oakland Hills Country Club, Royal Palm Yacht and Country Club (past commodore 1994), Loch Lomond Golf Club, Heathers Club. Republican. Avocation: golf. Home: 789 Upper Scotsborough Way Bloomfield Hills MI 48304-3827 Address: 2100 Queen Palm Rd Boca Raton FL 33432

GAGLIARDI, UGO OSCAR, systems software architect, educator; b. Naples, Italy, July 23, 1931; came to U.S., 1956; s. Edgardo and Lina (Valenzuela) G.; m. Anna Josephine Italiano, July 7, 1954 (div. May 1972); children: Oscar Marco, Alex Piero. Diploma in Math. and Physics, U. Naples, Italy, 1951; DEng in Elec. Engring., U. Naples, 1954. Chief scientist U.S. Air Force, Hanscom AFB, Mass., 1965-66; rsch. fellow Harvard U., Cambridge, Mass., 1966—67, lectr., 1967—74, prof. practice computer engring., 1974-83, Gordon McKay prof. practice computer engring., 1983—2000; v.p. tech. ops. Interactive Scis., Inc., Braintree, Mass., 1968-70; dir. engring. Honeywell Info. Systems, Waltham, Mass., 1970-75; pres. Gen. Systems Group, Salem, N.H., 1975—; chmn. Ctr. for Software Tech., Inc., 1982-99; vis. prof. Harvard Grad. Sch. Design, 2000—. Mem. NAS rsch. coun. panel Nat. Computer Systems Lab. (formerly Inst. Computer Scis. and Tech.), Nat. Inst. Standards and Tech. (formerly Nat. Bur. Standards), 1985-91, chmn., 1988-91. Fulbright scholar Columbia U., 1955-56. Office: Harvard U 335 Gund Hall 48 Quincy St Cambridge MA 02138 Address: General Systems Group 280 Perry Oliver Rd Wells ME 04090-6937 Office Phone: 207-646-9694. Personal E-mail: uog@focus.com. Business E-Mail: uog@deas.harvard.edu.

GAGLIARDO, MICHAEL ROBERT, music educator, conductor; b. Alton, Ill., Dec. 9, 1969; s. Robert Gene and Judith Ann Gagliardo; m. T. Melcia Barnhill, Mar. 27, 1999. MusB cum laude, Ea. Ill. U., 1993; MusM, Ball State U., 1996. Mktg., prodn. assoc. St. Louis Symphony Orch., 1992—94; music dir., conductor Etowah Youth Orch., Gadsden, Ala., 1995—. Conductor, adminstr. Youth Symphony Orch. E. Ctrl. Ind., Munice, 1993—95; asst. conductor Ball State U. Symphony Orch., Munice, Ind., 1994—95; dir. Gadsden Cmty. Sch. for Art, 1998—2001; adj. faculty Jacksonville (Ala) State U., 1999—; music dir., conductor Jacksonville State U. Orch, 1999—. Pres., bd. dirs. Humane Soc. Etowoh County, Gadsden, 2005. Recipient Citizenship award, Ball State U. Sch. Music, 1995, Outstanding Young Alumnus, Ea. Ill. U., 1997. Mem.: Conductors' Guild, Music Educators Nat. Conf., Ala. Symphony Orch. League (mem. youth orch. divsn. 1995—2001), Ala. Orch. Assn. (pres. 1999—2003), Am. String Tchrs. Assn. (pres. Ala. chpt. 2004—). Avocation: golf. Office: Etowah Youth Orch 501 Broad St Gadsden AL 35901

GAGNE, DAVID WARD, music educator; b. June 3, 1949; BA, Columbia U., 1971; MA, CUNY, 1980, PhD, 1988. Assoc. music dir. Dance Theatre of Harlem, N.Y.C., 1971-77; faculty Munnes Coll. Music, N.Y.C., 1978—. Assoc. prof. Queens Coll., CUNY, 1988—. Home and Office: 211 W 106th St Apt 14B New York NY 10025-3688

GAGNE, ERIC, professional baseball player; b. Montreal, Can., Jan. 7, 1976; Pitcher L.A. (Calif.) Dodgers, 1999—. Named to All Star Team, 2002, 2003, 2004; recipient Cy Young award, Nat. League, 2003, Rolaids Relief award, 2003, Espy Award for Record Breaking Performance, ESPN, 2004. Achievements include MLB record of 84 consecutive saves. Office: 1000 ElysianPark Ave Los Angeles CA 90012

GAGNE, MARY, academic administrator; Dir. Tex. Acad. Leadership in the Humanities Lamar U., Beaumont, 1998—. Recipient Blue Ribbon awards U.S. Dept. Edn., 1986-87, 90-91, Exec. Educator Best Prin. award, Nat. Tchg. award NCEA, Coca Cola Educator of Distinction award. 2000. Address: PO Box 10062 Beaumont TX 77710-0062 E-mail: gagneml@hal.lamar.edu.

GAGNIER, JOSEPH C., artist; b. Detroit, Oct. 18, 1929; s. Joseph A. Gagnier and Virginia F. De Buhl; m. Huguette M. Filion, Feb. 3, 1952 (div. 1969); children: Denise, Marcel, Michelle, Maurice, Monique, Paul. Student, U. Mich., 1957, Mich. State U., 1958. Musician Am. Fedn. Musicians, Detroit, 1954-80; mason contractor Gagnier & Assocs., St. Clair Shores, Mich., 1952-60, 85-90; landscape arch. Gagnier & Brox, Lockport, N.Y., 1960-85; profl. ski instr. Boyne Mt. Lodge, Boyne Falls, Mich., 1962-79; artist Jack Pine Studios, Roscommon, Mich., 1985—. Instr. painting, watercolor Kirtland C.C., Roscommon, 1990-91. Composer (music) Have a Merry Christmas, 1989 (Billboard Mag. award 1993). Mem. Am. Watercolor Soc. (assoc. mem.), Midwest Watercolor Soc. (life mem.), Rotary (pres. 1980-81). Avocation: writing biographical and political novels. Home: 4571 M 18 Roscommon MI 48653

GAGNON, CRAIG WILLIAM, lawyer; b. St. Cloud, Minn., Dec. 19, 1940; s. Marvin Sylvester and Signa Gunhild (Johnson) G.; children: Nicole, Jeffrey, Camille; m. Pam Peglow, Nov. 8, 1980; children: Claire, Jillian, Jane. BA, U. Minn., 1964; JD magna cum laude, William Mitchell Coll. Law, 1968. Bar: Minn. 1968, U.S. Dist. Ct. Minn. 1968, U.S. Tax Ct. 1972, U.S. Supreme Ct. 1970. Ptnr. Oppenheimer, Wolff & Donnelly, Mpls., 1968—. Chmn. bd. Equity Bank; bd. dirs. XOX Corp., First Fla. Bank. Trustee William Mitchell Coll. Law, St. Paul. 1989—, chmn. bd., 1999-2000. Named Alumnus of Notable Achievement, U. Minn. Fellow Am. Coll. Trial Lawyers; mem. Metro Breakfast Club (pres. 1993), Am. Bd. Trial Advocates (assoc.), Am. Law Inst. Avocations: hunting, fishing, golf. Home: 4807 Sunnyside Rd Edina MN 55424-1109 Office: Oppenheimer Wolff & Donnelly 45 S 7th St Ste 3400 Minneapolis MN 55402-1609 E-mail: cgagnon@oppenheimer.com.

GAGNON, ELEANOR MOSER, literature and language educator, history educator; b. Middletown, Conn. d. Theodore Pomeroy and Beatrice Johanna (Perkins) Moser; m. John Harvey Gagnon, Apr. 22, 1995. BA in History, Conn. Coll., 1979; MAT in History, Brown U., 1980. Faculty Kent Pl. Sch., Summit, NJ, 1980—91, Greenwich Country Day Sch., Conn., 1991—. Exec. dir. Kent Pl. Sch. Summer Camp, 1988—91; asst. dir. mid. sch. divsn. Kent

Pl. Sch., 1986—89, trustee emeritus, 1992—. Creator Greenwich Country Day Sch. Hole in the Wall Gang Camp Walkthon, 1993—. Named Oustanding Am. History Tchr. of Yr. for State of Conn., DAR, 2003. Mem.: ASCD, Nat. Coun. History Edn., Medieval Acad. Am., Phi Delta Kappa. Republican. Avocations: running, singing, reading, horseback riding, needlepoint. Home: 233 Oaklawn Ave Stamford CT 06905 Office: Greenwich Country Day Sch Old Ch Rd Greenwich CT 06830 Office Phone: 203-863-5620.

GAGNON, RONALD ADELARD, library director; b. Beverly, Mass., 1956; s. Adelard Amedee and Theresa Alice Gagnon; m. Ann Margaret Morris, 1991; children: Daniel Adelard, Ellen Alice. BSBA, Salem (Mass.) State Coll., 1978; MS in Libr. and Info. Sci., Simmons Coll., Boston, 1979. Cataloger Peabody Inst., Danvers, Mass., 1979-80, head tech. svcs., 1980-85, North Shore C.C., Beverly, 1985-88; network adminstr. North of Boston Libr. Exch., Beverly, 1988-93, exec. dir., 1993—. Bd. dirs. CLSI Ea. Region Users, 1990-94; strategic planning com. Mass. Bd. Libr. Commrs., 1993-94; mem. steering com. Innovative Consortium Ptnrs., 2004. Contbr. articles to Library Journal, 1981-91. Town meeting mem. Town of Danvers, 1978—82, 1994—; adv. com. EBSCO pub. Libr. Com., 2005—; bd. dirs. Danvers Hist. Soc., 1988—91. Mem. ALA, Assn. Specialized and Coop. Libr. Agys. (interlibr. coop. and networking sect.), New Eng. Libr. Assn., Mass. Libr. Assn. (legis. com. 2004—), Friends Peabody Inst. Roman Catholic.

GAGNON, STEWART WALTER, lawyer; b. Beaumont, Tex., Jan. 29, 1949; s. Stewart Paul and Helen Anne (Payne) G.; m. Lynn Bass, July 29, 1972; children— Ashley Lynn, Jason Stewart. Student, Trinity U., 1967-69; B.A., U. Houston, 1971; J.D., S. Tex. Coll. Law, 1974. Bar: Tex. 1974, U.S. Dist. Ct. (so. dist.) Tex. 1975, U.S. Ct. Apls. (5th cir.) 1975, U.S. Supreme Ct. 1976. Assoc. firm Fulbright & Jaworski, Houston, 1974-83, participating assoc., 1983—87, ptnr., 1987—, and head, family law dept.; mem. family & law coun. State Bar of Tex., 1990—, Supreme Ct. Commn. on Child Support Guidelines; master/referee Harris County Dist. Cts., Houston, 1977—. Asst. scoutmaster Boy Scouts Am., Troop 642, Houston, 1970—; mem. State Dem. Exec. Com., Tex., 1984-90; mem. Houston Found. Bd. Pub. Trust, 1982-90; lectr. Spring Branch Ind. Sch. Dist., 1976—; mem., bd. dirs. Sam Houston Area coun. Boy Scouts Am. Recipient Award of Merit, Boy Scouts Am., 1982, Silver Beaver award, 1983, Dan R. Price award for Outstanding Contbns. to Family Law in the State of Tex., 1994. Fellow Am. Acad. Matrimonial Lawyers; mem. Houston Bar Assn., Tex. Bar Assn. (dist. 4 com. on admissions), Gulf Coast Family Law Specialists Assn. (dir., pres. 1986—), Tex. Acad. Family Law Lawyers (v.p., pres. 1988), Gulf Coast Legal Found. (bd. dirs., pres. 1991), Houston Volunteer Lawyers Program, 1987-88; Presbyterian. Office: Fulbright & Jaworski LLP 1301 McKinney St Houston TX 77010-3031 Office Phone: 713-651-5151. Office Fax: 716-651-5246. Business E-Mail: sgagnon@fulbright.com.

GAGOSIAN, ROBERT B., chemist, educator; b. Medford, Mass., Sept. 17, 1944; m. Susan Gagosian; children: Travis, Alex. SB in Chemistry, MIT, 1966; PhD in Organic Chemistry, Columbia U., 1970; hon. degree, L.I. Univ., 2000, Northeastern U., 2000. Asst. scientist Woods Hole Oceanog. Instn., Mass., 1972-76, assoc. scientist, 1976-82, sr. scientist, 1982—, chmn. dept. chemistry, 1982-87, assoc. dir. rsch., 1987-92, sr. assoc. dir., dir. rsch., 1992-93, acting dir., 1993, dir., 1994, pres., dir., 2002. Vis. lectr. dept. geology and geophysics Yale U., 1975, cons., lectr. in field; mem. numerous vis. coms. and rsch. panels NSF, Office Naval Rsch., univs. and rsch. orgns. in U.S. and fgn. countries; mem. corp. Bermuda Biol. Sta. for Rsch., Sea Edn. Assn. Contbr. chpts. to books, articles to profl. jours. Vis. scholar U. Wash., 1983, Australian Inst. Marine Scis., 1983; vis. fellow Australian Nat. U., 1983; William Evans fellow, U. Otago, Dunedin, New Zealand, 1987. Mem. Am. Chem. Soc., AAAS, Geochem. Soc. Am., Am. Geophys. Union, European Assn. Organic Geochemists, Sigma Xi. Office: Woods Hole Oceanographic Inst Fenno House MS 40A Woods Hole MA 02543 E-mail: rgagosian@whoi.edu.

GAHAGAN, THOMAS GAIL, obstetrician, gynecologist; b. Brush Valley, Pa., Apr. 14, 1938; s. Ben D. and Zula C. (Brown) G.; m. Mary A. Miller, Dec. 23, 1960; children: David, Diane, Kevin, Keith. BA, Washington and Jefferson Coll., 1960; MD, U. Pa., Phila., 1964. Diplomate Am. Bd. Ob/Gyn. Intern U. Ky., Lexington, 1964-65, resident in ob/gyn., 1965-68; group practice Dr. Jones and Kelch P.A., Newark, Ohio, 1970-71, Naples (Fla.) Ob/Gyn., 1971-85; pvt. practice Naples, 1985-99; ret., 1999. Capt. USAF, 1968-70. Fellow ACOG, Fla. Ob-Gyn. Soc.; mem. AMA, Am. Cancer Soc. (life, bd. dirs. Collier unit 1973-93, bd. dirs. Fla. div. 1976-91, pres. 1986-87, St. George medal 1990), Fla. Med. Assn., Collier County Med. Soc. (exec. com. 1989-94, pres.-elect 1991-92, pres. 1992-93). Republican. Presbyterian. Avocations: scuba diving, flying, golf, skiing, fishing. Personal E-mail: tggahagan@cs.com. *The secret to my enjoyment of life has been keeping my priorities in order.*

GAHALA, ESTELLA MARIE, writer, consultant; b. Alva, Okla., Mar. 28, 1929; d. Ivan Grant Crouse and Margaret Estella Beck; m. Dale Lowell Lange, Apr. 18, 1998; m. John W. Gahala, Nov. 27, 1964 (dec. Aug. 1, 1989). BA magna cum laude, Wichita (Kans.) State U., 1953; MA, Middlebury (Vt.) Coll., 1963; PhD, Northwestern U., 1980. Tchr. Highland Pk. HS, Topeka, 1953—57, Amarillo (Tex.) HS, 1957—60, Glenbrook North HS, Northbrook, Ill., 1960—64; dept. chmn. Evanston (Ill.) Township HS, 1964—73; dir. curriculum Lyons Township HS, LaGrange, Ill., 1973—84; author, cons. Scott Foresman Pub., Glenview, Ill., 1984—94, McDougal Littell Pub., Boston, 1994—. Pres. Gahala Assocs., Pk. Ridge, Ill., 1980—96. Author: Son et Sens, 1984, Dis-moi, 1993, En Español, 2004; contbr. articles to profl. jours. Chpt. pres. Am. Assn. Tchrs. French, 1970—72, mem. exec. coun., 1976—81; vol. Albuquerque (N.Mex.) Mus. Art, 1987—2003, Presbyn. Hospice Care, Albuquerque, 1991—2003. Named Chevalier Palmes Académiques, French Ministry Edn., 1975. Mem.: Am. Coun. Fgn. Langs. Democrat. Avocations: art, genealogy, working with homeless and abused women. Home and Office: 2315 Madre Drive NE Albuquerque NM 87112 E-mail: egahala@aol.com.

GAHAM, JAMES HERBERT, retired dermatologist; b. Calexico, Calif., Apr. 25, 1921; s. August K. and Esther (Choudoin) G.; m. Anna Kathryn Luiken, June 30, 1950 (dec. May 1987); children: James Herbert, John A., Angela Joann; m. Gloria Boyd Flippin, July 29, 1989. Student, Brawley Jr. Coll., 1941-42; AB, Emory U., 1945; MD, Med. Coll. Ala., 1949. Diplomate: Am. Bd. Dermatology (dir. 1977-87, v.p. 1985-86, pres. 1986-87, Disting. Service medal 1987); diplomate in dermatopathology Am. Bd. Dermatology and Am. Bd. Pathology. Intern Jefferson-Hillman Hosp., Birmingham, Ala., 1949-50; resident in dermatology VA Center and UCLA Med. Center, 1953-56; clin. asst. instr. in medicine UCLA, 1954-56; Osborne fellow and NRC fellow in dermal pathology Armed Forces Inst. Pathology, Washington, 1956-58, vis. scientist, 1958-69, chmn. dept. dermatopathology, 1980-88; registrar Registry of Dermatopathology, Armed Forces Inst. Pathology, 1980-88, also program dir. dermatopathology, 1979-88; program dir. dermatopathology Walter Reed Army Med. Center, Washington, 1979-88; asst. prof. dermatology and pathology Temple U., 1958-61, assoc. prof., 1961-65, prof. dermatology, 1965-69, assoc. prof. pathology, 1965-67, prof. pathology, 1967-69; prof. medicine, chief div. dermatology, prof. pathology, dir. sect. dermal pathology and histochemistry U. Calif., Irvine, 1969-78; chief dermatology U. Calif. Med. Ctr., Irvine, 1977-78; prof. emeritus Coll. Medicine, U. Calif., 1978—; head sect. dermatology Orange County (Calif.) Med. Center, 1969-73; cons. dermatology VA Hosp., Long Beach, Calif., 1969-73, chief dermatology sect., 1973-78, acting chief med. service, 1976; cons. dermatology, dermal pathology Regional Naval Med. Center, San Diego, 1969-82, Long Beach, 1969-78, Camp Pendleton, Calif., 1972-78, Meml. Hosp. Med. Center, Long Beach, 1972-86, Fairview State Hosp., Costa Mesa, Calif., 1969-78; cons. for career devel. for rev. clin. investigator applications VA Central Office, Washington, 1973-78; Disting. Eminent physician VA physician and dentist-in-residence program, 1980-88; mem. organizational com. Am. Registry Pathology, Armed Forces Inst. Pathology, Washington, 1976-77, mem. exec. com., 1977-78; prof. dermatology, clin. prof. pathology Uniformed Services U. of Health Scis., Bethesda, Md., 1979-88, prof. emeritus, 1989—; program dir. dermatopathology Naval Hosp. and Scripps Clin. and Rsch. Found., San Diego, 1991-94; head divsn. dermatopathology, dept. pathology Scripps Clinic and Rsch. Found., LaJolla, Calif., 1988-94, ret., 1994. Sr. author: Dermal Pathology, 1972; contbr. articles to profl. publs. Served with M.C. USNR, 1949-53. Named Disting. Alumnus, Med. Coll. Ala., 1994; recipient ASDP 3d ann. Walter R. Nickel Award for Excellence in Teaching of Dermatopathology, Hilton La Jolla (Calif.) Torrey Pines Hotel, 1999. Mem. AMA (accreditation coun. for grad. med. edn., 1977-87, residency rev. com. for dermatology 1977-87, chmn. 1984-87, cert. of merit 1960), Soc. Investigative Dermatology (life), U.S. and Can. Acad. Pathology (life), Am. Soc. Investigative Pathology (life, emeritus mem. 1995), Am. Dermatol. Assn. (hon., v.p. 1986-87, Essay award 1958), Am. Soc. Dermatopathology (hon., pres. 1975-76, Founder's award 1990, rep. to bd. of mem. Am. Registry Pathology 1988-92), Dermatopathology Club (pres. 1980-81), Assn. Mil. Dermatologists (life), Am. Acad. Dermatology (life, dir. 1974-77, 82, v.p. 1980-81, rep. to bd. mems. Am. Registry Pathology 1977-78, hon. mem. San Francisco 2000), N.Am. Clin. Dermatologic Soc. (hon.), 1973, Pa. Acad. Dermatology, Pacific Dermatol. Assn. (dir. 1972-75, hon. mem. 1981), Dermatology Found. (Leader's Soc. and Annenberg Circle), Washington Dermatol. Soc. (spl. hon.), Phila. Dermatol. Soc. (pres. 1967-68, hon mem. 1994), San Diego Dermatol. Soc., Cutaneous Therapy Soc., Cosmos Club, Alpha Omega Alpha. *I have achieved far more than I dreamed possible but it could only happen in America. Being generally optimistic, enthusiastic and persistent has resulted in my serving society in a positive way.*

GAHAN, BRIAN C., petroleum engineer, chemical engineer, research scientist, business developer; b. Sandwich, Ill., Sept. 18, 1962; s. Joe Eugene and Judith Lynn Gahan; m. Cindy Ann Scholl, July 5, 1997; children: Liam Curtis, Ethan Riley, Megan Catherine. BSc in Petroleum Engring., Marietta Coll., 1984; MBA in Fin., Katz Grad. Sch. of Bus., U. Pitts., 1985; M in Chem. Engring., Armour Coll. of Engring. and Sci., Ill. Inst. Tech., 2002. Lic. profl. engr., Ohio, Ill., 2003. Technician Amerada Hess, Newburg, ND, 1982; engr. Conoco, New Orleans, 1983; petroleum engring. officer Pitts. Nat. Bank (now PNC Bank), 1985—91; mgr. engring. and tech. devel. Gas Tech. Inst., Des Plaines, Ill., 1991—; owner Enterprise Aviation. Mem.: AIAA, Am. Mensa, Inc., Exptl. Aircraft Assn., Internat. Soc. Optical Engring., Laser Inst. Am., Am. Assn. Petroleum Geologists, Am. Inst. Chem. Engrs. (sec., Chgo. sect. 2002—03, treas. Chgo. sect. 2003—04, program chair 2004—05, chair elect 2005—06), Soc. Petroleum Engrs. (dir. Pitts. sect. 1990—91, chair 1989—90, program chair 1988—89, treas. 1987—88, tech. com. drilling 1997—2000, 2002—05), Aircraft Owners and Pilots Assn., Am. Mensa, Inc, Pi Epsilon Tau (sec., treas. 1983—84), Kappa Mu Epsilon, Sigma Xi, Lambda Chi Alpha. Republican. Roman Catholic. Avocations: private pilot, history, baseball. Office: Gas Tech Inst 1700 South Mt Prospect Rd Des Plaines IL 60018 Office Phone: 847-768-0931. Business E-Mail: bgahan@alumni.pitt.edu. E-mail: brian.gahan@gastechnology.org.

GAIHA, VISHNU DAS, cardiologist; b. New Delhi, May 2, 1945; arrived in U.S., 1969; MBBS, All India Inst. Med. Scis., 1968. Diplomate Am. Bd. Internal Medicine, Am. Bd. Cardiology, bd. cert. Am. Bd. Interventional Cardiology, 2002. Intern Albert Einstein Med. Ctr., Phila., 1969-70; resident internal medicine Northwestern U. Med. Ctr., Chgo., 1970-72; fellow cardiologist U. Mich. Hosps., Ann Arbor, 1972-74; attending physician active cons. St. Francis Hosp., Evanston, Ill., 1974—. Attending physician, cons. Swedish Covenant Hosp., Rush N. Shore Hosp., 1974—, Evanston Hosp., 2000—. Fellow Am. Coll. Cardiologists (cert.), Am. Coll. Chest Physicians, Soc. Internat. Cardiology. Office: 800 Austin St Ste 602 Evanston IL 60202-3446 Fax: 847-491-0949. Office Phone: 847-491-1977. E-mail: vgaiha100@hotmail.com.

GAIL, MITCHELL H., science foundation executive; b. Lexington, Ky., July 10, 1941; married. BA magna cum laude, Harvard U., 1962, MD cum laude, 1968; MS in Math. Statistics, George Washington U., 1973, PhD in Math. Statistics, 1977. Rsch. dept. biochemistry Harvard U. Sch. Medicne, Boston, 1964-65; Knox fellow Cambridge (Eng.) U., 1962-63; intern Beter Bent Brigham Hosp., Boston, 1968-69; rsch. assoc. in cell biology NIH, Nat. Cancer Inst., 1969-72; rschr. lab. for computer scis. Mass. Gen. Hosp., Boston, 1968; med. statis. investigator clin. and diagnostic trials sect. NIH, Nat. Cancer Inst., 1972-85, head epidemiol. methods sect., 1985—, chief biostatistics br. divsn. cancer etiology, 1994-95, chief biostatistics br. divsn. cancer epidemiology/genetics, 1995—. Chmn. adv. com. to editors of Jour. of Controlled Clin. Trials, 1989, mem. editorial bd. 1987-94; vis. lectr. U. Pitts., 1991; vis. prof. internal medicine, U. Va., 1989; adj. prof. dept. biostatistics, Johns Hopkins U., 1988—; mem. external adv. bd. to Ctr. for AIDS Rsch., U. Wash., 1989-93; mem. adv. bd. biostatistics dept. Harvard U., Sch. Pub. Health, 1995; Charles Odoroff Meml. lectr., U. Rochester, 1996. Mem. editorial bd. Jour. AIDS, 1988—; contbr. articles to profl. jours. Recipient Spiegelman Gold medal for health statistics, Snedocor award for applied statis. rsch., Howard Temin award for AIDS rsch. Fellow AAAS, Am. Statis. Assn. (chmn. biostatistiacs sect. 1986, bd. dirs. 1994-96, former pres.); mem. Internat. Statis. Inst., Am. Soc. for Clin. Investigation. Soc. for Clin. Trials (chmn. program com. 1981, bd. dirs. 1981-85), Soc. for Epidemiol. Rsch., Biometric Soc. (regional adv. bd. 1981-84), Washington Statistical Soc. (chmn. biostatistics program 1982), Internat. Statis. Inst., Internat. Chinese Statis. Assn. (hon.), NAS, Inst. of Medicine. Phi Beta Kappa. Office: Divsn of Cancer Epidemiology and Genetic 6120 Executive Plaza South # 8032 Rockville MD 20852-4909 Office Phone: 301-496-4156. Office Fax: 301-402-0081. Business E-Mail: gailm@mail.nih.gov.

GAILEY, DOUGLAS MITCHELL, music educator; b. Salt Lake City, June 22, 1958; s. Myron Vern and Lois Belle Gailey; m. Jolene Dalton, July 18, 1987; children: Joshua Dalton, Justin Douglas. BA, U. Wash., 1984; MusM, U. Utah, 1986. Cert. tchr. Wash., 1991. Music educator Bingham H.S., South Jordan, Utah, 1986—91, Port Angeles H.S., Wash., 1991—. Named Rookie of Yr., Utah Music Educators Assn., 1986—87; recipient Disting. Band Dir. award, Am. Sch. Band Dirs. Assn., 1998. Mem.: North Olympic Music Educators Assn. (pres. 2003, 2004—), Wash. Music Educations Assn. (assoc.; North Olympic pres. 1994—96). Non-Partisan. Avocations: fishing, backpacking, skiing. Home: 173 Alice Rd Port Angeles WA 98363 Office: Port Angeles High Sch 304 E Park Ave Port Angeles WA 98362 Office Phone: 360-565-1536. E-mail: doug_gailey@pasd.wednet.edu.

GAILEY, JOAN DALE, retired finance educator; b. Beaver Falls, Pa., May 10, 1940; d. Irvin D. and Elizabeth Jane (Hollander) Anderson; m. Ronald L. Gailey, Aug. 15, 1957; 1 child, Ronald. BSBA, Geneva Coll., 1975; MBA, Youngstown State U., 1980; PhD, U. Pitts., 1987. Libr. tech. Community Coll. Beaver County, Monaca, Pa., 1969-74; customer liaison, floor supr. LTV Steel, Aliquippa, Pa., 1975-79; instr. Youngstown (Ohio) State U., 1980-83; asst. prof. bus. mgmt. Kent State U., East Liverpool, Ohio, 1984-91, assoc. prof. bus. mgmt., 1992—, prof. bus. mgmt., 1998—, prof. Trumbull campus Warren, Ohio, 2001—02, prof. East Liverpool campus, 2003, prof. emeritus, 2003. Cons. in bus. mgmt., 1988—; dir. Kent State East Liverpool Bus. Resource Ctr. Abstract editor Interface, 1994, 95, 96, 97, proceedings editor, 1998; co-editor: Humanities and Technology Rev., 1999—; contbr. articles to profl. jours. Mem. Rochester (Pa.) Area Planning Commn., 1989, Rochester Area Mktg. Com., 1990; tutor Adult Lit. Coun., Monaca, 1984-91; mem. adv. bd. Ret. Sr. Vol. Program, Lisbon, Ohio, 1990, vice chair, 1993-2000, facilitator Columbiana County Mini-Loan Fund, 1994-96. Recipient Kent State Teaching Devel. award, 1990, Kent State Profl. Devel. award, 1992; tchg. coun. grantee Kent State U., 1997-98, Summer award Univ. Tchg. Coun., 1999. Mem. Am. Edn. Rsch. Assn. (editor newsletter 1993-94, program chair 1992), Nat. Assn. Indsl. Tech., Midwest MLA, Ohio Bus. Tchrs. Assn., Humanities and Tech. Assn. (exec. bd. dirs. 1997—), Assn. for Bus. Comm., Alpha Mu (Outstanding Mktg. Tchr. 1983). Office: Kent State U East Liverpool OH

GAILEY, THOMAS CHANDLER (CHAN), JR., college football coach; b. Gainesville, Ga., Jan. 5, 1952; m. Laurie Gailey; 2 children. BS in Phys. Edn., U. Fla., 1974. Grad. asst. U. Fla., 1974-75; defensive backfield coach Troy State U., 1976-79, head coach, 1983-84; defensive backfield coach Air Force, 1979-82; asst. coach Denver Broncos, NFL, 1989-90, offensive coord., wide receivers coach, 1989-90; head coach Birmingham Fire, WFL, 1991-92, Samford U., 1993; wide receivers coach Pitts. Steelers, NFL, 1994-95, offensive coord., 1996-98; coach Dallas Cowboys, 1998-99; offensive coord. Miami Dolphins, 2000—01; head coach Ga. Tech., 2002—. Office: Georgia Tech Athletic Assn 150 Bobby Dodd Way NW Atlanta GA 30332-0455

GAILIUS, GILBERT KEISTUTIS, manufacturing executive; b. Boston, June 21, 1931; s. Joseph B. and Mary K. Gailius; m. Lillian P. Romanskis, Sept. 6, 1954; children: Gregory, Laura, Louise, Gilbert, Linda, Gary. BS in Bus. Adminstrn., Suffolk U., 1958; MBA, Boston Coll., 1962. Plant controller, staff asst. corp. controller Continental Group, N.Y.C., 1954-66; v.p. fin. Foster Grant Co., Inc., Leominster, Mass., 1966-77, Midland Glass Co., Cliffwood, N.J., 1977-78, Am. Biltrite Inc., Wellesley Hills, Mass., 1978—99, v.p. strategic planning, 2001, now bd. dirs. Also bd. dirs. Served with U.S. Army, 1952-54. Mem. Fin. Execs. Inst. Office: Am Biltrite Inc 57 River St Wellesley MA 02481-2013

GAILLARD, GEORGE SIDAY, III, architect; b. Miami, Fla., Apr. 24, 1941; s. George Siday and Sarah Margaret (Crawford) G.; m. Charlalee Bailey, 1965 (div. 1969); m. Sylvia Gayle Bridgewater, July 18, 1977; 1 child, Barron Matthew. BS, Ga. Inst. Tech., 1965; postgrad., Ga. State U. Registered architect Ga. Sole propr. Fox Magnanimus, Atlanta, 1971—78, Gaillard & Assocs., Atlanta, 1978—81, 1983—2004; mgr. design dept. Deca Inc., Miami, 1982, ret., 2004; prin., owner GIII Enterprises, 2005—. Sculpture exhibited in group shows at Piedmont Arts Festival, 1971, 73. Cubmaster Cub Scouts Am., Stone Mountain, Ga., 1988-89. With USMCR, 1962-68. Mem. AIA (chmn. liaison com. So. Coll. Tech. for Atlanta chpt. 1989-90), Huguenot Soc. S.C., Clan Lindsay Assn. U.S.A. Inc. (Ga. rep. 1989-95), St. Andrew's Soc. Atlanta (bd. dirs. 1996-98, interim v.p. 2002), Clan Gun Soc. N.Am. Avocations: reading, camping, constructing and competing with blackpowder rifles.

GAILLARD, MARY KATHARINE, physicist, educator; b. New Brunswick, N.J., Apr. 1, 1939; d. Philip Lee and Marion Catharine (Wiedemayer) Ralph; children: Alain, Dominique, Bruno. BA, Hollins (Va.) Coll., 1960; MA, Columbia U., 1961; Dr du Troiseme Cycle, U. Paris, Orsay, France, 1964, Dr-es-Sciences d'Etat, 1968. With Ctr. Nat. Rsch. Sci., Orsay and Annecy-le-Vieux, France, 1964-84, head rsch. Orsay, 1973-80, Annecy-le-Vieux, 1979-80, dir. rsch., 1980-84; prof. physics, sr. faculty staff Lawrence Berkeley lab. U. Calif., Berkeley, 1981—. Morris Loeb lectr. Harvard U., Cambridge, Mass., 1980; Chancellor's Disting. lectr., U. Calif., Berkeley, 1981; Warner-Lambert lectr. U. Mich., Ann Arbor, 1984; vis. scientist Fermi Nat. Accelerator Lab., Batavia, Ill., 1973-74, Inst. for Advanced Studies, Santa Barbara, Calif., 1984, U. Calif., Santa Barbara, 1985; group leader L.A.P.P., Theory Group, France, 1979-81, Theory Physics div. LBL, Berkeley, 1985-87; sci. dir. Les Houches (France) Summer Sch., 1981; cons., mem. adv. panels U.S. Dept. Energy, Washington; cons. Nat. Sci. Bd., 1996-97, 2002, bd. dirs., 1997-2002. Co-editor: Weak Interactions, 1977, Gauge Theories in High Energy Physics, 1983; contr. articles to profl. jours. Recipient Thibaux prize U. Lyons (France) Acad. Art and Sci., 1977, E.O. Lawrence award, 1988, J.J. Sakurai prize for theoretical particle physics, APS, 1993; Guggenheim fellow, 1989-90. Fellow Am. Acad. Arts and Scis., Am. Phys. Soc. (mem. various coms., chair com. on women, J.J. Saburai prize 1993); mem. AAAS, NAS, Am. Philos. Soc. Office: U Calif Dept Physics Berkeley CA 94720-0001

GAINER, AARON, systems analyst; s. Richard and Gwen Gainer. BSN, Tex. Woman's U.; MS in Health Informatics, U. Tex. RN Tex., 1996. Nurse The Meth. Hosp., Houston, nurse educator, sys. analyst, 2002—. Mem.: Sigma Theta Tau (assoc.). Office: The Methodist Hospital 6565 Fannin MS stb2-02 Houston TX 77030 Office Phone: 281-300-8744. Personal E-mail: againer@iwon.com.

GAINER, RONALD LEE, lawyer; b. Lansing, Mich., Aug. 7, 1934; s. Asher Leroy and Gladys Irene (Harvey) G.; m. Alice Louise Sherwood, June 15, 1957; children— Gregory Sherwood, Geoffrey Scott. BA, Mich. State U., 1956; JD, U. Mich., 1959. Bar: N.Y. 1960, D.C. 1963, U.S. Supreme Ct. 1963. Atty. appellate sect., criminal div. Dept. Justice, Washington, 1963-69, dep. chief legis. and spl. projects, 1969-73, chief legis. and spl. projects, 1973-75, dir. Office of Policy and Planning, 1975-77; dep. asst. atty. gen. Office for Improvements in Adminstrn. of Justice, 1977-81, Office of Legal Policy, 1981-83, dep. assoc. atty. gen., 1984-85, assoc. dep. atty. gen., 1985-86, dep. assoc. atty. gen., 1986-89; ptnr. Gainer, Rient and Hotis (and successor Gainer and Rient), Washington, 1990—2002; consulting atty. on internat. criminal fraud, 2003—. U.S. expert mem. UN Com. on Crime Prevention and Control, 1979-92; designated mem. U.S. Sentencing Commn., 1985-88; bd. dirs., mem. adv. com. Internat. Centre Criminal Law Reform and Criminal Justice Policy, 1992—. Editorial bd.: Criminal Law Forum, 1989—. Served to capt. U.S. Ar, 1960-63. Recipient Disting. Svc. award U.S. Atty. Gen., 1973. Mem. Am. Law Inst., Internat. Soc. for Reform of Criminal Law (bd. dirs., mem. mgmt. com., 1989—), Internat. Assn. Prosecutors, Internat. Assn. Penal Law, D.C. Bar Assn., Cosmos Club. Home: 3000 N Monroe St Arlington VA 22207-5371 Office Phone: 202-408-8000. E-mail: rlg@gainer.us.

GAINES, BARRY JOSEPH, English literature educator; b. Chgo., May 4, 1942; s. Gregory and Miriam (Davis) G.; m. Janet Colee Howe, Mar. 15, 1974; children: Gwendolyn Loren, Jason Micah Howe. BA, Rice U., 1965; MA, U. Wis., 1966, PhD, 1970. Prof. English lit. U. Tenn., Knoxville, 1970-79, U. N.Mex., Albuquerque, 1979—. Theater reviewer Albuquerque Jour. Author: (book) Sir Thomas Malory: An Anecdotal Bibliography of Editions, 1990; co-editor: (book) A Yorkshire Tragedy, 1986, Romeo and Juliet, 2000, Antony and Cleopatra, 2001; assoc. editor: Shakespeare Studies, 1974-93; mem. editl. bd.: Medieval and Renaissance Drama in England, 1983—; contbr. articles to lit. jours. Pres. Congregation Albert, Albuquerque, 1989-90. Recipient Disting. Educators award Pub. Svc. Co. of N.Mex. Found., 1992; Fulbright-Hays exch. scholar, 1987. Mem. MLA (chair del. assembly steering com. 1984-85), Shakespeare Assn. Am. (various offices), Phi Eta Sigma (Excellence in Tchg. award 1975), Phi Kappa Phi (hon., pres. 1997-98). Jewish. Home: 12809 Northern Sky Ave NE Albuquerque NM 87111-8089 Office: U NMex Dept English Albuquerque NM 87131-0001 E-mail: bjgaines@unm.edu.

GAINES, BENNETT L., utilities executive; married; 1 child. BA in Socioecons., Baldwin-Wallace Coll.; MBA, U. Phoenix. With IBM Corp., Minn., Ariz., Ky., NY and Asia, 1978—91; regional sales mgr., dir. mktg. Hamilton-Hallmark Corp., Phila. and Phoenix, 1991—94; v.p. consumer ops. McKesson, Dallas, 1994—98; corp. dir. strategic sourcing EDS Corp., Dallas, 1998—2000; corp. dir. supply and operating svc. LT&E Energy Corp., Louisville, 2000—01; with Cinergy Corp., Cin., 2001—, v.p., chief tech. officer, 2003—. Bd. dirs. Family and Children's Counseling Ctr., Louisville; rep. corp. contbns. United Way; bd. dirs. Am. Sports Inst., Mill Valley, Calif. Office: Cinergy Corp 139 E 4th St Cincinnati OH 45202

GAINES, BOYD, actor; b. Atlanta, May 11, 1953; Diploma, Julliard Sch. Performances include (stage) Spring Awakening, 1978, Oliver Oliver, 1984, The Double Bass, 1985, The Heidi Chronicles, 1988, Philadelphia, Here I Come!, 1988, She Loves Me, 1993 (Antoinette Perry award for leading actor in a musical 1994) (film) Fame, 1980, Porky's, 1982, The Sure Thing, 1985, Heartbreak Ridge, 1986, Call Me, 1988, Ray's Male Heterosexual Dance Hall, 1988, The Grass Harp, 1995, I'm Not Rappaport, 1996, (TV) One Day at a Time, 1981-84, Evergreen, 1985, Remington Steele, 1985, LA Law, 1986, Hotel, 1984, 1985, & 1986, Spenser: For Hire, 1988, Pidgeon Feathers, 1988, The Days and Nights of Molly Dodd, 1989, Piece of Cake, 1990, A Woman Named Jackie, 1991, Anything But Love, 1992, Murder She Wrote, 1992, Law & Order, 1993, 1995, & 1997, Frasier, 1994, Caroline in the City, 1997, Remember WENN, 1997, The Education of Max Bickford, 2001 & 2002, 100 Centre Street, 2001 & 2002, Queens Supreme, 2003; reader for audio books.

GAINES, BRENDA, retired financial services company executive; b. Chicago, 1949; Formerly with U.S. Dept. Housing & Urban Develop., Chgo.; former head Chgo. Housing Authority; dep. chief staff Office of Mayor, Harold Washington, Chgo., 1985—87; advanced through co. in govt. and cmty. rels. to sr. v.p. residential lending Citibank, Chgo., 1988—92; sr. v.p. Diners Club N.Am. (subsidiary of Citigroup), Chgo., 1992—99; pres. Diners Club N.Am., Chgo., 1999—2004. Mem. Diners Club Internat. Global bd.; bd. dirs. CNA Financial. Named one of 50 Most Powerful Black Executives in Am., Fortune, 2002, Chicago's 100 Most Influential Women, Crain's Chicago Business, 2004.

GAINES, CHERIE ADELAIDE, lawyer; b. Queens, N.Y., May 17, 1935; d. Charles Oscar and Billie (Robinson) Gaines; m. Eugene Merwyn Swann, Apr. 15, 1960 (div. Oct. 1978); children— Liana Jane, Eugene Michael, Elliott Mark. B.A., Barnard Coll., 1956; J.D., U. Pa., 1960. Bar: Calif. 1963, N.Y. 1981. Assoc. prof. law Golden Gate U., San Francisco, 1970-71; city atty. Berkeley, Calif., 1971; asst. prof. law U. San Francisco Law Sch., 1971-73; asst. regional atty. EEOC, San Francisco, 1973-79, regional atty., N.Y.C., 1979-81; dep. gen. counsel N.Y.C. Housing Authority, 1981-88; exec. dir. Bedford Stuyvesant Cmty. Legal Svcs., Bklyn., 1988-2001, The Ctr. for Jewish-Christian-Muslim Understanding, Inc., Irvington, N.Y., 2002—; practice law, San Francisco, 1963-65; chief atty. Alameda County Legal Aid Soc., Oakland, Calif., 1965-70; asst. to asst. regional adminstr. HUD, San Francisco, 1970. Founder, Phoenix Elem. Sch., Berkeley, 1969. rep. World Assembly of Youth, UN Commn. on the Status of Women, 1955; bd. dirs., treas., chmn. mgmt. com. Consumers Coop., Berkeley, 1972-76; bd. dirs. ACLU Berkeley-Albany chpt., Berkeley, 1968, San Francisco Regional Council, Berkeley, 1978. Recipient Commendation plaque Alameda Affirmative Action Com., 1971, Alameda County Human Relations Commn., 1973, Assn. Real Property Brokers, 1975. Mem. Calif. State Bar (commn. of profl. competence 1973-76, med. malpractice commn. 1972), N.Y. State Bar, Charles Houston Law Club (v.p. 1979). Episcopalian. E-mail: moimeme@att.net.

GAINES, FRANCIS PENDLETON, III, judge; b. Lexington, Va., Sept. 24, 1944; s. Francis Pendleton Jr. and Dorothy Ruth (Bloomhardt) G.; m. Mary Chilton, Dec. 19, 1967 (div. Aug. 1992); children: Elizabeth Chilton, Edmund Pendleton, Andrew Cavett. Grad., Woodberry Forest Sch., Va., 1962; BA in Hist., U. Ariz., 1967; LLB, U. Va., 1969. Bar: U.S. Dist. Ct. (Ariz.) 1969, Ariz. 1969, U.S. Ct. Appeals (9th cir.) 1972, U.S. Supreme Ct. 1975. Assoc. Evans, Kitchel & Jenckes, Phoenix, 1969-75, ptnr., 1975-89, Fennemore Craig, Phoenix, 1989-99; judge Superior Ct. of Ariz., Phoenix, 1999—; assoc. presiding civil judge Maricopa County Superior Ct., 2001—05, Maricopa County Complex Civil Litigation Ct., 2003—. Panel arbitrators N.Y. Stock Exch., 1984-99, NASD, 1984-99; judge pro tem Ariz. Ct. Appeals, 1994-95, Maricopa County (Ariz.) Superior Ct., 1994-99; mem. State Bar Disciplinary Hearing Com., 1991-94, chair, 1995-97; mem. nat. litig. panel U. Va. Sch. Law; mem. Ariz. Commn. on Judicial Performance Review, 2001—; lectr. and panelist CLE programs. Author: Punitive Damages-A Railroad Trial Lawyers Guide, 1985. Chmn. bd. govs. All Saints' Day Sch., Phoenix, 1990—91; sr. warden All Saints' Episcopal Ch., 1994—97, parish chancellor, 1997—99, diversity preceptor, 1999—2003; standing com. Episcopal Diocese of Ariz., 1997—2001. Recipient Outstanding Alumnus award, U. Az., 2002. Fellow: Ariz. Bar Found., Am. Bar Found.; mem.: ABA, Nat. Conf. State Trial Judges (coms. on jury mgmt. and bus. and comml. cts.), Securities Industry Assn., Nat. Assn. R.R. Trial Counsel (exec. com. Pacific Region, v.p. 1997—98), Maricopa County Bar Assn., State Bar Ariz. (civil practice and procedure com. 2000—, professionalism course oversight com. 2001—), U. Ariz. Pres.'s Club, Univ. Club. Republican. Episcopalian. Office: Superior Ct Ariz 201 W Jefferson St Phoenix AZ 85003-2205 Office Phone: 602-506-3940. Business E-Mail: pgaines@superiorcourt.maricopa.gov.

GAINES, IRVING DAVID, lawyer; b. Milw., Oct. 14, 1923; s. Harry and Anna (Finkelman) Ginsburg; m. Ruth Rudolph, May 22, 1947 (dec. Apr. 5, 1979); children: Jeffrey S., Howard R., Mindy S. Gaines Pearce; m. Lois Shier, Nov. 25, 1979. BA, U. Wis., Madison, 1943; JD, 1947; postgrad., U. Pa., 1943-44. Bar: Wis. 1947, U.S. Dist. Ct. (ea. dist.) Wis. 1947, U.S. Supreme Ct. 1954, U.S. Ct. Appeals (7th cir.) 1954, U.S. Dist. Ct. (we. dist.) Wis. 1970, Fla. 1971, U.S. Dist. Ct. (so. dist.) Fla. 1972, U.S. Dist. Ct. (mid. dist.) Fla. 1976, U.S. Ct. Appeals (11th cir.) 1981. Pvt. practice, Milw., 1947—72; ptnr. Gaines & Saichek, S.C. (and predecessor firm), Milw., 1972-78; sr. ptnr. Gaines Law Offices, S.C., Milw., 1979—. Arbitrator N.Y. Stock Exch., 1988—, Nat. Assn. Securities Dealers, 1988—, Am. Stock Exch., 1988—; mediator Wis. Ct. of Appeals, Dist. I. Contbr. articles to profl. jours. Bd. vis. U. Wis. Law Sch., 1987—96, Milw. County Cir. Ct. Commn., 1997—2005. Served with U.S. Army, 1943—46. Mem.: ATLA (state committeeman 1981—83, lectr.), ABA (com. current lit. on real property law, com. law and medicine negligence sect., various coms. title ins. litig. and real estate), Bar Assn. U.S. Ea. Dist. of Wis., Am. Arbitration Assn. (arbitrator 1966—, nat. panel arbitrators), Milw. Bar Assn. (exec. com. 1974—77, cts. com., econs. of law com., past chmn. unauthorized practice of law com., past chmn. negligence sect., lectr. programs, seminars, bench-bar com., appellate bench bar com.-civil), Wis. Acad. Trial Lawyers (pres. 1958—59, 1970—71, lectr.), 7th Fed. Cir. Bar Assn., State Bar Assn. Wis. (bd. govs. 1982—85, publs. com. 1982—91, past com. ethics, rsch. planning and earlier settlement coms., lectr. CLE seminars, convs., dist. com. state bd. lawyer regulation 2003—), Fla. Bar Assn. (bd. editors Fla. Bar Jour. 1972—84). Office: 312 E Wisconsin Ave Ste 208 Milwaukee WI 53202-4305 Home: 1600 W Green Tree Rd Apt 218 Milwaukee WI 53209 Office Phone: 414-271-1938.

GAINES, JAMES EDWIN, JR., retired librarian; b. Dalton, Ga., Feb. 21, 1938; s. James Edwin and Olivia (McCarty) Gaines; m. Sally Martin, Nov. 27, 1965 (div. May 1985); children: Thomas Martin, Robin Jeannette, Steven McCarty; m. Elizabeth Hood, July 28, 1990. AB, Emory U., 1961, MLS, 1964; PhD, Fla. State U., 1977. Tchr. English Marist Coll. H.S., Atlanta, 1961-62; grad. library asst. Emory U., Atlanta, 1962-64; asst. to head of pub. services U. Cin., 1964-65; asst. cataloger Antioch Coll., Yellow Springs, Ohio, 1965-68; dir. library Birmingham-So. Coll., Birmingham, Ala., 1968-74; head librarian Va. Mil. Inst., Lexington, 1976-93; ret., 1994. Contbr. Mem. Com. on Fgn. Rels., Charlottesville, Va., 1982—91; sec. ARC, Rockbridge County, Va., 1993—98, Rockbridge Disability Svcs. Bd., 1993—. Mem.: ALA, Va. Libr. Assn. (chmn. coll. and univ. sect. 1979—80), So. Assn. Colls. and Schs. (vis. committeeman 1979—89), Kiwanis (sec. 1985—92, 1999—2001, v.p. 2001—02, pres. 2002—03, sec. 2003—04). Democrat. Presbyterian. Home: 9 Edmondson Ave Lexington VA 24450-1903 E-mail: jegaines@rockbridge.net.

GAINES, JERRY LEE, retired secondary school educator; b. Seminole, Okla., Feb. 18, 1940; s. Frank Gaines and Jane M. (Crowe) Gring; m. Lorraine Louise Paulson, Oct. 7, 1961; children: Paul Martin, Mark Edwin. AA, Pasadena City Coll., 1960; BA, Calif. State U., L.A., 1964; MA, Calif. State U., Long Beach, 1969. Tchr. bus. Rolling Hills High Sch., Rolling Hills Estates, Calif., 1965-91, Palos Verdes Peninsula High Sch., Rolling Hills Estates, 1991—2002. Coord. driver edn. Palos Verdes Peninsula Unified Sch. Dist., Palos Verdes Estates, Calif., 1970-91, mentor tchr., 1984-93. Co-author driver edn. workbook; contbr. articles to traffic safety publs. Chmn. San Pedro (Calif.) Citizens Adv. Com., 1985-88; pres. South Shores Homeowners Assn., San Pedro, 1986-90, 95-96, San Pedro and Peninsula Homeowners Coalition, 1990-93; commr. City of L.A. Charter Reform Commn., 1997-99, City of L.A. Planning Commn., 2000-02; County of L.A. Workforce Investment Bd., 2002—; bd. dirs. South Bay Credit Union, 1997—. With USN, 1960-62. Mem. NEA, Calif. Tchrs. Assn., Nat. Bus. Edn. Assn., Calif. Bus. Edn. Assn., Am. Driver and Traffic Safety Edn. Assn. (bd. dirs. 1982-88), Calif. Assn. Safety Edn. (pres. 1982-83, 1998-2000), Elks, Lions, Phi Delta Kappa. Avocations: travel, model railroading. Home: 2101 W 37th St San Pedro CA 90732-4707 Personal E-mail: jgaines852@aol.com.

GAINES, LA DONNA ADRIAN See SUMMER, DONNA

GAINES, RALPH DEWAR, JR., lawyer, farmer; b. Cartersville, Ga., July 10, 1925; s. Ralph Dewar Gaines and Bessis Ellen Shaw; m. Mary Sue Pafford, July 21, 1951; children: Ralph Dewar III, Charles P., Mary Susannah, Priscilla Shaw, L. Shaw. BBA, Tulane U., 1946; JD, U. Ala. Sch. Law, 1949. Bar: Ala. 1949, U. S. Dist. Ct. (no. dist.) Ala. 1958, U. S. Supreme Ct. 1978. Sr. ptnr. Gaines, Gaines and Rasco P.C., Talladega, Ala., 1949—. Pres. Talladega County Bar Assn., 1973, Ala. Def. Lawyers Assn., 1973-74; moderator, spkr. Ala. Civil Justice Reform Com., 1986-87; chmn. Farrah Law Soc. U. Ala., 1990-92; pres. Law Sch. Alumni Assn. U. Ala., 1994. Pres. Talladega Kiwanis Club, 1954, Talladega C. of C., 1959, Talladega United Fund, 1963. Lt. USN, 1943-46. Fellow ABA, Am. Coll. Trial Lawyers, Ala. Law Found. Democrat. Baptist. Avocation: raising polled hereford cows. Office: Gaines Gaines and Rasco PC PO Box 275 Talladega AL 35161-0275

GAINES, RUTH ANN, secondary school educator; BA in Drama and Speech, Clarke Coll.; MA in Dramatic Art, U. Calif., Santa Barbara. Tchr. drama East High Sch., Des Moines, 1971—. Host Classroom Connection Cable TV; former TV/radio prodr., talk show host TCI of Ctrl. Iowa, WHO; diversity facilitator Heartland Area Edn. Agy., Des Moines, 1979—; instr. speech and drama Des Moines Area C.C., 1971—. Bd. dirs. Very Spl. Arts, Hospice of Ctrl. Iowa, Westminster Ho.; former bd. dirs. YWCA of Greater Des Moines, Polk County Mental Health Assn., Drama Workshop, Des Moines Tutoring Ctr.; vice chair City Wide Strategic Plan, 1994-95; state senate candidate, 1994; racial justice coord. YWCA, 1992-93; chair Cross Cultural Rels., Des Moines Area Religious Coun., 1988-89; dir. religious edn. St. Ambrose Cathedral, 1981-83; grad. Leadership Iowa Class of 1997. Recipient Wal-Mart Tchr. of Yr., 1998, Iowa Tchr. of Yr., 1998, Angel in Adoption award, 1999, Friends of Iowa Civil Rights Commn. Tchr. of Yr. award, 2000, U. Iowa's Phyllis M. Yeager Commitment to Diversity award, 2001, I'll Make Me a World in Iowa Heritage Legacy, 2002, Des Moines Bus. Records' Woman of Influence, 2002, USA Today's All USA Tchr. Recognition 3d Team, 2002; grad. Greater Des Moines Leadership Inst., 2002; inducted into Nat. Tchr. Hall of Fame, 2003. Mem. Iowa Edn. Assn., Des Moines Edn. Assn., Delta Kappa Gamma, Phi Delta Kappa, Delta Sigma Theta, Delta Kappa Pi. Home: 3501 Oxford St Des Moines IA 50313-4562 Office: East High Sch 815 E 13th St Des Moines IA 50316-3499

GAINES, STEVEN S., writer; Graduate, NYU. Rock and roll music critic NY Daily News. Author: Marjoe: The Life of Marjoe Gortner, 1973, The Club, 1980, Heroes and Villains: The True Story of the Beach Boys, 1986, Simply Halston, 1991, Obsession: The Lives and Times of Calvin Klein, 1994, Philistines at the Hedgerow: Passion and Property in the Hamptons, 1998, The Sky's the Limit: Passion and Property in Manhattan, 2005; co-author: (with Alice Cooper) Me, Alice, 1976, (with Peter Brown) The Love You Make: An Insider's Story of the Beatles, 2002; contbr. editor, NY Mag. Mailing: c/o Author Mail Little Brown & Co 1271 Ave of Americas New York NY 10020*

GAINES, WEAVER HENDERSON, lawyer; b. Ft. Meade, S.D., Aug. 31, 1943; s. Weaver Henderson and Bertha Louise (Harris) G. AB in Philosophy, Dartmouth Coll., 1965; LLB, U. Va., 1968. Bar: N.Y. 1969, Pa. 1979, U.S. Dist. Ct. (so. dist.) N.Y. 1973, U.S. Dist. Ct. (ea. dist.) N.Y. 1975, U.S. Ct. Appeals (2d cir.) 1975. Assoc. Dewey, Ballantine, Bushby, Palmer & Wood, N.Y.C., 1970-79; sr. staff counsel INA Corp., Phila., 1979; asst. gen. counsel, sec. Thyssen-Bornemisza Inc., N.Y.C., 1979-82, v.p. strategic projects, 1982-85; v.p., dep. gen. counsel Mut. of N.Y., N.Y.C., 1985-86, sr. v.p., gen. counsel, 1986-90, exec. v.p., gen. counsel, 1990-92; pres. Unified Mgmt. Corp., 1989-90; chmn. Ixion Biotechnology, Inc., Alachua, Fla., 1993—2005, CEO, 1993—2002; v.p., mng. dir. Americas Biotech Distributor, LLC, 2005—. Bd. dirs. Unified Fin. Svcs., Inc., Voyetra Turtle Beach, Inc., Americas Biotech Distributor, LLC, BIO Fla. Inc., Fla. Rsch. Consortium, Inc., Eagle Pines Acad.; vis. prof. Sch. Law U. Va., 2003—; adv. coun. Keck Grad. Inst. Life Scis. Bd. dirs. N.Y. Lawyers for Nixon, 1972; sr. advisor Bush/Quayle '92. Capt. U.S. Army, 1968-70, Vietnam. Decorated Bronze Star. Mem. ABA, Assn. Bar City N.Y., N.Y. Athletic Club, Haile Plantation Golf and Country Club. Republican. Episcopalian. Office: Americas Biotech Distributors LLC 13709 Progress Blvd Box 28 Alachua FL 32615-9495 Office Phone: 386-462-3961. Personal E-mail: weaver.gaines@worldnet.att.net. Business E-Mail: weaver.gaines@americasbiotech.com.

GAINETDINOV, RAUL RADIKOVICH, pharmacologist, researcher; b. Mishkino, Bashkiria, Russia, Sept. 1, 1964; s. Radik Akhmetovich Gainetdinov and Lilia Masgutovna Gainetdinova; m. Tatyana Dmitrievna Sotnikova; 1 child, Bulat Raulevich. MD, 2-nd Moscow Med. Inst., Russia, 1988; PhD, Inst. of Pharmacology, Moscow, 1992. Sr. rschr. Inst. of Pharmacology, Moscow, 1994—2004; asst. rsch. prof. Duke U., Durham, NC, 2000—. Contbr. chapters to books, articles to profl. jours. Recipient Young Investigator award, Internat. Soc. Neurochemistry, 1993, Investigator award, Tourette Syndrome Inc., 1997. Mem.: NY Acad. of Sci., European Behavioral Pharmacology Soc., Soc. for Neuroscience. Achievements include development of novel pharmacotherapies for schizophrenia, ADHD; patents pending in field; research in cocaine abuse, Parkinson's disease, schizophrenia. Avocations: chess, fishing. Office: Duke Univ CARL Bldg Rm 487 Research Dr Durham NC 27710 Office Fax: 919-681-8641. Business E-Mail: r.gainetdinov@cellbio.duke.edu.

GAINEY, LILAH LEIGH, librarian; b. Lubbock, Tex., Nov. 15, 1950; d. Will Allison and Bertha Beatrice G. B. Music. Edn., Lubbock Christian Coll., 1974; M.Ed., Tex. Tech. U., 1980; M.L.S., Sam Houston State U., 1982. Tchr. Crosbyton Elem. Sch. (Tex.), 1974-78; tchr.Levelland (Tex.) Pub. Schs., 1979-80; grad. teaching asst. Sch. Library Sci., Huntsville, Tex., 1981-82; librarian Abilene Christian U., 1982-95, Ea. N.Mex. U., 1996—. Mem. com. svc. computer and tech. Ea. N.Mex. U., 1997—, scholarship com., 2003—, campus devel. staff com., 2005—, leadership program, 2004-05, profl. senate, 2005—; svc. adv. com. Amigos Lib. Svc., 2000-01; chmn. libr. consortium Llano Estacado Info. Access Network, 1999—; chmn. Reading is Fundamental, 2001-03; coord. Meals on Wheels, 2000—. Contbr. articles to profl. jours. Mem. ALA (Jr. Mems. Roundtable, publicity chmn. 1985-87), Tex. Library Assn. (dist. 1 sec. 1983-84, pres. 1986-87)), Sam Houston Library Sch. Alumni Assn. (v.p. 1982-83, pres. 1983-84) AAUW, Ea. N.Mex. U. Women (pres. 2005—), N.Mex. Libr. Assn. (membership com., presenter), Delta Kappa Gamma. Office Phone: 505-562-2640. Business E-Mail: lilah.gainey@enmu.edu.

GAINEY, ROBERT MICHAEL, professional hockey coach, former player; b. Peterborough, Ont., Can., Dec. 13, 1953; Hockey player Montreal Canadiens, 1973-89; coach, player Les Ecureuils, Epinal, France; head coach, gen. mgr. Minn. North Stars, NHL, 1990-96; coach Dallas Stars, 1993—96, v.p., gen. mgr., 1996—2001, consultant, 2002; exec. v.p., gen. mgr. Montreal Canadiens, 2003—. Recipient Frank J. Selke award as Best Defensive Forward, 1977-78, 78-79, 79-80; Conn Smythe trophy as Most Valuable Player Nat. Hockey League Playoffs, 1978-79; elected to Hockey Hall of Fame, 1992. Office: Montreal Canadiens 1275 St Antoine St West Montreal PQ Canada H3C 5L2

GAINOR, THOMAS EDWARD, bank executive; b. St. Paul, Oct. 13, 1933; s. Joseph Paul and Teresa Cecilia (Whelan) G.; m. Janan Rose Nolan, Aug. 8, 1964; children: Mary, Michael, John, Daniel. BS, Marquette U., 1955; postgrad., Stonier Grad. Sch. Banking, Rutgers U., 1965-67, Stanford U. Exec. Program, 1977; PhD in Internat. Rels. and Diplomacy (hon.), Am. Grad. Sch. Internat. Rels. and Diplomacy, Paris, 1999. With Fed. Res. Bank of Mpls., 1958-93, asst. v.p., 1967-72, v.p., 1972-75, sr. v.p. ops., 1975-78, 1st v.p., COO, 1978-93. Bd. dirs. Am. Bancorp., 1994-96. Bd. dirs. Mpls. United Way, 1974-83, v.p., 1974-77; bd. dirs. Vis. Nurse Svc., 1967-75, pres., 1971-72; trustee Visitation Sch., 1983-89, v.p., 1985, chmn., 1986-88; mem. Commn. Archdiocesan Programs, 1983-89, chmn., 1986-87; trustee St. Joseph's Ch., 1985—; trustee St. Thomas Acad., 1989-98, chmn., 1992-98; bd. dirs. St. John Vianney Sem., 1986-2002, Cath. Charities, 1990-96; pres. Cath. Cmty. Found., 1994-2001, sec., 2002-03; internat. adv. coun. Am. Grad. Sch. Internat. Rels. and Diplomacy, Paris, 1997—; bd. dirs. Total Life Care Ctrs., 1998—, v.p., 1999-2001, pres., 2002-04. Served as officer USNR, 1955-58. Mem. Stanford Alumni Assn., Marquette U. Alumni Assn., Naval Res. Assn. Clubs: Six o'Clock (pres. 1982). Roman Catholic. E-mail: tjgainor@aol.com.

GAINSBURG, ROY ELLIS, publishing executive; b. Bklyn., May 1, 1932; s. Herbert Harry Gainsburg and Etta (Stein) Kornfeld; m. Vicki Bloye, July 12, 1957; children: Julie, Jeanne. AB, Brown U., 1954; LLB, Harvard U., 1957. Bar: NY 1957. From assoc. to ptnr. Szold & Brandwen, N.Y.C., 1957-87; exec. v.p. St. Martin's Press Inc., N.Y.C., 1987, pres., 1987-97, part-time v.p. adminstrn., 1997—. V.p. adminstrn. Holtzbrinck Pubs. and Tor Books; bd. dirs., exec. v.p. Macmillan Acad. Pub., Inc. Bd. dirs. The Partnership for the Homeless, N.Y.C., 1997—, chair, 2001—04. Democrat. Home: 157 Ralston Ave South Orange NJ 07079-2344 Office: Holtzbrinck Pubs 175 5th Ave New York NY 10010-7848 Office Phone: 646-307-5478. Personal E-mail: rgainsburg@verizon.net. Business E-Mail: roy.gainsburg@hbpub.com.

GAISER, ROBERT RAYMOND, obstetric anesthesiologist, educator; b. Pt. Pleasant, New Jersey, Sept. 18, 1962; s. Alfred and Eleanor Gaiser; m. Randi Berkowitz, Aug. 13, 1992; children: Matthew Thomas, Kimberly Beth. MD, Columbia U., N.Y., 1984—88. Diplomate in anesthesiology Am. Bd. of Anesthesiology, 1993. Assoc. prof. of anesthesia U. of Pa., Phila., 1992—. Den leader Boy Scouts of Am., Mt. Laurel, NJ, 2001—04. Recipient Tchr. of the Yr., Dept. of Anesthesia, 1993, 1996, Lindback Award for Edn., 1997, Outstanding Clin. Tchr., Graduating Med. Students, 1999—2000, Tchr. of the Yr., Dept. of Anesthesia, 2000, Internat. Anesthesia Rsch. Soc. Award, 2004. Mem.: Soc. of Obstetric Anesthesia (assoc.), John Morgan Honor Soc. (assoc.). Achievements include research in multiple publications concerning obstetric anesthesia. Home: 8 Edinburgh Ln Mt Laurel NJ 08054 Office: Univ of Pa 3400 Spruce St Philadelphia PA 19104 Office Phone: 215-662-3773. Office Fax: 215-615-3898. Business E-Mail: gaiserr@uphs.upenn.edu.

GAISER, TED JOSEPH, academic administrator, minister; b. Bluffton, Indiana, June 23, 1961; s. Noel Eugene and Grace Bernice (Klausky) Gaiser. BA history, So. CT. State U., Hamden, CT., 1986; MTS, Boston U. Sch. of Theology, 1988; MBA, Boston Coll. Carroll Sch. of Mgmt., Chestnut Hill, Mass., 1994; PhD sociology, Boston Coll. Grad. Sch. of A and S, Chestnut Hill, MA., 2000. Cert. Ordained Episcopal Diocese of Mass., 2001. Dep. dir. Corp. Design Found., Boston, 1988—90; rsch. and fin. mgr. Children's Hosp., Boston, 1990—93; grad. asst. Boston Coll., Chestnut Hill, Mass., 1993—96; sr. strategic fin. analyst, Partners Health Care, Boston, 1997; project dir. Boston Coll., Chestnut Hill, Mass., 1998, project mgr., 1999; dir. info. svc. Justice Resource Inst., Boston, 2000; dir. acad. rsch. svc. Boston Coll., Chestnut Hill, Mass., 2000—. Author: (jour. article) Soc. Sci. Computer Rev., 1997. Bd. mem. Saturday's / Sunday's Bread, Boston, 1986—99; com. mem. Brighton Main St., Brighton, Mass., 1999—; bd. mem. Supported Employment Program, Boston, 1998—. Mem.: Am. Sociological Assn. Episcopalian. Avocation: old home restoration. Home: 8 Glenmont Rd Brighten MA 02135-3113 Office: Boston Coll 140 Commonwealth Ave Chestnut Hill MA 02467 Business E-Mail: gaiser@bc.edu.

GAISSER, JULIA HAIG, classics educator; b. Cripple Creek, Colo., Jan. 12, 1941; d. Henry Wolseley and Gertrude Alice (Lent) Haig; m. Thomas Korff Gaisser, Dec. 29, 1964; 1 child, Thomas Wolseley. AB, Brown U., 1962; MA, Harvard U., 1966; PhD, U. Edinburgh, Scotland, 1966. Asst. prof. Newton (Mass.) Coll., 1966-69, Swarthmore (Pa.) Coll., 1970-72, Bklyn. Coll., 1973-75; assoc. prof. dept. Latin Bryn Mawr (Pa.) Coll., 1975-84, prof., 1984—. Martin Classical lectr. Oberlin Coll., 2000. Author: Catullus and his Renaissance Readers, 1993, Pierio Valeriano On the Ill Fortune of Learned Men, 1999, Catullus in English, 2001; editor Bryn Mawr Latin Commentaries, 1983—. Mem. Mid-East sel. com. Marshall Scholarships, Washington, 1975-89, chmn., 1984-89; mem. mng. com. Intercollegiate Ctr. for Classical Studies in Rome, Stanford, Calif., 1984-92, chmn., 1988-92. Decorated MBE; named Marshall scholar, U. Edinburgh, 1962—64, Phi Beta Kappa Vis. scholar, 1996—97, ACLS Travel grantee, 1985, fellow, ACLS, 1989—90, NEH sr. fellow, 1985—86, 1993—94, 1999; recipient NEH summer stipend, 1977, rsch. grantee, Am. Philos. Soc., 1980, 1993. Mem. Am. Philol. Assn. (dir. 1985-88, pres. 2000), Renaissance Soc. Am., Internat. Neo Latin Soc., Am. Philos. Soc. Office: Bryn Mawr Coll Dept Latin Bryn Mawr PA 19010

GAITHER, GEORGE A., education educator, researcher; b. Crawfordsville, Ind., May 23, 1968; s. Robert A. Gaither and Mary F. McElroy; m. Karin M Baer, May 7, 1994; children: Dakota J., Noah G., Savannah C. BA, U. South Fla., Tampa, Fla., 1994; MA, U. N.D., Grand Forks, N.D., 1996, PhD, 2000. Intern Med. U. S.C., Charleston, SC, 1999—2000; asst. prof. psychology Ball State U., Muncie, Ind., 2000—. Editl. bd. mem. Jour. of Trauma Practice, 2003—; mem. Ball State U. Instl. Rev. Bd., Muncie, Ind., 2003—; faculty advisor Dept. of Psychol. Sci., Ball State U., Muncie, Ind., 2001—; facilitator Ball State U. Office for Tchg. & Learning Advancement, Muncie, Ind., 2004—; faculty advisor BSU Chpt. of Psi Chi Nat. Honor Soc., Muncie, Ind., 2003—05; reviewer Jour. of Traumatic Stress, 2000—. Den leader Cub Scout Pack 5, Muncie, Ind., 2004. Specialist U.S. Army, 1987—90, Ft. Carson, Colo. Recipient Psi Chi Faculty Advisor of the Yr., Midwestern Region, Psi Chi Nat. Honor Soc., 2005, Scientist-Practitioner Award, Med. U. of SC. Psychology Internship Program, 2000, Hon. Discharge, US Army, 1990; grantee New Faculty Internal Rsch. Grant, Ball State U., 2002, Bldg. the Four-Year Commitment, Lilly Endowment Departmental Retention Initiative, 2003, Summer Assessment Grant, Ball State U. Office of Academic Assessment and Instl. Rsch., 2002. Mem.: Midwestern Psychol. Assn., Am. Psychol. Soc., Soc. for the Sci. Study of Sexuality (Student Rsch. Grant 1995 & 1999), Internat. Acad. of Sex Rsch. (assoc.). Office: Dept of Psychol Sci Ball State Univ Muncie IN 47306 Office Phone: 765-285-1694. Office Fax: 765-285-8980. Business E-Mail: ggaither@bsu.edu.

GAITHER, GEORGE MANNEY, marketing consultant; b. Mineola, NY, Sept. 21, 1930; s. Roscoe Bradley and Frances Bullitt (Williams) G.; m. Dorothy Wineman Streater, Apr. 4, 1953; children: Neal, George, Anne, Emee, Bruce. B in Journalism, U. Mo., 1952. From gen. mgr. to pres. Internat. Rsch. Assocs., Inc., N.Y.C., 1955-71; pres., founder Gaither Internat., Inc., Stamford, Conn., 1971-96; cons. GMG Cons., Winchester, Va., 1997—. Lt. U.S. Army, 1952-55, Korea. Mem. Market Rsch. Coun. Republican. Avocation: writing. Home: 2628 Windwood Dr Winchester VA 22601-6418 Office Phone: 540-723-6892. E-mail: gmg@visuallink.com.

GAITHER, JAMES C., lawyer; b. Oakland, Calif., Sept. 3, 1937; s. Horace Rowan Jr. and Charlotte Cameron (Castle) G.; m. Susan Good, Apr. 30, 1960; children: James Jr., Whitaker, Reed, Kendra. BA in Econs., Princeton U., 1959; JD, Stanford U., 1964. Bar: Calif. 1964, U.S. Dist. Ct. D.C. 1965, U.S. Dist. Ct. (no. dist.) Calif. 1965, U.S. Ct. Appeals (D.C. cir., 7th cir., 9th cir.), 1965, U.S. Supreme Ct. Law clk. to chief justice Earl Warren, Washington, 1964-65; spl. asst. to asst. atty. gen. John W. Douglas, Washington, 1965-66; staff asst. Pres. Lyndon B. Johnson, Washington, 1966-69; atty. Cooley Godward LLP, San Francisco, 1969-71, ptnr., 1971—2000, mng. ptnr., 1984-90, sr. counsel, 2000—; mng. dir. Sutter Hill Ventures, 2000—. Cons. to sec. HEW, 1977, chmn. ethics adv. bd., 1977—80; bd. dirs. Levi Strauss & Co., San Francisco, Kineto, Milpitas, Calif., Siebel Sys., San Mateo, nVidia Corp., Santa Clara, Satmetrix, Foster City, Calif., Hewlett Found.; former chair James Irvine Found.; chair Carnegie Endowment for Internat. Peace; former trustee The RAND Corp. Editor: Stanford Law Rev., 1963—64. Former pres. bd. trustees, Stanford (Calif.) U.; mem. exec. com. bd. vis. Sch. Law Stanford U.; former chmn. bd. trustees Branson Sch., Ross, Calif., Ctr. for Biotech. Rsch. San Francisco; past trustee Family Svc. Agy. San Francisco, St. Stephens Parish Day Sch., Belvedere, Calif., The Scripps Rsch. Inst.; past trustee, chmn. protem Marin Cmty. Found, Marin County, Calif.; past pres. bd. trustees Marin County Day Sch., Corte Madera; past pres. bd. trustees Marin Ednl. Found., San Rafael; past treas., trustee Rosenberg Found.; past v.p., trustee, vice chmn. San Francisco Devel. Fund; past chmn. Dean's Adv. Coun. Stanford Law Sch., chmn. capital campaign; Inst. Capt.

USMC, 1959-61. Recipient Disting. Pub. Svc. award HEW, 1977, Stanford Assocs. award Stanford U., 1989, 97; named Entrepreneur of Yr. Harvard Bus. Sch., 1979. Fellow Am. Acad. Arts and Scis.; mem. ABA, Calif. Bar Assn., San Francisco Bar Assn., Order of Coif, Phi Delta Phi (province 12). Democrat. Presbyn. Avocations: tennis, hiking, camping, fishing, photography. Office: Sutter Hill Ventures 755 Page Mill Rd # A-200 Palo Alto CA 94304

GAITHER, JOHN FRANCIS, accountant, consultant; b. Louisville, Oct. 26, 1918; s. Thomas R. and Marice F. Gaither; m. Marjilee Schaeffer, Nov. 26, 1942 (dec.); children: John Francis Jr., James M.; m. Catherine W. Cox, June 18, 2002. BCS, U. Notre Dame, 1941. CPA, Ind., Ky., Ill. Controller Evansville (Ind.) div. Whirlpool Corp., 1946-56; cons. Gaither, Rutherford & Co., CPAs, 1954-93; city contr., dep. mayor City of Evansville, 1972-76. Lectr., seminar leader and cons. in health care industry; legis. contact Am. Hosp. Assn., AICPA. Author: Financial Management of Medical Laboratories; contbr. articles to profl. jours. Past pres. Buffalo Trace coun. Boy Scouts Am.; mem. adv. com. Ind. Vocat. Rehab.; past trustee Brescia U., St. Benedicts Convent; past mem. regional cmty. adv. coun. Ind. U. Med. Sch.; past chmn. community adv. coun. Evansville Ctr. Med. Edn.; past chmn. Ind. Select Com. Ednl. Fin., past chmn. Ind. Utility and Energy Regulation Adv. Commn.; vice chmn. Ind. Health Facilities Fin. Authority; dir., officer Nat. Coun. Health Facilities Fin. Authorities; past mem. Ind. Transp. Coordinating Bd.; past Gov.'s rep. Ind. Hosp. Rate Rev. Commn.; past officer YMCA, Cancer Soc., Serra Club. Officer USNR, 1941-46. Recipient various awards Boy Scouts Am., other civic groups. Mem. AICPA, Ind. Assn. CPAs, Ill. Assn. CPAs, Ky. Assn. CPAs, Evansville Assn. CPAs, Inst. Mgmt. Accts. (past pres. Evansville), Ind. Assn. Cities and Towns Controllers Div. (past pres.), Ind. Soc. Chgo. (v.p.), SAR, Soc. J. Gaither Descendants Found. (pres.), Internat. Soc. Descendants of Charlemagne, First Families of Va., Evansville Country Club, Rotary Internat. Republican. Home: 730 S Colony Rd Evansville IN 47714-0636 Office: PO Box 8408 Evansville IN 47734-8408 Personal E-mail: johng730@aol.com.

GAITHER, JOHN FRANCIS, JR., lawyer, health products executive; b. Evansville, Ind., Mar. 31, 1949; s. John F. and Marjilee G.; m. Christine Luby, Nov. 26, 1971; children: John F. III, Maria Theresa. BA in Acctg., U. Notre Dame, 1971, JD, 1974. Bar: Ind. 1974, Ill. 1975, U.S. Ct. Appeals (7th cir.) 1975, U.S. Ct. Mil. Appeals 1977. CPA, Ind. Law clk. to Hon. Wilbur F. Pell, Jr. Ct. of Appeals 7th Cir., Chgo., 1974-76; assoc. atty. Bell, Boyd & Lloyd, Chgo., 1979-82; sr. atty. Baxter Healthcare Corp., Deerfield, Ill., 1982-83, asst. sec., sr. atty., 1983-84, asst. sec., asst. gen. counsel, 1984-85; sec., assoc. gen. counsel Baxter Internat. Inc., Deerfield, 1985-87, sec., dep. gen. counsel, 1987-91; v.p. law/devel. Baxter Diagnostics Inc., Deerfield, 1991-92; v.p. law, strategic planning Baxter Global Businesses, Deerfield, 1992-93; dep. gen. counsel, v.p. strategic planning Baxter Internat. Inc., Deerfield, 1993-94, corp. v.p., corp. devel., 1994-2001; v.p., sec., gen. counsel Global Healthcare Exch., LLC, Westminster, Colo., 2001—03; sr. v.p., sec., gen. counsel NeighborCare, Inc., Baltimore, Md., 2003—. Editor-in-chief Notre Dame Lawyer, 1973-74; contbr. articles to profl. jours. Lt. comdr. USNR, 1976-79. Mem. ABA, Ill. Bar Assn., Ind. Bar Assn., Chgo. Bar Assn., Ind. Assn. CPAs. Avocations: sailing, skiing. Office: NeighborCare Inc 601 E Pratt St Baltimore MD 21202 Office Phone: 410-528-7404. E-mail: john.gaither@neighborcare.com.

GAITHER, WILLIAM SAMUEL, civil engineering executive, consultant; b. Lafayette, Ind., Dec. 3, 1932; s. William Marcius and Susan Frances (Kirkpatrick) G.; m. Robin Cornwall McGraw, Aug. 1, 1959; 1 dau., Sarah Curwen. Student, Purdue U., 1950—51; BS in Civil Engring, Rose Poly. Inst., 1956; M. Sci. Engring. (Arthur Le Grand Doty fellow), Princeton, 1962, MA (Ford Found. fellow), 1963, PhD (Ford Found. fellow), 1964. Registered profl. engr., Del., Penn. Engr. Dravo Corp. (marine constrn.), Pitts., 1956-60; supt. Myer Corp., Neenah, Wis., 1960-61; supervising engr., chief engr. port and coastal devel., pipeline div. Bechtel Corp., San Francisco, 1965-67; assoc. prof. coastal engring. dept. U. Fla. at Gainesville, 1964-65; mem. faculty U. Del. at Newark, 1967-84, assoc. prof. civil engring., 1967-70, prof. civil engring., 1970; prof., dean U. Del. at Newark (Coll. Marine Studies), 1970-84, also dir. sea grant coll. program; pres., prof. trustee Drexel U., Phila., 1984-87, Weston Inst., West Chester, Pa., 1988-93; Inner City Consortium, Inc., 1993-94; owner Gaither & Assocs., Tucson, 1993—. Trustee Mut. Assurance Co., 1985-96; mem. marine bd. NRC, 1975-81; chmn. Gov.'s Oil Transp. Study Com., 1971-73; mem. Gov.'s Task Force Marine and Coastal Affairs, 1970-72, Gov.'s Coun. Sci. and Tech., Del., 1970-72; bd. dirs. Roy F. Weston, Inc., 1974-91, vice chmn., 1988-91; bd. dirs. Phila. Electric Co., 1985-89; mem. ocean affairs adv. com. U.S. Dept. State; mem. Commn. on the Future, Rose-Hulman Inst. Tech., 1991-93; mem. Cyberfab.net. LLC, 1999—. Chmn. adv. coun. dept. civil engring. Princeton U., 1973-84; bd. dirs. University City Sci. Ctr., 1984-93, Penjurdel Coun., 1984-2000, Ednl. Found. of Chester County, 1989-92; pres., dir. Soc. John Gaither Desc., Inc., 1984-87; port warden Phila. Maritime Mus., 1987-93; founding dir., sec. Internat. Consciousness Rsch. Labs., 1996—; vestryman Ch. St. Andrew and St. Monica, 1987-93, chmn. fin. com. 1991-96; bd. dirs., mem. exec. com. Phila. H.S. Acads., Inc., 1988-93; chmn. bd. govs. Environ. Tech. Acad., 1988-93; prin. sponsor Delaware Valley Sci. Fairs, 1990-93. Pvt. U.S. Army, 1953. Recipient Disting. Achievement award Rose Poly. Inst., 1975, Disting. citizenship award News Jour. Papers, Del., 1975, Norman Sollenberger award Princeton U., 1983; named to Lambda Chi Alpha Alumni Hall of Fame, 1996; named hon. citizen of Lewes, Del., 1980. Fellow: ASCE (chmn. offshore policy com. 1979—84); mem.: Nat. Water Rsch. Inst. (rsch.adv. bd. 1991—2002), Acad. Sci. Phila. (bd. dirs. 1989—92), Sea Grant Program Instns. (pres. 1973—74), Del. Acad. Scis. (pres. 1971—72), Ariz. Sr. Acad., Cosmos Club. Home and Office: 7719 S Galileo Ln Tucson AZ 85747-9605 Office Phone: 520-647-7267. E-mail: gaitherws@cox.net.

GAJARSA, ARTHUR J., federal judge; b. Norcia, Italy, Mar. 1, 1941; arrived in U.S., 1949; m. Melanie E. Gajarsa. BSEE, Rensselaer Polytech. Inst, 1962; JD, Georgetown U., 1967; MA in Econs., Cath. U., 1968. Bar: U.S. Patent Office 1963, DC 1968, U.S. Dist. Ct. DC 1968, U.S. Ct. Appeals (DC cir.) 1968, Conn. 1969, U.S. Supreme Ct. 1971, DC Superior Ct. 1972, U.S. Ct. Appeals (DC cir.) 1972, U.S. Ct. Appeals (9th cir.) 1974, U.S. Dist. Ct. (no. dist.) N.Y. 1980. Patent examiner U.S. Patent Office, Dept. Commerce, 1962—63; patent adviser USAF, Dept. Def., 1963—64, Cushman, Darby & Cushman, 1964—67; law clk. to Judge Joseph C. McGarraghy U.S. Dist. Ct. (D.C.), Washington, 1967—68; atty. office gen. counsel Aetna Life and Casualty Co., 1968—69; spl. counsel, asst. to commr. Indian affairs Bur. Indian Affairs, Dept. Interior, 1969—71; assoc. Duncan and Brown, 1971—72; ptnr. Gajarsa, Liss & Sterenbuch, 1972—78, Gajarsa, Liss & Conroy, 1978—80, Wender, Murase & White, 1980—86; ptnr., officer Joseph, Gajarsa, McDermott & Reiner, P.C., 1987—97; judge U.S. Ct. Appeals Fed. Cir., Washington, 1997—. Contbr. articles to profl. jours. Trustee Rensselaer Neuman Found., 1973—, Found. Improving Understanding of Arts, 1982—96, Outward Bound, 1987—96, Rensselaer Polytech. Inst., 1994—; gov. John Carroll Soc., 1992—99; regent Georgetown U., 1995—2000, bd. dirs., 2000—. Recipient Sun and Balance medal, Rensselaer Polytech. Inst., 1990, Rensselaer Key Alumni award, 1992, Albert Demers Fox award, 1999, Gigi Pieri award, Camp Hale Assn., 1992, 125th Anniversary medal, Georgetown U. Law Ctr., 1995, Order of Commendatore, Republic of Italy, 1995, Alumni Fellows award, Rensselaer Alumni Assn., 1996, Paul Dean award, Georgetown U., 1999. Mem.: Am. Judicature Assn., DC Bar Assn., Nat. Italian Am. Found. (bd. dirs. 1976—99, gen. counsel 1976—89, pres. 1989—92, vice-chair 1993—96), Fed. Cir. Bar Assn. Office: US Ct Appeals Fed Cir 717 Madison Pl NW Washington DC 20439-0002

GAJDA, AMY, columnist, educator, writer; d. Louise and Leo Gajda; m. David Douglas Meyer; children: Michael Meyer, Matthew Meyer. BA, U. Mich., 1983; JD, Wayne State U., 1991. Legal commentator Ill. Nat. Pub. Radio Stas., Ill., 1999; prof. legal writing U. Ill. Coll. Law, Champaign, 1999—. Mem.: Ill. Associated Broadcasters Assn. (7 awards 1999—2003), Assn. Legal Writing Dirs. (sec.-treas. 2003—04). Office: U Il Coll Law 504 East Pennsylvania Ave Champaign IL 61820 Office Phone: 217-333-5461. E-mail: agajda@law.uiuc.edu.

GAJDUSEK, ROBERT ELEMER, writer, retired language educator; b. Yonkers, N.Y., Apr. 18, 1925; s. Karl Abysius and Mahtil Gajdusek; m. Juliz Lee Terry, Dec. 26, 1949 (div. Sept. 1952); 1 child, Mark Robert; m. Bettye-jo Sode, 1952 (div. Sept. 1966); m. Linda Carol Nusbaum, Oct. 20, 1966 (div. Jan. 1998); 1 child, Karl Lawrence. BA magna cuma laude, Princeton U., 1949; MA, Columbia U., 1950, postgrad., U. Calif., Berkeley, Kans. U., George Washing U., San Francisco State U. Tchg. asst. English U. Calif., Berkeley, 1950—52; instr. English Kans. U., Lawrence, 1952—54; asst. to assoc. prof. George Washington U., Washington, 1955—65; assoc. prof. Hunter Col., N.Y.C., 1965; prof. San Francisco State U., 1965—92, prof. emeritus. Author: Hemingway in His Own Country, 2002; contbr. articles tto profl. jours. Pvt. 1st class U.S. Army, 1943—46, POW. Recipient Lifetime Achievement and Enduring Excellencein Belles Lettres and Hemingway Studies award, Nick Adams Soc., 1999, Extraordinary Achievement in Hemingway Studies award, Hemingway Soc., 1999. Avocations: travel, art. Home: 2305 Vakkecutis La Jolla CA 92037-3144 E-mail: robinegaj@aol.com.

GAJL-PECZALSKA, KAZIMIERA J., retired surgeon, pathologist, educator; b. Warsaw, Nov. 15, 1925; came to U.S., 1970; d. Kazimierz Emil and Anna Janina (Gervais) Gajl; widowed; children: Kazimierz Peczalski, Andrew Peczalski. Student, Jagiellonian Univ., Cracov, Poland, 1945-47; MD, Warsaw U., Poland, 1951, PhD in Immunopathology, 1964. Diplomate Polish Bd. Pediatrics, Polish Bd. Anatomic Pathology, Am. Bd. Pathology. Attending pediatrician Children's Hosp. for Infectious Diseases, Warsaw, Poland, 1953-58, head, pathology lab., 1958-65; adj. prof. Postgrad. Med. Sch., Warsaw, Poland, 1965-70; fellow U. Minn., Mpls., 1970-72, asst. prof. dept. pathology, 1972-75, assoc. prof. dept. pathology, 1975-79, prof. dept. pathology, 1979-00, dir. immunophenotyping and flow lab., 1974-00, dir. cytology dept. pathology, 1976-95; ret., 2000. Author chpts. to book; contbr. of numerous papers to profl. jours. Fellow WHO, Paris, 1959, London, 1962, Paris, 1967, U.S. Pub. Health Svcs. fellow, 1968-69; recipient Scientific Com. award Polish Ministry of Health and Social Welfare, 1964. Mem. Am. Soc. Experimental Pathology, Am. Soc. Cytology, Internat. Acad. Pathology, British Soc. Pediatric Pathology, Polish Soc. Pathology, Polish Soc Pediatricians. Roman Catholic. Avocations: music, skiing.

GAJRAJ, NOOR, anesthesiologist, educator; b. London, United Kingdom, Nov. 4, 1959; s. Harold and Mary Gajraj; m. Serena Wang, May 26, 2002; 1 child, Gavin. MD, King's Coll., London, 1978—83; fellow of royal coll. anaesthetists, King's Coll., 1978—83. Cert. Bd. cert. anesthesiology, pain mgmt., hospice and palliative care medicine, and addiction medicine. Assoc. prof. U. Tex. Southwestern Med. Ctr., Dallas, 1996—2004. Author more than 100 scientific articles. Fellow: Royal Coll. Anesthesiologists. Office: Baylor Ctr for Pain Mgmt 5575 warren Pkwy 220 Frisco TX 75034 Office Phone: 214-618-3686. E-mail: noorgajraj@aol.com.

GALAGANOV, MISHA, music educator; b. Russia, Feb. 17, 1970; s. Pavel and Anna Galaganov; m. Talya Bernstein Galaganov. MusB, Jerusalem Rubin Acad., 1994; MusM, Rice U., Houston, 1998, DMA, 2003. Cert. artist So. Meth. U., 1996, profl. violin performer Min-Vody Musical Coll., Russia, 1989. Asst. prof. of viola Tex. Christian U., 2000—; condr., string orch. Youth Orch. of Greater Fort Worth, 2001—, dir. of chamber music program, 2002—. Musician (soloist, ensemble performer): (concerts) Solo And Chamber Music Performances; co-dir.: (festival) Chamber Music Roundup in Fort Worth, 2003—. Youth orch. condr., dir. youth chamber music program, tchr. Scholar Full tuition scholarship and stipend, Rice U., 1996—2003, So. Meth. U., 1994—96, Full tuition scholarship, Jerusalem Music Acad., 1991—94. Office: Texas Christian Univ Fort Worth TX Office Phone: 817-257-6619. Business E-Mail: m.galaganov@tcu.edu.

GALAINENA, M. DAVID, lawyer; b. Cleve., Nov. 9, 1957; BA magna cum laude, Tulane U., 1980; JD, U. Notre Dame, 1983. Bar: Ill. 1983. Ptnr. Winston & Strawn LLP, Chgo., 1995—, mem. exec. com. Mem.: Phi Beta Kappa. Office: Winston & Strawn LLP 35 W Wacker Dr Chicago IL 60601-9703 Office Phone: 312-558-7442. Office Fax: 312-558-5700. E-mail: dgalainena@winston.com.

GALAMBOS, JOHN THOMAS, internist, medical educator; b. Budapest, Hungary, Oct. 29, 1921; came to U.S., 1947; m. Eva G. Cohn; children: Sharon Tobae Galambos McDuff, John Douglas, Michael Robert. BS, U. Ga., 1948; MD, Emory U., 1952. Diplomate Nat. Bd. Med. Examiners, Am. Bd. Internal Medicine, Am. Bd. Gastroenterology. Intern Barnes Hosp., St. Louis, 1952-53; resident U. Chgo. Clinics, 1953-55; dir. gastroenterology teaching program Emory U. Sch. Medicine, Atlanta, 1957-92, dir. gastroenterology labs., 1958-92, dir. div. digestive diseases, 1966-92. Dir. Gastroenterology Clinic Grady Hosp., Atlanta, 1957-92; mem. adv. bd. Nat. Inst. Digestive Diseases, NIH, Washington, 1985-88 Author: Cirrhosis, 1979, Digestive Diseases, 1983; author or co-author 36 book chpts.; contbr. 165 articles to profl. jours. Fellow ACP, Am. Coll. Gastroenterology (pres. 1975), Am. Gastroenterol. Assn., Am. Assn. for Study Liver Diseases, Internat. Assn. for Study Liver Diseases, Alpha Omega Alpha. Republican. Jewish. Avocation: sailing. Office: 95 Collier Rd NW Ste 4075 Atlanta GA 30309-1751 Office Phone: 404-355-3200. E-mail: jgalamb@emory.edu.

GALAMBOS, THEODORE VICTOR, civil engineer, educator; b. Budapest, Hungary, Apr. 17, 1929; s. Paul and Magdalena (Potzner) G.; m. Barbara Ann Asp, June 25, 1957; children: Paul, Ruth, Ronald, John. BSCE, U. ND, 1953, MSCE, 1954; PhD in CE, Lehigh U., 1959; Dr. honoris causa, Tech. U., Budapest, 1982; PhD (hon.), U. ND, 1998; DSc (hon.), U. Minn., 2001. Registered profl. engr., Pa., Minn., Mo. From asst. to assoc. prof. civil engring. Lehigh U., Bethlehem, Pa., 1959-65; prof. Washington U., St. Louis, 1965-81, head dept., 1970-78; prof. U. Minn., Mpls., 1981-96, emeritus prof., 1997—. Cons. engr. Steel Joist Inst., Myrtle Beach, S.C., 1965-2003; vis. prof. U.S. Mil. Acad., West Point, 1990. Author, co-author 4 books in field; editor 1 book; contbr. over 100 articles to profl. jours. Served with U.S. Army, 1954-56. Recipient T.R. Higgins award Am. Inst. Steel Constrn., 1981. Mem. ASCE (hon., Norman medal 1983, Shortridge Hardesty award 1988, E.E. Howard award 1992, OPAL award 2002, Walter P. Moore award 2004, Nathan M. Newmark medal 2004), NAE, Internat. Assn. Bridge and Structural Engrs. Democrat. Baptist. Avocation: photography. Home: 4375 Woodale Ave Minneapolis MN 55424-1060 Office: U Minn Civil Engring Dept Minneapolis MN 55455 Business E-Mail: galam001@tc.umn.edu.

GALAN, LEONIDEZ VINDOLLO, architect; b. Poblacion, Phillipines, Aug. 8, 1948; s. Juan Garcia Galan and Maria Victoria (Vergara) Vindollo; m. Adoracion Cipriaso Galan; children: John Patrick C., Denise Victoria. BS in Architecture, Calumpit Inst., Philippines; BS in Arch., Far Ea. U., 1965; MS in Archtl. Tech., Columbia U., 1973. Structural detailer Le Messuer Assoc. Engrs., St. Louis, 1968—69; arch. designer Port Authority N.Y. & N.J., 1969—85, task leader arch., 1985—. Cons. various cos.; pres. John Dendor Realty Corp.; asst. prof. arch. design NYU, N.Y.C.; asst. prof. Angeles Tech. Author: World Trade Center Book at Tenants Development, 1985. With U.S. Army, 1965—68, Vietnam. Mem.: Illuminating Engring. Soc., Foreign Policy Assn., Constrn. Specification Inst., Am. Inst. Architects, Colonial Williamsburg, Nat. Trust Hist. Preservation, Lions (bde. dirs.). Roman Catholic. Avocations: tennis, bowling, swimming, dance, boxing. Home: 179-15 Dalny Rd Jamaica Estates Jamaica NY 11432 Office: Port Authority NY & NJ One World Trade Ctr Rm 1933 New York NY 10048

GALANDIUK, SUSAN, colon and rectal surgeon, educator; b. NYC, Mar. 6, 1957; d. Joseph and Dora (Neu) G.; m. Hiram C. Polk Jr., Dec. 22, 1991. BS cum laude, SUNY, Albany, 1976; MD summa cum laude, Julius Maximilians U., Wuerzburg, Germany, 1982. Diplomate Am. Bd. Surgery, Am. Bd. Colon and Rectal Surgery. Surg. intern Chirurgische Univ. Klinik, Julius Maximilians U., Wuerzburg, Germany, 1982-83, Cleve. Clinic Found., 1983-84, surg. resident, 1984-88; Price fellow in surg. rsch., dept. surgery U. Louisville, 1988-89, colon and rectal surgery fellow dept. surgery, 1989-90, instr. dept. surgery, 1990-91, asst. prof. dept. surgery, 1991-96, assoc. prof., 1996-2001, program dir. sect. colon and rectal surgery, 1999—, prof., 2001—; dir. Price Inst. Surg. Rsch., 2001—. Presenter in field. Editl. bd. Digestive Surgery, Mayor Clin. Procs., Diseases Colon Rectum, Archives of Surgery; contbr. chpts. to books, articles to profl. jours. Chmn. fund raising com. ARC, Louisville, 1993, 1995—97, bd. dirs., 1997—2000, chmn. bd., 2001—03; bd. mem. Fund for the Arts, 1996—2003; chair med. adv. com. Ky. chpt. Crohn's and Colitis Found. Am., Louisville, 1993—97, 1999—2003. William E. Lower Fellow Thesis prize Cleve. Clinic Found., 1986. Fellow ACS, AAUP, Am. Soc. Colon and Rectal Surgeons (mem. chmn. rsch. found. young rschrs. com. 1996—, mem. program com. 1994-96, trustee rsch. found., 2001—, membership com., 2000—); mem. AMA, Am. Med. Women's Assn., Am. Soc. Microbiology, Assn. Acad. Surgery, Assn. Women Surgeons, Collegium Internat. Chirurgiae Digestivae, Jefferson County Med. Soc., Ky. Med. Assn. (mem. cancer com.), Louisville Surg. Soc., Hiram C. Polk Jr. Surg. Soc., Ohio Valley Soc. Colon and Rectal Surgeons, Priestly Soc., Soc. Surgery of Alimentary Tract, Soc. Am. Gastrointestinal Endoscopic Surgeons, Soc. Surg. Oncology (mem. corp. rels. and issues, govt. affairs coms.), Southea. Surg. Congress (councillor 1997-99), Surg. Infection Soc., Soc. Univ. Surgeons, Am. Soc. Gastrointestinal Endoscipists, Ctrl. Surg. Assn., Western Surg. Assn., Am. Gastroent. Assn., So. Surg. Assn., Am. Gastroenterol. Assn., Am. Soc. Human Genetics, Am. Soc. Clin. Oncology, Assn. Program Dirs. in Colon & Rectal Surgery, Soc. Pelvic Surgeons, Surg. Biol. Club I. Greek Catholic. Office: U Louisville Dept Surgery 550 S Jackson St Louisville KY 40202-1622 Office Phone: 502-852-4568. E-mail: S0gala01@gwise.louisville.edu.

GALANIS, JOHN WILLIAM, lawyer; b. Milw., May 9, 1937; s. William and Angeline (Koroniou) G.; m. Patricia Caro, Nov. 29, 1969; children: Lia Galanis Economou, William, Charles, John. BBA cum laude, U. Wis., 1959; JD, U. Mich., 1963; postgrad. (Ford Found. grantee), London Sch. Econs., 1964. Bar: Wis. 1965; CPA, Wis. Assoc. firm Whyte & Hirschboeck S.C., Milw., 1964-68; sr. v.p., gen. counsel, sec. MGIC Investment Corp. and Mortgage Guaranty Ins. Corp., Milw., 1968-88; ptnr. Galanis, Pollack, Jacobs & Johnson, S.C., Milw., 1988—. Assoc. editor: Mich. Law Rev, 1962-63. Bd. visitors Law Sch. U. Mich., Sch. Bus. U. Wis.; past chmn. Milw. Found.; bd. dirs., past pres. Milw. Boys' and Girls' Club; pres. Family Svc. Milw. Recipient Disting. Svc. award Internat. Inst., Hope Chest award Nat. MS Soc., Disting. Alumni award Milw. Boys' Club, Disting. Svc. award Milw. Civic Alliance Club, 1989, Ellis Island Medal of Honor, 2005. Mem. ABA, Wis. Bar Assn., Milw. Bar Assn., AHEPA, PDG, Order of Coif, Milw. Athletic Club, Blue Mound Golf and Country Club. Greek Orthodox. Home: 1200 Woodlawn Cir Elm Grove WI 53122-1639 Office: Galanis Pollack Jacobs & Johnson 2 Plaza East Ste 560 330 E Kilbourn Milwaukee WI 53202 Office Phone: 414-271-5400. Business E-Mail: jwg@gpjlaw.com.

GALANT, HERBERT LEWIS, lawyer; b. N.Y.C., Oct. 16, 1928; s. Charles A. and Bertha (Rosenberg) G.; m. Fern Judith Laikin, Feb. 10, 1957; children: Peter B., John M., Amy E. BA cum laude, U. Wis., 1949; LLB magna cum laude, Harvard U., 1952; LLM, NYU, 1960. Bar: N.Y. 1955, U.S. Dist. Ct. (so. dist.) N.Y. 1956, U.S. Ct. Appeals (2d cir.) 1959. Assoc. Fried, Frank, Harris, Shriver & Jacobson, N.Y.C., 1955-61, ptnr., 1962-95, co-chair, 1992-95, of counsel, 1995—. Editor: Harvard U. Law Rev., 1950—52. Mem. Tenafly Twp. (N.J.) Bd. Ethics, 1978-88, Tenafly Twp. Planning Bd., 1997-2000, 04-. 1st lt. USAF, 1952-54. Mem.: Assn. Bar City of N.Y., Harvard U. Club (N.Y.C.). Democrat. Jewish. Home: 150 Tekening Dr Tenafly NJ 07670-1219 Office: Fried Frank Harris Shriver & Jacobson 1 New York Plz Fl 22 New York NY 10004-1980 Office Phone: 212-859-8000. E-mail: herbgala@aol.com.

GALANTE, EDWARD G., oil industry executive; b. Inwood, N.Y. BS in Civil Engring, Northeastern U. Various positions Exxon Co., U.S.A., 1972—88, mgr., refinery Baton Rouge, 1988—92; chief exec., gen. mgr. Esso Caribbean and Ctrl Am., Coral Gables, Fla., 1992—95; exec. asst. to chmn. Exxon Corp., 1995—97; chmn., mng. dir. Esso Pub. Co. Ltd., Bangkok, 1997—99; exec. v.p. ExxonMobil Chem. Co., Houston, 1999—2001; sr. v.p. Exxon Mobil Corp., Irving, Tex., 2001—. Dir., Nat. Coun. Northeastern U.; bd. dirs. Coun. of the Ams. and Jr. Achievement Internat.; bd. trustees U.S. Coun. for Internat. Bus. Office: Exxon Mobil Corp 5959 Las Colinas Blvd Irving TX 75039-2298

GALANTE, JORGE OSVALDO, orthopedic surgeon, educator; b. Buenos Aires, Dec. 18, 1934; arrived in U.S., 1958; m. Sofija Kabliauskas; 1 child, Charles. BA, Colegio Nacional de Buenos Aires, 1952; MD, U. Buenos Aires, 1958; DMSc, U. Goteborg, Sweden, 1967. Diplomate Am. Bd. Orthopedic Surgery. Resident in orthopaedics U. Ill., Chgo., 1960-64; assoc. investigator bioengineering lab. U. Goteborg, 1964-67; asst. prof. orthopedic surgery U. Ill. Med. Ctr., Chgo., 1967-70, assoc. prof., 1970-72; lect. in orthopedics U. Ill. Abraham Lincoln Sch. Medicine, Chgo., 1972—; adj. rsch. prof. U. Ill. Circle, Chgo., 1972—, mem. graduate faculty, 1974—; prof., chmn. dept. orthopedic surgery Rush-Presbyn.-St. Luke's Med. Ctr., Chgo., 1972-94; prof. anatomy Rush Med. Coll., Chgo., 1977—; dir. Rush Arthritis and Orthopedic Inst., 1994—. Assoc. prof. exptl. orthopedics. U. Goteborg, 1969—. Contbr. articles to profl. jours. Recipient Kappa Delta award Am. Acad. Orthopedic Surgery, 1970, Clemson (S.C.) U. award, 1975, Steindler award Orthopedic Rsch. Soc., 1990, Zimmer Award for Disting. Achievement in Orthopedic Rsch. Bristol-Myers Squibb, 1996. Office: Rush-Presbyn-St Luke's Med Ctr 1725 W Harrison Chicago IL 60612-3833 Office Phone: 312-432-2344. Personal E-mail: jgalante@aol.com.

GALANTE, JOSEPH A., bishop; b. Philadelphia, Pa., July 2, 1938; BA, St. Charles Seminary, Phila.; JCD, Lateran U., Rome; MA in Spiritual Theology, U. St. Thomas, Rome. Ordained priest Roman Cath. Ch. 1964, bishop 1992. Asst. pastor Our Lady of Consolation Parish, 1964—65, St. John of the Cross, Roslyn, 1965; Bishop's sec., Diocesan Master of Ceremonies Diocese of Brownsville, Tex., 1968—72, vicar for religious, Diocesan newspaper editor, 1969—72; asst. vicar for religious Archdiocese of Phila., 1972—79; resident Good Shepherd Parish, 1972—73; defender of The Bond Archdiocesan Tribunal, Phila., 1972—74; chaplain Catholic Home for Girls, St. Vincent's Residence, 1972—81; prof. Canon Law St. Charles Seminary, 1974—77, Mary Immaculate Seminary, Northampton, Pa., 1975—78; vicar for religious Archdiocese of Phila., 1979—87; chaplain Convent of the Handmaids of the Sacred Heart, Haverford, Pa., 1981—87; undersec. Congregation for Institutes of Consecrated Life & Societies of Apostolic Life, Rome, 1987—92; aux. bishop Diocese of San Antonio, 1992—94; bishop Diocese of Beaumont, Tex., 1994—99; coadjutor bishop Diocese of Dallas, 2000—04; bishop Diocese of Camden, NJ, 2004—. Pres. Nat. Conf. for Vicars of Religious, 1976—80; spkr. in field. Religious affairs com. Canon Law Soc. Office: Diocese of Camden PO Box 708 631 Market St Camden NJ 08101*

GALANTER, EUGENE, psychologist, educator; b. Phila., Oct. 27, 1924; s. Max and Sarah (Honigman) G.; m. Patricia Anderson, Dec. 22, 1962; children: Alicia, Gabrielle, Michelle. AB, Swarthmore Coll., 1950; A.M., U. Pa., 1951, PhD, 1953. From instr. to prof. psychology U. Pa., 1952-62; research fellow Harvard U., 1955-56, Center Advanced Study Behavioral Scis., 1958-59; chmn. dept. psychology U. Wash., 1962-64, prof., 1964-66; Joseph Klingenstein vis. prof. social psychology Columbia U., N.Y.C., 1966-67, prof. psychology, 1967—. Cons. NIH, NSF, also to industry; mem. Coun. for Biology in Human Affairs; chmn. commn. on biology, learning and behavior Salk Inst.; founder Children's Computer Sch., 1980, sold to CompuServe, 1984; founder, chmn. bd. dirs. Children's Progress Inc., 1999—. Author: Plans and Structure of Behavior, 1960, 2d edit., 1986, CD edit., 2005, New Directions in Psychology, 1962, Textbook of Elementary Psychology, 1966, Kids & Computers: The Parents' Microcomputer Handbook, 1983, Kids & Computers: Elementary Programming for Kids in BASIC, 1983, Kids & Computers: Advanced Programming Handbook, 1984;

editor: Handbook of Mathematical Psychology, 3 vols., 1963-64, Readings in Mathematical Psychology, 2 vols., 1963-65, Psych Tech Notes, 1988, version 2.1, 1994. Served with AUS, 1942-46. Decorated Bronze Star, Croix de Guerre with Palm France. Fellow AAAS, APA, Acoustical Soc. Am., N.Y. Acad. Scis.; mem. Eastern Psychol. Assn., Assn. Aviation Psychologists (pres. 1970-71), Human Factors Soc., Internat. Soc. for Psychophysics, Sigma Xi (past chpt. pres.). Achievements include patent in field. Office: Columbia U 360 Engring Terr 1190 Amsterdam Ave # 5501 New York NY 10027-7054 Office Phone: 212-280-4382. Business E-Mail: EG53@columbia.edu.

GALANTER, MARC, psychiatrist, educator; b. N.Y.C., Sept. 17, 1941; s. Jacob and Ada (Simms) G. BA, Columbia U., 1963; MD, Albert Einstein Coll. Medicine, 1967. Diplomate Am. Bd. Psychiatry and Neurology with added qualifications in addiction psychiatry; cert. Am. Soc. Addiction Medicine. Intern UCLA Hosp., 1967-68; resident in psychiatry Albert Einstein Coll. Medicine-Bronx Mcpl. Hosp. Ctr., 1968-71, fellow in community psychiatry, 1972-73, clin. instr., 1972-74, dir. Drug and Alcohol Cons. Service, 1972-75, career tchr. drug abuse and alcoholism Nat. Inst. on Alcohol Abuse and Alcoholism, Nat. Inst. Drug Abuse, 1973-76, asst. prof., 1974-78, dir. div. alcoholism and drug abuse, 1975-87, assoc. prof., 1978-83, prof. dept. psychiatry, 1983-87; prof. psychiatry, dir. div. alcoholism and drug abuse NYU Sch. Med., 1987—; dir. addiction divsn., rsch. scientist Collaborating Ctr. WHO, 1987-98, dep. dir. Collaborating Ctr., 1998—. Clin. assoc. Lab. Clin. Psychopharmacology, NIMH, Washington, 1970-72; instr. psychiatry residency program St. Elizabeth's Hosp.; presenter at profl. confs. U.S., Can., Thailand, Germany, Japan, India, Kenya and Italy; chmn. Nat. Conf. on Alcohol and Drug Abuse Edn., 1977; program chmn. Internat. Conf. Med. Edn. in Alcohol and Drug Abuse, WHO and Assn. Med. Edn. and Rsch. in Substance Abuse, 1982, founder, pres., 1976-77; dir. Lab. Alcoholism and Drug Abuse WHO. Editor: Ofcl. Sci. Procs. of Nat. Coun. on Alcoholism, 1978-80, Alcohol and Drug Abuse in Medical Education, 1980, (book series) Currents in Alcoholism, 1979, 80, 81, Recent Developments in Alcoholism; mem. editl. bd. Am. Jour. Drug and Alcohol Abuse, 1978—; assoc. editor jour. Alcoholism Clin. and Exptl. Rsch., Am. Jour. of Addictions, 1979, Jour. Substance Abuse Treatment, 1995—; co-editor: Advances in the Psychosocial Treatment of Alcoholism, 1984; editor-in-chief Substance Abuse Jour., 1978—; author: Network Therapy for Alcohol and Drug and Abuse, 1993, 2nd edit., 1999, Cults: Faith, Health and Coercion, 1989, 2nd edit., 1999. Recipient Psychopharmacology award Am. Psychol. Assn., 1972; Career Tchr. award in drug abuse and alcoholism NIMN, 1973-77, Organon Tchg. awad Am. Psychiat. Assn., 1999; ann. Book award Commonwealth Fund, 1978-82, Macarthur medal Assn. Med. Edn. and Rsch., 1994. Fellow Am. Psychiat. Assn. (chmn. panel on alcoholism, nat. task force on psychiat. treatment 1983—, mem. task force on cults 1977-80, mem. com. on alcoholism, chmn. com. on addiction edn. 1992—, chmn. com. on religion 1985-90, Gold Achievement award 1993, bd. dirs. pub. group 1998–, Seymour Vastermark Edn. awrd 2002), Am. Soc. on Addiction Medicine (bd. dirs. 1986—, sec. 1995-97, pres. elect 1997-99, pres. 1999-2001); mem. AAAS, Am. Bd. Psychiatry and Neurology (vice chair com. on added qualifications in addiction psychiatry 1992-98), Rsch. Soc. on Alcoholism (sec. 1983-85), N.Y. Acad. Medicine (addiction com. 1985—), N.Y. State Task Force on Dual Psychiat. and Addictive Disorders (task force chmn. 1986-89, 93), N.Y. Psychiat. Soc., Am. Acad. Addiction Psychiatrists (v.p. 1987-89, pres. 1991-93, bd. dirs. 1986—), Nat. Inst. Alcohol Abuse and Alcoholism (Nat. Adv. Coun. 1997—). Office: Div Alcoholism & Drug Abuse NYU School of Medicine 550 First Avenue New York NY 10016 Office Phone: 212-887-4093, 212-263-6960.

GALANTUCCI, BRUNO, research scientist; b. Milan, July 13, 1969; s. Mario Galantucci and Anna Keller. PhD in Cognitive Sci., U. Padua, 2001; PhD in Exptl. Psychology, U. Conn., 2004. Rsch. asst. Max Planck Inst., Njimegen, Netherlands, 1993—96; grad. asst. U. Padua, Italy, 1997—98, U. Conn., Storrs, Conn., 1998—2004; rsch. scientist Haskins Labs., New Haven, 2004—. Contbr. scientific papers to profl. profl. and acad. jours. Office: Haskins Labs 300 George St New Haven CT 06511 Office Phone: 203-865-6163.

GALARIA, NOREEN AHMAD, physician, medical researcher, consultant; b. Toronto; d. Feroz and Mahmooda Ahmad; m. Irfan Ibrahim Galaria; 1 child, Alina. BSc with honors suma cum laude, Mcmaster U., 1996; MD suma cum laude, U. Western Ontario, 1998, Jefferson Med. Ctr., 2001. Bd. cert. NY. Pathology fellow Jefferson Med. Coll., Phila., 1999; intern Rochester Gen. Hosp., NY, 2002, physician, 2001—02, Strong Meml. Hosp., Rochester, 2002—. Organizer Med. Supplies for Bosnia, London, 1998; healthcare cons. Gerson Lehrman, Rochester, 2004; spkr. in field. Author: Resolving Quandries in Dermatology, Pathology and Dermatopathology II, 2000, Treatment of Skin Disease, 2002; contbr. articles to periodicals;, editor chpt. to books. Physician Jeff Hope, Phila., 1999—2000; advisor Muslim Youth Group, Rochester, 2001—; event organizer Iraq Earthquake Relief, 2004. Recipient Laser and Cosmetic fellowship, 2005; Laser Medicine fellow. Mem.: Soc. Investigative Dermatology, Am. Acad. Dermatology. Muslim. Achievements include created Smart Start, safety program for elementary students, 1998. Avocations: swimming, photography, canoeing. Office: Strong Meml Hosp 601 Elmwood Ave 697 Rochester NY 14642

GALASK, RUDOLPH PETER, obstetrician, gynecologist; b. Fort Dodge, Iowa, Dec. 23, 1935; s. Peter Otto and Adeline Amelia (Maranesi) G.; m. Gloria Jean Vasti, June 19, 1965 BS, Drake U., 1959; MD, U. Iowa, 1964, MS, 1967. Diplomate Am. Bd. Obstetrics and Gynecology. Research fellow in microbiology U. Iowa, Iowa City, 1965-67, resident in ob-gyn., 1967-70, asst. prof., 1970-74, asst. prof. microbiology, 1973-74, assoc. prof. obstetrics and gynecology microbiology, 1974-78, prof., 1978—, chmn. exec. com. Coll. Medicine, 1992-93, prof. dermatology, 1999—. Cons. various pharm. and diagnostic cos. Editor: Infectious Diseases in the Female Patient, 1986-89; contbr. numerous articles to profl. jours. Served to staff sgt. USNG, 1954-64 Recipient I.D.S.O.G./Ortho McNeil award for outstanding contbns. to field of infectious diseases in ob-gyn., A.P.G.O. Excellence in Tchg. award, 1997, I.D.S.O.G. Founders award, 2004; named one of Ams. Top Drs., 2000, Ams. Top OB/GYN, 2002, Ams. Top Drs. for cancer, 2005; numerous grants to study the efficacy of various antibiotics and chemotherapeutics. Fellow Am. Gynecol. and Obstet. Soc., Am. Coll. Obstetricians and Gynecologists, Infectious Disease Am.; mem. AAAS, Cen. Assn. for Obstetricians and Gynecologists, Infectious Disease Soc. for Ob-Gyn. (pres. 1982-84, founding mem.), Soc. Gynecol. Investigation (coun. 1987-90), Queens Gynecol. Soc. (hon.), Tex. Assn. Obstetricians and Gynecologists (hon.), Am. Soc. Microbiology, Izaac Walton League, Ducks Unltd. Club (sponsor), Sigma Xi. Roman Catholic. Office: Univ Iowa Hosps Dept Ob-Gyn Iowa City IA 52242 E-mail: rudolph-galast@uiowa.edu. *Power is a perception that lasts a moment but respect is a legacy that lasts forever.*

GALASSO, FRANCIS SALVATORE, materials scientist; b. Monson, Mass., Apr. 26, 1931; s. Paul and Rubino (Cirillo) G.; m. Lois E. Wood; children: Cynthia Egolf, Gary Galasso. BS, U. Mass., 1953; MS, U. Conn., 1957, PhD, 1960. Prin. scientist United Techs. Rsch. Ctr., East Hartford, Conn., 1974-77, sr. material scientist, 1977-85, mgr., 1985-91; owner Galasso Tech. Assocs., Manchester, Conn., 1991—; chief materials United Techs. Rsch. Ctr., East Hartford, Conn., 1960-74. Mem. adv. bd. Chem. Rubber Co., 1971—; cons. in space experiments NASA, Huntsville, Ala., 1971-77; vis. prof. U. Conn., Storrs, 1985—. Author 6 books; contbr. articles to profl. jours. patentee in field. Coach Manchester Little League, 1960-75, v.p., 1970-84, pres., 1984=88, mem. bd. govs. adv. com. on accreditation, 1988-90. 1st lt. USAF, 1953-55. Fellow Am. Ceramic Soc.; mem. AIME, Am. Chem. Soc., Am. Legion, Army-Navy Club, Sigma Xi. Democrat. Roman Catholic. Office: 13 Green Manor Rd Manchester CT 06040-3342 E-mail: locyngar@aol.com.

GALBRAITH, JAMES MARSHALL, lawyer, corporate financial executive; b. Iowa City, Oct. 4, 1942; s. John Semple and Laura (Huddleston) G.; m. Margaret Rodi, Aug. 19, 1966; children: Margaret Laura, Katherine Lou, Robert James. BA, Pomona Coll., 1964; JD, Stanford U., 1967. Bar: Calif. 1968. Assoc. Gibson, Dunn & Crutcher, Los Angeles, 1967-68; ptnr. Rodi, Pollock, Pettker, Galbraith & Cahill, Los Angeles, 1968-84, of counsel, 1984—2003; pres. Bell Helmets Internat., Inc., San Marino, Calif., 1980-84; ptnr. Palm Properties Co., San Marino, Calif., 1979—2001. Pres., dir. Van de Kamp's Bakers, Inc., San Marino, Calif., 1984—87; ptnr. Huntington Hotel Assocs., San Marino, 1986—95; pres. Crestmont Fin. Svcs., Inc., 1991—2004, Crestmont Investments, LLC, 1996—. Author: In the Name of the People, 1977, The Money Tree, 1982, Fear of Failure, 1993, Patient Power, 1995; mem. bd. editors Stanford Law Rev., 1965-67. Trustee Pomona Coll., 1987-89, hon. trustee, 1989—; trustee, mem. exec. com. Children's Hosp. L.A., 1986-91, hon. trustee, 1991—; mem. Soc. of Fellows, Huntington Libr. Art Gallery and Bot. Gardens, 1982—; mem. Young Pres. Orgn., 1979-93. Mem. State Bar Calif., Phi Beta Kappa. Clubs: California (L.A.), Valley Hunt (Pasadena). Episcopalian. Home: 1640 Oak Grove Ave San Marino CA 91108-1109 Office: 2600 Mission St San Marino CA 91108-1676

GALBRAITH, JOHN KENNETH, retired economist; b. Iona Station, Ont., Can., Oct. 15, 1908; s. William Archibald and Catherine (Kendall) Galbraith; m. Catherine Atwater, Sept. 17, 1937; children: Alan, Peter, James. BS, U. Guelph, 1931, LLD (hon.); MS, U. Calif., 1933, PhD, 1934; postgrad., Cambridge (Eng.) U., 1937—38; LLD (hon.), Bard Coll., U. Calif.; LLD (hon.), Miami U.; LLD (hon.), U. Mass., U. Mysore, Brandeis U., U. Toronto, U. Sask., U. Mich., U. Durham, R.I. Coll., Boston Coll., Hobart and William Smith Colls., Albion Coll., Tufts U., Adelphi Suffolk Coll., Mich. State U., Louvain U., Oxford U., U. Paris, Carleton Coll., U. Vt., Queens U., Moscow State U., Harvard U., Smith Coll. London Sch. Economics, others. Rsch. fellow U. Calif., 1931—34; instr. and tutor Harvard U., 1934—39; asst. prof. econs. Princeton U., 1939—42; econ. adviser Nat. Def. Adv. Commn., 1940—41; asst. adminstr. in charge price div. OPA, 1941—42, dep. adminstr., 1942—43; mem. bd. of editors Fortune Mag., 1943—48; lectr. Harvard U., 1948—49, prof. econs., 1949—75, Paul M. Warburg prof. econs., 1959—75, ret., 1975. Hon. fellow Trinity Coll., Cambridge U.; hon. prof. U. Geneva; U.S. amb. to India, 1961—63. Author: numerous books including, American Capitalism, 1952, A Theory of Price Control, 1952, The Great Crash, 1955, The Affluent Society, 1958, The Liberal Hour, 1960, Economic Development, 1963, The Scotch, 1964, The New Industrial State, 1967, Indian Painting, 1968, Ambassador's Journal, 1969, Economics, Peace and Laughter, 1971, A China Passage, 1973, Economics and the Public Purpose, 1973, Money: Whence It Came, Where It Went, 1975, The Age of Uncertainity, 1977; author: (with Nicole Salinger) Almost Everyone's Guide to Economics, 1978; author: Annals of an Abiding Liberal, 1979, The Nature of Mass Poverty, 1979, A Life in Our Times, 1981, The Anatomy of Power, 1983, The Voice of the Poor: Essays in Economic and Political Persuasion, 1983, A View From the Stands, 1986, Economics in Perspective: A Critical History, 1987; author: (with Stanislav Menshikov) Capitalism, Communism and Coexistence, 1988; author: (novels) The Triumph, 1968, A Tenured Professor, 1990, The Culture of Contentment, 1992, A Journey Through Economic Time, 1994, A Short History of Financial Euphoria, 1993, The Good Society, 1996, Name-Dropping From F.D.R. on, 1999, The Essential Galbraith, 2001, The Economics of Innocent Fraud, 2004; contbr. to econ. and sci. jours. Dir. U.S. Strategic Bombing Survey, 1945, Office of Econ. Security Policy, State Dept., 1946. Recipient Medal of Freedom, 2000; fellow, Social Sci. Rsch. Coun., 1937—38. Fellow: Am. Acad. Arts and Letters (pres. 1984—87); mem.: AAAS, Ams. for Dem. Action (chmn. 1967—68), Am. Agrl. Econ. Assn., Am. Econ. Assn. (pres. 1972), Saturday, Century. Home: 30 Francis Ave Cambridge MA 02138-2010 Office: Harvard U 206 Littauer Ctr Cambridge MA 02138 Fax: 617-496-1200.*

GALBRAITH, JOHN ROBERT, insurance company executive; b. Portland, Oreg., Oct. 18, 1938; s. Maurice Kerr and Margaret Ione (Veach) G.; m. Maureen McKovich, Oct. 2, 1971 (div. Mar. 1978); children: Margaret Maureen, Marc Ryan; m. Betty Jean Irelan, Dec. 11, 1987. BA, Willamette U., 1960; MBA, U. Washington, 1962. CPA, Oreg. Staff acct. Ernst & Young, Portland, 1962-65; treas. First Pacific Corp., Portland, 1965-71; v.p., treas. Geo McKovich Cos., Palm Beach, Fla. and L.A., 1971-80; v.p., chief fin. officer SAIF Corp., Salem, Oreg., 1980-82; exec. v.p., CFO Liberty N.W. Ins. Corp., Portland, 1983—, bd. dir. Bd. dir. Helmsman Mgmt. Svcs. N.W., Inc., Portland, 1987—. Bd. dirs. Liberty Health Plan, Inc., Portland, 1992—. With Army N.G., 1957-66. Mem. AICPAs, Fin. Exec. Inst., Fla. Ins. CPAs, Calif. Soc. CPAs, Oreg. Soc. CPAs, Multnomah Athletic Club. Republican. Office: Liberty NW Ins Corp One Liberty Ctr Portland OR 97232-2038 Home: 8004 Castlehill Rd Birmingham AL 35242-7226

GALBRAITH, MARIAN, elementary school educator; Tchr. West Side Mid. Sch., Reading and Lang. Arts Dept., Groton, Conn., 1991—, various U., 1986—96; with Conn. State Dept. Edn., Fist Assessment Devel. Lab. Served various com. State Dept. Edn., 1986—93. Bd. dirs. Nat. Edn. Assn., 1993—99. Office: West Side Mid Sch Reading and Lang Arts Dept 250 Brandegee Ave Groton CT 06340

GALBRAITH, NANETTE ELAINE GERKS, forensic and management sciences company executive; b. Chgo., June 15, 1928; d. Harold William and Maybelle Ellen (Little) Gerks; m. Oliver Galbraith III, Dec. 18, 1948; children: Craig Scott, Diane Frances. BS with high honors with distinction, San Diego State U., 1978. Diplomate Am. Bd. Forensic Document Examiners. Examiner of questioned documents San Diego County Sheriff's Dept. Crime Lab., San Diego, 1975-80; sole prop. Nanette G. Galbraith, Examiner of Questioned Documents, San Diego, 1980-82; pres., examiner of questioned documents Galbraith Forensic & Mgmt. Scis., Ltd., San Diego, 1982-97; cons., 1997—. Keynote spkr. Internat. Assn Forensic Scis., Adelaide, South Australia, 1990. Contbr. articles to profl. jours. including Jour. Forensic Scis., Forensic Sci. Internat., Internat. Jour. Forensic Document Examiners. Fellow: Am. Acad. Forensic Scis. (del. to Peoples Rep. of China 1986, USSR 1988, questioned documents sect.); mem.: Southwestern Assn. Forensic Document Examiners (charter), Am. Soc. Questioned Document Examiners (life; jour. editl. bd. 2000—), 1909 Univ. Club San Diego, Southwestern Yacht Club (life), Phi Kappa Phi. Republican. Episcopalian. Personal E-mail: nggalbrait@aol.com.

GALBRAITH, RUTH LEGG, retired dean, home economist; b. Lecompte, La., Nov. 5, 1923; d. Byron S. and Dora Ruth (Lindley) Legg; m. Harry W. Galbraith, June 16, 1950; 1 son, Allan Legg. BS, Purdue U., 1945, PhD, 1950. Chemist E.I. duPont de Nemours, Waynesboro, Va., 1945-46; textile chemist Gen. Electric Co., Bridgeport, Conn., 1946-47; teaching asst. Purdue U., 1947-48, research fellow, 1948-50; prof. textiles and clothing U. Tenn., Knoxville, 1950-55; asso. prof. U. Ill., Urbana, 1956-64, prof., 1964-70. chmn. textiles and clothing div., 1962-70; prof., head consumer affairs dept. Auburn (Ala.) U., 1970-73; dean Sch. Home Econs., head home econs. research, 1973-85. Mem. task force on quality of living Dept. Agr., 1967-68; mem. nat. adv. com. Flammable Fabrics Act, 1971-73; mem. U.S. Dept. Agr. Com. of Nine, 1981-83, chmn., 1983 Mem. editorial bd.: Research Jour. Home Econs., 1973-77, chmn. policy bd., 1978-80; contbr. articles to profl. jours. Recipient Disting. Alumni award Purdue U., 1970 Fellow Am. Inst. Chemists; mem. Am. Home Econs. Assn. (chmn. agy. mem. unit 1975-76, chmn. research sect. 1978-80, Outstanding Home Economist award 1984), Ala. Home Econs. Assn. (pres. 1983-84), Am. Assn. Textile Chemists and Colorists, Am. Chem. Soc., ASTM (3d v.p. com. D-13 textiles 1975-79), Assn. Adminstrs. Home Econs., Nat. Council Adminstrs. Home Econs., AAUW, Sigma Xi, Omicron Nu, Phi Kappa Phi, Delta Kappa Gamma. Home: 368 Singleton St Auburn AL 36830-6317

GALBRAITH, WILLIAM BRUCE, internist, educator; b. Romeo, Mich., Oct. 21, 1930; s. Bruce McKenzie and Helen Athelene (Stringham) G.; m. Jo Anne Fetterly Ames, June 27, 1953; children: Elise, Susan, Scott. BS, Ariz. State U., 1953; MD, George Washington U., 1957. Diplomate Am. Bd. Internal Medicine. Internship Good Samaritan Hosp., Phoenix, 1957-58; residency U. Iowa Hosps. and Clinics, Iowa City, 1958-61; instr. internal medicine U. Iowa Coll. Medicine, Iowa City, 1961-63, asst. prof., 1963-65, dir. gen. medicine tng. program, 1994-96, assoc. internal medicine, 1994-95; prof. clin. internal medicine U. Iowa, Iowa City, 1995-97, prof. emeritus, 1998—; owner Internists P.C., Cedar Rapids, Iowa, 1965-93, pres., 1986-93. Bd. dirs. Am. Bd. Internal Medicine, Phila., 1992-96. Trustee Mercy Med. Ctr., Cedar Rapids, 1997—; trustee Meth-Wick Cmty., 1999—, chair, 2005—; founding chmn. Cmty. Health Free Clinic, Cedar Rapids, 2002— Fellow ACP/ASIM (gov. for Iowa 1979-83, Laureate award 1988, master 1997); mem. Alpha Omega Alpha. Avocation: flyfishing. Personal E-mail: WGalbra66@aol.com.

GALDA, DWIGHT WILLIAM, finance company executive; b. Bklyn., Dec. 19, 1942; s. Fred C. and Audrey D. G.; children: Cynthia A., Gregory J.; m. Suzanne Galda, May 20, 2004. BA, Widener U., 1964; MBA, Tex. Christian U., 2000; MPA, MS, U. Tex., 2002. ChFC; accredited estate planning cons., cert. Nat. Assn. Securities Dealers, registered Prin. and Nat. Panel Arbitration. Rep. United Svcs. Planning Assn. and Ind. Rsch. Agy., Ft. Worth, 1983-86; dist. exec. USPA and IRA, Ft. Worth, 1986-92, regional exec., 1992-96, prin., 1990-96, Carefree (Ariz.) Capital Mgmt. and Rsch., Carefree, Ariz., 1997—. Ind. cons. Dwight W. Galda Consultancy, 1985-, adf. econ. prof., Western Internat. U., 2003-. Contbr. articles profl. jours.; creator U.S. Army Opposing Force Program, 1976. Lt. col. U.S. Army, 1964-82; Army attache U.S. Embassy, Cambodia, 1973-75. Recipient Pace award Dept. of Army, 1976, 77, Legion of Merit, Bronze star with V and 2 oak leaf clusters, Meritorious Svc. medal 4 oak leaf clusters, air medal with V and 4 oak leaf clusters, Vietnamese Cross of Gallantry with Silver star, Cambodian Nat. Def. Svc. medal. Fellow Chartered Fin. Analysts Inst.; mem. Phoenix Chartered Fin. Analysts Soc. Episcopalian. Avocations: running, chamber music, travel. E-mail: dgalda@att.net.

GALE, DIANE, music educator; b. Boston, Mass., Mar. 19, 1957; d. Charles Levine and Caroyln Ada Kaitz; m. Allen Gale, Jan. 10, 1987. BA, St. Joseph Coll., 1981; MS, C.W. Post Coll. Long Island U, 1987; student, Stony Brook U, 1988—. Piano tchr. SPTF, Suffolk County, NY, 1987—; music tchr. Solomon Schaeher Day Sch., Commache, NY, 1994—2002; adj. piano, voice NYSSMA, NY, 1998—; children's choir dir. Conglist. Ch. of Patchoque (N.Y.), 1999—; music tchr. Connetiguot Sch., Bohemar, NY, 2002—. Soprano I Long Island Symphonic Choral Assn., Bay Area Fine Arts BAFFA. Home: 33 Gabon Lane Coram NY 11727-1416

GALE, FOURNIER JOSEPH, III, lawyer; b. Mobile, Ala., Aug. 3, 1944; s. Fournier J. Jr. and Clara (Beckham) G.; m. Louise Smith, Aug. 7, 1965; children: Carolyn, Jeanette. BA, U. Ala., 1966, JD, 1969; postgrad., Oxford U., summer 1968. Bar: Ala. 1969. From assoc. to ptnr. Cabaniss, Johnston, Gardner, Dumas & O'Neal, Birmingham, Ala., 1969-84; ptnr. Maynard, Cooper & Gale, PC, Birmingham, 1984—. Bd. dirs. McWane, Inc., Birmingham; gen. counsel, bd. dirs. Bus. Coun. Ala., Birmingham, 1977—; bd. dirs., So. Rsch. Inst.; mem. Ala. Permanent Study Commn. on Judiciary, 1977-83; mem. Jefferson County Jud. Nominating Commn., 1993-2000; chmn. Ala. Commn. on Higher Edn., 1998-2003; spl. counsel to Gov. Don Siegelman, 1999-2002. Mem. Leadership Birmingham, 1986-87; pres. U. Ala. Law Sch. Found., 1987-89. Mem. ABA (standing com. on environ. law, standing com. on fed. judiciary), Birmingham Bar Assn. (pres. 1989), Ala. Young Lawyers Assn. (pres. 1976-77), Am. Judicature Soc. (bd. dirs. 1980-85), Jud. Conf. Ala., Am. Bar Found., Kiwanis. Roman Catholic. Home: 2937 Southwood Rd Birmingham AL 35223-1232 Office: Maynard Cooper & Gale PC 2400 Amsouth Harbert Plz Birmingham AL 35203-2600 Office Phone: 205-254-1000. Business E-Mail: galefo@mcglaw.com.

GALE, JAMES DARREN, nuclear energy industry executive; b. San Antonio, Tex., Feb. 26, 1961; s. Darrel Dee and Coleen Elaine Gale; m. Marsha B. Hall, Dec. 30, 1983; children: Derek Jameson, Madeline Elizabeth. BS in Nuc. Engring., Kans. State U., 1983, MS in Nuc. Engring., 1984; MBA, Averett Coll., 1996. Technician Gen. Atomic, San Diego, 1984—86; team leader Advanced Nuc. Fuels, Richland, Wash., 1986—91; v.p. U.S. region steam generator svc.s Framatome ANP, Lynchburg, Va., 1991—. Adv. bd. dept. nuc. engring. Fla. U., Gainesville, 2000—; pres. found. bd. dirs. Ctr'. Va. Gov.'s Sch. Sci. Tech., Lynchburg, 2002—. Mem. ch. coun. Holy Cross Cath. Ch., Lynchburg, 2001—03. Recipient 1st-team Acad. All-Am. Football Team, Coll. Sports Info. Dir. of Am., 1981, 1st-team Acad. All-Am. Football Team, Coll. Sports Info. Dirs. Am., 1982, Mem. Blue Key, Kans. State Chpt. Blue Key, 1981-82; scholar Leader of Tomorrow, Dane G. Hansen Found., 1979—82, Inst. Nuc. Power Ops., 1981, 1982, Student-Scholar, Big Eight Athletic Conf., 1983. Mem.: Boonsboro Country Club, Phi Kappa Phi. Roman Catholic. Achievements include development of Gadolinia absorber. Avocations: golf, running, basketball, reading, travel. Home: 100 Fairfax Court Lynchburg VA 24503 Office: Framatome ANP 155 Mill Ridge Rd Lynchburg VA 24502-4341 Office Phone: 434-832-2804. E-mail: darren.gale@framatome-anp.com.

GALE, JEFFREY, management consultant, business educator; b. Chgo., Aug. 13, 1948; s. Burton and Shirlee Gale; m. Julane Marx, Aug. 29, 1987; 1 child, Brandon. PhD of Mgmt., UCLA, 1976, JD, 1975; SM Mgmt., MIT, 1971, SB Mgmt., 1970. Bar: Calif. 1975; cert. Broker Calif. Dept. Real Estate, 2000. Asst. prof. bus. adminstrn. U. Wash., Seattle, 1977—84; asst. prof. mgmt. U. Tex. Dallas, Richardson, 1984—85; prof. mgmt. Loyola Marymount U., LA, 1985—. Mgmt. cons., Sherman Oaks, Calif., 1977—; v.p. internat. svcs. David French and Assocs., LLC, El Segundo, Calif., 1999—. Mem.: Internat. Assn. for Bus. and Soc., Acad. Internat. Bus., Acad. Mgmt. D-Liberal. Jewish. Avocations: travel, theater, films. Home: 3761 Whitespeak Dr Sherman Oaks CA 91403 Office: Loyola Marymount Univ 1 Loyola Marymount Dr Los Angeles CA 90045-2659 Office Phone: 310-338-7406. Office Fax: 310-338-3000. E-mail: jgale@lmv.edu.

GALE, JOHN A., state official; b. Omaha, Nebraska, 1940; m. Carol Gale; children: David, Elaine, Steve. BA in govt. internat. relations, Carleton Coll., Northfield, Minn., 1962; JD in govt. internat. relations, Univ. Chgo. Law Sch., Northfield, Minn., 1965. Sec. state State of Nebr., 2000—; pvt. practice of law 30 yrs.; elected state chmn. Nebr. State Rep. Party, 1986; asst. U.S. atty. Lincoln, 1971; legis. asst. Wash., DC, 1968; asst. U.S. atty. Omaha, 1965. Republican. Office: NE Sec State State Capitol Ste 2300 Lincoln NE 68509 Office Phone: 402-471-2554. Business E-Mail: sos08@nol.org.

GALE, JOSEPH H., federal judge; b. Smithfield, Va., 1953; s. Robert Whitfield and Charlotte H. G. AB, Princeton U., 1976; JD, U. Va., 1980. Atty. Dewey, Ballantine, Bushby, Palmer & Wood, N.Y.C., Washington, 1980-83, Dickstein, Shapiro & Morin, Washington, 1983-84; legis. counsel Senator Daniel P. Moynihan, Washington, 1985-88; adminstrv. asst. and tax counsel Hon. Daniel P. Moynihan, Washington, 1989, chief counsel, 1990-92; chief tax counsel Senate Finance Com., Washington, 1993-94, minority chief of staff, 1995; judge U.S. Tax Ct., Washington, 1996—. Dillard fellow U. Va. Office: US Tax Court 400 2nd St NW Washington DC 20217-0002

GALE, NEIL JAN, Internet company executive, computer scientist, consultant; b. Chgo., Jan. 12, 1960; s. Jack and Adele Gale. AA in Computer Sci., Wright Coll., 1980; D of Bus. Mgmt. (hon.), London Inst. Applied Rsch., 1993; diploma, Academia Argentina de Diplomacia, 1994; diploma (hon.), Institut Des Affaires Internationales, Paris, 1994; D of Bus. Mgmt. (hon.), World Acad., Monchengladbach, Germany, 1994. Mgr. Gen. Fin. Co., Chgo., 1980-84; mktg. mgr. Midland Fin. Co., Chgo., 1984-85; mktg. dir. Diamond Mortgage Corp., Chgo., 1985-86; sr. fin. analyst McKay Mazda-Nissan, Evanston, Ill., 1987-88; pres., CEO, Nat. Consumer Credit Cons., Chgo., 1988—; webmaster Everything Internet (merger with Millenium Techs. Inc. 1998), Naperville, Ill., 1996-98; pres. DrGale.com, Carol Stream, Ill., 1998—. Hon. prof. bus. mgmt. Inst. des Hautes Etudes Econs. et Sociales, Brussels, 1993; hon. prof. fin. Australian Inst. Coordinated Rsch., 1994; mem. adv. coun. Internat. Biog. Ctr., Cambridge, Eng.; mem. bd. govs., Continental gov. Am. Biog. Inst., 1990—, mem. rsch. bd. advisors, 1989—; notary pub. Ill., 1986-90; bd. dirs., amb. Ill. affiliate U.S. Woman's C. of C., 2002—; bd. dirs. U.S. Dept. of Peace Coaliton, 2003—. Contbr. articles to profl. jours. First aid chmn. Walk with Israel, 1977; notary pub., Ill., 1986-90; mem. computer com. Village of Hanover Park, Ill., 1997-2000; mem. bd. advisors U.S. Women's C. of C., 2002-. Decorated Knight of Order of San Ciriaco;

recipient Bus. in Urban Environment award Chgo. Bd. Edn. and Ill. Bell Tel. Co., 1978, Outstanding Achievement award Chgo. Pub. Libr., 1979. Mem. Auto Credit (hon.), Friendship Cir. Club (treas. 1976-78). Avocation: collecting antique Chicago postcards and books. Home and Office: DrGale dot com PMB 208 780 W Army Trail Rd Carol Stream IL 60188-9297 Office Phone: 800-736-1036. Personal E-mail: drgale@drgale.com.

GALE, ROBERT LEE, retired literature educator, critic; b. Des Moines, Dec. 27, 1919; s. Erie Lee and Miriam (Fisher) G.; m. Maureen Dowd, Nov. 18, 1944; children: John Lee, James Dowd, Christine Ann. BA, Dartmouth Coll., 1942; MA, Columbia U., 1947, PhD, 1952. Lectr. Columbia U., N.Y.C., 1947-48; instr. U. Del., Newark, 1949-52; asst. prof. U. Miss., Oxford, 1952-56, assoc. prof., 1956-59; asst. prof. U. Pitts., 1959-60, assoc. prof., 1960-65, prof. Am. lit., 1965-87; ret., 1987. Fulbright prof. Inst. Univ. Orientale, Naples, Italy, 1956-58, U. Helsinki, Finland, 1975. Author: Thomas Crawford, 1964, The Caught Image: Figurative Language in Henry James, 1964, Richard Henry Dana, Jr., 1969, Francis Parkman, 1973, Plots and Characters in Mark Twain, 1973, John Hay, 1978, Luke Short, 1981, Will Henry, 1984, Louis L'Amour, 1985, rev. edit., 1992, A Henry James Encyclopedia, 1989, Matt Braun, 1990, A Nathaniel Hawthorne Encyclopedia, 1991, The Gay Nineties: A Cultural Dictionary of the 1890s in the U.S., 1992, A Cultural Encyclopedia of the American 1850s, 1993, A Herman Melville Encyclopedia, 1995, An F. Scott Fitzgerald Encyclopedia, 1998, A Sarah Orne Jewett Companion, 1999, A Dashiell Hammett Companion, 2000, An Ambrose Bierce Companion, 2001, A Lafcadio Hearn Companion, 2002, A Ross Macdonald Companion, 2002, A Mickey Spillane Companion, 2003, A Henry Wadsworth Longfellow Companion, 2003; contbr. articles to profl. jours., chpts. to books, revs. Served with U.S. Army, 1942-46, ETO. Mem. MLA, Phi Beta Kappa. Home: 131 Techview Ter Pittsburgh PA 15213-3820 Office Phone: 412-683-7872.

GALE, STAN, real estate company executive; b. L.I., N.Y. 3 children. BA, MBA, Rollins Coll. With Daniel Gale Agy., 1973—76, Grubb & Ellis, 1976—85; pres. Sammis Co. N.E., 1985; chmn. The Gale Co., Florham Pk., NJ, CEO; co-owner N.Y. Yankees, N.J. Devils, N.J. Nets. Office: The Gale Co 100 Campus Drive Ste 200 Florham Park NJ 07932

GALE, STANLEY WILLIAM, psychiatrist; b. Mpls., Apr. 30, 1947; s. Harvey and Florence (Lapp) G.; children: Shawna, Greg. BS, Yale U., 1970, JD, 1974, MD, 1975. Asst. psychiatrist N.Y. Hosp., N.Y.C., 1975-78; pvt. practice Providence, 1978—. Mem. staff Butler Hosp., Providence, Miriam Hosp., Providence, Women's & Infant's Hosp., Providence, R.I. Hosp., Providence. Mem. Am. Psychiat. Assn., R.I. Med. Soc. Office Phone: 401-831-7756.

GALE, THOMAS MARTIN, university dean; b. Green Bay, Wis., May 16, 1926; s. Thomas Griswold and Carrie (Danz) G.; m. Mary Margaret Hardman, May 28, 1960; children— Thomas Hardman, John Martin. BA, U. Calif. at Berkeley, 1949, MA, 1950; PhD, U. Pa., 1958. Dean Coll. Arts and Scis. N.Mex. State U., 1971-91, bd. dirs. Acad. for Learning in Retirement, 1991—, ret., 1991, acting provost, 2001. With Border Books Festival, 1996-2000. Chmn. N.Mex. Humanities Coun., NEH, 1972-77; chmn. Las Cruces Am. 2000 Task Force, 1991-98; vice-chmn. N.Mex. Commn. on Higher Edn., 1997-99; pres. bd. dirs. N.Mex. State U. Found., 2001-03., bd. dirs. Las Cruces Pub. Sch. Found., 2002-; With AUS, 1944-46. Social Sci. Rsch. fellow, 1952-53, 53-54; Huntington Libr. fellow, 1959; Fulbright fellow Peru, 1960; recipient N.Mex. Disting. Svc. award, 2002. Mem. Phi Beta Kappa, Phi Alpha Theta. Clubs: Rotarian. Home: 3115 Majestic Rdg Las Cruces NM 88011-4603

GALEF, HAROLD ROBERT, psychiatrist; b. N.Y.C., June 6, 1928; s. Joseph and Adelaide Irene (Obadiah) G.; m. Bernice Schutzer, May 26, 1983; m. Winifred Betty Kron, Sept. 17, 1950 (dec. 1969); children: Deborah, David. A.B., Syracuse U., 1948; M.A., Columbia U., 1949; M.D., Chgo. Med. Sch., 1953. Diplomate Am. Bd. Psychiatry. Intern, USPHS Hosp., S.I., N.Y., 1953-54; resident in psychiatry Hillside Hosp., 1956-57, Bronx Mcpl. Hosp. Ctr., 1957-59; practice psychiatry, N.Y.C., 1959—; clin. assos. prof. psychiatry Albert Einstein Med. Coll., Scarsdale N.Y., 1959—; supr., tng. analyst Westchester Ctr. for Psychotherapy and Psychoanalysis, White Plains, N.Y., 1978—, dir. 1995-98. Served with USPHS, 1953-56. Fellow Am. Psychiat. Assn., Am. Acad. Psychoanalysis; mem. Westchester Psychiat. Soc. (exec. coun. 1974-76). Avocations: chorale; foreign languages; etymology; reading; music. Home and Office: 15 Roosevelt Pl Scarsdale NY 10583-5909 Office Phone: 914-472-4982.

GALEF, SANDRA RISK, state legislator, educator; b. LaCrosse, Wis., May 7, 1940; d. William P. and Christine Risk; m. Steven Allen Galef, Mar. 30, 1963 (dec.); children: Gregory Todd, Gwendolyn. BS, Purdue U., 1962; MS in Edn., U. Va., 1965. Tchr. Albemarle Schs., Charlottesville, Va., 1962-65, Scarsdale (N.Y.) Schs., 1965-67; mem. Westchester County Bd. Legislators, 1980-93, minority leader, 1984-93; mem. N.Y. State Assembly, Dist. 90, 1993—, chair com. on librs. and ednl. tech. Bd. dirs. Children's Hosp. Found., 1998—, Bethel Nursing Home, 1999—2003; bd. dirs. United Way No. Westchester, 1973—, pres., 1979-80, v.p., 1975-79; trustee Ossining (N.Y.) Pub. Libr., 1975-80, Briarcliff (N.Y.) Nursery Sch., 1974-76; pres. chpt. LWV, 1973-75; chair Ossining Youth Employment Svc., 1977-80; bd. dirs Day Care Coun. Westchester, 1976-79; pub. affairs chair Jr. League Westchester-on-Hudson, Tarrytown, 1978-80, mem. tng. com., 1980-85; mem. adv. bd. Children's Village, Dobbs Ferry, N.Y., 1984—, Interfaith Coun. for Action, Ossining, 1983—; mem. Ossining Upward Bound Substance Abuse Coun., 1984—, Ossining Restoration Com., 1975-77; mem. nominating com. White Plains chpt. ARC, 1985-86; bd. dirs. Phelps Meml. Hosp. Ctr., Vis. Nurse Svcs. Westchester. Recipient Harold J. Marshall award United Way No. Westchester, 1981. Mem. N.Y. Assn. Counties (v.p. 1984-85, pres. 1985, mem. steering com. 1989-92, Legislator of Yr. 1993), Westchester Mcpl. Planning Fedn. (bd. dirs. 1982—), Westchester 2000 (mem. task force 1985), Ossining C. of C. Avocations: gardening, sewing, crafts, decorating. Office: 2 Church St Ossining NY 10562-4802 Office Phone: 914-941-1111. E-mail: galefs@assembly.state.ny.us.

GALEL, SUSAN ALPERT, transfusion medicine; MD, Harvard U., Boston, 1979. Diplomate Am. Bd. Pediat., Am. Bd. Pediatric Hematology/Oncology. Med. dir. Stanford Med. Sch. Blood Ctr., Palo Alto, CA, Calif., 1987—. Office: Stanford Med Sch Blood Center 800 Welch Rd Palo Alto CA 94304

GALEMA, JOSEPH M., music director; b. Lafayette, Ind., Sept. 30, 1954; s. Joseph Martin Galema, Sr. and Lois Mae Galema. BA, Calvin Coll., 1976; MusM, U. Mich., 1978, D Musical Arts, 1982. Asst. organist Christ Ch. Grosse Pointe, Grosse Pointe Farms, Mich., 1978—81; organist First English Evang. Luth. Ch., Grosse Pointe, 1981—82; asst. for adminstrn. and music USAF Acad., USAF Academy, Colo., 1982—84, assoc. music dir., 1984—89, sr. music dir., acad. organist, 1989—. Musician: (recital) Am. Inst. Organbuilders 27th Nat. Conv., Organ Hist. Soc. Nat. Conv., Region VI Am. Guild Organists Conv., (service organist) 73rd Nat. Episcopal Conv. Eucharist; contbr. articles to profl. jours. Named to, Outstanding Young Men Am., 1985; recipient Palmer Christian award, U. Mich., 1987. Mem.: Am. Guild Organists, Am. Choral Dirs. Assn., Assn. Anglican Musicians. Episcopalian. Avocations: travel, reading. Home: 2672 Hatch Cir Colorado Springs CO 80918-6020 Office: Cadet Chapel Ste 100 2348 Sijan Dr U S A F Academy CO 80840-8280 Office Phone: 719-333-7846. Personal E-mail: joegalema@aol.com. Business E-Mail: joseph.galema@usafa.af.mil.

GALES, SAMUEL JOEL, retired civilian military employee, counselor; b. Dublin, Miss., June 14, 1930; s. James McNary McNeil and Alice Francis (Smith) Brouds-Gales; m. Martha Ann Jackson (div. Jan. 1978); children: Samuel II (dec.), Martha Diane Townsend, Katherine Roselein, Karlmann Von, Carolyn B., Elizabeth Angelica McCain. BA, Chapman Univ., 1981, MS, 1987. Ordained Eucharist minister, Episcopal Ch., 1985; cert. tchr., Calif.; registered parliamentarian. Enlisted U.S. Army, 1948, advanced through grades to master 1st sgt., 1969, ret., 1976; tchr. Monterey (Calif.) Unified Sch. Dist., 1981-82; civilian U.S. Army Directorate of Logistics, Ft. Ord, Calif., 1982-93; collateral EEOC counselor Dept. Def., U.S. Army, 1987-93; instr. AARP Driver Safety Program, 2001—. Peer counselor, 1982-84. Active Family Svc. Agy., Monterey, 1979-85; rep. Episc. Soc. for Ministry on Aging, Carmel, Calif., 1980-86, Task Force on Aging, Carmel, 1983-87, vestryman, 1982-85, 91-94; ombudsman Monterey County Long-Term Care Program, Calif. Dept. for the Aging, 1993-97; vol. guide Monterey Bay Aquarium Found., 1994—, vol. docent Bay Net, Ctr. for Marine Conservation, Monterey Bay Nat. Marine Sanctuary, 1997-2003. Decorated Air medal. Mem.: Am. Inst. Parliamentarians (registered parliamentarian), Am. Legion (post comdr. 1973—74), Nat. Assn. Parliamentarians (pres. 2000—01, pres. Pi Gamma unit Calif. State Assn. 2000—01), Nat. Assn. Ret. Fed. Employees (pres. chpt. 579 1999—2000), Calif. State Assn. Parliamentarians (dir. Pacific area 2005—), Toastmasters, Forty and Eight (chef-de-gare 1979, 1980), Comdr.'s Club Calif. (pres. Outpost 28 1981—82), Monterey Chess Club. Republican. Avocation: classical music. Home: PO Box 919 1617 Lowell St Seaside CA 93955-3811 Office Phone: 831-394-4520. Personal E-mail: samuelg875@aol.com.

GALESI, DEBORAH LEE, artist; b. Paterson, NJ, Oct. 08; d. John Michael Galesi and Ethel Marchitti; m. Samuel Corbinelli, Oct. 3, 1997. BFA, U. Colo.; studied with, Raymond Whyte and Gene Scarpentoni, NY, Ben Long, Florence; MA, Villa Schifanoia/Inst. Florence. One-woman shows include Lo Sprone, Florence, Italy, 1983, Spinetti Gallery, Florence, 1985, Benvenuti Gallery, Venice, 1986, Salaria Gallery, Spoleto, 1987, Lo Spirale, Prato, Italy, 1988, Traghetto Gallery, Venice, 1987; works exhibited at U. Colo., Boulder, 1980, NY Gallery, NYC, 1981, NJ Gallery, 1981, U. Avignon, France, 1981, Sieve Art Expo, Pontassieve, Italy, 1984, Cenacolo Gallery, Florence, 1985, Modigliani Gallery, Milan, 1990, Art Expo, Verona, 1990, Palazzo Congressi, Salsomaggiore, 1995, Palazzo, Florence, 1996, Montserrat Gallery NY, 1997; represented in permenent collections Montserrat Gallery Chelsey, NYC; contbr. articles to profl. jours. Vol. Natural Resource Def. Coun., Washington, Pacific Whale Found., Hawaii, Ctr. for Marine Conservation, Washington, WWF, Greenpeace. Nat. Art Ctr. award, NY, 1978, others; recipient Stewardess of Ctr. of Light and Harmony award, Sierra Club. Mem. Ptnrs. of Destiny. Avocations: scuba diving, music, rollerblading, chinese painting, piano. Office: PMB 523 PO Box 959 Kihei HI 96753-0959

GALI, HARIPRASAD, research scientist; arrived in U.S., 1996; s. Rajesham and Balaxmi Gali; m. Kavitha Gali, Dec. 17, 1999. BSc, Osmania U., Hyderabad, India, 1993; MSc, U. Hyderabad, India, 1995; PhD, U. Mo., 1999. Postdoctoral fellow U. Mo. Health Care, Columbia, 1999—2002; rsch. scientist Lynntech, Inc., College Station, Tex., 2002—. Contbr. to jours. more than 56 articles and abstracts on target-specific radiopharms. for diagnosis and therapy of cancers. Grantee Small Bus. Innovative Rsch.; Jr. Rsch. fellow, Coun. Sci. & Indsl. Rsch. India, 1994, U. Grants Commn. India, 1995, Summer Rsch. fellow, Jawaharlal Nehru Ctr. Advanced Sci. Rsch., 1994—95. Mem.: Am. Chem. Soc. (assoc.), Soc. Nuc. Medicine (assoc.). Achievements include patents in field; patents pending in field. Office: Lynntech Inc 7607 Eastmark Dr Ste # 102 College Station TX 77840 Office Phone: 979-693-0017.

GALIGARCIA, CARMEN MARIA, artist, educator; b. Havana, Cuba, Mar. 31, 1936; came to U.S., 1967, naturalized, 1972; d. Estefano Gregorio and Lilia (Del Castillo) G.; m. Juan Manuel Velasco, Nov. 28, 1934 (div. Oct. 1980); 1 child, Nelson Ignacio; m. John Sidney Michael Albert, Feb. 21, 1988. BS, Sch. Commerce Havana, 1957, Sch. Plastic Art San Alejandro, Havana, 1960; BFA in Art, BS in Art Edn., Fla. Internat. U., 1995. Cert. tchr., Fla. Analyst for wide body aircraft Ea. Airlines, Miami, Fla., 1972-91; tchr. fine arts Sunset Sr. H.S., Miami, 1995—. Ofcl. poster artist South Fla. Orchid Soc. One woman shows include Galeria Teodora Braga, Belem, Brazil, 1980, Big Five Club, Miami, 1982-83, 86, Equus Art Gallery, Miami Beach, 1992, Galeria Vanidades, Miami Springs, 1996, others; group shows include Embassy Gallery, Miami, 1987, Centre Art Gallery, Indpls., 1988, Palais de Luxembourg, Paris, 1988, IX Internat. Biennial, Valparaiso, Chile, 1989, Inst. Cultural Domecq, Mexico City, 1990, First Salon L.Am. Religious Paintings, 1992, Mus. Sci., 1985-94, others. Bd. dirs. Fla.-Israel Cultural Soc., Miami, 1987—. Recipient 1st prize for watercolors South Fla. Orchid Soc., 1985, 86, 87, 1st hon. mention for watercolors Nat. Capital Orchid Soc., 1991. Mem. Nat. Mus. Women in Arts, Nat. Trust for Hist. Preservation. Republican. Roman Catholic. Avocations: music, reading, travel, writing. Home: 14001 SW 92nd Ave Miami FL 33176-7117

GALIL, ZVI, engineering educator; b. Tel Aviv; m. Bella S. Galil; 1 child, Yair. BS in applied math., Tel Aviv U., 1970, MS in applied math., 1971; PhD in computer sci., Cornell U., 1975. Postdoctoral rsch. IBM Thomas J. Watson Rsch. Ctr., Yorktown Heights, NY, 1975—76; mem. computer sci. faculty Tel Aviv U., 1976—82, chmn. dept. computer sci., 1979—82, prof., 1981—82, Columbia U., 1982—, Morris and Alma A. Schapiro Prof. Engring., 1985—, Julian Clarence Levi Prof. Math. Methods and Computer Sci., 1987—, chmn. dept. computer sci., 1989—95, dean The Fu Found. Sch. of Engring. and Applied Sci., 1995—. Bd. guarantors The Italian Acad. for Advanced Studies in Am. at Columbia U., NYC; editor-in-chief Jour. of Algorithms, 1988—, SIAM Jour. on Computing, Soc. for Indsl. and Applied Math., 1992—. Author: over 200 rsch. papers; editor: (book) Computational Algorithms on Strings. Fellow: Assn. for Computing Machinary (mem., former chair, Automata and Computability Theory group); mem.: NAE. Office: 500 W 120th St MC 4714 New York NY 10027

GALIN, TAD, SR., home business owner; b. Yurovka, Kyiv, Ukraine, Dec. 8, 1930; came to U.S., 1958, naturalized. s. Josef and Janina (Piotrowska) Przegalinski; m. Alice Soroki, May 20, 1959 (dec. Sept. 1967); m. June Ashton, June 6, 1968; children: Tad, Joseph. Lic. mortgage broker, Fla.; cert. Dietary Supplement Health Edn. Act, Am. Nutraceutical Assn. Driver's license tng. exams tchr. Lang. Sch., Cleve., 1958; with Cleaners Hanger Factory, Cleve., 1958—63; indsl. diamond specialist Felker Mfg. Co., Torrence, Calif., 1963—65; owner Lake Heating & Air Conditioning, Pontiac, Mich., 1967, Instant Credit, Flint, Mich., 1968, Remnant Market, Clarkston, Mich., 1969, Warehouse Carpet, Oxford, Mich., 1970—73; home builder Mich., 1973; owner Scientific Meditation Inst. Am., Ft. Lauderdale, 1976, Sci. of Life Ch., 1976; direct distbr. Amway Corp., Ada, Mich., 1975—86; regional v.p. A.L. Williams, Atlanta, 1988; with Nat. Safety Assocs., Memphis, 1989—; regional dir. Nat. Telephone Co., Irvine, Calif., 1991—95; co-founder, presdl. dir. Legacy for Life, Palm Bay, Fla., 1995—. Author: Stalin, Hitler & I, 2001; patentee in field. With U.S. Army, 1952-57, Korea. Avocation: classical guitar. Home: 1300 NW 15th Ave Apt 7 Boca Raton FL 33486-1160 E-mail: Tad@tadgalin.com.

GALINAT, WALTON CLARENCE, research scientist; b. Manchester, Conn., Dec. 9, 1923; m. Elizabeth Ruth Warren, 1945; children: David W., Alice R. BS with honors, U. Conn., 1949; MS, U. Wis., 1951, PhD, 1953. Asst. in genetics Conn. Agrl. Experiment Sta., 1946-50; asst. in agronomy Wis. Agrl. Experimenbt Sta., 1950-53; rsch. fellow, rsch. assoc. Bussey Inst. Harvard U., 1953-64; assoc. prof. Waltham Field Sta. U. Mass., 1964-68, prof. Suburban Experiment Sta., 1968-90, prof. emeritus plant and soil scis., 1990—. With USCG, 1943-46. Recipient Disting. Econ. Botanist award Soc. Econ. Botany, 1994; Disting. Lifetime Achievement in Sci. and Art award U. Mass., 2001. Fellow AAAS. Office: Suburban Experiment Sta U Mass 240 Beaver St Waltham MA 02452-8096 Office Phone: 781-891-0650 x36.

GALINDO, DONALD VERNON, artist; b. Oakland, Calif., Apr. 21, 1925; s. Robert Eli and Josephine G. AB, U. Calif., Berkeley, 1946; BA in Edn., Calif. Coll. Arts and Crafts, 1951, MFA, 1955. Spl. secondary tchr. art credential, Calif. Tchr. art and U.S. history Sequoia Union High Sch., Redwood City, Calif., 1955-56; instr. art Coll. of San Mateo, Calif., 1956-87. Freelance artist, Calif., 1954—; judge Walnut Creek (Calif.) Art Festival, 1954, art shows San Francisco Bay area, 1954-80. One-man retrospective show CSM Gallery, 1976; exhibited in group shows, 1954-85; interviewee Sta. KCSM TV. Lt. USNR, 1944-47, 52-54. Recipient 1st prize for painting Sather Gate Art Festival, Berkeley, Calif., 1954, cert. of merit San Francisco Mayor's Hire the Handicapped Com. Mem. Calif. Tchrs. Assn., Los Californianos Genealogy and Hist. Assn., Coll. of San Mateo Ret. Faculty Assn. Republican. Avocations: collecting small sculptures, early california history, swimming, show horse investing, rodeos. Home: 1268 Rosita Rd Pacifica CA 94044-4223 Office Phone: 650-355-0385.

GALINSKY, DEBORAH JEAN, county official; b. Oakland, Calif., Jan. 22, 1951; d. Jerome James and Barbara Ann (Ball) G.; m. William H. Furr III, Sept. 27, 1997; 1 child by previous marriage, Lauren Rachel Lipscomb. BSW, Bowie State U., 1978. Cert. housing counselor. Substitute tchr. Anne Arundel County Schs., Ft. Meade, Md., 1972-74; addictions counselor Dept. of Health, Ellicott City, Md., 1977-78; coord. dept. Citizens Svcs., housing program specialist Housing and Cmty. Devel., Ellicott City, 1979; coord. youth teen devel. County of Howard, Ellicott City, 1978—; tchr. Rapides Parish Sch. Bd., Pineville, La., 1996—, arts and crafts youth tchr., 1997. Rep. Inter-Agy. Com., Ellicott City, 1990-93; computer instr. Aerie; tchr. Cabrini Sch., Alexandria, La. Author homeownership programs. Vol. Bethany United Meth. Ch., Ellicott City, 1987; tchr. Woodland Presbyn. Ch., Pineville. Fellow Nat. Assn. Housing and Revel. Ofcls.; mem. Nat. Fedn. Housing Counselors, Assn. Cmty. Svcs. (counselors rep.). Democrat. Avocations: dance choreographing, creative art crafts, water aerobics, bicycling, camping. Office: County of Howard Housing & Comm Devel Dept 3450 Court House Dr Ellicott City MD 21043-4330

GALINSKY, GOTTHARD KARL, classicist, educator; b. Strassburg, Alsace, Feb. 7, 1942; came to U.S., 1961, naturalized, 1971; s. Hans Karl and Edith (Margenburg) G.; children Robert Charles, John Anthony. BA, Bowdoin Coll., 1963; MA, Princeton U., 1965, PhD, 1966. Instr. classics Princeton U., 1965-66; mem. faculty U. Tex., Austin, 1966—, prof. classics, 1972—, chmn. dept., 1974-90, Armstrong Centennial prof., 1985-91, Cailloux Centennial prof., 1991—, Disting. tchg. prof., 1999—, chmn. grad. assembly, 1977-79, chmn. faculty senate, 1981-82. Dir. summer seminars NEH, 1975, 76, 83-85, 97 2002, 05; dir. residential seminar, 1977-78, dir. Collaborative Sch. Project, 1987-89, cons., 1976-78, 80-98; classicist-in-residence Am. Acad. Rome, 1972-73, vis. scholar, 1991; mem. adv. coun. Classical Sch., 1967—, chmn., 1982-85, mem. classical jury, 1970-71; lectr. U.S.-U.K. Edn. Commn., 1973; regional chmn. Mellon Humanities Fellowships, 1982-90; nat. lectr. Phi Beta Kappa, 1989-90; vis. Mellon prof. Tulane U., 1995; vis. prof. U. Nacional de La Plata, 1997; vis. prof. Gutenberg U. Mainz, Germany, 1998, Inst. Advanced Study, Princeton, 2000, U. Tex. Inst. for the Humanities, 2001. Author: Aeneas, Sicily and Rome, 1969, Tibulli Carmina, 1971, The Herakles Theme, 1972, Perspectives of Roman Poetry, 1974, Ovid's Metamorphoses, 1975, The Interpretation of Roman Poetry, 1992, Classical and Modern Interactions, 1992, Augustan Culture, 1996, Cambridge Companion to the Age of Augustus, 2005; mem. editl. bd. Classical World, 1973-76, Vergilius, 1973—, Classical Jour., 1991-98, Auster, 1996—. Mem. Leadership Austin, 1983-84. Fellow Am. Coun. Learned Socs., 1968-69, Fulbright fellow, 1972-73, Guggenheim fellow, 1972-73, NEH fellow, 1993-94; recipient Teaching Excellence award U. Tex., 1970, 76, 99, Robert W. Hamilton Author award U. Tex., 1997; Humboldt Found. sr. rsch. award, 1993, reinvitation award, 1998. Mem. Am. Philol. Assn. (Teaching Excellence award 1979, dir. 1980-83), Archaeol. Inst. Am., Classical Assn. Midwest and South (pres. 1980-81), Vergilian Soc. Am. (trustee 1972-76, v.p. 1976-77), Assn. Depts. Fgn. Langs. (exec. com. 1980-83, pres. 1983) Home: 4508 Edgemont Dr Austin TX 78731-5224 Office: U Tex Dept Classics Austin TX 78712-0308 Office Phone: 512-471-8504. Business E-Mail: galinsky@mail.utexas.edu.

GALINSON, MURRAY LAWRENCE, bank executive, director; b. Mpls., May 8, 1937; s. Louis and Kay Galinson; m. Elaine Galinson, Dec. 22, 1959; children: Laura, Jeffrey, Richard. BA, U. Minn., Mpls., 1958; at, Stanford U. Law Sch., 1958—59; JD, U. Minn., Mpls., 1961; PhD, U.S.I.U., San Diego, 1976; JD (hon.), Calif. Western Law Sch., 2001. Bar: Minn., Calif. Asst. U.S. attorney U.S. Dept. Justice, Mpls., 1961—62; ptnr. Mullin, Galinson & Swirnoff, 1963—70; prof. law Calif. Western Law Sch., San Diego, 1971—83; dep. campaign dir. Mondale for Pres., Washington, 1983—84; pres. and CEO San Diego Nat. Bank, San Diego, 1984—98, chmn. bd. dir., 1998—. Bd. dir. Price Smart Corp., San Diego, 1st Dental Health. Bd. dir. Weingart Found., L.A., Calif., 1998—, Price Charities, San Diego, 1998—, Calif. Western Law Sch., 1995—, San Diego Jewish Cmty. Found., 2000—, Calif. State U., Long Beach, 2001—, chmn., 2004—. Democrat. Jewish. Office: The Price Group Ste 520 7979 Ivanhoe Ave La Jolla CA 92038

GALIPEAU, PETER ARMAND, councilman; b. Willimantic, Conn., July 26, 1963; s. Joseph Denis and Theresa Dorothy (Gratton) G.; m. Susan Lynn Arbogast, June 23, 1990; 1 child, Jennifer Lynn. BS magna cum laude, Ea. Conn. State U., 1989. Regional mktg. mgr. Tele-Media Corp., Willimantic, 1989-91; advt. account exec. Time Warner, Norwalk, Ohio, 1991—2002; owner Seneca Video Prodns., Tiffin, Ohio, 1992—. City councilman at large Tiffin City Coun., Ohio, 1998—; chmn. Materials and Equipment Com., Tiffin, 1998-99; mem. Law and Cmty. Planning Com., Tiffin, 1998-99, 2002—, Fin. Com., Tiffin, 1998—, chmn. pers. and labor rels. com., 2000—; mem. Recreation and Pub. Property Com., Tiffin, 2000-2001; rep. ADA Adv. Com., Tiffin, 2000-01; mem. Revolving Loan Fund Com., Tiffin, 1998-99. 2002—; mem. Tiffin Parks and Recreation Bd., 1993-94, Hebron (Conn.) Rep. Town Com., 1990-91; softball coach Tiffin Ponytail Softball League, 1993—; v.p. Seneca County (Ohio) Young Reps., 1992-94; elected mem. Seneca County Ohio Rep. Ctrl. Com., 2002—. Avocations: genealogy, home renovations, gardening, drumming, playing bass guitar. Home: 108 Clinton Ave Tiffin OH 44883-1620 Office: Seneca Video Prodns 108 Clinton Ave Tiffin OH 44883-1620

GALIVAN, JOHN HENRY, biochemist, educator, public health officer, research administrator; b. Albany, N.Y., June 19, 1939; s. John Henry and Mary Hortense (Sullivan) G.; m. Nancy Lynn Stiehler, Jan. 24, 1982; children: Amanda, Brendan, Julie, Kate. BS, Union U., 1960; MS, SUNY Albany, 1963; PhD, Albany Med. Coll., 1967. Postdoctoral fellow Scripps Clinic and Rsch. Found., La Jolla, Calif., 1967—70; rsch. scientist Wadsworth Labs. N.Y. State Dept. Health, Albany, 1970—2003, dir. pathology lab. Wadsworth Labs., 1990—92; dir. divsn. clin. scis. Wadsworth Labs State Dept. Health, Albany, 1992—94; dir. divsn. molecular medicine N.Y. State Dept. Health, Albany, 1994—98, dep. dir. oncology Wadsworth Ctr., 1984—2003, dir. rsch. Wadsworth Labs., 1998—2003; co-dir., mem. exec. leadership com. Ordway Rsch. Inst., 1998—2003; prof. SUNY, Albany, 1985—2003, adj. prof., 2003—; sr. health rsch. svc. Wadsworth Labs., 2001—03, mem. exec. coun., 1992—2003, cons. From assoc. prof. to prof. biochemistry and molecular biology Albany Med. Coll., 1978-2003; vis. scientist Wadsworth Ctr., 2003-05; rsch. advisor Ordway Rsch. Inst., 2003-; mem. exptl. therapeutics study sect. Nat. Cancer Inst., Bethesda, Md., 1985-89, cons., 1983-97; exec. coun. U. Albany Sch. Pub. Health, 1989-91; mem. internat. sci. com. Folic Acid Symposium, Berchtesgaden, Germany, 1995-97, Washington, 2000-2001; mem. task force on rsch. agenda N.Y. State Dept Health, 1995-2000; mem. Internat. Clin. Chemistry Sci. Com., Basel, Switzerland, 1996-97; internat. adv. bd. Folic Acid Symposium, Washington, 2000-2001; disting. lectr. Med. U. So. Ala., Med. U. Ohio, U. Cin. Sch. Medicine. Assoc. editor Jour. Cellular Pharmacology, 1992-96; mem. editl. bd. Biofocus, 1995-99; contbr. numerous articles to profl. publs., chpt. to book. Mem. N.Y. State Legis. Com.; dir. N.Y. State Breast Cancer Tax Checkoff; mem. rsch. agenda task force N.Y. State Dept. Health; mem. ex officio com. Ctr. for Nanobiotech., Cornell U., 1998—2002. Recipient Recognition award N.Y. State Dept. Health Commrs., 2003; NIH grantee, 1976-2003. Mem.: AAAS, NY Acad. Scis., Fedn. Am. Soc. Exptl. Biology, Am. Assn. Cancer Rsch., Caroline Seymour Assn. (v.p. 1998—), Preservation Soc. Newport, Mus. Fine Arts Boston, Sail Newport. Home: 66 Kay St Newport RI 02840 E-mail: galivan@msn.com.

GALKIN, ROBERT THEODORE, company executive; b. Providence, Sept. 18, 1926; s. Athur Sherman and Shirley (Mann) G.; m. Wini Blacher, Nov. 2, 1952; children: Ellen Lee Kenner, Jane S. Litner, Debra L. Krim. BA,

Brown U., 1949; postgrad., Oxford U., 1950. Sales mgr. Natco Products Corp., West Warwick, R.I., 1949-60; v.p. Natco Products, West Warwick, 1960-75, pres., 1975-94; chmn. bd., 1994—; pres. Natco Home Fashions, 1994—, Norwood Devel. Corp., 1965—, Valley Industries, 1970—, Valley Hydro, 1984—, Arctic Devel., 1965—, New England Warehouse Co., 1984—, NPC South, Dalton and Chatsworth, Ga., 1985. Active devel. of low power hydroelectric in R.I., leader in recycling industry, R.I., Ga., 1975—. City coun. Good Govt. Candidate, Cranston, 1956; mem. adv. bd. Bryant Coll. Inst. Family Enterprise. With USN, 1944-45. Recipient Williams award for outstanding contbns. to Brown U. Mem. Naval War Coll. Assn., Ledgemont Country Club, Goat Island Yacht Club, Brown Club, R.I. Commodores., Pres.'s Cir. Brown U., Univ. Club. Office: Natco Products Corp 155 Brookside Ave West Warwick RI 02893-3802

GALKIN, SAMUEL BERNARD, orthodontist; b. Newark, Feb. 9, 1933; s. Saul J. and Mollie (Kleinberg) G.; m. Gail Beth Elkin, Feb. 26, 1972; children: Scott David, Seth Paul. Student, U. Conn., 1951-54; DDS, Temple U., 1958; MS in Histology, cert. grad. orthodontics, U. Ill., 1963; cert. in craniomandibular disorders, U. Medicine and Dentistry of N.J., 1989. Diplomate Am. Bd. Orthodontics. Group practice orthodontics, Woodbridge, N.J., 1963—; staff orthodontist J.F.K. Community Hosp., Edison, N.J., 1966—, with cleft palate com., 1971—, dir. dental dept., 1979—; staff Woodbridge Health Ctr., 1967—, with dental adv. com., 1971—; dir. dept. dentistry John F. Kennedy Med. Ctr., Edison, 1979-81; staff orthodontist Perth Amboy (N.J.) Gen. Hosp., 1986—, dir. dept. dentistry, 1990—; staff orthodontist Rahway Hosp., N.J., 1986—. Asst. prof. orthodontics N.J. Coll. Medicine and Dentistry, Jersey City, 1963-73; mem. panel physicians N.J. Crippled Children Program, 1971—; dentist Woodbridge Twp. Sch., 1989—. Chmn., Woodbridge Twp. Debutante Ball, 1970; bd. dirs. Woodbridge Twp. YMCA. Lt. Dental Corps, USN, 1958-61. Mem. ADA, Mid. Atlantic Soc. Orthodontists (chmn. clinics 1969-72), N.J. Dental Soc., Middlesex County Dental Soc., Am. Soc. Dentistry for Children, Am. Assn. Orthodontists, Am. Lingual Orthodontic Assn. (charter), Am. Assn. Dental Schs., Am. Acad. Head, Neck, Facial Pain and TMJ Orthopedics, N.E. Craniomandibular Soc., N.J. Craniomandibular soc. (charter), Am. Acad. Orofacial Pain, Am. Acad. Oral Medicine, Alpha Omega (chpt. v.p. 1969—), Omicron Kappa Upsilon. Home: 3 Dorset Rd Colonia NJ 07067-3101 Office: 711 Amboy Ave Woodbridge NJ 07095-3139 Office Phone: 732-750-2600.

GALL, CRAIG F., music educator; b. Sheboygan, Wis., June 11, 1968; s. Fred E. and Marlene A. Gall. MusB in Music Edn. magna cum laude, Lawrence U. Conservatory Music, 1990. Dir. bands Washington Jr. HS, Kenosha, Wis., 1990—96, Kimberly HS, Wis., 1996—. Trombonist Green Bay Packer Band, Wis., 1988—, Big Band Reunion, Appleton, 1997—; music dir., condr. Kenosha Pops Concert Band, Wis., 1992—; euphonium Dorf Kapelle, 2002—. Ch. organist Friedens Ch., Port Washington, Wis., 1984—. Recipient Cert. Excellence Tchg., Kenosha Sch. Bd. Mem.: Wis. Sch. Music Assn., Music Educators Nat. Conf. Office: Kimberly HS W2662 Kennedy Ave Kimberly WI 54136

GALL, ERIC PAPINEAU, internist, educator; b. Boston, May 24, 1940; s. Edward Alfred and Phyllis Hortense (Rivard) G.; m. Katherine Theiss, Apr. 20, 1968; children: Gretchen Theiss Gall, Michael Edward. AB, U. Pa., 1962, MD, 1966. Cert. Am. Bd. Internal Medicine, 1972, in rheumatology Am. Bd. Internal Medicine, 1974. Asst. instr. U. Pa., Phila., 1970-71, post doctoral trainee, fellow, 1971-73; asst. prof. U. Ariz., Tucson, 1973-78, assoc. prof., 1978-83, prof. internal medicine, 1983-94, prof. surgery, 1983-94, prof. family/community medicine, 1983-94, chief rheumatology allergy and immunology, 1983-93, dir. arthritis ctr., 1986-94; prof. medicine Rosalind Franklin Univ. Medicine & Sci., The Chgo. Med. Sch., North Chicago, Ill., 1994—, prof. microbiology and immunology, 1994—, chmn. dept. medicine, 1994—, chief rheumatology divsn., 1994-98, assoc. dean clin. affairs, 1996-97, dir. metabolic bone unit, 1998—. Author, editor: Rheumatoid Arthritis: Illustrated Guide to Path DX and Management of Rheumatoid Arthritis, 1988, Rheumatic Disease: Rehabilitation and Management, 1984, Primary Care, 1984; editor Clin. Care in The Rhematic Diseases, 1996; contbr. numerous articles to profl. jours. Chmn. med. and scientific com. Arthritis Found., Tucson, 1979-81; mem. Ill. Partnership for Arthritis; chair profl. edn. task force Ill. Dept. Pub. Health, 2001—. Major U.S. Army, 1968—70. Decorated Bronze Star; recipient Addie Thomas Nat. Svc. award Arthritis Found., 1988. Master ACP (coun. Ill. chpt. 1995—, Laureate award 2002); fellow Am. Coll. Rheumatology (founding chair ednl. materials com. 1986-96, edn. coun. 1991-96, bd. dirs. 1992-95, chmn. rehab. sect. 1992-95), Chgo. Inst. Medicine; mem. AMA (rep. sect. on med. schs. 1995—), Arthritis Health Professions Assn. (nat. pres. 1982-83), Am. Assn. Med. Colls., Am. Fedn. Clin. Rsch., Inst. Medicine of Chgo., Ctrl. Soc. Clin. Investigation, Arthritis Found. (nat. vice chmn. 1982-83, chmn. profl. edn. com. 1996-2001, blue ribbon com. on quality of life, trustee Greater Chgo. chpt. 1997—, exec. com. 1998—, bd. dir. 1997—, treas. 2003—), Assn. Profs. Medicine, Ill. Med. Soc. (del. 2002-04), Lake County Med. Soc. (treas. 1998-99, sec. 2000—, pres. 2002-03), Sigma Xi, Alpha Omega Alpha (counselor Chgo. Med. Sch. chpt., 1995—, regional counselor 1998—), Alpha Epsilon Delta. Roman Catholic. Avocation: photography. Office: The Chgo Med Sch Dept Medicine 3333 Green Bay Rd North Chicago IL 60064-3037 Office Phone: 847-578-8644. Business E-Mail: eric.gall@rosalindfranklin.edu. *Academic medicine provides the ideal opportunity to help patients, help touch and shape the lives of hundreds of students and trainees, and to add to the fund of knowledge in one's world.*

GALL, HELEN LOUISE, retired elementary school educator; b. Port Huron, Mich., Jan. 27, 1930; d. James Stanley and Marguerite Elizabeth (Fuerst) Burns; m. George Thomas Gall, Jly 19, 1952; children: Peggy Eileen, Kirk Patrick. AA, Community Coll. Port Huron, 1949; BA, Western Mich. U., 1951; MA, Eastern Mich. U., 1978; cert. in reading, Mich. State U. Cert. elem. tchr., Mich. Tchr. Waterford Twp. (Mich.) Sch. Sys., 1951-53; tchr., rep. sch. Port Huron Area Sch. Dist., 1953-58; tchr. Port Huron, Mich., 1961-93; ret., 1993. Mem. Port Huron Edn. Assn. negotiating team for tchr. contracts, 1971, 88. Vol. fundraiser Port Huron Hosp., participant Health O'Rama and Festival of Trees Christmas project; vol. fundraiser Mercy Hosp., 1986-99; troop leader Girl Scouts U.S., Kalamazoo, 1950-51, Port Huron, 1959-62; chmn. scholarship com. League Cath. women, 1995-96, advisor to scholarship com., workshop participant, bd. dirs., 1994-98; tchr. catechism chs. Port Huron, 1963-72; mem. parish coun. St. Stephen's Cath. Ch., 1973-81, chair fin. bd., ecumenical minister, 1980-99, sponsor, instr. adult edn., 1986-97, publicity chair St. Anne's Alter Soc., 1996-99; charter mem. St. Christopher Cath. Ch., Marysville, Mich.; mem. caucus Dave Bonior Commn.; precinct del. Dem. Com., 1987-98, liaison, 1992-93; active appeal dr. Cath. Svcs. Archdiocese of Detroit, 1988-97; mem. Port Huron Area Sch. Millage Com., 1988-93, St. Clair Coun. Sr. Citizens; cand. County Commr. St. Clair County, 1994; bd. dirs. Coun. on Aging, 1993—; vol. steering com. Comprehensive Cmty. Health Models, St. clair County. Mem. AAUW, Mich. Assn. Ret. Sch. Personel (life, scholarship com. 1994-96), Port Huron Edn. Assn. (exec. bd. 1980-93, treas., pres. vice chair Coun. on Polit. Affairs, rep. on millage proposals-legis. on Ptrns. in Edn Reform at state level in Lansing, rep. nat. NEA convs.), Cath. Social Svcs. Assn. (life), League of Cath. Women St. Clair County (chmn. Christmas project 1995), Black River Boat Club (exec. bd., treas. 1974-88), Am. Legion Women's Aux. Avocations: boating, basketball, bowling, biking, travel, bridge, camping. Home: 3212 Waldheim Dr Port Huron MI 48060-2320 Office: 2588 Michigan Rd Port Huron MI 48060-2446

GALL, JOHN R., lawyer; b. San Francisco, 1945; BA, Miami U., 1967; JD, Ohio State U., 1970. Bar: Ohio 1971. Ptnr. Squire, Sanders & Dempsey, Columbus, Ohio. Office: Squire Sanders & Dempsey 1300 Huntington Ctr 41 S High St Columbus OH 43215-6101 Business E-Mail: jgall@ssd.com.

GALL, JOSEPH GRAFTON, biologist, researcher, educator; b. Washington, Apr. 14, 1928; s. John Christian and Elsie (Rosenberger) G.; m. Dolores Marie Hogge, Sept. 17, 1955 (div. 1982); children: Lawrence, Barbara.; m. Diane Marie Dwyer, July 17, 1982. BS, Yale, 1949, PhD, 1952. Faculty U. Minn., 1952-63, prof., 1963; prof. biology and molecular biophysics Yale, 1963-83; staff dept. embryology Carnegie Instn., Balt., 1983—, Am. Cancer Soc. prof. developmental genetics, 1984—. Mem. cell biology study sect. NIH, 1963-67, chmn., 1972-75; chmn. bd. sci. counselors Nat. Inst. Child Health and Human Devel., NIH, 1986-90; mem. Yale Corp., 1989-95. Contbr. articles profl. jours. Recipient E.B. Wilson award Am. Soc. Cell Biology, 1983, Wilbur Cross medal Yale U., 1988, V.D. Mattia award Roche Inst. Molecular Biology, 1989, Purkinje medal Czech Acad. Scis., 1999. Mem. AAAS (Mentor award for lifetime achievement 1996), Am. Soc. Cell Biology (pres. 1967-68), Genetics Soc. Am., Nat. Acad. Scis., Am. Acad. Arts and Scis., Am. Philos. Soc., Accademia Nazionale dei Lincei, Soc. Developmental Biology (pres. 1984-85, Lifetime Achievement award 2004). Home: 107 Bellemore Rd Baltimore MD 21210-1314 Office: Carnegie Instn Dept Embryology 3520 San Martin Dr Baltimore MD 21218 Office Phone: 410-246-3017. E-mail: gall@ciwemb.edu.

GALL, MARY SHEILA, former federal agency administrator; 2 children. BA, Rosary Hill Coll., 1971; MS in Edn., Old Dominion U., 1998. Staff mem. various mems. of Senate and Ho. of Reps., 1971-79; sr. legis. analyst study com. Ho. of Reps., 1980-81; dep. domestic policy adviser Office of V.P. of U.S., 1981-86; counselor to dir. U.S. Office Pers. Mgmt., 1986-89; asst. sec. human devel. svcs. HHS, Washington, 1989-91; commr. U.S. Consumer Product Safety Commn., Washington, 1991—2004. Chair Pres.'s Task Force on Adoption, 1987-89. Dir. rsch. George Bush for Pres. campaign, 1979-80; mem. Reagan-Bush Presdl. campaign and transition team, 1980-81; tchr. Sunday sch. Republican.

GALL, MEREDITH DAMIEN (MEREDITH MARK DAMIEN GALL), education educator, writer; b. New Britain, Conn., Feb. 18, 1942; s. Theodore A. and Ray (Ehrlich) G.; m. Joyce Pershing, June 12, 1968; 1 child, Jonathan. AB, EdM, Harvard U., 1963; PhD, U. Calif., Berkeley, 1968. Sr. research assoc. Far West Lab. for Ednl. Research and Devel., San Francisco, 1968-75; assoc. prof. edn. U. Oreg., Eugene, 1975-79, prof., 1980—, dept. head for tchr. edn., 2002—. Author: Handbook for Evaluating and Selecting Curriculum Materials, 1981, (with K.A. Acheson) Techniques in the Clinical Supervision of Teachers, 5th edit., 2002, (with J.P. Gall) Making the Grade, rev. 2d edit., 1993, (with W.R. Borg and J.P. Gall) Educational Research: An Introduction, 7th edit., 2002, (with J.P. Gall, D.R. Jacobsen, and T.L. Bullock) Tools for Learning: A Guide to Teaching Study Skills, 1990, (with W.R. Borg and J.P. Gall) Applying Educational Research, 4th edit., 1999, 5th edit., 2005; editor: (with B.A. Ward) Critical Issues in Educational Psychology, 1974; cons. editor Jour. Rsch. in Rural Edn., Forum for Reading, Jour. Exptl. Edn. Grantee, USPH, 1963—64. Fellow Am. Psychol. Assn.; mem. ASCD, Am. Ednl. Research Assn., Oreg. Ednl. Research Assn. (pres. 1985-86), Phi Delta Kappa (Dist. I Meritorious award 1978). Home: 4810 Mahalo Dr Eugene OR 97405-4609 Office: U Oreg Coll Edn Eugene OR 97403 Business E-Mail: mgall@uoregon.edu.

GALL, SIMONE ELLEN, music educator; b. Elyria, Ohio, Sept. 7, 1950; d. Rudy and Dorothy Maravich; m. Steven Joseph Gall, June 30, 1974; children: Julie Jeannine, Melanie Nicole. B of Music Edn., Bowling Green State U., 1972. Vocal music tchr. K-6 Elyria City Schs., 1972—78; vocal music tchr. K-8 Amherst (Ohio) Exempted Village Schs., 1985—; dir. Amherst Comty. Chorus, 1996—. Dir. St. George Serbian Orthodox Ch. Choir, Lorain, Ohio, 1980—2000; dir. music Sandstone Summer Theater, Amherst, 1995—97. Named Lorain Internat. Queen, Lorain Internat. Festival, 1968. Mem.: Music Educators Nat. Conf., Ohio Edn. Assn. Democrat. Avocations: performing at retirement centers and nursing homes, singing and playing for weddings, organizing class reunions. Home: 764 Terra Ln Amherst OH 44001 Office: Amherst Jr H S 548 Milan Ave Amherst OH 44001 E-mail: simonegall51@aol.com.

GALL, STANLEY ADOLPH, immunologist, researcher; b. Bismarck, N.D., May 31, 1936; s. Adolph and Wilma Thelma (Nickisch) G.; m. Florence Marie Ketterling, Aug. 17, 1958; children: Stanley, Kathryn Louise, Mark Allan, Thomas Andrew. BA, U. Minn., 1958, MD, 1962. Diplomate Am. Bd. Ob-Gyn. Intern U. Oreg. Hosp., Portland, 1962-63; resident in ob-gyn U. Minn. Hosp., Mpls., 1963-66; asst. prof. ob-gyn U. Miami, Fla., 1968-73; assoc. prof. ob-gyn Duke U. Med. Ctr., Durham, N.C., 1973-78, prof., 1968—, dir. divsn. perinatal medicine; prof. ob-gyn, assoc. head dept. ob-gyn U. Ill. Coll. Medicine, 1985-89; prof. U. Louisville, 1989—, chmn. dept. ob-gyn., 1989—2000. Contbr. articles to profl. jours. Capt. M.C., U.S. Army, 1966-68. Fellow ACOG; mem. Soc. Gynecol. Oncology, Soc. Gynecol. Investigations, Infectious Diseases Soc. Ob-Gyn, Ctrl. Assn. Obstetricians and Gynecologists, Soc. Maternal Fetal Medicine. Lutheran. Office: U Louisville Dept Ob-Gyn 550 S Jackson St Louisville KY 40202-1622 Office Phone: 502-852-5811. Business E-Mail: sagall@louisville.edu.

GALLAGER, ROBERT GRAY, electrical engineering educator; b. Phila., May 29, 1931; s. Jacob Boon and May (Gray) G.; m. Ruth Atwood, Oct. 19, 1957 (div. July 1981); children: Douglas, Ann, Rebecca; m. Marie Tarnowski, July 18, 1981. BEE, U. Pa., 1953; MEE, MIT, 1957, ScD, 1960. Mem. tech. staff Bell Telephone Labs., Murray Hill, N.J., 1953-54; rsch. asst. MIT, Cambridge, Mass., 1956-60, asst. prof., 1960-64, assoc. prof., 1964-67, prof., 1967—. Co-dir. Lab. Info. and Decision Systems, 1986-96; chmn. adv. com. NSF Div. on Networking and Comm. Rsch. and Infrastructure, Washington, 1989-92; mem. adv. coun. Elec. Engring. Dept., U. Pa., 1991-93; chair adv. com. Elec. Engring. Dept., The Technion, Haifa, Israel, 1999. Author: Information Theory and Reliable Communication, 1968, Discrete Stochastic Processes, 1995; co-author Data Networks, 1987, 2d edit. 1992; patentee in field. Recipient Gold medal Moore Sch., U. Pa., 1973, Harvey prize The Technion, 1999, Eduard Rhein Basic Rsch. award, 2002; Guggenheim fellow, 1978, Marconi fellow, 2003. Fellow IEEE (Baker prize 1966, Medal of Honor 1990); mem. AAAS, NAS, NAE, Infor. theory Soc. of IEEE (bd. govs. 1965-72, 79-88, pres. 1971, Shannon Award 1983). Avocations: piano, skiing. Home: 13 Strawberry Cove Gloucester MA 01930-4128 Office: MIT Dept Elec Eng/Comp Sci Rm 32-D628 Cambridge MA 02139 Business E-Mail: gallager@mit.edu.

GALLAGHER, BRIAN, editor-in-chief; b. 1949; Employed The Jour. News, Westchester County, 1971—80, Gannett News Svc., Washington, 1980—83, mng. editor, 1983—86; employed USA Today, McLean, Va., 1986—91, editl. writer, 1991—99, editl. page editor, 1999—2002, 2004—, exec. editor, 2002—04. Office: USA Today Executive Editor 7950 Jones Branch Dr Mc Lean VA 22102

GALLAGHER, BRIAN JOHN, lawyer; b. Bklyn., Oct. 24, 1939; s. John Joseph and Margaret R. Gallagher; m. Mary Loughney, Sept. 10, 1966; children: Amanda, Ian. BS, Fairfield U., 1961; JD, Fordham U., 1964; postgrad., NYU Law Sch., 1969-70. Bar: N.Y. 1965, U.S. Dist. Ct. (so. dist.) N.Y. 1967, U.S. Ct. Appeals (2d cir.) 1971, U.S. Dist. Ct. (ea. dist.) N.Y. 1974, U.S. Ct. Appeals (11th cir.) 1982, U.S. Ct. Appeals (D.C. cir.) 1986. Asst. U.S. Atty. So. Dist. N.Y., 1967-71; ptnr. Kronish, Lieb, Weiner & Hellman, LLP, N.Y.C., 1976—. Mayor Village of Pelham Manor, N.Y., 1995-97, trustee, 1989-95. Mem. ABA, N.Y. State Bar Assn., Assn. Bar City N.Y., Fed. Bar Coun., Larchmont (N.Y.) Yacht Club, Williams Club, N.Y. Athletic Club. Office: 1114 Avenue Of The Americas New York NY 10036-7703 E-mail: bgallagher@klwhHp.com.

GALLAGHER, CAROL JOY, bishop; b. San Diego, Calif., Dec. 24, 1955; d. Donald K. and Elizabeth Anne (WalkingStick) Theobald; m. Mark Paul Gallagher, 1975; children: Emily, Ariel, Phoebe. BA in Writing and Communication, Antioch Coll., Balt.; MDiv, Episcopal Div. Sch., Cambridge, Mass., 1989; ThM, Princeton Theol. Sem., 1998; PhD in Urban Affairs and Pub. Policy, U. Del., 2004. Ordained priest, 1990; asst. Cathedral of the Incarnation, Balt., St. Martin's Ch., Radnor, Pa.; priest-in-charge Trinity Ch., Collingdale, Pa.; rector St. Anne's Ch., Middletown, Del., 1996—2002; consecrated bishop, 2002; bishop suffragen Episcopal Diocese of So. Va., 2002—. Mem. editl. bd. First Peoples Theology Jour. Episcopalian. Office: Episcopal Diocese of So Va 600 Talbot Hall Rd Norfolk VA 23505 Office Phone: 757-423-8287. Office Fax: 757-440-5354.*

GALLAGHER, CYNTHIA, artist, educator; b. N.Y. BFA in Painting, Phila. U. of Arts, 1972; MFA in Painting, Queens Coll., 1974. Instr. N.Y. Inst. Tech., N.Y.C., 1974-88; adj. prof. CUNY, Queens Coll., N.Y.C., 1974—90; instr. foundations dept. Parsons Sch. Design, 1994—2001. Critic Brown U., 1994, R.I. Sch. Design, 1994, Cooper Union for Advancement of Sci. and Art, 1994; selection com. vis. artists Fashion Inst. Tech., 1992-93; graphics cons. N.Y. State Found. Arts, 1978; vis. critic NYU, N.Y.C., N.Y., 1974-75; adj. asst. prof. Phila. (Pa.) Coll. Art, 1976—, Fashion Inst. Tech., N.Y.C., N.Y., 1976—; instr. summer sch. music and art Yale U., Norfolk, Conn., 1980—. One-woman shows include 55 Mercer St., N.Y.C., 1976, 1978, Grace Borgenicht Gallery, 1981, Luise Ross Gallery, 1988, Edward Thorden Gallery, Gothenborg, Sweden, 1989, Charles More Gallery, Phila., 1990, 1991, Mary Ryan Gallery, N.Y.C., 1992, Espace Crois, Barangnon, Toulouse, France, 1993, Johnson & Johnson, New Brunswick, N.J., 1998, exhibited in group shows at Weatherspoon Mus., Greensboro, N.Y.C., 1982, Castelli Graphics, N.Y.C., 1983, Bess Culter Gallery, 1984, Parrish Art Mus., Southampton, L.I., N.Y., 1991, Tiffany's, N.Y.C., 1993, Inst. for Art and Urban Resources, Inc., L.I. City, N.Y., 1982, Nat. Mus. Women in the Arts, Washington, 1996, Montclair (NJ) Mus. Art, 1997, Represented in permanent collections Met. Mus. Art, N.Y.C., Best Inc., Citibank, 1st Nat. Bank Chgo., Home Ins. Co., Owens Corning Corp., Salomon Bros., Shearson-Lehman Am. Express, N.Y.C., San Francisco, Skadden, Arts, Slate, Meagher and Flom, Johnson, Nat. Mus. of Women in the Arts, Whitney Mus. Am. Art, Met. Mus. Art, Nat. Women's Mus., Washington, D.C.; contbr. articles to profl. jours. Mem. adv. bd., bd. dirs. YWCA Elsa Mott Ives Gallery, 1992, curator, 1993. Grantee, Creative Artists Pub. Svc. Program, 1981—82, Nat. Endowment for Arts, 1983—84, 1989—90, N.Y. Found. for Arts, 1989—90.

GALLAGHER, EDWARD PETER, foundation executive; b. San Francisco, Mar. 23, 1951; s. Edward Owen and Virginia Anne (Scully) G. BA, U. Calif., 1976; MBA, Columbia U., 1982. Dir. comm. Wolf Trap Farm Pk. for Performing Arts, Vienna, Va., 1977; program mgr. Smithsonian Instn., Washington, 1977-79; sr. program mgr. Smithsonian Inst., Washington, 1979-81; dir. membership Mus. Modern Art, N.Y.C., 1983-90, dir. devel., 1986-87; dir. NAD, N.Y.C., 1990-96; pres. Am.-Scandinavian Found., N.Y.C., 1996—; also trustee. Cons. Cooper Hewitt Mus., N.Y.C., 1982-83; Yorkville Common Pantry, N.Y.C.; knight 1st class Norwegian Royal Order of Merit. Mem. Internat Commn. Mus., Am. Assn. Mus. Home: 666 W End Ave # 21 F New York NY 10025-7357

GALLAGHER, EUGENE BENNETT, sociologist, medical educator; b. Lancaster, Pa., Mar. 25, 1929; s. Joseph and Dorothy (Bennett) G.; m. Carol Thompson, Dec. 22, 1951 (div. July 1975); children: David Travis, Robert Thompson; m. Marilyn Milne, Aug. 20, 1977. BS, Lehigh U., 1949; MA, Harvard U., 1954, PhD, 1958. Lectr. Boston U., 1960-62; prof. U. Ky., Lexington, 1962—2003. Vis. prof. Bristol (Eng.) U., 1969-70, King Faisal U., Damman, Saudi Arabia, 1979-80, United Arab Emirates U., Al Ain, 1990, 97; rschr. NIH, Bethesda, Md., 1975-76. Author, editor: Patienthood in the Mental Hospital, 1964, Infants, Mothers and Doctors, 1977, Health and Health Care in Developing Countries, 1993, Global Perspectives on Health Care, 1995, Culture, Society, and Illness, 1996, Toward a Global Sociology of Health and Medicine, 2001. Fellow Am. Coun. Learned Socs., Washington, 1950; recipient Fulbright Rsch. award, 1996-97. Fellow: Am. Sociol. Assn.; mem.: Internat. Sociol. Assn. (pres. rsch. com. 1994—2002). Democrat. Office: U Ky Dept Behavioral Sci Lexington KY 40536-0001 Office Phone: 440-774-4497. E-mail: gallagher@oberlin.net.

GALLAGHER, GARY W(AYNE), educational services executive; b. Ponca City, Okla., May 13, 1954; s. Linden B. and Lenna J. (Greenshields) Wilson; m. Carole B. Stewart, May 1, 1979 (div. Mar. 1994); children: Heather, Danielle; m. Jani B. Viljoen, Aug. 5, 1998; children: Trevor, Derek, Stephen. BA in Polit. Sci., L.Am. Area Studies cert., Okla. State U., 1975, MS in Curriculum Studies, Supt. and Prin. Adminstrv. cert., Okla. State U., 1995, postgrad., 1995—. Tchr. Ponca City Pub. Schs., Okla., 1987—88; instr. transitional sch. and work program for seriously emotionally disturbed children Am. Legion Children's Home, Ponca City, 1988—89; instr. social scis. Olive Pub. Schs., 1989—90; instr. social scis. and tech. applications Ponca City Pub. Schs., 1990—98; founder, curriculum theorist Advanced Academics, Ponca City, 1999—2001; dir. comml. mktg. Okla. ops. Applied Techs. divsn. Sci. Rsch. Corp., 2002—03; dir. bus. devel. Applied Marine Tech., Inc., Ponca City, 2003—. Gov.'s Commendation for Volunteerism, 1993, 94; named Okla. Tech. Tchr. of the Yr., Tech. and Learning Mag., 1990. Mem. ASCD, NAESP, Am. Assn. Sch. Adminstrs., Nat. Assn. Secondary Sch. Prins., Internat. Internet Learning Assn., Internat. Soc. Tech. in Edn., Nat. Coun. Social Studies (instrnl. media/tech. com.), Am. Ednl. Rsch. Assn., Nat. Youth Leadership Coun., Okla. Alliance for Geog. Edn., Internat. Assn. Sch. Bus. Ofcls., Okla. Coun. Social Studies, Okla. Hist. Soc., Assn. Ednl. Comm. and Tech., Assn. Childhood Edn. Home: 1813 E Hartford Ave Ponca City OK 74604-2521 Office Phone: 580-761-2660. Personal E-mail: gwg@cableone.net. Business E-Mail: ggallagher@amti.net.

GALLAGHER, J. PATRICK, JR., insurance company executive; b. Chgo., 1952; Degree, Cornell U., 1974. From v.p. ops. to pres. Arthur J. Gallagher & Co., Itasca, Ill., 1985—90, pres., 1990—, CEO, 1995—, bd. dir. Office: Arthur J Gallagher & Co Two Pierce Place Itasca IL 60143

GALLAGHER, JAMES C., lawyer; b. Lyndonville, Vt., June 16, 1945; BA, Tufts U., 1967; JD, Cornell U., 1971. Bar: Vt. 1971, U.S. Dist. Ct. Vt. 1972, U.S. Ct. Appeals (2d cir.) 1977, U.S. Supreme Ct. 1984, N.H. 1986, U.S. Dist. Ct. N.H. 1986, U.S. Dist. Ct. (no. dist.) N.Y. 1986. With Downs Rachlin & Martin P.C., Littleton, N.H. Bd. dirs. Lyndon Inst., pres. bd. trustees, 1994—2003; trustee Vt. Legal Aid. Editor Cornell Law Review, 1970-71. Mem. ABA, N.H. Bar Assn., Vt. Bar Assn. (treas. 1999-, pres.-elect 2004-), Def. Rsch. Inst., Am. Bd. Trial Advocates. Office: Downs Rachlin & Martin PC PO Box 78 PO Box 560 Littleton NH 03561-0560

GALLAGHER, JOHN FRANCIS, education educator; s. John Charles Edward and Marion (McKeon) G.; m. Georgiana Frances Cole; children: Kristen Marie, John David. BA in Philosophy, Mary Immaculate Coll.; STD in Theology, U. Fribourg, Switzerland; MS in Indsl. Rels., EdD, Rutgers U. Instr. Mary Immaculate Coll., Northampton, Pa., 1962-65; asst. prof. Coll. St. Vincent De Paul, Boynton Beach, Fla., 1965-69, pres., 1966-70, assoc. prof., 1969-70; advisor instructional resources SUNY, Plattsburgh, 1970-71; dean humanities Brookdale Community Coll., Lincroft, N.J., 1971-73, v.p. acad., 1973-81; dir. Rockland Campus Iona Coll., New Rochelle, NJ, 1981-83, dean Sch. Gen. Studies, 1983-89, provost, v.p. acad. affairs, 1989-95, prof. edn., 1995—2005, prof. emeritus edn., 2005—. Coll. evaluation team NJ Dept. Higher Edn., Trenton, 1975-77, NY State Edn. Dept., Albany, 1980—; coord. coll. activities to achieve accreditation by Nat. Coun. for Accreditation of Tchr. Edn., 1999—2005; chief instnl. rep. Am. Assn. Colls. Tchr. Edn., 1999—2005. Chair County Arts Festival, Monmouth County, N.J., 1972; trustee Monmouth County Arts Coun., Red Bank, N.J., 1973-76. Mem. Am. Ednl. Studies Assn., Philosophy of Edn. Soc., Soc. for History Edn., Mid. States Assn. Colls. and Scis. (coll. evaluation team 1976—), Phi Delta Kappa. Avocations: photography, classical music, tennis. Office: Iona Coll Dept Edn New Rochelle NY 10801 Personal E-mail: glgr115@aol.com. Business E-Mail: jgallagher@iona.edu.

GALLAGHER, M. CATHERINE, English literature educator; b. Denver, Feb. 16, 1945; d. John Martin and Mary Catherine Sullivan; m. Martin Evan Jay, July 6, 1974; children: Margaret Shana, Rebecca Erin. BA, U. Calif., Berkeley, 1972, MA, 1974, PhD, 1979. Asst. prof. U. Denver, 1979-80, U. Calif., Berkeley, 1980-84, assoc. prof., 1984-90, prof., 1990—. Author: The Industrial Reformation of English Fiction, 1985, Nobody's Story, 1994, The Body Economic, 2005; co-author: The Making of the Modern Body, 1987,

Practicing New Historicism, 2000; editor Representation, 1983—. Guggenheim fellow Guggenheim Found., 1989; fellow NEH, 1990, ACLS, 1990, Mem. MLA (del. assembly mem. 1985-86, exec. com. lit. criticism divsn. 1991-94), Am. Acad. Arts and Scis., Acad. Lit. Studies, Brit. Studies Assn., The Dickens Soc. Office: U Calif Dept English Berkeley CA 94720-0001 Business E-Mail: cgall@berkeley.edu.

GALLAGHER, MAGGIE, columnist; B, Yale Univ., 1982. Articles editor Nat. Review; sr. editor City Jour., Manhattan Inst.; pres. Inst. for Marriage and Pub. Policy, Washington. Syndicated columnist; author: Enemies of Eros, 1989, The Abolition of Marriage, 1995. Sr. fellow, Ctr. for Social Thought. Mailing: Universal Press Syndicate 4520 Main St Kansas City MO 64111*

GALLAGHER, MICHAEL DAVID, federal agency administrator; BA, U. Calif. Berkeley; JD, U. Calif. LA. Bar: Wash. With Perkins Coie, LLP; adminstrv. asst. to Congressman Rick White, 1995—97; mng. dir. govt. rels. AirTouch Comm., Inc., Bellevue, Wash.; v.p. state pub. policy Verizon Wireless, Bellevue, Wash., 1998—2000; dep. chief of staff policy to sec. of commerce U.S. Dept. Commerce, Washington; dep. asst. sec. comm. & info. Nat. Telecomm. & Info. Adminstrn. U.S. Dept. Commerce, Washington, 2001—02, acting asst. sec., 2003—04, asst. sec., 2004—. Office: Nat Telecomm and Info Adminstrn US Dept Commerce Hoover Clark Hoover Bldg 14th St and Constitution Ave NW Rm 4898 Washington DC 20230 Office Phone: 202-482-1840.*

GALLAGHER, MICHAEL L., lawyer; b. LeMars, Iowa, Apr. 14, 1944; BA, Ariz. State U., 1966, JD, 1970. Bar: Ariz. 1970. Maj. league scout N.Y. Mets, 1967—70; atty. Snell & Wilmer, Phoenix, 1970—78, Gallagher & Kennedy, Phoenix, 1978—. Judge pro tem Maricopa County Superior Ct., 1979, Ariz. Ct. Appeals, 1985; Amerco, U-Haul; bd. dirs. Ariz. Pub. Svc. Co., Omaha World Herald Co., Pinnacle West Capital Corp., Action Performance, Inc. Chmn. gov.'s adv. com. profl. football, 1981-87, mayor's adv. com. profl. sports, 1984-91; bd. dirs. Maricopa County Sports Authority, 1989; bd. visitors law sch. Ariz. State U., 1979; dir. Valley of the Sun YMCA, chmn., 1995, Phoenix Suns Charities, 2002; trustee Peter Kiewit Found. Fellow Internat. Acad. Trial Lawyers. Office: Gallagher & Kennedy PA 2575 E Camelback Rd Phoenix AZ 85016-9225 Office Phone: 602-530-8000. E-mail: mlg@gknet.com.

GALLAGHER, MICHAEL ROBERT, retired consumer products company executive; b. Cedar Rapids, Iowa, Jan. 21, 1946; s. John Robert and Mabel Helen (Slaymaker) G.; m. Linda Katherine Nebb, Oct. 25, 1975; children: Megan Elizabeth, John William, Edward Michael. BS, U. Calif., Berkeley, 1967, MBA, 1968. Brand mgr. Procter & Gamble Co., Cin., 1968-72; various positions Clorox Co., Oakland, Calif., 1972-77; pres., gen. mgr. Clorox Can., Vancouver, B.C., advt. mgr. household products div., 1980-81, gen. mgr. household products div., 1982-84; pres. consumer products div. Lehn & Fink/Sterling Drug, Montvale, N.J., 1984-85; sr. v.p. Lehn & Fink Products, Montvale, N.J., 1985-87, exec. v.p., 1987-88; pres., chief exec. officer L&F Products Inc. (formerly Lehn & Fink), Montvale, N.J., 1989-95; pres., CEO Reckitt & Colman Inc., Montvale, 1995; CEO Playtex Products Inc., Westport, Conn., 1995—2004, ret., 2004. Bd. dirs. Allergan, 1998—, AMN Healthcare Svcs., 2001—04. Vice chmn. United Way Bergen County, N.J., 1985-87, bd. dirs., 1989-96, chmn. bd. dirs. 1993-95, chmn. Golden Ball, 1990; sports chmn. Cancer Care of Am., 1989; mem. exec. coun. Boy Scouts Am., Bergen County, 1990-95, bd. dirs. Haas Sch. Bus., U. Calif., Berkeley, 2002—; trustee St. Luke's Sch., 1998—. Mem. Soap and Detergent Assn. (bd. dirs. 1992-95), Grocery Mfrs. Assn. (bd. dirs. 1997-2004), Assn. Sales and Mktg. Cos. (bd. dirs. 2001-04).

GALLAGHER, PATRICIA E., government agency administrator; BA in Pub. Adminstrn. and Urban Studies, Elmhurst Coll., Ill.; MA in Pub. Policy Analysis, Northwestern U. Prin. P. Gallagher & Assocs., Chgo.; mgr. Chgo. River Devel. Plan; asst. commr. open space planning City of Chgo. Dept. Planning, dep. commr. strategic planning, 1999—2001; exec. dir. Nat. Capital Planning Commn., Washington, 2001—. Contbr. articles to profl. jours. Loeb fellow, Harvard U., 1999—2000. Office: Nat Capital Planning Commn 401 9th St NW Washington DC 20576 Office Phone: 202-482-7200.

GALLAGHER, PATRICK FRANCIS XAVIER, public relations executive; b. Cleve., Feb. 9, 1952; s. Patrick Francis and Eileen (Brennan) G.; m. Anne Platek, May 3, 1980; children: Molly Anne, Kate Louise. Student, Holy Cross Coll., Worcester, Mass., 1970-72; BA, U. Pa., 1974; MBA, Cleve. State U., 1991. Accredited in pub. rels. Staff editor Penton Pub. Co., Cleve., 1975-80, editor, 1980-83; mgr. corp. communications Leaseway Transp. Corp., Cleve., 1983-84, dir. pub. rels., 1984-85; sr. account exec. Edward Howard & Co., Cleve., 1985-89, v.p., 1990-94, sr. v.p., 1994—. Part-pres. Project LEARN, Cleve. Mem. Pub. Rels. Soc. Am., Nat. Investor Rels. Inst. (past pres. Cleve.-No. Ohio chpt.), CFA Soc. Cleve. Office: Edward Howard & Co 7th Fl 1360 E 9th St Fl 7 Cleveland OH 44114-1716

GALLAGHER, PHILIP, electronics executive; BA, Drexel Univ.; cert. in supplier base mgmt., Calif. Inst. Tech. With electronic components group Avnet, Inc., 1983, v.p. of sales and ops. for N. Am., 1996—2000, S.W. area dir., L.A. regional mgr., dist. mgr., sales mgr., and account mgr.; exec. v.p. sales and mktg. Avnet Electronics Mktg. Americas, 2000—01; pres. of the semiconductor dist. specialist bus. unit Avnet Cilicon, 2001; sr. v.p., global bus. devel. Avnet Electronics Mktg., Phoenix, 2002—. Vol. Arizona's Make A Difference Day, Ariz. Office: Avnet Inc 2211 S 47th St Phoenix AZ 85034

GALLAGHER, RICHARD SIDNEY, lawyer; b. Minot, N.D., May 10, 1942; s. J.W.S. and Esther T. (Tappon) G.; m. Ann Rylands Larson, June 24, 1972; children: Elizabeth, Catherine. BSBA, Northwestern U., 1964; JD, Harvard U., 1967. Ptnr. Foley & Lardner LLP, Milw., 1967—, chmn. tax & individual planning dept. Bd. dirs. Badger Meter Found., Milw. Bd. chmn. Milw. Youth Symphony Orchs., Milw., 1980-82, Milw. County Performing. Arts Ctr., Milw., 1986-91; dir. Curative Rehab. Ctr., Milw., 1988-93, United Performing Arts Fund, 1991-99, Blood Ctr. S.E. Wis., Milw. Youth Arts Ctr.; pres. Donors Forum of Wis., 1997-2000. Lt. comdr., USN, 1967-69, Vietnam. Fellow Am. Coll. Tax Counsel, Am. Coll. Trust & Estate Coun., Am. Law Inst.; mem. ABA (chmn. exempt orgns. com., sect. of taxation 1989-91, governing coun. sect. taxation, 2005-, chmn. com. adminstrn. trusts & estates, sect. probate & trust law 1996-98). Office: Foley & Lardner LLP US Bank Ctr 777 E Wisconsin Ave Milwaukee WI 53202 Business E-Mail: rgallagher@foley.com.

GALLAGHER, ROBERT E., risk management marketing company executive; b. 1923; CEO Arthur J. Gallagher & Co., Itasca, Ill., 1963-94, chmn. bd. Office: The Gallgher Ctr Two Pierce Pl Itasca IL 60143-3141 Fax: 630-285-4000.

GALLAGHER, ROBERT P., bank executive; s. Robert P. Sr. and Renata Gallagher. BA in Econs., Williams Coll., 1988; MBA in Fin., NYU, 1992. Lending officer Scotiabank, N.Y.C., 1992—94; sr. v.p., team leader U.S. Corp. Fin. dept. Mizuho Corp. Bank Ltd., N.Y.C., 2003—. Avocations: golf, tennis, auto restoration, squash.

GALLAGHER, ROBERT PATRICK, lawyer; b. Bryn Mawr, Pa., Sept. 16, 1945; s. Patrick J. and Esther Humphries (Conlin) G.; m. Cathie Greene, Jan. 12, 1976. BA, George Washington U., 1968, JD, 1971. Bar: D.C. 1972, Pa. 1971, U.S. Supreme Ct. 1986. Trial atty. U.S. Dept. Justice, Washington, 1971-74; directing atty. Micronesian Legal Svcs. Corp., Palau, 1974-75; counsel for ERISA litigation U.S. Dept. Labor, Washington, 1976-82; sr. counsel Groom Law Group, Chartered, Washington, 1982—. Condr. seminars in field. Contbr. articles on employee benefits issues to legal jours. Office: Groom Law Group Chtd Ste 1200 1701 Pennsylvania Ave NW Washington DC 20006-5893

GALLAGHER, TERRENCE VINCENT, editor; b. Phila., Nov. 22, 1946; s. Harold John and Marie Elizabeth (Kershaw) G.; m. Eileen Rose Small, Dec. 26, 1971; children: Sean Terrence, Elizabeth I. BS in Journalism, Temple U., 1971. With Chilton Co., Radnor, Pa., 1971-94; asst. editor Product Design and Devel. mag, 1971-73; mng. editor Internat. Product Digest, 1973-74; editor-in-chief Instrument and Apparatus News mag., 1974-84, Hardware Age mag., 1984-94, Decorative Products World, 1989-94, Outdoor Power Equipment Mag, 1989-94, Garden Supply Retailer mag., 1989-94; editorial dir. Chilton's Home and Yard Care Group, 1989-94; chmn. editorial bd. Chilton Co., 1980-83; contbg. editor Tennis U.S.A., 1974-75; pres. Gallagher Communications, 1994—. Served to 1st lt. U.S. Army, 1966-69, Vietnam. Decorated Bronze Star with 2 V devices; Vietnamese Cross of Gallantry. Home: 141 Chaps Ln West Chester PA 19382

GALLAGHER, THOMAS C., diversified manufacturing executive; b. 1948; With SP Richards Co., 1983, Genuine Parts Co., 1963—, exec. v.p., 1989-90, pres., COO, dir., 1990—2004, pres., CEO, dir., 2004—05, chmn., CEO, 2005—. Bd. dir. Oxford Industries, STI Classic Funds. Office: Genuine Parts Co 2999 Circle 75 Pkwy NW Atlanta GA 30339-3050*

GALLAGHER, THOMAS WILLIAM, lawyer; b. Chgo., Dec. 30, 1947; s. William P. and Frances M. (Battle) G.; m. Catherine I. Schlageter, Aug. 28, 1971; children: Jennifer, Kimberly, Courtney, Allison, Thomas, Abigail, Patrick. BS in Econs., Xavier U., 1969; JD, No. Ky. U., 1974. Bar: Ohio 1975. Trust adminstr. Toledo Trust, 1974-76; atty. Royer, Gallagher & Morgan, Toledo, 1976-78, Frank W. Cubbon Jr. & Assoc. Co., L.P.A., Toledo, 1978-87; ptnr. Huffman, Gallagher, Schlageter & Breier, Toledo, 1987-90; atty., ptnr. Williams, Jilek, Lafferty & Gallagher, Toledo, 1990—. Lectr. Fornoff Seminar Series, Ohio Acad. Trial Lawyers, Toledo and Lucas County Bar Assn. With USAR, 1969-74. Mem. Assn. Trial Lawyers Am., Ohio Acad. Trial Lawyers (trustee 1987—), Ohio State Bar Assn., Toledo Bar Assn., Toledo Trial Lawyers Assn. Office: Williams Jilek Lafferty Gallagher & Scott 416 N Erie St Ste 500 Toledo OH 43624-1696

GALLAGHER, TIMOTHY J., newspaper editor; Grad., U. N.Mex. Reporter, editor El Paso Herald-Post, The Albuquerque Tribune, N.Mex., editor, 1986—95; v.p., editor Ventura (Calif.) County Star, 1995—2000, pres., editor, 2000—00, pres., pub., 2004—. Office: Ventura County Star 5250 Ralston St Ventura CA 93003-7392

GALLANT, GEORGE WILLIAM, political scientist; b. Boston, Nov. 14, 1931; s. George William and Gladys Mary (Dalby) G.; m. Joan Cornelia Crimmins, Nov. 6, 1954; children: Judith Cornelia, Nicole Marie. AB cum laude, Boston Coll., 1952; MA, Georgetown U., 1965; PhD, Fordham U., 1971; grad., various specialized mil. schs. Commd. 2d lt. U.S. Army, 1952, advanced through grades to col., 1975; svc. in Eng., Fed. Republic Germany and Vietnam; asst. prof. U.S. Mil. Acad., West Point, N.Y., 1967-70; head Soviet and Asian communist rsch. sects. and divsns. Dept. Def., 1970-75; Soviet cons. and translator, 1975—. Adj. faculty mem. polit. sci. Stonehill Coll., North Easton, Mass., 1977-85, asst. prof., 1985-91, assoc. prof., 1991-97, dir. Stonehill Coll.-Yaroslavl State U. (Russia) Exch. Program, 1993-97, ret., 1997. Contbr. articles to profl. jours.; creator TV programs. Rep. Stoughton Town Meeting, 1975—, chmn. mcpl. ops. com. Decorated Legion of Merit (2), Bronze Star. Mem. Am. Assn. for Advancement Slavic Studies, Am. Polit. Sci. Assn., Assn. U.S. Army, Ret. Officers Assn., Cape Cod Ret. Officers Assn., Boston Coll. Alumni Club, Sigma Iota Rho, Phi Beta Kappa, Alpha Lambda Sigma (hon. mem. Beta Xi chpt.). Address: 303 Morton St Stoughton MA 02072-3239

GALLARDO, MIGUEL E., psychologist; b. San Antonio, July 5, 1974; s. Frank Epsinoza and Evangelina Robles Gallardo. BS, Tex. Christian U., 1996; D of Psychology, Calif. Sch. Profl. Psychology, 2001. Cert. trainer Stanford U., 2003. Dir. sexual offenders program Santa Anita Family Svcs., 1998—2001; intern UCLA Counseling Ctr., L.A., 2000—01; staff psychologist, lectr. Counseling Ctr., Dept. Social Ecology U. Calif., Irvine, 2001—04. Asst. prof. grad. sch. edn. and psychology Pepperdine U., 2003—05; mem. adv. bd. Am. Sch. Profl. Psychology, Argosy U., 2004—; mem. exec. coun. Nat. Inst. Multicultural Competence, Nat. Planning and Implementation Com., 2004—. Contbr. articles to profl. jours. Mem.: APA (chair program com. ind. practitioners 2004—05, mem. early career psychologists com. 2005—, Campus Rep. Yr. award 1999), Nat. Latino Behavioral Health Assn., Orange County Psychol. Assn. (bd. dirs. 2003—), Calif. Latino Psychol. Assn. (pres. 2004—), Nat. Latino Psychol. Assn. (chair chpt. devel. com. 2004—), Calif. Psychol. Assn. (chair pubs. com. 2002—05, chair diversity com. 2005—, Bronze Psi award 2000). Roman Catholic. Avocations: running, golf, basketball, movies. Office: Pepperdine U 18111 Von Karman Ave Ste 209 Irvine CA 92612

GALLARDO, SANDRA SILVANA, television producer; b. Bronx, Jan. 13, 1947; d. Edward Francis and Grace (Mallory) G.; m. Gerald O'Connor, Jan. 21, 1968 (div. 1978); m. Billy Burrows, Sept. 21, 1985. Student, HB Studio, N.Y.C., 1964—72, CCNY, 1964—66. CEO Gallardo Studios, North Hollywood, Calif., 1980—; pres. Camellia Prodns., Studio City, Calif., 1987—. Guest spkr. IRS, Hollywood, Calif., 1990. Prodr., dir., writer The Acting Class, 1988; author: The Winning, 1998, Acting for Success, 1999, 2d edit., 2005 (Academic World Star); actress (film) Solar Crisis, The Windwalker, Death Wish II, Out of the Dark, The Tin Angel; (TV) Prison Stories: Women on the Inside, Calendar Girl Murders, The People vs. Inez Garcia, Days of Our Lives, NYPD Blue, Lou Grant, ER, Babylon 5, Providence, Strong Medicine, Golden Girls, Ressurection Blvd., Kingpin; appeared on stage in American Mosaic Recipient Bronze Star halo So. Calif. Motion Picture Coun., 1985, Golden Eagle award Nosotros, 1989. Mem. SAG (guest spkr. 1988-96), Am. Fedn. TV Arts Scis., Am. TV Arts & Scis., Equity. Avocations: writing, paddle tennis, hiking, museums. Studio: #641 11288 Ventura Blvd Studio City CA 91604 Office: Camellia Prodns #641 11288 Ventura Blvd Studio City CA 91604 Office Phone: 818-752-2588. Personal E-mail: sgalla2222@aol.com.

GALLAS, MARTIN HANS, librarian; b. Berlin, Nov. 23, 1947; came to U.S., 1953; s. Ernst Gallas and Kate Lesser; m. Myoung Ok Lee, Dec. 23, 1977; children: Monica, Matthew. AA, Springfield (Ill.) Coll., 1971; AB, U. Ill., 1973, MLS, 1974. Reference libr. Starved Rock Libr. Sys., Ottawa, Ill., 1979—81; libr. dir. Springfield Coll., Ill., 1974—79, Oakland City U., Ind., 1981—86, Ill. Coll., Jacksonville, 1986—. With U.S. Army, 1965-68. Avocation: shortwave radio. Office: Ill Coll Schewe Libr 1101 W College Ave Jacksonville IL 62650-2212 Office Phone: 217-245-3020. Business E-Mail: gallas@ic.edu.

GALLAS, PHILIP S., lawyer; b. Kansas City, Mo., July 23, 1953; AB, Wash. U., 1975; JD, Am. U., 1978. Bar: DC 1978, US Ct. Internat. Trade 1982, US Ct. Appeals Fed. Cir. 1982. With Classification and Value Divsn., Office of Regulations and Rulings US Customs Svc., 1978—80; Antidumping Order Compliance Divsn., Internat. Trade Adminstrn. US Dept. Commerce, 1980—84; assoc. Grunfeld, Desiderio, Lebowitz, & Silverman, Washington, 1984—96, of counsel, 1996—98; ptnr. Sandler, Travis & Rosenberg, PA, Washington, 1998—2004, head internat. trade practice; ptnr. Sonnenschein Nath & Rosenthal LLP, Washington, 2004—. Mem.: Washington Customs Brokers and Freight Forwarders Assn., Customs and Internat. Trade Bar Assn. Office: Sonnenschein Nath & Rosenthal Ste 600, E Tower 1301 K St NW Washington DC 20005 Office Phone: 202-408-6430. Office Fax: 202-408-6399. Business E-Mail: pgallas@sonnenschein.com.

GALLASPY, DIXIE, interior designer, innkeeper; b. Franklinton, La., Dec. 12, 1934; d. Fred Whithurst and Camille Gardner Yates; m. John Norman Gallaspy, June 14, 1958; children: John Whithurst, Gardener Weeks, Leland Redding. BA in Interior Design, Tex. Woman's U., 1957; floral degree, Tex. A&M Coll., 1985. Cert. interior designer, La. Dir. interior design Mullers Dept. Store, Lake Charles, La., 1958-60; draftsperson Gabriel & Reames AIA, Lake Charles, 1960-61; owner Dixie's Designs & Flowers, Bogalusa, La., 1962—; interior design dir. Gulf State Theatre, New Orleans, 1978-84, United Artists Cinemas, Dallas, 1979-80, Alfalfa Video Stores, Hammond, La., 1986-91; owner Smoky Creek Plantation Bed and Breakfast Inn, Bogalusa. Chairperson United Way of Bogalusa, 1983, Meth. Ch. Pasonage, 1972—; tchr. New Day Sunday Sch. Meth. Ch., 1972—; mem. Bogalusa Civic League, 1995—, M.A.S.H. Ladies Mardi Gras Riding Group, 1985—; vol. Rest Haven Nursing Home, 1969—; bd. dirs. Washington Parish Fair Assn., 1983-86; foun. and dir. Smoky Creek Summer Sch. for Girls, Bogolusa, 1985—. Named Woman of Yr. Bus. and Profl. Women's Club, 1977, Citizen of Yr. Bogalusa Daily News, 1983, First Queen Magic City Carnival Assn., 1981. Mem. Am. Soc. of Interior Designers (bd. dirs. La. chpt. 1975-80). Republican. Avocations: aerobic dance, organ and piano, gardening, floral arranging, reading. Home: 1737 Gaylord Dr Bogalusa LA 70427-4056 Office: Smoky Creek Plantation 1500 Youngs Rd Bogalusa LA 70427-4040 Fax: 504-735-1550.

GALLATIN, CHARLES THOMAS, music educator; b. St. Paul, Minn., June 1, 1967; s. Thomas John and Carol Jane Gallatin; m. Jennifer Ann Snodgress, July 30, 1994; children: Joseph, John. BA in Music Edn., ND State U., 1991; MusM, Ball State U., 1995. Music tchr. Herman-Norcross Cmty. Schs., Herman, Minn., 1991—93, Blackford County Schools, Hartford City, Ind., 1995—. Grantee, Blackford Cmty. Found., 1999, 2000. Mem.: Ind. Fedn. Tchrs., Am. Choral Directors Assn., Ind. Bandmasters Assn., Music Educators Nat. Conf. Avocations: bicycling, travel, scuba diving, kayaking, fishing.

GALLATIN, JAMES ALLEN, music educator; b. Cedar Rapids, Iowa, Sept. 18, 1939; s. Melvin Herman Gallatin and Janet Elizabeth Miller; m. Jane Lynch Lynch, July 29, 1967; children: Christofa Lyn Letsom, Margaret Fahey Leeman. BS in Organ, Old Dominion Coll., Norfolk, VA, 1969; MusM, Western Mich. U., 1976; PhD in Music, U. of Cin. Coll. Conservatory of Music, 1980. Organist Emmanuel Episcopal Ch., Virginia Beach, Va., 1958—59; organist & choir master Larchmont Bapt. Ch., Norfolk, Va., 1964—67; organist & choirmaster St. Christopher's Episcopal Ch., Portsmouth, Va., 1967—69, St. Paul's Episcopal Ch., Norfolk, Va., 1970—74; organist First Congl. Ch., Mich., 1975—76; organist & choirmaster Westlake Presbyn. Ch., Mich., 1975—76, St. Paul's Episcopal Ch., Newport, Ky., 1977—80; music dir. Sacred Heart Ch., Norfolk, Va., 1980—. Musician: (recital) Kalamazoo Bach Festival, Miller Auditorium Recital Series, Water Front Arts Festival. Bd. mem. Pro Musica, Norfolk, Va., 1986—89. Sp-4 U.S. Army, 1960—63, Dougway Proving Grounds. Decorated Dougway Proving Grounds Cert. of Achievement Post Comdr. Mem.: Organ Hist. Soc. (assoc.), Am. Guild of Organists (assoc.; bd. mem. 1985—86). Home: 1405 Azalea Ct Norfolk VA 23507 Office: Sacred Heart Church 520 Graydon Ave Norfolk VA 23507 Office Phone: 757-625-6763. Personal E-mail: ja.gallatin@verizon.net. E-mail: j.gallatin@verizon.net.

GALLEGLY, ELTON WILLIAM, congressman; b. Huntington Park, Calif., Mar. 7, 1944; m. Janice Shrader; four children. Student, Calif. State U., L.A., 1962—63. Businessman, real estate broker, Simi Valley, Calif., from 1968; mem. Simi Valley City Coun., 1979; mayor City of Simi Valley, 1980-86; mem. U.S. Congresses from 21st (now 24th) Calif. dist., 1986—; chmn. internat. rels. subcom. internat. terrorism; judiciary com.; resources com.; select com. intelligence. Mem. Congl. Human Rights Caucus, Congl. Fire Svcs. Caucus, Congl. Task Force on Tobacco and Health, Congl. Task Force on Alzheimers Disease, other congl. caucuses include Automotive, Fight and Control Methamphetamine, Friends of Animals, Wine caucus, Diabetes caucus, Fairness caucus, House Renewable Energy and Energy Efficiency caucus, Older Ams. caucus; chmn. Task Force on Urban Search and Rescue; past vice-chmn., chmn. Ventura County Assn. govts., Calif. Bd. dirs. Moorpark Coll. Found. Republican. Office: US Ho Reps 2427 Rayburn Hob Washington DC 20515-0524

GALLEGO, GUILLERMO, industrial engineer, researcher; b. Mexicali, Mex., Jan. 24, 1957; s. Guillermo Gallego and Adriana (Noriega) Correa; m. Monica Alejandra Romero, June 9, 1984; children: Guillermo, Claudia, Miguel. BA, U. Calif., San Diego, 1980; MS, Cornell U., 1986, PhD, 1988. Asst. prof. Columbia U., N.Y.C., 1988-93, assoc. prof., 1994—. Cons. Northwest Airlines, 1993-94. Assoc. editor IIE Transactions, 1993—, Mgmt. Sci., 1994—, Ops. Rsch., 1994—, Naval Rsch. Logistics, 1994—. Grantee NSF, 1991—. Mem. Informs, IIE-Transactions (sr.), Phi Beta Kappa, Omega Rho. Republican. Roman Catholic. Home: 42-12 Union St Fair Lawn NJ 07410-5627 Office: Columbia U 500 W 120th St New York NY 10027-6623

GALLERANO, ANDREW JOHN, lawyer; b. Houston, Dec. 2, 1941; s. Andrew H. and Victoria J. (LaNasa) G.; m. Evelyn Cornelius, June 6, 1964; children: Kelly Lynn, Wendy Michelle. BA, U. Tex., Austin, 1964; JD, South Tex. Coll. Law, 1968. Bar: Tex. 1968, U.S. Supreme Ct. 1973. Asst. atty. gen., State of Tex., 1968-71; regional atty. Montgomery Ward & Co., 1971-72; v.p. Foley's, div. Federated Dept. Stores Inc., 1972-79; v.p., gen. counsel, sec. Nat. Convenience Stores Inc., Houston, 1979-89, sr. v.p., gen. counsel, sec., 1989-96; ptnr. Baker, Boldt & Gallerano, Dripping Springs, Tex., 1996-2000; v.p., gen. counsel K.C. Engring., Inc., Austin, Tex., 2000—03, DuBois, Bryant, Campbell & Schwartz, Austin, 2003—. Adj. prof. South Tex. Coll. Law, 1973-75; mem. adv. coun. U. Tex. Coll. Bus., 1993-98. Pres. S. Tex. Hosp. Fin. Agy., 1979—; mem. devel. bd. U. Tex. Health Sci. Ctr., Houston, 1978-93; bd. dirs. YMCA, 1973-86, 90-92, Assn. Cmty. TV, 1974-80; chmn. bd. trustees Star of Hope Mission, 1990-96. Mem. Tex. Bar Assn. (grievance com. 1986-89), U. Tex. Ex-Students Assn., Houston Retail Mchts. Assn. (bd. dirs. 1973—, pres. 1976-78), Tax Rsch. Assn. (bd. dirs. 1975-92). Office: DuBois Bryant Campbell & Schwartz 700 Lavaca Ste 1300 Austin TX 78701 Office Phone: 512-457-8000.

GALLI, JOHN RONALD, physicist, educator; b. Salt Lake City, Oct. 10, 1936; s. John Lester and Ella Mae (Lewis) G.; m. Marica Lee Jackson, Mar. 21, 1960 (div. July 1, 1977); children: Shawnee Sue Galli Hansen, Sherri Kay Galli Bond; m. Cheryl Maur Corley, June 2, 1978; children: Debora Maur Galli Baird, Diana Lynn Galli Marsden, John David Galli. PhD in Physics, U. Utah, 1963. Physicist Naval Weapons Ctr., China Lake, Calif., summer 1958, 59, Aerojet Gen., Downy, Calif., 1963; prof. Physics Weber State U., Ogden, Utah, 1963—, dept. chair physics, 1964-70, 83-95, dean Coll. of Sci., 1995—2003. Inventor: Mechanical Twisting Cat, 1993; contbr. various publs. and presentations, 1963-95. Mem. Golden Key, Am. Assn. Physics Tchrs., Phi Kappa Phi. Mem. Lds Ch. Avocations: skiing, golf, travel. Business E-Mail: jrgalle@weber.edu.

GALLI, JOSEPH, JR., consumer products company executive; BS in Bus. Adminstrn., U. NC, 1980; MBA, Loyola Coll., Balt., 1987. With Black & Decker, 1980—99; pres. Amazon.com, 1999—2000; CEO VerticalNet, 2000—01; CEO, pres. Newell Rubbermaid Inc., 2001—. Office: Newell Ctr 29 E Stephenson St Freeport IL 61032-0943

GALLIAN, JOSEPH ANTHONY, mathematics professor; b. New Kennington, Pa., Jan. 5, 1942; s. Joseph Anthony Gallian and Alvira Helen (Gardner) Strauss; m. Charlene Toy, May 29, 1965; children: William, Ronald, Kristin. BA, Slippery Rock State U., 1966; MA, U. Kans., 1968; PhD, Notre Dame U., 1971. Vis. asst. prof. Notre Dame (Ind.) U., 1971-72; asst. prof. U. Minn., Duluth, 1972-76, assoc. prof., 1976-80, prof., 1980—. Nat. coord. Math. Awareness Month, 2003; adv. bd. Math. Horizens, 1993—; chmn. Math. and Computer Sci. Divsn. Coun. Undergraduate Rsch. Author: Contemporary Abstract Algebra, 1990, 5th edit., 2002, For All Practical Purposes, 6th edit., 2003, Principals and Practices of Mathematics, 1997; editor: American Mathematical Society, 2000; assoc. editor Math. Mag., 1981-85, Am. Math. Monthly, 1992—, MAA OnLine, 1997—. Fellow Coun. Undergraduate Rsch., 2002. Mem.: Math. Assn. Am. (2d v.p. 2002—, Trevor Evans award 1996, Deborah and Franklin Tepper Haimo award 1993, Allendoerfer award 1977). Home: 1522 Triggs Ave Duluth MN 55811-2742 Office: Univ Minn Dept Math and Stats Solon Campus Ctr 140 1117 University Dr Duluth MN 55812-3000

GALLIANO, NESSIE VOISIN, elementary school educator; b. Houma, La., Jan. 14, 1957; d. Wiltz Anthony and Velma Marie Voisin; m. Stephen Anthony Galliano, June 21, 1986. BS, Nicholls State U., 1979; MS, Memphis State U., 1981; MS in Edn., La. State U., 1995. Cert. tchr. sci La. Petroleum geologist Amoco Prodn. Co., New Orleans; lab. tchr. Memphis State U.; tchr. Buras (La.) High Sch., St. Alphonsus Cath. Sch., Greenwell Springs, La., Our Lady of Mercy Cath. Sch., Baton Rouge. Mem.: Nat. Sci. Assn., La. Sci. Tchrs. Assn., Nat. Pastoral Musicians. Office Phone: 225-924-1054. E-mail: mrsg777@yahoo.com.

GALLIGAN, THOMAS C., JR., dean, law educator; AB, Stanford U., 1977; JD, U. Puget Sound (now Seattle U.), 1981; LLM, Columbia U., 1986. With Lane Powell Moss & Miller, Seattle; prof. law Paul Hebert Law Ctr. La. State U., Dale E. Bennett prof. law, 1997, exec. dir. La. Jud. Coll., 1996-98; dean, prof. law U. Tenn., Knoxville, 1998—, Elvin E. Overton Disting. prof. law, 2002—. Spkr. on legal topics to various groups, 1987—. Co-author: Legislation and Jurisprudence on Maritime Personal Injury Law, 1997, Louisiana Tort Law, 1996, supplemented 1997, 2000, 01, 02, Personal Injury in Admiralty, 2000, Admiralty in a Nutshell, 4th edit., 2000, Tort Law: Cases, Materials, and Problems, 3d edit., 2002, Cases and Materials on Maritime Law, 2003; contbr. articles to law revs. and acad. jours. Recipient John Minor Wisdom award for acad. excellence in legal scholarship Tulane Law Rev., 1996-97. Office: 1505 W Cumberland Ave Ste 278 Knoxville TN 37996-0001 Fax: 423-974-6595. Office Phone: 865-974-4241. E-mail: galligan@libra.law.uth.edu.

GALLIMORE, MARGARET MARTIN, poet; b. Winston Salem, Mar. 20, 1947; d. Holland Henry and Dallas Cornell (Robbins) Martin; m. Elmer Harold Holden Jr., Feb. 14, 1965; children: Andrew Harold, Amy Darlene, John Alan; m. Timothy Milton Gallimore, May 9, 1986. Student, High Point (N.C.) Coll., 1988. With AT&T Network Sys., Winston-Salem, 1965-69, 73-75, prodn. operator, 1979-89; real estate salesperson Lambe-Young Real Estate Co., Kernersville, NC, 1975-79; leasing cons. Vinyard Gardens Apt./S.E. Atlantic Properties, Winston-Salem, 1994-95; comm. assoc. AT&T Phone Ctr., Winston-Salem, 1995-96; real estate salesperson Triad Piedmont Properties, Kernersville, 1996; real estate broker, 1996—; asst. cmty. mgr. Lindsey Manor Apts./Steven D. Bell & Co., Kernersville, 1997; kitchen asst. child nutrition dept. Winston-Salem/Forsyth County Schs., 2001—. Author poetry. Mem. Nat. Women's History Mus., Pope John Paul II Cultural Ctr. Recipient Editors Choice awards (2) Nat. Libr. of Poetry, 1995, 97; named to Internat. Poetry Hall of Fame, Nat. Libr. Poetry, 1996. Mem. Internat. Soc. Poets (Disting. mem.).

GALLIN, JOHN I., medical researcher; b. NYC, Mar. 25, 1943; s. Nathaniel Mitchel and Helen (Cohen) G.; m. Elaine Barbara Klimerman, June 23, 1966; children: Alice Jennifer, Michael Louis. BA (cum laude), Amherst Coll., 1965; MD, Cornell U. Med. Sch., 1969; ScD honoris causa, Amherst Coll., 1988. Diplomate Nat. Bd. Med. Examiners. Intern medicine Bellevue Hosp., N.Y.C., 1969-70, asst. resident, 1970-71; teaching asst., instr. in medicine NYU Sch. Medicine, 1970-74, 74-81; clin. assoc. lab. clin. investigation Nat. Inst. Allergy and Infectious Diseases, NIH, Bethesda, Md., 1971-74, sr. investigator lab. clin. investigation, 1975-91, dir. div. intramural rsch., 1985-94, chief lab. of host defenses, 1991—2003; dir. NIH Warren Grant Magnuson Clin. Ctr., 1994—; assoc. dir. clin. rsch. NIH, 1994—. Asst. surgeon gen., rear adm. USPHS ret.; guest lectr. and spkr. in field. Editor: Principles and Practice of Clinical Research, 2002; co-editor: Inflammation, Basic Principles and Clinical Correlates, 1988, 3d edit., 1999; contbr. numerous articles to profl. jours. mem. editl. bd. various profl. jours. Recipient Rsch. award Am. Fedn. for Clin. Rsch., 1984, Squibb award Infectious Diseases Soc. Am., 1987, Disting. Svc. medal USPHS, 1992, Physician Exec. of Yr. award USPHS, 2001. Fellow Infectious Diseases Soc. Am.; mem. Inst. Medicine of NAS, Assn. Am. Physicians, Am. Soc. for Clin. Investigation, Am. Fedn. for Med. Rsch., Internat. Immunocompromised Host Soc. (pres. 1992-94), Am. Assn. Immunologists, Soc. for Leukocyte Biology (Marie T. Bonazinga award 2002). Office: NIH Bldg 10/2C 146 10 Center Dr MSC 1504 Bethesda MD 20892-1504 Business E-Mail: jig@nih.gov.

GALLIS, JOHN NICHOLAS, retired military officer, executive leadership training consultant; b. Pitts., Dec. 18, 1944; s. John Vincent Glade (dec.) and Sylvia Delores (Rizzo) Friedman (dec.); m. Carole Campbell, June 17, 1967; children: J. Christopher, Robin Noel. AS in Edn., No. Va. C.C., 1975; BS in Healthcare Adminstrn., George Washington U., 1977; MPA, Pa. State U., 1980. Enlisted USN, 1962, advanced through grades to capt., 1995; outpatient svcs. officer Submarine Med. Ctr., New London, Conn., 1974-76; patient adminstrn. officer Naval Hosp., Phila., 1977-80; officer-in-charge Naval Med. Clinic, Willow Grove, Pa., 1980-82; hosp. corpsman/dental technician rating assignment officer Bur. Naval Pers., Arlington, Va., 1982-85; dir. for adminstrn. Naval Hosp., Phila., Va., 1985-88; dir. leadership course Naval Sch. Health Scis., Bethesda, Md., 1988-91; adj. faculty leadership dept. U.S. Naval Acad.; assignment officer Med. Svc. Corps, Arlington, Va., 1991-93; exec. officer Naval Acad. Med. Clinic, Annapolis, Md., 1993-96; leadership and splty. tng. Naval Sch. Health Scis., Bethesda, 1996-98; cons., instr. Navy Medicine Ctr. Orgnl. Devel., Bethesda, 1999-2000; adj. faculty Nat. Fire Acad., Emmitsburg, Md., 2000—. Recipient Meritorious Svc. medal (3 awards), Navy Achievement medal, Navy Commendation medal (5 awards), Submarine Svc. badge. Fellow (life) Am. Coll. Healthcare Execs. Republican. Roman Catholic. Avocations: teaching, workshop. Home: 727 Suellen Dr King Of Prussia PA 19406 also: 3 Dewey Dr Annapolis MD 21401 E-mail: gallis@starpower.net.

GALLIVAN, JOHN WILLIAM, retired publishing executive; b. Salt Lake City, June 28, 1915; s. Daniel and Frances (Wilson) G.; m. Grace Mary Ivers, June 30, 1938 (dec.); children: Gay, John W. Jr., Michael D., Timothy. BA, U. Notre Dame, 1937. With Salt Lake Tribune, 1937—, promotion mgr., 1942-48, asst. pub., 1948-60, pub., 1960-84; pres. Kearns-Tribune Corp., 1960-86, chmn. bd., 1984-99; dir., exec. com. Tele-Communications, Inc., 1989-2000, ret., 2000—. Pres. Silver King Mining Co., 1960-97. Pres. Utah Symphony, 1964-65. Mem. Sigma Delta Chi, Bohemian Club (San Francisco). Clubs: Nat. Press (Washington); Alta (Salt Lake City), Salt Lake Country (Salt Lake City), Rotary (Salt Lake City). Home and Office: 1665 White Pine Canyon Rd Park City UT 84060 Personal E-mail: jwgallivan@comcast.net.

GALLMAN, KELLY ANN, music educator, musician; b. Savannah, Ga., June 29, 1971; d. Lawrence Bruce and Sandra Lee Hennessy; m. M Steven Gallman, June 21, 2004; 1 child, Robert Justin Welch. B Music Edn., Stetson U., 1993. Musician Brevard Symphony Orch., Melbourne, Fla., 1994—; music tchr. Enterprise Elem., Port St. John, Fla., 1994—95; itinerant strings tchr. Brevard County Schools, Melbourne, Fla., 1995—, chmn. All-County Mid. Sch. Orch., 2001—. Musician St. Mary's Ch., Rockledge, Fla., 2003—05. Mem.: Ctrl. Fla. Musicians Assn., Fla. Music Educators Assn., Fla. Orch. Assn. (dist. chmn. 1999—2001). Roman Catholic. Avocations: home improvement, crafts, auto racing, music. Home: 988 Kings Post Rd Rockledge FL 32955 Office Phone: 321-639-3897.

GALLO, ANTHONY ERNEST, playwright, economist; b. Vandergrift, Pa., Feb. 3, 1939; s. Dominic and Sara (Raso) G.; divorced; 1 child, Thomas Augustus. BA, Coll. William and Mary, 1961; MBA, U. Pa., 1963; postgrad., U. Pitts., 1966-70. Investment analyst Pitts. Nat. Bank, 1963-66; instr. mktg. and stats. Duquesne U., Pitts., 1964-69; instr. mktg. U. Pitts., 1965-69; instr. money and banking St. Vincent Coll., Latrobe, Pa., 1966-69; asst. prof. econs. Allegheny C.C., Pitts., 1966-70; econ. cons. SBA, Washington, 1967—; bus. economist Bur. Econ. Analysis/U.S. Dept. Commerce, Washington, 1970-71; sr. economist Econ. Rsch. Svc./USDA, Washington, 1971-2000. Propr. Capitol Hill Victorian Restorations, Washington, 1970-90. Econs. editor U.S. Food Mktg. Rev., 1984-2001; contbr. 300 articles to profl. and govt. jours.; writer (plays) Eugenio, 2002, Margherita, 2003, Death, (opera librettos) Eugenio, 2003, Margherita, 2003, Solomon, 2005; librettist, lyricist. Mem. Capitol Hill Restoration Soc., Washington, 1972—, mem. endowment bd., 1999; mem Capitol Hill Garden Club, Washington, 1972—; commr. Vandergrift Mcpl. Authority, 1965-67; pres. Civic League, Vandergrift, 1965-70; mem. governing coun., endowment bd. Holy Rosary Ch. With U.S. Army, 1963. Named Outstanding Civic Leader, Jaycees, Vandergrift, 1967. Mem. Cosmos Club (endowment advisor 1996—2001), Arts Club Washington (endowment bd. 1996-99), John Carroll Soc., Red Circle, U.S. Food Distbn. Rsch. Soc. (bd. dirs. 1994-97), Wharton Sch. Club (bd. dirs. 1991—), Italian Cultural Soc. (bd. dirs. 1994-97), Playwright's Forum, Writers Ctr., Charter Theatre, Dramatists Guild, Am. Composers Forum, Am. Music Ctr. Women in Film, Wash. Screenwriter's Group, Washington Area League Arts. Roman Catholic. Avocations: reading, gardening, swimming, dance, historic preservation, bridge. Home: PO Box 15414 Washington DC 20003-0414 Office Phone: 202-544-6973. E-mail: agallo2368@aol.com.

GALLO, DAVID MICHAEL, history professor, religious studies educator; b. Worcester, Mass., Sept. 30, 1957; s. Albert Gaetano and Eleanore Frances (Harpie) Gallo. BA, Assumption Coll., Worcester, Mass., 1979; MDiv, Weston S.J. Sch. Theology, Cambridge, 1984; ThM, Harvard U., 1985; PhD, Boston Coll., Chestnut Hill, 1993. Instr. religious studies Tampa Cath. H.S., Fla., 1980—81; lectr. history and religious studies Assumption Coll., Worcester, Mass., 1991—92, asst. prof. history, 1992—2001, Coll. Mt. St. Vincent, Riverdale, NY, 2001—. V.p. religious affairs Assumption Coll., Worcester, Mass., 1999—2000; chaplain Coll. Mt. St. Vincent, Riverdale, NY, 2001—. Mem.: North Am. Soc. Ct. Studies, Sacred Mil. Constaninian Order of St. George (Capellán Caballero con Merito 1998). Roman Catholic. Avocations: weight training, theater, opera, music. Home: 4F 104 W 74th St New York NY 10023 Office: Coll Mt St Vincent 3401 Riverdale Ave Riverdale NY 10471 Office Phone: 718-405-3747. Fax: 718-405-3747.

GALLO, DONALD ROBERT, retired literature educator; b. Paterson, N.J., June 1, 1938; s. Sergio and Thelma Mae (Lowe) G.; m. C.J. Bott, Feb. 14, 1997; 1 child, Brian Keith; 1 stepchild, Christian Perrett. BA in English, Hope Coll., 1960; MAT in English Edn., Oberlin Coll., 1961; PhD in English Edn., Syracuse U., 1968. English tchr. Bedford Jr. High Sch., Westport, Conn., 1961-65; rsch. assoc. Syracuse (N.Y.) U., 1965-67; from asst. prof. to assoc. prof. edn. U. Colo., Denver, 1968-72; reading specialist Golden Jr. High Sch., Jefferson County Pub. Schs., Colo., 1972-73; prof. English Cen. Conn. State U., New Britain, 1973-97. Instr. composition Onondaga C. C., Syracuse, 1967; vis. faculty grad. liberal studies program Wesleyan U., 1983; staff writer reading assessment Nat. Assessment Ednl. Progress, Denver, 1972-73; speaker in field; cons. to schs. and librs. Mem. editl. bd. Nat. Coun. Tchrs. English, 1985-88; compiler, editor: Speaking for Ourselves, 1990, Speaking for Ourselves, Too, 1993; editor: Connections: Short Stories by Outstanding Writers for Young Adults, 1989, Visions: Nineteen Short Stories by Outstanding Writers for Young Adults, 1987, Center Stage: One-Act Plays for Teenage Readers and Actors, 1990, Sixteen: Short Stories by Outstanding Writers for Young Adults, 1984, Books for You, 1985, Authors' Insights: Turning Teenagers into Readers and Writers, 1992, Short Circuits: Thirteen Shocking Stories by Outstanding Writers for Young Adults, 1992, Within Reach: Ten Stories, 1993, Join In: Multiethnic Short Stories by Outstanding Writers for Young Adults, 1993, Ultimate Sports: Short Stories by Outstanding Writers for Young Adults, 1995, No Easy Answers: Short Stories About Teenagers Making Tough Choices, 1997, Time Capsule: Short Stories About Teenagers Throughout the Twentieth Century, 1999, On The Fringe, 2001, Destination Unexpected, 2003, First Crossing: Stories About Teen Immigrants, 2004; author: Presenting Richard Peck, 1989, Bookmark Reading Program, Seventh and Eighth Grade Texts and Workbooks, 1979, Heath Middle Level Literature, 1995; co-author: (with Sarah K. Herz) From Hinton to Hamlet: Building Bridges Between Young Adult Literature and the Classics, 1996, rev. and expanded, 2005; interviewer of authors for Authors4Teens.com website. Recipient Disting. Svc. award Conn. Coun. Tchrs. English, 1989, ALAN award Assembly on Lit. for Adolescents of the Nat. Coun. Tchrs. English, 1992, Cert. of Merit award Cath. Libr. Assn., 1995, Ted Hipple Svc. award ALAN, 2001. Mem. Nat. Coun. Tchrs. English, Assembly on Lit. for Adolescents, Ohio Coun. Tchrs. English Lang. Arts (named an Outstanding English Lang. Arts Educator 2003), Soc. Children's Book Writers and Illustrators, Authors Guild. Avocations: gardening, cooking, travel, photography. Address: 34540 Sherbrook Park Dr Solon OH 44139-2046 E-mail: gallodon@aol.com.

GALLO, ERNEST, vintner; b. 1909; widowed. Co-owner, chmn. bd. dirs. E & J Gallo Winery, Modesto, Calif., 1933—. Office: E & J Gallo Winery 600 Yosemite Blvd Modesto CA 95354*

GALLO, JOAN ROSENBERG, lawyer; b. Newark, Apr. 28, 1940; BA in Psychology, Boston U.; postgrad., We. Md. Coll.; postgrad, We. Grad. Sch. Psychology; JD magna cum laude, U. Santa Clara, 1975. Bar: Calif. 1975. Assoc. with Cynthia Mertens U, Santa Clara, Calif., 1975-76; sr. law clk. U.S. Dist. Ct., Calif., 1976-78; assoc. Decker and Collins, San Jose, Calif., 1978-79; from dep. city atty. to city atty. City of San Jose, 1979-2000; ptnr. Terra Law LLP, San Jose, 2000—02, Realty Law, LLP, San Jose, 2002—03; of counsel Hopkins & Carley, 2004—. Mem. Psi Chi. Office: Hopkins & Carley 70 S First St San Jose CA 95113 Office Phone: 408-286-9800. Business E-Mail: jgallo@hopkinscarley.com.

GALLO, JON JOSEPH, lawyer; b. Santa Monica, Calif., Apr. 19, 1942; s. Philip S. and Josephine (Sarazan) G.; m. Jo Ann Broome, June 13, 1964 (div. 1984); children: Valerie Ann, Donald Philip; m. Eileen Florence, July 4, 1985; 1 child, Kevin Jon. BA, Occidental Coll., 1964; JD, UCLA, 1967. Bar: Calif. 1968, U.S. Ct. Appeals (9th cir.) 1968, U.S. Tax Ct. 1969. Assoc. Greenberg, Glusker, Fields, Claman & Machtinger, L.A., 1967-75, ptnr., 1975—. Bd. dirs. USC Probate and Trust Conf., L.A., 1980—, UCLA Estate Planning Inst., chmn. 1992—. Contbr. articles to profl. jours. Fellow Am. Coll. Trust and Estate Counsel; mem. ABA (chair Generation Skipping Taxation com. 1992-95, co-chair life ins. com. 1995—), Internat. Acad. Estate and Trust Law, Assn. for Advanced Life Underwriting (assoc. mem.). Avocation: photography. Office: Greenberg Glusker Fields Claman & Machtinger LLP Ste 2100 1900 Avenue Of The Stars Los Angeles CA 90067-4502

GALLO, JOSEPH ANTHONY, physical therapist, educator, personal trainer; b. Medford, Mass., June 14, 1968; s. Anthony M. and Phyllis Gallo. BS in Phys. Edn. and Athletic Tng., W.Va. U., 1989; Master of Phys. Therapy, U. of Del., 1993; DSc, Rocky Mountain U. of Health Professions, Utah, 2004. Cert. Athletic Trainer Nat. Athletic Trainer's Assn. Bd. of Cert., 1990, Physical Therapist NH. Bd. of Allied Medicine, 1993; Physical Edn. Tchr. Cert. Commonwealth of Mass., 1990. Head athletic trainer Burlington H.S.; rehab. seminar spkr. Ind. Contractor, Londonderry, NH; lectr. and clin. supr. Keene State Coll. Athletic Tng. Program, Keene, NH, 1993—96; dir. of tennis ops. Summer's Edge Inc, Medford, Mass., 1993—2004; clin. athletic trainer, phys. therapist Performance Rehab, INC, Nashua, NH, 1994—; prof., program dir. Hesser Coll. Phys. Therapist Asst. Program, Manchester, NH, 1996—. Rehabilitaion electromedical device consulting Ind. Contractor, Londonderry, NH, 2001—. John Spiker Athletic Tng. scholar, W.Va. U., 1989. Mem.: Nat. Athletic Trainer's Assn. Avocations: tennis, running, reading, travel, exercise. Home: 433 Pendleton Ln Londonderry NH NH 03053 Office: Hesser Coll 3 Sundial Ave Manchester NH 03103 Office Phone: 603-668-6660. Home Fax: 603-537-9943. E-mail: jgallo@hesser.edu.

GALLO, JOSEPH E., vintner; b. 1941; Various positions E&J Gallo Winery, South San Francisco, 1962—, now co-pres. & CEO. Office: E & J Gallo Winery 600 Yosemite Blvd Modesto CA 95354*

GALLO, ROBERT CHARLES, research scientist; b. Waterbury, Conn., Mar. 23, 1937; s. Francis Anton Gallo, Louise Mary (Ciancuilli) Gallo; m. Mary Jane Hayes, July 1, 1961; children: Robert, Marcus, Caroline. BA in biology, Providence Coll., 1959, DSc (hon.), 1974; MD, Jefferson Med. Coll., 1963; 20 hon. degrees univs. in US, Belgium, Italy, Argentina, Peru, Israel, Sweden, Germany, Mex., Ireland. Intern, resident medicine U. Chgo., 1963-65; clin. assoc. med. br. Nat. Cancer Inst. NIH, Bethesda, Md., 1965-68, sr. investigator human tumor cell biology br., 1968-69, head sect. cellular control mechanisms, 1969-72, chief lab. tumor cell biology, 1972—95; founder, dir. Inst. Human Virology, U. Md., Balt., 1996—, dir. Basic Sciences Divsn.; prof. Medicine, Microbiology and Immunology, Sch. Medicine U. Md., Balt. Adj. prof. genetics George Washington U.; adj. prof. biology Johns Hopkins U., Balt., hon. prof. biology, 1985—; hon. prof. medicine Karolinska Inst., Stockholm, 1998—; US rep. to world com. Internat. Comparative Leukemia and Lymphoma Assn., 1981—; mem. bd. govs. Franco Am. AIDS Found., 1987, World AIDS Found., 1987; sr. cons. HIV/AIDS China CDC, 2005—. Author: (book) Virus Hunting, 1991; author: (or co-author) more than 1,100 sci. papers. With USPHS, 1965—68. Named to Nat. Inventors Hall of Fame, 2004; recipient Dameshek award, Am. Hematol. Soc., 1974, CIBA-GIEGY award in biomed. sci., 1977, 1988, Superior Svc. award, USPHS, 1978, Meritorious Svc. medal, 1983, Disting. Svc. medal, 1984, First F. Stohlman lecture award, Am. Soc. Hematol., 1979, Albert Lasker award for basic biomed. rsch., 1982, 1986, Abraham White award in biochem., George Washington U., 1983, First Otto Herz award for cancer rsch., Tel Aviv U., 1982, Griffuel prize, Assn. for Cancer Rsch., France, 1983, GM award in cancer rsch., 1984, Gruber prize, Am. Soc. Investigative Dermatology, 1984, Lucy Wortham prize in cancer rsch., Am. Soc. for Surg. Oncology, 1984, Gold medal, Am. Cancer Soc., 1984, Berla Internat Sci. prize, India, 1985, Hammer prize for cancer rsch., 1985, Gairdner prize for biomed. rsch., Can., 1987, spl. award, Am. Soc. Infectious Disease, 1986, Gold Plate award, Am. Acad. Achievement, 1987, Lions Humanitarian award, 1987, Japan prize in sci. and tech., 1988, Ciba Corning award, 1993, 1st Dale McFarlin award for rsch., Internat. Soc. Human Retrovirology, 1994, 1st Gustav Embden award, U. Frankfurt, 1996, Pomesa award, 1996, 1st award, Internat. Soc. Blood Transfusion, 1997, Nomura prize for AIDS and Cancer Rsch, Japan, 1998, Warren Alpert prize, Harvard U., 1998, Paul Erlich award, Germany, 1999, Hero in Medicine award, Can, 2000, Frank Annunzio sci. award, Washington, 2000, Prince Asturias prize, Spain, 2000, 1st award, Ireland C. of C. and USA, 2001, Seminal contbrns. to field of Human Retrovirology award, Internat. Soc. HTLV, 2001, award, Internat. Retrovirology Assn., 2001, World Health award, Pres. M. Gorbachev Found., 2001, Austria, 2001, Archimedes prize in sci., Italy, 2003, Ellis Island Medal of Honor, 2005. Mem.: NAS, Fedn. for Advanced Edn. in Scis., Am. Fedn. Clin. Rsch., Am. Soc. Microbiology, Am. Assn. Cancer Rsch., Biochem. Soc., Am. Microbiology Soc., Am. Soc. Biol. Chemists, Am. Soc. Clin.Investigation, Internat Soc. Hematology, Inst. Medicine, Royal Acad. Medicine of Spain (hon.), Royal Soc. Medicine (hon.), Royal Soc. Physicians of Scotland (hon.), Royal Soc. Medicine Belgium (sr.), Alpha Omega Alpha. Achievements include research on viruses, AIDS and Leukemia; co-discovery of AIDS virus, discovery of first and second human retroviruses and Interleukin-2 (IL-2); development of HIV blood test. Office: 725 W Lombard St Ste S307 Baltimore MD 21201-1009 Office Phone: 410-706-8614. E-mail: gallo@umbi.umd.edu.

GALLO, SERGIO ROBERTO, music educator, researcher; b. Sao Paulo, Brazil, Aug. 12, 1963; came to U.S., 1993; s. Waldomiro and Cleonice Gallo. Diplome d'excellence, Conservatoire Europeen, Paris, 1987; MM, U. Cin., 1995; DMA, U. Calif., Santa Barbara, 1998. Tchg. asst. U. Calif., Santa Barbara, 1995-97; adj. prof. piano Millikin U., Decatur, Ill., 1997-98; asst. prof. piano U. N.D., Grand Forks, 1998—, coord. cultural exch. program dept. music, 1999-2000. Performer piano recitals, 1985—. Recipient Erno Daniel Meml. prize U. Calif., 1997; grantee CD recording U. N.D., 1999. Mem. N.D. Music Tchrs. Assn., Coll. Music Soc. Roman Catholic. Avocations: travel, reading. Office: U ND Dept Music Grand Forks ND 58202-7125 E-mail: sergio_gallo@und.nodak.edu.

GALLO, WILLIAM VICTOR, cartoonist; b. N.Y.C., Dec. 28, 1922; s. Francisco and Henrietta (Caballero) G.; m. Dolores Rodriguez, Mar. 13, 1950; children: Gregory, William. With N.Y. Daily News, 1941—, sports cartoonist, sports columnist, 1960—, assoc. sports editor, 1984—. One-man show, Spectrum Fine Arts Gallery, N.Y.C., 1981; works represented in permanent collection, Baseball Hall of Fame, Cooperstown, N.Y., Syracuse U. archives. Served with USMC, 1942-45. Named best sports cartoonist, Nat. Cartoonist Soc., 1969—73, 1984—86; named to Yonkers Hall of Fame, 1984, Westchester Hall of Fame, 1984, Boxing Hall of Fame, Canostota, N.Y., 2001; recipient 19 Page One awards, N.Y. Newspaper Guild, 1965—86, Elzie Segar award, 1976, Alumni Achievement award, Sch. Visual Arts, 1977, Power of Printing award, 1977, Long and Meritorious award, The Baseball Writers of Am., 2004. Mem. N.Y. Boxing Writers (pres.), Nat. Cartoonists Soc. (pres., Milt Caniff Lifetime Achievement award 1999), Baseball Writers, Profl. Football Writers, Turf Writers, N.Y. Press Assn., (award 1986), Soc. Silurians, Soc. Illustrators. Home: 1 Mayflower Dr Yonkers NY 10710-3801 Office: NY Daily News 450 W 33rd St New York NY 10001-2603 *Everything has to start with a dream. First the dream, and then the chasing of it. I pity the person who doesn't own a dream.*

GALLOMBARDO, ANGELA DALE, elementary school educator; b. Terrytown, N.Y., Mar. 30, 1962; d. Angelo Anthony Gallombardo and Audrey Dale. BS in Visual Comm., Lyndon State Coll., 1984; MST in Elem. Edn., Fordham U., 1994, MS in Edn., 2002. 2d grade tchr. PS 65, Bronx, 1994—99; tchr. tech. IS 129, Bronx, 1999—2002; 2d grade tchr. PS 179, Bronx, 2003—. Recipient Excellence in Tchg. awards, NYC Chancellor's Dept., 1997—99. Democrat. Home: 11th St New York NY 10009

GALLOP, JANE (JANE ANNE GALLOP), women's studies educator, writer; b. Duluth, Minn., May 4, 1952; d. Melvin Gordon and Eudice Zelda (Titch) G.; children: Max Blau Gallop, Ruby Gallop Blau. BA, Cornell U., 1972, PhD, 1976. Lectr. French Gettysburg (Pa.) Coll., 1976; asst. prof. Miami U., Oxford, Ohio, 1977-81, assoc. prof., 1981-85; prof. women's studies Rice U., Houston, 1985-87, Autrey prof., 1987-90; prof. English U. Wis., Milw., 1990-92, Disting. prof., 1992—. NEH vis. prof. Emory U., Atlanta, 1984-85; Hill vis. prof. U. Minn., Mpls., 1987; dir. seminar for coll. tchrs. NEH, Milw., 1985, 88; instr. Sch. of Criticism and Theory, Dartmouth Coll., 1991. Author: Intersections, 1981, The Daughter's Seduction, 1982, Reading Lacan, 1985, Thinking Through the Body, 1988, Around 1981, 1992, Feminist Accused of Sexual Harassment, 1997, Anecdotal Theory, 2002, Living with His Camera, 2003; editor: Pedagogy, 1995, Polemic, 2004. Guggenheim fellow, 1983-84. Mem. MLA. Office: Dept English Univ Wis - Milw PO Box 413 Milwaukee WI 53201-0413 Office Phone: 414-229-6402. Business E-Mail: jg@uwm.edu.

GALLOPOULOS, GREGORY STRATIS, lawyer; b. Detroit, Oct. 8, 1959; s. Nicholas E. and Mary Frances Gallopoulos; m. Christa L. Gallopoulos. AB with highest distinction, U. Mich., 1981, JD magna cum laude, 1984. Bar: Ill. 1984, US Dist. Ct. No. Dist. Ill. 1984, Supreme Ct. Ill. 1984, US Dist. Ct. Ea. Dist. Mich. 1988, US Ct. Appeals 7th Cir. 1990, US Supreme Ct. 1992, US Tax Ct. 1995, US Ct. Fed. Claims 1995, US Ct. Appeals 9th Cir. 1996, US Ct. Appeals Fed. Cir. 2001. Assoc. Jenner & Block LLP, Chgo., 1984-91, ptnr., 1992—, firm co-chair tax controversy practice, firm mng. ptnr., 2005—. Author: Preserving Error for Appeal in Illinois, 1990. Dir. Newscoverage Unlimited; bd. mem. Lincoln Pk. Presbyn. Ch. Mem. ABA, 7th Cir. Bar Assn., Order of Coif, Phi Beta Kappa. Presbyterian. Office: Jenner & Block LLP 1 IBM Plz Chicago IL 60611-7603 Office Phone: 312-923-2754. Office Fax: 312-840-7754. Business E-Mail: ggallopoulos@jenner.com.

GALLOWAY, GALE LEE, oil and gas executive, rancher; b. Pearsall, Tex., Jan. 10, 1930; s. Gerald Glenn and Vida Olga (Tate) G.; m. Connie Bird, July 30, 1965; children: Georgia Gayle, Michael W., Tara Lee. BBA in Econs., Baylor U., 1952; postgrad., Tex A&I U., 1953-54, South Tex. Law Sch., 1960-63. Fin. analyst, landman, gas contracts rep., mgr. gas supply Tenneco, Houston, 1954-65; sr. v.p. Coastal States Gas, Houston, 1964-73; chmn., pres., CEO Celeron Corp., Lafayette, La., 1973-86; chmn. bd. Entex Inc., Houston, 1987-89, San Antonio, 1994—. Chmn. bd. La. Intrastate Gas, Houston, 1989, GLG Energy, Inc., Austin, Tex., 1989—, Gas Transmission Ltd., London, 1989—; dir. Goodyear Tire & Rubber, Akron, Ohio; mem. adv. com. to bd. dirs. MBank; mem. adv. com. U.S. Senator Commn. Oil and Gas; mem. Interstate Oil Compact Commn. Bd. dirs. Boy Scouts Am., La. Assn. Bus. and Industry, La. State U. Found., Baylor Coll. of Medicine, DeBakey Med. Found.; council trustees Gulf South Research Inst.; chmn. bd. regents

Baylor U.; bd. regents Milsaps Coll. Officer USAF, 1952—54. Recipient Carnegie Hero medal Life Saving award, 1982, W.R. White Meritorious Svc. award, 1982, Tex. award for hist. preservation Tex. Hist. Commn., 1994, Disting. Alumni award Baylor U., Silver Beaver award, Boy Scouts Am.; named Baylor U. Hall of Fame, 1983 Mem. La. Assn. Ind. Producers and Royalty Owners (pres., bd. dirs.), Mid-Continent Oil and Gas Assn. (v.p., exec. com.), Nat. Petroleum Refiners Assn., Am. Petroleum Inst., Calif. Ind. Producers Assn., Ind. Producers Assn. Am., Interstate Natural Gas Assn. Am., Pub. Affairs Research Council, Natural Gas Men Houston, Greater Lafayette C. of C. (bd. dirs.), Natural Gas Men New Orleans, Am. Gas Assn. (bd. dirs.), Austin C. of C. Clubs: City, Petroleum; Austin Country, University (Austin). Home: 4100 Waters Edge Dr Austin TX 78731-5103 Office: 1224 Clear Rock Ranch Rd Johnson City TX 78636 Office Phone: 830-868-7429.

GALLOWAY, JANICE, writer, editor; b. Kilwinning, Scotland, Dec. 2, 1956; d. James and Janet (McBride) G.; 1 child, James Alexander Galloway McNaught. MA, Glasgow U., 1978. Tchr. Strathclyde Regional Coun., Ayrshire, Scotland, 1980-90. Music critic. Editor (with Hamish Whyte): New Writing Scotland, 1990, 1991, 1992; author: The Trick is to Keep Breathing, 1990, Foreign Parts, 1994, Where You Find It, 1996, Clara, 2002 (Saltire book of yr., 2002), Boy Book See, 2002; author: (with sculptor Anne Bevan) +Rosengarten, 2004; librettist (with sculptor Anne Bevan): Pipelines, librettist (with composer Sally Beamish): Operas Monster. Recipient Mind/Allan Lane prize, 1990, Cosmopolitan/Perrier award, 1991, E.M. Forster award in lit. Am. Acad. Arts and Letters, 1994, McVitie's prize for Scottish Writer of the Yr., 1994, Saltire prize, 2002; Times Literary Supplement Rsch. fellow Brit. Libr., 1999. Office: care Jonathan Cape 20 Vauxhall Bridge Rd London SW1 6RB England also: care Derek Johns AP Watt Agy 20 John St London WCIN 2DR England E-mail: sarah@galloway.itol.org.

GALLOWAY, JOE, professional football player; Degree in Bus./Mktg., Ohio State U. Wide receiver Seattle Seahawks, 1995-2000, Dallas Cowboys, 2000—03, Tampa Bay Buccaneers, 2004—. Sponsor group of students at each Seattle home game Galloway Express; appeared on Wheel of Fortune with proceeds from his spins benefiting Make-A-Wish Found. Named NFL Offensive Rookie of Yr., Coll. and Pro Football Newsweekly, 1995, Consensus All-Rookie choice, 1995, AFC Offensive Player of Week, 1995, AFC Spl. Teams Player of Month, 1995; Nat. Football Found. scholar athlete; Nat. Assn. Collegiate Dirs. of Athletics scholar. Office: c/o Tampa Bay Buccaneers 1 Buccaneer Place Tampa FL 33607

GALLOWAY, JOSEPH LEE, JR., writer, journalist; b. Bryan, Tex., Nov. 13, 1941; s. Joseph L. and Marian D. (Dewvall) G.; m. Theresa Magdalene Null, Sept. 9, 1966 (dec. Jan. 1996); children: Lee T., Joshua J; m. Karen M. McCray, Oct. 24, 1998 (div. Mar., 2005). Grad., Refugio, Tex., 1959; DHL (hon.), St. Mary's Coll., Newburgh, N.Y., 2003; D of Journalism (hon.), Norwich U., Vt., 2005. Reporter Victoria (Tex.) Advocate, 1959-61, United Press Internat., Kansas City, Mo., 1961, bureau chief Topeka, 1962-64, war correspondent South Vietnam, 1965-66, correspondent Tokyo, 1966-68, bureau chief Jakarta, Indonesia, 1968-73, mgr. South Asia New Delhi, 1973-74, mgr. southeast Asia Singapore, 1974-75, bureau chief Moscow, 1976-80, L.A., 1980-82; west coast editor U.S.News & World Report, L.A., 1982-84; assoc. editor U.S. News, Washington, 1984-86, sr. editor, 1986-90, sr. writer, 1990—2001; spl. cons. to Sec. of State U.S. Dept. State, Washington, 2001—02; sr. mil. corr. Knight Ridder Newspapers, Washington, 2002—; syndicated columnist Chgo. Tribune Media Svcs. Syndicate. Co-author: Triumph Without Victory, 1992, We Were Soldiers Once...and Young, 1992 (movie We Were Soldiers based on book, 2002). Dir. No Greater Love, Washington, 1990—; bd. adv. Vietnam Vets. Meml. Fund; adv. bd. Nat. Infantry Found., Sch. Humanities & Social Scis., The Citadel, Charleston, SC, Mus. America's Wars, Manassas, Va Decorated Bronze Star with V device; recipient Nat Mag. award Am. Soc. Mag. Editors, 1991, Nat. News Media award Vet. of Fgn. Wars of U.S.A., 1992, Excellence in Arts award Vietnam Vets. Am., 1999, U.S. Infantry Assn. Order St. Maurice, 2000, U.S. Armor Assn.'s Order St. George, 2001, Denig Memorial Disting. Svc. award U.S.M.C. Combat Corr. Assn., 2001, Stanley Larsen award, 25th Div. Assn., 2002, Abraham Lincoln award, Union League Club, Phila., 2005, Tex McCreary Media award, Congl.Medal of Honor Soc., 2005. Mem. Soc. Profl. Journalists, Overseas Press Club, 7th Cavalry Assn., 1st Cavalry Divsn. Assn. Avocations: travel, fly fishing, birdwatching. Office: 700 12th St NW # 1000 Washington DC 20005 Office Phone: 202-383-6000. Business E-Mail: jgalloway@krwashington.com.

GALLOWAY, JUDY A., deputy commissioner; BS in Bus. Adminstrn., Ga. State U.; postgrad., U. Colo., Denver. Program specialist Atlanta Regional Office, Dept. Health and Human Svcs.; deputy regional commr., ACF-Region VIII office Adminstrn. Children and Families, U.S. Dept. Health and Human Svcs., 1998—2000, deputy regional commr., Office of Early Childhood Programs, 2000—.

GALLOWAY, KATHELENE ENGRID, artist, educator; b. Pocatello, Idaho; d. Rulon Kidd adn Engelina Engrid (Kruger) G. BFA, Boise (Idaho) State U., 1995; MFA, Ind. State U., Terre Haute, 1998. Instr. art Ea. Oreg. U., La Grande, 1998—. Office: Ea Oreg U 1 Univ Blvd La Grande OR 97850 E-mail: kgallow@eou.edu.

GALLOWAY, KENNETH FRANKLIN, engineering educator; b. Columbia, Tenn., Apr. 11, 1941; s. Benjamin F. and Carrie (Dowell) G.; m. Dorothy Elise Lamar; children: Kenneth Jr., Carole A. BA, Vanderbilt U., 1962; PhD, U. S.C., 1966. Rsch. assoc. Ind. U., Bloomington, 1966-67, asst. prof., 1967-72, assoc. prof., 1972; rsch. physicist Naval Weapons Support Ctr., Crane, Ind., 1972-74; tech. staff Nat. Bur. Standards, Gaithersurg, Md., 1974-77, chief sect., 1977-79, chief divsn., 1980-86; prof. elect. engring. U. Md., 1980-86; prof., dept. head elect. and computer engring. U. Ariz., Tucson, 1986-96; dean engring., prof. elec. engring. Vanderbilt U., Nashville, 1996—. Contbr. articles to profl. jours. Sci. and Tech. fellow U.S. Dept. Commerce, 1979-80. Fellow IEEE (gen. chmn. Nuc. and Space Radiation Effects Conf. 1985, v.p. Nuc. and Plasma Sci. Soc. 1990, chmn. radiation effects com. 1991-94, chmn. engring. rsch. and devel. policy com. 1994, gen. chmn. Internat. Electron Devices Meeting 1997), AAAS, Am. Phys. Soc.; mem. Am. Soc. Engring. Edn., Sigma Xi, Eta Kappa Nu, Tau Beta Pi. Office: Vanderbilt U Sch Engring VU Sta B 351826 Nashville TN 37235-1826 Office Phone: 615-322-0720. Business E-Mail: kenneth.f.galloway@vanderbilt.edu.

GALLOWAY, MARGARET ELLIS, secondary school educator; b. Cleve., July 20, 1943; d. Ted and Hallie Marie (Herman) Ellis; m. John Martin Galloway, Feb. 17, 1985 (div. 1988); 1 child, John Edward Peterson. AB, Allegheny Coll., 1965; MA, Ball State U., 1977. Cert. elem. tchr., prin., supr., Ohio. Tchr. Cleve. Pub. Schs., 1965, Lubbock (Tex.) Ind. Sch. Dist., 1966-68, Cleve. Pub. Schs., 1971-72, Austin (Tex.) Ind. Sch. Dist., 1973-75; instr. City Colls. Chgo., European Br., Ramstein, Federal Republic of Germany, 1977-78; tchr. Gahanna Jefferson Pub. Schs., Ohio, 1978-80; tchr.-coordinator Bexley City Schools, Ohio, 1980—. Chmn. Social Studies dept., Bexley City Schs., 1985—, North Cen. Eval., 1987—; coorinator Gifted Program, 1980—; instr. Basics, 1982-86. Presenter speech workshops Ohio Assn. Gifted Children, 1983, 84, 85; contbr. articles in field. Danforth scholar, Bexley City Schs., Ohio State U., 1987. Mem. Assn. for Supervision & Curriculum, Ohio Assn. for Gifted Children, Consortium of Coordinators of Gifted, Cen. Ohio Assn. for Gifted Childen, Phi Delta Kappa. Republican. Presbyterian. Avocations: singing, reading, walking. Home: 655 Vancouver Dr Westerville OH 43081-3421 Office: Bexley Jr High Sch 250 S Cassingham Rd Columbus OH 43209-1805

GALLOWAY, SISTER MARY BLAISE, mathematics professor; b. Mendota, Ill., June 30, 1933; d. Otto William and Rita Irene (Cannon) G. BS in Math., St. Joseph's Coll., 1965; MS in Math. Edn., U. Ill., 1970; MS in Adminstrn., U. Notre Dame, 1985. Tchr. elem. edn. St. Augustine Sch., Richmond, Mich., 1952—58, Holy Rosary Sch., Duluth, Minn., 1958—65; asst. prin. Sacred Heart Acad., Springfield, Ill., 1983—85, co-prin., 1985—87; instr. math. Marian Cath. H.S., Chicago Heights, Ill., 1965—75, 1990—2002; ret., 2003; instr. math., chair math. dept. Marian Cath. H.S., Chicago Heights, Ill., 1975—83, asst. prin., 1987—90, tutor math., 2003—. Mem. curriculum com., adv. bd., registrar Marian Cath. H.S., Chicago Heights, 1987-90, faculty coun., 1994-2001, math tutor, 2002-. Recipient Disting. Life Svc. award, Marian Cath. H.S. Alumni Assn., 2002; grantee, U. Ill., 1990, Ohio State U., 1992, Ill. State U., 1992, 1995. Mem. Nat. Coun. Tchrs. Math., Ill. Coun. Tchrs. Math., Math. Tchrs. Assn. Chgo. (Master Tchr. 1994, pres. 1996-98). Roman Catholic. Avocations: gardening, music, reading. Home and Office: 700 Ashland Ave Chicago Heights IL 60411-2073 E-mail: srblaise@marianchs.com.

GALLOWAY, PATRICIA DENESE, civil engineer; b. Lexington, Ky., June 14, 1957; d. Howard John and Maudine Lou (Jones) Frisby; m. Kris Richard Nielsen, Mar. 16, 1987. BS in Civil Engring., Purdue U., 1978; MBA, N.Y. Inst. Tech., 1984; postgrad., Kochi U. Tech., Japan, 2003—. Registered profl. engr. Ky., N.Y., N.J., Ariz., Wis., Wyo., Fla., Wash., Colo., Pa., Man., Can., Australia. Project engr., insp. CH2M Hill, Milw., 1978-79, master program scheduler, 1979-81; sr. cons. Nielsen-Wurster Group, N.Y.C., 1981-83, sr. engr., 1983-84, v.p., 1984-85, prin., exec. v.p., 1985-99, pres., 1999-2000, CEO, pres., 2001—04, CEO, 2004—. Lectr. Columbia U., U. Wis.-Madison; vis. prof. Kochi U. Tech.; presenter to numerous orgns; ptnr. Unionville Vineyards, Ringoes, N.J.; pres. Unionville Aviation; gen. ptnr. Unionville Ranch, L.L.C., Wash.; chief exec. Nielson-Wurster Asia Pacific, Melbourne, Australia, 2001—; bd. dirs. Civil Engring. Rsch. Found., mem. adv. bd., mem. exec. com., 2001—. Contbr. articles to profl. jours. Named one of Top 10 Women in Constrn., Engring. New Record, 1986, one of Top 10 Women, Glamour Mag., 1987, 88, White House fellow regional finalist, 1990, Ky. Col., Gov. Patten, Sts. of Ky., 2002; named to Lafayette H.S. Hall of Fame, 2001; recipient Nat. Leadership Coun. Capital award, 1990, Engr. of Yr. award Mercer County Profl. Engrs., 1990, Nat. Leadership award Profl. Women in Constrn., 1995, Fed. Infrature Design award Whitehouse Commn., 1999, Upward Mobility award Soc. Women Engrs., 2003, Tribute to Women in Industry award, YWCA, 2004; named Disting. Engring. Alumnus, Purdue U., 1992, Celebration of Women, NAE, 2000. Fellow ASCE (instr. constrn. claims course, bd. chair task com. on women in civil engring. 1998—2000, internat. dir., bd. dirs. 1992-95, chmn. membership com. 2001—, pres.-elect 2003—, pres., bd. dirs. 2004 (1st woman); mem. NSF (dir. engring. 2004-), YWCA (Tribute to Women award), Am. Assn. Engring Socs., Nat. Soc. Professional Engrs., Am. Arbitration Assn., Professional Women in Construction, The Acad. Experts, UK, The Inst. Engrs., Australian Fellow, Soc. Women Engrs. (pres. Wis. chpt. 1980, pres. N.Y. chpt. 1982, Disting. New Engr. 1980, Mobility award 2003-), Project Mgmt. Inst. (dir. pub. bd.), Am. Assn. Cost Engrs., Am. Nuclear Soc., Garden State Wine Growers Assn. (pres. 1990-92), Somerset County C. of C. (most outstanding woman in bus. and industry 1987), Purdue Engring. Alumni Assn. (bd. dirs., 1975-2001), Toastmasters, Sigma Kappa (fin. com. 1993-97), Tau Beta Pi. Republican. Methodist. Avocations: scuba diving, cross country skiing, hiking, horseback riding, wine making. Office: Nielsen-Wurster Group 719 Second Ave Ste 700 Cle Elum WA 98922 Fax: 609-497-3412. Office Phone: 206-386-5250. E-mail: patnwg@aol.com.

GALLOWAY, ROBERT EDWARD, retired municipal official; s. Carl Henry and Marie Victorine Galloway; m. Sharon Leigh Brauns, Nov. 6, 1989; children from previous marriage: Angela, Gregory 1 stepchild from previous marriage, Stan Bouslog. BS, Western Ill. Tchrs. Coll., 1951; MS, Western Ill. U., 1965. Jr. h.s. tchr.; h.s. tchr.; part-time jr. coll. tchr.; juvenile ct. officer Lee County, Iowa, 1965—96; part-time tchr. Culver-Stockton Coll., 1991—. Bd. dirs. Learning Disability Assn., Iowa. Pres. Keokuk (Iowa) Libr. Bd., Keokuk Art Ctr.; mem. city coun. City of Keokuk, 1985—89; bd. dirs. Van Buren County Hist. Soc., 2005—. Served with USN, 1945—46, served with USN, 1951—53. Recipient Tchr. of Yr. award, Stockton Coll. Student Govt., 2004, Iowa Helping Hand award, Learning Disability Assn., 2004. Mem.: Phi Delta Kappa. Avocations: fishing, gardening, travel, reading, golf. Home: 16677 Hwy 1 Keosauqua IA 52565 Office: Culver-Stockton Coll One College Hill Canton MO 63435 Office Phone: 217-288-6513 ext. 6513. Office Fax: 217-288-6617. Business E-Mail: rgalloway@culver.edu.

GALLOWAY, THOMAS D., dean; B.A., Westmont Coll., Santa Barbara, 1962; M.U.P., U. of Washington, 1969, PhD, 1972. Research assoc., Center for Research U. of Kansas, 1972, assist. prof., Sch. of Architecture & Urban Design, 1971—74, assoc. dir. & sr. research assoc., Inst. for Soc. & Environ. Studies, 1973—75, assoc. prof., Sch. of Architecture & Urban Design, 1975—80, dir. grad. prog. in urban planning, 1974—80, assoc. dean, Sch. of Architecture & Urban Design, 1979—80; dir. & prof. Grad. Sch. of Community Planning & Urban Affairs, U. of Rhode Island, 1980—85; dir. Design Research Inst., Iowa State U., 1985—92; dean & prof. College of Design, Iowa State U., 1985—92; dean coll. architecture Ga. Inst. Tech., Atlanta, 1992—. Office: Ga Inst Technology Coll Arch 247 4th St Atlanta GA 30332-0001

GALLOWAY, WILLIAM JEFFERSON, retired foreign service officer; b. Throckmorton, Tex., Oct. 21, 1922; s. James Thomas and Ottis Virgil (Marrs) G.; m. Elizabeth Alice Cox, June 3, 1950; children— Jeff, Mary Elizabeth. BS, Tex. A&M U., 1943. Fgn. affairs officer Dept. State, 1948-50; spl. asst. to U.S. ambassador to NATO, London, Paris, 1950-53; spl. asst. to counselor Dept. State, 1953-56, 1st sec. Vienna, 1956-59, spl. asst. to dir. gen. fgn. service Washington, 1959-64; assigned Nat. War Coll., 1964-65; 1st sec., counselor polit. affairs Am. embassy, London, Eng., 1965-74; exec. asst. to under sec. state Dept. State, Washington, 1974-80, cons., 1980—. Served to capt. AUS, 1943-48. Home: The Jefferson 900 N Taylor St Apt 723 Arlington VA 22203 Personal E-mail: wmjgallo@earthlink.net.

GALLOWAY, WILLIAM RODNEY, military officer; b. Warner Robins, Ga., June 21, 1966; Student leadership training, 1988—89; student, Airman Leadership Sch., 1992. Cert. clin. radiol. tech. Am. Registry Clin. Radiol. Tech., radiologic tech. Am. Registry Radiologic Tech. Sgt. USAF, 1988—96; US Mil. Hist. First 5X; leadership instr., 1992—96; unit historian 116th Tac Hosp., 1991—94, non-commn. officer in charge radiol. dept., 1992—94; rschr. Relevant Time Rsch. Industries. Recipient Longevity Svc. award, Outstanding Unit award, Physicians Recognition award, AMA. Mem.: Am. Legion, Am. Soc. Registered Technologists, Nat. Mil. Family Assn., Air Force Assn. Republican. Christian. Business E-Mail: williamrgalloway.research@langley-va.us.

GALLOWAY-EDGAR, BARBARA RUTH, pastor; b. San Antonio, Tex., Nov. 30, 1956; d. Bruce Carlson Galloway and Helen Christine Ziegler; m. James L. Galloway-Edgar, May 27, 1978; children: Mitchell, Meghan. BA, Southwestern U., 1978; MTh, So. Meth. U., 1983. Assoc. pastor 1st United Meth. Ch., New Braunfels, Tex., 1983-86, pastor Ganado, Tex., 1986-89, Pearsall, Tex., 1989-93, Jefferson United Meth. Ch., San Antonio, 1993-96; dist. supt. San Angelo (Tex.) Dist., United Meth. Ch., 1996—2002. Del. Gen./Jurisdictional Conf., 1999-04; bd. ordained ministry S.W. Tex. Ann. Conf., San Antonio, 1999—. Elder United Meth. Ch., ministerial alliance, 1996—; trustee Southwestern U., Georgetown, Tex., 1997—. Mem. PEO Internat. (scholar 1998), Delta Zeta. Avocations: reading, writing, listening. Office: 205 James St Boerne TX 78006-2303

GALLUP, DAVID CRAIG, artist; b. St. Louis, July 12, 1967; s. Roger Smith and Dorothy Rae Gallup; m. Rosalind Alexis Bray, Sept. 23, 1995. BFA, Parsons Sch. Design, L.A., 1990. Chief studio asst. to Hiro Yamagata Club Pensee, Malibu, Calif., 1994—99. One-man shows include 52 California Sunsets- The Waning of the 20th Century, Malibu Magic, exhibited in group shows at Calif. Art Club 91st Gold Medal Juried Exhbn., Pasadena Hist. Mus., 2001, 92d Gold Medal Show, Pasadena Hist. Mus., 2002, 93d Gold Medal Juried Exhbn., Pasadena Mus. of Calif. Art, 2003, Mus. Cultural Art, 2002, 2003. Mem.: Landscape United Nature Artists (pres. 2002—), Calif. Art Club (bd. dirs. 2003—, v.p. 2003—), Conejo Valley Painters Assn. (pres., founder 1999—). Achievements include invention of luminous color wheel.

GALLUP, JOHN GARDINER, retired paper company executive; b. Bridgeport, Conn., Oct. 31, 1927; s. Prentiss Brownell and Evelyn (Crocker) G.; m. Paula Burgee, June 10, 1951; children: Susan, Paula, Bruce. AB, Dartmouth Coll., 1949; William Pynchon hon. degree in Humanics, Springfield Coll., 1998. Dept. mgr. J.B. White Co., Greenville, S.C., 1951, Castner Knott Dept. Store, Nashville, 1951-52; asst. store mgr. A.T. Gallup, Inc., Holyoke, Mass., 1952-55; with Strathmore Paper Co., Westfield, Mass., 1955-92, prodn. mgr., 1968-70, pres., div. mgr., 1970-92. Dir. Bank of New Eng.-West, Springfield, Mass.; chmn. Mass. Ventures, Inc. Mem. George Bush Campaign Com., 1979; chmn. Baystate Med. Center, Springfield, 1979-82; chmn. Baystate Health Systems, Inc., 1982-83; bd. dirs. Jr. Achievement Western Mass., 1979; trustee Springfield Coll., 1979-91; chmn. Valley 2,000; trustee Community Found. W. Mass., Beveridge Found; commr. Mass. Commn. Jud. Conduct; trustee St. Andrew's Ch. Longmeadow, Econ. Devel. Coun. West Mass.; dir. Willie Ross Sch. for Deaf. Served with USMC, 1945-47. Mem. Boston Paper Trade Assn. (pres. 1979), Am. Paper Inst. (exec. com. cover and text paper group 1979-91), Greater Springfield C. of C. (vice chmn. 1985-88, chmn. 1988-91, vol. econ. devel.), Visiting Nurses Assn. (bd. dirs.), Corp. fur Bus., Work and Learning (bd. dirs.), Cmty. Svc. Learning (bd. dirs.), World Affairs Coun. (bd. dirs.), Springfield Orch. Assn. (pres.), Associated Industries Mass. (hon. dir.), Century Club. Clubs: Longmeadow (Mass.) Country, Colony (Springfield). Episcopalian. Home and Office: 64 Cambridge Cir Longmeadow MA 01106-2828

GALLUP, PATRICIA, computer company executive; Grad., U. Conn., 1979. Chmn. PC Connection, Inc., Milford, Mass., 1982—, CEO, 2002—, pres., 2003—. Named Entrepreneur of Yr., Ernst & Young, 1998, 2003, N.H. High Tech. Coun., 2003; named one of Top 50 Women Bus. Owners in U.S., Working Woman, 2000—03. Office: PC Connection Inc Rt 101A 730 Milford Rd Merrimack NH 03054-4631

GALLUZZO, JAY A., lawyer; b. 1974; BA magna cum laude, U. Pa., 1996; JD, Columbia U., 1999. Bar: NY 2000. Law clk. to Hon. Charles L. Brieant So. Dist. NY, 1997—99; assoc. Skadden, Arps, Slate, Meagher & Flom, LLP, 2000—03; sr. v.p., gen. counsel, sec. Warnaco Group, Inc., NYC, 2003—. Office: Warnaco Group Inc 501 Seventh Ave New York NY 10018 Office Phone: 212-287-8282. Office Fax: 212-287-8275. Business E-Mail: jgalluzzo@warnaco.com.

GALOS, ERNEST PETER GABRIEL, lawyer; b. South Bend, Ind., Sept. 5, 1964; BA in History, U. Notre Dame, 1986; JD, Ind. U., 1989. Bar: Ill. 1989, Ind. 1991. Asst. state's atty. Vermilion County State's Atty., Danville, Ill., 1990-91; assoc. Noell & Assocs. Law Office, South Bend, Ind., 1991-96; pvt. practice South Bend, 1996—; dep. pub. defender, 1998—. Bd. dirs. Legal Svcs. Program of Northern Ind., South Bend. Mem. Saint Joseph County Bar Assn., Ind. State Bar Assn. Avocation: running. Office: 618 E Colfax Ave South Bend IN 46617-2827

GALOWICH, RONALD HOWARD, real estate investment executive, venture capitalist; b. Peoria, Ill., Feb. 18, 1936; s. Louis J. and Leah (Kahn) G.; m. Eleanor Bernstein, June 16, 1957 (div. Aug., 1977); children: Jeffrey, Robert, Pamela; m. Susan E. Loggans, Sept. 11, 1977 (div. Apr. 1988); m. Linda L. Kroupa, Oct. 18, 2000. BS in Commerce and Law, U. Ill., 1957, JD, 1959. Bar: Ill. 1959, U.S. Supreme Ct. 1963. Pres. Twin Oaks-Burr Oaks Realty, Joliet, Ill., 1961-81; ptnr. Galowich & Galowich, Joliet, Ill., 1960-81; dir. real estate ops. Pritzker & Pritzker, Chgo., 1981-90; chmn. Madison Realty Group, Inc., Chgo., 1985—, Madison Group Holdings, Inc., Chgo., 1990—; founder, chmn. Initiate Sys., Inc. (formerly Madison Info. Technologies, Inc.), Chgo., 1994—. Co-founder, dir. First Health Group Corp. (formerly Health Care Compare Corp.), Downers Grove, Ill., 1982—2005; commr. Ill. Supreme Ct., 1968-70. Chmn. devel. com. Joliet Greater YMCA, 2002—; bd. visitors U. Ill. Coll. Law, 1996—, pres., 1998—2000; mem. leadership com. Cancer Inst., Rush-Presbyn. St. Lukes Med. Ctr., Chgo., 1993—; bd. dirs. Athletes Against Drugs, 1992—. Fellow Am. Judicature Soc., Ill. Bar Found.; mem. ABA, Ill. Bar Assn., Urban Land Inst., Chgo. Bar Assn. Jewish. Avocation: pilot. Home: 1248 N Astor St Chicago IL 60610-2308 Office: Madison Group Holdings Inc 200 W Madison St Ste 2300 Chicago IL 60606-3463 E-mail: rhgalo@ix.netcom.com, rgalowich@initiatesystems.com.

GALPERIN, BORIS, mathematician, physicist, oceanographer, educator; b. Kiev, Ukraine, Nov. 25, 1952; came to U.S., 1983. s. Avraham and Haya (Goldgor) G.; m. Shlomit Sat, July 31, 1980; children: Michael, Daphne Aviyah. BA, Latvian State U., Riga, Latvia, 1975; PhD, Technion, Haifa, Israel, 1982. Engr., mathematician Mechanization and Automation Office, Kiev, 1975-76, Riga, 1976-77; teaching asst. Technion, Haifa, 1977-82; rsch. assoc. Technion-Israel Inst. Tech., Haifa, 1982-83; vis. rsch. staff mem. Princeton (N.J.) U., 1983-85, mem. rsch. staff, 1985-89; assoc. prof. U. South Fla., St. Petersburg, 1989—. Cons. to various industries. Contbr. articles to profl. jours. and books. NSF grantee, 1987, 90, Office Naval Rsch. grantee, 1990, 92, Army Rsch. Office grantee, 1990, Fla. Sea grantee NOAA, 1991, USGS grantee, 1992, 93, 94. Mem. AIAA (assoc.), Am Geophys. Union, The Oceanography Soc., Am. Phys. Soc. Office: U of South Fla Marine Sci 140 7th Ave S Saint Petersburg FL 33701-5016

GALPERIN, MICHAEL Y., microbiologist; s. Yuri I. Galperin and Natalia Galperina; m. Olga Galperina, Oct. 21, 1989; children: Natalia Nikitina, Maria. PhD, Moscow State U., 1987. Staff scientist NCBI, NLM, NIH, Bethesda, Md., 1996—. Author: (textbook) Sequence-Evolution-Function. Computational Approaches in Comparative Genomics. Office: NCBI NLM Nat Insts of Health 8600 Rockville Pike Bethesda MD 20894 Business E-Mail: galperin@ncbi.nlm.nih.gov.

GALSTON, ARTHUR WILLIAM, biology professor; b. N.Y.C., Apr. 21, 1920; s. Hyman and Freda (Zaks) G.; m. Dale Judith Kuntz, June 27, 1941; children: William Arthur, Beth Dale. BS, Cornell U., 1940; MS, U. Ill., 1942, PhD, 1943. Rsch. plant physiologist emergency rubber project Calif. Inst. Tech., 1943-44, sr. rsch. fellow, 1947-50, assoc. prof. biology, 1951-55; instr. Yale U., 1946-47, prof. plant physiology, 1955-65, prof. biology, 1965-72, Eaton prof. botany, 1973-90, emeritus prof., 1990, dir. div. biol. scis., 1966-66, sr. rsch. biologist, 1990—, chmn. dept. botany, 1961-62, chmn. dept. biology, 1985-88, lectr. in polit. sci., 2003—. Cons. ctrl. rsch. dept. E.I. duPont de Nemours & Co., 1956-78, Plant Resources Venture Funds, 1983-89, NASA, 1988-94; mem. divsn. biology and agr. NRC, 1963-66, 85-88, mem. com. on space biology and medicine, 1983-86; Einstein prof. Faculty Agr. Hebrew U., Jerusalem, 1980; vis. scientist Plant Breeding Inst., Cambridge, Eng., 1983; vis. fellow Wolfson Coll., Cambridge U., 1983; vis. scholar Riken Inst., Japan, 1988-89. Author: Life of the Green Plant, 1961; author: (with Peter J. Davies and Ruth L. Satter) 3d edit., 1980; Principles of Plant Physiology, 1952; author (with Peter J. Davies): Control Mechanisms in Plant Development, 1970; author: Daily Life in People's China, 1973, Green Wisdom, 1981, Life Processes in Plants, 1994; editor: New Dimensions in Bioethics, 2001, Expanding Horizons in Bioethics, 2005; mem. editl. adv. bd. World Book Science Year, 1976—78, Pesticide Physiology and Biochemistry, 1978—88, Plant Growth Regulation, 1983—93, Chem. Engring. News, 1977—78, Environment, 1979—83; contbr. sci. articles. Served as ensign USNR, 1944-46; mil. govt. Okinawa. Guggenheim fellow Stockholm, Paris, Sheffield, Eng., 1950-51; Fulbright fellow Canberra, Australia, 1960-61; Sci. Faculty fellow NSF, London, 1967-68. Fellow AAAS (chmn. com. on meetings 1956-59, life mem.); mem. Am. Soc. Plant Physiologists (sec. 1955-57, v.p. 1957-58, pres. 1963-64), Internat. Assn. Plant Physiology (sec.-treas. 1961-67), Bot. Soc. Am. (editl. bd. 1959-61, 72-76, pres. 1967-68), Fedn. Am. Scientists (coun. 1973-76), Am. Soc. Biochemists, Molecular Biol., Am. Soc. Photobiology, Am. Inst. Biol. Scis., Am. Acad. Arts & Scis. Office: Molecular Cellular & Devel Dept Biology Yale U New Haven CT 06520-8103 Home: 200 Leeder Hill Dr Apt 410 Hamden CT 06517-2749 Office Phone: 203-432-3509. Business E-Mail: arthur.galston@yale.edu.

GALSTON, WILLIAM ARTHUR, political scientist, educator; b. Bklyn., Jan. 17, 1946; s. Arthur William and Dale Judith (Kuntz) G.; m. Miriam, Sept. 15, 1968; 1 child, Ezra Moses. BA, Cornell U., 1967; MA, U. Chgo., 1969, PhD, 1973. Asst. prof. dept. govt. U. Tex., Austin, 1973-80, assoc. prof. dept. govt., 1980-82; issues dir. Mondale Pres. Campaign, Washington, 1982-84; dir. econ. and social programs Roosevelt Ctr. Am. Policy Studies, Washington, 1985-88; prof. sch. pub. affairs U. Md., College Park, 1988—, Saul I. Stern Prof. Civic Engagement, dir. Inst. Philosophy and Pub. Policy, interim dean, Md. Sch. Pub. Policy; dep. asst. to pres. domestic policy The White House, Washington, 1993—95. Vis. fellow Instn. Social and Policy Studies, Yale U., 1980-81; cons. Temple for Gov. Campaign, 1982; mem. adv. bd. Ford/Aspen-Wye Rural Econ. Policy Project, 1989-92; mem. selection com. rural policy fellowships Woodrow Wilson Nat. Fellowship Found., 1989-91; cons. and spkr. in field. Author: Kant and the Problem of History, 1975, Justice and the Human Good, 1980, A Tough Row to Hoe: The 1985 Farm Bill and Beyond, 1985, Liberal Purposes, 1991 (Spitz prize 1993), Rural Development in the United States, 1995, Liberal Pluralism, 2002, The Practice of Liberal Pluralism, 2004; editor Virtue, 1992, Philosophical Dimensions of Public Policy, 2002; mem. editl. bd. Ethics, 1991—, Nomos, 1991—, Prospectives on Politics, 2002-; contbr. numerous articles to profl. jours. Advisor Gore for Pres. Campaign, Washington, 1988, 2000; chief speechwriter John Anderson Nat. Unity Campaign, Washington, 1980; mem. working group on bicentennial bill of rights Wilson Ctr., 1990-91. Sgt. USMC, 1969-70. Fellow Danforth Found., 1967-68, NEH, 1980-81, Woodrow Wilson Ctr., 1991-92. Mem. Am. Polit. Scis. Assn. (program chmn. normative polit. theory sect. 1992), Conf. Study Polit. Thought, Am. Soc. Polit. and Legal Philosophy (program chmn. ann. mtng. 1989), Phi Beta Kappa. Democrat. Jewish. Home: 5616 Durbin Rd Bethesda MD 20814-1014 Office: Van Munching Hall U Md College Park MD 20742-1821 E-mail: bgalston@umd.edu.

GALTON, STEPHEN HAROLD, lawyer; b. Tulare, Calif., Dec. 23, 1937; s. Harold Parker and Marie Rose (Tuck) Galton; m. Grace Marilyn Shaw, Aug. 15, 1964; children: Mark(dec.), Bradley, Jeremy, Elisabeth. BS, U. So. Calif., 1966, JD, 1969. Bar: Calif. 1970, U.S. Ct. Appeals (9th cir.) 1973, U.S. Dist. Ct. (no. dist.) Calif. 1973, U.S. Dist. Ct. (cen. dist.) Calif. 1970, U.S. Dist. Ct. (ea. and so. dists.) Calif. 1973. Assoc. Martin & Flandrick, San Marino, Calif., 1970-71, ptnr., 1971-72; assoc. Booth, Mitchell, Strange & Smith, L.A., 1973-77, ptnr., 1978-85; sr. ptnr. Galton & Helm, L.A., 1986—. Contbr. articles to profl. jours. Named Super Lawyer, LA Mag., 2005. Mem. ABA (litigation, tort, ins. sects.), Am. Bd. Trial Advs., Calif. State Bar Assn. (del. 1974-81, chair fed. cts. com.), Wilshire Bar Assn. (pres. 1986-87), Los Angeles County Bar Assn. (trustee 1987-89). Episcopalian. Office: Galton & Helm 500 S Grand Ave Ste 1200 Los Angeles CA 90071-2624 Office Phone: 213-629-8800. E-mail: sgalton@galtonhelm.com.

GALVAN, MAX, humanities educator; b. Wanta, Aycucho, Peru, Apr. 13, 1939; arrived in U.S., 1961; s. Guillermo and Benedicta (Gonzalez) Galvan; m. Monika Heimerl, Aug. 11, 1964; children: Irmgard, Elba, Rafael, Rodrigo, Maxine. PhD, Hofstra Univ., Hempstead, NY, 1985; EdD, Rutgers Univ., New Brunswick, NJ, 1984; MS, CW Post Coll. LIU, New York, NY, 1979; MA, CUNY, New York, NY, 1974. Cert. PD LIU, 1979. Tchr. PS 128, X9, Bronx, NY, 1978—80; rsch. asst. prof. Rutgers Univ., New Brunswick, NJ, 1980—83; multicultural dir. Hempstead Pub. Sch., Hempstead, NY, 1984—94; prof. Five Towns Coll., Dix Hills, NY, 1999—. Asst. prof. C.W. Post Coll., Greenvale, NY, 1975—79, NYU, 1981—83, Hofstra U., Hempstead, NY, 1984—88. SP4 U.S. Army, 1962—65. Fellow Goethe Fellowship, CUNY/ Kiel, Germany, 1979. Avocations: writing, painting, music, reading, skiing. Home: 1582 Briard St Wantagh NY 11793 Personal E-mail: mgalvan@optonline.net.

GALVANI, PAUL B., lawyer; b. Nov. 28, 1938; s. John J. and Helen (Bransfield) G.; m. Sheila Dacey, June 24, 1967; children: Jill G. Finnerty, Susan D. BA, Williams Coll., 1960; JD, Harvard U., 1964. Bar: Mass. 1964, N.Y. 1965, U.S. Tax Ct. 1965, U.S. Dist. Ct. (so. and ea. dists.) N.Y. 1966, U.S. Dist. Ct. Mass. 1970, U.S. Dist. Ct. Nebr. 1978, U.S. Dist. Ct. Calif. (no. dist.) 1992, U.S. Ct. Appeals (2d cir.) 1966, U.S. Ct. Appeals (1st cir.) 1970, U.S. Ct. Appeals (9th cir.) 1993, U.S. Supreme Ct. 1981. Law clk. U.S. Dist. Ct. (so. dist.) N.Y., N.Y.C., 1964-66, asst. U.S. atty., 1966-70; assoc. Ropes & Gray, Boston, 1970-75, ptnr., 1975—. Fellow: Am. Coll. Trial Lawyers; mem.: Boston Bar Assn., Am. Law Inst. Office: Ropes & Gray One International Pl Boston MA 02110-2624

GALVIN, CHARLES O'NEILL, law educator; b. Wilmington, NC, Sept. 29, 1919; s. George Patrick and Marie (O'Neill) G.; m. Margaret Edna Gillespie, June 29, 1946; children: Katherine Marie, George Patrick, Paul Edward, Charles O'Neill, Elizabeth Genevieve. BSc, So. Meth. U., 1940; MBA, Northwestern U., 1941, JD, 1947; SJD, Harvard U., 1961; LLD, Capital U., 1990, So. Meth. U., 2005. Bar: Ill. 1947, Tex. 1948, U.S. Dist. Ct. (no. dist.) Tex. 1948, U.S. Tax Ct. 1949; CPA, Tex. Pvt. practice, Dallas, 1947-52; from asst. to assoc. prof. So. Meth. U., Dallas, 1952-55, prof., 1955-82, dean Sch. Law, 1963-78; Centennial prof. law Vanderbilt U., Nashville, 1983-90, Centennial prof. emeritus, 1990—, exec. in residence, 1990-93; of counsel Haynes and Boone, LLP, Dallas, 1994—. Thayer tchg. fellow Harvard U., 1956-57; vis. prof. U. Mich., 1957, Duke U., 1979, Pepperdine U., 1980; Raymond Rice Disting. vis. prof. U. Kans., 1990; adj. prof. law U. Tex., 1995-97; Disting. prof. law emeritus So. Meth. U., 1996—; trustee Am. Tax Policy Inst., 1992-97. Author: Estate Planning Manual, 1987; tax editor Oil and Gas Reporter; co-editor: Texas Will Manual, 1972—. Chmn. Dallas County Cmty. Action, Dallas 1970-72; pres. Cath. Found., Dallas, 1963-67. Served to lt. comdr. USNR, 1942-46. Recipient Disting. Alumnus award So. Meth. U., 1984, Alumnus Merit award Northwestern U., Chgo., 1993, John Rogers award Southwestern Legal Found., Dallas, 1997, McGill award Cath. Found., 1997. Fellow Am. Bar. Found., Tex. Bar Found. (Outstanding Fifty Yr. Lawyer award 2004), Dallas Bar Found.; mem. AICPA, ABA, Tex. Bar Assn., Dallas Bar Assn., Am. Law Inst. (life), Am. Judicature Soc., Tex. Soc. CPA's, Order of Coif, Am. Tax Policy Inst., U.S. Supreme Ct. Soc. (trustee), Tex. Supreme Ct. Soc. (trustee), Phi Delta Theta, Beta Gamma Sigma. Roman Catholic. Home: 4240 Twin Post Rd Dallas TX 75244-6741 Office: Haynes and Boone LLP 3000 Bank of Am Plz 901 Main St Dallas TX 75202-3789 Personal E-mail: cogalvin@swbell.net.

GALVIN, CHRISTINE M., lawyer; b. Rochester, N.Y., Apr. 17, 1954; d. Willard Harold and Shirley (Oster) G.; m. Raphael E. Rettig, Aug. 14, 1982. BS cum laude, U. N.H., 1976; JD, Albany Law Sch., Albany, 1982. Bar: N.Y. 1983, U.S. Dist. Ct. (no. dist.) N.Y. 1983. Assoc. Kouray & Kouray, Schenectady, N.Y., 1982-88; pvt. practice Schenectady, 1988-89; assoc. Gordon, Siegel, Mastro, Mullaney, Gordon & Galvin, PC, Schenectady, 1989-91, ptnr., 1991—. Com. on character and fitness of Appellate Divsn. of State of N.Y., 3d Jud. Dept., 2000—. Chmn. planning bd. Town of Wright, N.Y., 1990-94, mem. master plan com., 1991-98, zoning bd. appeals, 1997-2002; bd. dirs. Hispanic Outreach Svcs., 1998—; bd. trustees Albany Inst. History and Art, 2002—. Mem. N.Y. State Bar Assn., N.Y. State Trial Lawyers Assn., Capital Dist. Trial Lawyers Assn. (bd. dirs. 1998-2000), Schenectady County Bar Assn. (bd. dirs. 1993-96), Capital Dist. Women's Bar Assn. (bd. dirs. 1994-98). Office: Gordon Siegel Mastro Mullaney Gordon & Galvin PC 9 Cornell Rd Airport Pk Latham NY 12110-1481 E-mail: cgalvin@gordonsiegel.com.

GALVIN, CHRISTOPHER BRIAN, former electronics company executive; b. Chgo., Mar. 21, 1950; s. Robert Galvin; m. Cynthia Galvin; 2 children. BA in polit. sci., Northwestern U., 1973, MBA, 1977. With Motorola, Inc., 1973—2003; v.p. mktg. sales and services Tegal Corp., 1983—84, v.p. and gen. mgr. US ops., 1984—85; v.p. and dir. Comm. Sector Paging Divsn. Motorola, Inc., Boynton Beach, Fla., 1985—88, sr. v.p. Schaumberg, Ill., 1988—89, chief corp. staff officer, 1988—90, bd. dirs., 1988—2003, exec. v.p., 1989—90, sr. exec. v.p., asst. COO, 1990—93, pres., COO, 1993—97, CEO, 1997—2003, chmn., 1999—2003. Bd. dirs. US China Bus. Coun., chmn., 2003—04; mem. Hong Kong Chief Exec's Coun. Internat. Advisors. Bd. counselors Bechtel Corp.; trustee Northwestern U., Am. Enterprise Inst.; adv. bd. mem. Nat. Underground R.R. Freedom Ctr., Am. Soc. Engring Edn. Mem.: Am. Soc. Corp. Execs., Bus. Roundtable.

GALVIN, JOHN ROGERS, retired army officer, law educator; b. Wakefield, Mass., May 13, 1929; s. John James and Mary Josephine (Rogers) G.; m. Virginia Lee Brennan, June 5, 1961; children: Mary Jo, Elizabeth Ann, Kathleen Mary, Erin Elizabeth. BS, U.S. Mil. Acad., 1954; MA, Columbia U., 1962; postgrad., U. Pa., 1964-65; grad., Command and Gen. Staff Coll., 1966. Commd. 2d lt. U.S. Army, 1954, advanced through grades to gen.; mil. asst. to Supreme Allied Comdr. Europe, 1974-75; comdr. DISCOM, chief of staff 3d Infantry div., Germany, 1975-78; asst. div. comdr. 8th Infantry div., 1978-80; comdg. gen. 24th Infantry div., Ft. Stewart, Ga., 1981-83, also post comdr.; comdg. gen. VII U.S. Corps, Stuttgart, Fed. Republic Germany, 1983-85; comdr. in chief U.S. So. Command, Quarry Heights, Panama, 1985-87; supreme allied comdr. Europe, comdr.-in-chief U.S. European Command, 1987-92; ret., 1992; Olin disting. prof. nat. security studies U.S. Mil. Acad., West Point, N.Y., 1992-93; disting. vis. policy analyst The Mershon Ctr., Ohio State U., 1994-95; dean Fletcher Sch. Law and Diplomacy, Tufts U., Boston, 1995-2000; dean emeritus, 2000—. Author: The Minute Men, 1967, Air Assault, 1969, Three Men of Boston, 1976. Former bd. dirs. Wesleyan Coll. Fletcher Sch. of Law and Diplomacy fellow, 1972-73; decorated Silver Star, Legion of Merit, DFC, Bronze Star. Mem. Ctr. for Creative Leadership (past bd. govs.), Seligman (bd. dirs.), Am. Coun. on Germany (chmn. emeritus bd. dirs.), Inst. for Def. Analyses (trustee, 1995-2002). Roman Catholic. Home: 2714 Lake Jodeco Cir Jonesboro GA 30236-5329

GALVIN, KATHLEEN MALONE, communications educator; b. N.Y.C., Feb. 9, 1943; d. James Robert and Helen M. (Sullivan) G.; m. Charles A. Wilkinson, June 19,1973; children: Matthew, Katherine, Kara. BS, Fordham U., 1964; MA, Northwestern U., 1965, 80, PhD, 1968. Tchr. Evanston (Ill.) Township High Sch., 1967-72; asst. prof. Northwestern U., Evanston, 1968-73, assoc. prof., 1973-78, prof., 1978—, assoc. dean, 1988-2001. Presenter workshops in field. Author: Listening by Doing, 1986, multiple handbook chpts. family communication; sr. author: Family Communication, 6th edit., 2004; co-author: Person to Person, 5th edit., 1996, Basics of Speech, 4th edit., 2004; co-editor: Making Connections, 3d edit., 2002, Communication Works!, 2000; contbr. articles to profl. jours.; developer, instr. 26-video series on Family Communication (PBS Adult Satellite Sys.). Office: Northwestern U Comm Studies Dept 2240 N Campus Dr Evanston IL 60208-3545 Business E-Mail: k-galvin@northwestern.edu.

GALVIN, KERRY A., lawyer; b. Greenville, SC, Jan. 27, 1961; BS in fgn. svc. cum laude, Georgetown U., 1983; JD cum laude, U. Mich., 1986. Bar: Tex. 1986. Assoc. Mayor Day & Caldwell, Houston; joined legal dept. as fin. counsel Lyondell Chem. Co., Houston, 1990, named assoc. gen. counsel, sec., 1998, assoc. gen. counsel internat. legal affairs Maidenhead, England, v.p., gen. counsel, sec. Houston, 2000—02, sr. v.p., gen. counsel, sec., 2002—. Office: Lyondell Chem Co 1221 McKinney St Ste 700 Houston TX 77010

GALVIN, MATTHEW REPPERT, psychiatry educator; b. Seattle, July 24, 1950; s. Ralph B. and Virginia (Reppert) G.; children: Joseph, Sarah, Erin; m. Margaret Gaffney. AB with honors, Ind. U., 1975, MD, 1979. Diplomate Am. Bd. Adolescent Psychiatry, Am. Bd. Psychiatry and Neurology. Asst. prof. Ind. U. Med. Ctr., Indpls., 1984-95, clin. assoc. prof., 1995—. Staff psychiatrist Larue Carter Meml. Hosp., Indpls., 1984-88, assoc. dir. youth svcs., 1988, acting dir., 1988-90; child psychiatrist Riley Child Psychiatry Svcs., Indpls., 1990-98, Pleasant Run Children's Home, 1998-2001, St. Vincent Stress Ctr., 2001—, Children's Bureau Inc., 2001—, Ind. Sch. for the Blind, 2003—; vol. faculty Riley Child Psychiatry and Ind. U. Med. Ethics Program. Author: Ignatius Finds Help, A Story about Psychotherapy, 1988, Otto Learns About Medicine, 1988, 3d edit., 2001, A Story About Grown-ups Helping Children, 1988, Clouds and Clocks, A Story for Children Who Soil, 1989; co-author: Sometimes Y, A Story for Families with Gender Identity Issues, 1993, The Conscience Celebration, 1998, Right vs. Wrong: Raising a Child with a Conscience, 2000, Rachel and the Seven Bridges of Coscience-Berg, 2002; editorial staff Conscience Works; contbr. articles to profl. jours. With M.C., U.S. Army, 1970-73, Vietnam. Fellow Am. Psychiat. Assn.; mem. Am. Acad. Child Adolescent Psychiatry, Am. Soc. Adolescent Psychiatry, Nat. Alliance Against Mental Illness (affiliate), Ind. Coun. Child and Adolescent Psychiatry (treas. Indpls. chpt. 1986-89, pres. elect 1989-90, pres. 1990-91).

GALVIN, MICHAEL FRANCIS, state agency administrator, arborist; b. Lynn, Mass., Nov. 15, 1960; s. Neil Downing Galvin and Barbara Jean Lee; m. Christy Lynn Reddecliff, Aug. 10, 2002; m. Wendy Allyn Tucker, July 14, 1984 (div. June 30, 1998); children: Dylan Michael, Sean Quincy. Student, Ea. Nazarene Coll., Mass., 1978—80. Roadside Tree Care Expert State of Md., 1992, cert. Arborist Internat. Soc. of Arboriculture, 1994, Pesticide Applicator State of Md., 1994. Author: (jour. paper) Jour. of Arboriculture. Bd. mem. Mid-Atlantic Chpt., Internat. Soc. of Arboriculture, Haymarket, Va., 1999—2003, pres., 2002—03; bd. mem. U. Md. Urban Forestry Adv. Bd., Coll. Park, 2000—03, Mid-Atlantic Ctr. for Excellence in Urban Cmty. Forestry, Keystone Coll., La Plume, Pa., 2001—03. Recipient President's Citation, Mid-Atlantic Chpt., Internat. Soc. of Arboriculture, 2001. Mem.: Md. Electric Reliability Tree Trimming Coun., Am. Stds. Com. A300 (assoc.; usda-fs alt. 2000—03), Internat. Soc. of Arboriculture (Mid Atlantic chpt.) (assoc.; certification liaison 1999—2003). Achievements include development of Strategic urban forests assessment protocol; uses high resolution (= 1 m) satellite imagery, interpreted using color and texture, to determine spatial distribution of trees in urban areas; Particpatedin devel. of USDA-Forest svcs. urban forest health monitoring street tree assessment protocol. Avocation: music. Home: 1771 S Ritchie Hwy Annapolis MD 21401 Office: Maryland Dept of Natural Resouces 580 Taylor Ave Annapolis MD 21401 Office Phone: 410-260-8531. Office Fax: 410-260-8595. E-mail: mgalvin@dnr.state.md.us.

GALVIN, MICHAEL JOHN, JR., lawyer; b. Winona, Minn., July 8, 1930; s. Michael John Sr. and Margaret Elizabeth (O'Donohue) G.; m. Frances Dennis Culligan, Sept. 7, 1957; children: Sean, Kevin, Kathleen, Nora, Mary, Margaret, Patricia. BA, U. St. Thomas, 1952; LLB, U. Minn., 1957. Bar: Minn. 1957, U.S. Dist. Ct. Minn. 1957, U.S. Supreme Ct. 1961. With sales and svc. Badger Machine Co., Winona, 1950-56; mgr. Oaks Hotel Inc., Winona, 1950-56; ptnr. Briggs & Morgan, P.A., St. Paul, 1957—. Pres. St. Paul Winter Carnival Assn., 1970; sec. St. Paul Area C. of C., 1968-71; trustee U. St. Thomas, 1978-85, Coll. St. Catherine, St. Paul, 1999—; nat. chmn. U. Minn. Law Sch. Ptnrs. in Excellence Program, 2000-01; chmn. Indianhead Coun. Boy Scouts Am., 2003—. Lt. USAF, 1952-54, USAFR, 1954-60. Named Oustanding Young Man, City St. Paul, 1964, Boss of Yr., St. Paul Jaycees, 1990; recipient Disting. Alumnus award, U. St. Thomas, 1983, Great Living St. Paulite award, St. Paul Area C. of C., 2000, Eugene and Mary Fry Cmty. award, Cretin-Derham Hall Schs., 2000, Disting. Alumnus award, U. Minn. Law Sch., 2001, Monsignor James Lavin award, U. St. Thomas, 2003. Mem. ABA (labor and employment law sect.), Minn. Bar Assn. (treas. 1991-93, pres.-elect 1993, pres. 1994-95, chair labor and employment law sect. 1984), Ramsey County Bar Assn. (exec. coun. 1965-68, 83-86, pres. 1984-85), Minn. Vol. Attys. Corp. (pres. 1993-94), Univ. Club (pres. 1962), Minn. Club (pres. 1971), St. Paul Athletic Club (pres. 1986), St. Paul Area C. of C. (bd. dirs. 1995—, chmn. 1997-98). Republican. Roman Catholic. Office: Briggs & Morgan 2200 1st Nat Bank Bldg Saint Paul MN 55101 Office Phone: 651-808-6553. Business E-Mail: mgalvin@briggs.com.

GALVIN, WILLIAM FRANCIS, state official; b. Brighton, Mass., Sept. 17, 1950; m. Eileen Galvin. Degree cum laude, Boston Coll., 1972; JD, Suffolk U., 1975. Bar: Mass., Fed. Aide Gov.'s Coun., 1972; state rep. Mass. Gen. Ct., 1975-91; vice-chmn. Congl. Redistricting Com., 1981-83; chmn. Govt. Regulations Com., 1983-91; sec. of state Commonwealth of Mass., Boston, 1995—. Democrat. Office: State House, Room 337 Boston MA 02133-1000 E-mail: cis@sec.state.ma.us.

GALWAY, SIR JAMES, flutist; b. Belfast, Northern Ireland, Dec. 8, 1939; s. James Galway and Ethel Stewart (Clarke) G.; m. 1965 (div.), 1 child; m. Anna Christine Renggli, 1972 (div.), 3 children; m. Jeanne Cinnante, 1984. Student, Royal Coll. Music, Guildhall Sch. Music, London, Conservatoire National Superieur de Musique, Paris; MA (hon.), Open U., Eng., 1979; MusD (hon.), Queen's U., Belfast, 1979, New Eng. Conservatory Music, 1980. Prin. guest conductor London Mozart Players. Flutist, Wind Band of Royal Shakespeare Theatre, Sadler's Wells Orch., 1960-65, Royal Opera House Orch., BBC Symphony Orch.; prin. flutist London Symphony Orch., 1966, Royal Philharm. Orch., 1967-69; prin. solo flutist Berlin Philharm. Orch., 1969-75; internat. solo performer and condr., 1975-; U.S. debut, 1978; U.S. performances with Nat. Symphony Orch., NY Philharmonic, Houston Symphony Orch., San Diego Symphony, Cinn. Pops Orch. Boston Symphany Orch., 2004-2005; recordings include works of C.P.E. Bach, J.S. Bach, Beethoven, Corigliano, Danzi, Dvorak, Feld, Franck, Mozart, Quantz, Prokofiev, Nielsen, Reinecke, Rodrigo, Stamitz, Telemann, Vivaldi, Khachaturian; recordings include Annie's Song, The Classical James Galway, The Concerto Collection, Dances for the Flute, The Enchanted Forest: Melodies from Japan, Galway at the Movies, Greatest Hits Vol 1, Vol. 2, Vol. 3, James Galway and the Chieftains In Ireland, Galway at 50: A Portrait of James Galway, Winter's Crossing, 1998, James Galway Plays Lowell Liebermann, 1998, 60 Years, 60 Flute Masterpieces, Vols. 1-4, 1999, A Song of Home: An American Musical Journey, 2002, A Windham Hill Wedding Album, 2003, Andrea Immer Presents: Chardonnay, Shellfish, & Schubert, 2003, Best Classics 100, 2004, Quiet on the Set: James Galway at the Movies, 2004, numerous others; author: James Galway: An Autobiography, 1978, Flute, 1982, James Galway's Music in Time, 1983, Masterclass, 1987, others; several TV appearances including The Tonight Show, Good Morning America, CBS This Morning, Live with Regis and Kathie Lee, Sesame Street, Live from Lincoln Center. Pres. Flutewise (vol. nonprofit ogrn.). Decorated officer Order Brit. Empire, 1977; recipient Grand Prix du Disque, 1976, Order of the British Empire award, 1979; Record of Yr. awards Cash Box and Billboard mags., Pres. Merit award Recording Acad., 2004; named Musician of Yr., Musical Am., 1997; knighted 2001. Fellow Royal Coll. Music, Birmingham Schs. Music. Avocations: swimming, walking, films, theater, computers. Address: IMG Artists Lovell House 616 Chiswick High Rd London W4 5RX England*

GALWAY, RICHARD E., JR., state supreme court justice; b. Manchester, NH, 1944; m. Anita Galway; 2 children. BA, U. N.H., 1966; Fulbright scholar, U. Leeds, England, 1966—67; JD, Boston U. Law Sch., 1970. Bar: N.H. 1970. Atty. worker's compensation law Devine, Millimet & Branch, Manchester, NH, 1970—95; judge NH Superior Ct., 1995—2004; justice NH Supreme Ct., 2004—. Author: Worker's Compensation Law in New Hampshire, 1990, New Hampshire Worker's Compensation Manual, 2nd Edition, 1993. Mem.: ABA, Nashua Bar Assn., N.H. Bar Assn. (pres. 1981—82). Office: NH Supreme Ct 2 Noble Dr Concord NH 03301

GALYEAN, RICHARD DAVID, music educator, director; b. Galax, Va., Dec. 16, 1956; s. David Edgar and Vera Imogene Galyean; m. Cathy L. Lowe, July 1, 1978; children: Kristen Anne, Matthew Todd. BA, Radford U., 1981; MS in Music Edn., Radford (Va.) U., 2002. Dir. band Pennington (Va.) H.S. Band, 1982—83, Galax (Va.) H.S. Band, 1983—2001; instr. music U. Va., Wise, Va., 2002—, dir. band, 2002—. Reinactment of civil war in Geettysburg Pa. Mem.: Music Educators Nat. Conf. (assoc.). Independent. Methodist. Avocations: golf, walking. Home: 202 Holly St Galax VA 24333 Office: UVA-Wise Bands One College Ave Wise VA 24293 Personal E-mail: rdg3y@uvawise.edu.

GALYON, JAMES WILLIAM, minister; b. Urbana, Ill., Apr. 25, 1967; s. William and Dedra Galyon; m. Sharon Lynn Young, Dec. 14, 1991; children: Jenna, Jameson, Jonathan. AA, Mo. Bapt. Coll., 1988, BA, 1990; MA, Tyndale Theol. Sem., 1993; MDiv in Bibl. Langs., Southwestern Bapt. Theol. Sem., 1998; cert. in ordination, 1999; student, Billy Graham Sch. Evangelism, 2002; PhD, Southwestern Bapt. Theol. Sem., 2005. Pastor Sand Flat Bapt. Ch., Cleburne, Tex., 1999—2002, New Prospect Bapt. Ch., Nemo; pres. Gt. Awakening Ministries, Ft. Worth, 2002—; sr. pastor First Bapt. Ch., Frederick, Okla., 2004—. Contbr. article to profl. jour. Pres. Mo. Bapt. Coll. Bapt. Student Union, St. Louis, 1987—90, Southwestern Theol. Fellowship, Ft. Worth, 1997—98, 1999—2000. Mem.: North Am. Patristic Soc., Evang. Missionary Soc., Evang. Theol. Soc., Lions Club. Baptist. Avocations: golf, darts. Office Phone: 800-687-7724.

GAMARNIK, MOISEY YANKELEVICH, solid state physicist; b. Khmelnizky, Ukraine, USSR, Nov. 3, 1936; s. Yankel Khaymovich and Polya Iserovna (Gendelman) G.; m. Yevgeniya Adolfovna Lubomirskaya, Nov. 3, 1965; children: Yan, Alexander. Candidate of Scis. Phys.-Math., U. Kharkov, USSR, 1984, DSc Phys.-Math., 1992. Tchr. Pilyava (USSR) secondary sch., 1959-60, Kiev (USSR) Secondary Sch. N96, 1960-62; rschr., engr. Inst. Geol. Scis. Acad. Sci., Kiev, 1962-69, sr. rschr. Inst. Geochemistry and Physics Minerals, 1969-85, scientist, 1985-89, sr. scientist, 1989-93; crystallophysicist Instrumentation Tech. Assocs., Exton, Pa., 1994-98; assoc. prof. dept. materials engring. Drexel U., Phila., 1995-2001; x-ray crystallographer DuPont Pharms. Exptl. Sta., Wilmington, Del., 1999-2000; crystallophysicist Nanoscale Phases Rsch., Bensalem, Pa., 2000—. Contbr. articles to Phys. State Sollids. Grantee Internat. Sci. Found., 1995, NSF, 1997. Mem. Internat. Union Crystallography. Achievements include research in problem of structure and properties of small crystal particles and nanophase substances and research in problem of crystallization and structure of proteins. Home: 632 Longfellow Ct Warminster PA 18974-2065 E-mail: mgamarnik@comcast.net.

GAMBARDELLA, MARY JO, secondary school educator, music educator; b. N.Y.C., May 3, 1958; d. James Edward and Josephine Frances O'Toole; m. Thomas R. Gambardella, Oct. 31, 1981; children: Michael, Matthew, Regina, Mark. BA in Eng., Iona Coll., 1980; MA in Religious Studies, Providence Coll., 2003. Tchr. St. Raymond Acad., Bronx, NY, 1980—81, St. Francis Sch., Warwick, RI, 1995—98; tchr., music dir. Bishop Hendricken H.S., Warwick, 1998—. Mem. St. Benedict's, Warwick; music dir. St. Benedict's Children's Choir, Warwick. Mem.: Nat. Assn. Music Edn., R.I. Music Educators Assn., Nat. Cath. Educators Assn., Nat. Pastoral Musicians. Roman Catholic. Avocations: reading, music, theater. Home: 76 Mill Cove Rd Warwick RI 02889 Office: Bishop Hendricken HS 2615 Warwick Ave Warwick RI 02889 Office Phone: 401-739-3450.

GAMBARDELLA, THOMAS M., lawyer; b. Jamaica, NY, Mar. 28, 1954; BA magna cum laude, St. John's U., 1976, JD, 1979. Bar: NY 1980, US Dist. Ct. Ea., So., & No. Districts NY, US Ct. Appeals 2nd Cir. Ptnr. Wilson, Elser, Moskowtiz, Edelman & Dicker LLP, White Plains, NY, co-chmn. firm profl. liability practice team. Mem.: ABA, NY State Bar Assn. Office: Wilson Elser Moskowitz Edelman & Dicker LLP 3 Gannett Dr White Plains NY 10604 Office Phone: 914-323-7000 ext. 4523. Office Fax: 914-323-7001. Business E-Mail: gambardellat@wemed.com.

GAMBARI, IBRAHIM AGBOOLA, diplomat, international organization official; b. Ilorin, Kwara State, Nigeria, Nov. 24, 1944; m. Fatima Oniyangi, 1969; 2 children. Attended, Kings Coll., Lagos, Nigeria; BSc in Polit. sci. with a specialty in Internat. Rels., London Sch. of Econ.; MA in Polit. sci./Internat. Rels., Columbia U., 1970, PhD in Polit. sci./Internat. Rels., 1974; LHD (hon.), U. of Bridgeport (Conn.), 2000. Lectr. CUNY, NY, 1969-74; asst. prof. SUNY, Albany, 1974-77; sr. lectr. Ahmadu Bello U., Zaria, Nigeria, 1977-80, assoc. prof., 1980-83, prof., 1983-89; chmn. dept. polit. sci. U. in Zaria, 1982—83; dir.-gen. Nigerian Inst. Internat. Affairs, 1983-84; min. for fgn. affairs Govt. of Nigeria, 1984-85; resident scholar Rockefeller Found. Bellagio (Italy) Study and Conf. Ctr., Bellagio, 1989; amb., permanent rep. of Nigeria UN, NYC, 1990—99, pres., security coun., 1994, 1995, under-sec. gen., special advisor on Africa, 1999—2002, spl. rep of sec.-gen. for Angola, 2002. Vis. prof. Johns Hopkins U. Sch. Advanced Internat. Studies, Howard U., Washington, Georgetown U., Washington; rsch. fellow Brookings Inst., Washington, 1986—89; hon. prof. Chugsan U., Guangzhou, China, 1985; guest scholar Wilson Ctr. Internat. Scholars

Smithsonian Inst., Washington; chair Nat. Seminar Commemorate 25th Anniversary OAS, Lagos, Nigeria, 1988, UN Spl. Com. Against Apartheid, UN Spl. Com. on Peacekeeping Ops., 1990—99; led several UN missions, including the Spl. Com. against Apartheid mission to South Africa, Security Coun. missions to South Africa, Burundi, Rwanda and Mozambique; trustee UN Inst. Tng. and Rsch., 1993—99; pres. exec. bd. UNICEF, 1999; founder Savannah Centre for Diplomacy, Democracy and Development, Abuja, Nigeria. Author: (book) Party Politics and Foreign Policy in Nigeria During the First Republic, 1981, Theory and Reality in Foreign Policy Decision Making: Nigeria After the Second Republic, 1989, Political and Comparative Dimensions of Regional Integration: The Case of ECOWAS, 1991. Named to Society of Scholars, John's Hopkins U., 2002.

GAMBEE, ROBERT RANKIN, investment banker; b. N.Y.C., Aug. 26, 1942; s. Sumner and Eleanor Elizabeth (Brown) G.; m. Elizabeth Gregory Heard, 1991; children: Robert Gregory, Claire Elizabeth Fay. Grad., Phillips Exeter Acad.; AB, Princeton U., 1964; MBA, Harvard U., 1966. Assoc. corp. fin. White, Weld & Co., N.Y.C., 1966-71, v.p., 1971-73, Schroder Capital Corp. affiliate J Henry Schoder Wagg-London, N.Y.C., 1973-78, Atlantic Capital Corp. affiliate Deutsche Bank AG, Frankfurt, Germany, 1978-84; 1st v.p. Deutsche Bank Securities Inc., 1985-91, dir., 1992—. Prin. N.Y. Stock Exch., 1971—, Nat. Assn. Securities Dealers, 1971—; v.p. Apollo, Atlas, Hercules, Hermes, Mercury, Olympus, Orion, Pegasus, Taurus, Titan and Zeus Instl. Investments, Inc., 1984-92; COO, sec. Germany Fund, Inc., 1986—, The New Germany Fund, Inc., 1990—, The Future Germany Fund, Inc, 1990-95, The Ctrl. European Equity Fund, Inc., 1995—; v.p., sec. Deutsche Funds Inc., 1997-2000, Deutsche Bank Investment Mgmt. Inc., 1995—; dir. Deutsche Bank AG and Bankers Trust Co., 1999—, Deutsche Bank Securities, Inc., 2002—. Author, photographer: Nantucket Island, 1973, rev. edit., 1974, 81, paper edit., 1978, 87, 89, color edits., 1986, 88, 98, Manhattan Seascape: Waterside Views Around New York, 1975, Exeter Impressions (intro. by Nathaniel Benchley), 1980, Princeton in Color (intro by Robert F. Goheen), 1987, paperback edit., 1988, 2d rev. edit., 1993, 98, A Wall Street Christmas, 1989, rev. edit., 1990, Nantucket in Color, 1992, 94, 96, paperback edit., 1996, Wall Street-Financial Capital, 1999, Nantucket Impressions, 2001. Trustee Dwight-Englewood Sch., 1978-85, Elizabeth Morrow Sch., 1990—, Rye (N.Y.) Art Ctr., 1993—, Rye Presbyn. Ch., 1998-2001. Mem. Soc. Colonial Wars, Princeton Alumni Assn. Nantucket (v.p., sec.), Princeton Club N.Y. (gov.), Nantucket Yacht Club, Univ. Club. Republican. Presbyterian. Home: Wendover Rd Rye NY 10580

GAMBERINO, WILLIAM, psychiatrist; B.S., Pa. State U., 1989; M.D., Ph.D., Pa. State U., Hershey, 1996. Cert. psychiatrist Am. Bd. Psychiatry and Neurology. Resident dept. psychiatry U. Fla., Gainesville, 1996—2000; pvt. practice Ocala, Fla., 2000—. Braddock scholar, Pa. State U., 1985—89. Mem.: Fla. Psychiat. Soc. (sec./treas. local chpt. 2004—05), Phi Beta Kappa, Alpha Omega Alpha.

GAMBET, DANIEL G(EORGE), academic administrator, minister; b. June 9, 1929; Student, DeSales Hall Sch. Theology, 1953-57; AB in Latin and Greek, Niagara U., 1954; MA in Latin and Greek, Cath. U. Am., 1957; PhD in Classical Studies, U. Pa., 1963, postgrad. in higher edn. adminstrn, 1964; LHD (hon.), Lehigh U., 1986; HHD (hon.), Moravian Coll., 1988; DD (hon.), Lafayette Coll., 1994, Muhlenberg Coll., 1999. Ordained priest Roman Catholic Ch. (Order of Oblates of St. Francis de Sales), 1957; tchr. Latin Father Judge High Sch., Phila., 1957-58; dean of men. instr. Latin, French and German Salesianum Sch., Wilmington, Del., 1958-61; instr. history Oblate Coll., Childs, Md., 1962-64, St. Mary's Coll., Wilmington, 1962-64; acad. dean, instr. Latin and history Allentown Coll. of St. Francis de Sales, 1965-70, v.p., acad. dean, instr. Latin, 1970-72, v.p., 1972-78, pres., 1978—99, pres. emeritus, 1999—. Provincial Eastern Province Oblates of St. Francis de Sales, 1972-78; mem. Allentown Diocesan Bd. Edn., 1978-81, chmn., 1968-70, 79-81; pres. bd. trustees DeSales Hall Sch. Theology, 1972-77; pres. bd. dirs. Salesianum Sch., 1972-77; chmn. vis. com. dept. classica Lehigh U., 1977-85; mem. instl. survey com. Commn. for Ind. Colls. and Univs. in Pa., 1977-81, chmn. instl. survey com., 1980-81, exec. com., 1980-89; exec. com. Found. Ind. Colls., 1984—; chmn. vis. com. for religious studies Lehigh U., 1985-94; bd. dirs. Pa. Power and Light Co. Trustee Allentown Coll. of St. Francis de Sales, 1972-99; bd. dirs. Better Bus. Bur. of Ea. Pa., 1978, United Way of Lehigh County, 1979-88, Health East Inc., 1987-91, Moravian Acad., 1991-98, Ben Franklin Mfrs. Resource Ctr., 1994-97, Lehigh Valley Cmty. Fedn., 1996—; exec. com. Minsi Trails coun. Boy Scouts Am., 1980; trustee Valley Youth House, 1991-97; vice-chmn. bd. dirs. Lehigh Valley Hosp. Ctr., 1983-88. Mem. Pa. Assn. Colls. and Univs. (bd. dirs. 1994-99), Lehigh Valley Assn. Ind. Colls. (bd. dirs. 1978-99, chmn. 1980-81), Ctr. for Agile Pa. Edn. (chair bd. dirs. 1996-99), Assn. Governing Bds. Univs. and Colls., Allentown-Lehigh County C. of C. Home and Office: DeSales U Office of the Pres Emeritus 2755 Station Ave Center Valley PA 18034-9568 Office Phone: 610-282-4135. Business E-Mail: daniel.gambet@desales.edu.

GAMBETTI, PERLUIGI, pathologist; Grad., Liceo Classico Imola, Bologna, 1952; MD magna cum laude in Humanities, U. Bologna, Italy, 1959. Resident in neurology Neurol. Hosp. of U. Bologna Sch. Medicine, 1961—63; fellow in neuropathology Institut Bunge, Antwerp, Belgium, U. Rome, Italy, U. Pa., Phila., asst. prof. dept. pathology, 1969—72, assoc. prof. depts. pathology and neurology, 1972—77; prof. and dir. divsn. neuropathology Case Western Res. U. Sch. Medicine and Univ. Hosps. of Cleve., 1977—. Contbr. articles to profl. jours. Office: Case Western Reserve Univ Inst Pathology 2085 Adelbert Rd Cleveland OH 44106

GAMBILL, JAN-MICHAEL CHARLES, professional tennis player; b. Spokane, Wash., June 3, 1977; s. Chuck and Diane Gambill. Professional tennis player, 1996—; team player Davis Cup, 1997. Model Ford Modeling Agy. Named One of 50 Most Beautiful People in World, People Mag., 2000.

GAMBILL-SMITH, BOBBI JO, art educator, art business owner; MA in Art Edn., Ohio U., 1979. Cert. tchr. Ohio Dept. Edn. Secondary art educator Logan (Ohio)-Hocking Sch. Dist., 1980—; art educator Lancaster (Ohio) City Schs., 2000—. Exhibited in group shows at Columbus Art League Juried Exhbn., 1990. Named to Talented and Gifted Hall of Fame, Ohio U., 1999; Martha Holden Jennings scholar, 1995. Fellow: Ohio Art Edn. Assn. (pres. 1999—2001, past pres. 1999—, Disting. Fellow 2000, Ohio Art Educator of Yr. 2000, Disting. fellow 2000, Secondary Art Educator of Yr.); mem.: Nat. Art Edn. Assn. (nat. conv. program coord., naea 2005—, Presdl. Appointment 2006), Delta Kappa Gamma, Kappa Delta Pi, Phi Kappa Phi. Home: 621 Oak Hollow Way Lancaster OH 43130 Office: Lancaster City Schs/Thomas Ewing Jr 825 E Fair Ave Lancaster OH 43130 Personal E-mail: artisart@fairfieldi.com.

GAMBINO, RICHARD JOSEPH, materials engineer; b. N.Y.C., May 17, 1935; BA, U. Conn., 1957; MS, Polytech Inst. N.Y., 1976. Phys. sci. U.S. Army Signal Rsch. Lab., Ft. Monmouth, NJ, 1958—60; metallurgist Pratt & Whitney Aircraft divsn. United Aircraft Corp., 1960—61; rsch. staff mem. T.J. Watson Rsch. Ctr., IBM, Yorktown Heights, NY, 1961—93; prof., lab. dir. SUNY, Stony Brook, 1993—. Pres. MesoScribe Technologies, Inc., 2002—. Recipient Nat. Medal of Tech., 1995. Fellow: IEEE; mem.: IEEE Magnetic Soc., Nat. Acad. Engring., Materials Rsch. Soc., Am. Vacuum Soc. (thin film divsn. bd.), Tau Beta Pi, Sigma Xi. Home: 148 Sycamore Cir Stony Brook NY 11790-3161 Office: Dept Material Scis & Engng State U NY 107 Engineering Bldg Stony Brook NY 11794-2275 Office Phone: 631-632-9513. Business E-Mail: rgambino@ms.cc.sunysb.edu.

GAMBINO, S(ALVATORE) RAYMOND, lab administrator, educator; b. N.Y.C., Oct. 13, 1926; s. Salvatore Benedict and Rose (Ragona) G.; m. Madeline Russo, Apr. 5, 1953; children: Catherine Rose Garroni, Stephen Raymond. BS, Antioch Coll., 1948; MD, U. Rochester, 1952. Diplomate Am. Bd. Pathology. Labs. dir. Englewood (N.J.) Hosp., 1961-68; prof. pathology Columbia U., N.Y.C., 1968-82; dir. chemistry labs. Presbyn. Hosp., N.Y.C., 1968-77; labs. dir. St. Luke's-Roosevelt Hosp., 1978-82; chief med. officer, exec. v.p. MetPath, Inc., Teterboro, N.J., 1983-94, exec. v.p., chief med. officer emeritus, 1994—. Adj. prof. pathology Columbia U., N.Y.C., 1983—; mem. Corning (N.Y.) Mgmt. Group, 1984-94; bd. dirs. Ciba-Corning, 1988-94. Co-author: Beyond Normality, 1975; editor: (newsletter) Lab Report for Physicians, 1979-98. Mem. Englewood Cliffs (N.J.) Sch. Bd., 1966-69. Served with USN, 1945-46. Mem. Am. Soc. Clin. Pathologists (editor check sample program 1968-93), Alpha Omega Alpha. Roman Catholic. Avocations: walking, writing, travel. Office: Quest Diagnostics Inc 1300 E Newport Ctr Dr Deerfield Beach FL 33442 E-mail: doclab@aol.com.

GAMBITTA, RICHARD ANTHONY, political science professor; b. Oneida, N.Y., Aug. 28, 1946; s. Anthony Gamuel and Alice (Jones) G.; Sherry, Oct. 10, 1998; 1 child, Leon Antonio; stepson: Travis Michael Culpepper. BA, Syracuse U., 1970; MA, 1974, PhD, 1976. Assoc. prof. U. Tex., San Antonio, 1982—, discipline coord., grad. advisor of record, 1993-97, chair dept. polit. sci. and geography, 2001—, dir. Inst. Law and Pub. Affairs, 2001—. Pres. Gambitta Rsch. Assocs., San Antonio, 1986—; Fulbright sr. lectr. Chinese U. Hong Kong, 1984-85; cons. KPMG/Tex. Online, Austin, 2001-03; cons., report author Tex. Dept. Transp., San Antonio, 1986-88; cons., pollster numerous polit. candidates and media, Tex., 1986—. Contbr., editor articles to profl. jours. Recipient Frederick Douglass award U. Tex., 2004; Rsch. fellow NEH, Madison, Wis., 1979-80; Fulbright scholar, Hong Kong, 1983-85; Piper professorship Minni Stevens Piper Found., Tex., 1990. Mem. Am. Polit. Sci. Assn., ACLU, Internat. Assn. Philosophy of Law and Social Philosophy, San Antonio Dem. League. Democrat. Avocation: running. Home: 7605 Hummingbird Hill San Antonio TX 78255 Office: U Tex 6900 N Loop 1604 N San Antonio TX 78245 Office Fax: 210-458-5430. Business E-Mail: richard.gambitta@utsa.edu.

GAMBLE, DESIRATA, artist, poet; b. Wilkesboro, NC; d. Robert Lee and Mary Etta Gamble; m. David Bullins, Feb. 14; 1 child, Zoe Bullins. AA with honors, Surry C.C., Dobson, N.C., 1983; BA in Psychology, U. N.C., Wilmington, 1985, BA in Studio Arts, 2001; postgrad., U. Ga., 1985—87. Ordained to ministry Apostolic Ch. Proofreader Joan S. Northrop, Wilmington, 1984—85; artist U. N.C., Wilmington, NC, 1996—2002; artist transp. MerleFest, Wilkesboro, NC, 1994—2005; prof. arts in art Buxton U., England, 2003; with Apollo Apostilic Svcs., 2005—. One-woman shows include The Morning Dew, Winston-Salem, N.C., 1997—98, Claude Howell Gallery, Wilmington, 1998, 1999, The Deluxe, Wilmington, N.C., 1998—99, The Beanstalk, Boone, NC, 1999—2001, Daughtry's Old Books, Wilmington, NC, 2003, 2004, 2005, William Vance Nichols/Wilkes Art Gallery, Wilkesboro, NC, 2003; artist, poet: Sights of the Wind, Her White Hair Peeps and We Heard the Music for Miles, 1985 (Book award for poetry U. N.C. Wilmington); Represented in permanent collections Daniel Hall, Wilkes C.C., Wilkesboro, NC, River Valley Animal Foods, Harmony, NC; author: numerous poems. Named State-wide Hon. Mention for the Lyricist, A Violet Letter from Frannie, 2005. Mem.: AAUW, Smithsonian Inst., Acad. Am. Poets, Nature Conservancy, Southeastern Ctr. for Contemporary Art, Ala. State Poetry Soc. Office Phone: 336-921-2569. E-mail: gambled1@excite.com.

GAMBLE, E. JAMES, lawyer, accountant; b. Duluth, Minn., June 1, 1929; s. Edward James and Modesta Caroline (Reichert) G.; m. Lois Kennedy, Apr. 3, 1954; children: John M., Martha M., Paul F. AB, U. Mich., 1950, JD, 1953. Bar: Mich. 1953, D.C. 1980; CPA, Mich. Tax acct. Ernst & Ernst, Detroit, 1957-59; assoc. Dykema, Gossett, Spencer, Goodnow & Trigg, Detroit, 1959-67; ptnr. Dykema Gossett, Detroit, 1967-94, Gamble, Rosenberger & Joswick LLP, Bloomfield Hills, 1994—. Adj. prof. law Wayne State U., Detroit, 1964-79; adj. lectr. law U. Mich., Ann Arbor, 1979-81, 93; co-reporter, prin. draftsman Uniform Principal and Income Act (1997); mem. adv. com. Restatement of the Law, 3rd, Property, Wills and Other Donative Transfers, Restatement of the Law, 3rd, Trusts; counsel Mich. State Bd. Accountancy, Lansing, 1973-77. Author: (handbook) The Revised Uniform Principal and Income Act, 1966; contbr. articles to profl. jours. Trustee Rehab. Inst., Inc., Detroit, 1961-84, chmn. bd. trustees, 1974-77; bd. dirs., sec. Jr. Achievement Southeastern Mich., 1973-86; trustee Walsh Coll. Accountancy and Bus. Adminstrn., Troy, Mich., 1975-87, Alma (Mich.) Coll., 1981-91; mem. Fin. and Estate Planning Coun. Detroit, bd. dirs., 1969-76, pres., 1975. Lt. USN, 1953-57. Recipient Bronze Leadership award Jr. Achievement, Inc., 1985 Fellow Am. Coll. Tax Counsel, Am. Coll. Trust and Estate Counsel (bd. regents 1988—, chmn. estate and gift tax com. 1989-92, pres. 1998-99), Academician, Internat. Acad. Estate and Trust Law (exec. coun. 2001-04), Am. Bar Found. (life), Mich. State Bar Found.; mem. ABA (mem. spl. com. on profl. rels. with AICPA 1968-70), Mich. Bar Assn. (mem. various coms.), Detroit Bar Assn. (chmn. taxation com. 1968-74), Detroit Bar Assn. Found. (trustee, treas. 1973-79), Birmingham Athletic Club, Leland Country Club. Presbyterian.

GAMBLE, GEOFFREY, academic administrator; Degree in English, Fresno State Coll., 1965, M Linguistics, 1971; PhD Linguistics, U. Calif., Berkeley, 1975. Cert. specialist in Native Am. linguistics. Vice provost Washington State U.; provost, sr. v.p. U. Vt.; pres. Mont. State U.-Bozeman, 2000—. Office: Mont State U-Bozeman 211 Montana Hall Bozeman MT 59717-2420

GAMBLE, MICHAEL F., human resources generalist; BA in Mktg. and Comms., Bowling Green State U., Ohio, 1985. Cert. blackbelt Sigma Six, 2000, mediation 2000, profl. human resources Soc. Human Resource Mgmt. Ops. supr. and labor rels. specialist Ryder Distbn. Resources, Cleve., 1987—89; ter. mgr. employee rels. Norrell Svcs., Cleve., 1990—94; employee rels. mgr. Charter One Bank, 1995—97; human resources and union rels. mgr. Gen. Electric Quartz, Inc., Willoughby, 1997—2000; corp. human resources mgr. Werner Co., Greenville, Pa., 2000—01; human resources officer Nat. City Bank, Cleve., 1994—95, v. p. human resources, 2001—03; dir. human resources Revlon, Oxford, NC, 2004—. Bd. mem. Cuyahoga County Workforce Devel. Mem.: Soc. Human Resource Mgmt. Address: 8816 Cochran Ct Wake Forest NC 27587 Office Phone: 919-603-2592. Business E-Mail: michael.gamble@revlon.com.

GAMBLE, RAYMOND WESLEY, marriage and family therapist, clergyman; b. East Orange, N.J., Feb. 11, 1933; s. Kenneth Nelson and Lillian Clare (Apgar) G.; m. Margaret Gamble, Sept. 11, 1954 (div. 1964); children: Karen F., Roy B.; m. Penelope Louise Hansen, Nov. 19, 1979; 1 child, Wesley B. BA, Houghton (N.Y.) Coll., 1956; MDiv, Union Theol. Sem., Richmond, Va., 1960; postgrad., Yale U., 1967; D Ministry, Columbia Theol. Sem., Decatur, Ga., 1990. Ordained to ministry Presbyn. Ch., 1960. Student chaplain Va. State Penitentiary, 1958-60; asst. pastor Immanuel Presbyn. Ch., Lake Park, Fla., 1960-62; founder, pastor Westminster Presbyn. Ch., Palm Beach Gardens, Fla., 1962-67; exec. dir. Mental Health Assn. Palm Beach County, West Palm Beach, 1967-73; pvt. practice marriage and family therapy, West Palm Beach, Stuart, Fla., 1973—; founder, sr. pastor Palm City (Fla.) Presbyn. Ch., 1984—2003. Guest instr. Indian River Community Coll., 1978; cons., chaplain Lake Hosp., Lake Worth, Fla., 1973-75; chaplain Savannas Hosp., Port St. Lucie, Fla., 1986—2004; program dir., aftercare counselor narcotic addict rehab. program NIMH, West Palm Beach, 1969-73. Active numerous drug abuse rehab. programs, Palm Beach County; past mem. Com. for Mental Health Edn.; active Presbytery Tropical Fla., 1960—; past mem. ch.-coll. coun. Montreat Coll., 1988-96; past bd. dirs. Alcohol and Drug Abuse Coun. Palm Beach County, North County Drug Abuse Bd., Boca Raton (Fla.) Drug Abuse Found.; past pres. Drug Abuse Rehab. Team, Inc. Mem. Am. Assn. for Marriage and Family Therapy (clin.), Am. Assn. Christian Counselors. Avocations: sport fishing, horticulture. Home and Office: 288 NE Alice St # 101S Jensen Beach FL 34957-6006

GAMBLE, ROSANNE FULCOMER, computer scientist, educator; b. Easton, Pa., Nov. 8, 1963; d. William Earl F. and Rose Jenny (Petrei) Shankweiler; m. Michael Todd Gamble, Aug. 26, 1989. BS, Westminster Coll., 1986; MS, Washington U., 1988, DSc, 1992. Rsch. asst. dept. computer sci. Ctr. for Intelligent Computing Systems Washington U., St. Louis, 1986-92; asst. prof. computer scis. U. Tulsa, 1992—. Contbr. articles to profl. jours. Mem. Assn. for Computing Machinery, Am. Assn. for Artificial Intelligence, IEEE, IEEE Computer Soc., Sigma Xi. Avocations: golf, gardening. Office: U Tulsa 600 S College Ave Tulsa OK 74104-3126

GAMBLE, THEODORE ROBERT, JR., investment banker; b. St. Louis, Sept. 18, 1953; s. Theodore Robert and Rispah Adele (Dowse) Gamble; m. Susan Lee Stupin, Mar. 3, 1984. AB, Princeton U., 1975; MArch, Harvard U., 1977, MBA, 1979. Assoc. Morgan Stanley & Co., Inc., N.Y.C., 1979-84, v.p., 1984-86, prin., 1986-87; pres. Prescott Group Inc., N.Y.C., 1987—, mng. dir., 1999—, Transwestern Comml. Svcs., LLC, N.Y.C., 1999—2002. Mem. bus. com., mem. vis. com. Met. Mus. Art; bd. dirs., exec. v.p. Greater N.Y. coun. Boy Scouts Am.; bd. dirs. N.Y. Hist. Soc., Coll. Arms Found.; mem. vis. com. Mary Inst. St. Louis Country Day Sch.; mem. vestry St. Thomas Ch., N.Y.C.; co-chmn. adv. com. real estate devel., chmn. vis. com. Grad. Sch. Design Harvard U.; vice chancellor, bd. govs. Am. Soc. Order St. John of Jerusalem. Mem.: Young Mortgage Bankers Assn., Real Estate Bd. N.Y., Internat. Assn. Corp. Real Estate Execs., Assn. Fgn. Investors Real Estate, Nat. Assn. Real Estate Investment Trusts, Urban Land Inst. (mem. comml. and retail devel. coun., mem. internat. com.), Internat. Coun. Shopping Ctrs., The Pilgrims, Coral Beach and Tennis Club (Bermuda), City Club (Miami), Harvard Club (N.Y.C., Boston), Princeton Club (bd. govs., mem. exec. com., v.p. fin.), Doubles Club, Brook Club, Links Club, Knickerbocker Club, Univ Club, Racquet and Tennis Club, River Club. Republican. Episcopalian. Home: 860 UN Plaza New York NY 10017 Office: The Prescott Group Inc 666 Fifth Ave 26th Fl New York NY 10103 Personal E-mail: trgamblejr@msn.com. Business E-Mail: trgamblejr@prescott-group.com.

GAMBLE, THOMAS ELLSWORTH, academic administrator; b. Chgo., Nov. 14, 1941; s. Slade LeBlount and Anna Marie VanDuzer G.; m. Donna Kay Dersch, Nov. 3, 1973; children: Brendan, Shari, Oscar, Rebecca, Slade, Aubrey, David, Donna. BA in Biology, Northwestern U., 1964; MEd in Ednl. Psychology, U. Ill., 1970, PhD in Higher Ednl. Adminstrn., 1973. Asst. to dean student pers. U. Ill., Urbana-Champaign, 1968-71, asst. prof. edn., 1972, asst. dean Coll. Medicine, 1972—76, assoc. prof. Coll. Medicine Chgo., 1976—83; exec. asst. to chancellor U. Ill. Med. Ctr., Chgo., 1976-78, asst. chancellor, 1976—83; dean intercampus affairs Ill. Ea. C.C., Olney, 1983-84; dean of instrn. Wabash Valley Coll., Mt. Carmel, Ill., 1984—89, dean of coll., 1989-90; pres. Dodge City (Kans.) C.C., 1990-95, Joliet (Ill.) Jr. Coll., 1995-98, Brevard C.C., Cocoa, Fla., 1999—. Asst. prof. U. Ill. Coll. Edn., 1972-77; assoc. prof. U. Ill. Coll. Medicine, 1982-83; pres. Kans. Jayhawk C.C. Athletic Conf., 1993-94, Ill. N4C C.C. Athletic Conf., 1996-97. Contbr. articles to profl. jours. Bd. dirs. Kans. Newman Coll., Wichita, 1994-96, U.S. Naval Inst., 1968—, Jr. Achievement East Ctrl. Fla., Econ. Devel. Com. Fla. Space Coast, Brevard County Workforce Devel. Bd., Brevard C.C. Found.; chmn. Fla. Coun. Pres., 2003-04; mem. Am. Coun. on Edn., Commn. on Life Long Learning, 2002-05; mem. policy adv. bd. Fla. Solar Energy Ctr.; mem. First Bapt. Ch. Merritt Is., Fla. Capt. USNR, 1964-87, ret. Mem. VFW (life), Am. Assn. Cmty. Colls. (commn. on econ. and workforce devel. 2005—), Am. Coun. Edn., Fla. Assn. Colls. and Univs., Fla. Assn. C.C.'s, Fla. Space Rsch. Inst., Fla. Sterling Coun., Inc. (bd. dirs.), U. Ill. Coll. Edn. Alumni Assn. (life, sr. advisor, pres. 1988-90), Rotary, Beta Beta Beta, Chi Gamma Iota, Kappa Delta Pi, Phi Delta Kappa, Phi Kappa Phi. Avocations: non-fiction reading, children, classical music, naval science. Office: Brevard CC Office of Pres 1519 Clearlake Rd Cocoa FL 32922-6598 Office Phone: 321-433-7000. Business E-Mail: gamblet@brevardcc.edu.

GAMBLE, VANESSA N., historian; b. May 20, 1953; BA, Hampshire Coll., 1974; MD, U. Pa., 1983, PhD, 1987. Asst. prof. history of medicine, science and family medicine U. Wis., Madison, 1989-93, assoc. prof., 1994—; dir. Ctr. for the Study of Race and Ethnicity in Medicine U. Wis. Sch. of Medicine, Madison, 1996—. Office: Ctr for Study of Race/Ethnicity in Medicine U Wis 1300 University Ave Madison WI 53706-1510

GAMBLIN, WILLIAM BASIL, JR., editor; b. Madisonville, Ky., Mar. 22, 1969; s. William Basil Sr. and Anna Ruth (Ezell) Gamblin; m. Myra Elaine Howell, Oct. 6, 2001. AA, Madisonville (Ky.) C.C., 1990. News dir. WTTL-AM/WZEZ-FM, Madisonville, Ky., 1992—93, 1997—2003; instrnl. asst. Hopkins County Bd. Edn., Madisonville, Ky., 1994—98; asst. news editor Union County Adv., Morganfield, Ky., 1998—2000; sports editor Bowling Green (Ky.) Daily News, 2000; team mgr. Sykes Enterprises, Morganfield, Ky., 2000—02; paginator, reporter, photographer Navarre (Fla.), 2002—03; instrnl. devel. AST, Inc., Pensacola, 2003—; news dir. WTTL-AM/WZEZ-FM, 2003—04; sports editor Santa Rosa Press Gazette, 2005—. Syndicator of sports crosswords, Ky., 1993—94; contract photographer Associated Press, Fla., 2003—04. Author: (mag. feature) Touring News, 1998. Youth precinct chair Hopkins County Dems., Madisonville, Ky. Recipient Best Investigative Story, Ky. Press Assn., 2000, 3d Pl. Sports Columnist, 2001, 3d Pl. Spot News Picture, Fla. Press Assn., 2004, Honored for investigative reporting, paginating and spot news photography, 2004. Mem.: Wesley Meml. United Meth. Men's Club (sec. 2002—, 2004), Hon. Order of Ky. Cols., Wesley Meml. United Meth. Men's Club. Methodist. Avocations: writing, photography, music. Home: 4823 Tealwood Dr Pace FL 32571 Office: Advance Sys Tech Inc 6629 Elva St Milton FL 32570 Office Phone: 850-623-2120. E-mail: billgjr@bellsouth.net.

GAMBOA, GEORGE CHARLES, retired oral surgeon, educator; b. King City, Calif., Dec. 17, 1923; s. George Angel and Martha Ann (Baker) G.; m. Winona Mae Collins, July 16, 1946; children: Cheryl Jan Gamboa Granger, Jon Charles, Judith Merlene Gamboa Hiscox. Pre-dental cert., Pacific Union Coll., 1943; DDS, U. Pacific, 1946; MS, U. Minn., 1953; AB, U. So. Calif., 1958, EdD, 1976. Diplomate Am. Bd. Oral and Maxillofacial Surgery. Fellow oral surgery Mayo Found., 1950-53; clin. prof. grad. program oral and maxillofacial surgery U. So. Calif., L.A., 1954-99; assoc. prof. Loma Linda (Calif) U., 1958-99, chmn. dept. oral surgery, 1960-63; pvt. practice oral and maxillofacial surgery San Gabriel, Calif., 1955-93. Dir. So. Calif. Acad. Oral Pathology, 1995-2002. Mem., past chmn. first aid com. West San Gabriel chpt. ARC. Fellow Am. Coll. Dentists, Am. Coll. Oral and Maxillofacial Surgeons (founding fellow), Pierre Fauchard Acad., Am. Inst. Oral Biology, Internat. Coll. Dentists, So. Calif. Acad. Oral Pathology (pres. 2001); mem. Doctors' Mayo Soc., Calif. Assn. Oral and Maxillofacial Surgeons, Am. Assn. Oral and Maxillofacial Surgeons, Internat. Assn. Oral Surgeons, So. Calif. Soc. Oral and Maxillofacial Surgeons, Western Soc. Oral and Maxillofacial Surgeons, Am. Acad. Oral and Maxillofacial Radiology, Marsh Robinson Acad. Oral Surgeons, Profl. Staff Assn. L.A. County-U. So. Calif. Med. Ctr. (exec. com. 1976-99), Am. Cancer Soc. (Calif. div., profl. edn. subcom. 1977-90, pres. San Gabriel-Pomona Valley unit 1989-90), Am. Dental Assn. (sci. session chmn. sect. on anesthesiology, 1970), Calif. Dental Soc. Anesthesiology (pres. 1989-94), Calif. Dental Found. (pres. 1991-93), Calif. Dental Assn. (jud. coun. 1990-96), So. Calif. Acad. Oral Pathology (dir. 1995-2002, pres. 2000-01), San Gabriel Valley Dental Soc. (past pres.), Xi Psi Phi, Omicron Kappa Upsilon, Delta Epsilon. Seventh-Day Adventist. Home: 1102 Loganrita Ave Arcadia CA 91006-4535

GAMBOA, LUCITO G., pathologist; b. Pampanga, Philippines, Jan. 7, 1929; came to U.S., 1952; s. Serapion M. and Jacinta L. Gamboa; m. Sylvia V. Roque, Sept. 18, 1953; children: Richard, Virginia Majer, Debra Jorgensen. MD, U. Santo Tomas, Manila, 1952; MS, U. Colo., 1955. Diplomate Am. Bd. Pathology. Dir. pathology and clin. labs. Edgewater Hosp., Chgo., 1958-69, 80-90; dir. blood bank and sr. pathologist Little Co. of Mary Hosp., Evergreen Park, Ill., 1969-80; mem. staff Ctrl. Valley Gen. Hosp., Hanford, Calif., 1990—. Contbr. numerous articles to profl. jours. Bd. dirs. Chgo. Dist. Tennis Assn., 1973-76. Recipient Disting. Physician award Philippine Med. Soc. Chgo., 1966. Mem. Assn. Philippine Physicians in Am. (pres., founder 1972-74, Disting. Svc. award 1975), Assn. Philippine Pathologists in Am. (pres., founder 1970-72), Dove Canyon Country Club. Avocations: golf, tennis, photography, travel. Home: 18 Golf View Dr Dove Canyon CA 92679-3802 Office: Ctrl Valley Gen Hosp 1025 N Douty St Hanford CA 93230-3722 Office Phone: 949-888-8368. E-mail: lgamboamd@aol.com.

GAMBOA, NORMAN ARMANDO, conductor, educator; b. Cartago, Costa Rica, Oct. 21, 1972; arrived in U.S., 1996; s. Armando Gamboa and Aurelia Barquero. MusB, Baylor U., Waco, Tex., 2001; MusM, U. Nev. Las Vegas, 2003. Assoc. condr. Orquesta Filarmonica de Medellin, Medellin, Colombia, 2002—04; music dir. Waco Symphony Youth Orch., Waco, Tex., 2003—04; dir. orchestras Washburn U., Topeka, 2004—. Home: 2745 SW Villa W Dr # 707 Topeka KS 66614 Office: Washburn Univ 1700 SW College Ave Topeka KS 66621 Office Phone: 785-670-1887. E-mail: norman.gamboa@washburn.edu.

GAMBONE, VICTOR, JR., internist, geriatrician; b. Phila., Aug. 28, 1949; s. Victor Emmanuel and Eleanor Joyce (Porambo) G. BS, Pa. State U., 1971, MD, 1975. Diplomate Am. Bd. Quality Assurance and Utilization Rev. Physicians, Am. Bd. Internal and Geriatric Medicine; cert. med. dir. in long term care. Intern then resident in internal medicine U. S.Fla., Tampa, 1975-78, practice medicine internal medicine and geriatrics Dunedin, Fla., 1978—; med. dir. Evercare (United Health Group), Olosmar, Fla., 1996—; project coord. Fla. Med. Quality Assurance, Inc., Tampa, 2000—. Med. dir. Hospice Care, Inc., Pinellas County, 1982—86; chmn. dept. internal medicine Mease Health Care, Dunedin, Fla., 1989; med. dir. Stratford Ct. Health Ctr., Palm Harbor, Fla., 1991—, St. Mark Village, 1993—, Mease Continuing Care, Dunedin, Fla., 1993—, Spanish Gardens Nursing Ctr., Dunedin, Fla., 1994—98, East Bay Nursing Ctr., 1996—2005, Sylvan Health Ctr., 1996—2002, Manor Care Nursing Ctr., Dunedin, Fla., 1996—2001, Bayview Nursing Pavillion, Clearwater, 1996—99, Arbors of Safety Harbor, 1997—98, Mariner Health Belleair, 1997—98, Sabal Palms Health Care Ctr., Largo, Fla., 1997—99, Morton Plant Rehab. Ctr., 1998—2000, Largo Health Care Ctr., 1999—, Drew Village Rehab. and Nursing Ctr., Clearwater, Fla., 1998—99, Oak Manor Village, Largo, Fla., 1999, Encore Sr. Village, Clearwater, Fla., 1999—2004. Author: Post Operative Recall of Intra-Operative Events, 1975 (rsch. award U. Miami Med. Sch.). Fellow: ACP; mem.: AMA, Fla. Med. Assn., Fla. Geriatrics Soc., Fla. Med. Dirs. Assn. (pres. 2003—05), Am. Geriatrics Soc., Am. Med. Dirs. Assn. Office: Evercare 601 Brooker Creek Blvd Oldsmar FL 34677 Office Phone: 727-799-5041. E-mail: Victor.Gambone@verizon.net.

GAMBRELL, DAVID HENRY, lawyer; b. Atlanta, Dec. 20, 1929; s. E. Smythe and Kathleen (Hagood) G.; m. Luck Coleman Flanders, Oct. 16, 1953; children: Luck Coleman, David Henry, Alice Kathleen Hagood, Mary Latimer. BS, Davidson Coll., 1949; JD cum laude, Harvard U., 1952. Bar: Ga. 1951. Pvt. practice, Atlanta, 1952-54, 56—; teaching fellow Harvard Law Sch., 1954-55; partner firm Gambrell & Stolz, LLP, 1963—. U.S. senator from Ga. to succeed Richard B. Russell Coms. on Banking and Space, 1971-72. Bd. editors: Am. Bar Assn. Jour, 1969-70. Chmn. Ga. Gov.'s Com. on Postsecondary Edn., 1978-79; bd. dirs. Nat. Legal Aid and Defender Assn., 1965-69; chmn. Dem. Party of Ga., 1970-71; trustee Ga. Legal History Found., 1996—, Lawyers Found. of Ga., 1997-2003; bd. dirs. Buckhead Coalition, Inc., 2003—. Mem. ABA (ho. of dels. 1975), Atlanta Bar Assn. (pres. 1965-66), State Bar Ga. (pres. 1967-68, Disting. Svc. award 2002), Lawyers Club Atlanta, Ga. C. of C. (bd. dirs. 1989-92), N.C. Soc. Cin., Ga. Hist. Soc. (bd. curators 1999-2001), Met. Club (Washington), Piedmont Driving Club, Commerce Club, Capital City Club, Peachtree Golf Club, Sigma Alpha Epsilon, Omicron Delta Kappa. Democrat. Presbyterian. Home: 3205 Arden Rd NW Atlanta GA 30305-1918 Office: Gambrell & Stolz LLP 3414 Peachtree Rd NE #1600 Atlanta GA 30326-1164 Office Phone: 404-577-6000. E-mail: dgambrell@gambrell.com.

GAMBRELL, JAMES BRUTON, III, lawyer, educator; b. Rochester, Minn., Jan. 17, 1926; s. James Bruton Gambrell and Martha Judson Corley; m. Helen Jeanette Roddy, Aug. 12, 1950; children: Jamey, Gretchen, James Bruton IV. BS in Mech. Engring, U. Tex., 1949; MA in Econs, Columbia U., 1950; LL.B., N.Y. U., 1957. Bar: D.C. 1957, Okla. 1958, Calif. 1961, N.Y. 1967, Tex. 1976. Mem. staff Tex. Legis. Coun., Austin, 1950; instr. econs. Baylor U., Waco, Tex., 1950-51; mem. tech. staff (engr.) Bell Tel. Labs., Murray Hill, NJ, 1951-53, mem. patent staff N.Y.C., 1953-57; admitted to practice before U.S. Patent Office, 1954; asst. patent atty. Well Surveys, Inc., Tulsa, 1957-59; assoc. Townsend & Townsend, San Francisco, 1959-61; spl. asst. to commr. patents, dir. office legis. planning U.S. Patent Office, Washington, 1961-63; ptnr. Fowler, Knobbe & Gambrell, Santa Ana, Calif., 1963-66; prof. law NYU, N.Y.C., 1966-76, patent counsel, 1967-76; prof. law U. Houston, 1976-82; ptnr. Pravel, Gambrell, Hewitt, Kimball & Krieger, Houston, 1976-92, Gambrell, Wilson & Hamilton, Austin, Tex., 1993-95, Akin, Gump, Strauss, Hauer & Feld L.L.P., Austin, Tex., 1995-2000; vis. prof. law U. Tex., Austin, 2000—. Cons. to Practicing Law Inst., N.Y.C., 1966-71, cons. to Commn. Revision Fed. Ct. Appellate System, 1974, Energy and Rsch. Adminstrn., 1976; commr. patents Patent Adv. Com., 1968-72. Author: Patent Law Perspectives, 2d edit., 6 vols., 1970-88; editor: Orange County Bar Bull., 1965-66; mem. adv. bd.: Patent, Trademark and Copyright Jour., 1972-86, 94—. Lt. (j.g.) USNR, 1943-46. Mem. ABA, Calif. Bar Assn., Tex. Bar Assn., Am. Intellectual Property Law Assn. (bd. mgrs. 1977-80), Intellectual Property Panel of Experts, Am. Arbitration Assn., Ctr. for Pub. Resources. Home: PO Box 584 Hunt TX 78024-0854 Office: Roddy Tree Ranch State Hwy 39 Hunt TX 78024 Office Phone: 830-367-5137. E-mail: jim@gambrell.org.

GAMBRELL, LUCK FLANDERS, corporate financial executive; b. Jan. 17, 1930; d. William Henry and Mattie Moring (Mitchell) Flanders; m. David Henry Gambrell, Oct. 16, 1953; children: Luck G. Davidson, David Henry, Alice Kathleen, Mary G. Rolinson. Grad., St. Mary's Coll., 1948; AB, Duke U., 1950; diplome d'etudes françaises, L'Institut de Touraine, Tours, France, 1951. Chmn. bd. dirs. LFG Co., 1960—. Mem. State Bd. Pub. Safety, 1981—90, Chpt. Nat. Cathedral, Washington, 1981—85, World Svc. Coun. YWCA, 1965—; chmn. bd. dirs. Student Aid Found., Atlanta, 1992—99; life mem. bd. councilors Carter Ctr., Emory U.; mem. bd. advisors Emory U., 2001—04; coun. mem. Presbytery Greater Atlanta, 1988; elder First Presbyn. Ch., Atlanta; bd. dirs. Atlanta Symphony Orch., 1982—85. Recipient East Ga. Coll. Student Ctr. named in her honor, Swainsboro, Ga., 2002. Mem.: Atlanta Jr. League, Alpha Delta Pi.

GAMBRELL, RICHARD DONALD, JR., endocrinologist, educator; b. St. George, SC, Oct. 28, 1931; s. Richard Donald and Nettie Anzo (Ellenburg) G.; m. Mary Caroline Stone, Dec. 22, 1956; children: Deborah Christina, Juliet Denise. BS, Furman U., 1953; MD, Med. U. SC, 1957. Diplomate Am. Bd. Obstetrics and Gynecology, Diplomate Div. Reproductive Endocrinology. Intern Greenville Gen. Hosp., S.C., 1957-58, resident, 1961-64; commd. USAF, 1958, advanced through grades to col., chmn. dept. ob-gyn, cons. to surgeon gen. USAF Hosp. Wiesbaden, Germany, 1966-69, chief gynecologic endocrinology Wilford Hall USAF Med. Ctr. Lackland AFB, Tex., 1971-78, ret., 1978; clin. prof. ob-gyn and endocrinology Med. Coll. Ga., Augusta, 1978—2001; practice medicine specializing in reproductive endocrinology Augusta, 1978—. Fellow in endocrinology Med. Coll. Ga., 1969-71; mem. staff Westlawn Bapt. Mission Med. Clinic, San Antonio, 1972-78; assoc. clin. prof. U. Tex. Health Sci. Ctr., San Antonio, 1971-78; internat. lectr.; mem. ob-gyn. adv. panel U.S. Pharmacopeial Conv., 1986-90; mem. sci. adv. bd. Nat. Osteoporosis Found., 1988-91. Co-author: The Menopause: Indications for Estrogen Therapy, 1979, Sex Steroid Hormones and Cancer, 1984, Unwanted Hair: Its Cause and Treatment, 1985, Estrogen Replacement Therapy, 1987, Hormone Replacement Therapy, 3rd edit., 1992, 6th edit., 2005, Estrogen Replacement Therapy Users Guide, 1989, 2d edit., 1997; mem. editl. bd. Jour. Reproductive Medicine, 1982-85, Maturitas, 1982-99, The Female Patient, 1992—, Menopause: Jour. of the N.Am. Menopause Soc., 1995—; mem. editl. bd. Internat. Jour. Fertility, 1986-91, assoc. editor, 1988-91; contbr. articles to med. jours., chpts. to books. Deacon, Sunday sch. tchr. Baptist Ch., 1971—; mem. sci. adv. bd. Nat. Osteoporosis Found., 1988-91. Recipient Chmn.'s Best Paper in Clin. Rsch. from Tchg. Hosp. award Armed Forces Dist. Am. Coll. Ob-Gyn., 1972, 88, Host award, 1977, Chmn.'s award, 1978, Purdue-Frederick award, 1979, Outstanding Exhibit award Am. Fertility Soc., 1983, Am. Coll. Obstetricians and Gynecologists award, 1983, Thesis award South Atlantic Assn. Ob-Gyn., Winthrop award Internat. Soc. Reproductive Medicine, 1985, Chmn.'s Best Paper award Pan Am. Soc. for Fertility, 1986, Outstanding Sci. exhibit award Am. Acad. Family Physicians, 1986, 87, 92, Boston, 1994, New Orleans, 1996, Merit award ACS, 1994, Cert. of Appreciation for Sci. Exhibit, 1995, Best Doctors for Women award Good Housekeeping, 1997; named to Hall of Fame, Lloyd Meml. H.S., Erlanger, Ky., 1996. Fellow ACOG (mem. subcom. on endocrinology and infertility 1983-86, Kermit Krantz award 2000); mem. Pacific N.W. Ob-Gyn Soc. (hon.), So. Med. Assn. (2nd place Sci. Exhibit award 1992), Am. Fertility Soc., Ga. Obstetric and Gynecologic Soc., Tex. Assn. Ob-Gyn., Augusta Obstetric and Gynecologic Soc., San Antonio Ob-Gyn. Soc. (v.p. 1975-76), Chilean Soc. Ob-Gyn. (hon.), South Atlantic Assn. Obstetricians and Gynecologists (v.p. 1997-98, pres.-elect 1998-99, pres. 1999-00), Soc. Obstetricians and Gynecologists of Can. (hon.), Internat. Family Planning Rsch. Assn., Internat. Menopause Soc. (mem. exec. com. 1981-84), Internat. Soc. for Reproductive Medicine (program chmn. 1980, pres. 1986-88), Am. Assn. of Pro-Life Obs. and Gyn. (exec. bd. 1995—), Christian Med. and Dental Assn., Am. Geriat. Soc. (mem. editl. bd. 1981-83), N.Am. Menopause Soc. (Ortho-McNeil Pharm. Rsch. award 2001), Nat. Geog. Soc., Phi Chi, Alpha Epsilon Delta. Home: 3542 National Ct Augusta GA 30907-9517 Office: 903 15th St Augusta GA 30901-2607

GAMBRELL, SARAH BELK, retail executive; b. Charlotte, N.C., Apr. 12, 1918; d. William Henry and Mary (Irwin) Belk; m. Charles Glenn Gambrell (dec.); 1 child, Sarah Belk Gambrell Knight. BA, Sweet Briar Coll., 1939; D in Humanities (hon.), Erskine Coll., 1970, U. N.C., Asheville, 1986, Furman U., 1997, Johnson C. Smith U., 2003. Dir. Belk Inc., 1947—. Bd. consulators Erskine Coll. and Sem.; trustee Queens U., Charlotte, NC; nat. bd. asset mgmt. and devel. com. YWCA; hon. trustee Cancer Rsch. Inst.; hon. trustee emeritus Princeton (N.J.) Theol. Sem.; bd. dirs. Parkinson's Disease Found., N.Y.C., N.C. Cmty. Found., Raleigh, Charlotte Philharmonic Orch., N.C. Transp. Mus., Spencer, NC; hon. bd. dirs. YWCA, N.Y.C.; bd. dirs. YWCA of Ctrl. Carolinas. Recipient Algernon Sydney Sullivan award, Queens U., Charlotte, N.C. Mem. Fashion Group, Inc. (N.Y.C.), Jr. League Charlotte, Nat. Soc. Colonial Dames, DAR. Home: 300 Cherokee Rd Charlotte NC 28207-1908 Office: Belk Inc 2801 W Tyvola Rd Charlotte NC 28217-4500

GAMBRO, MICHAEL S., lawyer; b. N.Y.C., July 15, 1954; s. A. John and Rose A. (Grandinetti) G.; m. Joan L. Thurneyssen, Aug. 9, 1980; children: Dana E., Merrill R., Christopher J. BS summa cum laude, Tufts U., 1976; JD, Columbia U., 1980. Bar: N.Y. 1981, U.S. Dist. Ct. (so. dist.) N.Y. 1981, U.S. Dist. Ct. N.J. 1981, N.J. 1983, Calif. 1988. Assoc. Cadwalader, Wickersham & Taft, LLP, N.Y.C., 1980—86, ptnr., 1987—88, L.A., 1988—94, N.Y.C., 1994—. Bd. govs. Comml. Mortgage Securities Assn.; trustee Our House Found., Inc. Harlan Fiske Stone scholar, 1978-79, 1979-80. Mem. ABA, Phi Beta Kappa, Psi Chi. Office: Cadwalader Wickersham & Taft 100 Maiden Ln New York NY 10038-4818 Office Phone: 212-504-6825. Business E-Mail: michael.gambro@cwt.com.

GAMELLI, RICHARD LOUIS, surgeon, educator; b. Springfield, Mass., Jan. 18, 1949; married; 3 children. AB in Chemistry magna cum laude, St. Michael's Coll., Colchester, Vt., 1970; MD, U. Vt., 1974. Diplomate Nat. Bd. Med. Examiners, Am. Bd. Surgery (dir. 1993); lic. surgeon, Ill. Straight surg. intern. Med. Ctr. Hosp. Vt., 1974-75, surg. resident PG-II, PG-III, PG-IV, 1975-79; asst. prof. surgery U. Vt. Coll. Medicine, 1979-85, assoc. prof., 1985-89, prof., 1989-90, dir. surg. rsch. labs. dept. surgery, 1985-90, dir. house staff tng. program., 1985-89, vice chmn. dept. surgery, 1985-90, chmn. sect. gen. surgery, 1989; attending surgeon Med. Ctr. Hosp. Vt., 1979-90, dir., founder burn program, 1980-90, dir. nutritional support svcs., 1980-88, dir. resident teaching conf., 1983-90, assoc. surgeon-in-chief, 1985-89; prof. depts. surgery and pediatrics Strich Sch. Medicine, dir. Shock-Trauma Inst., chief burn ctr., dir. surg. rsch. Foster G. McGaw Hosp. Loyola U. Med. Ctr., Maywood, Ill., 1990—, now chmn, prof., dept. of surgery. Chmn. quailty assurance com. burn ctr. Loyola U. Med. Ctr., 1990—, infection control com., 1990—, rsch. com. coun., 1990—, surg. rsch. com., 1991—, intensive care unit com., 1991—, EMS bldg. com., 1991—, med. chmn. nutrition com., 1992—, managed care task force, 1993—, commitment to teaching task force, 1993—, OR/PAR com., 1995—, MD/PhD steering com., 1998—, med. exec. com., 1998-2000; Dr John C. Hartnett lectr. St. Michael's Coll., 1983; mem. spl. study sect. NIH, 1991. Co-author: Trauma 2000, 1992, A Compendium of Slides on Surgical Infections, 1992; co-editor: Clinical Surgery, 1987, Early Care of the Injured Patient, 1990, Essentials of Clinical Surgery, 1991; mem. editorial bd., reivewer Jour. Trauma, 1984—, Essentials Clin. Surgery, 1988—, Clin. Surgery, 1990—, Shock, 1993—; reviewer Circulatory Shock, Surgery, Jour. Surg. Rsch.; contbr. 172 articles to profl. jours., 16 chpts. to books. Recipient Dr. James E. DeMeules 1st Annual Rsch. award U. Vt. Dept. Surgery, 1990, Disting. Acad. Achievement award U. Vt., 2000; grantee NIH, 1981-84, 89-93, Ethicon, Inc., 1988-90, Genetech., Inc., 1988-89, Amgen, Inc., 1989-90, U. Ill., Chgo., 1991. Fellow ACS (vice chmn. Vt. state com. on trauma 1984-86, chmn. Vt. state com. on trauma 1986-91, sec.-treas. Vt. state chpt. 1987-90, subcom. on publs. 1987-90, exec. com. 1991-93, reviewer com. on trauma verification/consultaion program for hosps., 1991, 92, 93 chmn. audit com. 1992, 93, bd. dirs. 1992, cons., beta test site NTRACS, 1993); mem. Am. Burn Assn. (instr., dir. advanced burn life suuport course 1988—, regionalization com. 1992—, chair region V. 1992—, beta test site registry 1993, 1st v.p.), N.Am. Burn Soc. (pres. 1991), Shock Soc., Soc. for Leukocyte Biology, Soc. Univ. Surgeons (chmn. com. on social and legis. issues 1990-93, exec. com. 1990-93), Surg. Infection Soc. (edn. com. 1988—, chmn. fellowhsip com. 1990—), Surg. Biology Club III, Ea. Assn. for Surgery Trauma (exec. com. 1991-93, bd. dirs. 1992, chmn. audit com. 1992, 93), Internat. Soc. for Burn Injuries, John H. Davis Soc. (founding., bd. dirs. 1988—, coun. 1988-90, sec.-treas. 1990-92, pres. 1993—), New England Surg. Soc. Office: Loyola U Med Ctr Dept Surgery 2160 S 1st Ave Maywood IL 60153-3304

GAMER, CARLTON EDWIN, music educator, composer; b. Chgo., Feb. 13, 1929; s. Carl Wesley Gamer and Alice Clara Michael; m. Eleanor Everett; 1 child, Michael. MusB, Northwestern U., 1950; MusM, Boston U., 1951. Instr. The Colo. Coll., Colorado Springs, 1954—60, asst. prof., 1960—66, assoc. prof., 1966—74, prof., 1974—94, prof. emeritus, 1994—; vis. lectr., vis. prof. Princeton U., NJ, 1974, 1981, sr. fellow coun. of humanities, 1976—76; vis. prof. U. Mich., Ann Arbor, 1982—82. Adv. coun., dept. music Princeton U., 1987—93; jour. editl. bd. Perspectives of New Music, 1972—. Composer: (instrumental music) Sonata for Violin and Piano, Piano Raga Music, (orchestral music) Arkhe; contbr. articles to profl. jours. Vice-chmn. Pikes Peak Justice & Peace Commn., Colorado Springs, Colo., 2001—04. Fellow Asia Soc. Fellowship, 1962-1963, MacDowell Colony Fellowship, 1976. Mem.: Am. Music Ctr., Soc. Music Theory, Soc. Composers, Inc. Quaker. Avocations: travel, fitness, languages.

GAMET, DONALD MAX, appliance company executive; b. Mapleton, Kans., Feb. 21, 1916; s. Carl Adolph and Pearl May (McClanahan) G.; m. L. Pauline Fleming, Apr. 14, 1938 (dec. Dec. 1981); children: Merilyn Kay Gamet Paris, Carleton Lenoir, Kathy Lynn Gamet Stephenson; m. Marilyn Lang, Jan. 15, 1983. BBA, Ft. Hays State Coll., 1938; MBA, U. Kans., 1939, JD, 1942. CPA, Mo. Staff acct. Arthur Andersen & Co., Kansas City, Mo., 1942-46, mgr., 1946-54, ptnr., 1954-78, mng. ptnr. Kansas City office, 1956-70, vice chmn. tax practices Chgo., 1970-77, sr. ptnr., 1977-78; cons. Kansas City, 1978-84; v.p.-treas. Chgo. Pacific Corp. (merged with Maytag 1989), 1984-85, exec. v.p. fin., 1985-87, spl. cons. to chief exec. officer, 1987-89, ret., 1989. Bd. dirs. ANUHCO, Inc., Overland Park, Kans. Pres., chmn. bd. dirs. Heart Am. United Funds, Met. Kansas City, 1967-68, chmn. spl. reorgn. study com., 1980-84; mem. adv. bd. Salvation Army Kansas City, 1982-84; mem. personnel com. Village United Presbyn. Ch., 1982-84; pres., bd. dirs. Estate Planning Council Kans., 1962-63, Minority Supplier's Devel. Council Kansas City, 1983-84; bd. dirs., mem. exec. com., treas. Civic Council Kansas City, 1967-70; bd. dirs., chmn. long range planning com. Geriatric Resources Corp. Kansas City, 1982-84; bd. dirs. Metro Kansas City C. of C., 1962-70, pres., 1969-70; bd. dirs. Kansas City Indsl. Found., 1968-70, Jr. Achievement Kansas City, 1960-65. Named Boss of Yr., Met. Kansas City Jaycees, 1962; recipient Alumni Achievement award Ft. Hays State Coll., 1969. Mem. AICPA, Kansas City Club. Republican. Home: 12921 Riggs Rd Apt 102 Shawnee Mission KS 66209

GAMET, SUE ANN, music educator; b. Watertown, N.Y., Feb. 5, 1959; d. Wayne Edwin and Barbara Grace Stark; m. Craig Alan Gamet, Aug. 28, 1982; children: Steven Patrick, Diana Marie. B in Music Edn., Potsdam State U., 1981, M in Music Edn., 1988. Cert. permanent tchg. cert. N.Y. Pvt. voice and piano tchr., Rodman, NY, 1981—; vocal tchr. grades 7-12 Montpelier (Vt.) City Schs., 1981—82; pvt. tchr. Belleville, NY, 1982—83; vocal tchr. grades K-6 South Jefferson Ctrl. Sch., Adams, NY, 1983—93, vocal tchr. grades 5-8, 1993—95, vocal tchr. grades 9-12, 1995—. Ch. organist, choir dir. United Ch. of Christ, Rodman, 1997—2000; tech. in music rep. Model Schs. N.Y. State, 1999—; adj. music prof. Jefferson C.C., Watertown, NY, 2000—. Mem.: N.Y. State Sch. Music Assn. (bi-county condr. 1990, 1997, music tech. com. 2002—), Internat. Assn. Jazz Educators, Music Educators Nat. Conf., Am. Choral Dirs. Assn. Republican. Methodist. Avocations: golf, travel, camping, cross country skiing. Home: 13420 Whitford Rd Rodman NY 13682-2156

GAMMON, JAMES ALAN, lawyer; b. Keokuk, Iowa, Jan. 30, 1934; s. Tench Temme and Helen Dolores Gammon; m. Joanne Mott, Aug. 31, 1957; children— Daniel, Thomas, Matthew, Kelly, Timothy. BS in Commerce cum laude, U. Notre Dame, 1956; JD, Georgetown U., 1959. Bar: D.C. 1959. Assoc. McGrath & McGrath, Washington, 1959-62; ptnr. Molnar & Gammon, Washington, 1962-72; sole practice Washington, 1972-76; ptnr. Gammon & Tierney, Washington, 1976, Gammon & Grange, Washington, 1977-89, of counsel, 1989—; pres. Gammon Media Brokers Inc., Washington, 1981-98; chmn. Gammon Media Brokers, LLC, Phoenix, 1998—. Mem. Fed. Comms. Bar Assn., Christian Legal Soc., Nat. Assn. Media Brokers (pres. 1989-91). Republican. Avocation: body building. Office: 8280 Greensboro Dr Fl 7 Mc Lean VA 22102-3807 E-mail: jag@gg-law.com.

GAMMON, MALCOLM ERNEST, SR., surveying and engineering executive; b. Chattanooga, Tenn., Sept. 7, 1947; s. George A. and Frances Helen (Conway) G.; m. Glenna Dee Shirk, June 5, 1971; children: Malcolm Ernest Jr., Christopher Brian. BS, Miss. State U., 1970. Ops. mgr. Pyburn & Odom, Inc., Baton Rouge, 1970-84; chief exec. officer, prin. owner Hydro Cons., Inc., Baton Rouge, 1984—. Tech. contbr. (textbook) 4567 Review Questions for Surveyors, 11th edit., 1985, Elementary Surveying, 8th edit., 1989. State chmn. La. Trig Star Program, Baton Rouge, 1988-89; mem. adv. bd. La. Math. Coalition. Fellow Am. Congress on Surveying and Mapping (dir., cert. hydrographer, mem. bd. dirs. 1998-2003, mem. hydrographer cert. bd.); mem. Am. Congress on Surveying and Mapping Hydrograher Cert. Bd.; mem. La. Soc. Profl. Surveyors (registered, pres. 1990), Miss. Assn. Profl. Surveyors (registered), Nat. Soc. Profl. Surveyors (profl. mem.), Ark. Soc. Profl. Surveyors (registered), Ala. Profl. Land Surveyors (registered). Home: 19021 Saint Clare Dr Baton Rouge LA 70810-7979 Office: Hydro Cons Inc 10275 Siegen Ln Baton Rouge LA 70810-4926 Business E-Mail: egammon@hydroconsultants.com.

GAMMON, SAMUEL RHEA, III, association executive, former ambassador; b. Tex., Jan. 22, 1924; m. Mary Renwick. BA, Tex. A. and M. U., 1946; A.M., Princeton U., 1948, PhD, 1953. Instr. Emory U., 1952-54; joined Fgn. Service, Dept. State, 1954; served in Milan and Palermo, Italy, 1954-58; with Dept. of State, 1959-63; detailed fgn. affairs aide to Vice Pres. Lyndon Johnson, 1963; consul gen. Asmara, Ethiopia, 1964-67; counselor for polit. affairs Rome, 1967-70; detailed USIA dep. asst. dir. for W. Europe, 1970-71; exec. asst. to undersec., 1971-73; dep. exec. sec. State Dept., 1973-75; minister counselor Am. Embassy, Paris, 1975-78; ambassador to Mauritius Port Louis, 1978-80; exec. dir. Am. Hist. Assn., 1981-94. Pres. Nat. Humanities Alliance, 1986-88; bd. dirs. Consortium Social Sci. Assns., 1981-94, Truman Libr. and Inst., 1982-94, Assn. for Diplomatic Studies, 1986—. Served to Capt. AUS, 1943-46, 1950-52. Mem. Am. Fgn. Svc. Protective Assn. (bd. dirs. 1991—, pres. 1992—).

GAMMONS, PETER, columnist, commentator; b. Boston, Apr. 9, 1945; s. Edward Babson and Betty (Allen) G.; m. Gloria Fay Trowbridge, Aug. 24, 1968. BA, U. N.C., 1969. Writer, columnist Boston Globe, 1969-86; sr. writer Sports Illustrated, 1982-90; Major League Baseball studio analyst ESPN, 1988—, columnist, 1990—. Contbr. articles to numerous newspapers; author: (book) Beyond the Sixth Game. Named to Major League Baseball Hall of Fame. Home: 36 Glen Rd Brookline MA 02445-7721 Office: ESPN Sports Television ESPN Plaza Bristol CT 06010-1099*

GAMORAN, REUBEN, candy company executive; B of Acctg., Northwestern U.; MBA, U. Chgo. CPA Ill. With William Wrigley Jr. Co., Chgo., 1985, assoc. treas., v.p. fin., v.p., controller, 2001—04, cheif fin. officer, 2004—. Office: William Wrigley Jr Co 410 N Michigan Ave Chicago IL 60611

GAMSON, JOSHUA PAUL, sociology educator, writer; b. Ann Arbor, Mich., Nov. 16, 1962; s. William Anthony and Zelda (Finkelstein) G. BA, Swarthmore Coll., 1985; MA, U. Calif., Berkeley, 1988, PhD, 1992. Asst. editor Moment Mag., Boston, 1985-86; tchr. h.s. The Cambridge Sch., Weston, Mass., 1986-87; instr. U. Calif., Berkeley, 1992, lectr., 1993; asst. prof. Yale U., New Haven, 1993—98, assoc. prof., 1998—2002, U. San Francisco, 2002—. Author: Claims to Fame: Celebrity in Contemporary America, 1994, Freaks Talk Back: Tabloid Talk Shows and Sexual Nonconformity, 1998, Fabulous Sylvester, 2005; contbr. articles to profl. jours. Activist, media coord. Act Up/San Francisco, 1988-90. Spencer fellow Woodrow Wilson Nat. Fellowship Found., 1991-92, Regents-Intern fellow U. Calif., 1987-92, program on non-profit orgns. fellow Yale U., 1994. Mem. Am. Sociol. Assn. (coun. mem. coun. on stats. of lesbians, gays and bisexuals in sociology 1995—, Fund for the Advancement of the Discipline award 1995), Ea. Sociol. Assn. Office: Univ San Francisco 2130 Fulton Street San Francisco CA 94117*

GAMST, FREDERICK CHARLES, social anthropologist; b. NYC, May 24, 1936; s. Rangvald Julius and Aida (Durante) G.; m. Marilou Swanson, Jan. 28, 1961; 1 child, Nicole Christina. AA, Pasadena City Coll., 1959; AB, UCLA, 1961; PhD, U. Calif., Berkeley, 1967. Instr. anthropology Rice U., Houston, 1966-67, asst. prof., 1967-71, assoc. prof., 1971-75; prof. dept. anthropology U. Mass., Boston, 1975—2001, chmn. dept. anthropology, 1975-78, assoc. provost for grad. studies, 1978-83, prof. emeritus, 2001—. Cons. in social rels., human factors and ops. to R.R. industry, 1970—; acting dir. Houston Inter-Univ. African Studies Program, 1969-71, Behavioral Sci. Grad. Program, Rice U., 1974-75; mem. Joint Internat. Observer Group (for observation of Ethiopian elections), 1992; mem. com. on human factors for railroads and other fixed guideway transp. sys. Transp. Rsch. Bd., 1999—; adj. prof. anthropology U. Wyo., 2001—. Author: Travel and Research in Northwestern Ethiopia, 1965, The Qemant: A Pagan-Hebraic Peasantry of Ethiopia, 1969, Peasants in Complex Society, 1974, The Hoghead: An Industrial Ethnology of the Locomotive Engineer, 1980, Highballing with Flimsies: Working under Train Orders, 1990; editor: Studies in Cultural Anthropology, 1975, Letters from the United States of North America on Internal Improvements, Steam Navigation, Banking, Etc., 1990, Anthropology Quar., Golden Anniversary Spl. Issue on Indsl. Ethnology, 1977, (with Edward Norbeck) Ideas of Culture: Sources and Uses, 1976, Meanings of Work: Consideration for the Twenty-First Century, 1995, Early American Railroads: Franz Anton Ritter von Gerstner's Die Innern Communicationen (1842-1843), 2 vols., 1997, (video documentary) T-Time: The History of Mass Transit in Boston, 1984; contbr. articles and revs. to profl. publs., chpts. to books. Adv. com Quincy Quarries Hist. Site, Met. Dist. Commn. Mass., 1987—2001; bd. dirs. Cheyenne Depot Found., 2002—, sec. bd. dirs., 2002—. N.Y. State Regents scholar 1954-58, UCLA scholar 1959-60, Haynes Found. scholar 1960-61; Woodrow Wilson Nat. fellow 1961-62, Ford Found. Fgn. Area fellow 1962-63, Social Sci. Rsch. Coun. and ACLS Fgn. Area fellow 1963-66; Rice U. rsch. grantee 1967, NSF grantee 1970-72, NIMH grantee 1972-74, others. Fellow AAAS, Am. Anthrop. Assn. (Conrad Arensberg award 1995, Festschrift Session honoring life's work 2002), Soc.

Applied Anthropology, Royal Anthrop. Inst. Gt. Britain and Ireland; mem. Sci. Rsch. Soc., Ry. and Locomotive Hist. Soc. (dir., editor 4 vol. Franz Anton Ritter von Gerstner project 1988-), Indsl. Rels. Rsch. Assn., Soc. for History Tech., Lexington Group in Transp. History, Ry. Fuel and Operating Officers Assn., Am. Assn. R.R. Supts., Soc. Anthrop. Work (pres. 1984-87, bd. dirs. 1987-90), Internat. Union Anthrop. and Ethnol. Scis. (chmn. curriculum com. Commn. Study of Peace 1983-86), Assn. for Study Lang. in Prehistory (bd. dirs. 1988-), Mass. Tchrs. Assn. (mem. exec. com. Faculty Staff Union 1996-2001), Cheyenne Mus. Depot Mus. Found. (bd. dirs. 2002-, sec. bd. dirs. 2003-04, sec. 2003-04, v.p. bd. dirs. 2004-). Office: U Mass Dept Anthropology Harbor Campus Boston MA 02125-3393 Personal E-mail: fcgamst@aol.com.

GAN, CHENNY QUAN, music educator, musician; b. Nanning, Guangxi Province, China, May 11, 1981; arrived in U.S., 1989; d. Haiyan Gan and Grace Gang Wang. BA with hons. in Studio Art and Music, Wesleyan Coll., 2002; MusM in Piano Performance, U. N.C., 2004, MM in Accompanying, 2005. Recipient First Pl. award, Warner Robins Art Assn., 1998, Concerto Competition winner, U. N.C., 2003; fellow Minority Travel Fellowship, Am. Musicological Soc., 2003; scholar Adele Marcus Found. Scholarship, Wintergreen Music Festival, 2003, Pierce Talent Scholarship in the Fine Arts, Wesleyan Coll., 1998-2002, Mary Bowden Smith-Addy Music Scholarship, 1999-2000, Vera Watson Music Scholarship, 2001, Grad. Keyboard Scholarship, Atlanta Music Club, 2002. Mem.: Ga. Music Educators Assn. (winner all state piano auditions 2001), Greensboro Music Tchrs. Assn. (winner young artists competition 2004), Greensboro Ctr. Arts, Music Tchrs. Nat. Assn., Soc. Ethnomusicology, Coll. Music Soc. (Presenter at local and nat. chapters 2002-present), Am. Musicological Soc. (Minority Travel Scholarship 2003), Greensboro Chinese Assn., Phi Kappa Phi Honor Soc. (life Grad. Fellowship 2002). Daoist-Buddhist. Achievements include research in Chinese music notation; Daoist ritual music; the Trobairitz; Gyorgy Ligeti's piano etudes; Zemlinsky's opera Der Kreidekreis and Orientalism; Buddhist temples in Greensboro N.C. Avocations: swimming, travel, languages, philosophy, singing. Personal E-mail: chenny@iname.com.

GANAPATHY, SUBHASHINI, research scientist; d. Ganapathy Lalgudi and Pattu Ganapathy; m. Sasanka Prabhala, Apr. 4, 2004. B of Engring., U. Madras, 1999; MS in Engring., Wright State U., 2001, PhD in Engring., 2002. Software engr. Intel Corp., Phoenix, 2001—02; rschr. Wright State U., Dayton, Ohio, 2002—. Chair, jud. rev. panel Wright State U., Dayton, 2003—05. Fellow, Wright State U., 1999—2001, 2002—04; grantee, 2003; scholar, 2003—04. Mem.: Inst. Indsl. Engrs. Office: Wright State U 3640 Colonel Glenn Hwy Dayton OH 45435 Personal E-mail: subhashini_g@hotmail.com.

GANAS, PERRY SPIROS, physicist; b. Brisbane, Australia, June 20, 1937; came to U.S., 1968, naturalized, 1975; s. Arthur and Lula (Grivas) G. BS, U. Queensland, Australia, 1961; PhD, U. Sydney, 1968. Postdoctoral rsch. assoc., instr. U. Fla., 1968-70, vis. asst. rsch. prof., 1972, vis. assoc. rsch. prof., 1979-80, vis. assoc. prof. physics, 1978; prof. physics Calif. State U., L.A., 1970—2001, emeritus prof., 2001—. Adj. faculty U. So. Calif., 1985-86, East L.A. Coll., 1988-2004; vis. prof. physics UCLA, summer 1987, 91, 92; referee Astrophys. Jour., Astron. and Astrophysics. Contbr. articles to profl. jours. Mem. AAUP, Congress of Faculty Assns., Am. Phys. Soc., Sigma Xi. Home: 11790 Radio Dr Los Angeles CA 90064-3615 Office: Calif State U Physics Dept Los Angeles CA 90032 Office Phone: 323-343-2121. Business E-Mail: pganas@calstatela.edu.

GANAWAY, GEORGE KENNETH, psychiatrist, researcher; b. Davenport, Iowa, Mar. 22, 1946; s. Kenneth Joseph and Elizabeth Earl (Baker) G.; m. Elzada Lawson, Dec. 27, 1969; children: Heather, Erin. BS in Clin. Psychology, Duke U., 1968; MD, Emory U., 1973; grad., Emory Psychoanalytic Inst., 2001. Diplomate Am. Bd. Psychiatry and Neurology; lic. physician, Ga. Resident in psychiatry Emory Affiliated Hosps., Atlanta, 1973-76; pvt. practice in gen. adult and adolescent psychiatry Atlanta, 1976—; regional med. advisor Social Security Disability Program, 1997—; pvt. practice psychoanalysis, 2001—; founder, program dir. Ridgeview Ctr. for Dissociative Disorders, Smyrna, Ga., 1987-96; med. cons. dissociative disorders Ridgeview Inst., 1996—; asst. prof. psychiatry Emory U. Sch. Medicine, Atlanta, 1976-80, clin. asst. prof. psychiatry, 1981—, Morehouse Sch. Medicine, Atlanta, 1990—; tchg. faculty Emory Psychoanalytic Inst., 1997—, assoc. tchg. analyst, 2002—. Psychiat. cons. Disability Adjudication br. Social Security Adminstrn., Atlanta, part-time, 1980-87, Douglas County Mental Health Clinic, Douglasville, 1977-81, South Cobb Mental Health Ctr., Austell, Ga., 1978-80, Atlanta Depression Clinic of Ctr. Metabolic Studies, 1976-77, others; ann. chmn. S.E. Regional Conf. Dissociative Disorders, 1987-96; courtesy staff Ridgeview Inst. Asst. editor Dissociation: Progress in Dissociative Disorders, 1988-98; assoc. editor Internat. Jour. Clin. and Exptl. Hypnosis, 1995-96; mem. editl. adv. bd. Insight mag.; editl. reviewer Am. Jour. Psychiatry, Child Abuse and Neglect: The Internat. Jour., Jour. Psychology and Theology, Jour. Nervous and Mental Disease, Dissociation: Progress in the Dissociative Disorders; contbr. articles to profl. jours., chpts. to textbooks of psychiatry. Sci. adv. bd. False Memory Syndrome Found., 1992—. Fellow: Am. Psychiat. Assn. (Disting. fellow), Internat. Soc. for Study of Dissociation (task force on stds. of practice 1991—96); mem.: Internat. Psychoanalytical Assn., Atlanta Psychoanalytic Soc. (pres. 2005—, chair sci. program com. 2001—03, pres.-elect 2003—05), Ga. Psychiat. Physicians Assn., So. Med. Assn., Am. Psychoanalytic Assn. Avocations: sailing, collecting maritime antiques. Office: D-201 5064 Roswell Rd NE Ste 201D Atlanta GA 30342-2266 Office Phone: 404-252-4525. Business E-Mail: gganawa@emory.edu.

GANCZARCZYK, JERZY JOZEF, engineering educator, consultant; b. Tarnow, Poland, May 25, 1928; emigrated to Can., 1969; s. Kazimierz G. and Franciszka (Adamczyk) Ganczarczyk; m. Elizabeth B. Sawczynska, Aug. 7, 1956; 1 dau., Magdalena-Lynn Ganczarczyk Hamilton. MA Sci. in Engring., Silesian Tech. U., Gliwice, Poland, 1950, D.Sc. in Engring., 1956; Habilitation, Warsaw Tech. U., Poland, 1962. Diplomate: registered profl. engr., Ont. Research engr. Silesian Tech. U., 1951-56, sr. lectr., 1956-63; head tech. lab. Hydroproject Cons., Gliwice, 1956-63; v.p., research prof. Water Mgmt. Research Inst., Warsaw, 1964-69; prof. civil engring. U. Toronto, 1969—. Cons. Bio-San Cons., Warsaw, 1968-69; mem. panel of experts WHO, Geneva, 1966-72; pres. J. Ganczarczyk & Assocs., Toronto, 1975— Author: Activated Sludge Treatment, 1966, 1969, 1983; inventor utilization of desulfurization slag, 1983, controlled inhibition of nitrification, 1988. Recipient award Ministry of Constrn., Warsaw, 1968; recipient Polish State award, Warsaw, 1969 Fellow Royal Soc. Health; mem. Water Environ. Fedn., Internat. Assn. Water Quality, Assn. Environ. Engring. Profs. Roman Catholic. Home: 83 Edenbridge Dr Islington ON Canada M9A 3G5 Office: U Toronto Dept Civil Engring Toronto ON Canada M5S 1A4 Business E-Mail: ganc@civ.utoronto.ca.

GAND, GAYLE, chef; m. Rick Tramonto. Ry chef, owner Tru, Chgo., 1999—; chef Jam's, N.Y.C., 1985, Gotham Bar & Grill, N.Y.C., Strathallen Hotel, Rochester, NY, Carlos', Highland Park, Ill.; pastry chef The Pump Room, Chgo.; chef Cafe 21, Chgo., Bice, Chgo., Bella Luna, Chgo., Stapleford Park, London, Charlie Trotter's, Chgo.; chef, owner Trio, Chgo., 1993, Brasserie T, Chgo., 1995, Vanilla Bean Bakery, Chgo., 1996—98. Appeared on TV programs: Baker's Dozen, Chef du Jour, Ready, Set, Cook!, Cooking With Julia. Named one of Top Ten Best New Chefs, Food & Wine, 1994; recipient award, James Beard Found., 2001.

GANDEK, JEAN DAVIS, secondary school educator; b. Nashua, N.H., June 21, 1931; d. Townsend King and Helen Georgette (Butler) Davis; m. Andrew Gandek, Nov. 20, 1954 (dec. Aug. 1988); children: Barbara Lynne, Kathryn Lynne. BA, Mt. Holyoke Coll., 1952; MA, Columbia U., 1954. Rsch. technician Rockefeller Inst. for Med. Rsch., N.Y.C., 1952-53, 54-56, Alfred I. du Pont Inst., Wilmington, Del., 1956-57; substitute tchr. Seaford (Del.) Sch. Dist., 1977-93. Tutor Del. Tech. and C.C., Georgetown, 1993-02. Leader, cons., organizer Girl Scouts U.S.A., Seaford, 1970-81; v.p. Friends Seaford Dist. Libr., 1985-87; bd. commrs. Seaford Dist. Libr., 1987-96, v.p., 1988-90, treas., 1990-96; mem. Sussex County Libr. Adv. Coun., 1996-02, pres., 2001-02; mem. State Del. Coun. Librs., 2003—. Recipient Friend of Seaford Edn., Seaford Bd. Edn., 1987. Mem. AAUW (edn. rep. Del. div. 1984-86, Seaford chpt. 1991-92, Ednl. Found. gift in her honor Del. div. 1986, Seaford 1989), Phi Beta Kappa. Unitarian Universalist. Avocations: reading, knitting, crossword puzzles, travel. Home: 745 Woodlawn Ave Seaford DE 19973-1237

GANDER, JOHN EDWARD, biochemistry educator; b. Roundup, Mont., Mar. 9, 1925; s. Loren Dwight and Blanche Lenore (Mackay) G.; m. Dorothy Alice Hoffman, Jan. 1, 1951; children: Sharon Lee, Peggy Corinne, Linda Kay. BS in Agr, Mont. State U., 1950; MS in Biochemistry, U. Minn., 1954, PhD, 1956. Asst. prof. chemistry Mont. State U., Bozeman, 1955-58; asst. prof. agrl. biochemistry Ohio State U., Columbus, 1958—62, assoc. prof., 1962—64, U. Minn., St. Paul, 1964—68, prof. biochemistry, 1968—84; prof., chmn. dept. microbiology and cell sci. U. Fla., 1984-89, prof., 1989-97, prof. emeritus, 1997—; guest scientist Los Alamos Nat. Lab., 2001—. Mem. external site visit rev. teams for Dept. Energy, USDA, NIH, 1979-93. Contbr. chpts. to books, articles to profl. jours. and encys. Served with USAAF, 1943-46. Recipient Research Career award NIH, 1966-71; research grantee USPHS, 1960-69, 74-87; research grantee NSF, 1957-75, 80-84 Mem. AAAS, Am. Soc. Biochemistry and Molecular Biology, Am. Chem. Soc., Am. Soc. Microbiology, Masons. Presbyterian. Home: 4219 Rancho Grande Pl NW Albuquerque NM 87120-5337 E-mail: jgander12@comcast.net.

GANDHI, HAREN S., chemical engineer; b. Calcutta, India, May 2, 1941; m. Yellow Gandhi; 2 children. BSc in Chem. Engring., U. Bombay, 1963; MSc in Chem. Engring., U. Detroit, 1967, D in Chem. Engring., 1971. With Ford Motor Co., Dearborn, Mich., 1967—, rsch. engr., 1967, various rsch. engring. and staff scientist positions, mgr. dept. chem. engring. Ford Rsch. Lab., head emission and fuel economy core team, 1997, Ford tech. fellow. Mem. adv. com. Ministries of Industry and Environment. Contbr. numerous articles to profl. jours. Named Chem. Engr. of Yr., AIChE, 1984; recipient Nat. Medal Tech., US Dept. Commerce, 2002, Crompton Lanchester Medal, Instn. Mech. Engrs., 1988—89, Tech. Innovation award, Discover Mag., 1990, Exxon award Excellence in Catalysis, Nat. Assn. Sci. and Tech., 1994, Partnership New Generation of Vehicles Medal, 1997. Mem. NAE. Achievements include more than 40 U.S. patents; development of the monolithic three-way catalyst; pioneering research in catalysts for alternative fuels, oxygen components in three-way catalysts, poisoning of automotive catalysts, and novel catalyst formulation strategies. Office: 20000 Rotunda Dr Rm 3437 Dearborn MI 48124-3958

GANDHI, HITESH N., physician, investor; b. Mumbai, Maharashtra, India, Aug. 24, 1976; s. Narayan Vasudev and Shashi Narayan Gandhi; m. Kavita Hitesh Gajria, July 9, 2001. MB, B of Surgery, Dr. D.Y. Patil Med. Coll., Mumbai, India, 2000; M of Health Adminstrn., Va. Commonwealth U., 2004. Cert. Series 63, NASD, 2004, Series 65, NASD, 2004. Intern Rajawadi Hosp., Mumbai, India, 1999—2000; house surgeon Dr. B. Nanavati Hosp., Mumbai, India, 2000—01; grad. asst. Va. Commonwealth U., Richmond, 2001—03; adminstrv. resident MediCorp Health Sys., Fredericksburg, Va., 2003—04. Website creator (website) www.gandhidental.com. Recipient Gold Medal in Physics, Chemistry, Indian H.S., 1994; CFA scholarship, Va. Commonwealth U., 2002. Mem.: Maharashtra Med. Coun., Healthcare Fin. Mgmt. Assn., Inst. of Mgmt. Accts. (CMA, CFM). Home: Apt 1612 520 W Franklin St Richmond VA 23220 Personal E-mail: drhngandhi@hotmail.com.

GANDHI, OM PARKASH, electrical engineer; b. Multan, Pakistan, Sept. 23, 1934; came to U.S., 1967, naturalized, 1975; s. Gopal Das and Devi Bai (Patney) G.; m. Santosh Nayar, Oct. 28, 1963; children: Rajesh Timmy, Monica, Lena. BS with honors, Delhi U., India, 1952; MSE, U. Mich., 1957, Sc.D., 1961. Rsch. specialist Philco Corp., Blue Bell, Pa., 1960-62; asst. dir. Cen. Electronics Engring. Rsch. Inst., Pilani, Rajasthan, India, 1962-65, dep. dir., 1965-67; prof. elec. engring., rsch. prof. bioengring. U. Utah, Salt Lake City, 1967—, chmn. elec. engring., 1992-2000. Cons. U.S. Army Med. R & D Command, Washington, 1973-77; cons. to microwave and telecom. industry and govtl. health and safety orgns.; mem. Commns. B and K, Internation Union Radio Sci.; mem. study sect. on diagnostic radiology NIH, 1978-81. Author: Microwave Engineering and Applications, 1981; editor: Engineering in Medicine and Biology mag., 1987, Electromagnetic Biointeraction, 1989, Biological Effects and Medical Applications of Electromagnetic Energy, 1990; contbr. over 200 articles to profl. jours. Recipient Disting. Rsch. award U. Utah, 1979-80. Microwave Pioneer award IEEE-MTT Soc., 2001, Gov.'s medal for sci. and tech. State of Utah, 2002; grantee NSF, NIH, EPA, USAF, U.S. Army, USN, N.Y. State Dept. Health, others. Fellow IEEE (editor spl. issue Procs. IEEE 1980, co-chmn. com. on RF safety stds. 1988-97, Tech. Achievement award Utah sect. 1975, Utah Engr. of Yr. 1995), Am. Inst. for Med. and Biol. Engring.; mem. Electromagnetics Acad., Bioelectromagnetics Soc. (bd. dirs. 1979-82, 87-90, v.p., pres. 1991-94, d'Arsonval award 1995). Office: Univ Utah Dept Elec Engring 3280 Merrill Engring Salt Lake City UT 84112 Office Phone: 801-581-7743. E-mail: gandhi@ece.utah.edu.

GANDOLF, RAYMOND L., media correspondent; b. Norwalk, Ohio, Apr. 2, 1930; s. Raymond L. Gandolf and Rose (Brenner) Gandolf Neller; m. Blanche Haywood Cholet, Oct. 13, 1956; children— Alexandra, Jessica, Victoria, Amanda, Susanna BS in Speech, Northwestern U., 1951. Actor, 1951-62; writer, producer WCBS-TV, N.Y.C., 1963-65; writer, corr. CBS News, N.Y.C., 1965-82; corr. ABC News-Sports, N.Y.C., 1982-92, host Our World, 1986-87. Panel mem. Dictionary of Contemporary Usage, 1985 Recipient Peabody award U. Ga., 1980, Dupont award Columbia U., 1981, Emmy award, 1987. Mem. AFTRA, Writers Guild Am.

GANDOLFI, WILLIAM R., SR., management consultant; Student, Ill. State U., Ill. Valley CC, Oglesby. From corp. facilities mgr. to corp. dir. planning and devel. K's Merchandise, 1984—93; pres. Strategic Tng. and Cons. Assoc. (formerly GCI Cons. and Tng. Assoc.), 1993—; COO, CFO ESI, 1995—99; program mgr., inst. mgr. Parkland Coll. Bus. Devel. Ctr., 1999—2003. Mem.: AMA, ASTD. Home: 304 N Columbia Ave Oglesby IL 61348

GANDOLFINI, JAMES, actor; b. Westwood, N.J., Sept. 18, 1961; m. Marcy Wudarski, 1999 (div. 2002); 1 child. Student Rutgers U. Actor: (films) A Stranger Among Us, 1992, Mr. Wonderful, 1993, Italian Movie, 1993, True Romance, 1993, Money for Nothing, 1993, Angie, 1994, Terminal Velocity, 1994, Le Nouveau Monde, 1995, Crimson Tide, 1995, Get Shorty, 1995, The Juror, 1995, Night Falls on Manhattan, 1997, She's So Lovely, 1997, Perdita Durango, 1997, Fallen, 1998, The Mighty, 1998, A Civil Action, 1998, Wild Flowers, 1999, 8MM, 1999, A Whole New Day, 1999, The Mexican, 2001, The Man Who Wasn't There, 2001, The Last Castle, 2001, Surviving Christmas, 2004; (TV films) 12 Angry Men, 1997; (TV series) Gun, 1997, The Sopranos, 1999— (Emmy award best actor drama, 2000, 2001, 2003, Golden Globe best actor drama, 2000, Screen Actors Guild award best actor drama, 2000, 2003, TV Critics Assoc. award, 1999, 2000, 2001); (Broadway plays) A Street Car Named Desire. Named one of Top 20 Entertainers of 2001, E!; recipient Joe DiMaggio award, Xaverian HS, 2005. Office: c/o United Talent Agy 9560 Wilshire Blvd Ste 500 Beverly Hills CA 90212*

GANDY, GERALD LARMON, rehabilitation counseling educator, psychologist, writer; b. Thomasville, Ga., Feb. 9, 1941; s. Larmon Brinkley and Ruby Wylene (Vickers) G.; m. Patricia Kay Haltiwanger, Jan. 22, 1966. BA, Fla. State U., 1963; MA, U. S.C., 1968, PhD, 1971. Lic. profl. counselor, Va.; lic. clin. psychologist, Va.; nat. cert. rehab. counselor; nat. cert. counselor; nat. registered psychologist; cert. profl. qualification in psychology Assn. of State and Provincial Psychology Bds. Profl. counselor U. S.C. Counseling Ctr., Columbia, 1968-70; counseling psychologist VA Regional Office, Columbia, 1970-75, chief counseling psychologist, 1974-75; ind. cons., prof. emeritus Med. Coll. Va., Va. Commonwealth U., Richmond, 1996—, prof., program dir., 1975-95. Chair nat. com. on undergrad. rehab. edn. Nat. Coun. on Rehab. Edn., 1984-89; mem. numerous state and govt. adv. coms., 1970—; cons. in field. Author: Mental Health Rehabilitation, 1995; co-author: Rehabilitation and Disability, 1990; co-author/editor: Rehabilitation Counseling and Services, 1987, Counseling in the Rehabilitation Process, 1999; co-editor: International Rehabilitation, 1980, 89; contbr. numerous articles to profl. jours. Faculty pres. Sch. of Community and Pub. Affairs, VA Commonwealth U., 1989-93. Capt. U.S. Army, 1963-66. Recipient Disting. Svc. award Sch. of Community and Pub. Affairs, 1988, School and U. Leadership award, 1993. Fellow Internat. Acad. of Behavioral Medicine, Counseling and Psychotherapy (diplomate); mem. APA, ACA, World Fedn. for Mental Health, Phi Kappa Phi. Home and Office: Highland Springs 300 Southern Ct Richmond VA 23075-1519 Office Phone: 804-737-6089. Business E-Mail: ggandy@vcu.org.

GANDY, H. CONWAY, retired judge, state official; b. Washington, Nov. 3, 1934; s. Hoke and Anne B. (Conway) G.; m. Carol Anderson, Aug. 29, 1965; children: Jennifer, Constance, Margaret. BA, Colo. State U., 1962; JD, U. Denver, 1968. Bar: Colo. 1969, U.S. Dist. Ct. Colo. 1969. Pvt. practice, Ft. Collins, Colo., 1969-81; adminstrv. law judge divsn. adminstrv. hearings State of Colo., Denver, 1981-99. Bd. dirs. Foothills-Gateway Rehab. Ctr., 1970-80, Colo. State Bd. Dental Examiners, 1976-81; Dem. candidate for Colo. Senate, 1974, dist. atty., 1976; trustee Internat. Bluegrass Music Assn. Trust Fund, 1990—; pres. Colo. chpt. Nat. Assn. Adminstrv. Law Judges, 1985-86. With USN, 1954-58. Mem. Sertoma (Centurion award 1973, Tribune award 1975, Senator award 1977, 79, sec. Honor club 1977-78, pres. Ft. Collins club 1978-79, pres. Front Range club 1988-89). Home: 724 Winchester Dr Fort Collins CO 80526-2636 Personal E-mail: hcgcag@comcast.net.

GANDY, KIM ALLISON, feminist organization executive, lawyer; b. Bossier City, La., Jan. 25, 1954; d. Alfred K. and Roma Rae (Young) Gandy; m. Christopher Lornell; children: Elizabeth Cady, Katherine Eleanor. GBS, La. Tech. U., 1973; JD, Loyola U., 1978. Bar: La. 1978, U.S. Dist. Ct. (ea. and we. dists.) La. 1980, U.S. Supreme Ct. 1981, U.S. Ct. Appeals (5th cir.) 1982. Mgr. South Ctrl. Bell Tel. Co., New Orleans, 1973—77; asst. dist. atty. Orleans Parish, New Orleans, 1978—79; sole practice New Orleans, 1979—. Guest lectr. in field. Treas. ERA United Coalition La., 1977—78; chmn. New Orleans del. La. Dem. Conv., 1980, 1982; vice chmn. New Orleans del., 1984; dir. Women's Lobby Network, 1980—85; founder Greater New Orleans Assn. Dem. Women, 1984. Named New Orleans Outstanding Young Career Woman, New Orleans Bus. and Profl. Women, 1980; named one of New Orleans 100 Women in Forefront, 1986; recipient Law Alumni award, Loyola U., 1976, Milton Sheen award, 1978. Mem.: ABA, Assn. Women Attys., La. Trial Lawyers Assn., La. Bar Assn., NOW (nat. sec. 1987—91, exec. v.p. 1991—2001, pres. 2001—, Mid-South reg. dir. 1983—87, Woman of Yr.). Office: NOW 1700 Highland Dr Silver Spring MD 20910 Business E-Mail: president@now.org.

GANDY, MAURICE EDWARD, language educator, writer; b. Ely, Nev., Sept. 21, 1941; s. Maurice Edwin and Esther Ruth (Hutson) G.; m. Janice Kay Mitchell, Dec. 27, 1970; children: Maribeth, Megan Claire. BA in English, U. Ariz., 1966; MA in English, Ariz. State U., 1971. Instr. English Bishop State C.C., Mobile, Ala., 1979—. Adj. instr. English U. South Ala., Mobile, 1973—; sponsor and moderator creative writing and bus. writing seminars; contract feature writer Mobile Register, 1991—. Author: (poetry books) An Uncharted Inch, 1982, The Calpocalypse—A Cinovepoem, 1992; contbg. author: Literary Mobile, 2002; contbr. works to ref. publs. and poetry to anthologies. Recipient Hon. mention Writer's Digest Nat. Contest, 1988, 92. Mem. Nat. Coun. Tchrs. English, Soc. Children's Books Writers and Illustrators, Ala. Coun. Tchrs. English, Gulf Coast Assn. Creative Writing Instrs. Episcopalian. Avocation: fitness training. Home: 320 N University Blvd Mobile AL 36608 Office: Bishop State CC 351 N Broad St Mobile AL 36603-5898 E-mail: mgandy1110@aol.com.

GANDY, SAM, neurologist, neuroscientist, educator; b. Chesterfield, S.C., Nov. 3, 1956; s. Sam Evans Gandy and Millie Frances King; m. Michelle E. Ehrlich, Feb. 7, 1987. BS in Chemistry summa cum laude, Charleston So. U., 1976; MD, PhD in Molecular and Cellular Biology, Med. U. S.C., 1982. Diplomate Am. Bd. Psychiatry and Neurology. Intern dept. medicine Presbyn. Hosp., N.Y.C., 1982—83; vis. clin. fellow Coll. Physicians and Surgeons Columbia U., Columbia-Presbyn. Med. Ctr., N.Y.C., 1982—83; resident and clin. assoc. neurology N.Y. Hosp.-Cornell Med. Ctr., N.Y.C., 1983—86; rsch. assoc. lab. molecular and cellular neuroscience Rockefeller U., N.Y.C., 1986—91, asst. prof. lab. molecular and cellular neuroscience, 1991—92; asst. prof., lab. dir., asst. attending neurologist dept. neurology and neuroscience N.Y. Hosp.-Cornell Med. Ctr., N.Y.C., 1992—93, assoc. prof., lab. dir., assoc. attending neurologist dept. neurology and neuroscience, 1993—97; rsch. scientist Nathan S. Kline Rsch. Inst. Psychiat. Rsch. and prof. psychiatry and cell biology NYU Sch. Medicine, Orangeburg and N.Y.C., 1997—2001; dir. Farber Inst. Neurosciences and prof. dept. neurology, dept. psychiatry and human behavior, and dept. biochemistry and molecular biology Jefferson Thomas Jefferson U., Phila., 2001—. Ad hoc site visit mem. Nat. Inst. Neurol. Diseases and Stroke, 1993; dir. molecular basis of human neurol. diseases Cold Spring Harbor Labs, 1996—; adj. prof. Rockefeller U., N.Y.C., 1997—; vis. disting. prof. U. We. Australia, Perth, 1999—2000. Assoc. editor Alzheimer's Disease and Associated Disorders, 2003, cons. editor Jour. Clin. Investigation, 2003, mem. editl. adv. bd. Alzheimer's Disease and Associated Disorders, 1992—, Neurodegenerative Diseases, 2003; contbr. articles to numerous profl. jours.; reviewer in field, investigator in field. Fellow, Huntington's Disease Found., 1986—87; Glorney-Raisbeck fellow, N.Y. Acad. Medicine, 1986—87. Mem.: Am. Fedn. Aging Rsch. (mem. nat. sci. adv. coun. 1995, mem. rsch. com. 1996—2001), Fisher Found. Alzheimer's (chair sci. adv. bd. 2001—03), Alzheimer's Assn. (vice chair nat. med. and sci. adv. coun. 2001—), Rotary (chair CART grant award com. 2000—). Office: Farber Inst Neurosciences Thomas Jefferson U 900 Walnut St JHN 467 Philadelphia PA 19107 Home: 616 S American St Philadelphia PA 19147

GANEK, DAVID KENT, investor; s. Howard L. and Judie Ganek; m. Danielle DiGiacomo, Oct. 13, 1990; children: Harrison, Nicholas. Grad., Franklin & Marshall Coll., 1985. Risk arbitrage trader Donaldson Lufkin & Jenrette, NYC; ptnr. SAC Capital Advisors LLC, Stamford, Conn.; co-founder, prin. Level Global Investors LP, Greenwich, Conn., 2003—. Named one of Top 200 Collectors, ARTnews mag., 2004. Avocation: Collector contemporary art & photography. Office: Level Global Investors LP 537 Steamboat Rd Greenwich CT 06830*

GANEM, DONALD E., immunologist; AB, MA, Harvard U., 1972, MD, 1977. Asst. prof. microbiollogy, immunology and medicine U. Calif., San Francisco, 1982—88, assoc. prof. microbiology and medicine, 1988—90, prof. microbiology and medicine, 1990—; assoc. investigator Howard Hughes Med. Inst., San Francisco, 1991—94, investigator, 1995—. Recipient Soma Weiss award for med. student rsch., Harvard Med. Sch., 1975, Leon Resnick prize for rsch., 1977, Kaiser award for excellence in basic sci. tchr., 1986, Acad. Senate Tchg. award, U. Calif., 1986, 2d Yr. Students' Tchg. award for small group tchg., 1986, 2d Yr. Students' Tchg. award for excellence in lecturing, 1987, 1989, 1991; scholar Harkness scholar, Harvard Med. Sch., 1972. Fellow: Am. Acad. Arts and Scis.; mem.: Am. Acad. Microbiology, Inst. of Medicine (life), Alpha Omega Alpha. Office: Univ of Calif-San Francisco Box 0414 UCSF San Francisco CA 94143-0414*

GANESAN, RAJESH, industrial engineer, researcher; b. Madras, Tamil Nadu, India, Apr. 28, 1975; s. Ganesan Srinivasan and Vimala Ganesan; m. Vijayalakshmi Sampath, June 4, 2003. B of Tech. (hon.), U. Calicut, India, 1996; M in Indsl. Engring., U. South Fla., Tampa, 2002, PhD in Indsl. Engring., 2005; M in Math., U. South Fla., 2004. Registered internal quality sys. auditor for ISO 9000, Indian Inst. Quality Mgmt. Sr. quality engr. Robert Bosch Corp., Bangalore, India, 1996—2000; project mgr. NSF's K-12 project U. South Fla., Tampa, 2002—. Mem. indsl. engring. adv. bd. U. South Fla., Tampa, 2002—. Contbr. articles to profl. jours. Liaison U.-Hillsborough sch.

dist. partnership for enriching elem. sch. edn. U. South Fla., Tampa, 2002—05. Coll. Merit scholar, Cen. Bd. Secondary Edn., Govt. of India, 1992, Nat. Inst. Tech., U. Calicut, 1993. Mem.: Am. Soc. for Quality, Inst. Ops. Rsch. and Mgmt. Sci., Inst. Indsl. Engrs., Pi Mu Epsilon. Achievements include patents pending for wavelet based identification of delamination defect in chemical mechanical planarization (CMP) using nonstationary acoustic emission signal; online end point detection in CMP using SPRT of wavelet decomposed sensor data. Office Phone: 703-993-1693. Personal E-mail: ggrr888@yahoo.com.

GANG, HENRY, dean, lab administrator, director, biochemist; b. Fiume, Italy, Jan. 3, 1934; s. Alexander and Lea Gang; m. Denise Elbaze, Oct. 11, 1966; children: Rina B., Judith, Rebecca M. Student in chemistry, U. Vienna, 1962; MS in Chemistry, U. Bern, Switzerland, 1963, PhD in Chemistry and Biochemistry, 1965. Lic. lab. dir. NY. Assoc. rsch. scientist dept. psychiatry and neurology NYU, 1966—68; assoc. rsch. scientist Mt. Sinai Med. Ctr., N.Y.C., 1968—71; dir., clin. rsch. asst. prof. Hosp. for Joint Diseases, N.Y.C., 1971—80; asst. prof. pathology Mt. Sinai Sch. Medicine, N.Y.C., 1971—79, lab. dir., 1973—80; asst. prof. pathology U. Medicine and Dentistry, Newark, 1980—89; lab. dir., clin. asst. rsch. prof. St. Michael's Med. Ctr., Newark, 1980—89; lab. dir. forensic toxicology Bendiner & Schlesinger, N.Y.C., 1989—93; lab. dir. Town Clin. Labs., Ltd., Cedarhurst, NY, 1993—94; pres., clin. dir. tech. and sci. devel. Advanced Analytical Sys., Inc., Yonkers, NY, 1993—; lab. dir., tech. dir. Enzo Clin. Labs., Farmingdale and N.Y.C., 1995—99; assoc. dir. lab. Biochem. Tech. Lab. Inc., Riverdale, NY, 1997—; acting dean Maimonides U., Miami Beach, 2003—. Spkr. in field. Contbr. numerous articles to profl. jours. V.p., nat. sec. Religious Zionists Am., 1980—; nat. treas., fin. sec., assoc. v.p. Nat. Coun. Young Israel, N.Y.C., 1990—; dep. mem. Zionist Gen. Coun., 1997—2002. Fellow: Nat. Acad. Clin. Biochemistry; mem.: NY Acad. Scis., Am. Acad. Scis., Am. Chem. Soc., Am. Acad. Forensic Scis., Am. Acad. Bioanalysts, Clin. Ligand Assay Soc., Am. Assn. Clin. Chemistry (Best Abstract award 1999). Achievements include patents for new blood plasma expander, automated consecutive reaction analyzer, novel drugs of abuse assays cofactors and flame inhibiting and retarding chemical process and system for general use; research in chemical fire retardants and extinguishing compositions. Office: Biochem Tech Lab 5622 Broadway Bronx NY 10463 Personal E-mail: drhgang@aol.com.

GANG, ROBERT C., lawyer; b. Huntington, WVa., Jan. 19, 1948; AB in history, Princeton Univ., 1969; JD, Univ. Va., 1972. Bar: RI 1972, Mass. 1985, Fla. 1986, US Dist. Ct. (RI dist.) 1973. Shareholder, co-chair nat. public fin. practice Greenberg Traurig LLP, Miami. Dir. Fla. Grand Opera. Mem.: Fla. Bar Assn., Nat. Assn. Bond Lawyers. Office: Greenberg Traurig LLP 1221 Brickell Ave Miami FL 33131 Office Phone: 302-579-0886. Office Fax: 305-579-0717. Business E-Mail: gangr@gtlaw.com.

GANGEMI, COLUMBUS RUDOLPH, JR., lawyer, educator; b. Phila., Aug. 6, 1947; BA, Villanova U., 1969, JD, 1973; doctoral fellow, Temple U., 1970. Bar: Ill., U.S. Dist. Ct. Ill. (no. dist.), U.S. Supreme Ct., U.S. Ct. Appeals (1st, 3rd, 5th-8th, 10th, 11th cir.). Assoc. to mng. ptnr. Winston & Strawn LLP, Chgo., 1973—, nat. head labor and employment rels. practice, mem. exec. com. Spl. Ill. asst. atty. gen. 1991-94; adj. prof. Ill. Benedictine Coll., Lisle, Ill., 1988—; instr. Nat. Inst. Trial Advocacy Northwestern U.; mem. labor and employee rels. com. Chgo. Assn. Commerce and Industry, 1979-90. Contbr. articles to profl. jours. Bd. dirs. Ill. State C. of C.; v.p., bd. dirs. Easter Seal Soc. Chgo., 1983-89. Fellow Coll. Labor and Employment Lawyers; mem. ABA (nat. labor rels. bd. practice com. 1976-), Chgo. Bar Assn. Republican. Office: Winston & Strawn LLP 35 W Wacker Dr Chicago IL 60601-9703 Office Phone: 312-558-5811. Office Fax: 312-558-5700. E-mail: cgangemi@winston.com.

GANGOPADHYAY, PARTHA, management consultant; b. India; PhD in Econs., U. Sydney, 1993; Diploma in Mgmt., Indian Inst. Mgmt. Asst. to v.p. Blue Star Ltd., India, 1984-85; instr., grad. asst. U. Iowa, Iowa City, 1987-92; asst. prof. St. Cloud (Minn.) State U., 1992-95, assoc. prof., 1995—. Cons. Kennedy Western U., Cheyenne, Wyo., 1998—. Referee Fin. Rev., Internat. Rev. of Econs. and Fin., Quar. Jour. Bus. and Econs., Jour. Econs. and Bus.; contbr. articles to profl. jours. Participant St. Cloud Leadership Program, 1996-97. Recipient Gold medal Jadavpur U., 1981; Govt. of India Nat. Merit scholar, 1976. Mem. Fin. Mgmt. Assn., Midwest Fin. Assn., So. Fin. Assn., Southwestern Fin. Assn., Delta Sigma Pi, Beta Gamma Sigma. Avocations: chess, music, Karate. Office: St Cloud State U Coll Bus Fin/Ins/Real Estate 720 4th Ave S Saint Cloud MN 56301-4442 Home: 2406 18th Ave SE Saint Cloud MN 56304-7400

GANGSTAD, JOHN ERIK, lawyer; b. New Brunswick, N.J., May 16, 1948; s. Edward Otis and Ruth Margaret (Fletcher) G.; m. Cynthia Diane Coffman, July 5, 1974; children: Allison, Erik, Amy. BA, U. Tex., 1970, JD, 1974. Bar: Tex. 1974, U.S. Dist. Ct. (no. dist.) Tex. 1974. Assoc. Turner, Hitchins, McInnery, Webb & Hartnett, Dallas, 1974-76, ptnr., 1977-81, Brown McCarroll & Oaks Hartline, L.L.P., Austin, Tex., 1982-2000, Bickerstaff, Heath et al., Austin, 2000—. Partnership com. State Bar Tex., 1981-98. Bd. dir. Found. for the Homeless, Austin, 1988—. With USNG. Mem. ABA, Tex. Bar Assn., Order of Coif. Presbyterian. Avocations: golf, reading. Home: 7925 Cobblestone Dr Austin TX 78735 Office: Bickerstaff Heath et al 1700 FrostBank Plz 816 Congress Ave Ste 1700 Austin TX 78701-2443 Office Phone: 512-404-7827. E-mail: jgangstad@bickerstaff.com.

GANGULEE, AMITAVA, physicist, consultant; b. Rajshahi, India, Apr. 26, 1941; arrived in U.S., 1962; s. Hiren C. and Maya Gangulee; m. Suzanne G. Lorant, Oct. 7, 1989. BE, Calcutta Univ., Calcutta, India, 1961; ScM, Brown Univ., Providence, R.I., 1964; ScD, M.I.T., Cambridge, Mass., 1967; MBA, Pace Univ., N.Y., 1989. Diploma stat. quality control, India, 1962. Gordon McKay fellow Harvard Univ., Cambridge, Mass., 1962; rsch. staff mem. M.I.T., Cambridge, Mass., 1964—67; assoc. dir. rsch. ENSM, Paris, 1980; staff scientist IBM Rsch. Ctr., Yorktown Hts., NY, 1967—86; owner, pres, Logic Sci. and Innovations, Sudbury, Mass., 1995—2004; owner A. Gangulee, Sudbury, Mass., 2004—. Contbr. scientific papers over 60. Achievements include patents for. Avocation: photography.

GANGULY, JIBAMITRA, science educator; s. Santosh Kumar and Bivaranee Ganguly; m. Sucheta Roy, Dec. 14, 1966; children: Rajib, Sujoy. PhD, U. of Chgo., 1962—66. Prof. of geosciences U. of Ariz., Tucson, 1986—, assoc. prof. of geosciences, asst. prof. of geosciences, 1975—81; rsch. geophysicist U. of Calif., Los Angeles, 1972—85; asst. prof. of chemistry Birla Inst. of Tech. & Sci., Pilani, India, 1971—72; officer, csir scientists' pool Jadavpur U., Calcutta, India, 1967—69; post-doctoral rsch. staff Yale U., New Haven, 1967—69; sci. officer Bhaba Atomic Energy Establishment, Bombay, 1961—62. Recipient Rsch. Prize, Alexander von Humboldt Found., Germany, 2002. Mem.: Am. Geophys. Union. Democrat. Hindu. Achievements include research in thermodynamics and kinetics of high pressure and/or temperature processes in the Earth and asteroids. Avocations: music, sports. Office: Geosciences University of Arizona 1040 East Fourth Street Tucson AZ 85721 Office Phone: 520-621-6006. Business E-Mail: ganguly@geo.arizona.edu.

GANGWAL, RAKESH, airline executive; b. Calcutta, India, July 25, 1953; arrived in U.S., 1977, permanent resident; s. K. P. and C. D. Gangwal; m. Shobha Agarwal, Mar. 16, 1983. ME, Indian Inst. Tech., 1975; MBA, U. Pa., 1979. With cen. planning dept. Philips India Ltd., Calcutta, 1975-77; fin. analyst Ford Motor Co., Dearborn, Mich., 1979-80; assoc. Booz, Allen & Hamilton, Chgo., 1980-84; mgr. strategic planning United Airlines, Chgo., 1984-85, dir. flight bus. plans, 1985-86, v.p. flight adminstrn., 1986-87, v.p. revenue mgmt., 1987-94; exec. v.p. planning and devel. Air France, 1994-96; pres., CEO, U.S. Airways Group Inc., Arlington, Va., 1996—. Bd. dirs. Boise Cascade Corp.; bd. dirs. Air Transport Assn., Indian CEO High Tech Coun. Office: US Airways Group Inc 2345 Crystal Dr Arlington VA 22227-0001

GANIS, SIDNEY, film company executive, producer; Sr. v.p. Lucasfilm; pres. worldwide mktg. Paramount Pictures, pres. motion picture group; various positions including pres. worldwide mktg. Columbia/TriStar Motion Pictures; vice chmn. Columbia Pictures. Founder Out of the Blue Entertainment. Actor: (films) All the President's Men, 1976, Little Nicky, 2000, Anger Management, 2003, Montgomery West and the Wings of Death, 2003; exec. prodr.: (TV films) Great Movie Stunts: Raiders of the Lost Ark, 1981, The Making of Raiders of the Lost Ark, 1981, The Making of Indiana Jones and the Temple of Doom, 1984; prodr.: (films) Deuce Bigalow: Male Gigolo, 1999, Big Daddy, 1999, Mr. Deeds, 2002, The Master of Disguise, 2002. Mem.: Acad. Motion Picture Arts and Scis. (bd. govs. 1973—77, 1979—81, 1992—, pres. 2005—). Office: Acad Motion Picture Arts and Scis 8949 Wilshire Blvd Beverly Hills CA 90211-1972*

GANJIANPOUR, RAMIN, orthopedist, consultant; BA, Calif. State U., Northridge, 1991; MD, Ohio State, Columbus, 1995. Resident orthop. surgery, Albany, NY, 1995—2001; fellow joint replacement L.A., 2001—02; pvt. practice Holy Cross Hosp., L.A., 2002—03. Adv. bd. Dept. of Orthopedics, L.A., 2002—. Fellow: Am. Bd. of Orthopedics; mem.: Alpha Omega Alpha. Achievements include patents for modular hip endoprosthesis. Avocation: weightlifting. Office: Bone and Joint Inst #241 11550 Indian Hills Rd Mission Hills CA 91345

GANLEY, JAMES POWELL, retired ophthalmologist; b. Altadena, Calif., Apr. 25, 1937; s. Joseph Harrington and Ruth Alice (Carr) G.; m. Anne Hay Hunter, Aug. 7, 1965; children: Anne Hay, Susan Powell, Katherine Carr, Elizabeth Pearson. BS in Biology, Mt. St. Mary's Coll., 1959; MD, Georgetown U., 1963; MPH, Johns Hopkins U., 1969, DPH, 1972. Diplomate Am. Bd. Med. Examiners, Am. Bd. Preventive Medicine (fellow), Am. Bd. Ophthalmology (fellow). Intern Washington Hosp. Ctr., 1963-64; resident in ophthalmology SUNY Upstate Med. Ctr., Syracuse, 1965-68; resident in preventive medicine Johns Hopkins U., Balt., 1969-71; sr. staff fellow Nat. Eye Inst., NIH, Bethesda, Md., 1971-74; asst. prof. ophthalmology U. Ariz. Med. Ctr., Tucson, 1974-80; assoc. prof., dept. head La. State U. Med. Ctr., Shreveport, 1980-82, asst. dean clin. affairs, 1981-87, prof., head dept., 1982-97, prof., 1998—2004. Sci. adv. panel Onchocerciasis Control Program, WHO, Geneva, Switzerland, 1974-79; med. adv. bd. Internat. Eye Found., Bethesda, 1974-77, bd. dirs., 2004—; ophthalmic drugs adv. com. FDA, HEW, Rockville, Md., 1976-82; epidemiol. and disease control study sect. NIH, 1982-86. Author: book chpts., procs.; editor: Ophthalmic Epidemiology, 1993—; editl. bd. Sightsaver, Nat. Soc. to Prevent Blindness, 1982—86, Evidence-Based Eye Care, 1999—. Bd. dirs. Northwest Lions Eye Bank, Shreveport, 1987. Lt. USN, 1964-65. Mem. Am. Coll. Preventive Medicine, Am. Acad. Ophthalmology (com. rsch. regulatory agys. and fed. sys. 1986-91, chmn. 1990-91), Internat. Soc. Geog. Ophthalmology (pres. 1982-88, treas. 1988—, exec. bd. 1988—), Am. Coll. Epidemiology, La. Assn. Blind (bd. dirs. 1980-96, 1st vice chmn., sec. exec. bd. 1989-91, chmn. bd. 1992-93), Shreveport Med. Soc. (bd. dirs. 1990-96, 2d v.p. 1993, 1st v.p. 1994, pres. 1995), Assn. Rsch. in Vision and Ophthalmology (program planning com. 1993-96, internat. mems. com. 2001-04), Revs. Rsch. NIH. Republican. Roman Catholic. Avocations: swimming, sailing. Personal E-mail: drganley@comcast.net.

GANLEY, OSWALD HAROLD, retired director; b. Amsterdam, The Netherlands, Jan. 28, 1929; came to U.S., 1947, naturalized, 1952; s. Eric Harold and Emily (Auerbach) G.; m. Gladys Dickens, Sept. 3, 1950; children: Robert C., Delia A. AB, Hope Coll., 1950; MS, PhD, U. Mich., 1953; MPA, Harvard U., 1965. Cert. physician asst. Rsch. asst. Walter Reed Inst., 1953-55; rsch. assoc. Merck Inst. Therapeutic Rsch., Rahway, N.J., 1955-60; asst. dir. internat. rels. Merck, Sharp and Dohme Rsch. Labs., Rahway, 1960-64; head tech. div. Bur. Internat. Sci. and Tech. Affairs, State Dept., 1965-66, head European affairs, 1966-69; sci. attaché Am. Embassy, Rome and Bucharest, 1969-73; dir. Soviet and Eastern European sci. and tech. affairs State Dept., Washington, 1973-75; diplomatic advisor to sci. adv. to pres. Washington, 1973-78; dep. asst. sec. for tech. affairs State Dept., Washington, 1975-78; rsch. assoc. John F. Kennedy Sch. Govt. Harvard U., Cambridge, Mass., 1978-80, lectr. pub. policy, 1980—94; exec. dir. Harvard Program Info. Resources Policy, 1980-94; physician assoc. in cardiology Med. Ctr. Duke U., Durham, 1997—2000, ret., 2000. With The Healing Place of Wake County Clinics, 2001—; prin. investigator rsch. N.C. Physicians Health Program, 2002—, bd. dir., 2002—; lectr. in field. Author: To Inform or to Control?, 1982, 2d edit., 1989, The Global Political Impact of VCRs, 1987; contbr. articles to sci. jours. Bd. dirs. Jaycees, 1958-60, Am. Hosp., Rome, Fulbright Commn., 1970-73, Ctr. Info. Policy Rsch., 1992—; dir. pub. rels. CD, Plainfield, N.J., 1962-64. Served with AUS, 1953-55, USPHS Res., 1956-84. Sci. and Pub. Policy fellow Harvard U., 1964-65 Fellow Am. Acad. Physician Assts., Am. Acad. Microbiology; mem. Am. Physiol. Soc., Am. Soc. Microbiology, Assn. Mil. Surgeons, N.C. Med. Soc., Sigma Xi. Clubs: Circolo Catoniere Tevereremo (Rome); Cosmos; Harvard (N.Y.C.). Home: 408 N Estes Dr Chapel Hill NC 27514-7629 Office Phone: 919-838-9800. Personal E-mail: ohganley@cs.com.

GANN, PAMELA BROOKS, academic administrator; b. 1948; BA, U. N.C., 1970; JD, Duke U., 1973. Bar: Ga. 1973, N.C. 1974. Assoc. King & Spalding, Atlanta, 1973; 1975assoc. Robinson, Bradshaw & Hinson, P.A., Charlotte, 1974; asst. prof. Duke U. Sch. Law, Durham, 1975—78, assoc. prof., 1978—80, prof., 1980—99, dean, 1988—99; pres. Claremont McKenna Coll., Claremont, Calif., 1999—. Vis. asst. prof. U. Mich. Law Sch., 1977; vis. assoc. prof. U. Va., 1980 Author: (with D. Kahn) Corporate Taxation and Taxation of Partnerships and Partners, 1979, 83, 89; article editor Duke Law Jour. Mem. Am. Law Inst., Coun. Fgn. Rels., Order of Coif, Phi Beta Kappa Office: Claremont McKenna Coll Office Pres 500 E 9th St Claremont CA 91711-5903 Office Phone: 909-621-8111. Business E-Mail: pamela.gann@mckenna.edu.

GANNON, SISTER ANN IDA, retired philosophy educator; b. Chgo., 1915; d. George and Hanna (Murphy) G. AB, Clarke Coll., 1941; A.M., Loyola U., Chgo., 1948, LL.D., 1970; PhD, St. Louis U., 1952; Litt.D., DePaul U., 1972; L.H.D., Lincoln Coll., 1965, Columbia Coll., 1969, Luther Coll., 1969; LHD, Augustana Coll., 1969; L.H.D., Marycrest Coll., 1972, Ursuline Coll., 1972, Spertus Coll. Judaica, 1974, Holy Cross Coll., 1974, Rosary Coll., 1975, St. Ambrose Coll., 1975, St. Leo Coll., 1976, Mt. St. Joseph Coll., 1976, Stritch Coll., 1976; LHD, Stonehill Coll., 1976, Elmhurst Coll., 1977, Manchester Coll., 1977, Marymount Coll., 1977; L.H.D., Governor's State U., 1979; LHD, Seattle U., 1981, St. Michael's Coll., 1984, Nazareth Coll., 1985, Holy Family Coll., 1986, Keller Grad. Sch. Mgmt., Our Lady of Holy Cross Coll., New Orleans, 1988. Mem. Sisters of Charity, B.V.M.; tchr. English St. Mary's High Sch., Chgo., 1941-47; residence, study abroad, 1951; chmn. philosophy dept. Mundelein Coll., 1951-57, pres., trustee, 1957—75, prof. philosophy, 1975-85, emeritus faculty, 1987—, archivist, 1986—. Contbr. articles philos. jours. Mem. adv. bd. Sec. Navy, 1975—80, Chgo. Police Bd., 1979—89; bd. dirs. Am. Coun. on Edn., 1971—75, chmn., 1974—75; nat. bd. dirs. Girl Scouts USA, 1966—74, nat. adv., 1976—85; trustee St. Louis U., 1974—87, Ursuline Coll., 1978—92, Cath. Theol. Union, 1983—89, DeVry, Inc., 1987—98, Duquesne U., 1989—91, Montay Coll., 1993—95, Mundelein Coll., 1957—75; bd. dirs. Newberry Libr., 1976—, WTTW Pub. TV, 1976—, Parkside Human Svcs. Corp., 1983—89. Recipient Laetare medal, 1975, LaSallian award, 1975, Aquinas award, 1976, Chgo. Assn. Commerce and Industry award, 1976, Hesburgh award, 1982, Woman of Distinction award Nat. Conf. Women Student Leaders, 1985, Outstanding Svc. award Coun. Ind. Colls., 1989, Woman of History award for edn. AAUW, 1989; named One of 100 Oustanding Chgo. Women, Culture in Action, 1994, Alpha Sigma Nu, 1996. Mem. Am. Cath. Philos. Assn. (exec. coun. 1953-56), Assn. Am. Colls. (bd. dirs. 1965-70, chmn. 1969-70), Religious Edn. Assn. Am. (pres. 1973, chmn. bd. 1975-78), North Cen. Assn. (commn. on colls. and univs. 1971-78, chmn. exec. bd. 1975-77, bd. dirs.), Assn. Governing Bds. Colls. and Univs. (bd. dirs. 1979-88, hon. bd. dirs. 1989-92). Home: Wright Hall 6364 N Sheridan Rd Chicago IL 60660-1726 Office: Gannon Ctr Piper Hall 6525 N Sheridan Rd Chicago IL 60626-5344 Office Phone: 773-508-8450. Business E-Mail: aganno2@luc.edu.

GANNON, JOHN SEXTON, lawyer, management consultant, arbitrator, mediator; b. East Orange, NJ, Apr. 7, 1927; s. John Joseph and Agnes (Sexton) G.; m. Diane Ditchy, Aug. 11, 1951; children: Mary Catherine, John, Lanie Elizabeth, James. BA, U. Mich., 1951; JD, Wayne State U., Detroit, 1961. Bar: Mich. 1962, Tenn. 1971, U.S. Ct. Appeals (6th cir.) 1977, U.S. Dist. Ct. (mid. dist.) Tenn. 1989; Rule 31 approved mediator Tenn. Supreme Ct. Labor negotiator, mgr. employee rels. Chrysler Corp., Highland Park, Mich., 1951-61; labor counsel, mgr. employee rels. Ex-Cell-O Corp., Highland Park, 1961-65; assoc. Constangy & Powell, Atlanta, 1966; v.p. employee rels., labor counsel Werthan Industries, Nashville, 1967-80; ptnr. Dearborn & Ewing, Nashville, 1980-90; pvt. practice Nashville, 1991—. Mem. adj. faculty Owens Sch., Vanderbilt U., Nashville, 1975—85; instr. Soc. Human Resource Mgmt. Profl. cert. program Mid. Tenn. State U., 1993—2000; pres. Employee Rels. Svcs., Nashville, 1987—; chair bd. dirs. Elk Brand Mfg. Co. Inc., Nashville, 2002—. Contbr. articles to profl. jours. Mem. Birmingham (Mich.) Bd. Zoning Appeals, 1963-66; mem. Human Rels. Commn., Nashville, 1979-89; chmn. Tenn. Citizens for Ct. Modernization, Nashville, 1979-80; chmn. Pvt. Industry Coun., Nashville, 1986-95. With USN, 1945-47. Mem. ABA, FBA (former chmn. sr. lawyers divsn. mediation and arbitration com.), Tenn. Bar Assn., Nashville Bar Assn., Nat. Orgn. Social Security Claimants Reps., Am. Arbitration Assn. (panel employment mediators and arbitrators), Indsl. Rels. Rsch. Assn., Hillwood Country Club, Kiwanis. Home: 216 Jackson Blvd Nashville TN 37205-3300 Office Phone: 615-386-7003. Personal E-mail: jg216@msn.com.

GANNON, ROBIN BICKFORD, elementary school educator; d. David Ross and Clarice Avery Bickford; m. Glenn Lloyd Gannon, June 16, 1979; children: Jennifer Carol, Brooke Emily. BS, U. Vt., 1979, MEd, 1997. 1st grade tchr. Maple Grove Sch., Dittmer, Mo., 1980—82; 4th grade tchr. East Montpelier (Vt.) Sch., 1982—. Presenter in field. Author: Math Problems Exemplars, 2002, Science Problems Exemplars, 2003. Leader Girl Scouts US, East Montpelier, 1991—95; sch. postmaster East Montpelier, 1995—2000; Sunday sch. tchr. Orange, Vt., 1987—92. Named Tchr. of Yr., NSF, 1987; recipient Presdl. Excellence for Sci. Tchg. award, State of Vt. and Nat., 1999. Mem.: NEA, Nat. Sci. Tchrs. Assn., Vt. Reading Coun. Avocations: scrapbooks, knitting. Office: East Montpelier Sch 665 Vincent Flats Rd East Montpelier VT 05651 Office Phone: 802-223-7936. E-mail: rgannon@v32.org.

GANNON, THOMAS A., trucking executive; BS in Bus. Econs., Marquette U., 1976; JD, U. Wis., 1978. Vice chmn. Schneider Nat. Inc., Green Bay, Wis. Office: Schneider Nat Inc PO Box 2545 Green Bay WI 54306-2545

GANNON, TOM, paper company executive; CFO Riverwood Internat., Atlanta; exec. v.p. comml. ops., 1999—. Office: Riverwood International Corp 814 Livingston Ct SE Marietta GA 30067-8940

GANOE, CHARLES STRATFORD, banker, consultant; b. Abington, Pa., July 16, 1929; s. Robert L. and Leonette (Rehfuss) G.; m. Frances-Sue Williams, Apr. 2, 1960; children: F. Hemsley, Alice N. BA, Princeton U., 1951; MBA, U. Pa., 1952. With Fidelity Bank (now Wachovia Bank), Phila., 1952—, asst. treas., 1956—60, asst. v.p., 1960—61, v.p., 1961—66, sr. v.p., 1966—69, exec. v.p., 1969—75, sr. exec. v.p., dir., 1975—79; exec. v.p. N.Y. Bank for Savs., N.Y.C., 1979—82; sr. v.p. Am. Express Internat. Banking Corp., N.Y.C., 1982—84, 1st Am. Bank of N.Y., N.Y.C., 1984—91; mng. dir. FMS Group inc., Blue Bell, Pa., 1991—94; pres. Ganoe Assocs., LLC, Princeton, NJ, 1995—. V.p. Co. for Investing Abroad (became Fidelity Internat. Corp., merged into Fidelity Internat. Bank 1972), 1963-65, pres., bd. dir., 1965-72; bd. dir., chmn. exec. com. Fidelity Internat. Bank, N.Y.C., 1970-79; mem. adv. com. Export-Import Bank U.S., 1973-74. Co-author: Offshore Lending by U.S. Commercial Banks; contbr. articles to profl. jours. Class agt. Class of 1951 Princeton U., 1954-56, treas., 1956-61, v.p., 1981-85, pres., 1985-86; bd. dirs. Phila. Coun. for Internat. Visitors, 1963-69, chmn., 1969-73; mem. Phila. Dist. Export Coun., 1966-75. Mem. Bankers Assn. for Fgn. Trade (bd. dirs. 1969—, v.p. 1971-72, exec. v.p. 1972-73, pres. 1973-74), Robert Morris Assocs. (now RMA-Risk Mgmt. Assocs.)(past pres. Phila. chpt., Duning Meml. awards 1962, 65, 68), Greater Phila. C. of C. (sec. 1960-64, treas. 1960-70, bd. dirs. 1960-73, mem. adminstrv. com.), Wharton Grad. Sch. Alumni Assn. (past pres.), Coun. Fgn. Rels., Merion Cricket Club (Haverford, Pa.), Princeton Club (N.Y.C.), Princeton (N.J.) Elm Club, Ausable Club (St. Huberts, N.Y.), Delta Psi. Home: 23 Constitution Hl W Princeton NJ 08540-6752 Office: Ganoe Assocs 475 Wall St Princeton NJ 08540-1509 Office Phone: 609-497-4740. E-mail: cganoe@erols.com.

GANONG, WILLIAM F(RANCIS), physiologist, educator; b. Northampton, Mass., July 6, 1924; s. William Francis and Anna (Hobbet) G.; m. Ruth Jackson, Feb. 22, 1948; children: William Francis III, Susan B., Anna H., James E. AB cum laude, Harvard U., 1945, MD magna cum laude, 1949; DSc (hon.), Med. Coll. Ohio, 1995, Ohio State U., 2003. Intern, jr. asst. resident in medicine Peter Bent Brigham Hosp., Boston, 1949-51, asst. in medicine and surgery, 1952-55; research fellow medicine and surgery Harvard U., 1952-55; asst. prof. physiology U. Calif., San Francisco, 1955-60, assoc. prof., 1960-64, prof., 1964-82, Jack D. and Deloris Lange prof., 1982-91, Lange prof. emeritus, 1991—, faculty research lectr., 1968, vice chmn. dept., 1963-68, chmn., 1970-87. Cons. Calif. Dept. Mental Hygiene. Author: Review of Medical Physiology, 22nd edit., 2005, Physiology: A Study Guide, 3d edit., 1989; editor: (with L. Martini) Neuroendocrinology, vol. I, 1966, vol. II, 1967, Frontiers in Neuroendocrinology, 1969, 71, 73, 76, 78, 80, 82, 84, 86, 88, (with S. McPhee and V. Lingappa) Pathophysiology of Disease, 4th edit., 2003; editor-in-chief Neuroendocrinology, 1979-84; co-editor Frontiers in Neuroendocrinology, 1990-2002. Served with U.S. Army, 1943-46; served to capt. M.C. 1951-52. Recipient Boylston Med. Soc. prize Harvard U., 1949, A.A. Berthold medal, 1985, Lifetime Achievement award High Blood Pressure Rsch. Coun., Am. Heart Assn., 1995; named Disting. Svc. mem. Am. Assn. Med. Colls., 1988. Fellow: AAAS; mem.: Soc. for Neurosci., Internat. Brain Rsch. Orgn., Chilean Endocrine Soc. (corr.), Endocrine Soc. (Disting. Educator award 2002), Soc. Exptl. Biology and Medicine (councillor 1989—93), Am. Soc. for Gravitational and Space Biology (bd. dirs. 1984—87), Assn. Chairmen Depts. Physiology (pres. 1976—77), Am. Physiol. Soc. (pres. 1977—78), Internat. Soc. Neuroendocrinology (hon.; v.p. 1976—80). Home: 710 Hillside Ave Albany CA 94706-1022 Office: U Calif Dept Physiology San Francisco CA 94143

GANS, BRUCE MERRILL, physiatrist, educator, health facility administrator; b. NYC, Jan. 15, 1947; s. Murray and Bessie Jean (Schnitzer) G.; m. Linda Sharon Aberbach, June 22, 1969; children: Rebecca, Jeremy. BSEE, Union Coll., Schenectady, 1968; MS, BMEE, MD, U. Pa., 1972; MS, U. Wash., 1976. Diplomate Am. Bd. Phys. Medicine and Rehab. (bd. dirs.). Intern Phila. Gen. Hosp., 1972-73; resident in phys. medicine and rehab. U. Wash., 1973-76, instr. Seattle, 1976-78; from asst. prof. to prof., chair dept. phys. medicine/rehab. Tufts U. Sch. Medicine, Boston, 1978-88; physiatrist-in-chief New Eng. Med. Ctr., Boston, 1978-88; pres. Rehab. Inst. Mich., Detroit, 1989-99; chair dept. phys. medicine and rehab. Wayne State U. Sch. Medicine, Detroit, 1989-99; sr. v.p. Detroit Med. Ctr., 1989-99, North Shore-Long Island Jewish Health Sys., 1999—2001; chair dept. phys. medicine and rehab. L.I. Jewish Med. Ctr., Parker Jewish Inst., North Shore U. Hosp., 1999—2001; exec. v.p., chief med. officer Kessler Rehab. Corp., West Orange, 2001—03; chief med. officer Kessler Inst. for Rehab., West Orange. Bd. dirs. Greenery Rehab. Group, Inc., Newton, Mass., 1988-93. Editor: Principles and Practice of Rehabilitation Medicine, 4th edit., 2004; editl. bd.: Jour. Head Trauma Rehab., 1988—92. Trustee Met. Ctr. for High Tech., Detroit, 1989-94; bd. dirs. Health and Retirement Properties Trust, 1995-99, Five Star Quality Care, Inc., 2002—. Fellow Am. Acad. Phys. Medicine and Rehab. (bd. dirs., pres. 2004); mem. Am. Hosp. Assn. (chair governing coun. sect. for rehab. 1992), Assn. Acad. Physiatrists (pres. 1993), Am. Rehab. Assn. (bd. dirs. 1995-97), Am. Med. Rehab. Providers Assn. (bd. dirs. 1997—). Avocations: computers, reading, video. Office: Kessler Inst Rehab 1199 Pleasant Valley Way West Orange NJ 07052 Office Phone: 973-324-3658. E-mail: bgans@kessler-rehab.com.

GANS, CURTIS B., think-tank executive; AB, U. N.C., 1959. Dir., v.p. Com. for the Study of the Am. Electorate, 1977—; reporter Miami News, UPI. Cons. Woodrow Wilson Ctr. Internat. Scholars, Nat. Com. for Effective Congress. Contbr. articles to reviews including The Atlantic, Public Opinion, The Washington Monthly, The Nation, The New Republic, Social Policy, The N.Y. Times Book Rev., Book World, books and anthologies; guest Today, Good Morning Am., All Things Considered, The McNeil-Lehrer Report. Served with USMC Res. Avocation: baseball.

GANS, DENNIS JOSEPH, information technology manager, financial analyst; b. Yokohama, Japan, Sept. 7, 1949; came to U.S., 1951; s. Harry Leo and Hope Lorene (Everett) G.; m. Carolyn Johnson O'Grady, 1986; 1 child, Erik Christopher. BS in Bldg Constrn. (Engring./Mgmt.), Tex. A&M U., 1971. Project mgr. D.C.B., Inc., 1972-73, 78-79, 86-87; quality control engr. Martin Zachry, Kwajalein, Marshall Islands, 1975-76; co-owner B.G.S.Y. Enterprises, Denver, 1975; project mgr. State of Colo., 1977-78, 79-80; co-owner Denver Skatewear, 1978-80; mgr. scheduling Morrison Knudsen, Zaire, 1980-82; constrn. engr. Bechtel Internat., Jubail, Saudi Arabia, 1982; project mgr. Village at Breckenridge (Colo.) Resort, 1984-86; sr. buyer Hewlett Packard Co, Roseville, Calif., 1988-91, bus. analyst, 1991-95, sys. analyst, 1995—99, logistics specialist, 1999—2001, sys./bus. consultant, 2001—. Elem. sch. vis. scientist. Deacon, Presbyn. Ch. U.S.A.; mem. Comty. Archtl. Com. Mem. Tex. A&M U. Assn. Former Students, Sierra Club. Republican. Avocations: golf, personal computers, photography, model rocketry, astronomy. Home: 851 Sunfish St Lakeway TX 78734-4411 E-mail: gans@jps.net.

GANS, EUGENE HOWARD, cosmetic and pharmaceutical company executive, consultant; b. Dec. 17, 1929; married, 1953; 2 children. BS, Columbia U., 1951, MS, 1953; PhD, U. Wis., 1956. Lab. asst. Columbia U., 1951—53; sr. scientist group leader Hoffman-LaRoche, Inc., NJ, 1956—60; head new product devel. sect. Vick Div. R&D Labs. Richardson-Merrell, NY, 1960—64, asst. dir. devel., 1964—67, dir., 1967—71; dir. rsch. Vicks Personal Care div. Richardson-Vicks div. Proctor-Gamble, Shelton, Conn., 1972—76, v.p., dir. R&D, 1976—87; pres. Hastings Assocs., Westport, Conn., 1987—, Lincoln Techs., Westport, 1989—. Chmn. proprietary drug task group FDA, 1976—86; chmn. sci. adv. com. Cosmetic, Toiletry and Fragrance Assn., Washington, 1984—86; chmn. Consumer Health Products Assn. task group FDA, 1996—2003; chmn. ctrl. rsch. Medicis Pharm. Co., Phoenix, 1992—2002, sr. advisor, 2002—. Mem.: Soc. Investigative Dermatology, Am. Acad. Dermatology, Am. Chem. Soc., Am. Pharm. Assn., Sigma Xi. Address: 5101 N Casa Blanca Dr #223 Scottsdale AZ 85253-6988 Office Phone: 203-221-2023, 203-221-2023. Personal E-mail: egans48845@aol.com. Business E-Mail: egans@medicis.com.

GANS, HERBERT J., sociologist, educator; b. Cologne, Germany, May 7, 1927; arrived in US, 1940, naturalized, 1945; s. Carl M. and Elise (Plaut) G.; m. Louise Gruner, Mar. 19, 1967; 1 son, David. PhB, U. Chgo., 1947, MA, 1950; PhD, U. Pa., 1957, DSc (hon.), 2003. Planner pvt. and pub. planning agys., Chgo. and Washington, 1950-53; from lectr. to assoc. prof. urban studies and planning U. Pa., 1953-64; from asso. prof. to adj. prof. sociology Tchrs. Coll., Columbia, also sr. staff scientist Center Urban Edn., 1964-69; prof. sociology and planning Mass. Inst. Tech., also Mass. Inst. Tech.-Harvard Joint Center for Urban Studies, 1969-71; prof. sociology Columbia (Ford Found. Urban chair), 1971—; Robert S. Lynd prof. sociology Columbia U., 1985—. Sr. fellow Gannett Ctr. for Media Studies, fall 1985-86, Media Studies Ctr., 1996-97; vis. scholar Russell Sage Found., 1989-90; film critic Social Policy mag., 1971-78; cons. Ford Found., HEW, Nat. Adv. Commn. Civil Disorders. Author: The Urban Villagers, 1962, 2d edit., 1982, The Levittowners, 1967, 1982, People and Plans, 1968, More Equality, 1973, Popular Culture and High Culture, 1974, rev. edit., 1999, Deciding What's News, 1979, 25th Anniversary edit., 2004, Middle American Individualism, 1988, 1991, People, Plans and Policies, 1991, 2d edit., 1994, The War Against the Poor, 1995, 1996, Making Sense of America, 1999, Democracy and the News, 2003; co-editor: On the Making of Americans, 1979; editor: Sociology in America, 1990; adv. editor Jour. Am. Inst. Planners, 1965—75, Jour. Contemporary Ethnography, 1971—, Am. Jour. Sociology, 1972—74, Society, 1971—76, Social Policy, 1971—, Pub. Opinion Quar., 1972—86, Jour. Comm., 1974—91, Jour. Ethnic and Racial Studies, 1977—89, 1995—2003, Internat. Ency. Comm., 1984—88, The Am. Sociologist, 1991—95, Georgetown Jour. Fighting Poverty, 1992—, Critical Studies in Mass Comm., 1992—96, Rose Monograph Series, 1998—, Qualitative Sociology, 1998—2001. Bd. dirs. Ams. for Dem. Action, 1969-75, Met. (formerly Suburban) Action Inst., 1974-85, Human Serve Inst., 1987—, Workers Def. League, 1992—, Working Today, 1995—, Rsch. Coun. Jt. Project on Equality, 1996—, Nat. Jobs for All Coalition, 1996. With AUS, 1945-46. Recipient Excelsior award SUNY, Albany, 1987, award for disting. contbn. to media and media studies Freedom Forum Media Studies Ctr., 1995; Guggenheim fellow, 1977-78, Rsch. fellow German Marshall Fund, 1984. Fellow Am. Acad. Arts and Scis.; mem. Am. Sociol. Assn. (exec. coun. 1968-71, pres. 1988, Lynd award for lifetime contbn. to rsch. cmty. and urban sociology sect. 1992, Pub. Understanding Sociology award 1999, Disting. Career award Internat. Migration Sect. 2004), Ea. Sociol. Soc. (pres. 1972, Merit award, 1995), Sociol. Rsch. Assn., German Sociol. Assn. (hon.). Office: Columbia U 404 Fayerweather Hall New York NY 10027 Business E-Mail: hjg1@columbia.edu.

GANS, NANCY FREEMAN, lawyer; b. Phila., Nov. 26, 1943; d. Milton V. and Phyllis Freeman; m. Jerome S. Gans, June 21, 1964; children: Lisa Michelle, Rachel Marie, Shira Jeanne. BA with highest honors, U. Rochester, 1965; postgrad., Georgetown U., 1967-68; JD, Harvard U., 1970. Bar: Mass. 1970, U.S. Supreme Ct. 1975, U.S. Dist. Ct. Mass. 1996. Assoc. Sullivan & Worcester, Boston, 1970-73, Law Offices of Richard A. Glaser, Natick, Mass., 1983-84; ptnr. Gans & Stedman, Wellesley, Mass., 1985-92, Moulton & Welburn, Boston, 1993-97, Moulton & Gans, LLP, Boston, 1997—. Lectr., tchg. asst. Harvard Law Sch., Harvard Med. Sch., Mass. Mental Health Ctr., Emmanuel Coll., Boston Inst. for Psychotherapy, 1970-75. V.p., trustee, chmn. ednl. policy com., chmn. nominating com., chmn. recruitment com., chmn. by-law revision com., chmn. negotiation com., mem. exec. com., mem. long range plan steering com., mem. budget com., mem. Purim ball host com. Solomon Schechter Day Sch., 1982-96; legal cons. confidentiality in group psychotherapy task force Northeastern Soc. for Group Psychotherapy, 1991; dir. Boston Inst. for Psychotherapy, 1992-96. Sr. Kennedy fellow Harvard U., 1973-75. Mem. Mass. Bar Assn., Mass. Bar Found., Phi Beta Kappa.

GANS, SAMUEL MYER, temporary employment service executive; b. June 10, 1925; s. Arthur and Goldie (Goldhirsh) G.; m. Ada S. Zuckerman, Aug. 1, 1948; children: Gary M., Jeffrey R. Grad. in acctg., Pierce Jr. Coll., 1949. Pub. acct., 1949-55; sales exec., 1955-58; franchise owner, pres., CEO Manpower, Inc., Pennsauken, N.J., 1958-86; owner Micrographic Svcs. Inc., Pennsauken, 1975—. With Allstate Svcs., Inc., County Maintenance Corp., Affiliated Personnel Svc.; owner Antique & Classic Cars Storage Garage, Inc., Voorhees, N.J.; franchise cons.; instr. motivation courses. V.p. exec. bd. United Fund Camden County; v.p., bd. dirs. So. N.J. Coun., ARC Camden County, Nat. Conf. Christians and Jews; bd. mgrs. Am. Cancer Soc. Camden County; active Boy Scouts Am., Employer Legis. Com., Camden County Bicentennial Com., Score and Ace programs, Camden, YMCA, Allied Jewish Appeal, World Affairs Coun.; mem. N.J. Gov.'s Mgmt. Commn., 1971; trustee Camden County Heart Assn., Camden County Mental Health Assn.; exec. bd., founder Big Bros. Assn. Camden County; pub. rels. com. U.S. Savs. Bonds, Camden and Trenton. With USNR, 1943-46. Mem. Nat. Assn. Temp. Svcs. (chpt. rels. com. 1973), Nat. Soc. Pub. Accts., Camden County C. of C., S. Jersy Pub. Rels. Assn. (pres. 1967), S. Jersy Mfg. Assn. (exec. bd., treas.), S. Jersey Personnel Assn. (treas.), Cherry Hill C. of C. (bd. dirs., v.p.), Better Bus. Bur. Camden County, Adminstrv. Mgmt. Soc., N.J. Assn. Temp. Svcs. (pres. 1970-72, bd. dirs.), S. Jersey Purchasing Agts. Assn., Assn. Manpower Franchise Owners, Jewish War Vets., Dolphin Beach Condo Club, Masons, Lions (pres. Camden chpt. 1972-73, Lion of the Yr. 1977), Shriners, B'Nai B'Rith. Jewish. Office: 3801 Marlton Pike Camden NJ 08110-6312

GANSKE, J. GREG, former congressman, plastic surgeon; b. New Hampton, Iowa, Mar. 31, 1949; s. Victor Wilber and Mary Jo (O'Donnell) G.; m. Corrine Mikkelson, 1976; children: Ingrid, Briget, Karl. BA, U. Iowa, 1972, MD, 1976. Diplomate Am. Bd. Plastic Surgery, Am. Bd. Surgery. Intern U. Colo. Med. Ctr., Denver, 1976-78; resident in gen. surgery U. Oreg. Health Sci. Ctr., Portland, 1978-81, chief resident in gen. surgery, 1981-82; resident in plastic surgery Harvard Med. Sch., Boston, 1982-84; chief resident plastic surgery Brigham and Women's Hosp. and Children's Hosp., 1983-84; pvt. practice Des Moines, 1984-94; mem. U.S. Congress from 4th Iowa dist., Washington, 1994—2002; mem. energy and commerce com. Staff Iowa Luth. Hosp., Iowa Meth. Med. Ctr., Mercy Hosp. Med. Ctr. Lt. col. M.C., USAR, 1984—. Fellow ACS, Am. Soc. Plastic and Reconstructive Surgeons; mem. AMA, Am. Assn. Plastic Surgeons, Iowa Med. Soc., Iowa Soc. Plastic and Reconstructive Surgeons, Am. Assn. Hand Surgery, Am. Soc. Surgery Hand, Am. Cleft Palate-Craniofacial Assn. Republican. Roman Catholic. Office Phone: 515-265-4414.

GANSKE, LYLE G., lawyer; b. Toledo, 1959; BSBA summa cum laude, Bowling Green State Univ., Ohio, 1981; JD with honors, Ohio State Univ., 1984. Bar: Ohio 1984. Law clk. Judge Craig Wright, Ohio Supreme Ct., 1985; ptnr., chair, global mergers & acquisitions practice Jones Day, Cleve. Author: numerous articles in profl. publications. Mem.: Order of Coif. Office: Jones Day North Point 901 Lakeside Ave Cleveland OH 44114-1190 Office Fax: 216-579-0212.

GANSLER, JACQUES SINGLETON, public policy educator; b. Newark, Nov. 21, 1934; BE, Yale U., 1956; MSEE, Northea. U., 1959; MA in Polit. Econ., New Sch. for Social Rsch., 1972; PhD in Econs., Am. U., 1978. Engring. mgr. Raytheon Corp., 1956-62; program mgr. Singer Corp., 1962-70; v.p. ITT Corp., 1970-72; dep. asst. def. sec. U.S. Govt., 1972-77; exec. v.p., dir. TASC, Inc., 1977-97; undersec. of def. for acquisition, tech. and logistics U.S. Govt., 1997—2001; prof., Robert C. Lipitz chair Sch. Pub. Affairs, U Md., 2001—. Vis. scholar at Kennedy Sch. of Govt. Harvard U., 1984-97; hon. prof., Indsl. Coll. of Armed Forces; vis. prof. U. Va. Author: The Defense Industry, 1980, Affording Defense, 1989, Defense Conversion: Transforming the Arsenal of Democracy, 1995; contbr. author to 22 books on nat. security, rsch. and devel. mgmt, and pub. adminstr.; contbr. articles to profl. jours. Office: U Md Sch Pub Affairs Van Munching Hall College Park MD 20742-0001 Office Phone: 301-405-4794. Business E-Mail: jgansler@umd.edu.

GANSLER, ROBERT, professional soccer coach; b. Mucsi, Hungary, July 1, 1941; came to U.S., 1952; m. Nancy Gansler; children: Robert, Michael, Peter, Daniel. Grad., Marquette U., 1964. Coach Univ. Wis., Milwaukee, 1984—88, US Under-19 Men's Soccer Team, 1979—82, US Under-20 Men's Soccer Team, 1987—89, Milwaukee Rampage, 1996—98; head coach US Men's Soccer Team, 1989—91, Kansas City Wizards/MLS, 1999—. Named Coach of Year, Major League Soccer, 2000. Office: Kansas City Wizards 2 Arrowhead Dr Kansas City MO 64129

GANSON, BARBARA ANNE, history professor; b. Fresno, Calif., Sept. 8, 1953; d. Richard Cyril Ganson (Gredecky) and Elaine M. Wapperer; m. Marcelino Rivas, May 28, 1977 (div. Mar. 1, 1990). BA with distinction, San Jose State U., 1981; MA in Latin Am. studies, U. Tex., 1984, PhD in History, 1994. Assoc. prof. history Fla. Atlantic U., Davie, 1994—; dir. curriculum Gustavus McLeod's Solo Pole to Pole Expdn., Washington, 2002—. Author: The Guarani Under Spanish Rule in the Rio de la Plata (Outstanding Acad. Title, Choice, 2003). Fellow Pioneer Aviators in Celebration of the Centennial of Flight, Wolf Aviation Fund, 2003—04. Mem.: Southwestern Hist. Assn. (pres. 2002—03), Phi Kappa Phi (pres. univ. chpt. 2001—03). Home: 1414 Fletcher St Hollywood FL 33020 Office: Fla Atlantic U 2912 College Ave Davie FL 33314 Office Phone: 954-236-1114. Business E-Mail: bganson@fau.edu.

GANT, DONALD ROSS, investment banker; b. Long Branch, N.J., Oct. 5, 1928; s. Raymond LeRoy and Evelyn (Ross) G.; m. Jane Harriet Taylor, Sept. 12, 1953; children: Laura R., Christopher T., Sarah R., Alison A. BS, U. Pa., 1952; MBA, Harvard U., 1954. Assoc. Goldman, Sachs & Co., N.Y.C., 1954-64, ptnr., 1965-90, ltd. ptnr., 1990-99, sr. dir., 1999—. Bd. dirs. Diebold, Inc., Canton, Ohio, Stride Rite Corp., Lexington, Mass.; mem. vis. com. Harvard Bus. Sch., 1991—97. Served with U.S. Army, 1946-48. Republican. Presbyterian. Home: PO Box 83 New Vernon NJ 07976-0083 Office: Goldman Sachs & Co 85 Broad St New York NY 10004-2456 E-mail: don10285@cs.com.

GANT, LEON ANTHONY, II, lawyer; b. Nashville, Aug. 9, 1947; s. Leon Simon and Gloria Marietta (Darensburg) G.; m. Sharon Denise Horner, May 31, 1986; children: lauren Renae, Bree Ann. BA in Comms., Mich. State U., 1976; JD, Wayne State U., 1982. Bar: Mich. Pvt. practice, Detroit, 1983-84; staff atty. Wayne County Neighborhood Legal Svcs., Detroit, 1984-92, mng. atty. bankruptcy, 1992-97, mng. atty. Bankruptcy, Cmty. Opportunity Program Svcs. and AIDS Law Ctr., 1993-97; sr. ptnr. Gant & Taylor, Detroit, 1997—. Pres. web devel. Vortex Svcs., Inc., Detroit, 1996—; guest lectr. ACLU, Detroit, 1996; mem. faculty trial advocacy summer clinic Drake U., Des Moines, 1990; mem. faculty Inst. for CLE, Ann Arbor, Mich., 1996—; mem. pro bono involvement com. State Bar Mich., 1991-97. Author/developer websites. Mem. ABA, Wolverine Bar Assn., Consumer Bankruptcy Assn., HTML Authors Assn., Internat. Soc. Office: Gant & Taylor PLC 65 Cadillac Sq Rm 2215 Detroit MI 48226-2869

GANT, LINDA GAYLE, elementary school educator; b. Mineola, Tex., Dec. 8, 1947; d. Brooks Conway and Arrie Lou (Wicker) Duncan; m. Ronald Herman Gant, July 15, 1968; children: Shannon Gant Sonoda, Shane Stuart. Lic. cosmetologist, Icenhower U. Socmetology, 1968; AAS, Eastfield Coll., 1980; BS, U. Tex., Dallas, 1983; MEd, Tex. A&M U., 1986. Cosmetologist George AFB, Victorville, Calif., 1968—69; tchr. Mesquite (Tex.) Ind. Sch. Dist., 1979—. Pub. Readers Are Leaders Co., Mesquite, 1999—, author, illustrator, 1994—, greeting card designer, 1995—; spkr. in field. Author, illustrator: children's book Readers Are Leaders, 1999. Faculty mem. McDonald Mid. Sch. PTA, 1983—92. Scholar, Ret. Tchrs. Assn., Dallas, 1982. Mem.: Mesquite Edn. Assn., Tex. Area Artists. Avocations: drawing, reading, swimming, training dogs, needlecrafts. Home: 908 Ashland Dr Mesquite TX 75149-6002 Office: Readers Are Leaders 908 Ashland Dr Mesquite TX 75149-6002 E-mail: rlgant@airmail.net.

GANT, NORMAN FERRELL, JR., obstetrician, gynecologist, educator; b. Wichita Falls, Tex., Feb. 16, 1939; s. Norman Ferrell and Eleanor (Taylor) Gant. BA, North Tex. State U., Denton, 1962; MD, U. Tex., 1964. Diplomate Am. Bd. Ob-Gyn. (exec. dir.). Intern Parkland Meml. Hosp., Dallas, 1964—65, resident, 1965—68; mem. faculty U. Tex. Southwestern Med. Sch., Dallas, 1968—, prof. obstetrics and gynecology, 1976—, chmn. dept., 1977—83. Bd. dirs. Am. Bd. Ob-Gyn., Inc., 1993—; v.p. Internat. Soc. for Study of Hypertension in Pregnancy, 1992—94. Co-author: Williams Obstetrics; contbr. articles to med. jours. Recipient Outstanding Alumnus award, U. North Tex., 1998. Fellow: Am. Coll. Ob-Gyn., Royal Coll. Ob-Gyn.; mem.: Inst. Medicine, Southwestern Gyn. Assembly (pres. 1993), Am. Bd. Ob-Gyn. (maternal-fetal medicine, examiner for ob-gyn. and maternal-fetal medicine bds., mem. exec. com., credentials com.), Dallas-Ft. Worth Obstet. and Gynecol. Soc., Tex. Assn. Ob-Gyns., Dallas County Med. Assns., Soc. Gynecol. Investigation (pres. 1991). Address: Am Bd Ob-Gyn 2915 Vine St Dallas TX 75204-1045 Office Phone: 214-871-1619. Business E-Mail: ccash@abog.org.

GANT, PEGGY CATHLEEN, secondary school educator; b. Reno, Nev., Sept. 19, 1955; d. James Sloan and Joanne Francis (MacDonald) Doyle; m. Christopher Gant, Jan. 7, 1978. BS, U. Nev., Reno, 1977, MS, 1988. Cert. secondary tchr., Nev. Sci. tchr. Swope Middle Sch., Reno, 1978-87; biology tchr. Sparks (Nev.) High Sch., 1988—. Tchr. Outdoor Edn., Reno, summers, 1979-86; sci. rsch. project advisor Washoe County Sch. Dist., Reno; mem. secondary sci. curriculum revision com., Nev. Math. and Sci. Alliance Steering Com.; mem. program selection com. Dept. Energy; scholarship chair North Valley High Sch, 2000—. Grantee NIH; recipient Milken Family award, 1992; named Nev. Educator of Yr., 1992; fellow Am. Soc. Biol. Chemists, 1987; recipient award Sigma Xi, 1984. Mem. NEA, Washoe County Tchrs. Assn., Washoe County Sci. Tchrs. Assn., Phi Kappa PHi, Delta Delta Kappa, Delta Kappa Gamma. Republican. Roman Catholic. Avocations: snow and water skiing, bicycle touring, aerobics, weight training. Home: 7230 Lingfield Dr Reno NV 89502-9661 Office: Sparks High Sch 820 15th St Sparks NV 89431-0987

GANTER, SUSAN LYNN, association administrator, former mathematics educator; b. Waynesboro, Va., Jan. 29, 1964; d. Dorrance Lynn and Gertrude M. (Kirschner) G. B.Music Edn., BS in Math. Sci., So. Meth. U., Dallas, 1986; MA in Math., U. Calif., Santa Barbara, 1988; PhD in Math. Edn., U. Calif., 1990. Grad. math. instr. U. Calif., Santa Barbara, 1986-88; math. instr. Santa Barbara City Coll., 1988-90; asst. prof. math. Western Wash. U., Bellingham, 1990; dir. for program for promotion of inst. change Am. Assn. for Higher Edn.; math. sci. faculty Worcester Polytechnic Inst.; assoc. prof., math. sci. Clemson U., SC, 1999—2004; exec. dir. Assn. of Women in Sci., Washington, 2004—. Contbr. articles to profl. jours. Santa Barbara City Coll. faculty enrichment grantee, 1990, U. Calif.-Santa Barbara grantee, 1989. Mem. Nat. Coun. Tchrs. Math., Math. Assn. Am., Am. Math. Soc., Wash. Math. Coun., Soc. for Indsl. and Applied Math., Western Wash. U. Collegiate Chorale, Music Acad. of the West Opera, Kappa Mu Epsilon, Kappa Delta Pi, Mu Phi Epsilon. Roman Catholic. Avocations: singing, hiking, swimming. Office: Assn for Women in Sci Ste 650 1200 New York Av NW Washington DC 20005

GANTI, APAR KISHOR, oncologist, researcher; s. Surya Prakash Rao and Sundari Ganti; m. Ketki K. Tendulkar, Feb. 10, 2001. MBBS, B.J. Med. Coll., Pune, India, 1996, MD, 1999. Resident in clin. pharmacology B. J. Med. Coll., Pune, India, 1996—99; resident in internal medicine U. N.D. Sch. of Medicine and Health Scis., Fargo, 2000—03; clin. fellow U. of Nebr. Med. Ctr., Omaha, 2003—. Lectr. in clin. pharmacology Dr. D. Y. Patil Med. Coll. for Women, Pune, Maharashtra, India, 1999—2000; presenter in field. Contbr. articles to profl. jours. (2nd Am. Soc. Cardiology, 2002); author: (presentation) American Society of Geriatric Cardiology, presenation, (presentation) European Hematology Association. Mem.: ACP (assoc.), Am. Soc. of Blood and Marrow Transplantation (assoc.), Am. Soc. of Clin. Oncology (assoc.), Am. Soc. of Hematology (assoc.), Alpha Omega Alpha. Hindu. Avocation: reading.

GANTT, ALVIN JACK, JR., music minister; s. Alvin Gantt and Hazel Leslie Quick; m. Shirley M. Gantt, Aug. 18, 1962; children: Stephanie Lynn, Adrienne Leigh. AA, Gardner-Webb U., 1960; BA, Carson-Newman Coll., 1962; M in Ch. Music, Southwestern Bapt. Theol. Sem., 1966. Min. music Pendleton St. Bapt. Ch., Greenville, SC, 1965—71, Wienca Rd. Bapt. Ch., Atlanta, 1972—84, Tabernacle Bapt. Ch., Carrollton, Ga., 1984—. Pres. Ga. Bapt. Ch. Music Conf., Atlanta, 1993—94; chmn. Christian Index, Atlanta, 1997. Contbr. articles to profl. jours. Music leader Kiwanis Internat., 1968—71; fundraising mem. Pine Bloom Soc., Atlanta; mentor Carroll County Mentoring Program, 1997—; vol. svc. youth choir tour Fgn. Mission Bd. South Am.; chaplain Tanner Med. Ctr., Carrollton, Ga. Recipient Leadership award, Ga. Bapt. Ch. Music Conf., 1999, So. Bapt. Ch. Music Exec. Com., 1977—79, 1984—86. Mem.: Music Educators Nat. Conf., Am. Choral Dirs. Assn., Am. Guild English Handbell Ringers, Atlanta Chorister Guild (pres., exec. com.). Baptist. Avocations: reading, fishing, art, mentoring. Home: 108 Stonewall Dr Carrollton GA 30117

GANTZ, BRUCE JAY, otolaryngologist, educator; b. N.Y.C., May 18, 1946; m. Mary Katherine DeJong; children: Ellen Katherine, Jessica Rose, Jay Alexander. BS in Gen. Sci., U. Iowa, 1968, MD, 1974, MS in Otolaryngology, 1980; fellow neurotology, U. Zürich, Zurich, 1981-82. Asst. prof. dept otolaryngology U. Iowa Coll. Medicine, Iowa City, 1980-84, assoc. prof., 1984-87, prof., 1987—; interim head dept. otolaryngology head & neck surgery U. Iowa Hosps. & Clinics, Iowa City, 1993-95, head dept. otolaryngology head & neck surgery, 1995—. Mem. adv. bd. Deafness Research Found. Sci., 1988—. Mem. editl. bd. Am. Jour. Otology, Laryngoscope, Skull Base Surgery, Operative Techniques in Otolaryngology-Head and Neck Surgery, Anales De Otolarnolaringo-logica Mexicana, Annals Otolaryngology, Rhinology and Laryngology; contbr. articles to profl. jours. Recipient Tchr.-Investigator Devel. award Pub. Health Svc., 1981-86, Program Project award NIH, 1985—; clin. rsch. ctr. grantee NIDCD, 1990, 95. Mem.: AMA, NAS Inst. Medicine, Collegium Oto-Rhino-Laryngologicum Amictuae Sacrum, Am. Otological Soc., Am. Neurotology Soc. (v.p. 1994—96, pres.-elect 1996—97, pres. 1997—98), Soc. Univ. Otolaryngologists, Am. Acad. Otolaryngology-Head and Neck Surgery, Deafness Rsch. Found. (state chmn. 1985—), Assn. Rsch. in otolaryngology (pres. 1995). Office: U Iowa Hosps & Clinics 200 Hawkins Dr Iowa City IA 52242-1078

GANTZ, CARROLL MELVIN, industrial design consultant, consumer product designer; b. Sellersville, Pa., Sept. 9, 1931; s. Melvin Charles G. and Leona Alberta (Hornberger) Barner; m. Lorraine Sachs, Mar. 5, 1955; children: Erika Christine, Mitchell Allen. B.F.A., Carnegie Mellon U., 1953. Head indsl. design Hoover Co., North Canton, Ohio, 1956-72; mgr. indsl. design Black & Decker, Inc., Towson, Md., 1972-81, dir. indsl. design household products group Shelton, Conn., 1981-86; prof., head dept. design Carnegie Mellon U., Pitts., 1987—92; established Carroll Gantz Design, 1992; designer canal boat St. Helena II, Canal Fulton, Ohio, 1967-70; dir. Am. Canal Soc., York, Pa., 1974-79. Author: Design Chronicles. Significant Mass Produced Products of the 20th Century, 2005. Bd. dirs. Stark County Hist. Soc., 1970. Served with Security Agy. U.S. Army, 1953-56. Recipient Design award Indsl. Designers Inst., 1961, Indsl. Design Excellance award, 1995; Brashear scholar, 1949. Fellow Indsl. Designers Soc. Am. (pres. 1979-80, chmn. bd. 1981-82); mem. SAR, Omicron Delta Kappa, Tau Sigma Delta Republican. Achievements include patents for original Black & Decker Dustbuster, 1978; 28 others.

GANTZ, DAVID ALFRED, lawyer, academic administrator; b. Columbus, Ohio, July 30, 1942; s. Harry Samuel and Edwina G.; m. Susan Beare, Aug. 26, 1967 (div. Feb. 1989); children: Stephen David, Julie Lorraine; m. Catherine Fagan, Mar. 28, 1992. AB, Harvard U., 1964; JD, Stanford U., 1967, M in Jud. Sci., 1970. Bar: Ohio 1967, D.C. 1971, U.S. Ct. Internat. Trade 1983, U.S. Ct. Appeals (9th cir.) 1972, U.S. Supreme Ct. 1972. Asst. prof. law U. Costa Rica, San Jose, 1967-69; law clk. U.S. Ct. Appeals, San Francisco, 1969-70; asst. legal advisor U.S. Dept. State, Washington, 1970-77; ptnr. Cole & Corrette, Washington, 1977-83, Oppenheimer Wolff & Donnelly, Washington, 1983-90, Reid & Priest, Washington, 1990-93, of counsel, 1993-97, Dorsey & Whitney, 1997-99; Samuel M. Fegtly prof. law, dir. inter trade law program U. Ariz. Coll. Law, Tucson, 1993—; assoc. dir. Nat. Law Ctr. for Inter-Am. Free Trade, 1993—. Panelist U.S.-Can. Free Trade Agreement, 1989-92, Am. Arbitration Assn., 1996—, NAFTA, 1994—; judge OAS Adminstrv. Tribunal, 1987-95; adj. prof. Georgetown U. Law Ctr., 1982-93; vis. prof. law George Washington U., 2003-04. Contbr. numerous articles on internat. law to profl. jours. Pres. Potomac River Sports Found., 1992-94. Mem. ABA, Am. Soc. Internat. Law, Potomac Boat Club (Washington, bd. dirs. 1986-93). Office: Ariz James E Rogers Coll Law 1201 E Speedway Blvd Tucson AZ 85721 Office Phone: 520-621-1801. Business E-Mail: gantz@law.arizona.edu.

GANTZER, MARY LOU, medical products executive; d. Richard John and Mary Jane (Capistrant) G. B in Chemistry, U. Minn., 1972, MS, 1976; PhD in Chemistry, U. Va., 1980. Instr., postdoctoral fellow dept. chemistry U. Va., Charlottesville, 1980—81; rsch. scientist diagnostics divsn. Miles, Inc., Elkhart, Ind., 1981—84, sr. rsch. scientist, 1984—86, staff scientist, 1986—87, supr. R&D, 1987—91, project mgr., 1991—98, coord. clin. and outcomes rsch., 1996—98; dir. clin. and sci. affairs Dade Behring, Inc., Newark, Del., 1998—2004, v.p., clin. and sci. affairs, 2004—. Mem. in Mgmt. del. to People's Republic of China, 1988; bd. dirs. Clin. and Lab.

Stds. Inst. (formerly Nat. Comm. for Clin. Lab. Stds.), 2003-. Contbr. articles to chemistry jours.; patentee in field. Mem. Am. Assn. Clin. Chemistry (chmn. Chgo. sect. 1988, chair long range planning com. 1993-95, bd. editors Clin. Chem. News 1993-95, pres. 2002, Chmn.'s award 1988), Am. Heart Assn. (profl. mem.), Soc. Chest Pain Ctrs. Roman Catholic. Avocation: needlecrafts. Office: Dade Behring Inc (MS709) PO Box 6101 Newark DE 19714-6101

GANTZOS, ROBERT A., dentist; b. Toledo, Feb. 26, 1937; s. Ariqyrios Demetri Gantzos and Stascia Marguerite Poweirza; m. Mary Catherine MacDowell, Aug. 29, 1971; 1 child, Ryan; children: Robin, Nonny, Robert II. BA in History, U. Mich., 1959, DDS, 1964. Pvt. practice, Toledo, 1964—. Author: (book) Bullhunk Army, 2000. Mem.: Dental Soc. Office: 2428 Sylvania Ave Toledo OH 43613

GANULIN, JUDY, public relations professional; b. Chgo., May 2, 1937; d. Alvin and Sadie (Reingold) Landis; m. James Ganulin, June 23, 1957; children: Stacy Ganulin Clark, Amy Ganulin Lowenstein. BA in Journalism, U. Calif., Berkeley, 1958. Copywriter-sec. Joe Connor Advt., Berkeley, 1958; exec. sec. Prescolite Mfg. Co., Berkeley, 1958-59; info. officer Office of Consumer Counsel, Sacramento, 1959-61; pub. rels. positions various polit. campaigns, Fresno, Calif., 1966; adminstrv. asst., editor, mktg. Valley Pubs., Fresno, 1971-80; staff asst. to county supr. Bd. Suprs., Fresno, 1980-82; field rep. Assemblyman Bruce Bronzan, Fresno, 1982-84; prin. Judy Ganulin Pub. Rels., Fresno, 1984—. Speaker new bus. workshop SBA/Svc. Corps Ret. Execs., Fresno, 1990—. Active Hadassah, Fresno, 1975—; pres. Temple Beth Israel Sisterhood, Fresno, 1976; panelist campaign workshop Nat. Women's Polit. Caucus, Fresno, 1994, 2001, publicity chmn. ctrl. Caifl. chpt., 1999—2000; mem. C. of C. Art and Wine Festival Com., 1999—2000, Juvenile Justice Ctr. Task Force, 2001, Valley Women's Polit. Fund; bd. dirs. Temple Beth Israel, Fresno, 1972—75, Planned Parenthood Ctrl. Calif., Fresno, 1986—91, Empty Bowls, Sr. Companion Program. Mem. Pub. Rels. Soc. Am. (accredited pub. rels. practitioner, pres. Fresno/Ctrl. Valley chpt. 1994), Am. Mktg. Assn. (pres. ctrl. Calif. chpt. 1987-88), Calif. Press Women, Fresno Advt. Fedn., Fresno Comm. Network (v.p., pres. 1991-93), Fresno C. of C. (mem. mktg. com. 1988-), Fresno Comm. Network (formerly Pub. Rels. Roundtable) . Democrat. Avocations: travel, reading, cooking. Office: Judy Ganulin Pub Rels 1117 W San Jose Ave Fresno CA 93711-3112 Office Phone: 559-222-7411. Personal E-mail: jganulin@comcast.net.

GANZ, AXEL, publishing executive; b. Auggen, Germany, July 25, 1937; m. Renate von Plotho; 1 child. Editor Burda Publ., 1963—70, Bauer Publ. Group, 1971—78; joined as founding pres. French subsidiary Prisma Press Gruner + Jahr, 1978; founder Gruner + Jahr UK, 1986, Gruner + Jahr Italia, 1989, Gruner + Jahr Polska, 1993; mem. exec. bd. Gruner + Jahr Worldwide, 1991—, pres. internat. mag. divsn., 1991—2003, pres. mag. divsn. France and USA, 2004—; pres. internat. mag. divsn. Gruner + Jahr USA Publ.; chmn., CEO Prisma Presse, France. Office: G+J USA Publ 375 Lexington Ave New York NY 10017-5514

GANZ, DAVID L., lawyer; b. NYC, July 28, 1951; s. Daniel M. and Beverlee (Kaufman) G.; m. Barbara Bondanza, Nov. 3, 1974 (div. 1978); m. Sharon Ruth Lamnin, Oct. 30, 1981 (div. 1996); children: Scott Harry, Elyse Toby, Pamela Rebecca; m. Kathleen Ann Gotsch, Dec. 28, 1996. BS in Fgn. Svc., Georgetown U., 1973; JD, St. John's U., 1976. Bar: N.Y. 1977, D.C. 1980, N.J. 1985; cert. mediator U.S. Dist. Ct. (N.J.). Assoc. Regan, Dorsey & De Riso, Flushing, N.Y., 1977-79; ptnr. Durst & Ganz, N.Y.C., 1979-80; mng. ptnr. Ganz, Hollinger & Towe, N.Y.C., 1981-98, Ganz & Hollinger, N.Y.C., 1999—. Exec. com. Industry Coun. Tangible Assets, Washington, 1983—, bd. dirs.; pres. World Mint Coun., 1993-95; cons. in field. Author: A Critical Guide to the Anthologies of African Literature, 1973, A Legal and Legislative History of 31 USC Sec 342d-324i, 1976, The World of Coin Collecting, 1980, 3d edit., 1998, The 90 Second Lawyer, 1996, The 90 Second Lawyer's Guide to Selling Real Estate, 1997, How to Get an Instant Mortgage, 1997, Planning Your Rare Coin Retirement, 1998, Guide Commemorative Coin Values, 1999, Official Guide to America's State Quarters, 2000, rev. edit., 2002; corr. Numis. News Weekly, 1969-73, 96—, asst. editor, 1973-74, spl. corr., 1974-75, columnist, 1969-76, 96—; contbg. editor, columnist COINage Mag., 1974—; columnist Coin World, 1974-96, COINS Mag., 1973-83; contbr. articles to profl. jours. Presdl. appointee Annual Assay Commn., 1974; bd. dirs. Georgetown Libr. Assocs., Washington, 1982-2005, Bialystoker Home & Infirmary for the Aged, NYC, 2001—, Care Plus N.J. Inc., 2003—; active N.Y. County Draft Bd., 1984, Bergen County, NJ, 1985-2005, vice chair, 1996-2005; mem. Citizens Commemorative Coin Adv. Com. U.S. Treas., 1993-96; sec., mem. Zoning and Adjustment Bd., Fair Lawn, NJ, 1988-92, chmn., 1993-97; elected mem. Dem. County Com. Bergen County, 1988-96, borough coun. Borough of Fair Lawn, 1998—, mayor, 1999—, Bergen County freeholder, 2003—, vice-chmn., 2005; atty. Zoning Bd. Adjustment, Paramus, 2002-2003. Decorated Order of St. Agatha (Republic of San Marino) Fellow Am. Numis. Soc. (life); mem. Am. Numis. Assn. (life, legis. coun. 1978-81, 83-95, elected bd. govs. 1985-95, v.p. 1991-93, pres. 1993-95), Assn. of Bar of City of N.Y. (com. on state legis. 1987-90), N.Y. State Bar Assn. (mem. civil practice com., chmn. subcom. 1978-84), Profl. Numis. Guild Inc. affiliated mem. 1989—, gen. coun. 1981-92), Am. Soc. Internat. Law, Nat. Assn. Coin and Precious Metals Dealers (assoc. mem., gen. coun. 1981-85), Flushing Lawyers Club (pres. 1982-83). Democrat. Jewish. Avocation: coin collecting/numismatics. Office: Ganz & Hollinger PC 1394 3rd Ave New York NY 10021-0404 Office Phone: 212-517-5500. Personal E-mail: davidlganz@aol.com.

GANZ, HOWARD LAURENCE, lawyer; b. NYC, Apr. 3, 1942; s. Myron and Beatrice (W.) Ganz; children: Beth, David. BA, Colgate U., 1963; LLB, Columbia U., 1966. Bar: N.Y. 1966, U.S. Dist. Ct. (so. dist.) N.Y. 1968, U.S. Dist. Ct. (ea. dist.) N.Y. 1969, U.S. Dist. Ct. (no. dist.) Calif. 1984, U.S. Ct. Appeals (3rd cir.) 1974, U.S. Ct. Appeals (4th cir.) 1985, U.S. Dist. Ct. (9th cir.) 1984, U.S. Dist. Ct. (D.C. cir.) 1986, U.S. Supreme Ct. 1986. Law clk. to Hon. Marvin E. Frankel U.S. Dist. Ct., N.Y.C., 1966-68; assoc., ptnr. Proskauer Rose LLP, N.Y.C., 1968—, mem. exec. com., 1990—93, co-chmn. Labor and Employment Law Dept., 2004—. Articles editor: Columbia Law Rev. Named One of 100 Best Lawyers in NY NY Mag., 1995, One of Best Lawyers in America, 1987—, One of Am.'s Leading Lawyers for Bus., Chambers USA, 2004-05, One of Best Lawyers in NY NY mag., 2005. Fellow Coll. Labor and Employment Lawyers; mem. Fed. Bar Coun., NY State Bar Assn., NY County Lawyers Assn., Assn. of Bar of City of NY (chair com. on sports law 2003-05). Office: Proskauer Rose LLP 1585 Broadway New York NY 10036-8299 Office Phone: 212-969-3035. Office Fax: 212-969-2900. Business E-Mail: hganz@proskauer.com.

GANZ, JULIAN, JR., retail executive; b. Dec. 1929; m. JoAnn Ganz. Pres. McMahan Furniture Stores, LA. Trustee LA County Mus. Art, Nat. Gallery Art, Washington, DC. Office: McMahan Furniture Stores 2237 Colby Ave Los Angeles CA 90064 Home: 137 S Rockingham Ave Los Angeles CA 90049*

GANZ, LOWELL, scriptwriter, television producer; b. NYC, Aug. 31, 1948; s. Irving and Jean (Farber) G.; m. Jeanne Russo, Dec. 26, 1976; 3 children. Student, Queens Coll., N.Y.C. Adj. prof.grad. film screenwriting USC. TV work includes: story editor The Odd Couple, ABC, 1972-74, producer Happy Days, ABC, 1975, 79-81, Laverne & Shirley, ABC, 1976-78, exec. producer Busting Loose, 1978-79, Joanie Loves Chachi (also dir.), 1982, all Paramount TV, (with Babaloo Mandel) Makin' It, ABC, 1979, Gung Ho, ABC, 1986, Knight and Daye, NBC, 1986, A League of Their Own, CBS, 1993, (pilots) Herndon, NBC, 1983, Take Five, CBS, 1987, Channel 99, CBS, 1987, Hiller and Diller, 1997; dir. TV series The Bad News Bears, 1979; screenwriter: (with Babaloo Mandel) Night Shift, 1982, Splash (Nat. Film Critics Screenplay of Yr. award), 1984, Spies Like Us, 1985, Gung Ho, 1986, Vibes, 1988, Parenthood, 1989, City Slickers, 1991, A League of Their Own, 1992, Mr. Saturday Night, 1992, Greedy, 1994, (with Dan Aykroyd and Babaloo Mandel), City Slickers II: The Legend of Curly's Gold, 1994, Forget Paris, 1995, Multiplicity, 1996, Father's Day, 1997, Edtv, 1999, Where the Heart Is, 2000, Robots, 2005, Fever Pitch, 2005.*

GANZARAIN, RAMON CAJIAO, psychoanalyst; b. Iquique, Chile, Apr. 18, 1923; s. Eusebio Ganzarain and Maria Cajiao; m. Matilde Vidal Soto, Oct. 10, 1953; children: Ramon, Mirentxu, Alejandro. BS, St. Ignacio Coll., Santiago, Chile, 1939; MD, U. Chile, Santiago, 1947; postgrad., Chilean Psychoanalytic Inst., 1947-50, cert. tng. analyst, 1953. Assoc. prof. psychiatry U. Chile, Santiago, 1955—68, dir. dept. med. edn., 1962—68; prof. depth psychology, sch. psychology Cath. U., Santiago, 1962—68; dir. Chilean Psychoanalytic Inst., Santiago, 1967—68; tng. analyst Topeka Inst. Psychoanalysis, 1968—87; dir. group psychotherapy svcs. Menninger Found., Topeka, 1978—87; geog. tng. analyst Columbia U. Ctr. for Psychoanalytic Tng. and Rsch., Atlanta, 1987; assoc. prof. psychiatry Emory U., Atlanta, 1988—; tng. analyst Emory U. Psychoanalytic Inst., 1988—; geog. tng. analyst Fla. Psychoanalytic Inst., 2000—. Interviewed by CNN on numerous topics concerning trauma and/or the Middle East conflict; lectr. on incest www.khecjc.org. Author: Fugitives of Incest, 1988, Object Relations Group Psychotherapy, 1989; contbr. articles to profl. jours., chapters to books. Fellow: Am. Group Psychotherapy Assn. (bd. dirs. 1984—87, 1993—96); mem.: AMA, Topeka Psychoanalytic Soc. (pres. 1985—87), Atlanta Psychoanalytic Soc., Kans. Med. Soc., Am. Psychoanalytic Assn., Internat. Psychoanalytic Assn., Internat. Assn. Group Therapy (bd. dirs., exec. counselor 1986). Roman Catholic. Avocations: music, swimming, photography, writing, collecting antarctic stamps. Office: Emory U Psychoanalytic Inst Dept Psychiatry PO Box AF Atlanta GA 30337-0503 Office Phone: 404-636-1415. Personal E-mail: rganzarain@aol.com.

GANZEL, DEWEY ALVIN, English language educator; b. Albion, Nebr., July 5, 1927; s. Dewey Alvin Ganzel Sr. and Frances Gross; m. Carol Henderson, July 27, 1955; children: Rebecca, Catherine, Emily. BS, U. Nebr., 1949; MA, U. Chgo., 1954, PhD, 1958. Prof. English Oberlin (Ohio) Coll., 1958-97. Chair Oberlin City Coun., 1976-84. Served in U.S. Navy, 1945-47, PTO. Fulbright scholar, 1952-53, 55-56. Office: Oberlin Coll Rice Hall Oberlin OH 44074 Business E-Mail: dewey.ganzel@oberlin.edu.

GANZI, VICTOR FREDERICK, publishing executive; b. NYC, Feb. 14, 1947; s. Walter John and Gertrude (Meyer) G.; m. Patricia Frances Martin, July 10, 1971; children: Danielle Martin, Victoria Louise. BS, Fordham U., 1968; JD, Harvard U., 1971; LLM in Taxation, NYU, 1981. Bar: NY 1973, U.S. Dist. Ct. (so. and ea. dists.) NY 1975, US Ct. Appeals (2d cir.) 1975, US Tax Ct. 1975; CPA, Colo. Tax acct. Touche Ross & Co., Denver, 1971-73; assoc. Rogers & Wells, NYC, 1973-78, ptnr., 1978-86; mng. ptnr. Rogers & Wells (now Clifford Chance Rogers & Wells), 1986-90; v.p., sec., gen. counsel Hearst Corp., NYC, 1990—92, CFO, chief legal officer, sr. v.p., 1992—97; pres. Hearst Books/Bus. Pub. Group, 1995—99; exec. v.p Hearst Corp, NYC, 1997—2002; COO Hearst Corp., NYC, 1998—2002, pres., CEO, 2002—. Bd. dirs. Palm Mgmt. Corp., NYC, PGA Tour, Inc., ESPN, NYC, IMI Sys. Inc., N.Y.C, NYC, Econ. Devel. Corp., Olsten Corp.; mem. Coun. future of Law Sch., NYU Sch. Law; chmn. Hearst Argyle TV, 2003—; spkr. in field. Bd. dirs. William Randolph Hearst Found., Hearst Found.; trustee Whitney Mus. Am. Art. Mem. ABA, AICPA, Colo. Soc. CPAs, Sky Club, Cherry Valley Club (Garden City, NY). Office: The Hearst Corp 959 8th Ave New York NY 10019-3795*

GAO, DENGLIANG, geologist, researcher; b. QianLing, Anhui, China, July 6, 1962; came to U.S., 1992; s. Rongtai and Jiaoying (Shi) G.; m. Lantong Zhai, Nov. 18, 1991. BS in Geology, Hefei (China) U. of Tech., 1983, MS in Geology, 1986, W.Va. U., 1994; PhD in Geology, Duke U., 1997. Lectr. Tongji U., Shanghai, China, 1986-91; tchg. asst., rsch. asst. W.Va. U., Morgantown, 1992-94; rsch. asst. Duke U., Durham, N.C., 1994-97; geologist Exxon Prodn. and Rsch. Co., Houston, 1997—. Editor: (textbook) Introductory Geology, 1990; contbr. articles to profl. jours. including Shanghai Geology, Earthquake Geology, North China Earthquake Scis. Recipient Sci. and Tech. Progress prize Nat. Edn. Commn. of China, 1991. Mem. AAAS, Am. Geophys. Union, Am. Assn. Petroleum Geologists, Geol. Soc. Am. Achievements include research on active fracture system in Shanhai that was successfully tested and confirmed by a 3.7 magnitude earthquake as predicted by active fault system; subsurface geologic structures and their control on petroleum (oil and gas) in central Appalachian Basin. Home and Office: Exxon Prodn Rsch Co Houston TX 77252

GAO, HONG, music educator; arrived in U.S., 1994; d. Lan Yang and Huiting Gao; m. Paul K. Dice, May 29, 1994; 1 child, Alida Dice. BA, Ctrl. Conservatory Music, Beijing, 1990. Faculty dept. music Carleton Coll., Northfield, Minn., 2003—. Composer: (commns.) Am. Composers Forum, The Jerome Found., Twin Cities Pub. TV, Ragamala Music and Dance Theater, Walker Art Ctr. and Theater Mu; performer: Lincoln Ctr. Festival, San Francisco Jazz Festival, Smithsonian Instn., Next Wave Festival, Festival d'Automne a Paris, Internat. Festival Perth, Festival de Teatro d'Europa, St. Paul Chamber Orch., Heidelberg (Germany) Philharmonic, Women's Philharmonic, Portland (Maine) Symphony, numerous others. Recipient First prize, Hebei Profl. Young Music Performers Competition, Asian Pacific award; Artist fellow for performing musicians, Mcknight, Minn., 1998, 2000, Artist Assistance fellow, Minn. State Arts Bd., Leadership Initiatives in Neighborhoods grantee, St. Paul Cos., 2000, Travel and Study grantee, Jerome Found. Office: Carleton Coll One N College St Northfield MN 55057 Office Phone: 507-646-4475. Business E-Mail: ghong@carleton.edu.

GAO, KEMING, psychiatrist; b. Weifang City, China, Nov. 10, 1959; s. Yufeng Gao and RuiLan Yu; m. Qifang Liu, Mar. 22, 1985; children: Gao, Hui, Winni. MD, Weifang Med. Coll., 1985; PhD, Shanghai (China) Med. U., 1994. Instr. Weifang Med. Coll., 1985—88, Shanghai Med. U., 1991—94; postdocoral fellow La. State U. Med. Ctr., Shreveport, 1994—96; rsch. assoc. U. Chgo., 1996—2000; resident MetroHealth Med. Ctr., Cleve., 2000—. Vis. fellow Internat. Brain Rsch. Orgn.-Croucher Found., 1994. Bipolar Rsch. fellow, U. Hosp. Cleve. Case Sch. of Medicine, 2004. Mem.: Internat. Brain Rsch. Orgn., Am. Psychiat. Assn., Soc. Neurosci. Office: MetroHealth Med Ctr 11400 Euclid Ave Ste 200 Cleveland OH 44106

GAO, MING, materials scientist, consultant; b. Shanghai, Dec. 10, 1936; came to U.S., 1979; s. KeJi Gao and ErXian Zhu. BS, Shanghai Jiao Tong U., 1959; MS, Lehigh U., 1982, PhD, 1983. Instr. Shanghai Jiao Tong U., China, 1959-78, assoc. prof., 1978-79, prof., 1985; vis. scholar Lehigh U., Bethlehem, Pa., 1979-80, rsch. asst., 1980-83, rsch. scientist, sr. rsch. scientist, 1987-92, prin. rsch. scientist, 1992-97; vis. prof. Santa Clara (Calif.) U., 1985-87; engring. advisor, cons. Mobil E&P Tech. Ctr., Dallas, 1998-99; sr. rsch. specialist Exxon Mobil Upstream Rsch. Co., Houston, 1999—2001; global integrity svcs. chief engr. GE PII Pipeline Solutions, Houston, 2001—. Author: Fractography & Failue Analysis, 1978; contbr. articles to profl. jours. Recipient grant NSF, 1992-95, 95-98, grant FAA, 1993-97, grant Air Force Office of Sci. Rsch., 1992-97. Mem. ASM Internat., ASTM, Sigma Xi. Achievements include development of fundamental understanding of mechanical, metallurgical and chemical aspects of subcritical crack growth (namely, hydrogen embrittlement, stress corrsion cracking, high-temperature crack growth, and corrosion fatigue) in ferrous alloys, aluminum alloys, titanium alloys, nickel-base alloys, and intermetallics. Office: PII Pipeline Solutions GE Power Systems 2707 North Loop West Ste 600 Houston TX 77008 E-mail: ming.gas@og.ge.com, ming1014@aol.com.

GAO, PENG, research scientist; PhD, SUNY, 2003. Engr. Chengdu Inst. Mountain Disaster and Environment, China, 1993—97; postdoctoral rschr. U. Calif., Davis, 2003—. Office: U Calif One Shields Ave Davis CA 95616

GAO, WEIMIN M., microbiologist, phytopathologist; b. Daxian, Sichuan Province, China, Apr. 29, 1965; s. Zhiji J. Gao and Chensheng S. Zhao; m. Xi Wang, June 12, 1968; children: Bide (Peter) B, Bijei (Anthony) B. BS, Sichuan U., 1986; MS, Beijing Agrl. U., 1993; PhD, Pa. State U., 2001. Instr. Beijing Agrl. U., 1986—91; lectr. China Agrl. U., 1991—97; rsch. asst. Pa. State U., University Park, 1997—2001; rsch. assoc. Oak Ridge Nat. Lab., Tenn., 2001—. Ext. educator China Agrl. U., 1986—97. Recipient Honor Tchr. for Tchg. Excellence, Beijing Agrl. U., 1988, Lester P. Nichols Meml. award, Pa. State U., 1999, Student Travel award, Genetics Soc. Am., 1999; fellow, Pa. State U., 1997—2001. Mem.: Am. Soc. Microbiology, Am. Phytopathological Soc. Home: 219 W Fairview Rd Oak Ridge TN 37830 Office: Oak Ridge Nat Lab Building 1505 MS 6038 Oak Ridge TN 37831 Personal E-mail: wxg118@yahoo.com.

GAO, WENZHONG, science educator, researcher; s. Deen Gao and Ailian Shen; m. Dana Zhao; children: Ted, Tommy. PhD, Ga. Inst. Tech., 2002. Asst. rsch. prof. Miss. State U., Starkville, 2002—. Author: (jour. article) Transactions on Energy Conversion. Mem.: IEEE. Achievements include research in hybrid electric vehicle, electric machines, power systems modeling, simulation, design, and analysis. Office: Center For Advanced Vehicular Systems Miss State Univ Starkville MS 39759 E-mail: wg42@msstate.edu.

GAOLACH, BRAD WAYNE, academic administrator, director; b. Detroit Lakes, Minn., Apr. 25, 1967; s. James P Klepetka and Janet M Schroeder; m. Collene J Rasmussen, June 14, 2000. PhD, U. of Wash., 2001; MS, NC State U., 1995; BS, U. of Wash., 1992; BA, U. of Wash., Seattle, WA, 2001. Legislative asst. Minn. State Rep., St. Paul, 1989—89; rsch. asst. Dept. of Zoology, U. of Wash., Seattle, 1989—92; area ext. agt. Wash. State U. Ext., Renton, Wash., 2001—, interim dir., 2003—. Systems programer Self Employed, Seattle, 1992—92; vis. scientist Internat. Rice Rsch. Inst., Los Banos, Philippines, 1995—95; affiliate faculty Dept. of Entomology, Wash. State U., Pullman, Wash., 2002—. Author: (book chapter) Sixth International Symposium on Molecular Plant-Microbe Interactions; contbr. articles to prof. jours. Mem. Western Wash. Horticulture Assn., Wash., 2002—04, Cultivating Success Adv. Bd., Wash., 2002—04; advisor King County Agrl. Commn., Seattle, Wash., 2001—04; mem. King Conservation Dist., Renton, Wash., 2001—04; adv. King County Noxious Weed Bd., Seattle, Wash., 2001—04. Recipient Charlotte Cornell Crary award for Excellence in Tchg. Introductory Biology, U. of Wash., 2000; fellow Achievement Rewards for Coll. Scientist (ARCS), Achievement Rewards for Coll. Scientist (ARCS), Seattle, 1996-1998, Pre-doctoral Fellowship, NSF, 1993-1997, Math. Biology Tng. Grant, Dept. of Zoology, U. of Wash., 1999; grantee Organic control options for flea beetles on arugula, Western Sustainable Agr. Rsch. and Edn., 2003—04, Tng. Environ. Stewards: Integrating Water Quality & Quantity Edn. from Mountain to Ocean, USDA, 2002—05, King County Agrl. Drainage Maintenance, King County, Wash., 2001—06, Use of Cover Crops to Control Insect Pests in Brassicaceae crop prodn., Organic Farming Rsch. Found., 2000, Wash. State Commn. on Pesticide Registration, 2000, Food $ense: King County, Food Stamp Nutrition Edn. Program, 2003, Farming for the Future: Bringing the next generation of farmers to the land, Western Sustainable Agrl. Rsch. and Edn., 2003-2005, Conservation Tools for Landowners, Wash. Dept. of Ecology, 2003-2004, Bioagents for Invasive Weed Species Project, US Forest Svc., 2003-2004, Integrating Biol. Control into Cole Crop Prodn. in the Pacific NW, Western Sustainable Agrl. Rsch. and Edn., 2002-2005; scholar Rsch. Assistantship, NC Agrl. Rsch. Svc. / Coll. of Agr. & Life Sciences, 1992. Mem.: Wash. Sustainable Food and Farming Network, Entomol. Soc. of Am., Phi Sigma, Phi Beta Kappa. Office: Washington State University Extension 919 SW Grady Way Suite 120 Renton WA 98055 Office Phone: 206-205-3110. E-mail: gaolach@wsu.edu.

GAONA, ARLENE, secondary school educator; b. Paterson, NJ, Apr. 26, 1958; d. Grossman Frieda and Grossman Paul; m. J. Gaona, July 24, 1983; children: Sara, Rebecca. BA, Rowan U., NJ, 1980; MA, Georgian Ct. U., NJ, 1991. Cert. Spl. Edn. NJ, 1981, Early Childhood NJ, 1980, Elem. Edn. NJ, 1980. Tchr. Rocking Horse Day Sch., Passaic Park, NJ, 1980, No. Valley Regional Dist., Demarest, NJ, 1980—82; h.s. resource tchr. Fair Lawn H.S., NJ, 1982—84; spl. ed tchr. Wall H.S., NJ, 1984—. Author: (presentation) Teaching At Risk Youth (Governor's Grant for New and Innovative Tchg., 1993). V.p., pres. Temple Beth Am, Lakewood, NJ, 2000—, pres., 2005. Recipient Finalist Miss Teenage NJ., Miss Teenage NJ., 1975; grantee Penpal project, Wall Found. for Ednl. Excellence, 2000, 2003. Mem.: Wall Twp. Edn. Assn., NEA, NJ. Ednl. Assn., Rising Star Parents Assn. Jewish. Avocations: travel, theater, dance. Office: Wall High Sch PO Box 1199 Wall NJ 07719 Office Phone: 732-556-2000. Personal E-mail: mamagaona@aol.com. E-mail: agaona@wall.k12.nj.us.

GAPPA, JUDITH M., academic administrator; Student, Wellesley Coll., 1957-60; BA in Music, George Washington U., 1968, MA in Musicology, 1970; EdD in Ednl. Adminstrn., Utah State U., 1973; cert. Inst. for Ednl. Mgmt., Harvard U., 1980. Lectr. George Washington U., Washington, 1968-69; dir. fine arts program The York Sch., Monterey, Calif., 1970; program cons. Western Interstate Commn. for Higher Edn., Boulder, Colo., 1973; coord. affirmative action program Utah State U., Logan, 1973-75, dir. affirmative action/equal opportunity programs, asst. prof., 1975-77, 78-80, project dir., 1979-81; sr. staff assoc. Nat. Ctr. for Higher Edn. Mgmt. Systems, Inc., Boulder, 1977-78; assoc. v.p. for faculty affairs, dean of faculty, prof. San Francisco State U., 1980-91; sr. assoc. Am. Assn. Higher Edn., 1995-97; prof. Purdue U., West Lafayette, Ind., 1991—, v.p. human rels., 1991-98. Served on numerous coms., couns. Utah State U., San Francisco State U.; cons. Assn. Governing Bds., 1994, U. Mich., Duluth, 1992, Calif. State U. Human Resources Mgmt. Office, 1992, Am. U., Washington, 1987, No. Rockies Consortium for Higher Edn. Conf., 1985, So. Utah State Coll., 1982, Nat. Ctr. for Rsch. in Vocat. Edn., 1980-81, Hood Coll., 1982-84, Am. Insts. for Rsch. in Behavioral Scis., 1980-81; condr. workshops on edn. Co-author: The Invisible Faculty, 1993; mem. editl. bd. Rev. of Higher Edn., 1994-97; contbr. numerous articles to profl. jours. Grantee Lilly Endowment, 1995, United Techs. Corp., 1992, TIAA-CREF/Lilly Endowment, 1990, Calif. State U., 1985, San Francisco State U., 1981, HEW, 1979-81, Nat. Inst. Edn., 1977, Utah State U., 1977, Fed. workshop grant, 1976, State of Utah, 1975, 76. Mem. Western Assn. Schs. and Colls. (accreditation team mem. Calif. State U.-L.A. 1990), Am. Assn. for Higher Edn. (sr. assoc. Washington chpt. 1995-97), Assn. for Study of Higher Edn. (nat. adv. bd. ASHE-ERIC Higher Edn. Report Series 1990-91, editl. bd. Rev. of Higher Edn. 1994-97, nominating com. 1986-87, program com. for 1986 nat. conf., membership com. 1982-84, conf. com. 1983, editl. bd. Rev. of Higher Edn. 1994-97), Am. Coun. on Edn. Nat. Identification Program (No. Calif. state coord. 1988-91). Office: Purdue Univ Coll Edn 1446 Liberal Arts Rd West Lafayette IN 47907-1075

GARABEDIAN, BETTY MARIE, retired elementary school educator; b. Worcester, Mass., June 24, 1928; d. Henry L. and Marie A. (Holquist) Olson; m. Peter Garabedian, Aug. 20, 1960. BA in humanities, Bob Jones U., 1950; MEd, Boston U., 1961. Elem. tchr. Town of Shrewsbury, Mass., 1950-54, remedial reading tchr., 1950-57; elem. supr. Auburn, Mass., 1957-67; elem. tchr. grades 5th & 6th and music tchr. Douglas, Mass., 1967-87. Pres. Shrewsbury Tchrs. Club Assn., 1954-56, Auburn Tchrs. Assn., 1960-61. Recipient Horace Mann Outstanding Tchr. award, State of Mass., 1985-86. Mem. Boston U. Alumni, AAUW, Christian Appalachian Project; Delta Kappa Gamma (pres. 1961-62). Baptist. Avocations: sacred, Gospel, and classical music, reading the Bible, non-fiction/biographies, hospitality.

GARABEDIAN, CHARLES, artist; b. Detroit, 1923; MFA, UCLA, 1961. Solo shows include LaJolla (Calif.) Mus. Art, 1966, CeJee Gallery, N.Y., 1966, 67, Eugenia Butler Gallery, L.A., 1970, Newspace Gallery, L.A., 1974, Whitney Mus. Am. Art, N.Y.C., 1976, Broxton Gallery, L.A., 1976, L.A. Louver Gallery, Venice, Calif., 1979, 83, 86, 89, 90, 92, 94, 96, LaJolla Mus. Contemporary Art, 1981, Ruth S. Schaffner Gallery, Santa Barbara, Calif., 1982, Rose Art Mus., Waltham, Mass., 1983, Hirschl & Adler Modern Mus., N.Y.C., 1984, Gallery Paule Anglim, San Francisco, 1985, 93, 98, numerous others; exhibited in group shows at numerous mus. including Rose Art Mus., The High Mus., Atlanta, 1980, Emanuel Walter Gallery, San Francisco, 1981, LaJolla Mus. Contemporary Art, 1981, Mizumo Gallery, L.A., 1981, Mandeville Art Gallery, San Diego, Oakland Mus. Art, 1981, Brooke Alexander Gallery, N.Y., 1982, Kunst Mus., Luzern, 1983, Fresno Art Ctr., 1983, Tibor de Nagy Gallery, N.Y.C., 1983, Hirshhorn Mus. and Sculpture Garden, Smithsonian Instn., Washington, 1984, Newport Harbor Art Mus., Calif., 1984, El Museo Rufino Tamayo, Mexico City, 1984, L.A. Mcpl. Art Gallery, 1984, L.A. Louver, Venice, 1985, Whitney Mus. Art, 1986, DiLaurenti

Gallery, N.Y., 1986, R.C. Erpf Gallery, N.Y., 1987, N.Y. State Mus., Albany, 1987, Richard Green Gallery, 1988, Bklyn. Mus. Art, 1989, James Corcoran Gallery, 1991, Riva Yares Gallery, Scottsdale, Ariz., 1994, Hirschl & Adler Mus., 1996, Mcpl. Art Gallery L.A., 1997; pub. collections include Met. Mus. Art, N.Y.C., Whitney Mus. Am. Art, Mus. Contemporary Art, L.A., Rose Art Mus., San Diego Mus. Contemporary Art, L.A. County Mus. Art Staff sgt. USAF, 1942-45. John Simon Guggenheim Meml. Found. fellow, 1979, Nat. Endowment for the Arts fellow, 1977. Dealer: L A Louver 45 Venice Blvd Venice CA 90291 Office Phone: 310-822-4955.

GARABEDIAN, PAUL ROESEL, mathematics professor; b. Cin., Aug. 2, 1927; s. Carl A. and Margaret (Roesel) G.; m. Gladys Rappaport, Oct. 22, 1949 (div. 1963); m. Lynnel Marg, Dec. 31, 1966; children: Emily, Catherine. AB, Brown U., 1946; A.M., Harvard U., 1947, PhD, 1948. Asst. prof. math. U. Calif.-Berkeley, 1949-50; asst. prof. Stanford U., Calif., 1950-52, assoc. prof., 1952-56, prof., 1956-59; prof. math. Courant Inst., NYU, 1959—; dir. Courant Math. and Computing Lab. Dept. Energy, 1972-78, dir. div. computational fluid dynamics, 1978—. Mem. editl. bd. Internat. Jour. Computational Fluid Dynamics, Applicable Analysis; contbr. articles to profl. jours. NRC fellow, 1948-49, Sloan Found. fellow, 1961-63, Guggenheim fellow, 1966, 81-82, Fairchild Disting. scholar Calif. Inst. Tech., 1975; recipient Pub. Service Group Achievement award NASA, 1976, Boris Pregal award N.Y. Acad. Scis., 1980. Fellow Am. Phys. Soc.; mem. NAS (Applied Math. and Numerical Analysis prize 1998), Am. Acad. Arts and Scis., Am. Math. Soc. (Birkhoff prize 1983), Soc. Indsl. and Applied Math. (von Karman prize 1989). Home: 60 E 8th St Apt 9K New York NY 10003-2101 Office: New York University 251 Mercer St New York NY 10012-1110 Office Phone: 212-998-3237. Business E-Mail: garabedi@cims.nyu.edu.

GARABEDIAN-URBANOWSKI, MARTHA ANN, foreign language educator; b. Whitinsville, Mass., Dec. 8, 1953; d. Charles and Sadie (Madanjian) G.; m. William John Urbanowski, Jr., June 8, 1991. BA summa cum laude, Worcester State Coll., 1975; MA, U. Conn., 1978, PhD, 1984. Grad. tchg. asst. in Spanish U. Conn., Storrs, 1975-79; vis. asst. prof., lectr. Spanish Assumption Coll., Worcester, Mass., 1984-90; prof. Spanish Western New Eng. Coll., Springfield, Mass., 1990—. Adj. prof. Spanish, Worcester State Coll., fall 1985. Contbr. articles to profl. jours. The Josefina Romo-Arregui Meml. scholar U. Conn., Storrs, 1983. Mem. MLA, N.E. MLA, Am. Coun. on the Tchg. Fgn. Langs., Am. Assn. Tchrs. Spanish and Portuguese, Mass. Fgn. Lang. Assn., Worcester Art Mus., The Smithsonian, Libr. Congress, Phi Kappa Phi, Kappa Delta Pi. Armenian Evangelical. Avocations: golf, music, art, reading, travel. Home: 21 Pine Ridge Rd Southbridge MA 01550-2139 Office: Western New Eng Coll 1215 Wilbraham Rd Springfield MA 01119-2612

GARAFALO, LYNNE MARY, audiologist, speech pathology/audiology services professional; b. Boston, Apr. 29, 1954; d. Ralph Dominic and Maria Lenore (Tedeschi) G.; m. Robert Joseph Dalicandro, Mar. 22, 1975 (div. Dec. 1982); m. Edwin Joel Furman, Dec. 31, 1995. BS, Northeastern U., 1977, MS, 1992. Cert. clin. competence; lic. speech/lang. pathologist and audiologist. Speech pathologist Worcester (Mass.) Pub. Schs., 1978-90, audiologist, 1992—. Mem. traumatic brain injury team Worcester Pub. Schs., 1995—, co-founder hard of hearing program, 1995—, mem. ctrl. auditory processing com., 1998—, cochlear implant team, 2000—. Com. mem. Yankee Homecoming, Newburyport, Mass., 1992-94. Mem. Am. Speech and Hearing Assn. (ACE award 1999), Mass. Speech-Hearing Assn. Avocations: athletics, travel. Home: 8 Goulding Rd Sterling MA 01564

GARAGIOLA, JOE, JR., baseball team executive; m. Noel Garagiola; children: Meredith, Valerie, Natalie, Christopher. BA cum laude, U. Notre Dame, 1972; JD, Georgetown U., 1975. Bar: Ariz., Calif., N.Y. Gen. counsel, asst. to pres. N.Y. Yankees, N.Y.C.; ptnr. Gallagher and Kennedy, Phoenix, 1982—; chmn. bd. dirs. Phoenix Met. Sports Found., 1985-87; v.p., gen. mgr. Ariz. Diamondbacks (profl. baseball expansion team), 1995—. Vice chmn. Gov.'s Cactus League Task Force, Phoenix; mem. Mayor's profl. baseball com.; chmn. Maricopa County (Ariz.) Sports Authority, Ariz. Baseball Commn. Bd. dirs. Am. West Airlines Ednl. Found., Phoenix Meml. Hosp. Recipient Inst. Human Rels. award, Am. Jewish Com., 1998. Office: c/o Ariz Diamondbacks 401 E Jefferson St Phoenix AZ 85004-2438*

GARANZINI, MICHAEL J., academic administrator; b. St. Louis; BA in Psychology, St. Louis U., 1971; MA in Am. Civilization, NYU, 1978; MDiv, Weston Sch. Theology, 1980; STM in Moral Devel., U. Calif., Berkeley, 1981, PhD in Psychology and Religion, 1986. Part-time faculty mem. U. San Francisco, 1984—86, asst. prof. dept. psychology, 1986—88, asst. prof. dept. ednl. psychology Sch. Edn., 1986—88; assoc. prof. edn. St. Louis U., 1988—98, acting v.p. student devel., 1991—92, asst. acad. v.p., 1992—93, acting acad. v.p., 1993—94, acad. v.p., 1994—98; vis. prof. counseling Fordham U., 1998—99; spl. asst. to the pres., acting chair dept. psychology Georgetown U., 1999—2001; pres. Loyola U., Chgo., 2001—. Vis. prof. psychology and family studies grad. divsn. Gregorian U., 1986. 88. Author: The Attachment Cycle: An Object Relations Approach to the Healing Ministries, 1987, Child-Centered Schools: An Educator's Guide to Family Dysfunction, 1995. Office: Loyola Univ Chgo Office of the Pres 820 N Michigan Ave Chicago IL 60611

GARAUFIS, NICHOLAS G., district court judge; b. Paterson, N.J., 1948; AB, Columbia Coll., 1969; JD, Columbia U., 1974. Assoc. Chadbourne & Parke, 1974-75; asst. atty. gen. N.Y. State, 1975-78; pvt. practice Queens, N.Y., 1978-86; counsel to Hon. Claire Shulman/Pres. of Borough of Queens, N.Y.C., 1986-95; chief counsel FAA, Washington, 1995-2000; judge ea. dist. U.S. Dist. Ct., Bklyn., 2000—. Office: US Dist Ct Ea Dist NY 225 Cadman Plz E Brooklyn NY 11201

GARB, HOWARD NEIL, clinical psychologist, educator; b. Chgo., Jan. 27, 1955; s. Julius and Suzanne Rhoda (Weinberg) G.; m. Flora Horowitz, Sept. 20, 1981; children: Merrick, Leanna. BA in Psychology with high distinction, U. Ill., 1977, MA, 1981, PhD, 1983. Lic. psychologist Bur. Profl. and Occupl. Affairs, Pa. NIMH postdoctoral fellow Northwestern U., Evanston, Ill., 1983-84; clin. psychologist VA Health Care Sys., Pitts., 1984—2003; clin. instr. psychiatry U. Pitts., 1984-99, clin. asst. prof., 2000—02, clin. assoc. prof., 2002—03; chief Psychology Rsch. Svc. Wilford Hall Med. Ctr., Lackland AFB, Tex., 2003—. Author: Studying the Clinician, 1998; contbr. articles profl. jours. Psychol. Bull., popular sci. mags. Sci. Am. Fellow APA (divsn. 12 clin. psychology sect.); mem. Soc. for Sci. of Clin. Psychology (sect. III). Jewish. Achievements include description of the validity of judgments made by mental health professionals; description of occurrence of race bias and gender bias in clinical assessment; description of reasons why clinicians have trouble learning from clinical experience. Avocation: jazz music. Home: 3670 Hunters Cliff San Antonio TX 78230 Office: Psychology Rsch Svc Wilford Hall Med Ctr 2200 Bergquist Dr Ste 1 San Antonio TX 78236-5300 Office Phone: 210-671-4084. E-mail: howard.garb@lackland.af.mil.

GARBACZ, GREGORY A., lawyer; b. Columbus, Ind., May 21, 1967; s. Gerald G. and Jane Elizabeth (Snyder) Garbacz; m. Lauren Krause, Sept. 17, 1995; children: Luke, Matthew. BA in Govt. and Law, Lafayette Coll., 1989; JD, Washington and Lee U., 1993. Shareholder, COO Klinedinst PC, San Diego, 1993—. Contbr. articles to profl. jours. Office: Klinedinst PC 777 S Figueroa Ste 4700 Los Angeles CA 90017-3584 Business E-Mail: ggarbacz@klinedinstlaw.com.

GARBARINI, WILLIAM NICHOLAS, pharmaceutical executive; b. Somerville, N.J., Oct. 24, 1969; s. William Nicholas and Janet L. Garbarini; m. Maureen Elizabeth Murphy, June 10, 1995; children: Dana Marie, William Nicholas. BS in Econs., Coll. N.J., 1992; MBA in Pharm. Studies, Fairleigh Dickinson U., 2002. Profl. sales rep. Glaxo SmithKline, Research Triangle Park, NC, 1993—96; account supr. Lowe Healthcare Worldwide, N.Y., 1996—98; product mgr. Key Pharmaceuticals Schering-Plough Corp., Kenilworth, NJ, 1998—2000; dir. client svcs. Caresoft, Inc., Sunnyvale, Calif., 2000—01; dir. mktg. sr. Ferring Pharmaceuticals Inc., Suffern, NY, 2001—. Named Premier Performer, Burroughs Wellcome Co., 1994—95; recipient Dir. Leading Change award, 1995. Mem.: Excellence Club, Delta Mu Delta, Phi Kappa Psi (chpt. pres. 1991—92). Roman Catholic. Avocations: music, baseball, golf. Home: 32 Dunham Avenue Cranford NJ 07016 Office: Ferring Pharmaceuticals Inc 400 Rella Boulevard Suite 300 Suffern NY 10901 Office Phone: 845-770-2640. Office Fax: 845-770-2662. E-mail: william.garbarini@ferring.com.

GARBATY, THOMAS JAY, retired English language educator; b. Jan. 10, 1930; BA, Haverford Coll., 1951; MA, U. Pa., 1954, PhD, 1957. Asst. prof. English Dept. Clemson U., 1957-60; mem. faculty dept. English, U. Mich., Ann Arbor, 1960-93, prof. 1971-1993, prof. emeritus, 1993—. Vis. prof. U. Bern, Switzerland, 1970-80; TV commentator, PBS. Contbg. author Variorum Chaucer, 1970-90; asst. editor: Middle English Dictionary, 1960-61; mem. editl. bd. Genre, Envoi; editor Medieval English Lit., 1984—; contbr. to Medieval England, an Encyclopedia and Modern Language Assn. Approaches to Teaching the Canterbury Tales; reviewer, contbr. articles to profl. jours. Recipient Amoco Tchg. award, 1968, State of Mich. Tchg. Excellence award, 1990, First Biennial award U. Mich. Students with Disabilities, 1991. Mem. MLA (life, chmn. divsn. on Chaucer 1976), Medieval Acad., New Chaucer Soc., Phi Beta Kappa. Home: 2981 Hickory Ln Ann Arbor MI 48104-2840 Office: U Mich Dept English Ann Arbor MI 48109 E-mail: tgarbaty@umich.edu.

GARBER, ALAN MICHAEL, internist, educator, economist; s. Harry Garber; m. Anne Yahanda, Oct. 9, 1988. AB in Econs. summa cum laude, Harvard Coll., 1976, AM in Econs., 1977, PhD in Econs., 1982; MD, Stanford U., 1983. Diplomate Am. Bd. Internal Medicine. Cons. Inst. Medicine, Washington, 1979-80; clin. fellow Med. Sch. Harvard U., Boston, 1983-86, rsch. fellow John F. Kennedy Sch. Govt. Cambridge, Mass., 1986; staff physician VA Palo Alto (Calif.) Health Care System, 1986—; rsch. assoc. Nat. Bur. Econ. Rsch., Palo Alto, Calif., 1986—, dir. health care program Cambridge, 1990—; asst. prof. Stanford (Calif.) U., 1986-93, assoc. prof., 1993-98, dir. Ctr. Health Policy/Ctr. Primary Care and Outcomes Rsch., 1997—, prof. medicine, 1998—, Henry J. Kaiser jr. prof., endowed chair; contractor Office Tech. Assessment, Washington, 1987-88, 89-92. Chair Med. & Surgical Prodedures Panel Medicare Coverage Adv. Com., 1999—2003; mem. Nat. Adv. Coun. Aging, 2004—, chair, 2005—. Grad. fellow NSF, 1976, Henry J. Kaiser faculty fellow Kaiser Found., 1989-92. Fellow ACP, Acad. Health; mem. Inst. Medicine of NAS, Soc. Med. Decision Making (trustee 1989-91), Am. Econ. Assn., Am. Fedn. Clin. Rsch. (nat. councillor 1991-96), Soc. Gen. Internal Medicine, Am. Soc. for Clin. Investigation, Assn. Am. Physicians, Internat. Health Econs. Assn. Office: Primary Care Outcomes Rsch Ctr Health Policy 117 Encina Commons Stanford CA 94305-6019 Office Phone: 650-723-0920. Business E-Mail: garber@stanford.edu.

GARBER, BETH CAROL, early childhood educator, music educator; b. Miami Beach, Fla., Oct. 1, 1952; d. Seymour Albert Bender and Marian Jane Ascher; m. Harold Garber, Feb. 19, 1984; 1 child, Mathew Eric. BS in Edn., U. Hartford, 1974; MA in Student Personnel Svcs., Kean Coll. N.J., 1981; MA in Rehab. counseling, Seton Hall U., South Orange, N.J., 1985. Cert. tchr. handicapped N.J., 1975, student personnel svc. instr. N.J., 1982, rehab. counselor N.J., 1985, elem. tchr. N.J., 1991. Resource rm. tchr. Lafayette Mid. Sch., Elizabeth, NJ, 1975—78, Battin Career Ctr., Elizabeth, NJ, 1978—81; learning resource ctr. tchr. Union County Regional High Schs., Springfield, NJ, 1981—83; rehab. specialist Ctrl. Rehab. Assocs., Freehold, NJ, 1985—87; music specialist tchr. Sundance Sch., North Plainfield, NJ, 1988—90; nursery dir., lead tchr. Bayonne Jewish Cmty. Ctr., NJ, 1990—91; music tchr. TMR program Jointure for Cmty. Adult Edn., Bound Brook, NJ, 1992—95; head tchr., music specialist Wee People, Bound Brook, NJ, 1991—96; music specialist Jewish Edn. Assn., Ctr. for Spl. Edn., Whippany, NJ, 1996—; head tchr., music dir. Mountain Top Presch. and Kindergarten, Warren, NJ, 1996—. Ednl. cons. Teen Parent Program, Elizabeth, NJ, 1978; Judaic programming cons. Mountain Top Presch. and Kindergarten, Warren, NJ, 1996—, mentor, 2000—01. Vol. Somerset County Food B ank, Bound Brook, NJ; mem. Somerset County Mental Health Players, Bridgewater, NJ; coord. Interfaith Hospitality Network, Temple Beth-El, Hillsborough, NJ, 2002—, founding mem. adult choir, mem., past pres. Sisterhood, 1996—98. Named Outstanding Child Care Profl., Somerset Alliance for the Future, 1993; fellowship, Seton Hall U., 1983. Mem.: Nat. Assn. Edn. of Young Children, N.J. Assn. for Edn. of Young Children, Rho Chi Sigma (pres. 1983—84). Avocations: guitar, family and friends, reading, travel, performing in community theater.

GARBER, DONALD, Major League Soccer commissioner; b. 1960; married; 2 children. BA Business, Journalism, State University of New York, College at Oneonta. Marketing mgr. NFL Properties, 1984—88, dir., marketing, 1988—90, v.p., business development and special events, 1990—96; pres. NFL International, 1996—99; commissioner Major League Soccer, 1999—. Mem.: National Soccer Hall of Fame Board of Trustees, United States Soccer Foundation, United States Soccer Federation Executive Committee. Office: c/o MLS 110 E 42nd st 10th Fl New York NY 10017*

GARBER, MORRIS WILLIAM, retired pharmacist, historian, educator; b. Passaic, NJ, Dec. 5, 1928; s. Louis and Ethel S. Garber; m. Phyllis Joan Gruber, Aug. 6, 1959; children: Miriam Beth, Joshua Seth. BSc in Pharmacy, Rutgers U., 1952, MA in History, 1958, PhD in History, 1968. Registered pharmacist 1953. History instr. Rutgers U., New Brunswick, NJ, 1960—68, asst. prof. history, 1968—72; pharmacist Two Guys, Manalapan, NJ, 1972—81, Lane Drugs, Lakewood, NJ, 1982—88, Cunningham Pharmacy, Hightown, NJ, 1988—97; ret. Rev. editor NJ History, Newark, 1973—76. Cpl. U.S. Army, 1953—55, Korea. Mem.: Orgn. Am. Historians, Am. Hist. Assn., Nat. Cmty. Pharmacists Assn. Jewish. Home: 4 Lowell Rd Manalapan NJ 07726

GARBER, PAUL WILLIAM, lawyer; b. Boston, Nov. 16, 1934; s. Rubin Elias and Sarah Rose Garber. AB in Medieval History magna cum laude, Harvard Coll., 1956, JD, 1961; diploma in Command and Staff, U.S. Naval War Coll., 1967, diploma in Naval Warfare, 1970. Registered Land Court Title Examiner, 1966. Atty. Garber and Garber, Esqs., Boston, 1961—, pres.; consul. Consulate of Chile, Boston, 1974—. Author: (with Philip C. Garber) The Political Constitution of Chile-An English Translation, 1981; contbr. articles to profl. jours. Pres. constn. chpt. Naval Res. Assoc., 1973-75, Navy Chpt. 5 Res. Officers Assn., 1979, First Region Naval Res. Assn., 1980, exec. v.p. 1971-72, Club Chileno, hon. pres., 1974-80, dir. Alumni Assoc., West End House, 1963-99, Scholarship Com., 1976-99, bd. dirs. Eastern Mass. chpt. Navy League U.S., 1976-85; judge Adv. Mass. Bay Coun., NLUS, 1985-99, dir. emeritus, 1999—; trustee USS Constitution Mus., 2003—. Capt. USNR, 1956-86. Decorated Navy Achievement medal USN, knight comdr. order Bernardo O'Higgins, Govt. Chile, 1979, grand officer, 1999. Mem.: Naval War Coll. Found. (life), Surface Warfare Assn. (life), USS Constn. Mus. (life), Navy League U.S. (life), Medieval Acad. Am. (life), USN Inst. (life), Mil. Officers Assn. Am. (life), Boston Athenaeum (life), Caleuche Club Litoral Valparaiso, Wardroom Club, Harvard Club of Boston. Avocations: gardening, reading, antiquarian rsch. Office: Consulate of Chile 1 Bernardo O'Higgins Cir Brighton MA 02135 Office Phone: 617-232-0416. E-mail: conchile.org@comcast.net.

GARBER, ROBERT EDWARD, lawyer, insurance company executive; b. N.Y.C., Jan. 4, 1949; s. Edward Robert and Estelle (Rosenberg) G.; m. Mary Ellen Roche, Jan. 17, 1981; 1 child, Edward Thomas AB, Princeton U., 1970; JD, Columbia U., 1973. Bar: N.Y. 1974. Law clk. U.S. Dist. Ct. (so. dist.), N.Y.C., 1973-75; assoc. Debevoise, Plimpton, Lyons & Gates, N.Y.C., 1976-79; assoc. counsel, v.p. Irving Trust, N.Y.C., 1979-82, sr. v.p., 1982-87; gen. counsel Irving Bank Corp. and Irving Trust Co., N.Y.C., 1987-89; sr. v.p., dep. gen. counsel Equitable Life Assurance Soc. U.S., N.Y.C., 1989-93; sr. v.p., gen. counsel Equitable Cos., Inc. and Equitable Life Assurance Soc. U.S., 1993-94, exec. v.p., gen. counsel, 1994-99; exec. v.p., chief legal officer Equitable Life Assurance Soc. U.S., 1999—2001; exec. v.p., gen. counsel AXA Fin., Inc., 1999—2001. Served to capt. USAR, 1970-78 Home: 45 Sturgis Rd Bronxville NY 10708-5012

GARBER, SAMUEL B., lawyer, retail executive; b. Chgo., Aug. 16, 1934; s. Morris and Yetta G.; m. Marietta C. Bratta; children: Debra Lee, Diane Lori. JD, U. Ill., 1958; MBA, U. Chgo., 1968. Bar: Ill. 1958. Ptnr. Brown, Dashow and Langluttig, Chgo., 1960-62; corp. counsel Walgreen Co., 1962-69; gen. counsel, exec. asst. to the pres. Carlyle & Co., 1969-73; dir. legal affairs Stop & Shop Co., Inc., 1973-74; v.p., gen. counsel Goldblatt Bros., Inc., 1974-76; v.p., sec., gen. counsel, dir. Evans, Inc., 1976-99, pres., CEO, 1999-2000; prof. mgmt. DePaul U., 1975—; prin. The Garber Group, Bus. Cons. and Turnaround Management Firm, Chgo., 2000—. Adj. prof. bus. law grad. sch. bus. U. Chgo., 1993; arbitrator N.Y. Stock Exch., 1996, Chgo. Merc. Exch., 1996, Am. Stock Exch., 1997, Nat. Futures Assn., 1997; columnist Garber's Gurus, Tribune Media Svcs., 1999-2001. With U.S. Army, 1958-60. Mem. ABA, NYSE (arbitrator 1996—), Am. Arbitration Assn. (arbitrator 1993, mediator 1994—), Nat. Retail Fedn., Ill. Retail Mchts. Assn., Beta Gamma Sigma. Home: 2626 N Lakeview Ave Chicago IL 60614-1809 Office: DePaul U 1 E Jackson Blvd Ste 7010 Chicago IL 60604-2287 Business E-Mail: thegarbergroup@yahoo.com, sgarber@depaul.edu.

GARBIN, ALBENO PATRICK, sociology educator; b. Girard, Ill., June 20, 1932; s. Cipriano and Angelina (Sommavillia) G.; m. Carol Townsend Nichols, Sept. 3, 1969; children: Angela Marie, Tina Ann, A. Patrick, Carol Anne. AB, Blackburn Coll., 1956; MA, La. State U., 1959, PhD, 1963. Instr., asst. prof. sociology U. Omaha, 1961-64; asst. prof. Fla. State U., Tallahassee, 1964-66; assoc. prof., specialist occupation edn. Ohio State U., Columbus, 1966-68; prof. sociology U. Ga., Athens, 1968-97, prof. emeritus, 1997—. Served in U.S. Army, 1954—56. Recipient rsch. award Am. Personnel and Guidance Assn., 1977, Excellence in Undergrad. Tchg. award U. Ga., 1978, meritorious svc. award Ga. Soc. Assn., 1991. Mem. Am. Sociol. Assn., So. Sociol. Soc., Ga. Sociol. Assn. (v.p. 1984-85, pres.1986-87). Democrat. Roman Catholic. Avocations: gardening, photography. Home: 85 Timberland Trail Arnoldsville GA 30619-2216 Office: U Ga Dept Sociology Athens GA 30602 Office Phone: 706-542-3218. Business E-Mail: algarbin@arches.uga.edu. *Hard work is a requisite, but luck can be very helpful! A loving wife and family make it all worthwhile.*

GARBIS, MARVIN JOSEPH, judge; b. Balt., June 14, 1936; s. Samuel and Adele E. (Warshaw) G.; m. Phyllis Lorraine Zaroff, Aug. 27, 1961; children: Kendall Rose, Jason Anders, Kerri Jill. BES., Johns Hopkins U., 1958; JD, Harvard U., 1961; LLM, Georgetown U., 1962. Bar: D.C. 1961, Md. 1962. Trial atty. Tax Div., Dept. Justice, Washington, 1962-67; sole practice Balt., 1967-71; ptnr. Garbis, Marvel & Junghans, Balt., 1971-86, Melnicove, Kaufman, Weiner, Smouse & Garbis, Balt., 1986-88, Johnson & Gibbs, Washington, 1988-89; judge U.S. Dist. Ct. Md., 1989—. Lectr. U. Md. Law Sch., 1970-85, NYU Fed. Tax Inst., 1970, 74, 79, 87-88; adj. prof. Georgetown U. Law Sch., 1978-80, U. Balt. Law Sch., 1982—; adviser on tax procedure study, jud. com. U.S. Senate, 1969-70; mem. adv. commr. to commr. IRS, 1982; mem. adv. coun. U.S. Claims Ct., 1982—; mem. Md. Inst. for Continuing Profl. Edn. for Lawyers, 1978-80, pres., 1980-82; vis. scholar Fed. Ct. of Australia, 1998. Author: (with Frome) Procedures in Federal Tax Controversy, 1968, (with Schwait) Tax Refund Litigation, 1971, Tax Court Practice, 1974, (with Struntz) Cases and Materials on Federal Tax Procedure, Civil and Criminal, 1981, (with Junghans and Struntz) Federal Tax Litigation, 1985, (with Struntz and Rubin) Cases and Materials on Tax Procedure and Tax Fraud, 2d edit., 1987, (with Rubin and Morgan) Cases and Material on Tax Procedure and Tax Fraud, 3d edit., 1991; contbr. articles to profl. jours. Recipient Jules Ritholz Meml. Merit award, 1996; E. Barrett Prettyman fellow, Georgetown Law Sch., 1961—62. Mem. Fed. Bar Assn. (pres. Balt. chpt. 1972-73, nat. vice chmn. tax com. 1974-76), Md. Bar Assn. (chmn. tax sect. 1970-71, chmn. continuing legal edn. 1973-80), ABA (chmn. ct. procedure com., tax sect. 1975-77), Balt. Bar Assn. (bd. govs. 1974-79), Fed. Cir. Bar Assn. (bd. dirs. 1985—). Am. Law Inst., Md. Inst. Continuing Profl. Education Lawyers (pres. 1981-82) judge. Office: US Dist Ct 101 W Lombard St Ste 530 Baltimore MD 21201-2605 E-mail: judge_garbis@mdd.uscourts.gov.

GARBUS, MARTIN SOLOMON, lawyer; b. Bklyn., Aug. 8, 1934; s. Solomon and Anna (Washinsky) G.; m. Sarina Tang, June 24, 1995; children from previous marriage: Cassandra, Elizabeth. BA, Hunter Coll., 1955; JD, NYU, 1959. Bar: N.Y. 1960, U.S. Supreme Ct. 1962, U.S. Ct. Appeals (2d, 3d, 5th cirs.) 1970, U.S. Tax Ct. 1975. Mem. faculty Columbia U., NYC, 1968-78, Yale U., New Haven, 1969; ptnr. Frankfurt Garbus Klein & Selz, NYC, 1978—2002, Davis & Gilbert LLP, NYC, 2003—. Assoc. dir. Civil Liberties Union, 1967-69; faculty mem., Columbia U., 1968, Yale U. 1978; lectr. Stanford Law Sch., Harvard Law Sch., Practising Law Inst. on criminal, civil, libel, communications law and trial techiques, 1960-84; apptd. adv. to Chinese team on creation of intellectual property laws Chinese Govt., 2004; instr. Tsinghua U. Beijing; spkr. in field. Author: Ready for the Defense, 1971, Traitors and Heroes, 1987, Tough Talk: How I Fought For Writers, Comics, Bigots, and the American Way, 1998, Courting Disaster: The Supreme Court and the Unmaking of America Law, 2002; TV appearances include: 60 Minutes, Dateline, Good Morning America, Charlie Rose Show; commentator: NBC, ABC, CBS, PBS, CNN, Fox News Channel, Court TV; contbr. numerous articles to law revs. and to NY Times, Washington Post, LA Times, and others. Mem. Mayor's Select Com. on Criminal Justice, Criminal Law, 1972-75, Internat. Law, 1976-78. Named Legendar, Time Mag.; named one of Top 10 Litigators, Nat. Law Jour., Best Lawyers in NY, NY Mag. Mem. ABA, ACLU (bd. dirs. 1986-89), Bar Assn. NYC (mem. comm. and medial law com.) Achievements include representing well-known authors, publishers, actors, playwrights, directors, producers, and motion picture studios; being selected as a consultant on media and communications by Canada, England, Australia, the former Soviet Union, Czechoslovakia, Poland, China, and Hungary. Office: Davis & Gilbert LLP 1740 Broadway New York NY 10019 Office Phone: 212-468-4883. Office Fax: 212-468-4888. E-mail: mgarbus@dglaw.com.

GARCEAU, JO MILLS, writer; b. Portland, Oreg., Nov. 10, 1932; d. M. Pierre Mills and Mary Elizabeth Kies. BA in Polit. Sci., U. of Oreg., 1953; MA in Human Values, San Francisco Theol. Sem., 1982. Exec. sec. The Boeing Co., Seattle, 1959—65; campaign dir. Dan Evans for Gov. Com., Spokane, Wash., 1968; asst. to the gov. Office of the Gov. State of Wash., Olympia, Wash., 1969—72, cabinet dir., 1972—76; campus min. The Evergreen Coll. Campus Ministry, Olympia, 1977—82; asst. min. Ananda Ch., Nevada City, Calif., 1982—89; writer Boring, Oreg., 1990—; customer svc. assoc. PacifiCorp, Portland, 1996—. Chmn. affirmative action com. State of Wash., Olympia, 1973—77, mem. intergovtl. pers. adv. coun., 1975—77. Chmn. budget com. United Way, Olympia, Wash., 1974—78; v.chmn. 47th Legis. Dist. Rep. Party, Renton, Wash., 1960—63; co-chmn. Dan Evans for Gov. Legis. Com., Renton, 1963—64, Treadwell for Congress Com., Spokane, Wash., 1967; chmn. The Evergreen Coll. Campus Ministry, Olympia, 1976—78; dir. parish renewal project St. Michael's Parish, Olympia, 1981—82; bd. dir. Wash. Coun. of Ch., Seattle, 1977—82. Fellow Walden fellow, 1998; grantee, State of Oreg., 1949—51; scholar Hazel P. Schwering scholarship, U. of Oreg., 1952. Mem.: Nat. Assn. Securities Dealers (arbitrator 2003—), Willamette Writers (asst. treas. 2002), Pacific N.W. Writers, Oreg. Astrological Soc. Liberal. Buddhist. Avocations: car camping, astrology, psychology, spirituality.

GARCHIK, LEAH LIEBERMAN, journalist; b. Bklyn., May 2, 1945; d. Arthur Louis and Mildred (Steinberg) Lieberman; m. Jerome Marcus Garchik, Aug. 11, 1968; children— Samuel, Jacob BA, Bklyn. Coll., 1966. Editorial asst. San Francisco Chronicle, 1972-79, writer, editor, 1979-83, editor This World, 1983-84, columnist, 1984—; also author numerous book and movie reviews, features and profiles. Author: San Francisco; the City's Sights and Secrets, 1995; panelist (radio quiz show) Minds Over Matter; contbr. articles to mags. Vice pres. Golden Gate Kindergarten Assn., San

Francisco, 1978; pres. Performing Arts Workshop, San Francisco, 1977-79; bd. dirs. Home Away From Homelessness, 1994-99. Recipient 1st prize Nat. Soc. Newspaper Columnists, 1992. Mem. Newspaper Guild. Democrat. Jewish. Home: 156 Baker St San Francisco CA 94117-2111 Office: San Francisco Chronicle 901 Mission St San Francisco CA 94103-2905 Business E-Mail: lgarchik@sfchronicle.com.

GARCIA, ADOLFO RAMON, lawyer; b. Havana, Cuba, Nov. 5, 1948; came to U.S., 1961; s. Adolfo Damian and Luz I. (Garcia) G.; m. Elizabeth Ensor, July 17, 1971; children: Andrew, Laurence. AB magna cum laude, Harvard U., 1971; JD, Georgetown U., 1974. Bar: N.Y. 1975, Mass. 1981. Assoc. Cahill Gordon & Reindel, N.Y.C., 1974-79, Choate, Hall & Stewart, Boston, 1979-82; sr. ptnr. McDermott, Will & Emery, Boston, 1982—2003; ptnr., co-head internat. practice group Ropes & Gray, Boston, 2003—. Bd. dirs. Certified Oil Co., Carboclor Industrias Quimicas S.A., Sol Petrolgo, S.A., Healthcare Assocs., Inc. Co-chmn. legal affairs com., bd. dirs. Internat. Bus. Ctr. New Eng. Inc., Boston, 1983-87; past chmn. and pres., bd. dirs. Boston Ctr. for Internat. Visitors, 1981-86; active Mass. Internat. Trade Coun., Boston, 1984-86; v.p., dir. New Eng.-Latin Am. Bus. Coun; v.p. & dir. New England-Latin Am. Bus. Council. Mem. Internat. Bar Assn., Boston Bar Assn. (co-chmn. pvt. internat. law sect. 1982-86), InterAm. Bar Assn., Essex County Club, Manchester (Mass.) Yacht Club. Republican. Home: October Hill Prides Crossing MA 01965 Office: Ropes & Gray One Internat Pl Boston MA 02110-2624 Office Phone: 617-951-7468. Office Fax: 617-951-7050. Business E-Mail: agarcia@ropesgray.com.

GARCIA, ALVARO DANIEL, veterinarian, consultant; b. Montevideo, Uruguay, Sept. 4, 1953; s. Alberto Morenes Griñi Garcia and Ninón del Carmen Lamothe; m. Cristina Renee Lammers, Apr. 10, 1981; children: Federico Mario, Carmela Alejandra. DVM, U. Uruguay, Montevideo, 1975—83; MS, U. Minn., Saint Paul, 1987—87, PhD, 1997. Assoc. prof. and dept. head animal nutrition Coll. Vet. Medicine U. Uruguay, Montevideo, 1997—2000; ext. dairy specialist and assoc. prof. S.D. State, Brookings, 2001—. Nutritionist Solsire S.A., Montevideo, Uruguay, 1997—2001; dairy ext. specialist PARMALAT, 1997—2000, Cooperativa Ruralista Agropecuaria de Colonia, Colonia Valdense, 1997—2001. Author: (ednl. materials) comparative coop. and dairy herd mgmt. sys.in dairy prodn. (Award of Excellence at US Nat. Partners of the Americas Conv. Atlanta, Ga., 1994). Recipient Deans award., Coll. of Agr. and Biol. Scis. S.D. State, 2002, cert. of Merit Cmty. Svc., S.D. Ext. Specialist Assn., 1993. Mem.: Profl. Dairy Heifer Growers Assn. (assoc.), Am. Dairy Sci. Assn. (assoc.), Gamma Sigma Delta (assoc.). Achievements include research in effects of temperature, moisture, and aeration on heat damage in alfalfa haylage; energy balance in grazed and confined lactating dairy cows. Office: SD State Univ 113 Dairy/Microbiology Bldg PO Box 2104 Brookings SD 57007 Office Phone: 605-688-5488. Home Fax: 605-688-6276; Office Fax: 605-688-6276. E-mail: alvaro.garcia@sdstate.edu.

GARCIA, ANDREW B., chemical engineer; b. Las Cruces, N.Mex., Apr. 22, 1949; s. Rudolf A. and Margaret (Rivera) Garcia; m. Katherine D. Montano, July 5, 1974 (dec. Aug. 1996); children: Lauren, Alexandra; m. Elaine Rose Richards, Nov. 29, 2002. BS in Chem. Engring. with honors, N.Mex. State U., Las Cruces, 1972; MBA, St. Mary's Coll., Moraga, Calif., 1979; postgrad., U. Calif., Berkeley, 1994. Registered environ. assessor; cert. hazardous materials mgr. Design engr. Gen. Electric Co., San Jose, Calif., 1972-75; chem. engr. Chevron Chem. Co., Richmond, Calif., 1975-78; supr. Chevron Corp., San Francisco, 1978-80; supply product mgr. Chevron USA Inc., Walnut Creek, Calif., 1980-89; project mgr. Chevron Land & Devel. Co., San Francisco, 1989-93; environ. project mgr. Alameda County, Oakland, Calif., 1993-95; environ. support mgr. Computer Scis. Corp., Edwards AFB, Calif., 1995-99; due diligence coordinator Greenberg Farrow Architecture, Inc., 2000; site project mgr. Knight Piesold, 2000-2001; sr. engr., project mgr. MACTEC, 2001—. Park and recreation commr. City of Martinez, Calif., 1984-89; mem. citizens adv. bd. City of Martinez, 1989-91, former faithful navigator Knights of Columbus. Mem.: Project Mgmt. Inst., AIChE. Roman Catholic. Achievements include reputation for being expert on the site cleanup and due diligence; successful management of multimillion dollar projects. Home: 28420 Rock Canyon Dr Santa Clarita CA 91390 E-mail: garciaA1@aol.com.

GARCIA, ANDY, actor; b. Havana, Cuba, Apr. 12, 1956; m. Maria Lorido Garcia, 1982; 4 children. Student, Fla. Internat. U.; DFA (hon.), St. John's Univ., 2000. Actor: (films) Guaguasi, 1979, Blue Skies Again, 1983, The Mean Season, 1985, 8 Million Ways to Die, 1986, The Untouchables, 1987, Stand and Deliver, 1987, American Roulette, 1988, Black Rain, 1989, Internal Affairs, 1990, The Godfather III, 1990 (Oscar nominee best supporting actor, 1999, Golden Globe nominee, 1999), Dead Again, 1991, Hero, 1992, Jennifer 8, 1992, When a Man Loves a Woman, 1994, Steal Big Steal Little, 1995, Things to Do in Denver When You're Dead, 1996, Night Falls on Manhattan, 1997, The Disappearance of Garcia Lorca, 1997, Hoodlum, 1997, Desperate Measures, 1999 (ALMA award, 1997), Lakeboat, 1999, Ocean's 11, 2001, Confidence, 2002, Blackout, 2003, Twisted, 2004, Modigliani, 2004, Lazarus Child, 2004, Ocean's Twelve, 2004; actor, prodr.: (TV) Swing Vote, 1999, (film) Just the Ticket, 1999, The Man From Elysian Fields, 2002, The Unsaid, 2002; dir., prodr.; (films) Cachao, Like His Rhythm There Is No Other, Cachao.Goza Mi Mambo Cubano; music prodr.: (album) Cachao Master Sessions, vol. I (Grammy award 1994), Cachao Master Sessions, Vol. II (Grammy nominee 1995), Just the Ticket soundtrack, 4 songs for Steal Big, Steal Little soundtrack, Cachao-Cuba Linda, 2000(nominated for Latin Grammy, 2000, Grammy, 2001), For Love or Country: The Arturo Sandoval Story soundtrack, 2000, Cachao-Anora Si, 2003. Recipient Harvard Univ. Found. award, Star on Hollywood Walk of Fame, Hispanic Heritage award for Arts, Father of Yr. award Father's Day Coun., ALMA award, PRISM award; named Nat. Assn. of Theater Oweners Star of Yr.; nominated for Oscar and Golden Globe for Godfather III, Spirit of Hope award, 2001, Oscar de la Hoys Found. Champion award, 2000, Palm Springs Film Festival Desert Palm award, 2002, Imagen Found. Creative Achievement award, 2002, LA's BEST Focus on Family award, 2002, RP Internat. Film Artist of Vision award. Office: Paradigm Talent Agency 500 5th Ave Fl 37 New York NY 10110-3799*

GARCIA, ANGELA G., lawyer; b. Manila, Philippines, 1960; BA cum laude, Mount Holyoke U., 1982; MPhil, U. Cambridge, 1984; JD cum laude, Georgetown U., 1989. Bar: N.Y. 1990, D.C. 1990, U.S. Dist. Ct. (so. and ea. dists.) N.Y. 1994, U.S. Ct. Appeals (2d cir.) 1996. Law clk. Hon. James Belson D.C. Ct. Appeals, 1989—90; atty. Skadden, Arps, Slate, Meagher & Flom LLP, N.Y., 1990—97, ptnr., 1997—. Office: Skadden Arps Slate Meagher & Flom LLP Four Times Sq New York NY 10036 Office Phone: 212-735-3000.

GARCIA, ASTRID J., newspaper executive; b. Caguas, Puerto Rico, Sept. 6, 1950; m. Robert Gillespie; children: Robert, Richard. BA with distinction, Barnard Coll., 1972; JD, Bklyn. Law Sch., 1980. Bar: N.Y. 1980. Dir., lighting designer various theatres, N.Y.C., 1972-74; equal employment opportunity specialist Gen. Svcs. Adminstrn. Fed. Govt., Region II, N.Y.C., 1974-76; paralegal So. Dist. N.Y. U.S. Atty.'s Office, N.Y.C., 1976-80; atty. Puerto Rican Legal Def. and Edn. Fund, N.Y.C., 1980-81, NLRB, N.Y.C. and Hartford, Conn., 1981-85; mgr. employee rels. dept. human resources The Hartford Courant, 1985-87; asst. dir. human resources The Miami (Fla.) Herald, 1987-90; v.p., dir. employee rels. St. Paul Pioneer Press, 1990-94; sr. v.p. human resources and labor, dir. labor rels. Jour. Comm., Milw., 1994-97; sr. v.p. ops. Milw. Jour. Sentinel, 1997—. Mem. N.Y. Bar Assn. Office: Milw Jour Sentinel PO Box 661 Milwaukee WI 53201-0661 Home: 16360 Los Gatos Almaden Rd Los Gatos CA 95032-3618

GARCIA, SISTER BEATRICE MARIE, director, secondary school educator; b. L.A., Aug. 8, 1948; d. Benjamin Quiroz and Guadalupe G. Garcia. BA, Russell Coll., 1971; MA in Religious Studies, U. San Francisco, 1982. Cert. tchr. Calif., 1971. Tchr. religious studies Mercy High Sch., San Francisco, 1971—74, Marian High Sch., Imperial Beach, 1974—75, Mercy High Sch., 1975—79; tchr. religious studies, dept. chair Bishop Conaty Meml. High Sch., L.A., 1979—86; tchr. religious studies, dir. campus ministry San Gabriel Mission High Sch., 1986—2001, St. Paul High Sch., Santa Fe Springs, 2001—. Mem. Archdiocesan Religion Com., L.A., 1983—; mem. religious stds. com. Archdiocesan, 2000—. Co-author: Doing Great Campus Ministry, 2003. Mem.: ASCD, Nat. Cath. Edn. Assn., Cath. Campus Ministry Assn., Religious Edn. Assn. Avocations: crafts, photography. Office: St Paul High Sch 9635 Greenleaf Ave Santa Fe Springs CA 90670 Office Phone: 562-698-6246 719.

GARCIA, BEATRICE MAUDE, social worker; b. Boston, Jan. 18, 1929; d. George Louis and Beatrice Lawrence (White) Joughin; m. Edward P. Black, June 4, 1950 (dec.); children: Victoria, Edward, Barbara; m. Marvin Victor Aquirre, May 10, 1956 (div.); children: Deborah (dec.), Michael; m. Peter Charles Garcia, Aug. 13, 1961. BA in Anthropology with honors and distinction, Sonoma State U., 1971; MA in Anthropology, San Francisco State U., 1979; postgrad., Sonoma State U., 1982—. Coord. Boyle Heights Coalition, L.A., 1953-55; dir. Truman Boyd Housing Assn., Long Beach, Calif., 1961-63; med. records supr. Crestview Hosp., Petaluma, Calif., 1979-81; investigator, ombudsman Sonoma County Ombudsman, Santa Rosa, Calif., 1984—88; dir. sr. svcs. Ctrl. YMCA, San Francisco, 1988-90; dir. case mgmt. East Valley Sr. Ctr., North Hollywood, Calif., 1994-98, regional mgr. Region VII, long term care ombudsman L.A., 2001—. Sec. Red Banks Oaks Assn., 1998—, Dem. Club High Desert, 1999—; organizer campaigns Dem. Orgn., Santa Maria, Calif., 1964, Vallejo, Calif., 1968. Mem. AAUW (sec. Antelope Valley chpt. 1999—), No. Calif. Manx Assn. (adminstrv. 1999—). Democrat. Episcopalian. Avocations: reading, travel, antiques. Home: 4030 Lexington Ct Palmdale CA 93552-4356 Office Phone: 661-945-5563.

GARCIA, CASTELAR MEDARDO, lawyer; b. Conejos, Colo., June 3, 1942; s. Castelar M. Sr. and Anna (Vigil) G.; m. Mary Elizabeth Miller, Apr. 1, 1967; 1 child, Victoria Elisabeth. BA, Adams State Coll., 1965; JD, U. Colo., 1976. Bar: Colo. 1977, U.S. Dist. Ct. Colo. 1977, U.S. Ct. Appeals (10th cir.) 1983, U.S. Ct. Appeals (4th cir.) 1988, U.S. Supreme Ct. 1984. Human resources counselor State of Oreg., Klamath Falls, 1966-68; regional dir. Colo. Civil Rights Com., Alamosa, 1970-73; dep. dist. atty. Denver, 1977-80; chief dep. dist. atty., 1980-84; pvt. practice Alamosa, Colo., 1984—; owner Cumbres Ranch. Town atty., Manassa, Colo., 1984—; commr. Colo. Dept. Hwys., 1991, Colo. Dept. Transp., 1991—; chmn. Colo. Transp. Commn., 1996-2001. Mem. Colo. delegation to Cam Real Trade Corridor Consortium between U.S., Can. and Mex. With U.S. Army, 1968-70, Vietnam. Decorated Purple Heart. Mem. Colo. Bar Assn., Hispanic Bar Assn., San Luis Valley Bar Assn., Caminos Antiquos Scenic By-way Assn. (founder). Republican. Roman Catholic. Office: 701 Main St Alamosa CO 81101-2554 Office Phone: 719-587-0997. Office Fax: 719-587-9209. Business E-Mail: slulaw@fom.net.

GARCIA, CLAUDIA, graphics designer; d. Angelina and Florentino Garcia. AA, LA Valley Coll., Van Nuys, Calif., 2000. Cert. Duet Lyric Chyron. Graphic designer, deko operator Sta. KJLA-TV, LA, 1999—; deko operator G4TechTV, LA, 2001—04. Promos Sta. KJLA-TV, LA, 1999—, web adminstr., 2001—. Graphic designer, operator (best variety show) LATV Live (Imagen Award Best Variety Show, 2002), graphic designer (variety show) (Imagen Award Best Variety Show, 2003). Participant UFW Mar., Watsonville, Calif., 1997—98. Green Party. Roman Catholic. Avocations: music, films, politics, travel. Office: Kjla-Latv 2323 Corinth Ave Los Angeles CA 90064 Office Phone: 310-943-5288. Office Fax: 310-943-5299. Personal E-mail: rockera33@yahoo.com.

GARCIA, ELISA DOLORES, lawyer; b. Bklyn., Nov. 8, 1957; d. Vincent Garcia, Jr. and Dolores Elizabeth (Canedo) Marmo; m. John Jay Hasluck, Feb. 28, 1987; children: Brooke Elisabeth, John Neville. BA, MS, SUNY, Stony Brook, 1980; JD, St. John's U., 1985. Bar: N.Y. 1986. Cons. Energy Devel. Internat., Pt. Jefferson, N.Y., 1980-83; assoc. Willkie Farr & Gallagher, N.Y.C., 1985-89; sr. counsel GAF Corp./Internat. Specialty Products, Wayne, N.J., 1989-94; regional counsel for L.Am., Philip Morris Internat., Rye Brook, N.Y., 1994-2000; exec. v.p., gen. counsel Domino's Pizza, LLC, Ann Arbor, Mich., 2000—. Mem. Glen Rock (N.J.) Planning Bd., 1992-95, chmn., 1994-95. Mem. ABA, N.Y. State Bar Assn., Mich. Bar Assn., Assn. Corp. Counsel Assn. (pres. Mich. chpt.). Roman Catholic. Avocations: gardening, scuba diving. Office: Domino's Pizza LLC PO Box 997 30 Frank Lloyd Wright Dr Ann Arbor MI 48106-0997 E-mail: garciae@dominos.com.

GARCIA, F. CHRIS, academic administrator, political scientist, educator; b. Albuquerque, Apr. 15, 1940; s. Flaviano P. and Crucita A. Garcia; m. Sandra D. Garcia; children: Elaine L., Tanya C. BA, U. N.Mex., 1961, MA in Govt., 1964; PhD in Polit. Sci., U. Calif., Davis, 1972. Prof. U. N.Mex., Albuquerque, 1970—, pres., 2002—03, prof., 1970—, dean arts coll., 1980—87, acad. v.p., 1987—90, provost, 1993, 1998—2000; founder Zia Rsch. Assocs., Inc., Albuquerque, 1973-94, also chmn. bd. dirs. Cons.-evaluator North Ctrl. Assn. Higher Learning Commn., 1994—. Author: Political Socialization of Chicano Children, 1973, La Causa Politica, 1974, The Chicano Political Experience, 1977, State and Local Government in New Mexico, 1979, New Mexico Government, 1976, 81, 94, Latinos and the Political System, 1988, Latino Voices, 1992, Pursuing Power, 1997. Mem. charter rev. com. City of Albuquerque, 1999, Albuquerque Goals Commn.; bd. dirs. Nat. Hispanic Cultural Ctr., 2002—04. With N.Mex. Air N.G., 1957—63, hon. comdr., 2005—. Recipient Disting. Svc. award, Am. Polit. Sci. Assn., 2001. Mem. Western Polit. Sci. Assn. (pres. 1977-78), Am. Polit. Sci. Assn. (v.p. 1994-95, exec. coun. 1984-86, sec. 1992-93, Disting. Svc. award 2001), Am. Assn. Pub. Opinion Rsch., Coun. Colls. of Arts and Sci. (bd. dirs. 1982-85), Nat. Assn. State Univs. and Land Grant Colls. (coun. acad. affairs 1987-90, exec. com. 1989), Western Social Sci. Assn. (exec. coun. 1973-76), Phi Beta Kappa, Phi Kappa Phi, Gold Key. Home: 1409 Snowdrop Pl NE Albuquerque NM 87112-6331 Office: U N Mex Polt Sci Dept Social Scis Bldg 2053 Albuquerque NM 87131-1121 Office Phone: 505-277-5217. E-mail: cgarcia@unm.edu.

GARCIA, HENRY FRANK, supply management and project management consultant and trainer; b. San Antonio, Aug. 29, 1943; s. Henry V. and Lucia (Dominguez) G.; m. Rose Lozano, Feb. 28, 1970; children: John Henry, Rebecca. BA in Psychology, St. Mary's U., San Antonio, 1969, MA in Econs., 1974. Cert. purchasing mgr., Tex. Buyer purchasing Southwest Rsch. Inst., San Antonio, 1967-70, asst. mgr. purchasing, 1970-74, mgr. purchasing, 1974-78, asst. dir. materials mgmt., 1978-80, dir. corp. travel, 1980-87, dir. materials mgmt., 1980-87; dir. fin. and adminstrn. Ctr. for Nuc. Waste Regulatory Analyses, San Antonio, 1987—2003; ret., 2003; cons., trainer Asentrene. Instr. U. Tex., San Antonio, 1976-77; instr. materials mgmt. and econs., San Antonio Coll., 1975-83; instr. econs. St. Marys U., San Antonio, 1976-81; adj. prof. econs. Webster U., San Antonio, 1980—. Contbr. articles to profl. jours. Chmn. San Antonio Regional Minority Purchasing Council, 1983. Mem. Nat. Purchasing Inst. (pres. 1979-80, Outstanding Svc. award 1986), Nat. Assn. Purchasing Mgmt. (cert., v.p. dist. II 1987-89, Pro-D Man of Yr. award 1985, Congrove Outstanding Mem. award 1991, President's award 1994, J. Shipman Gold Medal award 1998), Purchasing Mgmt. Assn. San Antonio (pres. 1981-82, Conway L. Holmes award 1984, James H. Lieberman award 2000), Nat. Bus. Travel Assn. (v.p. 1985-86), Nat. Assn. Bus. Economists (pres. local chpt. 1978), Project Mgmt. Inst. (pres. 2005—). Democrat. Roman Catholic. Office: Asentrene PO Box 782474 San Antonio TX 78278-2474 Office Phone: 210-493-1971. Personal E-mail: hfgarcia@asentrene.com.

GARCIA, HUMBERTO SIGIFREDO, prosecutor, lawyer; b. Harlingen, Tex., June 7, 1944; s. Porfirio and Margarita (Herrera) G.; m. Lana Cheryl Caswell, Aug. 9, 1975. BA, Lamar U., 1974; JD, U. Tex., 1977. Bar: Tex. 1978, U.S. Dist. Ct. (ea. dist.) Tex. 1978, U.S. Dist. Ct. (so. dist.) Tex. 1979, U.S. Ct. Appeals (5th cir.) 1979, U.S. Supreme Ct. 1982. Ptnr. Mehaffy, Garcia & Bradford, Beaumont, Tex., 1977-83; asst. U.S. atty. ea. dist. US Dept. Justice, 1983—2002, U.S. atty. Puerto Rico dist., 2002—. Instr. Lamar U., Beaumont, 1980-83; bd. dirs. Western State Bank, Denton, Tex. Served to capt. USMC, 1968-71. Mem. ABA, Fed. Bar Assn., Tex. Bar Assn, Kappa Sigma. Republican. Presbyterian. Avocations: long distance running, fishing, photography, cars, golf. Office: Torre Chardon Ste 1201 350 Carlos Chardon Ave San Juan PR 00918 Office Phone: 787-766-5656. E-mail: h.garcia@usdoj.gov.

GARCIA, JOHN, psychologist, educator; b. Santa Rosa, Calif., June 12, 1917; married; 3 children. BA, U. Calif., Berkeley, 1948, MA, 1949, PhD, 1965. Teaching asst. U. Calif., Berkeley, 1949-51; psychologist U.S. Naval Radiol. Def. Lab., San Francisco, 1951-58; tchr. biol. sci. Oakland (Calif.) Pub. Schs., 1958-59; asst. prof. psychology Calif. State Coll., Long Beach, 1959-65; assoc. biologist, neurosurg. svc. Mass. Gen. Hosp., Boston, 1965-68; prof. psychology, chmn. psychobiology program SUNY, Stony Brook, 1968-71, chmn. dept., 1971-72; prof. U. Utah, Salt Lake City, 1972-73; prof. psychology and psychiatry UCLA, 1973-87, emeritus prof. psychology and psychiatry, 1987—. Recipient Lifetime Achievement award for neurosci., Soc. for Neurosci., 1998. Fellow Soc. Exptl. Psychologists (Howard Crosby Warren medal 1978); mem. AAAS, APA (Disting. Sci. Contbn. award 1979), Nat. Acad. Scis., Am. Psychol. Soc. (William James fellow), N.Y. Acad. Scis., Western Psychol. Assn. (pres. 1991—), Phi BEta Kappa, Sigma Xi. Address: PO Box 1217 La Conner WA 98257

GARCIA, JULIA THERESA, secondary school educator; b. N.Y.C., Aug. 30, 1923; d. Ignatius Colletti-Riena and Julia Pendeleur; m. Frank Leonard Garcia, May 26, 1949 (dec. Aug. 1995); children: Julia, Frank, Annette. BA, Hunter Coll., 1951; MA, Columbia U., 1956. Cert. tchr. chemistry N.Y., asst. prin. supervision phys. scis. N.Y. Tchr. gen. sci. Alfred E. Smith Jr. H.S. Bd. Edn. N.Y.C., tchr. chemistry Alfred E. Smith H.S., asst. prin. supervision phys. scis. Alfred E. Smith H.S., prin. summer sch. Alfred E. Smith H.S. Bd. examiner sci. and math. Bd. Edn. N.Y.C., 1984—89. Active Diabetic Assn. Recipient award for dedicated svc. to children, N.Y.C. Sci. Chmn.'s Assn., 1989. Mem.: Am. Assn. Scientists, Phi Delta Kappa, N.Y.C. Acad. Sci.

GARCIA, JULIET VILLARREAL, university administrator; m. Oscar E. Garcia; two children. BA in Speech, English, U. of Houston, 1970, MA in Speech, English, 1972; PhD in Communications & Linguistics, U. of Texas Austin, 1976. Teaching asst. U. of Houston, 1970—72; Instr. Pan American Univ. at Edinburg, 1972; teaching asst. U. of Texas Austin, 1974—76; adj. prof. Pan American U. Brownsville, 1977—79; instr. Tex. Southmost Coll., 1972—74, 1976—81, dir. TSC Self-Study, 1979—81, dean, arts and sciences, 1981—86, pres., 1986—92, U. Tex. at Brownsville, Tex. Southmost Coll., 1992—. Bd. dirs. Fed. Res. of Dallas/San Antonio br. of Tex. Commerce Bancshares Inc.; past bd. dirs. Am. Coun. Edn., chmn. bd. dirs. 1995. Bd. dirs. Carnegie Found. for Advancement of Teaching, Pub. Welfare Foun.; vice-chair adv. com. on Fin. Aid; appointed mem. White House Initiative on Ednl. Excellence for Hispanic-Ams. Named Woman of Distinction Nat. Conf. of Coll. Women Student Leaders, 1995, one of most influential Hispanics Hispanic Bus. Mag. Office: U Tex & Tex Southmost Coll Office of Pres 80 Fort Brown St Brownsville TX 78520-4956*

GARCIA, JUNE MARIE, librarian; b. Bryn Mawr, Pa., Sept. 12, 1947; d. Roland Ernest and Marion Brill (Hummel) Traynor; m. Teodosio Garcia, July 17, 1928; children: Gretchen, Adrian. BA, Douglass Coll., 1969; MLS, Rutgers U., 1970. Reference libr. New Brunswick (N.J.) Pub. Libr., 1970-72, Plainfield (N.J.) Pub. Libr., 1972-75; br. mgr. Phoenix Pub. Libr., 1975-80, extension svcs. adminstr., 1980-93; dir. San Antonio Pub. Libr., 1993-99; CEO, CARL Corp., Denver, 1999-2001; v.p., chief amb. TLC/CARL, Denver, 2001—02; mng. ptnr. Dubberly Garcia Assocs., 2002—, E-Learn Librs., Inc., Nashville and Denver, 2004—. Recipient Productivity Innovator award, City of Phoenix, 1981. Mem. ALA (life, coun. 1986-90, 93-2001, pres. Pub. Libr. Assn. 1991-92, new stds. task force 1983-87, goals, guidelines and stds. com. 1986-90, chairperson 1987-90, resource allocation com. 1998-99), Freedom to Read Found. (bd. dirs.), Ariz. State Libr. Assn. (pres. 1984-85, Libr. of Yr. award 1986, Pres.'s award 1990), Pub. Libr. Internat. Network (exec. dir.), Beta Phi Mu. Office: 1195 S Harrison St Denver CO 80210 Office Phone: 303-757-7420. Business E-Mail: jgarcia@dubberlygarcia.com.

GARCIA, LUIS F., social worker, photographer; b. Nogales, Ariz., Sept. 28, 1963; s. Francisco and Amanda E. Garcia; children: Vania, Fernando. BA, Our Lady of the Lake U., San Antonio, 1988. Press Photographer Am. Image Press, Wash., D.C., 1988, Profl. Photographer N.Y. Inst. of Photography, 2000, Master Photographer Internat. Freelance Photographers Assn., 2002. Social worker Sunnyvale Cmty. Svcs., Sunnyvale, Calif., 1997—2002; program mgr. Interfaith Cmty. Svcs., Escondido, Calif., 2002—. Photography calendar, China: Portraits of a Timeless land, photography, Climb Against the Odds/ Breast Cancer Fund, 2003. Cons. Breast Cancer Fund, San Francisco, 2000—03. Recipient Star award for Creativity, Leadership, and Collaboration, United Way of Silicon Valley, Vida award for Outstanding Svc., Who's Who in Photography, Recognition Press, 1998—2000. Personal E-mail: lgarcia@interfaithservices.org.

GARCIA, MARC ANTHONY, diplomat; b. Bklyn., June 1962; s. Carlos Antonio and Yolande (Price) G.; m. Shegurah Rolle; 1 child, Christina Chanel. BA, Hampton Inst., 1984; postgrad., SUNY, Albany, 1986, Cen. Mich. U., 1991. Legis. aide N.Y. State Assembly, Albany, 1984-85; commd. 2d lt. U.S. Army, 1982; advanced through grades to lt. col. USAR; officer UN Hqrs. Secretariate, N.Y.C., 1985; program monitor N.Y. state exec. dept. USAR, N.Y. Air N.G., NY, 1985—86; spl. agt. N.Y. field office U.S. Dept. of State, N.Y.C., 1987-89, 1998—2002; attaché fgn. svc. U.S. Dept. State, Washington, 1986—. Cons. Garcia, Garcia and Peoples, Ltd., Ft. Greene, N.Y., 1989—; bd. dirs. Ital Internat., Cambria Heights, N.Y.; officer of Provost Marshall, Ft. Buchanan, P.R., 1993; observer Olympics, Seoul, Korea, 1988, Atlanta, 1996; detail agt. U.S. Presdl. Inaugural, 1988; mem. Presdl. Security Adv. Unit, Haitian govt., 1994. Author: (monograph) Caribbean Basin Initiative, 1984; contbr. articles to crime prevention series. Advocate Nat. Orgnl. for Victims Assistance, Washington, 1986—; county committeeman Kings County Com., 1984-86; assoc. Am. Mus. Natural History, Bklyn., 1985; inspector N.Y. Bd. Elections, 1984-85; catechist Archdiocese of Bklyn., 1980; Am. Security Coun. Found. Ednl. grantee Va. Army N.G., 1981, 95. Mem. NAACP, VFW (mem.-at-large), DAV (life), Am. Fgn. Svc. Assn., Mil. Police Regtl. Assn. (mem.-at-large), Mil. Civil Affairs Regtl. Assn. (mem.-at-large), Am. Polit. Sci. Assn., Nat. Org. Black Law Enforcement Execs. (assoc.), Assn. MBA Execs. (mem.-at-large), Joint Ctr. for Polit. Studies (assoc.), Fed. Law Enforcement Officers Assn. (spl. agt.), Res. Officer Assn., Hampton Inst. Alumni Assn. (booster 1984-89), Blacks in Govt. Fgn. Affairs (Washington chpt.), Fraternity, Inc. (life), Ft. Hamilton Officers Club, Ft. Monroe NCO Club (asst. mgr. 1982), Masons Scottish Rite, Prince Hall Affiliates, Am. Legion, Alpha Phi Alpha (past chmn. internat. bros. affairs). Democrat. Roman Catholic. Avocation: radio telephone operator. Home: 19701 E Country Club Dr Aventura FL 33180 E-mail: marc.garcia@us.army.

GARCIA, MARCELO HORACIO, engineering educator, consultant; b. Cordoba, Argentina, Apr. 22, 1959; came to U.S., 1983; s. Juan Carlos Jose and Beatriz Alba Garcia; m. Estela Beti Rodriguez-Canga, May 17, 1984; children: Blas Ignacio, Emma Paina. Diploma in Engring., U. Litoral, Santa Fe, Argentina, 1982; MS in Civil Engring., U. Minn., Mpls., 1985; PhD in Civil Engring., 1989. Registered profl. engr., Argentina. Tech. asst. Agua y Energia Electrica, Santa Fe, Argentina, 1979-85; rsch. asst. St. Anthony Falls Lab., Mpls., 1983-87; rsch. fellow, 1988-89; asst. prof. U. Ill., Urbana, 1990-96, assoc. prof., 1996—2000, prof., 2000—. Cons. Govt. Taiwan, Taipei, 1993, U.S. Army of Engrs., Vicksburg, Miss., 1993—, Electricite de France, Toulousse, 1996; tech. adv. U.S./Taiwan Sedimentation, Washington, 1992-94; vis. prof. U. Litoral, Santa Fe, Argentina, 1993—, Calif. Inst. Tech., Pasadena, 1997-; disting. lectr. Hokkaido River Disaster Prevention Inst., Japan, 1990; guest lectr. U. Essen, Germany, 1995. Author: Environmental Hydrodynamics, 1996; contbr. articles to profl. jours. Recipient Karl Emil Hilgard hydraulics prize ASCE, N.Y.C., 1996, Alvin Anderson award U. Minn., Mpls., 1989; named Disting. Vis. Prof. U. Genoa, Italy, 1993. Mem. ASCE (Walter L. Huber Rsch. prize 1998), Am. Geophys. Union, Internat.

Assn. for Hydraulic Rsch., Internat. Water Resources Assn., Sigma Xi. Achievements include development of the first model for sediment mixtures transport by turbidity currents in the ocean. Office: U Ill 205 N Mathews Ave Urbana IL 61801

GARCIA, MARIA LUISA, biochemist, researcher; b. Valladolid, Spain, Oct. 9, 1953; came to U.S., 1979; d. Baldomero and Dolores (Garcia) G.; m. Gregory Kaczorowski, June 21, 1982. PhD, Autonoma U., Madrid, 1979. Sr. rsch. biochemist Merck & Co., Rahway, NJ, 1985—87, rsch. fellow, 1987—91, sr. rsch. fellow, 1991—97, sr. investigator, 1997—2003, disting. sr. investigator, 2003—. Invited speaker, presenter papers in field. Contbr. numerous articles and revs. to profl. jours.; patentee in field. Mem. AAAS, Am. Soc. Biol. Chemists, Biophys. Soc., N.Y. Acad. Sci. Home: 5 Ashbrook Dr Edison NJ 08820-4318 Office: Merck Rsch Labs PO Box 2000 Rahway NJ 07065-0900 Personal E-mail: maria_garcia@merck.com.

GARCIA, MELVA YBARRA, counseling administrator, educator; d. Estanislaso B and Ofelia M Ybarra; m. Frank Garcia, Dec. 28, 1974; children: Ruben Jesus, Luis Francisco, Ramon Estanislado. Student, San Francisco State U., 1969—72; B.A. in Sociology, Calif. State U., Hayward, 1974, MS in Counseling, 1983; PhD (hon.), U. Calif.-Berkeley, 1992. Cert. cmty. coll. counselor Calif., 1986, student pers. workers credential Calif., 1986. Dir. Chicano student counseling ctr. Wash. State U., Pullman, 1984—86; Chicano studies advisor U. of Calif., Berkeley, 1987—92; counselor/instr. Chabot Coll., Hayward, Calif., 1992—. Co-author (counseling manual) Counseling Chicanos: The Affects of Racial and Cultural Stereotype, 1985. Mem. Self-Help for the Hard of Hearing, 2001—; sponsor Children's Internat., Kansas City, Mo., 2002—; mem. La Alianza, Hayward, Calif., 1993; mentor Puente Program, Chabot Coll., 1992—; advisor Wash. State U.; ptnr. Spl. Olympics, 1995—; assoc. mem. Nat. Coun. of La Raza, Washington, 2000—. Mem.: Assn. Main United Farm Workers, So. Law Poverty Ctr., Chabot-Las Positas Faculty Assn., Faculty Assn of Calif. Cmty. Colls., Chicano/Latino Edn. Assn. (mem., 1992-present, co-chair 1998—99), NACADA. D-Liberal. Catholic. Avocations: travel, aerobics. Office: Chabot College 25555 Hesperian Blvd Hayward CA 94545 E-mail: mgarcia@chabotcollege.edu.

GARCIA, MICHAEL J., prosecutor, former federal agency administrator; b. 1961; BA, SUNY; MA, Coll. William & Mary; JD, Union U. Atty. Cahill Gordon & Reindel, Manhattan, NY, 1989—90; law clk. to Hon. Judith S. Kaye N.Y. State Ct. Appeals, 1990—92; asst. US atty. (So. dist.) NY US Dept. Justice, 1992—2001; asst. sec. export enforcement US Dept. Commerce, Washington, 2001—02; commr. Immigration and Naturalization Svc. US Dept. Justice, Washington, 2002—03; asst. sec. Bur. Immigration and Customs Enforcement US Dept. Homeland Security, Washington, 2003—05; US atty (So. dist.) NY US Dept. Justice, NYC, 2005—. Office: US Atty One St Andrews Plz New York NY 10007*

GARCIA, MINERVA A.F., microbiologist, research and clinical laboratory scientist; b. Santiago, Dominican Republic, Nov. 1, 1959; arrived in U.S., 1969; d. Seferino Frias and Lydia Hernandez; m. Jose N. Garcia, Aug. 25, 1985; 1 child, James. BS in Biology, St. Francis Coll., 1984; postgrad. Wagner Coll. Bacteriologist, S.I., NY. Poet Anthologies, 1994, Newspapers and Mags. Recipient award, Anaerobic Bacteriology, 1992, Mayor's scholarship, N.Y.C. Honor Citation award. Mem.: AAUW, Alliance for Prudent Use of Antibiotics, Am. Chem. Soc., N.Y. Acad. Scis., Am. Soc. Microbiology. Home: 29 Pontiac St Staten Island NY 10302-2213 Office: Beth Israel Med Ctr 1st Ave at 17th St New York NY 10003 E-mail: pferre@si.rr.com.

GARCIA, OFELIA, dean; b. Havana, Cuba, Feb. 12, 1941; d. Ramon Garcia-Castro and Nieves (Gomez de Molina) Garcia. Student, Escuela de Bellas Artes, Havana, 1958-60; BA, Manhattanville Coll., 1969; MFA, Tufts U., 1972; postgrad., Duke U., 1973-75; D. Fine Arts (hon.), Atlanta Coll. Art, 1991. Asst. prof., art dept. chair, div. dir. humanities and fine arts Newton (Mass.) Coll., 1969-75; dir. studio art Boston Coll., Chestnut Hill, Mass., 1975-76; exec. dir. The Print Club, Phila., 1978-86; critic Pa. Acad. Fine Arts, Phila., 1982-86; pres. Atlanta Coll. Art, 1986-91, Rosemont (Pa.) Coll., 1991—95; sr. fellow Am. Coun. on Edn., 1995—97; dean, coll. arts and comm., prof. William Paterson U., 1997—. Visual arts panelist State Coun. of the Arts, Pa. and N.J., 1985-86, Ga., 1990-91; mem. vis. com. dept. art and architecture Lehigh (Pa.) U., 1990-96; bd. mgrs. Haverford Coll., 1992—2004. Artist exhibitions of prints and drawings; curator, juror numerous nat. and internat. or regional art exhibitions. Nat. pres. Women's Caucus for Art, 1984-86; bd. dirs. Am. Coun. on Edn., 1993-96; co-chair Mayor's Commn. for Women, City Phila., 1992-97; Arts Adv. Com. Barnes Found. Bd., 1992-95; trustee Jersey City Mus., 2000—, chair, 2001—; bd. dirs. Caths. for Free Choice, 2000—, Artpride NJ, 2005—. Recipient Am. Bookbuilders prize Boston Mus. Sch., 1969, Park Found. award, 1974; Kent fellow Danforth Found., 1975-80. Fellow Soc. for Values Higher Edn.; mem. Coll. Art Assn. Am. (bd. dirs. 1986-90, bd. coms. 1986-92), Commn. on Women in Higher Edn., Am. Coun. on Edn. (chair 1990-91), So. Assn. Colls. and Schs. (accreditation evaluator 1990-91), ArtTable, Inc. Roman Catholic. Office: William Paterson U 300 Pompton Rd Wayne NJ 07470-2152 Office Phone: 973-732-2232. E-mail: garciao@wpunj.edu.

GARCIA, OSCAR NICOLAS, computer science educator; b. Havana, Cuba, Sept. 10, 1936; s. Oscar Vicente and Leonor (Hernandez) G.; m. Diane Ford Journigan, Sept. 9, 1962; children: Flora, Virginia. BSEE, N.C. State U., 1961, MSEE, 1964; PhDEE, U. Md., 1969. Engr. IBM Corp., Endicott, N.Y., 1962-63; asst. prof. Old Dominion U., 1963-66, assoc. prof., 1969-70; research asst., instr. U. Md., 1966-69; assoc. prof. U. South Fla., Tampa, 1970-75, prof. computer sci., chmn. dept., 1975-85; prof. dept. elec. engring. and computer sci. George Washington U., Washington, 1985-95; disting. NCR prof. Wright State U., Dayton, Ohio, 1995—2003, chmn. dept. computer sci. and engring., 1995—2003; founding dean Coll. Engring. U. North Tex., Denton, 2003—. Dir. interactive sys. program in info., robotics and intelligent sys. divsn. Computer and Info. Sci. and Engring. Directorate, Intergovtl. Pers. Act, NSF, Washington, 1992-94; cons. and lectr. in field. Author: (with Y.T. Chien) Knowledge-Based Systems: Fundamentals and Tools, 1991. Fellow IEEE (bd. dirs. 1984-85, 2005—, mem. U.S. activities bd. 1984, Profl. Leadership award 1991, Richard M. Emberson award 1994), Computer Soc. of IEEE (pres. 1981-83, awards com. chmn. 2002-03, bd. govs. 2003—, sec. bd. govs. 2003-04, Richard E. Merwin Disting. Svc. award 1988, Meritorious Svc. award 1991), AAAS; mem. Assn. Computing Machinery, Am. Soc. Engring. Edn., Am. Assn. Artificial Intelligence, Sigma Xi, Eta Kappa Nu, Phi Kappa Phi, Tau Beta Pi. Office: U North Tex Coll Engring PO Box 310440 Denton TX 76203-0440 Home: 120 W El Paseo St Denton TX 76205-8590 Office Phone: 940-565-4300.

GARCIA, PATRICIA A., lawyer; b. New Orleans, Feb. 18, 1956; d. Martin F. and Shirley (Polders) G. BA in History, U. New Orleans, 1976; JD, Loyola U., New Orleans, 1980. Bar: La. 1980, U.S. Tax Ct. 1982, U.S. Dist. Ct. (ea. dist.) La. 1984, U.S. Dist. Ct. (mid. dist.) La. 1986. Staff atty. office of chief counsel IRS, Washington, 1980-82; law clk. U.S. Ea. Dist. Ct. of La., New Orleans, 1983-86; assoc. Law Office of Eric A. Holden, New Orleans, 1986-89; ptnr. Holden & Garcia, New Orleans, 1990—2001; private practice, 2001—. Bd. dirs. La. Ctr. for Law and Civic Edn., 1992-96, pres., 1994-95, New Orleans Legal Assistance Corp., 1995-2000. Co-chair No/AIDS Task Force, 1997-01, sec./treas., 1994-97. Mem. ABA (comm. chair, exec. com. young lawyers divsn. 1990-91, gen. practice sect. gen. practice link conf. team 1994-99, vice chair sole practitioners and small firms com. 1990-92, vice chair law students com. 1991-96, vice chair law sch. curriculum com. 1991-94, La. dist. gov. 1979-80, project dir. model project for effective delivery of law-related edn. to low income families 1985-87, project dir. com. on substance abuse, chmn. delivery of legal svcs. com. young lawyers divsn. 1987, chmn. law student outreach com. 1988-91, asst. editor Affiliate mag. 1988-90, liaison to law student divsn. 1987-91, recipient Gold Key award 1980, regional coord. state and local bar liaison com. 1992-98, standing com. on Gavel awards 1994-97, project dir. com. on substance abuse 1994-97, ann. mtg. 1994 host com., ho. dels. 1994, 97-2000), La. Bar Assn. (chmn. law week 1986, mem. young lawyers sect. 1986-92, Achievement award 1985, 86, 87, mem. local and splty. bars com. 1992-98), New Orleans Bar Assn. (1st v.p. 1990-91, pres.-elect 1991-92, pres. 1992-93, chmn. TV com. 1992-98, com. on drugs and violence 1992-96, vice chmn. young lawyers sect. 1984-86, chmn. 1987-88, chmn. membership com. 1988-91, exec. com. 1988-94, vice chmn. increasing membership com. 1986-87, pub. rels. com. 1984-92, project grantee 1985-87), La. Ctr. for Law and Civic Edn. (pres. 1994-95, v.p. 1993-94, bd. dirs. 1992-96). Democrat. Roman Catholic. Home: 35 Dove St New Orleans LA 70124 Office: PO Box 24098 New Orleans LA 70184-4098 Office Phone: 504-288-3539. E-mail: pagarcia@pagarcialaw.com.

GARCIA, PAUL R., lawyer; AB Polit. Sci. & Hispanic Studies, Vassar Coll., 1987; JD, U. Chgo., 1992. Bar: Ill. 1992, U.S. Dist. Ct. No. Ill. Assoc. atty. Pattishal McAuliffe Newbury Hilliard & Geraldson, Chgo., 1992—94, Kirkland & Ellis, Chgo., 1994—96; asst. U.S. atty. U.S.D.O.J., Chgo., 1996—2001; ptnr., co-chair firm diversity com. Kirkland & Ellis, Chgo., 2001—. Mem.: Hispanic Nat. Bar Assn., Hispanic Lawyers Assn. Ill., Chgo. Council Lawyers, Internat. Trademark Assn. Office: Kirkland & Ellis 200 E Randolph Dr Chicago IL 60601 Office Phone: 312-861-2327. Office Fax: 312-861-2200. Business E-Mail: pgarcia@kirkland.com.

GARCIA, PHILIP A., insurance company executive; B in Acctg., Grove City Coll. CPA. From corp. acct. to mgr. internal audit Erie (Pa.) Indemnity Co., 1981—88; dept. mgr. life acctg. Erie Family Life Ins. Co., 1988—93; sr. v.p., contr. Erie Cos., 1993—97; exec. v.p., CFO Erie Ins. Group, 1997—. Bd. dirs. Hamot Health Found., Hamot Med. Ctr., Warner Theatre Preservation Trust, Bayfront Eastside Task Force, Erie Arts Coun. Mem.: AICPA, Fin. Exec. Inst., Pa. Inst. CPAs. Office: Erie Ins Group 100 Erie Insurance Pl Erie PA 16530

GARCIA, RAFAEL JORGE, retired chemical engineer; b. Havana, Cuba, July 2, 1933; came to U.S., 1962; s. Rafael and Martha Teresa (Suarez) G.; m. Amelia Fernandez, Feb. 23, 1958; children: Amelia Maria, Rafael Jorge Jr. BA, Columbia Coll., 1954; BSChE, La. State U., 1957; MS in Environ. Engring., Johns Hopkins U., 1975. Registered profl. engr., Ind., Ky., La., Md.; registered environ. mgr. Chem. engr. Freeport Sulphur Co., New Orleans, 1957—58; prodn. supt. Litografia Garcia Muniz, Havana, 1958—62; chem. engr. Am. Sugar Refining Co., Balt., 1962—63, House of Seagram, Balt., 1963—80, chief ecology engr. Louisville, 1981—97; cons. environ. regulatory affairs, 1998—; pres. Garcia Environ., 1997—. Mem. Am. Inst. Chem. Engrs., Instrument Soc. Am., St. Matthews Lions (pres. 1986-87). Republican. Roman Catholic. Home: 912 Lake Forest Pkwy Louisville KY 40245-5126 Personal E-mail: rj@garcia.win.net.

GARCIA, RAYMOND ARTHUR, lawyer; b. Chgo., Sept. 30, 1930; s. Raymond and Evelyn (Rathbun) G.; m. Yvonne Emily Garcia, July 7, 1955; children: Gregory Arthur, Curt Jonathan. BA, U. Ill., 1952; JD, Southwestern U., L.A., 1966. Bar: Calif. 1967, U.S. Dist. Ct. (ctrl. dist.) 1967, U.S. Ct. Appeals (9th cir.) 1967, U.S. Supreme Ct. 1974. Statistician Quaker Oats, L.A., 1953-55; asst. to pres. J.J. Haggarty's Stores, Beverly Hills, Calif., 1955-63; asst. contr. Seibu Dept. Stores, L.A., 1963-64; contr. Gourmet Concessions, L.A., 1964-65; audit rev. spl. U.S. Dept. Def., Bklyn., 1966; contr. Child Bros., L.A., 1967; dep. pub. defender Los Angeles County, L.A., 1967; sr. house counsel Baskin Robbins, Inc., Burbank, Calif., 1970-71; atty. Cohen England Whitfield, Oxnard, Calif., 1975-79; atty. in pvt. practice Thousand Oaks, Calif., 1968-70, 72—. Mayor, councilman City of Thousand Oaks, 1968-72; mem. So. Calif. Assn. Govt., L.A., 1968-72; pres. Thousand Oaks Sister City, 1994-97; bd. dirs. Conejo Youth Employment, pres., 1993-94; bd. dirs. ARC, pres., Ventura, 1993. Named Man of Yr. Conejo C. of C., 1972. Republican. Lutheran. Avocations: bowling, golf. Office: 516 Pensfield Pl Ste 104 Thousand Oaks CA 91360

GARCIA, RON B., securities trader, professional golfer; b. Donora, Pa., July 23, 1948; s. Angel Michael and Margaret Garcia; m. Karen Warner, Nov. 26, 1977; children: Courtney Elizabeth, Ron B. Jr. BA in Math., U. S. Fla., 1970. Head golf profl. Cedaebrook Golf Club, Smithton, Pa., 1970—72, Waynesville (N.C.) Country Club, 1972—74, Connestee Falls Country Club, Brevard, NC, 1974—82; dir. golf Keowee Key Country Club, Salem, SC, 1982; tchg. profl. Crooked Creek Golf Club, Hendersonville, NC, 1984—97, Hendersonville, 1992—2004. Profl. golfer PGA Tour, 2002; owner The Pro's Ice Cream Shop, Hendersonville, 1983—92. Author: Another Blessing From Lourdes, 2002. Mem.: PGA (class A mem.). Roman Catholic. Achievements include longest hole in one in world, 1973; aced 305 yard par 4 hole number 15th at Waynesville Country Club using 3 wood; double eagle on par 5 11th hole at Connestee Falls Country Clubusing a driver and eight iron; set five course records during 1970-1981. Avocations: golf, sports fan. Home and Office: PO Box 1817 Hendersonville NC 28793

GARCIA, RUDOLPH, lawyer; b. Phila., June 22, 1951; s. Rudolph Sr. and Assunta Rita (Marrara) G.; m. Randi Ellen Pastor, Aug. 3, 1980; 1 child, Jonathan P. BA magna cum laude, Temple U., 1974, JD cum laude, 1977. Bar: Pa. 1977, U.S. Dist. Ct. (ea. dist.) Pa. 1977, U.S. Ct. Appeals (3d cir.) 1982, U.S. Supreme Ct. 1982. Assoc. Wright, Thistle & Gibbons, Phila., 1977-78, Saul Ewing LLP, Phila., 1978-84, ptnr., 1984—. Judge pro tem Phila. Ct. Common Pleas. Fellow: Acad. Adv.; mem.: ABA (del. 2003—), Phila. Assn. Def. Counsel, Phila. Bar Assn. (chmn. local rules subcom. 1988—92, chmn. state civil com. 1999, bd. govs. 2000—02, chair fed. cts. com. 2004, bd. govs. 2004—05, chair state civil litigation sect. 2005), Pa. Bar Assn., Justinian Soc. (bd. govs. 1999—, vice-chancellor 2002—), Phi Beta Kappa. Avocations: computers, photography, golf. Home: 235 Lloyd Ln Wynnewood PA 19096-3323 Office: Saul Ewing LLP 1500 Market St 38th Fl Philadelphia PA 19102-2186 Office Phone: 215-972-1961. E-mail: rgarcia@saul.com.

GARCIA, SANTIAGO, cardiologist; b. Buenos Aires, Capital Federal, Argentina, May 23, 1975; s. Santiago Ricardo Garcia and Ana Maria Cortese; m. Mariana Canoniero, Apr. 12, 2002. MD, U. Buenos Aires, 1999. Diplomate Buenos Aires, Argentina, 2000. Mem. staff U. Miami, Fla., 2002—; chief med. resident VA Med. Ctr., Miami, Fla., 2005—. Recipient Sponge award, U. Miami, 2003. Mem.: ACP (assoc.), Am. Heart Assn. Achievements include research in the TIMI risk score correlates with extension and severity of coronary artery disease in patients with Non-ST segment elevation acute coronary syndromes.

GARCIA, SERAFIN MONTEALTO, physician; b. Sariaya, Philippines, Nov. 12, 1943; came to U.S., 1962; s. Zacarias and Roberta (Montealto) G.; children: John, Linda, Kimberly. BS, Columbia Union Coll., 1969; MD, Loma Linda U., 1973. Diplomate Am. Coll. Physicians. Chmn. bd. dirs. Covina Valley Cmty. Hosp., 1978-98; pres., adminstr. Glendale (Calif.) Home Health Care, 1988—; pres. Calif. Mobile X-Ray, Glendale, 1988—; chmn. bd. dirs. Thompson Meml. Med. Ctr., 1993-95. Bd. dirs. ARC, Glendale, 1996—. Avocations: tennis, golf, bicycling, skiing. Office: Glendale Home Health Care 601 E Glenoaks Blvd Ste 108 Glendale CA 91207-1760

GARCIA, SERGIO, professional golfer; b. Castellon, Spain, Jan. 9, 1980; Joined PGA, 1999; winner 19 events as amateur; winner Catalonian Open; winner Murphy's Irish Open, 1999; winner Linde German Masters, 1999; winner Mastercard Colonial and Buick Classic, 2001, Trophee Lancome and Nedbank Golf Challenge, 2001, Canarias Open de Espana and Kolon Cup Korean Open, 2002, Mercedes Championship, 2002, Nedbank Golf Challenge, 2003, EDS Bryon Nelson Championship and Buick Classic, 2004; co-winner Dunhill Cup title; finished 2nd Casio Open; mem. Ryder Cup, 1999, 2002, 2004, Dunhill Cup, 1999—2000. Record holder as youngest Ryder Cup participant, youngest player to make cut Turespana Open Mediterranea, 1995, youngest winner European Amateur Championship, 1995. Office: PGA Tour Box 109601 100 Ave of Champions Palm Beach Gardens FL 33410

GARCIA, SUSAN BREAUX, multi-media specialist, consultant; m. Gerard Garcia; children: Brandon, Caroline, Benjamin. BS in English Edn. magna cum laude, La. State U., 1973, MLS, 1977. Cert. secondary English, libr. sci. tchr. La. Elem. sch. libr. Iberia Parish Sch. Sys., Jeanerette, La., 1974—82, HS libr., 1982—93, dist. libr., media specialist supr. New Iberia, La., 1993—. Cons. storytelling Iberia Parish Sch. Sys., New Iberia, 1978—; cons. libr. sci. U. Southwestern La., Lafayette, 1995—2002, adj. instr. libr. sci.; storyteller. From pres. to sec. Entre Nous Club, Jeanerette, 1976—2005, chmn. Reading is Fundamental Project, 1979—2005; bd. dirs., sec. Friends of Iberia Parish Libr., New Iberia, La., 1998—2005; lector St. John the Evangelist Ch., Jeanerette, 1980—2005, mem. parish coun., 1999—2001. Named Outstanding Young Educator of La., La. Jaycees, 1980, Outstanding Young Educator, Jeanerette Jaycees, 1980, Outstanding Club Mem., Entre Nous Club, 1987, 1991, 2005; recipient Achievement award, Nat. Coun. Tchrs. English, 1970; scholar, La. State U. Alumni Fedn., 1970—73; Nat. Merit scholar, Texaco Merit scholar, Nat. Merit Scholarship Corp., 1970—73. Mem.: ALA, Title I Spl. Interest Coun., La. Reading Assn., Internat. Reading Assn., La. Libr. Assn., La. Assn. of Parish Textbook Administrs. (sec. 1999—2002), Alpha Beta Alpha, Alpha Lambda Delta, Beta Phi Mu, Phi Kappa Phi. Roman Catholic. Avocations: reading, storytelling, travel. Office: Iberia Parish Sch Sys 325 Provost St Jeanerette LA 70544 Office Phone: 337-364-7641.

GARCIA, VERONICA, school system administrator; BA, MA, EdD in Edn. Leadership, U. N.Mex. Exec. dir. N.Mex Coalition of Sch. Adminstrs.; supt. Santa Fe Pub. Schs.; regional supt. Albuquerque Pub. Schs.; sec. edn. N.Mex Pub. Edn. Dept., 2003—. Named one of Top Ten Hispanic Woman in N.Mex, N.Mex Legis., 2000; recipient Educator of Yr., N.Mex Rsch. and Study Coun., 2003. Office: NMex Pub Edn Dept 300 Don Gaspar Ave Santa Fe NM 87501-2752 Office Phone: 505-827-5800. Office Fax: 505-827-6696. E-mail: vcgarcia@ped.state.nm.us.*

GARCIA-BOLAO, JAIME MANUEL, music educator, linguist; b. Figueras, Gerona, Spain, Jan. 11, 1972; s. Francisco Garcia Rodriguez and Mercedes Bolao Diez; life ptnr. Neosha Ansherese Pringle. BA in Music, BA in Spanish, Fla. State U., 1996, BA in Russian. Founder, CEO Key Notes Piano Studio, Tallahassee, 1996—; translator State of Fla., Tallahassee, 2003—. Democrat. Office: Key Notes Piano Studio PO Box 12473 Tallahassee FL 32317 Office Phone: 850-322-8746. Personal E-mail: jgarciabolao@aol.com.

GARCIA-BUÑUEL, LUIS, neurologist; b. Madrid, Feb. 24, 1931; came to U.S., 1955; s. Pedro Garcia and Concepcion Buñuel; m. Virginia May Hile, June 30, 1960. BA, BS, U. Zaragoza, Spain, 1949; MD, U. Zaragoza, 1955. Diplomate Am. Bd. Psychiatry and Neurology. Resident neurology Georgetown U., Washington, 1955-59; postdoctoral fellow Washington U., St. Louis, 1959-61; asst. prof. neurology Thomas Jefferson U., Phila., 1961-67; assoc. prof. U. N.Mex., Albuquerque, 1967-72, U. Oreg. Health Scis. Ctr., Portland, 1972-84; chief neurology svc. Portland VA Med. Ctr., 1972-84; pvt. practice, Phoenix, 1984—; chief staff Carl T. Hayden VA Med. Ctr., Phoenix, 1984-96. Contbr. articles to sci. jours., including Nature, Sci., Neurology, Jour. Neurol. Sci. Lt. Spanish Air Force, 1952-55. Fellow Am. Acad. Neurology (sr. mem.), Sigma Xi. Unitarian Universalist. Avocations: painting, computer art, steel-welded sculpture. Home and Office: 128 N French Dr Prescott AZ 86303 E-mail: luisgbunuel@direcway.com.

GARCIA-GRANADOS, SERGIO EDUARDO, portfolio manager, writer, historian; b. June 11, 1942; s. Jorge and Miriam Garcia-Granados; m. Elizabeth Bentley, Apr. 3, 1973; children: Tatiana, Sybil. Law degree with honors, 1960-66, U. San Carlos, Guatemala, 1966; postgrad., U. Paris Inst. Scis. Politique, Paris, 1966-68. Bar: 1968. Rsch. assoc. Hague Acad. Internat. Law, 1969, Internat. Bur. Fiscal Documentation, Amsterdam, 1969-70; ptnr. law firm Saravia y Muñoz, Guatemala City, 1970-80; v.p. sales mgr. Merrill Lynch Capital Markets Internat., N.Y.C., 1982-88; v.p. resident mgr. internat. div. Shearson Lehman Hutton, N.Y.C., 1988-89; portfolio mgr. Lehman Bros., Miami, Fla., 1989—99; sr. portfolio mgr. UBS, Miami, 1999—. Lectr. tax problems in Central Am. Common Market, U. San Carlos, bus. orgns.,U. Landivar, Globalization of Capital Markets, Guatemalan Mgmt. Assn., 1991; bd. dirs. Miami Soc. Fin. Analysts, 1996—, Miami Symphony Orch., 2004—. Co-author: Cuaderno de Memorias (1900-1922), Artemis-Edinter, 2000, Reminiscencias (1944-51); author: Academia de Geografia e Historia, Revista Anales, 1999, El Siglo de las Luces Anales, 2002, Libre Crezca Fecunda (1729-1821), Editorial Magna Terra - Guatemala, 2005; organizer, 1st editor loose-leaf corp. taxation in Latin Am., Amsterdam, 1970. Bd. dir. Patronato de Bellas Artes, 1977—84, Guatemala Nat. Theatre Directorate, 1979—80, Miami (Fla.) Symphony Orch., 2004—, Cuban Mus. Art, trustee, 1991—99. Mem. Colegio de Abogados, Internat. Fiscal Assn. (gen. coun. 1972-80), Am. Soc. Internat. Law., CFA Inst., Miami Soc. Fin. Analysts (treas. 2000-2005, pres. 2005—), Acad. Geografia e Historia Guatemala. E-mail: sggranados@aol.com.

GARCIAPARRA, NOMAR (ANTHONY NOMAR GARCIAPARRA), professional baseball player; b. Whittier, Calif., July 23, 1973; m. Mia Hamm, 2003. Student, Ga. Tech. Shortstop Fla. St. League, Sarasota, Fla., 1994, Ea. League, Trenton, NJ, 1995, Internat. League, Pawtucket, 1996, Boston Red Sox, 1996—2004, Chicago Cubs, 2004—. Named Am. League Rookie Player of the Yr., The Sporting News, 1997, Baseball Writers' Assn. Am., 1997, Player's Choice Am. League Outstanding Rookie; named to Am. League All-Star Team, 1997, 1999, 2000, 2002, 2003. Achievements include being a mem. of U.S. Olympic Baseball Team, 1992; led Am. League in Batting Avg., 1999 (.357), 2000 (.372); led Am. League in Hits (209), 1997. Office: c/o Chicago Cubs Wrigley Field 1060 W Addison St Chicago IL 60613

GARCIA-SOSA, ICELINI, physician, educator; b. Mexico City, Feb. 21, 1978; d. Alfonso Garcia-Gutierrez and Martha Elena Sosa-Torres. MD, Nat. Autonomous U. Mexico, Mexico City, 2003. Fgn. med. grad. cert. Ednl. Commn. for Fgn. Med. Grads., 2004. Chief of interns Gen. Hosp. Manuel Gea Gonzalez, Mexico City, 2001—02; rschr. social svc. Nat. Inst. Med. Scis. and Nutrition Salvador Zubiran, Mexico City, 2002—03; post grad. tng. physician SUNY Downstate Med. Ctr., Bklyn., 2004—, clin. asst. instr., 2004—. Mem. Creativity Clinic Nat. Inst. Psychiatry, Mexico City, 2003—04. Mem. Chakrasambara Meditation Ctr., N.Y.C., 2004—05. Mem.: Assn. Women Psychiatrists, Am. Psychiat. Assn. Office: SUNY Downstate 450 Clarkson Ave Brooklyn NY 11215 Office Phone: 718-270-2902.

GARCIA Y CARRILLO, MARTHA XOCHITL, pharmacist; b. Austin, Tex., Dec. 7, 1919; d. Alberto Gonzalo and Guadalupe Eva (Carrillo) Garcia; m. Jerjes José Rodriguez, Oct. 9, 1943 (dec. 1987); children: Marie Eugenia, Jerjes Alberto, Nicanor Francisco. BS in Pharmacy, U. Tex., 1944. RPh, Tex. Retail pharmacist Ward Drug Store, Austin, Tex., 1952-57, Sommer's Drug Store, San Antonio, 1957-62, Skillern's Drug Store, Dallas, 1962-66; hosp. pharmacist Brackenridge Hosp., Austin, 1968-75; retail pharmacist Thorp Lane Pharmacy, San Marcos, Tex., 1975-77, The Pharmacy, San Marcos, 1975-79, MHMR Pharmacy, Austin, 1975-78, Ace Drug Co., Austin, 1979-82; ret. Contbg. author: The New Handbook of Texas, 1996. Recipient Citation of Achievement Tex. State Bd. Pharmacy, 1996. Mem. Am. Pharm. Assn. (emeritus mem.), Tex. Pharmacy Assn., Capitol Area Pharmacy Assn., Tex. State Hist. Assn., Ex-Students Assn. U. Tex. (life, Golden Anniversary cert. 1994). Republican. Avocations: reading, playing piano, current events, pharmacy medicine. Home: 21107 Ridgeview Rd Lago Vista TX 78645-4617

GARD, MARK ALVIN, music educator; s. Alvin and Zenora Gard. B in Music Edn., McPherson Coll., 1984; M in Music Edn., Wichita State U., 2000. Tchr. secondary music Hillcrest Sch., Jos, Nigeria, 1986—91; secondary vocal music tchr. Field Kindley H.S., Coffeyville, Kans., 1991—. Dir. Coffeyville Cmty. Children's Choir, 1997—. Bd. dirs. Coffeyville Cultural Arts Coun., 1992—2002; alumni bd. McPherson (Kans.) Coll., 1999—2002. Named Secondary Educator of the Yr., Coffeyville Area C. of C., 1998; recipient Involve award, Uniserv SE, 2001, Excellence in Edn., Coffeyville CC, 1999. Mem.: NEA, Kans. Music Educators Assn. (S.E. Kans. choral chairperson 1999—2001), Kans. Choral Dirs. Assn. (S.E. Kans. rep. 2001—,

2001—04), Music Educators Nat. Conf. (S.E. Kans. choral chairperson 1999—2001). Office: Field Kindley HS 1100 W 8th St Coffeyville KS 67337 Office Phone: 620-252-6410. E-mail: gardm@cvilleschools.com.

GARD, TOBY, computer graphics designer; s. John and Pat Gard. Lead graphic artist, creator of character Lara Croft for Tomb Raider Core Design, Derby, England, 1993—97; co-founder Confounding Factor, Bristol, England, 1997—2004; sr. designer, Tomb Raider team Crystal Dynamics, Palo Alto, Calif., 2004—. Lead graphic artist, creator of characters (computer games) Tomb Raider, 1996, lead graphic designer, creator Galleon, 2004. Office: Crystal Dyamics 64 Willow Pl Menlo Park CA 94025

GARDEBRING, SANDRA S., academic administrator; Grad., Luther Coll., Decorah, Iowa; JD, U. Minn. Dir. Region 5 U.S. EPA; commr. Minn. Pollution Control Agy., Minn. Dept. Human Svcs.; judge Minn. Ct. Appeals; assoc. justice Minn. Supreme Ct., 1991-98; v.p. univ. rels. U. Minn., 1998—2004; v.p. univ. advancement Calif. Polytech. State Univ., San Luis Obispo, 2004—. Bd. dirs. Nature Conservancy of Minn., Regions Hosp. Hearth Connection, Greater Mpls. Conv. and Visitors Assn. Mailing: 1055 Capistrano Ct San Luis Obispo CA 93405

GARDELLA, FRANCIS JOHN, mathematics professor; b. S.I., Jan. 1, 1943; s. Frank C. and Margaret G. Gardella; m. Gail Gardella, Aug. 24, 1968; children: Jennifer, Derek. BS in Math., Fordham U., 1964; MA in Edn., Lehigh U., Bethlehem, Pa., 1966; MA in Math., Bklyn. Coll., 1971; EdD in Math. Edn., Rutgers U., 1974. Tchr. math. Pa. and NJ schs., 1964—73; math supr. several NJ schs., 1974—94; assoc. prof. math. edn. and math. Hunter Coll.-CUNY, 1994—, exec. dir. Ctr. for Math. Learning and Tchg., 2002—. Cons. in math., 1975—. Author: (book series) Math Problem Solver, 1999, Problems Plus, 1995, 4 other math. textbooks; co-author: Mathematical Connections, 1992. Recipient Disting. Svc. award Rutgers U. Grad. Sch. Alumni Assn., 2000, LADAS award for excellence in tchg. Hunter Coll. Sch. Edn., 2001. Mem. Nat. Coun. Tchrs. Math., Assn. Math. Tchrs. N.J. Roman Catholic. Avocations: golf, tennis, history. Home: 30 Yorktown Rd East Brunswick NJ 08816 Office: Hunter College-CUNY 695 Park Ave New York NY 10021

GARDENIER, JOHN STARK, statistician, philosopher, researcher, writer; b. Portland, Maine, Apr. 10, 1937; s. John Stark and Lucia Esther (Christensen) G.; m. Margaret Elizabeth Mann, Jan. 26, 1962 (dec. 1976); children: Brenda Anne Marshall, Patricia Suzanne Depew, Linda Marie Sievering-Albrecht, Pamela Lee Antoun; m. Turkan Emine Kumbaraci, June 18, 1977; children: George Halil Bonneval, Jason Celal Stark. BA, Yale U., 1959; MS, George Washington U., 1968, DBA, 1973. Tech. staff Computer Scis. Corp., Falls Church, Va., 1968-69; sr. analyst CONSULTEC, Rockville, Md., 1969-71; ops. rsch. analyst USCG, Washington, 1971-90; survey statistician Nat. Ctr. Health Stats., Hyattsville, Md., 1990—2003; ret., 2003. Adj. assoc. prof. George Washington U., 1980-81; prof. lectr. Am. U., Washington, 1982-84; cons. in field. Comdr. USN, ret. Recipient Silver medal U.S. Dept. Transp., 1983, Dir.'s award CDC/Nat. Ctr. for Health Stats., 2000. Mem. AAAS (profl. soc. ethics group), Am. Statis. Assn. (com. profl. ethics 1994-96, chair com. profl. ethics 1996-99, vice chair com. reps. 2002—, rep. to AAAS sect. history and philosophy of sci. 2002—), Nat. Assn. of Sci. Writers, Naval Res. Assn Avocations: music, golf. Home: 115 St Andrews Dr NE Vienna VA 22180-3660 Office Phone: 703-319-3981. E-mail: drgarden@verizon.net.

GARDENIER, TURKAN KUMBARACI, statistician, researcher; b. Istanbul, Turkey, Nov. 10, 1941; arrived in U.S., 1958; d. Celal and Aysel (Triandafilidu) K.; m. John Stark Gardenier, June 18, 1977; children: Pamela Lee, George HalilBonneval, Jason Celal Stark. AB, Vassar Coll., 1961; MA, Columbia U., 1962, PhD, 1966. Ops. rsch. scientist IIT Rsch. Inst., Chgo., 1966-68; asst. prof., chmn. Middle East Tech. U., Ankara, Turkey, 1968-70; vis. scientist Brookhaven Nat. Labs., Upton, L.I., NY, 1970-71; assoc. dir. Pfizer Pharms., N.Y.C., 1971-73; asst. prof. N.Y. State Maritime Coll., Bronx, NY, 1973-78; health scientist U.S. EPA, Washington, 1978-81; assoc. prof. Am. U., Washington, 1982-84; pres. Pragmatica Corp., Vienna, Va., 1982—. Tech. cons. Analytic Services Corp., Arlington, Va., 1982-90; expert U.S. Energy Info. Adminstrn., Washington, 1982-84; statis. expert EEO, 1990—, statis. cons. Engring. Computer Optecnomics, Annapolis, Md., 1977—; cons. C.R. Cushing Co., Marine Engring., N.Y.C., 1974-77. Organizer, pub. Symposium on Data Efficiency Design; preprocessing pub. Garden-ear Math./Stat. Series for Quanititative Literacy. Corp. mem. Am. Friends of Turkey, McLean, Va., 1983-89; com. mem. World Mut. Service Com., N.Y.C., 1982—; bd. dirs., v.p. Friends of Am. BoardSchs. in Turkey, 1986-88, Am. Turkish Assn., Washington, 1988-90, Washington parents rep. Foxcroft Sch., Middleburg, Va., 1981-84. Grantee, NSF, 1980, CENTO, 1969, NIH/NCI, 1997-2000. Mem. Am. Statis. Assn. (audio-visual graphics com. 1979), Ops. Rsch. Soc. Am. (fin. com. 1980), Soc. Computer Simulation (assoc. editor jour. 1980-84), Soc. Risk Analysis (fin. com. 1980), AAAS (symposium organizer 1979-2003). Avocations: swimming, photography, music composition, multi-media training. Address: Pragmatica Corp 115 St Andrews Dr NE Vienna VA 22180-3660 Office Phone: 703-319-9009. E-mail: drgarden@erols.com.

GARDEZI, SYED A., medical researcher; b. Multan, Punjab, Pakistan, June 19, 1970; s. Syed Arif Raza and Sajida Gardezi; m. Anila Mushtaq; children: Mishaal, Maham. M.B.B.S., Allama Iqbal Med. Coll., Lahore, 1995. Diplomate 1997. Postdoctoral fellow M.D. Anderson Cancer Ctr., Houston, 1997—2001, Baylor Coll. Medicine, Houston, 1998—2001; pvt. practice Amarillo, Tex., 2001—. Author: Vitamin D Endocrine System Structural, Biological, Genetic and Clinical Aspects, 2000. Recipient Young Investigators award, Leo Pharms., 2000. Mem.: Am. Soc. Bone and Mineral Rsch. Home: 7905 Triumph Pl Amarillo TX 79119 Office: MD Anderson Cancer Ctr & Baylor Coll Holcombe Blvd Houston TX 77713

GARDIN, JULIUS MARKUS, cardiologist, educator; b. Detroit, Jan. 14, 1949; s. Abram and Fania (Toba) G.; children: Adam Lev, Tova Michal, Margot Anne. BS with high distinction, U. Mich., 1968, MD cum laude, 1972. Diplomate Am. Bd. Internal Medicine; cert. cardiovascular diseases. Intern then resident in medicine U. Mich., Ann Arbor, 1972-75; fellow in cardiology Georgetown U., Washington, 1975-77; dir. cardiology noninvasive lab., staff cardiologist Lakeside VA Med. Ctr., Chgo., 1977-79; staff cardiologist Northwestern U., Chgo., 1977—79, asst. prof. Med. Sch., 1978—79; dir. cardiology noninvasive lab. Irvine Med. Ctr. U. Calif., Orange, 1979-2000, from asst. prof. to assoc. prof. Irvine Med. Ctr., 1979—89, prof., 1989-2000, chief cardiology Irvine, 1994-99; acting chief cardiology Long Beach (Calif.) VA Med. Ctr., 1982—84; prof. Wayne State U., Detroit, 2000—; St. John Guild disting. chair, chief div. cardiology St. John Hosp. and Med. Ctr., Detroit, 2000—. Co-editor: Textbook of Two-Dimensional Echocardiography, 1983; assoc. editor: Update on Cardiovascular Diagnostics, 1982, Am. Jour. Cardiac Imaging, 1985-97, Preventive Cardiology, 2000, 05; mem. editl. bd. Archives of Internal Medicine and Chest, 1978-88, Am. Jour. Noninvasive Cardiology, 1985-95, Am. Jour. Cardiology, 1987-94, 97—, Cardiovascular Imaging, 1988—, Echocardiography, 1985—, Jour. Am. Coll. Cardiology, 1990-94, 2001-05, Am. Jour. Geriatric Cardiology, 1992—, Am. Jour. Sports Medicine, 1998-2004, Jour. Am. Soc. Echocardiography, 1992-2001; cardiovasc. area editor Jour. Clin. Ultrasound, 1989-94; contbr. articles to profl. jours. Maj. Med. Svc. Corps USAR. Grantee Am. Heart Assn., 1980-84, 99-2002, Nat. Heart Lung and Blood Inst., 1988—; named one of Best Drs. in Am. Woodward White Publs., 1994--, Am.'s Top Drs. Castle Connolly Publs., 2002--. Fellow ACP, Am. Coll. Cardiology (physician workforce adv., health care reform and echocardiography coms., 1993-99), Am. Heart Assn. (coun. clin. cardiology, coun. epidemiology and prevention, coun. cardiovascular radiology, ACC/AHA/ACP-ASIM task force to update guidelines for mgmt. of patients with chronic stable angina 1998-99, 2001-02), Soc. Geriat. Cardiology (v.p. 1990-92, pres. 1992-93); mem. Internat. Cardiac Doppler Soc. (bd. dirs., chmn. Pan-Am. sect. 1984—, v.p. 1988-90, pres. 1990-92), Am. Soc. Echocardiography (bd. dirs., treas. 1989-91, v.p. 1991-93, pres. 1993-95, chmn. nomenclature and stds. 1991-95, chmn. task force on standardized echo report 1999-2002, co-chmn. writing group on vascular imaging 2001—), U. Mich. Med. Ctr. Alumni Assn. (bd. govs. 1979-81), Phi Beta Kappa, Alpha Omega Alpha, Phi Delta Epsilon. Jewish. Office: St John Hosp and Med Ctr PBII Ste 470 22201 Moross Rd Detroit MI 48236 Office Phone: 313-343-6390. Business E-Mail: julius.gardin@stjohn.org.

GARDINER, E. NICHOLAS P., personnel director; b. Boston, June 19, 1939; s. John Pennington and Juliana (Geszty) G.; m. Judith Beck, Jan. 19, 1975 (div. Sept. 1981); m. Sigrid Becker Bron, Mar. 19, 1987; stepchildren: Christian Bron, Eric Edouard Bron. BA, Yale U., 1961; PMD, Harvard Bus. Sch., 1971. Gen. mgr. W.R. Grace & Co., N.Y.C., 1965-70, Envases Sanmarti div. W.R. Grace & Co., Lima, Peru, 1967-70; dir. corp. devel., N.Y. Internat. Basic Economy Corp., 1970-72, v.p., N.Y., 1974-78; v.p. Cen. Nat. Corp., 1973, Boyden Assocs., N.Y.C., 1979-80, ptnr., 1980-83, sr. v.p., 1982-83; pres., chief exec. officer Haley Internat. Inc., N.Y.C., 1984-87; mng. dir. Gardiner Stone Hunter Internat. Inc., N.Y.C., 1987-92; exec. Paul Ray & Co., N.Y.C., 1992-93; pres. Eric Salmon & Ptnrs. Inc., N.Y.C., 1993-95, Gardiner Internat., N.Y.C., 1995—, Gardiner, Townsend & Assocs., N.Y.C., 1998—2002. Dir. Radio Free Europe/Radio Liberty Fund.; dir. Am. Coun. on Germany, French-Am. Found. Served to 1st lt. USMCR, 1961-64. Mem. Inst. Francais des Rels. Internat., Royal Inst. Internat. Affairs, The Brook, Racquet and Tennis Club, Jesters Club, Polo Club (Paris). Republican. Episcopalian. Home: One White Pine Rd Sloatsburg NY 10974-2650 Office: Gardiner Internat 645 5th Ave 18th Flr New York NY 10022-6018 Office Phone: 212-546-6263. E-mail: ng@gardinerint.com.

GARDINER, HOBART CLIVE, petroleum company executive; b. Boston, Jan. 12, 1929; m. Patricia Williams, Oct. 14, 1950. BA, Yale U., 1950; postgrad., U. Central Caracas, Venezuela. Various mgmt. positions Esso Standard Oil Co. S.A., Havana, Cuba, 1954, Panama City, Panama, 1954, San Salvador, El Salvador, 1954-56, Guatemala City, Guatemala, 1956, country mgr. San Jose, Costa Rica, 1956-57, Tegucigalpa, Honduras, Brit. Honduras, 1957-60; asst. employee rels. mgr. Esso Interamerica Inc., Coral Gables, Fla., 1960; pres., gen. mgr. Esso Standard Oil Co., S.A., San Juan, P.R., 1960-62; v.p. Internat. Petroleum Co. Ltd., Bogota, Colombia, 1962-64, ops. mgr. Talara, Peru, 1964-66; pres. Esso Std. Oil (Chile), Santiago, 1966-69; L.Am. area advisor Standard Oil Co. N.J., N.Y.C., 1969-71; v.p. Esso Standard Oil Co. C.Am., Panama, San Salvador, El Salvador, 1971-74; gen. mgr. Esso Chile, Uruguay and Paraguay, Montevideo, Uruguay, 1974-77; pub. affairs program mgr. Exxon Corp., N.Y.C., 1977-79; asst. gen. mgr. Esso Caribbean, Coral Gables, Fla., 1979-81; v.p. fin. and adminstrn. Internat. Exec. Svc. Corps., Stamford, Conn., 1982-84, v.p. L.Am. and Caribbean, 1984-90, exec. v.p., 1990-93, pres., CEO, 1993—2003; ret., 2003. With USMC, 1950—52. Mem.: Country Club Fairfield. Episcopalian. E-mail: gardiner_hobart_c@sbcglobal.net.

GARDINER, JOHN ANDREW, political science educator; b. Niagara Falls, N.Y., July 10, 1937; s. William Cecil and Anne Charlotte (Hicks) G.; m. Jane Enstrom, Nov. 6, 1993; children: Margaret, Allison, Barrett. BA, Princeton U., 1959; MA, Yale U., 1962; LLB, Harvard U., 1963, PhD, 1966. Bar: Mass. 1963. Asst. prof. U. Wis., Madison, 1965-68; assoc. prof. SUNY, Stony Brook, 1968-69; chief rsch. planning Nat. Inst. Justice, Washington, 1969-71, dir. rsch. ops., 1971-73, asst. dir., 1973-74; prof. polit. sci. U. Ill., Chgo., 1974—, head dept. polit. sci., 1974-76, dir. office social sci. rsch., 1987—2002, acting assoc. dean Liberal Arts and Scis., 1991—92, 2000—02. Author: Fraud Control Game, 1984, Decisions for Sale, 1978, Politics of Corruption, 1970, Traffic and the Police 1969; contbr. articles to profl. jours. V.p. Ill. Citizens for Better Care, Chgo., 1988—90; rsch. dir. Chgo. Ethics Project, 1986—88. Rsch. fellow Am. Judicature Soc., 1985-86. Mem. Phi Beta Kappa. Office: U Ill Pol Sci M/C 276 1007 W Harrison St Chicago IL 60607-7137 E-mail: gracelan@uic.edu.

GARDINER, JOHN JACOB, adult education educator, writer, philosopher; b. Tel Aviv, Feb. 6, 1946; arrived in U.S., 1952; s. Leon and Zipora Zucker; m. Joanna Meredith Winslow, 1967 (div. 1998); children: James, Katharine. BA, U. Fla., 1967, PhD, 1973; postgrad., U. Oreg., 1978, Stanford U., 1983. Tchr., dept. chair Keystone Heights (Fla.) Sch., 1968-72; instr., asst. to v.p. acad. affairs U. Fla., Gainesville, 1973-75; asst. prof. edn. The Citadel, Charleston, SC, 1975-77; prof., dept. chair Okla. State U., Stillwater, 1979-91, Seattle U., 1991—. Assoc. in edn. Harvard U., 1985; vis. asst. prof. Fla. State U., Tallahassee, 1977-78, U. Oreg., Eugene, 1978-79; chair bd. Pacific N.W. Postdoctoral Inst., Seattle, 1995-99; bd. dir. Internat. Leadership Assn., Conflict Resolution Inst., Human Connection Inst., Ctr. for Advanced Study of Leadership, U. Md., College Park; co-founder All Russia Leadership Devel. Ctr., Novosibirsk, 1999-2000; mem. exec. com. Internat. Leadership Assn., 2001-03. Co-author: UNESCO Guide, 1991, Insights on Leadership, 1998, Building Leadership Bridges, 2003. Recipient Svc. to State award Gov. and Ho. of Reps., 1991; fellow W. K. Kellogg Found., 1972-73; grantee James McGregor Burns Leadership Acad. Ctr. for Advanced Study of Leadership, 1998. Mem. Am. Coun. Edn. (bd. dir. Nat. Leadership Group 1985-96), Assn. Study of Higher Edn. (bd. dir. 1983-85), Am. Ednl. Rsch. Assn. (bd. dirs. divsn. J 1983-85), Vashon Island Rotary Club (pres. 2000-01, dist. 5030 gov. 2003-04, permanent fund chair dist. 5030, 1996-2002, strategic advisor ann. program 2005—) Avocations: walking, reading, gardening, public speaking. Office: Seattle U 413 Loyola Hall Broadway and Madison Seattle WA 98122 Office Phone: 206-296-6171. Business E-Mail: gardiner@seattleu.edu.

GARDINER, JOY WENDY, conservator, educator; b. Woodbury, N.J., Feb. 12, 1955; d. Laura Ann and J. Willard Gardiner; m. Harold Kalmus, June 7, 1986; 1 child, Grace Gardiner Kalmus. BFA, Moore Coll. Art, Phila., 1973—77; MS, U. Del., Newark, 1985—88. Pvt. textile conservator, Phila., 1989—91; asst. textile conservator Winterthur Mus., Garden & Libr., Del., 1990—95, assoc. textile conservator, 1995—2000, textile conservator, 2000—05, asst. dir., conservation, 2001—; adj. asst. prof., art conservation U. Del., Newark, 1991—. Bd. dirs., sec. N.Am. Textile Conservation Conf., Albany, NY, 2002—. Contbr. articles to profl. jours. Bd. dirs. Arden Cmty. Recreation Assn., Del., 2003—05; membership co-chair Arden Club, Del., 2002—05. NEA Fellow in Costume and Textiles Conservation, NEA, 1988—89. Mem.: Am. Inst. for Conservation of Hist. & Artistic Works (assoc.; vice chair, textile splty. group 1998—99, chair, textile splty. group 1999—2000, treas., textile splty. group 1991—92). Avocations: reading, cross country skiing, snorkeling. Home: 2215 Little Ln Arden DE 19810 Office: Winterthur Mus Garden & Libr 5105 Kennett Pike Winterthur DE 19735 Office Phone: 302-888-4612. E-mail: jgardiner@winterthur.org.

GARDINER, JUDITH KEGAN, English language and women's studies educator; b. Chgo., Dec. 17, 1941; d. Albert and Esther (Oswianza) Kegan; divorced; children: Viveca, Carita. BA, Radcliffe Coll., 1962; MA, Columbia U., 1964, PhD, 1968. Prof. English, gender and women's studies U. Ill., Chgo., 1969—, acting dir. women's studies, 1989, 91, dir. gender and women's studies program, 2004—. Author: Rhys Stead Lessing, 1989; editor: Provoking Agents, 1995, Masculinity Studies and Feminist Theories, 2002; editor Feminist Studies, 1989—; also articles. Organizer Newberry Libr. Feminist Lit. Criticism Group, Chgo., 1985-95. Fellow, NEH, 1988. Office: U Ill Dept English M/C 162 601 S Morgan St Chicago IL 60607-7120 E-mail: gardiner@uic.edu.

GARDINER, LESTER RAYMOND, JR., retired lawyer; b. Salt Lake City, Aug. 20, 1931; s. Lester Raymond and Sarah Lucille (Kener) G.; m. Janet Ruth Thatcher, Apr. 11, 1955; children: Allison Gardiner Bigelow, John Alfred, Annette Gardiner Weed, Leslie Gardiner Crandall, Robert Thatcher, Lisa Gardiner West, James Raymond, Elizabeth Gardiner Smith, David William, Sarah Janet Boyden. BS with honors, U. Utah, 1954; JD, U. Mich., 1959. Bar: Utah 1959, U.S. Dist. Ct. Utah 1959, U.S. Ct. Appeals (10th cir.) 1960. Law clk. U.S. Dist. Ct., 1959; assoc. then ptnr. Van Cott, Bagley, Cornwall & McCarthy, Salt Lake City, 1960—67; ptnr. Gardiner & Johnson, Salt Lake City, 1967—72, Christensen, Gardiner, Jensen & Evans, 1972—78, Fox, Edwards, Gardiner & Brown, Salt Lake City, 1978—87, Chapman & Cutler, 1987—89, Gardiner & Hintze, 1990—92; CEO and pres. Snowbird Ski and Summer Resort, Snowbird Corp., 1993—97; prin., mgmt. cons. Ray Gardiner Assocs., 1998—2003. Reporter, mem. Utah Sup. Ct. Com. on Adoption of Uniform Rules of Evidence, 1970-73, mem. com. on revision of criminal code, 1975-78; master of the bench Am. Inn of Ct. I, 1980-90; mem. com. bar examiners Utah State Bar, 1973; instr. bus. law U. Utah, 1965-66; adj. prof. law Brigham Young U., 1984-85. Mem. Republican State Central Com. Utah, 1967-72, mem. exec. com. Utah Rep. Party, 1975-78, chmn. state convs., 1980, 81; mem. Salt Lake City Bd. Edn., 1971-72; bd. dirs. Salt Lake City Pub. Library, 1974-75; trustee Utah Sports Found., 1987-91; bd. dirs. and exec. com. Salt Lake City Visitors and Conv. Bur., 1988-91, 93-98; mem., chmn. bd. dirs. Inst. Outdoor Recreation and Tourism Utah State U., 1997-03. Served to 1st lt. USAF, 1954-56. Mem. Utah State Bar Assn. Mem. Lds Ch. Office: Ray Gardiner Assocs 93 Laurel St Salt Lake City UT 84103-4349

GARDINER, PAMELA NAN, performing company executive; m. David Edward Miller, 1974 (div. 1988); m. Anton Labuschagne, 1998 (div. 1999). BA, U. Wis.; MA, Columbia U.; JD, Case Western Res. U. Bar: Ohio 1975, Wis. 1982, Fla. 1999. Asst. trust officer Cleve. Trust Co., 1975-78; asst. dean acad. affairs Coll. Letters and Sci. U. Wis., 1978-84; exec. dir. Madison Festival of the Lakes, 1984-88, Miami City Ballet, Fla., 1988—, Gardiner & Fix LLC, Arts and Entertainment Atty., 2002—. Bd. dirs. Miami Performing Arts Ctr. Found., Miami Beach Prodn. Industry Coun. Office: Miami City Ballet 2200 Liberty Ave Miami Beach FL 33139-1641

GARDINER, T(HOMAS) MICHAEL, artist; b. Seattle, Feb. 5, 1946; s. Thomas Scott Gardiner and Carolyn Virginia (Harmer) Bolin; m. Kelly Michelle Floyd, Mar. 7, 1981 (div. Dec. 1983); m. Diana Phyllis Shurtlieff Rainwater, Sept. 26, 1986; children: Rita Em, Nigel Gus. BA in Philosophy, Sulpician Sem. N.W., Kenmore, Wash., 1969; student, Cornish Inst. Arts, 1971—73. Seaman Tidewater Barge, Camas, Wash., 1969; pari-mutuel clk. Longacres Racetrack, Renton, Wash., 1969-92; dock worker Sealand, Inc., Seattle, 1970. Tchr. Coyote Jr. H.S., Seattle, 1989-95, Sch. Visual Concepts, Seattle, 1990-95; tchr., vis. artist Ctrl. Wash. U., Ellensburg, 1991; installer fine art Artech, Seattle, 1999—. Represented in permanent collections Ballard H.S., Seattle, Microsoft Corp., Stoel Rives LLP, Stokes Lawrence PS, Seattle Water Dept., Nordstrom, Seattle City Light, Mus. of N.W. Art, LaConner, Wash., Sultan (Wash.) Sch. Dist., King County Portable Works Collection, SAFECO Ins. Co., Seattle, City of Portland Collection, 1988, Highline Sch. Dist., Seattle, U. Wash. Med. Ctr.; commns. include ARTp Metro Art Project, Seattle, interior painting Villa del Lupo restaurant, Vancouver, B.C., Can.; illustrations included in The New Yorker Mag., Am. Illustration 13, The Seattle Times. Recipient Best Design award Print Mag., 1985; Nat. Endowment for Arts fellow, 1989. Democrat. Roman Catholic. Home and Office: 3023 NW 63rd St Seattle WA 98107-2566 E-mail: gardiner@speakeasy.net.

GARDINER, WILLIAM CECIL, JR., chemist, educator; b. Niagara Falls, N.Y., Jan. 14, 1933; s. William Cecil and Annie Charlotte (Hicks) G.; children— Grace, Charlotte, Amy Louise; m. Regina R. Monaco, July 15, 1991. AB, Princeton U., 1954; postgrad., U. Heidelberg, 1954-55, U. Göttingen, 1955-56; PhD, Harvard U., 1960. Instr. chemistry U. Tex., Austin, 1960-62, asst. prof., 1962-66, assoc. prof., 1966-72, prof., 1972—. Cons. on chemistry of combustion reactions to govtl. agencies. Contbr. articles on rates of chem. reactions to tech. jours. Fulbright fellow, 1954-55, 75-76; Guggenheim fellow, 1975-76; Humboldt fellow, 1979, 82; Thyssen fellow, 1983; Lady Davis prof., 1985. Fellow Japan Soc. for Promotion Sci; mem. Am. Chem. Soc., Am. Phys. Soc., AAAS, Combustion Inst., Phi Beta Kappa, Sigma Xi. Office: Univ Tex Dept Chemistry/Biochemistry WEL 2 406 MC A5300 Austin TX 78712

GARDINER, WILLIAM DOUGLAS HAIG, bank executive, director; b. Chatham, Ont., Can., Apr. 21, 1917; s. William Henry and Elsie May (Armstrong) G.; m. Jean Elizabeth Blatchford, Sept. 5, 1945; children: Donald W. B., Campbell D., Gregory F. Grad., Kennedy Collegiate Sch., Windsor, Ont. Asst. gen. mgr. Royal Bank of Can., Montreal, 1961-64, Vancouver, 1964-67, v.p., dist. gen. mgr., 1967-73, dep. chmn., exec. v.p. Toronto, 1973-77, vice chmn., dir., 1977-80; pres. W.D.H.G. Fin. Assocs. Ltd., Vancouver. Served to lt. comdr. RCNVR. Decorated Order of Canada. Mem.: Shaughnessy Golf Club. Presbyterian. Home: 3115 W 49th Ave Vancouver BC Canada V6N 3T3

GARDINO, VINCENT ANTHONY, broadcast executive; b. NYC, Sept. 19, 1953; s. Anthony John and Carmelina Mary (Boglia) Gardino. BA in History magna cum laude, St. Francis Coll. V.p. NY sales mgr., dir. spl. programming and sales Metro Radio Sales, NYC, 1976-79; acct. exec. Sta. WABC-AM Radio, NYC, 1979-81; dir. ABC Radio Network, NYC, 1981-85, ABC Direction and Entertainment Radio Networks, 1981-85; pres., COO Selcom Radio, NYC, 1985—; v.p., gen. sales mgr. Sta. WOR-AM, NYC, 1985-95; v.p. ea. sales CNBC, 1995-98; exec. dir. corp. underwriting sales Sta. WNYC-FM, Sta. WNYC-AM, 1998—. Cons. DEI, Inc., 2001—; adj. assoc. prof. comm., arts St. Francis Coll., NY, 2003—. Mem. founders cir. Lower East Side Tenement Mus.; mem. parish coun. St. Malachy's Ch.; trustee St. Francis Coll., 2005—; bd. dirs. Kaplan Cancer Ctr., NYU Med. Ctr. Mem.: Mus. Broadcasting, Internat. Radio and TV Soc., Columbus Citizens Found., Inc., Famija Piemonteisa, NY Athletic Club. Roman Catholic. Avocations: tennis, golf, skiing, historical autograph collecting. Office: WNYC AM/FM 1 Centre St New York NY 10007-1602 Business E-Mail: vgardino@wnyc.org.

GARDNER, ANDREW WILLIAM, healthcare educator; s. William Oliver Gardner, Ray Kirk (Stepfather) and Helen Irene Ratcliff; m. Polly Sue Montgomery. BS, U. Calif., Fullerton, 1980—83; MS, Purdue U., West Lafayette, Ind., 1984—86; PhD, Ariz. State U., Tempe, 1986—90. Postdoctoral rsch. fellow, divsn. endocrinology, nutrition, and metabolism U. Vt., Burlington, 1990—93; asst., assoc. prof., divsn. gerontology U. Md., Balt., 1993—2001; prof., health and exercise sci. U. Okla., Norman, 2002—. Contbr. articles to profl. jours. Grantee, NIH, 1991—93, 1994—99, 2000—05. Fellow: Am. Coll. Angiology, Soc. for Vascular Medicine and Biology; mem.: Gerontol. Soc. Am., Internat. Soc. Aging and Phys. Activity, Am. Assn. Cardiovasc. and Pulmonary Rehab., Am. Coll. Sports Medicine. Office: Univ Okla 1401 Asp Av Room 110 Norman OK 73019 Office Phone: 405-325-1371. Office Fax: 405-325-0594. E-mail: awgardner@ou.edu.

GARDNER, ARNOLD BURTON, lawyer; b. N.Y.C., Jan. 3, 1930; s. Harry P. and Ruth G. (Gutfreund) G.; m. Sue Shaffer, Aug. 24, 1952; children—Jonathan H., Diane R. BA summa cum laude, U. Buffalo, 1950; LL.B., Harvard U., 1953. Bar: N.Y. State bar 1954. Assoc. firm Kavinoky Cook LLP (and predecessor), Buffalo, 1953—58, ptnr., 1958, sr. ptnr., 1977. Mem. Buffalo Bd. Edn., 1969-74, pres., 1971-72; mem. nat. bd. govs. Am. Jewish Com., 1972-95, nat. v.p., 1986-89; chmn. N.Y. State Edn. Dept. Task Force on Tchr. Edn. and Certification, 1975-77; trustee SUNY, 1980-99, vice chmn., 1991-95; bd. govs. Hebrew Union Coll., Jewish Inst. Religion, Cin., 1981-87; trustee N.Y. State Archives, 1994—; mem. N.Y. State Bd. Regents, 1999—. With U.S. Army, 1954-56. Recipient Cmty. Service award NCCJ, 1974, 88; named Lawyer of Yr. U. Buffalo Sch. of Law, 1994. Mem. N.Y. State Bar Assn., Erie County Bar Assn., Am. Law Inst. Clubs: Buffalo. Office: Kavinoky Cook LLP 726 Exchange St Ste 800 Buffalo NY 14210 Office Phone: 716-845-6000.

GARDNER, CLYDE EDWARD, healthcare executive, consultant, educator; b. Steubenville, Ohio, Oct. 8, 1931; s. Peter D. and Louella Mary (Gillespie) G.; m. Patricia Jackson, Oct. 4, 1953 (div. Dec. 1977); 1 child, Bruce Stephen. BA, San Francisco State U., 1969, MS, 1971. Adminstr. Gardner Convalescent Hosp., Napa, Calif., 1955-68; exec. dir. Haight Ashbury Free Med. Clinic, San Francisco, 1970-71; lectr. San Francisco State U., 1969-71; dir. planning and rsch. divsn. N. Country Com. on Area Wide Health Planning, Canton, N.Y., 1971-77; prof. Gov.'s State U., University Park, Ill., 1977-83; sr. ptnr. Health Care Cons., Park Forest, Ill., 1983-86; exec. dir. Mahoning Shenango Area Health Edn. Network, Youngstown, Ohio, 1986-90; pres., CEO Mahoning Edn. and Tng. Network, Youngstown, Ohio, 1990-92, Health

Sci. Assocs., Tucson, 1992—. Adj. prof. SUNY, Canton, 1975-76, Youngstown State U., 1987-90; bus. rep. Apollo Coll., 1994-95; rschr. FMR Rsch.; artist in residence Gardner Studio, 1994-2002; lectr. San Francisco State U., 1969-71. Author: Data Book for Health and Institutional Planning, 1981; author of numerous pub. health planning, health edn. studies and funded pvt., state and fed. health care grants, 1971-90. Pres. Found. I Ctr. for Human Devel., Harvey, Ill., 1978-83, U. Profls. of Ill., Chgo., 1982-83; bd. dirs. Blue Cross/Blue Shield Drug and Alcohol Benefit Study, Chgo., 1980-83; coord. pub. rels. and resource devel. VISTA; vol. Habitat for Humanity, Vista Leadership Corp, Tucson, 1997-98 Recipient Recognition award Ill. Dangerous Drugs Commn., 1980, 81, Outstanding Svc. award U. Profls. Ill., 1983-84, Outstanding Svc. award Ill. Fedn. Tchrs., 1983. Mem. Disabled Artist Assn. (bd. dirs., chair resource devel. com. 1992-93). Democrat. Avocations: painting, writing.

GARDNER, DALE RAY, lawyer; b. Broken Arrow, Okla., May 8, 1946; s. Edward Dale and Dahlia Faye (McKeen) G.; m. Phyllis Ann Weinschrott, Dec. 27, 1969. BA in History, So. Ill. U., 1968; MA in History, St. Mary's U., San Antonio, 1975; JD, Tulsa U., 1979. Bar: Okla. 1979, Colo. 1986, Tex. 1991, U.S. Ct. Mil. Appeals 1988, U.S. Ct. Claims 1989, U.S. Dist. Ct. (no. dist.) Okla. 1981, U.S. Dist. Ct. Colo. 1986, U.S. Dist. Ct. (so. dist.) Tex. 1992, U.S. Ct. Appeals (10th cir.) 1986, U.S. Dist. Ct. (ea. dist.) Okla. 2003, U.S Supreme Ct., 2004. Pvt. practice, Sapulpa, Okla., 1979-80, 94—; asst. dist. atty. child support enforcement unit 24th Dist. Oklahoma, Sapulpa, 1980-86, 94-95; pvt. practice Aurora, Colo., 1986-91, Houston, 1991-94; mng. atty. Hyatt Legal Svcs., Aurora, 1988-89; city atty. City of Sapulpa, Okla., 1996-99. Author: Immigration Act of 1965: The Preliminary Results, 1974, Teapot Dome: Civil Legal Cases that Closed the Scandal, 1989. Mem. Child Support Enforcement, Sapulpa, 1980-86, 94-96; trustee United Way, Sapulpa, 1985, 95, subchair for attys. campaign, 2000, 2002; Domestic Violence Counsel, Sapulpa, 1985; chmn. bd. trustees, elder, deacon 1st Presbyn. Ch., Sapulpa, 1985. Capt. U.S. Army, 1969-75, Vietnam., lt. col Res., judge adv., ret. Mem. Okla. Bar Assn., Tex. Bar Assn., Colo. Bar Assn., Creek County Bar (pres. 2003), Gold Coat Club (pres.), Sertoma (pres. Sapulpa 1985, pres. Collumbine 1988, 90, Sertoman of Yr. 1985), Rotary Internat. Democrat. Avocations: fishing, post card collecting. Home: 1533 Terrill Cir Sapulpa OK 74066-2567 Office: 7 S Park St Sapulpa OK 74066-4219 Office Phone: 918-224-0404. Personal E-mail: ltcja@sbcglobal.net.

GARDNER, DONNA RAE (DIEHL), education educator; b. Johnstown, Pa., Sept. 25, 1954; d. G. Edwin and Hilda M. (Batley) D.; m. William W. Gardner. BS in Edn., Geneva Coll., 1976; MEd, U. Pitts., 1984; EdD, U. Ga., 1997. Cert. tchr., Pa. Substitute 2d and 3d grade tchr. Portage (Pa.) Elem./Mid. Sch., 1976-77, 3d grade tchr., 1977-86, 2d grade tchr., 1986-87; assoc. prof. to full prof. Toccoa Falls (Ga.) Coll., 1987—. Chair Curriculum Rev. Com. for Accelerated Christian Edn.; spkr. in field. Editor (newsletter) Chalk Talk, Pew Pal; contbr. revs., articles to profl. publs., and ch. newsletter. Mem. choir First Alliance Ch., Toccoa, 1989-92, 96—; storyteller Stephens County Schs., Toccoa. Grantee U. Ga., 1991-92, Ga.'s Educators Profl. Devel. Mem. Internat. Reading Assn., Nat. Coun. Tchrs. English, Ga. Assn. Colls. Tchr. Edn., Ga. Assn. Ind. Colls. Tchr. Edn. Office: Toccoa Falls Coll PO Box 875 Toccoa Falls GA 30598 Business E-Mail: dgardner@tfc.edu.

GARDNER, EDWARD TYTUS, III, information technology executive; b. Dayton, Ohio, July 1, 1949; s. Edward Tytus Jr. and Elizabeth (Paxton) G.; m. Margaret L. workman, Dec. 27, 1984; children: Lindsay Elizabeth, Christopher Workman, Edward Earnshaw. BS, Denison U., Granville, Ohio, 1973; MS, Ohio U., 1975, PhD, 1978. Asst. prof. W.Va. State Coll., Institute, 1978-82; chmn., CEO Cambridge Ednl., South Charleston, W.Va., 1982-2000; CEO Jaguar Ednl., Charleston, W.Va., 2002—. Pres., co-founder Systems Software Assocs., Inc., 1982-90; adj. asst. prof. W.Va. State Coll., 1978-81; instr. Ohio U., Athens, 1972-78. Contbr. articles to profl. jours. Office: Jaguar Ednl PO Box 389 Charleston WV 25322-0389

GARDNER, ELMER CLAUDE, academic administrator; b. Marmaduke, Ark., Jan. 16, 1925; s. O.A. Gardner and Edna (Sutton) Rowe; m. Delorese Tatum, June 17, 1945 (dec.); children: Phyllis, Rebecca, Claudia, David; m. Glenda Jacobs, Sept. 10, 2002. AA, Freed-Hardeman Coll., 1944; BS, Abilene Christian U., 1946; MA, SW Tex. State U., 1947; postgrad., George Peabody Coll., 1951; LLD (hon.), Magic Valley Christian Coll., 1962, Pepperdine U., 1969; LittD (hon.), Okla. Christian U., 1969; HHD (hon.), Morehead State U., 1973; LLD (hon.), Freed-Hardeman U., 1990. Chmn. dept. edn. and psychology Freed-Hardeman U., Henderson, Tenn., 1949-56, registrar, 1950-68, dean, 1956-69, v.p., 1969, pres., 1969-90, chancellor, 1990-92, pres. emeritus, 1992—; chancellor Ga. Christian Sch., 1993—, Crowley's Ridge Coll., 2002—. Bd. dirs. Chester County Bank, Henderson; col. on former Gov. McWherter's staff, 1988—. Editor: Brigance's Sermons, 1951, Van Dyke's Sermons, 1971; contbr. numerous articles to Gospel Advocate and other publs. Former commr. Edn. Commn. of States, 1991; mem. pub. svcs. coun. Tenn. State Cert. Commn., 1988-91; past pres. Heritage Towers Bd., Henderson; past chmn. Crime Stoppers of Henderson and Chester County. Named Civitan of Yr., Civitan Internat., Henderson. Mem. Tenn. Coll. Assn. (pres. 1986-87), Chester County C. of C. (founder), Alpha Chi. Democrat. Mem. Ch. of Christ. Home and Office: 372 E Mill St Henderson TN 38340-2428

GARDNER, EMERSON N., JR., military officer; b. Chestertown, Md., Oct. 16, 1951; Grad. cum laude, Duke U., 1973; grad., Basic Sch., Def. Lang. Inst., Command and Staff Coll., Armed Forces Staff Coll., Norwegian Def. Coll. Commd. 2d lt. USMC, 1972, advanced through grades to maj. gen., 2003, helicopter pilot; White Ho. liaison officer, presdl. helicopter commd. pilot, 1980-85; commdg. officer 26th MEU, 1996-98; staff officer 9th Marine Amphibious Brigade, Okinawa, Japan, 1986-87; asst. chief of staff for ops. and logistics Allied Forces No. Europe, Kolsas, Norway and High Wycombe, England, 1993-95, High Wycombe, Eng., 1994-95; asst. dep. chief of staff aviation USMC, 1998-2000, dep. comdr. Marine Forces Atlantic, 2000—02, dir. ops. U.S. Pacific Command, 2002—. Decorated Def. Superior Svc. medal., Legion of Merit with Gold star, Def. Meritorious Svc. medal, Air medal; Olmsted scholar, 1978, Germany. E-mail: egardner@hq.pacom.mil.

GARDNER, EVERETTE SHAW, JR., information sciences educator, consultant, author; b. Osceola, Ark., Oct. 3, 1944; s. Everette Shaw and Evelyn (Fletcher) G.; m. Mary Ann Sihelnik, May 28, 1966; children: Cynthia Anne, Stacey Diane. BBA, Memphis State U., 1966; MBA, U. N.C., 1974, PhD, 1978. Commd. ensign USN, 1966, advanced through grades to comdr., 1980, ret., 1986; assoc. prof. U. Houston, 1987-88, chmn. dept. of decision and info. scis., 1988-95, prof., 1989—, dir. Ctr. Global Mfg., 1991—. Bd. dirs., pres. Gardner Rsch., Inc., Sugar Land, Tex., 1987—; cons. NASA Johnson Space Ctr., Houston, 1988-89, Shell Oil Co., Houston, Continental Airlines, Houston, 1993—, Continental Micronesia, Guam, Delta Airlines, Atlanta, 1997-2000, Hawaiian Airlines, Honolulu, 2000—, Texaco, Houston, Pennzoil, Houston, Arthur Andersen, Houston, Exxon Co. USA, Houston, Compaq Computers, Houston, Frito-Lay, Dallas, Southwestern Bell, Houston, Centel Comm., Houston, Sys. Evolution, Houston, Tenneco, Houston, Spring Comm., L.A., Alamo Water Refiners, San Antonio, Houston Livestock Show and Rodeo, Oil and Gas Consultants Inc., Tulsa, 1996-99, Telecheck Svcs. Inc., Houston, 1997-99, Randalls Food Markets, Inc., Houston, 1997-99, Trees Inc., Houston, 1999-2000, Tex. Industries, Inc., Houston, 2001—. Co-author: Quantitative Approaches to Management, 1993; author: (software) Autocast: Business Forecasting System, 1992, The Spreadsheet Forecaster, 1994, The Spreadsheet Quality Manager, 1993; assoc. editor Internat. Jour. of Forecasting, 1985-97, Mgmt. Sci., 1987-91, Interfaces, 1987-92; contbr. articles to profl. jours.; columnist Lotus mag., 1986-92. Bd. dirs. Women's Home Houston, 1992-97; mem. Republican Nat. Com. Mem. NRA, La. Shooting Assn., Tex. State Rifle Assn., Internat. Inst. Forecasters (pres. 1990-92, dir. 1987-94), Inst. for Ops. Rsch. and Mgmt. Scis., Operational Rsch. Soc., U.S. Naval Inst., Am. Prodn. and Inventory Control Soc. (bd. dirs. Houston chpt. 1997-98), Ret. Officers Assn., Sons. of Confederate Vets., Mus. of Confederacy Richmond Va., Confederate Meml. Hall New Orleans. Presbyterian. Avocations: competitive pistol shooting, tennis, gardening, civil war history. Office: U Houston 4800 Calhoun Rd Houston TX 77204-6021 E-mail: EGardner@uh.edu.

GARDNER, GARY A., lawyer; b. Glen Cove, NY, Mar. 10, 1959; BS, US Naval Acad., 1982; JD, St. John's U., 1994. Ptnr. Wilson, Elser, Moskowitz, Edelman & Dicker LLP, NYC. Served USN, 1977—89. Recipient USN Meritorious Unit Commendation, Coast Guard Unit Commendation. Mem.: ABA (aviation law sect.), Lawyer Pilot's Bar Assn. Office: Wilson Elser Moskowitz Edelman & Dicker LLP 23rd Fl 150 E 42nd St New York NY 10017-5639 Office Phone: 212-490-3000 ext. 2770. Office Fax: 212-490-3038. Business E-Mail: gardnerg@wemed.com.

GARDNER, H. MCINTYRE, diversified financial services company executive; BA, Dartmouth Coll, 1983. With corp. and instl. client group Merrill Lynch & Co., 1983—87; pres., CEO various comsumer products cos., 1987—2000; pres. Hanover Assocs., Inc., 1991—94; head ins. group Merrill Lynch & Co., 2001, various positions pvt. client bus., 2000—01, CEO global pvt. client, 2002—02, sr. v.p. N.Y.C., 2001—. Pres. Hanover Assocs., Inc., 1991—94. Office: Merrill Lynch & Co 4 World Fin Ctr New York NY 10080

GARDNER, HOWARD ALAN, travel company executive, writer, editor; b. Rockford, Ill., June 24, 1920; s. Ellis Ralph and Leanor (Roseman) Gardner; m. Marjorie Ruth Klein, Sept. 29, 1945; children: Jill, Jeffrey. BA, U. Mich., 1941. With advt. dept. Chgo. Tribune, 1941-43; mgr. promotion dept. Esquire mag., 1943-46; advt. mgr. Mrs. Klein's Food Products Co., 1946-48; pres. Sales-Aide Svc. Co., 1948-56, Gardner & Stein, 1956-59, Gardner, Stein & Frank, Inc., Chgo., 1959-83, Fun-derful World, Chgo., 1983—. Mem.: Connoisseurs Internat., Nat. Geog. Soc., Am. Geog. Soc., Confrerie de la Chaine des Rotisseurs (Bailli Honoraire, officier, comdr.), Travel Industry Assn. Am., Mid-Am. Club, Internat. Club, Carlton Club, Travelers' Century Club, Phi Beta Kappa. Home: 100 E Bellevue Pl Chicago IL 60611-1157 Office: Fun-derful World 100 E Bellevue Pl Chicago IL 60611-1157 Office Phone: 312-944-4061.

GARDNER, HOWARD EARL, psychologist, educator, writer; b. Scranton, Pa., July 11, 1943; s. Ralph and Hilde (Weilheimer) G.; m. Ellen Winner; children: Kerith, Jay, Andrew, Benjamin. AB summa cum laude, Harvard U., 1965, PhD, 1971; MA, Wheaton Coll., 2002; hon. degree, Curry Coll., 1992, New Eng. Conservatory of Music, 1993, Ind. U., 1995, Moravian Coll., 1996, Cleve. Inst. of Music, 1996, Salem State Coll., 1996, L.I. U., 1997, Macalester Coll., 1997, Tel-Aviv U., 1998, Princeton U., 1998, Pa. State U., 1998, Ithaca Coll., 1999, Conn. Coll., 1999, McGill U., 1999, U. Hartford, 2000, Mass. Sch. Profl. Psychology, 2000, Nat. U. Ireland, 2001, U. Toronto, 2001, U. Urbino, Italy, 2003; hon. (hon.), East China Normal Univ., 2004. Lectr. edn. Harvard U., Cambridge, Mass., 1971-86, co-dir. Project Zero, 1972-2000, prof. edn., 1986-98—, Hobbs prof. cognition and edn., 1998—, affiliated prof. psychology, 1987—. Prof. neurology Boston U. Sch. Medicine, 1984-87, adj. prof. neurology, 1987-05; rsch. psychologist Boston VA Med. Ctr., 1978-93; hon. prof. East China Normal U., 2004. Author: The Shattered Mind, 1975, Art, Mind and Brain, 1982, Frames of Mind, 1983 (Best Book award Am. Psychol. Assn. 1984), The Mind's New Science, 1985 (William James award 1988), To Open Minds, 1989, The Unschooled Mind, 1991, Multiple Intelligences, 1993, Creating Minds, 1993, Leading Minds, 1995, Extraordinary Minds, 1997, The Disciplined Mind, 1999, Intelligence Reframed, 1999, (with M. Csikszentmihalyi and W. Damon) Good Work, 2001, (with W. Fischman, B. Solomon and D. Greenspan) Making Good, 2004, Changing Minds, 2004. Bd. dir. Mus Modern Art, 2005—, Spencer Found., 2001—. Recipient Grawemeyer award in edn., 1990, Disting. Svc. medal Columbia U. Tchr.'s Coll., 1994, Pa. Gov.'s award in humanities, 1994, McGovern award Smithsonian Inst., 1998, Walker prize Boston Mus. of Sci., 1999, Samuel T. Orton award Internat. Dyslexia Assn., 1999, medal of the Pres. of Italy, 2001; MacArthur Prize fellow, 1981, Guggenheim Found. fellow, 2000; rsch. grantee numerous govtl. and pvt. founds. Fellow AAAS; mem. Am. Acad. Arts and Scis., Phi Beta Kappa. Office: Harvard U Grad Sch Edn Larsen Hall Cambridge MA 02138 Office Phone: 617-496-4929. Business E-Mail: hgasst@pz.harvard.edu.

GARDNER, HOWARD GARRY, pediatrician, educator; b. Gary, Ind., Oct. 5, 1943; s. Oscar and Anita (Arenson) G.; m. Judith (Geen), June 21, 1986; children: Molly, Joseph. BA, Ind. U., 1965, MD, 1968. Intern, resident St. Louis U., 1969-73; pvt. practice Hinsdale (Ill.) Pediatrics, 1973-79, DuPage Pediatrics, Darien, Ill., 1979—; attending staff Hinsdale Hosp., 1973—, chmn. dept. pediatrics, 2000—02; courtesy staff Childrens Meml. Hosp., Chgo., 1988—. Clin. prof. dept. pediatrics Loyola U. Sch. of Medicine, Maywood, 1983-2002; chmn. dept. pediatrics Hinsdale Hosp., 1983-85, 2000-02; prof. clin. pediatrics Northwestern U. Med. Sch.; med. adv. bd. YMCA of the USA, Chgo., 1989—. Mem. editl. bd. Pediatric News, 1990—; contbr. articles to profl. jours. Co-chmn. med. adv. bd. DuPage Easter Seal Ctr., Villa Park, Ill.; past, founding mem. bd. dirs. Loyola Ronald McDonald House; co-founder, past pres. Ill. Child Passenger Safety Assn.; mem. med. adv. bd. Pathways Awareness Found.; officer, steering com. DuPage Interagy. Coun. on Early Intervention. Lt. USN, 1969-71. Recipient Outstanding Clin. Tchr. award Loyola Med. Sch., 1978, Tchr. of Yr. Hinsdale Hosp. Family Practice Residency, 1981, Chgo. Caring Physician's award Met. Chgo. Health Care Coun., 1987, Buckle Up Am.! award Ill. Coalition for Safety Belt Use, 1991, Parent and Child Edn. Soc. 20th Anniversary Achievement award, 1992, Outstanding Vol. award West Suburban United Way, 1999, Carol Sanicki Crystal Heart award Easter Seals, DuPage, 2002. Fellow Am. Acad. Pediat. (past pres. Ill. chpt., past mem. nat. nominating com., instnl. rev. bd., com. on injury and poison prevention, Pisani Pediatrician of Yr. award 1986); mem. Chgo. Pediat. Soc. (past pres., Archibald Hoyne Pediatrician of Yr. 1994), Ill. Maternal and Child Health Coalition (bd. dirs., pres., 2000-2002, Advocacy award 1996), DuPage County Med. Soc. (bd. dirs.). Democrat. Jewish. Avocations: reading, skiing, photography. Office: DuPage Pediatrics 1306 Plainfield Rd Darien IL 60561-5038 Office Phone: 630-810-0900. E-mail: ggard4922@aol.com.

GARDNER, JAMES RICHARD, pharmaceutical company executive; b. Wellsville, N.Y., Nov. 18, 1944; s. James Myers and Adelaide (Stockman) G.; m. Linda Marie Cuomo, Oct. 14, 1967; children: Alexandra K., Mindy M. BS in Engring., U.S. Mil. Acad., 1966; M in Pub. Adminstrn., Princeton U., 1968, PhD, 1977; MBA, L.I. U., 1977; grad., U.S. Army War Coll., 1989. Commd. 2d lt. U.S. Army, 1966, advanced through grades to maj., 1976, resigned, 1977; staff asst. Office of U.S. Atty. Gen., 1973; asst. prof. U.S. Mil. Acad., West Point, NY, 1974—77; dir. agrl. planning Pfizer, Inc., N.Y.C., 1977—81, dir. corp. strategic planning, 1981—89, sr. dir. corp. strategic planning, 1988—94, v.p. corp. investor rels., 1994—. V.p. Pfizer Found., N.Y.C., 1985-99; mem. faculty U.S. Army Command Gen. Staff Coll., 1986-92; mem. adv. coun. Inst. for Internat. Regional Studies, Princeton U., 1987—; mem. adv. coun. Dept. Astrophysical Scis. Princeton U., 1992-99; head USAR polit. and mil. affairs div. Dept. Army, 1989-92; mem. adv. coun. Coll. Sci. Pa. State U., 1999—; mem. adv. bd. The Neuropathy Assn., 2000—, chmn., 2005—; mem bd. vis. Dept Astronomy Pa. State U., 2001—. Author: (with others) American National Security, 1981, Business Competitor Intelligence, 1984; editor: Handbook of Strategic Planning, 1986; contbr. articles to profl. jours. Strategic planning com. United Way of Tri-State, NYC, 1984-87; dir. adminstrn. Pfizer Inc. United Way campaign, NYC, 1985-87; bd. dirs. Greater NY couns. Boy Scouts Am., 1988-2000; NYC chmn. Nat. Eagle Scout Assn., 1989-92. Col. USAR, 1988-93. Decorated Bronze Stars (3), Air medals, Rep. Vietnam Gallantry Cross with Silver Star, Army Ranger; Recipient George Washington medal The Freedoms Found., Valley Forge, Pa., 1970, Silver Beaver award Boy Scouts Am., 1991, Disting. Eagle award, 1992; named Hon. Alumnus Pa. State U., 2004. Mem. Planning Forum (pres. N.Y.C. chpt. 1985-86), N.Am. Soc. Corp. Planning (nat. v.p. 1984-85), West Point Soc. N.Y. (bd. dirs. 1984-91, v.p. 1986-88, pres. 1988-90), Nat. Investor Rels. Inst. (bd. dirs. N.Y.C. chpt. 1995-97), U.S. Mil. Acad. Assn. Grads. (strategic planning com. 1992-96), Phi Kappa Phi. Republican. Roman Catholic. Avocations: youth activities, woodworking, astronomy, outdoor sports. Home: 40 Brundige Dr Goldens Bridge NY 10526-1416 Office: Pfizer Inc 235 E 42nd St New York NY 10017-5755

GARDNER, JANET PAXTON, journalist, film producer; b. Dayton, Ohio, Sept. 6, 1940; d. Edward Tytus and Mary Elizabeth (Paxton) G.; m. George Karl Debreczeny, Sept. 10, 1964 (div. Feb. 1970); 1 child, Karl Philip; m. George Edward Bradshaw Morren, Jr., Nov. 6, 1980. BFA in Art and Architecture, Cooper Union, 1965; MFA in Film Prodn., NYU, 1971; postgrad., Columbia U., 1976. Film editor, assoc. prodr. Sta. WRC-TV, NBC, Washington, 1972; asst. film editor NBC News, N.Y.C., 1973-74; newswriter, field prodr. NewsCenter4 NBC, N.Y.C., 1974-75; freelance film editor CBS News, N.Y.C., 1976-79; staff reporter, feature writer The Plain Dealer, Cleve., 1979-81; edn. columnist, editor Glamour mag., N.Y.C., 1981-82; staff writer Asbury Park Press, Neptune, N.J., 1985-86; press officer UN, 1989; owner, mgr. prodr. The Gardner Documentary Group, N.Y.C., 1991—. Mem. adj. faculty journalism Univ. Coll., Rutgers U., Newark, 1988-92, Montclair State Coll., Upper Montclair, N.J., 1992; mem. L.A. Times pub.-prof. exch. program, 1989. Prodr., dir., writer documentary videos The United Nations: It's More Than You Think, 1991, Vietnam: Land of the Ascending Dragon, 1993, Children of the Night & Starting Over, 1994, A World Beneath The War, 1996, Dancing Through Death: The Monkey Magic & Madness of Cambodia, 1999, Precious Cargo: Vietnamese Adoptees Come of Age, 2001, Siberian Dream, 2004; editor CBS News documentary film The Black Robes, 1978; prodr. Preparing To Give Birth, 1977, Choices in Childbirth, 1977, (film) Inside Ladies Home Jour., 1970; contbr. to NY Times, Phila. Inquirer, Boston Globe, Newsday, The Nation, Glamour, Working Women, New Woman, Diversion, Health Week, Indochina Newsletter, NJ Monthly, also others. Co-chair peace and social order com. Religious Soc. of Friends, Princeton, N.J., 1994; participant U.S.-Indochina Reconciliation Project Del. to Vietnam, 1987, to Cambodia, 1990. Nominee Emmy award Outstanding Hist. Programming, NATAS, 1997; recipient spl. citation, Edn. Writers Assn., 1983, 2d place award for news reporting, N.J. Press Women, 1990, 1st place award for newspaper feature writing, 1990, cert. of merit, Media & Methods mag., 1992, Lowell Thomas award for video on Vietnam, Soc. Am. Travel Writers Found., 1993, Bronze Apple award, Nat. Edn. Film and Video Festival, 1993, Golden Eagle award, CINE, 1994, 1999, 2001, 2004, Spl. Jury award, 2001, Silver Apple award, Nat. Edn. Film and Video Festival, 1997, Best Feature Reporting TV award, Soc. Profl. Journalists N.Y. chpt. Deadline Club, 1998, 2001, Bronze medallion (nat. award), Sigma Delta Chi, Best Feature Reporting TV award, Soc. Profl. Journalists N.Y. chpt., 2001, award, Chgo. Internat. Film Festival, 2002; fellow Woolrich writing fellow, Columbia U. Sch. Gen. Studies, 1976. Mem. Soc. Profl. Journalists (juror nat. mag. awards 1985, scholastic press awards 1986, chief juror editl. writing awards 1988), Investigative Reporters and Editors, Internat. Documentary Assn., North Jersey Press Club (2d place award for bus. feature writing 1990, 1st place award 1991, 1st place award for best documentary 1992, 2d place award for feature photography 1993), N.Y. Women in Film and TV. Office: Ste 2420 330 W 42d St New York NY 10036-6902

GARDNER, JASON P., immunologist, biologist; s. John and Meryl Gardner; m. Patcharin Sophia Ranauro, Oct. 10, 1998; 1 child, Isabelle Sophia. BA, MA, Cambridge (Eng.) U., 1991; PhD, Oxford (Eng.) U., 1995. Postdoctoral fellow Harvard Medcal Sch., Boston, 1995—97; prin. rsch. scientist Chiron Corp., Emeryville, Calif., 1997—2000; sr. investigator Progenics Pharms., Inc, Tarrytown, NY, 2000—. Scholar Wellcome Trust, 1991—95; Nessel Gene Therapy fellow, Harvard Med. Sch., 1998, Small Bus. Innovation grantee, NIH and NCI, 2001—04. Mem.: AAAS. Office: Progenics Pharms Inc 777 Old Saw Mill River Rd Tarrytown NY 10591 Office Phone: 914-789-2833.

GARDNER, JERRY LEE, financial consultant; b. Long Beach, Calif., Sept. 8, 1943; s. Don Gerard and Carol (Sorenson) G.; m. Rita Frandsen, May 29, 1969; children: Marc Don, Edward David, Victor John, Denise, Joyce, John Mackay, Michael Christopher. BA, Brigham Young U., 1971; MA, Calif. State U., Sacramento, 1973; postgrad., U. Calif., Davis, 1998-99. Account exec. duPont Glore Forgan & Co., Sacramento, 1973-74, E.F. Hutton & Co., Sacramento, 1974-84; sr. investment advisor Am. Savs., Sacramento, 1984-89; fin. cons. The Golden 1 Credit Union, Sacramento, 1989—. Mem. Leaders Coun., Mass. Fin. Svcs., Boston, 1993—2004; mem. Kite & Key Club, Franklin Templeton Group, San Mateo, Calif., 1993—2004; v.p. LDS Bus. Assocs., 1992—94. Mem. Valley Choral Soc., 2000—03; living history reinactor Old Sacramento Living History Assn., 2000—03. With U.S. Army, 1965—68, Vietnam. Recipient MVP award, Fin. Network Investment Corp., 1994—95, Century Club, 1996—2000, Amb. Club, 2001, Gov.'s award, 2002, Asst. VP award, XCU Capital Corp., 2004. Mem.: Fin. Planning Assn., United Families Internat., BYU Mgmt. Soc. (bd. dirs. 1990—). Mem. Lds Ch. Avocations: travel, history of california, violin, guitar. Office: The Golden 1 Credit Union 6507 4th Ave Sacramento CA 95817-2611 Office Phone: 916-443-3965. E-mail: jgardner@golden1.com.

GARDNER, JOEL ROBERT, writer, historian; b. N.Y.C., May 12, 1942; s. Stephen H. and Diana (Schneider) G.; m. Holly Alpine Phelps, July 7, 1980. BA, Tulane U., 1962; MA, UCLA, 1966. Assoc. editor The Riverdale (N.Y.) Press, 1966-68; oral historian UCLA Oral History Program, 1971-80, La. State Archives, 1980-82; asst. dir. La. Divsn. of the Arts, 1983-85; dir. Perkins Ctr. for the Arts, 1985-87; pres. Gardner Assocs., Cherry Hill, N.J., 1987—. Cons. The Pew Charitable Trusts, 1988-94, Robert Wood Johnson Found., 1991—, John D. and Catherine T. MacArthur Found., 1994—. Author: Oral History for Louisiana, 1980, 75 Years of Good Taste: A History of the Tasty Baking Company, 1990, A History of the Pew Charitable Trusts, 1991, (with others) In the Company of Writers, 1991, Neighbor Caring for Neighbor, 1996; editor: Built in Louisiana, 1985, Oral History and the Law, 1985. Bd. dirs. N.J. Com. for the Humanities, 1991-94, sec., 1993-94; pres. Trenton Cmty. Mus. Sch., 1999—. Mem. Oral History Assn. (bd. dirs. 1982-83), Oral History for Middle Atlantic Region (v.p. 1991-92, pres. 1992-93), Rotary (Garden State club 1998—). Democrat. Jewish. Office: 210 E Miami Ave Cherry Hill NJ 08034

GARDNER, JOHN HOWLAND, III, neurologist; b. New Haven, Conn., Oct. 1, 1931; s. John Howland Jr. and Ruth (Huntley) G.; m. Anne Kates Larkin, Apr. 23, 1960; children: Elizabeth Larkin Gardner Milgram, Helen Douglass Gardner. Student, Harvard U., 1949-52; MD, Yale, 1956. Diplomate Am. Bd. Psychiatry and Neurology. Intern Stanford, 1956-57; asst. to assoc. resident in medicine Strong Mem. Hosp., Rochester, N.Y., 1957-59; resident in neurology Boston City Hosp., 1959-61; resident in neuropathology Strong Mem. Hosp., Rochester, N.Y., 1961-62; officer in charge in neurology USAF Hosp. Keesler AFB, Biloxi, Miss., 1962-64; asst. prof. Case Western Res. U. Sch. Med., Cleve., 1965-67; asst. clin. prof. Case Western Res. U. Sch. Medicine, Cleve., 1967-83, assoc. clin. prof., 1983-98, emeritus assoc. prof. neurology, 1998—; chief of neurology St. Luke's Hosp., Cleve., 1967-85; neurologist U. Suburban Health Care Ctr., Cleve., 1975-96. Pres. Greater Cleveland Chpt. Epilepsy Fdn. Am., 1973-75; chmn. Mediation Comm. Acad. Med. Cleveland, 1982-84. Vestryman, St. Paul's Episcopal Church, Cleveland Hts., 1980-82. Capt. USAF, 1962-64. Decorated Commendation Medal, USAF. Fellow Am. Acad. Neurology; mem. AMA, Acad. Med. Cleveland, Ohio State Med. Assn., Yale Alumni Assn. (v.p. Cleve. 1988—). Avocations: skeet shooting, photography, hunting, music, sailing.

GARDNER, JOSEPH LAWRENCE, editor, writer; b. Willmar, Minn., Jan. 26, 1933; s. Elmer Joseph and Margaret Eleanor (Archer) G.; m. Sadako Miyasaka, Feb. 25, 1967; children: Miya Elise, Justin Lawrence. Student, U. Portland, Oreg., 1951-52; BA summa cum laude, U. Oreg., 1955; MA (Woodrow Wilson fellow), U. Wis., 1956. Researcher, writer, asst. editor, mng. editor Am. Heritage Books div. Am. Heritage Pub. Co., Inc., N.Y.C., 1959-65; editor Am. Heritage Jr. Library and Horizon Caravel Books, 1965-68; mng. editor Newsweek Books div. Newsweek Inc., N.Y.C., 1968-70, editor, 1971-76; sr. staff editor Reader's Digest Gen. Books, N.Y.C., 1976-81, group editor gen. reference, 1982-84; dir. internat. book pub.

Reader's Digest Assn., Inc., 1984-88; pres., editorial dir. Gardner Assocs., 1989—. Author: Labor on the March, 1969, Departing Glory, Theodore Roosevelt as Ex-President, 1973; editor: Newsweek Condensed Books and book series, including Wonders of Man, Milestones of History, The Founding Fathers, World of Culture, 1971-76, The World's Last Mysteries, 1978, Reader's Digest Wide World Atlas, 1979, Reader's Digest Atlas of the Bible, 1981, Eat Better, Live Better, 1982, Mysteries of the Ancient Americas, 1986, Reader's Digest Atlas of the World, 1987, Great Mysteries of the Past, 1991, The Story of Jesus, 1993, Who's Who in the Bible, 1994, Complete Guide to the Bible, 1998; contbg. editor Through Indian Eyes, 1996. Bd. dirs. Friends of Scarsdale Library, 1976-81, v.p., 1979-81; trustee Scarsdale Adult Sch., 1978-84, treas., 1981-83; trustee Scarsdale Pub. Library, 1983-84, 86-91, pres., 1989-91. Served with AUS, 1956-58. Mem. PEN, Phi Beta Kappa, Sigma Delta Chi, Phi Kappa Psi. Home and Office: 2667 Lake View Ter E Los Angeles CA 90039 E-mail: jlgardner@worldnet.att.net.

GARDNER, JUDITH WARREN, retired elementary educator; b. Hartford, Conn., Oct. 4, 1940; d. Henry Stanley and Madeline Warren; m. Fred Marvin Gardner, Dec. 28, 1963; children: Warren, Charles, Kevin, Eric. BA, Mt. Holyoke Coll., 1962; MEd, U. Hartford, 1976. Cert. profl. educator, Conn. Pre-kindergarten tchr. Hebron (Conn.) Elem. Sch., 1977-78; elem. tchr. Hopewell Sch., Glastonbury, Conn., 1978-94, Hebron Ave. Sch., Glastonbury, Conn., 1994—2003, ret., 2003—. Cons. dept. psychology U. Hartford, 1989; rep. Internat. Ctr. Adv. Com., Glastonbury, 1990-92; framework com. mem. East Hartford (Conn.) Glastonbury Magnet Sch., 1992; Glastonbury team leader Yale U. East Asian Group Project in China and Taiwan, New Haven, 1992-93. Author: (with others) A Look At Contemporary Chinese Culture in Taiwan Through the Family: Case Studies for the Classroom, 1994; co-author: (tchr. manual) Grade 3 Sci. Notebook, 1987-88. Recipient Celebration of Excellence award State of Conn. and So. New Eng. Tel. Co., 1988, Commendation awards Glastonbury Bd. Edn., 1989, 91, 93; grantee Glastonbury Bd. Edn., and PTO, 1986-89, 93, fellow Programs Internat. Edn. Resources, 1996. Mem. NEA, Conn. Edn. Assn., Glastonbury Edn. Assn. (elem. v.p. 1996-99), Conn. Sci. Suprs. Assn., Tchr. Fund Com., Book Club (founding mem.), Parent Tchr. Student Orgn. (mini-grant com. 1991-93). Avocations: reading, gardening. Home: 1A Stevens Way Durham NH 03824 Personal E-mail: fredjudygardner@comcast.net.

GARDNER, KERRY ANN, librarian; b. Honolulu, May 19, 1955; d. Byron Patton and Claire Gardner. BA in Polit. Sci. magna cum laude, Temple U., 1976; MA in L.Am. Studies, U. Ariz., 1983, MLS, 1990. Documents libr. FMC Corp., Chgo., 1977-78; grad. rsch. asst. U. Ariz., Tucson, 1983-86; rsch. cons., 1983-92; libr. asst. I Phoenix Pub. Libr., 1988-89; mgr. faculty resource libr., English 2d lang. U. Ariz. Ctr., 1989—90; project mgr. U. Ariz., 1990-92; mgr. faculty resource libr., English 2d lang. U. Ariz. Ctr., 1991—92; pub. svcs. libr. Bryan Wildenthal Meml. Libr., Sul Ross State U., Alpine, Tex., 1992-95; libr. dir. Am. U., Dubai, United Arab Emirates, 1995-96; literacy libr. Sterling Mcpl. Libr., Baytown, Tex., 1996-98; libr. Valle Verde campus, El Paso C.C., Tex., 1998—, co-head libr., 2001—02. Indexer Hispanic Am. Periodicals Index, 1995; maintain GPO Access Web site, 1998—. Contbr. articles to profl. publs. Tchr. English Literacy Vols. Am., 1991-92, 96-98; mem. Friends of the El Paso Pub. Libr., 2004-05 Named Libr. of Yr., Border Regional Libr. Assn., 2001; grad. scholar, U. Ariz., 1976—77, 1981—82. Mem.: NEA, ALA, Tex. C.C. Tex. Assn., Border Regional Libr. Assn. (chair publicity com. 1999—2002, chair. Libr. of the Yr. com. 2002—03), Assn. Coll. and Rsch. Librs., Tex. Libr. Assn. (legis. com. coll. and univ. librs. divsn. 1993—94), Beta Phi Mu. Avocations: travel, birding. Office: El Paso C C Valle Verde Campus PO Box 20500 El Paso TX 79998-0500

GARDNER, LENANN MCGOOKEY, management consultant; d. James Lester McGookey; m. Ken Reidy, Mar. 24, 2001; 1 child, Lindsay Erica McGookey Gunther. MBA, Harvard U., 1976. V.p. mktg. MNC Fin., Balt., 1990—91; pres. LM Gardner Mgmt. Consulting, Inc., Albuquerque, 1992—. Dir. of mktg., advt. and strategic planning Blue Cross Blue Shield, Balt., 1988—89. Chair devel. com., bd. dirs. Cuidando Los Ninos, Albuquerque, 2003—04. Mem.: Am. Mktg. Assn. (Profl. Svcs. Marketer of the Yr. 1996), Harvard Club. Office: LM Gardner Mgmt Consulting Inc 11024 Montgomery NE # 308 Albuquerque NM 87111 Office Phone: 505-828-1788. E-mail: lenann@youcansell.com.

GARDNER, MARVIN ALLEN, JR., pastoral and clinical psychologist; b. Washington, Mar. 15, 1943; s. Marvin Allen and Lillian Gertrude (McCracken) G.; m. Donna Frances Craven, Mar. 16, 1962 (div. 1987); children: Stephen Gregory, Sarah Elizabeth; m. Laura Churchill Mink, May 21, 1988; children: Charles Treadway, Laura Faith. BA with honors, U. Md., 1964; MDiv cum laude, Va. Theol. Sem., 1967; DMin, Wesley Theol. Sem., Washington, 1979; PhD, The Union Inst. and Univ., Cin., 1991. Lic. profl. counselor, lic. clin. psychologist, diplomate Am. Assn. Pastoral Counselors, D.C.; ordained priest Anglican Cath. Ch. Curate Ascension Episcopal Ch., Mt. Vernon, N.Y., 1967-69; rector St. Paul's Episcopal Ch., Waldorf, Md., 1969-76; pastoral counselor Pastoral Counseling and Cons. Ctrs. of Greater Washington, Oakton, Va., 1976-81; co-dir. Marriage and Family Inst., Washington, 1981-84; dir. Family & Marriage Assocs., La Plata, Md., 1984-86, Capital Hill Ctr. of Pastoral Counseling & Cons. Ctrs., Oakton, 1986-94; faculty and supr. Inst. for Pastoral Psychotherapy, Oakton, 1993-97; rector Holy Family Anglican Ch., Gaithersburg, Md., 1993-96, St. Thomas of Canterbury Anglican Cath. Ch., Roanoke, Va., 1997—; pvt. practice Washington, 1994—96; pvt. practice pastoral and clinical psychology Manassas Group, Roanoke, 1999—2002; dir. Pastoral Inst. Greater Roanoke, 1997—; Canon to Ordinary DMAS, 2001—04, Met. of the Anglican Cath. Ch., 2001—04. Mem. Bd. Profl. Counseling, Washington, 1993-95; adj. asst. prof. pastoral counseling Loyola Coll., Columbia, Md., 1993-96; cert. med. expert Office of Hearings and Appeals Social Security Adminstrn., 1999—; faculty, bd. dirs. St. Augustine's Inst., Charlotteville, Va., 2004—. Author: Pastoral Excellence in Pastoral Counselor Education and Training, 1991; contbr. articles to profl. jours. Decorated knight comdr. Order of Sts. Constantine and Helen. Mem. APA, Am. Assn. Pastoral Counselors (diplomate, chmn. bd. govs. rsch. com. 1992-95, Writing and Rsch. award 1991), Am. Assn. Marriage and Family Therapy, Am. Assn. Christian Counselors, Va. Acad. Clin. Psychologists. Office Phone: 540-345-6030. E-mail: drmarvgardner@cox.net.

GARDNER, MURRAY BRIGGS, pathologist, educator; b. Lafayette, Ind., Oct. 5, 1929; s. Max William and Margaret (Briggs) G.; m. Alice E. Danielson, June 20, 1961; children: Suzanna, Martin, Danielson, Andrew. BA, U. Calif., Berkeley, 1951; MD, U. Calif., San Francisco, 1954. Intern Moffitt Hosp., San Francisco, 1954-55; resident in gen. practice Sonoma County Hosp., Santa Rosa, Calif., 1957-59; resident in pathology U. Calif. hosps., San Francisco, 1959-63; faculty U. So. Calif. Sch. Medicine, Los Angeles, 1963-81, prof. pathology, 1973-81, U. Calif., Davis Sch. Medicine, 1981—, chmn. dept. pathology, 1982-90. Contbr. chpts. to books, numerous articles in field to profl. jours. Served to lt. M.C. USNR, 1957-59. NIH grantee, 1968— Fellow AAAS; mem. Coll. Am. Pathologists, Internat. Acad. Pathology. Home: 8313 Maxwell Ln Dixon CA 95620-9662 Office: Ctr of Comparative Medicine U Calif Davis Davis CA 95616 E-mail: mbgardner@ucdavis.edu.

GARDNER, PETER JAGLOM, lawyer, publishing executive; b. NYC, 1958; s. Ralph David and Natalie (Jaglom) G.; m. Victoire Taittinger, 1984; children: Evan, Emma, Nadya, Parker. BA, Middlebury (Vt.) Coll., 1980; JD, M in Environ. Law magna cum laude, Vt. Law Sch., 1999; M in Intellectual Property Law, Franklin Pierce Law Ctr., 2002. Pres. Transatlantic Comml. Svcs. Corp., 1985-90; pub. Northern Centinel, Kinderhook, NY, 1991—98; pres., CEO Centinel Co., 1991—2004; pvt. practice Hanover, NH, 2004—. Rsch. fellow Vt. Law Sch., 2002—04; vis. scholar Tuck Sch., Dartmouth Coll., 2002—04; rsch. fellow Franklin Pierce Law Ctr., 2004—. Mem. editl. bd. N.H. Bar Jour., 2002—; contbr. articles to profl. jours. Trustee Ford Sayre Meml. Ski. Coun., 2000—03; bd. overseers Hitchcock Found., 2003—. Mem.: Internat. Fedn. Intellectual Property Attys., Howe Libr. Corp., Am. Intellectual Property Law Assn., Licensing Execs. Soc. (USA and Can. chpts.), Frank Rowe Kenison Inn of Ct. (treas. 1999—2001), Vt. Bar Assn., N.Y. Bar Assn., N.H. Bar Assn. (sec. intellectual property law sect. 2002—03, vice-chmn. 2003—04, chmn. 2004—05), ABA, Overseas Press Club.

GARDNER, RAYMOND ALAN, webmaster, writer; b. Schenectady, N.Y., Feb. 28, 1943; s. George and Alice S. Gardner; children: Eva, John, Craig. AAS in Computer Info. Sys., Schenectady County C.C., 2000; AAS in Telecomm. Mgmt., C.C. of the Air ForceC., 1999; AAS in Electronics Tech., USN, 1965. Divsn. mgr. Sears Roebuck & Co., Albany, NY, 1970—78; gen. mgr. DG Petroleum Equipment Distbr., Schenectady, NY, 1978—93; web and database developer R Gardner Enterprises, Schenectady, NY, 1994—2000; web developer USAF, Randolph AFB, San Antonio, Tex., 2000—02. Author: (Book) The Cause of Liberty, 1997. Vol. St Jude Children's Hosp. Telethon, Schenectady, 1997—2000; database developer N.Y. State Emergency Mgmt. Office, Albany, NY, 1999—2000; Bd. dirs. Highlands at Woodlake Homeowners Assn., 2002. TSgt. (E-6) NY Air N.G., 1994—2002. Decorated Air Force Commendation medal with oak leaf cluster; recipient Svc. to Civil Authorities award, State of N.Y., 2000, Mil. Outstanding Vol. Svc. medal, 2002. Mem.: San Antonio Living History Assn. (webmaster 2001, v.p. 2002). Episcopalian. Avocations: golf, gardening, walking, art. Home: 5004 Crestwood Hill Dr San Antonio TX 78244 Office: R Gardner Enterprises 5004 Crestwood Hill Dr San Antonio TX 78244 Personal E-mail: rgardnertx@prodigy.net.

GARDNER, RICHARD KENT, retired librarian, educator, consultant; b. New Bedford, Mass., Dec. 7, 1928; s. Francis and Millicent Annetta (Kent) G. AB cum laude, Middlebury Coll., Vt., 1950; Dipl. Litt., U. Paris, 1954; MS in Library Sci., Western Res. U., 1955; PhD, Case Western Res. U., 1968. Asst. libr. Case Inst. Tech., 1955-57; library adviser Mich. State U. adv. group pub. adminstrn. to Govt. South Vietnam, 1957-58; libr., assoc. prof. Marietta Coll., Ohio, 1959-63; founding editor Choice: Books for Coll. Libraries, Middletown, Conn., 1963-66; lectr., assoc. prof. Case Western Res. U. Sch. Libr. Sci., 1966-69; prof. agrege Ecole de Bibliotheconomie, U. Montreal, Canada, 1969-70, dir., 1970—72, prof. titulaire, 1970—72; editor Choice: Books for Coll. Libraries, Middletown, Conn., 1972-77; prof. Grad. Sch. Library and Info. Sci. UCLA, 1977-82; prof. titulaire Ecole de Bibliotheconomie, U. Montreal, Canada, 1982—93, dir., 1982—87; ret., 1993. Internat. libr. edn. cons., 1966-93. Author: Cataloging and Classification of Books, with the Vietnamese Decimal Classification, 1958, rev. edit., 1966, Opening Day Collection, 1965, rev. edit., 1974, Education for Librarianship in France: An Historical Survey, 1968, Library Collections: Their Origin, Selection, and Development, 1981 (Blackwell award 1982), Education of Library and Information Professionals: Present and Future Prospects, 1987; also articles. Mem. Forest Press com. Lake Placid Ednl. Found., 1972-87; trustee Russell Library, Middletown, 1975-77. Served with AUS, 1951-53 Mem. ALA, Ohio Library Assn. (exec. bd. 1962-63), Can. Library Assn., Assn. Coll. and Research Libraries (Spl. Presdl. Recognition award, 2005), Music Library Assn., Ohio Coll. Assn. (v.p. librarians sect. 1962-63, pres. 1963), Corp. des Bibliothecaires professionsals du Que. (adminstrv. council 1970-72), Tudor Singers Montreal (v.p. 1970-72), Assn. internat. des ecoles des scis. de l'information Home: 1890 East 107th Street #507 Cleveland OH 44106 E-mail: rkgardn@sbcglobal.net.

GARDNER, RICHARD NEWTON, diplomat, lawyer, educator; b. NYC, July 9, 1927; s. Samuel I. and Ethel (Elias) G.; m. Danielle Luzzatto, June 10, 1956; children: Nina Jessica, Anthony Laurence. AB magna cum laude, Harvard U., 1948; JD, Yale U., 1951; PhD, Oxford U., 1954. Bar: NY 1952. Corr. UP, 1946-47, AP, 1948; teaching fellow internat. legal studies Harvard Law Sch., 1953-54; with Coudert Bros., NYC, 1954-57; assoc. prof. law Columbia U., 1957-60, prof., 1960-61, 65-66, Henry L. Moses prof. law and internat. orgn., 1967—77, 81—; sr. counsel Morgan, Lewis & Bockius, 1997—; U.S. amb. to Italy Am. Embassy, Rome, 1977-81, U.S. amb. to Spain Madrid, 1993-97. Dep. asst. sec. state internat. orgns. Dept. State, 1961-65; vis. prof. U. Istanbul, 1958, U. Rome, 1967-68; dep. U.S. rep. UN Com. on Peaceful Uses of Outer Space, 1962-65; U.S. alt. del. 19th UN Gen. Assembly; sr. adviser U.S. del. to 20th and 21st UN Gen. Assemblies; U.S. alt. del. 55th UN Gen. Assembly; rapporteur UN Com. Experts on Econ. Restructuring, 1975; mem. Pres.'s Commn. on Internat. Trade and Investment Policy, 1970-71, U.S. Adv. Com. on Law of Sea, 1971-76; cons. to sec.-gen. UN Conf. on Human Environment, 1972, UN Conf. Environment and Devel., 1992; mem. pres.'s adv. com. Trade Policy and Negotiations, 1998-2002. Author: Sterling-Dollar Diplomacy, 1956, New Directions in U.S. Foreign Economic Policy, 1959, In Pursuit of World Order, 1964, Blueprint for Peace, 1966, (with Max F. Millikan) The Global Partnership: International Agencies and Economic Development, 1968, In Pursuit of World Order, 1980, Negotiating Survival: Four Priorities after Rio, 1992, Mission Italy: On the Front Lines of the Cold War, 2005; note editor: Yale Law Jour, 1950-51. Bd. dirs. Ditchley Found., Salzburg Seminar. Served with AUS, 1945-46. Recipient Detur prize for disting. scholarship Harvard U., 1948, Arthur S. Flemming award, 1963; Harvard Club scholar, 1944, Rhodes scholar, 1951-53. Mem. ABA, UN Assn. (dir.), Assn. Bar City NY, Council Fgn. Relations, Am. Acad. Arts and Scis., Am. Philosophical Soc., Phi Beta Kappa, Order of Coif, Century Assn, Met. Club. Clubs: Century Assn. (NYC); Met. (Washington). Office: Columbia U Sch Law JG Room 824 435 W 116th St New York NY 10027-7297 Office Phone: 212-854-4635. E-mail: rgardn@law.columbia.edu.*

GARDNER, ROBERT, financial services executive; b. Dec. 19, 1949; s. Sam and Edythe (Berman) G.; m. Barbara Paccione, Apr. 21, 1975; children: Theodore Mathew, Jessica Andrea. BA in Philosophy, Hunter Coll., 1978. Account exec. Merrill Lynch & Co., N.Y.C., 1977-80; v.p. Lehman Bros., N.Y.C., 1980-89; v.p. investments Prudential Securities, N.Y.C., 1989-97, 1st v.p., retirement planning advisor, 1998—. Mem. Internat. Assn. Fin. Planning. Avocations: golf, reading. Office: Prudential Securities Inc PO Box 4355 Manhasset NY 11030-4355

GARDNER, ROBIN PIERCE, engineering educator; b. Charlotte, N.C., Aug. 17, 1934; s. Robin Brem and Margaret (Pierce) G.; m. Linda Jean Gardner, Oct. 21, 1976. B.Ch.E., N.C. State U., 1956, MS, 1958; PhD, Pa. State U., 1961. Scientist Oak Ridge Inst. Nuclear Studies, 1961-63; research engr., asst. dir. measurement and controls lab. Research Triangle Inst., Research Triangle Park, N.C., 1963-67; research prof. nuclear engring. and chem. engring., dir. Center Engring. Applications of Radioisotopes, N.C. State U., 1967—. Cons. Oak Ridge Inst. Nuclear Studies, Research Triangle Inst., Oak Ridge Nat. Lab., Internat. Atomic Energy Agy., NASA, AEC, TVA, Alcoa. Author: (with Ralph L. Ely, Jr.), Radioisotope Measurement Applications in Engineering, 1967; regional editor Applied Radiation and Isotopes, Jour. Fine Particle Soc., Nuc. Geophysics; contbr. articles to sci. jours. Served to 1st lt. AUS, 1956. Recipient Alcoa Found. Disting. Rsch. award N.C. State U. Sch. Engring., 1986, Alumni Disting. Grad. Professorship award, 1996, R.J. Reynolds award for excellence in tchg. and rsch., 1998; Centennial fellow Coll. Earth and Mineral Scis., Pa. State U., 1996. Fellow Am. Nuc. Soc. (Radiation Industry award isotopes and radiation divsn. 1984), Am. Nuc. Soc., Am. Soc. Engring. Edn. (Glenn Murphy award for Outstanding Nuc. Engring. 2003), Sigma Xi, Phi Kappa Phi, Phi Lambda Upsilon. Home: 3005 Randolph Dr Raleigh NC 27609-6941 Office: NC State U Ctr Engring Applications of Radioisotope Dept Nuclear Engring Raleigh NC 27695-0001 Business E-Mail: gardner@ncsu.edu.

GARDNER, RULON E., Olympic athlete; b. Afton, Wyo., Aug. 16, 1971; s. Reed and Virginia Gardner. Grad., Ricks Coll., 1991; BS in Phys. Edn., U. Nebr., 1996. Greco-Roman wrestler Olympic Games, Sydney, 2000, Athens, 2004; ret., 2004. Named USA Wrestling Greco-Roman Wrestler of Yr., 2000, Flag Bearer, Closing Ceremonies, Olympics, Sydney, 2000, Amateur Wrestling News Man of the Year, 2000, USA Wrestling Man of Yr., 2001, USOC Sportsman of Yr., 2001, James E. Sullivan Award-Amateur athlete of the year, 2001; named one of Top 100 Most Powerful in sports, Sporting News, 2000; named to Ricks Coll. Athletic Hall of Fame, 2001, Wyo. Sports Hall of Fame, Athlete of Yr., 2001; recipient Best Original Score award, USA Today's Sports, 2000, Arete award, U.S. Olympic Spirit award, 2001, ESPY award for Male U.S. Olympic Athlete of Yr., 2001, Jesse Owens award, 2001, USOC Citizenship through Sports Alliance award, 2001. Achievements include Nat. Jr. College Athletic Champion, 1991; Nat. Champion, Greco-Roman, 1995, 1997, 2001; World Cup Champion, Greco-Roman, 1996; Pan-American Champion, 1998; Vantaa Cup Champion, Finland, 1998; Sr. Greco-Roman Championship Belt Series champion, 1998; Winter Classic Champion, 1999; Gold Medal, 120kg Greco-Roman Wrestling, Sydney Olympic Games, 2000; Gold Medal, World Wrestling Championships, 2001; Champion, Kurt Angle Classic, 2003; Bronze medal, 120kb Greco-Roman Wrestling, Athens Olympic games, 2004. Office: c/o USOC 1 Olympic Plaza Colorado Springs CO 80909

GARDNER, RUSSELL MENESE, lawyer; b. High Point, N.C., July 14, 1920; s. Joseph Hayes and Clara Emma-Lee (Flynn) G.; m. Joyce Thresher, Mar. 7, 1946; children: Winthrop G., Page Stansbury, June Thresher. AB, Duke U., 1942, JD, 1948. Bar: Fla. 1948, U.S. Ct. Appeals (5th cir.) 1949, U.S. Tax Ct. 1949, U.S. Supreme Ct. 1985. Ptnr. McCune, Hiaasen, Crum, Gardner & Duke and predecessor firms, Ft. Lauderdale, Fla., 1948-90, Gunster, Yoakley, & Stewart, 1990—. Bd. govs. Shepard Broad Law Ctr. Nova S.E. U. Trustee Mus. of Art, Inc., Ft. Lauderdale, pres., 1964-67; bd. dirs. Stranahan House, Inc., 1981—, pres., 1983-85; bd. dirs. Ft. Lauderdale Hist. Soc., 1962—, pres. 1975-85, pres. emeritus, 1985—; mem. estate planning council Duke U. Sch. Law; bd. dirs., vice chmn. Broward Performing Arts Found., Inc., 1985—. Served to lt. USNR, 1943-49. Fellow Am. Coll. Trust and Estate Counsel; mem. ABA (real property, probate, trust sect.), Am. Judicature Soc., Fla. Bar Assn. (probate, guardianship rules com. 1978-2002, probate law com.), Broward County Bar Assn. (estate planning council), Coral Ridge Country Club, Lauderdale Yacht Club, Tower Club. Republican. Presbyterian. Office: PO Box 14636 Fort Lauderdale FL 33302-4636 E-mail: rgardner@gunster.com.

GARDNER, SHEA NICOLE, computational biologist, bioinformaticist; BA, Princeton U., Princeton, New Jersey, 1991; PhD, U. Calif., 1997. Rsch. assoc. Imperial Coll., Ctr. Population Biology, Ascot, England, 1997—99; Lawrence fellow Lawrence Livermore (Calif.) Nat. Lab., 1999—2002, bioinformaticist, 2002—. Office: Lawrence Livermore Nat Lab 7000 East Ave Livermore CA 94550 Business E-Mail: gardner26@llnl.gov.

GARDNER, SHERYL PAIGE, gynecologist; b. Bremerton, Wash., Jan. 24, 1945; d. Edwin Gerald and Dorothy Elizabeth (Herman) G.; m. James Alva Beat, June 20, 1986. BA in Biology, U. Oreg., 1967, MD cum laude, 1971. Diplomate Am. Bd. Ob-Gyn. Intern L.A. County Harbor Gen. Hosp., Torrance, Calif., 1971-72, resident in ob-gyn., 1972-75; physician Group Health Assn., Washington, 1975-87; pvt. practice Mililani, Hawaii, 1987—. Med. staff sec. Wahiawa (Hawaii) Gen. Hosp., 1994-95. Mem. Am. Coll. Ob-Gyn., Am. Soc. Colposcopy and Cervical Pathology, Hawaii Med. Assn., N.Am. Menopause Soc., Sigma Kappa, Alpha Omega Alpha. Democrat. Avocation: environmental, peace and social concern groups. Office: 95-1249 Meheula Pkwy Ste B10A Mililani HI 96789-1763 Office Phone: 808-625-5277.

GARDNER, STAN A., school librarian, educator; s. Charles Herbert Gardner; m. Katherine Ellerton, Aug. 24, 1985; children: Genelle, Christopher. BA in Social sci., Ctrl. Wash. State Coll., 1972; MA in Libr. sci., U. Mich., 1975; PhD in Info. sci., cert. of Advanced Study, U. North Tex., 1992. Instrnl. svcs. libr. Pioneer C.C., Kansas City, Mo., 1975—78; dir. libr. for the blind and physically handicapped Kans. City Pub. Libr., 1979—80; dir. learning resources ctr. Timberline campus Colo. Mountain Coll., Leadville, 1980—85; head media libr. Sultan Qaboos U. Libr., Al-Khod, Oman, 1986—89; asst. commr. librs. Mo. Dept. Higher Edn., Jefferson City, 1989—94; asst. state libr. Mo. Office Sec. of State, Jefferson City, 1994—96; libr. dir. Wayne State Coll., Nebr., 1996—. Author: A Descriptive Study of Statewide Bibliographic Databases. Libr. commn. adv. coun. Nebr. Libr. Commn., Lincoln, 1997—2003. Mem.: ALA, Mountain Plains Libr. Assn., Nebr. Media Assn., Nebr. Libr. Assn. Office: Wayne State Coll Conn Library 1111 Main St Wayne NE 68787 Office Phone: 402-375-7257. Office Fax: 402-375-7538. Business E-Mail: stgardn1@wsc.edu.

GARDNER, STEPHEN HENRY, lawyer; b. Dallas, Aug. 5, 1951; s. Willard Henry and Mary Frances (Brown) G.; m. Kathi Buchanan Child, Sept. 2, 1972 (div. Dec. 1977); m. Margaret Grace Bonner, Dec. 11, 1982; children: James Bonner, Mary Elizabeth. BA with honors, U. Tex., 1972, JD, 1975. Bar: Tex. 1976, N.Y. 1983, U.S. Supreme Ct. 1980, U.S. Ct. Appeals (2d cir.) 1984, U.S. Ct. Appeals (5th cir.) 1978, U.S. Ct. Appeals (7th cir.) 1999, U.S. Ct. Appeals (8th cir.) 1990, U.S. Ct. Appeals (9th cir.) 1993, U.S. Ct. Appeals (D.C. cir.) 1988, U.S. Dist. Ct., Ark. (ea. and we. dists.) 1986, U.S. Dist. Ct., Ill. (middle and no. dists.) 1999, U.S. Dist. Ct., N.Y. (ea. and so. dists.) 1983, U.S. Dist. Ct., Tex. (we. dist.) 1977, U.S. Dist. Ct., Tex. (no. dist.) 1984, U.S. Dist. Ct., Tex. (so. dist.) 1993, U.S. Dist. Ct., Tex. (ea. dist.) 2002. Staff atty. Legal Aid Soc. of Cen. Tex., Austin, 1975—81; students atty. U. Tex., Austin, 1982; asst. atty. gen. State of N.Y., N.Y.C., 1982—84, State of Tex., Dallas, 1984—91; of counsel Nat. Consumer Law Ctr., 2002—. Fellow Consumer Law Ctr., Boston, 1980-81; coun. mem. Consumer Adv. Coun. of the Fed. Res. Bd., Washington, 1986-89. Contbr. articles to profl. jours. Bd. dir. Legal Svcs. of North Tex., Dallas, 1987-89. Adm. Tex. Navy. Recipient Good Old Boy award Tex. Women's Polit. Caucus, 1987, Marvin award Nat. Assn. Attys. Gen., 1988, Hall of Fame award Ctr. for Sci. in the Pub. Interest, 1991. Mem. Tex. Bar Assn., Honorable Order of Ky. Cols., N.Y. State Bar Assn. Democrat. Home: 3230 Bryn Mawr Dr Dallas TX 75225-7645 Office: Ctr for Sci in Pub Interest 6060 N Central Expy Ste 560 Dallas TX 75206 Business E-Mail: steve@consumerhelper.com.

GARDNER, STEVEN, instructional designer; b. Springfield, Mo., Nov. 8, 1950; s. Arthur Daniel and Elizabeth Irene Gardner; life ptnr. Kenny Kightlinger. Cert. instrnl. technologist. Corp. tng. specialist BlueCross and BlueShield of Mo., Springfield, 1996—2002; instrnl. designer WellPoint Health Networks, Springfield, 2002—. Mem. Ozarks Literacy Coun., Springfield, 2000—01. Sgt. e-5 U.S. Army, 1970—76. Fellow, Acad. for Healthcare Mgmt., 2002. Democrat. Mem. Disciples Of Christ. Avocations: travel, wine, computers, reading. Office: WellPoint Health Networks 3534 East Sunshine Springfield MO 65804 E-mail: steve.gardner@wellpoint.com.

GARDNER, THOMAS NEVILLE, communications educator; b. New Orleans, La, July 7, 1946; s. Edward Neville and Margaret Agnes (Guess) G.; m. Karen Levine, Mar. 12, 1994; m. Jennifer N. Johnston, Dec. 22, 1979 (div. Aug. 1990); children: Sarah Rose Johnston-Gardner, Koby Leor Gardner-Levine. BA in Sociology, U. Va., 1971; MA in Journalism, U. Ga., 1981; MPA, Harvard U., 1985; PhD in Comm., U. Mass., 2005. Chmn. So. Student Organizing Com, Nashville, 1967-69; rsch. dir. Va. Rsch. Inst., Charlottesville, Va., 1971-73; media specialist Atlanta Jr. Coll., Ga., 1975-77; teaching asst. journalism U. Ga., Athens, Ga., 1977-79; reporter, columnist Montgomery Advertiser, Ala., 1980-83; pub. rels. dir. Ala. State Employees Assn., Montgomery, Ala., 1983-84; dir. comm. Union Concerned Scientists, Cambridge, Mass., 1985-87; pub. affairs officer Harvard U. Div. Sch., Cambridge, Mass., 1987-88; sr. editor Harvard Inst. Internat. Devel., Cambridge, Mass., 1988-92; pres., comm./edit. cons. Thomas N. Gardner & Assoc., Cambridge and Amherst, Mass., 1992—. Tchg. asst. comm. dept. U. Mass., Amherst, 1993—96; mng. dir. Media Edn. Found., 1996—2001; asst. prof. comm. Westfield State Coll., 2001—. Author: Rah's Hidden Treasure, 1992, SSOC: A Brief History of the Southern Student Organizing Committee, 2002; contbr.: We Won't Go, 1967; mng. editor: Reforming Economic Systems in Developing Countries, 1991. Bd. dirs. Men's Resource Ctr. Recipient 1st Prize Photography So. Regional Coun., Atlanta, 1978, Govt. Reporting award Ala. State Employees Assn., Montgomery, 1982. Mem. Soc. Profl. Journalists, Nat. Comm. Assn. Office: Westfield State Coll Dept Comm Westfield MA 01086-1630

GARDNER, TIMOTHY JOSEPH, surgeon, educator; b. Phila., Dec. 6, 1938; s. Joseph Thomas and Elva (Flynn) G.; m. Nina Hooton, July 4, 1964; children: Julie, Joseph, Emily, Nicholas. BA, Georgetown Coll., 1962; MD, Georgetown U., 1966. Intern Johns Hopkins Hosp., Balt., 1966-67, asst. resident in surgery, 1967-68, 71-74, rsch. fellow cardiac surg. lab., 1970-71, chief resident, 1974-75, chief resident in cardiac surgery, 1975-76, asst. prof., 1976-80, assoc. prof., 1980-86; prof. Johns Hopkins U. Sch. Medicine, 1986-93, Hosp. U. Pa., Phila., 1993—, chief divsn. cardiothoracic surgery, 1993—. Speaker in field; vis. prof. Royal Australasian Coll. Surgeons, Hobart, Tasmania, 1994, Royal Prince Alfred Hosp., Sydney, 1989, U. Kans. Sch. Medicine, 1984, Children's Hosp. Phila., 1981. Contbr. articles to profl. jours.; guest editl. reviewer: Jour. Thoracic and Cardiovascular Surgery, 1981-83, Circulation, 1983-91; book reviewer: Annals Thoracic Surgery, 1985-89. With U.S. Army, 1968-70. Fellow ACS, Am. Coll. Cardiology; mem. Am. Surg. Assn., Assn. for Acad. Surgery, Balt. City Med. Soc., Med. and Chirurgical Faculty Md., So. Thoracic Surg. Assn., Soc. Thoracic Surgeons, Soc. Univ. Surgeons, Am. Assn. for Thoracic Surgery, So. Surg. Assn., Am. Surg. Assn., Am. Heart Assn. (mem. coun. on cardiovasc. surgery), Am. Bd. Med. Specialists (chair, dir. thoracic surgery). Office: U Pa Health Sys 6 Silverstein Pavil 3400 Spruce St Philadelphia PA 19104-4227

GARDNER, WILFORD ROBERT, physicist, researcher; b. Logan, Utah, Oct. 19, 1925; s. Robert and Nellie (Barker) G.; m. Marjorie Louise Cole, June 9, 1949; children: Patricia, Robert, Caroline. BS, Utah State U., 1949; MS, Iowa State U., 1951, PhD, 1953; DSc (hon.), Ohio State U., 2003. Physicist U.S. Salinity Lab., Riverside, Calif., 1953-66; prof. U. Wis., Madison, 1966-80; physicist, prof., head dept. soil and water sci. U. Ariz., Tucson, 1980-87; dean coll. natural resources U. Calif., Berkeley, 1987-94, dean emeritus, 1994—; adj. prof. Utah State U., 1995—. Author: Soil Physics, 1972. Served with U.S. Army, 1943-46. Recipient Hon. Faculty award, U. Ghent, Belgium, 1972, Centennial Alumnus award, Utah State U., 1986; NSF Sr. fellow, 1959, Fulbright fellow, 1971—72. Fellow: AAAS, Am. Soc. Agronomy; mem.: NAS, Soil Sci. Soc. Am. (pres. 1990, Rsch. award 1962), Internat. Union Soil Sci. (hon.), Internat. Soil Sci. Soc. (pres. physics commn. 1968—74). Personal E-mail: colegardner@comcast.net.

GARDNER, WILLIAM ALBERT, JR., pathologist, medical products executive; b. Sumter, SC, Aug. 2, 1939; s. William A. and Betty Lee (Kennedy) G.; m. Kathryn Ann Medlin, June 30, 1960; children: Mary Elizabeth, Kathryn Lee, William Dylan. BS, Wofford Coll., 1960; MS in Anatomy, Med. Coll. S.C., 1963, MD, 1965. Diplomate: Am. Bd. Pathology. Intern Johns Hopkins Hosp., Balt., 1965-66, asst. resident, 1966-67, fellow in pathology, 1965-67; asst. resident Duke U., Durham, N.C., 1967-68, chief resident, 1968-69, instr. pathology, 1968-69; chief lab. service VA Hosp., Charleston, SC, 1969—76; asst. prof. pathology Med. U. S.C., 1969-72, assoc. prof., 1972-76; prof. pathology Vanderbilt U., Nashville, 1976-81, vice chmn. dept. pathology; chief lab. service VA Hosp., Nashville, 1976-81; prof., chmn. dept. pathology U. South Ala., Mobile, 1981—2002, Locke disting. prof. pathology, 1994—2002, emeritus prof., 2002—, asst. v.p. for risk adminstrn., 2001. Pres. health svc. found. U. South Ala., Mobile, 1988-91, assoc. dean clin. affairs, 1997—; pres., CEO Internat. Registry Pathology; exec. dir. Am. Registry Pathology, 2002-. Contbr. articles on oncology, urology, parasitology and pathology to profl. jours. Recipient Outstanding Teaching award Med. U. S.C., 1975, Disting. Alumnus award Med. U. S.C., 1988; named to Alumni Assn. Centennial Recognition list, 1992; Fulbright scholar, 1996. Fellow Am. Soc. Clin. Pathologists, Coll. Am. Pathologists (del. for govtl. pathology); mem. AMA, Internat. Acad. Pathology (v.p., chair fin. com. 1994—, internat. councillor 1994—), U.S.-Can. Acad. Pathology (v.p., pres.-elect 1993-95, pres. 1995-96, mem. fin. com. 1996—), Acad. Clin. Lab. Physicians and Scientists, Ala. Med. Assn., Assn. Pathology Chmn. (coun., pres. 1992-94), Armed Forces Inst. of Pathology (mem. sci. adv. bd. 1996—, chair sci. adv. bd., 1997—), Alpha Omega Alpha. Methodist. Office: Am Registry Pathology PO Box 8188 Silver Spring MD 20907 Business E-Mail: gardnerw@afip.osd.mil.

GARDNER, WILLIAM MICHAEL, state official; b. Manchester, N.H., Oct. 26, 1948; s. William George and Mildred Irene (Claus) G.; m. Kathleen Gordon, May 21, 1978; children: William Gordon, Kathleen Meghan. BA, U. N.H., 1970; diploma, London Sch. Econs., 1972; ME, U. N.C., Greensboro, 1973; MPA, Harvard U., 1985. Mem. N.H. Ho. of Reps., Concord, 1973-76; sec. state State of N.H., Concord, 1976—. Chmn. N.H. Mcpl. Records Bd., 1978—; pres. Nat. Assn. Secs. State, 1998—99. Editor: Towns Against Tyranny: Hills Borough County New Hampshire During the American Revolution 1775-83, 1976, New Hampshire: The State That Made Us a Nation, 1989; co-author: Why New Hampshire? The First-in-the-Nation Primary State, 2003. Mem. exec. com. Hillsborough County, N.H., 1973-74; chmn. Manchester Del., 1974-75; trustee Belanger-Gardner Found., Bishop's U., Can., 1985—. Democrat. Roman Catholic. Office: Office Sec State 107 N Main St State Ho Rm 204 Concord NH 03301-3222

GARDOM, GARDE BASIL, former lieutenant governor of British Columbia; b. Banff, Alta., Can., July 17, 1924; s. Basil and Gabrielle Gwladys (Bell) G.; m. Theresa Helen Eileen Mackenzie, Feb. 11, 1956; children: Kim Gardom Allen, Karen Gardom MacDonald, Edward, Brione Gardom MacDonald, Brita Gardom McLaughlin. BA, LLB, U. BC, Vancouver, Can., 1949, LLD (hon.), 2003. Called to bar 1949. With Campbell, Brazier & Co., 1949; sr. ptnr. Gardom & Co., Vancouver, 1960-75; apptd. Queen's Counsel, 1975; mem. BC Legis. Assembly for Vancouver-Point Grey, 1966-87; atty. gen. BC, 1975-79; min. intergovtl. rels., 1979-86; policy cons. Office of Premier, 1986-87; agt. gen. BC, 1987-92, Europe; mem. Premier's Econ. Adv. Coun., 1988-91; lt.-gov. BC, 1995—2001; dir. Brouwer Claims Can., 2002—. Dir. Justitute Inst. BC. Hon. patron Royal BC Mus., Drug Edn. Svcs., BCAA Traffic Safety Found.; hon. dir. Boys and Girls Club Vancouver; hon. chmn. Bibl. Mus. Can.; mem. Campaign for Constrn.; rowing facilitator U. BC; v.p. Pacific Alzheimer Rsch. Found.; mem. adv. coun. BC Cmty. Achievement awards. Decorated Order of BC; named to BC Sports Hall of Fame, 1995; named Freeman of City of London, 1992; hon. col. BC Regiment. Mem. Can. Bar Assn., BC Law Soc., Heraldry Soc. Can., Royal United Svcs. Inst. Vancouver, Govt. Ho. Garden Soc., Brook Ho. Soc., Royal Commonwealth Soc., Vancouver Lawn Tennis and Badminton Club, Union Club BC, Knight of Justice, Order St. John, Royal Overseas Club, Can. Club Vancouver (hon. vice patron, dir. life mem.), Vancouver Club, Phi Delta Theta. Anglican. Home Fax: 604-267-9525.

GARELICK, MARTIN, retired transportation executive; b. Rochester, NY, May 18, 1924; s. Samuel and Esther (Gerber) G.; m. Betty J. Mann, Jan. 18, 1951. BSC.E., Purdue U., 1947. With Milw. Rd. R.R., 1947-78, asst. v.p. mktg. devel. and planning Chgo., 1973-76, v.p. ops., 1976-78; exec. v.p., chief operating officer AMTRAK, Washington, 1978-80; v.p. Wyer, Dick & Co., Chgo., 1980-82; v.p., gen. mgr. N.J. Transit Rail Ops., Newark, 1982-84; dir. Kyle Rys., Inc., Scottsdale, Ariz., 1979-97; ret., 1997. With U.S. Army, 1943—46. Mem. Am. Soc. Traffic and Logistics, Am. Assn. R.R. Supts., Tau Epsilon Phi. Jewish. Home: 20876 Del Luna Dr Boca Raton FL 33433-1788 Personal E-mail: garelick@worldnet.att.net.

GAREY, DONALD LEE, oil industry executive; b. Ft. Worth, Sept. 9, 1931; s. Leo James and Jessie (McNatt) G.; m. Elizabeth Patricia Martin, Aug. 1, 1953; children: Deborah Anne, Elizabeth Laird. BS in Geol. Engring., Tex. A&M U., 1953. Registered profl. engr., Tex. Reservoir geologist Gulf Oil Corp., 1953-54, sr. geologist, 1956-65; v.p., mng. dir. Indsl. Devel. Corp. Lea County, Hobbs, N.Mex., 1965-72, dir., 1972-86, pres., 1978-86; v.p., dir. Minerals, Inc., Hobbs, N.Mex., 1966-72, pres., dir., 1972-86, CEO, 1978-82; mng. dir. Hobbs Indsl. Found. Corp., 1965-72, dir., 1965-76; v.p. Llano, Inc., 1972-74, exec. v.p., COO, 1974-75, pres., 1975-86, CEO, also dir., 1978-82; pres., CEO Pollution Control, Inc., 1969-81. Pres. NMESCO Fuels, Inc., 1982-86; chmn., pres., CEO Estacado, Inc., 1986—, Natgas Inc., 1987—; pres. Llano Co2, Inc., 1984-86; cons. geologist, geol. engr., Hobbs, 1965-72. Chmn. Hobbs Manpower Devel. Tng. Adv. Com., 1965-72; mem. Hobbs Adv. Com. for Mental Health, 1965-67; chmn. N.Mex. Mapping Adv. Com., 1968-69; mem. Hobbs adv. bd. Salvation Army, 1967-78, chmn., 1970-72; mem. exec. bd. Conquistador coun. Boy Scouts Am., Hobbs, 1965-75; vice chmn. N.Mex. Gov's Com. for Econ. Devel., 1968-70; bd. regents Coll. Southwest, 1982-85. Capt. USAF, 1954-56. Mem. AIPG, AAPG, SPE of AIME. Home: 315 E Alto Dr Hobbs NM 88240-3905 Office: Broadmoor Tower PO Box 5587 Hobbs NM 88241-5587 Office Phone: 505-393-6300.

GAREY, PATRICIA MARTIN, artist; b. State College, Miss., Nov. 11, 1932; d. Verey G. Martin and Eva Myrtle Jones; m. Donald L. Garey, Aug. 1, 1953; children: Deborah Anne Garey Furst, Elizabeth Laird Garey Jones. BS in Costume Design, Tex. Women's U., 1953; MFA, Tex. Tech. U., 1973; postgrad. in art history, Two-Dimensional Studio Art, 1970-73. Prodn. mgr. Cox Advt. Agy., Roswell, N.Mex., 1958-63; art instr. Coll. of Southwest, Hobbs, N.Mex., 1967-69, 72-73, prof. art history, art appreciation, 1974-76; studio artist Hobbs, 1976—; prof. art/painting and drawing N.Mex. Jr. Coll., 1997-98. Instr. Cloudcroft Artists Sch., N.Mex., 1991; prof. drawing, painting N.Mex. Jr. Coll.; prof. art hist. Coll. of Southwest, 1999—2001; rep., drawing instr. Villa Maria Ctr. for the Arts, Perugia, Italy, 1996; apptd. N.Mex. Arts Commn., 1999; artist-in-residence N.Mex. Art Commn., Santa Fe, 1975—76. Artist (one-woman shows) Sand Hills Mus., Kermit, Tex., 1968, N.Mex. Jr. Coll., Hobbs, 1969, 1985, Coll. of SW, 1974, 1979, Sangre de Cristo Arts Ctr., Puebl, 1979, U. Tex. of Permian Basin, Odessa, 1980, N.Mex. Jr. Coll., (represented by) Sylvia Ullman Am. Crafts, Cleve., Design Today, Lubbock, Tex., (exhibitions) Roswell Mus. Art, Four Women Artists of Hobbs, N.Mex., 1966, Lubbock Mcpl. Garden and Arts Ctr., 1966, Laguna Gloria Art Mus., 1968—, Southeastern N.Mex. Small Painting Exhibit, 1975 (2d pl., 1966, 2d pl. Graphics, 2d pl. Sculpture, 2d pl. Acrylics, 1st pl. Ceramics, 1st pl. Drawing, 2d pl. Painting), Americas Gallery, Taos, 1974, Blair Gallery, Santa Fe, 1976, Mus. Fine Arts, 1976, Tex. Tech. U. Grad. Show, 1977, Little Rock Art Ctr., Ark., 1978, Hills Gallery, Santa Fe, 1979, Llano Estacado Art Assn., Dallas Mus. Fine Art, 1986, 1987, 1988, 1990, Beaux Arts Ball Art Auction, 1990, Okla. City Mus. Art nat. drawing competition, Little Rock Art Ctr., El Paso Sun Carnival, Tex., Govs. Gallery, State Capitol, Santa Fe, 1997, L.E.A.A., Hobbs, N.Mex., 1999 (Best of Show, 1st pl. watercolor), (permanent collections) Home Scis. Dept., Tex. Tech. U., The Round House/State Capitol, Santa Fe, Villa Maria Ctr. for the Arts, Raimondi Collection, Perugia, Italy, docent Meadows Mus. of Art So. Meth. U., Dallas, 1990, Govs. Invitiational, Govs. Gallery, 1996, 35 Clay Workers of N.Mex., artist (exhibitions) Southeastern N.Mex. Small Painting Exhibit, 1976, 1987, 1988, 1990, (permanent collections) State Capitol, Santa Fe, N.Mex. Jr. Coll.; represented by, DeLis Backdoor Gallery, N.Mex. Arts commr. State of N.Mex., 1999—2002, N.Mex. Arts Commn., 1999—2003; artistic bd. S.W. Symphony, Hobbs, 1987—99; Bd. dirs. The Bridge Breast Ctr., Dallas, 1992—93, Llano Estacado Art Assn. Recipient Best of Show award for mixed media Llano Estacado Art Assn. Regional Show, Hobbs, N.Mex., 1996, Best of Show award for ceramics, 1999, 1st pl. award for watercolor, 1999, Best of Show for oil painting, 2004 Mem. Delta Phi Delta, Chi Omega. Democrat. Methodist. Avocations: swimming, cooking, classical music, book collecting. Studio: 315 E Alto Dr Hobbs NM 88240-3905 also: Piney Woods Cloudcroft NM 88350 Office Phone: 505-393-8683.

GARFIELD, ERNEST, bank executive, consultant; b. Colorado River, Ariz., July 14, 1932; s. Emil and Carmen (Ybarra) G.; m. Betty Ann Redden, Apr. 18, 1953; children: Laural, Jeffery Alan. BS, U. Ariz., 1975; B of Internat. Mgmt., Am. Grad. Sch., Phoenix, 1975, M of Internat. Mgmt., 1976. Owner Garfield Ins. Agy., Tucson, 1962-70; senator State of Ariz., Phoenix, 1967-68, dep. treas., 1970-71, treas., 1971-74; commr. Ariz. Corp. Commn., Phoenix, 1974-79; chmn. United Bancorp Systems, Inc., Phoenix, 1979—, Interstate Bank Developers, Inc., Scottsdale, 1994—. Chmn. The White House Conf. on Energy, Com. on Energy Policy of Nat. Assn. Regulatory Utility Commn.; pres. Western Conf. Pub. Svc. Commns.; mem. Ad Hoc Com. on Regulatory Reform, Electric and Nuclear Energy Com. Mem. Ariz. Kidney Found., Multiple Sclerosis Soc., Rep. Senatorial Inner Circle, 1989; mem. Pres. Bush Task Force, 1989; mem. adv. bd. St. Joseph's Hosp., Phoenix; mem. establishment com. Pima County Jr. Coll., Tucson; mem. orgn. com. Pima County Halfway House, Tucson; chmn. Ariz. Gov. Commn. on Rape Prevention, 1988, Nat. Commn. on Rape Prevention, 1990—; commr. Ariz. Gov. Commn. on Violence Against Women, 1993-2003; active Ariz. Gov.'s Sexual Assault Task Force; dir. Ariz. Sexual Assault Network; bd. dirs. Ariz. Cactus-Pine coun. Girl Scouts U.S.; mem. Men Against Violence Network. With U.S. Army, 1952-55. Recipient Outstanding Young Men Ariz. award, Press Club award; named to U.S. Arty. Hall of Fame, 1999. Mem.: Thunderbird Internat. Banking Inst. (mem. adv. coun. 1990—), Ariz-Mex. C. of C. Republican. Roman Catholic. Avocation: graphology. Home and Office: 8442 N 72nd Pl Scottsdale AZ 85258-2762 E-mail: egarfield@qwest.net.

GARFIELD, LESLIE JEROME, real estate executive; b. N.Y.C., Mar. 23, 1932; s. Jack and Anne (Weinert) G.; m. Johanna Rosengarten, Sept. 28, 1960; children: Clare Louisa, Jed Herbert, Cory Alexander. BA, U. Wis., Madison, 1953; MA, Harvard U., 1956; MBA, Columbia U., 1958. V.p. Pease & Elliman, Inc., N.Y.C., 1965—68, William A. White & Sons, Inc., N.Y.C., 1968—78; pres. Leslie J. Garfield & Co., Inc., N.Y.C., 1978—. Vice-chmn., bd. dirs. Internat. Print Ctr. Chmn. bd. dirs. N.Y. Youth Symphony, 1986—, pres. bd. dirs., 1975-86; bd. dirs. Carnegie Hill Neighbors, N.Y.C., 1985—; coun. Elvehjem Mus. Art Com. prints and illustrated books Mus. Modern Art; bd. overseers Mus. Fine Arts, Boston. Mem. Real Estate Bd. N.Y. (chmn. sales brokers com. 1985-86), Century Assn., Nat. Arts Club, Grolier Club (coun.). Avocation: collecting 20th century works on paper. Office: Leslie J Garfield and Co 505 Park Ave New York NY 10022-9332 E-mail: lesliejre@aol.com.

GARFIELD, ROBERT EDWARD, journalist; b. Phila., Pa., June 20, 1955; s. Samuel M. Garfield and Nancy G. Rowen; m. Carla Patricia Cain, Dec. 16, 1977; children: Kathryn Sarah, Allison Patricia, Ida Rose; m. Milena Trobozic, Mar. 11, 2001. BA, Pa. State U., 1977. Reporter Reading Times, Pa., 1977-81, Wilmington News-Jour., Del., 1981-82; columnist USA Today, Washington, 1982-85, Crain News Svc. and Advt. Age, Washington, 1985—; corr. Nat. Pub. Radio, 1986—. Analyst ABC News, 1999-2005; co-host On the Media, Nat. Pub. Radio, 1999—. Host Ad Age Reports program Fin. News Network, 1989-91; polit. advt. analyst CBS This Morning, 1992; contbg. writer Washington Post Mag., 1985-97; corr. Here and Now, Sta. WETA-TV, 1995; contbg. editor Civilization Mag., 1996-98; contbg. columnist U.S.A. Today, 1995-98; contbr. CNBC "Power Lunch", 1996-99, Adam Smith's Money Game, 1998; author: Waking Up Screaming from the American Dream, 1997, And Now a Few Words from Me, 2003. Recipient Keystone award Pa. Newspaper Pubs. Assn., 1981, Best of Gannett award Gannett Co. Inc., 1982, journalism award Saatchi & Saatchi/Compton Advt., 1984, 85, award Am. Soc. Bus. Press Editors, 1994, Neal award Am. Bus. Press, 1996, Internat. Radio award NY Festivals, 2003, RTNDA Edward R. Murrow award, 2003, Arthur Rowse award Nat. Press Club, 2003, Peabody award U. Ga., 2005. Mem. Nat. Press Club. Jewish.

GARFIELD, WINIFRED L., nursing administrator; b. Fredericksted, St. Croix, V.I., July 28, 1941; d. Walter Antonio and Idalia Crystalia (Stephens) L.; m. Victor Conrad Garfield, June 30, 1968; children: Vilma Cecilia, Victor Conrad, Vynette Crystine, Vivicka Celeste. RN, St. Lukes Sch. Nursing, Ponce, P.R., 1962; grad. anesthesiology for nurses, Harlem Hosp. Sch., 1966. RN, CRNA, AANA. Staff nurse Knud Hansen Hosp., St. Thomas, V.I., 1962-64, nurse anesthetist, 1966-70, nurse anesthetist supr., 1970-89, respiratory therapy instr., 1976-77; campus nurse U. of V.I., St. Thomas, V.I., 1979-82; first aid instr., trainer ARC, St. Thomas, V.I., 1973-80; supr. anesthesia and respiratory svc. St. Thomas Hosp., St. Thomas, V.I., 1980-89; exec. dir. V.I. Bd. of Nurse Licensure, St. Thomas, V.I., 1989—. Nurse cons. Educare Sch., Inc., 1970—, asst. dir., 1980—. Recipient Disting. Nurse Cons. award Dept. of Health Office of Commr., 1982, named Nurse of the Year V.I. Licensed Practical Nurse Assn., 1986. Mem. V.I. Nurses Assn. (v.p. 1963-64), Chi Eta Phi (historian, 1963-64), Eta Phi Beta (Alpha Chi chpt). Democrat. Roman Catholic. Avocations: reading, gardening, travel. Home: 394-140 Anas Retreat Charlotte Amalie VI 00803 Office: VI Bd of Nursing Licensure Veterans Dr Sta Charlotte Amalie VI 00803

GARFIELD-WOODBRIDGE, NANCY, writer; b. N.Y.C. d. Solomon and Betty Silbowitz; m. George Charles Woodbridge, Apr. 20, 1980; children from previous marriage: Maurice Garfield, Joshua Garfield. BA in Lit., Bennington Coll., 1955; MS in Edn., Hofstra U., 1972, postgrad., 1973. Cert. tchr. K-8, English 7-9 N.Y. Editl. asst. Wenner Gren Found. Anthropol. Rsch., N.Y.C., 1952—55; picture editor Forbes Mag., N.Y.C., 1955—56; editor-in-chief The Gifted Child Mag., N.Y.C., 1957—58; v.p. Info. Retrieval Systems, Great Neck, NY, 1958—72; rsch. assoc. to v.p. and editor N.Y. Inst. Tech., Westbury, 1972—73; dir. spl. projects Girl Scouts of USA, N.Y.C., 1973—2000; children's author, 2000—. Spkr. v.p.'s task force on youth employment, Little Rock, 1979, gov.'s conf. on juvenile justice, Baton Rouge; presenter Edn. Commn. for the States, Denver, 1979. Author: The Tuesday Elephant, 1968, The Dancing Monkey, 1970, Juvenile Justice, 1981; contbr. articles to profl. jours. and mags. Vol. Kennedy Kenya Airlift Program, N.Y.C., 1962, Biafran Refugee Campaign, N.Y.-London, 1967; fundraiser Sara's Ctr. Very Spl. Arts Festival, L.I. to Washington. Scholar Breadloaf Writers Conf., Vt., 1967. Mem.: Acad. Am. Poets, The Author's Guild, Milford Fine Arts Coun., Soc. Children's Book Writers and Illustrators. Avocations: travel, reading, opera, painting, photography.

GARFIN, LOUIS, retired actuary; b. Mason City, Iowa, June 7, 1917; s. Sam and Etta (Larner) G.; m. Clarice Fagen, Apr. 11, 1943 (dec. Apr. 8, 2004); children: Eugene Arthur, Erica. Student, Mason City Jr. Coll., 1934-36; BA, State U. Iowa, 1938, MS, 1939, PhD, 1942. Instr. USAAF, Scott Field, Ill., 1942-43; instr. math. Ill. Inst. Tech., Chgo., 1943, U. Minn., 1943-44; actuary Oreg. Ins. Dept., Salem, 1946-52; assoc. actuary Pacific Mut. Life Ins. Co., Los Angeles, 1952-62, actuary, 1962-64, v.p., chief actuary, 1964-82, cons. actuary, 1982-90; ret., 1990. Bd. dirs. Calif. Health Decisions, 1989-95, chairperson, 1993-94, Laguna Beach Cmty. Clinic, 1989-93; treas. Laguna Canyon Found., 1990-99, Mykonos Village, 1999—. Fellow Soc. Actuaries; mem. Am. Acad. Actuaries (v.p. 1976-78), Internat. Congress Actuaries (dir. 1977-80), Actuarial Club Pacific States (pres. 1967-68), Los Angeles Actuarial Club (pres. 1959-60), Am. Math. Soc., Phi Beta Kappa, Sigma Xi. Home: 4013 Arcadia Way Oceanside CA 92056-5139 Personal E-mail: lgarfin@cox.net.

GARFINKEL, ALAN, language educator; b. Chgo., Sept. 6, 1941; s. Bernard D. and Tillie (Schaffner) G.; m. Sonya Pickus, July 10, 1965; children: Eli Louis, Noah Baruch. BA, U. Ill., 1961, MA, 1963; PhD, Ohio State U., 1969. Tchr. Spanish Waukegan (Ill.) Twp. H.S., 1964-65; asst. prof. Okla. State U., Stillwater, 1969-72, Purdue U., West Lafayette, Ind., 1972-74, assoc. prof., 1974-93, prof., 1993—. Cons. Cath. U. of Chile, Santiago, 1976; vis. scholar U. Queensland, Brisbane, Australia, 1993; fgn. expert Beijing Fgn. Studies U., People's Republic China, 2000; cons. in field. Co-author: Modismos al Momento, 1978, Trabajo y Vida, 1983, Explorando en la Casa de los Monstruos, 1997, Navidad en España, 2002, Let's Get Together, 2003; contbr. articles to profl. jours. Bd. dirs. Congregation Sons Abraham, Lafayette, 1986-93; committeeman Dem. Party, West Lafayette, 1993-99. Recipient Sr. Lectr. award Fulbright Commn., 1978, Acad. Specialist award U.S. State Dept., 1985, Tchr. Ctr. award U.S. Dept. Edn., 1978-81. Mem. Am. Coun. Teaching Fgn. Langs. (nat. textbook com. 1992), Ind. Fgn. Langs. Tchr.'s Assn. (pres. 1993-95), Lafayette Adult Resource Acad. (mem. adv. bd.), Lafayette Daybreak Rotary Club (Rotarian of the Yr.) 1997-98, Phi Delta Kappa (del., chpt. pres. 2000—). Jewish. Avocation: philatelist. Home: 2229 Carberry Dr West Lafayette IN 47906-1943 Office: Purdue U FLL 640 Oval Dr West Lafayette IN 47907-2039 E-mail: alangarf@purdue.edu.

GARFINKEL, BARBARA ANN, pianist, educator, musicologist; b. Elizabeth, N.J., Dec. 19, 1931; d. Irving and Lillian (Treister) Slavin; m. Burton Garfinkel, June 28, 1952; children: Steven, Joan Struss. BS in Edn., Boston U., 1953. Cert. vocal music instr., piano instr. Pvt. piano tchr., Millburn, N.J., 1949-52, Livingston, N.J., 1968-90; elem. sch. tchr. Nahant (Mass.) Pub. Schs., 1953-54, Maplewood (N.J.) Pub. Schs., 1954-56; profl. pianist, vocalist, 1984—. Music tchr. Downs Syndrome Children, Livingston, 1982-85; choir dir. Daughers of Miriam, Clifton, N.J., 1986, Cranford (N.J.) Home Continuing Care, 1990. Composer liturgical and show music; performer one woman shows vocal and piano. Vol. pianist Grotta Nursing Home, West Orange, N.J., 1988-93; judge teen piano finalists Garden State Art Ctr., Holmdel, N.J., 1985-95; local leader Dem. Party, Livingston, 1990—; v.p. Christ Hosp. Auxiliary, Jersey City, 1980-85; instrs. Russian, Israeli, Chinese immigrants, 1980-93; diplomat World Jewish Congress, 1995—. Mem. N.J. Music Tchrs. Assn., Schumann Music Study Club (program chair 1994-95), Pro Musica Hon. Music Club, Pi Lambda Theta. Avocations: swimming, boating, gardening, writing, movies. Home: 7 Fowler Dr West Orange NJ 07052-2149

GARFINKEL, BARRY HERBERT, lawyer; b. Bklyn., June 19, 1928; s. Abraham and Shirley (Siegel) G.; m. Gloria Lorenz, Feb. 16, 1969; children— David, James, Paul. BSS, CCNY, 1950; LLB, Yale U., 1955. Bar: N.Y. State 1955, U.S. Supreme Ct. 1959. Law clk. to Hon. Edward Weinfeld U.S. Dist. Ct., N.Y.C., 1955-56; assoc. Skadden, Arps, Slate, Meagher & Flom, N.Y.C., 1956-61, ptnr., 1961-2000, of counsel, 2000—. Trustee, chmn. Practising Law Inst., Law Ctr. Found. of N.Y. U. Sch. Law Aperture Found., program com. 2d. Cir. Jud. Conf. Mng. editor: Yale Law Jour. Bd. dirs., former dir. Jewish Mus., Legal Aid Soc.; former trustee N.Y. Community Trust; pres. coun. Mus. City of N.Y.; chmn. lawyers' div., spl. gifts campaign United Jewish Appeal/Fedn. Jewish Philanthropies, 1979-81; mem. print com. Whitney Mus., Com. on Rsch. Libraries N.Y. Pub. Lib. Recipient Torch of Learning award Am. Friends of Hebrew U., 1983, Brandeis Distingish. Community Svc. award Brandeis U., 1985. Fellow: Am. Bar Found., Coll. of Commercial Arbitrators, Am. Coll. Trial Lawyers; mem.: ABA, Am. Law Inst., N.Y. State Bar Assn., Assn. of Bar of City of N.Y. (exec. com., judiciary com., past chmn. fed. cts. com.), Am. Arbitration Assn., Yale (N.Y.C.), Yale Club (N.Y.C.). Home: 211 Central Park W New York NY 10024-6020 Office: Skadden Arps Slate Meagher & Flom 4 Times Sq Fl 24 New York NY 10036-6595 Office Phone: 212-735-2500.

GARFINKEL, HARMON MARK, retired specialty chemicals company executive; b. Bklyn., May 20, 1933; s. Samuel and Elsie (Schwartz) G.; m. Lorraine Plawsky, Mar. 4, 1956; children: Elyse, Michelle. BA, Bklyn. Coll., 1957; PhD, Iowa State U., 1960; postgrad. program for mgmt. devel., Harvard U. Bus. Sch., 1973. Dir. bio-organic tech. Corning Inc., N.Y., 1973-74, dir. applied chemistry and biology, 1974-75, dir. biomed. and chem. tech., 1975-78, dir. research, 1978-85; v.p. R&D Engelhard Corp., Edison, N.J., 1985-95, cons., 1995—. Instr. math. Elmira Coll., 1964. Patents and publs. in field. Mem. Am. Chem. Soc., Am. Phys. Soc., Am. Inst. Chemists, Am. Ceramic Soc. Republican. Jewish. Home: 3836 Outlook Ct Jupiter FL 33477-1309 Office Phone: 561-744-2963. E-mail: Harmgarf@aol.com.

GARFINKEL, JANE E., lawyer; b. NYC, Dec. 2, 1952; d. Albert E. and Rita H. (Halpern) G.; m. Louis F. Solimine, May 20, 1979. BA, Wheaton Coll., 1974; MA, U. Mich., 1975, JD, 1979. Bar: Ohio 1980. Assoc. Smith & Schnacke, Cin., 1980-88, ptnr., 1988-89, Thompson Hine LLP, Cin., 1989—. Office: Thompson Hine LLP 312 Walnut St Ste 1400 Cincinnati OH 45202-4089 Office Phone: 513-352-6530. Business E-Mail: jane.garfinkel@thompsonhine.com.

GARFINKEL, LAWRENCE SAUL, academic administrator, educator, television producer; b. NYC, Mar. 9, 1932; s. Benjamin and Rose (Rochkind) G.; m. Adrienne Rederer, June 26, 1960; children: Andrew, Rodger, Craig. BS in Art Edn., NYU, 1953, MA in Higher Edn., 1955, postgrad. in Edn. Comm., 1975. Tchr., supr. art, prin. high schs. West Hempstead Pub. Schs., N.Y., 1954-56, dir. related arts, 1957-69, dir. cmty. rels., 1961-71; prof. edn. adminstrn. and comm., dir. instrnl. comm. program Hofstra U., Hempstead, N.Y., 1969-76; dir. summer television & media insts.; dir. gifted programs Sachem Pub. Schs., Lake Ronkonkoma, N.Y., 1978-79; dir. ednl. comm. Coll. Dentistry, Kriser Dental Ctr., NYU, 1979-91, ret.; adj. prof. dept. speech Baruch Coll., CUNY, 1980-91, Adelphi U., Stern Coll.-Yeshiva U., St. Johns U., Temple U., N.Y. Inst. Tech.; adj. prof. dept. media arts C.W. Post-L.I. U., 1991—. Adj. assoc. prof. art dept. Nassau C.C.; cons. bd. regents N.Y. State

Edn. Dept., Ctr. Urban Edn., N.Y.C. Pub.: Restorative Dentistry, 1985; illustrator: Classroom Television, 1970; illustrator N.Y. Times, John Huston Prodns., Century Theatres, Nat. Audio Visual Assn., and numerous publs.; editl. cartoonist Merrick Life; asst. prodr. WPIX-TV, programming Dumont Network; pub. Garson Assocs.; contbr. articles to profl. jours. Coord. youth edn. Mothers Against Drunk Driving, Long Island Area, 1997-99; bd. dirs. Hist. Soc. Merricks, 1983— pres., 2001-; bd. dirs. Higher Edn. Assn. TV, 1972; v.p. Health Equities, N.Y.C.; oral historian Bi Centennial Commn., 1975. Nominee, Woodrow Wilson Found.; named alt., Fulbright award; recipient Grad. Arch award medal, NYU, scholarship masters NYU, numerous awards, Nat. Com. Sch. Pub. Rels.; grad. tchg. fellow, NYU. Mem. N.Y. Acad. Sci., L.I. Art Tchrs. Assn. (pres. 1967-68), Nat. Com. Art Edn. (co-pres. 1967). Avocations: illustrating, lecturing on communications theory, arts, visual literacy, nostalgia therapy. Home and Office: Garson Assocs 172 Babylon Tpke Merrick NY 11566-4407

GARFINKEL, LEE, advertising agency executive; married; 2 children. BA, CUNY. From copywriter to exec. v.p., exec. creative dir. Levine, Huntley, Schmidt & Beaver; exec. v.p., sr. creative dir., also dir. BBDO; chief creative officer, chmn. Lowe, Lintas & Ptnrs., N.Y.C., 1992—2001; worldwide creative chief D'Arcy Masius Benton & Bowles, 2001—03; chmn., chief creative officer DDB New York, 2003—. Stand-up comedian and musician. Named 1986 East Coast All-Star Team as Best TV Copywriter, Adweek, Creative Dir. of Yr. on 1994 Nat. Creative All-Star Team; selected ann. Forty Under Forty feature Crain's New York Bus.; named one of top three creative dirs. as well as number one copywriter in U.S., Winners mag., 1989; inducted in Am. Advt. Fedn. Hall of Achievement. Mem. One Club for Art and Copy (bd. dirs., pres. 1992-95). Avocations: song writing, collecting guitars, animated art, cars. Office: DDB New York 437 Madison Ave New York NY 10022*

GARFINKLE, ELAINE MYRA, writer; b. Canton, Ohio, July 24, 1936; d. Clifford and Dora Adelman Margolis; m. Jack George Garfinkle, Dec. 27, 1959; 1 child, Marcia Lizabeth. Gen. mgr., editor, pub. Stark Jewish News, Inc., Canton, 1970—83; owner, writer, rschr. Canton Writing Svc., 1978—90; pres., treas. Marce Pubs., Inc., Canton, 1979—83; owner, rschr. Leo Rsch. unlimited, Canton, 1979—83; cmty. rels. supr. Goodwill Rehab., Canton, 1984—87; advt. exec. Cmty. Newspapers, Massillon, Ohio, 1987—91. Historian, pub., compiler, author Through the Years, the Informal History of the Canton, Ohio, Area Jewish Community 1870-2004, 70 vols. Program presenter area nursing homes, 1999—2003; historian on local spl. PBS program on history of Canton, Ohio; adv. U.S. Holocaust Meml. Mus.; supporter Goodwill's Amb. of Goodwill; bd. mem., publicity chair Canton chpt. Hadassah; trustee Cleve. Jewish Genealogy Soc.; advocate for spl. edn., sr. adult and consumer product affairs; mem., supporter Stark County Hist. Soc., McKinley Mus.; vol. and program presenter Canton Jewish Cmty. Ctr. Mem.: Friends of Ctr. Jewish History, Ohio Libr., Am. Friends Hebrew U., Leo Baeck Inst., Friends North Canton, YIVO Inst. Jewish Rsch., Am. Jewish Hist. Soc., Canton Jewish Cmty. Fedn. (edn. com. mem., Outstanding Svc. award 1996—2002), Internat. Jewish Women (life; past pres., treas.), Am. Heart Assn. (cmty. rels. com. 1992—96, Outstanding Svc. award 1992—96), Am. Sephardi Fedn., Nat. Geographic Soc., Hadassah (program presenter 2003, former edn. com. mem., bd. mem., publicity chair Canton chpt.), Anti-Defamation League, Women's League Conservative Judaism, Shaaray Torah Sisterhood (former social action chmn.). Jewish. Avocations: photography, practical psychology, music, reading, studying Jewish history.

GARFUNKEL, ART, singer, actor; b. Forest Hills, N.Y., Nov. 5, 1941; m. Kim Cermak, September 18, 1988; 1 child, James Arthur. BA, Columbia, 1965, MA, 1967. Former mem. team, Simon and Garfunkel; recs. with Simon include Bridge Over Troubled Water, Sounds of Silence, Dangling Conversation, Homeward Bound, I Am a Rock, Mrs. Robinson, others; now soloist: albums as soloist include Angel Clare, 1973, Breakaway, 1975, Watermark, 1978, Fate For Breakfast (Doubt for Dessert), 1979, Scissors Cut, 1981, Simon & Garfunkel The Concert in Central Park, 1982, (with Amy Grant) The Animals' Christmas, 1986, Lefty, 1988, Garfunkel, 1989, UP Till Now, 1993, Across America, 1997, Songs from a Parent to a Child, 1997, Everything Waits to be Noticed, 2002; films include Catch-22, 1970, Carnal Knowledge, 1971, Bad Timing...A Sensual Obsession, 1980, Good to Go, 1986. Recipient Grammy awards for Mrs. Robinson, 1969; 6 Grammy awards for Bridge Over Troubled Water, 1970; inducted into Rock & Roll Hall of Fame, 1990. Address: care Mary Ellen Kirby 12182 Daugherty Dr Zionsville IN 46077-8716*

GARG, SUNIR, ophthalmologist, retina surgeon; MD, U. Mich., 2002. Fellow Wills Eye Hosp., 2004; asst. prof. Washington U., St. Louis, 2004—. Office: Washington U St Louis 660 S Euclid Campus Box 8096 Saint Louis MO 63110

GARIBALDI, OSCAR M., lawyer; b. Buenos Aires, June 22, 1946; came to U.S., 1974; s. Oscar Maria Alvaro Garibaldi and Zulema Edith Alvarez; m. Norma Lidia Blomqvist, Mar. 19, 1971; children: Anne Patricia, Oscar Andrew, Diana Lynne. BA, U. Buenos Aires, 1964, LLB, JD, 1971; LLM, Harvard U., 1975, postgrad., 1975-79. Bar: D.C. Ptnr. Garibaldi, Garibaldi & Garibaldi, Buenos Aires, 1973-74; vis. asst. prof. law Cornell Law Sch., Ithaca, N.Y., 1976-78; lectr. U. Va. Law Sch., Charlottesville, 1979-81; assoc. Covington & Burling, Washington, 1979-85, ptnr., 1985—. Contbr. chpts. to books, articles to profl. jours. Romulo Gallegos fellow Inter-Am. Commn. on Human Rights, 1973; Ford Found. grantee, 1978. Mem. Am. Soc. Internat. Law, Federalist Soc., Md. Assn. Scholars. Republican. Avocations: history, philosophy, woodworking. Office: Covington & Burling 1201 Pennsylvania Ave NW Washington DC 20004-2401

GARIL, HERBERT, lawyer, arbitrator; b. N.Y.C., June 10, 1927; s. Max and Sarah Garil; m. Dec. 5, 1954; children: Cindi, Marla, Scott. LLB, St. John's U., N.Y.C., 1951. Bar: N.Y. Ptnr. Reibstein & Garil, 1953-74, Garil & Meyerson, Franklin Square, N.Y., 1974—. With U.S. Army, 1945-47. Mem. ATLA, New York County Lawyers Assn., N.Y.C. Trial Lawyers Assn., Queens County Lawyers Assn., Nassau County Lawyers Assn., VFW. Avocations: stained and cut glass, gardening. Office: Garil & Meyerson 1040 Hempstead Turnpike Franklin Square NY 11010

GARING, IONE DAVIS, civic worker; b. Huntsville, Ala., Jan. 8, 1930; d. Drury McNary and Ione (Thompson) Davis; m. John Seymour Garing, Apr. 26, 1952; children: John Davis, Susan Carolyn. BSc in Edn. cum laude, Ohio State U., 1951. Tchr. Columbus (Ohio) Pub. Schs., 1952-54, Upper Arlington Pub. Sch., Columbus, 1957-58; libr. Newton (Mass.) Libr., 1955; interviewer audits and surveys Elmo Roper, Boston, 1956. Adv. com. Sch. Com. on Spl. Edn., Lexington, Mass., 1979-80; adv. bd. Cary Meml. Libr., Lexington, 1989— Active Town Meeting, Lexington, 1980-2002, Lexington 2020 Vision Study, 2001; exec. bd. Lexington Dem. Com., 1987-89, mem., 1986—; del. Mass. Dem. Convs., 1986, 88, 90, 92, 94, 96, 98, 2000, 2002; exec. bd. Friends Coun. on Aging, 1986, PTA's, 1965-79; vol. Meals on Wheels, 1985-89; pres. United Meth. Women, Lexington, 1973-75; bd. dirs. Meth. Weekday Sch., 1971-80, chmn. bd. dirs., 2004—; co-organizer 1st town-wide hazardous waste collection in U.S., Lexington, 1983; vol. Lexington Hist. Soc., 1978—; co-founder, chmn. Friends of Cary Meml. Libr. Orgn., 1990-97, bd. dirs., 1990—; founding mem., treas., Precint 8 Residents Assn., 1996-05. Mem. LWV (pres. Lexington 1983-85), AAUW (Mass. long range planning com.), DAR (vice regent 1977-80, Mass. chmn. scholarships and loan com. 1980-83), Florence Crittenton League, Outlook Club (pres. 1985-87, chmn. scholarships com. 1990-2002), Lexington Field and Garden Club (chmn. Wednesday Workshop 1998-2000, 2d v.p. 2000-02), North Shore Rock and Mineral Club (Peabody, Mass.), Brookline Bird Club, Minute Man Nat. Pk. Assn., Alpha Chi Omega. Avocations: conservation, gardening, bird watching, genealogy, travel. Home: 157 Cedar St Lexington MA 02421-6507

GARINGER, LOUIS DANIEL, religion educator; b. Johnson City, Tenn. s. Merrion X. and Hilda (Gasteiger) G.; m. Joanne Mazna, June 21, 1958. AB, U. Tenn., 1947, JD, 1949; MA in Govt, Harvard, 1957. Staff writer Christian Sci. Monitor Youth Forums, Boston, 1949-51; teaching fellow, tutor govt. Harvard, 1955-58; assoc. dir. Salzburg Seminar in Am. Studies, 1958-60; editorial writer Christian Sci. Monitor, 1965-67, religious affairs editor, 1967-71; research, 1971-72; assoc. prof. polit. sci. and religion Principia Coll., Elsah, Ill., 1973-86; dir. Found. Bibl. Research, Charlestown, N.H., 1987-88. Vis. scholar Boston U. Sch. Theology, 1980, Grad. Theol. Union, Berkeley, Calif. Contbr. articles to profl. jours. Served with AUS, 1951-53. Recipient Religious Pub. Relations Council merit award, 1969; William E. Leidt award for religious reporting, 1970 Mem. Scarabbean, Pi Kappa Phi, Phi Kappa Phi, Phi Eta Sigma, Sigma Delta Pi, Phi Alpha Eta. Home: 105 Spaulding Hill Rd West Chesterfield NH 03466-3120 *Unless religion means a deep and heartfelt love for God and man expressed in very concrete and practical ways, unless it cuts to the very core of our being and radically changes our lives, it is worth little or nothing.*

GARLAND, CARL WESLEY, chemist, educator; b. Bangor, Maine, Oct. 1, 1929; s. Cecil G. and Blandena Couillard (Wadell) G.; m. Joan A. Donaghy, July 30, 1955; children: Leslie J., Andrew E. BS, U. Rochester, 1950; PhD, U. Calif.-Berkeley, 1953. Instr. chemistry U. Calif.-Berkeley, 1953; faculty MIT, 1953—, assoc. prof. chemistry, 1959-68, prof. chemistry, 1968-98; prof. emeritus, 1998—. Vis. prof. U. Calif., San Diego, 1972, U. Rome, 1974, Cath. U. Leuven, Belgium, 1977, Ben Gurion U., Israel, 1980, U. Paris, 1981, 82, U. Bordeaux, France, 1990; chmn. Gordon Rsch. Conf. Orientational Disorder in Crystals, 1984. Author: (with J.W. Nibler, D.P. Shoemaker) Experiments in Physical Chemistry, 7th edit., 2003; editor: Optics and Spectroscopy, 1960-81, Liquid Crystals, 1991-95; contbr. over 200 articles to profl. jours. A.P. Sloan fellow, 1954-60; Guggenheim fellow, 1963 Fellow Am. Acad. Arts and Sci.; mem. Am. Phys. Soc. Home: 4 Edward St Belmont MA 02478-2343 Office: MIT Rm 2-121 Cambridge MA 02139-4307 E-mail: cgarland@mit.edu, carlwgarland@aol.com.

GARLAND, CEDRIC FRANK, epidemiologist, educator; b. La Jolla, Calif., Nov. 10, 1946; s. Cedric and Eva (Caldwell) Garagliano. BA, U. So. Calif., 1967; MPH, UCLA, 1970, DrPH, 1974. Asst. prof. Johns Hopkins U., Balt., 1974-81; prof. Sch. Medicine U. Calif., La Jolla, 1981—. Contbr. chpts. to books, articles to profl. jours. Recipient Aristotle award for acad. excellence UCLA, 1974, Golden Apple award for Tchg. Excellence Johns Hopkins U., 1980, Environ. Health Coalition Disting. Svc. award, 1984, NIH Rsch. Career award, 1982. Fellow Am. Coll. Epidemiology; mem. Physicians for Social Responsibility (chmn. info. resources 1982—), Soc. Epidemiol. Rsch., Sierra Club (chmn. Save Our Shore 1982—, Disting. Achievement award 1984). Roman Catholic. Achievements include work with Dr. Frank Garland and Dr. Edward Gorham who together played a role in establishing the association between deficiency of vitamin D and calcium, and risk of intestinal, breast, and ovarian cancer; this group also played a role in establishing that ultraviolet A is a cause of human melanoma. Office: U Calif Dept 0631C Dept Family & Preventive Medicine 9500 Gilman Dr La Jolla CA 92093-0631 Business E-Mail: cgarland@ucsd.edu.

GARLAND, DAVID WILLIAM, law and sociology educator; b. Dundee, Scotland, Aug. 7, 1955; s. David Watt and Elizabeth (Gray) G.; m. Anne Jowett, July 21, 1984; children: Kasia Jowett Garland, Amy Elizabeth Jowett Garland. LLB with first class honors, Edinburgh U., Scotland, 1977, PhD in Socio-Legal Studies, 1984; MA in Criminology, Sheffield U., Eng., 1978. Lectr. Edinburgh U., Scotland, 1979-90, reader, 1990-92, prof., 1992—97; prof. law NYU Sch. Law, NYC, 1997—, Arthur T. Vanderbilt prof. law, 2001—; also prof. sociology NYU. Vis. reader Leuven U., Belgium, 1983; Davis Fellow history dept. Princeton U., 1984-85; vis. prof. Boalt Hall Sch. Law, U. Calif., Berkeley, 1985, 88, NYU Sch. Law, 1992-93, Global law program prof., 1995-97. Author: Punishment and Welfare: A History of Penal Strategies, 1985, Punishment and Modern Society: A Study in Social Theory, 1990, The Culture of Control: Crime and Social Order in Contemporary Society, 2001; co-editor (with R. Sparks): Criminology and Social Theory, 2000. Fellow Royal Soc. Edinburgh.; mem. Law & Soc. Assn., Am. Soc. Criminology (Sellin-Glueck Award, 1993). Mem. Labour Party. Avocations: reading, skiing, squash, cinema, music. Office: NYU Sch Law Vanderbilt Hall Rm 340 40 Washington Sq S New York NY 10012-1099 Office Phone: 212-998-6337. E-mail: david.garland@nyu.edu.*

GARLAND, HOWARD, psychology professor; b. Bklyn., June 22, 1946; s. Murray and Norma (Luft) G.; m. Eileen Mary Cohen, Aug. 21, 1968; children: Eric Lee, Adam Marc. BA, Bklyn. coll., 1968; MS, Cornell U., 1971, PhD, 1972. Asst. prof. Upsala Coll., East Orange, N.J., 1972-74; prof. U. Tex., Arlington, 1974-88; vis. prof. U. Ill., Champaign, 1985-86; prof., chair U. Del., Newark, 1988—. Contbr. over 30 articles to profl. jours. Mem. Internat. Assn. Applied Psychology, Am. Psychol. Soc., Soc. I/O Psychology, Acad. Mgt. Home: 9 Falling Tree Ct Newark DE 19711-7462 Office: U Del 118 Lerner Hall Newark DE 19716 Office Phone: 302-831-1760. Business E-Mail: garlandh@udel.edu.

GARLAND, JAMES C., academic administrator; b. Columbia, Mo., Aug. 11, 1942; BA in Physics, Princeton U., 1964; D in Solid State Physics, Cornell U., 1969; postgrad., Cambridge U., 1969-70. Asst. prof. physics Ohio State U., 1970-75, assoc. prof. physics, 1975-80, prof., 1980-96, chairperson dept. of physics; pres. Miami U., Oxford, Ohio, 1996—. Acting vice pres. for rsch. and grad. studies Ohio State U., dir. materials rsch. lab., 1986-90; pres., bd. dirs. Ohio State U. Rsch. Found., 1982-83; First Fin. Bancorp; First Nat. Bank of SW Ohio. Contbr. articles to profl. jours. Recipient numerous rsch. grants; postdoctoral fellowship NSF. Fellow Am. Phys. Soc. Office: Miami U McGuffey Hall Oxford OH 45056*

GARLAND, JOHN W., III, psychiatrist; b. Griffin, Ga., June 12, 1938; s. John W. Jr. and Lucy Deal Garland; m. Sylvia Parker, June 20, 1964; children: Eleanor Garland Simerly, William C., Stephen D. BS, U. Ga., 1960; MD, Med. Coll. Ga., 1964. Diplomate Am. Bd. Psychiatry and Neurology. Intern medicine U. Va. Hosp., Charlottesville, 1964—65, resident psychiatry, 1965—68; pvt. practice N.E. Ga. Psychiat. Group, N.E. Ga. Med. Ctr., Gainesville, 1970—. Chmn. bd. dirs. Lakeview Acad., Gainesville, 1986—92. Maj. Med. Corps. U.S. Army, 1968—70. Fellow: Am. Psychiat. Assn. (disting. life), So. Psychiat. Assn. (life; fellow); mem.: Hall County Med. Soc. (pres. 1976—77), Ga. Psychiat. Assn. (pres. 1979—80, Psychiatrist of Yr. 1978). Episcopalian. Avocations: reading, golf, church activities. Office: 664-A Lanier Park Dr Gainesville GA 30501 Office Phone: 770-534-0088. Personal E-mail: jwgarlandmd@aol.com.

GARLAND, LARETTA MATTHEWS, psychologist, nursing educator; b. Jacksonville, Fla. d. Wilburn L. and Clyde-Marian (Chamberlin) Matthews; m. John B. Garland, Mar. 2, 1946; children: John Barnard, Brien Freeling, Amy-Gwin. Diploma, Fla. State Sch. Nursing, 1942; BSN, Emory U., 1950, MA, 1953; BA in Edn., U. Fla., 1951; cert. cardiovascular nurse specialty, Tex. Med. Ctr., 1965; EdD, U. Ga., 1975; postgrad. in counseling and guidance, Ga. State U., 1969; grad. cert. in gerontology, 1981. Cert. nat. counselor. Office and staff nurse, Lakeland, Fla., 1942, 45; nurse ARC, Buffalo, 1956; asst. prof. nursing Med. Coll. Ga., 1965-67; instr. Emory U., 1952-54, assoc. prof., 1967-71, prof., 1972-86, prof. emeritus, 1987—. Ednl. psychologist, dir. gerontol. nurse practitioner program, 1978-80, asst. to dean, 1983-86. Author: (with Carol Bush) Coping Behavior and Nursing, 1982; contbr. articles to profl. jours. With Nurse Corps, U.S. Army, 1942-45. Decorated 2 Bronze Stars; recipient Outstanding Tchg. award Emory U. Sch. Nursing Grad. Srs., 1977, Appreciation award So. Region Constituent Leagues, Nat. League for Nursing award, 1987, Mabel Korsell award of appreciation Ga. League Nursing, 1987, Spl. Recognition award Ga. Nurses Assn., 1988, 90, Nurse of Yr. award, 1992, Appreciation award Ga. Assn. Nursing Students, 1990, Van de Vrede award Ga. League Nursing, 1993; HEW fellow, 1967-68. Mem. APA, AACD, ANA, Ga. Assn. Nursing Students (hon.), Nat. League Nursing, Bs. and Profl. Women, China Burma India VA Assn. (mem. nat. bd. 1993—), 14th Air Force Asssn. (Flying Tigers), Hump Pilots Assn., Ormond Beach Womens Club, Ormond Beach Hist. Trust, Nat. Assn. Women Vet. (steering com.), Women in Mil. Svc. Meml. Found. (charter), ARC Nurses, Panhellenic Assn., Hist. Trust, Alpha Chi Omega, Sigma Theta Tau, Kappa Delta Pi, Alpha Kappa Delta, Omicron Delta Kappa. Office: Emory U Nell Hodgson Woodruff Sch Atlanta GA 30322-0001

GARLAND, MERRICK BRIAN, federal judge; AB summa cum laude, Harvard U., 1974, JD magna cum laude, 1977. Bar: D.C. 1979, U.S. Dist. Ct. D.C. 1980, U.S. Ct. Appeals (D.C. and 9th cirs.) 1980, U.S. Ct. Appeals (4th cir.) 1983, U.S. Ct. Appeals (10th cir.) 1996, U.S. Supreme Ct. 1983. Law clk. to Hon. Henry J. Friendly U.S. Ct. Appeals (2d cir.), N.Y.C., 1977—78; law clk. to Justice William J. Brennan Jr. U.S. Supreme Ct., Washington, 1978—79; spl. asst. to atty. gen. U.S. Dept. Justice, Washington, 1979—81, assoc. ind. counsel, 1987—88, asst. U.S. atty., 1989—92, dep. asst. atty. gen., criminal divsn., 1993—94, prin. assoc. dep. atty. gen., 1994—97; judge U.S. Ct. Appeals (D.C. cir.), Washington, 1997—; from assoc. to ptnr. Arnold & Porter, Washington, 1981—89, ptnr., 1992—93. Lectr. Harvard U. Law Sch., 1985—86; mem. com. on jud. br. U.S. Jud. Conf. Author: Deregulation and Jud. Rev., Harvard Law Rev., 1985, Antitrust and State Action, Yale Law Jour., 1987, Antitrust and Federalism, Yale Law Jour., 1987. Mem. bd. overseers Harvard U. Mem.: Am. Law Inst., Phi Beta Kappa. Office: US Court of Appeals 333 Constitution Ave NW Washington DC 20001-2866

GARLAND, RICHARD ROGER, lawyer; b. Princeton, Ill., Aug. 20, 1958; s. Louis Roger and Irene Marie (Tonozzi) G. BA in Polit. Sci. summa cum laude, U. S. Fla., 1979; JD with honors, U. Fla., 1982. Bar: Fla. 1982, U.S. Dist. Ct. (mid. dist.) Fla. 1983, U.S. Ct. Appeals (11th cir.) 1987, U.S. Supreme Ct. 1988, U.S. Ct. Appeals (fed. cir.) 1995; Fla. Bar cert. in appellate practice, 1995. Instr., supr. appellate advocacy U. Fla., Gainesville, 1981-82; assoc. Dickinson, O'Riorden, Gibbons, Quale, Shields & Carlton, Venice, Fla., 1983-85, Sarasota, Fla., 1986-90; ptnr., sr. atty. Dickinson & Gibbons, Sarasota, Fla., 1991—. Pres. parish coun. San Pedro Cath. Ch., North Port, Fla., 1986-92; mem. Sarasota County Libr. Adv. Bd., 1999-2001. Mem. ABA, Fla. Bar Assn., Sarasota County Bar Assn. (editor newsletter 1991-93, bd. dirs. 1994-96, treas. 1996-97, sec. 1997-98, v.p. 1998-99, pres.-elect 1999-2000, pres. 2000-01), Judge John M. Scheb Am. Inn of Ct. (treas. 1998-99, counselor 1999-2000, pres.-elect 2000-01, pres. 2001-02, master historian 2004—), U. South Fla. Alumni Assn., Sarasota County Gator Club (bd. dirs. 2001-05, v.p. 2002-03), Phi Kappa Phi, Pi Sigma Alpha Democrat. Roman Catholic. Office: Dickinson & Gibbons PA 1750 Ringling Blvd Sarasota FL 34236-6836 Office Phone: 941-366-4680. Business E-Mail: rgarland@dglawyers.com.

GARLAND, ROBERT LEE, secondary school educator, writer; b. Chgo., Feb. 26, 1932; BA, UCLA, 1953; MA, Calif. State U., 1962; postgrad., U. Calif., Berkeley, Nat. U. Mex., Mexico City, Stanford U., Singapore U., U. N.C., Charlotte. Educator L.A. Sch. Dist., 1957-91. Mem. various coms. Los Angeles Schs., 1970-91. Contbr. articles on travel and edn. to jours. Served with U.S. Army, 1955-57. Nat. Def. Edn. Act scholar U.S. Govt., 1966, Fulbright scholar, U.S. Govt., 1967, Freedoms Found. scholar, 1982, 86; Robert Taft fellow, 1977, 81, 86, 88; NEH fellow Carnegie-Mellon U., 1990. Mem. NEA, Nat. Council Social Studies (com. chmn. 1980—), Fulbright Alumni Assn., Navy League of U.S., Steamship Hist. Soc., Am. Film Inst., Naval Inst., Big Band Soc. Am., Calif. Hist. Soc. Clubs: Travelers Century.

GARLAND, SYLVIA DILLOF, lawyer; b. N.Y.C., June 4, 1919; d. Morris and Frieda (Gassner) Dillof; m. Albert Garland, May 4, 1942; children: Margaret Garland, Paul B. BA, Bklyn. Coll., 1939; JD cum laude, N.Y. Law Sch., 1960. Bar: N.Y. 1960, U.S. Ct. Appeals (2d cir.) 1965, U.S. Ct. Claims 1965, U.S. Supreme Ct. 1967, U.S. Customs Ct. 1972, U.S. Ct. Appeals (5th cir.), 1979. Assoc. Borden, Skidell, Fleck and Steindler, Jamaica, N.Y., 1960-61, Fields, Zimmerman, Skodnick & Segall, Jamaica, 1961-65, Marshall, Brater, Greene, Allison & Tucker, N.Y.C., 1965-68; law sec. to N.Y. Supreme Ct. justice Suffolk County, 1968-70; ptnr. Hofheimer, Gartlir & Gross, N.Y.C., 1970—. Asst. adj. prof. N.Y. Law Sch., 1974-79; mem. com. on character and fitness N.Y. State Supreme Ct., 1st Jud. Dept., 1985—, vice chmn., 1991—. Author: Workman's Compensation, 1957, Labor Law, 1959, Wills, 1962; contbg. author: Guardians and Custodians, 1970; editor-in-chief Law Rev. Jour., N.Y. Law Forum, 1959-60 (svc. award 1960); contbr. articles to mag. Trustee N.Y. Law Sch., 1979-90, trustee emeritus, 1991—; pres. Oakland chpt. B'nai Brith, Bayside, N.Y., 1955-57. Recipient Disting. Alumnus award N.Y. Law Sch., 1978, Judge Charles W. Froessel award N.Y. Law Sch., 1997. Mem. ABA (litigation sect., family law sect.), N.Y. State Bar Assn. (family law sect.), Queen's County Bar Assn. (sec. civil practice 1960-79), N.Y. Law Sch. Alumni Assn. (pres. 1976-77), N.Y. Law Forum Alumni Assn. (pres. 1963-65). Jewish. Home: 425 E 58th St New York NY 10022-2300

GARLAND, WILLIAM JAMES, physicist, educator; b. St. John's, Nfld., Can., July 26, 1948; B in Engring. Physics, McMaster U., Hamilton, Ont., Can., 1970, M in Engring. Physics, 1971, PhD in Chem. Engring., 1975. Registered profl. engr., Ont. Design engr. Ont. Hydro, Toronto, Can., 1975-79; design specialist Atomic Energy of Can. Ltd., Mississauga, Ont., 1979-83; assoc. prof. McMaster U., 1983-97, chmn. dept. engring. physics, 1988-94, prof., 1997—; dir. McMaster Nuclear Reactor, 1994-95. Cons. System Analytics, Burlington, Ont., 1982—. Mem. Am. Nuclear Soc., Can. Nuclear Soc., Assn. Profl. Engrs. Ont. Office: McMaster U Dept Engring Physics 1280 Main St W Hamilton ON Canada L8S 4L7 Office Phone: 905-525-9140 ext. 24925. Business E-Mail: garlandw@mcmail.cis.mcmaster.ca.

GARLIN, JEFF, actor; b. Chgo., June 5, 1962; Actor: (TV series) The Computer Wore Tennis Shoes, 1995, The Love Bug, 1997, Mad About You, 1997—99, Curb Your Enthusiasm, 2000, Late Friday, 2001—02, What About Joan, 2001, (voice) Crank Yankers, 2003, Sleepover, 2004; (films) Straight Talk, 1992, Hero, 1992, RoboCop 3, 1993, Little Big League, 1994, Senseless, 1998, Austin Powers: The Spy Who Shagged Me, 1999, Bounce, 2000, Self Storage, 2000, The Third Wheel, 2002, Full Frontal, 2002, Daddy Day Care, 2003, (TV appearances include) Larry David: Curb Your Enthusiasm, 1999, Comedy Central Roast of Denis Leary, 2003. Office: 1100 Avenue of the Americas New York NY 10036

GARLOFF, SAMUEL JOHN, psychiatrist; b. Erie, Pa., Nov. 14, 1947; BS, Mansfield (Pa.) State Coll., 1969; MS, Johns Hopkins U., 1974; DO, Phila. Coll. Osteo. Medicine, 1978. Flexible intern Walter Reed Army Med. Ctr., Washington, 1978-79; resident in psychiatry Dwight David Eisenhower Army Med. Ctr., Ft. Gordon, Ga., 1981-84; officer in charge USA Health Care Clinic, Rock Island, Ill., 1980-81; divsn. psychiatrist Ft. Hood, Tex., 1984-86; pvt. practice, Pottsville, Pa., 1986-93; med. dir. counseling ctr. Good Samaritan Regional Med. Ctr., Pottsville, 1988-96, asst. med. dir., 1988-91, med. dir., 1991-94, v.p. med. affairs, 1994-97; med. dir. regional devel. Behavioral Health Ctrs., Pottsville, 1998-99; med. dir. partial hospitalization program Miners Meml. Med. Ctr., Coaldale, Pa., 1999-2001; psychiatrist Access Svcs., Orwigsburg, Pa., 1999—. Clin. cons. III Corps Drug and Alcohol Program, Ft. Hood, Tex., 1984-86; psychiat. cons. Turning Point, Pottsville, Pa., 1986-88, med. dir., 1988-91; psychiat. cons. Luzerne County MH/MR, Hazleton, Pa., 1987-88, Operation Plus Adolescent Partial Hospitalization Program, Pottsville, 1987-95. Chmn. spl. gifts com. St. Joseph Ctr. for Spl. Learning, Pottsville, 1989; bd. dirs. Good Samaritan Found., Pottsville, 1989-95, sec. 1993-95; bd. dirs. Schuylkill unit Am. Cancer Soc., 1990-91, St. Joseph's Ctr. Spl. Learning Devel. Bd., 1990-93, Mansfield Univ. Found., 1991-2002, AIDSNET, 1991-92; chair physician divsn. Schuykill United Way, Pottsville, 1994-98, e-physician online adv. bd., 2000—. Maj. M.C., U.S. Army, 1978-86. Recipient Achievement award, Hosp. Assn. Pa., 1993. Fellow Am. Coll. Med. Quality (bd. cert., treas. Pa. chpt. 1993-95, sec. 1995-97, v.p. 1997-99, pres. 1999—, columnist 1996—, Disting. fellow award 1996), Am. Acad. Pain Mgmt. (bd. cert.); mem. Am. Osteo. Assn., Am. Coll. Neuropsychiatrists, Internat. Assn. Med. Specialists, Nat. Coalition Physicians Against Family Violence, Pa. Osteo. Med. Assn.

(vice chmn. dist. 11 1997-98, trustee 1998—), Pa. C. of C., Schuylkill County C. of C., N.E. Pa. Regional Health Care Coalition (physician adv. com. 1998—). Home: 343 Spring Run Ct Etters PA 17319-8945 Personal E-mail: drsam1usa@netscape.net.

GARLOUGH, WILLIAM GLENN, marketing executive; b. Syracuse, N.Y., Mar. 27, 1924; s. Henry James and Gladys (Killam) Garlough; m. Charlotte M. Tanzer, June 15, 1947; children: Jennifer, William, Robert. BEE, Clarkson U., 1949. With Knowlton Bros., Watertown, NY, 1949—67, mgr. mfg. svcs., 1966—67; v.p. planning, equipment systems div. Vare Corp., Englewood Cliffs, NJ, 1967—69; mgr. mktg. Valley Mould divsn. Microdot Inc., Hubbard, Ohio, 1969—79, dir. corp. devel., 1977—78; v.p. corp. devel. Am. Bldg. Maintenance Industries, San Francisco, 1979—83; pres. The Change Agts. Inc., Walnut Creek, Calif., 1983—2005, Holland, Mich., 2005—. Bd. dirs. My Chef Inc.; mem. citizens adv. com. Watertown Bd. Edn., 1957. Ruling elder Presbyn. Ch.; bd. dirs. Watertown Cmty. Chest, 1958—61. With USMCR, 1942—46. Mem.: TAPPI, Assn. Corp. Growth (pres. San Francisco chpt. 1984—85, v.p. chpts. west 1985—88), Am. Mktg. Assn., Internat. Sanitary Supply Assn., Bldg. Svc. Contractors Assn., Inst. Mgmt. Cons. (cert.), Am. Mgmt. Assn., Clarkson Alumni Assn. (Watertown sect. pres. 1955), Am. Contract Bridge League (life master), No. N.Y. Transp. Club, No. N.Y. Contract Club (pres. 1959), Marine's Meml. Club, Mensa, Lincoln League (pres. 1958), Tau Beta Pi. Office: The Change Agts Inc Ste 402 145 Columbia Ave Holland MI 49423-2978 Office Phone: 616-886-7370.

GARMAN, DAVID KLINE, federal agency administrator; b. Greensboro, N.C., May 29, 1957; s. Jack Donald and Jane (Holtzclaw) G. BA in Pub. Policy, Duke U., 1979; MS in Environ. Sciences, Johns Hopkins U., 1995. Legis. aide Senator Stone U.S. Senate, Washington, 1980-81, legis. asst. Senator Murkowski, 1981-85, chief of adminstrn., exec. asst., 1986-90, profl. staff mem. intelligence com., 1991-92, spl. projects dir. Senator Murkowski, 1993-94, profl. staff subcom. energy R & D, 1995—2001; asst. sec., energy efficiency & renewable energy U.S. Dept. Energy, Washington, 2001—05, acting under sec energy, sci. & the environment, 2004—05, under sec energy, sci. & the environment, 2005—. Republican. Office: US Dept Energy Forrestal Bldg 1000 Independance Ave SW Rm 7A-219 Washington DC 20585-0001

GARMAN, RAY FILLMORE, occupational physician, director; s. Wynona Hudson Garman; m. Eugenie (Gigi) Virginia Moravec, Aug. 16, 1958; children: Ray Fillmore III, Scott Clayton, Andrew Seitz. AB, Johns Hopkins U., Balt., 1957; MD, George Wash. U., Washington, DC, 1961; MPH, Med Coll. Wis., Milw., 1995. Cert. in internal medicine U. Penna Grad. Sch. Medicine, Phila., 1962, Am. Bd. Internal Medicine, 1968, in pulmonary diseasese Am. Bd. Internal Medicine, 1974, in occupl. medicine Am. Bd. Preventive Medicine, 1996. Pulmonary medicine physician Guthrie Clinc/Robert Packer Hosp., Sayre, Pa., 1972—81, chief pulmonary medicine, 1981—90, med. dir., 1991—95; chief occupl. medicine and environ. health Lexington Clinic, Ky., 1995—99; med. dir. Gen. Electric Appliance Divsn., Bloomington, Ind., 1999—2000; clincal med. dir. Toyota Motor Mfg., Georgetown, Ky., 2000—04; assoc. prof., dir. occupl. med. training U. Ky., Lexington, 2004—. Sr. aviation med. examiner FAA, Lexington, 1977—; pres. Bradford County Med. Soc., Sayre, Pa., 1979—80; instr. quality process Quality Coll. (Crosby), Winter Park, Fla., 1989—90. Mem. Lexington Children's Mus., 1995—99; treas. Lex-Fayette Urban County Airport Bd., Lexington, 2003, sec., 2002, chmn., 2004—05; vice chair-med. Lexington Arts & Cultural Coun., 2000—04; pres. Lexington Opera Soc., 2005, bd. dirs.; pres. Lexington Kennel Club, 2002—05; survey chair Lexington Forum, 1997—2005. Capt. USAF, 1963—66, Brig Gen. Reserve, mobilization asst. to surgeon AF material command USAF, chief flight surgeon USAF. Decorated Golden Cross of Royal Order of Phoenix King of Greece, Legion of Merit USAF. Mem.: Am. Coll. Physician Exec., Jefferson Club (Louisville), Lexington Club, Lafayette Club (membership chmn. 1999—99). Home: 1214 Richmond Rd Lexington KY 40502-1614 Office: Univ Ky Coll Pub Health 200 Washington Ave Lexington KY 40536 Office Phone: 859-257-5166. Business E-Mail: ray.garman@uky.edu.

GARMAN, RITA B., state supreme court justice; b. Aurora, Ill., Nov. 19, 1943; children: Sara Ellen, Andrew Gil. BS in Economics, U. Ill., 1965; JD with distinction, U. Iowa, 1968. Asst. state atty. Vermilion County, 1969—73; pvt. practice Sebat, Swanson, Banks, Lessen & Garman, 1973; assoc. cir. judge, 1974—86; cir. judge Fifth Jud. Cir., 1986—95, presiding cir. judge, 1987—95; judge Fourth Dist. Appellate Ct., 1996—2001; justice Ill. Supreme Ct., 2001—. Mem.: Ill. Judge's Assn., Vermilion County Bar Assn., Iowa Bar Assn., Ill. State Bar Assn. Office: 3607 N Vermilion Ste 1 Danville IL 61832 also: Ill Supreme Ct State of Ill Bldg 160 N LaSalle St Chicago IL 60601

GARMANY, CATHARINE DOREMUS, astronomer; b. N.Y.C., Mar. 6, 1946; d. Edwin and Janet (MacMaster) Doremus; children: Richard, Jeffrey. BS, Ind. U., 1966; MS, U. Va., 1968, PhD, 1971. Rsch. assoc. U. Va., Charlottesville, 1971-73; rsch. assoc. Joint Inst. for Lab Astrophys. U. Colo., Boulder, 1977-84, sr. rsch. assoc. Joint Inst. for Lab Astrophys., 1984-2000; dir. Fiske Planetarium, 1991-2000; dir. astronomy Astronomy, Oracle, Ariz., 2000—03, NOAO, 2004—. Contbr. articles to profl. jours. Recipient Annie J. Cannon award AAUW, AAS, 1976; grantee NASA, NSF. E-mail: garmany@hnoao.edu.

GARMEL, MARION BESS SIMON, retired arts journalist; b. El Paso, Tex., Oct. 15, 1936; d. Marcus and Frieda (Alfman) Simon; m. Raymond Lewis Garmel, Nov. 28, 1965 (dec. Feb. 1986); 1 child, Cynthia Rogers; 1 stepchild, Christine Blum. Student, U. Tex., El Paso, 1954-55; BJ, U. Tex., Austin, 1958. Exec. sec. Nat. Student Assn., Phila., 1958-59, pub. rels. dir., 1960-61; sec. World Assembly Youth, Paris, Brussels, 1959-60; dictationist Wall Street Jour., Washington, 1961; libr., staff writer Nat. Observer, Silver Spring, Md., 1961-70; art critic Indpls. News, 1971-91, editor Free Time sect., 1975-91, critic radio and TV, 1991-95; theater critic Indpls. Star and News, 1995-99; television critic Indpls. News, 1995-99; theater critic Indpls. Star, 1999—2002, ret., 2002. Mem. Nat. Fedn. Press Women (1st Place Critics award 1974), Ind. Soc. Profl. Journalists (1st place criticism 2002), Hadassah Women's Zionist Orgn. Am. (life), Woman's Press Club Ind. (1st Place Critics award 1995, 2002). Jewish. Avocation: tennis. Home: 226 E 45th St Indianapolis IN 46205-1712 E-mail: mgarmel@earthlink.net.

GARMER, WILLIAM ROBERT, lawyer; b. Balt., May 8, 1946; s. William M. and Grace (DeLane) G.; 1 child, Lindsey DeLane; m. Kimberly Nichols. BA, U. Ky., 1968, JD, 1975. Bar: Ky. 1975, U.S. Dist. Ct. (ea. and we. dists.) Ky. 1977, U.S. Ct. Appeals (6th cir.) 1980, U.S. Supreme Ct. 1979. Law clk. to chief judge U.S. Dist. Ct. (ea. dist.) Ky., Lexington, 1975-76; assoc. prof. law litigation skills and health care law U. Ky. Law Sch., Lexington, 1981—; ptnr. Garmer & O'Brien, LLP, Lexington, 1984—. Contbr. articles to profl. jours. Elder Presbyn. Ch., chmn. Ky. Dem. Party, 2004. Staff sgt. USAF, 1969-73. Fellow: Am. Coll. Trial Lawyers; mem.: ATLA (bd. govs. 1996—, chair coun. state pres. 1995), ABA, So. Trial Lawyers Assn., Ky. Acad. Trial Attys. (bd. govs. 1984—89, treas. 1990, sec. 1991, v.p. 1992, pres. 1994, named Ky. Trial Lawyer of Yr. 1998), Fayette County Bar Assn., Ky. Bar Assn. (com. on specialization and cert. 1982—, litigation com. 1989—), Roscoe Pound Found., Phi Delta Phi (named One of Best Lawyers in Am. 1989—). Democrat. Office: Garmer & O'Brien LLP 141 N Broadway Lexington KY 40507-1230 Office Phone: 859-254-9352. E-mail: bgarmer@garmerobrien.com.

GARN, SUSAN LYNN, middle school art educator; b. Astoria, Oreg., July 12, 1948; d. Everett Leslie and Jeanne Esther (Linquist) G. BA in Art, U. Nev., Reno, 1970; MEd in Ednl. Adminstrn. and Higher Edn., U. Nev., Las Vegas, 1990. Tchr. art Desert Sands Unified Sch. Dist., Indio, Calif., 1973-74; art. resource tchr. Trinity County Schs., Weaverville, Calif., 1974-75; multi-subject tchr., primarily in visual arts, digital art edn. Clark County Sch. Dist., Las Vegas, 1975-80, 87—; tchr. English, reading Jordan Sch. Dist., Sandy, Utah, 1982-84; lead community sch coord. Lincoln County Sch. Dist., Newport, Oreg., 1984-87. Sole propr. Sue Garn and Kids Art, Las Vegas, 1988-98; presenter at profl. confs.; long term substitute tchr. Chemawa Indian Sch., Salem, Oreg., 1984. Work displayed at Educators as Artists exhibit, 1990, 92, 93, 2001, 02, 03, 04. Bd. dirs. Las Vegas Indian Ctr., 1996-99. Named Tchr. of Yr. Nev. State PTA, 1990; Excellence in Edn., CCSD, 1991, South West Region Disting. Star, CCSD, 2004. Mem. Art Educators So. Nev., Am. Indian C. of C, Nat. Art Edn. Assn., Art Educators Nev. Avocations: german short haired pointer, wirehaired terrier and weimaraner dogs, travel, movies, art. Home: 3709 El Jardin Ave Las Vegas NV 89102-3821 Office: James Cashman Mid Sch 4622 W Desert Inn Rd Las Vegas NV 89102 Office Phone: 702-321-0543. Personal E-mail: sgarninlv@hotmail.com.

GARNAR, MARTIN LUTHER, librarian; b. Huntington, N.Y., Oct. 22, 1971; s. Richard Luther and Joan Doreen Garnar; life ptnr. Edward Dennis Scholz, June 25, 1994. M of Libr. and Info. Svcs., U. Denver, 2000; MA in History, SUNY at Binghamton, 1995, BA in History and Geography, 1993. Reference libr. Dayton Meml. Libr. Regis U., Denver, 1999—. Chair intellectual freedom com. Colo. Assn. Librs., Englewood, 2000—03. Contbr. articles to profl. jours. Mem.: Intellectual Freedom Com., ALA (chair Eli M. Oboler book award com. 2002—04, chair IFRT membership promotion com. 2004—05, chair IFC privacy subcom. 2005—), Intellectual Freedom Round Table, Phi Beta Kappa. Democrat. Unitarian Universalist. Home: 11764 Bradburn Blvd Westminster CO 80031 Office: Regis University Mail Stop D-20 3333 Regis Blvd Denver CO 80221-1099 Office Phone: 303-964-5459. E-mail: mgarnar@regis.edu.

GARNER, ALBERT HEADDEN, investment banker; b. Memphis, Dec. 17, 1955; s. Jesse B. Jr. and Noella (Headden) Garner; children: Cyrus Dalton, Shelby Harris, Pleasant Noel. BS in Engring., Princeton U., 1977. Assoc. Devel. and Resources Corp., N.Y.C., 1977-79, Lazard Freres & Co., N.Y.C., 1979-83, v.p., 1984-88; gen. ptnr. Lazard Freres & Co. LLC, N.Y.C., 1989-95, mng. dir., 1995—. Elder 1st Presbyn. Ch., N.Y.C.; bd. dirs. Prospect Park Alliance. Home: 1510 Albemarle Rd Brooklyn NY 11226-4506 Office: Lazard Freres & Co LLC 30 Rockefeller Plz Fl 59 New York NY 10112-5900 Business E-Mail: al.garner@lazard.com.

GARNER, ALGEAN, II, healthcare company administrator, consultant; s. Algean and Charmaine Garner. BA in Psychology summa cum laude, Shaw U., 1993; PhD in Psychology, Ill. Sch. Profl. Psychology, 2001. Lic. clin. psychologist Ill., 2005. Psychology intern Houston Ind. Sch. Dist., 1997—98; assessment coord. Shelia Jenkins and Assocs., Houston, 1998—2000; post doctoral fellow ADAPT Counseling, Houston, 2000—02; dir. comprehensive svcs. Nr. North Health Svc. Corp., Chgo., 2002—. Bd. mem. Houston Psychol. Assn., 1998—2002, Houston Assn. Marriage and Family Therapist, 2001—02; presenter in field. Mem.: APA. Avocations: cooking, health and fitness. Office Phone: 312-337-1073 236. Personal E-mail: agarnerii@sbcglobal.net.

GARNER, BRYAN ANDREW, law educator, consultant, writer; b. Lubbock, Tex., Nov. 17, 1958; s. Gary Thomas and Mariellen (Griffin) G.; m. Pan Anurugsa, May 26, 1984; children: Caroline Beatrix, Alexandra Bess. BA, U. Tex., 1980, JD, 1984; LLD (hon.), Thomas M. Cooley Law Sch., 2000. Bar: Tex. 1984, U.S. Ct. Appeals (5th cir.) 1985, U.S. Dist. Ct. (no. dist.) Tex. 1986. Law clk. to judge U.S. Ct. Appeals (5th cir.), Austin, Tex., 1984-85; assoc. Carrington, Coleman, Sloman & Blumenthal, Dallas, 1985-88; dir. Tex./Oxford Ctr. for Legal Lexicography U. Tex. Sch. Law, Austin, 1988-90; adj. prof. law So. Meth. U., Dallas, 1990—. Vis. assoc. prof. law U. Tex., 1988—90; pres. LawProse, Inc., 1990—; vis. scholar U. Salzburg, 1995, 98, U. Glasgow, 1996, U. Cambridge, England, 1997; chmn. plain-lang. com. State Bar Tex., 1989—95; lectr. in field; cons. in field. Author: A Dictionary of Modern Legal Usage, 1987, A Dictionary of Modern Legal Usage, 2d edit., 1995, The Elements of Legal Style, 1991, Guidelines for Drafting and Editing Court Rules, 1996, A Dictionary of Modern American Usage, 1998, Securities Disclosure in Plain English, 1999, The Winning Bried, 1999, Legal Writing in Plain English, 2001, The Redbook: A Manual on Legal Style, 2002; editor: Scribes Jour. Legal Writing, 1989—2000, Tex, Our Texas, 1984, Black's Law Dictionary, 1996, Black's Law Dictionary, 7th edit., 1999, A Handbook of Basic Law Terms, 1999; A Handbook of Business Law Terms, 1999; editor: A Handbook of Family Law Terms, 2001; mem. editl. bd.: Tex. Law Rev., 1984; contbr. articles to profl. jours. Recipient Henry C. Lind award, Assn. Reporters Judicial Decisions, 1994, Clarity award, State Bar Mich, 1997, Outstanding Young Tex. Ex. award, 1998. Fellow: Tex. Bar Found.; mem.: ABA, Tex. Bar Assn. (chmn. plain lang. com. 1990—), Am. Law Inst. (commn. on bylaws & coun. rules 1993—94), Scribes (exec. bd. 1990—2001, pres. 1997—98), Dictionary Soc. N.Am., Am. Dialect Soc., Philos. Soc. Tex., Friars (abbot 1981—84), Bent Tree Country Club, Phi Beta Kappa. Republican. Avocation: golf. Home: 6478 Lakehurst Ave Dallas TX 75230-5131

GARNER, CARLENE ANN, fundraising consultant; b. Dec. 17, 1945; d. Carl A. and Ruth E. (Mathison) Timblin; m. Adelbert L. Garner, Feb. 17, 1964; children: Bruce A., Brent A. BA, U. Puget Sound, 1983. Adminstrv. dir. Balletacoma, 1984-87; exec. dir. Tacoma Symphony, 1987-95; prin. New Horizon Cons., Tacoma, 1995-98; co-owner Stewardship Devel., 1998—. Cons. Wash. PAVE, Tacoma, 1983-84. Treas. Coalition for the Devel. of the Arts, 1992-94; pres. Wilson High Sch. PTA, Tacoma, 1983-85; chmn. Tacoma Sch. Vol. Adv. Bd., 1985-87; pres. Emmanuel Luth. Ch., Tacoma, 1984-86, chmn. future steering com., 1987-93; sec.-treas. Tacoma-Narrows Conf., 1987-98; vice chmn. Tacoma Luth. Home, 1996-98; pub. mem. Wash. State Bd. Pharmacy, 1993-98. Mem. N.W. Devel. Officers Assn. (chair Tacoma/Pierce County com. 1994-96), Jr. Women's Club Tacoma (pres. 1975-76, pres. Peninsula dist. 1984-86), Gen. Fedn. Women's Club-Wash. State (treas. 1988-90, 3d v.p. 1990-92, 2d v.p. 1992-94, 1st v.p. 1994-96, pres. 1996-98, Clubwoman of Yr. 1977, Outstanding FREE chmn. Gen. Fedn. 1982), Commencement Bay Woman's Club (pres. 1990-92), Gen. Fedn. of Women's Club (bd. dirs., chair nat. conv. 1995, state pres. 1996-98, chair cmty. improvement program 1998-2000, treas. 2000—02, rec. sec. 2002-04, 2d v.p. 2004—). Lutheran.

GARNER, CHARLES WILLIAM, educational administration educator, consultant; b. Pine Grove Mills, Pa., Apr. 18, 1939; s. Adam Krumrine and Blanche Ella (Gearhart) G.; m. Karyl J. Packer, Sept. 8, 1962; children: Ronald Adam, Juliet Paige. Student, U.S. Navy Electronics Airborne Sonar Sch., 1959; BS in Bus. Edn., Pa. State U., 1965, MEd in Higher Edn. Adminstrn., 1968, EdD in Vocat. Indsl. Edn., 1974. Cert. govt. fin. mgr. Adminstrv. asst. dept. psychology Pa. State U., 1965-75; asst. prof., site adminstr. March AFB, Calif. for So. Ill. U., 1975-77; asst. prof., coordinator Ft. Knox Ctr.- U. Louisville, 1977-78; assoc. prof., acting vice dean Rutgers U., Camden, N.J., 1978-79, assoc. prof. urban edn., chmn. dept. edn. Univ. Coll. New Brunswick, N.J., 1978-81, assoc. prof. vocat. tech. edn. Grad. Sch. Edn., 1981—, chmn. dept. vocat. tech. edn., 1982-85, assoc. prof. edn. adminstrn., 1985—, exec. dir. Vocat. Edn. Resource Ctr., 1983-88, dir. continuing edn., 1987-89, program chair edn. adminstrn., 1990-96; cons. CWG Assocs., McElhattan, Pa., 1989—; pres. Penn State Auto Repair, Inc., Williamsport, Pa., 1997-2000. Author: Accounting and Budgeting in Public and Nonprofit Organizations: A Manager's Guide, 1991, Financial Management of School Districts in New Jersey: For School Leaders, 1996, Education Finance for School Leaders: Strategic Planning and Administration, 2004, (with R. Garner) The Service Consultant: Working in an Automotive Facility 2005; contbr. articles to profl. jours.; co-editor: Occupational Edn. Forum, 1979-85; editl. reader Jour. Indsl. Tchr. Edn., 1981; producer, host talk show pilot for pub. TV, 1979; producer, host: TV tape series Rutgers U.: Current Issues in Vocat. Edn., 1979; editor edn. sect. Pub. Budgeting and Financial Management, 1995, The Service Consultant: Woring in an Automotive Facility, 2005. Bd. dirs., treas. Cerebral Palsy League of Union County, N.J., 1996-99. With USN, 1959-62. Grantee N.J. Dept. Edn. Divsn. Vocat. Edn., 1978-88; grantee HEW, 1979-80. Mem.: AAUP, DAV (life), Nat. Soc. for Study of Edn., Spl. Needs Pers. (exec. coun. 1980—81, pres. 1981—82), Non-Commd. Officers Assn. (life), Elks (exalted ruler 1972—73), Epsilon Pi Tau (trustee 1983—88), Omicron Tau Theta, Phi Delta Kappa. Home: PO Box 456 Mc Elhattan PA 17748 Office: Rutgers U Dept Ednl Theory Admin New Brunswick NJ 08903 Office Phone: 732-932-7496 ext. 8217. E-mail: wgarner@rci.rutgers.edu. *Our influence in life is determined by the good deeds we do rather than by the emotions that we feel.*

GARNER, DANIEL C., lawyer; b. Austin, Tex., Jan. 18, 1950; BS, Tex. A&M U., 1972; JD with high honors, Tex. Tech. U., 1975. Bar: Tex. 1975. Shareholder Geary, Stahl & Spencer, Dallas, Jenkens & Gilchrist, P.C., Dallas, 1991—, firm leader fin. services practice group. Topics editor: Tex. Tech. Law Review, 1974-75. Mem. ABA, Dallas Bar Assn., Tex. State Bar Assn., Tex. Assn. Bank Counsel. Office: Jenkens & Gilchrist PC 1445 Ross Ave Ste 3200 Dallas TX 75202-2799 Office Phone: 214-855-4794. Office Fax: 214-855-4300. Business E-Mail: dgarner@jenkens.com.

GARNER, DIRK A., music educator, conductor; b. Charleston, Ill., Nov. 5, 1969; s. Donald Paul and Suellyn Lindsey Garner; m. Emily Mills Truckenbrod, July 14, 1999; 1 child, Aidan Paul Truckenbrod. Dr. in Musical Arts, U. of Iowa, 1999. Dir. of choral activities Southeastern La. U., Hammond, La., 1999—2002; dir. of choral studies Okla. State U., Stillwater, Okla., 2002—. Mem.: Am. Choral Dirs. Assn. (dist. rep.; chair, repertoire and standards 1999—2005). Democrat. Avocations: reading, cooking, singing, travel. Office: Okla State Univ 123 Scpa Stillwater OK 74074 Office Phone: 405-744-8992. Personal E-mail: gdirk@okstate.edu.

GARNER, DOUGLAS, music educator; s. Don and Katie Garner. BS in Music Edn., Pa. State U., 1997. Cert. K-12 music, chorus, band, orch. Music educator, choral dir. Mifflin County Sch. Dist., Lewistown, Pa., 1997—. Mem.: Pa. Music Educators Assn., Am. Choral Dirs. Assn. Office: Indian Valley Mid Sch 125 Kish Rd Reedsville PA 17084

GARNER, FRADLEY HAMILTON, freelance/self-employed writer, editor; b. Potsdam, N.Y., June 20, 1926; s. L. Hamilton and Geneva Van Bergen Garner; children: Luke, Glen, Nicholas. Pregrad, 24th Corps U., Seoul Korea, 1946; BS in Psychology, St. Lawrence U., Canton, N.Y., 1950; MA in Cultural Anthropology, Colgate U., Hamilton, N.Y., 1970; postgrad., SUNY, Potsdam, 1950, Northwestern U., Evanston, Ill., 1951. Divsnl. pub. rels. mgr. Pfizer, Inc., N.Y.C., 1955-60; freelance writer, editor, film/video narrator Denmark, 1960—. Author: Environment Denmark, 1972, Walt Disney's Donald Duck's Fritidsbok, 1976, Greenland: Arctic Denmark, 1977, Jakobshavn/Ilulissat: A Town in Greenland, 1977, Walt Disney's The Haunted Hotel, 1978; co-founder, editor Scoot mag., 1955; assoc. editor Family Health mag., 1969; internat. editor, columnist Ecology Today, 1971-72, Environment mag., 1973-77; editor: TMI World, 1988; chief translator, copy editor: Danish Music Review., 1994-95, Katalog, the Danish Jour. Photography and Video; appeared in film The Prince of Jutland, 1994; country editor, writer Insight Guide Denmark, 2000—; covered Denmark's dogsled patrol Sirius in No. Greenland for Internat. Edits. Reader's Digest; Nordic-Tanganyika project in Dar es Salaam, Tanzania for Scanorama mag.; Denmark contbr. DownBeat, Jersey Jazz, 2000-, humor columnist, Abroad Mag., 2004; contbr. numerous articles to profl. jours. and gen. mags.; narrator over 500 indsl., sci. and gen. documentary films and videos; bassist Copenhagen Symphony Orch., 1995-. Bd. dirs. HOF Internat. Edn. Program, 2000—. Named Denmark amateur Runner of Yr., (Aarets Eremitageløber), 1995. Mem. Fgn. Press Assn. in Denmark. Home: Ordruphøjvej 32 DK-2920 Charlottenlund Denmark Office Phone: +45-3964-1315. Office Fax: +45-3964-1315. Personal E-mail: fradgar@get2net.dk.

GARNER, HARVEY LOUIS, computer scientist, consultant, engineering educator; b. Lake, Colo., Dec. 23, 1926; s. Homa and Violet (Thuelin) Garner; m. Yvonne Lillian King, Aug. 7, 1949; children: Susan Ann, Harvey Thomas. BS, U. Denver, 1949, MS, 1951; PhD, U. Mich., 1958. Engr. with devel. MIDAC and MIDSAC computers U. Mich., 1951-55, from instr. to assoc. prof. elec. engring., 1955—63, prof., 1963-70; dir. Info. Sys. Lab., 1960-64, Sys. Engring. Lab., 1964-66, acting chmn. dept. comm. scis., 1965-67, prof. computer and comm. scis., 1967-70; prof. elec. engring. Moore Sch. Elec. Engring., 1970-86, dir., 1970-76, Microelectronics and Computer Tech. Corp., Austin, 1984-88; cons. sys. design and computer arithmetic, 1988—. Gen. chmn. Islands Applications Conf., Tokyo, 1972, 1st Nat. Computer Conf. and Exhbn., 1973. Contbr. articles to profl. jours. With USNR, 1945—46. Fellow: IEEE; mem.: AAAS, Am. Assn. Artificial Intelligence, Assn. Computing Machinery (apptd. nat. lectr. 1965), Sigma Xi, Sigma Pi Sigma, Eta Kappa Nu. Home and Office: 7400 Rockberry Cv Austin TX 78750-7920

GARNER, JAMES (JAMES SCOTT BUMGARNER), actor; b. Norman, Okla., Apr. 7, 1928; m. Lois Clarke, Aug. 17, 1956; children: Kimberly, Gretta, Scott. Student, N.Y. Berghof Sch., U. Okla. Motion picture debut in Toward the Unknown; Actor: (films) include Sayonara, 1957, Shoot-out at Medicine Bend, 1957, Darby's Rangers, 1958, Up Periscope, 1959, Cash McCall, 1960, The Children's Hour, 1962, The Great Escape, 1963, The Americanization of Emily, 1964, 36 Hours, 1964, The Thrill of It All, Move Over Darling, The Art of Love, 1965, A Man Could Get Killed, 1966, Duel at Diablo, 1966, Mister Buddwing, 1966, Grand Prix (also exec. prodr.), 1966, Hour of the Gun, 1967, How Sweet It Is, 1968, Marlowe, 1969, Support Your Local Sheriff, 1971, Support Your Local Gunfighter, 1971, Skin Game, 1971, They Only Kill Their Masters, 1972, One Little Indian, 1973, HEALTH, 1979, The Fan, 1980, Victor/Victoria, 1982, Tank, 1984, Murphy's Romance, 1985, Sunset, 1987, Fire in the Sky, 1993, Maverick, 1994, My Fellow Americans, 1996, Twilight, 1998, Space Cowboys, 2000, Atlantis: The Last Empire (voice), 2001, Divine Secrets of the YaYa Sisterhood, 2002, The Notebook, 2004; (TV series) include Maverick, 1957-60, Nichols, 1971-72, Rockford Files (Emmy award for oustanding lead actor in a drama series, 1977), 1974-80, Man of the People, 1991, Chicago Hope, 2000, 8 Simple Rules...for Dating My Teenage Daughter, 2003-; (miniseries) Space, 1985, Streets of Laredo, 1995, Century of Country, 1999, Shake, Rattle and Roll: An American Love Story, 1999; (TV movies) include The Long Summer of George Adams, 1982, Heartsounds, 1984, Promise (also exec. prodr. Emmy for outstanding comedy/drama spl., 1987), 1986, My Name Is Bill W. (also exec. prodr.), 1989, Decoration Day, 1990 (Golden Globe Award for Best Performance by an Actor in a Mini-Series or Motion Picture Made for TV, 1991), Barbarians at the Gate, 1993 (Golden Globe Award for Best Performance by an Actor in a Mini-Series or Motion Picture Made for TV), Breathing Lessons, 1994, The Rockford Files: I Still Love LA, 1994, The Rockford Files: A Blessing in Disguise, 1995, The Rockford Files: Punishment and Crime, 1996, The Rockford Files: Friends and Foul Play, 1996, The Rockford Files: If the Frame Fits, 1996, The Rockford Files: Godfather Knows Best, 1996, Dead Silence, 1997, The Rockford Files: Murder and Misdemeanor, 1997, Legalese, 1998, The Rockford Files: If It Bleeds.It Leads (also prodr.), 1999, One Special Night, 1999, The Last Debate, 2000, Roughing It, 2002. Joined U.S. Mcht. Marine; served with U.S. Army, Korea. Decorated Purple Heart; recipient Clio award for Polaroid commls., 1978, SAG 41st Annual Lifetime Achievement award, 2005. Office: c/o Eight Simple Rules ABC Stage 6 500 S Buena Vista St Burbank CA 91521-2901

GARNER, JAY MONTGOMERY, retired military officer; b. Arcadia, Fla., Apr. 15, 1938; s. James Harley and Consuello Adelaide (Pooser) G.; m. Mary Connie Kreigh, Dec 30, 1958; 1 child, Lori Lee Gibson. BA, Fla. State U., 1962; MA, Shippensburg U., 1983; attended, Air Defense Artillery Sch., Marine Corps. Command and Staff Coll., US Army War Coll., US Army Air Defense Sch., Ft. Bliss, Tex., 1962, Defense Lang. Inst., SW br., Ft. Bliss, 1966-67, Air Defense Artillery Officer Advanced Course, US Army Air Defense Sch., 1969, Vietnam Tng. Ctr. Fgn. Svc. Inst., Dept. State, Washington, 1970-71, Marine Corps. Command and Staff Coll., Quantico, Va., 1974-75, US Army War Coll. Carlisle Barracks, Pa., 1982-83. Commd. 2d lt. US Army, 1962, advanced through grades to lt. gen., 1994, ret., 1997, asst. platoon leader to platoon leader to exec. officer, Battery C, 3d Missile Battalion, 7th Artillery, US Army Europe, 1962-64, inactive Army Nat. Guard, 1964-65, ops. officer 53d Artillery Brigade Maxwell AFB, Ala., 1965-66, asst. subsector advisor, later dep. dist. sr. advisor adv. team 58, mil. assistance command Viet Nam Vietnam, 1967-68, comdr. Battery B, 5th Battalion, 7th Artillery, US Army Air Defense Commd. Franklin Lakes, N.J.,

1968, chief, programs br., logistics divsn., office mil. assistance, US Army So. Command Ft. Amador, Panama, 1969-70, dist. sr. advisor, adv. team 36, military assistance commd. Vietnam, 1971-72, S-3, then plans, tng. officer, reserve component study, later S-3, 1st Battalion, 3d Air Defense Artillery, 101st Airborne Divsn. (Airmobile) Ft. Campbell, Ky., 1972-74, staff officer, firepower divsn., requirements directorate, later asst. exec. officer, office dept. chief staff ops. Washington, 1975-78, comdr. 1st Basic Combat Tng. Battalion, tng. and doctrine command, 1978-79, comdr. 2d Battalion, 59th Air Defense Artillery, 1st Armored Division, US Army Europe, 1979-81, comdr. 108th Air Defense Artillery Brigade, 32d Army Air Defense Command, US Army Europe, 1984-86, dir. force requirements (combat support systems) office of dep. chief of staff ops. and plans Washington, 1986-88, dep. commdg. gen. US Army Air Defense Artillery Ctr., asst. commandant US Army Air Defense Artillery Sch. Ft. Bliss, 1988-90, dep. commdg. gen. V Corps. US Army Europe, 7th Army, 1990-91, commdg. gen. joint task force BRAVO, 1991, asst. dep. chief staff ops. and plans force devel. Office of Dep. Chief of Staff Ops. and Plans Washington, 1992-94; commdg. gen. U.S. Army Space and Strategic Def. Command, 1994-96; asst. vice chief of staff U.S. Army, 1996-97; dir. Office of Reconstruction and Humanitarian Assistance, Iraq, 2003. Pres. SY Tech. (now SYColeman Corp.), 1997—2004; mem. bd. dirs. Digital Fusion, Inc., 2005—. Decorated DSM with oak leaf cluster, Def. Superior Svc. medal with oak leaf cluster, Legion of Merit with 4 oak leaf clusters, Bronze Star, Air medal, Meritorious Svc. Medal, Joint Svc. Commendation Medal, Army Commendation Medal, Combat Infantryman Badge. Democrat. Episcopalian. Avocations: health, exercise.

GARNER, JENNIFER ANNE, actress; b. Houston, Apr. 17, 1972; d. Bill and Pat Garner; m. Scott Foley, Oct. 19, 2000 (div. Mar. 30, 2004); m. Ben Affleck, June 29, 2005. BFA, Dennison U., 1994. Actor: (TV miniseries) Danielle Steele's Zoya, 1995, Dead Man's Walk, 1996; (TV films) Harvest of Fire, 1996, The Player, 1997, Rose Hill, 1997, Aftershock: Earthquake in New York, 1999; (TV series) Swift Justice, 1996, Law & Order, 1996, Spin City, 1996, Fantasy Island, 1998, The Pretender, 1999, Significant Others, 1998, The Time of Your Life, 1999—2000, Alias, 2001— (Emmy nominee for outstanding lead actress in a drama, 2002, 2003, 2004, 2005, Golden Globe award for best actress in a television series, 2001, Saturn award for best actress in a television series, 2003, SAG award for outstanding performance in a drama series, 2005); (films) Deconstructing Harry, 1997, Washington Square, 1997, Mr. Magoo, 1997, In Harm's Way, 1997, Nineteen Ninety-Nine, 1998, Dude, Where's My Car, 2000, Pearl Harbor, 2001, Rennie's Landing, 2001, Catch Me if You Can, 2002, Daredevil, 2003, 13 Going On 30, 2004, Elektra, 2005.*

GARNER, JIM D., state official, lawyer; b. Coffeyville, Kans., June 14, 1963; s. Wayne W. and Carol L. Garner. AA with honors, Coffeyville C.C., 1983; BA in History with distinction, U. Kans., 1985, JD, 1988. Bar: Kans. 1988, U.S. Dist. Ct. Kans. 1988, U.S. Ct. Appeals (10th cir.) 1990, U.S. Supreme Ct. 2003. Jud. clk. for Dale E. Saffels U.S. Dist. Judge, Kans., 1988-90; atty. Hall, Levy, Lively, DeVore, Belot and Bell, Coffeyville, 1990-92; pvt. practice Coffeyville, 1992—; mem. Kans. Ho. of Reps., 1991—2003, minority leader, 1999—2003; sec. Kans. Dept. Labor, 2003—. Bd. dirs. Nat. Assn. State Workforce Agys.; mem. Program for Emerging Polit. Leaders, Darden Sch. of Bus., U. Va., 1994, Bowhay Inst. for Legis. Leadership Devel., Coun. of State Govts., U. Wis., 1995. Active cmty. co-chair, City of Coffeyville's Youth Focus Task Force, 1998; adv. com. Youth and Bus. Tng. Program; bd. dirs. Hospice Care Inc., Coffeyville, 1993-97, Pioneer chpt. ARC, 1998—2003; mem. leadership Coffeyville Class of 1995; mem. legis. adv. bd. Dem. Leadership Coun., 1999-2002; mem. bd. govs. U. Kans. Law Sch., 2000-02. Mem. Kans. Bar Assn., Order of Coif, Phi Alpha Theta, Phi Kappa Phi, Lions, Rotary. Office: 114 W 9th St Coffeyville KS 67337-5810 Home: Po Box 1184 Lawrence KS 66044-8184 Business E-Mail: jim.garner@dol.ks.gov.

GARNER, JOSEPH PAUL, animal scientist; b. Cheshire, United Kingdom, 1973; s. Alan and Griselda Garner. BA in Biol. Scis. and Zoology with honors, MA in Biol. Scis. and Zoology, New Coll., Oxford U., 1995; Phd, Oxford U., 1999. Postdoctoral rschr. U. Calif., Animal Sci., Davis, Calif., 1999—2004; asst. prof. Purdue U., Animal Scs., West Lafayette, Ind., 2004—. Ordinary coun. mem. Internat. Soc. for Applied Ethology, 2003—. Contbr. articles to sci. jours. Office: Purdue Univ Animal Scis 125 South Russell St West Lafayette IN 47907 Office Phone: 765-494-1780. Business E-Mail: jgarner@purdue.edu.

GARNER, JUDI COCHRON, retired elementary school educator; b. Nashville, Apr. 22, 1937; d. Edwin Ferris and Marjorie (Goebel) Cochron; m. John W. Garner, Nov. 24, 1960; 1 child, David Edwin. BS, U. Tenn., 1959; MEd, Mid. Tenn. State U., 1976. Cert. tchr. Tenn. Level III tchr. Tenn. Bd. of Edn., Nashville, 1985—2001; ret., 2001. Mem. Jackson-Madison Edn. Assn. (sec. Madison chpt. 1974-75, chmn. membership com. 1975-90, pub. rels. com. 1986-90). Home: 59 Raines Springs Rd Jackson TN 38301-7763

GARNER, JUNE BROWN, journalist; b. Detroit, July 19, 1923; d. Simpson and Vela (Wilkerson) Malone; m. Warren C. Garner, June 28, 1961; 1 dau., Sylvia G. Mustonen. Student, Wayne State U., 1941. Columnist, classified advt. mgr. Mich. Chronicle, Detroit, 1945-74; columnist Detroit News, 1974-87, Mich. Chronicle, 1990-92; CFO Warren Garner Realty, Southfield, Mich., 1992-96; reading tchr. North Tazewell (Va.) Elem. Sch., 1996—. Author: June Brown's Guide to Let's Read, 1981, June Brown's Tool Kit, 2000. Founder The Let's Read Summer Sch., 1980—. Recipient Best Column awards Detroit Press Club, 1971, 72, Nat. Newspaper Pubs. Assn., 1968, 69, Sch. Bell award Mich. Edn., Assn., 1989, Am. Promise award, 1999, Tazewell County Pub. Sch. award, 1998. Mem. S.W. Va. Reading Coun. Methodist. Home: PO Box 444 Prairie Du Chien WI 53821-0444 E-mail: june_garner@hotmail.com.

GARNER, MABLE TELOLA, health facility administrator; b. Sharon, Miss., June 11, 1931; d. Annie B. (Johnson) Garner; 1 child, Wendel Orson Siggers. BA, Fisk U., 1953; MD, Meharry Med. Coll., 1959; MTH, Springhill Coll., 1996. Diplomate Am. Bd. Clin. Pathology, 1967, Am. Bd. Anatomical Pathology, 1968. Intern Meharry Med. Coll., Nashville, asst. prof. pathology, 1968; resident in pathology Hubbard Hosp./Meharry Med. Coll., Nashville, 1963—66; sr. resident anataomny clin. and pathology VA Hosp., Nashville, 1966—67; USPHS spl. postdoctoral fellow dept. biochem. hypertension rsch. Case Western Res. U., Cleve., 1969—70; dir. health cons. Fayette St. Clinic Ltd., Shaw, Miss., 1979—. Mem.: Alpha Omega Alpha.: PO Box 798 Shaw MS 38773-0798 Office Phone: 662-754-2314.

GARNER, MELVIN C., lawyer; b. Phila., Feb. 9, 1941; BSEE, Drexel U., 1964; MSEE, NYU, 1968; JD, Bklyn. Law Sch., 1973. Bar: N.Y. 1974, U.S. Supreme Ct. 1977, U.S. Patent and Trademark Office. Prin., procurement and litig. patent, trademark, trade secret and copyright matters Darby & Darby, N.Y.C. Sr. editor Bklyn. Law Review; bd. mem. Nat. Inventors Hall Fame, 2001—. Named one of Am. Top Black Lawyers, Black Enterprise Mag., 2003. Mem.: ABA, Am. Intellectual Property Law Assn. Edn. Found. (v.p. 2001—02, sec. 2002—03, trustee 2003—), Am. Intellectual Property Law Assn. (vice chmn. com. on elec. and computer law 1998—99, bd. dirs. 1999—2002, second v.p. 2002—03, first v.p. 2003—04, pres. elect 2004—05), N.Y. Intellectual Property Law Assn. (chmn. com. on trade secret law and practice 1990—96, bd. 1997—98, sec. 1998—2000, second v.p. 2000—01, first v.p. 2001—02, pres. elect 2002—03, pres. 2003—04), Assn. Bar City of N.Y., Eta Kappa Nu. Office: Darby & Darby 805 Third Ave New York NY 10022-7513 Office Phone: 212-527-7700. Office Fax: 212-527-7701. Business E-Mail: mgarner@darbylaw.com.

GARNER, PATRICIA ANN, elementary school educator; d. Harold Ervin and Doloris Malinda Novotny; m. Allen Wayne Garner; children: Jodi Lynn Garner Hundley, Tami Jo Garner Satterthwaite. BS, U. Wis., Milw.; M in Edn., Olivet Nazarene U., Bourbonnais, Ill., 2003. Cert. tchr. Ill. 7th grade tchr. West Bend (Wis.) Pub. Schs., 1975—76; tchr.'s aide O'Fallon (Ill.) Dist. #90, 1987—88; substitute tchr. St. Clair County, Belleville, Ill., 1988—89; elem. tchr. Mascoutah (Ill.) Dist. #19, 1989—92, 1993—, Shiloh (Ill.) Dist. #85, 1992—93. Mem., honored queen Jobs Daus., West Bend, 1964—71; bd. Christian edn. O'Fallon United Ch. of Christ, 1988—90, supt. Sunday sch., 1991—2003. Mem.: NEA (com.). Avocations: reading, music, theater, movies, baseball. Office: Mascoutah Sch Dist #19 533 N 6th St Mascoutah IL 62258 Office Phone: 618-566-2152.

GARNER, PHIL, b. Jefferson City, Tenn., Apr. 30, 1949; m. Carol; children: Eric, Bethany, Ty. BS, U. Tenn., Knoxville, 1973. Profl. baseball player Oakland Athletics, 1973-76, Pitts. Pirates, 1977-81, Houston Astros, 1981-87, L.A. Dodgers, 1987, San Francisco Giants, 1988; coach Houston Astros, 1989-91; mgr. Milw. Brewers, 1991-99, Detroit Tigers, 1999—2002, Houston Astros, 2004—. Named to All-Star team, 1976, 80, 81. Office: c/o Houston Astros Union Station at Minute Maid Park 501 Crawford ste 400 Houston TX 77002

GARNER, ROBBY GLEN, software research executive, roboticist; Student, Floyd Coll., 1980-81, U. Ga., 1981-84, State U. West Ga., 1986-86, 96, Kennesaw State U., 1996-97. Clk., repair technician Garner's TV, Radio Shack Dealer, 1975-81; data entry clk. Star Mfg., 1985-86; adminstr. UNIX sys. Quality Ctrl. Lab. Henkel Chems., Cedartown, Ga., 1988-91; pres. Robitron Software Rsch., Inc., 1987—; staff roboticist FringeWare, Inc., 1995—. Developer, ptnr. Data Access Corp., Miami; presenter in field. Co-prodr., performer Poe Boy Jam 85; founding mem. Flux Oersted band; featured roboticist BBC MegaLab 98 Turing Test. Lt. col. USAF. Recipient Loebner prize Cambridge Ctr. for Behavioral Studies. Achievements include creation of FRED. Address: 223 Lawson Ave Cedartown GA 30125-2320 E-mail: robitron@fringeware.com.

GARNER, ROBERT EDWARD LEE, lawyer; b. Bowling Green, Ky., Sept. 26, 1946; s. Alto Luther and Katie Mae (Sanders) G.; m. Suzanne Marie Searles, Aug. 22, 1981; children: Jessica Marie, Abigail Lee. BA, U. Ala., Tuscaloosa, 1968; JD, Harvard U., 1971. Bar: Ga. 1971, U.S. Dist. Ct. (no. dist.) Ga. 1974, U.S. Ct. Appeals (5th cir.) 1974, U.S. Ct. Appeals (11th cir.) 1981, Ala. 1982, U.S. Ct. Appeals (4th cir.) 1991, S.C. 1992. Assoc. Gambrell, Russell & Forbes, Atlanta, 1972-76, ptnr., 1976-80, Haskell, Slaughter & Young and predecessors, Birmingham, Ala., 1981-88, mng. ptnr., 1986-87, of counsel, 1988-90; gen. counsel, sec. Builders Transport, Inc., 1988-90; ptnr. Nelson, Mullins, Riley & Scarborough, Atlanta and Columbia, S.C., 1991-96; mem. Haskell Slaughter Young & Rediker, LLC, Birmingham, 1996—, mng. ptnr., 2000—02. 1st lt. JAGC, USAF, 1971-72. Mem. ABA (com. on fed. regulation of securities, subcom. on disclosure matters and continuous reporting, subcom. on securities registration, ad hoc com. on pub. co. info. practices), State Bar Ga., Ala. State Bar, Birmingham Bar, S.C. Bar, U. Ala. Alumni Assn., Harvard U. Alumni Assn., Am. Soc. Corp. Secs. (mem. tech. com.), Phi Alpha Theta, Pi Sigma Alpha. Republican. Home: 284 Kings Crest Ln Pelham AL 35124-2846 Office: Haskell Slaughter Young & Rediker LLC 2001 Park Pl North Ste 1400 Birmingham AL 35203-2618 Office Phone: 205-251-1417. Business E-Mail: relg@hsy.com.

GARNER, RONALD A., automotive technology educator; s. Charles William and Karyl Jane Garner; m. Cindy Louderback; children: Steven, Jessica, Rachel, Kevin. AAS, Lehigh U., 1989; BS, Pa. State U., 1993, MS, 1996, PhD, 1999. Prof. Pa. Coll. Tech., Williamsport, 1993—, head nat. cert. automotive mgmt. program. Cons. Tech. Bus. Solutions, Lock Haven, Pa., 1998—; mem. NATEF Cert. Team, Arlington, Va., 1998—. Author: The Service Consultant: Working in an Automotive Facility, 2005, (tng. manual) Refrigerant, Recycling and Reclamation, 2001. Mem.: Nat. Assn. Indsl. Tech. (cert. automotive tech. mgmt.), N.Am. Coun. Automotive Tchrs. (v.p. 1997—98), Clinton Country Club, Elks. Avocation: golf. Office: Pa Coll Tech 1 Coll Ave Williamsport PA 17701 Office Phone: 570-321-6730. E-mail: rgarner@pct.edu.

GARNER, SHIRLEY IMOGENE, retired music educator; b. Silverton, Oreg., June 8, 1932; d. Julius Edgar and Amelia Christine (Preszler) Herr; m. Steven Mead Garner, Feb. 24, 1952 (div. Dec. 15, 1987); children: Shelia Christine Garner-Ward, Mark Steven. MusB with honors, Univ. Oreg., Eugene, 1957. Elem. tchr. Springfield USD, Oreg., 1957—58; vocal music tchr. Berkeley USD, Calif., 1958—61, San Jose USD, Calif., 1961—66; lit. tchr. Napa USD, Calif., 1966—67; vocal music tchr. San Jose USD, Calif., 1968—99, ret., 1996, part-time tchr., 1996—99. Choir dir. various ch., Oreg., Calif., 1955—83, Pilgrim Haven Ret. Home, Los Altos, Calif., 1969—72, The Fun Time Singers, Campbell, Calif., 2000—02. Edn. adv. com. Restoration of the Statue of Liberty and The Bicentennial of the Constitution, Washington, 1986; vol. Castillero Music Performance. Recipient Hall of Fame award, Youth Focus., Inc., 1993, Appreciation cert., Calif. State Assembly, 1993, Cert. Recognition, Calif. State Senate, 1993, Svc. Pub. Edn., Masonic Lodge, Spl. Citation award, Hawaii-Calif. Elks Assn. Mem.: Music Educators Nat. Conf. Presbyn. Achievements include started Castillero Middle Sch. annual music performance at the San Jose Ctr. for performing arts with 6 choirs and profl. performer in 1989; Nov. 2004 was the 16th annual performance in morning /afternoon and pub. evening performance with about 450 students-6 choirs, 2 bands. orchr. and dance team. Avocations: gardening, flower arranging, reading. Home: 1085 Tasman Dr Space 805 Sunnyvale CA 94089 Personal E-mail: shigarner@aol.com.

GARNER, SHIRLEY NELSON, language educator; b. Waxahachie, Tex., Aug. 8, 1935; d. Cleo and Ruby D. Nelson; m. Frank L. Garner, Nov. 24, 1972; children: Hart Phillip, Celia Ann. AB magna cum laude, U. Tex., 1957; MA, Stanford U., 1966, PhD, 1972. Instr. Stanford (Calif.) U., 1964-65, instr., asst. to dir. fresh composition, 1967-70; asst. prof. U. Minn., Mpls., 1972-76, assoc. prof., 1976-86, assoc. mem. faculty Women's Studies, 1980—, prof., 1986—, chair Women's Studies, 1989-90, dir. Ctr. Advanced Feminist Studies, 1990-94, chair English dept., 1994—2000, assoc. dean grad. sch., 2001—. Editor: (with Personal Narratives Collective) Interpreting Women's Lives: Feminist Theory and Personal Narratives, 1989, (with Madelon Sprengnether) Shakespearean Tragedy and Gender, 1995, Antifeminism in the Academy, 1996, (with VeVe Clark, Ketu Katrak, and Margaret Higonnet) Is Feminism Dead?, 2000; editor, contbg. author: (with Clare Kahane and Madelon Sprengnether) The (M)other Tongue: Essays in Feminist Psychoanalytic Interpretation, 1985; contbg. author: Bad Shakespeare: Revaluations of the the Shakespeare Canon, 1988, Seduction and Theory: Readings of Gender, Representation and Rhetoric, 1989, Shakespeare's Personality, 1989, Novel Mothering, 1991, Feminism and Psychoanalysis, Feminism and Philosophy: Essential Readings in Theory, Reinterpretation and Application, 1992, The Intimate Critique: Autobiographical Literary Criticism, 1993; founder, mem. editl. bd. Hurricane Alice, 1983—; mem. editl. bd. Signs, 1992—; contbr. articles, revs. to profl. jours. Recipient Horace T. Morse-Amoco Found. award, 1982, Pres.'s award for outstanding svc., 1999; Phillips Petroleum Found. scholar, 1953-57; Woodrow Wilson fellow, 1959-60, Sorptimists' fellow, 1965-66, 66-67; grantee U. Minn. 1974-76, 81, 87-88, Bush Sabbatical, 1984-85, Office Internat. Edn., 1988, CLA, 1981, 84-90, UROP, 1991-92; named to U. MInn. Avcad. Disting. Tchrs., 1999. Mem. MLA (co-chair Marriage and the Family in Shakespeare divsn., Shakespeare sect. 1979, chair 1980-82, chair/co-chair various seminars, symposia), Nat. Women's Studies Assn., Midwest Modern Lang. Assn. (sec. Shakespeare sect. 1972, chair 1973, nominations com. 1974-77, sec. Women and Lit. sect. 1978-79, chair 1980-81, nomination com. Women and Lit. sect. 1981-84), Shakespeare Assn. Office: U Minn English Dept 207 Church St SE Minneapolis MN 55455-0134 Office Phone: 612-824-6789. Business E-Mail: sngarner@umn.edu.

GARNER, STEVEN C., radiologist, emergency physician; m. Anne Garner; 2 children. Grad., Chgo. Med. Sch. Diplomate Am. Bd. Radiology, Am. Bd. Emergency Physicians, cert. aviation med. examiner. Chief med. officer St. Vincent Hosp. & Med. Ctr., NY; sr. v.p. St. Vincent Cath. Med. Ctrs.; intern Brookdale Med. Ctr., Bklyn.; resident Mt. Sinai Hosp.; asst. prof. radiology N.Y. Med. Coll. Cons. N.Y.P.D; cons. U.S. customs dept. N.Y. JFK Internat. Airport, pres. med. ctr. Host (TV series) Ask The Doctor; contbr. Fox News Channel; author: column in Bklyn. (N.Y.) Tablet. Fellow: Am. Acad. Emergency Physicians; mem.: Am. Coll. of Radiology (nat. emergency radiology com.), Am. Heart Assn. (edn. com., cert. fed. aviation med. examiner). Office: 88-25 153 Rd St Jamaica NY 11432 Business E-Mail: asgarner@optonline.net.

GARNER, TED, artist; b. Seattle, Feb. 10, 1957; s. James C. and Beatrice (Medicine) G.; m. Suzanne Martin, Sept. 27, 1986. BFA, Kans. City Art Inst., 1982. Artist, 1974—. V.p. Warrior Women, Inc., Wakpala, S.D.. 1996—; lectr. Iowa State U., Ames, 1982, DePauw U., Greencastle, Ind., 1997, Smithsonian Instn., Washington, 1993; vis. artist, lectr. Oberlin, 1992. One-man shows include C.N. Gorman Mus., U. Calif.-Davis, 1978, 2001, The Grayson Gallery, Chgo., 1983, Jan Cicero Gallery, Chgo., 1994, 98, Sacred Circle Gallery Am. Indian Art, Seattle, 1997; sculpture commn. Field Mus. Natural History, Chgo., 1991, City of Chgo., 1996. Recipient Martin and Doris Rosen award Appalachian State U., 1992, Purchase award Eiteljorg Mus. Western Art, 1996; Jerome Found. fellow, 2003. Avocation: electric and double bassist. Home: 1538 W Cortez St Chicago IL 60622-3955 Office: Ted Garner Artist 1544 N Sedgwick St Chicago IL 60610-1223 Office Phone: 312-944-0610. E-mail: tedgarner@mac.com.

GARNER, WILLIAM MICHAEL, lawyer; b. Huntington, W.Va., Sept. 28, 1949; s. William Max Garner and Celeste (Eichling) Neuffer; m. Christine Ann McElligott, Aug. 18, 1997. AB, Columbia U., 1971; JD, NYU, 1975. Bar: N.Y. 1976, N.J. 1994, Minn. 1997, U.S. Dist. Ct. (so. dist.) N.Y. 1977, U.S. Dist. Ct. (ea. dist.) N.Y. 1980, U.S. Dist. Ct. N.J. 1994, U.S. Dist. Ct. Minn. 1998, U.S. Ct. Appeals (2d cir.) 1980, U.S. Ct. Appeals (11th cir.) 1985, U.S. Ct. Appeals (7th cir.) 1993. Assoc. Hughes Hubbard & Reed, N.Y.C., 1976-80, Rivkin, Sherman & Levy, N.Y.C., 1980-84; ptnr. Schnader, Harrison, Segal & Lewis, N.Y.C., 1985-97, Dady & Garner, P.A., Mpls., 1997—. Author: Franchise and Distribution Law and Practice, 1990; editor Franchise Law Jour., 1988-93; contbr. articles to publs. Fellow Am. Bar Found.; mem. ABA, Assn. of Bar of City of N.Y. Home: 1815 Summit Ave Saint Paul MN 55105-1835 Office: Dady & Garner PA 4000 IDS Ctr 80 S 8th St Minneapolis MN 55402-2100 E-mail: wmgarner@dadygarner.com.

GARNETT, DOUGLAS ACREE, financial analyst, researcher; b. Caroline, Va., Aug. 11, 1928; s. James Richard Garnett and Mary Ella Acree; m. Natalie Rebecca Davis, Nov. 4, 1953; children: Michael Keith, Susan Jeanine Garnett-Rogers. Student, Bryan Coll., Dayton, Tenn., 1947—48; grad., Am. Inst. Banking, Richmond, Va., 1969. Check processing clk. Fed. Res. Bank, Richmond, Va., 1947—52, check processing supr., 1953—77, banking supr. dir., bond acct. analyst, 1978—87. Author, editor (book) Garnett Family: Ancestors and Descendants of Joseph B. Garnett, Sr., 2000. Avocation: gardening. Home: 5431 Claridge Dr Chesterfield VA 23832-7324 Office Phone: 804-276-0400.

GARNETT, GRIFFIN TAYLOR, lawyer, writer; b. Washington, Aug. 15, 1914; s. Griffin Taylor and Susie Lee (Crump) G.; m. Harriet Waddy Brooke, Sept. 21, 1938; children: Griffin Taylor III, Thomas Brooke. BA, U. Richmond, 1936; LLB, Nat. U. Law Sch., 1940. Bar: Va. 1940, D.C. 1945. Asst. clk. U.S. Dist. Ct., Washington, 1939-41; ptnr. Radigan & Garnett PC, Arlington, Va., 1995—2002. Author: (short stories) Pleasant Living, 1993, (novel) The Sandscrapers, 1995, Taboo Avenged, 1997, Sam's Legacy, 2003. Past mem. retirement bd. Arlington (Va.) Pub. Utilities Commn. Sr. lt. U.S. Navy, 1943-46, PTO. Mem. Va. Bar Assn., Arlington Bar Assn. (pres. 1960), U.S. Landing Ships Medium Assn. (life), Washington Golf and Country Club (pres. 1971). Republican. Episcopalian. Avocations: golf, cruising, reading, creative writing, music. Home: 900 N Taylor St # 904-020 Arlington VA 22203 Office: Radigan & Garnett PC 2009 N 14th St Ste 408 Arlington VA 22201 E-mail: sandscape@aol.com.

GARNETT, KEVIN, professional basketball player; Profl. basketball player Minn. Timberwolves, 1995—. Named MVP, NBA All-star Game, 2003, NBA MVP, 2004; named to NBA All-Rookie Second team, 1995—96, All-NBA Third team, 1999, USA Basketball Sr. Nat. team, 1999, All-NBA First team, 2000, All-NBA Second team, 2001, 2002, 2005, 8 NBA All-star Games, NBA All-Defensive team, 2000—05; recipient Gold medal, U.S. Men's Olympic Basketball team, 2000, Espy Award for Best NBA Player, 2004. Achievements include 1st NBA player to recieve 3 consecutive player of the month honors. Office: Minn Timberwolves 600 1st Ave N Minneapolis MN 55403-1400*

GARNETT, STANLEY IREDALE, II, utilities executive, lawyer; b. Petersburg, Va., Aug. 11, 1943; s. Stanley Arthur and Edith (Keirstead) G.; m. Beverly Jackson; children: Matthew S.A., Andrew F.W., Christie, Alfred. BA, Colby Coll., 1965; MBA, U. Pa., 1967; JD, NYU, 1973. Bar: N.Y. 1974. Sr. fin. analyst Standard Oil Co. of N.J., N.Y.C., 1967-70; assoc. Milbank, Tweed, Hadley & McCloy, N.Y.C., 1973-81; v.p.-legal and regulatory Allegheny Power Sys., Inc., N.Y.C., 1981-90, v.p. fin., 1990-94, sr. v.p. fin., 1994-95; sr. advisor Putnam, Hayes & Bartlett, 1996-97, 98-00; exec. v.p. Fla. Progress Corp., St. Petersburg, 1997-98; ptnr. PA Consulting Group, 2000—04; prin., owner Garnett Consulting Group, Inc., 2004—. Bd. dirs. Bay Corp Holdings, Inc. Vice chmn. Episcopal Ch. Bldg. Fund. Joseph P. Wharton scholar, 1965-67. Mem. ABA, N.Y. State Bar Assn. Republican. Episcopalian. Home: 2504 Sunset Way Saint Petersburg Beach FL 33706-4127 Business E-Mail: stangarnett@aol.com.

GARNETTE, CHERYL PETTY, government agency administrator; BS in Math., MA in Measurement and Stats., U. Md. With Model Secondary Sch. for the Deaf; dir. tech. in edn. programs Office Innovation and Improvement U.S. Dept. Edn., Washington. Com. dir. Assn. for Ednl. Comm. and Tech. Editor: (Rsch. Notes column) Jour. Ednl. Computing Rsch. Office: US Dept Edn Rm 522G Capitol Pl 555 New Jersey Ave NW Washington DC 20208

GARNETT-WOOTSON, ERIKA TAMIKA, social worker, educator; b. Phila., Pa. d. Elliott Tyler and Barbara Elizabeth Garnett; m. Derek Anthony Wootson (div.); 1 child, Trez Ernotine. BA with hons. in African-American Studies, Temple U., 2001, MA with hons. in African-American Studies, 2004. Coord. AmeriCorps Chester (Pa.) Youth Build, 1997—98; rep. student svcs. Temple U., Phila., 1999—2001; facilitator workshop Blaque Ins., Detroit, 2001—03; adv. youth Covenant House, Phila., 2003—04. Mem.: Youth Build USA (adv. bd. Chester chpt. 2004), Golden Key. Democrat. Akan. Avocations: writing, acting. Home: 7635 Thouron Ave Philadelphia PA 19150 Office: Covenant House PA 31-43 E Armat St Philadelphia PA 19144

GARNIER, JEAN-PIERRE, pharmaceutical executive; married; three children. PhD in Pharmacology, U. Louis Pasteur, France, 1972; MBA, Stanford U., 1974. Various positions to pres. U.S. Pharms. Products Divsn. Schering-Plough Corp., 1975-89, 89-90; pres. Smithkline Beecham, Phila., 1990-93, pres. N.Am. pharm., 1993—94, chmn. pharms., 1994—95, COO, 1995—2000, CEO, 2000—01, bd. dirs., 1992—2001; CEO GlaxoSmith-Kline, 2001—. Trustee Eisenhower Exch. Fellowships, Inc.; former bd. dirs. Phila. Mus. of Art, Mass. Eye and Ear Hosp., others. Decorated Chevalier de la Legion d'Honneur, 1997; recipient Communicator of Yr. award Internat. Assn. Bus. Communicators, 1993; recipient Fulbright Association's Lifetime Achievement Medal. Mem. Am. Soc. French Legion of Honor, United Technologies Corp. (bd. dirs.), The Acad. of Natural Scis. (emeritus trustee), Am. Found. for Pharm. Edn. (past bd. dirs.), French/Am. C. of C., others. Avocations: tennis, ping pong/table tennis, squash, golf, wind surfing. Office: GlaxoSmithKline Box 7929 One Franklin Plz Philadelphia PA 19101-7929

GARNISS, JOAN BREWSTER, musician, educator; b. Bangor, Maine, Aug. 10, 1940; d. William Ayer Brewster and Constance Miriam (Witham) Page; adopted d. Woodrow Evans Page; m. Howard Freeman Garniss, Aug. 26, 1962; children: Gretchen, Jonathan. MusB, Boston U., 1962, MusM, 1991. cert. music tchr., Music Tchr. Nat. Assn. Pvt. practice, Dover-Foxcroft, Maine, 1954-58, Hingham, Mass., 1963-65, Waltham, Mass., 1974—. Frequent adjudicator evaluator student events, Mass.; frequent adjudicator evaluator, NH. Musician: (albums) En blanc et noir, 2001; accompanist Wintersauce Chorale, 1984—86, Duo Con Anima, 1987—; musician: U. Mass., 1988—. Co-founder, pres. Waltham Band Parents, 1979-82, Waltham Music Festival, 1994-97; pres. Friends Waltham Pub. Libr., 1980-83 (bd. dir. 1980-89, 1995—); trustee Waltham Pub. Libr., 1986—, co-chmn. fundraising com., 1995-96; dir. children's choir, All Saints Ch., 1963-66; vol. Boston Pub. Sch., 1969-73; active City Coun. Citizens Com. Transp., Waltham, 1977 Mass. Cultural Affairs Coun. grantee, 1988-89. Mem. UUA/MA N.E. Dist. (human rels. chmn. 1967-70), LWV (v.p. 1979-83, pres. 1983-85, sec. 1997-2003, bd. dir., 2003—, Outstanding Mem. award, 1995), Music Tchrs. Nat. Assn.(rep. East Divsn. Cmty. Outreach, 1995-97,) Ind. Music Tchr. Forum oversight com., 1997-99, Mass. Music Tchrs. Assn. (v.p. 1987-91, pres.-elect 1991-93, pres. 1993-97, immediate past pres. 1997-99), New England Piano Tchr. Assn. (co-chmn. junior recitals com. 1982-88, student master class 1988-90, dir. 1988-90, chair Ensemble Festival, 2000-05), Mass. Libr. Trustees Assn., Lexington Music Club, Mu Phi Epsilon, Pi Kappa Lambda. Avocations: needlecrafts, travel, reading. E-mail: jbgarnissstudio@aol.com.

GAROFALO, JANEANE, actress, comedienne; b. Newton, N.J., Sept. 28, 1964; BA in History and Am. Studies, Providence Coll. Co-anchor Air America, 2004—. TV appearances include The Ben Stiller Show, 1992-93, The Larry Sanders Show, 1992-97, Saturday Night Live, 1994-95, Comedy Product, 1995, emcee, prodr., (movies) Late for Dinner, 1991, Armistead Maupin's Tales of the City, 1993, Reality Bites, 1994, Bye Bye Love, 1995, Cold Blooded, 1995, The Truth about Cats and Dogs, 1996, HBO 1 Hour Special, 1997; appearances include (films) The Cable Guy, 1996, Larger Than Life, 1996, Sweethearts, 1997, Touch, 1997, Romy and Michele's High School Reunion, 1997, Cop Land, 1997, Clay Pidgeons, 1997, The Matchmaker, 1997, Permanent Midnight, 1998, Dog Park, 1998, Half Baked, 1998, Thick as Thieves, 1999, Steal This Movie, 1999, The Minus Man, 1999, Dogma, 1999, Can't Stop Dancing, 1999, 200 Cigarettes, 1999, Mystery Men, 1999, Steal This Movie, 2000, The Independent, 2000, Titan A.E., 2000, The Adventures of Rocky and Bullwinkle, 2000, The Cherry Picker, 2000, Wet Hot American Summer, 2001, The Search for John Gissing, 2001, The Laramie Project, 2002, Martin and Orloff, 2002, Big Trouble, 2002, Manhood, 2003, Wonderland, 2003, Nobody Knows Anything, 2003, Ash Tuesday, 2003, Junebug and Hurricane, 2004, Jiminy Glick in La La Wood, 2004; radio talkshow co-host (with Sam Seder) The Majority Report, Air America Radio, 2004-; co-author (with Ben Stiller) Feel This Book, 2000. Office: UTA Inc 9560 Wilshire Blvd Fl 5 Beverly Hills CA 90212-2401*

GAROFOLO, RONALD JOSEPH, secondary education drafting and architecture educator; b. Omaha, July 10, 1949; s. Salvator A. and Louise (Marino) G.; m. Pamela J. Garofolo, Oct. 22, 1971; children: Amy, Timothy. BS in Secondary Edn., U. Nebr., 1971, MS, 1975, cert. in ednl. adminstrn., 1993. Indsl. edn. tchr. Bryan Jr. High Sch., Omaha, 1971-78; archtl. drafting tchr. Tech. High Sch., Omaha, 1978-84, Bryan Sr. High Sch., Omaha, 1984—. Recipient Alice Buffett Outstanding Tchr. award, 1988, Norwest Bank Outstanding Tchr. award, 1990, Tchr. Excellence award (Nebr.), Internat. Tech. Edn. Assn., 1992. Mem. NEA (rep. nat. assembly del.), Internat. Tech. Edn. Assn. (Tchr. Excellence award 1993), Nebr. State Edn. Assn. (state del. assembly del.), Nebr. Indsl. Tech. Edn. Assn. (Tchr. of Yr. 1992, Nebr. Coaches Assn. (mem. adv. com., tennis rep., Tennis Coach of Yr. 1992), Omaha Edn. Assn. (bd. dirs.), Nat. High Sch. Athletic Coaches Assn. (mem. nat. tennis com.), Phi Delta Kappa. Office: Bryan Sr High Sch 4700 Giles Rd Omaha NE 68157-2641

GAROIAN, CHARLES RICHARD, artist, educator; b. Fresno, Calif., Nov. 7, 1943; s. Kurken Makhtesi and Satenig Suzanne (Bezdigian) G.; m. Sherrie Elyce Alexanian, Jan. 27, 1968; children: Jason Aram, Stephanie Tamar. BA in Visual Art, Calif. State U., Fresno, 1968, MA in Visual Art, 1969; PhD in Edn., Stanford U., 1984. Art instr. and art curriculum coord. Los Altos (Calif.) High Sch., 1969-86; vis. lectr. U. Wash., Seattle, summer 1977; edn. dir. Pa. State U., Palmer Mus. of Art, University Park, 1986-90, asst. dir., 1990-91; assoc. prof. art edn. Sch. Visual Arts, Pa. State U., University Park, 1991—; dir. Sch. Visual Arts Pa. State U., University Park, 1999—. Exhibits include San Francisco Mus. Modern Art, 1974, Charles Garoian, San Jose Mus. Art, 1975, Rites of Sculpture, Berkeley Mus. Art, 1976, New Adventures: Time and Space, Wash. State U., 1982; contbr. articles to profl. jours. Bd. dirs. Cen. Pa. Festival of Arts, State College, 1988-90; chmn. Com. for Pub Sculpture, 1988-91. Named Tchr. of the Yr. Mountain View/Los Altos High Sch. Dist., 1976; Pa. Coun. on Arts grantee, 1986, 87, 88, 90, 91; recipient Creative Programming award Nat. U. Continuing Edn. Assn., 1990, 91. Mem. Nat. Art Edn. Assn., Coll. Art Assn. Fluent in Armenian. Office: School of Visual Arts Penn State University 210 Patterson Building University Park PA 16802-2502 Office Phone: 814-865-0444. Office Fax: 814-865-1158. E-mail: crg2@psu.edu.*

GARON, PHILIP STEPHEN, lawyer; b. Duluth, Minn., Nov. 11, 1947; s. Lawrence and Helen (Cohen) G.; m. Phyllis Sue Ansel, Mar. 22, 1970; children: Edward B., Sara B. BA summa cum laude, U. Minn., 1969, JD summa cum laude, 1972. Bar: Minn. 1972, D.C. 1973, U.S. Dist. Ct. Minn. 1974. Assoc. Covington & Burling, Washington, 1972-74, Faegre & Benson, Mpls., 1974-79, ptnr., 1980—. Mem. mgmt. com. Faegre & Benson, 1992-2004, chmn., 2001-04; mem. U.S. Law Firm Group, 2004—, pres., 2005. Co-author: Minnesota Corporation Law & Practice, 1996, 2d edit., 2004 (Burton award for legal writing 2001). Bd. dirs. Herzl Camp, Webster, Wis., 1985-91, Beth El Synagogue, Mpls., 1989-99, v.p., 1993-96; bd. vis. U. Minn. Law Sch., 2003-. Mem. Minn. Bar Assn. (pres. exec. coun. bus. law sect. 1996-97). Avocations: tennis, reading, bridge. Office: Faegre & Benson 2200 Wells Fargo Ctr 90 S 7th St Ste 2200 Minneapolis MN 55402-3901 Office Phone: 612-766-8101. Business E-Mail: pgaron@faegre.com.

GARON, RICHARD JOSEPH, JR., political organization worker; b. Bronxville, N.Y., Sept. 9, 1948; s. Richard Joseph Sr. and Jeane Helen (Schlemmer) G.; m. Karen Barclay, Jan. 15, 1972; children: Cynthia Beth, Timothy Michael. BA, Hartwick Coll., 1972; MA, NYU, 1975, PhD, 1983. Legis. asst. U.S. rep. Benjamin A. Gilman, Washington, 1977-79, adminstrv. asst. U.S. rep., 1985-89; staff cons. House Com. on Fgn. Affairs, Washington, 1983-85; staff asst. House Com. on Post Office & Civil Svc., Washington, 1979-83, dep. minority staff dir., 1989-92; Rep. chief of staff House Com. on Fgn. Affairs, Washington, 1993-95; chief of staff House Com. on Internat. Rels., Washington, 1995—2001; writer, 2001—. NYU scholar, 1976-77. Republican. Presbyterian. Home: 11526 Gunner Ct Woodbridge VA 22192-5745 E-mail: rgaron@comcast.net.

GARONZIK, SARA ELLEN, stage producer; b. Phila., Jan. 12, 1951; d. Milton and Bernice (Kohn) Garonzik. BA in Spanish cum laude, Temple U., 1972. Producing artistic dir. Phila. Theatre Co., 1982—. Bd. dirs. Arts and Bus. Coun. Greater Phila., Phila. Theatre Co., Theatre Alliance Greater Phila. Recipient prize, Sigma Delta Pi, 1972, award of Honor, Alumnae Assn. Girls H.S., 1997. Office: Phila Theatre Co 230 S 15th St Philadelphia PA 19102 Office Phone: 215-985-1400. Business E-Mail: sgaronzik@phillytheatreco.com.

GAROSSHEN, PAULETTE SHARON, writer; b. Aschnutt, Mass., July 31, 1951; children: Charolotte Sharon Romagnano, Sonya Lynn, Nicholas J. Grad. h.s. Author (self publisher): Book I. Office Phone: 1-860-334-8873.

GARR, DAVID ROSS, physician, educator; b. Boston, Mass., Sept. 6, 1946; s. Fred Manuel and Ida Shuman Garr; m. Deborah Camille Williamson, Dec. 10, 1976; children: Joshua, Rebecca. BA in Chemistry, Duke U., 1968, MD, 1972. Diplomate Am. Bd. Family Medicine. Resident family practice Highland Hosp., Rochester, NY, 1972—75; med. dir. Family Medicine Group of Tooele, Utah, 1975—81; dir. learning resources family practice residency Mercy Med. Ctr., Denver, 1981—85; clinician, prof., assoc. dean cmty. medicine Med. U. S.C., Charleston, 1985—, exec. dir. SC Area Health Edn. Consortium, 2003—. Office: Med Univ SC PO Box 250814 19 Hagood Ave Ste 802 Charleston SC 29425

GARR, SALLY D., lawyer; b. Atlanta, Ga., June 10, 1952; BA magna cum laude, Ga. State U., 1977; JD cum laude, U. Ga., 1980. Bar: Ga. 1980, DC 1980, US Dist. Ct. (DC, Md., Colo., ea. Mich., no. Ill. dist), US Ct. Appeals (4th, 6th, DC cir.), US Supreme Ct. Former assoc. gen. counsel, labor & personnel Amtrak, Washington; ptnr., Employment Law, Litigation & Dispute Resolution practices, mem. mgmt. com. Patton Boggs LLP, Washington. Office: Patton Boggs LLP 2550 M St NW Washington DC 20037-1350 Office Phone: 202-457-6525. Office Fax: 202-457-6315. Business E-Mail: sgarr@pattonboggs.com.

GARR, TERI (ANN), actress; b. Lakewood, Ohio, Dec. 11, 1949; m. John O'Neil, Nov. 1993 (div. 1996); 1 adopted child, Molly. Began career as dancer performing with San Francisco Ballet at age 13; in original road show co. of West Side Story; stage appearances include One Crack Out, 1978, Broadway, 1978, Ladyhouse Blues, 1979, Night of 100 Stars II, 1985; appeared in films including Viva Las Vegas, Head, 1968, Maryjane, 1968, Moonshine War, 1970, The Conversation, 1974, Young Frankenstein, 1974, Won Ton Ton, The Dog Who Saved Hollywood, 1976, Oh God!, 1977, Close Encounters of the Third Kind, 1977, Mr. Mike's Mondo Video, 1979, The Black Stallion, 1979, Honky Tonk Freeway, 1981, The Escape Artist, 1982, Tootsie, 1982, One From the Heart, 1982, The Sting II, 1983, The Black Stallion Returns, 1983, Mr. Mom, 1983, Firstborn, 1984, After Hours, 1985, Miracles, 1987, Out Cold, 1988, Let It Ride, 1989, Short Time, 1990, Waiting for the Light, 1990, Mom and Dad Save the World, 1992, Ready to Wear, 1994, Dumb and Dumber, 1994, Michael, 1996, A Simple Wish, 1997, Changing Habits, The Definite Maybe, 1997, Kill the Man, 1999, Dick, 1999, The Sky is Falling, 2000, Life Without Dick, 2001; TV movies include Doctor Franken, 1980, Prime Suspect, 1982, The Winter of Our Discontent, 1983, To Catch a King, 1984, Intimate Strangers, 1986, Fresno, 1986, Pack of Lies, 1987, Teri Garr in Flapjack Floozie, 1988, Drive, She Said (Trying Times), 1987, Mother Goose Rock n Rhyme, Stranger in the Family, 1991, Deliver Them From Evil: The Taking of Alta View, 1992, Fugitive Nights: Danger in the Desert, 1993, Ronnie and Julie, 1996, Casper Meets Wendy, 1998, Half a Dozen Babies, 1999, A Colder Kind of Death, 2001; regular on TV series The Sonny and Cher Comedy Review, 1974, Good and Evil, 1991, Good Advice, 1994, Duckman, 1994, The Women of the House, 1995, Double Jeopardy, 1996, Nightscream, 1997, Murder Live!!, 1997; other TV appearances include Law and Order, 1976, Fresno, Late Night with David Letterman, the Frog Prince, Tales From the Crypt, Friends, 1997-98; guest appearances include Murphy Brown, 1993, Frasier, 1995, Sabrina, the Teenage Witch, 1997, ER, 1999, Felicity, 2001, Life with Bonnie, 2003. Office: William Morris Agy 151 S El Camino Dr Beverly Hills CA 90212-2775

GARRAHAN-MASTERS, MARY PATRICIA, retired social worker, writer; b. Phila., June 6, 1951; d. Francis Edward and Mary Patricia McElduff Garrahan; m. Thomas Anthony Masters Mastrangelo, June 5, 1995 (div. Feb. 2000). Student, Georgetown U., 1971-72, Facultad Filosofia y Letras, Madrid; BA in Sociology with honors, Villanova (Pa.) U., 1973; M in Social Sci., M in Law and Social Policy, Bryn Mawr (Pa.) Coll., 1983. Geriat. case worker Schuylkill County Area Agy. on Aging, Pottsville, Pa., 1974-79; social svc. dir. Dowden Nursing Home, Newtown Sq., Pa., 1980-84; dir. admissions St. Francis County Ho., Darby, Pa., summer 1981; tchr. Delaware County Coll., Media, Pa., 1984; med. social worker VA Med. Ctr., Lebanon, Pa., 1985-88, Phila., Pa., 88-90. Part-time staff coord. Garrahan Equipment Inc., Havertown, Pa., 1973-92; part-time social worker Delta-T Home Health Agy., Bryn Mawr, 1992-97. Contbr. poetry to Lynx mag. Villanova U. Assoc. mem. Rep. Nat. Com., Washington, 1993-99; Eucharistic minister St. Richard's Roman Cath. Ch., Barnesville, Pa., 1974-79. Mem. Internat. Hypnosis Hall Fame Guild Inc., Nat. Assn. Ret. Fed. Employees, Soc. Friends of Touro Synagogue (assoc. mem.), Alpha Zeta Delta. Home: 2707 Stoneham Dr West Chester PA 19382-6649

GARRARD, JUDITH T., principal, elementary school educator; b. Butler, Pa., Sept. 6, 1960; d. William J. and Rue Ann Moore; children: Erin, Evan. AA, Palm Beach Jr. Coll., 1982; BA, Fla. Atlantic U., 1985, EdM, 1995. Tchr. Hagen Rd. Elem. Sch., Boynton Beach, Fla., 1985—95, Roosevelt Mid. Sch., West Palm Beach, Fla., 1995—97, asst. prin., 1997—2001; prin. Glade View Elem. Sch., Belle Glade, Fla., 2001—04, Seminole Tr. Elem. Sch., West Palm Beach, 2004—. Cons. Coun. Ednl. Change, Miami, Fla., 2004—. Mem. Migrant Assn. So. Fla., Boynton Beach, 1985—95; bd. dirs. Boys and Girls Club Glades Area, Belle Glade, 2001—04. Recipient Lifetime Profl. Educator award, Soka Gakkai Internat.-USA, 1998. Mem.: Internat. Reading Assn., Assn. Supr. and Curriculum Devel., Nat. Assn. Elem. and Secondary Prin. Avocations: reading, houseplants. Office: Seminole Tr Elem Sch 4075 Willow Pond Rd West Palm Beach FL 33417

GARRARD, PATRICIA RENICK, middle school educator; b. Miami, Fla., Mar. 9, 1950; d. Ralph Apperson and Elizabeth (Henry) Renick; m. Walter Martin Garrard, Dec. 29, 1972; children: Elizabeth, Danielle. BA, Fla. State U., 1972. Tchr. St. Lawrence Sch., North Miami Beach, Fla., 1972—73, Citrus Grove Jr. H.S., Miami, Fla., 1973—76, Hialeah Jr. H.S., Fla., 1977—79; tchr. lang. arts Pioneer Mid. Sch., Cooper City, Fla., 1979—, chair dept. lang. arts, 1996—. Tchr. cons. South Fla. Writing Project, Ft. Lauderdale, 2001—. Mem.: Nat. Coun. Tchrs. English, Fla. Coun. Tchrs. English, Broward Coun. Tchrs. English, Alpha Chi Omega (province officer 1987—93), Kappa Delta Pi. Roman Catholic. Home: 10427 SW 53 St Fort Lauderdale FL 33328 Office: Pioneer Middle Sch 5350 SW 90th Ave Cooper City FL 33328

GARREANS, LEONARD LANSFORD, protective services official, criminal justice professional; b. Glenwood, Iowa, Mar. 25, 1942; s. Ernest Lyle and Kathryn Hermine (Seeger) G.; m. Wanda Marian Ackley, Aug. 24, 1963; children: Kirk Anthony, Debra Renee, David Lance, Diana Jasmine. BSE summa cum laude, John Brown U., 1973; MSE, State Coll. Ark., 1974; postgrad., U. Ark., 1978-79; PhD, Internat. U., Independence, Mo., 1984. Cert. secondary tchr., guidance counselor, jailer, lic. police instr. Draftsman Pacific Pumping Co., Oakland, Calif., 1963; chem. operator Allied Chem. Corp., El Segundo, Calif., 1963-69; asst. swimming coach John Brown U., Siloam Springs, Ark., 1972-73; grad. asst. State Coll. Ark., Conway, 1973-74; tchr./coach, dir. athletics The Alliance Acad., Quito, Ecuador, 1974-78; teaching asst. U. Okla. Summer Inst. Linguistics, Norman, 1979-81; dir. guidance and counseling Lomalinda High Sch. Summer Inst. Linguistics, Colombia, 1981-87; internat. trainer, cons. Summer Inst. Linguistics, Dallas, 1987-89, pers. devel. officer, 1989-93; cmty. supervision officer Dallas County, State of Tex., Dallas, 1993-95; literacy proctor Dallas County Cmty. Supervision and Corrections Dept., 1999—2003; detention officer, tng. officer, acting supr. Richardson (Tex.) Police Dept., 1995—2003; ind. contract driver, 2003—. Internat. dir. of intercultural comm. course Summer Inst. Linguistics, Dallas, 1988-89. Vol. probation officer Benton County (Ark.) Juvenile Youth Authority, 1970-72; mem. Jaycees, 1970. With USMC, 1960-63. Mem. Am. Assn. Ret. Persons. Republican. Evangelical. Avocations: hiking, camping, reading, motorcycling. Home: 7346 Cave Dr Dallas TX 75249-1303 *Nothing in life is more important than one's relationship to God. Anything I may have accomplished in this life has been the direct result of God working through me. To God be the glory!.*

GARRELICK, JOEL MARC, acoustical scientist, consultant; b. N.Y.C., May 20, 1941; s. Samuel J. Garrelick and Phyllis Weidenbaum; m. Renee Brosell, Dec. 22, 1963; children: Kevin, Jenine, Daniel. BCE, CCNY, 1963, ME, 1965; PhD, CUNY, 1969. Lectr. CCNY, 1968-69; scientist Cambridge (Mass.) Acoustical Assocs., 1969-75, corp. scientist, 1976-97; sr. corp. scientist Cambridge Acoustical Assocs./ Anteon Corp., 1998—2002; prin. scientist Applied Phys. Sci. Inc., 2002—. Contbr. articles to profl. jours. Fellow Acoustical Soc. Am.; mem. ASME. Office: APS Inc 4 Muzzey St Lexington MA 02421 E-mail: jgarrelick@aphysci.com.

GARRELS, ANNE, news correspondent; b. July 2, 1951; m. Vint Lawrence Garrels. Grad., Harvard U., 1972. Various positions ABC News, 1975—85, Moscow bur. chief, Ctrl. Am. corr., 1984—85; State Dept. corr. NBC News, 1985—88; fgn. corr. Nat. Pub. Radio, Washington, 1988—. Recipient Alfred I. duPont-Columbia U. award, 1992, duPont-Columbia award, 1996, Whitman Bassow award, Overseas Press Club, 1999, Alumnae Recognition award, Radcliffe Assn., 2002, Courage award, Internat. Women's Media Found., 2003, George K. Polk award for radio reporting, 2004; Edward R. Murrow fellow, Coun. on Fgn. Rels., 1996. Mem.: Com. to Protect Journalists (bd. mem.). Office: NPR 635 Massachusetts Ave NW Washington DC 20001-3753

GARRELS, SHERRY ANN, lawyer; b. Chgo., Feb. 5, 1956; d. William Henry and Jacqueline Ann G.; m. Timothy Anthony Marion, Aug. 1, 1987 (div. June 1988); 1 child, William Garrels-Marion; 1 child, Georgianna Garrels-Rogers. BA, Barat Coll., 1980; certificate, Trinity Coll., 1989; JD, Western State U., 1990. Bar: Calif. 1992, U.S. Dist. Ct. (ctrl. dist.) Calif. 1992, U.S. Dist. Ct. (no. dist.) Calif. 1993, U.S. Dist. Ct. (so. dist.) Calif. 1996, U.S. Ct. Appeals (9th cir.) 1994, U.S. Tax Ct. 1996. Pvt. practice, Huntington Beach, Calif., 1992—; judge pro tem West Justice Ctr., Westminster, Calif., 1998—. Arbitrator Nat. Panel Consumer Arbitrators, Huntington Beach, 1996, State Panel Consumer Arbitrators, Huntington Beach, 1996, Better Bus. Bureau, 1996—, U.S. C. of C., 1996, Huntington Beach C. of C., 1996. Editor The Dictum, 1989. Active 4th of July Exec. Bd., Huntington Beach, 1996—. Mem. Assn. Trial Lawyers, L.A. Trial Assn., Orange County Bar Assn., St. Bonny Golf Classic (dir. 1991-97), Delta Theta Phi. Republican. Presbyterian. Avocations: swimming, golf, scuba diving. Office: 5942 Edinger Ave Ste 113-702 Huntington Beach CA 92649-1763 also: West Justice Ctr 8141 13th St Westminster CA 92683-4593 Fax: 714-374-0104.

GARRETSON, HENRY DAVID, neurosurgeon; b. Woodbury, N.J., June 8, 1929; s. O.K. and Mary Marjorie (Davis) G.; m. Marianna Schantz, July 4, 1964; children: John, Steven. BS, U. Ariz., 1950; MD, Harvard U., 1954; PhD, McGill U., 1968. Diplomate: Am. Bd. Neurol. Surgery (mem. 1981-87, vice chmn. 1985-86, chmn. 1986-87. Surg. intern Royal Victoria Hosp., Montreal, 1954-55; resident Montreal Neurol. Inst., 1959-63; asst. prof. neurosurgery McGill U., Montreal, 1966-71; prof. U. Louisville, 1971-98, prof. emeritus, 1998—, chmn. divsn. neurol. surgery, 1971-93, chmn. dept. neurol. surgery, 1993-97, assoc. dean clin. affairs Sch. Medicine, 1975-79, dir. neuroscis. programs Sch. Medicine, 1979-82. Individual practice medicine, specializing in neurosurgery, Montreal, 1963-71; with Grantham & Garretson, Louisville, 1971-90, Neurosurgery Inst. Ky., 1990-2000. Contbr. numerous articles, abstracts, editorials, presentations in field. Served with USNR, 1955-58. Fellow ACS; mem. AAAS, AMA, Am. Assn. Neurol. Surgeons (bd. dirs. 1983-85, sec. 1985-86, pres. elect 1986-87, pres. 1987-88), Am. Acad. Neurol. Surgery (pres. 1991-92), Congress Neurol. Surgeons, Ky. Neurosurg. Soc., Ky. Surg. Soc., Louisville Surg. Soc., Ky. Med. Assn., Soc. Neurol. Surgeons, Soc. U. Neurosurgeons (pres. 1983-84), So. Neurosurg. Soc. (pres. 1986-87), Jefferson County Med. Soc., Phi Beta Kappa, Phi Kappa Phi, Sigma Xi. Home: 517 Tiffany Ln Louisville KY 40207-1438 Office: Univ Louisville Dept Neurosurgery 210 E Gray St #1102 Louisville KY 40202-3907

GARRETT, BRAD, actor, comedian; b. Woodland Hills, Calif., Apr. 14, 1960; m. Jill Diven, 1999; 2 children. Actor in films including: Jetsons: The Movie (voice), 1990, Casper (voice), 1995, Suicide Kings, 1997, George B., 1997, Postal Worker, 1998, A Bug's Life (voice), 1999, Sweet and Lowdown, 1999, An Extremely Goofy Movie (voice), 2000, Facade, 2000, Stuart Little 2, 2002, The Country Bears (voice), 2002, Finding Nemo (voice), 2003, The Trailer, Garfield (voice), 2004, The Moguls, 2005, The Pacifier, 2005; TV films include: The Bears Who Saved Christmas, 1994, Don King: Only in America, 1997, Hooves of Fire (voice), 1999, Club Land, 2001, Bleacher Bums, 2002, Gleason, 2002, Legend of the Lost Tribe, 2002; TV series include: The Transformers (voice), 1984, Rock 'n' Wrestling (voice), 1985, First Impressions, 1988, Where's Waldo (voice), 1991, Eek! the Cat (voice), 1992, Biker Mice From Mars (voice), 1993, Bonkers (voice), 1993, 2 Stupid Dogs (voice), 1993, Pursuit of Happiness, 1995, Project G.e.e.K.e.R. (voice), 1996, Mighty Ducks (voice), 1996, Everybody Loves Raymond, 1996-2005 (Emmy award best sup. actor comedy series, 2002, 2003), Nightmare Ned, 1997, Toonsylvania (voice), 1998; TV guest appearances include: Roseanne, 1991, The Fresh Prince of Bel-Air, 1994, Lois & Clark: The New Adventures of Superman, 1996, Mad About You, 1996, Seinfeld, 1996, Superman (voice), 1996, 97, Murphy Brown, 1998, The King of Queens, 1998, Batman: The Animated Series, 1992; appeared on Broadway in Chicago, 2002. Office: Metropolitan Talent Agy 4526 Wilshire Blvd Los Angeles CA 90010-3801*

GARRETT, BYRON V., government agency administrator, director; s. Franklin R. and Yvonne W. Garrett. BA in Human Rels., High Point U., 1994; MA in Orgnl. Mgmt., U. Phoenix, 2002; attending, Pepperdine U., 2002—. Pres., CEO Life Works Internat., Phoenix, 1996—2000; CEO Prog. Schs., Inc., Phoenix, 2000—03; divsn. dir. Gov.'s Divsn. Cmty. & Youth Devel., Phoenix, 2003—05; policy advisor & dir. Gov.'s Office Faith & Cmty. Initiatives, Phoenix, 2005—. Commr. Human Rels. Commn., Phoenix, 1997—99, Phoenix Youth & Edn. Commn., 2005. Author: (book) The ABC's of Life, (leadership anthology) Go! MAD!, Teen Power & Beyond, Lead Now or Step Aside!. Policy advisor African Am. Strategic Leadership Alliance, Phoenix, 2002—05; pastor civic and cmty. affairs Greater Prog. Christian Ch., Phoenix, 1998—2005; mem. nat. coun. on youth policy Nat. Network for Youth, DC, 2004—; committeeman Ctrl. City Village Planning Com., 2000—03; mem. Ariz. SAVES, Phoenix, 2004—, Terracita Homeowners Assn., Phoenix, 2005—. Recipient Recognition award, Maricopa Cmty. Colls. Black Profls. Alliance, 2003, City of Phoenix Youth Workforce Coun., 2005, Pres.'s award, Greater Phoenix YMCA, 2004, award of Distinction, Phoenix HBCU Alumni Bd., 2004; Sr. Leadership fellow, TRI Leadership Resources, 1997—, Nigeria Group Study Exch. Team fellow, Rotary Internat., 1998. Mem.: Nat. Assn. Black Sch. Educators, Nat. Assn. Elem. Sch. Prins., Nat. Forum Black Pub. Adminstrs. (Phoenix Chpt.), Ariz. Chpt. of Nat. Black MBA Assn. Independent. Avocations: travel, shopping, swimming, bowling. Office: Office of Gov Janet Napolitano 1700 W Washington St Phoenix AZ 85007 Personal E-mail: byron@byrongarrett.com.

GARRETT, CHARLES GEOFFREY BLYTHE, physicist, consultant; b. Ashford, Kent, Eng., Sept. 15, 1925; came to U.S., 1950, naturalized, 1989; s. Charles Alfred Blythe and Laura Mary (Lotinga) G. BA in Natural Scis., Trinity Coll., Cambridge U., Eng., 1946; MA in Natural Scis., PhD in Physics, Cambridge U., 1950. Instr. physics Harvard U., 1950-52; mem. tech. staff Bell Labs., Murray Hill, N.J., 1952-54, supr., 1955-56, dept. head, 1960-69; dir. AT&T Bell Labs., Murray Hill-Morristown, N.J., 1969-87. Chmn. Gordon Conf. on non-linear optics, 1964 Author: Magnetic Cooling, 1954, Gas Lasers, 1963; contbr. articles to profl. jours.; patentee in field Named knight of Sovereign Order St. John of Jerusalem (Orthodox) Fellow: IEEE (life), Am. Phys. Soc.; mem.: Guild of Carillonneurs in N.Am. Episcopalian. Avocations: piano, harpsichord, carillon, restoring 18th century houses and older Rolls-Royce cars. Home: 7 Fithian Ln East Hampton NY 11937-2605

GARRETT, CHRISTER S., academic administrator; b. Middletown, N.Y., Mar. 23, 1962; s. Stephen A. and Marta G.; m. Claudia H., Jun. 12, 1999. BA, Univ. Calif., Santa Barbara, 1984; PhD, Univ. Calif., L.A., 1994. Vis. prof. Monterey (Calif.) Inst. Internat. Studies, 1994-99; exec. dir. european studies Univ. Wis., Madison, 1999—. Bosch fellow Bosch Found., Stuttgart, 1994-95, Fulbright fellow Fulbright Found., 1997-98. Fellow Rotary; mem. Bosch Found. (pres. 2001—), Fulbright Alumni Assn. (Wis. chpt., exec. bd. 1999—), Phi Beta Kappa. Home: 4710 Odana Rd Madison WI 93940 E-mail: cgarrett@chorus.net.

GARRETT, E. SCOTT, congressman, lawyer; b. Englewood, N.J., July 9, 1959; m. Mary Ellen Garrett; 1 child, Jennifer. BA in Polit. Sci., Montclair State Coll., 1981; JD, Rutgers U., 1984. Atty. Sellar, Richardson, Stuart and Chisholm; assembly mem. dist. 24 N.J. State Assembly, 1990—2002, asst. majority leader, 2000—02; mem. 108th U.S. Congress, 5th Dist., NJ, 2002—, mem. budget com., fin. svc. com. Labor and transportation com. N.J. State Assembly; of counsel Kelly, Gaus & Holub. Past pres. Sussex County Big Brothers; past dir. Sussex County Rep. Chmns. Club. Mem.: NJ Defense Assn., Sussex County Bar Assn., NJ Bar Assn. Republican. Office: US Ho of Reps 1641 Longworth Ho Office Bldg Washington DC 20515*

GARRETT, ELIZABETH, law educator, academic administrator; b. Oklahoma City, June 30, 1963; d. Robert D. and Jane (Thompson) G. BA in History with spl. distinction, U. Okla., 1985; JD, U. Va., 1988. Bar: Tex. 1988, D.C. 1989. Law clk. to Hon. Stephen Williams U.S. Ct. Appeals (D.C. cir.), 1988-89; law clk. to Hon. Thurgood Marshall U.S. Supreme Ct., 1989-90; legal adviser to Hon. Howard M. Holtzman Iran-U.S. Claims Tribunal, The Hague, The Netherlands, 1990-91; legal counsel, legis. asst. Senator David L. Boren, 1991-93, legis. dir., tax counsel, 1993—94; vis. assoc. prof. Univ. Va., 1994—95; asst. prof. Univ. Chgo. Law Sch., 1995—99, prof., 1999—2003, dep. dean, 1999—2001; vis. asst. prof. Harvard Univ., 1998; vis. prof. Ctrl. European Univ., 1999—2003, Interdisciplinary Ctr. Law Sch., Tel Aviv, 2001, Calif. Inst. Tech., 2004, Univ. Va., 2001, Univ. So. Calif. Law Sch., 2002; dir. USC-Caltech Ctr. Study Law & Politics, 2003—; vice provost acad. affairs USC, 2005—; Sydney M. Irma prof. pub. interest law, legal ethics and polit. Sci. Calif. Inst. Tech., 2005—; vice provost acad. affairs U. So. Calif., 2005—. Bd. dir. Initiative & Referendum Inst. Articles editor U. Va. Law Rev.; contbr. articles to profl. jours.; mem editl. bd. Election Law Journal Ewing fellow U. Okla. Fellow, Am. Bar Found.; mem. ABA, Am. Law & Econ. Assn., Fed. Bar Assn., Tex. Bar Assn., D.C. Bar Assn., Order of Coif, Mortar Bd., Phi Beta Kappa, Chi Omega. Office: The Law Sch Univ So Calif Los Angeles CA 90089 Office Phone: 213-740-0064. Business E-Mail: vpaa@usc.edu.

GARRETT, GEORGE PALMER, JR., language educator, writer; b. Orlando, Fla., June 11, 1929; s. George Palmer and Rosalie (Toomer) G.; m. Susan Parrish Jackson, June 14, 1952; children: William, George, Rosalie. AB, Princeton U., 1952, MA, 1956, PhD, 1985; DLitt (hon.), U. South, 1995. Asst. prof. English Wesleyan U.; writer-in-residence, resident fellow in creative writing Princeton U., 1964-65; former assoc. prof. U. Va.; prof. English Hollins Coll. Va., 1967-71; prof. U. S.C., Columbia, 1971-73, Princeton U., 1974-78, U. Mich., 1979-80, 83-84; Hoyns prof. creative writing U. Va., Charlottesville, 1984—2001; prof. Bennington Coll., 1980; Coal Royalty chair U. Ala., 1994. Author: The Reverend Ghost: Poems (Poets of Today IV), 1957, King of the Mountain, 1958, The Sleeping Gypsy and Other Poems, 1958, The Finished Man, 1959, Which Ones Are the Enemy, 1961; (poems) Abraham's Knife, 1961, In the Briar Patch, 1961; (plays) Sir Slob and the Princess, 1962, Cold Ground Was My Bed Last Night, 1964; (screenplays) The Young Lovers, 1964, The Playground, 1965, Frankenstein Meets the Space Monster, 1965, Do, Lord, Remember Me, 1965, For a Bitter Season, 1967, A Wreath for Garibaldi, 1969, Death of the Fox, 1971, The Magic Striptease, 1973, Welcome to the Medicine Show, Postcards/Flashcards/Snapshots, 1978, To Recollect a Cloud of Ghosts: Christmas in England 1602-03, 1979, Luck's Shining Child: Poems, 1981, The Succession: A Novel of Elizabeth and James, 1983, The Collected Poems of George Garrett, 1984, James Jones, 1984, An Evening Performance: New and Selected Short Stories, 1985, Poison Pen, 1986, Understanding Mary Lee Settle, 1988, Entered from the Sun, 1990, The Sorrows of Fat City, 1992, Whistling in the Dark, 1992, My Silk Purse and Yours, 1992, The Old Army Game, 1994, The King of Babylon Shall Not Come Against You, 1996, Days of Our Lives Lie in Fragments, 1998, Bad Man Blues, 1998, Going to See the Elephant, 2001, Southern Excursions, 2003, Double Vision, 2004, A Story Goes With It, 2004; editor New Writing From Virginia, 1963, The Girl in the Black Raincoat, 1966, The Sounder Few, 1971, Film Scripts I-IV, 1971, Craft So Hard to Learn, 1973, The Writer's Voice, 1973, Intro V, 1974, Intro 6: Life As We Know It, 1974, Intro 7: All of Us and None of You, 1975, Botteghe Obscure Reader, 1975, Intro 8: The Liar's Craft, 1977, Intro 9: Close to Home, 1978, Eric Clapton's Lover, 1990, The Wedding Cake in the Middle of the Road, 1992, Elvis in Oz, 1992, That's What I Like (About the South), 1993, The Yellow Shoe Poets, 1999. Served in occupation of Trieste, Austria and Germany. Recipient Rome prize AAAL, 1958-59, Sewanee Rev. fellow poetry, 1958-59, Am. Acad. and Inst. of Letters award, 1985, T.S. Eliot award Ingersoll Found., 1990, Pen/Malamud award, 1990, Hollins Coll. medal, 1992, U. Va. Pres.'s Report award, 1992, Aiken-Taylor award, 1999, Gov.'s award Commonwealth of Va., 2000, Lifetime Achievement award Libr. Va., 2004, Cleanth Brooks medal, 2005; named Cultural Laureate of Va., 1986, Poet Laureate of Va., 2000; Ford Found. grantee in drama, 1960, Nat. Found Arts grantee, 1966; Guggenheim fellow, 1974, resident fellow Bellagio Ctr., 2000. Fellow: Am. Acad. in Rome; mem.: PEN, MLA, Fellowship So. Writers (vice chancellor 1988, chancellor 1993—97, Cleanth Broutis medal), Poetry Soc. Am., Writers Guild Am. East, Authors League. Democrat. Episcopalian. Home: 1845 Wayside Pl Charlottesville VA 22903-1630 Office Phone: 434-979-5366. Personal E-mail: gpg@virginia.edu.

GARRETT, GORDON HENDERSON, lawyer; b. Charleston, S.C., Aug. 26, 1937; s. Gordon Hughes and Oleda (Henderson) G.; m. Margaret Moore Wilcox, Nov. 2, 1969; children: Elizabeth Wilcox, Caroline Henderson, Gordon Hughes. BS in Commerce, The Citadel, 1959; JD, U. S.C., 1966. Bar: S.C. 1966, U.S. Supreme Ct. 1966, U.S. Ct. Appeals (4th cir.) 1979. Law clk to chief judge U.S. Dist. Ct., Charleston, S.C., 1965-67; pvt. practice Charleston, S.C., 1967—. Mnging. editor, survey editor, mem. editorial bd. S.C. Law Rev., 1965-66. Mem. S.C. Senate, 1969-72; chmn. Charleston, Berkeley and Dorchester Coun. on Alcohol and Drug Abuse, 1973-74; past bd. dirs. Legal Aid Soc., Charleston; mem. S.C. Gov's. Task Force on Corrections. Capt. AGC, U.S. Army, 1959-62. Mem. ABA, S.C. Bar (real estate sect.), Assn. Citadel Men (life). Democrat. Episcopalian. Home: 87 Rutledge Ave Charleston SC 29401-1724 Office: 1075 E Montague Ave Charleston SC 29405-4825

GARRETT, LAURIE, journalist, global health scholar; b. L.A., Sept. 8, 1951; d. Banning and Lou Ann (Pierose) G. BA in biology with honors, U. Calif., Santa Cruz, 1975; postgrad. work in dept. bacteriology and immunology, U. Calif., Berkeley; PhD (hon.), Wesleyan Ill. U., U. Mass., Lowell, 2002. Sci. reporter KPFA, Berkeley, Calif.; with Calif. Dept. Food and Agr.; freelance journalist So. Europe, E. Africa, 1979; freelance reporter, 1980-88; sci. corr. Nat. Public Radio, 1980—88; health and sci. writer Newsday, N.Y.C., 1988—2004; sr. fellow in global health Coun. Fgn. Relations, 2004—. Vis. fellow Harvard Sch. Pub. Health, 1992-93; Editor-at-large, SEED Mag., 2003-. Author: The Coming Plague: Newly Emerging Diseases in a World Out of Balance, 1994, Betrayal of Trust: The Collapse of Global Public Health, 2000 (George C. Polk Award for Best Book, 2000, Nat. Book Critics Award finalist, 2000, Madeline Dane Ross Award, Overseas Press Club of Am., 2001, First Prize Med. Book Competition, Brit. Med. Assn., 2002); contbr. articles to periodicals including Omni, Washington Post, L.A. Times, Foreign Affairs, Vanity Fair, others; frequent guest appearances on Dateline, Jim Lehrer Newshour, ABC Nightline, The Charlie Rose Show, BBC, NPR, CNN, others; contbr. reports including Science Story (George Foster Peabody Broadcasting Award, 1977), Hard Rain: Pests, Pesticides, and People (Edwin Howard Armstrong Award in Broadcast Journalism, 1978), The VDT Controversy (Best Consumer Journalism Award, Nat. Press Club, 1982), Why Children Die in Africa (Meritorious Achievement Award in Radio, San Francisco Media Alliance, 1983, First Prize in Radio, World Hunger Alliance, 1987), AIDS in Africa (J.C. Penney/Mo. Journalism Cert. Merit, Award of Excellence, Nat. Assn. Black Journalists, 1989), Breast Cancer (Best Beat Reporter, Deadline Club N.Y., 1993, First Place Award, Soc. Silurians, 1994), AIDS in India (Bob Considine Award, Overseas Press Club of Am. 1995), Ebola (Madeleine Dane Ross Award, Overseas Press Club of Am., 1996, Pulitzer Prize in Explanatory Journalism, 1996), Crumbled Empire, Shattered Health (George C. Polk Award for Internat. Reporting, 1998), Orphans of AIDS (First Place in Internat. Reporting, NY Assn. Black Journalists, 2000). Named Times Mirror Journalist of Yr., 1996, Alumna of Yr., U. Calif., Santa Cruz, 1996, Champion of Prevention, Centers for Disease Control and Prevention, 1997; recipient Award of Excellence, Nat. Assn. Black Journalists, 1989, Spl. Citation for Outstanding Journalism, AAAS, 1995, Disting. Achievement Award, Ednl. Press Assn. of Am., 1996, Presdl. Citation, APHA, 1996, Pub. Health Hero Award, NYC Dept. Health, 2000, Victor Cohn Prize for Excellence in Med. Sci. Reporting, Coun. for the Advancement of Sci. Writing, 2000, Rsch. in Action Award, Treatment Action Group, 2002. Mem.: Nat. Assn. Sci. Writers. Achievements include Only person ever to be awarded the George Polk Award for Journalism, the George Foster Peabody Award for Broadcasting, and the Pulitzer Prize. Office: Coun Fgn Rels Harold Pratt House 58 E 68th St New York NY 10021

GARRETT, LELAND EARL, nephrologist, educator; b. Spartanburg, S.C., Jan. 8, 1949; s. Leland Earl and Mary Lillian (Butler) G.; m. Sarah Anne Pryor, Aug. 13, 1970 (div. 1978); 1 child, Katherine; m. Nancy Jean Swenson, May 3, 1980; children: Christopher, Jennifer. BS, N.C. State U., 1971; MD, Med. U. S.C., 1976. Commd. 2d lt. USAF, 1971, advanced through grades to lt. col., 1985, ret., 1991; intern Wilford Hall, USAF Med. Ctr., 1976-77; resident USAF Med. Ctr., 1977-79; fellowship Duke U. Med. Ctr., 1979-81; pvt. practice Wake Nephrology Assocs., Raleigh, N.C., 1991—. Clin. prof. medicine U. N.C., Chapel Hill, 1998—. Contbr. articles to profl. jours. Chair-elect Urban Ministries, 2000—01, chmn., 2001—02; mem. adv. chmn. N.C. affiliate Nat. Kidney Found., Charlotte, 1994—2001; med. dir. Open Door Clinic, 1996—98; chmn. Carolina Renal Care, 2000—02; pres. med. staff Raleigh Cmty. Hosp., 2000—02; data chair, bd. dirs. Southeastern Kidney Coun., Raleigh, 1993—97, 1998—, treas., 2000—01, chmn., 2002—; bd. dirs. South Tex. Organ Bank, San Antonio, 1984—86, Urban Ministries, 1997—, treas., 1998—2000; bd. dirs. Carolina Renal Care, 1999—2002. Named Physician of Yr. N.C. affiliate Nat. Kidney Found., 1995. Fellow ACP, Am. Soc. Nephrology, Internat. Soc. Nephrology. Anglican. Avocation: medical informatics. Office: Wake Nephrology Assocs 3604 Bush St Raleigh NC 27609-7511 Office Phone: 919-876-7807. E-mail: legarret@wakenephrology.com.

GARRETT, MARSHALL LEE, anesthesiologist, educator; b. Sacramento, 1951; m. Carol E. Kolbo, June 21, 1986; children: Mackenzie Lee, Lane Christian, William James. BA cum laude, U. of the South, 1972; MD, Creighton U., 1978. Diplomate Am. Bd. Anesthesiology. Intern St. Mary Med. Ctr., Long Beach, Calif., 1978—79; resident in anesthesiology U. Fla., Gainesville, 1979—81; chief fellow cardiothoracic anesthesiology Clevel. Clin. Found., 1988-89; anesthesiologist Cypress Fairbanks Med. Ctr., Houston, 1993—. Assoc. prof. U. Calif. Med. Ctr., Davis, 1983—85, Thomas Jefferson U., Phila., 1985—86. Bible Study fellow. Mem.: Harris County Med. Assn., Tex. Med. Assn., Soc. Cardiothoracic Anesthesiologists, Am. Soc. Anesthesiologists, Phi Beta Kappa.

GARRETT, MATTHEW LANGLEY, music educator; b. Spartanburg, S.C., Nov. 10, 1970; s. Joe Albert and Janet Richards Garrett; life ptnr. Aurelio Manuel Valente, Jan. 2, 1998. MusB in Edn., Fla. State U., 1993; MusM, Boston (Mass.) U., 2000. Cert. tchr. Mass. Choral dir. Mulberry (Fla.) HS and Mid. Sch., 1993—95, Conway Mid. Sch., Orlando, Fla., 1995—98; condr. Vocal Apprenticeship Program Handel and Hayon Soc., Boston, 2000—; choral dir. Hanover (Mass.) Mid. Sch., 2001—03, Hanover (Mass.) HS, 2001—. Leader Music Dept. Hanover (Mass.) Schs., 2002—. Guest condr.: Boston Pub. Schs., 2001—02, Southeastern Mass. Sch. Bandmasters Assn., 2003, 2004. Team sponsor AIDS Walk Boston, 2001—. Mem.: Chorus Am., Mass. Music Educators Assn., Am. Choral Dirs. Assn. (co-chmn. honor choir 2002—04). Democrat. Avocations: music, reading, travel, skiing. Office: Hanover High School 287 Cedar St Hanover MA 02339 Office Phone: 781-878-5450.

GARRETT, NANCY FALES, playwright, educator; b. Bryn Mawr, Pa., July 10, 1943; d. Haliburton and Katharine Ladd Fales; m. Jared Christopher Martin, June 8, 1963 (div. 1972); 1 child, Christian Mastrangelo Martin; m. Kent Garrett, Jan. 21, 1979; 1 child, Kabir William Richard. BA, Barnard Coll., N.Y.C., 1965; MA, Sarah Lawrence Coll., Bronxville, N.Y., 1967. Playwriting tchr. St. Ann's Sch., Bklyn., 1975—; workshop leader West Kortright Ctr., East Meredith, NY, 1987—; dir. Shakespeare in the Valley, East Meredith, NY, 1988—; adj. faculty mem., English N.Y. Tech. Coll., CUNY, Bklyn., 2000—02. Vis. artist Alaska Bd. Edn., Juneau, 1985. Mem. editl. bd. St. Ann's Rev., Bklyn., 2003—; author: (novels) Payback, 1980, (plays) How They Made It, 1969, Predicates: A Dance, 1971, Passion and Garbage, 1972, Surviving Death in Three Acts, 1973, Casserole: An Illusion, 1974, Ark, 1975, Zone of Middle Dimensions, 1977, Nicole Willing, 1978, Indianhead, 1979, Playing in Local Bands, 1982, The Secret Life of Women, 1985, A Hotel Room Somewhere on 8th Avenue, 1984, Long Distance, 1983, The Puppy Show, 1987, Some Sweet Day, 1985, The Northern Kingdom, 2003 (Best Play award Downtown Urban Theater Festival, 2004), (libretto for opera) Dora, 1990, (screenplays) The Stranger, 1990; co-author (with Joie Lee) Farmville, 2004; dir.: (plays) Surviving Death in Three Acts, 1973, Playing in Local Bands, 1985, A Hotel Room Somewhere on 8th Avenue, 1984; co-dir.(with Deborah Dobski): The Stranger, 1992, Dora, 2001, The Northern Kingdom, 2004. Fellow, NEA, 1979, Eugene O'Neill Theater Ctr., 1982, NY Found. for the Arts, 1989. Office: 122 Ashland Pl 9J Brooklyn NY 11201

GARRETT, REGINALD HOOKER, biology professor, researcher; b. Roanoke, Va., Sept. 24, 1939; s. William Walker and Lelia Evelyn (Blankenship) G.; m. Linda Joan Harrison, Mar. 15, 1958 (div.); children: Jeffrey David, Randal Harrison, Robert Martin; m. Catherine Leigh Touchton, June 12, 1989 (div.). BS, Johns Hopkins U., 1964, PhD, 1968. Asst. prof. biology U. Va., 1968-73, assoc. prof., 1973-82, prof., 1982—. Guest prof. U. Paul Sabatier, France, 2003; cons. in field. Author textbooks; contbr. articles to profl. jours. NIH fellow, 1964-68; Fulbright Hays fellow, 1975-76; Thomas Jefferson vis. fellow, 1983; grantee NIH, NSF Mem. Am. Soc. Biochemistry and Molecular Biology, Am. Soc. Microbiology, Am. Soc. Plant Physiology, Soc. Gen. Physiology, Sigma Xi, Phi Lambda Upsilon, Phi Sigma Office: U Va Dept Biology Gilmer Hall Charlottesville VA 22904 Office Phone: 434-982-5494. Business E-Mail: rhg@virginia.edu.

GARRETT, RICHARD G., lawyer; b. NYC, Oct. 16, 1948; BA magna cum laude, Emory U., 1970, JD, 1973. Bar: Ga. 1973, Fla 1979; U.S. Dist. Ct. (no. dist.) Ga. 1973, (so. dist.) Fla. 1979, U.S. Dist. Ct. (so. dist. trial bar) Fla. 1979; U.S. Ct. Appeals (5th cir.) 1974; U.S. Ct. Appeals (9th. cir., 11 cir.) 1981; U.S. Supreme Ct. 1981. Program dir., instr. rsch., writing and advocacy Emory U. Sch. Law, 1972-73; gen. counsel Greenberg, Traurig, Miami, Fla., prin. shareholder, 1978—. Past chmn. litigation dept., exec. com. bd. dirs. Greenberg, Traurig, Miami. Editor Emory Law Journal, 1972-73. Recipient 1st place and Best Brief award Region V Nat. Moot Ct. Competition, 1972. Mem. ABA, The Fla. Bar Assn., State Bar Ga., Omicron Delta Kappa, Order of the Barristers. Office: Greenberg Traurig LLP 1221 Brickell Ave Miami FL 33131-3224 Office Fax: 305-579-0717. Business E-Mail: garrettr@gtlaw.com.*

GARRETT, ROBERT, investment banker, director; b. Morristown, N.J., Feb. 27, 1937; s. Harrison and Grace Dodge (Rea) G.; m. Jacqueline E. Marlas, July 10, 1965; children: Robert Jr., Johnson. AB, Princeton U., 1959; MBA, Harvard U., 1965. V.p. Smith, Barney & Co., N.Y.C., 1965-69, Robert Garrett & Sons, N.Y.C. and Balt., 1969-71; 1st v.p. Smith, Barney, Harris Upham & Co., N.Y.C., 1972-78; sr. v.p. Smith, Barney Real Estate Corp., N.Y.C., 1978-84; exec. v.p. Security Capital Corp., N.Y.C., 1978-85; pres. Robert Garrett & Sons Inc., N.Y.C., 1986—. Pres. AdMedia Ptnrs. Inc., 1990-2005, founder, mng. dir. 2005—; bd. dirs. Mickelberry Corp.; chmn. bd. dirs. Penn Virginia Corp. Trustee Cleveland H. Dodge Found., Abell Found., N.Y. Bot. Garden, Adirondack Mus. With AUS, 1959-63. Mem. Univ. Club of N.Y., Nantucket Yacht Club, Knickerbocker Club of N.Y. Republican. Episcopalian. Home: 800 Park Ave New York NY 10021-2760 Office: 444 Madison Ave New York NY 10022-6903 Office Phone: 212-759-1870.

GARRETT, SANDY LANGLEY, school system administrator; b. Muskogee, Okla., Feb. 8, 1943; 1 child, Charles Langley (Chuck). BS in Elem. Edn., Northeastern U., Tahlequah, Okla., 1968, MS in Counseling, 1980; grad. John F. Kennedy Sch. Govt., Harvard U., 1989. Lic. tchr., adminstr., supt. std., Okla. Tchr. Hilldale Schs., Muskogee, Okla., 1968-80; coord. gifted program Hillsdale Schs., Muskogee, Okla., 1980-82; coord. gifted and talented State Dept. Edn., Oklahoma City, 1982-85, dir. rural edn., 1985-87, exec. dir. ednl. svcs., 1987-88, state supt. pub. instrn., 1991-95; sec. edn. Gov.'s Office, Oklahoma City, 1988—; supt. pub. instrn. Okla. Dept. Edn., Oklahoma City, 1991—. Chair State Bd. Edn., Oklahoma City, 1991—, State Vo-Tech. Edn., Oklahoma City, 1991—; bd. dirs. So. Regional Edn. Bd.; regent Okla. Colls., 1991—; mem. Nat. Coll. Bd. Equality Project; chair. Okla. Lit. Initiatives Commn.; mem. So. Regional Ednl. Bd. Co-author: (curriculum guide) Gifted Galaxy; mem. editorial bd. Rural and Small Schs.; contbr. articles to profl. jours. Co-chair Dem. Party, Muskogee, 1978; del. Dem. Nat. Conv., N.Y.C., 1980, 82; mem. Leadership Okla., 1990. Recipient Cecil Yarbrough award, 1989, Claude Dyer Legis. award, 1989. Mem. Muskogee County Ednl. Assn., Delta Kappa Gamma, Phi Delta Kappa, Delta Kappa Gamma. Methodist. Avocations: tennis, swimming, computer programming, travel, politics. Office: State Dept Edn 2500 N Lincoln Blvd Oklahoma City OK 73105-4503*

GARRETT, SCOTT T., medical products executive; BS in Mech. Engring., Valparaiso U.; MBA, Lake Forest Grad. Sch. Mgmt. Various positions Baxter Internat., Am. Hosp. Supply Corp.; chmn. Dade Behring, 1994—97; interim CEO Kendro Lab. Products, L.P., 2000; CEO Garrett Capital Advisors; pres., clin. diagnostic divsn. Beckman Coulter, Fullerton, Calif., 2002—03, pres., COO, 2003—05, pres., CEO, 2005—. Chmn. LifeStream Internat.; vice chmn. Kendro Lab. Products; dir. Inovision Holdings, Sunol Molecular Corp., Biotrin Holdings plc, Ability One Corp., Lake Forest Hosp. Found.; mem., adv. bd. Radius Ventures. Office: Beckman Coulter 4300 N Harbor Blvd PO Box 3100 Fullerton CA 92834-3100*

GARRETT, SHARON, health services company executive; B in Econs., MPH, PhD, UCLA. Formerly with Hyatt Med. Enterprises, VA, Am. Heart Assn., Cath. Hosp. Assn., Calif. Dept. Health Svcs.; former dep. dir. UCLA Med. Ctr.; chief info. officer The Walt Disney Co., 1989—2000; exec. v.p. enterprise svcs. PacifiCare Health Systems, Inc., Cypress, Calif., 2000—. Bd. dirs. Ross Stores, Corio. Office: PacifiCare Health Systems Inc 5995 Plaza Dr Cypress CA 90630

GARRETT, STEVEN LURIE, physicist; b. LA, Apr. 3, 1949; s. Fred Ellis and Vivian Dorothy (Lurie) Garrett. BS in Physics, UCLA, 1970, MS in Physics, 1972, PhD in Physics, 1977. Asst. prof. Naval Postgrad. Sch., Monterey, Calif., 1981-85, assoc. prof., 1985-88, prof., 1988-95; United Techs. prof. of Acoustics Pa. State Univ., State College, Pa., 1995—. Rosen prof. Technion, Haifa, Israel, 1985; cons. in field, 1982—. Contbr. Fellow, Miller Inst. Basic Rsch. in Sci., 1978—81. Fellow: Acoustical Soc. Am. (Hunt fellow 1978, Silver Medal in Phys. Acoustics and Engring. Acoustics 1993); mem.: Soc. Audio Engrs., Sigma Xi. Achievements include patents in field. Home: PO Box 10271 State College PA 16805-0271 Office: Grad Program in Acoustics PO Box 30 State College PA 16804-0030 Office Phone: 814-863-6373. Business E-Mail: sxg185@psu.edu. E-mail: garrett@thermoacousticscorp.com.

GARRETT, THEODORE LOUIS, lawyer; b. New Britain, Conn., Sept. 4, 1943; s. Louis and Sylvia (Greenberg) G.; m. Bonnie Garrett, Nov. 27, 1968; children— Brandon, Natalie. BA, Yale Coll., 1961—65; JD, Columbia Law Sch., 1965—68. Bar: NY 1968, DC 1971, US Supreme Ct. 1973, all eleven US Cts. Appeals. Law clk. to Judge J. Joseph Smith US Ct. Appeals for 2d Circuit, 1968-69; spl. asst. to asst. atty. gen. William H. Rehnquist US Dept. Justice, DC, 1969-70; law clk. to Chief Justice Warren E. Burger US Supreme Ct., 1970-71; assoc. Covington & Burling, DC, 1971-76, ptnr., 1976—, co-chmn. Environ. Practice Group. Editor, prin. author: Corporate Counsel Environmental Law Guide, 1993; author: Environmental Law and the Eleventh Amendment, 2000, Downwind Ozone: Clearing the Air, 2004; co-author: Clean Air Act Desk Book, 1991; contbg. author: A Practical Guide to Environmental Law, 1987, Liability for Hazardous Waste Sites Under CERCLA, 1988, Practice Under the New Federal Sentencing Guidelines, 4th edit., 2001, Environmental Dispute Handbook, 1991, Environmental Litigation, 2d edit., 1999; editor, contbg. author: The Environmental Law Manual, 1992, RCRA Policy Documents, 1993, RCRA Practice Manual, 2d edit., 2004; contbr. articles to profl. jours. Editl. bd. Chem. Waste Lit. Reporter; environment adv. com. Columbia Law Sch.; hazardous waste com. Ctr. Pub. Resources. Named One of 100 Most Influential US Lawyers, Nat. Law Jour., 1994. Mem. ABA (sect. environ., energy and resources chair 2000-01, mem. exec. com. 1995-2001, exec. bd. Environ. Lawyer, adv. bd. ABA Jour., contbg. author Trends, mem. task force on superfund reform, liaison standing com. on environ. law, chair environment and natural resources section, 2000-01), D.C. Bar Assn. (steering com. environment, energy and natural resources sect., 1991-97, co-chair 1992-94, chair coun. on sects, 94-95). Avocations: piano, tennis, woodworking, gardening. Office: Covington & Burling 1201 Pennsylvania Ave NW PO Box 7566 Washington DC 20044-7566 Office Phone: 202-662-6000. Office Fax: 202-662-6291. Business E-Mail: tgarrett@cov.com.

GARRETT, THOMAS W., retired career officer; b. Jan. 2, 1947; B, US Mil. Acad., West Point, NY; M in counseling Psychology, Duke U.; grad., Armed Forces Staff Coll., Army War Coll. Commd. officer US Army, commdg. Aviation Brigade of the 101st Airborne Division (Air Assault) during Desert Storm, advanced through grades to maj. gen., deputy commdg. gen. of I Corps, human resources dir., commdg. gen. Total Army Pers. Command, 1997—, asst. divsn. comdr. of the 101st Airborne; commdg. gen. US Army Personnel Command, Alexandria, Va.; ret. US Army; risk mgmt. dir., commdg. gen. US Army Safety Ctr.; assoc. Navigator Develop. Group, Inc., Enterprise, Ala. Taught behavioral science and leadership West Point; chief of staff US Army Aviation Ctr. and Sch.; prin. ptnr. Broad River Group, LLC; staff mem. Inst. for Def. Analysis. Office: Navigator Develop Group Inc 116 S Main St Ste 214 PO Box 310069 Enterprise AL 36330-0069 Office Phone: 334-347-7612. Office Fax: 334-347-2582.

GARRETT, WENDELL, antiques appraiser, historian, editor; BA in Am. History, UCLA; MA, Winterthur Program, U. Del.; MA in Am. History, Harvard U. Worked with the Adams Papers Mass. Hist. Soc., 1959—66; asst. editor The Diary and Autobiography of John Adams (4 vols.); assoc. editor first 2 vols. of Adams Family correspondence; editor, pub. The Magazine Antiques, 1966—90; sr. v.p., Americana Sotheby's, N.Y.C., 1990—; regular feature appraiser PBS' Antiques Roadshow. Editor: John Adams diary, 1965; author: Classic America: The Federal Style & Beyond, 1992, George Washington's Mount Vernon, 1999; co-author (with David Larkin): Victorian America: Classical Romanticisim to Gilded Opulence, 1993; author: American Home: From Colonial Simplicity to the Modern Adventure, 2001. Chmn., bd. trustees Thomas Jefferson Meml. Found., Monticello, 1987—93. Recipient Henry Francis du Pont award for Disting. Contbn. to the Am. Arts, 1994. Office: Sothebys 1334 York Ave New York NY 10021 Home: 279E 44th St Apt 18C New York NY 01001 Office Phone: 212-606-7137.

GARRETT, WILBUR (BILL GARRETT), magazine editor; b. Kansas City, Mo., Sept. 4, 1930; s. Clay Dean and Cecil Zora (Melton) Garrett; m. Lucille Hall, Dec. 26, 1950; children: Michael Dean, Kenneth Lewis. BJ, U. Mo., 1954; LittD (hon.), U. Miami. With Nat. Geog. Mag., 1954—90, editor, 1980—90; faculty photojournalism workshop U. Mo., 1963, 1964, 1969, 1970, 1973, 1974, 1975, 1977, 1978, 1979, 1980, 1994; editor Cosmos Jour., 1995—98. Mem. XIX Olympiad Cultural Com.; bd. dirs. Congentrix Energy, Inc., Nat. Geographic Soc., 1980—90, rsch. and exploration com., 1981—90; bd. advisors Corbis Prodns., Inc., Ptnrs. for Livable Cmtys. Designer (photog. exhbn.) U.S. Pavilion, N.Y.'s World Fair, 1965, designer, prodr. (exhibitions) Nat. Geog. Soc. Exhbns. 23d, 24th, 25th Picture of Yr. Competition. Bd. govs. The Nature Conservancy, 1988—98, Am. Land Conservancy; trustee W. Eugene Smith Meml. Fund; founder, pres. La Ruta Maya Conservation Found., 1990; bd. dirs. Heritage U.S.A. With USNR, 1946—52. Decorated Order of the Quetzal Guatemala; recipient Newhouse citation, U. Syracuse, 1963, Nat. Mag. awards for Excellence, 1984, 1989, 1990, 1991, Leadership Medal, UN Environ. Programme, 1990, Chevron Environ. award, 1990, La

Pluma Plata, Pres. of Mex., 1990, Rotondi award, Italy, 1998. Mem.: Cosmos Club (Washington). Home and Office: 209 Seneca Rd Great Falls VA 22066-1108 E-mail: billgarret@aol.com.

GARRIGLE, WILLIAM ALOYSIUS, lawyer; b. Camden, N.J., Aug. 6, 1941; s. John Michael and Catherine Agnes (Ebeling) G.; m. Jeannette R. Regan, Aug. 15, 1965 (div.); children: Maeve Regan, Emily Way; m. Rosalind Chadwick, Feb. 17, 1984; 1 child, Susan Chadwick. BS, LaSalle U., 1963; LLB, Boston Coll., 1966. Bar: N.J. 1966, U.S. Dist. Ct. N.J., U.S. Ct. Appeals (3rd cir.) 1973, U.S. Supreme Ct., 1973; cert. civil trial atty., N.J.; cert. civil trial adv., Nat. Bd. Trial Advocacy; diplomate Am. Bd. Profl. Liability Attys. Assoc. Taylor, Bischoff, Neutze & Williams, Camden, NJ, 1966-67, Moss & Powell, 1967-70; ptnr. Garrigle and Palm, Cherry Hill, 1970—. Sr. counsel Am. Coll. Barristers. With USAR, 1959-67. Mem. ABA, N.J. State Bar Assn., Burlington County Bar Assn., Camden County Bar Assn., Internat. Assn. Def. Counsel, Def. Rsch. Inst., N.J. Def. Assn., Am. Bd. Trial Advs. (diplomate; pres. South Jersey chpt. 2001), Fedn. of Ins. and Corp. Counsel, Trial Attys. N.J., Camden County Inn of Ct. (master of the bench, chmn. 1989-96, treas. 1996-2004), Tavistock Country Club. Home: 223 E Main St Moorestown NJ 08057-2905 Office: Garrigle and Palm 1415 Route 70 E Ste 311 Cherry Hill NJ 08034-2237 Office Phone: 856-427-9300. Personal E-mail: garrigle@aol.com.

GARRIOTT, OWEN KAY, astronaut, scientist; b. Enid, Okla., Nov. 22, 1930; m. Evelyn Long; children by previous marriage: Randall O., Robert K., Richard A., Linda S. BSEE, U. Okla., 1953; MS, Stanford U., 1957, PhD, 1960; DSc (hon.), Phillips U., Enid, 1973. NSF fellow Cambridge (Eng.) U., Radio Research Sta., Slough, Eng., 1960-61; asst. and assoc. prof. elec. engring. Stanford U., 1961-65; astronaut, scientist Johnson Space Ctr. NASA, Houston, 1965-86, sci. pilot Skylab-3, 1973, dep. dir. Sci. and Applications Directorate, 1974-76, dir. Sci. and Applications Directorate, 1976, asst. dir. for space and life scis., 77-78, mission specialist on first Spacelab flight, 1983, project scientist Space Sta. Program, 1984-86; v.p. Space Programs Teledyne Brown Engring., Huntsville, Ala., 1988-93; co-founder Enid (Okla.) Arts and Scis. Found., 1993; adj. prof. lab. for structural biology U. Ala. in Huntsville. Served with USN, 1953-56. Recipient Disting. Svc. medal NASA, 1973, Gold medal City of Chgo., 1974, Robert J. Collier trophy, 1974, V.M. Komarov diploma Fedn. Aeronautique Internationale, 1974, Robert H. Goddard Meml. trophy, 1975; inducted into Okla. Hall of Fame, 1980, U.S. Astronaut Hall of Fame, 1997, Okla. Mil. Hall of Fame, 2000. Fellow Am. Astronautical Soc., AIAA (assoc.); mem. IEEE, Am. Geophys. Union, Assn. Space Explorers, Internat. Acad. Astronautics, Astronaut Scholarship Found. (past chmn. bd. dirs.), Sigma Xi, Tau Beta Pi, Eta Kappa Nu.

GARRIS, CHARLES ALEXANDER, mechanical engineer, educator; b. Pomona, Calif., Feb. 2, 1944; s. Charles Alexander and Kathleen Ann (White) G.; m. Eugenia Dolores Cardenas, Sept. 11, 1971; children: Charles Alexander, Eugenia Catalina. B Engring., SUNY, N.Y.C., 1965; MS, SUNY, Stony Brook, 1968, PhD, 1971. Registered profl. engr.; registered patent agt. Va. Rsch. chief mech. engr. dept. Venezuela Inst. Sci. Rsch., Caracas, 1971-73, chief mech. engring., 1976-78; rsch. assoc. MIT, Cambridge, 1973-76; prof. engring. George Washington U., Washington, 1978—; program dir. NSF. Cons. in field. Contbr. articles to engring. publs.; patentee in field. Fellow: AIAA, ASME, Am. Soc. Engring. Edn., Sigma Xi, Pi Tau Sigma. Roman Catholic. Avocations: bicycling, boating, swimming. Office: George Washington U Dept of Mech and Aerospace Engring Washington DC 20052-0001 Home: 2125 Twin Mill Ln Oakton VA 22124-1022 Office Phone: 202-994-3646. Business E-Mail: garris@gwu.edu.

GARRIS, MICHAEL JACK, lawyer; b. Ann Arbor, Mich., May 24, 1954; s. Jack John and Helen (Cazepis) G. BA, U. Mich., 1976; JD, Wayne State U., 1979. Bar: Mich. 1979, Fla. 1980, U.S. Dist. Ct. (ea. dist.) Mich. 1979. Ptnr. Garris, Garris, Garris & Garris, PC, Ann Arbor, 1979—. Mem. Washtenaw County Trial Lawyers, Mich. Trial Lawyers Assn., Assn. Trial Lawyers Am., ABA. Greek Orthodox. Office: Garris Garris Garris & Garris PC 300 E Washington St Ann Arbor MI 48104-2000

GARRISH, THEODORE JOHN, lawyer; b. Detroit, Jan. 6, 1943; s. Theodore and Adella Beatrice (Kimball) Garrish; m. Joy Ann Ziegler, Aug. 4, 1967 (div. 1979); children: Theodore John, Amelia Sutter. AB, U. Mich., 1964; JD cum laude, Wayne State U., 1968. Bar: Mich. 1969, DC 1972. Trial atty. U.S. Dept. Justice, Washington, 1969-72; pub. opinion analyst Com. for Reelection of Pres., Washington, 1972; chief advt. substantiation FTC, Washington, 1973-74; asst. spl. counsel to Pres. Washington, 1974; asst. to sec. U.S. Dept. Interior, Washington, 1976, legis. counsel, 1981-82; gen. counsel Consumer Product Safety Commn., Washington, 1976-78; ptnr. Deane, Snowdon, Shutler, Garrish & Gherardi, Washington, 1978-81; gen. counsel Dept. Energy, Washington, 1983-85, asst. sec., 1985-89; fed. insp. Alaska Natural Gas Transp. Sys., 1986-89; Wash. counsel Flanagan Group, 1989-91; pres. Brewery Mgmt. Co., 1989-94, Kent Island Investment Co., 1989-91, chmn., 1991-94; mng. ptnr. Wild Gooose Brewery, 1989-91, dir., 1994-98; v.p. Hospitality Assocs., Washington, 2002—. Mem. U.S. Adminstrv. Conf., Washington, 1976—78, Washington, 1983—85, Pres.'s Commn. Catastrophic Nuc. Accidents, 1988—90; sr. v.p. Am. Nuc. Energy Coun., 1991—94; v.p. Nuc. Energy Inst., 1994—2000; energy program mgr. Bechtel Nat., Inc., 2001—03; dep. dir. Office Civilian Radioactive Waste Mgmt., Dept. Energy, Washington, 2003—05; v.p. fed. ops. and strategic planning CH2M Hill, 2005—. Advisor Nat. Policy Forum, 1994—96; dir. Nat. Energy Resources Orgn., 1987—2001, counsel, 2001—03; asst. to group dir. Pres. Inaugural Com., 1973, dep. exec. dir., 1981; mem. adv. com. human concerns Rep. Nat. Com., 1979; del. Mich. Rep. Conv., 1966. Mem.: DC Bar Assn., Mich. Bar Assn., Fed. Bar Assn., Alpha Delta Phi. Congregationalist. Home: 103 Chesapeake Ave Annapolis MD 21403-3305 Office: 555 11th St NW Washington DC 20004 Office Phone: 202-586-6850, 202-393-2426. Personal E-mail: tedco2000@hotmail.com.

GARRISON, ANN MCBRAYER, retired gift and antique shop owner; b. Lawrenceburg, Ky., Aug. 19, 1925; d. Wesley and Emma Lee (Van Arsdell) McBrayer; m. Rumsey Elliott Garrison, Mar. 8, 1947 (div. Feb. 1964); 1 child, Elliott Wesley. Student, U. Ky., 1943-45. Tchr. music, piano, voice, dance, Lawrenceburg, Ky., 1945-75; continuity writer Sta. WVLK, Lexington, Ky., 1964-65; labor market analyst Ky. State Govt., Frankfort, 1965-82; antique dealer Annie's Gifts and Antiques, Lawrenceburg, 1977—. Author: Going Home, Come In, Mrs. Murphy, cook book A Taste of Mama's Cooking, verse Silhouettes. Mem. Ky. Fedn. Music Clubs, 1945-75, Ky. Hist. Soc., Frankfort, 1965—, Harrison Fisher Soc., 1965—, Kate Greenway Soc., 1965—. Mem. DAR, Tenure Club, Lawrenceburg Mchts'. Assn., Phi Beta, Kappa Delta, Anderson Humane Soc. Democrat. Methodist. Home: 135 Broadway And Elm Lawrenceburg KY 40342

GARRISON, ANNE-MARIE DICKINSON, middle school educator; b. Fredericksburg, Va., May 21, 1947; d. Robert DuVal and Anne (Dawideit) Dickinson; m. Gary Leroy Garrison, Dec. 23, 1972; children: Stephen, Christine. BA in Math., Duke U., 1969. Cert. tchr., Va. Tchr. Stafford (Va.) County Schs., 1972—. Mem. Fredericksburg Full Gospel Fellowship. Mem. Nat. Coun. Math. Tchrs Republican. Avocation: reading. Home: 1525 Clover Dr Fredericksburg VA 22407-4820 Office: Stafford Mid Sch 101 Spartan Ln Stafford VA 22554-5453 Office Phone: 540-658-6210.

GARRISON, ARLENE ALLEN, academic administrator, engineering educator; BA in Liberal Arts, U. Tenn., 1975, PhD in Analytical Chemistry, 1981, BSEE, 1988. Instr. analytical chemistry, grad. rsch. asst. U. Tenn., Knoxville, 1975-81, rsch. assoc., 1981, sr. electonic design engr. dept. chemistry, 1985-89, rsch. asst. prof. dept. chemistry, 1989—; dir. measurement and control engring. ctr. Coll. Engring. U. Tenn., Knoxville; licensing exec. U. Tenn., Knoxville, 1998-99, dir. industry programs and tech. transfer, 1999-2000, asst. v.p., 2000—. Mem. NRC bd. assessment for Nat. Inst. Standards and Tech., Panel for Chem. Sci. and Tech., 1996-2001; mem. chemistry dept. alumni steering com. U. Tenn. Knoxville, 1994—; participant in NATO Advanced Study Inst. on Analytical Applications of Fourier transform infrared to Molecular and Biolog. Systems, Florence, Italy, 1980; organizer insl. spectroscopy symposium Internat. Conf. on Raman Spectroscopy, Hong Kong; co-chair Soc. Photo-Optical Instrumentation Engrs. conf. on optical methods for chem. process control, 1994; sci. bd. Iternat. Forum Process Analytical Chemistry, 1993-2002; presenter in field. Contbr. over 29 articles to profl. jours. Chair bd. trustees Fountain City United Meth. Ch., 1991-94; sec. Wesley Found. Bd., 1992-93; bd. dirs. Appalachian Sci. Fair, 1993-2003, WATTec, 1994-96, Discovery Ctr., 1995-98; mem. Pub. Bldg. Authority, 1995—, chair, 2000-02, Tenn. Econ. Coun. Women, 2002—. Recipient Chancellors Citation for extraordinay cmty. svc., 1993. Mem. Soc. for Applied Spectroscopy (Meggars award 1982), Soc. of Photo Instrumentation Engrs., Coblentz Soc. (bd. mgrs. 1989-92, pres. 1997-98), Am. Chem. Soc. (sec. East Tenn. sect. 1988-90, chair-elect 1991, chair 1992, steering com. divsns. chem. edn. and analytical chemistry, chair Williams Wright award com. 1991, 92). Phi Beta Kappa, Phi Kappa Phi, Alpha Lambda Delta, Tau Beta Pi. Office: U Tenn Office Rsch 1534 White Ave Knoxville TN 37996-1529 Business E-Mail: garrison@utk.edu.

GARRISON, BARBARA JANE, chemistry professor; b. Big Rapids, Mich., Mar. 7, 1949; BS, Ariz. State U., 1971; PhD in Chemistry, U. Calif., Berkeley, 1975. Rsch. fellow in chemistry Purdue U., Lafayette, Ind., 1975-77; lectr. U. Calif., Berkeley, 1977-78; from asst. prof. to assoc. prof. Pa. State U., University Park, 1979-86, prof. chemistry, 1986—, head dept. chemistry, 1989-94, Disting. prof. chemistry, 2000—02, Shapiro prof. chemistry, 2002—. Vis. asst. prof. Purdue U., 1978-79; vis. assoc. chemistry Calif. Inst. Tech., 1985-86. Alfred P. Sloan Found. rsch. fellow, 1980. Fellow Am. Phys. Soc., Am. Vacuum Soc.; mem. Am. Chem. Soc. (Francis P. Garvan - John M. Olin medal 1994). Office: Pa State U Dept Chemistry 104 Chemistry Bldg University Park PA 16802-4615

GARRISON, CAROL Z., academic administrator; b. Upper Montclair, N.J. BA, U. N.C., Chapel Hill, 1974; MS in nursing, U. Ala., Birmingham, 1976; PhD, U. N.C., Chapel Hill, 1982. Cert. nurse practitioner, U. Ala. Birmingham, 1978. Asst. prof. nursing U. Ala., Birmingham, 1976—78, U. N.C., 1978—82; faculty U. S.C., 1982—92, prof. and chair epidemiology and biostatistics, 1992—97, assoc. provost, 1994—97, dean grad. sch., 1994—97; provost U. Louisville, 1997—2002, acting pres., 2002; pres. U. Ala., Birmingham, 2002—. Office: AB 7070 1530 3rd Ave S Birmingham AL 35294-0110

GARRISON, DAVID EARL, artist; b. Jacksonville, Ill., Mar. 23, 1940; s. James Enger and Grace Heart Garrison; children: David Alan, Steven Boyd, Todd Spencer. Grad., Am. Acad. Art, 1969; BA, Iowa Wesleyan Coll., 1987. Cons. youth Iowa Arts Coun., 1985—2001; tchr. pastel workshops Pastel Soc. Am., 1996—2005. Exhibitions include Oil Painters Assn., Chgo., San Antonio, Hudson Valley Art Assn., White Plains, N.Y., Pastel Soc. Am. and Art du Pastel En Normandie in France, Yvetot and Vernon, 2002, Butler Inst. Am. Art, Youngstown, Ohio, 2003, Art du Pastel En France at Centre Philippe, Vernon, 2003. Mem.: Hudson Valley Art Assn., Am. Artist Profl. League, Nat. Soc. Mural Painters, Am. Impressionist Soc., Mural Painters of USA, Pastel Soc. Am. Avocation: tennis. Home and Studio: Garrison Art Studio 831 S Garfield Burlington IA 52601 Office Phone: 319-753-0809. E-mail: cniore@aol.com.

GARRISON, DAVID LACEY, JR., oil industry executive; b. Houston, July 12, 1945; s. David Lacey and Marie Bel (Gardiner) G.; m. Pamela Jean Reid Adger, Mar. 7, 1970 (div. July 1975); 1 child, James Gardiner; m. Robin Childers, Apr. 2, 1977; children: Robert Adam, Susan Alexandra. LLD, La Academia Mexicana, Mexico City, 1991. Landman Chapman Oil Co., Houston, 1978; ptnr. J.A. Bel et al, Lake Charles, La., 1964—; pres. Garrison Oil Co., Houston, 1979—84, Lakeside Exploration Corp., Houston, 1984—. V.p., bd. dirs. Lacassane Co., Inc., Lake Charles, 1990—. La. commr. of Indian Affairs, Baton Rouge, 1972—75; vice-chmn. Sam Houston Area coun. Boy Scouts Am., 1995—, bd. dirs. So. Region, 1999—; bd. dirs. Nat. Cath. Com. on Scouting, 1997—2001. Decorated knight comdr. Pontificial Order St. Gregory the Gt. (Vatican City), knight grand comdr. Equestrian Order of the Holy Sepulchre, knight grand cross with gold star with collar Sacred Mil. Constantinian Order of St. George, knight sovereign Mil. Order of Malta (Rome), knight of justice Most Venerable Order of St. John (U.K.). Roman Catholic. Avocations: hunting, fishing. Home: 3731 Olympia Dr Houston TX 77019-3029 Office: Garrison Properties 3939 Essex Ln Ste 100 Houston TX 77027-5190 E-mail: dlgarrison@houston.rr.com.

GARRISON, ELIZABETH JANE, artist; b. Elmira, N.Y., Feb. 11, 1952; BFA, Ringling Sch. Art and Design, 1973; postgrad., Mansfield U., 1976-78; MS, Fla. State U., 1980. Exhibits include Mus. Contemporary Art, The Netherlands, Mus. Fine Arts, St. Petersburg, Fla., Renwick Gallery, The Smithsonian Inst., Washington, and others; represented in permanent collections Yale U. Art Gallery, New Haven, Conn., Kunstgewerbe Mus., Berlin, Honolulu Acad. Arts, Mus. Fine Arts, Houston. Nat. Endowment Arts fellows, 1981, 88; Saltonstall Found. grantee, 1996. Home: 317 Elm St Ithaca NY 14850-3018

GARRISON, GENEVA, retired administrative assistant; b. Bowling Green, Ky., Feb. 14, 1933; d. Claude Harrison and Helen (Bohannon) Garrison; m. Marion Murphey Dare, Jr., Aug. 1955 (div. Mar. 1972); 1 child, Marcus Glenn. AAS, U. Louisville, 1975, BLS summa cum laude, 1977. Tchr. behavior disorders, learning disabilities, mentally handicapped Jefferson County Schs., Louisville, 1974—77; coord. parent edn. project U. Louisville, 1977—79; exec. sec. to dir. AHES Western Ky. U., Bowling Green, 1980, sec., asst. to dir. devel., 1980—84, exec. sec. to exec. v.p. adminstrv. affairs, 1984—87, sec. to pres., 1987—89; ret., 1989. Part-time crisis counselor LifeSkills Inc., Bowling Green, 1993—96. Author: (poetry) to profl. jours. Recipient Omicron Delta Kappa Outstanding Grad. Sr. award, U. Louisville, 1978. Mem.: AAUW, DAR, Warren County Ret. Tchrs. Assn., Ky. Ret. Tchrs. Assn., So. Appalachian Nature Photography Club, Internat. Soc. Poets, Phi Kappa Phi (scholar 1978). Avocations: photography, walking, reading, travel. Home: 733 Newman Way Bowling Green KY 42104-3810

GARRISON, GUY GRADY, librarian, educator; b. Akron, Ohio, Dec. 17, 1927; s. Grady and Emma (Dodson) G.; m. Joanne Ruth Sergeant, Mar. 22, 1964; 1 dau., Anne Olivia. BA, Baldwin-Wallace Coll., 1950; MS, Columbia U., 1954; PhD, U. Ill., 1960. Mem. staff Oak Park (Ill.) Pub. Library, 1954-58; head reader services Kansas City (Mo.) Pub. Library, 1960-62; prof., dir. library research center Grad. Sch. Library Sci., U. Ill., 1962-68; prof., dean Coll. Info. Studies, Drexel U., 1968-87, Alice B. Kroeger prof., 1987-91, dean emeritus, prof. emeritus, 1992—. Contbr. articles to profl. jours. Served with AUS, 1950-52. Mem. ALA, Assn. for Library and Info. Sci. Edn., Beta Phi Mu. Home: 731 Limehouse Rd Wayne PA 19087-2856 E-mail: guy.garrison@drexel.edu.

GARRISON, JOHN RAYMOND, organization executive; b. Bridgeton, NJ, Jan. 30, 1938; s. Raymond Wilson and Clara Ella (Moore) G.; m. Sally Anne Woodruff, Sept. 10, 1960; children: Glenn Thomas Wilson, Matthew Moore. AB, Harvard U., 1960; MPA (scholastic award), NYU, 1964. Adminstrv. asst. N.Y. State Banking Dept., 1962-63; planner N.J. Dept. Econ. Devel. and Conservation, 1963-64; sr. planner N.Y. State Office Regional Devel., 1964-66; mem. staff Gov. N.Y. State Exec. Chamber, 1966-71; program sec. Office of Lt. Gov., NY, 1971-73; dep. commr. adminstrn. N.Y. State Health Dept., 1973-75; exec. v.p. Hosp. Assn. N.Y. State, 1975-78; CEO Nat. Easter Seal Soc., 1978—90, Am. Lung Assn., N.Y.C., 1990—2001, Cherish Our Children Internat., Shiloh, NJ, 2001—; pres. J.R. Garrison and Assocs., 2001—. Bd. dirs. Internat. Union Against TB and Lung Disease, 1996—2003, World No Tobacco Day, 1999—, Health Care Choices, 1997—; mem. Nat. Bd. for Respiratory Care, 2003—. Mem.: Harvard Club (NYC). Office: JR Garrison and Assocs PO Box 209 Shiloh NJ 08353 Office Phone: 856-453-1288. Personal E-mail: jrg@jrgarrison.com.

GARRISON, LARRY RICHARD, accounting educator; b. Kansas City, Mo., Jan. 10, 1951; s. Robert Milton and Virginia Claire (Huntington) G.; m. Sheila Caroline Murry, Aug. 10, 1973. BBA, Cen. Mo. State U., 1973; MS in Acctg., U. Mo., 1982; PhD, U. Nebr., 1986. CPA, Mo. Mgr. Garrison & Co., CPAs, Kansas City, 1973-79; controller G.F. & F. Enterprises, Kansas City, 1979-82; instr. U. Nebr., Lincoln, 1983-86; prof. U. Mo., Kansas City, 1986—. Exec. dir. Tax Policy Rsch. Project. Contbr. articles to profl. jours. Recipient Disting. Teaching award U. Nebr., 1984-85. Mem. Am. Inst. CPA's, Am. Taxation Assn., N.Am. Acctg. Soc. (past pres.), Mo. Assn. Acctg. Educators (past pres.), Mo. Soc. CPA's (Outstanding Educator of Yr. award 1999, Pierson Tchg. award), Am. Acctg. Assn., Beta Alpha Psi, Beta Gamma Sigma. Office: U Mo 5100 Rockhill Rd Kansas City MO 64110-2481

GARRISON, MAURICE ALLEN MARTIN, missionary, minister; b. Margie, Minn., Sept. 4, 1924; s. Edward Richard and Malvina Anna (Brown) G.; 1 foster child, Simeon Ben. BS(med.), U. Minn., 1946, BA cum laude, 1947; STB, Gen. Theol. Sem., N.Y.C., 1952, STM, 1954; grad., Macalester Coll., St. Paul, 1943. Ordained priest, Episc. Ch., 1953. Lectr. St. Andrew's Sem., Manila, The Philippines, 1953-57; founder St. Mary's Sem., Odibo, Namibia, 1962-66; lectr. St. John's Sem., Lusaka, Zambia, 1967; prin. Codrington Coll., Barbados, 1969-70; lectr. Trinity Coll., Legon, Ghana, 1979-85, St. Paul's Theol. Coll., Limuru, Kenya, 1985-87, St. Mark's Theol. Coll., Dar es Salaam, Tanzania, 1987-89, 92-94; apptd. missionary Episc. Ch. U.S.A., 1953-57, 80-90, ret., 1990. Curate Trinity Ch., N.Y.C., 1957-61, 72-73; parish priest Resurrection Ch., N.Y.C., 1970-71, Church House, Khartoum, Sudan, 1981, St. Matthew Ch., Addis Ababa, Ethiopia, 1985; chaplain Bklyn. House of Detention, 1968-75; asst. priest Transfiguration Ch., N.Y.C., 1990, 99-2002, St. Mary the Virgin Ch., N.Y.C., 1998-2002. V.p. Am. Indian Cmty. House, N.Y.C., 1975; bd. edn. Sch. Dist. 9, N.Y.C., 1975; asst. priest St. Mary the Virgin, 1993-2001, Ch. of the Transfiguration, 1995—. With U.S. Army, 1943-46. Canonry award Diocese of Kumasi, 1979; named Sr. Episc. Missionary, World Mission Com. Episcopal Ch. Ctr., 1990. Home: 102 Washington Ave Brooklyn NY 11205

GARRISON, RAY HARLAN, lawyer; b. Allen County, Ky., Aug. 6, 1922; s. Emmett Washington and Ollie Irene (Keen) G.; m. Eunice Anne Bolz, Oct. 7, 1961. BA, Western Ky. U., 1942; MA, U. Ky., 1944; postgrad., Northwestern U., 1945-46; JD, U. Chgo., 1949. Bar: Ky. 1951, Ill. 1962, U.S. Ct. Appeals 1962, U.S. Tax Ct. 1962, U.S. Ct. Internat. Trade 1968, U.S. Supreme Ct. 1980. Tax acct. Ky. Dept. Revenue, Frankfort, 1943, supr. escheats, 1944-45, fiscal analyst, 1945; research asst. Bur. Bus. Rsch., U. Ky., Lexington, 1943-44; research assoc. Fedn. Tax Adminstrs., Chgo., 1946-52; spl. atty. U.S. Dept. Treasury, St. Louis, 1952-57, spl. asst., 1957-59, asst. regional counsel, 1959-61; sr. counsel Internat. Harvester Co., Chgo., 1961-86; gen. tax atty. Navistar Internat. Corp., Chgo., 1986-88, cons. atty., 1989—; gen. counsel Balmoral Racing Club, Inc., Crete, Ill., 1990—. Lectr. Loyola U., Chgo., 1949-51; del. Ill. Constl. Conv., 1969-70 Contbr. articles to various publs. Mem. Ill. Racing Bd., 1975-88; mem. adv. bd. Ill. thoroughbred Breeders Fund, 1976-80; hon. mem. coun. state taxation (COST), Washington. Mem. ABA, NAM (taxation com. 1969-88), Ill. Mfrs. Assn. (taxation com. 1969-88), Motor Vehicle Mfrs. Assn. (taxation com. 1963-88), Ill. Bar Assn., Ky. Bar Assn., Chgo. Tax Club, South Suburban Geneal. and Hist. Soc. (bd. dirs. 1973-77), Ky. Hist. Soc., Mecklenburg Hist. Assn., Cumberland Valley Civil War Heritage Assn. (adv. bd.), Filson Club, Beta Gamma Sigma. Methodist. Home and Office: 848 Braemar Rd Flossmoor IL 60422-2204 Office Phone: 708-798-6681.

GARRISON, RICHARD NEIL, artist; b. Ft. Bidwell, Calif., Nov. 26, 1912; s. John Henry and Vera Calista (Bell) G.; m. Ruth Geraldine George, Mar. 1, 1932 (div. Jul. 1968); m. Jeanne Trimble, Oct. 12, 1968. Student, Visalia (Calif.) Jr. Coll., 1930-32. Dir. Art League of Manatee Co., Bradenton, Fla., 1964-70. Author book of poetry, 1996, 95, 97. Mem. Art League of Manatee County, Longboat Key Art Ctr. Republican. Home: 260 47th St W Bradenton FL 34209-2830

GARRISON, ROBERT FREDERICK, astronomer, educator; b. Aurora, Ill., May 9, 1936; s. Robert W. and Dorothy I. (Rydquist) G.; m. Ada V. Mighell, June 7, 1957 (div. 1980); children: Forest L., Alexandra, David C.; life ptnr. Susanna E. Jacob, 1982. BA in Math., Earlham Coll., 1960; Postgrad., U. Wis., 1961-62; PhD in Astronomy and Astrophysics, U. Chgo., 1966. Research assoc. Mt. Wilson and Palomar Obs., Pasadena, Calif., 1966-68; asst. prof. U. Toronto, Ont., Can., 1968-74, assoc. prof. Ont., 1974-78, prof. astronomy, 1978—2001, prof. emeritus, 2001—, assoc. dir. D. Dunlap Obs.; dir. U. Toronto So. Obs., Chile, 1970-98. Bronowski lectr., 1987; Sigma Xi lectr., 1988—90. Editor: The MK Process and Stellar Classification, 1984; co-editor: The MK Process at Fifty Years: A Powerful Tool for Astrophysical Insight, 1994; subject The Garrison Festschrift, 2003; contbr. articles to profl. jours. Bd. dirs. Bruce Trail Assn., 1975—76. With USMC, 1954—56. Recipient Dean's award Lifetime Achievement as Outstanding Tchr., 2001, Queen's Golden Jubilee medal, 2003. Mem.: Royal Can. Inst. (v.p. 1991—93, pres. 1993—94), Internat. Astron. Union (pres. com. 45 on stellar classifications 1985—88), Royal Astron Soc. Can. (v.p. 1996—2000, pres. 2000—02, Svc. award 2005), Am. Assn. Variable Star Observers, Astron. Soc. Pacific, Am. Astron Soc. (Shapley lectr. 1985—), Can. Astron. Soc. (coun. 1978—81), U. Chgo. Club Can. (v.p. schs. 1982—88, pres. 1988—90). Office: David Dunlap Obs 123 Hillsview Dr Richmond Hill ON Canada L4C 1T3 Business E-Mail: garrison@astro.utoronto.ca.

GARRISON, SUSAN KAY, lawyer; b. Renton, Wash., Sept. 6, 1952; d. Walter Raymond and Rose Faye (Wilson) G.; m. William W. Mayer Jr., Aug. 4, 1973 (div. July 1988); 1 child, Jonathan William Mayer; m. Michael J.J. Campbell, Oct. 22, 1993; 2 stepchildren: Michael Sean and Andrew Jack Campbell. BA in Sociology cum laude, Gettysburg Coll., 1974; JD, Villanova U., 1980, LLM in Taxation, 1988. Assoc. Dechert Price and Rhoads, Phila., 1980-83, Surrick and Gollatz, Media, Pa., 1983-86; pvt. practice Media, 1986—. Exec. trustee Garrison Family Found., Media, 1990—; pres., bd. mem. Nat. Abortion Rights Action League Pa., Phila., 1986-94. Mem. com. Middletown Twp. (Pa.) Open Space Commn., 1984-86; bd. dirs. Clara Bell Duvall Edn. Fund, Phila., 1987-90, NARAL-Pa. Found.,1994—; nat. coord. Nat. Evang. Women's Caucus, Chgo., 1990-91; commr. Delaware County Women's Commn., Media, 1989-92; pres. Friends of Delaware County Women's Commn., Media, 1990-96; trustee Media-Providence Friends Sch., 1988-99; dir. The Ctr. Found., 1995—; chair Reps. Choice Pa., 1995—; mem. Delaware County Planning Commn., 1997—; mem. adv. bd. Women's Assn. Women's Alternatives, Inc., 1997—; commr. Pa. Commn. for Women, 1998—; bd. dirs. Pa. Ct. Apptd. Spl. Advocates Assn., 1998—. Mem. ABA, Nat. Assn. Women and Law, Nat. Women History Network, Nat. Assn. Commn. for Women (bd. dirs. 1998—), Delaware County Estate Planning Coun., Pa. Bar Assn., Delco Bar Assn. Republican. Office: 220 N Jackson St Media PA 19063-2807

GARRISON, TRUITT B., architect; b. Lubbock, Tex., Apr. 6, 1936; s. Miles Elisha and Iva J. (Greenway) G.; m. Joyce Ann Ward, June 27, 1959; children: Todd Michael, Craig Mitchell. BArch, Tex. Tech U., 1962; postgrad., Grad. Sch. Design Exec. Program, Harvard U., 1971. Registered architect, 42 states. With Welton Becket & Assocs., Houston, 1962-63; sr. v.p. Caudill Rowlett Scott, Houston, 1963—, also dir.; sr. v.p., dir. ops. Internat. Group CRS Sirrine, 1963-97, cons., 1997—. Bd. dirs. Global Group; exec. v.p., gen. mgr. archtl. svcs. divsn. CRSS Architects, Inc., 1988, pres., 1990, exec. v.p., 1992-94; exec. v.p. CRSS Inc. Peace Shield Divsn., 1994-96, cons., 1997-99; mem. bd. Houston Architecture Found., 1992-96. Pres. bd. Epernay Homeowners Assn., 1978—; sec. bd. Happy Hill Farm Acad., 1999—; chmn. bd. dirs. HHF&A, 2001—02; mem. fin. com. Celebrate Arch., 1994—96, 1998; mem. De Cordova City Coun., 2000—03; alderman City of DeCordova, 2000; bd. dirs. St. Lukes Meth. Ch., 1970—71, Epernay Homeowners Assn., 1977—86, DeCordova Bend Estates Homeowners Assn., 1999—2000, Happy Hill Farm Acad. With U.S. Army, 1958—59. Named Officer of Yr. Caudill

Rowlett Scott, 1980 Fellow: AIA; mem.: Nat. Coun. Archtl. Registration Bds., Tex. Soc. Architects, DeCordova Bend Estates Country Club (bd. dirs., pres. 1999—). Home and Office: 4917 Rio Vista Dr Granbury TX 76049-5172

GARRISON, WAYNE, transportation executive; Plant mgr. J.B. Hunt Transport Svcs., Inc., Lowell, Ark., 1976, v.p. fin., 1978, exec. v.p., 1979, pres., 1982, chmn., 1995—. Office: JB Hunt Transport Svcs Inc 615 JB Hunt Corporate Dr Lowell AR 72745

GARRISON, WILLIAM LLOYD, retired cemetery executive; b. Ridgway, Pa., Dec. 26, 1939; s. Lloyd and Mary Rebecca (Morrow) G.; m. Mary Jo Florio, May 30, 1964 (div. Mar. 2002), m. Mary Jo L. Mlakar, Jan. 21, 2005; children: David, Mark. BA in Psychology, Ohio Wesleyan U., 1962; postgrad., Garrett Theol. Sem., 1962—63, U. Pa., 1963—64; MSW, Fla. State U., 1967; MS in Mgmt., Case Western Res. U., 1976. Caseworker Mcpl. Ct. Chgo., 1963-64, United Cerebral Palsy Assn., Phila., 1964-65; psychiat. social worker Bellefaire, Shaker Heights, Ohio, 1967-74; dir. pers. and tng. Ctr. Human Svcs., Cleve., 1974-81, dir. resource devel., 1981-83; exec. dir. Cleve. Soc. for the Blind, 1983-85, Cleve. Eye Bank, 1983-85; exec. v.p. Lake View Cemetery Assn., Cleve., 1985-87, pres., CEO, 1987—2005; v.p. Lake View Cemetery Found., Cleve., 1988—2005. Adj. prof. Sch. Applied Social Sci., Case Western Res. U., 1974-80; v.p. E.A. Mabry Inc., Akron, Ohio, 1970-2001; chmn. agri-bus. adv. com. Cleve. Pub. Schs., 1990-2005, bus. adv. directorate, 1991-97. Numerous positions including ongoing and most recently Boy Scouts Am., coun. exec. bd., 1981—, mem. nat. coun., 1989—, cubmaster, 1997—, region nominating com., 1997—, nat. cub scout com. vice chmn., 1999—2005, v.p. cub scouting, 2003—04, dist. chmn., 2004—, nat. venture scout com., 2005—; pers. com. Lake Erie coun. Girl Scouts U.S., 1982—89; active Big Bros., Cleve., 1968—73; pres. Mayfield Heights Homeowners Assn., 1974—84, Cuyahoga County Reach Out Counseling Svcs., trustee, 1977—95, pres., 1991—95; mem. del. assembly United Way Svcs. of Cleve., 1987—95; trustee Alta HSE. Cmty. Ctr., 1994—2000, Ctr. for Families and Children, 1995—2002; co-founder, v.p. East Cleveland Pks. Assn., 1998—, pres., 2002—; co-chair civic divsn. United Way Campaign, 1999—2001; founder, pres. East Cleveland Twp. Cemetery Found., 2001—; bd. dirs. Garfield Meml. United Meth. Ch., 1979—81, vice chair pastor/parish rels. com., 1999—2000. Recipient Dist. award merit, Boy Scouts Am., 1980, Silver Beaver award, 1984, Silver Antelope award, 1994, 4-Way Test award, Rotary Club Cleve., 2000, hon. mention, No. Ohio LIVE award of achievement, 1994, 2002, Whitney M. Young award, 2005; fellow, Menninger Found. Mem. NASW, Acad. Cert. Social Workers, Soc. Human Resource Mgmt., Pers. Accreditation Inst., Internat. Cemetery and Funeral Assn. (cert. cemetery exec. 1997, membership com. 1993-2000, strategic planning com. 1994-96, hist. cemetery adv. com. 1994-2004, dir. 2003-), Ohio Assn. Cemetery Supts. and Ofcls. (exec. bd. 1992-97, v.p. 1993, pres.-elect 1994, pres. 1995-96), Greater Cleve. Cemetery Assn. (pres. 1987-90), Nat. Eagle Scout Assn., Greater Cleve. Pers. Coun., Social Agys. Employees Union (pres. 1970-73), Greater Cleve. Growth Assn., St. Luke's Hosp. Assn., Cleve. U. Cir. Inc., Am. Soc. Assn. Execs., Assn. Fundraising Profls., Cleve. Restoration Soc., Ohio Assn. Hist. Socs. and Museums, N.E. Ohio Intermus. Coun., Ohio Hist. Soc., Am. Field Svc., Cleve. Playhouse Club, Rotary (trustee Cleve. club 1993-96, v.p. 1996, pres. 1997-98, del. 88th Rotary Internat. conv. Glasgow, Scotland, 89th Indpls., 96th Chgo.), Cleve. Rotary Found. (trustee 1997-99, v.p. 1999-2000, pres. 2000-01), Hist. Cemetery Alliance (co-founder), Internat. Fellowship of Scouting Rotarians, Univ. Club, Delta Tau Delta, Phi Mu Alpha.

GARRISON, WILLIAM LOUIS, civil engineering educator; b. Nashville, Apr. 20, 1924; s. Sidney Clarence and Sara (Elisabeth) McMurry; s. Marcia Fordyce Stanley, Aug. 31, 1938; children: Sara, Ann, Helen, Deborah, James, Jane, John. BS, Peabody Coll., 1946, MS, 1947; PhD, Northwestern U., 1950. From asst. prof. to prof. dept. geography U. Wash., Seattle, 1950-60; prof. dept. geography, civil engrng. Northwestern U., Evanston, Ill., 1960-67, dir. transp. ctr., 1965-67; dir. ctr. for urban studies U. Ill., Chgo., 1967-69; Weidlein Prof. Environ. Engrng. U. Pitts., 1969-73; dir. Inst. for Transp. Studies U. Calif., Berkeley, 1973-81, prof. civil engrng., 1981—. Cons. U.S. Bur. Pub. Rds., Washington, 1960-68; bd. govs. Regional Sci. Research Inst., Phila., 1964—; adv. com. on econs. NSF, Washington, 1958-63; panel on values of social sci. research Nat. Sci. Bd., Washington, 1963-64. Author: Geographical Impact of Highway Improvements, 1960, Tomorrow's Transportation, 2000; author, editor Jour. Transp. Tech., 1985, The Transportation Experience, 2005; editor: Quantitative Geography, 1969; articles in field. Served to capt. USAF, 1943-46. Recipient Disting. award U. Coun. of Transp. Rsch. Ctrs., 1999. Mem. Transp. Research Bd. (chmn. 1972-73, Roy C. Crum award 1973), Regional Sci. Assn. (pres. 1960), ASCE, Assn. Am. Geographers (Outstanding research award 1958), AAAS. Home: 10 Rancho Diablo Dr Lafayette CA 94549-2722 Office: U Calif Dept Civil Engring Berkeley CA 94720-1712 Business E-Mail: garrison@newton.berkeley.edu.

GARRISON-FINDERUP, IVADELLE DALTON, writer, educator; b. San Pedro, Calif., Oct. 4, 1915; d. William Douglas and Olive May (Covington) Dalton; m. Fred Marion Garrison, Aug. 8, 1932 (dec. Nov. 1984); children: Douglas Lee, Vernon Russell, Nancy Jane; m. Elmer Pedersen Finderup, Apr. 8, 1994 (dec. Oct. 1997). BA, Calif. State U., Fresno, 1964; postgrad., U. Oreg., 1965, U. San Francisco, 1968. Cert. secondary tchr., Calif. Tchr. Tranquillity (Calif.) H.S., 1964-78, West Hills Coll., Coalinga, Calif., 1970-74. Lectr. in field. Author: Roots and Branches of Our Garrison Family Tree, 1988, Roots and Branches of Our Dalton Family Tree, 1989, The History of James' Fresno Ranch, 1990, 3d edit., 1993, There is a Peacock on the Roof, 1993; (with Vernon R. Garrison) William Douglas Dalton, a Biography, 1995, Sam (The Cat That Thought He Was a Boy), 1997, Amanda and Her Feathered Friends, 1997, Freddy Goes on a Trailer Outing, 1998, David Learns to Count, 1998, Laura and the Lizard: a fairy tale, 2001, A Mystery Story, 2005. Mem. DAR (sec. 1987-89, regent 1989-91, regent Fresno chpt. 1999-2001, scholarship chmn. 2002, 05, nat. recognition for excellence in cmty. svc. Cert. of Award 1995), Nat. Trust for Hist. Preservation, Frazier Clan N.Am., Fresno City and County Hist. Soc. (life), Fresno Archaeology Soc. (sec. 1994), Children of the Am. Revolution (life patriot, sr. pres. 1991-97), Westerners Internat., Fresno Gem and Mineral Soc., Thora # 11 Dannebrog, Friends of the Libr. (Fresno), Chaffee Zool. Gardens of Fresno, Archaeol. Inst. Am. (San Joaquin Valley chpt., charter mem.), Fresno County Archaeol. Soc, Fresno Met. Mus., Baker Hist. Mus. (life). Republican. Lutheran. Avocations: quilting, knitting. Office: Garrison Libr 3427 Circle Ct E Fresno CA 93703-2403

GARRISON-JACKSON, ZINA, retired professional tennis player; b. Houston, Nov. 16, 1963; m. Willard Jackson. Mem. U.S. Olympic tennis team, 1988 (Bronze Medal in Singles and Gold Medal in Doubles - with Pam Shriver). Winner tournaments including Wimbledon Jr. Singles, 1981, U.S. Open Jr. Singles, 1981, U.S. Open Doubles Title (with Mary Joe Fernandez), 1993, Can. Doubles, 1986, 87, Birmingham, 1990; finalist Wimbledon, 1990. Office: c/o USTA 70 W Red Oak Ln White Plains NY 10604-3602 also: c/o Advantage International 1751 Pinnacle Dr Ste 1500 Mc Lean VA 22102-3833

GARRISS, PHYLLIS WEYER, music educator, performer; b. Hastings, Nebr., Dec. 25, 1923; d. Frank Elmer and Mabelle Claire (Carey) Weyer; m. William Philip Garriss, Aug. 28, 1954; children: Daniel, Meredith, Margaret. AB, MusB, Hastings Coll., 1945; MusM, U. Rochester, 1948. Instr. DePauw U., Greencastle, Ind., 1948-51; assoc. prof. music Meredith Coll., Raleigh, N.C., 1951-94, assoc. prof. emerita, part-time prof., 1994—. Instr. Cannon Music Camp, Appalachian State U., Boone, N.C., 1973-98; vis. instr. Ball State U., Muncie, summers 1951, 53; dir. Lamar Stringfield Chamber Music Camp, Meredith Coll., 1980—; bd. dirs. Raleigh Symphony Orch., Raleigh Chamber Music Guild; mem. various symphonic groups as violinist, including Roanoke Symphony, Raleigh Civic Symphony, Duke U. Symphony, Tri-City Chamber Orch., Raleigh Symphony Orch., Capital Chamber Music Ensemble. Mem. Raleigh Civic Coun., 1958-60; bd. dirs. Raleigh Cmty. Mus. Sch., 1993-97, N.C. Fedn. Music Clubs, 1988-96; mem. PEO. Recipient Medal of Arts, City of Raleigh Arts Commn., 1987. Mem. Am. String Tchrs. Assn. (corr. sec. 1950-54, Disting. Svc. award 1979), Music Tchrs. Nat. Assn., Music Educators Nat. Conf., Local 500 Musicians Assn. (bd. dirs. 1980—), Raleigh Music Club (pres. 1958-60, 93-95), Pi Kappa Lambda, Mu Phi Epsilon. Democrat. Presbyterian. Avocations: cooking, travel. Home: 3400 Merriman Ave Raleigh NC 27607-7004 Office: Meredith Coll 3800 Hillsborough St Raleigh NC 27607-5237 Office Phone: 919-760-2821. Business E-Mail: garrissp@meredith.edu.

GARRITY, VINCENT FRANCIS, JR., lawyer; b. Phila., July 26, 1937; s. Vincent Francis and Anne (Glenn) G.; m. Maryellen O'Brien, May 8, 1965; children: Vincent III, Ellen, Christopher, Elisa. AB cum laude, Coll. of Holy Cross, Worcester, Mass., 1959; LLB, Harvard U., 1962. Bar: Pa. 1963, U.S. Dist. Ct. (ea. dist.) Pa. 1963. Assoc. Duane, Morris & Heckscher, Phila., 1963-70; ptnr. Duane, Morris LLP, Phila., 1970—2002, co-chmn. bus. law dept., 1981—94, of counsel, 2003—. Disting. practitioner in residence Cornell Law Sch., 2001; adj. prof. Sch. Law Temple U., 1996—, Law Sch. U. Va., 2004; lectr. .in law Sch. Law., U. Pa., 1999—; presenter, panelist in field; lectr. in field. Contbr. numerous articles to profl. jours. With USAR, 1962—68. Fellow Am. Bar Found.; mem. ABA (com. on corp laws bus. law sect. 1983-89, participant in preparation Model Bus. Corp. Act; vice chmn. 1991-95, chmn. 1995-98, com. on negotiated acquisitions), Pa. Bar Assn. (chmn. sect. corp. banking and bus. law 1981-83, vice chmn. Title 15 task force on 1988 Pa. Bus. Corp. Law 1983-2004, chmn., 2005—, Spl. Achievement award 1982), Am. Law Inst. (elected), Merion Golf Club (Ardmore, Pa.), Union League Phila Roman Catholic. Home: 118 Derwen Rd Bala Cynwyd PA 19004-2710 Office Phone: 215-979-1242. Business E-Mail: garrity@duanemorris.com.

GARROTT, CARL LEE, foreign language educator; b. Indpls., Dec. 4, 1948; s. George Richard and Rosie (Diggs) G. BA, Ky. State U., 1970; MA, Tenn. State U., 1974; EdS, Western Ky. U., 1977; EdD, U. Ky., 1985; postgrad., U. Guadalajara (Mex.), 1999—2000, Inst. de Filologia Hispanica, 1990, 91, 93, Monteverde Inst., Costa Rica, 2002—03. Instr. Cath. High Sch., Frankfort, Ky., 1969-70, Christian County Schs., Hopkinsville, Ky., 1974-81; prof. Chowan Coll., Murfreesboro, N.C., 1984-95; assoc. prof. Hampton U., 1995-98; prof. Va. State U., 1998—. Author: (monograph) The Thinking Man in France, 1977, (book) José Martí Poesía, Cuentos, Teatro, 2001, A systematic Approach to Teaching Intonation Patterns in French, 2003; contbr. articles to profl. jours. Donor Sci. Enrichment Scholarship, Hertford County, 1984-91, 93; founder African-Am. Forum, Franklin, Southampton, 1987—. Sgt. U.S. Army, 1971-73. Woodrow Wilson Found. fellow, 1970, U. Ky. fellow, 1970-71, 81-84; grantee Ford Found., Starr Found., Va. Found. Humanities; faculty rsch. grantee Hampton U. Mem. MLA, Am. Assn. Tchrs. Spanish and Portuguese, Am. Assn. Tchrs. French, N.E. Conf. on the Tchg. Fgn. Langs., Am. Assn. for Applied Linguistics, Coll. Lang. Assn., Afro-Latin Am. Rsch. Assn., Internat. Assn. Appllied Linguistics, County Alliance for Sci., Cmty. Concert Assn., Alpha Phi Alpha, Alpha Mu Gamma. Democrat. Baptist. Avocations: shortwave radios, internat. travel. Office: Va State Univ Dept Langs and Lit Petersburg VA 23806 Office Phone: 804-524-5168. E-mail: cgarrott@vsu.edu.

GARROTT, FRANCES CAROLYN, architectural technician; b. Bowling Green, Ky., Mar. 10, 1932; d. Irby Reid and Carrie Mae (Stahl) Cameron; m. Leslie Othello Garrott, Oct. 12, 1951 (dec. Feb. 1978); adopted children: Carolyn Maria, Karen Roxana children: Dennis Leslie, Alan Reid; m. Raymond William Scerbo, May 31, 1978 (div. Oct. 1990). Student, Fla. State U., 1951, St. Petersburg Jr. Coll., 1962—74; grad., Pinellas Vocat. Tech. Inst., 1975. With Sears, Roebuck and Co., Rapid City, S.D., 1951-52, St. Petersburg, Fla., 1961-62; bookkeeper Ohio Nat. Bank, Columbus, 1953-54, Sunbeam Bakery, Lakeland, Fla., 1955-56; with Christies Toy Sales, Pennsauken, N.J., 1958-60; exec. sec. Gulf Coast Automotive Warehouse, Inc., Tampa, Fla., 1970-73, office mgr., 1975-78; sec., treas., chief pilot, co-owner Tech. Devel. Corp., St. Petersburg, Fla., 1970-78. Freelance archtl. draftsman and designer, archtl. cons., constrn. materials estimator, Lakeland, Fla., 1995—, Seminole, Fla., 1975—95. Fla. judge Vocat. Indsl. Clubs Am. Skills Olympics, 1986. Nat. Assn. Women in Constrn. scholar, 1974. Mem. Nat. Assn. Women in Constrn. (scholar 1974), Alpha Chi Omega. Democrat. Home: 8156 Timberidge Loop W Lakeland FL 33809-2357

GARROW, DAVID JEFFRIES, historian, author; b. New Bedford, Mass., May 11, 1953; s. Walter and Barbara Mae (Fassett) G.; m. Virginia Darleen Opfer, Dec. 15, 2003. BA, Wesleyan U., Middletown, Conn., 1975; MA, Duke U., 1978, PhD, 1981. Instr. polit. sci. Duke U., Durham, N.C., 1978-79; vis. mem. Sch. Social Sci., Inst. Advanced Study, Princeton, N.J., 1979-80; asst. prof. polit. sci. U. N.C., Chapel Hill, 1980-84; assoc. prof. polit. sci. City Coll. N.Y., CUNY Grad. Ctr., 1984-87, prof., 1987-91. Vis. fellow Joint Ctr. Polit. Studies, Washington, 1984; sr. advisor Eyes on the Prize: Am.'s Civil Rights Yrs., PBS TV documentary broadcast, 1985-90; bd. dirs. Martin Luther King Jr. Papers Project, King Ctr., Atlanta; fellow 20th Century Fund, 1991-93; James Pinckney Harrison vis. prof. history Coll. William and Mary, 1994-95; disting. historian in residence Am. U., 1995-96, disting. Presdl. prof., Emory U., 1997—. Author: Protest at Selma: Martin Luther King and the Voting Rights Act of 1965, 1978 (Chastain award 1979), The FBI and Martin Luther King, Jr.: From "Solo" to Memphis, 1981, Bearing the Cross: Martin Luther King, Jr. and the Southern Christian Leadership Conference, 1986 (Pulitzer Prize for Biography 1987, Robert F. Kennedy book award 1987), Liberty and Sexuality: The Right to Privacy and the Making of Roe v. Wade, 1994; editor: The Montgomery Bus Boycott and the Women Who Started It: The Memoir of JoAnn Gibson Robinson, 1987; co-editor: The Eyes on the Prize Civil Rights Reader, 1987, 91, The Forgotten Memoir of John Knox, 2002; contbr. articles to publs. and profl. jours. Recipient NEH grant, 1984-85, Ford Found. grant, 1979-80, Lyndon B. Johnson Found. grant, 1979-80, Eisenhower World Affairs Inst. grant, 1985-86. Phi Beta Kappa. Democrat. Avocations: bicycling, hiking. Home and Office: Emory U Law Sch Atlanta GA 30322-2770

GARRUTO, RALPH MICHAEL, biomedical anthropologist, biologist, educator; b. Binghamton, NY, Nov. 20, 1943; s. Ralph Anthony and Josephine Janet (DiMartino) G.; children: Jessica Anne, Jason Michael, John Ralph. BS, Pa. State U., 1966, MA, 1969, PhD, 1973. Postdoctoral fellow NIH, Bethesda, Md., 1972-73, staff, then sr. staff fellow, 1973-78, from rsch. biologist to supervisory rsch. biologist, 1978—2003; adj. prof. med. genetics Coll. Medicine U. South Ala., Mobile, 1982—; adj. sr. scientist biol. anthropology Pa. State U., University Park, 1985—95; prof. biomedical anthropology neurosci. SUNY, Binghamton, 1997—, assoc. dir. Inst. Biomed. Tech., 2000—, dir. biomed. anthropology program, 2002—; adj. clin. prof. pathology Upstate Med. U., Syracuse, 1998—. Participant anthropol. and biomed. fieldwork, Asia, Pacific Islands, L.Am., 1969—; mem., NIH rep. U.S. Nat. Com. U.S. Man and the Biosphere Program, 1993-95; founding mem. bd. trustees Nat. Mus. Health and Medicine Found., Washington, 1989-91; exec. sec. Commn. on Aging and the Aged, Zagreb, Yugoslavia, 1985-89; cons. WHO, 1987; chair selection com. Paul T. Baker Disting. lectr. in human biology and anthropology Pa. State U., 1986-98; Wellcome Found. lectr., vis. prof. U. Mich., Dearborn, 2001. Co-editor: Biological Anthropology and Aging: Perspectives on Human Variation over the Lifespan, 1994, Dermatoglyphics: Science in Transition, 1991; contbr. articles on neurodegenerative disorders, neurosci. and aging to profl. jours.; patentee bil. agts. Recipient Commendation for Rsch., Guam Legislature, 1987, Spl. Achievement award, 1990, Merit award NIH, 1991, Dir.'s award, 1993; Wenner-Gren Found. leadership grantee, 1986, grantee, 1993-95; Alumni fellow Pa. State U., 1987. Fellow AAAS, Am. Coll. Epidemiology, Am. Dermatoglyphics Assn. (sec.-treas. 1981-82, pres. 1987-89, disting. achievement award 1995), Human Biology Assn. (pres./pres.-elect 1993-96, exec. com. 1991-93), Internat. Assn. of Human Biologists (pres. 1999-2002, Gorjanović-Krambergeri medal 1999-2000, Franz Boas Disting. Achievement award 2005), Internat. Genetic Epidemiology Soc. (founding fellow), NAS, Third World Acad. Scis. (assoc.); mem. Soc. for Neurosci., World Fedn. Neurology (rsch. com. on neurepidemiology). Avocations: field trialing, environmental projects. Business E-Mail: rgarruto@binghamton.edu.

GARRY, JAMES B., historian, naturalist, storyteller, writer; b. Taylor, Tex., Apr. 28, 1947; s. Mahon Barker and Grace (Dellinger) G. BS, U. Mich., 1970, MS, 1975. Part-time wilderness guide, naturalist Triangle X Ranch, Moose, Wyo., 1969-75; community organizer, media cons., tchr. Hobart St. Project, Detroit, 1974-75; media specialist, lobbyist Powder River Basin Resource Coun., Sheridan, Wyo., 1975-76; pvt. practice media and polit. cons. Big Horn, Wyo., 1976-78; video and film artist-in-residence Wyo. Coun. on the Arts/Sheridan Coll., Sheridan, 1978-80; mem. staff Great Plains Lore and Natural History, Big Horn, 1980—. Storyteller Buffalo Bill Hist. Ctr., Cody, Wyo., 1980—; tchr. Yellowstone (Wyo.) Inst., summers 1986—; tour study leader, rsch. collaborator Smithsonian Instn., Washington, 1984—. Co-author: Writing About Wildlife, 1974; author, editor: Buck: Stories by Lloyd Buck Bender, 1984, This Ol' Drought Ain't Broke Us Yet But We're All Bent Pretty Bad, 1992, The First Liar Never Has a Chance: Curly, Jack and Bill (and Other Characters of the Hills, Brush and Plains), 1994; storyteller in field. 2d lt. U.S. Army, 1970. Recipient Spl. Heritage award Old West Trail Found., 1983; named one of Individual Humanist of Yr., Wyo. Coun. for Humanities, 1986. Democrat. Roman Catholic. Avocation: nature. Office: Great Plains Lore & Natural History PO Box 2165 Cody WY 82414-2165

GARRY, JOHN THOMAS, II, lawyer; b. Albany, N.Y., Dec. 12, 1923; s. Joseph A. II and Jean Theresa (Cramond) G.; m. Mary Regina Hoffman (dec.); children: John, Michael, Regina, Maureen, Suzanne, Patricia; m. Claire Baynes, 1989. Student, Cornell U., 1942-43; BA, St. Bernadine of Siena Coll., 1949; LLB, JD, Union U., 1952. Bar: N.Y. 1952, U.S. Supreme Ct. 1952. Asst. corp. counsel City of Albany, 1953-55, asst. dist. atty., 1955-58; dist. atty. Albany County, 1958-68; sr. ptnr. Garry & Cahill, Albany, 1968—. Exec. chmn. Dem. Cen. Com., Albany, Albany Big Bros./Big Sisters Am., 1971; trustee Siena Coll., Loudonville, N.Y., 1987-97; mem. Empire State Art Commn., 1990-95, N.Y. State Plz. Art Commn. Served with USAAF, 1943. Decorated Air medal. Mem. ABA, N.Y. State Bar Assn. (character com. admission), Albany County Bar Assn., Am. Judicature Soc., Internat. Narcotic Enforcement Officers Assn., N.Y. State Dist. Attys. Assn. (v.p. 1967), St. Bernadine of Siena Coll. Alumni Assn. (pres. 1964, trustee 1989-97), Am. Legion, VFW, KC (Grand Knight 1956). Clubs: Wolfert's Roost Country. Lodges: K.C., Elks.

GARSCADDEN, ALAN, physicist; b. Glasgow, Scotland, June 10, 1937; came to U.S., 1962; s. Andrew and Sarah Florence (Black) G.; m. Avril Margaret Thompson Garscadden, Jan. 24, 1962; children: A. Graeme, A.K. Neil, A.K. Gael, A.E. Hilary. BS (hon.), Queens U., Belfast, Ireland, 1958; PhD in Physics, 1962. Rsch. physicist Aerospace Rsch. Labs, Wright-Patterson AFB, 1962-73; lab. dir., 1973-75; rsch. physicist Aero Propulsion and Power Divsn., 1975-91; chief scientist Aero Propulsion Directorate, 1991-94, Wright Lab., 1995-97, Propulsion Directorate/Air Force Rsch. Lab., Wright-Patterson AFB, 1997—, Edwards AFB, Calif., 1997—. Adj. prof. physics Air Force Inst. Tech., Wright Patterson AFB, 1969—; bd. dirs. Von Karman Inst., Brussels; trustee Ohio Aerospace Inst., 1996-98. Contbr. articles to profl. jours. Commr. Planning Commn., Village of Yellow Springs, 1985-96. Decorated Disting. Svc. medal USAF; recipient Presdl. Meritorious award, 2003; fellow, Air Force Rsch. Lab. Fellow IEEE, AIAA, Am. Phys. Soc. (Will Allis prize 2002), Inst. Physics (U.K.). Avocation: history of colonial science. Office: AFRL/PR Air Force Rsch lab 1950 5th St Wright Patterson Afb OH 45433-7251 Office Phone: 937-255-2246. Business E-Mail: alan.garscadden@wpafb.af.mil.

GARSH, THOMAS BURTON, publisher; b. New Rochelle, N.Y., Dec. 12, 1931; s. Harry and Matilda (Smith) G.; m. Beatrice J. Schmidt; children: Carol Jean, Thomas Burton, Janice Lynn. BS, U. Md., 1955. Edn. rep. McGraw Hill Book Co., N.Y.C., 1959-68; mktg. mgr. D.C. Heath & Co., Boston, 1969-71; dir. mktg. Economy Co., Oklahoma City, 1971-72; sr. v.p. Macmillan Pub. Co., N.Y.C., 1972-78; pres. Am. Book Co., N.Y.C., 1978-81; founder, pres., dir. Am. Ednl. Computer, Inc., Palo Alto, Calif., 1981-86. Founder, chmn., chief exec. officer OmnyEd Corp., Palo Alto, 1987-91; pres. Silver Burdett & Ginn divsn. of Simon and Schuster, 1991-92; dir. Fifty Plus Fitness Assn., Palo Alto, Calif. Publ. Homes and Land of Santa Clara, 1998—. Mem. county council Boy Scouts Am., 1963-65; mem. ch. council on Interracial Affairs, 1966-68, pres., 1967; vice-chmn. Madison County Democratic Party, 1967. Mem. Assn. Am. Pubs., Profl. Bookman's Assn., Omicron Delta Kappa, Sigma Alpha Epsilon. Clubs: Cazenovia Country (founder). Home: 401 Old Spanish Trl Portola Valley CA 94028 E-mail: tnb401@aol.com.

GARSON, ANDREW S., lawyer; b. N.Y.C., Nov. 12, 1952; m. Virginia Geiss, June 15, 1981; children: Danielle M, Sara A. BA with honors in Am. History, Clark U., Worcester, Mass., 1974; JD, Boston U., 1978. Bar: Mass. 1978, N.Y. 1979, cert.: Nat. Bd. Trial Attys. (Specialist Civil Litigation). Asst. dist. atty. Kings County Dist. Atty., Bklyn., 1978—82; assoc. trial atty. Martin Clearwater & Bell, N.Y.C., 1982—88; trial atty./ptnr. Belair & Evans, N.Y.C., 1988—99; sr. ptnr. Garson Gerspach DeCorato & Cohen, N.Y.C., 2000—. Lectr. in field; mem. editl. bd. "Ob-Gyn Malpractice Prevention". Contbr. articles to profl. jours. Mem.: ATLA, N.Y. State Bar Assn., N.Y. State Trial Lawyers Assn. Avocation: triathlon competition. Office: Garson Gerspach DeCorato & Cohen LLP 110 Wall St Fl 10 New York NY 10005 Office Phone: 212-742-8700. E-mail: garson@ggdclaw.com.

GARSON, ARNOLD HUGH, publishing executive; b. Lincoln, Nebr., May 29, 1941; s. Sam B. and Celia (Stine) Garson; m. Marilyn Grace Baird, Aug. 15, 1964; children: Scott Arnold, Christopher Baird, Gillian Grace, Megan Jane. BA, U. Nebr., 1964; MS, UCLA, 1965. Reporter Omaha World-Herald, 1965-69, Des Moines Tribune, 1969-72, city editor, 1972-75; reporter Des Moines Register, 1975-83, mng. editor, 1983-88; editor San Bernardino (Calif.) County Sun, 1988-96; pub., pres. Sioux Falls (S.D.) Argus Leader, 1996—; v.p. Gannett Pacific Newspaper Group, 2000—. Past pres. S.D. Symphony Orch., bd. dirs.; mem. adv. bd. Neuharth Ctr. U. S.D. Recipient Pub. Svc. Reporting award, Am. Polit. Sci. Assn., 1969, Mng. Editors Sweepstakes award, Iowa AP, 1976, John Hancock award for excellence in bus. and fin. journalism, 1979, Calif.-Nev. AP award for column writing, 1995. Mem.: S.D. Newspaper Assn. (past pres.). Jewish. Home: 5 S Riverview Hts Sioux Falls SD 57105-0252 Office: Sioux Falls Argus Leader PO Box 5034 Sioux Falls SD 57117-5034

GARSON, ARTHUR, JR., dean, medical educator; b. NYC; m. Suzan Garson; 2 children. Grad., Princeton U., 1970; MD, Duke U., 1974; MPH, U. Tex., Houston, 1992. V.p. Tex. Children's Hosp.; fellow in pediat. cardiology Baylor Coll. Medicine, 1979, chief pediat. cardiology, 1988, sr. v.p., dean acad. ops., 1995; assoc. vice chancellor health affairs Duke U., 1992; dean, v.p. U. Va. Sch. Medicine, 2002—. Mem. White House Adv. Panel on Health Sys. Improvement; chair quality nat. adv. coun. Agy. Healthcare Rsch. Mem.: Assn. Acad. Health Ctrs., U. Hosps. Consortium, Assn. Am. Med. Colls. (adv. panel on healthcare delivery), Am. Coll. Cardiology (pres. 2000—01, trustee, mem. govt. rels. com., mem. quality of care com.). Office: U Va Health Sys PO Box 800793 Charlottesville VA 22908 E-mail: garson@virginia.edu.

GARSON, GARY WAYNE, lawyer; b. NYC, Oct. 16, 1946; s. Norman and Pearl (Milikowski) G.; m. Bernice Susan Schumer, June 17, 1967; children: Burt M., Lauren L. BA, Queens Coll., 1967; JD, Bklyn. Law Sch., 1970. Bar: NY 1971. Assoc. Lord, Day & Lord, NYC, 1970-79; asst. gen. counsel Loews Corp., NYC, 1979-85, dep. gen. counsel, 1985—2002, v.p., 1988—2002, sr. v.p., sec., gen. counsel, 2002—. Mem. NYC Bar Assn. (com. on uniform state laws 1974-77, com. on mcpl. affairs 1978-81). Avocation: sailing. Office: Loews Corp 667 Madison Ave Fl 7 New York NY 10021-8087

GARSON, SUSAN JULEEN, medical/surgical nurse, small business owner, writer, pediatrics nurse, personal trainer; b. Anaheim, Calif., July 1, 1965; d. William Francis Harke and Sandra Lee Enstrom; m. Mark Allen Garson, Dec. 31, 1997; children: Mitchel Liam, Jared Quade. ASN, Santa Fe C.C., 1997; cert. in forensic nursing, Kaplan Coll., 2004. RN 1997. With Westwind Travel Agy., Santa Fe, 1988—97; emergency rm. registration clk. Presbyn. Hosp.,

Santa Fe, 1996—97; RN, hosp. fl. nurse Salem Hosp., Oreg., 1997—, RN, sexual assault RN coord., 1998—, med.-surg. fl. nurse, 1998—. Owner Garson Publs., 2003—; originator, facilitator Mom's Connection Salem Hosp., 2004—05, mem. child abuse and fatality rev. team, Oreg., 2003—05, mem. multidisciplinary and sexual assault team, 2003—05, mem. multidisciplinary team, Dallas, 2003—05. Author, pub. Pattern Setting for Childhood Health, 2004. Vol., educator Dist. Atty.'s Victim Assistance Program; bd. dirs. YMCA, 2005—. Scholarship, Dr. & Mrs. Brown, Santa Fe, 1995—97. Mem.: Internat. Assn. Forensic Nursing (sexual assault nurse examiner), Pacific N.W. Booksellers Assn. Avocations: exercise, writing, volunteering to help crime victims. Home: 2884 Laurelwood Ct NW Salem OR 97304 Office: Garson Publs PO Box 5775 Salem OR 97304 Office Phone: 503-363-1477. Office Fax: 503-363-1417. E-mail: susangarson@quest.net.

GARSTANG, ROY HENRY, astrophysicist, educator; b. Southport, Eng., Sept. 18, 1925; came to U.S., 1964; s. Percy Brocklehurst and Eunice (Gledhill) G.; m. Ann Clemence Hawk, Aug. 11, 1959; children: Jennifer Katherine, Susan Veronica. BA, U. Cambridge, 1946, MA, 1950, PhD, 1954, Sc.D., 1983. Research assoc. U. Chgo., 1951-52; lectr. astronomy U. Coll., London, 1952-60; reader astronomy U. London, 1960-64, asst. dir. Obs., 1959-64; prof. astrophysics U. Colo., Boulder, 1964-94, chair faculty assembly, 1988-89, prof. emeritus, 1994—; chmn. Joint Inst. for Lab. Astrophysics, 1966-67. Cons. Nat. Bur. Standards, 1964—73, Internat. Commn. Illumination, 1990—; v.p. commn. 14 Internat. Astron. Union, 1970—73, pres., 1973—76; Erskine vis. fellow U. Canterbury, New Zealand, 1971; vis. prof. U. Calif., Santa Cruz, 1971. Editor: Observatory, 1953-60; Contbr. numerous articles to tech. jours. Recipient Excellence in Svc. award, U. Colo., 1990. Fellow Am. Phys. Soc., AAAS, Optical Soc. Am., Brit. Inst. Physics, Royal Astron. Soc.; mem. Am. Astron. Soc., Royal Soc. Scis. Liege (Belgium). Achievements include rsch. on atomic physics and astrophys. applications; calculation of atomic transition probabilities, atomic spectra in very high magnetic fields and magnetic white dwarf stars; modelling of light pollution. Home: 830 8th St Boulder CO 80302-7409 Office: U Colo Boulder CO 80309-0440 Office Phone: 303-492-7795. Personal E-mail: garstang@earthlink.net. *It is a privilege to help others to learn about the wonderful universe in which we live.*

GARSTEN, JOEL JAY, gastroenterologist; b. N.Y.C., Jan. 10, 1948; s. Richard Maxwell and Gertrude Ann (Perlberg) G.; m. Marion Susan Moscovitz, July 10, 1971; children: Bryan David, Lauren Roberta. BA in Biology, CUNY, 1968; MD, Georgetown U., 1973. Resident in internal medicine Cornell-Coop. Hosps. Program, N.Y.C., 1973-76; fellow gastroenterology Yale Affiliated Gastroenterology Program, New Haven and Waterbury, Conn., 1976-78; gastroenterologist Gastroenterology Assocs. of Waterbury, 1978-90; physician, mng. ptnr. Digestive Disease Ctr. of Conn., 1990—; dir. sect. of gastroenterology Waterbury Hosp. Health Ctr., 1990—; assoc. dir. Yale Affiliated GI fellowship program Waterbury Hosp. and Hosp. of St. Raphael, New Haven and Waterbury, 1990-2000; clin. instr. internal medicine Yale U. Sch. Medicine, New Haven, 1978, asst. clin. prof., 1981, assoc. clin. prof., 1987—. Med. dir. Liberty Health Plan, Naugatuck, Conn., 1987-89, Physicians Health Plan, Trumbull, Conn., 1989-90, med. adv. bd., 1990-92. Contbr. articles to profl. jours. Med. adv. chmn. Crohn's and Colitis Found., WTBY Satelite, Waterbury, 1990—; resource speaker Waterbury Celiac Group, Thomaston, Conn., 1990—, Am. Cancer Soc., 1991—; prin. investigator multiple drug trials. Fellow ACP, Am. Coll. Gastroenterology; mem. Am. Soc. for Liver Disease, Conn. Soc. Internal Medicine (pres. sect. gastroenterology 1996-98), Am. Soc. Internal Medicine, Am. Gastroenterology Assn., Am. Soc. Parenteral and Enteral Nutrition, others. Achievements include introduction of home parenteral nutrition of sclerotherapy, esophageal stenting, percutaneous gastrostomy, other endoscopic techniques to Waterbury; prin. investigator in drug rsch. trials (chosen for Best Drs. in the N.E.). Home: 47 Harvest Ct Cheshire CT 06410-1844 Office: Digestive Disease Ctr Conn 60 Westwood Ave Waterbury CT 06708-2460 Office Phone: 203-574-3007.

GART, HERBERT STEVEN, communications executive, producer; b. Phila., June 11, 1937; s. Jack and Celia (Miller) G.; m. Lillian Allen Jay, Aug. 12, 1969; 1 child, Heather Joy. Student, Temple U., 1955—59. Pres. BSM Prodns., Inc., N.Y.C., 1965—70, Herbert S. Gart Mgmt., Inc., N.Y.C., 1963—84, Whitfeld Music, Inc., N.Y.C., 1965—90, Rainbow Collection, Ltd., N.Y.C., 1971—. Personal mgr.: (1963—) Bill Cosby, Buffy Sainte-Marie, Jose Feliciano, Jesse Colin Young, The Youngbloods (Gold Record award Rec. Industry Assn. Am. and RCA Records 1968), Don McLean (5 Platinum Record awards Rec. Industry Assn. Am. and United Artists 1972), Andy Breckman (3 Emmy awards 1982, 85), Peter Tork (The Monkees), Ed Begley Jr. (several Emmy nominations), Jack Bruce (Cream), Felix Pappalardi (Mountain), Tim Hauser (Manhattan Transfer), Tommy West (Jim Croce), The Persuasions, Headsoup, Alix Dobkin (feminist leader) Roger Davidson, Roxy Dawn, Ashley Cleveland, (record prodn.) (1965—) Janis Ian (Gold Record award Rec. Industry Assn. Am. and Columbia Records 1975, 9 nominations for and 3 Grammy awards won Nat. Acad. Rec. Arts and Scis. 1975), Dick Feller, Roy Buchanan, Charlie Daniels, Mississippi John Hurt, Felix Pappalardi, Roger Davidson. Office: The Rainbow Collection Ltd 3324 Emory Dr Marietta GA 30062 Business E-Mail: yes@therainbow.com.

GARTEN, DAVID BURTON, lawyer; b. Iowa City, Mar. 23, 1952; s. William B. and Linda (Laird) G.; m. Anita Wallner, Mar. 12, 1983. BA summa cum laude, honors in Econs., Yale U., 1974, JD, 1977. Law clk. to Hon. Anthony M. Kennedy U.S. Ct. Appeals (9th cir.), Sacramento, 1977-78; assoc. Kirkland & Ellis, Chgo., 1979-84, ptnr., 1984-90; v.p., gen. counsel NL Industries Inc., Houston, 1990—. Mem. Phi Beta Kappa. Avocations: skiing, golf. Office: NL Industries Inc 16825 Northchase Dr Ste 1200 Houston TX 77060-6012

GARTEN, JEFFREY E., dean, marketing professional; BA, Dartmouth Coll., 1968; MA, Johns Hopkins U., PhD, 1980. Mng. dir. Lehman Brothers and the Blackstone Group, N.Y.C., 1979-92; undersec. commerce internat. trade Pres. Clinton, Washington, 1993-95; dean Yale Sch. Mgmt., New Haven, Conn., 1995—. Bd. dirs. Aetna Corp., Calpine Energy Corp., Credit Suisse Asset Mgmt., CarMax, Inc. Author: A Cold Peace: America, Japan, Germany and the Struggle for Supremacy, 1992, The Big Ten: The Big Emerging Markets and How They Will Change Our Lives, 1997, The Mind of the CEO, 1997-2001, The Politics of Fortune: A New Agenda for Business Leaders, 2002; editor: World View: Global Strategies for the New Economy, 2000; columnist Bus. Week Mag.; contbr. articles to profl. jours. Capt. U.S. Army Special Forces. Office: Yale School of Management PO Box 208200 New Haven CT 06520-8200

GARTEN, MORRIS L., lawyer; b. Balt., Feb. 1, 1967; BA, Franklin and Marshall Coll., 1989; JD, U. Balt., 1995. Bar: Md. 1995, DC 1998. Law clk. Balt. County, Md. Cir. Ct., 1995—96; atty. Fedder & Garten, Balt. Mem.: ABA, Md. State Bar Assn., Balt. County Bar Assn., Bar Assn. Balt. City, Franklin and Marshall Coll. Alumni Assn., Associated Jewish Cmty. Fedn. Balt. (chmn. 2000—01, pres. 2004—). Office: Fedder & Garten 36 S Charles St Ste 2300 Charles Ctr S Baltimore MD 21201 Office Phone: 410-539-2800. Office Fax: 410-659-0543.

GARTENBERG, SEYMOUR LEE, retired recording industry executive; b. NYC, May 27, 1931; s. Morris and Anna (Banner) G.; m. Anna Stassi, Feb. 18, 1956 (dec. Feb. 3, 1998); children: Leslie, Karen, Mark; m. Phyllis H. Hecker, Mar. 14, 1999. BBA cum laude, CCNY, 1952, LHD (hon.), 1996. Asst. contr. Finlay Straus, Inc., N.Y.C., 1950-56; contr. Tappin's Inc., Newark, 1956; sr. v.p. Columbia House divsn. CBS, N.Y.C., 1956-65; v.p. fin. Columbia Records divsn. CBS, N.Y.C., 1965-67; exec. v.p. Columbia House divsn. CBS, N.Y.C., 1967-73; pres. CBS Toys Divsn., Cranbury, N.J., 1973-78; v.p. CBS/Columbia Group, N.Y.C., 1978—; sr. group v.p. CBS Records Group, 1979-87; exec. v.p. CBS Records Inc., 1987-91; ret., 1991. Mem.: Am. Mgmt. Assn., Inst. Mgmt. Accts., Mill Island Civic Assn. Personal E-mail: garten@optonline.net.

GARTENHAUS, SOLOMON, physicist, educator; b. Kassel, Germany, Jan. 3, 1929; came to U.S., 1937, naturalized, 1943; s. Leopolt and Hanna (Brandler) G.; m. Johanna Lore Weisz, Aug. 30, 1953; children: Michael M., Kevin M. BS, U. Pa., 1951; MS, U. Ill., 1953, PhD, 1955. Instr. Stanford U., 1955-58; faculty physics Purdue U., Lafayette, Ind., 1958—, prof., 1963—; asst. dean Grad. Sch., 1972-77, sec. of faculties, 1980—. Disting. vis. prof. USAF Acad., Colo., 1977-78; dir. Purdue-Ind. Studienprogram, U. Hamburg, W. Ger., 1979-80; cons. Lockheed, summers 1958-60; officer, dir. Advanced Research Corp., 1961-65 Author: Elements of Plasma Physics, 1964, Physics-Basic Principles, 1975; contbr. articles to profl. jours. Fellow Am. Phys. Soc.; mem. N.Y. Acad. Scis., Am. Assn. Physics Tchrs., Phi Beta Kappa, Sigma Xi. Home: 2102 S 9th St Lafayette IN 47905-2132 Office: Purdue U Dept Physics Lafayette IN 47907 Business E-Mail: garten@physics.purdue.edu.

GARTH, BRYANT GEOFFREY, lawyer, educator; b. San Diego, Dec. 9, 1949; s. William and Patricia (Feild) G.; m. Gwendolyn Sessions; children: Heather, Andrew, Daniela. BA magna cum laude, Yale U., 1972; JD, Stanford U., 1975; PhD, European U. Inst., Florence, Italy, 1979. Bar: Calif. 1975, Ind. 1988. Law clk. to judge U.S. Dist. Ct. (no. dist.) Calif., San Francisco, 1978-79; asst. prof. Ind. U., Bloomington, 1979-82, assoc. prof., 1982-85, prof., 1985-92, dean Law Sch., 1986-90; dir. Am. Bar Found., Chgo., 1990—2004, sr. rsch. fellow, 2004—. Cons. Ont. Law Reform Commn., 1984-85, 94, World Bank Argentina Project, 1993-94, World Bank Ecuador Project, 2003; vis. assoc. prof. U. Mich., Ann Arbor, 1983-84; bd. dirs. Internat. Human Rights Law Inst.; mem. bd. visitors Stanford U. Law Sch., 1993-2000. Author: Neighborhood Law Firms for the Poor, 1980; co-editor: Access to Justice: A World Survey, 1978, Access to Justice: Emerging Issues and Perspectives, 1979, Dealing in Virtue, 1996, Internationalization of Palace Wars, 2002; contbr. articles to profl. jours. V.p. H.G. & K.F. Montgomery Found. Rsch. grantee NSF, 1982, 91, 92, 95, 99, 2001, Nat. Inst. Dispute Resolution, 1985, Ind. Supreme Ct., 1989, Italian Coun. Rsch., 1989, Keck, 1995, MacArthur, 1997. Mem.: Law and Soc. Assn., Am. Law Inst. Democrat. Office Phone: 312-988-6575. Business E-Mail: bggarth@abfn.org.

GARTH, LEONARD I., judge; b. Bklyn., Apr. 7, 1921; s. Frank A. and Anne F. Goldstein; m. Sarah Miriam Kaufman, Sept. 6, 1942; 1 child, Tobie Gail Garth Meisel. BA, Columbia U., 1942; postgrad., Nat. Inst. Pub. Affairs, 1942—43; LLB, Harvard U., 1952. Bar: N.J. 1952. Mem. firm Cole, Berman & Garth (and predecessors), Paterson, NJ, 1952—70; judge U.S. Dist. Ct. for Dist. N.J., Newark, 1970—73; U.S. cir. judge Ct. Appeals for 3d Cir., 1973—; lectr. Inst. Continuing Legal Edn.; lectr., coadj. mem. faculty Rutgers U. Law Sch., 1978—98, Seton Hall Law Sch., 1980—95. Mem. N.J. Bd. Bar Examiners, 1964—68; mem. com. on revision gen. and admiralty rules Fed. Dist. Ct. N.J.; former mem. com. on fin. disclosure Jud. Conf. U.S.; adv. bd. Fed. Cts. Study Com. Pres.; trustee Harvard Law Sch. Assn. N.J., 1958—63; adv. bd. Law and Soc. Major of Ramapo Coll. 1st lt. U.S. Army, 1943—46. Mem.: FBA, ABA (N.J. fellows, appellate judges conf.), Am. Law Inst., Passaic County (N.J.) Bar Assn. (pres. 1967—68). Office: Ct Appeals ML King Jr Fed Bldg 50 Walnut St Rm 5040 Newark NJ 07102-3506 also: 20613 US Courthouse Philadelphia PA 19106 E-mail: chambers_of_judge_leonard_garth@ca3.uscourts.gov.

GARTHOFF, RAYMOND LEONARD, retired diplomat, diplomatic historian, researcher; b. Cairo, Mar. 26, 1929; parents Am. citizens; s. Arnold Alexander and Margaret Louise (Frank) G.; m. Vera Alexandrovna Vasilieva, Sept. 16, 1950; 1 child, Alexander Raymond. AB, Princeton U., 1948; MA, Yale U., 1949, PhD, 1951. Rsch. staff RAND Corp., Washington, 1950-57; estimates officer CIA, Washington, 1957-61; with U.S. Dept. of State, Washington, 1961-79, ambassador, 1977-79; sr. fellow Brookings Instn., Washington, 1980-94. Author: Detente and Confrontation, 1985, rev. edit., 1994, Deterrence and Revolution in Soviet Military Doctrine, 1990, The Great Transition, 1994, Reflections on the Cuban Missile Crisis, 1987, rev. edit. 1989, A Journey through the Cold War, 2001, 11 other books; editor, co-author 80 books; contbr. over 100 articles to profl. jours. Recipient Arthur S. Flemming award Jaycees, 1965, Superior Honor award Dept. of State, 1965, Disting. Honor award, 1972, Wilbur L. Cross medal Yale U., 1992. Mem. Coun. Fgn. Rels., Am. Assn. for Advancement of Slavic Studies, Soc. for Historians of Am. Fgn. Rels., Internat. Inst. for Strategic Studies, Acad. Polit. Sci., Assn. Diplomatic Studies. Home: 1901 Wyoming Ave NW Apt 14 Washington DC 20009

GARTHWAITE, GENE RALPH, historian, educator; b. Mt. Hope, Wis., July 15, 1933; s. Ralph Albert and Merle I. (Quarne) G.; div.; children: R. Andrew, Alexander, Martin. BA, St. Olaf Coll., 1955; postgrad., U. Chgo., 1958-59; PhD, U. Calif., 1969; MA, Dartmouth Coll., 1987. From instr. to prof. history Dartmouth Coll., Hanover, N.H., 1968-98, chair Asian studies, 1980-92, chair history dept., 1992-96, Jane & Raphael Bernstein prof. in Asian studies, 1998—. Author: Khans and Shahs, 1983, The Persians, 2004; contbr. articles to profl. jours. Capt. USAF, 1955-58. Grantee Social Sci. Rsch. Coun., NEH, 1979-80, 91-93. Mem. Middle East Studies Assn. (dir. 1968—), Soc. Iranian Studies (exec. sec. 1969—), Phi Beta Kappa. Democrat. Episcopalian. Avocation: gardening. Office: Dartmouth Coll Dept History Hanover NH 03755 Office Phone: 603-646-2594. E-mail: gene.r.garthwaite@dartmouth.edu.

GARTHWAITE, THOMAS LEONARD, city health department administrator; b. Port Allegany, Pa., July 8, 1947; 2 children. AB, Cornell U.; MD, Temple U., 1973. Intern Med. Coll. Wis. Affiliated Hosp., 1973—74, resident, 1974—76; with Veterans Health Adminstrn., 1976—87, chief of staff, 1987—95, dep. undersec. for health, 1995—2000, undersec. for health, 2000—02; assoc. prof., medicine Med. Coll. Wis., 1985—95, assoc. dean, 1987—95; dir., chief med. officer L.A. Co. Dept. Health Svcs., 2002—. Office: Dept Health Svcs 313 N Figueroa St Los Angeles CA 90012

GARTLAND, ALICE JOHNSON, artist; b. Phila., Jan. 27, 1922; d. Nelson Vincent Johnson and Alice Marie McDonald; m. Henry Joseph Gartland, Apr. 15, 1944; children: Kevin Henry, Michael Henry, Sean Henry. Student, Mary Washington Coll., 1945-46, George Washington U., 1950, Santa Fe C.C., 1971-72, Fla. C.C. With U.S. Govt., Phila., 1940—42, Petersburg, Va., 1942—44; tchr. Fla. C.C., Jacksonville, 1989-90; writer, columnist Art Scene Beaches Leader Newspaper, Jacksonville, 1991—. Exhibitions include St. Augustine Art Assn., 1994, Beaches Fine Arts Guild, 1990 (1st Prize), Gainesville Fine Arts Guild, 1980, Art League, Washington, 1975, 1984, Fla. Capitol, Tallahassee, 2001, one-woman shows include Cultural Ctr., Alantic Beach, Fla., 2003—04, Art Ctr., Jacksonville Beach, Fla., 1990, 1998. Pres., founder Beaches Art Found., Jacksonville, 1990; pres. Beaches Fine Arts Guild, Jacksonville; bd. dirs., 1st v.p. Beaches Area Hist. Soc., Jacksonville, 1995-2000; bd. dirs., chmn. cultural bd. City of Atlantic Beach, Fla., 1995-2000, 03; apptd. by mayor Cultural Coun. City of Jacksonville, 2002—; bd. dirs. Beaches Fine Arts Coun., Jacksonville Beach, Fla., City Grants Com., Jacksonville, 1991, 92; mem. cultural coun. Jacksonville, Fla., 2001—. Recipient Monetary award Jacksonville Comty. Found., 1994; named Beaches Arts Ctr. scholarship in her honor, 2005. Mem. Nat. Soc. Arts and Letters (pres., v.p. Fla. chpt.). Republican. Roman Catholic. Avocations: reading, gardening, painting. Home: 1140 Seminole Rd Atlantic Beach FL 32233-5505

GARTLAND, JOHN JOSEPH, physician, writer; b. Phila., Nov. 16, 1918; s. John Joseph and Jane Madelyn (Lafferty) G.; m. Madelyn T. Duffy, Jan. 5, 1944; children: Lynn, Barbara, John Jr., Patricia, Mary Ellen. AB, Princeton U., 1941; MD, Jefferson Med. Coll., 1944. Diplomate Am. Bd. of Orthopaedic Surgery. Chief orthopaedic surgery Meth. Hosp., Phila., 1960-68, Lankenau Hosp., Phila., 1968-70; James Edward prof., chmn. dept. of orthopaedic surgery Jefferson Med. Coll., Thomas Jefferson U., Phila., 1970-85, dir. office departmental rev. Jefferson Med. Coll., 1986-89, univ. med. editor, 1990—. Author: Fundamentals of Orthopaedics, 1965, 4th edit., 1986, Medical Writing and Communicating, 1993; contbr. numerous articles to profl. jours. Trustee Thomas Jefferson U., 1996-2002. Served to capt. U.S. Army, 1945-47. NIH grantee, 1971-74. Fellow Am. Acad. Orthopaedic Surgeons (pres. 1979-80), Am. Orthopaedic Assn.; mem. Coun. Med. Splty. Socs. (pres. elect 1987, pres. 1988), Overbrook Golf Club (Bryn Mawr, Pa.), Alpha Omega Alpha, Sigma Xi. Democrat. Roman Catholic. Avocations: tennis, writing. Office: Thomas Jefferson U 1710 Edison Bldg 130 S 9th St Philadelphia PA 19107 Office Phone: 215-503-4042.

GARTMAN, JOHN E., lawyer; BS in elec. engring. with highest honors, U. Tex., 1983, JD with honors, 1986. Bar: Calif., Va., DC. Judicial clk. to Honorable Giles S. Rich, US Ct. Appeals Fed. Circuit, 1988—90; ptnr. Brown & Bain, P.A., Fish & Richardson, 1993—98, mng. prin. San Diego, 1998—. Adj. prof. law Santa Clara U. Sch. Law, 1995—96. Contb. patents editor Fed. Circuit Bar Jour., 1990—98; contbr. articles to jour. Named one of Nation's Magnificent 7, IP's Best Young Trial Lawyers, IP Worldwide, 2002, Calif. Top 25 IP Lawyers, Daily Jour., Top 25 Intellectual Property Atty. Calif., 2003, 2004. Office: 12390 El Camino Real San Diego CA 92130 Office Phone: 858-678-4313. Business E-Mail: gartman@fr.com.

GARTNER, HAROLD HENRY, III, lawyer; b. L.A., June 23, 1948; s. Harold Henry Jr. and Frances Mildred (Evans) Gartner; m. Denise Helene Young, June 7, 1975 (div. 2003); children: Patrick Christopher, Matthew Alexander. Student, Pasadena City Coll., 1966-67, George Williams Coll., 1967-68, Calif. State U., Los Angeles, 1969; JD cum laude, Loyola U., Los Angeles, 1972. Bar: Calif. 1972, U.S. Dist. Ct. (ctrl. dist.) 1973, U.S. Ct. Appeals (9th cir.) 1973. Assoc. Hitt, Murray & Caffray, Long Beach, Calif., 1972; dep. city atty. City of L.A., 1972-73; assoc. Patterson, Ritner & Lockwood, L.A., 1973-79; mng. ptnr. all offices Patterson, Ritner, Lockwood, Gartner & Jurich, L.A., Bakersfield, and San Bernardino, Calif., 1991—. Instr. law Ventura Coll., 1981. Recipient Am. Jurisprudence award Trusts and Equity, 1971. Mem. ABA, Am. Bd. Trial Advocates, Calif. Bar Assn., Ventura County Bar Assn., Nat. Assn. Def. Counsel, Assn. Am. Bd. Trial Advocates, So. Calif. Def. Counsel, Ventura County Trial Lawyers Assn. Clubs: Pacific Corinthian Yacht. Republican. Avocations: sailing, scuba diving, flying. Home: 272 Camino Toluca Camarillo CA 93010 Office: Patterson Ritner Lockwood Gartner & Jurich 3580 Wilshire Blvd Ste 900 Los Angeles CA 90010 Office Phone: 213-487-6240. Personal E-mail: hgartner@dock.net.

GARTNER, JOAN J., elementary school educator; b. Havre De Grace, Md., Nov. 20, 1943; d. Lawrence S. and H. Lucille (Sauer) Pruett; m. Jerry E. Gartner, Dec. 17, 1965; children: Robert Tyler, Chad Eric, Cory Lynn. BS in Edn., Pittsburg (Kans.) State U., 1978, MS in Edn., 1984. Cert. tchr., reading specialist, Kans. Classrm. tchr. combination classrooms Unified Sch. Dist. 506, Altamont, Kans., 1979-95, tchr. TitleI Chap. I remedial reading and math., 1995—. Mem. com. on book selection Unified Sch. Dist. 506, 1985, 91. Chmn. sec. Altamont Recreation Commn. 1978-86; sec. Altamont Libr. Bd., 1985-89 Mem. NEA, Kans. Edn. Assn. (Apple award 1992), Internt. Reading Assn., Kans. Reading Assn. (del.), S.E. Kans. Reading Assn. (xec., v.p., pres.), Nat. Soc. Tole and Decorative Painters, Tchrs. Using Whole Lang. Avocations: painting, reading, sewing, walking, travel, auctions. Office: Mound Valley Grade Sch 402 Walnut Mound Valley KS 67354

GARTNER, JOHN D., clinical psychologist, educator; m. Claude Guillemard. BA in Psychology magna cum laude, Princeton U., 1979; MS in Clin. Psychology, U. Mass., 1982, PhD in Clin. Psychology, 1985. Lic. psychologist, Md. Postdoctoral fellow in treatment personality disorders N.Y. Hosp.-Cornell Med. Ctr., N.Y.C., 1985-87; instr. dept. psychology U. Mass., Amherst, 1981-85; asst. prof. dept. pastoral counseling, dir. doctoral rsch. Loyola U., Balt., 1987-90; clin. asst. prof. dept. psychology Johns Hopkins U., Balt., 1991—, asst. prof. div. med. psychology in psychiatry, 1992—, clin. supr. Student Mental Health Ctr., 1991-92, clin. supr. outpatient dept. Sch. Medicine, 1993—; pvt. practice, Balt. and Columbia, Md., 1987—. Mem. courtesy staff Sheppard and Enoch Pratt Hosp., 1989—; psychotherapist Psychol. Svcs. Ctr., U. Mass., 1980-84, family therapist learning intervention family therapy team, 1981-82; psychology extern Northampton VA Med. Ctr., 1982-83; clinician emergency svcs. div. Franklin-Hampshire Cmty. Mental Health Ctr., 1982-84; presenter in field, 1990—; clin. cons. Archdiocese of Balt., 1988-89, Md. Synod, Luth. Ch. Am., 1988-89, Pastoral Counseling Svcs. Md., Balt., 1989-93. Editor: (with M. Finn) Object Relations: Theory and Religion: Clinical Applications, 1993; author: The Hypomanic Edge, 2005; contbg. editor Jour. Psychology and Theology, Jour. Pastoral Counseling; contbr. articles to profl. jours. Bd. dirs. Ctr. for Social Rsch., Washington, 1991—. Rsch. grantee Prison Fellowship, 1989-90. Mem. APA (program chmn. div. psychology of religion 1993), Md. Psychol. Assn., Balt. Soc. for Psychoanalytic Studies (pres. 1991-93, dir. edn. 1993—). Office: Gibson Bldg 6525 N Charles St Ste 143 Baltimore MD 21204-6829 also: Grosvenor Century Plz 10632 Little Patuxent Pkwy Columbia MD 21044-3273*

GARTNER, LAWRENCE MITCHEL, pediatrician, medical college educator; b. Bklyn., Apr. 24, 1933; s. Samuel and Bertha (Brimberg) G.; m. Carol Sue Blicker, Aug. 12, 1956; children— Alex David, Madeline Hallie. AB, Columbia U., 1954; MD, Johns Hopkins U., 1958. Intern pediatrics Johns Hopkins Hosp., 1958-59; resident pediatrics Albert Einstein Coll. Medicine, 1959-60, chief resident, 1960-61, instr. pediatrics, 1962-64, asst. prof., 1964-69, assoc. prof., 1969-74, prof., 1974-80, dir. divsn. neonatology, 1967-80, dir. divsn. pediatric hepatology, 1967-80; dir. clin. research unit Rose F. Kennedy Ctr., 1972-80; attending physician Hosp. of Albert Einstein Coll. Medicine, 1967-80; prof. dept. pediatrics U. Chgo. Pritzker Sch. Medicine, 1980-98, prof. dept. obstetrics and gynecology, 1995-98, prof. emeritus pediatrics and obstetrics and gynecology, 1998—; chmn. dept. pediatrics, med. dir. Wyler Children's Hosp., U. Chgo. Med. Ctr., 1980-93. Chmn. Physician's Breastfeeding Network of Ill., 1993-98. Contbr. articles to med. jours. and textbooks. Pediatrician-of-the-Yr. award Ill. chpt. Am. Acad. Pediatrics, 1995; recipient award NIH, 1967-74; Appleton Century Crofts prize, 1956; Mosby book award, 1958. Mem. AAAS, Am. Pediatric Soc. (chmn. coun. 1989-90), Soc. Pediatric Rsch., Perinatal Rsch. Soc., Am. Assn. Study Liver Disease, Chgo. Pediatric Soc. (editor 1990-91, treas. 1992-93, sec. 1993-94, v.p. 1994-95, pres. 1995-96), Am. Acad. Pediatrics (chair breastfeeding workgroup 1994-2000, chair exec. com. sect. on breastfeeding 2000—), N.Am. Soc. Pediatric Gastroenterology (pres. 1974-75), The Milk Club (chmn. 1994-96), Acad. Breastfeeding Medicine (founding bd. dirs. 1994-95, editor newsletter 1995-2000, v.p. 1997-98, pres., 1998-99), LaLeche League Internat., Phi Beta Kappa, Alpha Omega Alpha. Personal E-mail: gart@uchicago.edu.

GARTNER, MICHAEL GAY, editor, baseball executive, television executive; b. Des Moines, Oct. 25, 1938; s. Carl David and Mary Marguerite (Gay) Gartner; m. Barbara Jean McCoy, May 25, 1968; children: Melissa, Christopher (dec.), Michael. BA, Carleton Coll., 1960; JD, NYU, 1969; LittD (hon.), Simpson Coll., 1984; LLD (hon.), James Madison U., 1989; LittD (hon.), Grand View Coll., 1990, Iowa Wesleyan Coll., 1997; LLD (hon.), Drake U., 2001. Bar: NY, Iowa. With Wall St. Jour., N.Y.C., 1960—74, page one editor, 1970—74; exec. editor Des Moines Register and Tribune, 1974—76, editor, 1976—82, editl. chmn., 1982—85, v.p., 1975—76, exec. v.p., 1977, pres., COO, 1978—85; editor Courier-Jour. and Louisville Times, 1986—87; gen. news exec. Gannett Co., 1987—88; pres. NBC News, 1988—93; editor, co-owner Ames (Iowa) Daily Tribune, 1986—99; chmn., majority-owner Iowa Cubs, 1999—; chmn., co-owner New West Newspapers, 2000—. Bd. dirs. Creative Loafing, Inc. Chmn. Vision Iowa, 2000—05; hon. trustee Simpson Coll.; mem. Pulitzer Prize Bd., 1982—92, chmn., 1991—92; trustee Freedom Forum Newseum, Washington; bd. dirs. World Food Prize; pres. Iowa Bd. Regents, 2005—. Recipient Pulitzer prize for editl. writing, 1997; fellow, Harvard U. Inst. Politics, 1994. Mem.: Am. Soc. Newspaper Editors (pres. 1986—87), Assn. Bar City N.Y., Iowa Bar Assn., ABA, Garden of Gods Club, Wakonda Club. also: 366 W 11th St New York NY 10014-6225 Office: One Line Dr Des Moines IA 50309-4631 Home: 100 Market St Des Moines IA 50309 E-mail: mgartner@iowacubs.com.

GARTNER, MURRAY, lawyer; b. N.Y.C., Sept. 23, 1922; s. Leo and Celia G.; m. Anne Ellis Thompson, June 9, 1961; children: Marion Moreau, Thomas Murray. AB, NYU, 1942; LLB, Harvard U., 1945. Bar: N.Y. 1946, Calif. 1948. Law clk. to assoc. justice Robert H. Jackson U.S. Supreme Ct., Washington, 1945-47; assoc. Pillsbury, Madison & Sutro, San Francisco,

1947-51; lectr. law Hastings Coll. Law, San Francisco, 1948; asst. to gen. counsel U.S. rep. in Paris, Econ. Coop. Adminstrn. Mut. Security Adminstrn., 1951-53; assoc. Roosevelt, Freidin & Littauer, N.Y.C., 1953-59; ptnr. Poletti, Freidin, Prashker & Gartner (and predecessors), N.Y.C., 1959-85, Proskauer Rose, LLP, N.Y.C., 1985-2000. Trustee Children's Aid Soc., 1971-2004. Office: Proskauer Rose LLP 1585 Broadway New York NY 10036-8299

GARTNER, STEVEN J., lawyer; b. Westwood, NJ, Nov. 22, 1959; BSBA, Georgetown U., 1981; JD magna cum laude, St. John's U., 1984. Bar: NY 1985, NJ 1986. Assoc. Willkie Farr & Gallagher LLP, London, 1988—90, ptnr., Corp. and Fin. Svcs. Dept. NYC. Office: Willkie Farr & Gallagher LLP 787 Seventh Ave New York NY 10019 Office Phone: 212-728-8222. E-mail: sgartner@willkie.com.

GARTON, CHARLES, classics educator; b. Leeds, Eng., Aug. 13, 1926; came to U.S., 1965; s. John Charles and Mary Garton; m. Hilary Joan Smithers, Jan. 9, 1960; children: Hugh James Lauriston, Christopher John. BA, Cambridge (Eng.) U., 1949, MA, 1953; postgrad., U. Basle, Switzerland, 1949, Brit. Sch. at Rome, 1950. Asst. lectr. classics U. Hull, Eng., 1951-53; lectr. classics U. Newcastle-upon-Tyne, 1953-65; assoc. prof. classics SUNY, Buffalo, 1965-72, prof. classics, 1972-91, prof. emeritus, 1991—. Author: Personal Aspects of the Roman Theater, 1972, Lincoln School: A Summary Honours Board, 1988; editor and trans. John Clarke's Orationes et Declamationes, 1972, The Metrical Life of Saint Hugh, 1986, co-editor and trans. Theophylact, On Predestined Terms of Life, 1978, Germanos, On Predestined Terms of Life, 1979, Robert Froriep: Aspects of the Tongue, 1982; editor: Arethusa, 1968—71, Arethusa Monographs, 1985—91; assoc. editor: Arethusa, 1974—85; contbr. numerous articles to profl. jours. Sub-lt. Bris. Royal Navy, 1946. Porson scholar U. Cambridge, 1949, Charles Oldham scholar, 1949-50. Mem. Lincoln Record Soc., Classical Assn. of Eng. and Wales (mem. coun. 1956-57). Home: 568 Seabrook Dr Williamsville NY 14221 E-mail: cgarton@worldnet.att.net.

GARTON, LINDA ANN, musician; b. Eau Claire, Wis., Dec. 19, 1971; d. Richard W. and Marilyn D. (Moxness) Duerst; m. Ryan Coe Garton, Aug. 27, 1994. B in Music, St. Olaf Coll., Northfield, Minn., 1993; M of Music, U. Neb., 1995, Northwestern U., 1997. Piano faculty Trinity U., Deerfield, Ill., 1995-99; lectr. in music theory, asst. to dean Northwestern U., Evanston, Ill., 1999—2001, dir. student affairs Sch. Music, 2002—. Co-author: (books) Beginning Piano 1&2, Intermediate Piano 1&2. Mem. MTNA, Soc. Music Theory, Music Theory Midwest, Coll. Music Soc., Pi Kappa Lambda.

GARTON, RANDALL K., music educator, church organist; b. Lincoln, Nebr., Apr. 19, 1982; s. Darwin Dan and Vicki Sue Garton. Music, Doane Coll., 2004. Cert. Tchr. Nebr., 2004. Dir. of music United Luth. Ch., Lincoln, Nebr., 2001—; music tchr. Freeman Pub. Schs., Adams, Nebr., 2004—. Mem.: Nebr. Edn. Assn. Lutheran. Avocations: hunting, fishing, composing, travel. Home: 5444 Garland Lincoln NE 68504 Office Phone: 402-988-2525.

GARTON, ROBERT DEAN, state legislator; b. Chariton, Iowa, Aug. 18, 1933; s. Jesse Glenn and Ruth Irene (Wright) G.; m. Barbara Hicks, June 17, 1955; children: Bradford, Brenda. BS, Iowa State U., 1955; MS, Cornell U., 1959. Pers. rep. Cummins Engine Co., Columbus, Ind., 1959-61; owner Garton Assocs. Mgmt. Cons., Columbus, 1961-96; v.p. profl. devel. Ivy Tech. State Coll., Columbus, 1996—; mem. Ind. Senate, Indpls., 1970—, minority caucus chmn., 1976-78, majority caucus chmn., 1978-80, pres. pro tempore, 1980—. Bd. dir. Rural Water Sys. Mem. exec. com. Nat. Conf. State Legislatures, 1989-92; chmn. Mid-West Conf. State Legislatures, Coun. State Govts., 1984-85, mem. gov. bd., 1985—; chmn. Ind. Civil Rights Commn., 1969-70; mem. exec. com. Nat. Fedn. Young Reps., 1966; trustee Franklin Coll., 1998—; bd. dirs. Independent Colls. of Ind., 2001—, State Legis. Leaders Found., 2003—. With USMCR, 1955-57. Co-recipient Legislator of the Yr. award, Ind. Civil Liberties Union, 2000, William M. Bulger Excellence in State Legis. Leadership award, 1999; named Hon. Citizen, Iowa, 1962, Tenn., 1977, winner internat. speech contest, Toastmasters, 1962, Small Bus. Champion, Ind. Small Bus. Coun., 1997, Pub. Servant of the Yr., Ind. Assn. Rehab. Facilities, 2000; named one of 5 Outstanding Young Men in Ind., 1968; recipient Man of Yr., Ind. Rep. Mayor's Assn., 1991, Disting. Svc. award, Jr. C. of C. Columbus, 1968, Guardian Small Bus. award, Nat. Fedn. for Ind. Bus., 1990, 1993, 1994, Lee Atwater Leadership award, Nat. Rep. Legislator Assn., 1991, Outstanding Pub. Svc. award, Podiatric Assn., 1993, United Sr. Action Legis. Leadership award, 1994, Outstanding Govt. Leader award, Apt. Assn. Ind., 1998, Freedom of Road award, ABATE of Ind., 2000, Senator of Yr. award, Ind. Primary Health Care Assn., 2001, Friend of Edn. award, N. Ctrl. Bus. Edn. Assn., 2001, Disting. Pub. Svc. award, Am. Legion, 2001, Pub. Sector award, Benjamin Harrison Medallion, 2001, Benjamin Harrison medallion, 2001, Friend of Autism award, 2001, Legislator of Yr., Trial Lawyers Assn., 2003. Mem. Rotary, Beta Theta Pi. Office: Ivy Tech State Coll PO Box 1111 Columbus IN 47202-1111 Business E-Mail: bgarton@ivytech.edu.

GARTON, THOMAS WILLIAM, lawyer; b. Ft. Dodge, Iowa, Jan. 19, 1947; s. H. Boyd and Ruth A. (Porter) G.; m. Marcia K. Hoover, June 21, 1969; children: Geoffrey, Matthew. BA, Carleton Coll., 1969; JD magna cum laude, U. Minn., 1974. Assoc. Fredrikson & Byron, PA, Mpls., 1974-80, shareholder, 1980—, chmn. corp. practice group. Adj. prof. William Mitchell Coll. Law, St. Paul, Minn., 1977-80, U. Minn. Law Sch., Mpls., 1980; bd. dirs. RS/Eden Programs; presenter continuing legal edn. seminars on tax, mergers and acquisitions, and bus. planning, 1977—. With U.S. Army, 1969-71. Mem. ABA (tax sect.), Minn. Bar Assn. (dir. tax coun. 1987-89). Office: Fredrikson & Byron PA 200 S Sixth St Ste4000 Minneapolis MN 55402-1425 E-mail: tgarton@fredlaw.com.

GARTRELL, DONALD EVERETT, lawyer; b. Washington; s. Everett A. and Martha (Buchanan) G.; m. Sarah Burgess, June 17, 1967; children: Bryce B., Molly B. BA in Econs., Ohio Wesleyan U., 1962; LLB, Vanderbilt U., 1965. Bar: Tenn. 1965, N.H. 1968. Staff judge advocate USAF, Dow AFB, Maine, 1965-68; assoc., ptnr. Sulloway, Hollis, Godfrey & Soden, Concord, N.H., 1968-74; mem., dir. Gallagher, Callahan & Gartrell, Concord, N.H., 1975—. Moderator Town of Warner, NH, 1972—98; trustee Gould Acad., Bethel, Maine, 1994—2001; bd. trustees N.H. Hist. Soc.; bd. dirs. Concord Area Chpt. Am. Red Cross. Fellow N.H. Bar Found.; mem. ABA, New Hampshire Bar Assn. (bd. govs. 1980-82, chair real property, probate and trust sect. 1978-80), Merrimack County Bar Assn., Concord Rotary Club (pres. 1980-81). Republican. Avocations: sailing, skiing, hiking. Office: Gallagher Callahan & Gartrell PC PO Box 1415 214 N Main St Concord NH 03301-5050 Office Phone: 603-228-1181. Business E-Mail: gartrell@gcglaw.com.

GARTZ, ROLF FRITZ, foundation administrator; b. Bonn, Germany, Dec. 23, 1940; s. Fritz and Hildegard (Rhein) G.; m. Christel Anneliese Overgahr gen. Willebrand, Aug. 7, 1970; 1 child, Stephan. Student, Bonn and Cologne U., Germany, 1964—69; DSc in Cell Biology, Bonn U., 1969; PhD (hon.), State U. Social Scis., Moscow, 2000. Civil servant, govt. dir., Germany, 1970-90; mng. chmn. Eduard Rhein Found., Hamburg, Germany, 1990—. Bd. dirs. Prof. Rhein Found., Koenigswinter, Germany, 1987—; academician Internat. Informatization Acad., 2000; hon. prof. internat. bus. sch. MIRBIS, 2003. Decorated Cross of the Order of Merit Fed. Republic of Germany; recipient Sputnik medal Russian Fedn. Cosmonautics, 2000, Highest Order of Merit, Internat. Informatization Acad., 2001. Mem. AAAS, N.Y. Acad. Scis., Assn. German Natural Scientists and Physicians, German Soc. Cell Biology, European Cell Biology Orgn., Max Planck Soc. for Advancement of Sci., Fedn. Biochemical Soc., Internat. Union Biochemistry and Molecular Biology. Avocations: hunting, riding. Home and Office: Eduard Rhein Stiftung Alex von Humboldt Str 6 D-56727 Mayen Germany

GARTZ, WILLIAM FREDERICK, architect; b. Chgo., Nov. 12, 1953; s. Frederick Samuel and Lillian Louise (Korschetz) G. BA in Edn., U. Wash., 1976; MArch, U. Wis., Milw., 1983. Registered architect, Wash. Project architect McCool McDonald Architect, Seattle, 1976-77, Morse Stafford Architects, Seattle, 1977-80, Davis & Fatica, Milw., 1982-83; prin. Callison Architecture Inc., Seattle, 1984—. Prin. Gartz Architects, Seattle, 1983-84. Prin. works include Inn at Semi-Ah-Moo, Blaine, Wash., 1987, Carillon Point-Woodmark Hotel, Kirkland, Wash., 1988, internat. resorts, Thailand, The Philippines, Malaysia, 1996-98, Westin Palms Resort, Orlando, Fla., ski resorts Big Mountain, Jackson Hole, Schweitzer Mountain, Mammoth Mountain, 1996-2001. Chmn. crime com. Capitol Hill Community Coun., 1978-79; pres. Phinney Ridge Community Coun. 1991-92. Mem. AIA (honor award Colo. 1987, Seattle chpt. 1988). Avocation: hiking. Home: 6748 1st Ave NW Seattle WA 98117-4827 Office: Callison Architecture Inc Ltd 1420 5th Ave Ste 2400 Seattle WA 98101-1345 E-mail: bgartz@callison.com.

GARVENS, ELLEN JO, art educator, artist; b. Omro, Wis., Aug. 15, 1955; d. Leonard Kenneth and Eugenia Mary (Wetter) G.; m. James Patrick Phalen, Oct. 18, 1988; children: Cole Garvens Phalen, Mason Garvens Phalen. BS in Art, U. Wis., 1979; MA, U. N. Mex., 1982, MFA, 1987. Asst. prof. of art Oberlin (Ohio) Coll., 1990-94; assoc. prof. art U. Wash., Seattle, 1994—. Artist: one person shows include: Humboldt State, 2000, Jayne H. Baum Gallery, N.Y.C., 1986, 89, 93, Wooster (Ohio) Mus. of Art, U. R.I., Kingston. Recipient Wis. Women in Arts award Madison, 1978, Fullbright Hays scholarship Internat. Comm. Agy., Washington, 1979-80; grantee, NEA, Washington, 1986, HC Powers grant, Oberlin Coll., 1991, Royalty Rsch. Fund grant, U. Wash., 1996, Artist Trust Washington State fellowship, 2000—. Home: 19518 67th Ave NE Kenmore WA 98028-3447 Office: U Wash Sch of Art PO Box 353440 Seattle WA 98195-3440 E-mail: elgarv@u.washington.edu.

GARVER, FREDERICK MERRILL, industrial engineering executive; b. Indpls., Mar. 25, 1945; s. Clyde Louis and Elizabeth Kemp (Finch) G.; m. Ruth Sikkema, Nov. 8, 1969. BS, Western Mich. U., 1967; postgrad., Grand Valley State U., 1976-77; MS, Western Mich. U., 1990. Cert. mfg. engr. Methods analyst Boeing Co., Seattle, 1968-69; indsl. engr. Wolverine World Wide, Inc., Rockford, Mich., 1969-72; mgr. indsl. engring. Leigh Products Inc., Coopersville, Mich., 1972-77; dir. indsl. engring. Integrated Metal Techs., Spring Lake, Mich., 1977-79; mgr. mfg. engring. Haworth Inc., Holland, Mich., 1979-88, Hart & Cooley, Inc., Holland, 1988-92; mfg. engr. Trumark Inc., Lansing, Mich., 1992-94; sr. adv. process engr. Walker Mfg. Inc., Grass Lake, Mich., 1994-97; sr. mfg. engr. Pridgeon and Clay Inc., Grand Rapids, Mich., 1997—. Mem. Inst. Indsl. Engrs. (sr.), Soc. Mfg. Engrs. (sr., ad hoc govt. relations com.), Chem. Coaters Assn., Assn. Bus. Advocating Tariff Equity, Assn. Finishing Processes, Precision Metal Forming Assn. Western Mich. (dir.-at-large 2000—2003), Jaycees (treas. Ithaca, Mich. chpt. 1971). Forming Assn. We. Mich. (vice chmn., 2003-). Republican. Avocations: computers, skiing, tennis. Home: 9466 Tannis Rd Clarksville MI 48815-9727 Office: Pridgeon and Clay Inc 50 Cottage Grove SW Grand Rapids MI 49507-1685 E-mail: fgarver@pridgeonandclay.com.

GARVER, ROBERT VERNON, retired research physicist; b. Mpls., June 2, 1932; s. Walter Burdette and Daveda Margaret (Hansen) G.; m. Shirley Marie Phillips, June 15, 1957; children: Debra, Douglas, Daniel, Mary, Jennifer. BS, U. Md., 1956; M.E.A., George Washington U., 1968. Physicist Harry Diamond Labs., Washington, 1956-69, supervisory physicist, 1969-89. Program mgr. Army High Power Microwave Hardening Tech., 1982-89; cons. Weinschel Engring., Gaithersburg, Md., 1970-75; chmn. electromagnetic effects subcom. DoD VHSIC Qualification Com., 1981-89; pvt. cons., 1989-95; sr. engr. Xeta Internat. Corp., Crystal City, Va., 1990-95; cons. Envisioneering, Inc., Dahlgren, Va., 2000-05; developer Leap Flight Tech., The Garver Product Co., 2000-. Author: Microwave Diode Control Devices, 1976; inventor Microwave Diode Switch; patentee in field. Elder Presbyn. Ch., Germantown, Md., 1975. Served with U.S. Army, 1953-54. Fellow: IEEE (editor Jour. Solid State Cirs. 1969—73, mem. nat. adminstrv. com. profl. group microwave theory and techniques); mem.: Toastmasters. Republican. Home and Office: 2393 Bear Den Rd Frederick MD 21701-9328

GARVER, THOMAS HASKELL, curator, consultant, writer; b. Duluth, Minn., Jan. 23, 1934; s. Harvie Adair and Margaret Hope (Foght) G.; m. Natasha Nicholson, Apr. 13, 1974. BA, Haverford Coll., 1956; MA, U. Minn., 1965. Asst. to dir. Krannert Art Mus., U. Ill., Urbana, 1960-62; asst. dir. fine arts dept. Seattle World's Fair, 1962, Rose Art Mus., Brandeis U., Waltham, Mass., 1962-68; dir. Newport Harbor Art Mus. (now Orange County Mus. Art), Calif., 1968-72, 77-80; curator exhbns. Fine Arts Mus. of San Francisco, 1972-77; dir. Madison (Wis.) Art Ctr., 1980-87; asst. prof. Calif. State U., 1970-71, 79-80. Curator art collection Rayovac Corp., Madison, 1985-2001; organizing curator O. Winston Link Mus., Roanoke, Va., 2001-04. Author: Twelve Photographers of the American Social Landscape, 1967, Just Before the War: Urban American from 1935-41, 1968, The Paintings of George Tooker, 1985, rev. edit., 1992, The Last Steam Railroad in America: Photographs by O. Winston Link, 1995; exhbn. catalogues including Robert Rauschenberg, 1969, Tom Wesselmann, 1971, Reginald Marsh, 1972, Joseph Raffael, Paintings From the California Years, 1977, George Herms, 1978, 83, Nathan Oliveira, 1984, George Tooker, Paintings, 1983-87, 88, Mind and Beast: Contemporary Artists and the Animal Kingdom, 1992, Flora: Contemporary Artists and the World of Flowers, 1995, Trains that Passed in the Night: The Railroad Photographs of O. Winston Link, 1998, WATER: Contemporary Artists Who Use Water as a Theme in Their Art, Gibbes Mus. of Art, Charleston, S.C., 1999. Trustee U.S.S. Mass. Meml. Commn., Fall River, 1965-68; trustee South Coast Repertory Co., Costa Mesa, Calif., 1970-72; trustee Wis. Citizens for Arts, 1985-87; steering com. Archives Am. Art, San Francisco, 1977-80; active Newport Beach Art Commn., 1978-79, Madison Com. for Arts, 1984-87. Mem. Western Assn. Art Mus. (pres. 1970-71, trustee 1970-73), Art Mus. Assn. Am. (pres. 1979-82, trustee 1979-85). Home and Office: 1962 Atwood Ave Madison WI 53704-5221 Office Phone: 608-246-3967. E-mail: thgart@aol.com.

GARVERT, MELINDA LEE, lawyer; b. Manhattan, Kans., Dec. 17, 1954; d. Asel W. and Joanne L. (Cribbs) Harder; m. Thomas L. Garvert, June 28, 1986; children: Luke, Michael, Alex, Rachel. BS, Kans. State U., 1976; JD, Washburn Sch. Law, 1980. Bar: Kans. 1980, Colo. 1988. Assoc. McDonald, Tinker, Skaer, Quinn & Herington, Wichita, Kans., 1980-86; pvt. practice Garden City, Kans., 1986—, Colorado Springs, Colo., 1988—. Adv. bd. mem. Covenant Internat., Colorado Springs, 1994—. Mem. ABA, Kans. Bar Assn., Colo. Bar Assn., Am. Acad. Adoption Attys., Garden City C. of C., Better Bus. Bur. (Colorado Springs). Office: PO Box 50317 Colorado Springs CO 80949-0317

GARVEY, JANE, public relations executive; BA, Mount Saint Mary Coll.; MA, Mount Holyoke Coll.; fellowship program for pub. leaders, Harvard U. Assoc. commr. Mass. Dept. Pub. Works, Boston, commr., 1988-91; dir. Logan Internat. Airport, Boston, 1991-93; dep. adminstr. Fed. Hwy. Adminstrn. U.S. Dept. Transp., Washington, 1993-97, acting adminstr. Fed. Hwy. Adminstrn., 1997, apptd. 14th adminstr. FAA Washington, 1997—2003; exec. v.p., chmn. APCO Worldwide, 2003—. Lectr., rsch. scientist Ctr. for Transp. and Logistics, MIT, 2003—. Office: APCO 1615 L St NW, Ste 900 Washington DC 20036

GARVEY, JEFFREY MATTHEW, medical librarian, educator; b. N.Y.C., Sept. 7, 1950; s. James W. and Mary Lou (Hendren) G.; m. Elaine Perry, Sept. 2, 1974; children: James W., Robert P., Todd M. BA, Colgate U., 1972; MLS, Syracuse U., 1974. Dir. libr. svcs. Samaritan Med. Ctr., Watertown, N.Y., 1974—. Libr. cons. various orgns., 1980—; bd. dirs. Family Counseling Svc. of Northern N.Y., 2004—, treas., 2004—. Bd. dirs. Watertown Family YMCA, 1997—, chmn. fin. devel. com., 2000—. Recipient award for outstanding svc. in librarianship North Country Regional Centennial Commn., N.Y. Libr. Assn., 1990, 7th Ann. award for excellence in libr. svc. North Country Reference and Rsch. Resources Coun., 1997. Mem.: Nat. Network Librs. of Medicine (regional adv. com. Mid. Atlantic Region 2002—), Med. Libr. Assn. (pres. Upstate N.Y.-Ont. chpt. 0202). Home: 24189 County Route 159 Watertown NY 13601-5702 Office: Samaritan Med Ctr 830 Washington St Watertown NY 13601-4099 Office Phone: 315-785-4191. Business E-Mail: jgarvey@northnet.org.

GARVEY, JOANNE MARIE, lawyer; b. Oakland, Calif., Apr. 23, 1935; d. James M. and Marian A. (Dean) Garvey. AB with honors, U. Calif., Berkeley, 1956, MA, 1957, JD, 1961. Bar: Calif. 1962. Assoc. Cavaletto, Webster, Mullen & McCaughey, Santa Barbara, Calif., 1961-63, Jordan, Keeler & Seligman, San Francisco, 1963-67, ptnr., 1968-88, Heller, Ehrman, White & McAuliffe, San Francisco, 1988—. Bd. dirs. Mex.-Am. Legal Def. and Ednl. Fund; chmn. Law in Free Soc., Continuing Edn. Bar; mem. bd. councillors U. So. Calif. Law Ctr. Recipient Paul Veazy award, YMCA, 1973, Internat. Women's Yr. award, Queen's Bench, 1975, honors, Advs. Women, 1978, CRLA award, Boalt Hall Citation award, 1998, Judge Lowell Jensen Cmty. Svc. award, 2001, Margaret Brent award, 2003, Latcham State and Local Disting. Svc. award, 2003. Fellow: Am. Bar Found.; mem.: ABA (gov., state del., chmn. SCLAID, chmn.delivery legal svcs.), Calif. Women Lawyers (founder), Am. Law Inst., San Francisco Bar Assn. (pres., pres. Barristers), Calif. State Bar (v.p., gov., tax sect., del., Jud Klein award, Joanne Garvey award), Phi Beta Kappa, Order of Coif. Democrat. Roman Catholic. Home: 16 Kensington Ct Kensington CA 94707-1010 Office: 333 Bush St San Francisco CA 94104-2806 Office Phone: 415-772-6729. Business E-Mail: joanne.garvey@hellerehrman.com.

GARVEY, JOHN HUGH, dean, law educator; b. Sharon, Pa., Sept. 28, 1948; s. Cyril T. and Claudia C. (Evans) G.; m. Jeanne Barnes Walter, Aug. 30, 1975. AB, U. Notre Dame, 1970; JD, Harvard U., 1974. Bar: Ky. 1976, U.S. Supreme Ct. 1982. Law clk. to chief judge U.S. Ct. Appeals (2d cir.), N.Y.C., 1974-75; assoc. Morrison & Foerster, San Francisco, 1975-76; asst. prof. Coll. Law U. Ky., Lexington, 1976-79, assoc. prof. Coll. Law, 1979-80, prof. Coll. Law, 1981-94; Univ. Rsch. prof. Coll. Law, 1989-90, Ashland prof., 1990-94; prof. Notre Dame Law Sch., South Bend, Ind., 1994-99; dean Boston Coll. Law Sch., Chestnut Hill, 1999—. Asst. to Solicitor Gen., U.S. Dept. Justice, Washington, 1981-84; vis. prof. law sch. U. Mich., Ann Arbor, 1985-86; chmn. constl. law sect. Assn. Am. Law Schs., Washington, 1991-93, chmn. law and religion sect., 1998-99. Author: Modern Constitutional Theory, 1989, 5th edit., 2004, The First Amendment, 1992, 2d edit., 1995, What Are Freedoms For?, 1996. Recipient Alpha Sigma Nu Jesuit Book Award, 2004; fellow Danforth Found., 1970. Mem. Am. Law Inst., Assn. Am. Law Schs. (exec. com. 2004—). Office: Boston Coll Law Sch Stuart HseM307 885 Centre St Newton Center MA 02459 Office Phone: 617-552-4340. E-mail: john.garvey.1@bc.edu.

GARVEY, RICHARD ANTHONY, retired lawyer; b. N.Y.C., Jan. 10, 1950; s. James Joseph Garvey and Janet Mary (Mooney) Rowse. AB, Boston Coll., 1972; JD, Harvard U., 1975. Bar: N.Y. 1976. Assoc. Simpson Thacher & Bartlett, N.Y.C., 1975-82, ptnr., 1982—93, 1997—2003, of counsel, 2003—. Mem. ABA, N.Y. State Bar Assn., Assn. Bar City N.Y., Phi Beta Kappa. Home: Apt 7D 105 Fifth Ave New York NY 10003 Office: Simpson Thacher & Bartlett 425 Lexington Ave New York NY 10017 Office Phone: 212-455-2578. Business E-Mail: rgarvey@stblaw.com.

GARVICK, KENNETH RYAN, broadcast engineer, announcer, educator; b. Akron, Ohio, Apr. 11, 1945; s. Kenneth Rodger and Dorothy Lillian G. Diploma, DeVry Inst. Tech., Chgo., 1966, Cleve. Inst., 1970, diploma, 1981. Cert. electronic technician. Electronic repairman RCA Consumer Electronics, Indpls., 1966—70; compilation technician Howard W. Sams & Co., Indpls., 1970—73; broadcast engr. Sta. WIBC/WNAP Fairbanks Broadcasting, Indpls., 1973; announcer, engr. Stas. WHYT-AM, WNON-FM, 1974—76; transmitter engr. Sta. WISH-TV, Indpls., 1976—79; instr. electronics Arsenal Tech. H.S., Indpls., 1979—82; announcer, engr. Stas. WSVL AM/FM, 1979—81; instr. various schs., Ohio, 1987—2005; announcer, engr. Sta. WMAN-AM, 1994—95. Author: Gerberich Descendants from York, PA, 1987; contbr. articles to profl. jours. With Signal Corps U.S. Army, 1966-72, Vietnam. Mem. Soc. Broadcast Engrs., Arsenal Tech., Radio Club (sec. 1979-82). Republican. Avocations: film history, amateur radio, bicycling. Address: 210 Fiftieth Ave Ter W Bradenton FL 34207-2741

GARVIN, ANDREW PAUL, computer company executive, writer; b. N.Y.C., July 24, 1945; s. Gene G. and Nora (Sheldon) London; m. 2d Linda Gail Bernstein, Oct. 1, 1983; children: Kira, Jeffrey. BA, Yale U., 1967; MS, Columbia U., 1968. Corr. Newsweek mag., N.Y.C., 1967-68; v.p. Four Elements, Inc., N.Y.C., 1968-69; co-founder, pres. FIND SVP, Inc., N.Y.C., 1970—, Info. Clearing House, Inc., N.Y.C., 1970—2004. Author: How to Win With Information, 1983, The Art of Being Well Informed, 1996. Chmn. Nat. Info. Conf. and Expn., Washington, 1979. Mem. Info. Industry Assn. (dir. 1979-82 Product of Yr. award 1974), Assn. Info. Mgrs. (dir. 1978-82), Am. Mktg. Assn., Am. Mgmt. Assn., Spl. Libraries Assn., St. Elmo Soc. (treas. 1974-81), Young Pres.' Orgn. Home: 401 E 89th St New York NY 10128 Office: FIND SVP 625 Avenue Of The Americas New York NY 10011-2095 E-mail: agarvin@findsvp.com.

GARVIN, C(LARENCE) ALEXANDER, JR., economics professor; b. Clarksville, Tenn., Sept. 1, 1921; s. Clarence Alexander and Lena (Medcalf) G.; m. Alice Esther Hand, Sept. 4, 1970. BA in English, U. Tenn., 1942, PhD in Econs., 1973; MA in Internat. Rels., U. Chgo., 1948; MA in Math., U. Pitts., 1983. Adj. instr. mktg. Austin Peay State U., Clarksville, 1960-61; lab. instr. acctg. Vanderbilt U., Nashville, 1964-65; grad. teaching asst. in econs. U. Tenn., Knoxville, 1966-69; assoc. prof. econs. Indiana U. Pa., 1969-75, prof., 1975—; ptnr., gen. mgr. Garvin Furniture Co., Clarksville, 1948-62; mem. senate Indiana U. Pa., 1976-78, chmn. senate subcom. for faculty rsch., 1976-78. Vis. fellow Sch. Econs. and Social Studies, U. East Anglia, Norwich, Eng., 1979-80; vis. prof. Am. U. in Cairo, 1984-86; presenter in field. Contbr. articles to profl. jours. Bd. dirs. Indiana U. Pa. Found., chmn. investment com., 1978-81; vestryman Trinity Episcopal Ch., Clarksville, 1961-62; vestryman Christ Episcopal Ch., Indiana, 1975-78, sr. warden, 1977-78, del. to dist. and diocesan conv., 1978-82; trustee Episcopal Diocese Pitts., 1978-81; vestryman St. Peter's Episcopal Ch., Blairsville, Pa., 1987-90, jr. warden, 1989-90, sr. warden, 1991—; Episcopal lay reader and minister, 1977—. Lt. USNR, 1942-46. Scholar Vanderbilt U., 1964-65. Mem. AAUP (pres. Indiana chpt. 1975-76), Am. Econ. Assn., Am. Math. Assn., Royal Econ. Assn., We. Econ. Assn., Ea. Econ. Assn. (area rep. 1974-78) Atlantic Econ. Assn. (exec. com. 1990—, chair disting. speaker adv. bd. 1992—), Pa. Econs. Assn. (bd. dirs., sec.-treas. 1973-78), Omicron Delta Epsilon, Beta Gamma Sigma. Home: 293 N 7th St Indiana PA 15701-1809 Office: Indiana U Pa Dept Econs Indiana PA 15701

GARVIN, FLORENCE WARD, management consultant; b. Ft. Sam Houston, Tex., Oct. 6, 1928; d. Edward Joseph and Florence Emily (Bock) Ward; m. Sheldon R. Rappaport, Mar. 2, 1950 (div. July 1969); children: Bruce Ward, Lisa Lynn; m. Stefan J. Garvin, Oct. 3, 1981. BA, Our Lady of Lake U., San Antonio, 1949; postgrad., Trinity U., San Antonio, 1949-50. Co-founder, asst. to pres. Pathway Sch., Norristown, Pa., 1961—68; adminstrv. dir. Neurosurg. Clinic for Children, Media, Pa., 1968—70; v.p. for devel. Vanguard Schs., Haverford, Pa., 1970—72; asst. to pres. Elwyn (Pa.) Inst., 1972—75; pvt. practice Media, 1976—78; cons. employee rels. dept. E.I. DuPont de Nemours & Co., Inc., Wilmington, Del., 1978—85, sr. bus. assoc. internat. dept., 1985—89, mgr. bus. rels. devel., 1989—90, mgr. internat. human resources devel. human resources dept., 1990—94. Dir. spl. project Gabriella and Paul Rosenbaum Found., 1997—2001; mng. dir. Rose Tree media Ednl. Found., 2000—01; cons. Del. County Office of Adult Svcs., 2003—04. Charter mem., bd. dirs. Montgomery County Mental Health Clinics, 1956-72; bd. dirs. Phila. United Fund, 1969-72; bd. mgrs., sec. Garrett-Williamson Found., 1973-81; trustee Wilmington Coll., 1979—, Curtis Inst. Music, 1985-92; devel. com. Mercy Haverford Hosp., 1994-95; policy coun. Del. County Head Start, 1994-96; pres. bd. dirs. AIDS Task Force/Phila. Cmty. Health Alternatives, 1994-96; bd. dirs. Mary Campbell Ctr., Wilmington, 1978-81, Pacific Rim Bus. Coun., 1994-96, Nationalities Svc. Ctr., 1996-98, Green Cir. Program, 1996-98, East Side Charter Sch.,

Wilmington, Del., 1996-98; pres. bd. dirs. Delaware County AIDS Network, 1999-2002; v.p. bd. dirs. Media Fellowship House, 2003-04 Home: 2 Yarmouth Ln Media PA 19063-4327 Office Phone: 610-565-7348.

GARVIN, GLENN A., writer; b. Bklyn., Apr. 5, 1948; s. Murray H. and Rose Garvin; m. Ellen Cogan, July 15, 1973 (div. Oct. 5, 1973); m. Leslie Mines, Mar. 20, 1980 (div.). BBA in Mktg., U. Miami. Dept. store mgr. Bloomingdales Retail Dept. Store, N.Y.C., Alexanders Dept. Store, Rego Park, NY, Herman's World of Sports, Valley Stream, NY; toys and sporting goods salesman Krotman & Berk, N.Y.C.; house salesman Mego Toys Co., N.Y.C., customer svc. mgr.; collector Dictograph Security Sys., Florham Park, NJ; freelance writer East Meadow, NY. Author poetry. Vol. Spl. Olympics, L.I., NY, 1996—, United Cerebral Palsy, Roosevelt, L.I., 1997—. Jewish. Avocations: piano, games.

GARVIN, MICHELE M., lawyer; b. Nov. 8, 1952; BA, Coll. William & Mary, 1974; MA, Boston Coll., 1977, PhD Sociology, 1981; JD, Suffolk Univ., 1987. Bar: Mass. 1988. Assoc. to ptnr. corp. dept. Ropes & Gray, Boston, 1988—, chmn. health care practice group. Contbr. articles to profl. jours., chapters to books. Mem.: ABA, Mass. Bar Assn., Boston Bar Assn., Jackson Hole Task Force on HCCPs. Office: Ropes & Gray 1 International Pl Boston MA 02110-2624 Office Phone: 617-951-7495. Office Fax: 617-951-7050. Business E-Mail: michele.garvin@ropesgray.com.

GARWIN, RICHARD LAWRENCE, physicist; b. Cleve., Apr. 19, 1928; married; 3 children. BS in Physics, Case Western U., 1947, DSc (hon.), 1966; MS, U. Chgo., 1948, PhD in Physics, 1949. Instr. to asst. prof. physics U. Chgo., 1949-52; physicist T.J. Watson Ctr. IBM, Yorktown Heights, NY, 1952-65, dir. applied rsch., 1965-66, lab. dir., 1966-67, fellow, 1967-93, fellow emeritus, 1993—; Phillip D. Reed sr. fellow for sci. and tech. Coun. on Fgn. Rels., N.Y.C., 1994—2004. Cons. Los Alamos (N.Mex.) Sci. Lab., 1950-93, Sandia Nat. Lab., 1994—, U.S. govt. on matters of military technology, arms control, etc.; mem. com. Pres.'s Sci. Adv. Com., 1962-65, 69-72, cons., 1958-62; mem. Def. Sci. Bd., 1966-69; adj. prof. physics Columbia U., 1957—; prof. pub. policy Harvard U., Cambridge, 1979-81, vis. prof. applied physics, 1974; adj. rsch. fellow, Kennedy Sch. of Govt., Harvard U.; mem. scientific adv. group to the Joint Strategic Target Planning Staff; commr. "Rumsfeld" Commn. to Access the Ballistic Missle Threat to the U.S.; chmn., Arms Control and Nonproliferation Adv. Bd., Dept. State, 1993-2001. Contbr. articles to profl. jours.; co-author: Nuclear Weapons and World Politics, 1977, Nuclear Power Issues and Choices, 1977, Energy: The Next Twenty Years, 1979, Science Advice to the President, 1980, Managing the Plutonium Surplus: Applications and Technical Options, 1994, Feux Folles et Champignons Nucleaires, 1997; co-author: (with Georges Charpak) Megawatts and Megatons: A Turning Point in the Nuclear Age?, 2001. Recipient Wright prize for interdisciplinary scientific achievement, 1983, Ettore Majorana-Erice Sci. for Peace award Ettore Majorana Ctr., 1991, R.V. Jones Intelligence award U.S. Govt. Fgn. Intelligence Cmty., 1996, Enrico Fermi award, 1997, Nat. Medal of Science award, 2002. Fellow Am. Phys. Soc.(chmn., panel on pub. affairs, 1978), IEEE, Am. Acad. Arts and Sciences (Scientific Freedom and Responsibility award, 1988); mem. NAS, NAE, Inst. of Medicine, Am. Philos. Soc., Council of the Inst. for Strategic Studies, 1977-85, Coun. Fgn. Relations, Am.; chmn., Arms Control and Nonproliferation advisory bd, 1993-2001; bd. dir. Fedn. Am. Scientists.; mem. Pugwash, Pugwash Coun. Achievements include patents in field.

GARWOOD, JULIE, writer; b. 1946; Author: (novels for young adults) A Girl Named Summer, 1985, (as Emily Chase) What's A Girl to Do, 1985, (historical romance novels) Gentle Warrior, 1985, Rebellious Desire, 1986, Honor's Splendor, 1987, The Lion's Lady, 1988, The Bride, 1989, Guardian Angel, 1990, The Gift, 1990, The Prize, 1991, The Secret, 1992, Castles, 1993, Saving Grace, 1993, Prince Charming, 1994, For the Roses, 1995, The Wedding, 1996, One Pink Rose, One White Rose, One Red Rose, Come the Spring, 1997, The Wedding, 1998, Ransom, 1999, Heartbreaker, 2000, Killjoy, 2002, Murder List, 2004 (Publishers Weekly Bestseller). Office: PO Box 7574 Leawood KS 66207-0574*

GARWOOD, NAOMI FUJI, education educator; d. Harry Ichiro and Susie Shizu Omaye; m. Ronald David Garwood, Aug. 15, 1981; children: Sarah Joy, Emily Faith. BA in Diversified Edn., Biola Coll., La Mirada, Calif., 1977; MS in Edn., SUNY, Brockport, 1984. Cert. tchr. nursery to 6th grade NY, 1984, reading tchr. NY, 1984. First grade tchr. Valley Pk. Bapt. Sch., Sepulveda, Calif., 1979—81; fifth grade tchr. North Bapt. Christian Sch., Rochester, NY, 1981—82; substitute tchr. Rochester City Sch. Dist., 1982—84; reading resource tchr. Rush Henrietta Ctrl. Schools, Rochester, 1984—85; coord. cmty. learning ctr. Roberts Wesleyan Coll., Rochester, 1986—90, asst. prof. of edn., 1990—. Mem. cmty. dialogue coun. Churchville Chili Ctrl. Sch. Dist., NY, 1999—2005; mem. Churchville Chili Sports Booster Club, NY, 1998—2002; Pearce 4 kids task force mem. Pearce Meml. Ch., North Chili, NY, 2001—05. Recipient Barbara Muller Award for Tchg. Excellence, Roberts Wesleyan Coll., 2002. Mem.: Assn. Supervision and Curriculum Devel., Internat. Reading Assn. Methodist. Avocations: reading, travel. Office: Roberts Wesleyan Coll 2301 Westside Dr Rochester NY 14624 Office Phone: 585-594-6437. Office Fax: 585-594-6806. E-mail: garwoodn@roberts.edu.

GARWOOD, WILLIAM LOCKHART, federal judge; b. Houston, Tex., Oct. 29, 1931; s. Wilmer St. John and Ellen Burdine (Clayton) Garwood; m. Merle Castlyn Haffler, Aug. 12, 1955; children: William Lockhart, Mary Elliott. BA, Princeton U., 1952; LLB with honors, U. Tex., 1955. Bar: Tex. 1955, U.S. Supreme Ct. 1959. Law clk. to judge U.S. Ct. Appeals (5th cir.), 1955—56; mem. Graves, Dougherty, Hearon, Moody & Garwood (and predecessor firms), Austin, Tex., 1959—79, 1981; justice Supreme Ct. Tex., Austin, 1979—80; judge U.S. Ct. Appeals (5th cir.), 1981—97, sr. judge, 1997—; dir. Anderson, Clayton & Co., 1976—79, 1981, exec. com., 1977—79, 1981. Mem. adv. com. on appellate rules Jud. Conf. U.S., 1994—2001, chair, 1997—2001. Pres. Child and Family Svc. of Austin, 1970—71, St. Andrew's Episcopal Sch., Austin, 1972; bd. dirs. Cmty. Coun. Austin and Travis County, 1968—72, Human Opportunities Corp. Austin and Travis County, 1966—70, Mental Health and Mental Retardation Ctr. Austin and Travis County, 1966—69, United Fund Austin and Travis County, 1971—73; mem. adv. bd. Salvation Army, Austin, 1972—. With U.S. Army, 1956—59. Fellow: Tex. Bar Found. (life); mem.: Tex. Law Rev. Assn. (pres. 1990—91, dir. 1986—96), Am. Law Inst. (life), Chancellors, Phi Delta Phi, Order of Coif. Episcopalian. Office: US Ct Appeals Homer Thornberry Jud Bldg 903 San Jacinto Blvd Austin TX 78701-2451

GARY, JAMES M., lawyer; b. Jonesboro, Ark. BA, Ouachita Bapt. Univ., 1977; JD, Univ. Ark., 1980. Bar: Ark. 1980, Tex. 1998, US Supreme Ct., Us Ct. of Appeals (5th, 8th cir.), US Dist. Ct. (no., so., ea., we. dists.) Tex., US Dist. Ct. (ea., we. dists.) Ark. Now ptnr., head, labor and employment practice group Akin Gump Strauss Hauer & Feld LLP, Austin, Tex. Editl. rev. bd. Tex. Employment Adv., Employer Resource Inst., 1999—2003, contbr. articles to profl. publications. Mem.: ABA, Fed. Bar Assn., Austin Human Resource Mgmt. Assn. (mentor), Soc. for Human Resource Mgmt., Phi Alpha Delta. Office: Akin Gump Strauss Hauer & Feld LLP Ste 2100 300 W Sixth St Austin TX 78701-2916 Office Phone: 512-499-6297. Office Fax: 512-703-1112. Business E-Mail: jgary@akingump.com.

GARY, JONATHAN MARK, academic administrator; b. Dallas, July 13, 1971; s. Alvin Lynn and Judy Bergstrom Gary; m. Emily Greer, Aug. 10, 2002. MusB in Piano performance, Ouachita Bapt. U., Arkadelphia, Ark., 1993; MusM i in Piano Performance and Pedagogy, Baylor U., Waco, Tex., 2000; Performance Cert., Stanislawa Moniuski Music Acad., Gdansk, Poland, 1995. Professional Kindermusik Educator Kindermusik Internat., NC, 1999. Dir. fine arts inst. and after sch. program EOAC Waco Charter Sch., 1995—2000; asst. dir. U. Mary-Hardin Baylor Conservatory, Belton, Tex., 2000—. Asst. music dir., organist Lakewood Christian Ch., Waco, 2002—. Dir. ops. Christian Cultural Awareness Assistance League, Houston, 2000—03. Scholar, Baylor U., 1996—99. Mem.: Tex. Music Tchrs. Assn., Ctrl. Tex. Music Tchrs. Assn. (chair sonata festival 2000—03), Nat. Guild Piano Tchrs. Coll. Musicians, Music Tchrs. Nat. Assn. (Star award 2000), Phi Mu Alpha Sinfonia (pres. 1992—93). Avocations: travel, gardening, piano, organ, weightlifting. Office: Univ Mary Hardin-Baylor Box 8012 900 Coll St Belton TX 76513 also: 4212 Red River Cir Temple TX 76504-4927

GARY, MARC, lawyer; b. Englewood, N.J., July 14, 1952; BA summa cum laude, Northwestern U., 1974; JD, Georgetown U., 1977. Bar: Va. 1977, D.C. 1978, U.S. Ct. Appeals (D.C. cir. and 4th cir.) 1978, U.S. Dist. Ct. D.C. 1978, U.S. Supreme Ct. 1982, U.S. Ct. Appeals (6th cir.) 1983, U.S. Dist. Ct. Md. 1985, U.S. Ct. Appeals (9th cir.) 1989. Ptnr. Mayer, Brown & Platt, Washington; assoc. independent counsel Office of Independent Counsel, Washington, 1990—92; v.p., assoc. gen. counsel Bell South Corp., Atlanta, 2000—04, gen. counsel, 2004—. Mem. regulatory agy. task force Pres'. pvt. sector survey cost control, 1982-83. Contbr. articles to profl. jours. Bd. dirs., coun. trustees Am. Friends of Hebrew U., 1995-2000; nat. bd. dirs. United Synagogue of Conservative Judaism, 1994—; bd. dirs. D.C. Jewish Cmty. Ctr., 1990-2000. Named a Fellow, Am. Bar Found., 1999; named One of 10 Outstanding In-House Counsel, Corp. Counsel mag., 2002. Mem. ABA, D.C. Bar (pub. dvc. activities com., steering com., antitrust, trade rresolution and consumer affairs sect.), Va. State Bar, Washington Coun. Lawyers (bd. dirs. 1982-2000), Phi Eta Sigma. Office: Bell South Corp Ste 1700 1155 Peachtree St NE Atlanta GA 30309

GARY, RICHARD DAVID, lawyer; b. Richmond, Va., Apr. 25, 1949; s. Morton Nathan and Blanche (Rudy) G.; m. Linda Levene, Aug. 6, 1972; children: Brent Ryan, Lauren Renee. AB in Econs., U. N.C., 1971; JD, U. Va., 1974. Bar: Va. 1974. From assoc. to ptnr.,r egulated industries & govt. rels. Hunton & Williams LLP, Richmond, 1974—, and mem. exec. com. Guest lectr. law Coll. William and Mary, Williamsburg, 1983-90, U. Va. Law Sch., 2004-2005; guest lectr. telecom. Va. Commonwealth U., 2004. Pres. Beth Sholom Home Ctrl. Va., Richmond, 1989-91; chmn. Beth Sholom Home Va., 1991-92; v.p. Jewish Cmty. Fedn. Richmond, 2002—. Recipient Disting. Svc. award Beth Sholom Home Ctrl. Va., 1984. Mem. ABA (pub. utilities sect. coun. mem.), Va. State Bar (chmn. adminstrn. law sect. 1982-83), Va. Bar Assn., Richmond Bar Assn., Fed. Comm Bar Assn., Fed. Energy Bar Assn. Avocation: sports. Office: Hunton & Williams Riverfront Plz East Twr PO Box 1535 Richmond VA 23219-1535 Home: 121 Countryside Ln Richmond VA 23229-7336 Office Phone: 804-788-8330. Office Fax: 804-788-8218. Business E-Mail: rgary@hunton.com.

GARY, WILLIE E., lawyer; b. Eastman, Ga., July 12, 1947; s. Turner and Mary Ella (McNarr) G.; m. Gloria R. Gary, Aug. 25, 1978; children: Kenneth, Sekou, Ali, Kobie. BA in Bus. Adminstrn., Shaw U., 1971; JD, N.C. Cen. U., 1974. Bar: Fla., admitted to practice: US Dist. Ct. (So. Dist.) Fla., US Dist. Ct. (Mid. Dist.) Fla. Pvt. practice, Martin County, Fla., 1975-1976; ptnr. Gary, Williams & Parenti, Finney, Lewis, Stuart, Fla., Ft. Pierce, Fla., 1976—. Chmn. bldg. fund Evergreen Bapt. Ch. of Indiantown, mem. adult choir; past pres. Young Men's Progressive Assn. of Martin County; chmn. bd. trustees Shaw U.; mem. NAACP, Urban League, Civitan Internat., Fla. Guardsmen, Inc., United Way of Martin County, Martin Mem. Hosp. Found. Coun.; contbr. to various charities. Named Role Model of Yr. Bethune-Cookman Coll., 1989, one of two Coll. Alumni of Yr. United Negro Coll. Fund, 1989; recipient Learned Hand Award, Am. Jewish Com., 1996, Golden Trumpet Award, Turner Broadcasting Co., 1997, Horatio Alger Award, Horatio Alger Soc., 1999; named one of Am.'s Top Black Lawyers, Black Enterprise Mag., 2003. Mem. ABA, Martin County Bar Assn., St. Lucie Bar Assn., Fla. Bar Assn. (past mem. bd. govs.), Nat. Bar Assn. (past pres. Fla. chpt., Lawyer of Yr.), Fla. Acad. Trial Lawyers, Am. Trial Lawyers Assn., Million Dollar Verdict Club, Phi Alpha Delta. Office: Gary Williams & Parenti Waterside Profl Bldg 221 SE Osceola St Ste 300 Stuart FL 34994-2289 also: 320 S Indian River Dr Fort Pierce FL 34950

GARZA, ANTONIO O., ambassador; BBA, U. Tex., Austin, 1980; JD, So. Meth. U., 1983. Formerly of counsel Garza & Garza, Brownsville, Tex.; judge Cameron County Ct., Tex., 1988—94; sec. state State of Tex., 1995-97; atty. Bracewell & Patterson, LLP, 1997—98; commr. Tex. R.R., 1998—2001; US amb. to Mex. US Dept. State, Mexico City, 2002—. Dir. parks adv. bd. Tex. Parks and Wildlife Commn.; past mem. State Job Tng. Coord. Coun., Census Complete Count Com., U.S. Marshall Selection Com.; conferee jud. conf., U.S. Ct. Appeals (5th cir.), 1986.; mem. presdl. del. Fed. Elections, El Salvador, 1991; mem. del. to Poland/Hungary, Am. Coun. Young Polit. Leaders, 1993; spkr. in field. Past dir. United Way So. Cameron County; past pres. Rio Grande Valley Big Bros./Big Sisters; dir. Brownsville Adult Lit. Coun. Cameron County; active H.O.S.T. program Brownsville Ind. Sch. Dist.; coach soccer and jr. varsity basketball. Names One of Five Outstanding Young Texans Exes, 1989, One of Five Outstanding Young Texans, 1990. Office: US Embassy Paseo de la Reforma 305 06500 Colonia Cuauhtemoc Mexico Mailing: US Dept State 8700 Mexico City Pl Washington DC 20521-8700*

GARZA, CUTBERTO, nutrition educator; b. San Diego, Tex., Aug. 26, 1947; s. Cutberto and Diamantina (Salinas) G.; m. Yolanda, Mar. 21, 1970; children: Luis-Andres, Carlos-Daniel, Ariel-Abram. BS summa cum laude, Baylor U., 1969; MD, Baylor Coll. Medicine, 1973; PhD, MIT, 1976. Asst. prof. Baylor Coll. Medicine, Houston, 1977-85, assoc. prof., 1984-86, prof., 1986-88, Cornell U. Divsn. Nutritional Sci., Ithaca, NY, 1988—. dir., 1988—98, 2003—; vice-provost Cornell U., 1998-2000; dir. food nutrition program UN Univ., Cornell U., 1998—. Chmn. Inst. Medicine Food and Nutrition Bd., Washington, 1995-2002; mem. WHO expert adv. panel on nutrition; adv. com., chmn. Nat. Dietary Guidelines, 2000. Contbr. articles to profl. jours. on normal growth of young children, Nutritional Mgmt. of Prematures, Comparison of Energy Expenditure, Energy Expenditure and Deposition. Bd. dirs. Tex. Rehab. Commn., Houston, 1985-88; mem. N.Y. State Pub. Health Coun., 1990-98. Recipient Disting. Achievement award Baylor U., 1986, Alan S. Feinstein World Hunger prize for Edn. and Rsch., Brown U., 1996, Lydia J. Roberts prize U. P.R., 1993. Mem. AAAS, NAS (nat. assoc.), Inst. of Medicine, Am. Soc. Clin. Nutrution, Am. Inst. Nutrition, Am. Pediatric Soc., Soc. Pediatric Rsch. Roman Catholic. Achievements include definition of energy requirements of infants, identification of functional outcomes of infants fed human milk or formula. Office Phone: 607-254-5144.

GARZA, ED, former mayor; b. San Antonio; m. Anna Laura Garza. Student in bus. adminstrn., U. Tex., Austin; B in Landscape Architecture, MS in Land Devel., Tex. A&M U. With various planning, devel., real estate fin., landscape architecture, and architecture firms; dir. land planning and devel. Internat. Waterfront Group, San Antonio; elected dist. 7 rep. San Antonio City Coun.; elected mayor City of San Antonio, 2003—. Adj. prof. U. Tex., San Antonio, St. Mary's U.; v.p. N.Am. Internat. Trade Corridor Partnership (NAITCP). Mem. San Antonio Trees Bd., CEOs for Cities, Urban Land Inst.; Fannie Mae; Internat. Coun. of Shopping Ctrs.; adv. bd. Nat. League of Cities, 2000—, nominating com., 2003—; bd. advisors Nat. Assn. Latino Elected and Appointed Ofcls. (NALEO); past bd. dirs. Jefferson Neighborhood Assn., Woodlawn Lake Neighborhood Assn.; bd. dirs. Hispanic Elected Local Ofcls., 1998—, pres.; bd. dirs. San Antonio Water Sys., City Pub. Svc., Tex. Municipal League. Named one of 40 Under 40 Rising Stars, San Antonio Bus. Jour., 1996. Office: City Hall PO Box 839966 San Antonio TX 78203-3966

GARZA, EMILIO MILLER, federal judge; b. San Antonio, Aug. 1, 1947; s. Antonio Peña and Dionisia (Miller) Garza. BA, U. Notre Dame, 1969, MA, 1970; JD, U. Tex., 1976. Assoc. Clemens, Spencer, Welmaker & Finck, San Antonio, 1976—82, ptnr., 1982—87; dist. judge 225th Dist. Ct., Bexar County, San Antonio, 1987—88, U.S. Dist. Ct. (we. dist.) Tex., San Antonio, 1988—91; judge U.S. Ct. Appeals (5th cir.), San Antonio, 1991—. Adv. coun. U. Tex. San Antonio Coll. Fine Arts and Humanities, 1992—98; adv. bd. Phoenix Inst., 1992—; bd. advisors Hispanic Law Jour. U. Tex. at Austin Sch. Law, 1992—96; adv. com. Notre Dame Law Sch., 1998—; bd. dirs. Symphony Soc. San Antonio, 1987—89; mem. Century Club San Antonio, 1987—88. Capt. USMC, 1970—79, active duty USMC, 1970—73. Mem.: San Antonio Bar Assn., State Bar Tex. Office: 8200 I-10 W Ste 501 San Antonio TX 78230 also: US Ct Appeals 600 Camp St New Orleans LA 70130*

GARZA, ERIK DAVID, lawyer; b. La Jolla, Calif., Apr. 14, 1974; s. Gumaro Garza and Marie Siegmund; m. Chelsie King Garza, July 4, 2002; 1 child, Megan Elizabeth. BS in Biomed. Sci., Tex. A&M U., 1997; JD, Seton Hall U., 2000. Bar: Tex. 2000, U.S. Ct. Appeals (5th cir.) 2000, U.S. Dist. Ct. (no. and so. dists.) Tex. 2001, U.S. Dist. Ct. (we. dist.) Tex. 2002, U.S. Dist. Ct. (ea. dist.) Tex. 2003, U.S. Supreme Ct. 2003. Atty. Royston, Rayzor, Vickery & Williams LLP, Houston, 2000—. Mem.: Am. Intellectual Property Law Assn., Southeastern Admiralty Law Inst., Maritime Law Assn. U.S. Office: Royston Rayzor Vickery & William LLP 1001 McKinney Ste 1100 Houston TX 77007 Office Phone: 713-224-8380. Office Fax: 713-225-9945. Business E-Mail: erik.garza@roystonlaw.com.

GARZA, RUDY A., lawyer; b. San Antonio, Aug. 30, 1952; s. Rudy A. and Maria (Villareal) G.; m. Connie Jo Dupuy, May 23, 1980; children: Thomas, Christine, Cassandra, Daniel. BS with high honors, U. Tex., 1974, JD, 1977. Bar: Tex. 1977, U.S. Dist. Ct. (we. dist.) Tex. 1979, U.S. Ct. Appeals (5th cir.) 1980, U.S. Supreme Ct. 1988; bd. cert. Tex. Bd. of Legal Spec., Civil Trial Law, Personal Injury Trial Law. Ptnr. Tinsman and Houser, San Antonio, 1977-86, Garza, Moore & Lazor, San Antonio, 1987—, Garza & Lazor, 1995—. Mem. Bexar County Dem. Exec. Com., 1984-86, bd. trustees Boerne Independent School Dist., 1991-99 (pres. 1996-98). Named Tex. Superior Lawyer, Tex. Monthly Mag., 2004. Fellow Tex. Bar Found.; mem. State Bar Tex. (grievance com. San Antonio 1985-89), San Antonio Bar Assn. (bd. dirs. 1986—, treas. 1987—), Tex. Bar Assn., Tex. Trial Lawyers Assn., San Antonio Young Lawyers Assn. (bd. dirs. 1982-83, sec. 1983-84, pres. 1985-86), San Antonio Inn of Ct. (master, sec.). Roman Catholic. Avocations: golf, chess. Office: Garza & Lazor PC 2400 Bank of America Plz San Antonio TX 78205 Office Phone: 210-225-2400.

GARZA-LOZANO, NEREYDA, language educator; b. Matamoros, Mexico, June 20, 1961; arrived in U.S., 1984; d. Ignacio Garza and Ninfa Lozano; children: Aideé Karina Lara-Garza, Lizabeth Viridiana Lara-Garza. BS magna cum laude in Social Sci., Matamoros, 1980; AA in Liberal Arts, Fresno City Coll., 1994; BA in Spanish, Calif. State U., Fresno, 1995, MA in Spanish, 1997. Elem. sch. tchr. Miguel Hidalgo Sch., Ebano, Mexico, 1980—84; part-time Spanish instr. Calif. State U., Fresno, Calif., 1997—99; full time Spanish instr. Fresno City Coll., 1999—. Sec. Ctrl. Valley Foreign Lang. Assn., Fresno, 2001—02; presenter in field. Contbr. articles to profl. jours. Coord. cultural activities Fresno City Coll., 1999—, coord. Cinco de Mayo activities, 2001—03; coord. Latin Film Festival Arte Am., Fresno, 2003. Grantee Mexican Am. Studies, NEH, 1999, Fulbright, Chile, 2000, Spanish Embassy Women's Lit. Seminar, Alcala de Henare, Spain; McNair scholar, Calif. State U. Fresno, 1997. Mem.: Latino Faculty Assn. (v.p. 2002—03), Calif. Lang. Tchrs. Assn., Am. Assn. Tchrs. Spanish and Portuguese, Phi Kappa Phi. Republican. Roman Catholic. Avocations: hiking, camping, films, travel. Office: State Ctr CC 1101 E University Ave Fresno CA 93741 E-mail: ngarza@fresnocitycollege.edu.

GARZARELLI, ELAINE MARIE, economist; b. Phila., Oct. 13, 1952; d. Ralph J. and Ida M. (Pierantozzi) G.; BS, Drexel U., 1973, MBA, 1977, Ph.D, 1992. With A.G. Becker, N.Y.C., 1973-84, v.p., economist, 1975-84, mgn. dir., 1984; ptnr., portfolio mgr. Lehman Bros. Inc., 1984-94; prin. Garzarelli Internat. Inc., Delray Beach, Fla., 1994—; lectr. in field. Named Businesswoman of Yr. Fortune Mag., 1987, # 1 in Quantitative Analysis, Instl. Investor Annual Contest. Mem. Nat. Assn. Bus. Economists, Women's Fin. Assn., Am. Statis. Assn., Women's Bond Assn. Developer Sector Analysis (econometric model for predicting industry profits and stock price movements, also predicted stock market crash of 1987).

GARZIA, SAMUEL ANGELO, lawyer; b. Highland Park, Mich., July 7, 1920; s. Angelo and Josephine G.; m. Josephine Lupo, June 6, 1946; children: Sanuel Angelo, Sandra Jo, Frank. JD, Wayne State U., Detroit, 1943. Bar: Mich. 1943. Asst. friend of ct., Wayne County, Mich., 1946-48; practice law Detroit, 1948-97; sr. ptnr. Vandeveer Garzia, 1960-97. Served with AUS, 1943-45, ETO. Decorated Bronze Star; Croix de Guerre Luxembourg). Mem. ABA, Mich. Bar Assn., Detroit Bar Assn. (dir. 1976-83), Oakland Bar Assn., Assn. Def. Counsel Mich. (1st pres. 1966-67), Internat. Assn. Ins. Counsel, Am. Coll. Trial Lawyers, Am. Legion (judge advocate Mich. 1958) Roman Catholic. Home: 5229 Greenbriar Ct West Bloomfield MI 48323-2322 Office: 1450 W Long Lake Rd Troy MI 48098-6330

GARZIONE, JOHN EDWARD, physical therapist; b. Newburgh, N.Y., Jan. 3, 1950; s. John Edward and Della Elizabeth (Gentila) G.; m. Anita Louise Hirschman, Sept. 21, 1974; children: Adriana, Katrina. AAS, Orange County C.C., Middletown, N.Y., 1970; BS, Ithaca Coll., 1973; D in Physical Therapy, Boston U., 2005. Mem. staff phys. therapy Chenango Meml. Hosp., Norwich, N.Y., 1973-74; sr. phys. therapist N.Y. State Vets. Home, Oxford, N.Y., 1974-86; CEO Chenango Therapeutics, Norwich, 1975—; lic. examiner N.Y. State, 1976-86; cons. phys. therapy Broome Devel. Ctr., Binghamton, N.Y., 1985—, Upstate Home for Children, Milford, N.Y., 1986-88, Hospice Chenango County, Norwich, 1991—. Adj. instr. Czenovia Coll., 1982-87, Ithaca Coll., 1993-94; clin. instr. EMPI Corp., 1996—; cons. BlueCross/Blue Shield, Utica, 1998-2001, YMCA, Norwich, N.Y., 2000; guest lectr. electrotherapy Utica Coll., 2000; presenter in field. Contbr. articles to profl. jours. Bd. dirs. STRIDE, 2000-04. Mem. Am. Phys. Therapy Assn. (sec. pain mgmt. spl. interest group 1996-2001, v.p. 2001-04), Am. Coll. Sports Medicine, Am. Acad. Pain Mgmt. (diplomate; clin. assoc., Continuing Edn. Excellence award 1996, 99, 2000, 01, 02, 03), N.Y. Acad. Scis., Lions (v.p. 1990). Congregationalist. Home: PO Box 451 Sherburne NY 13460-0451 Office: Chenango Therapeutics Country Club Rd Norwich NY 13815-1613 Office Phone: 607-334-6273. Personal E-mail: jgarzione@mkl.com.

GASBARRO, PASCO, JR., lawyer; b. Providence, Apr. 3, 1944; m. Mary Alyce McNamara, May 30, 1967; children: Pasco, John A., Christopher E. AB, Brown U., Providence, 1966; JD, Boston U., 1969. Bar: R.I. 1969, U.S. Dist. Ct. R.I. 1971, Mass. 1972, U.S. Dist. Ct. Mass. 1974. Law clk. R.I. Supreme Ct., Providence, 1969-70; atty. R.I. Legal Svcs., Providence, 1970-71, New Eng. Elec., Westborough, Mass., 1971-76; counsel Narragansett Elec. Co., Providence, 1976-79; asst. gen. counsel New Eng. Elec., Westborough, 1979-83; ptnr. Hinckley, Allen & Snyder LLP, Providence, Boston, Concord, NH, 1983—. Del. White House Conf. on Small Bus., 1995; mem. adv. bd., Advanced Technol. Mfg. Ctr. Former chmn. adv. coun. R.I. Small Bus. Devel. Ctr.; mem. adv. bd. Advanced Tech. and Mfg. Ctr. Mem. ABA, R.I. Bar Assn., Brown Club of R.I. Office: Hinckley Allen & Snyder LLP 1500 Fleet Ctr Providence RI 02903-2319 Office Phone: 401-274-2000.

GASH, JUDSON ROY, radiology educator; b. Tacoma, Wash., Feb. 26, 1965; s. Sydney S. Gash and Nellie P. Bishop; m. Cynthia H. Hofstetter; children: Ryan, Taylor, Christian. BS, Coll. of Charleston, 1986; MD, USC, Columbia, 1994; Radiology Residency, Wake Forest U., 1990—94. Cert. Am. Bd. Radiology, 1994. Assoc. prof. radiology U. Tenn., Knoxville, 1997—. Named Tchr. of Yr., U. Tenn. Med. Ctr. Knoxville, 2001, Best Dr. in Knoxville, City View Mag., 2003, 2004, 2005; recipient Med. Sch. Valedictorian (magna cum laude), USC, 1994, Joan Kershner and Frank Farley Leadership Award, 1990. Mem.: Soc. Uroradiology, Soc. Computed Body Tomography and Magnetic Resonance, Radiologic Soc. N.Am., Am. Roentgen Ray Soc. Office: Univ Tenn Medl Ctr 1924 Alcoa Hwy Knoxville TN 37920 Office Fax: 865-544-9038. Personal E-mail: jgash@mc.utmck.edu.

GASH, LAUREN BETH, lawyer, state legislator; b. Summit, N.J., June 11, 1960; d. Ira Arnold and Sondra Regina (Stetin) G.; m. Gregg Allen Garmisa, June 12, 1983; children: Sarah, Benjamin. BA in Psychology, Clark U., 1982; JD, Georgetown U., 1987. Bar: Ill. 1989. Projects dir. U.S. Senator Alan Dixon, Washington, 1981-83; statewide constituency coord., dir. Women for

Simon, U.S. Senator Paul Simon, Chgo., 1990; aide State Rep. Grace Mary Stern, Highland Park, Ill.; atty. Prairie State Legal Svcs., Waukegan, Ill.; mem. Ill. State Ho. of Reps., chair judiciary-criminal com. Mem. women's health adv. bd. Highland Park Hosp., southeast adv. bd Coll. Lake County, JUF govt. agencies divsn. campaign cabinet, 1999, chair, Highland Park 2000 com., human needs subcom. Women in Law as 2d Career grantee; recipient Disting. Svc. award Ill. Com. for Honest Govt., 1996, Best Legis. Record Voting award Ind. Voters Ill., 1996; named Legis. of Yr. Alliance for the Mentally Ill, 1997. Mem. Ill. State Bar Assn. (mem. com. cmty. involvement), Formerly Employed Mothers at the Leading Edge (co-founder North Shore chpt.), Chgo. Women in Govt. Rels., Women Employed, Ravinia PTA (bd. dirs., polit. action chair), Com. for Interdist. Cooperation, North Shore Synagogue Beth El (social action com.) LWV (bd. dirs. Highland Park chpt., bd. dirs. Lake County chpt.). Avocations: flute, french, spanish. also: 2052-I Stratton Bldg Springfield IL 62706-0001 Office: 1345 Forest Ave Highland Park IL 60035-3456

GASH, SONDRA REGINA, writer; b. Paterson, N.J., Dec. 7, 1934; d. Sol and Frieda Stetin; m. Ira Arnold Gash, Mar. 30, 1958; children: Lauren Beth, Amy Leah. BA, Univ. of Penn., 1956. Journalist Freelance, NJ, 1965—80; tchr. artist in sch. Varous schs. in N.Y. & N.J., 1980—; writing skill training coord. Labor Edn. Ctr. Rutgers Univ., New Brunswick, NJ, 1980—83; creative writing coord. Women's Resource Ctr., Summit, NJ, 1992—; pvt. tchr. in creative writing Various N.J. Schs. and groups, 1992—. Author: Silk Elegy, 2002 (Paterson Poetry Prize Finalist, 2003); contbr. articles to profl. jours. Principal for the Day P.E.N.C.I.L., N.Y.C., 1999. Fiction in Creative Writing fellow, N.J. State Coun. on Arts, 1986, Creative Writing Poetry grantee, 1991, Dodge Found. fellow in Creative Writing, 1999, Puffin Found. grantee, 2005. Avocations: reading, walking, travel. Home: 4 Mountain Rd Lebanon NJ 08833-4622

GASICH, WELKO ELTON, retired aerospace transportation executive, management consultant; b. Cupertino, Calif., Mar. 28, 1922; s. Elija J. and Catherine (Paviso) Gasich; m. Patricia Ann Gudgel, Dec. 28, 1973; 1 child, Mark David. AB cum laude in Mech. Engring. (Bacon scholar), Stanford U., 1943, MS in Mech. Engring., 1947, cert. in fin. and econs. (Sloan exec. fellow), 1967; Aero. Engr., Calif. Inst. Tech., 1948. Aerodynamicist Douglas Aircraft Co., 1943-44, supr. aeroelastics, 1947-51; chief aero design Rand Corp., 1951-53; chief preliminary design aircraft divsn. Northrop Corp., Los Angeles, 1953-56, dir. advanced systems, 1956-61, v.p., asst. gen. mgr. tech., 1961-66, corp. v.p., gen. mgr. Northrop Ventura divsn., 1967-71, corp. v.p., gen. mgr. aircraft divsn., 1971-76, corp. v.p., group exec. aircraft group, 1976-79, sr. v.p. advanced projects, 1979-85, exec. v.p. programs, 1985-88, ret., 1988; aerospace cons. Encino, Calif., 1988—. Author: (book) 40 Years of Ferrari V-12 Engines, 1990. Chmn. adv. coun. Stanford Sch. Engring., 1981—83; past. mem. adv. coun. Stanford Grad. Sch. Bus.; chmn. United Way, 1964; chmn. Scout-O-Rama, L.A. coun. Boy Scouts Am., 1964, chmn. explorer scout exec. com., 1963—64. Served to lt. USN, 1944—46. Fellow: AIAA, Soc. Automotive Engrs.; mem.: NAE, Navy League, Stanford Grad. Sch. Bus. Alumni Assn. (pres. 1971), Bel Air Country Club, Conquistadores del Cielo Club. Republican. Achievements include patents in field. Office: 10900 Chalon Rd Los Angeles CA 90077

GASIOR, MARIANNE F., lawyer, consultant; d. Joseph and Rosemary Gasior. JD, Univ. Pitts. Sch. Law, 1986. Bar: Pa. 1987. Assoc., corp. and litig. Thorp, Reed & Armstrong, Pittsburgh, 1986—88; assoc. atty., law & corp. affairs Duquesne Light Co., Pittsburgh, 1988—89; corp. atty. Kennametal, Inc., Latrobe, Pa., 1989—90; atty., cons. pvt. practice, Pittsburgh, 1990—. Chmn., CEO, dir. SpringWater Sanctuary, Inc., Pittsburgh, 2003—; with Dept. Ops., Rsch. & Fgn. Agr. US Ho. Subcom., 1991—95. Contbr. articles to profl. jours. Vol. Animal Legal Def. Fund, Pittsburgh, 1986—2003. Recipient Cavallo award for moral courage, Cavallo Found., 1993, Change the World award, Apple Computer, Inc., 1993; grantee Iraqgate grant, Fund Constl. Govt., 1993, Deer Creek Found., 1993. Achievements include conducting legal and nuclear non-proliferation work profiled in Time, Business Week, Wall Street Journal, Washington Post, CNN, NBC Dateline, CBS Sunday Morning and ABC Nightline. Avocations: photography, exercise, music. Office: Atty at Law 420 Atlantic Ave Pittsburgh PA 15221

GASKA, CHRISTINE, accountant; b. Queens, N.Y., June 25, 1965; d. Basil and Helen (Bulgarides) Palmeri. AS cum laude, Nassau Community Coll., 1985; BBA, Hofstra U., 1987. Staff acct. H.G. Toys, Inc., Long Beach, N.Y., 1987-88; project acct. Johansen Orgn., Hauppauge, N.Y., 1988-91; acct. Cashtek Corp., Melville, N.Y., 1991-94, Yusen Air & Sea Svc. Inc., Garden City, N.Y., 1994-98, Masonite Internat., Tampa, Fla., 1998—. Avocations: travel, reading, computer, movies, theme parks. Home: 9311 Mangrove Ct Tampa FL 33647 Office: Masonite Internat Ste 950 1 N Dale Mabry Hwy Tampa FL 33609-2771 Office Phone: 813-877-2726. E-mail: bcgaska@centuryfla.com.

GASKELL, CAROLYN SUZANNE, librarian; b. Glen Cove, N.Y., Aug. 14, 1954; d. Duane Uson and Betty Jane G. BA, Pacific Union Coll., 1976; MA, U. Denver, 1977. Circulation libr. Walla Walla Coll., College Place, Wash., 1978-89, dr. librs., 1989—. Mem. ALA, Assn. Seventh-day Adventist Librs. (pres.-elect 1991-92, pres. 1992-93), ACRL (v.p., pres. elect Wash. state chpt. 1995-96). Avocations: hiking, flower arranging. Office: Walla Walla Coll Peterson Meml Libr 204 S College Ave College Place WA 99324-1139

GASKELL, IVAN GEORGE ALEXANDER DE WEND, art museum curator; b. Weston-super-Mare, Somerset, U.K., Feb. 26, 1955; came to U.S., 1991. s. William George Keith de Wend and Johanna Catharina (van Leeuwen) G.; m. Jane Susan Whitehead, May 9, 1981; 1 child, Alexander Leo Ralph de Wend. Attended, Worcester Coll., Oxford, 1973-76, Courtauld Inst. Art, London, 1976-80; MA in Modern History, Oxford U.; MA in History of Western Art, London U.; PhD in History of Art, Cambridge U. Rsch. fellow, acad. curatorial asst. Warburg Inst. London U., 1980-83; fellow Wolfson Coll. Cambridge U., 1983-91, mem. faculty architecture, history of art, 1983-91; sr. lectr. fine arts Harvard U., Cambridge, Mass., 1991—, head dept. paintings and sculpture Fogg Art Mus., 1991—, Margaret S. Winthrop curator of paintings, 1991—, sr. lectr. history, 2002—; 8. Presenter papers at numerous internat. confs., 1978—; chair seminars in field; lectr. Royal Acad., Nat. Gallery, London, Courtauld Inst. Art, 1982—. Author: The Thyssen-Bornemisza Collection: Dutch and Flemish Painting, 1990, Vermeer's Wager: Speculations on Art History, Theory and Art Museums, 2000; co-editor: The Language of Art History, 1991, Landscape, Natural Beauty and the Arts, 1993, Explanation and Value in the Arts, 1993, Nietzsche, Philosophy and The Arts, 1998, Vermeer Studies, 1998, Sketches in Clay for Projects by Gianlorenzo Bernini, 1999, Performance and Authenticity in the Arts, 1999, Politics, Aesthetics and The Arts, 2000; joint gen. editor: Cambridge Studies in Philosophy and the Arts, 1988-2000; contbr. articles, revs. to profl. jours. Mem. Coll. Art Assn., Am. Soc. for Aesthetics (trustee). Avocation: sight-seeing. Office: Harvard U Fogg Art Mus 32 Quincy St Cambridge MA 02138-3845 Office Phone: 617-496-4252. E-mail: ivan_gaskell@harvard.edu.

GASKILL, JOHN WILLIAM, secondary school educator; b. Wendell, Idaho, Oct. 18, 1945; s. Charles William and Mae Merton (Hundley) G.; m. Lanae Anelda Reece, Feb. 2, 1968; children: William, Malinda, Jason, Cynthia, Jonathan. BA, Coll. of Idaho, 1967; MA in Teaching History, U. Idaho, 1972. Cert. secondary tchr., Oreg. Social studies tchr. Ontario (Oreg.) Jr. H.S., 1967-89, Ontario H.S., 1989-99; subst. tchr., 1999—. Mem. leadership team Ontario Sch. Dist., 1989-94, mem. curriculum coord. team, 1992-94; mem. social studies curriculum com. Oreg. State Dept. of Edn., Salem, 1987-89; counselor Ontario City, 2000—. Mem. scout com. 2d ward LDS Ch., Ontario, 1985-87; charter treas. Malheur Hist. Soc., Ontario, 1971, pres., 1972-73. Mem. Oreg. Coun. for Social Studies, Oreg. Geog. Alliance. Republican. Home: 1006 SW 6th Ave Ontario OR 97914-3308

GASKILL, PAMELA JO., retired elementary school educator; d. Robert Rex Doerrer and Jeanne Arlene Scott; m. Richard S. Gaskill; children: Melissa Garland, Scott, Molly McKinley. BA, Bowling Green State U., 1965; MA, Ohio State U., 1969, PhD, 2002. Elem. tchr. Columbus (Ohio) Pub. Sch., 1965—69, Dublin (Ohio) City Sch., 1982—2004; adj. prof. Ohio State U., Columbus, 2002—; ret., 2004. Staff Theory Into Practice, Columbus, 2004—. Contbr. chapters to books, articles to profl. jours. Recipient Golden Apple award, Ashland Oil, Ohio, 1990, Golden Shamrock award, Dublin City Sch., 1996; grantee, Ohio State U., 2001. Mem.: APA, Dublin Educators Assn., Nat. Educators Assn., Am.Edn. Rsch. Assn., Phi Kappa Phi. Mem. Ch. Of Christ. Avocations: reading, knitting. Home: 2550 Starford Dr Dublin OH 43016 Office: Ohio State Univ 141 Ramseyer Hall 29 W Woodruff Ave Columbus OH 43210

GASKIN, FELICIA, biochemist, educator; b. Carlisle, Pa., Jan. 17, 1943; d. Joseph A. and Wanda J. (Rakowski) G.; m. Shu Man Fu, Nov. 29, 1969; children: Kai-Ming, Kai-Mei. AB in Chemistry, Dickinson Coll., Carlisle, Pa., 1965; MA in Organic Chemistry, Bryn Mawr Coll., 1967; PhD in Biochemistry, U. Calif., San Francisco, 1969. Postdoctoral fellow Stanford U., Palo Alto, Calif., 1969-71; rsch. assoc. Rockefeller U., N.Y.C., 1971-72, Columbia U., N.Y.C., 1972-74; asst. prof., then assoc. prof. Albert Einstein Coll. Medicine, N.Y.C., 1974-82; prof. Sch. Medicine U. Okla., Oklahoma City, 1982-88, U. Va., Charlottesville, 1988—. Mem. Okla. Med. Rsch. Found., 1982-88. Contbr. articles to profl. jours. Recipient rsch. career devel. award NIH, 1975-80; Nat. Inst. Neurol. Diseases and Stroke spl. fellow, 1972-74. Mem. AAAS, Am. Soc. Biochemistry and Molecular Biology, Soc. Neurosci. Office: U Va Sch Medicine Box 800203 Charlottesville VA 22908-0001

GASKINS, KAREN D., management consultant, research scientist; b. Ft. George Meade, Md., Mar. 23, 1953; d. Melvin Whittier Gaskins Sr. and Geneva K. Hill. AA in Nursing, Prince George's C.C., Largo, Md., 1978; BS in Psychology and Neurosci., U. Md., 2000. Substitute tchr. Prince George's Pub. Schs., Upper Marlboro, Md., 1998—2005. Freelance writer, orgnl. devel., social svc. worker, inventor, linguist Indo-European langs., cognitive psychology. Mem. Healing Waters, Inc., Ponderosa Project, KDG Assocs., Inc. Mem. Noetic Sci. (neuroscientist), Am. Psychol. Soc. E-mail: millicent71@yahoo.com.

GASNER, DONN ALLAN, music educator; b. Madison, Wis., Mar. 24, 1958; s. Allan Arnold and Dorothy Mae Gasner; m. Renee Phyllis Fillingsness, June 30, 1984; children: Jocelyn, Olivia. MusB, U. Wis., Whitewater, 1981. Cert. instrumental music and vocal music edn. K-12. Elem. band dir./H.S. marching band dir. Ft. Atkinson Pub. Schs., Wis., 1981—84; dir. of bands Horicon H.S., Wis., 1984—. Chmn. North Ctrl. Assn. Sch. improvement team Horicon H.S., 1997—2000; percussion instr. Wis. Sch. Music Assn. State Honors Band, Madison, 1985; guest condr. summer band camp U. Wis., Whitewater, 1982; percussion instr. Wis. Sch. Music Assn. State Honors Orch., 2005. Dir.: (plays) Oliver, 1992, West Side Story, 1996, Seven Brides For Seven Brothers, 2000; actor, dir.: (plays) Fiddler on the Roof, 2002, The Music Man, 2005. Fellow Kohl Tchr. fellow, WEAC/DPI, 1989. Mem.: NEA, Horicon Edn. Assn. (pres. 1995—96), Wis. Edn. Assn., Nat. Band Assn. (bd. dirs. Wis. chpt. 1982—86), Wis. Sch. Music Assn. (guest clinician 1981—2002, mem. coun., Master Adjudicator 2003, Will Schmid scholar 2001). Home: 718 Neitzel St Horicon WI 53032 Office: Horicon HS 841 Gray St Horicon WI 53032 Personal E-mail: dagasner@charter.net. E-mail: dgasner@horicon.k12.wi.us.

GASPAR, ANNA LOUISE, retired elementary school educator, consultant; b. Chgo., May 12, 1935; d. Miklos and Klotild (Weiss) G. BS in Edn., Northwestern U., 1957. Cert. elem. tchr., Calif. Tchr. 6th grade Pacific Palisades Elem. Sch., L.A., 1957-58; tchr. 1st grade Eastman St. Elem. Sch., L.A., 1959, Glassell Park, L.A., 1959-62, Stoner Ave. Elem. Sch., L.A., 1962-67; 2nd-4th grade tchr. Brentwood Elem. Sch., L.A., 1967-78; tchr. 4th and 5th grades Brockton Ave. Elem. Sch., L.A., 1978-90; vol., established Swakopmund Tchrs. Resource Ctr., Peace Corps, Namibia, 1991-93; tchr. English, Atlantic Sr. Primary Sch., Swakopmund, Namibia, 1992; career info. cons. Peace Corps., 1991—; substitute tchr. Hebrew Acad./Pre-Primary, Las Vegas, 1994-2000. Mem. Elderhostel Programs in Alaska, 2000, Victoria BC, 2000, Hungary, 2001, Banff Ctr. Can. 2002, Mpls., 2002, San Francisco, 2002, Phoenix Valley, 2003, Santa Fe, 2003, Taos, N.Mex., 2003, Albuquerque, 2003, Boulder, Colo., 2004, Williamstown, Mass., 2005, North Adams, Mass., 2005, Willamstown, Mass., 2005, North Adams, Mass., 2005; mem. Bet Knesset Bamidbar Temple. Mem.: Calif. State Ret. Tchrs. Assn., So. Nev. Peace Corps Assn., Peace Corps, Northwestern U. Alumni Assn. Democrat. Jewish. Avocations: world travel, playing piano, art, collecting costume dolls, folk music. Home: 2700 Hope Forest Dr Las Vegas NV 89134-7322 Personal E-mail: agaspar1@cox.net.

GASPARETTI, LORENZO E., lawyer; b. Beloit, Wis., Oct. 15, 1962; m. Rita Gasparetti; 3 children. BA, U. Calif., Berkeley, 1984, JD, 1988. Bar: Calif. 1988, DC 1995. Assoc. Crosby Heafey Roach & May (combined with Reed Smith in 2003), LA, 1988—96, ptnr., 1996—2003, Reed Smith LLP, LA, 2003—, So. Calif. practice group leader litig. group. Mem.: Italian-Am. Lawyers Assn. Avocations: travel, music, photography, tennis. Office: Reed Smith LLP 355 S Grand Ave, Ste 2900 Los Angeles CA 90071 Office Phone: 213-457-8038. Office Fax: 213-457-8080. Business E-Mail: lgasparetti@reedsmith.com.

GASPAR-MARTINS, ISMAEL, Angolian diplomat, former government minister, business executive; b. Luanda, Angola, Jan. 12, 1940; s. Sebastao and Antonia (Brandao) Gaspar-M.; m. Luzia de Jesus, Sept. 27, 1968; children: Henda, Giza, Ulanga, Luziela. B in Econ., Lycoming Coll., Pa.; completed post-graduate studies in Econ., U. Mannheim, Germany, 1969; attended, receiving a diploma in econ. develop., Oxford U., 1969—71. Research officer on agricultural development policies in Africa UN Rsch. Inst. for Social Develop., Geneva, 1971—72; served with the United Nations Conference on Trade and Development (UNCTAD), 1972—75; external and economic affairs adviser President of Angola., 1975; gov. Central Bank of Angola, 1976—77; min. fin. Gov. of Angola, 1977—82, min. external commerce, 1982—87; exec. dir. African Development Bank, Abidjan, Cote d'Ivoire, 1989—95; founding mem. and co-pres. Angola-South Africa C. of C. and Industry, 1996—; mng. dir. Gaspar Martins and Assocs. Internat. Bus. Cons.; served on Southern African Development Cmty. Task Force, World Economic Forum Summit, 1996—2000; permanent rep.-Gov. of Angola UN, NY, 2001—. Econ. cons. Min. Ext. Affairs, Luanda, 1987-89; exec. dir. Am. Devel. Bank, Abidjan, Ivory Coast, 1989-95; mng. dir. Jaspar-Marthias & Assocs., Johannesburg, 1995—. Del. Popular Assembly, 1980-87, head del. So. Africa Devel. Cmty., 1980-87. Mem. Rotary, World Econ. Forum (task force 1997—), Angola-South Africa C. of C. Industry (co-chmn. 1998—). Methodist. Avocations: gym, tennis, reading, jazz. Office: Permanent Mission of the Republic of Angola to the UN 125 E 73rd St New York NY 10021 Office Phone: 212-861-5656. Office Fax: 212-535-2850.

GASPAROVICH, SANDRA, secondary school educator; b. Peoria, Ill., Apr. 8, 1947; d. Richard Lee and Lucille Ann (Gorman) Augusburger; m. M. Stephen Gasparovich, June 7, 1969; children: Stephen, Scott. BS, Western Ill. U., 1969, student. Cert. quest instr. Tchr. East Peoria (Ill.) Elem. Sch., 1969-75, Ctrl. Jr. High. Sch., East Peoria, 1977—2003. Coord. East Peoria Drug Prevention. Recipient Cert. of Appreciation USDA; named Sci.-Math. Tchr. of Yr., 1988; named Tchr. of Yr., Marvin Hult Health Edn. Ctr., 2003. Mem. NEA, Ill. Edn. Assn., Ill. Tchrs. Assn., East Peoria Elem. Edn. Assn., NSTA, ISTA (Sci. Tchr. of the Yr., 2001), Sigma Xi. Home: 4920 W Woodwind Ct Peoria IL 61607-1322 Personal E-mail: gasparsk@aol.com.

GASPARRINI-ETHERIDGE, CLAUDIA, publishing executive, research scientist, writer; b. Genova, Italy, Apr. 25, 1941; arrived in US, 1984; d. Corrado and Tina (Pizzuti) G.; m. James K. Etheridge, Oct. 15, 1998. D in Earth Scis., U. Rome, 1965; cert. in English, U. Cambridge, Eng., 1965, Pitman Inst., London, 1965. Sr. tech. U. Toronto, Can., 1966-67, rsch. asst., 1967-70, rsch. assoc., 1970-72; phys. scientist II Geol. Survey Can., Ottawa, 1973; rsch. scientist Nat. Inst. for Metallurgy (now Mintek), Johannesburg, 1974-75; ind. cons. Toronto, 1976; pres., owner Minmet Sci. Limited, Toronto, 1977—, Jacksonville, Fla., 1982-86, Tucson, 1986—2000, The Space Eagle Pub. Co., Inc., Toronto, Tucson, 1986—, 1987—; writer, pub., 1989—. Adviser Chinese chpt. Internat. Precious Metals Inst., 1996—2000; guest lectr. U. Heidelberg, 1990, 91, Inst. Precious Metals, Kunming, China, 1984, U. Padua, U. Florence, 1995; presenter in field; assoc. Amazon.com, 2003—. Author: Gold and Other Precious Metals-The Lure and the Trap, 1989, How to Get the Most Out of the Legal System Without Spending a Fortune, 1990, Gold and Other Precious Metals-From Ore to Market, 1993, Murder of the Mind-The Practice of Subtle Discrimination, 1993, Murder of the Mind-The Practice of Subtle Discrimination, rev. 2d edit., 1996, When You Make the Two One, 1994, When You Make the Two One, rev. 2d edit., 1996; author: (as Gloria J. Duv) How to Run a Successful Mail Order Business by Defrauding the Public, 1995; author: Deceit-The Fad of the Nineties, 1997, Gold and Other Precious Metals-Occurrence, Extration, Applications, 2000, From Darkness to Light, 2001, Mechanics-Doctors, Does the Quality of Their Assistance Justify the Fees?, 2002, Subtle Discrimination, 2003, The Enemy Within, 2003, The Wrath of the Devil, 2004; mem. bd. editors: Chinese mag. Gold Sci. and Tech., 1996—2000; contbr. articles to profl. jours. and books. Scientist Sci. by Mail Program, Boston Mus. Sci., 1991-92; mem. rsch. bd. advisors Am. Biog. Inst., Raleigh, N.C., 1990—; hon. mem. Internat. Biog. Ctr. Adv. Coun., Cambridge, Eng., 1992—. Recipient Cert. Appreciation Outstanding Svc. Internat. Precious Metals Inst., 1994; named hon. mem. organizing com. Internat. Conf. on Precious Metals, Kosice, Slovakia, 1995. Avocations: classical music, computers and computer applications, collecting books, crystals, precious and semi-precious stones. Home and Office: 9880 East Sterling View Tucson AZ 85749 Office: Minmet Sci Ltd/ The Space Eagle Pub Co Inc 1210 Sheppard Ave E # 200 North York ON Canada M2K 1E3 also: Via Ugo de Carolis 62 00136 Rome 00136 Italy Office Phone: 520-760-0155. Personal E-mail: claudiaetherigde@thespaceeagle.net.

GASPER, GEORGE, JR., mathematics professor; b. Hamtramck, Mich., Oct. 10, 1939; s. George Gregory and Anastasia Gasper; m. Brigitta Gasper, July 1, 1967; children: Karen, Kenneth. BS, Mich. Technol. U., 1962; MA, Wayne State U., 1964, PhD, 1967. Predoctoral traineeship NASA, 1966-67; vis. lectr. U. Wis., Madison, 1967-68; postdoctoral fellow U. Toronto, Ont., Can., 1968-69, vis. asst. prof., 1969-70; asst. prof. math. Northwestern U., Evanston, Ill., 1970-73, assoc. prof., 1973-77, prof., 1977—. Co-author: Basic Hypergeometric Series, 1990; assoc. editor Jour. Math. Analysis and Applications, 1985-95, The Ramanujan Jour., 1995—. Fellow Alfred P. Sloan Found., 1973-75. Mem. Am. Math. Soc., Soc. Indsl. and Applied Math. (assoc. editor Jour. Math. Analysis 1984-85, vice chair activity group on orthogonal polynomials and spl. functions 1993-95). Office: Northwestern U Dept Math Lunt Bldg Evanston IL 60208-0001

GASPER, JO ANN, social services administrator, consultant; b. Providence, Sept. 25, 1946; d. Joseph Siegleman and Jeanne Van Matre Shoaf; m. Louis Clement Gasper, Sept. 21, 1974; children: Stephen Gregory, Jeanne Marie, Monica Elizabeth, Michelle Bernadette (dec.), Phyllis Anastasia, Clare Genevieve. BA, U. Dallas, 1967, MBA, 1969. Adminstrv. asst. U. Dallas, 1964-68; asst. dir. adminstrn. Britian Convalescent Ctr., Irving, Tex., 1964-68; pres. Medicare Ctrs., Inc., Dallas, 1968-69; bus. mgr., treas. U. Plano, Tex., 1969-72; ins. agt. John Hancock Ins. Co., Dallas, 1972-73; systems analyst Tex. Instrument, Richardson, 1973-75; pvt. practice acctg., bus. cons. McLean, Va., 1976-81; editor, pub. Congl. News for Women and the Family, McLean, Va., 1978-81, Register Report, McLean, Va., 1980-81; dep. asst. sec. for social services policy HHS, Washington, 1981-85; exec. dir. White House Conf. on Agys., HHS, Washington, 1982-85; dep. asst. sec. for population affairs HHS, Washington, 1985-87; policy advisor to under sec. U.S. Dept. Edn., Washington, 1987-88, cons.; pres. Franklin Pk. Assocs., 1989—; exec. dir. Nat. Assn. for Abstinence Edn., 1989-94; mgr. TSR, 1995-98. Tchr. Grapevine-Colleyville Ind. Sch. Dist., 1998—. Co-chmn. St. John's Refugee Resettlement Commn., Va., 1977; bd. dirs., treas. Coun. Inter-Am. Security, Washington, 1978-80; active Fairfax County Citizens Coalition for Quality Child Care, Va., 1979-80; del. White House Conf. on Families, Va., 1979-80; mem. U.S. adv. Inter-Am. Commn. on Women, OAS, 1982-85; U.S. del. XVI Pan Am. Child Congress, Washington, 1984; mem. nat. family policy adv. bd. Reagan-Bush Campaign, 1980; mem. City of Colleyville Planning and Zoning Comm., 2000-02. Recipient Eagle Forum award, 1979, Wanderer Found. award, 1980, Bronze medal HHS, 1982; named Outstanding Conservative Woman, Conservative Digest, 1980, 81 Mem. Exec. Women in Gov. (treas. 1985, sec. 1986) Roman Catholic. Office Phone: 817-498-2671. Personal E-mail: joanngasper@yahoo.com.

GASPER, RUTH EILEEN, real estate executive; b. Valparaiso, Ind., July 16, 1934; d. Reuben John and Effie (Wesner) Tenpas; m. Ralph L. Gasper, May 25, 1957. Student, Purdue U., 1952—56; BA, Govs. State U., 1982. Analyst computer sys. Leo Burnett Advt., Chgo., 1958-69; nat. adminstr. registrars Sports Car Club Am., Denver, 1977-79; pres. Ainslie Inc., Port Orange, Fla., 1982—. Mem. North River Commn. Housing Com., Chgo., 1982-83, fin. com. Mayor's Task Force on Homelessness City of Chgo. Area coord. Concerned Action party, Lansing, Ill., 1977; chief race registrar Ind. N.W. Region Sports Car Club Am., 1969-80; co-founder, Single Rm. Operators Assn., 1987-98; treas. Sand Dollar Home Owners Assn. Inc. Mem. Dolphin Beach Club Condo Assn., Fantasy Island II Condo Assn. (sec.). Avocations: sports car racing, classical music. Personal E-mail: regasper@earthlink.net.

GASPERONI, ELLEN JEAN LIAS, interior designer; b. Rural Valley, Pa.; d. Dale S. and Ruth (Harris) Lias; student Youngstown U., 1952-54, John Carrol U., 1953-54, Westminster Coll., 1951-52; grad. Am. Inst. Banking; m. Emil Gasperoni, May 28, 1955; children: Sam, Emil, Jean Ellen. Mem. Coeurde Coeur Heart Assn., Orlando Opera Guild, Orlando Symphony Guild. Mem. Jr. Bus. Women's Club (dir. 1962-64), Sweetwater Country Club (Longwood, Fla.); Lake Toxaway Golf and Country Club (N.C.). Presbyterian. Home: 1126 Brownshire Ct Longwood FL 32779-2209 also: 92 Cold Mountain Rd Lake Toxaway NC 28747-9630

GASPERONI, EMIL, SR., realtor, real estate developer; b. Hillsville, Pa., Nov. 13, 1926; s. Attico and Rose Mary (Sarnicola) G.; m. Ellen Jean Lias, May 28, 1955; children: Samuel Dale, Emil Attico, Jean Ellen. Diploma in real estate, U. Pitts., 1957. Owner, pres. Gasperoni Real Estate, New Castle, Pa., 1956-63, Ft. Lauderdale, Fla., 1965-86, Gasperoni Internat. Group, Longwood, Fla., 1986—. Founder, chmn. bd. Fill-R-Up Auto Wash Systems Inc., Ft. Lauderdale, 1967-72. With U.S. Army, 1945-46, ETO. Mem. Nat. Inst. Real Estate Brokers, Fla. Assn. Mortgage Brokers, Sweetwater Country Club, Lake Toxaway Country Club (NC). Home: 1126 Brownshire Ct Longwood FL 32779 Office: 931 Wekiva Springs Rd Longwood FL 32779-2501 Office Phone: 407-774-9434. Personal E-mail: gaspgroup@aol.com. Business E-Mail: gasperoni@commercialrealtyfla.com.

GASQUE, DIANE PHILLIPS, mortgage manager; b. Madison, Wis., Mar. 31, 1954; d. Codie Odel and Ruth Elaine (Oimoen) Phillips.; m. Wyndham Henry Burriss, Feb. 5, 1977 (div. 1989); m. Allard Harrison Gasque, Nov. 14, 1992; 1 child, Folline Elaine Gasque. BA, Midlands Tech., Columbia, S.C. Cert. Notary S.C. With inventory control Oxford Industries, Columbia, S.C.; processing agent NCR, Columbia, S.C.; comml. loan officer S.C. Nat., Columbia, S.C.; personnel dir. Witten Sales, Columbia, S.C.; funding agt. Resource Bankshares Mortgage Group, 1995—, sr. specialist. Mem.: Order of Confederate Rose. Republican. Presbyterian. Avocations: bowling, coin collecting/numismatics. Home: 3728 Linbrook Dr Columbia SC 29204-4438 Fax: (803) 741-3595. Office Phone: 803-462-8147. E-mail: dgasque@sc.rr.com.

GASS, GERTRUDE ZEMON, psychologist, researcher; b. Detroit; d. David Solomon and Mary (Goldman) Zemon; m. H. Harvey Gass, June 19, 1938; children: Susan, Roger. BA, U. Mich., 1937, MSW, 1943, PhD, 1957. Lic.

clin. psychologist Mich. Mem. faculty Merrill-Palmer Inst., Detroit, 1958-69, lectr., 1967; mem. faculty Advanced Behavioral Sci. Ctr., Grosse Pointe, Mich., 1969-72; pvt. practice clin. psychology Birmingham, Mich., 1972—. Adj. prof. psychology U. Detroit, 1969-75; cons. Continuum Ctr. Oakland U., Rochester, Mich., 1961-77, Traveler's Aid, Detroit, 1959-75; pres. Shapero Sch. Nursing, Detroit, 1967-72, cons. 1958-78; psychol. cons. Physician's Ins. Co. of Mich., 1988—, mgmt. Mich. Bell Telephone, 1979-82. Mem. Adv. Com Sch. Needs, 1954-56; trustee Sinai Hosp. Detroit, 1972-99; bd. dirs. Tribute Fund United Cmty. Svcs., 1955-67. Fellow Am. Assn. Marriage-Family, Am. Orthopsychiatric Assn. (v.p. 1975-76), Mich. Psychol. Assn.; mem. Am. Psychol. Assn., Psychologists Task Force (v.p. 1977-84), Mich. Inter-Profl. Assn. (pres. 1976-78), Mich. Assn. Marriage Counselors (1979-80, pres. 1979-80), Mental Health Adv. Svc., Blue Cross and Blue Shield of Mich., Phi Kappa Phi, Pi Lambda Theta. Home and Office: 6155 E Longview Dr East Lansing MI 48823

GASS, JOHN D., oil industry executive; b. Key Biscayne, Fla., Apr. 1952; BS in civil engring., Vanderbilt U., 1974; MS in civil engring., Tulane U., 1980. Design engr. Chevron U.S.A., New Orleans, 1974—88; ops. mgr. Amoseas Indonesia Inc., Jakarta, 1988—91; field project mgr. U.K. Alba Field Devel. project Chevron, 1991—94; profit ctr. mgr. Chevron U.S.A. Prodn. Co., Bay Marchand, La., 1994—96; mng. dir. Chevron Australia Pty Ltd., Perth, 1996—2001; mng. dir. Southern Africa strategic bus. unit Chevron, Luanda, Angola, 2001, Chevron Texaco Corp., Luanda, Angola, 2001—03, v.p. San Ramon, Calif., 2003—; pres. Chevron Texaco Global Gas, 2003—. Bd. dirs. Sasol Chevron Holdings Ltd., LG-Caltex Oil Corp. Mem.: Soc. Petroleum Engr., Am. Soc. of Civil Engr. Office: ChevronTexaco Corp 6001 Bollinger Rd San Ramon CA 94583-2324*

GASS, MANUS M., accountant, construction executive; b. Montreal, Que., Can., June 28, 1928; came to U.S., 1948, naturalized, 1953; s. Maurice and Bertha (Silverberg) G.; m. Estella L. Gass; children: Thomas Evan, Winifred Caitlyn. Student, McGill U., 1945-48; BBA cum laude, CCNY, 1953. CPA, N.Y. Pres., dir. Buitoni Foods Corp., South Hackensack, N.J., 1966-86; chief exec. officer Stavola Constrn. Inc., Tinton Falls, N.J., 1989—. Dir. Buitoni Perugina Inc., N.Y.C., Perugina Chocolates & Confections Inc., Little Ferry, N.J.; acct. Am. Jewish Tercentenary Com., 1953-54 Chmn. River Edge-Oradell United Jewish Appeal, 1964-65, 67-76; mem. Shade Tree Commn., River Edge, 1987—; bd. govs. Hackensack Med. Center. Mem. Am. Inst. C.P.A.s, N.Y. State Soc. C.P.A.s, Fin. Execs. Inst. Home: 184 Woodland Ave River Edge NJ 07661-2321

GASS, STEVEN, librarian; BS, MIT, Cambridge, Mass., 1972; MLS, Simmons Coll., Boston, Mass., 1978. Head libr. and bibliographer, engring. libr. Stanford U. Libr. and Academic Info. Resources, Stanford, Calif., 1990—99; head, sci. and engring. resource group Stanford U. Libr. and Academic Info. Resources, Stanford, Calif., 1997—99; head, engring. libr. MIT, Cambridge, Mass., 1999—2000, head, engring. and sci. libraries, 2000—02; assoc. dir. for pub. services MIT Libr., Cambridge, Mass., 2002—. Adj. faculty, grad. sch. of libr. and info. sci. Simmons Coll., Boston, 2002—; adj. faculty, sch. of libr. and info. sci. San Jose State U., San Jose, Calif., 1990—99; libr. adv. coun. Inst. of Elec. and Electronic Engrs., Piscataway, NJ, 1999—2001; libr. adv. com. Optical Soc. of Am., Washington, 1994—; chair, engring. libraries divsn. Am. Soc. for Engring. Edn., Washington, 1994—95. Contbr. articles pub. to profl. jour. Mem.: ALA, Spl. Libraries Assn., Am. Soc. for Engring. Edn. (chair, engring. libr. divsn. 1994—95, Homer I. Bernhardt Disting. Svc. Award 1998). Office: MIT Libr Bldg 14S-216 77 Mass Ave Cambridge MA 02139 Office Phone: 617-253-7058. Office Fax: 617-253-8894. Business E-Mail: sgass@mit.edu.

GASS, WILLIAM H., writer, educator; b. Fargo, N.D., July 30, 1924; s. William Bernard and Claire (Sorensen) G.; m. Mary Patricia O'Kelly, 1952 (div.); children: Richard, Robert, Susan; m. Mary Alice Henderson, 1969; children: Elizabeth, Catherine. AB, Kenyon Coll., 1947, LHD (hon.), 1973, 85; PhD, Cornell U., 1953. Instr. philosophy Coll. of Wooster, Ohio, 1950-54; asst. prof. Purdue U., Lafayette, 1954-60, assoc. prof., 1960-66, prof. philosophy, 1966-69, Washington U., St. Louis, 1969-79, David May Disting. Univ. prof. in humanities, 1979-99; dir. Internat. Writers Center, 1990—2001. Vis. lectr. U. Ill., 1958-59; mem. Rockefeller Commn. on Humanities, 1978-80; mem. literature panel Nat. Endowment for the Arts, 1979-82. Author: Omensetter's Luck, 1966, In the Heart of the Heart of the Country, 1968, Willie Masters' Lonesome Wife, 1968, Fiction and the Figures of Life, 1970, On Being Blue, 1974, The World Within the Word, 1978, The Habitations of the Word: Essays, 1984, The Tunnel, 1995, Finding a Form, 1996, Cartesian Sonata, 1998, Reading Rilke, 1999, Tests of Time, 2002; contbr. to periodicals including N.Y. Rev. of Books, N.Y. Times Book Rev., New Republic, TriQuar., Salmagundi, others. Office: 6304 Westminster Pl Saint Louis MO 63130

GASSAWAY, WILLIAM BROOKS, retired manufacturing executive, writer; b. Memphis, May 11, 1921; s. Tandy Brooks and Lula Nisbet Gassaway; children: Carol Gassaway Goode, Julie Gassaway Tatum. BS in Aeronautical Engring., Miss. State, Starkville, 1943. Mktg. mgr. Hamilton Beach, Racine, Wis., 1946—64; pres. Tenn. Bolt and Screw Co., Memphis, 1966—91; creator and prodr. Day-Stretcher Sys., Memphis, 1991—93; author New South Pub., Memphis, 1999—. Author: Roadmap to Become a Millionaire, 2005. Elder Second Presbyn. Ch., Memphis, 1984—2004. Capt. Air Force, 1943—45, PTO. Named to Hall of Fame, Nat. Indsl. Fastener Show, 1988. Mem.: Kiwanis Club of Memphis (hon.). Achievements include patents for outside air conditioning unit compressor bolt which supports exterior compressor system. Personal E-mail: billgsswy02@aol.com.

GASSER, JONATHAN S., prosecutor; b. NYC, 1958; BA, Brandeis Univ., 1979; JD, Bklyn. Law School, 1986. Bar: New York 1988, U.S. Dist. Ct. Interim US atty. Dist. SC US Dept. Justice, Columbia, 2005—. Office: 1441 Main St Ste 500 Columbia SC 29201

GASSER, MICHAEL J., consumer products company executive; BA, Ohio Northern U. CPA Ohio. Internal auditor Greif, Inc., 1979—81, controller, 1981—88, v.p., finance, 1988—94, mem. bd. dir, 1991—, vice chmn., COO, 1994, chmn., CEO, 1994—. Office: c/o Greif Inc 425 Winter Rd Delaware OH 43015*

GASSERE, EUGENE ARTHUR, lawyer, investment company executive; b. Beaumont, Tex., Oct. 20, 1930; s. Victor Eugene and Althea June (Haight) G.; m. Mary Alice Engelhard, Aug. 4, 1956; children— Paul, John, Anne. BS, U. Wis., 1952, JD, 1956; postgrad., Oxford U., 1956-57. Bar: Wis. bar 1956. Asst. counsel Wurlitzer Co., Chgo., 1958-61, Campbell Soup Co., Camden, N.J., 1961-65; asst. to pres. Thilmany Pulp & Paper Co., Kaukauna, Wis., 1966-68; with Skyline Corp., Elkhart, Ind., 1968-92, v.p., gen. counsel, asst. sec., 1973-92, ret., 1992—. Pres., bd. dirs. Elkhart Urban League, 1972-73, Elkhart Symphony, 1975-76, Elkhart Concert Club, 1976-77. Served with U.S. Army, 1952-54. Mem. Wis. Bar Assn., Phi Mu Alpha. Home: PO Box 165 Mindoro WI 54644-0165 Office: Skyline Corp 2520 Bypass Rd Elkhart IN 46514-1584 E-mail: pelt2ridge@centurytel.net.

GASSON, JUDITH C., research scientist; m. David Kronemyer; children: Andrew, Lauren. BS in microbiology, Colo. State Coll., 1973; PhD in physiology, U. Colo., 1979; postdoctoral, Salk Inst., 1979—82. With UCLA Jonsson Comprehensive Cancer Ctr., 1983—, dir., 1995—; prof. medicine and biol. chemistry UCLA Sch. Medicine. Pres. Jonsson Cancer Ctr. Found., 1995—. Recipient Scholar award, Leukemia Soc. Am., 1988, Stohlman Scholar award, 1991, Women of Sci. award, UCLA, 1991, Am. Soc. Clin. Investigation award, 1994. Office: UCLA Jonsson Comprehensive Cancer Ctr 8-684 Factor Bldg 10833 Le Conte Ave Box 951781 Los Angeles CA 90095-1781

GASTIL, RAYMOND WESLEY, urban designer; b. Cambridge, Mass., Nov. 21, 1958; s. Raymond Duncan and Jeannette Carr Gastil. BA in Comparative Lit., Yale U., 1980; MArch, Princeton U., 1991. Dir. regional design program Regional Plan Assn. N.Y., N.J., and Conn., N.Y.C., 1991-95; exec. dir. Projects Pub. Architecture Van Alen Inst., N.Y.C., 1995—. Mem. profl. architecture adv. com. Parsons Sch. Design, N.Y.C., 1996—; vis. lectr. Pratt Inst., Bklyn., 1997, U. Pa., Phila., 2000; panelist N.Y. Coun. Arts, N.Y.C., 2000-02. Author: Beyond the Edge: New York's New Waterfront, 2002, (with Robert A. M. Stern) Modern Classicism, 1988; contbg. author: The Italian Garden: Art, Design, and Culture, 1996, New York, 2001; contbg. writer Blueprint Mag., 1987-90. Mentor N.J. Inst. Tech., Newark, 1997-98; mem. steering com. Pier 40 Cmty. Design, N.Y.C., 1999; mem. adv. bd. U. Va. Sch. Architecture, 2002—. Fellow Inst. Urban Design; mem. AIA (assoc.; mem. oculus publ. com. N.Y. chpt. 1999-2000). Office: Van Alen Inst 30 W 22d St New York NY 10010 E-mail: rgastil@vanalen.org.

GASTMANN, ALBERT LODEWIJK, retired political science professor, retired language professor, writer; b. Arnhem, The Netherlands, Oct. 28, 1919; s. Lodewijk A. Gastmann and Petronella M. Uhlenbeck. BA, Columbia Coll., 1949; MA, Columbia U., 1953, PhD, 1963. Clerical officer Netherlands Embassy, Chungking, China, 1943—46; tchr. Abraham Lincoln Am. Sch., Lima, 1950—53; instr. modern langs. Trinity Coll., Hartford, 1954—57, asst., assoc. prof. polit. scis., 1957—75; prof., lectr. Law Sch. Netherlands Antilles, Curacao, 1975—79; prof. Trinity Coll., Hartford, 1975—91, ret., 1991. Author: The Politics of Surinam and The Netherlands Antilles, 1968 (German Honor Soc. Delta Phi Alpha award), Urbanization Planning and Development in Caribbean, 1989, (with Scott MacDonald) Mitterand's Headache, 1984, A History of Credit and Power in the Western World, 2001; contbr. articles to profl. jours., chpts. to books. Served Netherlands Armed Svcs., 1941—43. Mem. Caribbean Studies Assn. U.S. (founding mem.), Pi Gamma Mu, Delta Phi Alpha. Home: 244 Avery Heights Hartford CT 06106-4092 Office: Trinity Coll Polit Sci 300 Summit St Hartford CT 06106

GASTON, JOSEPH, minister, educator; arrived in U.S., 1986; s. Denizard and Marie T. Gaston; m. Marie Yanick Eugene, Dec. 26, 1981; children: Mardochee, Nathaniel, Eunice, Timothee. BS in Econs., State U. Haiti, Port-au-Prince, 1982; MA in Christian Edn., So. Bapt. Theol. Sem., Louisville, 1997; PhD in Ch. Edn. and Leadership, So. Bapt. Theol. Sem., 2003. Economist, analyst Econ. Dept. Haiti, Port-au-Prince, 1981—83; tchr. various h.s., Haiti and U.S., 1980—95; minister, prof. various, 1979—2001; leadership trainer Haitian Ministries USA, 1995—; leadership devel. dir. Fla. Bapt. Conv., Jacksonville, 2002—. Chair Nat. Christian Leadership, 2002. Mem.: AAUP, N.Am. Christian Edn. Assn. Baptist. Office: Florida Baptist Conv 1230 Hendricks Ave Jacksonville FL 33065

GASTON, MARGARET ANNE, retired finance educator; b. Regina, Sask., Can., Aug. 28, 1930; Came to U.S., 1948. d. William Julius and Mary Josephine (Collins) Grogan; m. Robert F. Gaston, 1955 (dec. Mar. 1970); 1 child, Robert. BA in Bus. Edn., Ctrl. Wash. U., 1959; MEd, We. Wash. U., 1972; postgrad., Boston U., 1984. Cert. tchr. K-12, cert. vocat. tchr., Wash. Bus. educator Manson Sch. Dist., Wash., 1956—59; instr. K-12 Eastmont Sch. Dist., East Wenatchee, Wash., 1959—63; instr., chmn. dept. bus. Skagit Valley Coll. Whidbey Campus, Oak Harbor, Wash., 1970—90; ret., 1990. Part-time instr. bus. edn. Wenatchee Valley Coll., 1959-65. Contbr. articles to profl. jours. Fellow Western Wash. U., Bellingham, 1968-69. Mem. AAUW, NEA, Wash. Edn. Assn., Bus. and Profl. Women, Delta Pi Epsilon, Beta Sigma Phi. Home: 20 Little Mountain Estates 2610 E Section St Mount Vernon WA 98274-6100

GASTON, MARILYN HUGHES, health facility administrator; b. Cin. children: Amy Marie, Damon Allen. AB in Zoology, Miami U., Oxford, Ohio, 1960; MD, U. Cin., 1964. Diplomate Am. Bd. Pediats. Intern Phila. Gen. Hosp., 1964—65; resident in pediat. Childrens Hosp. Med. Ctr., Cin., 1965—67, asst. dir. out-patient dept., 1967—68, Convalescent Hosp. for Children, Cin., 1968—69; med. dir. Lincoln Heights (Ohio) Health Ctr., 1969—72; dir. Sickle Cell screening clinic Cin. Health Dept., 1972—76; med. expert Nat. Heart, Lung & Blood Inst./NIH, Bethesda, 1976—79; commd. 2d lt. USPHS, 1979—89; dir. divsn. medicine Bur. Health Professions, Rockville, Md., 1989—90; dir., asst. surgeon gen., assoc. adminstr. for bureau Bur. Primary Health Care, Rockville, Md., 1990—2002; chief medical officer National Minority Health Month, 2002; co-dir. Gaston Porter Health Improvement Ctr., Potomac, Md., 2002—. Instr. pediats. U. Cin. Coll. Medicine, 1967—68, asst. clin. prof. divsn. cmty. pediats., 1968—70, asst. prof. pediats., 1970—76, assoc. prof. pediats., 1976—77; asst. clin. prof. pediats. Cin. Tech. Coll., 1974—76, Howard U. Coll. Medicine, 1978—91, Uniformed Svcs. U. the Health Scis., 1987—; attending pediatrician Children's Hosp. Med. Ctr., 1969—76, attending pediatrician and clinician, 1969—76, dir. med. staff, 1969—76; attending pediatrician Bethesda Hosp., 1974—76; pediatrician Hosp. Albert Schweitzer Deschapelles, Haiti, 1967; presenter, lectr., spkr. in field. Author: AL Bibliography: Comprehensive Sickle Cell Centers, 1977; co-author (with C.L. Calhoun), 1981; author: Management and Therapy of Sickle Cell Disease, 1984, 1988, Prime Time: The African American Woman's Complete Guide to Midlife Health and Wellness, 2003; author: (with others) Newborn Screening for Sickle Cell Disease and Other Hemoglobinopathies, 1989; contbr. articles to profl. jours. Co-chair Nat. Sickle Cell Dirs., 1974; med. advisor Sickle Cell Awareness Group, 1971—77, State Crippled Children's Svcs., 1975—77; bd. trustees Child Health Assn., 1974—77; bd. dirs. U. Cin. Found., 1989—. George Washington U. Life Scis., 1993—, U. Md. Ctr. for Minority Rsch. External Adv. Bd., 1993—, Komen Found. for Breast Cancer, Wellesley Ctr. for Women, Nat. Black Women's Health Project. Named Woman of the Yr. in Medicine, Harriet Tubman Black Women's Dem., 1976; named one of Outstanding Young Women in Am., 1973, Outstanding Black Women in Cin., 1974; named to Ohio Women's Hall of Fame, 1990; recipient Phyllis Wheatley award, State of Ohio, 1975, Hildrus A. Poindexter award, Pub. Health Svcs., 1990, State of Ohio Gov.'s award, 1987, Disting. Alumnae award, U. Cin., 1989, Pub. Health award, D.C. Health Care for the Homless Project, Inc., Nathan Davis award, AMA. Mem.: APHA, AAAS, Inst. of Medicine/NAS, N.Y. Acad. Scis., Am. Med. Women's Assn., Am. Pediat. Soc., Am. Soc. Hematology, Nat. Med. Assn. (Living Legend award), Nat. Assn. Med. Minority Educators, Am. Acad. Pediats., Alpha Kappa Alpha, Sigma Delta Epsilon. Office: Gaston Porter Health Improvement Ctr 8612 Timber Hill Ln Potomac MD 20854*

GASTON, PAUL LEE, academic administrator, language educator; b. Hattiesburg, Miss., Aug. 23, 1943; s. Paul Lee and Ruth (Gooch) Gaston; m. Eileen Margaret Higgins, June 29, 1968; children: Elizabeth, Tyler Lee(dec.). BA, S.E. La. U., 1965; MA, U. Va., 1966, PhD, 1970. Ordained min. Episcopal Ch., 1990. Prof. English So. Ill. U., Edwardsville, 1969-88, assoc. v.p., 1984-88; dean Coll. Arts and Scis. U. Tenn., Chattanooga, 1988-93; provost, exec. v.p. No. Ky. U., Highland Heights, 1993-99; provost Kent (Ohio) State U., 1999—. Author: W. D. Snodgrass, 1978, Concordance Conrad, Arrow of Gold, 1980; contbr. articles to profl. jours. Chair, bd. dirs. Ohio Learning Network, Ohio Lik. Mem.: Nat. Assn. State U. and Land Grant Colls., Assn. Specialized and Profl. Accreditors, Phi Beta Kappa. Democrat. Avocations: softball, hiking, calligraphy. Office: Kent State U Office of Provost PO Box 5190 Kent OH 44242-0001 Office Phone: 330-672-2220. Business E-Mail: pgaston@kent.edu.

GASTWIRTH, DONALD EDWARD, lawyer, literary agent; b. N.Y.C., Aug. 7, 1944; s. Paul and Tillie (Scheinert) G. BA, Yale U., 1966, JD, 1974. Bar: Conn. 1979, U.S. Dist. Ct. Conn. 1981. Mem. advt. staf New Yorker mag., N.Y.C., 1967-68; v.p. Reader's Press, New Haven, 1968-74, dir., 1968-75; exec. v.p. Mainstream TV Studio, New Haven, 1974-77, dir., 1974-79; pres. Quasar Assocs., New Haven, 1979-89; account exec. Bache Halsey Stuart Shields Inc., New Haven, 1977-79; ptnr. Gastwirth, McMillan & Still, New Haven, 1981-84; pres. Don Gastwirth & Assocs. Literary Agy., New Haven, 1984—. Adj. prof. law Thomas Jefferson Sch. Law, 1996-99; lectr. in field; advisor fund raising, mem. benefit com. John Steinbeck Lit. Project, 1986-94; assoc. fellow Trumbull Coll., Yale U., 1991—. Assoc. prodr. Yankee Fishing (TV series, 1995-98); contbr. to Nat. Rev., Wall St. Jour., New Haven Register; mem. bd. advisors Yale Lit. Mag., 1987-94, Touchstone Mag., 1990-95, 98-99. Trustee Yale Ctr. for Parliamentary History, 1995-2002; bd. dirs. Chancel Opera Co. Conn., New Haven Downtown Soup Kitchen. Mem.: PEN Writers Assn., ABA, Writers Guild Am., Berzelius Soc., Lambs Club, Yale Club (N.Y.), Elizabethan Club. Home and Office: 265 College St New Haven CT 06510-2420 Office Phone: 203-562-7600. Business E-Mail: donlit@snet.net.

GASTWIRTH, GLENN BARRY, medical association administrator; b. N.Y.C., Sept. 18, 1946; s. Milton and Janette (Wasserman) G.; m. Joy Ann Binstock, Nov. 29, 1969; children: Sara Beth, Bradley Aaron. BA, Ohio State U., 1968; postgrad., NYU, 1968-69; Dr.Podiatric Medicine, N.Y. Coll. Podiatric Medicine, N.Y.C., 1974. Diplomate Am. Bd. Podiatric Surgery. Pvt. practice podiatry, Southgate, Mich., 1975-86, Tri-County Family Podiatrists, Pontiac, Mich., 1979-86; dir. sci. affairs Am. Podiatric Med. Assn., Bethesda, Md., 1986-92, dep. exec. dir., 1992—98; editor-in-chief Jour. Am. Podiatric Med. Assn., 1989-91; exec. editor, 1991—; exec. dir. Am. Podiatric Med. Assn., Bethesda, Md., 1998—. Surgical residency Kern Hospital, Detroit; predoctoral fellow preventive medicine NYU Sch. of Medicine. Pres. Cold Spring Sch. PTA, Potomac, Md., 1988-90; bd. dirs. Nat. Coun. on the Aging, 1996—; chair del. coun. Nat. Voluntary Orgns. for Ind. Living for the Aging. NIH fellow, 1968-69; N.Y.C. Dept. Pub. Health fellow, 1970. Fellow Am. Coll. Foot Surgeons, Am. Coll. Podiatric Med. Rev. (sec. 1990—); mem. Mich. Podiatric Med. Assn. (pres. 1981-82, Legion of Merit 1982), Am. Pub. Health Assn. (sect. council mem. 1972-74), Am. Diabetes Assn., Am. Podiatric Med. Assn. (ho. of dels. 1973-74, 80-86, Disting. Svc. citation 1996). Avocations: running, writing. Office: Am Podiatric Med Assn 9312 Old Georgetown Rd Bethesda MD 20814-1646

GATANAS, HARRY D., career officer; b. Bklyn., Mar. 21, 1947; Commd. officer U.S. Army, advanced through grades to brig. gen.; commdg. officer White Sands Missile Range White Sands (N.Mex.) Missile Range, 1998-99; comdg. gen. Army Test and Evaluation Command, Alexandria, Va, 1999—.

GATCH, JERALD V., music educator; b. Baton Rouge, La., Jan. 4, 1963; m. Sidney Marie Adickes, Dec. 29, 1987; children: Katherine Victoria, Alexander Bull. MusB in Edn., U. of S.C., 1985, MusM, 1987. Freelance musician, SC, 1985—; dir. of bands Lexington (S.C.) HS, 1993—. Condr. S.C. Philharm. Youth Orch., Columbia, 2002—; choir dir. Lexington (S.C.) United Meth. Ch., 1993—. Recipient Legion of Honor, John Philip Sousa Found., 2001. Mem.: S.C. Band Dirs. Assn. (chmn.various coms. 1991), Am. Sch. Band Dirs. Assn., Nat. Band Assn. (corr. Citation Excellence 1996, 1998, 2000, 2001, 2002, Cert. of Merit 2002), Phi Beta Mu. Republican. Avocations: golf, fishing, skiing. Office: Lexington High School Bands 2463 Augusta Highway Lexington SC 29072 E-mail: jgatch@lexington1.net.

GATCH, MILTON MCCORMICK, JR., library director, clergyman, educator; b. Cin., Nov. 22, 1932; s. Milton McCormick and Mary (Curry) G.; m. Ione Georganna White, Aug. 25, 1956; children: Ione Waite, Lucinda McCormick, George Crosby White. AB, Haverford Coll., 1953; student, U. Cin. Sch. Law, 1953-55; BD, Episc. Theol. Sch., Cambridge, Mass., 1960; MA, Yale U., 1961, PhD, 1963. Ordained priest Episc. Ch., 1961. Chaplain Wooster Sch., Danbury, Conn., 1963-64; chaplain, chair humanities dept. Shimer Coll., Mt. Carroll, Ill., 1964-67; assoc. prof. English No. Ill. U., DeKalb, 1967-68; prof. English U. Mo., Columbia, 1968-78, chair dept., 1971-74; prof. ch. history Union Theol. Sem., N.Y.C., 1978-98, acad. dean and provost, 1978-89, dir. Burke Libr., 1990-98, emeritus, 1998—; priest-in-charge Chapel of St. James Fisherman, Wellfleet, Mass., 1976—2005. Mem. coun. Coll. of Preachers, 1992-98; vis. fellow Emmanuel Coll., Cambridge, 1991; Bonhöffer vis. prof. Humboldt U., Berlin, 1998. Author: Death: Meaning and Mortality in Christian Thought and Contemporary Culture, 1969, Loyalties and Traditions: Man and His World in Old English Literature, 1971, Preaching and Theology in Anglo-Saxon England, 1977, So Precious a Foundation: The Library of Leander van Ess, 1996, The Yeats Family and the Book, 2000, Eschatology and Christian Nurture, 2000; contbr. numerous articles on antiquarian, bibliographical medieval subjects. With U.S. Army, 1955-57. NEH sr. fellow, 1974-75. Fellow Soc. of Antiquaries London, Medieval Acad. Am. (del. to Am. Coun. Learned Socs. 1981-93); mem. Internat. Soc. Anglo-Saxonists (founding, mem. adv. bd. 1980-85), Am. Coun. Learned Socs. (bd. dirs. 1992-93), Early English Text Soc., Bibliog. Soc., Bibliog. Soc. Am., Am. Printing History Assn. (trustee 1995-99), Yale Libr. Assocs. (trustee 1999-2003, 2004—), Century Assn., Grolier Club. Democrat. Avocations: book collecting, gardening, photography. Office Phone: 212-213-6990. E-mail: mac@miltongatch.us.

GATELY, MARK DONOHUE, lawyer; b. Balt., Jan. 6, 1952; s. Bernard Patrick and Margret (Donohue) G.; m. Rosemary Connolly, Dec. 27, 1986; children: Maeve Donohue, Harry John Connolly, Fiona Anne McCourt. BA, U. Md., 1974, JD, 1977. Bar: Md. 1977, U.S. Dist. Ct. Md. 1978, U.S. Ct. Appeals (4th cir.) 1978, U.S. Ct. Appeals (D.C. cir.) 1981, D.C. 1982, U.S. Supreme Ct. 1994, U.S. Ct. Appeals (3d cir.) 1988, U.S. Dist. Ct. (D.C. cir.) 1991, U.S. Ct. Appeals (7th cir.) 1993. Law clk. to Hon. C. Stanley Blair U.S. Dist. Ct. Md., Balt., 1977-78; asst. atty. gen. Office Md. Atty. Gen., Balt., 1980-81; assoc. Miles & Stockbridge, Balt., 1978-84, ptnr., 1984-2000, chair litigation dept., 1992-2000; ptnr. Hogan & Hartson, 2000—. Fellow Am. Coll. Trial Lawyers, Internat. Acad. Trial Lawyers, Am. Bd. Trial Advs.; mem. Order of Coif. Office: Hogan & Hartson LLP 111 S Calvert St Ste 1600 Baltimore MD 21202 Office Phone: 410-659-2700. Business E-Mail: mdgately@hhlaw.com.

GATES, ALEXANDER E., geologist, educator; b. N.Y., Apr. 23, 1957; s. David and Frieda Gates; m. Melinda Ernst (div.); children: Colin, Jasper, Maxine, Thomas. MS, Va. Poly. Inst. and State U., 1981, PhD, 1986; BS, SUNY, Stony Brook, 1979. Exploration geologist Chevron USA, Inc., New Orleans, 1981—83; vis. asst. prof. Lafayette Coll., Easton, Pa., 1986—87; sr. scientist N.Y. State Geol. Survey, Albany, 1990—91; asst. prof. Rutgers U., Newark, 1987—93, assoc. prof., 1993—99, prof., 1999—. Sci. content advisor Liberty Sci. Ctr., Jersey City, 1994—98, Palisades Interstate Pk. Commn., Bear Mountain, NY, 1997—; chief sci. content advisor Newark Mus., 1999—2003. Author: (book) Encyclopedia of Earthquakes and Volcanoes, A-Z Biographies of Earth Scientists; editor: (volume) Geologic Controls on Radon, The Tectonics of the Appalachian Belt, 5 profl. vols.; pub. 53 profl. papers. Henry Rutgers Rsch. fellow, Rutgers U., 1987-1988. Fellow: Geol. Soc. Am.; mem.: Am. Geophys. Union, Geol. Assn. N.J. (pres. 2005—), Nat. Assn. Geosci. Tchrs. (pres. ea. sect. 2004—05). Office: Rutgers U 101 Warren St Room 136 Newark NJ 07102 Office Phone: 973-353-5034. E-mail: agates@andromeda.rutgers.edu.

GATES, BILL (WILLIAM HENRY GATES III), computer software company executive; b. Seattle, Wash., Oct. 28, 1955; s. William H. and Mary M. (Maxwell) G.; m. Melinda French, January 1, 1994; Jennifer Katherine, Rory John, Phoebe Adele. Grad. high sch., Seattle, 1973; student, Harvard U., 1973-75. Co-founder Traf-O-Data Co., Seattle, 1972—73, Microsoft Corp. (formerly Micro Soft), Albuquerque, 1975; gen. ptnr. Microsoft Corp., 1975—77, pres., 1977—82, chmn. bd., 1981—, exec. v.p. development activities, 1982—83, chief software architect Redmond, Wash., 1999—; founder Corbis, 1989. Bd. dirs. ICOS Corp., 1990—, Berkshire Hathaway Inc., 2004—. Author: The Future, 1994, The Road Ahead, 1995, Business at the Speed of Thought, 1999. Founder William H. Gates Found., 1994—2000; co-founder Gates Learning Found. (formerly Gates Library Found.), 1997—2000, Bill and Melinda Gates Found., 2000—. Recipient Howard Vollum award, Reed Coll., Portland, Oreg., 1984, Nat. medal Tech. U.S. Dept. Commerce Tech. Adminstrn., 1992, Hon. Knighthood, UK, 2005; named CEO of Yr., Chief Executive mag., 1994; named one of Top 200 Collectors, ARTnews Mag., 2004, one of 100 Most Influential People, Time Mag., 2005. Avocation: Collector 19th Century Am. Art. Office: Microsoft Corp 1 Microsoft Way Redmond WA 98052-8300

GATES, BRUCE CLARK, chemical engineer, educator; b. Richmond, Calif., July 5, 1940; s. George Laurence and Frances Genevieve (Wilson) G.; m. Jutta M. Reichert, July 17, 1967; children: Robert Clark, Andrea Margarete. BS, U. Calif., Berkeley, 1961; PhD in Chem. Engring., U. Wash., 1966. Rsch. engr. Chevron Rsch. Co., Richmond, Calif., 1967-69; from asst. prof. to assoc. prof. U. Del., Newark, 1969-77, prof. chem. engring., 1977-85, H. Rodney Sharp prof., 1985-92, assoc. dir. Ctr. Catalytic Sci. & Tech., 1977-81, dir. Catalytic Ctr. Sci. & Tech., 1981-88; prof. chem. engring. U. Calif., Davis, 1992—2003, disting. prof., chmn. engring., 2003—. Basic energy sci. adv. com. Dept. of Energy, 2004—. Author: Catalytic Chemistry, 1992; co-author: Chemistry of Catalytic Processes, 1979; co-editor: Metal Clusters in Catalysis, 1986, Surface Organometallic Chemistry, 1988, Advances in Catalysis, 1996—. Recipient Sr. Rsch. award Humboldt Found., U. Munich, 1998; Fulbright Rsch. grantee Inst. Phys. Chemistry U. Munich, 1966-67, 75-76, 83-84, 90-91; Sr. Humboldt Found. fellow Inst. Phys. Chemistry, U. Munich, 1998-99, 2002 Mem.: AIChE (Alpha Chi Sigma award 1989, William H. Walker award 1995, R.H. Wilhelm award 2002), Catalysis Soc. N.Am. (bd. dirs. 1997—), Am. Chem. Soc. (Del. sect. award 1985, Petroleum Chemistry award 1993, G.A. Somorjai award for creative rsch. in catalysis 2004). Achievements include research in catalysis, surface chemistry and reaction kinetics, chemical reaction engineering, petroleum and petrochemical proccesses, catalysis by solid acids, zeolites, soluble and supported transition-metal complexes and clusters, catalytic hydroprocessing. Office: U Calif Dept Chem Engring & Materials Sci Davis CA 95616 E-mail: bcgates@ucdavis.edu.

GATES, CHARLES WOODLEY, SR., city official; b. Dayton, Ohio, Jan. 14, 1943; s. Theodore and Nellie M. (Black) G.; m. Nina J. Wright, Sept. 27, 1969; children: Charles W. Jr., Stephanie L. BSBA, U. Dayton, 1965. Acct. NCR Corp., Dayton, 1966-68, asst. sect. head mktg. and acctg., 1968-70; asst. contr. Montgomery County Community Action Agy., Dayton, 1970; airport compt. City of Dayton, 1970-75, supt. airport adminstrn., 1975-89; dir. aviation City of Austin, Tex., 1989-98, dir. aviation fin. and adminstrn., 1998—. Sec. West Area YMCA, Dayton, 1979-89; bd. dirs. Dayton Area YMCA, 1985-89, Austin Area Urban League, 1992—. Recipient nat. achiever's award Airport Minority Adv. Coun., 1991, Outstanding Black in Govt. award BOSS, 1991; named Outstanding Man of Yr. AME Ch., Ctrl. Tex. Annual Conf., 1998. Mem. Am. Assn. Airport Execs., Airport Operators Coun. Internat. (econ. com. 1974—), Sigma Pi Phi. Office: Austin Dept Aviation 3600 Presidential Blvd Austin TX 78719-2363 Office Phone: 512-530-2214.

GATES, CHRIS, not-for-profit developer, political organization worker; Degree with hons. in Econs., U. Colo.; MPA, Harvard U. Comms. dir. Piton Found.; aide Gov. Richard Lamm, Colo.; pvt. practice cons.; v.p. Nat. Civic League, 1987—95, pres., 1995—; chmn. Colo. State Dem. Party, Denver. Spkr. in field; vis. scholar U. East Anglia, Norwich, England. Active Coun. Advancement Citizenship, Calif. Ctr. Civic Renewal, Inst. Regional Cmty.; co-chmn. Saguaro Seminar. Fellow: Nat. Acad. Pub. Adminstrn. Mailing: Colorado Democratic Party chmn 777 Santa Fe Drive Denver CO 80204 Office: National Civic League 1445 Market St Ste 300 Denver CO 80202-1717

GATES, GREGORY ANSEL, lawyer; b. Cortland, N.Y., Sept. 25, 1953; s. Herbert Ansel and Mary (O'Connor) G.; m. Margaret Anne Schell, Aug. 9, 1975; children: Ryan Mary, Connor Ansel. BA, SUNY, Oswego, 1975; JD, Albany Law Sch. Union U., 1978. Bar: N.Y. 1979, U.S. Dist. Ct. (no. dist.) N.Y. 1979, U.S. Dist. Ct. (no. dist.) Calif. 1985, U.S. Ct. Appeals (2d cir.) 1993, U.S. Supreme Ct. 1994. Assoc. Levene Gouldin and Thompson, Binghamton, N.Y., 1979-84, ptnr., 1984-85, Hickey, Sheehan and Gates, Binghamton, N.Y., 1985--. Mem. Continuing Edn. Adv. Com., Binghamton, 1982-87. Commn. of Elections Broome County Gov., Binghamton, 1984-97, town justice, 1997—; pres. Broome County Magistrates Assn., 2002-2004; dir. Broome Sports Found., 1987--; counsel Broome County Dem. Com., 1984-87. Mem. ABA, N.Y. Bar Assn., Assn. Trial Lawyers Am., Broome County Bar Assn. (dir. 1988-91). Democrat. Roman Catholic. Avocations: hockey, golf, travel. Office: Hickey Sheehan and Gates PO Box 2124 Binghamton NY 13902-2124 Office Phone: 607-723-1990.

GATES, HENRY LOUIS, JR., English language educator; b. Keyser, W.Va., Sept. 16, 1950; s. Henry-Louis and Pauline Augusta (Coleman) G.; m. Sharon Lynn Adams, Sept. 1, 1979; children: Maude Augusta Adams, Elizabeth Helen-Claire. BA summa cum laude, Yale U., 1973; MA in English Lang. and Lit., U. Cambridge, Eng., 1979, PhD in English Lang. and Lit., 1979; hon. degrees, Dartmouth Coll., 1989, U. W.Va., 1990, U. Rochester, 1990, U. N.H., 1991, Harvard U., 1991, Manhattan C.C., 1992, Bryant Coll., 1992, George Washington U., 1993, Williams Coll., 1993, U. Mass., Boston, 1993, Bates Coll., 1995, Macalester Coll., 1995, Emory U., 1995, Colby Coll., 1995, Purchase Coll., 1995, Bard Coll., 1995, Bethany Coll., 1995, N.Y.U. Sch. Visual Arts, 1996, Haverford Coll., 1996, Nazareth Coll., 1996, U. Palacky, Czech Republic, 1996, Lawrence U., 1997, N. Ctrl. Coll., 1997, L.I. Univ., 1997, Pace U., 1998, Toronto U., 1998, Fairleigh Dickinson U., 1999, Potomac State U., 1999, Hamilton Coll., 1999, U. St. Thomas, Minn., 1999, City Coll. San Francisco, 2000, Cmty. Coll. Phila., 2000, Colgate U., 2001, U. Benin, 2001, U. Ill., Chgo., 2002, R.I. Sch. Design, 2002, U. Ala., 2002. Lectr. English and Afro-Am. studies Yale U., New Haven, 1976-79, asst. prof., 1979-84, assoc. prof., 1984-85; prof. English, comparative lit. and Africana studies Cornell U., Ithaca, N.Y., 1985-88, W.E.B. DuBois prof. lit., 1988-90; John Spencer Bassett prof. English and Lit. Duke U., 1990-91; W.E.B. DuBois prof. humanities, prof. English Harvard U., 1991—. Chair Dept. of Afro-Am. Studies, 1991—, dir. W.E.B. DuBois Inst., 1991—; pres. Afro-Am. Acad. 1984—; mem. Pulitzer Prize Bd., 1997-, chmn., 2005-. Author: Figures in Black, 1987, Signifying Monkey, 1988, Loose Canons, 1992, Colored People: A Memoir, 1994, (with Cornel West) The Future of the Race, 1996, Thirteen Ways of Looking at a Black Man, 1997, Wonders of the African World, 1999, Africana: The Encyclopedia of the African American Experience, 1999, (with Cornel West) The African-American Century, 2000, Little Known Black History Facts, 2000, The Trials of Phillis Wheatley: America's First Poet and Her Encounters with the Founding Fathers, 2003; editor: Black is the Color of the Cosmos: Charles T. Davis's Essays on Black Literature and Culture, 1942-81, 1982, Our Nig, 1983, The Slave's Narrative, 1985, Black Literature and Literary Theory, 1985, Race, Writing, and Difference, 1986, The Classic Slave Narratives, 1987, The Souls of Black Folk, 1989, Reading Black, Reading Feminist, 1990, Bearing Witness, 1991, The Norton Anthology of African American Literature, 1996, The Dictionary of Global Culture, 1997, Hannah Crafts, The Bondwoman's Narrative, 2002; series editor: Oxford-Schomburg Library of the 19th Century Black Women, 1988; co-editor: Encarta Africana Encyclopedia, 1999 (Outstanding Contbn. to Pub., Black Caucus of Am. Libr. Assn., 2000); co-editor, mem. editl. bd. Transition, 1991—; mem. editl. bd. Black Am. Lit. Forum, 1981-86, Am. Quar., 1981, Studies in Am. Fiction, 1981, Porteus, 1984—, Diacritics, 1985—, Publs. of MLA, 1987, Critical Inquiry, 1987, Cultural Critique A/B. Trustee Whitney Mus. Am. Art. Recipient MacArthur prize MacArthur Found., 1981—, Faculty prize Yale Afro-Am. Cultural Ctr., 1984, Am. Book award 1989, Anisfield-Wolfe Book award, 1989, Zora Neale Huston prize, 1986, George Polk award for social commentary, 1993, Lillian Smith Book award, Chgo. Tribune Heartland award West Virginia of Yr. award, 1994, Nat. Humanities medal, 1998, Tchrs. Coll. Medal for Disting. Svc., Columbia U., 2000, Jefferson lectr., 2002. Mem. Am. Acad. Arts and Scis., African Lit. Assn., Am. Studies Assn., MLA, Assn. for Study of Afro-Am. Life and History, Coll. Lang. Assn., PEN, Caribbean Studies Assn., Coun. on Fgn. Rels., Lincoln Ctr. Theatre (bd. dirs.), Century Club, Elizabethan Club, Phi Beta Kappa. Episcopalian. Avocations: jazz, pocket billiards. Office: Harvard U Dept Afro-Am Studies Barker Ctr 12 Quincy St Cambridge MA 02138-3804

GATES, JAMES DAVID, retired professional society administrator; b. East Cleveland, Ohio, July 9, 1927; s. James Adelbert and Margaretta (Voigt) G.; m. Carol Marie Schreiber, June 9, 1956; children: David, Keith, Robert. AB, Hiram (Ohio) Coll., 1951; MA, Columbia, 1956; EdD, George Washington U., 1975. Tchr. Maple Heights (Ohio) City Schs., 1951-61; profl. asst. Nat. Council Tchrs. Math., Reston, Va., 1961-63, exec. sec., 1963-76, exec. dir., 1976-95. Mem. faculty U. Va., 1963-66, George Washington U., 1966-75; assoc. dir. Math. Scis. Edn. Bd., Ctr. for Sci., Math., and Engring. Edn., Nat. Rsch. Coun., 1997-99. Mem. Va. Coalition Math. and Sci.; bd. dirs. MathCounts Found.; sec.-treas. Jr. Engring. Tech. Soc. Served with AUS, 1945-46. Fellow AAAS; mem. NEA, ASCD, Nat. Coun. Suprs. Math., Nat. Coun. Tchrs. Math., Math. Assn. Am., Assn. State Suprs. Math., Benjamin Banneker Assn., Assn. Math. Tchr. Educators, Am. Math. Assn. Two-Yr. Colls., Rotary. Home: 11303 Fieldstone Ln Reston VA 20191-3905 E-mail: jamgate@aol.com.

GATES, JANE CAROL, artist, writer, referral service proprietor, landscape designer; b. Providence, Aug. 6, 1948; d. Robert Leonard Schwartz and Grace Adrian Black. BFA, R.I. Sch. Design, 1970; cert., Academia Di Perugia, Italy, 1971. Cert. community coll. instr., Calif. Songwriter, performer Red Bus Internat. Music Pub., London, 1971-76; freelance writer, illustrator various advt. and pub. relations agys., London, Boston, San Diego, 1975-82; project mgr. Ctr. Human Resources, Irvine, Calif., 1983-84; pres., tng. program developer Gates & Croft, Los Angeles, 1983—; founder, pres. Createmps Inc., Los Angeles and Boston, 1985—; landscape designer/contractor Gates & Croft Horticultural Design, 1998—. Composer numerous recorded and pub. popular songs, 1971-76 (grand prize composition Yamaha World Popular Song Festival, Tokyo, 1972, 3d prize best song internat. Luxembourg Radio Festival, 1973); author: (children's book series) Adventures of Dat and Sidney, 1976; exhibited paintings and prints London, Boston, Los Angeles, 1971-81. Mem. Artists Equity Assn., The Performing Right Soc. (Eng.). Avocations: swimming, horticulture.

GATES, JEFF, writer; b. Chgo., Mar. 4, 1946; s. James Edward and Harriet Reed G.; m. Jeffrey Jr., Erin Christine, Michael Taylor. BA, U. Va., 1968; JD, U. Calif., San Francisco, 1975. Bar: Calif. Counsel Hewitt Assocs., Chgo., 1978-80, U.S. Sentate Com. Fin., Washington, 1980-87; of counsel Finley, Kumble, Washington, 1987-88; counsel Kelso & Co., N.Y.C., 1988-90; ptnr. Powell, Goldstein, Frazer & Murphy, Washington, 1990-92; pres. The Gates Group, Atlanta, 1992—, Shared Capitalism Inst., Atlanta, 1998—. Author: the Ownership Solution, 1998, Democracy At Risk, 2000. 1st lt. U.S. Army, 1968-70. Home: 570 Cress St 1266 W Paces Ferry Rd NW # 284 Laguna Beach CA 92651 E-mail: Jeffgates@mindspring.com.

GATES, MAHLON EUGENE, retired research and development company executive, retired military officer; b. Tyrone, Pa., Aug. 21, 1919; s. Samuel Clayton and Elsie (Nieweg) G.; m. Esther Boone Campbell, July 4, 1972; children by previous marriage: Pamela Townley, Lawrence Alan. BS, U.S. Mil. Acad., 1942; MS, U. Ill., 1948; postgrad., Command and Gen. Staff Coll., 1957, Army War Coll., 1962, Harvard U., 1965. Commd. 2d lt. U.S. Army, 1942, advanced through grades to brig. gen., 1966; area engr. Iran, Gulf Dist., 1960-61; chief, engr. br., officer Personnel Directorate, Dept. Army, 1963-64; gen. staff Dept. Army, 1964-66; comdg. gen. Cam Ranh Bay, Vietnam, 1966-67; dir. constrn. Vietnam, 1967; dir. research, devel. and engring. Army Materiel Command, Washington, 1971; ret., 1972; mgr. Nev. ops. office AEC now Dept. Energy, Las Vegas, 1972-82; sr. v.p. S.W. Rsch. Inst., San Antonio, 1982-89, ret., 1989. Leader US sci. team to N.W. Territories during recovery ops. for crashed nuclear-powered Russian satellite, 1978. Past pres. Boulder Dam Area council Boy Scouts Am.; past chmn. adv. bd. Clark County C.C. Decorated D.S.M., Legion of Merit, Bronze Star, Air medal; Army Distinguished Service Order 1st class Govt. Vietnam; Meritorious Service award; named Meritorious Exec. ERDA. Home: 1 Towers Park Ln Apt 2011 San Antonio TX 78209-6439 Personal E-mail: ink1942@aol.com. *Cherish the past; do not worship it.*

GATES, MARY ELIZABETH, musician, director, retired music educator; b. Warsaw, Ill. d. Walter Ernest Scott and Edna Mae Reynolds; m. Paul L. Gates (dec.); children: Stephen, Elizabeth, Philip, Christopher. BA, Carthage Coll., 1952; MA, Northwest Mo. State U., 1970. Organist/dir. music Christ Episcopal Ch., Springfield, Mo., 1988—2005; ret. pub. sch. music educator. Mem.: Keyboard Club (v.p. 1989—2005), Am. Guild Organists. Office: Christ Episcopal Church 601 E Walnut Springfield MO 65806

GATES, MARY ELIZABETH EVANS, secondary educator; b. Blacksburg, Va., Jan. 11, 1937; d. Frank Henderson and Mary Alice (Cromer) Evans; m. Gerald Paul Gates, June 18, 1960; 1 child, Lisa Pauline. BA in Edn. magna cum laude, Radford (Va.) U., 1958; MA in Edn. with honors, George Washington U., Washington, 1982. Tchr. Great Bridge High Sch., Chesapeake, Va., 1958-61; tchr., communication specialist Granby High Sch., Norfolk, Va., 1961—. Tutor athletes community, Granby High, Norfolk, 1980-90. Leader Girl Scouts, Chesapeake, Va., 1976-78; poll worker Republicans, Norfolk, 1966-67; Sunday sch. tchr. First Ch. of God, Norfolk, 1960-90, chmn. bd. Christian edn., 1972, 76, 88, 91. Ford Found. grantee, 1980. Fellow DAR, Internat. Reading Assn., Va. Athletic Dirs. Wives (hospitality chair 1987, tour dir. 1990), Secondary Reading of Va.; mem. Delta Kappa Gamma (membership chair 1988-91). Avocations: gardening, athletics, music. Home: 1904 Windjammer Ct Virginia Beach VA 23454-1427 Office: Granby High Sch 7101 Granby St Norfolk VA 23505-4097

GATES, MELINDA FRENCH, foundation administrator; b. Dallas, Tex., 1964; m. Bill Gates, Jan. 1, 1994; 3 children. BS in Computer sci. and Econ., Duke U., 1986, MBA, 1987. With Microsoft Corp., 1987—96; co-founder Bill & Melinda Gates Found., Seattle, 2000—. Bd. dir. drugstore.com, The Wash. Post Co., 2004—. Bd. trustee Duke U., 1996—2003; former co-chair Wash. State Gov. Commn. on Early Learning. Named one of Most Powerful Women, Forbes mag., 2005. Mem.: Bilderberg Group. Roman Catholic. Office: Bill & Melinda Gates Found PO Box 23350 Seattle WA 98102*

GATES, MILO SEDGWICK, retired construction company executive; b. Omaha, Apr. 25, 1923; s. Milo Talmage and Virginia (Offutt) G.; m. Anne Phleger, Oct. 14, 1950 (dec. Apr. 1987); children: Elena Motlow, Susan Gates Suman, Virginia Lewis, Anne Symington, Milo T.; m. Robin Templeton Quist, June 18, 1988; stepchildren: Robert L. Quist, Catherine Brisbin, Sarah Mazzocco. Student, Calif. Inst. Tech., 1943-44; BS, Stanford U., 1944, MBA, 1948. With Swinerton & Walberg Co., San Francisco, 1955—, pres., 1976—, chmn., 1988-96, ret. Bd. dirs., trustee Children's Hosp. San Francisco; trustee Grace Cathedral, San Francisco; bd. dirs. Calif. Acad. Scis. Lt. (j.g.), USNR, 1944-46. Mem. Pacific-Union Club, Bohemian Club. Republican. Home: 7 Vineyard Hill Rd Woodside CA 94062-2531

GATES, MIMI GARDNER, museum director; b. Dayton, Ohio, July 30, 1942; BA, Stanford U.; MA in Oriental and Chinese studies, U. Iowa; PhD in art hist., Yale U. Curator Asian art dept. Yale U. Art Gallery, New Haven, 1975—87, dir., 1987—94; Illsley Ball Nordstrom dir. Seattle Art Mus., Wash., 1994—. Instr. Chinese art hist. and mus. studies Yale U.; faculty mem. U. Wash.; chair Fed. Indemnity panel The Nat. Endowment, 1999—2002. Contbr. Bones of Jade, Soul of Ice: The Flowering Plum in Chinese Art, 1985, co-curator Stories of Porcelain, From China to Europe, 2000, Ancient Sichuan: Treasures from a Lost Civilization, 2001. Bd. mem. Downtown Seattle Assn., YWCA. Mem.: Assn. Art Mus. Dirs. (past pres.). Office: Seattle Art Mus 100 University St Seattle WA 98101*

GATES, PETER P. MCN., lawyer; b. N.Y.C., Dec. 27, 1934; s. John Monteith Gates and Ellen Houghton; m. Joan Bryan, Oct. 10, 1957; children: Peter NcNair, Courtlandt Dixon, Katharine Gates Warner. BA, Harvard U., 1956; LLB, Columbia U., 1963. Bar: N.Y. 1963, U.S. Ct. Appeals (2d cir.) 1966, U.S. Dist. Ct. (so. dist.) N.Y. 1973. Assoc. Carter, Ledyard & Milburn, N.Y.C., 1963-71, ptnr., 1971—2004, of counsel, 2005—. With U.S. Army, 1957-60. Mem. ABA, N.Y. State Bar Assn., N.Y. County Bar Assn., Assn. of Bar of City of N.Y., Down Town Assn. (pres. 1991-96). Home: 325 E 57th St New York NY 10022-2935 Office: Carter Ledyard & Milburn 2 Wall St New York NY 10005-2072 E-mail: gates@clm.com.

GATES, R. JORDAN, meteorologist; From Europe controller to exec. v.p., CFO, treas. Expeditors Internat. of Washington, Seattle, 1991—2000, exec. v.p., 2000—, CFO, 2000—, treas., 2000—, dir. Office: Expeditors International of Washington 1015 3rd Ave 12th Fl Seattle WA 98104

GATES, RICHARD DANIEL, retired manufacturing company executive; b. Trenton, Mo., Mar. 27, 1942; s. Daniel G. and Effie Wright (Johnson) G.; m. Jean Gates, Jan. 26, 1966; 1 child, Daniel Wright. BS, U. Mo., 1964; M.C.S., Rollins Coll., Winter Park, Fla., 1968; postgrad., Harvard U., 1976. Mgmt. assoc. Western Electric Co., N.Y.C., 1964-66; bus. mgmt. adminstr. Martin Marietta Aerospace Co., Orlando, Fla., 1966-68, chief indsl. engring., 1968-69; fin. analyst Martin Marietta Co., N.Y.C., 1969-70, sr. acct., 1970-71; controller Dragon Cement Co., divsn. Martin Marietta Co., 1971-72, N.E. divsn. Martin Marietta Aggregates Co., 1972-73; asst. controller, then asst. treas. Rubbermaid, Inc., Wooster, Ohio, 1973-79, treas., 1979-80, v.p., treas., 1980-91, sr. v.p., bus. devel., investor rels. and corp. communications, 1991-98; ret., 1998. Pres. The Rubbermaid Found., Wooster. Mem. Wooster City Fin. Task Force, All Am. City Com.; chmn. Wooster Growth Assn.; active local Cub Scouts.; adviser Art Center, chmn. maj. indsl. capital campaign Boy Scouts Camp; trustee, chmn. Wayne Ctr. Arts; mem. parents' com. St. Paul's Sch., Wesleyan U. Mem. Nat. Assn. Corporate Treas., Main St. Wooster Inc. (bd. trustees), Beta Gamma Sigma, Omicron Delta Kappa. Clubs: Harvard Bus. Sch, Wooster Country (bd. dirs.). Home: 4751 Gulf Shore Blvd N 1606 Naples FL 34103 Mailing: Ste 9-470 88005 Overseas Hwy Islamorada FL 33036

GATES, ROBERT MICHAEL, academic administrator, former CIA Director; b. Wichita, Kans., Sept. 25, 1943; married; 2 children. BA, Coll. William and Mary, 1965; MA, Ind. U., 1966; PhD in Russian and Soviet History, Georgetown U., 1974. Joined, various positions, including intelligence analyst, asst. nat. intelligence officer CIA, Washington, 1966-74; staff Nat. Security Coun. The White House, Washington, 1974-79; various positions, including officer nat. intelligence CIA, Washington, 1979-82, dep. dir. for intelligence, 1982-86, chmn. nat. intelligence coun., 1983-86, acting dir., 1986-87, dep. dir., 1986-89, dir., 1991—93; asst. to pres., dep. nat. security affairs The White House, Washington, 1989-91; interim dean, Sch. of Govt & Public Svcs Texas A&M U., College Station, Tex., 1999—2001, pres., 2002—. Bd. dir. Fidelity Funds, NACCO Industries, Inc., Brinker Internat., Inc., Parker Drilling Co., Inc. Author: (books) From the Shadows: The Ultimate Insider's Story of Five Presidents and How They Won the Cold War, 1996. With USAF, 1966-68. Recipient President's Citizens medal, Nat. Intelligence Disting. Svc. medal, Disting. Intelligence medal (2), Intelligence medal of merit, Arthur S. Flemming award presented annually to ten most outstanding young men and women in the Fed. Svc. Office: Off of Pres Texas A&M Univ 1246 TAMU College Station TX 77843-1246

GATES, STEPHEN FRYE, lawyer, oil industry executive; b. Clearwater, Fla., May 20, 1946; s. Orris Allison and Olga Betty (Frye) Gates; m. Laura Daignault, June 10, 1972. BA in Econ., Yale U., 1968; JD, MBA, Harvard U., 1972. Bar: Fla. 1972, Mass. 1973, Ill. 1977, Colo. 1986. Assoc. Choate, Hall, and Stewart, Boston, 1973-77; atty. Amoco Corp., Chgo., 1977-82, gen. atty., 1982-86; regional atty. Amoco Prodn. Co., Denver, 1987-88; asst. treas. Amoco Corp., Chgo., 1988-91, assoc. gen. counsel, corp. sec., 1991-92; v.p. Amoco Chem. Co., 1993-95; v.p., gen. counsel Amoco Corp., Chgo., 1995-98; exec. v.p., group chief of staff BP Amoco, London, 1999-2000; sr. v.p., gen. counsel, sec. FMC Corp., Chgo., 2000—01; ptnr. Mayer, Brown, Rowe,and Maw, Chgo., 2002—03; sr. v.p., gen. counsel Conoco Phillips, Houston, 2003—. Bd. dirs. Nat. Legal Ctr. Pub. Interest, Washington, 1999—, Internat. Inst. for Conflict Prevention and Resolution, N.Y.C., 2003—. Trustee Newberry Libr., Chgo., 1998—, Appleseed Found., 2003—; mem. adv. coun. Chgo. Schweitzer Urban Fellows Program, 1996—2000; mem. adv. bd. Chgo. Vol. Legal Svcs. Found., 1996—98; mem. Chgo. Crime Commn., 2000—03, bd. dirs., 2000—03; bd. dir. Houston (Tex.) Grand Opera, 2003—. Knox fellow, 1972—73. Fellow: Am. Bar Found., Royal Soc. Arts (London); mem.: ABA, Assn. Gen. Counsels, Yale Club, Chgo. Club, Univ. Club. Office: Conoco/Phillips 600 N Dairy Ashford Houston TX 77079 Business E-Mail: steve.gates@conocophillips.com.

GATES, SUSAN INEZ, magazine publisher; b. San Francisco, Jan. 14, 1956; d. Milo Sedgewick and Anne (Phelger) Gates. BA in English, French magna cum laude (hon.), U. Colo., 1978; MS in Journalism, Columbia U., 1983. With GEO Mag., N.Y.C., 1978—79, New York Mag., N.Y.C., 1981—82, Ladd Assoc., N.Y.C., 1983—85, Mc Namee Cons., N.Y.C., NY, 1986—88; founding pub. BUZZ Mag., L.A., 1989—97; co chmn. Mind Over Media, L.A., 1997—. Mem.: Phi Beta Kappa. Personal E-mail: sigates@adelphia.net.

GATES, VIOLA R., writer; b. St. Joseph, Mo., Oct. 13, 1931; d. Howard and Elsie (Lynch) Bennett; m. James E. Gates, May 7, 1949; children: Barbara Gates Bauguess, Nancy Gates Davis. Student, U. Denver, 1959—60; AA, U. Chgo., 1968; student, U. Colo., 1981—83. Tchr. piano pvt. practice, 1961—85, Brico Studios, Denver, 1970—82, Hamilton Mid. Sch., 1983—85, Englewood Christian, 1983—85. Author: Snow Storm, Journey to Center Place, 1996, Amanda's Gone; co-author: Winning Works, 1992. Ch. pianist, choral dir. Mem.: Denver Area Music Tchrs., Colo. State Music Tchrs. Assn., West Wind Writers, Nat. Writers Assn. (2d pl. award 1991), Brico Symphony Guild (sec.). Avocation: exploring ancient Pueblos. Home: 2149-A Hartford Way Montrose CO 81401

GATES, WILLIAM HENRY, SR., foundation administrator, retired lawyer; b. Bremerton, Wash., Nov. 30, 1925; m. Mary Maxwell (dec. 1994); children: Kristianne, Bill, Libby; m. Mimi Gardner, 1996. BS, U. Wash., 1949, LLB, 1950. Bar: Wash. 1950. Ptnr. Preston, Gates & Ellis (formerly Shidler & King), Seattle, 1964—98; founder Tech. Alliance, 1995—; co-chair The Bill & Melinda Gates Found., Seattle, 2000—. Mem. U. Wash. Bd. Regents, 1997—. U.S. Army, 1943—46. Recipient Am. Judicature Soc. Herbert Harley award, 1992, Lifetime Achievement award, Am. Law mag., 2005. Fellow Am. Bar Found.; mem. ABA (state del. 1975-78, 87-93), Seattle-King County Bar Assn. (pres. 1969-70), Wash. State Bar Assn. (pres. 1986-87, bd. govs. 1972-75), Nat. Conf. Bar Pres. (pres. 1982-83); mem. bd., Judicial Adminstrn., Wash. State Supreme Ct., 1993-1995, Am. Acad. Arts & Sciences, 2003-Office: Bill & Melinda Gates Found PO Box 23350 Seattle WA 98102

GATEWOOD, WILLARD BADGETT, JR., retired historian, writer; b. Pelham, NC, Feb. 23, 1931; s. Willard Badgett and Bessie Lee (Pryor) G.; m. Mary Lu Brown, Aug. 9, 1958; children: Willard Badgett III, Elizabeth Ellis. BA, Duke U., 1953, MA, 1954, PhD, 1957. Asst. prof. history East Tenn. State U., 1957-58, East Carolina U., 1958-60; assoc. prof. N.C. Wesleyan Coll., 1960-64; prof. U. Ga., 1964-70; Alumni Disting. prof. history U. Ark., 1970-98, ret., 1998, provost and chancellor, 1984-85. Author: Theodore Roosevelt and the Art of Controversy, 1970, Smoked Yankees, 1971, Black Americans and the White Man's Burden, 1975, Slave and Freeman, 1979, Free Men of Color, 1982, Aristocrats of Color, 1990, Arkansas Delta, 1993; mem. bd. editors Ga. Rev., 1968-70, Jour. Negro History, 1972-74, Ark. Hist. Quar., 1992-94. Bd. dirs. Winthrop Rockefeller Found., 1990-96. Recipient Parks Excellence in Teaching award Phi Alpha Theta, 1970, Michael Rsch. award, 1967; Outstanding Teaching award Omicron Delta Kappa, 1979, rsch. award U. Ark. Alumni Assn., 1980, Gingles award Ark. Hist. Assn., 1982, Chancellor's medal, 1994, Ledbetter prize, 1994; Truman Libr. fellow, 1963; Acad. Arts and Scis. grantee, 1962. Mem. So. Hist. Assn. (pres. 1986-87), Ark. Hist. Assn., Orgn. Am. Historians, Phi Beta Kappa. Presbyterian. E-mail: wgatewood@cox-internet.com.

GATH, JEAN MARIE, architectural firm executive; BS, SUNY, New Paltz; M in City and Regional Planning, Pratt Inst. Prin. Hardy, Holzman, Pfeiffer Assocs. LLP, N.Y.C., 2001—03, ptnr., dir. planning, 2003—. Fellow: Inst. for Urban Design; mem.: Soc. for Coll. and Univ. Planning, Am. Planning Assn. Office: HHPA 19th Fl 902 Broadway New York NY 10010

GATHRIGHT, HOWARD T., lawyer; b. Phila., May 3, 1935; s. Howard W. and Rose (McGurk) G.; m. Natalie Acquaviva, June 22, 1963 (div. May 1991); children: Donna Marie, Gary Thomas. BA, U. Pa., 1957; JD, Temple U., 1963. Bar: Pa. 1964, Alaska, 2001, U.S. Dist. Ct. Pa. 1964, U.S. Supreme Ct. 1968. Ptnr. Pratt, Gathright & Brett, P.C., Doylestown, Pa., 1964-78; with Gathright & Leonard, Doylestown, Pa., 1990—. Asst. dist. atty. of Bucks County, Pa., 1966-69; solicitor Doylestown Twp., Pa., 1970-75, New Hope Sewage Project of Bucks County Water and Sewer Authority, 1971-76; bd. dirs. Bean, Mason & Eyer, Doylestown. Bd. dirs. Am. Lung Assn., 1970—; pres. Bucks County Estate Planning Coun., 1972; active Bucks County Emergency Health Coun., Inc., 1977-79; apptd. by gov. to Bucks County Spl. Trial Ct. Nominating Commn., 1987. Served in U.S. Army, 1957, USAR, 1958-63. Mem. ABA, Phila. Bar Assn., Pa. Bar Assn., Bucks County Bar Assn. (pres. 1986-87), Assn. Trial Lawyers Am., Pa. Trial Lawyers Assn., Cen. Bucks C. of C. (pres. 1975, chmn. bd. dirs. 1976, Man of Yr. 1975). Democrat. Roman Catholic. Avocations: golf, tennis. Address: PO Box 2163 Bethel AK 99559 Fax: 907-543-1230. E-mail: UofPa@hotmail.com.

GATHRIGHT, JOHN BYRON, JR., colon and rectal surgeon, educator; b. Oxford, Miss., Sept. 29, 1933; s. J. Byron Sr. and Connie (Love) G.; m. Barbara Cooper, Sept. 19, 1959; children: John Byron III, Lin, John Miles, Peter C. BS, U. Miss., 1955; MD, Northwestern U., 1957. Diplomate Am. Bd. Colon and Rectal Surgery (pres. 1989-90), Am. Bd. Surgery. Intern Charity Hosp., New Orleans, 1957-58, resident in gen. surgery, 1958-62; fellow in colon & rectal surgery Alton Ochsner Med. Found., New Orleans, 1962-63; mem. staff So. Bapt. Hosp., New Orleans, 1963-69, Ochsner Found. Hosp., New Orleans, 1969-97, chmn. colon and rectal surgery dept.; clin. prof. surgery Tulane U., New Orleans, 1991—. Vis. surgeon So. La. Med. Ctr., Houma, 1977-97; trustee, exec. com., bd. dirs. Alton Ochsner Med. Found., 1980-97. Assoc. editor Diseases of the Colon and Rectum, 1977-93, Perspectives in Colon and Rectal Surgery, 1987-97, Colon and Rectal Surgery Outlook, 1987-97; mem. bd. editors Current Concepts in Gastroenterology, 1980-89. Fellow ACS (grad. edn. com. 1981-89, Am. Soc. Colon and Rectal Surgeons (pres. 1989-90), Soc. Coloproctology of Eng. and Ireland (hon.), Internat. Soc. Univ. Colon and Rectal Surgeons (sec. 1990-2002), Mex. Soc. Colon and Rectal Surgeons (hon.). Republican. Presbyterian. Avocations: boating, photography. Personal E-mail: jbeegee2@cox.net.

GATI, TOBY T., lawyer; b. Bklyn., July 27, 1946; m. Charles Gati; 2 children; 3 stepchildren. BA, Pa. State U., 1967; MA in Russian Lit., Columbia U., 1970, M in Internat. Affairs, 1972. Rsch. asst, project dir., dep. v.p., v.p., sr. v.p. UN Assn. of the U.S.A., 1972-93; spl. asst. to the pres. for nat. security affairs Nat. Security Coun., sr. dir. for Russia, Ukraine and Eurasian States, 1993; asst. sec. for intelligence and rsch. Dept. State, Washington, 1993-97; sr. internat. advisor Akin Gump Strauss Hauer & Feld LLP, Washington, 1997—. Commentator CNN Headline News and CNN; cons. ABC World Tonight, 1986, Ford Found., 1987-89, BDM Internat., 1989; mem. Coun. on Fgn Rels., Internat. Inst. for Strategic Studies. Office: Akin Gump Strauss Hauer & Feld LLP Ste 400 1333 New Hampshire Ave NW Washington DC 20036-1564 Home: 2123 O St NW Washington DC 20037-1008 Office Phone: 202-887-4422. Business E-Mail: tgati@akingump.com.

GATI, WILLIAM EUGENE, architect, educator; s. John and Edith Gati. Student, The Juilliard Sch. of Music, 1965-77; BS in Architecture, CCNY, 1980, BArch cum laude, 1982; MS in Urban Planning, CUNY, 1985. Registered architect, NY, NJ. Freelance designer, N.Y.C., 1978-83; designer Urban Living, Inc., N.Y.C., 1983-84, Robert L. Henry, Architect, N.Y.C., 1984-86, Glass & Assocs., N.Y.C., 1986-87; prin. architect William E. Gati, RA, AIA, N.Y.C., 1987—; prin. Architecture Studio, N.Y.C., 1991—; writer Home Editor Resident Publs., 1995-97. Prof. architecture N.Y. Inst. Tech., Old Westbury, 1985-89; instr. religious architecture Cooper Union, N.Y.C., 1989; instr. architecture St. John's U., N.Y.C., 1995—96; curator Fundamentals of Architecture, N.Y. Inst. Tech., 1987; vice chair, prof. Design Ctr., Queens, N.Y.; lectr. in field. Archtl. designs include offices for Here's Life, N.Y.C., alterations to Calvary Bapt. Ch., N.Y.C., El Eden Ch., Bklyn., Living Word Christian Ctr., N.Y.C., All Saints Ch., Queens, N.Y.C., Dr. Aviles Med. Ctr., Queens, Tampellini Residence, Queens, Beninen Residence, Queens, Khafi Residence, Queens, expansion for Flushing Christian Sch., Queens, N.Y., Faith Assembly Ch., Queens, P.S. 68 annex, Queens, Perkovich Residence, Queens, Kaufman Residence, L.I., Cardinal Residence, Mas, Lindas Natural Kitchen, Queens, Resurrection Ch., Bklyn., Dr. Peter Chin's Med. Offices, Queens, Dr. Peter Murowski's Med. Offices, Queens, Dr. Larry Weinstein med. offices, Quantum Feet Store, Queens, Greenberg Residence, Queens, Parson Residence, Queens, Malik Residence, Queens, Benenati Residence, Queens; author: Solar Energy Techniques, 1979 (AIA Recognition 1979), Frank L. Wright, 1981, Theory of Modern Architecture, 1981, Boston's Pub. Space, 1985, Vacant Lots, Architectural League N.Y.C., 1987; contbg. illustrator Jonathan Friedman Creations in Space, Fundamentals of Architecture; columnist Queens AIA. Chmn. religious architecture com., organized series: Places for Worship, N.Y.C. 1990; planning bd. Kew Gardens; dir. Queens Design Ctr. Recipient Design award, Queens County Builder's Assn., 2002, Builders award, 2002. Mem. AIA (mem. religious arch. com. N.Y.C., v.p. and pres. Queens chpt., head coms., bd. dirs. N.Y. State chpt.), Mcpl. Art Soc. (assoc.), Archtl. League (assoc.), CCNY Alumni Assn. (v.p. 1983-92), N.Y. Arts Group, Christian Architects Fellowship (pres.). Avocations: photography, chess, piano, art. Office: 11231 84th Ave Jamaica NY 11418-1321 Office Phone: 718-805-2797. E-mail: wgati@williamgati.com, wgati@architecturestudio.us.

GATISON, KAREN ANN, private school educator; b. Bridgeport, Conn., Apr. 1, 1953; d. Harold George and Teresa Mary Russer; children: Jonathan Isaiah, Denise Nicole. AS in Office Tech. and Mgmt., Ctrl. Fla. C.C., Ocala, 1992, AA in Bus. Mgmt., 1994; BA in Bus. Mgmt., St. Leo Coll., 1996. Tchr. Cambridge Acad., Ocala, Fla., 1996—. Bd. dirs. Help Agy. Forest, Silver Springs, Md. Mem.: NAFE, Nat. Bus. Edn. Assn., Nat. Women's History Project, Nat. Coun. Tchrs. Math., Phi Beta Lambda (profl. divsn. 1995—, historian 1993—94, Most Valuable Mem. 1994).

GATJE, ROBERT FREDERICK, architect, writer; b. Bklyn., Nov. 27, 1927; s. Frederick Christopher and Erna Henrietta (Kelting) G.; m. Barbara Mansfield Wright, Oct. 20, 1956 (div. Aug. 1981); children: Alexandra Lord, Marianna Gatje Perrier, Margot Gatje Small. B.Arch., Cornell U., 1951; Fulbright scholar, Archtl. Assn. Sch. Architecture, London, 1951-52. Architect Gatje, Papachristou Smith (formerly Marcel Breuer Assocs.), N.Y.C., 1953-56, assoc., 1956-87, ptnr., 1965-87, dir. Paris office, 1964-66; ptnr. Richard Meier and Ptnrs., N.Y.C., 1987-95. Architect: Broward County Main Library, 1980; co-architect: IBM France Research Center, 1962, Ski Town, Flaine, France, 1969, IBM Mfg. Center, Boca Raton, Fla., 1969, Armstrong Rubber Co. Hdqrs, New Haven, 1969, Baldegg (Switzerland) Convent, 1972, Mundipharma GmbH Hdqrs, Limburg, Ger., 1975; author: Marcel Breuer, A Memoir, 2000. Trustee Deep Springs Coll., Calif., 1974-82, N.Y. Hall of Sci., 1985-96, N.Y. Found. for Arch., 1994-96; pres. Telluride Assn., 1953-55; bd. dirs. Franklin and Eleanor Roosevelt Inst. With C.E., AUS, 1946-47. Telluride scholar, 1947-51; Skidmore, Owings and Merrill scholar, 1950-51; recipient Clifton Beckwith Brown medal Cornell U. Coll. Architecture, 1951, Charles Goodwin Sands medal, 1951 Fellow AIA (pres. N.Y. chpt. 1975-76, Sch. medal 1951); mem. Ordre des Architectes Francais, Century Assn., Am. Arbitration Assn. Democrat. Home: 1040 5th Ave Apt 6A New York NY 10028-0137 Office Phone: 212-861-7906. E-mail: bobgatje@earthlink.net.

GATLIN, JUSTIN, track and field athlete, Olympic track and field athlete; b. Brooklyn, NY, Feb. 10, 1982; Student, Univ. of Tennessee, St. Augustine's College. Professional runner, 2002—; mem. U.S. Track and Field Olympic Team, Athens, 2004. Achievements include NCAA Outdoor Champion, 100m, 200m, 2001, 2002, Indoor Champion, 60m, 200m, 2002, 60m, 2003; U.S. Champion, Indoor 60m, 2003; World Champion, Indoor 60m, 2003; Gold medal, 100m, Athens Olympic games, 2004. Office: c/o USOC 1 Olympic Plaza Colorado Springs CO 80909

GATONS, ANNA-MARIE KILMADE, government official; b. Albany, N.Y., Oct. 21, 1946; d. Daniel Joseph Jr. and Tomasina (Fallone) Kilmade; m. Robert A. McCarthy, Sept. 3, 1967 (div. Apr. 1990); children: Daniel Kilmade McCarthy, Kevin Michael McCarthy; m. Paul K. Gatons, July 28, 1991. BA, Coll. of St. Rose, 1970. Staff support positions HUD, Washington, 1976-79, mgmt. analyst, 1979-81, staff budget analyst, 1981-83, chief of the budget and legislation coord. br., 1983-91, dir. exec. secretariat, 1992-95; dir. exec. secretariat for atty. gen. Dept. of Justice, Washington, 1995—2001; corr. mgmt. officer Office of Asst. Atty. Gen. for Adminstrn., Washington, 2001—02; dir., exec. sec. Immigration and Naturalization Svc., Washington, 2002—03; dir., exec. secretariat U.S. Immigration and Customs Enforcement, Dept. Homeland Security, Washington, 2003—. Mem. St. Rose Alumni Assn. Roman Catholic. Avocations: reading, needlecrafts, decorating. Home: 7705 Huntsman Blvd Springfield VA 22153-3912 Office: US Immigration and Customs Enforcement Exec Secrt Rm 7045 Dept of Homeland Sec 425 I St NW Washington DC 20530 Office Phone: 202-514-2829. E-mail: akilmade@aol.com.

GATTERMEYER, DANIEL J., lawyer; b. Hamilton, Ohio, May 4, 1958; s. Eugene and Mary L. (Hoelle) G.; m. Pamela J. Sloan; children: Tyler, Todd, John, Morgan. BA, Ohio U., 1980; JD, Case Western Reserve U., 1983. Pvt. practice, Hamilton, 1983—; asst. prosecutor Butler County Prosecutor's Office, Hamilton, 1985-2000, atty., 2000—. Mem. Butler County Bd. Elections. Chmn. Butler County Dem. Party; edn. commn. St. Peter in Chains Ch., Hamilton, 1996—; coach West Side Little League, SAY Soccer, Hamilton. Democrat. Roman Catholic. Avocations: basketball, hockey. Office: 2 S 3rd St Ste 405 Hamilton OH 45011-6052

GATTI, EUGENE ANTHONY, immunologist, pediatrician; b. Camden, N.J., June 14, 1955; MD, Georgetown U., 1982. Diplomate Am. Bd. Allergy & Immunology, Am. Bd. Pediatrics. Resident pediatrics Thomas Jefferson U. Hosp., Phila., 1982-85, fellow allergy & immunology, 1985-87; immunologist West Jersey Hosp., Voorhees, N.J., 1987—, Cooper Hosp., Camden, 1987—. Mem. AMA, Am. Acad. Allergy and Immunology, Am. Acad. Pediatrics, Am. Coll. Allergy & Immunology. Home: 1135 Washington Ave Haddonfield NJ 08033 Address: 54 E Main St Marlton NJ 08053-2180 Office Phone: 856-988-0570. E-mail: eagatti@hotmail.com.

GATTI, LEONARD J., communications executive; married; 2 children. BS in Acctg., Villanova U. CPA. Ptnr. PricewaterhouseCoopers LLP, Washington, Phila. and Florham Park, NJ; v.p. fin. reporting Comcast Corp., Phila., 2003—. Mem.: AICPA (mem. task force on cost capitalization), NJ Inst. CPAs, Pa. Inst. CPAs. Office: Comcast 1500 Market St Philadelphia PA 19102

GATTING, CARLENE J., lawyer; b. Hartford, Conn., Apr. 12, 1955; d. Charles W. and Jean A. (Murkowicz) G. BS, U. Conn., 1977; JD, Rutgers U., 1983. Counsel Skadden, Arps, Slate, Meagher & Flom, N.Y.C., 1987—2001. Mem. ABA. Address: 26 Cow Bay Edgartown MA 02539 E-mail: cjgatting@msn.com.

GATTIS, DAN MOORE, lawyer, state representative, rancher; b. Austin, Tex., Dec. 1, 1967; s. Dan Allred and Karen Busby Gattis; m. Shana Lee Nugent, Oct. 20, 2001; 1 child, Sterling Jack. BS in Agr. Econ., Tex. A&M U., 1990; JD, South Tex. Coll. Law, Houston, 1994. Bar: Tex. 1994. Assoc. Tucker, Hendryx & Gascoyne, Houston, 1994—95; asst. county atty. Williamson County Attys. Office, Georgetown, Tex., 1996—99; asst. dist. atty. Williamson County Dist. Attys. Office, Georgetown, 2000—02; pvt. practice Georgetown, 2003—; state rep. Dist. 20 Tex. Ho. Reps., Austin, 2003—. Owner Law Office of Dan Gattis; pres. Gattis Cattle Co., LLC; co-founder, owner NewTrick Entertainment, Inc., Zim Speed Comm., Inc. Republican. Baptist. Office: PO Box 527 Georgetown TX 78627 Office Phone: 512-377-9442. Business E-Mail: dan@dangattis.com.

GATTIS, SARAH BREWER, retired history educator; b. Siler City, N.C., Aug. 19, 1925; d. George Ernest and Bertha (Russell) Brewer; m. David Lawrence Frady, Dec. 20, 1945 (div. 1950); children: Russell Allen, Susan Gayle Frady Price; m. Clyde Hughes Gattis, Apr. 1953 (dec.). BA, MA, U. N.C., 1962, postgrad., 1964-72. Cert. tchr., N.C. Instr. history Barton Coll. (formerly Atlantic Christian Coll.), Wilson, N.C., 1962-65, asst. prof., 1965-68, assoc. prof. history, 1968-90, ret., 1990. Adviser to Wilson City Coun., 1985—. Mem. AAUP, Am. Hist. Soc., So. Hist. Soc., Pi Gamma Mu. Democrat. Baptist. Home: 3710 Starship Ln Wilson NC 27893-1532 Office: Barton Coll Lee St Wilson NC 27893

GATTO, JOHN TAYLOR, educational consultant, educator; b. Monongahela, Pa., Dec. 15, 1935; s. Andrew Michael Mario and Frances Virginia (Zimmer) G.; m. Janet MacAdam, Dec. 29, 1961; children: Briseis Lucrezia, Raven Taylor. BS, Columbia U., 1959; MA, Hunter Coll., 1971; postgrad., Cornell U., 1954, 55, 86, U. Pitts., 1956, Yeshiva U., 1963, Calif. State U., 1984, Lehman Coll., 1987, Reed Coll., 1990. Cert. secondary tchr., N.Y. Copywriter Ted Bates Advt., N.Y.C., 1960-61; screenwriter Lotus Prodns., N.Y.C., 1961-62; instr. in English N.Y.C. Bd. Edn., 1962-71; lectr. Queens Coll., N.Y.C., 1971-76; dir. The Lab Sch., N.Y.C., 1976-91; pres. Oxford Ednl. Cons., Oxford, N.Y., 1991—. Songwriter (ASCAP listed), N.Y.C., 1967-72; ednl. cons. Bd. Higher Edn., N.Y.C., 1971-76; script cons. Marvel Comics, DC Comics, N.Y.C., 1972-73; sr. staff designer Huckleberry Designs, N.Y.C., 1976—; pres. Lava MT Records; adv. bd., Nat. Coalition Alternative Cmty. Schs., 1998—, Nat. TV Turnoff Week, 1999. Author: One Flew Over the Cuckoo's Nest: A Critical Study, 1975, Howard Phillips Lovecraft: A Critical Study, 1976, The Adventures of Snider, the CIA Spider, 1979, Are You My Father? An Odyssey Across the Barren Land of Adoption and Homelessness, 1990, Dumbing Us Down: The Hidden Curriculum of Compulsory Schooling, 1991, The Exhausted School, 1992, A Different Kind of Teacher, 2001, The Underground History of American Education, 2002, rev. edit., 2005, The Fourth Purpose: An Investigation of Modern Schooling, 2003, Curriculum of Power, 2005; contbr. articles to jours. and newspapers; composer Ballads of Sorrow and Sadness, 1968, Iphigenia in Aulis, 1969; recordings include Richard Nixon's Checkers Speech, 1976, Two Attacks on the Media, 1977, The Rats in the Walls, 1978, The Haunter of the Dark, 1979; author (filmscript) The Fourth Purpose, 2000 Founder The I.S. 44 Market, sch. fundraiser, N.Y.C.; dist. leader N.Y. Conservative Party, 1973—, state Committeeman, 1978—; candidate N.Y. State Senate, Albany, 1986, 88, 90; candidate for pres. Manhattan Borough, N.Y.C., 1989; mem. adv. bd. TV-Free Am., 1995—; sec. edn. Libertarian Party Shadow Cabinet, 1993—. Nominee Pres.'s Vol. Action award, 1984; recipient Citizen of the Week award Assn. for a Better N.Y., 1986, 1st prize Nat. Writing Contest Geraldine Dodge Found. and Tchrs. Coll., Columbia U., 1990, Spectrum Medal World Soc. Achievement of Human Potential, 1993, Alexis de Tocqueville award, 1998; named N.Y.C. Tchr. of Yr., Coun. Chief State Sch. Officers and Nat. Assn. Secondary Sch. Prins., 1989, N.Y. State Senate Resolution, 1990, N.Y. Alliance for Pub. Edn., 1991, N.Y. State Tchr. of Yr., Encyclopedia Brittanica, 1990, N.Y. State Edn. Dept., 1991; NEH grantee, 1983, 86, 90; N.Y. Tchr. Consortium grantee, 1984; Coun. for Basic Edn. Ind. Study fellow, 1984; Lehman Coll. fellow, 1987; Mario Salvadori fellow Inst. for the Built Environment, CUNY, 1989, Snowbird fellow Met. Life Ins. Co., 1990; commendations from Pres. Ford, Pres. Carter, Pres. Reagan, N.Y. Gov. Cuomo, N.Y. Mayors Koch and Dinkins. Fellow Scholars Cir., Chenango Upland Pistol Club (pres. 1975-2003, Qua Qua award 2004), Marshall Chess Club, Audubon Soc., U.S. Mycol. Soc., Scottish Heritage Assn., Working Press of the Nation Roman Catholic. Avocations: pistol-hunting, mycology, chess, ancient religions, graphoanalysis. Office: 235 W 76th St New York NY 10023-8210 Home: PO Box 562 Oxford NY 13830-0562 Office Fax: 212-721-6124.

GATTO, LOUIS CONSTANTINE, educational association administrator; b. Chgo., July 4, 1927; s. Louis S. and Marie (Bacigalupo) Gatto; m. Kathleen M. Paquette, July 7, 1951 (dec.); children: Christine Gatto Glasgow, Beth Gatto Roberts, Mark, Gregory, Janine, Sandra Gatto Minniear; m. Marilyn R. Bennett, Feb. 9, 1991 (dec.). Student, Amherst Coll., 1945-46; BA, St. Mary's Coll., Minn., 1950; postgrad., U. Minn., 1950-51; MA, DePaul U., 1956; PhD, Loyola U., Chgo., 1965; LittD (hon.), Marian Coll., Indpls., 1989; LHD (hon.), Martin U., Indpls., 1996. Speech asst. St. Mary's Coll., 1949-50; staff artist TV Times, Mpls., 1950-51; chmn. dept. English Zion-Benton H.S., Ill., 1951-56; tchr. New Trier H.S., Winnetka, Ill., 1956-57; instr. English St. Josephs Coll., Rensselaer, Ind., 1957-58, asst. prof., 1958-63, assoc. prof. Medieval and Renaissance lit., 1963-66, prof., 1966-71, asst. acad. dean, dir. summer session, 1967, acad. dean, 1968, v.p. acad. affairs, 1969-71; pres., prof. English Marian Coll., Indpls., 1971-89; dir. spl. projects, cons. svc. Independent Colls. of Ind., 1989—; amb. Independent Colls. Ind. Found., 1989—91; dir. Ind. Compact, 1989-99, West Point liaison officer, 1990—, dir. Operation Expanded Horizons, 1992—. Mem. Ind. N.W. Consortium Pvt. and Pub. Instns., 1968—71; selection com. Ind. Fulbright Found., 1968—70; mem. cmty. adv. coun. Indpls. Pub. Schs., 1976—77; mem. policy adv. coun. parent/child devel. project Bank St. Coll. Edn., 1976—79; mem. Hist. Landmarks Found. Ind., 1973—89; mem. long range devel. plan adv. com. Ind. Vocat. Tech. Coll., 1985—86; mem. adv. com. Alcohol Safety Action Project, 1972—75; mem. exec. com. adv. bd. Ctr. Econ. Edn., Ind. U.-Purdue U., Indpls., 1978—89; mem. exec. com. Ind. Conf. Higher Edn., 1973—75, 1978—81, 1987—89, pres., 1979—80; chmn. Consortium Urban Edn., 1974—75, pres., 1975—89; dir. spl. projects Ind. Conf. Higher Edn., 1992—94, exec. sec., 1994—; adv. We. Hemisphere Inst. Security Coop., 2004—. Contbr. articles to profl. jours. With Army War Coll., 1974; bd. dirs., treas. Associated Colls. Ind., 1976—78, v.p., 1984—86; mem. Benjamin Harrison Meml. Commn., 1987—91; vice chair Hamilton County ARC, 1999; mem. adv. bd. Sta. WYFI; mem. gov.'s commn. Hoosier Celebration, 1988; Ind. lobbyist Ind. Higher Edn., 1989—90; chmn. Ind. Ameritech. Partnership Awards Program, 1990—95; asst. dir. Ednl. Facilities Auth., 1991—93, exec. dir., 1994—; mem. Senator Lugar's merit selection com. West Point, 1995—; mem. adv. com. 21st century scholars program State Student Assistance Commn., 1998—2002; mem. adv. com. Ind. Coun. Quality Tchg. Student Learning, 2000—02; bd. dirs. Greater Indpls. Progress Com., ARC, Hosp. Audiences Inpls., 1974—76, Ind. Higher Edn. Telecom. Sys., 1987—95, Hamilton County ARC, Ind. Colls. and Univs. Ind., chmn., 1979—80, 1986—88; advisor Western Hemisphere Inst. Security Cooperation, 2004—. With AUS, 1945—46, with N.G., 1947—50. Recipient Sagamor of the Wabash award, State of Ind., 1980, 1989, Outstanding Svc. award, Ind. Health Careers, 1983, Cir. award, Ind. Coalition Blacks in Higher Edn., 1986, Oustanding Contbns. award, Army Career And Alumni Assn., 1994, Sponsor's award commitment to Hoosier Vets., Vets. Day Coun. Indpls., 2004; fellow ACE, 1966—67. Mem.: Nat. Assn. Higher Ednl. Facilities Authorities (v.p. 2002—03, pres. 2004—05), Ind. Conf. Higher Edn. (Dedicated Svc. award 1994), Am. Coun. Edn. (Ind. coord. fellow program 1999—), Friends of West Point Membership, West Point Soc. Ind., Heslar Naval Armory Club (life), Alpha Phi Omega. Home: 24 Apple Tree Cir Fishers IN 46038-1110 Office Phone: 317-875-3395. Personal E-mail: iefa@msn.com.

GATTO, PAUL ANTHONY, artist; b. Bklyn., Sept. 19, 1929; s. James Vincent and Pauline Gatto; m. Isabelle Anne Favuzzi, Sept. 14, 1957; children: Jeanne, Patrice. Student, St. John's U., 1951—53. Lic. ind. inst. adjuster N.Y. Mem. art studio staff Traeger Phillips, N.Y.C., 1947; with acct. office Gen. Adjustment Bur., Inc., 1947—51, fire ins. adjuster, 1953—72; artist Farmingdale, 1972—. One-man shows include Utah Pagaent of Art, American Fork, Utah, Hudson Valley Art Assn., White Plains, N.Y., Springville Mus., Utah, LIAR Heckscher Mus., N.Y., Qgunquit Art Ctr., Maine, Represented in permanent collections Citibank, A&S Dept. Store, AIG, Bishop Molloy High Sch., South Oaks Hosp., Kramer Ln. Sch., Man-hassett High Sch., Meth. Ch. Pres., trustee Farmingdale Pub. Libr.; bd. dirs. Farmingdale C. of C., Main St. Bus. Assn. Sgt. U.S. Army, 1951—53. Mem.: Rotary (bd. dirs. 2002). Avocations: piano, guitar, jazz. Studio: 300 Main St Farmingdale NY 11735

GATTONE, PAUL, lawyer; b. Chgo. BS in Polit. Sci., History, Univ. Ariz., JD, 1988. Founder So. Ariz. People's Law Ctr., Tucson, 1990—. Named one of Tucson's Best, Tucson Weekly, 2002. Mem.: Nat. Law Guild (exec. v.p.). Office: Southern Ariz People's Law Ctr 611 N 4th Ave Tucson AZ 85705 Mailing: Exec VP Nat Lawyers Guild 4th Fl 143 Madison Ave New York NY 10016 Office Phone: 520-218-5541.

GATZKE, DONALD FRANK, architecture educator; BA in Polit. Sci., U. Wis., 1972, MArch, 1979; grad. exec. leadership program, Ctr. for Creative Leadership, Colorado Springs. Cert. Wash., La., Nat. Coun. Archtl. Registration Bds. Tchr. U. Wis., Milw., Tuskegee U., Ala.; asst. prof. Tulane U., 1987, dean Sch. Arch., 1997—2004; assoc. prof. arch. U. Tex., Arlington, 2004—, dean Sch. Arch., 2004—. Exhibitions include Visions of Home: Designs for Affordable Housing in the Bronx, Bronx Mus. Arts, 1990—91. Recipient Design award, AIA, Ala. Coun., East Ala. Chpt., Excellence in Tchg. award, Tulane Sch. Arch., 1993, Design Studio award, ACSA, 1996. Mem.: AIA. Office: Univ Tex Arlington Sch Arch Box 19108 701 S Nedderman Dr Arlington TX 76019-0108

GAU, GEORGE W., dean; BS, U. Ill., Urbana-Champaign, 1969, MS, 1971, PhD in fin., 1975. Asst. prof. fin. U. Okla., 1975—79; asst. to assoc. prof. U. British Columbia, 1979—88; joined faculty McCombs Sch. Bus., U. Tex., Austin, 1988, chair fin. dept., 1992—2002, founding dir. Ctr. Real Estate Fin., 1999—2002, George S. Watson Centennial professorship in real estate, J. Ludwig Mosle Centennial Meml. professorship in investments and money mgmt., dean, 2002—. Co-editor: (book) North American Housing Markets into the Twenty-First Century, 1983; contbr. articles in acad. and profl. jour. Recipient Adv. Coun. award for tchg. innovation, CBA Found., 1994. Fellow: Homer Hoyt Inst., Urban Land Inst.; mem.: Am. Real Estate and Urban Econ. Assn. (past pres., Rsch. award 1990). Office: McCombs Sch Bus Univ Tex Austin TX 78712-1178 Office Phone: 512-471-5921. Office Fax: 512-471-7725. Business E-Mail: ggau@mail.utexas.edu.

GAUB, ALBRECHT FRIEDRICH, music educator; b. Stuttgart, Germany, May 14, 1967; arrived in US, 2004; s. Eberhard and Erika (Mack) Gaub. MA in Musicology and Slavic Studies, U. Hamburg, Germany, 1993, PhD in Musicology, 1997. Free lectr. U. Hamburg, 1997—99; fellow McGill U., Montreal, 1999—2000; music editor A-R Editions, Inc., Middleton, Wis., 2004—; freelance writer, musician, 2001—04. Author: The Collective Opera Ballet Mlada, 1998; composer: Utyos, 1997. With German Army, 1986—87. Grantee, German Acad. Exch. Svc., 1999—2000; Travel grant, Hamburgische Wissensch. Stiftung, Germany, 1994, 2003. Mem.: So. Conf. on Slavic Studies, Assn. for Musikforschung, Am. Musicol. Soc. (adjudicator 2000—02). Avocations: music, photography, movies, languages. Home: Apt 411 4817 Sheboygan Ave Madison WI 53705 Office: A-R Editions Inc Ste 180 8551 Research Way Middleton WI 53562

GAUCH, EUGENE WILLIAM, JR., retired air force officer; b. Newark, Dec. 6, 1922; s. Eugene William and Wilhelmina Katrina (Beiswenger) G.; m. Beryl Merle Walker, Jan. 15, 1947 (dec. Oct. 1995); children: Kathryn A. (Mrs. Jerry T. Stansfield), Tracey L. Enlisted as pvt. USAAF, 1942; advanced through grades to brig. gen. USAF, 1972; assigned Okinawa, World War II and Korean War; tng. and standardization officer SAC, Offutt AFB, Neb., 1955-59; ops. staff officer 72 Bombardment Wing, Ramey AFB, P.R., 1959-63; asst. exec. sec. to air staff bd. Office Vice Chief Staff Air Force, Washington, 1963-67; asst. chief staff, exec. to comdr. 7th Air Force, Vietnam, 1967-68; faculty Nat. War Coll., 1969; exec. to comdr. Hdqrs. Tactical Air Command, Langley AFB, Va., 1969-70, chief staff, 1970-72; comdr. 834th Air Div., Little Rock AFB, 1972-74; dir. automated mobility requirements DSC/Plans and Ops., Hdqrs. USAF, Washington, 1974—75; ret. USAF, 1975. Decorated Legion of Merit with 3 oak leaf clusters, D.F.C., Air medal with 4 oak leaf clusters, Air Force Commendation medal. Home: 628 Owl Way Sarasota FL 34236-1928

GAUCHER, JANE HEYCK, retail executive; b. Houston, Feb. 11, 1936; d. Theodore Richard and Gertrude Paine (Daly) Heyck; m. Donald Holman Gaucher, June 15, 1957 (dec.); children: Susan Heyck Merrill, Beverly Jane. AB cum laude, Brown U., Providence, 1957. Mgr. Bride and Groom Registry

Berings, Houston, 1990-99; asst. mgr. Pavillon Christofle, Houston, 1999—2002; mktg. rep. dinnerRings, 2002—. Pres. Antique Study Group, Houston, 1974—75. Bd. dirs. Jr. League Houston, 1963, sustaining bd., 1990-93; mem. Kinkaid Sch. Alumni Bd., Houston, 1995-98, Mus. So. History Bd., 2000-. Avocations: tennis, running, golf, mah jongg, bridge. Home: 1905B Potomac Dr Houston TX 77057-2921

GAUCHER, KIM ELIZABETH, artist, art director; b. Bklyn., July 17, 1960; d. Clifford Prior Marvin and Lilliane M. Gaucher; m. Steven Scot Srebrenick, Sept. 6, 1998; 1 child, Dylan Kent Srebrenick. AA in Fine Arts, Miami Dade C.C., 1982; postgrad., Parsons Sch. of Design, N.Y.C., 1986; postgrad. studies in computer graphics, Sch. Visual Arts, N.Y.C., 1991; postgrad. studies in painting, drawing, Pratt Inst., N.Y.C., 1993; studies painting, drawing, sculpture, Art Students League, N.Y.C., 1995. Graphic urban designer, model maker Downtown Devel. Authority, N.Y.C., 1982-84; graphic artist Simplicity Pattern Co., Inc., N.Y.C., 1984-85; graphic designer, draftsperson CEO, Inc., N.Y.C.; exhibit designer ECOFA, Inc., Long Island, N.Y., 1986-87; graphic artist, design asst. Rolling Stone Mag., N.Y.C., 1987-90; graphic artist and design asst. Sony Music Entertainment, Inc Creative Svcs., N.Y.C., 1991-97; art dir. PACE Comm., Greensboro, N.C., 1998—. Free lance desgner KEG Designs, N.Y., Miami, 1983-98. Exhbns. at Mary Wolfson Art Gallery, Miami, 1984, Arnold & Sheila Aronson Gallery, N.Y., Sculpture, 1986; several paintings in private collections, 1984—. Mem. NOW at Pro-Choice Rally, 1995, 96. Recipient Creativity award for Album Design, Art Direction Mag., 1995. Mem. NAFE. Avocations: knitting, hiking, swimming, roller blading, bike riding. Office: Pace Comm 1301 Carolina St Greensboro NC 27401-1090

GAUDEAMUS, See JORDAN, JOHN

GAUDET, JEAN ANN, retired librarian, educator; b. Oakland, Calif., Dec. 28, 1949; d. Edwin Joseph and Teresa Maureen (McDonnell) G. BS, Madison Coll., Harrisonburg, Va., 1971; MLS, George Peabody Coll. for Tchrs, Nashville, 1973. Libr., gifted edn. tchr. Prince William County Schs., Manassas, Va., 1971—2003, ret., 2003. Chmn. PSHS Site-Based Mgmt. Com., Dumfries, Va., 1989-92, 98-2001; chmn. Cmty. Choir, Woodbridge, Va., 1983-85; citizen ambassador People to People, Russia and Poland, 1992, China, 1993, 2000, Australia, 1994. Named Prince William Assn. for Edn. of Gifted Tchr. of Yr., 1998. Mem. ALA, Va. Edn. Media Assn., Va. Assn. for Edn. of Gifted, Delta Kappa Gamma (sec. 1994—), Beta Phi Mu, Alpha Beta Alpha. Home: 16820 Francis West Ln Dumfries VA 22026-2110 Office Phone: 703-221-4514. Personal E-mail: gaudetja@cs.com.

GAUDIERI, ALEXANDER V. J., art historian, consultant, museum director; b. 1940; divorced; 1 child. BA, Ohio State U., 1962; diploma, Sorbonne U. Paris, 1962; postgrad., Colgate U., 1963; MBA in Internat. Fin., Am. Grad. Sch. Internat. Commerce, 1965; MA, NYU, 1976. Internat. banking officer Marine Midland Bank, N.Y.C., 1965-71; with Sotheby Parke Bernet, 1972—; dir. Telfair Acad. Arts and Scis., Savannah, Ga., 1977-83; dir. Montreal (Can.) Mus. Fine Arts, 1983—88; art historian, art cons., 2003—. Adj. prof. mus. studies program Grad. Sch. Arts and Scis., NYU; dir. Samuel F.B. Morse hist. site Locust Grove, Poughkeepsie, N.Y., 1995-96. Mem. bd. sponsors Attingham Park Program, Eng.; bd. dirs. Young Concert Artists, N.Y.C. Barton Kyle Yount scholar. Mem. Assn. Art Mus. Dirs., Am. Assn. Mus. (accreditation commn.), Brit. Nat. Trust, Soc. Archtl. Historians. Office: PO Box 3 Palm Beach FL 33480 Office Phone: 561-832-6005. E-mail: gaudieri@bellsouth.net.

GAUDINO, MARIO, physician, pharmaceutical company executive, scientist; b. Buenos Aires, May 22, 1918; came to the U.S., 1945, naturalized, 1966; s. Nicolas M. and Maria Teresa (Ferrari) G.; m. Ann Murray, Sept. 24, 1947 (div. Jan. 1983); children: David, Brian; m. Judith A. Jenkins, May 19, 1984. Asst. Inst. Histology and Embryology, U. Buenos Aires, 1936; asst., rsch. asst. Inst. Physiology, 1937-42, chief lab. biol. physics, 1944; resident, chief resident Ramos Mejia Hosp., Buenos Aires, 1941-44; Millet and Roux fellow Argentine Assn. for Advancement Sci., 1943; asst., attending physician Inst. Semiology, Nat. Clin. Hosp., Buenos Aires, 1944-46; fellow Argentine Nat. Cultural Commn., 1945; Sauberan fellow Argentine Assn. Advancement Sci., 1946; physiol. rsch. fellow NYU, U.S. State Dept., Dazian Found. Med. Rsch., 1946-49; asst. prof. Tex. U., 1949; chmn. dept. biol. physics U. La Plata Med. Sch., Argentina, 1950-51; attending physician Ctrl. Inst. Cardiology, Buenos Aires, 1950-51; assoc. dir. med. writing and advt. Lederle Labs. divsn. Am. Cyanamid Co., N.Y.C., 1951-52; rsch. assoc., prof. dept. surgery NYU, 1952-55, adj. assoc. prof. surgery, rsch., 1955-57; established investigator Am. Heart Assn., N.Y.C., 1954-57; med. dir. Abbott Labs Internat. Co., Abbott Universal Ltd., Chgo., 1957-61; assoc. prof. dept. medicine Northwestern U., 1959-61; assoc. med. dir. Pfizer Internat. Inc., N.Y.C., 1962-67; assoc. dir. advanced clin. rsch. Internat. Merck Sharp & Dohme Rsch. Labs., Rahway, N.J., 1967-70, dir., 1970-71, sr. dir. clin. rsch. internat. med. affairs area, 1971-74; dir. med. compliance drug regulatory affairs CIBA-GEIGY Pharms., Summit, NJ, 1974-80, assoc. dir. med. svcs. med. affairs dept., 1980—89, dir. med. cons. svcs., 1989—96, ind. expert, 1997—. Clin. asst. prof. medicine Cornell U., N.Y.C., 1971-77. Fellow N.Y. Acad. Scis.; mem. AMA, Internat. Soc. Nephrology, Am. Fedn. Clin. Rsch., Am. Soc. Nephrology, Am. Soc. Clin. Pharmacology and Therapeutics, Am. Physiol. Soc., Am. Acad. Clin. Toxicology, Acad. Medicine N.J., Summit Med. Soc., Soc. for Exptl. Biology and Medicine, Microcirculatory Soc., Jockey Club, Argentine Yacht Club, Univ. Club, Buenos Aires Rowing Club. Home and Office: 3 Brainerd Rd Summit NJ 07901-1410

GAUDIO, GASTON, professional tennis player; b. Buenos Aires, Dec. 9, 1978; s. Norberto and Marisa Gaudio. Profl. tennis player ATP Tour, 1996—. Achievements include Winner of 3 singles titles: Barcelona, 2002, Mallorca, 2002, Roland Garros, 2004; Winner of 1 doubles title: (w/ Estoril) Vina del Mar, 2004. Office: c/o ATP Tour Internat Hdqs 201 ATP Tour Blvd Ponte Vedra Beach FL 32082

GAUDREAU, RUSSELL A., JR., lawyer, educator; b. Weymouth, Mass., Feb. 25, 1943; s. Russell A. and Jean (Sandwen) G.; m. Elizabeth Flanagan, Dec. 26, 1966; children: Russell A. III, Seth F. BA, U. Mass., Amherst, 1965; JD cum laude, Suffolk U., 1968; LLM in Taxation, NYU, 1969. Law clk. to Hon. Harold R. Tyler, Jr., U.S. Dist Ct. (so. dist.) N.Y., 1969-70; assoc. Ropes & Gray, Boston, 1970-79, mng. ptnr. Washington, 1990-94, ptnr. tax & benefits dept. Boston, 1979—, head benefits consulting practice group. Adj. prof. law Bentley Coll., 1978-80; adj. prof. law Boston U. Law Sch., 1980—; adj. prof. law Georgetown U. Law Ctr., 1991—; frequent spkr. in field. Editor-in-Chief Suffolk U. Law Rev. Bd dirs. Handel and Haydn Soc.; trustee Suffolk U. Fellow: Am. Coll. Employee Benefits Counsel; mem.: ABA (tax. sect., com. employee benefits), Boston Bar Assn., DC and Boston ERISA and Tax Discussion Groups, D.C. Bar Assn., New Eng. Benefits Coun. (dir.). Office: Ropes & Gray One International Pl Boston MA 02110-2624 Office Phone: 617-951-7261. Office Fax: 617-951-7050. Business E-Mail: russell.gaudreau@ropesgray.com.

GAUEN, PATRICK EMIL, news correspondent; b. St. Louis, July 15, 1950; s. Louis Otto and Wilma Ellen (Rogers) G.; m. Patti Lynn Seib, Dec. 8, 1972 (div. 1992); children: Bethany, Heather; m. Karen Earhart, July 11, 1992; 1 stepchild, Christopher Stephenson. Student, So. Ill. U., 1968-70. Reporter, photographer Collinsville (Ill.) Herald, 1969-72, news editor, 1972-78; reporter St. Louis Globe-Democrat, 1978-84, mng. editor, 1984-85; reporter Ill. affairs St. Louis Post-Dispatch, 1985-89, polit. corr., 1989—, pub. safety team leader, 2000—; faculty univ. coll. Washington U., St. Louis, 1991—2001. Pub. safety reporting team leader St. Louis Post Dispatch, 2000. Recipient Outstanding Med. News Series award Ill. State Med. Soc., 1970, Best Feature Story award Suburban Newspapers Am., 1971, Best News Story award Suburban Newspapers Am., 1973, Best Spot News Story award UPI Editors Ill., 1972, Best Pub. Svc. Reporting award Ill. Press Assn., 1974, Best Feature Story award, 1975, Bar-News Media award Bar Assn. Met. St. Louis, 1987, Bob Hardy award Southern Ill. Chiefs of Police and Southwestern Law Enforcement, 1996, Terry Hughes award St. Louis chpt. Newspaper Guild, 1996, Liberty Bell award Madison County Bar Assn., 1999. Mem. Mid-Am. Press Inst. (bd. dirs. 1985—), Press Club Met. St. Louis (bd. dirs. 1985—), Sigma Delta Chi (bd. dirs. St. Louis chpt. 1985—, chpt. pres. 1985-86, 86-87). Avocations: reading, photography. Home: 30 Meadowlark Ln Highland IL 62249-3000 Office: St Louis Post Dispatch 900 N Tucker St Saint Louis MO 63101 Office Phone: 314-340-8154. E-mail: pgauen@postdispatch.com.

GAUFF, LISA, broadcast journalist; b. Seattle; d. Joseph F. and Patricia A. (Lee) G. BA in Comm., U. Wash., 1987; MA in Journalism and Pub. Affairs, Am. U., 1988. Pub. info. asst. King County Coun., Seattle, 1985-86; reporter Sta. KUOW-FM, Seattle, 1985-86; news anchor Sta. KCMU-FM, Seattle, 1986-87; TV field prodr. Group W/Newsfeed Network, Washington, 1988-89; anchor, reporter Capitol TV, Washington, 1989-90, Newschannel 8, Washington, 1991-93; prodr., writer Sta. WJLA-TV, Washington, 1990-91; weekend anchor Sta. WHTM-TV, Harrisburg, Pa., 1993-94; morning anchor Sta. WJW-TV, Cleve., 1994-97; traffic anchor Sta. KNX-AM, L.A., 1998—2001, pub. rels. cons., 2001—. Freelance reporter KCBS-TV, KABC-TV, UPN-TV, Fox TV, Sunworld, Satellite News, Media Gen., NPR Radio, Shadow Broadcasting, 1988-89; ind. video prodr., 1989-91. Host, editor TV documentary Coming to Terms, 1993. Bd. dirs. NE Ohio AAU Baseball Com., 1995-96; moderator Ohio Acad. Decathalon, Cleve., 1995, 96; vol. United Way, Cleve., 1995, 96; honorary chair Women's Ctr. Greater Cleve., 1995; celebrity spokesperson Cleve. Christian Home for Children, 1995. Recipient John Merriman award Writer's Guild Am., 1988, Appreciation cert. United Negro Coll. Fund, 1995, 96; named One of 20 Top Women in Media, Washington D.C. Tchrs. Assn., 1993. Mem. NATAS, AFTRA. Avocations: art history, skiing, quiz shows. Office: Sta KNX-AM 6121 W Sunset Blvd Los Angeles CA 90028-6423

GAUFF, SUSAN TYRRELL, marketing and human resources executive; b. Hackensack, N.J., Oct. 19, 1946; d. Donald Eugene and Henrietta Dorothy (Benson) Tyrrell; m. James Anthony Gauff, Apr. 13, 1973; children: James Timothy, Janet Gauff Anthos, David Phillip. Student, Centenary Coll., 1967. Coord. market rsch. Warner-Lambert, Morris Plains, N.J., 1967-69; coord. pub. rels. Western Union Corp., N.Y.C., 1969-73; pvt. cons. practice in communications Princeton, N.J., 1973-75; asst. mgr. advt. Electronic Assocs., Inc., West Long Branch, N.J., 1975-79; dir. communications Mohawk Data Scis., Parsippany, N.J., 1979-83, Franklin Computer Corp., Pennsauken, N.J., 1983-84; dir. advt. and sales promotion Racal-Milgo, Miami, Fla., 1984-86; dir. corp. communications Siemens Info. Systems, Boca Raton, Fla., 1986-90; dir. mktg. communications Siemens Pvt. Communications Systems and Rolm Systems, Santa Clara, Calif., 1990-91; sr. dir. market and corp. communications Siemens Rolm Comm. Inc., Santa Clara, Calif., 1991-95; v.p. comm. Lexmark Internat., Inc., Lexington, Ky., 1995-97; sr. v.p. people and comm. Sarnoff Corp., Princeton, NJ, 1997—2002; mng. prin. The Growth Solutions Group, Princeton, NJ, 2002—. Mem. bus. adv. bd. Rider U. Named one of Outstanding Young Women of Am., 1971, Marketer of Yr., Advt. Age, 1995; recipient Tribute to Women in Industry award, 1993, Delaware Valley Human Resources Dept. of Yr., 2000. Mem. Bus. Mktg. Assn. (cert., chpt. pres. 1988-89, internat. v.p. media rels. com. 1989-90, internat. sec. 1990-92, internat. treas. 1994-95), Assn. Nat. Advertisers, Pub. Rels. Soc. Am., N.J. State C. of C., N.J. Tech. Coun., NJ 300, Soc. for Human Resources Mgmt., N.J. Human Resources Planning Group, Cherry Valley Country Club (bd. dirs. 2002—). Avocation: golf. Home: 16 Otter Creek Rd Skillman NJ 08558 Office Phone: 609-577-7370. Business E-Mail: susan@predictivehiring.com, susan@growth-solutions.group.com.

GAUGER, BETH LYNN, literature and language educator; b. New Ulm, Minn., Feb. 18, 1964; d. Warren Lee and Nereda Ruth Marti; m. Randy Lee Gauger, June 26, 1988; children: Michael, Melissa. BS in Edn., Dr. Martin Luther Coll., 1986. Tchr. Timothy Luth. Sch., St. Louis Park, Minn., 1986—90; tchr., chair English dept. West Luth. High Sch., Plymouth, 1995—. Sec. Twin Cities Luth. Grade Sch. Athletic League, Mpls., 1988—89. Treas. Timothy Ladies Soc., St. Louis Park, 1991—95, pres., 2002—04, 2004—05. Fellow: Am. Soc. Newspaper Editors; mem.: Minn. High Sch. Press Assn., Minn. Coun. Tchrs. English, Journalism Edn. Assn., Nat. Coun. Tchrs. English, Student Press Law Ctr. Lutheran. Avocations: reading, gardening, crafts, scrapbooks, travel, sports. Office: West Luth High Sch 3350 Harbor Ln N Plymouth MN 55447

GAUGHAN, EUGENE FRANCIS, lawyer, retired accountant; b. Aug. 31, 1945; s. Eugene Francis and Ruth Mae (Webster) Gaughan; m. Arlene Barber, July 8, 1972 (dec. May 1981); m. Margaret Duffy, Jan. 2, 1983. AB, Coll. Holy Cross, 1967; MBA, Rutgers U., 1968; postgrad., Duke U., 1989; MME, INSEAD, France, 1990; JD, Seton Hall U., 2004. CPA N.Y., N.J., Conn., Fla. Staff acct. Price Waterhouse LLP, N.Y.C., 1968—70, sr. acct., 1970—72, mgr., 1972—78, sr. mgr., 1978—79, ptnr., 1979—98, PricewaterhouseCoopers, N.Y.C., 1998—99, World Firm Coun. Ptnrs., N.Y.C., 1987—90. Mem. supr. bd. Price Waterhouse Ea. Europe, 1991—97; trustee Lenox Hill Hosp.; bd. dirs. Manhattan Eye, Ear and Throat Hosp. Mem.: ABA, AICPA, N.Y. County Lawyers Assn., Suffolk County Bar Assn., Assn. Bar City of N.Y., N.Y. State Soc. CPAs (bd. dirs. 1986—89), N.J. State Bar Assn., N.Y. State Bar Assn., Doonbeg Golf Club, Laurel Links Country Club, KC. Roman Catholic. Home: Apt 7B 164 E 72nd St New York NY 10021-4363 also: 33 Niamogue Ln PO Box 1675 Quogue NY 11959-1675 Personal E-mail: lawefg@aol.com.

GAULDIN, ROBERT L., music educator, composer; b. Vernon, Tex., Oct. 30, 1931; s. Robert L. and Lula Mae Gauldin; m. Barbara Jane Hullender, May 30, 1953; children: Elizabeth Ann, Phillip Vincent, Cecilia Jeanne, Angela Lynne. BM Composition, N. Tex. State U., Denton, 1952; MA Music Theory, Eastman Sch. of Music, Rochester, N.Y., 1956; PhD Music Theory, U. Rochester, 1958; DM (hon.), William Carey Coll., Hattiesburg, Miss., 1990. Prof. music William Carey Coll., Hattiesburg, Miss., 1958—63; from asst. prof. to prof. Eastman Sch. of Music, Rochester, NY, 1963—97, prof. emeritus, 1998—2005. Coord. contemporary music project Eastman Sch. of Music, Rochester, NY, 1966—68; vis. prof. music Oxford U., 1984—85; mem. rev. bd. Jour. of Music Theory Pedagogy, 1985—2000. Author: (textbook) Practical Introduction to 16th Century Counterpoint, Practical Introduction to 18th Century Counterpoint, 1988, Harmonic Practice in Tonal Music, 1997, 2004; contbr. articles to music theory jours., papers to nat. and regional convs. Cpl. U.S. Army, 1953—56. Named to Keynote Speaker, AMS/SMT Nat. Conv., Seattle, 2004; recipient 1st prize quartet Berkshire competition, Tanglewood, Mass., 1968, Lifetime Achievement award, de Stwolinski Ctr., Kans. City, Kans., 2002. Mem.: Coll. Music Soc., Theory Soc. N.Y. State (v.p. 1981—83), Soc. for Music Theory (v.p., pres. 1988—94). Baptist. Avocations: astronomy, Southwestern Cooking, chess. Home: 379 Wellington Ave Rochester NY 14619 Office: Eastman Sch of Music 26 Gibbs St Rochester NY 14604 Office Phone: 585-274-1554. E-mail: Bobgauldin@aol.com.

GAULIN, KENNETH, writer, photographer; b. Providence, R.I., July 2, 1940; s. Joseph Edward and Josephine (DiStefano) G.; m. Holly McNeely, Aug. 20, 1966 (div. 1972). BFA, RISD, 1965. Dir. film unit Rusk Inst. NYU Med. Ctr., N.Y.C., 1965-68; designer, film maker Rsch. and Design Inst., Providence, 1968-72; dir. audio visual archive Knoll Internat., N.Y.C., 1972-78; writer, designer, photographer Cambridge, Mass., 1978—. Lectr. Harvard Grad. Sch. Design, 1976, R.I. Sch. Design, 1988, 94, Am. Acad., Rome, 1990, Wentworth Inst. Tech., 1992-94; mktg. programs cons. Willowbee & Kent Travel Co., Boston, Mass., 1997—; designer film exhibit Teaching Occupl. Therapy, 1966; bd. dirs. Cambridge (Mass.) Art Assn. Author: Grand Luxe: The Transatlantic Style, 1988, (with others) Contemporary Designers, 1984; two-man photography show at Am. Acad., Rome, 1991; group show at Centennial Banners Am. Acad., Rome, 1994. Address: 100 Memorial Dr Cambridge MA 02142-1332

GAULKE, EARL H., publisher, clergyman, editor; b. Milw., July 18, 1927; s. Albert and Olga (Reinhardt) G.; m. Margaret Elaine Preuss, Aug. 5, 1951; children: Cheryl, Stephen. BS in Edn., Concordia U., River Forest, Ill., 1950; BA, MDiv, Concordia Sem., St. Louis, 1956; MA, Washington U., St. Louis, 1965, PhD, 1970; DD, Concordia U., Irvine, Calif., 1995. Ordained minister Lutheran Ch., 1956. Prin., tchr. Pilgrim Luth. Sch., Santa Monica, Calif., 1950-52; tchr., dept. head Detroit Luth. High Sch., 1956-57; assoc. pastor Faith Luth. Ch., L.A., 1957-58; editor bd. of parish svcs., 1958-75; dir. editorial svcs. Luth. Ch.-Mo. Synod, St. Louis, 1975-92; v.p. editl. Concordia Pub. House, St. Louis, 1992—. Vis. instr. Washington U., U. Mo., St. Louis, Concordia Sem., Concordia Coll., Mpls.; rsch. assoc. Ctrl. Lab. (CEMREL), St. Louis, 1967-68. Author: You Can Have A Family, 1975, First Chance for the Church, 1978; contbr. articles to profl. jours. Recipient Epphatha award Detroit Inst. for Deaf, 1992. Mem. Am. Edn. Assn., Luth. Edn. Assn. (exec. editor 1978-79, Christus Magister 1989). Avocations: gardening, making wine. Home: 2447 Camberwell Ct Des Peres MO 63131-2118 Office: Concordia Pub House 3558 S Jefferson Ave Saint Louis MO 63118-3910 E-mail: earl.gaulke@cph.org.

GAULKE, MARY FLORENCE, library administrator; b. Johnson City, Tenn., Sept. 24, 1923; d. Gustus Thomas and Mary Belle (Bennett) Erickson; m. James Wymond Crowley, Dec. 1, 1939; 1 son, Grady Gaulke (name legally changed); m. 22nd, Bud Gaulke, sept. 1, 1945 (dec. Jan. 1978); m. 3rd, Richard Lewis McNaughton, Mar. 21, 1983 (div. 1995). BS in Home Econs., Oreg. State U., 1963; MS in L.S., U. Oreg., 1968; Phd in Spl. Edn., 1970. Cert. std. pers. supr., std. handicapped learner, Oreg. Head dep. home econs. Riddle Sch. Dist. (Oreg.), 1963-66; libr., cons. Douglas County Intermediate Edn. Dist., Roseburg, Oreg., 1966-67; head resident, head counselor Prometheus Project So. Oreg. coll.ect, Ashland, summers 1966-68; supr. librs. Medford Sch. Dist. (Oreg.), 1970-73; instr. psychology So.Oreg. Coll., Ashland, 1970-73; libr. supr. Roseburg Sch. Dist., 1974-91; resident psychologist Black Oaks Boys Sch., Medford, 1970-75. Mem. Oreg. Gov.'s Coun. Librs., 1979. Author: Vo-Ed Course for Junior High, 1965; Library Handbook, 9167, Instructions for Preparation of Cards for All materials Cataloged for Libraries, 1971, Handbook for Training Library aides, 1972. Coord. Laubach Lit. Workshops for High Sch. Tutors, Medford, 1972. Fellow Internat. Biog. Assn. (life); mem. ALA, So Oreg. Libr. Fedn. (sec. 1971-73), Oreg. Libr. Assn., Pacific N.W. Libr. Assn., Am. Biog. Inst. (lifetime dep. gov. 1987—), Internat. Biog. Ctr. (hon., adv. coun. 1990), Delta Kappa Gamma (pres. 1980-82), Delta Kappa Gamma (pres. 1980-82), Phi Delta Kappa (historian, rsch. rep.). Democrat. Methodist. Office: 119 Orchard Ln Ashland OR 97520-9627 also: 2122 Ramona 366 Casa Grande AZ 85222 also: 14904 Birch St Long Beach WA 98631 Office Phone: 210-213-8833. Personal E-mail: ggmum1@earthlink.net.

GAULT, JEFFREY WAYNE, air transportation executive; b. Kansas City, Mo., Sept. 10, 1948; s. Wayne Clark and Phyllis Gault; m. Rose Godefroy, Mar. 21, 1974; children: Jacqueline Hickenbottom, John C., Claire J. BS, U.S. Mil. Acad., 1970; MPA, U. Okla., 1977; MA in German Lang. and Lit., Middlebury Coll., 1979; MA in Nat. Security and Strategic Studies, U.S. Naval War Coll., 1991. Commd. 2d lt. U.S. Army, 1970, advanced through grades to col.; comdr. 4th Battalion, 1st AD Artillery, Neubruecke, Germany, 1987—89; dep. comdr. 11th Air Def. Brigade, Riyadh, Saudi Arabia, 1990—91; dir. dept. tactics U.S. Air Def. Sch., Ft. Bliss, Tex., 1991—94; comdr. U.S. Army Forces, Dhahran, Saudi Arabia, 1993—94, U.S. Army Garrison, Ft. Bliss, 1994—96; chief of staff U.S. Army, Ft. Bliss, 1996—99, ret., 1999; program mgr., sr. cons. Computer Sci. Corp., Arlington, Va., 1999—2002; exec. Boeing Co., 2002—. State dir. Vets. for Earley for Gov., Richmond, Va., 2001; county chmn., mem. state steering com. Vets. for George Bush, Farifax County, Va., 2000, state dir., 2004; bd. dirs. El Paso (Tex.) Sch. Dist. Fund, El Paso, 1996—99, Yucca Coun. Boy Scouts Am., El Paso, 1995—99, Greater El Paso C. of C., El Paso, 1996—99. Decorated Cross of Honor Govt. of Germany; recipient Mayor's award for civic leadership, Office of Mayor, El Paso, 1999. Mem.: VFW, DAV. Republican. Presbyterian. Home: 7430 Spring Summit Rd Springfield VA 22150 Office: Boeing Corp 1421 Jefferson Davis Hwy Arlington VA 22202

GAULT, ROBERT MELLOR, lawyer; b. Pitts., Sept. 3, 1945; s. James Edward and Laura (Mellor) G.; m. Mary Joan Donnelly, Sept. 18, 1983; children: Sarah, Laura, Matthew. BA, Williams Coll., 1968; JD, U. Mich., 1971. Bar: US Dist. Ct. (We. Dist.) Wash. 1972, US Ct. Appeals (9th Cir.) 1972, Mass. 1973, US Dist. Ct. (Mass.) 1974, US Ct. Appeals (1st Cir.) 1974, US Supreme Ct. 1977, US Ct. Appeals (DC Cir.) 1983, US Ct. Appeals (7th Cir.) 1984. Law clk. US Dist. Ct. (We. Dist.) Wash., Seattle, 1971-73; assoc. Mintz, Levin, Cohn, Ferris, Glovsky, and Popeo, PC, Boston, 1973-78, mem., 1978—, chmn. Employment, Labor, Benefits, Sect. Former mem. adv. bd. Law Firm Resources Project. Bd. dirs. Greater Boston Legal Svcs., 1982—95, Greater Boston Food Bank, 2000—. Office: Mintz Levin Cohn Ferris Glovsky & Popeo PC 1 Financial Ctr Fl 39 Boston MA 02111-2657 Office Phone: 617-348-1643. Office Fax: 617-542-2241. Business E-Mail: rgault@mintz.com.

GAUMER ERICKSON, AMY SUE, special education educator; b. Oberlin, Kans., Oct. 11, 1975; d. W. James and Judy B. Gaumer; m. Clayton R. Erickson, June 18, 2005; children: Alexandria N. Erickson, Chase W.R. Erickson, Isabelle L. Erickson. BS in Psychology and Spl. Edn. (hon.), McPherson (Kans.) Coll., 1998; MS in Spl. Edn. Transition (hon.), U. Kans., 2004. Cert. multicategorical spl. edn. Kans. State Dept. Edn., 1998, lic. psychology Kans. State Dept. Edn., 1998, cert. tchr. ESL Kans. State Dept. Edn., 2003, reading specialist Kans. State Dept. Edn., 2004. Tchr. Jefferson Acad., Broomfield, Colo., 1998—2000, McLain Cmty. H.S., Arvada, Colo., 1999—2000, Gardner-Edgerton (Kans.) H.S., 2000—02; grad. rsch. asst. U. Kans., Lawrence, Kans., 2002—. Recipient Ednl. Travel award, U. Kans., 2003—05, Outstanding Master's Project award, 2004; grantee, U.S. Dept. Edn., 2002—; scholar, U. Kans., 2003—; Kans. Tchr. scholarship, Kans. State Dept. Edn., 1994—98, Presdl. scholarship, McPherson Coll., 1994—98. Mem.: Am. Assn. on Mental Retardation (1st Pl. Rsch. award 2003), Am. Ednl. Rsch. Assn., Coun. Exceptional Children. Achievements include design of database of community-based transition programs; research in high-stakes testing and college admission policies; nontraditional high school exit certificates; community-based transition supports and services. Avocations: racquetball, travel. Office: Transition Coalition 521 JR Pearson Hall 1122 West Campus Rd Lawrence KS 66045

GAUNAURD, GUILLERMO C., physicist, researcher, engineer; b. Havana, Cuba, July 19, 1940; arrived in US, 1961, naturalized; s. Celestino Carlos and Ana Marie (Herrera) G.; m. Marlene Jane Johnson, June 10, 1967. AB in Math., Cath. U. Am., Washington, 1964; BSME, Cath. U. Am., 1966, MS, 1967, PhD in Physics/Acoustics, 1972. Cons. engr. Ocean Systems Inc. (div. Union Carbide), Arlington, Va., 1966-68; sr. cons. engr. Litton Industries Inc., College Park, Md., 1968-71; rsch. physicist, sci. and tech. materials dept. Naval Surface Warfare Ctr., White Oak and Carderock Divsns., West Bethesda, Md., 1971-2000; sr. physicist, sensors and electron devices directorate Army Rsch. Lab., Adelphi, Md., 2001—. Lectr. U. Md. Sch. Engring., College Park, 1983-92, Cath. U. Am. Sch. Engring., Washington, 1974-78. Contbr. over 400 articles to profl. sci. jours., chpts. to books and conf. procs.; patentee in field. Mem. Randolph Hills Civic Com., Rockville, Md., 1971—. Recipient various publ. awards and sci. excellence medals; grantee Office Naval Rsch., 1967—; Fellow Nat. Defense Edn. Act, 1967-70. Fellow ASME, IEEE (editor IEEE Jour. Oceanic Engring. 1987—, assoc. editor IEEE Jour. Ultrasonics, Ferroelectrics and Frequency Control 1992—), Acoustical Soc. Am. (various offices, assoc. editor Linear Acoustics 2002—), Washington Acad. Scis.; assoc. fellow AIAA; mem. SPIE, Philos. Soc. Washington, Optical Soc. Am., Internat. Union Math. Physics, Am. Acad. Mechanics, Washington Soc. Engrs., N.Y. Acad. Scis., Sigma Xi, Tau Beta Pi. Avocations: photography, classical music. Home: 4807 Macon Rd Rockville MD 20852-2348 Office: Army Rsch Lab Code AMSRD-ARL-SE-RU Microwaves Br 2800 Powder Mill Rd Adelphi MD 20783-1197 Office Phone: 301-394-1357. Personal E-mail: electron20@aol.com. Business E-Mail: ggaunaurd@arl.army.mil.

GAUNCE, MICHAEL PAUL, insurance company executive; b. Paris, Ky., Oct. 17, 1949; s. Paul D. and Mary E. (Gardner) Gaunce; m. Annette Beauchamp Gaunce. BA, U. Ky., 1971. Agt., mgr. Equitable Life N.Y., Lexington, Ky., 1972-74; agt., regional mgr. Assn. Ins. Marketers, Inc., Indpls., Cin., South Bend, Ind., 1974-77; pres., chmn. Ins. Corp. Am., Indpls., 1977—. Chmn. bd. dirs. Argent Ins. Corp., Alternative Healthcare Marketers, Inc.; bd. dirs., past chmn. Brokers Ins. Corp., bd. dirs., Brokers Ins. Agy., Ins. Corp., Agy. Mgmt. Corp.; cons. adv. bd. Blue Cross/Blue Shield, Indpls., 1982—89; mem. adv. bd. Acordia, Inc., Indpls., 1996—98; mem. adv. group Trustmaker Ins. Co., 2000. Active Rep. Nat. Com. Mem.: Ind. Assn. Employee Benefit Cons. (pres. 1984—88), Seymour C. of C., Franklin C. of C., Greenwood C. of C., Elks. Republican. Avocations: fishing, swimming, reading, investments, travel. Office: Ins Corp Am 5140 Commerce Cir Indianapolis IN 46237-9744

GAUNT, JASPER MICHAEL PHILIP, curator; b. Rome, Nov. 16, 1963; s. David Philip Keppel Gaunt and Rose Jocelyn Oakeshott. MA Lit. Humaniores, Merton Coll., Oxford, Eng., 1986; MA, PhD, Inst. of Fine Arts, N.Y., 2002. Curator greek and roman art Michael C. Carlos Mus., Atlanta, 2002—. Contbr. articles pub. to profl. jour. Recipient Edwards Prize for Greek and Latin Lit., Oxford U., 1984. Mem.: Soc. for the Promotion of Hellenic Studies. Office: Michael C Carlos Mus 571 South Kilgo Cir Atlanta GA 30322 Office Phone: 404-727-1146. Office Fax: 404-727-1091. Personal E-mail: jgaunt@emory.edu.

GAURON, PAUL R., lawyer; BA, Bowdoin Coll., 1969; JD, Harvard Univ., 1972. Bar: Mass. 1972. Ptnr., energy practice group Goodwin Procter LLP, Boston, chair, bus. law dept, mem. exec. com. Knight of Malta. Mem.: Mass. Bar Assn., Boston Bar Assn., Phi Beta Kappa. Office: Goodwin Procter LLP Exchange Pl 53 State St Boston MA 02109 Office Phone: 617-570-1484. Office Fax: 617-523-1231. Business E-Mail: pgauron@goodwinprocter.com.

GAUSE-SNELSON, D., music educator; MusB, U. Nev., 1986, MEd, 1992, EdD, 1995, MusM, 2000. Adj. faculty C.C. So. Nev., Las Vegas, 1987—90, tchg. asst., 1990—95, prof. music, 1995—. Adj. faculty U. Nev., Las Vegas, 1989. Composer: (music) paradox sweet, a jazz suite, 2004, desert dawning, 2005; musician: (plays) Mamma Mia, We Will Rock You, The Full Montey, Beauty and The Beast, (live on Las Vegas Strip) The Wayne Brady Show, The Bill Acosta Show, Shirley Bassey, numerous others in Las Vegas. Named Outstanding Faculty, C.C. So. Nev. Arts Dept., 1999; grantee, Nev. Arts Coun., 2003, 2002, 2004, Nat. Endowment for the Arts, 2004. Mem.: Internat. Clarinet Assn. (performer 2005), Musicians Union. Office: Community Coll So Nev Music J-1-A 3200 E Cheyenne North Las Vegas NV 89030

GAUSS, JOHN A., former federal agency administrator, retired naval officer; b. Salem, Mass. BS in Engring. and Physics, Cornell U., 1969; M of Philosophy, Naval Postgrad. Sch., 1976, PhD in Electronics Engring. Commd. ensign USN, 1969, advanced through ranks to rear adm.; various assignments to comdr. Def. Info. Systems Agy., Arlington, Va., 1994-97; dir. Allied & Fleet Requirements Divsn. Space, Info. Warfare Command & Control Directorate, Washington, 1997—2001; asst. sec. and chief info. officer for info. and tech. U.S. Dept. Veterans Affairs, Washington, 2001—03. Decorated Def. Disting. Svc. medal, Legion of Merit (3 times), Meritorious Svc. medal, Navy Achievement medal.

GAUSS, KARL FREDERIK, internist, educator, geriatrician; b. Elmira, NY, July 19, 1956; s. Louis H. and Agnes L. (Yacubic) G.; m. Paula A. Tuite, Aug. 14, 1982; children: Erich Louis, Kurt William, Elsa Katarina. BS in Biology summa cum laude, SUNY, Geneseo, 1981; MD with honors, SUNY, Syracuse, 1985. Diplomate Am. Bd. Internal Medicine, Am. Bd. Geriat. Resident in internal medicine SUNY Health Sci. Ctr., Syracuse, 1985—88, asst. clin. instr. dept. internal medicine, 1988—95, clin. asst. prof., 1995—; pvt. practice Cortland, NY, 1988—; med. dir. Cortland Meml. Nursing Facility, Cortland, 1997—; chmn. dept. geriat. Cortland Meml. Hosp., Cortland, 2001—, chmn. dept. medicine, 2002—04. Pres. PHI Aeromed. Cons., Inc., Cortland, 1989-95; attending physician, mem. med. staff Cortland Meml. Hosp., 1988—, chmn. dept. internal medicine, 1989-93; dir., staff physician Moravia (N.Y.), Health Ctr., 1992-93; cons. physician Tully (N.Y.) Hill Drug and Alcohol Rehab. Ctr., 1990-92; aviation med. examiner Cortland County, 1988—; profl. and sci. presenter in field. Exhibited in group shows at Everson Art Mus., Syracuse, 1986, NY State Fair, Syracuse, 1992 Fellow ACP; mem. Am. Geriat. Soc., Flying Physicians Assn. (bd. dirs. 1994), N.Y. State Med. Soc. (Cortland County del. 1988-90), Cortland County Med. Soc. (pres. 1992—), Aircraft Owners and Pilots Assn, Harley Owners Group, Porsche Club of Am., BMW Owners Group Republican. Avocations: sailing, flying, high performance driving, motorcycling. Office: Cortland Internist Assocs 6 Euclid Ave Ste H Cortland NY 13045-1291

GAUSTAD, EDWIN SCOTT, historian, educator; b. Rowley, Iowa, Nov. 14, 1923; s. Sverre and Norma (McEachron) G.; m. Helen Virginia Morgan, Dec. 19, 1946; children: Susan, Glen Scott, Peggy Lynn. BA, Baylor U., 1947; MA, Brown U., 1948, PhD, 1951. Instr. Brown U., 1951-52, Am. Council Learned Socs. scholar in residence, 1952-53; dean Shorter Coll., 1953-57; prof. humanities U. Redlands, 1957-65; assoc. prof. history U. Calif., Riverside, 1965-67, prof., 1968-89, prof. emeritus, 1989; prof. Princeton (N.J.) Theol. Sem., 1991-92, Auburn U., 1993. Vis. prof. Baylor U., 1976, U. Calif., Santa Barbara, 1986, U. Richmond, 1987. Author: The Great Awakening in New England, 1957, New Historical Atlas of Religion in America, new edit., (with P.L. Barlow), 2001, Religious History of America, revised edit., (with Leigh E. Schmidt), 2002, Dissent in American Religion, 1973, Baptist Piety: The Last Will and Testimony of Obadiah Holmes, 1978, 2005, George Berkeley in America, 1979, Faith of Our Fathers, 1987, 2004, Liberty of Conscience: Roger Williams in America, 1991, Revival, Revolution, and Religion in Early Virginia, 1994, Sworn on the Altar of God: A Religious Biography of Thomas Jefferson, 1996, Church and State in America, 1998, 2d edit., 2003, Memoirs of the Spirit, 1999, Roger Williams: Prophet of Liberty, 2001, (with Mark Noll) Documentary History of Religion in America, 2 vols., 3d edit., 2003, Benjamin Franklin: Inventing America, 2004, Roger Williams, 2005, (with others) Unto a Good Land, 2005. Served to 1st lt. USAAC, 1943-45. Decorated Air medal; Am. Council Learned Socs. grantee, 1952-53, 72-73; Am. Philos. Soc. grantee, 1972-73 Mem. Am. Soc. Ch. History (pres.), Orgn. Am. Historians, Phi Beta Kappa. Democrat. Baptist. E-mail: egaustad@aol.com.

GAUT, C. CHRISTOPHER, gas company executive; b. 1957; BA in Engring. Sci., Dartmouth Coll.; MBA in Fin., U. Pa. Various fin. mgmt. positions Amoco Corp.; ptnr. Pacific Asset Capital; pres., COO, CFO ENSCO Internat., Inc., Dallas, 1988—2003; exec. v.p., CFO Halliburton, Houston, 2003—. Mem.: Fin. Execs. Internat., Internat. Assn. Drilling Contractors (mem. exec. com.). Office: ENSCO 500 N Akard St Ste 4300 Dallas TX 75201-3331

GAUTAM, AJAY, pharmaceutical executive; b. New Delhi, July 12, 1975; s. Anand Swarup and Chanderkala Gautam. B of Tech., Indian Inst. Tech., 1998; PhD, Baylor U., 2001; MBA, Rice U., 2003. Investment assoc. Momentum Equity Group, Houston, 2003—04; sr. prin. Pfizer Inc., New London, Conn., 2004—. Guest editor Current Cancer Drug Targets, Netherlands, 2001—02. Mem.: Am. Soc. Gene Therapy, Sigma Xi. Achievements include patents for aerosol delivery of gene and drug combinations for lung cancer treatment. Office: Pfizer Inc 50 Pequot Ave New London CT 06320 Office Phone: 860-581-0690. E-mail: ajay.gautam@pfizer.com.

GAUTHIER, DOREEN ANN, librarian; b. Davenport, Iowa, July 18, 1941; d. Clifford H. and Dorothy H. Wildman; m. William E. Gauthier, July 18, 1989. BA, Midland Coll., Fremont. Nebr., 1972; grad. cert., U. Omaha, 1972; MA, U. South Fla., 1996. Children's libr. Keene Meml. Libr., Fremont, Nebr., 1967-77; circulation libr. Pompano Beach (Fla.) Libr., 1978-79; libr. dir. Lighthouse Point (Fla.) Libr., 1979—. Dir. Fla. Pub. Libr. Assn., Lakeland, 1992—98. Mem. ALA, Fla. Libr. Assn., Broward County Libr. Assn. Episcopalian. Home: 1990 NE 32nd Ct # 44 Lighthouse Point FL 33064-7684 Office: Lighthouse Point Library 2200 NE 38th St Ste A Lighthouse Point FL 33064-3913 Office Phone: 954-946-6398. Personal E-mail: gauthid22@hotmail.com.

GAUTHIER, SERGE GASTON, neurologist; b. Montreal, Que., Can., Sept. 18, 1950; s. Gaston and Suzanne (Tremblay) G.; m. Louise Gauthier; children: Eric, Judith. BA, Coll. Ste-Marie, 1969; MD, U. Montreal, 1973; neurology, McGill U., 1977. Fellow Med. Rsch. Coun. Can., 1976-78; staff Montreal Neurol. Hosp. and Inst., 1978-86; dir. McGill Ctr. for Studies in Aging, Verdun, 1987-97, dir. Alzheimer unit, 1997—; and prof., Neurology and Neurosurgery, Psychiatry, and Med. McGill U., Verdun. Contbr. articles on treatment of Alzheimer's disease to med. jours. Recipient Prix Galien Canada, 1997, Sr. Scientist award, Med. Coun. of Canada, 1997. Office: McGill U Ctr Studies Aging 6825 Blvd La Salle Verdun PQ Canada H4H 1R3 E-mail: serge.gauthier@mcgill.ca.

GAUTIER, DICK, actor, writer; b. Los Angeles, Oct. 30, 1937; s. Aldoma Napoloeon and Marie Antionette Gautier; children: Christine, Rand, Denise; m. Tess Hightower, Dec. 2003. Student pub. schs., Los Angeles. Comedian, hungry i, San Francisco; appeared in N.Y.C. supper clubs including Blue Angel, Bonsoir, Coconut Grove; starred on Broadway as Conrad Birdie in Bye Bye Birdie, 1960-62 (Tony award and Most Promising Actor nominee); appeared in motion pictures including Billy Jack Goes to Washington, Divorce, American Style, Ensign Pulver, Manchu Eagle, Fun with Dick and Jane; played Hymie in series Get Smart; starred in TV series Mr. Terrific, CBS, It's Your Bet, NBC, Can You Top This?, Here We Go Again, ABC; starred as Robin Hood in TV series When Things Were Rotten, ABC, 1975; author: The Art of Caricature, 1985, The Creative Cartoonist, 1988, The Career Cartoonist, 1992, Actors as Artists, 1992, Drawing and Cartooning 1001 Faces, A Child's Garden of Weirdness, 3 books art instrn., 1992, Musicians as Artists, 1994; (screenplay) Uncle Sam; contbg. writer to numerous TV situation comedies; composer numerous songs. Active in Thalians Charity. Served with Spl. Services br. USN. Mem. Actors Equity Assn., AFTRA, Screen Actors Guild, ASCAP, Am. Guild Variety Artists. Office: 11333 Moorpark St Studio City CA 91602-2618 E-mail: DICK@DICKGAUTIER.com.

GAUTIER, JEAN, biomedical researcher; DSc, U. Toulouse, 1987. Dir. rsch. CNRS, Nice, France, 1984—2004; assoc. mem. Rsch. Inst. Molecular Biology, Nutley, NJ, 1993—95; assoc. prof. Columbia U., N.Y., 1995—. Contbr. articles to profl. jours. Grantee, Nat. Cancer Inst. Office Phone: 1-212-305-9586.

GAUTO, NELSON FERNANDO, plastic surgeon, consumer products company executive; b. Asuncion, Paraguay, Sept. 20, 1964; s. Mamerto and Maria Selva Gauto. BS in Major Biology, U. Asuncion, Paraguay, 1982; MD, Sch. Med. Scis., Paraguay, 1988. Cert. in med. scis. Ednl. Commn. Fgn. Med. Grads., 1991, plastic surgeon Royal Coll. Surgeons Can., 1999. Pres. So. Ill. Plastic Surgery, Herrin, Ill., 2001—, Aesthetic and Rejuvenation Ctr., Mt. Vernon, Ill., 2003—. Pro bono reconstructive surgeon US, overseas. Recipient Dept. of Surgery Rsch. Day award, Dalhousie U., 1999. Master: Grand Lodge Ill., Grand Lodge Mass.; fellow: Royal Coll. Surgeons Can.; mem.: AMA, Am. Soc. Aesthetic Plastic Surgery, Mass. Med. Soc., Ill. Med. Soc., Soc. Latin Am. Plastic Surgeons N.Am. (pres. 2004—), Can. Aesthetic Soc. Plastic Surgery, Am. Soc. Plastic Surgeons. Roman Catholic. Achievements include research in effect of vascular supply on bone graft healing in the canine tibial segmental osteotomy model; vascular study for breast reconstruction, and vascular delay in the canine rectus abdominis muscle flap. Avocations: travel, hiking, soccer. Office: So Ill Plastic Surgery 3307 Logan Dr Herrin IL 62948 Office Phone: 618-998-9600. Office Fax: 618-998-9611. Personal E-mail: nfgauto@yahoo.com.

GAUTREAUX, GABRIELLE, academic administrator, literature and language professor; b. Houma, La., Apr. 26, 1958; d. Edwin Joseph and Alberta M. (Pierce) Gautreaux; m. Hugh David Allen, Feb. 12, 1988. BA in English, Nicholls State U., 1981; MA in English, La. State U., 1983. Grad. tchg. asst. La. State U., Baton Rouge, 1981—83, instr. English, 1984—86, U. New Orleans, 1986—, chair freshman English, 1995—2002, dir. press, 2003—, asst. vice chancellor acad. and student affairs, 2004—. Co-author: Reading Matters, 1998, Reading and Writing Our World, 2002, Reading Life, 2005. Scholar, La. Endowment Humanities, 2000, 2002, 2003, U. New Orleans, 2001. Mem.: Modern Lang. Assn., Nat. Coun. Tchrs. English. Democrat. Avocations: reading, cooking. Office: U New Orleans Office Acad Affairs 2000 Lakeshore Dr New Orleans LA 70148

GAUVEY, SUSAN KATHRYN, judge; b. Van Wert, Ohio, Mar. 1, 1948; d. Richard David and Asta Walburga (Frericks) G.; m. David E. Kern, May 10, 1975; children: Megan E. Gauvey-Kern, Kevin C. Gauvey-Kern, Elizabeth H. Gauvey-Kern. Student, Georgetown U., 1968-69; BA cum laude Polit. Sci., Rosary Coll, River Forest, Ill., 1970; JD, Northwestern U., 1973; postgrad. Mental Hygiene, Johns Hopkins U., 1976-77. Bar: Wash. 1974, Md. 1975. Law clerk to fed. dist. ct. judge We. Dist. Ct., Seattle, Wash., 1973-74; staff atty. Mental Health Law Project Legal Aid Bur., Balt., 1975-77, chief Mental Health Law Project, 1977-79; asst. atty. gen. Dept. Health and Mental Hygiene Office of Atty. Gen., Balt., 1979-81, asst. atty. gen. Civil Divsn., 1981-86, prin. counsel trial litigation, 1984-86; with litigation divsn. Venable, Baetjer and Howard L.L.P., Balt., 1986-96; magistrate judge U.S. Dist. Ct. for Md., Balt., 1996—. Contbr. articles to profl. jours. Chair bd. dirs. Marian House for Women. Mem. Nat. Assn. Women Judges, Wranglers Law Club, Lawyers' Roundtable. Democrat. Office: US Courthouse 101 W Lombard St Baltimore MD 21201-2605 Office Phone: 410-962-4953. Business E-Mail: mdd_skgchambers@mdd.uscourts.gov.

GAVENDA, J(OHN) DAVID, physicist; b. Temple, Tex., Mar. 25, 1933; s. Edward and Rose Katherine (Machalek) G.; m. Janie Louise Yeoman, Dec. 22, 1952; children— Victor Joseph, Philip Martin. Student, U. Chgo., 1950-51; BS, U. Tex., Austin, 1954, MA, 1956; PhD, Brown U., 1959. Asst. prof. physics U. Tex., Austin, 1959-62, assoc. prof., 1962-65, assoc. prof. physics and edn., 1965-67, prof., 1967-99, prof. emeritus, 1999—. Contbr. articles on physics of metals and electromagnetic wave propagation to profl. jours. Sr. rsch. fellow Inst. Study of Metals, U. Chgo., 1963, NATO sr. fellow in sci. U. Oslo, 1969. Fellow: Am. Phys. Soc., Tex. Acad. Sci.; mem.: AAUP, AAAS, Am. Assn. Physics Tchrs. (Robert N. Little award 1988, Disting. Svc. citation 1997), Phi Beta Kappa, Sigma Xi. Democrat. Baptist. Home: 7317 Blue Heron Cove Volente TX 78641-6140 Office: Univ Tex Dept Physics 1 University Sta C1600 Austin TX 78712-0264 Office Phone: 512-471-3201. E-mail: gavenda@physics.utexas.edu.

GAVER, DONALD PAUL, mathematician, educator; b. St. Paul, Minn., Feb. 16, 1926; s. Donald Paul and Dorothea Haman Gaver; m. Frances Rouse; children: Elizabeth, Donald III, William. SB, MIT, 1950, SM in math. & econs., 1951; PhD in math., Princeton U., 1956. Mathematician Westinghouse Rsch. Labs, 1956—61, adv. mathematician, 1961—68; vis. assoc. prof. statistics Stanford U., 1961—62; vis. prof. ops. rsch. U. Calif., Berkeley, 1967—68; prof. mathematical stats. Carnegie-Mellon U., 1966—71; disting. prof. ops. rsch. Naval Postgraduate Sch., Monterey, Calif., 1971—. Recipient Koopman Award, Ops. Rsch. Soc. Am., 1991, Am. Men of Sci., The Richard W. Hamming Award for Interdisciplinary Achievement, 2001. Fellow: Am. Statis. Assn. (assoc. editor JASA 1965—68, vis. lectr. 1970—75, bd. dirs. 1978—80, chmn. com. on Nat. Security 1995—97), Inst. Math. Stats., Royal Statis. Soc., Inst. for Ops. Rsch. and Mgmt. Sci., Am. Assn. for Advancement Sci.; mem.: Ops. Rsch. Soc. Am. (ORSA) (vis. lectr. prog. 1970—80, past coun. mem. & treas., chmn. ORSA/TIMS Group, Coll. Applied Propability). Office: Naval Postgrad Sch USN Dept Operat Rsch Monterey CA 93943 Office Phone: 831-656-2605. Business E-Mail: dgaver@nps.edu.

GAVER, FRANCES ROUSE, lawyer; b. Lexington, Ky., Mar. 13, 1929; d. Colvin P. Rouse and Elizabeth Turner Sympson; m. Donald Paul Gaver, Jan. 24, 1953; children: Elizabeth, Donald, William. BA, Wellesley Coll., 1950; MA, U. Pitts., 1968; JD, Monterey (Calif.) Coll. of Law, 1986. Bar: Calif. 1986, U.S. Dist. Ct. (no. dist.) Calif. 1986; cert. specialist in probate, estate planing and trust law, Calif. Assoc. Hoge, Fenton, Jones & Appel, Monterey, 1986-93, Fenton & Keller, Monterey, 1993-97; ptnr. Johnson, Gaver & Leach, Monterey, 1997-99, of counsel, 2000—. Bd. dirs. Carmel (Calif.) Unified Sch. Dist., 1973-81, Monterey Coll. of Law, 1991-97, Legal Svcs. for Srs., Seaside, Calif., 1994-2000; bd. dirs. Monterey Peninsula Coll. Found., 2000-. Mem. Monterey County Bar Assn. Avocations: playing recorder, swimming. Office: Johnson Gaver & Leach LLP 2801 Monterey Salinas Hwy Monterey CA 93940-6401 Business E-Mail: fgaver@jglllp.com.

GAVERAS, HARRY, architect; b. N.Y.C., Feb. 9, 1971; s. Christos and Kyriaki Gaveras. BArch, Cooper Union U., 1993; MArch in Urban Design, Harvard U., 1997. Registered arch., Greece, NY. Pres. Propylaea Arch. Atelier, N.Y.C., 2000—. Co-founder Founds. Design Internat., N.Y.C., 1993—97; guest critic Huble Inst. Fine Arts, Wuhan, China, 2003; vis. critic and instr. Harvard U. Grad. Sch., 2003; vis. prof. Ctrl. Acad., Beijing, 2004. Orpheus Assn. Traveling grantee, 1992. Mem.: AIA (co-chairperson emerging N.Y. archs. com. N.Y. chpt. 2005—), Cooper Union Alumni (coun. mem.), Harvard Club N.Y.C. Avocations: painting, writing, travel. Office: Propylaea Arch Atelier 795 E 135th St Bronx NY 10454 Personal E-mail: harry@propylaea.com.

GAVIAN, PETER WOOD, securities analyst; b. Brewster, Mass., Dec. 8, 1932; s. Sarkis Peter and Ruth Millicent (Wood) G.; children: Sarah, Deborah Gavian Costolloe, Margaret Elizabeth. BA, Yale U., 1954; MBA cum laude, Harvard U., 1959. Chartered fin. analyst; accredited sr. appraiser; bus. valuation; USCG master's lic. Assoc. McKinsey & Co., N.Y.C., 1959-61; sec./treas. Greater Washington Investors, 1961-64, 70-71; v.p. fin. NUS Corp., Washington, 1965-66; asst. to group v.p. internat. Carborundum Co., Niagara Falls, N.Y., 1966-68; pvt. investment banker Washington, 1968—; pres. Corp. Fin. of Washington, Inc., 1976—. Expert witness in bus. valuation, 1980—; lectr. Am. U., Washington, 1978-80; independent trustee Calvert Group Funds, Bethesda, Md., 1980—, chair investment policy com., 2003—. Contbr. articles to profl. jours. Vol. varsity sailing coach U.S. Naval Acad., 1981-89; bd. dirs. ACLU, Va., 1993-95, Episcopal Diocese Washington, St. Anna's Home, Inc., 2004—. Lt. USN, 1954-57. Mem. Washington Soc. Investment Analysts (pres. 1978-79), Am. Soc. Appraisers (pres. Washington chpt. 1998-99), CFA Inst., New Providence Club. Avocations: ocean sailing, amateur radio. Home: 12 B3 Spa Creek Landing Annapolis MD 21403 Office Phone: 410-626-2567. E-mail: peter.gavian@verizon.net.

GAVIN, DONALD GLENN, lawyer, educator; b. Newark, Oct. 12, 1942; s. Louis Brooks and Elizabeth (Nievert) Gavin; m. Irene Dunn, Nov. 25, 1965; children: Andrew Scott, Mitchell Bryant. BS in Econs., U. Pa., 1964, JD, 1967; LLM, George Washington U., 1972. Bar: Pa. 1967, D.C. 1972, Va. 1973. Law clk. Ct. Common Pleas, Phila., 1967—68; assoc. to ptnr. Lewis, Mitchell & Moore, Washington and Vienna, Va., 1972—74; founding ptnr. Wickwire, Gavin P.C., Washington, L.A. and Vienna, 1974—. Lectr. in field. Contbr. articles to profl. jours. To capt. JAG U.S. Army, 1968—72. Mem.: ABA (mem., past nat. chmn. coun. pub. contract law sect., chmn. fed. grant legis., policies and remedies com., past chmn. grant coordination com., past chmn. environ. law com.), Phila. Bar Assn., Va. State Bar Assn., D.C. Ct. Fed. Claims Com., Fed. Bar Assn. Office: Wickwire Gavin International Gateway 8100 Boone Blvd Ste 700 Vienna VA 22182-7732 Office Phone: 703-790-8750.

GAVIN, JAMES RAPHAEL, III, biochemist; b. Oviedo, Fla., Nov. 23, 1945; m. Annie Ruth Jackson, June 19, 1971; children: Hakkim, Lamar. BS in Chemistry, Livingstone Coll., Salisbury, N.C., 1966; PhD in Biochemistry, Emory U., 1970; MD, Duke U., 1975. Diplomate Am. Bd. Internal Medicine, Nat. Bd. Med. Examiners. With USPHS, 1971—; staff assoc. diabetes br. NIH, Bethesda, Md., 1971-73; intern dept. pathology Duke U., Durham, N.C., 1975-76; intern dept. internal medicine Barnes Hosp., St. Louis, 1976-77, resident dept. internal medicine, 1977-78, asst. physician, 1978-85, assoc. physician, 1985-87; prof. medicine, chief diabetes sect. U. Okla. Health Scis. Ctr., Oklahoma City, 1988-89, William K. Warren prof. diabetes studies, 1989-91; sr. scientific officer Howard Hughes Med. Inst., Chevy Chase, Md., 1991—. Asst. prof. medicine Washington U., St. Louis, 1978-85, dir. RIA core lab., diabetes, rsch., tng. ctr., 1978-87, assoc. prof., 1985-87; George H. Howard, Jr. lectr. Meharry Med. Coll., 1988; Dr. Martin L. King, Jr. lectr. Washington U., 1988; Zollicofer vis. prof. U. N.C., 1990, Ralph Landes lectr., 1996; George H. Hamwi Meml. lectr. Ohio State Coll., 1991; Marty Alpern lectr. Henry Ford Hosp., 1991; Edward Hook Disting. lectr. U. Va., Charlottesville, 1994; Roerig Diabetes vis. prof. U. Hawaii Med. Ctr., Honolulu, 1995; mem. med. sci. adv. com. Juvenile Diabetes Found. Internat., 1981; mem. adv. com. minority med. faculty devel. program Robert Wood Johnson Found., 1983-93, nat. program dir., 1992—, sr. program cons., 1987—, nat. program dir. minority med. edn. program, 1987-93,; bd. trustees, 1996—; mem. adv. com. ctr. drugs biologics FDA, 1986-90; mem. Nat. Diabetes Adv. Bd., 1988-92; spl. reviewer endocrinology study sect. NIDDK, 1989-91, chmn. study sect. initiative diabetes minorities, 1991, chmn. study sect. intervention minorities diabetes, 1993, chmn. spl. rev. group prevention type 2 diabetes, 1994, chmn. investigator's working group diabetes minorities, 1995, mem. data monitoring bd. diabetes prevention program, 1995—; mem. com. increasing minority participation in health professions Inst. Medicine, Washington, 1992-94; mem. bd. overseers urban inst. Liberty Med. Ctr., Balt., 1993; mem. adv. coun. Miles Inst. Health Care Comm., 1994—; chmn. diabetes adv. bd. Bayer Pharm., Inc., 1995—; mem. steering com. Nat. Diabetes Edn. Program, 1995—; various vis. prof. Author: (chpt.) Immunopharmacology, 1977, Introduction to Endocrine Investigation: Techniques and Concepts, 1987, Key Issues in Minority Education: Research Directions and Practical Implications, 1989; co-author: (chpt.) Advances in Human Growth Hormone Rsch., 1973; mem. editl. bd. Am. Jour. Physiology, 1982-88, Am. Jour. Med. Sci., 1989-94, Acad. Medicine, 1994—; contbr. articles to Endocrinology, Sci., Biochemistry Biophysics Rsch. Comm., Nature New Biology, Jour. Biol. Chem., Jour. Clin. Endocrinology Metabolism, Pharmacology Rev., Israel Jour. Med. Sci., Jour. Pediat., Jour. Exptl. Medicine, Metabolism, Archives Internal Medicine, Jour. Applied Physiology, Obstetrics Gynecology, Diabetes, Am. Jour. Physiology, Am. Jour. Medicine, Nephron, Diabetes Edn., Bone, Am. Jour. Nursing, Diabetologia, Brain Rsch., Acta Diobetol, Preventive Medicine, Internat. Jour. Obesity, Diabetes Forecast, Am. Clin. Climatol. Assn., Patient Care. Founder, bd. dirs. Alpha Edn. Found. Bd., St. Louis, 1988—; mem. Okla. State Student Loan Authority, 1989-90; bd. trustees Okla. Sch. Sci. Math. Found., 1991—. Elk's scholar, 1962; recipient traineeship award NSF, 1966-70, Spl. Achiever award St. Louis Sentinel Newspaper, 1982, Disting. Alumnus award Nat. Assn. Opportunity Higher Edn., 1987, Excellence award Okla. Alliance Affirmative Action, 1988, Daniel Hale Williams award Chgo. Med. Assn., 1993, E.E. Just award Am. Soc. Cell Biology, 1995—; USPHS Predoc. fellow, 1970, Hastings Inst. Ethics Life Scis. fellow, 1971-75, Washington U. Sch. Medicine fellow, 1978-79; named Outstanding African Am. in Medicine, Aetna, 1993. Mem. Am. Assn. Physicians, Am. Diabetes Assn. (mem. rsch. com. St. Louis affiliate 1982-84, chmn. patient edn. com. 1982-86, v.p. 1985-86, mem. nat. com. scientific programs 1986-89, vice-chmn. 1987-88, chmn. 1988-89, pres.-elect Okla. affiliate 1989-90, pres. 1990-91, mem. nat. com. budget fin. 1989-91, nat. v.p. 1991-92, pres.-elect 1992-93, pres. 1993-94, immediate past pres. 1994-95, bd. dirs. rsch. found. 1994-95, chmn. workgroup reclassification diabetes 1995—, Outstanding Clinician 1990, Banting medal 1994), Am. Fedn. Clin. Rsch., Am. Soc. Acad. Black Surgeons, Am. Soc. Clin. Investigation, Assn. Acad. Minority Physicians, Ctrl. Soc. Clin. Rsch., Assn. Am. Physicians, So. Soc. Clin. Rsch., Endocrine Soc., Am. Clin. Climatol. Assn., Inst. Medicine, Sigma Xi, Alpha Omega Alpha, Beta Kappa Chi, Alpha Phi Alpha (life, William Alexander Cmty. Leadership award 1982), Omicron Delta Kappa, Sigma Pi Phi. Office: Howard Hughes Med Inst 4000 Jones Bridge Rd Chevy Chase MD 20815-6789

GAVIN, JOHN NEAL, lawyer; b. Chgo., Aug. 31, 1946; s. John Anthony and Mary Anne (O'Donnell) G.; m. Louise A. Sunderland, June 16, 1979; children: Anne, Matthew. AB, Coll. of Holy Cross, Worcester, Mass., 1968; JD, Harvard U., 1975. Bar: Ill. 1975. Law clk. to Hon. Charles M. Merrill U.S. Ct. Appeals (9th cir.), San Francisco, 1975-76; atty. office of legal counsel U.S. Dept. Justice, Washington, 1976-79; ptnr. Hopkins & Sutter, Chgo., 1981-2001, Foley & Lardner, Chgo., 2001—. Served to lt. USNR, 1968-71. Mem. ABA, Chgo. Bar Assn. Office: Foley & Lardner 321 N Clark St Chicago IL 60610 Office Phone: 312-832-4544. Business E-Mail: jgavin@foley.com.

GAVIN, MARY JANE, medical and surgical nurse; b. Prairie Du Chien, Wis., Sept. 1, 1941; d. Frank Grant and Mary Elizabeth Wolf; m. Alfred William Gavin, Nov. 9, 1963; children: Catherine Heidi Elizabeth, Carl Alfred Eric. Student, North Cen. Coll., Naperville, Ill., 1959-61; BS, RN, U. Wis., 1964; postgrad., Deepmuscle Tng. Ltd., 1980; postgrad. in deep muscle therapy. RN, Wis. Staff nurse U. Wis. Hosps., Madison; RN home response VA, Milw. Unit chair Badger Girls State, 1991—; mem. Wis. Am. Legion Aux.; mem. task force for handicapped Eastside Wis. Evang. Luth. Ch., Madison, 1993. U. Wis. scholar. Mem. Monona Grove Am. Legion Aux. (pres. Unit 429 1990—2005). Home: 702 Fairmont Ave Madison WI 53714-1424

GAVIN, PAULA LANCE, investment company executive; b. Nassau, N.Y., July 25, 1945; d. Paul P. and Gisela M. (Saume) Lance; m. John J. Gavin, July 23, 1983; children: Jennifer, Jason. BA, U. Del., 1967. With AT&T, N.J., 1967-90; pres. YMCA of Greater N.Y., N.Y.C., 1990—2004; with Jacobson Ptnrs., N.Y.C., 2004—. Bd. dirs. Childtime Learning Centers, Novi, Mich., 2002—. Bd. dirs. N.Y.C. Partnership and C. of C. Named to U. Del. Wall of Fame, 1998. Office: Jacobson Ptnrs 595 Madison Ave New York NY 10022

GAVIN, ROBERT MICHAEL, JR., education consultant; b. Coatesville, Pa., Aug. 16, 1940; s. Robert Michael and Helen Regina (Finnegan) G.; m. Charlotte Marie Dugan, June 2, 1962; children— Anne, Patricia, Robert, Charles, Sean. BA, St. John's U., Collegeville, Minn., 1962; PhD, Iowa State U., 1966; DSc (hon.), Haverford Coll., 1986, St. John's U., 1996. Mem. faculty Haverford (Pa.) Coll., 1966-84, prof. chemistry, 1975-84, dir. computing, 1979-80, provost, dean faculty, 1980-84, interim pres., 1996-97; pres. Macalester Coll., St. Paul, 1984-96, Cran Brook Ednl. Cmty., Bloomfield Hills, Mich., 1997—2001; ret., 2001. Bd. dirs. Hartford Funds, St. John's U., Minn.; chmn. bd. Hartford Mutual Funds, 2004-. Author papers in field. Pres. Haverford Twp. Sch. Bd., 1975. Recipient Dreyfus Tchr.-Scholar award, 1973; NSF fellow, 1969-70 Democrat. Roman Catholic. Home: 751 Judd St Marine On Saint Croix MN 55047 Personal E-mail: robertgavinjr@aol.com.

GAVIN, STEVEN J., lawyer; b. Teaneck, NJ, Feb. 17, 1960; BA, Yale U., 1982; JD, Stanford U., 1985. Bar: Ill. 1985, U.S. Dist. Ct. Ill. (no. dist.) 1986. Assoc. to ptnr. Winston & Strawn LLP, Chgo., 1985—. Bd. dirs. LINK Unlimited. Mem.: Phi Beta Kappa. Office: Winston & Strawn LLP 35 W Wacker Dr Chicago IL 60601-9703 Office Phone: 312-558-5979. Office Fax: 312-558-5700. E-mail: sgavin@winston.com.

GAVIRIA TRUJILLO, CESAR, former international organization administrator, former president of Colombia; b. Pereira, Colombia, Mar. 31, 1947; m. Ana Milena Muñoz Gómez; children: Simón, María Paz. BA in Econs., U. de Los Andes, Bogotá; JD (hon.), U. Libre de Colombia, 1990; Degree (hon.), Northeastern U., 2002. Chief of planning Dept. of Risaralda, 1969; mem. council Pereira, 1970-74; asst. to chief Nat. Planning Dept., 1971-72; dir. Transformadores T.P.L., SA, 1972-73; mem. Ho. of Reps., 1974-90; mayor Pereira, 1975-76; dep. min. of devel. Republic of Colombia, Bogota, 1978-79; pres., third commn. Ho. of Reps., 1980-81, pres., 1983-84; adj. dir. Liberal Party, 1986; min. of fin. and pub. credit Republic of Colombia, Bogota, 1986-87, min. of interior, 1987-89, pres., 1990-94; sec. gen. Orgn. Am. States, Washington, 1994—2004. La Intervención del Estado en la Economía, Aspectos Políticos del Plan de Integración Nacional, Deuda Pública Latinoamericana; columnist El Tiempo. Recipient W. Averell Harriman Democracy award, 2002, Nat. Dem. Inst. Democracy award, 2002.

GAVRAS, CONSTANTIN See COSTA-GAVRAS

GAVRILOFF, KATRINA, writer; b. Erie, Pa., Aug. 5, 1978; d. Perry Richard and Susan Loraine Gavriloff. BA in English, Pa. State U., 2000. Asst. support technician Am. Online, Inc., Reston, Va., 2000—01; sr. tech. writer Am. Online, Inc. Systems Ops., Reston, Va., 2001—. Tool com., tool documentation, aided in tng. new writers Am. Online, Inc., Multi-departmental, Reston, Va., 2002—03; spkr. Pa. State U. Mem.: Soc. Tech. Communication. Avocations: travel, reading, theater. Personal E-mail: wutangaler@aol.com.

GAVRITY, JOHN DECKER, retired insurance company executive; b. S.I., NY, Oct. 26, 1940; s. John S. and Eleanor R. (Decker) G.; m. Camille Appello, April 16, 1998; children: John, Joseph. BS, Wagner Coll., 1963. From staff to assoc. actuary U.S. Life, N.Y.C., 1963-74; from actuary to exec. v.p., fin. actuary USLIFE Corp., N.Y.C., 1975-97, exec. v.p., chief actuary, 1997-98; ret., 1998. Fellow Soc. Actuaries; mem. Am. Acad. Actuaries. Republican. Roman Catholic. Home: 688 New Dorp Ln Staten Island NY 10306-4933

GAWECKI, MARCIA ELIZABETH, artist, writer; b. Boston, Sept. 11, 1960; d. Frederick Mark Gawecki and Peggy Rose Knepper. BA in Advt., U. Nebr., 1982. Propr., artist Pop Art Portraits, Temecula, Calif., 1985—; health info. specialist Douglas County Health Dept., Omaha, 1990—92; advt. copywriter Mut. of Omaha Ins. Co., 1992—95; pubs. editor Oriental Trading Co., Omaha, 1995—98; freelance writer Chgo. Sun Times, Chgo. Reader, Arena Cultural, La Raza Newspapers, New Arts Examiner Mag., Chgo., 1998—2001; English instr. Lingmatec Inst., Santiago, Chile, 2001—02; editor News Rev. Newpaper, Santiago, 2002—03; propr., artist pop art portraits Idyllwild, Calif. Author: (art book) Birds of Prey: Works by Artist Lorna Marsh, 2000, (column) On the Town with Marcia, 1983; editor, writer: weekly column News Rev. Newspaper, 2002—03; portrait of Bill Cosby, portrait of Andy Warhol, Make-A-Wish Found., Omaha, 1986. Vol. Nat. Marrow Donor Program, Omaha, 1991; mem. Addy awards rev. com. Omaha Fedn. Advt., 1988—89; vol. writer, artist Watanabe Wellness Ctr., Nebr. AIDS Project, Omaha, 1996—98. Mem.: Friends or Art and Music, Chile, Art Alliance of Idyllwild, Temecula WRiters' Group. Roman Catholic. Avocations: Spanish, drawing, painting, photography. Office: Pop Art Portraits 54225 Pine Crest Ave Idyllwild CA 92549 Office Phone: 951-659-0477.

GAWOSKI, JOHN MICHAEL, physician; s. Michael and Julia (Podsiadlo) Gawoski. BS, MS, MIT, 1973; MD, McGill U., Montreal, 1978; DTMH, London Sch. Hygiene & Tropical Med., 2002. Cert. Am. Bd. of Path., Anatomic and Clin. Path. 1985. Sec. head, spl. chem. Lahey Clinic, Dept. Lab. Medicine, Burlington, Mass., 1986—. Fellow: Royal Soc. Tropical Medicine Hygiene, Coll. Am. Path.; mem.: Am. Soc. Tropical Medicine Hygiene, Nat. Acad. Clin. Biochemistry, Sigma Xi. Office: Lahey Clin Dept Lab Medicine 41 Mall Rd Burlington MA 01805 Office Phone: 781-744-8935. E-mail: john.m.gawoski@lahey.org.

GAY, DARRELL S., lawyer; b. Bklyn., July 20, 1955; BA, Fordham Univ., 1976; JD, Columbia Univ., 1979. Bar: NY 1982, Mass. 1980, US Dist. Ct. (so. and ea. dists. (NY) 1987, US Dist. Ct. (we. and no. dists. (NY) 1992, US Ct. Appeals (2d cir.) 2003. Atty. NLRB, 1979—84; dir. labor rels. Met. Hosp., 1984—85; mng. ptnr. DSGay Law Group PLLC, NYC; ptnr., head U.S. Labor & Employment Law practice Coudert Bros. LLP, NYC, 2003—. Commr. NY State Civil Svc. Commn., 1991—94; dir. Labor Rels. Met. Hosp. Editor (writing & rsch.): Human Rights Law Rev. Former chmn. Coalition of Black Profl. Orgns. Named one of Forty Under Forty People to Watch in the 90's, Crain's NY; Charles Evans Hughes fellow. Fellow: Am. Bar Found.; mem.: ABA, Nat. Bar Assn., Assn. Bar City of NY, Minority Corp. Counsel Assn. (found. mem.), Com. Minority Labor Attys. (found. mem.), Nat. Employment Law Coun. (found. mem., coord.). Office: Coudert Bros LLP 1114 Ave of the Americas New York NY 10036 Office Phone: 212-626-4549. Office Fax: 212-626-4120. Business E-Mail: dgay@coudert.com.

GAY, DAVID EDWARD RYAN, economist; b. Bryan, Tex., Sept. 19, 1945; s. John Gordon and Emma Louise (Ryan) G.; B.A., Tex. A&M U., 1968; Ph.D. (NDEA fellow), 1973; postdoctoral Kans. U., 1974, U. Chgo., 1979, U. Miami, 1980. Asst. prof. econs. U. Ark., Fayetteville, 1973-77, assoc. prof., 1977-83, prof., 1983—; vis. scholar U. Glasgow (Scotland), 1975, Hoover Instn. Stanford U., 1975; vis. assoc. prof. DePaul U., 1979; vis. assoc. prof. U. Colo., 1980, Tex. A&M U., 1980-81; vis. prof. Brigham Young U., 1983-84, Justus-Liebig U., Giessen, Germany, 1993; vis. prof. Higher Sch. Econ, Moscow, 1993, Pvt. Inst. Internat. Bus. Studies, Munich, 1994, Consort Internat. Bus. Studies, Italy; rsch. fellow Internat. Ctr. Econs., Turin, Italy, 1994, 96-97, 2002; co-dir. UA Tchr. and Faculty Support Ctr., 1999-2002. Bd. dirs. N.W. Ark. Community Concerts, 1975-76, Tex. A&M Opera and Performing Arts Soc., 1972-73; bd. govs. Ark. Union, 1977-79, Tex. A&M Commn. on Visual Arts, 1982—; Outstanding Econ. Grad., coll. Lib. Arts, Tex. A&M U., 1995, Recipient Disting. Achievement in Svc., Tchg., Svc. Ark. Alumni Assn., 1996-2004. Mem. Am. Econ. Assn., Am. Fin. Assn. (life), Assn. Pvt. Enterprise Edn. (mem. exec. com. 1993-97, 2000--, pres.1995-96, Kent-Aronoff award 2003), Eastern Econ. Assn. (founding, life), Pub. Choice Soc., Royal Econ. Soc. (life), So. Econ. Assn. (life), Southwestern Econs. Assn. (pres. 1981-82), Southwestern Soc. Economists (v.p. 1986-87, pres. 1988-89, Outstanding Educator award 2002), Southwestern Social Sci. Assn. (exec. coun. 1981-83, 1985-2005, sec. 1985-86, v.p. 1986-87, pres. 1988-89, membership dir. 1991-2005), Western Econ. Assn. (life), Western Social Sci. Assn. (exec. coun., pres. 1983-84, appreciation award 1985, 1990, 30th anniversary appreciation award 1988), Mid-South Acad. Econs. and Fin. (exec. council, pres. 1986-87), Missouri Valley Econ. Assn. (dir., exec. com. 1984-86, 93-95, pres. 1992-93), Southwestern Fedn. Administrn. Disciplines (v.p. 1989-90, pres. 1990-91, mem. exec. coun. 1991-96), Mont Pelerin Soc., Assn. for Arid Land Studies (v.p. 1987-89, pres. elect 1989-90, pres. 1990-91, 2002-2003), Sigma Xi, Beta Gamma Sigma (chpt. sec. 1985-89, outstanding UA honor soc. 1988, 2d place nat. award 1989, 1997-2002, 1st place 1990), Alpha Kappa Psi (adviser 1977-79), Phi Kappa Phi, Omicron Delta Epsilon (advisor 1986—), Phi Beta Delta (chpt. pres. 1991-93, pres-elect 2001-02, pres. 2002-2003). Republican. Methodist. Mem. editorial bd. Ark. Bus. and Econ. Rev., 1976-98, Bus. and Econ. Perspectives, 1984-91, Social Sci. Quar., 1982-99, dep. editor, 1984-93, Jour. Bus. Strategies, 1987-1993, Social Science Jour., 1987-2000; contbr. articles to profl. jours.

GAY, DOUGLAS MACKENZIE, pharmacologist; b. Ilion, NY, May 7, 1959; s. Raymond Edward and Alice (Fean) G.; m. Carol Ann Houser Gay, June 2, 1984; children: Elizabeth Ann, Stephanie Marie, Rebecca Danielle. BS in Pharmacy, Albany (N.Y.) Coll. of Pharmacy, 1982. Grad. intern Fay's Inc., Liverpool, N.Y., 1982-83, staff pharmacist Dewitt, N.Y., 1983, Mohawk Valley Gen. Hosp., Ilion, N.Y., 1983-85, Fay's Inc. # 127, Utica, N.Y., 1985-87, supervising Pharmacist, 1987-93, Fay's Inc. # 35, Ilion, N.Y., 1993-96, Eckerd Inc. # 5081, Ilion, N.Y., 1996—. Fay's Drugs Spkrs. group, Fay's Inc., Ilion, N.Y., 1992-96; peer rev. cons. Eckerd Drugs, 1999—; judge Eckerd Drugs Quiz Show, 1993—, Exec. bd. Gen. Herkimer coun. Boy Scouts Am., Revolutionary Trails coun., 2002—. Mem. Am. Pharm. Assn., Elks (chaplain Ilion lodge 1995-96, esquire 1996-97, loyal knight 1997-98, leading knight, 1998-99, exalted ruler 1999-2000, trustee 2000—, chmn. drug awareness N.Y. State ctrl. dist. 1995—). Avocations: camping, travel, snowmobiling, reading, photography. Home: PO Box 326 Ilion NY 13357-0326 Office: Eckerd Drugs # 5081 45 Central Plz Ilion NY 13357-1701

GAY, E(MIL) LAURENCE, lawyer; b. Bridgeport, Conn., Aug. 10, 1923; s. Emil Daniel and Helen Lillian (Mihalich) Gulyassy; m. Harriet A. Ripley, Aug. 2, 1952; children: Noel L., Peter C., Marguerite S., Georgette A. BS, Yale U., 1946; JD magna cum laude, Harvard U., 1949. Bar: N.Y. 1950, Conn. 1960, Calif. 1981, Hawaii 1988. Assoc. Root, Ballantine, Harlan, Bushby & Palmer, N.Y.C., 1949—52; mem. legal staff U.S. High Commr. Germany, 1952—53; law sec. fo David W. Peck, presiding justice appellate divsn. 1st dept. N.Y. Supreme Ct., N.Y.C., 1953—54; assoc. Debevoise, Plimpton & McLean, N.Y.C., 1954—58; v.p., sec.-treas., gen. counsel Hewitt-Robins, Inc., Stamford, Conn., 1958—65; pres. Litton Gt. Lakes Corp., N.Y.C., 1965—67; sr. v.p. fin. AMFAC, Inc., Honolulu, 1967—73, vice chmn., 1974—78; fin. cons. Burlingame, Calif., 1979-82; of counsel Pettit & Martin, San Francisco, 1982—88, Goodsill, Anderson, Quinn & Stifel, Honolulu, 1988—. Editor: Harvard Law Rev., 1948—49. Pres. Honolulu Symphony Soc., 1974—78; officer, dir. numerous arts and ednl. orgns.; bd. dirs. Loyola Marymount U., 1977—80, San Francisco Chamber Soloists, 1981—86, Honolulu Chamber Music Series, 1988—. 1st lt. U.S. Army, 1943—46. Mem.: ABA, Hawaii State Bar Assn., Phi Beta Kappa. Republican. Roman Catholic. Avocations: music, literature. Home: 1159 Maunawili Rd Kailua HI 96734-4641 Office: Goodsill Anderson Quinn & Stifel 1099 Alakea St #1800 Honolulu HI 96814 Office Phone: 808-547-5641. Business E-Mail: egay@goodsill.com.

GAY, ESMOND PHELPS, lawyer; b. New Orleans, Sept. 15, 1952; s. Charles Fenner and Harriott (Phelps) G.; m. Marian Enochs, June 6, 1981; children: Jacqueline Elinor, Marian Phelps. AB, Princeton (N.J.) U., 1975; JD, Tulane U., 1979. Bar: La. 1979, U.S. Dist. Ct. (ea. dist.) La. 1979, U.S. Ct. Appeals (5th cir.) 1986. Assoc. Christovich & Kearney, New Orleans, 1979-84, ptnr., 1985—. Mem. ABA (ho. of dels. 2004—, State Bar Tex., Internat. Bar Assn., La. Bar Assn. (pres. 2000-01), New Orleans Bar Assn. (bd. dirs. 1997-99), Fed. Ins. and Corp. Counsel (chmn. maritime law com.), La. Assn. Def. Counsel (bd. dirs. 2003—), Def. Rsch. Inst. Home: 237 Hector Ave Metairie LA 70005-4117 Office: Christovich & Kearney 601 Poydras St Ste 2300 New Orleans LA 70130-6078 E-mail: engay@christovich.com.

GAY, JOHN MARION, retired federal agency administrator, financial analyst; b. Sept. 23, 1936; s. John Henry and LolaBell (Collins) Gay; m. Rebecca Jane Gay; children: John Marion II, Dierdre, Michael, Michelle-(dec.), Steven, Christina. BA, Tex. So. U., 1956; MSW, U. Richmond, 1968; BS, Fla. Meml. Coll., 1976; MBA, Nova U., 1977. Cert. tchr. Fla. Compensation analyst SE Banks, N.A., Miami, Fla., 1976—78; personnel job analyst Kaiser Transit Group, Miami, 1978—80; tribal adminstr. Miccosukee Indians, Everglades Nat. Park, Fla., 1980—81; tchr. Broward County Schs., Fort Lauderdale, Fla., 1981—83, Dade County Schs., Miami, 1983—84; from postal employee to postal inspector US Postal Svc., North Miami Beach, Fla., 1984—96; postal inspection svc. detail US Postal Svc. DHQ, North Miami Beach, 1996—2003; ret. Corp. coord. United Negro Coll. Fund, Dade County, Fla., 1977; bd. govs. Tuskegee Airmen Nat. Mus. With USAF, 1956—59. Recipient Honor award, Alpha Kappa Mu, 1974, award, Fla. Meml. Coll. Alumni Assn., 1978; scholar Max Fleischmann, United Negro Coll. Fund, 1975. Fellow: NEA; mem.: Nat. Assn. Postal Suprs., Tuskegee Airmen, Inc. Democrat. Avocations: bowling, tennis, writing. Home: 373 NW Irma Ave Lake City FL 32055-335 Office Phone: 954-336-5236. E-mail: jongay36@bellsouth.net.

GAY, PETER, historian, educator, writer; b. Berlin, June 20, 1923; came to U.S., 1941, naturalized, 1946; s. Morris Peter and Helga (Kohnke) G.; m. Ruth Slotkin, May 30, 1959; stepchildren: Sarah Khedouri, Sophie Glazer Cohen, Elizabeth Glazer. BA, U. Denver, 1946; MA, Columbia U., 1947, PhD, 1951; LHD (hon.), U. Denver, 1970, U. Md., 1979, Hebrew Union Coll., Cin., 1983, Clark U., 1985, Suffolk U., Boston, 1987, Tufts U., 1988; LHD (hon.), Tavistock Inst., 1999; LHD (hon.), U. Ill., 2003. Faculty Columbia U., N.Y.C., 1947-69, prof. history, 1962-69, William R. Shepherd prof. history, 1967-69; prof. comparative European intellectual history Yale U., New Haven, 1969—, Durfee prof. history, 1970-84, Sterling prof., 1984-93, Sterling prof. emeritus, 1993—; dir. Ctr. for Scholars and Writers N.Y. Pub. Libr., 1997—. Dir. Ctr. Scholars and Writers N.Y. Pub. Libr. Author: The Dilemma of Democratic Socialism: Eduard Bernstein's Challenge to Marx, 1952, Voltaire's Politics: The Poet as Realist, 1959, The Party of Humanity: Essays in the French Enlightenment, 1964, A Loss of Mastery: Puritan Historians in Colonial America, 1966, The Enlightenment: An Interpretation, vol. I, The Rise of Modern Paganism, 1966, Weimar Culture: The Outsider as Insider, 1968, The Enlightenment, vol. II, The Science of Freedom, 1969, The Bridge of Criticism: Dialogues on the Enlightenment, 1970; author: (with R.K. Webb) Modern Europe, 1973; author: Style in History, 1974, Art and Act, 1976, Freud, Jews, and Other Germans, 1978, Education of the Senses, 1984, Freud for Historians, 1985, The Tender Passion, 1986, A Godless Jew: Freud, Atheism, and the Making of Psychoanalysis, 1987, Freud: A Life for Our Time, 1988, A Freud Reader, 1989, Reading Freud: Explorations and Entertainments, 1990, The Cultivation of Hatred, 1993, The Naked Heart, 1995, Pleasure Wars, 1998, My German Question: Growing Up in Nazi Berlin, 1998, Mozart, 1999, Schnitzler's Century: The Making of Middle-Class Culture, 1815-1914, 2001, Savage Reprisals, Bleak House, Madame Bovary, Buddenbrooks, 2002. Fellow Am. Coun. Learned Soc., 1959-60, Ctr. Advanced Study Behavioral Scis., 1963-64; Guggenheim fellow, 1967-68, 77-78; Overseas fellow Churchill Coll., Cambridge, 1970-71; Rockefeller Found. fellow, 1979-80; Wissenschaftskolleg zu Berlin, 1984; recipient First Amsterdam prize in Hist. Sci., 1991. Mem. Am. Philos. Soc., Am. Inst. Arts and Letters (gold medal in history 1996), Ctr. for Scholars and Writers (dir. emeritus), N.Y. Pub. Libr., Phi Beta Kappa. Home: 270 Riverside Dr 8C New York NY 10025 E-mail: petergay@verizon.net.

GAY, ROBERT DERRIL, behavioral health consultant; b. Savannah, Ga., June 23, 1939; s. Roscoe Degomar and Mollie Ann (Jones) G. BA, Oglethorpe U., 1962; MA, Emory U., 1966, PhD, 1984. Dep. dir. Divsn. Mental Health and Mental Retardation Ga. Dept. Human Resources, Atlanta, 1975-77, asst. commr., 1977-78, dir. Divsn. Mental Health and Mental Retardation, 1978-81; dep. dir. DeKalb County Health Dept., Decatur, Ga., 1981-94; dir. DeKalb Community Mental Health, Mental Retardation and Substance Abuse Svc. Bd., Decatur, 1994—2004; ind. cons., 2004—. Vis. instr. Oglethorpe U., 1966, 67, 85-94, Emory U. Sch. Nursing, 1970; mem. Ga. Gov.'s Coun. on Devel. Disabilities, 1978-81, Ga. Gov.'s Coun. on Mental Health and Mental Retardation, 1978-81, DeKalb County Coun. on Devel. Disabilities, 1981-2004 Bd. dirs. St. Joseph's Mercy Care Svcs., 1994-2000. Mem. Am. Sociol. Assn. So. Sociol. Soc., Ga. Sociol. Assn., Nat. Assn. State Mental Health Program Dirs. (bd. dirs. 1978-81, pres. 1990-91), Atlanta Mercy Mobile Health Program (bd. dirs. 1987-94, chair 1991-94). Home: 2295 Dunwoody Xing Apt I Atlanta GA 30338-7332

GAY, SARAH ELIZABETH, lawyer; b. Cambridge, Mass., May 24, 1950; d. Frank Smith and Jane (Spencer) Fussner; m. Kirk D. Gay; 1 child, John Russell. BA, Harvard/Radcliffe, 1972; JD, U. Oreg., 1975. Bar: Alaska 1976, U.S. Dist. Ct. Alaska 1976, U.S. Ct. Appeals (9th cir.) 1976, U.S. Supreme Ct. 1980. Assoc. Ely, Guess & Rudd, Anchorage, 1975—77; asst. atty. gen. natural resources sect. State of Alaska, Anchorage, 1977—88, asst. atty. gen. oil spill sect., 1989—91, supr. natural resources sect., 1991—93; corp. counsel Alaska Safari, Inc., Alaska's Valhalla Lodge, Inc., Anchorage, 1993—; pvt. practice Anchorage, 1993—. Workshop leader U. Oreg. Law Sch., Eugene, 1989; chmn. Anchorage Mcpl. Airports Adv. Com., 1990-93; food safety adv. com. Dept. Environ. Conservation, State Alaska, 2000—, mem. com. Alaska Bar Examiners, 1984-2005 Mng. bd. editor U. Oreg. Law Rev., Eugene, 1975. Citizens' adv. bd. Land Conservation & Devel. Bd., Salem, Oreg., 1975. Mem. Alaska Bar Assn. Law Examiners, Phi Delta Phi. Avocations: commercial pilot, sport fish lodge operator. Address: Valhalla Lodge Nondalton AK 99640 Office Phone: 907-294-2250. Business E-Mail: sarah@valhallalodge.com.

GAY, SUSAN MATTHEWS, publishing professional; b. Atlanta, Dec. 14, 1954; d. Brinton Bizzelle, Jr. and Evelyn (Ward) G.; m. Jonathan P. Andrews, Dec. 14, 1991; children: Katherine Rose Andrews, Paul Brinton Andrews. BS, Presbyn. Coll., 1976; MA, Emory U., 1980. Continuing edn. coord. Emory U. Sch. of Medicine, Atlanta, 1976-79; editor Ctrs. for Disease Control, Atlanta, 1979; editor, sr. editor Butterworth Pubs., Inc., Boston, 1979-82; sr. editor to exec. editor Grune & Stratton, Inc., N.Y.C., 1982-85; exec. editor J.B. Lippincott, Inc., Phila., 1986-88; exec. editor to editor-in-chief Mosby, Inc., Phila., 1988-95; v.p., pub. Williams and Wilkins (Waverly, Inc.), Balt. and Phila., 1995-99; pres., CEO InfoBrand Pub. Inc., Phila., 1999—. Spkr. Thomas Jefferson Med. Coll., Phila., 1997, others. Co-author: (book) Clinical Methods Learning System, 1979. Sec. Presbyn. Coll. Alumni Assn., Clinton, S.C., 1980-81; bd. dirs. New Gulph Children's Ctr., Villanova, Pa., 1996-98, Found. for Architecture, Phila., 1989-91. Mem.: Am. Med. Pubs. Assn. (pres. 2000—01), Am. Med. Writers Assn. (bd. dirs., chmn. audiovisual sect. 1978—85). Avocations: historic architecture, design, gourmet cooking. Office Phone: 610-581-7468.

GAY, WILLIAM ARTHUR, JR., thoracic surgeon; b. Richmond, Va., Jan. 16, 1936; s. William Arthur and Marion Harriette (Taylor) G.; m. Frances Louise Adkins, Dec. 17, 1960; children— William Taylor, Mason Arthur. BA, Va. Mil. Inst., 1957; MD, Duke U. Med. Sch., 1961. Resident, general surgery Duke U. Med. Ctr., Durham, NC, 1961—63, 1965—69, resident, thoracic surgery, 1969—71; clin. assoc. Nat. Heart, Lung, and Blood Inst., 1963—65; asst. prof. surgery Cornell U. Med. Coll., N.Y.C., 1971—74, assoc., prof., 1974—78; cardiothoracic surgeon-in-chief N.Y. Hosp., 1976—84; prof., chmn. dept. surgery U. Utah Sch. Medicine, 1984—92; v.p. for health scis. U. Utah, 1990—91; thoracic surgeon Washington U. Sch. Medicine, St. Louis. Prof. surgery Sch. Medicine Washington U., St. Louis; exec. dir. Am. Bd. Thoracic Surgery. Contbr. articles to profl. jours. With USPHS, 1963—65. Recipient Career Scientist award, Irma T. Hirschl Charitable Trust, 1972. Mem. ACS, Soc. Vascular Surgery, Soc. Thoracic Surgeons, Am. Assn. Thoracic for Surgery (treas. 1989-94), Am. Surg. Assn., Soc. Univ. Surgeons (treas. 1977-80), Western Thoracic Surgical Assn., Am. Bd. Thoracic Surgeons (chmn., 1995-97, sect.-treas., 2000, exec. dir.). Office: Washington U Sch Medicine 3180 Queeny Tower 1 Barnes Jewish Hospital Plz Saint Louis MO 63110-1013 also: Am Bd Thoracic Surgery 633 N St Clair St Ste 2320 Chicago IL 60611 Office Phone: 314-747-1315, 312-202-5900. Office Fax: 314-367-8459, 312-202-5960. E-mail: gayw@msnotes.wustl.edu.

GAY, WILLIAM INGALLS, veterinarian, health science association administrator; b. Sussex, N.J., Jan. 25, 1926; s. William David and Dorothy Julia (Ingalls) G.; m. Millicent Ruth Chapman, June 10, 1948. DVM, Cornell U., 1950; grad., Fed. Exec. Inst., 1972. Diplomate Am. Coll. Lab. Animal Medicine. Pvt. practice vet. medicine, Richmond Hill, N.Y., 1950-52; chief animal hosp. sect. lab. aids br. divsn. research services NIH, Bethesda, Md., 1954-63, asst. chief lab. aids br. divsn. research services, 1962-63, asst. chief animal resources br. divsn. research facilities and resources, 1964-65; program dir. comparative medicine Nat. Inst. Gen. Med. Scis., NIH, 1966-67, program adminstr. radiology and physiology tng. programs, 1966, chief research grants br., 1967-70, acting assoc. dir., 1970; assoc. dir. extramural programs Nat. Inst. Allergy and Infectious Diseases, NIH, 1970-80, dir. animal resources program, divsn. research resources, 1981-88; cons. ROW Svcs., Rockville, Md., 1989-98; pvt. practice Bethesda, Md., 1999—. Mem. com. on primates Inst. Lab. Animal Resources, NRC, 1961-63, chmn. subcom. on cat standards, 1963-64, mem. standards com., 1965-66; program chmn. Internat. Symposium on Lab. Animals, 1969 Author numerous papers on expt. surgery and lab. animal research.; editor: Methods of Animal Experimentation, 7 vols. Mem. sci. adv. bd. Mark L. Morris Found., 1966-71, trustee, 1971-84; mem. grants adv. council The Seeing Eye, 1971-74. Served as Lt. Vet. Corps, AUS, Walter Reed, 1952-54. Recipient Superior Service cert. HEW, 1975, NIH Dir's. award, 1983, Superior Service award USPHS, 1987, Spl;. Recognition award Am. Assn. Accreditation Lab. Animal Sci., 2003. Mem. AVMA (sec.-treas. D.C. chpt. 1957-58, v.p. 1962, pres. 1963), AAAS, Am. Assn. Lab. Animal Sci. (dir. 1961-69, program chmn. 1962-64, exec. bd. 1963, 66, nat. pres. 1968, chmn. awards com. 1969, Griffin award 1971, pres. Washington br. 1962, chair Gala 2000 com., Lifetime Achievement award 2003), Am. Assn. Lab. Animal Sci., NIH Alumni Assn. (bd. dirs. 1994, v.p. 1995-98, pres. 1999-2002), Phi Zeta, Cosmos Club.

GAY, WILLIAM TOLIN, lawyer; b. Everett, Wash., July 4, 1957; s. Warren Truman and Mary Margaret (McDonald) G.; m. Lori Rika Inano, May 14, 1988; 1 child, Christopher Tolin. JD, U. Wash., 1982, MBA, 1983, LLM,

1984. Bar: Wash. 1983, Calif. 1989, U.S. Dist. Ct. (we. dist.) Wash. 1983, U.S. Ct. Appeals (9th cir.) 1983, U. S. Dist. Ct. (so. dist.) Calif. 1989. Assoc. Blakemore & Mitsuki, Tokyo, 1984-87, Baker & McKenzie, Tokyo, 1987-88, Graham & James, L.A., 1988-91, Bryan Cave, Irvine, Calif., 1991-95; ptnr. McIntyre Burns & Gay, Costa Mesa, Calif., 1996-97, Snell & Wilmer, Irvine, 1998—. Mem. Tech. Coast Adv. Group, Calif., 1996. Mem.: Calif. Bar Assn. (chair cyberspace law com. 2001—02). Office: Snell & Wilmer LLP 1920 Main St Ste 1200 Irvine CA 92614-7230 E-mail: wtgay@swlaw.com.

GAYDA, MICHAEL D., lawyer; b. Phila., Sept. 23, 1954; BS econ., U. Pa., 1976; JD, Boston U. Sch. Law, 1979. Bar: Calif. 1979, Pa. 1981. Sr. v.p., gen. counsel, sec. Premcor Inc., Old Greenwich, Conn. Mem.: State Bar Calif., Fed. Energy Bar Assn., ABA. Office: Premcor Inc 1700 E Putnam Ave Ste 400 Old Greenwich CT 06870 Office Phone: 203-698-7500. Office Fax: 203-698-7925.

GAYDOS, JOEL CARL, physician; b. Edenborn, Pa., 1942; s. Joseph and Ann G.; m. Charlotte Ann Klaus, 1965; children: Kathryn, Joseph, Steven, Jennifer. AB, W.Va. U., 1964, MD, 1968; MPH in Epidemiology, U. Pitts., 1972. Diplomate Nat. Bd. Med. Examiners, Am. Bd. Preventive Medicine. Intern Walter Reed Gen. Hosp., Washington, 1968-69, resident in gen. preventive medicine, 1972-74; commd. 2d lt. U.S. Army, 1964, advanced through grades to col.; mil. physician Med. Corps, 1968-97; dir. occupl. and environ. health U.S. Army Environ. Hygiene Agy., Aberdeen Proving Ground, Md., 1983-85; occupl. health cons., chief preventive medicine cons. divsn. Dept. of the Army Office of the Surgeon Gen., Falls Church, Va., 1985-89; assoc. prof., assoc. dean acting Uniformed Svcs. U. of the Health Scis., Bethesda, Md., 1989-93; dir. clin. preventive medicine U.S. Army Ctr. for Health Promotion and Preventive Medicine, Aberdeen Proving Ground, Md., 1994-97; dir. pub. health practices Dept. of Def. Global Emerging Infections Surveillance & Response Sys., 1997—; sr. scientist Henry M. Jackson Found., Rockville, Md., 1997—. Adj. prof. Uniformed Svcs. U. Health Scis., 1999—, George Washington U., Washington, 2000—. Contbr. chapters to books, articles to profl. jours. Decorated Def. Superior Svc. medal, Legion of Merit. Fellow Am. Coll. Preventive Medicine, Am. Coll. Occupational & Environ. Medicine, Infectious Diseases Soc. Am.; mem. AMA, Soc. for Epidemiologic Rsch., Assn. Tchrs. Preventive Medicine, Am. Soc. Tropical Medicine & Hygiene, Assn. Mil. Surgeons of U.S. Office: Walter Reed Arm Inst Rsch Divsn Preventive Medicine 503 Robert Grant Ave Silver Spring MD 20910-7500 Business E-Mail: joel.gaydos@na.amedd.army.mil.

GAYDOS, TIM J., artist; b. NYC, Dec. 6, 1941; s. John Alfred and Lili Kallay Gaydos; children: Paloma, Sabrina. Student, U. Calif., Berkeley, 1959—61, Acad. Di Belli Art, 1962—63. Exhibitions include Butler Inst. Am. Art, Montclair Art Mus., Jersey City Mus., Bergen Mus., Represented in permanent collections NYC Cow Parade Sculpture, Butler Inst. Am. Art, Montclair Art Mus., Jersey City Mus., Bergen Mus. Fellow, N.J. State Coun. Arts, 1993—94. Mem.: N.J. Watercolor Soc., Pastel Soc. Am., Am. Watercolor Soc. (Gold medal 1995, Silver medal 2002). Avocation: soccer. Home: PO Box 9108 Paterson NJ 07509

GAYLE, CAROL, history educator, educational association administrator; b. Atlanta, July 18, 1936; d. William Thomas and Margot Gayle; m. Thomas Moodie (div.); m. William Moskoff, July 23, 1983; children: Elizabeth, Kate, David, Moodie. BA, Swaethmore Coll., 1958; MA, Columbia U., 1963. Instr. history Polytech. Inst. Bklyn., 1963—65, Lake Forest Coll., Ill., 1966—96, assoc. prof., 1996—. Cons. in field, spkr. Co-editor: (book) Economic History of Europe: Twentieth Century, 1968; co-author: Cast Iron Architecture in America, 1997. Dep. voter registrar Lake County, Ill., 1980—. Grantee Ford Found. Area Studies grant, Ford Found., 1960—63. Mem.: Am. Hist. Assn., Am. Assn. Advancement Slavic Studies, Phi Beta Kappa. Avocation: history preservation. Home: 148 Washington Cir Lake Forest IL 60045 Office Phone: 847-735-5083. Business E-Mail: gayle@lfc.edu.

GAYLE, GIBSON, JR., lawyer; b. Waco, Tex., Oct. 15, 1926; s. Gibson and Elsie (Little) G.; m. Martha Jane Wood, May 29, 1948; children: Sally Ann, Alice, Gibson III, Jane, Philip. AB, LLB, Baylor U., 1950; D Human Medicine (hon.), Baylor Coll. Medicine, 1991. Bar: Tex. 1950. Since practiced in, Houston; sr. ptnr., chmn. exec. com. Fulbright & Jaworski., 1979-92; adj. prof. U. Tex. Law Sch. Instr. U. Houston Law Sch., 1951-55. Bd. editors: Am. Bar Assn. Jour, 1967-72. Trustee M.D. Anderson Found.; bd. govs. Harris County Ctr. for Retarded, 1956-76; Tex. Med. Ctr. Inc., Leon Jaworski Found.; bd. dirs., pres. Am. Bar Endowment, 1970-80; chmn. Baylor Coll. Medicine, 1982-91, trustee, 1977—. 2d lt. F.A. AUS, 1945-47. Recipient Knight of Legion award, Rep. France, 2004. Fellow Am. Bar Found. (dir. 1978-79), Tex. Bar Found. (chmn. 1968-69); mem. ABA (chmn. jr. bar conf. 1959-60, ho. of dels. 1960-62, 63—, sec. 1963-67), Houston Bar Assn., State Bar Tex. (dir. 1966-69, pres. 1976-77), Houston C. of C. (dir. 1979-87) Home: 11727 Broken Bough Cir Houston TX 77024-5115 Office: Fulbright & Jaworski LLP 1301 Mckinney St Ste 5100 Houston TX 77010-3031 Personal E-mail: ggayle@fulbright.com.

GAYLE, HELENE D., pediatrician, public health physician; b. Buffalo; BS in Psychology cum laude, Columbia U., 1976; MD, U. Pa., 1981; MPH, John Hopkins U., 1981. Diplomate Am. Bd. Pediats. Intern then resident in pediats. Children's Hosp. Nat. Med. Ctr., Washington, 1981-84; epidemic intelligence svc. officer br. epidemiology divsn. nutrition Ctr. Health Promotion and Edn., 1984-86; preventive medicine resident divsn. evaluation and rsch. office internat. health program Ctrs. Disease Control Ga. State Dept. Health, 1986-87; med. epidemiologist pediats. and family studies sect., AIDS program Ctrs. Disease Control, 1987-89, acting spl. asst. minority HIV policy coordination office dep. dir. (HIV), 1988-89, asst. chief sci., 1989-90, chief internat. activity divsn. HIV/AIDS Atlanta, 1990-92, assoc. dir. Washington, 1994-96; agy. AIDS coord., chief divsn. HIV-AIDS Agy. Intl. Devel., Washington, 1992-94; dir. Nat. Ctr. HIV, Sexually Transmitted Diseases and Tb Prevention Ctrs. Disease Control, Atlanta, 1995—2001; dir. HIV, Tb, reproductive health Bill and Melinda Gates Found., 2001—. Lectr. Sch. Medicine Morehouse U., 1987—92; lectr. masters in pub. health program Emory U., Atlanta, 1989, 90, clin. asst. prof. cmty. medicine, 1996—; cons. WHO, others; bd. dir. Africa Am. inst. Global Health Coun., Internat. Ctr. Rsch. in Women; adj. assoc. prof. Sch. Pub. Health U. Wash. Contbr. articles to profl. jours. Adm. USPHS. Merit scholar, 1981; recipient Henrietta and Jacob Lowenburg prize, 1981, Model Excellence award Colgate-Palmolive Co., 1992, Medal of Excellence Columbia U., 1996, Sec. Award Disting. Svc. US Dept. Health and Human Svcs., 1999, Disting. Svc. Award Nat. Med. Fellowships, 2003, Disting. Alumnus Award, John Hopkins U. Sch. Pub. Health; named Barnard Woman of Achievement Barnard Coll., 2001, Mem. AAS, AMA, APHA, Am. Coll. Epidemiology, Internat. AIDS Soc., Soc. Against AIDS in Africa, Inst. Medicine, Coun. Fgn. Rels. Mailing: PO Box 23350 Seattle WA 98102 E-mail: heleneg@gatesfoundation.org.

GAYLE, MONICA, broadcast journalist; b. Wenatchee, WA, Mar. 3, 1960; BA Journalism, Wash. State U., 1982. Anchor, gen. assignment reporter Sta. KUSA-TV, Denver, 1986—89, Sta. KNSD-TV, San Diego, 1990—92; co-anchor CBS News Up to the Minute, N.Y.C., 1992-93, CBS Morning News, N.Y.C., 1993—97; anchor Sta. WJBK-TV, Detroit, 1997—. Recipient 4 Emmys, 2 Golden Mic awards and 3 Sigma Delta Chi awards. Office: WJBK FOX 2 Box 2000 Southfield MI 48037-2000

GAYLES, JOSEPH NATHAN, JR., medical association administrator, not-for-profit fundraiser, chemist; b. Birmingham, Ala. s. Joseph Nathan Webster and Ernestine Gayles; children: Jonathan, Monica Gayles Dorsey. AB summa cum laude, Dillard U., 1958, LL.D. (hon.), 1983; PhD, Brown U., 1963; postgrad., Oreg. State U., 1962-63, U. Uppsala, Sweden, 1965; D.Sc (hon.), Morehouse Sch. Medicine, 2000. Asst. prof. chemistry Oreg. State U., 1962-63; Woodrow Wilson teaching asso., asst. prof. chemistry Morehouse Coll., 1963-66, assoc. prof. chemistry, 1969-71, founding dir. med. edn. project, 1971-75, founding dir. Sch. Medicine, 1975-77, prof. Sch. Medicine, 1971-77; pres. Talladega (Ala.) Coll., 1977-83; v.p., research prof. medicine Morehouse Sch. Medicine, Atlanta, 1983-97; chmn., CEO Gayles and Assocs., Inc., Fund Raising Cons., 1983—; cons. v.p. Clark Atlanta U., 1996-98; v.p. advancement Sojourner Douglass Coll., 2002—. Staff scientist, project dir. IBM Research Lab., San Jose, Calif., 1966-69 Contbr. articles to profl. jours. Bd. dirs. Woodrow Wilson Nat. Fellowship Found., 1978-98, Rotary Internat., 1991—; bd. overseers Sch. Medicine, Morehouse Coll., 1977-81; bd. dirs. Coun. for Internat. Exchange Scholars, 1979-83; mem. Gov.'s Commn. on Future of Ala. in Yr. 2000, 1982-83; trustee Morehouse Coll., 1976-77, Talladega Coll., 1977-83, Morehouse Med. Coll., 1981-83; mem. nat. adv. coun. divsn. rsch. resources NIH, 1980-85; bd. visitors MIT, 1981-88. Woodrow Wilson fellow, 1958-59; Dreyfus Found. Tchr.-scholar, 1972; recipient Tchr. of Yr. award Morehouse Coll., 1976; Alumnus of Yr. award Dillard U., 1977; Presdl. Leadership award Morehouse Sch. Medicine, 1986 Mem. Am. Phys. Soc., Am. Chem. Soc., Nat. Assn. Equal Opportunity in Higher Edn. (bd. dirs. 1979-82), Sigma Xi, Phi Beta Kappa, Alpha Phi Alpha. Office: Gayles and Assoc Inc 1515 Austin Rd SW Atlanta GA 30331-2205 E-mail: j_gaylen@yahoo.com.

GAYLIN, NED L., psychologist, educator; b. Cleve., May 2, 1935; s. Harry C. and Fay I. G.; m. Rita Atran, June 30, 1957; children: Hilarie C., Ann E., Jed J., Daniel S. BA, U. Chgo., 1956, MA, 1961, PhD, 1965. Counselor Bellefaire Children's Home, Cleve., 1953, Sonja Shankman Orthogenic Sch., Chgo., 1954-56; group worker, supr. Jewish Community Ctrs. Chgo., 1957-60; grad. rsch. asst. Com. Human Devel., U. Chgo., 1959-60; intern Inst. Juvenile Rsch., Chgo., 1960-61, staff psychologist, 1965-68; intern Counseling and Psychotherapy Rsch. Ctr., U. Chgo., 1961-63; grad. teaching asst. dept. psychology U. Chgo., 1961-63; psychol. cons. State Ill., Rockford, 1961-64; psychotherapist, cons. Counseling and Psychotherapy Rsch. Ctr., U. Chgo., 1963-65, psychol. cons., lectr., 1965; lectr. dept. social sci. S.E. Jr. Coll., Chgo., 1965-66; psychol. cons. Peace Corps, No. Ill. U., DeKalb, 1966-68; chief psychologist S.W. Suburban Mental Health Assn., LaGrange, Ill., 1966-68; psychol. cons. Virginia Frank Child Devel. Ctr., Chgo., 1966-68; child clin. rsch. psychologist NIMH, Bethesda, Md., 1968-70; lectr., cons. Washington Sch. Psychiatry, 1968-72; chmn. dept. family and community devel. Coll. Human Ecology U. Md., College Park, 1970-77, prof., dir. family therapy tng. Coll. Health and Human Performance, 1977—2003, prof. emeritus, 2003—. Mem. rsch. com. Md. Community Coordinated Child Care, 1970-75. Author: Family, Self, and Psychotherapy, 2001; contbr. articles in field to profl. jours. USPHS grantee, 1961-63; U. Chgo. fellow and scholar, 1954-56, 58-60; State Ill. edn. and tng. grantee, 1963-65 Mem. APA, Nat. Coun. on Family Rels., Am. Assn. Marriage and Family Therapy, Groves Conf. on the Family, Assn. for Devel. of Person-Centered Approach, Sigma Xi. Home: 4617 Norwood Dr Chevy Chase MD 20815-5348 Office: Univ Md 1210 Marie Mount Hall College Park MD 20742-7515 Office Phone: 301-405-4006. Business E-Mail: gaylin@umd.edu.

GAYLIN, WILLARD, physician, educator; b. Cleve., Feb. 23, 1925; s. Harry C. and Fay (Baumgard) Gaylin; m. Betty Schofer, June 15, 1947; children: Joan Deborah, Ellen Andrea. AB, Harvard U., 1947; MD, Western Res. U., 1951. Lic. psychiatrist N.Y. Intern Cleve. City Hosp., 1951—52; resident psychiatry Bronx VA Hosp., 1952—54; faculty Columbia Psychoanalytic Sch., 1956—, clin. prof. psychiatry, 1972—; adj. prof. psychiatry Union Theol. Sem.; adj. prof. psychiatry and law Columbia Sch. Law, 1970; founder The Hastings Ctr., Briarcliff Manor, NY, 1970—, chmn. bd., 1970—96. Author: The Meaning of Despair, 1968, In The Service of Their Country: War Resisters in Prison, 1970, Partial Justice: A Study of Bias in Sentencing, 1974, Caring, 1976; author: (with others) Doing Good: The Limits of Benevolence, 1978; author: Feelings: Our Vital Signs, 1979, The Killing of Bonnie Garland: A Question of Justice, 1982, The Rage Within: Anger in Modern Life, 1984, Rediscovering Love, 1986, Adam and Eve and Pinocchio, 1990, The Male Ego, 1992, The Perversion of Autonomy, 1996, Talk Is Not Enough: How Psychotherapy Really Works, 2000, Hatred: The Psychological Descent into Violence, 2003; contbr. articles to profl. jours. Bd. dirs. Helsinki Watch., Nat. Bd. Planned Parenthood. Served with USNR, 1943—45. Recipient George E. Daniels medal of Merit for contbns. to psychoanalytic medicine, 1973, Elizabeth Cutter Morrow lectureship, Smith Coll., 1970; fellow Chubb, Yale U., 1972. Fellow: Am. Psychiat. Assn.; mem.: N.Y. Psychiat. Soc., Am. Psychoanalytic Assn., Inst. Medicine NAS. Fax: 914-478-8212. Office Phone: 914-478-2712. E-mail: willgaylin@aol.com.

GAYLOR, DONALD HUGHES, surgeon, educator; b. Bklyn., Apr. 17, 1926; s. Norman Hunter and Frances (Hughes) G.; m. Joan Winifred Power, Apr. 3, 1948; children: David, Christopher, Steven, Susan, Timothy. AB, U. Rochester, 1946, MD, 1949. Diplomate Am. Bd. Surgery, Am. Bd. Thoracic Surgery. Commd. lt. (j.g.) USN, 1949, advanced through grades to capt. M.C., 1966; intern U.S. Naval Hosp., Phila., 1949-50; student flight surgeon Sch. Aviation Medicine, Pensacola, Fla., 1950-51; flight surgeon U.S. Naval Sta., Trinidad, B.W.I., 1951-53; resident gen. surgery U.S. Naval Hosp., St. Albans, N.Y., 1953-57; postgrad. fellow surgery Royal Victoria Hosp., McGill U., Montreal, Can., 1957; resident thoracic surgery U.S. Naval Hosp., St. Albans, N.Y., 1957-59; resident cardiovascular surgery St. Francis Hosp., Roslyn, N.Y., 1958; staff thoracic surgeon U.S. Naval Hosp., Portsmouth, Va., 1959-64; surgeon U.S.S. Enterprise, 1964; staff thoracic surgeon U.S. Naval Hosp., Nat. Naval Med. Ctr., Bethesda, Md., 1964-65, chief thoracic and cardiovascular surgery, 1965-68; chief surgery, exec. officer U.S.S. Repose, 1968-69; exec. officer Naval Med. Sch., Bethesda, Md., 1969-72; ret., 1972; clin. assoc. surgery U. Pa. Sch. Medicine, 1976-90; prof. clin. surgery Hahnemann U. Sch. Medicine, 1986-96. Chief surgery Allentown (Pa.) Hosp., 1972-90, Sacred Heart Hosp., 1973-76, Lehigh Valley Hosp. Ctr., 1974-90. Contbr. articles to profl. jours. Fellow ACS; mem. AMA, Am. Thoracic Soc., Am. Trauma Soc. (pres. Pa. divsn. 1979-83, treas. 1985-91), Soc. Thoracic Surgeons (founding), Pa. Assn. for Thoracic Surgery, Assn. Mil. Surgeons U.S., Am. Trauma Soc. (founding mem.). Roman Catholic. Home and Office: 3761 Devonshire Rd Allentown PA 18103-9628 E-mail: capdonjo@earthlink.net.

GAYLOR, WILLIAM E., III, lawyer; b. Sarasota, Fla., Jan. 16, 1964; s. William E. Jr. and Phyllis F. Gaylor. BA, Asbury Coll., 1986; JD, Am. U., 1989; LLM, U. Miami, 1990. Bar: Fla. 1989. Assoc. Isphording Korp & Payne, Venice, Fla., 1990-92; ptnr., shareholder Muirhead, Gaylor & Steves LLP, Venice, 1992—. Adj. prof. Manatee C.C., 1996—; active Cmty. Found. of Sarasota County, Sarasota, 1992. Past pres., bd. mem. Cmty. Found. Sarasota County, 1999—; pres. New Coll. Libr. Assn., Sarasota, 1999—. Mem. ABA, Fla. Bar Assn., Sarasota County Bar Assn. (pres. probate and trust law sect. 1997-98). Avocations: scuba diving, traveling. Bus. Office: Muirhead Gaylor & Steves LLP 901 Ridgewood Ave Venice FL 34292-1938 E-mail: cgaylor@ewol.com, cgaylor@home.com.

GAYNOR, ELLEN ROSE, hematologist; b. Chgo., 1948; MD, U. Wis., 1978. Cert. Am. Bd. Internal Medicine, 1982, in Med. Oncology 1985, in Hematology 1986. Intern Loyola U. Med. Ctr., Maywood, Ill., 1978—79, resident, 1979—82, fellow, oncology, 1980—81; fellow, hematology and oncology U. Chgo., 1982—84; assoc. prof. Loyola U., Stritch Sch. Medicine, Maywood, Ill. Office: Loyola Univ Health Sys 2160 S First Ave Maywood IL 60153

GAYNOR, JOSEPH, chemical engineer, management consultant; b. N.Y.C., Nov. 15, 1925; s. Morris and Rebecca (Schnapper) G.; m. Elaine Bauer, Aug. 19, 1951; children: Barbara Lynne, Martin Scott, Paul David, Andrew Douglas. B in Chem. Engring., Poly. Inst., 1950; MS, Case Western Res. U., 1952, PhD, 1955. Rsch. asst. Case Inst., Cleve., 1952-55; with Gen. Engring. Labs. GE, Schenectady, NY, 1955-66, mgr. R & D sect., 1962-66; group v.p. rsch. Bell & Howell Co., 1966-72; mgr. comml. devel. group, mem. pres.' office Horizons Rsch., Inc., Cleve., 1972-73; pres. Innovative Tech. Assocs., Ventura, Calif., 1973—; mem. nat. materials adv. bd. com. NAS; chmn. conf. com. 2d internat. conf. on bus. graphics, 1979; program chmn. 1st internat. congress on advances in non-impact printing techs., 1981; mem. adv. com. 2d internat. congress on advances in non-impact printing techs., 1984; chmn. publs. com. 3rd internat. congress on advances in non-impact printing techs., 1986; chmn. internat. conf. on hard copy media, materials and processes, 1990. Editor: Electronic Imaging, 1991, Procs. Advances in Non-Impact Printing Technologies, Vol. I, 1983, Vol. II, 1988, 3 spl. issues Jour. Imaging Tech., Proc. Hard Copy Materials Media and Processes Internat. Conf., 1990; delivered invited keynote address NIP-17 Digital Printing Techs. Internat. Conf., 2001; patentee in field. Served with U.S. Army, 1944-46. Fellow AAAS, AIChE, Imaging Sci. and Tech. Soc. (sr., gen. chmn. 2nd internat. conf. on electrophotography 1973, chmn. bus. graphics tech. sect. 1976—, chmn. edn. com. L.A. chpt. 1978—), Am. Soc. Photobiology, Sigma Xi, Tau Beta Pi, Phi Lambda Upsilon, Alpha Chi Sigma. Home: 108 La Brea St Oxnard CA 93035-3928 Office: Innovative Tech Assocs 3639 Harbor Blvd Ste 203E Ventura CA 93001-4255 Office Phone: 805-650-9353. Personal E-mail: joseph.gaynor@adelphia.net.

GAYNOR, KEVIN ALLEN, lawyer; b. Cambridge, Mass., Oct. 5, 1948; s. William Joseph and Ruth Claire (Krepelka) G.; m. Cathy Thayer Cook, Oct. 20, 1973. BA, U. Conn., 1970; JD, U. Va., 1973. Bar: Conn. 1973, D.C. 1978, Conn. 1974, Md. 1978, U.S. Dist. Ct. D.C. 1978, U.S. Ct. Appeals (1st cir.) 1985, U.S. Ct. Appeals (D.C. cir.) 1978. Assoc. Thompson, Weir and Barclay, New Haven, 1973-74; atty. U.S. EPA, Washington, 1975-76; assoc. Nixon, Hargraves, Devans & Doyle, Washington, 1977-82; atty., asst. sect. chief U.S. Dept. Justice, Washington, 1983-87; ptnr. Venable, Baetjer, Howard & Civiletti, Washington, 1988-1993, Vinson & Elkins, Washington, 1993—. Adv. bd. Environ. Counselor, Chesterland, Ohio, 1989—. Co-author: Regulation of Chemical, 1982; contbr. articles to profl. jours. Sec. Rockburn Land Trust, Elkridge, Md., 1989—. Mem. ABA (vice chmn. natural resources com. 1989—), D.C. Bar Assn., Environ. Law Inst., Md. Bar Assn., Nat. Hist. Trust, Md. Conservation Found. Avocations: hiking, land conservation, running, biking. Office: Viscon & Elkins LLP Willard Office Bldg 1455 Pennsylvania Ave NW, Ste 600 Washington DC 20004

GAYNOR, SUZANNE MARIE, healthcare executive, researcher; b. Jan. 10, 1941; d. Howard Aloyousis and Irene Marie (Dunn) Gaynor; m. John Michael Hayes, May 26, 1962 (div. 1982); children: Marguerite Hayes, Jennifer Hayes, Christopher Hayes. Diploma in nursing, Fitzgerald-Mercy Sch. Nursing, 1961; BS, Marymount U. Va., 1977, MBA, 1981; DrPH, U. Mich., 1991. RN Pa., Va. Svc. coord. Upjohn Health Care, Washington, 1972—74, tng. coord., 1974—75; health intern U.S. Senate, Washington, 1977; health analyst Am. Blood Commn., Arlington, Va., 1977—79, dir. regionalization program, 1979—83, cons., 1983; dir. regional svcs. Greater NY Blood Program, N.Y.C., 1983—89; mem. faculty Mt. Sinai Sch. Medicine, 1989—2003; mem. interacy. tech. com. Working Group on Blood Resources and Blood Substitutes Dept. HHS, 1981—83; mem. subcom. on blood supply and blood svcs. Com. on Pub. Health N.Y. Acad. Medicine, 1984—; mem. Blood Bank Task Force Region II, Regional Comprehensive Hemophilia Treatment Ctrs.; sr. environ. health policy analyst, Office of Healthy Homes and Lead Hazard Control U.S. Dept. HUD, Washington, 2004—. Co-founder, chmn. East Harlem Asthma Working Group, Inc., N.Y.C., 1996—; mem. East Harlem Asthma Working Group, Inc. Housing Subcom., N.Y.C., 1998—; co-founder, chmn. CUES Asthma Working Group, N.Y.C., 2000—; mem. Manhattan Consortium for Children with Spl. Health Car Needs, N.Y.C., 2000—; mem. asthma working group Ctr. for Urban Epidemiol. Studies NY Acad. Medicine, 1996—; mem. com. on environ. N.Y.C. Asthma Partnership, 2001—, mem. steering com., 2000—02, chmn. com. on the environ., 2001—02; mem. pediat/child health subcom. East Harlem Cmty. Health Com., 1995—2002. Contbr. articles to profl.jours. Discussion leader Jr. Great Books, Arlington, 1974—75; bd. dirs. LWV, 1973—76, mem. bd. dirs., study com., membership com., 1971—76. Recipient Plaque for Recognition of Svc., Am. Blood Commn., 1983—83, Healthy Housing award, Indoor Environ. Health and Tech. Conf., 2003; grantee, NHLBI,SBIR, 2003—; PEW fellow, U. Mich. Grad. Sch. Pub. Health, 1986—91, Health Homes Demonstration grant, HUD, 2003—, Healthy Homes, Healthy Families grant, EPA, 2002—. Mem.: Assn. Tchrs. Preventive Medicine, APHA, NOW, NAFE, Assn. for Health Svcs. Rsch., Coun. Cmty. Blood Ctrs. (membership com.), Am. Assn. Blood Banks (dist. adv. group), Internat. AIDS Soc., Am. Soc. Law and Medicine, Delta Sigma Epsilon. Roman Catholic. Avocations: reading, travel, music, theater. Office: HUD Office Health Homes & Lead Hazard Control 451 7th St 520 Rm P-3206 Washington DC 20410

GAYOSKI, KATHLEEN MARY, counselor, minister; d. Thomas and Katherine Ida Gayoski. MA in Psychology and Religion, Andover Newton (Mass.) Theol. Sch., 2000; DEdn., Elfinstone Coll., 2004. Cert. cert. holistic health counselor; RN Mass., cert. epidemiologist, CDC; ordained min. Universal Life Ch., 1997; cert. Reiki master tchr. Crystal Crossing Holistic Resource Ctr., Tapas accupressure technique Tapas Assn., Mass., Am. Soc. Alternative Therapists C.O.R.E. Counselor Inst. Transformational Studies, batter's treatment counselor EMERGE/Mass., Nat. Crisis Responder, Debriefer and Chaplain Nat. Office of Victims Assistance, traumatic bereavement specialist, 1999, and death notification specialist MADD, 1979. Psychiat. RN specialist Mass. Dept. Mental Health, Taunton, 1971—72; RN, health prevention specialist, alcohol rehab. counselor South Miami (Fla.) Hosp., 1972—73; state epidemiologist, RN Mass. Dept. Pub. Health, Boston, 1973—97; coord., traumatic bereavement specialist and trainer Project REACH, Ctr. for Health and Human Svcs., Inc, New Bedford, Mass., 1997—2002; ordained min., crisis chaplain Tender Spirit Ministries, Rochester, Mass., 1997—; cert. holistic health counselor, profl. lectr. and educator Eagle Feathers Healing Arts Garden, Wareham, Mass., 2002—. Poet, author, clay artist Eagle Feathers Healing Arts Garden, 2002—; poet, author, artist Tender Spirit Ministries, 1997—; author Mass. Med. Assn., Boston, 1995. Com. mem. Rochester Meml. Sch., 1982—88; commr. Rochester Pk. Dept., 1988—91; chair South Ea. Ednl. Collaborative, New Bedford; publicity dir. Rochester Cmty., East Freetown, Mass., 1985—88; chaplain, counselor World AIDS Day; minister Old North Rochester Congregational Ch., 2004—. Named to Wall of Tolerance, 2003; recipient cert. appreciation, Bur. Family and Cmty. Health, Mass. Dept. Pub. Health, 1997, Silent No More cert. appreciation, U.S. Dept. Justice, 1999, Cert. of Achievement, MADD, 1999, cert. recognition for spiritual care for Egyptian Air Crash, ARC, 1999, letter appreciation for svc. response, Can. Consulate, 1999, cert. recognition for svc. to edn., ORPEA for crisis intervention and bereavement counseling, Old Rochester Regional Sch. Dist., 2000, cert. recognition, Sen. Edward M. Kennedy, U.S. Senate, Washington, 2001. Mem.: Nat. Office Victims Assistance Crisis Response Team, Greater New Bedford Trauma Response Team, Am. Soc. Alternative Therapists, Sisters of Mercy of the Ams. (assoc.; poet, author, nat. lectr.). Avocations: travel, writing, reading, expressive clay figures, hiking. Office: Eagle Feathers Healing Arts Garden 191 Main St Wareham MA 02571 Office Phone: 508-245-2860. E-mail: efhealingarts@aol.com.

GAYOSO, MICHAEL, JR., lawyer; b. Waterbury, Conn., June 14, 1972; s. Michael A. and Yoly H. Gayoso; m. Candace Michael Brewster, June 10, 2000; children: Garrett, Zachary, Gabriella. BA in Philosophy, Pontifical Coll. Josephinum, 1994; JD, Washburn U., 1999. Bar: Kans. 1999, U.S. Dist. Ct., Kans. 1999, U.S. Ct. of appeals (10th cir.) 1999. Assoc., legal intern Rork Law Office, Topeka, 1996—2000; ptnr. Law Office of Gayoso & Brewster, Girard, Kans., 2000—05, Meek, Battitori & Gayoso, 2005—. Author: (criminal law seminar) Aggressive Pretrial Tactics in the Defense of Drug-Related Offenses, 2000. Named Oral Advocate, Am. Coll. Trial Lawyers Kans., 1999; Pres.' scholar, Washburn U., 1996. Mem.: Kans. Bar Assn., Kans. Assn. Criminal Def. Lawyers, Crawford County Bar Assn.l (pres. 2004), Phi Alpha Delta. Roman Catholic. Office: Meek Battitori & Gayoso 127 S Summit St Girard KS 66743 Office Phone: 620-724-8239. Office Fax: 620-724-6105. Business E-Mail: mgayoso@cpol.net.

GAYVORONSKY, LUDMILA, artist, educator; b. Kharkov, Ukraine, Dec. 4, 1939; arrived in U.S., 1980; d. Pavel Nikanorovich Nikitin and m. Eva Lazarevna Skibityanskaya; m. Alexander Vitalievich Eremenko, June 9, 1996; 1 child, Gleb. Diploma in meteorology, Hydrometeorol. Inst. Ukraine, 1961; PhD of Geography, World Meteorol. Ctr. Moscow, 1965; BFA, Acad. Fine Art Moscow, 1968. Engr.-climatologist Climatol. Obs., Samara, Russia, 1961—62; engr.-agrometeorologist World Meteorol. Ctr., Moscow, 1965—66; editor Inst. Tech. Info., Moscow, 1966—69, chief editor,

1969—79; instr. fine art Sts. Cosmas & Damian Human Svcs. Ctr., S.I., NY, 1983—93; prof. fine art Lebanon Coll., NH, 1997—. Artist stage art constrn. for Childrens Week, Lincoln Ctr., N.Y.C., 1990, wall mural for Sinergia, Inc., N.Y.C., 1992-93, wall mural Town of Newport, N.H., 1998, backdrop panel Dicken's Fair, 1997. Recipient Gold medal Festival of Art, Moscow, 1968, Jurors prize distinction Spring Art Competition, Moscow, 1969, medal of honor Ukrainian Inst. Am., N.Y.C., 1988, cert. of appreciation USCG, Governors Island, N.Y., 1989, Jurors prize distinction Sunapee (N.H.) Art Fair, 1999; named acad. knight Acad. Verbano, Italy, 1999. Mem. World Phenomenological Inst. (artist-in-residence 1997—), N.H. Art Assn., Acad. Fine Arts, Acad. Verbano (Italy). Mem. Orthodox Ch. Of Am. Home: 26 Church St Newport NH 03773-1908 E-mail: ludmila.gayvoronsky@verizon.net.

GAZAWAY, BARBARA ANN, music educator, art educator; b. Lebanon, Pa., Jan. 7, 1942; d. Ammon Mark Brubaker and Margaret (Lesher) Dierwechter; m. Hal Prentiss Gazaway; children: Farideh Dunford, Ramin Dunford, Ammon Dunford, Lavada Kahumoku, Rene Dunford. BS in Music Edn., West Chester State U., 1963; cert. in elem. edn., Brigham Young U., 1979. Cert. Multiple Subject Tchg. Credential 1984, type A tchg. cert. 1990. Elem. music tchr. Oxford (Pa.) Sch. Dist., 1963—65; elem. classroom tchr. Lebanon (Pa.) Sch. Dist., 1965—67; elem. music tchr. U.S. Dept. Edn., European Area, Bad Kreuznach, Germany, 1968—70, elem. classroom tchr. Darmstadt, Germany, 1972—74, elem. music tchr. Alconbury, England, 1974—75; instrumental music instr. Lebanon (Pa.) Cath. H.S., 1976—78, h.s. music tchr., 1976—77; music instr. Brigham Young U., Provo, Utah, 1978—79; elem. vocal music tchr. Bennett Valley Union, Santa Rosa, Calif., 1987—89; elem. vocal music instr. Anchorage Sch. Dist., 1990—2000; pvt. music studio practice, 2001—. Owner, dir. Millcreek Nursery Sch., Newmanstown, 1975—76; instr. Homestay Am. Japanese Exch. Program, Santa Rosa, Calif., 1987; show pianist Marquee Theater, Santa Rosa, Calif., 1985—85; governess, Stuttgart, Germany, 1967—68; opermädchen Internat. Student Info. Svc., Mautern, Austria, 1967; singer, waitress The Harbor View, Martha's Vineyard Is., Mass., 1964; singer, baker, pianist The Inn, Mt Gretna, Pa., 1963; active Experiment in Internat. Living Home Stay Program, Switzerland, 1962; gasthaus worker Am. Student Info. Svc., Feldkirch, Austria, 1965; pres. Internat. Reading Assn. Campus Chpt. Singer: Sister Quartet, 1956—64. Family Coun. sec. Anchorage Pioneer Home, 2001—02; sec. Alpine Condominium Assn., Anchorage, 2001—02; chair Beautification Com., Anchorage, 2001—02; co-tchr. Divorce Care for Kids, Anchorage, 2004—; co-chair County Rep. Com., Santa Rosa, 1984—84; co-chair mission com. Trinity Christian Reformed Ch., Anchorage, 2001—02, co-facilitator divorce recovery program, 1999—, co-facilitator adult divorce care program, 1999—. Mem.: NEA, Internat. Reading Assn. (pres.), Music Educators Nat. Conv. Avocations: travel, hiking, reading, gardening, cooking. Home and Studio: 8620 Boundary Ave Anchorage AK 99504 Office Phone: 907-338-8111. Personal E-mail: gazaway_barbara@hotmail.com.

GAZDA-GRACE, PATRICIA ANN, counseling administrator, educator; d. Stanley Thomas and Mary Gazda; m. James A. Grace, June 21, 1975. BA in English Secondary Edn., State U. Coll., Oneonta, N.Y., 1972; MA in Guidance cum laude with distinction, Colgate U., Hamilton, N.Y., 1977; EdD in Ednl. Theory and Practice, Binghamton U., N.Y., 1999; post grad. in Reality Therapy/Control Therapy, 1990—. Cert. permanent sch. dist. adminstr. N.Y., permanent sch. counselor N.Y., permanent secondary edn. N.Y. Tchr. English North Sr. H.S., Binghamton, NY, 1972—80; counselor East Mid. Sch., 1980—82; tchr. English Binghamton H.S., 1982—84; counselor Binghamton City Sch. Dist., 1984—93; assoc. prin. and guidance dept. chair Binghamton H.S., 1993—; dir. curriculum and instrn. Binghamton City Schs., 2002. Counselor coord. H.S. equivalency program Binghamton City Sch. Dist., NY, 1979—93, prin. summer enrichment program, 1989—92, advanced placement testing coord., 2000—; social studies dept. chair Binghamton H.S., 1993—99, internat. baccalaureate program coord., 1997—; instr. counselor edn. program State U. Coll., Oneonta, 1996; adj. prof. sch. edn. and human devel. Binghamton U., 2000—. Contbr. articles to profl. jours. Mem. St. Vincent de Paul Ch. Couper scholar, Binghamton U., 1991. Mem.: AAUW, Am. Ednl. Rsch. Assn., Harpur Forum, Vestal Hills Country Club (bd. dir.), Kappa Delta Phi, Phi Delta Kappa. Avocations: golf, travel, writing. Mailing: 31 Main St Binghamton NY 13905-3107

GAZERRO, G. JOHN, JR., lawyer; b. West Warwick, R.I., Sept. 11, 1940; s. G. John and Lucy (Petrarca) G.; m. Carolyn M. DiPippo, Nov. 22, 1969; children: John Francis, Kerra Lynn. BA, Providence Coll., 1962; JD, Boston U., 1965. Bar: R.I. 1965, U.S. Dist. Ct. R.I. 1969, U.S. Supreme Ct. 1972. Chief inheritance tax, divsn. of taxation State of R.I., 1966-69, asst. atty. gen. Providence, 1969-73; town solicitor Town of West Warwick, R.I., 1978-80, 88-92, Town of Coventry, R.I., 1980-86; ptnr. Gazerro & Richardson, Warwick, 1984—. Bd. trustees, gen. counsel Centreville Savs. Bank, West Warwick, 1984. Treas. Rep. Town Com., West Warwick, 1969-77, legal counsel, 1977-88; mem. exec. com. Rep. State Com., Providence, 1968-82; bd. dirs. Kent County Mental Health, Warwick, 1976-78; mem. bd. incorporators Kent County Hosp., Warwick, 1984-90. Mem. R.I. Bar Assn. Avocations: skeet shooting, trap shooting, hunting. Home: 15 Magnolia Ln Coventry RI 02816-6634 Office: Gazerro & Richardson 1551 Centerville Rd Warwick RI 02886-4251

GBKURUVILLA, KOLLANPARAMPIL, electrical engineer; b. Kodukulanji, Kerala, India, July 20, 1943; came to U.S., 1988; s. Thomas and Susanna (Idicula) K.; m. Elizabeth Kuruvilla, Oct. 23, 1967 (dec. Jan. 1971); 1 child, Susan, m. Santha Mathew, Feb. 12, 1972; children: Babita, Nandita, Oscar. BSc in Engring., Kerala U., 1965; PhD, Kennedy Western U., 1997; postgrad., Trinity Coll./Theol. Sem., Newburgh, Ind., 1998—. Lectr. in elec. engring. Mar. Athanasius Coll. Engring., Kerala, 1965-66; elec. engr., exec. engr. Kerala State Electricity Bd., Trivandrum, 1966-87; elec. engr. Zambia Electricity Supply Corp., Lusaka, 1972-75; chief power sta. Soiedade Hidroelectrico do Révue, Mininstry of Power, Chimoio, Mozambique, 1979-81; project engr., design engr. Southeastern Pa. Transp. Authority, Phila., 1989—. Author: In Nature's Lap, 1995, A Smell of Africa (Safe in his Arms), 1998, It's Spring in America, 1999; inventor in field of safety and security measures; patentee in field. Nat. assoc. Libr. of Congress. Named Citizen of Yr., Hutt River Province, Australia, 1994, 96. Mem. Instn. Engrs. India, World Affairs Coun. of Phila., Handi Ham Club. Achievements include invention of in field of safety and security measures; patents for in field. Avocations: reading, music, painting, writing, amateur radio, reading, music, reading about nature, painting, amateur radio, writing. Home: 133A Dawn Dr Lansdale PA 19446-5251 Office: Southeastern Pa Transp Authority 1234 Market St Ste 13 Philadelphia PA 19107-3721 Office Phone: 215-580-8247. Personal E-mail: KuruvillaIII@gmail.com. Business E-Mail: wkuruvilla@septa.org.

GE, JIANHUA, information technology manager; BSME, Zhejiang U., Zhejiang, 1984; MS, Zhejiang U., Zhejiang Univ., 1987; PhD, Zhejiang U., Zhejiang, 1990. Sr. engring. specialist Am. GNC, Simi Valley, Calif., 1995—2001; project mgr. Impact Tech., Rochester, NY, 2002—. Author: Analysis and Synthesis for Fault Tolerant Control Systems (Awards from U. Press, China, 1995); contbr. scientific papers pub. to profl. jour. Recipient Rsch. Achievement Award, Nat. Edn. Commn. of China, 1994; Alexander von Humboldt Rsch. Fellow, Alexander von Humboldt Found., 1994, fellow, Fed. Ministry for Rsch. and Tech., Germany, 1993. Mem.: IEEE (electronics). Achievements include research in Outstanding Young Tchg. Award from Zhejiang Univ., 1992; papers publ. in Automatica, European Jour. of Ctrl., Internat. Jour. of COntrol. Home: 6489 Trefoil Ave Oak Park CA 91377

GEAKE, RAYMOND ROBERT, psychologist; b. Detroit, Oct. 26, 1936; s. Harry Nevill and Phyllis Rae (Fox) G.; m. Carol Lynne Rens, June 9, 1962; children: Roger Rens, Tamara Lynne, William Rens. BS in Spl. Edn., U. Mich., 1958, MA in Guidance and Counseling, 1959, PhD in Edn. and Psychology, 1963. Coord. child devel. rsch. Edison Inst., Dearborn, Mich., 1962-66; dir. psychology dept. Plymouth (Mich.) State Home and Tng. Sch., Mich. Dept. Mental Health, 1966-69; pvt. practice ednl. psychology Northville, Mich., 1969-72; mem. Mich. Ho. of Reps., 1973-76, Mich. Senate, 1977-98; investigator, dir. Mich. Office of Children's Ombudsman, 1999—2002; commr. Mich. Racing, 2002—04. Adj. asst. prof. edn./psychology dept. Madonna Coll., Livonia, Mich., 1984-86. Co-author: Visual Tracking, A Self-instruction Workbook for Perceptual Skills in Reading, 1962. Trustee-at-large Schoolcraft C.C., 1969-72, chmn. bd. trustees, 1971-72; vice chmn. nat. adv. com. on mental health and illness of elderly HEW, 1976-77; vice chmn. human svcs. com., assembly fed. issues Nat. Conf. State Legislatures, 1994-95. Recipient Recognition award Found. for Improvement of Justice, 1993. Fellow Mich. Psychol. Assn.; mem. NEA (life), APA, Rotary. Republican.

GEALT, MICHAEL A., environmental microbiologist, educator; b. Phila., Nov. 27, 1948; s. Edward Leonard Gealt and Lillian Rose Brenner; m. Maryjanet McNamara, Jan. 2, 1981; 1 child; m. Antonia Malandrucco, May 12, 1967 (div. 1977); 2 children. BA, Temple U., 1970; PhD, Rutgers U., 1974. Rsch. assoc. Med. Sch. Rutgers U., Piscataway, N.J., 1974-76; postdoct. assoc. Inst. Cancer Rsch., Phila., 1976-78; asst. prof. biol. scis. Drexel U., Phila., 1978-84; assoc. prof., 1984-90; prof., 1990-2000; dir. Sch. Environ. Sci., Engring. and Policy, 1994-2000; dean Sch. Engring., Math. and Sci. Purdue U. Calument, Hammond, Ind., 2000—, prof. biology, 2000—. Contbr. articles to profl. jours. Grantee EPA, 1983, 85, 89, NSF, 1981, 94, 97, USAF, 2002. Mem. AAAS, Am. Soc. Microbiology (chair environ. and applied micro divsn. 1995), Am. Soc. Cell Biology, Assn. Environ. Engrs. & Science Profs., Am. Assn. Higher Educ., Am. Soc. Engring. Educ., Sigma Chi. Avocations: motorcycles, photography. Office: Purdue U Calumet Sch Engring Math and Sci 2200 169th St Hammond IN 46323-2068 Office Phone: 219-989-2468. Business E-Mail: gealt@calumet.purdue.edu.

GEAN, THOMAS C., lawyer, former prosecutor; b. 1962; BA, U. Ark.; JD, Vanderbilt U. Atty. Alston and Bird, Atlanta, 1988—92, Gean, Gean and Gean, Ft. Smith, Ark., 1992—96; prosecuting atty. Sebastian County Dist. Atty.'s Office, 1997—2001; U.S. atty. western dist. Ark. U.S. Dept. Justice, 2001—04; v.p. legal dept., chief legal compliance officer Wal-Mart Corp., Bentonville, Ark., 2004—. Office: Wal-Mart Corp 702 SW 8th St Bentonville AR 72716

GEARAN, MARK D., former federal agency administrator; m. Mary Herlihy; children: Madeleine, Kathleen. BA cum laude, Harvard U., 1978; JD, Georgetown U., 1991. Press sec. Robert F. Drinan, Mass., 1978; reporter Fitchburg (Mass.) Sentinel, 1978-79; press sec., chief of staff Rep. Berkley Bedell, Iowa, 1980-83; dir. Mass. Office Fed. Rels. Gov. Michael Dukakis, 1983-87, 88-89; hdqs. press sec. Dukakis for Pres. Campaign, 1987-88; exec. dir. Dem. Gov. Assn., 1989-92; sr. advisor Clinton for Pres. Campaign, 1992-93; dep. dir. Presdl. Transition Team, Washington, 1992-93; asst. to President U.S., dir. comm. White House, Washington, 1993-95; dir. The Peace Corps, Washington, 1995-99. Office: Peace Corps Office of the Director 1111 20th St NW Washington DC 20526-0002

GEAREN, JOHN JOSEPH, lawyer; b. Wareham, Mass., Sept. 1, 1943; BA, U. Notre Dame, 1965; MA (Rhodes Scholar), Oxford U., 1967; JD, Yale U., 1970. Bar: Ill. 1972. Ptnr. Mayer, Brown & Platt, Chgo., 1970—. Democrat. Roman Catholic. Home: 179 Linden Ave Unit 2 Oak Park IL 60302-1661 Office: Mayer Brown & Platt 190 S La Salle St Ste 3100 Chicago IL 60603-3441 E-mail: jgearen@mayerbrown.com.

GEARHART, PAMELA CAUM, conductor, educator, musician; b. Altoona, Pa., July 21, 1934; d. Russell Gerhart and Martha Treese Caum; m. Livingston Hawley Gearhart, Nov. 25, 1955; children: Kim Russell, Martha Almitra, Fritz Peter. Diploma, Curtis Inst. Music, Phila., 1955. Instr. music dept. SUNY, Buffalo, 1958—69, asst. prof. music dept., 1969—75; asst. prof. Ithaca (N.Y.) Coll. Sch. Music, 1975—77, Dana prof. music, 1977—93, Dana prof. emerita, 1994—. Condr., founder Buffalo (N.Y.) Youth Orch., 1960—75; cons. Shawnee Press Inc., Delaware Water Gap, Pa., 1965—79; condr. Ithaca (N.Y.) Youth Orch., 1977—93. Co-founder, condr., tchr. Youth Makes Music, Ala., 1972—82. Recipient Outstanding Achievement as condr., violinist and tchr., N.Y. Fedn. of Music Clubs, 1976. Mem.: N.Y. State Sch. Music Assn., Am. String Tchrs. Assn., Music Educators Nat. Convention. Democrat. Unitarian Universalist. Avocation: collecting political memorabilia. Home: 425 Richard Pl Ithaca NY 14850-3130 Office Phone: 607-273-8033.

GEARHEART, GALEN GRANT, pharmacist, educator; b. Martin, Ky., July 13, 1962; s. Burnice Jennings Gearheart and Edna Martin Gearhart; m. Kathy S. Slone, Dec. 19, 1984; children: Ryan, Alexis. BS in Pharmacy, D Pharmacy, U. Ky., 1986. Lic. pharmacist, cert. geriatric pharmacist. Supr. outpatient pharmacy Potter Med. Clinic, Lackey, Ky., 1986—87; commd. officer USAF, 1987, advanced through grades to maj., 1997, resigned, 1997; chief clin. pharmacy svcs. Malcom Grow USAF Med. Ctr., Clinton, Md., 1987—90; asst. chief pharmacy svc. Huntington (W.Va.) VA Med. Ctr., 1990—94; chief clin. pharmacy svcs. Keesler USAF Med. Ctr., Biloxi, Miss., 1994—97; clin. edn. cons. Pfizer Inc., Ashland, Ky., 1997—2000, assoc. team mgr. clin. edn. Mid-Atlantic region Reston, Va., 2000—03, regional team mgr. clin. edn., 2003—. Author: Safe Use of Your Medications, Drug Utilization Evaluation: A Practical Guide, exhbns. in field. Fellow: Am. Soc. Cons. Pharmacists; mem.: Am. Pharmacists Assn., Am. Mgmt. Assn., Am. Soc. Health Sys. Pharmacists. Republican. Baptist. Avocation: travel. Office: Pfizer Inc 11921 Freedom Dr Ste 300 Reston VA 20190 Home: 544 Rugby Ct Purcellville VA 20132 Office Phone: 540-338-8304. Home Fax: 540-338-8304. E-mail: G3FARMD@aol.com.

GEARY, DAVID PATRICK, criminal justice educator, consultant, writer; b. Milw., May 20, 1928; s. Cornelius John and Madeline (Cushway) G.; m. Mary Ann Delavan, June 19, 1954; children: Patrick, John, Daniel, Peter. BS, LaVerne U., L.A., 1971; MPA, U. So. Calif., 1972; PhD, Marquette U., 1979; postgrad., U. Mich., 1980. Cert. life teaching credential, Calif. Police officer City of Greendale, Wis., 1950-55; chief police City of Hales Corners, Wis., 1955-61, City of Salem, Oreg., 1961-65, City of Ventura, Calif., 1965-72; assoc. prof. criminal justice U. Wis., Milw., 1972-76, U. South Fla., Tampa, 1976-79, U. Nev., Reno, 1979-82, Va. Commonwealth U., Richmond, 1982—2003, pres. faculty senate, 1989, emeritus faculty, 2003—. Mem. vis. faculty Ventura Coll., 1966-72, Carthage Coll., Kenosha, Wis., 1974; cons. Commn. on Accreditation for Law Enforcement Agys., Fairfax, Va., 1990; cons. to Va. State Police, 1994, Richmond Va. Police, 1996—; cons. to city atty. and police dept. City of Dallas, 1990; cons. to atty. gen. City of Birmingham, 1991; cons. to postal insp. U.S. Postal Svc., Washington, 1992; cons. to City of Richmond, 1996—. Author: How To Deliver Death News, 1981; editor: Community Relations, 1976; also articles. Gen. chmn. Arts in Justice, Anderson Gallery, Richmond, 1989. With U.S. Maritime Svc., 1944-46. Named Outstanding Young Man, U.S. Jaycees, Hales Corners, 1965; rsch. fellow U.S. Govt. Law Enforcement Assistance Adminstrn., 1976. Mem. AAUP (pres. Va. Commonwealth U. chpt. 1987, 94), Va. Assn. Criminal Justice Educators (pres. 1985-87), Va. Internat. Human Rights and Responsibilities Found., Inc. (founder 1998). Home: 7678 Yarmouth Dr Richmond VA 23225-2145 Office Phone: 804-320-1494. Business E-Mail: nocon@vcu.org. *Don't let the barbarians get you. Don't let them injure your body, but more important don't let them get into your head and make you one of them.*

GEARY, HILARY R., society editor; d. J. Jeffrey Roche and Sidney B. Wood; m. John W. Geary II, Apr. 28, 1973 (dec. 1995); children: Alfred, John; m. Peter Green, 2000 (div. 2002); m. Wilbur Ross, Oct. 9, 2004. Student, Finch Coll. Society editor Quest Mag. Mem.: Southampton Rose Soc. Office: QUEST Media 920 Third Ave 6th Fl New York NY 10022 Office Phone: 646-840-3404 ext. 106. Office Fax: 646-840-3408.*

GEARY, PATRICK JOSEPH, security and emergency planning administrator, writer; b. Milw., Mar. 6, 1957; s. David Patrick and Mary Ann (Delavan) G. BS, Va. Commonwealth U., 1984; MA, U. Richmond, 1987, U.S. Naval War Coll., 2000. Operations security cert. profl. Tech. publs. writer Dept. Def. Security Inst., Richmond, Va., 1987—88; ops. security officer David Taylor Naval Rsch. Ctr., Bethesda, Md., 1988—91, Space and Naval Warfare Sys. Command, Arlington, Va., 1991—92; divsn. head office of security Naval Sea Sys. Command, Arlington, 1992—2002; dir. Office of Security and Continuity Planning Dept. of Treasury, Washington, 2002—03; sr. analyst emer. mgmt. policy and planning Dept. Treasury, IRS, 2003—. Pres. Ybor City Jaycees, Tampa, Fla., 1979, Reno Jaycees, 1980-81; regional/dist. dir. Nev. Jaycees, Reno, 1981-83; co-campaign mgr. state assembly Rep. Party of Nev., Reno, 1982; senator Jaycees Internat., Coral Gables, Fla., 1983, life mem.; active West End Jaycees Richmond, 1983-98. Decorated superior civilian svc. medal Dept. Navy, 1995; recipient Charles Kulp meml. award U.S. Jaycees, 1981, Nat. Interagy. award for individual achievment in ops., 1998; Albright grad. fellow U. Richmond, 1985. Mem. NRA, KC, Nat. Def. Indsl. Assn. (life), Ops. Security Profls. Soc. (life, charter, nat. bd. dirs. 1995-2004, pres. 2000-2003), Nat. Assn. Parliamentarians, Nat. Mil. Intelligence Assn. (life), U.S. Naval War Coll. found. (alumni life), Va. Commonwealth U. Alumni Assn. (life), Pi Sigma Alpha, Alpha Phi Sigma. Roman Catholic. Avocations: water-skiing, basketball, football, parliamentary procedure, pistol shooting. Home: 7035 Devereux Circle Dr Alexandria VA 22315

GEARY, WILLIAM JOHN, entreprenuer, researcher, film director; b. Kingston, N.Y., May 2, 1954; s. Robert William and Janet Isabelle Cochrane-Geary. Student, Hope Coll., 1972-76; BA, Thomas Edison State, 1993; MA, NYU, 2000. Intern Phila. Mus. Art, 1974-75; project mgr., project coord. Food Co-operative Farming Project, New Paltz, N.Y., 1978-79; support mem., culinary staff Sands Hotel, Atlantic City, N.J., 1980-85; group leader Lower Kensington Eviron. Ctr., New Castle, Del., 1985; support mem., culinary staff Showboat Hotel, Atlantic City, 1987-93. Artist Urban Outreach/Phila. Mus. Art, 1974-75; researcher Dat Matrix, Atlantic City, 1990-93. Spokesperson Friends of the Mountain, New Paltz, 1979. Protestant. Avocations: reading, swimming, skiing, chess. E-mail: wgeary8089@aol.com.

GEBALLE, THOMAS RONALD, astronomer; b. Seattle, Nov. 16, 1944; s. Ronald and Marjorie Louise Geballe; m. Carole Gem Leach, June 11, 1967; children: Annere Lee, Matthew Thomas. BA, U. Calif., 1967, PhD, 1974. Rsch. fellow U. Calif., Berkeley, 1974—75, Leiden U., Netherlands, 1975—77; Carnegie fellow The Observatories, Pasadena, Calif., 1977—81; from astronomer to assoc. dir. UK Infrared Telescope, Hilo, Hawaii, 1981—98; sr. scientist Gemini Obs., Hilo, 1998—. Bd. dirs. East Hawaii Cultural Coun., Hilo, 1992—. Mem.: Astron. Soc. of the Pacific, Am. Astron. Soc., Hawaii Concert Soc. (pres. 1992—). Office: Gemini Obs 670 N A'Ohoku Pl Hilo HI 96720

GEBAUER, KURT MANFRED, management executive; b. Paterson, N.J., Dec. 12, 1951; s. Werner and Edna Julie (Harris) G.; . Cheryl Lawton, Oct. 24, 1981. BA, Burknell U., 1974. Gen. mgr. Sta. WUDO, Lewisburg, Pa., 1973-74; v.p. New Sound Assocs., Lewisburg, 1974-75; ops. mgr. Sta. WCRV, Washington, N.J., 1975-76; pres. WTS Corp., Rockaway, N.J., 1976—. Product mgr. BestWare, Inc., 1994-95, dir. internat. ops., 1995-96, mng. dir. MYOB (now MYOB US, Inc.) product line, 1996-99; internet & E strategist MYOB Global Technology, 1999—; personal and bus. mgr. Light, 1980-82; N. Am. tour mgr. Cleo Laine/John Dankworth, 1980-82, bus. and concert mgr., 1983-93; East Coast tour mgr. Henry Mancini, 1980-86; cons. Warren Broadcasting Co. (WFMV-FM), Blairstown, N.J., 1977-79, Cam Kay, Inc., 1979-84 1st Nat. Bank of Hope, N.J., 1986-88; dir. Sonoma-Hope, Inc., 1984—, Keynight Pty. Ltd., 1988-93, Consolidated Libr. Assocs., Inc., 1989-96, Distinctive Artists Mgmt., Inc., 1990-95. Sound. designer A Little Night Music, Mich. Opera Theater, 1983, Lady in Waiting, Houston Ballet, 1984, The Merry Widow, Mich. Opera Theater, 1984; prodr. DRG album Cleo at Carnegie: The 10th Anniversary Album, 1986 (Grammy award for best female jazz vocalist 1995), RCA Victor album Woman to Woman, 1989, Blues and Sentimental, 1993, Golden Records albums: Cleo Laine Live in Manhattan, 2001, Quintessential Cleo, 2001. Mem. Pi Delta Epsilon. Office: WTS Inc 10 Bank St Ste 55 Rockaway NJ 07866-3428

GEBAUER, PHYLLIS VICTORIA FELTSKOG, writer, educator; b. Chgo., Ill., Oct. 17, 1928; d. Gustave Moritz Emmanuel and Ethel Wilhelmina Feltskog; m. Frederick August Gebauer, Dec. 2, 1950 (dec. Apr. 1998). BS in Spanish, Northwestern U., 1950; MA in Spanish, U. Houston, 1966. Procedures coord. Boeing, Renton, Wash., 1957—60; spanish tchr. Bellevue Sch. Dist., Bellevue, Wash., 1963—64; tchr. Lennox Sch. Dist., Lennox, Calif., 1966—67, San Dieguito Dist., Cardiff, Calif., 1967—68; spanish tchr. Highline Sch. Dist., Seattle, 1969—70; filmmaker Gebauer Prodns., Santa Barbara, Calif., 1970—74; freelance writer, 1974—; instr. writers program U. Calif., L.A., 1989—. Workshop leader Santa Barbara Writer's Conf., Santa Barbara, 1980—, So. Calif. Writer's Conf., San Diego, 1989—93, San Diego State U. Writer's Conf., San Diego, 1995—. Author: The Pagan Blessing, 1979; contbr. articles to profl. jours., stories to mags. Named Outstanding Tchr., UCLA Ext., 1992; recipient Bronze plaque, Columbus Ohio Film Festival, 1974. Mem.: Dorothy L. Sayers Soc., Pen Ctr. U.S.A. West (exec. v.p. 1984—87), Sigma Delta Pi, Phi Sigma Iota, Phi Beta Kappa. Democrat. Unitarian Universalist. Avocations: swimming, reading, movie going.

GEBBIE, KRISTINE MOORE, health science educator, health official; b. Sioux City, Iowa, June 26, 1943; d. Thomas Carson and Gladys Irene (Stewart) Moore; m. Lester N. Wright; children: Anna, Sharon, Eric. BSN, St. Olaf Coll., 1965; MSN, UCLA, 1968; DPH, U. Mich., 1995. Project dir. USPHS Tng. Grant, St. Louis, 1972—77; coord. nursing St. Louis U., 1974—76, asst. dir. nursing, 1976—78, clin. prof., 1977—78; adminstr. Oreg. Health Div., Portland, 1978—89; sec. Wash. State Dept. Health, Olympia, 1989—93; coord. Nat. AIDS Policy, Washington, 1993—94; assoc. prof. Sch. Nursing Columbia U., 1994—; assoc. prof. Oreg. Health Scis. U. Portland, 1980—90. Chair secretarial panel on evaluation of epidemiologic rsch. activities U.S. Dept. Energy, 1989—90; mem. Presdl. Commn. on Human Imunodeficiency Virus Epidemic, 1987—88. Author (with Deloughery and Neuman): Consultation and Community Orgn., 1971; author: (with Deloughery) Political Dynamics: Impact on Nurses, 1975; author: (with Scheer) Creative Teaching in Clinical Nursing, 1976. Bd. dirs. Lusth. Family Svcs. Oreg. and S.W. Wash., 1979—84, Oreg. Psychoanalytic Found.1, 1983—87. Recipient Disting. Alumna award, St. Olaf Coll., 1979; scholar Disting. scholar, Am. Nurses Found., 1989. Fellow: Am. Acad. Nursing; mem.: Am. Soc. Pub. Adminstrn. (Adminstrn. award II 1983), N.Am. Nursing Diagnosis Assn. (treas. 1983—84), Inst. Medicine, Am. Pub. Health Assn. (exec. bd.), Assn. State and Territorial Health Ofcls. (pres. 1984—85, exec. com. 1980—87, McCormick award 1988). Office: Columbia U Sch Nursing 630 W 168th St New York NY 10032-3702 Business E-Mail: KMG24@columbia.edu.

GEBERTH, FRANCES WHITE, painter; b. Mt. Vernon, N.Y., May 9, 1925; d. Milo J. and Frances Bame White; m. William J. Geberth, June 27, 1948; children: Elizabeth, Deborah. Student, Parsons Sch. Design, 1946-48. Pub.'s asst. Moore-Robbins Pub., N.Y.C., 1943-45; display advt. Macy Newspapers, White Plains, N.Y., 1945-46; propr. Summer Gallery, Harwich Port, Mass., 1985-87, Fo'cas'le House Gallery, Harwich Port, Mass., 1987—. Illustrator: A Quest for Good Eating, 1994, To Always Persevere, 1995. Chair Arts Lottery Coun., Harwich, 1984-90; mem. Archtl. Adv. Bd., Harwich, 1990-94. Mem. Guild Harwich Artists, Harwich Hist. Soc. (mus. chair 1996-98, 2001-03, pres. 1999-2000, 2004, newsletter editor 2002—), Gen. Soc. Mayflower Descs., Creative Arts Ctr. Avocation: antique costume identification and preservation. Home and Office: Fo'cas'le House Gallery 35 Wendys Way Harwich MA 02645-2507 Office Phone: 508-432-5907. Personal E-mail: fgeberth@capecod.net.

GEBHARD, LAVERNE ELIZABETH, retired accounting educator; b. Milw., Aug. 30, 1936; d. Frank and Helen Gebhard. BS, Marquette U., 1958, MBA, 1964. CPA, cert. internal auditor, cert. cost analyst, cert. mgmt. acct. Internal auditor Fed. Res. Bank Chgo., 1958-60; gen. acct. City Products, 1960-61; tchr. bus. Milw. Pub. Schs., 1961-65; from instr. to lectr. to sr. lectr.

U. Wis., Milw., 1966-93; cons. New Berlin, Wis., 1993—. CMA exam. adminstr. ICMA-Milw. site, Montvale, N.J., 1984-97. Contbr. articles to profl. jours. Vol. advisor Milw. Hist. Soc., La Farge Learning Ctr., others. Recipient Citizen Ambassador award People to People, Inc., 1991—. Mem. Inst. Internal Auditors, Wis. Inst. CPAs (ch. bd. dirs. 1984—, mem. numerous coms., cons. 1984-86), Inst. Mgmt. Accts., Beta Gamma Sigma, Delta Pi Epsilon, Beta Alpha Psi (faculty advisor, founder). Avocations: travel, reading, tennis, continuing education, volunteer work. Home: 12685 W Bobwood Rd New Berlin WI 53151-6975 E-mail: gebhard3@netzero.com.

GECELTER, GARY RAYMOND, gastrointestinal surgeon, researcher; b. Johannesburg, S. Afica, Aug. 18, 1958; came to U.S., 1993; s. Louis and Sybil (Win) G.; m. Jacqueline Naomi Gittleson, Jan. 29, 1986; children: Ryan J., Rachel C., Amy M. MBBCh, U. Witwatersrand, Johannesburg. Intern Johannesburg Hosp., 1982, attending surgeon, 1992-93; surg. resident U. Witwatersrand, Johannesburg, 1985-90, fellow in gastroenterology, 1990-92; asst. prof. surgery SUNY, Stony Brook, 1993-98; chief gen. surgery L.I. Jewish Hosp., New Hyde Park, N.Y., 1998—. Oper. rm. dir. Stony Brook U. Hosp., 1994-98, chmn. med. exec. bd., 1998 Mem. editl. bd. S. African Jour. Surgery, 1989-90; contbr. articles to profl. jours. Lt. S. African Med. Corps, 1983-84. Fellow ACS, Coll. Surgeons; mem. Soc. Gastrointestinal Endoscopic Surgeons. Jewish. Avocations: golf, tennis, jogging, piano. Office: LI Jewish Med Ctr 270-05 70th Ave New Hyde Park NY 11040

GECHTOFF, SONIA, artist; b. Phila., Sept. 25, 1926; d. Leonid and Etya (Freedman) G.; children: Susannah Kelly, Miles Kelly. BFA, Phila. Mus. Sch. Art, 1950. Instr. painting, drawing Calif. Sch. Fine Art, 1957-58; adj. asst. prof. art NYU, 1960—70; lectr. Queens Coll., N.Y.C., 1970-74; assoc. prof. U. N.Mex., 1974-75. Artist-in-residence Skidmore Coll., summers 1988, 89, 90, Adelphi U., N.Y., 1991, 93; vis. artist Chgo. Art Inst., 1989. One-woman shows include DeYoung Mus., San Francisco, 1957, Ferus Gallery, L.A., 19157, 59, Poindexter Gallery, N.Y.C., 1959, 60, Cortella Gallery, N.Y.C., 1976, 78, Gruenebaum Gallery, N.Y.C., 1979, 80, 82, 83, 85, 87, Witkin Gallery, N.Y.C., 1984, 89, Kraushaar Gallery, N.Y.C., 1990, 92, 95, Fine Arts Gallery, San Francisco, 1991, Adelphi U., 1993, Skidmore Coll., N.Y., 1995, Harrison Mus. Art, Utah, 1996; group shows include Guggeneim Mus., N.Y.C., 1954, San Francisco Mus. Art, 1953-58, Brussels World's Fair, 1958, 1st Paris Biennale, 1959, Whitney Mus., N.Y.C., 1959. 60, Sao Paulo Biennale, 1961, Nat. Gallery Am. Art Smithsonian Instn., 1976, Mus. Modern Art, N.Y.C., 1977, Aldrich Mus. Contemporary Art, Ridgefield, Conn., 1981, Bennington Coll., Vt., 1985, Weatherspoon Gallery, Greensboro, 1987, Gruenebaum Gallery, 1987, The Butler Inst. of Am. Art: 56th Nat. Mid-Yr. Exhbn., Youngstown, Ohio, 1992, Santa Cruz (Calif.) Mus., 1993, Laguna Art Mus., Laguna Beach, Calif., 1996, San Francisco Mus. Modern Art, 1996; represented in permanent collections, San Francisco Mus. Modern Art, Guggenheim Mus., Mus. Modern Art, Met. Mus., N.Y.C., Balt. Mus. Art, Harrison Mus. Art at Utah State U., Worcester (Mass.) Art Mus., Laguna (Calif.) Art Mus.; also pvt. and corp. collections. Ford Found. fellow Tamarind Inst., L.A., 1963; recipient Purchase awards San Francisco Mus. Art, 1955-59; grantee Esther and Adolph Gottlieb Found., 1987, Mid. Atlantic NEA, 1988, Pollock-Krasner Found., 1994, Richard Florsheim Art Fund, 1994. Mem. Nat. Acad. Design. Mailing: c/o Kraushaar Galleries 724 Fifth Ave New York NY 10019 *I have, since my early twenties, always thought of myself as a painter. As the mother of two children (now adults), I was able to work on my paintings and to develop my art continuously. My life is my work.**

GECKER, JAMES M., lawyer; b. Milwaukee, Wis., July 1, 1947; BA, U. Calif., Berkeley, 1971; JD cum laude, U. Wis., 1974; MSIR, Loyola U., Chgo., 1984. Bar: Ga. 1974, Ill. 1976, Wis. 1977, Ohio 1978, US Ct. Appeals, 5th, 6th & 7th Cirs., US Ct. Appeals, Fed. Cir., US Dist. Ct., Ea. Dist. Mich., US Dist. Ct., No. Dist. Ill. Ptnr. Katten Muchin Zavis Rosenman, Chgo. Mem.: ABA. Office: Katten Muchin Zavis Rosenman 525 W Monroe St Chicago IL 60661 Office Phone: 312-902-5586. Office Fax: 312-577-8825. E-mail: james.gecker@kmzr.com.

GECKLE, DAVID ALAN, music educator, director; b. Mt. Pleasant, Pa., Mar. 18, 1969; s. Ronald and Dana Geckle; m. Leigh Ann Bowman, June 6, 1992; children: Cassandra Rae, Benjamin David, Christopher Jaison. BS in Music Edn., Ind. U., Pa., 1992. Band dir., music tchr. Serra Cath. H.S., White Oak, Pa., 1997—99, Clairton (Pa.) Edn. Ctr., 1999—. Home: 109 Layfette Cir Irwin PA 15642 Office: Clairton Edn Ctr 501 Waddell Ave Clairton PA 15025

GECKLE, GEORGE LEO, III, language educator; b. Danbury, Conn., Dec. 2, 1939; s. George Leo and Dorothy Marion (Hill) G.; m. Justine Virginia Carroll, Aug. 19, 1961 (dec. Nov. 26, 2002); children: George, Richard. AB, Middlebury Coll., 1961; MA, U. Va., 1962, PhD, 1965. Asst. prof. English U. Wis., Madison, 1965-68, U. S.C., Columbia, 1968-70, assoc. prof. English, 1970-74; prof. English U S.C., Columbia, 1974—2002; dir. honors program U. S.C., Columbia, 1970-73, dir. English grad. studies, 1974-76, 77-78, chmn. English dept., 1978-87. Author: John Marston's Drama, 1980, Tamburlaine and Edward II: Text and Performance, 1988; editor: Twentieth Century Interpretations of Measure for Measure, 1970, Measure for Measure, Shakespeare: The Critical Tradition, 2001. Fulbright grantee sr. prof. category U. Bamberg, Fed. Republic Germany, 1984-85; recipient 1st Jo Ann Boydston Essay prize Assn. for Documentary Editing, 1995. Mem. MLA, South Atlantic MLA, Shakespeare Assn. Am., Southeastern Renaissance Conf. (pres. 1985-86). Home: 5925 Timle Ln Columbia SC 29206-1629 Office: U South Carolina Dept English Humanities Bldg Columbia SC 29208-0001

GECKLE, ROBERT ALAN, manufacturing executive; b. Newtown, Conn., July 12, 1944; s. George Leo and Dorothy Marion (Hill) G.; m. Katherine Bernarda Landry, July 22, 1967; children: Sarah Nicole, Robert Alan Jr. BA in Econs., Middlebury Coll., 1967; MBA in Mktg., U. Pa., 1969. Sales mgr. Branson Cleaning Equipment Co., Stamford, Conn., 1969-71, product mgr. Shelton, Conn., 1971-73, dir. mktg., 1973-75, gen. mgr., 1975-78, pres., 1978-86, Branson Ultrasonics Corp., Danbury, Conn., 1987-94; pres., CEO Scan-Code, Inc., Rocky Hill, Conn., 1994-97; pres. Fluid and Power Systems Group, Textron, Providence, 1997—2002; adv. dir. Investcorp Internat., 2002—. Bd. dirs. Neptune Techs. Group, SI Corp., Playpower Corp. Contbr. articles on ultrasonics to profl. jours.; patentee in field. Bd. dirs. Danbury Health Systems, 1988—, mem. fin. com.; mem. Pres.'s Club, 1988—. Mem. Conn. Bus. Industry Assn. (bd. dirs. 1991, exec. com., 1992), Ridgewood Country Club, Danbury C. of C. Republican. Roman Catholic. Avocations: golf, gardening. Office: Investcorp Internat 280 Park Ave New York NY 10017

GECKLE, TIMOTHY J., lawyer; b. 1952; m. Bernadette Geckle; children: Caroline, Noelle. BA in religion, Catholic U. Am., 1974, MA in religion, 1979; JD, U. San Francisco, 1984. Bar: 1985. Lawyer Piper & Marbury, 1985—91; corp. counsel The Ryland Group, Calabasas, Calif., 1991-95, v.p., dep. gen. counsel, 1995-97, v.p., corp. counsel, sec., 1997, sr. v.p., gen. counsel, sec., 1997—. Office: The Ryland Group Inc 24025 Pk Sorrento Ste 400 Calabasas CA 91302

GECKLER, RICHARD DELPH, retired metal products executive; b. Toledo, Nov. 4, 1918; s. Maurice T. and Edith (Payne) G.; m. Elaine Mary Campbell, June 27, 1965; 1 child, Elaine Demian; 1 child by previous marriage, Carole Faye (Mrs. Gene Hendrix). AB, DePauw U., 1939. Chem. engr. Standard Oil Co., Ind., 1939-45; with Aerojet-Gen. Corp., Calif., 1945-68, v.p., mgr. solid rocket plant, Sacramento, 1956-63, corp. v.p., El Monte, 1963-68; chmn. bd., chief exec. Aerojet Delft Corp., 1968-69; pres. Marquardt Co., 1972-73, Pitter Metal Products, Inc., 1972-89, J.L. Mallard Co., 1972-89, Geckler Industries, Inc., 1972—2003; ret., 2003. Asst. dir. strategic weapons Office Sec. Def., 1964-66 Recipient Meritorious Pub. Service citation Navy Dept., 1961 Fellow Am. Inst. Aeros. and Astronautics; mem. Am. Chem. Soc., Am. Math. Soc., Am. Assn. of Artificial Intelligence, The Athenaeum, Phi Beta Kappa. Home: 7450 Olivetas Ave # C245 La Jolla CA 92037-4902 E-mail: pgeckler@mac.com.

GECZI, PAUL C., financial consultant, bank executive; MBA in Internat. Bis. and Fin., Prague Sch. Econ., Czech Republic; M in Comml. Banking with distinction, So. Meth. U., Dallas, Tex. Dept. mgr. to v.p. and loan officer Republic Nat. Bank, Dallas, 1973—80; v.p. and dept. mgr. MBank, 1981—85; v.p. and sr. credit officer Bank of Dallas, 1985—87; v.p. and dir. nat. accounts EDS Corp., 1987—88; v.p. and southwestern rep. Security Pacific Trade Finance Corp., N.Y.C., 1988—99; mmg. agt. FDIC/Resolution Trust Co., Dallas, 1989—90; chief rep. and mgr. Komercni Banka, N.Y.C., 1994—2000; self-employed cons., 1991—94, 2000—. Instr. Am. Inst. Banking, 1974—79, Southwestern Grad. Sch. Banking, 1980—85, 1991—94, So. Meth. U., Dallas, Grad. Sch. Banking, Moscow, 1995, U. Pa., Phila., 1996—2000, European Inst., Washington, 1998; CEO Victoria Savings of San Antonio, 1989—90. Address: 9727 Trevor Dr Dallas TX 75243-2315

GEDA, YONAS ENDALE, psychiatrist, researcher; s. Endale Geda Wakenie and Almaz Genemie Korbie; m. Tigist W. Tsegaye, Oct. 7, 1994; children: Ezra, Abigail. MD, Haile Selassie/Addis Ababa U., Ethiopia, 1991. Diplomate Am. Bd. Neurology and Psychiatry. Gen. med. practitioner Armed Forces Gen. Hosp., Addis Ababa, 1991—93; intern in internal medicine Wright State U., Dayton, Ohio, 1995—96; resident in psychiatry Mayo Clinic, Rochester, Minn., 1996—2000, fellow in behavioral neurology, 2000—01, neuropsychiatrist, 2001—. Recipient merit award, Laughlin Found., 1999, Mayo Brothers Dist. Fellowship Award. Ethiopian Orthodox Christian. Office: Mayo Clinic 200 1st St SW Rochester MN 55905 Business E-Mail: geda.yonas@mayo.edu.

GEDDES, BARBARA SHERYL, communications executive, consultant; b. Poughkeepsie, NY, May 27, 1944; d. Samuel Pierson and Dorothy Charlotte (Graham) Brush; m. James Morrow Geddes, Feb. 24, 1968 (div. Dec. 1980); 1 child, Elisabeth. BA, Skidmore Coll., 1968. Project leader Four-Phase Systems, Cupertino, Calif., 1976—77, Fairchild Co., San Jose, Calif., 1979—80; mgr. tech. publs. Mohawk Data Scis., Los Gatos, Calif., 1977—79; project mgr. Advanced Micro Computers, Santa Clara, Calif., 1980—81; mgr. tech. publs. Sytek Inc., Mountain View, Calif., 1981—83; v.p. comms. sys. Strategic Inc., Cupertino, 1983—86; pres., mng. ptnr. Computer and Telecomms. Profl. Svcs., Mountain View, Calif., 1986—89; v.p. corp. mktg., sec. First Pacific Networks, Sunnyvale, Calif., 1988—94; pres. Auration, Inc., Palo Alto, 1994—; v.p. mktg., corp. sec. Tachyon Semiconductor Corp., San Jose, 1999—. Cons. H-P, Varian, Aydin Energy, Chemelex, also others, 1972—; v.p. Conf. Recorders, Santa Clara, 1975—77; advisor Tele-PC, Morgan Hill, Calif., 1983—88. Editor: Mathematics/Science Library, 7 vols., 1971; contbr. numerous articles to profl. jours. Advisor Los Altos Hills Planning Commn., Calif., 1978—79; mem. Santa Clara County Adoptions Adv. Bd., 1971—73, Las Cumbres Archtl. Control Commn., Los Gatos, 1983. Named N.Y. State Regents merit scholar, 1962. Mem.: Women in Comms. (pres. San Jose 1983—84), Bus. and Profl. Advt. Assn., Nat. Soc. for Performance and Instrn., Assn. for Computing Machinery (editor 1970—72). Democrat. Home: 10072 Senate Way Cupertino CA 95014-5710 Personal E-mail: sherry@netmagic.net.

GEDDES, LESLIE ALEXANDER, engineering educator, forensic engineer, physiologist; b. Scotland, May 24, 1921; s. Alexander and Helen (Humphrey) G.; m. Irene P. Bloomer; 1 child, James Alexander; m. La Nelle E. Nerger, Aug. 3, 1962. BEE, MEngring., ScD (hon.), McGill U.; PhD in Physiology, Baylor U. Med. Coll. Demonstrator in elec. engring. McGill U., 1945, research asst. dept. neurology, 1945-52; cons. elec. engring. to various indsl. firms Que., Can.; biophysicist dept. physiology Baylor Med. Coll., Houston, asst. prof. physiology, 1956-61, assoc. prof., 1961-65, prof., 1965-74; dir. Lab. of Biophysics, Tex. Inst. Rehab. and Research, Houston, 1961-65; prof. physiology Coll. Vet. Medicine, Tex. A. and M. U., College Station, 1965-74, prof. biomed. engring., 1969-74; Showalter Disting. prof. bioengring. and elec. engring. Purdue U., West Lafayette, Ind., 1974-91, Showalter Disting. prof. emeritus, 1991—. Cons. NASA Manned Spacecraft Center, Houston, 1962-64, USAF, Sch. Aerospace Medicine, Brooks AFB, 1958-65; expert witness, 1981—. Author: 22 books; cons. editor: Med. and Biol. Engring., 1969—, Med. Research Engring., 1964-74, Med. Electronics and Data, 1969—; mem. editorial bd.; Jour. Electrocardiology, 1968—, med. instr., 1974—; contbr. over 800 articles to bioengring. Mem. Soc. Free Space Floaters, 1961. With Can. Army OTC. Recipient Ctrl. Ind. Corp. award for Commercialization, 2003—04, Corp. Vitae award, Am. Heart Assn., 2005. Fellow: IEEE (Lee De Forest award 2001, Leadership award, Edison gold medal, IEEE 3d Millennium award, World of Difference award), AAAS (Am. Heart Vital award 2005), Royal Soc. Medicine, Am. Inst. for Med. and Biol. Engring., Am. Coll. Cardiology, Nat. Acad. Forensic Engrs., Australasian Coll. Physicists in Biology and Medicine; mem.: NAE, NSPE, Am. Physiol. Soc., Assn. for Advancement Med. Instrumentation (Leadership award), Biomed. Engring. Soc., Tex. Soc. Profl. Engrs., Radio Club Am., Phi Zeta, Tau Beta Pi, Sigma Xi. Achievements include patents for Holder 23 U.S. patents. Home: 400 N River Rd Apt 701 West Lafayette IN 47906-3131 Office: Purdue U POTR Bldg West Lafayette IN 47907-2022 Office Phone: 765-494-2995. Business E-Mail: geddes@ecn.purdue.edu.

GEDDES, ROBERT, architect, educator; b. Phila., Dec. 7, 1923; s. Louis J. and Kay (Malmed) G.; m. Evelyn Basse, June 15, 1947; children: David, Ann. Student, Yale U., 1941-46; M.Arch., Harvard U., 1950; LHD, N.J. Inst. Tech., 1998, U. N.Y., 1999. Sr. ptnr. Geddes-Brecher Qualls Cunningham (architects), Phila., 1954-89, Princeton, 1965-89; pvt. practice Robert Geddes, Arch., Princeton and N.Y.C., 1990-99; prof. architecture and civic design U. Pa., 1951-65; prof. architecture, dean Sch. Architecture Princeton U., 1965-82, William Kenan prof., 1968-89; Henry Luce prof. architecture, urbanism and history NYU, 1989-98; univ. lectr. U. London, 1972-98; pvt. practice Geddes Archs., 2000—. Dir. Manville Corp., Butler Mfg. Co.; chmn. adv. bd. design Redevel. Authority Phila., 1959-66; bd. dirs. Citizens Council City Planning, Phila., 1961-63, Urban America, Inc.; cons. Regional Plan Assn., N.Y.; advisor on architecture and urban design, U.S. Delegation to UN, Habitat II Conf., Istanbul, 1996; founder, co-chmn. Princeton Future Inc., 2000—. Contbr. articles on architecture to Ency. Brit., 1974-79; editor Principles and Precedents, Process Architecture jour., 1985; prin. works include Moore Sch. Elec. Engring, U. Pa., 1958, Police Hdqrs, Phila., 1962, resident halls U. Del., 1966, U. Pa., 1967, housing projects, Westchester, Pa., also, Phila. and, Trenton, 1966-77, U. Pa. Med. Sch. and Hosp., 1978-84, dining hall and acad. bldg., Sch. Natural Scis., 2001, Inst. for Advanced Study, Princeton, 1971, humanities and social scis. bldg., So. Ill. U., Carbondale, 1968-74, Stockton State Coll, 1971-75, Corning (N.Y.) Downtown Renewal, 1975; master plan and design Liberty State Park, N.J., 1975-77, lab. bldgs., Mobil Corp., 1981, J. B. Speed Art Mus., Louisville, 1983; Muhlenberg Coll. Library, 1986, Center City plan, Phila., 1985-87, Hosp. U. Pa., 1987, Pub. Safety Bldg., White Plains, N.Y., 1985—, Franklin Inst., Phila., 1987-90, Stern Sch. Bus. NYU, 1987-93, Alexanderpolder urban design, Rotterdam, 1993; co-dir. Crosstown 116 Upper Manhattan HUD U. Partnership, 1997; editor: Cities in Our Future, 1997. Fellow, N.Y. Inst. for the Humanities, 1989—, Appleton Traveling fellow Harvard U., 1950-51; recipient Design awards Progressive Architecture, First Design award, 1958; 2d prize Nat. Opera House, Sydney, Australia, 1958; first prize Internat. Town Planning Competition for Expansion of Vienna, Austria, 1971, award for Excellence in Archtl. Edn. ACSA-AIA, 1984. Fellow for design AIA (dir. edn. research project 1965-67, pres. N.Y. chpt. 1997, Nat. First Honor award 1960, 77, Archtl. Firm award 1979, Gold medals Phila. chpt., Design medals Pa. Soc., medals N.J. Soc., pres. N.Y. chpt. 1997); mem. Harvard Grad. Sch. Design Alumni Assn. (past pres.). E-mail: rgeddes@earthlink.net.*

GEDELA, SATYANARAYANA, pediatrician, neurologist; s. Satyamnaidu and Narayanamma Gedela; m. Sailatha Gullapalli, Aug. 15, 1990; children: Kaushik, Sravya. Pre-univ. course, Andhra U., Visakhapatnam, India, 1981—83; MB BChir, Andhra U., 1990; MD in Pediats., U. Health Scis., 1994. Completion of cert. specialist tng. Royal Coll. of Pediat. and Child Health U.K., bd. cert. pediats. Am. Bd. of Pediats. Attending pediatrician SagaraDurga Hosp., Visakhapatnam, 1994—95; house staff mem. Wigan and Billinge Royal Infirmary, Wigan, England, 1995—97; specialist registrar North West Deanery, Manchester, England, 1997—2001; house staff mem. Brookdale U. Hosp., N.Y.C., 2001—03; child neurology fellow Childrens Hosp. of Pitts., 2003—. Named Best Outgoing Pediat. Resident, Pediat. Emergency Dept., 2003. Mem.: Indian Acad. of Pediats. (assoc.), Royal Coll. of Physicians of London (assoc.), Am. Acad. of Pediats. (assoc.), Am. Acad. of Neurology (assoc. neurology resident scholarship 2005), Child Neurology Soc. (assoc.). Office: Childrens Hosp Pitts 5th Ave Pittsburgh PA 15213 Office Phone: 412-692-6207. Personal E-mail: satyanarayana.gedela@chp.edu.

GEDEON, LUCINDA HEYEL, museum director; b. Port Chester, N.Y., Oct. 13, 1947; d. Philip H. and Isabel (Oldham) H.; m. Francis A. Sprout, Feb. 8, 1987. BA, Calif. State U., Long Beach, 1978; MA, UCLA, 1981, PhD, 1990. Asst. curator Grunwald Ctr. UCLA, 1978-81, asst. dir. Grunwald Ctr., 1981-83, acting dir. Grunwald Ctr., 1983-85; chief curator Ariz. State U. Art Mus., Tempe, 1985-91; dir. Neuberger Mus. SUNY, Purchase, 1991—2004, Vero Beach Mus. of Art, Fla., 2004—. Author: (exhbn. catalogues) Tamarind: Los Angeles to Albuquerque, 1985, Fiber Concepts, 1989 (book) The Art of Leonard Lehrer, 1986; gen. editor: Melvin Edwards Sculpture: A Thirty Year Retrospective, 1993, Shared Beginnings Separate Passages: A Retrospective of the Work of Carol Anthony and Elaine Anthony, 1996, June Wayne; A Retrospective, 1997, Elizabeth Catlett Sculpture: A Fifty-Year Retrospective, 1998, Marisol, 2001, Toshiko Takaezu, 2001, Grace Hartigan, 2001; contbr. articles to profl. jours. Chairperson Tempe Mcpl. Arts Commn., 1989-90; bd. dirs. Balboa Art Conservation Ctr., San Diego, 1986-91, ArtTable, N.Y., 1995-98, Westchester Arts Coun., 1998-2004. Recipient Individual Arts award Westchester Arts Coun., 2002, Chancellor's award Excellence, SUNY, 2002; Edward A. Dickson History of Art fellow UCLA, 1984, Afro-Am. Studies fellow, 1984. Mem. Am. Assn. Mus., Assn. Art Mus. Dirs. Office: Vero Beach Mus Art 3001 Riverside Pk Dr Vero Beach FL 32963 Office Phone: 772-231-0707 ext. 113. Business E-Mail: lgedeone@vbmuseum.org.

GEDEVANISHVILI, SHALVA, materials scientist, researcher; b. Tbilisi, Georgia, Feb. 15, 1964; s. Vsevolod and Eliso Gedevanishvili; m. Lela Kometiani, Feb. 28, 1993; children: Alexander, Anna. BS, Tbilisi Tech. U., 1986; PhD in Metall. Engring., Inst. Metallurgy, Tbilisi, 1990. Rsch. scientist Inst. Metallurgy, Tbilisi, 1990—93; post doctoral rschr. U. Calif., Davis, 1993—96; rsch. assoc. Pa. State U., State College, 1996—99, Philip Moris USA, Richmond, Va., 1999—2001; rsch. scientist Chrysalis Techs. Inc., Richmond, Va., 2001—02, Philip Morris USA, Richmond, Va., 2002—. Contbr. articles to profl. jours. Recipient Innovations in Real Materials award, Internat. Union Materials Rsch. Socs., 1998, 1st pl., Internat. Metallographic Soc., 2000. Mem.: Am. Soc. Metals Internat., Materials Rsch. Soc., Am. Ceramic Soc. Achievements include four Russian patents, three US patent, one US patents pending; research in materials synthesis, development of inorganic advanced materials. Avocations: photography, travel.

GEDJEYAN, HOVANNES JOHN, real estate broker; b. Yerevan, Armenia, June 20, 1956; arrived in U.S., 1976; s. Minas Mike and Zvart Joyce Gedjeyan; m. Gaiane D. Astvatsatrian, Apr. 22, 1983; children: Minas Mike, Zvart Joyce. Import/export The Milinger Co., Valencia, Calif., 1989—; life ins. broker Dept. Ins., Glendale, Calif., 1986—, Santa Monica, 1987—; real estate broker Dept. Real Estate, Glendale, 1988—. Mem.: Awesome A Shrine Club (1st v.p.), Al Malaikah Temple (nobel), Scottish Rite, Masons. Republican. Avocations: painting, travel, hunting, swimming. Office: Magic Realty 409 S Glendale Ave #200 Glendale CA 91205

GEDWED, WILLIAM J., insurance company executive; Bd. dir. UICI, 2000—, pres., CEO, 2003—. Chmn. The MEGA Life and Health Insurance Co, Mid-West Nat. Life Insurance Co. of Tenn.; dir. NMC Holdings, Inc. Office: c/o UICI 9151 Grapevine Hwy North Richland Hills TX 76180*

GEE, CHUCK YIM, dean; b. San Francisco, Aug. 28, 1933; s. Don Yow Elsie (Lee) G. AA, City Coll. of San Francisco, 1953; BSBA, U. Denver, 1957; MA, Mich. State U., 1958; PhD (hon.), China Acad. Chinese Cultural U., 1972; D of Pub. Svc. (hon.), U. Denver, 1991. Assoc. dir. Sch. of Hotel and Restaurant Adminstrn. U. Denver, 1958-68; cons. East West Ctr., Honolulu, 1968-74; assoc. dean and prof. Sch. of Travel Industry Mgmt. U. Hawaii, 1968-75, dean and prof. Sch. Travel Industry Mgmt., 1976-99, interim dean Coll. Bus. Adminstrn., 1998-99, dean emeritus, 2000—. Vis. prof. Sch Bus. and Commerce, Oreg. State U., 1975; hon. prof. Nankai U., Tianjin, China, 1987—, Shanghai Inst. Tourism, 1994-2003, Dept. Tourism Huaqiao U., Xiamen, China, 1995—, Shanghai Normal U., 2004—; cons. Internat. Sci. and Tech. Inst., Washington, 1986-90, cons. on tourism development, Jiaojuo, Henan Province, Xiamen City, Fujian Province, China, 2004-; trustee Pacific Asia Travel Assn. Found., San Francisco; chmn. Govs. Tourism Tng. Coun., Honolulu, 1989-92, chmn., 1992-96, chmn. industry coun. PATA, 1994-96, PATA Human Resource Devel. Coun., 1996-99, chmn. PATA Coun. on Ednl. Devel. and Certification, 2000-02; mem. State Workforce Devel. Coun., 1997-98, Pacific Asia Travel Assn. Human Resource Devel. Coun., 1996-98; acad. Inst. Cert. Travel Agts., Wellesley, Mass., 1989—; mem. Coun. on Hotel, Restaurant Edn., 1967-2000, Honolulu Commn. on Fgn. Rels., 1979-98; mem. Pacific Asian Affairs Coun.; sr. acad. adv. China Tourism Assn. Cons., Inc., 1993—; adv. World Tourism Orgn. Internat. Tourism Edn. and Tng. Ctr., 1991-2000; external examiner sch. accountancy and bus. Nanyang Tech. U., Singapore, 1996-98; bd. dirs. ProjectonNet.com. Author: Resort Devel. and Mgmt., 1988, 2d edit., The Story of PATA, 2d edit., co-editor, 2001; co-author: The Travel Industry, 1988, 3d edit., 1997, Profl. Travel Agency Mgmt., 1990, Internat. Hotels: Devel. and Mgmt., 1994; editor: Internat. Tourism: A Global Perspective, 1997; founding dir., Hong Kong, China, Hawaii Chamber of Commerce, 1998-; mem. adv. bd. Asian Hotelier mag., 1997-99, Get2Hawaii.com, 2001-04. Bd. dirs. Hawaii Visitors Bur., 1993-95, Kaukini Med. Ctr., Honolulu, 1986-95, KMC, 1996-2005, Travel and Tourism Adv. Bd., U.S. Dept. Commerce, Washington, 1982-90, Pacific Rim Found., Honolulu, 1987-93, vice-chmn. Tourism Policy Adv. Coun., Dept. Bus. and Econ. Devel., Honolulu, 1978-92; chmn. Kaukini Geriat. Care, Inc., bd. dirs., 1992-95; trustee Pata Found., 1984-95, Kuakini Health System, 1988-2003, 2005—; consulting com. Beijing Inst. Tourism, 1992—; v.p. Hawaii Vision 2020, 1992-93; mem. Mayor's Task Force on Waikiki Master Plan, 1992-93; devel. bd. Miss Hawaii Scholarship Pageant, 1993-; workforce devel. coun. Hawaii Dept. of Labor and Indsl. Rels., 1996-98; bd. dirs., Cmty. Enterprises, Hawaii Dept. Edn., 1997—. Served with U.S. Army, 1953-55. Named State Mgr. of Yr., State of Hawaii, 1995; named one of 100 Who Made a Difference in Hawaii during 20th Century, Star Bull., 1999; recipient NOAH award, Acad. Tourism Orgns., 1987, Gov.'s Proclamation honors, State of Hawaii, 1998, 1999, 2003, Dean Chuck Yim Gee Excellencein Film Achievements award, 2004; grantee Chuck Yim Gee-Hawaii Scholarship Endowment established in his honor, Nat. Tourism Found., 2001; Chuck Yim Gee Tech. Learning Ctr. at U. Hawaii named in his honor, 2003. Mem. Acad. for Study of Tourism (emeritus), Pacific Asia Travel Assn. (hon. life Hawaii chpt., bd. dirs. 1993-96, chmn. industry coun. 1994-96, 50th Anniversary Hall of Honors, 2001, Grand award 1991, Life award 1990, Presdl. award 1986), Travel Industry Am. (Travel Industry Hall of Leaders award 1988), China Tourism Assn. (award of excellence 1992), China-Hawaii C. of C. (founding dir. 1998), Hong Kong-China-Hawaii C. of C. (bd. dirs. 1999—), Golden Key. Office: U Hawaii Sch Travel Industry Mgmt 2560 Campus Rd Honolulu HI 96822-2217 Office Phone: 808-956-8148. Business E-Mail: cgee@hawaii.edu.

GEE, DAVID E., academic administrator; BS, Muskingum Coll., 1966; MA, U. Bridgeport, 1974, Columbia U., 1969, EdD, 1988. Supt. Queensbury (N.Y.) Union Free Sch. Dist., Western Suffolk Bd. Coop. Ednl. Svcs., Dix Hills, NY, 1998—2004; asst. prof. ednl. leadership SUNY, New Paltz, NY, 2004—. Exec. com. liaison Leadership Adv. Com., Suburban Schs. Adv. Com.; mem. Am. Assn. Sch. Adminstrs./N.Y. State Resolutions Com. Mem.: N.Y. State Coun. Sch. Supts. (pres. 1999—2000), Am. Assn. Sch. Adminstrs. (pres. 2005—06, presenter, presider nat. confs., chair fin. com., mem. governance com., mem. new bldg. com., past chair suburban schs. adv. com., mem. exec. dir.'s nat. adv coun., mem. blue ribbon evaluation task force, mem. women administrators adv. com., leadership adv. com.). Mailing: Am Assn Sch Adminstr 801 N Quincy St Ste 7000 Arlington VA 22203-1730 Office Phone: 703-528-0700. Office Fax: 703-841-1543.

GEE, ELWOOD GORDON, academic administrator; b. Vernal, Utah, Feb. 2, 1944; s. Elwood A. and Vera (Showalter) Gee; m. Elizabeth Dutson, Aug. 26, 1968 (dec. Dec. 1991); 1 child, Rebekah; m. Constance Bumgarner, Nov. 26, 1994. BA, U. Utah, 1968; JD, Columbia U., 1971, EdD, 1972. Asst. dean U. Utah, Salt Lake City, 1973—74; jud. fellow U.S. Supreme Ct., Washington, 1974—75; assoc. dean Brigham Young U., Provo, Utah, 1975—79; dean W.Va. U., Morgantown, 1979—81, pres., 1981—85, U. Colo., 1985—90, Ohio State U., Columbus, 1990—97, Brown U., Providence, 1998—2000; chancellor Vanderbilt U., Nashville, 2000—. Bd. dirs. Nabisco, Inc., Hasbro, The Limited, Dollar Gen. Corp., Massey Energy Corp., Gaylord Entertainment Co., Jason Found., Nat. Hospice Found., Kresge Found.; mem. Pres. Coun. for Imagining Am., Christopher Isherwood Found., Bus.-Higher Edn. Forum. Author: Education Law and Public Schools, 1975, Law and Public Education, 1980, Violence, Values and Justice in American Education, 1982, Fair Employment Practice, 1982. Recipient Good Guy award, Nashville Women's Polit. Caucus, 2004; fellow, W.K. Kellogg, 1971—72, Mellon fellow, 1977—78. Mem.: ABA, Adminstrv. Conf. U.S., Phi Kappa Phi, Phi Delta Kappa. Mem. Lds Ch. Office: Vanderbilt U Chancellors Office 211 Kirkland Hall Nashville TN 37240 E-mail: gordon.gee@vanderbilt.edu.*

GEE, JAY EDWARD, microbiologist, researcher; s. Jimmy and Louise Gee. BS, Miss. State U., Starkville, 1987; PhD, U. Ala., Birmingham, 1992. Rsch. assoc. Baylor Coll. of Medicine, Houston, 1992—95; rsch. fellow Institut de Génétique Moléculaire, Montpellier, France, 1996—97; tchr. Webb (Miss.) Twp. H.S., 1998—2000; master instr. New Horizons Computer Learning Ctr., Houston, 2000—02; rsch. biologist Ctrs. Disease Control & Prevention, Atlanta, 2002—. Contbr. scientific papers to profl. jours. Fellow, Nat. Agy. AIDS Rsch., France, 1996—97. Mem.: Am. Soc. Microbiology, Toastmasters (v.p. edn. (Dogwood chpt.) 2004, sec. dist. 56 2001—02). Achievements include research in differentiation of Burkholderia mallei and B. pseudomallei based upon 16S rRNA gene sequence. Office: Ctrs Disease Control & Prevention MS D11 1600 Clifton Rd NE Atlanta GA 30333 Office Phone: 404-639-4936.

GEE, ROBERT LEROY, agriculturist, dairy farmer; b. Moorhead, Minn., May 25, 1926; s. Milton William and Hertha Elizabeth (Paschke) G.; m. Mae Valentine Erickson, June 18, 1953 BS in Agronomy, N.D. State U., 1951, postgrad., 1955, Colo. A&M U., 1954. Farm labor controller Minn. Extension Service, Clay County, 1944-45, county 4-H agt., 1951-57; rural mail carrier U.S. Postal Service, Moorhead, Minn., 1946-47; breeder registered shorthorn cattle and registered southdown sheep Moorhead, Minn., 1950-63; owner, operator Gee Dairy Farm (Oak Grove Farm), Moorhead, Minn., 1957—. Asst. prof. status U. Minn., 1951-57; bd. dirs. Red River Valley Devel. Assn., Crookston, Minn., v.p., 1992—; treas. Red River Milk Producers Pool, Minn., ND, 1968-78; chmn. bd. Cass Clay Creamery Inc., Fargo, ND, 1982-85, 92-95, v.p., 1990-91; mem. Nat. Dairy Promotion Bd., Washington, 1984-88. Treas. Oakport Twp., 1974-82, supr., 1986-2002, v.p., 1987-2002; mem. Clay County Planning and Zoning Commn., 1991-2000, vice chmn., 1992-96, chmn., 1996-2000; mem. Clay County Bd. Adjustment, 1995-2000, chmn., 1996-2000. With USN, 1945-46. Recipient Grand Champion Farm Flock award Man. Expn., 1960, Clay County's Outstanding Agriculturist award, 1996; named Clay County King Agassiz, Red River Valley Winter Shows, 1966, Grand Champion forage exhibit Red River Valley Winter Shows, 1979, 82; co-recipient Clay County Dairy Farm Family of Yr. award Red River Valley Dairymen's Assn., 1979. Mem. Minn. Milk Producers Assn. (bd. dirs. 1977-88, 93-97, sec. 1972-78, treas. 1977-87), Minn. Assn. Coops. (bd. dirs. 1984-96), State Coop. Assn. (dairy council 1975-96), Am. Farm Bur. Fedn., Nat. Farmers Union, Kragnes Farmers Elevator Assn., Red River Valley Livestock Assn., Am. Shorthorn Breeders Assn., Am. Southdown Breeders Assn., Holstein-Friesian Assn. Am. Republican. Mem. United Ch. of Christ. Club: Agassiz (v.p. 1979-81, pres. 1981-82) (Moorhead) Avocations: hunting, fishing, skiing. Home and Office: 8595 2nd St N Moorhead MN 56560-7103

GEE, ROBERT NEIL, law librarian; b. Miami, Okla., June 22, 1956; s. Robert Sanford and Nancy Ann (Neil) G. AA, Tulsa Jr. Coll., 1976; BA, U. Okla., 1978, JD, 1981; LLM, George Washington U., 1984. Bar: Okla. 1981, U.S. Suprem Ct. 1986, D.C. 1989. Legal reference specialist Library of Congress, Washington, 1984-94; chief law libr. pub. svcs. Law Libr. of Congress, Washington, 1994—. Mem. ABA (recipient Silver Key cert. 1981), Fed. Bar Assn., Am. Assn. Law Librs., Okla. Bar Assn., Am. Judicature Soc., D.C. Bar Assn., Phi Delta Phi. Avocations: reading, travel, current events.

GEE, SHARON LYNN, funeral director, educator; b. Berea, Ohio, Jan. 11, 1963; d. Donald Edward Gee and Janet Lee Floyd. Cert. in mortuary sci., Wayne State U., 1986, BS Psychology, 1987. Mortuary sci. lic. Mich., Nat. Bd. Cert. Funeral Dir. Mgr., funeral dir. Pixley Funeral Home, Keego Harbor, Mich., 1996—; lectr. instr. dept. mortuary sci. Wayne State U., Detroit, 1996—2003, asst. prof. embalming, 2003—. Recipient Residential Beautification award, City of Royal Oak, Mich., 1993. Mem.: West Bloomfield C. of C., Tri City Bus. Assn., Mich. Embalmers Soc. (pres. 2000—), Mich. Funeral Dirs. Assn., Nat. Funeral Dirs. Assn. (pursuit of excellence achievement award 1997—), Optimist Internat., Keego Harbor Chpt. (Keego Harbor chpt.), A-Dock Sailing Club. Avocations: sailing, circa 1910 home renovation and restoration. Office: Pixley Funeral Home Godhardt-Tomlinson Chapel 2904 Orchard Lake Rd Keego Harbor MI 48320 Business E-Mail: ad7158@wayne.edu.

GEEKER, NICHOLAS PETER, lawyer, judge; b. Pensacola, Fla., Dec. 15, 1944; BA in English, La. Poly. Inst., 1966; JD, Fla. State U., 1969. Bar: Fla. 1969, U.S. Dist. Ct. 1970, US. Supreme Ct., 1980. Assoc. firm Merritt & Jackson, Pensacola, 1969; law clk. U.S. Dist. Judge D.L. Middlebrooks, Tallahassee, 1970-73; asst. state atty. Fla. 1st Jud. Circuit, 1973; asst. U.S. atty. No. Dist. Fla., 1973-76, U.S. atty., 1976-82; sole practice Pensacola, Fla., 1982-85; circuit judge Fla. 1st Jud. Circuit, 1985—. Mem. Fed.-State Joint Com. on Law Enforcement. Mem. Fla. Bar Assn., Fla. Trial Lawyers Assn. (editor Newsletter 1975), Phi Delta Phi. Office: 190 Government St Pensacola FL 32501-5773 Office Phone: 850-595-4439.

GEELAN, JOHN, lawyer; BA, U. Notre Dame, 1986; JD cum laude, Am. U., 1990. Bar: NY 1991. Law clerk to Hon. A. Andrew Hauk US Dist. Ct., Ctrl. Dist. Calif., 1990—91; ptnr. Employment & Labor Law Group Kaye Scholer LLP, NYC. Recipient Thurgood Marshall Award. Mem.: Assn. Bar of City NY. Office: Kaye Scholer LLP 425 Park Ave New York NY 10022 Office Phone: 212-836-8121. E-mail: jgeelan@kayescholer.com.

GEENTIENS, GASTON PETRUS, JR., former construction management consultant company executive; b. Garfield, N.J., Apr. 6, 1935; s. Gaston Petrus and Margaret (Piros) G.; m. Barbara Ann Chamberlin, Oct. 14, 1960; children: Mercedes Frith, Faith Piros. BSCE, The Citadel, 1956. Registered profl. engr., 15 states. Plant engr. Western Elec. Co., Inc., Kearny, N.J., 1956-58, owner's rep. N.Y.C., 1960-64; v.p. Gentyne Motors, Inc., Passaic, N.J., 1958-60; project engr. Ethyl Corp., Baton Rouge, La., 1964-65; mgr. Timothy McCarthy Constrn. Co., Atlanta, 1965; asst. to v.p. A.R. Abrams, Inc. and Columbia Engring., Inc., Atlanta, 1965-66; supr. engring. and constn. Litton Industries, N.Y.C., 1966-71; pres. G.P. Geentiens Jr., Inc., Charleston, S.C., 1971-82; gen. ptnr. Engineered Enterprises Co., Charleston, 1973-76; dir. Cayman Broadcasting Assocs., Cayman Islands, B.W.I., 1977-82. Mem. Ramapo (N.Y.) Republican Com., 1961-64. Served to 1st lt. C.E., AUS, 1956-58. Mem. ASCE, Tau Beta Pi. Home: 1219 Pembrooke Dr Charleston SC 29407-7748

GEER, DEREK HUNTER, electrical engineer, photographer; b. Albuquerque, Dec. 17, 1957; s. Hunter Lee Geer and Mary Louise (Shambaugh) Maes; m. Jennifer Dovre Schilling, May 25, 1985. BSEE, U. N. Mex., 1985. Electronics engineer Hewlett Packard, San Diego, 1986-91, 94-98, VORAD Safety Sys., San Diego, 1992-93. Pres. Citizens Commn. on Human Rights, San Diego, 1994; tutor Literacy Campaign, San Diego, 1995. Recipient Internat. Youth Achievement award Internat. Biographical Ctr., Cambridge, England, 1985; mem. design team of first comml. radar for cars, 1993, main electronics designer first Hewlett Packard color copier, 1996. Mem. IEEE. Mem. Ch. Scientology. Office: Geer & Geer Engring PMB 201 11835 Carmel Mountain Rd # 1304 San Diego CA 92128-4609

GEER, JOHN FARR, retired religious organization administrator; b. N.Y.C., Oct. 15, 1930; s. William Montague and Edith Jaffray (Farr) G.; m. Carolyn Boston, June 25, 1954; children: Jennifer, Evelyn, John Farr. BA, Princeton U., 1952; LLB, Columbia U., 1957. Bar: N.Y. State 1957. Asso. firm Sullivan & Cromwell, N.Y.C., 1957-65, Whitman & Ransom (and predecessor firms), N.Y.C., 1965-67, ptnr., 1967-73; v.p., gen. counsel, sec. Am. Standard Inc., N.Y.C., 1973-89, ret., 1989; sr. v.p., gen. counsel, sec. The Church Pension Fund, N.Y.C., 1991-97. Trustee Protestant Episcopal Soc. for Promoting Religion and Learning in State N.Y., 1960-82, treas., 1968-82; trustee Gen. Theol. Sem., 1980-95, vice chmn. bd. trustees, 1986-95; mem. Corp. for Relief Widows and Children of Protestant Episcopal Clergymen in State of N.Y., 1960—2003, treas., 1967-98. 1st lt. F.A. AUS, 1952-54, Korea. Mem. Phi Delta Phi. Clubs: Princeton (N.Y.C.). Episcopalian. Home: 151 Central Park W New York NY 10023-1514

GEER, RONALD LAMAR, mechanical engineer, consultant, retired oil industry executive; b. West Palm Beach, Fla., Sept. 2, 1926; s. Marion Wood and Bertha (Lightfoot) G.; m. Geneva Yvonne Chappell, Dec. 24, 1951; children— Ronald Lamar, Mark Randall. B.M.E., Ga. Inst. Tech., 1951. With Shell Oil Co., 1951—, sr. staff mech. engr., head office Houston, 1969-71, cons. mech. engr., 1971-86. Mem. various govt., univ. adv. coms. Contbr. articles on petroleum drilling and prodn. to profl. jours.; patentee petroleum drilling and prodn. equipment; mem. Shell Oil Co. team recognized in Offshore Tech. Conf. Disting. Achievement award to co., 1971, for individuals, 1984. Recipient Robert Earll McConnell award Am. Inst. Mech. Engrs., 1995; named to Offshore Energy Ctr. Pioneer Engring Tech. Hall of Fame, 1999, Offshore Energy Ctr. Industry Pioneer Hall of Fame, 2002. Mem. Nat. Acad. Engring., NRC (marine bd.), Nat. Security Indsl. Assn. (petroleum panel, research and engring. adv. com.), ASME (hon.), Marine Tech. Soc., Am. Petroleum Inst., Model-A Ford Club Am., Classic T-Bird Club Internat., Thistle Class Assn., Pi Tau Sigma. Republican. also: 430 Covered Bridge Ln # 135 Sky Valley GA 30537-2593

GEERDES, JAMES D(IVINE), retired chemicals executive; b. Davenport, N.D., Apr. 13, 1924; s. William A. and Martha (Buchholz) G.; children: Andrew B., Margaret BS, N.D. State U., 1949, MS, 1950; PhD, U. Minn., 1953. Instr. biochemistry U. Minn., 1950-53; research chemist E.I. duPont de Nemours & Co., Inc., Richmond, Va. and Seaford, Del., 1954-58, group supr., 1958-60, tech. supr., 1960-62, research asso., 1962-64; dir. research Entoleter, Inc., Hamden, Conn., 1964-65, exec. v.p., 1965-66, pres., 1966-67; asst. to v.p. fibers divsn. Allied Chem. Corp., N.Y.C., 1967, asst. to pres., 1967-68, exec. v.p., 1968, pres., 1968-71; pres., dir. Alrac Corp., Stamford, Conn., 1971-73, Geerdes Industries, Richmond, Va., 1971—; pres. Geerdes Internat., Inc., Richmond, Va., 1981—2005, ret., 2005. Pres. Geerdes Internat. Assocs., Inc., Manasses, Va., 1993—. Contbg. editor jour. Fiber Producer, Fiber World, Internat. Fiber Jour.; contbr. articles to profl. jours. Advisor bd. dirs. Richmond Children's Museum. Served to 1st lt. C.E. AUS, 1943-46. Mem. Textile Inst., Del. Acad. Sci., Am. Chem. Soc., AAAS, Textile Research Inst., Fiber Soc., Sigma Xi, Phi Kappa Phi, Gamma Sigma Delta, Gamma Alpha. Achievements include patents in field. Home: 1508 Westshire Ln Richmond VA 23238

GEERKIN, SUSAN MARY, art educator; d. Joseph William and Mary Ann Geerkin. BA in English Lit., BFA in Painting, SUNY, Oswego, 1993; MS in Art Edn., Buffalo State Coll., 2004. Part time art tchr. Regionalized Sch. of Immaculate Conception, Eden, NY, 1999—2002, St. Bonaventure Elem. Sch., West Seneca, NY, 2000—03, St. John Vianney Sch., Orchard Park, NY, 2000—03, St. Agatha's Sch., South Buffalo, NY, 2002—03; art tchr. Nativity of Our Lord Sch., Orchard Park, NY, 2003—. Asst. curator N.Y. Collects Buffalo State Exhbn., Burchfield-Penney Art Ctr., 2003—04. Contbr. exhbn. catalog. D-Conservative. Roman Catholic. Office: Nativity of Our Lord Sch S 4414 S Buffalo St Orchard Park NY 14127 Office Phone: 716-662-7572. Personal E-mail: susangee4@hotmail.com. Business E-Mail: sgeerkin@nativityschool.net.

GEERMAN, RUBEN DANIEL, music educator, elementary school educator; b. Santa Cruz, Aruba, June 16, 1951; s. Eduardo and Johanna Geerman; m. Caroline Van Gelder, Oct. 17, 1981; children: Erin, Alejandro. Degree in Elem. Edn., Aruban Pedagogical Acad., 1972; diploma in Profl. Music, Berklee Coll. Music, 1981; MusM, U. Bridgeport, 1989. Cert. music educator Nat. Bd. Profl. Tchg. Standards, 2005. Tchr. Maria Goretti Coll., Paradera, Aruba, 1972—74; dir. Aruban Music Sch., Oranjestad, Aruba, 1981—85; rschr. Ministry of Culture, Oranjestad, 1985—86; tchr. mid. sch. music Greens Farms Acad., Westport, Conn., 1986—89; tchr. music Dade County Pub. Schs., Miami, Fla., 1989—. Named Tchr. of Yr., Rockway Mid. Sch., 2005. Mem.: Music Educators Nat. Conf. Office: Rockway Middle School 9393 SW 29th Terrace Miami FL 33155 Office Phone: 305-221-8212. Personal E-mail: rgeerman@berklee.net.

GEERTZ, CLIFFORD JAMES, anthropology educator; b. San Francisco, Aug. 23, 1926; s. Clifford James and Lois (Brieger) G.; m. Hildred Storey, Oct. 30, 1948 (div. 1981); children: Erika, Benjamin; m. Karen Blu, 1987. AB, Antioch Coll., 1950; PhD, Harvard U., 1956, LL.D. (hon.), 1974; L.H.D. (hon.), No. Mich. U., 1975, U. Chgo., 1979, Bates Coll., 1980, Knox Coll., 1982, Brandeis U., 1984, Swarthmore Coll., 1984, New Sch. for Social Research, Yale U., 1987, Williams Coll., 1991, Princeton U., 1995, Cambridge (Eng.) U., 1997; L.H.D. (hon.), Colby Coll., 2003. From asst. prof. to prof. dept. anthropology U. Chgo., 1960-70; prof. dept. social sci. Inst. for Advanced Study, Princeton, N.J., 1970—, Harold F. Linder prof. social sci., 1982-2000, prof. emeritus, 2000—; Eastman prof. Oxford U., 1978-79. Author: The Religion of Java, 1960, Peddlers and Princes, 1963, The Social History of an Indonesian Town, 1965, Islam Observed, 1968, The Interpretation of Cultures, 1973, (with H. Geertz) Kinship in Bali, 1975, (with L. Rosen and H. Geertz) Meaning and Order in Moroccan Society, 1979, Negara: The Theatre State in Nineteenth-Century Bali, 1980, Local Knowledge, 1983, Works and Lives, 1988, After the Fact, 1995, Available Light, 2000. Served with USNR, 1943-45. Recipient Asian Cultural prize, 1992, Bintang Jasa Utama, Govt. of Indonesia, 2002, award Republic of Indonesia; Nat. Acad. Scis. fellow, 1973—. Fellow AAAS, Am. Philos. Soc., Am. Acad. Arts and Scis., Brit. Acad. (corr.); mem. Am. Anthrop. Assn., Assn. for Asian Studies, Middle East Studies Assn. Office: Inst for Advanced Study Princeton NJ 08540 E-mail: geertz@ias.edu.

GEESEMAN, ROBERT GEORGE, lawyer; b. Shreveport, La., Oct. 23, 1944; s. George Robert and Cora (Hamilton) Glasgow; m. Rosemary Monahan, Aug. 19, 1967; 1 child, Regan Glasgow. BA, Yale U., 1966; JD, U. Mich., 1969. Bar: Pa. 1969, U.S. Dist. Ct. (we. dist.) Pa. 1969, U.S. Supreme Ct. 1973, U.S. Tax Ct. 1979. Assoc. Blaxter, O'Neill, Houston & Nash, Pitts., 1969-75; ptnr. Lynch, Lynch, Carr & Kabala, Pitts., 1975-81, Lynch, Kabala & Geeseman, Pitts., 1981, Kabala & Geeseman, Pitts., 1981—2002; spl. counsel Fox, Rothschild, L.L.P., Pitts., 2002—. Lectr. tax law and employee benefits. Mem.: ABA (mem. closely held bus. com. sect. taxation, bd. editors Withdrawal Retirement and Disputes, bd. editors What You and Your Firm Should Know), Pitts. Inst. Legal Medicine, Allegheny County Bar Assn., Pa. Bar Assn., John's Island Country (Vero Beach, Fla.), Rivers Club, Mory's Club (New Haven), Phi Delta Phi. Address: Fox Rothschild LLP 625 Liberty Ave Fl 29 Pittsburgh PA 15222-3110 Office Phone: 412-391-1334.

GEFFE, PHILIP REINHOLD, electrical engineer, consultant; b. Napa, Calif., Oct. 22, 1920; s. Eugene Carl and Mary Rebecca (Woliston) G.; m. Barbara Ann Wean; children: Bethann, Philip, Timur. Student, Calif. Inst. Tech., 1947-49. Chief filter engr. Triad Transformer Corp., Venice, Calif., 1952-56; dir. engring. Hycor, Inc., Sylmar, Calif., 1957-60; sr. staff engr. Axel Electronics Inc., Jamaica, N.Y., 1962-65; fellow engr. Westinghouse Electric Corp., Balt., 1965-74; staff engr. Lynch Communication Systems, Inc., Reno, 1974-80, Scientific-Atlanta, Inc., Atlanta, 1980-85, K&L Microwave, Inc., Salisbury, Md., 1985-87; ind. cons., 1988—; sr. engr. PULSE divsn. Technitrol, San Diego, 1997—; ret., 2003. Cons. in field, 2001—02. Author: Simplified Modern Filter Design, 1963; contbr. articles to profl. jours.; patentee in field. Master U.S. Chess Fedn. New Windsor, N.Y., 1968 Fellow IEEE; mem. AAAS Address: 28789 Calle De La Paz Murrieta CA 92563-5790 E-mail: p_geffe@yahoo.com.

GEFFEN, DAVID, recording company executive, producer; b. Bklyn., Feb. 21, 1943; s. Abraham and Batya (Volovskaya) Geffen. Student, CUNY. Agt. with William Morris, N.Y.C., 1964—68, Ashley Famous, 1968; exec. v.p., agt. Creative Mgmt. Assocs., 1969; founder (with Laura Nyro) and pres. Tuna Fish Pub. Co.; pres. Geffen-Roberts, Inc., 1970—71, Asylum Records, 1970—73, Elektra-Asylum Records, 1973—76; vice-chmn. Warner Bros. Pictures, 1974, v.p., 1975; exec. asst. to chmn. Warner Comm., 1977; founder, pres., chmn. Geffen Records & Geffen Film Co., L.A., 1980—89; founder, pres. David Geffen Co., 1990—95; co-founder (with Jeffrey Katzenberg & Steven Spielberg) Dreamworks SKG, Universal City, 1995—. Mem. faculty Yale U., 1978; apptd. Regent U. Calif., Govt. Calif., 1980—87; bd. councilors USC Sch. Cinema-TV. Prodr.: (films) Personal Best, 1982, Risky Business, 1983, After Hours, 1985, Lost in America, 1985, Little Shop of Horrors, 1986, Beetlejuice, 1988, Men Don't Leave, 1990, Interview with the Vampire, 1994; co-prodr.: (plays) Master Harold...and the Boys, 1982, Cats, 1982, Good, 1982, Dreamgirls, 1983, Social Security, 1986, Madam Butterfly, 1988 (9 Tony awards including best play), (musical) Miss Saigon. Bds. dirs. Los Angeles County Art Mus. Named one of Top 200 Collectors, Artnews Mag., 2004, 50 Most Powerful People in Hollywood, Premiere mag., 2005, World's Richest People, Forbes mag., 2002—05. Avocation: Collector of Modern Art. Office: Dreamworks SKG 100 Universal City Plz Bldg 477 Universal City CA 91608*

GEFFNER, DONNA SUE, speech pathology/audiology services professional, audiologist, educator; d. Louis and Sally (Weiner) Geffner. BA magna cum laude, Bklyn. Coll., 1967; MA, NYU, 1968, PhD (NDEA fellow), 1970; postgrad., Advanced Inst. Analytic Psychology, 1973—75; EdD (hon.), Providence Coll., 2003. Asst. prof. Lehman Coll., 1971-76; assoc. prof. dept. speech St. John's U., 1976-81, prof., 1982—. Dir. Speech and Hearing Ctr., 1976—, chmn. dept. speech comm. scis. and theater, 1983—92, developer M.A. program in speech pathology, 1984, developer Au.D audiology and doctoral consortia, 2004, dir. grad. program in speech-lang. pathology and audiology, 1992—; pvt. practice, 1980—; cons. to corp. execs.; TV prodr. and hostess NBC, 1977—78, CBS, 1978—79; mem. N.Y. State Licensure Bd., 1993—97. Issue editor: Jour. Topics Lang. Disorders, 1980; editor: ASHA monograph, 1987; author: What Professionals Need to Know About Attention Deficit Hyperactivity Disorder, 2005, The Listening Inventory, 2005; contbr. articles to profl. jours., chapters to books. Recipient Emmy nomination for outstanding instrnl. program, 1978, award, Pres.'s Com. Employment Handicapped, Disting. Achievement award, N.Y.C. Speech-Lang.-Hearing Assn., 1994, Honors, L.I. Speech-Lang.-Hearing Assn., 1998; grantee, CUNY Rsch. Found., 1972, N.Y. State Dept. Edn., 1976—78. Fellow: Am. Speech, Lang. and Hearing Assn. (legis. councillor 1978—87, 1988—90, 1990—94, v.p. acad. affairs 1995—97, pres.-elect 1998, pres. 1999, past pres. 2000, ednl. standards bd. 1992—94); mem.: Coll. Bd. Com. on Literacy, Am. Guidance Svc. (mem. bd. advisors), Audiology Study Group N.Y., N.Y. State Speech and Hearing Assn. (pres. 1978—80, honors). Office: St John's U Speech and Hearing Ctr 8000 Utopia Pkwy Jamaica NY 11432-1343 Business E-Mail: geffnerd@Stjohns.edu.

GEFKE, HENRY JEROME, lawyer; b. Milw., Aug. 4, 1930; s. Jerome Henry and Frances (Daley) G.; m. Caroline Ann Lawrence, June 25, 1955 (div. Jan. 1968); children: Brian Lawrence, David Jerome; m. Mary Clare Nuss, Aug. 28, 1976; children: Lynn Marie, James Scott. BS, Marquette U., 1952, LLB, 1954; postgrad., Ohio State U., 1955—56. Bar: Wis. 1954, Tax Ct. U.S 1969; C.P.A., Wis. Acct.-auditor John G. Conley & Co. (C.P.A.s), Milw., 1956-59; with J.I. Case Co., Racine, Wis., 1959-68, corp. sec., asst. gen. counsel, 1965-68; assoc. Maier & Mulcahy, S.C., Milw., 1968-69; prin. Mulcahy, Gefke & Wherry, S.C., Milw., 1969-73; individual practice law Milw., 1973—. Corp. officer, dir. various bus. corps. Pres., bd. dirs. Big Bros., Greater Racine, 1965-67; trustee Racine County Instns., 1960-63; bd. dirs., sec., legal counsel Racine Transitional Care, Inc., 1973-76; bd. dirs., legal counsel Our Home Found., Milw., 1979-82; bd. dirs. Racine County Mental Health Assn., 1963-67, Alliance for Mentally Ill Milw. County, 1986-88; bd. dirs., sec., legal counsel Glendale Econ. Devel. Corp., 1996—; bd. dirs. Glendale Bus. Coun., 1996-97; bd. dirs. Glendale C. of C., Inc., 1997—, treas., 1998-00, pres. 2000-02. Mem. Wis. Bar Assn., Milw. Bar Assn., Wis. Inst. CPA's, Delta Sigma Pi, Delta Theta Phi. Home and Office: 5521 N Lydell Ave Milwaukee WI 53217-5042 Office Phone: 414-332-1200. Personal E-mail: hjgjdcpa@aol.com. Business E-Mail: hjgjdcpa@sbcglobal.net.

GEH, HANS-PETER, retired library director, consultant; b. Frankfurt am Main, Germany, Feb. 11, 1934; s. Peter and Maria Geh; m. Roswitha Dieterich, Aug. 31, 1968. MA, U. Bristol, Eng., 1963; PhD, U. Frankfurt am Main, 1963. Subject specialist City and Univ. Libr., Frankfurt am Main, 1962—69; dir. Libr. Sch., Frankfurt am Main, 1967—69, Stuttgart, Germany, 1970—80, Württemberg State Libr., Stuttgart, 1970—97, prof., 2003—. Hon. prof.; cons. UNESCO, 1971—; chmn. libr. assns. and lit. socs., Germany, 1965—. Author: Insular Policy in England before the Tudors, 1964; co-editor jours., 1965—; also articles. Trustee Bibliotheca Alexandrina, Egypt. Decorated Order of Merit (Germany). Mem. Internat. Fedn. Libr. Assns. and Instns. (pres. 1985-91); European Found. for Libr. Coop. (pres. 1991-95); hon. mem. numerous internat. libr. assns. Avocation: travel. Home: Hebbergstrasse 76/1 70794 Filderstadt Germany Office: Württemberg State Libr Konrad-Adenauer-Strasse 8 70049 Stuttgart Germany Personal E-mail: gehhp@t-online.de.

GEHA, ALEXANDER SALIM, cardiothoracic surgeon, educator; b. Beirut, June 18, 1936; came to U.S., 1963; s. Salim M. and Alice I. (Hayek) G.; m. Diane L. Redalen, Nov. 25, 1967; children— Samia, Rula, Nada BS in Biology, Am. U. Beirut, 1955, MD, 1959; MS in Surgery and Physiology, U. Minn.-Rochester, 1967; MS (privatum), Yale U., 1978. Asst. prof. U. Vt., Burlington, 1967-69; asst. prof. Washington U., St. Louis, 1969-73, assoc. prof., 1973-75, Yale U., New Haven, 1975-78, prof., chief cardiothoracic surgery, 1978-86, Case Western Res. U. and Univ. Hosp. of Cleve., 1986-98; Jay L. Ankeney prof. cardiothoracic surgery Case Western Res. U., 1994-98; pres. Univ. Cardiothoracic Surgeons, Inc., Cleve., 1986—2001; prof., chief cardiothoracic surgery U. Ill. Med. Ctr., Chgo., 1998—; chief cardiothoracic surgery Mt. Sinai Hosp. Med. Ctr., Chgo., 2000—. Cons. VA Hosp., West Haven, Conn., 1975-86, VA Hosp., Cleve., 1986-98, Westside VA Hosp., Chgo., 1998—, Cleve. Met. Health Med. Ctr., 1986-98, Mt. Sinai Med. Ctr., Cleve., 1990-98, Waterbury Hosp., 1976-86, Sharon Hosp., 1981-86, Michael Reese Hosp., 2002—; mem. study sect. Nat. Heart Lung and Blood Inst., 1981-85. Editor: Glenn's Thoracic and Cardio-vascular Surgery, 4th edit. 1983, 5th edit. 1991, 6th edit. 1996; editor Basic Surgery, 1984. Bd. dirs. New Haven Heart Assn., 1981-85 Mem. AMA, Assn. Clin. Cardiac Surgery (chmn. membership com. 1978-80, sec.-treas. 1980-83, pres. 1988), Am. Heart Assn. (bd. dirs. 1981-85. councils on basic sci., cardiovascular surgery), Am. Coll. Chest Physicians (steering com. 1980-84), Am. Assn. Thoracic Surgery, Am. Coll. Cardiology, ACS (chmn. coordinating com. on edn. in thoracic surgery, chmn. 1992-95), Am. Lung Assn., Am. Physiol. Soc., Am. Surg. Assn., Assn. Acad. Surgery, Central Surg. Assn., Chgo. Inst. Medicine, European Assn. Cardiothoracic Surgery, Internat. Soc. Heart and Lung Transplantation, Internat. Soc. Cardiovascular Surgery, Lebanese Order Physicians, New Eng. Surg. Soc., Pan Am. Med. Assn., Halsted Soc., Soc. Thoracic Surgeons (govt. rels. com., manpower com., program com., edn. and resources com.), Soc. for

Vascular Surgery, Soc. Univ. Surgeons, Chgo. Surg. Soc., also others. Home: 854 W Fullerton Ave Chicago IL 60614-2413 Office: ILL Chgo 840 S Wood St Chicago IL 60612-7321 Office Phone: 312-996-4942. Business E-Mail: ageha@uic.edu.

GEHAN, MARK WILLIAM, lawyer; b. St. Paul, Dec. 19, 1946; s. Mark William and Jean Elizabeth (McGee) G.; m. Lucy Lyman Harrison, Aug. 25, 1971; children: Mark Harrison, Alice McGee. BA, U. Notre Dame, 1968; JD, U. Minn., 1971. Bar: Minn., 1972; U.S. Supreme Ct., 1989. Asst. county atty. Ramsey County Atty.'s Office, St. Paul, 1972-76; prosecutor, Met. Area Dist. Urban County Attys. Bd., St. Paul, 1976-77; ptnr. Collins Buckley Sauntry & Haugh, St. Paul, 1978—. Bd. dirs. Minn. State Bd. Pub. Def., St. Paul, 1982-90. Pres. St. Paul Charter Commn., 1986-94. Mem. Minn. Bar Assn. (pres. 1998-99), Ramsey County Bar Assn. (pres. 1990-91). Avocations: scuba diving, tennis, guitar. Office: Collins Buckley Sauntry & Haugh First Nat Bank Bldg 332 Minnesota St Ste W1100 Saint Paul MN 55101-1379 Office Phone: 651-227-0611. E-mail: mgehan@cbsh.net.

GEHL, RAYMOND HAROLD, psychiatrist, educator; b. Newark, Dec. 9, 1916; s. Philip Morris and Bertha (Schoenstadt) G.; m. Gita Rabin, Sept. 2, 1943; children: Richard, Leonard. BA, U. Mich., 1937, MD, 1940. Diplomate Am. Bd. Psychiatry and Neurology. Intern Kings County Hosp., Bklyn., 1940-42; resident in psychiatry VA Hosp., Lyons, N.J., 1946-48; trainee in psychoanalysis N.Y. Psychoanalytic Inst., N.Y.C., 1948-52; pvt. practice, West Orange, N.J., 1953—. Adj. prof. Rutgers U. Sch. Social Work, New Brunswick, N.J., 1952-58; cons. VA Hosp., East Orange, N.J., 1954-84, Montclair (N.J.) Family and Child Agy., 1955-80; mem. bd. med. advisors Essex County Mental Hosp., Cedar Grove, N.J., 1972-79; clin. prof. psychiatry U. Medicine and Dentistry N.J., Newark, 1979—; clin. assoc. prof. psychiatry NYU Med. Sch., N.Y.C., 1980—, tng. analyst dept. psychiatry and psychoanalysis, 1969—. Co-author: The Graphomotor Projection Technique, 1954; contbr. articles to med. jours. Maj. M.C., USAAF, 1942-46, PTO. Recipient Disting. Teaching award U. Medicine and Dentistry N.J., 1982, 89-90. Fellow Am. Psychiat. Assn. (life); mem. AMA (life), Internat. Psychoanalytic Assn., Am. Psychoanalytic Assn. (pub. rels. com., exec. coun. 1961-63, 65-67), N.J.Psychoanalytic Soc. (founder, pres. 1960-61, 66-67, 72-74, 88-90, chmn. nominating com., by-laws com. 1990), N.J. Psychoanalytic Found. (pres.). Jewish. Home: Claridge House II Apt 10 NE Verona NJ 07044 Office: 111 Northfield Ave West Orange NJ 07052-4795

GEHL, WILLIAM D., manufacturing executive; b. 1947; Bar: Wis., Fla. With The Ziegler Co., Inc., West Bend, Wis., 1978-92, sr. v.p., gen. counsel, 1985-92, exec. v.p., COO, gen. counsel, sec., 1990-92, also bd. dirs.; dir. Gehl Co., 1987—, chmn. nominating com., mem. compensation and benefits com., pres., CEO, 1992—, also chmn. bd. dirs. Office: Gehl Co PO Box 179 143 Water St West Bend WI 53095-3400

GEHLBACH, GRETCHEN D., literature and language educator, psychologist, educator; b. Cin., June 5, 1940; d. C. Mexwell and Gladys Gray Dieffenbach; 1 child, Derrick R. AB in English, Centre Coll., 1962; MEd, U. Cin., 1963. Instr. English Princeton City Schs., Cin., 1963—65, Clark County Schs., Springfield, 1965—67; instr. English, psychology Canal Winchester Schs., 1973—. Avocations: photography, travel, reading. Office: Canal Winchester High Sch 300 Washington St Canal Winchester OH 43110

GEHR, JUDITH ANN, mathematician, educator; d. Leonard Herbert and Naomi Ruth Estep; m. James Edwin Gehr, Sept. 3, 1977; 1 child, Leza Rae Owens. BS, Clarion State Coll., 1972; MS, We. Md. Coll., 1988. Tchr. Manchester Elem., Md., 1974—90, N. Carroll Mid. Sch., Hampstead, Md., 1990—; adj. prof. McDaniel Coll., Westminster, Md., 1999—. Chaperon sch. events, Hampstead, 1990—; mem. Md. Assessment Consortium, Frederick, Md., 1991—95, Tchr. Advisory Council, Westminster, 1999—; coord. Math. Intervention Program, Hampstead, 1999—; mentor, tchr., trainer Performance Learning Svcs. Recipient Tchr. of Yr. award, Md. & Carroll County, 1996, Md. Council, 1997, Westminster C. of C., 1997. Mem.: Md. Council Tchrs. Math., Assn. Supervision & Curriculum Development, Nat. Council Tchrs. Math., N. Carroll PTO. Avocations: reading, exercise. Home: Box 512 2300 Bachman Valley Rd Manchester MD 21102 Office: N Carroll Mid Sch 2401 Hanover Pike Hampstead MD 21074

GEHRES, JAMES, retired lawyer; b. Akron, Ohio, July 19, 1932; s. Edwin Jacob and Cleora Mary (Yoakam) G.; m. Eleanor Agnew Mount, July 23, 1960. BS in Acctg., U. Utah, 1954; MBA, U. Calif.-Berkeley, 1959; JD, U. Denver, 1970, LLM in Taxation, 1977. Bar: Colo. 1970, U.S. Dist. Ct. Colo. 1970, U.S. Tax Ct. 1970, U.S. Supreme Ct. 1973, U.S. Ct. Appeals (10th cir.) 1978, U.S. Ct. Claims 1992. Atty. IRS, Denver, 1965-80, atty. chief counsel;s office, 1980—2002; ret., 2002. Contbr. articles to profl. jours. Treas., dir. Colo. Fourteeners Initiative. With USAF, 1955-58, capt. Res. ret. Mem. ABA, Colo. Bar Assn., AICPA, Colo. Soc. CPAs, Am. Assn. Atty.-CPAs, Am. Judicature Soc., Order of St. Ives, The Explorers Club, Am. Alpine Club, Colo. Mountain Club, Colo. Mountain Club Found. (bd. dirs., pres.), Beta Gamma Sigma, Beta Alpha Psi. Democrat. Office: 935 Pennsylvania St Denver CO 80203-3145 E-mail: jimgehres@yahoo.com.

GEHRICH, LEONORA SUPPAN, artist, musician, German literature educator; arrived in US, 1963; d. Josef Cornelius and Josefine Maria Suppan; m. Heinz-Guenter Gehrich; children: Alan, Brian, Colleen. Diploma, Acad. Music, Vienna, 1958; MusM, Ind. U., 1965; PhD, Quincy U., 1988. Cert. performer Ind. U., 1965. Asst. prof. Western Ill. U., Macomb, 1965—68; artist-in residence Culver-Stockton Coll., Canton, Miss., 1968—75, Quincy U., 1977—2005. Musician, pianist (concerts), Austria, Germany, France, Italy, Poland, Hungary, Eng., Portugal, Can., Costa Rica, Mex., Holland, Czech Republic. Recipient City of Quincy Arts award, 1995. Mem.: Am. Coll. Musicians, Muddy River Opera (mem. bd. 2003), Hist. Soc. Avocations: sailing, tennis, swimming. Office: Quincy U 1800 College Ave Quincy IL 62301 Office Phone: 217-228-5460. Office Fax: 217-885-3024. Business E-Mail: ggehrich@msn.com.

GEHRIG, EDWARD HARRY, electrical engineer, consultant; b. Portland, Oreg., Oct. 31, 1925; s. Henry Oscar and Selma Victoria (Charf) G.; m. May 20, 1950; children: Cynth Ann, Nanette Lou, Timothy Alexander. BA in Physics, Reed Coll., 1948; BSEE, Stanford U., 1949; MSEE, Oreg. State U., 1951. Registered profl. engr., Oreg. Physicist AEC, 1950-52; head system planning Bonneville Power Adminstrn., Portland, 1963-72, chief transmission design, 1972-76, chief R & D, 1976-81; ind. cons. Lake Oswego, Oreg., 1982—. Participant Electric Power Rsch. Inst. and GE Project UHV; designer, distbr. for Lindal Cedar Homes, Seattle, 1987—. Patentee in field; contbr. articles to profl. jours. Chmn. Lake Grove Zoning Bd., Lake Oswego, Oreg., 1962-64; elder First Presbyn. Ch., Portland; coach basketball, soccer, Lake Grove. Sgt. U.S. Army, 1944-46, ETO. Recipient Meritorious Svc. award Dept. of Interior, 1979. Fellow IEEE. Democrat. Avocations: woodcraft, golf. Home: PO Box 2062 Lake Oswego OR 97035

GEHRIG, LEO JOSEPH, retired surgeon; b. Mapleton, Minn., Apr. 25, 1918; s. Paul P. and Marcella (Hund) G.; m. Marillyn May Nelson, June 10, 1944; children: Gregory Paul, Mark Nelson. BS, U. Minn., 1942, MB, 1944, MD, 1945. Diplomate Am. Bd. Surgery, Am. Bd. Thoracic Surgery. Intern Salt Lake County Gen. Hosp., Salt Lake City, 1944-45; resident New Eng. Deaconess Hosp., Boston, 1947-50; with USPHS, 1945-70, advanced through grades to rear adm., ret., 1970, chief chest surgery unit S.I., NY, 1950-52, resident, 1952-55, chief thoracic surgery Seattle, 1955-57, asst. chief divsn. hosps. Washington, 1957-59, dep. chief, 1959-60, program officer bur. med. svcs. Washington, 1960-61; med. dir. Peace Corps, Washington, 1961-62; asst. surgeon gen., dep. chief Bur. Med. Svcs., 1962-64, chief bur., 1964-65, dep. surgeon gen., 1965-68; dir. office internat. health HEW, 1968-70; assoc. dir. Washington svc. bur. Am. Hosp. Assn., 1970-72, v.p., 1972-75, sr. v.p., dir. Washington office, 1978—80. Dir. rsch. Health Rsch. Edn. Trust, 1985—89. Bd. dirs. St. Lukes Inst., Silver Spring, Md., 1988—2002. Recipient U.S. Disting. Svc. medal. Fellow ACS, Am. Coll. Thoracic Surgery; mem. AMA, Am. Heart Assn., Assn. Mil. Surgeons, USPHS Clin. Soc., Am. Pub. Health Assn., Mil. Officer Assn. Am. (bd. dirs. Alexandria, Va. 1990-97), Alpha Omega Alpha. Home: 4535 Alton Pl NW Washington DC 20016-2023 Personal E-mail: ljgehrig@msn.com.

GEHRING, DAVID AUSTIN, cardiologist, physician, health facility administrator; b. Bryn Mawr, Pa., Dec. 6, 1930; s. Harry Rittenhouse and Anne Gardiner (Bozarth) G.; m. Joan Helen Lotz, June 7, 1953 (div. Aug. 1982); children: David, Paul, Peter, Sue, Barbara, Eric; m. Victoria Marie Damiano, Sept. 2, 1982 (dec. May 2000); children: Theresa, Judy Lynne, Michael Austin; m. Rose Y. Barron, May 5, 2001. BA magna cum laude, U. Pitts., 1952, MD, 1956; grad., Naples Sch. of Real Estate, Fla., 2000. Diplomate Am. Bd. Internal Medicine; cert. geriatric medicine. Commd. USN, 1956, advanced through grades to lt. comdr., intern, then resident in internal medicine U.S. Naval Hosp. Phila., 1956-60, mem. staff internal medicine U.S. Naval Hosp., 1960-61, chief internal medicine heart sta. U.S. Naval Hosp. Annapolis, Md., 1961-63, resigned, 1963; cardiologist K.G.E. Med. Group, Woodbury, NJ, 1963—82; cardiologist, pres. Hobbs Cardiology, P.A., Hobbs, N.Mex., 1982-86; med. dir. Polk (Pa.) Ctr., 1986-91; physician, chief grade VA Med. Ctr., Coatesville, Pa., 1991-97, assoc. chief of staff for ambulatory care, 1993-96, chief med. svc., 1995-96, chief primary care and chief of staff, 1995-96, chief of staff, 1995-96, cardiologist, 1996-97; assoc. med. dir. for correctional med. svcs. South Jersey, 1997-98; site med. dir. South Woodstate Prison, 1997-98; clin. dir. Del. Hosp. Chronically Ill, 1998-99; clin. dir. long term care pub. health divsn. State of Del., 1998-99; physician VA Clinic, Naples, Fla., 2002—. Clin. dir. Del. Hosp. for Cronically Ill, Smyrna, 1998—99; v.p. Regent Park Villas II Assoc., Inc., Naples, Fla., 1999—2000, pres., 2000—01; realtor VIP Lodge McKee Realtors, 2000—01, VIP Lodge McKee, 2000—01; sect. chief VA Med. Ctr., Salisbury, NC, 2001—02, occupl. health physician, 2002, mem. ethics com., 2001—02, mem. hosp. disaster com., 2002, chair small pox com., 02; testing cardiologist Anthropometrics United Med. Group, Cherry Hill, NJ, 1974—82; clin. asst. prof. medicine Temple U. Hosp., Phila., 1975—82; adj. asst. prof. medicine Jefferson Meml. Coll., 1981—82; chief cardiac rehab. unit Lea Regional Hosp., Hobbs, 1982—86; chief med. svcs. 829th Sta. Hosp., USAR, Lubbock, Tex., 1984—86; cons. cardiology, Oil City, Pa., 1986—91; staff Franklin (Pa.) Regional Med. Ctr., 1986—90, Oil City Area Health Ctr., 1986—91; teaching staff St. Joseph Hosp., Lancaster, Pa., 1991—97; clin. preceptor U. Pa. Sch. Nursing, 1993—96; cons. Southeastern Vets. Ctr., Spring City, Pa., 1997—98, Providence Med. Ctr., Media, 1997—98; others; assoc. med. dir. Correctional Med. Svcs. South Jersey, 1997—98; mem. adult protective svcs. coun. State of Del., 1998—99; mem. profl. devel. com. Naples Area Bd. Realtors, 2000—01, mem. complaint rev. com., 2000—01; chair pharmacy and therapeutics com. Dept. Health and Social Svcs., State of Del., 1998—99; mem. pharmacy and therapeutics com. for VISN 6 dept. Vet. Affairs, 2001—02; cons. in field. Author: EKG Workbook, 1972, EKG Workbook I, 1978; contbr. articles to profl. jours. Project dir. 23 Greater Del. Valley Reg. Med. Program, Pa., 1971—75; mem. ACLS Inst. and affiliated faculty Pa. Heart Assn., 1986—98, bd. dirs. N.W. chpt., 1988—90; bd. dirs. Inst. Christianna Hosp., Del., 1998—99; bd. dirs. adv. com., chmn. personnel com. med. health, rehab., drugs and alcohol Venango County, Franklin Parl, Pa., 1986—90, pres., 1988—89; mem. Health Care Adv. Com. to Congressman William F. Clinger, Jr., 23d Dist., 1989—91, Naples Mus. Art, 2000—; patron Philharmonic Ctr. for Arts, 1998—, Carolina Opera, 2001—03; lector St. Joseph Ch., Oil City, 1987—91, eucharistic min., 1990—92, Swedesboro, NJ, 1992—93, Sacred Heart Ch., Mt. Ephraim, 1994—99, lector, 1998—99. Lt. col. USAR, 1983—90. Recipient Outstanding Svc. award Am. Cancer Soc. N.J., 1967, Benjamin Berkowitz award N.J. Heart Assn., 1975, Nat. Def. Svc. medal, 1975, USAR Components Achievement medal, 1988, Letter of Commendation USAR, 1988, 90, Pres.'s medal of Merit, Rep. Task Force, 1984Letter of Commendation Sec. of Vets. Affairs, 1994; Cert. of Appreciation, Sec. of State N.Mex., 1982, Venango County Commrs., 1987, 88, 89, 90, Polk Ctr. award of Merit, 1991, Spl. Contbn. award and Mgr. of Yr. award VAMC Coatesville, 1996, Spl. Contbn. award, VA Med. Ctr., Salisbury, NC, 2002. Fellow ACP (life, Recognition awards 1967-70), Am. Coll. Cardiology, Am. Coll. Chest Physicians, Coll. Physicians Phila., Am. Coll. Clin. Pharmacology; mem. AMA, Am. Geriat. Soc., St. Jude Soc., Holy Name Soc., Assn. Miraculous Medal (promoter 1987—), Venango County Med. Soc. (pres. 1989-91), Assn. Mil. Surgeons, Mil. Officers Assn. Am., Am. Coll. Physician Execs., Mil. Officers Assn. Am. (life), Mil. Officers Club Collier County Fla. (dir.), Am. Legion, Collier County Mil. Officers Club, KC. Republican. Roman Catholic. Avocations: stamp collecting/philately, reading, walking, swimming, opera. Home: 2347 Butterfly Palm Dr Naples FL 34119 Office: VA Primary Care Clinic Ste 101 2685 Horseshoe Dr S Naples FL 34109 Office Phone: 239-659-9188. E-mail: docdave@earthlink.net.

GEHRING, FREDERICK WILLIAM, mathematician, educator; b. Ann Arbor, Mich., Aug. 7, 1925; s. Carl E. and Hester McNeal (Reed) G.; m. Lois Caroline Bigger, Aug. 29, 1953; children: Kalle Burgess, Peter Motz. BSE in Elec. Engring., U. Mich., 1946, MA in Math, 1949; PhD (Fulbright fellow) in Math, Cambridge U., Eng., 1952, ScD, 1976; PhD (hon.), U. Helsinki, Finland, 1977, U. Jyväskylä, 1990, Norwegian U. Sci. & Technology, 1997. Benjamin Peirce instr. Harvard U., Cambridge, Mass., 1952-55; instr. math. U. Mich., Ann Arbor, 1955-56, asst. prof., 1956-59, assoc. prof., 1959-62, prof., 1962-96, T.H. Hildebrandt prof. math., 1984-96, prof. emeritus, 1996, chmn. dept. math., 1973-75, 77-84, disting. univ. prof., 1987—; hon. prof. Hunan U., Changsha, People's Republic of China, 1987. Vis. prof. Harvard U., 1964-65, Stanford U., 1964, U. Minn., 1971, Inst. Mittag-Leffler, Sweden, 1972, Mittag-Leffler, Sweden, 1990; Lars Onsager prof. Norwegian Tech. Hochschule, Norway, 1995; chair program in Geo Function Theory, Math. Scis. Rsch. Inst., Berkeley, 1986. Editor Duke Math. Jour., 1963-80, D. Van Nostrand Pub. Co., 1963-70, North Holland Pub. Co., 1970-94, Springer-Verlag, 1974-2002; editl. bd. Procs. Am. Math. Soc., 1962-65, Ind. U. Math. Jour., 1967-75, Math. Revs., 1969-75, Bull. Am. Math. Soc., 1979-85, Complex Variables, 1981—, Mich. Math. Jour., 1989-98, Annales Academiae Scientiarum Fennicae, 1996—, Conformal Geometry and Dynamics, 1997—, Computational Methods and Function Theory, 2001—; contbr. numerous articles on rsch. in pure math. to sci. jours. With USNR, 1943-46. Decorated comdr. Finnish White Rose; NSF fellow, 1959-60; Fulbright fellow, 1958-59; Guggenheim fellow, 1958-59; Sci. Rsch. Coun. sr. fellow, 1981; Humboldt fellow, 1981-84; U. Auckland Found fellow, 1985; Finnish Acad. fellow U. Helsinki, 1989. Mem. NAS, Am. Acad. Arts and Scis., Assn. Women in Math., Math. Assn. Am., Am. Math. Soc. (coun. 1969-75, 80-83, trustee 1983-93, mem. editl. bd. 1997-98), Inst. for Math. and Its Applications (gov. 1981-84), Swiss Math. Soc., Finnish Math. Soc., London Math. Soc., Finnish Acad. Sci., Royal Norwegian Soc. Scis. and Letters. Home: 2139 Melrose Ave Ann Arbor MI 48104-4067 E-mail: fgehring@umich.edu.

GEHRING, WALTER JAKOB, biology professor, geneticist; b. Zurich, Switzerland, Mar. 20, 1939; s. Jakob and Marcelle (Rebmann) G.; m. Elisabeth Lott, Jan. 31, 1964; children: Stephan, Thomas. Diploma in Zoology, U. Zurich, 1963, PhD, 1965; PhD honoris causa, U. Torino, Italy, 2003, U. Nuevo Léon, Mex., 2003. Rsch. assoc. U. Zurich, 1963-67; postdoctoral fellow Yale U., New Haven, Conn., 1967-69, assoc. prof., 1969-72; prof. U. Basel, Switzerland, 1972—. Assoc. editor: Jour. Exptl. Zoology, Mechanisms of Devel., Trends in Genetics, Growth & Differentiation. Recipient Otto Nägeli prize Zurich, 1982, Warren Triennial Harvard Med. Sch., Cambridge, Mass., 1986, Dr. Albert Wander prize City of Bern, Switzerland, 1986, Charles Léopold Mayer prize Inst. of France, Paris, 1986, Louis Jeantet prize for medicine City of Geneva, 1987, Prix d'Honneur, Moet Hennessy Louis Vuitton, 1993, Newcomb Cleve. prize AAAS, 1994-1995, Otto Warburg-medaille, 1996, Paul Wintrebert prize U. Pierre and Marie Curie, 1996, March of Dimes prize Devel. Biology, 1997, Karl von Frisch prize German Zool. Soc., 2000, Kyoto prize Inamori Found., 2000, Preis der Alfred Vogt Stiftung zur Förderung der Augenheilkunde, Zürich, 2001, Premio Balzan, Fondazione Internat. Premio E. Balzan, 2003. Mem. AAAS, NAS, European Molecular Biology Orgn., European Devel. Biology Orgn., Deutsche Akademie der Naturforscher Leopoldina, Academia Europaea, Genetics Soc. Am., Internat. Soc. for Developmental Biology, Swiss Soc. for Cell Biology, Molecular Biology and Genetics, Am. Soc. for Developmental Biology, Human Genome Orgn., Royal Soc. London (fgn.), Acad. Scis. (fgn.), Sigma Xi. Avocations: birdwatching, photography. Home: Hochfeldstrasse 32 CH-4106 Therwil Switzerland Office: U Basel Biozentrum Klingelbergstrasse 70 CH-4056 Basel Switzerland E-mail: walter.gehring@unibas.ch.

GEHRINGER, RICHARD GEORGE, publishing executive; b. Newark, Oct. 31, 1949; s. George John and Constance Mary (Volz) G.; m. Phyllis Jean Salerno, Nov. 13, 1977; children: Alexandra Rane, Skyler George. BS, U. S.C., 1972; MBA, St. John's U., Jamaica, N.Y., 1976. Cert. cash mgr.; cert. treasury profl. Mgmt. trainee Avdel Corp., Teterboro, N.J., 1972-74; purchasing analyst Resistoflex Corp., Roseland, N.J., 1974-76; staff acct. McGraw-Hill Pub. Co., Hightstown, N.J., 1976-78; fin. analyst corp. real estate McGraw-Hill, Inc., N.Y.C., 1978-79; bus. mgr., corp. real estate McGraw-Hill Inc., N.Y.C., 1979-80; asst. contr. McGraw-Hill Book Co., N.Y.C., 1980-81; contr. Oxford U. Press Inc., Fair Lawn, N.J., 1981-86, v.p., CFO N.Y.C., 1986—90, Cary, NC, 1990—95, sr. v.p., CFO N.Y.C., 1995—. Fin. advisor Pi Kappa Alpha, Columbia U., N.Y.C., 1988-89; bd. dirs. Fin. Execs. Inst., Dickens Pen & Inc., Books Alive!. Mem. Fin. Execs. Inst., Inst. Mgmt. Accts., Treasury Mgmt. Assn., Bldg. Owners' and Mgrs.' Assn. of Greater N.Y., N.C. Citizens for Bus. and Industry, Raleigh C. of C., Assn. for Fin. Profls. Republican. Roman Catholic. Office: Oxford U Press Inc 198 Madison Ave New York NY 10016-4341 E-mail: rggehringer@aol.com.

GEHRKE, CHARLES WILLIAM, biochemistry professor; b. N.Y.C., July 18, 1917; s. Henry Edward and Louise (Mader) G.; m. Virginia Dorothy Horcher, Dec. 25, 1941; children: Charles William (dec.), Jon Craig, Susan Gay. BA in Biochemistry, Ohio State U., 1939, BS in Edn, MS in Biochemistry and Bacteriology, Ohio State U., 1941, PhD in Agrl. Biochemistry, 1947. Prof., head dept. chemistry Missouri Valley Coll., Marshall, Mo., 1942-49; instr. agrl. chemistry Ohio State U., Columbus, 1945-46; assoc. prof. agrl. chemistry U. Mo., Columbia, 1949-54, prof. biochemistry, 1954-87, prof. emeritus, 1987—, mgr. Expt. Sta. Chem. Labs., 1954-87, dir. interdisciplinary chromatography Mass Spectrometry Facility, 1982-87; founder, chmn. bd. dirs. Bioscis. and Tech. Internat., Inc., 1992. Founder, chmn. bd. dirs. Analytical Biochemistry Labs., Columbia, 1968-92, dir., 1992—; USA co-chmn. colloquium on A Lunar-Based Chem. Analysis Lab., 1989, 93; co-investigator lunar samples NASA, 1969-75; lectr., Japan, China, Taiwan, The Philippines, Hong Kong, 1982, 87, France, Germany, Eng., Norway, Sweden, Switzerland, Italy, Egypt, 1986, 89. Author: 75 Years of Chromatography--A Historical Dialogue; author-editor: Amino Acid Analysis by Gas Chromatography, 3 vols., 1987, Chromatography and Modification of Nucleosides, 3 vols., 1990, A Lunar-Based Chemical Analysis Laboratory, 1993, A Lunar-Based Analytical Laboratory, 1997, Chromatography a Century of Discovery, 2001; mem. editl. bd. Jour. Chromatographic Sci., Jour. Chromatography; contbr. more than 270 articles to sci. jours. Recipient Faculty Alumni Gold medal award U. Mo., 1975, Chromatography Meml. medal Sci. Council on Chromatography of USSR Acad. Scis., 1980, Ohio State Alumni Profl. Achievement award, 2001; Ohio State Outstanding scholar, 1996. Fellow Am. Inst. Chemists, Assn. Ofcl. Analytical Chemists (Harvey W. Wiley award 1971, chmn. Magruder standard sample subcom. 1958-79, bd. dirs., mem. editl. bd. 1979-82, pres.-elect 1983, pres. centennial yr. 1984); mem. AAAS, Am. Soc. Biol. Chemists, Am. Chem. Soc. (pres. Mo. sect. 1958-59, 78-79, Spencer award 1980, Midwest Chemist award 1986, Dal Nogare award in chromatography 1995, U. Mo. Faculty Retiree of Yr. award 1993, nat. award in separations sci. and tech. 1999, Nat. award in Chromatography 2000), Am. Dairy Sci. Assn. (chmn. com. on protein nomenclature 1961-62), Fedn. Am. Socs. Exptl. Biology, Internat. Soc. Study of Origin of Life, N.Y. Acad. Sci., Cosmopolitan Luncheon Club (chmn. adv. com. 1976—), Sigma Xi. Home: 708 Edgewood Ave Columbia MO 65203-7410 Office: Cancer Rsch Ctr 3501 Berrywood Dr Columbia MO 65201-6570 Office Phone: 573-442-4964.

GEHRLEIN, WILLIAM VINCENT, business professor; b. Erie, Pa., June 8, 1946; s. Vincent Francis and Eunice Mae (Knauff) G.; m. Sheila Eileen Lawson, Nov. 25, 1973 (div. May 1991); m. Barbara Elaine Eller, June 29, 2001. BS in Physics, Gannon Coll., 1968; MS in Physics, Pa. State U., 1972, PhD in Bus. Adminstrn., 1975. Postdoctoral fellow Pa. State U., State College, Pa., 1975-77; asst. prof. Clarkson Coll., Potsdam, N.Y., 1977-78; assoc. prof. U. Del., Newark, 1978-81, prof. of bus. adminstrn., 1981-2001. Mem. editl. bd.: Social Choice and Welfare; guest editor: Spl. Issue of Annals of Opers. Rsch., 1990, 97; author: Operations Management Cases, 2003; contbr. numerous articles to profl. jours.; mem. bd. assoc. editors Inst. of Indsl. Engrs., 1985. With U.S. Army, 1968-70. Fellow Ctr. for Advanced Study, U. Del., 1988; grantee NSF, 1978. Mem. Internat. Soc. for Social Choice and Welfare (exec. coun.), Opers. Rsch. Soc. of Am. Avocations: running, fishing, genealogy. Office: Dept Bus Adminstrn Univ Del Newark DE 19716 Business E-Mail: wvg@udel.edu.

GEHRY, FRANK OWEN, architect; b. Toronto, Ont., Can., Feb. 28, 1929; arrived in U.S., 1947; s. Irving and Thelma (Caplan) Gehry; m. Berta Aguilera, Sept. 11, 1975; children: Alejandro, Samuel; children: Leslie, Brina. BArch, U. So. Calif., 1954; postgrad., Harvard U., 1956—57; DFA (hon.), RI Sch. Design, 1987, Otis Art Inst. at Parsons Sch. Design, 1989; Doctorate of Visual Arts (hon.), Calif. Inst. Arts, 1987; DEng (hon.), Tech. U. Nova Scotia, 1989; HHD (hon.), Occidental Coll., 1993; doctorate (hon.), Whittier Coll., 1995, Calif. Coll. Arts and Crafts; DAgr (hon.), Southern Calif. Inst. Architecture, 1997; LLD (hon.), U. Toronto, 1998. Registered profl. architect, Calif. Designer Victor Gruen Assocs., LA, 1953—54, planning, design and project dir., 1958—61; project designer, planner Pereira & Luckman, LA, 1957—58; prin. Frank O. Gehry & Assocs. (succeeded by Gehry & Krueger, Inc., now Gehry Partners, LLP), Santa Monica, Calif., 1962—. William Bishop chair Yale U, 1979, Charlotte Davenport Professorship in Architecture, 82, 85, 1987—89, 1999; Eliot Noyes chair Harvard U., 1984; vis. scholar Fed. Inst. Tech., Zürich, Switzerland, 1996—97; vis. prof. UCLA, 1998. Prin. works include Loyola Law Sch., LA, 1978—92, Temporary Contemporary Mus., 1983, Calif. Aerospace Mus., 1984, Frances Goldwyn Regional Br. Libr., Hollywood, Calif., 1986, U.C.I. Info. and Computer Sci./Engring. Rsch. Lab. and Engring Ctr., Irvine, Calif., 1986—88, Vitra Internat. Mfg. Facility and Design Mus., Weil am Rhein, Germany, 1989, Chiat/Day Hdqs., Venice, Calif., 1991, Advanced Tech. Labs. Bldg., U. Iowa, Iowa City, 1992, U. Toledo Ctr. for Visual Arts, Toledo, Ohio, 1992, Walt Disney Concert Hall, LA, 1993, Frederick R. Weisman Art Mus., Mpls., 1993, Vitra Internat. Hdqs., Basel, Switzerland, 1994, Am. Ctr., Paris, 1994, Team Disneyland Adminstrn. Bldg., Anaheim, Calif., 1995, EMR Communication and Tech. Ctr., Bad Oeynhausen, Germany, 1995, Nationale-Nederlanden Bldg., Prague, Czech Republic, 1996, Guggenheim Mus., Bilbao, Spain, 1997, Vontz Ctr. for Molecular Studies, U. Cin., Ohio, 1999, Der Neue Zolihof, Dusseldorf, Germany, 1999, DG Bank Hdqrs., Berlin, Germany, 2000, Experience Music Project, Seattle, 2000, Bard Coll. Ctr. for the Performing Arts, Annandale-on-Hudson, NY, 2001, The Walt Disney Concert Hall, LA, 2002, Peter B. Lewis Weatherhead Sch. Mgmt. Case Western Reserve U., Cleve., 2003, Ray and Maria Stata Ctr., MIT, Cambridge, Mass., 2003, and several others, selected exhbn. designs, Art Treasures of Japan, LA County Mus. Art, 1965, Assyrian Reliefs, 1966, Billy Al Bengston Retrospective, 1968, Treasures of Tutankhamen, 1978, Avant-Garde of Russia 1910-1930, 1980, Seventeen Artists in the Sixties, 1981, German Expressionist Sculpture, 1983, Degenerate Art, 1994, Exiles & Emigrés, 1997, The Art of the Motorcycle, Solomon R. Guggenheim Mus., NY, 1998, Guggenheim Mus., Bilbao, Spain, 1999; work featured in major architectural publs. including Newsweek, Time, Forbes, Economist, Vanity Fair, Art in America, Wall Street Jour., NY Times, LA Times, Washington Post, Le Monde, L'Express, El Correo and Frankfurter Allgemeine. Trustee Hereditary Disease Found., Santa Monica, Calif., 1970—. Named Hon. Consul, City of Bilbao, Spain, 1997, Chancellor, 1998; recipient Arnold W. Brunner Meml. prize in architecture, AAAL, 1983, Pritzker Architecture prize, Hyatt Found., 1989, Wolf prize in art, Wolf Found., 1992, Praemium Imperiale award, Japan Art Assn., 1992, Dorothy and Lilian Gish award, 1994, Nat. Medal of Arts, Nat. Endowment of the Arts, 1998, Friedrich Kiesler prize, Friedrich Kiesler Found., 1998, Gold medal, Royal Architectural Inst. Canada, 1998, Lotus medal of Merit, Lotos Club, 1999, Gold medal, Am. Inst. of Architects, 1999,

Lifetime Achievement award, Am. for the Arts, 2000. Fellow: Am. Inst. Architects, AAAS, AAAL; mem.: Royal Acad. Arts (hon. academician 1998), Nat. Acad. Design (academician 1994), Am. Acad. Rome (trustee 1989). Office: Gehry Partners LLP 12541 Beatrice St Los Angeles CA 90066*

GEIBEL, SISTER GRACE ANN, university president; b. Sept. 17, 1937; BA in Piano and Music Edn., Carlow Coll., 1961; MA in Music Edn., U. Rochester, 1967, PhD in Music, 1975. Tchr. elem. and high schs., 1959-67; ch. musician, 1972-80; assoc. prof. and co-chmn. music dept. Carlow Coll., Pitts., 1981-82, acting acad. dean, 1982-83, dean, 1983-88, v.p. acad. affairs, 1984-88, pres., 1988—2005. Mem. adv. bd. Pitts. Symphony Soc.; bd. dir. Oakland Cath. H.S., Urban League Pitts., Penn. Econ. League. Office: Carlow Univ Office of the Pres 3333 5th Ave Pittsburgh PA 15213-3109 Business E-Mail: geibelga@carlow.edu.

GEIER, KATHLEEN T., human resources specialist; b. Akron, Ohio, Aug. 7, 1956; BS, Heidelberg Coll., 1978. Indsl. engr., various human resources positions Goodyear Tire and Rubber Co., Akron, Ohio, 1978—86; ops. mgr. Cosmoflex (subsidiary of Goodyear Tire and Rubber Co.), 1986—90, plant mgr., pres. Mt. Pleasant, Iowa, 1992—94; bus. ctr. mgr. Goodyear Tire and Rubber Co., St. Marys, Ohio, 1990—92, dir. salaried human resources end employment practices Akron, Ohio, 1994—95, dir. human resources employment practices and systems, 1995—96, dir. human resources ctrl. svcs. N.Am. bus. unites and corp. staff, 1996—99, dir. human resources Europe, Africa, Middle East region Brussels, sr. v.p. human resources Akron, 2002—. Office: Goodyear Tire and Rubber Co 1144 E Market St Akron OH 44316-0001 Office Phone: 330-796-2121. Office Fax: 330-796-2222.*

GEIER, PHILIP HENRY, JR., advertising executive; b. Pontiac, Mich., Feb. 22, 1935; s. Philip Henry and Jane (Gillen) G.; m. Faith Power, children: Hope Smith, Johanna Howard. BA, Colgate U., 1957; MS, Columbia U., 1958. With McCann-Erickson, Inc., Cleve., 1958-60, NYC, 1960-68; chmn. McCann-Erickson Internat. U.K. Co., London, 1969-73; exec. v.p. McCann-Erickson Europe, 1973-75; vice chmn. internat. ops. McCann Worldwide, London, 1973-75; vice chmn. internat. Interpublic Group of Cos., Inc., NYC, 1975-77, pres., chief operating officer, 1977-80, chmn., chief exec. officer, 1980—2001, pres., 1985—2000, chmn. emeritus. Bd. dirs. AEA Investors, Inc., Alcon Labs. Inc., Fiduciary Trust Internat. Inc., Foot Locker, Inc., Mettler-Toledo Internat. Inc., IAG Rsch. Inc. Dir. Sch. of Am. Ballet, Internat. Tennis Hall of Fame; bd. overseers Meml. Sloan-Kettering Cancer Ctr., Columbia U. Bus. Sch.; trustee Whitney Mus. of Am. Art, Autism Speaks. Mem.: Doubles (NYC); River (NYC); Sloane (London); Hurlingham (London). Address: The Geier Group 70 E 55th St New York NY 10022 Office Phone: 646-840-6721. Business E-Mail: pgeier@geiergroup.com.

GEIER, PHILIP OTTO, III, volunteer, director, academic administrator; b. Cin., 1948; s. Philip O. Jr. and Susanne (Ernst) G.; m. Amy Yeager, Dec. 27, 1975; children: Katherine, Elizabeth, Christopher. BA in Am. Civilization with honors, Williams Coll., 1970; attended, U. Paris, 1973; MA in History, Syracuse U., 1975, PhD in Am. Studies and History, 1980. Instr. history and Am. studies Dickinson Coll., Carlisle, Pa., 1976-77; Fulbright lectr. U. Paris-Sorbonne, 1977-78; interim exec. dir. French-Am. Found., N.Y.C., 1978-79; assoc. dir. Am. Farm Sch., Thessaloniki, Greece, 1979-82; v.p. external affairs World Learning, Brattleboro, Vt., 1982-93; pres., dir. United World Coll.-USA, Montezuma, N.Mex., 1993—2005; exec. dir. Davis United World Coll. Scholars Program, 2005—; spl. advisor to pres. Middlebury Coll., 2005—. Bd. dirs. Fulbright Prize Com., Washington, Pine Manor Coll., United World Coll.; chair social Svcs. and Internat. Exch. Commn. 2d U.S.-USSR Emerging Leaders Summit, Moscow and Sochi, 1990, del. to 1st Commn., Phila., 1988; mem. Coun. Fgn. Rels., Pacific Coun. on Internat. Policy, L.A. Supply Corps officer, USN, 1970-72, Vietnam. Fulbright award Fed. Republic of Germany, 1988. Avocations: international relations, outdoor recreation. Office: Middlebury Coll 14 Chapel Rd Middlebury VT 05753

GEIGEL, PATRICK RAYMOND, secondary school educator, coach; s. William V. and Sally Geigel; m. Laura J. Habeck, Oct. 25, 1986; children: Brent Patrick, Drew William. BS in Edn., Silver Lake Coll., 1982, MA in Edn., 1993. Cert. in edn. Wis. Educator New Holstein (Wis.) H.S., 1982—99, Kiel (Wis.) H.S., 1999—. Basketball coach New Holstein H.S., 1986—98, Lakeland Coll., Sheboygan, Wis., 1998—99; basketball coach, mentaor facilitator Kiel H.S.; COG facilitator U. Wis., Green Bay, 1996—99. Mem.: ASCD, Fellowship of Christian Athletes, Wis. Basketball Coaches Assn. Office: Kiel HS 210 Raider Heights Kiel WI 53042 Office Phone: 920-894-5136. Personal E-mail: pgeigel@kiel.k12.wi.us.

GEIGER, ALBERT J., JR., retired radiologist; b. Elberton, Ga., 1929; s. Albert James and Sara Frances (Asbury) G.; m. Laura Marvine Gillespie, June 10, 1956; children: Albert J. III, Laura E. Geiger Hornsby, Suzanne C. Geiger Ballenger. AB, Princeton U., 1951; MD, Emory U., 1955. Bd. cert. radiology, 1965; diplomate Am. Bd. Radiology. Intern Grady Meml. Hosp., Atlanta, 1955-56; resident in radiology Emory U. Hosp., 1958-61; rsch. fellow USPHS Nat. Cancer Inst., 1959-60; staff St. Anthony's Hosp., St. Petersburg, Fla. Adv. bd. St. Petersburg (Fla.) Jr. Coll. Sch. Radiologic Tech., 1990-95. Recipient Disting. Citizen award, West Ctrl. Coun. Boy Scouts Am., 2002, Silver Beaver award, West Ctrl. Fla. Coun. Boy Scouts Am., 2003. Mem. AMA, Fla. Med. Assn., Fla. Radiology Soc., Radiol. Soc. N.Am., So. Med. Assn., Pinellas County Med. Soc. (bd. govs. 1984-87, Achievement award 1982), St. Anthony's Hosp. Med. Alumni, Rotary Club St. Petersburg (pres. 1970-71). Republican. Methodist.

GEIGER, ALEXANDER, lawyer; b. Kosice, Czechoslovakia, May 21, 1950; came to U.S., 1965; s. Emil and Alice (Brickmann) G.; m. Helene R. Mortar, May 28, 1972; children: Theodore, Aviva. AB, Princeton U., 1972; JD, Cornell U., 1975. Bar: N.Y. 1976, U.S. Dist. Ct. (we. dist.) N.Y. 1976, U.S. Supreme Ct. 1980, U.S. Ct. Appeals (2d cir.) 1985, U.S. Tax Ct. 1986. Assoc. Nixon, Hargrave, Devans & Doyle, Rochester, N.Y., 1975-82; sr. ptnr. Geiger & Rothenberg, Rochester, 1982—. Adj. asst. prof. St. John Fisher Coll., Rochester, 1977-78. Mem. N.Y. State Bar Assn., Monroe County Bar Assn., Assn. Trial Lawyers Am., Rochester Inns of Ct. (master). Jewish. Home: 227 Brittany Ln Pittsford NY 14534 also: 30 Newport Pkwy # 3009 Jersey City NJ 07310 Office: Geiger & Rothenberg 45 Exchange Blvd Ste 800 Rochester NY 14614-2093 also: Geiger and Rothenberg 30 Vesey St 4th Fl New York NY 10007 Business E-Mail: ageiger@geigroth.com.

GEIGER, DAVID E, engineer; b. Passaic, NJ, May 28, 1954; s. Gordon R and Norma B Geiger; children: Jesse David, Andrea Nicole. BEE with honors, Stevens Inst. Tech., 1976, MEE, 1989; cert. in bus. adminstrn., Heriot-Watt U., Scotland, 2002. Registered profl. engr., NJ. Engr. Universal Mfg., Paterson, NJ, 1976, Transistor Devices, Cedar Knolls, NJ, 1976—77; mem. tech. staff ITT Def. Commn. Divsn., Nutley, NJ, 1977—79; art dir. Hudson Studios, Totowa, NJ, 1981—83; engr. KDI Electronics, Whippany, NJ, 1983—84, Western Union Telegraph Co., Upper Saddle River, NJ, 1984—85, Merrimac Industries, West Caldwell, NJ, 1985, Con Edison of NY, 1987—2000; owner, home inspector Hip Home Inspections, 2004—. Author: Change Happens: What Direction for NNJM:, 1995 (Mensa award, 1995). Mem.: Am. Mensa Ltd. Republican. Roman Cath. Avocations: hiking, pen pals. Mailing: P O Box 3577 Wayne NJ 07474 Personal E-mail: commish123@juno.com.

GEIGER, JAMES NORMAN, lawyer; b. Mansfield, Ohio, Apr. 5, 1932; s. Ernest R. and Margaret L. (Bauman) G.; m. Paula Hunt, May 11, 1957; children: Nancy G., John W. BA, Ohio Wesleyan U., 1954; JD, Emory U., 1962, LLD, 1970. Bar: Ga. 1961, U.S. Dist. Ct. (mid. dist.) Ga. 1966, U.S. Ct. Appeals (5th and 11th cirs.) 1980, U.S. Dist. Ct. (so. dist.) Ga. 1983. Ptnr. Henderson, Kaley, Geiger and Hunt, Perry, Ga., 1962—64, Nunn, Geiger and Hunt, Perry, 1964—72, Geiger & Geiger, PC and prececessors, 1972—. Bd. visitors Westfield Schs., 2003—; trustee Westfield (Ga.) Schs., 1970—74, bd. visitors, 2003—; mem. civilian adv. bd. Warner Robins AFB, 1976; chmn. coun. ministries Perry United Meth. Ch., 1970—71, mem. adminstrv. bd., 1968—. Capt. USAF, 1954—57. Mem.: ABA, Perry C. of C. (pres. 1976, 1990), South Ga. C. of C. (bd. dirs.), Houston County Bar Assn., Ga. Bar Assn., Perry Club Coun. (pres. 1967), Perry Kiwanis (pres. 1968, Man of Yr. 1968), Phi Sigma Alpha, Phi Delta Phi. Methodist. Home: 1910 Northside Rd Perry GA 31069-2223 Office: Geiger & Geiger 1007 Jernigan St Perry GA 31069-3325 Office Phone: 478-987-2952. Business E-Mail: geigerj@alltel.net.

GEIGER, JOHN GRIGSBY, editor, writer, reporter; b. Ithaca, N.Y., Jan. 20, 1960; s. Kenneth Warren and Shirley Frances (Gilchrist) G.; m. Marina Jimenez, Oct. 15, 1999; 1 child, John Alvaro. BA, U. Alberta, 1981. Weekly columnist Edmonton Sun, 1981-83, reporter, 1983-86, Edmonton Jour., 1986-87, columnist, 1987-95, edtl. writer, 1995-98; dep. nat. editor Nat. Post, 1998-99, acting nat. editor, 1999-2000, fgn. editor-UN, 2000, rev. editor, 2000—04, editorials editor, 2004—. Co-author: Frozen in Time: The Fate of the Franklin Expedition, 1987 (best seller in U.K., Germany, Canada), Dead Silence, 1993 (best seller Canada), (children's book) Buried in Ice, 1992; editor: Empire of the Bay, 1989; author: Chapel of Extreme Experience, 2003, Nothing is True Everything is Permitted, 2004. Recipient Edward Dunlop award of excellence, Edward Dunlop Found., 1984; St. Clair Balfour fellow Massey Coll. Fellow: Royal Can. Geog. Soc., Explorers Club. Episcopalian. Office: Nat Post 300-1450 Don Mills Rd Toronto ON Canada M3B 3R5 Fax: 416-442-2212. E-mail: jgeiger@nationalpost.com.

GEIL, WILMA JEAN, librarian; b. Pitts., May 24, 1939; d. George Andrew and Elfrieda (Hemker) G. BA, Swarthmore Coll., 1961; MLS, U. Ill., 1964, MusM, 1967. Assoc. music librarian U. Ill., Urbana, 1963—2001; ret., 2001. Co-author: Resources of American Music History, 1981; contbr. articles to profl. jours. Mem. Music Libr. Assn. (bd. dirs. 1983-85, rec. sec. 1988-90), Soc. Am. Music (sec. 1975-83, spl. issues coord. Am. Music 1983-89, bd. dirs. 1997-1999, Disting. Svc. award 2003). Home: 60 N Kuakini St No 1 B Honolulu HI 96817

GEILFUSS, C. FREDERICK, II, lawyer; b. Aug. 5, 1953; BA cum laude, Williams Coll., Williamstown, Mass., 1975; MA in econs., U. Wis., 1976, JD cum laude, 1979. Bar: Wis. 1979, U.S. Ct. Appeals, seventh cir. 1979, U.S. Supreme Ct. 1982, U.S. Dist. Ct., Ea. Dist. Wis. 1983. Law clk. Hon. Judy Harlington Wood, Jr., U.S. Ct. Appeals, 7th Cir., 1979-80; atty., appellate staff Civil divsn. U.S. Dept. Justice, Washington, 1980-83; atty. Foley & Lardner LLP, Milw., 1983, ptnr., chmn. health care bus. counseling. Co-author: chpt. Long-Term Care Facilities: Regulation. Mem.: State Bar Wis., Nat. Health Lawyers Assn., ABA, Wis. Psychol. Found. (mem. 1992—), Curative Rehabilitation Svc. (mem. 1993—, chmn. 1997—99, 1997—), Milw. County War Meml. Inc., Columbia Coll. Nursing (mem. 1995), Grand Ave. Club (mem. 2000—, 1998—), Gardner Found. (mem. 1993—), Milw. County Marcus Ctr. Performing Arts (mem. 1990—, chmn. 1998—2001), Order Coif. Office: Foley & Lardner LLP 777 E Wisconsin Ave Milwaukee WI 53202-5306 Office Phone: 414-297-5650. Office Fax: 414-297-4900. Business E-Mail: fgeilfuss@foley.com.

GEILING, LOUISE ELIZABETH, elementary school educator, secondary school educator; b. New Milford, N.J., Aug. 25, 1934; d. Samuel and Susan Lagrotteria; m. Jacob V. Geiling, Apr. 17, 1960 (dec. Apr. 1998); children: Janet Darvin, Lois Nagie. BS, Montclair State U., N.J., 1955; MA, Montclair State U., 1959; postgrad., William Paterson Coll., Monmouth Coll. Cert. tchr. K-8, tchr. 9-12 in social studies, geography, guidance counselor. Tchr. 4th grade Roosevelt Sch., River Edge, NJ, 1955—56; tchr, reading specialist, guidance counselor Bergenfield Jr./Sr. H.S., NJ, 1956—60; tchr. learning disabilities, elem. and mem. child study team River Vale Schs., 1971—81, tchr. gifted and talented, 1981—85, elem. tchr., 1985—94; substitute tchr. grades K-8 Waldwick Bd. Edn. and Allendale Bd. Edn., NJ, 1994—2001. Contbr. poetry to profl. pubs. CCD tchr. Assumption Parish, Emerson, NJ, 1962—64; tchr. CCD St. Elizabeth Parish, Wyckoff, NJ; leader Girl Scouts U.S., Park Ridge, NJ, 1971—73. Recipient A+ Tchr. award, Students of River Vale, 1990. Mem.: AAUW (charter, v.p. 1962—64), Jr. Women's Club (v.p. 1965—67). Roman Catholic. Avocations: piano, bridge, writing, sports. Home: 181 Mabie Ct Mahwah NJ 07430

GEIMAN, J. ROBERT, lawyer; b. Evanston, Ill., Mar. 5, 1931; s. Louis H. and Nancy O'Connell-Crowe G.; m. Ann L. Fitzgerald, July 29, 1972; children: J. Robert, William Patrick, Timothy Michael. BS, Northwestern U., 1953; JD, Notre Dame U., 1956. Bar: Ill. 1956, U.S. Ct. Appeals (7th cir.) 1956, U.S. Supreme Ct. 1969. Assoc. Eckert, Peterson & Lowry, Chgo., 1956-64; ptnr. Peterson, Lowry, Rall, Barber & Ross, Chgo., 1964-70, Peterson & Ross, Chgo., 1970-96, of counsel, 1996—. Mem. com. on civil jury instructions Ill. Supreme Ct., 1979-81. Case editor Notre Dame Law Rev., 1956. Bd. advisors Cath. Charities of Archdiocese of Chgo., 1973-96. Fellow Internat. Acad. Trial Lawyers, Am. Coll. Trial Lawyers, Ill. Bar Found.; mem. ABA (aviation com., tort and ins. practice sect. 1980-90), Ill. Bar Assn. (sec. 1969-70, sec. bd. govs. 1969-71), Chgo. Bar Assn. (aviation law com. 1970-73), Bar Assn. of 7th Fed. Ct. (meetings com. 1968-70, vice chmn. membership com. 1973-75), Soc. Trial Lawyers, Cath. Lawyers Guild of Chgo. (bd. advisors 1973-96), Law Club Chgo., Chgo. Athletic Assn. (pres. 1973). Republican. Home: 900 SW Bay Point Cir Palm City FL 34990-1758 Office: Peterson & Ross 200 E Randolph St Ste 7300 Chicago IL 60601-7012

GEIRSSON, JONAS, dentist; b. Reykjavik, Iceland, June 6, 1961; s. Geir Christensen and Gudrun Edvaldsdottir; m. Hafdis Dogg Hafsteinsdottir, Sept. 3, 1988; children: Trausti Jonasson, Dagmar Elsa Jonasdottir. DDS, U. Iceland, Reykjavik, 1982; MS, U. N.C., Chapel Hill, 2004. Cert. in operative dentistry State of N.C., 2004. Forensic dentistry The Icelandic Identification Com., Reykjavik, 1993—2001; mem. bd. com. Icelandic Dental Assn., Reykjavik, 1997—2001. Office: Tannlaeknastofa Jonasar Geirssonar Kirkjubraut 28 Akranes 300 Iceland Office Phone: +354 431 2355. Office Fax: +354 431 2365. E-mail: tennu@simnet.is.

GEIS, GEORGE SAMUEL, management consultant; MBA, JD, U. Chgo. Mgmt. cons. McKinsey & Co., L.A., 1997—. Mem. Calif. Bar Assn. Office: McKinsey & Co 400 Hope St Los Angeles CA 90071 E-mail: george_geis@mckinsey.com.

GEIS, JEROME ARTHUR, lawyer, law educator; b. Shakopee, Minn., May 28, 1946; s. Arthur Adam and Emma Mary (Boegemann) G.; m. Beth Marie Bruger, Aug. 11, 1979; children: Jennifer, Jason, Joan, Janice. BA in History magna cum laude, St. John's U., Collegeville, Minn., 1968; JD cum laude, U. Notre Dame, 1973; LLM in Taxation, NYU, 1975. Bar: Minn. 1973, U.S. Dist. Ct. Minn. 1973, U.S. Tax Ct. 1973, U.S. Ct. Appeals (8th cir.) 1973. Law clk. Minn. Supreme Ct., St. Paul, 1973-74; assoc. Dudley & Smith, St. Paul, 1975-76, Briggs & Morgan P.A., St. Paul, 1976-79, chief tax dept., 1983-95. Adj. prof. tax law William Mitchell Coll. of Law, St. Paul, 1976-83. Columnist Minn. Law Jour., 1986-89, Bench & Bar, 1990—; editl. cons.: Sales and Use Tax Alert; former reviewer Summary Reporter: Finance and Commerce, Minnesota State Bar Assn.; corr. State Tax Notes. Bd. dirs. Western Townhouse Assn., West St. Paul, 1979, St. Matthews Cath. Ch., West St. Paul, 1981; adv. bd. Minn. Inst. of Legal Edn., 1984—2002. Served to specialist 4th class U.S. Army, 1969-71. Fellow Am. Coll. Tax Counsel; mem. ABA, Am. Law Inst., Tax Inst. Am. (chmn. sales and use tax commn. 1988-90), Nat. Tax Assn., Am. Judicature Soc., Minn. Bar Assn. (bd. dirs. tax coun. sect. 1984-93, 94-97, 99—, chmn. 1990-91), Ramsey County Bar Assn., Minn. Taxpayers Assn. (bd. dirs. 1988—), Inst. Property Taxation, Supreme Ct. Hist. Soc., Nat. Assn. State Bar Tax Sects. (exec. com. 1993—), Citizens League, Minn. Club (bd. dirs. 1997-2000), Federalist Soc., Kiwanis (bd. dirs. 2000-02). Home: 1116 Dodd Rd Saint Paul MN 55118-1821 Office: Briggs & Morgan PA 2200 1st St N Saint Paul MN 55109-3210 Office Phone: 651-808-6409. E-mail: JGeis@Briggs.com.

GEIS, MILTON ARTHUR, painter, writer; b. Milw., Jan. 31, 1926; s. Edgar Gustave and Olga Louise (Jennrich) Geis; m. Donna Ellen Holtz, Aug. 21, 1954; children: Joseph Patrick, Kalen Ann. BFA, Webster U., St. Louis, 1983; MFA, Syracuse U., N.Y., 1986. Scenic artist WTMJ-TV, Milw., 1950—52; art dir. WBAY-TV, Green Bay, Wis., 1953—55, WXIX-TV, Milw., 1955—58; dir., design KMOX-TV, St. Louis, 1959—85; instr. Maryville U., St. Louis, 1988—90. Exhibitions include McCaughen and Burr Fine Arts Gallery, Hallmark Corp., Kans. City, Tex. Tech. U., Centenary Coll, Shreveport, La., Milw. Art Ctr., Chgo. Art Inst. Mem.: Audubon Artists (Silver Medal of Honor 1991), Watercolor U.S.A. Honor Soc., Nat. Watercolor Soc. (The Strathmore Award 1982, 1984, 1985). Avocations: writing, reading, history. Home: 162 Ameren Way Apt 830 Ballwin MO 63021

GEIS, STEPHEN ANTHONY, music educator; b. Cin., July 11, 1952; m. Monica D. Geis, May 1, 1963; children: David, Jason. MusB, U. Cinn. Coll. Conservatory Music, 1974. Band dir. Elder HS, Cin., 1974—2005. Mem.: Ohio Music Educator's Assn. Home: 1038 Coronado Ave Cincinnati OH 45238 Office: Elder HS 3900 Vincent Ave Cincinnati OH 45205 Office Phone: 513-921-3744. Business E-Mail: geis.s@elderhs.org.

GEISEL, CAMERON MEADE, JR., brokerage house executive; b. Harrisburg, Pa., Oct. 7, 1937; s. Cameron Meade and Dorothy Mae G.; m. Martha L. Frohring, Sept. 3, 1977 (dec.); children: Melissa Ellen, Gregory Stuart, Andrew Frohring, Martha Bliss; m. Saskia Hessler, Sept. 8, 1991. BA, Bucknell U., Lewisburg, Pa., 1960; grad. Sch. Credit and Fin. Mgmt., Harvard U., 1970; Advanced Mgmt Program, Harvard Bus. Sch., 1985. With Phila. Nat. Bank, 1961-86, asst. v.p., then v.p., 1965-77, sr. v.p., 1977-86. Bd. dirs. Hessler Properties, Inc. Trustee Lankenau Hosp. Found., Fox Chase Cancer Ctr., Cardigan Mountain Sch. Corp., Morris Arboretum. 2d lt. inf. U.S. Army, 1960-61. Mem. U.S. Coun. Internat. Bus. (trustee, exec. com.), Merion Golf Club, Merion Cricket Club, Phila. Club, Racquet Club (Phila.), Royal Ashdown Forest Golf Cloub, Royal and Ancient Golf Club of St. Andrews, Honourable Co. of Edinburgh Golfers, Loblolly Pines Golf Club, Sunningdale Golf Club. Republican. Episcopalian. Home: 1411 Youngsford Rd Gladwyne PA 19035-1232

GEISEL, HAROLD WALTER, diplomat; b. Chgo., May 11, 1947; s. Gustav and Stefi Geisel; m. Susan L. Gordon, Oct. 2, 1983; children: Jacqueline Julie, Katherine Louise. BA in History, Johns Hopkins U., 1968; MBA, U. Va., 1970. Commd. fgn. service officer Dept. State, 1970, adminstrv. officer Washington, 1973-75; 1st sec. Am. embassy, Bern, Switzerland, 1975-78, Bamako, Mali, 1978-80; adminstrv. officer Dept. State, Washington, 1980-82; consul gen. U.S. consulate gen., Durban, South Africa, 1982-85; mem. NATO Def. Coll., Rome, 1985-86; adminstrv. counsellor Am. Embassy, Rome, 1986-88, adminstrv. minister-counsellor Bonn, 1988-92, adminstrv. minister-counselor Moscow, 1992-93; exec. asst. to under-sec. Dept. State, Washington, 1993-94, deputy inspector gen., 1994-95, dep. asst. sec. for info. mgmt., 1995-96, amb. to Mauritius, Seychelles, and Comoros, 1996-99, sr. negotiator, 1999-2000; acting dep. asst. sec. logistics mgmt. Dept. State A/LM, Washington, 2001—; head U.S. Dels. to U.S.-Chinese COCA Negotiations, 2002. Jewish. E-mail: hwgeisel@mindspring.com.

GEISELMAN, LUCYANN, college president; m. Robert L. Harrington; 1 child, Gabriella. BA in Religion, MA in Theology, Tex. Christian U.; PhD in Edn., U. Chgo. Former v.p. Eisenhower Med. Ctr., Rancho Mirage, Calif.; v.p. for planning and Advancement Calif. Inst. of Arts, 1989-91; pres. Mt. Vernon Coll., Washington, 1991—.

GEISELMAN, PAULA JEANNE, psychologist, educator; b. Ohio, June 30, 1944; d. Paul and Rosemary (Dawson) Parsley. AB in Psychology with honors, Ohio U., 1971, MS in Exptl. Psychology, 1976; PhD in Physiol. Psychology, UCLA, 1983. Adj. asst. prof. UCLA, 1986-91; dir. psychophysiol. rsch. UCLA Sch. Medicine, 1986-91; assoc. prof. dept. psychology La. State U., Baton Rouge, 1991—; adj. assoc. prof. Pennington Biomed. Rsch. Ctr. La State U., Baton Rouge, 1991—. Lectr. in field. Reviewer for Sci. Jour., Am. Jour. Physiology, Physiology and Behavior, Brain Research Bulletin, Appetite: Determinants and Consequences of Eating and Drinking; contbr. numerous articles to profl. jours. Mem. Soc. Neurosci., AAAS, N.Am. Assn. Study of Obesity, Women in Neurosci., Assn. Acad. Women, Am. Psychol. Assn., Am. Psychol. Assn., Eastern Psychol. Assn., Western Psychol. Assn. (head of physiol. psychol., chair. Animal Feeding and Behavior paper session 1981), Assn. Advancement Psychology, Internat. Brain Research Orgn., World Fedn. Neuroscientists, Brit. Brain Research Assn. (hon.), European Brain and Behavior Soc. (hon.), N.Y. Acad. Scis., Sigma Xi, Psi Chi. Achievements include rsch. on the behavioral, nutritional and physiological mechanisms of energy, appetite and body weight regulation in humans and animal models; on the role of the liver, gut, vagus, sympathetic nervous system, enteric and pancreatic hormones in the control of food intake and body weight; on the role of macronutrients (especially carbohydrates and fats and their breakdown products) in the control of food intake and body weight; on the physiological and nutritional control of ingestive behavior in females across the estrous and menstrual cycles; on an animal model of anorexia nervosa; on meal-patterning analysis; on human taste psychophysiology, especially in smokers and in women across the menstrual cycle; on the relationship between smoking, food intake, and body weight control; and on patient compliance. Office: La State U Psychology Dept Pennington Biomed Rsch Ctr 6400 Perkins Rd Baton Rouge LA 70808-4124

GEISENDORFER, JAMES VERNON, religious writer, researcher; b. Brewster, Minn., Apr. 22, 1929; s. Victor H. and Anne B. (Johnson) G.; m. Esther Lillian Walker, Sept. 23, 1949; children: Jane, Karen, Lois. Student, Augustana Coll., 1950-51, Augsburg Coll., 1951-54, Orthodox Luth. Sem., 1954-55; BA, U. Minn., 1960; LLD, Burton Coll. and Sem., 1961. Grain buyer Pillsbury Mills, Inc., Worthington, Minn., 1947-48; acct. Boote Hatcheries, Worthington, 1949-50; night supr. Strutwear, Inc., Mpls., 1951-52; dispatcher Chgo. and North Western Ry., 1953-54; office mgr. Froedtert Malt Corp., Mpls., 1955-56, Nat. Automotive Parts Assn., 1957-60; sr. creative writer Brown & Bigelow, St. Paul, 1960-72; religious rschr., writer, 1972—. Rsch. cons. Inst. for the Study of Am. Religion; mem. panel of reference Chelston Bible Coll., New Milton, Eng. Author: (with J. Gordon Melton) A Directory of Religious Bodies in the United States, 1977, Religion in America, 1983, Religion USA, 1989; mem. editl. bd. Biog. Dictionary Am. Cult and Sect Leaders; contbr. articles to profl. jours.; cons. editor Directory of Religious Organizations in the United States, 1977. Recipient Amicus Poloniae medal Polish Ministry of Culture and Edn., 1969. Mem. AAAS, Am. Acad. Religion, Acad. Ind. Scholars, Wis. Evang. Luth. Synod Hist. Inst., Augustana Hist. Soc., Royal Anthrop. Inst., Ea. Territorial Hist. Soc. (charter), Medieval Acad. Am., Renaissance Soc. Am., George Eliot Fellowship, Wis. Acad. Scis., Arts and Letters, Aristotelian Soc., Hegel Soc. Am., Sixteenth Century Studies Conf., Am. Cath. Philos. Assn., N.Am. Conf. on Brit. Studies, Internat. Soc. for Comparative Study of Civilizations, Religous Rsch. Assn., Internat. Assn. Greek Philosophy, Brit. Soc. Philosophy Religion, Inst. Interdisciplinary Rsch., Inst. for Advanced Studies in Culture, Thomas More Law Ctr., Chs. of God Hist. Soc., Am. Friends the Vatican Libr. Lutheran. Address: 1001 Shawano Ave Green Bay WI 54303-3020

GEISER, ELIZABETH ABLE, publishing company executive; b. Phillipsburg, N.J., Apr. 28, 1925; d. George W. and Margaret I. (Ross) G. AB magna cum laude, Hood Coll., 1947. Promotion mgr. coll. dept. Macmillan Co., N.Y.C., 1947-54; promotion mgr. R.R. Bowker, N.Y.C., 1954-60, sales mgr., 1960-67, dir. mktg., 1967-70, v.p., 1970-73, sr. v.p., 1973-75, sr. v.p., pub. book divsn.; adj. prof., dir. U. Denver Pub. Inst., 1976—; sr. v.p. Gale Rsch. Co., 1976-91, cons., 1991—. Cons. Excerpta Medica, Elsevier, 1976-82; lectr. pub. procedures Radcliffe Coll., 1966-75; lectr. schs. libr. sci. U. Wash., U. So. Calif.; panel mem. TV series Living Library, 1970 Editor: The Business of Book Publishing, 1985; contbr. Manual of Bookselling, 1969. Trustee Hood Coll., 1993-99. Inducted into Publishing Hall of Fame, 1988. Mem. Assn. Am. Pubs. (exec. coun. prof. and scholarly pub. divsn. 1989-91, adv. coun. Frankfurt book fair 1971, sch. and libr. promotion and mktg. com. 1972-76, bd. dirs. 1982-85), ALA (pres. exhibits roundtable 1968-70, bd. dirs. exhibits roundtable 1968). Presbyterian. Home: 3329 E Bayaud Ave Denver CO 80209 Office: Pub Inst 335 E 51st St Apt 5E New York NY 10022-6765 Office Phone: 212-752-8652. E-mail: egeiser@worldnet.att.net.

GEISER, ROBERT NEIL, computer scientist; b. Cleve., Jan. 20, 1961; s. Roger Neal and Betty Lou (Keiner) G.; m. Laura Jane Burkholder, June 18, 1983; children: Jessika Christen, Benjamin, Matthew. BS in Acctg., AS in Data Processing, U. Akron, 1982. CPA, Ohio; cert. data processor, Ohio. Acct., programmer G&S Titanium, Inc., Wooster, Ohio, 1979-83, cons., 1983-93; computer specialist, acct. Hall, Kistler & Co., Canton, Ohio, 1983-88; owner Computer Productivity Assistance, Wooster, 1988—2000; MIS dir. G&S Titanium, Inc., Wooster, 1988—2000, v.p. fin., 2000—. Group leader Appalachia Service Project Home Repair, various locations, 1984-87; mem. Grace Brethren. Mem. AICPA, Ohio Soc. CPAs (chmn. local computers in practice 1987-88, mem. statewide computers in practice panel 1987-95), Nat. Assn. Accts. (Mem. of Yr. award 1984-85), Assn. of the Inst. for Cert. of Computer Profls. Republican. Avocations: backpacking, boy scout leading, web page design, reading and studying the bible. Home: 9520 E Moreland Rd Apple Creek OH 44606-9448 Office: G&S Titanium Inc 1550 Spruce St Wooster OH 44691-4600 Office Phone: 330-263-0564. Business E-Mail: gsbob@gstitanium.com.

GEISER, THOMAS CHRISTOPHER, lawyer, insurance company executive; b. Bern, Switzerland, Aug. 13, 1950; came to U.S., 1952; s. Henry Abraham and Pia Margaret (Tschudin) G.; m. Catherine Barlow Yeakle, Oct. 20, 1973 (div. Mar. 1983); m. Donna Lea Schweers, Jan. 3, 1987; 1 child, Kelsey Schweers. BA, U. Redlands, Calif., 1972; JD, U. Calif., San Francisco, 1977. Bar: Calif. 1978. Atty. Internat. Bur. Fiscal Documentation, Amsterdam, The Netherlands, 1977-78; assoc., ptnr. Hanson, Bridgett, Marcus, Vlahos & Stromberg, San Francisco, 1979-85; ptnr. Epstein, Becker, Stromberg & Green, San Francisco, 1985-90, Brobeck, Phleger & Harrison, San Francisco, 1990-93; sr. v.p., gen. counsel, sec. WellPoint Health Networks Inc., Woodland Hills, Calif., 1993-96, exec. v.p., gen. counsel, sec., 1996—2005. Mem. Am. Health Lawyers Assn., Calif. Soc. Health Care Attys., Order of Coif. Office Phone: 310-451-4807. Personal E-mail: thomasgeiser@aol.com.

GEISINGER, JANICE ALLAIN, accountant; b. Iroquois County, Ill., June 21, 1927; d. Carl Oliver and Constance Kathryn (Risser) Irps Allain; m. Robert Bond Geisinger, Oct. 17, 1947 (div. 1976); children: Jacque K., Holly D., Terry Joe. AA, Blackburn U., Carlinville, Ill., 1947. Lab. technician Mich. Health Lab., East Lansing, 1947-48; with Southwestern Bell Telephone, Tulsa, 1948-49; bookkeeper Geisinger Ent., Dallas, 1951-69; salesman Earl Page Real Estate, Irving, Tex., 1969-71; food purchaser Town & Country vending, Dallas, 1971-75; bookkeeper/sec. Belco C & I Wiring Inc., Irving, 1976-85; leasing bookkeeper Copiers Etc., Inc., Dallas, 1985-89; bookkeeper Kennedy Elec. Inc., Mesquite, Tex., 1989; ret., 1990. Cons. Ross Mech., Irving, 1989—; bookkeeper Metroplex Dental Group (now Dr. Julian M. Chong), 1990—, Limpede, Inc., 1999—. Crew leader Census Bur., Dallas, 1990. Mem. Am. Contract Bridge Assn. Avocations: flying, gardening, knitting, rug making. Home: 1216 E Grauwyler Rd Irving TX 75061-5031

GEISINGER, KIM ROBERT, pathologist, educator; s. Karl William Geisinger Sr. and Florence Geisinger. BS, Drexel U., 1972; MD, Med. Coll. Pa., 1976. Diplomate Am. Bd. Pathology. Dir. catology Wake Forest U. Med. Ctr., Winston-Salem, 1986—, dir. surgl. pathology, 1990—. Prof. pathology Wake Forest U., 1990—. Author: Modern Cytopathology, 2004. Office: Wake Forest Univ Med Ctr Med Ctr Blvd Winston Salem NC 27157-1072 Business E-Mail: kgeis@wfubmc.edu.

GEISLER, THOMAS MILTON, JR., lawyer; b. Orange, N.J., Jan. 16, 1943; s. Thomas M. and Helen K. (Thomas) G.; m. Sarah Ann Farrell Geisler, Aug. 6, 1977; children: Sarah C., Ann. C. AB in Math. (cum laude), Harvard Coll., Cambridge, Mass., 1965; JD, Harvard Law Sch., Cambridge, Mass., 1968. Bar: NJ, NY, Conn., U.S. Dist. Ct. (2d cir.), U.S. Supreme Ct. Asst., base legal officer U.S. Naval Submarine Base, New London, Conn., 1969-71; appellate def. counsel Naval Appellate Review Activity, Washington, 1971-72; assoc. Shearman & Sterling, N.Y.C., 1973-80, ptnr., 1980-91; pvt. practice N.Y.C., 1991-96, New Haven, Conn., 1994—. Dir., bd. dirs. Friends of Harvard Law Record, Cambridge, Mass., 1997—. Author: Am. Jur. Proof of Facts 3d, 1995, 1996, 1998, 1999, 2001; editor: Trial Practice Newsletter, 1986—2001. Lt., USNR, 1969-72. Recipient Litigation Star ABA Litigation Sect., 1997, Navy Achievement award USN, Washington, 1971. Mem. ABA (trial practice com.), Conn. Bar Assn., Harvard Club of So. Conn. (dir.), Harvard Club of N.Y.C., Quinnipiack Club, Madison Beach Club. Presbyterian. Avocations: tennis, squash, theater, concerts. Office: 205 Church St Ste 508 New Haven CT 06510 E-mail: T1827@aol.com.

GEISMAR, RICHARD LEE, communications executive; b. Paterson, N.J., Aug. 22, 1927; s. Sylvan and Marjorie (Leeser) G.; m. Patricia Willard, Nov. 27, 1954; children: John, Elisabeth, Nancy. B in Mgmt. Engring., Rensselaer Poly. Inst., 1949; MBA, Harvard, 1951. With DuMont TV Network, 1951-55, Metromedia, Inc. (and predecessors), N.Y.C., 1955-69, also bd. dirs.; pres., dir. Reeves Telecom Corp., 1969-70; comm. cons. BGW Assocs., Inc., 1970-84; chmn. Broad St. Comm. Corp., 1971-84; pres. Broad St. Ventures, 1984-98; chmn. Broad St. TV, 1989-96. Bd. dirs., treas. Greenwich chpt. ARC, mem. state svc. coun, 1992-96; bd. dirs., treas. Greenwich Adult Day Ctr., Inc., 1997-2005. Served with USNR, 1945-46. Mem. Riverside Yacht Club, Sigma Xi. Republican. Congregationalist. Home: 18 Hidden Brook Rd Riverside CT 06878 Personal E-mail: daddick37@aol.com.

GEISS, ROGER WILLIAM, pathologist, medical educator; b. Jersey City, Sept. 13, 1947; s. Robert William and Eleanor Gladys Rich; m. Agnes Josephine Meadows, Aug. 5, 1972 (dec.); m. Dianne Louise Welch, Sept. 13, 1980; children: Kevin James Easter, Kenneth David. BSc in Biology, Georgetown U., 1969; MD, Cornell U., 1975. State med. license, Colo., Iowa, Miss.; Am. Bd. Pathology; cert. in anatomic pathology, clin. pathology, cytopathology. Intern in pathology Meml. Hosp. Med. Ctr., Long Beach, Calif., 1975-76; resident in anatomic pathology U. Chgo. Hosps. and Clinics, Chgo., 1976-78; resident in clin. pathology U. Ariz. Health Sci. Ctr., Tucson, 1978-80, fellow in anatomic pathology, 1980-81; assoc. pathologist Clin. Pathologists, Inc., Colorado Springs, 1981-82, Morgantown Pathology Con., W.Va., 1982-84; asst. prof. pathology U. W.Va. U. Med. Ctr., Morgantown, 1984—89, Creighton U. Med. Ctr., Omaha, 1989—95; assoc. prof. pathology U. Miss. Med. Ctr., Jackson, 1995—. Dep. coroner El Paso County, Colorado Springs, 1981-82; dep. med. examiner Monongalia County, W.Va., 1984-89; consulting pathologist Mercy Hosp., Corning, Iowa, 1989-92, designated forensic pathologist State of Miss., Jackson, 2000—. Contbr. articles to profl. jours. including Am. Jour. Otology, 1991, Bulletin of Pathology Edn., 1994, So. Med. Jour., 1996, Modern Pathology, 1999, Pathology Education, 2001, Archives of Pathology and Laboratory Medicine, 2002, 04. Mem. Golden Apple award Creighton U., Omaha, 1993, Alpha Omega Alpha award Creighton U., 1994. Fellow Coll. Am. Pathologists, Am. Soc. Clin. Pathologists; mem. W.Va. Assn. Pathologists (sec./treas. 1988-89), Group Rsch. Pathology Edn. (pres. 1999-2001), Internat. Acad. Pathology, Internat. Assn. Med. Sci. Educators. Avocations: photography, travel, distance running. Home: 6295 Old Canton Rd #2A Jackson MS 39211 Office: Dept Pathology U Ill Coll Medicine 1 Illini Dr Box 1649 Peoria IL 61656-1649 Office Phone: 601-984-1532. E-mail: rgeiss@pathology.umsmed.edu.

GEISSBUHLER, STEPHAN, graphics designer; b. Zofingen, Kanton Aargau, Switzerland, Oct. 21, 1942; arrived in US, 1967; s. Theodor and Ruth (Schneider) Geissbuhler; m. Elissa Beth Feuerman, June 26, 1983; children: Alexander Charles, Benjamin Adam;children from previous marriage: Marc Phillip, Christopher Luke. MA, Sch. Design Basel, 1964. Designer J.R. Geigy A.G., Basel, Switzerland, 1964-67; assoc. prof., dept. chmn. Phila. Coll. Art, 1967-73; design cons. Murphy-Levy-Wurman Architects, Phila., 1968-71; designer/assoc. Anspach-Grossman-Portugal, Inc., NYC, 1973-75; assoc. ptnr. Chermayeff & Geismar, Inc., NYC, 1975-79, ptnr., 1979—2005, C & G Ptnrs., 2005—. Mem. faculty improvement Fed. Graphics, Washington, 1976—; vis. lectr. field. With Swiss Army, 1962—67. Recipient nat. prize applied art, Fed. Govt. Switzerland, 1966, 1967, Gold medal, NY Art Dirs. Club, 1984, Gold medal, Lifetime Achievement award, Am. Inst. Graphic Arts, 2005. Mem.: Alliance Graphique Internat. (pres. US membership 1993—2000), Group Environ. Edn., Am. Ctr. Design, Am. Inst. Graphic Arts (v.p., dir. 1980—83, pres. NY chpt. 1984—86), NY Art Dirs. Club. Methodist. Office: C & G Ptnrs Inc 116 East 16th St New York NY 10003 Office Phone: 212-532-4460. Business E-Mail: steff@cgpartnersllc.com.

GEISSINGER, FREDERICK WALLACE, finance company executive; b. Huntingdon, Pa., Oct. 3, 1945; s. Harry Lloyd and Elizabeth Gertrude Geissinger; m. Anne Beth Lawrenz, Feb. 14, 1970 (div.); children: Amy Elizabeth, Jacqueline Marie. AB, Dartmouth Coll., 1967; MBA, U. Chgo., 1969. Lic. in securities and real estate, N.Y.C. Corp. banking officer Chase Manhattan Bank, N.Y.C., 1969-74, dir. corp. planning, 1974-76, asst. gen. mgr. Tokyo, 1976-80, chief staff Western Hemisphere N.Y.C., 1980-83, budget dir., 1983-86, sr. v.p. real estate, 1986-90; exec. v.p. Daiwa Securities Am. Inc., N.Y.C., 1990-92; prin. Geissinger and Assocs., N.Y.C., 1993; CEO Am. Gen. Land Devel. Inc., Houston, 1994-95, Am. Gen. Mortgage and Land Devel. Inc., 1995; chmn., CEO Am. Gen. Finance, Evansville, Ind., 1995—; vice chmn., group exec. Am. Gen. Corp., Houston, 1998—. Trustee Pelham (N.Y.) Bd. Edn., 1983-86. Mem. Urban Land Inst. (coun. 1986—), Real Estate Bd. N.Y., Pelham Country club (bd. govs. 1987-92, pres. 1990-92). Republican. Presbyterian. Avocations: skiing, golf, tennis, coaching girls soccer, classical music.

GEIST, GEORGE F., judge; b. Pottsville, Pa., June 18, 1955; BA cum laude, Ursinus Coll.; JD, Rutgers U. Sch. Law. Assembly mem. dist. 4 N.J. State Assembly, 1992—2004; apptd. workers' compensation judge Burlington County, 2004—. Atty. Chmn. Camden County Rep. Com., 1983-91. Office: Burlington Twshp Municipal Ct 851 Old York Rd Burlington NJ 08016

GEIST, KATHE STERNBACH, art history, cinema and English educator, writer; b. Lansing, Mich., Mar. 6, 1948; d. Robert John and Margaret Antoinette Geist; m. Steven Sternbach, Feb. 14, 1991. BA, U. Mich., 1970, PhD, 1981. Prof. Ill. State U., Normal, 1983-88, Koryo Coll., Nagoya, Japan, 1991-93, Bentley Coll., Waltham, Mass., 1993-97, Mass. Coll. of Pharmacy and Health Scis., Boston, 2001—02, Showa Boston Inst., 2003—. Panel chair Soc. for Cinema Studies, New Orleans, 1986, Coll. Art Assn., Houston, 1988; editor Asian Cinema Studies Soc., 1986-88; consumer advocate. Author: Cinema of Wim Wenders, 1988; contbr. chpts. to books and articles to profl. jours. Mem. exec. bd. Friends of the Muddy River, 1997—; coord. Brookline Artists Open Studios, 1997-2002. Personal E-mail: foxbrook3@yahoo.com.

GEISTFELD, MARK, law educator; b. 1958; BA, Lewis and Clark Coll., 1980; MA, U. Pa., 1981; JD, Columbia U., 1989, PhD, 1990. Bar: NY 1990. Assoc. Dewey Ballantine, NYC, 1990—91, Simpson Thacher & Bartlett, NYC, 1992; law clk. to Hon. Wilfred Feinberg US Ct. Appeals 2nd Cir., NYC, 1991—92; asst. prof. NYU Law Sch., 1992—95, assoc. prof., 1995—97, prof., 1997—, Crystal Eastman prof. law. Vis. scholar Columbia U., 1992. Office: NYU Sch Law Vanderbilt Hall Rm 411A 40 Washington Sq S New York NY 10012-1099 Office Phone: 212-998-6683. E-mail: geistfeld@juris.law.nyu.edu.

GEISTFELD, RONALD ELWOOD, retired dental educator; b. St. James, Minn., Nov. 9, 1933; s. Victor E. and Viola (Becker) G.; m. Lois N. Tolzman Wilkens, June 15, 1955 (div. June 1974); m. Annette L. Swenson, Jan. 14, 1977; children: Shari, Mark, Steven, Ann, Leah, Erik. AA, Bethany Jr. Coll., 1952; BS, U. Minn., 1954, DDS, 1957. Pvt. practice dentistry, Northfield, Minn., 1959-72; clin. asst. prof. dentistry U. Minn. Sch. Dentistry, Mpls., 1969-72, assoc. prof., 1972-82, chmn. dept. operative dentistry, 1978-87, prof., 1982-97, prof. emeritus, 1997; dir. quality programs Pentegra Dental Group, Inc., 1998-2000. Dental cons. Hennepin County Med. Ctr., Mpls., 1975-96, VA Hosp., Mpls., 1977-96, VA Hosp. St. Cloud, Minn., 1978-96, Human Performance and Informatics Inst., Atama, Japan, 1990-95, K-9 Dental Sys. Quidnunc Australia Pty. Ltd., 1994-95, Metro Dental Group, Mpls., 1995-2000, The Dentists Ins. Co., 1995-99, VGM Expert Systems, 1996-98, Met. Life Ins. Co., 1996—, Pentegra Ltd., 1997-2000; mem. resource faculty for Bush faculty devel. program on excellence and diversity in teaching U. Minn., 1993-94; founder Global Network for Systematic Healthcare, 2003. Pres. PTA, Northfield, 1965, Arts Guild, Northfield, 1968; bd. dirs., chairperson Rice County Health and Sanitation Bd., Faribault, Minn., 1966-74; bd. dirs. Northfield Bd. Edn., 1969-74; pres. Roseville Luth. Ch., 1987-88. Capt. U.S. Army, 1957-59. Am. Coll. Dentists fellow, 1972; recipient Prof. of Yr. award Century Club, 1996-97. Mem. Am. Dental Assn. (chairperson operative dentistry sect. 1979-80, curriculum cons. 1981-88, grants and spl. projects request evaluator 1988-92, Am. fund for Dental Health, edit. review bd. JADA 1992-96), Minn. Dental Assn. (ethics com. 1969-76, chairperson sci. and ann. sessions com. 1984-86, spkr. house del. 1992-96, del. to ADA 1992-96, bd. dirs. 1992-96), Mpls. Dist. Dental Soc. (program chairperson 1978-79, peer rev. com. 1988-92, bd. dirs. 1979-80, 87-89, MDA del. 1989-92), Minn. Acad. Restorative Dentistry (pres. 1979-80), Minn. Acad. Gnathological Rsch. (pres. 1986-87), Am. Assn. Dental Schs. (chairperson operative dentistry sect. 1984-85, edit. rev. bd. 1984-88), Acad. Operative Dentistry (exec. council 1978-81, rsch. com. 1987-89), Am. Acad. Gold Foil Operators, Northfield C. of C. (treas. and chairperson 1968-70), Delta Sigma Delta, Omicron Kappa Upsilon (Theta chpt.). Lodges: Rotary (pres. Northfield 1972-73). Personal E-mail: RAGeist@aol.com.

GEITHNER, PAUL HERMAN, JR., retired banker; b. Phila., June 7, 1930; s. Paul Herman and Henriette Antonine (Schuck) G.; m. Irmgard (Hagedorn), Sept. 6, 1956; children: Christina, Amy, Paul. BA cum laude, Amherst Coll., 1952; MBA with distinction, U. Pa., 1957. Sec., treas. Ellicott Machine Co., Balt., 1964—68. V.p., sr. v.p., exec. asst. to the chmn., First Va. Banks, Inc., Falls Ch., 1968-85, pres., chief adminstrv. officer, 1985-95, bd. dir., vice chmn., 1986-95; pres. First Va. Life Ins. Co., 1974-96; bd. trustees Bridgewater Coll., Va., 1988—; dir. BB and T Bank Va., 2003—. Bd. dirs. Fairfax Symphony Orch., Va., 1988—2004, pres., 1991—92; sec.-treas. Fairfax Symphony Orch. Found., Va., 1999—; bd. dirs. Va. Coll. Fund, 1987—91; trustee Va. Banker Sch. Bank Mgmt., 1988—92. Lt. USNR, 1952—55. Mem. Va. Bankers Assn., (pres. 1992-93). Home: 4290 Highlands Bridge Rd Sarasota FL 34235 Personal E-mail: phgswim@comcast.net.

GEITHNER, TIMOTHY F., bank executive; m. Carole Sonnenfeld; children: Elise, Benjamin. BA in Govt. and Asian Studies, Dartmouth Coll., 1983; MA in Internat. Econ. and East Asian Studies, Johns Hopkins Sch., 1985. With Kissinger Assoc., Inc., 1985—88; dep. asst. sec. for internat. monetary and fin. policy US Dept. Treasury, 1995—96, sr. dep. asst. sec. for internat. affairs, 1996—97, asst. sec. for internat. affairs, 1997—98, under-sec. for internat. affairs, 1998—2001; dir. policy devel. and rev. dept. Internat. Monetary Fund, 2001—03; pres., CEO Fed. Res. Bank NY, NYC, 2003—. Adv. com. Ctr. for Global Devel.; coun. mem. Fgn. Rels.; chmn. com. payment and settlement sys. Bank for Internat. Settlements. Mem.: Econ. Club N.Y. (trustee), Coun. Fgn. Rels. Office: Fed Res Bank NY 33 Liberty St New York NY 10045

GEJDENSON, SAM, former congressman; b. Eschwege, Fed. Republic of Germany, May 20, 1948; m. Betsy Henley-Cohn; children: Mia, Ari stepchildren: Juri Henley-Cohn, Jesse Henley-Cohn. AS, Mitchell Coll., 1968; BA, U. Conn., 1970. Mem. Conn. State Ho. of Reps., 1974-78; coal broker, 1978-79; legis. liaison Conn. Office Policy and Mgmt., Hartford, 1979-80; mem. U.S. Congress from 2d Conn. dist., Washington, 1981-2001; owner & founder Sam Gejdenson Internat., 2001—. Democrat. Office: Sam Gejdenson International 84 Johnson Point Rd Branford CT 06405*

GEKELMAN, DIANA, dentist, dental educator, researcher; d. Edward and Margareta Gekelman; m. Jean-Sebastien El Kaim; 1 child, David Gekelman El Kaim. DDS, U. Sao Paulo, Brazil, 1993; specialization in endodontics, U. Sao Paulo, 1997, MS, 2000. Post-doctoral fellow lasers in dentistry U. Calif., San Francisco, 2000—02, asst. prof. clin. endodontics, 2002—. Presenter in field; spkr. nat. and internat. confs. Sci. reviewer (articles); contbr. articles to profl. jours. Grantee, Sao Paulo Found. Rsch., 1999—2000, Found. Sci. and Technol. Devel. Dentistry, 2000, Lares Rsch., 2001—02, Parnassus Funding, U. Calif., San Francisco Sch. Dentistry, 2004—05. Mem.: ADA, San Francisco Dental Soc., Calif. Dental Assn., Am. Assn. Endodontists, Am. Assn. Dental Rsch., Soc. Photo-Optical Instrumentation Engrs., Acad. Laser Dentistry, Internat. Assn. Dental Rsch. Office: Univ Calif San Francisco Sch Dentistry 707 Parnassus Ave San Francisco CA 94143-0758 E-mail: gekelmand@dentistry.ucsf.edu.

GELATT, CHARLES DANIEL, manufacturing executive; b. La Crosse, Wis., Jan. 4, 1918; s. Philo Madison and Clara (Johnson) G.; m. Jane Leicht, Mar. 6, 1942 (div. 1972); children: Sarah Jane Gelatt Gephart, Charles D., Philip Madison; m. Paula Jo Evans, Aug. 22, 1973 (div. 1978); m. Sue Anne Jimieson, Dec. 11, 1983. BA, MA, U. Wis., 1939. V.p. Gelatt Corp., La Crosse, 1940-52, pres., 1952-95, chmn., 1995—99; pres. No. Engraving Corp., Sparta, Wis., 1958-67, chmn., 1967-96, chmn. emeritus, 1996—; pres. N.E. Co. Ltd., 2000—. Trustee Northwestern Mut. Life Ins. Co., Milw., 1960-88, mem. exec. com., 1961-77; chmn. North Ctrl. Trust Co., La. Crosse, 1989-93; mem. bd. regents U. Wis., 1947-74, pres. bd. regents, 1955-57, v.p., 1964-68, pres., 1968-69; mem. Wis. Coordinating Com. for Higher Edn., 1955-59, 64-69, chmn., 1956; chmn. Assn. Governing Bds. Univs. and Colls., Washington, 1971-72; trustee Carroll Coll., Waukesha, Wis., 1971-79, Viterbo U., La. Crosse, 1972-2002; trustee Gundersen Found., La Crosse, 1973-95. Mem. Phi Beta Kappa. Office: PO Box 1087 La Crosse WI 54602-1087 Home (Summer): 30976 Old MIll Rd La Crescent MN 55947

GELB, ARTHUR, electrical and systems engineering executive; b. N.Y.C., Sept. 20, 1937; m. Linda Lewis; children: Ronald, Caren, Laurie. BEE, CUNY, 1958; MS in Applied Math., Harvard U., 1959; ScD in Systems Engring., MIT, 1961. Engr. Aviation Gas Turbine div. Westinghouse Electric Corp., Kansas City, Mo., 1956, Am. Dist. Telegraph Co., N.Y.C., 1957-58, Draper Lab., Cambridge, Mass., 1959; dept. mgr. Dynamics Research Corp., Stoneham, Mass., 1961-66; pres., chief exec. officer TASC (The Analytic Sciences Corp.), Reading, Mass., 1966-93, chmn., 1993-94, sr. chmn., 1994; pres. Four Sigma Corp., Lexington, Mass., 1995—. Chmn. adv. bd. Ctr. for Tech., Policy and Indsl. Devel., MIT, 1987-97; mem. MIT Corp., 1996—; mem. Lincoln Lab. Adv. Bd. Co-author: Multiple-Input Describing Fns., 1968, Applied Optimal Estimation, 1974; contbr. articles to profl. jours. Bd. dirs. Massport, Boston, 1977-85; bd. regents Higher Edn., Mass., 1989-90; mem. Higher Edn. Coord. Coun., Mass., 1990-95. Named Outstanding Young Engr. CUNY, 1969. Fellow AIAA, IEEE (bd. editors Control Systems Mag. 1981-91), AAAS; mem. Mensa. Avocations: music, tennis, golf, microcomputing, math. Office: Four Sigma Corp One Cranberry Hill Lexington MA 02421-7394

GELB, BRUCE STUART, city commissioner, consultant; b. NYC, Feb. 24, 1927; s. Lawrence M. and Joan Friedman (Hewett) G.; m. Lueza Denise Thirkield, June 6, 1953; children: John T., Joan H., Richard E., M. Constance. BA, Yale U., 1950; MBA, Harvard U., 1953. With Clairol Inc., 1950—51, 1957—61, v.p. mktg., 1961-65, exec. v.p., pres., 1965-76; brand mgr. Procter & Gamble, 1953-57; with Bristol-Myers Co., N.Y.C., 1957-89, sr. v.p., 1977-85, exec. v. p., 1981-84, pres. consumer products group, 1985-89; dir., vice-chmn. Bristol-Myers, 1985-89; dir. USIA, Washington, 1989-91; amb. to Belgium Brussels, 1991-93; NYC commr. UN Consular Corps and Internat. Bus., NYC, 1994—97; with UN Devel. Corp., 1994—. Sr. cons. Bristol Myers Squibb, 1997-2001. Life trustee Choate Rosemary Hall Sch.; active Pres.'s Arts and Humanities Com., 1989-91; trustee John F. Kennedy Ctr. for Performing Arts, 1989-91, Howard U., 1987-89, Woodrow Wilson Ctr.; vice-chair Madison Sq. Boys and Girls Club; pres. Woodrow Wilson Coun., 2003—, Coun. Am. Ambassadors, 2005—. Office: 345 Park Ave Ste 3-1 New York NY 10154-0037 E-mail: jojoricos@aol.com.

GELB, HAROLD SEYMOUR, manufacturing executive, consultant, entrepreneur; b. N.Y.C., Apr. 26, 1920; s. Daniel and Fanny (Gelb) G.; m. Sylvia M. Miller, Sept. 24, 1942; children: Richard, Alan. BBA, CCNY, 1941. CPA, N.Y. With S.D. Leidesdorf & Co. (CPAs), N.Y.C., 1943-78, mng. partner, 1969-78; sr. ptnr. Ernst & Young, N.Y.C., 1978-82; chmn. United Indsl. Corp., N.Y.C., 1995—2003. Past vice chmn. Citizens Budget Commn., N.Y.C., now trustee emeritus; past chmn. N.Y. State Bd. Pub. Accountancy. Pres. Bronx-Lebanon Hosp. Ctr., 1977; bd. dirs., v.p. S.D. Leidesdorf Found., 1969-80; trustee Accts. Found., 1973-80, Adelphi U., 1997—; bd. overseers Albert Einstein Med. Coll., 1977-79; bd. dirs., sec. Benjamin Cardozo Law Sch., 1977-89; mem. Gov.'s Task Force, Bus. Alliance with Edn., Mayor's Com. on Taxi Regulatory Issues, 1981-82. Recipient Disting. Cmty. Svc. award Brandeis U., 1978 Mem. AICPA (coun. 1970-76), N.Y. State Soc. CPAs (past v.p., bd. dirs.), Metropolis Country Club (White Plains), Town Club (Scarsdale). Home and Office: 181 Fox Meadow Rd Scarsdale NY 10583-2334

GELB, JUDITH ANNE, lawyer; b. NYC, Apr. 5, 1935; d. Joseph and Sarah (Stein) G.; m. Howard S. Vogel, June 30, 1962; 1 child, Michael S. BA, Bklyn. Coll., 1955; JD, Columbia U., 1958. Bar: N.Y. 1959, U.S. Dist. Ct. (so. and ea. dists.) N.Y. 1960, U.S. Ct. Appeals (2d cir.) 1960, U.S. Ct. Mil. Appeals 1962. Asst. to editor N.Y. Law Jour., N.Y.C., 1958-59; confidential asst. to U.S. atty. ea dist N.Y., Bklyn., 1959-61; assoc. Whitman & Ransom, N.Y.C., 1961-70, ptnr., 1971-93, Whitman Breed Abbott & Morgan LLP, N.Y.C., 1993-2000, Winston & Strawn LLP, NYC, 2000—. Mem.: ABA (individual rights sect., real property and trust law sect.), Assn. Bar City N.Y., N.Y. State Dist. Attys. Assn., N.Y. State Bar Assn. (trusts and estates com.), Fed. Bar Coun., Columbia Law Sch. Alumni Assn. (bd. dirs.), Princeton Club. Home: 169 E 69th St New York NY 10021-5163 Office: Winston & Strawn LLP 200 Park Ave New York NY 10166-0005 Business E-Mail: jgelb@winston.com.

GELB, LESLIE HOWARD, writer, lecturer, consultant; b. New Rochelle, N.Y., Mar. 4, 1937; s. Max and Dorothy (Klein) G.; m. Judith Cohen, Aug. 2, 1959; children: Adam, Caroline, Alison. AB magna cum laude in Govt. and cum laude in Philosophy, Tufts U., 1959; MA, Harvard U., 1961, PhD, 1964. Teaching fellow govt. and social scis., non-resident tutor Winthrop House, Harvard U., 1962-64, assoc. def. studies program, 1963-64; asst. prof. govt. Wesleyan U., Middletown, Conn., 1964-65; exec. asst. to U.S. Senator Jacob K. Javits, 1966-67; dep. dir. policy planning staff Dept. Def., Washington, 1967-68, dir., 1968, acting dep. asst. sec. def. for policy planning and arms control staff, 1968-69; dir. sec. def. Vietnam task force, 1967-68; sr. fellow Brookings Instn., Washington, 1969-73; corr. N.Y. Times, Washington, 1973-77; dir. bur. politico-mil. affairs Dept. State, Washington, 1977-79; sr. assoc. Carnegie Endowment for Internat. Peace, 1979-81; chmn. Carnegie Endowment Panel on Future U.S. Security and Arms Control, 1980-81; nat. security corr. N.Y. Times, 1981-86, dep. editorial page editor, op-editorial page editor, 1986-90, fgn. affairs columnist, 1991-93; pres. Coun. Fgn. Rels., 1993—2003, pres. emeritus, sr. fellow bd, 2003—. Bd. dirs. certain funds advised by Salomon Bros. Asset Mgmt., certain registered investment cos. advised by subs. of CIBC Oppenheimer Corp., britannica.com, The Nixon Ctr.; mem. The Trilateral Commn., 1993-2000; chmn. adv. bd. Emerging Europe Pvt. Equity Fund III. Author: The Irony of Vietnam: The System Worked, 1979, Anglo-American Relations, 1945-49, 1988; co-author: Our Own Worst Enemy: The Unmaking of American Foreign Policy, 1984; contbr. numerous articles to mags.; sr. cons. and producer "The Crisis Game," 1983 (Emmy, DuPont, Hood awards); sr. editor postwar history of U.S. "45/85," 1985 Trustee emeritus Tufts U., Carnegie Endowment for Internat. Peace; mem. adv. bd. Sch. Internat. and Pub. Affairs, Columbia U., 1997-2001; bd. dirs. James A. Baker III Inst. Pub. Policy; adv. mem. Ctr. Press, Politics and Pub. Policy, Harvard U. John F. Kennedy Sch. Govt., 1991-2001. Recipient Woodrow Wilson award, 1980, Page One award in explanatory journalism, 1985, Nat. Father of Yr. award U.S. Nat. Com. on Fathers and Mothers of Yr. Awards, 1993; mem. N.Y. Times Pulitzer Prize Winning Team, 1985. Fellow AAAS; mem. Internat. Inst. Strategic Studies, Coun. Fgn. Rels. Home: 150 E 69th St New York NY 10021-5704 Office: Coun Fgn Rels 58 E 68th St New York NY 10021-5953 E-mail: billwill15@earthlink.net.

GELB, RICHARD MARK, lawyer; b. N.Y.C., June 12, 1947; s. Harold Seymour and Sylvia Mildred (Miller) Gelb; m. Gail Kleven, July 29, 1973; 1 child, Daniel Kleven. BA, NYU, 1969; JD, Boston Coll., 1973. Bar: Mass.

1973, N.Y. 1975, D.C. 1975, U.S. Dist. Ct. (so. and ea. dists.) N.Y. 1975, U.S. Ct. Appeals (2d cir.) 1975, U.S. Dist. Ct. Conn. 1977, U.S. Ct. Appeals (1st cir.) 1978, U.S. Dist. Ct. Mass. 1978, U.S. Supreme Ct. 1980. Assoc. Proskauer Rose, LLP, N.Y.C., 1975-77; ptnr. Gelb & Gelb LLP, Boston, 1987—. Contbr. articles to profl. pubis. Mem. Mass. Bar Assn. (ethics com. 1991-96, civil litig. coun. 1994-96, chmn. bus. litig. com. 1992-94, assoc. editor Mass. Law Rev. 1982-87), Am. Inn of Ct. Found. (trustee 1994-98), Boston Inn of Ct. (co-pres. 1993-94), Boston Coll. Law Sch. Intellectual Property Am. Inns of Ct. (pres. 1998-2000, treas. 2001-02), Boston Coll. Law Sch. Alumni Coun. (v.p. comms. 2001-03), Suffolk U. Law Sch. Litig. Am. Inn Ct. (co-pres. 2002-05), Pi Sigma Alpha. Democrat. Jewish. Home: 60 Pine Hill Rd Swampscott MA 01907-2240 Office: Gelb & Gelb LLP 20 Custom House St Ste 1030 Boston MA 02110-3559 Office Phone: 617-345-0010. Business E-Mail: rgelb@gelbgelb.com.

GELBAND, HENRY, pediatric cardiologist; b. Austria, Aug. 31, 1936; came to U.S., 1941, naturalized, 1951; s. Herman and Charlotte (Rubin) G.; m. Ellen Brooke Charin, Aug. 26, 1962; children— Craig Harris, Mark Evan, Todd David. BA, Washington (Pa.) and Jefferson Coll., 1958; MD, Jefferson Med. Coll., Phila., 1962. Intern Beth Israel Hosp., Newark, 1962-63; resident in pediatrics Mt. Sinai Hosp., N.Y.C., 1965-67; fellow in pediatric cardiology Columbia U. Coll. Phys. and Surg., 1967-69, spl. research fellow in pharmacology, 1969-71; mem. faculty U. Miami (Fla.) Med. Sch., 1971—, prof. pediatrics, vice chmn. clin. affairs, 1976—, prof. pharmacology, 1977—; prin. investigator NIH grants, 1976—; vice chair dept. pediatrics U. Miami (Fla.) Med. Sch., 1995—. Vice pres. Ronald McDonald House, South Fla., Miami, 1978— Co-author: Infant and Child, 1977; contbr. articles to med. jours. Served as officer M.C. USNR, 1963-65. Mem. Am. Physiol. Soc., Soc. Pediatric Research, Am. Soc. Pharmacology and Exptl. Therapeutics, Internat. Study Group Research Cardiac Metabolism, Am. Acad. Pediatrics, Am. Heart Assn., Am. Coll. Cardiology, Internat. Coll. Pediatrics, Am. Coll. Chest Physicians, Fla. Assn. Pediatric Cardiology. Democrat. Jewish. Home: 181 Crandon Blvd Apt 406 Key Biscayne FL 33149-1549 Office: U Miami Med Sch PO Box 16820 Miami FL 33101-6820

GELBART, LARRY, scriptwriter, television producer, theater producer; b. Chgo., Feb. 25, 1928; s. Harry and Frieda (Sturner) G.; m. Pat Marshall, Nov. 25, 1956; children: Gary, Paul, Adam, Becky. LittD (hon.), Union Coll., Schnectady, N.Y., 1986; LHD (hon.), Hofstra U., 1999. Writer: for radio series The Eddie Cantor Show, 1946, Maxwell House Coffee Time with Danny Thomas, 1946, Duffy's Tavern, 1946, Command Performance, 1946-47, Jack Carson, 1947-48, The Jack Paar Show, 1949, The Joan Davis Show, 1949, The Bob Hope Show, 1949-52; for ballet, Peter and the Wolf, 1992; for theatre My L.A., 1950, The Conquering Hero, 1960, A Funny Thing Happened on the Way to the Forum, 1962 (Tony award with Burt Shevelove best musical play 1963), Sly Fox, 1976, One, Two, Three, Four, Five, 1988, City of Angels, 1989 (Drama Desk award best book of musical 1989, Tony award best musical, best book of musical 1990, Best New Musical citation NY Drama Critics Circle 1990, Outer Critics Circle award outstanding Broadway musical, contbn. to comedy award 1990, Edgar Allan Poe award best mystery play 1990), Mastergate, 1989 (Outer Critics Circle award contbn. to comedy 1990), (co-author) Jerome Robbins' Broadway, 1989; for films The Notorious Landlady, 1962, The Thrill of It All, 1963, (also co-producer) The Wrong Box, 1966, Not With My Wife You Don't, 1966, The Chastity Belt, 1968, A Fine Pair, 1969, Oh, God, 1977 (Acad. award nomination best screenplay material from another medium 1977, Edgar Allan Poe award, Mystery Writers Am. award, Writers Guild award), Movie, Movie, 1978 (Writers Guild award, Christopher award), Neighbors, 1981, Tootsie, 1982 (Acad. Award nomination best screenplay written directly for screen 1982, LA Film Critics award, NY Film Critics award, Nat. Soc. Film Critics award), (also exec. producer) Blame It on Rio, 1984, Bedazzled, 2000; writer, prodr., co-prodr. TV shows M*A*S*H, 1972-76 (Emmy award nomination outstanding writing comedy 1972, 75, Writers Guild Am. award 1972, 74, Emmy award outstanding comedy series 1973, Emmy award nominations outstanding comedy series 1974, 75, George Foster Peabody award 1975, Humanitas award), Roll Out!, 1973-74, Karen, 1975, United States, 1980, After M*A*S*H, 1983-84 (Emmy award nomination outstanding directing comedy series 1983); TV adaptation Mastergate, 1992; writer, exec. prodr. HBO film Barbarians at the Gate, 1993 (Outstanding Made-for-TV-Movie Emmy award, Best Made-for-TV-Motion Picture award The Am. TV Awards, Program of Yr., The TV Critics Assn., Cable Ace award, Writing in a Movie or Miniseries), Weapons of Mass Distraction, 1997; Best Teleplay awd., PEN Ctr. USA West, writer TV shows The All-Star Revue, 1950-53, The Red Buttons Show, 1952-55, Honestly, Celeste!, 1954, The Patrice Munsel Show, 1954-62, Caesar's Hour, 1955-57 (Emmy award nominations best comedy writing 1955, 56, 57), The Pat Boone Chevy Showroom, 1957-60, The Danny Kaye Show, 1963 (Emmy award nomination outstanding writing comedy or variety show 1963), The Marty Feldman Comedy Machine, 1972, (TV movie) And Starring Pancho Villa as Himself, 2003, Like Jazz, A New Kind of Musicial, 2003; author: Laughing Matters, 1998. Served with AUS, 1945-46. Recipient Lee Strasberg Lifetime Achievement in Arts and Sci. award, 1990, William S. Paley award for excellence in TV, Anti-Defamation League, 2001, citation for disting. svc., AMA, 2001. Mem. Dramatists Guild, Writers Guild Am. (award 1972, 74), ASCAP, Dir. Guild Am. Address: 807 N Alpine Dr Beverly Hills CA 90210-2901 E-mail: elsig@aol.com.

GELBER, DON JEFFREY, lawyer; b. L.A., Mar. 10, 1940; s. Oscar and Betty Sheila (Chernitsky) G.; m. Jessica Jeasun Song, May 15, 1967; children: Victoria, Jonathan, Rebecca, Robert. Student UCLA, 1957-58, Reed Coll., 1958-59; AB, Stanford U., 1961, JD, 1963. Bar: Calif. 1964, Hawaii 1964, U.S. Dist. Ct. (cen. and no. dists. Calif.) 1964, U.S. Dist. Ct. Hawaii 1964, U.S. Ct. Appeals (9th cir.) 1964, U.S. Supreme Ct. 1991. Assoc. Greenstein, Yamane & Cowan, Honolulu, 1964-67; reporter Penal Law Revision Project, Hawaii Jud. Council, Honolulu, 1967-69; assoc. H. William Burgess, Honolulu, 1969-72; ptnr. Burgess & Gelber, Honolulu, 1972-73; prin. Law Offices of Don Jeffrey Gelber, Honolulu, 1974-77; pres. Gelber & Wagner, Honolulu, 1978-83, Gelber & Gelber, Honolulu, 1984-89, Gelber, Gelber, Ingersoll, Klevansky & Faris, Honolulu, 1990-2002, Gelber, Gelber, Ingersoll & Klevansky, 2002--; legal counsel Hawaii State Senate Judiciary Com., 1965; adminstrv. asst. to majority floor leader Hawaii State Senate, 1966, legal counsel Edn. Com., 1967, 68; majority counsel Hawaii Ho. of Reps., 1974; spl. counsel Hawaii State Senate, 1983. Contbr. articles to legal publs. Mem. State Bar Calif., ABA (sect. bus. law), Am. Bankruptcy Inst., Hawaii State Bar Assn. (sect. bankruptcy law, bd. dirs. 1991-93, pres. 1993). Clubs: Pacific, Plaza (Honolulu). Office: Gelber Gelber Ingersoll & Klevansky 745 Fort Street Mall Ste 1400 Honolulu HI 96813-3877 Office Phone: 808-524-0155.

GELBER, LOUISE C(ARP), lawyer; m. Milton Gelber (dec.); children: Jack, Bruce, Julie McCoy. BA, JD, U. Calif., 1944. Bar: Calif. 1945, U.S. Dist. Ct. (so. dist.) Calif. 1945, U.S. Supreme Ct. 1965. Pvt. practice; commr. Calif. Bd. Examiners for Nursing Home Adminstrs.; adminstr. Calif. Dept. Consumer Affairs. Speaker local drug rehab. hosp.; mem. Vis. Nurses Bd.; commr. Calif. Adv. Cost Control to State Govt.; mem. temporary judge panel L.A. County; settlement officer dispute resolution svc. Pasadena Superior Ct. Mem. editorial staff U. Calif. Law Rev. Calif. nominee for State Assembly, 1992; judge pro tem Rio Hondo Mcpl. Ct.; pro bono Bd. Legal Aid; v.p. local PTA; mem., invocator Arcadia Coord. Coun.; bd. dirs. Foothill Apt. Assn., People-For People; active ARC, Community Chest, United Way, Boy Scouts Am., Girl Scouts U.S. Mem. ABA, Calif. Bar Assn., Foothill Bar Assn., L.A. County Bar ASsn., Pomona Valley Bar Assn., Citrus Bar Assn., Arcadia C. of C. (legis. com.), So. Calif. Women Lawyers (treas.), Pasadena C. of C., Bus. and Profl. Women Lawyers (past state legis. chmn., state legis. adv.), Order of Eastern Star, LWV, Sierra. Home and Office: 1225 Rancho Rd Arcadia CA 91006-2241 Office Phone: 626-355-1872. Personal E-mail: french.court@verizon.net.

GELBERG, LILLIAN, family medicine physician, educator; b. L.A., May 14, 1955; married; 3 children. BA, UCLA, 1977; MD, Harvard U., 1981; MSPH, UCLA, 1987. Diplomate Am. Bd. Family Practice. Robert Wood Johnson Found. clin. scholar UCLA/VA, 1984-86; asst. prof. UCLA, 1987-97, assoc. prof., 1997—, George F. Kneller prof. family medicine, 2001—. Contbr. chpts. to books, articles to profl. jours. Vol., com. chair various family clinics, Venice, Calif., 1984—. Recipient CAFP 1st Rsch. Excellence award, 2001; Robert Wood Johnson Found. scholar UCLA, 1984-86, Robert Wood Johnson faculty scholar, 1995-2001. Fellow Am. Acad. Family Physicians; mem. Soc. Gen. Internal Medicine, Assn. Health Svc. Rsch. (Young Investigator award 1995, Article of the Yr. award 1997), Soc. of Tchrs. of Family Medicine, Am. Pub. Health Assn., Inst. Medicine, 2004. E-mail: gelberg@ucla.edu.

GELBERMAN, RICHARD H., orthopedist, surgeon; b. N.Y.C., Nov. 27, 1943; MD, U. Tenn. Health Scis. Ctr., 1969. Diplomate orthopedic surgery and in hand surgery Am. Bd. Orthopaedic Surgery. Prof. orthop. surgery Harvard U. Med. Sch., Boston, 1987—94; Fred C. Reynolds prof. orthop. surgery Washington U. Sch. Medicine, St. Louis, 1995—. Mem.: Inst. Medicine, 2004, IOS, Am. Soc. Surgery of the Hand, Am. Orthop. Assn., Am. Acad. Orthop. Surgeons (pres. 2001—02). Office: Washington U Sch Medicine Ste 11300 One Barnes Hosp Plz Saint Louis MO 63110

GELBKE, CLAUS-KONRAD, nuclear physics educator; b. Celle, Germany, May 31, 1947; came to the U.S., 1976; s. Heinz and Gertraud Gelbke; m. Brigitte Zabeschek, Apr. 6, 1973; children: Susanne, Martin. Diploma für physik, U. Heidelberg, Germany, 1970, doctor rerum naturalium, 1973. Wissenschaftlicher asst. Max-Planck-Inst für Kernphysik, Heidelberg, 1973-76; physicist Lawrence Berkeley (Calif.) Lab., 1976-77; assoc. prof. physics Mich. State U., East Lansing, 1977-81, prof. physics, 1981-87, assoc. dir. nuclear sci. Nat. Superconducting Cyclotron Lab., 1987-90, disting. prof., 1990—, dir. Nat. Superconducting Cyclotron Lab., 1992—. Summer visitor Brookhaven Nat. Lab., Upton, N.Y., 1974, U. Washington, Seattle, 1975. Alfred P. Sloan fellow, 1979-83; Scholarship Studienstiftung des Deutschen Volkes, 1971-72; Humboldt Rsch. award U.S. Scis. Fellow Am. Physical Soc. Office: Mich State U Cyclotron Lab S Shaw Ln East Lansing MI 48824 E-mail: gelbke@nscl.msu.edu.

GELBOIN, HARRY VICTOR, biochemistry educator, researcher; b. Chgo., Dec. 21, 1929; s. Herman and Eva (Jurkowsky) Gelboin; m. Stella Bezansky, June 19, 1951; m. Marlena Maisels, Apr. 1, 1962; children: Michele Ida, Lisa Rebecca, Sharon Anna, Tamara Rachel. BA in Chemistry, U. Ill., 1951; MS in Biochemistry and Oncology, U. Wis., 1956, PhD in Biochemistry and Oncology, 1958; DSc (hon.), U. Inonu, Malatya, Turkey, 1999. Devel. chemist U.S. Rubber Co., Chgo., 1952-54; rsch. asst. McArdle Meml. Lab. for Cancer Rsch., U. Wis., 1954-58; biochemist lab. cellular pharmacology NIMH, 1958-60, biochemist lab. clin. sci., 1960-61; supervisory biochemist chemistry sect., diagnostic rsch. br. Nat. Cancer Inst., 1962-64, head chemistry sect., carcinogenesis studies br., 1964-66, chief lab. molecular carcinogenesis, div. cancer etiology, 1966—; adj. prof. Georgetown U., 1974-78. Bd. dirs. Internat. Soc. Polycyclic Aromatic Com.; keynote spkr. carcinogenesis Gordon Res. Conf., 1965; Franz Bielschowsky meml. lectr., Dunedin, New Zealand, 66; Smith Kline French hon. lectr. U. Fla., 1974, U. Mich., 1976; hon. lectr. Israel Cancer Soc. and U. Tel Aviv, Israel, 1983; keynote lectr. Internat. Conf. Carcinogenesis, Alghero, Italy, 1986; Nakasone hon. lectr. Japan Found. Promotion Sci., Tokyo and Osaka, Japan, 1989; keynote speaker U.S. organizer and co-chmn. Princess Takamatsu Cancer Symposium, Tokyo, 1990; vis. prof. Hebrew U., Jerusalem, 1985—86, 2000; plenary lectr. Glinos Found., Athens, 1996; cons. drug metabolism, toxicology and drug discovery; domestic and fgn. spkr. in field. Editor 8 profl. books; assoc. editor Cancer Rsch., 1968-79, 83-87, mem. editl. adv. bd., 1965-67; assoc. editor Biochem. Toxicology, 1984—; mem. editl. bd. Chemico-Biol. Interactions, 1969-75, Archives Biochemistry and Biophysics, 1969-76, Life Scis., 1976, Environ. Health Scis., 1976-78; contbr. and co-contbr. over 420 sci. papers to med. publs.; editor/co-editor 10 books, 8 patents. Recipient Superior Svc. award NIH, 1970, Claude Bernard award U. Montreal, 1970, New Horizons award Radiol. Soc. N.Am., 1970, Merit awards Sr. Sci. Svc. NIH, 1983, 85, EEO award NIH, 1989 Fellow: Amer. Coll. Clin. Pharmacol.; mem.: Internat. Soc. for Study Xenobiotics, Internat. Soc. for Preventive Oncology, Am. Soc. for Pharmacology and Exptl. Therapeutics, Am. Soc. Biol. Chemists, Am. Cancer Soc. (adv. com. on carcinogenesis, mem. coun. 1975—), Am. Assn. for Cancer Rsch., AAAS. Achievements include discovery of mechanism of carcinogenesis and cytochrome P450; microsomal P450 activation of chemicals to forms binding to proteins and DNA; describing the activation system for the initial stages of mutagenesis and carcinogenesis, activation for Ames mutagen detection system; development of isolation of specific inhibitory and immunoblotting monoclonal antibodies to each of human cytochrome P450 enzymes, system analyzing drug and xenobiotic metabolism for reduction of drug toxicity; drug discovery. Office Phone: 301-589-3678. Personal E-mail: HGG@helix.nih.gov.

GELDER, DONALD CLIFFORD BARNARD EDWARD, artist; b. Naples, N.Y., Apr. 17, 1933; s. Clifford Barnard and Ruby Alberta (Davis) G.; m. Sandra Lea Boyles Smith, June 9, 1962 (div. 1980); children: Sheril Lea, Andrea Beth, Victoria Lynn, Kristina Carol; m. Nancy Figuracion Gelder, Jan. 14, 1983; children: Ryan, Mary Alejandra Louise, William Alfred II. Diploma, Buffalo Fine Arts Acad., 1953. Stained glass designer Willet Studios, Phila., 1962-66, Frohe Stained Glass Studio, Buffalo, 1966-68, United Archtl. Svcs., Buffalo, 1968-75, The Judson Studios, L.A., 1975-82, Luxfer Studios, Toronto, Ont., Can., 1983-84, Gelder Studios, Naples, 1984—. Art lectr. Am. Sci. Glassblowers Soc., Phila., 1964, Depew (N.Y.) Mid. Sch., 1967. Freelance portrait painter. With U.S. Army, 1954-56. Recipient Gold Key award Scholastic Mags., 1949, Mural Commendation award Col. Howard Smigelow, 1955, Fannie Benjamin award Meml. Art Gallery, 1956, First Pl. award in crafts St. John's Ch., 1970. Mem. Am. Soc. Portrait Artists, Brit. Soc. Master Glass Painters, Portrait Soc. Am., Am. Portrait Soc. Republican. Baptist. Avocations: genealogy, piano music. Home: Hill Grove House 8205 West Hollow Rd Naples NY 14512 Studio: Gelder Studios 7 Main St Naples NY 14512 Office Phone: 585-374-2884. Personal E-mail: GelArt66@aol.com.

GELDER, JOHN WILLIAM, lawyer; b. Buffalo, Aug. 7, 1933; s. Ray Horace and Grace Catherine (Kelly) G.; m. Martha J. Kindleberger, June 12, 1953; William R., Mark S., Cathryn J. Gelder Brooks, Carolyn G. Gelder Bird BBA, U. Mich., 1956, JD with distinction, 1959. Bar: Mich. 1960, D.C. 1981, U.S. Supreme Ct. 1982. Assoc. Miller, Canfield, Paddock and Stone, P.L.C., Detroit, 1959-68, mng. ptnr., 1975-81, 90-93, ptnr., 1968-93, prin., 1994—. Bd. dirs. Tecumseh Products Co., 1989—. Asst. editor Mich. Law Rev., 1958, 59 Trustee, officer Herrick Found., Detroit, 1989—. Mem. State Bar Mich. (coun. mem. bus. law sect. 1984-90), Order of Coif, Bloomfield Hills Country Club. Home: 30845 River Crossing St Bingham Farms MI 48025-4656 Office: Miller Canfield Paddock & Stone PLC 840 W Long Lake Rd Ste 200 Troy MI 48098-6358 E-mail: gelder@millercanfield.com.

GELDRICH-LEFFMAN, HANNA, German/Spanish language and literature educator; b. Budapest, Hungary, Feb. 3, 1934; d. John and Bertha (Feigler) Geldrich; m. Peter Leffman, Mar. 11, 1978. BA, Mt. St. Agnes Coll., Balt., 1963; PhD, Johns Hopkins U., 1967. From asst. to assoc. prof. Mt. St. Agnes Coll., Balt., 1964-71; assoc. prof. Loyola Coll., Balt., 1971-79, prof., 1979—2004, dept. chair, 1971-89; emerita, 2000; ret., 2004. Author: (in German) Heine and the Latin-American Modernismo, 1971, The Dialogue of Marriage in Contemporary German and Latin American Short Stories, 1999; contbr. articles to profl. jours. Recipient Woodrow Wilson fellowship, 1963-64, Woodrow Wilson Dissertation fellowship, 1966. Mem. AAUP, Assn. Tchrs. German, Assn. Tchrs. Spanish, Am. Coun. Tchrs. Fgn. Langs., German Soc. Md. (scholarship com. 1976—), Soc. for History of Germans in Md. (v.p. 1979—), Goethe Soc. (pres. 1969-71).

GELEHRTER, THOMAS DAVID, medical educator, geneticist, educator; b. Liberec, Czechoslovakia, Mar. 11, 1936; married 1959; 2 children. BA, Oberlin Coll., 1957; MA, U. Oxford, Eng., 1959; MD, Harvard U., 1963. Intern, then asst. resident in internal medicine Mass. Gen. Hosp., Boston, 1963—65; rsch. assoc. in molecular biology NIAMD NIH, Bethesda, Md., 1965—69; fellow in med. genetics U. Wash., 1969—70; asst. prof. human genetics, internal medicine and pediatrics Sch. Medicine Yale U., 1970—73, assoc. prof., 1973—74, U. Mich., Ann Arbor, 1974—76, prof. internal medicine and human genetics, 1976—87, dir. divsn. med. genetics, 1977—87, chmn. dept. human genetics, 1987—2004, prof. human genetics and internal medicine, 1987—. Josiah Macy, Jr. Found. faculty scholar and vis. scientist Imperial Cancer Rsch. Fund Labs., London, 1979-80; vis. fellow Inst. Molecular Medicine; Keeley vis. fellow Wadham Coll., U. Oxford, Wellcome Rsch. Travel grantee, 1995. Mem. editl. bd. Jour. Biol. Chemistry, 1995-2000. Trustee Oberlin Coll., 1970-75; mem. adv. com. NIH Recontinant DNA, 2002-05. Rhodes scholar, 1957-59. Fellow AAAS, Am. Coll. Med. Genetics; mem. Am. Soc. Human Genetics (bd. dirs. 1994-96), Am. Soc. Clin. Investigation, Am. Soc. Biochemistry and Molecular Biology, Assn. Am. Physicians. Office: Univ Mich Med Sch Dept Human Genetics Box 0618 1241 Catherine St Ann Arbor MI 48109-0618 Office Phone: 734-764-5491. Business E-Mail: tdgum@umich.edu.

GELENBE, SAMI EROL, computer scientist, engineering educator; b. Istanbul, Turkey, Aug. 22, 1945; arrived in France, 1972; s. Ali Yusuf and Maria (Sacchet) G.; m. Deniz Arman, June 8, 1968; 1 child, Pamir. BSEE, Mid. East Tech. U., Turkey, 1966; MSEE, Poly. Inst. Bklyn., 1968, PhD, 1969; DSc, U. Paris, 1973; D of Engring. (hon.), U. Rome, 1996; PhD (hon.), Boğaziçi U., Istanbul, 2004. Asst. prof. U. Mich., Ann Arbor, 1970-72; prof. U. Liege, Belgium, 1972-79, U. Paris, 1979—. Sci. dir. Inria, Rocquencourt, France, 1973—82; sci. advisor Sec. State, Paris, 1984—86; chaired prof. Duke U., 1993—98; assoc. dean engring. U. Ctrl. Fla., 1998—2003, univ. chaired prof., 2001—03; chair tech. adv. bd. US Army Simulation and Tng. Command, 1999—2003; Dennis Gabor chair Imperial Coll., London, 2003, head of intelligent sys. and networks, chaired prof., 2003—. Author: (books transl. into Japanese and Korean) Analysis and Synthesis of Computer Systems, 1980, 1980, Introduction aux reseaux de files d' attente, 1982, Multiprocessor Performance, 1988, Concurrency Control in Distributed Databases, 1989, Introduction to Networks of Queues, 1999; mem. editl. bd.: Acta Info., 1978—, Performance Evaluation, 1979—, IEEE Transactions on Software Engring, 1979—92, Computer Comms., 1999—, Telecomm Systems, 1993—, Simulation Practice and Theory, 1996—, Computer Jour., Annales des Telecommunications, 2002—, Computational Mgmt. Sci., 2002—, Recherche Opérationnelle, 1994—; contbr. articles to profl. jours. Decorated chevalier and officer Order of Merit France, chevalier Palmes Académiques, France; recipient Silver Core award, IFIP, 1980, Sci. award, Parlar Found., Turkey, 1994, French Acad. Sci. award, Grand Prix France Telecom, 1996; fellow, Fulbright Found., 1966, Gordon McKay fellow, Harvard U., 1974. Fellow: IEE, ACM, IEEE (Meritorious Svc. award 1989, 1992); mem.: Acadmia Europaea, Eta Kappa Nu, Epsilon Pi Upsilon, Sigma Xi. Avocations: history, bicycling. Office: Imperial College London SW7 2BT England Office Phone: 44-207 594 6342. E-mail: e.gelenbe@imperial.ac.uk.

GELERNTER, DAVID H., critic, painter, educator; BA, MA in Classical Hebrew Lit., Yale U.; PhD in Computer Sci., SUNY. Prof computer sci. Yale U., New Haven; chief scientist Mirror Worlds Technologies. Mem. Nat. Coun. Arts., Nat. Endowment for Arts, 2002—. Cultural columnist NY Post, art critic Weekly Standard; author: Mirror Worlds, The Muse in the Machine: Computerizing the Poetry of Human Thought, 1994, 1939: The Lost World of the Fair, 1995, Drawing Life, 1997, Machine Beauty. Office: Nat Endowment Arts 1100 Pennsylvania Ave NW Washington DC 20506 Office Phone: 202-682-5400.*

GELFAND, DAVID R., lawyer; b. Bethpage, N.Y., 1963; BA, Vanderbilt Univ., 1984, JD, 1987. Bar: N.Y. 1988, D.C. 1990, US Dist. Ct. So. & Ea. N.Y., Ea. Dist. Wis., US Ct. Appeals Second, Fifth, Seventh & Eleventh Cir., US Supreme Ct. Assoc. Milbank Tweed Hadley & McCloy, N.Y.C., 1987—96, ptnr. & Nat. Litigation Dept. group leader, 1996—. Editor: Vanderbilt Jour. Transnational Law. Mem.: ABA, Assn. Bar City of N.Y. (mem. Com. Judicial Adminstrn.), D.C. Bar Assn. Office: Milbank Tweed Hadley & McCloy 1 Chase Manhattan Plz New York NY 10005-1413 Office Phone: 212-530-5520. Office Fax: 212-530-5219. Business E-Mail: dgelfand@milbank.com.

GELFAND, ELISSA D., French language and literature educator; b. N.Y.C., Jan. 26, 1949; d. Abe William and Frances (Gottesman) G.; m. James A. Glickman, Oct. 14, 1982; 1 child, Daniel Gelfand Glickman. BA in French, Barnard Coll., 1969; MA in French, Brown U., 1972, PhD in French, 1975. Instr. of English, Ecole Active Bilingue, Paris, 1973-75; asst., assoc. and full prof. French, Mt. Holyoke Coll., South Hadley, Mass., 1975—, Dorothy Rooke McCulloch prof. of French, 1992—. Chair French dept. Mt. Holyoke Coll., 1991-94, chair Women's Studies program, 1982-85. Author: Imagination in Confinement, 1983; co-author: French Feminist Criticism, 1985; contbr. articles to profl. jours. Andrew W. Mellow faculty fellow, 1979, Mellon teaching fellow, 1987; faculty rsch. fellow Mt. Holyoke Coll., 1976, 84, 87; rsch. grantee William H. Donner Found., 1982-86. Mem. MLA (regional del. 1987-89), N.E. MLA, Am. Assn. Tchrs. of French, Women's Caucus for the Modern Langs., Nat. Women's Studies Assn. Jewish. Avocations: film, running, food. Office: French Dept Mount Holyoke College South Hadley MA 01075

GELFAND, JEFFREY ALAN, physician, educator; b. N.Y.C., Sept. 13, 1946; s. Michael R. and Doris (Eichmann) G. BS, U. Pa., 1967; MD, Tufts U., 1971. Bd. cert. internal medicine, 1976, infectious diseases, 1980, allergy and immunology, 1981. Intern Johns Hopkins Hosp., Balt., 1971-72, resident, 1972-73, chief resident, 1976-77; rsch. fellow NIH, Bethesda, Md., 1973-76; asst. prof. Tufts Univ. Sch. Medicine, Boston, 1977-82, assoc. prof., 1982-90, prof., 1991—; vice chmn. dept. medicine New Eng. Med. Ctr., Boston, 1991, acting chmn., 1994-95, chmn. dept. medicine, physician-in-chief, 1995-98, dr. v.p. rsch. & technology, 1998—; dean rsch. Tufts U. Sch. Medicine, Boston, 1998-99; sr. attending physician Mass. Gen. Hosp., Boston, 1999—. Dean rsch. Tufts U. Sch. Medicine, Boston, 1998-99. Contbr. articles to profl. jours. Lt. commdr. USPHS, 1973-76. Office: Mass General Hosp 50 Staniford St Ste 801 Boston MA 02114-2696 Office Phone: 617-726-1796. Business E-Mail: jgelfand@partners.org.

GELFAND, JULIA MAUREEN, librarian; b. Cleve., Sept. 26, 1954; d. Lawrence Emerson and Miriam J. Ifland Gelfand; m. David Bruce Lang, Apr. 30, 1995. AB, Goucher Coll., 1975; MS in Libr. Sci., MA, Case Western Res. U., 1977. Reference libr. Penrose Libr. U. Denver, 1971-81; reference libr., bibiliographer U. Calif., Irvine, 1981-86, applied sci. and engring. libr., 1986—. Adj. faculty Sch. Info. Resources and Libr. Sci., U. Ariz., Tucson, 1998— Editor: (jour.) Grey Lit., 2000; co-editor: (jour.) Libr. Hi-Tech. News, 2001—. Bd. dirs. Orange County chpt. Am. Jewish Com., 1999—. Recipient U.S./UK Fulbright award Fulbright Commn., 1992-93, Literati award for excellence in Grey Lit., MCB Univ. Press, 1999, Literati award for leading editors MCB U. Press, 2003. Mem. ALA, AAAS, Am. Soc. Engring. Edn., Soc. Scholarly Pub., Internat. Fedn. Lib. Assns. (chmn. sci. tech. sect., 2001—). Democrat. Jewish. Business E-Mail: jgelfand@uci.edu.

GELFAND, LAWRENCE EMERSON, historian, educator; b. Cleve., June 20, 1926; s. Maurice Hirsch and Rachel S. (Shapiro) G.; m. Miriam J. Ifland, June 14, 1953; children: Julia M., Daniel B., Ronald S. BA, Western Res. U., 1949, MA, 1950; PhD, U. Wash., 1958. Asst. prof. history U. Hawaii, 1956-58; acting asst. prof. history U. Wash., 1958-59; asst. prof. history U. Wyo., 1959-62, U. Iowa, Iowa City, 1962-64, assoc. prof., 1964-66, prof., 1966-94, chmn. history dept., 1989-92; prof. emeritus, 1994—; vis. prof. U. Oreg., summer 1966, U. Mont., summer 1970, U. Wash., 1974. Mary Ball Washington prof. Am. History, Univ. Coll., Dublin, Ireland, 1987-88. Author: The Inquiry: American Preparations for Peace 1917-1919, 1963; contbr.; editor: A Diplomat Looks Back (Memoirs of Lewis Einstein), 1968, Essays on the History of American Foreign Relations, 1972, Herbert Hoover: The Great War and Its Aftermath 1914-1923, 1979; contbr. chapters to books, articles to profl. jours. Bd. curators State Hist. Soc. Iowa, 1970-72; mem. adv. bd. Nat. Archives for Region VI, 1968-74; chmn. Ctr. for Study Recent History of U.S., Iowa City, 1981-91; mem. rsch. and book prize com. Hoover Presdl.

Libr., 1996-99. Served with AUS, 1944-46. Decorated Purple Heart; Am. Council Learned Socs. grantee in Korean studies, summer 1951; Rockefeller Found. grantee, 1964-65. Mem. Am. Hist. Assn., Orgn. Am. Historians, Soc. for Historians of Am. Fgn. Relations (v.p. 1981, pres. 1982) Home: 1437 Oakcrest St Iowa City IA 52246-1622

GELFAND, NEAL, oil industry executive; b. Bronx, N.Y., Nov. 8, 1944; s. Daniel and Faye (Frank) G.; m. Jane Auerbach, Sept. 11, 1982; children: Alexandra, Laura. BS in Psychology, CCNY, 1965; MS in Indsl. Psychology, Western Mich. U., 1967; PhD in Organizational Psychology, U. Houston, 1972. Ptnr. Hay Assocs., N.Y.C., 1972-80; sr. v.p. human resources Amerada Hess Corp., N.Y.C., 1980—2004; pres. PondfieldGroup, LLC, Bronxville, NY, 2004—. Mem. APA, N.Y. Acad. Scis. Office: Pondfield Group LLC 14 Westway Bronxville NY 10708-4311 Office Phone: 914-316-7733. Business E-Mail: gelfandn@optonline.net.

GELFMAN, PETER TRUSTMAN, lawyer; b. New Rochelle, N.Y., Oct. 3, 1963; s. Robert William and Phyllis (Trustman) Gelfman; m. marguerite Gabrielle Dreifuss, Sept. 6, 1992; children: Justine Caroline, Max Sokoloff. AB magna cum laude, Harvard Coll., 1986; JD, Yale U., 1989. Bar: N.Y. 1989, DC 1990, U.S. Dist. Ct. (so. and ea. dists.) N.Y. 1990, U.S. Ct. Appeals (2d cir.) 1991. Assoc. Cravath, Swaine & Moore, N.Y.C., 1989-91; asst. U.S. Atty. U.S. Dist. Ct. (so. dist.) N.Y., N.Y.C., 1992-96; sr. atty. Westvaco Corp., N.Y.C., 1996-99; sr. assoc. gen. counsel Sequa Corp., N.Y.C., 1999—2005; dep. gen. counsel Rheem Mfg. Co., N.Y.C., 2005—. Mem. Town Village Civic Club, Scarsdale, NY, 1998—, co-chair edn. com., 1999—2001, 1st v.p., 2001—02, pres., 2002—03, past pres., 2003—04, chair nom. com., 2004—05; mem. bd. edn. Mt. Pleasant Cottage UFSD, Pleasantville, NY, 1999—; bd. ethics Scarsdale Village, 1999—2004; mem. legis. adv. com. Scarsdale Bd. Edn., 2000—02; mem. Scarsdale Bowl, 2001—03. Mem.: ABA, Assn. Bar City of N.Y., Am. Corp. Counsel Assn., Harvard Club (N.Y.C.). Office: Rheem Mfg Co 405 Lexington Ave New York NY 10174

GELFMAN, ROBERT WILLIAM, retired lawyer; b. N.Y.C., Jan. 22, 1932; s. Irving and Lillian (Meltzer) G.; m. Phyllis Trustman, Dec. 18, 1955; children: Lisa Jane (Mrs. Gary S. Matthews), Peter Trustman. BS, U. Pa., 1953; LL.B., Harvard U., 1956. Bar: N.Y. 1956, Mass. 1956. Ptnr. Battle Fowler LLP, 1974—99; ret. Dir. Graycor, Inc.; trustee Independence Savs. Bank, 1988-2004; adj. prof. Columbia U. Grad. Sch. Bus. Adminstrn., 1998-2004; past chmn. bd. dirs. Arrow Lock Corp.; mem. panel disting. neutrals CPR Inst. for Dispute Resolution. Former trustee, v.p. Jewish Bd. Guardians; past chmn. bd. Hawthorne Cedar Knolls Sch., past pres. bd. edn. Served to capt. USAF, 1957-60. Mem. Am. Law Inst., Am. Arbitration Assn. (mem. maj. real estate dispute panel of arbitrators), ABA, Assn. Bar City N.Y., N.Y. County Lawyers Assn. Clubs: Harvard (N.Y.C.); Metropolis Country (White Plains, N.Y.). Jewish. Home: 18 West Ln Greenwich CT 06831-2632

GELLAR, SARAH MICHELLE, actress; b. Apr. 14, 1977; d. Arthur and Roselen Gellar; m. Freddy Prinze Jr., 2002. Appearances include (TV movie) Invasion of Privacy, 1983, (TV series) All My Children (Daytime Emmy award for outstanding younger leading actress in a daytime drama series 1995) 1993-96, Buffy The Vampire Slayer, 1997-2003 (Saturn Award Best Genre TV Actress, 1999), (films) I Know What You Did Last Summer, 1997 (Blockbuster Entertainment award for favorite best supporting actress-horror, MTV Movie award for best breakthrough performance), Scream 2, 1997, Beverly Hills Family Robinson, 1997, Cruel Intentions, 1999, Simply Irresistable, 1999, Scooby Doo, 2002, Harvard Man, 2002, Scooby-Doo 2: Monsters Unleashed, 2004, The Grudge, 2004, numerous others, also TV commls. Avocations: Tae Kwon Do, kickboxing, gymnastics. Office: c/o Internat Creative Mgmt 8942 Wilshire Blvd Beverly Hills CA 90211-1934

GELLER, BARBARA, psychiatrist, researcher; b. N.Y.C., Apr. 21, 1939; MD, Yeshiva U., 1964. Diplomate Am. Bd. Psychiatry and Neurology 1971, Am. Bd. Psychiatry and Neurology in Child and Adolescent Psychiatry 1976. Resident in psychiatry NYU Bellevue Med Ctr., 1965—69; fell. in child psyc. NYU Bellevue Med. Ctr., 1974—76; prof. psychiatry Sch. Medicine, Wash. U., St. Louis, 1991—, Barnes Jewish Christian Hosp., St. Louis Children's Hosp. Contbr. over 100 articles to profl. jours. Recipient Nathan Cummings Found. Spl. Rsch. award, Am. Acad. of Child Psychiatry, 1995. Office: Washington U Sch Medicine Dept Psychiatry 660 S Euclid Ave Saint Louis MO 63110 E-mail: gellerb@medicine.wustl.edu.

GELLER, BUNNY ZELDA, poet, author, publisher, sculptor, artist, photographer; b. N.Y.C., May 21, 1926; d. Herman and Shirley (Shoenfeld) Juster; m. Lester Roy Geller; children: Judy Lynn, Robert Douglas, Sheryl Sue, Wayne Mitchell. Student, UCLA, 1944-46, Fla. Internat. U., 1989-97. Invited artist Pegasus Internat. Corp., N.J., 1981-85, Internat. Art Expo., N.Y., 1982-83; invited guest artist Broward County Main Lib., Ft. Lauderdale, Fla., 1988; pres. BZG Enterprises. Author: Bunny Geller Original Poetry, 1995, Destiny, 1995, Choices (poetry), 1996, The Monkey and the Parakeet (A Poetic Tale for Children), 1997, Kaleidoscope (poetry), 1997, Impressions (poetry), 1999, Bunny Geller Original Sculpture, 1985; one woman sculpture shows include Bowery Savings Bank, N.Y.C., 1978, Lynn Kottler Galleries, N.Y.C, 1978, Hollywood (Fla.) Art Mus., 1978-79, Broward County Main Libr., Fla., Hallandale Cultural Ctr., 1996; group exhbns. include All Broward Exhibit 78, Ft. Lauderdale, Fla., 1978, Old Westbury Hebrew Congregation, Westbury, N.Y., 1978, De Ligny Galleries, Ft. Lauderdale, Fla., 1979, 1983-84, Internat. Treas. Fine Art, Plainview, N.Y., 1978, 79, 80, 81, Artists Equity Assn. Hollywood (Fla.) Art Mus., 1979, Limited Edition Galleries, Bal Harbour, Fla., 1979, Temple Beth-El, Boca Raton, Fla., 1979, Expo 79, Pompano, Fla., 1979, Hilda Rindom Galleries, Hallendale, Fla, 1980, Jockey Club Art Gallery, Miami, 1980, 81, 83, 84, Gallery SO-HO 7, Ltd., Great Neck, N.Y., 1979-80, Exhibition of Fine Art Nassau Mus. of Fine Art Assn., 1985, Gallery at Turnberry, Turnberry Isle, Fla., 1980-81, Galleria Martin, Palm Beach, Fla., 1981, Contextual Fine Arts, Ft. Lauderdale, Fla., 1980-81, Art and Culture Ctr. of Hollywood (Fla.), 1981, Miami Convention Ctr., 1981, Anita Gordon Gallery, Inc., North Miami Beach, 1981, Collier Art Internat., Ltd., Westbury, N.Y., 1981, Tavistock Country Club, Haddonfield, N.J., 1982, Internat. Art Expo, N.Y.C., 1982, 83, Ohio All Arabian Show and Buckeye Sweepstakes, Columbus, 1982, West Elec. Co., Hopewell, N.J., 1982, Devon (Pa.) Arabian Horse Show, 1982, Bondstreet Art Gallery, Pitts., 1982, Blumka II Gallery, N.Y.C., 1982, Korby Gallery, Cedar Grove, N.J., 1982, Washington Internat. Horse Show, Gaithersburg, Md., 1982, Pegasus Internat. Corp., Pennington, N.J., 1981, 82, 83, 84, 85, Patricia Judith Art Gallery, Boca Raton, Fla., 1983-84, Panache Gallery, Ft. Lauderdale, Fla., 1983, The Nelson Rockefeller Collection, Inc., N.Y.C., 1983, Shorr Goodwin Gallery, N.Y.C., 1983, Carrier Found. Auxiliary, Belle Meade, N.J., 1983, First Annual Internat. Wildlife Exposition, Atlantic City, N.J., 1983, Amann Gallery, Inc., Palm Beach, Fla., 1984-85, Robert's One-of-a-Kind, Bal Harbour, Fla., 1984, Hallandale (Fla.) Pub. Lib., 1984-85, Galleria Camhi, Bar Harbor Is., Fla., 1984-85, Tatem Galleries, Ft. Lauderdale, Fla., 1984-85, Westbury (N.Y.) Meml. Lib., 1984, Trenton Country Club, 1984, Designers' Showcase 1985 Cashelmara, Glen Cove, N.Y., 1985, UN Conf., Nairobi, 1985, Hallandale Cultural Ctr., Fla., 1998; sculptures on permanent exhibits; featured in (book) Artists/USA, 1979-80, The Am. Album, Nat. Mus. Women Arts permanent collection, Washington, 1985, Art Expo N.Y. catalogue, 1982, 83, 92, Limited Collectors Edition, 1982, Town and Country mag., 1982, Gold Coast Life mag., 1983, Art in America mag., 1983-84, Sunstorm Arts Mag., 1984; represented in permanent collection Kushi Found.; Wrote words, music to song One World, 1989. Pres. Sisterhood Westbury Hebrew Congregation, Westbury, N.Y., 1967-69; judge Fine Art and Craft Show, Ft. Lauderdale, Fla., 1979-81; art adv. coun. Westbury Meml. Libr., 1990-94. Recipient 1st prize Carrier Found. Aux. 2d Ann. Arts Festival, 1983; named to Internat. Poetry Hall Fame, 1996, Merit award, Hallandale Beach, Fla., 2004; inducted into Internat. Libr. Photography, 2002. Mem. Nat. Mus. Women in the Arts (assoc.), Nat. Libr. Poetry (Editor's Choice award 1995, published in Best Poems of the 90s 1996), Internat. Soc. Poets (disting. mem. 1995, Poet of Merit 1995, semi-finalist symposium 1995, inducted into Internat. Poetry Hall of Fame 1996), Nat. Trust for Historic Preservation. Avocations: tennis, all sports, cultural events, national events, art shows. Home: 400 Diplomat Pkwy Apt 711 Hallandale Beach FL 33009

GELLER, DEBRA F., academic administrator, educator; BA cum laude, U. So. Fla., 1986; MBA, Calif. Coast U., 1998; EdD, UCLA, 2004. Cert. salary adminstrn. ACA/World at Work, 1999. Asst. to dir. nursing systems UCLA Med. Ctr., 1992—94; bus. officer campus human resources UCLA, 1994—99, chief adminstrv. officer student and campus life. Instr. L.A. City Coll. Chair, nominating com. Univ. Credit Union, 2001—02. Recipient Witness Program Wall of Fame, UCLA Sch. of Law. Mem.: Nat. Assn. Student Personnel Adminstr., Soc. Human Resource Mgmt., ACA/World at Work. Office: UCLA Box 951626 Los Angeles CA 90095-1626 E-mail: dgeller@saonet.ucla.edu.

GELLER, ESTHER (BAILEY GELLER), artist; b. Boston, Oct. 26, 1921; d. Harry and Fannie (Geller) G.; m. Harold Shapero, Sept. 21, 1945; 1 child, Hannah. Diploma, Sch. Boston Mus. Fine Arts, 1943. Tchr. Boston Mus. Sch., 1943, Boris Mirski Sch., 1945-49. Art cons. Leonard Morse Hosp., Natick, Mass. One-woman shows at Boris Mirski Art Gallery, Boston, 1945-46, 49, 52, 61, Addison Gallery Am. Art, Children's Art Centre, Andover, Mass., 1953-55, Mayo Gallery, Provincetown, Mass., 1958, Marion (Mass.) Art Centre, 1966, St. Mark's Sch., Southboro, Mass., 1969, Decenter Gallery, Copenhagen, 1969, Regis Coll., Weston, Mass., 1970, Am. Acad. Gallery, Rome, 1971, Newton (Mass.) Libr., 1973, Newton Art Centre, 1978, Artworks of Wayne, Providence, 1979, Stonehill Coll., Easton, Mass., 1986; 2-person show at The Ctr. for Arts in Natick, 2001; exhibited in group shows at San Francisco Mus., Va. Mus. Art, Chgo. Art Inst., Worcester Art Mus., U. Ill., Smith Coll., Inst. Contemporary Art, DeCordova Mus., USIA traveling show, USIS circulating exhbn., Far East, Boston Mus., Regis Coll., 1984, Danforth Mus. Art, 1995, Boston Ctr. for Arts, 1997, Firehouse Artists Show, Natiek, 1998, Univ. Place, Cambridge, 1999, Mass. State House, Boston, 2000, Boston U. Art Gallery, 2002, Visionary Decade Thorne-Sagendorph Art Gallery, Keene, N.H., 2003. Cabot fellow, 1949; Studios Am. Acad. fellow, 1949-50, 70-71, 75; MacDowell Colony-Yaddo fellow, 1945, 67, 69 Mem.: Arts Wayland Assn., Boston Visual Arts Union. Home: 9 Russell Cir Natick MA 01760-1223 Studio: 5 Summer St Natick MA 01760-4511

GELLER, ETHELL A., consulting clinical psychologist; b. Linz, Austria, Sept. 26, 1946; came to U.S., 1948; d. Abraham and Orinka (Brown) Avram; m. Ronald D. Geller, June 2, 1968. BA summa cum laude, Hunter Coll., 1970, MA, 1972; PhD, CUNY, 1977. Diplomate in Profl. Psychology Internat. Acad. Behavioral Medicine, Counseling and Psychotherapy. Prof. psychology Hunter Coll., N.Y.C., 1977-79; staff psychologist Albert Ellis Inst. for Psychotherapy, N.Y.C., 1979-89; pvt. practice clin. psychology, N.Y.C., 1980—. Rschr. in field. Contbr. articles to profl. jours. Mem. APA, N.Y. Acad. Scis., Am. Assn. Behavior Therapy, Soc. for Behavioral Medicine, Inst. for Rational Emotive Psychotherapy, Phi Beta Kappa. Avocations: cooking, martial arts, travel, languages, music. Office: 952 5th Ave New York NY 10021-1740 Office Phone: 212-861-7521.

GELLER, HAROLD ARTHUR, earth and space sciences executive, educator; b. Bklyn., June 14, 1954; s. Morris and Minnie (Kaplan) G. BS, SUNY, Albany, 1983; MA, George Mason U., 1992, ArtsD in C.C. Edn., 2005. Rsch. asst. SUNY at Downstate Med., Bklyn., 1972-74, CUNY at Bklyn. Coll., 1974-75; engring. aide FBI, Washington, 1977-78; lab. supr. ENSCO Inc., Springfield, Va., 1978-80; assoc. engr. Def. Systems Inc., McLean, Va., 1980-83; staff scientist, systems engr. Sci. Applications Internat. Corp., McLean, 1983-87, systems engr., 1988-90, sr. sys. engr., 1996-99; systems engr. Grumman Aerospace, Reston, Va., 1987-88; rsch. asst. Naval Rsch. Lab., George Mason U., 1990-91; project mgr. Rsch. and Data Systems Corp., Greenbelt, Md., 1991-92; dep. dir. Washington ops. Consortium Internat. Earth Sci. Info. Network, Washington, 1992-96; instr. physics and astronomy George Mason U., 1993—. Computer cons., Burke, Va., 1986—87. Commonwealth fellow, 1992-93. Mem.: AAAS, AIAA (chmn. corp. liason com. 1989—90, chmn. pub. affairs com. 1990—91), Astron. League (media rels. officer 2000—01), Assn. C. C. Coll. Educators (v.p. 2000—01), Potomac Geophys. Soc. (1st v.p. 1994—95, 2000—01, pres. 1995—96, 2001—02), Am. Geophys. Union, Am. Astron. Soc. Democrat. Jewish. Office: George Mason U Dept Physics 4400 University Dr Fairfax VA 22030-4444 Business E-Mail: hgeller@gmu.edu.

GELLER, JANICE GRACE, nurse; b. Auburn, Ga., Feb. 25, 1938; d. Erby Ralph and Jewell Grace (Maughon) Clack; m. Joseph Jerome Geller, Dec. 23, 1973; 1 child, Elizabeth Joanne. Student, LaGrange Coll., 1955-57; BS in Nursing, Emory U., 1960; MS, Rutgers U., 1962. Nat. cert. group psychotherapist; cert. clin. nurse specialist. Psychiat. staff nurse dept. psychiatry Emory U., Atlanta, 1960; nurse educator Ill. State Psychiat. Inst., Chgo., 1961; clin. specialist in mental retardation nursing Northville, Mich., 1962; faculty Coll. Nursing Rutgers U., Newark, 1962-63, faculty Advanced Program in Psychiat. Nursing, 1964-66; faculty Coll. Nursing U. Mich., Ann Arbor, 1963-64; faculty, Teheran (Iran) Coll. for Women, 1967-69; clin. specialist psychiat. nursing Roosevelt Hosp., N.Y.C., 1969-70; faculty, guest lectr. Columbia U., N.Y.C., 1969-70; supr. Dept. Psychiat. Nursing Mt. Sinai Hosp., N.Y.C., 1970-72; pvt. practice psychotherapy N.Y.C., 1972-77, Ridgewood, N.J., 1977-96. Faculty, curriculum coord. in psychiat. nursing William Alanson White Inst. Psychiatry, Psychoanalysis and Psychology, N.Y.C., 1974-84; mem. U.S. del. of Community and Mental Health Nurses to People's Republic of China, 1983. Contbr. articles to profl. jours.; editorial bd. Perspectives in Psychiat. Care, 1971-74, 78-84; author: (with Anita Marie Werner) Instruments for Study of Nurse-Patient Interaction, 1964. Mem. Bergen County Rep. Com., 1989. Recipient 10th Anniversary award Outstanding Clin. Specialist in psychiat.-mental health nursing in N.J., Soc. Cert. Clin. Specialists, 1982; Fed. Govt. grantee as career tchr. in psychiat. nursing, Rutgers U., 1962-63; cert. psychiat. nurse and clin. specialist, N.J., N.Y. Mem. AAAS, ANA (various certs.), N.C. Nurses Assn., Soc. Cert. Clin. Specialists in Psychiat. Nursing (chmn.), Coun. Specialists in Psychiat./Mental Health Nursing, Am. Group Psychotherapy Assn. (cert. group psychotherapist), Am. Assn. Mental Deficiency, World Fedn. Mental Health, Sigma Theta Tau. Address: 307 Chatterson Dr Raleigh NC 27615-3137 Fax: (919) 518-0495.

GELLER, JAY, humanities educator; AB, Princeton U., 1995; PhD, MA, Yale U., 2001. Asst. prof. U. Tulsa, Okla., 2002—. Author: (book) Jews in Post-Holocaust Germany. Bd. mem. Sherwin Miller Mus. of Jewish Art, Tulsa, Okla., 2003—. Mem.: Am. Hist. Assn. Office: U Tulsa 600 South College Ave Tulsa OK 74104 Office Phone: 918-631-2239. Office Fax: 918-631-2057.

GELLER, JEFFREY L., psychiatrist, educator; b. N.Y.C., 1948; MD, U. Pa., 1973; MPH, Harvard U., 1978. Bd. cert. psychiatry. Intern psychiatry Phila. Gen. Hosp., 1974; resident psychiatry Beth Israel Hosp., Boston, 1974—77, fellow, 1977—78; staff mem. U. Mass. Med. Ctr., Worcester; prof. psychiatry U. Mass. Med. Sch., Worcester, dir. pub. sector psychiatry. Co-author: Women of the Asylum, 1994; contbr. articles to profl. jours. Mem.: Am. Psychiat. Assn. (book rev. editor Jour., first person account column editor psychiat. svcs. Jour., mem. coun. on social issues and pub. policy, area 1 rep., Arnold J. Van Ameringen award 2003). Office: Univ Mass Med Sch Dept Psychiatry 55 Lake Ave North Worcester MA 01655

GELLER, KENNETH STEVEN, lawyer; b. NYC, Sept. 22, 1947; s. Edward and Sylvia R. (Tannenbaum) G.; m. Judith B. Ratner, Sept. 9, 1990; children: Eric Jonathan, Lisa Beth. BA magna cum laude, CCNY, 1968; JD magna cum laude, Harvard U., 1971. Bar: NY 1972, US Dist. Ct. (so. and ea. dists.) NY 1972, US Ct. Appeals (2d cir.) 1972, US Ct. Appeals (DC cir.) 1974, US Supreme Ct. 1975, US Ct. Appeals (10th cir.) 1976, DC 1986, US Ct. Appeals (6th cir.) 1987, US Ct. Appeals (4th cir.) 1987, US Ct. Appeals (9th cir.) 1988, US Ct. Appeals (5th and 11th cirs.) 1990, US Dist. Ct. DC 1991, US Ct. Appeals (3rd and 7th cirs.) 1991, US Ct. Appeals (Armed Forces) 1995, US Ct. Appeals (8th cir.) 1996, US Ct. Appeals (fed. cir.) 1999. Law clk. US Ct. Appeals (2d cir.), 1971-72; assoc. Nickerson, Kramer, Lowenstein, Nessen & Kamin, NYC, 1972-73; asst. spl. prosecutor Watergate Spl. Prosecution Force, Washington, 1973-75; asst. to solicitor gen. Dept. Justice, Washington, 1975-79, dep. solicitor gen., 1979-86; ptnr. Mayer, Brown, Rowe & Maw LLP (formerly Mayer, Brown & Platt), Washington, 1986—, mng. ptnr., 1995—. Mem. adv. bd. State and Local Legal Ctrs., 1986-92; mem. adv. com. on rules U.S. Ct. Appeals for Armed Forces, 1994-2000; mem. adv. com. on procedures Ct. Appeals D.C. Cir., 2000—. Co-author: (Stern, Gressman, Shapiro & Geller) Supreme Court Practice, 8th edit., 2002; contbg. author: Business and Commercial Litigation in Federal Courts, 1998; contbr. articles to profl. jours. Mem. vis. com. Harvard U. Law Sch.; trustee, chmn. publs. com. Supreme Ct. Hist. Soc. Recipient Younger Fed. Lawyer award FBA, 1981, Presdl. Disting. Exec. award. Office: Mayer Brown Rowe & Maw LLP 1909 K St NW Washington DC 20006-1152 Office Phone: 202-263-3000. E-mail: kgeller@mayerbrown.com.

GELLER, MARGARET JOAN, astrophysicist, educator; d. Seymour and Sarah Geller. AB, U. Calif., Bekeley, 1970; MA, Princeton U., 1972, PhD, 1975; DSc (hon.), Conn. Coll., 1995, Gustavus Adolphus Coll., 1997, U. Mass., Dartmouth, 2000. Rsch. assoc. Harvard Coll. Obs., Cambridge, Mass., 1978-80; asst. prof. Harvard U., Cambridge, 1980-83; astrophysicist Smithsonian Astrophys. Obs., Cambridge, 1983—. Goodspeed-Richardo lectr. U. Pa., 1992; Brickwedde disting. lectr. JHU, 1993; Hogg lectr. Royal Astro. Soc. Can., 1993; Bethe lectr. Cornell U., 1996; Hilldale lectr. U. Wis., 1999; NSF Disting. lectr., 2004. Contbr. articles to profl. jours.; mem. editl. bd. Sci., 1991—94. Named Libr. Lion, N.Y. Pub. Libr., 1997; recipient Newcomb-Cleve. prize, 1989—90, Klopsteg award, Am. Assn. Physics Tchrs., 1996, ADION medal, 2003; fellow, MacArthur Found., 1990—95. Fellow: AAAS, APS; mem.: NAS (coun. mem. 2000—03), Assoc. Univs. Rsch. in Astronomy (dir.-at-large), Am. Astron Soc. (councillor), Am. Acad. Art and Scis. (coun. mem.), Internat. Astron Union, Phi Beta Kappa (senator 1998—99). Office: Smithsonian Astrophys Obs 60 Garden St Cambridge MA 02138-1516

GELLER, MARVIN ALAN, meteorology educator, researcher; b. Boston, Mar. 19, 1943; s. James and Saide (Schlager) G.; m. Lynda Louise Grafinger, June 16, 1968; children: Stephanie, Steven. BS in Applied Math., MIT, 1964, PhD in Meteorology, 1969. From asst. prof. to prof. U. Ill., Champaign-Urbana, 1969-77; prof. U. Miami, Fla., 1977-80; rsch. scientist NASA Goddard Space Flight Ctr., Greenbelt, Md., 1980-84, chief Lab. for Atmospheres, 1984-89; prof., head Inst. for Terrestrial and Planetary Atmospheres SUNY, Stony Brook, 1989-2000, dean, dir. Marine Scis. Rsch. Ctr., 1998—2002, prof. atmospheric scis., 2002—. Contbr. articles to profl. jours. Fellow Am. Meteorol. Soc., Am. Geophys. Union (pres. atmospheric scis. sect. 2000-02); mem. Sci. Com. Solar-Terrestrial Physics (pres. 2000—), Nat. Assn. U.S. Nat. Acads. Democrat. Jewish. Avocations: golf, music. Home: 145 Oakwood Rd Port Jefferson NY 11777-1423 Office: SUNY-Stony Brook Msrc Stony Brook NY 11794-5000 Office Phone: 631-632-8686.

GELLER, ROBERT JAMES, advertising agency executive; b. NYC, May 5, 1937; s. Jerome and Pearl (Klein) G.; m. Lois Dee Fromkin, June 9, 1968; children: Richard Evan, Stephen Laurence. BS, CCNY, 1958. Account exec. Furman, Feiner & Co., NYC, 1958-62; media supr. Interpublic Group of Cos., NYC, 1962-64; asst. media dir. Foote, Cone & Belding, NYC, 1964-69; pres. Adforce, Inc., NYC, 1970-92, Robert J. Geller & Assocs., Inc., NYC, 1993—; pres., CEO Reel Am., Inc., NYC, 2000—03; mng. dir. Charter Media, 2002—; sec.-treas., CFO, Charter Digital Media Inc., 2005—. Contbr. numerous articles to profl. jours. Pres. Robert J. and Lois F. Geller Found. Mem. Assn. Nat. Advertisers (mgmt. policy com. 1980-92, corp. membership com. 1990-92), Am. Advt. Fedn. (bd. dirs., corp. membership com. 1989—, plans rev. com. 1990—, asst. sec. 1992—), Advt. Club NYC Republican. Home: 155 E 76th St New York NY 10021-2810 also: Parsonage Ln Sagaponack NY 11962 Office: Robert J Geller & Assocs Inc 708 Third Ave 29th Fl New York NY 10017 Office Phone: 212-351-3350. Personal E-mail: rjgeller@mindspring.com.

GELLER, SCOTT A., management consultant; BA in Pub. Adminstrn. and Pre-Law, Carthage Coll., 1986; MS in Healthcare Adminstrn. and Cmty. Mental Health and Counseling, LI U., US Mil. Acad., West Point, NY, 1990; post grad., Regis U., 2005—. Mgr. recruit new store openings, tng. and gen. mgr. devel. Pepsi Co.; asst. chaplain U.S. Army, West Point, Europe, Saudi Arabia, Ft. Lewis, Wash.; field assoc., coll. liaison and mktg. instr. Gen. Motors Ednl. Programs; exec. dir. sr. assisted living and memory care Sunrise Assisted Living, Inc.; mktg. cons. and nat. acct. exec. SALEM Comm. Corp.; adminstr. cmty.-based residential facility and gen. mgr. The Harbor Campus Lakeview Properties, LLC; regional mgr. and nat. healthcare adminstr. Sunwest Mgmt. Co.; pres. small bus. devel. Cow Country Enterprises. Decorated Army Commendation medal with Oakleaf Cluster, Southwest Asia Svc. medal with Bronze Star, Army Achievement medal, Nat. Defense medal. Mem.: Gamma Kappa Alpha. Address: PO Box 151 Appleton WI 54911 Office Phone: 920-277-1614. E-mail: scott@cowcountryenterprises.com.

GELLER, STEPHEN ARTHUR, pathologist, educator; b. Bklyn., Apr. 26, 1939; s. Sam John and Alice (Podber) G.; m. Kate Eleanor DeJong, June 24, 1962; children: David Phillip, Jennifer Lee. *Son, David P. Geller, is founder, president and CEO of WhatCounts, a Seattle-based unique e-mail marketing firm providing cutting-edge publishing technology through their ASP appliance, Managed Enterprise, and Agency Solutions. Daughter, Jennifer L. Geller, J.D., is a Development Officer with the Michael J. Fox Foundation for Parkinson's Research in New York City.* BA, Bklyn. Coll., 1959; MD, Howard U., 1964. Diplomate Am. Bd. Pathology, Nat. Bd. Med. Examiners. Intern Lenox Hill Hosp., N.Y.C., 1964-65; resident in pathology Mt. Sinai Hosp., N.Y.C., 1965-69; chief lab. Naval Hosp., Beaufort, S.C., 1969-71; asst. prof. pathology Mt. Sinai Med. Ctr., N.Y.C., 1971-75, assoc. prof., 1975-78, prof., 1978-84; chmn. dept. pathology Cedars-Sinai Med. Ctr., L.A., 1984—; prof. pathology UCLA, 1984—. Co-author: Histopathology, 1989, Biopsy Interpretation of the Liver, 2004; contbr. articles to profl. jours. Recipient Excellence in Teaching award CUNY, 1974, Golden Apple tchg. award Cedars-Sinai Med. Ctr., 1986, 2000, 02, 04. Fellow Coll. Am. Pathologists, Am. Soc. Clin. Pathologists; mem. Am. Assn. Study of Liver Diseases, Hans Popper Hepatopathology Soc., Calif. Soc. Pathologists (sec. 1989-91, v.p. 1991-93, pres. 1994-96), L.A. Soc. Pathologists (v.p. 1989-91, pres. 1992), N.Y. Pathol. Soc., Alpha Omega Alpha. Democrat. Jewish. Avocations: music, photography, writing fiction. Office: Cedars Sinai Med Ctr 8700 Beverly Blvd Los Angeles CA 90048-1865 Office Phone: 310-423-6632. Business E-Mail: geller@cshs.org.

GELLER, WILLIAM ALAN, criminologist, consultant, protective services official; b. Bklyn., June 4, 1950; s. Maurice and Shirley F.E. (Scherker) G.; m. Julia Marie Arment, Oct. 1, 1978. BA, SUNY, Buffalo, 1972; JD, U. Chgo., 1975. Bar: Ill. 1975, U.S. Dist. Ct. (no. dist.) Ill. 1975. Rsch. asst. U. Chgo., 1974—75; law clk. to Hon. Walter V. Schaefer Ill. Supreme Ct., Chgo., 1975-76; exec. dir. Chgo. Law Enforcement Study Group, 1976-81; project dir. Am. Bar Found., Chgo., 1981-86; dir. Louisa May Alleycat Music, 1985—; spl. counsel Chgo. Park Dist., 1986-88; assoc. dir. Police Exec. Rsch. Forum, 1987-97; dir. Geller & Assocs. Consulting, Wilmette, Ill., 1997—. Mem. Pres. Clinton's Transition Team (U.S. Dept. Justice search team mem.), 1992-93; staff Office Presdl. Pers., Washington, 1993; commr. Wilmette Fire and Police Commn., 1985-88; co-founder Cmty. Safety Initiative, 1994; cons. Local Initiatives Support Corp., 1995—, Nat. Inst. Justice, U.S. Dept. Justice, Washington, 1980—, Office of Cmty. Oriented Policing Svcs., U.S. Dept. Justice, 1994-2002, fellow Office of Cmty. Oriented Policy Svcs., 1999-2001; dep. atty. gen., 1993-94, civil rights divsn., 2001, NYC Police Dept., 1985-88, 93, FBI, Washington, 1986-96, L.A. Police Dept., 2005, Police Found., 1986-88, NYC Met. Transp. Authority, 1991, Boston Police Dept., 2002-04, Des Moines Police Dept., 2002, Detroit Police Dept., 2003, Albuquerque Police Dept., 1997, Charlotte-Mecklenburg Police Dept., 1998, 2003—, LA Police Dept, 2005, Seattle Police Dept., 1998, Fed. Signal Corp., 1990, Chgo. Police Bd., 1991-95, St. Louis Police Dept., 1991-97, Office of the Mayor, Washington, 1992-93, St. Louis, 1997-2001, Boulware & Assocs., 1992—,

U.S. Info. Agy., 1999, Burkhalter & Assocs., 1992-95, Washington Post, 1998, San Francisco Chronicle, 2005, Harvard U. Office Gen. Counsel, 1995, Ill. Criminal Justice Info. Authority, 1993; police chief exec. searcher Washington, Charlotte, NC, Detroit; rsch. adv. com. Chgo. Police Dept., 1983-86; mem. Cook County Sheriff's adv. com. on internal affairs, 1986; exec. com. Chgo. Ethics Project. Author: Split-Second Decisions: Shootings Of and By Chicago Police, 1981, Deadly Force: What We Know.A Practitioner's Desk Reference on Police-Involved Shootings in the United States, 1991, Police Violence: Understanding and Controlling Police Abuse of Force, 1996, And Justice For All, 1995, Managing Police Innovation, 1995; also many articles to profl. jours., mags., and newspapers; editor: Police Leadership in America: Crisis and Opportunity, 1985, Local Government Police Management, 1991, 2003; script cons. (TV show) L.A. Law, 1991; mem. expert adv. panel RAND Corp., 2002-03. Co-chmn. Citizens for Safety Vests, Chgo., 1982-83; adv. bd. March of Dimes Met. Chgo., 1983; bd. dirs. John Howard Assn., Chgo., 1978—99, Bus. and Profl. People for Pub. Interest, 1988—, Travel Light Theatre, Chgo., 1980-82; adv. bd. Yale U. Nat. Ctr. Children Exposed to Violence, 2000—; priority grants com. United Way Met. Chgo., 1990-92; task force on criminal justice studies, Clark-Atlanta U., 1991-95; mgr. Harvard Exec. Session on Drugs and Cmty. Policing, Cambridge, Mass., 1990-92. Recipient Richard J. Daley Police medal of honor, City of Chgo., 1983, commendation N.Y.C. Police Commr., 1986, commendation St. Louis Police Chief, 1997; grantee Nat. Inst. Justice, 1980, 84, 88, 90, 91, Chgo. Bar Found., 1980, Chgo. Cmty. Trust, 1976-80, 84, 85, Charles Stewart Mott Found., 1990, Edna McConnell Clark Found., 1998. Mem. ABA (com. on stds. for criminal justice 1983-86, prison and jail problems com. 1985-86), Internat. Assn. Chiefs Police, Police Exec. Rsch. Forum, NOBLE, Am. Soc. Criminology, Acad. Criminal Justice Scis. Home and Office: 2116 Thornwood Ave Wilmette IL 60091-1452 E-mail: wageller@aol.com.

GELLERT, GEORGE GEZA, food importing company executive; b. NYC, Apr. 15, 1938; s. Imre and Martha (Tessler) G.; m. Barbara Rubin, July 21, 1963; children— Andrew, Amy, Thomas. BS, Cornell U., 1960, MBA, 1962, LL.B., 1963. Bar: N.Y. State bar 1963. Atty. SEC, Washington, 1963-64; v.p., exec. v.p., pres. Atalanta Corp., N.Y.C., 1966—, chmn. bd., 1978—. Chmn. U.S.-Rumanian Econ. Council; bd. dirs. Am. Importers Meat Products Group. Trustee Cornell U., 1995-99, mem. Cornell U. Council. Served to 1st lt. Office Staff Judge AUS, 1964-66. Decorated Army Commendation medal; recipient Outstanding Alumni award Cornell U., 2000, Ellis Island Nat. Medal of Honor, 2001, Ernst & Young Master Entrepreneur of the Yr. award, 2001, George Washington award Am. Hungarian Found., 2004. Mem. Am. Importers Assn. (dir., exec. com. meat product group), Am. Assn. Exporters and Importers (bd. dirs.), Met. Pres.'s Orgn. Home: PO Box 213 New Vernon NJ 07976 Office: Atalanta Corp Atalanta Plz Elizabeth NJ 07206 Office Phone: 908-351-8000. Personal E-mail: ggellert@atalanta1.com.

GELLERT, JAY M., health and medical products executive; b. Mar. 13, 1954; BA, Stanford U., 1975. Dir. health services, County of San Mateo Calif. Dept. of Health Services; sr. v.p., COO Calif. Healthcare System, 1985-88; pres., CEO Bay Pacific Health Corp., 1988-91; dir. strategic advisory engagements Shattuck Hammond Ptnrs. Inc.; pres., COO Health Systems Internat. Inc. (merged with Found. Health. Corp. in 1996), 1996—97, Health Net, Inc. (formerly Found. Health Systems), 1997—98; pres., CEO Health Net, Inc., 1998—, bd. dirs., 1999—. Chmn., admin. simplification com. Coun. Affordable Quality Healthcare; bd. dirs. Am. Assoc. Health Plans, MedUnite, Inc., Miavita, Inc. Office: Health Net Inc 21650 Oxnard St Woodland Hills CA 91367-4901*

GELLERT, MICHAEL ERWIN, investment banker; b. Prague, Czechoslovakia, June 15, 1931; s. Oswald Rudolf and Grete (Petschek) G.; m. Mary Crombie, Jan. 11, 1969; children: John Matthew, Catherine Ann. BA, Harvard U., 1953; MBA, U. Pa., 1955. Exec. dir. Drexel Burnham Lambert and predecessor co., NYC, 1958-89; gen. ptnr. Windcrest Ptnr., NYC, 1967—. Bd. dirs. Six Flags, Inc., Oklahoma City, Seacor Holdings, NYC, Smith Barney World Funds, NY, Travelers Series Fund, Inc., NYC. Trustee Caramoor Ctr. for Mus. and Arts, Katonah, NY; chmn. bd. trustees Carnegie Instn. Washington; vice chmn. bd. trustees New Sch. U., NYC. With U.S. Army, 1955-57. Fellow: AAAS; mem.: Am. Acad. Arts and Sci. (trustee), Cosmos Club, The Field Club (Greenwich, Conn.), Penn Club (NYC), Harvard Club (NYC), Burning Tree Country Club (Greenwich). Office: Windcrest Ptnrs 122 E 42nd St New York NY 10168-0002 E-mail: mgellert@chelseacap.com.

GELLES, RICHARD JAMES, sociology professor, psychology professor, academic administrator; b. Newton, Mass., July 7, 1946; s. Sidney S. and Clara (Goldberg) G.; m. Judy S. Isacoff, July 4, 1971; children: Jason Charles, David Philip. AB, Bates Coll., 1968; MA, U. Rochester, 1971; PhD, U. N.H., 1973. Asst. prof. sociology U. R.I., Kingston, 1973-76, assoc. prof., 1976-81, prof., 1982-98, dean Coll. Arts and Scis., 1984-90; Joanne and Raymond Welsh chair child welfare/family violence Sch. of Social Policy and Practice, U. Pa., 1998—, dean, 2002—. Cons. Children's Hosp. Med. Ctr., Boston, 1973—98; lectr. Harvard Med. Sch., Boston, 1979-88, 95—98; rsch. dir. Louis Harris and Assocs., N.Y.C., 1981-82, cons., 1982-86; cons. Sage Pubs., Newbury Park, Calif., 1986—2004. Author: The Violent Home, 1974, Family Violence, 1979; co-author: Behind Closed Doors: Violence in the American Family, 1980, Intimate Violence, 1988, The Book of David, 1996. Mem. Am. Sociol. Assn. (chair family sect. 1985-86, recipient Disting. Contributions to Teaching award Sect. on Undergrad. Edn. 1979), Nat. Council Family Relations (chair rsch. and theory sect. 1989-91, v.p. publs. 1996-98). Jewish. Avocations: tennis, golf. Office: Sch Social Policy and Practice U Pa 3701 Locust Walk Philadelphia PA 19104-6214 Office Phone: 215-898-5541. Business E-Mail: gelles@sp2.upenn.edu.

GELLHORN, ALFRED, physician, educator; b. St. Louis, June 4, 1913; s. George and Edna (Fischel) Gellhorn; m. Olga Frederick, Aug. 4, 1939; children: Martha, Anne, Christina, Maria, Edna. Student, Amherst Coll., 1930—32, DSc (hon.), 1969; MD, Washington U., St. Louis, 1937; DSc (hon.), CCNY, 1979, SUNY, 1984, Albany Med. Coll., 1986, U. Pa., 1992. Diplomate Am. Bd. Internal Medicine. Gen. surg. tng. Barnes Hosp., St. Louis, 1937—39; gynecology trainee Passavant Meml. Hosp., Chgo., 1939—40; fellow Carnegie Instn. of Washington, Balt., 1940—43; instr., later asst. prof. physiology Coll. Physicians and Surgeons, Columbia U., N.Y.C., 1943—45, asst., then assoc. prof. pharmacology, 1945—48, assoc. prof. clin. cancer research dept. medicine, 1948—52, assoc. prof. medicine, 1952—58, prof. medicine, 1958—68; prof. medicine and pharmacology, dean Sch. Medicine, also dir. Med. Ctr. U. Pa., Phila., 1968—73; dir. Ctr. Biomed. Edn., City Coll., v.p. for health affairs CUNY, 1974—79, emeritus, 1979—; dir. med. affairs N.Y. State Dept. Health, Albany, 1983—96; rsch. dir., cons. diamond fund fell. prgm. Aaron Diamond Post Doctoral Rsch. Fell. Prgm., 1996—. Cons. Commonwealth Fund, NY, 1979—80, Aaron Diamond Found., 1987—; vis. prof. Harvard Sch. Pub. Health, 1980—83; physician Francis Delafield Hosp., N.Y.C., 1949—52, chief med. svc., 1952—68; vis. prof. medicine Albert Einstein Med. Sch.; dir. Inst. Cancer Rsch., Columbia; bd. regents Nat. Libr. Medicine. Mem.: ACP, Am. Soc. Biol. Chemistry, Inst. Medicine, Am. Soc. Pharm. and Exptl. Therapeutics, Am. Assn. Cancer Rsch. (pres. 1962—63), N.Y. County Med. Soc., Assn. Am. Physicians, Soc. for Clin. Investigation, Coll. Physicians Phila. Office: 90 Church St 13th Fl New York NY 10007 E-mail: axg08@health.state.ny.us.

GELLIN, GERALD ALAN, dermatologist; b. Bklyn., May 24, 1934; m. Lucille E. Gellin. AB, U. Pa., 1954; MD, NYU, 1958. Diplomate Am. Bd. Dermatology. Chief sect. dermatology VA Hosp., Bklyn., 1964-67; clin. prof. U. Calif. Med. Ctr., San Francisco, 1969—. Chief dermatology divsn. VA Hosp., Bklyn., 1963-67, San Francisco Gen. Hosp., 1969-73, Calif. Pacific Med. Ctr., 1986—2003. Contbr. articles to profl. jours. With USPHS, 1967-69. Fellow ACP. Office: 3838 California St San Francisco CA 94118-1522 Office Phone: 415-668-2400.

GELLIN, SLADE, engineering educator, consultant; b. Bklyn., Apr. 14, 1951; s. Jerry and Lillian Gellin; m. Marcia Ann Kulpa, June 27, 1976; children: Erika Lynne Griffin, Caren Elizabeth Gellin-Talledo, Jonathan Craig, Laura Michelle, Matthew David. BS, Columbia U., 1972; MS, Harvard U., 1973, PhD, 1977. Vis. asst. prof. U. Buffalo, 1976—80; sr. engr. Bell Aerospace Textron, 1980—92; lectr. Buffalo State Coll., 1993—97; sr. engr. ATSI, Inc., 1997—99; lectr. Buffalo State Coll., 1999—2000, asst. prof., 2000—. Lectr. U. at Buffalo, 1977—2000; engr. EGW Assocs., 1996—97; engrng. analyst/cons. Birdair, Inc., 1999—. Treas. TTA Booster Club, Tonawanda, NY, 1998—2000; meet entry chairperson, 1998—2002. Mem.: ASEE, ASME, NY State Engrng. Tech. Assn. (mech. interest group chair 2003—05). Achievements include development of Engineering software for applications. Avocation: urban rail transportation infrastructure. Office: Buffalo State Coll 1300 Elmwood Ave Buffalo NY 14222 Office Phone: 716-878-6002. Office Fax: 716-878-3033. E-mail: gellins@buffalostate.edu.

GELLINEK, CHRISTIAN JOHANN, language educator; b. Potsdam, Prussia, Germany, May 11, 1930; arrived in US, 1961; s. Christian Johann Michael and Margaretha C. (Lorenzen) Gellinek; m. Josepha E. Schellekens, June 27, 1975; children: Else, Saskia, Torsten, Jens. BA, U. Toronto, Ont., 1959, M.Edn., 1961; MA, Yale U., 1963, PhD, 1964; dr.phil.habil., Basel (Switzerland) U., 1974. Instr. Yale U., 1964—66, asst. prof., 1966—68, assoc. prof., 1968—70; prof., chmn. German dept. Conn. Coll., 1970—71; prof. German U. Fla., Gainesville, 1971-87; guest rschr. Inst. Vergleichende Stadtgeschichte, 1987—; guest prof. Salt Lake City, Basel, Poznan, Münster, Westphalia, The Hague, UCLA. Author 20 books including: Literature, History, Ethnology: Hugo Grotius, 1983, Stadtkultur, 1990, Philipp Scheidemann Cologne, 1994, Those Damned Dutch, 1996, Northwest Germany in Northeast Amterica, 1997, Christus in Amerika, 1999; co-author: (with H.W. Kelling) Avenues Towards Mormonism, 2001, Going Dutch — Gone American. Germans Settling North America, 2003, Young Schleiermacher and the Transatlantic Connection, 2004. Fulbright grantee, 1980-81, 85, 91. Mem. MLA. Calvinist. Avocations: walking, swimming. E-mail: gellinek@yahoo.com.

GELLING, PATRICIA I., reading educator; b. Rockville Ctr., NY, Oct. 21, 1950; d. James Christopher and Myrtle Hattie Egan; m. Gilbert Gelling, Apr. 14, 1973; children: Michael David, Brian Christian, Sara Elizabeth. BS summa cum laude, Molloy Coll., Rockville Ctr., NY; MS with distinction, Hofstra U., Hempstead, 1994. Cert. reading tchr. NY, 1994, special edn. tchr. NY, 1990, elem. edn. tchr. NY, 1990, reading recovery tchr. NYU, 1999. Reading tchr. Seaford Union Free Sch. Dist., NY, 1994—2000, reading chairperson, 2000—; reading recovery tchr. Seaford Manor Sch., 2000—. Literacy collaborative bldg. team Seaford Manor Sch., 2004—05; title I coord. Seaford Union Free Sch. Dist., 2003—. Religious edn. tchr. St. William the Abbot Ch., Seaford, 1986—93. Sidney J. Rausch Scholarship, Hofstra U., 1994. Mem.: Reading Recovery Coun. (assoc.), Nassau Reading Coun. (assoc.). Office: Seaford Union Free Sch Dist 1600 Washington Ave Seaford NY 11783 Office Phone: 516-592-4008.

GELLIS, WILLARD LEON, poet, language educator; b. N.Y.C., June 9, 1936; s. Harold and Edna Alperin G.; m. Jill Brody Gellis, Jun 15, 1965 (div. 1970); 1 child, Jenny B.; m. Shirley Routten, Aug. 21, 1981. AB in Lit. Art, Hofstra Coll., 1958; MA in Lit., U. Md., 1961; PhD in Lit., NYU, 1972. Cert. English tchr., N.Y. Univ. prof. Lockhaven (Pa.) Coll., 1965-66; univ. prof. Calumet campus Purdue U., Hammond, Ind., 1966-70; English tchr. spl. edn. N.Y.C. Pub. Schs., 1977-86; vis. tchr. SUNY, Farmingdale, 1988-89. Host Ideas and Images Pub. Access TV, Hamptons, and The Abiding Voice. Author 31 books including Tramping Dirtyside, 2000, Fire Rat, 1998 (Best Fiction 1996); (CD) No Grease on the Gump (Spoken Word), 1996, Under Algol, 2001, My Back Against the Wall, 2003, No Jive Haim, 2005. Poet Sch. of Cultural Arts. With USAR, 1954-58.

GELLIS, ZVI DAN, healthcare educator; PhD, U. Toronto, 1998. Asst. prof. SUNY, Albany, 1999—2005, assoc. prof., 2005—. Rsch. dir. Ctr. Mental Health and Aging, Albany, 1999—. Recipient Faculty Rsch. award, SUNY, Albany, 1999, Competitive Faculty Rsch. award, 2002, Summer Rsch. Inst. award on Aging, Nat. Inst. Aging, 2003, Behavioral Health Leadership award, St. Peter's Med. Ctr., 2004, Career Devel. award, NIMH, 2005—, R.C.T. Summer Rsch. Inst. award, 2005; grantee, John A. Hartford Found., 2002—04, NY State Office Mental Health, 2002—, NY State Coalition Aging, 2004—05, NY State Office Atty. Gen., 2004—; scholar, Hartford Found., 2002—04. Mem.: NASW, Soc. Social Work Rsch., State Soc. Aging NY, Gerontol. Assn. Am. Office: SUNY 1400 Washington Ave Albany NY 12222 Office Phone: 518-442-5152.

GELLMAN, GLORIA GAE SEEBURGER SCHICK, marketing professional; b. La Grange, Ill., Oct. 5, 1947; d. Robert Fred and Gloria Virginia (McQuiston) Seeburger; m. Peter Slate Schick, Sept. 25, 1978 (dec. 1980); 2 children; m. Irwin Frederick Gellman, Sept. 9, 1989; 3 children. BA magna cum laude, Purdue U., 1969; student, Lee Strasberg Actors Studio; postgrad., UCLA, U. Calif.-Irvine. Mem. mktg. staff Seemac, Inc. (formerly R.F. Seeburger Co.); v.p. V.I.P. Properties, Inc., Newport Beach, Calif.; pres. Glamglo Prodns. Host radio show Orange County Art Bytes, Sneak Previews from the Orange County Performing Arts Ctr.; prodr. corp. videos. Profl. actress, singer, artist, writer; TV and radio talk show hostess, Indpls.; performer radio and TV commls.; feature writer arts and entertainment column H mag., The Grand Tour mag.; co-prodr. Fullerton: Then and Now (PBS); exec. prodr. (video) Paris Air Show, 2003, Tibet: Beyond Mystique (PBS; 2004 Emmy finalist). Devel. officer mission media Orange County Philharm. Soc., bd. dirs. women's com.; mem. Orange County Master Chorale, Orange County Performing Arts Ctr., v.p., treas. Crescendo chpt. OCPAC Ctr. Stars, 1st v.p. membership; bd. dirs. Newport Harbor (Calif.) Art Mus., v.p. membership, mem. acquisition coun.; bd. dirs., mem. founders soc. Opera Pacific, mem. exec. com. bd. dirs.; patron Big Bros./Big Sisters Starlight Found.; mem. Visionaries Newport Harbor Mus., Designing Women of Art Inst. Soc. Calif.; past pres. Opera Pacific Guild Alliance; past pres. Spyglass Hill Philharm. Com.; v.p. Pacific Symphony Orch. League, chair endowment sect., spl. events chair; bd. dirs. Pacific Symphony Orch., v.p. cmty. affairs, vice chair vol. devel.; mem. UCI Found. of U. Calif. Irvine Bd., mem. devel. com., honors com., pub. affairs and advocacy com.; mem. social scis. dean's adv. coun. U. Calif., Irvine; chmn. adv. coun. Cold War Studies Ctr., Chapman U.; chmn. numerous small and large fundraisers; mem. com. Red Cross; mem. Fashionables of Chapman U.; bd. dirs. Sta. KOCE PBS TV; founder UCI Humanities Assocs.; bd. dirs., exec. com., nominating com., 25th anniversary com., devel. com., vice chmn. vol. devel. Pacific Symphony; pres. Symphony of 100; fundraising cons. Mission Media Pa.; dir. devel. Mission Media Ministries, Pa., 2005. Recipient Lauds and Laurels award U. Calif., Irvine, 1994, Gellman Courtyard Sculpture honoring contbn. to Sch. of Humanities, U. Calif., Irvine, Most Outstanding Vol. award Pacific Symphony, 2002, Most Outstanding Vol. award Pacific Symphony Orch. League, 2002; finalist Emmy award, 2004. Mem. AAUW, AFTRA, SAG, NATAS, Am. Acad. Television Arts & Scis., Internat. Platform Assn., Actors Equity, U. Calif.-Irvine Chancellor's Club, U. Calif.-Irvine Humanities Assocs. (founder, pres., bd. dirs.), Mensa, Orange County Mental Health Assn., Seneca Network, Balboa Bay Club, U. Club, Club 39, Islanders, Covergirls, Pacific Symphony Supper Club (founder), Pacific Symphony "Symphony 100" (pres., founder), Alpha Lambda Delta, Delta Rho Kappa. Republican. Home: PO Box 189 Sadsburyville PA 19369 Personal E-mail: glamglo@aol.com.

GELLMAN, RACHEL LEE, artist, educator; b. Rockville Centre, N.Y., May 30, 1950; d. Maurice Martin and Naomi (Colvin) G. BS, Cornell U., 1972. Vice pres. Interactive Picture Systems, N.Y.C., 1979-82; dir. computer art lab. L.I. U., Greenvale, N.Y., 1984-87; instr. Sch. Visual Arts, N.Y.C., 1983—2002. Artists Space grantee, N.Y., 1988. Mem. Spl. Interest Group Graphics. Democrat. Avocations: horse-back riding, tennis. Home and Office: 192 Bleecker St New York NY 10012-1448

GELLMAN, SAMUEL HELMER, chemist, educator; b. Evanston, Ill., Sept. 12, 1959; s. Aaron Jacob and Susanne Gellman; m. Julie Ann Plotkin, Dec. 30, 1990. AB, Harvard U., 1981; PhD, Columbia U., 1986. Postdoctoral fellow Calif. Inst. Tech., Pasadena, 1986-87; asst. prof. chemistry U. Wis., Madison, 1987-93, assoc. prof., 1993-95, prof., 1995—. Contbr. articles to Jour. Am. Chem. Soc., Nature. Office Naval Rsch. young investigator, 1990; NSF presdl. young investigator, 1991; Alfred P. Sloan fellow Alfred P. Sloan Found., 1993. Mem. AAAS, Am. Chem. Soc. (Arthur C. Cope scholar 1997). Office: U Wis Dept Chemistry 1101 University Ave Madison WI 53706-1322 E-mail: gellman@chem.wisc.edu.

GELL-MANN, MURRAY, theoretical physicist, educator; b. NYC, Sept. 15, 1929; s. Arthur and Pauline (Reichstein) Gell-Mann; m. J. Margaret Dow, Apr. 19, 1955 (dec. 1981); children: Elizabeth Sarah, Nicholas Webster; m. Marcia Southwick, June 20, 1992; 1 stepchild, Nicholas Southwick Levis. BS in Physics, Yale U., 1948; PhD in Physics, MIT, 1951; ScD (hon.), Yale U., 1959, U. Chgo., 1967, U. Ill., 1968, Wesleyan U., 1968, U. Turin, Italy, 1969, U. Utah, 1970, Columbia U., 1977, Cambridge U., 1980, Oxford (Eng.) U., 1992, So. Ill. U., 1993; ScD in Natural Resources (hon.), U. Fla., 1994; ScD (hon.), So. Meth. U., 1999. Mem. Inst. for Advanced Study, Princeton, NJ, 1951, 1955, 1967—68; instr. U. Chgo., 1952—53, asst. prof., 1953—54, assoc. prof., 1954, prof., 1956; assoc. prof. Calif. Inst. Tech., Pasadena, 1955—56, prof., 1956—67, Robert Andrews Millikan prof. physics, 1967—93, Robert Andrews Millikan prof. emeritus, 1993—; co-chmn. sci. bd. Santa Fe Inst., 1985-2000, visitor, 1992—93, disting. fellow, 1993—. Vis. prof. MIT, 1963, CERN, Geneva, 1971—72, Geneva, 1979—80, U. N.Mex., 1995—; vis. assoc. prof. Columbia U., 1954; overseas fellow Churchill Coll., 1966; mem. Pres.'s Sci. Adv. Com., 1969—72, Pres.'s Coun. of Advisors on Sci. and Tech., 1994—2001; mem. sci. and grants com. Leakey Found., 1976—88, mem. sci. adv. com., 1988—; chmn. bd. trustees Aspen Ctr. for Physics, 1973—79; founding mem. Santa Fe Inst., 1982, bd. trustee, 1984—, chmn. bd. dir., 1984—85, co-chmn. sci. bd., 1985—2000, prof. and disting. fellow, 1993—, prof., disting. fellow, 1993—; cons. Inst. Def. Analysis, Arlington, Va., 1961—70, Rand Corp., Santa Monica, Calif., 1956; mem. physics panel NASA, 1964, Coun. Fgn. Rels., 1975—, Los Alamos Sci. Lab., N.Mex., 1956—, visitor, N.Mex., 1975, 1992—93, Lab. fellow, N.Mex., 1982—; mem. adv. bd. Network Physics, 1999—; fel. Com. for the Scientific Investigation of Claims of the Paranormal, 1985—. Author (with Y. Ne'eman): Eightfold Way, 1964; author: The Quark and the Jaguar: Adventures in the Simple and the Complex, 1994; author: (with S. Lloyd) Entropy: Interdisciplinary Applications, 2004. Citizen regent Smithsonian Instn., 1974—88; trustee Wildlife Conservation Soc., 1994—; dir. J.D. and C.T. MacArthur Found., 1979—2002, chmn., World Environ. & Resources Com., 1982—97; bd. dirs. Calif. Nature Conservancy, 1984—93, Aero Vironment, Inc., 1971—, So. Calif. Skeptics, 1985—91, Lovelace Insts., 1993—95; mem. sci. adv. com. Conservation Internat., 1993—. Co-recipient Erice "Science For Peace" prize, 1989; named to UN Environ. Program Roll of Honor for Environ. Achievement, 1988; recipient E. O. Lawrence Meml. award, AEC, 1966, Franklin medal, Franklin Inst. Phila., 1967, Rsch. Corp. award, 1969, Nobel prize in Physics, 1969, Ellis Island Family Heritage award in Sci., Statue of Liberty-Ellis Island Found., Inc., 2005; fellow NSF postdoctoral, vis. prof., Coll. de France and U. Paris, 1959—60. Fellow: Am. Acad. Arts and Scis. (v.p. 1970—76, chmn. We. ctr. 1970—76), Am. Phys. Soc. (Dannie Heineman prize 1959); mem.: NAS (John J. Carty medal 1968), Irish Acad. Scis., Russian Acad. Scis. (fgn. 1993—), Indian Acad. Scis. (fgn. 1985—), Pakistan Acad. Scis. (fgn. 1985—), French Phys. Soc. (hon.), Royal Soc. London (fgn. 1975—), Conservation Internat. (sci. adv. com. 1993), Am. Philos. Soc., Coun. on Fgn. Rels., AAAS, Athenaeum (Pasadena), Cosmos Club (Washington), Century Assn., Explorers Club (N.Y.), Phi Beta Kappa, Sigma Xi. Achievements include contributions and discoveries concerning the classification of elementary particles and their interactions. Address: Santa Fe Institute 1399 Hyde Park Rd Santa Fe NM 87501 Office Phone: 505-984-8800. Office Fax: 505-982-0565. E-mail: mgm@santafe.edu.*

GELMAN, ANDREW RICHARD, lawyer; b. Chgo. s. Sidney S. and Beverly Gelman; m. Amy H., 1985; children: Stephen S., Adam P., Elizabeth F. BA, U. Pa., 1967; JD, U. Va., 1970. Bar: Va. 1970, Ill. 1971. Assoc. Roan & Grossman Law Firm, Chgo., 1971-74, McBride, Baker & Coles Law Firm (now Holland & Knight LLP), Chgo., 1974-77, ptnr., 1978—. Mem. com. on character and fitness of Ill. Supreme Ct., Chgo., 1979-95. Bd. dirs. Scholarship and Guidance Assn. Youth and Family Svcs., Chgo., 1979—, Children's Meml. Rsch. Ctr. of Children's Meml. Hosp., Chgo., 1991—, vice-chair, 1998—; chmn. Med. Rsch. Inst. Coun., 1983-86, 91-92; trustee Michael Reese Hosp. and Med. Ctr., Chgo., 1987-91. Recipient Weigle award Chgo. Bar Found., 1980. Mem. ABA (standing com. jud. selection, tenure and compensation 1982-87, pub. understanding about the law com. 1987-91, chair probate and estate planning com. gen. practice sect. 1994-97, commn. on mental and phys. disability law 1995-97), Chgo. Bar Assn. (past chmn. divsn. probate practice com., bd. mgrs. 1978-80, chmn. young lawyers sect. 1976-77), Chgo. Estate Planning Coun. Office: Holland & Knight LLP 131 S Dearborn St #30 Chicago IL 60603-5547 Office Phone: 312-715-5718. E-mail: andy.gelman@hklaw.com.

GELMAN, JON LEONARD, lawyer; b. Paterson, NJ, Mar. 14, 1946; s. Carl and Gussie (Weiss) G.; m. Nancy R. Sugarman, Oct. 2, 1971; children: Michael A., Jason L. BA, Rutgers U., 1967; JD, John Marshall Law Sch., 1971. Bar: N.J. 1971, U.S. Dist. Ct. N.J. 1971, U.S. Tax Ct. 1973, U.S. Ct. Appeals (D.C. cir.) 1973, U.S. Supreme Ct. 1974, U.S. Ct. Appeals (3d cir.) 1980, N.Y. 1985. Pvt. practice, Wayne, NJ, 1979—. Author: Workers' Compensation Law, 2000; contbg. author: Modern Workers Compensation, 2002; contbg. columnist N.J. Law Jour.; contbr. articles to profl. jours. Mem. ATLA, Nat. Orgn. Social Security Claimants Rep., Asbestos Litigation Group, NJ Trial Lawyers, DC Bar Assn., NJ Bar Assn. (workers' compensation sect.), Passaic County Bar Assn., Workplace Litig. Group (v.p.). Office: 1450 Valley Rd 1st Flr PO Box 934 Wayne NJ 07474-0934 Office Phone: 973-696-7900. E-mail: jon@gelmans.com.

GELMAN, LEONID MOISEEVICH, research scientist; b. Kiev, Ukraine, Apr. 15, 1949; s. Moisey Morduh-Leybovich and Mariya Grigorevna (Dubinskaya) G.; 1 child, Anna. MS with honors, Nat. Tech. U. Ukraine, 1972; PhD, Acoustical Inst., Moscow, 1987, DSc, 1993. Academician Russian Acad. Natural Scis., Ukrainian Acad. Scis. of Nat. Progress, Acad. Scis. of Applied Radioelectronics of Belarus, Russia, Ukraine; prof., sr. rsch. officer Cranfield U., England; with STI -Tech, Rochester, 2000, Modal Shop, Cin., 2000, Argonne Nat. Lab., Argonne, 2000. Vis. lectr. Cleve. U., 1996, U. Ill., 1996, Northwestern U., 1996, 97, Cornell U., 1996, GE, 1996, 2000, Boston U., 1997, Wayne U., Detroit, 1997, U. Mich., Ann Arbor, 1997, Binghamton U., 1998, Syracuse U., 1998, NASA Glenn Rsch. Ctr., 1997, Fed. Aviation Adminstrn., 1998, 2000, CUNY, 1998, U. Le Mans, France, 1998, Zhitomir U. Engrng. Tech., 1998, Tel-Aviv U., 1999, STI-TECH, Rochester, 2000, Argonne Nat. Lab., 2000, U. Ala., Birmingham, 2004; vis. prof. Technion, Israel, 1999, U. S.C., 2000, 01, Enitechnologie, Italy, 2001-02, U. S.C., 2004, Auburn U., 2004; mem. coun. conferment DSc, PhD, Nat. Tech. U. Ukraine, prin. investigator, chief designer grants contracts, mil. oriented rsch. developer, 1972-92. Contbr. more than 100 articles to profl. jours.; holder 17 patents. Recipient award U.S. Internat. Sci. Found., awards U.S. Civilian R&D Found., award U.S. MacArthur Found., award U.K. Dept. Trade and Industry, award Rolls-Royce plc., award Israel Lady Davis Fellowship Trust; Italian Landau-Volta fellowship, U. S.C. fellowship; grantee U.S. NRC, U.S. Nat. Acad. Scis. Fellow AIAA, Brit. Inst. of NDT; mem. SMART (U.K.), Acoustical Soc. Am. (award), Acoustical Soc. Japan, Russian Acoustical Soc., Ukrainian Soc. Nondestructive Testing, London Inst. EE, Internat. Inst. Acoustics Vibration, N.Y. Acad. Scis., U.K. Inst. Diagnostic Engr., Brit. Inst. Avocations: modern literature, sports, dance. Office: Cranfield U Sch of Engrng AMAC Cranfield Bedfordshire MK 43 0AL England Home: 3 Butterfields Wellingborough NN8 2P2 England Fax: 44 (0) 1234 750195. Office Phone: 44 (0) 1234 750111 ext. 5425. E-mail: gelmanlm@yahoo.com, L.Gelman@cranfield.ac.uk.

GELMANN, EDWARD PAUL, oncologist, educator; b. N.Y.C., May 31, 1950; m. Connie Sommers; children: Lauren R., Elyssa R., Emily B, Jonathan S. BS magna cum laude, Yale U., 1972; MD, Stanford U., 1976. Diplomate Nat. Bd. Med. Examiners, Am. Bd. Internal Medicine. Intern then resident U. Chgo. Hosps., 1976-78; med. staf fellow Nat. Cancer Inst., Bethesda, Md.,

1979-83, sr. investigator, 1983-88; adj. assoc. prof. microbiology Georgetown U., Washington, 1986-88, prof. medicine and cell biology, 1988—, chief med. oncology divsn., 1988-93, chief hematology/oncology divsn., 1993-95, vice chair Dept. Medicine, 1997-98. Dir. urologic oncology program Lombardi Cancer Rsch. Ctr., 1990-93, dir. prostate cancer program, 1993—, dir. prgram in growth regulation of cancer, 2001-, William M. Scholl Professorship in Oncology, 2002. Mem. editl. bd. jour. Blood, 1985-90, Cancer Rsch., 2004—; ad hoc reviewer jours.; contbr. 180 articles to profl. jours Sr. surgeon USPHS, 1978-88. Grantee Nat. Cancer Inst., 1990—. Fellow ACP; mem. AAAS, Am. Soc. Clin. Investigation, Am. Assn. Cancer Rsch., Am. Soc. Clin. Oncology. Office: Georgetown U 3800 Reservoir Rd NW Washington DC 20007-2196

GELPI, ALBERT JOSEPH, language educator, department chairman, critic; b. New Orleans, July 19, 1931; s. Albert Joseph and Alice Marie (Delaup) G.; m. Barbara Charlesworth, June 14, 1965; children: Christopher Francis Cecil, Adrienne Catherine Ardelle. AB, Loyola U., New Orleans, 1951; MA, Tulane U., 1956; PhD, Harvard U., 1962. Asst. prof. Harvard U., 1962-68; assoc. prof. Stanford U., 1968-74, prof. Am. lit., 1974-99, Wm. Robertson Coe prof. Am. lit., 1978-99, Coe prof. emeritus, 1999—, chmn. Am. studies program, 1980-83, 94-97, asso. dean grad. study and research, 1980-85, chmn. English dept., 1985-88. Author: Emily Dickinson: The Mind of the Poet, 1965, The Tenth Muse: The Psyche of the American Poet, 1975, A Coherent Splendor: The American Poetic Renaissance 1910-1950, 1987; editor: The Poet in America: 1650 to the Present, 1974, (with Barbara Charlesworth Gelpi) Adrienne Rich's Poetry, 1975, Wallace Stevens: The Poetics of Modernism, 1985, (with Barbara Charlesworth Gelpi) Adrienne Rich's Poetry and Prose, 1993, Denise Levertov: Selected Criticism, 1993, The Blood of the Poet: Selected Poems of William Everson, 1994; editor Cambridge Studies in American Literature and Culture, 1981-91, Living in Time: The Poetry of C. Day Lewis, 1998, The Wild God of the World: An Anthology of Robinson Jeffers, 2003, Wild God of Eros: A William Everson Reader, 2003, (with Robert J. Bertholf) The Letters of Robert Duncan and Denise Levertov, 2004. Served with U.S. Army, 1951-53. Guggenheim fellow, 1977-78 Mem. MLA, Am. Lit. Assn. Democrat. Roman Catholic. Home: 870 Tolman Dr Palo Alto CA 94305-1026 Office: Stanford U Dept English Stanford CA 94305

GELPI, ARMAND PHILIPPE, internist; b. Denver, Aug. 27, 1925; BS, U. Calif., Berkeley, 1946; MD, U. Calif., San Francisco, 1949. Diplomate Am. Bd. Internal Medicine. Intern Santa Clara Valley Med. Ctr., San Jose, Calif., 1949-50; asst. resident U. Calif. Med. Ctr., San Francisco, 1952-53, San Francisco Gen. Hosp., 1953-54; chief resident Santa Clara Valley Med. Ctr., 1954-55; staff physician VA Med. Ctr., Fresno, Calif., 1955-58, fellow hematology/oncology San Francisco, 1957-58; pvt. practice San Leandro, Calif., 1958-59; chief medicine Arabian Am. Oil Co., Dhahran, Saudi Arabia, 1959-68; trainee, immunology Stanford U., Palo Alto, Calif., 1967-68; med. dir. Charles E. Drew Health Ctr., East Palo Alto, Calif., 1968-70; assoc. med. dir. student health Stanford U., 1970-78, 79-81; physician specialist Stanford U. Med. Ctr., 1978-79, 81-83; staff physician NASA/Ames Rsch. Ctr., Mountain View, Calif., 1983-97; prof. emeritus Stanford U., 1987—. Attending physician Chaboya Clinic, San Jose, 1983-86, Dept. Veterans Affairs, Palo Alto, 1986-94. Vol. Sonoma Valley Sch. Dist., 1994—. Lt. med. corps USN, 1950-52. Home: 443 Dahlia Dr Sonoma CA 95476-8098 Personal E-mail: apgelpi@vom.com.

GELSINGER, PATRICK P., computer company executive; married; 4 children. AS in Elec. Engring., Lincoln Tech. Inst., 1979; BS in Elec. Engineering, Santa Clara U., 1983; MS in Elec. Engineering, Stanford U., 1985. Various positions, including design mgr. and chief architect original i486 microprocessor & gen. mgr. Pentium Pro, IntelDX2, Intel486 microporcessor. Intel Corp., 1979—92, dir. Platform Architecture Group, mgr. CAD methodologies, key contbr. on the original i386 and i286 chip design teams, responsible Intel ProShare video conferencing and Internet comm. product line, 1992—96, leader Desktop Products Group, chief tech. officer, Intel Architecture Group, sr. v.p., chief tech. officer, 1996—. Contbr. articles to profl. publs. Holds six patents and six applications in the areas of VLSI design, computer architecture and communications. Office: Intel Corp 2200 Mission College Blvd Santa Clara CA 95052

GELSTON, PHILIP A., lawyer; b. NYC, Aug. 26, 1952; AB cum laude, Harvard Univ., 1974, JD magna cum laude, 1977. Bar: NY 1978. Law clk., Hon. John Minor Wisdom US Ct. of Appeals, 5th Cir.; assoc. Cravath Swaine & Moore, LLP, NYC, 1978—84, ptnr., corp., 1984—. Supreme Ct. note editor Harvard Law Rev. Mem.: ABA, NY State Bar Assn., Bar of Assn. of City of NY, Phi Beta Kappa. Office: Cravath Swaine & Moore LLP Worldwide Plz 825 Eighth Ave New York NY 10019-7475 Office Phone: 212-474-1548. Office Fax: 212-474-3700. Business E-Mail: pgelston@cravath.com.

GELT, HOWARD BERNARD, lawyer; b. Mason City, Iowa, Jan. 19, 1943; s. Harry Gelt and Estelle Jean Lapiner; children: Ben, Anna. BSBA, U. Ariz., 1966; JD, U. Denver, 1969. Bar: Colo. 1969, U.S. Dist. Ct. Colo. 1969, U.S. Ct. Appeals (10th cir.) 1970. Asst. to dir. clin. edn. U. Denver Coll. Law, 1969-73; clin. instr. Duke U. Coll. Law, Durham, N.C., 1973-75; asst. to gov. State of Colo., Denver, 1975-77; assoc. Inman Flynn & Coffee, Denver, 1977-78, Atler Zall & Haligman, Denver, 1978-79; ptnr. Berenbaum & Weinshienk, Denver, 1980-92, Sherman & Howard, Denver, 1993-99, Shughart Thomson & Kilroy PC, Denver, 2000—. Chmn. Colo. Dem. Party, 1991—95. Avocations: skiing, tennis, basketball, reading, politics. Office: Shughart Thomson & Kilroy PC 1050 17th St # 2300 Denver CO 80265 Fax: 303 572-7883. Office Phone: 720-931-8143. Business E-Mail: hgelt@stklaw.com.

GELT, THEODORE ZVI, lawyer, director; b. Denver, Jan. 29, 1950; s. Louis Eleazar and Betty Goldie Gelt; m. Sharon Gelt, July 30, 1993; children from previous marriage: Timothy, Sarah. BA, U. Colo., 1972; JD, U. Denver, 1975; LLM, NYU, 1976. Bar: U.S. Tax Ct. Assoc. Atler, Zall & Haligman, P.C., Denver, 1975-77, Head, Moye, Carver & Ray, Denver, 1977; mem., dir. Silver and Gelt, Denver, 1977-81, Theodore Z. Gelt, P.C., Denver, 1981-82, Roath & Brega, Denver, 1982-88, Gelt, Fleishman & Sterling, Denver, 1989-99, Gelt & Grassgreen P.C., Denver, 1999—. Adj. prof. grad. tax program U. Denver, 1974—, asst. prof., 1978. Mem. ABA (partnership com. of tax sect.), Nebr. Bar Assn., Colo. Bar Assn. (exec. coun. of tax sect., sec., treas. 1980-81, vice chmn. 1981-82, chmn. 1982-83), Denver Bar Assn. Office: Gelt & Grassgreen PC 303 E 17th Ave Ste 910 Denver CO 80203-1262 Office Phone: 303-830-1200. Business E-Mail: gcg@gelttaxlaw.com.

GELTMAN, EDWARD ALAN, lawyer; b. Newark, Apr. 14, 1946; s. Donald and Muriel G.; m. Elizabeth Ann Glass, Jan. 2, 1989; children: Andrew, Jeffrey, Rachel. BA with honors, Franklin & Marshall Coll., 1968; JD with honors, George Washington U., 1971. Bar: D.C. 1971, U.S. Ct. Appeals (D.C. cir.) 1971, U.S. Supreme Ct. 1980. Trial atty. FTC, Washington, 1971-73; assoc., then ptnr. Nicholson & Carter, Washington, 1973-79; ptnr. Squire, Sanders & Dempsey, Washington, 1979—. Contbr. articles to profl. jours. Mem. ABA (antitrust sect.), Order of Coif. Office: Squire Sanders & Dempsey 1201 Pennsylvania Ave NW Washington DC 20004-2491 Office Phone: 202-626-6681. Business E-Mail: egeltman@ssd.com.

GELTZEILER, MICHAEL S., publishing executive; BA, U. Del., 1980; MBA, NYU. Former audit mgr., regional contr., sr. v.p., CFO NCH Promotional Svcs. Dun & Bradstreet, former asst. treas.; former sr. v.p., CFO Europe, Mid. East and Africa ACNielsen, Belgium, former contr., treas., also former sr. v.p., CFO; sr. v.p., CFO The Reader's Digest Assn., Inc., Pleasantville, NY, 2001—. Office: The Reader's Digest Assn Inc Reader's Digest Rd Pleasantville NY 10570

GELTZER, ROBERT LAWRENCE, lawyer, arbitrator, mediator, retired retail executive; b. N.Y.C., Jan. 27, 1945; s. Edward and Grace Theresa (DeFeo) G.; m. Elise Anne Lewis, Nov. 11, 1972; 1 child, Joshua Alexander. BA Biochemistry and Polit. Sci., Queens Coll., N.Y.C., 1965; JD, George Washington U. Law Sch., 1968; postgrad. in English Lit., CCNY. Bar: N.Y., 1969, U.S. Dist. Ct. (so. and ea. dists.), U.S. Ct. Appeals (2nd cir.), U.S. Supreme Ct., U.S. Ct. Mil. Appeals. Ptnr. Tendler, Biggins & Geltzer, N.Y.C., 1990—2002; sole practitioner, 2002—. Appointments include: Private Law Practice, 1968-71; Assoc. Atty. for Legal and Governmental Affairs for Allied Stores Corp., 1971-74; Sr. Atty. for J.C. Penney, 1974-84; Northeastern Regional Counsel, 1984-88; counsel firm Meyer, Suozzi, English & Klein, 1988-89. Admitted to N.Y. State Bar, 1969; U.S. Dist. Cts. Appeal (so. and ea. dists.) (2d cir.), 1974; U.S. Supreme Ct., 1976. Dir., Credit Specialist Program at Adelphi Univ., 1976-78; mem. ABA Bd. Govs., 1988-91, bd. program com., 1988-90, bd. ops. com., 1990-91, liaison commn. on mentally disabled, 1988-89, liaison standing com. on specialization, 1989-91, spl. com. on youth edn., 1988-91, spl. com. on pub. understanding about the law, 1988-91; House of Delegates, 1980-86, 88-93, 94-97; chair Task Force on Providing Mem. Benefits for Disabled Lawyers, 1991-93; mem. standing com. on pub. edn. about law, 1992-98; mem. Law Day Task Force, 1994-97, Nat. Conf. on Lawyers and Corp. fiduciaries, 1986-87; Standing Com. on Legal Drafting, 1979-82; Spl. Com. on Youth Edn. for Citizenship, 1982-86; chmn. Tellers Com., 1982-83; Conf. of Section Chairs, chair fiscal com., 1986-88; Annual Meeting Host Coms., mem. (1986), vice-chair, (1993); Coordinating Group on Bioethics and the Law, (1991-96); liaison to Standing Com. on Scope and Correlation of Work, 1988-91, mem. Standing Com., 1991-96, chair, 1994-95; corp. Com. of Resource Devel. coun., 1987-92; Sci. and Tech. Sect. (coun. mem. 1981-84, 91-93) sec., 1984-85, vice chair, 1985-86, chair-elect, 1986-87, chair, 1987-88; chair Nat. Conf. on Birth, Death & Law, 1987-88; Corp., Banking and Bus. Law Sect. (co-chmn. Corporate Counsel Com., mem. Consumer Fin. Svc. Commn., Long-Range Planning Com., Issues Affecting the Profession Com., Comml. Arbitration Com., 1992—), Bus. Bankruptcy Com., (1992—), Consumer Bankruptcy Com., (1992—); Individual Rights and Responsibilities Sect. (vice-chmn. Equal Protection of the Laws, mem. 1st Amendment Rights Com., 1992-97), Rights of the Elderly Com., (1992-97), Rights of Children Com., (1992-97); Economics of Law Practice Sect. (mem.); Family Law Sect. (mem.); Judicial Adminstrn. Div. (Exec. Com., Lawyers' Conf.; chair Membership Com., Jud. Compensation Com.; Litigation sect., 1st co-chair com. on corp. counsel, mem. class action com., liaison with ABA com.); co-chair Nat. Conf. on the Role of the Lawyer in the 1980s (1979-81). New York State Bar Assn. House of Delegates (1981-97); Exec. Com. At-Large Mem., (1992-95), state bar del., 1995-97, liaison to atty. and community com. juvenile justice commn., solo and small firm practitioners commn. and judicial evaluation commn.; Founder and 1st Chmn. Corp. Counsel Sect. (1981-83); chair Commn. to Provide Legal Svcs. to Middle Income Consumers (1995—); chair Unlawful Practice of Law Com. (1990-92), chair Solo and Small Firm Practitioner Task Force (1991-96); mem. Action Unit #5 pertaining to Regulatory Reform (1980-83); mem. Law Simplification Task Force (1982-88), chair Pub. Rels. Com., 1983-86; mem. AIDS and the Law Com. (1988-91); recipient Corp. Counsel of Yr. award (1989). Assn. of the Bar of the City of N.Y.: del. to N.Y. State Bar House of Delegates, 1988-92, mem. Profl. and Jud. Ethics Com. (1982-83); Sci. and Law Com. (1985-88); Children and the Law Com. (1985-88); N.Y. County Lawyers' Assn.: mem., bd. dirs. (1982-88); chmn. spl. projects com., 1992-96; mem. 75th Anniversary Steering Com. (1982-84); mem. Federal Legislation, State Legislation, Trade Regulation, and Alcoholism in the Profession committees; mem. Am. Law Inst.; life fellow Am. Bar Found. (fellow, vice chair N.Y. fellows, 1988-91, chair, 1991-96); fellow N.Y. Bar Found., ABA Young Lawyers' Div. (fellow, bd. dirs.); life mem., dir. N.Y. state chair (1979-82) of Am. Judicature Soc. Adjunct prof., Pace College. Mem. Am. Soc. for Polit. and Legal Philosophy; Am. Soc. for Legal History: General Com., Conf. on Personal Finance Law; speaker at various state and local bar assns. (Ark., Calif., Colo., Conn., Ill., Mich., N.J., N.Y., Pa., Va., W.Va. and various programs of practicing law instns. and ABA Nat. Insts.). Pro Bono General counsel for Nat. Kidney Found. (1981-91). Co-first male mem. of Nat. Assn. Women Lawyers. Bd. dirs. Fund for Justice and Edn. (1988-91), Community Action for Legal Svcs. (1988-90). Mem. Vol. Lawyers for the Arts. Past chancellor commander, past spl. dep. grand chancellor Knights of Pythias. Mem. American Jewish Com., Masons, Phi Epsilon Phi, Phi Delta Phi, George Washington U. Law Sch. Alumni Assn. Contbr. to various profl. jours. in areas of fed. and state consumer credit legislation, regulation, litigation and compliance, class action litigation, law firm mgmt., consumer, comml., gen. practice and state civil litigation issues affecting the legal profession. Fellow Am. Bar Found.; mem. Congregation Temple Emanu-El; mem. legal com., bicentennial com. Am. Jewish Com.; mem. Jewish Welfare Bd.; chair JC Penney Legal Dept.'s Ann. Blood Dr., 1979, 83; mem. Vol. Lawyers for the Arts; pro bono gen. counsel, chair legal com. Nat. Kidney Found. 1981-91. Mem. ABA (bd. govs. rep. N.Y. State 1988-91; mem. ho. of dels. 1980-86, 88-93, 95—; vice chmn. tellers com. 1981-82; chmn. 1982-83, bd. dirs. Am. Bar Retirement Assn. 1988-91, Nat. Jud. Coll. 1988-91, Fund. Justice and Edn. 1988-91; bd. govs. liaison standing com. on scope and correlation of work 1988-91, 91-96; spl. com. on youth edn. for citizenship 1982-86, mem. standing com. 82-86; commn. on public understanding about the law 1989-91; mem. steering com. on unmet legal needs of children 1996-97; chair task force on member benefits for disabled lawyers 1991-93; mem. standing com. on pub. edn. 1992-95; mem. law day working group 1994-95; chmn. fiscal com. conf. of sect. chairs 1987-89, Nat. Conf. on Birth, Death and Law, 1987-88, ann. meeting host coms. 1986, vice chair, 1993, coordinating group on bioethics and the law 1991-95; chmn. subcom. on liaison with state and local bars 1983-86; mem. young lawyers divsn., corp., banking and bus. law sect, litigation sect., sci. and tech. sect., gen. practice sect., individual rights and responsabilities sect., numerous other sects. and coms.), Am. Law Inst., Am. Judicature Soc. (life, mem. mem bership com. 1979-80, chair N.Y. State 1989-94), N.Y. State Bar Assn. (founder 1981, first chair corp. counsel sect. 1981-83, Corp. Counsel of Yr. award 1989; mem. at large exec. com. 1992-95, liaison, ho. of dels. 1981-87, 88-93, 95-97; mem. spl. com. alternat dispute resolution 1993—, numerous other coms., sects.), Assn. Bar City of N.Y., N.Y. County Lawyers' Assn., Fed. Bar Assn. Home: 115 E 87th St New York NY 10128-1136 Office Phone: 212-410-0100.

GELTZER, SHEILA SIMON, public relations executive; b. N.Y.C. d. Sidney E. and Bertie (Rome) Simon; m. Howard E. Geltzer, Sept. 10, 1967; children: Jeremy Niles, Gabriel Lewis. BA, Queens Coll., 1961. With Philip Lesly Co., N.Y.C., 1962-63, Benjamin Co., N.Y.C., 1963-68; ptnr. Simon and Geltzer, Inc., N.Y.C., 1968-74, Ries and Geltzer, N.Y.C., 1974-79; pres. Geltzer and Co., Inc., N.Y.C., 1979—2000; mng. dir., exec. prin. Publicis Dialog, N.Y.C., 2000—. Mem. Pub. Rels. Soc. Am. (counselors acad.), Women in Comms., Women in Pub. Rels., Nat. Coun. of Women, Abingdon Theater. Business E-Mail: sgeltzer@geltzerco.com.

GEMAN, STUART, mathematician; s. Harold and Dorothy Geman; children: Aaron, Jesse. PhD, MIT, Cambridge, 1973—77. Prof., divsn. applied math. Brown U., Providence, 1977—; CEO Math. Techs. Inc., Providence, 1996—2002, chief scientist, 2002—. Contbr. articles to profl. jours. Fellow: Inst. Math. Stats. (life). Achievements include patents in field. Office: Brown Univ Divsn Applied Mathematics Providence RI 02912 Office Phone: 401-863-3088.

GEMERY, HENRY ALBERT, economics professor; b. Shelton, Conn., Sept. 5, 1930; s. John and Mary (Benco) G.; m. Pamela Joyce Malcolm, Aug. 30, 1958; childen: John Malcolm, Pamela Ann. BS, So. Conn. State Coll., 1952; MBA, Harvard U., 1958; PhD, U. Pa., 1967; MA hon., Colby Coll., 1977. Asst. dir. admissions Colby Coll., Waterville, Maine, 1958-61, from instr. to Pugh Family prof. econs., 1961—2001, emeritus, 2001—. Assoc. Charles Warren Ctr., Harvard U., 1989—90. Contbg. author, co-editor: The Uncommon Market, 1979, Science Technology and Environment, 1994; author: monograph Emigration from the British Isles, 1980, European Emigration to North America, 1984. Served to 1st lt., C.E. U.S. Army, 1953—56. NDEA fellow, U. Pa., 1963—65, NIH postdoctoral fellow, 1968—69, Charles Warren fellow, Harvard U., 1982—83. Mem.: Internat. Union for Sci. Study of Population, Econ. History Assn., Cliometric Soc., Am. Econs. Assn. Home: 1185 Pond Rd Sidney ME 04330-2015 Office: Colby Coll Mayflower Hill Waterville ME 04901 Business E-Mail: hagemery@colby.edu.

GEMIGNANI, JOSEPH ADOLPH, lawyer; b. Hancock, Mich., Apr. 17, 1932; s. Baldo A. and Yolanda M.; m. Barbara A. Thomson, Sept. 5, 1953; children: Joseph, Jon. BSME, Mich. Technological U., 1953; JD, U. Mich., 1958. Bar: Wis. 1959, Mich. 1960, U.S. Dist. Ct. (ea. and we. dists.) Wis., U.S. Ct. Appeals (7th cir.), U.S. Ct. Appeals (fed. cir.). In-house counsel McGraw Edison Co., Milw., 1958-60; ptnr. Michael, Best & Friedrich, Milw., 1960—. 1st lt. USAF, 1953-55. Home: 616 E Day Ave Milwaukee WI 53217-4841 Office: Michael Best & Friedrich 100 E Wisconsin Ave Ste 3300 Milwaukee WI 53202-4108

GEMIGNANI, MICHAEL CAESAR, clergyman, retired secondary school educator; b. Balt., Feb. 23, 1938; s. Hugo J. and Dorothy G.; m. Carol A. Federico, June 30, 1962 (dec.); children: Stephen, Susan; m. Nilda B. Keller, May 18, 1985. BA, U. Rochester, 1962; MS, U. Notre Dame, 1964, PhD, 1965; JD, Ind. U., 1980. Bar: Ind. 1980, U.S. Dist. Ct. Ind. 1980, Maine 1987, U.S. Dist. Ct. Maine 1987, Tex. 1990; ordained to ministry Episcopal Ch., 1973. Asst. prof. math. SUNY, Buffalo, 1965-68; assoc. prof. Smith Coll., 1968-72; prof., chmn. dept. math. scis. Ind. U.-Purdue U., Indpls., 1972-81; dean Coll. Scis. and Humanities Ball State U., Muncie, Ind., 1981-86; dean Coll. Arts and Scis. U. Maine, Orono, 1986-88; sr. v.p., provost U. Houston-Clear Lake, 1988-91, prof. math. and computer sci., 1991-92; rector St. Paul's Episcopal Ch., Freeport, Tex., 1991—. Vicar St. Francis Episcopal Ch., Zionsville, Ind., 1974-79; pres. Met. Indpls. Campus Ministry, 1975-76, bd. dirs., 1974-81; mem. adv. bd. Ind. Office Campus Ministry, 1973-86, pres., 1983-85; chair divsn. spiritual formation Episcopal Diocese of Tex., 1997—; founder, chmn. bd. Brazosport Med. Ctr., 1999—. Author: books including Elementary Topology, 1967, 2d rev. edit., 1972, Introductory Real Analysis, 1970, Law and the Computer, 1981, Computer Law, 1985, Legal Guide for EDP Managers, 1989, To Know God: Small Group Exercises in Spiritual Formation, 2001, Spiritual Formation for Pastors Tending the Fire Within, 2002; composer; rsch., publs. in math. Mem. ABA, AAAS, Am. Math. Soc. (chmn. N.E. sect. 1970-71, chmn. Ind. sect. 1975-76), Scribes, Sigma Xi, Kappa Sigma. Business E-Mail: mgmign@hal-pc.org.

GEMMETT, ROBERT J., dean, English language educator; b. Schenectady, NY, Mar. 11, 1936; s. A James and Dorothy M. (MacFarlane) G.; m. Kendra B. Baxter, Jan 24, 1964; children: Stephen, Scott, David, Kerry. BA cum laude, Siena Coll., 1959; MA, U. Mass., 1962; PhD, Syracuse U., 1967. Instr. Clarkson U., N.Y.C., 1964-65; assoc. prof. English SUNY, Brockport, 1965-70, prof., 1970-92, 97—, chmn. dept., 1975-79, dean humanities, 1979-82, dean letters and scis., 1982-92; prof. English, provost, v.p. for acad. affairs SUNY Coll., Buffalo, 1992-97. Author: Poets and Men of Letters, 1975, William Beckford, 1977, Beckford's Fonthill: The Rise of Romantic Icon, 2003; editor: Biographical Memoirs of Extraordinary Painters, 1969, Dreams, Waking Thoughts and Incidents, 1971, The Consummate Collector, 2000. 2d lt. U.S. Army, 1959. Recipient Chancellor's Excellence in Tchg. award SUNY, 1975; fellow, rsch. grantee SUNY, 1967-69, 84-85. Office: SUNY Dept English Brockport NY 14220 Office Phone: 585-395-2476. E-mail: rgemmett@brockport.edu.

GEMORAH, SOLOMON, retired education educator, retired historian; b. Bklyn., May 22, 1936; s. Morris Gemorah and Miriam Moglensky. BA, Bklyn. Coll., N.Y., 1956; MA, N.Y. U., N.Y., 1962, PhD, 1965. Instr. Bklyn. Coll., 1965—68; assoc. prof. Coll. S.I., NY, 1968—2001; ret., 2001. Contbr. articles pub. to profl. jour. Mem.: Am. Hist. Assn. Home: 340 W 28th St APt 18E New York NY 10001

GEMUNDER, JOEL FRANK, healthcare company executive; b. NYC, July 15, 1939; s. Abraham and Frances (Kubrick) G.; m. Claudia Joan Hoffman (div. 1984); children: David Austin, Allison Paige. AB, CCNY, 1960; MBA, U. Chgo., 1962. Fin. analyst W. R. Grace & Co., N.Y.C., 1962-68, v.p. splty. products group, 1968-71; v.p. Chemed Corp., Cin., 1971-77, v.p., group exec. health care group, 1977-81, exec. v.p., 1981; pres. Omnicare, Inc., Cin., 1981—, CEO, 2001—, also bd. dirs. Cin. Bd. dirs. Chemed Corp., Cin., Datacare, Inc., Roanoke, Va., Cin., The John Bunn Co., Buffalo, Xorbox Corp., Buffalo, Sequoia Pharmacy Svcs., Inc., L.A., The Veterex Corp., Troy. Mich., Medarco Corp., Troy, Bignall Dental Supply, Grand Rapids, Mich., Labtronics, Inc., Palo Alto, Calif. Mem. Cin. Council World Affairs, 1986; trustee City of Hope, Cin., 1983. Recipient Spirit of Life award City of Hope, 1983. Mem. Cin. C. of C. (aviation com. 1981). Office: Omnicare Inc 1600 RiverCenter II 100 E RiverCenter Blvd Covington KY 41011-1555*

GENADER, ROBERT J., investment company executive; With Citibank; exec. v.p. Ambac Assurance, NYC, 1986—98, Ambac Financial Group Inc., NYC, 1991—98, dir., 1992—, vice chmn. Specialized Fin. Div., 1998—2000, vice chmn. Fin. Insurance Bus. Group, 2000—01, pres., COO, 2001—04, pres., CEO, 2004—. Mem.: Assn. of Fin. Guaranty Insurors (chmn. 1994—96). Office: Ambac Fin Group One State St Plz New York NY 10004 Office Phone: 212-668-0340. Office Fax: 212-509-9190.*

GENARO, DONALD MICHAEL, industrial designer; b. Hoboken, NJ, Feb. 22, 1932; s. Gustav G. and Margaret (DeMave) G.; m. Margaret Hermes, June 23, 1956; children: Susan, Karen. BID, Pratt Inst., 1957. Archtl. designer F.W. Fisher-Architects, N.J. and N.Y., 1951-52; indsl. designer Henry Dreyfuss Assocs., N.Y.C., 1957-63, assoc., 1963-68, ptnr., 1968-82, sr. ptnr., 1982-94; ret., 1994. Lectr., cons. in field. Designer of Trimline Phone; holder over 200 patents; contbr. numerous articles to profl. jours. Trustee, chmn., bd. dirs. Pascack Valley Hosp.; bd. dirs. Well Care Group, Inc. Represented in permanent collection at Mus. of Modern Art and Cooper-Hewitt (Smithsonian) Mus.; recipient Contemporary Achievement award Pratt Inst., 1970, Best Product Design 1983 Time Mag., Design award Indsl. Designers Soc. Am. and Indsl. Design Mag.; named one of 25 Best Designed Products Fortune Mag., 1977. Mem. Indsl. Designers Soc. Am.

GENBERG, IRA, lawyer; b. Newark, July 27, 1947; s. Jack and Ann (Lerman) G.; m. Rosemary Lawlor, Jan. 15, 1981; children: Jack Michael, Anne Rebecca. AB magna cum laude, Rutgers U., 1969; JD, U. Pa., 1972. Bar: Ga. 1972, D.C. 1978. Assoc. Haas, Holland, Levison & Gibert, Atlanta, 1972-75; ptnr. Stokes, Shapiro, Fussell & Genberg, Atlanta, 1975-87; ptnr., head litigation sect. Smith, Gambrell & Russell LLP, Atlanta, 1987—. Spkr. Seminar on Constrn. Litigation, Atlanta, 1985, Seminar on Constrn. Law, Atlanta, 1986; co-chmn. Seminar on Trying A Complex Constrn. Case, 1994. Contbr. articles to Constrn. Bus. Review Mag. Mem. ABA, Ga. Bar Assn., Atlanta Bar Assn., D.C. Bar Assn. Office: Smith Gambrell & Russell LLP 1230 Peachtree St NE Atlanta GA 30309-3592 Office Phone: 404-815-3638. Business E-Mail: igenberg@sgrlaw.com.

GENCO, ROBERT JOSEPH, immunologist, periodontist, educator, scientist; b. Silver Creek, N.Y., Oct. 31, 1938; s. Joseph A. and Santa G. (Barone) Genco; m. Sandra Clarke, Sept. 14, 1957; children: Deborah Genco Powell, Robert M., Julie Clarke Alford. DDS cum laude, SUNY-Buffalo Sch. Dentistry, 1963; PhD in Microbiology and Immunology, U. Pa., 1967. Resident, periodontology U. Pa., 1967; asst. prof. dept. oral biology Sch. Dental Medicine SUNY, Buffalo, 1967—69, assoc. prof., 1969—72, prof., 1972—, chmn. dept. oral biology, 1977—, Disting. Univ. Prof., dept. oral biology, 1990—; Disting. Univ. Prof., dept. microbiology Sch. Medicine and Biomedical Scis. SUNY, Buffalo. Editor-in-chief: Jour. Periodontology, 1988—, Annals Periodontology; contbr. to books and publications in the field. Recipient Gold medal for Excellence in Rsch., ADA, 1991, Basic Rsch. in Oral Sci. award, Internat. Assn. for Dental Rsch., Rsch. in Periodontal Disease award, Deans medal, George Thorn award. Fellow: AAAS (chmn. dental sect 1980); mem.: NAS, Am. Assn. Immunology, Am. Acad. Periodontology, Internat. Assn. Dental Rsch. (pres. 1991—92), Inst. Medicine, Am. Assn. Dental Rsch. Achievements include patents in field. Avocations: music, sports. Office: SUNY at Buffalo Periodontal Disease Rsch Ctr 135 Foster Hall 3435 Main St Buffalo NY 14214 Address: Sch Dental Medicine U Buffalo 115 Foster Hall Buffalo NY 14214 Business E-Mail: rgenco@buffalo.edu.

GENDELL, GERALD STANLEIGH, retired public relations executive; b. Stamford, Conn., June 14, 1929; s. Irving and Henrietta (Lund) G.; m. s. Marion F. Belvin, July 28, 1952; children: Carin Gaye, Danna Joyce, Adrian Leigh, Jeffrey Lund, David Blake, Marc Steven, Bradley Howard. BS, NYU, 1949. With Procter & Gamble Co., Cin., 1954-91, dir. community affairs and contbns., 1976-80, mgr. external affairs divsn., 1980, mgr. pub. affairs div., 1981—91, also pres., trustee Procter & Gamble Fund. Trustee Glen Manor Home, 1978-80, Queen City Housing Corp., Cin., 1981-89, Cin. Local Initiative Support Corp., The Spire Found., Jewish Fedn. So. Ariz.; vice chmn. bd. trustees Jewish Hosp. of Cin.; bd. dirs., trustee Nat. Coun. on Econ. Edn., 1985-91; mem. met. adv. coun. U. Cin.; mem. adv. coun. George Mason U. Sch. Law, 1988-91; mem. Cin. Mayor's Com. on Econ. Devel.; chmn. Found. for Pub. Affairs; mem. bd. overseers Hebrew Union Coll.; pres. Jewish Cmty. Found. of So. Ariz.; bd. dirs. Jewish Fedn. of So. Ariz., Ariz. Jewish Post. 1st lt. U.S. Army, 1950-53. Mem. Pub. Affairs Coun. Am. (bd. dirs. 1981-91, chmn. 1988-89), Greater Cin. C. of C. (vice chmn., mem. exec. com. 1981-87), Conf. Bd., Bankers Club (bd. govs. 1988-93). Personal E-mail: gendellgm@aol.com.

GENDLER, ELLEN, dermatologist; b. Bklyn., Feb. 15, 1956; MD, Columbia U., 1981. Diplomate Am. Bd. Dermatology. Resident in dermatology NYU Med. Ctr., N.Y.C., 1982—85; pvt. practice dermatology N.Y.C., 1985—. Clin. assoc. prof. dept. dermatology NYU Sch. Medicine, N.Y.C., 1990—. Office: 1035 Fifth Ave New York NY 10028

GENDRON, ANDREW, lawyer; b. North Brunswick, N.J., Oct. 6, 1960; s. Robert Emmett and Norma (Brunalli) G. AB, Georgetown U., 1982; JD, U. Md., 1986. Bar: DC, Md., US Ct. of Appeals, Fourth Circuit, US Dist. Ct., DC & Md. Assoc. Piper & Marbury, Balt., 1986-88, Goodell, DeVries, Leech & Gray, Balt., 1988—2001; ptnr., commercial litigation Venable LLP, Balt., 2001—. Mem. ABA, Md. State Bar Assn. (People's Pro Bono award), Bar Assn. Balt. City, Md. Assn. Def. Trial Counsel, Md. Inst. Continuing Profl. Edn. Lawyers (evidence programs com. 1985-86, contbg. author evidence program #1, 1986), Def. Rsch. Inst., Georgetown U. Alumni Assn. (fundraising chmn. class 1982, 1987—). Clubs: Georgetown Alumni Md. (dir. 1983-85). Democrat. Roman Catholic. Office: Venable LLP 2 Hopkins Plaza 1800 Mercantile Bank & Trust Bldg Baltimore MD 21201 Office Phone: 410-244-7439. Office Fax: 410-244-7742. Business E-Mail: agendron@venable.com.

GENDRON, GEORGE, magazine editor; With New York Mag.; editor-in-chief Boston Mag., Inc. Mag., Boston, 1983—2002; Kauffman Entrepreneur-in-Residence Clark Univ. Grad. Sch. Mgmt., Worcester, Mass., 2003—. Adv. bd. mem. Foundation Source; nat. dir. Initiatives for a Competitive Inner City. Mailing: Kauffman Entrepreneur-in-Residence Clark Univ 950 Main St Worcester MA 01610

GENDRON, MICHÈLE MARGUERITE MADELEINE, librarian; b. Paris, Mar. 15, 1947; came to U.S., 1950; d. Gerard Joachim and Denise Marie Louise (Le Morvan) G. BA, Orlinda Pierce Coll. for Women, Athens, Greece, 1969; MS, U. Ill., 1971. Libr. Free Libr. Phila., 1971-75, head, Kingsessing Br., 1975-76, head, Ramonita G. de Rodriguez Br., 1976-91, curator spl. collections ctrl. children's dept., 1991-92, head, lit. dept., 1992—. Cons. devel. Hist. Children's Lit. Collection Montgomery County-Norristown (Pa.) Pub. Libr., 1993-94; organizing mem. Pa. Libr. Assn.'s 1st Conf. Svcs. to Youth, Harrisburg, Pa., 1987-89, Women's Network's 1st Conf. on P.R. Woman in Phila., 1981. Author: (bibliographies) Booklist, 1983; contbr. bibliographies Destination World, 1979, Stories to Share, 1985. Trustee Legal Svcs. Fund Dist. Coun. 47 of Am. Fedn. State, County and Mcpl. Employees, 1985-95, mem. exec. bd. Local 2186, 1996—. Recipient Charles Scribner award Scribner Pub., 1976, Nat. Security Forum, Air War Coll., 1985. Mem. ALA (Assn. Libr. Svcs. Children, Mildred Batchelder award selection com. 1979-81, 85-87, internat. rels. com. 1981-85, chair 1984-85, libr. instrn. round table 1991-93), Pub. Libr. Assn. (mktg. to pub. librs. 1991—, svcs. to multicultural populations 1991, sec. exec. com. mktg. pub. libr. svcs. sect. 1995-96), Alliance Francaise de Phila., Franklin Inn Club, Beta Phi Mu. Roman Catholic. Office: Free Libr of Phila Lit Dept 1901 Vine St Philadelphia PA 19103-1116

GENDRON, SUSAN ANN, school system administrator; b. Tewksbury, Mass. m. Mark Gendron; children: Stacey, Matthew. BS in Elem. and Secondary Edn., MS in Ednl. Adminstrn., U. So. Maine, Gorham. From tchr. to supt. Scarborough Pub. Schs., Maine; supt. Windham Sch. Dist., 1997—2003; commr. of edn. State of Maine, Augusta, 2003—. Mem.: Maine Sch. Supts Assn. (Disting. Educator award 2001, Supt. of Yr. award 2002). Office: Commr of Edn State House Sta #23 Augusta ME 04333 E-mail: susan.gendron@maine.gov.*

GENECOV, DAVID GLENN, plastic surgeon; b. Dallas, Tex., Oct. 17, 1963; s. Edward Ray Genecov and Selma Jean Goldberg; m. Lisa Weinburger Genecov, Oct. 22, 1988; children: Michael, Max, Matthew, Megan. BA, U. Tex., Austin, 1985; MD, U. Tex., San Antonio, 1990. Diplomate Am. Bd. Surgery, Am. Bd. Plastic Surgery, lic. physician N.C., Tex. Intern in gen. surgery W.Va. Sch. Medicine, Morgantown, 1990—91, resident in gen. surgery, 1991—95, chief resident in gen. surgery, 1994—95; resident in plastic and reconstructive surgery Wake Forest/Bowman Gray Sch. Medicine, Winston-Salem, NC, 1995—97, chief resident in plastic surgery, 1996—97; craniomaxillofacial fellow Internat. Craniofacial Inst., Dallas, 1997—98. Mem. active staff Med. City Dallas Hosp., mem. pediat. adv. bd., 2001—, pediat. surgery sect. chief, 2002—, chmn. pediat. performance improvement com., 2002—03; mem. provisional staff Children's Med. Ctr. Dallas, Frisco (Tex.) Med. Ctr.; mem. courtesy staff Med. Ctr. Plano, Tex., Trinity Med. Ctr., Carrollton, Tex.; cons. Driscoll Children's Hosp., Corpus Christi, Tex., Presbyn. Hosp. Dallas; adj. asst. prof. dept. biomed. scis. Baylor Coll. Dentistry; clin. instr. dept. plastic surgery U. Tex. Southwestern Med. Sch.; mem. Coun. Health Care Advisors, 2001—; mem. adv. bd. Lorenz Surg. Cir. Surgeons, 2000—; lectr., presenter in field. Contbr. articles to profl. jours., chpts. to books. Bd. dirs. Congregation Shearith Israel, 1997—98, 2003—, patron divsn. chmn., 2002—. Named Johnson & Johnson Intern of Yr., 1991; named one of Nation's Top Surgeons, 2004; recipient Resident Rsch. award, Wound Healing Soc., Tucson, Ariz., 1996, Healthcare Affordability Hero of Yr. award, 2002. Fellow: Am. Coll. Surgeons, Am. Acad. Pediat.; mem.: AMA, Tex. Med. Assn., Internat. Soc. Craniofacial Surgeons, Dallas Med. Soc., Am. Soc. Aesthetic Plastic Surgeons, Am. Cleft Palate Assn., Am. Soc. Maxillofacial Surgeons (AMA plastic surgery caucus 2000—, AMA del. young physicians sect. 2000—, socioecon. com. 1999—, parliamentarian, trustee 2003—04), Am. Soc. Plastic Surgery (young plastic surgeons com. 1999—2003, regulatory evaluation com. 2001—02, vice chmn. entering practice com. 2001—03, young plastic surgeons steering com. 2001—03, profl. liability ins. com. 2002, pub. edn. com. 2002—, cranio/maxillofacial subcom. of internat. course 2003—, devel. com. 2003—). Avocations: triathlons, boating, skiing, golf. Office: Genecov Plastic Surgery Group PA 7777 Forest Ln Ste C717 Dallas TX 75230

GENEL, MYRON, pediatrician, educator; b. York, Pa., Jan. 6, 1936; s. Victor and Florence (Mowitz) G.; m. Phyllis Norma Berkman, Aug. 25, 1968; children: Elizabeth, Jennifer, Abby. Grad., Moravian Coll., 1957; MD, U. Pa., 1961; MA (hon.), Yale U., 1983; DSc (hon.), Moravian Coll., 1995. Diplomate Am. Bd. Pediat. Intern Mt. Sinai Hosp., N.Y.C., 1961-62; resident in pediat. Children's Hosp. Phila., 1962-64; trainee pediat. endocrinology Johns Hopkins Hosp., Balt., 1966-67; instr. pediat. U. Pa. Sch. Medicine, 1967-69, assoc. in pediat., 1969-71; trainee in genetics, inherited metabolic diseases Children's Hosp. Phila., 1967-69, assoc. physician, 1969-71; attending physician Yale-New Haven Hosp., 1971—; faculty Yale U. Sch. Medicine, New Haven, 1971—, dir. pediat. endocrinology, 1971-85, program dir. Children's Clin. Rsch. Ctr., 1971-86, prof., 1981—2004, prof. emeritus, 2004—, assoc. dean, 1985—2004, dir. Office Govt. and Cmty. Affairs, 1985—2004. Genetic adv. bd. State of Conn., 1979—82, 1994—; cons. subcom. investigations, oversight com. sci. and tech. U.S. Ho. of Reps., 1982—84; mem. adv. bd. New Eng. Congenital Hypothyroidism Collaborative; cons. Hosp. St. Raphael, Milford Hosp., Norwalk Hosp., Stamford Hosp., Danbury Hosp., Greenwich Hosp.; chmn. transplant adv. com. Office of Commr. Conn. Dept. Income Maintenance, 1984—92; health policy fellowship bd. Inst. Medicine, 1989—95; clin. rsch. roundtable Inst. Medicine NRC, 2000—04; mem fed adv com nat children's study NICHD/NIH, 2005—. Contbr. articles to profl. jours. Bd. dirs. Rsch. America!, 1997—2000. Capt. USAR, 1964—66. Robert Wood Johnson Health Policy fellow Inst. Medicine NAS, Washington, 1982-83; recipient ann. award Conn. Campaign Against Cooley's Anemia, 1979, Ann. Comenius Alumni award Moravian Coll., 1990, Abraham Jacobi Meml. award Am. Acad. Pediat. and AMA, 1999, Joseph W. St. Geme Leadership award Fedn. Pediat. Orgns., 2004. Fellow: AAAS; mem.: AMA (med. schs. sec. 1985—, coun. on sci. affairs 1994—2001, task force on fin. grad. med. edn. 1995, alt. del. governing coun., med. schs. sec. 1995—98, task force on privacy and confidentiality 1998—99, del. 1998—2002, chair 2003—04), APHA, Assn. Patient Oriented Rsch., N.Y. Acad. Medicine, Conn. Acad. Sci. and Engring. (coun. 2000—), Soc. Pediat. Rsch. (Disting. Svc. award 2003), Endocrine Soc. (rsch. initiative com. 1995—99, legis. affairs com. 2002—), Conn. United for Rsch. Excellence (chmn. steering com. 1989—90, pres. 1990—93, chmn. bd. dirs. 1993—94), Conn. Endocrine Soc., Nat. Assn. Biomed. Rsch. (bd. dirs. 1990—93, exec. com. 1991—93), Assn. Program Dirs. (pres.-elect 1980—81, pres. 1981—82), New Haven County Med. Assn. (bd. govs. 1990—2002, 2004—), Assn. Am. Med. Colls. (adminstrv. bd. coun. acad. socs. 1987—92, chmn.-elect coun. acad. socs. 1989—91, exec. coun. 1989—92, adv. panel on rsch. 1999—2003, Disting. Svc. mem. 2005), Am. Soc. Bone and Mineral Rsch., Am. Pediat. Soc., Am. Fedn. Med. Rsch., Am. Diabetes Assn. (co-recipient Jonathan May award 1979), Am. Coll. Preventive Medicine, Am. Coll. Nutrition, Am. Assn. Clin. Endocrinologists, Am. Acad. Pediat. (task force organ transplants, com. on fed. govt. affairs), Sigma Xi. Jewish. Office: Yale Sch Med PO Box 208081 New Haven CT 06520-8081 Office Phone: 203-785-6019, 203-393-2685. Business E-Mail: myron.genel@yale.edu.

GENEL, NOAH D., lawyer; b. N.Y.C., May 18, 1971; BA, Union Coll., Schenectady, N.Y., 1993; JD, Fordham U., 1998. Bar: N.Y. 1999, U.S. Dist. Ct. (so. and ea. dists.) N.Y. 1999. Assoc. Schulte Roth & Zabel LLP, N.Y.C., 1998—2001, Morvillo Abramowitz Grand Iason & Silberberg, PC, N.Y.C., 2001—. Mem.: ABA, The Assn. of the Bar of the City of N.Y., Nat. Assn. Criminal Def. Lawyers, N.Y. State Bar Assn. Office: Morvillo Abramowitz et al PC 565 Fifth Ave New York NY 10017 E-mail: ngenel@magislaw.com.

GENEREUX, L. JOSEPH, lawyer; b. 1952; BA in Polit. Sci., Grinnell Coll., 1974; MSc in Internat. Rels., London Sch. Econ., 1977; JD, Univ. Mich., 1981. Bar: Minn. 1982. And mem., mgrs. com. Dorsey & Whitney, Mpls., 1981—89, ptnr., chair, comml. banking practice group; chair, fin. svcs., 1989—. Staff Mich. Jour. Law Reform, 1980—81. Mem.: ABA (adv. com. law firm pro bono project 2000—), Legal Corps (pres., bd. dirs. 2004—), Minn. State Bar Assn. (co-chair, bus. law pro bono task force 2002—03), Minn. Legal Aid Soc. (pres 2003—, bd. dir.). Office: Dorsey & Whitney LLP Ste 1500 50 S Sixth St Minneapolis MN 55402-1498 Office Phone: 612-340-2888. Office Fax: 612-340-2868. Business E-Mail: genereux.joe@dorsey.com.

GENEST, JACQUES, nephrologist, clinical scientist, science administrator; b. Montreal, Que., Can., May 29, 1919; s. Rosario and Annette (Girouard) G.; m. Estelle Deschamps, Oct. 3, 1953; children: Paul, Suzanne, Jacques, Marie, Helene. BA, Coll. Jean de Brebeuf, Montreal, 1937; MD, U. Montreal, 1942; LLD (hon.), Queen's U., 1966, U. Toronto, Can., 1970; DSc (hon.), Laval (Can.) U., 1973, Sherbrooke U., 1974, Meml. U. Nfld., 1978, McGill (Can.) U., 1979, U. Ottawa, 1980, St. Francis Xavier U., 1983, SUNY, Buffalo, 1984, Rockefeller U., 1986, Concordia U., Montreal, 1986, Chinese Acad. Med. Scis., 1987, U. Montpelier, France, 1989. Resident in medicine and pathology Hôtel-Dieu Hosp., Montreal, 1942-45, cons. physician in nephrology, endocrinology and internal medicine, 1952-91; rsch. fellow Johns Hopkins Hosp., Balt., 1945-48, Harvard Sch. Chemistry, Boston, 1948, Rockefeller Hosp. Med. Rsch., N.Y.C., 1948-51; chmn. dept. medicine U. Montreal, 1962—65, prof. medicine, 1965-96; prof. exptl. medicine McGill U., Montreal, 1960-98; founder, 1st dir. Clin. Rsch. Inst. Montreal, 1965-84, adviser, 1984-94. Editor: (with Erich Koiw) Hypertension, 1972; (with Erich Koiw and Otto Kuchel) Hypertension: Physiopathology and Treatment, 1977, 83; (with Marc Cantin, Otto Kuchel, Pavel Hamet) 2d edit., 1983; author: One Ideal, One Life, 1998, L'Homme Seul. Decorated companion Order of Can., grand officer Ordre Nat. du Que.; recipient award Gairdner Found., 1963, Archambault medal Can. Assn. for Advancement Sci., 1965, Stouffer prize, 1969, Marie-Victorin Sci. prize Govt. of Que., 1977, Royal Bank award, 1980, Isaac Walton Killam award, 1986, Armand Frappier prize Govt. of Que., 1996, Patronat du Quebec prize, 1998, Grand Montrealais prize, 2000, FCAR award Govt. Que., 2001, Purkynje medal Czech Acad. Sci., 2002; named to Can. Med. Hall of Fame, 1994. Master ACP; fellow Royal Coll. Physicians and Surgeons Can. (James H. Graham award of merit 1993), Royal Soc. Can. (Flavelle medal and award 1968); mem. Assn. Am. Physicians, Am. Clin. and Climatol. Assn., Am. Heart Assn. (Disting. Scientist award 2003), Peripatetic Club. Roman Catholic. Home: 5955 Wilderton Ave PH-L6 Montreal PQ Canada H3S 2V1 Office: Inst de Recherches Cliniques Montreal PQ Canada H2W 1R7 Business E-Mail: jacgensr@sympatico.ca.

GENÉT, BARBARA ANN, accountant, travel company executive; b. N.Y.C., Oct. 14, 1935; d. Arthur Samuel and Louise Margaret (Scheider) G. Profl. cert. in acctg., U. Calif., La Jolla, 1995, student, 1996—; BS of Acctg., U. Phoenix, 2001; MBA, Keller Grad. Sch. Mgmt., 2003. Asst. to chmn. bd., asst. v.p. pub. rels. Brink's Inc., Chgo., 1976-78; co-owner, pres. Ask Mr. Foster, Chgo., 1982-90; with Profl. Cmty. Mgmt., Laguna Hills, Calif., 1990-92; travel counselor E.J. Brown & Assocs., San Diego, 1992-94; tchr.'s asst. U. Calif-San Diego, La Jolla, 1996—. Rep. Becker CPA-CMA Rev., San Diego, 1995—. Mem. campership cmty. coun. YMCA. Becker scholar, 1995, scholar Marks CPA Rev., 1996. Mem. Am. Soc. Woman Accts., Inst. Mgmt. Accts., Inst. Cert. Travel Agts., Order Ea. Star, Ladies of Shrine N.Am., Zonta Internat. of La Jolla (treas. 1998-2000, kids camp 2005). E-mail: barbaragenet@cox.net.

GENETSKI, CHRISTIAN S., lawyer; b. NYC, Aug. 28, 1970; BA magna cum laude, Birmingham-Southern Coll.; JD, Vanderbilt U., 1995. Bar: Ga. 1995, DC 2001. Assoc. King & Spalding, Atlanta; trial atty. Computer Crime and Intellectual Property Sect., Criminal Divsn. US Dept. Justice, Washington; assoc. Kirkland & Ellis, Washington, ptnr., 2002—03, Sonnenschein Nath & Rosenthal LLP, Washington, 2003—, vice chair Info. Security and Internet Enforcement Practice Group. Adj. prof. computer crime law Georgetown U. Law Ctr. Office: Sonnenschein Nath & Rosenthal LLP Ste 600, E Tower 1301 K St NW Washington DC 20005 Office Phone: 202-408-6463. Office Fax: 202-408-6399. Business E-Mail: cgenetski@sonnenschein.com.

GENETSKI, ROBERT JAMES, economist; b. N.Y.C., Dec. 26, 1942; s. Alex and Helen Genetski. BS, Ea. Ill. U., 1964; MA, NYU, 1968, PhD, 1972. Tchr. English St. Procopius Acad., Lisle, Ill., 1965-66; research analyst Nat. Econ. Research Assn., N.Y.C., 1967-68; lectr. econs. NYU, N.Y.C., 1969-70; econ. analyst Morgan Guaranty Trust Co., N.Y.C., 1970-71; sr. v.p., economist Harris Trust & Savs. Bank, Chgo., 1971-88; pres. Stotler Econs., Chgo., 1988-90; sr. v.p., chief economist The Chgo. Corp., 1990-91; pres. Robert Genetski & Assocs., 1991—; sr. mng. dir. Chgo. Capital, 1995-2000. Lectr. econs. NYU, 1969-70, U. Chgo., 1973; vis. prof. Wheaton (Ill.) Coll., 1986; mem. census adv. com. U.S. Dept. Commerce, 1983-86; bd. dirs. DNP Select Income Fund, Midwest Bank and Trust. Author: (with Beryl Sprinkel) Winning with Money, 1977, Taking the Voodoo out of Economics, 1986, 88, A Nation of Millionaires, 1997. Chmn. ednl. com. Sch. Bd. Dist. 25, West Chicago, Ill., 1973-79; bd. dirs. Ctrl. DuPage Health Svcs., 1988-94. Mem. Am. Statis. Assn., Am. Econ. Assn. (fin. com. 1983-), Nat. Assn. Bus. Economists (editor Newsletter 1978), Western Econ. Assn., Am. Bankers Assn. (econ. adv. com. 1980-83), U.S. C. of C. (econ. adv. com. 1985-) Office: 107 Park St Saugatuck MI 49453 Office Phone: 312-565-0112. Business E-Mail: rgenetski@classicalprinciples.com.

GENGA, JOHN MICHAEL, lawyer; b. Detroit, Apr. 28, 1962; BA, Stanford U., 1983; JD, U. Mich., 1986. Bar: Calif. 1986, U.S. Dist. Ct. (ctrl. and ea. dists.) Calif. 1987, U.S. Dist. Ct. (no. and so. dists.) Calif. 1988, U.S. Ct. Appeals (9th cir.) 1988, U.S. Supreme Ct. 1993, U.S. Ct. Appeals (10th cir.) 1997. Assoc. Jones, Day, Reavis & Pogue, L.A., 1986-88, Hill Wynne Troop & Meisinger, L.A., 1988-93; ptnr. Troop Steuber Pasich Reddick & Tobey, LLP, L.A., 1994—2000, Paul, Hastings, Janofsky & Walker LLP, San Francisco, chmn. entertainment practice group; founder, owner Genga & Assocs., Encino, 2004—. Mem. ABA, State Bar Calif., L.A. County Bar Assn. Office: Genga & Assocs PC 15821 Ventura Blvd Ste 525 Encino CA 91436 Office Phone: 818-444-4580. Business E-Mail: jgenga@gengalaw.com.

GENGLER, RICHELLE RUTH, musician, educator; b. Hoisington, Kans., Apr. 14, 1951; d. Richard Albert and Charlotte Ruth (Schepmann) Popp; m. Scott Edward Gengler, June 22, 1985; children: Shawn, Barry, Jeremy, Kristin, Jordan. AA, St. John's Coll., Winfield, Kans., 1972. Parish worker Holy Cross Luth. Ch., Memphis, 1972—73, Zion Luth. Ch., Chanute, Kans., 1973—75; sec. to divsn. atty. Exxon Co. U.S., Midland, Tex., 1980—88; sec. to dir. Cmty. Devel. Greater Hutchinson Kans. C. of C., 1975—76; pvt. piano instr. Midland, 1985—. Organist various Luth. chs., Midland, Odessa, Tex., 1980—2000; mem. handbell choir 1st Bapt. Ch., Midland, 2001—, Sunday sch. dir., 2002—, mem. benevolence com., 2003—. Mem.: Nat. Guild Piano Tchrs. (cert.), Midland Symphony Guild (newsletter chmn. 2004—), R. E. Lee Choir Booster Club, Nat. Fedn. Jr. Music Clubs (dist. 9 chmn. 2004—, cert.), Musicians Club Midland (pres. 2003—). Republican. Avocations: swimming, singing, counted cross stitch.

GENIA, VICKY, psychologist; b. N.Y.C., June 6, 1950; d. Vincent and Victoria (Bondzio) Auletta; m. Howard D. Genia Jr., Feb. 26, 1971 (div. Nov. 1984); 1 child, Howard D. III; m. Billy G. Witt, Jan. 11, 1985. BA in Math., Buffalo State Coll., 1971; MA in Psychology, U. No. Colo., 1981, D of Counseling Psychology, 1989. Lic. psychologist Md., Washington. Psychologist Ctr. Psychol. and Learning Svcs. Am. U., Washington, 1990—. Adj. prof. dept. psychology Am. U., 1995-96. Author: Counseling and Psychotherapy of Religious Clients, 1995; contbr. articles to profl. jours. With U.S. Army, 1974-76. Mem. Am. Psychol. Assn., Soc. Scientific Study Religion, Religious Rsch. Assn. Office: Am U 4400 Massachusetts Ave NW Washington DC 20016-8003

GENIESER, NANCY BRANOM, radiologist; b. Aurora, Ill., 1936; MD, Med. Coll. Pa., 1962. Diplomate Am. Bd. Radiology, Am. Bd. Diagnostic Radiololgy, Am. Bd. Pediatric Radiology. Intern Phila. Gen. Hosp., 1962-63; resident in radiology NYU Hosps., NYC, 1963-65; prof. radiology NYU Med. Ctr.; staff Bellevue Hosp., NYC; cons. Manhattan VA; prof. radiology NYU; assoc. dean, admissions and fin. aid NYU Sch. of Med., 2004—. Mem. Am. Coll. Radiologists, N.Y.C. Med. Soc., N.Y. Radiol. Soc., N.Y. State Radiol. Soc., Radiol. Soc. N.Am., Soc. Pediatric Rsch. Fax: 212-263-7666.

GENIESSE, ROBERT JOHN, lawyer; b. Appleton, Wis., Sept. 16, 1929; s. Arthur John and Rhoda (Miller) G.; m. Jane Elizabeth Fletcher, June 10, 1961; children: Julia Forrest, Thomas Guy. BA magna cum laude, Williams Coll., 1951; LLB cum laude, Harvard U., 1957. Bar: N.Y. 1958, D.C. 1982. Assoc. Debevoise and Plimpton, N.Y.C., 1957-61, 64-66, ptnr., 1966-94; asst. U.S. atty. So. Dist. N.Y., 1962-63, chief appellate atty., 1963-64. Editor Harvard Law Rev., 1955-57. Bd. dirs. Legal Action Ctr., N.Y., 1973-78, Environ. Def. Fund, 1974-82; trustee Williams Coll., 1974-87; trustee World Monuments Fund, 1993—, sec., gen. counsel, 1995—; trustee Nat. Bldg. Mus., 1994-2000, hon. trustee, 2000—; trustee Sterling and Francine Clark Art Inst., Williamstown, Mass., 1974-2001; pres., 1987-98; trustee Ringling Mus. Art, Sarasota, Fla., 2001—. 1st lt. Inf. U.S. Army, 1952-54. Mem. N.Y. State Bar Assn., D.C. Bar Assn., Soc. Alumni of Williams Coll. (pres. 1973-74), Phi Beta Kappa. Home: PO Box 516 Boca Grande FL 33921-0516 also: 2101 Connecticut Ave NW Apt 61 Washington DC 20008-1757 Office: Devevoise & Plimpton 555 13th St NW Ste 1100E Washington DC 20004-1163

GENINI, RONALD WALTER, retired history educator, historian; b. Oakland, Calif., Dec. 5, 1946; s. William Angelo and Irma Lea (Gays) G.; m. Roberta Mae Tucker, Dec. 20, 1969; children: Thomas, Justin, Nicholas. BA, U. San Francisco, 1968, MA, 1969. Cert. secondary edn. tchr., Calif.; adminstrv. svcs. credential. Tchr. Ctrl. Unified Sch. Dist., Fresno, Calif., 1970—2004, ret., 2004—. Judge State History Day, Sacramento, 1986-94; mem. U.S. history exam. devel. team Golden State, San Diego, 1989-93; securer placement of state-registered landmarks; guest appearance History Channel program "UFO Hotspots,", Jan. 2003; guest contbr. Time Line Films, 2005. Author: Romualdo Pacheco, 1985, Darn Right It's Butch, 1994, Theda Bara, 1996; contbr. articles to profl. jours.; cited as authority on Theda Bara by Ency. Brit. Online Am. Women in History, 1999, also on Romualdo Pacheco by Biog. Directory of Am. Congress. Bd. dirs. Fresno Area 6 Neighborhood Coun., 1973-74, Fresno City and County Hist. Soc., 1975-78, St. Anthony's sch. bd., Fresno, 1980-84; active Good Company Players, Fresno, 2000-01, San Joaquin Parkway and Conservation Trust, Utah Shakespeare Festival, Carmel Bach Festival Named one of Outstanding Young Educators Am., Fresno Jaycees, 1978; recipient recognition for Tchr. Cares award Calif. State Assembly and Fresno City Coun., 1996. Mem.: Mt. Vernon Ladies Assn., Calif. Ret. Tchrs. Assn., Smithsonian Inst., Arte de Americas. Democrat. Avocations: writing history, motion picture scriptwriting, commercial acting. Home: 1486 W Menlo Ave Fresno CA 93711-1305 E-mail: r_genini@yahoo.com.

GENIS, ALICE SINGER, psychologist; b. Vilnius, Lithuania, June 8, 1926; d. Nahum Signer and Miriam Singer (Smith) Galerkin; widowed; children: naomi Genis-Mazin, Robert Genis. Esq., Ludwig Maximillian U., Munich, 1950; BA, Pace U., 1974; MA, Mercy Coll., Dobbs Ferry, N.Y., 1978, Coll. of New Rochelle, 1983. Cert. sch. psychologist. Lab. tech. Queens Gen. Hosp., N.Y.C., 1952-55; with Daycare Ctr. Presbyn. Ch., Peekskill, N.Y., 1972-73; psychologist Mental Health Clinic, Peekskill, 1978-80; asst. sch. psychology Pines Bridge Sch., Yorktown, N.Y., 1980-82; biofeedback therapist Med. Cmty. Ctr., Cortland, N.Y., 1985-94; sch. psychologist BOCES, Yorktown, N.Y., 1983-85. Presenter in field. Contbr. articles to profl. jours. Vol. Hosp. Aux., Peekskill, 1962-98; com. Heart Fund Ball, Westchester, 1970s, 80s; pres. Norchester Hadassam, Peekskill, 1983-85, 88-91; mem. The Field Libr., Peekskill. Named Woman of Merit, Westchester Hadassh, White Plaines, N.Y., 1996; recipient New Life award Israel Bonds, Peekskill, 1979, Presl. awards Norchester Hadassah, 1985, 91. Mem. Nat. Assn. Sch. Psychologists, Biofeedback and Psychophysiology Performing Ctr. for the Arts. Avocations: music, piano, swimming, gardening, travel.

GENKIN, BARRY HOWARD, lawyer; b. Phila., Aug. 8, 1949; s. Paul and Pearl (Rosenfeld) G.; m. Marian (Block), Aug. 15, 1975; children: Matthew Todd, Kimberly Beth. BS (hon.), Pa. State U., 1971; JD (hon.), U. Balt., 1974; LLM in Taxation, Georgetown U., 1977. Bar: Pa. 1975, Wash. 1977, N.Y. 1995. Spl. counsel divsn. corp. fin. SEC, Washington, 1975—79; assoc. Blank Rome LLP, Phila., 1979—83, ptnr., 1983—, co-chmn. bus. and corp. dept., 1988—93, mem. mgmt. com., distribution com., 1997—, chmn., budget com., 1996—, mem. exec. com., finance ptnr., 2001—. Pres. bd. dirs. Smeal Bus. Sch., Pa. State U., 2003-; lectr. various orgns. Contbr. U. Balt. Law Rev., 1991—. Mem.: ABA, N.J. Savs. League, Pa. Savs. League, Pa. Bar Assn., Ace Country Club (bd. trustees), Omicron Delta Kappa, Heuisler Honor Soc. Office: Blank Rome LLP One Logan Sq Philadelphia PA 19103 Office Phone: 215-569-5514. Office Fax: 215-832-5514. Business E-Mail: genkin@blankrome.com.

GENKINS, GABRIEL, physician; b. Berlin, Mar. 20, 1928; came to U.S., 1940, naturalized, 1945; s. Arkady and Tamara (Schlesinger) G.; children: Karen Lee Genkins Fairbank, Steven M., Amy E. BS, NYU, 1949, MD, 1952. Diplomate Am. Bd. Internal Medicine, Am. Bd. Cardiology. Intern, resident Mt. Sinai Hosp., NYC, 1952-57; practice medicine specializing cardiology NYC; chief myasthenia gravis clinic rsch. labs. Mt. Sinai Med. Ctr., NYC, 1972—, clin. prof. medicine, 1973—; attending physician cardiology Mt. Sinai Hosp., NYC, 1973—; mem. nat. med. adv. bd. Myasthenia Gravis Found., 1956—, v.p. bd. dirs., 1973—. Contbr. articles to profl. jours., chpts. to books. Served with airborne inf., U.S. Army, 1945-46. Democrat. Office: 30 E 60th St New York NY 10022-1008 Office Phone: 718-268-5412. Business E-Mail: ggenkins@nycrr.com.

GENN, NANCY, artist; b. San Francisco; d. Morley P. and Ruth W. Thompson; m. Vernon Chathburton Genn; children: Cynthia, Sarah, Peter. Student, San Francisco Art Inst., U. Calif., Berkeley. Lectr. on art and papermaking Am. Ctrs. in Osaka, Japan, Nagoya, Japan, Kyoto, Japan, 1979-80; guest lectr. various univs. and art mus. in U.S., 1975—; vis. artist Am. Acad. in Rome, 1989, 94, 2001. One-woman shows include, De Young Mus., San Francisco, 1955, 63, Gumps Gallery, San Francisco, 1955, 57, 59, San Francisco Mus. Art, 1961, U. Calif., Santa Cruz, 1966-68, Richmond (Calif.) Art Center, 1970, Oakland (Calif.) Mus., 1971, Linda/Farris Gallery, Seattle, 1974, 76, 78, 81, LA Inst. Contemporary Art, 1976, Susan Caldwell Gallery, NYC, 1976-77, 79, 81, Nina Freudenheim Gallery, Buffalo, 1977, 81, Annely Juda Fine Art, London, 1978, Inoue Gallery, Tokyo, 1980, Toni Birckhead Gallery, Cin., 1982, Kala Inst. Gallery, Berkeley, Calif., 1983, Ivory/Kimpton Gallery, San Francisco, 1984, 86, Eve Mannes Gallery, Atlanta, 1985, Richard Iri Gallery, LA, 1990, Harcourts Modern and Contemporary Art, San Francisco, 1991, 93, 96, Am. Assn. Advancement of Sci., Washington, 1994, Anne Reed Gallery, Ketchum, Id., 1995, Michael Petronko Gallery, NY, 1997, Mills Coll. Art Mus., Oakland, Calif., 1999, Takada Gallery, San Francisco, 1999-2000, 03, Ulivi Gallery, Prato, Italy, 2002, Fresno Art Mus., Calif., 2003, Bolinas Mus., Calif., 2003, Inst. Italiano di Cultura, Chgo., LA, 2004, Inst. Italiano Di Cultura/Chgo. Art Inst., Flatfile Galleries, Chgo., Ill., 2005; group exhbns. include San Francisco Mus. Art, 1971, Aldrich Mus., Ridgefield, Conn., 1972-73, Santa Barbara (Calif.) Mus., 1974-75, Oakland (Calif.) Mus. Art, 1975, Susan Caldwell, Inc., NYC, 1974-75, Mus. Modern Art, NYC, 1976, traveling exhbn. Arts Coun. Gt. Britain, 1983-84, Inst. Contemporary Arts, Boston, 1977, J.J.Brookings Gallery, San Francisco, 1997, Portland (Oreg.) Art Mus., 1997—, Takada Gallery, San Francisco, 1999-2000, Leighton Glalery, Blue Hill, Maine, 2005; represented in permanent collections Mus. Modern Art, NYC, Achenback Found., Palace of the Legion of Honour, San Francisco, Albright-Knox Art Gallery, Buffalo, Libr. of Congress, Washington, Nat. Mus. for Am. Art, Washington, LA County Mus. Art, Art Mus. U. Calif., Berkeley, McCrory Corp., NYC, Mus. Art, Auckland, N.Z., Aldrich Mus., Ridgefield, Conn., (collection) Bklyn. Mus., (collection) U. Tex., El Paso, Internat. Ctr. Aesthetic Rsch., Torino, Italy, Cin. Art Mus., San Francisco Mus. Modern Art, Oakland Art Mus., LA County Mus., City of San Francisco Hall of Justice, Harris Bank, Chgo., Chase Manhattan Bank, NYC, Modern Art Gallery of Ascoli Piceno, Italy, Mills Coll. Art Mus., Oakland, Calif., Mills Coll. Art, Oakland, Calif., Leighton Gallery, Blue Hill, Maine, various mfg. cos., also numerous pvt. collections; commd. works include, Bronze lectern and 5 bronze sculptures for chancel table, 1st Unitarian Ch., Berkeley, Calif., 1961, 64, bronze fountain, Cowell Coll., U. Calif., Santa Cruz, bronze menorah, Temple Beth Am, Los Altos Hills, Calif., 17, murals and 2 bronze fountain sculptures, Sterling Vineyards, Calistoga, Calif., fountain sculpture, Expo 1974, Spokane, Wash; vis. artist Am. Acad., Rome, 1989. U.S./Japan Creative Arts fellow, 1978-79; recipient Ellen Branston award, 1952; Phelan award De Young Mus., 1963; honor award HUD, 1968 Home: 1515 La Loma Ave Berkeley CA 94708-2033 Office Phone: 510-849-4366.

GENNARI, F(RANK) JOHN, medical educator, educator; b. Jersey City, May 18, 1937; s. Frank and Amelia (Sargia) G.; m. Emily Hewson Michie, Sept. 15, 1958; children: John Hewson, Jennifer Meade, Amelia Sargia. BS cum laude, Yale U., 1959, MD, 1963. Diplomate Am. Bd. Internal Medicine, Am. Bd. Nephrology. Intern U. Va. Hosp., Charlottesville, 1963—64, resident in medicine, 1964—66; fellow in nephrology Tufts-New Eng. Med., Boston, 1968—71; asst. prof. Sch. Medicine Tufts U., Boston, 1971—75, assoc. prof. Sch. Medicine, 1975—79; prof. Coll. Medicine U. Vt., Burlington, 1979—, Robert F. and Genevieve B. Patrick prof. medicine Coll. Medicine, 2000—, dir. nephrology Coll. Medicine, 1979—2002, assoc. chair dept. medicine Coll. Medicine, 1987—92, 1996—, interim chair dept. medicine Coll. Medicine Burlington, 1993. Mem. Nephrology bd. Am. Bd. Internal Medicine, 1994-2000. Co-author: Acid-Base, 1981, Acid-Base Disorders, 1987; contbr. articles to profl. publs., chpts. to books. Mem. exec. com. Vt. Heart Assn., 1982-85; mem. exec. com. Vt. Kidney Assn., 1980—, pres., 1984-86; mem. merit rev. bd. VA, Washington, 1989-92. Capt. Med. Corps, USAF, 1966-68. Grantee NIH, 1971-91, Fogarty Internat., 1991. Fellow ACP; mem. Am. Fedn. Clin. Rsch., Am. Soc. Clin. Investigation, Am. Soc. Nephrology, Am. Physiol. Soc., Internat. Soc. Nephrology. Democrat. Avocations: skiing, hiking. Office: UHC Campus Fletcher Allen Health Care Rehab 2319 Burlington VT 05401

GENNAULA, CHARLES PAUL, family practice physician; b. Charleroi, Pa., Oct. 28, 1937; s. Charles G. and Mary (Tesi) G.; m. Shirley Karpinsky, July 18 1964; children: Charles, Kevin, Pamela. BS, U. Pitts., 1959, MD, 1963. Diplomate Am. Bd. Family Practice. Intern Southside Hosp., Pitts., 1963-64; pvt. practice Pitts. and Pleasant Hills, Pa., 1966—. Capt. USAF, 1964-66. Home: 360 Challen Dr Pittsburgh PA 15236-4559 Office: 67 Old Clairton Rd Pittsburgh PA 15236-3907 Office Phone: 412-655-3444.

GENNETT, TIMOTHY, academic administrator; b. Richmond, Ind., July 25, 1951; s. Henry and Barbara Milda (Collignon) G.; m. Sharon Gail Cox, Mar. 5, 1976. BS in Chemistry, Purdue U., 1973, MS in Indsl. Adminstrn., 1974, MSEd, 1984. Lic. amateur radio operator. Sales engr. Gulf Oil Corp., San Antonio, 1975-77; asst. mgr. residence halls Purdue U., West Lafayette, Ind., 1977-82, mgr. residence halls, 1982-90, asst. dir. residence halls, 1990-95, dir. facilities housing and food svcs., 1995—2003. Bd. dirs. Gennett Graphics, Lafayette, Ind.; presenter in field. Contbr. articles to profl. jours. Damage assessement coord. ARC, Tippecanoe County, Ind., 1998-2000. Named Vol. of Yr. Disaster Svsc. ARC, 1996 Mem. Assn. Higher Edn. Cable TV Adminstrs. (bd. dirs. 2000-04), Tippecanoe Amateur Radio Assn. (sec. 1995-97), Soc. Cable TV Engrs. Office: Purdue U 1225 3d St West Lafayette IN 47906-4205

GENOVA, DIANE MELISANO, lawyer; b. Aug. 8, 1948; d. Joseph Louis and Ines (Fiumana) Melisano; m. Joseph Steven Genova, Jan. 15, 1983; children: Anthony Robert, Matthew Edward. AB, Barnard Coll., 1970; postgrad., Harvard U., 1970-71; JD, Columbia U., 1975. Assoc. Milbank, Tweed, Hadley & McCloy, N.Y.C., 1975-80; v.p., asst. resident counsel Morgan Guaranty Trust Co. N.Y., N.Y.C., 1981-90, mng. dir., assoc. gen. counsel, 1990-2000, J.P. Morgan Chase & Co., N.Y.C., 2001—03; co-gen. counsel Investment Bank, 2003—. Harlan Fiske Stone scholar, 1972-75. Mem. Assn. of Bar of City of N.Y., N.Y. State Bar Assn., Internat. Swaps and Derivatives Assn. (bd. dirs. 1999—). Roman Catholic. Office: J P Morgan Chase & Co 270 Park Ave New York NY 10022 E-mail: genova_diane@jpmorgan.com.

GENOVA, JOSEPH STEVEN, lawyer; b. Red Bank, N.J., Nov. 12, 1952; s. M. Leonard and Margaret (Coons) G.; m. Janet Scott, May 18, 1974 (div. Dec. 1980); m. Diane Melisano Genova, Jan. 15, 1983; children: Anthony Robert, Matthew Edward. BA, Dartmouth Coll., 1974; JD, Yale U., 1977. Bar: N.Y. 1978, U.S. Dist. Ct. (no., so. and ea. dists.) N.Y., Calif. 1993. Assoc. Milbank, Tweed, Hadley & McCloy, N.Y.C., 1977-85, ptnr., 1986—. Ct. appointed arbitrator U.S. Dist. Ct. (ea. dist.) N.Y., 1986—; mediator U.S. Dist. Ct. (so. dist.) N.Y., 1992—. Bd. dirs. Legal Aid Soc., N.Y.C., 1995-2000; N.Y. Lawyers Pub. Interest, 1997—, Legal Svcs. N.Y.C., 2001—; apptd. N.Y. Chief Judge Pro Bono Review Com. (1990-94), Legal Svcs. Project., 1997-2000 Fellow Am. Bar Found., N.Y. Bar Found.; mem. ABA (Pro Bono Pub. award 1992, William Reece Smith award 1996, ABA Commn. on Iolta 1996-99), Assn. Bar City N.Y. (com. on housing and urban devel. 1982-85, com. on judiciary 1988-91, vice chmn. 1990-91, frequent interim mem., com. pro bono legal svcs., 1993-99, project on homelesness 2001—), N.Y. State Bar Assn. (com. on legal aid 1980—), chmn. 1986-91, pres.'s com. on access to justice 1990—, co-chmn. 1990-99, mem. task force on law guardian sys. 1989-99, mem. special com. future profession, 1998-2000), Fed. Bar Coun. (com. on 2d cir. cts. 1988-98, com. pub. svc. responsibility 1991—, chmn. 1994-2000, trustee 1998—2004, mem. 1st dept. disciplinary com. 2005-). Roman Catholic. Avocations: fishing, skiing. Office: Milbank Tweed Hadley & McCloy 1 Chase Manhattan Plz Fl 47 New York NY 10005-1413 Office Phone: 212-530-5532. Business E-Mail: jgenova@milbank.com.

GENOVESE, FRANCIS CHARLES (FRANK GENOVESE), economist, educator, editor-in-chief, writer; b. Toronto, Ont., Can., Feb. 16, 1921; came to U.S., 1946, naturalized, 1960; s. Francis A. and Florence M. (Ferguson) G.; m. Candace E. Moorhouse, June 17, 1944; children: Margaret, Steven, Jeremy, Michael. BA, U. Toronto, 1942, MA, 1946; PhD, U. Wis., 1953. Mem. faculty Babson Coll., Babson Park, Mass., 1955—87, dean Grad. Sch., 1962-73, prof. econs., 1962-87, prof. emeritus, 1987—; pres. Pleiad Corp., 1974-76. Advisor Ctrl. Bank Jordan, 1975; vis. prof. NYU, 1960-62; vis. faculty Brown U. Grad. Sch. Banking, 1962-64, Wellesley Coll., 1962; pres. Am. Jour. Econs. & Sociology, Inc., 1997-99. Editor: Lombard Street; editor in chief Am. Jour. Econs. and Sociology, 1989-97; dir. Babson-Bernays Competition, 1976; contbr. articles to profl. jours., newspapers. Active Dem. Town Com., 1978—; Nelson small bus. task force Ea. Boston Cmty. Devel. Corp., 1964-66; bd. dirs. Mass. Higher Edn. Loan Corp., 1978-81, Schalkenbach Found., 1983-99; corp. mem. Mass. Goodwill Industries, 1973-86; chmn. Am. adv. com. Mrs. Helena Kaushik Coll., 1999—. With Can. Army, 1944-45. Fellow, U. Wis., 1946—47. Mem. Am. Econ. Assn., Am. Fin. Assn., Can. Econ. Assn., Harvard Faculty Club. Unitarian Universalist. Home: 18 Massasoit Rd Wellesley MA 02481-2411 Office: Babson Coll Faculty Babson Park MA 02481-0310 Office Phone: 781-239-4339. Office Fax: 781-239-6465.

GENOWAYS, HUGH HOWARD, systematic biologist, educator; b. Scottsbluff, Nebr., Dec. 24, 1940; s. Theodore Thompson and Sarah Louise (Beales) G.; m. Joyce Elaine Cox, July 28, 1963; children: Margaret Louise, Theodore Howard. AB, Hastings Coll., 1963; postgrad., U. Western Australia, 1964; PhD, U. Kans., 1971. Curator Mus. of Tex. Tech U., Lubbock, 1972-76, lectr. Mus. Sci. Program, 1974-76; curator Carnegie Mus. Natural History, Pitts., 1976-86; dir. U. Nebr. State Mus., Lincoln, 1986-94; chair mus. studies program U. Nebr., 1989—95, 1997—2004, prof. state mus., 1986—2004, prof. mus. studies, 1989—2004, prof. natural resource scis., 1997—2003, prof. phased retirement program, 2003—. Author, editor:(with Michael A. Mares) Mammalian Biology in South America, 1982, (with Marion A. Burgwin) Natural History of the Dog, 1984; (with Mary R. Dawson) contbns. in Vertebrate Paleontology, 1984, Species of Special Concern in Pennsylvania, 1985, Current Mammalogy, 1987, 90, Biology of the Heteromyidae, 1993, Storage of Natural History Collections: A Preventive Conservation Approach, 1996, (with Robert J. Baker) Mammalogy: A Memorial Volume Honoring Dr. J. Knox Jones, Jr., 1996, (with Ted Genoways) A Perfect Picture of Hell: Eyewitness Accounts by Civil War Prisoners from the 12th Iowa, 2001, (with Lynne M. Ireland) Museum Administration: An Introduction, 2003 (with J.R. Baker J.W. Bickham and C.J. Phillips) Bats of Jamaica, 2005; founding editor: Collections: A Journal for Museum and Archives Professionals, 2003- (Best New Jour. any catagory 2004) . Packmaster Allegheny Trails coun. Boy Scouts Am., 1981-83, asst. scoutmaster, 1983-86. Co-recipient Acad. Freedom Coalition Nebr. award, 2004; awardgrantee Fulbright Found., 1964, NSF, 1977-86, R.K. Mellon Found., 1981-86, Smithsonian Fgn. Currency Program, 1983-84, Inst. Mus. Svcs., 1989-96, Nebr. Game and Park Commn., 2001—. Mem. Am. Soc. Mammalogists (pres. 1984-86, C. Hart Merriam award 1987, editor Spl. Pubs. 1995-96, historian 1997—, elected hon. mem. 2002, Hartley H. T. Jackson award 2004), Internat. Theriological Congress (steering com. 1985-2004), Southwestern Assn. Naturalists (pres. 1984-85, trustee 2003--), Am. Assn. Mus., Nebr. Mus. Assn. (pres. 1990-92, 1st Hugh H. Genoways Achievement award 1994, sec. 1997-2000), Assn. Systematics Collections (bd. dirs. 1993-94), Nat. Inst. for Conservation Cultural Property (bd. dirs. 1993-94), Sociedad Argentina para Estudio Mamiferos, Lincoln Attractions and Mus. Assn. (chair 1987-94), Soc. Systematic Biologists, Rotary (bd. dirs. Lincoln N.E. club 1990-92). Office: U Nebr-Lincoln State Mus W436 Nebraska Hall Lincoln NE 68588-0514 Office Phone: 402-472-2012. Business E-Mail: hgenoways1@unl.edu.

GENRICH, MARK L., retired foundation administrator; b. Buffalo, Aug. 28, 1943; m. Allison Forbes, 1967; children: Audrey, Liza, Colby. BA, Bucknell U., 1966. Editl. writer Palladium-Item, Richmond, Ind., 1970; writing exec. Bruce Eberle & Assocs., Inc., Vienna, Va., 1975-77; dep. editor editl. pgs. Phoenix Gazette, 1977-96; editl. writer, columnist The Ariz. Republic, Phoenix, 1996-98; dir. Warne Ctr. Goldwater Inst., Phoenix, 1998-2000; pub. rels. dir. Qwest Comm. Internat., Inc., 2000—02; dir. Ariz. Affairs, 2002—. Participant U.S. Army War Coll., Carlisle, Pa., U.S. Naval War Coll., Newport, R.I.; participant arms control, disarmament programs including Space & Arms talks, Geneva; chmn. New Tech. Com., Journalism in Edn. Com.; mem. various coms. Creator, host cable TV program focus on polit. figures; regional editor The Masthead. Grantee European Cmty. Visitor Programme, 1993; recipient highest honors editl. writing, newspaper design Ariz., Western Region; highest honor Maricopa County Bar Assn.; Hoover Inst. media fellow, 1985. Mem. Nat. Conf. Editl. Writers (bd. dirs., included vol. Editl. Excellence), First Amendment Cong. (bd. dirs.), Soc. Profl. Journalists/Sigma Delta Chi, ABA (com. prisons, sentencing). Avocations: coaching competitive soccer, tennis, photography, riding. Home: 130 W Pine Valley Dr Phoenix AZ 85023-5283 Office: Qwest Comm Internat Inc 4041 N Central Ave 11th Fl Phoenix AZ 85012

GENS, RALPH SAMUEL, electrical engineering consultant; b. Berlin, Nov. 25, 1924; s. Alexander and Renata Gens; m. Ida L. Mattson; children: Marilyn R., David A. BS in Elec. Engring., Oreg. State U., 1949. Registered profl. engr., Oreg. Engr. Bonneville Power Adminstrn., Portland, Oreg., 1949-80, chief, system engr., 1966-74, mgr. planning, research and devel., 1974-77, chief engr., asst. adminstr. for engring and constrn., 1977-80; cons. Portland, 1980—. Advisor NSF, 1971-76; mem. adv. com. Project UHV, 1968-79; mem. Electricity Commn. of Papua, New Guinea, 1981-88; chmn. energy rsch. adv. bd. U.S. Dept. Energy, 1984-85, mem., 1985-89; chmn. planning coordination com. of Western Systems Coordinating Coun., 1975-76. Contbr. articles to profl. jours.; patentee in field. Served as sgt. U.S. Army, 1943-46, PTO. Recipient Disting. Service award Dept. Interior, 1978. Fellow IEEE (chmn. surge protective devices com. 1971, chmn. Portland sect. 1968, William M. Harbishaw award 1984, Centennial medal 1984, medal for engrng. excellence 2003); mem. NAE, Internat. Conf. Large High Voltage Electric Systems (U.S. v.p. 1979-80, chmn. study com. system analysis and technique 1986-92, Atwood award 1990, Internat. honorary mem., 1992), Electric Power Rsch. Inst. (rsch. adv. com. 1977-80), Tau Beta Pi, Sigma Tau, Eta Kappa Nu, Pi Mu Epsilon.

GENSER, JARED MATTHEW, lawyer; b. New Haven, Conn., June 17, 1972; s. Sander Gary and Lyne Taylor Genser; m. Lisa Joy Noik, June 1, 2003. BS, Cornell U., 1995; MA in Pub. Policy, Harvard U., 1998; JD, U. Mich., 2001. Bar: Md. 2001, D.C. 2002, lic.: Law Soc. UK (solicitor England and Wales) 2005. Raoul Wallenberg scholar Hebrew U., Jerusalem, 1995—96; assoc. McKinsey & Co., Washington, 2001—03, DLA Piper Rudnick Gray Cary US LLP, Washington, 2003—. Pres. Freedom Now, Bethesda, 2001—. Named Pro Bono Lawyer of Yr., DLA Piper Rudnick Gray Cary US LLP, 2005; recipient John F. Kennedy Meml. award, Cornell U., 1995, Jane L. Mixer Social Justice award, U. Mich. Law Sch., 2001, Rising Star award, Harvard U. John F. Kennedy Sch. of Govt., 2002. Mem.: Am. Soc. Internat. Law. Office Phone: 202-302-4049. Personal E-mail: jmg11@cornell.edu.

GENSHAFT, JUDY LYNN, psychologist, educator; b. Canton, Ohio, Jan. 7, 1948; d. Arthur I. and Leona (Caghan) G. BA, U. Wis., 1969; MA, Kent State U., 1973, PhD, 1975. Lic. psychologist, Ohio. Sch. psychologist Canton (Ohio) City Schs., 1972-75; asst. prof. Ohio State U., 1976-81, assoc. prof., asst. chmn., 1981-85, prof., 1985—92, asst. chair, 1985-86, chair, 1987—92, presdl. intern, acting assoc. provost, 1986-87; dean Sch. Edn. SUNY, Albany, 1992-95, interim v.p. for acad. affairs, 1995-97, provost, v.p. acad. affairs, 1997-2000; pres. U. So. Fla., Tampa, 2000—. Psychiat. social worker Canton Mental Health Clinic, 1970-72; vis. prof. U. British Columbia, Vancouver, Can., 1976-81. Contbr. numerous articles and book chpts. to profl. publ. Mem. Ballet Met., Columbus, 1986; cons. League Against Child Abuse, Columbus, 1978—, Bur. Vocat. Edn., Columbus, 1980—; mem. adv. bd. Support for Talented Students, Columbus, 1985—; bd dirs. H. Lee Moffitt Cancer Ctr. and Rsch. Inst., Fla. High-Tech Corridor, Greater Tampa Bay C. of C., Tampa Bay Partnership, Coun. of 100 (chair-designate). Nat. Rsch. grantee, 1984-85; recipient Kathryn Schoen Endowment award, 1986, Huelsman award, 1988, Hon. award Ohio Dept. Edn., 1984, Disting. Affirmative Action award, 1991, Leadership award Nat. Sch. Devel. Coun., Shirley A. Ryals award, Prevent Blindness, 2003. Mem. Am. Psychol. Assn., Nat. Assn. Sch. Psychologist, (sec. 1983-85, Presl. award 1982, 85, 87), Am. Assn. Counseling and Devel., Internat. Assn. Sch. Psychologists, Ohio Sch. Psychologist Assn. (ethics chmn. 1985-86), Sigma Xi. Avocations: sports, reading. Office: U So Fla Pres Office 4202 E Fowler Ave Tampa FL 33620-8000

GENSLER, M. ARTHUR, JR., architect; b. N.Y.C., July 12, 1935; s. M. Arthur and Gertrude (Wilson) G.; m. Drucilla Cortell, Sept. 7, 1957; children— David, Robert, Kenneth, Douglas BA in Architecture, Cornell U., 1957. Lic. architect, 38 states. Jr. designer Shreve, Lamb & Harmon, N.Y.C., 1958-59; project mgr. Norman & Dawbarn, Kingston, Jamaica, 1959-60, Albert Sigal & Assocs., N.Y.C. and San Francisco, 1961-63, Wurster, Bernardi & Emmons, San Francisco, 1963-65; pres., founder Gensler & Assocs., Architects, San Francisco, 1966—, now chmn. Mem. adv. council, mem. bldgs. and properties com. Coll. Architecture, Cornell U., Ithaca, N.Y., 1981-83. Co-author: A Rational Approach to Office Planning. Bd. dirs. World Coll. West, Petaluma, Calif., 1984-87; bd. overseers U. Calif., San Francisco; trustee World Affairs Coun., 1990—. Wity C.E., U.S. Army, 1958. Recipient Charles Goodwin Sands award Cornell U. Coll. Architecture, 1958; named charter mem. Interior Design mag. Hall of Fame, Cornell Enterpeneurs of Yr., 1995. Fellow AIA, Internat. Interior Design Assn.; mem. Inst. Bus. Designers (Star award 1992), San Francisco Planning and Urban Rsch. Assn., Bldg. Mgrs. and Owners Assn., Bay Area Coun., Urban Land Inst., San Francisco C. of C. (bd. dirs. 1984-86, 94—), Bohemian Club, Univ. Club, Bankers Club, Presidio Club. Republican. Congregationalist. Office: 2 Harrison St Ste 400 San Francisco CA 94105*

GENT, ALAN NEVILLE, physicist, researcher; b. Leicester, Eng., Nov. 11, 1927; came to U.S., 1961, naturalized, 1972; s. Harry Neville and Gladys (Hoyle) G.; m. Jean Margaret Wolstenholme, Sept. 1, 1949; children: Martin Paul Neville, Patrick Michael, Andrew John; m. Ginger Lee, Sept. 4, 1997. BS, U. London, 1946, BS in Physics, 1949, PhD in Sci., 1955; DHC, U. Haute-Alsace, France, 1997; DSc (hon.), De Montfort U., Eng., 1998. Lab. asst. John Bull Rubber Co., Leicester, Eng., 1944-45; research physicist Brit. (now Malaysian) Rubber Producers' Research Assn., 1949-61; prof. polymer physics U. Akron, Ohio, 1961-88, Dr. Harold A. Morton prof. polymer physics and polymer engring., 1988-94; prof. emeritus, 1994—; dean grad. studies and research U. Akron, 1978-86. Vis. prof. dept. materials Queen Mary Coll., U. London, 1969-70; vis. prof. dept. chem. engring. McGill U., 1983; Hill vis. prof. U. Minn., 1985; cons. Goodyear Tire & Rubber Co., 1963-2002, Gen. Motors, 1973-87. Contbr. articles to profl. publs. Served with Brit. Army, 1947-49. Recipient Mobay award, Cellular Plastics divsn. Soc. of Plastics Industry, 1963, Colwyn medal Plastics and Rubber Inst. Gt. Brit., 1978, Adhesives award Com. F-11, ASTM, 1979, Internat. Rsch. award Soc. Plastics Engrs., 1980, Whitby award Rubber Chem. divsn. Am. Chem. Soc., 1987, Pub. Svc. medal NASA, 1988, Charles Goodyear medal Rubber Chem. divsn. Am. Chem. Soc., 1990; installed Ohio Sci. Tech. and Industry Hall of Fame, 1993. Mem. NAE, Soc. of Rheology (pres. 1981-83, Bingham medal 1975), Adhesion Soc. (pres. 1978-80, 3M award 1987, Pres.'s award 1997), Am. Phys. Soc. (chmn. divsn. high polymer physics 1977-78, High Polymer Physics prize 1996). Democrat. Office: U Akron Inst Polymer Science Akron OH 44325-3909 Office Phone: 330-972-7505. Business E-Mail: gent@uakron.edu.

GENT, PETER ROBERT, research scientist; b. Newcastle-under-Lyme, Staffordshire, England, Nov. 6, 1948; s. Robert James and Joan Gent. BSc, U. of Bristol, Eng., 1970; MSc, U. of Bristol, 1971, PhD, 1974. Scientist II Nat. Ctr. for Atmospheric Rsch., Boulder, Colo., 1979—83, scientist III, 1983—90, sr. scientist, 1990—. Adv. bd. on modeling Internat. Rsch. Inst. for Climate Prediction, N.Y.C., NY, 1997—99. Author 65 articles in various jours.; co-editor: Jour. Phys. Oceanography, 1988—91; assoc. editor Jour. Phys. Oceanography, 1992—. Recipient Disting. Achievement award for Climate Modeling, Nat. Ctr. for Atmospheric Rsch., 2004. Fellow: Am. Meteorol. Soc. (Fellow of Soc. 2004); mem.: Am. Geophys. Union. Achievements include research in Fundamental advances in global ocean circulation models used for climate studies and prediction. Fundamental advances in numerical models used to forecast El-Nino. Avocations: birdwatching, playing squash, cross-country skiing. Office: National Center for Atmospheric Research 1850 Table Mesa Dr Boulder CO 80307 Office Phone: 303-497-1355.

GENTILE, JOSEPH F., lawyer, educator; b. San Pedro, Calif., Jan. 15, 1934; s. Ernest B. and Icy Otie (Martin) Gentile; children: Kim Yvonne, Kevin James, Kelly Michele, Kristien Elyse, Kerri Nicole. BA cum laude, San Jose State U., 1955; JD, San Fernando Valley U., 1966; cert. in indsl. rels., UCLA, 1959; teaching credential, Calif. C.C., 1972; M.Pub. Adminstrn., U. So. Calif., 1976. Bar: Calif. 1967, U.S. Supreme Ct. 1972. Mem. indsl. relations staff Kaiser Steel Corp., Fontana Works, 1957-62; labor relations counsel Calif. Trucking Assn., Burlingame, Calif., 1964-68; acting dir. indsl. relations, labor relations counsel McDonnell Douglas Corp., Santa Monica, Calif., 1968-70; sr. partner Nelson, Kirshman, Goldstein, Gentile & Rexon, Los Angeles, 1970-76; individual practice, 1976—. Arbitration panel Fed. Mediation and Conciliation Svc., Calif. Counciliation Service; instr. bus. econs., indsl. rels. U. Calif. Ext., 1969-94, personnel and indsl. rels. San Bernardino Valley Coll., 1960-62, transp. Mt. San Antonio Coll., 1972-74; lectr. Loyola U., 1973-74, U. So. Calif., 1976-80; adj. prof. law Pepperdine U., 1981-2001; chmn. employee rels. commn. LA (Calif.) County, 1979—; employee rels. bd. City of LA, 2001—. Contbr. articles to profl. jours. Served with AUS, 1955-57. Mem. ABA, Calif. Bar Assn., Los Angeles County Bar Assn. (past chmn. exec. com. labor law sect.), Am. Arbitration Assn. (chmn. regional adv. coun., arbitration panel, nat. bd. dirs. 1985-91), Phi Sigma Alpha, Phi Alpha Delta. Office: PO Box 7418 Thousand Oaks CA 91359-7418 Office Phone: 805-499-4282.

GENTILE SACHS, VALERIE ANN, lawyer; b. Cleve., Aug. 4, 1955; d. John Charles and Doreen Phyllis (Neale) G. B.L.S., Bowling Green U., 1977; J.D., Case Western Res. U., 1981. Bar: Ohio 1981. Summer assoc. Arter & Hadden, Cleve., 1980, assoc., 1981-83; sec. Royal Petroleum Properties, Inc., Cleve., 1982-83; assoc. Baker & Hostetler, Cleve., M.A. Hanna Co., v.p., gen. counsel, sec. RELTEC Corp., 1997-2000; v.p., gen. counsel, Marconi Comm., Inc., 2000-01; exec. v.p., gen. counsel, 2001-02, gen. counsel, chief legal officer Marconi PLC, London, 2002-03; exec. v.p., gen. counsel, sec. Jo-Ann Stores, Inc., 2003-; Editor: Case Western Res. U. Law Rev., 1980-81, assoc. editor, 1979-80; assoc. editor Case Western Res. U. Jour. Internat. Law, 1978-79. Mem. Cleve. Citizens League, 1982-84; trustee Forest Hills Housing Corp., Cleve., 1982-84; mem. fgn. trade policy com. Cleve. World Trade Assn., 1982— . Mem. ABA, Ohio State Bar Assn., Cleve. Bar Assn., Alpha Epsilon Delta, Beta Beta Beta, Alpha Lambda Delta. Office: Jo Ann Stores Inc 5555 Darrow Rd Hudson OH 44236-4011 Office Phone: 330-656-2600 2156. Office Fax: 330-463-6675.

GENTINE, LEE MICHAEL, marketing professional; b. Plymouth, Wis., Feb. 18, 1952; s. Leonard ALvin and Dolores Ann (Becker) G.; m. Debra Ann Suemnicht, Dec. 29, 1973 (div. Nov. 2003); children: Amanda, Joshua, Jonathan. BBA, U. Notre Dame, 1974; MBA, DePaul U., 1977. Acct. Hurdman & Cranston, Chgo., 1974-75; sales rep. Sargento Cheese Inc., Plymouth, 1975-78, mktg. mgr., 1978-81, sr. v.p. mktg., 1981-84, exec. v.p. mktg., 1984-89, pres. consumer products divsn., 1989-97; mng. ptnr. Dairyland Investors Group LLP, Plymouth, Wis., 1997—; ptnr. Vintage Neighborhood LLC, 2004—. Adv. bd. Kaytee Products Inc., Chilton, Wis., 1994-98; bd. dirs. Sargento Foods Inc. Bd. dirs. Plymouth Softball Assn., 1980—; pres. Plymouth Indsl. Devel. Corp., 1981-85, Parish Coun., 1989-90; chmn. Plymouth Advancement Com., 1992-96, pres., 1992-2002; mem. adv. bd. St. Nicholas Hosp., 1998—; pres. Quit Qui Oc Athletic Alliance, Inc., 1999—; vice chmn. Elkhart Lake Tourism Commn., 1998-2004. Named One of 100 Best and Brightest Advt. Execs., Advt. Age, 1986. Mem. Am. Mktg. Assn., Sheboygan County C. of C. (bd. dirs. 1987-89), Beta Gamma Sigma. Roman Catholic. Avocations: softball, golf, home rehabilitation. Office: Dairyland Investors Group LLP 601 Eastern Ave Plymouth WI 53073-1913

GENTINO, ROBERT E., lawyer; b. Hartford, Conn., Dec. 9, 1954; s. Edward Joseph and Marjorie Jean (Kissinger) G. BA summa cum laude, U. Conn., 1976; JD, Cornell U., 1980. Bar: Calif. 1980, U.S. Dist. Ct. (ctrl. dist.) Calif. 1980, U.S. Ct. Appeals (9th cir.) 1986. Congl. intern U.S. Rep. William Cotter, Washington, 1975; assoc. Wyman, Bautzer, Rothman, Kuchel & Silbert, L.A., 1980-83; pvt. practice L.A., 1984—; judge pro tem Superior Ct. LA County, 1990—. Pro bono pub. counsel; law sch. moot ct. judge. Trustee Hollywood United Meth. Ch. Office: Ste 1950 10 Universal City Plz Universal City CA 91608-1074 Office Phone: 818-509-7272. E-mail: robert@gentinolaw.com.

GENTLE, KENNETH WILLIAM, physicist; b. Oak Park, Ill., Oct. 27, 1940; s. William and Cathryn Mary (Spence) G. BS, MIT, 1962, PhD, 1966. Asst. prof. dept. physics U. Tex., Austin, 1966-69, assoc. prof., 1970-75, prof. physics, 1976—, chair dept. physics, 1997-2001. Sloan fellow, 1973-75 Fellow Am. Phys. Soc. Home: 212 Buckeye Trl Austin TX 78746-4420 Office: Univ Tex Dept Physics Austin TX 78712 Office Phone: 512-471-7581. Business E-Mail: k.gentle@mail.utexas.edu.

GENTNER, DEDRE, psychology professor; PhD in psychology, U. Calif., San Diego, 1974. Sr. scientist Bolt Beranek and Newman; faculty mem. U. Wash., U. Ill., Urbana; prof. psychology, edn. and social policy Northwestern U., Evanston, Ill., 1990—. Fellow: Am. Acad. Arts and Scis. Office: Northwestern U 213 Swift Hall 2029 Sheridan Rd Evanston IL 60201 E-mail: gentner@northwestern.edu.*

GENTNER, JOSHUA D., lawyer; b. South Bend, Ind., Aug. 8, 1972; BA, Indiana U., 1994; JD cum laude, Northwestern U., 1997. Bar: Ill. 1997. Shareholder Vedder, Price, Kaufman & Kammholz, P.C. Mem.: Ill. State Bar Assn., Order of the Coif. Office: 222 N La Salle St Chicago IL 60601-1003 Office Phone: 312-609-7887. Office Fax: 312-609-5005. Business E-Mail: jgentner@vedderprice.com.*

GENTRY, ALBERTA ELIZABETH, elementary school educator; b. Richter, Kans., Feb. 18, 1925; d. John Charles and Dessie Lorena (Duvall) Briles; m. Kenneth Neil Gentry, June 1, 1947; children: Michal Neil, Alan Dale, Elisa Ann. BE, Emporia (Kans.) Tchrs. Coll., 1975. Cert. tchr., Kans. Tchr. Chippewa Rural Sch., Ottawa, Kans., 1943-44; prin., tchr. Pomona (Kans.) Grade Sch., 1944-47, tchr., 1960-61, Silverlake Rural Sch., Pomona, 1947-48, Hawkins Rural Sch., Ottawa, 1948-49, Davy Rural Sch., Ottawa, 1950-53, Eugene Field Sch., Ottawa, 1953-54, Centropolis Grade Sch., Ottawa, 1964, Appanoose Elem. Sch., Pomona, 1964-90, ret., 1990. Trainer student tchr., 1985-86. Author: Proven Ideas for Classroom Teachers, 1988. Project leader, supporter 4-H, Franklin County, Kans., 1963-67; den mother Boy Scouts Am., Ottawa, 1955-66; dir. Bible sch., tchr. Trinity Meth. Ch., Ottawa, 1955-70, supt., 1955-66, mem. choir, 1947—. Named to Kans. Tchrs. Hall of Fame, 1991. Mem. NEA, Kans. Tchrs. Assn., Kans. Edn. Assn., Alpha Delta Kappa (sec. 1988-90). Republican. Methodist. Avocations: bird watching, arts and crafts, family genealogy, flower gardening, music. Home: PO Box 2 Pomona KS 66076-0002

GENTRY, BERN LEON, SR., management consultant; b. Goldsboro, N.C., Sept. 9, 1941; s. Theodore Alfonso and Ruth Ester (Taylor) G.; m. Jane A. Price, Nov. 11, 1965; children: Michelle Lorraine, Bern Leon. Student, Rutgers U., 1959-61, Temple U., 1961-63, Cornell U., 1966-67, U. Okla., 1971. Tax acct. IRS, Phila., 1965-66; collection mgr., credit mgr., appliance store mgr., soft goods mdse. mgr. Sears, Roebuck & Co., Phila., 1966-71; program mgr., dir. nat. urban affairs U.S. Jr. C. of C., 1971-73, cons., 1973—; pres. Together, Inc., Tulsa, 1973—. Contbr. articles to profl. jours. Mem. nat. adv. bd. Boys Clubs Am., 1971—; mem. nat. Black alliance for grad. level edn. U. Mich.; past pres., bd. dirs. Tulsa Econ. Opportunity Task Force; pres. Community Service Agy.; bd. dirs. Jr. Achievement. Recipient award of accomplishment Sears Staff Sch., 1967; award of appreciation Black Peoples Unity Movement Econ. Devel. Corp., 1971; George Washington Honor medal Freedoms Found., 1974, 76; Keys to cities of Roanoke, Va.; Keys to cities of Baton Rouge, La.; Keys to cities of New Orleans; named Outstanding Young Man Camden, 1970; Outstanding Chpt. Pres. N.J. Jaycees; Outstanding Jaycee. Mem. Nat. Urban League, NAACP, Am. Mgmt. Assn., Nat. Assn. Human Rights Workers, Assn. Black Found. Execs., Nat. Assn. Pub. Relations Execs., Nat. Civil Service League, Nat. Assn. Community Devel., Nat. Assn. Vol. Services Coordinator, Camden Jaycees (pres. 1970-71), Tulsa Met. C. of C. Office: Together Inc PO Box 52528 802 E 6th St Tulsa OK 74120-3610

GENTRY, FRANCIS G., German language educator; b. June 8, 1942; s. Louise M. (Casey) Denehy; m. Edda Schrader, Oct. 27, 1972. BS in German and English cum laude, Boston Coll., 1963; MA in German, Ind. U., 1966, PhD in German, 1973. Instr. SUNY, Albany, 1969-74, asst. prof., 1974-75, U. Wis., Madison, 1975-80, assoc. prof., 1980-84, prof., 1984-91, Pa. State U., Univ. Park, 1991—; prof. emeritus U. Wis.-Madison, 2000, Pa. State U., 2003. Guest prof. Universität Freiburg, 1984; asst. to chair dept. German, U. Wis., Madison, 1980-84, chair, 1988-91, chair medieval studies program, 1986-89; head dept. German, Pa. State U., 1991-97; co-dir. Max Kade Inst. Forsgerman-Am. Rsch.; served on numerous coms. U.Wis., Madison, Pa. State U.; councillor Medieval Assn. of the Midwest, 1980-82, v.p., 82-83, pres., 83-84; chair various sects. Internat. Cong. on Medieval Studies, 1977—; mem. USA Fellowship Selection Com. (Freiburg), 1984-85, Fulbright Selection Com. (Freiburg), 1985, commn. for selection of summer stipend awards NEH, Washington, 1988, exec. com. German-Am. Inst. (Freiburg), 1984-85; lectr. in field. Author: Triuwe and Vriunt in the Nibelungenlied, 1975, Bibliographie zur frühmittelhochdeutschen Dichtung, 1992, (with James K. Walter) German Epic Poetry, 1995, (with Christopher Kleinhenz) Medieval Studies in North America: Past, Present, Future, 1982, (with others) Monatshefte, 1982, Medieval Tales, 1983, Festschrift for Frank Banta, 1988, Deutsche Literatur: Eine Sozialgeschichte, 1988, Gottfried von Strasburg, 1988, Studies in Medievalism, 1991, A Companion to Middle High German Lit. to the 14th Century, 2002, (with Winder McConnell, Ulrich Muller, Werner Wunderlich) The Nibelungen Tradition: An Encyclopedia, 2002, A Companion to the Works of Hartmann Von Ave, 2005; mem. edit. bd. Monatshefte, 1975-92, editl. cons. 1992—, book rev. editor, 1975-91; mem. edit. bd. Allegorica, 1976-86; German editor Studies in Medievalism, 1986-91; mem. nat. adv. bd. dirs. The German Quarterly, 1991-94; assoc. editor: Medieval Germany: An Encyclopedia, 1992—; co-editor: The Nibelungen Tradition: An Encyclopedia, 1993—; reviewer various profl. jours., including Monatshefte, German Studies, German Studies Rev., German Quarterly, Germanistik, Modern Lang. Jour., Speculum, Choice; author numerous scholarly articles, contbr. articles to profl. jours. Organizer Jr. Year in Freiburg 25th Anniversary Celebration, 1985; bd. dirs. Madison-Freiburg Sister City Assn., 1987-91, v.p., 1988-89, pres., 1989-91; adv. bd. dirs. Wis.-Hessen Ptnr. State Coun., 1990-91. Recipient Campion Disting. Alumnus award Boston Coll., 1977; Ind. U.-Kiel Universität Exch. fellow, 1964; fellow Inst. for Rsch. in the Humanities, 1977; Alexander von Humboldt-Stiftung fellow, 1978, 1982; Vilas Assoc. fellow U. Wis., Madison, 1986-88. Mem. Medieval Acad. Am. (chmn. local arrangements for ann. meeting 1989), Wolfram-von-Eschenbach-Gesellschaft, Alexander Von Humboldt Assn. Am. (pres. Pa. chpt. 1997—), Delta Phi Alpha (pres. Beta chpt. 1968), Alpha Sigma Nu, Alpha and Omega. Avocations: hiking, travel. Office Phone: 814-865-5481. Business E-Mail: FGG1@psu.edu.

GENTRY, JAMES ROBERT, education educator; b. Evanston, Ill., Nov. 15, 1945; s. Lonnie W Gentry and Goldie Lee Brumback-Gentry; m. Barbara June Wolfer, Nov. 29, 1968; children: Robin June Angemi, Dale James. AA in social sci., Citrus Coll., 1964; BS in social sci., Calif. State Poly. U., 1966; MA in hist., Calif. State U. at LA, 1968; PhD in hist., U. of Utah, 1985. Instr. of history Cascade Coll., Portland, Oreg., 1968—69; prof. of history Coll. of So. Idaho, 1969—, chmn. social sci. dept., 1997—. Contbr. articles to jours.; mem. editl. bd.: Idaho Yesterdays. Mem. Twin Falls County Hist. Preservation Commn., Idaho, 1987—97. Mem.: Am. Hist. Assn. (corr.), Phi Alpha Theta (corr.). Am. Bapt. Achievements include assisting in development and implementation of a J.A. & Kathryn Albertson grant under the Recreating Idaho colleges and schools of education initiative. Avocations: walking, movies, reading, canoeing. Home: 675 Alturas Dr N Twin Falls ID 83301-4334 Office: College Of Southern Idaho 315 Falls Ave Twin Falls ID 83301 Office Phone: 208-732-6864. Business E-Mail: jgentry@csi.edu.

GENTRY, JAMES WILLIAM, retired state agency administrator; b. Danville, Ill., Aug. 14, 1926; s. Carl Lloyd and Leone (Isham) G.; m. Dorothie Shirley Hechtlinger, Mar. 18, 1967; 1 stepdau., Susan Mushkin. AB, Fresno State Coll., 1948; MJ, U. Calif., Berkeley, 1956. Field rep. Congressman B.W. Gearhart, Fresno, Calif., 1948, Assemblyman Wm. W. Hansen, Fresno, 1950, sec., 1953-56; exec. asst. Calif. Pharm. Assn., L.A., 1956-69; asst. adminstr., dir. pub. info. So. Calif. Comprehensive Health Planning Coun., 1969-71, acting adminstr., 1971-72, exec. sec., 1972-73, Calif. Adv. Health Coun., 1973-85, fed. cons., 1986-88. Editor, pub. Calif. Pharmacy Jour., L.A., 1956-69; pub. rels. dir. PAID Prescriptions, 1963-64; dir. pub. info. Comprehensive Health Planning coun., L.A. County, 1969; fed. cons. Calif. Health Care Commn., 1973-75; acting pub. info. officer Calif. Office Statewide Health Planning and Devel., 1978-79, interim dir., 1983; mem. L.A. Civil Svc. Police Interview Bd., 1967-72, Calif. Health Planning Law Revision Commn.; asst. sgt.-at-arms Calif. State Assembly, 1950; exec. sec. Calif. Assembly Interim Com. on Livestock and Dairies, 1954-56; mem. adv. bd. Am. Security Coun.; former mem. Calif. Bldg. Safety Bd. Editor: Better Health, 1963-67, Orientation Conf. Comprehensive Health Planning, 1969, commentary, 1969-71, Program and Funding, 1972, Substance Abuse, 1972; editl. adv. Pharm. Svcs. for Nursing Homes: A Procedural manual, 1966. Mem. Fresno County Rep. Ctrl. Com., 1950; charter mem. Rep. Presdl. Task Force. Served to col. AUS, 1949-85, Korea, 1950-53. Decorated Legion of Merit, Bronze Star medal, Commendation Ribon with metal Pendant; recipient pub. awards Western Soc. Bus. Publs. Assn., 1964-67. Mem. Am. Assn. Comprehensive Health Planning, Pub. Rels. Soc. Am., Allied Drug Travelers So. Calif., L.A. Press Club, Mil. Police Assn., Mil. Officers Assn. Am., Res. Officers Assn. (life), Assn. US Army, US Senatorial Club, The Victory Svcs. Club of London, Pi Gamma Mu, Phi Alpha Delta, Sigma Delta Chi. Home: 1603 Patriots Colony Dr Williamsburg VA 23188-1341

GENTRY, MARGARET BURTON, retired elementary school teacher; b. Iva, SC, Oct. 19, 1939; d. Emory Goss and Olivia (Copeland) Burton; m. Aubrey Lee Gentry, July 5, 1981 (dec. Apr. 1991). AA, Anderson (S.C.) Coll., 1962; BS, East Tenn. U., 1964; Cert. Grad. Study, U. Ga., 1969-72; postgrad., Clemson U., 1969-72. Cert. tchr., Ga.; cert. poll mgr., 2002. Salesperson Browns Five and Ten Store, Iva, 1958-61; adminstrv. asst. SC Hwy. Dept., Anderson, 1962; spl. asst. to prof. govt. and history East Tenn. State U., Johnson City, 1962-64; tchr. grade 4 DeKalb County, Decatur, Ga., 1964-71; adminstrv. asst. Poinsettia Heat and Treat Co., Anderson, 1965; tchr. grade 4 Elbert County, Elberton, Ga., 1971-99; ret., 1999. Researcher for pictorial history of Iva Reviva Civic and Cmty. Devel., 1998-99; pres. Willing Workers Class, Iva, 1998—; del. Saluda Bapt. Assn., Iva, 1999—; cert. nat. poll mgr. for presdl. and local elections, 2000-. Work scholar Anderson Coll., 1960-62; named. Girls Aux. Queen Union Bapt. Ch., Iva, 1955. Mem. NEA, Ga. Assn. Edn. (rep. plant facility 1979-80, Gift/Letter of Appreciation 1999, cert. poll mgr. 2002), Ga. Retired Tchr., SC Retired Tchr., Elbert County Assn. Edn., Anderson County Ret. Educators Assn., Tartan Cross Soc. Republican. Baptist. Avocations: travel, sewing, genealogy, music, gardening. Home: 311 W Jackson St PO Box 474 Iva SC 29655-0474

GENTRY, ROBERT VANCE, physicist, researcher, writer; b. Chattanooga, July 9, 1933; s. Vance Ault and Sara Frances (Northington) G.; m. Patricia Ann Gentry, Jan. 20, 1953; children: Patricia Lynn, Michael Vance, David Wayne. BS in Physics, U. Fla., 1955, MS, 1956; D.Sc. (hon.), Columbia Union Coll., Takoma Park, Md., 1977. Nuclear engr. Gen. Dynamics Co., Ft. Worth, 1956-58; sr. engr. Martin Co., Orlando, Fla., 1958-59; instr. math. U. Fla., Gainesville, 1959-61, Walla Walla (Wash.) Coll., 1961-62; instr. physics Ga. Inst. Tech., 1962-64; research physicist Archeol. Research Found., Atlanta, 1965-66; mem. faculty Columbia Union Coll., 1966-84, assoc. prof. physics, 1977-84; cons. physicist, 1984-86; research physicist Earth Sci. Assocs., Knoxville, Tenn., 1986—; pres. The Orion Found., 1997—. Guest scientist chemistry div. Oak Ridge Nat. Lab., 1969-82, 89; hon. asst. res. prof. physics U. Tenn.-Knoxville, 1982-83. Author: Creation's Tiny Mystery, 1986, 2d edit., 1988, 3d edit., 1992, 4th edit., 2003; chief rschr. (video) Fingerprints of Creation (Telly award 1993), The Young Age of the Earth, 1994; contbr. articles to profl. jours. Grantee NSF, 1962, 1971-77, NASA, 1970-72. Mem. AAAS, Am. Phys. Soc., Am. Geophys. Union, N.Y. Acad. Scis., Sigma Xi (assoc.). Seventh-day Adventist. Achievements include discovery of polonium radioactive halos in granites, a new model of the universe to explain the Hubble redshift relation and the 2.7K Cosmic Blackbody Radiation without the use of spacetime expansion. Home: PO Box 12067 Knoxville TN 37912-0067 Office Phone: 865-947-4726. Personal E-mail: esa@halos.com. *To recognize that success in any field is not the result of chance or destiny but instead the reward of faithfully developing those talents endowed by the Creator provides the highest possible incentive for achieving that station in life for which each individual is uniquely fitted.*

GENTRY, VERNESSA DIANA, principal, consultant; b. Longview, Tex., July 19, 1959; d. Clarence and Helen Marie Carr; m. William Abbott Gentry, Aug. 23, 1980; children: William Bryan, Ashely Briana. AA, Tyler Jr. Coll., Tyler, Tex., 1979; BEd, Stephen F. Austin Coll., 1980, MEd, 1987, mid-mgmt. cert., 1994. Reading tchr. Mid. Sch., Longview, 1981-84, lang. arts tchr., 1984-86, sci. tchr., 1986-94, asst. prin. Henderson, 1994-96; prin. Tatum (Tex.) Mid. Sch., 1996-2000, Forest Park Mid. Sch., Longview, Tex., 2000—. Cons. Edn. Leadership, 1997. Mem. Tex. Middle Sch. Assn. (dir. region 5 1995—, dir. region 7 1995-2002, region 7 Prin. of Yr. award 1999), Delta Sigma Theta (Outstanding Educator award 1996). Avocations: reading, antique shopping, shopping at the mall. Home: RR 21 Box 91 Longview TX 75603-9428 Office: 1515 Lake Dr Longview TX 75601-4816 E-mail: vgentry@lisd.org.

GENTY, PHILIP, law educator; BA, Colorado Coll., 1977; JD, NYU, 1980. Atty. Prisoners' Legal Svcs., NY, NYC Dept. Housing, Preservation and Develop., Bedford-Stuyvesant Cmty. Legal Svcs. Corp.; faculty mem. Brooklyn Law Sch., 1987; clin. prof. Columbia U. Law Sch., 1989—. Mem. adv. group Fed. Resource Ctr. for Children of Prisoners. Office: Columbia Law Sch 435 W 116th St New York NY 10027 Office Phone: 212-854-3250. Office Fax: 212-854-3699. E-mail: pgenty@law.columbia.edu.

GENTZSCH, WOLFGANG, grid computing and networking service company ececutive; With Max Planck Inst. Physics, Germany, Siemens, Germany; head, computational fluid dynamics and supercomputing German Agency for Aerospace and Aeronautics, DLR; prof. mat. and computer sci. U. Applied Sciences, Regensburg, Germany, 1985—2000; cons. for many computing companies such as, IBM, Cray Computers and Digital Equipment Corp., 1985—2000; founder Genias Software (also called the Ctr. for Numerically Intensive Applications and Supercomputing), 1990—99; also founder of Genias Parallel Computing, Genias Benelux, Genias Internet, and Genias Graphics; founder Gridware (predecessor of Genias Software), 1999—2000; joined (with acquisition of Gridware) Sun Microsystems, Inc., 2000—04, sr. engring. dir. for grid computing, 2000—04; mng. dir. MCNC Grid Computing & Networking Svcs., Research Triangle Park, NC, 2004—. Spkr. in the field; adj. prof. Duke U., NC State U., U. NC, Charlotte. Author of 150 articles about computer science, numerical algorithms, engring. applications, and grid computing. Responsible for Sun Microsystem's grid computing vision, strategy and technology development. Gridware's technology became the foundation for the Sun Grid Engine, the world's leading distributed resource management software no used in over 10,000 departmental and enterprise grids worldwide. Office: MCNC Grid Computing & Networking Svcs PO Box 12889 3021 Cornwallis Rd Research Triangle Park NC 27709-2889

GENUNG, DAN BALDWIN, minister, writer; b. Prescott, Ariz., July 23, 1915; s. Dan Baldwin and Kathleen Farrell Genung; m. Frances Ulrich Genung, Oct. 1, 1942; children: David Dan, Linda Joy McKown, Carol Dale Wilson, Bruce Michael. BA, U. Ariz., 1938; MA, U. Chgo., 1940, degree, 1941, postgrad., 1952—53. Founding pastor All Peoples Christian Ch. and Ctr., L.A., 1942—56; pastor Oceanside (Calif.) First Christian Ch., 1957—64, Foothill Christian Ch., LaCrescenta, Calif., 1967—70, Mt. Hollywood Congregational Ch., L.A., 1970—84. Bd. dirs. L.A. Urban League; chmn. bd. YMCA, Verdugo Hills, Calif.; pres. Disciplined Order of Christ. Author: Death in His Saddlebags, 1992, A Street Called Love, 1999; contbr. articles to profl. jours. Mem.: Kiwanis (pres. 1981—82), Rotary (pres. 1963—64). Home: 614 W 8th St Claremont CA 91711

GEOFFROY, CHARLES HENRY, retired retail executive; b. Longford, Ireland, Sept. 25, 1926; came to U.S., 1927, naturalized, 1945; s. Francis Louis and Kathleen Elizabeth (Fetherston) G.; m. Alida Baird McClenahan, Apr. 24, 1954; children: Evan Lloyd, Mark Lee, Douglas Baird. BA, Haverford Coll., 1949; postgrad., U. Pa., 1950. With GM Ins. Corp., Phila., 1950-51; mgr. rsch. dept. Ward Wheelock Co., Phila., 1951-54; assoc. rsch. dir., account exec. Lennen & Newell, Inc., N.Y.C., 1954-59; account exec. Young & Rubicam, Inc., N.Y.C., 1959-64, v.p. L.A., 1965-67; pres., mng. dir. Young & Rubicam, Ltd., Toronto, Ont., Can., 1968-74; pres., dir. J.K. Gill Co. Ltd., Portland, Oreg., 1974-80; pres., chief operating officer Grantree Corp., Portland, 1980-83; pres. Rathcline Corp., Portland, 1984-86; chmn. Wide Travel Internat., Portland, 1986-94, ret., 1994. With AUS, 1945-46. Fellow Inst. Can. Advt.; mem. Portland Execs. Assn., Waverley Country Club, Arlington Club, Huguenot Soc. Great Britain and Ireland, Rotary. Personal E-mail: cgeoff8520@aol.com.

GEOFFROY, GREGORY L., academic administrator, educator; b. Honolulu, July 8, 1946; s. Glenn Gaylord and Lucille Lavaughn (Lewis) G.; m. Kathleen Carothers, Apr. 17, 1971; children: Susan, Janet, David, Michael. BS in Chemistry, U. Louisville, 1968; PhD in Chemistry, Calif. Inst. Tech., 1974. Asst. prof. dept. chemistry Pa. State U., University Park, 1974-78, assoc. prof. dept. chemistry, 1978-82, prof. dept. chemistry, 1982-88, head dept. chemistry, 1988-89, dean Eberly Coll. Sci., 1989-97; provost, sr. v.p. acad. affairs U. Md., 1997; pres. Iowa State U., 2001—. Bd. dirs. Assn. Advancement Res. Astro., Washington; cons. Union Carbide Corp., South Charleston, W.Va., 1984-95, ARCO Chem., Newtown Square, Pa., 1988-92. Author: Organometallic Photochemistry, 1979; contbr. articles to profl. jours. Recipient Tchr.-Scholar award Camille & Henry Dreyfus Found., 1978, fellowship John Simon Guggenheim Found., 1982. Fellow AAAS; mem. Am. Chem. Soc. (chair inorganic chemistry divsn. 1990). Avocations: mountain biking, skiing. Office: 1750 Beardshear Hall Ames IA 50011 Office Phone: 515-294-2042. Business E-Mail: president@iastate.edu.

GEOGA, DOUGLAS GERARD, real estate developer, lawyer; b. Detroit, Aug. 13, 1955; s. Christ and Virginia M. (Juras) G. AB, Harvard U., 1977, JD, 1980. Bar: Mich. 1980., Ill. 1984. Assoc. Miller, Canfield, Paddock and Stone, Detroit, 1980-83; devel. counsel Hyatt Devel. Corp., Chgo., 1983-85, gen. counsel, 1985-86, v.p., gen. counsel, 1986-88, sr. v.p., 1988-89, exec. v.p., 1989-94; pres. Hyatt Hotels Corp., Chgo., 1994—. Mem. Industry Real Estate Financing Adv. Coun. Bd. dirs. United Way of LaGrange (Ill.), United Way of Surburban Chgo.; mem. strategic planning com. United Way/Crusade of Mercy. Mem. ABA, Am. Hotel & Motel Assn. (trustee Ednl. Inst., chmn. govtl. affairs com.), U.S. Nat. Travel Orgn. (bd. dirs.), Travel Industry Assn. (past mem. travel and tourism govt. affairs coun.), Travel Bus. Roundtable, Urban Land Inst. (assoc.). Democrat. Roman Catholic. Office: Hyatt Hotels Corp 200 W Madison St Chicago IL 60606-3414

GEOGHEGAN, PATRICIA, lawyer; b. Bayonne, N.J., Sept. 9, 1947; d. Frank and Rita (Mihok) G. BA, Mich. State U., 1969; MA, Yale U., 1972, JD, 1974; LLM, NYU, 1982. Bar: N.Y. 1975. Assoc. Cravath, Swaine & Moore, N.Y.C., 1974-82, ptnr., 1982—. Mem. ABA, N.Y. State Bar Assn., Assn. of Bar of City of N.Y. Office: Cravath Swaine & Moore Worldwide Plz Fl 45 825 8th Ave New York NY 10019-7416 Office Phone: 212-474-1584. Office Fax: 212-474-3700. Business E-Mail: pgeoghegan@cravath.com.

GEORGAKAKOS, KONSTANTINE PETER, hydrologist, researcher; b. Athens, Greece, Sept. 12, 1954; came to U.S., 1977; MS, MIT, 1980, ScD, 1982. Postdoctoral rschr. NOAA-Nat. Rsch. Coun., Silver Spring, Md., 1982-85, rsch. hydrologist Office Hydrology, 1985; asst. prof. CEE U. Iowa, Iowa City, 1986-89, assoc. prof., 1989-94; dir., sr. rsch. hydrologist Hydrologic Rsch. Ctr., San Diego, 1994—; full rsch. hydrologist IV Inst. Oceanography U. Calif., San Diego, 1994—. Cons. Food & Agriculture Orgn. UN, Rome, 1995—; sci. rev. panelist Nat. Oceanography Atmosphere Adminstrn., Silver Spring, 1996; reviewer NSF, NOAA, NASA, Washington, 1986—. Editor Jour. Applied Meteorology, 1995, Jour. Hydrology, 1996; contbr. articles to profl. jours. Coach Little League Soccer Club Del Mar, San Diego, 1994—. Rsch. associateship Nat. Rsch. Coun., Washington, 1982; recipient Presdl. Young Investigator award NSF, Washington, 1987. Mem. ASCE (assoc. editor 1996—), Am. Geophys. Union (chair hydrology 1991-93), Am. Meteor. Soc. (chair hydrology sect. 1991-93, elected expert on the WMO Commn. Hydrology Working Group on Applications). Achievements include development of flash flood prediction system used nationally by U.S. Nat. Weather Svc., elucidated dynamics and scaling of rainfall and soil water, role of soil water in development of future land surface hydrologic response; performed integrated impact assessments of climate variability and temperature change; developed operational system for rain estimation from satellite multispectral data; developed the first regional flash-flood warning system in Central America (7 countries) in operation since 2004. Office: Hydrologic Rsch Ctr 12780 High Bluff Dr Ste 250 San Diego CA 92130-3017 Office Phone: 858-794-2726. Business E-Mail: kgeorgakakos@hrc-lab.org.

GEORGANAS, NICOLAS D., electrical engineering educator; b. Athens, Greece, June 15, 1943; s. Demetrios N. and Athanasia (Kotsovou) G.; m. Jacynthe Savard, June 17, 1972; children: Nikita, Emmanuel. Diploma in Engring., Nat. Tech. U. Athens, 1966; PhD summa cum laude, U. Ottawa, Ont., Can., 1970; PhD (hon.), U. Daermstadt, 2004. Registered profl. engr., Ont. Lectr., elec. engring. U. Ottawa, 1970-71, asst. prof., 1971-76, assoc. prof., 1976-80, prof., 1980—, chmn., 1981-84, dean engring., 1986-93, assoc. v.p. rsch., 2005—. Vis. prof. IBM, LaGaude, France, 1977-78, INRIA/Bull-Transac, Paris, 1984-85, Bell-No. Rsch., Ottawa, 1993-94, CRC, Ottawa, 1997. Author: Queueing Networks—Exact Computational Algorithms: A Unified Theory by Decomposition and Aggregation, 1989; contbr. over 100 articles to profl. jours., more than 200 conf. articles. Recipient Killam Prize for Engring., Can. Coun. for Arts, 2002. Fellow IEEE, Can. Acad. Engring., Royal Soc. Can., Engring. Inst. Home: 1915 Montereau Ave Gloucester ON Canada Office: U Ottawa Faculty Engring SITE 161 Pasteur St Ottawa ON Canada K1N 6N5 Office Phone: 613-562-5800 x 5270. Personal E-mail: n.georganas@ieee.org.

GEORGE, ALEXANDER ANDREW, lawyer; b. Missoula, Mont., Apr. 26, 1938; s. Andrew Miltiadin and Eleni (Efstathiou) G.; m. Penelope Mitchell, Sept. 29, 1968; children: Andrew A., Stephen A. BBA honors, U. Mont., 1960, JD, 1962; postgrad., John Marshall U., 1964-66. Bar: Mont. 1962, U.S. Ct. Mil. Appeals 1964, U.S. Tax Ct. 1970. Sole practice, Missoula, 1966—. Mem. adv. com. U. Mont. Tax Inst., 1973-76; adj. lectr. U. Montana Law Sch. Corp. Taxation. Pres. Missoula Civic Symphony, 1973; nat. dir. Assn. Urban and Cmty. Symphony Orch., 1974, Mont. Eye Endowment Found.; pres. Greek Orthodox Ch., 1978, 91. Served to capt. JAG U.S. Army, 1962-66. Recipient Jaycee Disting. Svc. award, 1973. Mem.: Mont. Soc. CPA, Mont. Law Found. (treas. 1986—92), Western Mont. Bar Assn. (pres. 1971, lifetime achievement award 1998), State Bar Mont. (pres. 1981), Glacier-Waterton Internat. Peace Pk. Assn. (bd. dirs. 1999—2002), Ahepa (pres. 1967, state gov. 1968), Rotary (pres. 1972, state chmn. found. 1977, membership com. chmn. 1978), Sigma Nu (alumni trustee 1966—71), Alpha Kappa Psi, Phi Delta Phi. Home: 4 Greenbrier Ct Missoula MT 59802-3342 Office: 210 N Higgins Ave Ste 234 Missoula MT 59802-4497 Office Phone: 406-728-4310. Business E-Mail: georgelaw@in-tch.com.

GEORGE, ALEXANDER LAWRENCE, political scientist, educator; b. Chgo., May 31, 1920; s. John and Mary (Sargis) G.; m. Juliette Lombard, Apr. 20, 1948; children: Lee Lawrence, Mary Lombard. AM, U. Chgo., 1941, PhD, 1958; DHL (hon.), U. San Diego, 1987; PhD (hon.), U. Lund, Sweden, 1994. Rsch. analyst OSS, 1944-45; dep. chief rsch. br. Info. Control divsn. Office Mil. Govt. for Germany, 1945-48; specialist study of decision-making and internat. rels. RAND Corp., Santa Monica, Calif., 1948-68, head dept. social sci., 1961-63; prof. polit. sci. and internat. rels. Stanford (Calif.) U., 1968—. Lectr. U. Chgo., 1950, Am. U., 1952—56; chmn. com. on Conflict Rrsolution NRC/NAS, 1995—2000. Author: (with Juliette L. George) Woodrow Wilson and Colonel House: A Personality Study, 1956, Propaganda Analysis, 1959, The Chinese Communist Army in Action, 1967; (with others) The Limits of Coercive Diplomacy, 1971; (with Richard Smoke) Deterrence in American Foreign Policy: Theory and Practice, 1974 (Bancroft prize for Deterrence in Am. Fgn. Policy 1975), Towards A More Soundly Based Foreign Policy: Making Better Use of Information, 1976, Presidential Decisionmaking in Foreign Policy, 1980, Managing U.S.-Soviet Rivalry, 1983; (with Gordon Craig) Force and Statecraft, 1983, 3rd edit., 1995; editor: (with others) U.S.-Soviet Security Cooperation: Achievements, Failures, Lessons, 1988, Avoiding War: Problems of Crisis Management, 1991, Forceful Persuasion, 1992, Bridging the Gap: Theory and Practice of Foreign Policy, 1993; (with William E. Simons) The Limits of Coercive Diplomacy, 2d. edit., 1994; (with Juliette L. George) Presidential Personality and Performance, 1998, (with Andrew Bennett) Case Studies and Theory Development in the Social Sciences, 2005. Mem. Carnegie Commn. on Preventing Deadly Conflict, 1993-97. Fellow Ctr. Advanced Study Behavioral Scis., 1956-57, 76-77, NIMH, 1972-73, MacArthur Prize, 1983-88, Disting. fellow U. S. Inst. Peace, 1990-91, 91-92; Founds. Fund for Rsch. in Psychiatry grantee, 1960, NSF rsch. grantee, 1971-73, 75-77; recipient award for behavioral rsch. relevant to prevention of nuclear war NAS, 1997, Johan Skytte prize in polit. sci., Uppsala U., Swden, 1998; Carnegie Corp. grantee, 1999. Mem. Am. Acad. Arts and Scis., Coun. on Fgn. Rels., Am. Polit. Sci. Assn., Internat. Studies Assn. (pres. 1973-74), Am. Philos. Soc., Phi Beta Kappa. Home: 944 Lathrop Pl Stanford CA 94305-1060 Business E-Mail: algeorge@stanford.edu.

GEORGE, ALFRED L., JR., medical educator, researcher; b. Batavia, NY, June 14, 1956; BA in Chemistry, Coll. of Wooster, Ohio, 1978; MD, U. Rochester, 1982. Diplomate Am. Bd. Internal Medicine, Am. Bd. Nephrology. Intern and resident in internal medicine Vanderbilt U. Hosps., Nashville, 1982—86; chief resident in medicine St. Thomas Hosp., Nashville, 1985—86; instr. medicine Vanderbilt U. Sch. Medicine, Nashville, 1985—86, asst. prof. dept. medicine nephrology and pharmacology, 1992—95; assoc. prof. medicine and pharmacology Vanderbilt U., Nashville, 1995—; postdoctoral fellow in clin. nephrology renal-elctrolyte sectl dept. medicine Hosp. of U. Pa., Phila., 1986—87; rsch. fellow dept. medicine and dept. biochemistry and biophysics U. Pa., Phila., 1988—91, rsch. assoc. dept. medicine and Inst. Neurol. Scis., 1991—92. Vis. postdoctoral fellow Inst. Suisse de Recherches Experimentales sur le Cancer, Lausanne, Switzerland, 1987—88. Mem. editl. bd.: Am. Jour. Physiology, 1996—, jour. reviewer: Neuron, —, Nature Genetics, —, Jour. Membrane Biology, —; Jour. Biol. Chemistry, —; jour. reviewer: Kidney Internat., —, Jour. Physiology, —. Mem.: AAAS, Biophys. Soc., Am. Heart Assn. (mem. coun. on kidney disease, established investigator award 1996), Am. Soc. Nephrology. Office: Vanderbilt U Med Ctr 21st And Garland Ave Bldg Ii Nashville TN 37232-0001

GEORGE, ARTHUR CHARLES, lawyer; b. Boston, Dec. 9, 1954; s. Charles Arthur and Diana Kanavos George; m. Soteria Liousas, May 22, 1983; children: Charles Arthur, Peter Arthur, Elizabeth Diana. BSBA, Boston U., 1976; JD, New Eng. Sch. Law, 1979. Bar: Mass. 1980, U.S. Dist. Ct. Mass. 1981, U.S. Ct. Appeals (1st cir.) 1981. Lawyer Arthur C. George, Esq., Randolph, Mass., 1980-86; ptnr. George & George, Stoughton, 1987—. Town counsel Town of Holbrook, Mass., 1986—; mem. Rep. Town Com., Holbrook, 1988—, chmn., 1990-2000; co-leader Adventurer's 4-H Club, Holbrook, 1988—; trustee Bridgewater State Coll., 1999—; chmn. Holbrook Rep. Town Com., 2004—; mem. adv. bd. Greek Inst. Recipient Cert. of Appreciation, Mass. Chpt. Black Rep. Coun., citation Mass. State Senate, 1995, Salute to Excellence award U. Mass. Ext. and Mass. 4-H Found., 1998, Lucem Diffundo Plate award Mayor of New Bedford, 2001. Mem. Mass. Bar Assn., Bar Assn. Norfolk County (coun. mem. 2004—), Ripon Soc. (nat. sec. 1992-94), Holbrook Sportsmen's Club. Avocations: research and policy, political speechwriting, chess, baseball. Office: 1st Fl 10 Cabot Pl Fl 1 Stoughton MA 02072-4600 Office Phone: 781-341-4430.

GEORGE, DAVID SANDERSON, Spanish language educator, writer; b. Mpls., Minn., Feb. 8, 1942; s. William Allen and LaVerne Helen Eloise George; m. Beatriz de Arruda Zonis, May 26, 1985; 1 child, Alexander Sanderson. PhD, U. Minn., 1981. Asst. prof. Spanish Middlebury (Vt.) Coll., 1978—85; prof. Spanish Lake Forest (Ill.) Coll., 1985—. Area studies presenter Cendant Intercultural, Chgo., 1991—; vis. scholar U. of Chgo. Ctr. for Latin Am. Studies, 1996—2001. Author: (drama criticism) Flash & Crash Days: Brazilian Theatre in the Post-Dictatorship Period; contbr. literary reference Latin American Writers, drama criticism Tradición, Modernidad y Posmodernidad, drama criticism La Dramaturgia en Iberoamérica: Teoría y práctica teatral; author: (play) À Mão Armada, (drama criticism) The Modern Brazilian Stage; translator: (short stories) Scent of Love, (novel) Early Mourning; author: (drama criticism) Grupo Macunaíma: Carnavalização e Mito; translator: (novel) Village of the Ghost Bells, (short stories) Bag of Stories; contbr. book of travel essays Travellers' Tales Brazil. Recipient fellowship for coll. tchrs., NEH, 1987—88, summer stipends, 1993, Oskar Nobiling Medal for contbns. to rsch. on Brazilian lit., Sociedade Brasileira de Língua e Literatura, 1998, fellowship for coll. tchrs., NEH, 1995, summer stipends, 2002; grantee summer seminars, 1989, 1994. Mem.: MLA, Latin Am. Studies Assn., Brazilian Studies Assn. Liberal. Avocations: reading, travel, bicycling. Office: Lake Forest Coll 555 N Sheridan Rd Lake Forest IL 60045 Personal E-mail: george@lfc.edu.

GEORGE, DAVID WEBSTER, architect; b. Tulsa, Dec. 26, 1922; s. Calvin Webster and Ollie (McReynolds) G.; m. Xena Ruth Gill, Nov. 25, 1950; 1 child, Molly Evelyn; m. Elizabeth Howard, Dec. 30, 1984. Student U. Okla., 1940-43, 46-48; BArch., NC State U., 1949. Assoc., Frank Lloyd Wright, Taliesin Assoc. Architects, Scottsdale, Ariz., 1947-48; assoc. Harwell Hamilton Harris, Ft. Worth, Tex., 1954-56; founding ptnr. Architects Partnership, and predecessor firm, Dallas, 1959— . Bd. dirs. Dallas Theater Ctr. Capt. AUS, 1942-46, 51-52. Fellow AIA; mem. Tex. Soc. Architects, Nat. Council Archtl. Registration Bds. Methodist. Club: Horseshoe Bay Country. Home and Office: 2980 Burney Ln Southlake TX 76092-2704 E-mail: tinkigeo@aol.com.

GEORGE, DEVERAL D., editor, journalist, advertising consultant; b. Dallas, Nov. 23, 1939; s. Jack Weldon and Lleen Lelia (Hume) G. Student, U. Tex., 1958-61; BA, North Tex. State U., 1964; P.BA, U. Houston, 1974. Copywriter advt. agys., Houston, Dallas, 1964-70; free lance journalist, 1970-73, 75-76; copy and creative dir. Schey Advt., Houston, 1973, Bruce Advt., Houston, 1973-75; editor-in-chief, v.p. Bus. and Energy Internat., Houston, 1976-80; editor Ultra mag., 1980-81; freelance journalist Houston, 1981-83, 84-85; editor Saudi Bus. Mag.; cons. Saudi Research and Mktg. Inc., Houston, Washington, and Jeddah, Saudi Arabia, 1983-84; writer, advt. cons. Dale Carnegie & Assocs., Garden City (N.Y.) and Houston, 1985-90; mng. editor internat. Offshore Mag., Houston, 1991-97; editor Schlumberger Oilfield Rev., 1997-98, Oil and Gas Online, Vertical Net, Horsham, Pa., 1998-2001, Houston, 1998-2001; owner, mng. editor Oil and Gas Internat., Houston, 2001—. Author: Cathedrals of Mexico, and Other Poems, 1963, The Erratic Pilgramage, 1973, The Whole World Cookbook, 1976, The Offshore Atlas, 1995; screenplays: The Monument, 1980, Armageddon, 1981; television series Treasure Hunt, 1984; editor: Worldwide Directory of Petroleum Ministries and National Oil Companies, 1995; mem. editl. bd. Xi'an Petroleum Inst., China. Del., Democratic Conv., 1972; mem. Houston Outdoor Group. Mem. ACLU, Am. Assn. Petroleum Geologists, Soc. Exploration Geophysicists, Geophys. Soc. Houston, Soc. Internat. Devel., N.Am. Congress on Latin Am., Amnesty Internat., Internat. Platform Assn., Ctr. for Study of Dem. Instns., Asia Soc., World Expeditionary Assn., Soc. Profl. Journalists-Sigma Delta Chi, Houston Press Club. Clubs: Houston Press. Home: 8310 Braesdale Ln Houston TX 77071-1228 Office: PO Box 710046 Houston TX 77071-1030

GEORGE, DONALD WARNER, online columnist and editor, freelance writer; b. Middlebury, Conn., June 24, 1953; s. Lloyd Foster and Vivian (Minor) G.; m. Kuniko Ninomiya, Apr. 24, 1982; children: Jennifer Ayako, Jeremy Naoki. BA, Princeton U., 1975; MA, Hollins (Va.) Coll., 1977. Tchg. fellow Athens (Greece) Coll., 1975-76, Internat. Christian U., Tokyo, 1977-79; TV talk show host Japan Broadcasting Corp., Tokyo, 1977-79; freelance writer, 1980-81; travel writer San Francisco Examiner, 1981-82, sr. editor Calif. Living mag., 1982-85, sr. editor Image mag., 1985-87, travel editor, 1987-95; cyber columnist, Global Network Navigator American Online, Berkeley, Calif., 1995-96; editor Salon Wanderlust Online Travel Mag., 1997-2000; global travel editor Lonely Planet Publs., 2001—. Editor: Wanderlust: Real-Life Tales of Adventure and Romance, 2000, A House Somewhere: Tales of Life Abroad, 2002, The Kindness of Strangers, 2003 (Best Travel Book of 2003, Ind. Publishers Assn., Bronze Medal in best travel book competition, Soc. Am.Travel Writers, 2003), By the Seat of My Pants: Humorous Tales of Travel & Misadventure, 2005; co-author (with Amy Greimann Carlson): Travelers' Tales: Japan, 2005. Recipient gold award Pacific Asia Travel Assn., 1987-94, 2001. Mem. Soc. Am. Travel Writers (Lowell Thomas award 1987-94, 2002). Office: Lonely Planet 150 Linden St Oakland CA 94607 E-mail: dgeorge@lonelyplanet.com.*

GEORGE, EDDIE (EDWARD NATHAN GEORGE), professional football player; b. Sept. 24, 1973; 1 child. BS in Landscape Architexture, Ohio State Univ. Running back Tenn. Oilers (now called Tenn. Titans), 1996—2004, Dallas Cowboys, 2004—. Founder Visions With Infinite Possibilities, 2000. Named NFL Rookie of Yr., 1996, NFL Pro Bowl, 1997—2000; recipient Heisman Trophy. Office: c/o Dallas Cowboys 1 Cowboys Pwky Irving TX 75063

GEORGE, ELIZABETH (SUSAN ELIZABETH GEORGE), writer; b. Warren, Ohio, 1949; Student, Foothill Cmty. Coll.; graduate, Univ. Calif., Riverside; M in counseling, psychology, Univ. Calif., Fullerton. English tchr. Mater Dei H.S., Santa Ana, Calif., 1974-75, El Toro (Calif.) H.S., 1975-87; creative writing tchr. Coastline Coll., Costa Mesa, Calif., 1988—, Irvine (Calif.) Coll., 1989, U. Calif., Irvine, 1990. Author: A Great Deliverance, 1989 (Anthony award, Agatha award, 1989, Le Grand Prix de Litterature Policiere, 1990), Payment in Blood, 1989, Well Schooled in Murder, 1990 (MIMI award, Germany), A Suitable Vengeance, 1991, For the Sake of Elena, 1992, Missing Joseph, 1993, Playing for the Ashes, 1994, In the Presence of the Enemy, 1996, Deception on His Mind, 1997, In Pursuit of the Proper Sinner, 1999, A Traitor to Memory, 2001, Remember, I'll Always Love You, 2001, I, Richard, 2002, A Place of Hiding, 2003, Write Away, 2004, A Moment on the Edge, 2004, With No One as Witness, 2005 (Publishers Weekly bestseller list). Named Orange County Tchr. of Yr. Mailing: c/o Trident Media fl 36 41 Madison Ave New York NY 10010*

GEORGE, EMERY EDWARD, foreign language and studies educator, writer; b. Budapest, Hungary, May 8, 1933; came to U.S., 1946, naturalized, 1954; AB, U. Mich., 1955, MA, 1959; postgrad., Fed. Rep. Germany, 1961-62; PhD, U. Mich., 1964. Instr. U. Ill., Champaign-Urbana, 1964-65, asst. prof. German, 1965-66, U. Mich., Ann Arbor, 1966-69, assoc. prof., 1969-75, prof., 1975-88, prof. emeritus, 1988—, faculty program in comparative lit., 1969—, faculty program Center for Russian and East European Studies, 1975—. Author: Hölderlin's Ars Poetica, 1973, Mountainwild: Poems, 1974, Black Jesus, 1974, A Gift of Nerve: Poems, 1966-77, 1978, Kate's Death, 1980, The Poetry of Miklós Radnóti: A Comparative Study, 1986, The Boy and the Monarch, 1987, Voiceprints, 1987; (essay) The Allegory of Spandau, 1990 (Kenyon Rev. 2d ann. nonfiction award 1991), Hölderlin and the Golden Chain of Homer, 1992, Blackbird: Poems on the World and Work of Franz Kafka, 1993, Valse Triste: Songs and Ballads, 1997, Hölderlin's Hymn Der Einzige, 1999, Compass Card: One Hundred Villanelles, 2000, Iphigenie in Manhattan: A Play in Five Acts, 2001, Iphigenie in Czestochowa: A Play in Five Acts, 2001, Orest: A Play in Five Acts, 2001, Iphigenie in Auschwitz: A Play in Five Acts, 2001; editor: Friedrich Hölderlin: An Early Modern, 1972, (with L.T. Frank) Husbanding the Golden Grain, 1973, Contemporary East European Poetry: An Anthology, 1983, expanded, 1993, (with D. E. Sattler) Friedrich Hölderlin, Homburger Folioheft (Frankfurter Hölderlin-Ausgabe, Supplement III), 1986, 93; also transls.; contbr. poetry, non-fiction prose, transls., articles, revs. to scholarly jours., lit. publs.; founding editor Mich. Germanic Studies; assoc. editor Russian Lit. Triquar.; mem. editl. bd. advisors Germano-Slavica, 1973-77; editl. bd. Mich. Monographs in the Humanities, 1979—, (yearbook) Cross Currents, 1986—. Served with M.I. U.S. Army, 1957-58. Recipient Avery and Jule Hopwood award in poetry U. Mich., 1960; Ottendorfer Meml. fellow, 1961; Am. Council Learned Socs. Publs. award, 1964; Rackham Publ. award U. Mich., 1973, 80; Hungarian PEN Research and Travel grant, 1979; IREX Exchange fellow to Hungary, 1981, Deutsche Forschungsgemeinschaft research and travel grantee, 1986. Fellow: Internat. Acad. Poets; mem.: MLA, Assn. Literary Scholars and Critics, Hungarian Writers Assn., Hungarian Acad. Scis., Shelley Soc. NY, Poetry Soc. Am., Hölderlin-Gesellschaft. Home: 16 Buckingham Ave Trenton NJ 08618-3312 Office Phone: 609-984-8375. E-mail: eegeorge@hotmail.com. *Listen carefully to language, to words;.try to write each day. Make no separation between writing and scholarship, between old and new literature. Monitor the eternal present. Try to achieve newness, a sense of experiment from within.*

GEORGE, FRANCIS EUGENE CARDINAL, cardinal; b. Chgo., Jan. 16, 1937; Ordained priest Roman Cath. Ch., 1963. Provincial ctrl. region Oblates of Mary Immaculate, 1973—74, vicar gen., 1974—86; bishop Diocese of Yakima, Wash., 1990—96; archbishop Archdiocese of Portland, Oreg., 1996—97, Archdiocese of Chgo., 1997—98, cardinal, 1998—. Chancellor Cath. Ch. Ext. U. St. Mary of Lake, 1997; mem. Congregation Divine Worship, Discipline of Sacraments, Congregation for Oriental Chs., 2001—, Congregation Insts., Consecrated Life, Socs. Apostolic Life, Pontifical Commn. for Cultural Heritage of Ch., 1999—, Pontifical Coun. Cor Unum, 1998, Congregation Evangelization of Peoples, Pontifical Coun. for Culture, 2004—; v.p. US Conf. Cath. Bishops, 2004—. Mem.: Coll. Cardinals. Roman Catholic. Office: Archdiocese of Chgo Pastoral Ctr PO Box 1979 Chicago IL 60690-1979 Office Phone: 312-751-8230.

GEORGE, FRANK WADE, small business owner, antiquarian book dealer; b. Austin, Tex., Aug. 22, 1918; s. Frank Wade and Rosa Scott (Slaughter) W.; m. Marjorie Ann Miller, Dec. 27, 1948 (div. Jan. 1955); children; Frank Wade III, Gregory Scott, Barbara Lee; m. Martha Jeanne Wagner, Feb. 8, 1964 (dec. 1996); m. Wenona Thoma, 1996. Student, Tex. Sch. Fine Arts, 1936-41, Mexico City Coll., 1947; BJ, U. Tex., 1948. Office mgr. Tex. Sch. Fine Arts, 1936-41; mgr. Austin Symphony Orch., 1946-48, Erie (Pa.) Philharmonic Orch., 1948-49, Birmingham (Ala.) Symphony Orch., 1949-50, Ala. Pops Orch., Birmingham, 1955-62, Town and Gown Theatre, Birmingham, 1962-65; pres. Birmingham Opera Co., 1973-75; owner Books! By George, Birmingham, 1981—. Co-founder Margo George Fashion Prodns., 1951, Hanna Antiques, 1981; participant Antiquarian Book Seminar, U. Denver, 1986. Pres. Rockwood Plantation Condominium Assn., 2001—; treas. Greater Birmingham Arts Alliance, 1971—75, Birmingham Opera Guild, 1971—74, So. Regional Opera, 1981—84; trustee Birmingham Symphony Assn., 1973—75; chmn. artist hospitality Arts Hall of Fame, Birmingham, 1974; judge nat. coun. auditions Met. Opera Assn., 1981; docent Birmingham Mus. Art, 1980—82. With USAF, 1941—45. Mem. Gideons Internat. (pres. 1980-83), Allegro Mus. Club (v.p. 1993-94), Ala. Symphonic Assn. (dir. speakers bur. 1995), Rockwood Plantation Condominium Assn. (pres. 2001—). Avocations: lay preaching, public speaking, reading, writing, travel. Home: 1851 Rockwood Rd Birmingham AL 35216-1425 Office: Books! By George 2424 7th Ave S Birmingham AL 35233-3318 Office Phone: 205-323-6036. Business E-Mail: booksbygeorge@aol.com.

GEORGE, GAY, lawyer; b. Hollywood, Calif., Mar. 3, 1955; d. Wallace Erby and Audrey Eva Elizabeth George. BS, Calif. Poly. U., 1977; MBA, U. Wyo., 1993, JD, 2001. Bar: Wyo. 2001. Peace Corps vol. U.S. Govt., Apia, Western Samoa, 1979—80; quality assurance mgr. Arnott's Biscuits, Auckland, New Zealand, 1981—88; R&D mgr. ETA Foods, Ltd., Auckland, 1988—99; tech. writer G&G Enterprises, Laramie, Wyo., 1991—98; law clk. to Hon. Barton R. Voigt Wyo. Supreme Ct., Cheyenne, 2001—03; corp. counsel Blue Cross Blue Shield Wyo., Cheyenne, 2003—. Contbr. chapters to books. Avocations: reading, films, theater, camping, backpacking. Office Phone: 307-432-2914. Business E-Mail: ggeorge@bcbswy.com.

GEORGE, GERALD WILLIAM, writer; b. Caldwell, Kans., Aug. 4, 1938; s. Chester Dale and Mildred M. (Jolitz) G.; m. Patricia Rae Woolsey, Sept. 23, 1961 (div. 1989); children: Brian William, Roxane Elizabeth; m. Carol Maryan Bell, Sept. 18, 1993. BA, U. Wichita, 1960; MA, Yale U., 1962. Instr. Bethany Coll., Lindsborg, Kans., 1962; reporter Salina (Kans.) Jour., 1962-64; staff writer The Nat. Observer, Washington, 1964-67; editl. assoc. Woodrow Wilson Nat. Fellowship Found., Princeton, NJ, 1967-68; spl. asst. to chmn. NEH, Washington, 1969-70; free-lance writer Washington, Netherlands, 1971-73; mng. editor book series Am. Assn. State and Local History, Nashville, 1973-78, dir., 1978-87, mem. steering com. endowment campaign, 1999—2001; free-lance writer, cons. to hist. orgns. Arlington, Va., 1987-90; exec. dir. Nat. Hist. Publs. and Records Commn., 1990-94; program devel. officer Coun. on Libr. Resources, Washington, 1995; exec. dir. Nat. Hist. Publs. and Records Commn., Washington, 1995-97; dir. commns. Nat. Archives and Records Adminstrn., College Park, Md., 1997-2000; spl. projects assoc. Coun. on Libr. and Info. Resources, Washington, 2000—03, ret., 2003. Author: Visiting History, Arguments Over Museums and Historic Sites, 1990, Imitations of Indonesia and Other Poems, 1997; co-author: Starting Right: A Basic Guide to Museum Planning, 1986, rev. edit., 2004; mng. editor: The States and the Nation; mem. editl. bd.: Ency. of the Am. West; contbr. articles to profl. jours. and mags. Woodrow Wilson fellow, 1960-61. Mem. Am. Assn. State and Local History, Nat. Trust Hist. Preservation, Soc. Am. Archivists, Kans. State Hist. Soc., Hist. Soc. Machias, Maine. E-mail: maryangeorge@msn.com.

GEORGE, JAMES EDWARD, accountant; b. Mt. George, Ark., May 22, 1943; s. Opal W. Sr. and Mildred M. G.; m. Corliss Ann, Sept. 3, 1965; children: J. Mark, Ty C., Ryan E. BA in Acctg., U. Ark., Little Rock, 1967; MS in Logistics, Air Force Inst. Tech., 1979; grad., Air Command and Staff Coll. of USAF, 1987, USAF Air War Coll., 1992. CPA, Ark. Commd. 2d lt. USAF, 1967, advanced through grades to capt.; commdr. Field Tng. Detachment, Mt. Clemens, Mich., Kadena AFB, Japan and Kunsan AFB, Korea, 1967-73; supr. maintenance Field Maintenance Squadron, Craig AFB, Ala., 1973-75; flightline br. chief Royal AFB, Bentwater, Eng., 1976-77; officer in charge quality control Tactical Fighter Wing, Royal AFB, Bentwater, 1977-78; left active duty USAFR, 1978, advanced through grades to lt. col., 1988, ret., 1994; pub. utility auditor Ark. Pub. Svc. Commn., Little Rock, 1979-98; exec. dir. Ark. State Bd. Pub. Accountancy, Little Rock, 1998—2003. Lectr. pub. utility income taxes and depreciation ea. utility rate Nat. Assn. Regulatory Utility Commrs., 1984—85; adj. faculty U. Ark., Ark., 1997—2003, Webster U., 1998—; acctg. adv. coun. U. Ark., Little Rock, 2002—. Bd. dirs. Brockington Rd. Ch. of the Nazarene, 1989—94, 1998—2002, 2004—05. Mem. AICPA (infol retrieval com. 1987-90), Ark. Soc. CPAs (pres. Ctrl. Ark. chpt. 1992-93, 95-96, chmn. membership com. 1991-93, bd. dirs. 1994-97, exec. com. 1996-97, chmn. public rels. com. 1997-2003, pub. rels. com. 2004—, Outstanding Ark. CPA in Industry and Bus. award 1995), Toastmasters (pres. Uptown chpt. 1985, Able Toastmaster award 1988), Officers Club (bd. dirs. Kadena AFB, Okinawa, 1971-72) Home: 720 Mill Creek Rd Higden AR 72067

GEORGE, JEAN CRAIGHEAD, author, illustrator; b. Washington, July 2, 1919; d. Frank Cooper and Carolyn (Johnson) Craighead; m. John L. George, Jan. 28, 1944 (div. Jan. 1964); children: Twig George Pittenger, John Craighead, Thomas Lothar. BA, Pa. State U., 1941. Reporter Washington Post, 1943-44; artist Pageant mag., 1945; reporter United Features, 1945-46; roving editor Reader's Digest, 1966-80; continuing edn. tchr. Chappaqua, N.Y., 1960-68. Author, illustrator: My Side of the Mountain, 1959, Summer of the Falcon, 1962, Gull Number 737, 1964, The Thirteen Moons, 1967-69, Coyote in Manhattan, 1968, River Rats, Inc., 1968, Who Really Killed Cock Robin, 1972, Julie of the Wolves, 1972, American Walk Book, 1978, Cry of the Crow, 1980, Journey Inward, 1982, The Talking Earth, 1983, One Day in the Alpine Tundra, 1984, How to Talk to Your Animals, 1985, One Day in the Prairie, 1986, Water Sky, 1987, (mus.) One Day in the Woods, 1988, The Shark Beneath the Reef, 1989, On the Far Side of the Mountain, 1990, One Day in the Tropical Rain Forest, 1990, The Missing 'Gator of Gumbo Limbo, 1992, The Fire Bug Connection, 1993, The First Thanksgiving, 1993, Dear Rebecca, Winter Is Here, 1993, Animals Who Have Won Our Hearts, 1994, Julie, 1994, To Climb a Waterfall, 1995, Acorn Pancakes & Dandelion Salad, 1995, There's an Owl in the Shower, 1995, Everglades, 1995, The Case of the Missing Cutthroat Trout, 1996, The Tarantula in My Purse, 1996, Look to the North, A Wolf Pup Diary, 1997, Julie's Wolf Pack, 1997, Arctic Son, 1997, Rhino Romp, 1998, Giraffe Trouble, 1998, Dear Katie, the Volcano Is a Girl, 1998, Survival Filmstrips, 1984, (film) My Side of the Mountain, 1965, Nature Filmstrips, 1978-80, One Day in the Woods Musical for Children (music by Chris Kubie), 1997, Elephant Walk, 1998, Gorilla Gang, 1999, Morning, Noon and Night, 1999, Frightful's Mountain, 1999, Snow Bear, 1999, How to Talk to Your Dog, 2000, How to Talk to Your Cat, 2000, Nutik, the Wolf Pup, 2001, Nutik & Amaoq Play Ball, 2001, Tree Castle Island, 2002, Cliff Hanger, 2002, Frightful's Daughter, 2002, Fire Storm, 2003, Charlie's Raven, 2004, Snowboard Twist, 2004, (musical) Julie of the Wolves, 2004, Luck, 2005. Recipient Aurianne award, 1957, Newbery Honor Book award, 1961, medal, 1973, Hans Christian Andersen Honor List award, 1964, Pa. State Woman of Yr. award, 1968, World Book award, 1971, Kerlan award, 1982, U. So. Miss. award, 1986, Washington Irving award, 1991, 92, Knickerbocker award, 1991, Washington Post Children's Book Guild award, 1998, Empire State award, 1998, runner-up Lamplighter award, 2002, Regina medal Cath. Libr. Assn., Literary Lights award for children's lifetime work Boston Pub. Libr., 2003, Ludington award Am. Paperback Assn., 2004, Lamplighter Hon. Book, 2005. Address: 20 William Pl Chappaqua NY 10514-3114 E-mail: jeangeorgemail@aol.com.

GEORGE, JOEY RUSSELL, lawyer; b. Bklyn., Oct. 8, 1963; s. Jonas and Celeste Dorothy (Russell) G. BA, Howard U., 1985; JD, Harvard U., 1988. Bar: N.Y. 1989, Conn. 1989, U.S. Dist. Ct. (so. and ea. dists.) N.Y. 1989, U.S. Supreme Ct. 1992. Asst. prosecutor Queens County Dist. Atty., Kew Gardens, N.Y., 1988-90; asst. gen. counsel Exec. Office of the Pres., Office Mgmt. and Budget, Washington, 1990-91; assoc. dir. for policy The White House, Washington, 1991-93; pvt. practice, 1993—94; chief staff, chief counsel com. govt. reform subcom. on govt. efficiency, fin. mgmt. and intergovtl. rels. U.S. Ho. Reps., Washington, 1995—2002; inspector gen. US Corp. for Nat. and

Cmty. Svc., Washington, 2002—04; inspector gen. for tax adminstrn. US Dept. Treasury, Washington, 2004—. Trustee Howard U., Washington, 1984-85; big brother Big Bros. Am. Cambridge, Mass., 1986-96; bd. advisers City Harvest, 1993-95. Mem. ABA (vice chmn. govt. ops. com., adminstrv. law sect. 1997-99), Ripon Soc. (pres. Harvard chpt. 1986-87, nat. v.p. 1987-88, bd. dirs. ednl. fund 1989-97, pres. ednl. fund 1993-97), Harvard Club, Univ. Club, Rotary Club of Washington D.C., Phi Beta Kappa, Pi Sigma Alpha, Phi Alpha Theta. Republican. Episcopalian.

GEORGE, JOHN ANTHONY, health corporation executive; b. New Kensington, Pa., July 11, 1948; s. Moses and Veronica (Raymond) G.; m. Leah Diane Vota, Oct. 30, 1971 (div. 1992); children: Jessica, Cara, John, Ethan; m. Carolyn D. Dozier, Sept. 22, 2000. BS, Duquesne U., Pitts., 1970; MBA, U. Pitts., 1973; MS in Taxation, Robert Morris Coll., Pitts. CFP. Asst. adminstr. mental health and mental retardation program Western Psychiat. Inst. and Clinic, Pitts., 1971-72; adminstrv. dir. Latrobe (Pa.) Area Hosp., 1973-76; asst. dir. Presbyn. U. Hosp., Pitts., 1976-80; owner, prin. George-Anstey Food Distributing Corp., Pitts., 1978-81; mgmt. cons. Arthur Young & Co., Pitts., 1980-82; exec. dir. Ea. Allegheny County Health Corp., 1982-85; pres. Alpha Health Network, 1985-88; pres., bd. dirs. Intergroup Svc. Corp., 1988—; mng. ptnr. Med. Benefit Svc., 1991—. Bd. mgrs. Health Coalition Ptnrs.; lectr. in field. Contbr. articles to profl. jours. Mem. Am. Coll. Health Care Execs., Am. Assn. Prepared Provider Orgns. Roman Catholic. Home: 5121 Ellsworth Ave Pittsburgh PA 15232-1419 Office: 401 Shady Ave Suite A207 Pittsburgh PA 15206-4450 Business E-Mail: jgeorge@igs-ppo.com.

GEORGE, JOHN MARTIN, JR., lawyer; b. Normal, Ill., Dec. 17, 1947; s. John and Ada George; m. Judy Ann Watts; children: Sarah, Michael. AB with high honors, U. Ill., 1970, AM, 1971; PhD, Columbia U., 1976; JD cum laude, Harvard U., 1982. Bar: Mass. 1982, U.S. Dist. Ct. Mass. 1983, Ill. 1984, U.S. Dist. Ct. (no. dist.) Ill. 1984, U.S. Ct. Appeals (11th cir.) 1987, U.S. Ct. Appeals (9th cir.) 1988, U.S. Ct. Appeals (7th cir.) 1992, U.S. Ct. Appeals (3d cir.) 2000, U.S. Ct. Appeals (6th cir.) 2005. Assoc. Hill & Barlow, Boston, 1982-84, Sidley & Austin (now Sidley, Austin, Brown & Wood), Chgo., 1984-89; ptnr. Sidley, Austin, Brown & Wood LLP (formerly Sidley & Austin), Chgo., 1989—. Mem. Leading Lawyers Network, 2004. Editor Harvard U. Law Rev., 1980-82. Sr. warden Trinity Ch., 1998-2000. Named to Hall of Fame, Unity H.S., 2005. Mem. ABA, Chgo. Bar Assn., Mid-Day Club, Phi Beta Kappa. Democrat. Episcopalian. Office: Sidley Austin Brown & Wood LLP Bank One Plz Chicago IL 60603-2003 Office Phone: 312-853-7550. E-mail: jgeorge@sidley.com.

GEORGE, JULIANNE MARY, music educator, conductor; b. Martinez, Calif., July 16, 1964; d. Robert Joseph and Marjorie C. George. BA, U. of the Pacific, Stockton, Calif., 1987. Tchr. instrumental music Sequoia Mid. Sch., Pleasant Hill, Calif., 1993—, chair dept., 2001—. Mem.: NEA, Calif. Tchrs. Assn., Music Educators Nat. Conf., Am. String Tchrs. Assn., Nat. Assn. String Educators, Internat. Assn. Jazz Educators, Calif. Music Educators Assn. Avocations: gardening, birdwatching. Home: 1025 Merrithew Drive Martinez CA 94553 Office: Sequoia Middle School 265 Boyd Road Pleasant Hill CA 94523 Office Phone: 925-934-8174. Office Fax: (925) 946-9063.

GEORGE, KATHERINE ELIZABETH, artist, educator; b. Palmerton, Pa., Nov. 16, 1970; d. Ralph William Jr. and Louise Marie Hill; m. Matthew Lee George, June 24, 1995; children: Megan Margaret, Abigail Elizabeth. BS in Edn., Kutztown U., 1992; MS in Edn., Millersville U., 1998. Cert. instnl. level II tchr. Pa. Secondary sch. art tchr. Annville (Pa.) -Cleona Sch. Dist., 1993—, theatrical set designer/painter, 2004—. Mem.: Pa. State Edn. Assn., Lebanon County Edn. Honor Soc. Independent. Evangelical Free Church. Avocations: writing, camping, drawing, painting, volleyball. Office: Annville-Cleona Sch Dist 500 South White Oak St Annville PA 17003 Office Phone: 717-867-7700. E-mail: kgeorge@acschools.org.

GEORGE, LILA GENE PLOWE KENNEDY, music educator; b. Sioux City, Iowa, Sept. 25, 1918; d. Eugene Preston Plowe and Lila Mazo Pickel; m. Richard Painter George; children: Eugenia, Richard Jr. BA in English and French, U. Okla., 1939, MusB in Theory, 1940; postgrad., Northwestern U., 1950, Columbia U., 1963—65; pvt. piano study with Egon Petri, Silvio Scionti & Edward Steuermann; pvt. composition study with Nadia Boulanger, Fontainebleau, France, 1971—78. Pvt. piano tchr., Oklahoma City, 1938—42, Talara, Peru, 1947—54, Houston, 1954—60, 1970—, Pelham Manor, NY, 1960—65. Soloist Oklahoma City Little Symphony, 1939, Houston Symphony, 1957; judge piano competitions Nat. Guild Piano Tchrs., Tex. State Music Tchrs. Recipient Houston Alumnae Music Leadership award, Sigma Alpha Iota, 2005. Mem.: Houston Tuesday Musical Club (pres. 1960), European Piano Tchrs. Assn., Am. Music Ctr. (composer), Sigma Alpha Iota (Music Leadership award Houston (Tex.) Alumnus chpt. 2005). Republican. Episcopalian. Avocation: genealogy. Home: 701 N Rusk Wharton TX 77488

GEORGE, MARY WIEDENBECK, reference librarian, educator; b. Ann Arbor, Mich., Jan. 23, 1948; d. Marcellus L. and Jane Kathryn (Young) Wiedenbeck; m. Emery Edward George, May 9, 1969. AB, U. Mich., 1969, AMLS, 1970, AM, 1975. Reference libr. U. Mich., Ann Arbor, 1970—80; head gen. and humanities reference divsn. Princeton U. Libr., NJ, 1980—2000, user edn. coord., 2000—01; interim dir. slide and photograph collections dept. art and archeology Princeton U., 2001—02, acting interlibr. svcs., libr., 2002, libr. instrn. coord., sr. rschr., 2002—05, sr. reference libr., 2005—. Adj. asst. prof. Coll. Info. Sci. and Tech. Drexel U., Phila., 1982-92, 96-2002; adv. bd. Bibliography Revision project MLA, NYC, 1978-80; mem. adv. bd. New Dictionary of the History of Ideas, 2003-04l lectr. dept. libr. and info. sci. Rutgers U., 2001-02; lectr. writing program Princeton U., 2002; speaker in field. Co-author: Learning the Library, 1982; co-editor Rsch. Strategies, 1983-90; contbr. chpt. to book. Recipient Hopwood award in writing U. Mich., 1969, Disting. Alumna award, 1987. Mem. ALA (Shera award for rsch. 1989). Office: Firestone Libr Princeton U One Washington Rd Princeton NJ 08544 Office Phone: 609-258-3254. Business E-Mail: mwgeorge@princeton.edu.

GEORGE, MELVIN DOUGLAS, retired university president; b. Washington, Feb. 13, 1936; s. Douglas Elmer and Catherine Evelyn (McNelly) G.; m. Meta Jane Barghusen, Aug. 17, 1958; children— Elizabeth Anne, Margaret Susan BA, Northwestern U., 1956; PhD, Princeton U., 1959. From asst. to assoc. prof. math. U. Mo., Columbia, 1960-67, prof., assoc. dean, 1967-70, v.p. acad. affairs, 1975-85; dean Coll. Arts and Scis. U. Nebr., Lincoln, 1970-75; pres. St. Olaf Coll., Northfield, Minn., 1985-94, pres. emeritus, 1994—; v.p. instnl. rels. U. Minn., Mpls., 1994-96; prof. math. emeritus U. Mo., Columbia, 1996—, interim pres., 1996-97, pres. emeritus, 1997—. Contbr. articles to profl. jours. Recipient Robert W. Martin award for Acad. Freedom, Mo. conf. AAUP, 1985 Mem. Am. Math. Soc., Math. Assn. Am. Lutheran. Avocations: music, swimming. Home: 1509 W Rollins Rd Columbia MO 65203-2378

GEORGE, NELSON, writer, film producer; b. Bklyn., 1957; BA, St. John's Univ. Reporter Amsterdam News, NYC, Billboard Mag., 1982—89; columnist, "Native Son" Village Voice, 1988—92. Author: (non-fiction) Where Did Our Love Go: The Rise and Fall of the Motown Sound, 1986, The Death of Rhythm & Blues, 1988, Elevating the Game: Black Men in Basketball, 1993, Buppies, B-Boys, Baps & Bohos: Notes on Post-Soul Black Culture, 1993, Blackface: African Americans in the Movies, 1994, Hip Hop America, 1998 (Am. Book award), (novels) Urban Romance, 1995, Seduced: Life & Times of a One Hit Wonder, 1996, One Woman Short, 2001, Show & Tell, 2001, Night Work, 2003, The Accidental Hunter, 2005; exec. prodr.: (films) Def by Temptation, 1990; assoc. prodr.: Just Another Girl on the IRT, 1992; assoc. prodr., writer: (films) Strictly Business, 1991; prodr.: CB4, 1993; supervising prodr. (TV series) The Chris Rock Show, 1997; exec. prodr.: (films) Everyday People, 2004; consulting prodr.: (TV films) Hip-Hop Honors, 2004; prodr.: (documentaries) The N Word, 2004 (co-recipient, Peabody award, 2005); exec. prodr.(and writer): A Great Day in Hip Hop, (short films) To Be A Black Man. Mailing: c/o Author Mail Simon & Schuster/Touchstone 1230 Ave Americas New York NY 10020*

GEORGE, NICHOLAS, lawyer, entrepreneur; b. Seattle, July 11, 1952; s. Harry and Mary (Courounes) G.; children: Harry Nicholas, James Michael. BA in Polit. Sci. cum laude, Whitman Coll., 1974; MBA in Mktg. and Corp. Planning, U. Chgo., 1979; JD, U. Puget Sound, 1989. Bar: Wash. 1991, U.S. Dist. Ct. (we. dist.) Wash. 1991, U.S. Ct. Appeals (9th cir.) 1991, U.S. Tax Ct. 1992, U.S. Dist. Ct. (ea. dist.) Wash. 1994, U.S. Supreme Ct. 1994. Fin. cons. Pacific Western Investment Co., Lynnwood, Wash., 1975-77; planning dir. Clinton Capital Ventures, Seattle, 1979-81; corp. planning mgr. Tacoma Boatbldg., 1981-83; pres. MegaProf Investors, Bellevue, Wash., 1983-89; practice trial-settlement law bus., Seattle, 1989—. Free-lance coll. counselor, Seattle, 1980—. Author: Legitimacy in Government: Ideal, Goal, or Myth? 1974. Bd. auditor St. Demetrios Greek Orthodox Ch., Seattle, 1982-83; bd. dirs. Hellenic Golfers Assn., Seattle, 1981-83. Mem. ABA, Assn. Trial Lawyers Am., Wash. State Bar Assn., Wash. Assn. Criminal Def. Lawyers, Wash. State Trial Lawyers Assn., Fed. Bar Assn., Nat. Assn. Criminal Def. Lawyers, Tacoma-Pierce County Bar Assn., Seattle-King County Bar Assn., Wash. Defender Assn., Wash. State Hist. Soc., Am. Inst. Archeol., Phi Alpha Delta. Greek Orthodox. Avocations: weightlifting, travel, family history, football coaching, writing. Home: 5007 80th St SW Lakewood WA 98499-4077 Office: 1919 N Pearl St Ste A2 Tacoma WA 98406 Office Phone: 253-272-7181. Business E-Mail: ngeorge@legalpaladin.com.

GEORGE, PATRICK JOSEPH, entertainment company executive; b. Worcester, Mass., Aug. 30, 1951; s. Joseph Patrick and Lucy Joanne (Zarette) G.; m. Laurie Anne Griggs, 1995; children: Kristen Lee, Sherilyn Ann. Student, U. Dijon, France, 1968; student, Worcester State Coll., 1969-71. Account exec. Recorder Group Pubs., Worcester, 1969-73; founder, owner, pub. Night Life mag., Worcester, 1973-74; pres., owner The Entertainment Agy., Spencer, Mass., 1968—, Innovative Artists Mgmt., Spencer, 1977-83. Named Outstanding Young Man of Am. U.S. Jaycees, 1979, 80, 81. Mem. Spencer Exchange Club (pres. 1983-84, 90-91, 2002-03). Office: The Entertainment Agy 172 Main St Spencer MA 01562-2117

GEORGE, PAUL M., law librarian, library director; b. 1952; AB magna cum laude, with high distinction in History, U. Ill., Urbana-Champaign, 1974; JD, Duke U., 1977; MLS, U. Ill., Urbana-Champaign, 1985. Bar: Ill. 1977. Atty. Land of Lincoln Legal Assistance Found., Champaign, Ill., 1977—84; reference libr. U. Southern Calif. Law Libr., 1985—88, head, pub. services, 1988—91, asst. dir., pub. services, 1991—94; assoc. libr., rsch. services Harvard U. Law Sch. Libr., 1994—2002, acting libr., 1999—2000; dir. Biddle Law Libr. and adj. law prof. U. Pa. Law Sch., Phila., 2002—. Mem.: So. Calif. Assn. Law Libraries (pres. 1994), Ill. State Bar, Am. Assn. Law Libraries, Phi Kappa Phi, Phi Beta Kappa. Office: U Pa Law Sch Biddle Law Libr 3400 Chestnut St Rm T-209 Philadelphia PA 19104-3406 Office Phone: 215-898-7488. Office Fax: 215-898-6619. Business E-Mail: pmgeorge@law.upenn.edu.*

GEORGE, PETER JAMES, economist, educator; b. Toronto, Sept. 12, 1941; s. Ralph Langlois and Kathleen May (Larder) G.; m. Gwendolyn Jean Scharf, Oct. 19, 1962 (dec. Mar. 1997); children— Michael James, Katherine Jane; m. Allison Mary Barrett, July 31, 1998. BA with honors, U. Toronto, 1962, MA, 1963, PhD, 1967; DU (hon.), U. Ottawa, 1995; D Hon. C. (hon.), Lviv Nat. Poly U., 2001; DLitt (hon.), Nipissing U., 2002. Lectr. McMaster U., 1965-67, asst. prof., 1967-71, assoc. prof., 1971-80, prof. econs., 1980—, assoc. dean grad. studies, 1974-79, dean social scis., 1980-89, pres., vice chancellor, 1995—; spl. lectr. U. Toronto, 1967; vis. lectr. U. Cambridge, 1974; economist Govt. of Ont., 1963; project mgr. Tanzania Tourist Corp., 1970-71; pres. Coun. Ont. Univs., Toronto, 1991-95; hon. prof. Beijing U. Sci. and Tech., 1998. Author: Government Subsidies and the Construction of the Canadian Pacific Railway, 1981, The Emergence of Industrial America: Strategic Factors in American Economic Growth Since 1870, 1982; Appointed to Ont. Coun. on Univ. Affairs, 1987-91. Decorated Order of Can., 1999; recipient Commemorative medal 125th Anniversary Confedn. of Can., 1993; recipient The Queen's Golden Jubilee medal, 2002. Mem. Can. Econs. Assn., Can. Hist. Assn., Am. Econ. Assn., Econ. History Assn., Econ. History Soc. Office: McMaster U Office Pres GH-238 1280 Main St W Hamilton ON Canada L8S 4L8 Office Phone: 905-525-9140 ext. 24340. Business E-Mail: presdnt@mcmaster.ca, pgeorge@mcmaster.ca.

GEORGE, PETER T., orthodontist, consultant; b. Akron, Ohio, 1929; s. Tony and Paraskeva (Ogrenova) G.; children: Barton Herrin, Tryan Franklin. BS, Kent State U., 1952; DDS, Ohio State U., 1956; Cert. in Orthodontics, Columbia U., 1962. Diplomate Am. Bd. Orthodontics. Pvt. practice orthodontics, Honolulu, 1962—2000; inventor, writer self-employed, 2003—. Cleft palate cons. Hawaii Bur. Crippled Children, 1963-90; asst. prof. Med. Sci. Editor Hawaii State Dental Jour., 1965-67. Mem. Hawaii Gov.'s Phys. Fitness Com., 1962-68; mem. Honolulu Mayor's Health Coun., 1967-72; mem. med. com. Internat. Weightlifting Fedn., 1980-84; chmn. bd. govs. Hall of Fame of Hawaii, 1984; bd. dirs. Honolulu Opera Theatre, 1986-91; chmn. bd. Hawaii Internat. Sports Found., 1988-91; U.S. Weightlifting coach, USSR, 1979, asst. coach Olympic Weightlifting team, 1980. Served to Capt. Dental Corps, U.S. Army, 1956-60, Silver medallist weightlifting, London, 1948; Olympic Gold medalist in weightlifting, Helsinki, 1952, Melbourne, 1956; six times world champion; recipient Disting. Service award Hawaiian AAU, 1968; Gold medal Internat. Weightlifting Fedn., 1976; named to Helms Hall of Fame, 1966; named to 100 Gold Olympians, 1996. Fellow Am. Coll. Dentistry, Internat. Coll. Dentistry; mem. Hawaii Amateur Athletic Union (pres. 1964-65), U.S. Olympians (pres. Hawaii chpt. 1963-67, 80-2000), Am. Assn. Orthodontists, Honolulu Dental Soc. (pres. 1967-68), Hawaii Dentists Assn. (pres. 1976), Hawaii Soc. Orthodontists (pres. 1972). Achievements include invention of first dental appliance to prevent sleep apnea; jetlogger, an anti jet lag instrument. Home and Office: 1649 Kalakaua Ave Ste 204 Honolulu HI 96826-2494 E-mail: pt.george@verizon.net.

GEORGE, RONALD M., state supreme court chief justice; b. L.A., Mar. 11, 1940; AB, Princeton U., 1961; JD, Stanford U., 1964. Bar: Calif. 1965. Dep. atty. gen. Calif. Dept. Justice, 1965-72; judge L.A. Mcpl. Ct., L.A. County, 1972-77, Superior Ct. Calif., L.A. County, 1977-87, supervising judge criminal divsn., 1983-84; assoc. justice 2d dist., divsn. 4 Calif. Ct. Appeal, L.A., 1987-91; assoc. justice Calif. Supreme Ct., San Francisco, 1991-96, chief justice, 1996—. Named Trial Judge of the Yr., L.A. Metropolitan News, 1983, Appellate Justice of the Yr., L.A. Trial Lawyers Assn., 1991, Person of the Yr., L.A. Metropolitan News, 1996; recipient St. Thomas More Medallion award, St. Thomas More Law Honor Soc., 1997, Judge Learned Hand award, 2000, Found. of the State Bar's Justice award, 2000, William H. Rehnquist award for Judicial Excellence, 2002, James Madison Freedom of Information award, Soc. of Professional Journalists, 2003, George Moscone award for Outstanding Public Service, Consumer Attorneys of L.A., 2003, William O. Douglas award, 2004. Mem. Calif. Judges Assn. (pres. 1982-83), Conf. Chief Justices (pres. 2003-04). Avocations: hiking, skiing, running. Office: Calif Supreme Court 350 McAllister St Fl 5 San Francisco CA 94102-4797 Office Phone: 415-865-7060.

GEORGE, ROSHNY, gastroenterologist; b. Kerala, India, July 28, 1973; d. George Mathew and Valsa George; m. Thomas Philip, Nov. 15, 1973. MD, Christain Med. Coll., Vellore, India, 1997. Ho. staff, resident Our Lady of Mercy Med. Ctr., Bronx, 2002—. Recipient Presdl. Poster award, Am. Coll. Gastroenterology., 2002. Mem.: AMA, ACP (assoc.), Med. Soc. State NY, Bronx County Med. Soc., Am. Assn. Physicians from India, Indian Med. Assn. (life). Personal E-mail: roshnygeorge@gmail.com.

GEORGE, ROY KENNETH, minister; b. Haskell, Tex., Sept. 23, 1934; s. Roy F. and Jimalee (Scott) G.; m. Patsy Sue Brasher, May 14, 1955; children: Janis Sue, Cheryl Anne. Ordained to ministry Assemblies of God Ch., 1959. Evangelist, U.S., Africa, Europe, Asia, 1954-63; pastor Highland Assembly of God Ch., Bakersfield, Calif., 1964-65, 1st Assembly of God Ch., Carlsbad, N.Mex., 1966-67, Sem. South Ch., Ft. Worth, 1968-73, Christian Ctr., Ashland, Oreg., 1973-74, 1st Family Ch., Albuquerque, 1974-93. Broadcaster religious radio and TV programs, including Moments with the Master, Sta. KKIM, Albuquerque, 1975-85; state exec. presbyter Assemblies of God N.Mex., 1976—; asst. dist. supt. Assemblies of God, 1981-93, dist. supt. N.Mex. dist., 1993—, mem. Gen. Presbytery, 1981—; mem. exec. bd. Am. Indian Coll. of the Assemblies of God, Phoenix, Ariz., 1993—. Contbr. articles to profl. jours. Bd. regents Southwestern Assemblies of God U. at Waxahachie, Tex., 1981—. Mem. Albuquerque Ministerial Assn., Greater Albuquerque Pentecostal Fellowship (pres. 1975-76), Rogue Valley Nat. Assn. Evangelicals (v.p. 1974-75), Civitains (chaplain 1969-73), Kiwanis (pres. Albuquerque club 1982-83, lt. gov. S.W. dist. 1985-86). Office: Assemblies of God NMex Dist 6640 Caminito Coors NW Albuquerque NM 87120-3119 E-mail: Revrkg@aol.com, nmaog@aol.com. *The only way to win in the Game of Life, is to overcome evil with good. To try to conquer evil by being bad is folly. The Game plan that wins, is when you return Good for Evil.*

GEORGE, SARAH B., museum director; Dir. Utah Mus. of Natural History, Salt Lake City. Office: Utah Mus Natural History U Utah 1390 E Pres Cir Salt Lake City UT 84112 E-mail: sgeorge@umnh.utah.edu.

GEORGE, THOMAS, artist; b. N.Y.C., July 1, 1918; s. Rube and Irma (Seeman) Goldberg; m. Lavergne Burton, July 16, 1951; children John R., Geoffrey T. BA, Dartmouth Coll., 1940. One-man shows include Feragil Gallery, N.Y.C., 1951, 53, Korman Gallery, N.Y.C., 1954, Dartmouth Coll., 1965, Contemporaries Gallery, N.Y.C., 1956, Bridgestone Mus., Tokyo, 1957, Betty Parsons Gallery, N.Y.C., 1959, 63, 65, 66, 68, 70, 72, 74, 76, 78, 81, Reid Gallery, London, 1962, 64, Del. Mus., 1971, 76, Henie-Onstad Art Mus., Oslo, 1971, Princeton U. Art Mus., 1975, Dartmouth Coll., 1979, 90, Nat. Gallery, Oslo, 1980, Maxwell Davidson Gallery, N.Y.C., 1983, 85, 88, 90, Riis Gallery, Oslo, 1982, 84, 86, 88, 90, Hood Art Mus., Dartmouth Coll,1990, Snyder Fine Art, N.Y.C., 1991, Snyder Fine Art, N.Y.C., 1991, 93, 96, Julian Hartnoll Gallery, London, 1993, Williams Gallery, Princeton, 1997, 99, Mercer County (NJ) Coll., 2002; retrospective exhbns. N.J. State Mus., 1987, Princeton U. Art Mus., 2005; group exhbns. include Met. Mus. Art, N.Y.C., Am. Fedn. Arts, Mus. Modern Art, N.Y.C., Whitney Mus. Ann., N.Y.C., Carnegie Internat., Pitts., Pa. Acad., Japan Internat. Biennial Art, Tokyo, White House, Lausanne (Switzerland) Mus.; represented in permanent collections Whitney Mus., Mus. Modern Art, N.Y.C., Bklyn. Mus., Tate Gallery, London, Nat. Coll. Fine Arts at Smithsonian Instn., Washington, Chase Manhattan Coll., N.Y.C., Library of Congress, Bridgestone Mus., Hood Art Mus., Dartmouth Coll., Lausanne Mus. Art, Mus. Fine Arts, Houston, U. Calif. Art Mus., Berkeley, Santa Barbara Mus. Fine Arts, Okla. Art Ctr., U. Calif. Mus., Santa Clara, Yale U. Art Gallery, Flint (Mich.) Inst., N.J. State Mus., Rose Art Mus., Brandeis U., Heine-Onstad Art Mus., San Francisco Mus. Art, Del. Art Mus., Nat. Gallery, Oslo, Princeton Art Mus., Inst. Advanced Study, Princeton, many corp. collections; fellow, Edward MacDowell Colony, vis. artist, U. Tex., 1978, artist-in-residence, Dartmouth Coll., 1979 (Recipient purchase prize Bklyn. Mus. 1955, Ford Found. 1961, Whitney Mus. Ann. Am. Painting 1962, N.J. State Mus. 1971, Purchase prize N.J. State Mus. 1971, Olympic games Poster/Print Commn. 1974). Served with USNR, 1942-45. Recipient Presdl. medal Dartmouth Coll., 1991; Princeton Arts Coun. award, 1992, 2000; Rockefeller Found. grantee, 1957. Address: 1087 The Great Rd Princeton NJ 08540-4801 *A good artist must work hard all his life. He must know his craft and, most important of all, he must feel deeply about something in life.*

GEORGE, THOMAS FREDERICK, academic administrator; b. Phila., Mar. 18, 1947; s. Emmanuel John and Veronica Mather (Hansel) G.; m. Barbara Carol Harbach, Apr. 25, 1970. BA in Chemistry and Math., Gettysburg (Pa.) Coll., 1967; MS in Chemistry, Yale U., 1968, PhD, 1970. Rsch. assoc. MIT, 1970; postdoctoral fellow U. Calif., Berkeley, 1971; mem. faculty U. Rochester, N.Y., 1972-85, prof. chemistry, 1977-85; dean Faculty Natural Sci. and Math., prof. chemistry and physics SUNY-Buffalo, 1985-91; provost, acad. v.p., prof. chemistry and physics Wash. State U., Pullman, 1991-96; chancellor, prof. chemistry and physics U. Wis., Stevens Point, 1996—2003, U. Missouri, St. Louis, 2003—; Disting. vis. lectr. dept. chemistry U. Tex., Austin, 1978; lectr. NATO Advanced Study Inst., Cambridge, Eng., 1979; Disting. speaker dept. chemistry U. Utah, 1980; Disting. lectr. Air Force Weapons Lab., Kirtland AFB, N.Mex., 1980; mem. com. recommendations U.S. Army Basic Sci. Research, 1978-81; lectr. NATO Summer Sch. on Interfaces under Photon Irradiation, Maratea, Italy, 1986; organizer NSF workshop on theoretical aspects of laser radiation and its interaction with atomic and molecular systems Rochester, N.Y., 1977; vice chmn. 6th Internat. Conf. Molecular Energy Transfer, Rodez, France, 1979; chmn. Gordon Rsch. Conf. Molecular Energy Transfer, Wolfeboro, N.H., 1981. Adj. rsch. prof. physics Korea U., Seoul, 1994-99, vis. prof. physics, 1994-2003; Dow lectr. polymer sci. U. Detroit Mercy, 1996; mem. program com. Internat. Conf. on Lasers, San Francisco, 1981-83, ACS Symposium on Recent Advances in Surface Sci., Rochester sect., 1982, Internat. Laser Sci. Conf., Dallas, 1985, external rev. com. for chemistry Gettysburg Coll., 1984, awards com. ACS Procter and Gamble student prizes in chemistry, 1982-83, Free-electron Laser peer rev. panel Am. Inst. Biol. Sci. Med., alt., bd. trustees alt. Calspan-UB Rsch. Ctr., 1989-91; organiser APS Symposium on Laser-Induced Molecular Excitation/Photofragmentation, N.Y., 1987; co-organizer ACS Symposium on Phys. Chemistry High-Temp. Superconds., L.A., 1988; co-organizer MRS Symposium on High-Temperature Superconductors, Alfred, N.Y., 1988; chmn. SPIE Symposium on Photochemistry in Thin Films, L.A., 1989; mem. internat. program adv. com. Internat. Sch. Lasers and Applications, Sayanogorsk, East Siberia, USSR, 1989; lectr. on chemistry at cutting edge Smithsonian Instn./Am. Chem. Soc., Washington, 1990; Musselman lectr. Gettysburg Coll., 1999; Disting. lectr. Korean Acad. Sci. and Tech., 2003; mem. internat. adv. com. Xth Vavilov Conf. Nonlinear Optics, Novosibirsk, USSR, 1990; Am. coord. NSF Info. Exchange Seminar for U.S.-Japan Program of Cooperation in Photoconversion and Photosynthesis, Honolulu, 1990; mem. program com. Optical Soc. Am. Topical Meeting on Radiative Processes and Dephasing in Semiconductors, Coeur d'Alene, Idaho, 1998; mem. sci. com. Sixth Brijuni Internat. Conf. on Interdisciplinary Topics in Physics and Chemistry, Brijuni Isles, Croatia, 1998; mem. superregional steering com. Wis. Econ. Summit, 2000; mem. exec. bd. N.Y. State Inst. on Superconductivity, 1990-91; mem. ONT/ASEE rev. panel for Engring. Edn. postdoctoral fellowship program, 1990; mem. rev panel rsch. experiences for undergrads of sci. and tech. rsch. ctrs., NSF, 1989, mem. rev. panel grad. res. traineeships NSF, 1992; cons., lectr. in field. Co-author: (with Blackwell) Notes in Classical and Quantum Physics, 1990, (with Kluwer) Fundamentals in Chemical Physics, 1998; mem. editl. bd. Molecular Physics, 1984-90, Jour. Cluster Sci., 1989-97; mem. adv. bd. Jour. Phys. Chemistry, 1980-84; mem. adv. editl. bd. Chem. Physics Letters, 1979-81, Chem. Materials, 1989; mem. editl. bd. Jour. Quantum Nonlinear Phenomena (Soviet jour), 1991-96, Nova Jour. Theoretical Physics, 1996-97; editor-at-large Marcel Dekker, 1989; editor: Photochemistry in Thin Films, 1989; co-editor Internat. Jour. Theoretical Physics, Group Theory, and Nonlinear Optics, 1999—; co-editor: Chemistry of High-Temperature Superconductors, Vol. I, 1987, vol. II, 1988, ACS Symposium Series, Computational Studies of New Materials, 1999, Optics of Nanostructural Materials, 2001, Modern Topics in Chemical Physics, 2001; feature editor Jour. of Optical Soc. of Am., Spectrochimica Acta, Optical Engring.; contbr. over 630 articles to profl. jours. Tchr., scholar Camille and Henry Dreyfus Found., 1975-85; bd. mgrs. Buffalo Mus. Sci., 1986-92; mem. exec. bd. N.Y. State Inst. on Superconductivity, 1990-91; mem. canvassing com. ACS; mem. external rev. com. for chemistry Gettysburg Coll., 1984; mem. NEASC site visit team Boston U., ten-yr. accreditation, 1989; bd. dirs. Wash. State Inst. for Pub. Policy, 1991-96; trustee Wash. State U. Found., 1991-96; bd. dirs. Wash. Tech. Ctr., 1992-96; mem. exec. com. Northwest Acad. Forum, 1992-96, chmn. 1994-95; mem. rev. panel Grad. Rsch. Traineeships, NSF, 1992, mem. rev. panel for sci. and tech. ctr. proposals, 1998, rev. panel for preproposals for sci. and tech. ctrs., 1998; mem. Project 435 Dist. Leadership Coun., Wis. Assn. Biomed. Rsch. and Edn./Research America!, 1997; mem. Commn. on the Future of

Gettysburg Coll., 1997-98; bd. dirs. Portage County Bus. Coun., 1998-2003, Stevens Point Area YMCA, 1998—2003, v.p., 2002-2003, United Way Portage County, Wis., 1997—, chmn. 1999 campaign, pres., 2002-2004, Tech. Alliance State Wash., 1996, U. Wis.-Stevens Point Found., 1996-2003, Paper Sci. Found., 1996-2003, St. Michael's Hosp., Stevens Point, 1999-2003, Distributed Learning Workshop, Midwestern Higher Edn. Commn., 1999-2003, 2005-, Wis. Ctr. Acad. Talented Youth, 2001—, Marathon County Ptnrs. in Edn., 2002, Civic Progress, 2003-, Ctr. for Emerging Tech., 2003—, St. Louis (Mo.) Mercantile Libr., 2003, John W. Berringer III Nat. RR Libr., 2004, Christian Hosp., 2004—, United Way of Greater St. Louis, 2004—, Mo. Coun. Pub. Higher Edn., 2004—, St. Louis (Mo.) Merc. Libr., 2003—, John W. Barriger III Nat. R.R. Libr., 2004—; bd. trustees/dirs. (alt.) Assoc. Western Univs., 1993-96; bd. dirs. alt. Joint Ctr. Higher Edn., Spokane, 1996; mem steering com. Ctr. for Advanced Tech. in Healthcare Instruments and Devices, 1988-90; with Midwestern Higher Edn. Commn., 1999-2003; exploring chair Mushkodany dist. Wis. Samoset coun. Boy Scouts Am., 1998, fin. chair, 1999, pres., 2002-03; bd. dirs. trustee WiSys Tech. Found., 2000-, Mo. Bot. Garden, 2003-; exec. bd. Greater St. Louis Area coun. Boy Scouts Am., 2004-; bd. commrs. Acad. Advanced Distributed Learning Lab. (UW-US Dept. Def.), 2001; adv. coun. Ednl. Directories Unltd., 2001—; mem. adv. bd. New Economy Workforce Coalition, Wausau, 2001, Mo. Coun. Pub. Higher Edn., 2003—; steering com. St. Louis Regional Competitiveness Coun. Initiative, 2004—; mem. Mo. Coun. Pub. Higher Edn., 2003—. Sloan fellow, 1976-80, postdoctoral fellow, 1990, Guggenheim fellow, 1983-84; recipient Disting. Alumni award Gettysburg Coll., 1987, Disting. Alumnus award Friends Ctr. Sch., 2003. Fellow AAAS, Soc. Photo-Optical Instrumentation Engrs., Am. Phys. Soc., N.Y. Acad. Scis., Inst. Superconductivity (steering com. 1987-91); mem. Am. Chem. Soc. (exec. com. phys. div. 1979-82, 85-89, 94-97, vice chmn. 1985-86, chmn.-elect 1986-87, chmn. 1987-88), Outstanding Contbns. to Chemistry award 2002, Am. Chem. Soc., Am. Assn. State Colls. and Univs. (acad. affairs subcom. on sci. edn. rsch. and tng., coun. state reps.), Wis. Assn. for Biomed. Rsch. and Edn., European Phys. Soc., Royal Soc. Chemistry (Marlow medal and prize 1979), Korean Acad. Sci. and Tech. (fgn.), Phi Beta Kappa, Sigma Xi (exec. com. U. Rochester 1984-85). Office: U Mo-St Louis Office of the Chancellor One Univ Blvd Saint Louis MO 63121-4499 Office Phone: 314-516-5252. Business E-Mail: tfgeorge@umsl.edu.

GEORGE, TIMOTHY MERRILL, neurosurgeon; b. Bklyn., Oct. 17, 1960; s. Carey and Gracie Mae (Gallman) G.; m. Sonya Denise Jacobs, Aug. 18, 1984; 1 child, Kevin Randall James. BA, Columbia U., 1982; MD, N.Y. U., 1986. Diplomate Nat. Bd. Med. Examiners. Asst. resident in surgery Yale U., New Haven, 1986-87, asst. resident in neurological surgery, 1987—93; trainee, pediatric neurosurgery Children's Mem. Hosp., 1993—95; faculty mem. Duke U. Med. Ctr., Durham, 1995—. Rsch. assoc. Dept. Neuroanatomy Yale U., 1988—. Author: Symposium on Critical Care, 1989, Surgical Management of Supratentorial Gliomas: Contemporary Neurosurgery, 1989, Current Management of Aneurysmal Subasachnoid Hemorrhage, 1989, Lateral Ventricular Tumors: Complication Avoidance in Neurosurgery, 1990; designer (invention) Intracranial Localizer, 1988. Mem. NAACP, 1977-82. Recipient Merck Manual award Merck, Sharp & Dohme, 1986; named One of Outstanding Young Men in Am., 1990. Mem. AMA, Am. Assn. Neurol. Surgeons, Congress Neurol. Surgeons, Nat. Med. Assn. Avocations: disc jockey, basketball, music, jazz. Office: Duke U Med Ctr Div Neurosurgery Box 3272 Durham NC 27710 E-mail: georg017@mc.duke.edu.

GEORGE, WALTER EUGENE, JR., architect; b. Wichita Falls, Tex., Oct. 28, 1922; s. Walter Eugene and Mamie Alta (Evans) G.; m. Mary Carolyn Hollers Jutson, May 20, 1980. B.Arch., U. Tex., 1949; M.Arch., Harvard U., 1950. Designer Wiltshire and Fisher (architects), Dallas, 1950-51; partner Pendley, George and Bowman (architects and engrs.), Austin, 1952-57; asst., then assoc. prof. architecture U. Tex., 1956-62; prof. architecture, chmn. dept. U. Kans., 1962-67; dean Coll. Architecture, U. Houston, 1967-69; practice of architecture Austin, 1969—71, 1974—; resident architect Colonial Williamsburg, Va., 1971-73; sr. lectr. engring. U. Tex., Austin, 1975-96, San Antonio Conservation Soc. prof. architecture San Antonio, 1997—2004. Served as pilot USAAF, 1943-46, ETO. Decorated Air medal with oak leaf cluster, Purple Heart; recipient 2d award 1st ann. Southwestern furniture competition, Dallas Mus. Fine Arts, Mont San Michele and Chartres award, 1949, D.B. Alexander Lifetime Acheivement award, Heritage Soc. Austin, Tex., 2005. Fellow: AIA; mem.: Tex. Soc. Archs. (Edward J. Romieniec award for outstanding archtl. educator 2001), Soc. Archtl. Historians, Archaeol. Inst. Am., Tau Sigma Delta. Episcopalian. Office: PO Box 4426 Austin TX 78765-4426

GEORGE, WARREN S., labor union administrator; b. Pitts. m. Janice George; 3 children. Bus operator Critchlow Bus Lines, 1956—63; mem. Local 85, Amalgamated Transit Union, 1963—76, pres., fin. sec., treas., 1970—75; internat. v.p. Amalgamated Transit Union, 1975—93, internat. exec., v.p., 1993—2002, internat. pres., 2003—. Office: ATU 5025 Wisconsin Ave NW Washington DC 20016-4139 Office Phone: 202-537-1645. Office Fax: 202-244-7824.

GEORGE, WILLIAM WALLACE, former manufacturing executive; b. Muskegon, Mich., Sept. 14, 1942; s. Wallace Edwin and Kathryn Jean (Dinkeloo) G.; m. Ann Tonnlier Pilgram, Sept. 6, 1969; children: Jeffrey, Jonathan. BS in Indsl. Engring. with honors, Ga. Inst. Tech., 1964; MBA with high distinction, Harvard U., 1966. Asst. to asst. sec. Dept. Def., Washington, 1966-68; spl. civilian asst. to sec. Navy, Washington, 1968-69; with Litton Industries, 1969-78, dir. long-range planning Cleve., 1969-70, v.p., 1976, Litton Microwave Cooking Products, Mpls., 1970-71, exec. v.p., 1971-73, pres., 1973-78; v.p. corp. devel. Honeywell, Mpls., 1978-80, exec. v.p., 1983-87; pres. Honeywell Europe (S.A.), 1980-82, Indsl. Automation, 1987, Space and Aviation Systems, Mpls., 1988-89; pres., chief oper. officer Medtronic Inc., Mpls., 1989-91, CEO, 1991—2002, chmn., 1996—2002. Bd. dirs. Dayton-Hudson, Imation., Goldman Sachs Group, Inc., Target Corp. and Novartis AG; sr. lecturer, Harvard Bus. Sch., prof. leadership and governance, Internat. Inst. Mgmt. Devel., 2002-2003, visiting prof. tech. mgmt., Ecole Polytechnique Federale de Lausanne, 2002-2003, exec.-in-residence, Yale Sch. Mgmt., 2003 Bd. dirs. Am. Red Cross, Minn. Symphony Orch., 1976-80, United Way, Minn. 1976-79, 96—, nat. chmn., Belgium, 1982-83, campaign chair, 1997; bd. dirs., pres., treas. Guthrie Theater, 1977-84; vice-chmn. United Theol. Sem., 1977-80, Abbott-Northwestern Hosp., 1984—, vice-chair, 1989-91, chair, 1991-93, Health Span, 1989-94; trustee Macalaster Coll., 1987-93, Allin Health Sys., 1994—, vice-chair, 1997—, Mlps. Inst. Arts, 1993—, chmn. Minn. Thunder Pro Soccer, 1994—. Recipient Meritorious Civilian Service Award Sec. Navy, 1969 Mem. Sigma Chi (Internat. Balfour award 1964, trustee 1971-77, Disting. Alumni award Harvard U., 1997). Clubs: Minneapolis, Minikahda. Episcopalian. Home: 2284 W Lake Of The Isles Pky Minneapolis MN 55405-2434 Office: George Family Found 1818 Oliver Ave S Minneapolis MN 55405

GEORGES, PETER JOHN, lawyer; b. Wilmington, Del., Sept. 8, 1940; s. John Peter and Olga Demetrius (Kazitoris) G. BS in Chemistry, U. Del., 1962; JD, John Marshall Law Sch., 1970; LLM in Patent and Trade Regulations, George Washington U., 1973. Bar: Ill. 1970, U.S. Ct. Appeals (fed. cir.) 1972, D.C. 1973, U.S. Supreme Ct. 1973, Del. 1977. Chemist engring. labs Bell & Howell Co., Chgo., 1966; patent coordinator Armour & Co., Chgo., 1967; patent agt., atty. UOP Inc., Chgo., 1968-71, Washington counsel Arlington, Va., 1972-77; ptnr. Kile, Gholz, Bernstein & Georges, Arlington, 1977-78; assoc., then ptnr. Law Office Sidney W. Russell, Arlington, 1978-83; mng. officer Breneman & Georges (and predecessor law firms), Alexandria, 1983—; founding ptnr. Lenastri Properties and Joanastri Properties, Alexandria, Va. Served to 1st lt. USMC, 1963-65, Vietnam. Mem. Ill. Bar Assn., D.C. Bar Assn., Del. Bar Assn., Fed. Cir. Bar Assn., Assn. Am. Hellenic Lawyers Soc. Home: 1637 13th St NW Washington DC 20009-4302 Office: Breneman & Georges 3150 Commonwealth Ave Alexandria VA 22305-2712

GEORGESCU, PETER ANDREW, retired advertising executive; b. Bucharest, Romania, Mar. 9, 1939; came to US, 1954, naturalized, 1954; s. V.C. Rica and Lygia (Bocu) G.; m. Barbara Anne Armstrong, Aug. 21, 1965; 1 son, Peter Andrew. AB cum laude, Princeton U., 1961; MBA, Stanford U., 1963. With Young & Rubicam, Inc., NYC, 1963—2000, dir. mktg., 1977-79, exec. v.p. Cen. Region Chgo., dir., 1979-82; pres. Young & Rubicam Internat., NYC, 1982-86, Young & Rubicam Advt., NYC, 1986—94; pres., CEO Young & Rubicam Inc., 1994—2000; CEO, chmn. bd. dirs. Young & Rubicam Inc, to 1999, chmn. emeritus, 2000—. Bd. dirs. Briggs & Stratton, Inc.; Toys R Us; Levi Strauss Co.; EMI. Bd dir. Am. Assn. Advt. Agencies, Internat. Advt. Assn., Inc.; adv. bd. mem. Stanford Bus. Sch.; bd dir. A Better Chance, NY Philharm. Named to Adv. Hall of Fame, 2001. Mem. Coun. on Fgn. Rels., Links Club, River Club, Racquet Club, Casino Club, Brooks Club.

GEORGESON, GARY ERNEST, engineer; b. Santa Barbara, Calif., July 25, 1959; s. Stanton Berneil and Phyllis Jean Georgeson; m. Lorraine Ellen Songs, Feb. 18, 1984; children: Nathaniel, Jonathan, Rachel. BS in mech. engring., U. Calif. at Santa Barbara, 1981, MS in mech. engring., 1982, PhD in materials sci., 1985; MA in theology, Fuller Theol. Seminary, 1992. Post doctoral rschr. U. Calif., 1985—88; destructive eval. focal The Boeing Co., Seattle, 1988—, assoc. tech. fellow, 2002—04, tech. fellow, 2005—. Co-chair Spie Internat. Conf., 1998—; expert rev. Australian Rsch. Coun., 1996—. Pastor Vineyard Cmty. Ch., 1990—. Mem.: Am. Soc. of Composites, Am. Soc. of Non-Destructive Evaluation. Achievements include patents for. Avocations: hiking, running, surfing, camping, reading. Home: 145 So 258th Federal Way WA 98003 Office: Boeing Co P O Box 1707 MC4E-96 Seattle WA 98124

GEORGI, HOWARD, physics professor; b. San Bernardino, Calif., Jan. 6, 1947; married, two children. BA magna cum laude with high honors, Harvard Coll., 1967; PhD, Yale U., 1971. Rsch. fellow Harvard U., Cambridge, Mass., 1971-73, jr. fellow Soc. of Fellow, 1973-76, assoc. prof. physics, 1976-80, prof. physics, 1980—, sr. fellow, 1982-98, chmn. dept. physics, 1991-94. Co-chair com. on women in sci. and engring. NRC, 1996-99; master Leverett House, 1998—. Author: Lie Algebras in Particle Physics, 1981, Weak Interactions and Modern Particle Theory, 1984, The Physics of Waves, 1993; editor: Physics Letters B, 1982—. NSF postdoctoral fellow 1971-73, Alfred P. Sloan Found. fellow, 1976-80, Am. Phys. Soc. Divsn. Particles and Fields fellow, 1994; recipient Dirac medal Abdus Salam Internat. Ctr. Theoretical Physics, 2000, Levenson Meml. Tchg. award, 1999, 2004, Phi Beta Kappa Tchg. award, 2002. Fellow Am. Acad. Arts and Scis., Am. Phys. Soc. (com. on status of women in physics 1994-97, exec. com. Forum on Edn. 1995-98, Sakurai prize 1995); mem. NAS. Office: Harvard Univ Lyman Lab Of Physics Cambridge MA 02138 E-mail: georgi@physics.harvard.edu.

GEORGIEVA, RENNIE T., medical librarian; b. Lubimetz, Bulgaria; arrived in U.S., 1997; d. Tono Nikolov Tonchev and Milka Mihailova Toncheva; m. Goshko A. Georgiev, Nov. 4, 1984; 1 child, Maria. MA, Sofia (Bulgaria) U., 1996. Head libr. Nat. Inst. Meteorology, Sofia, 1980—96, APA, Washington, 2000—. Mem.: Spl. Libr. Assn., Med. Libr. Assn. Avocations: travel, tennis, reading. Office: APA 750 1st St NE Washington DC 20002

GEORGIOU, ATHENA PASTRAS, psychologist; d. Petrangelos and Iralia Pastras; m. George Costas Georgiou; children: Evridiki, Iralia. BA in Psychology, The George Wash. U., 1976; MA in Psychology, Cath. U. Am., 1979; MA in Sch. Psychology, Towson (Md.) U., 1999, cert. in Advanced Studies, 2000. Cert. sch. psychologist State of Md., 2000. Attache adminstrn. Emb. Greece, Washington, 1976—92; cons. dept. Personnell The World Bank, Washington, 1992—96; tchr. Greek Sch. St. George, Bethesda, Md., 1996—2000; psychologist Prince George's Pub. Sch. Sys., Adelphi, Md., 2000—. Bd. dirs. Greek Sch. St. George, 1986—92. Mem.: NEA, Nat. Assn. MultiCultural Edn., Nat. Assn. Sch. Psychologists, Md. Sch. Psychology Assn. Avocations: dance, singing, swimming, reading, languages. Home: 9509 Linden Avenue Bethesda MD 20814 Office: Prince George's County Public Schools 8909 Riggs Road Adelphi MD Office Phone: 301-431-5630.

GEORGITIS, JOHN, allergist, educator; b. Columbus, Ohio, June 19, 1950; s. William James and Mary Helen (Wyman) G.; children: Nancy Lynn, Kathryn Mary, Matthew Walter. BA, Bowdoin Coll., Brunswick, Maine, 1972; MD, U. Vt., 1976. Diplomate Am. Bd. Pediatrics, Am. Bd. Allergy and Immunology. Resident in pediatrics James Whitcomb Riley Hosp., Indpls., 1976-78, pulmonology fellow, 1978-79; allergy fellow SUNY, Buffalo, 1979-81, rsch. asst. prof., 1981-84; assoc. prof. Bowman Gray Sch. Medicine, Winston-Salem, N.C., 1984-94, prof., 1994-2000, dir. Allergy and Immunology program, 2000—. Dir. allergy and immunology tng. program Bowman Gray Sch. of Medicine, Winston-Salem, 1987-2000; sect. chief Pediatric Allergy, Immunology and Respiratory Medicine, Wake Forest U. Sch. Medicine, 2000—. Office: Wake Forest U Sch Medicine Med Ctr Blvd Winston Salem NC 27157-0001

GEORGOPOULOS, APOSTOLOS, neuroscientist, neurologist, educator; b. Patras, Greece; MD, D of Physiology, U. Athens. Joined faculty Johns Hopkins U., 1976, prof., 1986; Am. Legion Brain Scis. chair, dir. Minneapolis Veteran Affairs Med. Ctr. U. Minn., 1991—; prof. neuroscience, neurology and psychiatry U. Minn. Med. Sch. Grantee McKnight Presdl. Endowed Chair, U. Minn., 2004. Mem.: Inst. Medicine, Nat. Acad. Scis. Office: U Minn Dept Neuroscience 6-145 Jackson Hall 321 Church St Minneapolis MN 55455

GEORGOULIS, MANOLIS KONSTANTINOS, physicist; b. Sykiada, Chios, Greece, Aug. 14, 1969; s. Konstantinos Demetrios and Eirini K Georgoulis; m. Despoina M Stefaniorou, Sept. 1, 1974; 1 child, Konstantinos Emmanouil. B, Aristotle U. Thessaloniki, 1993, PhD, 2000. Rsch. assoc. JHU/APL, Laurel, Md., 2001—03, sr. profl. staff physicist, 2003—. Contbr. articles to profl. jours. Lt. Hellenic Army, 1998—2000. Fellow, European Astrophysy. Doctoral Network, 1996—97; IKY scholar, Found. Scholarships Hellenic State, 1996—2000. Mem.: Am. Geophys. Union, Hellenic Astron. Soc., Am. Astron. Soc. (assoc.; Solar Physics Divsn.). Achievements include research in Solar and Space Physics, Space Weather. Office: Jhu/Apl 11100 Johns Hopkins Rd Laurel MD 20723 Office Phone: 240-228-5508. Office Fax: 240-228-0386. E-mail: manolis.georgoulis@jhuapl.edu.

GEPFORD, BARBARA BEEBE, retired nutrition educator; b. Buffalo, N.Y., Sept. 2, 1930; d. Kenneth Hildreth and Martha Bell (Griswold) Beebe; m. William George Gepford, Dec. 28, 1952; children: David, Scott, Joanna, Andrea. BS in Home Econs. Edn., Iowa State U., 1952. Nutrition instr. Sidon Girl's Sch., Lebanon, 1953-56; instr. textiles and clothing Beirut Univ. Coll., Lebanon, 1955-56, 62-63; nutrition cons. Hong Kong Coun. of Social Svcs., 1967-71; commd. fraternal worker Presbyn. U.S.A., Lebanon, Hong Kong, 1953-71; mgr. Lila's Fabric Store, Cambridge, Ohio, 1973-74. Overseas missionary advisor to Assembly Coun. of Presbyn. Ch., U.S.A., 1971-72. Elder Presbyn. Ch., New Concord, Ohio, 1974-79, mem. com. on Ministry, Detroit, 1987-94; pres. Presbyn. Women of Littlefield Ch., 1987-89; vice-moderator Presbyn. Women of Presbytery of Detroit, 1985-87, moderator, 1997-99; synod of covenant women's rep. Churchwide Coordinating Team of Presbyn. Women, 1999-2002; chair Presbyn. Women Triann. Global Exch. to Africa, 2002-03; advisor YWCA Head Start Program, Dearborn, Mich., 1988-91; bd. dirs. YWCA, 1985-96, pres., 1993-95. Named Ohio Mother of the Yr., Am. Mothers Com., New Concord, 1978. Mem., AAUW (bd. dirs. 87-89, internat. rels. area rep.). Democrat. Avocations: reading, gardening, sewing, knitting. Home: 9421 Westwind Dr Livonia MI 48150-4530 E-mail: barbbgepford@msn.com, wiamfrd@msn.com.

GEPHARDT, DICK (RICHARD ANDREW GEPHARDT), lawyer, former congressman; b. St. Louis, Jan. 31, 1941; s. Louis Andrew and Loreen Estelle (Cassell) Gephardt; m. Jane Ann Byrnes, Aug. 13, 1966; children: Matthew, Christine, Katherine. BS, Northwestern U., 1962; JD, U. Mich., 1965. Bar: Mo. 1965. Atty. Thompson & Mitchell, St. Louis, 1965-76; Dem. committeeman 14th ward, St. Louis, 1968—71, alderman, 1971-76; mem. US Congress from 3d dist. Mo., 1977—2005; US House Majority Leader, 1989—94; US House Minority Leader, 1995—2003; candidate for Dem. presdl. nomination, 1987—88, 2003—04; sr. counsel DLA Piper Rudnick Gray Cary US LLP, Washington, 2005—. Co-author (with Michael Wessel): An Even Better Place: America in the 21st Century, 1999. Pres. Children's Hematology Rsch. Assn., St. Louis Children's Hosp., 1973-76. Served to capt. Air Nat. Guard, 1965—71. Mem.: Metro St. Louis Bar Assn., Mo. Bar Assn., Boy Scouts Am., Am. Legion, Mid-Town Club (St. Louis), Kiwanis. Democrat. Office: DLA Piper Rudnick Gray Cary US LLP 1200 19th St NW Washington DC 20036

GEPHARDT, DONALD LOUIS, academic administrator; b. St. Louis, Mar. 27, 1937; s. Louis Andrew and Loreen Estelle (Cassell) G.; m. Zenaida Otero Gephardt, June 10, 2000; children from previous marriage: Lisa Diane, Francis Joseph. B Music Edn., Drake U., 1959; BS, Juilliard Sch., 1961, MS, 1962; EdD, Washington U., St. Louis, 1978. Clarinet instr. Henry Street Settlement Music Sch., N.Y.C., 1961-64; music tchr. Wantagh (N.Y.) Elem. Schs., 1962-67; music tchr., band and orch. dir. W.C. Mepham High Sch., Bellmore, N.Y., 1967-70; assoc. prof. music, band and jazz ensemble conductor Nassau C.C., Garden City, N.Y., 1970-83, chmn. music dept., 1977-83, dean instrn., 1984-90; dean Coll. Fine and Performing Arts, Rowan U., Glassboro, N.J., 1990—, acting exec. v.p., provost, 1994-95. Clarinetist Des Moines Symphony Orch., 1956-59, Aspen (Colo.) Festival Orchestra, 1959-60, Henry Schuman's Wind Ensemble Workshop, 1965-69, L.I. Symphony Orch., 1970-82; clarinetist Seuffert Band, 1962-90, Great Neck (N.Y.) Symphony, 1967-80; contbr. articles to profl. jours. Bd. dirs. L.I. Symphony, 1980-82; surrogate spkr. Richard Gephardt for Pres., 1987-88, 2004. Mem. Music Educators Nat. Conf. (chpt. advisor 1970-83, 2-yr. coll. chmn. Ea. divsn. 1982-83), N.Y. State Sch. Music Assn. (chmn. rsch. 1982-84), N.J. Music Educators Assn., Alliance for Arts Edn. N.J. (past pres.), Nassau Music Educators Assn. (rec. sec. 1968-69, 1st v.p. 1969-70, pres. 1970-71), Coll. Music Soc., Internat. Coun. of Fine Arts Deans (pres.-elect 2001-02, pres. 2003-05, past pres. 2005—), Arts Edn. Partnership (steering com.), Phila. Arts Edn. Partnership (bd. dirs. 2004—), Phi Mu Alpha Sinfonia. Democrat. Avocations: cooking, reading. Office: Rowan U NJ Coll Fine-Performing Arts Glassboro NJ 08028 Office Phone: 856-256-4551. Business E-Mail: gephardt@rowan.edu.

GERACHIS, GEORGE MATTHEW, lawyer; b. Washington, DC, Dec. 7, 1957; BA with high distinction, U. Va., 1979, JD, 1983. Bar: Tex. 1983, US Tax Ct. Ptnr., mem. firm mgmt. com., co-head Tax Sect., leader Fed. Tax Controversy and Litig. practice Vinson & Elkins LLP, Houston. Mem.: ABA, Internat. Fiscal Assn., Houston Bar Assn. Office: Vinson & Elkins LLP First City Tower 1001 Fannin St, Ste 2300 Houston TX 77002-6760 Office Fax: 713-758-1056. E-mail: ggerachis@velaw.com.

GERACI, RICHARD V., military officer, government agency administrator; BS in Mgmt., Park Coll.; M.Mgmt., Webster U.; MS in Systems Mgmt., Fla. Inst. Tech.; MA in Nat. Security Affairs and Strategic Studies, U.S. Naval War Coll. Commd. 2d lt. U.S. Army, 1975—, advanced through grades to brig. gen.; platoon leader, battery exec. officer, asst. ops. officer 3d Battalion 32nd Army Air Def. Command, Germany; Patriot plans and future war plans officer, G3 32d AADCOM; battalion ops. officer 1st Bn. 7th ADA (PATRIOT; brigade ops. officer and dep. brigade comdr. 94th ADA Brigade; battalion ops. officer 3d Battalion 1st ADA, Tng. Brigade, Ft. Bliss, Tex.; garrison ops., plans, tng., mobilization officer Installation Support Activity, U.S. Army, Aberdeen Proving Grounds, Md.; dep. commdg. gen. Army Space Command and Ops., U.S. Army Space and Missile Def. Command, Colorado Springs, Colo. Decorated Legion of Merit, Meritorious Svc. medal, silver and 2 bronze oak leaf clusters, Army Commendation medal with 2 oak leaf clusters, Army Achievement medal with 1 oak leaf cluster, S.W. Asia Svc. medal, Saudi-Kuwaiti Liberation medal, Kuwaiti Liberation medal. Office: HQ US Army Space Command 350 Vandenberg St Colorado Springs CO 80914-4999

GERACI, ROBERT PAUL, historian, educator; b. Buffalo, N.Y., Oct. 1, 1962; s. Robert Paul and Patricia Ann Geraci. BA, Swarthmore Coll., 1984; MA, U. Calif., Berkeley, 1989, PhD, 1995. Post-doctoral fellow Woodrow Wilson Internat. Ctr. for Scholars, Washington, 1994—95, Harvard U., Cambridge, Mass., 1995—96; asst. prof. history U. Va., Charlottesville, 1996—2002, assoc. prof. history, 2002—. Author: Window on the East: National and Imperial Identities in Late Tsarist Russia, 2001; co-editor, author: Of Religion and Empire: Missions, Conversion, and Tolerance in Tsarist Russia, 2001. Grantee Individual Advanced Rsch. Opportunity, Internat. Rsch. and Exchanges Bd., 2003—04; Mellon Fellowship in the Humanities, Woodrow Wilson Nat. Fellowship Found., 1987—94, Dissertation fellow, Social Sci. Rsch. Coun., 1992—93, Post-Doctoral fellow, 1996, Long-Term Rsch. Exch. grantee, Internat. Rsch. and Exchanges Bd., 1991—92, rsch. grantee, Nat. Coun. for Eurasian and East European Rsch., 2003—04. Mem.: Am. Assn. for the Advancement Slavic Studies, Am. Hist. Assn., Phi Beta Kappa. Home: 1311 Delaware Ave SW #S-638 Washington DC 20024 Office: Univ Va PO Box 400180 Charlottesville VA 22904-4180 Office Phone: 434-924-6984. Office Fax: 434-924-7891. Business E-Mail: geraci@virginia.edu.

GERAGHTY, DIANE C., law educator; BA, U. California; MA, U. Chgo., 1967; JD, Northwestern U. Faculty mem. Loyola U. Chgo., 1977—, prof. law, dir. Civitas ChildLaw Ctr., acting dean, 2004—05. Author: Juvenile Law Benchbook, Vols. I and II, 2001; co-author: Training the Lawyer to Represent the Whole Child: In re Pena, 2003; mem. editl. bd. Ill. Child Welfare; contbr. articles to law jours. Named Juvenile Justice Pioneer, 2000; recipient Livingston Hall Juvenile Justice Award, ABA, 2001, Leonard Jay Schrager Award, Chgo. Bar Found., 2003. Mem.: Ill. State Ct. Improvement Project (co-chair), Ill. Juvenile Justice Initiative (hon. bd. mem.), Citizens Com. on Juvenile Ct. (chair), Chgo. Children's Advocacy Ctr. (bd. mem., co-chair Strategic Planning Com.), Am. Civil Liberties Union (mem. Nat. Bd. Dirs.). Office: Loyola U Chgo Sch Law 1 E Pearson St Rm 506 Chicago IL 60611 E-mail: dgeragh@luc.edu.

GERAGHTY, PATRICK D., lawyer; b. Woodside, NY, Jan. 9, 1970; BA, SUNY, Stony Brook, 1992; JD, NY Law Sch., 1995. Bar: NJ 1995, NY 1996, US Dist. Ct. Dist. NJ 1996, US Dist. Ct. Ea. & So. Districts NY 1996. Ptnr. Wilson, Elser, Moskowitz, Edelman & Dicker LLP, NYC. Office: Wilson Elser Moskowitz Edelman & Dicker LLP 23rd Fl 150 E 42nd St New York NY 10017-5639 Office Phone: 212-490-3000 ext. 2524. Office Fax: 212-490-3038. Business E-Mail: geraghtyp@wemed.com.

GERAGHTY, THOMAS F., law educator; b. 1944; AB, Harvard U., 1966; JD, Northwestern U., 1970. Bar: Ill. 1970. Staff atty. Northwestern U. Legal Clinic, Chgo., 1970—73, co-dir., 1973—75, dir., 1976—; assoc. prof. Northwestern U. Sch. of Law, 1976—79, prof., 1979—, asst. dean, 1977—81, assoc. dean, 1981—. Tchg. team leader Midwest regional session Nat. Inst. Trial Advocacy; bd. dirs. Legal Assistance Found., Chgo., Chgo.-Cook County Criminal Def. Consortium, Chgo. Coun. of Lawyers. Contbr. articles to profl. jours. Mem.: Chgo. Bar Assn. (Leonard Jay Schrager Award of Excellence 2003), Am. Inst. Trial Advocacy (Robert F. Oliphant Award 1994, Disting. Svcs. Award 1997). Office: Northwestern U Law Sch 357 E Chicago Ave Chicago IL 60611-3069*

GERAGOS, MARK JOHN, lawyer; b. L.A., Oct. 5, 1957; BA, Haverford Coll., 1979; JD, Loyola Marymount U., 1982. Mng. ptnr. Geragos & Geragos, L.A.; with Calif. Legis. Assembly Resolution, 2003. Legal cons. CNBC, MSNBC, Fox News Svc., CNN; spkr. in field; owner Magnaband.net, TheJusticeSystem.net, VoteAcrossAmerica.com, ItsAboutFinance.com. Named Profl. of Yr. award, Am. Profl. Soc., 2004; recipient Jerry Giesler Meml. award, Criminal Cts. Bar Assn., 1999, Humanitarian of the Yr. award, Mexican Am. Grocers Assn., 2001, Joseph Rosen Justice award, Criminal Cts. Bar Assn., 2002, Resolution award for pioneering work in internet TV, Calif. Legis. Assembly, 2003, Profl. of Yr. award, Am. Profl. Soc., 2004. Mem.: LA County Bar Assn. (mem. jud. appointments com., mem. outstanding trial jurist award com. 1992—93, jud. com. 1994—), State Bar Calif. Office: Geragos & Geragos Two California Plaza 350 S Grand Ave 39th Fl Los Angeles CA 90071 Office Phone: 213-625-3900. Business E-Mail: geragos@geragos.com.

GERAKITIS, RICHARD, lawyer; b. Atlanta, Ga., 1956; AB magna cum laude, Univ. Ga., 1978; JD, Mercer Univ., 1981. Bar: Ga. 1981. Assoc. Cashin, Morton & Mullins, 1981—85, ptnr., 1986—97; ptnr., practice group leader, labor and employment Troutman Sanders LLP, Atlanta, 1997—. Named a Super Lawyer, Atlanta Mag., 2004, Legal Elite in labor/employment, Ga. Trend Mag., 2004. Mem.: Atlanta Bar Assn., Nat. Coll. Trial Advocacy (instr. 1996—98), State Bar Ga., Old Warhorse Lawyers Club. Office: Troutman Sanders LLP One Logan Sq Ste 5200 600 Peachtree St NE Atlanta GA 30308-2216 Office Phone: 404-885-3328. Office Fax: 404-962-6568. Business E-Mail: richard.gerakitis@troutmansanders.com.

GERALD, BARRY, retired radiology educator, neuroscientist; b. Greenville, Miss., Feb. 10, 1934; s. Louis Elmo and Eula (Mitchell) G.; m. Marjorie Brown, Aug. 6, 1955; children: Lucy Gerald Cook, Lee, Paul. Student, U. Miss., Oxford, 1951-54; MD, U. Miss., Jackson, 1958. Diplomate Am. Bd. Radiology. Intern Hermann Hosp., Houston, 1958-59, resident in radiology, 1959-62; fellow in pediatric radiology Children's Hosp. Med. Ctr., Cin., 1962-64; mem. faculty dept. radiology U. Ark., Little Rock, 1964-65, 67-69; dir. radiology dept. Children's Hosp. Med. Ctr., Oakland, Calif., 1965-66; mem. faculty dept. radiology U. Tenn. Coll. Medicine, Memphis, 1969—2004, prof., chmn. dept., 1979-95; fellow in neuroradiology Tufts-New Eng. Med. Ctr., Boston, 1971-72, interim chair dept. radiology, 2004—. Dir. radiology dept. Le Bonheur Children's Hosp., Memphis, 1983-88, 1991-2002; acting dir. radiology dept. St. Jude Children's Rsch. Hosp., Memphis, 1985-87; trainee Nat. Cancer Inst., 1960-62. Contbr. articles to med. jours., chpts. to books. Fellow Am. Coll. Radiology; mem. Am. Soc. Neuroradiology, Soc. for Pediatric Radiology, Radiol. Soc. N.Am. (councillor 1980-85), Am. Roentgen Ray Soc., Southeastern Neuroradiologic Soc. (founder, pres. 1977-78), So. Radiologic Conf. (pres. 1975-76). Avocations: tennis, american history. Home: 694 Clanlo Dr Memphis TN 38104-5067 Office: U Tenn Dept Radiology 800 Madison Ave Memphis TN 38103-3400 E-mail: bgerald@utmem.edu.

GERALD, MICHAEL CHARLES, pharmacy educator; b. N.Y.C., Nov. 20, 1939; s. Tobias Gerson and Ruby Rose (Weinstock) G.; m. Gloria Elaine Gruber, Jan. 31, 1965; children— Marc Jonathan, Melissa Suzanne. B.S. in Pharmacy, Fordham U., 1961; Ph.D., Ind. U., 1968. Registered pharmacist, N.Y. Postdoctoral fellow USPHS, U. Chgo., 1968-69; asst. prof. Coll. Pharmacy Ohio State U., Columbus, 1969-74, assoc. prof., 1974-80, prof., 1980-93, prof. and assoc. dean., 1984-93; dean, prof. Sch. Pharmacy U. Conn., Storrs, 1993-02; prof., 2002—. cons. WHO, Geneva, 1983-84; mem. adv. panel U.S. Pharmacopeia Com. Revision, Washington, 1980-85. Author: Pharmacology: An Introduction to Drugs, 2d edit. 1981, Nursing Pharmacology and Therapeutics, 2d edit. 1988, The Poisonous Pen of Agatha Christie, 1993; (co-author) The Nurse's Guide to Drug Therapy: Drug Profiles for Patient Care, 1984, Editor: Instruction in Pharmacology: New Approaches and New Faces, 1979. Mem. FDA Drug Abuse Adv. Com., 1993—. Served to 1st lt. USAF, 1963-65. USPHS fellow Ind. U., 1965-68; Gustavus A. Pfeiffer Meml. Research fellow Am. Found. Pharm. Edn., 1983-84. Fellow Acad. Pharm. Scis. (sect. sec. 1975-77, sect. v.p. 1978-79). (sect. sec. 1975-77, sect. v.p. 1978-79); mem. Am. Assn. Colls. of Pharmacy (bd. dirs. 1980-82), Am. Soc. Pharmacology and Exptl. Therapeutics, N.Y. Acad. Scis., Soc. Neurosciences. Avocations: photography, reading, music, walking Office Phone: 860-486-5416. Business E-Mail: michael.gerald@uconn.edu.

GERALDSON, RAYMOND I., JR., lawyer; b. Racine, Wis., Oct. 19, 1940; s. Raymond I. Sr. and Evelyn (Thorpe) G.; m. Melinda Paine, June 13, 1964; children: Amy Geraldson-Bhote, Raymond I. III. BA, DePauw U., 1962; JD, Northwestern U., 1965. Bar: Ill. 1965, D.C. 1966, U.S. Dist. Ct. (no. dist.) Ill. 1967. Ptnr. Pattishall, McAuliffe, Newbury, Hilliard & Geraldson, Washington, 1965-67, Chgo., 1967—. Adj. prof. John Marshall Law Sch. 1978—; lectr. in field. Contbr. articles on trademark law to profl. jours. Trustee Kendall Coll., 1985—, chmn., 1990-2000. Mem. ABA, Ill. State Bar Assn. (coun. sect. intellectual property law 1978-82, chmn. 1980-81), Chgo. Bar Assn., 7th Cir., Intellectual Property Law Assn. Chgo. (bd. dirs. 1984-86, 92-93, pres. 1991-92), Internat. Trademark Assn. (bd. dirs. 1985-87), Am. Intellectual Property Law Assn., Lawyers for Creative Arts (hons. coun. 1994—, bd. dirs. 1974-94, pres. 1976-78), Lawyers Club Chgo., Econ. Club Chgo., Sunset Ridge Country Club, Union League Club of Chgo., Chi. Office: Pattishall McAuliffe Newbury Hilliard & Geraldson 311 S Wacker Dr Ste 5000 Chicago IL 60606-6631

GERARD, BARBARA, visual artist, educator; b. N.Y.C., Apr. 21, 1943; d. Arthur and Edith (Perrone) De Bernarda; m. Marvin Hartenstein, Sept. 18, 1976; 1 son by aprevious marriage, David Gerard. BS, NYU, 1963; MA, 1966, postgrad., 1972—; profl. diploma, City Coll. CUNY, 1975; postgrad., Columbia U., 1977-79. Graphic designer C.A. Parshall Advt. Agy., N.Y.C., 1962; art tchr. Herman Ridder Jr. High Sch., N.Y.C., 1963-65; art chmn., 1967-70; freelance desinger Sam Muggeo Advt. Inc., 1965-67; program counselor recruitment, tng. Spanish-speaking tchrs. N.Y.C. Bd. Edn., 1970-72; program coord. bilingual pupil svcs. Ctr. Bilingual Edn., 1972-75; dir. bilingual tchr.-intern program, 1975-79; dir. Ctr. Dissemination, 1979-81; dir. Project MASTER, 1983-87; spl. asst. to dep. chancellor, 1988-89; dir. staff devel., 1989-91; dir. staff and curriculum devel. office multi-cultural edn., 1991—; owner, v.p. George Gerard Assocs., Inc., Port Washington, N.Y., 1981-83. Adj. prof. Nova Southeastern U., 1995—, Hunton Coll., Queens Coll., L.I. U.; cons. Yeshiva U., Pace U., 1973, Aspiria of N.Y., 1974, Children's TV Workshop - Sesame St., 1975; adj. lectr. CCNY, 1973-74, N.Y.U., 1974-75, Coll. New Rochelle, 1974-75, Upsala U., Sweden, 1994, Hunter Coll., 1994--, Nova Southeastern U., 1996--, LIU, 1999-2002, The City Coll., 2001-03; cons., participant WNBC-TV, 1970, 75, 79. Contbr. articles to profl. jours.; one woman ships inlcude Lincoln Inst. Gallery, N.Y., 1968, Henry Hicks Gallery, Bklyn., 1976, Second Story Spring St. Gallery, N.Y., 1976, Viridian Gallery, N.Y., 1977, 79; group shows include Loeb Student Ctr. Gallery, N.Y.C., 1962, 63, Riverdale Cmty. Gallery, N.Y., 1965, Environment Gallery, N.Y.C., 1969, Metamorphosis, N.Y., 1970, Concepts II, N.Y.C., 1971, Uion Carbide, N.Y., 1872, Lever House, 1973, Westchester Arts Soc., White Plains, N.Y., 1973, Gillary Gallery, Jericho, Long Island, 1974, Manhattan Savs. bank, 1976, Bklyn. Acad. Music, 1976, Pvt. Viewings/The Erlichs, The Colins, 1976, Gallery 91, Bklyn., 1976, Henry Hicks Gallery, Bklyn., 1975, 76, 77, Lincoln Ctr., Avery Fisher Hall, N.Y.C., 1976, second Story Spring St. Gallery, 1976, Bergdorf Goodman, White Plains, 1976, First Women's Bank, 1976, 80, Viridian Gallery, 1976, 77, 80, Womanart Gallery, 1976, Norman Kramer Gallery, Danbury, Conn., 1976, Mfrts. Hanover Bank, N.Y., 1977, 80, Union of Maine Artists, Portland, 1977, Northeastern U., Boston, 1978, Verd Internat. Gallery, East Hampton, 1978, Women in the Arts Gallery, 1979, Rensselaer Inst., Troy, 1979, Marie Pellicone Gallery, 1981, N.Y. Tech. Coll., 1982, guild Hall Mus., 1983, 84, Gov. of N.Y. - World Trade Ctr., 1985, Marte Previti Gallery, 1986, South Street Gallery, Guild Hall Mus., 1987, N.Y. Tech. Coll., 1988, CUNY, 1989; represented in permanent collections Mus. Contemporary Crafts, N.Y.C., BBD&O Advt., Inc., N.Y.C., Guild Hall, East Hampton; also pvt. collections. Chmn. Pres.'s Task Force on Bilingual edn., 1972; bd. dirs. Nat. Assn. Italian-Am. Dirs., 1982; v.p. Italian Bilingual Bicultural Educators Assn., 1982. HEW/Fed. govt. ESEA Title VII grantee, 1975-79; recipient Nat. Scene Award for Achievement in Arts and Culture, 1979. Mem. NEA, Nat. Assn. Bilingual Edn., Nat. Assn. Italian-Am. Women (bd.dirs. 1987—, pres. 1990-93), N.Y. State Assn. Bilingual Edn., coun. supervisory Adminstrs., NOW, Am. Coun. Arts, Coalition of Women Artists Orgn., Assn. Artist-Run Galleries, Women in the Arts, Advt. Women N.Y., Women Bus. Owners N.Y. Office: 30 Waterside Plz Apt 29F New York NY 10010-2626 E-mail: gerardba1@aol.com.

GERARD, JAMES WILSON, publishing consultant; b. Chgo., May 16, 1935; s. Ralph Waldo and Margaret (Wilson) G. Student, U. Vt., 1955, Roosevelt U., 1955-59. Ptnr. UNIPUB, N.Y.C., 1962-77; pres. Brookfield (Vt.) Pub. Co., 1977—. Bd. dirs. Renouf Pub. Co., Ltd. Mem. Am. Assn. Scholarly Pub., Les Ambassadeurs Club. Democrat. Office: Brookfield Mktg Inc 1517 Sagebrush Rd Palm Springs CA 92264 Office Phone: 760-320-8663. Personal E-mail: jgerard@dc.rr.com.

GERARD, JULES BERNARD, law educator; b. St. Louis, May 20, 1929; s. John Baptist and Faith Vera (Clinton) G.; m. Camilla Roma Smith, Aug. 8, 1953; children: Lisa, Karen Julia. Student, Iowa State Coll., 1947-49; AB, Washington U., St. Louis, 1957, JD, 1958. Bar: N.Y. 1959, U.S. Supreme Ct. 1979. Assoc. Donovan, Leisure, Newton & Irvine, N.Y.C., 1958-60; asst. prof. law U. Mo., Columbia, 1960-62; asst. prof., assoc. prof. law Washington U., 1962-67, prof., 1967-99, prof. emeritus, 1999—. Author: Local Regulation of Adult Businesses, 1992, Proposed Washington D.C. Amendment, 1979, (with others) Sum and Substance Constitutional Law, 1976, (with others) Federal Land Use Law, 1986; editor: 100 Years of 14th Amendment, 1973; editor-in-chief Washington U. Law Quar., 1958; contbr. articles to profl. jours., chpts. to books. Mem. Mo. Adv. com. U.S. Commn. on Civil Rights, 1987-92. Served to 1st lt. USAF, 1950-54 Mem. ABA. Republican. Avocations: collecting scrimshaw and antique photographica, photography. Home: 1564 Yarmouth Point Dr Chesterfield MO 63017-5639 E-mail: gerard@law.wustl.edu.

GERARD, LEO W., labor union executive; b. Sudbury, Ont., 1947; LLD (hon.), Laurentian U., 1994; attended, Canadian Labour Congress Labour Coll., 1996—98. Staff rep. United Steelworkers Am. USWA, 1977, internat. sec.-treas., 1993—2001, internat. pres., 2001—; dir. Dist. 6 Ont., Canada, 1985—91; nat. dir. Can., 1991—93; chmn. Steelworkers Health and Welfare Fund, 1996—98; with Heartland Labor Capital Funds. Contbr. articles to profl. pubs.

GERARD, ROY DUPUY, retired oil company executive; b. New Orleans, Sept. 14, 1931; s. Lester Charles and Helene (Dupuy) G.; m. Minnie Harper, May 17, 1958; children: Roy Dupuy Jr., Nannette Gerard Helmcamp, Carl, Denise Ingram. BSChemE, La. State U., 1953, MSChemE, 1958. Chemist, technologist various plants Shell Chem. Co., Houston, La., N.Y., Calif., 1958-69; dept. head Shell Devel. Co., Emeryville, Calif., 1969-71, dir. indsl. chems. and petrochems. Houston, 1973-75, mgr. chem. R & D, 1975-77, gen. mgr. Westhollow rsch., 1982-90; pres. Saudi Petrochem. Co., Al Jubail, Saudi Arabia, 1980-82; mgr. logistics econs., supply and econs. and mktg. Shell Oil Co., Houston, 1971-73, gen. mgr. engring. products, 1977-80, v.p. health, safety and environ., 1990-92, ret., 1992; pvt. investor, stocks, bonds, etc., 1992—. Mem., vice chmn. coun. environ. affairs Conf. Bd., 1991—; mem., chmn. chem. engring. vis. com. U. Tex., Austin, 1985-87; mem. chem. engring. vis. com. La. State U., Baton Rouge, 1987-90, mem. dean's adv. com., 1990-2001; mem. chem. engring. vis. com. Tex. A&M U., College Station, 1989, U. Tenn., Knoxville, 1989 1st lt. C.E., U.S. Army, 1954-56. Mem. AICE, Coun. for Chem. Rsch. (chmn. 1991—), Am. Indsl. Health Coun. (bd. dirs., exec. com. 1990—), Am. Petroleum Inst. (health and environ. gen. com. 1990—), Northgate Country Club, Raveneaux Country Club (Spring, Tex.). Republican. Roman Catholic. Avocations: fishing, golf, woodworking. Personal E-mail: rgerard914@aol.com.

GERARD, SUSAN JANE, secondary school educator; b. Spokane, Wash., Feb. 8, 1962; d. Michael Arthur and Jane Carol (Sheppard) Hussey; m. Thomas Roy Gerard, Dec. 20, 1986; children: Andrew Thomas, Stephen Michael, Kymberley Sue. BA in History and Edn. with honors, Gonzaga U., 1984, MA in Tchg. and History, 1987, postgrad., 1990, Ea. Wash. U., 1990. Cert. tchr., adminstrn., Wash. Tchr. social studies Lewis and Clark H.S., Spokane, 1984—, freshman track coach, 1984-88, debate coach, 1986-88, mem. sch. care team, 1985—. Adj. prof. edn. Whitworth Coll., 1995—; advanced placement European history essay exam grader, 1996—, table leader, 2002—; mem. sch. attendance discipline com., 1995—, sch. faculty adv. group leader, site coun., 2000-03; coll. bd. faculty cons., workshop presenter, 1998—; racial and cultural equality adv. Lewis and Clark HS, Spokane, Wash., 1996—. Author: A.P. Teacher's Guide to European History, 1998; contbr. articles to profl. publs. Voter registrar Spokane County Election Bd., 1983—; leader, Cub Scouts, 1996-2001, Girl Scouts Am., 2002—; chmn. com. Boy Scouts Am., 2002—05. Named Wash. State Profl. Woman of Yr., 1997, Tchr. of Yr., VFW, 1998; Cataldo acad. scholar Gonzaga U., 1984-87; recipient 20th Century achievement award, Cambridge, 1998, Outstanding Scholar award Cambridge Press, 1999, Disting. Tchr. award Spokane Pub. Schs., 2004. Mem. ASCD, NEA, Wash. Edn. Assn., Spokane Edn. Assn. (bldg. rep. 1985-87), Am. Hist. Assn., Phi Alpha Theta, Kappa Delta Pi, Alpha Sigma Nu. Roman Catholic. Avocations: camping, family activities, cooking, reading. Home: 14025 E 23rd Ave Veradale WA 99037-9330 Office: Lewis and Clark HS 521 W 4th Ave Spokane WA 99204-2692

GERARD, WHITNEY IAN, lawyer; b. N.Y.C., Oct. 31, 1934; s. Harold Todd and Beatrice Roma (Meyer) G.; m. Marion Lehane, Apr. 1, 1966; children: Ian Alexandre, Stefan Meredith. AB, Princeton U., 1956; JD, Harvard U., 1963. Bar: N.Y. 1964. Wine exporter Alexis Lichine et Cie, Bordeaux, France, 1956-58; wine cons. S.S. Pierce Co., Boston, 1960-75; assoc., then ptnr. Alexander and Green, N.Y.C., 1963-84; ptnr., chmn. internat. practice comm. Chadbourne and Parke LLP, N.Y.C., 1984—. Bd. dirs. U. Cape Town Fund, Inc., N.Y.C., Dreyfus Liquid Assets, Inc., The Dreyfus Fund, Inc., Dreyfus Worldwide Dollar Money Market Fund, Inc., Dreyfus Lifetime Portfolios, Inc., Dreyfus Short Intermediate Mcpl. Bond Fund, Dreyfus Short Intermediate Govt. Fund. and other Dreyfus funds. 1st lt. USAF, 1958-60. Mem. ABA, N.Y. State Bar Assn., Internat. Bar Assn., Univ. Club, Ancient Order of Beefeaters (Chief Warder 1965-90). Democrat. Avocations: classical music, ballet, theater, mountain hiking, literature. Home: 940 Park Ave New York NY 10028-0311 also: 102 W Center Rd West Stockbridge MA 01266-9378 Office: Chadbourne & Parke LLP 30 Rockefeller Plz New York NY 10112-0129 Office Phone: 212-408-5265.

GERARD-SHARP, MONICA FLEUR, communications executive; b. London, Oct. 4, 1951; came to U.S., 1975; d. John Hugh Gerard-Sharp and Doreen May (Kearney) Dewhurst; m. Ali Edward Wambold, Nov. 21, 1981; children: Marina, Daniela, Dominica. BA in Philosophy and Lit. with honors, U. Warwick, Eng., 1973; MBA in Fin., Mktg. and Internat. Bus., Columbia U., 1980. Editor Inst. Chem. Engrs., London, 1973-74; sub-editor TV Times, London, 1974-75; press officer, editor UN, N.Y.C., 1975-78; bus. mgr. Time-Life Video, N.Y.C., 1980-81; mgr. fin. analysis Time-Life Films, N.Y.C., 1981; v.p. T.V.I.S., N.Y.C., 1982-83; dir. strategy and devel. HBO, ATC, N.Y.C., 1984-85; asst. treas., officer Time Inc., N.Y.C., 1985—87; pub. Travel Today and other mags. Fairchild Pubs. subs. Capital Cities/ABC, N.Y.C., 1987-88; dir. video programming Fairchild Pubs., Capital Cities/ABC, N.Y.C., 1988-89; pub. Entrée and Home Fashions Mags., N.Y.C., 1988-90; pres. Monali Inc., N.Y.C., 1991—. Cons. UN Bus. Council, N.Y.C., 1979; bd. rep. U.S.A. Network, N.Y.C., 1983-85. Editor: Everyone's United Nations, 1977; contbg. editor Asia Pacific Forum, 1976-77; contbr. articles to profl. jours. and mags., 1973-78. Treas. Help the Aged, Eng.; nat. devel. bd. Chances for Children, 1995-, pres. 2001-2003; adv. bd. Am. Mus. Natural History, 1998—; pres. bd. Am. Friends of Royal Ct. Theatre, 1998-2000. Bronfman fellow, 1979-80. Mem. Nat. Acad. Cable Programming, Am. Film Inst., Beta Gamma Sigma. Roman Catholic. Avocations: antiques, photography, wildlife. Home: Deer Park 128 Sunset Hill Rd Pleasant Valley NY 12569 Office: Monali Inc 26 E 80th St New York NY 10021-0110

GERASIMCHUK, NIKOLAY, chemistry professor; MS in Chemistry, Kiev State U., Ukraine, 1981; PhD, U. Kans., 1996. Asst. prof. dept. chemistry Kiev State U., Ukraine, 1986—90, 1991—92; rsch. asst. U. Kans., Lawrence, 1993—94, tchg. asst. chemistry dept., 1995; rsch. asst. Kans. Advanced Synthesis Lab., 1995—96; rsch. assoc. ND State U., 1997—98; from rsch. assoc. to rsch. chemist Pharmacyclics, Inc., Sunnyvale, Calif., 1998—2001; asst. prof. dept. chemistry SW Mo. State U., Springfield, 2001—. Reviewer in field. Contbr. articles to profl. jours. Chmn. inorganic chemistry sect. Am. Chem. Soc., 2003. Achievements include patents for useful properties of synthesized coordination compounds; patents pending for. Home: 1117 W woodbine St Springfield MO 65803

GERATHY, E. CARROLL, retired insurance company executive, real estate developer; b. Long Island City, NY, June 25, 1915; s. Joseph Hewson and Emma E. (Donady) G.; m. Julia F. Gill, Sept. 7, 1942; children: Nancy, John; m. Joyce K. Baker, Dec. 31, 1972; children: Stephen Baker, Nancy Baker; m. Betty Ann Durkin, Jan. 27, 1984. MBA, U. Chgo., 1962. C.L.U. With McKesson & Robbins, Inc., 1933-48; with Prudential Ins. Co. Am., 1948-78, sr. v.p., 1964-78; project dir. Hilton Hawaiian Village, Hilton Hotels Corp., 1979-81, Third Newark Gateway Urban Renewal Assn., 1981-91. Mem. N.J. C. of C., Canoe Brook Country Club (N.J.). Home: 42 Knob Hill Dr Summit NJ 07901-3051

GERATY, LAWRENCE THOMAS, academic administrator, archaeologist, educator; b. St. Helena, Calif., Apr. 21, 1940; s. Thomas Sinclair and Hazel Mae (McVicker) G.; m. Gillian Anne Keough, Aug. 5, 1962; children: Brent, Julie. BA, Pacific Union Coll., 1962; MA, Andrews U., 1963, BD, 1965; PhD, Harvard U., 1972. Pastor 7th Day Adventist Ch., Calif., 1962-66; instr. old testament Andrews U., Berrien Springs, Mich., 1966-72, asst. prof. archaeology and history, 1972-76, assoc. prof. archaeology and history, 1976-80, prof., 1980-85; curator S.H. Horn Archaeol. Mus., Berrien Springs, Mich., 1976-85; dir. Inst. Archaeology Andrews U., Berrien Springs, 1981-85; pres. Atlantic Union Coll., Lancaster, Mass., 1985-93, La Sierra U., Riverside, Calif., 1993—. Project dir. Excavation of Tell Hesban, Jordan, 1973-76, Madaba Plains Project, Jordan, 1984—; v.p. Am. Ctr. of Oriental Rsch., Amman, 1985—. Editor, contbr. articles to profl. jours. Bd. dirs. Thayer Symphony Orch., Lancaster, Mass., 1985-93; mem. Edn. Forum of Clinton, Mass., 1990-93. Fulbright fellow, 1970-71, Robert H. Pfeiffer fellow, 1970-71; grantee Ford Found., 1969-70, Ctr. Field Rsch., 1976, NEH, 1979. Mem. Soc. Bibl. Literature (pres. 1988-90), Archeol. Inst. Am., Clinton C. of C. (bd. dirs. 1985-92), Riverside C. of C. (bd. dirs. 1996—), Raincross Club, Employers Group (bd. dirs. 1996—). Seventh-Day Adventist. Office: La Sierra U Office Pres 4700 Pierce St Riverside CA 92505-3332

GERB, BERNARD, lawyer; b. Gloversville, N.Y., Aug. 20, 1925; s. Joseph and Theresa G.; m. Alice Kirman, Nov. 24, 1957; children— Andrew Alan, Jane Laurel, B.E.E., Cornell U., 1950; J.D., Rutgers U., 1955. Bar: N.Y. 1955, U.S. Supreme Ct. 1956. Ptnr., Ostrolenk Faber, Gerb, & Soffen, N.Y.C., 1955-86; dir. T. K. Communications, Inc., Metuchin, N.J., Wm. Steinen Mfg. Co., Parsippany, N.J. Mercer County Democratic Committeeman, Princeton, N.J., 1983-88. Served with U.S. Army, 1944-46. Mem. N.Y. Patent Law Assn., N.J. Patent Law Assn., Am. Patent Law Assn., N.Y. State Bar Assn., ABA, Phi Alpha Delta. Clubs: Princeton Democratic. Home: 127 Meadowbrook Dr Princeton NJ 08540-3664

GERBA, CHARLES PETER, microbiologist, educator; b. Blue Island, Ill., Sept. 10, 1945; s. Peter and Virginia (Roulo) G.; m. Peggy Louise Scheitlin, June 6, 1970; children: Peter, Phillip. BS in Microbiology, Ariz. State U., 1969; PhD in Microbiology, U. Miami, 1973. Postdoctoral fellow Baylor Coll. Medicine, Houston, 1973-74, asst. prof. microbiology, 1974-81; assoc. prof. U. Ariz., Tucson, 1981-85, prof., 1985—. Cons. EPA, Tucson, 1980—, World Health Orgn., Pan Am. Health Orgn., 1989—; advisor CRC Press, Boca Raton, Fla., 1981—. Editor: Methods in Environmental Virology, 1982, Groundwater Pollution Microbiology, 1984, Phage Ecology, 1987, Pollution Sci., 1996; contbr. numerous articles to profl. and sci. jours. Mem. Pima County Bd. Health, 1986-92; mem. sci. adv. bd. EPA, 1987-95. Recipient McKee medal Water Environ. Fedn., 1996; named Outstanding Research Scientist U. Ariz., 1984, 92, Outstanding Rsch. Team, 1994. Fellow AAAS (environ. sci. and engring.), Am. Acad. Microbiology, Am. Soc. Microbiology (divsn. chmn. 1982-83, 87-88, pres. Ariz. chpt. 1984-85, councilor 1985-88); mem. Internat. Assn. Water Pollution Rsch. (sr. del. 1985-91), Am. Water Works Assn. (A.P. Black award 1997), Water Quality Assn. (Hon. Mem. award 1998). Achievements include research in environmental microbiology, colloid transport in ground water, wastewater reuse and risk assessment. Home: 1980 W Paseo Monserrat Tucson AZ 85704-1329 Office: U Ariz Dept Microbiol & Immunol Wat Tucson AZ 85721-0001 Office Phone: 520-621-6906. Business E-Mail: gerba@ag.arizona.edu.

GERBASI, KATHLEEN CARRESE, psychologist, educator; b. Ithaca, N.Y., Oct. 19, 1949; d. Dominic Ralph and Jacqulyn Faye Carrese; m. Thomas Ross Gerbasi; children: Julianna Faye Kaden, Alexandra Marie, Margaret Elizabeth. BA in Psychology, U. Rochester, 1971; PhD, U.Rochester, 1976. Animal Assisted Therapy DePaul U./ People Animals Nature, 2001. Instr., psychology Niagara County C.C., Sanborn, NY, 2000—; resource coord. Soc. and Animals Forum, Washington Grove, Md., 2001—. Dir. rsch. and edn. People Animals Nature, Naperville, Ill., 2001—. Coun. mem. Internat. Soc. for Anthrozoology, 2003; vol. Nursing home, Lewiston, NY, 1999—2003. Recipient Innovations in Tchg. Award, Niagara County C.C., 2001, 2003, 2004; SUNY Conversions in Disciplines grant, 2004. Mem.: APA, Internat. Soc. for Anthrozoology (coun. mem. 2003), Animal Behavior Soc., Am. Sociol. Assn., Am. Psychol. Soc. Achievements include patents for Mailing/Display Device. Home: 601 Sherwood Ct Lewiston NY 14092 Office: Niagara County Cmty Coll Saundersettlement Rd Sanborn NY 14132 Office Phone: 716-614-6764. Personal E-mail: kcgerbasiphd@earthlink.net.

GERBER, DAN, writer; b. Grand Rapids, Mich., Aug. 12, 1940; s. Daniel F. and Dorothy Scott G.; m. Virginia Hartjen Gerber, Aug. 12, 1961 (div. Jan. 1992); children: Wendie Elizabeth, Frank Daniel, Tamara Yeager; m. Debra West Gerber, Sept. 14, 1996. BA, Mich. State U., 1962. Author: A Second Life, 2001, others; author of short stories and poems. Democrat. Buddhist. Avocations: fly fishing, auto racing, hiking, writing. Address: PO Box 371 Driggs ID 83422-0371

GERBER, DARYL JEFFREY, lawyer; b. Hershey, Pa., Jan. 14, 1951; s. George A. and Winifred J. (Heilman) G.; m. Pamela L. Boger, Aug. 26, 1972; children: Erin B., Kelly B., Joshua D. BA, Millersville (Pa.) State U., 1972; JD, Villanova U., 1975. Ptnr. Brandt & Gerber, Palmyra, Pa., 1975—. Gen. counsel Pa. Sports Hall of Fame, Lebanon, Pa., 1990—. Named Dist. Sertoman of Yr. East Central Pa. Dist., Lancaster, 1995. Mem. Hershey-Palmyra Sertoma Club (chmn. bd. 1997—), Hearlsay Fund, Inc. (pres. 1994-96), Four Diamonds Adv. Bd. Avocations: flying, skiing, biking, golf. Office: Brandt & Gerber 46 E Main St Palmyra PA 17078-1729

GERBER, DEAN N., lawyer; b. Chgo., Ill., Dec. 4, 1959; married. BS magna cum laude, U. of Delaware, 1982; JD cum laude, U. of Ill., 1985. CPA Ill., 1984; bar: Ill. 1985. Joined Chapman & Cutler; assoc. atty. Vedder, Price, Kaufman & Kammholz, 1991, shareholder, 1992—, chair equipment fin. practice group. Mem.: Omicron Sigma Delta, Phi Kappa Phi. Office: Vedder Price Kaufman & Kammholz 222 N LaSalle St Chicago IL 60601*

GERBER, DOUGLAS EARL, classics educator; b. North Bay, Ont., Can., Sept. 14, 1933; s. Earl Jacob and Bertha (Cox) G.; m. Joan Isobel Warner, Nov. 22, 1986; 1 dau., Allison S. BA, U. Western Ont. (Can.), London, 1955, MA, 1956; PhD, U. Toronto, 1959. Lectr. Greek U. Toronto, 1958-59; mem. faculty dept. classics U. Western Ont., London, 1959-99, assoc. prof., 1964-69, prof., 1969-99, chmn. dept., 1969-97, vice provost for acad. affairs, 1984-86, W.S. Fox chair of classics. Author: A Bibliography of Pindar, 1513-1966, 1969, Euterpe: An Anthology of Early Greek Lyric, Elegiac and Iambic Poetry, 1970, Emendations in Pindar, 1513-1972, 1976, Pindar's Olympian One: A Commentary, 1982, Lexicon in Bacchylidem, 1984, Greek Iambic Poetry, 1999, Greek Elegiac Poetry, 1999, A Commentary on Pindar Olympian Nine, 2002; editor Greek Poetry and Philosophy; Studies in Honor of Leonard Woodbury, 1984, A Companion to the Greek Lyric Poets, 1997. Mem. Classical Assn. Canada (treas. 1960-62, pres. 1988-90), Am. Philol. Assn. (editor trans. 1974-82), Classical Assn. Middle West and South, Classical Assn. (Gt. Britain). Home: 2 Grosvenor St London ON Canada N6A 1Y4 Office: U Western Ont Dept Classics London ON Canada N6A 3K7 E-mail: degerber@uwo.ca.

GERBER, JACK, artist; b. Phila., May 19, 1927; s. Benjamin Samuel and Jean (Ginzberg) G. Student, Pa. Acad. Fine Arts, Phila., 1949-53. Curator Phila. Water Color Club; juror Sketch Club Phila., 1987, 90, Artists' Equity, 1985, Perkins Ctr. for the Arts, 1984, others. One-person shows include Roger LaPelle Gallery, Phila., 1983, 84, Pavilion Galleries, Mt. Holly, N.J., 1990, Congregation Beth Orr, 1995, Plastic Club, Phila., 1995, Library of the Swedenborg Acad., Pa., 1996, The Hill Sch., Pottstown, 1997, Rodger Lapelle Gallery, Phila., 2000; exhibited in group shows at Pa. Acad. Fine Arts, Phila. Mus. Art, The Library of Congress, Rutgers Nat. Drawing Show, Nat. Acad. Design, 1988, 90, Allentown Mus., 2000, Phila. City Hall, 2000. Recipient numerous prizes at art shows; Phila. Bd. Edn. scholar; Branywine Workshop fellow, 1983. Mem. Am. Color Print Soc. (First prize 1996), Phila. Watercolor Club, Phila. Sketch Club, Plastic Club (Gold medal 1997), The Woodmere Mus. (Harry A. Harris award 1997), Phila. Mus. Art. Democrat. Home: 540 W Chew Ave Philadelphia PA 19120-2229

GERBER, JOEL, federal judge; b. Chgo., July 16, 1940; s. Peter H. and Marcia L. (Weber) G.; m. Judith R. Smilgoff, Aug. 18, 1963; children— Jay Lawrence, Jeffrey Mark, Jon Victor BSBA, Roosevelt U., Chgo., 1962; JD, DePaul U., Chgo., 1965; LL.M., Boston U., 1968. Bar: Ill. 1965, Ga. 1974. Trial atty. IRS, Boston, 1965-72, staff asst. to regional counsel Atlanta, 1972-76, dist. counsel Nashville, 1976-80, dep. chief counsel Washington, 1980-83, acting chief counsel, 1983-84; judge U.S. Tax Ct., Washington, 1984—99, 2000—04, sr. judge, 1999—2000, chief judge, 2004—; gen. counsel ATF Credit Union, Boston, 1968-70; lectr. Vanderbilt U. Sch. Law, Nashville, 1976-80. Lectr. U. Miami Grad. Law Sch., 1986-90. Recipient awards U.S. Treasury Dept., 1979, 81, 82; Presdl. Meritorious Exec. Rank award, 1983. Office: US Tax Ct 400 2nd St NW Rm 432 Washington DC 20217-0002

GERBER, KAREN JOYCE, project planning consultant; b. Detroit, Dec. 30, 1955; d. Arthur William and Joan Joyce Konarske; m. Vincent John Gerber, Sept. 22, 1978; children: Jason, Alison. BS, Mich. Technol. U., 1978; MS, Colo. Sch. Mines, 1991. Cert. in advanced project mgmt. Engring. technician ALCOA, Inc., Massena, N.Y., 1976-77; metall. engr. Rockwell Internat., Golden, Colo., 1978-81, planning analyst, 1981-83, advanced engr., 1983-85, sr. engr., 1985-87, prin. engr., 1987-90; sr. prin. engr. EG&G, Inc., Golden, 1990-92, program mgr., 1992-95; pres., founder Strategies and Solutions, Arvada, Colo., 1995—; trainer Project Mgmt. Careertrack, Boulder, 1998-99. Mem. steering com. Jefferson County Sch. to Career, Golden, 1996-99; mem. adv. bd. Sch.-to-Career, Arvada, 1997—. Author booklets and articles. Mem. Leadership Jefferson County, Lakewood, Colo., 1997-98. Recipient Do-er of Deeds award Dept. Energy, Golden, 1992. Mem. NAFE, Denver-Metro C. of C., Nat. Spkrs. Assn., Project Mgmt. Inst., Toastmasters Internat. (mem. energetics, club pres. 1996-97, Outstanding Toastmaster 1997). Avocations: mentoring, hiking, camping, public speaking.

GERBER, LARRY GEORGE, historian, educator; b. L.A., Oct. 27, 1947; s. Max N. and Sara Gerber; m. Viena Louise Katainen, Oct. 23, 1980; 1 child, Michael Spinello. BA, U. Calif., Berkeley, 1968, MA, 1969, PhD, 1979. Lectr. European divsn. U. Md., Heidelberg, Germany, 1979—80; vis. asst. prof. U. Ariz., Tucson, 1980—82; vis. asst. prof. history Brown U., Providence, 1982—83; prof. history Auburn U., Ala., 1983—. Author: (historical monographs) The Limits of Liberalism: Josephus Daniels, Henry Stimson, Bernard Baruch, Donald Richberg and the Development of the Modern American Political Economy, The Irony of State Intervention: American Industrial Relations Policy in Comparative Perspective, 1914-1939, 2005; contbr. articles to profl. jours. Mem. Ala. Holocaust Commn., 2000—. Mem.: AAUP (chair nat. com. on governance 1995—98, 1st v.p. 2002—), Am. Assn. Univ. Pres. (pres. Ala. conf. 1991—93), Ala. Coun. Coll. and Univ. Faculty Pres. (pres. 1994—95), Phi Beta Kappa. Office: Auburn Univ History Dept Auburn AL 36849-5207 Office Phone: 334-844-6646. Office Fax: 334-844-6673. E-mail: gerbelg@auburn.edu.

GERBER, MELANIE K., lawyer; b. Jersey City, May 27, 1947; BA, Univ. Md., 1973; JD, Georgetown Univ., 1988. Bar: DC 1989, Pa. 1989, Supreme Ct. Pa., US Dist. Ct. (DC dist.), US Ct. Appeals (DC cir.), US Supreme Ct. Assoc. Morrison & Foerster, Washington; exec. dir. Legal Resource Ctr. for Housing & Cmty. Devel., Washington; pub. svc. counsel Patton Boggs LLP, Washington. Mem. oper. com. Whitman-Walker Legal Svc.; mem. adv. bd. DC Employment Justice Ctr.; mem. legal adv. bd. Capital Area Immigrants Rights Coalition; mem. editl. bd. Law Firm Pro Bono Project; vol. mentor Georgetown Univ. Law Ctr.; mem. regional leadership council Lawyers for Children Am.; mem. Legal Svc. Providers Consortium. Recipient Mayor's Arts award, DC Commn. on Arts & Humanities, 2003, Legal Assistance Disting. Svc. award, Sept. 11 Pro Bono Legal Relief Project, 2002, Servant of Justice award, Legal Aid Soc., 2001. Mem.: Washington Lawyers' Com. for Civil Rights (Vincent E. Reed award 2004, Outstanding Achievement award, Immigration & Refugee Rights 2003, Outstanding Achievement award, Equal Employment Opportunity 2000), Pa. Bar Assn., DC Bar (award for Pro Bono Work 2001). Office: Patton Boggs LLP 2550 M St NW Washington DC 20037-1350 Office Fax: 202-457-6315, 202-457-6312. Business E-Mail: mgerber@pattonboggs.com.

GERBER, MURRY S., utilities, gas, oil executive; b. 1953; BA with honors in Geology, Augustana Coll.; MS in Geology, U. Ill. Geologist Shell Oil, 1978, various mgmt. positions for exploration programs in the continental US, Alaska and the offshore Gulf of Mexico, gen. mgr. planning and finance Shell Exploration and Production, 1991—95, treasurer; CEO and co-creator of Shell affiliate formed from subs. of Shell Oil Co. and Tejas Gas Corp. Coral Energy, 1995—98; pres., CEO Equitable Resources, Inc., Pitts., 1998—, chmn., 2000—. Bd. mem., mem. exec. com. BlackRock, Inc., 2000—; bd. mem. Westport Resources Corp.; mem. Nat. Petroleum Coun. Bd. dirs. United Way of Allegheny County, 1999; chmn. bd. Education Policy and Issues Center, Pitts., 2001—; host com. chmn. Nat. Urban League Conference, Pitts., 2003. Recipient CEO Communicator of the Year Renaissance award, Pitts. Chap. Public Relations Society of Am., 2003, Frieda Shapira award, Heritage Health Found., 2003. Mem.: Pa. Roundtable (vol. chmn. early childhood initiative effort), Am. Gas Assn. (Com. on Security, Infrastructure Integrity and Reliability 2001—). Office: Equitable Resources Inc One Oxford Ctr Ste 3300 301 Grant St Pittsburgh PA 15219

GERBER, ROBERT EVAN, judge; s. Milton M. and Miriam G. BS with high honors, Rutgers U., 1967; JD magna cum laude, Columbia U., 1970. Bar: N.Y. 1971, U.S. Dist. Ct. (so. and ea. dists.) N.Y. 1972, U.S. Ct. Appeals (2d cir.) 1973, U.S. Ct. Appeals (9th cir.) 1974, U.S. Ct. Appeals (10th cir.) 1975, U.S. Ct. Appeals (11th cir.) 1983, U.S. Supreme Ct. 1983, U.S. Ct. Appeals (5th cir.) 1987, U.S. Ct. Appeals (6th cir.) 1989, U.S. Ct. Appeals (3d cir.) 1997. Assoc. Fried, Frank, Harris, Shriver & Jacobson, N.Y.C., 1970-71, 72-78, ptnr., 1978-2000; judge U.S. Bankruptcy Ct. (so. dist.) N.Y., N.Y.C., 2000—. Served to 1st lt. USAF, 1971-72. James Kent scholar, 1970, Harlan Fiske Stone scholar, 1969. Mem. ABA, Assn. Bar City N.Y. (sec. spl. com. on energy 1974-79), Fed. Bar Coun., Am. Bankruptcy Inst., Nat. Conf. Bankruptcy Judges, Tau Beta Pi. Office: US Bankruptcy Ct US Custom House One Bowling Green New York NY 10004 Office Phone: 212-668-5660.

GERBER, ROBERT SCOTT, lawyer; b. Lansing, Mich. s. Arnold William and Carol L. Gerber. BA with high honors, U. Mich., 1984, M of Pub. Policy, 1985; JD cum laude, Harvard U., 1988. Bar: Calif. 1988, US Dist. Ct. (so. dist.) Calif. 1989, US Dist. Ct. (ctrl. dist.) Calif. 1991, US Ct. Appeals (9th cir.) 1992, US Dist. Ct. Ariz. 1994, US Supreme Ct. 2000. Econ. devel. analyst Mich. Dept. Commerce, 1984-85, City of San Diego, 1985; summer assoc. Riker, Danzig, Scherer, Hyland & Perretti, Morristown, N.J., 1986, Lillick, McHose & Charles, San Diego, 1987, Debevoise & Plimpton, NYC, 1987; law clk. Hon. Rudi M. Brewster U.S. Dist. Ct. (so. dist.) Calif., San Diego, 1988-89; assoc. Sheppard, Mullin, Richter & Hampton LLP, San Diego, 1989-97, ptnr., 1997—. Contbr. articles to profl. jours. Active San Diego Vol. Lawyer Program, 1989—; judge pro tempore Small Claims Ct., Mspl. Ct. Calif., San Diego Jud. Dist., 1994—; mem. Calif. Jud. Nominees Evaluation Commn., 2004—; bd. dirs. ch. coun. Christ Evang. Luth. Ch., Pacific Beach, Calif., 1991—94, 1995—96, long range planning com., 1994—95. Master: Am. Inns of Ct.; mem.: ABA (asst. editor-in-chief profl. liability com. newsletter 1994—), San Diego Def. Lawyers, Assn. Bus. Trial Lawyers, State Bar Calif. (ct. rules com. 1992—, fed. rules subcom. 1991—92, exec. com. litig. sect. 1995—, treas. 1996—97, sec. 1997—, vice chair 1998—99, chair 1999—2000). Avocations: fine wines, collecting movies, golf. Office: Sheppard, Mullin, Richter & Hampton LLP Ste 300 12544 High Bluff Drive San Diego CA 92130 Office Phone: 858-720-8907. Office Fax: 858-509-3691. Business E-Mail: rgerber@sheppardmullin.com.

GERBER, ROGER ALAN, lawyer, consultant; b. Bklyn., Jan. 27, 1939; s. Edward and Anne (Rothstein) G.; m. Jane E. Satlow, Sept. 20, 1964; children: Dina Huebner, Deborah Tor, Tamar Gerber. BA magna cum laude (Rufus Choate scholar), Dartmouth Coll., 1959; JD, Harvard U., 1962. Bar: N.Y. 1963. Real estate atty. ABC, Inc., 1965-68; assoc. Kaye, Scholer, Fierman, Hays & Handler, other law firms, 1968-75; v.p., gen. counsel ISS Internat. Service System, Inc., N.Y.C., 1975-83; v.p., sec., gen. counsel Meyers Parking System, Inc., N.Y.C., 1975-89, sr. exec. v.p., chief oper. officer, 1989-95, also bd. dirs., 1981-91; pres. Meyers Realty Co., N.Y.C., 1982-95. Abritrator Am. Arbitration Assn., 1973—; bd. dirs. Nat. Parking Assn., 1991-92; mem. adv. bd. Mid. East Forum, 1995—; bd. dirs. Jewish Inst. for Nat. Security Affairs, 1995—. Treas. Scarsdale (N.Y.) Democratic Com., 1977-83; v.p., exec. com. Bd. Jewish Edn., Greater N.Y., 1977—; bd. trustees PEF-Israel Endowment Fund, 1997-2004; bd. dirs. Conf. Jewish Social Studies, 1975-93, Jewish Conciliation Bd., N.Y.; class agt. Dartmouth Coll. Mem. N.Y. State Bar Assn., Phi Beta Kappa. Clubs: Harvard (N.Y.C.). Home: 26 Sage Ter Scarsdale NY 10583-2045 Office Phone: 212-983-4414. E-mail: RG26@aol.com.

GERBERDING, JULIE LOUISE, federal agency administrator; b. SD, 1956; m. David Rose. BA in chemistry and biology, MD, Case Western Reserve U., Cleve.; MPH, U. Calif., Berkeley, 1990. Intern and resident in internal medicine U. Calif., San Francisco, fellow in clin. pharmacology and infectious diseases; assoc. clin. prof. medicine Emory U.; assoc. prof. medicine, epidemiology and biostatistics U. Calif., San Francisco; founder, dir., Epidemiology Prevention and Interventions Ctr. San Francisco Gen. Hosp., 1987—98; dir., divsn. healthcare quality promotion CDC, Atlanta, 1998—2001, acting deputy dir. sci., 2001—02, dir., 2002—; adminstr. Agency for Toxic Substances and Disease Registry (ATSDR), 2002—. Dir., Prevention Epicenter U. Calif., San Francisco; mem., bd. scientific counselors CDC, mem., HIV adv. com., mem., scientific program com.; mem. Nat. Conf. Human Retroviruses; cons. NIH, AMA, Occupational Safety and Health Adminstrn., Nat. AIDS Commn., U.S. Congress, and WHO.; assoc. clin. prof. medicine (infectious diseases) Emory U. Edtl. bd. Annals of Internal Medicine, assoc. editor Am. Jour. Medicine, contbr. to profl. pubs. and textbooks. Named one of Most Powerful Women, Forbes mag., 2005. Fellow: Infectious Diseases Soc. Am. (chair and co-chair com. profl. devel. and diversity, mem. nominations com., co-chair. annual program com.); mem.: Am. Epidemiology Soc., Am. Coll. Physicians, Soc. for Healthcare Epidemiology Am. (mem. AIDS/Tuberculosis com., bd. acad. counselor), Am. Soc. Clin. Investigation, Alpha Omega Alpha, Phi Beta Kappa. Achievements include first female director for the CDC. Avocations: scuba diving, reading, gardening. Office: CDC 1600 Clifton Rd NE 214 Atlanta GA 30333*

GERBERDING, MILES CARSTON, lawyer; b. Decatur, Ind, Oct. 25, 1930; s. Arnold H. and Luella E. (Lapp) G.; m. Ruth H. Hostrup, Aug. 20, 1955 (dec. Mar. 1992); children: Karla M. Smith, Greta E. Cowart, Kent E., Brian K.; m. Joan W. Fackler, Jan. 2, 1993; stepchildren: Stephen W. Fackler, Deborah E. Holbrook. BS, Ind. U., 1954, JD, 1956. Bar: Ind. 1956, US Dist. Ct. (so. and no. dists.) Ind. 1956, Mich. 1984. Ptnr. Nieter & Smith, Ft. Wayne, Ind., 1956-58, Barrett, Barrett & McNagny, Ft. Wayne, 1958-85, Barnes & Thornburg, Ft. Wayne, 1985-97; pvt. practice Frankfort, Mich., 1998—. Lectr., writer Ind. Continuing Legal Ednl. Forum. Contbr. articles to profl. jours. Pres. Luth. Assn. Elem. Edn., 1968-69; vice chmn., mem. Ind. Supreme Ct. Commn. on Continuing Legal Edn., sec.; bd. dirs. Big Bros., Ft. Wayne, Jr. Achievement, Ft. Wayne, United Way Allen County; pres. Concordia Ednl. Found., Greater Ft. Wayne C. of C. Found.; chmn. bd. visitors Ind. U. Sch. Law, Bloomington, 1984-85, mem. 1979-94; vice chmn. United Way of Allen County Campaign, 1990-92, chmn., 1992-93, dir., 1992-98; trustee Boys and Girls Club Ft. Wayne; sec. Willoughby Rotary Found., 1999—. With USMC, 1950-52. Decorated UN medal, Korean Svc. medal with star; recipient Christus Magister award Luth. Edn. Assn., 1971, Disting Svc. award Ind. U. Sch. Law, 1999; named Grad. of Yr., Concordia Alumni Assn., 1993, named Citizen of Yr. Benzie County C. of C., 2003. Fellow: Mich. Bar Found., Ind. Bar Found. (dir.), Am. Coll. Trust and Estate Counsel, Am. Coll. Tax Counsel, Am. Bar Found.; mem.: VFW, ABA (rep. Nat. Conf. Lawyers and CPAs 1980—86, nominating com., ho. dels. credentials com., chmn. Ind. del. 1985—94, ho. dels. mem. com., standing com. on bar svc., budget officer Sr. Lawyers divsn., com. on pub. understanding about law, med. profl. liability com., coordinating com. on outreach, vice-chmn. com. on state and local bars-sr. lawyers divsn., marital deduction com. taxation sect.), Korean War Vets. Assn., Nat. Conf. Bar Pres. (exec. coun. 1983—86), Ind. CLE Forum (pres. 1978—79), Am. Judicature Soc., Allen County Bar Found. (former bd. dir., sec.), Lawyer-Pilot Bar Assn., Allen County Bar Assn. (dir.), Benzie County Bar Assn. (pres. 1999—2000), State Bar Mich. (coun. 1998—, treas. Sr. Lawyers 1999—2000, chmn.-elect 2000—01, chmn. 2001—02, Mich. del to ABA ho. of dels. 2004—06, com. on mandatory CLE, com. on quality profl. life), Ind. Bar Assn. (pres. 1979—80, del. ABA 1979—94), Am. Legion, Benzie Area Hist. Soc. (dir.), TerraLex (former co-vice chmn. N.Am., dir. 1993—96), Frankfort Rotary Club, Arcadia Lions Club. Republican. Lutheran. Home: 17726 N Ridgewood PO Box 6 Arcadia MI 49613-0006 Office: PO Box 272 Frankfort MI 49635-0272 also: PO Box 118 Arcadia MI 49613-0118 Office Phone: 231-352-9526. E-mail: mcgerb@bignetnorth.net.

GERBERDING, WILLIAM PASSAVANT, retired university president; b. Fargo, N.D., Sept. 9, 1929; s. William Passavant and Esther Elizabeth Ann (Habighorst) G.; m. Ruth Alice Albrecht, Mar. 25, 1952; children: David Michael, Steven Henry, Elizabeth Ann, John Martin. BA, Macalester Coll., 1951; MA, U. Chgo., 1956, PhD, 1959. Congl. fellow Am. Polit. Sci. Assn., Washington, 1958-59; instr. Colgate U., Hamilton, N.Y., 1959-60; research asst. Senator E.J. McCarthy, Washington, 1960-61; staff Rep. Frank Thompson, Jr., Washington, 1961; faculty UCLA, 1961-72, prof., chmn. dept. polit. sci., 1970-72; dean faculty, v.p. for acad. affairs Occidental Coll., Los Angeles, 1972-75; exec. vice chancellor UCLA, 1975-77; chancellor U. Ill., Urbana-Champaign, 1978-79; pres. U. Wash., Seattle, 1979-95. Cons. Dept. Def., 1962, Calif. Assembly, 1965. Author: United States Foreign Policy: Perspectives and Analysis, 1966; co-editor, contbg. author: The Radical Left: The Abuse of Discontent, 1970. Trustee Macalester Coll., 1980—83, 1996—2001, Gates Cambridge Trust, U. Cambridge, England, 2000—. With USN, 1951—55. Recipient Distinguished Teaching award U. Calif., Los Angeles, 1966; Ford Found. grantee, 1967-68 Office: Univ Wash PO Box 352800 Seattle WA 98195-2800

GERBERICH, SUSAN GOODWIN, epidemiologist, educator, medical researcher; b. Cortland, N.Y. d. Arthur George and Elizabeth Pratt Goodwin; m. William Warren Gerberich; children: Bradley Kent, Brian Keith, Beth Clarice. BS summa cum laude, U. Minn., 1975, MS, 1978, PhD, 1980. Prof. U. Minn., Mpls., 1983—; dir. Regional Injury Prevention Rsch. Ctr., Mpls., 1987—, Ctr. for Violence Prevention and Control, Mpls., 1994—. Pres. Gerberich, Inc., Shorewood, Minn., 1985—; cons. Injury Prevention/Epidemiology, 1985—; cons. Nat. Inst. for Occupl. Safety and Health and Ctrs. for Disease Control. Contbr. articles to profl. jours. Trauma adv. com. Minn. Dept. of Health, Mpls., 1999—, mem. Brain and Spinal Cord adv. com., 1993—. Named to Blue Ribbon Panel Nat. Inst. for Occpl. Safety and Health, Washington, 1990-93, 96, Ctr. for Disease Control, Atlanta, 1986-91. Mem. APHA (gov. coun. 1994-96,98-2003), Injury Control and Emergency Health Svcs. (Exellence in Sci. award 2004), Soc. for Epidemiol. Rsch. Avocations: tennis, golf, sailing, rollerblading. Office: EHS/SPH/U Minn/MMC 807 420 Delaware St SE Rm 1156 Minneapolis MN 55455-0374 Office Phone: 612-625-5934. E-mail: gerbe001@umn.edu.

GERBI, SUSAN ALEXANDRA, biology professor; b. N.Y.C., 1944; d. Claudio and Jeannette Lena (Klein) Gerbi; m. James Terrell McIlwain, Apr. 10, 1976. BA, Barnard Coll., 1965; MPhil, Yale U., 1968, PhD, 1970. NATO and Jane Coffin Childs Fund fellow Max-Planck Institut fur Biologie, Tubingen, Germany, 1970—72; asst. prof. biology Brown U., Providence, 1972—77, assoc. prof., 1977—82, prof., 1982—. Dir. grad. tng. program in molecular and cell biology, 1982-87, asst. dir. grad. program in molecular biology, cell biology and biochemistry, 1987-89, vice-chair sect. molecular, cellular and devel. biology, 1990-94, chair dept. molecular biology, cell biology and biochemistry, 1994-2004; vis. assoc. prof. Duke U., Durham, N.C., 1981-82; mem. genetics research grants rev. panel NSF, 1979-80; mem. genetic basis of disease com. NIH, 1980-84. Contbr. articles to profl. jours. Dist. commr. Palmer River Pony Club, 1973—75. N.Y. State Regents scholar, 1965; NIH fellow, 1966—70; NIH research grantee, 1974—, research career devel. award, 1975-80; recipient Gov.'s award for sci. achievement State of R.I., 1993. Mem. Fedn. Am. Socs. Exptl. Biology (pub. policy com. 1994-97, chair consensus conf. on grad. edn. 1996), Assn. Am. Med. Colls. (pub. policy com. 1994-98, chair grad. rsch. edn. and tng. group 1999), Am. Soc. for Cell Biology (program chair 1986, council mem. 1988-90, pub. policy com. 1991-97, pres. 1993), Soc. for Devel. Biology, Genetics Soc., RNA Soc., Sigma Xi (nat. lectr.). Office: Brown Univ Biomedical Divsn Providence RI 02912-0001 Office Phone: 401-863-2359. E-mail: susan_gerbi@brown.edu.

GERBIE, ALBERT BERNARD, obstetrician, gynecologist, educator; b. Toledo, Nov. 20, 1927; s. Louis and Fay (Green) G.; m. Barbara Hirsch, June 29, 1952; children: Gail Diane, Stephen Ralph. MD, George Washington U., 1951. Intern Michael Reese Hosp., Chgo., 1951-52; preceptorship in Ob-Gyn under Drs. R.A. Reis, J.L. Baer, E.J. DeCosta, Chgo., 1952-55; practice medicine specializing in Ob-Gyn Chgo., 1955—; mem. faculty Northwestern U. Med. Sch., Chgo., 1952—, prof. Ob-Gyn, 1972—, dir. continuing grad. edn., 1975—. Mem. staff Northwestern Meml. Hosp., 1955—; chief divsn. ob-gyn. Children's Meml. Hosp.; v.p., dir. Am. Bd. Ob-Gyn, 1976—, chmn. 1988—, pres. 1990, historian, 1998; chmn. liaison com. for ob-gyn., 1989; rep. Am. Bd. Med. Specialties; bd. dirs. Chgo. Maternity Ctr., Found. for Excellence in Women's Health Care. Author textbooks; assoc. editor Surgery, Gynecology, and Obstetrics, Am. Jour. Ob-Gyn.; editor ACOG Current Jour. Rev.; contbr. chpts. to books, articles to profl. jours. Served with U.S. Army, 1946-47. Mem. ACS (bd. govs.), ACOG (chmn. learning resources commn.), AMA, Am. Gynecol. Soc., Am. Assn. Obstetricians and Gynecologists, Am. Gynecol. and Obstet. Soc., Am. Bd. Med. Specialties, Am. Coll. Sports Medicine, Ctrl. Assn. Ob-Gyn, Soc. Human Genetics, Southwestern Ob-Gyn. Soc., Chgo. Gynecol. Assn. (pres. 1977-78), Skokie Valley Figure Skating Club, (pres. 2003). Office: Ste 900 251 E Huron St Chicago IL 60611-4814

GERDA, JANICE JOYCE, education educator; b. Columbus, Jan. 18, 1967; d. Jerome Joseph Gerda and Joyce Eileen Gerda (nee Murphy). BA in Comm. Sci., Case Western Res. U., Cleve., 1989; MEd in Adult Learning Develo., Cleve. State U., 1993; PhD in Higher Edn. Adminstrn., Bowling Green State U., Ohio, 2004. Hall dir. Grinnell Coll., Grinnell, Iowa, 1991—93; asst. dean of students U. of Va., Charlottesville, 1993—99; asst. prof. Kent State U., Kent, Ohio, 2003—. Mem.: History of Edn. Soc., AAUW, Nat. Assn. of Student Pers. Adminstrs., Am. Coll. Pers. Assn., Nat. Trust for Hist. Preservation. Avocations: genealogy, civil war history, local history. Home: 555 W Grant St Kent OH 44240 Office: Kent State University 404 White Hall Kent OH 44242

GERDEMANN, JAMES WESSEL, plant pathologist, educator; b. Warrenton, Mo., Nov. 13, 1921; s. Carl Edward and Cora Wilhelmina (Wessel) G.; m. Janice Mae Olbrich, July 2, 1949; children— Stephen, Dale, Glenn. BA, U. Mo., 1945, MA, 1946; PhD, U. Calif., Berkeley, 1948. Teaching asst. U. Mo., Columbia, 1945-46; research asst. U. Calif., Berkeley, 1946-48; prof. plant pathology U. Ill., Urbana, 1948-81, prof. emeritus, 1981—. Author: Taxonomy of the Endogonaceae, 1974; condr. research in field; contbr. writings to publs. Recipient Ruth Allen award, 1977, Funk award, 1977, excellence in undergrad. teaching award U. Ill., 1976 Fellow Am. Phytopathol. Soc.; mem. Am. Mycol. Soc. Home: PO Box 391 Yachats OR 97498-0391

GERDES, DAVID ALAN, lawyer; b. Aberdeen, S.D., Aug. 10, 1942; s. Cyril Fredrick and Lorraine Mary (Boyle) G.; m. Karen Ann Hassinger, Aug. 3, 1968; children: Amy Renee, James David. BS, No. State Coll., Aberdeen, 1965; JD cum laude, U. S.D., 1968. Bar: S.D. 1968, U.S. Dist. Ct. S.D., 1968, U.S. Ct. Appeals (8th cir.) 1973, U.S. Supreme Ct. 1973. Assoc. Martens, Goldsmith, May, Porter & Adam, Pierre, S.D., 1968-73; ptnr. successor firm May, Adam, Gerdes & Thompson, Pierre, 1973—. Chmn. disciplinary bd. S.D. Bar, 1980-81, mem. fed. practice com. U.S. Dist. Ct., S.D., 1986-91, 1994-2000; mem. fed. adv. com. U.S. Ct. Appeals (8th cir.), 1989-93; bd. dirs. U.S.D. Law Sch. Found., 1973-84, pres., 1979-84. Mng. editor U.S.D. Law Rev., 1967—68; author: Physician's Guide to South Dakota Law, 1982. Chmn. Hughes County Rep. Ctrl. Com., 1979-81; del. Rep. State Conv., co-chair platform com., 1988, 90; state ctrl. committeeman, 1985-91. Served to lt. Signal Corps, AUS, 1965-68. Mem. ABA, Nat. Coun. Bar Pres., Internat. Assn. Def. Counsel, Assn. Def. Trial Attys., Am. Judicature Soc., Am. Bd. Trial Advocates, State Bar S.D. (chmn. professionalism com. 1989-90, pres. 1992-93), Pierre Area C. of C. (pres. 1980-81), S.D. C. of C. (bd. dirs. 1998-2004), Lawyer-Pilots Bar Assn., Def. Rsch. Inst., Am. Soc. Med. Assn. Counsel, Kiwanis, Elks. Republican. Methodist. Office: May Adam Gerdes & Thompson PO Box 160 503 S Pierre St Pierre SD 57501-0160 Office Phone: 605-224-8803.

GERDES, NEIL WAYNE, library director, educator; b. Moline, Ill., Oct. 19, 1943; s. John Edward and Della Marie (Ferguson) G. AB, U. Ill., 1965; BD, Harvard U., 1968; MA, Columbia U., 1971; MA in Libr. Sci., U. Chgo., 1975; DMin, U. St. Mary of the Lake, 1994. Ordained to ministry Unitarian Universalist Assn., 1975. Copy chief Little, Brown, 1968-69; instr. Tuskegee Inst., 1969-71; libr. asst. Augustana Coll., 1972-73; edit. asst. Library Quar., 1973-74; libr., prof. Meadville Theol. Sch., Chgo., 1973—; libr. program dir. Chgo. Cluster Theol. Schs., 1977-80; dir. Hammond Libr., 1980—; prof. Chgo. Theol. Sem., 1980—. Affiliated minister 1st Unitarian Church, Chgo., 2002—. Mem. exec. bd. Sem. Coop. Bookstore, Chgo., 1982-2002, Ctr. for Religion and Psychotherapy, Chgo., 1984-97, Ind. Voters of Ill., 1986-89, Hyde Park-Kenwood Cmty. Orgn., Chgo., 1988-89; pres. Hyde Park-Kenwood Interfaith Coun., 1986-90, Inst. for Spiritual Leadership, 2000—; chair libr. coun. Assn. Chgo. Theol. Sch., 1984-88, 96-98, LGBT Religious Archive Network, 2002—; trustee Civitas Dei Found., 1994—; mem. alumni coun. Harvard Divinity Sch., 1999—, sec., 2001—. Mem. ALA, Am. Theol. Library Assn., Chgo. Area Theol. Library Assn., Unitarian Universalist Mins. Assn. (sec., treas. nat. body 1990-94), Assn. Liberal Religious Scholars (sec., treas. 1975—), Phi Beta Kappa Office: Chgo Theol Sem Hammond Libr 5757 S University Ave Chicago IL 60637-1507 Office Phone: 773-752-5757. Business E-Mail: ngerdes@ctschicago.edu.

GERDES, RALPH DONALD, fire safety consultant; b. Cin., Aug. 11, 1951; s. Paul Donald and Jo Ann Dorothy (Meyer) G. BArch, Ill. Inst. Tech., 1975. Registered architect, Ill. Architect Schiller & Frank, Wheeling, Ill., 1976; sr. assoc. Rolf Jensen & Assocs., Inc., Chgo., 1976-84; pres. Ralph Gerdes & Assocs., Inc., Indpls., 1984-88, chmn., 1988—; gen. mgr. Ralph Gerdes Cons., LLC. Lectr. Purdue U., Ind. U., Ill. Inst. Tech., Butler U., Ball State U.; bd. dirs. Ind. Fire Svcs. Inst. Co-author: Planning and Designing the Office Environment, 1981. Recipient Joel Polsky prize Am. Soc. Interior Designers, 1983. Mem.: AIA (bldg. performance and regulations com., liaison to Nat. Fire Protection Agy.), ASHRAE, Archs. and Engrs. Bldg. Ofcls. (bd. dirs. 1994—, Ind. code devel. com.), Ind. Fire Safety Assn. (bd. dirs. 1986—92, pres. 1989—91, bd. dirs. 1994—95), Internat. Code Coun., Nat. Fire Protection Assn. (tech. coms., stds. council), Soc. Fire Protection Engrng.

(assoc.; exec. com. Ind. chpt. 1992—, pres. 1995—96), Indpls. Soc., Maple Creek Country Club. Roman Catholic. Home: 556 Lockerbie Cir N Indianapolis IN 46202-3600 Office: 5510 S East St Ste E Indianapolis IN 46227

GERDING, THOMAS GRAHAM, medical products executive; b. Evanston, Ill., Feb. 11, 1930; s. Louis Henry and Helen Frances (Graham) G.; m. Beverly Ann Starnes, June 18, 1955; children: Mark, David, Gail, Gene Ann. Student, U. Notre Dame, 1948-49; BS in Pharmacy, Purdue U., 1952, MS, 1954, PhD, 1960, D (hon.), 2002. From instr. to asst. prof. Purdue U., West Lafayette, Ind., 1956-61; dir. product devel. Pitman-Moore divsn. Dow Chem., Indpls., 1962-64; tech. dir. new products Glenbrook Labs., N.Y.C., 1964-66; dir. product devel. Sterling-Winthrop Rsch. Inst., Rensselaer, N.Y., 1966-70; v.p. rsch. and devel. Calgon Consumer Products, Rahway, N.J., 1970-77; v.p., dir. rsch. and devel., quality assurance, consumer affairs, engring. Johnson & Johnson Products Inc., New Brunswick, N.J., 1977-88; pres. Thomas G. Gerding, Inc., Georgetown, Tex., 1988-96; dir. Drug Dynamics Inst. U. Tex., Austin, 1988-95; pres. Newform Devel. Labs., Inc., Georgetown, Tex., 1993—. Deans adv. coun. Purdue U. Sch. Pharmacy, 1996—2001, U. Tex. Coll. Pharmacy, 2002—. Sgt. U.S. Army Med. Svc. Corp, 1954-56. Recipient Disting. Alumni award, Purdue U., 1984, Best Friend award, U. Tex., 2002. Mem.: Am. Assn. Pharm. Scientists, Am. Chem. Soc., Berry Creek Country Club, Union League Club (Chgo.). Republican. Achievements include research in pharmaceutics, wound care and unique drug delivery systems; 6 patents. Home: 340 Shell Spur Georgetown TX 78628 Office: Newform Devel Labs Inc 340 Shell Spur Georgetown TX 78628

GERDNER, LINDA ANN, nursing researcher, educator; b. Burlington, Iowa, Sept. 17, 1955; d. Richard Paul and Edna Marie Gerdner. AA, Southeastern C.C., 1975, ADN, 1977; BSN, Iowa Wesleyan Coll., 1980; MA, U. Iowa, 1992, PhD, 1998. RN, Iowa, Ark., Minn. Staff devel. coord. Elm View Care Ctr., Burlington, Iowa, 1985—88, DON, 1988—89; tchg./rsch. asst. U. Iowa Coll. Nursing, Iowa City, 1989-92; nursing faculty Grand View Coll., Des Moines, 1992-93; project dir. Nat. Caregiver Tng. Project, U. Iowa Coll. Nursing, 1992-97, predoctoral fellow, 1996-98; postdoctoral fellow/faculty dept. psychiatry U. Ark. Med. Scis., VA Med. Ctr., Little Rock, 1998—2000; asst. prof. U. Minnesota Sch. Nursing, 2001—. Presenter in field; cons. Alverno Health Facility, Clinton, Iowa, 1997—2000. Mem. referee panel Clin. Nursing Rsch., 1997—, Western Jour. Nursing Rsch., 1998—, Jour. Gerontol. Nursing, 1999—, Internat. Jour. Geriatric Psychiatry, 2000—, Internat. Psychogeriatrics, 2002—, Alzheimer's Disease and Related Disorders, 2002—, Nursing Research, 2003—; contbr. chapters to books, articles to profl. jours. AARP Andrus Found. grad. fellow in gerontology Assn. Gerontology in Higher Edn., 1996-97, Rsch. award Am. Soc. Aging, 1999, mini-fellowship ethnogeriatrics, Stanford U., Palo Alto, Calif., 2004-. Mem.: ANA, Coun. Nursing and Anthropology, Am. Assn. Geriatric Psychiatry, Midwest Nursing Rsch. Soc. (Outstanding Poster award 1993), Mid-Am. Contress on Aging (Best Grad. Paper award 1994), Am. Geriatric Soc., Internat. Psychogeriatric Assn. (task force on behavioral and psychol. symptoms of dementia 1999—, scientific advisory com. 2001, IPA/Bayer Rsch. award 1999), Sigma Theta Tau (Best of Image award 1997). Avocations: reading, travel, walking, music, photography. Home: 1160 Cushing Cir Apt 318 Saint Paul MN 55108 Office: Weaver-Densford Hall 308 Harvard St SE Minneapolis MN 55455-0353 E-mail: gerdn001@umn.edu.

GERDTS, WILLIAM HENRY, art history educator; b. Jersey City, N.J., Jan. 18, 1929; s. William Henry and Suzanne (Zanowick) G.; m. Elaine Evans, Apr. 4, 1953 (div. 1962); 1 child, Jeffrey Evans Dee; m. Abigail Booth, July 23, 1976. BA, Amherst Coll., 1949; MA, Harvard U., 1950, PhD, 1966; LHD (hon.), Amherst Coll., 1992; DFA (hon.), Syracuse U., 1996. Resident dir. Hist. Myers House, curator Norfolk (Va.) Mus., 1953-54; curator paintings and sculpture Newark (N.J.) Mus., 1954-66; prof. art history U. Md., College Park, 1966-69; v.p. Coe Kerr Gallery, N.Y.C., 1969-71; prof. art history CUNY, 1971-99, prof. emeritus, 1999—, acting exec. officer art history PhD program, 1977-79, exec. officer, 1979-85. Vis. lectr. Johns Hopkins U., Balt., 1969-71; adj. prof. Rutgers U., New Brunswick, N.J., 1975, Washington U., St. Louis, 1977; mem. adv. bd. Archives Am. Art, Smithsonian Instn., N.Y.C., 1981—. Author: American Still-Life Painting, 1971, American Neo-Classic Sculpture: The Marble Resurrection, 1973, The Great American Nude: A History in Art, 1974, A Man of Genius: The Art of Washington Allston, 1979, Masters of the Humble Truth: Masterpieces of American Still Life, 1801-1930, 1981, American Impressionism, 1984, rev., 2001, The Art of Henry Inman, 1987; (with James L. Yarnall) The National Museum of American Art's Index to American Art Exhibition Catalogues From the Beginning through the 1876 Centennial Year, 6 vols., 1986, Art Across America: Regional Painting in America through 1920, 3 vols., 1990, others. Summer Rsch. grantee U. Md., 1968, Mellon Found., 1974; Guggenheim Found. fellow, 1980, Am. Philos. Soc. fellow, 1980. Office: CUNY Grad Ctr 365 5th Ave New York NY 10016-4334

GERE, JAMES MONROE, civil engineering educator; b. Syracuse, N.Y., June 14, 1925; s. William S. and Carol (Hixson) G.; m. Janice M. Platt, June 1, 1946; children— Susan M., William P., David S. BS, Rensselaer Poly. Inst., 1949, MS, 1951; PhD, Stanford, 1954. Registered profl. engr., Calif., N.Y. Instr. Rensselaer Poly. Inst., 1949-51; faculty Stanford U., 1954—; prof. civil engring., 1962—; assoc. dean Sch. Engring., 1960-67, exec. head dept. civil engring., 1967-72. Cons. and lectr. in field, 1954— Author 7 textbooks in field, also tech. papers. Served with USAAF, 1943-46, ETO. Fellow ASCE; mem. Am. Soc. Engring. Edn., Earthquake Engring. Research Inst., Sigma Xi, Tau Beta Pi.

GERE, RICHARD, actor; b. Phila., Aug. 31, 1949; m. Cindy Crawford, 1991 (div.); m. Carey Lowell, 2002; 1 child, Homer James Jigme. Attended, U. Mass. Played trumpet, piano, guitar and bass and composed music with various musical groups. acting appearances with Provincetown Playhouse in Great God Brown, Camino Real, Rosencrantz and Guildenstern are Dead; off-Broadway prodn. Killer's Head, Richard Farina: Long Time Coming and Long Time Gone, Back Bog Beast Bait; in Broadway prodn. Taming of the Shrew; London and Broadway prodns. Midsummer Night's Dream; Broadway prodns. Habeas Corpus, Bent; on Broadway Soon, Grease; appeared in and composed music for Volpone at Seattle Repertory Theatre; film debut in Report to the Commissioner, 1975; other films include Baby Blue Marine, 1976, Looking for Mr. Goodbar, 1977, Days of Heaven, 1978, Blood Brothers, 1978, Yanks, 1979, American Gigolo, 1980, An Officer and a Gentleman, 1982, Breathless, 1983, Beyond the Limit, 1983, The Cotton Club, 1984, King David, 1985, Power, 1986, No Mercy, 1986, Miles from Home, 1988, Internal Affairs, 1990, Pretty Woman, 1990, Rhapsody in August, 1991, Final Analysis, (also exec. prodr.) 1992, Sommersby, 1993, Mr. Jones, 1993, Intersection, 1994, First Knight, 1995, Primal Fear, 1996, Red Corner, 1997, The Jackal, 1997, An Alan Smithee Film: Burn Hollywood Burn, 1998, Runaway Bride, 1999, Autumn in New York, 2000, Dr. T and the Women, 2000, The Mothman Prophecies, 2002, Unfaithful, 2002, Chicago, 2002, Shall We Dance?, 2004; TV movie Strike Force, 1975, And the Band Played On, HBO, 1993 (Emmy nomination, Supporting Actor - Special, 1994), AFI's 100 Years...100 Movies, 1998; author: Pilgrim Photo Collection, 1998; exec. prodr. (films) Final Analysis, 1992, Mr. Jones, 1993, Sommersby, 1993; TV guest appearance Kojak, 1973. Alfred P. Sloan Found. fellow, 1941—43, Tax Found. fellow, 1943—44.

GEREAU, MARY CONDON, political corporate executive; b. Winterset, Iowa, Oct. 10, 1916; d. David Joseph and Sarah Rose (Stack) Condon; m. Gerald Robert Gereau, Jan. 14, 1961. Student, Mt. Mercy Jr. Coll., 1935-37; BA, U. Iowa, 1939, MA, 1941. Program dir. ARC, India, 1943-45; dean of students Eastern Mont. Coll., 1946-48; supt. pub. instrn. State of Mont., 1948-56; sr. legis. cons. NEA, 1967-73; dir. legis. Nat. Treasury Employees Union, 1973-76; legis. asst. to Senator Melcher Mont., 1976-86; pres. Woman's Party Corp., 1991—. Co-chmn. Truman Commerative Com., 1994—. Contbr. articles on state govt. and edn. to profl. jours. Nat. chmn. Equal Rights Ratification Coun.; pres. Coun. Chief State Sch. Officers, 1956; exec. bd. Rural Edn. Assn., 1953—56; mem. campaign staff Kennedy, Johnson, Humphrey, Jackson; v.p. Nat. Women's Party, 1984—91; mem. Westmoreland Dem. com.; bd. dir. Coun. Chief State Sch. Officers, 1953—56. Named Conservationist of Yr. Mont. Conservation Coun., 1952, Roll Call Cong. Staffer of Yr., 1985; recipient Disting. Svc. State Sch. Officers, 1956, medal of honor Vet. Feminists of Am., 2000. Mem. U.S. Congress Burro Club (pres. 1983-84), Mont. State Soc. of Wash. Office Phone: 804-224-8000. Personal E-mail: gereau@verizon.net.

GEREIGHTY, ANDREA SAUNDERS, diversified financial services company executive, poet; b. New Orleans, July 20, 1938; d. Andrew Jackson and Jeanne Teresa (Martin) Saunders; m. Dennis Anthony Gereighty Jr., May 19, 1959 (wid.); children: Deni Ann, David Dennis, Peggy T. Cert., Exeter Coll., Oxford, Eng., 1972; BA, U. New Orleans, 1974, MA in English with distinction, 1978. Cotton analyst Anderson-Clayton, Metairie, La., 1956; records retrieval profl. Shell Oil Co., New Orleans, 1956-60; census coord. St. Vincent De Paul Ch., New Orleans, 1960-65; bldg. funds dir. St. Francis Xavier Ch., Metairie, 1965-70; tchr. spl. edn. Deckbar Elem. Sch., Jefferson, La., 1966-70; tchr. English Chalmette (La.) H.S., 1971-73; assoc. prof. English dept. U. New Orleans, 1973-75; tchr. secondary edn. Berlin-Am. H.S., 1980-81; owner, founder, CEO New Orleans Field Svcs. Assocs., 1974—. Guest speaker Delgado Coll., New Orleans, 1989; guest presenter Rabouin Vo-Tech., New Orleans, 1980; lectr., guest presenter poetry at New Sarpy Sch., 1994-95; guest presenter St. Mark's Episcopal Ch., Latter Libr., N.O. Pub. Libr., others. Author: (public opinon polls book) Asking Q's, 1980; (poetry) Illusions and Other Realities, 1974, Restless for Cool Weather, 1990, Season of the Crane, 1994; publ., editor Desire Street, 1997—; author numerous poems. Recipient Coda award Poets and Writers, 1983, Poetry award of honor Nat. League Am. Pen Women, 1973, Deep South Writers, 1984, 88, 90, 92, 94, 95, 96, 97, 98, 99, 2d place award Nuyarikin Poet's Cafe, N.Y.C., Ellipsis Poetry prize, 1983, 85, 87, 90, other poetry awards. Mem. Am. Mktg. Assn., Mktg. Rsch. Assn., Nat. Geneal. Soc., Jefferson Geneal. Soc., Geneaol. Soc. of New Orleans, New Orleans Poetry Forum (dir. 1990—), New Orleans Track Club. Democrat. Roman Catholic. Avocations: poetry, jogging, genealogy, dogs, camping. Office: New Orleans Field Svcs 257 Bonnabel Blvd Rear Office Metairie LA 70005-3738

GEREN, PETE (PRESTON M. GEREN), civilian military employee, former congressman; b. Ft. Worth, Jan. 29, 1952; m. Beckie Ray; children, Tracy, Annie, Mary. Student, Ga. Inst. Tech., 1970—73; BA, U. Tex., 1974, JD, 1978. Atty. pvt. practice, 1978-83; exec. asst. to senator Lloyd Bentsen US Senate, 1983-85; mem. 101st-104th Congresses from Tex. 12th dist., Washington, 1989-96; sr. v.p. Pub. Strategies, Inc., Ft. Worth, 1997-98, atty., 1997-99, Ft. Worth, 1999—2001; spl. asst. to the sec. US Dept. Def., Washington, 2001—05, acting sec. USAF, 2005—. Bd. dirs. Dallas/Ft. Worth Airport, 1999—2001. Office: USAF 1670 Air Force Pentagon Washington DC 20330*

GERETY, PETER LEO, archbishop; b. Shelton, Conn., July 19, 1912; s. Peter Leo and Charlotte (Daly) Gerety. Student, St. Thomas Sem., Bloomfield, Conn., 1934, Sem. St. Sulpice, Paris, 1939. Ordained priest Roman Catholic Ch., 1939. Asst. pastor, New Haven, 1939—42; dir. Blessed Martin de Porres Interracial Ctr., 1942—56; pastor New Haven, 1956—66; coadjutor bishop Portland, Maine, 1966—; apostolic adminstr., 1967—; bishop, 1969—74; archbishop of Newark, 1974—86; archbishop emeritus, 1986—. Roman Catholic. Address: St John Vianney Residence 60 Home Ave Rutherford NJ 07070-1760 Office Phone: 201-460-1369. Business E-Mail: abgerety@verizon.net.

GERETY, ROBERT JOHN, microbiologist, researcher, pediatrician, pharmaceutical executive; b. Jersey City, Oct. 16, 1939; s. James Leo and Helen (Beck) G.; m. Joan Imelda Grant, Feb. 3, 1967; children: Andrew, Kathleen, Nancy. BA with spl. honors, Rutgers U., 1962; MA, Stanford U., 1966, PhD, 1971; MD, George Washington U., 1970. Diplomate Nat. Bd. Med. Examiners. Rsch. assoc. dept. med. microbiology Stanford (Calif.) U. Med. Sch., 1969-70; intern in pediatrics Stanford U. Hosp., 1970-71, resident, 1974-75; staff assoc. Lab. Viral Immunology, NIH, Bethesda, Md., 1971-72; staff assoc. Bur. Biologics, FDA, Bethesda, 1972-73, dir. hepatitis br., 1973-84, assoc. dir. medicine and sci., chief infectious diseases br., 1984-85; exec. dir. virus & cell biology Merck Rsch. Labs., West Point, Pa., 1985-89, chief clin. evaluation of vaccines and antiviral drugs, 1985-89; v.p. devel. ops. Biogen, Inc., Cambridge, Mass., 1989-93; v.p. pharm. ops. Immulogic Pharm. Corp., Waltham, Mass., 1993-94, CEO, pres. and dir., 1994-96; v.p. devel. and regulatory affairs ORAVAX, Cambridge, Mass., 1997-99; exec. v.p. corp. devel. Cell Gate Inc., Sunnyvale, Calif., 1999-2000; v.p. regulatory affairs and clin. ops. Inhale Therapeutic Sys., San Carlos, Calif., 2000—02; v.p., head proprietary products Nektar Therapeutics, San Carlos, 2002—. Adj. prof. medicine Jefferson Med. Sch., Phila., 1985; Plenary lectr. Internat. Symposium on Viral Hepatitis and Liver Disease, London, 1987; mem. U.S. Army Med. R&D Adv. Bd., 1987; mem. AIDS subcom. Nat. Inst. Allergy and Infectious Diseases, 1988; mem. Nat. Vaccine Adv. Com., 1990-92, sci. bd. Oravax, Cambridge, Mass., 1991-94, numerous others; participant confs., symposia and workshops. Editor: Non-A, Non-B Hepatitis, 1981, Hepatitis A, 1984, Hepatitis B, 1985; mem. editl. bd. Biols., 1990-94; contbr. over 200 articles to sci. jours. Med. dir. USPHS, 1970-85. Recipient commendation medal USPHS, 1975, Outstanding Svc. medal, 1982, Disting. Svc. medal, 1985; Patriotic Svc. award U.S. Dept. Treasury, 1983; Henry Rutgers fellow, 1961-62, fellow NIH, 1962-65, Calif. Tb and Health Assn., 1964-67, U.S. Health Professions scholar and microbiology fellow, 1966-70. Fellow Infectious Disease Soc. Am.; mem. AMA, Am. Soc. for Microbiology, Am. Acad. Pediatrics, Am. Assn. Immunologists, William Beaumont Soc., Henry Rutgers Soc., Internat. assn. for Biol. Standards, Internat. Soc. Interferon Rsch. Achievements include development and/or approval of vaccine against Hepatitis A and Hepatitis B, pediatric vaccines including Hemophilus Influenza B and varicella, and Biogen's beta interferon product to treat multiple sclerosis (Avonex); patents for Inactivation of Non-A, Non-B Hepatitis Agent; Hepatitis B Immune Globulin used to Inactivate Hepatitis B Virus in Injectable Biological Products; Detection of Non-A, Non-B Hepatitis Associated Antigen; Heat Treatment of a Non-A, Non-B Hepatitis Agent to Prepare a Vaccine; Hepatitis B Core Antigen Vaccine; Hepatitis B Core Antigen Vaccine Made by Recombinant DNA; Purified Antigen from Non-A, Non-B Hepatitis Causing Factor: Screening Test for Reverse Transcriptase Containing Viruses in human blood. Home: 1850 Sand Hill Rd Apt 10 Palo Alto CA 94304-2144 Office Phone: 650-631-5046. Business E-Mail: rgerety@ca.nektar.com.

GERETY, TOM, academic administrator, lawyer, educator, philosopher; b. NYC, July 22, 1946; m. Adelia Moore, Oct. 7, 1972; children: Finn, Carrick, Amias, Rowan. BA, Yale U., 1969, MPhil, 1974, JD, PhD, Yale U., 1976; MA, Amherst Coll., 1995; LLD (hon.), Williams Coll., 1995; LHD, Doshisha U., 1996; LLD (hon.), Wesleyan U., 2001. Tchr. Peru project Joint Ctr. Urban Studies Harvard-MIT, Lima, 1966—67; bilingual tchr. Boston Pub. Schs., 1970—71; assoc. lectr. philosophy, master's asst. Morse Coll. Yale U., New Haven, 1972—74; asst. prof., fellow Ctr. Profl. Ethics Chgo. Kent Coll. Law, Ill. Inst. Tech., 1976—78; prof. law U. Pitts., 1978—86; dean, Nippert prof. Coll. Law U. Cin., 1986—89; pres., prof. philosophy Trinity Coll., Hartford, Conn., 1989—94, Amherst Coll., 1994—2003; exec. dir., Brennan prof. Brennan Ctr. for Justice, NYC, 2003—. Vis. asst. prof. Ind. U. Sch. Law, Bloomington, 1977—78; vis. prof. constl. law and jurisprudence Stanford U. Sch. Law, 1983—84; occasional appellate litigation in constl. law ACLU, 1981—; chair New Engl. Small Coll. Athletic Conf., 1991—92, 2000—01; chair bd. dirs. Consortium on Financing Higher Edn., 1993—95; testimony before the Senate Judiciary Com., Subcom. on Constitution on various proposed amendments. Writer, cons., on-air corr., fundraiser Visions of the Constitution, Nat. Endowment for Humanities TV series in constl. law, 1985—88, commentaries in various media Washington Post, Boston Globe, Chgo. Tribune, Christian Sci. Monitor, L.A. Times, MacNeil Lehrer Report, Nat. Pub. Radio; contbr. articles to profl. jours. Bd. mem. Internat. Rescue Com., 1989—2003, Save the Children U.S., Conn. State Bd. Edn., 1992—94. Fellow Kent fellow, Danforth Found., 1972—76, Woodrow Wilson fellow, 1983. Office: Brennan Ctr for Justice 12th Fl 161 Avenue of the Americas New York NY 10013

GERGECEFF-COOPER, LORRAINE, artist, consultant; b. Ill. d. Harry Robert and Grace Johnson; m. George William Gergeceff (dec. 1984); m. John Cooper, Jr., May 30, 1992 (dec. 2002); children: Jill Gergeceff Lohnes, Jon Rice Gergeceff. Cert., Internat. Sommerakad., Salzburg, Austria, 1962, Sch. Landscape Painting, Dordogne, France, 1973; BS, So. Ill. U., 1953; MFA, U. Guanajuato, San Miguel Allende, Mex., 1970. Tchr., gallery dir. Ursuline Acad., Oakland, Mo., 1962-70; instr. McKendree Coll., Lebanon, Mo.; artist Forum Creative Dynamics, St. Louis, 1995, Unique Paintings, Webster Groves, Mo., 1997-98; owner LorPaint Gallery, Webster Groves, 1998—. Cons. JDR 3 Through Awareness Classroom Environment; founder, dir. Ursuline Art Gallery, Oakland, Mo. Author: Careers in Art, Self Designed Fabrics; one woman shows at Kinsella Gallery, Long Art Gallery, Ursuline Art Gallery, Notre Dame Coll., University City Libr., St. Louis U.; group shows include St. Louis Art Mus., Art Mus. St. Louis, Bellas Artes, Cuernavaca, Mex., Mus. Arts and Scis., Mo. Hist. Soc., Spete Kukla Gallery, Samos, Greece, Internat. Acad. Fine Arts, Salzburg, Austria, Highland Gallery, Atlanta, St. Louis Artists' Guild, 2002, Galeria Osman, Mex., Creative Art Gallery, St. Louis, 2001, 02, Centro Cultural El Nigromante, San Miguel de Allende, Mex., Art Expo '96, Webster Groves, Mo., Nat. Mus. Women in the Arts, Mo. Water Colo Assn., St. Peter's Cultural Art Ctr., 2001, 2002, 2003, Oil and Acrylic Nat. Exhbn., 2001, Collector's Choice, St. Louis, 2002, 2003, CJ Mggs Art Gallery, 2002, Oil and Acrylic Nat. Exhibit, 2002. Backer Repertory Theater, Webster Groves, Mo., 1996—. Best of Show Kinsella Gallery, Long Art Gallery, Ursuline Art Gallery; recipient prize St. Louis Artists' Guild, 1969, 71, 75; named Outstanding Secondary Educator, 1971. Mem. St. Louis Art Mus., Chgo. Art Inst., Guild of Opera Theater, Art St. Louis, St. Lousi Artists' Guild (spl. events, prize 1969, 71, 75), St. Louis Watercolor Soc. (signature), Soc. Multi Media Layerists. Avocations: travel, sailing, reading. Address: LorPaint Gallery 16 N Gore Ave Ste 201 Webster Groves MO 63119-2315 E-mail: lorpaint@aol.com.

GERGELY, TOMAS, astronomer; b. Budapest, Hungary, Oct. 14, 1943; came to U.S., 1976, naturalized, 1982; s. Tibor and Magda (Szilasi) G.; m. Ana Lajmanovich, Mar. 6, 1970; children: Gabriela S., Esteban A., Daniel M. Licenciado in Physics, U. Buenos Aires, 1967; PhD in Astronomy, U. Md., 1974. Asst. prof. Nat. Tech. U., Buenos Aires, 1974, rschr., 1975; rsch. assoc. U. Md., College Park, 1976-81, sr. rsch. assoc., 1981-82, assoc. rsch. sci., 1982-85; astrophysicist NASA Hdqs., Washington, 1985-86; mgr. electromagnetic spectrum NSF, 1986—. Mem. U.S. del. to World Adminstrv. Radio Conf., 1987, 92, World Radio Comm. Conf., 1995, 97, 2000, 03. Editor: (with others) Radio Physics of the Sun; contbr. articles to profl. jours. Recipient Young Scientist award French Govt., 1976. Mem. Internat. Astron. Union, Am. Astron. Soc., Internat. Radio Physics Union. Home: 8217 Windsor View Ter Rockville MD 20854-4028 Office: NSF Divsn Astron Scis 4201 Wilson Blvd Arlington VA 22230-0001 Office Phone: 703-292-4896. Business E-Mail: tgergely@nsf.gov.

GERGEN, DAVID RICHMOND, federal official, magazine editor; b. Durham, NC, May 9, 1942; s. John Gergen; m. Anne Gergen, 1967; children: Christopher, Katherine. BA, Yale U., 1963; LLB, Harvard U., 1967. Staff asst. Nixon Adminstrn., Washington, 1971-72, spl. asst. to Pres., chief White House writing/research team, 1973-74; spl. comm. counsel to Pres. Ford White House, Washington, 1975-77, dir. comm. staff, 1981, dir. comm. to Pres. Reagan, 1981-84, counselor to Pres. Clinton, 1993-94, spl. advisor to Pres. and Sec. of State, 1994-95; resident fellow Am. Enterprise Inst.; mng. editor Am. Enterprise Inst. Public Opinion mag., Washington, 1977-81; resident fellow Inst. Politics, John F. Kennedy Sch. Govt., Cambridge, Mass., 1983-85; dir., Ctr. for Pub. Leadership John F. Kennedy Sch. Govt., Cambridge, Mass., prof. pub. svc.; mng. editor U.S. News & World Report, Washington, 1985-86, from editor to editor-at-large, 1986-93, 96—; weekly polit. analyst MacNeil/Lehrer News Hour, 1987-93. Weekly contbr. Newshour with Jim Lehrer; vis. prof. Duke U. Mem.: Trilateral Commn., Coun. on Foreign Relations. Office: JFK Sch Govt Harvard U 79 JF Kennedy St Cambridge MA 02138

GERHARD, LEE CLARENCE, geologist, educator; b. Albion, N.Y., May 30, 1937; s. Carl Clarence and Helen Mary (Lahmer) G.; m. Darcy LaFollette, July 22, 1964; 1 dau., Tracy Leigh. BS, Syracuse U., 1958; MS, U. Kans., 1961, PhD, 1964. Exploration geologist, region stratigrapher Sinclair Oil & Gas Co., Midland, Tex. and Roswell, N.Mex., 1964-66; asst. prof. geology U. So. Colo., Pueblo, 1966-69, assoc. prof., 1969-72; assoc. prof., asst. dir. West Indies Lab. Fairleigh Dickinson U., Rutherford, N.J., 1972-75; asst. geologist State of N.D., Grand Forks, 1975-77, geologist, 1977-81; prof., chmn. dept. geology U. N.D., Grand Forks, 1977-81; mgr. Rocky Mountain div. Supron Energy Corp., Denver, 1981-82; owner, pres. Gerhard & Assocs., Englewood, Colo., 1982-87; prof. petroleum geology Colo. Sch. Mines, Denver, 1982—2004, Getty prof., 1984-87; state geologist, dir. geol. survey State of Kans., Lawrence, 1987-99, prin. geologist, 1999—2005; prin. Gerhard & Assocs., 2005—; founder, co-dir. Energy Rsch. Ctr., U. Kans., 1990-94. Presdl. appointee Nat. Adv. Com. on Oceans and Atmosphere, 1984-87. Contbr. articles to profl. jours. Served to 1st lt. U.S. Army, 1958-60. Danforth fellow, 1970-72; named to Kans. Oil and Gas Hall of Fame, 2002. Fellow Geol. Soc. Am.; mem. Am. Assn. Petroleum Geologists (hon. mem., Disting. Svc. award 1989, Journalism award 1996, pres. divsn. environ. geosci. 1994-95, hon. mem. divsn. environ. geosci. 1998, v.p. diversified affairs 2003-04, Pub. Outreach award 1999, 2003), Am. Inst. Profl. Geologists, Rocky Mountain Assn. Geologists, Colo. Sci. Soc., Kans. Geol. Soc. (hon.), Sigma Xi, Sigma Gamma Epsilon. Home: 1628 Alvamar Dr Lawrence KS 66047-1714 Personal E-mail: leeg@sunflower.com.

GERHARDT, CAROL ASHBY, artist; b. Wabash, Ind., Aug. 10, 1946; d. Dale Martin Ashby and Helen Irene Harper; 4 children from previous marriage. BS, U. Houston, 1986, postgrad., 1994—96. Exec. dir. Penguin Photography Studio, Houston, 1986—87, photographer, 1987—90; photojournalism faculty North Harris County Coll., Houston, 1990—92; art faculty Houston Ind. Sch. Dist., 1992—2003. Exhibitions include UN/UNIFEM, Marias do Mundo, Brazil, 2001, Diverse Works Art Space, Houston, 1996.

GERHARDT, E. ALVIN, JR., retired museum director; b. Lynchburg, Va., Oct. 15, 1930; s. Earl Alvin and Georgia Burton Gerhardt; m. Sally Tazewell Flournoy, Sept. 10, 1955; children: Beth, Fritz, Tom, Anna. BS in Bus., Davidson Coll., 1951; postgrad., Lebanon Valley Coll., 1952, Columbia U., 1955; MA in Mus. Studies, SUNY, 1974. Salesman Murphy, Brill & Sahner, Inc., NYC, 1954—56; sales mgr., treas. Lynchburg (Va.) Hosiery Mills, Inc., 1956—73; exec. dir. Rocky Mount Mus., Piney Flats, Tenn., 1974—92; mus. dir., tchr. Tusculum (Tenn.) Coll., 1992—2000. Pres., officer Lynchburg Hist. Soc., 1960—73, Tenn. Assn. Mus., Nashville, 1975—79, SE Mus. Conf., Atlanta, 1977—86; pres., founding dir. Va. Assn. Mus., Richmond, 1967—73; founding chmn. mus. assessment program Inst. Mus. Svcs. and Am. Assn. Mus., 1980—87; founding mem., bd. dirs. World's Fair Hospitality Assn., Knoxville, Tenn., 1979—83; chmn., officer Upper East Tenn.-SW Va. Tourism Coun., 1977—81; bd. dirs. Assn. Living History, Farms and Agrl. Mus., Ohio, 1990—93. 1st lt. inf. U.S. Army, 1951—53. Decorated Combat Inf. badge; recipient James Short award, SE Mus. Conf., 1993, Millenium award, Tenn. Assn. Mus., 2000, Schlebecker award, Assn. Living History, Farms and Agrl. Mus., 2003. Mem.: Am. Assn. Mus. (coun. mem. 1979—89), Am. Assn. for State & Local History (bd. exec. com. 1986—92). Presbyterian. Avocations: history, photography, genealogy. Home: 139 Onks Ln Jonesborough TN 37659 Personal E-mail: alvin.gerhardt@att.net.

GERHARDT, FRITZ, ecologist, educator, researcher; b. Lynchburg, Va., Sept. 25, 1961; s. Earl Alvin and Sally Flournoy Gerhardt; m. Amy Kristin Acker, July 21, 2001. BA, Grinnell Coll., 1983; MFS, Harvard U., 1993. Biol. technician U. S. Fish & Wildlife Svc., Anchorage, 1987—91; rsch. and tchg. asst. Harvard U., Cambridge, 1991—94, Dartmouth Coll., Hanover, NH,

1994—97; field biologist, prin. Langlois Mountain Inst., Strafford, Vt., 1997—99; rsch. and tchg. asst. U. Colo., Boulder, 1999—. Tchg. asst. Oreg. Inst. Marine Biology, Charleston, 1998; vis. instr. Middlebury Coll., Vt., 1998. Fellow, Dartmouth Coll., 1994—97, U. Colo., 2001; scholar, Harvard U., 1991—93. Mem.: Soc. Conservation Biology, Ecol. Soc. Am., Am. Inst. Biol. Sci. Achievements include research in factors structuring natural communities, including the effects of physiography, natural and human disturbances, and global change on the structure and composition of plant communities. Avocations: travel, woodworking, gardening. Home: 58 Burger Rd Chelsea VT 05038-4401

GERHARDT, LESTER A., engineering educator, dean; b. Bronx, N.Y., Jan. 28, 1940; s. David and Mary G.; m. Karen Rita Zimmerman, Sept. 2, 1961; children: Brian, Douglas. BEE, CUNY, 1961; MSEE, SUNY, Buffalo, 1964, PhD, 1969; Doctorate (hon.), Danish Tech. U., 2000. Engr., asst. dir rsch. Bell Aerospace, Buffalo, 1961-70; assoc. prof. Rensselaer Polytechnic Inst., Troy, N.Y., 1970-74, prof., 1974—, chmn. elect., computer and systems engring. dept., 1975-86, dir. CIM Program, 1986-91, assoc. dean engring., 1991—, v.p. rsch. adminstrn. and fin., 2003—, acting dean engring., 2004—. Acting dir. Ctr. for the Mfg. Productivity, 1991-92, founding dir., 1979-80, dir. Ctr. for indsl. Innovation, 1993—; nat. del. NATO, 1980—, chair Rsch. Collaborative Grants Programme; mem. AFSB com. on Robotics and Artificial Intelligence, 1986-89, mem. com. Tactical Communications Nat. Acad. Scis.; mem. adv. bd. N.Y. Gov. Carey's Panel on Telecommunications, NSF, chair. adv. bd.; active internat. cons. to industry, the gov't, and other Universities. Recipient Inventor of Yr. award N.Y. State Intellectual Property Law Assn., 1997, Rsch. adminstrn. award Engring. Rsch. Coun., 2002. Fellow: ASEE (chmn. engring. rsch. coun. 1996—98, bd. dirs. 1996—98, inaugural award for rsch. adminstrn. engring. rsch. coun. 2002). Avocations: sailing, photography, tennis. Office: Rensselaer Poly Inst Deans Office Sch Engring JEC 3002 Troy NY 12180 E-mail: gerhal@rpi.edu.

GERHART, EUGENE CLIFTON, lawyer; b. Bklyn., Apr. 7, 1912; s. Herman Eugene and Mary Elizabeth (Hamilton) G.; m. Mary Richardson Schreiber, Mar. 30, 1939; children: Catherine Gerhart Landon, Virginia Gerhart Mason. AB, Princeton U., 1934; LLB, Harvard U., 1937. Bar: N.J. 1938, N.Y. 1945. Practiced in, Newark, 1938-43, Binghamton, N.Y., 1946—; counsel firm Coughlin & Gerhart, Binghamton; sec. to Judge Manley O. Hudson, Secretariat/League of Nations, Geneva, 1934; lectr. bus. law U. Newark, 1942-43, Triple Cities Coll., 1946-48, Harpur Coll., Endicott, N.Y., 1953-55; lectr. indsl. and labor relations Cornell U., Ithaca, N.Y., 1946; dir., gen. counsel Columbian Mut. Life Ins. Co., 1949-83, acting pres., 1969-70, chmn. bd., 1970-82. Mem. coun. SUNY, Cortland, 1967-77, chmn., 1971-77; mem. Select Task Force on Ct. Reorgn. N.Y. State Senate; mem. jud. nominating com. 3d Jud. Dept., State of N.Y.; mem. N.Y. Unified Ct. Sys. Judicial Records Disposition and Archives Devel. Com. Author: American Liberty and Natural Law, America's Advocate: Robert H. Jackson, Robert H. Jackson: Lawyer's Judge, 2003, Arthur T. Vanderbilt: The Compleat Counsellor, Quote It!, Quote It II, The Lawyer's Treasury, Quote It Completely!, 1998, World Reference Guide to more than 5500 Memorable Quotations from Law and Literature, 1998; spl. contbg. author: Law Office Econs. and Mgmt, 1962—; mem. editl. bd. Quar. Report of Conf. on Personal Fin. Law, 1965; contbr. articles to legal, other publs. Chmn. Harpur Forum SUNY, Binghamton, 1983-84. Lt. USNR, 1943-46. Fellow Am. Bar Found., Am. Coll. Probate Counsel, N.Y. State Bar Found.; mem. ABA (editor Jour. 1946-67, Ross Essay award 1946), Internat. Assn. Ins. Counsel, Assn. Life Ins. Counsel, Am. Judicature Soc., Am. Law Inst., N.Y. State Bar Assn. (editor-in-chief jour. 1961-97, editor-in-chief emeritus 1997—, Disting. Svc. award 1998), Assn. Bar City N.Y., Broome County Bar Assn. (pres. 1961-62, Lifetime Achievement award 1995), Selden Soc., Broome County Princeton Alumni Assn., Harvard Law Sch. Assn. Upstate N.Y. (pres. 1955-57), Scribes (pres., dir. 1966-67), St. Andrew's Soc. Clubs: Rotary (pres. 1969-70), Cosmos, Oteyokwa Lake (pres. 1971-73), Nassau, Harvard of N.Y, Princeton of N.Y. Republican. Home: 34 W End Ave Binghamton NY 13905-4026 Office: 20 Hawley St Binghamton NY 13901-3216

GERHART, JAMES BASIL, physics professor; b. Pasadena, Calif., Dec. 15, 1928; s. Ray and Marion (van Deusen) G.; m. Genevra Joy Thomesen, June 21, 1958; children: James Edward, Sara Elizabeth. BS, Calif. Inst. Tech., 1950; MA, Princeton, 1952, PhD, 1954. Instr. physics Princeton, 1954-56; asst. prof. physics U. Wash., Seattle, 1956-61, assoc. prof., 1961-65, prof., 1965-98, prof. emeritus, 1998—. Exec. officer Pacific Northwest Assn. for Coll. Physics, 1972-94, bd. dirs., 1965-99, chmn., 1970-72; governing bd. Am. Inst. Physics, 1973-76, 78-81. Recipient Disting. Teaching award U. Wash. Regents and Alumni Assn., 1982, Ann. Gerhart lectr., 1997. Fellow Am. Phys. Soc, AAAS; mem. Am. Assn. Physics Tchrs. (sec. 1971-77, v.p. 1977, pres.-elect 1978, pres. 1979, Millikan medal 1985). Home: 5859 NE Park Point Dr Seattle WA 98115-7852 E-mail: gerhart@dirac.phys.u.wahington.edu.

GERICKE, PAUL WILLIAM, minister, educator; b. St. Louis, Apr. 8, 1924; s. Orville Herman and Irma Rose (Reinhart) G.; m. Jean Fisher, Feb. 18, 1953; 1 child, Michael Paul. BSEE, Washington U., St. Louis, 1949; BD, So. Bapt. Theol. Sem., 1960; ThD, New Orleans Bapt. Theol. Sem., 1964; MA, U. New Orleans, 1972. Ordained to ministry So. Bapt. Conv., 1952. Instr. electronics USAF, 1949; calibration engr. Emerson Electric Co., St. Louis, 1950; asst. pastor Calvary Bapt. Ch., St. Louis, 1951-53, Forest Ave. Bapt. Ch., Kansas City, Mo., 1954; pastor First Bapt. Ch., Marceline, Mo., 1955-56, New Hope Bapt. Ch., St. Louis, 1957, Summit Park Bapt. Ch., Louisville, 1959-60, Logtown (Miss.) Bapt. Ch., 1960-64; asst. prof., dir. libr. svcs. New Orleans Bapt. Theol. Sem., 1965-73, assoc. prof., dir. libr., 1973-91, assoc. prof. comms., dir. Comm. Ctr., 1991-92, dir. rsch. and planning, 1992-93, prof. comms. N. Ga. Campus, 1993, acad. counselor, 1993—, dir. of libr., 1993—99, prof. comms. emeritus, 1999—. Mgr. Sta. WSBN-FM, New Orleans, 1979-85, chmn., 1985-92; bd. dirs. religious access channel REACH, New Orleans, 1985-93. Author: The Preaching of Robert G. Lee, 1967, The Ministers Filing System, 1971, Sermon Building, 1973, Crucial Experiences in the Life of D.L. Moody, 1978, Pastor's Library, 1986, Great Preachers of the Church, 1996, Prince of Preachers: The Abortle Paul, 2005. Served with AC USNR, 1942-46. Mem. Am. Radio Relay League, Theta Xi. Republican. Avocation: amateur radio. Home: 482 Sletten Dr Lawrenceville GA 30045 *My life has been completely changed by a personal encounter with Jesus Christ in 1951. Through faith in Him as Savior and Lord, I received a new life, a new sense of values, a new purpose in life, and a new hope both for this life and the life to come. My purpose now is to seek first the kingdom of God and all the other things I need will be given unto me.*

GERIG, MARK S., counselor, educator; b. Fort Wayne, Ind., July 30, 1954; s. Paul R. and Christine J. Gerig; m. Michelle A. Keim, July 26, 1980; children: Brandon, Lauren. BA, Purdue U., 1980; MA, Trinity Evangelical Divinity Sch., 1983; PhD, U. Toledo, 1991. Lic. mental health counselor Ind., psychologist Mich. Therapist Cath. Social Svcs., Defiance, Ohio, 1983—88, Luth. Social Svcs., Ft. Wayne, Ind., 1988—90; outpatient program supr. Ea. Upper Peninsula Mental Health Ctr., Sault Ste. Marie, Mich., 1992—93; assoc. prof., dir. MA counseling program Bethel Coll., Mishawaka, Ind., 1993—, mental health counselor, 1993—96. Prof. Summit Christian Coll., Ft. Wayne, 1987—91. Contbr. articles to profl. jours. Mem. AIDS Task Force, Sault Ste. Marie, 1992—93, Homeless Task Force, Sault Ste. Marie, 1992—93, Stop Child Abuse Now, Sault Ste. Marie, 1992—93; coach Irish Youth Hockey League, South Bend, Ind., 1995—2000; v.p. Riley H.S. Hockey Club, South Bend, Ind., 2003—04, pres., 2004—05. Named Mental Health Counselor of Yr., Ind. Counseling Assn., 2003. Mem.: Christian Assn. Psychol. Studies, Am. Psychol. Assn., Am. Counseling Assn., Am. Mental Health Counselors Assn. (profl. issues com. 2004—), Ind. Mental Health Counselors Assn. (chair profl. devel. 1998—99, editor newsletter 1999—2004, pres. 2000—02). Avocations: ice hockey, fishing, bicycling, hiking. Home: 611 W Grove St Mishawaka IN 46545 Office: Bethel Coll Dept Counseling 1001 W McKinley Ave Mishawaka IN 46545

GERIKE, ERNEST LUTHER, clergyman; b. Tripp, S.D., Nov. 13, 1917; s. Henry Frederick William and Clara Marie (Bornhoeft) G.; m. Vera Martha Roschke, June 11, 1944 (dec. 1999); children: Mary Ann Richard, James Walter, Kenneth John. BA, Concordia Sem., St. Louis, 1940, MDiv, 1944. Ordained to ministry, Luth. Ch. Pastor St. Paul Luth. Ch., East St. Louis, Ill., 1944-49, St. Andrew Luth. Ch., St. Louis, 1949-61; head pastor Trinity Luth. Ch., Bloomington, Ill., 1961-85, pastor emeritus, 1985—; supply pastor Cen. Ill. Area, 1985—. Advisor So. Ill. Luth. Women's Missionary League, East St. Louis, 1948, 49; v.p., bd. dirs. Cen. Ill. Dist. of Luth. Ch.-Mo. Synod, Springfield, 1964-85. Contbr. articles to profl. jours. Chmn. bd. dirs. Mid-Ill. Area Health Planning, Bloomington, 1984; com. mem. McLean County United Way, Bloomington, 1982-92. Mem. McLean County C. of C. (hosp. clergy staff liaison 1989-93), Kiwanis. Republican. Avocations: model trains, sports. Home: 2025 East Lincoln St Apt 1324 Bloomington IL 61701-5995 Office: Trinity Luth Ch 801 S Madison St Bloomington IL 61701-6464

GERINGER, JOHN MICHAEL, economist, educator; b. Indpls., Nov. 13, 1958; s. R.J. and J.A. Geringer BS, Ind. U., 1980; MBA, U. Wash., 1983, PhD, 1986. Vis. asst. prof. Portland (Oreg.) State U., 1983-84; asst. prof. So. Meth. U., Dallas, 1985-87, U. Western Ont., London, 1987-92; prof. Calif. Poly. U., San Luis Obispo, 1992—. Vis. prof. Helsinki Sch. Econs. & Bus. Adminstrn., 1993—, Bond U., Gold Coast, Australia, 1996, Monterey (Calif.) Inst. Internat. Studies, 1996—2000, China Europe Internat. Bus. Sch., 2005—. Author: Joint Venture Partner Selection, 1989; co-author: Business Policy, 1992, International Business, 10th edit., 2005. Recipient decade award Acad. Internat. Bus., 1999. Mem. Acad. Mgmt., Strategic Mgmt. Soc., Licensing Execs. Soc., We. Acad. Mgmt., Assn. Japanese Bus. Studies. Office: Cal Poly Coll Business San Luis Obispo CA 93407 Office Phone: 805-756-1755.

GERJUOY, EDWARD, physicist; b. Bklyn., May 19, 1918; s. Abraham and Clara (Hirsch) G.; m. Clark Jacqueline Reid, Aug. 26, 1940; children: Neil, David Leif. BS cum laude, CCNY, 1937; MA, U. Calif., Berkeley, 1940, PhD, 1942; JD magna cum laude, U. Pitts., 1977. Bar: Calif. 1977, Pa. 1978. Assoc. dir. sonar analysis group Divsn. War Research, Columbia, 1942-46; mem. faculty U. So. Calif., Los Angeles, 1946-51; vis. assoc. prof. N.Y. U., 1951-52; mem. faculty U. Pitts., 1952-58, 64-82, prof. physics, 1964-82, prof. emeritus, 1982—; mem. Pa. Environ. Hearing Bd., 1982-86, cons. hearing examiner, 1987-89; of counsel Rose, Schmidt, Hasley & DiSalle, Pitts., 1987-2001. Mem. rsch. staff Gen. Atomic div. Gen. Dynamics Corp., San Diego, 1958-62; dir. plasma and space applied physics RCA Labs., Princeton, N.J., 1962-64; cons. Westinghouse Rsch. Labs., 1952-58; mem. adv. com. health physics divsn. Oak Ridge Nat. Labs., 1967-71, chmn. com., 1971-74; assoc. Tucker Arensberg Very & Ferguson, Pitts., 1978-80; vis. fellow Joint Inst. Lab. Physics, U. Colo., Boulder, 1970; vis. sci. USSR Acad. Sci. Lebedev Inst., Moscow, 1972; hearing examiner Pa. Environ. Hearing Bd., 1980-81; vis. scholar Stanford Math. Dept., 1987; cons. EPA, 1977-81,; cons. atty. Reed, Smith, Shaw & McClay, Pitts., 1993-2004; adj. prof. U. Pitts. Law Sch., 2000. Author: (with A. Yaspan) Reverberation, in series The Physics of Sound in the Sea, 1968; editor: Physics Text Series, 1960-62, Jour. Comments on Atomic and Molecular Physics, 1971-74, Jurimetrics Jour. of Law Sci. and Tech., 1980-87; contbr. chpts. and numerous articles to tech. and legal lit. Bd. dirs. Pitts. ACLU, 1975-80, 92-95, vice-chmn., chair-elect, chair Am. Phys. Soc. Forum on Physics and Soc., 1994-97; bd. dirs. Pitts. Group Against Smog and Pollution, 2002—04. Fellow AAAS, Am. Phys. Soc. (panel on pub. affairs 1976-79, 94-96, chmn. 1981, governing coun. 2000—03, audit com. 2002-04, chair com. on internat. freedom of scientists 2004), Inst. Physics, Phys. Soc. (Eng.); mem. ABA (chmn. phys. scis. com., sect. sci. and tech. 1976-77, coun. sci. and tech. 1977-80, 84, 87-91), Phi Beta Kappa, Sigma Xi, Order of Coif. Achievements include first predictions of interference in Zeeman Effect allowing magnetic dipole and electric quadrupole transitions, and (with others) of beats between photons of different frequencies; first derivation of transition rates in many-particle collisions from a purely time-independent formalism; first development (with others) of routine procedure for constructing variational estimates of very wide class of quantities. Home: 400 Richland Ln Pittsburgh PA 15208-2732 Office: Univ Pitts Dept Physics 100 Allen Hall Pittsburgh PA 15260 Office Phone: 412-624-2737. Business E-Mail: gerjuoy@pitt.edu. *I have tried to avoid overspecialization, while not letting myself descend into dilettantism. I believe I have succeeded in these endeavors. The last phase of my career, embarking on a law degree at age 56, earning the degree and passing the bar at 59, and then being employed full time as a judge in environmental disputes, probably is an extreme example of career restlessness. I am not sorry to have strayed from a straight line career path, and it has kept me feeling young in my so-called golden years. Nevertheless— and this is more a comment about the present world than about me— I do not believe I would advise young men today to be guided by me.*

GERKE, THOMAS A., communications executive, lawyer; BBA, U. Mo., Columbia; MBA, Rockhurst Coll.; JD, U. Mo., Kansas City. Ptnr. Smith, Gill, Fisher & Butts, Kansas City; sr. atty. US Sprint, 1994—97, various mgmt. pos. in legal, including asst. v.p.-legal, corp. transactions, 1997—99, v.p.-legal gen. bus. and tech., 1999—2000; corp. sec., assoc. gen. counsel Sprint Corp., Overland Park, Kans., 2000—02, v.p.-bus. devel., strategic planning and alliances in the Global Markets Group, 2002—03, exec. v.p.-gen. counsel and external affairs, 2003—. Office: 6200 Sprint Pkwy Overland Park KS 66251

GERKENS, HENRY H., trucking executive; m. Marcia Gerkens; 3 children. Degree, Adelphi U. CPA. V.p., CFO LSHI, 1988—94, exec. v.p., CFO, 1994—2001, pres., CFO, 2001, pres., COO, 2001—; also bd. dirs.; v.p., CFO Landstar Sys., Inc., Jacksonville, Fla., 1993—94, exec. v.p., CFO, 1994—2001, pres., CFO, 2001, pres., COO, 2001—04, bd. dirs., pres., CEO, 2004—. Mem.: AICPA, N.Y. State Soc. CPAs. Office: Landstar Sys 13410 Sutton Park Dr S Jacksonville FL 32224*

GERKEY, STEPHEN J., management consultant, writer, speech-language educator, consultant; b. Eau Claire, Wis., Sept. 14, 1943; d. Joseph Thomas and Mary Jane (Lawrence) G. BA, U. Wis., Eau Claire, 1966; MA, Mich. State U., 1967; PhD, Ind. U., 1977. Cert. project mgr. IBM Corp., 1998, archives and records mgr. State Hist. Soc. of Wis., 1979. Instr. English U. Wis., Eau Claire, 1967-70, 76; assoc. instr., lectr. Ind. U., Bloomington, 1971—75; home sch.-coord. West Ctrl. Wis. Native Am. Comty., Inc., Eau Claire, 1977-78; archives asst. State Hist. Soc. of Wis., Eau Claire, 1978-79; chmn. dept. English, journalism, drama McDonell Ctrl. H.S., Chippewa Falls, Wis., 1981-82, dir. writing program, 1980-82; owner, prin. cons. NMB Assocs., Santa Fe, 1982—; sr. cons. BDM Internat., Albuquerque, 1995-96; project mgr. IBM Corp., Santa Fe, sys. change leader, 1997-98, edn. consulting practice leader, 1998-99; sr. business intelligence cons., 2000—02. Adj. asst. prof. English Iowa State U., Ames, Iowa, 1982-84; asst. prof. English Ea. N.Mex. U., Portales, 1984-88; asst. prof. bus. Ea. N.Mex. U., Portales, 1988-90, assoc. prof. bus., 1990-92; dir. N.Mex. Ctr. Tchg. Excellence, Ea. N.Mex. U., Portales, 1990-92; sr. rsch. and policy analyst, N.Mex. Legislature, Santa Fe, 1992-93; edn. summits steering com. Office N.Mex. Gov., Santa Fe, 1990-93; chair N.Mex.'s Govs., Edn. Renewal Task Force, Edn. Commn. States, Santa Fe, 1991-92; tchr. N.Mex. Author: Sources for the Study of Chippewa Valley History: A Preliminary Bibliography, 1977, A Manual for Full-Time Tutors, 1978, N.Mex. Gov.'s Edn. Summit Reports, 1991, 92, 93, The Navajo Code Talkers, 1996; assoc. editor rsch. and legis. ops. Capitol Govt. reports, Santa Fe, 1993-95; contbr. articles to profl. jours. including N.Mex. Jour. Reading, 1989. V.P. Roosevelt County Humane Soc., 1985-92; v.p., pres. faculty senate Ea. N.Mex. U., Portales, 1986-89. Hobbs Found. Doctoral fellow, 1969; Ind. U. scholar, Bloomington, 1971; Ea. New Mex. U. Faculty Devel. grantee. Mem.: Sigma Tau Delta (life; pres. 1964—65). Avocations: triathlons, road racing. Home and Office: 314 N 14th St Memphis TX 79245-2720 E-mail: sgerkey@nwol.net.

GERLACH, DOUGLAS ELDON, financial writer, Internet developer; b. Columbus, Ohio, May 19, 1963; s. Eldon Chloral and Judith Ann (Benadum) G.; 1 child. BA, Bennington (Vt.) Coll., 1985. Sr. editor, co-creator website Nat. Assn. of Investors Corp., 1995—; founder, editor-in-chief Investorama-.com, N.Y.C., 1995-2000; internet bus. analyst First Albany Corp., N.Y.C., 1997-98; sr. editor Armchair Millionaire.com, New York, NY, 1998—. Cons. editor Mutual Funds mag., 2000—. Actor: Investor's Web Guide, 1997; author: Complete Idiot's Guide to Online Investing, 1998, 2d edit., 2000, The Armchair Millionaire, 2001, Investment Clubs for Dummies, 2001; contbr. articles to mags. Recipient Disting. Svc. award Investment Edn. Inst., 1996. Mem. Nat. Writers Union, Computer Press Assn., Pioneer On-Line Investment Club (pres. 1994—), Am. Assn. of Individual Investors (life), Nat. Assn. of Investor Corp. Computer Group (bd. dirs. 1995—), Mensa.

GERLACH, JAMES WILLIAM, congressman; b. Ellwood City, Pa., Feb. 25, 1955; s. Jack Allen and Helen (Fitzgerald) G.; m. Karen Devanna, 1980; children: Katie, Jimmy, Robby. BA, Dickinson Coll., 1977, JD, 1980. Bar: Pa. Pvt. practice, Downingtown, Pa.; mem. Pa. Ho. of Reps., Dist. 44, Harrisburg, 1991-94; legis. aide Pa. Senate, Harrisburg, 1978-80; mem. Pa. Senate, Dist. 44, Harrisburg, 1995—2002, 108th Congress, 6th Dist., 2003—; mem. small bus. com., transportation com. Recipient Guardian of Small Bus., Nat. Fedn. Ind. Bus. Mem.: Lions (bd. dirs. Downingtown), Pa. Bar Assn., Chester County Agr. Devel. Coun., Sigma Chi. Republican. Home: 1230 Pottstown Pike Ste 4 Glenmoore PA 19343-9533 Office: Senate Box 203044 168 Capitol Bldg Harrisburg PA 17120*

GERLACH, JEANNE ELAINE, English language educator; b. Charleston, W.Va., Oct. 20, 1946; d. Lafayette and Edith Lorraine (Robinson) Marcum; m. Roger Thomas Gerlach Sr., Dec. 30, 1966; children: Roger Thomas Jr., Kristen Elaine. BS, W.Va. State Coll., Institute, 1974; MA, W.Va. State Coll., 1979; EdD, W.Va. U., 1985, U. North Tex., 1992. Lang. arts tchr. Ohio County Schs., Wheeling, W.Va., 1974-79; English instr. West Liberty (W.Va.) State Coll., 1979-82; continuing edn. instr. Seattle Pacific U., 1982-85; asst. prof. English W.Va. U., Morgantown, 1985-86, Tarrant County Jr. Coll., Ft. Worth, 1986-88; dir. Communications Unlimited, Dallas, Pitts., 1986—; assoc. prof. English edn. W.Va. U., Morgantown, 1989-97, spl. asst. to the provost, 1994-97, dir. ctr. women's studies, 1993-94; dean coll. edn. U. Tex., Arlington, 1997—, assoc. v.p. K-16 initiatives, 2003—. Cons. to bus. and corps., 1986—; co-dir. advanced writing project W.Va. U., Morgantown, 1989, lang. arts camps, 1988, 89, 90, young writers inst. Editor: English Internat.; contbr. articles to profl. jours. Mem. LWV, W.Va. DAR, Young Republicans, W.Va.; participant Leadership Tex., 2005. Recipient 1st place Creative Writing award, W.Va. Women's Clubs, 1976, Great Tex. Woman award, Ft. Worth Bus. Press, 2002; Faculty Devel. grantee, W.Va. U., 1989. Mem. AAUW, AAUP, Nat. Coun. Tchrs. English (chair women's com. 1986—, chair nominating com. 1988-89, Outstanding Tchr. in Coll. of Human Resources and Edn. award W.Va. U. 1992, Rewey Belle Inglis award 1992), Am. Ednl. Rsch. Assn., W.Va. U. Alumni Assn. (sec. 1990, pres.), Nat. Women's Studies Assn., Nat. Soc. Daus. Am. Revolution. Republican. Methodist. Avocations: tennis, golf, poetry, photography, doll collecting. Office Phone: 817-272-7185. E-mail: gerlach@uta.edu.

GERLAI, ROBERT T., behavioral neuroscientist, behavioral geneticist; b. Budapest, Hungary, May 17, 1960; arrived in U.S., 1996; married. MSc, Hungarian Acad. Scis., Budapest, 1984, PhD, 1988. Asst. prof. Etvos Lorand U., Budapest, 1987—90; vis. prof. U. Toronto, Canada, 1990—91; scientist Mount Sinai Hosp. Rsch. Inst., 1991—96, Genentech, Inc., South San Francisco, 1996—2000; sr. rsch. scientist Lilly Rsch. Labs., Indpls., 2000—. Mem. reviewing panel NIH, 1999—. Editor: (textbook) Ethology I, 1987, Ethology II, 1987, (sci. handbook) Handbook of Molecular-Genetic Techniques for Brain and Behavior Research, 1999, (sci. jour.) Genes, Brain and Behavior, 2001, (spl. issue sci. jour.) Molecular Behavior Genetics of the Mouse, 2001, Behavioral Neurogenetics, 2002; editor: (review editor) (sci. jour.) Con. Bd. Cognitive Processing. Recipient Travel award, SOROS Found., 1986, 1988, 1989, 1990, Fellow award, Clin. Rsch. Soc. Toronto, 1994; fellow postdoctoral fellow, Network Ctrs. Excellence, 1991—93, Med. Rsch. Coun. Can., 1993—95; grantee, Otka, 1989—93. Mem.: Soc. Neuroscience, Internat. Behavioral Neuroscience Soc. (U.S.councillor 1998—2001), Internat. Behavioral Neural Genetics Soc. (treas. 1998—2002).

GERLICK, HELEN J., tax practitioner, accountant; b. Denver, Dec. 11, 1931; d. JAmes Jeffries and Margaret (Fitzwater) Farrell; m. Jerald James Gerlick, Aug. 25, 1950; children: Michael James, Daniel Lee, Kenneth Dwayne. Grad., Barnes Bus. Sch., 1950, H&R Block Sch., 1974. CPA, Cert. Tax Preparer. Acctg. clerk Colo. Teamsters, Denver, 1956; ins. div. NSLI, Denver, 1956-58; assoc. St. Lukes Acctg., Denver, 1958; acctg. office mgr. Mundix Control Systems, Denver, 1964-83; tax preparer H & R Block, Denver, 1977-79; acct., tax preparer Gerlick's Tax Svc., Wheat Ridge, Colo., 1979—. Mem. NAFE, Am. Bus. Women's Assn. (named Women of Yr. 1977, 81, 94), Nat. Assn. Tax Practitioners, Nat. Pub. Accts. Assn., Pub. Accts. Soc. of Colo. Democrat. Lutheran. Avocations: teaching at senior center, painting, collecting and making porcelain dolls. Home and Office: 4601 Robb St Wheat Ridge CO 80033-2536

GERLITS, FRANCIS JOSEPH, lawyer; b. Chgo., Mar. 29, 1931; s. John T. and May (Cameron) G.; m. Suzanne Long, June 20, 1953; children: Kathleen, Karen, Mary Cameron, Francis Jr. Ph.B., U. Notre Dame, 1953; JD, U. Chgo., 1958. Bar: Ill. 1958. Ptnr. Kirkland & Ellis, Chgo., 1964-95, of counsel, 1995; gen. counsel Internat. Harvester Co. (now Navistar Internat. Corp.), Chgo., 1985-90. Mem. ABA, Order of Coif, Tavern Club, Chicago Club Office: Kirkland & Ellis 200 E Randolph St Fl 54 Chicago IL 60601-6636 Office Phone: 312-861-2070.

GERMAIN, CLAIRE MADELEINE, law librarian, educator, lawyer; b. Chaumont, France, Sept. 22, 1951; d. Pierre and Jeanne (Despujols) G.; m. Stuart M. Basefsky, Aug. 16, 1976; 1 child, Nicolas. Licence-es. lettres, U. Paris, 1971, LLB, 1974; M in Comparative Law, La. State U., 1975; M in Law Librarianship, U. Denver, 1977. Reference librarian Duke U. Law Library, Durham, N.C., 1977-80, head reference librarian, 1982-84, asst. librarian, sr. lectr. comparative law, 1984-89, assoc. dir., sr. lectr. comparative law, 1989-93; Edward Cornell law libr., prof. law Cornell U., Ithaca, N.Y., 1993—. Research fellow Max Planck Inst., Hamburg, Federal Republic of Germany, 1980. Author: Germain's Transnational Law Research: A Guide to Attorneys, 1991, (with Szladits) Guide to Foreign Legal Materials, French, 2d edit., 1985; contbr. and editor articles to profl. jours. Mem. ABA, Am. Assn. Law Librs. (chair fgn. law sect. 1985-86, v.p., pres.-elect 2004—, chair-elect sect. librs. 2003-), Am. Assn. Law Schs. (chmn. libr. and tech. com., chmn. elect libr. sect. 2003—). Roman Catholic. Office: Cornell Law Libr Myron Taylor Hall Ithaca NY 14853 E-mail: cmg13@cornell.edu.

GERMAIN, GALE INOFF, research psychologist; b. Washington, June 19, 1946; d. Victor and Arlene Inoff; m. Ronald Nathan Germain, June 9, 1985; 1 child, David Aaron. BA with high honors, U. Md., College Park, 1968. Rsch. psychologist NIMH at NIH, Bethesda, Md., 1968—. Contbr. articles to profl. jours. Mem.: Phi Beta Kappa. Avocations: painting, reading, travel. Home: 10404 Crossing Creek Rd Potomac MD 20854 Office: NIMH at NIH Child Psychiatry Br Rm 3N202 Bldg 10 10 Center Dr MSC1600 Bethesda MD 20892-1600 Office Phone: 301-435-4504. Office Fax: 301-402-0296. Business E-Mail: ggermain@mail.nih.gov.

GERMAIN, MARIE-LINE, education educator; b. Maisons-Laffitte, Franc3e, Nov. 6, 1970; arrived in US, 1995; d. Christian Robert Germain and Geraldine Fruit. BS, Stirling U., Scotland, 1992; MS, U. Nanterre-Paris X, 1993; PhD, Barry U., 2005. Career advisor Coll. St. Joseph, Asnieres, France, 1990—95; prof. higher edn. Enghien-Les-Bains, Val d'Oise, France, 1994; lectr. U. Miami, Coral Gables, Fla., 2000—; mem. faculty, chmn. dept. City Coll., Miami, Fla., 2001—; instr. U. St. Francis, Miami, 2004—. Author conf. procs., chpts. to books, articles and papers in field. Mem.: MLA, Acad. Human Resource Develop., Am. Ednl. Rsch. Assn., Am. Resort Devel. Assn., So. Mgmt. Assn., Soc. Indsl. and Orgnl. Psychology, Toastmasters Internat.

Office: City Coll 9300 S Dadeland Blvd Office 700 Miami FL 33156 Home: 6271 N Waterway Dr Miami FL 33155 Office Fax: 305-666-9243. Personal E-mail: mgermain99@hotmail.com. Business E-Mail: mgermain@citycollege.edu.

GERMAN, DONALD FREDERICK, physician; b. San Francisco, Oct. 2, 1935; m. Marilyn Sue King; children: Susan, Charles, Donald. BS, U. San Francisco, 1956; MD, U. Calif., San Francisco, 1960. Diplomate Am. Bd. Pediats., Am. Bd. Allergy and Immunology. Intern Kaiser Found. Hosp., San Francisco, 1960-61, resident in pediats., 1963-65, resident, fellow in allergy, 1966-68; staff pediatrician Kaiser Med. Ctr., Santa Clara, Calif., 1965-66, staff allergist, 1968-69; chief dept. allergy Kaiser Permanente Med. Ctr., San Francisco, 1969-99, allergy staff physician, 1999—. Clin. prof. pediatrics U. Calif. Med. Sch., San Francisco, 1991—; bd. dirs. Asthma, Allergy and Immunology Found. No. Calif. Capt. USAF, 1961-63. Fellow Am. Acad. Pediats., Am. Coll. Allergy and Immunology, Am. Acad. Allergy and Immunology; mem. Calif. Soc. Allergy and Immunology (past pres.). Avocations: running, hiking, fly fishing, travel. Office: Karser Dept Allergy 1635 Divisadero St 101 San Francisco CA 94115 Office Phone: 415-833-3780. Personal E-mail: ofgerman2@yahoo.com. Business E-Mail: donald.german@kp.org.

GERMAN, ELAINE, physician; b. Newark, Apr. 1, 1927; d. Nathan and Fanny (Kasen) Utal; m. Philip Eli German, Nov. 25, 1948 (Sept. 1998); children: Ted, Matthew. BA, U. Wis., 1947; MD, NYU, 1953. Diplomate Am. Bd. Internal Medicine, Am. Bd. Endocrinology and Metabolism. Intern Maimonides Hosp., Bklyn., 1953-54, resident, 1954-55, Montefiore Hosp., Bronx, N.Y., 1957-58; rsch. fellow Columbia U./Goldwater Meml. Hosp., N.Y.C., 1955-57; internist Montefiore Med. Group, Bronx, N.Y., 1958-67; chief sect. medicine Bird S. Coler Hosp., N.Y.C., 1968-70; asst. dir. medicine Hosp. for Joint Diseases, N.Y.C., 1971-74; dir. medicine and med. edn. Helene Fuld Med. Ctr., Trenton, N.J., 1974-79, United Hosps., Newark, 1980-92; instr. medicine Columbia Coll. Phys. and Surg., N.Y.C., 1955-57; asst. prof. medicine N.Y Med. Coll., N.Y.C., 1967-71; assoc. prof. clin. medicine Mt. Sinai Sch. Medicine, N.Y.C., 1972-74; prof. medicine Hahnemann Med. Coll., Phila., 1974-80; clin. prof. medicine U. Medicine and Dentistry N.J.-N.J. Med. Sch., Newark, 1980-92. Contbr. articles to profl. jours. Mem. Coalition for Peace, Princeton, N.J. Recipient Women's Med. award NYU-Bellevue Med. Sch., 1953. Fellow ACP; mem. AAAS, N.Y. Acad. Medicine, Am. Diabetes Assn., Phi Beta Kappa. Avocations: reading, travel, classical music. Home: 8 Autumn Hill Rd Princeton NJ 08540-2910

GERMAN, JUNE RESNICK, lawyer; b. N.Y.C., Feb. 24, 1946; d. Irving and Stella (Weintraub) Resnick; m. Harold Jacob German, May 31, 1974; children: Beth Melissa, Heather Alice, Bret. *Paternal grandparents, Frank and Rebecca Resnick, immigrated from Russia. Frank Resnick served in the Russian cavalry and established a textile business in the United States. Maternal grandfather, Aaron Isaac Weintraub, immigrated from Poland and owned a grocery business in Coney Island. Maternal grandmother, Martha Weintraub, an accomplished pianist, played at dance halls and silent movies. Father, Irving Resnick, was a chemical engineer recruited by the Manhattan Project. He solved a complex technical problem involving the use of the gaseous diffusion process to enrich uranium to weapons grade thereby advancing the development of the atomic bomb. Mother, Stella Resnick, taught early education. Husband, a graduate of Princeton University and Columbia College of Physicians and Surgeons, practices internal medicine and has been a nationally ranked tennis player. Daughter Beth is a senior communications specialist for The Getty Center. Daughter Heather has received her M.S.W. degree. Son Bret is a high school student* BA, U. Pa., 1965; JD, NYU, 1968. Bar: N.Y. 1968, U.S. Dist. Ct. (ea. and so. dists.) N.Y. 1974, U.S. Ct. Appeals (2d cir.) 1973, U.S. Supreme Ct. 1973. Atty., sr. atty., supervising atty. Mental Health Info. Svc., N.Y.C., 1968-77; atty., advisor Course in Human Behavior Mems. of N.Y. State Judiciary, Nassau and Suffolk County, 1980; pvt. practice Huntington, N.Y., 1985—. *June Resnick German brought several test cases which guaranteed rights to mentally disabled persons in the civil and criminal justice system, including a landmark case which established that, in New York State, civil involuntary patients have (a) a right to treatment, (b) a right to be treated in a facility that is least restrictive of their liberty, and (c) a right not to be transferred to a correctional facility. She has written several articles pertaining to the rights of the mentally disabled and has prepared amicus curiae briefs to the United States Supreme Court in the fields of mental health and environmental law.She has successfully represented the "Mi Casa" orphanage, an organization caring for 500 Guatemalan children, in litigation to recover funds wrongfully seized by the United States* Contbg. author: Bioethics and Human Rights, 1978, Mental Illness, Due Process and the Acquitted Defendant, 1979; contbr. chpts. to books, articles to profl. jours. Chmn. Citizen's Ad Hoc Com. Constrn. of the Dix Hills Water Adminstrn. Bldg., Huntington, N.Y., 1985-90; mem. Citizens Adv. Com. for Dix Hills Water Dist., Huntington, 1992—; dir. House Beautiful Assn. at Dix Hills, 1986—, Citizens for a Livable Environment and Recycling, Huntington, 1989-93; active Suffolk County (N.Y.) Dem. Com., 1986—, Deer Park Avenue Task Force, Town of Huntington, 1997-98, Dix Hills Revitalization Com., 1999-2000. Mem. Suffolk County Bar Assn. Jewish. Avocations: tennis, hiking, travel. Office: 150 Main St Huntington NY 11743-6908 Office Phone: 631-271-8711. Personal E-mail: junegerman@hotmail.com.

GERMAN, KATHERINE L., international consultant; b. Reading, Pa., May 10, 1947; d. John Elmer and Mabel Berdella (Feick) G.; m. L. Denton Crews, Aug. 4, 1983. BA, Pa. State U., 1969; MEd, Bowling Green State U., 1971; cert. advanced studies, Harvard U., 1985; PhD, U. Ill., 1981. Tchr., coord. Eastwood Jr. High sch., Lucky, Ohio, 1971; dir. Comms. Ctr. North Shore C.C., Beverly, Mass., 1971-74, div. chair, 1974-79, asst. academic dean Lynn, Mass., 1979-88; acad. v.p. Endicott Coll., Beverly, 1988-89; v.p. Devel. Inst., Boston, 1989—. Reader U.S. Dept. Edn., Washington, 1980—; speaker and cons. in field. Contbr. articles to profl. jours. Vol. King's Chapel, Boston, 1982-91. Recipient Pride of Performance award Commonwealth of Mass., 1985. Mem. ASTD, Internat. Reading Assn., Am. Ednl. Rsch. Assn., Am. Assn. Higher Edn., Mass. Women in Pub. Higher Edn., Phi Delta Kappa. Avocations: swimming, music, theater, writing, tennis. Home and Office: 150 Staniford St Apt 331 Boston MA 02114-2591

GERMAN, RANDALL MICHAEL, materials scientist, educator; b. Bainbridge, Md., Nov. 12, 1946; s. Eugene Knox and Helen (Schrufer) G.; m. Carol Jean Hosmer, Dec. 21, 1968; children: Eric, Garth. BS in Materials Sci., San Jose State U., 1968; MS in Metall. Engring., Ohio State U., 1971; PhD in Materials Sci., U. Calif., Davis, 1975; cert. mgmt. devel., Hartford Grad. Ctr., 1979; Doctorate (hon.), U. Carlos III de Madrid. Materials scientist Battelle Columbus Labs., Columbus, Ohio, 1968-69; tech. staff Sandia Nat. Lab., Livermore, Calif., 1969-77; dir. R&D Mott Metall. Corp., Farmington, Conn., 1977-78; dir. rsch. J.M. Ney Co., Bloomfield, Conn., 1978-80; Hunt prof. Rensselaer Poly. Inst., Troy, N.Y., 1980-91; Brush chair prof. materials Pa. State U., University Park, 1991—. Founder Six Cos., Inc., Troy, 1989—, Xform; dir. PIM Symposium, 1990—. Author: Powder Metallurgy Science, 1984, 2d edit., 1994, Liquid Phase Sintering, 1985, Powder Packing Characteristics, 1989, Injection Molding, 1990, Sintering Theory and Practice, 1996, Injection Molding of Metals and Ceramics, 1997, Powder Metallurgy of Iron and Steel, 1998. PIM Design and Applications, 2003; contbr. numerous articles to profl. jours.; patentee in field. Named Hon. Prof. N.E. U. Tech., 1985, Disting. Alumni U. Calif., 1990, Penn State Engring. Soc. Outstanding and Premiere Rschr. award, 1995. Fellow ASM Internat. (chmn. Geissler award 1983), Am. Powder Metallurgy (spkr., organizer, bd. dirs.); mem. Minerals, Metals, Materials Soc. (chmn. 1983-85), Am. Ceramic Soc., Materials Rsch. Soc., Alpha Sigma Mu (hon.). Avocation: bicycling.

GERMAN, SUSAN LEE, secondary school educator; b. Aberdeen, SD, Feb. 16, 1951; d. William Garth and Mae Elaine (Raisanen) Holmes; m. F. Walter Kalbus, June 2, 1973 (div.); children: Andrew, Rachel, Matthew; m. Charles John German, Jan. 2, 1988. BS, Valley City State Coll., 1973. Cert. tchr., N.D. Music tchr. Lisbon (ND) Pub. Schs., 1973—87, Fullerton Pub. Sch., ND, 1988—93, Monango Pub. Sch., ND, 1989—91; ind. music tchr. Oakes, ND, 1987—97; tchr. music Oakes Pub. Sch., 1997—. Dist. dir. N.D. Jaycettes, 1979-80, regional dir., 1980-83, state pres., 1982-83; regional chaplain U.S. Jayceetes, 1983-85; v.p. Active Arts, Inc., 1990, pres., 1991; mem. Guelph Cmty. Band. Named Outstanding Regional Dir., U.S. Jayceettes, 1981, 82, Mem. Country Rose Homemakers (historian 1990—). Democrat. Lutheran. Avocations: sports, concerts, flower gardening, crafts, reading. Home: 106 3d Ave Ludden ND 58474 Office: Oakes Pub Sch 804 Main Ave Oakes ND 58474 Business E-Mail: sgerman@oakes.k12.nd.us.

GERMAN, WILLIAM, newspaper editor; b. N.Y.C., Jan. 4, 1919; s. Sam and Celia (Norack) G.; m. Gertrude Pasenkoff, Oct. 12, 1940 (dec. 1998); children: David, Ellen, Stephen. BA, Bklyn. Coll., 1939; MS, Columbia U., 1940; Nieman fellow, Harvard U., 1950. Mng. editor KQED, Newspaper of the Air, 1968; editor Chronicle Fgn. Service, 1960-77; reporter, asst. fgn., news, mng., exec. editor, editor San Francisco Chronicle, 1940-2000, editor emeritus, 2000—. Lectr. U. Calif., Berkeley, 1946-47, 68-70 Editor: San Francisco Chronicle Reader, 1962. Bd. trustees World Affairs Coun. Served with AUS, 1943-45. Mem. AP Mng. Editors Assn., Am. Soc. Newspaper Editors, Commonwealth Club of Calif. (pres. 1995). Home: 150 Lovell Ave Mill Valley CA 94941-1883 Office: San Francisco Chronicle 901 Mission St San Francisco CA 94103-2905 E-mail: wgerman@sfchronicle.com.

GERMANI, ELIZABETH A., lawyer; b. Portland, Maine, Aug. 19, 1963; BA, Boston Coll., 1985; JD, U. Maine Sch. Law, Portland, 1988. Bar: N.H. 1988, Maine 1989. Assoc. atty. Sulloway & Hollis, Concord, N.H., 1988-92, Friedman & Babcock, Portland, 1992-96; ptnr. Friedman Babcock & Gaythwaite, Portland, 1996—99, Germani & Riggle LLC, Portland, 1999—. Office: Germani & Riggle LLC 93 Exchange St Portland ME 04101-4164 Office Phone: 207-773-7455.

GERMANN, GARY STEPHEN, lawyer; b. Evansville, Ind., Sept. 12, 1948; s. Henry Luther and Esther Louise (Gerichs) G.; m. Beth Coppel, Dec. 27, 1971; children: Mark, David, Matthew, Sarah. BA, Purdue U., 1970; JD, Valparaiso U., 1973. Bar: Iowa 1973, Ind. 1973, U.S. Dist. Ct. (no. dist.) Ind. 1977, U. Ct. Appeals (7th cir.) 1989, U.S. Supreme Ct. 1989. Dep. pros. atty. Prosecutor's Office, Valparaiso, Ind., 1973-74, chief dep. pros. atty., 1974-77; assoc. Harris and Welsh, Chesterton, Ind., 1977-78; pros. atty. Porter County, Valparaiso, 1978-82; pvt. practice, Portage, Ind., 1982—. Assoc. prof. Valparaiso U., 1977. High sch. tchr., elder-trustee 1st Presbyn. Ch., Valparaiso, 1977—; bd. dirs. YMCA, Valparaiso, 1976-80; vol. Am. Cancer Soc., Valparaiso, 1987—; mem. Cmty. Sys. Wide Response Team, Valparaiso, 1994—. Mem. Ind. Bar Assn., Ind. Pub. Defender Coun., Porter County Bar Assn. (pres. 1986). Avocations: basketball, soccer. Office: 3437 Airport Rd Portage IN 46368-5107

GERMANN, RICHARD P(AUL), pharmaceutical company chemist, chemicals executive; b. Ithaca, NY, Apr. 3, 1918; s. Frank E.E. and Martha Minna Marie (Knechtel) G.; m. Malinda Jane Plietz, Dec. 11, 1942; 1 child, Cheranne Lee. Student, U. N.Mex., 1938-39; BA, U. Colo., 1939, postgrad., 1940-41, Western Res. U., 1941-43, Brown U., 1954. Chief analytical chemist Taylor Refining Co., Corpus Christi, 1943-44; rsch. devel. chemist Calco Chem. divsn. Am. Cyanamid Co., 1944-52; devel. chemist charge pilot plant Alrose Chem. Co. divsn. Geigy Chem. Corp., 1952-55; new product devel. chemist, rsch. divsn. W.R. Grace & Co., Clarksville, Md., 1955-60; chief chemist soap-cosmetic divsn. G.H. Packwood Mfg. Co., St. Louis, 1960-61; coord., promoter chem. product devel. Abbott Labs., North Chicago, Ill., 1961-71; internat. chem. cons. to mgmt., 1971-73; pres. Germann Internat. Ltd., 1973-82, Ramtek Internat. Ltd., 1973-2000. Real estate broker, 1972-90; cons. major Japanese chem. cos., 1971-85; cons. dept. chemistry Bowling Green (Ohio) State U., 1988. Author: The Technical Man of the Sea of Change, 1965, Decontamination of Plant Wastes--An Overview, 1969, Science's Ultimate Challenge--The Re-evaluation of Ancient Occult Knowledge, 1978, Science and Innovation, 1993; patentee in U.S. and fgn. countries on sulfonamides, vitamins, detergent-softeners and biocides. Rep. Am. Inst. Chemists to Joint Com. on Employment Practices, 1969-72; vestryman St. Paul's Episc. Ch., Norwalk, Ohio, 1978-81, chmn. adminstrn. and long-range planning commn., 1980-81, The Ch. of Light, Friends of the Norwalk Pub. Libr., 1996-97, pres., 1997-99; trustee Svcs. for the Aging, Inc., 1982-94, treas., 1992-93, pres., 1994; mem. nutritional coun. Ohio Dist. Five Area Agy. on Aging, 1983-84; sr. adv. Ohio Assn. Ctrs. for Sr. Citizens, Inc., 1982-90; bd. dirs. Christie Lane Industries, 1981—2005, chmn., 1988-94; mem. com., sec. Huron County Disaster Svcs. Agy., 1987-89. Fellow AAAS, Am. Inst. Chemists (chmn. com. employment rels. 1969-72), Chem. Soc. (London); mem. Am. Chem. Soc. (councilor 1971-73, chmn. membership com. chem. mktg. and econs. divsn. 1966-68, chmn. program com. 1968-69, del. at large for local sects. 1970-71, chmn. 1972-73, chmn. Chgo. program com. 1966-67, chmn. Chgo. endowment com. 1967-68, dir. Chgo. sect. 1968-72, chmn. awards com. 1972-73, sec. chem. mktg. and econs. group Chgo. sect. 1964-66, chmn. 1967-68), Am. Numastic, Internat. Sci. Found., Sci. Rsch. Soc. Am., Comml. Chem. Devel. Assn. (chmn. program com. Chgo. conv. 1966, mem. fin. com. 1966-67, ad hoc com. of Comml. Chem. Devel. Assn. and Chem. Market Rsch. Assn. 1968-69, co-chmn. pub. rels. Denver conv. 1968, chmn. membership com. 1969-70, mem. directory com. 1967-68, employment com. 1969-70), Nat. Security Indsl. Assn. (com. rep. ocean sci. tech. com., maintenance adv. com., tng. ad. com. 1962-70), Midwest Planning Assn., Am. Assn. Textile Chemists and Colorists, Am. Pharm. Assn., Midwest Chem. Mktg. Assn., Am. Mgmt. Assn., N.Y. Acad. Scis., Internat. Platform Assn., Am. Meteorol. Soc., Water Pollution Control Fedn., Lake County Bd. Realtors, World Future Soc., Midwest Planning Assn., Am. Fedn. Astrologers, Washington Astrological Assn. (v.p. 1959-60), Ancient Astronaut Soc., Am. Philatelic Soc., Am. Numismatic Assn., Am. Rose Soc., AARP (pres. Huron county Firelands chpt. #4110 1986-88, chmn. legis. com. 1988-90, active project vote, pres. 1997-98, bd. dirs. 1998—), Friends Norwalk Pub. Libr. (sec. 1997-98, pres. 1998-2000), Chemists Club (N.Y.C., Chgo.), Torch Club, Toastmasters, Lions (sec. Allview, Md. 1956-57), Kiwanis, Masons, (32nd degree, Knights Templar, Rotary, Gamma Delta (pres. Cleve. chapt. 1941-42), Sigma Xi, Alpha Chi Sigma (chmn. profl. activities com. 1968-70, pres. Chgo. chpt. 1968-70). Home and Office: 394 Cleveland Rd #11H Norwalk OH 44857-8500 *Total knowledge, whether it be in business, science, history, or religion, is a mirage. That which we believe to be true today will be subject to continuous modification throughout all eternity as understanding of the universe continues to expand. This belief has made my life an adventure in which I have attempted to find the many "reasons why" which determine the way we think and live. It is obvious that all the fields in question are interrelated in many ways. History shows that dogma in any discipline or a lack of knowledge of the past has always inhibited or prevented man's spiritual, scientific or material growth. The incorrect beliefs thus perpetuated become the cross we bear that prevents us in no small part from living our lives to the fullest during our short stay here on earth. Since I believe that there is a hidden reason for everything that happens during our lifetime, logic tells me that in the eons to come each soul will continue its adventures through many rebirths both here on this earth and on earths in many distant galaxies far out in the universe as God allows us to increase our knowledge of the real reason for our existence.*

GERMANO, MARY CATHERINE, writer; b. Washington, D.C., Dec. 16, 1949; d. Robert F. and Mary C. (Lahatte) Pierozak; m. Donald J. Germano, May 26, 1973; children: David, Peter, Michael, Mary. BS, St, Bonaventure U., 1972; MLS, Rutgers U., 1975. Libr. Lincoln 1st Bank, Rochester, N.Y., 1975-81, Gates-Chili (N.Y.) Sch. Dist., 1981; pvt. practice Fairport, N.Y., 1988—. Author: Silent Witness, 1993. Mem. special edn. com. Fairport (N.Y.) Sch. Dist., 1992-95, regional trauma oversight com. Strong Meml. Hosp. Trauma Ctr., Rochester, N.Y., 1994—; bd. dirs. Perinton Vol. Ambulance Corps., Fairport, 1996-98. Mem. Mystery Writers Am., Am. Trauma Soc., Authors' Guild. Avocations: reading, gardening. Home: 48 South Ave Fairport NY 14450-2454 Office: 48 South Ave Fairport NY 14450-2454

GERMANO, WILLIAM PAUL, publisher; b. Yonkers, N.Y., Oct. 10, 1950; s. William Peter and Edna Mary (Gilmore) G.; m. Diane Grace Gibbons, July 21, 1973; 1 child, Christian. BA in English, Columbia U., 1972; PhD in English, Ind. U., 1981. Editor Columbia U. Press, N.Y.C., 1980-83, editor in chief, 1983-85; v.p., editorial dir. Routledge, Chapman and Hall Inc., N.Y.C., 1986-92, Routledge, Inc., N.Y.C., 1992-96, v.p., dir. pub. humanities, 1996—. Author: Getting It Published: A Guide for Scholars and Anyone Else Serious About Serious Books, 2001, From Dissertation to Book, 2005. Bd. suprs. The English Inst. Mem. MLA, PEN. Home: 33 Riverside Dr New York NY 10023-8012 Office: Routledge 270 Madison Ave New York NY 10016 Business E-Mail: william.germano@taylorandfrancis.com.

GERMANY, DANIEL MONROE, aerospace engineer; b. Lake Village, Ark., Sept. 14, 1937; s. Jones Harry and Sara (Farrar) G.; m. Edie Germany; children: Cheryl Germany, Danel Germany, Dianne Germany, Randy Robertson, Rick Robertson, Vaughn Loiuse. BSM.E., Miss. State U., 1959. Aerospace systems engr. NASA Marshall Space Flight Center, Huntsville, Ala., 1960-78; tech. exec. asst. to assoc. adminstr. of shuttle transp. systems NASA Hdqrs., Washington, 1978-79, dir. orbiter programs, 1979-81; asst. mgr. Orbiter Project Office Johnson Space Ctr., Houston, 1982, mgr. Flight Equipment Project Office, 1983-85, dep. mgr. Space Sta. Project Office, 1985-86, dep. mgr. Orbiter and GFE Projects Office, 1987-90, mgr. Orbiter and GFE Projects Office, 1990-95; ind. aerospace cons., 1995-97; program dir. Honeywell Aerospace, Houston, 1997—2002. Aerospace cons., 2002—. Republican.

GERMANY, JOHN FREDRICK, lawyer; b. Daviston, Ala., Jan. 16, 1923; s. Thomas Brooks and Aldora Toles (Finley) G.; m. Mary Ellen Cook, June 15, 1951; children: Sue Ellen Germany Lucas, John Jr., Jan Fielder Germany Gruetzmacher, Lindsey Brooks Robbins. BA, U. Fla., 1943; JD, Harvard U., 1950; LLD (hon.), Stetson U., 1974. Bar: Fla. 1950, U.S. Dist. Ct. (mid. dist.) Fla., 1951, D.C., 1981. Assoc. Fowler, White, Gillen, Yancey & Humkey, Tampa, Fla., 1950-52; ptnr. Coles, Himes & Germany, Tampa, 1952-59; judge 13th Jud. Cir., Tampa, 1959-66; ptnr. Knight, Jones, Whitaker & Germany, Tampa, 1966-68, Holland & Knight, Tampa, 1968—. Asst. county atty. Hillsborough County, Tampa, 1955-59; legal asst. to gov. State of Fla., 1955-57. Served to 1st lt. U.S. Army, ETO, PTO. Downtown Tampa Pub. Libr. renamed John F. Germany Pub. Libr., 1999. Fellow ABA (state chmn.); mem. Atty.'s Liability Assurance Soc. Ltd. (bd. dirs.), Univ. Club (pres. 1964-65), Tampa Club (pres. 1983-85), Ye Mystic Krewe of Gasparilla King. Democrat. Episcopalian. Avocations: reading, travel, walking. Office: Holland & Knight PO Box 1288 Tampa FL 33601-1288 E-mail: jgermany@hklaw.com.

GERMON, GEORGE, small business owner; Degree, R.I. Sch. of Design; Dates in Culinary Arts (hon.), Johnson and Wales Univ., 2000. Chef, co-owner Al Forno Restaurant, Providence, 1975—. Appeared (TV series) Julia Child's Kitchen with Master Chefs, Baking with Julia, Martha Stewart Living, David Rosengarten's Grilling, Cooking Live Primetime (Sarah Moulton); co-author: CUCINA SIMPATICA:Robust Trattria Cooking. Actively involved Providence Pub. Libr., R.I. Food Bank, R.I. Projects Aids, R.I. Ballet. Named Rising Stars of Am., James Beard Found.; named one of The Ten Best Chefs in Am., Food and Wine; recipient World's Restaurant for causal dining, Internat. Herald Tribune, Disting. Restaurants of North Am., Conde Nast Traveler's, 1992—2003, Hall of Fame award, Nations Restaurant News, Ivy award, Insegna del Ristorante Italiano, Italian Ministries of Agrl. and Foriegn Trade, 1999. Achievements include he has taught disting. venues as Degustibus (Macy's N.Y.C.), Bristol Farms Draegers and Fetzer Vineyards in Calif., La Varence in W.Va; in Italy he teaches regularly at Capezzana Estate in Tuscany and Hotel Cipriani in Venice. Office: 577 South Main St Providence RI 02903

GERMOND, JACK, columnist; b. Boston, 1928; m. Alice Germond, 1994. BA in journalism & history, U. of Mo. Reporter Gannett Newspapers, chief-Washington Bureau; reporter The Washington Star, Baltimore Sun; columnist Nat. Jour.; semi-regular panelist The McLaughlin Group; political analyst CNN; panelist Inside Washington. Co-author (with Jules Witcover): Blue Smoke & Mirrors: How Reagan Won and Why Carter Lost the Election of 1980, 1981, Wake Us When It's Over: Presidential Politics of 1984, 1985, Whose Broad Stripes and Bright Stars? The Trivial Pursuit of the Presidency, 1989, Mad As Hell: Revolt at the Ballot Box, 1992; author: Fat Man in A Middle Seat: Forty Years of Covering Politics, 2002, Fat Man Fed Up: How American Politics Went Bad, 2004. Democrat. Atheist. Office: 520 6th St Washington DC 20003*

GERMROTH, PETER, biologist, educator; b. Frankfurt, Hessen, Germany, Dec. 15, 1958; came to US, 1998; m. Jennifer R. Langford, Aug. 7, 1998. Dr. phil. nat., Goethe U., Frankfurt, 1990. Tchg. cert. Hessen, Germany. Researcher Max Planck Inst. Brain Rsch., Frankfurt, 1987-90; tchr. Goethe Sch., Frankfurt, 1993-98; tchr. biology North Shore Country Day Sch., Winnetka, Ill., 1999-2001. Adj. lectr. Pensacola (Fla.) J. Coll., 1999, 2001—02, Okaloosa Walton C.C., Niceville, 1999, Niceville, 2001—02; lectr. Hillsborough C.C., 2002—. Editor, translator: Spectrum Akademischer Verlag, 1988-98, The Forebrain in Non-Mammals, 1990; mem. editl. bd., contbr. Neuropsychology, German edit., 1993; contbr. articles to profl. jours. Bd. dirs., pub. rels. officer Hessischer Philologen Verband, Wiesbaden, Germany, 1992-98. Mem.: Nat. Sci. Tchrs. Assn., Human Anatomical and Phys. Soc., Soc. German Physicians and Scientists. Avocations: reading, writing, scuba diving. Office: Hillsborough Community Coll Dale Mabry Campus 4001 Tampa Bay Blvd Tampa FL 33614 Office Phone: 813-253-7278. E-mail: pgermroth@hccfl.edu.

GERNAND, BRADLEY ELTON, archivist, librarian; b. Hugo, Okla., Aug. 29, 1964; s. Charles D. Jr. and Mary Ellen (Akins) G. BA, U. Okla., 1985, MA, 1987, postgrad., 1987—. Archivist Western History Collections, Norman, Okla., 1982-89, Nat. Archives of U.S., Washington, 1989—91, Libr. of Congress, Washington, 1991—2001; libr. mgr. Inst. for Def. Analyses, Alexandria, Va., 2001—. Lachenmeyer Media fellow U. Okla., 1985-87. Independent. Baptist. Avocations: photography, reading, history. Office: Inst for Def Analyses 4850 Mark Center Dr Alexandria VA 22311-1882

GERNER, LEONARD ARTHUR, elementary school educator, minister; b. Crete, Neb., July 12, 1918; s. James Thomas and Albie Olga Gerner; m. Betty Jim Blake, June 24, 1946 (div. 1953); m. Marie Kathryn Henry, 1964. BA, Doane Coll., 1946; MEd, East Tex. State Coll., 1953. Cert. tchr. Tex., adminstrn. Tex. Tchr., coach, prin. Ector ISD, Tex., 1949—59; tchr., coach Bonham ISD, Tex., 1959—85, substitute tchr., 1985—2000; lay spkr. First United Meth. Ch., Bonham, 1974—2004, min. visitation, 2001—04. Trustee COMPASS Ministries, Bonham, Tex., 1997—2004; mem. Bonham ISD improvement coun., 2002—04. Mem. Lion Club Bonham, 1983—85; mem., trustee Jubilee Singers, Bonham, Tex., 1997—2004; mem. city zoning bd., 2002—04; mem. exec. com. Fannin County Ret. Sr. Vol. Program, 1999—2004; mem. Fannin Networking Group. Primary flight instr. USAF, 1943—44. Named to Fannin County Sports Hall of Fame, Bonham, Tex., 1993—2004. Mem.: Fannin County Tchrs. Assn., Tex. State Tchrs. Assn. (life). Republican. Methodist. Avocations: fishing, gardening, reading, music. Home: 520 E 13th Bonham TX 75418

GERNON, ROBERT L., state supreme court justice; b. Sabetha, Kans., July 29, 1943; children: Rebecca Gernon Wilson, Kristin Gernon Olson. BSBA, U. Kans.; JD, Washburn U., 1969; LLM in Jud. Process, U. Va., 2001. Asst. atty. Shawnee County, presentence investigator; probation officer; pvt. practice, 1970—79; atty., county counselor Brown County, 1971—75; judge 22d Dist., 1979—88, adminstrv. judge, 1981—88; mem. Ct. Appeals, 1988—2002; justice Kans. Supreme Ct., Topeka, 2003—. Trial advocacy instr. U. Kans. Sch. Law; chmn., program coord. ann. program Ann. Survey of Law Com.; faculty advisor Nat. Jud. Coll.; spkr. in field; mem. task force on permanency planning U.S. Supreme Ct. Fellow: Kans. Bar Found., Am. Bar Found.; mem.: Kans. Dist. Judges' Assn. (mem. legis. com.), Kans. Bar Assn.

(continuing legal edn. com. 1986—, mem., past chair pub. info. com., mem. com. on professionalism, Outstanding Svc. award 1991, Professionalism award 2001). Office: Kans Jud Ctr 301 W 10th Topeka KS 66612*

GERO, ANTHONY GEORGE, securities and commodities trader; b. London, May 31, 1936; came to U.S., 1947; s. Stephen Gero and Ilona (Braun) Von Rieger; m. Joan Selinger, Nov. 20, 1969 (div. 1980); m. Gale Gendason, Feb. 14, 1989; 1 child, Danielle Joy. BS, NYU, 1959; cert., Investment Bankers Inst. U. Pa., 1965. Reporter USIS Chilean Eartquake Relief/Am. Embassy, 1959-60; ptnr. Goodbody & Co., 1960-64, Charles Plohn & Co., N.Y.C., 1964-67; v.p., dir. Internat. First Hanover Corp., N.Y.C., 1967-69; v.p. Drexel Burnham & Co., N.Y.C., 1971-80; 1st v.p. Prudential Securities, N.Y.C., 1981—2003; sr. v.p. Legg Mason Wood Walker Inc., NYC, 2003—. Mem. U.S. Dept. Commerce, Nat. Def. Exec. Res., 1989—; bd. dirs. Commodity Clearing Corp.; arbitrator Nat. Assn. Securities Dealers, N.Y. Stock Exch., 1992—. Author: Precious Metals, 1985. Dir., treas. children's fund Commodities Exch. Ctr., N.Y.C., 1980—; chmn. NYMEX Charitable Trust, N.Y.C., 1990-95; dir. Futures Options for Kids, 1995—. Recipient Cert., Holocaust Meml., 1991. Mem. Internat. Precious Metals Inst. (dir. 2000—), N.Y. Produce Exch., N.Y. Merc. Exch. (bd. dirs., treas. N.Y.C. chpt. 1974—), Commodity Exch. (bd. dirs. 1995), N.Y. Coffee, Sugar and Cocoa Exch., N.Y. Cotton Exch. (bd. dirs. 1995), Commodity Floor Brokers and Traders Assn. (chmn. 1990—), Investment Brokers Assn., Ret. Westchester County Police Revolver League, Westchester County Sheriff's Assn., N.Y. Police Res. Assn., Securities Industry Assn. (swaps and derivatives commn.), Police Res. Assn. N.Y.C., N.Y. State Troopers Alumni Assn., Am. Radio Relay League. Republican. Avocations: photography, amateur radio, chess. Home: 180 East End Ave New York NY 10128-7763 Office: Legg Mason Inc 58th Fl One Chase Manhattan Plz New York NY 10005 Office Phone: 212-428-4846. Business E-Mail: aggero@leggmason.com.

GERONA, CARLA, historian, educator; b. Madrid; d. Juan and Isolina Gerona; m. Robert Desrochers; children: Ellison, Alejandro. BA in History cum laude, Columbia U., 1991; MA in History, U. Calif., Irvine, 1992, Johns Hopkins U., 1994, PhD in History, 1998. Asst. prof. Otterbein Coll., Westerville, Ohio, 1997—99, Ea. Ill. U., Charleston, 1999—2000, U. Tex., Dallas, 2001—. Presenter in field. Author: Night Journeys: The Power of Dreams in a Transatlantic Quaker Culture, 2004. Early Am. History fellow, U. Calif., Irvine, 1991—92, Mellon Rsch. fellow, The Va. Hist. Soc., 1996, Wood Inst. Rsch. fellow, Coll. Physicians of Phila., 1996, Gest Rsch. fellow, The Quaker Collection at Haverford Coll., 1996, Albert J. Beveridge grantee, Am. Hist. Assn., 1996, Mellon Postdoctoral Rsch. fellow, Newberry Libr., Chgo., 2001. Address: 6649 Catalpa Trl Plano TX 75023

GERONEMUS, ROY G., dermatologist; b. Hollywood, Fla., Mar. 5, 1953; BA in Biology, Harvard U., 1975; MD, U. Miami Sch. Medicine, 1979. Diplomate Am. Bd. Dermatology 1983. Intern internal medicine Beth Israel Med. Ctr., NY, 1979—80; resident dermatology NYU Med. Ctr. Skin-Cancer Unit, 1980—83, Bellevue Hosp., NY, 1980—83, Manhattan VA Hosp., NY, 1980—83; chief resident and tchg. asst. dept. dermatology NYU Med. Ctr.-Skin and Cancer Unit, NY, 1982—83, Mohs Surgery fellow, Mohs Surgery Unit, dept. dermatology, 1983—84; assoc. prof. dermatology, chief of surgery and laser sects. of skin and cancer unit, dept. dermatology NYU Med. Ctr., NY, clin. prof. dermatology, dept. dermatology; dir., skin laser divsn., assoc. attending surgeon, dept. plastic surgery N.Y. Eye and Ear Infirmary; dir. Laser and Skin Surgery Ctr. N.Y. Contbr. to publications and chapters in books. Named Top Dermatologist in America, Woodward and White's Listing. Fellow: N.Y. Acad. Medicine, Am. Soc. for Laser Medicine and Surgery (v.p. 2003—04, pres. 2005—06, Ellet Drake Lectureship award 2001, presdl. citation 2002), Am. Acad. Cosmetic Surgery, Am. Acad. Dermatology (presdl. citation 2000, Golden Triangle award 2003); mem.: AMA, Dermatology Found., Assn. of Surgical Faculty, N.Y. County Med. Soc., Soc. for Investigative Dermatology, Internat. Soc. for Dermatologic Surgery, Am. Soc. for Dermatologic Surgery (pres. elect 2001—02, pres. 2002—03). Office: Laser and Skin Surgery Ctr NY 317 E 34th St New York NY 10016 Office Phone: 212-686-7306. Office Fax: 212-686-7305. Business E-Mail: mail@laserskinsurgery.com.

GEROSA, PETER R., automotive executive; BA, U. Conn.; post grad., U. Ill., 1983, Harvard U., 1990. With GM Oldsmobile Div., 1964, asst. gen. sales. mgr., 1984; gen. sales svc. mgr. GM Cadillac Div., 1986; regional gen. mgr. GM N.E. Region Vehicle Sales Svc, Mktg., 1999, GM North Ctrl. Region, 2000; v.p. GM North Am., 2003—. Office: GM Corp 300 Renaissance Ctr PO Box 300 Detroit MI 48265-3000*

GEROU, PHILLIP HOWARD, architect; b. Natick, Mass., July 20, 1951; s. James Francis and Enid (Meymaris) G.; m. Cheri Rodgers, Nov. 24, 1979; children: Gregory Bedford, Sara Christine. BArch, U. Nebr., 1974, MArch, 1975. Designer, owner Gerou & Assocs. Ltd., Evergreen, Colo., 1986—. Design cons. Kilimanjaro Children's Hosp., Tanzania, 1988-91, World Alpine Ski Championships, Vail, Colo., 1988. Pres. Colo. Soc. of Architects Ednl. Fund., Denver, 1986; del. State Rep. Assembly, Denver, 1986; trustee Rockland Community Ch., Denver, 1986-89. Recipient Citation award Nat. Assn. of Remodeling Industry, 1991, 96, Design Excellence Wood, Inc., 1990, Citation award, 1990. Fellow AIA (pres. Colo. chpt. 1986, bd. dirs. 1981-87, nat. dir. 1991-94, nat. v.p. 1995, dir. Nat. Ethics Coun. 1997—2002, chmn., 2001—02, conf. chair Western Mountain region design conf. 1990, Spl. Recognition award 1990), Nat. Coun. Archtl. Adminstrn. Bds. (examiner 1985). Republican. Mem. United Ch. of Christ. Avocations: skiing, travel, architectural design. Office Phone: 303-674-4177. E-mail: phil@gerou.net.

GERRARD, JOHN M., state supreme court justice; b. Schuyler, Nebr., Nov. 2, 1953; BS, Nebr. Wesleyan U., 1976; MPA, U. Ariz., 1977; JD, U. of Pacific, 1981. Pvt. practice, Norfolk, 1981-95; city atty. City of Battle Creek, Nebr., 1982-95; justice Nebr. Supreme Ct., Lincoln, 1995—. Co-chair Minority and Justice Task Force; chair Nebr. Supreme Ct. Gender Fairness Implementation Com., Gender Fairness Implementation Com. Fellow: Nebr. Bar Found.; mem.: Nebr. State Bar Assn. (Nebr. State Bar Assn. Standing Com. on Professionalism). Office: Nebr Supreme Ct 2219 State Capitol Lincoln NE 68509-8000

GERRARD, KEITH, lawyer; b. Malden, Mass., Feb. 8, 1935; s. William Francis and Mary Ethel (Compton) Gerrard; stepchildren: Elizabeth Perera, Jonathan Perera; children: Jessica, Beth. AB, Harvard U., 1956; LLB, Harvard U. Law Sch., 1963. Bar: Wash. 1963. Assoc. Perkins Coie, Seattle, 1963—70, ptnr., 1970—. Served to lt. USAF, 1956—59. Fellow: Am. Coll. Trial Lawyers; mem.: ABA, Seattle-King County Bar Assn., Wash. State Bar Assn., Rainier Club (Seattle). Office: Perkins Coie 1201 3rd Ave Fl 40 Seattle WA 98101-3029 Office Phone: 206-359-8462. Business E-Mail: kgerrard@perkinscoie.com.

GERRAS, STEPHEN JOSEPH, military officer, psychologist; b. Reading, Pa., June 23, 1960; s. Charles Stephen and Anne Christina Gerras; m. Ann Catherine Kelliher, Oct. 12, 1991; children: Joshua Stephen, Zachary Charles. PhD., Pa. State U., State Coll., Pa., 1992; BS, West Point Acad., West Point, NY, 1982; M Strategic Studies, U.S. Army War Coll., Carlisle Barracks, PA, 2002; MS, Pa. State U., State Coll., Pa., 1991. Bn. comdr. 24th Transp. Bn., Fort Eustis, Va., 1998—2001; liaison officer to Turkish mil. Office of Def. Cooperation, Ankara, Turkey, 2002—04; prof. US Army War Coll., 2004—. Mem., army chief of staff strategic leadership task force U. S. Army War Coll., Carlisle Barracks, Pa., 2001—02. Author article to profl. jours. Lt. col. U.S. Army, 1982—2003. Recipient Douglas MacArthur Leadership Award, U.S. Army Command and Gen. Staff Coll., 1996. Mem.: Soc. of Indsl. and Orgnl. Psychologists. Avocations: travel, weightlifting, reading. Office Phone: 717-245-3571. Personal E-mail: stevegerras@hotmail.com. Business E-Mail: stephen.gerras@us.army.mil.

GERRISH, BRIAN ALBERT, theologian, educator, minister; b. London, Aug. 14, 1931; s. Albert and Doris (King) G.; children from previous marriage: Carolyn, Paul; m. Dawn Ann De Vries, Aug. 3, 1990; 1 child, Heather. BA, Queens' Coll., Cambridge, Eng., 1952, MA, 1956; cert., Westminster Coll., Cambridge, 1955; S.T.M., Union Theol. Sem., N.Y.C., 1956; PhD, Columbia U., 1958; D.D. (hon.), U. St. Andrews, Scotland, 1984. Ordained to ministry Presbyn. Ch., 1957. Asst. pastor West End Presbyn. Ch., N.Y.C., 1956-58; tutor philosophy of religion Union Theol. Sem., N.Y.C., 1957-58; instr. ch. history McCormick Theol. Sem., Chgo., 1958-59, asst. prof., 1959-63, assoc. prof., 1963-65; assoc. prof. hist. theology U. Chgo., 1965-68, prof., 1968-85, John Nuveen prof., 1985-96, John Nuveen prof. emeritus, 1996—. Disting. Svc. prof. theology Union Theol. Sem., Va., 1996—2002; Cunningham lectr. U. Edinburgh, Scotland, 1990. Author: Grace and Reason: A Study in the Theology of Luther, 1962, Japanese transl. 1974, 2d edit., 1979, Tradition and the Modern World: Reformed Theology in the Nineteenth Century, 1978, The Old Protestantism and the New: Essays on the Reformation Heritage, 1982, A Prince of the Church: Schleiermacher and the Beginnings of Modern Theology, 1984, 2001, Korean transl., 1988, Grace and Gratitude: The Eucharistic Theology of John Calvin, 1993, 2002, Continuing the Reformation: Essays on Modern Religious Thought, 1993, Saving and Secular Faith: An Invitation to Systematic Theology, 1999, The Pilgrim Road: Sermons on Christian Life, 2000; editor: The Faith of Christendom: A Source Book of Creeds and Confessions, 1963, Reformers in Profile, 1967, 2d edit., 2004, Reformatio Perennis: Essays on Calvin and the Reformation in Honor of Ford Lewis Battles, 1981, Reformed Theology for the Third Christian Millennium: The 2001 Sprunt Lectures, 2003; co-editor: Jour. Religion, 1972-85; contbr. articles to profl. jours. Am. Assn. Theol. Schs. faculty fellow, 1961; Guggenheim fellow, 1970; Nat. Endowment Humanities fellow, 1980 Fellow Am. Acad. of Arts and Scis.; mem. Am. Soc. Church History (pres. 1979), Am. Theol. Soc. (Midwest divsn. pres. 1973-74). Home: 9142 Sycamore Hill Pl Mechanicsville VA 23116-5806

GERRITSEN, HENDRIK JURJEN, physics professor, researcher; b. The Hague, The Netherlands, Jan. 19, 1927; came to U.S., 1957; s. Hendrik Pieter and Augusta (Koopmans) G.; m. Lida Buitelaar, June 13, 1955 (div. 1968); children: Robert (dec.), Steven, Albert (dec.), Leon; m. Heide Robertson Hoppe, Dec. 28, 1978, (div. 2002); m. Maria Emilio, Jan. 17, 2003. AB in Physics and Chemistry, U. Leiden, 1948; PhD in Physics, 1955. Scientist RCA Labs., Zurich, Switzerland, 1955-57, Princeton, N.J., 1957-67; lectr. electrophysics Chalmers U., Sweden, 1961-62; prof. physics Brown U., Providence, 1967-97, prof. emeritus, prof. rsch., 1997—; prof. physics U. Utrecht, Netherlands, 1974, U. Karlsruhe, W. Germany, 1981-82; cons. Polaroid Corp., Cambridge, Mass., 1968-70; prin. investigator U.S. Bur. Mines, Brewster, Pa., 1970-76, Honeywell, Mpls., 1980-87, NSF, Dept. Energy and AERG., 1968-98; cons. Krieger Corp., Providence, 1986-89. Dir. Ladd Observatory, Providence, 1985-89. Contbr. sci. articles to profl. jours., 1968—; patentee in field. Vis. IREX scholar, Baltic Republics. Fulbright grantee Rostock, Germany, 1995, 96. Mem. Fedn. Am. Scientists, Union of Concerned Scientists, Profl. Photographers Soc. Am. (hon.), Am. Optical Soc., Celestial Observers (hon.), Sigma Xi. Office: Brown U Physics Dept Hope/George St Providence RI 02912 Office Phone: 401-863-1488. Business E-Mail: gerritsen@physics.brown.edu.

GERRITSEN, MARY ELLEN, vascular and cell biologist; b. Calgary, Alta., Can., Sept. 20, 1953; came to U.S., 1978; d. Thomas Clayton and Alice Irene (Minton) Cooper; m. Paul William Gerritsen, May 24, 1975 (div. 1977); m. Thomas Patrick Parks, Oct. 11, 1980; children: Kristen, Madelene. BSc summa cum laude, U. Calgary, 1975, PhD, 1978. Postdoctoral fellow U. Calif., San Diego, 1978-80; asst. prof. N.Y. Med. Coll., Valhalla, 1981-86, assoc. prof., 1986-90; sr. staff scientist Pharm. divsn. Bayer Corp., West Haven, Conn., 1990-93, head inflammation exploratory rsch., 1990-96, prin. staff scientist, 1993-97; vis. scientist Harvard U., 1996; assoc. dir. cardiovasc. rsch. Genentech, South San Francisco, 1997—2001; sr. dir. Millennium Pharms., South San Francisco, 2003—04, Molecular Pharm., Exelixis Inc., South San Francisco, 2004—. Cons. Insite Vision, Alameda, Calif., 1987-89, Boehringer Ingelheim Pharms., Ridgefield, Conn., 1985-88, Xoma, Berkeley, Calif, 2003-04, Frazier Health Care Ventures, Palo Alto, Calif, 2003—, Macusite, Union City, Calif., 2004—; adj. assoc. prof. N.Y. Med. Coll., 1990-99. Co-author: Masdevallias: Gems of the Orchid World, 2005; mem. editl. bd. Microvascular Rsch., 1988—96, Am. Jour. Physiology, 1983—, Am. Jour. Cardiovasc. Pathology, 1996—, Circulation Rsch., 1997—99, Endothelium, 1999—, editor-in-chief Microcirculation, 1993—98, cons. editor, 1998—, editor N.Am. Vascular Biology Orgn. Newsletter, —; contbr. articles to profl. jours. I. W. Killam Found. fellow, 1976, Med. Rsch. Coun. Can. fellow, 1978. Mem. Am. Soc. for Pharmacology and Exptl. Therapeutics, Am. Physiol. Soc., Assn. Rsch. on Vision and Ophthalmology, Am. Soc. Investigational Pathology, Soc. Leukocyte Biology, Am. Soc. Cell Biology, Microcirculatory Soc. (mem. coun. 1989-92, chairperson publs. com. 1991-93, Mary Weideman award 1985, Young Investigator award 1984), N.Am. Vascular Biology Orgn. (mem. steering com. 1993, mem. coun. 1994-97, editor-in-chief newsletter 1994-97, sec.-treas. 1997-99, pres. 1999, chair devel. com., 2004-05). Avocations: orchids, horticulture. E-mail: meg570@comcast.net.

GERRY, DALE FRANCIS, military officer, legislative staff member; b. Bangor, Maine, Apr. 18, 1950; s. Richard Woodman and Corrine (Paddock) G.; m. Dale Marie Ahearn, Dec. 22, 1976. BA, U. Maine, 1972. Dist. rep. Congressman William S. Cohen, Bangor, 1972-76, spl. asst., 1976-77, senate campaign coord. Portland, Maine, 1977-78; legis. asst. mil./communications/transp./maritime affairs Senator William S. Cohen, Washington, 1979-94; legis. dir. Senator William S. Cohen, 1995—96; sr. def. advisor Sens. William S. Cohen and Olympia J. Snowe, Washington, 1994-97; hon. dep. asst. sec. Mine and Undersea Warfare, USN, Washington, 1997-2001; lobbyis Strategic Mktg. Innovations, Inc., Washington, 2001—. Cons. polit. candidates. Bd. dirs. Maine State Ballet, Bangor, 1976-79. Recipient Disting. Pub. Svc. award, Dept. of Navy. Republican. Roman Catholic. Avocations: scuba diving, politics, music, theater, gardening. Home: 4708 Tecumseh St College Park MD 20740-2156 Office: SMI Inc 1020 19th St NW Washington DC 20036 Office Phone: 202-467-5459. Office Fax: 202-467-5469. Business E-Mail: Dale@StrategicMI.com.

GERRY, DEBRA PRUE, psychotherapist, recording artist, writer; b. Oct. 9, 1951; d. C.O. and Sarah E. Rawl; m. Norman Bernard Gerry, Apr. 10, 1981 (div. 1998); 1 child, Gisele Psyche Victoria. BS, Ga. So. U., 1972; MEd, Armstrong State U., 1974; PhD, U. Ga., 1989. Cert. Ariz. Bd. Behavioral Health Examiners. Spl. edn. tchr. Chatham County Bd. Edn., Savannah, Ga., 1972-74; edn. and learning disabilities resource educator Duval County Bd. Edn., Jacksonville, Fla., 1974-77; ednl. resource counselor spl. programs adminstr. Broward County Bd. Edn., Ft. Lauderdale, Fla., 1977-81; pvt. practice Scottsdale, Ariz., 1990—. Contbr. author coll. textbooks; contbr. articles to profl. jours.; prodr. musical album Welcome to this World. Vol., fundraiser, psychol. cons., group leader Valley AIDS Orgns., Phoenix, 1990-96; fundraiser Hosp. Health Edn. Programs, Scottsdale, 1992-93; mem. com. for women's issues Plz. Club, Phoenix, 1992-93; pres. Laissez Les Bon Temps Rouler, Wrigley Club, Phoenix, 1993-96; mem. bd. Sojourner' Ctr., 1996, exec. bd., 1997-98, v.p., 1999; exec. bd. Breast Found., Inc., Phoenix, 1997-98; appointee Ariz. Supreme Ct., Foster Care Rev. Bd., Phoenix, 1996-2001. Recipient Rudy award Shanti Orgn., 1991. Mem. APA, NOW, ACA, Internat. Soc. Poets (disting., Poet of Merit award 1996), Nat. Assn. Women Bus. Owners, Assn. for Multicultural Coun., Assn. for Specialists in Group Work, Mensa, Phi Delta Kappa, Kappa Delta Epsilon, Sigma Omega Phi, Kappa Delta Pi. Avocations: ballroom dancing, playing musical instruments, singing, travel, air sports. E-mail: dgerryphd@aol.com.

GERSH, DARREN, television correspondent; BA in English cum laude, Yale U., 1984. Prodr. documentary Roosevelt Ctr., Washington; news prodr. Sta. WJXT-TV, Jacksonville, Fla., 1987-88; assoc. prodr. Money Politics, Sta. WJLA-TV, Washington; Wash. bur. chief Nightly Bus. Report, Washington. Office: NBR 1325 G St NW Ste 1005 Washington DC 20005-3126

GERSHEL, ALAN M., prosecutor; b. Nov. 19, 1951; s. Marvin and Francine G.; m. Linda, Aug. 3, 1975; children: Jessica Sara, Bradley Ross. BS, Northeastern U., 1974; MS, Ind. State U., 1975; JD, U. Detroit, 1978. Bar: Mich. 1978, U.S. Ct. Appeals (6th cir.) Mich. 1980. Asst. atty., criminal chief ea. dist. U.S. Dept Justice, Detroit, 1993—, interim U.S. atty., 2000—01; currently adjunct prof. U. of Detroit Mercy Sch. of Law, Mich. Office: Assist US Atty 211 W Fort St 2001 Detroit MI 48226-3211

GERSHENGORN, MARVIN C, research scientist, director; MD, NYU. Prof. Weill Med. Coll. of Cornell U., NYC, 1983—2001; sci. dir. Niddk, Nih, Bethesda, Md., 2001—. Office: Niddk Nih 9000 Rockville Pike Bethesda MD 20892 Office Phone: 301-496-4128.

GERSHENGORN, MARVIN CARL, internist, researcher, educator; b. N.Y.C. MD, NYU, 1971. Diplomate Am. Bd. Internal Medicine. Intern Strong Meml. Hosp., Rochester, N.Y., 1971-72, asst. resident in medicine, 1972-73; asst. prof. medicine NYU Sch. Med., 1976-80, assoc. prof., 1980-83; prof. medicine Cornell U. Med Coll., N.Y.C., 1983-2001; Abby Rockefeller Mauze disting. prof. Weill Med. Coll. Cornell U.; sci. dir. divsn. Intramural Rsch. Nat. Inst. Diabetes & Digestive & Kidney Diseases, NIH, 2001—. Office: NIH Nat Inst Diabetes & Digestive & Kidney Diseases Bldg 10 Rm 9N222 Bethesda MD 20892-1818 Office Phone: 301-496-4128. Business E-Mail: marving@intra.niddk.nih.gov.

GERSHMAN, CARL SAMUEL, foundation administrator; b. N.Y.C., July 20, 1943; s. Joseph Saul and Josephine (Cohen) G.; m. Laurie Pfeffer, Jan. 25, 1970; children: Sarah, Joseph, Jacob. BA, Yale U., 1965; MEd, Harvard U., 1968. Researcher Anti-Defamation League of B'nai B'rith, N.Y.C., 1968; dir. rsch. A. Philip Randolph Inst., N.Y.C., 1969-71; exec. dir. Youth Inst. for Peace in the Mid. East, N.Y.C., 1971-74, Social Dems., U.S.A., N.Y.C., 1974-80; sr. rsch. fellow Freeedom House, N.Y.C., 1980-81; sr. counselor U.S. Mission to the U.N., N.Y.C., 1981-84; pres. Nat. Endowment for Democracy, Washington, 1984—. Author: Foreign Policy of American Labor, 1975; editor: Israel, the Arabs and the Middle East, 1972; mem. editorial bd. Washington Quarterly, 1988—, Society Mag., 1989—; contbr. articles to popular mags. and jours. Avocations: reading, jogging, travel. Office: Nat Endowment for Democracy 1101 15th St NW Ste 700 Washington DC 20005-5013

GERSHON, NINA, federal judge; b. Chgo., Oct. 16, 1940; d. David and Marie Gershon; m. Bernard J. Fried, May 15, 1983. BA, Cornell U., 1962; LLB, Yale U., 1965; postgrad., London Sch. Econs., 1965-66. Staff atty. NY Supreme Ct. (Appellate div.), 1966—68; asst. corp. counsel, Appeals div. State of NY, 1968—69; lectr. law and political sci. U. of Calif. San Diego, 1969—70; chief fed. appeals State of NY, 1972—75, chief consumer protection div., 1975—76; magistrate judge U.S. Dist. Ct. (so. dist.) N.Y., NYC, 1976—96; U.S. dist. judge Eastern Dist. N.Y., Bklyn., 1996—. Adj. prof. law Cardozo Sch. Law, 1986—88. Fulbright scholar. Office: US Courthouse 225 Cadman Plz E Brooklyn NY 11201-1818*

GERSHON, RICHARD A., commmunications educator; b. Apr. 20, 1952; s. Phillip and Sylvia Gershon; m. Casey, Aug. 25, 1978; 1 child, Matthew. BA in English, Goddard Coll., Plainfield, Vt., 1974; MEd in Edn., U. Vt., 1980; PhD in Mass Communication, Ohio U., 1986. Instr. English and Mass Communication Rice Meml. High Sch., Burlington, Vt., 1976-81; sr. bus. editor Telecom. Mag., Dedham, Mass., 1984-86; asst. prof. telecommunications SUNY, New Paltz, 1986-89; prof. telecommunications Western Mich. U., Kalamazoo, 1989—. Chair Policy and Planning Task Force for Greater Kalamazoon Telecity Project. Author: Transnational Media Corporation: Global Markets and Free Market Competition, 1997, Telecommunications Management: Industry Structures and Planning Strategies, 2001 (Nat. Cable TVs Mus.'s Book of Yr. award); contbr. articles to profl. jours. Mem. Broadcast Edn. Assn. (chair elect for internat. div.). Office: Western Mich U Dept Comm Kalamazoo MI 49008 E-mail: Richard.Gershon@wmich.edu.

GERSIE, MICHAEL H., insurance company executive; Actuarial trainee The Prin. Fin. Group, Des Moines, 1970, officer, 1975, sr. v.p., 1994, CFO, exec. v.p., 1996—. Office: The Prin Fin Group 711 High St Des Moines IA 50392-0001

GERSON, DONALD JEROME, computer scientist, consultant; b. N.Y.C., Apr. 26, 1934; s. Irwin I. Gerson and Helen Sacks; m. Barbara A. Jaques, Aug. 21, 1960 (dec. Oct. 1998); 1 child, Laura Melissa; m. Emma Sue Gaines, June 24, 2000. BA in Meteorology, N.Y.U., 1956; MS in Computer Sci., U. Md., 1975. Oceanographer Naval Oceanographic Office, Suitland, Md., 1956-78, Defense Mapping Agy., Bethesda, Md., 1978-83; imagery scientist CIA, Langley, Va., 1983-97; prin., owner Gerson Imaging Solutions, LLC, Silver Spring, Md., 1997—. Instr. George Washington U., Washington, 1983-88; U.S. rep. working group on sea ice World Meteorological Org., Geneva, 1975-77. Co-author: Processes in Marine Remote Sensing, 1982, Radius, Image Understanding for Imagery Intelligence, 1997; contbr. articles to profl. jours. Trustee Paint Br. Unitarian U. Ch. Recipient Goldsborough award for best tech. paper of yr., 1983, Intelligence Commendation medal CIA, 1997. Fellow: Royal Geog. Soc. (Eng.), Explorers Club (Wash. chpt. chmn. 1986—88); mem.: IEEE, Am. Soc. Media Photographers, Applied Imagery Pattern Recognition Com. (chmn. 1975—), Cosmos Club, Sigma Xi. Avocations: photography, racewalking, hiking, book collecting. Office Phone: 301-586-1990. E-mail: donald@GersonImagingSolutions.com.

GERSON, ELLIOT FRANCIS, foundation administrator; b. New Haven, July 15, 1952; s. Louis Lieb and Elizabeth (Shanley) G; children: Emily, Hilary, Alexander, Marissa, Jillian; m. Amy Shapiro, May 23, 1993. AB summa cum laude, Harvard Coll., 1974; BA with first class honors, Oxford U. (Eng.), 1976, MA, 1981; JD, Yale U., 1979. Bar: Conn. 1981, D.C. 1982, U.S. Dist. Ct. Conn. 1982, U.S. Ct. Appeals (D.C. cir.) 1982, U.S. Supreme Ct. 1985. Law clk. to judge U.S. Ct. Appeals, Washington, 1979; staff asst. to sec. Dept. Def. The Pentagon, Washington, 1979-80; law clk. to Justice Stewart U.S. Supreme Ct., Washington, 1980-81; assoc. Verner, Liipfert, Bernhard & McPherson, Washington, Hartford, Conn., 1981-83; dep. atty. gen. State of Conn., Hartford, 1983-86; v.p. Travelers Corp., Hartford, 1986-90, sr. v.p., 1990-93; pres. Travelers Ins. Co., 1993-95; exec. v.p. MetraHealth Cos., Inc., 1995-96, United Healthcare, 1996; pres. ETC, Inc., 1996—97, CEO, 1997-99, Lifescape, LLC, 1999-2000; pres. FHC Health Sys., Inc., 2000—03, ValueOptions, Inc., 2001—03; policy dir., nat. fin. chair Joseph I. Lieberman for Pres., Inc., Vienna, Va., 2003—04; exec. v.p. The Aspen Inst., 2004—. Bd. dirs. Bazelon Ctr. Mental Health Law, Fische Internat. Biomed. Rsch. Alliance. Editor: Conn. Law Tribune, 1986-88. Mem. Sec. State's Adv. Com. Internat. Law, Washington, 1984-86; mem. Gov's. Commn. Design Environ. Policy for Conn., 1969; dir. Eastern Conn. Develop. Coun. Inc., 1981-86, Hartford State Co., 1985-95, pres., 1990-93, Hartford Ballet, 1986-88, Greater Hartford Arts Coun., 1986-90, 94-95; mem. Conn. Humanities Coun., 1987-90; dir. Conn. Civil Liberties Union, 1987-89, Conn. Women's Ednl. and Legal Fund, 1987-91; staff mem. commn. Critical Choices Ams., 1973-74; mem. Council Fgn. Rels. Inc., N.Y.C., 1981-86, 98—, Yale Law Sch. Com. Pub. Interest Law, New Haven, 1983-85; elector Wadsworth Atheneum, Hartford, 1983-93; sec. Conn. Rhodes Scholar Selection Com., 1982-94; asst. Am. sec. Rhodes Scholarship Trust, 1976-79, Am. sec., Eng., 1998—; treas. Am. South African Scholarship Assn., Inc., 1986-94; trustee Conn. Pub. Broadcasting, 1988-92, Conn. Histo. Soc., 1993-95, The Shakespeare Theatre, Washington, 1996—; founding trustee Mandela Rhodes Found. (USA), 2005—; bd. dirs. Internat. Biomed. Rsch. Alliance, 2005—; trustee Hartford Courant Found., 1988-95, pres., 1992-94. Rhodes scholar 1974; recipient Sec. Def. Meritorious Civilian Service medal, 1980. Mem. Conn. Bar Assn. (long range planning com. 1984-87), Spee Club (pres. 1973-74, Cambridge, Mass.), Cosmos Club (Washington), River Bend Golf Club (Great Falls, Va.), Phi Beta Kappa. Democrat. Office: One Dupont Cir NW Washington DC 20036 Office Phone: 202-736-3841. Business E-Mail: elliot.gerson@aspeninstitute.org.

GERSON, IRWIN CONRAD, advertising executive; b. NYC, Mar. 18, 1930; s. Leon and Charlotte (Steinhause) G.; m. Lenore Greenblatt, Nov. 29, 1953; children: Jill Beth, Matthew Ted. BS, Fordham U., 1953; MBA, NYU, 1959; DHL, Albany Coll. Pharmacy, 1992, L.I. U., 2001. Ter. mgr. Wyeth Labs. divsn. Am. Home Products, 1956-58; account exec., supr. William Douglas McAdams, Inc., NYC, 1958-66, v.p., 1966-68, sr. v.p., 1969-70, exec. v.p., 1971-74, pres., 1974-86, chmn. bd., 1987-96, Lowe McAdams Healthcare, NYC, 1996-98, chmn. emeritus, 1999-2000. Instr. sales mgmt. Columbia Coll. Pharm. Sci., 1967-77; bd. dir. ANDRX Corp., Enzo Biochem. Inc.; bd. advisors, v.p. Lifelong Learning Soc., Fla. Atlantic U., 2000—. Editorial adv. bd.: US Jour. Drug and Alcohol Dependence, 1977-83. Trustee, bd. dirs. Chemotherapy Found., 1971-86; bd. dir. Nutritional Rsch. Found., 1977-85, Am. Found. for Pharm. Edn., 1996-2003, Conn. Grand Opera, 1983-93, Stamford Chamber Orch., 1985-93; mem. coun. overseers Arnold and Marie Schwartz Coll. Pharmacy and Health Sci., LI U., 1986-90, chmn., 1990-99; bd. trustees Bus. Publs. Audit of Circulation, 1988-95, vice chmn., 1992-93, chmn., 1993-94; bd. trustees LI U., 1989-99; trustee Albany Coll. Pharmacy, Union U., 1993-97. With AUS, 1954-56. Named to Med. Advt. Hall of Fame, 1999. Mem. Am. Assn. Advt. Agys. (bd. govs. NY coun. 1991-95, ea. region 1995-98), Pharm. Advt. Coun. (bd. dirs. 1974-84, treas. 1976-77, v.p. 1979-81), Alpha Zeta Omega. Home: 189 Spyglass Ln Jupiter FL 33477-4090 Office Phone: 561-307-8077.

GERSON, RALPH JOSEPH, manufacturing executive; b. Detroit, Nov. 30, 1949; s. Byron Hayden and Dorothy Mary (Davidson) G.; m. Erica Ann Ward, May 20, 1979. BA, Yale U., 1971; MSc, London Sch. Econs., 1972; JD, U. Mich., 1975. Bar: Mich. 1975, D.C. 1976, U.S. Dist. Ct. D.C. 1976, U.S. Ct. Appeals (D.C. cir.) 1976. Counsel Dem. Nat. Com., Washington, 1975-77; spl. asst. U.S. Spl. Trade Rep., Washington, 1978-79; counselor to spl. Middle East negotiator Office of Pres., Washington, 1979-80; ptnr. Akin, Gump, Strauss, Hauer and Feld, 1981-83, 85-87; dir. Mich. Dept. Commerce, Lansing, 1983-84; exec. v.p. Guardian Industries Corp., Auburn Hills, Mich., 1988—, also bd. dirs., 1988—; pres., CEO Guardian Internat. Corp., 1993—. Bd. dirs. Pistons-Palace Found., U.S. Spain Coun., Nat. Endowment for Democracy; chmn. Hungarian-U.S. Bus. Coun.; trustee Henry Ford Mus., Detroit Symphony Orch., Citizens Rsch. Coun. Mem. ABA, D.C. Bar Assn., Mich. Bar Assn., Coun. Fgn. Rels., World Pres. Orgn., Royal Automobile Club, Franklin Hills Country Club, Bloomfield Open Hunt Club, Yale Club of NYC. Office: Guardian Industries Corp 2300 Harmon Rd Auburn Hills MI 48326-1714

GERSON, STUART MICHAEL, lawyer; b. NYC, Jan. 16, 1944; s. James and Ethel (Cherney) G.; m. Pamela Somers, July 28, 1979; children: James Barker, Somers Elizabeth, Lindsey Dakota. BA in Polit. Sci., Pa. State U., 1964; JD, Georgetown U., 1967. Bar: D.C. 1968, N.Y. 1999, U.S. Ct. Appeals (DC cir.) 1972, U.S. Ct. Appeals (5th cir.) 1972, 81, U.S. Supreme Ct. 1974, U.S. Ct. Appeals (9th cir.) 1978, U.S. Ct. Appeals (2d cir.) 1979, U.S. Ct. Appeals (11th cir.) 1981, U.S. Ct. Appeals (6th cir.) 1982, U.S. Ct. Appeals (4th cir.) 1984, U.S. Ct. Appeals (3d cir.) 1985, U.S. Ct. Appeals (8th cir.) 1986, U.S. Ct. Appeals (1st, 7th, 10th, fed. cirs.) 1989. Asst. U.S. atty. City of Washington, 1972-75; assoc., then ptnr. Reed Smith Shaw & McClay, Washington, 1975-80; pvt. practice; ptnr. in charge litig. Epstein, Becker & Green, Washington, N.Y.C., 1980-89; asst. atty. gen. in charge civil divsn. U.S. Dept. Justice, Washington, 1989-93; acting Atty. Gen. U.S., 1993; atty. and head of litig. Epstein, Becker & Green, P.C., Washington and N.Y.C. Bd. dirs. Counsel for Ct. Excellence; mem. bd. legal advisors Heritage Found, Washington Legal Found., Nat. Legal Ctr. for the Pub. Interest; adj. prof. law Georgetown U., 1991. Contbr. articles to profl. jours. Gen. counsel Nat. Rep. Senatorial Com., Washington, 1985-86; sr. advisor presdl. campaign George Bush, 1988; leader transition team Office Pres. Elect, 1988; advisor Transition Office Pres. Elect, 2000; lay Eucharistic min. Capt. USAF, 1967-72. Decorated Meritorious Svc. medal. Fellow Am. Bar Found.; mem. ABA, D.C. Bar Assn. (steering com. litig. 1985-93), The Barristers (pres.), Am. Health Lawyers Assn., Am. Inns of Ct., Met. Club, Lawyers Club. Episcopalian. Avocations: competitive running, national track and field official, sailing, reading history. Office: Epstein Becker & Green PC 1227 25th St NW Ste 700 Washington DC 20037-1175 also: 250 Park Ave New York NY 10177-0001 Office Phone: 202-861-4180. Business E-Mail: sgerson@ebglaw.com.

GERSONY, WELTON MARK, pediatrician, cardiologist, educator; b. Syracuse, NY, Nov. 19, 1931; s. Irving and Ann (Cohen) G.; m. Susan; children: Neal, Anne, Richard, Deborah. AB, Syracuse U., 1954; MD, SUNY, Syracuse, 1958. Diplomate Am. Bd. Pediatrics, Sub Bd. Pediatric Cardiology. Intern Cleve. Met. Gen. Hosp., 1958-59, resident in pediatrics, 1959-61, Babies and Childrens Hosp., Cleve., 1959-61; fellow in cardiology Harvard U., 1963-65; asst. prof. pediatrics U. Tex., Dallas, 1965-68, Columbia U., 1968-71, assoc. prof., 1971-74, prof., 1974—, Alexander S. Nadas prof., 2000—. Dir. div. pediatric cardiology Columbia-Presbyn Med. Ctr., Columbia-Cornell Pediatric Cardiovasc. Ctr., 1999—; pres. faculty practice orgn., Coll. of Physicians and Surgeons, Columbia U., 2003-05; vis. dir. pediatric cardiology Gt. Ormond St. Hosp. Sick C hildren, London, 1984-85; organizer 2d World Congress Pediatric Cardiology, N.Y.C., 1985; chmn. steering com. World Congress Pediatric Cardiology and Cardiac Surgery, 1989-97, plenary lect., 2001, plenary chair, 2005; mem. Sub.-bd. Pediatric Cardiology, 1976-83, chmn., 1981-83, com. ofcl. examiners, 1983-90; cons. AMA, 1985—, Extram. Affairs Divsn. Nat. Heart Lung and Blood Inst., 1988—; vis. prof., named lectureships multiple U.S. and Foreign Med. Ctrs., 1982-2005; mem. adv. bd. Congress of Pediat. Cardiology Internat., 1998—; prin. investigator NIH grants, Natural History of Congenital Heart Defects, 1977, 93, Indonethacin Closure of Patent Ductus Arteviocus, 1983, Pediat. Heart Network, NIY/NHCBI, 2002—, chmn. publ. comm.; lectr. in field. Author: Nelson's Textbook of Pediatrics, 1983, 3d edit., 1991, Congenital Heart Disease in The Adult, 2001; assoc. editor: The American Heart Association Consultant, 2001; mem. editl. bd. Pediatric Cardiology, 1978-90, Jour. of Pediatrics, 1986-93, Jour. Am. Coll. Cardiology, 1990-94, Cardiology in the Young, 1990, Progress in Pediatric Cardiology, 1991—; editl. bd. Circulation, 1993-96, cons. editor, 1996-2001; internat. adv. bd. Japanese Circulation Jour., 1996-2002; contbr, revs, to profl. jours., chpts. to books. Mem. internat. com., bd. dirs. Internat. Cardiology Found., 1993—; mem. program com. Internat. Kawasaki Disease Chmn. Cardiology Symposium, 1989, 1992, 1995, 1998, 2001. Capt. M.C. U.S. Army, 1961—63. Falkner fellow U. Sydney, Australia, 1983; NIH grantee, 1977, 82, 83, 2002; named Practitioner of the Year, NY Presbyn. Hosp., 2005; recipient Disting. Practitioner award Coll. Physicians and Surgeons, 2005. Fellow Am. Coll. Cardiology, Am. Acad. Pediatrics; mem. AMA (accreditation coun. for grad. med. edn. 1994—), Soc. Pediatric Rsch., Am. Pediatric Soc., Am. Heart Assn. (pres. coun. cardiovascular disease in the young 1988-90, T. Duckett Jones lectr. 1998, Disting Achievement award 2003), Am. Fedn. Clin. Rsch., Harvey Soc., Assn. European Paediatric Cardiologists (corr.), Internat. Soc. for Adult Congenital Heart Disease, Am. Contract Bridge League (life master). Achievements include research on cardiovascular disease in infants, children and adults, natural history of congenital heart disease in children; patent ductus arteriosus in premature infants; persistence of the fetal circulation. Office: Columbia U 630 W 168th St New York NY 10032-3795

GERSPACH, THOMAS JOSEPH, lawyer; b. Mineola, NY, Dec. 16, 1960; s. John Charles and Claire Louise Gerspach; m. Eileen Elizabeth O'Reilly, Oct. 28, 1989; children: Ryan, Megan, Anne. BA, U. Notre Dame, 1983; JD, St. John's U. Sch. Law, 1987. Assoc. atty. Martin Clearwater & Bell, NYC, 1987—88; assoc., ptnr. Belair & Evans, NYC, 1988—99; founder, sr. ptnr. Garson, Gerspach, Decorato & Cohen, LLP, NYC, 1999—. Mem.: ATLA, NY Medical Defense Bar Assn., NY State Bar Assn. Avocations: coaching youth baseball, football, basketball and soccer, skiing. Office: Garson Gerspach Decorato & Cohen LLP 110 Wall St New York NY 10005 Office Phone: 212-742-8700. Business E-Mail: gerspach@ggdc.com.

GERST, PAUL HOWARD, physician; b. Sept. 24, 1927; s. David and Hilde (Werbel) G.; m. Elizabeth Carlsen, Aug. 3, 1957; children— Steven R., Jeffrey C., Andrew L. AB, Columbia U., 1948, MD, 1952. Diplomate: Am. Bd. Surgery, Am. Bd. Thoracic Surgery. Intern Columbia Presbyn. Med. Center, N.Y.C., 1952-53, resident, 1956-62, mem. staff, 1962—; instr. physiology U. Pa., 1955-56; practice medicine specializing in surgery N.Y.C., 1962—; asst. clin. prof. surgery Columbia U., 1964-72; prof. surgery Albert Einstein Coll. Medicine, 1972—2003. Dir. surgery Bronx-Lebanon Hosp. Ctr., NYC, 1964—2003 Contbr. articles to profl. jours. Served to 1st lt. U.S. Army, 1953-55. USPHS postdoctoral fellow, 1955-56; recipient Rsch. Career Devel. award, 1964-65. Fellow ACS; mem. Am. Physiol. Soc., N.Y. Soc. for Thoracic Surgery, N.Y. Surg. Soc., N.Y. Soc. for Cardiovasc. Surgery, Am. Heart Assn. Home: 141 Tekening Dr Tenafly NJ 07670-1218 Office: Bronx Lebanon Hosp Ctr 1650 Grand Concourse Bronx NY 10457-7606 Office Phone: 201-569-0018. Fax: 201-569-5198. Personal E-mail: pgerstfacs@aol.com.

GERSTAD, ROBIN LEE, conservator; b. N.Y.C., July 20, 1965; d. John Leif and Annabel Lee Gerstad; m. John Travis Wendel (div.); life ptnr. Neil Dempster Ostrander. BA in Latin Am. Studies, NYU, NYC, 1987; MSc in Hist. Preservation, Columbia U., NYC, 1998. Conservator, project mgr. Conservation & Sculpture Co., Bklyn., 1999—2000, Ehrenkrantz, Eckstut & Kuhn Archs., NYC, 2000—01, NYC Pks./Citywide Monuments Program, NYC, 2001—03, Conservation Solutions, Inc., Washington, 2003—. Recipient Lucy G. Moses award, NY Landmarks Conservancy, 2004, 14th Ann. Village award, Greenwich Village Soc. for HP, 2004, Best of 2004, NY Constrn., 2004. Mem.: Washington Conservation Guild, Assn. Preservation Tech., Am. Inst. Conservation (assoc.). Democrat. Achievements include Conservation of Washington Square Arch in New York City. Office Phone: 202-544-3257.

GERSTEIN, DAVID BROWN, manufacturing executive, professional sports team executive; b. N.Y.C., Jan. 30, 1936; s. Frank and May G.; m. Jane Ellen Bender, May 4, 1963; children: Mark, James. BS, Seton Hall U., 1959. With Thermwell Products Co., Paterson, N.J., 1958—, sales mgr., 1965-68, v.p., 1968-74, pres., 1974—. Prin. owner N. J. Nets NBA franchise, 1978—98; v.p. Lever Mfg. Co., Paterson; pres. Woodlowe Realty, Paterson, Wait Assocs., Paterson, Dim Assocs., Mahwah, N.J. Chmn. adv. council energy and conservation State of N.J.; co-chmn. athletic program Seton Hall U. Office: Thermwell Products Co Inc 420 Rte 17 S Mahwah NJ 07430 Mailing: 860 5th Ave New York NY 10021 Office Phone: 201-684-4440.

GERSTEIN, JOHN RICHARD, lawyer; b. Washington, May 5, 1951; s. Albert S. and Jean (Armes) G.; m. Georgia Strange, July 31, 1976; children: Georgia Steedly, John Richard Jr. AB in Psychology with high distinction and honors, U. Mich., 1972, JD magna cum laude, 1975. Bar: D.C. 1975. Assoc. Hogan & Hartson, Washington, 1975-82; ptnr. Casey, Scott & Canfield, Washington, 1982-84, Ross, Dixon & Masback, Washington, 1984—. Gen. counsel Internat. Systems Fin. Corp., 1983-86, Alt. Gas, Inc., Data Cons., Inc., 1983-87. Recipient Am. Jurisprudence award Adminstrv. Law, 1974. Mem. Def. Research Inst., Order of Coif, Phi Beta Kappa.

GERSTEIN, MORDICAI, illustrator, writer; b. LA, Nov. 24, 1935; s. Samuel and Fay Gerstein. Student, Chouinard Art Inst., 1953—56. Artist, animator United Prodrs. Am., LA, 1956—57; prin., owner Summer Star Prodns., N.Y., 1969—79. Author and illustrator: Arnold of the Ducks, 1983, Tales of Pan, 1986, The Seal Mother, 1986, The Mountains of Tibet, 1987, Beauty and the Beast, 1988, The Cataract of Lodore, 1990, The New Creatures, 1991, The Story of May, 1993, Jonah and theTwo Great Fish, 1997, Stop Those Pants!, 1998, The Wild Boy, 1998, Victor, 1998, Noah and the Great Flood, 1999, The Absolutely Awful Alphabet, 1999, Queen Esther, 2000, Fox Eyes, 2001, What Charlie Heard, 2002, Sparrow Jack, 2003, The ManWho Walked Between the Towers, 2003 (Caldecott award, 2004); author and illutrator The Old Country, 2005; illustrator: Dracula is a Pain in the Neck, 1983, FrankensteinMovedin on the Fourth Floor, 1987, Something Queer in the Wild West, 1997, A Hare Raising Tail, 2002, The Mixed-Up Mask Mystery, 2002, The Principal's on the Roof, 2003; author: (films) The Room, 1965, The Magic Ring, 1966 (Golden Eagle award CINE, 1967). Mailing: c/o Roaring Brook Books Millbrook Press 2 Old New Milford Rd Brookfield CT 06804*

GERSTENHBER, MURRAY, law educator, mathematics professor; b. New York, NY, May 6, 1927; s. Joseph Gerstenhaber and Pauline Rosenzweig; m. Ruth P. Zager, MD, June 3, 1956; children: David E. Gerstenhaber, Rachel R. Stern. BS, Yale, New Haven, CT, 1944—48; PhD in math, U. Chgo., 1948—51; JD, U. Pa., Phila., 1969—73. Bar: Pa. (Pa. bar) 1973. Prof. math. U. Pa., Phila., 1953—, prof. law, 1973—. Chmn., com. academic freedom, tenure, and employment security Am. Math. Soc., Providence, 2004—. Contbr. articles. Former trustee Solomon Schechter Day Schs., Phila. Cpl. Inf. U.S. Army, 1945—47, US, Germany. Fellow: Am. Assn. Advancement Sci.; mem.: ABA, Math. Assn. Am., Am. Math. Soc. (former coun. mem., editor). Jewish. Achievements include research in Algebraic Deformation Theory; Statistics For Law. Home: 237 Hamilton Rd Merion Station PA 19066-1102 Office: U Pa Dept Mathematics Philadelphia PA 19104-6395 Office Phone: 215-898-8178. Business E-Mail: mgersten@math.upenn.edu.

GERSTMYER, WILLIAM COLEY, architect, land use planner; b. Roanoke, Va., Oct. 30, 1956; s. Robert George Gerstmyer and Elouise Smith; m. Denise A. Pickering, Apr. 27, 1991; children: Aiden Arthur Robert, Marin Grace. BS in Landscape Architecture, U. Va., 1979, MArch, 1983. Registered architect, AIA, 1987, Nat. Coun. Archtl. Registrations Bd., 2004, Ill., 1987, Mass., 2004; LEED accredited profl. U.S. Green Bldg. Coun., 2004. Lectr. U. Va. Sch. of Architecture, Charlottesville, 1979; design critic U. Va. Summer Program, Vicenza, Italy, 1982—83; urban design fellow Deutsche Akademischer Austauschdienst, Freiburg, Germany, 1983; landscape arch. Jacobs/Ryan Assocs., Chgo., 1983—84; archtl. designer Holabird & Root, Chgo., 1984—85; assoc. prof. U. Tenn. Sch. of Art and Architecture, Knoxville, 1985—87; arch., graphic designer Design Boston, Cambridge, Mass., 1987—88; archtl. lead designer Stopfel/Miller Archs., Boston, 1989—91; planner, graphic designer Boston Olympic Organizing Com., Boston, 1991—94; archtl. designer Elkus/Manfredi Archs., Boston, 1994—96; sr. assoc., arch., project mgr. Sasaki Assocs., Watertown, Mass., 1997—2003; prin., arch., planner Design Partnership of Cambridge, Charlestown, Mass., 2003—. Urban planning fellow Rotary Internat., Quito, Ecuador. Building and site design, Merrimack Coll. Campus/Recreation Ctr. (New Eng. AIA Honor Award, 2001), national design competition, Inner City Housing Design (First Pl., 1985), international design competition, Sears Tower: A Late Entrance (Hon. Mention, 1984), regional design competition, Brockton Fed. Courthouse (First Pl., 1995). Mem. Women's Inst. for Housing and Econ. Devel., Boston, 2004—05; big brother Big Bros. Big Sisters, Charlottesville, Va., 1979—81. Mem.: Omicron Delta Kappa (life). Achievements include design of thin film rooftop solar panels. Avocations: soccer, sailing, poetry, painting, wooden toys. Home: 689 Bedford St Concord MA 01742 Office: Design Partnership of Cambridge 500 Rutherford Ave Charlestown MA 02129 Office Phone: 617-241-9800. Office Fax: 617-241-5143. Business E-Mail: wgerstmyer@design-partnership.com.

GERSTNER, JONATHAN NEIL, religious studies educator; b. Latrobe, Pa., Aug. 5, 1957; s. John H. and Edna Rachel Gerstner; m. Kathleen Jipping, June 20, 1987; children: Sarah Elizabeth, Jerusha Joy, Monica Kaye, Nathanael John, Micaia Eden. BA, Mich. State U., 1979; MA, U. Chgo., 1980, PhD, 1985. Ordained to ministry, Reformed Ch. in Am. Asst. prof. systematic and practical theology Payne Theol. Sem., Wilberforce, Ohio, 1986-89, acting acad. dean, 1988-89; exec. sec. Reformed Ch. in Can., Cambridge, Ont., 1989-94; prof. ch. history and apologetics Knox Theol. Sem., Ft. Lauderdale, Fla., 1994—98; prof. systematic theology and apologetics Knox Theol Sem., 1999; adj. prof. Ottawa Theol. Hall, Ottawa, Canada, 1997—2002, Sch. of Pastoral Studies, Rio de Janeiro, 1999—; dean and prof. of systematic theology and apologetics New Geneva Theol. Sem., Balt., 2001—02; corp. trainer MCI, Hunt Valley, Md., 2002—04; regional cons. in workforce devel. ACT Balt (Mid-Atlantic Region), 2004—; adj. faculty, dept. religious studies Coll. Notre Dame, Balt., 2004—. Mem. governing bd. Can. Coun. Ch., Toronto, Ont., Canada, 1989—94, Evang. Fellowship Can., Willowdale, Ont., Canada, 1989—94; bd. dir. Ligonier Ministries Can., Guelph, Ont., Canada, 1992—2002; radio program host, 1998—2002; sr. pastor Inverness Presbyn. Ch., Balt., 2000—02. Author: The Thousand Generation Covenant: Dutch Reformed Covenant Theology and Group Identity in Colonial South Africa, 1652-1814, 1991; (with others) Trust and Obey, 1996, Christianity in the History of South Africa, 1997, Onward Christian Soldiers, 1999. Grad. fellow Rotary Internat., 1983. Mem. Am. Acad. Religion, Am. Soc. Ch. History, Phi Beta Kappa, Phi Kappa Phi.

GERSTNER, LOUIS VINCENT, JR., retired information technology executive; b. Mineola, NY, Mar. 1, 1942; s. Louis Vincent and Marjorie (Rutan) G.; m. Elizabeth Robins Link, Nov. 30, 1968; children: Louis, Elizabeth. BA in Engring., Dartmouth Coll., 1963; MBA with hon., Harvard U. Bus. Sch., 1965; DBA (hon.), Boston Coll., 1994; LLD (hon.), Wake Forest U., 1997, Brown U., 1997, Notre Dame U., 2001; D of Engring. (hon.), Rensselaer Poly. Inst., 1999. Dir. McKinsey & Co., NYC, 1965-78; exec. v.p. Am. Express Co., NYC, 1978-81, vice-chmn. bd., 1981-83, chmn. exec. com., 1983-85, pres., 1985-89, chmn., CEO travel related svcs., 1985-89; chmn., CEO RJR Nabisco Inc., NYC, 1989-93; chmn. bd., CEO IBM, Armonk, NY, 1993—2002, dir., ret., 2002; chmn. The Carlyle Group, 2003—. Bd. dirs. Bristol-Myers Squibb Co.; mem. Pres.'s Nat. Security Telecom. Adv. Com., 1994-97, Adv. Com. for Trade Policy and Negotiations, 1995-2002; chmn. Computer Sys. Policy Project, 1999-2001; adv. bd. DaimlerChrysler, 2001—, Sony Corp., 2002—. Author: Who Says Elephants Can't Dance: Inside IBM's Historic Turnaround, 2002; co-author: Reinventing Education: Entrepreneurship in America's Public School, 1994. Bd. dirs. Meml. Sloan Kettering Hosp., 1978-89, 98—, vice-chmn., 2000—, United Negro Coll. Fund, 1987-91, Lincoln Ctr. for Performing Arts, 1984-2002, NY Times Co., 1986-97, AT&T, 1987-93, Caterpillar, 1984-89, Jewel Co., Melville Corp, Coun. Fgn. Rels., 1995-2005; trustee Joint Coun. on Econ. Edn., 1975-87, chmn. 1983-85; active Bus. Roundtable, 1991-98, The Bus. Coun., 1992; vice-chmn., bd. dirs. New Am. Schs. Devel. Corp., 1991-98; trustee NY Pub. Libr., 1991-96; bd. regents Smithsonian Instn., 1996-99; co-chmn. Achieve, 1996-2002, chmn. emeritus, 2003-; chmn. The Teaching Commn., 2003-; trustee Am. Mus. Natural History, 2004-. Recipient Cleveland E. Dodge Medal for disting. svc. to edn. Tchrs. Coll., Columbia U., Disting. Svc. to Sci. and Edn. award Am. Mus. Natural History, Award for Excellence in Bus., Engring. and Tech., John M. Olin Sch. of Washington U., 1999; named Knight of British Empire, 2001. Fellow Am. Acad. Arts and Scis., Am.-China Forum; mem. NAE Office: IBM Corp 20 Old Post Rd Armonk NY 10504-1709

GERSTNER, ROBERT WILLIAM, structural engineering educator, consultant; b. Chgo., Nov. 10, 1934; s. Robert Berty and Martha (Tuchelt) G.; m. Elizabeth Willard, Feb. 8, 1958; children: Charles Willard, William Mark. BS, Northwestern U., 1956, MS, 1957, PhD, 1960. Registered structural and profl. engr., Ill. Instr. Northwestern U., Evanston, Ill., 1957-59, research fellow, 1959-60; asst. prof. U. Ill., Chgo., 1960-63, assoc. prof., 1963-69, prof. structural engring., architecture, 1969-92, prof. emeritus, 1992—. Structural engr. cons., 1959—; mem. State of Ill. Structural Engring. Bd., 1992-94. Contbr. articles to profl. jours. Pres. Riverside Improvement Assn., 1973-77, 79-82. Mem. AAUP, ACLU, ASCE, Am. Soc. Engring. Edn., Structural Engrs. Assn. Ill. (bd. dirs. 1986-89, 92-94, sec. 1989-91, pres. 1991-92). Home: 2628 W Agatite Ave Chicago IL 60625-3011 E-mail: robertwgerstner@aol.com.

GERT, BERNARD, philosopher, educator; b. Cin., Oct. 16, 1934; s. Max and Celia (Yarnovsky) G.; m. Esther Libbye Rosenstein, Aug. 3, 1958; children: Heather Joy, Joshua Noah. BA, U. Cin., 1956; PhD, Cornell U., 1962. Instr. philosophy Dartmouth Coll., Hanover, NH, 1959-62, asst. prof. philosophy, 1962-66, assoc. prof., 1966-70, prof., 1970—, chmn. dept. philosophy, 1971—74, 1979—81, 1998—2001, Stone prof. intellectual and moral philosophy, 1981—92, 1998—, Eunice and Julian Cohen prof. ethics and human values, 1992-98. Vis. assoc. prof. philosophy Johns Hopkins U., Balt., 1967-68; vis. prof. philosophy Edinburgh U., fall 1974, Hebrew U. Jerusalem, 1985-86, Nacional U. de la Plata and U. Buenos Aires, Argentina, fall 1995, Ctr. Applied Philosophy Charles Sturt U., Canberra, Australia, 2004; adj. prof. psychiatry Dartmouth Med. Sch., 1976—; prin. investigator NIH, 1990-93. Author: The Moral Rules: A New Rational Foundation for Morality, 1970, 1973, 1975, German edit. 1983, Morality: A New Justification of the Moral Rules, 1988, Morality: Its Nature and Justification, 1998, revised edit., 2005, Common Morality, 2004; co-author: Philosophy in Medicine: Conceptual and Ethical Issues in Medicine and Psychiatry, 1982, Japanese edit. 1984; first author: Morality and the New Genetics: A Guide for Students and Health Care Providers, 1996, Bioethics: A Return to Fundamentals, 1997; editor: Hobbes' Man and Citizen, 1972, reprinted with revisions, 1991, Rationality, Rules, and Ideals: Critical Essays on Bernard Gert's Moral Theory, 2002; contbr. chpts. to books, articles to profl. jours. Recipient NSF-NEH Sustained Devel. award, 1980—84, Fulbright lectureship, Israel, 1985—86, Argentina, fall, 1995; fellow, NEH, 1969—70, Hastings Ctr., 1986—. Fellow Nat. Humanities Ctr. 2001-2002; mem. Am. Philos. Assn., Am. Soc. Polit. and Legal Philosophy, Soc. Ethics Across the Curriculim, Assn. Practical and Profl. Ethics. Avocations: squash, poker. Home: 8 Bridgman Rd Hanover NH 03755-1302 Office: Dartmouth Coll Dept Philosophy Hanover NH 03755 Office Phone: 603-646-2022. Business E-Mail: bernard.gert@dartmouth.edu.

GERTH, DONALD ROGERS, university president, educator; b. Chgo., Dec. 4, 1928; s. George C. and Madeleine (Canavan) G.; m. Beverly J. Hollman, Oct. 15, 1955; children: Annette, Deborah. BA, U. Chgo., 1947, AM, 1951, PhD, 1963. Field rep. S.E. Asia World Univ. Svc., 1950; asst. to pres. Shimer Coll., 1951; Admissions counselor U. Chgo., 1956-58; assoc. dean students, admissions and records, mem. dept. polit. sci. San Francisco St. U., San Francisco, 1958-63; assoc. dean instnl. relations and student affairs Calif. State Univ., 1963-64; chmn. commn. on extended edn. Calif. State Univs. and Colls., 1977-82; dean of students Calif. State U., Chico, 1964-68, prof. polit. sci., 1964-76, assoc. v.p. for acad. affairs, dir. internat. programs, 1969-70, v.p. acad. affairs, 1970-76, pres., prof. polit. sci. Dominguez Hills, 1976-84, pres., prof. pub. policy and adminstrn. Sacramento, 1984—2003, pres., prof. emeritus, 2003—; co-dir. Danforth Found. Research Project, 1968-69; coordinator Inst. Local Govt. and Public Service, 1968-70. Past chair Accrediting Commn. for Sr. Colls. and Univs. of Western Coll. Assn.; chmn. admissions coun. Calif. State U., 1974-03; bd. dirs. Ombudsman Found., L.A., 1968-71; lectr. U. Philippines, 1953-54, Claremont Grad. Sch. and Univ. Ctr., 1965-69; mem. World Trade Ctr. No. Calif., 1986-, chair, 1996-03; chmn. Calif. State U. Inst., 1997-98; pres. Internat. Assn. Univ. Pres. 1996-99; mem. coun., governing bd. UN U., 1998-04, vice chair, 2002-04. Co-author: The Learning Society, 1969; author, editor: An Invisible Giant, 1971; contbg. editor Education for the Public Service, 1970, Papers on the Ombudsman in Higher Education, 1979. Mem. pers. commn. Chico Unified Sch. Dist., 1969-76, chmn., 1971-74; adv. com. on justice pgorams Butte Coll., 1970-76; mem. Varsity Scouting Coun., 1980-84; chmn. United Way campaign Calif. State Univs., L.A. County, 1981-82; bd. dirs. Sacramento Area United Way, campaign chmn., 1991-92, exec. com., 1991-96, vice chmn., 1992-94, chmn.-elect, 1994-95, chmn., 1995-96; mem. bd. dirs. South Bay Hosp. Found., 1979-82; mem. The Cultural Commn., L.A., 1981-84; mem. com. govtl. rels. Am. Coun. Edn. Capt. USAF, 1952-56. Mem. Internat. Assn. Univ. Pres. (pres. 1996-99), Am. Polit. Sci. Assn., Am. Soc. Pub. Adminstrn., Soc. Coll. and Univ. Planning, Western Govtl. Rsch. Assn., World Affairs Coun. No. Calif., Assn. Pub. Adminstrn. Edn. (chmn. 1973-74), Western Polit. Sci. Assn., Am. Assn. State Colls. and Univs. (bd. dirs.), Calif. State C. of C. (edn. com.), Assn. Governing Bds. of Univs. and Colls., Calif. State U. Inst. (chmn. bd. dirs.), UN Ednl., Sci. and Cultural Orgn. (mem. adv. com.), UN U. Coun. (governing bd. 1998-04, vice chair 2001-04), Am. Coun. UN U. (chair 2004-). Democrat. Episcopalian. Avocations: tennis, skiing, reading. Home: 7132 Secret Garden Loop Roseville CA 95747-8339 Office: Calif State U 2000 State Univ Drive East Rm 3022 Libr Sacramento CA 95819-6039 Office Phone: 916-278-7400. Business E-Mail: dongerth@csus.edu.

GERTJEJANSEN, DOYLE, artist, educator; b. Tracy, Minn., Sept. 1, 1948; BA, Mankato State U., 1969; MFA, U. Minn., 1971. Instr. fine arts U. New Orleans, 1971-75, grad. coun., 1986-91, prof. fine arts, 1988—, chmn. dept. fine arts, 1995-97. Panelist Insts. and the ARtist Optima Studio, New Orleans, 1982; visual arts com. New Orleans Contemporary Arts Ctr., 1983—86; dir. Sculpture Front U. New Orleans, 1984—86, project dir. for traveling exhbn. So. Folk Images Univ. Senate, 1984, permanent art collection com., 1984—87; task force on pub. sculpture Downtown Devel. Dist. and Arts Coun. New Orleans, 1985; mem. downtown pub. art com. Arts Coun. New Orleans, 1986, mem. percent for art com., 1987—89, bd. dirs., 1988—89, mem. art-works artists steering com.; bd. dirs. New Orleans Contemporary Arts Ctr., 1996—99; chair visual arts com. N.D. Contemporary Arts Ctr., 1997—99. One-man shows include Augusta Coll. Fine Arts Gallery, Sioux Falls, S.D., 1968, Coffman Gallery U. Minn., Mpls., 1971, U. No. Ala., Florence, 1975, La. Crafts Coun., New Orleans, 1980, Arthur Roger Gallery, 1981, 1983, 1985, New Orleans Ctr. Performing Arts, 1984, Susan Abeline Gallery, Zurich, Switzerland, 1986, Galerie Simonne Stern Ltd., Atlanta, 1989, Galerie Simonne Stern, New Orleans, 1987, 1989, 1990, 1993, 1996, Conkling Gallery Mankato (Minn.) State U., 1989, exhibited in group shows at Galerie Simonne Stern, New Orleans, 1994, 1995, 1999, New Orleans Ctr. Contemporary Art, 1995, La. Arts and Sci. Ctr., Baton Rouge, 1995, Contemporary Arts Ctr., New Orleans, 1995, Positive Space Gallery, 1996, 1996, Delfina Studio Trust, London, 1996, Ctr. Contemporary Art, Winston-Salem, N.C., 1997, U. West Fla., 1997, D.C. Arts Ctr., Washington, 1998, Gunma Print Artists Assn., Maebshi City, Japan, 1999, numerous others. Represented in permanent collections Adams & Reese, New Orleans, Ariz. State U., Ark. Art Ctr., Hotel Intercontinental, New Orleans, Middleberg, Riddle & Gianna Attys., New Orleans Mus. Art, Pan Am. Life, New Orleans, Premier Bank, Baton Rouge, Scudder, Stevens and Clark, Boston, State St. Rsch. and Mgmt. Co., TJM Corp., New Orleans, Westminster, Corp., other pvt. collections. Recipient Artist of Yr. award, New Orleans Contemporary Arts Ctr. Century Club, 1993, South Ctrl. Artists award, Phi Kappa Phi, 1996; DeBois Faculty fellow, U. New Orleans Coll. Urban and Pub. Affairs, 1992, regional fellow, NEA/So. Arts Fedn., 1996, fellow, La. Divsn. Arts, 1998. Office: 1 Central Park W #43A New York NY 10023-7703

GERTLER, JANOS JOHN, electrical engineer, educator; b. Vienna, Sept. 9, 1936; came to U.S., 1981; s. Mor and Marta (Ungar) Gertler; m. Judit Andai, July 29, 1965; 1 child, Nicholas Balazs; m. Eva Anna Vas, Dec. 30, 2000. Diploma in engring., Tech. U., Budapest, Hungary, 1959; Candidate of Sci., Hungaraian Acad. Scis., Budapest, 1967, DSc, 1980. Rsch. assoc. Power Systems Rsch. Inst., Budapest, 1959-65; asst. prof. Tech. U., Budapest, 1965-67; postdoctoral fellow U. Toronto, Ont., Can., 1967-68; sr. rsch. assoc. Automation Rsch. Inst., Budapest, 1968-70, dep. dir., 1971-81; vis. prof., assoc. dean engring. Poly. Inst. N.Y., Bklyn., 1984-85; prof. George Mason U., Fairfax, Va., 1985—. Assoc. vis. prof. Case Western Res. U., Cleve., 1977, vis. prof., 1982-84; cons. Bailey Controls, Cleve., 1983-84, GM, Warren, Mich., 1989-96; plenary spkr. internat. confs., 1974, 86, 91, 92, 93, 94, 95, 00. Author: Fault Detection and Diagnosis, 1998; series editor Internat. Fedn. Automatic Control Procs., 1984-96; editor Ann. Revs. in Control, 1996—; contbr. articles to profl. jours. Fellow IEEE; mem. Hungarian Nat. Acad. Scis. (fgn. mem.), Internat. Fedn. Automatic Control (chmn. publ. bd. 1993-96, 96-99, advisor for life, 1999—). Achievements include rsch. in the theory and application of model-based diagnosis in engineering systems; development of generalized parity relation method; isolation-enhanced principal component analysis; application to car engines. Office: George Mason U Elec Engring Dept Fairfax VA 22030 Office Phone: 703-993-1604. Business E-Mail: jgertler@gmu.edu.

GERTLER, MENARD M., physician, educator; b. Saskatoon, Sask., Can., May 19, 1921; arrived in U.S., 1947, naturalized, 1953; s. Frank and Clara (Handelman) G.; m. Anna Paull, Sept. 4, 1943; children: Barbara Lynn, Stephanie Jocelyn, Jonathan Paull. BA, U. Sask., Saskatoon, 1940; MD, McGill U., Montreal, 1943, MS, 1946, DSc (hon.), 1998; DSc, NYU, 1960. Intern Royal Victoria Hosp., Montreal, Canada, 1943—44; resident Mass. Gen. Hosp., Boston, 1947—50; rsch. fellow in medicine Mass. Gen. Hosp., Harvard Med. Sch., 1947—50; dir. cardiology Francis Delafield divsn. Columbia Presbyn. Med. Ctr., N.Y.C., 1950—54; spl. rsch. fellow NIH, NYU Dept. Biochemistry, 1954—56; prof. Sch. Medicine, dir. cardiovascular rsch. Rusk Inst. NYU Med. Ctr., 1958—71; sr. med. examiner FAA, 1975; dir. Washington Fed. Savs. & Loan Assn., 1972—83; adj. prof. medicine McGill U., 1996—; clin. prof. medicine N.Y. Hosp.-Cornell Med. Ctr., attending physician. Prof. medicine Weill Med. Sch., Cornell U.; attending physician N.Y. Hosp./Presbyn. Hosp., 1998—; med. dir. Sinclair Oil Corp., 1958-68; internat. cons. cardiovascular diseases, social and rehab. svcs. HEW, Washington, 1968-92. Author: Coronary Heart Disease in Young Adults, 1954, Coronary Heart Disease, 1974; Contbr. articles to profl. jours. Pres. Friends of McGill U., 1983-2001; mem. dean's com. McGill U. Med. Sch. With M.C., Royal Can. Army, 1940-43. Recipient Founders Day award NYU, 1959, medal of honor McGill U., 1993, award of merit McGill U., 1993. Mem. Gallatin Assocs. NYU, Cosmos Club (Washington), Harvard Club (Boston), Univ. Club. Home and Office: 1000 Park Ave Apt 2C New York NY 10028-0934

GERTRUDE, KATY See WILHELM, KATE

GERTSENZON, GALINA, music educator; b. Paitygorsk, Russia, Apr. 3, 1946; arrived in U.S., 1981; d. Yefim Olshansky and Hana Berman; m. Igor Gertsenzon, Nov. 8, 1968; 1 child, Elena Gertsenzon Orujev. MusB, Baku Coll. Music, 1964; MusM, Gorky Conservatory, 1970. Prof. music Baku Coll. Music, Azerbaijan, 1970—81; with faculty music Smith Coll., Northampton, Mass., 1985—86; staff pianist U. Mass., Amherst, 1981—82; with music faculty Westfield State Coll., 1983—, Elms Coll., Chicopee, 1982—. Vol. Immingrant Resettlement Program, Springfield, Mass., 1981—. Democrat. Jewish. Avocations: travel, reading.

GERTZ, DAVID LEE, homebuilding company executive; b. Denver, July 30, 1950; s. Ben Harry and Clara (Cohen) G.; m. Bonnie Lee Schulein, June 2, 1973; children: Joshua, Eva. BS, U. Colo., 1972; MBA, U. Colo., Denver, 1993. Real estate broker Crown Realty, Denver, 1972-73; pres. Sunshine Plumbing Co., Lakewood, Colo., 1974-76, Sunshine Diversified, Inc., Lakewood, 1976—, Sunshine Master Builders, Ltd., Lakewood, 1990—. Sec.-treas. Wight Lateral Ditch Co., Lakewood, 1987-91. Builder Taylor Made semi-custom homes. Cub master Boy Scouts Am., Lakewood, 1989-91, asst. scout master, 1991-94; chmn. Parade of Homes com., 1999-2000, pres. Homebuilders Assn. of Metro Denver, 2004. Scholar, Evans Scholars, U. Colo., 1968-72. Mem.: Home Aid Denver (bd. dirs., pres.), Colo. Assn. Home Builders (bd. dirs., legis. com., accessability com.). Avocations: skiing, golf. Office: Sunshine Master Builders 7120 E Orchard Rd Englewood CO 80111 Office Phone: 303-932-9929. E-mail: dlgertz@sunshinemb.com.

GERTZ, SUZANNE C., artist; b. Chgo., Sept. 8, 1938; d. Henry A. Feldman and Helen Flanzer; m. Theodore G. Gertz, June 19, 1960; children: Craig M., Candace C., Scott W. Student, Art Inst. Chgo., 1960; BFA, Barat Coll., 1982. Exhibited in group shows at Art Inst. Chgo., San Jacinto Coll., Houston, 2001, New Horizons in Art, Chgo., Lake Forest Art Show, exhibitions include San Bernardino County Mus., Firehouse Gallery, N.Y., Evanston and Vicinity 12th Bienniel Exhbn., The Cmty. Gallery Art Coll. Lake County, Dittmar Gallery, Northwestern U., David Adler Cultural Ctr., Cindy Bordeau Gallery, others. Mem.: Cliff Dwellers Club. Democrat. Jewish. Home: 950 Benson Ln Libertyville IL 60048

GERUT, ZACHARY E., plastic surgeon; b. Boston, Mass., July 1, 1954; s. Leo and Anna Gerut; m. Robin Lynn Thun, Aug. 21, 1981; children: Benjamin, Talli, Maxie. BA, Brandeis U.; MD, U. Mass. Med. Sch. Diplomate Am. Bd. of Plastic Surgery, 1988, lic. NY, diplomate Nat. Bd. of Med. Examiners, 1981. Internship Montefiore Hosp., Albert Einstein Coll. of Medicine, N.Y.C., NY, resident gen. surgery, fellow, resident plastic surgery; burn fellow Bronx Municipal Hosp., N.Y.C.; chief resident plastic surgery Montefiore Hosp., Albert Einstein Coll. of Med. Contbr. articles various profl. jours. Fellow: Am. Coll. of Surgeons; mem.: Am. Soc. of Aesthetic Plastic Surgery, Am. Soc. Plastic and Reconstructive Surgery, Nassau Acad. of Medicine, Nassau County Med. Soc. Avocations: golf, tennis. Office: Zachary E Gerut MD 1245 Colonial Rd Hewlett NY 11557 Office Phone: 516-295-2100. Office Fax: 516-295-2487. E-mail: zger@optonline.net.

GERVAIS, CHERIE NADINE, small business owner; b. Marysville, Calif. d. Victor H. and Gladys A. (Poissant) Fehr; 1 child, Dublin M. Ryan. Student, Yuba Coll., Coll. of Marin, 1977, Sonoma State Coll., 1994, student, 2002. Owner, operator Grandma's Trunk Doll Hosp., San Francisco, 1969-72, San Rafael, Calif., 1972-92, Cherie's Doll Hosp., Petaluma, Calif., 1992-93. Model various local fashion shows, San Francisco and Marin County, Calif., 1973-87. Editor: U.F.D.C. Doll Convention Book; contbr. numerous poems to profl. publs.; paintings and sculptures exhibited at show in Petaluma Mus. Recipient many 1st, 2d and 3d place ribbons at doll shows, ribbons for quilts at fairs in Sonoma and Marin County, 1st place ribbons for paintings and sculptures Sonoma Fair, 1993, Best of Show Sonoma-Marin Fair, 2004, 1st and 2d ribbons, 2005; named Poet of Month, San Rafael (Calif.) Pointer News, 1975. Mem. Dolls from the Attic (pres. 1988-2002, v.p.), 101 Doll Club (pres. 1975-76), San Francisco Doll Club (pres. 1976-77), Women of the Moose. Democrat. Episcopalian. Avocations: painting, sculpting, writing, sewing. Home and Office: Cherie's Doll Hosp 45 La Cresta Dr Petaluma CA 94952-2460 Office Phone: 707-778-8534.

GERVAIS, SISTER GENEROSE, hospital consultant; b. Currie, Minn., Sept. 18, 1919; d. Philip Frederick and Elizabeth Eleanor (Sandgathe) Gervais. BS, Stout State U., Menomonie, Wis., 1945; M. Hosp. Adminstrn., U. Minn., 1954. Joined Sisters of St. Francis, Roman Catholic Ch., 1938; adminstrv. dietitian St. Marys Hosp., Rochester, Minn., 1948-50, adminstrv. asst., 1951-52, asst. adminstr., 1954-63, assoc. adminstr., 1963-71, hosp. adminstr., 1971-81, exec. dir., 1981-85, bd. trustees, 1968-86; hosp. cons., 1985-90. Cons. dietitian Mercy Hosp., Portsmouth, Ohio, 1950-51; bd. dirs. 1st Nat. Bank, Rochester, 1974-78, Fed. Res. Bank Mpls., 1978-86, St. Francis Med. Ctr., LaCrosse, Wis., 1979-87, S.E. Minn. Health Systems Agy., 1978-83, S.E. Minn. Health Coun., 1983-87, Unity Home Health Svcs., Inc., LaCrosse, 1994-95; v.p., sec. Family Health Ctr. LaCrosse, Inc., 1985-91, pres., 1991-93; mem. residency adv. bd. St. Francis-Mayo Family Practice, 1993-95; mem. v.p., bd. dirs. Caledonia Health Care Ctr., 1986-90; bd. dirs. Franciscan Health System, LaCrosse, 1987-94, mem., treas., bd. dirs. Franciscan Cmty. Programs 1985-94. Bd. dirs. United Way of Olmstead County, 1968-73, Sr. Citizens Svcs. Inc., Rochester, Minn., 1988-94, Diocese of Winona Found., 1991-2000; bd. dirs. Madonna Towers, Rochester, 1987—, chair, 1991-97, 2003—; bd. dirs. Olmstead County Hist. Soc., 1994-97; bd. dirs. Regina Med. Ctr., Hastings, Minn., 1996-02, Madonna Meadows, 2002—; pres. Poverello Found., Rochester, 1983—; bd. adv. Winona State U. Rochester Ctr., 1985-93; mem. fin. coun. Diocese of Winona, 1986-91; mem. Franciscan Skemp Healthcare Cmty. Bd., LaCrosse, 1995—. Decorated Lady of Equestrian Order of Holy Sepulchre, 1989; recipient Alumni Disting. Service award U. Wis.-Stout, 1978, Teresa of Avila award Coll. of St. Teresa, 1980, Outstanding Achievement award Rochester chpt. U. Minn. Alumni Assn., 1981, Women of Achievement in Area of Bus. award YWCA, 1985, Pro Ecclesiae et Pontifice medal, 1985, Service to Mankind award Sertoma 700 Club, 1987, Mayor's Medal of Honor City of Rochester, 1990, The Athena award, 1994, Outstanding Alumni award Coll. Human Devel., U. Wis.-Stout, 2001; named Boss of Yr., Rochester Jaycees, 1980, named in her honor Sister Generose Gervais Bldg. St. Marys Hosp., 1991; Paul Harris fellow Nat. Rotary Club, 1998. Mem. Cath. Health Assn. U.S. (trustee 1979, vice chair 1981-82, chair 1982-83, speaker membership assembly 1983-84), Am. Coll. Hosp. Adminstrs., Am. Hosp. Assn., Minn. Hosp. Assn., Minn. Conf. Cath. Health Facilities (past dir.), Rochester Area C. of C. Republican. Address: 1216 2nd St SW Rochester MN 55902-1906 Office Phone: 507-255-5158. Business E-Mail: hanson.sandra@mayo.edu.

GERVAIS, MARK G., physical education educator; b. Oct. 10, 1954; s. Joseph F. and Dorothy F. Gervais. B, N.E. Mo. State U., 1980; M, Ea. Ill. U., 1985. Asst. instr. N.E. Mo. State U., Kirksville, Mo., 1978—81; head wrestling coach Marist H.S., Chgo., 1981—82, tchr., 1982—2005, dept. chair health and phys. edn., 1995—2005. Named to Hall of Fame, Marist H.S., 2003; recipient Champnat Educator of Yr. award, Marist Bros., 2003, Heart of Sch. award, Marist H.S., 2005. Mem.: ASCD, AAHPERD, Ill. Wrestling Coaches Ofcls. Assn. (Coach of Yr. 1987, named to Hall of Fame 1995). Office: Marist High Sch 4200 W 115th St Chicago IL 60655 Office Phone: 773-881-5300.

GERVAIS, PAUL NELSON, foundation administrator, psychotherapist, public relations executive, author; b. Augusta, Maine, June 28, 1947; s. Adrien and Phyllis (Sullivan) G. B in Bible and Doctrine/Ministerial Studies, Berean Coll., 1975; M, U. Maine, 1987; M in Marriage and Family Therapy, Coll. Clin. Family Sci., 1988; cert. in Constl. Law, U. Maine, 1969; Dr., N.Am. Biblical Sem., Buffalo, 1987; M. in Marriage and Family, San Antonio Theol. Sem., 1988; PhD in Psychology, San Antonio Theol. Sem., St. Paul, 1989; PhD in Marriage and Family Therapy, Minn. Grad. Sch., 1990. Cert. behavioral analyst, clin. supr., registered clin. therapist, lic. marriage and family therapist, clin. profl. counselor, profl. counselor, pastoral counselor Maine. Reporter No. New Eng. divsn. News dept. NBC Radio divsn., N.Y.C., 1966-70; dir. pub. rels. Kennebec Valley Med. Ctr., Augusta, 1970-73, Penobscot Bay Med. Ctr., Rockport, Maine, 1973-74; pres., chmn. bd. dirs. Ministry of Miracles Evangelistic Assn., Maine, 1975—; staff clinician Augusta Police Dept. News dir. Maine Broadcasting Sys., Augusta, 1966—70; advisor, assoc. dir. pub. rels. State VA Svcs., Maine, 1969—70; family counselor Gracelawn Meml. Park, Auburn, Maine, assoc. dir., 1987, COO; pres., CEO Motivational Resources; behavioral scientist Augusta Police Dept. Pioneered one of first radio and TV health edn. programs from which proceeded other nat. and internat. programs in field; mental health columnist Maine Sunday Paper; internat. network TV guest. Active Rep. Nat. Com., Washington, 1987, Dole for Pres. exploratory Com., 1987—, also adv. com., 1987, steering com. Campaign Am., 1987-88; mem. Presdl. Task Force, Washington, 1989, Rep. Senatorial Inner Circle, 1989—, U.S. Senatorial Club, Washington, 1989-90, Nat. Rep. Senatorial Com., Washington, 1990; CEO Gracelawn Meml. Park, Auburn, Maine, 1988—; spl. advisor, dep. Kennebec County Sheriff's Office, also dep. sheriff. Recipient vice-presdl. Citation Office of U.S. V.P. Hubert Humphrey, 1968, Malcolm T. MacEachern Citation Am. Health Congress, 1973; cert. in pub. rels. Chgo. chpt. Am. Hosp. Assn.; Presdl. Medal of Merit Pres. George Bush, 1989. Fellow Profl. Assn. Christian Counselors and Therapists; mem. AACD, Am. Acad. Family Therapists (exec. dir.), Acad. for Eating Disorders, Nat. Assn. Anorexia Nervosa and Associated Disorders, Publicity Club Boston (disting. bell ringer award 1974), Nat. Christian Counselors Assn. (mem. licensing bd., chmn. legal com.), Am. Mental Health Counselors Assn., Maine Network Associated Profl. Practitioners, Maine Assn. for Counseling and Devel., Mensa. Baptist. Home and Office: Am Acad Profl Family Therapists 16 Julianne Ln Augusta ME 04330-6251 Business E-Mail: clinicdrpng@aol.com.

GERVAIS, RICKY, actor; b. Reading, Eng., June 25, 1961; Disc jockey XFM Radio Sta., London. Actor: (films) Dog Eat Dog, 2001, (voice) Valiant, 2005; (TV films) Legend of the Lost Tribe, 2002,: (TV series) The 11 O'Clock Show, 1998, Meet Ricky Gervais, 2000, The Office, 2001—03, Extras, 2005—; writer: TV series Bruiser, 2000, Meet Ricky Gervais, 2000, The Office, 2001—03, The Sketch Show, 2001; performer: (appeared in) Comic Relief, 2003, The Big Hair Do, 2003; author (illus. by Rob Steen): (children's books) Flanimals, 2005. Named No. 3 on the list, "British Culture's Top 50 Movers and Shakers", BBC 3, 2004; recipient O.K. Comedy award, 2003, Golden Globe for best comedic actor, 2003. Office: PFD 34-43 Russell St London WC2B 5HA England*

GERVAIS-GRUEN, ELIZABETH, lawyer; b. Papa, Hungary, Feb. 04; arrived in U.S., 1921; d. Samuel Friedmann and Vilma Kohn; m. Ralph Gervais, Feb. 7, 1970; m. Rudolph Gruen, Aug. 2, 1934 (div.); children: Richard Gruen, Robert Gruen, S. Daniel Gruen, David Gruen. Student, St. John's U., 1929—31, LLB, 1934. Bar: N.Y. 1936, N.Y. Supreme Ct. 1936, U.S. Supreme Ct. 1969. Law clk. Law Office of Samuel Newfield, 1934—36; ptnr. Rudolf Gruen and Elizabeth Gruen, 1936—38; asst. to town atty. James Dowsey, Jr. Nassau County, NY, 1938—40, asst. to county atty. James Dowsey, 1940—43; pvt. practice, 1943—58; pvt. practice Immigration and Naturalization Law, 1958—. Pres. Nassau County Women's Assn., 1968—70; bd. trustees Blumenthal Jewish Home, 1989—93; pres. Durham-Chapel Hill Jewish Fedn., 1988—90; chair Am. Affairs com. Hadassah, 1960—64, 1972—74; founder, mem. Women's Ctr., Chapel Hill, NC; chair, advisor youth activity com. Temple Beth El, Great Neck L.I., NY, chair, advisor Temple Teens, chair, advisor Coll. Youth com., pres. Sisterhood; mem. long-term planning com. Temple Beth Zion, Buffalo; chair women's group Judea Reform Congregation, Durham, NC, 1976—78, mem. long-term planning com., hon. chmn. Capitol Campaign. Recipient Sara Mutt Evans award, Jewish Fedn. and Cmty. Svc., 1992. Mem.: Commn.-Status of Women Attys. (Status of Women Attys. in N.C. com. mem.), N.C. Bar Assn. (chair Immigration and Nationality com. 1981—99), Am. Immigration Lawyers Assn. (chair N.C. chpt. 1980—84, bd. govs., founder N.C. chpt., hon. fellow 2002, Sam Williamson Mentor award 2000, Carolinas chpt. Mentor award in honor Elizabeth Gervais-Gruen established 1999, Elizabeth F. Gervais-Gruen Mentor award 1999, Pres.'s Commendation 1992). Avocations: reading, analyzing law, collecting Judaic artifacts, collecting ancient glass, collecting minerals and fossils, stamp collecting/philately. Office: 914 Crestwood Ln Chapel Hill NC 27517 Office Phone: 919-933-6810.

GERVASIO, RALPH J., JR., public relations executive; BA magna cum laude, U. Balt. Legis. asst., Washington, 1982-85; dir. govt. affairs dept. Profl. Homebuilders Assn., Annapolis; exec. dir. Ho. Dem. Rsch. Group; dir. Foley Govt. Rels., Annapolis, Md. Office: PO Box 61303 Potomac MD 20859

GERWICK, BEN CLIFFORD, JR., construction engineer, educator; b. Berkeley, Calif., Feb. 22, 1919; s. Ben Clifford and Bernice (Coultrap) Gerwick; m. Martelle Louise Beverly, July 28, 1941 (dec. Jan. 1995); children: Beverly Brian, Virginia Wallace, Ben Clifford III, William; m. Ellen Chaney Lynch, May 18, 1996. BS, U. Calif., 1940. With Ben C. Gerwick, Inc., San Francisco, 1946—, pres., 1952—88, chmn., 1988—2000, hon. chmn., sr. tech. cons., 2000—; exec. v.p. Santa Fe-Pomeroy, Inc., 1968—71; prof. civil engring. U. Calif., Berkeley, 1971—89, prof. emeritus, 1989—. Sponsoring mgr. Richmond-San Rafael Bridge substructure, 1953—56, San Mateo-Hayward Bridge, 1964—66; lectr. constrn. engring. Stanford U., 1962—68; cons. major bridge and marine constrn. projects; cons. engr. ocean structures and overwater bridges, also offshore structures. U.S., North Sea, Arctic Ocean, Japan, Australia, Indonesia, Arabian Gulf, China, Europe, Can., S.E. Asia, S.Am.; mem. Arctic Rsch. Commn., 1990—95. Author: (book) Russian-English Dictionary of Prestressed Concrete and Concrete Construction, 1966, Construction of Prestressed Concrete Structures, 1971, 2d edit., 1996, Construction and Engineering Marketing for Major Project Services, 1981, Construction of Marine and Offshore Structures, 1986, 2d edit., 2000; contbr. articles to profl. jours. Chmn. marine bd. NRC, 1978—80. With USN, 1940—46, comdr. USNR, ret. Named one of Top Engrs. in Past 125 Yrs., Engring. News Record, 2000; recipient Golden Beaver award, Beavers Constrn. Soc., 1974, Mörsch medal, Deutsche Beton Verein, Weisbaden, Germany, 1978, Blakely Smith Ocean Engring. medal, Soc. Naval Archs. and Marine Engrs., 1981, Lockheed Ocean Engring. award, Marine Tech. Soc., 1982, Citation, U. Calif., Berkeley, 1989, Internat. award, Japan Soc. Civil Engring., 2001, award, Swedish Concrete Soc., 1986. Fellow: ASCE (hon. Karp award 1976, G. Brooks Earnest award 1980, Peurifoy award 1989, Pres.'s award 1989, Disting. Constructor award 2000, Ralph B. Peck Lectr. award 2001, Outstanding Lifetime Achievement award 2001), Norwegian Concrete Soc. (Holand award 2002, Ivar Holand award 2002), Am. Segmental Bridge Inst., Nat. Acad. Constrn., Internat. Assn. Bridge and Structural Engrs., Deep Founds. Inst. (Disting. Svc. award 1996), Am. Concrete Inst. (hon.; dir. 1960, Turner award 1974, Corbetta award 1981, Franklin Inst. Brown award 1984, Offshore Tech. Rsch.Ctr. Honors award 1992, Ocean Tech. Pioneer award 2004); mem.: NAE, Nat. Acad. Engrs., Prestressed Concret Inst. (hon.; pres. 1957—58, Titan award 2004), Fédn. Internat. Procontrainte (pres. 1974—78, now hon. pres., Freyssinet medal 1982), Claremont Country Club (Oakland), Bohemian Club (San Francisco). Congregationalist. Home: 5727 Country Club Dr Oakland CA 94618-1717 Office: Ben C Gerwick Inc 20 California St Fl 4 San Francisco CA 94111-2607 Office Phone: 415-288-2730. E-mail: bcg@gerwick.com.

GERWICK-BRODEUR, MADELINE CAROL, marketing and timing professional; b. Kearney, Neb., Aug. 29, 1951; d. Vern Frank and Marian Leila (Bliss) Gerwick; m. David Louis Brodeur; 1 child, Aria Renée. Student, U. Wis., 1970-72, U. Louisville, 1974-75; BA in Econs. magna cum laude, U. N.H., 1979; postgrad., Internat. Trade Inst., Seattle. Cert. profl. cycles cons., 1995; cert. bus. astrologer. Indsl. sales rep. United Radio Supply Inc., Seattle, 1980-81; mfrs. rep. Ray Over Sales Inc., Seattle, 1981-82; sales engr. Tektronix, Inc., Kent, Wash., 1982-83; mktg. mgr. Zepher Industries, Inc., Burien, Wash., 1983-85, Microscan Systems Inc., Tukwila, Wash., 1986; market devel. URS Electronics, Inc., Portland, 1986-88; sr. product specialist Fluke Corp., 1989-95; owner Astro Cycles Cons. L.L.C., Seattle, 1995—; co-founder Polaris Business Guides LLC. Co-found. Polaris Bus. Guides LLC, 2001; bd. dirs., sec. Starfish Enterprises Inc., Tacoma, 1984-87; com. chmn. Northcon, Seattle and Portland, 1984-86, 88, 90; speaker to Wash. Women's Employment and Edn., Tacoma, 1983—. Writer daily column for Zodiac Zone, 1995-96, Online Noetic Network; author, pub. The Good Timing Guide; co-author The Complete Idiot's Guide To Astrology, 1997, Pocket Idiot's Guide to Horoscopes, 1998-2000, (annual) Good Timing Guides, 1997—. Bd. dirs. Kepler Coll. of Astrol. Arts and Scis., 1998-2000. Recipient Jack E. Chase award for Outstanding Svc. and Contbr. Northcon Founder's Orgn., 1988. Mem. Electronic Mfrs. Assn. (sec. 1982, sec.-treas. 1988, v.p. 1989), Inst. Noetic Scis., Internat. Soc. for Astrol. Rsch., Wash. State Astrol. Assn. (bd. dirs. 1996-98), Phi Kappa Phi. Avocations: writing, healing arts, metaphysics. Office: Polaris Business Guides PO Box 27065 Seattle WA 98165 Home: 201 S Macleod Ave Arlington WA 98223-1525 Office Phone: 877-524-8300 ext. 401. Business E-Mail: mgb@polarisbusinessguides.com.

GERY, JOHN ROY OCTAVIUS, secondary school educator, poet; b. Reading, Pa, June 2, 1953; s. Malcolm R. Dougherty and Eugenie Gunesh (Guran) Gery, Addison H. Gery, Jr. (Stepfather); m. Bilijana D. Obradovic, 2003; 1 child, Peter Malcom Obradovic. BA in English with honors, Princeton U., 1975; MA in English, U. Chgo., 1976; MA in Creative Writing, Stanford U., 1978. Lectr. English San Jose State U., 1977-79; lectr. Stanford U., 1977-79; from instr. to assoc. prof. U. New Orleans, 1979—95, prof. English, creative writing, 1995-2000, rsch. prof., 2000—, dir. creative writing, 1986—90, 1996. Vis. assoc. prof. U. Iowa, Iowa City, 1991, Iowa City, 93; dir. Philol. Assn. La., New Orleans, 1986—88, Ezra Pound Ctr. Lit., Brunnenburg Castle, Italy, 1990—; resident poet Cummington Cmty. Arts, 1993, Bucknell U., 2001, 03; bd. dir. New Orleans Poetry Jour. Press. Author: (poems) Charlemagne: A Song of Gestures, 1983, The Enemies of Leisure, 1995, Nuc. Annihilation and Contemporary Am. Poetry, 1996, various poems; co-translator: For the House of Torkom, 1999; author: (poems) American Ghost: Selected Poems, 1999, Davenport's Version, 2003, A Gallery of Ghosts, 2005. Treas. Educators Social Responsibility, New Orleans, 1982—90; co-chair polit. action New Orleans Progressive Alliance, 1986—90. Recipient Deep South Poetry awards, Deep South Writers Conf., 1984, 1987, Critics' Choice award for poetry, 1995—96, European award, Cir. Franz Kafka, 2000; Poetry fellow, Wesleyan U. Writers Conf., 1989, Creative Writing fellow, Nat. Endowment Arts, 1992—93, Artist fellow, La. Divsn. Arts, 2002. Mem.: MLA, Gulf Coast Assn. Creative Writing Tchr. (2d v.p. 1996—98), La. State Poetry Soc., Assoc. Writing Programs, Poets & Writers. Democrat. Avocations: jazz piano, travel, baseball, films, art. Office: U New Orleans Dept English Lakefront New Orleans LA 70148-2315 Office Phone: 504-280-6133. Business E-Mail: jgery@uno.edu.

GESKE, JANINE PATRICIA, law educator; b. Port Washington, Wis., May 12, 1949; d. Richard Braem and Georgette (Paulissen) Geske; m. Michael Julian Hogan, Jan. 2, 1982; children: Mia Geske Berman, Sarah Geske

Hogan, Kevin Geske Hogan. Student, U. Grenoble, U. Rennes; BA, MA in Tchg., Beloit Coll., 1971; JD, Marquette U., 1975, LLD, 1998, LLD (hon.), 1994; DHL (hon.), Mt. Mary Coll., 1999. Bar: Wis. 1975, U.S. Dist. Ct. (ea. & we. dists.) Wis. 1975, U.S. Supreme Ct. 1978. Tchr. elem. sch., Lake Zurich, Ill., 1970-72; staff atty., chief staff atty. Legal Aid Soc., Milw., 1975-78; asst. prof. law, clin. dir. Law Sch. Marquette U., Milw., 1978-81; hearing examiner Milw. County CETA, Milw., 1980-81; judge Milw. County Circuit Ct., Milw., 1981-93; justice Supreme Ct. Wis., 1993-98; disting. prof. law Marquette U. Law Sch., Milw., 1998—, interim Miles County exec., 2002, interim dean Sch. Law, 2002—03. Dean Wis. Jud. Coll.; mem. faculty Nat. Jud. Coll.; instr. various jud. tng. programs, continuing legal edn. Fellow ABA, mem. Am. Law Inst., Am. Arbitration Assn., Soc. Profls. in Dispute Resolution, Wis. Bar Assn., Wis. Assn. Mediators, Milw. Bar Assn., Nat. Women Judges Assn., 7th Cir. Bar Assn., Alpha Sigma Nu. Roman Catholic. Office: Marquette U Law Sch PO Box 1881 Milwaukee WI 53201-1881

GESKE, NORMAN ALBERT, museum director; b. Sioux City, Iowa, Oct. 31, 1915; s. Albert Geske and Delossa Stone; m. Jane Pope Geske, Sept. 18, 1968. BA, U. Minn., 1938; MA, NYU Inst. Fine Arts, 1953; DFA (hon.), Doane Coll., 1969. Dir. Hennepin County Historical Soc., Mpls., 1940—41; curator Walker Art Ctr., Mpls., 1947—50; asst. dir. U. Nebr. Art Galleries, 1950—53, acting dir., 1953—56; dir. Sheldon Meml Arts Gallery, U. Nebr., Lincoln, 1956—83, dir. emeritus, 1983—. Am. commr. XXXIV Biennale, Venice, Italy, 1968. Author: The Figurative Tradition in Recent American Art, 1968, The Graphic Art of Rudy Pozzatti, 1970, American Sculpture, 1970, Ralph Albert Blakelock, 1847-1919, 1975, Light and Color-Images from New Mexico, 1981, Art and Artists in Nebraska, 1983, Rudy Pozzatti: A Printmaker's Odyssey, 2002; co-author (with Karen Janovy): The American Painting Collection of the Sheldon Memorial Art Gallery, 1988. Bd. dirs. Mus. Nebr. Art, Kearney. Sgt. U.S. Army, 1940—44. Recipient Gov.'s Art award, Nebr. Arts Coun., 1979, Leonard Thiessen award, 2004, Disting. Svc. award, Kearney State Coll., 1980, Mayor's Arts award, City of Lincoln, 1987, Sowers award, Lincoln Found., 1990, Pioneer award, Nebraskaland Found., 2004. Mem.: Nebr. Art Assn., Assn. Art Museum Dirs. (hon.). Democrat. Home: 128 N 113th St Apt 408 Lincoln NE 68508

GESNER, LAWRENCE H., lawyer; b. NYC, 1958; BBA, George Washington U., 1980; JD cum laude, Georgetown U., 1983. Bar: DC 1983. Former ptnr. Arter & Hadden LLP, Washington; ptnr., real estate group Venable LLP, Washington, 2003—. Sr. lead articles editor Law and Policy in Internat. Bus., 1982—83. Mem.: ABA, DC Bar Assn. Office: Venable LLP 575 7th St NW Washington DC 20004 Office Phone: 202-344-4733. Office Fax: 202-344-8300. Business E-Mail: lhgesner@venable.com.

GESSAMAN, DONALD EUGENE, retired government executive; b. Dayton, Ohio, Nov. 11, 1939; s. Stanley Loran and Alma Elizabeth (Tevis) G.; m. Jane Alexander Giles, Oct. 16, 1965; 1 child, William Arthur. BS in Indsl. Mgmt., U. Cin., 1964; MS in Indsl. Engring., Stanford U., 1972. Exec. trainee Office of Sec. of Def., Washington, 1966; with nat security divsn., dep. divsn. chief Office Mgmt. and Budget, Exec. Office of Pres., Washington, 1967-90, dep. assoc. dir., 1990-95; cons. EOP Group, Inc., Washington, 1995—. Office: EOP Group Inc 819 7th St NW Washington DC 20001-3762

GESSAMAN, MARGARET PALMER, mathematician, educator, retired dean; b. Florence, Ariz., Oct. 7, 1934; d. William Lee Sr. and Lillian Maude (Henkle) Palmer; m. Paul Hayden Gessaman, June 11, 1965. BS, Mont. State Coll., 1956, MS, 1965, PhD, 1966. Statistician Fatstock Mktg. Corp., London, 1957-59; ops. researcher Richard, Thomas and Baldwin, Ebbw Vale, South Wales, 1959-60; market researcher Nestle Co., Inc., London, 1960-61; instr. Mont. State U., 1966-67; asst. prof. math. Ithaca Coll., 1967-70; asst. prof., assoc. prof., prof. math. U. Nebr., Omaha, 1970—, chmn. dept. math., computer sci., 1973-80, 98—, dean grad. studies rsch., 1980-93. Cons. grad. and rsch. activities, Coll. Bd., Chgo., 1981-88, Ednl. Testing Svc., Princeton, N.J., 1976-80, various govt. units, univs.; panelist NSF, Washington. Contbr. articles to profl. jours. Program chair Nebr. Commn. United Ministries in Higher Edn., Lincoln, 1976-81, 88-90. Mem. Coun. Grad. Schs. (bd. dirs.), Inst. Math. Stats., Am. Statis. Assn., Grad. Women in Sci.(nat. treas. 1994-95), Fulbright Assn., Mid-Am. State Univs. Assn. (chair 1984-89), Midwestern Assn. Grad. Schs. (chair-elect, chair, past chair 1986-89). Methodist. Avocations: travel, mayan history, cat lore.

GESSEL, GERALD EMERY, minister; b. Oklahoma City, May 8, 1952; s. Benjimen Francions Gessel and Edna Marion Wood; m. Minnie Pearl Buckaloo, July 24, 1971; children: Christopher Charles, David Ray, Jimmy Joe. Diploma in Ministerial, Berean U., 1996. With Fred Jones Mfg., Oklahoma City, 1977; founding pastor Indep. Full Gospel, Oklahoma City, 1982—90; pastor Elm Grove Assembly of God, Muskogee, Okla., 1997—99, Kiowa (Okla.) First Assembly of God, 1999—2001; with McAlester First Assembly, Okla., 2004—. Author: Perfect Soul Winner, 2002, A Healthy Church, 2003, If the Rapture Was Yesterday.

GESSNER, DONALD ROBERT, healthcare consultant; b. Duluth, Minn., Aug. 1, 1941; s. Lester Gessner and H. Viola Johnson; m. Stephanie Marie Dirtzu, Apr. 19, 1977; children: Lael Marie Wilder, D. (Donald) Robert Gessner II, Gayle Kari Cox. Student, U. Wis., Madison, 1959—61; BS in Acctg., U. Minn., 1963. CPA Minn. Lt. U.S. Army Medcial Svc. Corps, Colorado Springs, 1963—64; assoc. Stillman and Oase, CPA, Duluth, Minn., 1964—66; ptnr. Whitsitt, Gessner & Co., Duluth, 1966—73; v.p. PM Fla. East Coast, Inc., Fort Lauderdale, 1973—76; pres. PCI Profl. Consultants, Inc., Fort Lauderdale, 1977—92, D.R. Gessner, Inc., Park City, Utah, 1993—97; v.p., sr. cons. Profl. Mgmt. Milw., Inc., 1997—99; pres. Gessner & Co., Inc., Lecanto, Fla., 1999—. Del. Healthy Fla. Found., Orlando, 2003—03; nat. pres. Soc. of Profl. Bus. Consultants, Chicago, 1990—91; panel mem. Am. Arbitration Assn., Salt Lake City, 1992—97; com. chair, alt. commr. Utah Health Policy Commn., Salt Lake City, 1993—95. Contbr. articles to profl. jours. Mem. Gubernatorial appointment Minn. State Adv. Coun. for Vocat. Edn., St. Paul, 1968—70; candidate US Ho. of Representatives, FL05, Washington, 2002—02; treas., bd. mem. Ind. Sch. Dist. #709, Duluth, Minn., 1970—72; dir. Coral Ridge Ministries, Ft. Lauderdale, 1979—84; pres. Duluth Bus. U., Inc., 1964—73; treas. Lago Mar Country Club, Plantation, Fla., 1986—89; active Am. Nat. Bank, NA, Ft. Lauderdale, 1985—89. Mem.: AICPA, Inst. Cert. Healthcare Bus. Cons. (cert.), Minn. Soc. CPAs, Nat. Assn. Healthcare Cons. (life; pres. f/k/a soc. prof. bus. cons. 1990—91), Chi Psi. Avocations: golf, skiing. Home: 3399 W Pebble Beach Court Lecanto FL 34461-9303 Personal E-mail: drgessner@earthlink.net.

GEST, HOWARD, microbiologist, educator; b. London, Oct. 15, 1921; m. Janet Olin, Sept. 8, 1941 (dec. 1994); children: Theodore Olin, Michael Henry, Donald Evan; m. Virginia Davies Ollis, Jan. 6, 1998. BA in Bacteriology, UCLA, 1942; postgrad. in biology (Univ. fellow), Vanderbilt U., 1942; PhD in Microbiology (Am. Cancer Soc. fellow), Washington U., St. Louis, 1949. Rsch. asst. Metall. Lab. (Manhattan Project) U. Chgo., 1943; from jr. to assoc. chemist Clinton Labs. (Manhattan Project), Oak Ridge, 1943-46; Instr. microbiology Western Res. U. Sch. Medicine, 1949-51, asst. prof. microbiology, 1951-53, asso. prof., 1953-59; USPHS spl. research fellow in biology Calif. Inst. Tech., 1956-57; prof. Henry Shaw Sch. Botany, Washington U., 1959-64, dept. zoology, 1964-66; prof. Ind. U., Bloomington, 1966-78, disting. prof. microbiology, 1978—, disting. prof. emeritus microbiology, 1987—, adj. prof. history and philosophy of sci., 1983—, chmn. dept. microbiology, 1966-70, disting. faculty rsch. lectr., 1987. NSF sr. postdoctoral fellow Nat. Inst. Med. Rsch., London, 1965—66; Guggenheim fellow Imperial Coll., London, U. Stockholm, U. Tokyo; vis. prof. dept. biophysics and biochemistry U. Tokyo and Japan Soc. Promotion Sci., 1970; mem. study sect. bacteriology and mycology NIH, 1966—68, chmn. study sect. microbial chemistry, 1968—69, mem. study sect. microbial physiology and genetics, 1988—90; mem. com. microbiol. problems of man in extended space flight Nat. Acad. Scis.-NRC, 1967—69; Guggenheim fellow Imperial Coll., London, UCLA, 1979—80; 1st H.D. Peck lectr. U. Ga., 1994; Cummings lectr. Bucknell U., 1997. Fellow: AAAS, Am. Acad. Microbiology; mem.: Am. Acad. Arts and Scis., Am. Soc. Microbiology (hon.). Office: Ind U Dept Biology Bloomington IN 47405 Office Phone: 812-855-9612. Business E-Mail: hgest@bio.indiana.edu. E-mail: gest@indiana.edu.

GEST, HOWARD DAVID, lawyer; b. Bergenfield, NJ, Jan. 24, 1952; m. Lucy Acevedo; 1 child, Aaron. AB in Econs., U. Calif., Berkeley, 1974; JD, Hastings Coll., 1977. Bar: Calif. 1977. Staff atty. U.S. Ct. Appeals (9th cir.), San Francisco, 1977-78; asst. U.S. atty. Cen. Dist. Calif., L.A., 1978-83; ptnr. Sidley & Austin, L.A., 1983-99, Burhenn & Gest, L.A., 2000—. Office: Burhenn & Gest LLP Ste 2200 624 S Grand Ave Los Angeles CA 90017 Office Phone: 213-688-7715. Business E-Mail: hgest@burhenngest.com.

GEST, KATHRYN WATERS, public relations executive; b. Boston, Mar. 20, 1947; d. Mendal and Anna Waters; m. Theodore O. Gest, May 28, 1972; 1 child, David Mendal. BS, Northwestern U., 1969; MS, Columbia U., 1970. Reporter The Patriot-Ledger, Quincy, Mass., 1968; writer Europe desk Voice of Am., Washington, 1969; reporter St. Louis Globe-Democrat, 1970-77, Congl. Quar., Washington, 1977-78, news editor, 1978-80, asst. mng. editor, 1980-83, mng. editor, 1983-87; St. Louis corr. Time Mag., 1975-77, The Christian Sci. Monitor, 1976-77; press sec. to Sen. William S. Cohen, Washington, 1987-96; chmn., U.S. del. Internat. Labor Orgn. Tripartite Meeting on Conditions of Employment and Work of Journalists, Geneva, 1990; exec. v.p., dir. internat. issues Powell Tate, 1996—. Election observer Nat. Dem. Inst., Albania, 1996, Azerbaijan, 2003, Ukraine, 04. Recipient award for investigative reporting Inland Daily Press Assn., 1975 Bd. dirs. Nat. Press Found. Soc. Profl. Journalists, Women's Fgn. Policy Group, Internat. Women's Media Fund, Nat. Press Club. Office: Powell Tate 700 13th St NW Washington DC 20005-6618 E-mail: kgest@aol.com.

GESTELAND, TRACELYN K., vocalist, music educator; d. James S and Karen L Magyar; m. Thor H Gesteland, Dec. 23, 2000. MusB, U. Wis., Stevens Point, 1994; MusM, Chgo. Coll. of Performing Arts at Roosevelt U., 1997—99; D of Musical Arts, U. Houston, 2003. Lic. Teacher for Choral and General Music K-12 Wis., 1994. Choral condr. Chgo. Children's Choir, 1999—2003; tchg. fellow in voice U. of Houston, 2003—. Artistic dir. Vocal Arts Group, Houston, 2003—. Singer: (opera performances) Atlantic Coast Opera Festival. Recipient Hon. Mention in Advanced Vocal Competition, Nat. Assn. of Teachers of Singing (Ill. regional chpt.), 2000. Mem.: Am. Guild of Musical Artists. Personal E-mail: tracelyn@gesteland.net.

GESTON, MARK SYMINGTON, lawyer; b. Atlantic City, N.J., June 20, 1946; s. John Charles and Mary Tobiatha (Simmington) G.; m. Gayle Francis Howard, June 12, 1971 (div. Aug. 1972); m. Marijke Havinga, Aug. 14, 1976; children: Camille LaCroix, Robert L. LaCroix, Emily S. Geston. AB in History (with honors), Kenyon Coll., 1968; JD, NYU, 1971. Bar: Idaho, U.S. Ct. Appeals (9th cir.). With Eberle and Berlin, 1971—2003; atty. Stoel Rives LLP, Boise, Idaho, 2003—. Author: Lords of the Starship, 1967, Out of the Mouth of the Dragon, 1969, The Day Star, 1972, The Seige of Wonder, 1975, Mirror to the Sky, 1992, The Stronghold If, 1973; contbr. stories to Amazing Stories, Fantasy and Sci. Fiction. Recipient Kenyon Rev. prize for achievement in lit., Kenyon Coll., 1968; named Root-Tilden fellow NYU, 1968-71. Mem. Idaho State Bar Assn., Phi Beta Kappa. Avocation: writing. Office: Stoel Rives LLP 101 S Capitol Blvd Boise ID 83702 Office Phone: 208-387-4291. Business E-Mail: msgeston@stoel.com.

GESTRICH, THOMAS E., paper company executive; b. Pitts., 1946; Attended, U. Pitts., 1972. V.p., gen. mgr., beverage packaging Internat. Paper Co., Memphis, 1999—2001, sr. v.p., consumer packaging, 2001—. Office: Internat Paper Co 2400 Poplar Ave Memphis TN 38197

GESUALDI, LOUIS J., social sciences educator; b. Stamford, Conn., May 22, 1955; s. John and Catherine Pelli Gesualdi. BS in biology, BA in anthropology, U. Conn., 1978; MA in Sociology, St. John's U., 1980; PhD in Sociology, Fordham U., 1988. Tchr. Immaculata H.S., N.Y.C., 1980—82; adj. instr. Cathedral Coll., Queens, NY, 1983—86; instr. sociology dept. St. John's U., Jamaica, NY, 1986—90, asst. prof., 1992—2003. Author: The Italian Immigrants of Connecticut, 1997, (articles) various publications, 1997—2000. Mem. Human Rights Coun. of Queens, 1988—90. Recipient Assoc. Calandra scholar, Calandra Italian Am. Inst., 1998—2003, Hibernian Rsch. award, Cushwa Ctr. Notre Dame U., 1994. Mem.: Acad. Criminal Justice, Am. Sociol. Assn., Am. Italian Hist. Assoc. Office: St John's U 8000 Utopia Pkwy Jamaica NY 11439 Office Phone: 718-990-7435. Business E-Mail: gesualdl@stjohns.edu.

GESWEIN, GREGORY T., electronic company executive; married; 2 children. BBA, MBA in Fin., U. Cin. V.p., corp. contr., corp. treas. Mead Corp., Dayton, Ohio; sr. v.p., CFO Pioneer-Standard Electronics, Inc., Cleve., Diebold, Inc., North Canton, Ohio, 2000—. Office: Diebold Inc 5995 Mayfair Rd North Canton OH 44720-8077

GETCHELL, CHARLES WILLARD, JR., lawyer, publisher; b. LA, May 29, 1929; s. Charles Willard and Katharine (Fitch) G.; m. Angela Winthrop, Sept. 16, 1961; children: Katharine Chisholm, Emily Erskine, Sarah Fields. AB, Stanford U., 1951, JD, 1954. Bar: Calif. 1955, Mass. 1979, U.S. Dist. Ct. (no. dist.) Calif. 1960, Mass. 1983, U.S. Ct. Appeals, 9th cir. 1960, U.S. Supreme Ct. 1985. Atty. Air Materiel Force, Chateauroux, France, 1958-59; asst. U.S. atty. No. Dist. Calif., San Francisco, 1960-61; asst. mgr. Citibank, N.Y.C., Brussels, 1961-68; v.p. Wood Struthers & Winthrop, N.Y.C., Brussels, 1969-77; ptnr. Gray, Wendell, Chalmers & Dahlen, Boston, 1981-87; pub. The Ipswich (Mass.) Press, 1980—. Pres. Yorkham Timber Co., Inc., 1986-2000; chmn. Sabre Europe (Belgium); sec. Sabre Found., 1995—; sr. fellow Salzburg Seminar, 1997—. Translator: European Monetary Unity: For Whose Benefit? (Pascal Salin), 1980; contbr. articles and poetry to newspapers and mags. Mem. steering com. Bilderberg Meetings, The Hague, 1980—85; trustee Shore Country Day Sch., 1978—84; bd. dirs. Salzburg Seminar, 1985—89. Lt. j.g. USNR, 1955—58. Mem. Belgian Am, Ednl. Found.; fellow Mass. Hist. Soc., Tavern Club. Republican. Office: Ipswich Press PO Box 291 Ipswich MA 01938-0291

GETCHES, DAVID HARDING, lawyer, educator, dean; b. Abington, Pa., Aug. 17, 1942; s. George Winslow Getches and Ruth Erskine (Harding) Fossette; m. Ann Marks, June 26, 1964; children: Matthew, Catherine, Elizabeth. AB, Occidental Coll., 1964; JD, U. So. Calif., 1967. Bar: Calif. 1968, U.S. Supreme Ct. 1971, D.C. 1972, Colo. 1973. Assoc. Luce, Forward, Hamilton & Scripps, San Diego, 1967-69; directing atty. Calif. Indian Legal Services, Escondido, 1969-70; founding dir. Native Am. Rights Fund, Boulder, Colo., 1970-76; ptnr. Getches & Greene, Boulder, 1976-78; prof. U. Colo. Sch. Law, Boulder, 1978—, dean, 2003—; exec. dir. Colo. Dept. Natural Resources, Denver, 1983-87. Ptnr. MB Land Co., Centro Bldg. Devel. Co. Author: Water Law in a Nutshell, 1997; co-author: Cases and Materials on Federal Indian Law, 2005, Water Resources Management, 5th edit., 2002; contbr. articles to profl. jours. Bd. trustees Rocky Mountain Mineral Law Fedn. Mem. Wilderness Soc. (governing coun.), Defenders of Wildlife (bd. dirs.). Democrat. Office: U Colo Sch Law Boulder CO 80309-0401 Office Phone: 303-492-3084. Business E-Mail: lawdean@colorado.edu.

GETER, JENNIFER L., psychologist; b. Washington, Mar. 12, 1970; d. Robert James and Delores Marie Geter. BA, Speluan Coll., 1992; PsyD, Nova Southeastern U., 1997. Lic. clin. psychologist Bd. Examiners in Psychology/Tenn., 2002. Lead children and youth therapist, case mgr. Midtown Mental Health Ctr., Memphis, 1998—2003; clin. psychologist NIA Therapy Svcs., Memphis, 1999—2003; sch. psychologist Memphis City Schs., 2003—; owner, clin. psychologist Imani Psychol. Svcs., Memphis, 2003—. Singer: (church choir) Greater Cmty. Temple Voices, (gospel choir) Marc Cooper and Friends and Miami Mass Choir. Pres. Greater Cmty. Temple Voices, Memphis, 2002—05. Post Doctoral fellow, U. Tenn., 1997—98. Mem.: APA (assoc.). Mem. Church Of God In Christ. Avocations: music, basketball, swimming, travel. Office: Imani Psychol Svcs Ste 709 1407 Union Ave Memphis TN 38104 Office Phone: 901-726-5200. Personal E-mail: psyd4kids@aol.com.

GETER, RODNEY KEITH, plastic surgeon; b. Baton Rouge, La., Nov. 13, 1946; s. Argless William and Jewel Alma (Rudolph) G. BA in Chemistry with honors, U. Mo., 1975, MD, 1979. Resident in gen. surgery U. Mo., Columbia, 1979-83, fellow in microvascular surgery, 1983-84, resident in plastic surgery, 1984-86; pvt. practice Springfield (Mo.) Clinic, 1986—. Chmn. dept. surgery St. John's Regional Health Ctr., Springfield, 1992-94, chmn. two hosp. coms., 1994-97; v.p. med. staff St. John's Hosp., 1996-97, chmn. plastic surgery dept., 2000-02. Contbr. articles to profl. jours. Pres. Springfield Music Found., 1989—; leader troop 210 Boy Scouts Am., Springfield, 1995-98. Sgt. Spl. Forces, U.S. Army, 1968-71, Vietnam. Mem. Am. Soc. Plastic and Reconstructive Surgeons, Greene County Med. Soc., Mo. State Med. Assn., Phi Beta Kappa, Phi Lambda Upsilon. Avocations: playing keyboard in band, fishing, backpacking. Office: St Johns Clinic Plastic Surgery 1229 E Seminole Ste 340 Springfield MO 65804 Office Phone: 417-820-9330.

GETHERS, PETER (RUSSELL ANDREWS), writer, publishing executive; b. N.Y.C., Apr. 10, 1953; s. Steven and Judy (Harmatz) G. Student, U. Calif., Berkeley, U. London, UCLA. Exec. editor Bantam Books, N.Y.C., 1974-80; pub., editorial dir., v.p. Villard Books, N.Y.C., 1983-91; editor Random House, Inc., N.Y.C., 1980-83, v.p., editor-at-large, 1991—. Author: The Dandy, 1979, Getting Blue, 1987, The Cat Who Went to Paris, 1991, (as Russell Andrews): Gideon, 1999, Icarus, 2001, Aphrodite, 2003, Midas, 2005. Mem. Handgun Control, Inc., Klanwatch. Mem. Writers Guild Am., ACLU. Mailing: c/o Author Mail Mysterious Press-Warner 1271 Ave of the Americas New York NY 10020*

GETIS, ARTHUR, geography educator; b. Phila., July 6, 1934; s. Samuel J. and Sophie Getis; m. Judith M. Marckwardt, July 23, 1961; children: Hilary Hope Tarazi, Victoria Lynn, Anne Patterson Tibbetts. BS, Pa. State U., 1956, MS, 1958; PhD, U. Wash., 1961. Asst. instr. geography U. Wash., 1960-61; asst. prof. Mich. State U., 1961-63; faculty Rutgers U., New Brunswick, N.J., 1963-77, prof. geography, 1969-77, dir. grad. programs in geography, 1970-73, chmn. New Brunswick geography dept., 1971-73; prof. geography U. Ill., Urbana-Champaign, 1977-90, San Diego State U., 1990—, doctoral program coord., 1990-92, Stephen/Mary Birch Found. endowed chair geog. studies, 1992—2004, disting. prof. geography, 2004—, Albert W. Johnson univ. rsch. lectr., 1995; head dept. U. Ill., 1977-83, dir. Sch. Social Scis., 1983-84; centennial fellow Pa. State U., 1996; A. Robinson lectr. Ohio State U., 1999. Vis. lectr. Bristol U., Eng., 1966-67, UCLA, summers 1968, 74, U. B.C., 1969; vis. prof. Princeton U., 1971-74; vis. disting. prof. San Diego State U., 1989; mem. Regional Sci. Research Group, Harvard U., 1970; panelist NSF, 1981-83 Author: (with B. Boots) Models of Spatial Processes, 1978, Point Pattern Analysis, 1988, (with J. Getis and J.D. Fellmann) Geography, 1981, Human Geography, 7th edit., 2001, Introduction to Geography, 9th edit., 2004, (edited with J. Getis) The United States and Canada, 1995, 2d edit., 2001, The Tyranny of Data, 1996, (edited with M.M. Fischer) Recent Developments in Spatial Analysis, 1997, (with J. Mur and H. Zoller) Spatial Econometrics and Spatial Statistics; editor-in chief Jour. Geographical Systems, 1992—; contbg. editor, assoc. editor: Jour. Geography, 1972-74; mem. editl. bd. Nat. Geog. Rsch., 1984-90, Rsch. and Exploration, 1991-95, Geog. Analysis, 1991—, Papers in Regional Sci., 1999-02, Annals of Regional Sci., 1999—, Regional Rsch. Inst., 2003—; contbr. articles to profl. jours. Mem. Urbana Zoning Bd. Appeals, 1980-84; co-pres. Univ. High Sch. Parent-Faculty Orgn., 1982-83; bd. dirs. Univ. Consortium for Geog. Info. Scis., 1997-2004, pres.-elect, 2000-02, pres. 2002-03. Rutgers U. faculty fellow, 1970; East-West Center sr. fellow, 1974; NSF grantee, 1983-85, 1992-94, 99—, NIH grantee, 1999—; recipient Walter Isard award N.Am. Regional Sci. Coun., 1997. Fellow Western Regional Sci. Assn. (bd. dirs. 1992-97, pres. 1998-99); mem. Assn. Am. Geographers (grantee 1964-65, vis. scientist 1970-72, chair math. models and quantitative methods splty. group 1991-92, recipient award for disting. scholarship, 2002), Regional Sci. Assn. (pres. N.E. sect. 1973-74, bd. dirs. 1998-2004), Internat. Inst. Brit. Geographers, Internat. Geog. Union (sec. commn. math. models 1988-96), Sigma Xi. Home: 5135 Jumilla St San Diego CA 92124-1503 Office: San Diego State U Dept Geography San Diego CA 92182 Business E-Mail: arthur.getis@sdsu.edu.

GETMAN, WILLARD ETHERIDGE, lawyer, mediator; b. Cin., Jan. 31, 1949; s. Frank Newton and Dorothy Dill (Etheridge) G. BA, U. N.C., 1971; JD, Stetson U., 1974. Bar: Fla. 1974, N.Y. 1985, U.S. Dist. Ct. (so. dist.) Fla. 1975, U.S. Dist. Ct. (mid. dist.) Fla. 1996, U.S. Supreme Ct. 1997; County Ct. cert. mediator. Assoc., Law Offices John M. Callaway, Lake Worth, Fla., 1974-75; sole practice, West Palm Beach, Fla., 1976-80, Boynton Beach, Fla., 1980-93, Jacksonville, Fla., 1993—. mem./agt. Attys' Title Ins. Fund, Inc., Fla., Atty's. Real Property Coun. NE Fla., Inc. Mem. ABA, N.Y. State Bar Assn., Assn. Trial Lawyers Am., Fla. Bar (trust law com. 1975-76, summary rules com. 1980-84, probate and guardianship rules com. 1981-82), Jacksonville Bar Assn., Estate Planning Coun. N.E. Fla., Cedar Lake Club (Clayville, N.Y.), Trailside Lions, Elks, Moose, Masons, Shriners, Delta Theta Phi. Republican. Presbyterian. Home and Office: 567 Lazy Meadow Dr E Jacksonville FL 32225-3428 also: 38 Morgan St PO Box 477 Ilion NY 13357-0477

GETNICK, NEIL VICTOR, lawyer; b. Bklyn., Oct. 28, 1953; s. Irving Murray and Zita (Ellman) G.; m. Margaret Joan Finerty, May 21, 1978. BA in Govt. magna cum laude, Cornell U., 1975, JD, 1978. Bar: N.Y. 1979, U.S. Dist. Ct. (so. and ea. dists.) N.Y. 1983. Asst. dist. atty. trial divsn. N.Y. County, N.Y.C., 1978-81, asst. dist. atty. frauds bur., 1981-82; ptnr. Getnick & Getnick, N.Y., 1983—. Mem. Criminal Justice Act panel U.S. Dist. Ct. for So. Dist. N.Y., N.Y.C., 1984-89. Editor-in-chief: Civil Prosecution News, 1994-96. Recipient Pub. Citizenship award N.Y. Pub. Interest Rsch. Group, 1977. Mem. ABA (litigation and criminal law sects.), N.Y. State Bar Assn. (exec. com. comml. and fed. litigation sect., chair com. on civil prosecution), Assn. of Bar of City of N.Y., N.Y. County Lawyers Assn., Internat. Assn. Ind. Pvt. Sector Inspectors Gen. (pres. 1994—), Internat. Assn. of Ind. Pvt. Sector Inspectors Gen. (pres. 1994—). Office: Getnick & Getnick Rockefeller Ctr 620 5th Ave 4th Flr New York NY 10020-2457

GETS, LISPBETH ELLA, educational administrator; b. Jhelum, Pakistan, Mar. 18, 1931; arrived in USA, 1952, naturalized, 1955; s. Henry Ellis and Constance Selina (Bodell) Glenn; m. Terence Mathew Gets, Jan. 19, 1952; children: Erik Charles, Alison Beth, Hugh Malcolm, Adrienne Lea. AA, Santa Fe Cmty. Coll., 1973—74; BA (hon.), U. Fla., 1976; postgrad, 1977—89, MS, 1989. Cert. ednl. specialist Fla., 1989. Cert. adminstr., supr., Fla. Editl. asst. John Trundell Pub., London, 1950—52; exec. secretarial positions, various co. Chgo., Ft. Smith, Ark. and Jamestown, NY, 1952—58; tchr. spl. edn. Buchholz HS, Gainesville, Fla., 1976—81; asst. prin. Sidney Lanier Sch., Gainesville, 1981—83, 1987—2003; prin. Monarch Ctr. for Exceptional Students, Gainesville, 1983—87; inclusion specialist Alachua County Pub. Schs., 2003—. Named Tchr. of Yr., Gatorland chpt. Coun. for Exceptional Children, 1981. Mem.: Fla. Assn. Exceptional Sch. Adminstrs. (state chmn. 1988—90), Coun. Exceptional Children (chpt. pres. 1983—), Phi Delta Kappa. Democrat. Episcopalian. Home: 4601 NW 13th Ave Gainesville FL 32605-4534 E-mail: jblg31@aol.com.

GETTELFINGER, RON, labor union administrator; b. 1945; m. Judy Gettelfinger; 2 children. Grad., Ind. U. Mem. Local 862 United Auto, Aerospace, and Agrl., 1964—, dir. Region 3, 1992—98, v.p., 1998—2002, pres., 2002—. Office: UAW Solidarity House 8000 E Jefferson Detroit MI 48214 Office Phone: 313-926-5000.

GETTELMAN, ROBIN CLAIRE, media specialist; b. Milw., Jan. 6, 1952; d. Robert Otto and Virginia Mae (Proffit) G.; m. Ted Bayard Johnson, Sept. 25, 1976 (div. Jan. 1985). BS in Secondary Edn., U. Wis., 1974; MA in

Librarianship, U. Denver, 1975. Dir. instructional material ctr. Cripple Creek (Colo.)-Victor Sch. Dist., 1975-81; dir. Franklin Ferguson Meml. Libr., Cripple Creek, 1975-81; dir. instructional materials ctr. D.C. Everest Jr. High Sch., Schofield, Wis., 1981—; dist. media coord. D.C. Everest Area Schs., Schofield, 1988—. Reviewer Sch. Evaluation Consortium, Madison, Wis., 1986, Marshfield, Wis., 1987, reviewer, coord., Ashland, Wis., 1989; chair media com. D.C. Everest Area Schs., Schofield, 1988—; mem. Wis. Dept. Pub. Instrn. Task Force, 1998. Recipient Svc. award of the Yr., Franklin Ferguson Meml. Libr., 1981. Mem. Wis. Sch. Libr. Media Assn. (chair profl. devel. com. 1983, chair 1984, 85 confs. exec. bd. 1985), Wis. Ednl. Media Assn., Wausau Area Jaycees (community dir. 1986-87, chair cancer ski-a-thon 1987, chair 4th of July concessions 1989, Project Chmn. of the Month 1987), Sierra Club, Friends of Libr. Methodist. Avocations: skiing, physical fitness, walking, photography, travel. Home: 2405 Petunia Rd Wausau WI 54401-9351 Office: DC Everest Jr High Sch 1000 Machmueller St Schofield WI 54476-3811 E-mail: rgettelman@dce.k12.wi.us.

GETTIER, EDMUND LEE, III, retired humanities educator; b. Balt., Oct. 31, 1927; s. Edmund Lee and Clara Frances (Schuele) Gettier; m. Astrid Elizabeth Pfeiffer, Mar. 1957 (div. 1965); children: Evan E.(dec.), Elizabeth L., Edmund L. IV, Sheila A., David B.; m. Lucia Milda Mingela, July 8, 1966; children: Daina N., Jonathan M. BA, Johns Hopkins U., 1949; PhD, Cornell U., 1961. Instr. to asst. prof. philosophy Wayne State U., Detroit, 1957-67; assoc. prof. to prof. U. Mass., Amherst, 1967—2001, prof. emeritus, 2001—. With U.S. Army, 1953—55. Mellon Postdoctoral fellow, U. Pitts., 1964—65. Home: 77 Weatherwood Rd Amherst MA 01002-9802 Office: U Mass Dept Philosophy Amherst MA 01003 Office Phone: 413-545-0878. Business E-Mail: gettier@philos.umass.edu.

GETTIG, MARTIN WINTHROP, retired mechanical engineer; b. South Bend, Ind., Nov. 8, 1939; s. Joseph H. and Esther (Scheppele) G.; m. Nancy Caroline Buchannan, June 25, 1960 (dec. 1965). Student, Pa. State U., 1957-60, 89—. Process engr. Gettig Tech. Inc., Spring Mills, Pa., 1960-88. Inventor ultralight non-solid state miniature ignition systems for model aircraft employing small two cycle spark ignition engines. Staff sgt. Pa. N.G., 1961-67. Mem.: NRA, Acad. Model Awronautics, Soc. Antique Modelers and Model Airplanes, Model Engine Collectors Assn., Delta Phi. Republican. Lutheran. Home: PO Box 85 Boalsburg PA 16827-0085

GETTLER, BENJAMIN, lawyer, manufacturing executive; b. Louisville, Sept. 16, 1925; s. Herbert and Gertrude (Cohen) G.; m. Deliaan Angel, Mar. 1972; children: Jorian, Thomas, Gail, John, Benjamin. BA in Econs. with high honors, U. Cin., 1945; JD (Frankfurter scholar), Harvard U., 1948. Bar: Ohio 1949, U.S. Supreme Ct. 1955. Ptnr. Brown & Gettler, Cin., 1951—73, Gettler, Katz & Buckley, Cin., 1973—87; chmn. bd. Am. Controlled Industries Inc., Cin., 1973—86; chmn. bd. dirs., pres. Colorpac Inc., Franklin, Ohio, 1973—86; chmn. bd., pres. Vulcan Internat. Corp., Wilmington, Del., 1988—, Vulcan Corp., Clarksville, Tenn., 1988—; chmn. exec. com. Valley Industries, Inc., Cin., 1973—86; vice chmn. bd. Cin. So. R.R., 1987—91; chmn. bd. Trusthouse, Inc., Cin., 1987—. Chmn. bd. dirs. ACI Internat., Inc., Cin., 1990—; spl. counsel U. Cin., 1975-77, trustee, 1994-2003, vice chmn. bd., 1999-2000, chmn., 2000-2002; bd. dirs. PNC Bank, Ohio, 1988-96. Chmn. bd. Jewish Inst. Nat. Security Affairs, 1994-98, chmn. policy com., 1998—; chmn. Cin. Bonds for Israel, 1969; chmn. Nat. Israel Commn., Nat. Jewish Cmty. Rels. Adv. Coun., 1981-82; mem. Ohio, Ky. and Ind. Mass Transit Policy Com., 1970-75; pres. Cin. Jewish Cmty. Rels. Coun., 1978-80; trustee Jewish Hosp. Cin., 1978-92, chmn., 1991-92; chmn. Midwest Hosp. Sys., Inc., 1987-90, 92-93; pres. Jewish Found. Cin., 1995-99, chmn., 1999-2002; trustee Health Alliance Greater Cin., 1995-96, 2000-2001; chmn. Cin. Coalition for Reagan, 1980; co-chmn. Hamilton County Reagan Bush Campaign Ohio, 1984; chmn. Rep. Fin. Com., Hamilton County, 1991-92; mem. Hamilton County Rep. Policy Com., 1990—; trustee Rockwern Found., 1998—; trustee S.W. Ohio Regional Transit Authority, 2003—, chmn., 2004—. Capt. U.S. Army, 1955-56. Mem. ABA, Cin. Bar Assn., Shoe Last Mfrs. Assn. (pres. 1984-85), Footwear Industries Am. (bd. dirs. 1989-2000), Phi Beta Kappa, Omicron Delta Kappa. Clubs: Coldstream Country, Harvard. Office: Vulcan Corp 30 Garfield Pl Ste 1040 Cincinnati OH 45202-4322

GETTO, ERNEST JOHN, lawyer; b. Dubois, Pa., May 24, 1944; s. Ernest F. and Olga (Gagliardi) G.; m. Judith Payne, Aug. 19, 1967; children: Matthew Payne, Christopher Ernest, Sarah Elizabeth. BA, Cornell U., 1966; JD, Vanderbilt U., 1969. Bar: NY 1970, Calif. 1973. Assoc. Simpson Thacher & Bartlett, NYC, 1969-73; from assoc. to ptnr. Kadison, Pfaelzer, Woodard, Quinn & Rossi, LA, 1973-80; ptnr. Latham & Watkins LLP, San Francisco & LA, 1980—, chair litig. dept., 1991—95. Past bd. dirs. Calif. Pediatric and Family Med. Ctr., LA, Children's Hosp. of LA Rsch. Inst. Fellow Am. Coll. Trial Lawyers; mem. ABA, Calif. Bar Assn., LA Bar Assn., NY State Bar Assn., Assn. Bus. Trial Lawyers, Jonathan Club, Wilshire Country Club. Republican. Roman Catholic. Office: Latham & Watkins Ste 2000 505 Montgomery St San Francisco CA 94111-2562 Office Phone: 415-395-8189. Office Fax: 415-395-8095. E-mail: ernie.getto@lw.com.

GETTY, ESTELLE (ESTELLE SCHER), actress; b. NYC, July 25, 1923; m. Arthur Gettleman, Dec. 21, 1946; children: Barry, Carl. Student, New Sch. for Social Rsch., Herbert Berghof Studios; studied with Gerald Russak. Actress: numerous stage prodns. on and off Broadway including Death of a Salesman, The Glass Menagerie, All My Sons, 6 Rms Rv Vu, Blithe Spirit, Arsenic and Old Lace, I Don't Know Why I'm Screaming, Widows and Children, Torch Song Trilogy, 1981-83; (films) Team-Mates, 1978, Tootsie, 1982, Deadly Force, 1983, Mask, 1985, Mannequin, 1987, Stop! Or My Mom Will Shoot, 1992, Stuart Little, 1999, The Million Dollar Kid, 2000; (TV movies) No Man's Land, 1984, Victims for Victims: The Teresa Saldana Story, 1984, Copacabana, 1985, A Match Made in Heaven, 1997, The Sissy Duckling, 1999; (TV series) The Golden Girls, 1985-92, (Emmy award for outstanding supporting actress in a comedy series, 1988, Golden Globe award for best performance by an actress in a TV series - comedy/musical, 1986, Am. Comedy award for funniest supporting female performer in a TV series, 1991, 92), Golden Palace, 1992-93, Empty Nest, 1994-95; author: If I Knew Then What I Know Now...So What?, 1988. ret. 2000.

GETTYS, THOMAS WIGINGTON, medical researcher; BS in Biology, Lander Coll., 1978; PhD in Nutrition, Clemson U., 1984. Grad. rsch. asst. animal sci. dept. Coll. Agr. Clemson (S.C.) U., 1979—84; rsch. assoc. Howard Hughes Med. Inst., Dept. Molecular Physiology and Biophysics Vanderbilt U. Sch. of Medicine, Nashville, 1985—87; rsch. assoc. divsn. gastroenterology, dept. medicine Duke U. Med. Ctr., Durham, NC, 1987—90, rsch. asst. prof. divsn. gastroenterology, dept. medicine, 1990—, rsch. asst. prof. dept. cell biology, 1992—93; assoc. prof. medicine Med. U. S.C., Charleston, 1993—, assoc. prof. biochemistry and molecular biology, 1995—, prof. medicine, 2000—; prof., chief exptl. obesity divsn. Pennington Biomed. Rsch. Ctr., Baton Rouge. Contbr. articles to profl. jours., chapters to books. Recipient Rsch. award, Am. Diabetes Assn., 1996; fellow predoctoral rsch., Clemson U., 1981—82; grantee, NIH, 1990, 1994, 1996, 1998, USDA, 1997, 2000. Mem.: Am. Soc. Biochemistry and Molecular Biology, Sigma Xi. Office: Pennington Biomed Rsch Ctr 6400 Perkins Rd Baton Rouge LA 70808

GETZ, BERT ATWATER, investment company executive; b. Chgo., May 7, 1937; s. George Fulmer Jr. and Olive Cox (Atwater) G.; m. Sandra Maclean, July 17, 1958; children: Lynn Getz, George F., Bert A. Jr. BSBA, U. Mich., 1959. V.p. Globe Corp., Scottsdale, Ariz., 1960-74, pres., bd. dirs., 1974—, CEO, 1992—. Bd. dirs. Bank of Am., Ill., Dean Foods Co., Franklin Park, Ill., Ameritas Life Ins. Corp., Lincoln, bd. trustees, Mayo Found., Rochester (chmn. 2002—). Bd. dirs. Western Golf Assn., Golf, Ill., Ind. U. Found., Bloomington; chmn. bd. govs. Merit Club, Libertyville, Ill.; trustee Lawrenceville (N.J.) Sch., 1972—, pres. bd. dirs. 1984-90, trustee emeritus, 1990; trustee Ariz. Cmty. Found., Phoenix, 1978—, chmn. bd. dirs., 1981-89, chmn. emeritus, 1989. Mem. Phoenix Thunderbirds, Paradise Valley Country Club, John Gardiners Tennis Ranch, Merit Club, Sigma Chi, Theta Theta. Republican. Episcopalian. Avocations: tennis, golf. Home: 6335 W Highway 120 Libertyville IL 60048-9788 Office: Globe Corp 6730 N Scottsdale Rd Ste 250 Scottsdale AZ 85253-4416

GETZ, MELISSA B., secondary school educator; b. Balt., May 26, 1969; d. Stanley (adoptive father) and Kathy Getz. BS, Va. Poly. Inst. and State U., 1991; MS, U. Calif., Davis, 1994; tchg. cert., Calif. State U., Sacramento, 1995. Tchr. Berkeley (Calif.) H.S., 1995-96; sci. tchr. Tennyson H.S., Hayward, Calif., 1996—. Cluster leader, East Bay (Calif.) Biotech. Edn. Partnership, 1999-2002; girls tennis coach, Tennyson H.S., 1997-99, Sci. Explorations Club advisor, 2000-01. Bd. dirs. Bridgewater Homeowners Assn., Albany, Calif., 1999—. Mem. ASCD, Nat. Assn. Biology Tchrs. (life), Assn. Women in Sci. (Sacramento Valley and East Bay chpts.), Nat. Sci. Tchrs. Assn., Calif. Sci. Tchrs. Assn., Phi Beta Kappa. Home: 545 Pierce St # 1208 Albany CA 94706 Office: Tennyson H S 27035 Whitman St Hayward CA 94544 E-mail: ntropi@aol.com.

GETZ, MORTON ERNEST, medical facility director, gastroenterologist; b. Bklyn., May 22, 1930; s. Jacob Michael and Regina (Kohn) G.; m. Carol Washer, Aug. 12, 1956; children: Jacob Michael, Deborah Etta. AB, Emory U., 1950; MS, Purdue U., 1952; MD, Wake Forest U., 1956. Intern Jackson Meml. Hosp., Miami, Fla., 1956-57, resident in medicine, 1957-58; sr. surgeon NIH, Atlanta and Bethesda, Md., 1958-60; chief resident in medicine Jackson Meml. Hosp., 1960; NIH fellow in gastroenterology U. Miami, 1960-61; pvt. practice internal medicine and gastroenterology Coral Gables, Fla. Mem. courtesy staff South Miami Hosp., Bapt. Hosp., Drs. Hosp.; attending physician Cedars Med. Ctr. Contbr. articles to profl. jours. With USPHS, 1958-60. Mem. AMA, Am. Soc. Internal Medicine, Internat. Hospice Physicians, Am. Assn. Hospice and Palliative Medicine, Nat. Coun. Hospice Profls., Miami Fla. Gastroenterologic Soc., Dade County Soc. Internal Medicine, So. Med. Assn., Fla. Med. Assn., Dade County Med. Assn., Ind. Acad. Scis., N.C. Acad. Sci., Phi Rho Sigma. Democrat. Jewish. Avocations: art collecting, fishing. Office: Douglas Gardens Hospice 5200 NE 2d Ave Miami FL 33137 Office Phone: 305-762-3883. Personal E-mail: megetz@worldnet.att.net. Business E-Mail: mgetz@MJHHA.org.

GETZENDANNER, SUSAN, lawyer; b. Chgo., July 24, 1939; d. William B. and Carole S. (Muehling) O'Meara; children— Alexandra, Paul. BBA, JD, Loyola U., 1966. Bar: Ill. bar 1966. Law clk. U.S. Dist. Ct., Chgo., 1966-68; assoc. Mayer, Brown & Platt, Chgo., 1968-74, ptnr., 1974-80; judge U.S. Dist. Ct., Chgo., 1980-87; ptnr. Skadden, Arps, Slate, Meagher & Flom, Chgo., 1987—2002. Recipient medal of excellence Loyola U. Law Alumni Assn., 1981 Mem. ABA, Chgo. Council Lawyers. Office Phone: 312-944-2629. E-mail: sgetzendanner@mindspring.com.

GEUSIC, JOSEPH EDWARD, physicist; b. Nesquehoning, Pa., Nov. 21, 1931; s. Joseph John and Mary Martha (Kosch) Geusic; m. Irene Jean Hosak, July 18, 1953; children: Patricia, Mark, Michael, Mary Ellen, Robert, Joseph. BS in Physics, Lehigh U., 1953; MS in Physics, Ohio State U., 1955, PhD in Physics, 1958. Rsch. assoc. physics dept. Ohio State U., Columbus, 1955-58; mem. tech. staff AT&T Bell Labs., Murray Hill, N.J., 1958-62, supr. solid state laser group, 1962-66, head solid state optical device dept., 1966-70, head magnetics dept., 1970-84, head semiconductor laser dept., 1984-94; pres. Geusic Info. Svcs., Inc., 1996—. Adj. fellow Micron Tech. Advanced Research Inst. Contbr. more than 63 to profl. publs. Recipient R. W. Wood prize, Optical Soc. Am., 1993, Clinton J. Davisson Patent award trophy, AT&T, 1993. Fellow: IEEE (Quantum Electronics award 1992); mem.: Am. Inst. Physics, Sigma Xi. Achievements include first to demonstrate Nd/YAG laser and first continuous operating optical parametric oscillator; development of semiconductor lasers for terrestrial and undersea lightwave communication systems, magnetic bubble materials and devices; 75 patents in field. Home: 261 Lorraine Dr Berkeley Heights NJ 07922-2341 Personal E-mail: josephgeusic@comcast.net.

GEVERTZ, BRENDA DALE, social services administrator; b. Miami, Fla., Oct. 1, 1949; d. Alexander and Fanny Cohen Gevertz; m. Carl J. Rheins, July 8, 1979; children: Jason Rheins, Jaclyn Rheins. BS in journalism and comm., U. Fla., 1971; MS in applied social svcs., Case Western Reserve U., 1978; certificate in bus. mgmt., not for profit mgmt., Columbia U., 1999. Cert. MSSA Case Western Reserve. Dir. Hillel Found., Cin., 1973—79, Miami, Fla., 1973—79; staff assoc., spl. grants UJA-F, N.Y.C., NY, 1979—82; dir., student unit Suffolk Y-JCC, Commack, NY, 1982—84; dir., jewish outreach project Suffolk Assn. Jewish Schs., Commack, NY, 1984—86; rec. dir. No. Am. Jewish Students Appeal, Huntington, NY, 1986—95; dir. LI Program Svcs. UJA-Federation, N.Y.C., NY, 1995—2001; exec. dir. Jewish Comm. Svc. Assn. of No. Am., N.Y.C., NY, 2002—. Adv. bd. Brandis U., Hornstein Program, Waltham, Mass., 1987—95, Hewbrew Union Coll., HUC-JCS, Los Angeles, Calif., 1990—95. Author: (poetry) Jewish Woman Talk to God; editor: Journal of Jewish Communal Service; columnist: e-newsletter Newsletter-JCSA. Danforth fellowship, Danforth Found., 1976. Mem.: JOFA, Nat. Coun. Jewish Woman, Jewish Womens Task Force. Jewish. Achievements include first women to be named dir. of a Hillel Found. Avocations: cooking, needlecrafts, gardening, poetry, political activism. Office: JCSA 156 26St Ste 917 New York NY 10010 Office Phone: 212-532-0167. Office Fax: 212-532-1461. E-mail: brenda@jcsano.org.

GEVIRTZ, RICHARD NEIL, psychologist, educator; b. Chgo., Jan. 25, 1944; s. Palmer Edward and Florence (Miller) G.; m. Maureen Clifford, May 2, 1971; children: Sara, Elizabeth. BS, U. Wis., 1966; MA, DePaul U., 1969, PhD, 1971. Lic. psychologist, Calif.; cert. biofeedback clinician. Asst. prof. St. Mary's Coll., Winona, Minn., 1971-75, assoc. prof., 1975-79, Calif. Sch. Profl. Psychology, San Diego, 1980-89, prof., 1989—. Vis. scientist Mayo Clinic, Rochester, Minn., 1979-80; rsch. dir. Western Behavioral Scis. Inst., San Diego, 1980-83; pvt. practice/cons. Biofeedback Inst. of San Diego, 1988—; practice Ctr. for Applied Behavioral Svcs., 1996—. Contbg. author: T.M. Disorders, 1985; contbr. articles to profl. jours. Chmn. Heat in Industry Com., San Diego, 1981-88. Recipient Phalin Found. fellowship, 1970-71, Danforth fellowship, 1975. Office: Calif Sch Profl Psychology 10455 Pemenodo Rd San Diego CA 92131

GEWARTOWSKI, JAMES WALTER, retired electrical engineer; b. Chgo., Nov. 10, 1930; s. Joseph Walter and Irene Dorothy (Dziekanowski) G.; m. Marion Ruth Wakeman, June 23, 1956; children: Marion, Diane, Patricia, John, Karen. BS in Elec. Engring., Ill. Inst. Tech., 1952; S.M., MIT, 1953; PhD, Stanford U., 1958. Research asst. Stanford Electronics Lab., Calif., 1954-57; supr. microwave sources AT&T Bell Labs., Inc, Murray Hill, N.J., 1957-71, supr. high bit rate optical data link group Allentown, Pa., 1971-88, supr. SL optical relay/receiver group Breinigsville, Pa., 1988-89, ret. Co-author: Principles of Electron Tubes, 1965, Fundamentals of Electron Tubes, 1969; contbg. author: Microwave Semiconductor Devices and Their Circuit Applications, 1969; contbr. articles to profl. jours. Fellow IEEE (Browder J. Thompson Meml. prize 1960); mem. Sigma Xi, Tau Beta Pi, Eta Kappa Nu, Serra Internat. Republican. Roman Catholic. Home: 2908 Edgemont Dr Allentown PA 18103-5410

GEWEKE, JOHN FREDERICK, economics professor; b. Washington, May 11, 1948; s. Robert William and Winnifred Lois (Quies) G.; m. Lynne Marie Osborn, Aug. 22, 1970; 1 child, Andrew Robert. BS, Mich. State U., 1970; PhD, U. Minn., 1975. Asst. prof. U. Wis., Madison, 1975-79, assoc. prof., 1979-82, prof., 1982-83, Duke U., Durham, N.C., 1983-86, William R. Kenan Jr. prof., 1986-90, dir. Inst. Stats. and Decision Scis., 1987-90; prof. U. Minn., Mpls., 1990—99; McGregor Chair in econs. & stats. U. Iowa, 1999—. Editor Jour. Bus. and Econs. Stats., 1989-92; co-editor Jour. Applied Econometrics, 1993-2002, Jour. Econometrics, 2003-; assoc. editor Econometrica, 1984-88, 95-2002. Rsch. fellow Sloan Found., N.Y.C., 1982. Fellow Econometric Soc., Am. Statis. Assn.; mem. Am. Econ. Assn., Internat. Soc. for Bayesian Analysis (pres. 1999). Office: U of IA Dept Econs Iowa City IA 52242

GEWERTZ, BRUCE LABE, surgeon, educator; b. Phila., Aug. 27, 1949; s. Milton and Shirley (Charen) G.; children: Samantha, Barton, Alexis; m. Diane Weiss, Aug. 31, 1997. BS, Pa. State U., State Coll., 1968; MD, Jefferson Med. Coll., Phila., 1972. Diplomate Am. Bd. Surgery. Surg. resident U. Mich., Ann Arbor, 1972-77; asst. prof. U. Tex., Dallas, 1977-81; assoc. prof. U. Chgo., 1981-87, prof. surgery, 1988—, faculty dean med. edn., 1989-92, Dallas Phemister prof., chmn. dept. surgery, 1992—. Tchg. scholar Am. Heart Assn., Dallas, 1980-83; pres. Assn. Surg. Edn., 1983-84; dir. vascular surgery bd. Am. Bd. Surgery, 2001—. Author: Atlas of Vascular Surgery, 1989, 2005, Surgery of the Aorta and its Branches, 2000; editor Jour. Surg. Rsch., 1987-2002; patentee removable vascular filter. Recipient Jobst award Coller Surg. Soc., 1975, Coller award Mich. chpt. Am. Coll. Surgeons, 1975, Outstanding Sci. Alumnus award Pa. State U., 2003. Mem. Soc. Vascular Surgery, Midwestern Vascular Soc. (pres. 1993, 94-95), Soc. Clin. Surgery, Soc. Univ. Surgeons, Chgo. Surg. Soc. (treas. 1989-92, pres. 2005), Am. Surg. Assn., Point O'Woods Club (Benton Harbor, Mich.). Office: U Chgo MC 5029 5841 S Maryland Ave Chicago IL 60637-1463 Office Phone: 773-702-0881. Business E-Mail: gewertz@surgery.bsd.vchicago.edu.

GEWIRTZ, ELLIOT, lawyer; b. N.Y.C., Apr. 8, 1947; m. Barbara Gewirtz; children: Lisa D., Eric S. BA summa cum laude, Colgate U., 1969; JD cum laude, Harvard U., 1972; M in Pub. Adminstrn., Princeton U., 1973. Bar: N.Y. 1973. Assoc. Milbank, Tweed, Hadley & McCloy, N.Y.C., 1973—78, assoc. to ptnr.-in-charge Tokyo, 1978—84, ptnr. global transp. fin. dept. N.Y.C., 1984—. Mem.: ABA, N.Y. State Bar Assn., Assn. of the Bar of the City of N.Y. Home: 52 Greenacres Ave Scarsdale NY 10583-1436 Office: Milbank Tweed Hadley & McCloy 1 Chase Manhattan Plz Fl 47 New York NY 10005-1413 Office Phone: 212-530-5474. Office Fax: 212-530-5219. Business E-Mail: egewirtz@milbank.com.

GEWIRTZ, PAUL D., lawyer, educator; b. May 12, 1947; s. Herman and Matilda (Miller) Gewirtz; m. Zoë Baird, June 8, 1986; children: Julian, Alec. AB summa cum laude, Columbia U., 1967; JD, Yale U., 1970. Bar: D.C. 1973, U.S. Supreme Ct. 1976. Law clk. to Hon. Marvin E. Frankel US Dist. Ct (so. dist.) NY, 1970—71; law clk. to Justice Thurgood Marshal US Supreme Ct., Washington, 1971—72; assoc. Wilmer, Cutler & Pickering, Washington, 1972—73; atty. Ctr. Law and Social Policy, Washington, 1973—76; assoc. prof. then prof. Yale Law Sch., New Haven, 1976—, Potter Stewart prof. Law, 1992—, dir. The China Law Ctr., 1999—. Dir. Global Constitutionalism Project, 1996—; Spl. Rep. the Presdl. Rule of Law Initiative US Dept. of State, 1997—98; guest prof. Peking (China) U. Law Sch., 2003—; US rep. European Commn. on Democracy through Law, 1996—2000. Author: Law's Stories, 1996, The Case Law Sys. in Am., 1989; contbr. numerous articles to profl. jours. Mem.: Am. Law Inst., Coun. on Fgn. Rels. Office: Yale U Law Sch PO Box 208215 New Haven CT 06520-8215 Business E-Mail: paul.gewirtz@yale.edu.

GEWIRTZ-FRIEDMAN, GERRY, editor; b. N.Y.C., Dec. 22, 1920; d. Max and Minnie (Weiss) G.; m. Eugene W. Friedman, Nov. 11, 1945; children: John Henry, Robert James. BA, Vassar Coll., 1941. Editor Package Store Mgmt., 1942-44, Jewelry Mag., 1945-53; freelance editor promotion dept. McCall's Mag., Esquire, 1953-56; free-lance fashion and gifts editor Jewelers Circular Keystone, N.Y.C., 1955-71; editor, pub. The Fashionables, 1971-74, The Forecast, 1974—, Nat. Jeweler, Ann. Fashion Guide, 1976-80; editor, assoc. pub. Exec. Jeweler, 1980-83; editor The Fashion Source (formerly Internat. Fashion Index), N.Y.C., 1984—; freelance editor and mktg. specialist, 1995—. Ptnr. Gary Gewirtz-Editl. and Mktg.; free-lance editl. wrtier, 1995—. Corr. Internat. Mktg. News. Mem. exec. com. Inner City Council of Cardinal Cooke, N.Y.; chairperson women's task force United Jewish Appeal Fedn.; former bd. govs. Israel Bonds; former trustee Israel Cancer Research Fund, Central Synagogue; bd. dirs. Double Image Theater; former pres. women's aux. Brandeis U. Honored guest Am. Jewish Com., 1978; Israel Cancer Research Fund, 1978-81; recipient Disting. Community Service award Brandeis U., 1987; named to Jewelry Hall Fame, 1988. Mem. N.Y. Fashion Group, Nat. Home Fashions League (former pres.), Women's Jewelry Assn. (pres. 1983-87, named editor who has contbd. most to jewelry industry 1984, free lance editor). Home: 45 Sutton Pl S New York NY 10022-2444

GEWITZ, MICHAEL HAROLD, pediatrician; b. Jan. 20, 1949; m. Judith Lipshutz, May 12, 1973; children: Emily, Andrew. BA, Yale U., 1970; MD, Hahnemann U., 1974. Intern Children's Hosp. Phila., Phila., 1974—75, resident, 1975—76, Hosp. Sick Children, London, 1976—77; fellow Yale New Haven Hosp., 1977—79; dir. noninvasive cardiology Children's Hosp. Phila., 1979—83; asst. prof. pediat. Sch. Medicine U. Pa., Phila., 1979—83; chief pediat. cardiology N.Y. Med. Coll. and Westchester Med. Ctr., 1983—; dir. dept. pediat., chief pediat. cardiology Children's Hosp. Westchester, Valhalla, NY, 1991—; prof., vice chair dept. pediat. N.Y. Med. Coll., Valhalla, NY, 1992—; pres. med. staff Westch Med. Ctr., 1998—2002; physician in chief Maria Fareri Children's Hosp., Valhalla, 2004—, exec. dir., 2004—, chief pediat. cardiology, 1983—. Editor: (book) Primary Pediatric Cardiology, 1995; assoc. editor: (journal) Heart Diseases, 1999-2004. Fellow Am. Acad. Pediat., Am. Coll. Cardiology, N.Y. Acad. Medicine, Am. Heart Assn. (exec. com. cardiovasc. disease in young 1999—, com. Rheumatic fever, endocarditis and Kawasaki disease 1995—, vice chmn. 2001-04, chmn. 2004—), Am. Coll. Physician Execs.; mem. Pediat. Acad. Soc. Office Phone: 914-594-4370.

GEWURZ, ANITA TARTELL, medical association administrator; b. Buffalo, July 30, 1946; MD, Albany Med. Coll., 1970. Resident in pediat. U. Ill., Chgo., 1971—73; resident in allergy and immunology Rush-Presbyn.-St. Luke's Hosp., Chgo., 1974—76; fellow allergy and immunology Max Samter Inst., Grant Hosp., Chgo., 1976—77, Northwestern U. Med. Coll., Chgo., 1983—85; assoc. prof. immunology/microbiology, pediat. and internal med. Rush U. Med. Coll., Chgo., 1993—2003, prof. immunology/microbiology, pediat. and internal med., 2003—; physician Rush U. Med. Ctr., Chgo., 1974—. Chair, Tng. Program Dirs. Com. Am. Acad. Allergy, Asthma & Immunology, 2003—04; chair Am. Bd. Allergy and Immunology, 2005—. Office: Rush Univ Med Ctr 1725 W Harrison St Ste 117 Chicago IL 60612 Office Phone: 312-942-6296. Business E-Mail: agewurz@rush.edu.

GEX, LUCIEN MARION, III, (BEAU GEX), legislative staff member; b. New Orleans, Oct. 5, 1959; s. Lucien Marion Jr. and Nancy (Gould) G. BS, U. So. Miss., 1982. Registered appraiser. Claims adjuster Allstate Ins., Biloxi, Miss., 1985-89; dist. chief of staff Congressman Gene Taylor, Gulfport, Miss., 1989—. Appraiser Lucien M. Gex III Appraisals, Long Beach, Miss., 1999—. Mem. adv. bd. U. So. Miss., Hattiesburg, 2000—, St. Stanislaus H.S., 1999—. Mem. World Trade Club, Bay Waveland Yacht Club (dir.), Kappa Alpha. Roman Catholic. Home: 129 Markham Dr Long Beach MS 39560 Office: Congressman Gene Taylor 2424 14th St Gulfport MS 39501 Office Phone: 228-864-7670. E-mail: beaugex@mindspring.com, beau1@cableone.net.

GEYER, CATHERINE S., elementary school educator; d. Lowell E. and Marjorie L. Richardson; m. Alan M. Geyer, June 27, 1981. BS, Huntington Coll., Huntington, Ind., 1981; MA (hon.), St. Francis Coll., Fort Wayne, Ind., 1985; Kindergarten Endorsement, IPFW, Fort Wayne, Ind., 1993. 1st/ 2nd grade tchr. St. Peter Luth. Sch., Huntington, Ind., 1982—84; first grade tchr. Roanoke Elem. Sch., Roanoke, Ind., 1984—85, Horace Mann Elem. Sch., Huntington, Ind., 1985—87; second grade tchr. Roanoke Elem. Sch., Roanoke, Ind., 1987—88, kindergarten tchr., 1988—. Gen. edn. intervention com. Roanoke Elem. Sch., Roanoke, Ind., pub. law 221 com., 2002—, cheerleading coach, 1984—85, kendall dennis meml. fitness trail chmn., 1999—2000, pto treas., 1998—2000. Mem. Ladies of Harley, Fort Wayne, Ind., 1995—2005. Mem.: Little Turtle Reading Coun. (assoc.), Ind. Profl. Educators (assoc.). Republican. Lutheran. Office: Roanoke Elem Sch 423 West Vine St Roanoke IN 46783 Office Phone: 260-672-2806. Personal E-mail: cgeyer@hccsc.k12.in.us.

GEYER, GEORGIE ANNE, columnist, educator, commentator, writer; b. Chgo., Apr. 2, 1935; d. Robert George and Georgie Hazel (Gervens) G. BS, Northwestern U., 1956, LHD (hon.), 1993; postgrad., U. Vienna, Austria, 1956-57; LittD (hon.), Lake Forest Coll., 1980, Coll. Mt. St. Joseph, 1986, Notre Dame, 1986, Wilson Coll., 1987, Linfield Coll., 1987, St. Mary-of-the-Woods Coll., 1989, U. Indpls., 1991, Colby-Sawyer Coll., 1992, Franklin Coll., 1992, Cabrini Coll., 1994; LHD (hon.), Northwestern U., 1984, U. S.C., 1991, Rockhurst (Jesuit) Coll., Kansas City, 1992, Spring Hill Coll., 1993, Lebanon Valley Coll., 1994, Hofstra U., 1995, Loyola U., Chgo., 1996, Westminster Coll., 1996, Govs. State U., 1997, Notre Dame Coll., 1999, Knox Coll., 1999. Reporter Southtown Economist, Chgo., 1958; soc. reporter Chgo. Daily News, 1959-60, gen. assignment reporter, 1960-64, corr. Lat. Am., Ctrl. Am., Soviet Union, Middle East, Europe, 1964-75, roving fgn. corr. and columnist, 1967-75; syndicated columnist Los Angeles Times Syndicate, 1975-80, Universal Press Syndicate, 1981—; Lyle M. Spencer prof. journalism Syracuse U., 1977. Regular news commentator PBS' Washington Week in Review; questioner on Presdl. debate, Oct., 1984; steering com. Aspen Inst. Latin Am. Governance Project, 1981-82; commentator on the BBC; regular panelist Voice of America; sent by Internat. Communication Agy. on 3 worldwide speaking tours on Am. journalism: Nigeria, Zambia, Tanzania and Somalia, 1979, Philippines and Indonesia, 1981, Iceland, Norway, Belgium and Portugal, 1982; rep. Fulbright scholar program 40th anniversary, New Zealand, 1987; commencement speaker various colls., univs. including U. S.Carolina, Rockhurst Coll., St. Mary's Notre Dame; sr. fellow Annenburg Washington, 1992-93; columnist on fgn. policy, internat. affairs The Chgo. Tribune, The Wash. Times, Universal de Caracas, The Dallas Morning News, Diario las Americas, The Denver Post, others; speaker, lectr. in field. Author: The New Latins, 1970, The New 100 Years War, 1972, The Young Russians, 1976; (autobiography) Buying the Night Flight, (Weintal prize citation Sch. Fgn. Svc. Georgetown U. 1984, Chgo. Found. for Lit. award 1984), 1983, reissued, 1996, Guerilla Prince, The Untold Story of Fidel Castro, 1991, Waiting for Winter to End, An Extraordinary Journey Through Soviet Central Asia, 1994, Americans No More: The Death of Citizenship, 1996, Tunisia: A Journey Through the Country that Works, 2003, When Cats Reigned Like Kings: On the Trail of the Sacred Cats, 2004; subjects of interviews include Prince Sihanouk of Cambodia, Yassar Arafat, Anwar Sadat, King Hussein of Jordan, Pres. Khaddafy of Libya, the Ayatollah Khomeini, Sultan Qaboos of Oman, Pres. Juan Peron of Argentina, Pres. Siad Barre of Somalia, Prime Minister Mauno Koivisto of Finland, Anastasio Somoza, Jerzy Urban, Janusz Onyszkiewicz, Prime Minister Edward Seaga of Jamaica, Pres. Ronald Reagan, Pres. George Bush, others; discovered and had first interview with second most-wanted Nazi, Walter Rauff in Tierra del Fuego, Chile, 1966; found Dominican pres. Juan Bosch in hiding in P.R. during Dominican revolution, 1965; held by Palestinians as Israeli spy, 1973; imprisoned in Angola for writing about revolutionary government, 1976; contbr. chpts. to books, articles numerous pubs. Active Orgn. for S.W. Community Chgo., 1960-64; trustee Am. U., Washington, 1981-86; Coun. Fgn. Rels. Recipient 1st prize Am. Newspaper Guild, 1962; 2d prize Ill. Press Editors Assn., 1962; award for best writing on Latin Am. Overseas Press Club, 1967; Merit award Northwestern U., 1968; Nat. Headliner award Theta Sigma Phi, 1968; Maria Moors Cabot award Columbia U., 1970; Hannah Solomon award Nat. Council Jewish Women, 1973; Ill. Spl. Events Commn. Woman's award, 1975; Northwestern U. Alumni award, 1991; Fulbright scholar U. Vienna, 1956-57; Woodrow Wilson fellow Rollins Coll., Winter Park, Fla., 1982; Presdl. Citation award Am. Univ., 1985; Disting. fellow Mortar Bd. Nat. Sr. Honor Soc., Am. U., 1982, Sr. fellow Annenberg Washington Program, Washington, 1992-93; fellow Soc. Profl. Journalists, 1992; named Outstanding Illinoisian, Ill. State Assn., 2001; named to Hall of Fame of Soc. of Profl. Journalists, 2001, Stewart Alsop award Assn. Retired Intelligence Officers, 2001, Headliners Club Lifetime Achievement award, 2003, Woman Extraordiaire award Internat. Women Assn., 2004. Mem.: Chgo. Coun. Fgn. Rels. (bd. dirs.), Washington Inst., Women's Inst. for Freedom of Press, Internat. Soc. Polit. Psychology, Internat. Inst. Strategic Studies, Inst. Internat. Edn. (bd. dirs.), Women in Comm., Soc. Profl. Journalists, Cosmos Club (1st women mem.), Gridiron Club. Home and Office: The Plaza 800 25th St NW Washington DC 20037-2207 Personal E-mail: gigi_geyer@juno.com. *I have never compromised seriously on any ethical or moral principle, and I truly believe that the women of my generation can bring a new and cleansing element to American public life. Whatever I have accomplished I could not have done without profoundly analyzing myself: but I also find that in professional life the old injunction to " Know Thyself" reaches women more than men. It has been a constant struggle, often with little personal approval or backing, which I feel also adds to a woman's inner strength.*

GEYER, JAMES A, insurance company executive; BA in math., U. Conn. V.p. and chief actuary Aetna Inc., 2000—; various positions with Aetna's Individual Life Divsn., Corp. Acutarial, Employee Benefits Divsn., 1980; head of planning and fin. reporting Employee Benefits Divsn. Fellow: Soc. of Actuaries; mem.: Am. Acad. of Acutaries. Office: Aetna Inc 151 Farmington Ave Hartford CT 06156 Office Phone: 860-273-6304. Business E-Mail: geyerja@aetna.com.

GEYER, MARK ALLEN, healthcare educator, science educator, consultant; b. Portland, Dec. 19, 1944; s. Ralph Allen and Mary McLean Geyer; m. Athina Markou, Dec. 19, 1986. BA, U. Oreg. Hons. Coll., 1966; MA, U. Iowa, 1968; PhD, U. Calif. San Diego, La Jolla, 1972. Asst. rsch. psychobiologist U. Calif. San Diego, La Jolla, Calif., 1973—78, asst. prof. psychiatry, 1979—83, assoc. prof. psychiatry, 1983—89, prof. psychiatry, 1989—. Founder, sci. advisor San Diego Instruments, Inc., San Diego, 1981—; mng. editor Psychopharmacology, Springer Verlag, Heidelberg, Germany, 1991—; adj. prof. of neuroscis. U. of Calif. San Diego, La Jolla, Calif., 1995—; exec. editor Neuropharmacology, Elsevier, Amsterdam, The Netherlands, 2000—. Author over 280 rsch. pubs., over 40 pub. book chpts. Named ISI Highly Cited Rschr. in Neuroscience, Thomson Sci., 2004; recipient Rsch. Scientist awards, NIMH, 1983-2000; grantee Disting. Investigator award, NARSAD, 1996-1997, Monoamines & Hallucinogens' Effects on Rodent Behavior, Nat. Inst. on Drug Abuse, 1981-2005, Sensory Gating and Habituation in Schizophrenia, NIMH, 1987-2008, Devel. Models Gating Deficits in Schizophrenia, 1995-2005; Fogarty Internat. fellow, 1993-1994, Elected fellow, AAAS, 2004. Fellow: Internat. Behavioral Neuroscis. Soc. (pres. 2001—02), Am. Coll. Neuropsychopharmacology; mem.: Serotonin Club (pres. 2004—). Achievements include first to establishing valid animal model for identifying novel antipsychotic drugs. Office: U Calif San Diego 9500 Gilman Dr La Jolla CA 92093-0804 Office Phone: 619-543-3582. Office Fax: 619-543-2493. E-mail: mgeyer@ucsd.edu.

GEYER, MICHAEL, history professor; PhD, Albert Ludwigs U., Freiburg, Germany. Samuel N. Harper prof. history U. Chgo., 1986—. Guggenheim fellow, 2003. Office: U Chgo Dept History 1126 E 59th St Chicago IL 60637 Office Phone: 773-955-7204. E-mail: mgeyer@uchicago.edu.

GEYER, RICHARD DOUGLAS, librarian, poet; b. Detroit, June 23, 1964; s. John Richard Geyer and Mary Jennie Winiarczyk. BA, U. Minn., 1989; MLS, U. Mich., 1990. Libr. Adrian Coll., Adrian, Mich., 1991—, head libr., 1996—2001. Pub. Yellow Bat Press, Adrian, 2003—, editor, 2004—; dir. website Thomas Lovell Beddoes Text Archive, Adrian, 2004—. Author: XXX, The Phantasm of Despair, Sleepy Hollow, 1776; contbr. poetry to jours. and mags. Mem.: ALA, Am. Soc. Info. Sci. and Tech., Thomas Lovell Beddoes Soc. (bibliographer 2003—), Beta Phi Mu. Office: Adrian College 110 S Madison Adrian MI 49221 Office Phone: 517-265-5161. E-mail: rgeyer@adrian.edu.

GEYER, THOMAS POWICK, newspaper publisher; b. Phila., Dec. 13, 1946; s. John Alvin and Jean (Powick) G. BA, St. John's Coll., 1969. Reporter The Mercury, Pottstown, Pa., 1969-73; editor Internat. Data Corp., Waltham, Mass., 1974, The Eagle-Times, Claremont, N.H., 1975; editor, pub. The Daily Freeman, Kingston, N.Y., 1976-81; pres. Ingersoll Pubs. Co., Princeton, N.J., 1982-86; pub. New Haven Register, 1986-91, The Daily Record, Parsippany, N.J., 1991-98. Bd. govs. St. John's Coll., Annapolis, Md., 1991—; chmn. First Night, Morristown, N.J., 1993. Fellow Berkeley Coll. Yale, 1988—. Address: Apt 15J 54 W 16th St New York NY 10011-6342

GEYMAN, JOHN PAYNE, physician, educator; b. Santa Barbara, Calif., Feb. 9, 1931; s. Milton John and Betsy (Payne) Geyman; m. Eugenia Clark Deichler, June 9, 1956; children: John Matthew, James Caleb, William Sabin. AB in Geology, Princeton U., 1952; MD, U. Calif., San Francisco, 1960. Diplomate Am. Bd. Family Practice. Intern L.A. County Gen. Hosp., 1960—61; resident in gen. practice Sonoma County Hosp., Santa Rosa, Calif., 1961—63; pvt. practice specializing in family practice Mt. Shasta, Calif., 1963—69; dir. family practice residency program Cmty. Hosp. Sonoma County, Santa Rosa, 1969—71; assoc. prof. family practice, chmn. divsn. family practice U. Utah, 1971—72; prof., vice chmn. dept. family practice U. Calif., Davis, 1972—77; prof., chmn. dept. family medicine U. Wash., 1977—90, prof. family medicine, 1990—93, prof. family medicine emeritus, 1993—. Author: The Modern Family Doctor and Changing Medical Practice, 1971, Family Practice: Foundation of Changing Health Care, 1980, 2d edit., 1985, Flight as a Lifetime Passion: Adventures, Misadventures and Lessons, 2000, Falling Through the Safety Net: Americans Without Health Insurance, 2005; editor: Content of Family Practice, 1976, Family Practice in the Medical School, 1977, Research in Family Practice, 1978, Preventive Medicine in Family Practice, 1979, Profile of the Residency Trained Family Physician in the U.S, 1970—79, Funding of Patient Care, Education and Research in Family Practice, 1981, The Content of Family Practice: Current Status and Future Trends, 1982, Archives of Family Practice, 1980—82, Family Practice: An International Perspective in Developed Countries, 1983, Jour. Am. Bd. Family Practice, 1990—2003; founding editor Jour. Family Practice, 1973—90; co-editor: Behavioral Science in Family Practice, 1980, Evidence-Based Clinical Practice: Concepts and Approaches, 2000, Textbook of Rural Medicine, 2000, Health Care in America: Can Our Ailing System Be Healed?, 2002, The Corporate Transformation of Health Care: Can the Public Interest Still be Served?, 2004. Pres. Physicians for Nat. Health Program, 2005—. Served to lt. (j.g.) USN, 1952—55, PTO. Recipient Gold-Headed Cane award, U. Calif. Sch. Medicine, 1960, Alumnus of Yr. award, 1998. Mem.: Inst. Medicine NAS, Soc. Tchrs. Family Medicine, Am. Acad. Family Physicians. Unitarian Universalist. Home: 53 Avian Ridge Ln Friday Harbor WA 98250-8895 Business E-Mail: jgeyman@u.washington.edu.

GFELLER, DONNA KVINGE, clinical psychologist; b. Chgo., Jan. 15, 1959; d. Milton Melvin and Doris Ann (Chapman) Kvinge; m. Jeffrey Donald Gfeller, Aug. 2, 1986. BS in Biol. Scis., Ill. State U., 1980, MS in Clin. Psychology, 1984; PhD in Clin. Psychology, Ohio U., 1987. Lic. psychologist. Staff psychologist Cardinal Glennon Children's Hosp., St. Louis, 1986-87, sr. psychologist, 1988-89, dir. dept. psychology, 1990—. Mem. APA (divsn. clin. psychology, clin. child psychology), Soc. Pediatric Psychology, World Wildlife Fund. Avocations: travel, horseback riding. Office: Cardinal Glennon Children's Hosp 1465 S Grand Blvd Saint Louis MO 63104-1003

GFELLER, LISA ANNE, computer systems analyst; b. Aberdeen, Miss., May 24, 1959; d. Dewey Edward and Doris Louise (Ferguson) Gill; m. Daniel Dumitru Pope, May 12, 1979 (div. Sept. 1984); m. James Robert Gfeller, July 19, 1985; children: Jennifer, Kelly, Lindy, Melissa. Student, Judson Coll., 1977-79; BA in Math. and Computer Sci., So. Ill. U., 1981. Fin. planning asst. U.S. Planning Assn./Ind. Rsch. Assn., Jacksonville, N.C., 1982-84; mem. computer sales staff Computer Store, Jacksonville, N.C., 1984-85; sys. analyst Blue Cross/Blue Shield of Ala., Birmingham, 1985-93; ind. computer cons. Orlando, Fla., 1993-96; sys. analyst Blue Cross/Blue Shield of Ala., Birmingham, 1996—2002, mainframe svc. mgr., 2002—. Mem. career devel. com. Leadership Devel. Assn., Birmingham, 1992-93, adopt-a-sch. program tutor, 1990-92; poll watcher Bob McKee Election Campaign, Birmingham, 1986; discipleship tng. tchr. Eastside Bapt. Ch., Birmingham, 1990-93; chm. tech. Lakemont Sch. Adv. Coun., 1993-95; commr. Am. Soccer Club, 2000-2002. Mem. Triplet Connection of Birmingham (pres. 1992, sec. 1993). Republican. Avocations: sewing, piano, gardening, bicycling, soccer. Home and Office: 5329 Harvest Ridge Ln Birmingham AL 35242-3109

GHABBOUR, ELHAM A., research scientist, educator; arrived in U.S., 1993; d. Afifi A. Ghabbour and S. Abo-zid. BS, Alexandria U., Egypt, 1982, MS, 1988, PhD, 1995. Postdoctoral rsch. fellow Northeastern U., Boston, 1996—98, staff scientist, 1999—2001, sr. rsch. scientist, 2002—. Contbr. articles to profl. jours.; editor: Humic Substances: Structures, Properties and Uses, 1998, Understanding Humic Substances: Advanced Methods, Properties and Applications, 1999, Humic Substances: Versatile Components of Plants, Soil and Water, 2000, Humic Substances: Structures, Models and Functions, 2001, Humic Substances: Nature's Most Versatile Materials, 2004, Humic Substances: Molecular Details and Applications in Land and Water Conservation, 2004. Recipient Advanced Rsch. award, Barnett Inst., 1998, Innovation Rsch. award, 2000; grantee, USDA NRICGP, 2002. Fellow: Royal Soc. Chemistry; mem.: AAUP, Soil Sci. Soc. Am., Internat. XAFS Soc., Internat. Humic Substances Soc. (founder, nat. coord. Egyptian chpt. 1996—), Am. Chem. Soc., Internat. Soil Sci. Soc., Environ. Friends Soc., Phi Beta Delta (pres. NU chpt. 2002—), Sigma Xi. Office: Northeastern U Dept Chemistry Boston MA 02115-5000 Office Phone: 617-373-7988.

GHADRY, FARID N., political organization worker; b. Aleppo, Syria, June 18, 1954; arrived in Lebanon, 1964, arrived in US, 1975; m. Ahlam Ghadry; 4 children. B in Fin. & Mktg., Am. U., Washington, DC, 1979. With EG&G Intertech, Inc., 1979—81; founder, pres. Internat. TechGroup, Inc., 1983—89. Co-founder, pres. Reform Party of Syria, 2001—; bd. dirs. Norwood Sch., Bethesda, Md.*

GHAIM, BERHANE TEQUABO, mathematician, educator; b. Asmara, Eritrea, Nov. 14, 1968; s. Tequabo Ghaim and Hidat Gilamicheal; m. Alem Ghaim, May 18, 2002. B.S, Mt. Vernon Nazarene Coll., Ohio, 1994; MA, Kent State U., 1999, Ph.D, 2003. Grad. asst. Kent State U., Ohio, 1995—99, tchg. fellow, 1999—2003; asst. prof. Baldwin-Wallace Coll., Berea, Ohio, 2003—. Contbr. articles to profl. jours. Mem.: Math. Assn. Am., Am. Math. Soc. Avocations: travel, reading. Office: Baldwin-Wallace Coll 275 Eastland Rd Berea OH 44017 Office Phone: 440-826-2396. Office Fax: 440-826-6973. Business E-Mail: bghaim@bw.edu.

GHALI, ANWAR YOUSSEF, psychiatrist, educator; b. Cairo, May 30, 1944; arrived in U.S.A., 1974, naturalized, 1980; s. Youssef and Insaf Wahba (Soliman) G.; m. Violette Fouad Saleh, May 23, 1968; 1 child, Susie MD, Cairo U., 1966, DPM, 1970, DM, 1971; MPA, NYU, 1999. Diplomate Am. Bd. Psychiatry and Neurology; cert. adminstrv. psychiatry. Registrar in psychiatry Woodilee Hosp., Glasgow, Scotland, 1973-74; resident in psychiatry N.J. Med. Sch., Newark, 1974-77, instr., 1977-78, clin. asst. prof., 1978-79, asst. prof., 1979-83, clin. assoc. prof., 1983—; chief Outpatient Dept.-Community Mental Health Ctr., N.J. Med. Sch., Newark, 1978-86; dir. Emergency Psychiat. Svcs. Univ. Hosp., U. Medicine and Dentistry of N.J., Newark, 1986-87; med. dir. Profl. Counsel Ctr., Westfield, NJ, 1984-87; med. chief ambulatory psychiat. svcs. Elizabeth (N.J.) Gen. Hosp., 1987-89; dir. psychiat. tng. VA Med. Ctr., East Orange, NJ, 1989—2001, asst. chief psychiatry, 1990—91, assoc. chief psychiatry, 1991—2001; chmn. psychiatry Trinitas Hosp., Elizabeth, NJ, 2001—. Contbr. articles to profl. jours. Recipient Exceptional Merit award Coll. Medicine & Dentistry, Newark, 1981 Mem. AMA, Christian Med. Soc., Am. Psychiat. Assn., N.J. Psychiat. Assn., N.Y. Acad. Scis. Republican. Presbyterian. Home: 22 Benvenue Ave West Orange NJ 07052-3202

GHANI, CYRUS, lawyer; b. Sabzevar, Khorasan, Iran, Nov. 8, 1929; came to U.S., 1980; s. Qasem and Maryam (Ghaffouri) G.; m. Caroline Bennett, May 19, 1956; children: Ali Ghani, Vida Ghani Touran. BA, Wagner Coll., Staten Island, N.Y., 1954; JD, NYU, 1958. Head contract dept. Plan Orgn., Tehran, Iran, 1958-59; dep. mgr. legal dept. Indsl. Mining Devel. Bank Iran, 1959-63, mgr. legal dept., 1963-70; sr. ptnr. Ghani & Tavakoli, Tehran, Iran, 1964-79; legal cons. N.Y. and London, 1979-89. Mem. commn. drafting co. law, Iran, 1965-68. Author: Iran and the West, 1987, Iran and The Rise of Reza Shah, 1998, My Favorite Films, 2004; editor: 13 Vol. Memoirs of Ghassem Ghani, 1981-84. Mem. Century Club N.Y. Home: 360 E 72nd St New York NY 10021-4753

GHARIB, SUSIE, newscaster; b. N.Y.C., Nov. 27, 1950; d. Ali and Homa (Razzaghmanesh) G.; m. Fereydoun Nazem, Jan. 20, 1973; children: Alexander, Taraneh. BA magna cum laude, Case Western Res. U., 1972; M in Internat. Affairs, Columbia U., 1974. Reporter Cleve. Plain Dealer, 1972-73; assoc. editor Fortune Mag., N.Y.C., 1974-83; anchor, reporter Bus. Times/ESPN, N.Y.C., 1983-85; bus. reporter ABC News, N.Y.C., 1986-87; anchor Fin. News Network, N.Y.C., 1989-90, CNBC Network, Ft. Lee, N.J., 1993-98, Nightly Bus. Report, N.Y.C., 1998—. Moderator/host Xerox Corp., Stanford, Conn., 1989-95, KPMG Peat Marwick, N.Y.C., 1992-95; cons. Adam Smith's Money World/PBS, N.Y.C., 1987. Bd. dirs. First Fortis, Inc., 1991-2000, Ice Theatre of N.Y., 1988-90; trustee Case Western Res. U., 2005—. Mem. Fgn. Policy Assn., N.Y. Fin. Writers Assn., Overseas Press Club, Econ. Club N.Y. (trustee 2003—),Can. Western Reserve U. (Trustee, 2005-), Phi Beta Kappa. Democrat. Avocations: figure skating, tennis, classical piano. Home: 44 E 73rd St New York NY 10021-4173

GHAUSI, MOHAMMED SHUAIB, retired dean, electrical engineer, educator; b. Kabul, Afghanistan, Feb. 16, 1930; came to U.S., 1951, naturalized, 1963; s. Mohammed Omar; m. Marilyn Buchwold, June 12, 1961; children: Nadjya, Simine. BS summa cum laude, U. Calif., Berkeley, 1956, MS, 1957, PhD, 1960. Prof. elec. engring. NYU, 1960-72; head elec. scis. sect. NSF, Washington, 1972-74; prof., chmn. elec. engring. dept. Wayne State U., Detroit, 1974-77; John F. Dodge prof. Oakland U., Rochester, Mich., 1978-83, dean Sch. Engring. and Computer Sci., 1978-83; dean Coll. Engring., U. Calif., Davis, 1983-96, interim vice chancellor rsch., vice provost, dean grad., 1996-97; ret., 1997. Mem. adv. panel NSF, 1989. Author, co-author: Principles and Design of Linear Active Circuits, 1965, Introduction to Distributed-Parameter Networks, 1968, Electronic Circuits, 1971, Modern Filter Design: Active RC and Switched Capacitor, 1981, Electronic Devices and Circuits: Discrete and Integrated, 1985, Design of Analog Filters, 1990, Introduction to Electronic Circuit Design, 2003, also numerous articles.; cons. editor Van Nostrand Rinehold Pub. Co., 1968-71. Mem. disting. alumni rev. panel Elec. Engring. and Computer Sci. programs U. Calif., Berkeley, 1973; mem. external bd. visitors U. Pa., 1974. Recipient Outstanding Alumnus award in Elec. Engring. and Computer Sci., U. Calif., 1998. Fellow IEEE (chmn. edn. medal com. 1990-92, Centennial medal, Alexander von Humboldt prize 1983, circuits and systems soc. edn. award); mem. Circuits and System Soc. (v.p. 1970-72, pres. 1976), N.Y. Acad. Scis., Engring. Soc. Detroit, Sigma Xi, Phi Beta Kappa, Tau Beta Pi, Eta Kappa Nu. Business E-Mail: msghausi@uc.davis.edu.

GHAVAMIAN, REZA, surgeon, physician; BA, Boston U., Boston, 1987, MD, 1991; Residency in Urology, Umass Med. Ctr., Worcester, Mass., 1991—97; Fellow in Urologic Oncology, Mayo Clinic, Rochester, Minn., 1997—98. Cert. Bd.Urology Am. Bd. Of Urology, 2000, lic. Nat. Bd. of Med. Examiners Nat. Bd. of Med. examiners. Assoc. prof. of urology Montefiore Med. ctr. / Albert Einstein Coll. of Medicine, Bronx, NY, 1998—; dir. urologic oncology Montefiore med. ctr., Bronx, NY, 1998—2005; dir. urologic laparoscopic surgey Montefiore Med. ctr., Bronx, NY, 2001—05. Contbr. scientific papers over 20 pub. to profl. jour., chapters to books. Fellow: N.Y. Acad. of Medicine; mem.: N.Y. section of the AUA, Soc. of Urologic Oncology, Am. Urologic assn. Achievements include Tchr. of the Yr., 2001. Office: Montefiore Med ctr 3400 Bainbridge ave Bronx NY 10467 Office Phone: 718-920-8475. Office Fax: 718-547-2902.

GHAZARBEKIAN, SAHAK, retired civilian military employee; b. Meshed, Iran, Mar. 1, 1928; came to U.S., 1964; s. Vartan Ghazarbekian and Satenik Abrahamian; m. Bonnie J. Bakke (dec. Nov. 1988); m. Sonia Etmekjian. BS in Physics, U. Tehran, 1952; BA in Pub. Adminstrn., Am. U., Beirut, 1956; grad. diploma PA, Internat. Inst. Social Studies, The Hague, The Netherlands, 1962; postgrad., Princeton U., 1965. Adminstrv. officer U.S. Ops. Mission, Tehran, 1952-54; assoc. pub. adminstrn. advisor Joint U.S./Iran Govt., Tehran, 1954-58; dep. dir. Plan Orgn. Iran, Tehran, 1958-63, chief mgmt. bur., 1963-65; dir. gen. Office of Prime Min., Tehran, 1965-69; chief pub. adminstrn. sect. UN Econ. and Social Commn. for Asia and the Pacific, Bangkok, 1969-74, chief projects ops. office, 1974-77. Chief program coord. and monitoring office UN Asia and Pacific Commn., Bangkok, 1977-80; chief joint planning sect. UN Hdqs., N.Y.C., 1980-88; cons. in field, N.Y.C., 1988—. Contbr. articles to profl. jours. Mem. Ea. Regional Orgn. for Pub. Adminstrn., Manila, 1968-80. Recipient Svc. Citation of Distinction, Shah of Iran, 1967, 68, Order of Homayoun, Shah of Iran, 1968; Parvin fellow Woodrow Wilson Sch., Princeton U., 1964-65. Avocations: travel, history study, lecturing, translating. Home: 5 Archway Pl Forest Hills Flushing NY 11375-5255

GHERARDI, GHERARDO JOSEPH, pathologist; b. Lucca, Italy, July 1, 1921; came to U.S., 1933; s. Mario E. and Maria (Gilli) G.; m. Celeste Tranfaglia, Sept. 16, 1957; children: Roberta, Ronald, Mark, Peter. BA, Princeton U., 1942; MD, Columbia U., 1945. Diplomate Am. Bd. Pathology. Pathologist in charge, assoc. prof. pathology Tufts New Eng. Med. Ctr., Boston, 1954-70; assoc. prof. pathology Tufts Med. Sch., 1954-70; sr. pathologist Framingham (Mass.) Union Hosp., 1970-93; assoc. prof. pathology Boston U. Sch. Medicine, 1970—2003. Capt. AUS, 1945-48. Fellow Coll. Am. Pathologists; mem. N.E. Soc. Pathologists (past pres.).

GHERMAN, PAUL M., university librarian; BA, Wayne State U., Detroit, Mich.; MALS, U. Mich. Acting head humanities divsn. Wayne State U., 1971—72; pers. officer univ. libr. Pa. State U., 1972—74; asst. dir. adminstrv. svc. Iowa State U., 1977—85; univ. libr. Va. Poly. Inst. and State U., 1985—92; dir. libr. Kenyon Coll., Gambier, Ohio, 1992—96; univ. libr. Vanderbilt U., Nashville, 1996—. Mem.: ALA (Hugh C. Atkinson Meml. Award 2005). Office: Jean and Alexander Heard Libr Vanderbilt U 419 21st Ave S Nashville TN 37240-0007 Office Phone: 615-322-7120. Fax: 615-343-8279. E-mail: paul.m.gherman@vanderbilt.edu.

GHERTY, JOHN E., food products and agricultural products company executive; b. 1944; married. BBA, U. Wis., 1965, JD, 1968, MA, 1970. Lawyer corp. law dept. Land O' Lakes Inc., Arden Hills, Minn., 1970-79, asst. to pres., 1979-81, group v.p., 1981-89, pres., CEO, 1989—. Bd. dirs. CF Industries, Long Grove, Ill., Minn. Life Ins., St. Paul. Bd. dirs. Grad. Inst. Coop. Leadership, Greater Twin Cities United Way. Mem.: 4-H Found., Minn. Bus. Partnership (bd. dirs.), Nat. Coun. Farmer Coops. (bd. dirs.). Office: Land O'Lakes PO Box 64101 Saint Paul MN 55164-0101 also: 4001 Lexington Ave N Saint Paul MN 55126-2934

GHETTI, BERNARDINO FRANCESCO, pathologist, educator, neuroscientist; b. Pisa, Italy, Mar. 28, 1941; s. Getulio and Iris (Mugnetti) G.; m. Caterina Genovese, Oct. 8, 1966; children: Chiara, Simone. MD cum laude, U. Pisa, 1966, specialist in mental and nervous diseases, 1969. Lic. physician, Italy; cert. Edn. Coun. for Fgn. Med. Grads.; diplomate Am. Bd. Pathology. Postdoctoral fellow U. Pisa, 1966-70; rsch. fellow in neuropathology Albert Einstein Coll. Medicine, Bronx, NY, 1970-73, resident, clin. fellow in pathology, 1973-75, resident in neuropathology, 1975-76; asst. prof. pathology Ind. U., Indpls., 1976-77, asst. prof. pathology and psychiatry, 1977—78, assoc. prof. pathology and psychiatry, 1978—83, prof. pathology and psychiatry, 1983—91, assoc. dir. program in med. neurobiology, 1983—2000, assoc. dir. divsn. neuropathology, 1989-93, prof. pathology, psychiatry, med. and molecular genetics, 1991—97, dir. Alzheimer Disease Ctr., 1991—, dir. divsn. neuropathology, 1993—, Disting. prof. pathology and lab. medicine, psychiatry, med. and molecular genetics, neurology, 1997—. Mem. Nat. Inst. Neurol. Disorders and Stroke rev. com. NIH, 1985-89; mem. NIH Reviewers Res., 1989-93. Contbr. articles to profl. jours. Alzheimer's disease rsch. sci. rev. com. Am. Health Assistance Found., 1998—2002. Recipient Potamkin Prize, 1999, Laurea Houoris Causa, U. Siena, 2005. Mem. Internat. Soc.

Neuropathology (v.p. 2000-03, pres.-elect 2005—), Am. Acad. Neurology, Am. Neurol. Assn., Am. Assn. Neuropathologists (pres. 1996-97), Soc. Neurosci., Assn. Rsch. in Nervous and Mental Diseases, Internat. Brain Rsch. Orgn., Am. Soc. Cell Biology, Italian Soc. Psychiatry, Italian Soc. Neurology, Sigma Xi. Roman Catholic. Home: 1124 Frederick Dr S Indianapolis IN 46260-3421 Office: Ind U 635 Barnhill Dr Rm 138 Indianapolis IN 46202-5126 Office Phone: 317-274-7818. Business E-Mail: bghetti@iupui.edu.

GHEZ, ANDREA MIA, astronomy educator, physics educator; b. NYC, June 16, 1965; d. Gilbert and Susanne; m. Tom La Tourette, May 1, 1993; 1 child, Evan LaTourette-Ghez. BS, MIT, 1987; MS, Calif. Inst. Tech., 1989, PhD, 1993. Hubble postdoctoral fellow U. Ariz., Tucson, 1992-93; vis. rsch. scholar Inst. Astronomy, Cambridge, England, 1994; asst. prof. physics and astronomy UCLA, 1994-97, assoc. prof. physics and astronomy, 1997—. Recipient Young Investigator award NSF, 1994, Fullam Dudley award, 1995, Pierce prize, 1998, Maria Goeppert-Meyer award, Am. Phys. Soc., 1999, Sacker prize, Tel Aviv U., 2004, Gold Shield Faculty prize, UCLA, 2004; Pacific Telesis fellow, 1991, Sloan fellow, 1996, Packard fellow, 1996. Fellow: Am. Acad. Arts and Scis.; mem.: AAUW (Anne Jump Cannon award 1994), NAS, Am. Astron. Soc., Phi Beta Kappa. Achievements include discovery of formation of young low mass stars in multiple star systems; production of the first diffraction-limited image with the keck 10-m telescope (the largest telescope in the world); measurement of stellar motions which indicate the presence of a supermassive black hole at the center of our own galaxy. Home: 224 Barlock Ave Los Angeles CA 90049 Office: UCLA Dept Astronomy 405 Hilgard Ave Los Angeles CA 90095-1562

GHEZZI, SHERYL RAE, lawyer, real estate broker; b. Chgo., Nov. 12, 1955; d. Raymond Marion and Carol Jean G. BA, Lake Forest Coll., 1977; JD, John Marshall Sch. Law, 1984. Bar: Ill. 1984. Assoc. Hoffman, Burke & Bozick, Chgo., 1984-86; sole practice Chgo., 1986—. Faculty, family law divsn. Nat. Bus. Inst., 2004—; lectr. in field; human relations com. Village of Lincolnwood. Commr. human rels. commn. Village of Lincolnwood, 2005—; child's rep. Cir. Ct. Cook County, 1991—; bd. dirs. Lincolnwood Sch. Found., 2003—05. Mem. ABA, Ill. State Bar Assn. (mil. affairs com. 2002-05), Chgo. Bar Assn., Women' Bar Assn. Ill., Assn. Trial Lawyers Am., Assn. Family and Conciliation Cts., North Suburban Bar Assn. Roman Catholic. Office: 4433 Touhy Ste 301 Lincolnwood IL 60712 Office Phone: 847-675-7570. E-mail: sheryl@ghezzilaw.com.

GHIARDI, JAMES DOMENIC, lawyer, educator; b. Gwinn, Mich., Nov. 10, 1918; s. John B. and Margaret M. (Trosello) G.; m. Phyllis A. Lindmeier, Sept. 5, 1945; children— Catherine, Jeanne, Mary. PhB, Marquette U., 1940, LLB, 1942, JD, 1968. Bar: Wis. bar 1942. Prof. law Marquette U. Law Sch., Milw., 1946-89, prof. law emeritus, 1990—; research dir. Def. Research Inst., Milw., 1962-72; of counsel firm Kluwin, Dunphy, Hankin & McNulty, Milw., 1972-87. Author: Personal Injury Damages, Wisconsin, 1964, Punitive Damages, Vol. I, 1981, Vol. II, 1985; contbr. articles to profl. jours. Served to capt. Med. Adminstrv. Br. U.S. Army, 1942-45. Recipient award for teaching excellence Marquette U. Faculty, 1971, Edward A. Uhrig Found., 1971, Alumni of Yr. award Marquette U. Law Sch., 1971, Charles L. Goldberg award for outstanding pub. svc. Wis. Law Found., 1986, Charles C. Pinckney award for legal scholarship and svc. to the legal profession N.Y. Def. Bar Assn., 1986. Fellow Am. Bar Found.; mem. ABA (mem. ho. of dels. 1967-80, Disting. Prof. Torts and Ins. Law award Torts and Ins. Practice sect. 1989), Milw. Bar Assn. (Lifetime Achievement award 1993), State Bar Wis. (gov., mem. exec. com. 1962-72, pres. 1970-71), Am. Law Ins., Wis. Bar Found., Am. Legion. Office: Sensenbrenner Hall Marquette U Law Sch PO Box 1881 Milwaukee WI 53201-1881

GHIGLIONE, LOREN FRANK, newspaper editor; b. N.Y.C., Apr. 5, 1941; s. William John and Norma Rae (Whitney) G.; m. Nancy Ellen Geiger, Feb. 24, 1968; children: Jessica, Laura. BA, Haverford Coll., 1963; M of Urban Studies, LLB, Yale U., 1966; PhD in Am. Civilization, George Washington U., 1976. Asst. to dir. office of planning & analysis NEH, Washington, 1967-68; editor The News, Southbridge, Mass.; pres. Worcester County Newspapers, Southbridge, Mass.; former James M. Cox Chair in Journalism Emory U.; former dir. Sch. Journalism U. So. Calif., Annenberg Sch. Comm.; dean, prof. Medill Sch. Journalism, Northwestern U., 2001—. Bd. dirs. Maynard Inst., Oakland, Calif.; cons. Libr. of Congress, Washington, 1988—, Newseum, Arlington, Va., 1992—. Author books and contbr. chpts. and essays to books and articles to profl. jours.; mem. edit. bd. Newspaper Rsch. Jour., Athens, Ohio, 1990—. Trustee Worcester Art Mus., 1993—, Worcester Hist. Mus., 1990, Haverford (Mass.) Coll., 1992—; councillor Am. Antiquarian Soc., Worcester, 1993—. Congrl. fellow U.S. Congress, Washington, 1966-67, Freedom Forum Media Studies Ctr. fellow Columbia U., 1987-88, Joan Shorenstein Ctr. Harvard's John F. Kennedy Sch. Govt. fellow, 1988-89, Soc. Profl. Journalism fellow, 1990-91. Fellow Am. Acad. Arts and Scis.; mem. Am. Soc. Newspapers Editors (pres. 1989-90), New Eng. Soc. Newspaper Editors (pres. 1978-79), New Eng. Press Assn. (pres. 1984), Internat. Press Inst. (dir. Am. com. 1989-94), Coun. Fgn. Rels. Avocations: reading, wind surfing. Office: Medill School of Journalism Northwestern U 1845 Sheridan Rd Evanston Evanston IL 60208-2101 E-mail: ghiglion@northwestern.edu.*

GHIL, MICHAEL, atmospheric scientist, geophysicist; b. Budapest, Hungary, June 10, 1944; s. Louis and Ilona V. (Dobo) Cernat; m. Michèle J. Denizot, July 8, 1982; children: Emmanuel A., Mirella J. BSc cum laude, Technion-Israel Inst. Tech., Haifa, 1966, MSc in Mech. Engring., 1971; MS, NYU, 1973, PhD in Math., 1975. Rsch. asst. to instr. Technion-Israel Inst. Tech., Haifa, 1966-71; rsch. assoc. NASA Goddard Inst. Space Studies, NYC, 1975-76; rsch. asst. prof. math. Courant Inst. Math. Scis., NYC, 1976-79, rsch. assoc. prof. atmospheric sci., 1979-82, rsch. prof., 1982-86; prof. atmospheric sci. and geophysics UCLA, 1985—; prof. geoscis. Ecole Normale Superieore, Paris, 2002—. Chmn. dept. atmospheric scis., UCLA, 1988-92; dir. Climate Dynamics Ctr., UCLA, 1986-92, Inst. Geophys. Planet Physics UCLA, 1992-2003, Dept. Terre Atmosphere-Ocean, ENS, Paris, 2003-; disting. vis. scientist Jet Propulsion Lab., Calif. Inst. Tech./NASA, Pasadena, Calif., 1988—; Condorcet chair Ecole Normale Supérieure, Paris, 1995; Elf-Aquitaine/CNRS chair Acad. Scis., Paris, 1996, Collège de France, Paris, 1997. Author: Topics in GFD: Atmospheric Dynamics, Dynamo Theory and Climate Dynamics, 1987; editor: Turbulence and Predictability in Geophysical Fluid Dynamics and Climate Dynamics, 1985, Dynamic Meteorology: Data Assimilation Methods, 1981, Natural Climate Variability on Decade-to-Century Time Scales, 1995, Data Assimilation in Meteorology and Oceanography: Theory and Practice, 1997. Mem. adv. bd. Calif. Space Inst., San Diego, 1986-90; chmn. sci. adv. coun. Climate Sys. Modeling Program, Boulder, Colo., 1988—; bd. dirs. New Sun Found. Geneva, 1994-99, bd. govs. Weizmann Inst. Sci. Rehovot, Israel, 1995-2000. Recipient L.F. Richardson medal, European Geoscis. Union, 2004. Fellow Am. Meteorol. Soc. (profl. com. 1989-92), Am. Geophys. Union; mem. NRC (climate rsch. com. 1989-98), Soc. for Indsl. and Applied Math., Royal Astron. Soc. (assoc., hon.), Acad. Europaea (fgn.), Sigma Xi. Democrat. Jewish. Avocations: hiking, climbing, skiing, swimming, languages. Office: UCLA Inst Geophys Planet Phys 405 Hilgard Ave Los Angeles CA 90095-9000

GHIU, SILVANA MELANIA STEFANIA, environmental engineer; b. Constanta, Romania, Dec. 27, 1971; d. Gheorghe and Camelia Ghiu. BSc, U. Bucharest, 1995, MSc, 1996, Ctrl. European U., Budapest, 1998; PhD, U. So. Fla., 2003. EIT 2000. Rsch. asst. Engring. and Environment Rsch. Inst., Bucharest, 1995—97; safeguards officer asst. Nat. Commn. of Nuc. Activities Control, Bucharest, 1996—97; rsch. asst. U. So. Fla., Tampa, 1999—2003; environ. engr. HSA, Tampa, 2004—. Contbr. articles to profl. jours. Fellow, U. So. Fla. Coll. Engring., 1998—2001, 2001; Govtl. fellow, U. Bucharest, 1995—96, George Soros Found. fellow, Ctrl. European U., 1997—98, Channabasappa Meml. scholar, IDA, 2001. Mem.: Internat. Desalination Assn., North Am. Membrane Soc., Am. Membrane Tech. Assn., Am. Water Works Assn. (v.p. Fla. sect. 2001—03), Nat. Soc. of Profl. Engr., Phi Kappa Phi. Achievements include patents pending for submersible pump; research in equations governing the process of direct osmosis. Office: HSA 4019 E Fowler Ave Tampa FL 33617 Office Phone: 813-971-3882. Personal E-mail: silvanaghiu@yahoo.com. Business E-Mail: sghiu@hsa-env.com.

GHOGAWALA, ZOHER, neurosurgeon; b. Dhaka, Bangladesh, Nov. 3, 1966; s. Honed and Nema (Mohammed) G.; m. Tasneem Haidermota, June 16, 1991; 1 child. AB, Harvard U., 1987; MD, Harvard Med. Sch., 1991. Diplomate Am. Bd. Neurol. Surgeons. Resident Mass. Gen. Hosp., Boston, 1991—99; clin. asst. prof. neurosurgery Yale U., New Haven, 2001—. Mem. Am. Assn. Neurol. Surgeons, Congress Neurol. Surgeons. Mailing: 75 Holly Hill Ln Greenwich CT 06870 Office Phone: 203-661-3333.

GHOLSTON, ROBERT M., lawyer; b. Amarillo, Tex., May 17, 1936; s. John Edward Thurman Gholston and Lora Hodges; m. Sharon E. Crull, July 4, 1958 (div. Apr. 1982); children: Kevin M., Curtis M., Deborah A.; m. Bettie J. Wright, Apr. 28, 1983. AA, Amarillo Jr. Coll., 1956; BA, U. North Tex., 1958; JD, Ind. U., 1964. Bar: Ind. 1965, U.S. Dist. Ct. (so. dist.) Ind. 1965, U.S. Ct. Appeals (7th cir.) 1972, U.S. Supreme Ct. 1972. Assoc. Acher & Young, Franklin, Ind., 1965-66; ptnr. Acher & Gholston, Franklin, Ind., 1967-78, Young, Gholston & Young, Franklin, 1979-88; pvt. practice Franklin, 1988—. State legal counsel Ind. Jaycees, 1970-74; treas., v.p. and bd. dirs. local coun. Boy Scouts Am., 1978-88, dist. chmn., 1978-80; bd. dirs. Greenwood (Ind.) C. of C., 1978-80. Named Sagamore of Wabash, Gov. Ind., Ky. Col., Gov. Ky. Mem.: Johnson County Bar Assn. (sec-treas., v.p., pres.), Ind. State Bar Assn. (bd. mgrs. 1984—86). Republican. Lutheran. Avocations: reading, coin and stamp collecting, biking, hiking, camping. Home: 528 Delbrook Dr New Whiteland IN 46184-1302 Office: 120 W Madison St Franklin IN 46131-2126 Office Phone: 317-736-7768.

GHOSH, AJIT KUMAR, daycare administrator; b. Calcutta, India, May 20, 1922; arrived in U.S., 1987, naturalized, 1997; s. Rajendra Kumar and Uma Rani Ghosh; m. Sovana Sirkar, June 29, 1945; children: Baruna, Surajit. BSME, Bengal Engring. Coll., 1943. Asst. foreman Govt. Ctrl. Workshops, Kanpore, India, 1943; owner Gen. Engring. Co., Kanpore, 1943—46; lectr. applied mechanics Bengal Engring. Coll. U. Calcutta, Calcutta, India, 1946—48; with Dept. Prodn. and Design Office William Asquith et al., Birmingham, England, 1948—50; designer Newall Engring. Co. Ltd., Peterborough, England, 1950; chief process planning engr. Burn & Co., Howrah, India, 1951—54; works mgr. Ctrl. Engring. Orgn., Howrah, 1956—59; gen. mgr. Heavy Machine Tools Plant Heavy Engring. Corp., Ranchi, India, 1960—70; mng. dir. Rehab. Industries Corp., India, 1971—72; mem., CEO on-shore divsn. Oil & Natural Gas Commn., Dehradun, India, 1972—77; founder, mng. dir. Webel Toolsind Ltd., Calcutta, 1977—87; co-prin., owner Incare, Inc., Parsippany and Randolph, 1987—. Author: Practical Machine Design, 1969. Recipient Honor cert., Govt. India, 1963; scholar, U. Calcutta, 1940. Mem.: AARP, Instn. Engrs. India. Achievements include patents in field. Avocations: walking, cooking. Home: 25 Gilmar Rd Randolph NJ 07869 Office Phone: 973-989-8637.

GHOSH, ALOK, pharmaceutical executive; s. Benoy and Maya Ghosh; m. Alpana Ghosh; 1 child, Soham. MPharm, Jadavpur U., Calcutta, India, 1978. Officer develop. Bengal Immunity, Calcutta, India, 1978—84; mgr. formulation develop. Lupin Lab. Ltd., Bombay, 1984—88; mgr., Quality Assurance Astra AB, Bangalore, India, 1988—93; dir. corp. quality assurance Ranbaxy Lab Ltd., New Delhi, 1993—2001; v.p. ops. Ronbaxy Phar. Inc., North Brunswick, NJ, 2001—. Office: Ranbaxy Pharm Inc 1385 Livingston Ave North Brunswick NJ 08902 E-mail: alok.ghosh@ranbaxy.com.

GHOSH, AVIJIT, dean; m. Sara McLafferty; children: Smita, Priya. BS in chem. with honors, Calcutta U., 1970; postgrad. in mgmt., Xavier Inst., 1975; MA in geography, U. Iowa, 1977, PhD in geography, 1979. Asst. prof. mktg. Sch. Bus., U. Iowa, 1978—79; asst. to assoc prof. mktg. Leonard N. Stern Sch. Bus., NYU, 1980—91, dir. Ctr. Entrepreneurial Studies, 1991—95, vice dean profl. programs, 1994—2001, dep. dean, 1998—99; dean Coll. Bus., U. Ill., Urbana-Champaign, 2001—., assoc. editor: Jour. Retailing, 1983 (Best Article Yr., 1984); editor, 1985—91 (Best Article Yr., 1991); author: (books) Retail Management, 1990, 1994; co-author (with Sara McLafferty): Location Strategy for Retail and Service Firms, 1987; co-editor: Spatial Analysis and Location Allocation Models, 1987, Spatial Analysis in Marketing: Theory, Methods and Applications, 1991. Office: Coll Bus Univ Ill Urbana Champaign 1206 S Sixth St 260 Wohlers Hall Champaign IL 61820 Office Phone: 217-333-2747. Office Fax: 217-244-3113. Business E-Mail: ghosha@uiuc.edu.

GHOSH, BHASKAR KUMAR, statistics educator, researcher; b. Dibrugarh, India, Feb. 10, 1936; arrived in US, 1961; s. Saroj Kumar and Usha Rani (Bose) G.; m. Hedwig Graf, 1960; children: Monica, Anita, Rebecca. BSc, Calcutta U., 1955; PhD, London U., 1959. Statistician Atomic Power Constrn., London, 1959-60; asst. prof. U. London, 1960-61, Lehigh U., Bethlehem, Pa., 1961-63, assoc. prof., 1963-68, prof., 1968—. Vis. prof. MIT, Cambridge, Mass., 1968, Va. Tech., Blacksburg, 1978-80, U. Munster, Germany, 1986-87. Author: Sequential Tests of Statistical Hypotheses, 1970; editor: Handbook of Sequential Analysis, 1991; editor: Sequential Analysis, 1982-95. Recipient U.S. Sr. Rsch. Scientist award Alexander von Humboldt Found., 1986-87, 92. Fellow Royal Statis. Soc., Inst. Math. Statistics. Home: 1440 E University Ave Bethlehem PA 18015-4718 Office: Lehigh U Dept Math 14 E Packer Ave Bethlehem PA 18015-3175 Office Phone: 610-758-3722. Business E-Mail: bkg0@lehigh.edu.

GHOSH, NARENDRA NATH, research scientist; b. Bankura, West- Bengal, India, Jan. 1, 1970; s. Nanda Dulal and Purnima Ghosh; m. Swayang Probha (Biswas) Mar. 08, 1980. MSc in Chemistry, Indian Inst. Tech., Kharagpur, 1992—94, PhD in Chemistry, 1998. Rsch. scholar Indian Inst. Tech., Kharagpur, India, 1994—98; postdoctoral rschr. U. Del., Newark, 1998—2000; faculty dept. chemistry Birla Inst. Tech. and Sci., Pilani, India, 2000—02; postdoctoral rschr. U. Tenn., Knoxville, 2002—04, U. Ky., Lexington, 2004; mem. faculty dept. chemistry Birla Inst. Tech. and Sci. Pinali, India, 2005—. Chair Conf. on Materials for the New Millennium, India, 2000. Contbr. articles to profl. jours. Achievements include research in nanomaterials, mesoporous solids, polymer and inorganic chemistry. Home: BITS Gaca Campus 403726 India Office: Faculty Dept Chemistry Birla Inst Tech and Sci Pilani Goa Campu Goa Zuarinagar 403 726 India Office Phone: 011-91-832-2580318. Business E-Mail: naren70@yahoo.com. E-mail: ghosh@novell.chem.utk.edu.

GHOSH, SAMBHUNATH (SAM GHOSH), civil engineering educator, environmental engineer; BS, U. Calcutta, 1956; MS, U. Ill., 1963; PhD, Ga. Inst. Tech., 1970. Engr. Wiedeman & Singleton, Atlanta, 1963—65; mgr. bioengring. rsch. Gas Tech. Inst., Chgo., 1971—85; prof. civil engring. U. Utah, Salt Lake City, 1985—2000; prof. civil, agrl. and geol. engring. N.Mex State U., Las Cruces, 2000—01; pres. EnviroEnergetics, Salt Lake City, 1988—, EnviroEnergetics of Wis., Inc., 2005—. Recipient Ill. Energy award, 1985, Utah Gov.'s award for energy innovation, 1986, John Ericsson award and Gold medal in Renewable Energy U.S. Dept. Energy, 1994, George Bradley Gascoigne medal, Water Environment Fedn., 1996, Thomas R. Camp medal, Water Environment Fedn., Alexandria, Va., 2001. Home: 1281 E Federal Heights Dr Salt Lake City UT 84103-4325 Office: 1281 E Federal Heights Dr Salt Lake City UT 84103 Office Phone: 801-355-1429. Home Fax: 801-596-2166. Personal E-mail: sambhughosh@aol.com.

GHOSTLEY, DAVID CARL, psychologist, retired military officer; b. Fargo, ND, Dec. 29, 1955; s. James Garnet and Constance Mae; m. Rebecca June Anderson, Dec. 29, 1995; children: Mary, Kyle, Melody, Jesse, James, Kaitlynn. BA, Bemidji State U., 1985; MS, Troy U., 1994; DS in Psychology, Argosy U., 2003. Lic. psychologist Ala. State Bd. Exam., cert. forensic examiner Ala. Dept. Mental Health and Mental Retardation. Commn. officer U.S. Army, 1974—95; adj. faculty Embry Riddle Aeronautical U., Ala., 2003. Cons. Dale Med. Ctr., Ozark, Ala., 2004—, Southeast Ala. Med. Ctr., Dothan, 2004—. Contbr. scientific papers in field. Bd. mem. Local Chpt. Red Cross, 2005—. Capt. U.S. Army. Avocations: music, running, hiking. Home: 2806 Turner Cir Dothan AL 36303-2146 Office: Southwood Med Park 1841 Honeysuckle Rd Dothan AL 36305-4269 Personal E-mail: ghostley@mindspring.com.

GHOVANLOO, MAYSAM, engineer, educator; m. Azadeh N. Shahshahani, Sept. 8, 2001. BS, U. Tehran, Iran, 1990—94; MS, Amirkabir U. Tech., Tehran, Iran, 1994—97; PhD, U. Mich., Ann Arbor, 2000—04, MS, 2000—03. Sr. rsch. engr. IDEA Co. Ltd., Tehran, Iran, 1994—99; sr. engr. Ctr. for Repair and Reconstruction Med. Devices, Tehran, Iran, 1997—98; founder, CEO Sabz Nagar Rayaneh Co. Ltd., Tehran, Iran, 1998—99; rsch. asst. U. Mich., Ann Arbor, 2000—04; tech. intern Advanced Bionics Corp., Santa Clarita, Calif., 2002; asst. prof. N.C. State U., Raleigh, 2004—. Cons. Nitinol Devel. Corp., Fremont, Calif., 2004—. Contbr. articles to profl. jours. Grantee, N.C. State U., 2005. Mem.: IEEE, Tau Beta Pi. Achievements include patents pending for Frequency shift keying demodulation methods for wireless biomedical Implants; Three dimensional microassembly structures for micromachined planar microelectrode arrays; Shatter-proof microprobes; A compact large voltage compliance high output impedance programmable current source. Office: NC State Univ 2440 Campus Shore Dr Raleigh NC 27695 Office Phone: 919-513-1923. Office Fax: 919-515-2285. Business E-Mail: mghovan@ncsu.edu.

GHYSELS, ERIC, finance educator; s. Pierre Ghysels; m. Lutgart Van Zeghbroeck, June 19, 1981; children: Nicholas, Jonathan. PhD, Northwestern U., 1984. Edward M. Bernstein disting. prof. econs. U. NC, Chapel Hill, 2000—05, prof. fin. Kenan-Flagler Bus. Sch., 2000—05. Fellow: Am. Statis. Assn. (editor Jour. Bus. Econ. Stats.). Office: Univ NC Dept Economics Chapel Hill NC 27599 Office Phone: 919-966-5325.

GIACCONE, JASON MICHAEL, music educator, musician; b. Baton Rouge, June 4, 1976; s. Vincent Phillip Giaccone and Deborah Neely Farr, George Walter Farr (Stepfather) and Rhenda Newsom Giaccone (Stepmother); m. Jamie Colleen Riley, July 5, 1978. BFA, La. Tech U., 1999. Track bugler La. Downs, Bossier City, 1999—2000; assoc. dir. bands Jesuit H.S., New Orleans, 2001—. Musician: (trumpet/flugelhorn soloist) La. Tech U. Jazz Ensemble. Scholar, La. Tech U. Dept. Liberal Arts, 1994—99. Mem.: Phi Mu Alpha (music coord. 1996—97, v.p. 1997—98, pres. 1998—99). Independent. Roman Catholic. Home: 3301 W Esplanade Ave N Apt 15241C Metairie LA 70002-2600 Office: Jesuit High Sch New Orleans 4133 Banks St New Orleans LA 70119 Office Phone: 504-483-3935. Business E-Mail: giaccone@jesuitnola.org.

GIACCONI, RICCARDO, astrophysicist, educator; b. Genoa, Italy, Oct. 6, 1931; arrived in U.S., 1956, naturalized, 1967; s. Antonio and Elsa (Canni) Giacconi; m. Mirella Manaira, Feb. 15, 1957; children: Guia Giacconi Trutter, Anna Lee, Marc A. PhD, U. Milan, Italy, 1954; ScD (hon.), U. Chgo., 1983; laurea honoris causa in astronomy, U. Padua, 1984; ScD (hon.), Warsaw U., 1996; laurea honoris causa in physics, U. Rome, 1998; Dr Tech. and Sci. (hon.), U. Uppsala, 2000. Asst. prof. physics U. Milan, 1954—56; rsch. assoc. Ind. U., 1956—58, Princeton U., 1958—59; exec. v.p., dir. Am. Sci. & Engring. Co., Cambridge, Mass., 1959—73; prof. astronomy Harvard U.; also assoc. dir. high energy astrophysics divsn. Center Astrophysics, Smithsonian Astrophys. Obs./Harvard Coll. Obs., Cambridge, 1973—81; dir. Space Telescope Sci. Inst., Balt., 1981—92; prof. astrophysics Johns Hopkins U., 1981—99, U. Milan, Italy, 1991—99; dir.-gen. European So. Obs., Garching, Germany, 1993—99; pres. Assoc. Univs., Inc., Washington, 1999—2004; prof. Johns Hopkins U., 1999—. Richtmeyer meml. lectr. Am. Assn. Physics Tchrs., 1975; mem. space sci. adv. com. NASA, 1978—79, mem. adv. com. innovation study, 1979—; mem. NASA Astrophysics Coun., mem. adv. com. innovation study astronomy adv. com., 1979—; mem. high energy astronomy survey panel Nat. Acad. Scis., 1979—80, mem. Space Sci. Studies Bd., 1980—84, 1989—; mem. adv. com. Max-Planck Inst. für Physik und Astrophysik; chmn. bd. dirs. Instituto Guido Donegani, Gruppo Montedison, 1987—89; mem. vis. com. to divsn. of phys. scis. U. Chgo., U. Padua; chmn. ISC E-1 (galactic and extragalactic astrophysics) Com. on Space Rsch. (COSPAR), 1982—93; Russell lectr. Co-editor: X-ray Astronomy, 1974, The X-Ray Universe, 1985, author numerous articles and papers in field.; inventor x-ray telescope, discoverer of x-ray stars. Recipient Röntgen prize in astrophysics, Physikalish-Medizinische Gesellschaft, Wurzburg, Germany, 1971, Exceptional Sci. Achievement medal, NASA, 1971, 1980, Disting. Pub. Svc. award, 1972, 2003, Space Sci. award, AIAA, 1976, Elliot Cresson medal, Franklin Inst., 1980, Gold medal, Royal Astron. Soc., 1982, A. Cressy Morrison award, N.Y. Acad. Sci., 1982, Bruce medal, 1987, Heinneman award, 1987, Wolf Prize in Physics, 1987, Nobel prize in physics, 2002, Nat. medal of Sci., 2003; fellow, Fulbright, 1956—58. Mem.: Am. Philos. Soc., Royal Astron. Soc., Max-Planck Soc. (ext. mem.), Academia Nazionale dei Lincei (fgn.), Md. Acad. Sci. (sci. coun. 1982—), Internat. Astron. Union, Am. Acad. Arts and Scis., Italian Phys. Soc. (Como prize 1967), Am. Astron. Soc. (Henry Norris Russel lectr. 1981, Darwin lectr. Royal Soc. 1993, chmn. high energy astrophysics divsn., Helen B. Warner award 1966), NAS (rep. 1979—82), AAAS, Cosmos Club (Washington). Office: Johns Hopkins Univ Dept Physics and Astronomy 3400 N Charles St Baltimore MD 21218 Office Phone: 410-516-6021.

GIACHELLO, AIDA L., social worker; b. San Juan, PR; BA, Univ. Puerto Rico; AM, PhD in Sociology, Univ. Chgo. Assoc. prof. Jane Addams Coll. of Social Work, Univ. Ill., Chgo.; founder, dir. Midwest Latino Health Rsch., Training & Policy Ctr., Chgo., 1993—. Mem. study group Nat. Acad. Sci., Inst. Medicine, 2002—04; mem. intervention com., US-Mex. Border Diabetes Project Panamerican Health Org., 2002—; mem. planning com. Hispanic Cancer Genetic Rsch. Conf., 2002—03; mem. Nat. Latino steering com. on tobacco control Am. Legacy Found., 2000—; mem. Ill. Diabetes adv. com. Ill. Dept. Health & Human Svc., 1999—; bd. dir. Health & Med. Policy Rsch. Group, Chgo., 1985—. Contbr. articles to profl. jours. Bd. mem. Nat. Inst. for Diversity, Am. Hosp. Assn., 2001—03; mem. nat. survey com. on alternative med. NIH; mem. HIV/AIDS adv. com. Ctr. for Substance Abuse & Prevention, 1995—2000; mem. bd. adv. Catholic Charities, 1997—. Named one of 25 Most Influential Hispanics, Time Mag., 2005. Mem.: Am. Pub. Health Assn., Hispanic Nat. Inst. for Reproductive Health. Office: Midwest Latino Health Research Training & Policy Ctr Ste 636 DHSP Bldg 1640 W Roosevelt Rd Chicago IL 60608-6906*

GIACUMAKIS, GEORGE, JR., educator, administrator; b. New Castle, Pa., July 6, 1937; s. George, Sr. and Stavroula (Pappas) G.; m. Joan Elizabeth Gillies, Sept. 3, 1960; children— Stephen, Deborah, Mark, Andrew. B.A., Shelton Coll., 1959; M.A., Brandeis U., 1961, Ph.D., 1963. Chmn. Evang. Free Ch., Yorba Linda, Calif., 1969-73, 85—; chmn. SW dist., 1974-77; pres., exec. dir. Inst. Holy Land Studies, Jerusalem, 1978-84; editorial dir. Lockman Found., La Habra, Calif., 1985—; prof. history Calif. State U.-Fullerton, 1963-78, prof. lectr. history, 1985— . Author: The Akkadian of Alalah, 1970. Co-editor Young's Bible Dictionary, 1984. Contbr. articles to profl. jours. Mem. Conf. Faith and History, Evang. Theol. Soc., Am. Schs. Oriental Research, Am. Sci. Affiliation, Middle East Inst., Near East Archaeology Soc. Republican. Lodge: Rotary. Home: 17540 Monette Cir Yorba Linda CA 92886-5137 Office: Lockman Found, 900 S Euclid St La Habra CA 90631-6805

GIADROSICH, DONALD LOUIS, research scientist, retired electrical engineer; b. Oceans Springs, Miss., Apr. 5, 1932; s. Edward and Ella May Giadrosich; m. Diana Davidson, Jan. 20, 1956; children: Kirk, Dana, Keith, Kevin(dec.). BSEE, Miss. State U., 1957; MS in Sys. Analysis and Econs., U. Md., 1967. Sr. electronics engr. Hughes Aircraft Co., Culver City, Calif., 1959—64; dir. advanced rsch. and tech. U.S. Naval Weapons Sys. Analysis Office, Washington, 1964—66; dir. ctrl. sys. analysis group Joint Chiefs of Staff, Sandia Base, N.Mex., 1966—67; chief operational applications Tactical Air Warfare Ctr. USAF, Eglin AFB, Fla., 1967—76; dir. ops. analysis Hdqrs. USAF Europe, Ramstein AB, Germany, 1980—82; chief scientist, chief ops. analysis Air Warfare Ctr., Englin AFB, 1982—94; chief scientist, chief ops. analysis Tactical Fighter Weapons Ctr. USAF, Nellis AFB, Nev., 1976—80;

chief scientist, chief ops. analysis USAF Air Warfare Ctr., Eglin AFB, Fla., 1982—94; ret., 1994. Tech. advisor USAF Sci. Adv. Bd., Washington, 1982—94; mem. tech. adv. bd. Dept. Def. Joint Testing, Washington, 1982—94; mem. study group on live fire testing F-22 NRC, Washington, 1995. Author: Operations Research Analysis in Test and Evaluation, 1995; contbr. more than 30 articles to profl. publs. Coach Little League and other youth activities, Destin, Fla., 1967—76. Recipient Gen. Lewis H. Brereton award in Aerospace, Air Force Assn., 1986, Presdl. Rank award, Office of Pers. Mgmt., Washington, 1986, 1991, USAF Outstanding Civilian Career Svc. award, 1994. Mem.: Inst. Ops. Rsch. and Mgmt. Scis., Am. Legion. Achievements include contributions in modeling and simulation, electronic combat, intelligence synthesis, large scale military exercises, aircraft missile and weapons systems, armament and avionics, range systems. Home: 3811 Indian Trail Destin FL 32541

GIAEVER, IVAR, physicist; b. Bergen, Norway, Apr. 5, 1929; arrived in U.S., 1957, naturalized, 1963; s. John A. and Gudrun (Skaarud) Giaever; m. Inger Skramstad, Nov. 8, 1952; children: John, Anne Kari, Guri, Trine. Siv. Ing., Norwegian Inst. Tech., Trondheim, 1952; PhD (hon.), Rensselaer Poly. Inst., 1964, Union College, 1974; PhD U. of Oslo (hon.), 1976; PhD (hon.), Michigan Tech. U., 1976, Worcester Polytechnic Inst., 1977, Norwegian Inst. of Tech., 1985, Clarkson U., 1985, SUNY, 1985. Patent examiner Norwegian Patent Office, Oslo, 1953—54; mech. engr. Can. Gen. Electric Co., Peterborough, Canada, 1954—56; applied mathematician Gen. Electric Co., Schenectady, 1956—58, physicist Research and Devel. Ctr., 1958—88; Inst. prof. Rensselaer Poly. Inst., Troy, NY, 1988—; and pres. Applied BioPhysics, Inc., Troy, NY. Prof.-at-large Univ. Oslo, Norway, 1988—. Served with Norwegian Army, 1952—53. Recipient Nobel prize for Physics, 1973; fellow Guggenheim, 1970. Fellow: Am. Phys. Soc. (Oliver E. Buckley prize 1965); mem.: NAS, IEEE, Korean Acad. of Sci., Swedish Acad. of Engring., Norwegian Acad. Tech., Norwegian Acad. Sci., Am. Acad. Arts and Scis., Nat. Acad. Engring. (V.K. Zworykin award 1974), Norwegian Profl. Engrs. Achievements include experimental discoveries regarding tunneling phenomean in semiconductors and superconductors. Office: Rensselaer Poly Ins Physics Dept 110 8th St Troy NY 12180-3590 also: Pres Applied Biophysics Inc 1223 Peoples Ave Troy NY 12180 E-mail: giaevi@rpi.edu.*

GIAIMO, KATHRYN ANN, performing arts company executive; b. Milw., Jan. 20, 1961; d. Samuel Patrick and Marilyn Eunice G. BA, U. Minn., 1983; MA, NYU, 1989. Adminstrv. dir. Thalia Spanish Theatre, Sunnyside, N.Y., 1989—. Steering com. Coalition to Develop Young Theatre Audiences, N.Y.C., 1992; panelist Queens (N.Y.) Coun. Arts, 1992-93, Nancy Quinn Fund for Alliance of Resident Theatres, N.Y., 1994 and N.Y.C. Dept. of Cultural Affairs, 1997; performer Theater for a Greater Peace, Flying Bridge Prodns., 1993-97. Vol. Increase the Peace Vol. Corps., N.Y.C., 1992-93; mem. steering com. N.Y.C. Arts Coalition, 2002—. Recipient proclamation for women's history month N.Y.C. Coun., 2001. Mem. Kiwanis (sec. Sunnyside chpt. 1993-95). Office: Thalia Spanish Theatre PO Box 4368 41-17 Greenpoint Ave Long Island City NY 11104 E-mail: kgiaimo@thaliatheatre.org.

GIALANELLA, ALEX JUSTIN, bank executive, educator; b. New Rochelle, NY, Apr. 15, 1980; s. Al Anthony and Nancy Marie Gialanella; m. Jennifer Lynn Loiacono; 1 child, Alex Justin. BBA, Iona Coll., 2002, MBA, 2003; postgrad. studies, Fordham U., 2003—. Fin. analyst Bresnan Comm., White Plains, NY, 2003—04; asst. v.p. fin. Citigroup Pvt. Bank, NYC, 2004—; prof. fin. Iona Coll., New Rochelle, NY, 2003—; prof. econs. SUNY Westchester, Valhalla, 2004—. Mem.: Fin. Mgmt. Assn., Am. Econs. Assn. Roman Catholic. Avocations: chess, travel, gold. Home: 134 Highview Dr Carmel NY 10512 Office Phone: 718-248-8836. Personal E-mail: ag4602@aol.com. E-mail: alex.gialanella@citigroup.com.

GIALANELLA, DONALD GEORGE, broadcast executive, sound recording engineer, sculptor; b. Plainfield, N.J., June 9, 1956; s. Angelo George and Helena Joan (Kreminski) G.; m. Phyllis Clare Orlowski, June 25, 1988; children: Max Philip, Julian Andrew. Student, Montclair (N.J.) State U., 1974-77; BFA cum laude, Cooper Union, 1979. Art dir. South Coast Publs., San Diego, 1981-83; artist, animator ABC News/Sports, N.Y.C., 1983-84; assoc. network news graphics dir. ABC News, N.Y.C., 1984-85; broadcast graphics artistic dir. ABC Sports/Entertainment, N.Y.C., 1985—. Designer, producer (animation/graphics) Monday Night Football, 1990 (Emmy award 1990), (opening animation) Good Morning America, 1989. Recipient Elliot Lash Meml. prize Cooper Union, 1979, Page Design award Sigma Delta Chi, 1983, Gold Design award North County Press Club, 1984, Art Direction awards Art Direction mag., 1985; finalist Monitor Award Assn., 1986. Mem. Acad. TV, Arts and Scis. (Sports Emmy award 1990), Broadcast Designers Assn. Avocations: triathlons, biathlons. Home: 20 Sugar Ct Newtown CT 06470 Office: ABC Sports 47 W 66th St Fl 8 New York NY 10023-6201

GIALLORENZI, THOMAS GAETANO, optical engineer; b. NYC, Feb. 28, 1943; s. Amedeo and Eleanor (Spica) G.; m. Margaret Mary Marrin, Sept. 6, 1966; children: Thomas R., Kathy. BS in Engring. Physics, Cornell U., 1965, MS in Engring. Physics, 1966, PhD, 1969. Tech. staff Gen. Tel. & Electronics Lab., Bayside, N.Y., 1969-70; sect. head, optical techniques br. Naval Rsch. Lab., Washington, 1970-76, head optical techniques br., 1976-79, supt. optical scis. divsn., 1979—. Lectr. in field and at profl. soc. confs. Editor Jour. Lightwave Tech., 1983-88; contbr. over 80 articles to profl. jours.; over 30 patents in field. Mem. adv. bd. U. Va., 1986-92. Recipient Applied Sci. award Rsch. Soc. Am., 1973, Meritorious Civilian Svc. award USN, 1978, Conrad award USN, 1985, Disting. Exec. Rank award Pres. of U.S., 1990, 98, Meritorious Exec. Rank award Pres. of U.S., 1984, 2004, Disting. Civilian Svc. award Dept. Def., 1987. Fellow IEEE (assoc. editor Procs. 1990-95, Lightwave Comms. 1989-92, Harry Diamond award 1986, John Tyndell award 1990), IEEE Laser and ElectroOptics Soc. (pres. 1996), Optical Soc. Am. (editor Jour. Lightwave Tech. 1983-89, assoc. editor Applied Optics 1991-94); mem. Nat. Acad. Engring., U.S. Naval League (Albert Michelson award 1995, USN Rodger Easton award Office of Naval Rsch. 1998). Home: 8704 Side Saddle Rd Springfield VA 22152-2731 Office: Naval Rsch Lab Optical Scis Divsn Washington DC 20375-0001 Office Phone: 202-767-3171. Business E-Mail: nrl5600@ccf.nrl.navy.mil.

GIAMALIS, JOHN N, investment company executive; BSc, M of profl. accountancy, West Va. U. Sr. audit mgr. Deloitte & Touche; corp. contr., dir. fin. reporting, analysis The Hartford Fin. Svcs. Group, 1997, deputy contr., 1998, sr. v.p., 1998—, treas., 2002—. Mem.: Am. Inst. of CPAs (mem. fin. svcs. expert panel). Home: Hartford Fin Svcs Group Hartford Plaza 690 Asylum Ave Hartford CT 06115

GIAMATTI, PAUL, actor; b. NYC, June 6, 1967; s. Bart and Toni (Smith) Giamatti; m. Elizabeth Cohen, Oct. 13, 1997; 1 child. M in Fine Arts, Yale U. Actor: (films) Singles, 1992, Past Midnight, 1992, Mighty Aphrodite, 1995, Sabrina, 1995, Breathing Room, 1996, Donnie Brasco, 1997, Private Parts, 1997, My Best Friend's Wedding, 1997, Destructuring Harry, 1997, Dr. Dolittle, 1998, Saving Private Ryan, 1998, The Negotiator, 1998, Safe Men, 1998, The Cradle Will Rock, 1999, Man on the Moon, 1999, Big Momma's House, 2000, Duets, 2000, Storytelling, 2001, Planet of the Apes, 2001, Thunderpants, 2002, Big Fat Liar, 2002, American Splendor, 2003 (Nat. Bd. Rev. award Best Breakthrough Performance, 2003), Paycheck, 2003, Sideways, 2004 (Best Actor, NY Film Critics Circle award, 2004, Best Actor San Francisco Film Critics, 2004, Screen Actors Guild Award, outstanding performance by cast in motion picture, 2005), (voice) Robots, 2005, Cinderella Man, 2005; (TV films) Winchell, 1998, If These Walls Could Talk 2, 2000, The Pentagon Papers, 2003; TV appearances include: NYPD Blue, 1994; (voice) King of the Hill, 2001. Office: Endeavor Talent Agency 9701 Wilshire Blvd 10th Fl Beverly Hills CA 90212*

GIAMBASTIANI, EDMUND P., JR., career military officer; b. Canastota, N.Y., May 4, 1948; Grad. with leadership distinction, US Naval Acad., 1970. Commd. ensign USN, 1970, advanced through grades to admiral, 2005, various assignments including weapons officer, USS Puffer, 1971-75, enlisted program mgr., staff Navy Recruiting Command Hdqrs., 1975-78, flag aide to dep. comdr., 1975-78, engr. officer, USS Francis Scott Key, 1978-82, comdr. Submarine NR-1, 1982-85, mem. staff of Asst. Chief Naval Ops. for undersea warfare, 1985-86, spl. asst. to dep. dir. for intelligence, CIA, comdr. USS Richard B. Russell, 1987-90, fellow Chief Naval Ops. Strategic Studies Group, 1991, comdr. Submarine Devel. Squadron 12, 1991-93, jt. task group comdr., spl. warfare exercise, dir. strategy and concepts Naval Doctrine Command Norfolk, Va., currently dir. submarine warfare divsn. Washington, 1996-98, comdr. Submarine Force, U.S. Atlantic Fleet Norfolk, Va., 1998—2000, dep. chief of naval ops. for resources, warfare req. and assessments Washington, 2000—01; sr. mil. assist. to sec. US Dept. Def., Washington, 2001—02; comdr. U.S. Joint Forces Command (CDRUSJF-COM), Norfolk, Va., 2002—05; supreme allied comdr. Transformation (SACT) NATO, Brussels, 2003—05; vice chmn. Joint Chiefs of Staff US Dept. Def., Washington, 2005—. Decorated Legion of Merit with 3 gold stars, DSM with 2 gold stars. Office: US Dept Def 9999 JCS Pentagon Washington DC 20318*

GIAMBI, JASON GILBERT, professional baseball player; b. West Covina, Calif., Jan. 8, 1971; m. Dana Mandela, Nov. 9, 1996 (div.); m. Kristian Rice, Feb. 2002. Grad., Long Beach State U. 1st baseman U.S. Olympic Team, 1992, Oakland A's, Calif., 1992—2001, N.Y. Yankees, 2002—. Named Am. League MVP, 2000; named to U.S. Olympic Baseball team, Barcelona, Spain, 1992, Am. League All-star team, 2000—04. Avocations: off-roading, WWF. Office: NY Yankees Yankee Stadium 161st Street and River Avenue Bronx NY 10451

GIAMBRA, JOEL ANTHONY, municipal official; m. Michelle Giambra; children: Gabriella, Nicholas, Dominic, Joel Anthony. Student, Bryant & Stratton Bus. Inst., 1973; AAS in Bus. Adminstrn., Erie C.C., 1978. Legis. asst. Erie County Legis., Buffalo, 1975-76, cmty. aide, mem. citizens adv. com., 1976; sgt.-at-arms Buffalo Common Coun., 1976-77; dir. field ops. western N.Y. Carter/Mondale Re-Election Com., Buffalo, 1980; monitor/evaluator Divsn. Employment & Tng., Buffalo, 1982-90; comptroller City of Buffalo, 1990-2000; Erie County exec. Buffalo, N.Y., 2000—. Bd. dirs. Buffalo Fine Arts Acad.; mem. Loaned Exec. Club, United Way Buffalo & Erie County. Recipient Bus. First 40 under 40 award, 1995, Erie C.C. Found. Disting. Alumni award, Be-A-Friend Big Brother/Big Sister Program Dir.'s award, Disting. Svc. to Preservation award Landmark Soc. Niagara Frontier, 1984, Appreciation award Preservation Coalition Erie County, 1984, Man of Yr. award YMCA, 1998, Donald A. Miller Cmty. Svc. award, 2000, Man of Yr. award Buffalo Renaissance Found., 2000, Italian-Am. Achievement award Good Govt. Club, 2000, Abraham Lincoln Leadership award, 2000, Paul Harris Fellow Rotary Found. Rotary Internat., 2001, Erie Cmty. Coll. Light of Leadership award, 2002, Frank E. Van Lare award, N.Y. Water Environ. Assn., 2002, Buffalo award, Buffalo Niagara Assn. of Realtors, 2002; named Buffalo News Outstanding Citizen, 2001. Mem. NCCJ, N.Y. State Fin. Officers Assn. (bd. govs. 1992), West Side Bus. & Taxpayers' Assn. (Man of Yr. 20024), Forest Dist. Civic Assn., Jr. C. of C., Kiwanis Club Buffalo, Leadership Buffalo (adv. bd.), Romulus Club. Office: Erie County 95 Franklin St Buffalo NY 14202-3925 Business E-Mail: giambraj@bflo.co.erie.ny.us.

GIAMPIETRO, WAYNE BRUCE, lawyer; b. Chgo., Jan. 20, 1942; s. Joseph Anthony and Jeannette Marie (Zeller) G.; m. Mary E. Fordeck, June 15, 1963; children: Joseph, Anthony, Marcus. BA, Purdue U., 1963; JD, Northwestern U., 1966. Bar: Ill. 1966, U.S. Dist. Ct. (no. dist.) Ill. 1966, U.S. Ct. Appeals (7th cir.) 1967, U.S. Tax Ct. 1977, U.S. Supreme Ct. 1971. Assoc. Elmer Gertz, Chgo., 1966-73; mem. firm Gertz & Giampietro, Chgo., 1974-75; pvt. practice, 1975-76; ptnr. Poltrock & Giampietro, 1976-87, Witwer, Burlage, Poltrock & Giampietro, 1987-94, Witwer, Poltrock & Giampietro, Chgo., 1995—2002, Stitt, Klein, Daday, Aretos & Giampietro LLC, Arlington Heights, Ill., 2003—. Former cons. atty. Looking Glass divsn. Traveler's Aid Soc.; gen. counsel First Amendment Lawyers Assn., 2000—. Contbr. articles to profl. jours. Pres. Chgo. 47th Ward Young Republicans, 1968; bd. dirs. Ravenswood Conservation Commn.; gen. counsel First Amendment Lawyers Assn. Lutheran. Avocation: stamp collecting/philately. Home: 23 Windsor Dr Lincolnshire IL 60069-3410 Office: Stitt Klein Daday Aretos & Giampietro LLC 121 S Wilke Ste 500 Arlington Heights IL 60005 Office Phone: 847-590-8700. Business E-Mail: wgiampietro@skdaglaw.com.

GIANCARLO, CHARLES H., computer company executive; BSEE, Brown U.; MSEE, U. Calif., Berkeley; MBA, Harvard U. Co-founder, former v.p. mktg. Adaptive Corp.; former v.p. mktg. and corp. devel. Kalpana, Inc.; v.p. bus. devel. Cisco Systems, Inc., San Jose, Calif., 1994—98, sr. v.p. global alliances, 1998—99, sr. v.p., gen. mgr. switching, voice and storage, 1999—2003, chief tech. officer, 2004—05, chief develop. officer, 2005—; pres. Cisco-Linksys, LLC, 2003—; chair Cisco Enterprise Bus. Coun. Founder ATM Forum; leader, Voice Technology and Global Gov. Solutions Cisco Systems, Inc.; former head Cisco Service Provider Bus. Coun.; co-chair Cisco Enterprise Bus. Coun. Patentee in field. Achievements include holding multiple patents in the areas of ATM and voice technologies. Office: Cisco Systems Inc 170 W Tasman Dr San Jose CA 95134*

GIANCOLA, JAMES J., bank executive; Grad., Harvard U.; postgrad., Suffolk U., Boston; student, U. Colo. Pres. Gainer Bank, Ind.; exec. v.p. CNB Bancshares, Inc., 1992, pres., COO, 1994. Cmty. work U. So. Ind., U. Evansville, Evansville Dance Theatre, United Way, Leadership Evansville. Mem. Methodist Temple. Office: CNB Bancshares Inc PO Box 778 Evansville IN 47705-0778

GIANCOTTI, FILIPPO GIUSTO, molecular biologist, educator; b. Rome, Mar. 25, 1958; MD, U. Torino, Italy, 1981, PhD, 1987. Diplomate Italian Bd. Hematology/Oncology. Intern and resident dept. hematology U. Torino Sch. Medicine, 1979—83; sr. rsch. fellow La Jolla (Calif.) Cancer Rsch. Found., 1987—91; asst. prof. Sch. Medicine, NYU, 1991—96, assoc. prof., 1996; assoc. prof. Sch. Medicine Cornell U., N.Y.C., 1996—2000, prof. Sch. Medicine, 2000—; assoc. prof. cell biology and genetics Weill-Cornell Grad. Sch. Biomed. Scis., 1996—2000, prof., 2000—. Cons. NIH, 1994—; assoc. mem. Sloan-Kettering Inst. Meml. Sloan-Kettering Cancer Ctr., 1996—2000, mem., 2000—. Contbr. articles to profl. jours. including, Cell, European Molecular Biology Orgn. Jour., Jour. of Cell Biology. Recipient Lucille P. Markey Charitable Trust award, 1992—96, Established Investigatorship award, Am. Heart Assn., 1996—; fellow Sr. postdoctoral fellow, European Molecular Biology Orgn., 1987—89, postdoctoral, European Orgn. for Rsch. and Treatment Cancer and Nat. Cancer Inst., 1987—89, Am. Cancer Soc., 1989—90, Arthritis Found., 1990—93, Whitehead Presdl., 1992—93. Mem.: ASCB, AAAS. Achievements include patent on novel fibronectin receptor. Office: Cell Biology Program Box 216/1275 York Ave Meml Sloan-Kettering Cancer New York NY 10021 Home: #9B 170 2nd Ave New York NY 10003-5754

GIANELLONI, MELBA DUKES, artist; b. Birmingham, Nov. 21, 1914; d. Edward Homer and Pearl Lucile (Cotton) Hildreth; m. John Benjamin Baenen, Feb. 28, 2001; 1 child, Alan Thomas Dukes. BFA, Tulane U.; MA, Thompson Edn. Direct. Home: 1342 Bridlebrook Dr Casselberry FL 32707

GIANINNO, SUSAN MCMANAMA, advertising executive; b. Boston, Dec. 25, 1948; d. John Carroll and Barbara (Frances) Magner; m. Lawrence John Gianinno, June 7, 1970; 1 child, Alexandra Christin. BA in English Lit. and Psychology cum laude, Boston Coll., 1970; MA in Ednl. Psychology, Northwestern U., 1973; postgrad. in behavioral scis., U. Chgo., 1974-78. Psychiat. asst. Quinn Psychiat., Pavilion St Elizabeth's Hosp., Brighton, Mass., 1967-70; research assoc. com. human devel., dept behavioral scis. U. Chgo., 1973-79; resident adv. U. Chgo. Housing Systems, from 1979; research assoc., then research supr. Needham, Harper and Steers Advt. Inc., Chgo., 1979-80, dir. life style rsch., from 1981; v.p., dir. creative rsch. Young & Rubicam NY, then sr. and exec. v.p., dir. rsch. svcs., 1982-86, exec. v.p., dir. mktg., 1986-90, exec. v.p., worldwide group dir., 1990-92, exec. v.p. worldwide acct. mng. dir., 1992-94; exec. v.p., sr. dir. BBDO, NYC, 1994; chief branding officer D'Arcy; chairwoman, CEO Publicis USA, 2003—. Contbr. papers, reports to profl. jours. Trustee Boston Coll. Univ. scholar U. Chgo., 1975-77 Office: Publicis USA 4 Herald Sq 950 Sixth Ave New York NY 10001 Office Phone: 212-279-5550. Office Fax: 212-279-5560.*

GIANLORENZI, NONA ELENA, art dealer, painter; b. Virginia, Minn., July 20, 1939; d. Teto Nicholas and Lena Dora (Zini) Gianlorenzi; m. George Michael Devlin, July 20, 1966 (dec. Feb. 1990); children: Gian Loren Kjellesvig Waering, Helena Nicole Devlin Seidel. BA, Bklyn. Coll./CUNY. Painter self employed, N.Y.C., 1960—; asst. dir. Am. Art Gallery, N.Y.C., 1961-67; owner, dir. Asage Art Gallery, N.Y.C., 1977-88; pvt. art dealer Art Space Inc., Bklyn., 1989—. Tchr. art and aesthetics St. Francis Sch. Deaf, Bklyn., 1968-71, Mt. Carmel, Queens, N.Y., 1968-71, Charles Borromeo Sch., Bklyn., 1968-71. Ford fellow, 1992-94, Loy fellow, 1992-94; Art Studio scholar, 1961. Address: 415 Rugby Rd Brooklyn NY 11226-5611

GIANNETTI, LOUIS DANIEL, film critic, educator; b. Natick, Mass., Apr. 1, 1937; s. John and Vincenza (Zappitelli) G.; m. Justine Ann Gallagher, Sept. 7, 1963 (div. 1980); children: Christina, Francesca. BA, Boston U., 1959; MA, U. Iowa, 1961, PhD, 1967. Asst. prof. English Emory U., Atlanta, 1966-70; prof. English and film Case Western Res. U., Cleve., 1970—2001, prof. emeritus English and film, 2002—. Author: Understanding Movies, 1972, rev. 10th edit., 2004, Godard and Others, 1975, Masters of the American Cinema, 1981, (with S. Eyman) Flashback, 1986, 5th rev. edit., 2005. Democrat. Office: Case Western Res U Dept English Euclid Ave Cleveland OH 44106-2706 Office Phone: 216-595-0360. E-mail: louisgiannetti@aol.com.

GIANNETTI, STEPHEN P., publishing executive; BA, Dickinson Coll., Carlisle, Pa. Ea. regional mgr. Reader's Digest; advt. dir. Prevention, 1993—96, assoc. pub., 1996—98, publisher Emmaus, Pa., 1998—2000; v.p., pub. Nat. Geog. Mag., N.Y.C., 2000—; group pub. Nat. Geog. Mags., 2002—. Advisory bd. position Make-A-Wish Found. New York. Mem.: Am. Advt. Fedn., Consumer Healthcare Products Assn. Office: National Geographic 711 Fifth Ave New York NY 10022*

GIANNETTI, THOMAS LEONARD, lawyer; b. Stamford, Conn., June 7, 1947; s. Thomas and Lucille Giannetti; m. Charlene Canape, Jan. 12, 1974; children: Joseph, Theresa. BS, Yale U., 1968; MSEE, Carnegie-Mellon U., 1970; JD, George Washington U., 1976. Bar: N.Y. 1977, U.S. Dist. Ct. (so. and ea. dists. N.Y.) 1978, U.S. Ct. Appeals (fed. cir.) 1984, U.S. Dist. Ct. (no. dist.) Calif. 1993, U.S. Supreme Ct. 1996, U.S. Patent and Trademark Office 1975. Engr. Westinghouse Electric Corp., Pitts. and Phila., 1968-73; assoc. Fish & Neave, N.Y.C., 1976-86, ptnr., 1986—. Mem. ABA, Am. Intellectual Property Law Assn. N.Y. Intellectual Property Law Assn., Assn. of Bar of City of N.Y., Fed. Cir. Bar Assn., Yale Club (N.Y.C.). Home: 1158 5th Ave New York NY 10029-6917 Office: Fish & Neave Fl 50 1251 Avenue of the Americas New York NY 10020-1105

GIANNI, GASTON LOUIS, JR., federal agency administrator; b. Steubenville, Ohio, Aug. 12, 1942; m. Sue Jones; 3 children. BS in Acctg., Franciscan U. Steubenville, 1964; postgrad., Pa. State U., 1980, Harvard U., 1989. Various positions to sr. exec. Gen. Acctg. Office; inspector gen. Fed. Deposit Ins. Corp., 1996—2004; ret. Mem., past chair audit com., vice chair Pres.'s Coun. on Integrity and Efficiency, 1999-2004. With D.C. Nat. Guard, 1964-70. Mem. Inst. Mgmt. Accts., Assn. Govt. Accts., Inst. Internal Auditors, Cert. Govt. Auditing Profls. Office: Fed Deposit Ins Co Office Inspector Gen 801 17th St NW Washington DC 20434-0002

GIANNINI, A. CHRISTINA, costume designer, set designer; d. Francis F. and Marion (Mills) Giannini; m. Andrea Brass (div.). BA, Rutgers U., 1959; postgrad., Birmingham Coll. Arts and Crafts, Eng., 1959—60, Zurich Opera Studio, 1963—64. Costume scenic collaborator Festival of Two Worlds, Spoleto, Italy, 1964—76; costume designer Hartford Stage Co., 1969, Pa. Ballet, 1971—89, Trinity Sq. Repertory Theatre, 1972—73, Roundabout Theatre, 1975—89, Joffrey Ballet, 1975—78, Spoleto Festival USA, Charleston, SC, 1977—78, Actors Studio, 1980, South St. Theatre, 1981, SUNY, Purchase, 1984, Ballet Hispanico, 1985—88, Ballet du Nord, France, 1986, AMAS Repertory Theatre, 1986—87, Hong Kong Ballet, 1988—89, Hong Kong Acad. Performing Arts, 1988—89, Puerto Rican Traveling Theatre, 2002; costume designer for 12 ballets Alvin Ailey Dance Theatre, 1969—82; resident designer Chautaugua Dance, 1990—2005, Casa Blanca the Dance, Char. J. Cliford premier, China, 2005. Costume designer: (Broadway plays) Me and Thee, 1965; Three Men on a Horse, 1969; (plays) Tickles by Tuchkolsky, 1977; Swan Song, 1986. Recipient Oscar for best costume designer, Don Quixhote, Venezuela, 1996, The Nutcracker, Venezuela, 1997. Mem.: United Scenic Artists Union. Republican. Episcopalian. Avocations: boating, sailing, kayaking, skiing, skating. Home and Office: 210 W 101st St 16J New York NY 10025 Office Phone: 212-666-3649.

GIANNINI, A. JAMES, psychiatrist, educator, researcher, author; b. Youngstown, Ohio, June 11, 1947; s. Matthew and Grace Carla (Nistri) G.; children: Juliette Nicole, Jocelyn Danielle. BS, Youngstown State U., Ohio, 1970; MD, U. Pitts., 1974; postgrad., Yale U., 1974-78, U. London, 1996-97. Diplomate Nat. Bd. Med. Examiners. Intern St. Elizabeth Med. Ctr., Youngstown, 1974, assoc. dir. family medicine, psychiatry, 1978-80; resident in psychiatry Yale U., New Haven, 1975-78, chief resident, 1977-78; assoc. psychiatrist Elmcrest Psychiat. Inst., Portland, Conn., 1976-78; acting ward chief Conn. Mental Health Ctr., New Haven, 1977; assoc. dir. family medicine, psychiatry St. Elizabeth Med. Ctr., Youngstown, 1978-80; from asst. prof. to assoc. prof. dept. psychiatry N.E. Ohio Med. Coll., 1978-84, program dir., 1980-88, prof., 1984-90, vice-chmn., 1985-89; assoc. clin. prof. dept psychiatry Ohio State U., 1983-89, clin. prof., 1989-96; chmn. depts. psychiatry and toxicology Western Res. Care System Hosp., 1985-87, med. dir. toxicology, 1987; acting dir. dual diagnosis unit Youngstown Osteo. Hosp., 1987—2000; pres., corp. med. dir. Chem. Abuse Ctrs., Inc., Ohio and Mich., 1987—2004; med. dir. substance abuse svcs. Cmty. Mental Health Ctr. of Mid. Ga., Dublin, 2004—; lt. col. M.C., U.S. Army, 2004—. Dir. alumni schs. com. Yale U., New Haven, 1997-2005; vis. prof. Inst. for Scis. Comm. and Sci. Edn., Columbia Coll., Chgo., U. Naples, Italy, 1990; examiner in psychology LaTrobe U., Bundoora, Australia, 1988-89; sr. mentor U. Pitts., 2001—05, U. Pitts. Alumni Recruitment Team, 2005-; sr. cons. Fair Oaks Hosp., Summit, N.J., 1979, Regent Hosp., N.Y.C., 1981-96, chmn. Nat. Adv. Council Prevention and Control of Rape, NIMH, Rockville, Md., 1983-86, spl. reviewer mood disorders com., 1995-97; mem. drug abuse clin., behavioral and rsch. rev. com. Nat. Inst. Drug Abuse, Rockville, Md., 1987-88; chief forensic psychiatrist Mahoning County Prosecutor, 1989-97; Am. Participant USIA Drug Abuse program to Cyprus, Italy, Can., Barbados, St. Lucia and Yugoslavia, 1990-94; panelist Renaissance Weekend, Hilton Head and Charleston, S.C., 1997—; cons. Smith-Kline Labs., McNeil Labs., Excerpta Medica Pubs., Amino Labs., Fund for Am. Renaissance; dir. clin. rsch. Princeton Diagnostic Labs., South Plainfield, N.J., 1987-89; med. dir. med. adv. bd. Neurodata Inc., 1987-89, pres., 1989-2004, med. dir. Chem. Abuse Ctrs. Inc., 1987, corp. med. dir., 1987-97; spl. reviewer initial review group, 1995-97, health, behavior and prevention review com. NIH, Rockville, Md.; ethics com. Mahoning County Mental Retardation Bd., Youngstown, Ohio, 1995-98, treas. 1996-97, vice-chmn., bd. treas., 1997-98; psychiatrist emeritus Stony Lodge Hosp., Briar Cliff Manor, NY; book reviewer Psychiat. Times, 2000—. Author: (with Henry Black) Psychiatric, Psychogenic, Somatopsychic Disorders, 1978; (with Robert Gilliland) Neurologi and Neuropsychiatric Disorders, 1983; (with Andrew Slaby) Overdose and Detoxification Emergencies, 1983; Biological Foundation of Clinical Psychiatry, 1988, (with Andrew Slaby) Drugs of Abuse, 1989, 2d edit., 1996, Comprehensive Laboratory Services in Psychiatry, 1986; (with Philip Jose Farmer) Red Orc's Rage, 1991; (with Andrew Slaby) The Eating Disorders, 1993, 2d edit., 1997, Drugs of Abuse, 2d edit., 1998, Drug Abuse: A Family Guide to Recognition and Treatment, 1999; contbr. numerous articles to profl. jours. Vice chmn. Mahoning County (Ohio) Mental Health Bd., 1982-84, chmn., 1984-86; councilor Nat. Italian Am. Found. Recipient Physician's Recognition award, 1978—, rsch. award Fair Oaks Hosp., 1979, bronze award Brit. Med. Assn., 1983, Outstanding Leadership award Mahoning County Mental Health Bd., 1986, Silver Rose award Assn. Italiano Donati d'Organo, Milan, 1990, Excellence award Yale U. Admissions Com., 2002. Fellow: APA (disting. 2003—), Am. Coll. Clin. Pharmacology (sec.-treas. Ohio chpt. 1990—97, nat. govt. affairs com. 1990—2003, steering coun., exec. com. Ohio chpt. 1990—, pres. 1997—2004, nat. edn. com. 2003—04), Acad. Medicine, Royal Acad. Medicine (Eng.), N.J. Acad. Medicine; mem.: Royal Soc. Medicine (sub-dean 2005—), Ga. Psychiat. Assn., Acad. Clin. Psychiatry, N.Y. Acad. Scis., Royal Coll. Medicine, European Neurosci., Brit. Brain Soc., Soc. Neurosci., Am. Psychiat. Assn. (fellow 1989—2003, disting. fellow 2003—), Dublin C. of C., Youngstown C. of C. (vice-chmn. health com. 1986—89, chmn. 1989—96), Dublin Country Club, Atrium Club (Warren, Ohio), Yale Club (Cleve., Pitts.), Youngstown Club, Domus (London), Swim and Racquet Club (Poland, Ohio), Cercola di Corso (Florence, Italy), Morey's (New Haven), Sigma Xi. Republican. Roman Catholic. Office: 463 Deer Creek Trail Dublin GA 31021-3248 Office Phone: 478-278-3736. Personal E-mail: abalard2@aol.com.

GIANNINI, ANTOINETTE FRANCES, music educator, researcher; b. Worcester, Mass., Sept. 9, 1923; d. Domenic Giannini and Mary Margaret Amato-Giannini. MusB, Boston U., 1945, MA, 1948; postgrad., Juilliard Sch., N.Y.C., Columbia U. Dir. music pub. schs., Spencer, Mass., 1948—51; tchr. Worcester Pub. HS, 1958—91; instr. music history Worcester, 1962—91; ret., 1991. Concert pianist, NY. Mem.: Nat. Guild Piano Tchrs. (adjudicator 1965—94), Mu Phi Epsilon. Independent. Roman Catholic. Home and Studio: 196 Pakachoag St Auburn MA 01501

GIANNINI, VALERIO LOUIS, investment banker; b. NYC, Feb. 7, 1938; s. Gabriel M. and Luisa M. (Casazza) G.; m. Linda Martin, Oct. 6, 1979; children: Martin Louis, Alexander Elliot, Charles Gabriel. BSE, Princeton U., 1959. With Kidder Peabody & Co., NYC, 1961-64; sr. cons. IIT Rsch. Inst., Chgo., 1964-66; sec. Giannini-Voltex, LA, 1966-68; pres. V.L. Giannini & Co., LA, 1968-76; chmn. Namco Chems., Inc., 1975; dir. White House ops., Washington, 1977-78; dep. spl. asst. to Pres. for adminstrn. White House, 1979-80; dep. asst. sec. Dept. Commerce, Washington, 1980-81; prin. Cumberland Investment Group, NYC, 1981-87; pres. Numex Corp., 1986-87; CEO, Geneva Bus. Network, Inc., Irvine, Calif., 1987-90. Adj. prof. Argyros Sch. Bus., Chapman U., 2001; founder Eurosearch Ptnr., Newport Beach, Calif., 1990; prin. Newcap Ptnr., 1995; bd. dir. Dudek & Assoc., Pro-Dex, Inc., Lynx Ednl. Found. Pres. Lido Jr. Sailing Found., 2000-03; bd. dirs. Lynx Ednl. Found. Lt. USNR, 1959-61 Mem. N.Y. Yacht Club, Newport Harbor Yacht Club. Office: 1122 Bristol St Costa Mesa CA 92626 Office Phone: 714-241-8686. E-mail: vgiannini@att.net.

GIANNINY, OMER ALLAN, JR., retired humanities educator; b. Charlottesville, Va., Dec. 5, 1925; s. Omer Allen and Frances Belle (Bussenger) G.; m. Jean Claire Post, July 31, 1948; children: Donald Hagen, James Emory, Peter Arnold, Robert Matthew, Gary Lee. BME, U. Va., Charlottesville, 1947; MEd, U. Va., 1958, EdD, 1967; postgrad., Rutgers U., 1947-48. Registered profl. engr., Va. Refinery engr. Esso Std. Oil Co., Linden, N.J., 1947-51; rsch. engr. U. Va., Charlottesville, 1953-56, asst. prof. Sch. Engring., 1955-65, 67-71, lectr., 1965-67, assoc. prof. humanities Sch. Engring., 1971-82, prof. humanities Sch. Engring., 1982-93, chmn., 1979-80, 90-93, prof. emeritus, 1993—. Ednl. cons. Newport News Shipbuilding, Va., 1962, Inst. Textile Tech., Charlottesville, 1984-2001. Co-author: Thomas Jefferson's Rotunda Restored, 1981. Served to lt. USNR, 1942-46, 51-53. Mem. Am. Soc. Engring. Edn. (dir. 1980-82), Soc. History Tech. (group chmn. 1983-85), The Raven Soc., Phi Beta Kappa, Tau Beta Pi, Phi Delta Kappa. United Methodist. Home: 1711 King Mountain Rd Charlottesville VA 22901-3047 Personal E-mail: agianniny@earthlink.net.

GIANNOPOULOU, ATHINA, physician, surgeon; b. Xanthi, Greece, May 12, 1962; came to U.S., 1990; d. Alexandros and Pipina (Papanikas) Giannopoulou; m. Nick Kanopoulos, Feb. 28, 1992; 1 child, Tasos Kanopoulos. MD with honors, U. Thessaloniki, Greece, 1987. Diplomate Am. Bd. Plastic and Reconstructive Surgery. Resident in gen. surgery Theagenio Med. Ctr., Thessaloniki, 1987-90; rsch. fellow Duke U. Hosp., Durham, N.C., 1991-92; resident in gen. surgery U. N.C. Hosps., Chapel Hill, 1992-96, resident in plastic surgery, 1996-98; fellow aesthetic and oculoplastic surgery Paces Plastic Surgery, Atlanta, 1998-99; pvt. practice Faces Plastic Surgery, Chapel Hill, N.C., 1999—. Contbr. articles to profl. jours. Avocations: skiing, swimming, gourmet cooking, fashion design. Home: 3723 Dairy Pond Pl Durham NC 27705 Office: 1515 W NC Hwy 54 Ste 130 Durham NC 27707 Office Phone: 919-419-8319. E-mail: facesps@aol.com.

GIANNOTTI, ROBERT ANTHONY, music educator; b. Bronx, NY, Dec. 17, 1972; s. Robert S. and Mary T. Giannotti. MusB, Crane Sch. Music SUNY, Potsdam, 1995; MA, SUNY, Stony Brook, 1999. Cert. Music Tchr. N.Y., 2000. Band dir. Massapequa (N.Y.) Sch, Bands, 1995—. Adjudicator NY State Sch. Music Assn., NY, 1997—. Mem.: NY State Band Dirs. Assn., Nat. Band Assn., NY State Sch. Music Assn., Internat. Assn. Jazz Educators, Music Educators Nat. Conf., Internat. Trumpet Guild. Home: 73 Cedar Dr Bay Shore NY 11706 Office: Massapequa HS 4925 Merrick Rd Massapequa NY 11758 Personal E-mail: rgiannotti@yahoo.com.

GIANNULLI, MOSSIMO, designer, apparel business executive; b. June 4, 1963; s. Gene and Nancy; m. Chris Clausen, 1988 (div. 1995); 1 child, Gianni; m. Lori Loughlin, 1997; children: Isabella Rose, Olivia Jade. Student, Orange Coast Cmty. Coll., U. So. Calif. Founder Mossimo Inc., Irvine, Calif., 1987, chmn. bd., 1988—, pres., 1988—98, 2000—02, CEO, 1995—96, 2000—; signed exclusive contract Target, 2000. Appeared in (music video) Janet Jackson's "You Want This?", 1994. Recipient Orange County Entrepreneur of Yr. award, 1992, Fashion Performance award, 1996. Office: Mossimo Inc 2016 Broadway Blvd Santa Monica CA 90404

GIANOPOULOS, JOHN GEORGE, obstetrician; b. 1952; MD, Loyola U., Stritch Sch. Medicine, Maywood, Ill., 1977. Cert. Am. Bd. Obstetrics and Gynecology, 1984, in Maternal and Fetal Medicine 1985. Resident, ob-gyn. Loyola U. Med. Ctr., Maywood, Ill., 1977—81, fellow, maternal fetal medicine, 1981—83; Mary Isabelle Caestecker prof., chmn. dept., ob-gyn. Loyola U., Stritch Sch. Medicine, Maywood, Ill., 1997—. Office: Loyola Univ Sch Medicine 2160 First Ave Maywood IL 60153 Business E-Mail: jgianop@lumc.edu.

GIANOPULOS, JIM, film company executive; b. Bklyn. JD, Fordham U. Bus. affairs RCA/Columbia Pictures Internat. Video, RCA Selectavision; sr. v.p. bus. affairs and internat. video divsn. Paramount Pictures, 1988—91; exec. v.p. internat. Carolco Pictures, 1991—92; pres. Twentieth Internat. TV, 1992—94, Twentieth Century Fox Internat. and Pay TV, 1994—2000; co-chmn. Fox Filmed Enteraintment, L.A., 2000—. Named one of 50 Most Powerful People in Hollywood, Premiere mag., 2004—05. Office: Fox Filmed Entertainment 10201 W Pico Blvd Los Angeles CA 90035 Office Phone: 310-277-2211. Office Fax: 310-203-1558.*

GIANTURCO, DELIO E., management consultant, educator, author; b. Washington, Sept. 28, 1940; s. Elio and Valentine (McGillycuddy) G.; m. Mary Elizabeth Jordan, Jan. 31, 1961; children: Lisa, Grace, Mark. BS in Fgn. Trade, Georgetown U., 1963; MA, George Washington U., 1967. Staff asst. to Robert J. Corbett of Pa. U.S. Ho. of Reps., Washington, 1960-62, legis. asst. to Robert L.F. Sikes of Fla., 1962-63; sr. v.p. guarantees, ins. and exporter credits, treas., comptroller, exec. v.p., vice chmn., 1st v.p., dir. Export-Import Bank, Washington, 1963-77; pres. First Washington Assocs., 1978—. Dir. Fgn. Credit Ins. Assn., N.Y.C., 1971-76; adj. prof. George Mason U., 1995—. Office: First Washington Assocs 1501 Lee Hwy Ste 102 Arlington VA 22209-1147 Personal E-mail: fwa@mindspring.com.

GIANTURCO, PAOLA, communications consulting company executive; b. July 22, 1939; d. Cesare and Verna Bertha (Daily) G.; m. David Sanderson Hill, Mar. 12, 1988; 1 child from previous marriage, Scott Sangster. BA, Stanford U., 1961; postgrad., U. So. Calif., 1971. Dir. pub. rels. Joseph Magnin, San Francisco, 1961-67; dir. pub. rels., acct. exec. Hall & Levine Advt. Agy., L.A., 1968-73, v.p., acct. supr., 1973-76, sr. v.p., 1977-82; v.p. Dancer Fitzgerald Sample, 1982-87; exec. v.p., mgmt. supr. Saatchi and Saatchi, 1988-91; pres. The Gianturco Co., Mill Valley, Calif., 1991—. Co-developer, instr. exec. insts. on women and leadership Stanford U., 1994-95. Co-author, photographer: In Her Hands: Craftswomen Changing the World, 2000, paperback edit., 2004; author, photographer Celebrating Women, 2004. Past bd. dirs. The Country Schs., Above the Line Homeless Teen Shelter, 1996-98; bd. dirs. Internat. Nature & Cultural Adventures, The Crafts Ctr., vice-chair, 1999, chair, 2000-01; bd. dirs. Assn. Women in Devel., 1998-2000. Home and Office: 30 Cecily Ln Mill Valley CA 94941-3300 Personal E-mail: pgianturco@aol.com.

GIARDINA, ELSA GRACE VONNA, cardiologist, educator; b. Newark, Aug. 1, 1941; d. John and Elsa (Freda) G.; m. Alan L. Saroff, June 1, 1974; 1 child, John Saroff. AB, Bryn Mawr Coll., 1961; MD, NY Med. Coll., 1965. Diplomate Am. Bd. Internal Medicine, Am. Bd. Cardiology; cert. internal medicine, cardiovascular disease. Resident Roosevelt Hosp., N.Y.C., 1965-69; cardiology resident Columbia Presbyn. Med. Ctr., N.Y.C., 1969-71, NIH cardiovascular pharmology fellow, 1971-72; asst. prof. medicine Columbia U., N.Y.C., 1972-79, assoc. prof. medicne, 1980-87, prof. medicine, 1987—. Mem. cardiorenal adv. com. Food & Drug Adminstrn., Rockville, Md., 1984-88; mem. pharmacology study sect. NIH, Bethesda, Md., 1989-93; dir. Ctr. for Women's Health, Columbia-Presbyn. Med. Ctr., N.Y.C., 1994—. Contbr. articles to profl. jours. Bd. dirs. Sarnoff Endowment for Cardiovascular Sci., 2000—. Fellow: ACP, Heart Rhythm Soc., Am. Heart Assn., Am. Coll. Cardiology. Office: Columbia U 630 W 168th St New York NY 10032-3795 Office Phone: 212-305-6154. Business E-Mail: evg1@columbia.edu.

GIBALA, RONALD, metallurgical engineering educator; b. New Castle, Pa., Oct. 3, 1938; s. Steve Anthony and June Rose (Frank) G.; m. Janice Claire Grichor; children: Maryellen, Janice, David, Kristine. BS, Carnegie Inst. Tech., 1960; MS, U. Ill., 1962, PhD, 1964. Engring. technician Crane Co., New Castle, Pa., 1956-59; engr. U.S. Steel Rsch. Labs., Monroeville, Pa., 1960; rsch. asst. U. Ill., Urbana, 1960-64; asst. prof. metallurgy Case Western Res. U., Cleve., 1964-69, assoc. prof., 1969-76, prof. metallurgy and materials sci. and macromolecular sci., 1976-84, co-dir. materials rsch. lab., 1981-84; dir. metallurgy program NSF, 1982-83; prof., chmn. dept. materials sci. and engring. U. Mich., Ann Arbor, 1984-94, L.H. and F.E. Van Vlack prof. materials sci. and engring., 1998—2004, L.H. and F.E. Van Vlack prof. emeritus, 2004—. Dir. electron microbeam analysis lab. U. Mich., Ann Arbor, 2002—04. Contbr. articles to profl. jours.; editor: Hydrogen Embrittlement and Stress Corrosion Cracking, 1984. Pres. Woodhaven Hills Homeowners Assn., 1989—91. Recipient Alfred Noble prize ASCE, 1969, NASA Materials Sci. Divsn. Paper award, 1992; Tech. Achievement award Cleve. Tech. Socs. Council, 1972; vis. research fellow C.E.N.G. Labs., Grenoble, 1973-74; Matthias fellow Los Alamos Nat. Lab., 1991-92, Disting. Merit award U. Ill., 1998; vis. scientist Sandia Nat. Labs., 1998-99. Fellow: TMS (bd. dirs. 1981—87), Am. Soc. Metals Internat. (life; chpt. chmn. 1975—76, Outstanding Young Mem. Cleve. chpt. 1971); mem.: AAAS, Am. Ceramic Soc., Materials Rsch. Soc. (councillor 1995-97 1995—97, v.p. 1998, pres. 1999), Suburban Ski (pres. 1981—82), Alpha Sigma Mu, Tau Beta Pi, Sigma Xi. Democrat. Home: 1543 Stonehaven St Ann Arbor MI 48104-4149 Office: U Mich Dept Materials Sci Engring Ann Arbor MI 48109-2136 Office Phone: 734-936-0178. Business E-Mail: rgibala@umich.edu.

GIBALDI, LOUIS MILO, composer, marketing professional; b. Bklyn., Aug. 28, 1951; s. Louis Anthony Gibaldi and Beatrice Terry Guarneri; m. Elizabeth Anne Dehner, Nov. 12, 1999 (div. Jan. 2002). BA, Hofstra U., 1973; cinema/film scoring, NYU The New Sch., 1974. Nat. dir. Cal-Ctrl. Mktg. Corp., Ft. Lauderdale, Fla., 1984—90; pres./CEO Med. Digest Mag., Ft. Lauderdale, 1990—; CEO/founder Restaurant Tour Interactive, Winter Pk., Fla., 1997—, Gourmet Records, Winter Pk., Fla., Gourmet Media Corp., Winter Pk., 2000—, ESP Entertainment, Winter Pk., 2000—, The Cutler Edge, Inc., Winter Pk., 2001—; founder/pres. MovieMusicBank.com, L.A., 2005. Dir. Video Composites Corp., Beverly Hills, 1976—80; chmn. bd. The Cutler Edge, Inc., 2000—; creator/prodr. Musicofthestars.com. Co-arranger: films Godspell (grammy award, 1971). Mem.: ASCAP. Avocations: piano, guitar, photography, filmmaking, design. Office Phone: 407-599-4400. Personal E-mail: lmgibaldi@earthlink.net.

GIBANS, JAMES DAVID, architect; b. Akron, Ohio, Feb. 10, 1930; s. Myer Jacob and Sylva (Hirsch) G.; m. Nina Freedlander, July 16, 1955; children: David Myer, Jonathan Samuel, Amy, Elisabeth. BA, Yale U., 1951, BArch, MArch, Yale U., 1954. Architect George K. Raad & Assocs. et al, San Francisco, 1958-63; project architect Ward and Schneider, Cleve., 1964-68; sr. assoc. William A. Gould and Assocs., Cleve., 1968-74, Don M. Hisaka and Assoc., Cleve., 1974-76; pvt. practice architecture Cleve., 1976-81; v.p. Teare Herman & Gibans, Inc., Cleve., 1981-89; v.p., treas. Herman Galvin Gibans, Inc., Cleve., 1989-91, HGG, Inc., Cleve., 1991-94, Herman Gibans Fodor, Inc., 1994—2000, v.p., 1994—. Faculty Edn. for Aesthetic Awareness Cleve. State U., 1977—79. Mem. Cleve. Landmarks Commn., 1993—, chmn., 2004—; trustee, mem. exec. com., 1st v.p. Cleve. Chamber Music Soc., 1970—78; mem. adv. bd. Environ. Resource Ctr. Cleve. Pub. Libr., 1973—76; mem. design rev. com. Shaker Sq. Hist. Dist., 1991—93; bd. dirs. Cleve. Soc. Contemporary Art, 1985—86, Friends of Shaker Sq., 1994—96, Shaker Sq. Area Devel. Corp., 1996—, v.p., 1996—97, treas., 1997—2001, pres., 2001—03; trustee Cleve. Found. for Arch., 1999—2003, chair focus com., 1999—2001, pres., 2001—03; bd. dirs. Bulldogs on the Cuyahoga, 2002—. Served with U.S. Army, 1955—57. Fulbright grantee, 1954-55. Fellow AIA (sec. Cleve. chpt. 1972-74, bd. dirs. 1984-86, treas. 1989, v.p. 1990, pres. 1991); mem. Architects Soc. Ohio (trustee 1975-76, bd. dirs. 1985-88), Cleve. City Club, Fulbright Assn. (bd. dirs. N.E. Ohio chpt. 1995-99, treas. 1998-99), N.E. Ohio Jazz Soc. (bd. dirs. 1991-96, v.p. 1993-95, pres. 1995-96), Rowfant Club (chair bldgs. and furnishings com. 2002—, coun. of fellows, 2005-, bd. dirs. 2005—). Democrat. Jewish. Avocations: music, art, jogging, cross country skiing. Home: 13800 Shaker Blvd # 1108 Cleveland OH 44120-1585 Office: Herman Gibans Fodor Inc 1304 W 6th St Cleveland OH 44113-1304 Office Phone: 216-696-3460. Business E-Mail: jgibans@hgfarchitects.com.

GIBARA, SAMIR G., tire manufacturing executive; b. Cairo, Egypt, Apr. 23, 1939; B in bus. adminstrn., Cairo U., 1960; M in internat. bus. and fin., Harvard U., 1964; attended, Kellogg Grad. Sch. Mgmt. Exec. Program, Northwestern U., 1985. Mgmt. trainee Goodyear Tire & Rubber Co., Akron, Ohio, 1964, v.p. European region, v.p. French operations, v.p., strategic planning and bus. devel., acting v.p., fin., chief fin. officer, 1992, exec. v.p., N. Am. tire oper., 1994, pres., COO, chmn., 1996—2003, ret., CEO, 1996—2002, mem. bd. dir., 1995—; head Goodyear Morocco; pres. Goodyear Canada; v.p. mktg. Internat. Harvester. Adv. Internat. Trade Ctr., Brussels; econ. adv. Moroccan Govt. Delegation to the U.S.; v.p., bd. mem. Am. C. of C., France; vis. prof., bus. univ. throughout Europe and U.S.; bd. dirs. Internat. Paper Co., Sumitomo Rubber Indus., Kobe, Japan, 1999—2003; exec. com. Rubber Mfr. Assn., mem. bus. coun., mem. bus. roundtable, mem. exec. mgmt. assn.; mem. Ohio Roundtable, Akron Reg. Devel. Bd.; bd. trustees Summa Health Sys., Cleveland Symphony Orchestra; past chmn. Summit County United Way Campaign, Ohio. Named Bus. Person Yr., France-Am. C. of C., Luxembourg C. of C., hon. alumnus, Univ. Akron; recipient knighted, French Order Nat. Merit, inducted, Am. Acad. Achievement. Office: Goodyear Tire & Rubber Co 1144 E Market St Akron OH 44316-0002

GIBB, GINARI RENE, psychiatrist; d. Delores Morse and Rogelio Edwin Gibb; m. Michael Price, July 12, 1996; children: Evan Michael Price, Norman Louis Price, Corey Thomas Price. BS, Vanderbilt U., Nashville, 1995, Clark Atlanta U., Atlanta, 1996; MD, Meharry Med. Coll., Nashville, 2003. Diplomate Fedn. Of State Med. Boards, 2003. Office asst. Gibb Ins. Agy., Atlanta, 1988—93; dormitory asst. Vanderbilt U. Residential Affairs Dept, Nashville, 1992—95; adminstrv. asst. Mike's Electronics and More, 1997—2003; rschr. dept. psychiatry Meharry Med. Coll., 2002—03; resident physician dept. psychiatry Vanderbilt U. Med. Ctr., 2003—04, Morehouse Sch. Of Medicine, Atlanta, 2004—. Del. and rep. (Meharry chpt.) Am. Med. Student Assn., Nashville, 1999—2001; profl. in residence Hazelden Nat. Assn. Of Alcoholism And Drug Abuse Counselors, Center City, Minn., 2004; residency recruiting adv. com. dept. psychiatry Morehouse Sch. Of Medicine, Atlanta, 2004—; student advisor curriculum com. Meharry Med. Coll., Nashville, 2001—03. Mem. spl. events com. Apec Learning Ctr., Atlanta, 2004—; mem. steering com. and vol. tutor St. Vincent De Paul Cath. Sch., Nashville, 2001—03. Recipient Protection of Human Rights Cert., Nat. Inst. Mental Health, 2004; scholar, Clark Meml. Scholarship Fund, 2000—01; Meharry Assn. Office Personnel scholarship, Meharry Med. Coll., 2000—01. Mem.: AMA, Nat. Inst. Mental Health, Am. Psychiat. Assn. (Psychodynamic Psychotherapy Continuing Med. Edn. Cert. 2005), Ga. Psychiat. Physicians Assn. (Annual Meeting Resident Scholarship 2005), Delta Sigma Theta (chaplain, v.p. and treas. 1994—2000, Vol. of Yr. 1994—95). Achievements include research in forensic investigation and clinical consequences of violence and murder within families. Avocations: catering special events, gardening, roller skating, tutoring at local schools, national public radio. Office: Morehouse Sch Medicine Psychiatry 720 Westview Dr SW Atlanta GA 30310 Office Phone: 404-756-1440. Office Fax: 404-756-1471. E-mail: ggibb@msm.edu.

GIBB, ROBERTA LOUISE, lawyer, artist; b. Cambridge, Mass., Nov. 2, 1942; d. Thomas Robinson Pieri and Jean Knox Gibb. BS, U. Calif., La Jolla, 1969; JD, New Eng. Sch. Law, 1982. Bar: Mass. 1978. Legal aide Mass. State Legis., 1973; practice law Mass., 1980—. Assoc. MIT, 1972—85. Author: To Boston With Love, 1980, The Art of Inflation, 1981, The Art of Economics, 1982; co-prodr.: (documentaries) Lovins on the Soft Path; Exhibited in group shows at Geraci Galleries, Rockport, Mass., 1996—2005, Rockport Art Assn. Gallery, Rockport, 1996—2005, Represented in permanent collections, Nat. Art Mus. Art, Indpls.; prodr.: (documentaries) Where the Spirit Leads, 2001—; Albert Einstein, Pres. Carter, Pres. Johnson, Pres. Reagan, Mother Theresa, Eleanor Roosevelt, The Marathon, Fire Dancers, Birth, Olympia, The Family, The Left Handed Squash Player, Basketball, Germain Gliddin, others. Bd. dir. Essex County Environ. and Conservation, Rockport, Mass., 1980-85; adv. MGH Day Lab. Women winner Boston Marathon, 1966-68, 1st woman to run Boston Marathon, 1966; named to Road Runners of Am. Hall of Fame, 1982 Mem.: Inst. Study of Natural Sys. (founder, pres. 1976—), Rockport Art Assn., Mass. Bar, Nat. Sculpture Soc. (assoc.), Boston Athletic Assn.

GIBBES, WILLIAM HOLMAN, lawyer; b. Hartsville, S.C., Feb. 25, 1930; s. Ernest Lawrence and Nancy (Watson) G.; m. Frances Hagood, May 1, 1954; children: Richard H., William H. Jr., Lynn. BS, U. S.C., 1952, LLB, 1953. Bar: S.C. 1953, U.S. Ct. Mil. Appeals 1954, U.S. Dist. Ct. S.C. 1956, U.S. Supreme Ct. 1959, U.S. Ct. Appeals (4th cir.) 1965. Asst. atty. gen., Columbia, S.C., 1957-62; ptnr. Berry & Gibbes, Columbia, 1962-68, Berry, Lightsey, Gibbes, Columbia, 1968-72; mem. Gibbes Law Firm, P.A., Columbia, 1972—; house of dels. S.C. Bar, 1994-96. Chief judge U.S. Army Legal Svcs. Agy., 1980-83. Author: Control of Highway Access - Its Prospects and Problems, Legal Dimensions of Community Health Planning, 1969, Manual for Fee Appraisors, 1960; contbr. articles to S.C. Law Review, Law Rev. Digest, 1960. Chmn. bd. dirs. U. S.C. YMCA, 1956-60. Brig. gen. JAGC, USAR 1980-83. Recipient Legion of Merit, U.S. Army, 1983. Mem. ABA (mil. laws com. 1984-90, meml. com.), S.C. Bar Assn. (exec. com. 1961-62), Am. Bd. Trial Advocates (sec.-treas. 1994-95, pres.-elect 1995-96, pres. 1996-97), Judge Advs. Assn. (pres. 1982-83), Richland County Bar Assn., S.C. Credit Ins. Assn. (gen. counsel 1963-94), Tarantella Club, Caprician Club, Summit Club, Doonbeg (Ireland) Golf Club, Forest Lake Country Club, Kiawah Island Club, Kappa Sigma Kappa, Omicron Delta Kappa, founding mem. Doonberg Golf Club, Cnty. Clare Ireland, 2002. Episcopalian. Home: 35 Avian Tr Columbia SC 29206-4965 Personal E-mail: billgibbes@aol.com.

GIBBINS, BOB, lawyer; b. Seminole, Okla., Feb. 27, 1936; s. Robert Lee and La-Ceile Rene (Shackelford) G.; m. Suzanne K. Gibbins (div. Oct. 1975); children: Bob Jr., Steven, Jenny Durbin, Kyndall Krebs; m. Pam Reed, Feb. 26, 1982. BBA, U. Tex., 1958, LLB, 1961. Bar: Tex. 1961, U.S. Dist. Ct. (no. dist.) Tex. 1961, U.S. Ct. Appeals (5th cir.) 1971, U.S. Supreme Ct. 1974, Colo. 1991; diplomate Am. Bd. Trial Advs., Am. Bd. Profl. Liability Attys. Assoc. Morehead, Sharpe, Tisdale & Gibbins, Plainview, Tex., 1961-71; ptnr. Gibbins & Spivey, Austin, Tex., 1971-76; pvt. practice, Austin, 1976-78; sr. ptnr. Gibbins, Wash and Bratton, Austin, 1978-79, Gibbins, Burrow, Wash & Bratton, Austin, 1979-81, Gibbins, Burrow & Bratton, Austin, 1981-86, Gibbins & Bratton, Austin, 1986-89, Gibbins, Winckler & Bayer, Austin, 1989-91, Gibbins, Winckler & Harvey, Austin, 1991-97; pvt. practice law Austin, 1997—. Co-author: Texas Practical Guide: Personal Injury, 1988, Products Liability Litigation: Trial Strategy, 1988. Recipient War Horse award So. Trial Lawyers Assn., 1991, Faculty Svc. award, Univ. Tex. Sch. of Law, 1992; Bob Gibbins endowed presdl. scholarship named in his honor U. Tex. Sch. of Law, Austin, 1991. Fellow Internat. Acad. Trial Lawyers (bd. dirs. 1993-97), Internat. Soc. Barristers, State Bar Tex., Coll. of the State Bar Tex.; mem. Assn. Trial Lawyers Am. (pres. 1991-92, Lifetime Achievement award 1998, Champion of Justice award 1999), Nat. Bd. Trial Advocacy (civil trial adv.), Am. Bd. Trial Advocates (pres. Austin chpt. 1981), Trial Lawyers for Pub. Justice (bd. dir.s 1993), Tex. Trial Lawyers Assn. (dir. emeritus). Office: Gibbins Law Office 1411 West Ave Ste 200 Austin TX 78701-1537

GIBBON, MARY-LYNN, special education educator; b. La Jolla, Calif., Feb. 5, 1955; d. Leslie and Edith Gertrude Swaim; m. Mark Jeffrey Gibbon, Mar. 12, 1987; children: Shawna Odet Pedro, William Leslie Lower. BS, Excelsior Coll., Albany, N.Y., 1993—95; MA in Edn., Chapman U., Victorville, Calif., 1995—97; MA in Spl. Edn., Azusa Pacific U., Victorville, Calif., 2002—04. Cert. Early Childhood Generalist Nat. Bd. for Profl. Tchg. Standards, 2001. Substitute tchr. Dept. Def. Dependent Schs., Baumholder, Germany, 1993—94, Barstow Unified Sch. Dist., Calif., 1995—96; elem. tchr. Lenwood Sch., Barstow, Calif., 1996—97, Hinkley Sch., Barstow, Calif., 1997—2002, mid. sch. spl. edn. tchr., 2002—04; sixth grade spl. edn. tchr. Barstow Intermediate Sch., Calif., 2004—. Bus. action plan com. mem. Barstow Unified Sch. Dist., Calif., 1996, report card revision adv. bd. mem., 1999—2000, schoolwide assessment rev. & revision adv. com. mem., 1999—2000, mem. sci., social studies standards adoption adv. com., 2000; tchr. participant Goldstone Apple Valley Radio Telescope, NASA, Barstow, Calif., 2002—04. Vol. Police Activities League, Barstow, Calif., 1997—2003. Grantee, Barstow Rotary Club, 1996. Mem.: Delta Kappa Gamma - Zeta Omicron (assoc.), Pi Lambda Theta (hon.). Conservative. Roman Catholic. Avocations: reading, travel. Office: Barstow Unified Sch Dist 551 So Ave H Barstow CA 92311 Office Phone: 760-255-6304.

GIBBONS, CELIA VICTORIA TOWNSEND (MRS. JOHN SHELDON), editor, publisher; b. Fargo, N.D. d. Harry Alton and Helen (Haag) Townsend; m. John Sheldon Gibbons, May 1, 1935; children: Mary Vee, John Townsend. Student, U. Minn., 1930-33. Advt. mgr. Hotel Nicollet, Mpls., 1933-37; contbg. editor children's mags., 1935—; ptnr. Youth assocs. Co., Mpls., 1942-65; pub. art dir. Mines and Escholier mags., 1954-65; founder Bull. Bd. Pictures, Inc., Mpls., 1954, pres., 1954—. Founder Periodical Litho Art Co., Mpls., 1962, pres., 1962-65; artist Cath. Boy mag., 1938; artist, designer book Palaces That Went To Sea, 1990; chief photographer Cath. Miss mag., 1955; cons., contbg. editor Nereus Pub. Co., 1998-. Mem. Women's aux. Mpls. Symphony Orch.; mem. Ft. Lauderdale (Fla.) Art Mus.; Rep. chairwoman Golden Valley, Minn., 1950; alt. del. Hennepin County Rep. Conv., 1962. Mem. Mpls. Inst. Arts, Internat. Inst., St. Paul Arts and Sci., Art Guild Boca Raton, Woman's Club, Minikahda Club, Deerfield Beach Women's Club. Home: 1416 Alpine Pass Tyrol Hills Minneapolis MN 55416 Office: 1057 Hillsboro Mile Hillsboro Beach FL 33062

GIBBONS, DONA ALDEN COE, electrical engineer; b. Springfield, Mass., Mar. 9, 1975; s. Arthur Coe and Virginia Elaine Fife Gibbons. BEE, B in Computer Engring., Coop. Edn. BEE, Coop. Edn. B of Software Engring., Auburn U., 2000. Cert. profl. Comptia Network, 03. Thinkpad product specialist, server qas analyst IBM Personal Sys. Group, Research Triangle Park, NC, 1996—98; goverment contract U. S. Army - Ft. Benning, Columbus, Ga., 1999—2002; network specialist - instl. support earmy Troy State U. - SE Regions, Columbus, Ga., 2002—. Mem.: IEEE, Math. Assn. Am., Assn. Supervision and Curriculum Devel., Assn. for Computing Machinery, Auburn Alumni Assn. Home: 1081 Lee Rd 439 Salem AL 36874 Office: Troy State Univ - Southeast Region 506 Manchester Expressway Suite B-15 Columbus GA 31904 Personal E-mail: gibboda@netscape.net. Business E-Mail: gibbonsd@troy.edu.

GIBBONS, GREGORY DENNIS, minister; b. Saginaw, Mich., May 23, 1953; s. Everett Durward and Doris Lorraine (Miller) G.; m. Susan Rae Schulz, Jan. 17, 1982; children: Stephanie Grace, Michael Everett, Naomi Susan, Matthew Gregory, Christopher Donald. BA, Northwestern Coll., Watertown, Wis., 1975; MDiv, Wis. Luth. Sem., 1979. Ordained to ministry Luth. Ch., 1979. Pastor Cross of Glory Luth. Ch., Baton Rouge, 1979-81, Good Shepherd Luth. Ch., West Bend, Wis., 1981-85, Mt. Zion Luth. Ch., Kenosha, Wis., 1985-94, Lola Park Luth. Ch., Redford, Mich., 1994—. Mem. S.E. Wis. Bd. of Evangelism, Milw., 1989—93; mem. nominating com., 1990; chmn. So. Pastoral Conf., Kenosha, 1990—; dir., vice chmn. Shoreland Luth. H.S., 1988—94; bd. regents Huron Valley Luth. H.S., 1995—98; bd. dirs. Mich. Lutheran Seminary Found., 2000—. Bd. dirs. Glen Eden Meml. Pk., 2000—. Republican. Home: 29522 Oakview St Livonia MI 48154-4464 Office: Lola Park Luth Ch 14750 Kinloch Redford MI 48239-3118 Office Phone: 313-532-8655. *The only thing that's truly important in life is sharing Jesus Christ as our crucified and risen Savior. That makes a difference, not only for this life but for all eternity.*

GIBBONS, JAMES ARTHUR, congressman; b. Reno, Dec. 16, 1944; s. Leonard A. and Matilda (Hancock) G.; m. T. Dawn Sanders-Snelling, June 21, 1986; children: Christopher, Jennifer, James A. Jr. BS in Geology, U. Nev., Reno, 1967, MS in Mining Geology, 1973; JD, Southwestern U., 1979. Bar: Nev. 1982, admitted to practice: US Dist. Ct. Nev. 1982. Hydrologist U.S. Fed. Water Master, Reno, 1963-67; geologist Union Carbide Co., Reno, 1972-75; comml. pilot Western Airlines, Inc., L.A., 1979—86; pilot Delta Airlines, Salt Lake City, 1986—96; sr. land mgr., atty. Homestake Mining Co., Reno, 1980-82; pvt. practice Reno, 1982—; mem. U.S. Congress from Nev. 2nd dist., 1997—, mem. armed svcs. com., homeland security com., mem. com. in intelligence, vice chmn. com. on resources. Contbr. Mem. Nev. Coun. on Econ. Edn., 1986; mem. Nev. State Assembly, 1988-94. Lt. col. Nev. Air Nat. Guard, Persian Gulf, 1990-91; with USAF, 1967-72. Decorated DFC. Mem. Assn. Trial Lawyers of Am., Nev. Trial Lawyers Assn., Rocky Mt. Mineral Law Found., Comml Law League Am., Am. Inst. Mining Engrs., Nev. Landman's Assn. (chmn. 1981-82, cons. atty. 1982-83). Republican. Avocation: flying. Office: US Ho Reps 100 Cannon Ho Office Bldg Washington DC 20515-0001 E-mail: mail.gibbons@mail.house.gov.*

GIBBONS, JOHN HOWARD (JACK GIBBONS), federal official, physicist; b. Harrisonburg, Va., Jan. 15, 1929; s. Howard K. and Jessie Diana (Conrad) G.; m. Mary Ann Hobart, May 21, 1955; children: Virginia Neil, Diana Conrad, Mary Marshall. BS in Math. and Chemistry, Randolph-Macon Coll., 1949, ScD (hon.), 1977; PhD in Physics, Duke U., 1954, ScD (hon.), 1997; PhD in Humane Letters and Sci. (hon.), Ill. Inst. Tech., 1994; PhD in Sci. (hon.), Mt. Sinai Med. Sch., 1995; ScD (hon.), U. Delaware, 1996, U. Md., 1997. Physicist and group leader nuclear geophysics Oak Ridge Nat. Lab., 1954-69, dir. environ. program, 1969-73; dir. Energy Conservation Office, Fed. Energy Adminstrn., Washington, 1973-74; prof. physics, dir. Energy, Environ. and Resources Center, U. Tenn., Knoxville, 1974-79; dir. Office of Tech. Assessment, U.S. Congress, 1979-92; asst. to Pres. for sci. and tech. Exec. Office of the Pres., Washington, 1993-98; dir. of sci. and tech. policy Exec. Office of Pres., Washington, 1993-98; Karl T. Compton lectr. MIT, 1998-99; sr. fellow NAE, 1999-2000; sr. advisor U.S. Dept. State, 1999-2000, Nat. Acad. Engring., 1999—. Energy and resources com. Aspen Inst., 1979—; mem. adv. com. Stanford U. Sch. Engring., 1984—87, Electric Power Rsch. Inst., 1986—92; mem. Carnegie Corp. Sci., Tech. and Govt. Task Force on Long Term Goals and Priorities, 1990—92; bd. dirs. Supercritical Combustion Tech. Interstate Gen. LP, Dynamac Corp., Action LLC, Black Rock Forest Consortium; mem. coun. advisors Nat. Renewable Energy Lab., 1998—; pres. Resource Strategies, 1998—; mem. internat. adv. bd. com. on internat. programs Nat. Acads., 2001—, divsn. advisor divsn. on phys. scis. and engring., 2001—; mem. strategic adv. com. Gas Tech. Inst., 2003—; mem. steering com. Nat. Climate Assessment, 1998—2001; mem. adv. bd. MIT Innovations Tech./Governance/Globalization Jour., 2005—; chmn. bd. Population Action Internat., 2003—. Author: This Gifted Age: Science and Technology at the Millennium, 1997; contbr. articles to profl. jours. Chmn. bd. assocs. Randolph-Macon Coll., Ashland, Va., 1980-83, trustee, 1977-79; bd. dirs. World Resources Inst., 1998-2005. Decorated comdr. Ordre des Palmes Academiques (France), officer's cross Order of Merit (Germany); recipient Disting. Svc. award Fed. Energy Adminstrn., 1974, Pub. Svc. award Fedn. Am. Scientists, 1990, Disting. Alumni award James Madison U., 1993, Life Achievement in Sci. award Commonwealth of Va., 1995, First Seymour Cray High Performance Computing Industry Recognition award, 1997, Disting. Svc. medal NASA, 1998. Fellow: NSF (Disting. Pub. Svc. award 1998), AAAS (bd. dirs. 1988—90, Philip Hauge Abelson prize 1993), Am. Assn. Engring. Socs. (chmn.'s award 1998), Am. Phys. Soc. (Leo Szilard award for physics in pub. interest 1991), Assn. for Women in Sci.; mem.: NAE (Arthur Bueche award 1998), Am. Assn. Engring. Socs., Am. Philos. Soc., N.Y. Acad. Scis. (bd. govs. 1998—2002), Coun. Fgn. Rels., Cosmos Club, Sigma Pi Sigma (John P. McGovern Sci. and Soc. award and medal 1997), Pi Mu Epsilon, Omicron Delta Kappa, Pi Gamma Mu, Phi Beta Kappa, Sigma Xi (pres. 2000—01). Episcopal. Avocations: hiking, farming, conservation, non-governmental organizations (ngo's). Home: PO Box 379 The Plains VA 20198 Office Phone: 540-253-9843. E-mail: jackgibbons@direcway.com. *My formal training in physics, backed by a liberal arts education, enabled me to drink deeply from the sweet spring of basic research for many years. When I took leave from disciplinary research and became immersed in analysis of socio-technical issues, it was a most discomforting step. But having taken it, the new challenges were not only enlivening, but also surprisingly susceptible to the problem-solving approaches I had learned in science. The lessons: (1)Training in physics is an effective instrument to learn how to solve many kinds of problems; (2)A change in professional direction about every decade or so is a great tonic; (3)Attacking issues from fresh perspectives is a natural ingredient of creativity.*

GIBBONS, JOHN JOSEPH, lawyer, retired federal judge; b. Newark, Dec. 8, 1924; s. Daniel Lehane and Julia (Murray) G.; m. Mary Jeanne Boyle, Apr. 19, 1952; children: Daniel J., Mary E., Nora F., Richard G., Deirdre E., Maude A., David C. BS, Holy Cross Coll., 1947, LL.D., 1970; LLB cum laude, Harvard U., 1950; LLD, Seton Hall U., 1980, Suffolk U., 1982. Bar: N.J., 1950. Ptnr. Crummy, Gibbons & O'Neill, Newark, 1953-70; cir. judge U.S. Ct. of Appeals (3d cir.), 1970-90, ret. judge; spl. counsel Crummy, Del Deo, Dolan, Griffinger & Vecchione, Newark; dir. Gibbons, Del Deo, Dolan, Griffinger & Vecchione, Newark; chief judge U.S. Ct. Appeals (3d cir.), 1987-90. Richard J. Hughes prof. Constl. law Seton Hall U., 1989—; adj. prof. Rutgers U., Suffolk U., Duke U.; mem. N.J. Bd. Bar Examiners, Trenton, 1959-64, chmn., 1963-64; mem. Gov.'s Select. Commn. on Civil Disorders, N.J. Coun. Against Crime; mem. vis. com. Law Sch., U. Chgo. Contbr. articles in field. Trustee Practicing Law Inst., 1973—; trustee Holy Cross Coll., 1970— . Served to lt. (j.g.) USNR, 1943-46. Named Lawyer of the Year, N.J. Law Jour., 2004; recipient Lifetime Achievement award, Am. Law mag., 2005. Fellow Am. Bar Found.; mem. ABA (ho. of dels. 1968), N.J. Bar Assn. (pres. 1967-68), Essex County Bar Assn. (trustee 1961-64), Holy Cross Coll. Gen. Alumni Assn. (trustee, v.p. 1967-70) Office: Gibbons Del Del Griffinger & Vecchione One Riverfront Plz Newark NJ 07102-5496 Office Phone: 973-596-4733. Business E-Mail: jgibbons@gibbonslaw.com.

GIBBONS, JOHN MARTIN, JR., physician, educator; b. N.Y.C., Feb. 25, 1933; s. John Martin and Mary Frances (Darr) G.; m. Mary Therese Peyser, Dec. 26, 1955; chidlren: Catherine Way, Mary Sloan, John M. III, Fredericka Kerr, Myles. AB, Holy Cross Coll., 1954; MD, Georgetown U., 1958. Diplomate Am. Bd. Ob-Gyn., Am. Bd. Maternal and Fetal Medicine. Intern and resident ob-gyn Saint Vincent's Hosp., N.Y.C., 1958—63; from asst. to assoc. prof. ob-gyn. U. Conn., Farmington, 1970—78, prof. ob-gyn., 1978—. Chief dept. ob-gyn. Fordham Hosp., N.Y.C., 1968-70; dir. dept. ob-gyn. Saint Francis Hosp. and Med. Ctr., Hartford, Conn., 1970-93, sr. v.p. for med. affairs, 1993-99; mem. adv. coun. Nat. Inst. Child Health and Human Devel., 2001-05. Mem. Capital Area Health Consortium Bd., 1978-2000; mem. exec. com. Combined Hosps. Fund, 1978-82, Mt. Sinai Hosp. Bd., 1990-95; mem. Bristol Hosp. Bd., 1997-2004, 2005-; mem. Hartford Ballet Bd., 1978-83, hon. mem., 1983-95, v.p., 1993-95, pres., 1995-97; mem. Hartford Stage Bd., 1999-2003; mem. Med. Delivery Sys., Inc., 1985-88, Greater Hartford Arts Coun., 1988-92, 95-97; corporator Wadsworth Atheneum, 1987-97; overseer Bushnell Meml. Hall, 1990—. Capt. USAR, 1961-68. Fellow ACOG (dist. treas. 1987-91, dist. vice chmn. 1991-94, nat. fin. com. 1992-00, dist. chmn. 1994-97, nat. treas. 1997-00, pres.-elect 2002-03, pres. 2003-04, immediate past pres. 2004-05), ACS, Soc. Maternal-Fetal Medicine, Obstet. Soc. Boston; mem. Conn. State Med. Soc. (sec. ob-gyn., vice chmn. 1979-82, chmn. 1982-85), Hartford Med. Soc., Hartford Golf Club, Harvard Club of N.Y.C., Lotos Club (N.Y.C.). Office: Saint Francis Hosp Med Ctr 114 Woodland St Hartford CT 06105-1208 Office Phone: 860-714-4456. Business E-Mail: jgibbons@stfranciscare.org. E-mail: jgibbonsmd@hotmail.com.

GIBBONS, JULIA SMITH, federal judge; d. John Floyd and Julia Jackson (Abernathy) Smith; m. William Lockhart Gibbons, Aug. 11, 1973; children: Rebecca Carey, William Lockhart Jr. BA, Vanderbilt U., 1972; JD, U. Va., 1975. Bar: Tenn. 1975. Law clk. to judge U.S. Ct. Appeals, 1975-76; assoc. Farris, Hancock, Gilman, Branan, Lanier & Hellen, Memphis, 1976-79; legal advisor Gov. Lamar Alexander, Nashville, 1979-81; judge 15th Jud. Cir., Memphis, 1981-83, U.S. Dist. Ct. (we. dist.) Tenn., Memphis, 1983—2002, chief judge, 1994-2000; judge U.S. Ct. Appeals (6th cir.), Memphis, 2002—. Fellow: Memphis and Shelby County Bar Found., Tenn. Bar Found., Am. Bar Found.; mem.: Memphis Bar Assn., Phi Beta Kappa, Order of Coif. Presbyterian. Office: US Ct Appeals 970 Federal Bldg 167 N Main St Memphis TN 38103-1816

GIBBONS, MARK, state supreme court justice; BA, U. Calif., Irvine, 1972; JD, Loyola U., L.A., 1975. Assoc. atty. Woofter & Bilbray, 1975—86; partner Bilbray & Gibbons, 1976—85, Gibbons & Berman, 1985—90, Oshins & Gibbons, 1990—95; of counsel Streich Lang, 1995—96; judge Clark County Dist. Ct., Nev., 1996—98, presiding judge civil divsn., 1998—2001; chief judge 8th Jud. Dist. Ct., Nev., 2001—02; assoc. justice Nev. Supreme Ct., Carson City, 2003—. Advisory mem. Senior Citizens Law Project Las Vegas City Council, 1995, chair of advisory mem. Senior Citizens Law Project, 1998—2001. Mem.: Nev. Bar Assn., Clark County Bar Assn. Office: Nev Supreme Ct 201 Carson St Carson City NV 89701-4702

GIBBONS, MARY PEYSER, civic volunteer; b. N.Y.C., Dec. 15, 1936; d. Frederick Maurice and Catherine Mary (McKelvey) Peyser; m. John Martin Gibbons; children: Catherine Way, Mary Sloan, John, Fredericka Kerr, Myles. Trustee Wadsworth Atheneum, 1978-99, hon. trustee, 2000; trustee Hartford Art Sch., 1985-95; regent U. Hartford, 1988-2004; bd. dirs. Hartford Ballet, 1981-95, Conn. Valley Girl Scouts, 1994-95, U.S. Found. World Fedn., Friends of Museums, 1990—; vol. Com. Art Mus., U.S. and Can., 1982-91; pres. Am. Assn. Mus. Vols., 1983-91, adv. bd. mem., 1991—; corporator St. Francis Hosp., 1990—, Hartford Ballet, 1995-97, Conn. Inst. for the Blind; mem. alumnae bd. divs. Convent of the Sacred Heart, 91th St., N.Y.C. Mem. Hartford Golf Club, Town and County Club. Office: Sefton & Sheil Ltd 1130 Prospect Ave Hartford CT 06105-1124

GIBBONS, MILES JOSEPH, JR., foundation administrator; b. Scranton, Pa., June 25, 1935; s. Miles J. and Claire (Kennedy) G.; m. Carole Forker; children: Miles D., Elisabeth D. BA, Dickinson Coll., Carlisle, Pa., 1957; JD, Georgetown U., 1964; postgrad., Harvard U., 1996. Cost acct. U.S. Steel, Johnstown, Pa., 1957-60; acct. RCA Svc. Co., Alexandria, Va., 1961-64; atty. Keating, Waterval and Johnson, Falls Church, Va., 1964-65; staff atty. AMP Inc., Harrisburg, Pa., 1965-68; counsel to minority leader Ho. of Reps. Commonwealth of Pa., Harrisburg, 1968-70; assoc. atty. Morgan, Lewis and Bockius, Harrisburg, 1968-71, ptnr., 1971-81, of counsel, 1981-84; exec. dir. The Helen F. Whitaker Fund, Mechanicsburg, Pa., 1984—, The Franklin H. and Ruth L. Wells Found., Machanicsburg, 1983—; CEO, pres. The Whitaker Found., Rosslyn, Va. and Mechanicsburg, Pa., 1981-2000. Mem. sch. bd. Northern York County Sch. Dist., Dillsburg, Pa., 1984-88; chair problem solving com. United Way of Capital Region, Harrisburg, 1990-91; bd. dirs. United Way of Pa., 1994-95; bd. dirs. South Ctrl. Pa. Housing Devel. Found., Harrisburg, 1990-95, mem. exec. com., 1991-95; bd. dirs. Coun. for Pub. Edn., Harrisburg, 1989-92, The Fredricksen Found., Mechanicsburg, Pa., 1990—; mem. adv. bd. Milton S. Hershey Med. Sch., 1992-98; vol. Big Bros./Big Sisters, Harrisburg, 1990-95; co-chair Found. Exec. Rountable, Harrisburg, 1989-99; bd. dirs. Capital Campaign Review Com., Harrisburg, 1989—, chair, 1992—. Recipient Pub. Svc. award Messiah Coll., 1997, Founder's Day award Lebanon Valley Coll., 1999. Mem. Rotary Club Harrisburg (pres. 1988-89, Community Svc. award 1990). Office: The Helen F Whitaker Fund 4718 Old Gettysburg Rd Mechanicsburg PA 17055-4378 E-mail: mgibbons@whitaker.org.

GIBBONS, PAMELA R., professional athletic trainer; b. Orange, Calif., May 16, 1965; d. Donna L. and Greg S. Crandall (Stepfather), Richard P. Gibbons; 1 child, Savana R. AS in Sports Med./Athletic Tng., Rancho Santiago C.C., 1985; BS in Phys. Edn. and Athletic Tng., Calif. State U., 1989; MA in Ednl. Leadership and Adminstrn., Chapman U., 2001. Cert. athletic trainer 1989, cardiopulmonary resuscitation instr. ARC, 1985, lifeguard tng. instr. ARC, 1996, adv. first aid, basic first aid, basic lifesaving ARC, 1998, first aid for pub. safety personnel instr. ARC, 1998. Head athletic trainer Los Alamitos (Calif.) H.S., 1988—91; personal trainer, fitness instr. Los Caballeros Sports Village, 1990—91; legal asst., investigator Juvenile Law Ctr., Santa Ana, Calif., 1991—94; asst. athletic trainer Chapman U., Orange, 1991—98, head women's swimming coach, 1993—96, head athletic trainer, 1998—. Instr./instr.'s aid Rancho Santiago C.C., 1984—90; substitute tchr. Los Alamitos H.S., 1988—91; part time faculty Chapman U., 1994—; lifeguard tng. instr. City of Orange, 1996—2000; approved clin. instr. Chapman U., 2003—. Mem. ARC. Mem.: Far West Athletic Trainers' Assn., Coll. Athletic Trainers Soc., Nat. Athletic Trainers' Assn. Office: Chapman U One University Dr Orange CA 92866 Office Phone: 714-997-6640. Business E-Mail: gibbons@chapman.edu.

GIBBONS, PATRICK CHANDLER, physicist, researcher; b. Washington, Dec. 18, 1943; s. Myles Francis and Margaret Mack (Chandler) G.; m. Jane Elizabeth Forsell, Aug. 17, 1968; children: Elizabeth Jane, Jonathan Myles, Jane Chandler, Katherine Forsell. BS, Georgetown U., 1965; PhD, Harvard U., 1971. Physics instr. Princeton (N.J.) U., 1971-73, asst. prof. physics, 1973-76, Washington U., St. Louis, 1976-79, assoc. prof. physics, 1979-89, prof. physics, 1989—. Contbr. articles to Philos. mag., Jour. Non-Crystal Solids. Trustee Univ. Hills Subdivsn., University City, Mo., 1984-87. Mem. Am. Phys. Soc., Univ. City Swim Club (pres. 1988-90, 94-95), Sigma Xi, Phi Beta Kappa. Office: Washington U PO Box 1105 Saint Louis MO 63188-1105 Office Phone: 314-935-6271.

GIBBONS, PETCH, real estate company executive; Grad., U. Md., 1976. With Barnes, Morris, Pardoe & Foster, 1980—97, pres., 1990—97; exec. mng. dir. Insignia, Washington, 1997—2001; pres., CEO Advantis GVA, Washington, 2001—. Trustee U. Md. Coll. Park Found.; mem. adv. bd. Real Share, Washington. Office: Advantis GVA Ste 800 1747 Pennsylvania Ave Washington DC 20006

GIBBONS, REX VINCENT, geologist; b. Lumsden, Nfld., Can., Feb. 12, 1946; s. Clayton Manuel and Nita Mildred (Vincent) G.; m. Marjorie Stagg, May 20, 1966; children: Kim, Emily, Vince. BA in Edn., BSc, Meml. U. of Nfld., 1967, MSc in Geology, 1969; PhD in Geology, Calif. Inst. Tech., 1974. Registered profl. geologist, Nfld. Rsch. scientist NASA/Johnson Space Ctr., Houston, 1974-76; sr. geologist Nfld. Dept. Mines & Energy, St. John's, 1976-89; mem. Ho. of Assembly, St. John's West, Nfld., 1989-97, minister of mines and energy, 1989-94, 96-97, minister of natural resources, 1994-96; exec. v.p., sr. geosci. cons. Jacques Whitford Environment Ltd., Nfld. Geoscis. Ltd., St. John's, Canada, 1997—2004; sr. v.p. Jacques Whitford Ltd., St. John's, 2004—. Bd. dirs. Terra Nova Gold Inc. Contbr. articles to profl. jours.; assoc. editor Geosci. Canada, 1980-85. Mem. Avalon Consol. Sch. Bd., St. John's, 1982-89, chmn., 1986-89; bd. mgmt. St. James United Ch., 1983-87; bd. regents Meml. U. of Nfld., 1978-81; bd. dirs. Nfld. Lung Health Found., Nfld. Sci. Ctr., Nfld. Ocean Industries, 1998-2001, St. John's Bd. Trade, 1998-2000. Nat. Rsch. Coun. Can. grad. bursary, 1968-69; Nfld. Govt. grad. fellow, 1967-68; Centenary scholar, 1966-67. Mem.: Assn. Profl. Engrs. and Geoscientists of Nfld., Can. Inst. Mining, Metallurgy & Petroleum (councillor, nat. v.p. 1982—87, nat. pres. 2001—02). Liberal. Avocations: fly fishing, curling, canoeing, hunting, genealogy. Home: 34 Spratt Pl Saint John's NL Canada A1E 4M2 Office: Jacques Whitford Ltd 607 Torbay Rd Saint John's NL Canada A1A 4Y6 Office Phone: 709-576-1458. Personal E-mail: rex@rexgibbons.com.ca.

GIBBONS, ROBERT BUTLER, JR., retired military officer; b. Sumter, S.C., Sept. 20, 1947; s. Robert Butler Gibbons Sr. and Dorothy Jean (Welsh) Gibbons; m. Patricia Theodora Atkins, July 7, 1970 (div. Aug. 1983); 1 adopted child, Carole Gibbons Taylor children: Robert Butler III, Hannah Gibbons Tremer; m. Jean Claire Kennedy Burttram, June 24, 1984; 1 stepchild, Paige Burttram Belt. AS in Bus. Mgmt., Victor Valley Coll., 1986; grad., Nat. Am. Legion Coll., 2000. Entered USAF, 1966, ret., 1989; chief security various internat. security cos., 1990—99; comdr. Am. Legion Dist. 11, SC, 1998—2000; 1st 2d, 3d, and 4th dept. vice comdr. Am. Legion, 2000—03, S.C. dept. comdr., 2003—04, Am. Legion Americanism Commn., SC, 2004—08. Chmn. Clarendon County Planning Commn., Manning, SC, 1998, 1999, Clarendon County GOP, Manning, SC, 2002—, Clarendon County Planning Commn., Manning, 2003—04; candidate for SC Senate Dist 36, 1996, 2004. Mem.: VFW (life), Am. Air Mus. Brit., Disabled Am. Vets. (life), Am. Legion (life), Air Force Assn. (life), La Soc. Des Quarante Hommes Et Huit Chevaux, Sumter Voiture 1254 (Voiture of Yr. 2003, Grand Voiture of Yr. 2004), Mason Fidelity Lodge. Republican. Methodist. Avocations: collecting models of presidents homes and European castles, gardening, travel. Home: PO Box 19 6877 Salem Rd New Zion SC 29111 Office Phone: 843-659-8793.

GIBBONS, ROBERT EBBERT, university official; b. Sharon, Pa., Nov. 15, 1940; s. Thomas Michael and Mary Jane (Ebbert) G.; m. Patricia Arlene Fox, Aug. 18, 1962; children: Patrick, Timothy, Roberta, Aaron. BS, John Carroll U., 1962; MA, Bowling Green State U., 1963, PhD, 1967. Pres. Viterbo Coll., La Crosse, Wis., 1980-91; asst. prof. English Our Lady of the Lake U., San Antonio, 1969-72, chmn. English dept., 1972-74, dir. humanities div., 1974-77, exec. asst. to pres., 1977-80, exec. v.p., 1991-99, prof. English, 1991—, pres., 2001—02. Bd. dirs. Wis. Found. of Ind. Colls., Milw., 1980-91, pres., 1987-88; mem. USCC Com. on Cert. and Accreditation, 1988-94, vice chair, 1991-93. Mem. Phi Kappa Phi. Roman Catholic. Home: 3518 Hunters Gate St San Antonio TX 78230-2820 Office: Our Lady of the Lake U 411 SW 24th St San Antonio TX 78207-4689

GIBBONS, ROBERT JOHN, lawyer; b. Bklyn., Dec. 3, 1944; s. David Thomas and Virginia Marie G.; m. Judith Ann Borst, Nov. 23, 1968; children: Robert, Sharon, Suzanne. BA, St. John's U., Jamaica, N.Y., 1966; JD, Fordham U., 1969. Bar: N.Y. 1970. Assoc. Mudge, Rose, Guthrie, Alexander & Ferdon, NYC, 1969-76; ptnr. Wood, Dawson et al, NYC, 1976-77, Debevoise & Plimpton LLP, NYC, 1977—, co-head Project Fin. Practice Group. Trustee New Canaan County Sch., Conn., 1983-91, pres. bd. trustees, 1988-91; bd. dirs. New Canaan Baseball Inc., 1982-88, New Canaan Field Club; mem. Utilities Commn. Town of New Canaan, 1986-90. Mem. ABA, N.Y. State Bar Assn., Assn. of Bar of City of N.Y. Home: 221 Michigan Rd New Canaan CT 06840-2223 Office: Debevoise & Plimpton LLP 919 3rd Ave Fl 47 New York NY 10022-6225 Office Phone: 212-909-6303. Office Fax: 212-909-6836. E-mail: rjgibbons@debevoise.com.

GIBBONS, ROBERT PHILIP, management consultant, director; m. Mary Jane M. Jamieson, June 12, 1965; children: Laura Ann, Robert John. BSME, Stevens Inst. Tech., 1955; MS in Indsl. Mgmt., Purdue U., 1959. Ptnr. Touche Ross Co., N.Y.C., 1959—74; v.p., gen. mgr. Carborundum Co., Niagara Falls, NY, 1975—78, Main Hurdman, N.Y.C., 1978—84, Zolfo, Cooper & Co., N.Y.C., 1984—86; ptnr. Gibbons, Quintero & Co., N.Y.C., 1986—90, Gibbons & Co,., Tenafly, NJ, 1990—. Apptd. trustee U.S. Trustee and U.S. Bankruptcy Ct. Contbr. Am. Mgmt. Assn. Mgmt. Handbook, 1970. Bd. dirs., chmn. audit com., compensation com. Weldotron Corp., 1974—91. With U.S. Army, 1956—58. Mem.: Turnaround Mgmt. Assn., Am. Bankruptcy Inst., Inst. Mgmt. Cons. (cert.), Am. Prodn. and Inventory Control Soc. (cert.). Office: Gibbons and Co 118 Fisher Rd Mahwah NJ 07430 Office Phone: 201-760-0567.

GIBBONS, SAM MELVILLE, former congressman, business executive; b. Tampa, Fla., Jan. 20, 1920; s. Gunby and Jessie Kirk (Cralle) G.; m. Martha Hanley, Sept. 14, 1946; children: Clifford, Mark, Timothy. JD, U. Fla., 1947. Bar: Fla. 1947. Mem. Fla. Ho. of Reps., 1952-58, Fla. Senate, 1958-62, 88th-104th Congresses from 7th (now 11th) Fla. dist., 1962-96; ranking minority mem. ways and means com. U.S. Ho. Reps, chmn. ways and means com., 1994-95, mem. joint taxation com. Washington, 1996—; chmn. Gibbons & Co., Washington, 1996—. Founder, 1st pres. U.S. Fla. Found., 1958. Served to maj. AUS, 1941-45, ETO. Decorated Bronze Star; named Outstanding Young Man Tampa Jr. C. of C., 1954; recipient President's award Tampa C. of C., 1955; featured in Tom Brokaw book The Greatest Generation and Steve Ambrose's "D" Day. Mem. Tampa Bar Assn. (dir.), Hillsborough Bar Assn. (dir.), Greater Tampa C. of C. (dir.) Democrat. Presbyterian (deacon). Office: PO Box 1037 Mc Lean VA 22101-1037

GIBBONS, WILLIAM JOHN, lawyer; b. Chgo., Jan. 22, 1947; s. Edward and Lottie (Gasiorek) G.; children: Maximilian Clay, Bartholomew David, Ariel Katherine. BA, Northwestern U., 1968, JD, 1972. Bar: Ill. 1972, U.S. Dist. Ct. (no. dist.) Ill. 1972, U.S. Ct. Appeals (9th cir.) 1980, U.S. Supreme Ct. 1982, U.S. Ct. Appeals (7th cir.) 1984, U.S. Ct. Appeals (3d cir.) 2002. Assoc. Kirkland and Ellis, Chgo., 1972-76; ptnr. Hedlund, Hunter and Lynch, Chgo., 1976-82, Latham and Watkins, Chgo., 1982—, mng. ptnr. Chgo. office, 1995-2000. Served with USAR, 1968-74. Mem.: ABA, Chgo. Coun. Lawyers, Seventh Cir. Bar Assn., Chgo. Bar Assn. (chair class action com. 1994—95), Riverpark Club (Chgo.). Home: 1515 S Prairie # 913 Chicago IL 60605-3024 Office: Latham & Watkins Sears Tower Ste 5800 Chicago IL 60606-6306 Office Phone: 312-876-7706. Business E-Mail: william.gibbons@lw.com.

GIBBONS, WILLIAM REGINALD, JR., poet, writer, translator, editor; b. Houston, Jan. 7, 1947; s. William Reginald and Elizabeth (Lubowski) G.; m. Virginia Margaret Harris, June 8, 1968 (div. July 1982); m. Cornelia Maude Spelman, Aug. 18, 1983. AB, Princeton U., 1969; MA, Stanford U., 1971, PhD, 1974. Instr. Spanish Rutgers U., Brunswick, N.J., 1975-76; lectr. creative writing Princeton U., 1976-80, Columbia U., N.Y.C., 1980-81; prof. English Northwestern U., Evanston, Ill., 1981—, chair English, 2002—05, editor TriQuarterly Evanston, Ill., 1981-97; prof. MFA Program for Writers Warren Wilson Coll., 1989. Author: Roofs Voices Roads, 1979 (Quar. Rev. prize), The Ruined Motel, 1981, Saints, 1986, Maybe It Was So, 1991, Five Pears or Peaches, 1991, William Goyen: A Study of the Short Fiction, 1991, Sweetbitter, 1994, Sparrow: New and Selected Poems, 1997, Homage to Longshot O'Leary, 1999, It's Time, 2002; translator: Selected Poems of Luis Cernuda, 1978, Guillén on Guillén, 1979, (with Charles Segal) Euripides' Bakkhai, 2001, (with Charles Segal) Sophokles' Antigone, 2003; editor: The

Poet's Work, 1979; (with G. Graff) Criticism in the University, 1985, The Writer in Our World, 1986, Fiction of the Eighties, 1990, Thomas McGrath: Life and the Poem, 1991, New Writing from Mexico, 1992. Woodrow Wilson fellow Stanford U., 1969-70; Fulbright fellow Spain, 1971-72; Guggenheim fellow, 1983-84; NEA fellow, 1984; Ill. Arts Coun. fellow, 1988; recipient Translation prize Denver Quar., 1977, Short Story award Tex. Inst. Letters, 1986, Carl Sandburg award, 1992, Anisfield-Wolf Book award, 1995, Jesse Jones award Tex. Inst. Letters, 1995, Ill. Arts Coun. Lit. awards, 1996, 97, Balcones Poetry prize, 1998, Best Book of Poetry award Tex. Inst. Letters, 2003, O.B. Hardison Jr. Poetry prize Folger Libr., 2004. Mem. PEN Am. Ctr., Poetry Soc. Am. (John Masefield Meml. award 1991), Associated Writing Programs (bd. dirs. 1984-87), The Guild Complex (bd. dirs. 1989—). Office: Northwestern U Dept English Univ Hall 215 Evanston IL 60208-0001 Office Phone: 847-491-7294. E-mail: rgibbons@northwestern.edu.

GIBBS, ANTONY (TONY GIBBS), film editor; Editor: (films) The Loneliness of the Long Distance Runner, 1962, A Taste of Honey, 1962, Tom Jones, 1963, The Luck of Ginger Coffey, 1964, The Knack...And How to Get It, 1965, The Loved One, 1965, Petulia, 1968, Performance, 1970, Walkabout, 1971, (with Robert Lawrence) Fiddler on the Roof, 1971, Jesus Christ Superstar, 1973, Rollerball, 1975, The Sailor Who Fell from Grace with the Sea, 1976, A Bridge Too Far, 1977, (with Graeme Clifford) F.I.S.T., 1978, Yesterday's Hero, 1979, (with George Trirogoff) Butch and Sundance: The Early Days, 1979, (with Anne V. Coates and Stanley Warnow) Ragtime, 1981, The Dogs of War, 1981, Bad Boys, 1983, Dune, 1984, Agnes of God, 1985, Tai-Pan, 1986, Russkies, 1987, Stealing Home, 1988, (with Lou Lombardo) In Country, 1989, The Runner, 1990, The Taking of Beverly Hills, 1992, The Man Without a Face, 1993, Don Juan DeMarco, 1995, Ronin, 1998, Reindeer Games, 2000, (TV movies) Devlin, 1992, A Case for Life, 1996, Crime of the Century, 1996, George Wallace, 1997, James Dean, 2001. Office: 15691 Royal Ridge Rd Sherman Oaks CA 91403-4208

GIBBS, BEATRICE ESTHER, librarian; b. Malden, Mass., Oct. 16, 1918; d. Joseph S. and Della N. (Rainen) G.; m. Howard Konowitch (dec. 1976); children: Paula, Bonnie, Marian, Ben. BA, Tufts U., 1969; MA, Rowan State U., 1972. Tchr. Mid. Twp., Cape May Courthouse, N.J., 1964-75; libr., head children svcs. Cape May County Libr., Cape May Courthouse, 1975-84; libr. Montgomery County Libr., Bethesda, Md., 1985—. Conducted weekly WCMC TV program, 1976-84; dir. Children's Resource Ctr., 1994-96. Columnist: (book rev.) Gazette. Pres. PTA, Wildwood, N.J., 1964-70; leader Girl Scouts Am., Wildwood, 1964-70; dir. Coop Nursery, Wildwood, 1966-70. With USN, 1942-45. Mem. ALA, NCJW, Cape May County Art League (v.p. 1960-65), Cape May County Hist. Soc. (sec. 1965-68), Montgomery Libr. Staff Assn., Women in the Arts Mus., Corcoran Mus., Phillips Collection, Smithsonian Donor, Tufts Alumni Assn., Internat. Reading Assn., Internat. Board Books for Young Children (del.), Am. Legion, Primetimers. Avocations: travel, photography, museums, music, art. Home: 8100 Connecticut Ave Apt 523 Chevy Chase MD 20815 Office: Montgomery County Library 5501 Massachusetts Ave Bethesda MD 20816-1932

GIBBS, DAVID GEORGE, retired food processing company executive; b. Vancouver, B.C., Can., May 5, 1925; s. Albert Edward and Florence (Bedford) G.; m. Lenore Joyce De Geer, Oct. 7, 1949; 1 dau., Susan Caroline. Grad. high sch.; MBA, Simon Fraser U., 1975. C.G.A., Can. Audit clk. Price Waterhouse (chartered accountants), 1943-46; with Kelly Douglas Co. Ltd., Vancouver, 1946-89, controller, 1965-89, v.p., 1975-89. Elected bd. dirs., elected pres. Western Lettuce Now Inc., 1996. Treas. Burrard Yacht Club, Coalition to Eliminate Abuse of Srs., D.K.G.D. Enterprises Ltd. Named Ky. col., 1968 Mem. Fin. Execs. Inst., B.C. Hot House Growers Assn. (bd. dirs. 1998-2002). Clubs: Capilano Lions (charter pres. 1977), Masons. Home: 956 Belgrave St North Vancouver BC Canada V7R 1Z2

GIBBS, DENIS LAUREL, radiologist; b. Wayne, Mich., Mar. 6, 1945; s. Laurel Pierce and Alwyn Marie (Larson) G.; m. Paula Kay Lynn, Sept. 6, 1974 (div. Aug. 1988); children: Jeremy Paul, Matthew Ryan, Kevin Christopher, Denis Patrick; m. Kathleen Marie DeLaFuente, July 9, 1989; 1 child, Andrew Zachery. BS, Andrews U., Berrien Springs, Mich., 1967, postgrad., 1967-69; DO, Kansas City Coll. Osteopathic Medicine, 1974. Diplomate Am. Bd. Radiology. Intern, radiology resident Doctors' Hosps., Columbus, Ohio, 1974-78, staff radiologist, 1978; chmn. dept. radiology Rocky Mountain Hosp., Denver, 1978-88, vice chief of staff, 1982, chief of staff, 1983, 84; chmn. dept. radiology Colo. Plain Med. Ctr. Regional Trauma Ctr., Ft. Morgan, 1988—2002, vice chief of staff, 1992—93; staff radiologist, VICE CHMN. DEPT. Lakeland Med. Ctr., Niles, Mich., 2002—, radiologist, vice chair of dept., 2002—. Med., legal cons., Colo., 1979—, Calif., 1979—, Fla., 1979—; consulting radiologist East Morgan Hosp., Luth. Health Sys., Brush, Colo., 1988—2002; CEO IRS Radiology Cons., P.C., Ft. Morgan, 1988—2002, Interstate Radiology Services, Henderson, Nev., 2002—; v.p. Niles Imaging Physicians, Mich., 2002—. Med. reviewer Post Grad. Medicine. Mem. Am. Osteopathic Assn., Am. Osteopathic Coll. Radiology, Am. Roentgen Ray Soc., Nat. Assn. Seventh-Day Adventist Osteopaths, Colo. Med. Soc., Soc. Nuclear Medicine Physicians. Republican. Avocations: snorkeling, skin diving, racquetball, sports car enthusiast and owner, travel. Office: PO Box 820 Niles MI 49120

GIBBS, FREDERICK WINFIELD, lawyer, communications executive; b. Buffalo, Mar. 22, 1932; s. Walter L. M. and Elizabeth Mari (Georgi) G.; m. Josephine Janice Jarvis, Dec. 20, 1954; children: Michael, Mathew, Robyn. BA cum laude, Alfred U., 1954; JD with Tax honors, Rutgers U., 1989. Bar: Pa. 1989, N.J. 1989, U.S. Dist. Ct. N.J. 1989. With N.Y. Tel. Co., 1954-65, ITT, 1965-86; mng. dir. ITT Standard Electrica, S.A., 1971-75; chief exec. officer ITT Standard Electrica, Brazil, 1975-77; exec. dir. ops. ITT Communications Ops. Group ITT Comm. Ops. Group, 1977; corp. v.p. ITT, 1977-80; pres. U.S. Tel. and Tel. Corp., 1977-79, exec. dir., sr. group exec., 1980-86; dir. System 12, ITT, 1979-80; exec. v.p. ITT, 1980-86, ITT Telecom. Corp., 1983-86; pvt. practice law Pemberton, N.J., 1989-95; founding ptnr. Gibbs & Gregory Attys. at Law, Pemberton, 1995—. Cons. ITT, 1986-89, The World Bank/IFC, 1989—; pres. Mulberry Hill Enterprises, 1989—; bd. dirs. ACT Mfg., eOn Comm. Inc. Trustee Alfred U., 1981—; trustee Whitesbog Found., 1996—, pres. bd. trustees, 2000—; mem. planning bd. Barnegat Light, N.J., 1992-2002; elected Borough Coun., Barnegat Light, 1992, re-elected, 1995, 98; bd. dirs. Burlington County Red Cross, 1999—, Our Gang Players, Inc. Named Hon. Citizen of Rio de Janeiro, 1973; inducted to Alfred Univ. Athletic Hall of Fame, 1993. Mem. ABA, N.J. Bar Assn., Pa. Bar Assn., Burlington County Bar Assn., Barnegat Light Taxpayers Assn. (v.p. 1989-90, pres. 1990-92), Rotary Internat. (bd. dirs. Pemberton club 1996-97, v.p. 1997-98, pres. 1999-00, Pemberton Rotarian of Yr. 1996-97). Home: 12 E 17th Street Rd Barnegat Light NJ 08006 Office Phone: 609-893-9600. E-mail: gng@comcast.net.

GIBBS, JAMES ALANSON, geologist; b. Wichita Falls, Tex., June 18, 1935; s. James Ford and Clovis (Robinson) G.; m. Judith Walker, June 18, 1966; children: Ford W., John A. BS, U. Okla., 1957, MS, 1962. Lic. geoscientist Tex. Geologist Calif. Co., New Orleans, 1961-63, Lafayette, La., 1963-64; cons. geologist, oil prodr. Dallas, 1964—. Chmn. Five States Energy Co., 1984—. Author: Finding Work as a Petroleum Geologist: Hints to the Jobseeker, 1984, Becoming an Independent Geologist: Thriving in Good Times and Bad, 1999. Trustee Inst. for Study Earth and Man, So. Meth. U. Lt. USNR, 1957-59. Recipient Regents award U. Okla., 1996. Mem. AAAS, Am. Geol. Inst. (trustee, William B. Heroy Disting. Svc. award 1994), Geol. Soc. Am., Dallas Geol. Soc. (pres. 1975-76, hon. mem. 1986), Am. Assn. Petroleum Geologists (sec. 1983-85, pres. 1990-91, found. trustee 1998—, Disting. Svc. award 1987, hon. mem. 1995), Am. Inst. Profl. Geol., Ind. Petroleum Assn. Am., Nat. Petroleum Coun., Houston Geol. Soc., West Tex. Geol. Soc., Soc. Ind. Profl. Earth Scientists (past chmn. Dallas chpt., hon. mem. 1999), Dallas Country Club, Dallas Petroleum Club, Explorers Club, Sigma Xi, Sigma Gamma Epsilon, Phi Delta Theta. Republican. Methodist. Home: 3514 Caruth Blvd Dallas TX 75225-5001 Office: 4925 Greenville Ave Ste 1220 Dallas TX 75206-4015 Office Phone: 214-363-3008. E-mail: jagibbs@fivestates.com.

GIBBS, JAMES HOWARD, broadcast executive; b. Dover, Ohio, Jan. 3, 1929; s. Howard James and Berniece Ruth (Spahr) Gibbs; m. Bettye Jean Porter, Nov. 10, 1956 (dec. June 7, 2003); children: Charles Kenneth(dec.), Tammy Ann. Grad. H.S., Dover, 1947. Announcer KWED Radio, Sequin, Tex., 1947-48; owner KIVY Radio, Crockett, Tex., 1948—2003; news dir. Sta. WFAA-TV, Dallas, 1956-57. Home: 111 Valley Ln Crockett TX 75835-1325 Office: KIVY Radio PO Box 1109 Crockett TX 75835-1109 E-mail: jhgibbs@pcstx.net.

GIBBS, JAMES R., oil industry executive; With Frontier Oil, 1982—, pres., COO, 1987—, CEO, 1992—, also chmn. bd. dir., 1999—. Mem. bd. dir. Smith Internat. Inc.; adv. dir. Frost Nat. Bank, Houston; dir. Talon Internat. Office: Fronteir Oil Ste 600 10000 Memorial Dr Houston TX 77024-3411 Office Phone: 713-688-9600. Office Fax: 713-688-0616.*

GIBBS, JOE JACKSON, professional football coach; b. Mocksville, N.C., Nov. 25, 1940; BS, San Diego State U., 1964, MS, 1966. Asst. coach San Diego State U., 1966, Fla. State U., 1967-68, U. So. Calif., 1969-70, U. Ark., 1971-72, St. Louis Cardinals, NFL, 1973-77, Tampa Bay Buccaneers, 1978, San Diego Chargers, 1979-80; head coach Washington Redskins, 1981-93, 2004—; sports commentator NBC, 1993—98; team owner NHRA Top Fuel, Pro Stock with Funny Car, 1994—, NASCAR, 1994—. Announcer NBC; race car owner. Coached Washington Redskins to Super Bowl Championship, 1982, 88, 91. Office: c/o Washington Redskins 21300 Redskin Park Dr Ashburn VA 20147

GIBBS, JUNE NESBITT, state legislator; b. Newton, Mass., June 13, 1922; d. Samuel Frederick and Lulu (Glazier) Nesbitt; m. Donald T. Gibbs, Dec. 8, 1945 (dec. 2001); 1 child, Elizabeth. BA in Math., Wellesley Coll., 1943; MA in Math., Boston U., 1947; postgrad. computer sci., U. R.I., 1981-84. Mem. from R.I. Rep. Nat. Com., 1969-80, sec., 1977-80; mem. R.I. Senate, Dist. 48, Providence, 1985—2003, R.I. Senate, Dist 12, 2003—. Mem. def. adv. com. Women in Svcs., 1970-72, vice chmn., 1972 Mem. Middletown Town Coun., 1974-80, 82-84, pres., 1978-80. Lt. (j.g.) USNR, 1943-46. Avocation: windsurfing. Home: 163 Riverview Ave Middletown RI 02842-5324 Office: Senate Minority Office State House Providence RI 02903 Office Phone: 401-222-2708. Business E-mail: sen-gibbs@rilin.state.ri.us. *To help restore faith in our government every elected official must constantly seek to do all he can for the people he serves and continually guard against doing anything which is self-serving or takes personal advantage of his office in any way.*

GIBBS, KATHERINE HARVIN, secondary school educator; b. Norfolk, Va., Mar. 24, 1956; d. Hugh Wilson and Toby Brown Harvin; m. James R. Gibbs Jr., Aug. 2, 1993. BA, Wesleyan Coll., 1978; MEd, Ga. State U., 1987. Tchr. Houston County Schs., Perry, Ga., 1980—83, Fulton County Schs., Atlanta, 1987—90, Henry County Schs., McDonough, 1990—2001, instructional lead tchr., 2001—. Mem.: ASCD, Ga. Assn. Supervision and Curriculum Devel., Profl. Assn. Ga. Educators. Home: 336 Golden Acres Dr Stockbridge GA 30281 Office: Eagles Landing High Sch 301 Tunis Rd Mcdonough GA 30253

GIBBS, LAWRENCE BLAIR, lawyer; b. Hutchinson, Kans., Aug. 31, 1938; married; 2 children. BA, Yale U., 1960; JD, U. Tex., 1963. Assoc., then ptnr. Branscomb, Gary, Thomason & Hall, Corpus Christi, Tex., 1963-72; dep. chief counsel IRS, Washington, 1972-73, acting chief counsel, 1973, asst. commr., 1973-75; ptnr. Johnson and Swanson, Dallas, 1976-86; commr. IRS, Washington, 1986-89; ptnr. Johnson & Gibbs, Washington and Dallas, 1989-94; mem. Miller & Chevalier, Washington, 1994—. Bd. advisors Taxation Mergers & Acquisitions. Trustee So. Fed. Tax Inst. Mem. ABA (vice chmn. adminstrn. sect. taxation 1991-92), FBA, State Bar Tex. (chmn. taxation sect. 1978-79), D.C. Bar Assn., Am. Law Inst., Communities Found. Tex. Adv. Bd., Am. Coll. Trust and Estate Counsel (bd. regents 1990-96). Office: Miller & Chevalier 655 15th St NW Ste 900 Washington DC 20005-5799 Office Phone: 202-626-6005. E-mail: lgibbs@milchev.com.

GIBBS, MARTIN, biologist, educator; b. Phila., Nov. 11, 1922; s. Samuel and Rose (Sugarman) G.; m. Svanhild Karen Kvale, Oct. 11, 1950; children: Janet Helene, Laura Jean, Steven Joseph, Michael Seland, Robert Kvale. BS, Phila. Coll. Pharmacy, 1943; PhD, U. Ill., 1947. Scientist Brookhaven Nat. Lab., 1947-56; prof. biochemistry Cornell U., 1957-64; Abraham S. and Gertrude Berg prof. biology, chmn. dept. Brandeis U., Waltham, Mass., 1965-93. Cons. NSF, 1961-64, 69-72, NIH, 1966-69, Cosmos Club, 1984; mem. corp. Marine Biol. Lab., Woods Hole, Mass., 1970, RESA lectr., 1969; NATO cons. fellowship bd., 1968-70; mem. Coun. Internat. Exch. of Scholars, 1976-82; chmn. adv. com. selection Fulbright Scholars for Eastern Europe; adj. prof. Bot. Inst., U. Munster, Fed. Republic of Germany, 1978, 80, 87; adj. prof. dept. botany U. Calif., Riverside, 1979-89. Author: Structure and Function of Chloroplasts, 1970, Crop Productivity-Research Imperatives, 1975, Crassulacean Acid Metabolism, 1982, Crassulacean Acid Biosynthesis and Function of Plant Lipids, 1983, Crop Productivity-Research Imperative, Revisited, 1985, Hungarian-USA Binational Symposium on Photosynthesis, 1986; editor-in-chief: Plant Physiology, 1963—92, assoc. editor: Physiologie Vegetale, 1966—76, Ann. Rev. Plant Physiology, 1966—71. Recipient Charles Reid Barnes award, 1984, Adolph E. Gude award, 1993, Martin Gibbs medal, 1993, U. Ill. Achievement award, 1996, Gold medal Bulgarian Acad. Scis.; Alexander von Humboldt fellow, 1987. Mem. NAS, AAUP, Am. Soc. Plant Physiologists (Barnes, Gude, Gibbs medal), Russian Soc. Plant Physiologists (hon. life mem.), Am. Acad. Arts and Scis., Am. Soc. Biochem. Molecular Biology, Can. Soc. Plant Physiologists (hon. life), Acad. Scis. France. Home: 32 Slocum Rd Lexington MA 02421-5622 Personal E-mail: mgibbs8912@aol.com.

GIBBS, MITCHELL WAYNE, lawyer; b. Metairie, La., Sept. 5, 1965; s. Stanley Kenneth and Linda Ann (Schachter) G. BA, U. New Orleans, 1988; JD, Tulane U., 1992. Pvt. practice, New Orleans, 1992—; pub. defender Indigent Def. Bd., Gretna, La., 1994—2001. Bd. dirs. Carrollton Village Condominium. Mem. City Park Tennis Club. Avocations: tennis, art. Office: FNBC Bldg Ste 1800 210 Baronne St New Orleans LA 70112-1722 Fax: 504-525-4380.

GIBBS, PATRICIA HELLMAN, physician; b. Boston, Oct. 22, 1958; d. Frederick Warren and Patricia Christina (Sander) H.; m. Richard D. Gibbs, Dec. 22, 1984; children: Ruth, Samuel, Matthew, Kate, Frank. BA summa cum laude, Williams Coll., 1982; MD, Yale U., 1987. Diplomate Am. Bd. Family Practice. Intern, resident in family practice U. Wash., Seattle, 1987-90; ptnr. Tricia Gibbs, MD and Richard Gibbs, MD, San Francisco, 1990-95; co-founder, med. dir. San Francisco Free Clinic, 1993—. Supervising physician San Francisco Ballet, 1990-95. Co-author: Medical and Orthopedic Issues of Active and Athletic Women-Skiing, 1993, Spine Care-Dance, 1993. Founder Sugar Bowl Acad., 1999. Women's scholar Williams Coll., 1982, Class of '25 Athlete scholar, 1982; named Family Physician of Yr., Calif. Acad. Family Physicians, 1998. Mem. AMA, Am. Acad. Family Physicians, Phi Beta Kappa, Sigma Xi. Avocations: distance running, ski racing, computers. Office: San Francisco Free Clinic 4900 California St San Francisco CA 94118-1115 E-mail: pgibbs@sttc.org.

GIBBS, PATRICIA M, academic administrator; d. John R Gibbs and Mary Lou Connery. BA, Coll. of St. Catherine, 1981—85, MA, 1996. Coord. of student life Coll. of St. Catherine, St. Paul, 1987—93, dir. of student life, 1993—96, asst. dir. of admission, 1996—97, assoc. dir. of admission, 1997—98; assoc. dir. of admission and fin. aid Coll. of St. Catherine-Mpls., Minneapolis, Minn., 1998—99; dean of enrollment services Stephens Coll., Columbia, Mo., 1999—2002; v.p. for enrollment services and student affairs Wesleyan Coll., Macon, Ga., 2003—. Instr. Wesleyan Coll., Macon, Ga., 2003—, Stephens Coll., Columbia, Mo., 1999—2002, Coll. of St. Catherine, St. Paul, 1999. Avocations: golf, running. Office: Wesleyan Coll 4760 Forsyth Rd Macon GA 31210 Office Phone: 478-757-5206. Office Fax: 478-757-4030.

GIBBS, ROBERT T. (TOM GIBBS), sculptor, consultant; b. Dubuque, Iowa, Sept. 17, 1942; s. Robert Francis and Norma Margaret (Kieffer) Gibbs; m. Dorothy Christena Burbach, June 8, 1968; 1 child, Jennifer Marie. BA in Art, Loras Coll., Dubuque, 1964; MA in Sculpture, U. Iowa, 1969, MFA in Sculpture, 1970. Instr. art Clarke Coll., Dubuque, 1968-69; asst. prof. art Ariz. State U., Tempe, 1970-72. Supr sculpture installations Hemmeter Develop Corp, Kauai, Hawaii, 1988; mem creative artists' planning project Iowa Arts Coun, Des Moines, 1988, mem visual arts adv panel, 1985—86. Comn, Tweed Mus, Duluth, Minn, 1989, Molly Rose Gallery, Coral Gables, Fla, 1993, Univ Dubuque, 1992, Morningside Col, 1992, commn., Univ Cent Ark, 1994, Univ Northern Iowa, 1995, Pier Walk, Chicago, 1998, Pyramid Sculpture Park, Hamilton, Ohio, 2003, U. Miami, Coral Gables, 2005. Witness Cong Hearing, Reauthorization of NEA, Washington, 1980. Recipient Honorable Mention, Nat Vietnam War Mem Design Co, Washington, 1981, Gov's Award for serv to arts, Gov Iowa, Des Moines, 1989; grantee, Iowa Arts Coun, 1977. Mem.: Nat Sculpture Soc. Avocation: computers. Home and Office: 1333 Kaufmann Ave Dubuque IA 52001-3162 Office Phone: 563-556-4230. E-mail: tomgibbs@mchsi.com.

GIBBS, RONALD STEVEN, obstetrician/gynecologist; b. Phila., Mar. 31, 1943; MD, U. Pa., 1969. Intern Hartford (Conn.) Hosp., 1969-70; resident ob.-gyn. U. Pa. Hosp., Phila., 1970-74; fellow maternal-fetal medicine U. Tex. Health Ctr., San Antonio, 1976-78; obstetrician-gynecologist Univ. Hosp. U. Colo., Denver, 1989—; prof., chmn. dept. ob.-gyn. U. Colo., Denver, 1989—, E. Stewart Taylor chair ob-gyn. Dir., treas, Am. Bd. of Obstetric and Gyn., 1999-2004, Residency Review Com., 1997-2003. Mem. ACOG, AMA, Am. Gynecologic and Obstetric Soc. (pres.-elect), Infectious Disease Soc. Am., Infectious Disease Soc. Ob/Gyn, Soc. Gynecologic Investigation, Soc. Perinatal Obstetrics (bd. dirs.). Office: U Colo Health Sci Ctr 4200 E 9th Ave # Denver CO 80220-3706

GIBBS, SARAH PREBLE, biologist, educator; b. Boston, May 25, 1930; d. Winthrop Harold and Edith Dorothea (Hill) Bowker; m. Robert H. Gibbs, June 9, 1951 (div. 1962); 1 dau., Elizabeth Dorothea; m. Ronald J. Poole, Feb. 2, 1963 (div. 1980); 1 son, Christopher Harold. AB, Cornell U., 1952, MS, 1954; PhD, Harvard U., 1962. Research assoc. Inst. Animal Genetics Edinburgh U., 1963-65; asst. prof. botany McGill U., Montreal, Que., Can., 1966-69, assoc. prof. biology, 1969-74, prof., 1974-98, Macdonald prof. bot., 1998, Macdonald emeritus prof., 1999—. Recipient Darbaker prize, Bot. Soc. Am., 1975, Gilbert Morgan Smith medal, NAS, 2003; fellow, NSF, 1958—61, NIH, 1961—63. Fellow: AAAS, Royal Soc. Can.; mem.: Can. Assn. Univ. Tchrs., Phycol. Soc. Am. (award of excellence 1999), Am. Soc. Cell Biology, Phi Kappa Phi, Sigma Xi, Phi Beta Kappa. Home: 70 Henley Ave Montreal PQ Canada H3P 1V3 Office: McGill U Dept Biology 1205 Avenue Docteur Penfield Montreal PQ Canada H3A 1B1

GIBBY, DIANE LOUISE, physician, plastic surgeon; b. Miami, Feb. 5, 1957; d. John and Mabel (Kunce) G.; m. Rodney J. Rohrich, July 3, 1990; children: Taylor Rodney, Rachel Nicole. BS, Duke U., Durham, N.C., 1975; MD, U. Miami, 1980. Diplomate Am. Bd. Gen. Surgery, Bd. Plastic and Reconstructive Surgery. Clin. asst. prof. U. Tex. Southwestern, Dallas, 1987—; pvt. practice plastic surgery Med. City Dallas, 1987—. Founder Women's Ctr. for Plastic and Reconstructive Surgery, 1992. Fellow Am. Coll. Surgeons; mem. Am. Soc. Plastic and Reconstructive Surgeons, Am. Med. Soc., Tex. Soc. Plastic Surgeons, Dallas Soc. Plastic Surgeons, Aesthetic Soc. Office: 7777 Forest Ln Ste C820 Dallas TX 75230-2552 Office Phone: 972-566-6323. Business E-Mail: dgmdpa@aol.com.*

GIBBY, MABEL ENID KUNCE, psychologist; b. St. Louis, Mar. 30, 1926; d. Ralph Waldo and Mabel Enid (Warren) Kunce; student Washington U., St. Louis, 1943-44, postgrad., 1955-56; B.A., Park Coll., 1945; M.A., McCormick Theol. Sem., 1947; postgrad. Columbia U., 1948, U. Kansas City, 1949, George Washington U., 1953; M.Ed., U. Mo., 1951, Ed.D., 1952; m. John Francis Gibby, Aug. 27, 1948; children— Janet Marie (Mrs. Kim Williams), Harold Steven, Helen Elizabeth, Diane Louise (Mrs. Roderick Rohrich), John Andrew, Keith Sherridan, Daniel Jay. Dir. religious edn. Westport Presbyn. Ch. Kansas City, Mo., 1947-49; tchr. elementary schs., Kansas City, 1949-50; high sch. counselor Arlington (Va.) Pub. Schs., 1952-54; counselor adult counseling services Washington U., 1955-56; counseling psychologist Coral Gables (Fla.) VA Hosp., 1956—; counseling psychologist Miami (Fla.) VA Hosp., 1956—, chief counseling psychology sect., 1982-86; sr. psychologist Office Disability Determination Fla. Hdqrs., 1987-94. Sec. bd. dirs. Fla. Vocat. Rehab. Found. Recipient Meritorious Service citation Fla. C. of C., 1965, President's Com. on Employment of Handicapped, 1965; commendation for meritorious service Com. on Employment of Physically Handicapped Dade County, 1965, named Outstanding Rehab. Profl., 1966, 81; named Profl. Fed. Employee of Year, Greater Miami Fed. Exec. Council, 1966; Outstanding Fed. Service award Greater Miami Fed. Exec. Council, 1966; Fed. Woman's award U.S. Civil Service Commn., 1968, Community Headliner award Theta Sigma Phi, 1968, Outstanding Alumni award Park Coll., 1968, Freedom award The Chosen Few, Korean War Vets. Assn., 1986; certificate of appreciation Bur. Customs, U.S. Treasury Dept., 1969, Fla. Dept. Health and Rehab. Services, 1970. Mem. Am., Dade County (past sec.) psychol. assns., Nat., Fla. (past dir. Dade County chpt.) rehab. assns., Nat. Rehab. Counseling Assn. (past sec.). Patentee in field. Home: 7107 Aberdeen Ave Dallas TX 75230-5406 E-mail: jfgpc@aol.com.

GIBBY-SMITH, BARBARA, psychologist, nurse; b. Woodburn, Oreg., Dec. 13, 1938; d. Chester Clifton and Marvel Elizabeth (Hill) Gibby; m. Roy Milton Smith, June 2, 1957 (div. June 1990); children: Thomas Clifton, Jeffery Shawn, Mark Anderson. ADN, Chemeketa C.C., Salem, Oreg., 1972; BS, SUNY, Albany, 1980; MS, Western Oreg. State Coll., 1982; D of Psychology, Pacific U., Forest Grove, Oreg., 1993. Diplomate Am. Bd. Profl. Disability Cons., Am. Bd. Specialist, Am. Bd. Forensics Medicine; cert. addiction examiner. Adminstr. Birch St. Manor, Dallas, Oreg., 1973—81; disability determination specialist State of Oreg. Workers' Compensation Dept., Salem, 1983—85; counselor Women's Crisis Ctr., Salem, 1986—88; rehab. counselor Employer Rehab. Svcs., Portland, Oreg., 1985—87; therapist, counselor Pacific U., Hillsboro, Oreg., 1988—89, Forest Grove, 1989—91; intern psychology Portland State U., 1991—92, Kaiser-Permanente, Salem, 1991—92; resident psychology Tillamook Counseling Ctr., Oreg., 1993—95; hosp. privileges psychology and medicine Quality Healthcare, Forest Grove, 1996—; pvt. practice clin. psychology Mountain View Counseling Ctr., Forest Grove, Oreg., 1993—. Group therapy counselor Women's Crisis Ctr., Dallas, 1982-83; eating disorders group therapy facilitator, Salem, 1986-88; nat. register Doctoral Addiction Examiner. Author: William G. Hill: Pioneer of Oregon, 2004. Active Women's Coalition Orgn., Salem, 1988—. Mem. APA, Am. Coll. Forensic Examiners (diplomate), Nat. Bd. Addiction Examiners (diplomate), Oreg. Psychol. Assn., Prescribing Psychologist Assn. (diplomate), Am. Mental Health Alliance (Oreg.). Democrat. Avocations: golf, bicycling, travel, geneology, walking. Office: Mountain View Counseling Ctr 1911 Mountain View Ln Ste 500 Forest Grove OR 97116-2248 Office Phone: 503-357-0206. Personal E-mail: barbpg@juno.com.

GIBERT, STEPHEN P., social studies educator; b. North Augusta, S.C., July 16, 1924; s. Paul C. and Helen B. Gibert; m. Cynthia L. Livingstone, June 8, 1968; children: Stephen Jr., Julia, Clare, Christopher, Jennifer. BA, Wofford Coll., 1948; MA, Harvard U., 1952; PhD, Johns Hopkins U., 1958. Prof. govt. Georgetown U., Washington, 1958—. Vis. prof., cons. U. Rangoon, Burma, 1961-62; dir. MS in fgn. svc. program Georgetown U., 1964-68, dir. nat. security studies program, 1977-2000; co-dir. village rsch. project in Thailand, U.S. Dept. Def. and Royal Thai Govt., Bangkok, 1971. Author: Soviet Images of America, 1977, (in Japanese) The America That Can Say No, 1994; author, editor: Security in Northeast Asia: Approaching the Pacific Century, 1988; co-author: Arms for the Third World: Soviet Military Diplomacy, 1969, East Asia in American Foreign Policy, 1990; co-editor: America and Island China: A Documentary History, 1989; mem. bd. editors Asian Perspective, Orbis, Comparative Strategy, Studies in Global Security, National Security Studies Quar. Mem. Gov. Reagan's Def. Adv. Group; active

Reagan presdl. campaign, 1980. Sgt. U.S. Army Air Corps, 1944-46, PTO. Mem. Internat. Inst. Strategic Studies (life), Cosmos Club (life). Episcopalian. Avocations: tennis, classical music. Office: Georgetown U 35th and O Sts NW Washington DC 20057 Home Fax: (202) 687-5858; Office Fax: (202) 687-5175. E-mail: giberts@georgetown.edu.

GIBLETT, ELOISE ROSALIE, retired hematologist; b. Tacoma, Wash., Jan. 17, 1921; d. William Richard and Rose (Godfrey) Giblett. BS, U. Wash., 1942, MS, 1947, MD with honors, 1951. Mem. faculty U. Wash. Sch. Medicine, 1957—, research prof., 1967—87, emeritus research prof., 1987—. Assoc. dir., head immunogenetics Puget Sound Blood Ctr., 1957—79, exec. dir., 1979—87, emeritus exec. dir., 1987—; former mem. several rsch. coms. NIH. Author: Genetic Markers in Human Blood, 1969; mem. editl. bd. numerous jours. including: Blood, Am. Jour. Human Genetics, Transfusion, Vox Sanguinis; contbr. over 200 articles to profl. jours. Recipient fellowships, grants Emily Cooley, Karl Landsteiner, Philip Levine and Alexander Wiener immunohematology awards, disting. alumna award, U. Wash. Sch. Medicine, 1987. Fellow: AAAS; mem.: NAS, Assn. Am. Physicians, Western Assn. Physicians, Am. Fedn. Clin. Rsch., Internat. Soc. Hematologists, Brit. Soc. Immunology, Am. Assn. Immunologists, Am. Soc. Hematology, Am. Soc. Human Genetics (pres. 1973), Alpha Omega Alpha, Sigma Xi. Home: 6533 53rd Ave NE Seattle WA 98115-7748 Office: Puget Sound Blood Ctr 921 Terry Ave Seattle WA 98104-1256

GIBLIN, JAMES CROSS, writer, publishing executive; b. Cleve., July 8, 1933; s. Edward Kelley and Anna Belle (Cross) G. BA, Case Western Res. U., 1954; MA, Columbia U., 1955. Asst. editor Criterion Books, N.Y.C., 1959-62; editor Lothrop, Lee & Shepard Co., N.Y.C., 1962-67; editor in chief Clarion Books, N.Y.C., 1967-79, pub., 1979-89, contbg. editor, 1989—. Author: The Scarecrow Book, 1980, The Skyscraper Book, 1981, Chimney Sweeps: Yesterday and Today, 1982 (Am. Book award 1983, Golden Kite award 1983), Fireworks, Picnics and Flags: The Story of the Fourth of July Symbols, 1983, Walls: Defenses Throughout History, 1984 (Golden Kite award 1985), The Truth About Santa Claus, 1985 (Boston Globe-Horn Book Nonfiction Honor Book award 1986), Milk: The Fight for Purity, 1986, From Hand to Mouth, 1987, Let There Be Light: A Book About Windows, 1988 (Golden Kite award 1989), Writing Books for Young People, 1990, The Riddle of the Rosetta Stone: Key to Ancient Egypt, 1990, The Truth About Unicorns, 1991, Edith Wilson: The Woman Who Ran the United States, 1992, George Washington: A Picture Book Biography, 1992, Be Seated: A Book About Chairs, 1993, Thomas Jefferson: A Picture Book Biography, 1994, When Plague Strikes: The Black Death, Smallpox, AIDs, 1995, The Dwarf, the Giant and the Unicorn: A Tale of King Arthur, 1996, Charles A. Lindbergh: A Human Hero, 1997 (Orbis Pictus Honor Book award 1998), The Mystery of the Mammoth Bones, and How it Was Solved, 1999, The Amazing Life of Benjamin Franklin, 2000 (Orbis Pictus Honor Book award 2001), The Century That Was: Reflections on the Last One Hundred Years, 2000, Fireworks, Picnics and Flags: The Story of the Fourth of July Symbols, rev. edit., 2001, The Life and Death of Adolf Hitler, 2002 (Robert F. Sibert Informational Book award 2003), Secrets of the Sphinx, 2004 (Orbis Pictus Honor Book award 2005), Good Brother, Bad Brother: The Story of Edwin Booth and John Wilkes Booth, 2005, The Giblin Guide to Writing Children's Books, 2005; also numerous articles and short stories. Mem. Authors Guild, Soc. Children's Book Writers and Illustrators (bd. dirs.). Avocations: travel, museum exhibits, movies, plays, walking. Home: 200 E 24th St Apt 1606 New York NY 10010-3919 Office Phone: 212-679-7126. E-mail: jcgiblin@aol.com. *Having written books for both children and adults, I find the juvenile field more stimulating and exciting because of the responsibility the children's writer has to his or her impressionable young readers. If the writer gives them solid, truthful, imaginatively treated books, he or she is contributing in a very real sense to their education and development.*

GIBLIN, LOUIS, lawyer; b. Omaha, Nov. 1, 1944; s. Richard and Mary (Mahoney) G.; m. Janis Schoblocher, May 20, 1977; 1 child, Marijo. AB in Econs., Creighton U., 1966; MBA, U. Chgo., 1968; cert. in investment mgmt., Princeton U., 1986; MS, Northwestern U., 1998; JD, cert. in employment law, Chgo.-Kent Coll. Law, LLM, 2004. Asst. v.p. No. Trust. Co., Chgo., 1968-73; v.p. MGIC Investment Corp., Milw., 1973-85; 1st v.p. Smith Barney Co., Milw., 1985-93. Chmn. fin. analyst seminar Northwestern U., Evanston, Ill., 1990; adj. faculty U. Wis., Milw., 1985—; adviser Financiers U. Wis., Milw., 1986-2002; sr. exam. grader Inst. CFAs, 1986-2003; cons. Fin. Svcs. Vol. Corp., Skoda Koncern, Czech Republic, 1993-2001. Founder Joint Univ./Soc. Scholarship program, CFA exam, 1988; trustee St. Stephen's Ch., Milw., 1989-99; chmn. investment com., fin. com., ops. com. United Way, Milw., 1989-2002; Oak Creek (Wis.) Housing Authority, Creighton U. Alumni Senate, 1991-99; adv. com. Creighton U.; bd. dirs. Creighton U. Alumni, 1993. Nominee Pulitzer Prize, 1985. Mem. Internat. Soc. Fin. Analysts (charter), Internat. Inst. Forecasters, N.Y. Soc. Security Analysts, Nat. Assn. Bus. Economists, Nat. Options and Futures Soc. (bd. dirs. 1986-93), Deutsch-Amerikanischer Nat. Kongress, North Atlantic Cultural Exch. League, Internat. Inst. Am. Host, Milw. Investment Analysts Soc. (bd. dirs. 1988-99), CFA Inst. (bd. dirs.), Milw. Investment Analysts Soc. (pres. 1989-90), Mensa. Home: 7468 S Logan Ave Oak Creek WI 53154-2234 Personal E-mail: lgi319@aol.com.

GIBLIN, PAMELA M., lawyer; b. N.Y.C., June 7, 1946; BA, U. Tex., 1967, JD, 1970. Bar: Tex. 1970. Mem. Jones, Day, Reavis & Pogue, Austin; ptnr. environ. dept. Baker Botts LLP, Austin, Tex. Gen. counsel Tex. Air Control Bd., 1970-76; chmn. Commn. on Electric Rates, Austin, 1975-76. Named a Texas Super Lawyer, Texas Monthly mag. & Law & Politics mag., 2003—04; named one of Top 50 Female Super Lawyers, 2003—04, Top 50 Regional & West Texas Region Super Lawyers, 2003—04; recipient Disting. Lawyer award, Travis County Bar Assn., 2003. Office: Baker & Botts LLP 98 San Jacinto Blvd Ste 1600 Austin TX 78701-4039 Office Phone: 512-322-2509. Office Fax: 512-322-8308. Business E-Mail: pam.giblin@bakerbotts.com.

GIBLIN, PATRICK DAVID, retired bank executive; b. St. Louis, July 24, 1932; s. Patrick Joseph and Ann Jane (Gill) G.; children: Mary Clare, Christopher, Gregory. BBA, Manhattan Coll., 1954; MBA, St. John's U., Jamaica, N.Y., 1965. Staff auditor KPMG Peat Marwick, N.Y.C., 1956-59; chief plant acct. div. Am. Machine & Foundry, Bklyn., 1959-63; with CBS, N.Y.C., 1963-73, controller electronic video rec. div., 1968-73, dir. corp. acctg., 1967-68; vice chmn., chief fin. officer CRESTAR Fin. Corp., Richmond, 1973-95; ret., 1995. Served with U.S. Army, 1954-56. Mem. Delta Mu Delta. Roman Catholic. Personal E-mail: pdg3silver@aol.com.

GIBLIN, THOMAS PATRICK, labor union administrator, political organization administrator; b. East Orange, N.J., Jan. 15, 1947; s. John Joseph and Theresa Elizabeth (Moran) G.; m. Mary Katherine Hughes, June 20, 1970; children: Thomas P. Jr., Noreen M., Edward M., Patrick F., Anne T. BA, Seton Hall U., 1969. Pres. Internat. Union of Oper. Engrs. Local 68, West Caldwell, NJ, 1975—2004, bus. mgr., 2004—; freeholder Essex County, Newark, 1977-78, 82-89, surrogate, 1990-93; chmn. Dem. Party State of N.J., 1993—2001; Dem. Chmn. Essex Co., Newark, 1993—2002. Candidate from 25th legis. dist. N.J. Assembly, 1973; treas. Essex County Dem. Com., Newark, N.J., 1979-82; alt. del. Dem. Nat. Conv., San Francisco, 1984, Atlanta, 1988, del. Chgo., 1996, LA, 2000; commr. N.J. Real Estate Commn., Trenton, 1979-82; lay adv. bd. St. Vincent Acad., 1984—; chmn. bd. trustees St. Barnabas Burn Found., 1989-93, United Way Essex, 1976-82, 89-95; bd. dirs. Essex unit Assn. Retarded Citizens, 1986-96; trustee North Jersey Blood Ctr., 1991-2003. Named Man of Yr. United Cerebral Palsy, 1980; recipient Cert. of Merit, U.S. Dept. of Labor, 1979, Community Svc. award Frontiers Internat., 1985, Humanitarian award, N.J. Blood Ctr., 1988. Mem. N.J. Ins. Underwriting Assn. (bd. dirs. 1982-90). Democratic. Roman Catholic. Avocations: reading, swimming, travel. Home: 40 Montague Pl Montclair NJ 07042-2820 Office: 11 Fairfield Pl West Caldwell NJ 07006

GIBNEY, FRANK BRAY, publishing executive, foundation administrator; b. Scranton, Pa., Sept. 21, 1924; s. Joseph James and Edna May (Wetter) G.; m. Harriet Harvey, Dec. 10, 1948 (div. 1957); children: Alex, Margot; m. Harriet C. Suydam, Dec. 14, 1957 (div. 1971); children: Frank, James, Thomas; m. Hiroko Doi, Oct. 5, 1972; children: Elise, Josephine. BA, Yale U., 1945; DLitt (hon.), Kyung Hee U., Seoul, Korea, 1974. Corr., assoc. editor Time mag., N.Y.C., Tokyo and London, 1947-54; sr. editor Newsweek, N.Y.C., 1954-57; staff writer, editorial writer Life mag., N.Y.C., 1957-61; pub., pres. SHOW mag., N.Y.C., 1961-64; pres. Ency. Brit. (Japan), Tokyo, 1965-69, TBS-Brit., Tokyo, 1969-75, vice chmn., 1976-99; v.p. Ency. Brit., Inc., Chgo., 1975-79; vice chmn., bd. editors Ency. Brit., Chgo., 1978—; pres. Pacific Basin Inst., Pomona Coll., Claremont, Calif., 1979—. Prof. Pomona Coll., 1997—; bd. dirs. U.S. Com. for Pacific Econ. Cooperation, 1988—, v.p., 1993-95; cons. com. on space and aeros. U.S. Ho. of Reps., Washington, 1957-59; vice chmn. Japan-U.S. Friendship Commn., 1984-90, U.S.-Japan Com. Edn. and Cultural Interchange, 1984-90. Author: Five Gentlemen of Japan, 1953, 3d edit., 2004, The Frozen Revolution, 1959, (with Peter Deriabin) The Secret World, 1960, The Operators, 1961, The Khrushchev Pattern, 1961, The Reluctant Space Farers, 1965, Japan: The Fragile Super-Power, 1975, 3rd edit., 1996, Miracle by Design, 1983, The Pacific Century, 1992, Korea's Quiet Revolution, 1993; co-author: The Battle for Okinawa, 1995; editor: The Penkovskiy Papers, 1965, Senso, 1995, Unlocking The Bureaucrats' Kingdom, 1998, The Nanjing Massacre, 1999, Rising Sun; Morning Calm, 2004. Served to lt. USNR, 1942-46. Decorated Order of the Rising Sun 3d Class Japan, Order of Sacred Treasure 2d Class Japan. Mem. Council on Fgn. Relations, Tokyo Fgn. Corr. Club, Japan-Am. Soc., Century Assn., Yale Club. Roman Catholic. Home: 1901 E Las Tunas Rd Santa Barbara CA 93103-1745 Office Phone: 909-607-8035. Personal E-mail: fgibney@silcom.com.

GIBNEY, JOHN, plastic surgeon, consultant, medical researcher; s. Sophia Margaret Wojewodzki and John Bertram Gibney; life ptnr. Margaret Mary Kane; children: Suzanne, Erica, Suzanne, Erica, Jonathan, Kara, Allison. BS, St. Peter's Coll., Jersey City, N.J., 1963—67; MD, U. N.J. Coll. Medicine, Newark, 1967—71; MBA, U. Ariz., Tempe, 1999—2001. Cert. in Plastic Surgery Am. Bd. Plastic Surgery, 1980. Plastic & reconstructive surgeon Cosmetic & Plastic Surgeons, Ltd., Scottsdale, Ariz., 1977—; adj. prof. biomedical engr. Ariz. State U., Tempe, 1990—. Owner, cons. Med. Malpractice Evaluators, Scottsdale, Ariz., 2002—. Contbr. chapters to books, articles to profl. jours. Bd. mem., treas. Vista Parc Cmty. Org., Scottsdale, Ariz., 2004—05; bd. mem. Busom Buddies Breast Cancer Support Orgn., Phoenix, 1986—2005; founder, bd. mem. Y-Me Breast Cancer Support Orgn., Scottsdale, Ariz., 1987—93. Capt. USAF, 1964—76. Fellow: ACS; mem.: Maricopa County Med. Soc. (assoc.), Soc. Biomed. Engrs. (assoc.), Am. Soc. Plastic Surgeons (assoc.). Conservative. Achievements include patents for autogenous pumping chamber for heart replacement; design of the duel chamber and tissue expanding breast reconstructive implant; research in tissue expansion and muscle transformation. Avocations: art, literature, cooking, gardening, bicycling. Office: Cosmetic & Plastic Surgeons Ltd 3501 N Scottsdale Rd #347 Scottsdale AZ 85251 Office Phone: 480-994-0537.

GIBNEY, LISA ANN, emergency management specialist; b. Des Moines, May 14, 1960; d. Charles Robert and Elizabeth Ann Sears; children: James Ramon, Aaron Michael. BA, U. Iowa, 1982. Workplace instr. ARC, Cedar Rapids, Iowa, 1987—92; tng. instr. Duane Arnold Energy Ctr., Palo, Iowa, 1992—96, emergency mgmt. specialist, 1996—. Emergency mgmt. liaison officer Linn County Emergency Mgmt. Agy., Cedar Rapids, Iowa, 1996—; contbr., coord. emergency mgmt. programs Emergency Mgmt. Support to Spl. Needs Populations, Support for Cmty. Emergency Mgmt. Programs, contbr. emergency mgmt. program support; contbr. emergency mgmt. programs Project Impact-Fed. Emergency Mgmt. Agy. Author: Grants Management. Vol. support FEMA Cmty. and Faith Based Organizations Initiatives, Washington, 2002—03; vol. fund distbn. Variety-The Childrens Charity of Iowa, Cedar Rapids, 1987—2005; coord. Linn County Project Impact Steering Com., Cedar Rapids, 1998—2000, Citizen Corps Coun., Cedar Rapids, 2000—05, Spl. Needs Adv. Coun., Cedar Rapids, 2003—05. Named Outstanding Citizen of Yr., Project Impact, 2000, Ofcl. Greeter for the Pres. of the US, USA Freedom Corps-Office of the White Ho., 2004; recipient Iowa Govs. award for volunteerism, 1999, Lumir Dostal, Jr. Outstanding Pub. Svc. award, Linn County Emergency Mgmt. Commn., 2004, Spl. Cert. Appreciation, Nuc. Energy Inst., 2004, Pres. Gold award for vol. svc., 2004, Innovation award for Special Needs-Medically Fragile Emergency Shelter Program, Iowa State Assn. Counties, 2005. Mem.: Internat. Assn. Emergency Mgrs. (award for Industry-Cmty. Partnership 2001), Iowa Emergency Mgr. Assn. (assoc.; cert. emergency mgr.). Avocations: meeting the needs of special populations, music, travel. Office: Duane Arnold Energy Ctr 3313 DAEC Dr Palo IA 52324 Office Phone: 319-851-7010. Business E-Mail: lisa.gibney@nmcco.com.

GIBRAN, KAHLIL, sculptor; b. Boston, Nov. 29, 1922; s. Nicholas and Rose (Gibran) G.; m. Jean English, July 1, 1957; children: Timothy; by previous marriage, Nicole. Student, Boston Mus. Sch., 1940-43. Exhibited widely as painter, 1949-52, life sized steel sculpture, 1953—, one person show bronzes, Cambridge Art Assn., 1977, Charlottesville, Va., 1993; exhbn.: Boston Arts Festival, 1985, Santa Fe, 1993, The Jean and Kahlil Gibran Collection, Danforth Mus. Art, Framingham, Mass., 2002-03; ann. exhbn. Bologna-Landi Gallery, East Hampton, L.I., N.Y., Denenberg Fine Arts, San Francisco, 1997, Contemporary Sculpture Chesterwood, 1997, St. Botolph Club, 1998, Art of the Spirit Forest Hills Cemetery, 1998, Copley Soc., 2001; included in Forum 49 Retrospective, Provincetown Art Assn., 1999; exhibited lifesize bronze Into the Millennium, Boston, 1999, commd. bronze plaque of Kahlil Gibran, Copley Sq., Boston, 1977, Judge Francis Ford, Fed. Ct. House, Boston, 1977, Judge Anthony Julian, Fed. Ct. House, Boston, Elliot Norton medal, Boston, 1983, bronze figure of Kahlil Gibran, Worcester State Coll., 1987, West Canton Street Child, Hayes Pk., Boston, 1992, Processional Cross All Soul's Episcopal Ch., San Diego, 1993, bronze plaque composer Amy Beach, 28 Commonwealth Ave., Boston; inventor Gibran Tripod, Mus. Modern Art collection; sculpture and painting show Copley Soc., 1994; represented in permanent collections Pa. Acad., Tenn. Fine Arts Ctr., Norfolk (Va.) Mus., Chrysler Mus., William Rockhill Gallery, Swope Gallery, Brockton Fine Arts Ctr.; author: Sculpture--Kahlil Gibran, 1970, (with wife Jean Gibran) Introduction to Lazarus and His Beloved, 1973, Kahlil Gibran, His Life and World, 1974, rev. edit., 1991; author: (monograph) Observations on the Reasons for the Cremona Tone, 1993. Pres. Kahlil Gibran Scholarship Fund, Boston, 1974. Recipient George Widener award Pa. Acad., 1958; Guggenheim fellow, 1959-61; award Nat. Inst. Arts and Letters, 1961; Grand prize Boston Arts Festival, 1964; John Gregory award sculpture, 1965; Gold medal Internat. Sacred Art Show, Trieste, Italy, 1966 Address: 160 W Canton St Boston MA 02118-1216

GIBSON, ANN EDEN, art historian, educator; b. Hagerstown, Md., Apr. 30, 1944; d. James Orville and Mary Ellen (Ellis) G.; m. H. Thomas Simmons; 1 child, Jessica; m. Allan Federman, Jan. 10, 1982 (dec.); children: Elizabeth, Michele. BS, Kent State U., 1965, MA, 1970, U. Pitts., 1978; PhD, U. Del., 1984. Tchr. art pub. schs., Hinckley and Wooster, Ohio, 1966-69; studio adj. Kent (Ohio) State U., 1969-72, Akron (Ohio) State U., 1970-72; art history adj. U. Pitts., 1979; instr. art Art Inst. Pitts., 1972-75, Point Park Coll., Pitts., 1975-79; assoc. prof. history art Yale U., New Haven, 1981-91; assoc. prof. art history SUNY, Stony Brook, 1992-98, acting chair dept. art, 1993-94; chair dept. art history U. Del., 1998—. Author: Issues in Abstract Expressionism, 1990, Abstract Expressionism: Other Politics, 1997, Judith Godwin, Style and Grace, 1997, Norman Lewis, Black Paintings, 1946-1977, 1998; guest editor (with Stephen Polcari), Art Journal; also articles. Andrew W. Mellon fellow Met. Mus. Art, 1981-83; Morse fellow Yale U., 1987-88, sr. fellow, 1990-91; Ailsa Mellon Bruce fellow Ctr. for Advanced Study in Visual Arts, Washington, 1990, postdoctoral fellow Smithsonian Instn., 1990-91, Getty Rsch. Fellow, Guggenheim Meml. Found. Fellow, 2004; recipient Distinguished Alumna award, U. Pitts., 1995. Mem. Internat. Assn. Critics, Coll. Art Assn., Phi Kappa Phi. Office: U Del Dept Art History 206 Mechanical Hall Newark DE 19716 Business E-Mail: agibson@udel.edu.

GIBSON, ARLENE JOY, headmaster; BA, Bryn Mawr Coll., 1965; MA, Georgetown U., 1969. Dir. middle sch. Bryn Mawr Sch., Balt., 1981-84; dir. lower sch. Holton Arms Sch., Bethesda, Md., 1984-87; headmistress Kent Place Sch., Summit, N.J., 1987-96; head of sch. Spence Sch., NYC, 1998—. Office: Spence Sch 22 E 91st St New York NY 10128-0657 E-mail: agibson@spenceschool.org.*

GIBSON, BARRY JOSEPH, magazine editor; b. Boston, Feb. 6, 1951; s. Joseph Wray and Marjorie Mitchell (Jacobs) G.; m. Jean Harley Reese, Oct. 11, 1980; 1 child, Michael Reese BA, U. Miami, 1973. Assoc. editor Salt Water Sportsman, Boston, 1977-81; assoc. boating editor Outdoor Life, N.Y.C., 1981-82; editor Directory for Boats, Accessories and Fishing Tackle, Boston, 1981-83, Salt Water Sportsman, Boston, 1981—2004, v.p., 1981-88. Adviser Internat. Commn. for Conservation Atlantic Tuna, Washington, 1986-89; mem. New Eng. Fishery Mgmt. Coun., 1987-96, chmn., 1992; cons. sport fishing industry. Contbr. numerous articles to profl. jours. Charter boat capt., Boothbay Harbor, Maine, 1971— Recipient Mako Outdoor Writer Yr., Mako Marine Inc., 1982 Mem. Outdoor Writers Assn. Am., New England Outdoor Writers Assn. (excellence in writing award 1982), Northeast Charterboat Capts. Assn. (founding mem. 1988—), Atlantic Sportfishing Assn. (bd. dirs. Natick, Mass. 1988-90). Clubs: Boothbay Harbor Tuna (pres. 1979). Avocation: sport fishing. Home: 19 Royall Rd East Boothbay ME 04544 Office Phone: 207-633-5929. Personal E-mail: barry.gibson6@aol.com.

GIBSON, BENJAMIN FRANKLIN, physicist; b. Madisonville, Tex., Sept. 3, 1938; s. Mitchell Osler and Christine (Bennett) G.; m. Margaret Alice Ferguson, July 20, 1968; children: James M., Michael W., Stuart W. BA, Rice U., 1961; PhD, Stanford U., 1966. Postdoctoral fellow Lawrence Livermore (Calif.) Nat. Lab., 1966-68; rsch. assoc. NAS, Nat. Bur. Stds., Gaithersburg, Md., 1968-70, CUNY, Bklyn., 1970-72; group leader, T-5 Los Alamos (N.Mex.) Nat. Lab., 1982-86, staff mem., 1972—; detailee Dept. of Energy Divsn. Nuclear Physics, 1980-81. Program adv. com. MIT Bates Electron Accelerator, Boston, 1985-89, 98—; mem. subatomic physics grant selection com. Can. Natural Scis. and Engring. Rsch. Coun., 1994-96, theory rev. panel NSF, 1997, 98. Co-editor: Three-body Force in the Three-Nucleon System, 1986, Procs. of LAMPF Workshop on pi K Physics, 1991, New Vistas in Physics with High-Energy Pion Beams, 1993, Properties and Interactions of Hyperons, 1994, Baryons '95, 1996, 20 Years of Meson Factory Physics: Accomplishments and Prospects, 1997, Procs. of PANIC05, 2005; assoc. editor Phys. Review C, 1988-02, editor, 2002—, mem. editl. bd., 1978-79, 87-88; mem. editl. bd. FEW Body Sys., 1986—; contbr. articles to profl. jours. Recipient Sr. Scientist Rsch. award Alexander von Humboldt Found., 1992; Japan Soc. Promotion of Sci. rsch. fellow Tohoku U., 1984; vis. fellow U. Melbourne, Australia, 1986, Flinders U., Adelaide, Australia, 1987, Murdoch fellow Inst. for Nuclear Theory, U. Wash., Seattle, 1992. Fellow Am. Phys. Soc., Few-Body Sys. Topical Group (vice chmn. 1990-92, chmn. 1992-93), Divsn. Nuc. Physics (sec.-treas. 1995—). Achievements include patents in field of epithermal-neutron well logging. Office: T-16 MS-B283 Los Alamos NM 87545-0001 Office Phone: 505-667-5059. Business E-Mail: bfgibson@lanl.gov.

GIBSON, CHARLES DEWOLF, broadcast journalist; b. Evanston, Ill., Mar. 9, 1943; s. Burdett and Georgiana (Law) G.; m. Arlene Joy Gibson, July 20, 1968; children: Jessica Law, Katherine Burdett. AB, Princeton U., 1965. Corr. RKO Radio, Washington, 1966; anchorman Sta.-WLVA-TV, Lynchburg, Va., 1967-69, Sta.-WMAL-TV (now WJLA-TV), Washington, 1970-73; corr. TVN, Inc., Washington, 1974-75, ABC News, Washington, 1975-80, Capitol Hill corr., 1981-87; co-host Good Morning Am. ABC TV, N.Y.C., 1987-98, 99—; co-host 20/20, 1999—. Nat. journalism fellow NEH, U. Mich., 1973-74. Office: Good Morning America 147 Columbus Ave New York NY 10023-5900*

GIBSON, COLVIN DONALD, human resources specialist; b. N.Y.C., Nov. 10, 1945; s. Beatrice White; m. Ann T. Tucker, June 15, 1985; 1 child: Rachel C. BA in History, Va. State Coll., 1968. Various positions Exxon Mobil Corp., Tex., La., 1971-88, coord. hdqrs. employee rels. Irving, Tex., 1991—97, advisor compensation and exec. programs, 1998—2000; sect. supr. Exxon U.S.A., Houston, 1984-88, benefits advisor, 1988; sr. cons. HR Staff Resources and Assocs. Inc., Irving, 2001—. Chmn. scouting com. Wheeler Ave. Bapt. Ch., Houston, 1978-86, scoutmaster, asst. scoutmaster; bd. dirs. Salvation Army, Irving, 1992-; chmn. Irving Cmty. Devel. Corp., former pres. Irving Black Arts Coun.; vice rector bd. dirs. Norfolk State U. Capt. U.S. Army, 1968-70. Mem. Nat. Soc. Stock Profls., Nat. Alumni Assn. Norfolk State U. (pres. 1983-87, dist. alumnus 1990), Rotary. Baptist. Avocations: travel, tennis, visual and performing arts. Home: 2110 Texas Ash Dr Irving TX 75063-3464 Office Phone: 972-402-9380.

GIBSON, EMMITT E., career officer; b. Feb. 7, 1944; Commd. officer U.S. Army, advanced through grades to maj. gen., commdg. gen. Aviation and Missile Redstone Arsenal, Ala., 1997-98, dep. dir. resources and requirements, 1998—. Office: FSRAD J-8 9000 Defense Pentagon Rm 1e962 Washington DC 20318-0001*

GIBSON, ERNEST WILLARD, III, retired state supreme court justice; b. Brattleboro, Vt., Sept. 23, 1927; s. Ernest William and Dorothy Pearl (Switzer) G.; m. Charlotte Elaine Hungerford, Sept. 10, 1960; children: Margaret, Mary, John. BA, Yale U., 1951; LLB, Harvard U., 1956. Bar: Vt. State's atty. Windham County, Vt., 1957-61; mem. Vt. Ho. of Reps., 1961-63, chmn. judiciary com., 1963; chmn. Vt. Pub. Svc. Bd., 1963-72; judge Vt. Superior Ct., 1972-83; assoc. justice Vt. Supreme Ct., 1983-97, ret., 1997. Chancellor Episcopal Diocese Vt., 1977-98, trustee, 1972-99, pres. bd. trustees, 1991-99, dep. to gen. conv., 1976-94. Served in U.S. Army, 1945-46, 51-53, Major Army Nat. Guard, 1956-71. Mem. Vt. Bar Assn. Avocations: bridge, tennis. Home: 11 Baldwin St Montpelier VT 05602-2110

GIBSON, EVERETT KAY, JR., aerospace scientist, geochemist; b. Seagraves, Tex., May 13, 1940; s. Everett Kay and Lillie Gertrude (Ivey) G.; m. Mary Morgan Shott, Oct. 13, 1973; 1 son, Bradford Pierce Gibson. BS, Tex. Tech U., Lubbock, 1963, MS, 1965; PhD, Ariz. State U., 1969. Instr. Tex. Tech. U., 1963-65; postdoctoral research assoc. NASA Johnson Space Center, Houston, 1969-70, space scientist, geochemist, 1970-91; sr. scientist NASA-Johnson Space Ctr., 1991—; vis. program mgr. NSF, Washington, 1979; mission sci. advisor Apollo 14; test dir. Lunar Receiving Lab. NASA, 1971, prin. investigator Lunar Sample Analysis Program, 1971-90, mem. Lunar Sample Analysis Planning Team, 1974-77, prin. investigator Planetary Geology Program, 1978-86, prin. investigator Mars Data Analysis Program, 1979-84, prin. investigation Exobiology Program, 1983—. Mem. U.S. Antarctic Meteorite Search Team, 1979-80; adj. prof. geology U. Houston, 1975-90; sr. Leverhulme vis. fellow Open U., Milton Keynes, Eng., 1984-85; cons. The Economist (London), BBC, London; interdiscipline scientist Mars Express/Beagle 2 Mission to Mars, European Space Agy., 2001—. Assoc. editor 5th, 6th, 7th, 8th, 9th and 12th Proc. Lunar and Planetary Sci. Conf., 1974-81; assoc. editor: Chondrules and Their Origins, 1983; contbr. articles to sci. jours. Bd. dirs. Clear Creek Basin Authority, Harris County, Tex., 1974-75; col. Commemorative Air Force, 1983—, life mem., 1987, aircraft sponsor, 1988, exec. officer, 1990-2002; exec. bd. Wings Over Houston Air Show, 1990—. Recipient award for lunar sci. team participation NASA Johnson Space Ctr., 1974, Manned Flight Awareness award, 1993, Laurel Space award Aviation Week and Space Tech., 1972, 97; recipient Exceptional Sci. Achievement medal NASA, 1997, Disting. Achievement award Ariz. State U., 1980, Silver Magnolia award Commemorative Air Force, 1993, 99, Ariz. State U. Hall of Fame award, 1998, Scientist of Yr. award Tex. Acad. of Sci., 2000. Fellow Meteoritical Soc. (sec. 1974-80, councilor 1987-90); mem. Am. Chem. Soc., Internat. Soc. for Study of Origin of Life, AAAS, Am. Geophys. Union, Sigma Xi, Phi Lambda Upsilon. Baptist. Home: 1015 Trowbridge Dr Houston TX 77062-2726 Office: NOW SR Astromaterials Rsch Office Nasa Johnson Space Ctr 2101 Nasa Rd 1 Houston TX 77058 E-mail: ekgmars@aol.com.

GIBSON, FLORENCE ANDERSON, talking book company executive, narrator; b. San Francisco, Feb. 7, 1924; m. V.H. Carlos Gibson, Aug. 30, 1947; children: Nancy Derwent, Christopher Carlos, Katherine Wayne Bolland, Diana Corona. Student, Finch Jr. Coll., N.Y.C., 1941—42; BA in Dramatic Lit., U. Calif., Berkeley, 1944; student, Neighborhood Playhouse, N.Y.C., 1944—45. Radio actress, San Francisco, 1944, 46, 47; chmn. Washington com. Am. Field Svc., 1958-60, 62-65, founder, chmn. Peruvian Com. Lima, 1960-62; treas., distbn. mgr. Living Garden and Concern 1975 calendars, 1971-75; sec. exec. com Fgn. Student Svc. Coun., 1973-76; narrator Talking Books Libr. of Congress div. for Blind and Physically Handicapped, 1975-96; narrator Recorded Books, Inc., 1979; founder, pres. Audio Book Contractors, Inc., 1982—. Actress Blithe Spirit, the USO Corp Show, 1944, Ah, Wilderness, 1946, Equity Libr. Theater, NYC, (TV series) Traffic Ct., others, narrator 1,020 unabridged books on cassette. Bd. dirs. Fgn. Student Svc. Coun., Concern, Inc., Rec. for the Blind, Children's Theater of Washington; vol. in occupational therapy Children's Hosp., Washington, 1949-50; vol. lobbyist student exch. program Am. Field Svc. Recipient Parents' Choice awards, 1983, 84, 86, Audiophile Earphone award, 1999; named Best Female Narrator, Book World, 1989; selected as A Notable Children's Recording, ALA, 1983, 87, 88, 89. Home: 4626 Garfield St NW Washington DC 20007-1025 Office: Audio Book Contractors Inc PO Box 40115 Washington DC 20016-0115 Office Phone: 202-363-3429. Personal E-mail: flogibsonabc@aol.com.

GIBSON, JAHNN HANSEN SWANKER, mental health nurse; b. Amsterdam, N.Y., Apr. 21, 1949; d. John Nichols and Andrienne M. (Hansen) Swanker; m. David Michael Gibson, Aug. 31, 1970; 1 child, Rebecca Lynne. BA in Psychology, Plattsburgh State, N.Y., 1971; AAS in Nursing, Adirondack Cmty. Coll., Glens Falls, N.Y., 1987. RN N.Y. Med. social worker Cohoes Meml. Hosp., NY, 1973; asst. residence mgr. Alternatives in Mankind, Saratoga Springs, 1980—83; RN Saratoga Hosp., 1987—89, Wesley Nursing Home, 1990—92, Fulton County, Johnstown, 1992—93, Lexington Ctr., Gloversville, 1993—98; RN psychiat. dept. St. Mary's Hosp., Amsterdam, 1999—, RN unit QI, 2001—. Author: Susan's Sailing Adventures, 2001; editor: (newsletter) Armchair Yachtsman, 1974—76; contbr. articles to perodicals. Chmn. svc. and rehab. Am. Cancer Soc., Saratoga Springs, NY, 1981—82; mem. Victorian Ball com. Johnstown Libr., 1997—98; pres. Johnstown Hist. Soc., 1998, coord. tea and fashion show, 1995—97; soup kitchen vol. Saratoga Springs, NY, 1990—92; treas. Ch. Women's Assn., Saratoga Springs, 1986. Mem.: Eclectic Soc. Study Club, Clio Study Club, Mayfield Yacht Club (long range planning com. 1973, sec. 1974—86, historian 1993—, Daniel C. Shepard award 1965, Ladies' Cup 1980, 1982, 1983, 1986, Bill Chatterton award 1996). Republican. Presbyn. Avocations: sailing, reading, history, writing, church choir. Home: 302 Melcher St Johnstown NY 12095

GIBSON, JANNETTE POE, educational consultant; b. Lubbock, Tex., Oct. 29, 1948; d. Hugh Miller and Norma Grace (Harrison) Poe; m. William Carroll Gibson, June 30, 1967; children: Darin L., Arminda L. Gibson Peery, Victoria L. Gibson Dixon. BS, East Tex. State U., 1971, MEd, 1981; postgrad., Tex. A&M U., Commerce, 1992—. Tchr. Como (Tex.)-Pickton Ind. Sch. Dist., 1971-77; tchr., cons. Diosese of Dallas, Diocese of Tyler, Tex., 1982-87; tchr., supr. Hyder Migrant Ctr., Dateland, Ariz., 1987-88; tchr., adult ESL edn. dir. Ariz. Western U., Hyder Campus, 1988-89; tchr. Sulphur Springs (Tex.) Ind. Sch. Dist., 1989-98; cons., presenter Multicultural/Migrant Edn., 1987—; edn. diagnostician Sulphur Springs ISD Spl. Edn. Dept., 1998—. Cons. ESL edn. and early childhood edn. and child devel. U.S. Dept. Edn., 1988-89; profl. adv. com. Sulphur Springs Ind. Sch. Dist., 1990, 92, 96; doctoral adv. bd. East Tex. State U., 1993-96; regional adv. com. migrant edn. Region V111 Svc., 1994-97, advisor Tex. Edn. Agy. assessments of ESL/LEP children, 1997-98; cons. for devel. of culture and lang. bias-free assessments to sch. dists. in Tex.; presenter in fields of migrant edn. and ESL; private cons. assessment in sch. dists., Tex. Mem. AAUW, NEA, Tex. State Tchrs. Assn., TAMU Doctoral Students Assn., TESOL, Classroom Tchrs. Assn. Tex., Tex. Ednl. Diagnosticians Assn., N.E. Tex. Assn. Ednl. Diagnosticians, Mensa, Alpha Chi, Phi Beta Kappa, Kappa Delta Pi. Democrat. Methodist. Avocations: reading, gardening. Office: 411 College St Sulphur Springs TX 75482-2809

GIBSON, JERRY LEIGH, oil industry executive; b. El Dorado, Ark., Jan. 24, 1930; s. Oscar Edward and Ruth (Coleman) G.; m. Alma Gail Peoples, Apr. 11, 1953; children: Sallie Gail, Gregory Leigh. BBA with honors, U. North Tex., 1951; MBA, So. Meth. U., 1956. With Exxon Mobil, 1952-59, 60-66, asst. to asst. comptr.; mgmt. cons. KPMG CPAs LLP, 1959; v.p., sec., treas. Riviana Foods Inc., Houston, 1966-69; pres., treas., CEO Intermedco Inc., Houston, 1969-73; pres., CEO Automated Fin. Svcs., Houston, 1973-75; v.p. fin. A-Z Internat. Tool Co., Houston, 1975-80; pres., CEO, owner JHJ Drilling Co., Houston, 1980-85; pres., CEO Kellywood Corp., Houston, 1986—. Tchr. acctg. So. Meth. U., 1956-57. With USAF, 1950-52. Home and Office: 6801 Auckland Ct Austin TX 78749-4136 Office Phone: 512-289-0804. Personal E-mail: jgibson14@austin.rr.com.

GIBSON, JOHN, news anchor, correspondent; B film sch., UCLA. Reporter Hollywood Reporter, LA, 1969-72, various locations, Calif., 1974-77; bur. chief, anchor Weekend Mag., Sta. KCRA-TV, San Francisco, 1979-89; anchor, corr. In Am., 1989-92; corr. NBC News, Burbank, Calif., 1992-94; West Coast corr. NBC News Channel, 1994—2000; anchor News Chat and InterNight, Playback MSNBC, NYC; host, The Big Story with John Gibson Fox News, NYC, 2000—. Office: Fox News Channel 1211 Ave of the Americas New York NY 10036*

GIBSON, JOHN ROBERT, federal judge; b. Springfield, Mo., Dec. 20, 1925; s. Harry B. and Edna (Kerr) G.; m. Mary Elizabeth Vaughn, Sept. 20, 1952 (dec. Aug. 1985); children: Jeanne, John Robert; m. Diane Allen Larrison, Oct. 1, 1986; stepchildren: Holly, Catherine. AB, U. Mo., 1949, JD, 1952. Bar: Mo. 1952. Assoc. Morrison, Hecker, Curtis, Kuder & Parrish, Kansas City, Mo., 1952-58, ptnr., 1958-81; judge U.S. Dist. Ct. (we. dist.) Mo., 1981-82, U.S. Ct. Appeals (8th cir.), 1982-94, sr. judge, 1994—. Mem. Mo. Press-Bar Commn., 1979-81; mem. com. on adminstrn. of magistrate sys. Jud. Conf. U.S., 1987-91, mem. security and facilities com., 1995-2001. Vice chmn. Jackson County Charter Transition Com., 1971-72; mem. Jackson County Charter Commn., 1970; v.p. Police Commrs. Bd., Kansas City, 1973-77. Served with U.S. Army, 1944—46. Recipient Citation of Merit award U. Mo. at Columbia Sch. of Law, 1994. Fellow Am. Bar Found.; mem. Mo. State Bar (gov. 1972-79, pres. 1977-78; Pres.' award 1974, Smithson award 1984), Kansas City Bar Assn. (pres. 1970-71), Lawyers Assn. Kansas City (Charles Evan Whittaker award 1980), Fed. Judges Assn. (bd. dirs. 1991-97), Phi Beta Kappa, Omicron Delta Kappa. Presbyterian. Office: US Ct Appeals 8th Cir 400 E 9th St Ste 1040 Kansas City MO 64106-2695*

GIBSON, JOHN ROBERT, software engineer; b. Murfreesboro, Tenn., Dec. 24, 1948; s. Donald Cotis Gibson and Sara Elizabeth Garner; m. Corinne de Marie Pallatto, Sept. 2, 1978 (div. July 1989). BSEE, U. Ala., 1973. Commd. 2d lt. USAF, 1973, advanced through grades to capt., 1977, resigned, 1983; computer programmer/analyst Computer Scis. Corp., Colorado Springs, Colo., Ridgecrest, Calif., 1984-90; sci. computer programmer Boeing Computer Support Svcs., Ridgecrest, 1990-91; computer engr. USAF, Edwards AFB, Calif., 1993-95; software tester EER Sys., Inc., Ridgecrest, 1996-97; software engr. EDO Tech. Svcs. Ops., Edwards AFB, 1997—2001; embedded programming AOA Inc., Westlake Village, Calif., 2002—04. Contbr. articles to profl. jours. Candidate for Calif. State Senate, Antelope Valley Libertarian Party, 2000, treas., 2000-02. Mem. Calif. Checker Assn. (pres. 1999-2005). Avocations: anime, checkers, coins, history, skiing. Home: 563 Hampshire Rd Apt 171G Westlake Village CA 91361-2228 E-mail: jrgibson_7@hotmail.com.

GIBSON, JOHN THOMAS, academic administrator, consultant; b. Montgomery, Ala., Sept. 19, 1948; s. Herman Farris and Lillian Christine (Payload) G.; m. Mayme Voncile Pierce, Jan. 31, 1970; children: John Thomas II, Jerard Trenton, Justin Tarrance, Shayla Voncile. BS, Tuskegee (Ala.) U., 1970, EdM, 1971; EdS, U. Colo., 1972, PhD, 1973; cert. in mgmt., Harvard U., 1982. Dir. lab. experiences Ala. State U., Montgomery, 1973-75, coord. fed. rels., 1975-76, area head edn. adminstrn., 1976-83, exec. asst. to pres., 1983-86; v.p. bus. and fin. Ala. A&M U., Huntsville, 1986-90, assoc. v.p. adminstrn., 1990-97, pres., 1996—. Cons. Ala. Edn. Assn., Montgomery, 1975-76, Montgomery County Bd. of Edn., 1976, Gray, Seay & Langford, Montgomery, 1976, Thomas, Means & Gillis, Montgomery, 1990-91; bd. dirs. Am. Coun. Edn., Ala. Sci. & Math. Inst.; chmn. bd. dirs. Sci. & Engring. Alliance. Contbr. articles to profl. jours. Exec. com. Ala. Dem. Party, Montgomery, 1976-78. Capt. U.S. Army, 1970-73. Named one of Outstanding Young Men of Am., 1983. Mem. Masons (32d), Optimists, Kiwanis, Kappa Alpha Psi (Svc. award 1980-82), Phi Delta Kappa (chair fin. com. 1983), Kappa Delta Pi. A.M.E. Avocations: tennis, swimming. Home: 151 Heritage Ln Madison AL 35758-7975 Office: Ala A&M U PO Box 1357 Normal AL 35762-1357 E-mail: jgibson@aamu.edu.

GIBSON, JOSEPH WHITTON, JR., retired chemical company executive; b. Norristown, Pa., Feb. 24, 1922; s. Joseph Whitton and Nellie (Dear) G.; m. Norma Jean Stewart, Sept. 21, 1946; children: Joseph Whitton, Winn S. Gobeil, Philip B. BS, Worcester Poly. Inst., 1944; postgrad., Princeton U., 1944, MIT, 1945. With E. I. duPont de Nemours & Co., Wilmington, Del., 1946-91, sr. research engr., 1961-79, sr. tech. specialist printing systems, imaging systems, 1979-91. Mem. pantyhose sizing com. Nat. Assn. Hosiery Mfrs., 1969-71. Contbr. articles to profl. jours. Treas. Mayfield Civic Assn.; v.p. Brandywine Babe Ruth; treas. Shellcrest Swim Club; IRS VITA vol., 1995—; vol. LPGA/AJGA, 1997—, US Census 2000, 1999—. Served to lt. USNR, 1944-46. Recipient Joseph W. Gibson Jr. award tech. excellence established duPont, 1992, Internat. Man of Yr. award Internat. Biog. Centre, Cambridge, Eng., Dateline Recognition award Chem. Heritage Found., Phila., Dupont Lavoisier award, 2000. Mem. Am. Assn. Textile Chemists and Colorists (mem. history and archives com. 1994—, Olney medal 1979), Am. Chem. Soc., Fiber Soc. (hon.), Internat. Platform Assn., Planetary Soc., Sigma Xi, Tau Beta Pi. Republican. Episcopalian. Achievements include the invention of thermosol dyeing, sparkle hosiery, synthetic leather, fish swimway, printing plates. Home: 1215 Hillside Blvd Wilmington DE 19803-4211

GIBSON, KATHLEEN RITA, anatomy and anthropology educator; b. Phila., Oct. 9, 1942; d. Keath Pope and Rita Irene (Shewell) G. BA, U. Mich., 1963; MA, U. Calif., Berkeley, 1969, PhD, 1970. Teaching assoc. U. Calif., Berkeley, 1965-69; lectr., adj. assoc. prof., then adj. prof. Rice U., Houston, 1973-2000; asst. prof. U. Tex. Health Sci. Ctr., Houston, 1970-73, assoc. prof., 1973-80, prof., 1980—, chair dept. basic sci., 1998—2002. Mem. com. on parenting behavior Social Sci. Rsch. Coun., N.Y.C., 1980-89; mem. fellowship rev. panel NSF, 1992-95; vis. fellow Cambridge U., 1993; vis. scholar Oxford U., 1996. Editor: (with M. Thames and K. Molokon) Genealogy and Demography of the West Main Cree, 1989, (with S. Parker) Language and Intelligence in Monkeys and Apes, 1990, 94, (with A. Petersen) Brain Maturation and Cognitive Development, 1991, (with Tim Ingold) Tools, Language and Intelligence in Human Evolution, 1993, 94, 98, (with Paul Mellars) Modelling the Early Human Mind, 1996, (with Hilary Box) Social Learning in Mammals: Comparative and Ecological Perspectives, 1999 (with Dean Falk) Evolutionary Anatomy of the Primate Neocartin, 2001; contbg. editor Anthropology Newsletter, 1990-93; contbr. articles, commentaries and abstracts in profl. jours. Conf. grantee Wenner Gren Found., 1990, Sloan Found., 1985, travel grantee NSF, 1984, 86, Brit. Soc. Devel. Biology, 1982. Fellow AAAS, Am. Assn. Phys. Anthropologists, Am. Assn. Anthropologists; mem. Am. Assn. Anatomists, Internat. Primatol. Assn., Am. Assn. Dental Schs. (chmn. sect. anatomical scis. 1990), Am. Anthropol. Assn. (chmn.-elect biolog. anthropology sect. 1994-96, chair 1997-98, co-chmn. com. on ethics, 1994-95, chair 1996, chair com. scientific comm. 1997, mem. exec. bd. 1997, 99—2002, chmn. assn. oper. com. 2000—02, mem. nominations com., 2002—), Lang. Origins Soc., Am. Assn. Primatologists (publs. com. 1987-89). Office: Dept Nueorology and Anatomy U Tex Houston Houston TX 77225

GIBSON, KENNETH E., entomologist; b. Kansas City, Mo., May 2, 1943; s. Elvan J. Gibson and Dorothy L. Petersen; m. Carol A. Wiese, Sept. 7, 1963; children: Lyndee C. Sperry, Keith E. MS, U. Mo., 1975. Entomologist USDA Forest Svc., Ogden, Utah, 1976—78, Missoula, Mont., 1978—. Co-author: A Field Guide to Diseases & Insect Pests of Northern & Central Rocky Mountain Conifers. Res. dep. sheriff Missoula County Sheriff's Dept., Missoula, Mont., 1982—2002. Staff sgt. US Army, 1966—70, Vietnam, USA. Mem.: Entomol. Soc. Am., Soc. Am. Foresters. Republican. Avocations: hiking, hunting, insect collecting. Home: 511 Simons Dr Missoula MT 59803 Office: USDA Forest Svc 200 E Broadway Missoula MT 59807 Office Phone: 406-329-3278. Office Fax: 406-329-3557. Personal E-mail: kgibson@fs.fed.us.

GIBSON, LISETTE L., elementary school educator, music educator; b. St. Louis, Dec. 14, 1945; d. Erwin L. and Anna Marie Lueker; children: Robert, Todd. BA, Concordia, River Forest, Ill., 1967; MA, U. Mich., 1989. Tchr. classroom grades 3 and 4, music educator grades 5-8 St. Paul Lutheran Ch. and Sch., Bay City, Mich.

GIBSON, MCGUIRE, archaeologist, educator; b. Bushwood, Md., Nov. 6, 1938; s. Thomas Laurie and Essie Mae (Owens) Gibson. BA, Fordham U., 1959; MA, U. Chgo., 1964, PhD, 1968. Asst. prof. anthropology U. Ill., Chgo., 1968-71; asst. prof. U. Ariz., Tucson, 1971-72; from asst. prof. to assoc. prof. U. Chgo., 1972—81, prof., 1981—. Ann. prof. Am. Schs. Oriental Rsch., Baghdad, Iraq, 1969—70; dir. Nippur Expdn., Iraq, 1972—, Dhamar Expdn., Yemen, 1978—98, Hamoukar Expdn., Syria, 1999—; chmn. Coun. Am. Overseas Rsch. Ctrs., 1984—88, treas., 1988—92, mem. exec. com., 1995—2001; pres. Am. Acad. Rsch. Inst. in Iraq, 2003—. Author: (book) The City and Area of Kish, 1972; editor: Irrigation's Impact on Society, 1974, Seals and Sealing in the Ancient Near East, 1977, The Organization of Power: Aspects of Bureaucracy in the Ancient Near East, 1987, Uch Tepe II, 1990, Nippur II, 1993; author, editor: book Excavations in Nippur, 12th Season, 1978, Uch Tepe I, 1981. Mem. UNESCO Fact-Finding Mission to Iraq, 2003; mem. arts com. Union League Civic and Arts Found., Chgo., 1984—86; mem. adv. bd. Chgo. Humanities Festival, 2003—. Recipient Yemeni Arch. Svc. award, 1998; grantee, Am. Numismatic Soc., 1966, Am. Philos. Soc., 1969, Nat. Geog. Soc., 1978, 1989, NSF, 1994, 2000, NEH, 1995—98. Fellow: Deutsche Orient-Gesellchaft, Royal Anthrop. Inst., Brit. Sch. Archaeology Iraq; mem.: AAAS, Civil War Landscapes Assn., Am. Assn. Rsch. Baghdad, Mid. E. Studies Assn., Am. Inst. Yemeni Studies, Am. Anthrop. Assn., Archaeological Inst. Am., Quadrangle Club. Democrat. Avocations: architectural restoration, study of oriental rugs. Office: U Chgo Oriental Inst 1155 E 58th St Chicago IL 60637-1540 Office Phone: 773-702-9525. E-mail: m-gibson@uchicago.edu.

GIBSON, MEL, actor, film director, producer; b. Peekskill, NY, Jan. 3, 1956; emigrated to Australia, 1968; s. Hutton and Anne Gibson; m. Robyn Moore June 7, 1980; children: Hannah, Edward, Christian, Willie, Louis, Milo, Tommy. Grad., Nat. Inst. Dramatic Art, Sydney, Australia, 1977; LHD (hon.), Loyola Marymount U., 2003. Founder Icon Prodns. Works include: (films) Summer City, 1977, Mad Max, 1979, Tim, 1979, Attack Force Z, Gallipoli, 1981, The Road Warrior (Mad Max II), 1982, The Year of Living Dangerously, 1983, The Bounty, 1984, The River, 1984, Mrs. Soffel, 1984, Mad Max Beyond Thunderdome, 1985, Lethal Weapon, 1987, Tequila Sunrise, 1988, Lethal Weapon II, 1988, Bird on a Wire, 1989, Hamlet, 1990, Air America, 1990, Lethal Weapon III, 1992, Forever Young, 1992, Maverick, 1994, Pocahontas, 1995 (voice only), Ransom, 1996, Father's Day, 1997, Conspiracy Theory, 1997, Lethal Weapon 4, 1998, The Million Dollar Hotel, 1999, Payback, 1999, Chicken Run, 2000 (voice only), The Patriot, 2000, What Women Want, 2000, Signs, 2002, We Were Soldiers, 2003, The Singing Detective (also prodr.), 2003; actor, dir.: The Man Without a Face, 1993; actor, dir., prodr.: Braveheart, 1995 (Golden Globe award for best dir. of film 1996, Acad. award for best dir. 1996, Acad. award for best picture of yr. 1996, Outstanding Directorial Achievement in Motion Picture award nominee Dir. Guild Am. 1996, Oscar award for Best Dir.); dir., screenwriter, prodr.: The Passion of the Christ, 2004; performed with Nimrod Theatre Co. in plays including Death of a Salesman, Romeo and Juliet, with South Australian Theatre Co., from 1978, appeared in plays including Oedipus, Henry IV, Cedoona; work in TV series includes The Sullivans, The Oracle (Australia); exec. prodr. (TV) The Three Stooges, 2000, Complete Savages, 2004-05, Clubhouse, 2004-05. Favorite Movie Actor, People's Choice award, 1997; named one of 50 Most Power People in Hollywood Premiere mag. 2003-05. Roman Catholic.*

GIBSON, MICHAEL ALLEN, music educator; b. Kansas City, Mo., Dec. 19, 1962; s. Harold, Jr. Eugene Gibson and Judith Kay McKown, Dianne Miller Gibson (Stepmother) and Curtis McKown (Stepfather); m. Melissa Upchurch Gibson, July 4, 1962; children: Megan Erin, Abigail Elizabeth. B of Music Edn., U. of Ga., 1985, M of Music Edn., 2002. Cert. performance-based tchg.cert. 5-yr. Ga. Profl. Stds. Commn. Band dir. Greene County Bd. of Edn., Greensboro, Ga., 1985—88, Fulton County Bd. of Edn., Atlanta, 1988—. Clinician, dir. Fulton County Jazz Workshop, Atlanta, 1993—94; tuba instr. Atlanta Summer Olympic Games Marching Band, 1994—95; low brass clinician Fulton County Elem. Band Clinic, Sandy Springs, Ga., 1999—2001; coord., host, dir. Nat. Mid. Sch. Assn. Honor Band, Atlanta, 2003; county honor band coord. Fulton County Schs., Atlanta, 1994—98. Composer: (composition for mid. sch. band) Step To The View (Superior Rating, GMEA Dist. V Large Group Festival, 2001), Step To The View 2. Lay leader Hapeville (Ga.) United Meth. Ch., 1995—97, instrumental ensemble dir., 2000—04, Stockbridge (Ga.) Bapt. Ch., 1989—92. Named Tchr. of the Yr., Palmetto H.S., 1989—90; recipient Yearbook Dedication award, Creekside H.S., 1993—94, Fulton County Mini grant, Fulton County Edn. Found., 1999—2000, 2000—01, Ga. Rep. for Band Composition Project award, Am. Composers' Forum, 2000—01. Mem.: Profl. Assn. of Ga. Educators (bldg. rep. 1994—98), Nat. Band Assn., Ga. Music Educators Assn. (sec. 1999—2000, coord. and host dist. solo and ensemble festival 2000—02, vice-chmn. dist. V 1992—93, various 1985 to present), Phi Kappa Phi, Kappa Delta Pi, Pi Lambda Theta, Phi Mu Alpha (treas. 1984—85). United Methodist Church. Avocations: music, miniatures/doll house design and construction, golf, gardening, assorted carpentry. Home: 126 Brookwood Estates Trl Stockbridge GA 30281 Office: 5340 S Trimble Rd Atlanta GA 30342 Personal E-mail: mikegibs@bellsouth.net. E-mail: gibsonm@fultonschools.org.

GIBSON, MILTON EUGENE, cardiologist; b. Laporte, Ind., July 11, 1939; s. Maurice Wayne and Mary Leola Gibson; m. Gloria Jean Birky, Aug. 12, 1961; children: Kevin Scott, Bradley Mark. BA, Valparaiso U., 1961; MD, Ind. U., 1965. Diplomate Am. Bd. Internal Medicine, Am. Bd. Cardiovasc. Disease, Am. Bd. Interventional Cardiology. Rotating intern Meml. Hosp. of South Bend, 1965—66; resident in internal medicine Meth. Hosp. Grad. Med. Ctr., 1968—70, fellow in cardiology, 1970—72; cardiologist Cardiology Assocs., Inc., South Bend, Ind., 1972-88, pres., 1984-88; cardiologist, pres. Heart Group, South Bend, 1988—2004; cardiologist South Bend Clinic, 2004—. Chmn. cardiac cath com. Meml. Hosp., South Bend, 1973-90, St. Joseph's Med. Ctr., South Bend, 1999-2001; chmn. dept. medicine Meml. Hosp., South Bend, 1976-79; asst. clin. prof. medicine Ind. U., Indpls., 1980—. Author: Heart Sounds and Murmurs, 1973; contbr. articles to profl. jours. Pres. Am. Heart Assn., Indpls., 1977, pres. St. Joseph County chpt., 1975; bd. dirs. Vis. Nurse Assn., South Bend, 1984; mem. adv. bd. South Bend Pops Orch., 1978. Capt. U.S. Army, 1966-68, Vietnam. Decorated Bronze Star; recipient Man of Yr. award St. Joseph County Heart Assn., 1976. Fellow Am. Coll. Cardiology, Am. Coll. Chest Physicians, Coun. Critical Cardiology, Am. Heart Assn.; mem. ACP. E-mail: megibso@comcast.net.

GIBSON, NIGEL C, education educator; s. Reginald Frederick and Rita Gibson; m. Esme Katharine Josephson, Apr. 25, 1986; 1 child, Aidan F. BSc with honors in econ., U. Coll. of Wales, 1977—80; MA in english and comparative lit., Columbia U., 1992—93, PhD in polit. sci., 1988—96. Asst. dir. of african studies Columbia U., NYC, 1997—2000; vis. scholar Emerson Coll., Boston, 2000—03, dir. of the honors program, 2003—. Rsch. assoc., dept. of african and african-am. studies Harvard U., Boston, 2000—; rsch. assoc. Africana Studies, Brown U., Providence, 2001—. Author: (book) Fanon: The Postcolonial Imagination; co-editor (with George C. Bond): (collection of essays) Contested Terrains and Constructed Essays: Contemporary Africa in Focus; co-editor: (with Andrew N. Rubin) (collection of critical essays) Adorno: A Critical Reader; editor: Rethinking Fanon: The Continuing Legacy, Jour. of Asian and African Studies. Office: Emerson Coll 120 Boylston St Boston MA 02116 Office Phone: 617-824-8769.

GIBSON, PAMELA HEMENWAY, elementary school educator; b. Rocky Mount, N.C., May 7, 1953; d. Robert Walter and Irene (Hodges) Hemenway; d. Elliott H. Gibson, Jr.; children: Deana Emily, Kimberly Nichole. BSEd, East Carolina U., 1976; postgrad., East Carolina Grad. Sch. Edn., 1982; MA in Reading Edn., N.C. State U., 1995—. Cert. reading, lang. arts, social studies tchr., elem. edn. Tchr. Tarboro (N.C.) City Schs., Wake County Pub. Schs., Raleigh, NC, Sampson County Schs., 1996; reading specialist Intercede to Succeed Chapel Hill (N.C.) Profl. Devel. Sch., 1996-98; exceptional children's tchr., I.E.P. chair Vance County Schs., 1998-2000; literacy and lang. arts specialist, grades 2-5 Wake County Pub. Schs., NC, 2000—01; with N.C. Dept. Corrections, 2001—03; tchr. Durham Pub. Schs., NC, 2004—. Cons. N.C. Dept. Pub. Instrn., 1991, test reader, editor, 1991; adviser/advisee planning com. West Cary Middle Sch. Task Force; coord. KEYS mentoring/vol. program E.O. Young Elem; reading instr., Vance Granville C.C., 2001, Dept. Corrections Divsn. Criminal Investigations, 2003, Durham Pub. Schs., 2003— Recipient PTSA Svc. award, Cert. of Svc. Girl Scouts U.S.; N.C. Vets. scholar. Mem. NEA, NCAE (treas. local unit, Tarboro Pace rep.), N.C. English Tchrs. Assn., N.C. Social Studies Coun., Internat. Reading Assn., Bus. and Profl. Women's Club, Gamma Sigma Sigma. Home: 110 Northington Pl Apt C Cary NC 27513-3268 Office Phone: 919-637-0659.

GIBSON, PAUL RAYMOND, investment company executive; b. Cathay, Calif., Apr. 10, 1924; s. Otto and Louella (Vestal) G.; m. Janice Elizabeth Carter, dec. 19, 1952; children: Scott C., Paula S. *Wife, Janice Carter Gibson, BA, University of Michigan, is retired but still an active life time member of the Time-Life Alumni Society, New York, NY. She has also worked at WGN radio station in Chicago and Blue Danube radio station in Salzburg, Austria. Daughter, Paula S. Gibson, BA, Northwestern University, 1982, currently is Human Resources Director at Charles Schwab. Son, Scott Carter Gibson, BA in Economics, University of Pennsylvania, 1980, is currently the Managing Director of Seabury Investment Banking and Transportation Advisors Group in New York. He has held executive positions at PanAmerican World Airways, New York Air, Continental Airlines, and TWA.* BS in Fgn. Svc., Georgetown U., 1956. With U.S. Govt., 1948-52; export mgr. Asia, Philip Morris Co., San Francisco, 1952-54; founder, v.p., gen. mgr. McGregor and Werner Internat. Corp., Washington, 1954-62; v.p., dir. McGregor and Werner Corp., 1955-62; v.p. fin. Parsons & Whittemore, Inc., N.Y.C., 1962-65; founder, pres. Paul R. Gibson & Assocs., Washington, 1965-70; mng. dir. Black Clawson Pacific Co., Sydney, Australia, 1970-72; pres. Envirotech Asia Pacific, Sydney, 1972-75, Envirotech Internat., Menlo Park, Calif., 1975-80; founder, pres. INTERACT, San Francisco, 1980-91; pres. The Manchester Group, Ltd., Washington, 1987-89; pres., mng. assoc. Projects Internat. Assocs., Inc., Washington, 1991—95; pres. Projects Internat., Inc., 1996—, Sustainable Project Mgmt. USA, 1994—. Mem. Pacific Basin Econ. Coun., 1975—, vice chmn. policy and planning U.S. sect., 1976-91, chmn. Vietnam Task Force, 1998-2000; mem., trustee San Francisco World Affairs Coun., 1980-91; mem. World Affairs Coun., Washington, 1998—2002. Served to sgt. USMC, 1941-45. Mem. Am. C. of C. Sydney (chmn. Asia-Pacific coun. Am. C. of C. 1973-74, mem. adv. com. 1975—), Dirs. Cir., Mus. Natural History Smithsonian Instn., Confrerie des Chevaliers du Tastevin (chevalier, sous commanderie de Washington 1992-2002), Rural Health Internat. (co-chmn. 2002—), Am. Nat. Club (Sydney). Home: 2631 Golfside Ct Naples FL 34110 Office: Projects Internat Inc 1800 K St NW Ste 1000 Washington DC 20006-2202 Office Phone: 202-333-1277. Personal E-mail: pgibson@protectsinternational.com.

GIBSON, RALPH H(OLMES), photographer; b. Jan. 16, 1939; Student in photography, U.S. Navy, 1956-60, San Francisco Art Inst., 1960-61; DFA (hon.), U. Md., 1991, Ohio Wesleyan U., 1997. Lectr. at numerous schs., museums. Exhibited photography in one-man shows including Madison (Wis.) Arts Ctr., 1975, Hoesch Mus., Duren, W. Ger., 1975, Castelli Graphics, N.Y.C., 1976, 80, 82, 91, Balt. Mus. Art, 1976, Van Reekum Galerji Mus., Apeldoorn, Netherlands, 1977, Swedish Mus. Photography, 1977, Mus. Modern Art, Oxford, Eng., 1977, Photographers Gallery, Melbourne, Australia, 1977, Robert Self Gallery, London, 1978, Mus. Modern Art, Brisbane, Australia, 1978, I.C.A. Mus. Art, Richmond, Va., 1979, Canon Gallery, Geneva, 1979, Grapestake Gallery, San Francisco, 1979, Kunstmuseum, Dusseldorf, Fed. Republic Germany, 1980, Night Gallery, London, 1980, Mus. Folkwang, Essen, Fed. Republic Germany, 1981, Mattingly Baker Gallery, Dallas, 1981, Sprengel Mus., Hanover, W. Ger., 1981, Cantieri Navali, La Giudeca, Venice, Italy, 1981, F.I.A.C., Paris, 1982, Olympus Gallery, London, 1892, Centre Georges Pompidou, Paris, 1982, Shadai Gallery, Tokyo, 1982, Sun Valley Ctr. for the Arts, Idaho, 1983, Seattle Art Mus., 1983, Weston Gallery, Carmel, Calif., 1984, Consejo Argentino de Fotografia, Buenos Aires, Argentina, 1985, Bouwfonds Hovelaken, The Netherlands, 1985, Castelli Uptown, N.Y.C., 1985, Galerie Agathe Gaillard, Paris, 1985, Leo Castelli Gallery, N.Y.C., 1985, 87, Ministry of Culture Hall, Marrakech, Morocco, 1986, Nat. Exhibit Hall, Moabane, Swaziland, 1986, Musee Carnavalet, Paris, 1986, Hellenic Ctr. Photography, Athens, 1987, Mus. Fine Arts, Alexandria, Egypt, 1987, Museo Archivi Alinari, Florence, Italy, 1987, Circulo de Bellas Artes, Madrid, 1987, Internat. Ctr. Photography, N.Y.C., 1987, Villa Medici, Rome, 1987, Mpls. Inst. Arts, 1988, Bibliotheque Nationale, Paris, 1988, Moderna Museet, Fotografiska Museet, Stockholm, 1989, Arts Club Chgo., 1989, Albin O. Kuhn Libr. and Gallery, U. Md., Balt., 1990, Musee Nicephore Niepce, Chalon Sue Soane, France, 1990, Princessehof Mus., Leuwarden, Holland, 1991, Okla. City Art Mus., 1991, Espace Photo Paris Audiovisuel, 1991, Photography House, Prague, 1992, Kunstverein Emmerich, Haus imm Park, 1996—, High Museum of Art, Atlanta, GA., 1997, MMK, Frankfurt, Germany, 1998, Maison Européenne De La Photographie, Paris, 1999; Greenville Cnty. Museum of Art, Greenville, Whitney Museum of American Art- N.Y.C., Ger., 1992, Boca Mus. Art, Boca Raton, Fla., 1993, 94, Butler Mus. Am. Art, Ohio, 1994, Frankfurt Kunstverein, 1996, Internat. Ctr. Photography 5-yr. world wide travelling exhbn., Villa Medici, Rome, 1986—, Mus. Carnavalet, Paris, 1986—, Leo Castelli Gallery, N.Y., Galerie Eric Van de Weghe, Brussels, Expo 1991, ICAC/Weston Gallery, Tokyo, others; exhibited in numerous group shows, including, Mus. Modern Art, N.Y.C., 1978, Hayden Gallery, MIT, Cambridge, 1978, Bologna Art Fair, Italy, 1978, Walker Art Center, Liverpool, Eng., 1978, Cleve. Mus. Art, 1978, Musée Marseilles, 1980, Addison Gallery of Art, Phillips Acad., Andover, Mass., 1981, Mus. Folkwang, Essen, 1981, San Francisco Mus. of Modern Art, 1982, 84, 85, Met. Mus. Art, N.Y.C., 1982, Whitney Mus. Art, N.Y.C., 1983, Houston Ctr. for Photography, 1983, Mus. Art, Phila., 1983, Denver Art Mus., 1984, Nat. Mus. Art, Washington, 1984, Sesnon Gallery, U. Calif.-Santa Cruz, 1984, Mus. of Modern Art, Paris, 1984, Pace-McGill Gallery, N.Y.C., 1985, Barbican Art Gallery, London, 1985, Bronx Mus., N.Y.C., 1985, Kunsterin, Stuttgart, Fed. Republic Germany, 1985, Musee Cantonal, Lausanne, Switzerland, 1985, Lehigh U., Pa., 1985, Gallery Hirondelle, N.Y.C., 1986, Villa Medici, Rome, numerous others; represented in permanent collections, including Nat. Gallery Ottawa, Ont., Can., Whitney Mus. Am. Art, Bibliotheque National de France, Paris, Mus. Modern Art, N.Y.C., Internat. Mus. Photography, George Eastman House, Rochester, N.Y., Fogg Art Mus., Boston, Met. Mus. Art, N.Y.C., Australian Nat. Gallery, Canberra, Nat. Gallery Victoria, Australia, Art Gallery South Australia, Victoria and Albert Mus., London, Mus. Modern Art, Brisbane, Fotografiska Museet, Moderna Museet, Stockholm, Sweden, Musee Reattu, Arles, France, G. Ray Hawkins Gallery, Los Angeles, Mus. Fine Arts, Alexandria, Egypt, Mus. Art, Athens, Greece; author: Apropos de Mary Jane, 1990, Chiaroscuro, 1990; author, illustrator: The Strip, 1966, The Hawk, 1968, The American Civil Liberties Union Calendar, 1969, The Somnambulist, 1970, Deja-vu, 1973, Days at Sea, 1975, Syntax, 1983, Tropism, 1987, Archive-Early Work, 1988; navarin editor: In-Situ, 1988, Les Cahiers des La Photographie, 1988, L'Histoire de France, 1991, Deux ex Machina, Taschen edits., 1999, Ex Libris Powerhouse edits., 2000, Light Strings, 2004, Refractions, 2005, Brazil, 2005, Piemonte, 2005. Decorated comdr. Ordre Arts et Lettres (France); recipient Leica medal of excellence award, 1988, grand medal City of Arles, France, 1994, Silver Plumb award Design Trust for Pub. Space, 2000; fellowship grantee Nat. Endowment for Arts, 1973, 75, 86-87, creative artists pub. svc. grantee N.Y. State. Coun. Arts, 1977, grantee Eastman Kodak Co., 1989, Murray and Isabella Rayburn Found., 1994; Guggenheim fellow, 1985-86. Address: 331 W Broadway New York NY 10013-2265 Office Phone: 212-334-1854. E-mail: lustrum@pipeline.com. *Photography is a way for measuring my perception-I trust my photographs and study them intensely. After working over forty years, I realize that the years of struggle are over. Now begin the years of struggle.*

GIBSON, REGINALD WALKER, federal judge; b. Lynchburg, Va., July 31, 1927; s. McCoy and Julia Ann (Butler) G.; 1 child, Reginald S. BS, Va. Union U., 1952; postgrad., Wharton Grad. Sch. Bus. Adminstrn., U. Pa., 1952-53; LL.B., Howard U., 1956. Bar: DC 1957, Ill. 1972. Agt. IRS, Washington, 1957-61; trial atty. tax div. US Dept. Justice, Washington, 1961-71; sr. tax atty. Internat. Harvester Co., Chgo., 1971-76, gen. tax atty., 1976-82; judge US Ct. Fed. Claims, Washington, 1982-95, sr. judge, 1995—. Mem. bus. adbv. council Chgo. Urban League, 1974-82. Served with AUS, 1946-47. Recipient cert. award U.S. Dept. Justice Atty. Gen., 1969, recipient spl. commendation U.S. Dept. Justice Atty. Gen., 1970, Wall St. Jour. award, 1952, Am. Jurisprudence award, 1956; named Alumni of Yr. Howard U. Sch. Law, 1984. Mem. DC Bar Assn., Chgo. Bar Assn., Fed. Bar Assn., Nat. Bar Assn., Claims Ct. Bar Assn., J. Edgar Murdock Am. Inn of Ct. (taxation com.). Clubs: Nat. Lawyers (Washington). Baptist. Office: US Ct Fed Claims 717 Madison Pl NW Washington DC 20439-0002

GIBSON, REX HILTON, lawyer; b. Galveston, Tex., May 17, 1963; BBA, So. Meth. U., 1985; JD, Southern Meth. U., 1988. Bar: Tex. 1988, U.S. Tax Ct. 1989, U.S. Ct. Claims 1992. Tax assoc. Exxon Co., U.S.A., Houston, 1988, tax atty., 1988-92, sr. tax atty., 1992, Exxon Co., Internat., Florham Park, NJ, 1992-95, Exxon Ventures (CIS) Inc., Houston, 1995-99; tax counsel ExxonMobil Internat. Ltd., London, 2000—01, ExxonMobil Devel. Co., Houston, 2001—03, ExxonMobil Exploration Co., Houston, 2003—. Bd. dirs. Internat. Tax and Investment Ctr.; mem. tax com. Petroleum Adv. Forum, 2000—05; mem. US-Russia Bus. Coun., 2001—05; vice-chair Caspian Mineral Taxation Com., 2003—05. Mem. ABA (taxation sect., natural resources com. 1995—, environ. taxes com. 1990—), State Bar Tex. (taxation sect., oil, gas & minerals law sect. 1989—), Houston Bar Assn. (taxation sect. 1995—), Houston Livestock Show and Rodeo Assn., U.S. Ski Team Found., Beta Alpha Psi. Avocations: skiing, hiking, fishing, golf. Office: ExxonMobil Exploration Co CORP GP4 428 16945 Northchase Dr Houston TX 77060 Business E-Mail: rex.h.gibson@exxonmobil.com.

GIBSON, ROGER, air transportation executive; B in Mgmt., St. Mary's Coll., Moraga, Calif. Joined United Airlines, 1967, held various mgmt. positions, v.p. N.Am. mountain region Chgo., 1995—. Bd. dirs. First Am. Funds, Met. State Coll. Denver Found., Nat. Jewish Med. Ctr. Bd. dirs. Denver Area Coun., Boy Scouts Am., Colo. Uplift, Colo. Ocean Journey, Denver Found. With USN, 1964—70. Office: United Airlines PO Box 66100 WH QSA Chicago IL 60666

GIBSON, RONALD P., finance company executive; BS in Bus. Mgmt., Va. Commonwealth U. Founder SNL Fin. LLC, Raleigh, NC, 1978—, mng. ptnr., 1978—; CEO Highwoods Properties, Raleigh, 1994—. Bd. dir. Highwoods Properties Inc., chmn. exec. com., mem. investment com., mem. fin. com. Office: Highwoods Properties Inc 3100 Smoketree Ct Ste 600 Raleigh NC 27604

GIBSON, SAMUEL NORRIS, educational association administrator, retired clergy; b. Troy, Ala., Sept. 2, 1926; s. Clarence Samuel Gibson and Annie Pearl Clark; m. Ellen Ruth Waldo, June 19, 1948 (div. Aug. 1972); children: Richard Waldo, Christopher Samuel; m. Ella Marie Booth, Oct. 28, 1972; stepchildren: Curtis David Schurman, Darryl John Schurman. *Samuel Norris Gibson wife, Ella Booth Gibson, distinguished educator, for twenty years Head of The University School, Pittsburgh, a private college preparatory school. Son, Richard; Guitar instructor, Pittsburgh High School for Creative and Performing Arts and local professional Band Leader, Married to Jolynn Gahan. Son, Christopher; for 26 years Ballet Performer and Instructor in Connecticut and accomplished electrician and photographer, Married to Lynne Watt. Descendent of Jonas Weed who arrived with Governor Winthrop to Massachusetts Bay colony in 1631 and later a Puritan founder of Stamford, Connecticut, and of Samuel Royal Gibson of South Carolina, a pioneer settler of Pike County, Alabama in 1831.* BS in Architecture, Ga. Inst. Tech., 1947; BD, Yale U., 1951, STM, 1955; PhD, U. Pitts., 1980. Exec. dir. Christian Assn. Pa. State U., State College, 1956—64; rsch. dir. Study of Meth. Campus Ministry, Nashville, 1964—66; exec. min. Univ. and city Ministries, Pitts., 1967—72; pres. Alternative Learning Lab., Pitts., 1971—77; exec. dir. East End Coop. Ministry, Pitts., 1978—82, United Meth. Ch. Union, Pitts., 1982—88; regional dir. Internat. Edn. Forum, Bay Shore, NY, 1989—97; pres. ASA Internat., Inc., Pitts., 1997—2003. Co-founder Youth Learning Ctr., 1971. Author: Public Policy in Alabama Higher Education, 1980, (booklet) The Windows of Calvary, 1989; editor: (booklets) You and the Communist Challenge, 1960, Riverfront Development Study, 1990. Trustee Otterbein Coll., Westerville, Ohio, 1984-89; pres. The Univ. Sch., Pitts., 1981-88; chair bd. trustees Calvary Meth. Ch., Pitts., 1991—; mem. exec. com. Nat. Campus Ministry Assn., 1967-70; co-founder, treas. The Dollar Energy Fund, Pitts., 1983-92; candidate Senate of Commonwealth of Pa., Pitts., 1975; mem., chair Allegheny Historic Preservation Soc., Pitts., 1989—; mem. steering com. Mayor's Commn. on Families, Pitts., 1986-90; alumni pres. Leadership Pitts., 1986—; pres. Pitts. East Rotary Found., 2001-05. With USNR, 1943-46. Area studies fellow Ford Found., 1953-54, campus ministry fellow Danforth Found., 1972-73 Mem. Ind. Ednl. Counselors Assn., Rotary (pres. Pitts. East chpt. 1984, 2001, Paul Harris fellow 1993), Longue Vue Club. Democrat. Avocations: folk songs, church architecture, genealogy, book collecting, gardening. Home: 29 Newgate Rd Pittsburgh PA 15202 Office: Gibson Enterprises Inc 7119 Church Ave Pittsburgh PA 15202 Office Phone: 412-761-5190. E-mail: sngibson35@hotmail.com.

GIBSON, SANDRA, painter, filmmaker; b. Portland, Oreg. BFA, RI Sch. Design, 1999; attended, Ecole des Beaux-Arts. Artist Whitney Biennial, Whitney Mus. Am. Art, 2004; dir.: (films) Cinematheque, ON, Pacific Film Archive, Anthology Film Archive, Rotterdam Film Festival, Ind. Exposure, Empire State Film Festival, Ann Arbor Film Festival, South Beach Animation Festival. Mailing: c/o Whitney Museum American Art 945 Madison Ave New York NY 10021 E-mail: sgibson31@hotmail.com.*

GIBSON, SCOTT RUSSELL, director; b. New Castle, Pa., Feb. 5, 1956; s. Earle A. and Barbara (Gormley) G.; m. Michele Moshier, May 10, 1980; children: Kathleen, Andrew, Benjamin, Noah. BSN with honors, Indiana U. Pa., 1989, MA in Adult Edn./ Comm. Tech., 2001, postgrad., 2004, RN Anesthetist Sch., Altoona, 1992-94. Cert. transplant technician, U.S. Navy Sch.; cert. emergency nurse 1989. Staff nurse Ind. (Pa.) Hosp., 1989-96; regional faculty BLS program Am. Heart Assn., 1989—; faculty instr. Ind. Vocat. Tech. LPN Sch., 1990-92; with infusion dept. Diamond Drugs, Inc., 1996-2000; staff nurse Ind. U. Pa., 2000—; asst. dir. Pechan Health Ctr., Ind., Pa., 2002—, interim dir., 2004—. Am. Heart Assn.-Cmty. Tng. Ctr. co-ord., 1995—. Mem. Am. Heart Assn., 1979, ARC, 1974. With USN, 1979-86. Mem. Emergency Nurses Assn. Business E-Mail: sgibson@iup.edu.

GIBSON, SIDNEY KAY, retired lawyer; b. Salina, Kans., Nov. 9, 1937; s. Melvin Merit and Katherine Pauline (Marlin) Gibson; m. Sandra Pauline Ogden, Dec. 21, 1959; children: Jeffery Merit, Russell Paul. Student, N.Mex. State U., 1955—58; BMus, U. Tex. El Paso, 1959, MEd, 1968; JD, St. Mary's U., San Antonio, 1971. Bar: Tex. 1971, U.S. Ct. Appeals (5th cir.) 1982. Tchr. El Paso Pub. Schs., 1959—68; assoc. H.T. Santiesteban and Assocs., El Paso, 1982—89; ret., 1989. Contbr. articles to law jours. Recipient Outstanding Scholastic Achievement award, 1968, 1970, Liech-Semaan award, 1970, James R. Norvell Moot Ct. award, 1970, Achievement award, State Jr. Bar Tex., 1970, Internat. Trial Lawyers Outstanding Achievement award, Art and Sci. Adv., 1970. Mem.: El Paso Bar Assn., State Bar Tex. Presbyterian. Home: 437 Stonebluff Rd El Paso TX 79912-3310

GIBSON, SLOAN D., IV, corporate financial executive; MA in econ., U. Mo.; grad., US Military Acad. Tchr. Stonier Grad. Sch. of Bkg.; with Bank South, First Union; comm. bkg. group head AmSouth, AmSouth Bk., 1993—97, sr. exec. v.p., 1994—2000, fin., comm. credit group head, 1997—99, CFO, fin. credit group head Birmingham, Ala., 1997—99; pres., CEO First Am. Nat. Bk., 1999; Tenn, Miss., La. bkg. group head AmSouth Bk., 1999—2000; CFO, fin. credit group head AmSouth, AmSouth Bk., 2000—. Vice chmn. AmSouth Bancorp, 2000—. Office: AmSouth Bancorp 1901 6th Ave N Birmingham AL 35203

GIBSON, SUSAN IRMA, plant biologist, educator; b. Takoma Park, Md., Dec. 10, 1960; d. Earl Doyle and Ursula Elisabeth Martha Gibson. BS in Biology and Chemistry, Stanford U., 1987; PhD, Cornell U., 1989. Adj. assoc. prof. Rice U., Houston, 2000—; assoc. prof. U. Minn., St. Paul, 2002—. Grantee NSF, Dept. of Energy, 1995-2006. Mem.: Am. Soc. of Plant Physiologists. Achievements include patent for dentification of a fatty acid desaturase gene from plants and use in altering seed oil composition. Office: Univ Minn 1500 Gortner Ave Saint Paul MN 55108 Office Phone: 612-624-7408.

GIBSON, VIRGINIA LEE, lawyer; b. Independence, Mo., Mar. 5, 1946; BA, U. Calif., Berkeley, 1972; JD, U. Calif., San Francisco, 1977. Bar: Calif. 1981. Assoc. Pillsbury, Madison & Sutro, San Francisco, 1980-83; ptnr. Chickering & Gregory, San Francisco, 1983-85, Baker & McKenzie, San Francisco, 1985—2001, White & Case, LLP, Palo Alto and San Francisco, 2001—. Mem. ABA (internat. law and practice sect., labor and employment law sect.), Nat. Assn. Stock Plan Profls., Nat. Ctr. for Employee Ownership, Calif. Bar Assn. (exec. com. tax sect. 1985-88), San Francisco Bar Assn. (internat. taxation sect.), Western Pension and Benefits Conf. (pres. San Francisco chpt. 1989-91, program com. 1984-88). Office: White & Case LLP 4 Embarcadero 24th Fl San Francisco CA 94111 also: White & Case LLP 5 Palo Alto Sq 3000 El Camino Real Palo Alto CA 94306 Business E-Mail: vgibson@whitecase.com.

GIBSON, WALKER, retired language educator, poet, writer; b. Jacksonville, Fla., Jan. 19, 1919; s. William Walker Sr. and Helen (Jones) G.; m. Nancy Close, 1942; children: David R., Susan M., William Walker. III, John S. B.A, Yale U., 1940; MA, U. Iowa, 1946. Rsch. asst. writers workshop U. Iowa, 1945-46; instr. English Amherst (Mass.) Coll., 1946-48, asst. prof., 1948-54, assoc. prof., 1954-57; assoc. prof., dir. freshman English Washington Square Coll. NYU, N.Y.C., 1957-61, prof., 1961-67; prof. English U. Mass., Amherst, 1967-87, dir. freshman English, 1967-70, dir. rhetoric program, 1970-72, dir. undergrad. studies in English, 1974-76, prof. emeritus, 1984. Lectr. Yale Summer Music Sch., 1948-56; dir. NYU Summer Inst. for Secondary Tchrs. English, 1962, NDEA Summer Inst. for Secondary Tchrs. English, NYU, 1965, Summer Seminars for Coll Tchrs, NEH, 1973-75; prof. summer intern teaching program Smith Coll., 1963-64, 66-67; vis. prof. Swarthmore Coll., 1965-66; prof. NDEA Summer Inst. at Mass., 1968, Bread Loaf Sch. English, Middlebury Coll., 1976, 77. Author: (verse) The Reckless Spenders, 1954 Come As You Are, 1957, (texts) Seeing and Writing: Fifteen Exercises in Composing Experience, 1959, Tough Sweet & Stuffy, 1966, Persona: A Style Study for Readers and Writers, 1969, (antholgy text) Poems in Progress, 1963; co-author: The Macmillan Handbook of English, 1960, 2nd edit, 1965; contbg. author: Traditions of Inquiry, 1985, The Legacy of Language, 1987, others; editor: Limits of Language, 1962, New Students in Two-Year Colleges, 1979; co-editor: The Play of Language, 1971; contbr. articles to profl. jours.; contbns. to TV and film include Sunrise Semester, CBS-TV, full-year course Modern Literature: British and American, 1962-63, semester course Studies in Style, 1966-67, film The Speaking Voice and the Teaching of Composition, 1963, videotapes on dramatic role-playing in student writing, 1971, 84; author numerous poems in publs. including The New Yorker, Harpers, Atlantic Poetry, others. 1st lt. U.S. Army Air Corps, 1941-45. Ford Found. fellow 1955-56; John Simon Guggenheim Found. fellow, 1963-64; grantee NEH, 1973-77. Mem. MLA (selection com. for scholar's libr. 1968-71, del. assembly 1976-77, exec. com. divsn. on tchg. of writing 1976-80, chmn. divsn. 1979), Nat. coun. Tchrs. English (commn. on curriculum 1962-65, chmn. coll. sect. 1969-71, pres. elect and pres. coun. 1971-73, com. pub. doublespeak 1972-90, chmn. emeritus assembly 1986-87, Disting. Lectr. award 1969, Disting. Svc. award 1988), CCCC (exec. com. 1966-69), 5 Coll. Learning in Retirement (pres. 1990-91). Avocations: reading, writing. Home: 38 Lessey St Amherst MA 01002-2118

GIBSON, WALTER MAXWELL, physics researcher; b. Enoch, Utah, Nov. 11, 1930; married, 1967; children. BS, Univ. Utah, 1954; PhD, Univ. Calif., 1956. Prof. physics SUNY, 1976-84, v.p. rsch. and dean grad. studies, 1984-86, prof. physics, 1988—. Mem. tech. staff Bell Telephone Labs, 1959-76; rsch. collaborator Brookhaven Nat. Labs., 1960—; adj. prof. Renesselear Polytech. Inst., 1963-76, Rutgers Univ., 1963-76 Editor: Radiation Effects, 1984-88. Fellow Am. Physics Soc.; mem. Am. Vacuum Soc., Sigma Xi, AAAS. Achievements include research nuclear and solid state physics, principally nuclear fission mechanism studies; principles and application of solid state detectors and interaction of charged particles with crystalline and amorphous media, surfaces, structure and dynamics. Office: SUNY-Inst for Partl Solid Int Accelerator Lab 1400 Washington Ave Albany NY 12222-0100

GIBSON, WILLIAM LEE, financial consultant; b. Newark, Dec. 1, 1949; S. Joseph Wilton Gibson and Margaret (Reynolds) Gibson Leavens; stepson William Barry Leavens, Jr.; m. Lorraine Wrightson Besch, July 10, 1982. BA in chemistry, Bucknell U., 1972; postgrad., Harvard Bus. Sch., 1977; MBA, NYU, 1987, Sch. of Advanced Fin. Mgmt., 1995. With Bur. Solid Waste Mgmt EPA, Cin., 1970-71; chemist Dow Chem. Co., Midland, Mich., 1972-75; mktg. cons. Westvaco, Charleston, S.C., 1976; sales rep. Diamond Shamrock Co., Cleve., 19777-79; market devel. specialist strategic planing and ventures operation GE, Pittsfield, Mass., 1979-81; mktg. programs mgr. Allied-Signal Corp., Morristown, N.J., 1981-86, mgr. tech. and bus. devel., 1986-91, sr. sales mgr., 1991-93; v.p. Merrill Lynch, Short Hills, N.J., 1994—. Former pres., trustee Hartford Family Found; v.p. Leavens Found. Trustee N.J. Symphony Orch.; treas. Coun. N.J. Grantmakers. Mem. Harvard Bus. Sch. Club N.Y., Harvard Club N.Y. Home: 8 Lone Oak Rd Basking Ridge NJ 07920-1613 Office: 51 John F Kennedy Pky Short Hills NJ 07078-2702

GIBSON, WILLIAM M., technology company executive; BA in Econs., Villanova U., 1966; grad. Exec. Edn. Program, Harvard U., 1979. With IBM, Applied Logic Corp., IIT Data Svcs., Chase Econometrics/Interactive Data Corp., Strategic Info. Inc.; with info. svcs. divsn. Ziff-Davis Corp.; COO Manugistics Group Inc., Rockville, Md., 1982, pres., 1982. Chmn. bd. dirs. Manugistics, 1986—. Recipient Entrepreneur of Yr. award Ernst & Young, 1997, High Tech Entrepreneur of Yr. award for Greater Washington region KPMG, 1997. Office: Manugistics Inc 9715 Key West Ave Rockville MD 20850-3915 Fax: 301-984-5370.

GIBSON, WILLIAM SHEPARD, retired insurance company executive; b. Bklyn., Jan. 2, 1933; s. William S. and Mary (Keeney) G.; m. Charmaine Wallett, May 26, 1967; children: Susan, Joshua, 1 stepdau., Tracy; children by previous marriage: William, Gregory. BS in Acctg., U. Ill., 1954, JD, 1959. Counsel Am. Ins. Assn., Chgo., 1963-69; asst. dir. ins. State of Ill., Chgo., 1969-71; v.p. midwest Am. Ins. Assn., Chgo., 1971-77; v.p., gen. counsel Continental Ins., N.Y.C., 1977-82; v.p. govt. affairs Continental Corp., N.Y.C., 1982-95; dep. supt. N.Y. Ins., N.Y.C., 1995-97; v.p. Peterson Worldwide, N.Y.C., 1997—2001; pres., CEO Interboro Mut. Ind. Ins. Co., 2002—04; ret. Chmn. bd. N.J. Auto Ins. Assn., Newark, 1983-89; chmn. Continental PAC, 1981-95; mem. N.Y. Motor Vehicle Indemnity Corp. Bd. dirs. Lower Manhattan Cultural Coun. Served with U.S. Army, 1954-56. Mem. ABA, Ill. State Bar Assn., N.Y. Bar Assn., Internat. Assn. Ins. Counsel, N.Y. Med. Malpractice Ins. Assn. Congregationalist. Home: 80 Warren St Apt 67 New York NY 10007-1039

GIBSON, WILLIAM WILLARD, JR., law educator; b. Amarillo, Tex., Mar. 5, 1932; s. William Willard and Genelle (Works) G.; m. Beth Smyth, July 31, 1953; children— William Willard, Michael Murray, Timothy Thomas, Elizabeth Mills. BA, U. Tex., Austin, 1954, LLB, 1956. Assoc. Gibson, Ochsner, Harlin, Kinney & Morris, Amarillo, Tex., 1956-60, ptnr., 1960-65; assoc. prof. U. Tex.-Austin Sch. Law, 1965-69, prof., 1969-76, Albert Sydney Burleson prof. law, 1976-83, Sylvan Lang prof. law, 1983-98, Sylvan Lang prof. emeritus, 1998—, dir. continuing legal edn., 1981-85, assoc. dean, 1979-86; Austin. Provost jud. edn. Supreme Ct. Tex., 1992-93. Author: Teaching Materials on Wills and Estates, 1967; Selected Provisions from Texas Statutes Pertaining to Wills and Estates, 1973; also articles Vice chancellor Diocese of Tex., Protestant Episcopal Ch. Recipient Leon Green award Tex. Law Rev. Assn. of Ex-Editors, Austin, 1983. Mem. Am. Coll. Real Estate Lawyers. Democrat. Avocations: walking, fishing, hunting. E-mail: bgibson@mail.law.utexas.edu.

GIDDENS, DON PEYTON, engineering educator, researcher; b. Augusta, Ga., Oct. 24, 1940; m. Karin Baldzer; 1 child, Eric. BS in aerospace engring., Ga. Inst. Tech., 1963, MS in aerospace engring., 1965, PhD in aerothermodynamics, 1967. Assoc. aircraft engr. Lockheed-Ga. Co., Atlanta, 1963; mem. tech. staff Aerospace Corp., San Bernardino, Calif., 1966-67; asst. prof. Ga. Inst. Tech., Atlanta, 1968-70, assoc. prof., 1970-77, prof., 1977-82, regents prof., 1982-92, chair dept. aerospace engring., 1988-92, dean Coll. Engring., 2002—; eminent scholar Ga. Rsch. Alliance; co-dir. Biomedical Tech. Rsch. Ctr. Ga. Inst. Tech./Emory U., Atlanta, 1987—92, prof., chair Wallace H. Coulter Dept. Biomedical Engring., 1997—2002, now Lawrence L. Gellerstedt Jr. Chair in Bioengineering; dean Whiting Sch. Engring. Johns Hopkins U., Balt., 1992-97. Contbr. numerous articles to profl. jours. Fellow: Am. Heart Assn. Arteriosclerosis, Thrombosis and Vascular Biology Coun., Am. Inst. Med. and Biol. Engineers (founding fellow, pres. 2004—), ASME; mem.: NAE. Avocation: whitewater canoeing. Office: Ga Inst Tech Coll Engring Adminstrn Bldg 225 North Ave NW Atlanta GA 30332-0360

GIDDENS-JONES, EMILY JANE, architectural and interior designer, consultant; b. Jackson, Miss., Sept. 18, 1924; d. Jasper Franklin and Erma Jane (Simmons) Giddens; m. William Everard Jones, Nov. 10, 1947 (div. July 1967). BA, Belhaven Coll., 1946; postgrad., Phila. Mus. Coll. Art, 1964. Dir. design Office Supply Co., Jackson, 1954-58; dir. design and prodn. Designers Fore Ltd., NYC, 1969-75, John F. Saladino, Inc., NYC, 1975-79; pres., CEO, owner Cross Quadrate Design, NYC, 1972—. Assoc. prof. interior design Post Coll., Waterbury, Conn., 1978-79; cons. Flexcon, Inc., Spencer, Mass., 1985-89; bd. dirs. Cornwall Assn., 2003— Contbr. articles to profl. jours. Sec. bd. dir. Cornwall (Conn.) Extras for Kids, 1993-2001 Honors Scholar Belhaven Coll., 1942-46. Mem. Chi Delta. Presbyterian. Avocations: reading, writing, music, composing, painting. Home: 49 Popple Swamp Rd Cornwall Bridge CT 06754-1137 Office: Cross Quadrate Design 138 E 38th St New York NY 10016-2646

GIDDON, DONALD B(ERNARD), psychologist, educator; b. Newark, May 1, 1930; s. William and Ruth (Franklin) G.; m. Phoebe L. Rothman, Aug. 28, 1955; children: David, Kenneth, Joanna, James. AB, Brown U., 1952; MA, Boston U., 1953; DMD, Harvard U., 1959; PhD in Psychology, Brandeis U., 1961. Lectr. psychology Brandeis U., 1954-71, 82-84, lectr. phys. edn., 1985-89; prof., chmn. dental ecology Harvard U., 1972-75, vis. prof., 1976-89, lectr., 1989-98, clin. prof. growth and devel., 1999—, lectr. health svcs. adminstrn. Sch. Pub. Health, 1972-75, asst. dean adminstrn. Sch. Dental Medicine, 1973-75; assoc. staff New Eng. Med. Center, 1964-73; assoc. prof., chmn. dept. social dentistry Tufts U., Boston, 1964-67, prof., chmn. dept. social dentistry, 1967-72, asst. dean, 1967-69, assoc. dean, 1969-71; dean NYU Dental Ctr., 1975-78, prof. epidemiology and health promotion,

1976—; prof. psychology Grad. Sch. Arts and Scis., prof. anesthesiology NYU Med. Center, 1976-80; prof. Faculty of Medicine, U. Groningen, The Netherlands, 1980-81. Cons. Astra Pharm. Products, Inc., 1960—, dept. medicine and surgery VA, 1966-69, med. rsch. cons., 1988-90, Peter Bent Brigham Hosp., 1975-76, Meml. Sloan-Kettering Cancer Ctr., 1976-78, psychologist dept. anesthesiology Brigham and Women's Hosp., 1979—; vis. prof. U. Gothenburg, Sweden, 1971, Royal Dental Coll., Aarhus, Denmark, 1972, U. Pa., 1972, medicine McGill Med. U., 1981-83, psychology Mass. Coll. Pharmacy and Allied Health Scis., 1984-89; clin. prof. NYU Med. Ctr., 1976—, Brookdale Hosp. Med. Ctr., 1977—, Goldwater Meml. Hosp., 1977-80, Brown U., 1989—, U. Ill., Chgo., 1994—, Health Scis. Ctr. Stony Brook U., 2004—; founding dir. Rsch. Inst., Royal Victoria Hosp., Montreal, Can., 1981-82; mem. NIH study sect. 2000—. Contbr. articles to profl. jours. Bd. dirs. Mass. Health Coun., 1965-70, pres., 1968-69; pres. Hamilton sch. PTA, Newton Lower Falls, Mass., 1963-64; trustee Emerson Coll., 1991-2000, Berkshire Opera, 1996—; mem. Com. on Univ. Resources, bd. overseers Harvard U., 1991—, NIH study sect., 2000—. Named Fulbright scholar, 1971. Fellow AAAS, APA, Acad. Behavioral Med. Rsch., Am. Pub. Health Assn., Am. Coll. Dentists, Internat. Coll. Dentists, Internat. Coll. Psychosomatic Medicine, Royal Soc. Medicine; mem. AAUP, Am. Statis. Assn., Internat. Assn. Study Pain, Am. Psychosomatic Soc., Am. Coll. Sports Medicine, Am. Dental Soc. Anesthesiology (assoc. editor 1965-72, chmn. ethics com. 1979-81), Behavioral Sci. in Dental Rsch. (pres. 1976-77), Internat. Assn. Dental Rsch. (pres. Boston sect. 1965-66), Am. Pain Soc. (dir. 1977-79), Soc. Behavioral Med., Soc. Psychophys. Rsch., Soc. Clin. and Experimental Hypnosis, Sigma Xi. Office: 277 Linden St Wellesley MA 02482-5900 Business E-Mail: donald_giddon@hms.harvard.edu.

GIDEL, ROBERT HUGH, real estate investor; b. Ft. Dodge, Iowa, Sept. 19, 1951; s. Wayne D. and Mary A. (Ziegler) G.; m. Linda Carol Lombardo, Oct. 23, 1976; children: Jill, Allison, Robert. BSBA, U. Fla., 1973. Comml. loan officer Century Bank, St. Petersburg, Fla., 1975-77; asst. v.p. N.Y. Life, Washington, 1977-81; exec. v.p. Heller Real Estate Fin. Co., Chgo., 1981-86; pres., mng. dir., bd dirs. Alex Brown Realty Advisors, Balt., 1986-90; mng. dir., bd. dirs. Alex Brown Kleinwort Benson Realty Advisors, Balt., 1990-93; pres., bd. dirs. Brazos Ptnrs. L.P., Dallas, 1993-99. Pres., COO, bd. dirs. ParagonGroup Inc., 1996-97; CEO, bd. dirs. Meridian Realty Trust VIII, 1997-98; mng. ptnr., bd. dirs. Liberty Ptnrs., 1999-2005; bd. dirs. Fortress Registered Investment Trust, Fortress Investment Fund II, Developers Diversified Realty Corp., Am. Indsl. Properties, 1997-2001, Lone Star Opportunity Fund I, II, III, IV, and V, Brazos Fund, 1996-2005, Global Signal Inc., U.S. Restaurant Properties, 2001-05; mem. exec. com. U. Fla. Ctr. Real Estate Studies; chmn. bd. LNR Holdings, 2005-. Contbr. articles to profl. publs. Bd. dirs. Gator Boosters, U. Fla. Found. Fellow Homer Hoyt Inst. Mem. Nat. Coun. Real Estate Investment Fiduciaries, Pension Real Estate Assn., Assn. Fgn. Investors in Real Estate, Nat. Assn. Real Estate Investment Trusts, Windermere (Fla.) Club. Republican. Home: 12552 Park Ave Windermere FL 34786 Office: Liberty Ptnrs 3001 N Rocky Point Dr E Ste 200 Tampa FL 37607 Office Phone: 813-281-4822. E-mail: RGidel@aol.com.

GIDEON, KENNETH WAYNE, lawyer; b. Lubbock, Tex., July 25, 1946; s. Melton Jean and Mary B. (Lanham) G.; m. Carol Almack, June 2, 1968; children: Christopher Lynn, Kevin Almack, Timothy Charles, Emily Susan BA, Harvard U., 1968; JD, Yale U., 1971. Bar: Tex. 1971, U.S. Tax Ct. 1971, U.S. Ct. Claims 1972, U.S. Supreme Ct. 1981, D.C. 1984. Assoc. Fulbright & Jaworski, Houston, 1971-78, ptnr., 1978-81, Washington, 1983-86; chief counsel IRS, Washington, 1981-83; ptnr. Fried, Frank, Harris, Shriver & Jacobson, Washington, 1986-89, 92-93; asst. sec. tax policy Dept. Treasury, Washington, 1989-92; ptnr. Wilmer, Cutler & Pickering, Washington, 1994-2000, Skadden, Arps, Slate, Meagher & Flom, 2000—. Mem. Spring Valley (Tex.) City Coun., 1978-79. Capt. U.S. Army, 1971-72. Fellow Am. Bar Found., Am. Coll. Tax Counsel (regent 1999-2004); mem. ABA (vice chair govt. rels. 1995-97, mem. coun. 1987-89, sect. taxation, chair, 2004-05), Am. Law Inst., Orgn. Econ. Cooperation and Devel. (Paris, vice chmn. com. on fiscal affairs 1990-92). Office: Skadden Arps Slate Meagher & Flom 1440 New York Ave NW Washington DC 20005-2111

GIDEON-HAWKE, PAMELA LAWRENCE, fine arts small business owner; b. NYC, Aug. 23, 1945; d. Lawrence Ian Verry and Lily S. (Stein) Gordon; m. Jarrett Redstone, June 27, 1964; 1 child, Justin Craig Hawke. Grad. high sch., Manhattan. Owner Gideon Gallery Ltd., L.A. and Las Vegas, 1975—. Pres. San Fernando Valley West Point Parents Club, 1990-93; mem. Rep. Congl. com. on tax reform, Rep. Congl. com. for small bus., State of Calif. Named Friend of Design Industry Designers West Mag., 1987, Bus. Woman of the Yr. for Calif., Rep. Congl. Com.; Knighted, Dame of Grace, Lady Pamela Gideon-Hawke, by order of St. John, Knights of Malta, 1999. Mem. Am. Soc. Interior Designers (publicist), Internat. Soc. Interior Designers (trade liaison 1986-88), Network Exec. Women in Hosp. (pres. Las Vegas chpt., pres. L.A. chpt. 2002-2004), Internat. Furnishings and Design Assn. (pres.), British Am. Business Coun. Avocations: ice-skating, fashion design, writing, cooking, law enforcement. Office: Gideon Gallery Ltd 8121 Lake Hills Dr Las Vegas NV 89128-7089 also: 8748 Melrose Ave Los Angeles CA 90069-5015 Office Phone: 310-657-4194. Personal E-mail: pamgideon@aol.com.

GIEBEL, MIRIAM CATHERINE, librarian, genealogist; b. Williamsburg, Iowa, Oct. 10, 1934; d. John Timothy and Helen Gertrude (Wright) Donahoe; m. William Herbert Giebel, Sept. 30, 1967; 1 child, Sara Ann Giebel Ward. BS, Marquette U., 1956; MLS, Rosary Coll., 1960; cert. in paralegal, Roosevelt U., , 1992; cert. in family history rsch., Brigham Young U., 1992. Asst. acquisitions dept. Marquette U. Libr., Milw., 1956—58; tech. svcs. libr. Chicago Heights Pub. Libr., Ill., 1953—63, ext., reference libr., 1974—99, vol. coord./webmaster, 1999—2000, webmaster, 2000—01, geneal. rschr., 2002—; libr. Little Co. Mary Nursing, Evergreen Park, Ill., 1963—64; asst. libr. hdqrs. ALA, Chgo., 1964—67. Mem.: DAR (chpt. registrar 1994—2001), Fedn. Bus. Profl. Women (state libr. chair 1994—96), Daus. Union Vets. 1861-1865 (historian John Butler chpt. 2004—), Daus. Colonial Wars, Dames Ct. Honor (historian Ill. soc. 2003—), Ill. Cameo Soc. of DAR (state v.p. 1996—99, state pres. 1999—2001), U.S. Daus. of 1812 (chpt. pres. 1991—97, Ill. state registrar 1994—97, Ill. state pres. 1997—99, nat. chair lineage and geneal. records 1997—2000, chpt. registrar 1997—, hon. state pres. life), Soc. Ind. Pioneers (life). Roman Catholic. Avocations: reading, personal genealogical research, Web surfing. Personal E-mail: mirgiebel@aol.com.

GIEBELHAUSEN, ROBIN JOAN, music educator; b. Peoria, Ill., Nov. 16, 1981; d. Richard William and Peggy Ann Giebelhausen. MusB, U. Ill., Champaign/Urbana, 2000—04. Cert. music tchr. Ill. State Bd. Edn., 2004. Asst. dir. Singsations Show Choir Camp, Morton, Ill., 2003—; gen. music tchr., choral dir. Libertyville Schs. Dist. 70, Ill., 2004—. Costume designer (musical theatre) Once Upon a Mattress, West Side Story, Merrily We Roll Along; dir.: (musical theatre) Fame; actor: Cinderella, How to Succeed in Business Without Really Trying. Recipient Warren H. Schuetz Award, U. Ill., 2002; scholar, Morton Area Players, 2000. Mem.: Am. Choral Dir.'s Assn. (assoc.), Music Educator's Nat. Conf. (assoc.). Office: Libertyville Sch Dist 70 1381 W Lake St Libertyville IL 60048 Office Phone: 847-362-9020 4726. Business E-Mail: rgiebelhausen@d70.k12.il.us.

GIEDT, BRUCE ALAN, paper company executive; b. Fargo, N.D., May 7, 1937; s. Alexander and Alice Mildred (Rognaldson) G.; m. Suzanna Tae Abbott, Apr. 30, 1963; children: Alex, Jeffrey, Marybeth; m. 2d, Gail Ann Platt. BA, U. Wash., 1959; MBA, Harvard U., 1965. From regional sales mgr. to v.p. service products bus. units Crown Zellerbach Corp., San Francisco, 1965—; pres. Champion Paper Distbrs., Inc., Riverside, Calif., 1981-87, Pioneer Packaging, Phoenix, 1987—, Woodale, Ill., 1997—. Author: The Future of Commercial Arbitration, 1965. V.p. exec. com. Keep Riverside AHead, econ. devel. com., bd. dirs.; exec. com. mem. Riverside C. of C., devel. com. Served to Capt. USAF, 1959-63. Evans scholar Western Golf Assn., 1967. Mem. Am. Paper Inst. (past com. chmn.), Elks. Republican. Lutheran. Home: 704 Foothills East cir Payson AZ 85541 Office: 730 E University Dr Phoenix AZ 85034-6509

GIEGENGACK, ROBERT, university administrator; b. Nov. 27, 1938; m. Francesca Marshall, May 14, 1967; children: Jonathan, Matthew, Catharine Hae Kyung. BA in Geology, Yale U., 1960, PhD in Geology, 1968; MS in Geology, U. Colo., 1962. Geologist prehist. expdn. to Nubia, Egypt Yale U., 1963-67, acting instr. dept. geology New Haven, 1966-67, asst. in rsch. Peabody Mus. Natural History, 1967-68; asst. prof. geology, landscape arch. and regional planning U. Pa., Phila., 1968-74, assoc. prof., 1974-86, chmn. dept. geology, 1978-85, 1998—, prof., 1987—, co-dir. Inst. for Environ. Studies, 1992-98. Geologo asesor Ministerio de Minas e Hidrocarburos, Venezuela, 1972, Ministerio de Energia y Minas, 1975-76. Contbr. articles to profl. jours. Bd. trustees The Canterbury Sch., New Milford, Conn., 1980-90, 91-95; bd. dirs. Sea Edn. Assn., Woods Hole, Mass., 1984—, A Better chance, Wallingford-Swarthmore (Pa.) Sch. Dist., 1992-95; adv. bd. dept. geol. scis. U. Colo., 1992—; councilor Yellowstone-Bighorn Rsch. Assn., Red Lodge, Mont., 1985—. Recipient Lindback Award for Disting. Tchg., 1979, Ira Abrams Disting. Tchg. award, 1994. Office: University of Pennsylvania Inst Environ Studies Dept Earth Environ Sci 240 S 33rd St Haden Hall Philadelphia PA 19104-3802

GIELOW, KATHLEEN LOUISE, career planning administrator, consultant, special education educator; b. Buffalo, July 8, 1951; d. James Elbert and Billie Elaine Robinson; m. Arthur William Gielow, Sept. 1, 1973; 1 child, James Arthur. BS in Edn., SUCNY, Buffalo, 1973, MS in Edn., 1979. Spl. edn. tchr. Buffalo Pub. Schools, 1974—98, career devel. coord., 1998—; edn1. founds. faculty SUCNY, Buffalo, 2001—, prin. investigator, 2002; entrepreneurship coord. Buffalo Employment and Tng. Ctr., 2002—; owner Queen Creations, 2005—. Profl. devel. provider various ednl. and cmty. orgns., NY, 1997—; profl. conf. workshop presenter, NY, 1998—; conf. workshop presenter Coun. of Gt. City Schs., San Francisco, 1999; careerzone trainer N.Y. State Dept. of Labor, 2000—; cons. Syracuse U., NY, 2001—; career plan trainer N.Y. State Edn. Dept., 2001—; edn. adv. bd. mem. N.Y. State Electric and Gas, Lancaster, 2001—. Editor: (career development best practices collec) Best Practices in Career Development; contbr. nysbest practices in career development Career Development in the Automotive Industry. Vol. Aids Cmty. Svcs., Aids Family Svcs., Buffalo, 1998—; eucharistic min. St. Joseph U. Cath. Ch., Buffalo, 2002—. Recipient Partnership Svc. Award, Sch. to Work Family Resource Ctr., 1998, Career and Tech. Educator Award, Buffalo Career and Tech. Educators Guild, 2002, Vol. of the Yr., AIDS Cmty. Services, 2003, Pathfinders award for forging partnerships between bus. and edn. in western NY, 2004, Entrepreneur award, Nat. Consortium for Entrepreneurship, 2004; grantee School-To-Work (for Buffalo Pub. Schools), NY State Edn. Dept., 1997-1999, Urban/Rural Opportunity Grant (for BPS), US Dept. of Labor, 1998-2003, Youth Entrepreneurship Matching Grant, Kidsway, Inc., 2000, Workforce Devel. Entrepreneurship Grant, Workforce Investment Bd. of Erie County, 2002, Tech Prep Planning Grant (for BPS), NY State Edn. Dept., 2002-2003, Cornell Workforce Devel. grantee, Cornell U., 2004. Mem.: Assn. for Career and Tech. Educators Adminstrs. (licentiate), Nat. Educators Assn. (licentiate), Buffalo Tchrs. Fedn. (licentiate). Roman Catholic. Avocations: scrapbooking, travel, reading, musical theater. Home: 300 Hamilton Blvd Kenmore NY 14217-1811 Office: Buffalo Pub Schs 2201 City Hall 65 Niagara Sq Buffalo NY 14202 Office Phone: 716-816-3656. Personal E-mail: klg7851@aol.com. E-mail: kgielow@buffalo.k12.ny.us.

GIERAS, JACEK FRANCISZEK, engineering educator, research scientist; b. Maleniec, Voivodship Piotrkow Tryb, Poland, Apr. 2, 1947; s. Stanislaw Gieras and Zofia Rychlewska-Gieras; m. Janina Omilianczyk, Sept. 25, 1975; children: Izabella Anna, Karolina Maria, Michael Benjamin. MSEE, Tech. U., Lodz, 1971; PhD, Tech. U., Poznan, Poland, 1975, DSc, 1980. Project engr. Factory of Loudspeakers Tonsil, Wrzesnia, Poland, 1971; lectr. Tech. U. Poznan, 1971-73, sr. lectr., 1973-75, asst. prof., 1975-77, Acad. Technology and Agr., Bydgoszcz, Poland, 1977-81, assoc. prof., dean, 1981-83, assoc. prof., head of dept., 1985-87, prof., 1987—. Vis. assoc. prof. Queen's U., Kingston, Ont., Can., 1983-85; prof. U. Cape Town, 1989-98; vis. prof. endowed chair in transp. sys. engring. U. Tokyo, 1996; guest prof. Chungbuk Nat. U., Korea, 1996-97; scientist United Technologies Rsch. Ctr., East Hartford, Conn., 1998—. Author: Special Purpose Electric Machines, 1983, Linear Induction Motors, 1990, Linear Induction Drives, 1994; author: (with M. Dabrowski) Induction Machines with Solid Rotors, 1977; author: (with W.H. Middendorf and R.H. Engelmann eds.) Handbook of Electric Motors, 1995, 2d edit., 2004; author: (with M. Wing) Permanent Magnet Motor Technology: Design and Applications, 1996, 2d edit., 2002; author: (with Z. Piech) Linear Synchronous Motor, 1999; author: (with R. Wang and M. Kamper) Axial Flux Permanent Magnet Machines, 2004; author: (with J. Lai and C. Wang) Noise of Polyphase Electric Motors, 2005; contbr. articles to profl. jours. Recipient Silver medal Polish Assn. of Elec. Engring., Poland, 1979; fellow Polish Ministry of Edn., 1976, 81, NSERC of Can., 1983, Italian Ministry of Sci. and Tech. Rsch., 1994, Merit awards U. Cape Town, 1995, 96, 97, 98. Fellow N.Y. Acad. Scis., IEEE; mem. Internat. Acad. Electrotech. Scis. Roman Catholic. Avocations: railways, music, overseas travel, home improvement. Address: United Tech Rsch Ctr Mail Stop 129-15 411 Silver Ln Hartford CT 06118-1127 also: Univ Cape Town Dept Elec Engring Rondebosch 7700 South Africa Office Phone: 860-610-7050. Personal E-mail: jgieras@cox.net. Business E-Mail: gierasjf@utrc.utc.com.

GIERER, VINCENT A., JR., tobacco and wine holding company executive; b. NYC, Oct. 21, 1947; s. Vincent A. Sr. and Isabel (McEwen) G.; m. Josephine Lindenmayer; children: Gregory, Vincent, Beth. BBA, Iona Coll., 1969. CPA, N.Y. Audit supr. Ernst & Whinney, White Plains, N.Y., 1971-77; dir. fin. reporting U.S. Tobacco Inc., Greenwich, Conn., 1978-83, controller, 1983-86, sr. v.p., chief fin. officer, 1986-88, exec. v.p., chief fin. officer, 1988-90, pres., chief operating officer, 1990-93; chmn., CEO U.S. Tobacco, Inc., Greenwich, Conn., 1993—; also bd. dirs. U.S. Tobacco Inc., Greenwich, Conn. Pres., UST Inc. Mem. Wilton (Conn.) Newcomers; mgr. Little League, Wilton. Served with U.S. Army, 1969-71, Vietnam. Mem. Am. Inst. CPA's, Am. Mgmt. Assn., Fin. Execs. Inst. Roman Catholic. Avocations: golf, gardening. Office: UST Inc 100 W Putnam Ave Greenwich CT 06830-5316*

GIESBRECHT, F. BRUCE, entertainment company executive; Founder, pres. RamSoft, Inc.; v.p. corp. info. systems, chief info. officer Hollywood Entertainment Corp., Wilsonville, Oreg., 1993—96, sr. v.p. product mgmt., 1996—98, sr. v.p. strategic planning, 1998—2000, exec. v.p. bus. devel., 2000—03, pres., chief operating officer, dir., 2004—, CEO, 2005—. Bd. dirs. Video Software Dealers Assn. Office: Hollywood Entertainment Corp 9275 W Peyton Ln Wilsonville OR 97070*

GIESBRECHT, MARTIN GERHARD, retired economics professor, musician; b. Newark, Aug. 25, 1933; s. Theodore Gerhard and Martha Margarete (Thurm) G.; m. Patricia Maxine Berlin, July 4, 1957 (dec. Sept. 2000); children: Lisa, Martin F., Theodore K. BA, Rutgers U., 1955; Dr. Oec. Publ., U. Munich, 1958; diploma internat. bus., German-Am. C. of C., 1991. Asst. prof. econs. Wilmington (Ohio) Coll., 1958-63, assoc. prof. econs., 1963-75, prof. econs., 1975-87, No. Ky. U., Highland Heights, 1987—98, prof. emeritus, 1998—. Bd. dirs. Econs. Assocs., Villa Hills, Ky.; mem. spkrs. bur. WMKV-FM, Cin., 2002—; econ. commentator WNKU, 1989—, WMKV, 1997—; cons. No. Ky. U. Met. Edn. and Tng. Svcs., 2003—. Author: The Evolution of Economic Society, 1972, Using Economics, 1976, Space Settlements, 1977, The Wealth of People, 1978, A Guide to Everyday Economic Statistics, 1990, 6th edit., 2003, A Guide to Everyday Economic Thinking, 1997. Chmn. Ohioans for the Merit Selection of Judges, Clinton County, 1979; mem. Cin. Silvers Jazz Quartet, 1995-, Over-the-Hill Gang, 1987-95, Bath House Five, 1958-89, The New Look Jazz Band, 1960-89, Riverboat Ramblers, 1970-74. Fellow Ford Found., Ind. U., 1964, Gen. Electric Found., U. Chgo., 1966, NSF, Miami U., 1971, NASA-Am. Soc. Engring. Edn., Stanford U., 1975; Danforth Found. assoc. Wilmington Coll., 1969-82; recipient award Am. Heart Assn., Clinton County, 1977, Excellence award Soc. Profl. Journalists, 1993, award of distinction The Communicator, 2001. Mem. Am. Econs. Assn., Ohioana Libr. Assn., Cin. Musicians Assn., Ea. Econ. Assn., Midwest Econ. Assn., Ky. Econ. Assn. (trustee 1989-92, 96—), Ohio Assn. Economists (pres. 1977-78), Ohio Acad. Sci., Amyotrophic Lateral Sclerosis Assn. (bd. dirs. Ky. chpt. 2001—), Am. Fedn. Musicians. Avocation: jazz clarinetist. Home: 2501 Kingston Ct Villa Hills KY 41017-3760

GIESE, ROBERT JAMES, minister; b. Eau Claire, Wis., Apr. 7, 1950; s. Walter H. and Doris B. (Kuhn) G.; m. Jo Ann P. Zutz, June 19, 1971; 1 child, Rachel. BS in Zoology, U. Wis., 1972; MDiv, Christ Sem.-Seminex, St. Louis, 1978; D Ministry in Pastoral Care and Counseling, Luth. Sch. Theology, Chgo., 1990. Ordained to ministry Evang. Luth. Ch. Am., 1979. Min. Christian Ministry in Nat. Pks., NYC, 1974-77; chaplain Bear Creek Boys Ranch, Lodi, Calif., 1978-79; pastor Trinity Luth. Ch., Rolling Meadows, Ill., 1979—. Exec. cons. Stephen Ministries, St. Louis, 1974-82; sec. Chgo.-Milw. Conf. Evang. Luth. Ch. Am., Chgo., 1983-85, v.p., 1985-86; youth adv. Luth. Social Svc., Chgo., 1987-88. Contbr. articles to profl. jour. Bd. dir. The Bridge Youth Svc., Palatine, Ill., 1983-87; pres., bd. dir. Racetrack Ministries, Arlington Heights, Ill., 1990-94, 2000—, v.p., 1994-2000; dean N.W. Conf. Chgo. Metro Synod ELCA, 1992-96, mem. nominating com. 1999-2001; mem. steering com. Rolling Meadows Tomorrow, 1995-99; mem. Rolling Meadows Bd. Ethics, 1997—2002, mem. sr. citizens' com., 1999—2002, mem. sr. housing com., 2003—. Mem. AACC, Racetrack Coalition. Home: 3203 Meadow Dr Rolling Meadows IL 60008-2728 Office: Trinity Luth Ch 3201 Meadow Dr Rolling Meadows IL 60008-2798 Office Phone: 847-398-7122. Personal E-mail: rjgiese@msn.com. *I believe that the more I am able to know and accept myself for who I am as God knows and accepts me for who I am through Christ, the more I will be enabled to know and accept those with whom I am called to minister.*

GIESE, WILLIAM HERBERT, tax accountant; b. Boston, Jan. 19, 1944; s. Robert Ewald and Harriet (Blaney) G.; m. Elaine Rabe, May 26, 1973; children: Amy Theiss, Katherine Clark, Lauren Stearns. BA, Amherst Coll., 1966; MBA, U. Pa., 1968. CPA. Staff acct. Price Waterhouse, Phila., 1968-70, sr. acct., 1970-73, mgr., 1973-79, ptnr., 1979-95; pres. William H. Giese, Ltd., Ardmore, Pa., 1995-97, Tax Counselors of Bryn Mawr, Inc., Pa., 1997-2000; ptnr. Tax Counsellors of Bryn Mawr, LLC, 2001—. Spkr. Wharton Tax Conf. Phila., 1988; bd. dirs. Verion, Inc., Exton, Pa. Treas. Dunwoody Home and Village, Newtown Square, Pa., 1988—2000; past pres. North Ardmore Civic Assn., Phila., Squash Racquets Assn., Bala Cynwyd; fin. chmn. U.S. Amateur Golf Tournament, 1989; past treas. U.S. Squash Racquets Assn., Bala Cynwyd; Bd. dirs. Dunwoody Home and Village, Newtown Square, Pa., 1998—2000; bd. dirs. Lankenau Found., Phila., 1990—2001. Mem. AICPA, Pa. Inst. CPA's, Merion Golf Club (Ardmore, Pa.), Merion Cricket Club (Haverford, Pa.), Phila. Racquet Club. Republican. Presbyterian. Avocations: squash, golf, tennis. Home: 133 Edgewood Rd Ardmore PA 19003-2507 Office: 101 S Bryn Mawr Ave Ste 360 Bryn Mawr PA 19010

GIESEN, RICHARD ALLYN, manufacturing executive; b. Evanston, Ill., Oct. 7, 1929; s. Elmer J. and Ethyl (Lillig) G.; m. Jeannine St. Bernard, Jan. 31, 1953; children: Richard Allyn, Laurie J., Mark S. BS, Northwestern U., 1951. Research analyst new bus. and research depts. Glore, Forgan & Co., Chgo., 1951-57; asst. to pres. Gen. Dynamics Corp., N.Y.C., 1957-60, asst. treas., 1960-61, asst. v.p. ops. and contracts, 1961-63; fin. cons. IBM Corp., 1963, exec. asst. to sr. v.p., 1964-65; treas. subs. Sci. Research Assocs., Inc., Chgo., 1965-66, v.p. fin. and adminstrn., 1966-67, exec. v.p., chief operating officer, 1967-68, pres., chief exec. officer, 1968-80; pres., chief exec. officer, chmn. exec. com., dir. Field Enterprises, Inc., Chgo., 1980-83; pres. RLM Investments, 1983-93; chmn., pres., CEO Am. Appraisal Assocs., Inc., 1984-93; chmn. Continental Pkg. Solutions, Chgo., 1988—; chmn., CEO Continere Corp., 1988—. Bd. trustees Asia House Funds, 1994-98. Bd. trustees Asia House Fund, 1994-98; mem. bus. adv. coun. Chgo. Urban League, 1968-83; prin. Chgo. United, 1980-83; dir. GATX, Inc., 1982-2000, JWT Group, 1980-1985; mem. adv. coun. Technol. Inst., Northwestern U.; mem. pres.'s coun. Nat. Coll. Edn., Evanston, Ill., 1977-86; bd. dirs. Am. Cancer Soc.; mem. adv. coun. J.L. Kellogg Grad. Sch. Mgmt., Northwestern U.; dir. Jr. Achievement Chgo., 1993-2002; trustee Chgo. Edn. TV Assn., 1975-81, Inst. Internat. Edn., 1971—, chmn. midwest adv. bd., 1997-2003. Mem. Chief Execs. Orgn., Webhannet Golf Club, Chgo. Club, Shoreacres Club (Lake Bluff, Ill.), Alpha Tau Omega, Beta Gamma Sigma. Office: Continental Pkg Solutions Inc 230 W Monroe Chicago IL 60606 Fax: 312-666-7501. E-mail: rag@continentalpackagingsolutions.com.

GIESEY, RALPH EDWIN, retired historian; b. Detroit, Jan. 7, 1923; s. William Carl and Mary Thomas Giesey. AB, Wayne U., Detroit, 1943, MA, 1947; PhD, U. Calif., Berkeley, 1954. Asst. Inst. for Advanced Study, Princeton, NJ, 1953—55; instr. Vassar Coll., Poughkeepsie, NY, 1955—56, U. Wash., Seattle, 1956—59; assoc. prof. U. Minn., Mpls., 1959—66; prof. U. Iowa, Iowa City, 1966—88. Vis. prof. Folger Libr., Washington, 1972; dir. d'études Ecole des Hautes Etudes en Scis. Sociales, Paris, 1985. Author: The Royal Funeral Ceremony in Renaissance France, 1960, The Juristic Basis of Dynastic Right to the French Throne, 1961, If Not, Not, The Oath of the Aragonese and the Legendary Laws of Sobrarbe, 1968, Francogallia by François Hotman, 1972, Cérémonial et puissance souveraine: France, XVe-XVII siècles, 1987, Rulership in France, 15th-17th Centuries, 2004; editor: Selected Studies by Ernst H. Kantorowicz. Lt. j.g. USN, 1943—46, PTO. Fellow, Am. Coun. Learned Socs., 1952—53, Am. Numis. Soc., 1954, Inst. for Advanced Study, 1964—65, 1975—76, Guggenheim Found., 1970, NEH, 1974—75; grantee, Am. Coun. Learned Socs., 1960, Rockefeller Found., 1962, Am. Philos. Soc., 1966; Fulbright fellow, 1951—52. Democrat.

GIESKES, HANS, information services and publishing executive; married; 3 children. BSBA, Netherlands Inst. Mktg. V.p. sales Elsevier Sci., Amsterdam, Netherlands, 1979—85; CEO Elsevier Sci. U.K., London, 1985—91, Bonaventura, Netherlands, 1992—96; pres., CEO LEXIS-NEXIS Group, Miamisburg, Ohio, 1997—2000; pres. Monster.com, Maynard, Mass., 2000—02; CEO Houghton Mifflin Co., Boston, 2002—03. Past pub. Elsevier, Netherlands; past mem. sales, tech. and gen. mgmt. staffs Elsevier Sci.; past vice chmn. legal divsn. LEXIS-NEXIS, Reed Elsevier, vice chmn. European divsn. Avocations: reading non-fiction, modern European history, yachting, gardening, golf, cricket.

GIESY, JOHN PAUL, JR., fisheries and wildlife educator; b. Youngstown, Ohio, Aug. 9, 1948; s. John Paul and Betty Jeane (Auld) G.; m. Susan Elaine Damerell, Sept. 5, 1970; 1 child, Emily Jeane. BS in Biology summa cum laude, Alma Coll., 1970; MS in Limnology, Mich. State U., 1971, PhD in Limnology, 1974. Instr. in biology Alma (Mich.) Coll., 1972; adj. asst. prof. in zoology U. Ga., 1976-80; instr. in biology U. S.C., Aiken, 1976; adj. asst. prof. biology Emory U., Atlanta, 1978-81; adj. asst. prof. environ. engring. U. Fla., 1978-81; adj. asst. prof. fisheries and wildlife Mich. State U., East Lansing, 1980, assoc. prof., 1981-85, prof., 1985-92, Univ. Disting. prof., 1993—, Univ. disting. prof. Vis. prof., chair ecolog. chemistry and geochemistry U. Bayreuth (Fed. Republic Germany), 1987-88, vis. scientist, 1989; vis. scientist Italian Hydrobiolog. Inst., Italian Nat. Rsch. Coun., Pallanza, 1989-90; cons., presenter, lectr. in field; appeared on various TV and radio programs. Editor: Microcosms in Ecological Research, 1980, Sediments: The Toxicity and Chemistry of In-Place Pollutants, 1990; mem. editorial bd. various publs. in field; contbr. articles to profl. publs., chpts. to books. Vol. Boy Scouts Am., 1983— Recipient Agrl. Recognition award Ciba Geigy, 1990, Willard F. Shepard award Mich. Water Pollution Control Assn., 1992, Voilenweider medal Can. Govt., 1994; NSF fellow, 1969, 70, Fulbright fellow, 1987-88. Mem. AAAS, ASME, ASTM, Am. Chem. Soc., Internat. Assn. Gt. Lakes Rsch. (bd. dirs. 1992—), Internat. Assn. Water Rsch., Internat. Humic Substances Soc., Internat. Soc. for Study of Xenobiotics, Internat. Soc. Ecotoxicology and Environ. Safety, Internat. Soc. Theoretical and Applied Limnology, Am. Fisheries Soc., Am. Inst. Biol. Scis., Am. Inst. Fisheries Rsch. Biologists, Am. Soc. Zoologists, Soc. Environ. Geochemistry and Health, Soc. Environ. Toxicology and Chemistry (pres. 1990, Founder's award 1995), Sigma Xi (pres. 1993, Meritorious Rsch. award). Office: Mich State U 13 Natural Resources East Lansing MI 48824-1222

GIFFEN, DANIEL HARRIS, lawyer, educator; b. Zanesville, Ohio, Feb. 11, 1938; s. Harris MacArtor and Anne Louise (Crawford) G.; m. Jane Louise Cayford, Nov. 23, 1963 (div. 1970); children: Sarah Louise, Thomas Harris; m. Linda Eastin, Aug. 19, 1972. AB, Coll. of William and Mary, 1960; MA, U. Pa., 1962, MA, 1967; testamur, U. Exeter, Eng., 1971; JD, Case Western Res. U., 1973. Bar: Ohio 1973. Corp. asst. U. Pa. Lippincott Libr., Phila., 1961-63; assoc. curator La. State Mus., New Orleans, 1963-64; sec. N.H. Hist. Soc., Concord, 1964-69; asst. dir. Syracuse (N.Y.) U. Arents Rsch. Libr., 1969-70; pvt. practice Cleve., 1973-99; asst. prof. law Cleve. State U., 1976-79; asst. prof. Kent (Ohio) State U., 1980-98, prof. emeritus, 1998—. Editor Walter Drane Co., Cleve., 1974-76; lectr. Monadnock C.C., Peterborough, N.H., 1968-69; vis. scholar London Libr., 1991-92. Author: Adventures in Vermont, 1969, Adventures in Maine, 1969, New Hampshire Colony, 1970; contbr. articles to profl. jours. Hon. life mem. Pres.'s Coun., Coll. William and Mary, 1980. Recipient Kenyon English Prize scholarship, 1956; fellow Heritage Found., 1959-60, Nat. Trust, 1959-61, 67, 73. Fellow Saltire Soc. (Scotland); mem. ABA, Ohio Bar Assn., Am. Soc. Interior Design, Am. Assn. Mus., Am. Assn. State and Local Historians, Nat. Trust, Soc. Archtl. Historians, Masons, Shriners. Episcopalian. Home: 6058 Mad River Rd Centerville OH 45459-1508

GIFFIN, GORDON D., former ambassador, lawyer; b. Springfield, Mass. m. Patti Alfred; 1 child, Kelley. BA, Duke U., 1971; JD, Emory U., 1974. Bar: Ga. 1974, DC 1979. Dir. legis. affairs, chief counsel to Senator Sam Nunn U.S. Senate, 1974-79; assoc. Hansell and Post, Atlanta, 1979-86; sr. ptnr. Long, Aldridge & Norman, Atlanta and Washington, until 1997; amb. to Can., Am. Embassy, Ottawa, Canada, 1997—2001; ptnr., co-chmn. pub. policy & regulatory affairs practice McKenna, Long & Aldridge LLP, Atlanta & Washington, 2001—. Former adj. prof. law Emory U. Sch. Law, Atlanta; bd. dirs. Overseas Pvt. Investment Corp., 1993-97. Treas. Senator Sam Nunn Campaign Com., 20 yrs.; with Senator Nunn and Gov. Clinton founder Dem. Leadership Coun., 1984, mem. bd., 1984-96; mem. com. to host Dem. Nat. Conv., Atlanta, 1988, chmn. site selection com., Chgo., 1996, gen. counsel, 1992, 96; presdl. elector, Ga., 1992, 96; chmn. Ga. Clinton primary campaign, 1992, Clinton-Gore Gen. Election Campaign, 1992; dep. dir. pers. White House Transition Team, 1992; sr. advisor on south, also chmn. Clinton-Gore effort in Ga., Clinton Reelection Campaign, 1996; active Atlanta Olympic Games Com., 1996; former mem. bd. dirs. Ga. C. of C., Trees Atlanta Found., Atlanta Hist. Soc., Atlanta Ballet. Named One of 100 Most Influential Georgians, Ga. Trend mag., 3 times. Democrat. Office: McKenna Long & Aldridge 1900 KSt NW Washington DC 20006-1108 Office Phone: 202-496-7500.*

GIFFIN, MARGARET ETHEL (PEGGY GIFFIN), management consultant; b. Cleve., Aug. 27, 1949; d. Arch Kenneth and Jeanne (Eggleton) G.; m. Robert Alan Wyman, Aug. 20, 1988; 1 child, Samantha Jean. BA in Psychology, U. Pacific, Stockton, Calif., 1971; MA in Psychology, Calif. State U., Long Beach, 1973; PhD in Quantitative Psychology, U. So. Calif., 1984. Psychometrician Auto Club So. Calif., L.A., 1973-74; cons. Psychol. Svcs., Inc., Glendale, Calif., 1975-76, mgr., 1977-78, dir., 1979-94; rschr. Social Sci. Rsch. Inst., U. So. Calif., L.A., 1981; dir. Giffin Consulting Svcs., L.A., 1994—. Instr. Calif. State U., Long Beach, Long Beach, 1989—90; tech. adv. com. on testing Calif. Fair Employment and Housing Commn., 1974—80, steering com., 1978—80; pres. Pers. Testing Coun. So. Calif., 1980, exec. dir., 82, 88, bd. dirs., 1980—92. Mem. APA, Soc. Indsl. Organizational Psychology. Home and Office: 260 S Highland Ave Los Angeles CA 90036-3027 Office Phone: 323-939-0246. E-mail: peggygiffin@cs.com.

GIFFIN, MARJIE G., writer; b. Columbia City, Ind., Nov. 22, 1951; d. Robert Edwards and Harriett (Brown) Gates; m. Kenneth Neal Giffin, May 17, 1975; children: Christopher, Matthew, Elisabeth Anne. AB in Lit. magna cum laude, Ind. U., 1974; MA in Lit., Butler U., 1982. Cert. tchr., Ind., 1974, gifted and talented edn., 2000. Advt. writer Curtis Pub. Co., Indpls., 1974-75; pub. rels. dir. Dept. Parks and Recreation, Indpls., 1975-76; comms. dir. Acad. Pub. Svc., Indpls., 1976-78; editor Wayne Twp. Sch. Dist., Indpls., 1983-88; assoc. faculty Ind. U./Purdue U., Indpls., 1992-94; freelance writer Indpls., 1978—; rschr./ writer W.B. Brown historical Project, 2001. Mem. grad. sch. arts/scis. alumni bd. Ind. U., 1976-78; bd. dirs. Indpls. Pub. Libr., 1985-86; adv. bd. Ind. U. arts/scis. newsletter, 1977-78. Author: Water Runs Downhill, 1981, If Tables Could Talk, 1988, A Walk Through Time, 1989. Indpls. Zoo, Indpls. Children's Mus.; bd. dirs. Marion County Welfare Bd., 1981-82, Sycamore Sch. Assn., 1998-2001. Honoree Girls, Inc., Indpls. Forum Series, 1991. Honoree Ind. Authors Day, 1990. Mem. Ind. Hist. Soc., Hist. Landmarks found., Acad. Am. Poets, Kappa Alpha Theta. Republican. Roman Catholic. Avocations: water sports, poetry, reading, history, writing. E-mail: mggiffin@aol.com.

GIFFIN, WALTER CHARLES, retired industrial engineer, educator, consultant; b. Walhonding, Ohio, Apr. 22, 1936; s. Charles Maurice and Florence Ruth (Davis) G.; m. Beverly Ann Neff, Sept. 1, 1956; children— Steven, Rebecca B. Indsl. Engring., MS, Ohio State U., 1960, PhD, 1964. Registered profl. engr., Ohio. Research engr. Gen. Motors Research Labs., Warren, Mich., 1960-61; research assoc. systems research group Ohio State U., Columbus, 1961-62, instr. indsl. and systems engring., 1962-64, asst. prof., 1964-68, assoc. prof., 1968-71, prof., 1971-87, prof. emeritus, 1987—; prof. engring. U. So. Colo., Pueblo, 1987-92; ret., 1992—. Cons. in field Author: Introduction to Operations Engineering, 1971; Transform Techniques for Probability Modeling, 1975; Queueing: Basic Theory and Applications, 1978 NASA Research grantee, 1978-83 Mem.: Expt. Aircraft Assn. (Oshkosh, Wis. and Pueblo, Colo.). Home: 419 Fairway S Dr W Pueblo CO 81007

GIFFORD, CARLA J., education educator; b. Spangler, Pennsyvania, July 19, 1956; d. William Carlton and Joann F. (Farrell) Rummel; m. Steven E. Gifford, Jan. 18, 1995; children: Rebecca Lynn, Mark Daniel. BS edn., Peru St. Coll., Peru, NE., 1995; libr. media specialist, U. Nebr., Omaha, Nebr., 1996—97. Cert. K-12 IA. and NE., 1995. Libr. media specialist St. James Seton Sch., Omaha, 1995—96, George Little Rock Sch., George, Iowa, 1997—2000; instr. N.W. IA. Cmty. Coll., Sheldon, Iowa, 1998—. Web devel. cons. Her Realm, Melvin, Iowa, 2000—01. Mem. Women's Aux. Am. Legion, Melvin, Iowa. Mem.: Women's Aux. Am. Legion (pres.), NEA. Avocations: violinist, pianist, tutoring children, tng. horses. Home: 5944 250th St Melvin IA 51350 Office: NW IA Cmty Coll Bus Divsn 603 W Park St Sheldon IA 51201-1060 Business E-Mail: GiffFylz@iowatelecom.net.

GIFFORD, CHARLES K., banker; b. Providence, Nov. 8, 1942; s. Clarence H. and Priscilla G.; m. Anne Gifford, Oct. 3, 1964; children: Ramsay, Charles, John, Jessica BA, Princeton U., 1964. Joined First Nat. Bank, Boston, 1966—67, loan officer, 1967—70, asst. v.p., 1970—73, v.p., 1973—78, first v.p., 1978, sr. v.p., 1979—81, exec. v.p., 1981—84, group exec. corp. banking group, 1984—87; vice chmn. Bank of Boston Corp. and First Nat. Bank of Boston (sub. of Bank of Boston), 1987—89, pres., 1989—95, chmn., CEO, 1995—99; pres., COO BankBoston and Fleet Fin. Group (merged), 1999—2001, CEO, 2001—02, chmn., 2002—04; chmn. emeritus Bank of Am., Boston, 2004—, bd. dirs., 2004—. Dir. NSTAR Corp. Bd. mem. Northeastern U., Boston Symphony Orchestra, WGBH Pub. Broadcasting, Jr. Achievement, Dana Farber Cancer Inst., Dana Farber/Ptnrs. Cancer Care, Greater Boston C. of C.; bd. dirs. Boston Pvt. Ind. Coun., Assn. Res. City Bankers; founding chmn. Success By 6, United Way, 1994-98; chmn. Boston Plan for Excellence in Pub. Schs. Mem. Greater Boston C. of C. (chmn.). Office: Bank of America 100 Federal St Boston MA 02110-2003

GIFFORD, DALE L., human resources executive; b. May 30, 1950; BA, U. Wis., 1971. With Hewitt Assocs. LLC, Lincolnshire, Ill., 1972—, mgr. Southwest and Midwest U.S. Market Groups, CEO, 1992—, chmn., 2002—. Fellow: Soc. Actuaries; mem.: Am. Acad. Actuaries. Office: Hewitt Associates 100 Half Day Rd Lincolnshire IL 60069-3242*

GIFFORD, DONALD ARTHUR, lawyer; b. Derry, N.H., Nov. 21, 1945; s. George Donald and Bertha Margaret (Gibbs) G.; m. Sandra Louise Robaldo, July 25, 1964; children: Adriana, Roy, Stacy. BA, U. South Fla., 1967; JD with high honors, Fla. State U., 1970. Bar: Fla. 1970, U.S. Dist. Ct. (mid. dist.) Fla. 1970, U.S. Dist. Ct. (no. dist.) Fla. 1981, U.S. Dist. Ct. (so. dist.) Fla. 1982, U.S. Ct. Appeals (5th cir.) 1975, U.S. Ct. Appeals (11th cir.) 1981. U.S. Supreme Ct. 1980. Assoc. Raymond, Wilson, Karl, Conway & Barr, Daytona Beach, Fla., 1972; law clk. U.S. Dist. Ct. (mid. dist.) Fla., Tampa, 1972-73; with Shackelford, Farrior, Stallings & Evans, P.A., Tampa, 1973—. Chair divsn. allocations United Way Greater Tampa, 1987-94, treas., 1991-93, pres., 1994-96; mem., trustee U.S. Fla. Found., 1986—, New Coll. Found., 1990-93. Fellow ABA (ho. of dels 1991-92), Am. Judicature Soc., Am. Bar Found.; mem. Fed. Bar Assn., Fla. Bar (bd. govs. 1989-95, mem. exec. com. 1993-94, chair legis. com. 1993-94, legis. com. 1995-98, mem. bd. legal specialization and edn.), Fla. Bar Found. (bd. dirs. 1996—, chair AOJ com.), Hillsborough County Bar Assn. (bd. dirs. 1981-90, pres. 1988-89), U. South Fla. Nat. Alumni Assn. (pres. 1976, bd. dirs. 1970-92, Outstanding Alumnus 1976, Outstanding Svc. award 1996), Fla. State U. Coll. Law Alumni Assn. (bd. dirs. 1982-96, pres. 1987-88), Greater Tampa C. of C. (gen. counsel, mem. exec. com., bd. govs.), Fla. State U. Alumni Assn. (bd. dirs. 1987—, chmn. 1992-94), F.L.A. Inc. (bd. dirs. 1995-98), Outback Bowl (mem. team rels. com. 1986-95), Tiger Bay Club (bd. dirs. 1988-92). Office: Shackleford Farrior Stallings & Evans PA PO Box 3324 Tampa FL 33601-3324

GIFFORD, DONALD GEORGE, dean, law educator; b. Medina, Ohio, July 26, 1952; s. George W. and Ruth Ann (Reed) G.; m. Nancy Ray Aten, Mar. 24, 1973; children: Rebecca, Caroline. BA, Wooster Coll., 1973; JD, Harvard U., 1976. Bar: Ohio 1976, Fla. 1984. Assoc. Gallagher, Sharp, Fulton, Norman & Mollison, Cleve., 1976-77; ptnr. Noble & Gifford, Millersburg, Ohio, 1977-79; asst. prof. law U. Toledo, 1979-82, assoc. prof. law, 1982-84; prof. U. Fla., Gainsville, 1984-89; assoc. dir. academic task force for rev. ins. and tort systems Fla. Gov.'s Office, Gainsville, 1986-88; dean, prof. law W.Va. U., Morgantown, 1989-92; prof. law U. Md., Balt., 1992—, dean, 1992-99. Contbr. articles to profl. jours.; author 3 books. Chmn. Gov.'s Lead Paint Poisoning Commn., Md., 1992-94; vice chair Md. Alt. Dispute Resolution Task Force, 1997-2000. Mem. Ohio Bar Assn., The Fla. Bar, Am. Law Inst. Office: U Maryland Sch Law 500 W Baltimore St Baltimore MD 21201-1602 Office Phone: 410-706-1843. E-mail: dgifford@law.umaryland.edu.

GIFFORD, FRANKLIN ANDREW, JR., meteorologist, consultant; b. Union City, N.J., May 7, 1922; s. F.A. and Hazel (Sheehan) G.; m. Eleanor Mary Frith, Aug. 7, 1943; children: Michael J., Robert K. BS, NYU, 1947; MS, Pa. State U., 1954, PhD, 1955. Area chief meteorologist Northwest Airlines, N.Y.C., 1945-50; rsch. meteorologist U.S. Weather Bur. (NOAA), Washington, 1950-55; dir. Atmospheric Turbulence Diffusion Lab. NOAA, Oak Ridge, Tenn., 1955-80. Cons. Los Alamos Nat. Lab., 1980—, U.S. NRC Adv. Com. on Reactor Safety, Washington, 1958-82; cons. Internat. Atomic Energy Agy., Vienna, 1966-82; mem. U.S.-USSR Bilateral Working Group on Air Pollution, 1974-75. Author: Meteorology and Atomic Energy, 1968; contbr. over 140 articles to profl. jours. Capt. USAF, 1943-45, ETO. Recipient Gold medal U.S. Dept. Commerce, 1963. Fellow AAAS, Am. Meteorol. Soc. (Contbn. to Applied Meteorology award 1990). Home: 708 Potomac Knolls Dr Mc Lean VA 22102-1422 E-mail: fagifford@aol.com.

GIFFORD, GAYLE LYNN, consultant; b. Hartford, Conn., Dec. 15, 1953; d. Russell William Gifford and Elsie (George) Forster; m. Jonathan Walker Howard, June 18, 1983; children: Emma G., Alexander G., Samuel G. AB magna cum laude, Clark U., 1975; MS mgmt., Antioch New England Grad. Sch., 1999. ACFRE (Advanced Cert. Fund Raising Exec.). Claims rep. Social Security Adminstrn., Providence, 1976-83; dir. devel. and comm. Plan Internat. USA, Warwick, R.I., 1983-90; dep. dir. Save the Bay, Providence, 1990-95. City yr. RI, Providence, 1995-96, pres. Cause & Effect Inc., Providence, 1996—. Founder, bd. dirs. R.I. Moblzn. for Survival, 1977-82, Recap, 1987-90; pres. Environ. Fedn. New Eng., 1992-94; mem. Women for Non-Nuclear Future, Providence, 1980-90, pres. edn. fund, 1988-90; bd. dirs. Am. Friends Svc. Com., Providence, 1977-8; bd. dirs. R.I. Women's Health Collective, 1995-96, R.I. Coun. Humanities, 2002—. Mem. Assn.of Fund-raising Profl., Internat. Assn. for Public Participation, Assn. of Fundraising Profl. (bd. dirs. R.I. chpt., 1997-2003, R.I. com. humanities 2002—), Phi Beta Kappa Democrat. Office: Cause and Effect Inc 178 9th St Providence RI 02906-2931

GIFFORD, GERALD FREDERIC, retired science educator; b. Chanute, Kans., Oct. 24, 1939; s. Gerald Leo and Marion Lou (Browne) Gifford; m. Cinda Jean Lowman, June 26, 1982. Student, Kans. U., 1957-60; BS in Range Mgmt., Utah State U., 1962, MS in Watershed Mgmt., 1964, PhD in Watershed Sci., 1968. Asst. prof. watershed sci. Utah State U., Logan, 1967-72, assoc. prof., 1972-80, prof., 1980-84, chmn. watershed sci. unit, 1967-84, dir. Inst. Land Reclamation, 1982-84; head range, wildlife and forestry U. Nev., Reno, 1984-92, chmn. environ. and resource sci. dept., 1992—94, prof. hydrology and natural resource mgmt., 1994—2000, ret., 2000. Exch. scientist NSF, Canberra, Australia, 1974; cons. in field. Author: (book) Rangeland Hydrology, 1981; assoc. editor: Jour. Range Mgmt., 1982—87, 1991—95, Arid Soil Rsch. and Rehab., 1985—90; contbr. scientific papers to profl. pubs. Mem.: Soil and Water Conservation Soc., Am. Water Resources Assn. Avocations: racquetball, antiques, garage sales. Home: 3880 Squaw Valley Cir Reno NV 89509-5663 Office Phone: 775-826-7932. Personal E-mail: fredandcinda@sbcglobal.net.

GIFFORD, JOHN F., computer company executive; Founded AMD, Sunnyvale, Calif., 1969, Maxim Integrated Products, Sunnyvale, 1983, chmn., pres., CEO, 1992—. Named one of Am.'s Most Powerful People, Forbes mag. Office: Maxim Integrated Products 120 San Gabriel Dr Sunnyvale CA 94086-5150

GIFFORD, JOHN IRVING, retired agricultural equipment company executive; b. Lockport, N.Y., July 23, 1930; s. John Jacob and Carrie (McAdam) G.; m. Sara Jane Bauer, Jan. 28, 1955; children: John Hutchins, James Scott. BS, Purdue U., 1952, MS, 1956. Sales trainee Am. Nat. Foods, Inc., L.A., 1956; economist Deere & Co., Moline, Ill., 1956-65, pers. adminstr., 1965-70, mgr. data svcs., 1970-96; stats. cons. to cos. and trade assns., 1996—. Bd. dirs., Rock Island (Ill.) sect. Easter Seal Found., 1981-87; v.p. coun., St. John Luth. Ch., Rock Island, 1981-82; pres., Rock Island Little League, 1981-82; v.p. Babe Ruth Baseball, Rock Island, 1983; mem. agrl. census adv. com. U.S. Dept. Commerce, 1997-98; mem. adv. com. stats. USDA, 1999-2004. 1st lt. U.S. Army, 1952-54, Korea. Recipient Leadership recognition Equipment Mfrs. Inst. Mem. Nat. Assn. Bus. Econs., Equipment Mfrs. Assn., Farm and Indsl. Equipment Inst., Constrn. Industry Mfrs. Assn., Outdoor Power Equipment Inst., Engine Mfrs. Assn., Internat. Farm Tractor Com., Internat. Harvesting Equipment Com. (chmn. statistics com. 1994-95), Rock Island (Ill.) Noon Kiwanis Club. Avocations: reading, golf. Office Phone: 309-788-5141. E-mail: gifford@revealed.net.

GIFFORD, JONATHAN LEWIS, finance educator; b. Pitts., July 3, 1954; s. Richard Louis and Ardelle (S.) Gifford. BSCE, Carnegie Mellon U., 1976; MSCE, U. Calif., Berkeley, 1979, PhD in Civil. Engring., 1983. Jr. engr. Kaiser Engrs., Oakland, Calif., 1976-77; intern U.S. OMB, Washington, 1981, Congl. Budget Office, Washington, 1982; cons. Office Tech. Assessment, U.S. Congress, 1982, 83; asst. prof. pub. mgmt. and policy Sch. Urban and Pub. Affairs, Carnegie-Mellon U., Pitts., 1983-88; prof. pub. mgmt. and policy George Mason U., Fairfax, Va., 1988—, dir. Master's in Transp. Policy, Ops., Logistics, 2000—. Cons. to industry and govt., 1985—; vis. assoc. prof. MIT, 1997. Author: Flexible Urban Transportation; assoc. editor: Public Works Management and Policy; mem. editl. adv. bd. Internat. Jour. Transport Mgmt.; script reviewer film Divided Highways; assoc. editor Public Works Management and Policy; contbr. articles to profl. jours. Fenwick fellow, 1991-92, Carnegie Mellon U. Rsch. awardee, 1985, 84-86, grad. fellow Inst. Transp. Studies, U. Calif., Berkeley, 1981-83. Mem. NRC (chair com. for rev. of U.S. Dept. Transp. Intelligence Transp. Sys. standards program, co-chair com. workshop on developing a regional concept for mng. surface transp. ops.), ASCE, Soc. for History of Tech., Transp. Rsch. Bd. (chair com. on transp. and land devel.), Assn. for Pub. Policy and Mgmt., Intelligent Transp. Soc. Am., Cosmos Club. Office: George Mason Univ Sch Pub Policy MS 3B1 3401 Fairfax Dr Arlington VA 22201 Office Phone: 703-993-2275. Business E-Mail: jgifford@gmu.edu.

GIFFORD, KATHIE LEE, television personality, vocalist; b. Paris, Aug. 16, 1953; d. Aaron Leon and Joan Epstein; m. Paul Johnson, 1976 (div. 1983); m. Frank Gifford, Oct. 18, 1986; children: Cody Newton, Cassidy Erin. Student, Oral Roberts U., Tulsa. Gospel singer; singer $100,000 Name That Tune Quiz Show; co-host Morning Show, 1985-88, LIVE with Regis and Kathie Lee, 1988-2000, spl. corr. The Insider, 2005-; author: The Quiet Riot, 1976, I Can't Believe I Said That, 1992, (with Regis Philbin) Cooking With Regis and Kathie Lee, 1993, Entertaining With Regis and Kathie Lee, 1994, Christmas With Kathie Lee, 1997; marketer clothing collection Kathie Lee for Plaza South; singer (albums): Sentimental, 1993, It's Christmas Time, 1993, Born for You, 2000, A Gentle Grace, 2004; sang Nat. Anthem, Super Bowl, 1995; host, co-writer, co-producer, CBS television special, Kathie Lee...Looking for Christmas, 1994.; co-writer (with David Pomeranz), Under the Bridge (play), 2004, Hurricane Amy, 2005 Office: The Insider Paramount Pictures 5555 Melrose Ave Los Angeles CA 90038 also: William Morris Agy 1325 Ave of Americas New York NY 10019*

GIFFORD, MARILYN JOYCE, emergency physician, consultant; b. Denver, Aug. 3, 1943; m. Leslie Arthur and Dorothy Marianne (Stevens) G.; m. Robert Bruce Caplan (div.); children: Eric Louis Caplan, Brian Matthew Caplan; m. Daniel Patrick McKenna, July 17, 1992. AA, Stephens Coll., Columbia, Mo., 1963; BS, Mich. State U., 1965; MD, Mt. Sinai Sch. Medicine, N.Y.C., 1971. Diplomate Am. Bd. Emergency Medicine. Emergency physician Longmont (Colo.) United Hosp., 1974-80, Boulder (Colo.) Cmty. Hosp., 1976-78; dir. emergency svcs. Meml. Hosp., Colorado Springs, Colo., 1980—. Physician advisor Colorado Springs Fire Dept., 1980—; bd. dirs. Nat. Registry Emergency Med. Technicians, Columbus, Ohio, 1983—. Co-author: Protocols for Prehospital Emergency Medical Care, 1984, Prehospital Emergency Care, 1996. Advisor E-911 Authority Bd., Colorado Springs, 1996—. Lt. USNR, 1971-72. Recipient Kim Langstaff Meml. award for excellence Region IV EMs Coun., 1986, Val. Wolhauer award for physician excellence Emergency Med. Technician Assn. Colo., 1982, Pres.'s Leadership award Nat. Assn. Emergency Med. Technicians, 1983, ACEP contbn. in EMS, 2001. Fellow Am. Coll. Emergency Physicians (chair EMS com. 1979-81, Colo. coun. 1978-85); mem. El Paso County Med. Soc. (pres. 1993-94). Avocation: skiing. Office: Meml Hosp 1400 E Boulder St Colorado Springs CO 80909-5599 Office Phone: 719-365-2000. Personal E-mail: marilyngifford@hotmail.com.

GIFFORD, MARJORIE FITTING, mathematician, educator, consultant; m. Frederick N. Fitting, Feb. 25, 1972 (dec. 1985); m. Forrest W. Gifford, May 28, 1988 (div. 1992). BS in Math., Mich. State U., PhD in Math. Edn., 1968; AM in Math., U. Mich., 1966; postgrad., U. Nev., Las Vegas, 1995—97. Cert. tchr., Mich., Calif. Tchr. math. in secondary schs., Mich., 1954-61; instr. Lawrence Inst. Tech., Southfield, Mich., 1961-68; grad. asst. Mich. State U., East Lansing, 1966-68; prof. emeritus math. and computer sci. San Jose State U., Calif., 1968-92; instr. math. U. Nev., Las Vegas, 1994—95; CEO Metier Cons., Kauai, 2004—. V.p. fin. Metra Instruments, San Jose, 1972—82; pres. Metier, San Jose, 1982—98; cons. San Jose Unified Sch., 1969—71. Author: (software) Math Test Generation, 1983; co-author: (book series) Computer Literacy Series, 1983-85, (book) Introduction to Geometry, 1996. Recipient Dean's award San Jose State U., 1982; J.C. Plant scholar Mich. State U., 1954; fellow NSF fellow, 1965-66, Paul Harris fellow; grantee Fulbright Found., 1985-86. Mem. Am. Math. Soc., Calif. Math. Coun., Rotary, Zeta Tau Alpha. Roman Catholic. Avocations: gardening, rafting, bridge, photography, painting.

GIFFORD, NELSON SAGE, finance company executive; b. Newton, Mass., May 3, 1930; s. Gordon Babcock and Hariette Rose (Dooley) G.; m. Elizabeth B. Brow, Nov. 12, 1955; children: Susan Helen, Ian Christopher, Diane Brow. AB, Tufts Coll., 1952; HHD (hon.), U. Mass., 1989; PhD (hon.), Tufts U., 1996. With Dennison Mfg. Co., Framingham, Mass., 1954-90, mem. acctg. staff, 1954-63, controller, 1964-65, gen. mgr., 1965-67, v.p., 1967-72, pres., 1972-86, chmn., 1986-90; vice chmn. Avery Dennison Corp., Boston, 1990-91; prin. Fleetwing Capital, Boston, 1992—. Bd. dirs. Nypro Inc., Clinton, Mass., MDT Group, Westford, Mass., Doble Engring., Watertown, Mass. Past bd. dirs. New Eng. Colls. Fund, Reed and Barton, Taunton, Mass., John Hancock Fin. Svcs., Boston, J.M. Huber Corp., Edison, N.J., NSTAR, Boston, Avery Dennison, Pasadena, Calif.; corp. mem. Newton Wellesley Hosp., Mass. Gen. Hosp.; past chmn. Wellesley Pers. Bd.; past trustee Woods Hole Oceanographic Inst., Mass., 1984-90; chmn. bd. trustees Tufts U., 1986-95. Lt. comdr. USNR, 1952-60. Mem. Silvanus Packard Soc., Mass. Bus. Roundtable (bd. dirs., vice chmn. 1982-88), Assoc. Industries Mass. (bd. dirs. 1976-86), Kittansett Club, Brae Burn Country Club, Beverly Yacht Club, Soc. Tufts Followes. Home: 14 Windsor Rd Wellesley MA 02481-6134 Office: Fleetwing Capital 75 Federal St Boston MA 02110-1913 Office Phone: 617-357-9175. E-mail: giffordn@msn.com.

GIFFORD, PROSSER, library administrator; b. NYC, May 16, 1929; s. John Archer and Barbara (Prosser) G.; m. Shirley Mireille O'Sullivan, June 26, 1954; children: Barbara, Paula, Heidi. BA, Yale U., 1951, PhD, 1964; BA, Oxford (Eng.) U., 1953, MA, 1958; LLB, Harvard U., 1956; MA, Amherst Coll., 1969, LHD, 1980; LLD, Doshisha U., Kyoto, Japan, 1979. Bar: DC 1956. Asst. to pres. Swarthmore Coll., 1956-58; asst. prof. history Yale, 1964-66; dir. 5 yr. B.A. program, 1965-66; dean faculty Amherst Coll., 1967-79, assoc. prof. history, 1967-69, prof. history, 1969-79; dep. dir. Woodrow Wilson Internat. Ctr. for Scholars, Washington, 1975-76, 80-87, acting dir., 1987-88; dir. scholarly programs Libr. Congress, 1990—. Chmn. Merton Coll. Charitable Corp., 1991—; Sir Thomas Bodley fellow Merton Coll., 2001. Co-editor, contbr.: Britian and Germany in Aftica, 1967, France and Britain in Africa, 1971, Transfer of Power in Africa, 1982, Decolonization and African Independence, 1988, Creating French Culture, 1995, Democracy and the Rule of Law, 2001. Trustee, Hotchkiss Sch., 1971-81, Concord Acad., 1972-78; chmn. bd. trustees Woods Hole Marine Biol. Lab., 1978-90. Rhodes scholar, 1951-53; Fgn. Area fellow No. Rhodesia, 1963-64 Mem. Assn. Yale Alumni (gov. 1972-77), Woods Hole Oceanographic Inst. (mem. corp.), Internat. House of Japan, India Internat. Ctr., Century Club, Cosmos Club, Elizabethan Club, Woods Hole Golf and Tennis Club, Quisset Yacht Club. Home: 59 Penzance Rd Woods Hole MA 02543-0005 Office Phone: 202-707-1517. E-mail: pgif@loc.gov.

GIFFORD, WILLIAM C., lawyer, educator; b. Aurora, Ill., Sept. 18, 1941; AB, Dartmouth Coll., 1963; LLB, Harvard U., 1966. Bar: Ill. 1966, D.C. 1968, N.Y. 1976, Paris 1994. Assoc., ptnr. Ivins, Phillips & Barker, Washington, 1967—74; assoc. prof. Cornell Law Sch., 1974—78; counsel, ptnr. Wilmer, Cutler & Pickering, 1978—83; ptnr. Davis Polk & Wardwell, N.Y.C., 1983—98, sr. counsel, 1999—; prof. law Cornell U. Law Sch., 2001—03. Vis. lectr. Yale Law Sch., 2003, Columbia Law Sch., 2004—. Author: International Tax Planning, 1974, 2d edit. (with W.P. Streng), 1979, (with E.A. Owens) International Aspects of U.S. Income Taxation, 1982. Office: Davis Polk & Wardwell 450 Lexington Ave New York NY 10017-3911 Office Phone: 212-450-4632. Business E-Mail: gifford@dpw.com.

GIFT, JAMES JOSEPH, aquatic toxicologist; BA in Biology, Harvard U, 1964; MA in Environ. Sci., Rutgers U., 1968, PhD in Environ. Sci., 1970. Lab. rsch. dir. Ichthyological Assocs., Brigantine, N.J., 1970-75; sr. v.p., dir.

sci. and tech. EA Engring., Sci. & Tech. Inc., Md., 1975-97; owner Quail's Roost Environ. Svcs., 1997—, Quail's Roost Photography, 1997—. Mem.: Am. Fisheries Soc. Achievements include direction of a multimedia assessment contrasting ocean disposal of sewage sludge with various land-based waste management options; direction of ocean site designation studies for New York City and other municipalities; preparation of the first Special Permit Application for ocean disposal of sewage sludge; direction of a wide variety of ecological and human health risk assessments; conducting of research on the physiological effects of thermal gradients of numerous marine, estuarine and freshwater fish species; award-winning nature photographer. Personal E-mail: jgift@comcast.net.

GIGER, MARYELLEN LISSAK, medical physicist; d. Frank and Margaret Lissak; m. Charles Giger; children: Megan, Jennifer, Charlie, Eric. BS summa cum laude, Ill. Benedictine Coll., 1978; MSc, U. Exeter, Eng., 1979; PhD, U. Chgo., 1985. Asst. prof. U. Chgo., 1986—91, assoc. prof., 1991—2000, prof., 2000—. Dir. advanced imaging program Cancer Rsch. Ctr. U. Chgo., 1994—, dir. grad. programs in med. physics, 1998—; presenter in field. Author: (manuscript in investigative radiology) Computerized Detection of Pulmonary Nodules in Computed Tomography Images (Stauffer Award, 1995), (manuscript in medical physics) Multifractal Radiographic Analysis of Osteoporosis (Sylvia Sorkin Greenfield Award, 1995); contbr. chapters to books, articles to profl. jours. Leader Girl Scouts, Elmhurst, Ill., 1994—2001. Recipient President's Scholarship award, Ill. Benedictine Coll., 1975, 1976, 1977, Rev. Shonka, O.S.B. Scholarship Award in Physics, 1977, First Pl. award Young Investigators' Symposium, Am. Assn. Physicists in Medicine, 1985, Jr. Faculty Rsch. award, Am. Cancer Soc., 1988, Faculty Rsch. award, 1991; grantee, Wendy Will Case Cancer Fund, 1989, NIH, Nat. Cancer Inst., 1989—95, 1999—2001, 2000—, 2001—, U.S. Army, DOD, 1993—96, 1996—2000, 1998—2001, 1999—2002; Rotary Internat. fellow, Rotary, 1978—79, Louis Block Rsch. grantee, U. Chgo., 1986, Am. Cancer Soc. Instl. grantee, 1986. Fellow: Am. Assn. Physicists in Medicine, Am. Inst. Med. Bioengring.; mem.: IEEE, Soc. for Computer Applications in Radiology, Assn. Univ. Radiologists, Internat. Soc. for Optical Engring. Achievements include first to in computer-aided diagnosis research; patents for computer-aided diagnosis for breast and lung cancer detection and diagnosis; assessment of breast cancer risk and assessment of osteoporosis. Office: U Chgo 5841 S Maryland Ave Chicago IL 60637 Business E-Mail: m-giger@uchicago.edu.

GIGGLEMAN, GENE FELTON, academic administrator, veterinarian; b. Dallas, Aug. 23, 1953; s. Gene Felton Giggleman and Linda Jean Long; m. Katherine Ann Lowe, May 31, 1975; children: Kristin Lane, Cynthia Lauren. DVM, Tex. A&M U., 1981. Prof. anat. sci. Parker Coll. Chiropractic, Dallas, 1992—, dean Ctr. Basic Sci., 1994—2000, dean acad. affairs, 2000—. Veterinarian In Home Vet. Care, Grapevine, Tex., 1990—. Worship team mem. Carroll Bapt. Ch., Southlake, Tex., 1996—2003. Cable Scholarship, Tex. A&M U., 1981. Mem.: Tex. Vet. Med. Assn. Conservative-R. Baptist. Avocations: herpetology, motorcycling. Home: 2105 Brentcove Dr Grapevine TX 76051 Office: Parker Coll Chiropractic 2500 Walnut Hill Ln Dallas TX 75229-5668 E-mail: ggiglman@parkercc.edu.

GIGLI, IRMA, dermatologist, educator, academic administrator; b. Cordoba, Argentina, Dec. 22, 1931; d. Irineo and Esperanza Francisca (Pons de Gigli) Gigli; m. Hans J. Muller-Eberhard, June 29, 1985. BA, Liceo Nacional Manuel Belgrano, Cordoba, 1950; MD, Universidad Nacional de Cordoba, 1957. Intern Cook County Hosp., Chgo., 1957—58, resident in dermatology, 1958—60; fellow in dermatology NYU, 1960—61; mem. faculty Harvard Med. Sch., 1967—75, asso. prof. dermatology, 1972—75; chief dermatology service Peter Bent Brigham Hosp., Robert B. Brigham Hosp., 1971—75; prof. dermatology and exptl. medicine N.Y. U. Med. Center, N.Y.C., 1976—82, mem. Irvington Houst Inst., mem. faculty N.Y. Grad. Sch. Med. Scis., dir. Asthma and Allergic Disease Center for Immunodermatology Studies, 1980—91; prof. medicine, chief div. dermatology U. Calif.-San Diego, 1983—95; prof. medicine and dermatology, vice chair medicine for sci. U. Tex. Health Sci. Ctr., Houston, 1995—; assoc. dir. Inst. Molecular Medicine for Prevention Human Diseases U. Tex., Houston, 1998—2003, dep. dir., 2003—, Walter and Mary Mischer prof. molecular medicine Houston, 1998—; dir. Rsch. Ctr. Immunology and Autoimmune Diseases, 1995—. Mem. Nat. Inst. of Allergy and Infectious Diseases Coun., 1978—79, bd. sci. counselors, 1997—; chmn. study sect. Allergy and Immunology Inst., NIH, 1978—83; mem. Guggenheim Found. Western Hemisphere and Phillippines Com. of Selection; adv. bd. NIH Fogarty Internat. Ctr., 1984—97. Bd. dirs. U.S. Civilian R&D Found. for the Ind. States of the Former Soviet Union. Recipient Rsch. award, Am. Cancer Soc., 1970—72, NIH, 1972—76, Disting. Profl. Woman of Yr. award, U. Tex. Health Sci. Ctr. at Houston, 2003, David Martin Carter Mentor award, Am. Skin Assn., 2005; grantee, Guggenheim Found., 1974—75. Mem.: Acad. Medicine, Engring. & Sci. Tex. (bd. dirs.), Am. Acad. Arts and Scis., Henry Kunkel Soc. (councilor 1999—), PEW Latin Am. Fellows Program in Biomed. Scis. (nat. adv. com. 1998—2005), Inst. Medicine/NAS, Am. Dermatol. Assn., Assn. Am. Physicians, Am. Acad. Allergy, Am. Acad. Dermatology, Am. Assn. Immunologists, Am. Soc. Clin. Investigation, Soc. Investigative Dermatology (hon.; pres. 1990—91, Stephen Rothman Meml. award 1996). Office: U Tex Health Sci Ctr Inst Molecular Medicine 2121 W Holcombe Blvd Houston TX 77030-3303

GIGLIO, JAMES NICHOLAS, humanities educator, writer; b. Akron, Ohio, Mar. 28, 1939; s. Frank Maris Giglio and Mary Matthew Naturale; m. Frances Theresa Jendrisak, June 19, 1965; children: Peter Jason, Anthony Matthew. BA, Kent State U., Ohio, 1961, MA, 1964; PhD, Ohio State U., 1968. Asst. prof. history SW Mo. State U., Springfield, 1968—73, assoc. prof. history, 1973—78, prof. history, 1978—2000, disting. prof. history, 2000—. Exam and table leader Advance Placement (AP) in U.S. History readings, Princeton, NJ, 1977—; editl. bd. mem. Presdl. Studies Quar., N.Y.C., 1992—99; evaluator manuscripts for various publs. Author: (books) H.M. Daugherty and the Politics of Expediency, 1978, Truman In Cartoon and Caricature, 1984, The Presidency of John F. Kennedy, 1991, John F. Kennedy: A Bibliography, 1995, Musial: From Stash to Stan the Man, 2001, Debating the Kennedy Presidency, 2003, many scholarly articles and reviews. Mem. apptd. by gov. State Hist. Records Bd., Jefferson City, Mo., 1985—87; past mem. task force of Mo. hist. records bd. Mo. State Archives, Jefferson City, Mo. Lt. U.S. Army, 1962—63, capt. USAR. Recipient Inducted into Mo. Writers Hall of Fame, 1997; grantee Rsch. grant, Truman Libr. Inst., 1978, 1982, Fellowship, Nat. Endowment for the Humanities, 1983, John F. Kennedy Libr. Found., 1991. Mem.: The Soc. for Am. Baseball Rsch., Orgn. of Am. Historians. Democrat. Roman Catholic. Achievements include Founder of Mid-Am. Conf. on history, a regional conf. that draws nat. Avocations: golf, fishing. Home: 1300 South Virginia Ave Springfield MO 65807 Office: Southwest Mo State U 90 S National Ave Springfield MO 65804 Office Phone: 417-836-5378. Personal E-mail: jng890f@smsu.edu.

GIGLIO, JULIE JEAN, psychiatrist; d. Kenneth Walter and Dorothy Marie Holoien; m. Mark Frederick Giglio, July 27, 1985; children: Kevin, Emily, Joshua. BA, Stanford U., 1982, MS, 1984; MD, U. Va., 1988. Diplomate Am. Bd. Psychiatry and Neurology, 1996. Intern U. Calif. Med. Ctr., Irvine, 1988—89, resident, 1989—91, fellow in child and adolescent psychiatry, 1991—93; individual and group therapist Olive Crest Treatment Ctrs., Orange County, Calif., 1989—91; pvt. practice Santa Ana, Tustin, Calif., 1992—. Outpatient psychiatry cons. Ctr. for Family Therapy, Orange, Calif., 1994—96; managed care child psychiatry MCC Behavioral Care, Santa Ana, Calif., 1995; managed care psychiatry Johnson & Johnson Psych Care, Newport Beach, Calif., 1996—98; group supr. for therapists Cath. Charities Orange County, Santa Ana, 1999—. Contbr. articles to profl. jours. Music and youth vol., elder, tchr. Irvine (Calif.) Presbyn. Ch., 1999—. Fellow: Am. Psychiat. Assn.; mem.: Orange County Psychiat. Soc. (com. mem.), Am. Acad. Child/Adolescent Psychiatry. Avocations: jogging, water-skiing, hiking. Office: Ste 203 161 Fashion Ln Tustin CA 92780 Office Phone: 714-730-1433.

GIGNILLIAT, WILLIAM ROBERT, III, lawyer; b. Sebring, Fla., Mar. 22, 1943; s. William Robert and Ann Josephine (Harris) G.; m. Rosemary Rebecca Bersch, May 29, 1971 (div. July 1979); 1 dau., Meigan Rebecca; m. Laura Crowell Lieberman, Mar. 20, 1984; children: William Robert, IV, Elizabeth Ann. BA, U. South, 1965; JD, Emory U., 1968. Bar: Ga. 1968, U.S. Dist. Ct. (no. dist.) Ga. 1970, U.S. Ct. Appeals (5th cir.) 1970, U.S. Supreme Ct. 1972, U.S. Ct. Appeals (11th cir.) 1982. Atty. Emory Neighborhood Law Office, Atlanta, 1967-71; ptnr. Mantegna, Gignilliat & Wiggins, Atlanta, 1974—75, Gignilliat, Manchel, Johnson & Wiggins, Atlanta, 1977-83; pvt. practice Atlanta, 1983—. Author: Contracts for Artists, 1983, Handbook on the Georgia Print Law, 1986, Art Law in Georgia, 2004, Contracts for Public Art, 1998; editor: An Artists handbook on Copyright, 1990. Bd. dirs. Ctr. Puppetry Arts, Atlanta, 1979-96, Hammonds House, Inc., 1995—; pres., chmn. bd. Words of Art, Inc., Atlanta, 1982-88; pres. Art Contracts, Inc., 1997—; founder, chmn. Met. Pub. Art Coalition, Inc., 2000-04; chmn. bd. People TV, Inc., 2004-05. Served with AUS, 1968-70. Mem. ABA, Ga. Vol. Lawyers for Arts (bd. dirs. 1988-90), Ga. Criminal Def. Lawyers Assn. (mem. trial advocacy program faculty 2002-05). Democrat. Office: 918 Ponce De Leon Ave NE Atlanta GA 30306-4212

GIGOT, PAUL ANTHONY, editor; b. San Antonio, 1955; AB in Govt., Dartmouth Coll., 1977. Editl. asst. Nat. Rev., 1978-79; reporter, editor Far Ea. Econ. Rev., 1979-80; reporter Wall St. Jour., 1980-82, Asia corr., 1982-84, editor editl. page Asian edit., 1984-86, columnist Potomac Watch, mem. editl. bd., 1987—2001, editl. page editor N.Y.C., 2001—. Recipient Pulitzer prize, 2000; White House fellow, 1986—87. Office: The Wall St Jour 200 Liberty St New York NY 10281-1003

GIKAS, PAUL WILLIAM, medical educator; b. Lansing, Mich., July 23, 1928; s. John and Minnie (Neumann) G.; m. Lois Suzanne Haglund, Dec. 27, 1952; children— Sandra Jane, Sarah Elizabeth, Paula Suzanne. AB, U. Mich., 1950, MD, 1954. Diplomate: Am. Bd. Pathology. Chief lab. service VA Hosp., Ann Arbor, Mich., 1960-68; mem. faculty U. Mich. Med. Sch., Ann Arbor, 1959—, assoc. prof. pathology, 1966-69, prof., 1969-95, prof. emeritus, 1995—, faculty rep. to Big Ten Intercollegiate Conf., Nat. Collegiate Athletic Assn., 1982-88, assoc. dean for admissions, 1990-97. Cons. Armed Forces Inst. Pathology, 1966-74 Author: The Accident Problem, 1976, Uropathology, 1976, Forensic Aspects of the Highway Crash, 1983; co-editor: The Prevention of Highway Injury, 1967. Mem. adv. com. traffic safety HEW, 1966-68; mem. Gov. Mich. Spl. Commn. Traffic Safety Mich., 1964; chmn. bd. dirs. Pub. Citizen, Inc., 1971-2002; co-trustee Center Study Responsive Law, Washington, 1969-71. Served to capt. M.C. AUS, 1956-58. Recipient Auto Safety award Med. Tribune, 1966-67, Distinguished Service award U. Mich., 1965, Disting. Svc. award U. Mich. Med. Ctr. Alumni Soc., 1998. Fellow Coll. Am. Pathologists, U.S. and Can. Acad. Pathology, Alpha Omega Alpha, Nu Sigma Nu. Lutheran. Achievements include rsch. with preservation of blood for transfusion by freezing and rsch. in pathogenesis of injury in highway crashes. Home: 1900 Mershon Dr Ann Arbor MI 48103-5939

GIL, GUILLERMO, prosecutor; Acting U.S. atty. Dept. Justice, Hato Rey, PR, 1993—2002, asst. U.S. atty. PR, 2002—. Office: US Attys Office Fed Bldg 350Carlos E Chardon Ave Hato Rey San Juan PR 00918*

GILANI, ROSHANAK SARBAZ, architect, consultant; d. Aboulghasem Sarbaz and Sekineh Nouri; m. Cyrous Asvadi Gilani, Jan. 5, 1968; children: Ryan Cyrous, Shannon Elizabeth. MS in Engring. Mgmt., Nat. Tech. U., Ft. Collins, Colo., 1989; BSEE, Calif. State U., Long Beach, 1990; MS in Sys. Design and Mgmt. (hon.), MIT, 2001. Fundamental engring., EIT/CA. Program analyst L.A. Culver City (Calif.) Dist., 1986—90; bus. process improvement and integration mgr. Xerox Corp., El Segundo, Calif., 1990—98, 1998—2003; enterprise bus. arch. Souther Calif. Edison, Rosemead, Calif., 2003—. Recipient Excellence Recognition award, 2004. Mem.: Xerox Mgmt. Assn. (pres. 1988—99, program chair 1987—88), Toastmasters (Competent Toastmaster 1987—2000). Home Fax: 310-375-8880. Business E-Mail: rgilani@alum.mit.edu.

GILBANE, THOMAS F., JR., building company executive; b. Providence, June 7, 1947; s. Thomas F. and Jean A. (Murphy) G.; m. Mary O'Donnell, June 9, 1973; children— Thomas F., Daniel, Martha, Michael Attended, Brown U.; BSBA in bus. mgmt., Babson Coll., 1970; MS in civil engring. and project mgmt., MIT, 1975; postgrad. in advanced mgmt., Harvard Bus. Sch., 1984. cert. in bldg. construction, RI Sch. of Design. Various positions Gilbane Bldg. Co., Providence, 1964-76, v.p., reg. mgr. Cleve., 1976-83, exec. v.p. Providence, 1983—2004, CEO, 2004—. Bd. dirs. Nynex, NY, New England Telephone, audit fin. com.; mem. Associated General Contractors (AGC)of Am. Private Industry Adv. Coun., chmn. AGC Nat./Reg. Contractor's Com. Alumni dir., mem. corp. Babson Coll., Wellesley, Mass., 1974-76; bd. dirs. Boy Scouts Am., Cleve., 1981-83, Providence, 1985—; trustee Greater Cleve. Roundtable, 1983-85; R.I. Assn. for Blind, Providence, 1985—; bd. dirs. United Way-Southeastern New Eng., Providence, 1985-93, campaign chmn. 1986; bd. dirs. United Way Am., 1994—, fin. com., 1994—; trustee City of Hope, 1984—, Catholic Charities, US Lacrosse Found; Served to 2d lt RI N.G., 1970-76. Recipient Spirit of Life award City of Hope, 1984 Mem. Alexis de Tocqueville Soc. Am. (nat. chmn. 1994—), In-Sight Pro Am., New Albany Country Club, Sigma Chi, Phi Kappa Si., Sigma XI, Clubs: Union (Cleve.); Agawan Hunt (East Providence, RI), Point Judith Country (Narragansett, RI, Hope, US Golf Assn. Sectional Affairs Com., Lodges: Knights of Malta. Roman Catholic. Avocations: golf, skiing, fishing. Office: Gilbane Bldg Co 7 Jackson Walkway Providence RI 02903-3694 Office Phone: 401-456-5900. Office Fax: 401-456-5404.

GILBERG, MARGOT D., secondary school Spanish educator; Tchr. Spanish St. Catherine Acad., Bronx, N.Y., chair dept. fgn. langs. Mem. Am. Coun. Tchrs. of Fgn. Langs., Am. Assn. Tchrs. Spanish and Portugese, N.Y. State Assn. Tchrs. Fgn. Langs.

GILBERG, MARK RICHARDSON, environmental scientist, director; b. San Francisco, July 20, 1953; s. Marvin Richard and Wilma Eileen Gilberg; m. Teresa Louise Bowman, Nov. 28, 1954; 1 child, Grace Marie. BS, Stanford U., 1977, MS; PhD, U. London Inst. Archaeology, 1982. Conservation scientist Can. Conservation Inst., Ottawa, 1982—87; sci. officer Australian Mus., Sydney, 1987—92; rsch. dir. Nat. Ctr. Preservation Tech. and Tng., Natchitoches, La., 1994—2002; pres. Conservation Processes Rsch., Phoenix, 2002—. Abstractor, art and archaeology tech. abstracts Getty Conservation Inst., L.A., 1994—2002; adj. prof. Ariz. State U., Phoenix, 2004—. Author: (book) Primer for the Rehabilitation and Renovation of Older and Historic Schools; editor: PTT Newsletter; contbr. articles to profl. jours. Usher St Francis Xavier Cath. Ch., Phoenix, 2004—05. Recipient Outstanding Svc. award, Nat. Pk. Svc., 2001, Oliver Torrey Fuller award, Assn. Preservation Tech. Internat., 2003. Fellow: Internat. Inst. Conservation; mem.: Am. Inst. Conservation (assoc.). Independent-Republican. Roman Catholic. Achievements include development of first practical methodology and protocols for the use of low oxygen atmospheres as an alternative to conventional chemical fumigants for the disinfestation of museum objects; practical methodology for use of thermal imaging for the detection of subterranean termites in historic structures; computer software program to model heat transfer through stained glass windows with protective glazing installed. Avocation: golf. Office: Conservation Processes Rsch 1129 West Orangewood Ave Phoenix AZ 85021 Office Phone: 602-757-1161. Personal E-mail: markgilberg@cox.net.

GILBERT, ALAN, conductor; b. NYC; Studies with Leon Kirchner, Peter Lieberson & Earl Kim, Harvard U.; studies with Masuko Ushioda, New England Conservatory of Music; studies with Otto-Werner Müller, Curtis Inst. of Music, Phila.; MusM, Juilliard Sch. Staff mem. The Cleveland Orch., 1994, asst. condr., 1995—97; music dir. Haddonfield Symphony, NJ, 1996—97; asst. concertmaster The Santa Fe Opera, Santa Fe, 1993—2001; chief condr. & artistic advisor Royal Stockholm Philharmonic Orch., 2000—; condr. & music dir. The Santa Fe Opera, Santa Fe, 2001—; principal guest condr. NDR Symphony Orch., Hamburg, 2004—. Guest condr. Orch. Philharmonique de la Radio, France, Tonhalle Orch., Orch. de la Suiss Romande, Bamberg Symphony, Phila. Orch., NY Philharmonic, Nat. Symphony Orch., Minnesota Orch., Atlanta Orch., Boston Orch., San Francisco Orch., Los Angeles Orch. Recipient Helen M. Thompson award, Am. Symphony Orch. League, 1994, First prize, Internat. Competition Mus. Performance, Geneva, 1994, Swiss prize, 1994, Bunkamura Orchard Hall award, 1994, Sir Georg Solti prize, 1994, Arts Conductors award, Seaver/Nat. Endowment for Arts, 1997. Office: Santa Fe Opera PO Box 2408 Santa Fe NM 87504-2408

GILBERT, ANITA RAE, psychologist, educator; d. Marie Olivia Love; children: Ray Bernard, Lorin D'Andrew. PhD, Wright Inst., Berkeley, Calif., 1981. Lic. clin. psychologist Calif., 2001. Psychology instr. San Francisco City Coll., 1976—78; psychologist Bayview Mental Health Svc., San Francisco, 1980—82; lectr. U. of Calif., San Francisco, 1982—86; neuropsychologist San Francisco Gen. Hosp., 1982—84; forensic psychologist Calif. Dept. of Correction, San Francisco, 1985—; lectr. Calif. State U., Hayward, 1993—96, San Francisco State U., 2003—; clin. program dir. Westside Cmty. Mental Health, San Francisco, 1987—88; psychol. testing program dir. Calif. Med. Facility-Vacaville, Calif., 1984—86. Cons. psychologist Calif. Dept of Mental Health, San Francisco, 1987—88; cons. Asian Am. Residential Treatment Ctr., San Francisco. Mentor Cath. Charities, San Francisco, 1995—98. Fellow Doctoral fellow, APA, 1978—80. Mem.: Soc. for Personality Assessment, APA (assoc.). Achievements include research in depression, women's studies, issues in neuropsychology. Avocations: yoga, travel, exercise program, painting, dance. Personal E-mail: dragilbert@aol.com.

GILBERT, BARBARA MARIE, literacy coach; b. Patapsco, Md., July 4, 1952; d. Leo Joseph and Margaret Theresa (White) Finn; m. C. Raymond Gilbert, Apr. 25, 1980; 1 child, Christen René. BA, Frostburg State U., 1974, MA, 1976. Cert. nat. bd. in literacy 2004. Tchr. Garrett County Schs., Oakland, Md., 1974—75, Carroll County Schs., Westminster, Md., 1975—90, Beaufort County Schs., SC, 1990—2000, literacy coach, 2000—. Staff development evaluator 100 Book Challenge Am. Reading Co., King of Prussia, Pa., 2003—. Pres. Friends of Bluffton Libr., SC, 2003; pres.-elect Kiwanis, Bluffton, 2005. Recipient Tchr. of Yr., M.C. Riley Elem. Sch., 1999, Bluffton Elem. Sch., 2001; Reading Program grant, Island Found., 2001, Comprehensive Sch. Reform grant, S.C., 2004. Mem.: Nat. Council Tchrs. English, Internat. Reading Assn. Methodist. Avocations: reading, bicycling, golf. Home: 37 Heritage Lakes Dr Bluffton SC 29910 Office: Bluffton Elem Sch 160 H E McCracken Cir Bluffton SC 29910

GILBERT, BENTLEY BRINKERHOFF, retired history professor, retired historian; b. Mansfield, Ohio, Apr. 5, 1924; s. John Hopkinson Gilbert and Mary Bentley Brinkerhoff; children: Bentley Brinkerhoff Jr., Margaret Mary, Louis Haviland, Francis Hopkinson; m. Elsie Louise Meyer, Jan. 1946 (div. 1967); m. Ellen Margaretta MacVeagh, 1968 (div. 1984). BA, Miami U. Ohio, 1949; MA, U. Cin., 1950; PhD, U. Wis., 1954. Instr. U. Cin., 1950-51; asst. prof. Colo. Coll., Colorado Springs, 1951-54, assoc. prof., 1954-67; prof. U. Ill., Chgo., 1967-97, dean Grad. Coll., 1971—72, chmn. dept. history, 1988-91, ret., 1997. Adv. bd. First Nat. Bank Mansfield, Ohio, 1967—84. Author: The Evolution of National Insurance in Great Britain: The Origins of the Welfare State, 1966, reprinted 1974, 97, Britain Since 1918, 1967, rev., 1980, British Social Policy, 1970, David Lloyd George: A Political Life, Vol. I, The Architect of Change 1863-1912, 1987, David Lloyd George: A Political Life, Vol. II, The Organizer of Victory 1912-1916, 1992 (Soc. Midland Authors award for biography), Britain 1914-1945: The Aftermath of Power, 1996; editor: The Heart of the Empire, 1973; editor Jour. Brit. Studies, U. Chgo., 1978-83; contbr. articles to profl. jours.; chpts. to books. Exec. com. Young Dems. Colo., Colorado Springs, 1961-67; vestryman St. Elisabeth Episcopal Ch., Glencoe, Ill., 1976-78. Tech. sgt. USAAF, 1942-45, PTO Grantee Am. Philos. Soc., 1961-72, U. Ill. Chgo., 1973; fellow Nat. Libr. Medicine, NIH, 1963-71, Guggenheim Found., 1973-74, U. Ill. Inst. for the Humanities, 1982-83. Fellow Royal Hist. Soc. Gt. Britain; mem. Univ. Club Chgo., Westbrook Country Club (Mansfield, Ohio). Avocations: reading, travel. Home: 681 Home Rd S Mansfield OH 44906-3363 Office: U Ill Chgo 601 S Morgan St # 922 Chicago IL 60607-7100

GILBERT, BRADLEY, professional tennis coach, former professional tennis player, former Olympic athlete; b. Oakland, Calif., Aug. 9, 1961; m. Kim Gilbert; 3 children: Zachary, Julian Elizabeth, Zoe. Student, Foothills Jr. Coll., Pepperdine. Ranked 9th in U.S. Tennis Assn., 1993; played in over 35 USTA tour events; coach Andre Agassi, 1994—2002, Andy Roddick, 2003—04; commentator ESPN. Co-author: (books) Winning Ugly, 1994, I've Got Your Back, 2004. Recipient Bronze medal Olympics, Seoul, 1988. Achievements include winning 20 profl. singles titles. Office: USTA 70 W Red Oak Ln White Plains NY 10604-3602

GILBERT, BRUCE FREDERIC, small business owner; b. Whitehall, Wis., Dec. 23, 1932; s. Frederic and Louise (Hahn) G.; m. Ellen Foster Strachan, June 28, 1968; children: James, Eric, Heidi, Sarah. BS, Marquette U., Milw., 1958. Chmn. bd., founder Cedar Lake Sand and Gravel, Hartford, Wis., 1962—; dir., founder, sec. Dodge Concrete, Inc., Watertown, Wis. Contbr. articles to profl. jours. Recipient ABC (Associated Builders and Contractors Assn.) High Stds. award, 1990. Mem. Assoc. Bldrs. and Contrs. of Wis. (dir. 1992), Aurora Rd. Businessman's Assn. (pres, dir. 1995—), Safari Club (dir. 1987—), Bean Club. Republican. Lutheran. Avocations: raising beef cattle, horses. Office: Cedar Lake Sand and Gravel 5189 Aurora Rd Hartford WI 53027-9550 also: Two Sleep Ranch Ten Sleep WY 82442 Office Phone: 262-644-5125.

GILBERT, BRUCE RAYMOND, urologist, educator; b. NYC; married, June 1974. PhD, NY Med. Coll., Valhalla, 1977; MD, Cornell U., NYC, 1983. Medical Diplomate NY, 1983. Assoc. clin. prof. urology Weill Cornell Med. Coll., NYC, 1989—, assoc. clin. prof. reproductive medicine, 2001—; assoc. clin. prof. urology SUNY, Stony Brook. Contbr. articles to profl. jours., over 100 chpts. to books. Fellow: ACS, Am. Acad. Reproductive Surgeons; mem.: Am. Acad. Med. Acupuncture (assoc.; dir. 2004—05), Am. Soc. Reproductive Medicine (assoc.), Am. Urol. Assn. (assoc.). Achievements include research in studies ongoing on cryopreservation of sperm and the use of medical acupuncture for urologic conditions. Office: Bruce R Gilbert MD PhD PC 900 Northern Blvd Suite 230 Great Neck NY 11021 Office Phone: 516-487-2700. Office Fax: 516-487-2007. E-mail: bruce.gilbert@verizon.net.

GILBERT, BRUCE RITS, lawyer; b. Milw., Apr. 8, 1954; s. Eugene George and Inez Laurel (Rits) Gilbert; m. Andrea L. Fenton, Aug. 13, 1981; children: Molly, Emily, Casey. BBA, U. Wis., Madison, 1976; JD, Antioch Sch. Law, 1981. Bar: DC 1981, US Dist. Ct. DC 1982, US Ct. Appeals DC cir. 1982, Pa. 1985. Assoc. Weissburg and Aronson, Washington, 1981-84, Case & Cohen, Washington, 1984-85; named gen. counsel-health care, asst. sec. Universal Health Services, Inc., King of Prussia, Pa., 1985, gen. counsel, 1991—. Bd. dirs. Fedn. Am. Hospitals (formerly Fedn. Am. Health Systems), chmn., 1997, treas., 2003—. Mem. ABA, Nat. Assn. Health Lawyers. Jewish. Office: Universal Health Services Inc Universal Corp Ctr 367 S Gulph Rd King Of Prussia PA 19406-0958

GILBERT, CHARLES RICHARD ALSOP, obstetrician, gynecologist, surgeon, educator; b. Phila., May 26, 1916; s. Chauncey McLean and Frances Marguerite (Young) G.; m. Helene Scher, Dec. 24, 1973; children: Anita Ivonne, Charles Richard Alsop Jr. MD, U. Va., 1944. Bar: Am. Bd. Abdominal Surgeons; diplomate: Am. Bd. Obstetrics and Gynecology. Rotating intern N.Y.C. Hosp., 1944-45, asst. resident in internal medicine, 1945-46; resident in surgery Nix Hosp., San Antonio, 1946; resident in gen. surgery, chief female abdominal surgery Ryder Meml. Hosp., Hunacao, P.R., 1952-55; house staff gynecology Johns Hopkins Hosp., Balt., 1948-49; asst. resident in obstetrics U. Md., 1949, chief resident in obstetrics, 1949-50, asst. resident in gynecology, 1950-51, chief resident in gynecology, 1951-52, assoc. in gynecology, instr. gynecol. pathology, 1952; asst. clin. prof. obstetrics and gynecology U. P.R., 1952-55, George Washington U., 1972-74, assoc. clin. prof. obstetrics and gynecology, 1974-93, clin. prof. ob/gyn. Washington,

1994—; chief gynecology Doctors Hosp., 1973—; sr. attending in obstetrics and gynecology Washington Hosp. Center. Instr. internal medicine Randolph Sch. Aviation, San Antonio, 1946; cons. U.S. Air Force in obstetrics, gynecology, female urology, 1952-54 Author: Childbirth-The Modern Guide to Expectant Mothers, 1960, Better Health for Women, 1964, Abdominal Pelvic Surgery, 1969; co-editor, editor: Symposiumon Abdominal Pelvic Surgery, 1966; contbr. articles to profl. jours.; Mem. editorial staff: Jour. Abdominal Surgery, 1964-74. Served with M.C. USAF, as chief internal medicine, 1946-48, Selfridge AFB, Mt. Clemens, Mich. Fellow ACS (founding fellow), Am. Coll. Obstetrics and Gynecology, Am. Soc. Abdominal Surgeons (teaching faculty 1964-74, mem. exec. com. 1964-74, v.p. 1969-70, pres. 1971-72), Internat. Coll. Surgeons (U.S. sect., regent, exec. com. 1981—, chmn. bd. regents 1983-84, sec. 1982-83, membership chmn. 1983, 2d pres.-elect 1985, pres.-elect 1986, pres. 1987-88, coordinator diplomatic relations 1985—, spl. advisor to pres. 1989-90, mem. internat. bd. govs. 1990, sec. N.Am. fedn. 1991-92, Regent of Yr. award 1981, emeritus 1992, bd. trustees 1993, 96-98, hon. fellow 1995); mem. Pan Am. Med. Assn., Med. Soc. D.C., AMA, Med. and Surgery Soc. Johns Hopkins Hosp., Douglass Obstet. and Gynecol. Soc., Nat. Rifle Assn., African Safari Club Washington (v.p. 1974-77, pres. 1977), Am. Outdoors Council (dir.), Hunting Hall of Fame Found. (dir. 1978), Jefferson Soc. Club: Boone and Crockett. Clubs: Boone and Crockett. Achievements include developing first audiovisual med. corr. teaching courses for continuing med. edn., 1973. Home and Office: 705 E Franklin Ave Silver Spring MD 20901-4707 Office Phone: 301-565-8821.

GILBERT, CREIGHTON EDDY, art historian; b. Durham, N.C., June 6, 1924; s. Allan H. and Katharine (Everett) G. BA, NYU, 1942, PhD, 1955; DHL (hon.), Adelphi U., 1990, U. Louisville, 1997. Assoc. prof. Brandeis U., 1961-65, Sidney and Ellen Wien prof. history of art, 1965-69; prof. Queens Coll. City U. N.Y., 1969-77; Jacob Gould Schurman prof. art history Cornell U., 1977-81; prof. Yale U., 1981-2000, prof. emeritus, 2000—. Fulbright sr. lectr. U. Rome, 1951-52; fellow Netherlands Inst. for Advanced Study, 1972-73; vis. prof. U. Leiden, 1974-75; Zacks Found. vis. prof. Hebrew U. Jerusalem, 1985. Author: Change in Piero della Francesca, 1968, History of Renaissance Art, 1972, The Works of Girolamo Savoldo, 1986, Poets Seeing Artists' Work: Instances from the Italian Renaissance, 1991, Michelangelo On and Off the Sistine Ceiling, 1994, Piero della Francesca et Giorgione: Problèmes d'Interpretation, 1994, Caravaggio and His Two Cardinals, 1995, The Saints' Three Reasons for Paintings in Churches, 2001, How Fra Angelico and Signorelli Saw the End of the World, 2002, Lex Amoris, 2005; editor: Italian Art 1400-1500, Sources and Documents, 1979, enlarged Italian edit., 1988; editor-in-chief: The Art Bull, 1980-85; translator: Complete Poems and Selected Letters of Michelangelo, 1963, 3d edit., 1979. Recipient Mather award Coll. Art Assn., 1964 Fellow Am. Acad. Arts and Scis., Ateneo Veneto (fgn.). Office: Yale U Dept Art History Box 208272 New Haven CT 06520-8272 Office Phone: 203-432-2678.

GILBERT, DAVID A., lawyer; b. 1944; BA, Brown U., 1966; JD, Boston Coll., 1969. Bar: Mass. 1969, Colo. 1982, US Dist. Ct. (Dist. Mass.). Ptnr., dir., Real Estate Sect. Mintz, Levin, Cohn, Ferris, Glovsky & Popeo PC, Boston. Overseer Newton-Wellesley Hosp. Mem.: Internat. Assn. Corp. Real Estate Execs. (past pres. New Eng. Chpt.), Boston Bar Assn., Mass. Bar Assn., ABA. Office: Mintz Levin Cohn Ferris Glovsky & Popeo PC One Financial Ctr Boston MA 02111 Office Phone: 617-348-1645. Office Fax: 617-542-2241. Business E-Mail: dgilbert@mintz.com.

GILBERT, DAVID ERWIN, academic administrator, physicist; b. Fresno, Calif., June 23, 1939; s. Erwin Azel and Hester (Almond) G.; m. Carolyn Faye Parker, June 24, 1960; children: Ronald David, Joan Elaine. AB, U. Calif.-Berkeley, 1962; MA, U. Oreg., 1964, PhD, 1968. Prof. physics Eastern Oreg. U., La Grande, 1968-98, dean. acad. affairs, 1977-83, pres., 1983-98; pres. emeritus. Vis. rschr. Obs. Paris, 1975-82; commr. N.W. Assn. Schs. and Colls., 1982-88. Contbr. articles on physics to profl. jours. V.p. Ea. Oreg. Regional Arts Coun., 1979-80; vice chair, bd. dirs. Oreg. Ed-Net, 1989-97, Oreg. Pub. Broadcasting Found., 1991-93; mem. Oreg. Task Force Superconducting Super Collider, 1987, Oreg. Pub. Broadcasting Commn., 1991-01, Oreg. Bd. Forestry, 1991-2002, chair, 1996-2002; mem. Gov.'s Transition Team, 1990, Oreg. visibility adv. com. Dept. Environ. Quality, 1990-91; bd. dirs. Blue Mountains Natural Resources Inst., 1990-98, N.E. Oreg. Area Health Edn. Ctr., Gov.'s Telecomms. Forum Coun., 1996-97; bd. dirs. Oreg. Agr. Found., 1998—, Keep Oreg. Green Assn., 1999-2001, Tillamook Forest Heritage Trust, 1999-2002, North Ctrl. U., Ariz., 2002—04. Grantee NATO; grantee Research Corp. U.S.A., U.S. Govt., pvt. founds. Mem. Am. Assn. Colls. and Univs. (bd. dirs. 1995-97, chmn. com. econ. and cmty. devel. 1990-92), Am. Assn. Physics Tchrs. (pres. Oreg. chpt. 1973-74), Pacific N.W. Assn. Coll. Physics (bd. dirs. 1970-74), Sigma Xi, Sigma Pi Sigma, Phi Kappa Phi. Democrat. Home: PO Box 36 Joseph OR 97846-0036 Personal E-mail: deg@starband.net.

GILBERT, DEBBIE ROSE, entrepreneur; b. Indpls., Jan. 18, 1961; d. James Taylor and Rosemary (Robinson) G. BA, Ind. U., 1994; diploma in computer literacy, St. Augustine Coll., 1995. Student typing asst. Shortridge H.S. Indpls. Pub. Schs./Bd. Schs. Commrs., 1978—79; substitute tchr. Indpls. Pub. Schs./Bd. Sch. Commrs., 1985—89, Washington Twp. Schs., Indpls., 1992; CHA housewatcher, clothes distbr. Inner Voice, Inc., Chgo., 1994—95; vol. Lakefront Single Room Occupancy Employment Program, Chgo., 1997—. Dep. registrar O.N.E./Bd. Election Commrs., Chgo., 1996—; mem. People for Am. Way, Chgo., 1995-96; mem. Access Living, Chgo., 1996—, So. Poverty Law Ctr., Tchg. Tolerance, Militia Task Force, Klanwatch Org., Montgomery, 1998—. Mem. ACLU, NOW, AAUW, NAACP, Nat. Mus. Women in Arts Orgn., Older Women's League, Voice of Midlife & Older Women, Mental Health Consumer Edn. Consortium, Inc. Democrat. Baptist. Avocations: modeling, singing, race walking, Bingo, reading. Home: 5012 N Winthrop Ave Apt 224 Chicago IL 60640-3124 Office: 4753 N Broadway Ste 632/808 Chicago IL 60640-4986

GILBERT, DONALD ROY, lawyer; b. Phila., June 6, 1946; BA, Stanford U., 1968; JD, U. Calif., 1971. Bar: Calif. 1972, Ariz. 1972. Ptnr., dir. Fennemore Craig, Phoenix, 1972—. Mem. ABA, State Bar Ariz., State Bar Calif., Maricopa County Bar Assn. Office: Fennemore Craig 3003 N Central Ste 2600 Phoenix AZ 85012-2913

GILBERT, DOUGLAS BRAINERD, telecommunications industry executive; b. Miami, Fla., July 4, 1957; s. Thomas Marshall Gilbert Jr. and Jeanne Brainerd; m. Susan M. Pace, Apr. 28, 2001; 1 child, Joshua Daniel. BA in Philosphy/Theology, Boston Coll., 1979; MDiv, Maryknoll Sch. of Theology, 1983; MA in Counseling, Duquesne U., 1995. Microsoft cert. sys. engr., cert. project mgmt. profl., cert. info. systems security profl. Cons. Worklife Solutions, Old Greenwich, Conn., 1997; assignment dir. Deloitte & Touche, LLP, N.Y.C., 1998-2000; sr. project mgr. Exodus Comms., Herndon, Va., 2000-01; svc. dir. Cable & Wireless, Sterling, Va., 2001—04; sr. project mgr. Netsec, Herndon, Va., 2004—. Chmn. bd. SMA African Art Mus., 1997-98; exec. bd. Internat. Liaison of Lay Vols. in Mission, Washington, 1988-90. Recipient Eagle Scout, Boy Scouts Am., 1974. Mem.: Internat. Info. Sys. Security Cert. Consortium, Project Mgmt. Inst. Republican. Roman Catholic. Avocations: travel, fishing, amateur radio. Office: Netsec 13525 Dulles Technology Drive Herndon VA 20171 Office Phone: 703-788-6391. E-mail: dbg1999@hotmail.com.

GILBERT, ELAYNE RHODA, writer; b. Bklyn., Oct. 22, 1940; d. Henry Albert and Sara Gilbert. *America's revolution interests the Russians because in the last century maternal grandfather gave grandmother a handmade tablecloth embroidered with the family name and "1776" on it which he brought over from the Ukraine.* BA, U. Miami, 1964, MA, 1972; AA, Miami Dade C.C., 1996. With Dade County Cir. and County Cts., 1980—84; pollworker Dade County Election Days, 1988, 1990—2000, Broward County Election Days, 2002, 2004—05. Author: (book) Keepin' Up Kulcher: John Adams and Sidney Lanier Build Pound's Cantos, 1972, 4th edit, 2005, These Had Thrones: Edward Coke's Impact on 'The Cantos', 2001, 2d edit., 2004, Ivory Dipping in Silver: Poetic Ideas Wrapped in Monographs and Murders, 2002, 2d edti., 2004. Active Broward County Election Days, 2002, 2004—05. Avocations: reading, theater, movies, music, book collecting. Home: 3725 South Ocean Dr Penthouse 20 Hollywood FL 33019

GILBERT, ELLEN EFFMAN, music educator, conductor; b. New London, Conn., May 21, 1969; d. David Garth and Elaine Avery Effman; m. Steven Dale Gilbert, Dec. 25, 1995; 1 child, Eliza Avery. BS in Music Edn., U. Conn., 1991, MMus, 1995; Kodaly cert. in Music Edn., HARTT Sch. of Music, Hartford, Conn., 2001—. Music educator, bilingual Bridgeport (Conn.) Pub. Schs., 1992—93; choral condr. Hartford (Conn.) Camerata Conservatory, 1996—98; music educator Hartford Pub. Schools, 1996—98; choral condr. U. Conn. Treblemakers Cmty. Music Sch. of the Arts, Mansfield, Conn., 2003—; choir dir. Old Mystic (Conn.) Bapt. Ch., 2000—; music educator Mystic (Conn.) Mid. Sch., 1998—. Choral chairperson Ea. Region Music Festival, Waterford, Conn., 2002—; clinician/adjudicator R.I. Music Educators Conf., 2001—04; panel discussion rep. Providence Coll., Providence, 2000—00; presenter/condr. Gt. East Adjudication Festivals, Agawam, Mass., 1998—; presenter Conn. Music Educator's Conf., 2001, 03, 04, All State Elem. Gen. Mus. Conf., 2003, Frankin Pierce Coll., 2003; chmn. Children's Choir Repetoire and Stds. for Am. Choral Dir. Assn. Singer: Prov. Performing Arts Ctr.; contbr. articles to profl. jours. Member-at-large Stonington (Conn.) Players Thespian Assn., 2003; bd. of Christian edn. Old Mystic Bapt. Ch.; sec. Kodaly Educators of So. New Eng., Hartford, Conn. Grantee Celebration of Excellence, State of Conn., 2000, World Music Drumming in the Classroom, Stonington Edn. Fund, 2002, Recorder Consort, 2000, 100 Best Cmtys. Music Edn., 2002; scholar Young Artist Competition, Nat. Assn. of Teachers of Singing, 1990. Mem.: Am. Choral Directors Assn. (assoc.; presenter Mid. Sch. Festival, West Hartford, Conn. 1999—2003), Kodaly Educators of So. New Eg. (assoc.; sec. 1994—99), Orgn. Am. Kodaly Educators (assoc.), Conn. Music Educators Conf. (assoc.; presenter, Hartford 2001, choral chairperson 2002—03, presenter 2003—), Music Educators Nat. Conf. (assoc.). Democrat. American Baptist. Office: Mystic Mid Sch 204 Mistuxet Ave Mystic CT 06355 Office Phone: 860-536-9613. E-mail: egilbert@stoningtonschools.org.

GILBERT, ELMER GRANT, engineering educator, control theorist; b. Joliet, Ill., Mar. 29, 1930; s. Harry A. and Florence A. (Otterstrom) G.; m. Lois M. Verbrugge, Dec. 27, 1973. BSEE, U. Mich., 1952, MSEE, 1953, PhD in Instrumentation Engring., 1956. Instr. U. Mich., Ann Arbor, 1954-56, asst. prof., 1957-59, assoc. prof., 1959-63, prof. aerospace engring., 1963—. Founder, Applied Dynamics Inc., Ann Arbor. Patentee computer devices, 1968-74. Fellow IEEE (Control Engring. Field award 1994), AAAS; mem. Nat. Acad. Engring., Soc. Indsl. and Applied Math. Office: U Mich Dept Aerospace Engring Ann Arbor MI 48109-2140 Office Phone: 734-764-3355. Business E-Mail: elmerg@umich.edu.

GILBERT, FREDERICK E., development planner, Africanist, consultant; b. Mpls., May 28, 1939; s. Eugene Lester and Anne Cecelia (Omlie) G.; m. Jane Arey, June 30, 1962; children: Erik O., Christopher A., Peter A. BA, U. Minn., 1961; MALD, Tufts U., 1963, PhD, 1976. Desk officer for Niger, Upper Volta, Cote d'Ivoire, Dahomey and Togo U.S. AID, Washington, 1974-76, asst. dir. Yaounde, Cameroon, 1976-80, chief Africa econ. policy and analysis Washington, 1980-81, dir. Sahel and West Africa, 1981-83, prin. officer Dar es Salaam, Tanzania, 1983-86, dep. mission dir. Khartoum, Sudan, 1986-88, mission dir., 1988-90, regional dir. Abidjan, Cote d'Ivoire, 1990-93; ind. cons., 1994-97; dir. Famine Early Warning Sys., 1998-2000; ind. cons. Falls Church, Va., 2000—. Mem. ACLU, Am. Fgn. Svc. Assn., Amnesty Internat., Sierra Club, World Resources Inst. (policy consultative group on natural resources mgmt. for Africa 1994-97). Episcopalian. Avocations: skiing, tennis, bicycling.

GILBERT, GLENN GORDON, retired linguistics educator; b. Montgomery, Ala., Sept. 17, 1936; s. William H. and Margaret (Christensen) G.; m. Erika Wrede, Aug. 8, 1964 (div. Nov. 1993); children: Alexander Martin, Christa Selene; m. Sharon Wright Pape, July 23, 1994. AB in German Lang. and Lit., U. Chgo., 1957; postgrad., U. Frankfurt, Fed. Republic Germany, 1957—59; Diplôme de la Langue Française with honors, Sorbonne, U. Paris, 1960; PhD in Linguistics, Harvard U., 1963. Instr. Germanic langs. and lits. U. Tex., Austin, 1963-66, asst. prof. Germanic langs., 1967-70; vis. asst. prof. linguistics Can. Summer Sch. Linguistics, U. Alta., Edmonton, summer 1966; Fulbright lectr. linguistics U. Marburg, Fed. Republic Germany, 1966-67; assoc. prof. So. Ill. U., Carbondale, 1970-74, prof., 1975—, chmn. dept. linguistics, 1987—89, 1999—2002; Fulbright lectr. linguistics U. Mainz, Fed. Republic Germany, 1973-74; Z.W.O. rsch. fellow in Creole langs. U. Nijmegen, Netherlands, 1984-85; ret., 2005. Active numerous univ. linguistics coms. and couns.; bd. dirs., mem. editl. bd., Ill. bus. rep. Papers in Linguistics, 1979-87; pres. Linguistic Rsch. Inc., 1983-87; numerous invited lectures. Founder, editor Journal of Pidgin and Creole Languages, 1985-2001; author: Linguistic Atlas of Texas German, 1972; editor: (books) Texas Studies in Bilingualism, 1970, The German Language in America, 1971, Pidgin and Creole Languages: Essays in Memory of John E. Reinecke, 1987, Pidgin and Creole Linguistics in the Twenty-First Century, 2002; co-editor (with Jacob Ornstein) Problems in Applied Educational Sociolinguistics, 1978; editor and translator: Pidgin and Creole Languages: Selected Essays by Hugo Schuchardt, 1980; editor: (book series) Studies in Ethnolinguistics, 1993-2003; contbr. numerous articles to profl. jours., chpts. to books; also revs. Translator, interpreter various cmty. orgns. NDEA fellow in Swedish, Harvard U., 1961-63; rsch. grantee U. Tex.-Austin, 1963-70, Nat. Carl Schurz Meml. Fund, 1968, So. Ill. U.-Carbondale, 1970-84, NEH, 1981, Am. Philos. Soc., 1982. Mem. Soc. Caribbean Linguistics, Soc. for Pidgin and Creole Linguistics. Home: 166 Union Grove Rd Carbondale IL 62903-7687 Office Phone: 618-536-3385. Personal E-mail: glenngilbert@msn.com.

GILBERT, HARRY EPHRAIM, JR., retired hotel executive; b. Phila., Feb. 1, 1931; s. Harry Ephraim and Anna (Chilton) G.; children: Ronald C., Glen G.; m. Jacqueline J. Newton. BS in Hotel Adminstrn., Pa. State U., 1954. Resident mgr. Benjamin Franklin Hotel, Phila., 1954-71, gen. mgr., 1971-77, Cherry Hill Inns, N.J., 1977-78, Holiday Inn-City Line, Phila., 1978-80, Colony Inn, New Haven, 1980-81; sr. oper. analyst, gen. mgr. Aramark Corp., Phila., 1981-00; ret., 2000. Lectr. Hotel Sch., Pa. State U., 1956-58, Drexel U., Phila., 1962-63 Bd. dirs. Saratoga Council Boy Scouts Am., 1983-86; bd. dirs. Saratoga Conv. and Tourism Bur., 1985—; mem. ch. council Luth. Ch., Saratoga Springs. Mem. N.Y. Hotel/Motel Assn., Phila. Hotel and Motor Inn Assn. (sec. 1971-72, v.p. 1973-74, pres. 1975-76), Pa. Hotel Restaurant Soc. (sec.-treas. 1973-74), Pa. Hotel Motor Inn Assn. (dir. 1975-76, treas. 1976-77), N.J. Hotel-Motel Assn. (dir. 1977-78), Hotel-Motel Greeter Internat., Pa. State Hotel Greeters (pres. 1952-54, 74-79), Phila. Press Assn., Pa. State Alumni Club Phila., Hotel Sales Mgrs. Assn., Chestnut St. Assn. (dir. 1971-76), Skal of N. Am. (treas. 1979-80, sec. 1980-86, v.p. 87-88) Clubs: Skal of North Am. (treas. 1979-80, sec. 1980-86, v.p. 1987-88). Home: 152 Fox Chase Dr Delran NJ 08075-2322 E-mail: hgilbert@webtv.net.

GILBERT, HOWARD ALDEN, retired economics professor; b. Spokane, Wash., Feb. 1, 1935; s. Alden Phineas and Hester Anne (Warner) G.; m. Lucille Dorothy Weaver, June 28, 1957; children: Douglas Alden, Daniel William, Dawnna Faye Gilbert Berndt, Debra Anne Gilbert La Croix. BA, Cen. Bible Inst., Springfield, Mo., 1957; BS, Wash. State U., 1961, MA, 1962; PhD, Oreg. State U., 1967; postgrad., Vanderbilt U., 1971. Asst. prof. S.D. State U., Brookings, 1966-70, assoc. prof., 1970-76, prof., 1976—2001; ret., 2001. Expert witness retained by various attys. Mem. Mensa (pres. S.D. chpt. 1989-91, v.p. 1992-94, v.p. 1996-97), Mortar Bd., Phi Kappa Phi (pres., v.p., sec., marshall), Pi Gamma Mu (sec., v.p., pres.), Gamma Sigma Delta (treas., pres.), Alpha Zeta, Omicron Delta Epsilon, Lambda Chi Alpha (head advisor 1967-97, ednl. advisor 1997—, order of merit, Alumni Hall of Fame). Democrat. Avocations: motorcycling, building restoration, running, piano, photography. Home: 708 8th St Apt 7 Brookings SD 57006-1559 Business E-Mail: purplesage@brookings.net.

GILBERT, HOWARD N(ORMAN), lawyer, director; b. Chgo., Aug. 19, 1928; s. Norman Aaron and Fannie (Cohn) G.; m. Jacqueline Glasser, Feb. 16, 1957; children: Norman Abraham, Harlan Wayne, Joel Kenneth, Sharon. PhB, U. Chgo., 1947; JD, Yale U., 1951. Bar: Ill 1951, U.S. Dist. Ct. (no. dist.) Ill. 1955, U.S. Ct. Appeals (7th cir.) 1956. Ptnr. Rusnak, Deutsch & Gilbert, Chgo., 1962-79, Aaron, Schimberg, Hess & Gilbert, Chgo., 1980-84; sr. ptnr. Holleb & Coff, Chgo., 1984-2000, Wildman, Harrold, Chgo., 2000—. Bd. dirs. Jewish Fedn. Met. Chgo., 1977-83; chmn. bd. dirs., pres. Mt. Sinai Hosp. Med. Ctr., Chgo., 1968-69; trustee Chgo. Hosp. Coun., 1979-84; mem. Bd. Jewish Edn., 1972-77; mem. vis. com. Coll. of U. Chgo., 1997-2003. Mem. ABA, Chgo. Bar Assn., Chgo. Coun. Lawyers, Ill. Soc. Health Lawyers, Standard Club, Bryn Mawr Country Club. Democrat. Jewish. Office: Wildman Harrold Allen & Dixon 225 W Wacker Dr Ste 3000 Chicago IL 60606-1224 Office Phone: 312-201-2722. Business E-Mail: gilbert@wildmanharrold.com.

GILBERT, J. PHIL, federal judge; b. 1949; BS, U. Ill., 1971; JD, Loyola U., Chgo., 1974. Ptnr. Gilbert & Gilbert, Carbondale, Ill., 1974-83, Gilbert, Kimmel, Huffman & Prosser, Carbondale, 1983-88; circuit judge First Jud. Circuit, Ill., 1988-92; fed. judge U.S. Dist. Ct. (so. dist.) Ill., Benton, 1992—, chief judge, 1993—2000. Spl. asst. atty. gen. Pub. Aid Enforcement Divsn., 1974-75; asst. city atty. City of Carbondale, 1975-78; active Nat. Coun. Govt. Ethics Laws, 1988—; mem. Ill. State Bd. Elections, 1982, vice chmn., chmn., 1983-85. Bd. dirs. Friends of Morris Libr., 1988—; active Edn. Coun. 100, 1989—, Boy Scouts Am. Mem. Ill. State Bar, Jackson County Bar Assn., Ill. Judges Assn. (mem. com. jud. retention), Phi Alpha Delta. Office: US Dist Ct 301 W Main St Benton IL 62812-1362

GILBERT, JAMES CAYCE, minister; b. Nashville, Feb. 26, 1925; s. Gettis and Delia Mae (Snyder) G.; m. Freda Mae Mitchell, Sept. 3, 1949; children—Elizabeth, Suzanne, Kathryn, Rosalie. BA, Bethel Coll., McKenzie, Tenn., 1945, D.D. (hon.), 1976; B.D., Cumberland Presbyn. Theol. Sem., McKenzie, 1947; MA, Scarritt Coll., Nashville, 1948. Ordained to ministry Cumberland Presbyn. Ch., 1944; asso. pastor West Nashville Cumberland Presbyn. Ch., 1947-48; pastor River Oaks Cumberland Presbyn. Ch., Houston, 1948-55, Trinity Cumberland Presbyn. Ch., Ft. Worth, 1956-64; pastor emeritus Trinity Cumberland Presbyn. Ch, Ft. Worth; exec. dir. Cumberland Presbyn. Children's Home, Denton, Tex., 1964-90, dir. devel., 1991-94, exec. dir. emeritus; moderator gen. assembly Cumberland Presbyn. Ch., 1979-80. Stated clk., Red River Presbytery of the Cumberland Presbyn. Ch., 1993—. Mem. Nat. Assn. Homes Children, Southwestern Assn. Children's Home (past pres.), Tex. Assn. Execs. Homes Children (past pres.), Lions, Masons, K.T. Home: 3720 W Biddison St Fort Worth TX 76109-2705

GILBERT, JAMES EASTHAM, academic administrator; b. Bridgeport, Conn., July 1, 1929; s. Carl Ludwig and Anna Maude (Eastham) G.; m. Betty Lee Blankenship, Aug. 26, 1953; 1 child, Gregory Eastham. BS in Psychology, U. N.Mex., 1952, MA in Psychology, 1959; PhD in Psychology, Am. U., 1969. Interviewer Va. State Employment Service, Alexandria, 1952-53; tng. officer Nat. Security Agy., Washington, 1953-55, rsch. psychologist Ft. Meade, Md., 1957-64, Hdqrs., Sec. to Air Staff, USAF, Washington, 1955-57; assoc. dean adminstrn. Northeastern U., Boston, 1964-71; assoc. vice-chancellor Ind. U.-Purdue U., Ft. Wayne, 1971-78; v.p. acad. affairs Pittsburg (Kans.) State U., 1978-86, interim pres., 1983; pres. East Stroudsburg (Pa.) U., 1986-96, pres. emeritus, 1996—; spl. asst. to provost Med. U. S.C., 1996—. NCES fellow, 1998, Robert Wood Johnson Exec. Nurse Fellow Mentor, 2003. Mem. Sigma Xi, Psi Chi, Phi Kappa Phi, Omicron Delta Kappa. Democrat. Home: 1296 Waterfront Dr Mount Pleasant SC 29464-9493 Office Phone: 843-792-2010. Business E-Mail: gilbertj@musc.edu.

GILBERT, JAMES FREEMAN, geophysics educator; b. Vincennes, Ind., Aug. 9, 1931; s. James Freeman and Gladys (Paugh) G.; m. Sally Bonney, June 19, 1959; children: Cynthia, Sarah, James. BS, MIT, 1953, PhD, 1956; D honoris causa, Utrecht U., 1994; D in Engring. (hon.), Colo. Sch. Mines, 2004. Research assoc. MIT, Cambridge, 1956-57; asst. research geophysicist Inst. Geophysics and Planetary Physics at UCLA, 1957, asst. prof. geophysics, 1958-59; sr. research geophysicist Tex. Instruments, Dallas, 1960-61; prof. Inst. Geophysics and Planetary Physics, U. Calif. San Diego, La Jolla, 1961—2001, assoc. dir., 1976-88, prof. emeritus, 2001—; chmn. grad. dept. Scripps Inst. Oceanography, La Jolla, 1988-91. Chmn. steering com. San Diego Supercomputer, 1984-86. Contbr. numerous articles to profl. jours. Recipient Arthur L. Day medal Geol. Soc. Am., 1985, Internat. Balzan prize, 1990; Fairchild scholar Calif. Inst. Tech., Pasadena, 1987; fellow NSF, 1956, Guggenheim, 1964-65, 72-73, Overseas fellow Churchill Coll. U. Cambridge, Eng., 1972-73. Fellow AAAS, Am. Geophys. Union (William Bowie med. 1999); Nat. Acad. Scis., European Union Geoscis. (hon.); mem. Seismology Soc. Am. (medal 2004), Am. Math. Soc., Royal Astron. Soc. (recipient Gold medal 1981), Acad. Nat. dei Lincei (fgn.), Sigma Xi. Home: 780 Kalamath Dr Del Mar CA 92014-2630 Office: U Calif Inst Geophysics Planetary Physics 0225 La Jolla CA 92093 Office Phone: 858-534-2470. Business E-Mail: fgilbert@ucsd.edu.

GILBERT, JAMES H., lawyer, former state supreme court justice; b. Minneapolis, Mar. 11, 1947; three children. BA, U. Minn., 1969, JD, 1972. Bar: Minn., 1972; Wis., 1984; U.S. Dist. Ct. Minn., 1974; U.S. Tax Ct., 1978; U.S. Ct. Appeals (8th cir.), 1989; U.S. Supreme Ct., 1988. Lawyer, v.p., mng. ptnr. Meshbesher, Singer, and Spence Ltd., Mpls., 1971—; assoc. justice Minn. State Supreme Ct., Mpls., 1998—2003; atty. James H. Gilbert Law Group, Minnetonka, 2003—. Park Commr. City of Orono, Minn., 1988—; bd. dir. Minn. Drug Abuse Resistance Edn. Inc.,(D.A.R.E.) Mem. Minn. Bar Assn. Avocations: skiing, hunting, golf, tennis, snowmobiling. Office: James H Gilbert Law Group 10159 Wayzata Blvd Ste 250 Minnetonka MN 55305

GILBERT, JEREMIAH ABRAHAM, education educator, writer; b. San Bernardino, Calif., July 3, 1971; s. James and Adrienne Gilbert. BA, Calif. State U. San Bernardino, 1992; MA, U. Calif. Riverside, 1996. Instr. San Bernardino Valley Coll., 1998—. Adj. prof. Chaffey Coll., Rancho Cucamonga, Calif., 2000—. Author: (poetry collection) In a Strange Land, 2003. Mem.: PEN USA. Home: PO Box 753 Bryn Mawr CA 92318-0753 Personal E-mail: jgilbert@jgweb.net.

GILBERT, JOHN B., retired electric and power company official; b. Wilmington, Del., Nov. 9, 1956; s. William Edgar and Helen (Ginn) G.; m. Meralyn Gilbert; children: Jamie, Amanda, Chris. BA, Rollins Coll., 1978; postgrad., U. Fla., 1980-82. Supr. corp. environ. affairs Savannah (Ga.) Electric and Power Co., 1982-96; ret., 1996. Recipient So. Superlative award So. Co., Atlanta, 1992. Mem. Navy League, Air Force Assn. Avocations: reading, computers, model building. Home: 118 W Gazebo Ln Savannah GA 31410-3949

GILBERT, JOHN OREN, insurance company executive; b. Morris, Minn., Aug. 30, 1942; s. Oren Lincoln and Thelma (Hall) G.; m. Marilyn Jean Erickson, Nov. 26, 1966; children: Brad, Erica. BA, U. Minn., Morris, 1964; MBA, U. Wis., Oshkosh, 1978, DSc (hon.), 2003. Asst. v.p. managerial reporting Aid Assn. for Luths., Appleton, Wis., 1981-85, asst. vp. info. mgmt., 1985-86, v.p. field svcs., 1986-90, v.p., gen. mgr., 1990-91, sr. v.p., mem. ins. svcs., 1992-94, exec. v.p., 1995—96, chmn., pres., CEO, 1997—2001; chmn. Thrivent Fin. for Lutherans, Mpls., 2002—. Mem. U. Wis. Alumni Assn. (Disting. Alumni award 1992), Beta Gamma Sigma. Lutheran. Avocations: travel, wood-working. Home: 524 River St Minneapolis MN 55401-2542 Office: Thrivent Fin for Lutherans 625 Fourth Ave S Minneapolis MN 55415-1665 Business E-Mail: john.gilbert@thrivent.com.

GILBERT, JUDITH ARLENE, lawyer; b. L.A., Jan. 9, 1946; d. Beril B. and dorothy Marilyn (Stern) G.; m. Joel Philip Schiff; children: Lauren Michelle, Jared Daniel. AB in Econs. magna cum laude, UCLA, 1967; JD, Harvard U., 1970. Bar: Calif. 1971. Assoc. Rosenfeld, Meyer & Susman, 1970-72; Quittner, Stutman, Treister & Glatt, L.A., 1972-74; Abeles & Markowitza and predecessors, Beverly Hills, Calif., 1974-76; sr. counsel legal dept., credit advice, spl. assets North Am. divsn. Bank of Am. Nat. Trust and Savings Assn., 1977-88; of counsel Denton, Hall, Burgin & Warrens, 1988-90; contract ptnr. Lewis, D'Amato, Brisbois & Bisgaard, 1990-92; spl. counsel Pettit & Martin, 1992-95; contract ptnr. Adams, Duque & Hazeltine, 1995-96; of counsel Arter & Hadden, L.A., 1996—. Judge pro-tem Mcpl. and Small Claims Ct.; mem. arbitration panel L.A. Superior Ct.; planning com. ann. meeting State Bar Calif., 1986-87, 94-95, also host com. ann. meeting, 1987; bd. dirs. Pub. Counsle, 1986-89; spkr. in field. Mem. L.A. County Com. Human Resources; active girl Scouts U.S.A., Cystic Fibrosis, City of Hope; bd. govs. Arthritis Found., 1989-94; bd. trustees, co-chair ritual com., libr. com. Temple Judea, 1993-94, edn. and mem. com., 1990-94; co-chair drugs in workplace task force Temple Emanuel, 1989-91; mem. steering com. drugs in workplace program Temple Emanuel-Jewish Fedn. Coun. Mem. ABA (litigation, internat., banking, corp. and comml. sects., comml. transactions litigation com., creditor's rights litigation com., bus. bankruptcy com., others), Calif. State Bar Conf. (bd. dirs. 1997—, exec. com. 1991-95, chair exec. com. and conf. dels. 1994-95, resolutions com. of state bar, 1986, 1988-90, del. 1972—, vice chair conf. com. living wills and right to die 1977, com. on rights and obligations of unmarried cohabitators 1978-80, and legal separation 1980-81), Los Angeles Bar Assn. (bd. trustees 1984-85, comml. law and bankruptcy, taxation and copyright sects., steering com., co-chair fund raising sub-com. 1986, pac to defeat Prop 61), Beverly Hills Bar Assn. (ex-officio mem. bd. govs, exec. com. 1986-87, res. 1985-86, del. to state bar conf. of dels. 1973-91, vice chair 1980, chair 1981, atty. fee disputes panel, numerous other positions), L.A. Bankruptcy Forum, Fin. Lawyers Conf., Women in Bus., Calif. Women Lawyers Assn., Women Lawyers Assn., Am. Bankruptcy Inst., Comml. Law League Am., Fed. Bar Assn., L.A. Copyright Soc., Thespians, Collegian Singers, Brick Muller Soc., UCLA Alumni Assn. (adv. bd., mem. scholarship bd.), Tower and Flame, Merchants, Sutherland (sec.-treas. 1968-69), Phi Beta Kappa, Gamma Delta Epsilon, Pi Gamma Mu, Omega Delta Epsilon, Phi Chi Theta, Delta Phi Epsilon. Office: Arter & Hadden 725 S Figueroa St Ste 3400 Los Angeles CA 90017-5434

GILBERT, KATHIE SIMON, economist, educator; b. Akron, Ohio, Feb. 28, 1943; d. John Nicholas and Bernadine Mary (Ilg) Simon; m. John Randalph Gilbert, Jr., Jan. 28, 1964; children: Mark Ivan, Adam Stacy. BA, U. Ala., 1964; MA, La. State U., 1966, PhD, 1972; grad. mgmt. devel. program, Harvard U., 1989. Assoc. prof. econs. Miss. State U., 1968-78, prof. econs., 1978-93, prof. polit. sci., 1981-93, dept. head econs. and fin., 1985-93; prof. econs. Western N.Mex. U., Silver City, 1993—, v.p. acad. affairs, 1994—99, spl. asst. for quality initiatives, 1999—. Vis. sr. econ. analyst Miss. Rsch. and Devel. Ctr., 1985—; mem. adv. bd. Deposit Guaranty Nat. Bank, Starkville; bd. dirs. Quality N.Mex., 2003—. Contbr. articles to profl. jours. Vice chmn. Miss. Internat. Women's Yr. Com., 1977; chmn. Miss. State U. Faculty Coun., 1986-87; trustee Ednl. Found., 1993-96; bd. dirs. Oktibbeha County United Way, 1990-93, Starkville Area Habitat for Humanity; active Miss. Gov. Pvt. Sector Action Coun., Oktibbeha County Dem. Exec. Com., 1976-80, 84-88, N.Mex. First, 1994—, ACE nat. identification program, N.M. coord., 1997-99. Am. Council on Edn. fellow, 1979-80; Miss. Com. for Humanities grantee, 1975, 83 Mem. Am. Econ. Assn., So. Econ. Assn., Miss. Econ. Coun., Southwestern Econ. Assn. (pres.), Nat. Women's Studies Assn., Southeastern Women's Studies Assn. (pres.), AAUW (pres. Starkville br. 1977-79, v.p. Miss. div. 1980-82, pres. 1982-84, pres. Grant county br. 1986-87, nat. bd. dirs. 1987-89), LWV (treas. Starkville chpt. 1981-83), Southwestern Social Sci. Assn. (sec., pres. 1993-94), Silver City Grant County Econ. Devel. Assn. (pres. 1999-2003), Miss. State U. Faculty Women's Assn. (pres. 1981-82, 88-89), Mortar Bd., Phi Kappa Phi, Omicron Delta Epsilon, Beta Gamma Sigma. Democrat. Roman Catholic. Home: 3451 Ursa Minor Silver City NM 88061-6200 Office: Western New Mex U College Ave Silver City NM 88062-0610

GILBERT, LEONARD HAROLD, lawyer; b. Hutchinson, Minn., Apr. 3, 1936; s. Sidney and Clara (Franzblau) Gilbert; m. Jean Buchman, Apr. 21, 1963; children: Jonathan Stuart, Suzanne Elaine. BA, Emory U., 1958; LLB, Harvard U., 1961. Atty. Carlton, Fields, Tampa, Fla., 1961-98, Holland & Knight, LLP, Tampa, 1999—. Bd. dirs. Gasparilla Sidewalk Art Festival, Tampa, 1970—74, United Way; trustee Tampa Bay Performing Arts Ctr., Lowry Park Zool. Soc., Univ. Cmty. Hosp.; chmn. Art Coun. Tampa, Tampa, 1973—74; mem. Hillsborough County Bicentennial Commn., Fla., 1973—76, Tampa Charter Revision Com., 1975; pres. Tampa Mus. Art, 1986—87; chmn. bd. fellows U. Tampa, 1986—87, trustee, 1987—2000. With USCGR, 1961—69. Fellow: Fla. Bar Found., Am. Bar Found.; mem.: ABA (chmn. sect. gen. practice 1979—80, ho. dels. 1980—90, chmn. creditors' rights com. corps. sect., mem. coun. sect. bus. law 2000—04, mem. coun. sr. lawyer divsn.), Eleventh Cir. Hist. Soc. (trustee, v.p.), Am. Coll. Comml. Fin. Lawyers (pres. 1999—2000), N.C. Banking Inst., Internat. Insolvency Inst. (bd. dirs., sec. 2000—), Internat. Bar Assn., Am. Coll. Bankruptcy (bd. dirs. 1997—2003), Am. Law Inst., Am. Judicature Soc. (bd. dirs.), Bar Assn. Hillsborough County (pres. 1974—75), Fla. Bar (chmn. sect. corp. banking and bus. law 1970—71, chmn. sect. gen. practice 1972—73, bd. govs. 1975—79, pres. 1980—81), Tampa C. of C. (bd. dirs.), Harvard Law Sch. Assn. Fla. (pres. 1986), Univ. Club, Ye Mystic Krewe Gasparilla, Kiwanis (pres. 1972), Tampa Club (pres. 1986—87). Office: Holland & Knight LLP PO Box 1288 Tampa FL 33601-1288 Office Phone: 813-227-6481. Business E-Mail: leonard.gilbert@hklaw.com.

GILBERT, LUCIA ALBINO, psychology educator; b. Bklyn., July 27, 1941; d. William V. and Carmelina (Cutro) Albino; m. John Carl Gilbert, Dec. 18, 1965; 1 child, Melissa Carlotta. BA, Wells Coll., 1963; MS, Yale U., 1964; PhD, U. Tex., 1974. Lic. psychologist, Tex. Supr. research info. G.S. Gilmore Research Lab., New Haven, 1964-67; tchr. St. Stephen Sch., Austin, Tex., 1967-69; asst. prof. Iowa State U., Ames, 1974-76, U. Tex., Austin, 1976-81, assoc. prof., 1981-86, prof., 1986—, dir. women's studies, 1994—. Author: Men in Dual Career Families, 1985, Sharing It All: The Rewards and Struggles of Two-Career Families, 1988, Two Careers/One Family: The Promise of Gender Equality, 1993, Gender and Sex in Counseling and Psychotherapy, 1999; editor spl. issue Parenting, Dual Career Families; assoc. editor Psychology of Women Quarterly, 1987—. Recipient Excellence in Teaching award U. Tex., 1981-86, Holland award, 1989, Carolyn Sherif award, 1998. Fellow AAUW, Am. Psychol. Soc., Am. Psychol. Assn. (rep. council 1980-83, 86-89, 93—); mem. Assn. Women in Psychology. Avocations: swimming, progressive country music, ecology, theater. Home: 4402 Balcones Dr Austin TX 78731-5710 Office: U Tex Dept Psychology Austin TX 78712

GILBERT, MARIE ROGERS, poet; b. Florence, SC, Jan. 27, 1924; d. Frank Mandeville and Marie Barringer Rogers; m. Richard Austin Gilbert, Apr. 24, 1946; children: Richard Austin Jr., Laurie Gilbert Sanford. BA in Psychology and Theater Arts, Rollins Coll., 1945. Read poetry at Spoleto Festival, Charleston, S.C., 1999. Contbr. poetry to anthologies including Word and Witness: 100 Years of North Carolina Poetry, 1999; author: Brookgreen Oaks, 1999, Connexions, 1994, Myrtle Beach Back When, 1989, Forever New, 1987, The Song and the Seed, 1983, From Comfort, 1981. Driver ARC, Florence Army Air Base, 1943-44; trustee St. Andrews Presbyn. Coll., Laurinburg, NC, 2002 Recipient Poet Laureate Sam Ragan Fine Arts award St. Andrews Presbyn. Coll., 1994, Fortner award St. Andrews Presbyn. Coll., 2003. Mem. Poetry Soc. N.C. (v.p., 1988-89, pres. 1990-92), Poetry Soc. S.C. (1st pl. for lyric poetry 1987, 90), N.C. Writers Conf., N.C. Writers Network, Colonial Dames of Am. in state of N.C. (sec. 1990-91, v.p. 1992-93), Jr. League. Avocation: poetry readings and seminars. Home: 2 Saint Simons Sq Greensboro NC 27408-3833

GILBERT, MELISSA, actors guild executive, actress; b. Los Angeles, May 8, 1964; d. Paul and Barbara (Crane) G.; m. Bo Brinkman (div.); 1 son, Dakota; m. Bruce Boxleitner, Jan. 1, 1995; stepchildren: Lee, Sam. Student, U. So. Calif. Actress: (TV movies) Little House on the Prairie, 1974, Christmas Miracle in Caulfield, U.S.A., 1977, The Miracle Worker, 1979, The Diary of Anne Frank, 1980, Splendor in the Grass, 1981, Little House: Look Back to Yesterday, 1983, Choices of the Heart, 1983, Little House: Bless All the Dear Children, 1984, Family Secrets, 1984, Little House: The Last Farewell, 1984, Choices, 1986, Penalty Phase, 1986, Family Secrets, Killer Instincts, Without Her Consent, Forbidden Nights, 1990, Blood Vows: The Story of a Mafia Wife, Joshua's Heart, 1990, Donor, The Lookalike, 1990, Conspiracy of Silence: The Shari Karney Story, 1992, With Hostile Intent, 1993, Shattered Trust, 1993, House of Secrets, 1993, Dying to Remember, 1993, Cries From the Heart, 1994, Against Her Will: The Carrie Buck Story, 1994, The Babymaker: The Dr. Cecil Jacobson Story, 1994, Danielle Steel's 'Zoya', 1995, Christmas in My Hometown, 1996, Seduction in a Small Town, 1996, Childhood Sweetheart, 1997, Her Own Rules, 1998, Murder at 75 Birch, 1999, Switched at Birth, 1999, A Vision of Murder: The Story of Donielle, 2000, Sanctuary, 2001, Then Came Jones, 2003; (TV series) Little House on the Prairie, 1974-82, Little House: A New Beginning, 1983, Stand By Your Man, 1992, Sweet Justice, 1994-95 (TV spls.) Battle of the Network Stars, 1978, 79, 81, 82, Celebrity Challenge of the Sexes, 1980, Circus Lions, Tigers and Melissa, Too, 1977, Dean Martin Celebrity Roast, 1984, (stage prodns.) Night of 100 Stars, 1982, The Glass Menagerie, 1985, A Shayna Maidel, 1987 (Outer Critics Circle Award), (feature films) Nutcracker Fantasy, 1979, Sylvester, 1985, Ice House, 1989. Mem.: SAG (pres. 2001—).

GILBERT, MICHAEL M., neuropsychiatrist; b. Orange, N.J. 3 children. BS in Psychology, U. Mich., 1938, MS in Psychology, 1940, MD, 1948, PhD in Psychology, 1949. Diplomate Am. Bd. Psychiatry and Neurology, 1955. Lab. asst. dept. psychology U. Mich., 1937—40; occupl. analyst U.S. Employment Svc., 1940—41; chief occupl. analyst rsch. and tech. svcs. Region III War Manpower Commn., 1941—44; pers. rsch. analyst war dept. Adj. Gen. Office, 1947; neuropsychiatrist pvt. practice, 1952—; sr. psychiatrist Fla. State Hosp., Chattahoochee, 1992. Adj. prof. Psychol. Inst., Miami, 1990. Contbr. articles profl. jours. Classification specialist U.S. Army, 1943—44, med. officer, psychiatrist USAF, 1950—51. Fellow: Acad. Psychosomatic Medicine; mem.: Am. Soc. Clinic Psychopharmacology, Soc. Med. Psychiatry, Fla. Psychol. Assn., Ea. Psychiat. Assn., Parkinson Found. (med. adv. bd.), Nat. Assn. Alcholism, So. Med. Assn., Fla. Med. Assn., AMA, Dade County Med. Assn., APA, Am. Psychiat. Assn., Sigma Xi. Achievements include research in psychotropic and analgesic drugs. Home: 22 W San Marino Dr Miami Beach FL 33139 E-mail: m22gilbert@juno.com.

GILBERT, NEIL ROBIN, social work educator, writer, consultant; b. N.Y.C., Sept. 18, 1940; s. Alan and Ida (Bedzin) G.; children: Evan Mallory, Jesse Arthur; m. Rebecca A. Van Voorhis, 2002; children: George Nathaniel, Nicole. BA, Bklyn. Coll., 1963; MSW, U. Pitts., 1965, PhD, 1968. Caseworker Interdepartmental Service Ctr., N.Y.C., 1963; dir. research Mayor's Com. on Human Resources, Pitts., 1967-69; prof. sch. social welfare U. Calif., Berkeley, 1969—, chmn. doctoral program, 1983—, acting dean sch. social welfare, 1986, 95-97, Milton and Gertrude Chernin prof. social welfare and social svcs., 1989—. Advisor Jour. Social Policy, 1982—. Author: Clients or Constituents, 1970, Capitalism and the Welfare State, 1983, (with others) Dimensions of Social Welfare Policy, 1974, 2d rev. edit., 1986, Dynamics of Community Planning, 1978, (with Barbara Gilbert) The Enabling State, 1989, Protecting Young Children from Sexual Abuse, 1989, Practical Program Evaluation, 1990, (with Jill Berrick) With the Best of Intentions, 1992, Welfare Justice, 1995, Transformation of the Welfare State, 2002; editor: (with Rebecca Van Voorhis) Activating the Unemployed; editor Social Welfare Series, 1977-83, Social Worker and Social Welfare Series, 1977—. Trustee Head Royce Sch., 1990-96; chair bd. dirs. Seneca Ctr. Fellow NIMH, 1966, U.N. Research Inst. for Social Devel., 1975; Fulbright scholar, U.S. Info. Agy, 1981; Fulbright Research fellow, London, 1981, Fulbright Western European scholar, 1987; recipient Medallion of Distinction U. Pitts., 1987. Mem. Nat. Assn. Social Workers, Assn. Pub. Policy Analysis and Mgmt. Avocations: skiing, moutaineering. Office: U Calif Sch Social Welfare Haviland Hl Berkeley CA 94720-0001

GILBERT, PAUL H., engineering executive, consultant; b. Healdsburg, Calif., Apr. 23, 1936; s. Lindley D. and Beatrice G.; m. Elizabeth A. Gilbert, July 13, 1963; children: Christopher, Gregory, Kevin. BSCE, U. Calif., Berkeley, 1959, MSCE, 1960. Registered profl. engr. in 17 states. Project mgr. Calif. State Water Project, Sacramento, 1959-68; officer U.S. Army Corp Engrs., Heidleberg, Germany, 1960-61, capt., 1961-68; project mgr. Parsons Brinckerhoff, N.Y.C., 1969-73, regional mgr./ptnr. San Francisco, 1973-85, dir. N.Y.C., 1973-98, sr. v.p., 1973—; vice chmn. Parsons Brinckerhoff Internat. Inc., 1973—99; chmn. bd. Parsons Brinckerhoff, N.Y.C., 1990-98, project dir. supercollider design and constrn. Dallas, 1990-95. Prin.-in-charge of award winning projects Glenwood Canyon I-70 tunnels, San Francisco Ocean Outfall, Seattle Bus. Tunnel, Hood Canal Floating Bridge and West Seattle High Level and Low Level Swing Bridges, others; Laser Interferometer Gravitational-Wave Obs. reviewer NSF, Washington, 1992—99; program mgmt. advisor Railtrack West Coast Modernization Project, London, GM Design Ctr. Modernization, Warren, Mich.; NRC spl. com. on rev. and oversigh U.S. Dept. Energy Project Mgmt. Program, 1999—2002; mem. U. Calif. Pres.'s Coun.; chmn. Project Mgmt. Panel for the UC Managed Three Nat. Labs., 2000—; mem. NRC Com. on Sci. and Tech. for Countering Terrorism; chmn. oversight com. for nat. radio astronomy obs. Atacama Large Millimeter Array Radio Astronomy Obs. Trustee Assoc. Univs., Inc., 1998—. Recipient Lincoln Art Welding award, 1964; named disting. engring. alumnus U. Calif., Berkeley, 1998. Fellow: ASCE (life Rickey medal 1969, Constrn. Mgmt. award 1994); mem.: Nat. Acad. Engring., Moles, Soc. Am. Mil. Engrs., Project Mgmt. Inst. Republican. Roman Catholic. Office: Parsons Brinkerhoff 999 3rd Ave Ste 2200 Seattle WA 98104-4020 Office Phone: 206-382-6357. Personal E-mail: gilbertp@pbworld.com.

GILBERT, RICHARD KEITH, education educator, researcher; b. St. Louis, Apr. 23, 1958; s. William Ray and Janice Sylvia (Rephlo) Gilbert. BA, U. Calif., Santa Barbara, 1981, MA, 1990, postgrad., 1993; PhD, U. So. Calif., 1997. Cert. secondary tchr. Calif. Rschr. Marine Sci. Inst., Santa Barbara, 1979-82; rschr., coord. Catalina Isl. Marine Inst., Calif., 1983-85; tchr. sci. LA Unified Sch. Dist., 1985-87; sci. and calculus educator Am. Internat. Sch., Johannesburg, 1987-89; rschr. psychotherapy U. Calif., Santa Barbara, 1990-92; cons. advanced tech. divsn. spl. projects Gen. Rsch. Corp., Santa Barbara, 1992-94; instr., rschr. U. So. Calif., LA, 1993—; head dept. sci. Valley HS, 2002—. Rschr., cons. Human Scis. Rsch. Coun., Pretoria, South Africa, 1995; cons. spl. project divsn. binary sys. and geog. area specialist Akela Corp., 1994; team leader, cons. Tertiary Edn. Linkages Project USAID, Pretoria, 1996; profl. expert rsch. and evaluation dept. alternative edn. L.A. County Office Edn.; adj. prof., rschr. U. So. Calif., 1993—; cons. tech. Capabilities, Assessment Geog. Info. Sys.; evaluator NSF, 1999—; adj. prof. rsch. U. Phoenix; evaluator MSP Projects NSF, 2002—; cons. UN Bangladesh Sci. Project, 2002; chair sci. dept. Hacienda La Punta Sch. Dist., 2002—; evaluator TPC programs NSF, 2003—; cons. South East Asia Mins. of Edn. Orgn., 2005—; facilitator organizational devel. tertiary edn. Republic Vietnam, CSEAME, 2005; mem edn. task force Hacuabde La Ponte, U. S.D. Active re-election campaign Hon. Robert Lagomarsino, Santa Barbara, 1992. Named Outstanding Tchr. Advanced Biol. Sci., NSF, Calif. State U. Northridge, 1986—87; recipient Outstanding Mentor award, NSF Rsch. Dir. Fellow Program, 2002—; Calif. State U. fellow, U. So. Calif. fellow, 1993, Eisenhower fellow in marine rsch., NSF, 2002—, Calif. Sci. Project fellow, 2002—, NSF fellow, 2002, Robotics edn. grantee, NASA. Mem.: AAAS, Am. Ednl. Rsch. Assn., Comparative Internat. Edn. Soc., NY Acad. Sci., Order Internat. Ambs., Phoenix Soc. (Outstanding Achievement award 1987), US Naval Inst., Phi Beta Delta. Presbyterian. Avocations: scuba diving, photography, music, climbing, trekking. Home: 7931 Caldwell Ave Whittier CA 90602 Office: 6285 Avenide Ganso Goleta CA 93117-5485 E-mail: richard.gilbert@mindspring.com.

GILBERT, RONALD RHEA, lawyer; b. Sandusky, Ohio, Dec. 29, 1942; s. Corvin and Mildred (Millikin) G.; children: Elizabeth, Lynne, Lisa; m. Wendy Wawrzyniak, Apr. 2, 2002; 1 stepchild, Joshua Sisco. BA, Wittenberg U., 1964; JD, U. Mich., 1967, postgrad., 1967-68, Wayne State U., 1973-74. Bar: Mich. 1968, U.S. Dist. Ct. (ea. and we. dists.) Mich. 1968, U.S. Ct. Appeals (6th cir.) 1968, U.S. Ct. Appeals (9th cir.) 1977, U.S. Ct. Appeals (7th cir.) 1984, U.S. Ct. Appeals (3d cir.) 1988, U.S. Ct. Appeals (4th cir.) 1989, U.S. Ct. Appeals (8th cir.) 1990, U.S. Ct. Appeals (10th cir.) 1991, U.S. Ct. Appeals (11th cir.) 1992, U.S. Ct. Appeals (2nd cir.), 1992. Assoc. prosecutor Wayne County, Mich., 1969; assoc. Rouse, Selby, Dickinson, Shaw & Pike, Detroit, 1969-72; ptnr. Charfoos, Christensen, Gilbert & Archer, P.C., Detroit, 1972-84; sole practice, 1984—. Instr. Madonna Coll., Detroit, 1977-81; mem. faculty Inst. Continuing Legal Edn., 1977—; speaker symposium on social security law Detroit Coll. Law, 1984; state bar grievance investigator; vol. chmn. Aquatic Injury Safety Found; mgr. web sites Found. for Spinal Cord Injury Prevention, Care and Cure (fscip.org), Found. for Aquatic Injury Prevention (aquaticisf.org). Co-author: Social Security Disability Claims, 1983; contbr. articles to legal jours. Founder, chmn. Aquatic Injury Safety Group, 1982-89, Found. for Aquatic Injury Prevention, 1988, Found. for Spinal Cord Injury Prevention, 1988; chmn. aquatic safety com. Nat. Safety Coun., 1987; data collection subcom. of Nat. Swimming Safety Com. for Consumer Products Safety Commn.; bd. dirs. Nat. Coordinating Coun. on Spinal Cord Injuries; patron Detroit Art Inst., Detroit Zool. Soc.; mem. Pres.' Club U. Mich.; mem. Detroit Council on World Affairs, 1968-73, Council for Nat. Coop. in Aquatics; mem. combined fed. campaign Nat. Health Agy. Mich.; founder Spinal Cord Injury Traumatic Brain Injury Adv. Com. Mich. Pub. Health Chronic Adv. Com.; co-founder Safe Kids Coalition Southeastern Mich.; mem. Nat. Safe Kids Coalition. Mem. ATLA, Mich. Trial Lawyers Assn., System Safety Soc., ABA, Mich Bar Assn., Detroit Bar Assn., Am. Arbitration Assn., Am. Judicature Soc., Nat. Spinal Cord Injury Assn. (sec. 1988, bd. dirs., exec. com., chmn. prevention com.), Nat. Head Injury Assn., Mich. Head Injury Assn., Am. Standards and Testing Materials (com. F-24 on water parks and playgrounds, mem. com. F-8), World Water Parks Assn., Nat. Environ. Health Assn., Nat. Pub. Health Assn., Nat. Eagle Scout Assn. (alumni), Blue Key, Pi Kappa Alpha, Pi Sigma Alpha, Pi Delta Epsilon, Fenton Rotary, Fenton Village Theatre, U. Mich. Club, Spring Meadows Country Club. Office Phone: 800-342-0330. Personal E-mail: rrgjedi@aol.com.

GILBERT, ROSE BENNETT, journalist; b. High Point, NC, July 11, 1938; d. Ellis Howard and Sadie B. (Vernon) Bennett; children: Scott Randolph, Bennett J. BA, Mary Washington Coll., 1960; postgrad., George Washington U., 1964—65. Reporter Richmond (Va.) News-Leader, 1960—64; editor 1,001 Decorating Ideas Mag., NYC, 1973—75; columnist Chgo. Tribune-Daily News Syndicate, 1975—77; v.p., ptnr. Sweet & Co., NYC, 1978—80; pres. Gilbert/Green Comm., NYC, 1980—90, RBG Comm., NYC, 1990—. Assoc. editor Country Decorating Mag., NYC; tchr. Maplewood/South Orange (NJ) Adult Sch., 1975—90; lectr. NY Sch. Interior Design, 1985—88; syndicated columnist Copley News Svc., San Diego, 1988—. Co-author: You-Do-It Book of Early American Decorating, 1978, Decorating Country-Style, 1980, Your Colors at Home, 1985, Manhattan-Style, 1990, Hampton Style, 1993; contbg. editor, columnist Cooking Light Mag., 2003—05. Fellow: Bd. Internat. Furnishings and Design Assn. (pres. 2001); mem.: Mary Washington Coll. Alumni Assn. (v.p. 1966—67). Episcopalian. Home: 73 Jefferson Ave Maplewood NJ 07040-1228 Office: 101 W 23d St Ste 2396 New York NY 10011 Office Phone: 212-674-5108. E-mail: rose.gilbert@att.net.

GILBERT, SARA, actress; b. Jan. 29, 1975; d. Harold Abeles and Barbara Gilbert. Actor: (TV series) Roseanne 1988-97, Twins, 2005, (TV movies) Sudie & Simpton, 1990, Calamity Jane, Broken Record, 1997, (TV spls.) ABC Weekend Spl., 1988, Valvolene Nat. Driving Test, 1989, 4th Ann. Am. Comedy Awards, 1990, Tom Arnold: The Naked Truth, 1991, In a New Light, 1992, 43 Ann. Foley's Thanksgiving Day Parade, 1992, CBS Schoolbreak Spls., 1992, (syndicated game show) Fun House, 1989, (talk show) At Rona's, 1989, (film) Poison Ivy, 1992, Outside Providence, 1998, Desert Blue, 1998, $30, 1999, Light It Up, 1999, The Big Tease, 1999, High Fidelity, 2000, Boys Life 3, 2000, Riding in Cars with Boys, 2001.

GILBERT, SCOTT FREDERICK, biologist, educator, author; b. N.Y.C., Apr. 13, 1949; s. Marvin Marshall and Elaine (Caplan) G.; m. Anne Marie Raunio, Dec. 30, 1971; children: Daniel, Sarah, David. BA, Wesleyan U., 1971; MA, PhD, Johns Hopkins U., 1976; PhD (hon.), U. Helsinki. Postdoctoral assoc. U. Wis., Madison, 1976-78, 1978-80; asst. prof. Swarthmore (Pa.) Coll., 1980-86, assoc. prof., 1986-92, prof., 1992—. Author: Developmental Biology, 1985, 88, 91, 94, 97, 2000, 03, Embryology, 1997; zoology editor Jour. Irreproducible Results, 1979-93, Com. de Patronage, Annales Hist. Philosophie Sci.; mem. editl. bd. Am. Jour. Med. Genetics, Jour. Exptl. Zoology, Internat. Jour. Devel. Biol., Ency. of Life Scis.; contbr. articles to sci. jours. Recipient Dwight J. Ingle award Perspectives in Biology and Medicine, 1984, medal of Francois I, Coll. de France, 1996; Guggenheim fellow, 1999. Fellow AAAS; mem. Soc. Devel. Biology (Viktor Hamburger prize 2002), Soc. Integrative Comparative Biology, Internat. Soc. for Differentiation (exec. bd.), Soc. Human Genetics, Hist. Sci. Soc., St Petersburg Soc. Naturalists (hon. fellow 2001, Kowalevsky prize 2004), Internat. Soc. Hist., Philos. Soc. Studies Biology, Phi Beta Kappa, Sigma Xi. Democrat. Jewish. Home: 224 Cornell Ave Swarthmore PA 19081-1932 Office: Swarthmore Coll Dept Biology 500 College Ave Swarthmore PA 19081-1306 Office Phone: 610-328-8049. Business E-Mail: sgilber1@swarthmore.edu.

GILBERT, SHARON, artist; b. Bklyn., Feb. 15, 1944; m. Vyt Bakaitis, Jan. 23, 1970; children: Elena Bakaitis, Ellery Bakaitis. BFA, Cooper Union, 1966. Author: Three Mile Island Reproductions, 1979, Waste, 1980, '80 Faces, 1980, A Nuclear Atlas, 1982, Poison America, 1988, Green the Fragile, 1989, Urgent Life, 1990, Action Poses, 1991, Urban Renewal, 1992, Working Time, 1994, Chemical Ways, 1997, Police (State) USA, 2001, So Quiet, 2003, Seeing Amsterdam, 2004; one-woman shows include Printed Matter, N.Y.C., 1980, Resnick Gallery, LI U., 1990, Rutgers U., New Brunswick, N.J., 1992, PABA Gallery, New Haven, 1999, Ctr. Book Arts, N.Y.C., 2002, Kanaal 10, Amsterdam, 2004, exhibited in group shows at Albert-Ludwig U., Freiburg, Germany, 1980, Ctr. George Pompidou, Paris, 1985, Mus. Modern Art, N.Y.C., 1988—90, Vasarely Mus., Budapest, Hungary, 1990, Bklyn. Mus. Art, 2004, Corcoran Gallery Art, Washington, 2005, others. Grantee, Carl Schurz Hans German-Am. Inst., Freiburg, 1980, Women's Studio Workshop, 1982, N.Y. Found. Arts, 1989, Artists Space, 1990, Puffin Found., 2005.

GILBERT, STEVEN JEFFREY, venture capitalist, screenwriter; b. N.Y.C., Apr. 6, 1947; s. Bernard and Ruth (Turner) G.; m. Anita Schneider, Apr. 25, 1987; children: Steven Turner, Anna Christina. BS in Econs., U. Pa., 1967; JD, Harvard U., 1970, MBA, 1972. Bar: Mass. 1970. Assoc. Morgan Stanley and Co., N.Y.C., 1972-76; v.p. Wertheim and Co., N.Y.C., 1976-78; mng. dir. E.F. Hutton, Internat., N.Y.C., 1978-80; pres., chief exec. officer Lion's Gate Films, Inc., L.A., 1980-82; gen. ptnr. Ctrl. Devel. Ptnrs., N.Y.C., 1982-83; mng. gen. ptnr. Chem. Venture Ptnrs., N.Y.C., 1983-88; mng. dir. Commonwealth Capital Ptnrs., N.Y.C., 1988—; mng. gen. ptnr Soros Capital, N.Y.C., 1992—; chmn. bd. Gilbert Global Equity Ptnrs., L.L.C., 1997—. Bd. dirs. A.C.X. Pacific, Inc., The Asian Infrastructure Fund, LCC Internat., Inc., Montpelier Re, CPM Holdings, True Temper Sports, Inc., J.O. Hambro Capital Mgmt. Group; trustee NYU Med. Ctr. Screenwriter Chapter XI, 1982. Mem. undergrad. bd. Wharton Sch.; bd. govs. Lauder Inst.; trustee Woodrow Wilson Internat. Ctr. for Scholars. Mem. Writers Guild Am., Young Pres. Orgn., Coun. on Fgn. Rels. E-mail: sgilbert@gilbertglobal.com.

GILBERT, WALTER, molecular biologist, educator; b. Boston, Mar. 21, 1932; s. Richard V. and Emma (Cohen) G.; m. Celia Stone, Dec. 29, 1953; children: John Richard, Kate. AB, Harvard U., 1953, AM, 1954; PhD, Cambridge U., 1957; DSc (hon.), U. Chgo., 1978, Columbia U., 1978, U. Rochester, 1979, Yeshiva U., 1981. NSF postdoctoral fellow Harvard U., Cambridge, Mass., 1957-58, lectr. physics, 1958-59, asst. prof. physics, 1959-64, assoc. prof. biophysics, 1964-68, prof. biochemistry, 1968-72, Am. Cancer Soc. prof. molecular biology, 1972-81, prof. biology, 1985-86, H.H. Timken prof., 1986-87, Carl M. Loeb Univ. prof., 1987—, chair dept. cellular and devel. biology, 1987-93; chmn. sci. bd. Biogen, 1978-83, co-chmn., supervisory bd., 1979—81, chmn. supervisory bd., chief exec. officer, 1981—84; vice chmn., bd. dirs. Myriad Genetics, Inc., 1992—; chmn. bd. dirs. Paratek Pharms., Inc., 1996—, Prolexis, Inc. (formerly Myriad Proteomics, Inc.), 2001—. V.D. Mattia lectr. Roche Inst. Molecular Biology, 1976; mem. bd. sci. govs. The Scripps Rsch. Inst., 1994-; bd dirs. ActivBiotics, Inc. 1997-; bd. dirs. Memory Pharms., Inc., mem. sci. adv. bd., 1998-; bd. dirs., mem. sci. adv. bd. Trankaryotic Therapies, Inc., 2000-; bd. dirs. HospitalCareOnline.com., Inc., 2001; chmn. bd. dirs., sci. adv. bd. Pintex Pharms., Inc., 1999; mng. ptnr. BioVentures Investors, 2001- Recipient U.S. Steel Found. NAS, 1968, Ledlie prize Harvard U., 1969, Warren triennial prize Mass. Gen. Hosp., 1977, Louis and Bert Freedman Found. N.Y. Acad. Scis., 1977, Prix Charles-Leopold Mayer Academie des Scis., Inst. de France, 1977, Nobel prize in chemistry, 1980, New Eng. Entrepreneur of Yr. award, 1991; co-winner Louisa Gross Horwitz prize Columbia U., 1979, Gairdner prize, 1979, Albert Lasker Basic Sci. award, 1979; Guggenheim fellow, 1968-69; hon. fellow Trinity Coll., Cambridge, U.K., 1991. Mem. Am. Phys. Soc., Nat. Acad. Scis., Am. Soc. Biol. Chemists, Am. Acad. Arts and Scis., Royal Soc. (fgn.), Harvard Soc. Fellows (chmn.). Office: The Biol Labs 16 Divinity Ave Cambridge MA 02138-2020*

GILBERT, WAYNE FRANCIS, surgeon, educator; b. Omak, Wash., May 15, 1960; MD, St. Louis U., 1987. Cert. in surgery. Intern U. Oreg. Health Scis.-U. Portland, 1987—88, resident, 1988—89, active staff, adj. asst. prof. surgery, 1996—; resident Legacy Emanuel-Kaiser Surgery, Portland, 1989—94; staff St. Vincent's Hosp., Portland, 1996—; active staff, adj. asst. prof. surgery Providence Portland Med. Ctr., 1996—; staff Southwest Wash. Med. Ctr., Vancouver, 1996—. Fellow ACS; mem. AMA, Soc. Am. Gastrointestinal Endoscopic Surgeons, Am. Med. Informatics Assn. Office: Kaiser Permanente Mother Joseph Plaza 9427 SW Barnes Rd Portland OR 97225-6606

GILBERT-BARNESS, ENID F., pathologist, educator; b. Sydney, Australia, May 31, 1927; arrived in U.S., 1952, naturalized, 1975; d. Christian Henry and Mabel (Milne) Fischer; m. James Bryson Gilbert, Aug. 12, 1954; children: Mary M., Elizabeth A., James C. (dec.), Jennifer E., Rebecca D.; m. Lewis Barness, July 5, 1987. MBBS, U. Sydney, 1950, MD, 1983; DSc (hon.), U. Wis., 1999; MD (hon.), U. Sydney, 1999. Diplomate Am. Bd. Pediat., Am. Bd. Clin. Pathology, Am. Bd. Anatomical Pathology, Am. Bd. Pediat. Pathology. Resident Children's Hosp., Boston, Phila., Washington, Brackenridge Hosp., Austin, Tex.; from asst. prof. to assoc. prof. U. W.Va., 1963-70; from assoc. prof. pathology and pediats. to prof. U. Wis., Madison, 1970-93, Disting. Med. Alumni prof., 1986-93, dir. pediat. pathology, 1970-93, prof. emeritus pathology and pediat., 1993—, Disting. Med. Alumni prof. emeritus, 1993—; prof. pathology, pediats. and ob-gyn. U. So. Fla., 1993—. Mem. editl. bds. Pediat. and Devel. Path. Med. jours., 1986—. Author: Introduction to Pathology, 1978, Genetic Aspects Developmental Pathology, 1987, Potters Pathology of the Fetus and Infant, 1997, Atlas Infant and Fetal Pathology, 1998, Metabolic Diseases, 2000, Atlas Embryo Fetal Pathology, 2004, Clinical Use of Pediatric Diagnostic Tests, 2003, Pediatric Autopsy Pathology, 2004; also numerous chpts., articles. Decorated Order of Australia; recipient Disting. Pathologist award, Royal Coll. Pathologists (Australia), 2001; grantee, NIH, 1972—92. Mem. Am. Soc. Clin. Pathology, Soc. Pediat. Pathology (pres. 1986-87), Internat. Acad. Pathology, Internat. Pediat. Pathology Assn. (pres. 1990-92), Teratology Soc., Cardiovasc. Soc. S.Am. (hon.), Am. Pediat. Soc., Am. Acad. Pediat., U.S. Can. Acad. Pathology, Arthur Purdy Stout Soc. Surg. Pathology, N.Y. Acad. Sci., Alpha Omega Alpha. Republican. Avocation: writing. Home: 3301 Bayshore Blvd #403 Tampa FL 33629 Office: Tampa Gen Hosp Dept Pathology Tampa FL 33601 Office Phone: 813-844-7565. Business E-Mail: egilbert@tgh.org.

GILBERT-JONES, GLENNA, artist, educator; b. New London, Conn., Sept. 24, 1923; d. Joseph and Florence (Scheyer) Fine; m. Harold N. Gilbert, Sept. 15, 1946 (div. 1973); m. John Paul Jones, June 30, 1990. BA, Hunter Coll., 1944. Tchr. Barnsdall Arts and Crafts Ctr., 1965—, Torrance Adult Sch., Torrance, Calif., 1983-88, Rustic Canyon Art, Santa Monica, Calif., 1983-90, Emerson H.S., Westchester, Calif., 1987-88. Represented in permanent collection Brand Libr., Glendale, Calif, Ventana Med. Sys., Oro Valley, Ariz. Mem. AAUW, Nat. Watercolor Soc. (signature). Avocation: photography. Home: 10384 N Fair Mountain Dr Tucson AZ 85737-9058

GILBERTSON, DAVID, state supreme court justice; b. Milw., Oct. 29, 1949; BA, S.D. State U., 1972; JD, U. S.D. Sch. of Law, 1975. Atty. priv. practice, SD, 1975—86; dep. state atty. Roberts County; city atty. City of Sisseton; judge SC Cir. Ct. (5th jud. cir.), Pierre, 1986—95; assoc. justice SD Supreme Ct., Pierre, 1995—2001, chief justice, 2001—. Mem. Civil Pattern Jury Instruction Com., 1986—99, Tribal-State Judges Forum, 1992. Mem.: S.D. Bar Assn. (mem. Judicial-Bar Liaison Com.), Brown County Bar Assn., Glacial Lakes Bar Assn., S.D. Judges Assn. (past pres.). Office: 500 E Capitol Ave Pierre SD 57501-5070

GILBERTSON, DAVID W., secondary school educator; s. Rodney B. and Joan C. Gilbertson; m. Debra Donn Black, July 5, 1986. BA in English, U. Mont., 1982. Cert. tchr. Mont., 1982. Tchr. english Laurel (Mont.) H.S., 2000—. Coach basketball Laurel (Mont.) H.S., 2000—, coach softball, 2001—. Mem.: Nat. Coun. Tchrs. English, Am. Soc. Curriculum Developers, Mont. Coaches Assn. (licentiate 20 Yr. award 2004), The Civil War Trust. Avocations: reading, civil war history. Office Phone: 406-628-7911.

GILBERTSON, ERIC RAYMOND, academic administrator, lawyer; b. Cleve., Mar. 5, 1945; s. Ewald R. and Esther V. (Johnson) G.; m. Cynthia F. Forrest, Jan. 25, 1974; children: Sara, Seth. BS, Bluffton Coll., 1966; MA in Econs., Ohio U., 1967; JD cum laude, Cleve. State U., 1970; DLitt (hon.), U. Mysore, Karnataka, India, 1993. Bar: Ohio 1970, Vt. 1984, U.S. Dist. Ct. (no. and so. dists.) Ohio 1971, U.S. Supreme Ct. 1981. Instr. econs. Kent State U., Ohio, 1969-70; law clk. Supreme Ct. of Ohio, Columbus, 1970-71; asst. atty. gen. State of Ohio, Columbus, 1971-73; exec. asst. to pres. Ohio State U., Columbus, 1973-79; assoc. Vorys, Sater, Seymore & Pease, Columbus, 1979-81; pres. Johnson State Coll., Vt., 1981-89, Saginaw Valley State U., University Center, Mich., 1989—. With Midland Tomorrow. Contbr. articles to profl. jours. Exec. com. Mich. Campus Compact; Pres. Coun. State Univs. Mich.; cmty. affairs com. Diocese Saginaw; active Bay County Bus. and Edn. Adv. Coun., Saginaw County Crime Prevention Coun., Vision Tri-County Steering Com.; trustee Citizens Rsch. Coun. Mich., 2003—. Mem. Am. Assn. State Colls. and Univs., Saginaw County C. of C., Torch Club, Saginaw Club, Bay City Country Club. Home: 7371 Glen Eagle Dr Bay City MI 48706-9316 Office: Saginaw Valley State U Office Of Pres University Center MI 48710-0001 E-mail: erg@svsu.edu.

GILBERTSON, JOEL WARREN, lawyer; b. Valley City, N.D., Nov. 9, 1949; s. Roy W. and Gwen D. (Haugen) G.; m. Jan Erikson, June 11, 1972; children: David, Lisa. BA, Concordia Coll., Moorhead, Minn., 1972; JD, U. N.D., 1975. Bar: N.D. 1976, U.S. Dist. Ct. N.D. 1976. Ptnr. Binek & Gilbertson, Bowman, N.D., 1976; atty. N.D. Supreme Ct., Bismarck, 1976-78; exec. dir. N.D. Bar Assn., Bismarck, 1978-81; ptnr. Pearce & Durick, Bismarck, 1981-97; exec. v.p., gen. counsel Ind. Cmty. Banks of N.D., 1997—. Served with U.S. Army N.G., 1972-78. Mem. N.D. Bar Assn. (bd. govs. 1989-95, pres. 1992-93), N.D. Bar Found. (vice chmn. 1982-84, chmn. bd. dirs. 1986-89), South Cen. Dist. Bar Assn. (pres. 1987-89). Republican. Lutheran. Avocations: piano, softball. Home: 1025 Crescent Ln Bismarck ND 58501-2463 Office: Ind Comty Banks ND PO Box 6128 Bismarck ND 58506-6128

GILBERTSON, JOHN T., lawyer; b. Madison, Wis., Aug. 26, 1962; BA, Mich. State U., 1984; JD, Wake Forest U., 1991; LLM in taxation, Georgetown U., 1999. CPA Mich., 1986; bar: Calif. 1993. With Ernst & Young; ptnr. Sonnenschein Nath & Rosenthal LLP, LA, 2000—. Mem.: Am. Health Lawyers Assn., State Bar Calif. Office: Sonnenschein Nath & Rosenthal LLP 601 S Figueroa St, Ste 1500 Los Angeles CA 90017 Office Phone: 213-892-5077. Office Fax: 213-623-9924. Business E-Mail: jgilbertson@sonnenschein.com.

GILBERTSON, PHILIP, academic administrator; BA in Comparative Lit., Augustana Coll., S.D., 1965; PhD in English, U. Ky., 1971. Prof. U. Idaho, 1969—73; tchg. and dept. chair positions Wartburg Coll., Iowa, 1973—79; chair humanities divsn. Tex. Luth. Coll., 1979—86; v.p. acad. affairs Doane Coll., Nebr., 1986—89, acad. dean, 1986—89, prof., 1986—89; dean Coll. Arts and Scis. Valparaiso U., Ind., 1989—96, prof., 1989—96; provost U. of the Pacific, Stockton, Calif., 1996—. Office: Office of the Provost Anderson Hall 2nd Fl Univ of the Pacific Stockton CA 95211

GILBOY, MARGARETTA, artist, educator; b. Phila., Aug. 10, 1943; d. James Anthony and Ida Rae (Reisbord) Gilboy; m. Lester Goldstein, Aug. 25, 1963 (div. June 1982); m. Frank Zadlo, Oct. 17, 1987 (div. May 2002). BFA, Phila. Coll. Art, 1965; MFA, U. Colo., 1981. Instr. art U. Colo., Boulder, 1980—84, 2002—03, Met. State Coll., Denver, 1983, Anderson Ranch, Aspen, Colo., 1984—89, CC Phila., 1985, Pa. Acad. Fine Arts, 1986—, U. of Arts, Phila., 1989—91, Art Students League Denver, 2003—. One-woman shows include J. Magnin, Denver, 1979, U. Colo., 1981, Boulder Ctr. Visual Arts, 1982, Marian Locks Gallery, Phila., 1984, 1988, Arvada (Colo.) Ctr. Arts Humanities, 1986, Robischon Gallery, Denver, 1988, Print Club, Phila., 1992, F.A.N. Gallery, 1992, 1994, 1996, Phila. Art Alliance, 1999, Del. Ctr. Contemporary Art, Wilmington, 2001, Celia Hirsch Gallery, Chappaqua, N.Y., 2003, Singer Gallery, Denver Jewish Cmty. Ctr., 2003, exhibited in group shows at Jocelyn Art Mus., Omaha, 1968, Denver Art Mus., 1979, Arvada Ctr. Arts and Humanities, 1979, 1984, Colorado Springs Art Ctr., 1981—82, Challenge Exhibit Fleisher Meml., 1986, Am. Drawing Biennial, Muscarelle Mus., Coll. William and Mary, 1988, Represented in permanent collections U. Colo., Phila. Mus. Art, Arcadia U., Denver Art Mus., Woodmere Mus., State Mus. Pa., Pa. Acad. Fine Arts, Bryn Mawr Coll., Wistar Inst., George Washington U. Sch. Medicine, Albert Einstein Med. Ctr., Phila. Recipient Eugene M. Kayden Arts award, 1983; Merit scholar, U. Colo., 1980, City of Boulder Arts grantee, 1985, Yaddo residency, 1986. Mem.: Coll. Art Assn. Home: 2741 S Sherman St Englewood CO 80110

GILBREATH, SARAH BURKHART GELBACH, health facility administrator; b. Hagerstown, Md., Feb. 21, 1913; d. George and Carolyne Backer (Knode) Gelbach; m. Ylan Kailo Kealoha, Aug. 21, 1936 (dec. Nov. 9, 1944); 1 child, Ylan K. Kealoha; m. Junious Dewey Gilbreath, Apr. 13, 1946. BS in Edn., NYU, 1942. RN N.Y., lifetime Red Cross nurse. Newspaper reporter Herald Mail Publ. Co., Hagerstown, 1929—31; supr., instr. N.Y.C. Dept. Hosps., Seaview, S.I., 1934—36, supr. dept. Kings County, Bklyn., 1936—39, supr., ednl. dir. Goldwater Rsch. Hosp. Welfare Island, 1939—41; asst. dir. nurses Goldwater Rsch. Hosp., Welfare Island, 1941—46; supr. Kendall Hosp. Dade County Hosp. Sys., Fla., 1948—64; supr. Morris County Nursing Home, Morris Plains, NJ, 1964—74. Author (under pen name S. Burkhart Gilbreath): (book) Prayers of the Amwell Valley, 1987, Henry Stafford Little, Lawyer, 1993, Professor Benjamin B. Warfield, Princeton Clergy, 1996, Prayerful Praise-Sing Again in the Garden, 1999; contbr. poetry to various publs. Nurse Army Res. Hosp. Unit, N.Y. Harbor, Governor's Island, NY, 1939—45. Republican. Presbyterian. Home: PO Box 217 Quincy PA 17247

GILCHREST, BARBARA ANN, dermatologist; b. Port Chester, N.Y., 1945; MD, Harvard U., 1971. Diplomate Am. Bd. Dermatology, Am. Bd. Internal Medicine. Intern Boston City Hosp., 1971-72, resident internal medicine, 1972-73, resident dermatology, 1973-76; fellow photobiology Harvard U., Boston, 1974-75; chief dermatology U. Hosp., Boston, Boston City Hosp. (now Boston Med. Ctr.); prof., chmn. dermatology Boston U. Sch. Medicine, 1985—. Mem. AAAS, Am. Acad. Dermatology, Assn. Am. Physicians, Am. Soc. for Clin. Investigation, Inst. Medicine, Soc. for Investigative Dermatology. Office: Boston U Sch Medicine Dermatology 609 Albany St # J507 Boston MA 02118-2515

GILCHREST, THORNTON CHARLES, retired association executive; b. Chgo., Sept. 1, 1931; s. Charles Jewett Gilchrest and Patricia (Thornton) Thornton; m. Barbara Dibbern, June 8, 1952; children: Margaret Mary, James Thornton. BS in Journalism, U. Ill., 1953. Cert. tchr., Ill. Tchr. pub. high sch., West Chicago, Ill., 1957; exec. dir. Plumbing-Heating-Cooling Info. Bur., Chgo., 1958-64; asst. to pres. A.Y. McDonald Mfg. Co., Dubuque, Iowa, 1964-68; exec. dir. Am. Supply Assn., Chgo., 1968-77, exec. v.p., 1977-82, Nat. Safety Coun., Chgo., 1982-83, pres., 1983-95; chmn. Internat. Safety Coun., Chgo., 1992-95. Pres. Nat. Safety Coun. Found. for Safety and Health, 1986-95. Bd. dirs. Prevent Blindness Am., 1993. With USN, 1953-55. Mem. Am. Soc. Assn. Execs., Chgo. Soc. Assn. Execs. Methodist.

GILCHREST, WAYNE THOMAS, congressman, secondary school educator; b. Rahway, N.J., Apr. 15, 1946; s. Arthur and Elizabeth Gilchrest; m. Barbara Rawley; children: Kevin, Joel, Katie. AA in Liberal Arts, Wesley Coll., 1971; BA in History, Del. State Coll., 1973; postgrad., Loyola Coll., Balt., 1984—. Tchr. social studies Warren Hills Jr. H.S., Washington, N.J., 1973-76; tchr. history St. Alban's City (Vt.) Elem. Sch., 1976-79, Kent County H.S., Worton, Md., 1979-90; mem. U.S. Congress from 1st Md. dist., 1991—; mem. resources com., transp. and infrastructure com., sci. com. Vol. Nat. Forest Svc., Bitterroot Nat. Forest, Idaho, 1986-87. Sgt. USMC, 1964-68, Vietnam. Decorated Purple Heart, Bronze Star. Mem. Kent Country Tchrs. Assn., VFW, Am. Legion, Mil. Order Purple Heart. Republican. Methodist. Office: US Ho of Reps 2245 Rayburn Hob Washington DC 20515-0001

GILCHREST, WILLIAM MONROE, music educator; b. Fitchburg, Mass., Apr. 13, 1980; s. Gary Paul and Gwenn Ellen Gilchrest; m. Anneliese May Seitz, July 12, 2003; 1 child, Amaya May. MusB, Gordon Coll., 2002. Music tchr. Robeson City Pub. Schs., Pembroke, NC, 2002—04, Charlotte Valley Ctrl. Sch., Davenport, NY, 2004—. Baptist. Home: 1179 County Hwy 5 Otego NY 13825

GILCHRIST, ANN ROUNDEY, medical/surgical nurse; b. Utica, N.Y., Dec. 21, 1948; d. William Gilchrist and Adele (Cobb) Roundey; married; children: Kristie Ann Hughes, Megean Elizabeth Hughes Holden. Student, Cazenovia Coll., 1967-68; LPN, Utica Sch. Practical Nursing, 1972; postgrad., Mohawk Valley C.C., 1972-75; ADN, SUNY, Morrisville, 1976; student in Forensic Nursing Specialist, Kaplan U., 2005. RN, Nev.; CNOR. Obstetrics and med., surg. staff nurse St. Elizabeth Hosp., Utica, 1972-76; asst. charge nurse CCU and ICU Mohawk Valley Gen. Hosp., Ilion, N.Y., 1976-78; staff nurse operating room Tucson Med. Ctr., 1978-80, El Dorado Hosp., Tucson, 1978-80; staff nurse oper. room and post anesthesia care unit Tucson Gen. Hosp., 1980-85; charge nurse oper. room Desert Springs Hosp., Las Vegas, Nev., 1985-87, staff nurse GI Lab., 1988-90; charge nurse GI Lab, staff nurse operating room Lake Mead Hosp., Las Vegas, 1991-93; supr. operating room Red Rock Surg. Ctr., Las Vegas, 1993-95; staff nurse Endoscopy Lab., Sunrise Flamingo Surg. Ctr., Las Vegas, 1995-97; RN case mgr. Home Side, at Odyssey Hospice, Las Vegas, 1998—; operating room RN Inst. Orthop. Surgery, Las Vegas, 2005—. Mem.: Assn. Hospice and Palliative Care Nurses. Avocations: professional doll artist, learther artist, ceramicist, equestrian. Home: 4552 Scott Ave Las Vegas NV 89102-8107 Office: 4011 Mcleod Dr Las Vegas NV 89121-4305 E-mail: annzart@msn.com.

GILCHRIST, ELLEN LOUISE, writer; b. Vicksburg, Miss., Feb. 20, 1935; d. William Garth and Aurora (Alford) G.; children: Marshall Peteet Walker, Jr., Garth Gilchrist Walker, Pierre Gautier Walker. BA in Philosophy, Millsaps Coll., 1967; postgrad., U. Ark., 1976; LittD (hon.), Millsaps Coll., 1987; LHD (hon.), U. So. Ill., 1988, U. Ark., 2000; PhD (hon.), Tulane U., 2005. Freelance writer, journalist. Commentator, morning edit. of news Nat. Pub. Radio, Washington, 1984, 85; Andrew W. Mellon fellow Tulane U., New Orleans, 2005; Zale writer in residence Newcome Coll. at Tulane, 2005. Author: The Land Surveyor's Daughter, 1979, In The Land of Dreamy Dreams, 1981, The Annunciation, 1983 (Book of Month Club alternate in U.S. and Sweden), Victory Over Japan, 1984 (Am. Book award, 1984), Drunk With Love, 1986, Falling Through Space, 1987, The Anna Papers, 1988, Light Can Be Both Wave and Particle, 1989, I Cannot Get You Close Enough, 1990 (Miss. Inst. Arts and Letters award, 1990, fiction award Miss. Libr. Assn., 1990), Net of Jewels, 1992, Starcarbon, 1994, Anabasis, A Journey to the Interior, 1994, The Age of Miracles, 1995, Rhoda, A Life in Stories, 1995, The Courts of Love, 1996, Sarah Conley, 1997, Flights of Angels, 1998, The CABAL and Other Stories, 1999, Collected Stories, 2000, I, Rhoda Manning, Go Hunting with My Daddy, 2002, The Writing Life, 2005, Nora Jane, A Life in Stories, 2005, (poems) Riding Out the Tropical Depression; contbr. short stories poems to literary publs. Named Woman of Yr., Chi Omega, 2001; recipient Poetry award, U. Ark., 1976, Craft in Poetry award, N.Y. Quar., 1978, Fiction award, The Prairie Schooner, 1981, Poetry award, Miss. Arts Festival, 1968, Saxifrage award, 1983, Fiction award, Miss. Acad. Arts and Sci., 1982, 1985, Am. Book award Victory Over Japan, 1984, J. William Fulbright prize, U. Ark., 1985, Lit. award, Miss. Inst. Arts and Letters, 1985, 1990, 1991, 2 Pushcart prizes, O. Henry Short Story award, 1995, Thomas Wolfe award, U. NC, Chapel Hill, 2004; grantee, NEA, 1979; Andrew Mellon fellow, Tulane U., 2005. Mem. Author's Guild.

GILCHRIST, GERALD SEYMOUR, pediatric hematologist, oncologist, educator; b. Springs, Transvaal, South Africa, May 25, 1935; arrived in U.S.A., 1962; s. David and Anne (Lipschitz) G.; m. Antoinette E. Besset, May 7, 1967; children: Daniel J., Michael A., Lauren D. MB BCh, U. Witwatersrand Med. Sch., Johannesburg, South Africa, 1957; Diploma in Child Health, Royal Coll. Physicians and Surgeons, London, 1961. Diplomate Am. Bd. Pediat. Intern Johannesburg Gen. Hosp., 1958-59; resident Transvaal Meml. Hosp. for Children and Baragwanath Hosp., Johannesburg, 1959-60; resident in pediatrics Hosp. for Sick Children, London, 1961; resident in pediat. Children's Hosp., Cin., 1962-63; fellow pediat., hematology/oncology Children's Hosp. of L.A., 1963-65, cons. hematology and blood banking, 1965-71, attending physician, 1968-71; asst. prof. pediat. U. So. Calif., L.A., 1966-71; assoc. prof. pediat. Mayo Med. Sch., Rochester, Minn., 1972-78, chmn. dept. pediat., 1984-96; cons. pediatric hematology/oncology Mayo Clinic and Found., Rochester, 1971-2000; prof. pediat. Mayo Med. Sch., Mayo Clinic and Found., Rochester, 1978-2000; Helen C. Levitt prof. Mayo Clinic and Found., Rochester, 1987-2000; prof. emeritus Mayo Found. and Med. Sch., 2000—. Mem. Commn. on Cancer ACS, 1982—85; bd. dirs. Hemophilia Ctr., Dept. Maternal and Child Health, Rockville, Md., 1978—2000; prin. investigator Children's Cancer Study Group Nat. Cancer Inst., Bethesda, 1981—99; mem. Accreditation Coun. Grad. Med. Edn. Residency Rev. Com. Pediat., 1997—2002. Co-author: You and Leukemia, 1976; contbr. chpts. to books, numerous articles to profl. jours. Med. advisor Northland Childrens Oncology Svcs., Rochester, Minn., 1978-80; bd. dirs. Minn. chpt. Nat. Hemophilia Found. Found., Mpls., 1981-84; chpt sec. Physicians for Social Responsibility, Rochester, 1982-85; bd. dirs. Nat. Childhood Cancer Found., 1990-97; chair med. and sci. adv. bd. Nat. Children's Cancer Found., 1995-97. Named to Children's Med. Ctr. Hall of Honor, Cin., 1994; recipient Joseph D. Early award, Nat. Hemophilia Found., 1997, Lifetime Achievement award, Minn., Dakotas Chpt. Nat. Hemophilia Found., 2000, Abraham Jacobi Meml. award, Am. Acad. Pediat., AMA, 2001. Fellow: Am. Acad. Pediat. (chmn. sect. on pediat. hematology-oncology 1988—90, chair coun. on sects. 1999—2002, com. on pediat. edn. 1999—2005, com. on pediat. workforce 2003—05); mem.: Am. Soc. Pediat. Hematology/Oncology (trustee 1996—98), Soc. Pediat. Rsch. Accrediation Coun. Grad. Med. Edn. (residency rev. com. pediat. 1997—2002), Am. Bd. Pediat. (chmn. sub-bd. pediat. hematology-oncology 1989—91, bd. dirs. 1990—91), Am. Pediat. Soc., Am. Soc. Hematology, Am. Soc. Clin. Oncology. Democrat. Jewish. Avocations: sailing, bicycling, kayaking, scuba diving.

GILCHRIST, HENRY, lawyer; b. Austin, Tex., Nov. 6, 1924; s. Gibb and Vesta (Weaver) G.; m. Patricia Ann Lynch, Nov. 24, 1951; children: Thomas Gibb, Terri Lynn. BS in Civil Engring., Tex. A&M U., 1948; LLB with honors, U. Tex., 1950. Bar: Tex. 1950, US Supreme Ct. 1971. Assoc. Douglass & McGuire, Pampa, Tex., 1951-52; co-founder Jenkens & Gilchrist, P.C., Dallas, 1952—, now of counsel, corp. & securities practice group. Mem. Rsch. Fellows Southwestern Legal Found., 1976—. Contbr. articles to profl. jours. Bd. dirs. Dallas County Heritage Soc., 1984-87, chmn. bd. trustees, 1978-81, Ctrl. Dallas Assn., exec. com., chmn., 1984-85, Dallas World Salute 1985—, chmn. pres., 1988-90, Theatre Three, 1986-87, Tex. A&M U. Pvt. Enterprise Rsch. Ctr., 1987—, Dallas Bus. Com. for Arts, exec. com. 1988—; adv. coun. Communities Found. Tex., Inc., Dallas Citizens Coun., mem. cultural arts task force; mem. planning and zoning commn. Town of Highland Park, Tex., 1976-84; mem. exec. com. Dallas Mus. Art Trustee and Audit Com., 1988—, chmn. 1988-91, TACA Inc., v.p. 1986-89; mem. devel. coun. Tex. A&M U. Coll. Liberal Arts; mem. Tex. A&M U. Commn. Visual Arts, 1982—, chmn. 1982-88; mem. exec. bd. So. Meth. U. Sch. Theology, 1992—; founder Park Cities Hist. Soc. Served U.S. Army, 1943—46. Mem.: ABA, Ctr. for Am. and Internat. Law, Dallas Bar Assn., Tex. State Bar Assn., Tex. Bar Found. (life), Greater Dallas C. of C. Methodist. Avocations: reading, walking, gardening. Office: Jenkens & Gilchrist PC Ste 3200 1445 Ross Ave Dallas TX 75202-2799 Office Phone: 214-855-4301. Office Fax: 214-855-4300. Business E-Mail: hgilchrist@jenkens.com.

GILCHRIST, JAMES MANNING, neurologist, researcher, educator; b. Keosauqua, Iowa, Nov. 7, 1954; s. James Manning and Ann Elizabeth (Harbison) G.; m. Maria Martha Del Beccaro, July 16, 1983; children: Cullen, Greer, James, Aidan. BS in Biology, U. Ill., 1976; MD, Loyola U., 1979. Diplomate Am. Bd. Psychiatry and Neurology with added qualifications in clin. neurophysiology, Am. Bd. Electrodiagnostic Medicine. Intern Evanston (Ill.) Hosp., 1979-80; resident in neurology Med. Coll. of Va., Richmond, 1980-83, fellow in electrophysiology, 1983-84; rsch. fellow Duke U., Durham, N.C., 1984-85, asst. prof. medicine, 1985-87; asst. prof. neurology Brown U., Providence, 1987-91, assoc. prof. neurology, 1991-98, prof. neurology, 1998—. Dir. Muscular Dystrophy Clinic, Providence; dir. EMG lab. R.I. Hosp., Providence. Editor: Prognosis in Neurology, 1998; mem. editl. bd., Muscle and Nerve, 2000-04, assoc. editor 2005—; contbr. articles to profl. jours. including Jour. Neurology, Jour. Muscle and Nerve, Jour. EEG and Clin. Neurophysiology, Jour. Archives Neurology, Jour. Annals Internal Medicine. Mem. Town Meeting of Dartmouth, Mass., 1991. Grantee Muscular Dystrophy Assn. Fellow Am. Acad. Neurology, Am. Assn. Electrodiagnostic Medicine; mem. AMA. Office: RI Hosp 593 Eddy St # 689 Providence RI 02903-4971 Office Phone: 401-444-8761. Business E-Mail: james_gilchrist@brown.edu.

GILCHRIST, JOHN MARK, otolaryngologist; b. Dallas, Dec. 10, 1959; s. Ronald Wallace Jr. and Patricia Gene G.; m. Melissa Paige LaBoon, Jan. 4, 1986; children: Sarah, Claire, Michael. BS, Wheaton (Ill.) Coll., 1982; MD, U. Okla., Oklahoma City, 1986. Diplomate Am. Bd. Otolaryngology. Intern U. Okla. Med. Ctr., 1986-87, resident otolaryngology, head and neck surgery, 1987-91; mem. staff Mercy Health Ctr., Oklahoma City, 1991—, Bapt. Med. Ctr., Oklahoma City, 1991—, Deaconess Hosp., Oklahoma City, 1991—; head, otolaryngology sect., dept. of surgery Mercy Health Ctr., Oklahoma City, 1995-2000; pvt. practice Okla. Otolaryngology Assocs., Inc., Oklahoma City, 1991—. Pres. Okla. Acad. of Otolaryngology, 1996-97. Mem. com. Young Life, Oklahoma City, 1987-97. Mem. AMA, Am. Acad. Otolaryngology-Head and Neck Surgery, Okla. Med. Assn., Okla. Acad. Otolaryngology (pres. 1996-97). Office: Okla Otolaryngology Assocs 4200 W Memorial Rd Ste 606 Oklahoma City OK 73120-8359 Office Phone: 405-755-1930. Business E-Mail: jmgilchristmd@oklahomaent.org.

GILCHRIST, WILLIAM AARON, architect; b. N.Y.C., Jan. 31, 1956; s. Johnie Aaron and Juanita Marcella (Hunt) G. BS, MIT, 1977, MArch, MS, MIT, 1982; postgrad., Harvard U., 1996. Registered arch., Ga., Ala., Nat. Coun. Archtl. Registration Bds. Project engr. H.J. Russell & Co., Atlanta, 1982-84, project mgr., 1987-88, project dir. Birmingham, Ala., 1988-90; br. mgr. H.J. Russel & Co., Birmingham, Ala., 1990-93; dir. planning and engring. City of Birmingham, 1993-97, dir. planning, engring. and permits, 1997—; architect intern Cherry Roberts Sullivan, Atlanta, 1984-87. Project dir. Birmingham Civil Rights Inst., 1988-91; mem. vis. com. dept. architecture MIT, Cambridge, 1997—; mem. adv. com. on cmty. devel. Auburn (Ala.) U., 1994—. Contbg. editor articles to Birmingham News, 1997—. Bd. dirs. Discovery 2000 Sci. Mus., Birmingham, 1991-93, Birmingham Festival of Arts, 1993—, Ala. Symphony Found., Birmingham, 1997-99. Recipient James C. Howland award Nat. League of Cities, 1995, Karl Taylor Compton prize, 1979, Chandler prize MIT, 1982; Aga Khan fellow MIT-Harvard U., 1981. Mem. AIA (Ala. state coun., mem. nat. task group regional urban design asst. team, mem. urban design com. 1999—), Am. Planning Assn. (del. 1996), Constrn. Specifications Inst., Urban Land Inst. (pub./pvt. partnership coun.), Kiwanis. Roman Catholic. Avocations: linguistics, photography, graphic arts, Aikido. Office: City of Birmingham 710 20th St N Birmingham AL 35203-2216

GILDEA, BRIAN MICHAEL, lawyer; b. New Haven, Nov. 1, 1939; s. Thomas Michael and Lillian Frances (Reilly) G.; children: Larysa Albina, Stefan Bohdan. AS, New Haven U., 1964; BA, Providence Coll., 1967; JD, Suffolk U., 1970. Bar: Conn. 1970, U.S. Dist. Ct. Conn. 1971, U.S. Ct. Appeals (2d cir.) 1975, U.S. Ct. Appeals (3d cir.) 1979, U.S. Ct. Appeals (5th cir.) 1984, U.S. Supreme Ct. 1975. Legal adviser City of Boston, 1969-70; assoc. Celentano, Ivey & Gery, New Haven, 1970-73; ptnr. Celentano & Gildea, New Haven, 1973-74; pvt. practice New Haven, 1974—. Bd. dirs. St. Mary's High Sch., New Haven, 1975-77; mem. Bethany (Conn.) Town Charter Commn., 1976; del. U.S./Japan Bilateral Session, 1988, U.S./China Joint Session on Trade and Econ. Law, 1987. With USAF, 1958-62. Recipient Svc. award Providence Coll., New Haven, 1979, Friar award St. Mary's Alumni Assn., 1980. Mem. ABA, Def. Rsch. Inst., Conn. Bar Assn., New Haven County Bar Assn., Am. Lawyers Assn. Democrat. Roman Catholic. Avocations: bicycling, tennis, skiing, photography. Office: 512 Blake St New Haven CT 06515-1287 Office Phone: 203-387-7493. E-mail: b.m.gildea@att.net.

GIL DE GIBAJA, SUSANA, artist, small business owner; b. Havana, Cuba, May 15, 1959; arrived in U.S., 1961; AA, Miami Dade C.C., 1982; BFA, Fla. Internat. U., 1985. Cert. legal sec. One-woman shows include Infinite Possibilities Gallery, Hollywood, Fla., 1996, I've Been Framed Gallery, Miami, 1996, Mus. New Arts, Ft. Lauderdale, Fla., 1996, 97, Art and Culture Ctr., Hollywood, Fla., 1998; contbr. articles to profl. publs. Mem. Vivas Las Artes, Broward Art Guild, Hollywood Art Guild, Miami Watercolor Soc. Republican. Roman Catholic. Avocations: bicycling, book collecting, reading. Office: 7417 W 30th Ct Hialeah FL 33018-5207 E-mail: sgbarral@aol.com.

GILDENHORN, JOSEPH BERNARD, lawyer, real estate company executive, retired diplomat; b. Washington, Sept. 17, 1929; s. Oscar and Celia (Koval) G.; m. Alma Lee Gross, June 28, 1953; children: Carol Winer, Michael Saul. BS, U. Md., 1951; LLB, JD, Yale U., 1954. Bar: D.C. 1954, U.S. Ct. Appeals (D.C. cir.) 1954, U.S. Supreme Ct. 1954. Ptnr. Brown, Gildenhorn & Jacobs, 1955—; vice chmn. D.C. Nat. Sovran Bank, Washington, 1979—89; amb. to Switzerland Dept. State, Bern, 1989—93; ptnr. The JBG Cos., 1960—. Adj. prof. George Washington U.; pres. JBG Properties, Inc., 1956-88; vice chmn. adv. bd. DC metro region BB&T Bank, 1985-2003; bd. dirs. Mills Corp.; DC chmn. George W. Bush for Pres., 2000; trustee U. Md. College Park Found., Inc.; chmn. bd. trustees Woodrow Wilson Internat. Ctr. for Scholars, 2002—. Mem. editl. bd. Yale Law Jour., 1954. D.C. campaign chmn. Bush-Quayle, 1988; past pres., bd. dirs. Hebrew Home Greater Washington, 1975-77; treas. Coun. Am. Ambassadors, 2000; bd. dirs. Washington Jewish Cmty. Found., Inst. for Study of Diplomacy, Georgetown U., Ctr. for Strategic and Internat. Studies, UN Watch, Geneva, Internat. Inst. Strategic Studies; bd. dirs. Am. Joint Distbn. Com., 1999—; pres. bd. dirs. Jewish Fedn. Greater Washington, 1988-89; vice chmn. D.C. Sports and Entertainment Commn., 1996-2003; participant Nat. Prayer Breakfast, 2000. With AUS, 1954-56. Named Washingtonian of Yr., Washingtonian mag., 1996, Philanthropist of the Yr., Nat. Soc. of Fundraising Execs., 2000; recipient David Ben Gurion award, State of Israel, 1977, B'nai B'rith Disting. Alumnus award, 1983, Hyman Goldman Humanitarian award, 1984, B'nai B'rith Humanitarian award, 1985, Ourisman Cmty. Svc. award, 1987, Ottenstein Cmty. Svc. award, 1991, Jewish Inst. for Nat. Security Affairs Leadership award, 1993, U. Md. Disting. Alumnus award, 1996, Leadership award, Washington Inst., 1999, Corp. Citizenship award, Woodrow Wilson Internat. Ctr. for Scholars, 2000. Mem. Order of Coif, Team 100, Presdl. Trust. Republican. Home: 2030 24th St NW Washington DC 20008-1608 Office: 4445 Willard Ave Ste 400 Chevy Chase MD 20815 Business E-Mail: jgildenhorn@jbg.com.

GILDER, GEORGE FRANKLIN, communications executive, writer; b. N.Y.C., Nov. 29, 1939; s. Richard Watson Gilder and Anne (Alsop) Palmer; m. Cornelia Ewing Brooke, Oct. 23, 1976; children: Louisa Ludlow, Mary Ellen Tiffany, Richard Brooke, Cornelia Chapin. AB, Harvard U., 1962. Editor Advance mag., 1960-64; assoc. editor The New Leader, 1966; speech writer for Gov. Nelson Rockefeller, 1964, 68, Gov. George Romney, 1967, Sen. Jacob Javits, 1968, Richard Nixon, 1968, Sen. Charles McCurdy Mathias, 1969-70, Ben C. Toledano, 1972, Sen. Robert Dole, 1976, David Rockefeller, 1980; pres. Gilder Tech Report. Author: The Party That Lost Its Head, 1965, Sexual Suicide, 1973, Naked Nomads: Unmarried Men in America, 1974, Visible Man, 1978, Wealth & Poverty, 1981, The Spirit of Enterprise, 1985, Microcosm, 1988, Life After Television, 1992; mem. editorial bd. Nat. Review, from 1978; contbr. to Forbes, National Review, Commentary, Wall St. Jour., other periodicals. With USMCR, 1958. Republican. Episcopalian.

GILDERHUS, MARK THEODORE, historian, educator; b. Rochester, Minn., Nov. 15, 1941; s. M.R. and Thea L. (Enderson) Gilderhus; m. Nancy Loutzenheiser, June 24, 1967; children: Kirsten, Lesley. AB, Gustavus Adolphus Coll., 1963; MA (NDEA Title IV fellow), U. Nebr., 1965, PhD, 1968. Asst. prof. Colo. State U., Fort Collins, 1968-72, assoc. prof., 1972-77, prof. history, 1977—, chmn. dept., 1980-93, John N. Stern disting. prof., 1996—97; Lyndon B. Johnson prof. history Tex. Christian U., 1997—. Editorial cons. jours. and pubs. Author: Diplomacy and Revolution: U.S.-Mexican Relations Under Wilson and Carranza, 1977, Pan American Visions: Woodrow Wilson in the Western Hemisphere, 1986, History and Historians, A Historiographical Introduction, 1987, 5th edit., 2000, The Second Century: U.S.-Latin American Relations Since 1889, 2000. Nat. Endowment for Humanities grantee, 1972 Mem. Orgn. Am. Historians, Am. Hist. Assn. (pres. 1996), Soc. Historians Am. Fgn. Rels., Conf. on Latin Am. History. Democrat. Unitarian Universalist. Home: 5112 Blue Sage Rd Fort Worth TX 76132-2009 Office: History Dept Tex Christian Univ Fort Worth TX 76129 Office Phone: 817-257-6299. Business E-Mail: m.gilderhus@tcu.edu.

GILDRED, THEODORE E., former diplomat, real estate developer; b. Mexico City, 1935; m. Heidi Copin. Grad., Stanford U., 1959; postgrad., Sorbonne, U. Heidelberg; grad. Sch. Internat. Rels. and Pacific Area Studies, U. Calif. Pres. Gildred Found., 1967; founder Torrey Pines Bank (now Wells Fargo Bank), San Diego, 1979; U.S. amb. to Argentina, 1986-89; founder, chmn. bd. The Lomas Santa Fe Group, San Diego, 1989—. Bd. dirs. N.Am. Airlines, Grad. Sch. Internat. Rels. and Pacific Area Studies, U. Calif., San Diego, Security Pacific Nat. Bank; spkr. in field. Recipient hon. command pilot wings Ecuadorian Air Force, Orden de Mayo al Mèrito, en Grado de Gran Cruz, Pres. Carlos Menem, Argentina, 1992. Office: 265 Santa Helena Ste 200 Solana Beach CA 92075-1547 Fax: 858-755-6821. E-mail: Tegildred@lsfg.com.

GILE, MARY STUART, state legislator, educational executive; b. Montreal, Que., Can., Mar. 24, 1936; d. William Gillies and Hazel Irene (Stuart) Sinclair; m. Robert Hall Gile, Mar. 29, 1974; children: D. Christopher, Julia Mary, Robertson Sinclair. BS, McGill U., 1957; EdM, U. NH, 1971; EdD, Vanderbilt U., 1982. Specialist phys. edn. Protestant Sch. Bd. Greater Montreal, 1957-64; kindergarten tchr. White Mountains Sch. Bd., Littleton, NH, 1965-67; dir. Open Door Kindergarten, Salem, NH, 1967-69; coord. State Follow Through, NH, 1969-80, Right to Read, NH, 1973-74; coord. US Sec.'s Initiative in Excellence; Chpt. 1 Edn. Consol. and Improvement Act, 1983-84; sr. cons. edn. State Dept. Edn., Concord, NH, 1969-85; v.p. edn. and devel. Acad. Applied Sci., Concord, NH, 1985-90; prof., dept. head early childhood edn. NH Tech. Inst., Concord, NH, 1990-98. State dept. staff assoc. to U. NH, Durham, 1970—74; mem. Gov.'s Task Force on Sexual Harassment, Concord, NH, 1981—83; chair Trust Fund for Prevention of Child Abuse and Neglect, NH, 1988—92; mem. state child abuse neglect prevention leadership team; mem. State Child Care Adv. Coun., NH, 1994—99; pres. faculty Tech. Inst. and C.C., NH, 1995—97; chmn. State Child Care Adv. Coun., NH, 1997—2001. Pres. Concord Parents and Children, 1977—82; chmn. Citizens Adv. Bd. to Cmty. Devel., 1978—82; bd. gov. Merrimack County United Way, 1983—88; pres. Assn. for Mental Health, NH, 1984—86; Founder Legis. Caucus for Young Children, NH, 1997—; elected to NH legis. Merrimack Dist. 38, 1996—; apptd. to exec. dept. and adminstrn., 1997—98; apptd. to children and family law, bd. dirs., 1997, 1999, 2001, 2003; U. NH Alumni Assn., 1999. Recipient cert. outstanding achievement NH State Bd. Edn., 1985, NH Dept. Children, Youth and Families award for exemplary leadership and svc., 1999, Providian Child Care leader award, 1999, Honoree DCYF Mary Stuart Gile Award presented to group committed to devel. leadership in early childhood. Mem. NH Assn. for Edn. Young Children (Svc. for Young Children award 1998), Phi Delta Kappa. Congregationalist. Avocations: skiing, music, theater, hiking.

GILES, ALLEN, pianist, composer, music educator; b. Cambridge, Mass., Dec. 26, 1924; s. Allen Lester and Clara Lillian (Collins) G.; m. Marilla Jane Roberts, May 26, 1950 (div. 1970); children: Marilyn, Andrea, Cynthia; m. Anne Watson Diener, Sept. 26, 1970 (div. 1996); 1 child, Katherine Anne. MusB in Piano, Boston U., 1946, MA in Music, 1949; EdD in Music Edn., Columbia U., N.Y.C., 1981. performing pianist, soloist and chamber musician, U.S., Europe, Japan, 1945—; adjudicator for competitions nationwide, 1956—. Pvt. piano tchr., Mass., N.Y., Calif., 1944—; head piano dept., assoc. dir. music dept. SUNY, Buffalo, N.Y., 1952-64; chair, music dept., dir. Inst. of Music Villa Maria Coll., Buffalo, 1964-68; prof. music, chair performing arts Golden West Coll., Huntington Beach, Calif., 1972-93, prof. emeritus, 1993-2000; exec. dir. South Bay Conservatory, Torrance, Calif., 1997-98; owner, pres. GME Piano Video, 1984—; artistic dir. Learning Ctr. for Arts Excellence, Torrance, Calif., 1999-2000; DVD annotator Media Hyperium/Pioneer Classics, 2000—; piano and musicianship tchr. Rivers Music Sch., Weston, Mass., 2001—05. Author: (books) Beginning Piano-An Adult Approach Vol. 1, 1978, Vol. 2, 1988, Beginning Piano Telecourse Student Study Guide, 1979; Learning To Play The Piano By Television, 1982; course designer, tchr. on camera (video series) Beginning Piano-An Adult Approach, 1978—; contbr. articles to profl. jours. Recipient Annual Piano Tchr. award SUNY, Fredonia, 1968; Radio and TV award for Noteworthy Achievement in Serious Music, Sigma Alpha Iota, 1980; named Master Tchr., Univ. Tex., Austin, 1986, Master Tchr. (piano), Music Tchrs. Nat. Assn., 1989. Mem. Music Tchrs. Nat. Assn., Nat. Piano Found., New Eng. Piano Tchrs. Assn. Home: 42 Windingwood Ln Lincoln MA 01773-4912 Office: GME Piano Video PO Box 6035 Lincoln MA 01773-4912 E-mail: gmegiles@comcast.net.

GILES, CONRAD LESLIE, ophthalmic surgeon; b. N.Y.C., July 14, 1934; s. Irving Samuel Giles and Victoria Ampole; m. Marilyn Toby Schwartz, June 20, 1955 (div. 1978); children: Keith Martin, Suzanne Speer, Kevin William, Brian Alan; m. Lynda Fern Schenk, Nov. 26, 1978; stepchildren: Jared Schenk, Jamie Schenk. MD, U. Mich., 1957, MS, 1961. Diplomate Am. Bd. Ophthalmology. Clin. assoc. NIH, Bethesda, Md., 1961-63; clin. asst. prof. Wayne State U. Sch. Medicine, Detroit, 1965-72, clin. assoc. prof. ophthalmology, 1973-89, clin. prof. ophthalmology, 1989—; chief ophthalmologist Children's Hosp. Mich., 1985-99, emeritus chief, 1999—, chief emeritus, 2000—. Contbr. articles to med. jours. Active Jewish Welfare Fedn., Detroit, 1981-86, pres., 1986-89; bd. govs. Jewish Agy. for Israel, 1995-2000; vice-chair United Jewish Communities, 2000-2002; vice chair Jewish Coun. Pub. Affairs, 2005—. Fellow: Am. Acad. Ophthalmology; mem.: AMA, Mich. State Ophthalmol. Soc., United Jewish Cmtys. (vice chair 2000—02), Mich. Jewish Conf. (pres. 1992—95), United Jewish Appeal Fedns. N.Am. (co-pres. 1997—99), Coun. Jewish Fedns. (v.p. 1992—95, treas. 1995—96, pres. 1996—99). Avocations: golf, tennis. Home: 6300 Westmoor Rd Bloomfield Hills MI 48301-1359 Office: 31500 Telegraph Rd Bingham Farms MI 48025 Office Phone: 248-594-6702. Personal E-mail: clgiles@sbcglobal.net.

GILES, EUGENE, anthropology educator; b. Salt Lake City, June 30, 1933; s. George Eugene and Eleanor (Clark) G.; m. Inga Valborg Wikman, Sept. 9, 1964; children: Eric George, Edward Eugene. AB, Harvard U., 1955, AM, 1960, PhD, 1966; MA, U. Calif., Berkeley, 1956. Diplomate Am. Bd. Forensic Anthropology (bd. dirs. 1996-2002). Instr. in anthropology U. Ill., Urbana, 1964-66, assoc. prof., 1970-73, prof., 1973-99, head dept. anthropology, 1975-80; asst. prof. Harvard U., Cambridge, Mass., 1966-70; assoc. dean Grad. Coll. U. Ill., 1986-89, assoc. dean Liberal Arts and Scis. Coll., 1995-99, prof. emeritus, 1999—. Editor: (with J.S. Friedlaender, jr. editor) The Measures of Man: Methodologies in Biological Anthropology, 1976. Served with U.S. Army, 1956-58. NSF postdoctoral fellow, 1967-68; NSF grantee, 1970-72, NIH grantee, 1965-68 Fellow Am. Anthropol. Assn., AAAS, Am. Acad. Forensic Scis. (T. Dale Stewart award 2004); mem. Am. Assn. Phys. Anthropologists (exec. com. 1973-76, v.p. 1979-80, pres. 1981-83, Charles R. Darwin Lifetime Achievement award 2005), Human Biology Assn. (exec. com. 1974-77), Phi Beta Kappa, Sigma Xi. Home: 1001 Ross Dr Champaign IL 61821-6631 Office: U Ill Dept Anthropology 607 S Mathews Ave Urbana IL 61801-3635 Office Phone: 217-333-0801. E-mail: e-giles1@uiuc.edu.

GILES, GLENN EVERETT, music educator, fine arts administrator; b. Boston, June 28, 1949; s. Dana Davis Giles and Jacquline Stella Zyla; m. Gloria J. Johnson; children: Dana Miller, Gregory Arthur. BS in Music Edn. with honors, Castleton State Coll., 1973; MusM in Instrumental Conducting with honors, U. Maine, 1996. Cert. music tchr. Vt. Music dir. Proctor (Vt.) Schools, 1973—74; band dir. Mt. St. Joseph Acad., Rutland, Vt., 1974—80; music educator Rutland Pub. Schools, 1974—81, fine arts supr., 1993—; furnishings salesman McAuliffe Office Products, Rutland, 1981—86, gen. mgr. so. vt., 1992—93; dir. of music Mill River Union H.S., N. Clarendon, Vt., 1986—92. Past pres. Vt. Music Educator Assoc., Music Educators Nat. Conv., Burlington, 1991—93; min. music, choir dir. Union Ch., Proctor, 1974; dir. wind ensemble Lakes Region Youth Orch., Rutland, 2000; band dir. Rutland City Band, 1985—95; bass trombonist Marble City Swing Band, Rutland; choir dir. Proctor Cmty. Chorus, 1980—2001; guest condr. various music dists., Vt. Dir. v.p. First Night Rutland, 1992—2001. Recipient Cmty. Arts award, Crossroads Arts Coun., 1993, Arts award, Vt. Alliance Arts Edn., 2002. Mem.: Masons (master 1989—90), Phi Kappa Lambda. Avocations: fishing, hunting, skiing, singing, boating. Office: Rutland Pub Schs 6 Church St Rutland VT 05701 Business E-Mail: ggiles@rutlandhs.k12.vt.us.

GILES, JAMES FRANCIS, financial executive; b. Teaneck, N.J., Aug. 16, 1954; s. James Francis Giles Sr. and Regina Bianca (Renzo) Micera. BA, Fairleigh Dickinson U., 1977, MBA, 1980, cert. webmaster skills, 1999; postgrad., NYU, 2004—04. Lic. real estate broker, N.J. Bus. mgr. Bradford Securities, Teaneck, 1977-78; self employed translator Emerson, N.J., 1978-82; real estate broker Micera Realty, Oradell, N.J., 1982-89, Nigito Realty, River Edge, N.J., 1989—; payroll adminstr. Butler Telecom, Montvale, N.J., 1996-97; pension adminstr. Nat. Assocs. Metro, Totowa, N.J., 1997-99; tchr. online courses in bus. and math. Colo. Tech. U., 2004—. Adj. prof., lectr. Bergen C.C., Paramus, NJ, 1985—, chmn. real estate adv. com., 1993—95; adj. prof. William Paterson U., Wayne, NJ, 1993—; adj. prof. math. Felician Coll., Lodi, NJ, 2001—; instr. online courses in bus. and math. Colo. Tech. U., 2004—. Roman Catholic. E-mail: jgilesmba@comcast.net.

GILES, JOE W., music educator; b. Clarksville, Tenn., Mar. 29, 1940; s. Emmett J. and Rubye Elizabeth Waters Giles. BS in Music Edn., Austin Peay State U., 1961, M with honors in Music Edn., 1972. Tchr. choral and gen. music Met. Nashville Pub. Sch., 1961—84; music cons. Tenn. Dept. Edn., Nashville, 1984—85, dir. arts edn., 1985—99; arts edn. cons. Ctr. Creative Arts, Clarksville, Tenn., 1999—2001; adj. faculty McLean Sch. Music, Mid. Tenn. State U., Murfreesboro, 2003—. Presenter in field; conductor De-Graffenried Chorale, 2001—. Vol. Nashville Pub. Libr., 1999—2001; mem. FIND-18, Nashville, 2003—05; lay reader Christ Ch. Cathedral, Nashville, 1992—97; founding bd. dirs. Tenn. Arts Acad., 1986—. Recipient Gov.'s award, State of Tenn., 1988, Friends award, Tenn Art Edn. Assn., 1988, Tenn. Art Edn. Assn., 1998. Mem.: Tenn. Music Educators (pres. 1980—82), Music Educators Nat. Conf. (divsn. pres. 1996—98, past nat. exec. bd. dirs.), Nat. Coun. State Supr. Music (pres. 1992—94), Kappa Delta Pi, Phi Beta Mu. Democrat. Episcopalian. Avocations: genealogy, travel, reading. Home: 4487 Post Pl Nashville TN 37205

GILES, KATHARINE EMILY (J. K. PIPER), retired administrative assistant, writer; b. Jackson Hole, Wyo., Jan. 9, 1938; d. William Lamar and Grace Hawley (Domrose) G.; children: Piper Lee Shanks, John Richard Hamlin. Diamond cert., Gemological Inst. Am., 1971. Adminstrv. asst. Matthiesen Equipment Co., San Antonio, 1993-96; driver USA Truck, Van Buren, Ark., 1996—. Top Gun, USA Truck, 148,900 accident free miles, 1997; 147,100, 1998. Author: The Marvelous Bean, 1989, The Lost Trident, 1991, The Missing Crystal, 1992, Jewel of Avalon, 1992, The Lost Kingdom, 1991, The Desert Sun, 1992, The Fire Sled, 1991, Knights of Glass, 1992, Black Pagoda, 1992, Memories from the Kitchen of Grace & Rich Williams, 1992, My Recipe Box, 2000. Home: 6700 Jefferson Paige Rd Lot 265 Shreveport LA 71119-4905

GILES, KATHLEEN C., headmaster; m. Ralph Giles; children: Kait, Daniel, Eileen. AB in English and Am. Lit. magna cum laude, Radcliffe Coll.; JD cum laude, Harvard Law Sch. Teaching intern Groton Sch., coach; assoc. Gaston Snow, Boston; law clerk to Chief Justice Vincent McKusick Supreme Judicial Ct., Maine; coll. advisor Groton Sch., 1985—96, asst. dean of academic affairs, 1996—2002, dean of academic affairs, 2002—03; head of sch. Middlesex Sch., Concord, Mass., 2003—. Mem.: Phi Beta Kappa. Office: Middlesex Sch 1400 Lowell Rd Concord MA 01742-9122*

GILES, MARJORIE BRIGGS, publishing executive, writer; b. Lancaster, Calif., Mar. 21, 1926; d. Lloyd Stephenson Briggs and Helen Huntington Ward; m. Sheldon Edward Reaume, Feb. 24, 1945 (dec. May 6, 1957); children: Kristina Marie Reaume children: Kurt Geoffrey Reaume; m. Robert Andrew Gordon, Dec. 20, 1965 (div.); 1 child, Robert Andrew Gordon; m. David Norman Giles, Apr. 24, 1993. BA, San Francisco State U., 1980. Writer Inkwell, Dobbins, Calif., 1974—; journalist Appeal Dem., Marysville, Calif., 1985—87. Author: (illustrated history) Changes in Harmony (History and Heritage Week, 1988); editor (publisher): (book) Under the Plum Tree: The Tao of Everything (Book of the Yr. finalist, Foreword Mag., 2001), (newsletter) Sci. & People Bull. #3; author: (essay) Pelican (2nd Pl. essay, 1996); author: (publisher) (history book) Gold Rivers of N. Calif.; editor: (newsletter) Enabled Courier, 1992—94. Judge Very Spl. Arts, Marysville, Calif., 1991—94; dir., design chair Main St. USA, Marysville, Calif., 1989—93. Mem.: Nat. Writer's Union, Calif. Writers Club (pres. 1997—99), Sigma Xi (assoc.). D-Liberal. Tao. Avocations: travel, music. Home and Office: PO Box 178 Dobbins CA 95935-0178 Office Phone: 530-692-1581. Personal E-mail: mbgiles@saber.net.

GILES, NORMAN HENRY, geneticist, science educator; b. Atlanta, Aug. 6, 1915; s. Norman Henry and Alice (Guerard) G.; m. Dorothy Lunsford, Aug. 26, 1939 (dec. Jan. 1967); children: Annette Guerard, David Lunsford; m. Doris Vos Weaver, Aug. 1, 1969 (dec. Aug. 2004); stepchildren: Gayle Weaver (dec.), Alix Weaver. AB, Emory U., 1937, ScD (hon.), 1980; MA, Harvard U., 1938, PhD, 1940; MA (hon.), Yale U., 1951. Instr. botany Yale U., New Haven, 1941-45, asst. prof., 1945-46, assoc. prof., 1946-51, prof., 1951-61, Eugene Higgins prof. genetics, 1961-72; Fuller E. Callaway prof. genetics U. Ga., 1972-86, emeritus, 1986—. Prin. biologist Oak Ridge Nat. Lab., 1947-50; cons. AEC, 1954-64; mem. genetics study sect. NIH, 1960-64, genetics tng. com., 1966-70; ednl. adv. bd. John Simon Guggenheim Meml. Found., 1977-86. Mem. editorial bd. Radiation Research, 1953-58, Am. Naturalist, 1961-64, Devel. Genetics, 1979-86. Bd. dirs. U. Ga. Research Found., 1979-85. Parker fellow Harvard U., 1940-41, Fulbright and Guggenheim fellow Genetics Inst., U. Copenhagen, 1959-60, Guggenheim fellow Australian Nat. U., Canberra, 1966; recipient Bicentennial Silver medallion U. Ga., 1984, Lamar Dodd award for rsch. U. Ga., 1985, Thomas Hunt Morgan medal Genetics Soc. Am., 1988. Fellow Am. Acad. Arts and Scis., AAAS; mem. Nat. Acad. Scis. (chmn. genetics sect. 1976-79), Genetics Soc. Am. (treas. 1954-56, pres. 1970), Bot. Soc. Am., Am. Soc. Naturalists (pres. 1977), Am. Inst. Biol. Scis., Genetics Soc. Japan (hon.), Royal Danish Acad. Scis. and Letters (fgn.), Am. Ornithologists Union, Phi Beta Kappa, Sigma Xi. Office: U Ga Dept Genetics Athens GA 30602-7223 E-mail: ngiles@uga.edu.

GILES, ROBERT EDWARD, JR., lawyer; b. Bremerton, Wash., Dec. 17, 1949; s. Robert Edward Sr. and Alice Louise (Morton) G.; m. Barbara Susan Miller, Aug. 21, 1971; children: Steven, William, Thomas, James. BA in Fin., summa cum laude, U. Washington, 1971, JD, 1974. Bar: Wash. 1974, US Tax Ct. 1974. From assoc. to fin. ptnr. Perkins Coie, Seattle, 1974-86, mng. ptnr., 1986—, chmn. mgmt. com. Bd. dirs. Jr. Achievement, Seattle, 1984—; bd. dirs., sec. Wash. Coun. for Econ. Edn., 1981-91; v.p., chief Seattle coun. Boy Scouts Am., 1996-2002; pres. Seattle (Wash.) Sports Commn., 2005. Capt. U.S. Army, 1974. Mem.: ABA, Seattle C. of C. (trustee 1994—97, 2000—02), Wash. State Bar Assn. Avocations: hiking, climbing. Office: Perkins Coie 1201 3rd Ave 48th Fl Seattle WA 98101-3029 Office Phone: 206-359-8536. Office Fax: 206-359-9000. Business E-Mail: rgiles@perkinscoie.com.

GILES, ROBERT HARTMANN, journalist, educator; b. Cleve., June 6, 1933; s. Robert Hamilton and Grace (Hartmann) G.; m. Nancy May Morgan, Feb. 6, 1960; children: David Morgan, Megan Elisabeth, Robert Hamilton II. BA, DePauw U., 1955; MS, Columbia U., 1956; D of Journalism (hon.), DePauw U., 1996. Reporter Newport News Daily Press, 1957-58; reporter Akron (Ohio) Beacon Jour., 1958-63, editorial writer, 1963-65, city editor, 1966-68, met. editor, 1968-69, mng. editor, 1969-73, exec. editor, 1973-76; spl. lectr. Sch. Journalism, U. Kans., 1976-77; exec. editor Gannett Rochester (N.Y.) Newspapers, 1977-81, editor, 1981-86; v.p., exec. editor Detroit News, 1986-89, editor, pub., 1989-97; sr. v.p. The Freedom Forum, 1997-2000; exec. dir. Media Studies Ctr., 1997-2000; curator Nieman Found. Harvard U., Cambridge, Mass., 2000—. Pres. Media Mgmt. Books Inc. Author: Newsroom Management: A Guide to Theory and Practice. Trustee William Allen White Found., U. Kans., 1978—. With AUS, 1956-58. Nieman fellow Harvard, 1965-66; co-recipient Pulitzer prize for local reporting, 1971, Scripps-Howard 1st Amendment award, 1978 Mem. AP Mng. Editors Assn. (pres. 1988), Am. Soc. Newspaper Editors (bd. dirs., treas. 1994, v.p. 1995, pres. 1996), Soc. Profl. Journalists, Found. Am. Comm. (chmn. 1993-97), Accrediting Coun. for Edn. in Journalism and Mass Comm. (pres. 1992-98), Alpha Tau Omega. Office: Harvard U One Francis Ave Cambridge MA 02138 Office Phone: 617-496-5827.

GILES, ROSCOE C., engineering educator; B in Physics, U. Chgo., 1970; PhD, Stanford U., 1975. Prof., dept. of elec. and computer engring. Boston U., dep. dir., Ctr. for Computational Sci. Exec. dir. Inst. for African Am. E-Culture; team leader Education, Outreach, and Tng. Partnership for Advanced Computational Infrastructure (EOT-PACI). Office: Ctr for Computational Sci Boston U 3 Cummington St Boston MA 02215 Office Phone: 617-353-6082. Office Fax: 617-358-2487.

GILES, WILLIAM ELMER, editor; b. Somerville, N.J., July 5, 1927; s. Elmer and Mary Jane (Reed) G.; m. Gloria Mastrangelo, June 4, 1949; children: William J., Michael E., Richard H. and Paul L. (twins), Joseph R. AB in Government, Columbia U., 1950, MS in Journalism, 1951. Reporter Plainfield Courier-News, N.J., 1946-47; copyreader, reporter Wall Street Jour., 1951- 58, mng. editor S.W. edit. Dallas, 1958-61, news editor Washington bur., 1961; an organizer nat. weekly newspaper Nat. Observer, 1961, editor, 1962-71; asst. gen. mgr. Dow Jones & Co., Inc.; pub. Dow Jones & Co., Inc. (Wall Street Jour. and Nat. Observer), 1971-76; dir. mgmt. programs, mem. Dow Jones mgmt. com., 1972-76; disting. editor in residence Baylor U., 1976; exec. editor Detroit News, 1976-77, editor, v.p., 1977-83; editor-in-residence, lectr. Mich. State U., East Lansing, 1983—; Sunday editor Singapore Monitor, 1984-85; v.p. Sandy Corp., Troy, Mich., 1985-87; prof. journalism La. State U., Baton Rouge, 1987-91, dir. Manship Sch.

Journalism, 1988-91; prof. So. U., Baton Rouge, 1992-97; mng. editor The Washington Times, 1997—2002; ret., 2002. Mem. Assn. Educators in Journalism and Mass Comm., Soc. Profl. Journalists, Nat. Press Club. Home: 85 Dogwood Trl London KY 40741-7536 Personal E-mail: billgiles75@hotmail.com.

GILES, WILLIAM (BILL) T., retail executive; BA in Acct. and Mgmt., Alfred U. With PriceWaterhouse LLP, 1981—90; dir. fin. reporting Melville Corp., 1990—91; from asst. controller to exec. v.p., CFO Linens'n Things Inc., Clifton, NJ, 1991—2000, exec. v.p., 2000—, CFO, 2000—. Office: Linens n Things Inc 6 Brighton Rd Clifton NJ 07015

GILFORD, STEVEN ROSS, lawyer; b. Chgo., Dec. 2, 1952; s. Ronald M. and Adele (Miller) G.; m. Anne Christine Johnson, Jan. 2, 1974; children: Sarah Julia, Zachary Michael, Eliza Rebecca. BA, Dartmouth Coll., 1974; JD, M of Pub. Policy Scis., Duke U., 1978. Bar: Ill. 1978, U.S. Dist. Ct. (no. dist.) Ill. 1978, U.S. Ct. Appeals (7th cir.) 1981, U.S. Ct. Appeals (D.C. cir.) 1984, U.S. Ct. Appeals (5th cir.) 1988, U.S. Dist. Ct. (ea. dist.) Mich. 1995. Assoc. Isham, Lincoln & Beale, Chgo., 1978—85, ptnr., 1985—87, Mayer, Brown, Rowe & Maw, Chgo., 1987—. Adminstrv. law editor Duke Law Jour., 1976-77. Participating atty. ACLU, 1983—2000; sec. Evanston (Ill.) YMCA, 1985, vice chmn., 1986—92; v.p. ACLU, Ill. chpt., 1995—96; elected mem. bd. edn. dist. 202 Evanston Twp. H.S., 1993—2005, v.p., 1995—96, 2003—04, pres., 1996—98, 2004—05, mem. joint task force on safety, 1995—96, chmn. fin. com., 2001—04; mem. Legal Aid Soc., 2001—, chmn., 2005—; mem. Met. Family Svcs., Evanston Skokie Valley Cmty. Adv. Bd., 1997; mem., bd. dirs. Met. Family Svcs., 1998—; mem. exec. com. ED-RED, 2002—05; bd. dir. Dem. Party Evanston, Ill., 2004—; bd. dirs. Evanston YMCA, 1982—92, 2005—; bd. dirs. Ill. ACLU, 1991—96; bd. dirs. Roger Baldwin Found., 1993—96. Mem. ABA, Ill. Bar Assn., Chgo. Bar Assn. Home: 2728 Harrison St Evanston IL 60201-1216 Office: Mayer Brown Rowe & Maw 190 S La Salle St Ste 3100 Chicago IL 60603-3441 Office Phone: 312-701-7909.

GILFOYLE, NATHALIE FLOYD PRESTON, lawyer; b. Lynchburg, Va., May 4, 1949; d. Robert Edmund and Dorothea Henry (Ward) Gilfoyle; m. Christopher Y.W. Ma, Sept. 9, 1978; children: Olivia Otey. Rohan James. BA, Hollins Coll., 1971; JD, U. Va., 1974. Bar: Mass. 1974, D.C. 1977. Staff counsel Rate Setting Commn., Boston, 1974-76; ptnr. Peabody, Lambert & Meyers, Washington, 1976-84, McDermott, Will and Emery, 1984-96; gen. counsel Am. Psychol. Assn., 1996—. Bd. dirs. ACLU Nat. Capital Area, Washington, 1980-83, St. Columbia's Nursery Sch., 1992-99, D.C. Bar Atty. Client Arbitration bd., chmn., 1994-95. Mem.: ABA, Mass. Bar Assn., Women's Bar Assn., DC Bar Assn. (legal ethics com. 1999—2001, gen. counsel 2002—04, bd. govs. 2004—). Office: APA 750 1st St NE Washington DC 20002-4241 Office Phone: 202-336-6186. Business E-Mail: ngilfoyle@apa.org.

GILG, MATTHEW RONALD, biology professor, researcher; b. Neligh, Nebr., May 2, 1972; s. Ronald Francis and Frances Jean Gilg; m. Lisa Elizabeth Wills, Sept. 9, 1998. BA, Hastings Coll., 1994; MS, Eastern Ill. U., 1996; PhD, U. S.C., 2002. Rsch. asst. prof. U. S.C., Columbia, 2002—03; asst. prof. U. N. Fla., Jacksonville, 2003—. Avocations: fishing, hunting. Office: U N Fla Dept Biology 4567 Saint Johns Bluff Rd S Jacksonville FL 32224

GILGEN, ALBERT RUDOLPH, psychologist, educator; b. Akron, Ohio, Sept. 19, 1930; s. Albert and Jeannette (Rufer) Gilgen; m. Carol E. Keyes, 1954; children: James D., Jeanne Elizabeth, Albert P. *Parents were Swiss immigrants. Wife, AB 1954 Bryn Mawr, MA 1964 Kent State, is a CPA who majored in Russian as an undergraduate and has co-authored or co-edited books on international and Russian psychology with Albert and Russian psychologists. Son Jim owns and manages a Cedar Falls store, Gilgen's Consignment Furnishings. Daughter Beth, married to Douglas Gerken, has a home day care center in Cedar Falls and is mother of 2 sons: Christopher and James. Son Bert is a music agent in Houston, Texas.* AB in Chemistry, Princeton U., 1952; MA in Psychology, Kent State U., 1963; PhD in Psychology, Mich. State U., 1965. Asst. then assoc. prof. Beloit Coll., Wis., 1965-73; prof., head of dept. U. No. Iowa, Cedar Falls, 1973-93, prof., 1993-2001, prof. emeritus, 2001—. Author: American Psychology Since World War II, 1982; co-author: Soviet and American Psychology During World War II, 1997; editor: Contemporary Scientific Psychology, 1970; co-editor: International Handbook of Psychology, 1987, Chaos Theory in Psychology, 1995, Post-Soviet Perspectives on Russian Psychology, 1996; contbr. articles to profl. jours. Served to lt. j.g. USN, 1952—55. Named Fulbright Exch. lectr., U. Coll. Galway, Ireland, 1971—72. Fellow: APA, Am. Psychol. Soc.; mem.: AAAS, Fulbright Alumni Assn. Avocations: reading, maintaining Victorian house. Home: 1107 Washington St Cedar Falls IA 50613-3069 Business E-Mail: albert.gilgen@uni.edu.

GILHAM, HANNA KALTENBRUNNER, writer; b. Linz, Austria, July 1, 1943; arrived in U.S., 1977; d. Werner and Marianne Kaltenbrunner; m. Royce Edward Gilham, Sept. 13, 1971. BA, East Carolina U., 1994. Office worker Teekanne, Salzburg, Austria, 1959—64; ground hostess Lufthansa, Frankfurt, Germany, 1965—66; distbr. Oefag Car Dealership, Salzburg, 1966—67; receptionist Europea Hotel Mirabell, Salzburg, 1968—71; writer, 1971—. Author: Sechsundsechzig Seiten, 1996, The Secret Rock, 1997, The King, Short Stories, 1998, Poetry, 1999, Elite, 2000, CET, Color Equals Time, 2000, Gravity, 2001, VS-VE=EA, 2002, Five Pieces, Five Narrative Renderings on Cloning, 2002, MS to VS-VE=EA, Mathematical Solution to Volume Sun Minus Volume Earth Equals Earth's Age, 2005. Roman Catholic. Avocation: painting. Home: 401 Summit St Greenville NC 27858

GILHOOLEY, DAN, artist, psychoanalyst; BA, MA, Hunter Coll.; MA in Psychoanalysis, Boston Grad. Sch.; Cert. in Psychoanalysis, Ctr. Modern Psychoanalytic Studies. Prof. art Suffolk County Cmty. Coll. Office: Asst Dean of Instruction Suffolk County Cmty College 121 Speonk-Riverhead Rd Riverhead NY 11901 E-mail: gilhood@sunysuffolk.edu.*

GILHOOLY, DAVID JAMES, III, artist; b. Auburn, Calif., Apr. 15, 1943; s. David James and Gladys Catherine (Schulte) G.; m. Camille Margot Chang, Aug. 23, 1983; children: David James, Andrea Elizabeth, Abigail Margaret, Peter Rodney, Hakan Yuatutsu, Kiril Shintora, Sorqan Subetei. BA, U. Calif., Davis, 1965, MA, 1967. Tchr. San Jose (Calif.) State Coll., 1967-69, U. Sask. (Can.), Regina, 1969-71, York U., Toronto, Ont., Can., 1971-75, 76-77, U. Calif.-Davis, summer 1971, 75-76, Calif. State U.-Sacramento, summers 1978-79; lectr. in field. One-man shows include San Francisco Museum Art, 1967, M. H. deYoung Meml. Mus., San Francisco, 1968, Matrix Gallery, Wadsworth Athenuem, Hartford, Conn., 1976, Mus. Contemporary Art, Chgo., 1976, Vancouver (B.C., Can.), Art Gallery, 1976, ARCO Ctr. for Visual Arts, L.A., 1977, Mus. Contemporary Craft, N.Y.C., 1977, E.B. Crocker Art Mus., Sacramento, 1980, St. Louis Mus. Art, 1981, Smith-Anderson Gallery, Palo Alto, 1985, San Jose Mus. Art, 1992, De Saisset Mus., Santa Clara U., 1999, Hallie Ford Mus. Art, Salem, Oreg., 2000; group shows include U. Calif.-Berkeley Art Mus., 1967, Inst. Contemporary Art, Boston, 1967, Whitney Mus. Am. Art, N.Y.C., 1970, 74, 81, Musee d'art de la Ville Paris, 1973, Chgo. Art Inst., 1975, San Francisco Mus. Art and Nat. Collection Fine Art, Washington, 1976-77, Stedelijk Mus., Amsterdam, Netherlands, 1979, Everson Mus. Art, Syracuse, N.Y., 1979, Whitney Mus. Am. Art, N.Y.C., 1981, Palm Springs Desert Art Mus., 1984, Oakland Mus., 1985, Stanford Mus. Art, 1987, Inst. Contemporary Art, Boston, 1994, DeSaisset Mus., Santa Clara, Calif., 1999, Hallie Ford Mus., Salem, Oreg., 2000; represented in permanent collections S. Bronfman Collection Can. Art, Montreal, Que., San Francisco Mus. Art, Phila. Mus. Art, Vancouver Art Gallery, Art Gallery Greater Victoria (B.C.), Albright-Knox Art Gallery, Buffalo, San Antonio Mus. Art, Oakland (Calif.) Mus. Art, Stedelijk Mus., Stanford U., Palo Alto, Calif., Australian Nat. Gallery, Canberra, Govt. Can., Calgary, Alta., Whitney Mus. Am. Art, Eugene (Oreg.) Ctr. Performing Arts. Can. Coun. grantee, 1975, 78. Mem. Royal Can. Acad. Republican. Mem. Ch. of Scientology. Office: 4385 Yaquina Bay Rd Newport OR 97365-9618 Personal E-mail: dgilhooly@earthlink.net.

GILINSKY, VICTOR, physicist; b. Warsaw, May 28, 1934; came to U.S., 1941, naturalized, 1948; s. Shlome Faywysh and Luba (Kantorowicz) G.; m. Madeleine Gilinsky, 2000; children from previous marriage: David, Anessa. BS in Engring. Physics, Cornell U., 1956; PhD in Physics, Calif. Inst. Tech., 1961. Physicist Rand Corp., Santa Monica, Calif., 1961-71, head dept. phys. sci., 1973-75; asst. dir. policy and program rev. AEC, Washington, 1971-73; mem. U.S. Nuclear Regulatory Commn., Washington, 1975-84, cons., 1984—. Mem. IEEE, Am. Phys. Soc., Internat. Inst. Strategic Studies, Internat. Conf. on Large Elec. Sys. E-mail: victor@gilinsky.com.

GILIOLI, ERIC LAWRENCE, lawyer; b. Cin., Sept. 9, 1957; s. Daniel Ettore and Helen Marie (Tiersch) G.; m. Vivia J. Chen. AB, Harvard Coll., 1979; JD, Fordham U., 1983; Giurisprudenza, U. Milan, 1996. Bar: N.Y. 1984, D.C. 1985, U.S. Dist. Ct. (so. and ea. dists.) N.Y., U.S. Ct. Internat. Trade. Ptnr. Curtis, Mallet-Prevost, Colt & Mosle, LLP, N.Y.C., Gilioli, Alemani, Bocchiola, Tamburini & Ptnrs., Milan. Mem. Am. C. of C. in Italy, Havard Club (N.Y.C.). Office: Curtis Mallet-Prevost Colt & Mosle 101 Park Ave Fl 34 New York NY 10178-0061 E-mail: egilioli@cm.p.com.

GILKES, CHERYL LOUISE TOWNSEND, sociologist, educator, minister; b. Boston, Nov. 2, 1947; d. Murray Luke Jr. and Evelyn Annette (Reid) Townsend. BA, MA, PhD, Northeastern U.; postgrad., Boston U., 1988. Lectr. Univ. Coll. Northeastern U., Boston, 1973-78; instr. sociology Boston State Coll., 1974-78, U. Mass., 1976; asst. prof. sociology Boston U., 1978-87; MacArthur assoc. prof. African-Am. studies and sociology Colby Coll., Waterville, Maine, 1989-2000, MacArthur asst. prof., 1987-89, MacArthur prof. African Am. studies and sociology, 2000—. Vis. lectr. Tufts U., 1974; rsch. assoc., vis. lectr. sociology of religion Harvard U. Div. Sch., 1981-82, vis. lectr. African-Am. religious studies, 1992-93; vis. lectr. Afro-Am. studies Simmons Coll., Chgo. Theol. Sem., 1989, Iliff Sch. Theology, 1989, Temple U., 1989; faculty fellow Bunting Inst., Radcliff Coll., 1982-84; vis. scholar Episcopal Div. Sch., 1992-93; fellow W.E.B. DuBois Inst. for Afro-Am. Rsch., Harvard U., Inst. Advanced Study Religion, Yale U., 1999-2000; host gospel music radio sta. WMHB Waterville, 2002—. Author: If It Wasn't for the Women...: Black Women's Experience and Womanist Culture in Church and Community, 2000; contbr. articles and revs. to profl. jours., chpts. to books. Sec. Cambridge Civic Unity Com., 1978-87; mem. adv. com. Schlessinger Libr., Radcliffe Coll., 1984-86; pres. Cambridge Black Cultural and Hist. Assn., 1978-87; parliamentarian, asst. dean congress Christian Edn. United Bapt. Conv., Mass., R.I. and N.H., 1986—; assoc. min. Union Bapt. Ch., Cambridge, Mass., 1982-97, asst. pastor, 1998—; mem. NAACP. Nat. Fellowships fund dissertation fellow, 1977-78, Socialization Tng. fellow Northeastern U., 1970-73. Fellow: Inst. Advanced Study Religion; mem.: NAACP, Urban League Ea. Mass., Assn. for Sociology of Religion, Soc. Study Black Religion, Soc. Sci. Study of Religion (exec. coun. 1995—97), Sociologists Women in Soc. (lectr. 2002—), Assn. Black Sociologists, Soc. Study of Sybolic Interaction, Am. Acad. Religion, Assn. Humanist Sociology, Soc. Study of Social Problems (v.p. 1990—91), Mass. Sociol. Assn., Ea. Sociol. Soc. (v.p. 1995—96), Am. Sociol. Assn. (Spivak dissertation fellow 1977—78, mem. coun. 1995—98), Delta Sigma Theta, Phi Kappa Phi. Office: Colby Coll Dept Sociology Waterville ME 04901

GILL, BECKY LORETTE, retired psychiatrist; b. Phoenix, Mar. 16, 1947; d. David Franklin and Lorette (Cooper) Brinegar; m. Jim Shack Gill, Jr., Aug. 5, 1978. BA in Biology, Stanford U., 1968; MD, U. Ariz., 1973. Diplomate Am. Bd. Psychiatry and Neurology, cert. addiction counselor, substance abuse residential facility dir., addictions specialist, clin. supr. Clerk typist Ariz. Med. Ctr. Med. Libr., Tucson, 1970, asst. ref. libr., 1971; surg. extern Tucson Med. Ctr., summer 1970; med. extern Fed. Reformatory for Women, Alderson, W.Va., 1972-73; commd. lt. USN, 1974, advanced through grades to capt., 1992; intern in medicine USPHS Hosp., Balt., 1973-74; resident in psychiatry Nat. Naval Med. Ctr., Bethesda, Md., 1974-77; head alcohol rehab. svc./substance abuse dept., staff psychiatrist Naval Hosp., Camp Lejeune, N.C., 1977-85, head alcohol rehab. svc./substance abuse dept., head psych. Millington, Tenn., 1985-88, head alcohol rehab. dept. Long Beach, Calif., 1988-94; head Navy Addictions Rehab. and Edn. Dept., Camp Pendleton, Calif., 1994-2001; ret., 2001. Mem. tumor bd. Naval Hosp., Camp Lejeune, 1977—85, watch officer Acute Care Clinic, Millington, 1985—86; cons. Tri-Command Consol. Drug and Alcohol Adv. Coun., 1977—85, phys. fitness program com., 1980—85, med. liaison substance abuse, 1982—85, drug/alcohol program advisor, cons., 1983—85; cons. Counseling and Assistance Ctr., 1985—88, mem. bioethics com., chmn. med. records utilization rev. com., 1985—88, mem. exec. com. med. staff, chmn., 1986—87; psychiat. cons. NAS Brig, 1986—88, mem. quality assurance com., mem. pharmacy and therapeutics com., dir. surg. svcs., 1986, mem. credentials com., commd. duty watch officer, 1986—87, dir. med. svcs., 1986—88, watch officer Acute Care Clinic, 1987—88; mem., preceptor to social worker Navy Drug and Alcohol Adv. Coun., 1987—88, mem. pos. mgmt. com., mem. commd. retention coun., 1988. Capt. USN. Decorated Legion of Merit. Mem.: Nat. Assn. Alcoholism and Drug Abuse Counselors, Addiction Profls. N.C. (chmn. pub. info. com. 1979—80, eastern regional v.p. 1981—82, chmn. fall meeting planning com. 1983, sec. 1984—85), Am. Soc. Addiction Medicine, Am. Acad. Psychiatrists Alcoholism and Addictions (founding mem.), U.S. Lawn Tennis Assn. (life), U. Ariz. Alumni Assn., VFW Aux., Stanford Alumni Assn., Stanford Cardinal Club, Am. Legion, Stanford Cap and Gown. Democrat. Avocations: tennis, swimming, jogging. Home: PMB 8187 PO Box 2428 Pensacola FL 32513-2428

GILL, CLAIR F., military career officer; b. Johnstown, Pa., July 7, 1943; m. Sherry Angello; children: Clair, Heidi, Christopher. Grad., U.S. Mil. Acad., 1965; MS in Civil Engring., U. Calif., Berkeley; postgrad., Harvard U.; grad., Command & Gen. Staff Coll., Army War Coll. Registered profl. engr., D.C. Commd. officer US Army C.E., 1965, advanced through grades to maj. gen., various positions, 1965-71, platoon leader, co. exec. officer, 307th Engr. Bn., 82nd Airborne Divsn., platoon leader, co. exec. officer, 8th Engr. Bn., 1st Cav Divsn. (Airmobile), aide de Camp to the Chief of Staff, I Field Force Vietnam, co. comdr., 103rd Engr. Co.; asst. exec. officer to dean US Mil. Acad., 1971-74; dir. facilities engring., dir. engring. and housing US Mil. Cmty. Activity, Ansbach, Germany; Bn. exec. officer 16th Engr. Bn, 1st Armored Divsn. US Army, Germany, 1977-79, comdr. 14th Engr. Battalion Ft. Ord, Calif., 1979; chief manpower and force programs analysis divsn. Office of the Chief of Staff, Washington; comdr. 7th Engr. Brigade VII Corps US Army, Germany; comdr. Pacific Ocean divsn. US Army C.E., Ft. Shafter, Hawaii; dep. chief staff, engr. US Army Europe and Seventh Army, Heidelberg, Germany; dir. resource mgmt. US Army Forces Command, Ft. McPherson, Ga.; engr. sch. comdt. and installation comdt. US Army Engr. Ctr., Ft. Leonard Wood; dep. asst. sec. Army for Budget Office of the Asst. Sec. of the Army; created and led, office of engring. and construction mgmt. US Dept. Energy, 1999—2001; chief of staff and resources/planning dir. Smithsonian Inst., Office of Facilities Engineering and Operations (OFEO), Washington, 2001—. Bd. dir. Army Engr. Assn. Decorated Legion of Merit with 3 oak leaf clusters, Bronze Star medal with 2 oak leaf clusters, Meritorious Svc. medal, Air medal, Vietnam Tech. Svc. medal (First Class), Ranger Tab, Parachutist Badge. Office: Smithsonian Inst Office Facilities Engring & Ops PO Box 37012 Washington DC 20013-7012

GILL, DAVID BRIAN, electrical engineer, educator; b. Columbus, Ohio, Oct. 23, 1957; s. Emery Jr. and Norma Jean Gill; m. Karen Marie Schaar, June 25, 1988. BSEE with highest distinction, Purdue U., 1978, MSEE, 1979, MBA, 1981. Registered profl. engr., Tex. Systems design engr. Owens-Ill., Toledo, 1976-80; engr. Tex. Instruments Def. Group, Dallas, 1981-84, lead engr., 1984-86, mem. group tech. staff, 1986-88, br. mgr., 1988-95, sr. mem. tech. staff, 1995—2001; sr. fellow Raytheon, 2001—. Instr. Purdue U., West Lafayette, Ind., 1978-80, Richland Coll. Engring. Lab., Dallas, 1982-96. Editor lab. manual Control Systems Workbook, 1979. Krannert scholar, 1981. Mem. Purdue Alumni Assn. (life), IEEE, Assn. Old Crows, Phi Eta Sigma, Tau Beta Pi, Eta Kappa Nu, Beta Gamma Sigma, Phi Kappa Phi. Avocations: golf, skeet shooting, hunting. Office: Raytheon 2501 W University Dr Mc Kinney TX 75071-2813

GILL, E. ANN, lawyer; b. Elyria, Ohio, Aug. 31, 1951; d. Richard Henry and Laura (Beeler) G.; m. Robert William Hempel, Aug. 4, 1973; children: Richard, Peter, Mary. AB, Barnard Coll., 1972; JD, Columbia U., 1976. Bar: N.Y. 1977, U.S. Supreme Ct. 1982. Assoc. Mudge, Rose, Guthrie & Alexander, NYC, 1976-77, Dewey Ballantine LLP, NYC, 1977-84, ptnr., 1985—2004, Thelen Reid & Priest LLP, NYC, 2004—. Mem. ABA, Nat. Assn. Bond Lawyers. Home: 255 W 90th St New York NY 10024-1109 Office: Thelen Reid & Priest LLP 875 Third Ave New York NY 10022 Office Phone: 212-603-2412. Personal E-mail: agill@thelenreid.com.

GILL, EVALYN PIERPOINT, editor, writer, publisher; b. Boulder, Colo. d. Walter Lawrence and Lou Octavia Pierpoint; m. John Glanville Gill; children: Susan Pierpoint, Mary Louise Glanville. Student, Lindenwood Coll.; BA, U. Colo.; postgrad., U. Nebr., U. Alaska; MA, Ctrl. Mich. U., 1968. Lectr. humanities Saginaw Valley State Coll., University Ctr., Mich., 1968-72; mem. English faculty U. N.C., Greensboro, 1973-74; editor Internat. Poetry Rev., Greensboro, 1975-92; pres. TransVerse Press, Greensboro, 1981—. Author: Poetry by French Women, 1930-1980, 1980, Dialogue, 1985, Southeast of Here: Northwest of Now, 1986, Entrances, 1996; editor: O. Henry Festival Stories, 1985, 87, Women of the Piedmont Triad: Poetry and Prose, 1989, Edge of Our World, 1990, A Turn in Time: Piedmont Writers at the Millennium, 1999. Bd. dirs. Eastern Music Festival, Greensboro, 1981-85, Greensboro Symphony, 1982-86, Greensboro Opera Co., 1982—, Weatherspoon Art Mus., 1980-; chmn. O Henry Festival, 1985, 95. Recipient numerous poetry prizes, Fortner award St. Andrews Coll., 1995, Altrusa Internat. Cmty. Arts award, Greensboro, 1998. Mem. MLA, Amn. Lit. Translators Assn., N.C. Poetry Soc., Phi Beta Kappa. Home: 2900 Turner Grove Dr N Greensboro NC 27455-1977

GILL, GAIL STOORZA, corporate professional; b. Yoakum, Tex., Aug. 28, 1943; d. Roy Otto and Ruby Pauline (Ray) Blankenship; m. Larry Stoorza, Apr. 27, 1963 (div. 1968); m. Ian M. Gill, Apr. 24, 1981; 1 child, Alexandra Leigh. Student, N. Tex. State U., 1961-63, U. Tex., Arlington, 1963. Stewardess Cen. Airlines, Ft. Worth, 1963; advt. and acctg. exec. Phillips-Ramsey Advt., San Diego, 1963-68; dir. advt. Rancho Bernardo, San Diego, 1968-72; dir. corp. communications Avco Community Developers, San Diego, 1972-74; pres. Gail Stoorza Co., San Diego, 1974—, Stoorza, Ziegaus & Metzger, San Diego, 1974—2002; CEO Stoorza, Ziegaus, Metzger, Inc. (now Stoorza Communications, Co.), 1993—2002; chmn. Stoorza/Smith, San Diego, 1984-85, Stoorza Internat., San Diego, 1984-85; CEO ADC Stoorza, San Diego, 1987—2001, Franklin Stoorza, San Diego, 1993—2001; chmn., CEO The Right Question, LLC. Columnist The San Diego Daily Transcript; bd. dirs. Security Bus. Bank, San Diego. Trustee San Diego Art Found.; bd. dirs. San Diego Found. for Performing Arts, San Diego Opera, Sunbelt Nursery Groups, Dallas; vice chmn. San Diego Convention Ctr. Corp.; mem. bd. San Diego Econ. Devel. Corp., Ind. Colleges of So. Calif. Named Small Bus. Person of Yr. Select Com. on Small Bus., 1984, one of San Diego's Ten Outstanding Young Citizens San Diego Jaycees, 1979; recipient Woman of Achievement award Women in Communications Inc., 1985, Human Unity award, Nat. Conf. Christians and Jews. Mem. Pubs. Soc. Am., Nat. Assn. Home Builders (residential mktg. com.), COMBO, Greater San Diego C. of C (chmn.), Young President's Assn., Arthur Page Soc; Clubs: Chancellors Assn. U. Calif. (San Diego), Pub. Relations, San Diego Press. Methodist.

GILL, GEORGE NORMAN, newspaper publishing company executive; b. Indpls., Aug. 11, 1934; s. George E. and Urith (Dailey) G.; m. Kay Baldwin, Dec. 28, 1957; children— Norman A., George B. AB, Ind. U., 1957. Reporter Richmond (Va.) News Leader, 1957-60; copy editor, reporter, acting Sunday editor, city editor, mng. editor Courier-Jour., Louisville, 1960-74; v.p., gen. mgr. Courier-Jour. and Louisville Times Co., 1974-79, sr. v.p. corp. affairs, 1979-80, pres., chief exec. officer, 1981-86. Chief exec. officer affiliates Standard Gravure Corp., WHAS, Inc., 1981-86; pres., pub. Courier-Jour. and Louisville Times Co., 1986-93. Served with USNR, 1954-56. Recipient Picture Editors award Nat. Press Photographers Assn., 1965 Mem. Am. Soc. Newspaper Editors, Asso. Press Mng. Editors, Alpha Tau Omega, Sigma Delta Chi. Home: PO Box 108 Pewee Valley KY 40056-0108 E-mail: gillg@BellSouth.net.

GILL, GEORGE WILHELM, anthropologist; b. Sterling, Kans., June 28, 1941; s. George Laurance and Florence Louise (Jones) Gill; m. Carol Anne Livesay, Aug. 11, 1962 (div. 1974); children: George Scott, John Ashton; m. Pamela Jo Mills, July 26, 1975 (div. 1988); children: Bryce Thomas, Jennifer Florence; m. Denise Ann Royer, Oct. 30, 2001. BA in Zoology with honors (NSF grantee), U. Kans., 1963, MPhil Anthropology (NDEA fellow, NSF grantee), 1970, PhD in Anthropology, 1971. Diplomate Am. Bd. Forensic Anthropology, 1978. Mem. faculty U. Wyo., Laramie, 1971—, prof. anthropology, 1985—, chmn. dept. anthropology, 1993—96, dir. Anthropology Mus., 1979—87. Forensic anthropologist law enforcement agys., 1972—; sci. leader Easter Island Anthrop. Expdn., 1981; chmn. Rapa Nui Rendezvous: Internat. Conf. Easter Island Rsch., U. Wyo., 1993. Author: articles, monographs; editor: (with S. Rhine) Skeletal Attribution of Race, 1990. Capt. U.S. Army, 1963—67. Recipient J.P. Ellbogen meritorious classroom tchg. award, 1983; rsch. grantee U. Wyo., 1972, 78, 82, Nat. Geog. Soc., 1980, Ctr. for Field Rsch. 1980, Kon-Tiki Mus., Oslo, 1987, 89, 94, 96, World Monuments Fund, 1989, Mus. Inventory and Curation co-grantee BLM, Bur. Reclamation, Wyo. DOT, Fish and Wildlife Svc., 1994-99. Fellow: Am. Acad. Forensic Scis. (sec. phys. anthropology sect. 1985—87, chmn. 1987—88); mem.: Wyo. Archaeol. Soc., Plains Anthrop. Soc., Am. Assn. Phys. Anthropologists. Republican. Unitarian. Office: U Wyo Dept Anthropology Laramie WY 82071 Office Phone: 307-766-6282. Business E-Mail: ggill@uwyo.edu.

GILL, GERALD LAWSON, librarian; b. Montgomery, Ala., Nov. 13, 1947; s. George Ernest and Marjorie (Hackett) G.; m. Nancy Argroves, Mar. 5, 1977 (div. 1982). AB, U. Ga., 1971; MA, U. Wis., 1973. Cert. profl. libr., Va. Cataloger James Madison U., Harrisonburg, Va., 1974-76, reference libr., 1976-87, bus. reference libr., 1987-99, govt. documents libr., 1998—2003, head of reference and govt. documents, 2003—, instr., 1974-80, asst. prof., 1980-90, assoc. prof., 1990—2002, prof., 2002—. Lectr., spkr. nat. and regional groups; cons. in field; mem. faculty senate James Madison U., 1975-79, 96-98, sec. curriculum and instrn. com., 1976-78, chair, 1978-79, univ. coun., 1996-98. Mem. editl. bd. James Madison Jour., 1977-80; reviewer Am. Reference Books Ann.; contbr. articles to profl. jours. Mem. libr. adv. com. State Coun. for Higher Edn. in Va., 1986-87; virtual Va. Coord. Mgmt. Bus. com. Mem. ALA (chmn. bus. reference svcs. com. 1984-86, sec. law and polit. sci. sect. 1982-85, chmn. bus. reference svcs. discussion group 1986-87, chmn. bus. reference in acad. librs. com. 1988-91, Gale Rsch. award 1991), AAAS, Am. Soc. for Info. Sci., Va. Libr. Assn. (coun. 1986-87, parliamentarian 1979, 81), Spl. Librs. Assn. (treas. Va. chpt. 1983-85, pres. 1986-87), World Future Soc., Harrisonburg C. of C., Sierra Club. Democrat. Roman Catholic. Avocations: art collecting, travel. Home: 326 Westfield Rd Charlottesville VA 22901-1660 Office: James Madison U Library Harrisonburg VA 22807-0001 E-mail: gillgl@jmu.edu.

GILL, GLENDA ELOISE, university educator; b. June 26, 1939; d. Melvin Leo and Olivia (Dunlop) Gill. BS, Ala. A&M Coll., 1960; MA, U. Wis., 1964; PhD, U. Iowa, 1981. Asst. prof. Simpson Coll., Indianola, Iowa, 1981—82; assoc. prof., dept. head Tuskegee U., Ala., 1982—83; assoc. prof. Winston-Salem State U., NC, 1984—90, Mich. Tech. U., Houghton, 1990—2000, prof. drama, 2000—. Presenter nat. and internat. confs. including The World Congress of Theatre, Stockholm, 1989, Dublin, 92, Eugene O'Neill Internat. Conf., France, 2003, Provincetown, Mass., 05. Author: White Grease Paint on Black Performers, 1988, No Surrender! No Retreat! African American Pioneer Performers of 20th Century American Theater, 2000; contbr. articles to profl. jours. Summer fellow Nat. Portrait Gallery The Smithsonian Instn.,

1990; NEH grantee,1974, 85, 89, 91; Rockefeller grantee, 1976, 77. Mem.: Assn. Theatre in Higher Edn., Eugene O'Neill Soc. Democrat. Baptist. Home: 1105 Quincy Cove Rd Houghton MI 49931

GILL, GORDON N., medical educator; b. Dec. 19, 1937; BA in Chemistry/Lit., Vanderbilt U., 1960, MD, 1963. Diplomate Am. Bd. Internal Medicine with subspecialty in endocrinology and metabolism. Internal medicine intern Vanderbilt U. Hosp., Nashville, 1963-64; resident Yale-New Haven Hosp., 1964-66; fellow postdoctoral fellow metabolism/endocrinology NIH/Yale U., 1966-68; spl. postdoctoral rsch. fellow NIH/U. Calif., San Diego, 1968-69; asst. prof. medicine U. Calif., San Diego, 1969-73, assoc. prof., 1973-78, prof. medicine, 1978—, chief divsn. endocrinology dept. medicine, 1971-83, chief divsn. endocrinology/metabolism, 1983-95, assoc. chair sci. affairs, 1992-95, chmn. faculty basic biomed. scis., 1995—2002, dean sci. affairs, 2001—03, interim dir. Moores/UCSD Cancer Ctr., 2003. Chmn. endocrinology study sect. NIH, 1979-80, chmn. task force on endocrinology, 1978, dir. tng. grant on exptl. endocrinology and metabolism, 1978-; prin. investigator interdisciplinary program to study macromolecules regulating growth and oncogenesis U. Calif., San Diego, 1988-95; chmn. Gordon Conf. on Hormone Action, 1979, Gordon Conf. on Peptide Growth Factors, 1990; mem. sci. adv. bd. BioCryst, 1990-; sci. and med. adv. bd. chair Whittier Inst., 1991-95; sci. adv. bd. Liver Ctr., U. Calif., San Francisco, 1991-95, Charles E. Culpepper Found., 1992—2001, Coun. for Tobacco Rsch. USA, 1991-97, ICN Pharms., 1992-; internat. adv. bd. dept. molecular and structural biology U. Grenoble, France, 1993-98; S. Richardson Hill vis. prof. U. Ala., Birmingham, 1991; Berlin lectr. Northwestern U. Sch. Medicine, 1994, sci. adv. bd. Chau, Kirsch Found., 2001-04. Mem. editl. bd. Jour. Cyclic Nucleotide and Protein Phosphorylation Rsch., 1974-84, Endocrinology, 1978-82, Am. Jour. Physiology, Cell Physiology, 1981-87, Jour. Biol. Chemistry, 1983-88, Jour. Cellular Biochemistry, 1984-89, Ann. Rev. Medicine, 1986-91, Analytical Biochemistry, 1980-92; editor Molecular and Cellular Endocrinology, 1974-92; cons. editor Jour. Clin. Investigation, 1992-97; sect. editor: Endocrinology, Best and Taylor Physiological Basis of Medical Practice, 11th-12th edits., Endocrinology and Metabolism, Cecil's Textbook of Medicine, 20th-22nd edit. Bd. dirs. Med. Rsch. and Edn. Found., The Agouron Inst., 1985—; mem. biochemistry and endocrinology sci. adv. com. Am. Cancer Soc., 1989-91; adv. com. Markey Charitable Trust, 1990-97; peer rev. com. Am. Heart Assn., 1991-96. Helen Hay Whitney Found. fellow, 1969-73; NIH Rsch. Career Devel. awardee, 1969-73, Merit award. Fellow ACP, Am. Acad. Arts and Scis.; mem. AAAS, Assn. Am. Physicians, Am. Fedn. Clin. Rsch., Am. Soc. Clin. Investigation, Am. Soc. Biol. Chemistry and Molecular Biology, Endocrine Soc., Western Assn. Physicians, Western Soc. for Clin. Investigation, Am. Soc. for Cell Biology, Phi Beta Kappa, Alpha Omega Alpha. Office: Univ Calif 9500 Gilman Dr La Jolla CA 92093-0650 Office Phone: 858-534-4310.

GILL, HENRY HERR, photojournalist; b. Detroit, July 21, 1930; s. Henry Herr and Esther (King) G.; m. Mary Jane Brown, Aug. 26, 1957. Student, Vincennes U., 1948, Northwestern U., 1949, Ind. U., 1951, McNeese State U., La., 1952, U. Miami, 1962. Mem. publ. staff U. Miami, 1960; fgn. service photographer, then dir. photography Chgo. Daily News, 1976; dir. photography Chgo. Sun-Times, 1978-83; pres., exec. editor Globalfoto/Roma, 1983-87; pres., film dir. Fotostar Prodns., 1987—. Lectr. in field, exhibitor of photographs, 1964- Co-author: Mississippi Notebook, 1964; photographer: film A War of Many Faces, 1965, The Cocaine Express, 1982. Recipient photo reporting award on Vietnam Nat. Headliners Club, 1967, Overseas Press Club award, 1967, 81, Emmy award for documentary Nat. Acad. TV Arts and Scis., 1965, Best News Picture of Yr. award Inland Press Assn., 1968, 69, Faculty citation Vincennes U., 1979, Baker Meml. Journalism award, 1980; named to Journalism Hall of Fame, 1994, Ind. Journalism Hall of Fame, 2004. Mem. Internat. Press Club (Chgo.), Headliner Club (Chgo.), Sigma Delta Chi (Disting. Journalism award 1965). E-mail: gattolv@earthlink.net.

GILL, INDERBIR SINGH, urologist, lapraroscopic surgeon; b. New Delhi, Sept. 5, 1958; came to U.S., 1989; s. Devinder Singh and Rajinder Kaur Gill; m. Navneet Kaur, Mar. 25, 1984; children: Tania, Karanvir Singh. MB BS, Govt. Med. Sch., Patiala, Punjab, India, 1980; MS, Dayawand Med. Coll., Ludhiana, Punjab, India, 1983; MCh, All India Inst. Med. Scis., 1987. Fellowship in renal transplantation Cleve. Clinic Found., 1989-91; resident in urology U. Ky., 1995; assoc. prof. urology U. Nebr. Med. Ctr., Omaha, 1995-97; head sec. laparoscopic and minimally invasive Cleve. Clinic Found., 1997—. Editl. reviewer Jour. of Urology, Jour. of Endourology, 1998, 99; co-author: Urology MCQs, 1987, 90. Mem. Am. Urol. Assn. Avocations: jogging, cricket, tennis. Office: Cleve Clinic Found A-100 9500 Euclid Ave # A-100 Cleveland OH 44195-0001

GILL, JAMIE W., librarian; d. John F. and Millicent E. Webster; m. Andrew J. Gill, Apr. 5, 2001. BS, SUNY, Geneso, NY, 1968; MLS, Kent State U., 1969. Library Media Specialist NY State, 1969. Reference libr. Buffalo & Erie County Pub. Libr., 1969—72; children's & young adult libr. Amherst Pub. Libr., Williamsville, NY, 1972—78, br. mgr., 1978—81; serials, tech. svcs. coord. Eckerd Coll., St. Petersburg, Fla., 1982—. V.p. Libr. & Info. Resources Network (LIRN), Largo, Fla., 2004—. Co-editor: Bibliographic Instruction in Practice, Mission Statements for College Libraries, Periodicals in College Libraries; contbr. chapters to books. Com. mem. CASA Amigas, St. Petersburg, Fla., 1994—99. Mem.: Fla. Chpt. of the Assn. of Coll. & Rsch. Librs. (sec. 1991—94), Assn. of Coll. & Rsch. Librs. (chair, publications com. 2002—05), Fla. Chpt. Assn. Coll. & Rsch. Librs. (sec. 2004—06). Office: Eckerd Coll 4200 54th Ave S Saint Petersburg FL 33711 Office Phone: 727-864-8206.

GILL, KAREN V., secondary school educator, consultant; b. Lexington, Ky., Mar. 12, 1968; d. Jack B. and Anita L. (Jones) Vinning; m. Scot A. Gill, June 8, 1991. BS, Transylvania U., 1990; MS, U. Ky., 1995; postgrad., Georgetown Coll., 1995—99. Cert. secondary sch. tchr. Ky., Nat. Bd., 2002. Tchr. physics Tates Creek H.S.; Lexington, Ky., 1990-92, Henry Clay H.S., Lexington, Ky., 1992—. Cons. Z-tek, Lexington, Ky., 1994—; mem. Physics Modeling Workshop, 1998—. Co-author: (CD-ROM) Physics Cinema Classics Teachers Guide, 1995. Mem. Am. Assn. Physics Tchrs. (physics tchr. resource agent 1996, workshop leader 1996—), Ctrl. Ky. Physics Alliance (planning com. 1991-96, Presdl. award 2003). Office: Henry Clay HS 2100 Fontaine Rd Lexington KY 40502-2014 Office Phone: 859-381-3624. Business E-Mail: kgill@fayette.k12.ky.us.

GILL, LIBBY, television executive; BA in Theater magna cum laude, Calif. State U., Long Beach. Mgr., publicist Embassy Comm. and Columbia Pictures TV, Calif., 1986-89; dir. primetime publicity Columbia Pictures TV/TriStar TV, Calif., 1989-92; v.p. publicity and promotion Sony Pictures Entertainment TV Group, Calif., 1992-94; v.p. pub. rels. west coast Turner Entertainment Group, Calif., 1994-96; sr. v.p. media rels. Universal TV Group, Universal City, Calif., 1996—. Pub. rels. cons. for non-profit orgns., including Deaf Arts Coun. Mem. TV Publicity Execs. Com. (former chmn.). Office: MCA TV 100 Universal City Plz Universal City CA 91608-1002

GILL, LINDA A., advertising executive; b. Buffalo, May 8, 1942; d. Elvin R. Albee and Marian Elizabeth Beardsley; m. W. Richard Davy, Apr. 4, 1964 (div. Oct. 1973); children: Ashley, Jennifer, Kit; m. Edward W. Fallon, June 14, 1992. AS, Endicott Coll., 1962; student, Rutgers U., 1984—85. Sales rep., account mgr. Ciba-Geigy Pharm., Summit, NJ, 1980—87; account supr., v.p. Bozell, N.Y.C., 1987—90; sr. v.p., mgmt. supr. FCB, N.Y.C., 1990—94; exec. v.p., mng. dir. Healthworld, N.Y.C., 1994—. Tchr. music/piano, 1979—87. Recipient Clio award, 1986. Mem.: Healthcare Mktg. and Comm. Coun., Healthcare Bus. Woman's Assn., Jr. League. Avocations: piano, golf, reading, horseback riding, mentoring. Office: Healthworld 100 6th Ave New York NY 10013 Business E-Mail: fallonle@aol.com.

GILL, MARGARET GASKINS, lawyer; b. St. Louis, Mar. 2, 1940; d. Richard Williams and Margaret (Cambage) Gaskins; m. Stephen Paschall Gill, Dec. 21, 1961; children: Elizabeth, Richard. BA, Wellesley Coll., 1962; JD, U. Calif., Berkeley, 1965. Bar: Calif. 1966. Assoc. Pillsbury, Madison & Sutro, San Francisco, 1966-72, ptnr., 1973-94, mem. mgmt. com., 1973-94, head corp. securities group, mem. assoc., rev. com., 1981-91, chair assoc., rev. com., 1988-91; sr. v.p. legal, external affairs & sec. AirTouch Communications, San Francisco, 1994—. Referee Calif. State Bar Ct., 1979-82; bd. dirs. Consolidated Freightways. Mem. steering com. Trinity Episcopal Ch., Menlo Park, Calif., 1980-82, com. to revise constitution, Diocese Calif., 1981-82; trustee St. Luke's Hosp. Found., San Francisco, 1983-93; mem. adv. coun. Ch. div. Sch. of the Pacific, 1986; bd. dirs. Episcopal Diocese Calif., 1989—; trustee San Francisco Ballet, 1991—; bd. dirs., gen. counsel United Way Bay Area, San Francisco, 1993-94. Fellow Am. Bar Found.; mem. ABA (spl. com. on internat. practice 1979-82, spl. com. negotiated acquisition 1988-90), Calif. Bar Assn. (corp. com. 1982-85, chairperson 1985, exec. com. 1985-88, vice chairperson 1987-88, chair nominating com. bus. law sect. 1988), San Francisco Bar Assn. Republican. Episcopalian. Office: Airtouch Communications 2999 Oak Rd #5 Walnut Creek CA 94597-2066

GILL, MICHAEL GERARD, music educator; s. Carl Robert and Marie Genevieve Gill; m. Lori Ann Cook, Aug. 10, 1991; children: Miles, Liam. MEd, Lesley U., 1999; MusB, U. Wyo., 1988; A in Music, Casper Coll., 1984. Lic. profl. tchg. Colo., 1999. Music tchr. Westlake Mid. Sch., Broomfield, Colo., 1990—; dist. music coord. Adams 12 Sch. Dist., Thornton, Northglenn, Colo.; freelance musician Denver, 1990—; music tchr. Lincoln Mid. Sch., Green River, Wyo. Adjudicator Colo. State Solo & Ensemble Festival, Various, Colo., 1990—; dept. chmn. Westlake Mid. Sch., Broomfield, Colo., 1990—; guest condr. No. League Honor Band, Sterling, Colo., 1999, Rocky Mountain Mid. Sch. Honor Band, Frisco, Colo., 2001—01. Author: (jour. article) Integrating Tech. in the Music Classroom, 1998. Mem.: Colo. Music Educators Assn., NEA, Nat. Bandmasters Assn., Music Educators Nat. Conf., Internat. Trumpet Guild, Denver Musicians Assn., Colo. Bandmasters Assn., Dist. Twelve Edn. Assn. Lutheran. Avocations: yoga, hiking, camping, bicycling. Office: Westlake Mid Sch 2800 W 135th Dr Broomfield CO 80020 Office Phone: 720-972-3229. Business E-Mail: mike.gill@adams12.org.

GILL, RICHARD F., construction engineering executive; Joined Shaw Group, 1997; founder, pres. Merit Industrial Constructors, Inc.; exec. v.p., COO Shaw Group, 1999—2003; pres. Stone & Webster, Inc., 2000—03; chmn. exec. com. The Shaw Group, Inc.; pres. Shaw Stone and Webster Nuc. Svcs., Baton Rouge. Office: The Shaw Group Inc 4171 Essen Ln Baton Rouge LA 70809

GILL, RICHARD LAWRENCE, lawyer; b. Chgo., Jan. 8, 1946; s. Joseph Richard and Dolores Ann (Powers) Gill; m. Mary Helen Walker, July 14, 1990; children: Kyla Marie, Matthew Joseph. BA, Coll. of St. Thomas, St. Paul, 1968; JD, U. Minn., 1971. Bar: Minn. 1971, U.S. Dist. Ct. Minn. 1971, U.S. Supreme Ct. 1979, U.S. Ct. Appeals (8th cir.) 1983, U.S. Ct. Appeals (4th cir.) 1990, Ill. 1992. Spl. asst. atty. gen. State of Minn., St. Paul, 1971-73; assoc. Maun, Hazel, Green, Hayes, Simon & Aretz, St. Paul, 1974-77; ptnr. Gill & Brinkman, St. Paul, 1978-84, Robins, Kaplan, Miller & Ciresi, Mpls., 1984—2002, of counsel, 2002—. Vol. Courage Ctr., Golden Valley, Minn., 1981—; youth football coach Maplewood (Minn.) Athletic Assn., 1978-80; youth basketball coach Orono (Minn.) Athletic Assn., 1999—; mem. athletics adv. bd. U. St. Thomas, 2002—. Mem. ABA, Minn. Bar Assn., Hennepin County Bar Assn., Ramsey County Bar Assn., Assn. Trial Lawyers Am., Minn. Trial Lawyers Assn., Town and Country Club, Windsong Golf Club. Avocations: skiing, tennis, golf. Office: Robins Kaplan Miller & Ciresi 800 Lasalle Ave Ste 2800 Minneapolis MN 55402-2015 Office Phone: 612-349-8430. Business E-Mail: rlgill@rkmc.com.

GILL, ROBERT TUCKER, lawyer; BA, Union U., 1969; JD, MA, Boston Coll., 1973. Bar: Ga. 1973, Mass. 1973, U.S. Ct. Appeals (1st and 5th cirs.) 1973, U.S. Supreme Ct. 1993. Staff atty. Ga. Indigents Legal Svcs., Savannah, Ga., 1973-74; assoc. Sherwin & Gottlieb, Fall River, Mass., 1974-75; ptnr. Parker, Coulter, Daley & White, Boston, 1975-95, Peabody and Arnold, Boston, 1995—. Chmn. Weston (Mass.) Transp. Commn., 1984—89; mem., chmn. Weston (Mass.) Cable TV Com., 1987-88; trustee Monsignor George V. Kerr Trust, Boston, 1988-2000. Mem. ABA, Am. Arbitration Assn. (panel of arbitrators), Mass. Bar Assn., Boston Bar Assn., State Bar of Ga., Mass. Trial Lawyers Assn., Wianno Yacht Club. Avocations: sailing, skiing. Office: Peabody & Arnold 30 Rowes Wharf Fl 6 Boston MA 02110-3339 Office Phone: 617-951-4706.

GILL, SARAH M., music educator; b. Terre Haute, Ind., Sept. 1, 1974; d. Gary Lee and Sally Jane Gill. MusB in performance, Millikin U., 1996; MusM in performance, U. N. Tex., 1998, MusM in musicology, 1999; MusD in performance, Fla. State U., 2002. Instr. flute Columbus State U., Columbus, Ga., 2000—01; asst. prof. Tex. A&M U., Kingsville, Tex., 2002—. Guest prin. flutist Orguesta Sinfonia de Udla, Monterrey, Mexico, 2001. Finalist Young Artist Competition, Nat. Flute Assn., 2004; recipient 1st prize Young Artist Competition, Flute Soc. of Ky., 2005. Mem.: Tex. Flute Soc., Tex. Music Educators Assn., Nat. Flute Assn. Office: Tex A&M U Dept Music MSC 174 700 U Blvd Kingsville TX 78363 Office Phone: 361-593-2823. Office Fax: 361-593-2816. E-mail: sarah.gill@tamuk.edu.

GILL, STEPHEN PASCHALL, retired physicist, mathematician; b. Balt., Nov. 13, 1938; s. Robert Lee and Charlotte (Olmsted) G.; m. Margaret Ann Gaskins, Dec. 21, 1961; children: Elizabeth Olmsted, Richard Paschall. BS, MIT, 1960; MA, Harvard U., 1961, PhD, 1964. Cons. hypersonic aerodynamics Raytheon Corp., Bedford, Mass., 1963-64; research physicist Stanford Research Inst., Menlo Park, Calif., 1964-65, head high energy gasdynamics, 1965-68, Physics Internat. Co., San Leandro, Calif., 1968-70, mgr. shock dynamics dept., 1970-72; founder, pres. Artec Assocs., Inc., Hayward, Calif., 1972-77, chief scientist, 1977-91; founder, pres. Votan Corp., Hayward, Calif., 1979-91, chief scientist, chmn. bd., 1981-85; ret., 1999. Founder, chief scientist Magnetic Pulse Inc., 1985-99. Mem. San Francisco Symphony Assn.; mem. San Francisco Mus. Art. Mem. IEEE, Am. Phys. Soc., Am. Math. Soc., MIT Alumni Assn., Sigma Xi, Delta Kappa Epsilon. Clubs: MIT. Republican. Episcopalian. Home: 32 Flood Cir Atherton CA 94027-2151 E-mail: stephen_p_gill@hotmail.com.

GILL, THOMAS GRANDON, information technology executive, educator; b. Boston, Apr. 26, 1955; s. Richard Thomas and Elizabeth B. Gill; m. Clare Ellen Barres, July 29, 1958; children: Thomas Richard, Jonathan Grandon. BA, Harvard Coll., 1975; MBA, Harvard U., 1982, D in Bus. Adminstrn., 1991. Pres. SnCorp, Inc., Dallas, 1982—83; sr. v.p. Agribus. Assocs., Wellesley Hills, Mass., 1983—86; assoc. prof. Fla. Atlantic U., Boca Raton, 1991—2001, U. South Fla., Tampa, 2001—. Author: (textbook) Introduction to Programming Using Visual C++.NET, (laminated study guides) CyberCue Cards, QuickStudy Guides, (case studies) HBS Pub., Prentice Hall; contbr. trade paperback MBA Handbook. Lt. Submarine Force USN, 1975—80. Scholar Baker scholar, Harvard U., 1982. Conservative. Home: 9226 Highland Ridge Way Tampa FL 33647-2299 Office: University of South Florida IS&DS Dept 4202 E Fowler Ave CIS1040 Tampa FL 33620-7800 Office Phone: 813-974-6755. Personal E-mail: grandon@grandon.com. E-mail: ggill@coba.usf.edu.

GILL, THOMAS JAMES, III, pathologist, educator; b. Malden, Mass., July 2, 1932; s. Thomas James and Marguerite (Capobianco) G.; m. Faith Libbie Etoll, July 8, 1961; children: Elizabeth Ruth, Thomas James IV, Christopher Gregory. AB summa cum laude, Harvard U., 1953, AM in Chemistry, MD, Harvard U., 1957. Diplomate Am. Bd. Pathology. Asst. in pathology Peter Bent Brigham Hosp., Boston, 1957-58; intern N.Y. Hosp.-Cornell Med. Center, 1958-59; jr. fellow Soc. Fellows Harvard U., 1959-62; mem. faculty Harvard U. Med Sch., 1962-71, asso. prof. pathology, 1970-71; prof. pathology, chmn. dept. U. Pitts. Med. Sch., 1971-90; pathologist-in-chief Univ. Health Ctr. Pitts., 1971-90, Maud L. Menten prof. exptl. pathology, 1988—98, prof. human genetics, 1988-98, prof. emeritus human genetics and exptl. pathology, 1999—; prof. clin. immunology for postgrad. studies U. Rijeka, Croatia, 1996—; fellow U. Pitts. Ctr. for Philosophy Sci., 1996—98, assoc., 1999—2001; vis. scholar in biology Harvard U., 1998-2001. Affiliate of Eliot House, Harvard Coll., 1998—; cons. to govt. and industry; mem. sci. adv. bd. St. Jude Children's Rsch. Hosp., Memphis, 1969-77, chmn., 1974-76; mem. allergy and immunology rsch. com. Nat. Inst. Allergy and Infectious Diseases, 1973-76; mem. med. rsch. svc. merit rev. bd. in immunology VA, 1976-79, chmn., 1977-79; mem. sci. adv. com. Damon Runyon-Walter Winchell Cancer Fund, 1978-81; mem. com. on animal models and genetic stocks NRC, 1978-86, chmn. com., 1983-86, mem. com. on rabbit genetic resources, 1979-80, mem. coun. Inst. Lab. Animal Resources, 1986-92, mem. com. on preservation of lab. animal resources, 1985-90, com. on transgenic animals, 1991-92; mem. surgery, anesthesiology and trauma study sect. NIH, 1983-84; sci. adv. com. on immunology and immunotherapy Am. Cancer Soc., 1986-88; mem. Armed Forces Epidemiol. Bd., 1966-72; adj. prof. U. Milan, 1990-92; nutrition found. Italy lectr. U. Milan, 1986-97; trustee Am. Bd. Pathology, 1981-92, life trustee, 1992—, pres., 1992; mem. Maternal and Child Health com. Nat. Inst. Child Health and Human Devel., 1992-96; chmn., 1995-96; mem. immunology task force Nat. Inst. Allergy and Infectious Diseases, 1996-98; mem. adv. com. for the Rat Genome Project and Rat EST Project, Nat. Heart, Lung, and Blood Inst., 1998; rsch. sci. Gen. Hosp., Mass., 2004-; instr. orthopaedic surgery Harvard Medical Sch., 2004-. Mem. editorial bd. several sci. and med. jours.; contbr. articles to profl. jours. Bd. dirs. Easter Seal Soc., Allegheny County, 1972-77, Univs. Asso. for Research and Edn. in Pathology, 1979-90 Recipient Lederle med. faculty award, 1962-65, rsch. career devel. award NIH, 1965-71, MERIT award NIH, 1992-2002, cert. of appreciation for patriotic civilian svc. Dept. Army, 1973, Spl. Qualification in Pathology: Immunopathology, 1983, Disting. Scientist award in genetics S.W. Found. for Biomed. Rsch., 1986, Charter with medal U. Rijeka, 1990, medal U. Pitts., 1990; named George H. Fetterman lectr. U. Pitts., 1981, George Hoyt Whipple lectr. U. Rochester, N.Y., 1984, Aron E. Szulman lectr. U. Pitts., 1993, Raymond O. Berry Meml. lectr. Tex. A&M U., 1995, Mühlblock lectr. Internat. Coun. for Lab. Scis., 1995, Spiridion Brusina award Croatian Soc. Natural Scis., 1997. Fellow Assn. Pathology Chairmen (pres. 1978); mem. AMA, Am. Assn. Immunologists, Am. Assn. Pathologists, Am. Soc. Molecular Biology and Biochemistry, Am. Soc. Human Genetics, Transplantation Soc. (v.p. 1982-84), Am. Soc. for Immunology of Reprodn. (v.p. 1988-89, Disting. Investigator award 1991, pres. 1995-96), Genetics Soc. Am., Internat. Acad. Pathology, Internat. Soc. Immunology of Reprodn. (pres. 1992-95, hon. pres. 1995—), Alps Adria Soc. for Immunology of Reprodn. (hon. pres. 1994—), Mass. Med. Soc., Harvard Club (Boston), Harvard Varsity Club. Business E-Mail: gilliii@massmed.org.

GILL, TINA, music educator; d. Rae Behlman; m. Leighton Gill, June 22, 1996; children: Julia, Abigail, Gareth. MusB, U. Miami, 1989; MusM, U. Mo., 1993. Cert. tchr. Fla., 1990. Dir. choral Palm Beach County Schs., Boynton Beach, Fla., 1989—94, Dade County Pub. Schs., Cutler Ridge, Fla., 1994—95, Broward County Pub Schs., Davie, Fla., 1995—. Music min. Cokesbury United Meth. Ch., Margate, Fla., 2000—. Mem.: Am. Choral Dirs. Assn. (assoc.; webmaster Fla. chpt. 1999—2005), Fla. Vocal Assn. (assoc.; dist. chmn. 2000—02), Music Educators Nat. Conf. (assoc.), Omicron Delta Kappa (life), Sigma Alpha Iota (life; student v.p. 1988—89). Republican. Episcopalian. Avocations: swimming, reading.

GILL, WILLIAM NELSON, chemical engineering professor; b. N.Y.C., Sept. 13, 1928; s. William Nelson and Frances (Murphy) G.; m. Chandlee Stevens, Aug. 13, 1982; children: Alison Louise, Christine Marie, Douglas Max, Max William. BSChemE, Syracuse U., 1951, MA, 1955, PhD, 1960. Field engr. Am. Blower Corp., 1951-55; mem. faculty Syracuse U., 1957-65, assoc. prof., 1963-65; prof. chem. engring., chmn. dept. Clarkson U., 1965-71; provost engring. and applied sci. SUNY, Buffalo, 1971-78, prof. chem. engring., 1982-87; Glenn Murphy Disting. prof. engring. Iowa State U., Ames, 1980-82; Russell Sage disting. prof. chem. engring. Rensselaer Poly. Inst., Troy, N.Y., 1987—. Cons. in field. Editor: Chem. Engring. Communications, 1979—; mem. editorial adv. bd. Fuel, Processing Tech.; mem. bd. cons. editors Elsevier Texts in Engring.; editor Chem. Engring. series Elsevier Sci. Pub. Co.; author numerous articles in field. Named Alumnus of Yr., Bklyn. Tech. H.S., 1977; recipient William H. Wiley Disting. Faculty award in recognition of outstanding tchg. and scholarship Rensselaer Poly. Inst., 1994; Fulbright-Hays sr. rsch. scholar Univ. Coll., London, 1977-78, U. Queensland, Australia, 1986-87, Best Paper award Interconnect Scis. & Tech., Techcon 96 Semiconductor Rsch. Corp., 1996, Lectureship award Chem. Eng. Divsn. ASEE, 1992, Best Paper award Interconnect Modeling and Simulation, Techcon 98, Semiconductor Rsch. Corp., 1998. Fellow AIChE; mem. AAAS, AAUP, Am. Chem. Soc., Am. Soc. Engring. Edn. (lectureship award chem. engring. divsn. for fundamental contbns. to chem. engring. theory and practice 1992), N.Y. Acad. Scis., Sigma Xi. Office: Rensselaer Poly Inst Chem Engring Ricketts Troy NY 12180 Office Phone: 518-276-2880. Business E-Mail: gillw@rpi.edu.

GILLAM, LINDA DAWN, cardiologist, researcher; b. Corner Brook, Nfld., Can., Sept. 23, 1952; d. Donald Samuel and Vera (Pieroway) G.; m. Vincent Charles DiCola, Aug. 30, 1985 (div. 1995); children: John William DiCola, Laura Ann DiCola. BS, McGill U., Montreal, Que., Can., 1972; MD, Queen's U., Kingston, Ont., Can., 1976. Diplomate Am. Bd. Internal Medicine, Am. Bd. Cardiovascular Disease. Intern U. Toronto, 1976; resident in medicine St. Michaels Hosp., Toronto, 1977-79; fellow in cardiology U. Toronto, 1979-81, Mass. Gen. Hosp., Boston, 1981-83; instr. in medicine Harvard U. Med. Sch., Boston, 1983-86; clin. asst. prof. medicine U. Conn., Farmington, 1986-95, clin. assoc. prof., 1995—. Dir. echocardiography U. Conn. Health Ctr., Farmington, 1986-90, Hartford (Conn.) Hosp., 1990—; spkr. in field. Contbr. articles to profl. jours. Rsch. grantee Can. Heart Assn. Fellow: Am. Heart Assn. (chair com. on women in cardiology 2000—, task force on guidelines for echocardiography, exec. com. coun. on clin. cardiology, ARDMS chair adult echo exam task force), Am. Coll. Cardiology (gov. 1996—99, chpt. pres. 1996—99, govt. rels. com. 1997—, mem. steering com. bd. govs., chair task force on comm., mem. awards com., editl. bd. website, program com., Pac bd. medicare carrier adv. com.); mem.: AMA, Am. Soc. Echocardiography (legis. and regulatory affairs com. 1993—2001, bd. dirs. 1995—98, com. on sonographer tng. 1997—, treas. 2001—), Am. Bd. Echocardiography, Conn. State Med. Soc. Avocations: ballet, opera, classical music, aerobics, tennis. Office: Hartford Hosp 80 Seymour St Hartford CT 06102-8000

GILLAM, MAC, physical education educator; b. Paducah, Ky., Apr. 1, 1945; s. Eugene Gillam and Katherine McKenzie; m. Elizabeth Engley, Dec. 21, 1992; children: Kenny, Lyndsey, John Thomas. BS, Jacksonville State U., 1968, MS, 1974; PhD, Fla. State U., 1978. Prof. Jacksonville State U., Ala., 1977—87, prof., dept. head, 1987—2001. Author: Training for Muscle Strength, 1981. Mem. Govs. Comm. Phys. Fitness, Ala., 1991—94; dist. chmn. People Against a Littered State, 1988—93. Home: 961 Alexandria-Jacksonville Rd Alexandria AL 36250

GILLANI, NOOR VELSHI, atmospheric scientist, researcher, educator; b. Arusha, Tanzania, Mar. 8, 1944; came to the U.S., 1963, naturalized, 1976; s. Noormohamed Velshi and Sherbanu (Kassam) G.; children: Michael, Michelle, Nicole. Cert. Edn., U. Cambridge, 1960; advanced level, U. London, 1963; AB cum laude, Harvard U., 1967; MSME, Washington U., St. Louis, 1969, DSc, 1974. Rsch. assoc. Washington U., St. Louis, 1975—76, rsch. scientist, 1976—77, asst. prof., 1977—80, assoc. prof., 1981—84, prof. mech. engring., 1984—91, faculty assoc. Ctr. Air Pollution Impact and Trend Analysis, 1979—91, dir. air quality spl. studies data ctr., 1981—88, dir., mech. engring. rsch. computing facility, 1988—90; pres. N.V. Gillani & Assocs., Inc., 1991—; prin. rsch. scientist UAH Nat. Space Sci. & Tech. Ctr. NASA, Ala., 1995—; adj. prof. atmospheric sci. U. Ala., Huntsville, 1995—. Vis. scientist Stockholm U., 1977, Brookhaven Nat. Lab., 1990—91, EPA/RTP, 1992—93, TVA Environ. Rsch. Ctr., 1994—95; organizer NATO CCMS 15th internat. tech. meeting on air pollution modeling and its applications, St. Louis, 1985; mem. Sci. Bd. NATO/Commn. for the Challenges of Modern Soc. Air Pollution Pilot Study, 1984—92; mem. tech. adv. bds. U.S. EPA, DOE and others, 1980—; hon. mem. Aga Khan Edn. Bd. for U.S.A. (AKEB/USA), 1987—90; vis. prof. NC State U., NC, 1993—94. Author: (with others) Critical Assessment Document on Acidic Depositions,

1984, EPA Criteria Document for Particulate Matter, 1994-95; editor: Air Pollution Modeling and Its Applications V, vol. 10, 1986; contbr. chpts. to book and articles to profl. jours. Dir., founder AKEB/USA Program (PIAR)for Parental Involvement in Children's Edn., 1987-97; pres. Pyar Found. for Humanitarian Assistance, 2000—. Scholar, Harvard Coll., 1963—67; Aga Khan travel grantee, 1961—63, grad. fellow, Washington U., 1967—74, rsch. grantee, EPA, DOE, Elec. Power Rsch. Inst., NASA, NOAA, NSF, TVA, Tex. Commn. Environ. Quality, 1978—. Mem. Am. Meteorol. Soc., Am. Chem. Soc., Am. Geophys. Union, Nat. Assn. for Edn. Young Children, N.Y. Acad. Scis. Achievements include research on superconductivity, bioengring., atmospheric scis., air pollution and Islamic humanism. Office: NASA-UAH Nat Space Sci and Tech Ctr 320 Sparkman Dr Huntsville AL 35805 Office Phone: 256-961-7942. E-mail: gillani@nsstc.uah.edu.

GILLECE, JAMES PATRICK, JR., lawyer; b. Annapolis, Md., May 26, 1944; s. James Patrick and Erna Virginia (Barling) G.; m. Jane C. Szczepaniak, Apr. 24, 1971 (div. 1998); children: Jessica K., Jocelyn J., Jillian N., James P. III, Juliette A., John M. Szczepaniak -Gillece; m. Rosa Beza, Feb. 12, 1999. BA, LaSalle U., 1966; JD, U. Notre Dame, 1969. Bar: Md. 1969, U.S. Dist. Ct. Md. 1969, U.S. Ct. Appeals (4th cir.) 1972, U.S. Supreme Ct. 1974, U.S. Ct. Appeals (7th cir.) 1992, U.S. Ct. Appeals (8th and 11th cir.) 1995, U.S. Ct. Appeals (D.C. cir.) 2000. Assoc. Piper & Marbury, Balt., 1969-77, ptnr., 1977-92, dir. poverty law program, 1971-72; ptnr. Miles & Stockbridge, Balt., 1992-93; prin. Miles and Stockbridge, Balt., 1994-98; ptnr. McGuire, Woods, Battle & Boothe, Balt., 1998—. Cons. Mercy Hosp. Dietitians Program, Balt., 1986-95. Mem. law adv. coun. U. Notre Dame, 1983—95; mem. Com. to Keep Supreme Bench Judges; trustee Everyman Theatre, 1996—; mem. com. for Mayor Kurt Schmoke, 1987; mem. Lawyers' Com. for Jerry Brown, 1976; mem. fin. com. Mayor Martin O'Malley, 2000—; bd. dirs. Balt. City Fair, 1984—88, Legal Aid Soc, Balt., Family Crisis Ctr., Balt. County, Inc., 1992—97, Everyman Theatre, 1995—, Justice for Children, 2004—. Mem. ABA, FBA, Am. Judicature Soc. (bd. dirs. 1988-90), Md. State Bar Assn. (Disting. Svc. award), Balt. Bar Assn., Notre Dame Law Assn. (pres. 1983-99, bd. dirs. 1977—, exec. coun., life mem.), U. Notre Dame Law Assocs., Internat. Childbirth Edn. Assn. (cons. 1987-97). Democrat. Roman Catholic. Home: 3809 Greenway Baltimore MD 21218-1826 Office: McGuire Woods Battle & Boothe 7 Saint Paul St Ste 1000 Baltimore MD 21202-1671 Fax: 410-659-4455. Office Phone: 410-659-4421. E-mail: jgillece@Mcguire.woods.com.

GILLELAND, JOHN ROGERS, technology company executive; b. Gadsden, Ala., Jan. 12, 1941; s. Earl Rogers and Margaret Eta Gilleland; m. Kim Denise Turos, Aug. 23, 1987. BS in Physics, Yale U., 1963; MS in Physics, U. Mich., 1964, PhD in Physics, 1969. Scientist Gulf Gen. Atomics, La Jolla, Calif., 1970-72, dir. Doublet III program, 1972-78, sr. v.p. fusion energy program, 1985-87; program dir. U.S.-Japan Fusion rsch. Collaboration, La Jolla, 1978-85; mng. dir. Internat. Thermonuclear Exptl. Reactor Project, Garching, Germany, 1987-91; v.p., chief scientist Bechtel Corp., San Francisco, 1991-98; pres., CEO Archimedes Tech. Group, San Diego, 1998—; dir. Archis, LLC, 2005—. Advisor space def. initiative Dept. Def., Washington, 1985-86; advisor Nat. Acad. Scis., Washington, 1984-87; chmn. bd. dirs. Archis, LLC. Named Young Engr. of the Yr. Am. Nuc. Soc., 1980; recipient Achievement award Am. Nuc. Soc., 1992. Avocations: cello, squash, art installation, philosophy, carpentry. Home: PO Box 9154 Rancho Santa Fe CA 92067-4154 Office: Archimedes Tech Group 5405 Oberlin Dr San Diego CA 92121-1700 Office Phone: 858-410-0759. E-mail: jgilleland@at-sd.com.

GILLEN, JAMES ROBERT, lawyer, insurance company executive; b. N.Y.C., Nov. 14, 1937; s. James Matthew and Katharine Isabel (Fritz) G.; m. Rita Marie Wahleithner, June 15, 1963 (div. 1992); children: Jennifer Elaine, Nancy Louise, Paula Anne; m. Edda Lya Pacheco, Dec. 10, 1994. AB magna cum laude, Harvard U., 1959, LLB cum laude, 1965. Bar: N.Y. 1966, N.J. 1975. Assoc. firm White & Case, N.Y.C., 1965-72; v.p., assoc. gen. counsel Prudential Ins. Co. Am., Newark, 1972-77, sr. v.p., assoc. gen. counsel, 1977-80, sr. v.p. pub. affairs, 1980-84, sr. v.p., gen. counsel, 1984-98. Mem. bd. trustees Columbia Inst. Investor Project, 1981—97; legal adv. com. N.Y. Stock Exch., 1986—89; mem. adv. bd. Ascertain Solutions, Inc., 2001—02. Trustee United Way Essex and West Hudson Counties, 1981-90, pres., 1986-88; mem. Mendham Twp. (N.J.) Bd. Edn., 1981-82; trustee N.J. Shakespeare Festival, 1991-99, Mendham Twp. Libr., 1979-82; dir., chmn. Neurol. Inst. N.J., 1998—. Lt. (j.g.) USN, 1959-62. Mem. ABA, N.J. Bar Assn., Assn. Life Ins. Counsel, Harvard Club (N.Y.C.), Morris Country Golf Club. Home: 72 Washington Valley Rd Morristown NJ 07960-3332 Personal E-mail: jrgillen@verizon.net.

GILLEN, KATHERINE ELIZABETH, librarian; b. Washington, May 16, 1951; d. Hugh Chisholm and Norma Marie (Provost) G. BS, U. Md., 1973, MLS, 1976; MA, U. Phoenix, 1989; grad., Citizens Police Acad., Mesa, Ariz., 1993, Air Command and Staff Coll., 1996; student, Kino Inst., 2004—06. Mem. Order of Preachers Laiety, Dominical Laiety. Librarian Maricopa County Community Coll., Phoenix, 1982-84; librarian reference and serials Mesa (Ariz.) Pub. Library, 1981-92; libr. mgr. Denver Pub. Libr., 1992; libr. dir. USAF, Luke AFB, Ariz., 1993—. Book reviewer Libr. Jour., 1988—, KLIATT, 1991—; contbr. short stories to mags.; pub.: Felicia's First Christmas, 1994. Class mem. Mesa Leadership Tng. and Devel., 1991-92; chair Luke Officers' Wives Club scholarship program, 1998-2003; lector Luke Cath. Cmty., 1997—; vice-chair Avondale Libr. Bd., 2002-05, chair, 2005—. Mem. AAAS (reviewer 1982—), ALA (v.p. Armed Forces Librs. Roundtable 1997-98, pres. 1998-99), Ariz. State Libr. Assn. (exec. bd. 1991-92, serials roundtable chmn. 1991-92), Serials Specialists of Maricopa County, Mensa. Avocations: flying, ballet, reading, ecological issues, animal rights. Home: 11301 W Orange Blossom Ln Avondale AZ 85323-3532

GILLEN, WILLIAM GARVER, psychologist; b. Decatur, Ill., Sept. 14, 1946; s. William Alexander and Charlotte May Gillen; m. Susan Bowles Gillen, Oct. 30, 1965; children: Elizabeth, Jonathon. BA, Millikin U., 1974; MA, U. Ill., 1976; PhD, Walden U., 2003. Cons. psychologist Rohi Patil, MD & Assocs., Decatur, Ill., 1989—; psychologist Drew Corp., Decatur, 1998—. Cons. in field. Adv. bd. Easter Seals, Decatur, 2005. Mem.: APA, Ill. Psychol. Assn. Home: 4207 East Lincoln Ave Decatur IL 62521

GILLER, EDWARD BONFOY, retired government official, retired military officer; b. Jacksonville, Ill., July 8, 1918; s. Edward Bonfoy and Ruth (Davis) G.; m. Mildred Florana Schmidt, July 2, 1943; children— Susan Ann, Carol Elaine, Bruce Carleton, Penny Marie, Paul Benjamin. BS in Chem. Engring, U. Ill., 1940, MS, 1948, PhD, 1950. Chem. engr. Sinclair Oil Refining Co., 1940-41; commd. 2d lt. USAAF, 1942; advanced through grades to maj. gen. USAF, 1968; pilot, 1941-46; chief radiation br. (Armed Forces Spl. Weapons Project), Washington, 1950-54; dir. research directorate Air Force Spl. Weapons Center, Albuquerque, 1954-59; spl. asst. to comdr. (Office Aerospace Rsch.), Washington, 1959-64; dir. sci. and tech. Hdqrs. USAF, 1964-67; asst. gen. mgr. for mil. application U.S. AEC, 1967-72; ret. USAF, 1972; asst. gen. mgr. for nat. security AEC, 1972-75; dep. asst. adminstr. for nat. security U.S. ERDA, 1975-77; rep. of Joint Chiefs of Staff to Comprehensive Test Ban Negotiations, Geneva, 1977-84; sr. scientist Pacific-Sierra Rsch. Corp., Arlington, Va, 1984-92; v.p. Trans Mar Inc., Spokane, Wash., 1992-96; cons. Sandia Nat. Labs., Albuquerque, 1990—2004, ret., 2004. Cons. in the field. Decorated Silver Star, D.S.M., Legion of Merit with oak leaf cluster, D.F.C., Air medal with 17 oak leaf clusters, Purple Heart; Croix de Guerre France). Fellow Am. Inst. Chemists; mem. Am. Inst. Chem. Engrs., Sigma Xi, Alpha Tau Omega. Episcopalian. Home: 14415 Soula Dr NE Albuquerque NM 87123-1941

GILLERAN, JAMES E., bank executive, former federal agency administrator; married; 2 children. Law degree, Northwestern Calif. U. CPA. Banking supt. State of Calif., 1989—94; chmn., CEO Bank of San Francisco, 1994—2000; dir. Office Thrift Supervision U.S. Dept. Treasury, Washington, 2001—05; pres., CEO Fed. Home Loan Bank of Seattle (Seattle Bank), 2005—. Chmn. state liaison coun. Fed. Fin. Instns. Examination Coun., 1991—92; chmn. Conf. State Banking Suprs., 1993—94, mem. bankers adv. coun., 2000. Office: Seattle Bank 1501 Fourth Ave Ste 1900 Seattle WA 98101

GILLERAN, PETER JOSEPH, retired art educator; b. Detroit, Aug. 9, 1921; s. Peter Joseph Gilleran and Vera Cinderalla Jeager; m. Anne Crow Gilleran; children: Peter, Margaret, Katherine. BA, Colo. Coll., 1949; MFA, Cranbrook Acad., 1950. Art tchr. Albright Art Sch., Buffalo, 1950—54, Cranbrook Art Acad., Mich., 1960—68; art prof. Wayne State U., Detroit, 1954—89; ret., 1989. Numerous art exhibitions, 1950—. Sgt. Army, 1942—45, China. Avocations: photography, book collecting.

GILLERS, STEPHEN, lawyer, educator, academic administrator; b. 1943; BA, Bklyn Coll., 1964; JD, NYU, 1968. Bar: N.Y. 1968. Law clk. to Hon. Gus J. Solomon, Oreg., 1968-69; assoc. Paul, Wiess, Rifkind, Wharton & Garrison, N.Y., 1969-71; pvt. practice NYC, 1973—78; assoc. prof. NYU, NYC, 1978—81, prof. law, 1981—, vice dean, 1999—2004. Mem. deptl. disciplinary com. N.Y. Supreme Ct., 1980-83. Editor: Looking at Law School, 4th edit., 1997, Regulation of Lawyers: Problems of Law and Ethics, 7th edit., 2005. Exec. dir. SALT, 1975-78, 78-80, bd. govs. Mem.: ABA (chair, joint com. lawyer regulation 2004—). Office: NYU Sch Law 40 Washington Sq S New York NY 10012-1099 Office Phone: 212-998-6264. Business E-Mail: stephen.gillers@nyu.edu.

GILLES, BRUCE CARLSON, civil engineer; b. Meadville, Pa., Sept. 4, 1936; s. August John and Lillian Maude (Carlson) G.; m. Carolyn Ann Hilsdon, Sept. 1, 1967; children: James, Thomas. BA, Gannon U., 1962; MEd, U. Pitts., 1965, postgrad., 1980-82; BSCE, Int Corr. Sch., 1974; postgrad., U. Pitts., 1963-65, 80-82. Quality control engr. Alaska pipeline Mich. Baker Engrs., Beaver, Pa., 1974; civil engr. trainee Cbgo. Bridge and Iron, Greenville, Pa., 1974-75; cons. Hendricks and Assocs., Erie, Pa., 1977-79; civil engr., asst. to v.p. Green Internat. Engrs., Sewickley, Pa., 1980-82; resident engr. Pitts. subway Parsons-Brinkerhoff, Pitts., 1983-86; asst. pub. works dir. USN, Adak (Alaska) Naval Sta., 1986; regional chief engr. Mazza Engrs., Aliquippa, Pa., 1986-91; chief quality assurance/quality control engr. Adak Alutian Constrn. Co., Anchorage, 1991-92; rsch. engr. Greiner Engrs., Denver, 1992—93; asst. rsch. engr. Monaloh Basin Engrs., Pitts., 1993—94; project mgr. Multi-Lynx Engrs., Inc., Pitts., 1994—99; rsch. engr. Warf Constrn., Anchorage, 1999—2001; cost engr. Laird Engrs., Erie, Pa., 2001—. Instr. weightlifting YMCA, Meadville, Pa., 1977—. Mem. ASCE (bd. dirs. N.W. Pa. br. 1990-91), NSPE. Republican. Methodist. Home: 373 Allegheny St Meadville PA 16335-1214

GILLESPIE, DANIEL CURTIS, SR., retired not-for-profit developer; b. Shamokin, Pa., Sept. 22, 1922; s. John F. and Verna E. (Erdman) G.; m. Juliet Warren Yearns, Oct. 7, 1950; children: Julia W., Daniel Curtis, David R. BS, Pa. State U., 1943; MS in Chem. Engring., U. Mich., 1948. Devel. engr. Tidewater Associated Oil Co., Bayonne, N.J., 1943-44; jr. scientist Manhattan Project, Los Alamos Sci. Lab., 1946; with Dorr-Oliver Inc., Stamford, Conn., 1948-82, v.p. mktg., 1973-75, exec. v.p., 1975-76, pres. and chief exec. officer, 1976-82, also dir.; v.p. bus. devel. Sohio Chems. & Indsl. Products Co., 1982-84; pres., chief exec. officer Metropool, Inc., 1985-87; cons., 1987-92; ret., 1992. Served with U.S. Army, 1944-46. Fellow Am. Inst. Chem. Engrs.; hon. mem. Process Equipment Mfrs. Assn., Southwestern Area Commerce and Industry Assn. Home: 18 Pepper Bush Cir Savannah GA 31411-3009

GILLESPIE, EDWARD MALCOLM, hospital administrator; b. Mpls., Oct. 19, 1935; s. Harold Livingston and Alice May (Thompson) G.; children: Karin, Timothy, Kenneth. BS, U. Minn., 1957, MPA, 1959, MHA, 1962. Engaged in refugee adminstrn., Linz, Austria, 1958-60; asst. adminstr. Luth. Med. Ctr., Denver, 1962-66; asst. gen. sec. Meth. Bd. Health and Welfare Ministries, Evanston, Ill., 1966-69; adminstr. Meth. Hosp., Rochester, Minn., 1969-74, Univ. Hosp., Augusta, Ga., 1974-91, pres. Health Advance, 1991-92. Bd. dirs. Augusta Area Mental Health, Augusta Speech and Hearing Ctr., St. John's Towers, CSRA Blood Assurance; chmn. hosp. divsn. certification coun. Meth. Health and Welfare. Bd. dirs. local United Way, Boy Scouts Am., Blue Cross Ga., Bankers First; chmn. Augusta Resource Ctr. on Aging, Brandon Wilde. Fellow ACHA; mem. Am. Hosp. Assn., Ga. Hosp. Assn. (chmn.), Rotary Internat. (bd. dirs. Augusta chpt.). Methodist. Home and Office: Health Advance 12 Shadow Brook Cir Augusta GA 30909-3749

GILLESPIE, EDWARD WALTER, former political organization administrator; b. Browns Mills, NJ, 1962; m. Catherine Hay; children: John Patrick, Carrie, Mollie Brigid. BA in Polit. Sci., Cath. U., 1983. Asst. to Rep. Andy Ireland, Fla., 1983—84; press spokesman Rep. Dick Armey, Tex., 1985—95; dir. comm. and congl. affairs Rep. Nat. Com., 1996; pres., CEO Policy Impact Communications, 1997—99; founder, prin. Quinn Gillespie & Assocs., Washington, 2000—; chmn. Rep. Nat. Com., Washington, 2003—05. Editor: Contract with America, 1995 (NY Times bestseller list, 1995). Comm. dir. Pres. George W. Bush Inauguration, 2001; mgr. Phila. conv. Rep. Nat. Com., 2000; sr. comm. advisor George W. Bush Presdl. Campaign, Austin, 2000, spokesman for Fla. election recount, 2001; gen. strategist Elizabeth Dole Senate Campaign, NC, 2002. Republican. Office: Quinn Gillespie & Assocs LLC Fl 5 1133 Connecticut Ave NW Washington DC 20036

GILLESPIE, GARY DON, physician; b. Jackson, Mich., Apr. 23, 1943; s. Harold Don and Marion Estella (Diemer) G.; m. Nancy Bliven Hinkle, June 29, 1969 (div. July 1980; children: Brian James, Julie Elizabeth; m. Elaine Marie Beard, July 25, 1984. BS, U. Mich., 1966, D of Medicine, 1971. Diplomate Am. Bd. Family Practice. Intern Edward W. Sparrow Hosp., Lansing, Mich., 1971-72, resident in family practice, 1971-74; physician Dept. Family Practice, USN Med. Corps., Orlando, Fla., 1974-76; pvt. practice Okemos, Mich., 1976—2001; ret., 2001. Chmn. continuing edn., dept. family practice Edward W. Sparrow Hosp., 1976-91; asst. clin. prof. dept. family practice Mich. State U. Coll. Medicine, East Lansing, 1981-2001. Lt. comdr. USN, 1974-76. Mem. AMA, Am. Acad. Family Physicians, Am. Bd. Family Practice, Mich. Acad. Family Physicians (treas. Capitol chpt. 1982-92). Republican. Avocations: reading, music, photography, travel, golf.

GILLESPIE, GEORGE JOSEPH, III, lawyer; b. NYC, May 18, 1930; s. George Joseph Jr. and Dorothy Elizabeth (McKenna) Gillespie; m. Eileen Tracy Dealy, July 27, 1955; children: Gail Gillespie Garcia, John D., Myles D., Eileen G. Fahey. AB magna cum laude, Georgetown U., 1952; LLB magna cum laude, Harvard U., 1955. Bar: N.Y. 1957. Assoc. Cravath, Swaine & Moore, LLP, N.Y.C., 1956-62, ptnr., trusts, estates, 1963—. Mem. bd. dirs. The Washington Post Co., 1974—; chmn. bd. White Mountains Holdings, Inc. Trustee, pres. John M. Olin Found., 1976—; pres. Pinkerton Found., 1971—, Arthur Ross Found., 1986—, William S. Paley Found., 1984—, Edward E. Ford Found., Edmond J. Safra Philanthropic Found.; trustee, sec. Mus. TV and Radio, 1997—; vice-chmn. exec. com. Madison Sq. Boys and Girls Club; chmn. emeritus, hon. life dir. Nat. Multiple Sclerosis Soc.; trustee Jackson Lab.; active Bar Harbor, Maine. Frederick Sheldon Travel fellow, Harvard U., 1955—56. Mem.: Century Assn., Portland Country Club, Am. Yacht Club, Double Eagle Club, Falmouth Country Club, Prouts Neck Country Club, Winged Foot Golf Club. Republican. Roman Catholic. Office: Cravath Swaine & Moore Worldwide Pla 825 8th Ave Fl 43 New York NY 10019-7475 Office Phone: 212-474-1700. Office Fax: 212-474-3700. Business E-Mail: ggillesp@cravath.com.

GILLESPIE, GERALD ERNEST PAUL, comparative literature educator, writer; b. Cleve., July 12, 1933; s. Francis and Nora Veronica (Quinn) G.; m. Adrienne Amalia Galante, Sept. 5, 1959. AB, Harvard U., 1956; postgrad., U. Tübingen, Germany, 1956—57; MA, Ohio State U., 1958, PhD, 1961; postgrad., U. Munich, 1960—61. Asst. prof. U. So. Calif., L.A., 1961-65; from assoc. prof. to prof. SUNY, Binghamton, 1965-74; prof. Stanford (Calif.) U., 1974—. Vis. prof. U. Pa., Phila, 1969, NYU, 1970, U. Minn., Mpls., 1978, Peking U., Beijing, 1985, U. East Anglia, Norwich, Eng., 1988, U. Munich, 1993, U. Hagen, Germany, 2002; hon. prof., Liaoning U., China. Author: German Baroque Poetry, 1971, Evolution of the European Novel, 1987, Garden and Labyrinth of Time, 1988, Proust, Mann, Joyce in the Modernist Context, 2003, By Way of Comparison, 2004, Echoland: Readings from Late Humanism to Postmodernism, 2005; author, editor: Herkommen und Erneuerung, 1976, Studien zum Werk D.C. von Lohenstein, 1983, German Theater Before 1750, 1992, Romantic Drama, 1994, Narrative Ironies, 1997, Mallarmé in the Twentieth Century, 1998, Romantic Nonfictional Prose, 2004; translator, editor: Night Watches, 1972, Puss-in-Boots, 1974, Bohemian Lights, 1976; editor: Littérature Comparée, Littérature Mondiale, 1991, Visions in History, 1995, Powers of Narration, 1995; mem. edtl. bd.: Comparative Lit., 1977—, Internationales Archiv, 1975—, Utrecht Studies in Comparative Lit., 1987-2004, Recherche Littéraire, 1991—, Literary Imagination, 1998-2004; co-editor: German Life and Letters, 1987-2004, advisor, 2005—. Andrew Mellon Found. fellow, 1966—67, John S. Guggenheim Found. fellow, 1967—68, NEH sr. fellow, 1973—74, vis. fellow Clare Hall, Cambridge U., Eng., 1979. Mem.: MLA (exec. com. comparative studies in romanticism and the 19th century 1982—87, mem. nat. program com. 1985—88, mem. exec. com. classical studies and modern lit. 1986—91), Calif. Assn. Scholars (bd. dirs. 1992—), Assn. Lit. Scholars and Critics (coun. 1998—2001), Renaissance Soc. Am., Brit. Comparative Lit. Assn., Am. Comparative Lit. Assn., Internat. Comparative Lit. Assn. (sec. 1979—85, mem. edtl. bd. bull. 1979—85, v.p. 1985—88, pres. 1994—97), Berliner Wissenschaftliche Gesellschaft (corr.). Office Phone: 650-723-3266, 650-856-9580.

GILLESPIE, J. MARTIN, sales and distribution company executive; b. Detroit, Sept. 27, 1949; s. John Martin and Shirley Ann (Rees) G.; children: Heather, Tara. BBA, Xavier U., 1971; MBA, U. Mich., 1973. Account exec. Foote Cone & Belding, Chgo., 1973-76, account supr., 1976-77; mktg. mgr. Hansen Corp., Walled Lake, Mich., 1977-80, gen. mgr., 1980-82; chmn., CEO Hansen Mktg. Svcs., Inc., Walled Lake, 1982—. Founder Hickory Stick Invitational Charity Tournament; bd. dirs. Xavier U. Alumni Assn., 2001—. Recipient Merit award Nat. Alliance Businessmen, 1973. Mem. Assn. MBA Execs., Am. Mgmt. Assn., Nat. Acad. TV Arts and Scis., Nat. Assn. Credit Mgmt., Nat. Bldg. Materials Distbn. Assn., Alpha Kappa Psi. Office: Hansen Mktg Svcs Inc PO Box 640 1000 Decker Rd Walled Lake MI 48390-0640 Office Phone: 248-669-2323.

GILLESPIE, JAMES DAVIS, lawyer; b. Elkin, N.C., Apr. 30, 1955; s. John Banner and Jerry Sue (Swaim) G.; m. Tommie Lee Johnson, Aug. 13, 1977 (div. Dec. 1995); 1 child, John Foster; m. Regina Lee Robinson, July 11, 1998. BA, U. N.C., 1977; JD, Samford U., 1980. Bar: N.C. 1980, U.S. Dist. Ct. (mid. dist.) 1982, U.S. Dist. Ct. (we. dist.) N.C. 1983, U.S. Ct. Appeals (4th cir.) 1984. Ptnr. Neaves & Gillespie, Elkin, 1980—. Mem. Surry-Yadkin Mental Health Authority, Mt. Airy, N.C., 1981-91, vice chmn., 1987-89, chmn. 1990-91. Bd. editors: Cumberland Law Rev., 1978-80. Commr. Town of Jonesville, N.C., 1983-85, mayor, 1985-93; mem. exec. com. N.W. Piedmont Coun. Govts., 1987, sec., 1988-89, chmn., 1990-91. Mem. ABA, Assn. Trial Lawyers Am., N.C. Bar Assn., N.C. Trial Lawyers Assn., Surry County Bar Assn., Elkin Jaycees (bd. dirs. 1981-83, v.p. 1983-84), N.C. Acad. Trial Lawyers, Greater Elkin-Jonesville C. of C. (charter, bd. dirs. 1987-90), Phi Alpha Delta, Soc. Curia Honoris. Democrat. Methodist. Avocations: tennis, basketball, reading, travel. Home: 516 Westbrook St Jonesville NC 28642-2658 Office: Neaves & Gillespie 124 W Main St Ste A Elkin NC 28621-3433 Office Phone: 336-835-2522. Personal E-mail: neavesgillespie@aol.com.

GILLESPIE, JOHN DAVID, political science educator, academic administrator; b. Oxford, NC, Sept. 22, 1944; s. Arthur S. and Pauline M. (Pittard) G.; m. Judi K. Flowers, June 11, 1966. BA, Wake Forest U., 1966, MA, 1967; PhD, Kent State U., 1973. Instr., history and polit. sci. Davidson C.C., Lexington, NC, 1967-70; asst. prof. Samford U., Birmingham, Ala., 1973-79; from assoc. prof. to prof. to Charles A. Dana prof. polit. sci. Presbyterian Coll., Clinton, SC, 1979—, v.p. academic affairs, dean of faculty, 1997-2005, former chmn. dept. polit. sci.; pres. SC Ind. Colls. Deans' Coun., 1999-2000; spkr. at colloquia, profl. confs. in field; interviewee Stas. ABC-TV, BBC-TV, CNN-TV, PBS-TV, NPR, and others; testimony expert in fed. and state ballot access cases. Author: Politics at the Periphery: Third Parties in Two-Party America, 1993. Contbr. chpts. to anthologies, articles to profl. jours.; former chmn. Laurens County Dem. Party, mem. SC Dem. Exec. Com., v.p. Ala. Polit. Sci. Assn., 1978-79, pres. SC Polit. Sci. Assn., 1985-86; NDEA Title IV fellow, 1970-73; grantee NEH 1978, Fulbright group project, China, 1988; Fulbright scholar, Tartu U., Estonia, 1997; named SC Prof. of Yr., 1993-94; Designated Exemplary Tchr., US Dept. Edn., 1996. Mem. Am. Polit. Sci. Assn., Internat. Soc. for Sci. Study Subjectivity. Presbyterian. Home: 103 Pinehurst Dr Clinton SC 29325-9553 Office Phone: 864-938-3761. Business E-Mail: dgillesp@presby.edu.

GILLESPIE, JOHN THOMAS, retired university administrator; b. Thunder Bay, Ont., Can., Sept. 25, 1928; came to U.S., 1954, naturalized, 1961; s. William and Jeannie (Barr) G. BA, U. B.C., 1948; MA, Columbia U., 1957; PhD, NYU, 1969. High sch. tchr., Powell River, B.C., Can., 1949-53; libr. Roslyn (N.Y.) Pub. Sch. Dist., 1955-63; mem. faculty Palmer Grad. Library Sch., C.W. Post Center, LIU, N.Y., 1963—, prof., 1975-80, dean, 1981-83; acad. v.p. C.W. Post Ctr., LIU, 1983-85; ret., 1985. Vis. prof. Syracuse (N.Y.) U., SUNY, Albany; cons. in field. Author: Juniorplots, 1966, Introducing Books, 1970, Young Phenomenon, 1971, Creating the School Media Program, 1973, A Model School Media Program, 1973, Paperback Books for Young People, 3d edit., 1987, More Juniorplots, 1977, Best Books for Children, Administering the School Library Media Center, 1983, Elementary School Paperback Collection, 1985, Senior High School Paperback Collection, 1986, Juniorplots 3, 1987, Seniorplots, 1989, Best Books for Junior High Readers, 1991, Best Books for Senior High Readers, 1991, Juniorplots 4, 1993, Middleplots 4, 1994, Best Books for Children, 5th edit., 1994, Guides to Library Collection Development, 1994, The Newbery Companion, 1996, 2d edit. 2000, Characters in Young Adult Literature, 1997, Guides to Library Collection Development for Children and Young Adults, 1997, Best Books for Children, 7th edit., 2001, supplement, 2003, Best Books for Young Teen Readers, 1999, Teenplots, 2003, Best Books for Middle and Jr. HIgh School Readers, 2004, Best Books for High School Readers, 2004, The Children's and Young Adult Literature Handbook, 2005. Mem. ALA, N.Y. Libr. Assn., Phi Delta Kappa, Kappa Delta Pi. Home: 360 E 72nd St New York NY 10021-4753 Personal E-mail: bestgill@aol.com.

GILLESPIE, MARCIA LOU, tax specialist, accountant, musician; b. Grand Rapids, Mich., Nov. 26, 1942; d. Peter James and Bernice Lucille (DeReus) Muyskens; m. Norman Wayne Edwards, Aug. 15, 1964 (div. Apr. 1977); 1 child, Cary Ann Edwards; m. Eugene Scott Gillespie, Jan. 31, 1988. BA cum laude, U. Pitts., 1973. Enrolled agt. IRS. Acct. San Jose (Calif.) Symphony, 1977-78; agt. Prudential Ins., San Jose, 1978-81; acct. MicroFocus, Palo Alto, Calif., 1981-83; pianist, accompanist Opera Soc., Jr. Colls., San Jose and Napa, Calif., 1976—; contr. Gaston Snow, Palo Alto, 1983; acct. Accountemps, San Francisco, 1983-85, Bernheim Co., San Francisco, 1985-93; acct., tax preparer M.L. Gillespie Tax Svc., Emeryville, Napa, Calif., 1993—. Mem. Better Bus Bur., Oakland, Calif., 1996-97. Sgt., mem. Army Band, U.S. N.G., 1977-2000. Mem. Nat. Assn. Enrolled Agts. Democrat. Avocations: tennis, bowling, home decorating. Office: 1834 1st St # 5 Napa CA 94559-2353 Personal E-mail: marciaea@sbcglobal.net.

GILLESPIE, MATTHEW DAMIEN, composer; b. Sylva, N.C., Jan. 25, 1977; s. James Lester Gillespie and Judith Lynn Fastenau. MusB, U. N.C., 1999; MusM, East Carolina U., 2004. Lectr. Sch. of Music East Carolina U., Greenville, NC, 2004—. Organist First Christian Ch., Robersonville, NC, 2003—. Composer: (songs) String Quartet No. 1, Three Songs, Movement for Viola and Electronic Sounds, Piano Rags, Five Canons for Flute, Clarinet and Violoncello. Office: East Carolina University School of Music 1001 East Fifth Street Greenville NC 27858-2500 Personal E-mail: ubiquitor@hotmail.com.

GILLESPIE, MICHAEL J., lawyer; b. Feb. 21, 1960; AB summa cum laude, Amherst Coll., 1982; JD, Harvard U., 1986. Bar: NY 1987. Assoc. Debevoise & Plimpton LLP, NYC, 1986—95, mem., 1995—, ptnr., co-chair Media and Tech. Group. Mem.: ABA, Assn City Bar NY. Office: Debevoise & Plimpton LLP 919 Third Ave New York NY 10022 E-mail: mjgillespie@debevoise.com.

GILLESPIE, ROBERT WAYNE, banker; b. Cleve., Mar. 26, 1944; s. Robert Walton and Eleanore (Parsons) G.; m. Ann. L. Wible, June 17, 1967; children: Laura, Gwen. BA, Ohio Wesleyan U., 1966; MBA, Case Western Res. U., 1968; postgrad., Harvard U., 1979. Credit analyst Soc. Nat. Bank, Cleve., 1968-70, v.p., 1970-76, sr. v.p., 1976-79; exec. v.p. Soc. Nat Bank, Cleve., 1979-81; vice-chmn., chief operating officer Soc. Nat. Bank, Cleve., 1981-83, pres., chief operating officer, 1983-85, CEO, 1985—, pres., 1987-94; pres., CEO, Key Corp., Cleve., 1995—, chmn., 1996—, CEO, 1996—. Trustee Case Western Res. U., Ohio Wesleyan U., Cleve. Mus. Art, Cleve. Initiative for Edn. and Musical Arts, Greater Cleve. Roundtable, Cleve. Tomorrow and North Coast Harbor; bd. dirs. Greater Cleve. Growth Assn. Office: Key Corp 127 Public Sq Cleveland OH 44114-1306

GILLESPIE, RONALD JAMES, chemistry professor, researcher, writer; b. London, Aug. 21, 1924; arrived in Can., 1958; s. James Andrew and Miriam (Kirk) G.; m. Madge Garner, July 5, 1950; children: Ann, Lynn. BSc, London U., 1945, PhD, 1949, DSc, 1957; LLD (hon.), Concordia U., Montreal, Can., 1988, Dalhousie U., Halifax, Can., 1988; D Honoris causa, U. des Scis. et Techniques du Languedoc, 1991; DSc (hon.), McMaster U., 1993. Asst. lectr. dept. chemistry U. Coll., U. London, 1948-50, lectr., 1950-58; assoc. prof. dept. chemistry McMaster U., Hamilton, Ont., Can., 1958-60, prof., 1960-87, prof. emeritus, 1988—, chmn. dept., 1962-65. Vis. prof. U. Manchester (Eng.), 1965-66, U. des Scis. et Techniques du Languedoc, Montpellier, France, 1972-73, U. Geneva, 1976, U. Göttingen, Fed. Republic Germany, 1978, Australian Nat. U., Canberra, 1979, U. Melbourne, Australia, U. Auckland, New Zealand, 1980, Panjab U., Chandigarh, India, 1983; Nyholm lectr. Chem. Soc., London, 1978; Gillespie lectr. U. Coll., London, 1990; Muetterties vis. scholar U. Calif., Berkeley, 1990. Author: Molecular Geometry, 1972, (with others) Chemistry, 1986, 2d edit., 1989, (with I. Hargittai) The VSEPR Model of Molecular Geometry, 1991, (with others) Atoms, Molecules and Reactions: An Introduction to Chemistry, 1994, (with P. Popelier) Chemical Bonding and Molecular Geometry: From Lewis to Election Densities, 2001; contbr. over 380 articles to profl. jours. Recipient Can. Centennial medal, 1967, Coll. Chemistry Tchr. award Mfg. Chemists Assn., 1972, Silver Jubilee award, 1977, Excellence in Teaching award McMaster u. Students Union, 1983, Izaak Walter Killam Meml. Prize of Can. Coun. for Pure Sci., 1987; Commonwealth Fund fellow Brown U., 1953-54. Fellow Royal Soc. London, Royal Soc. Can. (Henry Marshall Tory medal 1983), Royal Soc. Chemistry (Harrison Meml. medal 1953), Royal Inst. Chemistry, Chem. Inst. Can. (Noranda award 1966, Union Carbide award 1976, medal 1977); mem. Am. Chem. Soc. (N.E. Region award 1971, Tour Speaker of Yr. award 1971, Disting. Svc. award 1973, fluorine chemistry award 1981). Avocations: sailing, skiing, travel. Office: McMaster U Dept Chemistry Hamilton ON Canada L8S 4M1 Office Phone: 905-628-1502. Business E-Mail: ronald.gillespie@sympatico.ca.

GILLESPIE, SAMUEL H., III, lawyer, oil industry executive; b. N.Y.C., 1942; BA, Middlebury Coll., 1966; JD, Vanderbilt U., 1972. Bar: N.Y. 1973. Assoc. Milbank, Tweed, Hadley & McCloy, 1972-82, counsel, 1982-85; asst. gen. counsel Mobil Corp., Mobil South, 1985-87; asst. gen. counsel M&R divsn. Mobil Corp., 1987-89, asst. gen. counsel Exploration and Producing divsn., 1990-94; v.p., gen. cousnel Mobil Oil Corp., Fairfax, Va., 1994—, sr. v.p., gen. counsel; sr. v.p., gen. counsel, chief legal officer Unocal Corp., El Segundo, Calif. Office: Mobil Oil Corp 3225 Gallows Rd Fairfax VA 22037-0002 also: Onocal Corp 2141 Rosecrans Ave Ste 4000 El Segundo CA 90245

GILLESPIE, THOMAS STUART, investment company executive; b. Montreal, July 18, 1938; s. Alexander Robert and Lois Tully (O'Brien) G.; m. Caroline Pierce Doyle, June 28, 1963; children: Caroline Alexandra, Alexandra Olivia, Vanessa Margaret, Joshua William. BA, McGill U., 1959, BCL, 1963. Assoc., Ogilvy, Renault, Montreal, 1964-72, ptnr., 1972-89, sr. ptnr., 1989-2001; pres. Tyringham Investments Ltd., 2001—. Sec., bd. dirs. Bouverie Investments Ltd.; bd. dirs. Daily Mail and Gen. Trust plc, Imperial Tobacco Can. Ltd. Bd. dirs. Carnegie Instn. Can., Biomosaics Inc. Mem. Que. Bar Assn., Can. Bar Assn., Mt. Bruno Country Club, Orleans Fish and GameClub, Univ. Club, Tarratine Club Dark Harbor, Toronto Golf Club. Roman Catholic. Home: 48 Aberdeen Ave Westmount PQ Canada H3Y 3A4 Office: 1800 McGill College Ave Ste 2430 Montreal PQ Canada H3A 3J6 E-mail: tgillespie@tyringham.ca.

GILLESPIE, THOMAS WILLIAM, retired academic administrator, religious studies educator; b. LA, July 18, 1928; s. William A. and Estella (Beers) G.; m. Barbara A. Lugenbill, July 31, 1953; children: Robyn C., William T., Dayle E. BA, George Pepperdine Coll., 1951; BD, Princeton Theol. Sem., 1954; PhD, Claremont Grad. Sch., 1971; DD (hon.), Grove City Coll., 1984; ThD (hon.), Theol. Acad. Debrecen, Hungary, 1988; DTh (hon.), Karoli Gaspar Reformed U., Budapest, Hungary, 1994; DPhil (hon.), Soong Sil U., Seoul, Korea, 1994; DD (hon.), U. St. Andrews, Scotland, 1996; LHD (hon.), King Coll., Bristol, Tenn., 1999; DD (hon.), Edinburgh U., Scotland, 2004. Ordained to ministry Presbyterian Ch., 1954. Pastor 1st Presbyn. Ch., Garden Grove, Calif., 1954-66, Burlingame, Calif., 1966-83; pres., prof. N.T. Princeton (NJ) Theol. Sem., 1983—2004, emeritus prof, 2005—. Author: The First Theologians: A Study in Early Christian Prophecy, 1994. Chmn. bd. trustees Ctr. Theol. Inquiry, 1992—. With USMC, 1946-47. Recipient A.A. Hodge prize in systematic theology Princeton Theol. Sem., 1953; Disting. Alumnus award Claremont Grad. Sch., 1984; Disting. Alumnus award Pepperdine U., 1986, Princeton Theol. Sem., 2004. Mem. Soc. Bibl. Lit., Studiorum Novi Testamenti Societas, Rotary Internat. Republican.

GILLET, PAMELA KIPPING, special education educator; EdB in Elem. Edn., Chgo. Tchrs. Coll., 1963; MA in Mental Retardation, Northeastern Ill. U., 1966; PhD in Gen. Spl. Edn./Adminstrn., Walden U., 1976. Cert. elem. edn., early childhood edn., learning disabled, mental retardation, behavior disorders, supt., supr. and dir. spl. edn. 4th grade tchr. Dist. # 83 Mannheim, Franklin Park, Ill., 1963—64; h.s. spl. edn. tchr. Dist. # 207 Maine Twp., Park Ridge, Ill., 1964—67, prevocational coord., 1967—69, dept. chmn. spl. edn. dept., 1969—70; dir. EPDA tchr. tng. program Chgo. Consortium Colls. and Univs., Northwest Ednl. Coop., Palatine, Ill., 1970—71; prin. West Suburban Spl. Edn. Ctr., Cicero, Ill., 1971—73; supr. West Suburban Assn. Spl. Edn., Cicero, 1973—75; asst. dir. Northwest Suburban Spl. Edn. Orgn., Palatine, 1975—78, supt. Mt. Prospect, Ill., 1978—96; spl. edn. cons., 1996—. Adj. instr. Northeastern Ill. U., Chgo. State U., Corcordia Coll., Barat Coll., Nat. Coll. Edn., Roosevelt U.; mem. task forces ISBE, 1975—2007, cons. career edn. project, 1977—78, spl. edn. demandate study group, 1983—85; cons. Ednl. Testing Svc.; tchr. edn. coun. Northeastern Ill. U., 1981—97, dean's grant program, 1982—97; workshop leader, 1974—; lectr., cons. in field. Author: Auditory Processes, 1974, rev., 1992, Career Education for Children, 1978, Of Work and Worth: Career Education Programming for Exceptional Children and Youths, 1981; contbr. articles to profl. jours., chapters to books. Bd. dirs. Found. Exceptional Children, 1996—, pres., 1999—2004. Recipient Cmty. Svc. award, Am. Legion, 1976, 1980, Alumnus of Yr. award, Northeastern Ill. U., 1984, Learning Disabilities of Am. Contributors award, Coun. Understanding Learning Disabilities, 1992, Those Who Excel award of excellence, Ill. State Bd. of Edn., 1994, Outstanding Svc. award, Divsn. Mental Retardation and Devel. Disabilities, 1994, Sleznick award, Coun. of Admin. of Spl. Edn., 1996, Outstanding Contbr. award, Coun. Exceptional Children, 1996, Burton Blatt award, Divsn. on Metal Retardation and Devel. Disabilities, 1997, Spl. Edn. Leadership award, Ill. Adminstrs. of Spl. Edn., 1995, Outstanding Spl. Edn. Adminstr. of Yr. award, 1997. Mem.: Found. for Exceptional Children (pres. 2000—04, v.p. CEC Pioneers divsn. 2005—), Ill. Adminstrs. Spl. Edn. (pres. 1994—95), Coun. Exceptional Children (pres. Ill. chpt. 1975—77, bd. govs. 1977—80, pres. mental retardation divsn. 1983—85, bd. govs. 1986, exec. com. 1989—92, v.p. internat. 1992—93, pres.-elect 1993—94, pres. 1994—95, bd. govs. 1996—2000, bd. dirs. 2000—04, v.p. CEC pioneers divsn. 2005—, Meritorious Svc. award Ill. 1983), Am. Assn. Sch. Adminstrs. Home and Office: 413 Courtlea Oaks Blvd Winter Garden FL 34787

GILLETT, ANNETTE DAMRON, retired speech and forensics educator; b. L.A., Dec. 17, 1905; d. George Wilshire Damron and Florence Frances Helm; m. Cecil Gillett, June 15, 1934 (dec. Mar. 1969); 1 child, Charles Lucky. BA, U. Calif., Berkeley, 1926. Tchr. English and Spanish local high schs., Ramona, Calif., 1927-30, Cen. Union H.S., El Centro, Calif., 1931-57; tchr. speech Cen. Cmty. Coll., El Centro, Calif., 1931-57. Active Nevada County Task Force on Housing, Nevada City, Calif., 1998-2001; mem. cen. com. Nevada County Dems., 1990-98. Recipient Vol. Svc. award Calif. Ret. Tchrs. Assn., 1997. Mem. LWV (life, vol. svc. award 1996), AAUW (life, pres. 1975-77), Pi Lambda Theta (life). Avocations: hiking, fishing. Home: 50 Rockwood Dr Grass Valley CA 95945

GILLETT, GROVER, author; b. Whitewright, Tex., June 22, 1927; s. Grover Cleveland and Gertrude (Holland) G.; m. Mary Margaret Landress, Aug. 16, 1963. BBA, Tex. Tech. U., 1949; MBA, U. Tex., 1951; postgrad., Columbia U., 1953. CPA, Tex. Auditor Lumberman's Mutual Casualty Co., Dallas, 1954-56; operational auditor Dept. of Def., Dallas, 1956-58; self-employed CPA Dallas, 1958-64; asst. prof. McMurry Coll., Abilene, Tex., 1964-66; sr. internal auditor Ling-Temco-Vought Aerospace Corp., Dallas, 1966-67; instr. El Centro Coll., Dallas, 1967-96. Author: Personnel Policies of Public Accounting Firms in Texas, 1951, (booklet) Marriage Quotables, 1999, 73 other books and booklets. Bd. dirs. Twenty-One Turtle Creek Homeowners Assn., Dallas, 1996-98; mem. World Affairs Coun. With USN, 1945-46, Korea, lt. (j.g.) USNR ret. Mem. AICPA, Tex. Soc. CPAs, World Future Soc., Dallas UN Assn., S.W. Social Sci. Assn., Lions. Democrat. Unitarian Universalist. Avocations: reading, collecting antiques. Home and Office: Apt 1103 3883 Turtle Creek Blvd Dallas TX 75219-4426 E-mail: gmgillett@sbcglobal.net.

GILLETT, JAMES WARREN, ecotoxicology educator; b. Sept. 18, 1933; s. Ira Elijah and Atha Arthela (Morlan) Gillett; m. Mary Francis Hebert, Aug. 7, 1970; children: Grant Jameson, Iain; m. Mary Alexia Stuart, June 26, 1958 (div. Apr. 1970); children: John Stuart, Peter Warren. BS, U. Kans., 1955; PhD, U. Calif., Berkeley, 1962. Postdoctoral rsch. chemist U. Calif., Berkeley, 1962-64; asst. prof. agrl. chemistry Oreg. State U., Corvallis, 1964-69, assoc. prof., 1969-74; rsch. ecologist EPA/Environ. Rsch. Lab., Corvallis, 1974-81, rsch. environ. scientist, 1981-83; prof. ecotoxicology dept. natural resources Cornell U., Ithaca, N.Y., 1983—, dir. superfund basic rsch. program, 1992—2001. Dir. Inst. for Comparative and Environ. Toxicology, 1986-92, Risk Analysis Studies minor field of grad study. Editor, pub.: Biological Impact of Pesticides in the Environment, 1971; editor: Terrestrial Microcosms, 1979; editor: (jour.) Hazard Assessment, Environ. Toxicology & Chemistry, 1988-93; contbr. articles to profl. jours. Chmn. bd. Oreg. Mus. Sci. and Industry, 1969-71, Cmty. Action Program, 1970-72; sec. Willamette Soccer League, 1970-74; coach Corvallis Womens Soccer Team, 1979-81; pres., founder Esophagal Cancer Awareness Assn., 2002-. Summerfield scholar, 1951-54. Mem.: Soc. Risk Analysis, Soc. Environ. Toxicology and Chemistry (bd. dirs. 1984—88), Toastmasters (pres. 1974), Alpha Kappa Lambda. Office: Cornell U Dept Natural Resources 8b Fernow Hall Ithaca NY 14853 Office Phone: 607-255-2163. Business E-Mail: jwg3@cornell.edu.

GILLETT, MARY CAPERTON, military historian; b. Richmond, Va., Apr. 28, 1929; d. Lewis Hopkins and Mary Caperton (Horsley) Renshaw; m. Richard Clark Gillett, June 7, 1949; children: Richard Clark Jr., Glenn Douglas, Mary Caperton, Priscilla Elizabeth, Blakeney Diana. Student, Wellesley Coll., 1946-49; BA, Am. U., 1966, MA, 1971, PhD, 1978. Historian U.S. Navy Dept., Washington, 1966-69, U.S. Dept. Army, Washington, 1972-96. Author: The Army Medical Department, 1775-1818, 1981, The Army Medical Department, 1818-1865, 1988, The Army Medical Department, 1865-1917, 1995; contbr. articles to profl. jours. Mem. Am. Assn. for History of Medicine, Nat. Wildlife Fedn., We. Hist. Assn., The Nature Conservancy, The Wilderness Soc., The Sierra Club, Nat. Audubon Soc., Audubon Naturalist Soc. Avocations: backpacking, gardening. E-mail: mcgillett@mindspring.com.

GILLETT, RICHARD CLARK, JR., physician, educator, health facility administrator; b. Richmond, Va., Mar. 27, 1950; s. Richard Clark and Mary Caperton (Renshaw) G.; m. Barbara Jean Bolecek, Aug. 12, 1972; children: Douglas Clark, Ann Caperton. BA, U. Va., 1971, MD, 1977. Diplomate Am. Bd. Family Practice. Tchr. Prince William County Schs., Manassas, Va., 1971-72; resident Roanoke (Va.) Meml. Hosp., 1977-80; family physician Family Practice Clinic, Inc., Radford, Va., 1981-82; emergency physician Montgomery Regional Hosp., Blacksburg, Va., 1982-83; pvt. practice Radford, Va., 1983-85; asst. prof. family medicine, asst. dean continuing med. edn. East Tenn. State U., Johnson City, 1986-91; dir. med. edn. Columbus (Ga.) Regional Healthcare Sys., 1991-2000. Bd. dirs. Stewert Cmty. Home, Columbus, 1996-99, Human Experience Theater, Columbus, 1997, Springer Theater, Columbus, 1993-94, 99-00. Mem. AMA (rep. sect. on med. schs. Chgo., 1996-2000), Am. Assn. Family Physicians, Med. Assn. Ga. (mem. com. med. schs.), Muscogee County (Ga.) Med. Soc. Avocations: gardening, flying. Fax: 706-571-1604. E-mail: gillettrc@knology.net, clark.gillett@crhs.net.

GILLETT, VICTOR WILLIAM, JR., title insurance company executive; b. El Paso, Tex., Feb. 4, 1932; s. Victor William and Alice Cecelia (Kemper) G.; m. Anita Johanne Dexter, Mar. 1, 1975; children: Victor William III, Blake Andrew. BBA, Tex. A&M U., 1953. V.p., dist. mgr. Stewart Title Guaranty Co., Corpus Christi, Tex., 1955-61; pres., CEO, Stewart Title & Trust Co., Phoenix, 1961-77, dir., 1965-77; sr. v.p. nat. mktg. dir. Stewart Title Guaranty Co., Houston, 1977-91, dir., 1981-91, sr. v.p. Irvine, Calif., 1988-91; pres. Old Republic Title Co. Bell County, Temple, Tex., 1992—2001; ret., 2001. Dir. Stewart Info. Svcs. Corp., 1983-91. Bd. dirs. Ariz. Heart Assn., 1970-73; bd. dirs., sec. Phoenix Civic Improvement Corp., 1974-76. With AUS, 1953-54. Mem. Am. Land Title Assn. (gov. 1969-71), Temple C. of C. (former bd. dirs.), Rotary, Assn. U.S. Army (pres., bd. dirs. 1968), Former Students Assn. Tex. A&M U., 12th Man Found. (Tex. A&M U.). Home: 5007 Sterling Dr Temple TX 76502-7108

GILLETTE, CLAYTON P., law educator, academic administrator; b. 1950; BA, Amherst Coll., 1972; JD, U. Mich., 1975. Bar: NY 1977. Law clk. to Hon. J. Edward Lumbard US Ct. Appeals 2nd Cir., 1975—75; assoc. Cleary, Gottlieb, Steen & Hamilton, NYC, 1976—78; assoc. prof. Boston U. Sch. Law, 1978—84, prof., 1984—92, assoc. dean, 1990—92, Warren scholar mcpl. law; Perre Bowen prof. law U. Va. Sch. Law, 1992—2000; prof. NYU Sch. Law, 2000—02, Max E. Greenberg prof. contract law, 2002—, vice dean. Office: NYU Sch Law Vanderbilt Hall Rm 403 40 Washington Sq S New York NY 10012-1099 Office Phone: 212-998-6749. Office Fax: 212-995-4692. E-mail: gillette@juris.law.nyu.edu.

GILLETTE, EDWARD LEROY, radiation oncology educator; b. Coffeyville, Kans., May 21, 1932; s. Harold R. and Laura Belle (McLaughlin) G.; m. Carol J. Peterson, June 2, 1956 (div. Oct. 1981); children: William R., Jeffrey S., Timothy E., Jennifer L.; m. Sharon L. McChesney, Nov. 26, 1988. BS, DVM, Kans. State U., 1956; MS, Colo. State U., 1961, PhD, 1965. From instr. to prof. radiology and radiation biology Colo. State U., Ft. Collins, 1959-72, prof., 1972-2000, prof., chmn. emeritus, 2000—, dir. comparative oncology, 1974-98, chmn. dept. radiol. health scis., 1989-98, assoc. dean rsch. Coll. Vet. Medicine and Biomed. Sci., 1997-98; adj. clin. prof. dept. radiation oncology UCLA Med. Sch., 1998—. Adj. prof. dept. radiation oncology Duke U. Med. Coll., Durham, N.C.; bd. dirs. The Children's Hosp. Kempe Rsch. Ctr., Denver, 1984-90; vis. scientist M.D. Anderson Cancer Ctr. U. Tex., 1988. Assoc. editor Radiation Rsch., 1979-82, 86-90; assoc. editor, Internat. Jour. of Radiation Oncology Biology and Physics, 1990-95, mem. editl. bd., 1995—; contbr. articles to profl. jours. Bd. dirs. Colo. State Sci. Fair, 1984-90. 1st lt. U.S. Army, 1956-58. Recipient Outstanding Svc. to the Vet. Profession award Am. Animal Hosp. Assn., 1984, Ralston-Purina rsch. award, 1988, Kans. State U. Alumni Assn. Medallion award, 1999; U. Tex. fellow, 1968-69. Mem. AVMA, Am. Coll. Vet. Radiology (cert., pres. 1973-74), Am. Coll. Vet. Internal Medicine, Oncology (cert.), Am. Cancer Soc. (mem. exec. com. Colo. divsn. 1978-82, bd. dirs. Colo. divsn. 1984-90, pres. Larimer County chpt. 1977-81), Vet. Cancer Soc. (pres. 1982-84), Radiation Rsch. Soc. (councilor 1988-91), Am. Soc. Therapeutic Radiology and Oncology, Am. Assn. Cancer Rsch., Colo. State U. Alumni Assn. (Honor Alumnus award 1985), Rotary. Republican. Avocation: reading. Office: Colo State Univ Animal Cancer Ctr Fort Collins CO 80523-0001 Office Phone: 970-297-1278. Business E-Mail: edward.gillette@colostate.edu.

GILLETTE, FRANK C., JR., retired mechanical engineer; m. Jane Gillette; 3 children. BS in Mech. Engring., U. Fla. Mech. designer Pratt & Whitney, 1962-77, chief of structures, 1977-80, engring. mgr. YF119 program, dir. engring. programs F119 engine projects for Govt. Engines and Space Propulsion, 1980-95, dir. advanced mil. programs, 1995-97, dir.-chief engr. F119/JSF engine programs, 1997-98, ret., 1998. Mem. adv. bd. U. Fla. Coll. Engring.; cons. in field. Recipient Disting. Alumnus Disting. Svc. award U. Fla. Coll. Engring., Laurels award Aviation Week, 1991. Fellow ASME, AIAA (assoc.; Nat. Engr. of Yr. award 1991); mem. Soc. Automotive Engrs. (Cliff Garrett Turbomachinery Engring. award 1994). Achievements include design of the RL10 rocket chamber, the turbine section of the J58, F119 engine; management of the overall structural engineering effort of the J52, TF30, F100 rockets and preliminary design by the Nat. Acads., Air Force & Dept. Def. Aerospace Propulsion Commn.; patents in field. Home: 8325 Nashua Dr Palm Beach Gardens FL 33418 E-mail: fcgillette@yahoo.com.

GILLETTE, FRANKIE JACOBS, retired savings and loan association executive, federal agency administrator, social worker; b. Norfolk, Va., Apr. 1, 1925; d. Frank Walter and Natalie (Taylor) Jacobs; m. Maxwell Claude Gillette, June 19, 1976. BS, Hampton U., 1946; MSW, Howard U., 1948. Lic. clin. social worker; cert. jr. coll. tchr., life. Youth dir. YWCA, Passaic, N.J., 1948-50; dir. program Ada S. McKinley Community Ctr., Chgo., 1950-53; program dir. Sophie Wright Settlement, Detroit, 1953-64; dir. Concerted Services Project, Pittsburg, Calif., 1964-66, Job Corps Staff Devel., U. Calif., Berkeley, 1966-69; spl. program coordinator U.S. Community Services Adminstrn., San Francisco, 1969-83; pres. G & G Enterprises, San Francisco, 1985—. Chmn. bd. dirs. Time Savs. and Loan Assn., San Francisco, 1986-87. Commr. San Francisco Human Rights Commn., 1988-93; bd. dirs. Urban Econ. Devel. Corp., 1980-93, San Francisco Conv. and Visitors Bur.; trustee Fine Arts Mus. of San Francisco, 1993—; chmn. San Francisco-Abidjan Sister City Com., 1990—; founding bd. dirs. Mus. African Diaspora, 2002—. Mem. Nat. Assn. Negro Bus. and Profl. Women's Clubs (pres. 1983-87), The Links, Inc., Delta Sigma Theta, Inc. Office: G & G Enterprises 85 Cleary Ct Apt 4 San Francisco CA 94109-6518

GILLETTE, HYDE, retired brokerage house executive; b. Chgo., June 23, 1906; s. Edwin Fraser and Mabel (Hyde) G.; m. Marie Clarke Smith, Sept. 7, 1932 (dec. Sept. 28, 1994); 1 child, Marie Clarke Gerald. Grad., Exeter Acad., 1924; AB cum laude, Princeton U., 1928; MBA with distinction, Harvard U., 1930. With Glore, Forgan & Co., 1930-53, ptnr., 1950-53; dep. asst. and dep. under sec. USAF, 1953-57; asst. postmaster gen., bur. finance U.S. Post Office Dept., Washington, 1957-61; ptnr. Auchincloss Parker & Redpath, 1961-70; regional v.p. Thomson & McKinnon Auchincloss, Inc., Washington, 1970-73; v.p. Thomson McKinnon Securities, 1973-89, Prudential Securities, 1989-91. Exec. bd. Chgo. Area Project, 1936-53, chmn., 1948-53; bd. dirs., v.p. Nat. Capital area council Boy Scouts Am.; regent Nat. Eagle Scout Assn.; dir., vice chmn. budget com. Community Fund of Chgo., 1942; chmn. exec. com. Chgo. Opera Theatre, 1947; adv. bd. Dept. Public Welfare Ill., 1949-53; pres. Barrington Country Day Sch., 1941; v.p. Washington Heart Assn., 1961; bd. dirs. Am. Heart Assn., 1960-63. Served as lt. comdr. USNR, 1943-46. Recipient Exceptional Civilian Svc. award USAF, 1956; Disting. Svc. award U.S. Post Office Dept., 1960; disting. Eagle Scout Nat. award. Mem. Mayflower Descs., Soc. Colonial Wars, English Speaking Union (dir. 1977-86), Barrington Countryside Assn. (pres. 1949-50), Phi Beta Kappa. Clubs: Quadrangle (Princeton); Chevy Chase (Washington), Metropolitan (Washington); Beverly Yacht (Marion, Mass.), Kittanset (Marion, Mass.). Episcopalian. Home: Fox Hill Village 10 Longwood Dr Apt 404 Westwood MA 02090-1144

GILLETTE, JAMES R., construction executive; Grad., U. Ill., Urbana. CPA. Ptnr. Hood and Strong, 1974; CFO Swinerton Inc., 1983, pres., 1996—2003, CEO, 2003—, chmn. bd., 2004—. Bd. dirs. Norcal Waste Sys. Inc. Mem.: Associated Gen. Contractors of Am. Office: Swinerton Inc 260 Townsend St San Francisco CA 94107

GILLETTE, P. ROGER, physicist, systems engineer; b. Mt. Vernon, Iowa, May 12, 1917; s. Clinton Edgar and Celia (Rogers) G.; m. Bettelaine Dunbar, Apr. 26, 1947 (dec. Mar. 1986); children: Kenneth Lee, Sandra Jo. BA in Physics, Cornell Coll., 1937; BS in Engring. Physics, U. Ill., 1938, MS in Physics, 1939, PhD in Physics, 1942. Staff mem. Radiation Lab, MIT, Cambridge, Mass., 1942-45; rsch. engr. Sperry Gyroscope Co., Great Neck, N.Y., 1945-48; physicist Hanford Works Gen. Electric Co., Richland, Wash., 1948-50; sr. rsch. physicist SRI Internat., Menlo Park, Calif., 1950-92, ret. Co-author: Pulse Generators, 1948. Bd. dirs. Inst. for Continued Learning, Willamette U., Salem, Oreg., 2004—05, West Bay Opera Assn., Palo Alto, Calif., 1959—64, 1977—79, Inst. for Continued Learning, Willamette U., Salem, Oreg., 1996—98, 2004—05. Mem. AAAS, IEEE (sr. life), Am. Phys. Soc. (life), Am. Acd. Religion, Inst. on Religion in an Age of Sci., Sigma Xi, Phi Beta Kappa, Tau Beta Pi, Phi Kappa Phi. Achievements include development of pulse transformer theory, of system design concepts for command, control, communications and intelligence systems, electronic combat systems, and air combat training systems. Home: 2385 Crestview Dr S, Salem OR 97302-5373

GILLETTE, PATRICIA K., lawyer; b. L.A., Aug. 7, 1951; AB, Occidental Coll., 1973; JD cum laude, U. San Francisco, 1976. Bar: Calif., Am. Bar Assoc. In-house council Bank of Am.; atty. private practice; ptnr. Heller Ehrman LLP, San Francisco, 1990—. Co-chmn. labor and employment practice group Heller Ehrman LLP. Office: Heller Ehrman LLP 333 Bush St San Francisco CA 94104-2806 Office Phone: 415-772-6000.

GILLETTE, PAUL CRAWFORD, pediatric cardiologist; b. Winston-Salem, N.C., Dec. 1, 1942; s. Crawford Paul and Eileen Marie (O'Rourke) G.; m. Vicki Lynn Zeigler, 1992; 2 children. BA in Chemistry, U.N.C., 1965; MD, Med. Coll. S.C., 1969. Intern, then resident in pediatrics Baylor U. Coll. Medicine, Houston, 1969-71, fellow in pediatric cardiology and cell biophysics, 1971-74, mem. faculty, 1974-84, assoc. prof. exptl. medicine, 1977-84, prof. pediatrics, 1980-84, Med. U. S.C., Charleston, 1984-96, chmn. promotions com., dept. pediatrics, 1989-96; dir. S.C. Children's Heart Ctr., Charleston, 1984-96; med. dir. Cook Children's Cardiology, 1996—, Cook Childrens Cardiac Ctr., Fort Worth, Tex., 1996—. Dir. electrophysiology and electrocardiography Tex. Children's Hosp.; co-dir. Palmetto Heart Inst., 1988-96; mem. tng. grant manpower rev. com. Nat. Heart, Lung and Blood Inst., 1989-93, chmn., 1992-93. Co-author: A Guide to Pediatric Cardiac Dysrhythmias, 1980, Pediatric Cardiac Dysrhythmias, 1981, A Practical Guide to Cardiac Pacing, 1986, Pediatric Electrophysiology, Arrythmia and Pacing, 1990, Pediatric Cardiac Pacing, 1995, Clinical Pediatric Arrythmias, 1999, Cardiac Arrhythmias after Surgery for Congential Heart Disease, 2001; editl. bd. Circulation, Am. Heart Jour., Pediatric Cardiology, Jour. Am. Coll. Cardiology; contbr. articles to profl. jours. Mem. sports com., treas. St. Thomas More Sch., Houston; bd. dirs. Toler's Cove Homeowners Assn. Charleston, 1989-94, Ronald McDonald House of Ft. Worth, 2001—. Nat. Heart, Lung and Blood Inst. grantee; named Disting. Alumni, Medical Univ. S.C., 1991; recipient Rsch. award So. Med. Assn., 1994. Fellow Am. Acad. Pediatrics (exec. com. cardiology sect. 1979, ednl. grantee 1970, Young Investigator award 1975, trustee 1987—, chmn. rsch. rev. com. 1987-88 S.C. chpt.), Am. Coll. Cardiology (trustee 1984-90, learning ctr. com. 1984-88, strategic planning com. 1986-90, long range planning com. 1987-88, chmn. pacemaker com. 1990-95, mem. rsch. com. 1990—); mem. Soc. Pediatric Rsch., So. Soc. Pediatric Rsch., Southeastern Pediatric Cardiology Soc. (pres. 1987), N.Am. Soc. Pacing and Electrophysiology (pres. 1986-87, trustee 1987-90, program com. 1987, Pioneer in Cardiac Pacing and Electrophysiology award 1998, Healthcare Hero 2004, Tex. Super Doc 2004), Am. Heart Assn. (chmn. rsch. peer rev. com. S.C. chpt. 1989, chmn. rsch. com. 1990, pres.-elect Ft. Worth chpt. 1998-98, pres. 1998-99), Tex. Pediatric Soc., Harris County Med. Soc., Houston Cardiology Soc., North Tex. Electrophynology Soc., Houston Pediatric Soc., S.C. Med. Soc., Charleston County Med. Soc., Tarrant County Med. Soc. (bd. dirs. 2001—), S.C. Heart Assn. (rschr. of the yr. 1991), Alpha Omega Alpha, Phi Chi. Republican. Roman Catholic. Office: Cook Childrens Cardiac Ctr 901 7th Ave Ste 301 Fort Worth TX 76104-2724 Office Phone: 682-885-7940. E-mail: pgillette@cookchildrens.org.

GILLETTE, RICHARD GARETH, neurophysiology educator, researcher; b. Seattle, Feb. 17, 1945; s. Elton George and Hazel I. (Hand) G.; m. Sally A. Reams, Feb. 17, 1978 (div. Nov. 1988); 1 child, Jesse Robert. BS, U. Oreg., 1968; MS, Oreg. Health Sci. U., 1976, PhD, 1993. Rsch. asst. dept. otolaryngology Oreg. Health Sci. U., Portland, 1969-72, grad. rsch. asst., 1973-80; instr. neurosci. Western State Chiropractic Coll., Portland, 1981-85, asst. prof. neurosci., 1985-93, assoc. prof. neurosci., 1993-99, prof. neurosci., 1999—. Lectr. neurosci. sch. optometry Pacific U., Forest Grove, Oreg., 1985-86; grad. rsch. asst. Neurol. Sci. Inst. OHSU, Portland, 1988-93, vis. scientist, 1993—. Contbr. articles to profl. jours. NIH Predoctoral Tng. fellow Oreg. Health Sci. U., 1973-76, Tarter fellow Med. Rsch. Found. Oreg., 1989; NIH grantee, 1990-99. Mem. AAAS, Soc. for Neurosci., Am. Pain Soc., Internat. Assn. for Study of Pain. Avocations: history studies, vocal music performance. Office: WSCC 2900 NE 132nd Ave Portland OR 97230-3014 Business E-Mail: rgillette@wschiro.edu.

GILLETTE, ROBERT J., aerospace transportation executive; BS in Fin., Ind. U. With GE Plastics; v.p., gen. mgr. AlliedSignal Engring. Plastics; v.p. strategic growth, v.p., gen. mgr. Asia Worldwide aftermarket Garrett Engine Boosting Sys., pres., 2000—01; pres., CEO Honeywell Transp. Systems Honeywell Internat. Inc., Morristown, NJ, 2001—04, CEO, Honeywell Aerospace Phoenix, 2005—. Office: Honeywell Aerospace 1944 E Sky Harbor Cir N Phoenix AZ 85034

GILLETTE, W. MICHAEL, state supreme court justice; b. Seattle, Dec. 29, 1941; s. Elton George and Hazel Irene (Hand) G.; children: Kevin, Saima. AB cum laude in German, Polit. Sci., Whitman Coll., 1963; LLB, Harvard U., 1966. Bar: Oreg. 1966, U.S. Dist. Ct. Oreg. 1966, U.S. Ct. Appeals (9th cir.) 1966, Samoa 1969, U.S. Supreme Ct. 1970, U.S. Dist. Ct. Vt. 1973. Assoc. Rives & Rogers, Portland, Oreg., 1966-67; dep. dist. atty. Multnomah County, Portland, 1967-69; asst. atty. gen. Govt. of Am. Samoa, 1969-71, State of Oreg., Salem, 1971-77; judge Oreg. Ct. Appeals, Salem, 1977-86; justice Oreg. Supreme Ct., Salem, 1986—. Instructor constitutional and criminal law Portland State U., 1971—74; mem. bd. Oreg. Law-Related Education Project, 1980—88; mem. advisory com. Scholars for Constitution Project, 1984; prof. administrative, constitutional, and consumer law Nat. Jud. Coll. Bd. trustees Oreg. Museum of Science and Industry, 1977—80. Avocation: officiating basketball. Office Phone: 503-986-5705.

GILLETTE, WILLIAM, historian, educator; b. Bridgeport, Conn., Mar. 2, 1933; s. Samuel William and Lillian (Abeson) G.; m. Elisabeth L. Janes, May 23, 1971; children: Scott Douglas, Wendy Elisabeth. BS, Georgetown U., 1955; MA, Columbia U., 1956, postgrad., 1958-59; PhD, Princeton U., 1963. Instr. Ohio State U., 1962-64; acting asst. prof. U. Conn., Storrs, 1965-66; asst. prof. Bklyn. Coll. CUNY, 1966-67; asso. prof. Rutgers U., 1967-81, prof., 1981—. Fulbright prof. U. Salzburg (Austria), 1982-83, Japan Women's U. and Tsuda Coll., 1997-98. Author: The Right to Vote: Politics and the Passage of the Fifteenth Amendment, 1969, Retreat From Reconstruction, 1869-1879, 1979, Jersey Blue: Civil War Politics in New Jersey, 1995. Served with AUS, 1956—58. Social Sci. Research Council faculty fellow, 1970; recipient Landry award La. State U. Press, 1979, Chastain award So. Polit. Sci. Assn., 1980, award of merit Am. Assn. for State and Local History, 1996, McCormick award N.J. Hist. Commn., 1997; grantee Am. Philos. Soc., N.J. Hist. Commn. Mem. AAUP, N.J. Hist. Soc., Advs. for N.J. History. Democrat. Unitarian Universalist. Home: 43 South Dr East Brunswick NJ 08816-1134 Office: Rutgers U Dept History New Brunswick NJ 08901-1108 Office Phone: 732-932-6779.

GILLEY, MICKEY LEROY, musician; b. Natchez, Miss., Mar. 9, 1936; s. Arthur Philmore and Irene Frances (Lewis) G.; m. Vivian McDonald, Dec. 27, 1962; 1 son, Gregory Brent. Ptnr. Gilley's Club, Pasadena, Tex., 1971-89; owner Gilley's Theatre, Branson, Mo., 1990—; pres., owner Gilley's Tex. Cafe, 1992—, owner Myrtle Beach, SC, 1995—2000, Gilley's Rest., Pasadena, Tex., 2002—05. Appeared in night clubs in, Houston, New Orleans, Biloxi, Miss., Mobile, Ala., Lake Charles, La., 1957-59; appeared at, Nesadel Club, Houston, 1960-70. Named Most Promising Male Artist, Acad. Country Music 1974, Most Promising Male Artist, Record World 1974, Top New Country Singles Artist, Billboard 1974, Top New Male Vocalist in Album Category, Record World 1975, Most Promising Male Artist, Music City News 1976, Best Male Vocalist, Entertainer of Year, Acad. Country Music 1976; recipient Star in Walk of Fame on Hollywood Blvd., 1984, over 17 #1 records, Grammy award for Orange Blossom Special Nat. Acad. Rec. Arts and Scis., 1981. Mem. Country Music Assn., Acad. Country Music, AFTRA, Musicians Local 65. Clubs: Moose. Office: 3737 Lily St Pasadena TX 77505-2927 E-mail: mickey@gilleys.com.

GILLHAM, JOHN KINSEY, chemical engineering professor; b. London, Aug. 7, 1930; came to U.S., 1959, naturalized, 1968; s. Gerald Albert and Doris (Kinsey) G.; m. Helen Alyce Currier, Sept. 18, 1961; children: Matthew, Jane, Martha. BA, Cambridge U., 1953, MA, 1957; PhD in Chemistry, McGill U., Montreal, 1959. Research chemist Am. Cynamid Co., Stamford, Conn., 1958-65; vis. rsch. chemist Princeton (NJ) U., 1964-65, mem. faculty, 1965—, prof. chem. engring., 1975-98, prof. emeritus, 1998—. Cons. to chem. and polymer industries; vis. fellow Japan Soc. Promotion Sci., 1983; vis. scholar Chinese Acad. Scis., 1984; sci. exch. visitor USSR Acad. Scis./NAS, 1986. Author papers in field. Recipient 1st prize for best tech. paper Roon Found. Awards Competition of Fedn. Socs. for Coatings Techs., 1983, 89, Outstanding Rev. Paper award Electronics Components Conf. of IEEE, 1985. Fellow Soc. Plastics Engrs. (Internat. Rsch. award 1988, Best Paper award 1991, Founders award Polymer Analysis Divsn., 2005); mem. Am. Chem. Soc. (Borden award 1978, Doolittle award 1980, Roy W. Tess award 1996, fellow divsn. Polymeric Materials: Sci. and Engring. 2000), N.Am. Thermal Analysis Soc. (Mettler award 1978). Home: 11 Vernon Cir Princeton NJ 08540-5415 Office: Princeton U Dept Chem Engring Princeton NJ 08544-0001 Office Phone: 609-258-4690. E-mail: jkgillham@yahoo.com.

GILLHAM, NICHOLAS WRIGHT, geneticist, educator; b. NYC, May 14, 1932; s. Robert Marty and Elizabeth (Enright) G.; m. Carol Lenore Collins, June 2, 1956. AB, Harvard, 1954, A.M., 1955, PhD (USPHS fellow), 1962. From instr. to asst. prof. Harvard U., 1963-68; assoc. prof. zoology Duke U., 1968-72, prof., 1973-82, James B. Duke prof. biology, 1982—2002, chmn. dept. zoology, 1986—89, profl. emeritus, 2002—. Mem. biochemistry, molecular genetics and cell biology interdisciplinary cluster Pres.'s Biomed. Rsch. Panel, 1975; mem. study sect. in genetics NIH, 1976-80; mem. N.C. Gov.'s Bd. Sci. and Tech., N.C. Gov.'s Task Force on Sci. and Tech., chmn., bd. dirs. Am. Type Culture Collection, 1993-96. Author: (with R. Krueger and J. Coggin) Introduction to Microbiology, 1973, Organelle Heredity, 1978, Organelle Genes and Genomes, 1994, A Life Sir Francis Galton: From African Exploration to the Birth of Eugenics, 2001; mem. editl. bd. Genetics, 1975-78, Jour. Cell Biology, 1977-79, Intl. Review of Cytology, 1987-97; sr. editor Plasmid, 1977-86. Served to 1st lt. Med. Service Corps USAF, 1955-58. Postdoctoral fellow, 1962-63; Spl. fellow, 1967-68; Research Career Devel. Award grantee, 1972-77; all USPHS); Guggenheim fellow, 1984-85. Mem. Genetics Soc. Am., Sigma Xi. Office: Duke Univ Dept Biology DCMB Group PO Box 91000 Durham NC 27708-1000 Office Phone: 919-623-8160. E-mail: gillham@acpub.duke.edu.

GILLIAM, GEORGE HARRISON, lawyer; b. Alexandia, Va., July 26, 1942; s. Robert Skelton Jr. and Delia Bryan (Harrison) G.; m. Sara Wilson Brown, May 29, 1964 (div. 1984); children: Louise Bell Gilliam McGrady, Sara Carter Gilliam; m. Page O'Neill, May 6, 1985; children: Caroline Bryan Gilliam, George Harrison Gilliam Jr. BS, Columbia U., 1965; LLB, U. Va., 1968, MA in History, 1997. Bar: Va. 1968, U.S. Dist. Ct. (we. dist.) Va. 1968, U.S. Dist. Ct. (ea. dist.) Va. 1992. Assoc. Paxson, Marshall & Smith, Charlottesville, Va., 1968-72; ptnr. Paxson, Smith, Gilliam & Scott (now Scott & Kroner), Charlottesville, 1972-95. Bd. dirs. Ctrl. Fidelity Nat. Bank, Richmond, Va. Author: Business Entities, 1981, Racin', 1988. Chmn. State Bd. for Community Colls., Richmond, 1984-85, 87-88, Va. Pesticide Control Bd., Richmond, 1989-93, 7th Congl. Dist. Dem. Party, Va., 1980-83, 89-95. Mem.: ABA, Va. Bar Assn., Farmington Country Club (pres. 2002—03). Democrat. Episcopalian. Avocations: race car driving, skiing, golf. Office: 619 E High St Charlottesville VA 22902 E-mail: ghg4u@virginia.edu.

GILLIAM, JAMES L., architectural firm executive; BArch, U. So. Calif.; Degree in Liberal Arts, U. Redlands. Joined HMC Group, Ontario, Calif., 1978—, project arch., pres., CEO, 2000—. Found. bd. dirs. U. Calif. Riverside; bd. dirs. Coalition for Adequate Sch. Housing. Mem.: AIA (bd. dirs. Inland chpt., mem. Calif. coun. sch. com.). Office: HMC Group 3270 Inland Empire Blvd Ontario CA 91764-4854

GILLIAM, SAM, artist; b. Tupelo, Miss., Nov. 30, 1933; s. Sam and Estery C. (Cousins) G.; children: Stephanie, Melissa, Leah. BA, U. Louisville, 1955, MA, 1961, LHD (hon.), 1980; ArtsD (hon.), Northwestern U., 1990; numerous DFA (hon.). Instr. art Pub. Sch. Sys., Washington, 1958—67; instr. painting Corcoran Sch. Art, Washington, 1964—67, Md. Inst. Art, Baltimore, 1967—82; prof. painting U. Md., 1982—85, Carnegie Mellon U., Pitts., 1985—89. Exhibitions include "Arts on Line: Art Pub. Transit Spaces" Hayden Gallery, MIT, Cambridge, Mass., 1980, "Am. Abstraction Now" Va. Mus. Fine Arts, 1982, "Painting in South" Va. Mus. Fine Art, 1984, "Experienced Eye" Ownesboro Mus. Fine Art, Ky. 1988, African Am. Art from Collection, Phila. Mus. Art, 1990, "Golden Windows Inside Gold" an installation Whitney Mus. Am. Art, Phillip Morris, N.Y.C., 1993-1995, Baumgartner Galleries, Washington, 1994, 44th Biennian Exhbn. Contemporary Am. Painting, Corcoran Gallery Art, Washington, 1995; numerous one-man shows of paintings, include Univ. Gallery, U. Mass., Amherst, 1978, Dart Gallery, Chgo., 1979, Florence Dugl Gallery, N.Y.C., 1979, Nina Freudenheim Gallery, Buffalo, 1979, Hamilton Gallery of Contemporary Art, N.Y.C., 1979, U. Wis., Stevens Point, 1980, Hamilton Gallery Contemporary Art, 1981, Galerie Darthea Speyer, Paris, France, 1983, Alice Simsar Gallery, Ann Arbor, Mich., 1986, Davis/McClain Gallery, Houston, 1986, G H Dalsheimer Gallery, Baltimore, 1986, Robert Kidd Gallery, Birmingham, Mich., 1987, Carl Solway Gallery, Cin., 1987, Klein Gallery, Chgo., 1987, 88, Iannetti-Lanzone Gallery, San Francisco, 1988, Middendorf Gallery, Washington, 1989, Frederick Gallery, N.Y.C., 1991, Gallery Simmone Stern, New Orleans, 1991, Smith Andersen Gallery, Palo Alto, Calif., 1992, Whitney Mus., N.Y.C., 1993—; numerous group shows including Galerie Darthea Speyer, Paris, 1978, Dade County Library, Miami, Fla., 1978, Grey Gallery, N.Y.C., 1979, Hamilton Gallery of Contemporary Art, N.Y.C., 1979, Alternative Mus., Washington, 1980, SUNY, 1980, N.J. State Mus., Trenton, 1980, "Afro-Am. Abstraction" L.A. Municipal Art Gallery, 1982, "10+10+10" Corcoran Gallery Art, Washington, 1982, "Abstraction/Abstraction" Carnegie Mellon U. Art Gallery, Pitts., 1986, "Contemporary Visual Expressions" Anacostia Mus. Smithsonian Inst., Washington, 1987, "Looking South: Different Dixie" Birmingham Mus. Art, Ala., 1988; represented in numerous permanent collections including, Nat. Gallery Art, Washington, Mus. Modern Art, N.Y.C., Rockefeller Collection, N.Y.C., Corcoran Gallery Art, Washington, Howard U., Washington, Phillips Collection, Washington, Gallery Modern Art, Washington, Mus. African Art, Washington, IBM Co., Washington, Carnegie Inst., Pitts., Balt. Mus. Art, Art Inst., Chgo., Hirschhorn Mus. and Sculpture Gardern, Smithsonian Inst., Met. Mus. Art, Walker Art Ctr., Tate Gallery, London, Musée d'art Moderne de la Ville de Paris, France, Beymans Mus., Rotterdam, Holland, and others; commissions include "Circles, Circuits, Boxes" Fed. Sys. Commn., Chantilly, Va. 1990, "Windows Go Orange" (ee cummings), Am. Craft Mus., 1991, "Washington Coulours" Kaempfer Corp., Washington, 1991, "Riders Blue" Archer St. Sta., Met. Transit Authority, Jamica, N.Y.C., 1991, Norfolk, USAA Ins. Co., MARO Bldg. Norfolk, Va., 1992; pub. works include Phillips Collection, Nat. Collection Fine Arts, Howard U., Mus. Modern Art, Met. Mus. Art, Princeton U., Rutgers U., Madison Art Ctr. Bd. dir. Washington Project Arts, 1980—85; art com., bd. dir. Coll. Art Assn., 1985—88; pub. art work com., adv. bd. Anacostia Cmty. Orgn., 1987—88. Recipient Norman W. Harris Prize Award, Art Inst. Chgo., 1969, Disting. Alumnus Award, U. Louisville, 1975, Pres. Award, Md. Coll. Art & Design, 1987, Order Merit Award, U. Louisville Alumni Assn., 1987; grantee, Nat. Endowment Arts, 1967, 1989. Fellow: Washington Gallery Modern Art, 1968, Guggenheim, 1971. Office: c/o Workshop Inc 3145 Newark St NW Washington DC 20008*

GILLICE, SONDRA JUPIN (MRS. GARDNER RUSSELL BROWN), sales and marketing executive; b. Urbana, Ill. d. Earl Cranston and Laura Lorraine (Rose) Jupin; m. Gardner Russell Brown, Jan. 12, 1980; 1 child, Thomas Alan Gillice. BS, Lindenwood Coll., 1968; MBA, Loyola Coll., 1983. Pers. officer N.Y. Citibank, 1968-70, 1st Nat. Bank Chgo., 1970-72; mgr. human resources Potomac Electric Power Co., Washington, 1973-81; dir. pers. U.S. Synthetic Fuels Corp., Washington, 1981-86; v.p. human resources Guest Svcs., Inc., 1987-90, v.p. sales and mktg., 1990-93; sr. v.p. govt. rels. Drake Beam Morin, Inc., 1994-98; pres. RusSon, Inc., 1998—. Bd. govs. Nat. Coal Coun., exec. com. Bd. dirs. Nat. Womens Econ. Alliance, Life With Cancer; dir. Black Bear Energy Corp., Capital Speakers Club; treas. Arts for the Aging. Mem. AAUW (pres. Falls Church br.), Edison Electric Inst. (chair tng. and mgmt. devel. com.), Soc. for Human Resource Mgmt., Greater Met. Washington Bd. Trade, Soroptimists (pres. Washington chpt. 1979-80), DAR, Army Navy Country Club, Army Navy Club, Soc. Magna Charta Dames, Edgartown Yacht Club, Georgetown Club.

GILLIES, DONALD RICHARD, marketing and advertising consultant, educator; b. Sioux Falls, S.D., Jan. 14, 1939; s. Donald Franklin and Gladys O. (Gullickson) G.; m. Twyla Elaine Bloomquist, Apr. 7, 1962; children: Dawn, Trent, Tara. BA in Journalism/Advt., U. Minn., 1961. Writer, producer Sta. WCCO-TV, Mpls., 1954-60; mgmt. supr., sr. v.p., bd. dirs. Campbell-Mithun Advt., Mpls., 1960-86; pres., chief oper. officer Colle & McVoy Inc., Mpls., 1987-89; prin. Gillies group inc. (Gg), Minnetonka, Minn., 1989—. Adj. prof. U. St. Thomas, 1990-97, asst. prof., 2001—. Bd. dirs. Guthrie Theater, Mpls., 1979-84; ch. coun. Mt. Olivet Ch., Mpls., 1988-94; Midwest adv. rev. bd. BBB, 1996—. Mem. Am. Assn. Advt. Agencies (regional gov.), Minn. Advt. Fedn. (bd. dirs. 1973-76). Lutheran. Home and Office: Gillies group inc (Gg) 5942 Fairwood Ln Minnetonka MN 55345-6533 Business E-Mail: drgillies@stthomas.edu. E-mail: dongillies@prodigy.net.

GILLIG, PAULETTE MARIE, psychiatry educator, researcher; b. Boston, Mar. 24, 1949; d. Franklin Joseph and Marie Robichaud (Collins) G.; m. Douglas K. Fairobent, June 13, 1981. BA cum laude hons. psychology, SUNY, Buffalo; MA, PhD, Ohio State U., 1973; MD, Med. Coll. Ohio, 1977. Diplomate Am. Bd. Psychiatry and Neurology, Am. Bd. Geriat. Psychiatry. Resident in neurology Med. Coll. Ohio, 1978-79, U. Mich., Ann Arbor, 1979-81; resident in psychiatry Ohio State U., Columbus, 1981-83; med. dir. North Ctrl. Mental Health Ctr., Columbus, 1985; clin. asst. prof. Ohio State U., Columbus, 1983-85; asst. prof. U. Cin., 1985-90; assoc. prof. Wright State U., Dayton, 1990-2000, prof. psychiatry, 2000—; chief clin. officer Mental Health Drug and Alcohol Svcs. Bd., Champaign and Logan Cos., 1995—2005. Prof. rural psychiatry Ohio Dept. Mental Health, 1997—; strategic planning coun. Wright State U., Dayton, 1998—, faculty devel. com., faculty senate, 2004—. Founding Bd. Domestic Abuse and Violence Inst. of Dayton, 2000—; Patron Cin. Ballet Co., Xavier U., 1988—, Humane Soc. U.S., Dayton Opera Co., Cin. Symphony Orch., Sorg Opera Co., Middletown, Ohio, 1989—, Lebanon Police Children's Fund, 1995—, Balletech Ohio, 2002—, Warren County Animal Shelter, 2002—; chair Domestic Violence Rsch. Group, 1999-2002. Recipient Clin. Neuroscis. award, Med. Coll. Ohio; grantee Pruitt Found., 1992, Ohio Dept. Mental Health, 1995—. Fellow Am. Psychiat. Assn. (disting.; com. on poverty, homelessness, and psychiatric disorders 1999—); mem. Am. Assn. Women Psychiatrists, Am. Assn. Cmty. Psychiatrists (Midwestern rep. 2002—, chair training com., Moffic award 1999), Ohio Psychiat. Assn. (chmn. com. on minorities 1999-2002, Pres.'s award 2001), World Health Orgn. (dir. internat. classification diseases), Nat. Wildlife Fedn. (cert.), Univ. Club, Alpha Omega Alpha. Avocations: classical piano, opera, companion animals, ballet, horticulture. Office: Wright State U Dept Psychiatry PO Box 927 Dayton OH 45401-0927 E-mail: paulette.gillig@wright.edu.

GILLIGAN, CAROL, psychologist, writer; b. N.Y.C., Nov. 28, 1936; d. William Edward and Mabel (Caminez) Friedman; m. James Frederick Gilligan, June 12, 1960; children: Jonathan Mark, Timothy David, Christopher James. AB, Swarthmore Coll., 1958, degree (hon.), 1985; AM, Radcliffe Coll., 1961; PhD, Harvard U., 1964; degree (hon.), Regis Coll., 1983, Haverford Coll., 1987, Fitchburg State Coll., 1989, Wesleyan U., 1992, Smith Coll., 1999. Instr. U. Chgo., 1965-66; lectr. Harvard U., Cambridge, Mass., 1967-69, rsch. asst., 1969-70, asst. prof., 1970-78, assoc. prof., 1978-86, prof., 1986—; now Patricia Albreg Graham prof. gender studies NYU, 1997—2001; Laurie chair in Women's Studies Rutgers U., New Brunswick, N.J., 1986-87; Pitt Prof. U. Cambridge, England, 1992-93, vis. prof. England, 2004—05, fellow Jesus Coll., 2004—. Vis. prof. NYU Sch. Law; founding mem. Harvard Project on Women's Psychology and the Devel. of Girls, 1987—2001; co-dir., The Company of Women and Girls, 1991—96; mem. coun. scholars Erikson Inst. Ansten Riggs Ctr. Author, editor: (with J. Ward and J. Taylor) In a Different Voice, 1982, Mapping the Moral Domain: A Contribution of Women's Thinking to Psychological Theory and Education, 1988; author: Making Connections: The Relational Worlds of Adolescent Girls at Emma Willard School, 1990, (with Lyn M. Brown) Meeting at the Crossroads: Women's Psychology and Girls Development, 1992, (with J. Taylor and A. Sullivan) Between Voice and Silence: Women and Girls, Race and Relationship, 1995, The Birth of Pleasure: a new map of love, 2002; editor: Women, Girls and Psychotherapy: Reframing Resistance, 1991. Bd. dirs. Ms Initiative in Girls, Facing History & Ourselves. Sr. rsch. fellow Spencer Found., 1984—; Mellon Faculty fellow Bunting Inst.-Radcliffe Coll., 1982-83; recipient Grawemayer award U. Louisville, 1992, Heinz award, 1997. Mem.: APA, Assn. Women in Psychology, Nat. Acad. Edn. Democrat. Jewish. Avocations: music, piano, modern dance, theater. Office: NYU Sch Law 511 Vanderbilt Hall New York NY 10012 Office Phone: 212-998-6048. Business E-Mail: carol.gilligan@nyu.edu.

GILLIGAN, COURTNEY, lawyer; b. 1977; BS, biology & philosophy, Univ. Scranton, 1999; JD highest honors, George Washington Univ., 2002. Bar: N.J., Pa., U.S. Ct. Appeals 8th cir. Law clk. U.S. Ct. Appeals (8th cir.), Fargo, ND, 2002—03; law clk. to Hon. William H. Rehnquist U.S. Supreme Ct., Washington, 2003—04; assoc. Baker Botts LLP, Washington, 2004—. Editor (articles): The George Washington Law Review. Mem.: Order of the Coif. Office: Baker Botts LLP The Warner 1299 Pennsylvania Ave Washington DC 20004-2400

GILLIGAN, EDWARD P., diversified financial services company executive; Pres. corp. services American Express Co., N.Y.C., NY, 1996—2000, group pres., global corp. services, 2000—. Mem. Am. Express Global Leadership Team, Am. Express Planning and Policy Com.; bd. dirs. Ketera Tech. Office: Am Express Co World Fin Ctr 200 Vesey St New York NY 10285

GILLIGAN, KEVIN, manufacturing executive; b. Newburgh, N.Y. BA in Elecs. and Polit. Sci., Boston Coll. Sales rep. energy svc. bldg. svcs. divsn. Honeywell Internat., Inc., 1977—80, various sales mgmt. and mktg. positions, 1980—87, v.p., gen. mgr. bldg. control midwest area, 1988, v.p. bldg. control bus. Europe, 1989—94, pres. home and bldg. control, 1997—2001, pres., CEO automation and control solutions Moristown, NJ, 2001—. Office: Honeywell Internat Inc 101 Columbia Rd Morristown NJ 07962

GILLIGAN, SANDRA KAYE, private school director; b. Ft. Lewis, Wash., Mar. 22, 1946; d. Jack G. and O. Ruth (Mitchell) Wagoner; m. James J. Gilligan, June 3, 1972 (div. June 1998); 1 child, J. Shawn Gilligan. BS in Edn., Emporia State U., 1968, MS in Psychology, 1971; postgrad., Drake U., 1976, U. Mo., St. Louis, 1977-79. Tchr. Parklane Elem. Sch., Aurora, Colo., 1968-69, Bonner Springs (Kans.) Elem., 1970; stewardess Frontier Airlines, Denver, 1969; grad. teaching asst. Emporia (Kans.) State U., 1970-71; lead tchr. Western Valley Youth Ranch, Buckeye, Ariz., 1971-74; staff mem. program devel., lead tchr. The New Found., Phoenix, 1974; ednl. therapist Orchard Pl., Des Moines, 1974-76; ednl. cons. Spl. Sch. Dist. of St. Louis County, 1976-79; founding dir. The Churchill Ctr. and Sch. for Learning Disabilities, St. Louis, 1978—. Instr. Webster Coll., Webster Groves, Mo., 1978-80; adj. prof. Maryville Coll., St. Louis, summer 1985; mem. exec. com. Ind. Schs. of St. Louis; keynote spkr. Miss. Learning Disabilities Assn. Conv., 1991; site visitor blue ribbon schs. program U.S. Dept. Edn., 1992; mem. evaluation rev. Com. Ind. Schs. of Ctrl. States; cert. trainer Human Potential Seminars; exec. com. Ind. Schs. St. Louis; presenter in field. Recipient Spirit Care & Counseling award, 2004. Mem. Learning Disabilities Assn., Internat. Dyslexia Assn. (chpt. bd. dirs.), St. Louis Jr. League. Avocations: gardening, painting. Office: The Churchill Sch 1035 Price School Ln Saint Louis MO 63124-1596 Office Phone: 314-997-4343. E-mail: sgill@churchillschool.org.

GILLILAND, JOHN CAMPBELL, II, lawyer; b. Bellefonte, Pa., June 4, 1945; s. John Campbell and Miriam Ruth (Forsythe) G.; m. Karen Gardner, Nov. 2, 1997; children: Jennifer, John, David. BA, Pa. State U., 1967; JD, Georgetown U., 1971. Bar: Pa. 1971, Ind. 1979, Ky. 1991, Ohio 1992. Ptnr. McQuaide, Blasko & Brown, Inc., State College, Pa., 1974-79, DeFur, Voran, Hanley, Radcliff & Reed, Muncie, Ind., 1979-90; prin. Gilliland & Assocs., Covington, Ky., 1991-2000; sr. counsel Locke Reynolds LLP, Indpls., 2000—01; prin. Gilliland Law Office, Indpls., 2001—02; ptnr. Gilliland & Caudill, Indpls., 2002—. Lectr. econs. dept. Ball State U., Muncie. Bd. dirs. United Way Delaware County, v.p., 1983-85; bd. dirs. Vis. Nurses Assn.; v.p. Muncie chpt. ARC, 1983-85; bd. govs. Friends of Bracken Libr. Served to capt. U.S. Army, 1971-72. Fellow, Rotary Found., Queens Coll., Belfast, Ireland, 1968—69. Mem. ABA, Ind. Bar Assn., Ky. Bar Assn., Ohio Bar Assn., Am. Health Lawyers Assn., Ind. Soc. Hosp. Attys. (chmn. 1989), Pa. Soc. Hosp. Attys. (pres. 1978-79), East Ctrl. Ind. Pers. Assn. (bd. dirs.). Republican. Presbyterian. Home: 3446 Kenilworth Dr Indianapolis IN 46228 Office: 3905 Vincennes Rd Indianapolis IN 46268 Office Phone: 317-704-2400. Business E-Mail: jcg@gilliland.com.

GILLILAND, MICHAEL S., travel company executive; m. Shannon Gilliland; 2 children. BS in Elec. Engring., U. Kans., 1985; MBA, U. Tex., Dallas. With Lockheed Missiles and Space, Austin, Tex.; sr. v.p., gen. mgr., Sabre Bus. Travel Solutions Sabre Holdings, Southlake, Tex., exec. v.p., chief mktg. officer, 2000—02, group pres., Airlines Solutions bus., 2001—02, sr. v.p., gen. mgr., product mktg., pres., CEO, Travelocity, 2002—03, bd. dirs., pres., CEO, 2003—, chmn., 2004—. Office: Sabre Holdings 3150 Sabre Dr Southlake TX 76092*

GILLILLAND, THOMAS, art gallery director; b. Bladen, Nebr., Feb. 14, 1932; s. Whitney and Virginia (Wegmann) G.; m. Cora Lee Critchfield, Aug. 23, 1956; children: Shaun, Ruth, Virginia. Grad., Wentworth Mil. Acad., 1952; BA, Am. U., 1963, MA, 1967. Dep. dir. congl. liaison AID, Washington, 1969-75; congl. liaison officer USDA, Washington, 1975-76, dir. legis. affairs Animal and Plant Health Inspection Svc., 1976-83; dir. external affairs Fin. Mgmt. Svc. U.S. Dept. Treasury, Washington, 1983-93; owner Art in the Hand Gallery, St. Augustine, Fla., 1999—2000. Contbr. mag. articles. Mem.

Nat. Assn. Govt. Communicators (Blue Pencil award 1986), Soc. for Preservation and Encouragement of Barbershop Quartet Singing in Am., Nat. Press Club. Republican. Methodist. Home: 227 Mountain View Dr Willsboro NY 12996-3506

GILLINGHAM, BRYAN REGINALD, music educator; b. Vancouver, B.C., Can., Apr. 12, 1944; s. Reginald Pearce and Ethel Gladys (Collier) G.; m. Helen Campbell, Aug. 11, 1970 (div. 1980); children: Gregory, Sara; m. Susanna Catharine Burton, Oct. 29, 1984; children: Gwendolyn, Miranda, Jeremy. BA, U. B.C., 1966, MusB, 1968; MusM, U. London, 1972; PhD, U. Wash., 1976. Lectr. Mt. Allison U., Sackville, N.B., Can., 1972-73, U. Alta., Edmonton, Can., 1975-76; prof., chmn. Carleton U., Ottawa, Ont., Can., 1976-83. Dir. Inst. Medieval Music, Ottawa, 1985—. Author: The Polyphonic Sequences in Codex Wolfenbüttel 677, 1982, Saint-Martial Mehrstimmigkeit, 1984, Medieval Polyphonic Sequences, 1985, Modal Rhythm, 1986, Secular Medieval Latin Song, 1993, A Critical Study of Secular Medieval Latin Song, 1995, The Social Background to Secular Medieval Latin Song, 1998, Chant & Its Peripheries, 1998; editor (with Donald Beecher) Dovehouse early music edits.; contbr. articles and book revs. to profl. jours. Avocations: wine making, squash, cross country skiing. Office: Carleton U Dept Music Colonel By Dr Ottawa ON Canada K1S 5B6 Office Phone: 613-520-3791.

GILLINGHAM, ROBERT FENTON, economist, consultant; b. Newark, Nov. 13, 1944; s. Evan Stevenson and Eleanor (Fenton) G.; m. Deborah Lynn Wickham, 1989; children: James Stevenson, Sarah Eleanor. BA, Haverford Coll., 1965; PhD, U. Pa., 1973. Economist Bur. Labor Stats., Washington, 1968-73, chief price rsch. div., 1973-82, dep. assoc. commr., 1982-85; dir. office econ. analysis Dept. Treasury, Washington, 1985-88, dep. asst. sec. for econ. policy, 1988-98; cons. Internat. Monetary Fund, Washington, 1998—. Assoc. editor Jour. Bus. and Econ. Stats., 1982-93; contbr. articles to profl. jours. Mem. Am. Econ. Assn., Am. Statis. Assn., Econometric Soc., Western Econ. Assn. (bd. dirs. 1995-98), Conf. on Income and Wealth, Nat. Acad. Social Ins. Home: 20448 Tappahannock Pl Sterling VA 20165-4786 Office: Internat Monetary Fund 700 19th St NW Washington DC 20431-0001

GILLINGS, DENNIS B., medical products executive; Prof. biostats. U.N.C., Chapel Hill; cons. various pharm. cos.; founder, chmn., CEO Quintiles Transnat. Corp., Durham, N.C., 1982—. Named One of 15 Top Biotechnology Execs., Genetic Engring. News, 1994. Office: Quintiles Transnat Corp 4709 Creekstone Dr Ste 200 Durham NC 27703

GILLIO, VICKIE ANN, lawyer; b. Chgo., May 8, 1948; d. Rocco Robert and Viva Gene (Sherover) G. BA cum laude, St. Norbert Coll., 1969; JD, U. Ill., 1972. Bar: Pa. 1974, Ill. 1975, U.S. Dist. Ct. (southeast dist.) Pa. 1975, U.S. Dist. Ct. (no. dist.) Ill. 1978. Atty. Lehigh Valley Legal Svcs., Easton, Pa., 1974-78; with office of spl. counsel U.S. Merit Sys. Protection Bd., 1983-85; atty. in charge Chgo. field office Ill. Civil Svc. Commn., adminstrv. hearing officer, 1978-83; gen. counsel Waubonsee C.C., Sugar Grove, Ill., 1985-88, Kusper & Raucci, Chartered, Chgo., 1988-92, prin., 1990-92, Gillio & Assocs., Chgo., 1992—. Adj. prof. negotiations Chgo. Kent Coll. Law-Ill. Inst. Tech., 1987—; adj. prof. pub. law GPPA program Ill. Inst. Tech. Editor Newsletter of the C.C. Consortium, 1990-92. Mem. ABA (state and local govt. collective bargaining and employment sect., equal employment opportunity sect.), Ill. State Bar Assn. (co-editor newsletter edn.-law sect. 1994-95, past chair edn. law sect., coun.),adminstr. Law Section Coun., Women's Minority Com., Women's Bar Assn. Ill. (bd. dirs. 2000—), Justinians, (co-chair). Home: 210 Thornbrook Rd Dekalb IL 60115-2317

GILLIOM, JUDITH CARR, federal official; b. Indpls., May 19, 1943; d. Elbert Raymond and Marjorie Lucille (Carr) G. BA, Northwestern U., 1964; MA, U. Pa., 1966. Feature writer, asst. women's editor Indpls. News, summers 1961-63; rsch. asst. cultural anthropology Northwestern U., 1963-64, asst. instr. freshman English, 1964; editorial asst. to dir. div. cardiology Phila. Gen. Hosp., 1965-67; asst. to ophthalmologist-in-chief Wills Eye Hosp., Phila., 1967-69; editor, writer Nat. Assn. Hearing and Speech Agencies, Washington, 1969-70; free-lance speech writer White House Conf. Children and Youth, 1969-70; free-lance editor, writer, abstractor, 1971-78; free-lance speechwriter President's Com. Mental Retardation, 1971-78; from dir. publs. to dir. comm. Nat. Assn. Hearing and Speech Action, Silver Spring, Md., 1972-77; editor Hearing & Speech Action mag., 1969-70, 72-77; program mgr. Interagy. Com. on Handicapped Employees, 1978, dep. exec. sec., 1979-83; mgr. disability program Dept. Def., 1983—. Cons. U.S. Archtl. and Transp. Barriers Compliance Bd., 1976-77, Office Ind. Living for Disabled, HUD, 1977-78, Office for Handicapped Individuals, HEW, 1978, Women's com. Pres.'s Com. Employment Handicapped, 1985-86. Mem. Nat. Spinal Cord Injury Assn., 1970-90, editor, pub. conv. jour., 1974-82, bd. dirs. D.C. chpt., 1975-81, 89-90, nat. trustee, 1975-81, nat. bd. dirs., 1978-79; bd. dirs. Nat. Ctr. for a Barrier-Free Environment, 1979-84, v.p., 1980-81, pres., 1981-82; nat. bd. dirs., treas. League Disabled Voters, 1980-85; local bd. dirs. Easter Seal Soc. Disabled Children and Adults, 1985-90; active Montgomery County Commn. on People with Disabilities, 1989-95; mem. Taxicab Svcs. Adv. Com., 1995-99. Recipient Smittkamp award Nat. Paraplegia Found., 1976, Outstanding Svc. award Fed. Asian Pacific Am. Coun., 1990, Geico Pub. Svc. award, 1996, Civilian Career Svc. award Office of Sec. of Def., 1997, Outstanding Leadership award Fed. Asian Pacific Am. Coun., 2002; Woodrow Wilson fellow, 1965. Mem. Phi Beta Kappa, Delta Delta Delta. Home: 901 Arcola Ave Silver Spring MD 20902-3401 Office: Dept Def The Pentagon Rm 5D641 Washington DC 20301-4000 Office Phone: 703-571-9330. Business E-Mail: judy.gilliom@osd.mil.

GILLIOM, MORRIS EUGENE, social studies and global educator; b. Bluffton, Ind., Feb. 10, 1932; s. William Orel and Zella Leota (Gallimore) G.; m. Bonnie Lee Cherp, Dec. 29, 1956; children: Gregor William, Julia Lee. BA, Heidelberg Coll., 1954; MA, Ohio State U., 1958, PhD, 1962. Cert. tchr., Ohio. Tchr. social studies Cleve. Pub. Schs., 1956-59; instr. Ohio State U., Columbus, 1959-62; asst. prof. San Francisco State Coll., 1962-65, U. Chgo., 1965-66; from assoc. prof. to prof. social studies, global edn. Ohio State U., Columbus, 1966-95, prof. emeritus, 1995—, dir. social studies edn. program abroad, 1969-95. Cons. TraveLearn, Lakeville, Pa., group leader programs worldwide; group leader Smithsonian Instn. Programs to China. Author, sr. editor: Practical Methods for the Social Studies, 1977; author, co-editor: Perspectives of Global Education, 1981; contbr. chpts. to books, articles to profl. publs. Mem. Heidelberg Coll. Fellows, Heidelberg Coll. Global Edn. Adv. Coun. With U.S. Army, 1954—56. Recipient Disting. Tchg. award Ohio State U., 1985, Outstanding Alumni award, Heidelberg Coll., 2005; Malone fellow. Mem. Nat. Coun. Social Studies (coll. and univ. faculty assembly), Social Sci. Edn. Consortium (bd. dirs. 1986-90), Ohio Coun. Social Studies, Torch Club. Democrat. Avocations: photography, travel, skiing, reading. Home: 2495 Haverford Rd Columbus OH 43220-4203 Office: Ohio State U 1945 N High St Columbus OH 43210-1120 Fax: 614-451-1763. E-mail: gegilliom@mac.com.

GILLIS, ANDREW J., photographer; b. Ithaca, NY, Mar. 12, 1954; s. Paul Montrose and Mary Elizabeth Gillis. AB, Cornell U., 1976. Photographer, Ithaca, 1976—90; gallery dir. White Apple Gallery, Ithaca, 1978—89; co-founder, adminstr. State of the Art Gallery, Ithaca, 1989—95; co-founder Greater Ithaca Art Trail, 1999; owner Cascadilla Photography, Ithaca, 1990—. Office: Cascadilla Photography 618 Elmira Rd Ithaca NY 14850 Office Phone: 607-272-7386.

GILLIS, EDWIN, information technology executive; BA in govt., Clark U.; MA in internat. rels., U. So. Calif.; MBA, Harvard Bus. Sch. CPA, gen. practice ptnr. Coopers & Lybrand, 1976—91; CFO Lotus Devel. Corp., 1991—95; exec. v.p., CFO Parametric Tech. Corp., 1995—2002, VERITAS Software Corp., Mountain View, Calif., 2002—. Office: VERITAS Software Corp 350 Ellis St Mountain View CA 94043

GILLIS, JOHN LAMB, JR., lawyer; b. St. Louis, June 13, 1939; s. John L. and Carol (Randolph) G.; m. Nichola Mitchell, Aug. 1965; children: John Mitchell, Suzanne Lamb. Student, Brown U.; AB, Washington U., 1965; LLB, Stanford U., 1968. Bar: Mo. 1968. Ptnr., chmn. securities dept. Armstrong Teasdale LLP, St. Louis. Address: Armstrong Teasdale LLP 1 Metropolitan Sq Saint Louis MO 63102-2733 E-mail: jgillis@armstrongteasdale.com.

GILLIS, JOHN SIMON, retired psychologist, educator; b. Washington, Mar. 21, 1937; s. Simon John and Rita Veronica (Moran) G.; m. Mary Ann Wesolowski, Aug. 29, 1959; children: Holly Ann, Mark, Scott. BA, Stanford U., 1959; MS (fellow), Cornell U., 1961; PhD (NIMH fellow), U. Colo., 1965. Lectr. dept. psychology Australian Nat. U., Canberra, 1968-70; sr. psychologist Mendocino (Calif.) State Hosp., 1971-72; asso. prof. dept. psychology Tex. Tech U., Lubbock, 1972-76; prof. psychology Oreg. State U., Corvallis, 1976—2004, chmn. dept. psychology, 1976—84, 1997—2004; ret., 2004. Cons. VA, Ciba-Geigy Pharms., USIA, UN High Commn. for Refugees; commentator Oreg. Ednl. and Pub. Broadcasting System, 1978-79; Fulbright lectr., India, 1982-83, Greece, 1992, Kyrgyzstan, 2001; vis. prof. U. Karachi, 1984, 86, U. Punjab, Pakistan, 1985, Am. U., Cairo, 1984-86. Contbr. articles to profl. jours. Served with USAF, 1968-72. Ciba-Geigy Pharms. grantee, 1971-82 Roman Catholic. Home: 7520 NW Mountain View Dr Corvallis OR 97330-9106 Office: Oreg State U Dept Psychology Corvallis OR 97331 Business E-Mail: jgillis@orst.edu.

GILLIS, JOHN W., federal agency administrator; Grad., Calif. State U., L.A., U. So. Calif. Lt., asst. comdg. officer L.A. Police Dept., 1962—88; ret., 1988; dir. victims of crime U.S. Dept. Justice, Washington, 2001—. Commr. Calif. Bd. Prison Terms, chmn., 1991—93; mem. crime victims and corrections com. Calif. State Bar Assn.; mem. victim com. Am. Legis. Exch. Coun. Founding mem. Justice for Homicide Victims; founder Coalition of Victims Equal Rights, Victims and Friends United; active Memory of Victims Everywhere, Parents of Murdered Children. Named to Am. Plice Hall of Fame; recipient Nat. Crime Victim Svc. award, 1991, Spl. Commendation award, 1993. Achievements include being one of six Black students to integrate the University of Kentucky in 1954. Office: US Dept Justice Victims of Crime 810 7th St NW Washington DC 20531 Office Phone: 202-307-5983, 202-305-2984. Personal E-mail: jwgillis@aol.com.

GILLIS, MALCOLM (STEPHEN GILLIS), former academic administrator; b. Dothan, Ala., Dec. 28, 1940; s. Stephen Malcolm and Eva May (Mac Kinnon) Gillis; m. Elizabeth Cifers, Aug. 18, 1962; children: Eva Leanora, Heather Elizabeth, Stephen Malcolm. BA, U. Fla., 1962, MA, 1963; PhD, U. Ill., 1968; LLD (hon.), Rocky Mountain Coll., 1992. Asst. prof. econs. Duke U., Durham, NC, 1967—69; lectr. in econs. Harvard U., Cambridge, Mass., 1969—73, inst. fellow, 1974—84; prof. econs., pub. policy Duke U., 1984—93, dean grad. sch., vice provost acad. affairs, 1986—91, Z. Smith Reynolds Disting. prof. pub. policy, 1990—93, dean faculty arts and scis., 1991—93; pres. Rice U., Houston, 1993—2004, Irvin Kenneth Zingler prof. economics, 1998—2004. Com. on energy taxation NRC/NAS, 1979—80; coun. econ. policy Office of Gov. State of Alaska, Juneau, 1982—83; mem. seminar on Southeast Asia in world affairs Columbia U., 1982—84; adv. com. energy divsn. Oak Ridge Nat. Lab., 1984—87, chmn. adv. com., 1985—86; internat. adv. bd. KPMG Peat Marwick Policy Econs. Group, 1988—; cons. World Bank, Washington; Disting. Fulbright prof. Cath. U., Chile, 1989; adv. bd. Internat. Ctr. for Econ. Growth, 1986—, Inst. for Policy Reform, 1990—; so. regional adv. bd. Inst. Internat. Edn., 1993—; bd. dirs. Houston Advanced Rsch. Ctr.; presenter in field; bd. dirs. Fed. Res. Bank, Dallas. Author (with others): Fiscal Reform For Colombia, 1971, Taxation and Mining, 1978, Tax and Investment Policies for Hard Minerals, 1980, Economics of Development, 1983; editor: Export Diversification and the New Protectionism, 1981, Public Policy and Misuse of Forest Resources, 1988, The Value-Added Tax in Developing Countries, 1991; mem. editl. bd.: Pakistan Devel. Rev, 1977—80, Quar. Jour. Econs., 1978—79, co-editor; mem. editl. bd.: Tex. Bus. Rev., 1979—83, Pakistan Jour. Applied Econs., 1980—83, Comparative Econ. Studies, 1986—88, referee: various jours.; contbr. articles to profl. jours. Adv. Navajo Indian Nation, Ship Rock, N.Mex., 1983—84; trustee Found. for Hosp. Art, 1989, Francisco Marroquin Found., 1989—, Friends of Edn. in Chile, 1989—, United Way of Tex. Gulf Coast; vice-chmn. higher edn. sector Houston area U.S. Savs. Bond Campaign, 1994; bd. adv. Houston Symphony, 1995; chmn. March of Dimes Gulf Coast Walk Am., 1995; chmn. bd. trustees Ctr. for World Environ. and Sustainable Devel., 1969, 1975, 1983—87, Harvard Inst. Internat. Devel., 1984—; bd. dirs. Am. Forestry Assn., 1989—92; chair U.S. Savs. Bonds, Gulf Coast Region, 2002—04; bd. dirs. South Main Ctr. Assn., 1993—, Greater Houston Partnership, 1993—, St. Luke's Episc. Hosp., 1994—2003, Amigos de las Ams., Consortium on Financing Higher Edn., 1994—, Ind. Colls. and Univs. Tex., 1995—; exec. com. Houston Advanced Res. Ctr. Bd., 1994—, Assn. Am. Univs., 1993—; mem. Houston Lifestock Show and Rodeo; bd. dirs. Indo-Am. C. of C., 2000—, Houston Tech. Ctr., 1999—, BioHouston, 2000—, Tex. Aviation Hall of Fame, 1998—. Grantee, U.S. AID, Washington, 1986—87. Mem.: Houston Philos. Soc., Assn. Pub. Policy Analysis and Mgmt., Nat. Tax Assn., Am. Econ. Assn. Republican. Episcopalian.

GILLIS, MARVIN BOB, retired chemical executive, consultant; b. Treutlen County, Ga., Apr. 5, 1920; s. Bob Lee and Pearl (Gillis) G.; m. Helen Reed, Dec. 23, 1946; children: Margaret Susan, Marvin Reed, Kenneth Robert. BSA., U. Ga., 1940; PhD, Cornell U., 1947. Rsch. assoc. Cornell U., 1947-51; sr. rsch. chemist Internat. Minerals and Chem. Corp., from 1947, asst. dir. rsch., 1956-57, dir. rsch., 1957-64, dir. animal health and nutrition, 1964-66, div. v.p., 1966-70, corp. v.p., 1970-72, sr. v.p., 1972-82; pres., dir. IMC Chem. Group, Inc., 1976-78; pres. Animal Products Group, 1978-82, cons. to exec. office, 1982-86. Sec. Agrl. Rsch. Inst., NRC, 1958-59, v.p., 1960-62, 66-67, pres., 1962-63, 68-69, mem. Agrl. bd., 1962-67; bd. dirs. Animal Health Inst., 1966-69 Author numerous papers in field; patentee in field Served to 1st lt. USAAF, 1942—45. Decorated DFC with oak leaf cluster, Air medal with 3 oak leaf clusters. Mem. North Shore Country Club (Glenview, Ill.), Blue Key, Sigma Xi, Gamma Alpha, Alpha Zeta, Phi Kappa Phi. Baptist. Home: 2500 Indigo Ln 409 Glenview IL 60026

GILLISPIE, HAROLD LEON, minister; b. Levant, Kans., May 11, 1933; s. Harold Leon and Agnes Anne (Dryden) G. BA in Bus. Adminstrn., Kans. Wesleyan U., 1955. Youth dir. Cen. YMCA, Des Moines, 1957-61; exec. dir. West Des Moines br. YMCA, 1961-65; exec. dir. Aurora Br. YMCA, Denver, 1965-69, YMCA, McCook, Nebr., 1969-75, Junction City, Kans., 1975-79; owner H & R Block Franchise, Manhattan, Kans., 1979-91; lay pastor Presbyn. Ch., Oak Hill, Kans., 1996—; vice moderator Presbytery of No. Kans., 1999-00, moderator, 2000-01. Proofreader text H & R Block, Kansas City, Mo., 1986-92. Bd. dirs. Flint Hills Breadbasket, Manhattan, Kans., 1982-89, treas., 1987; bd. dirs. Big Bros. Big Sisters, Manhattan, 1981-85, pres., 1983-85; pres. Downtown Manhattan, Inc., 1986; bd. dirs. Manhattan Main Street, 1986-89; bd. dirs. Ecumenical Campus Ministry, Kans. State U., 1995-99, 2002-2005, chmn., 1996-98 Republican. Presbyterian. Avocations: theology, tennis, baking, working with youth. Home: 710 Bertrand St Manhattan KS 66502-5156 E-mail: pastogil@flinthills.com.

GILLISPIE, ROBERT J., lawyer; b. Washington, Aug. 25, 1943; s. Eugene Render and Gertrude (Pensock) G.; m. Susan Scott (div. Jan. 1977); children: Robert, Megan; m. Barbara Farrell, Oct. 23, 1982; children: Bradley, Todd John. BEE, Catholic U., 1965, JD magna cum laude, 1968. Bar: NY 1969, DC 1977, US Supreme Ct. 1977. Assoc. Mudge, Rose, Guthrie, Alexander & Ferdon, NYC, ptnr., 1977—95; ptnr., corp. dept., leasing & tax dept. Cahdbourne & Parke LLP, NYC, 1995—. Adj. prof. Rutgers U., 1972—76. Contbr.; lectr. in field, editor-in-chief Catholic U. Law Rev., 1967—68. Mem.: DC Bar, ABA, NY Bar Assn. Roman Catholic. Avocation: golf. Office: Chadbourne & Parke LLP 30 Rockefeller Plz New York NY 10112 Office Phone: 212-408-1154. Office Fax: 212-541-5369. Business E-Mail: rgillispie@chadbourne.com.

GILLISPIE, STEVEN BRIAN, systems analyst, researcher; b. Seattle, Oct. 19, 1955; s. Edwin B. and Claudia Mae (Cooper) G. BS in Physics with distinction, BS in Math., U. Wash., 1979, BS in Psychology, BA in Gen. Studies, U. Wash., 1983, MS in Math., 1998. Software specialist Fla. Computer Graphics, Seattle, 1983-84; data analyst coronary artery surgery study U. Wash., Seattle, 1985-87, sci. programmer dept. radiology, 1987-88, systems analyst dept. radiology, 1988—. Dir. devel. med. imaging software Viewbox, 1992; contbr. articles to profl. jours. Mem. Woodland Park Zool. Soc., Seattle, 1986—; contbg. mem. Nordic Heritage Mus., Seattle, 1991—; patron The High Desert Mus., Bend, Oreg., 1991—. Mem. Soc. for Indsl. and Applied Math., U. Wash. Alumni Assn. (life), So. Oreg. Hist. Soc. Office: U Wash Dept Radiology Box 356004 Seattle WA 98195-6004 E-mail: gillisp@u.washington.edu.

GILLISS, CATHERINE LYNCH, nursing educator; b. New Britain, Conn., Apr. 18, 1949; d. James A. and Lorraine Lynch; m. Thomas P. Gilliss, June 6, 1970. BS in Nursing, Duke U., 1971; MS in Nursing, Cath. U. Am., Washington, 1974; D of Nursing Sci., U. Calif., 1983; cert. adult nurse practitioner, U. Rochester, 1979. Staff and charge nurse Duke U. Med. Ctr., Durham, 1971, VA Hosp., Washington, 1971-72; asst. prof. U. Md., Balt., 1974-76, The Cath. U. Am., 1976-79; assoc. prof. U. Portland, Oreg., 1979-83; lectr. in nursing Sonoma State U., Rohnert Park, Calif., 1983-84; prof., chmn. dept. family health care U. Calif., San Francisco, 1984-98, prof. emeritus, 1999—; prof. Sch. Nursing, Yale U., New Haven, 1998—2004, dean Sch. Nursing, 1998—2004, Duke U., Durham, NC, 2004—; vice chancellor nursing affairs Duke U. Health System, 2004—. Chair NIH, Nat. Inst. Nursing Rsch. Study Sect., 1997-99. Co-author: Toward a Science of Family Nursing, 1989, The Nursing of Families, 1993; mem. editl. bd. Families, Systems and Health, 1994-98, jour. Family Nursing; contbr. articles to profl. jours. Bd. dirs. Conn. Inst. for Child Health and Devel., Am. Acad. Nursing, U. Calif. San Francisco Ctr. for the Health Professions. Recipient Disting. Alumna award Duke U., 1991; Pres.'s fellow U. Calif., 1983; Se. fellow Ctr. for Health Professions, 1996-99, Primary Care Policy fellow USPHS, 1993; Regent U. Portland, Oreg., 1994-2000. Fellow Am. Acad. Nursing (bd. dirs. 1999-2004); mem. ANA, Nat. Coun. on Family Rels., Nat. Orgn. Nurse Practitioner Faculty (pres. 1995), Primary Care Fellowship Soc. (pres. 1996-97). Office: Duke Univ Sch of Nursing DUMC 3322 Durham NC 27710

GILLMAN, DANIEL W., information scientist; b. Balt., Mar. 14, 1952; s. Robert D. and Katherine B. Gillman; m. Julie A. Black, Mar. 17, 1990; children: Ivan, Stephanie. BS in Math., U. Md., 1979, MA in Math., 1982. Mathematician U.S. Census Bur., Washington, 1982—88, info. scientist, 1988—2000, Bur. of Labor Stats., Washington, 2000—. Chair INCITS/L8 (Metadata) Standards Com., 1998—, UN/ECE Workgroup on Statis. Metadata, Geneva, 1999—. Editor, author: International Standard Specification and Standardization of Data Elements-Part 1, 1999, Technical Report Procedures for Achieving Metadata Registry Content Consistency, Part 3: Value Domains, 2004; tech. contbr. Metamodel for Management of Sharable Data, Metadata Registries-Part 3, 2003, 2d edit., 2005; contbg. author: Encyclopedia of Knowledge Management, 2005; contbr. numerous articles to profl. jours. Recipient Bronze medal, U.S. Dept. Commerce, 1999. Mem.: Data Documentation Initiative, Internat. Assn. for Social Sci. Info. Svc. Technologies, Am. Statis. Assn. Achievements include development of conceptual model for managing statistical metadata within U.S. and Canadian federal statistical offices. Office: Bureau of Labor Statistics 2 Massachusetts Ave NE Washington DC 20212 Office Phone: 202-691-7523. Business E-Mail: Gillman_D@BLS.gov.

GILLMAN, DEREK A., museum director, academic administrator; m. Yael Gillman; 3 children. MA, Oxford U., England; LLM, U. East Anglia, England. Curator British Mus.; keeper (dir.) Sainsbury Centre Visual Arts, U. East Anglia, Norwich, England; dep. dir. Nat. Gallery Victoria, Melbourne, Australia; exec. dir. & provost Pa. Acad. Fine Arts, Phila., 1999—2001, pres. & CEO, 2001—, pres., CEO, Edna S Tuttleman dir. Mem. Getty Trust Mus. Mgmt. Inst., 1991. Mem.: Norfolk Inst. Art & Design (gov. 1990—95). Office: Pennsylvannia Academy of Fine Arts 1301 Cherry St Philadelphia PA 19107 Office Phone: 215-972-2056. Business E-Mail: dag@pafa.org.

GILLMAN, LEONARD, mathematician, educator; b. Cleve., Jan. 8, 1917; s. Joseph Moses and Etta Judith (Cohen) G.; m. Reba Parks Marcus, Dec. 24, 1938; children: Jonathan Webb, Michal Judith. Diploma (fellow in piano 1933-38), Juilliard Grad. Sch. Music, 1938; BS, Columbia U., 1941, MA (Carnegie fellow math. statistics 1942-43), 1945, PhD, 1953. Asst. in math. dept. Columbia U., 1941-42, lectr., 1942-43; ops. analyst Tufts Coll., MIT, 1943-51; from instr. to assoc. prof. math. Purdue U., 1952-60; prof. math., chmn. dept. U. Rochester, 1960-69; prof. math. U. Tex., Austin, 1969-87, prof. emeritus, 1987, chmn. dept., 1969-73. Mem. Inst. Advanced Study, Princeton, 1958-60; cons. editor W.W. Norton Co., Inc., 1967-80. Author: (with Meyer Jerison) Rings of Continuous Functions, 1960, 76, You'll Need Math, 1967, (with Robert H. McDowell) Calculus, 1973, 78, Writing Mathematics Well, 1987; mem. editorial bd. Topology and Its Applications, 1971-94. Guggenheim fellow, 1958-59; NSF sr. post-doctoral fellow, 1959-60. Mem. Am. Math. Soc. (assoc. sec. 1969-71, mem. com. to monitor problems in commn. 1972-77), Nat. Coun. Tchrs. Math., Math. Assn. Am. (bd. govs. 1973-95, treas. 1973-86, pres.-elect 1986-87, pres. 1987-89, past pres. 1989-90, Lester R. Ford award for expository writing 1994, 2003, Yueh-Gin Gung and Dr. Charles Y. Hu award for disting. svc. to math. 1999). Home and Office: 1606 The High Rd Austin TX 78746-2236 Personal E-mail: lgillman@austin.rr.com.

GILLMOR, CHARLES STEWART, historian, researcher, educator; b. Kansas City, Mo., Nov. 6, 1938; s. Charles Stewart and Evelyn (Noland) G.; m. Rogene Marie Godding, Nov. 28, 1964; children: Charles Stewart III, Alison Bogue. BSEE, Stanford U., 1962; MA, Princeton U., 1966, PhD, 1968; postgrad., U. Colo., 1963. Ionospheric physicist Bur. Standards, Antarctica and Boulder, Colo., 1960-62; instr. history Wesleyan U., Middletown, Conn., 1967-68, asst. prof., 1968-72, assoc. prof., 1973-79, prof. history and sci., 1979—, chmn. dept. history, 1986-88, 91-94; cons. Office Sci. Edn., AAAS, 1973-75. Adv. com. Coun. Internat. Exch. Scholars, 1978—82; cons. NSF, 1983; Hennebach vis. prof. Colo. Sch. Mines, 1996—97; vis. prof. elec. engring. Stanford u., 1998—2001. Author: Coulomb and the Evolution of Physics and Engineering in 18th Century France, 1971, Fred Terman at Stanford, 2004; editor: The History of Geophysics, Vol. 1, 1984, Vol. 2, 1986, Vol. 4, 1990, Vol. 7, 1997; jour. editor: Transactions Am. Geophys. Union, 1983-86; mus. dir. Nutmeg Foxtrot-Jazz Orch., 1990-96; contbr. articles to profl. jours.; recording artist with Leo Records, 1998. Deacon Higganum Congl. Ch., Conn., 1978-96. Mt. Gillmor in Antarctica named in his honor, 1963; Social Sci. Rsch. Coun. grantee, 1971; NSF rsch. grantee, 1972-74, 75-77, 76-79; sr. Fulbright rsch. scholar Cambridge U., Eng., 1976; NASA History scholar, 1980-81; U.S.-France NSF research fellow, Paris, 1984-85; Joseph J. Malone fellow to Tunisia Nat. Coun. U.S.-Arab Rels., 1989; Smithsonian Instn. Lemelson fellow, 2005. Fellow Am. Phys. Soc. (sec.-treas. history of physics divsn. 1988-94, exec. com. 1996-98, chair 1997-98); mem. AAAS, IEEE, Am. Geophys. Union, History of Sci. Soc., Soc. History of Tech. (adv. coun. 1978-82), Sigma Xi. Home: 29 Spencer Rd Higganum CT 06441-4034 Office: Wesleyan Univ Dept History Middletown CT 06459-0002 Office Phone: 860-685-2378. E-mail: sgillmor@wesleyan.edu.

GILLMOR, HELEN, federal judge; BA, Queen's Coll. of CUNY, 1965; LLB magna cum laude, Boston U., 1968. With Ropes & Gray, Boston, 1968-69, Law Offices of Alexander R. Gillmor, Camden, Maine, 1970, Torkildson, Katz, Jossem, Fonseca, Jaffe, Moore & Hetherington, Honolulu, 1971-72; law clk. to Chief Justice William S. Richardson Hawaii State Supreme Ct., 1972; dep. pub. defender Office of Pub. Defender, Honolulu, 1972-74; dist. ct. judge per diem Family Ct. (1st cir.) Hawaii, 1977-83; per diem judge Dist. Ct., 1st circuit, 1983-85; pvt. practice Honolulu, 1985-94; district judge U.S. Dist. Ct. Hawaii, 9th circuit, 1994—. Counsel El Paso Real

Estate Investment Trust, 1969; lectr. U.S. Agy. Internat. Devel., Seoul, South Korea, 1969-70, Univ. Hawaii, 1975. Office: Prince J K Kuhio Fed Bldg 300 Ala Moana Blvd Rm C-400 Honolulu HI 96850-0400

GILLMOR, JOHN EDWARD, lawyer; b. Phila., Oct. 26, 1937; s. John Edward and Louise Ann (Porter) G.; m. Allis Dale Brannon, Aug. 17, 1968; children: Sarah, Abigail, Susan, Eleanor, John, Matthew. BA, Swarthmore Coll., 1959; LL.B., U. Pa., 1962. Bar: D.C. 1962, N.Y. 1963, Tenn. 1972, Pa. 1980. Assoc. Dewey Ballantine Bushby Palmer & Wood, 1962-63, 66-71; v.p., corp. counsel Hosp. Affiliates Internat., Nashville, 1971-78, sr. v.p., gen. counsel, 1978-79; staff v.p., asst. gen. counsel INA Corp., Phila., 1980; sr. v.p., gen. counsel INA Health Care Group, 1981; partner Gillmor, Mills & Gillmor, 1981-83; dir., exec. v.p. Health Am. Corp., 1983-86; ptnr. Gillmor, Anderson & Gillmor, 1986-89, Dearborn & Ewing, 1989-92, Boult, Cummings, Conners & Berry, Nashville, 1992—. Trustee U. Sch. Nashville, 1990-2002; bd. dirs. Nashville Opera Assn., 1996-2002, pres.; bd. dirs. Hoosier CARE, Inc., Am. Eagle Life Care Corp. With USMC, 1963-66. Mem.: ABA, Nashville Bar Assn., Nashville Bar Found., Tenn. Bar Assn. Republican. Home: 1700 Graybar Ln Nashville TN 37215-2106 Office: Boult Cummings Conners & Berry 414 Union St Ste 1600 Nashville TN 37219-1744 Office Phone: 615-252-2305. Business E-Mail: jgillmor@bccb.com.

GILLMOR, KAREN LAKO, state agency administrator; b. Cleve., Jan. 29, 1948; d. William M. and Charlotte (Sheldon) Lako; m. Paul E. Gillmor, Dec. 10, 1983; children: Linda D., Julie E., Paul Michael, Connor W., Adam S. BA cum laude, Mich. State U., 1969; MA, Ohio State U., 1970, PhD, 1981. Asst. to v.p. Ohio State U., Columbus, 1972-77, spl. asst. dean law, 1979-81, assoc. dir. Ctr. Healthcare Policy and Rsch., 1991-92; asst. to pres. Ind. Cen. U., Indpls., 1977-78; rsch. asst. Burke Mktg. Rsch., Indpls., 1978-79; v.p. pub. affairs Huntington Nat. Bank, Columbus, 1981-82; fin. cons. Ohio Rep. Fin. Com., Columbus, 1982-83; chief mgmt. planning and rsch. Indsl. Commn. Ohio, Columbus, 1983-86; mgr. physician rels. Ohio State U. Med. Ctr., Columbus, 1987-91; cons. U.S. Sec. Labor, Washington, 1990-91; mem. Regional Bd. Rev./Indls. Commn., Ohio, 1991-92; state senator Ohio Gen. Assembly, 1993-97; vice-chair State Employment Rels. Bd., 1997—. Legis. liaison Huntington Bancshares, Ohio, Ohio State U., Columbus; trustee Heidelberg Coll., 1999—, Rutherford B. Hayes Presd. Ctr., 2002—. Mem. adv. coun. The Childhood League Ctr., 2003—; nat. bd. dirs. Nat. First Ladies' Libr., 2004—; bd. dirs. Congl. Childcare Ctr., 2003—. Named Outstanding Freshman Ohio Legislator, 1994, Watchdog of the Treasury, 1994, 1996, Outstanding Nat. Freshman Legislator of the Yr., 1995; named to Rocky River HS Hall of Fame, 1998; recipient Pres. award, Ohio State Chriopractic Assn., 1994, Pub. Svc. award, Am. Heart Assn., 1995, Ctr. Advancement and Study of Ethics award, Capitol U. and Trinity Luth. Sem., 1996, cert. of Achievement, U.S. Dept. of Army, 1997, Friend of Medicine award, Ohio State Med. Assn., 1997, Legis. Achievement award, Ohio chpt. Am. Acad. Pediat., 1997, Spirit of Women award, 1999; grantee, Andrew W. Mellon Found., 1978, Carnegie Corp., 1978. Mem.: DAR, Coun. Advancement and Support Edn., Am. Assn. Higher Edn., Ohio Fedn. Rep. Women, Women's Roundtable, Women in Mainstream, Phi Delta Kappa. Methodist. Office: 65 E State St Ste 1200 Columbus OH 43215-4209

GILLMOR, PAUL E., congressman, lawyer; b. Tiffin, Ohio, Feb. 1, 1939; s. Paul Marshall and Lucy Jeannette (Fry) G.; m. Karen Lee Lako, Dec. 10, 1983; children: Linda Dianne, Julie Ellen, Paul Michael, Connor Sheldon, Adam William BA, Ohio Wesleyan U., Delaware, 1961; JD, U. Mich, 1964; LL.D. (hon.), Tiffin U., Ohio, 1985. Bar: Ohio 1965. Mem. Ohio Senate, 1967-89, minority leader, 1978-81, 83-85, pres., 1981-83, 85-88; mem. U.S. Congress from 5th Ohio dist., Washington, 1989—; mem. energy and commerce com., fin. svcs. com., dep. majority whip. Assoc. firm Tomb and Hering, Tiffin, 1967-88; bd. dirs. Old Fort Banking Co., Ohio. Pres. Ohio Electoral Coll., Columbus, 1984. Served to capt. USAF, 1965-67. Recipient Gov.'s award, Ohio, 1980; Phillips medal of pub. service Ohio U. Coll. Osteopathy, 1981; Exec. Order, Ohio Commodores Assn., 1981; Disting. Citizen award Med. Coll. Ohio, 1982; named Legislator of Yr., Ohio VFW, 1994. Mem. ABA, Ohio State Bar Assn., Nat. Republican Legislators Assn. (named Outstanding Legislator of Yr. 1983). Republican. Methodist. Office: US Ho of Reps Office House Mems 1203 Longworth Bldg Washington DC 20515-3505*

GILLMORE, TAMMY LYNN, literature and language professor; b. West Plains, Mo., Oct. 25, 1966; d. Ollie Jo and Wilford Friel; m. John Gillmore, Nov. 19, 2004; children: Holly Hernandez, Julie, Nathan. English Edn., Lyon Coll., 1985—89; Secondary Adminstrn., Ark. State U. English tchr. Sulphur Rock H.S., Sulphur Rock, Ark., 1995—. Recipient Indepedence County Tchr. of the Yr., Citizen's Bank, 2002, Outstanding Cooperating Tchr. award, Ark. Assn. of Tchr. Educators, 2004, Ark. Tchr. of the Yr. Regional Finalist, Ark. Dept. of Edn., 2002, 2004. Mem.: Ark. Coun. of Teachers of English and Lang. Arts, Nat. Coun. of Teachers of English, Assn. of Supervision and Curriculum. Home: 700 Mt Hermon Rd Charlotte AR 72522 Office: Sulphur Rock Sch Dist PO Box 98 Sulphur Rock AR 72579 Office Phone: 870-799-8088. Office Fax: 870-799-8099. Personal E-mail: tammygillmore@yahoo.com.

GILLOM, JENNIFER, professional basketball player; b. Abbeville, Miss., June 13, 1964; Grad., U. Miss., 1986. Basketball player Italian League, Milan, 1987—91, Ancona, 1991—94, Messina, 1995—96, Athens, Greece, 1996—97, Phoenix Mercury, WNBA, 1997—2002, Los Angeles Sparks, WNBA, 2003—. Named an Sports Hall of Fame, U. Miss., 1999; named to All WNBA 2nd Team, 1997, All WNBA 1st Team, 1998, Inaugural WNBA All-Star Team, 2000; recipient Gold medal, Pan Am. Games, 1987, Olympic Games, 1988, Nat. Distinction award, U. Miss., 1998, Kim Perrot Sportsmanship award, 2002, USA Basketball World Championship Team, 2002. Office: Phoenix Mercury 201 E Jefferson St Phoenix AZ 85004-2412

GILLON, PETER M., lawyer; b. Phila., Mar. 9, 1957; AB magna cum laude, Duke Univ., 1979; JD, Georgetown Univ., 1983. Bar: Fla. 1983, DC 1984. Shareholder, chair nat. insurance coverage and adv. practice, co-chair nat. environ. practice Greenberg Traurig LLP, Washington. Assoc. editor Tax Lawyer; contbr. articles to profl. journals. Mem.: ABA (chmn., subcom. bankruptcy and litig., litig. sect. com.). Office: Greenberg Traurig LLP Ste 500 800 Connecticut Ave NW Washington DC 20006 Office Phone: 202-331-3100. Office Fax: 202-331-3101. Business E-Mail: gillonp@gtlaw.com.

GILLUM, RODERICK D., automotive executive; b. Detroit; BA, Mich. State U., 1972; JCD, Northeastern U. Sch. Law, 1975; MS in Mgmt., Mass. Inst. Tech., 1985. Atty. Nat. Labor Rels. Bd., Detroit; with GM Corp., mgr. strategic planning, 1985—86, v.p., gen. coun., sec., 1988—93; sec. GM Bd. Dirs., 1986—88; chief pers. labor atty. GM Corp., 1988—97, v.p. corp. respsibility, diversity, 1997—. Admin. asst. Mich. Senator Arthur Cartwright. Mem.: ABA Coll. Labor Employment (fellow), New Detrot (bd.mem.), Mich. Colls. Found. (bd.mem.), Detroit Econ. Corp. (bd. mem.), Martin Luther King Jr. Nat. Meml. Project Found. (bd.mem.), Charles H. Wright Mus. African Am. His (bd.mem.), Harvard U. Kennedy Sch. Govt. (bd. mem.), Hispanic Assn. Corp. Responsibility (bd. mem.), Nat. Coun. LaRaza (bd. mem.), Congl. Black Caucus Found. (bd. mem.), Nat. Urban League (bd. mem.), Holcim Inc. (chair, audit com.). Office: GM Corp 300 Renaissance Ctr Detroit MI 48265-3000

GILMAN, ALAN B., restaurant company executive; b. South Bend, Ind., Sept. 24, 1930; s. Sol M. and Lee R. (Rintzler) G.; m. Phyllis Schrager, Feb. 16, 1951; children: Bruce, Jeffrey, Lynn. AB with highest honors (Raymond Charles Stoltz scholar), Ind. U., 1952, MBA (John H. Edwards fellow), 1954. With Lazarus Co. div. Federated Dept. Stores, Inc., Columbus, Ohio, 1954-64, div. mdse. mgr., 1961-64; with Sanger Harris div. Federated Dept. Stores, 1965-74, chmn. bd., chief exec. officer, 1970-74; corp. v.p. Federated Dept. Stores, 1974-80; with Abraham & Straus div. Federated Dept. Stores, 1975-80, chmn. bd., chief exec. officer, 1978-80; pres. Murjani Internat. Ltd., N.Y.C., 1980-85; pvt. investor, 1985-87; chmn. At Ease of Newport Beach (Calif.) Inc., 1988-91; pres., CEO Consol. Products Inc., 1992—2002; chmn. Steak 'n Shake Co., Indpls., 2002—. Vice-chmn. bd. dirs. Ind. U. Found., 2000-03, nat. chmn. ann. giving, 1983, presdl. search com., 1987-88; chmn. dean's adv. coun. Ind. U. Grad. Sch. Bus., 1976-86; dean's adv. coun. Coll. Arts and Scis., Ind. U., 1989—, pres.'s cabinet, 1995=2003; bd. dirs., pres., exec. com. Greater N.Y. Fund-United Way, 1984-87; bd. dirs., exec. com., chmn. strategic planning com. United Way of N.Y.C., 1982-88; dir. Corp. Comty. Coun., Indpls., 1992-2001, Greater Indpls. Progress Com., Kelley Restaurants, Inc.; trustee Com. for Econ. Devel. Recipient Humanitarian of Yr. award Juvenile Diabetes Found., 1979, Disting. Alumni Svc. award Ind. U., 1996. Mem. Young Pres. Orgn. 49'er, Ind. U. Acad. Alumni Fellows, World Bus. Council, Phi Beta Kappa Fellows, Phi Alpha Theta, Beta Gamma Sigma (charter mem. dirs. table) Office: The Steak and Shake Co 500 Century Bldg 36 S Penn Ave Indianapolis IN 46204 Office Phone: 317-633-4100. *Value intellectual curiosity, an open mind, the greater import of tomorrow over yesterday, and recognize rapid change as the definition of opportunity while maintaining a sense of humor and honest humility.*

GILMAN, ALFRED GOODMAN, pharmacologist, educator; b. New Haven, July 1, 1941; s. Alfred and Mabel (Schmidt) Gilman; m. Kathryn Hedlund, Sept. 21, 1963; children: Amy, Anne, Edward. BS, Yale U., 1962, DMS (hon.), 1997; MD, PhD, Case Western Res. U., 1969, DSc (hon.), 1995, U. Chgo., 1991, U. Miami, 1999. Pharmacology rsch. assoc. NIH, Bethesda, Md., 1969—71; from asst. prof. to assoc. prof. pharmacology U. Va., Charlottesville, 1971—77, prof., 1977—81, dir. med. sci. tng. program, 1979—81; prof. pharmacology, chmn. dept. U. Tex. Southwestern Med. Ctr., Dallas, 1981—, Raymond and Ellen Willie disting. chmn. molecular neuropharmacology, 1987—, regental prof., 1994—, acting dean, 2004—, dir. Cecil H. and Ida Green Comprehensive Ctr. for Molecular Computational and Sys. Biol., 2004—, interim dean Southwestern Med. Sch., 2004—; chmn. steering com. The Alliance for Cellular Signaling, 2000—. Mem. pharmacology study sect. NIH, 1977—81, mem. nat. adv. gen. med. scis. coun., 1992—95; bd. sci. counselors Nat. Heart, Lung and Blood Inst. NIH, 1982—86; sci. adv. com. Am. Cancer Soc., N.Y.C., 1982—86; adv. com. Lucille P. Markey Charitable Trust, Miami, 1984—96; sci. rev. bd. Howard Hughes Med. Inst., Bethesda, 1986—93; dir. Regeneron Pharmaceutics, 1989—, Eli Lilly and Co., Inc., 1995—; mem. vis. com. Sch. Medicine Case Western Reserve U., 1995—99; mem. sci. adv. bd. Huntsman Cancer Inst., U. Utah, 1995—2000, Ernest Gallo Clinic and Rsch. Ctr., U. Calif., San Francisco, 1996—2001. Editor The Pharmacological Basis of Therapeutics, 1975, 1980, 1985, 1990, cons. editor, 1996, 2001, contbr. over 240 articles to profl. jours. Recipient Poul Edvard Poulsson award, Norwegian Pharmacology Soc., 1982, Gairdner Found. Internat. Award, Can., 1984, Albert Lasker Basic Med. Rsch. award, 1989, Passano Sr. award, Passano Found., 1990, Waterford Biomed. Sci. award, Scripps Clinic and Rsch. Found., 1990, Basic Sci. Rsch. prize, Am. Heart Assn., 1990, City of Medicine award, Durham, N.C., 1991, Ciba-Geigy Drew award, 1991, Nobel prize in Physiology or Medicine, 1994, ACP award, 1995, Disting. Alumnus award, Case Western Reserve U., 1995, Am. Acad. Achievement award, 1995, Med. Honor award, Am. Cancer Soc., 1995. Mem.: NAS (Richard Lounsbery award 1987), Am. Acad. Arts and Scis., Inst. Medicine NAS, Am. Soc. Biol. Chemistry, Am. Soc. Pharmacology and Exptl. Therapeutics (John J. Abel award in pharmacology 1975, Louis S. Goodman and Alfred Gilman award 1990, Torald Sollman award 1997). Office: U Tex Southwestern Med Ctr Dept Pharmacology 5323 Harry Hines Blvd Dallas TX 75390-9041 Office Phone: 214-648-2370. E-mail: alfred.gilman@utsouthwestern.edu.

GILMAN, BENJAMIN ARTHUR, former congressman, lawyer; b. Poughkeepsie, N.Y., Dec. 6, 1922; s. Harry and Esther (Gold) G.; m. Jane Prizant, Oct. 19, 1952 (div. 1978); children: Jonathan, Harrison, Susan, David (dec.), Ellen (dec.); m. Rita Gail Keller Kelhoffer, Nov. 9, 1984 (div. 1996); m. Georgia Nickles Tingus, Jan. 12, 1997; children: Nicole, Peter. BS, SUNY, 1946; LLB, N.Y. Law Sch., 1950; degree (hon.), St. Thomas Aquinas Coll., 1977, Mercy Coll., 1984, Yeshiva U., 1995, Dominican Coll., 2003, U. Bridgeport, 2003, Inje U., South Korea, 2004. Bar: N.Y. 1952. Dep. asst. atty. gen. N.Y. Dept. Law, 1952-54, asst. atty. gen., 1954-55; ptnr. Gilman & Gilman, Middletown, NY, 1955-72; counsel N.Y. Assembly's Com. on Local Fin., 1956-64; mem. N.Y. State Assembly, 1967-72; congressman 93d-97th Congresses from 26th N.Y. dist., 1972-82, 20th dist. N.Y., 1983—2002; sr. counsel Finkelstein & Ptnrs., New Windsor, NY, 2003—04. Mem. Rep. Congl. Policy Com., 1997-2002; mem. Presdl. Commn. on World Hunger, 1978-80, co-chair Ad-Hoc Com. on Irish Affairs, Rep. Task Force on Handicapped and Task Force on Econ. Policy; mem. U.S.-Mex. Consultative Mechanism Subcom. on Narcotics Trafficing, co-founder Ho Select Com. on Narcotics; U.S. Congl. rep. to 36th session UN Gen. Assembly; pub. del. U.S. UN Mission 58th Gen. Assembly, 2003; mem. Spkrs.'s Task Force on Narcotics; chmn. House Task Force on Prisoners of War and Missing in Action, 1983-85; mem. World Hunger Yr. Bd.; mem. adv. com. N.Y. State Divsn. Youth's Start Ctr., 1962-67; mem. N.Y. State Southeastern Water Study Com., 1971-73, Lawyers' Com. for Civil Rights Under Law, 1963-75; mem. adv. com. Otisville Fed. Correctional Instn.; v.p., bd. dirs. Orange County Health Assn.; adv. coun. Lamont-Doherty Geol. Obs., Columbia U., 1979-82; chmn. House Internat. Com. on Fgn. Affairs, 1995-2001; bd. dirs. Co-Operation Ireland, U.S., 2004-. Bd. dirs. Bnai Zion, 2003-, Humpty Dumpty Inst., Nat. Legis. Office Jewish War Vets., 2000—; mem. chmn.'s adv. bd. U.S. Inst. for Peace; mem. Com. on Present Danger, 2005—, Haiti Internat. Assessment Com., Internat. Rep. Inst., 2005—; chmn. bd. dirs. Middletown Little League; bd. trustees Am. U. Antigua, 2005—; bd. visitors U.S. Mil. Acad., 1973-83; lt. col. USAAF, 1943-45, Japan; col. N.Y. Guard. Decorated D.F.C., Air medals; recipient Disting. Svcs. award HHS Adminstrn. Law Judges, 1980, Silver Beaver award Boy Scouts Am., 1994, Am. Hellenic Percles award, 1996, FBI and DEA Jt. award for promoting internat. fight vs. drugs and crime, 2000, Disting. Svc. award U.S. Dept. State, 2001, award Anti Defamation League, 2004; named to St. Thomas Aquinas Hall of Fame, 2004; established Grad. Sch. scholarships U. Belfast, No. Ireland, U. Limerick, Ireland; Benjamin A. Gilman Internat. Congl. Ann. Internat. Scholarship named in his honor, 2000. Mem. ABA, D.C. Bar Assn., N.Y. State Bar Assn., Assn. of Bar of City of N.Y., Middletown Bar Assn., Orange County Bar Assn., Assn. Trial Lawyers Am., VFW (past county comdr.), Am. Legion, Masonic War Vets. (lt. comdr.), Jewish War Vets., Forty and Eight, Air Force Assn., Internat. Narcotics Enforcement Officers, N.Y. Law Sch. Alumni (advisor), N.Y. Soc. in Washington (pres.), Grange, La Société des 40 Hommes et 8 Chevaux, Masons (33 deg.), Shriners (Capitol Hill pres.), Elks, DAV (hon.), Vietnam Vets. (hon.), Nat. Sojourners. Republican. Jewish. Achievements include the creation of the Gilman International Library at SUNY Orange County Community College named in his honor. Office: The Gilman Group 1625 K St Ste 1070 Washington DC 20006 Office Phone: 202-659-3333.

GILMAN, FRANCES H., science educator; b. Newton, Mass., May 29, 1952; s. Nicanor Garcia Montt and Frances Helen Martin; m. Steven Brian Gilman, Sept. 24, 1983; 1 child, Daniel Brian. BSc, Northeastern U., 1982; MSc, St. Joseph U., 1988. Cert. radiological tech. cert. North Eastern U., 1974. Staff radiological tech. Boston City Hosp., 1974—75, chief tech., 1975—83; tech. specialist Polaroid Corp., Boston, 1982—84; imaging system specialist Asta-Gevaeit, Ridgefield, NJ, 1985—87; clin. instr. Cmty. Coll. of Phila., 1989—98; instr. Thomas Jefferson U., Phila., 1993—2003, chair, asst. prof., 2003—. Mem.: Am. Soc. Radiol. Scis., Am. Assn. of Educators, Phila. Soc. of Radiol. Tech. (chair 1998—99, pres. 1995—96). Avocations: skiing, snorkeling. Home: 854 Penn Way West Chester PA 19382 Office: Thomas Jefferson U 130 south 9th Ste 1010 Philadelphia PA 19107 Business E-Mail: frances.gilman@jefferson.edu.

GILMAN, JOHN JOSEPH, research scientist; b. St. Paul, Dec. 22, 1925; s. Alexander Falk and Florence Grace (Colby) G.; m. Pauline Marie Harms, June 17, 1950 (div. Dec. 1968); children: Pamela Ann, Gregory George, Cheryl Elizabeth; m. Gretchen Marie Sutter, June 12, 1976; 1 son, Brian Alexander. BS, Ill. Inst. Tech., 1946, MS, 1948; PhD, Columbia, 1952. Research metallurgist Gen. Electric Co., Schenectady, 1952-60; prof. engring. Brown U., Providence, 1960-63; prof. physics and metallurgy U. Ill., Urbana, 1963-68; dir. Materials Research Center Allied Chem. Corp., Morristown, N.J., 1968-78; dir. Corp. Devel. Center, 1978-80; mgr. corp. research Amoco Co. (Ind.), Naperville, Ill., 1980-85; assoc. dir. Lawrence Berkeley Lab./U. Calif., Calif., 1985-87; sr. scientist Lawrence Berkeley Lab., Calif., 1987-93; adj. prof. UCLA, 1993—. Author: Micromechanics of Flow in Solids, 1969, Inventivity-The Art and Science of Research Management, 1992, Electronic Basis of the Strength of Materials, 2003; editor: The Art and Science of Growing Crystals, 1963, Fracture of Solids (with D.C. Drucker), 1963, Atomic and Electronic Structures of Metals, 1967, Metallic Glasses, 1973, Energetic Materials, 1993; editl. bd. Jour. Applied Physics, 1969-72; contbg. editor Materials Tech., 1994-99; contbr. over 325 papers, articles to tech. jours. Served as Ensign USNR, 1943-46. Recipient Mathewson gold medal Am. Inst. Metal Engrs., 1959, Disting. Service award Alumni Assn. Ill. Inst. Tech., 1962, Application to Practice award, 1985. Fellow AAAS, Am. Phys. Soc., The Materials Soc., Am. Soc. for Metals (Campbell lectr. 1966); mem. Nat. Acad. Engring., Phi Kappa Phi, Tau Beta Pi. Home: 2852 Forrester Dr Los Angeles CA 90064-4662 Office: UCLA 6532 Boelter Hl Los Angeles CA 90095-0001 Office Phone: 310-825-9608. Business E-Mail: gilman@seas.ucla.edu.

GILMAN, KENNETH B., retail executive; Formerly v.p., corp. contr. The Limited Inc., Columbus, Ohio, exec. v.p., chief fin. officer, 1987—93, vice chmn., chief adminstrv. officer, 1993—2001; vice chmn. Intimate Brands, Inc., Columbus, Ohio, 1998; CEO Lane Bryant, Reynoldsburg, Ohio, 2001; pres., CEO Asbury Automotive Group, Stamford, Conn., 2001—. Office: Three Landmark Square Ste 500 Stamford CT 06901*

GILMAN, RICHARD CARLETON, retired college president; b. Cambridge, Mass., July 28, 1923; s. George Phillips Brooks and Karen Elise (Theller) G.; m. Lucille Young, Aug. 28, 1948 (dec. 1978); children: Marsha, Bradley Morris, Brian Potter, Blair Tucker; m. Sarah Gale, Dec. 28, 1984 (dec. 1986). BA, Dartmouth Coll., 1944; student, New Coll., U. London, Eng., 1947-48; PhD (Borden Parker Bowne fellow), Boston U., 1952, LHD, 1969; LLD, Pomona Coll., 1966, U. So. Calif., 1968, Coll. Idaho, 1968; LHD, Chapman Coll., 1984, Occidental Coll., 1988. Teaching fellow religion Dartmouth, 1948; mem. faculty Colby Coll., 1950-56, assoc. prof. philosophy, 1955-56; exec. dir. Nat. Council Religion Higher Edn., New Haven, 1956-60; dean coll., prof. philosophy Carleton Coll., 1960-65; pres. Occidental Coll., L.A., 1965-88, pres. emeritus, 1988—; pres., mng. trustee S.W. Mus., L.A., 1994-95. Past mem. bd. dirs. Am. Coun. on Edn., Assn. Am. Colls., Assn. Ind. Calif. Colls. and Univs., Coun. for Fin. Aid to Edn., Coun. on Postsecondary Accreditation, Nat. Coun. Ind. Colls. and Univs., Ind. Coll. Funds Am.; mem. Intergovtl. Adv. Coun. on Edn., 1980-84; mem. president's commn. NCAA, 1984-86; exec. asst., counselor to sec. of edn., 1979-80; mem. Calif. Student Aid Commn., 1988-92. Bbd. dirs. Wellness Cmty.-Foothills, pres., 1996-98; past mem. bd. dirs. Calif. Mus. Found., Cape of Good Hope Found., Exec. Svc. Corp. Calif., S.W. Mus., L.A. World Affairs Coun. Fellow Soc. for Values in Higher Edn.; mem. Calif. C. of C. (past bd. dirs.), Calif. Club L.A., Twilight Club (Pasadena), Phi Beta Kappa. Home: 131 Annandale Rd Pasadena CA 91105-1405 Personal E-mail: rcgilman@earthlink.net.

GILMAN, RICHARD H., newspaper publishing executive; BA in Govt. and Journalism, U. Ariz., 1972; MBA, Harvard Bus. Sch., 1983. Positions including copy editor, asst. city editor, city editor Ariz. Daily Star, Tucson, 1970—78, asst. mng. editor, 1978—81; named asst. to v.p. circulation NY Times, NYC, 1983, positions in circulation, 1983—87, managerial positions in prodn., 1988—91, positions in systems & tech., 1991—92, v.p. systems & tech., 1992—93, sr. v.p. ops., 1993—99, added responsibility for circulation dept., 1998—99; pub. The Boston Globe, Boston, 1999—. Office: Boston Globe PO Box 2378 135 Morrissey Blvd Boston MA 02107-2378*

GILMAN, RONALD LEE, federal judge; b. Memphis, Oct. 16, 1942; s. Seymour and Rosalind (Kuzin) Gilman; m. Betsy Dunn, June 11, 1966; children: Laura M., Sherry I. BS, MIT, 1964; JD cum laude, Harvard U., 1967. Bar: Tenn. 1967, U.S. Supreme Ct. 1971. Mem. Farris, Mathews, Gilman, Branan & Hellen, Memphis, 1967—97; judge U.S. Ct. Appeals (6th cir.), 1997—. Judge Tenn. Ct. Judiciary, 1979—87; lectr. trial advocacy U. Memphis Law Sch., 1980—97; arbitrator, mediator Am. Arbitration Assoc., 1988—97; arbitrator NASD, 1993—97; referee Pvt. Adjudication Ctr., 1994—97. Contbr. articles to profl. jours. Regional chmn. ednl. coun. MIT, 1968—88; active Chickasaw coun. Boy Scouts Am., 1993—2000; mem. Leadership Memphis; bd dirs Memphis Jewish Home, 1984—87. Recipient Sam A. Myar Jr. Meml. award for outstanding svc. to legal profession and cmty., 1981. Mem.: ABA (ho. of dels. 1990—97), Am. Arbitration Assn. (mem. large, complex case panel 1993—97), Tenn. Bar Assn. (spkr. ho. of dels. 1985—87, pres. 1990—91), Memphis Bar Assn. (pres. 1987), Am. Coll. Trust and Estate Counsel, Am. Judicature Soc., Am. Law Inst., 6th Cir. Jud. Conf. (life). Democrat. Jewish. Office: Fed Bldg 167 N Main St Ste 1176 Memphis TN 38103-1824

GILMAN, SANDER LAWRENCE, German language educator; b. Buffalo, Feb. 21, 1944; s. William and Rebecca (Helf) G.; m. Marina von Eckardt, Dec. 28, 1969; children: Daniel, Samuel. BA, Tulane U., 1963, PhD, 1968; postgrad., U. Berlin and U. Munich, Ger.; LLD (hon.), U. Toronto, Ont., 1997. Lectr. German St. Mary's Dominican Coll., New Orleans, 1963-64; instr. Dillard U., New Orleans, 1967-68; asst. prof. Case Western Res. U., 1968-69; mem. faculty Cornell U., 1969-94, prof. German, 1976-94, prof. Near Eastern studies, 1984-91, prof. humane studies, 1984-87, Goldwin Smith prof., 1987-94, chmn. dept. German lit., 1974-81, 83-84; fellow dept. psychiatry Cornell U. Med. Coll., 1977-78; prof. history of psychiatry Cornell U., 1978-94; prof. German, history of sci. and psychiatry U. Chgo., 1994-2000, Henry R. Luce prof. Liberal Arts in Human Biology, 1995-2000, disting. svc. prof., 1999-2000; disting. prof. liberal arts & scis. and medicine U. Ill., Chgo., 2000—. O'Connor prof. Colgate U., 1982-83; Mellon prof. Tulane U., 1988, Old Dominion prof. English, Princeton U., 1988; Northrup Frye prof. of comparative lit. U. Toronto, Ont., Can., 1989; vis. prof. German lit. Free U. Berlin, 1989; vis. hist. scholar Nat. Libr. Medicine, 1991-92; vis. Rudolph prof. Jewish studies Syracuse (N.Y.) U., 1992; vis. prof. U. Witwatersrand, South Africa, 1994, U. Potsdam, 1996, U. Cape Town, 1996, Ctr. for Advanced Studies in the Behavioral Scis., 1996-97, Getty Inst. for Art and the Humanities, 1998, Am. Acad., Berlin, 2000-01. Author, editor.: Bertolt Brecht's Berlin, 1975, Nietzschean Parody, 1976, The Face of Madness, 1976, Klingers Werke, 1978, On Blackness Without Blacks, 1982, Begegnungen mit Nietzsche, 1981, Difference and Pathology, 1985, Jewish Self-Hatred, 1986, Oscar Wilde's London, 1987, Conversations with Nietzsche, 1987, Diseases and Representation, 1989, Sexuality: An Illustrated History, 1989, Nietzsche on Rhetoric and Language, 1989, The Jew's Body, 1991, Inscribing the Other, 1991, Rasse, Seuche, Sexualitat, 1992, Freud, Race, Gender, 1993, The Case of Sigmund Freud, 1993, Reading Freud Reading, 1993, Reemerging Jewish Culture in Germany, 1994, Jews in Today's German Culture, 1995, Health and Illness, 1995, Franz Kafka: The Jewish Patient, 1996, L'Autre et Le Moi, 1996, Smart Jews, 1996, Yale Companion to Jewish Writing and Thought in German Culture, 1997, Love and Marriage with Death, 1998, Creating Beauty to Cure the Soul, 1998, Making the Body Beautiful, 1999, Jurek Becker: Die Biographie, 2002; mem. editl. bd. Diacritics, 1971-72, Lessing Yearbook, 1974—, German Quar., 1977-86, Confinia Psychiatrica, 1978-80. Guggenheim fellow, 1972-73, IREX exch. fellow German Democratic Republic, 1976, Soc. for Humanities faculty fellow Cornell U., 1981-82, Nat. Libr. Medicine sr. historian, fellow, 1990-91, Ctr. for the Adv. Study of the Behaviorial Scis. fellow, Stanford, 1996-97, Am. Acad., Berlin, 2000—. Mem. MLA (pres. 1995), Lessing Soc., Am. Assn. Tchrs. German, Soc. Internat. d'Études Littéraires et Psychiatres, Internat. Assn. Germanists. Democrat. Jewish. Home: 5701 S Dorchester Ave Chicago IL 60637-1726 E-mail: sander34@aol.com.

GILMAN, SHELDON GLENN, lawyer; b. Cleve., July 20, 1943; BBA, Ohio U., 1965; JD, Case Western Res. U., 1967. Bar: Ohio 1967, Ky. 1971, Ind. 1982, Fla. 1984, DC 1985, Tenn. 1985, U.S. Supreme Ct. 1987. From assoc. to ptnr. law firms, Louisville, 1972—; ptnr. Lynch, Cox, Gilman &

Mahan, P.S.C., Louisville, 1987—. Gen. counsel Louisville Assn. Life Underwriters, 1977, 78, 90; adj. prof. law U. Louisville Sch. Law; spkr. in field. Author: Kentucky Estate Planning, 2d edit., 2003; contbr. articles to profl. jours. Bd. dirs., chmn. Louisville Minority Bus. Resource Ctr., 1975—80; bd. dirs., v.p., sec. Louisville Orch., 1982—85; bd. dirs. City of Devondale, Ky., 1976; pres. Congregation Adath Heshurun, 1986—88; bd. dirs. United Synagogue Cons. Judaism, NY, pres. Ohio Valley region. With JAGC U.S. Army, 1968—71. Fellow: Am. Bar Found., Am. Coll. Trust and Estate Counsel; mem.: ACLU (bd. dirs. 1998—), Louisville Employee Benefit Coun. (pres. 1980), Ky. Bar Assn. (mem. ethics com. 1982—, mem. ethics hotline com. 1990). Office: Lynch Cox Gilman & Mahan 500 W Jefferson St Ste 2100 Louisville KY 40202 Office Phone: 502-589-4215. Business E-Mail: SGilman@lcgandm.com.

GILMAN, SID, neurologist; b. L.A., Oct. 19, 1932; s. Morris and Sarah Rose (Cooper) G.; m. Carol G. Barbour. BA, UCLA, 1954; MD, 1957, FRCP, 2001. Intern UCLA Hosp., 1957-58; resident in neurology Boston City Hosp., 1960-63; from instr. to assoc. in neurology Harvard Med. Sch., 1965-68; from asst. prof. to prof. neurology Columbia U., N.Y.C., 1968-76, H. Houston Merritt prof. neurology, 1976-77; William J. Herdman prof. neurology U. Mich., Ann Arbor, 1977—, chair dept. neurology, 1977—2004, D. Denny-Brown disting. prof., 2005—. Cons. VA Hosp., Ann Arbor, 1977—; mem. peripheral and ctrl. nervous sys. drugs adv. com. FDA, 1983-85, 86-87, 90-94, chmn., 1996-2000, cons., 2000—; adj. attending neurologist Henry Ford Hosp., Detroit; mem. chronic disease adv. com. Mich. Dept. Pub. Health, 1988-94; mem. neurol. sci. rsch. and tng. com. NIH, 1971-73, mem. neurol. disorders program project B com., 1976-80, mem. sci. programs adv. com. Nat. Inst. Neurol. Diseases, Communicative Disorders and Stroke, 1982-84, mem. nat. adv. neurol. disorders and stroke coun., 1994-97; mem. clin. trials subcom. Nat. Adv. Neurol. Disorders and Stroke Coun., 2001—; dir. Mich. Alzheimer's Disease Rsch. Ctr., 1991—; mem. rsch. adv. coun. United Cerebral Palsy Found.; mem. sci. adv. coun. Nat. Ataxia Found., Nat. Amyotrophic Lateral Sclerosis Found., Inc.; mem. profl. adv. bd. Epilepsy Found. Am.; mem. rsch. adv. com. Nat. Multiple Sclerosis Soc., 1986-90; mem. exec. bd. Nat. Coalition for Rsch., 1989-95, Nat. Found. for Brain Rsch., 1989-95; mem. rsch. adv. com. Dana Alliance; mem. sci. adv. bd. Merck, Inc., 2000-04, PPD Devel., 1999—, INC Rsch., 2000—; Henry Russel lectr. U. Mich., 2001. Author: (with J.R. Bloedel and R. Lechtenberg) Disorders of the Cerebellum, 1981, (with S.W. Newman) Manter and Gatz's Essentials of Clinical Neuroanatomy and Neurophysiology, 10th edit., 2003, (with J.C. Mazziotta) Clinical Brain Imaging: Principles and Applications, 1992, Clinical Examination of the Nervous System, 2000; sect. editor editl. bd. Exptl. Neurology, Current Opinion in Neurology and Neurosurgery, Neurology, Annals Neurology, Jour. Neuropathology and Exptl. Neurology, Neurobase Arbor Pub. Co.; editor-in-chief MedLink Neurology, 1992, Contemporary Neurology Series, 1995—, Neurology Network Commentary, 1996-2000, Lancet Neurology Network, 2000-02, Exptl. Neurology, 2003—, Neurobiology of Disease, 2005—; contbr. articles to profl. jours. Dir. Mich. Dem. Program, 1994-2000. With USPHS, 1958-60. Recipient Lucy G. Moses prize Columbia U., 1973, Weinstein Goldenson award United Cerebral Palsy Assn., 1981, UCLA Alumni Profl. Achievement award, 1992, UCLA Med. Alumni Profl. Achievement award, 1992. Fellow AAAS, Royal Soc. of Medicine, Royal Coll. Physicians, Am. Acad. Arts and Scis.; mem. Am. Neurol. Assn. (hon.; 1st v.p. 1985-86, pres.-elect 1987-88, pres. 1988-89), Mich. Neurol. Assn. (pres. 1987-88), Soc. Clin. Investigation, Am. Physiol. Soc., Am. Assn. Neuropathologists, Soc. Neurosci., Am. Acad. Neurology (vice chmn. geriatric neurology subcom. 1992-94, chmn. 1994-96, chmn. Decade of Brain com. 1990-95, AB Baker award 2004), Am. Epilepsy Soc., Assn. Rsch. in Nervous and Mental Disease, Assn. Am. Physicians, Inst. Medicine, Nat. Acad. Scis., The Nat. Acads. (nat. assoc.), Assn. Am. Physicians, Phi Beta Kappa, Alpha Omega Alpha. Home: 3411 Geddes Rd Ann Arbor MI 48105-2518 Office: U Mich Dept Neurology 300 N Ingalls 3D15 Ann Arbor MI 48109 Office Phone: 734-936-1808. Business E-Mail: sgilman@umich.edu.

GILMAN, SUSAN JANE, writer; b. NY; married. Grad, Brown Univ., 1986; MFA in Creative Writing, Univ. Mich. Reporter Jewish Week newspaper; tchr., writing, lit., poetry, drama Univ. Mich., Eastern Mich. Univ.; commentator World News Radio, Washington; columnist, editor-at-large Hues mag. Author: Kiss My Tiara, 2001, Hypocrite in a Pouffy White Dress, 2005. Recipient NY Press Assn. award for feature writing. Mailing: c/o Author Mail Warner Books 1271 Ave of Americas New York NY 10020

GILMARTIN, CLARA T., volunteer; b. East Stroudsburg, Pa., Jan. 23, 1922; d. Harry and Clarissa (Snearley) Treible; m. John Gilmartin, Jan. 18, 1945 (dec. Feb. 1956); children: Ronald, Donald; m. William Gilmartin, Sept. 8, 2002. BA, Rutgers U., 1961, MA, 1966. Elem. sch. tchr. Union Beach (N.J.) Pub. Sch., 1956-61; lang. arts tchr. Holmdel Village (N.J.) Intermediate Sch., 1961-82; Fulbright exch. tchr. New Zealand, 1973-74; mem. adv. bd. Juvenile Conf. Com., 1986—. Chair bd. trustees Grace Meth. Ch., Union Beach, 1997—. Mem. Monmouth County Ret. Educators Assn., Am. Legion (Post 321 Color Guard, scholarship com., trustee, chaplain), Triad. Democrat. Home: 122 Dock St Union Beach NJ 07735

GILMARTIN, RAYMOND V., pharmaceutical company executive; b. Washington, Mar. 6, 1941; m. Gladys Higham; 3 children. BS in Elect. Engring., Union Coll., 1963; MBA, Harvard U., 1968. Sr. cons. Arthur D. Little Inc., 1968-76; v.p. corp. planning Becton Dickinson & Co., Paramus, N.J., 1976-79, pres. Becton Dickinson divsn., 1979-87, group pres., 1982-83, sr. v.p., 1983-86, exec. v.p., 1986-87, pres. Franklin Lakes, N.J., 1987-94, CEO, 1989-94; chmn., pres., CEO Merck & Co. Inc., Whitehouse Station, NJ, 1994—2005, spl. adviser to the bd. exec. com. Whitehouse, NJ, 2005—. Bd. dirs. Merck & Co. Inc., 1994-2005, Microsoft Corp., 2001-, Gen. Mills, Inc.; chmn. Inter-faculty initative in Health Policy. Trustee Healthcare Inst. NJ; bd. dirs. Alliance for Healthcare Reform, Am. Enterprise Inst.; Pharm. Rsch. and Mfrs. Am., Healthcare Leadership Coun.; chmn. United Negro Coll. Fund; active Bus. Coun., Bus. Roundtable, Pres. Export Coun.; mem. exec. com. Coun. on Competitiveness. Mem.: Internat. Fed. Pharm. Mfrs. Assn. (chmn.). Office: Merck & Co Inc 1 Merck Dr Whitehouse Station NJ 08889-0100

GILMER, ROBERT, mathematics professor; b. Pontotoc, Miss., July 3, 1938; s. Robert William and Lucy Marie (Jernigan) G.; m. Rachel Grace Colson, Aug. 24, 1963; children: David Patrick, Stephen Douglas. Student, Itawamba Jr. Coll., 1955-56; BS, Miss. State U., 1958; MS, La. State U., 1960, PhD, 1961. Instr., Miss. State U., Starkville, 1959, vis. prof., 1962; research instr. La. State U., Baton Rouge, 1961-62; vis. lectr. U. Wis., Madison, 1962-63; mem. faculty Fla. State U., Tallahassee, 1963—2003, prof. math., 1968—2003, Robert O. Lawton Disting. prof., 1981—2003, prof. emeritus, 2003—. Vis. prof. Latrobe U., Bundoora, Victoria, Australia, 1974, U. Tex., Austin, 1976-77; vis. rsch. prof. U. Conn., Storrs, 1982; visitor Inst. for Advanced Study, 1990; vis. scholar U. N.C., Chapel Hill, 1997. Author: Multiplicative Ideal Theory, 1967, 72, 92, Commutative Semigroup Rings, 1984; also articles; assoc. editor Am. Math. Mo., 1971-73; editorial bd. Jour. Communications in Algebra, 1974-85. Named Barrett Meml. Lectr., U. Tenn., Knoxville, 1994; Office Naval Rsch. fellow, 1962-63; Alfred P. Sloan Found. fellow, 1965-67; NSF grantee, 1965-89; Fulbright sr. scholar to Australia, 1974. Mem. Am. Math. Soc., Math. Assn. Am. (gov. Fla. sect. 1986-89, cert. meritorious svc. 1992). Baptist. Home: 2414 Perez Ave Tallahassee FL 32304-1329 Office Phone: 850-644-2295. E-mail: gilmer@math.fsu.edu.

GILMOR, JANE ELLEN, artist, educator; b. June 23, 1947; d. Fred Howard and Margery Ann (Maberry) F. BS, Iowa State U., 1969; MAT, U. Iowa, 1973, MA in Painting, 1976, MFA in Painting, 1977. Cert. secondary tchr. Iowa. Prof. art, chmn. dept. Mt. Mercy Coll., Cedar Rapids, Iowa, 1974—, dir. McAuley Gallery, 1978—81. Cons. Cedar Rapids Sch. Sys., 1979—83; lectr. in field. Exhibited in group shows at N.A.M.E. Gallery, Chgo., 1984, Renwick Gallery, Smithsonian Inst., Washington, 1981, Olbrick Gallery, Kassel, Germany, 1980, George Sand Gallery, L.A., 1977, Conn. Coll., New London, 1982, N.Y.C. FIT Galleries, 1980, A.I.R. Gallery, N.Y.C., 1987, 2002, Bernice Steinbaum Gallery, 1986, Fla. State U. Mus. Art, Tallahassee, 1986, Palazzo Vagnotti, Cortona, Italy, 1986, Minn. Mus. Art, St. Paul, 1986, Bemis Ctr. Cont Art, 1993, Des Moines Art Ctr., 2000, Olson Larsen Gallery, 2000, Artemesia Chgo., 2000, Women Artists in the U.S., Lisbon, Portugal, 2005. Bd. dirs. Cedar Rapids Mus. Art, 1977—80. Recipient Art in Architecture Purchase award, Iowa Arts Coun.; grantee, NEA, 1996, 2002; Visual Artist fellow, 1986, Guthrie fellow, Ireland, 1992, McKnight Artists fellow, 1997, Fulbright scholar, Evora, Portugal, 2003. Mem.: AAUP (v.p. Mt. Mercy chpt. 1977—79), Coll. Art Assn. Office: Mount Mercy College Cedar Rapids IA 52402 Office Phone: 319-363-1323.

GILMORE, ARTHUR WARHAM, retired aeronautical engineer; b. Louisville, Oct. 5, 1920; s. Frank Foster and Annie (Miller) Gilmore; m. Beverly Mary Snow, Dec. 11, 1948 (dec. July 11, 1995); children: David, Beverly, Richard, Paul; m. Katherine Purcell Thomas, Sept. 28, 1997. BA in Aeroengring., Rensselaer Poly. Inst., 1942; MS, U. Colo., 1956. Registered profl. engr., NY. Instr. aeroengring. Rensselaer Poly. Inst., Troy, NY, 1942—43; aerodynamicist Consol. Vultee, Ft. Worth, 1943—45; asst. product engr. Sperry Gyroscope, Lake Success, NY, 1945—47; sect. head, dir., mem. NACA rsch. adv. com. on aerodynamics Grumman Aero Corp., Bethpage, NY, 1948—77; dir. grad. studies indsl. mgmt. SUNY-Stony Brook, 1978—. Cons. L.I. Lighting Co., Hicksville, NY, 1978—79, Am. Assn. Engring. Soc., N.Y.C., 1977—84, Eaton Corp. AIL divsn., Deer Park, NY, 1984—85. Author: numerous tech. papers and reports. Chmn. Engring. Manpower Commn., 1975—77; mem. Suffolk County Econ. Devel. Com., 1979—80, Nat. Commn. Engring. Manpower, 1974. Mem.: Sigma Xi (assoc.). Democrat. Avocations: boating, swimming, hiking, model building. Home: 316 Oakwood Rd Port Jefferson NY 11777-1460 Personal E-mail: awg2000@worldnet.att.net.

GILMORE, CLARENCE PERCY, editor-in-chief, writer; b. Baton Rouge, Feb. 8, 1926; s. Clarence Percy and Clara (Cobb) G.; m. V. Elaine Oliver, 1985; children: Robert Dillard, Patricia Anne. Student, La. State U., 1942-44, 46-48. Reporter various radio, TV stas., 1948-56; free-lance mag. writer, 1956—; sci. editor Metromedia TV, 1967-84; exec. editor Popular Sci. Mag., 1971-80, editor-in-chief, 1980-89; dep. editorial dir. Times Mirror Mags., N.Y.C., 1989-92, ret., 1992. Cons. in field. With USNR, 1944-46. Recipient Claude Bernard sci. journalism award Nat. Soc. Med. Rsch., 1969, Albert and Mary Lasker Found. award, 1969, Howard W. Blakeslee award Am. Heart Assn., 1969, Spl. Commendation for med. journalism AMA, 1969, 70, Sci. Writing award for physics and astronomy Am. Inst. Physics, 1970, Sci. Writing award AAAS, 1980. Home: 19725 Creek Round Ave Baton Rouge LA 70817-1915 E-mail: kgilmore@cox.net.

GILMORE, H. JAMES, film producer, educator; b. Park Forest, Ill., Mar. 25, 1961; s. Harold James Gilmore, Jr. and Mary Emily Curtis; m. Sheryl Ann Christy, June 22, 1991; children: Grace, Griffin, Ronan. BA, Kalamazoo Coll., 1983; MA, U. Iowa, 1984. Writer/prodr. WSBT-TV, South Bend, Ind., 1985—86; field prodr. The Christian Sci. Monitor, Boston, 1986—88; coordinating prodr./dir. N.H. Pub. TV, Durham, 1989—95; exec. prodr. Acadia Pictures, St. Augustine, Fla., 1995—. Assoc. dir. Acadia Inst. Oceanography, Seal Harbor, Maine, 1992—; asst. prof. St. Joseph's Coll., Standish, Maine, 1999—2000, Flagler Coll., St. Augustine, 2000—. Prodr.: (documentary) Great Lakes/Toxic Lakes, 1987, Zimbabwe: A Racial Revolution, 1988 (Gold Plaque, Chgo. Intnl. Film Festival, 1988), The Rhino War, 1988; dir.: (documentary film) The Shipyard Dance, 1999, (editor) Alone Together, 1990 (AFI Robert M. Bennett Award, 1990), (writer, editor) Soul of a Woman: The Life & Times of Mary Baker Eddy, 1994 (Wilbur, Telly, 1994), Chronicle of an American Suburb, 2002, (film) Pale in Your Shadow, 1997 (Gold Aurora, 1998); prodr.: (documentary) Dare Not Walk Alone, 2005. Mem.: Assn. Ind. Video and Film, Internat. Documentary Assn., Univ. Film and Video Assn. (Award of Merit in Documentary Film 2002). Avocations: theater, piano, photography, travel. Office: Acadia Pictures Inc PO Box 1860 Saint Augustine FL 32085 E-mail: hjames@acadiapictures.com.

GILMORE, JENNIFER A.W., computer specialist, educator; b. San Fernando, Trinidad, Jan. 12, 1954; arrived in US, 1972, naturalized, 1993; d. Fitzroy Grant and Zelma (Williams) Oudkerk; m. Frederick R. Gilmore, June 17, 1983. BA, MA, Bklyn. Coll., 1984; BBA, MS, Baruch Coll., 1993; MBA, L.I. U., 1994; PhD, Walden U./Kennedy-Western U., 2001. Cert. Microsoft Office Specialist (MOS) 2002, Internet Computing Core (IC3) Certiport, 2003, IC3 Instr. Certiport, 2003, Online Tchr. U. MD Univ. Coll., 2003. COBOL programmer MetLife, N.Y.C., 1972-86; project mgr., human resources adminstrn. mgmt. info. sys. City of N.Y., 1990—. Adj. prof. NYC Coll. Tech., 1997, Kingsborough C.C., 1998, St. Francis Coll., Bklyn., 1998, Medgar Evers Coll., 1998, Borough of Manhattan C.C., 1998, Touro Coll., 1999—, Baruch Coll., 1999—2000, Monroe Coll., 1999—, U. Md., 2003—, Kaplan U., 2005—. Author: (books) A Case Study of Two System Development Projects and their Implementation, 2003, An Analysis of Computer and Telephone Usage in the New York City Metropolitan Area, 2003. Democrat. Adventist. Home: 47 Mckeever Pl Apt 16J Brooklyn NY 11225-2537 Office: NYC-HRA-MIS 15 Metrotech Brooklyn NY 11201 Personal E-mail: jgilmore102716560@yahoo.com.

GILMORE, JIM E., plastic surgeon; b. Agusta, Tes., July 23, 1937; s. James E. and Mildred Holcomb (Davis) Gilmore; m. Gay Lynne Chastain, Dec. 21, 1960; children: Annette K. Melton, Alyssa L., Scott C. Degree, Tex. A & M State U., 1955; BA, Stephen F. Austin State U., 1958; MD, U. Tex. SW Med. Sch., 1962. Cert. Am. Bd. of Otoloaryngology, 1970, Am. Bd. of Cosmetic Plastic Surgery, 1979, Am. Bd. of Facial Plastic and Reconstructive Surgery, 1991; proficiency in basic sci. State of Tex., 1960, Tex. State Bd. of Med. Examiners, 1962. Facial plastic and cosmetic surgeon Jim E. Gilmore MD and Assoc., Dallas, 1970—; rotating intern Meth. Hosp. of Dallas, Dallas, 1962—63; general surgery, OB-GTN Grand Forks AFB, ND, 1963—65; general surgery Meth. Hosp. of Dalland, Parkland Meml. Hosp., Tex., 1965—66; residency, otolaryngology- head and neck surgery Parkland Meml. Hosp., U. Tex. SW Med. Sch., Dallas, 1966—69; clin staff surgeon, facial plastic surgery Parkland Meml. Hosp. U. Tex. SW Med. Sch., Otolaryngology Dept., Dallas, 1969—88; clin. fellowship U. Tex. SW Med. Sch., Otolaryngology Dept., 1988—93; course instr. U. Chgo. Sch. of Medicine, 1998—2003. Surgical extern Meth. Hosp. of Dallas, Dallas, 1959—60. Contbr. articles various profl. jours.; presenter: various profl. conf. presentations. Bd. dirs. Dallas Mus. of Art; bd. mem. Greenhill's Found. Trustees for the Dallas Nature Ctr.; mem. North Dallas C. of C., Sierra Club; trustee The Dallas Opera. Cpt. USAF, 1963—65. Recipient award, Dallas Mid-Winter Dental Soc., 1982, Ex-Students award, Stephen F. Austin State U., 1984, Physician's Recognition award, AMA, 1984, Cert. of Excellence in Continuing Med. Edn. in Cosmetic Surgery, AACS, 1995, 1997; fellowship, Am. Acad. of Otolaryngology Head and Neck Surgery, 1970, Am. Acad. of Facial Plastic and Reconstructive Surgery, 1972, Am. Coll. of Surgeons, 1972, Am. Acad. Cosmetic Surgery, 1974, Internat. Coll. of Surgeons, 1983. Mem.: AMA (life), Tex. Soc. of Facila Plastic Surgery, Tex. Otolaryngological Assn., Tex. Med. Found., Tex. Med. Assn. and Section Otoloaryngology, Tex. Cosmetic Surgical Soc., Tex. Assn. of Otolaryngology, Head and Neck Surgery, Southern Med. Assn., Pan Am. Assn. of Otorhinolaryngology, Nat. Patient Safety Found., Internat. Soc. Cosmetic Laser Surgeons, Internat. Mus. of Surgical Sci., Internat. Fed. of Otorlinularyngological Soc., Internat. Coll. of Surgeons, Intramerican Soc. Cosmetic, Plastic and Reconstructive Surgery, Dallas County Med. Soc., Dallas Acad. of Otolaryngology, Cosmetic Surgery Found., Am. Soc. Liosuction Surgery, Am. Soc. Cosmetic Surgeons, Am. Coun. Otolaryngology, Am. Coll. of Surgeons, Am. Bd of Otolaryngology, Am. Bd Facial Plastic and Reconstructive Surgery, Am. Bd. Cosmetic Surgery, Am. Assn. Cosmetic Surgeons, Am. Acad of Otolaryngology, Head and Neck Surgery, Am. Acad. of Facial Plastic and Reconstructive Surgery, Am. Acad. of Cosmetic Surgery, Town North YMCA, The 500, Inc., The Dallas Symphony Assn., Theta Kappa Psi/Phi Delta Pi Nat. Med. Fraternity Webster Soc. Achievements include development of Jlift/Internal Face Lift. Avocations: archaeology, foreign lang. Office: Jim E Gilmore MD Assoc 6750 Hillcrest Plz Dr 215 Dallas TX 75230 Office Phone: 972-960-0950. Office Fax: 972-760-2417. E-mail: jim@jimgilmore.com.

GILMORE, JOAN MARIE, international marketing company executive; b. Glasgow, Mont., Apr. 2, 1959; d. John Dale and Marlice Ione (Hushagen) G. BA in English-Philosophy, St. Olaf Coll., 1979. Licensed USCG Master 100-Ton Capt., 1997. Mktg. rsch. analyst Energy Absorption Systems, Chgo., 1978; freelance photographer Mpls., 1980-83; store mgr. Frameyourself, Edina, Minn., 1983-84; planner, distbr. Dayton Hudson Dept. Store Co., Mpls., 1984-87; tchr. English, Miyagi Gakuin Jr.-Sr. High Sch., Sendai, Japan, 1987-88; pres. Japan Mktg. Group, Mpls., 1988—; co-owner Northern Breezes Sailing Sch., Mpls., 1999—2003. Author: (plays) The Party People, 1977, Summit at Sendai, 1988; editor: Elementary Physics, 1989; contbg. editor Northern Breezes Sailing Mag., 1999-2003. Tour guide Walker Art Ctr., Mpls., 1988-91; vol. art cataloguer Mpls. Inst. Art, 1988-92; edn. dir. Am. Sailing Assn., L.A., 2003-2004; fleet capt. Fairwind Yacht Club, L.A., 2003. St. Olaf Coll. Oxford U. fellow, 1978. Mem.: Am. Sailing Assn. (edn. dir. 2003—04), Fairwind Yacht Club (fleet capt. 2003). Avocations: collecting art, photography, interior-architectural design. Home and Office: Japan Mktg Group 400 Groveland Ave Apt 312 Minneapolis MN 55403-3243

GILMORE, JOSHUA DAVID, music educator, lay worker; b. Palm Beach Gardens, Fla., July 15, 1977; s. Michael Bruce and Grace Phelan Gilmore. BS in Music, Clearwater Christian Coll., Fla., 1999. Dir. vocal music Keswick Christian Sch., St Petersburg, Fla., 1999—2002; chair music dept. Calvary Christian H.S., Clearwater, Fla., 2002—. Minister of music First Bapt. Ch., Largo, Fla., 2000—02; youth minister Calvary Bapt. Ch., Clearwater, Fla., 2002—. Recipient Outstanding Musician award, Clearwater Christian Coll., 1999. Mem.: Music Educators Nat. Conf. Office: Calvary Christian HS 331 Pierce St Clearwater FL 33756 Office Phone: 727-449-2247. Office Fax: 727-461-5421. E-mail: gilmore.josh@cchs.us.

GILMORE, JUDITH MARIE, physician; b. Houston, Dec. 28, 1942; d. Howard Ray and Mary Gardner (Currier) G.; m. Richard E. Kelley, July 21, 1974 (div. 1981); 1 child, Lisa Kelley. BA, U. Maine, 1965; MA, NYU, 1968; MD, Woman's Med. Coll., 1972. Diplomate Am. Bd. Internal Medicine, Am. Bd. Endocrinology. Resident St. Vincent's Hosp., N.Y.C., 1972-74; fellow in endocrinology St. Raphael's Hosp., New Haven, 1974-75, West Haven VA-Yale Hosp., New Haven, 1975-76; pvt. practice Bridgeport, Conn., 1976-80, Cranston, R.I., 1986—; mem. staff St. Joseph's Hosp., Providence, 1986—; mem. cons. staff Newport (R.I.) Hosp., 1986—; mem. courtesy staff Roger Williams Hosp., Providence, 1994—, R.I. Hosp., Providence, 1995, Kent County Hosp., Pawtucket Meml. Hosp. Lt. comdr. USNR, 1980-86. Mem. ACP, AMA, Am. Assn. Endocrine, Am. Diabetes Assn., R.I. Endocrine Assn. Avocations: hiking, music, art. Office: 725 Reservoir Ave Ste 2 Providence RI 02910-4450 Office Phone: 401-943-5120. E-mail: JP1994@msn.com.

GILMORE, JUNE ELLEN, psychologist; b. Middletown, Ohio, Oct. 22, 1927; d. Linley Lawrence and Elizabeth Kathleen (Barker) Wetzel; m. John Lester Gilmore, July 6, 1945; children: John Lester Jr., Michael Edward. BS, Miami U., Oxford, 1961; MS, Miami U., 1964. Lic. psychologist, Ohio. Intern in psychology Hamilton (Ohio) City Schs., 1963-64; psychologist Talawanda, Shiloh, Trenton Schs., Butler County, Ohio, 1964-66, Franklin (Ohio) City Schs., 1966-72, Wapakoneta (Ohio) City Schs., 1972-76, Cin. City Schs., 1978-86; pvt. practice psychology, 1975-95; planner, evaluator Warren/Clinton Counties Mental Health Bd., Ohio, 1986-88; adj. instr. Wright State U., Dayton, Ohio, 1989-90. Co-author: Summer Children-Ready or not for School, 1986, The Rape of Childhood--No Time to be a Kid, 1990. Sec. Tri County Drug Coun., Lima, Ohio, 1975; chmn. Auglaize County Social Svcs., Wapakoneta, 1973-75; bd. dirs. Butler County Alcohol and Drug Addiction Svcs. Bd., 1990-97, sec., 1992-94. Mem. Ohio Sch. Psychologists Assn. (exec. bd. 1982-86), Southwestern Ohio Sch. Psychologist Assn. (pres.), Southwest Council Exceptional Children (Pres.), Nat. Assn. Sch. Psychologists, Ohio Psychol. Assn., Butler County Retired Tchrs. Assn. (newsletter editor 2002-04, pres. 2004), Butler County 648 Mental Health Bd. (bd. dirs. 1978-86, pres. 1983-84). Republican. United Methodist. Home and Office: 6120 Michael Rd Middletown OH 45042-9402

GILMORE, KATHI, state treasurer; b. Dec. 23, 1944; m. Richard Gilmore; children: Suzi, Barb, Jeff, Amy. Mem. N.D. Ho. of Reps. from Dist. 6, 1989-92; treas. State of N.D., 1993—. Mem. Bd. Tax Equalization, State Hist. Bd., State Investment Bd., Tchrs. Fund for Retirement Bd., State Canvassing Bd., Bd. of Univ. and Sch. Lands Mem.: Assn. Securities Profls. (hon. co-chair pension fund conf. 1994, Task Forces Orgnl. Planning and Coordinating Com. 1993), Retirement and Investment Office Internal Audit Com., Nat. Assn. State Treas. (pension com.). Democrat. Presbyterian. Office: State Treasurer 600 E Boulevard Ave Bismarck ND 58505-0660

GILMORE, MAURICE EUGENE, mathematics professor; b. N.Y.C., Jan. 2, 1938; s. Maurice Eugene and Mary Wells (Barnes) G.; m. Julie Anne Rogers, June 20, 1964 (div. 1989); children: Peter Barnes, Christopher Alan, Jessica Lynn; m. Cathi Leslie Sonneborn, Sept. 1, 1991. BA, Georgetown U., 1959; MS, Syracuse U., 1961; PhD, U. Calif., Berkeley, 1967. Instr. Northeastern U., Boston, 1966-68, asst. prof., 1968-72, assoc. prof., 1972-78, prof., 1978—, chmn. math. dept., 1975-88. Vis. prof. U. Tecnica Del Estado, Santiago, Chile, 1968, U. of Sussex, Falmer, U.K., 1989. Grantee, NSF, 1979, 1992, 1999, CNSF, 1999, Nellie Mae, 2001. Mem.: Assn. Tchrs. Math. Mass., Nat. Coun. Tchrs. Math., Am. Math. Soc., Math. Assn. Am. Office: Northeastern U 360 Huntington Ave Boston MA 02115-5000 Office Phone: 617-373-5675. Business E-Mail: gilmore@neu.edu.

GILMORE, MERLE, diversified financial services company executive; BSEE, U. Ill., 1970; MSEE, Fla. Atlantic U. Various positions Motorola, 1970—2000; indsl. ptnr. Ripplewood Holdings L.L.C., 2001—; pres. LKR Tech. Ptnrs., 2001—; chmn. D&M Holdings, North Barrington, Ill., 2002—. Bd. dir. Denon, Ltd., Proxim Corp. Bd. trustees Chgo. (Ill.) Ednl. TV Assn. Recipient Disting. Alumni award, U. Ill., 1998. Achievements include patents in field.

GILMORE, ROBERT WITTER, retired foundation administrator; b. College Corner, Ohio, Sept. 6, 1933; s. Robert Foster and Frances Elizabeth (Witter) G.; m. Sara Louise McIntosh, Dec. 23, 1956; children: Susan Lynne, Robert Riley, Christopher Edwin. EdB, Miami U., Oxford, Ohio, 1955; M in Social Work, Ohio State U., 1957. Exec. dir. United Way, Massillon, Ohio, 1960-64, St. Joseph, Mo., 1964-69, Dayton, Ohio, 1969-78, Cin., 1978-88, ret., 1988, cons., 1988—. 1st lt. U.S. Army, 1957-60. Named Man Of Yr. Jr. C. of C., St. Joseph, 1967. Mem. Assn. Cert. Profl. Social Workers (cert.), Queen City Club, Rotary, Masons, Sigma Chi. Avocation: golf. Home: 6424 Butler Israel Rd College Corner OH 45003-9797 also: 15653 Carriedale Ln Fort Myers FL 33912-3927

GILMORE, VOIT, travel company executive; b. Winston-Salem, NC, Oct. 13, 1918; s. John Merriman and Helen (Hensel) G.; m. Kathryn Kendrick, Jan. 21, 1945 (div. 1975); children: Kathryn, Geraldine, Susan, Peter, David.; m. Tatiana Dominick, July 4, 1982 (div. 1990); m. Josephine Baldwin, Nov. 23, 1990. BJ, U. N.C., 1939, M in Geography, 1985, PhD in Geography, 1987; grad., Nat. Inst. Pub. Affairs, Washington, 1940. Cert. travel counselor Inst. Cert. Travel Agts. Asst. to div. mgr. Pan Am. Airways, Miami, Fla., 1940-41; personnel mgr. Pan Am. Airways-Africa Ltd., Accra, Gold Coast, 1942-43; pub. relations dir. Pan Am. Airways, San Francisco, 1946-48; pres. Storey Corp. and affiliated cos., 1948-61, 64-83, Four Seasons Travel Service, Inc., 1971-95. Dir. U.S. Travel Svc., Washington, 1961-64, So. Nat. Bank of N.C., 1980-95; news corr. to Arctic, 1958, Antarctic, 1958, 60, 61, 63; mem. adv. coun. U.S. Travel and Tourism Adminstrn., 1990-96. Contbr. articles on polar exploration to newspapers, mags. Mem. town coun., mayor, Southern Pines, N.C., 1953-57; mem. N.C. Senate, 1965-69, N.C. Bd. Conservation and Devel., 1957-61; trustee U. N.C., Fayetteville, 1981-87; mem. Gov.'s Adv. Com. on Travel and Tourism, 1982, N.C. Forestry Adv. Com., 1986; candidate for U.S. Congress from 8th Dist. N.C., 1968; bd. dirs. U. N.C. Sch. Journalism Found., Chapel Hill; chmn. Clean N.C. 2000, 1999-01. Lt. (j.g.) USN, 1943-46, PTO. Recipient European Tourism Golden Helm award, West

Berlin, 1986, Parker award Travel Coun. NC, 1997, Order of Long Leaf Pine award Gov. NC, 2003, NC Pub. Svc. award Gov. NC, 2004; named to Travel Industry Assn. Hall of Leaders, 1988. Fellow Royal Geog. Soc. (life), Explorers Club (life); mem. Am. Soc. Travel Agts. (pres. 1988-90), Assn. of Am. Geographers, Am. Forestry Assn. (pres. 1973-75), Soc. Am. Travel Writers, Travel Coun. N.C. (pres. 1969-71), Bohemian Club, Cosmos Club, Country Club N.C., Heidelburg Prince Club. Home and Office: 1600 Morganton Rd D11 Pinehurst NC 28374-6842

GILMORE, W. FRANKLIN (FRANK GILMORE), academic administrator; BS, Va. Mil. Inst.; PhD in organic chemistry, MIT; postdoctoral study, Inst. Molecular Biophysics, Fla. State Univ. Prof., dept. chmn., rsch. prof. med. chemistry dept. Univ. Miss.; exec. v.p. W.Va. Univ. Inst. Tech.; chancellor Mont. Tech, Univ. Mont., Butte. Bd. dir. Butte-Silver Bow United Way, Butte Family YMCA; mem. Goldwater Scholarship Selection Com.; mem. NAPLEX steering com. Nat. Assn. Boards of Pharmacy. Mem.: Sigma Xi (past pres.). Office: Montana Tech Office of the Chancellor 1300 W Park St Butte MT 59701-8997*

GILMOUR, D(AVID) JAMES, financial analyst, systems analyst; b. Phila., July 10, 1947; s. James William and Florence Elizabeth (Weisbrod) Gilmour; m. Deborah Anne Kaufold, July 2, 1977. BS, Muhlenberg Coll., 1969; MS in Adminstrn., George Washington U., 1974; MBA, Temple U., 1981, MEd, 2005; MS, U. Pa., 1995, MPhil, 1998. Analyst Nat. Security Agy., Ft. Meade, Md., 1970-74; programmer, analyst Rohm & Haas Co., Phila., 1974-77; staff economist Sun Oil Co., Radnor, Pa., 1977-85; project leader Arco Chem. Corp., Phila., 1985-87; asst. v.p. Corestates Fin. Corp., Phila., 1987-98, cons., 1998—. Hon. amb. Ctr. Orgnl. Dynamics U. Pa., Phila.; MEd, PhD student asst., grad. rsch. asst. Temple U. Author: (book) An Economic Model of Core States Financial Corporation, 1994, How to Write Term Papers Real Good, 1996, The Corestates/University of Pennsylvania Strategic Planning Model, 1997, The Philadelphia Ethos, 1998, 1776 and All That: A Memorable History of Philadelphia, 2002. With USN, 1970—74. Mem.: NEA, NRA, NJ Edn. Assn., Pa. Edn. Assn., Clan Morrison Soc., Mensa, Beta Gamma Sigma, Alpha Tau Omega (exchequer 1965—69, Thomas Arcle Clark award 1969). Republican. Anglican. Achievements include co-inventor semi-automatic pistol. Home and Office: 15 Keats Rd Yardley PA 19067-3219 Office Phone: 610-888-9107. E-mail: djames_gilmour@hotmail.com, jgilmour@temple.edu.

GIL ORRIOS, ANGEL, theater director, lighting designer, translator; b. Cariñena, Zaragoza, Spain, Oct. 7, 1956; s. Angel Gil Sebastian and Cristina Orrios Ruiz; m. Soledad Lopez, Feb. 22, 1980; children: Sebastian Orrios, Mariana Orrios. MFA in Directing, Sch. Dramatic Arts, Zaragoza, Spain, 1974. Artistic dir. Royal Theatre Of Spain, NYC, 1980—85, Internat. Art Theatre Inst., NYC, 1995—99; artistic, exec. dir. Thalia Spanish Theatre, Sunnyside, NY, 2000—. Cultural corr. El Pais, NY, 1988—92; cons., lectr. in field. Dir.(prodr., set & lighting designer): (musical) Pablo Picasso's the Four Little Girls, Picasso's Guernica (Best Dir. and Best Prodn. award Assn. Critics of Entertainment, 2000); (plays) Ramos Perea's We Women Do It Better, Jardiel Poncela's Brake Four Hearts (Best Dir. award Assn. Critics of Entertainment, 2001), (writer, prodr., set & lighting designer): (musical) Maestro Jaurena's I Love Tango, Tangomania, Life's Tango, All That Tango (Best Musical Prodn. award Assn. Critics of Entertainment, 2001), (translator, prodr., set & light designer): (plays) Carlos Fuentes' The One-eyed Man Is King (Best Dir. and Best Prodn. award Hispanic Orgn. Latin Actors, 2003, Best Set Designer award Assn. Critics of Entertainment, 2003), Jaime Salom's Almost a Goddess, Calderon De La Barca's The Great Theatre of the World (Hola award for best dir. and best prodn., 2000). Recipient Prince Ferdinand award, Radio Juventud De Zaragoza, Spain, 1975, Silver medal, French Acad. Arts, Sci. and Letters, Paris, 1987, Best Short Film award, XVIII San Francisco Poetry Film Festival, 1993. Mem.: Spanish Soc. Authors, Composers & Publ., Dramatists Guild, Soc. Stage Dir. & Choreographers. Office: Thalia Spanish Theatre 41-17 Greenpoint Ave Sunnyside NY 11104 Office Phone: 718-729-3880. E-mail: angel@thaliatheatre.org.

GILPATRICK, RUSSELL O., dental educator, dean; married; 1 child, Nicholas. Degree, Chico State U.; DDS, U. Pacific Sch. Dentistry. Pvt. practice; mem. faculty U. Conn. Sch. Dentistry; joined faculty, Health Sci. Ctr. Sch. Dentistry, U. Tenn., 1988; prof. gen. dentistry Health Sci. Ctr. Sch. Dentistry, U. Tenn., 1993, chmn. gen. dentistry dept., exec. assoc. dean academic affairs, dean, 2003—. Recipient Outstanding Tchr. award, U. Tenn. Alumni Assn., 1992, Fellowship award, Tenn. Dental Assn., 2003. Office: U Tenn Health Sci Ctr 875 Union Ave Memphis TN 38163 Office Phone: 901-448-6202. Business E-Mail: rgilpatrick@utmem.edu.

GILPIN, PERI, actress; b. Waco, Tex., May 27, 1961; m. Christian Vincent, 1999; 2 children, Ava, Stella. Former student, Dallas Theatre Ctr., U. Tex., Brit.-Am. Acad., London. Owner prod. co. (with Jane Leeves) Bristol Cities. Actress (TV series) Frasier, 1993-2004 (SAG award outstanding performance ensemble, 2000), The Lionhearts (voice), 1998; (TV guest appearances) 21 Jump Street, 1988, Matlock, 1990, Wings, 1992, Designing Women, 1993, Cheers, 1993, Pride & Joy, 1995, The Outer Limits, 1996, Early Edition, 1996, Superman, 1998, Hercules (voice), 1998, Baby Blues, 2000, The Chris Isaak Show, 2001, King of the Hill (voice), 2003, Justice League (voice), 2003, I'm With Her, 2003; (TV movies) Fight for Justice: The Nancy Conn Story, 1995, The Secret She Carried, 1996, Laughter on the 23rd Floor, 2001, (films) Spring Forward, 1999, How to Kill Your Neighbor's Dog, 2000, Finaly Fantasty: The Spirits Within (voice), 2001; guest appearance Later with Greg Kinnear, 1994, Early Edition, 1996, The Outer Limits, 1995, Superman, 1996, Pride & Joy, 1995, Talk Soup, 1991, Matlock, 1986, 21 Jump Street, 1987. Office: William Morris Agy One William Morris Place Beverly Hills CA 90212-2775

GILPIN, ROBERT GEORGE, JR., political science professor; b. Burlington, Vt., July 2, 1930; s. Robert George and Beatrice (Sandspra) G.; m. Jean Millis, Aug. 13, 1955; children— Linda, Elizabeth, Robert. BA, U. Vt., 1952; MS, Cornell U., 1954; PhD, U. Calif., Berkeley, 1960. Fellow Harvard U., 1960-61; lectr. Columbia U., 1961-62; faculty Princeton U., 1962—68, prof. polit. sci., 1970-98, Eisenhower prof. internat. affairs, 1975-98, prof. emeritus, 1998—. Mem. Pres.'s Advisory Group Tech. and the Economy, 1975-76. Author: American Scientists and Nuclear Weapons Policy, 1962, France in the Age of the Scientific State, 1968, U.S. Power and the Multinational Corporation, 1975, War and Change in World Politics, 1981, The Political Economy of International Relations, 1987, The Challenge of Global Capitalism: The World Economy of the 21st Century, 2000, Global Political Economy: Understanding the International Economic Order, 2001; co-author (co-editor): Scientists and National Policy Making, 1964. Served with USNR, 1954-57. Congl. fellow, 1959-60, Guggenheim fellow, 1969, Rockefeller fellow, 1967-68, 76-77 Fellow AAAS; mem. Am. Polit. Sci. Assn. (v.p. 1984-85). Home: PO Box 105 Greensboro VT 05841 Personal E-mail: rggilpin@princeton.edu.

GILPIN, VICKY SUE, literature and language educator, principal; b. Decatur, Ill., Feb. 2, 1976; d. Daniel Gene and Ramona Lavonne Walker; m. David Edward Gilpin, Aug. 7, 1999; children: Shayna Punim, Talysyn, Merlyn, Sylas. A in Arts, Richland CC, 1996; BA in English and Theatre summa cum laude, Ea. Ill. U., 1999; M in Tchg. and Learning summa cum laude, Nova Southeastern U., 2003; postgrad., U. Phoenix, 2004—. Cert. Nat. Bd. Profl. Tchg. Stds. 2004. Stage mgr. Tibbet's Opera Ho., Coldwater, Mich., 1998; English tchr. Cerro Gordo HS, Ill., 2000—; poetry, creative writing instr. Coll. Youth/Richland CC, Decatur, 2001—02; speech and English tutor Richland CC, 2002—04; religious sch. prin., mem. bd. Temple B'nai Abraham, Decatur, 2003—, head English dept. Stage mgr. Richland Players, Decatur, 1994—2002, Merely Players, Decatur, 2001—02; sponsor hs activities Future Tchr. Soc., Student Coun., Cerro Gordo, 2001—; adj. English instr. Richland CC, Decatur, 2001—04. Book reviewer (TV book revs.), (online book revs.); dir.: (plays) The Rope (David L. and Audrey Jorns Directing Theory Theatre award, 1999). Mem. So. Poverty Law Ctr., Montgomery, Ala., 2004—05, Assn. Social Sci. Study Jewry, NYC, 2004—05, Assn. Jewish Studies, NYC, 2004—05. Recipient Tchr. of Yr., WalMart, 2003. Mem.: NEA, Ill. Edn. Assn., Ctr. Advancement Ethics and Character, Ill. Assn. Gifted Children, Phi Delta Kappa (Tchr. of Yr. 2003). Jewish. Avocations: reading, music, writing. Office: Cerro Gordo HS 300 East Durfee St Cerro Gordo IL 61818-0079 Office Phone: 217-763-2711 128. Personal E-mail: gilpin_vicky@hotmail.com.

GILROY, FRANK DANIEL, playwright; b. N.Y.C., Oct. 13, 1925; s. Frank B. and Bettina (Vasti) Gilroy; m. Ruth Dorothy Gaydos, Feb. 13, 1954; children: Anthony, John, Daniel. BA magna cum laude, Dartmouth Coll., 1950; postgrad., Yale Sch. Drama. Author became TV writer, (TV series) (originated) Burkes Law, (TV writer, scripts prod. on programs) Playhouse 90, U.S. Steel Hour, Omnibus, Kraft Theatre, Lux Video Theatre, Studio One; dir.(writer): 40 Gibbsville, 1975, The Doorbell Rang, 1977, Money Plays, 1997; author: (plays) Who'll Save the Plowboy? (presented off-Broadway, 1962), 1957, (completed) The Subject Was Roses, 1962, (presented on Broadway, 1964), 1962; presented (Broadway plays) That Summer-That Fall, 1967, The Only Game in Town, 1968, Last Licks, 1979, Any Given Day, 1993, (off Broadway plays) Contact With the Enemy, 1999, one-act (produced off-Broadway plays) The Next Contestant, 1978, Real to Reel, 1987, Match Point, 1990, A Way With Word, 1991, Give the Bishop My Faint Regards, 1992, Contact with the Enemy, 2000, Inspector Ohms, 2001; prodr.(writer, dir.): (films) Desperate Characters, 1970 (best screenplay award Berlin Film Festival), From Noon Till Three, 1977, The Gig, 1985, Once in Paris (original screenplay), 1978; writer, dir. (films) The Luckiest Man in the World, 1989; author: Present Tense, prod. off-Broadway, 1972, (novels) Private, 1970, (with Ruth Gilroy) Little Ego, 1970, From Noon till Three, 1973, (nonfiction) I Wake Up Screening-Everything You Need to Know About Making Independent Films Including A Thousand Reasons Not To, 1993, (screenplays) (with Russell Rouse) The Fastest Gun Alive, 1956, (with Beirne Lay Jr.) Gallant Hours, 1960, Desperate Characters, 1971, The Subject was Roses, The Only Game in Town, From Noon till Three, Once in Paris. Served with U.S. Army, 1943—46, ETO. Nominee Best Play N.Y. Drama Desk, 1999—2000; recipient Obie award for best Am. play, 1962, Outer Circle award, 1964, Drama Critics Circle award, 1964, N.Y. Theatre Club award, 1964—65, Antoinette Perry award, 1965, Pulitzer prize for drama, 1965. Mem.: Writers Guild Am., Dirs. Guild Am., Dramatists Guild (pres. 1969—71).

GILROY, TRACY ANNE HUNSAKER, lawyer; b. St. Louis, Aug. 13, 1959; d. Raymond Thomas Hunsaker and Dorothy Jayne Hunsaker Reilly. BA, U. Dayton, 1981; JD, St. Louis U., 1984. Bar: Mo. 1984, Ill. 1985. Atty. Mo. State Hwy. and Transp. Dept., St. Louis, 1984-89; of counsel Draheim & Pranschke, St. Louis, 1989-94; pvt. practice The Gilroy Law Firm, St. Louis, 1994—. Mem. ABA (strategic comms. bar svcs. standing com., reporter The Affiliate, bd. dirs. LPM solo divsn., chair solo and small firm practitioners 2002-04, chair, standing com. on solo & small firms), Mo. Bar Assn. (chair eminent domain com., legis. com., bd. govs. 1998—), St. Louis Bar Found. (pres. 1998-99), St. Louis Met. Bar Assn. (pres. 1997-98, chair young lawyers sect. 1993, chair legis. com. 1985-87, chair, vice-chair, chair trial sect., chair social com., chair auction com., media com., chair solo small firm cmty.), Woman Lawyers Assn. (mem.-at-large, chair legis. com. 1984-87, sec. 1987), Lawyers Assn., Assn. Trial Lawyers Am. Avocations: golf, skiing, running, writing, painting. Office: Gilroy Law Firm 1610 Des Peres Rd # 300 Saint Louis MO 63131-1813 Office Phone: 314-965-3536.

GILSON, ARNOLD LESLIE, retired engineering executive, consultant; b. Perrysburg, Ohio, Apr. 10, 1931; s. Leslie Clair and Velma Lillian (Hennen) G.; m. Phyllis Mary Seiling, Sept. 15, 1951 (dec. May 1982); children: David, Jeffrey, Luann, Suzanne. BSME, U. Toledo, 1962. Engr. Miller, Tillman & Zamis engrs., Toledo, 1962-67, regional mgr. Phoenix br., 1967-69; owner, mgr. ABS Tech. Svcs., Phoenix, 1969-98; ret. Patentee in several fields. With U.S. Army, 1952, Korea. Decorated Bronze Star; Commd. extraordinary minister, 1975. Mem. Nat. Mil. Intelligence Assn. (charter). Republican. Roman Catholic. Home: 8226 E Meadowbrook Ave Scottsdale AZ 85251-1739 E-mail: ADGILSON@JUNO.COM.

GILSON, JEROME, lawyer, writer; b. Chgo., Jan. 12, 1931; s. William George and Clara Margaret (Loewe) G.; m. Jamie Marie Chisam, June 19, 1955; children: Thomas, Matthew, Anne. AB, U. Mo., 1952; JD, Northwestern U., 1958. Bar: Ill. 1958, U.S. Dist. Ct. (no. dist.) Ill. 1958, U.S. Ct. Appeals (7th cir.) 1962, U.S. Supreme Ct. 1966, U.S. Ct. Appeals (3d cir.) 1967, U.S. Ct. Appeals (5th cir.) 1968, U.S. Ct. Appeals (fed. cir.) 1982, U.S. Ct. Appeals (11th cir.) 1985, U.S. Ct. Appeals (4th cir.) 1988, U.S. Ct. Appeals (8th cir.) 1994. Assoc. Rooks, Pitts, Fullagar & Poust, Chgo., 1958-63; ptnr. Brinks Hofer Gilson & Lione, Chgo., 1963—. Mem. faculty John Marshall Law Sch., Chgo., 1961-63; advisor Am. Law Inst.-Unfair Competition Law Restatement, Phila., 1986-91. Co-author (with Anne Gilson LaLonde): Trademark Protection & Practice, 1974—, also supplements; contbr. articles to profl. jours. Served as sgt. U.S. Army, 1952-55. Named as top trademark law practitioner in world Managing Intellectual Property, 1998. Mem. ABA, Internat. Trademark Assn. (reporter trademark rev. com. 1985-88, counsel 1991-94), Intellectual Property Law Assn. Chgo., Union League, Mich. Shores Club. Avocations: tennis, piano. Office: Brinks Hofer Gilson & Lione 445 N Cityfront Plaza Dr Chicago IL 60611-4316 Office Phone: 312-321-4205. E-mail: jgilson@brinkshofer.com.

GILSON, RONALD JAY, law educator; b. 1946; AB summa cum laude, Washington U., St. Louis, 1968; JD, Yale U., 1971. Bar: Calif. 1972. Law clk. to Hon. David L. Bazelon US Ct. Appeals DC Cir., 1971—72; assoc. to ptnr. Steinhart, Goldberg, Feigenbaum & Ladar, San Francisco, 1972-79; assoc. prof. law Stanford Law Sch., 1979-83, Charles J. Meyers prof. law and bus., 1991—; Marc and Eva Stern prof. law and bus. Columbia Sch. Law, NYC, 1992—. Co-dir. Legal Scholarship Network; vis. prof. law Yale Law Sch., 1982—83, U. Tokyo Sch. Law, 1996, Hebrew U., Jerusalem, 1998; vis. Henley Prof. law and bus. Columbia Sch. Law. & Grad. Sch. Bus., NYC, 1991—92; disting. Olin vis. prof. law U. Va. Law Sch., 1999; vis. scholar The Hoover Instn., 1988—89; resident scholar Rockefeller Study Ctr., Bellagio, Italy, 1998. Co-author: (with B. Black) (Some of) the Essentials of Finance and Investment, 1993, The Law and Finance of Corporate Acquisitions, 1995, (with J. Choper & J. Coffee) Cases and Materials on Corporations, 1999. Fellow: Am. Acad. Arts and Sciences; mem.: Am. Law and Economics Assn., Am. Law Inst. Office: Stanford Law Sch Crown Quadrangle 559 Nathan Abbott Way Stanford CA 94305-8610 also: Columbia U Sch Law 435 W 116th St New York NY 10027 Office Phone: 650-723-0614, 212-854-1655. Office Fax: 650-725-7663, 212-854-7946. Business E-Mail: rgilson@stanford.edu, rgilson@law.columbia.edu.*

GILSON, SUSAN LEE, performing arts educator; d. Izzy and Beatrice C. Westen; m. Robert Gilson, Dec. 6, 1970; 1 child, Tamara Shannon Piasecki. AA, Santa Monica City Coll., 1964. Profl. dancer Dance Ctr. West, LA, 1964—69; dance instr., staff choreographer Palomar Coll., San Marcos, Calif., 1974—, dir. outreach program, 1997—; owner Georgia's Sch. Dance, 1997—. Bd. dirs. Jazz Dance World Congress, Chgo., Calif. Rhythm Tap Project, San Diego; musical theatre choreographer Palomar Coll., San Marcos, 1975—. Co-prodr., choreographer Gershwin in Revue, 1993, Ballads, Blues & Boogie Woogie, 1994, Stompin' at the Brubeck, 1996. Mem.: Escondido C. of C., Downtown Bus. Assn. Avocations: travel, shopping, dance, designing costumes. Office: Palomar Coll 1140 W Mission San Marcos CA 92069 Office Phone: 760-745-6662 ext. 5304.

GILSTER, PETER STUART, lawyer; b. Carbondale, Ill., Dec. 10, 1939; s. John S. and Ruth Gilster; m. Carol Clevenger, June 30, 1968; children: John F., Thomas B. BS, U. Ill., 1962, JD, 1965. Bar: Ill. 1965, Mo. 1968, U.S. Dist. Ct. (ea. dist.) Mo. 1969, U.S. Patent Office 1970, U.S. Ct. Appeals (8th cir.) 1978, U.S. Supreme Ct. 1978, U.S. Ct. Customs and Patent Appeals 1980, U.S. Ct. Appeals (fed. cir.) 1983. Assoc. Koenig, Senniger, Powers & Leavitt, St. Louis, 1967-71, ptnr., 1971-72; patent atty. Monsanto Co., St. Louis, 1972-77; ptnr. Kalish & Gilster, St. Louis, 1977-96, Peper, Martin, Jensen, Michael and Hetlage, St. Louis, 1997-98, Blackwell, Sanders, Peper Martin, LLP, St. Louis, 1998-99; head patent sect. Kalish & Gilster Intellectual Property Group, St. Louis; chmn. internat. practice Peper Martin, 1998; officer, shareholder Greensfelder, Hemker & Gale, P.C. Intellectual Property Grp., 1999—; sr. patent counsel. Seminar lectr. U. Mo.-St. Louis, 1976-83, guest lectr., 2002, adj. prof., 2002-. Contbr. articles to profl. jours. Capt. USAR, 1966-67. Decorated Army Commendation medal. Mem. AIPLA, IEEE, AAAS, Ill. Bar Assn., Mo. Bar Assn. (patent, trademark, and copyright com.), Lawyer Pilots Bar Assn., Fed. Cir. Bar Assn., Bar Assn. Met. St. Louis (chmn. patent sect. 1975-76), Assoc. Pilots St. Louis (v.p. 1977-83, bd. dirs. 1975-87, 2002-04), World Affairs Coun. St. Louis (bd. dirs. 2000-03), Soc. Hispano-Am. St. Louis (bd. dirs. 1993-96, treas. 1994-96). Office: Equitable Bldg Ste 2000 10 S Broadway Saint Louis MO 63102 Office Phone: 314-241-9090. Business E-Mail: psg@greensfelder.com.

GILSTRAP, LIVIA LEE, psychology professor; b. Seattle, Wash., Mar. 2, 1974; d. Michael and Valerie Gilstrap. PhD, Cornell U., 2002. Asst. prof. U. Colo., Colorado Springs, 2002—. Mem.: Am. Psychology, Law Soc.

GIMBEL, ALFRED ADOLF, employee benefits professional; b. Ladendorf, Austria, Nov. 5, 1944; came to U.S., 1969; s. Adolf and Olga (Hiltz) G.; m. Judy Mae Adams, Mar. 22, 1968; children: Heidi Lynn, Shannon Noel. BSc, U. Man., 1965. Mgmt. trainee GM, Winnipeg, Man., Can., 1965-66; group underwriter, rep. Gt. West Life, Winnipeg, 1966-69, mgr. underwriting, group mgr., 1972-75; group mgr., dir. group sales IDS Life Ins. Co., Detroit and Mpls., 1969-72; cons., exec. v.p., sec.-treas. Byerly & Co., Inc., Denver, 1975—, also bd. dirs.; mgr. Rocky Mountain Region Watson Wyatt Worldwide, 1994—. Bd. dirs. Perry Park Met. Dist., Larkspur, Colo., 1986-88. Mem. Denver Rustlers, Optimist Internat., Perry Park Country Club. Republican. Lutheran. Avocations: golf, skiing, bicycling, reading. Home: 336 Saint Paul St Denver CO 80206-4335

GIMBEL, HERVEY WILLIS, public health physician, medical administrator; b. Calgary, Alta., Can., Nov. 25, 1926; s. Jacob Allen Gimbel and Ruth Helen Johnson; m. Ann Matterand Gimbel, Dec. 23, 1951; children: Shirley Tetz, Denise Job, Kenneth, Marlin, Beverly Kramer. BA, Walla Walla Coll., 1950; MD, Loma Linda U., 1955, MPH, 1978. Diplomate Nat. Bd. Medicine; cert. Am. Bd. Preventive Medicine. Med. dir. North Hill Med. Clinic, Calgary, 1957-82; assoc. prof. Loma Linda (Calif.) U., 1982-84; med. dir. Parkview Ctr. for Occupl. Medicine, Riverside, Calif., 1985-91, Rancho Canyon Occupl. Medicine, Temecula, Calif., 1991-2001, Steck Meml. Medica Ctr., Centralia, Wash., 2002. Cons. China Nat. Health Edn. Inst., Beijing, 1992—; dir. China-U.S.A. Health Project, Loma Linda, Calif., 1991—, Health Edn. Ctr., Calgary, 1969-82; guest prof. Huazhong U., Wuhan, China, 2002-2004. Contbr. articles to periodicals. Flight lt. Royal Can. Air Force Res., 1958—60. Named an Honored Alumus, Loma Linda U., 2005; recipient China Tobacco Control award Chinese Assn. Smoking and Health, 2000. Fellow Am. Coll. Preventive Medicine; mem. Am. Coll. Environ. and Occupl. Medicine, Med. Coll. Can. (licentiate), Delta Omega. Avocations: travel, photography, history. Home: 911 Landing Way Centralia WA 98531 Personal E-mail: gimbel@quik.com.

GIMBLETT, MAXWELL HAROLD, artist, art educator; b. Auckland, New Zealand, Dec. 5, 1935; s. Frank Harold and Dorathea Connon Gimblett; m. Barbara Diane Kirshenblatt, Aug. 17, 1964. Artist Max Gimblett Studio, NYC, 1972—. Trustee Len Lye Found., New Plymouth, Taranaki, New Zealand, 1990—; vis. artist Elam Sch. Fine Art, Auckland U., Auckland, 2004—, Auckland Boys Grammar Sch., Auckland, 2000—; vis. assoc. prof. of art and design Pratt Inst., Bklyn., 1979—88; chmn. East Coast Artists, NYC, 1996—98; j. paul getty assoc. The Getty Ctr. History Art and Humanities, Santa Monica, Calif., 1991—92; artist in residence Rockefeller Found., Study and Conf. Ctr., Bellagio, Lake Como, Italy, 1991; inaugural artist in residence Queensland U. Tech., Acad. Arts-Visual Arts, Brisbane, Australia, 1993. Exhibitions include Haines Gallery, San Francisco, Calif., Gow Langsford Gallery, Auckland, hatcher Projects, NYC, Auckland Art Gallery, Queensland Art Gallery, Brisbane, Australia, Ethan Cohen Fine Arts, NYC. Fellow, NEA, Washington, 1989; grantee, Queen Elizabeth II Arts Coun. of New Zealand, 1980, 1996. Achievements include Painting Fellowship, National Endowment for the Arts, Washington D.C. 1989; Grant, Queen Elizabeth II Arts Council of New Zealand, 1986. Home: 231A Bowery 3rd Floor New York NY 10002-1218 Home Fax: 212-254-7885. Personal E-mail: gimblett@maxgimblett.com.

GIMBRONE, MICHAEL ANTHONY, JR., research scientist, pathologist, educator; b. Buffalo, Nov. 16, 1943; married, 1971; 3 children. AB, Cornell U., 1965; MD, Harvard U., 1970. Intern, resident fellow Mass. Gen. Hosp., Boston, 1970-72; staff assoc. Nat. Cancer Inst., Bethesda, Md., 1972-74; resch. assoc. Harvard Med. Sch., Boston, 1974-76, from asst. prof. to assoc. prof., 1979-85, Elsie T. Friedman prof. pathology, 1985—; chmn. dept. pathology Brigham and Women's Hosp., Boston, 2001—. Cons. Nat. Heart, Lung and Blood Inst., NIH, 1976—; established investigator Am. Heart Assn., 1977-82; head Vascular Pathophysiol. Rsch. Lab., 1977-85; dir. vascular rsch. div. Brigham and Women's Hosp., 1985—, dir. Ctr. for Excellence in Vascular Biology. Recipient Achievement award in cardiovascular scis. Bristol-Myers Squibb, 2001. Fellow NIH, AAAS, Nat. Acad. of Scis., Am. Acad. Arts and Scis.; mem. Inst. of Medicine, Am. Heart Assn. (Basic Rsch. prize 1993), Am. Soc. Cell Biologists, Tissue Culture Assn., Am. Soc. Hematology, Am. Assn. Pathologists (v.p. 1991-92), Am. Soc. Invest. Pathology (pres. 1992-93), Am. Assn. Physicians, Fedn. Am. Socs. for Exptl. Biology (Exptl. Pathologist award 1982, bd. dirs. 1990-94), N.Am. Vascular Biology Orgn. (founding pres. 1994—, J. Allyn Taylor Internat. prize in medicine). Achievements include research in cardiovascular pathophysiology, especially atherosclerosis, thrombosis and inflammation, vascular cell biology. Office: Brigham and Womens Hosp Dept Pathology 75 Francis St Boston MA 02115 E-mail: mgimbrone@rics.bwh.harvard.edu.

GIMELSTOB, JUSTIN, professional tennis player; b. Livingston, N.J., Jan. 26, 1977; s. Barry and Patricia Gimelstob. Professional tennis player, 1996—. Winner, Men's Doubles USTA Challenger, Tiburon, Calif., 2003, winner, Men's Singles and Doubles, Forest Hills, NY, 04. Office: c/o USTA 70 W Red Oak Ln White Plains NY 10604-3602

GIMENES, SONIA REGINA ROSENDO, family therapist, psychologist; b. São Paulo, Brazil, Jan. 25, 1953; arrived in U.S., 1996; d. Joao Rosendo and Luzia Pragelis; m. Airton Jose Gimenes, May 7, 1976; children: Erika, Rodrigo. BS in Psychology, U. Mogi Cruzes, São Paulo, 1980; M in Sci. Psychology with honors, U. Americas, Mexico City, 1988; postgrad. in psychology; cert. in clin. psychology, U. Paulista, São Paulo, 1994. Registered family therapist intern Fla., lic. clin. psychologist Brazil. Family therapist intern Clinica Oira, Mexico City, 1987—88; psychologist intern Clinica Psicologia Objetivo, São Paulo, Brazil, 1994, Pontificia U. Cath., São Paulo, 1995; clin. psychologist Human Inst., São Paulo, 1995—96; family therapist Counseling and Hypnosis Inc., Miami, Fla., 1999—. Author: Domestic Violence, 2001; contbr. monography project Child Abuse, 1988, articles to profl. jours. Mem.: ACA, Am. Bd. Hypnotherapy, Am. Coll. Forensic Examiners, Am. Psychotherapy Assn., Rotary (chair new mems. 1998—, dir., chair found., vol. fight against domestic violence, Paul Harris medal of honor 1976). Avocations: music, dance, piano, arts and crafts. Office: Brickle Bayview Co Bus Ctr 80 SW 8th St Ste 2000 Miami FL 33130 Fax: 786-275-9514.

GIMENEZ, LUIS FERNANDO, physician, educator; b. Antofagasta, Chile, Mar. 3, 1952; came to U.S., 1979; s. Luis Sr. and Nelly (Basulto) G.; m. Diane Marie Salazar, Sept. 20, 1957; children: Luis Andres, Pilar Elizabeth, Nicholas Miguel, Catherine Anne. MD, U. Chile, Valparaiso, 1976. Diplomate Am. Bd. Internal Medicine, Am. Bd. Nephrology. Intern U. Chile Sch. Medicine, Valparaiso, 1975-76; resident U. Concepcion Sch. Medicine, Chile, 1976-77, U. Chile Sch. Medicine, Valparaiso, 1977-79; research fellow in nephrology Johns Hopkins U. Sch. Medicine, Balt., 1979-81; intern Johns Hopkins Hosp., Balt., 1981-82, resident, 1982-84, clin. fellow nephrology div., 1984-85; instr. Johns Hopkins U. Sch. Medicine, Balt., 1985-86, asst. prof. medicine, 1986—. Dir. dialysis unit The Good Samaritan Hosp., Balt., 1985—, chief renal div., 1990; mem. med. adv. bd. Am. Kidney Found., Balt., 1987—. Contbr. articles to profl. jours. Recipient Outstanding Civic Svc. award Chilean Med. Assn., Valparaiso, 1974. Mem. Am. Fedn. for Clin. Research., Am. Soc. Nephrology, Am. Coll. Physicians, Internat. Soc. Nephrology, Internat. Soc. Peritoneal Dialysis, Am. Coll. Clin. Pharmacology. Avocation: philatelist. Office: Johns Hopkins Hosp Renal Divsn 1830 Bldg Baltimore MD 21205-2109 Business E-Mail: lfimene@jhm1.edu.

GINDER, GORDON DEAN, internist, educator; b. Jacksonville, Ill., Feb. 20, 1949; s. Clyde Delbert and Helen L. Ginder; m. Georgianne Schuller, May 31, 1975. BS, U. Ill., 1971; MD, Johns Hopkins U., 1975. Resident Case Western Res. U., Cleve., 1975-77; rsch. assoc. NIH, Bethesda, Md., 1977-79; fellow U. Iowa, Iowa City, 1979-80, asst. prof. div. hematology oncology, 1980-85, assoc. prof., 1985-89, prof., assoc. dir., 1989-90; prof., dir. div. med. oncology U. Minn., Mpls., 1990-97; prof., dir. Massey Cancer Ctr. Med. Coll. Va. Commonwealth U., Richmond, 1997—. Lt. comdr. USPHS, 1977-79. Mem. Am. Soc. Hematology, Am. Fedn. Clin. Rsch., Cen. Soc. Clin. Rsch. (councillor 1989-92), Am. Soc. Clin. Investigation, Am. Assn. Cancer Rsch., Assn. Am. Physicians. Office: Massey Cancer Ctr PO Box 980037 401 College St Richmond VA 23298-5017 Office Phone: 804-828-0450. Business E-Mail: gdginder@hsc.vcu.edu.

GINDIN, WILLIAM HOWARD, retired judge; b. Perth Amboy, N.J., Sept. 1, 1931; s. Jac Paul and Belle Ruth (Steinberg) G.; m. Jane Hersh, June 24, 1954; children: Thomas L., Suzanne Hinsdale; m. Emily Shimkin, Dec. 25, 1965; children: Geoffrey A. Drucker, Janine Drucker Gordon. AB, Brown U., 1953; JD, Yale U., 1956. Bar: N.J. 1956, U.S. Supreme Ct. 1965, U.S. Ct. Appeals (3d cir.) 1980. Assoc. Gindin & Gindin, Plainfield, NJ, 1956—62, ptnr., 1962—82; adminstrv. law judge Newark, 1982—85; U.S. bankruptcy judge Trenton, NJ, 1985—90, 1999—2004; chief, 1990—98. Adj. prof. Rutgers Camden Law Sch., 1988-93; lectr. Inst. Continuing Legal Edn., Profl. Edn. Systems, Inc.; bd. govs. Nat. Conf. Bankruptcy Judges (3d cir.), 1989-92. Mem. editl. bd. N.J. Bar Assn. Jour., 1962-72. Mem. Plainfield Human Relations Commn., 1965-72, chmn., 1968-72; pres. Temple Sholom, Plainfield, 1979-81; regional v.p. Union Am. Hebrew Congregations, 1983-86; trustee Princeton Jewish Ctr.1994-96, Jewish Cmty. Found. of Mercer-Bucks 1998-2000; mem. Opera Festival of N.J. Fellow: Bankruptcy Inn of Ct. (pres. 1995—99), Am. Bar Found., Am. Coll. Bankruptcy; mem.: ABA, Am. Judicature Soc., N.J. Bar Assn., Mercer County Bar Assn., Union County Bar Assn., Plainfield Bar Assn., Assn. Fed. Bar (adv. bd.), Plainfield Rotary (Paul Harris fellow, pres. 1974—75). Home: 5839 Bromelia Ct Naples FL 34119-4798 E-mail: ebgindin@aol.com.

GINEPRI, ROBBY (ROBERT LOUIS GINEPRI), professional tennis player; b. Ft. Lauderdale, FL, Oct. 7, 1982; s. Rene and Nancy Ginepri. Profl. tennis player ATP Tour, 2001—. Achievements include winner, Newport, RI, 2003, Indpls., 2005. Office: c/o ATP Tour 201 ATP Boulevard Ponte Ponte Vedra Beach FL 32082

GINER, A. SILVANA, lawyer; b. 1959; BA cum laude, Univ. Mass., Amherst, 1982; JD, Stanford Univ., 1985. Bar: Mass. 1985. Assoc. to ptnr. Wilmer Cutler Pickering Hale & Dorr, Boston, 1985—, vice chmn. Private Client dept. Contbr. chapters to books. Trustee Boston Social Law Libr., Brain Sci. Found., Medfield, Mass.; mem. adv. bd. Commonwealth Coll., Univ. Mass. Amherst; overseer Opera Boston. Fellow: Am. Coll. Trust & Estate Counsel; mem.: Boston Estate Planning Council, Phi Beta Kappa. Office: Wilmer Cutler Pickering Hale & Dorr 60 State St Boston MA 02109 Office Phone: 617-526-6327. Office Fax: 617-526-5000. Business E-Mail: nan.giner@wilmerhale.com.

GINGERICH, NAOMI R., emergency room nurse; b. Linwood, Mich., Sept. 18, 1945; d. Leroy and Mary Alice (Driver) G. Diploma in Nursing, Kansas City (Mo.) Gen. Hosp., 1967. RN, Pa., Md., Fla., Mo.; cert. ACLS, BLS, PALS, TNCC, advanced trauma life support. Charge nurse emergency rm. Kansas City (Mo.) Gen. Hosp. and Med. Ctr., 1967-70, oper. rm. nurse, 1971-74; charge nurse emergency rm. Univ. Med. Ctr., Kansas City, Kans., 1970-73; oper. room charge nurse Lancaster (Pa.) Gen. Hosp., 1974-79, charge nurse emergency rm., 1979-88; staff nurse emergency room Preferred Nursing Pool, Balt., 1988-90; with home health care, emergency room Norrell Health Care, Sarasota, Fla., 1990-91; office nurse Landisville Family Practice, 1991-92; on-call night nurse Hospice of Lancaster County, 1992-98, pvt. duty nurse, 1998—2000; emergency rm. nurse Bothwell Regional Health Ctr., Sedalia, Mo., 2001—. Home: 13254 Mount Zion Rd Versailles MO 65084-4335 Office: Bothwell Regional Health Ctr 601 E 14th St PO Box 1706 Sedalia MO 65302-1705

GINGERICH, OWEN JAY, astronomer, educator; b. Washington, Iowa, Mar. 24, 1930; 3 children. BA, Goshen Coll., 1951; MA, Harvard U., 1953, PhD in Astronomy, 1962. Dir. obs. Am. U., Beirut, 1955-58, from instr. to asst. prof., 1955-58; lectr. astronomy Wellesley Coll., 1958-59; astrophysicist Smithsonian Astrophys. Obs., 1961-87, sr. astronomer, 1987-2000; from lectr. to assoc. prof. astronomy and history of sci. Harvard U., 1960-69, prof., 1969-2000, chmn. history of sci. dept., 1992-93, emeritus prof., 2000—. Astronomy cons. Harvard Project Physics, 1964-69; dir. ctrl. telegram bur. Internat. Astronomical Union, 1965-67, pres. commn. history astronomy, 1970-76, chmn. U.S. nat. com., 1982-84; Sigma Xi nat. lectr., 1971; George Darwin lectr. Royal Astron. Soc., 1971; adv. com. Ctr. Theol. Inquiry, Princeton, 1988-97; adv. bd. John Templeton Found., 1994-99, 2001-2003, trustee, 2003—. Assoc. editor: Jour. History Astronomy, 1975-; mem. editorial bd. Am. Scholar, 1975-80; dir. Harvard mag., 1978-85, incorporator, 1986—; contrb. over 500 publications to profl. jours. on model stellar atmospheres and history of astronomy. Overseer Boston Mus. Sci., 1979-96, 1998—2004. Decorated Order of Merit comdr. class People's Republic of Poland, 1981 Fellow AAAS (chmn. sect. L 1974, sect D 1981); mem. Academie Internationale d'Histoire des Sciences, Am. Acad. Arts and Scis., Am. Philos. Soc. (v.p. 1982-85, John F. Lewis prize 1976, councilor 1994-2000), Am. Astron. Soc. (chmn. hist. astronomy div. 1983-85, Doggett prize 2000, Edn. prize 2004), Royal Astron. Soc. Can. (hon.), Examiner Club, Phi Beta Kappa. Achievements include research on model stellar atmospheres (to 1971) and in history of astronomy. Office: Harvard-Smithsonian Ctr for Astrophysics Cambridge MA 02138 Office Phone: 617-495-7216. Business E-Mail: ginger@cfa.harvard.edu. *Our most earnest ambitions are in effect unspoken prayers-they define our deepest views on the meaning of life far more precisely than any outward profession of religion or ethics.*

GINGERY, PHILIP ALVAH, music educator; b. Greenville, SC, July 22, 1962; s. Gail Alvah and Alice Christman Gingery; m. Rebecca Leigh Adams, Aug. 16, 1986; children: Adam, Benjamin, William, Samuel, Sarah, Joseph, David. BA in Vocal Performance, Bob Jones U., 1985, MusM in Vocal Performance, 1987, Master's degree, 1999. Ordained to ministry Bible Bapt. Ch., 2001. Tchg. asst. Bob Jones U., Greenville, SC, 1985—87, pub. rels., adj. music faculty, 1987—89; dir. bands, choir West Chester Christian Sch., Pa., 1989—. Min. music Westside Bapt. Ch., Augusta, Ga., 1987—89, Bible Bapt. Ch., West Chester, 1989—; mem. Sacred Music Singers, Greenville, 1989—; adj. music faculty N.E. Bapt. Sch. Theology, Downingtown, Pa., 1995—. Recipient Grace Levinson medal, Bob Jones U., Greenville, 1985, Profl. Recognition award, Keystone Christian Edn. Assn., Harrisburg, Pa., 2001. Mem.: Nat. Assn. Tchrs. Singing, Am. Choral Dirs. Assn., Pa. Music Educators Assn. Avocations: music, golf, book collecting. Office: Bible Baptist Ch West Chester Christian Sch 1237 Paoli Pike West Chester PA 19380 Office Phone: 610-692-4492.

GINGHER, MERLENE C., occupational therapist, educator; b. Buffalo, N.Y. d. Earl George and Merna Bethene Gingher. BS, SUNY, Buffalo, N.Y., 1970, MS, 1975, EdD, 1989. Physical therapist Erie Co. Home Infirmary, Buffalo, 1970—75; instr. SUNY, Buffalo, 1975—76; occupl. therapist, dir. Indendent. Living Project, Buffalo, 1976—80; asst. prof. SUNY, Buffalo, 1980—91, D'Youville Coll., Buffalo, 1991—97, chairperson occupl. therapy, 1997—. Mem.: Program Dirs.Edn. Coun. (vice chairperson), Am. Occupl. Therapy Assn. Avocations: singing, reading. Office: D'youville Coll 320 Porter Ave Buffalo NY 14201 Office Phone: 716-829-7830.

GINGLES, MARJORIE STANKE, music educator; b. Bklyn., Jan. 30, 1938; d. E.C. and E.L. (Lewthwaite) Stromberg; m. Charles Frederick Stanke, Aug. 27, 1960 (div. Nov. 8, 1976); m. William Glen Gingles, Sept. 29, 1984. BS in Music Edn., W. Chester U., formerly W. Chester State Tchrs. Coll., 1959; MA in Edn., W. Chester U., formerly W. Chester State Tchrs. Coll., mem, 1969. Elem. music tchr. George Gray Elem. Sch., Wilmington, Del., 1959-60, Penn-Delco Pub. Schs., Aston, Pa., 1960-61; pvt. piano tchr. home studio Berwyn, Norwood, Devon, Malvern, Pa., 1963—; choral dir. Coterie Singers, Wayne, Pa., 1975-84; music dir. St. Francis-in-the-Fields Ch., Malvern, Pa., 1981-88; piano tchr. Acad. Cmty. Music, Fort Washington, Pa., 1997—. Mem. music com. Main Line Unitarian Ch, Devon, 1970—, chair music com., 1978-79; mem. music com. Dorothy Taubman Inst. Piano, Amherst Coll., 1988-97, adjudicator Pa. Govs. Sch. Arts, 1986; music dir. Pro-Arte Chorale, 1980-86, dir. world and area premieres of new works; instr. several vocal workshops in field; clinician PMTA Convention, 1999; presenter in field. Piano concert artist, Pa. and N.Y. State; duo pianist with William Gingles; performances (in Gingles Duo) Pa. Music Tchrs. Conv. Taubman Piano Study grantee Pa. Music Tchrs. Assn., 2000. Mem. Main Line Music Tchrs. Assn. (chair adult recitals, chair Prime Time Players). Unitarian-Universalist. Avocations: reading, swimming, decorating. Home and Office: 27 Cypress Ln Berwyn PA 19312-1004 Office Phone: 610-296-5908. Personal E-mail: wgingles@comcast.net.

GINGOLD, GEORGE NORMAN, insurance company executive, lawyer; b. N.Y.C., Aug. 2, 1939; s. Josef and Gladys (Anderson) G.; m. Anne Brenda Davis, July 7, 1963; children— Rachel June, David Bruce AB magna cum laude, Harvard U., 1960, JD, 1963. Bar: Ariz. 1964, Conn. 1968, Mass. 1989. Pvt. practice law, Phoenix, 1964-65; atty. SEC, Washington, 1965-67; counsel AEtna Life & Casualty, Hartford, Conn., 1967-94; counsel, corp. sec. AEtna Life Ins. and Annuity Co., Hartford, 1981-94; pvt. practice ins. securities law, 1994—. Mem. com. on securities regulation Am. Council of Life Ins., Washington, 1978-94, chmn., 1986-88; instr. Hartford Coll. for Women, 1983-95. Author articles in field Vice pres., bd. dirs. United Cerebral Palsy Assn., Hartford, 1980-87; vice chmn. West Hartford Human Rights Commn., Conn., 1975-79; pres. West Hartford PTA, 1976-78 Mem. ABA (mem. fed. regulation of securities com. 1978—), Am. Soc. Corp. Secs., Fed. Bar Assn. (pres. Hartford County chpt. 1974-76) Lodges: B'nai B'rith Unity (pres. 1971-72). Avocations: classical music, theater, chess. Office: PO Box 155 West Hyannisport MA 02672-0155 Personal E-mail: gingoldga@comcast.net.

GINGREY, JOHN PHILLIP, congressman; b. Augusta, Ga., July 10, 1942; m. Billie Ayers; children: Billy, Gannon, Phyllis, Laura Neill. BS in Chemistry, Ga. Inst. Tech., 1965; MD, Med. Coll. Ga., 1969. Resident in ob-gyn. Med. Coll. Ga., Augusta; practice medicine specializing in ob-gyn. Marietta, Ga.; mem. Ga. State Senate, Atlanta, 1999—2002, mem. banking and fin. instns. com., edn. com., retirement com., transp. com.; mem. 11th Dist. Ga. US Ho. Reps., 2003—. Mem. St. Joseph's Cath. Ch., Marietta; mem. Marietta Sch. Bd., 1993-97, also chmn.; bd. dirs. North Cobb divsn. Am. Cancer Soc. Mem.: GA. Ob-Gyn. Soc., Med. Assn. of Ga., Cobb County Med. Soc., AMA. Republican. Roman Catholic. Mailing: Marietta Dist Office 219 Roswell St Marietta GA 30060 Office: US House of Repr 119 Cannon House Office Bldg Washington DC 20515 Office Phone: 202-225-2931. Office Fax: 202-225-2944.*

GINGRICH, NEWT (NEWTON LEROY GINGRICH), former congressman; b. Harrisburg, Pa., June 17, 1943; s. Robert Bruce and Kathleen (Daugherty) G.; children: Linda Kathleen, Jacqueline Sue.; m. Jackie Battley, June 19, 1962 (div. Feb. 1981), m. Marianne Ginther, Aug. 1981 (div. 2000), children: Linda Kathleen, Jacqueline Sue; m. Callista Bissek, Aug. 18, 2000. BA, Emory U., 1965; MA, Tulane U., 1968, PhD in European History, 1971. Asst. prof. history W. Ga. Coll., Carrollton, 1970—78; mem. 96th-105th Congresses from 6th Ga. dist. U.S. Ho. Reps., Washington, 1979-99, speaker, 1995-99; founder The Com. for New Am. Leadership, Washington, Ctr. for Health Transformation; chmn. The Gingrich Group, 1999—; polit. analyst Fox News Network; sr. fellow Am. Enterprise Inst.; Disting. vis. fellow Hoover Instn. Speaker, chmn. emeritus GOPAC; co-founder Conservative Opportunity Soc., congl. mil. caucus, space caucus; mem. joint com. on printing, house adminstrn. com.; co-chmn. Leader's Task Force on Health, US Commn. on Nat. Security/21st Century, 1999-; adj. prof. Reinhardt Coll., Waleska, Ga., 1994-95. Author: To Renew America, 1995, Lessons Learned the Hard Way: A Personal Report, 1998, Winning The Future: A 21st Century Contract With America, 2005; (with Marianne Gingrich) Window of Opportunity, 1984, Renewing American Civilization, 1995, (with William R. Forstchen) Nineteen Forty-Five, 1995, Gettysburg: A Novel of the Civil War, 2003, Grant Comes East: A Novel of the Civil War, 2004, Never Call Retreat: Lee and Grant: The Final Victory, 2005 Named Man of Yr., 1995, Ga. Citizen of the Year, March of Dimes, 1995, Legislative Conservationist of the Year, Ga. Wildlife Found., 1998, Sci. Pioneer award, Sci. Coalition, 2001, Health Quality award, Nat. Com. for Quality Assurance, 2005, Nat. Minority Health Month Found. award, 2005. Mem. AAAS, Ga. Conservancy. Lodges: Kiwanis, Moose. Republican. Baptist. Office: Ctr for Health Transformation 1425 K St NW Ste 750 Washington DC 20005

GINIGER, KENNETH SEEMAN, publisher; b. N.Y.C., Feb. 18, 1919; s. Maurice Aaron and Pearl (Triester) G.; m. Carol Virginia Wilkins, Sept. 27, 1952 (dec. Aug. 1985); m. Bernice Dees Ellinger Cullinan, Apr. 13, 2002. Student, U. Va., 1935-39, N.Y. Law Sch., 1940-41. Ptnr. Signet Press, 1939-40; assoc. editor Arts and Decoration and The Spur, 1940-41; dir. pub. relations Prentice-Hall, Inc., 1946-49, editor-in-chief trade book div., 1949-52; v.p., gen. mgr. Hawthorn Books div., 1952-61; pres. Hawthorn Books, Inc., N.Y.C., 1961-65, K.S. Giniger Co., Inc., N.Y.C., 1965—, Consol. Book Pubs. div. Processing & Books, Inc., Chgo., 1969-74, Tradewinds Group div. IPC Ltd., Sydney, Australia, 1974-76. Lectr. New Sch. Social Rsch., 1948—49, NYU, 1979—81, adj. asst. prof., 1981—83, adj. assoc. prof., 1983—85; asst. to dir. CIA, 1951—52. Author: The Compact Treasury of Inspiration, 1955 (NCCJ Brotherhood Week citation), America, America, America, 1957, A Treasury of Golden Memories, 1958, (with Walter Russell Bowie) What Is Protestantism?, 1965, A Little Treasury of Hope, 1968, A Little Treasury of Comfort, 1968, A Little Treasury of Christmas, 1968, The Sayings of Jesus, 1968, (with Will Yolen) Heroes for Our Times, 1969, The Family Advent Book, 1979, Pope John Paul II: Pilgrim of Faith, 1987, (with Sir John Templeton) Spiritual Evolution, 1998; editor: Internat. Pub. News, 1983-91, European Bookseller Pub. World/Update Newsletter, 1991-92; mem. editorial bd.: RAM Reports, 1977-83, Communications and the Law, 1978-94. Sec. Com. Collective Security, 1952—65; nat. adv. bd. Found. Religious Action, 1956—94; dir. Layman's Nat. Bible Com., 1957—, pres., 1963—71, chmn., 1987—94, chmn. emeritus, 1994—; mem. adv. bd. Templeton Found., 1992—2000, 2004—, Am. Theater Wing, 1999. From pvt. to capt. AUS, 1941—45. Decorated French Legion of Honor. Mem. P.E.N., Garrick Club (London), Authors Club (London) Arts Club (London), Army and Navy Club (Washington), Players Club, Yale Club, Dutch Treat Club, Church Club (N.Y.C.), Phi Delta Phi. Republican. Episcopalian. Home: 1045 Park Ave New York NY 10028-1030 Office: 250 W 57th St New York NY 10107 Office Phone: 212-570-7499.

GINN, RONN, architect, urban planner, general contractor; b. Jacksonville, Fla., Apr. 17, 1933; s. Angus Theodore and Joan Adelaide (Bailey) G.; children: Sharon Lee, John Norman. AA, U. Fla., 1957, B.Arch., 1960, B.Landscape Architecture, 1961. Lic. Lic. bldg. ofcl. Fla. Urban design specialist Model Cities Adminstrn., HUD, Washington, 1967-68; pvt. practice landscape architecture, constrn., urban planning St. Petersburg, Fla., 1968—; pres. ARG Constrn. Corp., 1975-76, ARG Corp., 1977—, Ginn Corp., 1967-70, Atrium Corp., 1965-72. Urban design lectr. U. N.Mex., 1967; planning cons. State Dept., 1967-68; design cons. Am. Revolution Bicentennial Commn., 1967-69; vis. design critic Rice U., 1974; mem. Pinellas County (Fla.) Bd. Adjustments and Appeals, 1981-88; mem. Albuquerque Fine Arts Commn., 1965-67, St. Petersburg Design Goals Com., 1971-73; moderator radio program Design in Our Community WPKM, Tampa, Fla., 1971-72; founder, bd. dirs. Pinellas County Red Flag Charrette, 1972-76, Catalyst, St. Petersburg; bd. dirs. Fla. Council Clean Air, Fla. Red Flag Charrette; mem. Pinellas County Planning Council, 1972-73 Supervising architect, urban designer: Roswell (N.Mex.) Ctrl. bus. dist. redesign, 1964, Tucumcari (N.Mex.) ctrl. bus. dist. redesign, 1967, Treasure Island (Fla.) civic ctr. design, 1971; architect, urban designer, prin. Atrium One, Albuquerque, 1965-67; contbg. editor Urban Affairs Symposia, 1965-73; guest columnist St. Petersburg Evening Ind., 1974; important works include Albuquerque ctrl. bus. dist. redesign (nat. AIA award 1966), new town Fla. Ctr. (nat. Am. Soc. Landscape Architects award 1970), Brown residence (AIA merit award 1975), Penguin Restaurant, Treasure Island, Fla., 1973, Cross residence, 1974, Sheridan Gallery, 1974, Madeira Beach C. of C., 1975, Greenpepper Restaurant, 1975, Mixon Bldg., Ruskin, Fla., 1976, Congregation Beth Chai Synagogue, Seminole, Fla., 1979, Villa Dos Santos Master Plan, St. Petersburg Beach, Fla., 1979, Congregation Kol Ami Synagogue, Tampa, 1981, Markham residence, St. Petersburg, 1981, The Moorings, Tierra Verde, Fla., 1981, Ginn Residence, St. Petersburg, 1981, Congregation B'nai Israel Synagogue, Clearwater, Fla., 1981, Suncoast Seabird Sanctuary, St. Petersburg, 1982, Lilly Residence, Treasure Island, Fla., 1983, Anchor Bank Office Bldg., St. Petersburg, 1984, 1600 Pasadena Office Bldg., 1984 (nat. design patent), Lighthouse Harbor Marina, 1984, Tugaloo Environ. Edn. Ctr., 1989, Latorre Chiropractic Clinic, 1990, Johnnie Ruth Clarke Health Ctr., 1986, 92, Jakabosi Studio, 1995, Jakabosi residence, 2001, Santeeteah (N.C.) Town Hall, 1998, Graham County (N.C.) EMS Bldg., 2002, Graham County Adminstrn. Bldg. Design Studies, 2002, Graham County Vets. Meml. Plaza, 2002. Mayoral candidate City of Treasure Island, Fla., 1973; bldg. dir. City of Seminole, 1975-78; mem. Leadership St. Petersburg, 1978-79; mem. permitting task force City of St. Petersburg, 1999-2001. Named Spiffs Person of Courage, 1984; recipient numerous archtl., landscape architecture, urban design awards, Addy awards, 1981, 1982. Mem. AIA (nat. com. on regional devel. 1969-76, vice chmn., commr. pub. affairs Fla. chpt.), Am. Inst. Planners, Constrn. Specifications Inst., Am. Inst. Landscape Architects, So. Bldg. Code Congress, Fla. Planning and Zoning Assn., Nat. Eagle Scout Assn. (chpt. chmn.). Republican. Presbyterian. Office: Jakabosi-Ginn Arch PO Box 1541 Robbinsville NC 28771-1541 Office Phone: 828-479-2188. Personal E-mail: ronnginn@aol.com.

GINN, SAM L., telephone company executive; b. Saint Clair, Ala., Apr. 3, 1937; s. James Harold and Myra Ruby (Smith) G.; m. Meriann Lanford Vance, Feb. 2, 1963; children: Matthew, Michael, Samantha. BS, Auburn U., 1959; postgrad., Stanford U. Grad. Sch. Bus., 1968. Various positions AT&T, 1960-78; with Pacific Tel. & Tel. Co., 1978—, exec. v.p. network San Francisco, 1979-81, exec. v.p. services, 1981-82, exec. v.p. network services, 1982, exec. v.p., strategic planning and adminstrn., 1983, vice chmn. bd., strategic planning and adminstrn., 1983-84; vice chmn. bd., group v.p. PacTel Cos. Pacific Telesis Group, San Francisco, 1984-86; pres. Air Touch Commn., San Francisco, 1984-87; vice chmn. bd., pres., chief exec. officer PacTel Corp. Pacific Telesis Group, San Francisco, 1986; pres., chief operating officer Pacific Telesis Group, San Francisco, 1987-88, former chmn., pres., chief exec. officer; chmn. Air Touch Commn., San Francisco, 1993—, now chmn. bd., CEO. Mem. adv. bd. Sloan program Stanford U. Grad. Sch. Bus., 1978-85, mem. internat. adv. council Inst. Internat. Studies; bd. dir. 1st Interstate Bank, Chevron Corp., Safeway, Inc. Trustee Mills Coll., 1982— . Served to capt. U.S. Army, 1959-60. Sloan fellow, 1968 Mem.: Blackhawk Country (Danville, Calif.); World Trade, Pacific-Union; Rams Hill Country (Borrego Springs, Calif.), Bankers. Republican. Office: Ste 1400 400 S El Camino Real San Mateo CA 94402-1740

GINNEVER, CHARLES, artist; b. San Mateo, Calif., Aug. 28, 1931; s. Charles Albert and Helyne Ruth Ginnever; children from previous marriage: Jodi, Chloe. AA, San Mateo Jr. Coll., 1951; BFA, Calif. Sch. Fine Arts, 1957; MFA, Cornell U., 1959. Tchr. Cornell, Ithaca, NY, 1960—98, Bklyn. Mus., New Sch., Pratt Inst., Aspen, Dayton Art Inst., Newark Sch. Fine and Ind. Art, NJ, Vt. Studio Sch., U. Del., U. Calif., Berkeley, 1972; dir. art dept. Windham Coll., Putnyh, 1972. Cpl. USAF, 1950—51, Washington. Recipient Lifetime Achievement Lee Krasner award, 2000—03; Guggenheim fellow, NY, 1974, Artist grant, Nat. Endowment Art, Washington, 1975, Pollock/Krasner Artist grant, NY, 1999—, Emergency grant, Pollock/Krasner, 2004, Gottlieb Found., 2004. Home: PO Box 411 Putney VT 05346 Business E-Mail: ginnever@earthlink.net.

GINOBILI, MANU, professional basketball player; b. Argentina, June 28, 1977; Player Andino, La Rioja, Argentina, 1995—96, Olimpo de Bahía Blanca, Argentina, 1996—97, Basket Viola Reggio Calabria, Italy, 1998—2000, Kinder Bologna, Italy, 2001—02, San Antonio Spurs, 2002—. Player Argentina Nat. Olympic Team, Athens, Greece, 2002. Named Euroleague Finals MVP, 2001, Italian League MVP, 2000—01, 2001—02; named to NBA All-Star game, 2005. Achievements include mem. Argentina Olympic Gold Medal Men's Basketball team, 2002; mem. NBA Champion San Antonio Spurs, 2003, 2005; only player in NBA history to win Olympic Gold medal, NBA Championship, and Euroleague Championship. Office: c/o San Antonio Spurs 1 SBC Center San Antonio TX 78219*

GINOS, JAMES ZISSIS, retired research chemist; b. Hillsboro, Ill., Feb. 1, 1923; s. Zissis and Nicoletta M. (Sakellaris) G.; m. Chrisilla Katsas, June 13, 1947; children: Geoffrey, Milton. BA, Columbia U., 1954; MSChE, Stevens Inst. Tech., 1962, PhD in Organic Chemistry, 1964. Chemist Colgate Palmolive Co., Jersey City, 1953—57; chief chemist Diamond Shamrock Corp., Newark, 1957—58; project coord. Nopco Chem. Co., Harrison, NJ, 1959—64; asst. scientist Brookhaven Nat. Labs., Upton, NY, 1964—68; rsch. asst. prof. Mt. Sinai Sch. Medicine, N.Y.C., 1968—70; assoc. scientist Brookhaven Nat. Labs., 1970—74, scientist, 1974—75; rsch. assoc. prof. Cornell U. Med. Coll., 1975—92, assoc. rsch. prof. neurosci., 1989—92; ret., 1992. Sr. rsch. assoc. neuro-oncology Lab. Meml. Sloan-Kettering Cancer Ctr., N.Y.C., 1980-84, assoc. lab. mem., 1984-89, assoc. lab. mem. nuc. medicine cyclotron core, 1989-93. Contbr. articles to profl. jours. Mem. AAAS, Am. Chem. Soc., Am. Soc. Pharmacology and Exptl. Therapeutics, N.Y. Acad. Sci., Soc. Nuc. Medicine, Harvey Soc. Achievements include research on synthesis of radiopharmaceuticals labelled with shortlived positron emitting radioisotopes used in positron emission tomography; patentee in field. Home: 2222 Norwegian Dr Apt 38 Clearwater FL 33763

GINOZA, WILLIAM, former biophysics educator; b. L.A., Feb. 7, 1914; s. Shinkichi and Kame (Yamashiro) G.; m. Midori Sugita, Oct. 4, 1944 (dec. May 1987); children: Lillian, Donn. BA, U. Calif., Berkeley, 1937, MA, 1939; PhD, UCLA, 1952. Asst. rsch. biochemist dept. botany UCLA, 1952-55, rsch. scientist atomic energy commn., 1956-61; assoc. prof. dept. biophysics Pa. State U., University Park, 1961-67, prof., 1967-79, prof. emeritus, 1979—. Invited speaker ednl. instns. and sci. confs., including Internat. Congress Biochemistry, Vienna, 1958, Faraday Soc. meeting on nucleic acids, Birmingham, Eng., 1958; vis. fellow Yale U., New Haven, 1958-60; vis. prof. U. Kyoto, Japan, 1974. Co-author: Methods in Virology, Vol IV, 1968.; contbr. reviews to Ann. Reviews Nuclear Sci., Ann. Reviews Microbiology; contbr. articles to profl. jours. Fellow AAAS; mem. Biophys. Soc., Sigma Xi, Phi Lambda Upsilon. Achievements include illucidation of molecular structure of Tobacco Mosaic Virus and its RNA, mechanisms by which heat or high energy radiations destroy the biological functions of nucleic acids of viruses and bacteria. Home: 962 E McCormick Ave State College PA 16801-6529

GINSBERG, BARRY, lawyer; b. Bklyn., June 23, 1952; s. Samuel and Helen G.; m. Linda Mary Wagner, Nov. 29, 1979; children: Nathan W., Joanna W. BA cum laude, SUNY Buffalo, 1975, JD cum laude, 1980. Bar: Ill. 1980, N.Y. 1987; cert. fraud examiner. Counsel U.S. Ct. Appeals 7th cir., Chgo., 1980-82; assoc. Isham Lincoln & Beale, Chgo., 1982-87; asst. dist. atty. N.Y. County Dist. Atty., N.Y.C., 1987-94; ptnr. Arthur Andersen, N.Y.C., 1994-98; prin. Barry Ginsberg, Atty.-at-Law, N.Y.C., 1998-99; assoc. gen.

counsel, mng. dir. Decision Strategies/Fairfax Internat., N.Y.C., Stanford, Conn., 1999—2001; exec. mng. dir. Thacher Assocs., N.Y.C., 2002—. Coach Am. Youth Soccer Orgn., Dobbs Ferry, N.Y., 1992—. Mem. ABA (white collar crim com.), Internat. Assn. Ind. Pvt. Sector Inspectors Gen. (bd. dirs.), N.Y. State Bar Assn. (civil prosecuting com.), Assn. CFE's, Assn. of Bar of City of N.Y., N.Y. County Lawyers Assn. Avocations: running, weightlifting, kayaking, biking. Home: 15 Hollywood Dr Dobbs Ferry NY 10522-3008 Office: 330 W 42nd St 9th Floor New York NY 10036

GINSBERG, BARRY GAVRILLE, psychologist, marriage and family therapist; b. Bklyn., July 25, 1936; s. Elias Ginsberg and Lea Schwartz Epstein; m. Mindi Silverberg, Feb. 22, 1962; children: Joshua, Neil Daniel, Jeremy Marc. BS in Pharmacy, columbia U., 1958; MS in Edn./Clin. Sch. Psychology, CCNY, 1969; PhD in Human Devel. and Family Studies, Pa. State U., 1971. Diplomate Am. Bd. Profl. Psychology; lic. pharmacist, NY, NJ, Calif., Fla.; cert. tchr., NY; lic. psychologist, Pa., Mass.; cert. play therapist/supr., cert. marriage and family therapist; nat. cert. sch. psychologist. Pharmacist, mgr. Ginsberg Pharmacy, Bronx, N.Y., 1958-63; tchr. jr. and sr. h.s. N.Y.C. Bd. Edn., 1963-69; psychologist Bucks County Psychiat. Ctr., Chalfont, Pa., 1971-73; dir. child and family unit Lenape Valley Found., Chalfont, 1973-75, dir. cmty. svcs., 1975-78; psychologist dir. Ginsberg Assocs., Doylestown, Pa., 1978—; cons. and trainer, dir. Ctr. Relationship Enhancement, Doylestown, 1981—. Adj. assoc. prof. Temple U., 1975-85; cons. Bucks County Area Coun. Aging, 1988—, Bucks County Children and Youth, Doylestown, 1989—, Bucks County Head Start, Bucks County Assn. Retarded Citizens, Doylestown, 1982—; adj. prof. psychology Phila. Coll. Osteo. Medicine, 1997; adj. prof. clin. psychology Chestnut Hill Coll., 2000. Author: Relationship Enhancement Family Therapy, 1997, 50 Wonderful Ways to Be a Single Parent Family, 2002; columnist Parenting, 1988-89; co-host (cable TV) Parenting, 1994—. Bd. dirs. Big Bros./Big Sisters of Bucks County, 1972—, Bucks County Drug and Alcohol Commn., 1981-87, Network of Victims Asistance, 1990-95. Recipient Sterling Vol. award Ctrl. Bucks C. of C., 1996, Meritorious award Am. Bd. Profl. Psychology, 1992, Meritorious award Bucks County Drug and Alcohol Commn., 1987. Fellow APA (bd. dirs. divsn. family psychology, Meritorious awards divsn. family psychology 1986, 87, 88, 89), Pa. Psychol. Assn. (bd. dirs., pres. cmty. divsn.), Am. Assn. Marriage and Family Therapists (clin. mem., approved supr.), Ctrl. Bucks C. of C. (v.p., bd. dirs. 1975-89, chmn. parenting and family com. 1990—). Avocations: racquetball, folk dancing, nutcracker ballet. Office: Ctr Relationship Enhancement 70 W Oakland St Ste 313 Doylestown PA 18901 Office Phone: 215-348-2424. Personal E-mail: enhancerelations@aol.com.

GINSBERG, BARRY HOWARD, physician, researcher; b. Bklyn., May 9, 1945; s. Emanuel and Ruth (Friedman) G.; m. Marjorie Ellen Kanef, Aug. 20, 1967; children: Susan, David. BA, SUNY, Binghamton, 1965; PhD, Yeshiva U., 1971, MD, 1972. Intern Beth Israel Hosp., Boston, 1972-73, resident in internal medicine, 1973-74; fellow in endocrinology NIH, 1974-77; asst. prof. U. Iowa, Iowa City, 1977-82, assoc. prof. medicine and biochemistry, 1982—87, prof., 1988-90, assoc. dir. Diabetes-Endocrinology Rsch. Ctr., 1982-84, dir., 1984-86, co-dir. diabetes control and complications trial, 1984—86, dir., 1986-90; med. dir. worldwide diabetes healthcare Becton Dickinson and Co., Franklin Lakes, NJ, 1990—98; v.p. med. affairs BD Consumer Healthcare, 1999—2005. Adj. prof. medicine Robert Wood Johnson Coll. Medicine. Contbr. chpts. to med. books. Comdr. USPHS, 1974-77. Mem. Am. Fedn. Clin. Rsch., Endocrine Soc., Ctrl. Soc. Clin. Rsch., Am. Diabetes Assn. (pres. Iowa chpt. 1982-84, bd. dirs. 1982-85, bd. dirs. N.E. chpt. 1989—). Avocation: computer programming. Office: Becton Dickinson and Co 1 Becton Dr Franklin Lakes NJ 07417-1880 E-mail: barry_ginsberg@bd.com.

GINSBERG, DAVID LAWRENCE, architect; b. N.Y.C., Sept. 21, 1932; s. Harry Seaman and Zena (Sagal)S.; m. Emily (Boor), Dec. 29, 1969; children: Stuart Samuel, Daniel Paul, Laura Ruth. BArch, Cornell U., 1955. Ptnr. charge N.Y. offices Perkins and Will, N.Y.C., 1957-78; exec. v.p. Perkins and Will, Chgo., 1978-79; exec. v.p. and chief planning officer Columbia-Presbyn. Health Svc., Inc., N.Y.C., 1979-92; v.p. Columbia-Presbyn. Health Sys., Inc., N.Y.C.; dep. to pres. Presbyn. Hosp., N.Y.C., 1993-95; ptnr. Larsen, Shein, Ginsberg, and Snyder LLP, N.Y.C., 1995—. Mem. adv. group, asst. clin. prof. pub. health Columbia U., N.Y.C., 1979-97; sr. cons. U.S. Global Health Svc., 1992-94; mem. Nat. Healthcare Guidelines Com. Mem. parents coun. Washington U., St. Louis, 1988-91; mem. Scarsdale Planning Bd., 1980-90; sec. bd. trustees N.Y. Presbyn. Hosp. Infant and Child Care Ctr.; v.p., bd. dirs. Stephen Wise Free Synagogue. Recipient medal N.Y. Soc. Architects, 1955, award N.Y. Soc. for Health Planning, 1993, Modern Healthcare Design award. Fellow A1A (nat. guidlines revision com.); mem. APHA, Acad. Architecture for Health, Forum for Healthcare Planning, Am. Hosp. Assn., Assn. Am. Med. Colls., Soc. Hosp. Planning, Regional Planning Assn., Gargoyle Soc. Office: Larsen Shein Ginsberg & Snyder LLP 170 Varick St New York NY 10013-1221 Office Phone: 212-803-0300. Business E-Mail: dginsberg@Lsgsarchitects.com.

GINSBERG, DONALD MAURICE, physicist, researcher; b. Chgo., Nov. 19, 1933; s. Maurice J. and Zelda Ginsberg; m. Joli D. Lasker, June 10, 1957; children: Mark D., Dana L. BA, U. Chgo., 1952, BS, 1955, MS (NSF fellow), 1956; PhD (NSF fellow), U. Calif. at Berkeley, 1960. Mem. faculty U. Ill., Urbana, 1959-97, prof. physics, 1966-97, prof. emeritus, 1997—. Vis. scientist in physics Am. Assn. Physics Tchrs.-Am. Inst. Physics, 1965-71; vis. scientist IBM, 1976; mem. evaluation com. for Nat. High-Field Magnet Lab., NSF, 1977-79, 85, 91; mem. rev. com. for solid state sci. div. Argonne Nat. Lab., 1977-83, chmn., 1980; mem. rev. panel for basic energy scis. div. Dept. Energy, 1981 Editor: Physical Properties of High Temperature Superconductors, Vols. 1, 2, 3, 4, and 5, 1989, 90, 92, 94, 96; contbr. to Ency. Britannica, 1971, 82, 88, 94, 96, Concise Ency. of Magnetic and Superconducting Materials, 1992. Alfred P. Sloan rsch. fellow, 1960-64, NSF fellow, 1966-67; U. Ill. scholar, 1994; recipient Daniel C. Drucker award U. Ill. Engring. Coll., 1992. Fellow Am. Phys. Soc. (winner Oliver E. Buckley Consensed Matter Physics prize 1998); mem. AAAS, Phi Beta Kappa, Sigma Xi. Achievements include research and publications on low temperature physics, superconductivity, cryogenic instrumentation. Home: 2208 Grange Cir Urbana IL 61801-6607 Office: Loomis Lab 1110 W Green St Urbana IL 61801-9013

GINSBERG, ELIZABETH, artist, educator; b. NYC, 1942; BFA, R.I. Sch. design, 1964. Instr. R.I. Sch. Design, Providence, 1970-71; assoc. prof. Moore Coll. Art, Phila., 1971-86; mem. faculty Parson Sch. Design, N.Y.C., 1976-77. Lectr. Kyoto Fukikawa Coll. Art, Japan, U. Utah, Salt Lake city, R.I. Sch. Design; dir. travel/study program to Japan Moore Coll. Art, 1973. One-person shows include Seattle Pacific U., 1995, Bokushin Gallery, Tokyo, 1995, Casements Cultural Ctr., Ormond Beach, Fla., 1996, Pintsch Contemp. Art Mus., Germany, 1997; Ea. Mont. Coll., Billings, 1992, Anchorage Mus. History and Art, 1993, Witter Gallery, Storm Lake, Iowa, 1998-99, Iowa State U. Gallery, Ames, Iowa, 2001, Waldorf Gallery, Forest City, Iowa, 2001, Yavapai Coll., Prescott, Ariz., 2001, William Woods U., Fulton, Mo., 2001, TAI Gallery, NYC, 2001, 2003, Castello di Roncade, Roncade, Italy, 2004, Switzer Ctr. for the Arts, Fla, 2005, Southern Light Gallery, Amarillo Coll., Tex., 2005, Tai Gallery, N.Y., 2005, others; group shows include Marsha Mateyka Gallery, Washington, 1990, Nat. Acad. Scis., Washington, 1991, others; represented in permanent collections: Chase Manhattan Bank, N.A., NYC, Gallery Point, Tokyo, Union Carbide Corp., NYC, First Nat. City Bank, NYC, European-Am. Bank, NYC, U.S. Steel Corp., NYC, Am. Fedn. Savs., Orlando, Fla., First Options Chgo., Port Authority NY, Castello di Poncade, Italy, 2005, Southern Light Gallery, Tex., 2005, Chuo Koran Sha Corp., Tokyo, Security Pacific Nat. Bank, Carmichal, Calif., Davis, Polk, and Wardwell, NYC, A.P.F., NYC, Cigna Collectio, Phila Carnegie grantee, 1963-64, Moore Coll. Art, 1982; Textron fellow, 1965. Office: 5 Great Jones St New York NY 10012-1157

GINSBERG, ERNEST, lawyer, banker; s. Morris Henry and Mildred Florence (Slive) G.; m. Harriet Gay Scharf, Dec. 20, 1959; children: Alan Justin, Robert Daniel. BA, Syracuse U., 1953, JD, 1955; LLM, Georgetown U., 1963. Bar: N.Y. 1955, U.S. Supreme Ct. 1964. Pvt. practice law, Syracuse, 1957-61; mem. staff, office chief counsel IRS, Washington, 1961-63; tax counsel Comptr. of Currency, Washington, 1964-65, assoc. chief counsel, 1965-68; v.p. legal affairs, sec. Republic Nat. Bank N.Y., N.Y.C., 1968-74; sr. v.p. legal affairs, sec. Republic Nat. Bank, N.Y.C., 1975-86, exec. v.p., gen. counsel, sec., 1984-86, vice chmn. bd., gen. counsel, 1986-94, vice chmn. bd., 1990-99. Sr. v.p., sec. legal affairs Republic N.Y. Corp., N.Y.C., 1974-84, exec. v.p., gen. counsel, sec., 1984-86, vice chmn. bd., gen. counsel, sec., 1986-94, vice chmn. bd., 1986-99, also bd. dirs.; bd. visitors Syracuse U. Coll. Law, 1980-2005; bd. dirs. Safra Nat. Bank of N.Y., N.Y.C. Chmn. emeritus Roundabout Theatre Co., N.Y.C. With U.S. Army, 1955-57. Mem. Am. Bankers Assn. (bd. dirs. 1995-97), Am. Bankers Coun. (co-chmn. 1992-94), N.Y. State Bankers Assn. (pres. 1993-94), Bankers Roundtable (bd. dirs. 1995-97), Phi Sigma Delta, Phi Delta Phi. Office Phone: 305-936-9322.

GINSBERG, HERSH MEIER, rabbi, religious organization administrator; b. Vienna, July 8, 1928; s. Lazar Yonah Ginsberg and Perl Roth; m. Fradel Levy; children: Lazar Yonah, Meshulim, Chana. Dir. Union Orthodox Rabbis of U.S. and Can.; rabbinical ct. judge; dean Rabbi Jacob-Joseph Sch., N.Y.C., 1955-73. Founder Kolel Ohel Elemelech Rabbinical Coll., Jerusalem. Jewish. Office: Union Orthodox Rabbis US & Can 235 E Broadway New York NY 10002-5600

GINSBERG, MARC CHARLES, former diplomat, investment company executive; b. N.Y.C., Oct. 18, 1950; m. Janet Louise Ginsberg; two children. BA, MBA, Am. U.; JD, Georgetown U., 1978. Legis. asst. to Sen. Edward Kennedy, 1973-76; spl. asst. to under sec. of mgmt. Dept. State, 1977-80; dep. sr. adviser to Pres. for Middle East affairs, 1980-81; atty. Surrey & Morse, D.C., 1981-87, Galland, Kharasch, Morse & Garfinkle, D.C., 1987-93; U.S. amb. to Morocco, 1993-98; pres. Georgetown Global Investments Corp., Washington, 1998-2000; CEO, mng. dir. Northstar Equity Group Inc, Washington, 2000—. Contbr. FOX News Channel. Mem. ABA, D.C. Bar Assn. Office: Northstar Equity Group Inc 1615 L St NW Ste 900 Washington DC 20036-5623

GINSBERG, MYRON, computer scientist; b. Brockton, Mass., May 3, 1943; s. Frank and Evelyn Hazel (Spekin) Ginsberg; m. Judith Beverly Rosenbaum, Nov. 19, 1989; 1 child, Ellen Joy Hochberg. BA in Math., Boston U., 1965; MA in Math., Clark U., 1967; PhD in Computer Sci., U. Iowa, 1972. Instr. dept. computer sci. U. Iowa, Iowa City, 1969-72; from asst. prof. to assoc. prof. computer sci. So. Meth. U., Dallas, 1972-77, 77-79; NASA/ASEE rsch. fellow NASA Langley Rsch. Ctr, Hampton, Va., summer 1979, summer 2000; assoc. sr. rsch. scientist GM Rsch. Labs., Warren, Mich., 1979-81, sr. rsch. scientist, 1981-82, staff rsch. scientist, 1982-92; cons. sys. engr. EDS Advanced Computing Ctr., GM NAO R & D Ctr., Warren, 1992-96, EDS High Performance Computing Group, Troy, Mich., 1996-97; ind. cons. HPC Rsch. and Edn., Farmington Hills, Mich., 1997—. Mathematician U.S. Army Ballistics Rsch. Lab., Aberdeen Proving Ground, Md., 1964—67; data sys. analyst NASA Electronics Rsch. Ctr., Cambridge, Mass., 1968—69; adj. assoc. prof. U. Mich., Ann Arbor, 1990; mem. adv. bd. Cray Rsch. Fortran, 1991—92; grant rev. panelist NSF, 1992—93, 1996—97; GM/EDS rep. Supercomputing Automotive Applications Partnership, 1992—94; founder, first chmn. AUTOBENCH Project U.S. Coun. Automotive Rsch., 1995—96; mem. couns. advisors HPC area Gerson Lehrman Group, N.Y.C., 2002—. Editor: Supercomputers in the Auto Industry, 1985, Automotive Applications of Supercomputers, 1988, High-Speed and Large-Scale Computing: A Panoramic View, 1988, Automotive Applications of Vector/Parallel Computers: State-of-the-Art, 1992; contbr. articles to profl. jours.; mem. editl. bd. Computing Sys. Engring., 1988—93. Grantee, Mobil Oil Found., 1975, Alfred P. Sloan Found., 1975—78, U.S. Army C.E., 1977—78, NSF, 1977—79, 1983—84. Fellow: Assn. Computing Machinery (lectr., bd. dirs. SIGNUM, editor-in-chief SIGNUM newsletter 1976—80); mem.: ASME (lectr.), IEEE (sr.; program evaluator 2003—), Soc. Automotive Engr. (founder, 1st chmn. com. high performance computing stds. for automotive mfg. 1996—97, lectr., award for excellence in oral presentation 1985—87, Disting. Spkr. plaque 1988, Forest R. McFarland award 1994), Soc. Indsl. and Applied Math. (lectr. spl. group supercomputing), Computer Soc. of IEEE (lectr.), Sigma Xi (lectr.). Avocations: playing alto sax, tenor sax, soprano sax, clarinet and flute, listening to jazz and classical music. Office: HPC Rsch & Education 35764 Congress Rd Ste 100 Farmington MI 48335-1222 E-mail: m.ginsberg@ieee.org.

GINSBERG, MYRON DAVID, neurologist; b. Denver, Aug. 26, 1939; s. Morris Seymour and Evelyn (Fishman) G.; children: Deborah Mara, Emily Michelle. BA, Wesleyan U., 1961; MD, Harvard U., 1966. Intern, resident Harvard Med. Svc., Boston City Hosp., 1966-68; neurology resident, fellow Mass. Gen. Hosp., Boston, 1968-70, 72-73; staff assoc. Lab. Perinatal Physiology, NIH, Bethesda, Md., 1970-72; asst. prof., assoc. prof. dept. neurology U. Pa., Phila., 1973-79; assoc. prof. neurology U. Miami (Fla.) Sch. Medicine, 1979-81, prof. neurology, 1981—, dir. cerebral vascular disease rsch. ctr., 1981—, dir. neurotrauma clin. rsch. ctr., 1991-95, Peritz Scheinberg endowed chair of neurology, 1992—. Mem. study sect. NIH, Bethesda, 1982-86; nat. rsch. com. Am. Heart Assn., Dallas, 1986-91. Editor: Cerebrovascular Diseases, 16th Princeton Conf., 1989; editor Jour. Blood Flow and Metabolism, 1992-97; contbr. over 280 articles to profl. jours. Lt. comdr. USPHS, 1970-72. Fulbright scholar U.S. Govt., 1961-62; recipient Jacob Javits Neuroscience Investigator award NIH, 1985-92, Willis Lectr. award, Am. Stroke Assn., 2002, Disting. Scientist award Am. Heart Assn., 2003, Disting. Faculty Scholar award U. Miami, 2004. Fellow Am. Acad. Neurology; mem. Am. Neurol. Assn. (membership com. 1990-91), Am. Physiol. Soc., Internat. Soc. Cerebral Blood Flow & Metabolism (dir. 1985-89), Phi Beta Kappa, Alpha Omega Alpha. Office: U Miami Sch Medicine Dept Neurology D4-5 PO Box 016960 Miami FL 33101-6960 Office Phone: 305-243-6449.

GINSBERG, NORMAN ARTHUR, physician, educator; b. Chgo., May 28, 1946; m. Denise Ginsberg; children: Melinda, Sara. BA, So. Ill. U., 1968; postgrad., Ill. Coll. Pharmacy, 1968-69, U. Guadalerjara, 1969-72; MD, Chgo. Med. Sch., 1974. Diplomate Am. Bd. Ob-gyn. Intern Michael Reese Hosp. and Med. Ctr., Chgo., 1974-75, resident in ob-gyn., 1975-79, mem. staff, 1979—; pvt. practice in ob-gyn. Chgo. Mem. staff Northwestern Hosp. and Med. Ctr., 1984—; investigator 1st trimester diagnosis of inheritable diseases WHO. Bd. dirs. Nat. Abortion Rights League Ill. Fellow Am. Coll. Ob-gyn., Am. Soc. Human Genetics, Ctrl. Assn. Ob-gyn.; mem. AMA, Am. Fertility Soc., Chgo. Med. Soc. Achievements include pioneering of chorionic villi sampling in U.S.; first trimester screening for Down's Syndrome; pre-implantation genetis in U.S. Home: 1520 Eastwood Ave Highland Park IL 60035-2729 Office: Assn for Women's Health Care Ltd 30 N Michigan Ave Ste 607 Chicago IL 60602-3405 Office Phone: 312-726-3917.

GINSBURG, ALLEN J., lawyer; b. July 5, 1944; BS, Northwestern U., 1965, JD cum laude, 1968. Bar: Ill. 1969, U.S. Tax Ct. 1973; CPA, Ill. Ptnr.-in-charge Chgo. office DLA Piper Rudnick Gray Cary, Chgo. Address: DLA Piper Rudnick Gray Cary Ste 1900 203 N La Salle St Chicago IL 60601-1210 Office Phone: 312-368-4025. Office Fax: 312-630-5357. Business E-Mail: allen.ginsburg@dlapiper.com.

GINSBURG, CHARLES DAVID, lawyer; b. N.Y.C., Apr. 20, 1912; s. Nathan and Rae (Lewis) G.; m. Marianne Laïs; children by previous marriage: Jonathan, Susan, Mark. AB, W.Va. U., 1932; LLB, Harvard U., 1935. Bar: W. Va. 1935, U.S. Supreme Ct. 1940, D.C. 1946, U.S. Ct. Appeals (2d, 3rd, 4th, 7th, and Fed. cirs.) 1946, U.S. Claims Ct. 1960, U.S. Tax Ct. 1961. Atty. for public utilities div. and office of gen. counsel SEC, 1935-39; law sec. to Justice William O. Douglas, 1939; asst. to commr. SEC, 1939-40; legal adviser Price Stblzn. Div., Nat. Def. Adv. Com., 1940-41; gen. counsel Office Price Adminstrn. and Civilian Supply, 1941-42, OPA, 1942-43; pvt. practice law Ginsburg, Feldman and Bress, Washington, 1946-98; founding ptnr. Ginsburg, Feldman & Bress, 1946-98; sr. counsel firm Powell, Goldstein, LLP, 1998; adminstrv. asst. to Senator M.M. Neely, W.Va., 1950; adj. prof. internat. law Georgetown U. (Grad. Sch. Law), 1959-67. Dep. commr. U.S. del. Austrian Treaty Commn., Vienna, 1947; adviser U.S. del. Council Fgn. Ministers, London, 1947; Mem. Presdl. Emergency Bd. 166 (Airlines), 1966; mem. Pres.'s Commn. on Postal Orgn., 1967; chmn. Presdl. Emergency Bd. 169 (Railroads), 1969; exec. dir. Nat. Adv. Commn. Civil Disorders, 1967 Author: The Future of German Reparations; Contbr. to legal jours. Bd. mem., chmn. exec. com. Nat. Symphony Orch. Assn., 1960-69; bd. govs. Weizmann Inst., 1965 (hon. fellow 1972); mem. vis. com. Harvard-Mass. Inst. Tech. Joint Ctr. on Urban Studies, 1969; trustee St. John's Coll., 1969-76, chmn. bd., 1974-76; overseers com. Kennedy Sch. Govt. Harvard, 1971—; mem. coun. Nat. Harvard Law Sch. Assn., 1972—, gen. counsel Dem. Nat. Com., 1968-70. Served from pvt. to capt. AUS, 1942-46; dep. dir. econs. div. Office Mil. Govt., 1945-46; Germany. Decorated Bronze Star, Legion of Merit; recipient Presdl. Cert. of Merit. Mem. ABA, Fed. Bar Assn, Am. Law Inst., Coun. on Fgn. Rels., Met. Club, Army and Navy Club, Phi Beta Kappa. Democrat. Home: 619 S Lee St Alexandria VA 22314-3819 Office: 901 New York Ave NW Washington DC 20001-2505 Office Phone: 202-624-7356. Business E-Mail: dginsbur@pogolaw.com.

GINSBURG, DAVID, human genetics educator, researcher; b. Newburgh, NY, Aug. 11, 1952; s. Leonard and Ruth Helena Henrietta (Falkson) G.; m. Maureen Rose Kushinsky, June 7, 1981; children: Daniel William, Leah Beth. BA magna cum laude, Yale U., 1974; MD, Duke U., 1977. Diplomate Am. Bd. Internal Medicine, subspecialties in med. oncology and hematology; diplomate Am. Bd. Med. Genetics. Resident in pathology Presbyn. Hosp., San Francisco, 1977-78; intern, resident in internal medicine Peter Bent Brigham Hosp., Boston, 1978-81; fellow tng. program in hematology and med. oncology Brigham and Women's Hosp., Harvard Med. Sch., Boston, 1981-84; instr. medicine Harvard Med. Sch., Boston, 1984-85; asst. prof. dept. medicine U. Mich., Ann Arbor, 1985-89, assoc. prof. with tenure, 1989-93, assoc. prof. human genetics, 1989-93; asst. investigator Howard Hughes Med. Inst. Howard Hughes Med. Inst., Ann Arbor, 1985-89, assoc. investigator, 1989-93; prof. internal medicine and human genetics, 1993—; dir. divsn. med. genetics, dept. medicine, 1993—2002; investigator Howard Hughes Med. Inst., 1993—. Contbr. numerous articles to profl. jours. Fellow AAAS; mem. ACP, Am. Soc. Human Genetics, Am. Soc. Hematology (E. Donnall Thomas lectr. and prize 2000), Am. Heart Assn. (Sol Sherry lectr., 2002, Basic Rsch. prize 2003), Assn. Am. Physicians, Am. Soc. for Clin. Investigation (pres., 2002, ASCI award, 2004), Inst. Medicine, Am. Acad. Arts and Scis., Alpha Omega Alpha. Jewish. Office: Life Scis Inst Rm 5028 210 Washtenaw Ave Ann Arbor MI 48109 Business E-Mail: ginsburg@umich.edu.

GINSBURG, DOUGLAS HOWARD, federal judge; b. Chgo., May 25, 1946; Diploma, Latin Sch. Chgo., 1963; BS, Cornell U., 1970; JD, U. Chgo., 1973. Bar: Ill. 1973, Mass. 1982, U.S. Supreme Ct. 1984, U.S. Ct. Appeals (9th cir.) 1986. Assoc. Covington & Burling, Washington, 1972; law clk. to Hon. Carl McGowan U.S. Ct. Appeals, Washington, 1973—74; law clk. to Justice Thorogood Marshall U.S. Supreme Ct., Washington, 1974—75; prof. Harvard U., 1975—83; dep. asst. atty. gen. for antitrust divsn U.S. Dept. Justice, Washington, 1983—84; adminstr. for info. and regulatory affairs Exec. Office Pres., Office Mgmt. and Budget, Washington, 1984—85; asst. atty. gen. antitrust divsn. U.S. Dept. Justice, Washington, 1985—86; judge U.S. Ct. Appeals (D.C. cir.), 1986—, chief judge, 2001—. Vis. prof. law Columbia U., NYC, 1987—88; lectr. law Harvard U., Cambridge, Mass., 1988—89; disting. prof. law George Mason U., Arlington, Va., 1988—; Charles J. Merriam vis. scholar, sr. lectr. U. Chgo., 1990—, 1994. Author: Regulation of Broadcasting: Law and Policy Towards Radio, Television and Cable Communications, 1979, Antitrust, Uncertainty, and Technological Innovation, 1980; co-author: Regulation of the Electronic Mass Media, 1991; editor (with W. Abernathy): Government, Technology and the Future of the Automobile, 1980; contbr. articles to profl. jours. Recipient Casper Platt award, U. Chgo. Law Sch., 1972; Mecham scholar, 1970—73. Mem.: ABA (jud. rep. antitrust sect. coun. 2000—03), Mont Pelerin Soc., Am. Law and Econs. Assn., Am. Econ. Assn., Phi Kappa Phi, Order of Coif. Avocations: historic preservation, land conservation. Office: US Ct Appeals 333 Constitution Ave NW Washington DC 20001-2866*

GINSBURG, ESTELLE, artist; b. St. Louis; Student, U. Mo., Bklyn. Mus. Art Sch., Cornell U. Art lectr., tchr. Five Towns Music and Art Found., N.Y., Hewlett-Woodmere Sch. Dist., North Shore Community Arts Ctr., N.Y., Nassau Office Cultural Devel. in Sch. Program. One-woman shows include Cen. Hall Gallery, N.Y., Brentanos Gallery, N.Y., Town Hall Showcase, N.Y., Post Coll., N.Y., Port Washington Library, N.Y., Peninsual Pub. Library, N.Y., Nassau Library Systems, N.Y., Fine Arts Mus. Nassau County, N.Y.; exhibited in group shows at Hofstra U., N.Y., L.I. U., N.Y., N.Y. State Pavillion, Norfolk (Va.) Mus. Art, J. Walter Thompson Co., N.Y., Heckscher Mus., N.Y., Fordham U., N.Y., Nat. Acad., N.Y., Audobon Soc., N.Y., N.Y. Inst. Tech., Grad. Ctr. CUNY, Ball State U., Plaza Gallery, Rochester, N.Y., Royal Acad., Stockholm, Fontana Gallery, Pa., R.A.A. Gallery, N.Y.C., Cen. Art Gallery, N.Y., Brentanos Gallery, N.Y., Rhoda Ochs Gallery, N.Y., Art Resources, Ltd., N.Y., Isis Gallery, N.Y., Nancy Stien Gallery, N.Y.C.; represented in permanent collections C.W. Post Coll., N.Y., U. Mass., Amherst, Far Gallery, N.Y.C., Stony Brook U., N.Y., Avnet Gallery, N.Y., Tasca Gallery, N.Y.C., North Shore Arts Gallery, N.Y., Artium Gallery, N.Y., Lenid Gallery, N.Y., Off Broadway Gallery, N.Y., Kessler Gallery, Provincetown, Mass., Mus. of State U. N.Y., Stony Brook, C.W. Post Coll., N.Y., U. Mass., Amherst; represented in pvt. and pub. collections throughout U.S., Europe and South Am. Recipient Mixed Media award Heckscher Mus., N.Y., Five Towns Music and Art Found., N.Y., Port Washington Library Exhbn., N.Y., Sculpture award North Shore Juried Art Exhbn. Home and Office: 370 Longacre Ave Woodmere NY 11598-2417

GINSBURG, GERALD J., lawyer, management consultant; b. Poughkeepsie, N.Y., Aug. 29, 1930; s. Abraham and Anna (Murkoff) G.; children: Jason Andrew, Stephanie Carla. BS, Syracuse U., 1952; JD, Bklyn. Law Sch., 1958. Bar: N.Y. 1959. Pub. acct., 1954-59; v.p. fin. and ops., dir. Sheffield Watch Corp., N.Y.C., 1959-70, dir., 1967-70; exec. v.p., dir. Kurt Orban Co., Wayne, N.J., 1971-83; pres., dir. Pacific Marine Holdings Corp., 1983-87; pres. J&S Cons., Walnut Creek, CAlif. Dir. Ramapo Fin. Corp., Pilgrim State Bank Served with USNR, 1952-53. Mem. ABA, N.Y. Bar Assn. Office: PO Box 5314 Walnut Creek CA 94596-1314

GINSBURG, GILBERT J., lawyer, educator; b. Chgo., Aug. 26, 1936; s. Maurice I. and Sarah (Ginsberg) G.; m. Faith D. Rosenson, June 28, 1959; children: Yale Maurice, David Bennett, Benjamin Lavin, Raphael Natan, Herzl, Melissa. BA, U. Chgo., 1954, JD, 1957. Bar: D.C., Ill., U.S. Claims Ct., U.S. Ct. Appeals (2d cir., Fed. cir., D.C. cir.), U.S. Supreme Ct. Atty., advisor Army Corps. Engrs., Chgo., 1958-59; prof. law Army JAG Sch., Charlottesville, Va., 1959-62; atty. NASA Gen. Counsel Office, Washington, 1962-66; prof. law George Washington U., Washington, 1967-80, dir. govt. contracts, 1973-80; dean Touro Law Sch., N.Y.C., 1980-81; sr. ptnr. Epstein Becker & Green, Washington, 1981-96. Adj. prof. George Washington U., 1981—; co-dir. a-76 Inst.; speaker in field. Author: Federal Labor Standards, 1997, Employer's Guide to FLSA, 1993, FLSA Handbook, 1986, Pricing of Claims, 1999, Loss of Efficiency and Extended Overhead Claims, 1999, The Service Contract Act, 2005, others; contbr. articles to profl. jours. Pres. Yeshiva of Greater Washington, 1965-73, Young Israel, Washington, 1962-65, 75-80; bd. dirs. Touro Coll., 1971—. Capt. U.S. Army, JAGC, 1959-62. Mem. ABA, Fed. Bar Assn., Order of Coif. Democrat. Jewish. Avocations: swimming, bridge. Office: 1250 24th St NW Ste 350 Washington DC 20037-1124 Office Phone: 202-776-7772. Personal E-mail: gilgins@aol.com, profgins@aol.com.

GINSBURG, IONA HOROWITZ, psychiatrist; b. N.Y.C., Dec. 2, 1931; d. A. Eugene and Gertrude (Seidman) Horowitz; m. Selig M. Ginsburg, Aug. 15, 1954 (div. 1984); children: Elizabeth, Jessica. AB, Vassar Coll., 1953; MD, Columbia U., 1957. Diplomate Am. Bd. Psychiatry and Neurology. Pvt. practice, N.Y.C., 1961—; instr. psychiatry Columbia U., N.Y.C., 1961-81, asst. clin. prof. psychiatry, 1981-95, assoc. clin. prof. psychiatry, 1995—; psychiatrist student health svc. NYU, N.Y.C., 1978—2000. Cons.-liaison psychiatrist Columbia Presbyn. Med. Ctr., N.Y.C., 1982—. Contbr. articles to profl. jours. Med. adv. bd. Nat. Psoriasis Found. 1990-95. Recipient Josie Bradbury Travel award, Psoriasis Assn. Gt. Britain. Mem. Am. Soc. Adolescent Psychiatry, N.Y. Soc. Adolescent Psychiatry (pres. 1986, cert. of appreciation 1986), Am. Psychiat. Assn., Am. Psychosomatic Soc., Met. Coll. Mental Health Assn. (pres. 1980), Assn. Psychocutaneous Medicine N.Am. (sec.-treas. 1994-95, v.p. 1995-98, pres. 1998-2000). Office Phone: 212-289-5050.

GINSBURG, MARTIN DAVID, lawyer, educator; b. NYC, June 10, 1932; s. Morris and Evelyn (Bayer) Ginsburg; m. Ruth Bader, June 23, 1954; children: Jane, James. AB, Cornell U., 1953; JD, Harvard U., 1958; LLD (hon.), Lewis and Clark Coll., 1992, Wheaton Coll., 1997. Bar: N.Y. 1959, D.C. 1980. Practiced in N.Y.C., 1959-79; mem. firm Weil, Gotshal & Manges, N.Y.C., 1963-79; of counsel firm Fried, Frank, Harris, Shriver and Jacobson, Washington, 1980—; Charles Keller Beekman prof. law Columbia U. Law Sch., N.Y.C., 1979-80; prof. law Georgetown U. Law Center, Washington, 1980—; lectr. U. Leiden, The Netherlands, 1982; lectr. Salzburg Seminar Austria, 1984; mem. tax divsn adv. group Dept. Justice, 1980-81; mem. adv. group to Commr. Internal Revenue, 1978-80; mem. adv. bd. U. Calif. Securities Regulation Inst., 1973-91. Adj. prof. law NYU, 1967—79; vis. prof. law Stanford U., Calif., 1978, Harvard U., Cambridge, Mass., 1986, U. Chgo., 1990, NYU, 1993; cons. joint com. on taxation U.S. Congress, 1979—80, acad. advisor, 2000—01; chmn. tax adv. bd. Commerce Clearing House, 1982—94; mem. bd. advisors NYU/IRS Continuing Profl. Edn. Program, 1983—88, co-chmn., 1986—88; sub coun. on capital allocation, co-chmn. taxation expert group Competitiveness Policy Coun., 1993—95; chmn. tax adv. bd. Little, Brown, 1994—96; bd. dirs. Millennium Chems., Inc., 1996—2003, Chgo. Classical Rec. Found.; lectr. various tax insts. Co-author: Mergers, Acquisitions, and Buyouts, 4 vol., 2005; spec. editor: Structuring Venture Capital, Private Equity, and Entrepreneurial Transactions, 2005; contbr. articles to legal jours. Mem. vis. com. Harvard Law Sch., 1994—98. 1st lt. arty. U.S. Army, 1954—56. Recipient Chair named in his honor, Georgetown U. Law Ctr., 1986, Marshall-Wythe Medallion, Coll. of William and Mary Sch. Law, 1996, Outstanding Achievement award, Tax Soc. NYU, 1993, Viccenial medal, Georgetown U., 2000. Fellow: Am. Bar Found. (bd. dirs. 2000—03), Am. Coll. Tax Counsel; mem.: ABA (mem. com. corp. taxation, tax sect. 1973—, chmn. com. simplification 1979—81, mem. tax sect. coun. 1984—87, tax systems task force 1995—97), Assn. Bar City N.Y. (chmn. com. taxation 1977—79, mem. audit com. 1980—81), N.Y. State Bar Assn. (mem. tax sect. exec. com. 1969—, chmn. tax sect. 1975, ho. of dels. 1976—77), Am. Law Inst. (cons. Fed. Income Tax Project 1974—93). Office: 600 New Jersey Ave NW Washington DC 20001-2022 Office Phone: 202-639-7030. Business E-Mail: ginsbma@ffhsj.com.

GINSBURG, MAX, artist; b. Paris, France; s. Abraham and Rachel Ginsburg; m. Miryam Soman Ginsburg; children: Marc, Maya stepchildren: David, Liana. BFA, Syracuse U., 1953; MA, City Coll. of NY, 1963. One-man shows include Harbor Gallery, Cold Spring Harbor, NY, Reyn Gallery, NYC, Gallery 306, Phila., Franklin Mint, Pa., Syracuse U., exhibited in group shows at Invitational, Gallery Henoch, NY, 2004, Mus. of the City of NY, Am. Acad. and Inst. of Arts and Letters, NY, Nat. Acad. Design, Butler Inst., Ohio, Greenhouse Gallery, San Antonio, Tx., Hermitage Found. Mus., Norfolk, Va., Huntsville Mus. of Art, J. Wayne Stark Gallery, Tex., Mus. of Tex. Tech. U., Bergstron Mahler Mus., Wis., Danville Mus. of Fine Art and History, Va., USVC Woodbury Gallery, Utah, Represented in permanent collections New Britain Mus. of Am. Art, Conn., NY Cultural Ctr. Mus., Fairleigh Dickinson U., Soc. of Illustrators Mus. Collection, H.J. Heinz Co., Martin Luther King Labor Ctr. et. al.

GINSBURG, NORTON SYDNEY, retired geographer; b. Chgo., Aug. 24, 1921; s. Morris and Sarah (Ginsberg) G.; m. Diana Roselle Peterson, Aug. 12, 1973; children: Jeremy, Alexander. BA, U. Chgo., 1941, MA, 1947, PhD, 1949. Geographer U.S. Army Map Service, 1941-42; prof. geography U. Chgo., 1947-86, assoc. dean Coll., 1963-66, assoc. dean social scis., 1967-69; dean academic program, sr. fellow Center for Study Democratic Instns., Santa Barbara, 1971-74; chmn. dept. U. Chgo., 1978-85; retired, 1986; dir. Environment and Policy Inst. East-West Ctr., Honolulu, 1986-91. Cons. Social Sci. Research Council, Ency. Brit., Ford Found. East-West Center, Nat. Acad. Sci., NRC, SCOPE, UN, UNESCO Author: Atlas of Economic Development, 1961, The Urban Transition: American and Asian Experiences, 1990; co-author, editor: Pattern of Asia, 1958, Malaya, 1958, Essays on Geography and Economic Development, 1960, China: Urbanization and National Development, 1980, China: The 80s Era, 1984, Geographic Perspectives on the Wealth of Nations, 1986; co-author, editor: The Extended Metropolis in Asia, 1991; co-editor: The Ocean Yearbooks, 1978-96. Served to lt. USNR, 1942-46. Guggenheim fellow, 1983 Mem. Assn. Am. Geographers (pres. 1970-71), Quadrangle Club, Cosmos Club, Phi Beta Kappa, Sigma Xi. Home: 5550 S Shore Dr Chicago IL 60637

GINSBURG, PAUL, health facility administrator; Degree, Binghamton U.; PhD in Econs., Harvard U. Dep. asst. dir. Congl. Budget Office, Washington, 1978—84; sr. economist RAND, 1984—86; founding exec. dir. Physician Payment Rev. Commn., 1986—95; pres. Ctr. for Studying Health Sys. Change, Washington, 1995—. Mem. adv. bd. Nat. Inst. for Health Care Mgmt. Rsch. and Edn. Found., Washington, 2003—. Office: Ctr for Studying Health Sys Change 600 Maryland Ave SW Ste 550 Washington DC 20024 Business E-Mail: pginsburg@hschange.org.

GINSBURG, RUTH, state representative; b. Bklyn., July 18, 1931; m. George S.; two children. Grad., Bklyn. Coll., 1954. Mem. Mayor's Adv. Com. for Social Svc. Funding; mem. dist. 26 N.H. Ho. of Reps., 1996—. Mem. sci., tech. and energy com., children and family law com. N.H. Ho. Reps. Former mem. Nashua Sch. Bd.; bd. dirs. Nashua Children's Assn.; mem. Nashua Ethnic Awareness Com. Jewish. Office: NH State Legis State House Concord NH 03301

GINSBURG, RUTH BADER (JOAN RUTH BADER GINSBURG), United States Supreme Court Justice; b. Bklyn., June 23, 1933; d. Nathan and Celia (Amster) Bader; m. Martin David Ginsburg, June 23, 1954; children: Jane Carol, James Steven. AB, Cornell U., 1954; postgrad., Harvard Law Sch., 1956—58; LLB Kent scholar, Columbia Law Sch., 1959; LLD (hon.), Lund (Sweden) U., 1969; LLD (hon.), Am. U., 1981, Vt. Law Sch., 1984; LLD (hon.), Georgetown U., 1985; LLD (hon.), DePaul U., 1985, Bklyn. Law Sch., 1987, Amherst Coll., 1991; LLD (hon.), Rutgers U., 1991; LLD (hon.), Lewis and Clark Coll., 1992, Radcliffe Coll., 1994, NYU, 1994; LLD (hon.), Columbia U., 1994; LLD (hon.), Smith Coll., 1994, L.I. U., 1994, U. Ill., 1995; LLD (hon.), Brandeis U., 1996, Wheaton Coll., 1997, Jewish Theol. Sem. of Am., 1997; LLD (hon.), George Washington U. Law Sch., 1997; DHL (hon.), Hebrew Union Coll., 1988. Bar: N.Y. 1959, D.C. 1975, U.S. Supreme Ct. 1967. Law sec. to Hon. Edmund L. Palmieri U.S. Dist. Ct. (so. dist.) N.Y., 1959—61; rsch. assoc. Columbia Law Sch., N.Y.C., 1961—62, assoc. dir. project internat. procedure, 1962—63; asst. prof. Rutgers U. Sch. Law, Newark, 1963—66, assoc. prof., 1966—69, prof., 1969—72, Columbia U. Sch. Law, N.Y.C., 1972—80; judge U.S. Ct. Appeals, (DC cir.), Washington, 1980—93; assoc. justice U.S. Supreme Ct., Washington, 1993—. Phi Beta Kappa vis. scholar, 1973—74; fellow Ctr. for Advanced Study in Behavioral Scis., Stanford, Calif., 1977—78; lectr. Aspen (Colo.) Inst., 1990, Salzburg (Austria) Seminar, 1984; gen. counsel ACLU, 1973—80, bd. dirs., 1974—80. Author (with Anders Bruzelius): Civil Procedure in Sweden, 1965, Swedish Code of Judicial Procedure, 1968; author: (with H.H. Kay & K. M. Davidson) Text, Cases and Materials on Sex-Based Discrimination, 1974; contbr. numerous articles to books and jours. Named one of World's 100 Most Powerful Women, Forbes mag., 2004, Most Powerful Women, 2005. Fellow: Am. Bar Found.; mem.: AAAS, Coun. Fgn. Rels., Am. Law Inst. (coun. mem. 1978—93). Office: US Supreme Ct One First St NE Washington DC 20543*

GINSBURG, SIGMUND G., management and executive search consultant; b. NYC, Oct. 12, 1937; s. Saul and Rose (Rich) Ginsburg; m. Judith Ann Jacobson, July 4, 1965; children: Beth Alison, David Grant. BA magna cum laude, Dartmouth Coll., 1959; postgrad., London Sch. Econs., 1959-60; MPA, Harvard U., 1961. Mgmt. intern Office of Sec. of Def., Washington, 1961-62; asst. to pres. Hudson Inst., 1964; asst. mgr. pers. adminstrv. svcs., mgmt. analyst Port Authority of N.Y. and N.J., 1964-66; sr. mgmt. cons. and spl. asst. to dep. mayor Office of the Mayor, City of N.Y., 1966-67, asst. city adminstr., 1967-72; v.p. for adminstrn. and planning, treas. Adelphi U., Garden City, NY, 1972-78; v.p. for fin., treas. U. Cin., 1978-84, adj. prof. higher edn. adminstrn., bus. adminstrn., 1980-84; v.p. fin. and adminstrn. Barnard Coll., N.Y.C., 1984-94; v.p. bus. devel. Am. Mus. Natural History, N.Y.C., 1994, sr. v.p. fin. and bus. devel., 1995—2002; exec. v.p., dir. nonprofit practice DHR Internat., N.Y.C., 2003—; pres. Sigmund G. Ginsburg Cons., 2003—. Adj. asst. prof., lectr. CUNY, 1966—72; founder, dir. N.Y.C. Urban Fellows Program, 1969—72; adj. assoc. prof. Adelphi U., 1972—78; mem. City Mgrs. Working Rev. Com. Cin. 2000 Plan, 1979—82; mgmt. commentator Sta. WGUC, Cin., 1980; instr. Fordham U., 1985—95, New Sch. U., 1986, 91; adv. coun. Tchrs. Ins. and Annuity Assn.-Coll. Retirement Equities Fund, 1993—96; chmn. Am. Mus. Nat. History; project exec. Rose Ctr. Earth and Space, 1995—2000; lectr. profl. meetings; cons. in field. Co-author: Managing the Higher Education Enterprise, 1980; author: Management: An Executive Perspective, 1982, Ropes for Management Success: Climb Higher, Faster, 1984; editor: Paving the Way for the 21st Century: The Human Factor in Higher Education Financial Management, 1993, Managing with Passion: Making the Most of Your Job and Your Life, 1996; contbr. chapters to books, articles to profl. jours. Mem. citizens adv. com. Wyo. Bd. Edn., 1980. Lt. U.S. Army, 1962—64. Decorated Army Commendation medal; recipient Merit award, City. of N.Y., 1969, Neil O. Hines Publ. award, Nat. Assn. Coll. and Univ. Bus. Officers, 1992, Disting. Svc. award, N.Y.C. Urban Fellows Program, 1994; Littauer fellow, Harvard U., 1961. Mem.: Phi Beta Kappa. Office: DHR Internat 280 Park Ave 43d Fl West New York NY 10017

GINSPARG, PAUL, physicist; married; 2 children. AB in Physics, Harvard U., 1977; PhD in Physics, Cornell U., 1981. Asst. prof. physics Harvard U., 1984—86, assoc. prof. physics, 1986—90; mem. tech. staff Los Alamos Nat. Lab., 1990—2001; prof. physics, computer sci. Cornell U., 2001—. Vis. prof. CEN, Saclay, France, Princeton U.; vis. scientist Stanford Linear Accelerator Ctr.; vis. prof. U. Calif., Santa Barbara, vis. scientist, Berkeley; vis. prof. Hebrew U., Jerusalem. Contbr. articles to profl. jours. Named Outstanding Jr. Investigator, Dept. Energy, 1986—91; recipient Physics, Astronomy and Math award, Spl. Libr. Assn., 1998; fellow A.P. Sloane fellow, 1986—90; grantee MacArthur Found., 2002. Fellow: Am. Phys. Soc. Achievements include development of website www.arXiv.org. Office: Cornell U 325 Clark Hall Ithaca NY 14853

GINTAUTAS, JONAS, physician, scientist, administrator; b. Justinava, Lithuania, Oct. 3, 1938; came to U.S., 1967; s. Jonas and Elena (Zaveckaitė) Sinsinas; m. Kristina Zebrauskaite, June 13, 1970; children: Stasys, Pasaka, Vadas. PhD, Northwestern U., 1976; MD, U. Juarez, Mex., 1984; MBA, Century U., 1996. Assoc. prof. Tex. Tech. U., Lubbock, 1975-77; assoc. prof. and dir. rsch. Tex. Tech. U. Health Scis. Ctr., Lubbock, 1979-82; dir. basic and clin. rsch., prof. neurology The Brookdlae U. Hosp. Med. Ctr., N.Y.C., 1985—. Cons. Amtorg Corp., N.Y.C., 1987-94, Ralex Internat. Co., Boston, 1988-91, Arrow Biomed Inc., Metuchen, N.J., 1988—. Editorial cons. Jour. Aphasia Agnosia Apraxia, 1979—; contbr. articles on pharmacology, anesthesia and surgery to profl. jours. Charter mem. Rep. Presdl. Task Force, Washington, 1982—, Platinum mem., 2002–; mem. Nat. Rep. Senatorial Com., Washington, 1984—, U.S. Senatorial Club, Washington, 1984—; nat. campaign advisor Nat. Rep. Senatorial Com., Washington, 1995-96. Recipient Gold medal for rsch. in med. sci. Am. Biog. Inst., medal of honor Rep. Presdl. Task Force, 1982; rsch. grantee various pvt. and govtl. agys. Fellow Internat. Coll. Physicians and Surgeons (hon.); mem. Am. Biog. Inst. (dep. gov. 1987—), U.S. Senatorial Club (preferred). Roman Catholic. Avocations: woodworking, camping, scuba diving, fishing, reading. Home: 84-19 107th St Richmond Hill NY 11418-1140

GINTER, ALAN ERIC, music educator; b. Newark, Apr. 30, 1947; s. Morris and Sylvia (Teitelbaum) Ginter; m. Valerie Fennell, Oct. 16, 1971; children: Mark, Helene. BS in Comm. and Theater, Temple U., 1970; BFA in Music, Calif. State U., 1987, MFA in Music, 1990. Cert. tchr. Calif. Dir. music Palermo (Calif.) Sch. Dist., 1989—94; head music Santa Cruz Coop. Sch., Bolivia, 1994—95; chmn. music dept. Bilkant U. Prep. Sch., Ankara, Turkey, 1995—2000; music coord. Min. Edn. Ankara Coll., 2000—02; dir. instrumental music Jesuit HS, Carmichael, Calif., 2003—. Adj. prof. music South Tahoe CC, South Lake Tahoe, Calif., 2002—03; instrumental music tchr. South Tahoe HS, South Lake Tahoe, 2001—03; music dir. jazz program Sacramento Youth Symphony, 2005—; music dir. jazz band Internat. HS, The Hague, Netherlands, 1998. Composer: Yiddish Fantasy, 1993, Turkish Delight, 1995. Mem.: Calif. Music Educators Assn., Calif. Band Dirs. Assn., Music Educators Nat. Conf. Jewish. Avocations: music, hiking, reading, bicycling, swimming. Home: 271 Selby Ranch Rd #3 Sacramento CA 95864 Office: Jesuit HS 1200 Jacob Ln Carmichael CA 95608

GINTER, VALERIAN ALEXIUS, urban historian, educator; b. Chgo., Nov. 4, 1939; s. Valerian Adalbert and Bernice (Podraza) G.; m. Linda Garner Tadlock, Feb. 24, 1968 (div. 1973). BS in Speech, Northwestern U., 1962; postgrad., L.I. U., 1979—81. Investigator Acme Secret Svc. Ltd., Chgo., 1960-62; prodr., dir. Sta. WAAY-TV, Huntsville, Ala., 1965-68; comml. coord. CBS TV, NYC, 1968-70; buyer SSC&B Lintas Worldwide, Furman-Roth Inc., SFM Media Corp., NYC, 1970-79; prin. Ginter-Gotham Urban History, NYC, 1981—. Adj. lectr. Kingsborough C.C., NY, 1990—98, LaGuardia C.C., NY, 1998—. Author: Manhattan Trivia: The Ultimate Challenge, 1985; contbr. articles to profl. jours., The Ency. NYC, 1995. Cons., lectr. Mcpl. Art Soc., NY, 1975—2000, dir. video tng., St. Bartholomew's Cmty. House, NYC, 1974-77. With U.S. Army, 1962-65. Mem. Theatre Hist. Soc., Victorian Soc. Am., Nat. Trust Hist. Preservation, Soc. Archtl. Historians. Roman Catholic. Avocation: jazz accordionist. Home and Office: 50 W 72nd St Ste 312 New York NY 10023 Office Phone: 212-496-6859. Personal E-mail: gintgotham@aol.com.

GINTZLER, ALAN SCOTT, musician, writer; b. Bklyn., Mar. 24, 1956; s. Eugene and Phyllis Gintzler; m. Heather Harr; 1 child, Guthrie. BA, Brandeis U., Waltham, Mass., 1979. Music tchr. N.Y.C. Pub. Schs., 1980; guitar instr. N.Y.C., 1982—89, Santa Fe, 1992—2004; musician Chgo. Blues Soc., N.Y.C., 1985—2000; assoc. editor Scholastic, Inc., N.Y.C., 1989—92; journalist, editor Global Gourmet, N.Y.C., 1992—2001; author John Muir Publs., Santa Fe, 1992—94; pub. Fontanel Books, Santa Fe, 2001—04; freelance journalist Santa Fe, 1992—2004; musician Chgo. Blues Soc., N.Y.C. and N.Mex. Author: Just Causes, 1992; co-author: Bizarre & Beautiful Series, 1993; author: Rough and Ready Series, 1994, Angel Up My Sleeve, 2001. Recipient Ind. Pub. Book award for fantasy sci., IPPY, 2002. Mem.: Phi Beta Kappa. E-mail: mail@fontanelbooks.com.

GINYARD, CALEB NATHANIEL, III, government agency administrator; b. Jacksonville, Fla., Sept. 22, 1940; s. Caleb Nathaniel Ginyard Jr. and Janie Elnora (Flowers) Ginyard; divorced; children: Valleta, Desiree, Sean. Dipl. in heating and plumbing, Wilkesbarre Vocat. Tech. Sch., Pa., 1978. Cert. emergency med. tech. 1996. Emergency med. tech. Pa. State Turnpike, Wilkesbarre, 1961—78, maintenance engr., 1978—2002. Singer: Mistyaires, 1967—72; author, pub.: My Name is Caleb N. Ginyard, 2002. Vol. fireman Hanover Green (Pa.) Hose Co. #1, 1967—, vol. ambulance attendant, 1967—; mem. Civil Air Patrol, 1953—66. Mem.: Wyoming Valley Torch Club, Kiwanis, Masonic (dep. grand master Worshipful dist. 1982—89), Tyre Sq. Club (treas. 2004), Frank Albert Meml. Lodge (assoc.). Baptist. Avocations: ceramics, beaded jewlery, bowling. Home: 56 Cist St Hanover Township PA 18706

GINZBURG, VITALY LAZAREVICH, physicist; b. Moscow, Oct. 4, 1916; s. Lazar and Augusta G.; m. Nina Ginzburg, 1946; 1 child. PhD, Moscow U., 1940. With P.N. Lebedev Phys. Inst. Russian Acad. Scis., 1940—, dir. I.E. Tamm dept. theoretical physics, 1971-88, adv., head theoretical group in P.N. Lebedev Physical Inst., 1988—; prof. Gorky U., 1945-68, Moscow Tech. Inst. Physics, 1968—. Author: Theoretical Physics and Astrophysics, 1979, Waynflete Lectures of Physics, 1983; author: (with S.I. Syrovatskii) Origin of Cosmic Rays, 1964; author: Propagation of Electromagnetic Waves in Plasma, 1970; author: (with V.M. Agranovich) Crystal Optics with Spatial Dispersion and Excitons, 1984; author: (with V.N. Tsytovich) Transition Radiation and Transition Scattering, 1990; author: (in Russian) On Physics and Astrophysics, 1995; author: About Science, Myself and Others, 1997, 2001, 2003, The Physics of a Lifetime, 2001; contbr. Decorated Order of Lenin; recipient Manelstam prize, 1947, Lomonosov prize, 1962, USSR State prize, 1953, Lenin prize, 1966, M. Smoluchovskii Medal Polish Physics Soc., 1987, Bardeen prize, 1991, Wolf Found. prize, 1994, 95, Vavilov Gold medal, 1995, Big Lomonosov Gold medal, 1995, UNESCO-Nils Bohr Gold medal, 1998, Nicholson Medal Am. Phys. Soc., 1998, Nobel prize in physics, 2003. Fellow Indian Acad. Sci. (hon.); mem. Acad. Sci. USSR (elected people's dep. mem. of Soviet Parliament 1989) Royal Soc. (London), Royal Astronomy Soc. London (assoc., Gold Medal 1991), Academia Europaea, Internat. Acad. Astronautics, Royal Danish Acad. Sci. (fgn.), NAS. Address: PN Lebedev Phys Inst RAN Leninsky Prospect 53 119991 Moscow Russia Fax: 095-135-85-33. Business E-Mail: ginzburg@lpi.ru.

GINZEL, ANDREW H., artist; b. Chgo., July 14, 1954; s. Roland F. and Ellen (Laynon) G.; m. Kristin A. Jones, June 14, 1986. Student, SUNY, 1978-81, Bennington Coll., 1972-74. Sculpture faculty Sch. of Visual Arts, N.Y.C., 1986—. Artistic cons. Hudson River Park Conservancy, N.Y.C., 1997. Solo shows include: Polarities Kansas City Internat. Airport, 2004, Metronome Union Square South Project, N.Y.C., 1999, TZ'Art, N.Y.C., 1996, Acqario Romano, Rome, 1995, Madison Art Ctr., Wis., 1992-93, Three Rivers Arts Festival, Pitts., 1991, Mpls. Coll. of Art and Design, 1991, Damon Brandt Gallery, N.Y.C., 1990, Kunsthalle, Basel, 1989, others; commns. include: Oculus, MTA, N.Y.C., 1999, Olympic Arts Festival, Atlanta, 1996, Battery Park City, N.Y.C., 1992, Pa. Conv. Ctr., 1994, Oreg. Conv. Ctr., Portland, 1990, Kunsthalle, Basel, Switzerland, 1989; group shows include Contemporary Artists and the Am. Acad. in Rome, 1995, 96, Equitable Gallery, N.Y.C., 1996, Paine Webber Gallery, N.Y.C., 1994, The Drawing Ctr., N.Y.C., 1993-94, numerous others; selected collections include: Bklyn. Mus., Beckton Dickinson and Co., Franklin Lakes, N.J., Bklyn. Mus., Centro per L'Arte Contemporanea Luigi Pecci, Prato, Italy, Hoffmann-La Roche, Inc., Pacific Enterprises, L.A., Progressive Corp., Cleve., The Prudential Life Ins. Co., others. Recipient Visual Arts fellowship Nat. Endowment for the Arts, 1986, 94, awards Pollack-Krasner Found., 1994, Louis Comfort Tiffany Found., 1991, fellowship for Indo-Am. Coun. for Internat. Exch. of Scholars, 1990, numerous others in field. Fellow Am. Acad. in Rome (Rome prize 1994-95). Home: 289 Bleecker St New York NY 10014-4106

GIOBBI, EDWARD GIACCHINO, artist; b. Waterbury, Conn., July 18, 1926; s. Achille and Teresa (Gasparetti) G.; m. Elinor E. Turner, Feb. 14, 1959; children: Eugenia, Elizabeth, Chambless Martino. Student, Whitney Sch. Art, New Haven, 1946-47, Vesper George Sch. Art, Boston, 1947-50, Cape Sch. Art, Provincetown, Mass., summer, 1949-50, Art Students League, N.Y.C., 1950-51, 55-56, Acad. Fine Arts, Florence, Italy, 1951-54. One man shows include Ward Eggleston Gallery, N.Y.C., 1951, Mattatuck Mus., Waterbury, Conn., 1955, 78, Artists Gallery, N.Y.C., 1956, Contempories Gallery, N.Y.C., 1956, 60-61, 63, Heller Gallery, N.Y.C., 1957, 58, Brooks Meml. Art Gallery, Memphis, 1961, 72, 80, New Arts Ctr., London, 1964, 67, Bear Lane Gallery, Oxford, Eng., 1964, Queen Sq. Gallery, Leeds Gallery, 1964, Tirca Karlis Gallery, Provincetown, 1964-66, 67, Michelson Gallery, Washington, 1966, Alan Gallery, N.Y.C., 1966, Ark. Art Centre, Little Rock, 1966, Waddell Gallery, N.Y.C., 1967, Obelisk Gallery, Boston, 1968, Gertrude Kasle Gallery, Detroit, 1968, Hopkins Ctr., Dartmouth, 1972, Galleria del Obelisco, Rome, 1974, Crane Kalman Gallery, London, 1975, Neuberger Mus., Purchase, N.Y., 1977, 92, Gruenbaum Gallery, N.Y.C., 1977, (sculpture), 1979, Katonah (N.Y.) Gallery, 1978, Irving Gallery, Palm Beach, 1978, Norton Gallery, Palm Beach, 1988, Long Point Gallery, Provincetown, 1987, 93, Sta. Gallery, Katonah, 1989, Armstrong Gallery, N.Y.C., 1987, Alice Ringham Gallery, Memphis, 1980, Hudson River Mus., 1995; two-man shows include Galeries an der Reuss, Lucerne, Switzerland, 1953, Nexus Gallery, Boston, 1956, Hudson River Mus., 1995; group exhbns include Recent Drawings U.S.A. Mus. Modern Art, 1956, Am. Fed. Arts Travelling Show, 1956, 58, 61, 63, Whitney Mus. Ann., 1957-61, 66, Corcoran Gallery, 1958, Pa. Acad. Fine Arts, 1961, Young Am., Whitney Mus., 1961, 40 Painters Under 40, Whitney Mus., 1962, Figure USA, Mus. Modern Art, 1962, Art in Progress, Finch Coll., N.Y.C., 1967. Mem. adv. bd. Westchester Coun. Arts, Katonah Gallery. Served with inf. AUS, 1944-46, ETO. Recipient Emily Lowe award, 1951-52; Guggenheim fellow, 1972; decorated Combat Inf. Badge. Mem. NAD, Coll. NAD., Century Assn. (mem. adv. bd.). Address: 161 Croton Lake Rd Katonah NY 10536-1201*

GIOCONDA, THOMAS F., government agency administrator, retired military officer; BA in History, St. Joseph's U., 1970; grad., Squadron Officer Sch., 1974; MBA, U. Mont., 1975; grad., Air Command and Staff Coll., 1976; M in Edn1. Adminstrn., Seton Hall U., 1979; grad., Air War Coll., 1986. Commd. 2d lt. USAF, 1970, advanced through grades to brig. gen., 2001; stationed at Malmstrom AFB, Mont., 1970-75; asst. prof. aerospace studies AFROTC detachment 750 St. Joseph's U., Phila., 1975-76, prof., 1976-77, detachment comdr., detachment closure officer, 1976-77; adminstrn. officer, asst. prof. aerospace studies N.J. Inst. Tech., Newark, 1977-79; missile launch instr./evaluator Vandenberg AFB, Calif., 1979-83; mission analyst strategic programs Hdqs. SAC, Offutt AFB, Nebr., 1983, congl. liaison br. chief, action officer, 1983-85; congl. affairs and resources planner, dep. chief of staff plans and ops. Hdqs. USAF, Washington, 1985-89; comdr. ICMB Squadron, Whiteman AFB, Mo., 1989-91; dep. legis. asst. to chmn. joint chiefs of staff USAF, Washington, 1991-93; legis. asst. to chmn. joint chiefs of staff Washington, 1993-97; prin. dep. asst. sec. mil. application Dept. Energy, Washington, 1997-99, acting asst. sec. energy for defense programs, 1999—2001; ret., 2001; v.p. govt. programs Bechtel Nat. Inc., 2001—. Mem.: KC, Air Force Assn. (life), Mil. Officers Assn. Am. (life), Am. Legion (life), Soc. SAC (life), Kappa Delta Phi. Home: 4818 Hercules Ct Annandale VA 22003-4243 Office Phone: 202-828-7375. Business E-Mail: tfgiocon@bechtel.com.

GIOIA, ANTHONY ALFRED, mathematics professor; b. Torrington, Conn., Apr. 7, 1934; s. Patrick James and Eugenia (Mencuccini) G.; m. Sept. 25, 1954 (div. 1966); children: Patrick James II, Kathleen, Michael; m. Mary Patricia Rogers, Dec. 30, 1978. BA, U. Conn., 1955; MA, U. Mo., 1961, PhD, 1964. Instr. U. Mo., Columbia, 1964; asst. prof. Tex. Technol. U., Lubbock, 1964-66; assoc. prof. math. Western Mich. U., Kalamazoo, 1966-74, prof., 1975-96, prof. emeritus, 1996—. Referee math. jours. Author: Number Theory: An Introduction, 1972, Number Theory: An Introduction, 2001; co-editor Proc. Conf. on Arithmetic Functions, 1975; contbr. articles to math. jours. Bd. dirs. Comstock (Mich.) Community Ctr., 1987—. Rsch. grantee Tex. Technol. U., 1965, 66, Western Mich. U., 1975, NSF, 1977-78. Mem. Math. Assn. Am., Am. Math. Soc. (reviewer math. revs.), Fibonacci Assn. Home: 7230 N 41st St Augusta MI 49012-9662

GIOIA, (MICHAEL) DANA, poet, critic, cultural organization administrator; b. LA, Dec. 24, 1950; s. Michael and Dorothy (Ortiz) G.; m. Mary Hiecke, 1980; children: Michael (dec.), Theodore, Michael Frederick. BA, Stanford U., 1973, MBA, 1977; MA, Harvard U., 1975; PhD in Lit. (hon.), St. Andrews Coll., 2003; LittD (hon.), St. Andrew Presbyterian Coll., 2003; LHD (hon.), Lehigh U., 2003; LittD, West Chester U., 2003, Chapman U., 2005, U. Pacific, 2005; LittD (hon.), Seton Hall U., 2005. V.p. mktg. General Foods Corp., White Plains, N.Y., 1977-92; pres., bd. dirs. Story Line Press, 1992-2001; chmn. Nat. Endowment Arts, 2003—. Editor Sequoia mag., 1971-73, poetry editor, 1975-77; literary editor Inquiry mag., 1977-79, poetry editor, 1979-83; mem. bd. dirs. Wesleyan U. Writers Conf., 1985-99; commentator BBC Radio, 1992-2003; co-dir. West Chester Writers Conf., 1995-2002; music critic San Francisco mag., 1997-2003; librettist for opera Nosferatu, 2001; dir. Tchg. Poetry Conf., 2001-02; vis. writer John Hopkins U., Sarah Lawrence Coll., Colo. Coll., Wesleyan U. Author: (poetry) Daily Horoscope, 1986, The Gods of Winter, 1991, Interrogations at Noon, 2001

(Am. Book award, 2002), (criticism) Can Poetry Matter? Essays on Poetry an American Culture, 1992, 2d edit., 2002; editor: The Ceremony and Other Stories, 1984, Poems from Italy, 1985, New Italian Poets, 1991; co-editor: Literature: An Introduction to Fiction, Poetry and Drama, 2001, Longman Anthology of Short Fiction, 2001, Selected Short Stories of Weldon Kees, 2002, Twentieth-Century American Poetry, 2003, Disappearing Ink, 2004; translator: Eugenio Montale's Mottetti: Poems of Love, 1990; contbr. to periodicals including New Yorker, Atlantic, Washington Post, Hudson Rev., Poetry. Recipient Frederick Bock prize Poetry, 1986, Am. Book award, 2002. Mem. Poetry Soc. Am. (v.p. 1992-2003), Nat. Fed. Coun. on Arts and Humanities. Office: Nat Endowment for Arts 1100 Pennsylvania Ave NW Washington DC 20506 Office Fax: 212-682-5611.

GIOIA, DANIEL AUGUST, lawyer; b. Bellerose, N.Y., Dec. 23, 1950; s. Joseph Daniel and Concetta P. (Della Femina) Gioia; m. Helen Dumas, June 30, 1973; children: Martha Dumas Picarello, Thomas Joseph, David Albert, Carl Daniel. BA in Govt., Georgetown U., 1972; JD, Am. U., 1975. Bar: Ind. 1975, U.S. Dist. Ct. (no. and so. dist.) Ind. 1975. Ptnr. Spangler, Jennings & Dougherty, Merrillville, Ind., 1975—, mng. ptnr., 2002—. Adj. prof. med. malpractice Sch. of Law Valparaiso U., Ind., 1998—; mem. Commn. for C.L.E. Ind. Supreme Ct., 1992—98; mem. Conclave for Legal Edn., Ind. State Bar Assn., 1996, 2002. Mem.: Nat. Assn. Sports Officials, Lake County Bar Assn. (bd. mgrs. 1987—91, pres. 1990), Valpo Soccer Club (pres. 1992—98), Am. Inn of Ct. (pres. Calumet chpt. 2003—). Roman Catholic. Avocations: soccer referee and coach, gourmet cooking, coin collecting/numismatics. Home: 4221 Oak Grove Cir Valparaiso IN 46383-2084 Office: 8396 Mississippi St Merrillville IN 46410 E-mail: dhgioia@comcast.net, dgioia@sjdlaw.com.

GIOIELLA, SUSAN M., gifted and talented educator, director; b. Alexandria, Minn., Dec. 30, 1950; d. Joseph James and Eileen Clara Bauderer; m. Louis Anthony Gioiella, June 23, 1973; children: Julie, Joseph, Anthony, Stephen. BS in Edn., Bowling Green State U., 1973, MEd, 1999. Tchr. grades 2 and 3 Liberty St. Sch., Middletown, NY, 1973—75; tchr. grade 2 Toledo Christian Sch., 1990—98, coord., tchr. gifted edn., 1998—, dir. curriculum, 2003—, dir. presch., 2004—; tchr. Toledo Zoo, 2001—, Lourdes Coll., Sylvania, 2005—. Cons. gifted edn., Sylvania, 2002—. Recipient Exemplary Program Recognition, Assn. Christian Schs., 2001—02. Mem.: Sci. Edn. Coun. Ohio, Nat. Sci. Tchrs. Am., Nat. Assn. Gifted Children, Ohio Assn. Gifted Children. Office: Toledo Christian Schs Inc 2303 Brookford Dr Toledo OH 43614 Office Phone: 419-724-2111. E-mail: gioiella@toledochristian.com.

GIORDANENGO, SAM PETER, history professor; b. San Francisco, Aug. 3, 1971; s. Charles Peter and Marry Ellen Giordanengo; m. April Christine Muir, July 6, 1996; 1 child, Anne Frances. BA in Polit. sci. and History, U. Portland, 1993; MA in History, Ctrl. Wash. U., 1997. Instr. Armstrong Atlantic State U., Savannah, Ga., 1997—99, Yakima Valley C.C., Grandview, Wash., 1999—. Mem. city coun. City of Prosser, Wash., 2004—. Mem.: Fraternal Order Eagles. Republican. Christian Reformed. Avocation: scuba diving.

GIORDANO, ANDREW ANTHONY, retired naval officer; b. Passaic, NJ, May 17, 1932; s. Samuel and Sarah (Pollara) G.; m. Felice Rochman, Mar. 3, 1957; children: Andrew Anthony, II, Dean James, Catherine Lisa. BBA cum laude, CCNY, 1953; MBA with distinction, Harvard U., 1962; student, Naval War Coll., 1965; L.H.D. (hon.), Nat. U., San Diego, 1982. Commd. ensign U.S. Navy, 1953, advanced through grades to rear adm., 1978; supply officer U.S.S. Kitty Hawk, Vietnam, 1968-70; ops. officer Aviation Supply Office, Phila., 1970-72; dir. material div. Office of Chief of Naval Ops., Washington, 1977-81; comdr. Naval Supply Systems Command, Chief Supply Corps, 1981-84; sr. v.p. control and ops. Donaldson's of Mpls. unit Allied Stores, 1984-87; exec. v.p., CFO Lamonts Corp., 1987-93; assoc. prof. acctg. George Washington U., 1966-67, Nat. U., 1970-72; prin. The Giordano Group, Ltd., Arlington, Va., 1993—. Bd. dirs. Nomos, Inc., Dale Carnegie Assocs.; chmn., interim CEO, Jos. A. Bank, Inc. Treas., trustee Navy Marine Coast Guard Residence Found., 1993-98; pres., COO Graham Field, 1998. Decorated Legion of Merit, DSM; recipient Navy Civilian Svc. award, Disting. Grad. award Navy SC Found., 2004. Mem. NAS (Naval studies bd. 1996), Army-Navy Country Club (chmn. bd. govs. 1993-96). Roman Catholic. Address: PO Box 31059 Palm Beach Gardens FL 33420-1059 Office Phone: 561-776-6298. Personal E-mail: tggltd@aol.com.

GIORDANO, BILL A., psychotherapist; b. Newark, June 15, 1957; s. John and Marie Giordano. BA in Polit. Sci. cum laude, Fairleigh Dickinson U., Rutherford, N.J., 1979; postgrad. cert. in clin. social wk., NYU, 1982, MSW, 1992, postgrad., 2003—. LCSW N.Y. Case worker Cath. Charities, N.Y.C., 1982; social worker Bklyn. Bur. C.C., 1986—89; primary therapist South Beach Psychiat. Ctr., S.I., 1989—93; sr. therapist day tx. coord. H.S.S. Cmty. Cons. Ctr., N.Y.C., 1993—. Cons., Think Tank mem. On Step Inst., N.Y.C., 1998—; presenter in field. Mem. Dem. Nat. Com., 1976—; bd. trustees On Step Inst. Mental Health Rsch. Mem.: NASW, Phi Omega Epsilon. Achievements include research in on paternal instinct; symptoms of parental alienation and its implications for clinicians and patients; coordination of multicultural day treatment program; depression in men. Home: 98 Ann St Newark NJ 07105-3110 Office: On Step Inst 169 E 74th St New York NY 10021 E-mail: bgeo15@aol.com.

GIORDANO, DAVID ALFRED, retired internist, gastroenterologist; b. South Bend, Ind., Feb. 3, 1930; s. Alfred S. and Alice (Gracy) G.; m. Sally Kay Buchanan, Jan. 30, 1960; children: Steven David, Michael Bruce. BS, Northwestern U., 1951; MD, Ind. U., Indpls., 1955. Diplomate Am. Bd. Internal Medicine. Intern Univ. Hosp., Cleve., 1955-56; resident in internal medicine Ind. U. Med. Ctr., Indpls., 1958-60; instr. medicine Duke U. Med. Ctr., Durham, N.C., 1960-61, Ind. U. Med. Ctr., Indpls., 1961-63; cons. gastroenterology Vets. Hosp., Univ. Hosp., Indpls., 1961-63; pvt. practice Sarasota, Fla., 1963-99; ret., 1999. Active staff Sarasota Meml. Hosp., chief of staff, 1970-71, assoc. staff Drs. Hosp., Sarasota; mem. West Cen. Fla. Profl. Standards Review Orgn., 1976, Sarasota County Local Govt. Study Commn., 1967-69; sec. Sarasota County Comprehensive Health Planning Coun., 1969-70, exec. com., 1969-72; bd. dirs. Blue Shield, 1973-80, chmn. Governmental Affairs Com., 1978-80; rep. of state ins. commr. to Russia, Denmark, Sweden, Eng. and France, 1979. Contbr. articles to profl. jours. Med. advisor Planned Parenthood Assn., 1965-70; bd. dirs. Pines Sarasota, 2000—. Lt. comdr. USN, 1956-58. Fellow Am. Coll. Physicians (rep. Fla. coun. med. specialists 1973—, health and pub. policy com. 1987—, governing bd. 1987— Internist of Yr. Fla. chpt. 1997), Am. Coll. Gastroent.; mem. AMA, Fla. Soc. Internal Medicine (med. adv. coun. 1971-90), Fla. Gastroent. Soc. (pres. 1972), West Coast Acad. Internal Medicine (pres. 1977-78); Sarasota County Med. Soc. (co-chmn. peer review com. 1970-71), Fla. Med. Assn., Am. Soc. Internal Medicine, Fla. Med. Assn., Am. Soc. Gastrointestinal Endoscopy, Am. Gastroent. Assn. Avocations: sailing, tennis, nautical antiques. Home: 6 Lands End Ln Sarasota FL 34242-1148

GIORDANO, JOSHUA A., energy executive, consultant; s. Nicholas and Laura Giordano; m. Yuka Uebayashi, May 20, 2000. BA, Rutgers U., New Brunswick, NJ, 1992. Pres. Energistics LLC, N.Y., 2001—; sr. mgr. Caminus (Sungard Energy), New York, NY, 1999—2001. Risk mgr. Mitsubishi Corp., New York, NY, 1994—99. Achievements include development of Founder and pres. of Energistics LLC. Office: Energistics LLC 116 W 23rd St New York NY 10011 Office Phone: 646-375-2332. Office Fax: 646-349-1256. Business E-Mail: jg@energisticsllc.com.

GIORDANO, NICHOLAS ANTHONY, brokerage house executive; b. Phila., Mar. 7, 1943; s. Nicola and Aida (Gioioso) G.; m. Joanne M. Pizzuto, Oct. 21, 1967; children: Jeannine, Colette and Nicholas (triplets). BS, LaSalle Coll., 1965. CPA Pa. Mem. staff Price Waterhouse & Co., Phila., 1965-68; with various brokerage cos. Phila., 1968-71; controller stock exchange and stock clearing corp PBW (later Phila.) Stock Exch., Inc., 1971-72, v.p. ops., 1972-75, sr. v.p., 1975-76, exec. v.p., 1976-81, pres., CEO, 1981-97, bd. dirs. Cons. in field. Bd. trustees LaSalle U.; former chmn. bd. dirs. Mt. St. Joseph Acad.; trustee Am. U. Rome; trustee, bd. dirs. WT Mut. Fund, Kalmar Investments, Inc.; bd. dirs. Intricon Corp. (formerly Selas Corp.), Ind. Blue Cross. Mem.: Union League Phila. Office: PO Box 984 Blue Bell PA 19422-0984 Personal E-mail: nagiordano@yahoo.com.

GIORDANO, THOMAS HENRY, chemist, educator; b. Phila., Feb. 13, 1950; s. James A. and Margaret H. Giordano. BA in Chemistry, Millersville (Pa.) U., 1972; PhD in Geochemistry, Pa. State U., 1978. From postdoc. rschr. to prof. dept. geol. scis. N.Mex. State U., Las Cruces, 1977—98, dept. head dept. geol. scis., 1994—2003, prof. dept. geol. scis., 1998—, chmn. dept. beol. scis., 1994—2003. Vis. scientist, chemistry divsn. Oak Ridge Nat. Lab., 1987—93; vis. scientist dept. earth scis. U. Manchester, England, 1995. Editor: Ore Genesis and Exploration: The Roles of Organic Matter, 2000, Ore Geology Reviews, 1996. Mem.: N.Mex. Geol. Soc., Am. Geophys. Union, The Geochem. Soc. Roman Catholic. Home: 1914 LaJolla Ave Las Cruces NM 88005 Office: Dept Geol Scis NMex State Univ Box 3AB Las Cruces NM 88005 Office Phone: 505-646-2511.

GIORGADZE, TAMAR A., pathologist, physician; b. Tbilisi, Georgia, Apr. 6, 1960; d. Alfred G. Giorgadze and Venera O. Iosava; m. Archil G. Tsuladze, May 26, 1991. MD, Tbilisi State Med. Inst., 1982, PhD, 1987. Doctor of Medicine Tbilisi State Med. Inst., 1982, Anatomical and Clinical Pathology Diplomate, Am. Bd. of Pathology, 2002, Cytopathology Diplomate, Am. Bd. of Pathology, 2004, Board of Medicine Phisician License State of Mich., USA, 2002, lic. State of Tenn., Bd. of Med. Examiners, USA, 2005. Resident in oncology Tbilisi State Med. Inst., Chair of Oncology, Tbilisi, Georgia, sr. lab. asst., 1985—94; staff oncologist Rep. Cancer Ctr., Dept. of Pediatric Oncology, Tbilisi, Georgia, 1984—85; rsch. fellow Patho Lab Ltd, Sci. Pk., Kiryat-Weizmann, Rechovot, Israel, 1995—96; pathology resident East Tenn. State U., Dept. Pathology, James H. Quillen Coll. Med., Johnson City, Tenn., 1998—2001, chief resident, 2001—02, asst. prof., 2004—; surg. pathology fellow Dept. Pathology and Lab. Medicine Hosp. U. Pa., Philadelphia, 2002—03, cytopathology fellow, 2003—04. Sr. lab. asst. editl. bd. chair of oncology Tbilisi State Med. Inst., Tbilisi, Georgia, 1987—89; manuscript reviewer Hosp. U. Pa., Phila., 2003—04. Author: (scientific papers) Journals: Diagnostic Cytopathology, Archives Pathology and Laboratory Medicine, Journal of Cutaneous Pathology, Modern Pathology, Acta Cytologica, Pathology International, Reviews in Cardiovascular Medicine, Stomatology; contbr. chapters to books. Fellow: Coll. Am. Pathologists; mem.: Internat. Acad. Pathology, Am. Soc. Cytopathology, US, Can. Acad. Pathology. Orthodox Christian. Achievements include patents for Method of forming of the high oncoproctological risk groups; first to Innovative methodologies in cytopathology and endocrine pathology. Avocations: opera, art, reading, swimming, tennis. Office: East Tenn State Univ 1 Dogwood Ln Room B-30 Johnson City TN 37614 Office Phone: 423-439-6328. Business E-Mail: giorgadz@etsu.edu.

GIOSEFFI, DANIELA (DOROTHY DANIELA GIOSEFFI), poet, writer, playwright, critic; b. Orange, N.J., Feb. 12, 1941; d. Daniel Donato Gioseffi and Josephine Buzevska; m. Richard J. Kearney, Sept. 7, 1965 (div.); 1 child, Thea D. Kearney; m. Lionel B. Luttinger, June 6, 1986. BA, Montclair State Coll., 1963; MFA, Cath. U. of Am., 1966. Cons., poet Poets-in-the-Schs., Inc., N.Y.C., 1972-85. Freelance writer, lectr. at numerous univs. throughout U.S. and Europe; appeared on Nat. Pub. Radio, CBC, BBC; spkr. on world peace and disarmament, 1979—; keynote spkr. Am. Forum for Global Edn. Nat. Conf., Miami, Fla., 1994, State Coun. Tchrs. English conf., Orlando, Fla., 1995, So. Edn. Found. Internat. Conf. of Tchrs. of English, Atlanta, 1997, IV Feminist Internat. Book Fair, Barcelona, 1989, Miami Internat. Book Fair, 1990. Author: The Great American Belly, 1977, The Great American Belly, 4th edit., 1979; author: (collections of poems) Eggs in the Lake, 1979, Word Wounds and Water Flowers, 1995, Going On, 2000, Symbiosis, 2002; author: Earth Dancing: Mother Nature's Oldest Rite, 1981, Women on War: International Voices for the Nuclear Age, 1988 (Am. Book award, 1990), rev. edit., 2003, On Prejudice: A Global Perspective, 1993—, Dust Disappears: Translations of Carilda Oliver Labra of Latin America, 1995—, (short stories) In Bed With the Exotic Enemy, 1997—, (novella) The Psychic Touch, 1996—; author: (play) The Golden Daffodil Dwarf, 1988—, Care of the Body, 1988—, The Sea Hag in the Cave of Sleep, 1988—; author: (radio play) Fathers and Children, 1988—, 1998—; author: Going On: Poems Via Folios, 2002, Symbiosis: Poems, 2003, Women on War: International Writings From Antiquity to the Present, 2003; author: (short stories) Daffodil Dollars, —(PEN Short Fiction award, 1990, Lifetime Achievement award Assn. Italian Am. Educators, 2003); contbr. numerous periodicals and anthologies;, performer (stage presentations throughout U.S. and Europe), composer (and lyricist), singer (many concert series); creator The First Bklyn. Bridge Poetry Walk, 1972; verses carved in marble: Penn Sta., 2002; editor: poetry website www.PoetsUSA.com. Pres. Bklyn. Citizens for Sane Nuclear Policy, 1987—89; mem. exec. bd., chmn. media watch com. Writers and Pubs. Alliance for Nuclear Disarmament, 1978—91. Named Featured poet, The Peoples' Poetry Gathering: The Great Hall, Cooper Union, 2003; recipient World Peace award, Ploughshares Fund, 1989, 1999; grantee poetry and fiction, Creative Artists' Pub. Svc. Program - N.Y. State Coun. on Arts, 1971—77, Thanks Be to Grandmother Winifred Found., 1996. Mem.: Poet's House, Nat. Book Critics Cir., Actors Equity Assn., Acad. Am. Poets, PEN Am. Ctr. Office: Box 8G 57 Montague St Brooklyn NY 11201-3356 Office Phone: 718-643-3837. Personal E-mail: daniela@garden.net.

GIOVANIELLI, DAMON VINCENT, physicist, consultant; b. Teaneck, NJ, May 8, 1943; s. Dominick John and Marie Concetta (Conti) G.; m. Eleanor Ruth Rand, Aug. 18, 1968; children: Kira, Tina. AB, Princeton U., 1965; PhD in Physics, Dartmouth Coll., 1970. Instr. dept. engring. and applied sci. Yale U., New Haven, 1970-72; with Los Alamos (N.Mex.) Nat. Lab., 1972-93, leader physics divsn., 1987—93; ret., 1993; pres. Sumner Assocs., Sante Fe, 1993—; chmn. bd. dirs. La Mancha Co., 1997—. With J. Robert Oppenheimer Meml. Com. Contbr. articles to profl. jours. Mem. alumni schs. com. Princeton U.; trustee Coll. Santa Fe. Fellow AAAS, mem. AIAA, Am. Phys. Soc., Fusion Power Assocs., Sigma Xi. Episcopalian. Home: 12 Loma Del Escolar Los Alamos NM 87544-2524 Office: Sumner Assocs 100 Cienega St Ste D Santa Fe NM 87501-2003

GIOVANONI, STEPHEN FRANCIS, music educator; b. Urbana, N.Y., June 10, 1964; s. Richard Louis and Mary Josephine Giovanoni; m. Lisa Kay Sheridan, May 20, 1988; children: Matthew, Tyler. MusB, W.Va. U., 1986; MusM, U. North Tex., 1990. Cert. tchr. Tex. Saxophonist 323d Army Band, San Antonio, 1993—99; band dir. Comfort (Tex.) Ind. Sch. Dist., 1999—2001, LaVernia (Tex.) Ind. Sch. Dist., 2001—02; music instr. San Antonio Coll., 2000—02; saxophone instr. Tex. Luth. U., Seguin, 2001—02; dir. bands Wharton (Tex.) County Jr. Coll., 2002—. Saxophonist Al Sturchio Orch., San Antonio, 1993—2002; clinician various schs. in Tex.; saxophone performer various Tex. bands; arranger jazz band music. Served U.S. Army, 1993—99, Ft. Sam Houston. Mem.: Tex. Bandmasters Assn., Tex. Music Educators Assn. Avocations: music history, sports. Office: Wharton County Jr Coll 911 Boling Hwy Wharton TX 77488 E-mail: stepheng@wcjc.edu.

GIOVINAZZO, VIVIAN CURRY, writer; b. Gstaad, Switzerland, Dec. 7, 1945; arrived in U.S., 1949; d. Hugo Alexander and Beatrice Ferdinand (Wärtli) Curry; m. George Potts, Dec. 30, 1965 (dec.); m. Anthony Gioviazzo, Sept. 10, 1995 (dec. Apr. 18, 2002). HS, Lâchâtlaine, Switzerland, 1962—63; HS diploma, Edgewater High, Orlando, Fla.; student psychology. Author children's books; athletic (Tennis) Champion, Fla. and NY, 1950—59; author: (children's stories) Those Scary Dust Bunnies, 2001—02, Daddy, I Don't Want To Go To School, 2001—02, New Puppy on the Block, 2001—02, Bubbles for My Birthday, 2001—02. Named NY State Tennis Championship, FIA. Avocation: stamp collecting/philately. E-mail: vgiovin@wmconnect.com.

GIOVINCO, JOSEPH, non profit agency administrator, writer; b. San Francisco, Oct. 12, 1942; s. Joseph Bivona Giovinco and Jean Andrews; m. Sally Garey, Aug. 31, 1970 (div. Mar. 1982); 1 child, Gina Lorraine. BA, U. Oreg., 1964; MA in History, San Francisco State U., 1968; PhD in History, U. Calif., Berkeley, 1973. Asst. prof. history SUNY, Albany, 1974-76; instr. multicultural studies Sonoma State U., Cotati, Calif., 1976-79; exec. dir. Hist. Mus. Found., Sonoma County, Santa Rosa, Calif., 1977-80; exec. dir. no. Calif. affiliate Am. Diabetes Assn., San Francisco, 1980-81; exec. dir. San Francisco Sch. Vols., 1981-85, Calif. Hist. Soc., San Francisco, 1985-87; dir. Ctr. Advancement & Renewal of Educators, San Francisco, 1988—. Contbr. articles to profl. publs. Fellow, NEH and Harvard U., 1973; recipient scholarship U. Minn. Ctr. for Immigration History, Mpls., 1975; Rockefeller Found. grantee, 1977; recipient Covello prize Italian Am. Hist. Assn., 1976; named Alumnus of Yr., San Francisco State U., 1987. Roman Catholic. Avocations: rose gardening, classical music. Office: Ctr Advancement & Renewal Educators 25550 25th Ave San Francisco CA 94116

GIPSON, HARVEY LOFTON, lawyer; b. Memphis, Feb. 18, 1931; s. Raymond Turner and Frances Lenora (Boling) G.; m. Cara Evelyn Holland (dec. Feb, 1993); children: Gloria Ray Gipson Ingles, Harvey Lofton Jr, Ashley Gipson. BBA, Memphis State U., 1959; LLB, So. Law U., 1962. Asst. controller City Products, Memphis, 1959-61; internal auditor Plough Inc., Memphis, 1961-62; atty., charge legal dept. W.R. Grace & Co., Memphis, 1963-65; pvt. practice Memphis, 1965—. Divorce referee Shelby County, 2001—. Divorce ref. Shelby County, Tenn., 2004-; Staff sgt. USAF, 1951-55. Recipient Nat. Def. Medal, USAF, Reno, 1953, Good Conduct Medal, 1953. Mem. ABA, Tenn. Trial Lawyers Assn., Alchymia Shrine. Methodist. Office: PO Box 280741 Memphis TN 38168 Office Phone: 901-526-0252. Personal E-mail: HarveyGipson04@bellsouth.net.

GIPSON, JEFFERY, chemistry professor; b. Waco, Tex., Aug. 7, 1922; s. Jeffery and Johnnie (Donahue) G. BS, Tillotson Coll., 1944; MS, Howard U., 1949; PhD, U. Tex., 1955. Assoc. prof. chemistry So. U., Baton Rouge, 1954-59; prof. chemistry, chmn. dept. St. Augustine's Coll., Raleigh, N.C., 1959-76; prof. chemistry Va. Union U., Richmond, 1981—. Vis. prof. chemistry Met. State coll., Denver, 1974; vis. prof. sci. U. Va., Charlottesville, summer 1985; cons. USAID, Bangalore, India, 1965, 67; rsch. scientist DNA Lawrence Radiation Lab., Livermore, Calif., summer 1970; rsch. trichina Los Alamos (N.Mex.) Sci. Lab., summer 1971; mem. colloid chem. conf. U. So. Calif., L.A., summer 1983; environ. scientist U.S. EPA, Arlington, 1987, Chgo., 1988, Phila., 1989, 91, 92, Research Triangle Park, N.C., 1990, Phila., 1991-92. Editor: Experiments in Physical Science, 1989; contbr. articles to profl. jours. Sgt. U.S. Army, 1944-46, PTO, 50-51. Mem. AAAS, AAUP, Am. Assn. Retired Profs., Nat. Space Acad. Am. Legion. Avocations: walking, create science crosswords. Home: 8500 Hazen St Richmond VA 23235-3452

GIPSON, STEPHEN RICHARD, journalist, construction executive; b. Tacoma, Apr. 29, 1945; s. William Richard and Justina Pauline Gipson; m. Helen Therese Cory (div. Feb. 1981); 1 child, Mark Tyler. Diploma in acctg., Western Bus. Coll., 1974; degree in bus. law, Mt. Hood CC, Gresham, Oreg., 1975; studies in bus. admin., U. Md., 1966. Exec. v.p. Pioneer Optics, Beaverton, Oreg., 1974—76; founder, pres. Group Optical, Portland, Oreg., 1976—78; founder, CEO Gipson Optical & Safety, Portland, 1978—81; founder, publ. Comon Cents Newspaper, Cour d'Alene, Idaho, 1981—85; founder, pres. Gipson Bus. Cons., Portland, 1985—93, House Calls Contractors, Portland, 1993—2001; writer, pres. Gipson Lit. Svcs., Milton-Freewater, Oreg., 2001—; pres. Western Dolphin Pub., 2000—; CEO River Ratz New N.W. Regional Recreation Paper, 2004. Prin., owner Western Dolphin Gems, 2002—, Western Dolphin Wholesalers Jewelers, 2002—. V.p. Mid Atlantic Pistol & Rifle Club, 1965—66. With USAF, 1962—66. Mem.: Eagles, Am. Legion. Democrat. Methodist. Avocations: flying, skydiving. Home and Office: Gipson Lit Svcs PO Box 417 Milton Freewater OR 97862

GIRACELLO, ROBERT F., music educator, director, composer, musician; b. Hackettstown, NJ, Nov. 18, 1976; s. Vincent D. and Maureen F. Giracello; m. Rebecca D. Kampley, Feb. 21, 1976. BA in Music, Calif. State U., 2003. Composer: (symphony) Symphony No. 1: (Grand Prize; New Am. Symphony Soc., 2004), (choral music) 3 Landscapes for Choir (MACRO 2000 Composition Award, 2001); composer: (librettist) (opera) Nothing Spoken; author: (book of poetry) Now You See it & Sonnetine. Dir. of contemporary music San Rafael Cath. Ch., Rancho Bernardo, Calif., 2000—05. Recipient MACRO award for Composition, 2000, Best NY, NOVA Assn., 2004; Golden State scholar, State of Calif., 1996. Mem.: Nat. Pastoral Musicians. Roman Catholic. Avocations: baseball, writing, electronics. Home: 3200 Blossom Dr Perris CA 92571 Personal E-mail: imonkey@adelphia.net.

GIRAGOSIAN, C. CHRISTOPHER, lawyer; b. Richmond, Va., Oct. 15, 1951; BA in Math., magna cum laude, Washington & Lee Univ., 1973; JD, Univ. Richmond, 1976. Corp. counsel Bank of Va. (now Signet Bank), 1976—84; ptnr., capital fin., real estate Hunton & Williams LLP, McLean, Va. Mem.: ABA, Fairfax Bar Assn., Va. State Bar. Office: Hunton & Williams Ste 1700 1751 Pinnacle Dr Mc Lean VA 22102 Office Phone: 703-714-7426. Office Fax: 703-714-7410. Business E-Mail: cgiragosian@hunton.com.

GIRALDI, ROBERT NICHOLAS, film director; b. Paterson, N.J., Jan. 17, 1939; B.F.A., Pratt Inst., 1960. Assoc. creative dir. Young & Rubicam, N.Y.C., 1960-71; v.p., head creative dept. Della Femina, N.Y.C., 1971-73; ptnr. Ampersand Prodns., N.Y.C., 1973-74, dir.; pres. Giraldi Suarez Prodns., N.Y.C., 1974—. Head advt. and design, asst. dir. Sch. Visual Arts, N.Y.C., 1969-73, instr. 2002—; owner N.Y.C. restaurants, Vong, Lipstick Cafe, Patria, Gigino, Jean-Georges, Prime Las Vegas, The Mercer Kitchen, Bread Tribeca. Dir.: (play) Laughing on the Outside, 1982, (music videos) Say Say Say, 1983, Love Is a Battlefield, 1984, Hello, 1984, Don't Drive Drunk, 1984, Beat It (Michael Jackson), 1983, World Series (Baseball Hall Fame), (TV special) A Christmas to Remember with Dolly Parton and Kenny Rogers, 1985, (feature film) Hiding Out, 1987, (feature film) Dinner Rush with Danny Aiello, 2000, (short film) The Routine, 2002 (Best Drama award L.A. Internat. Short Film Festival), The Dream Begins for N.Y.C. 2012 Olympic Bid, 2002; art represented in permanent collection Mus. Modern Art, N.Y.C. Bd. dirs. Hamptons Internat. Film Festival, 2004-; appears in numerous ads against AIDS. Recipient numerous gold awards Art Dirs. Club N.Y., N.Y.C., numerous Andy awards Advt. Club N.Y., N.Y.C., numerous Clio awards, numerous One Show awards Copy Club N.Y., N.Y.C., numerous N.Y. Festival awards, numerous Mobius awards, Gold award Cannes Film Festival, 1974, 76, 79, 81, 88, 96, AICP MOMA gold award, 1992, 94, London Internat. Film Festival gold award, 1992, Italian Key awards, 1990, numerous other awards for excellence in advt., 1993-96, MTV Best Male Video award Will Smith's Just The Two of Us; Herschel Levit Scholarship award Pratt Inst., 1994; named to N.Y. Dir.'s Hall of Fame, 1991. Mem. Dirs. Guild Am. Roman Catholic. Office: Giraldi Suarez Prodns 149 Wooster St 2d Fl New York NY 10012-3327 *If you do quality you will always do quantity, but it never works the other way around.*

GIRARD, DENNIS PAUL, psychologist; b. Dracut, Mass., May 8, 1948; s. Sylva Joseph and Rita Pilotte Girard; m. Kathleen Curran, Oct. 20, 1979; 1 child, Lauren Elizabeth. BS, Hawthorne Coll., 1971; EdM, Suffolk U., 1974; EdD, Boston U., 1979. Lic. psychologist, health care provider Mass., diplomate clin. psychology Am. Bd. of Profl. Psychologist. Sr. psychologist South Shore Mental Health Ctr., Quincy, Mass., 1974-80; psychiatry instr. Tufts U. Med. Sch., Boston, 1977-87; cons. psychologist Westwood (Mass.) Lodge Hosp., 1980-85; courtesy staff/psychology and psychiatry McLean Hosp., Belmont, Mass., 1985-96; unit chief, mental health dept. of medicine Mass. Gen. Hosp./Boston Evening Med. Ctr., 1980—; clin. instr. psychology in dept. psychiatry, tutor Harvard Med. Sch., Boston, 1996—; clin. psychologist New England Bapt. Hosp., Boston, 1997—. Cons. Mass. Rehab. Commn., Boston, 1979—; adv. bd. Mass. Sch. of Profl. Psychology, Boston, 1999—; exec. bd. Internat. Coll. of Perscribing Psychologists, Miami, 1996—. Trustee, bd. dirs. Boston Evening Clin. Found., 2000—. Fellow Mass. Pscyhol. Assn.; mem. Am. Psychol. Assn., New England Pain Assn. Office: New England Bapt Hosp 125 Parker Hill Ave Ste 390 Boston MA 02120-2865

GIRARD, FRANCOIS, film director; b. Lac St-Jean, Que., Can. Founder, prin. Zone Prodns., 1988-92, Velvet Camera, 1988-92. Writer, dir. feature films including Cargo, 1990, Thirty Two Short Films About Glenn Gould, 1993 (Best Film prix Genie award, 1993, Best Dir. prix Genie award, 1993, Best photography prix Genie award, 1993, Best Editing prix Genie award, 1993, mention Festival of Festival Toronto, 1993, mention Festival du Film de Vancouver, 1993, Prize Figueira Da Foz Festival de Lisbonne, 1994, Badeira Paulista award Mostra de Sao Paulo, 1994), Peter Gabriel's Secret World, 1994 (Prix du Pub. Festival Internat. du Nouveau Cinéma Mtl., 1994, silver rose for best concert film Montreux Film Festival, 1995, Internat. Grammy award for Music Video long version, 1996); dir. medium-length films including Le Dortoir, 1991 (Internat. Emmy award, Gold FIPA, Gemeau award), Le Jardin des Ombres, 1993, After Othello, 1994, Souvenirs d'Othello, 1994; dir. short films including Das Brunch, 1983, Human Scope, 1984, Le Train, 1985, Monsieur Léon, 1986, Tango Tango, 1986, Montréal Danse, 1988, Mourir, 1988, Supect No 1, 1989, CCA, 1989, Vie Et Mort De L'Architecte, 1989; co-dir. short films including Distance, 1984; co-writer: Thirty Two Short Films About Glenn Gould; dir. various commls.; dir.: The Red Violin, 1998 (8 Genie awards including best film and best dir., Oscar for best original soundtrack). Office: c/o Chantal Neveu 1435 St Alexandre Ste 500 Montreal PQ Canada H3A 2G4 Office Phone: 514-937-3198. E-mail: chantal.neveu@videotron.ca.

GIRARD, JAMES EMERY, chemistry professor; b. Joliet, Ill., July 1, 1945; s. George I. and Mary C. (Jones) G.; children: Krista, Jon, Mark, Steven, Lauren, Alexis. BA, Lewis Coll., Lockport, Ill., 1967; PhD, Pa. State U., 1971. Research fellow Pa. State U., Univ. Park, 1967-71, postdoctoral fellow, 1971-72; NIH postdoctoral fellow U. Calif., San Diego, 1972-73, vis. prof., summer 1974; asst. prof. Coll. the Holy Cross, Worcester, Mass., 1973-77; staff scientist Gen. Elec. Co. Corp. Research and Devel. Ctr., Schenectady, N.Y., 1977-79; assoc. prof. The Am. U., Washington, 1979-84, prof., 1984—, chmn. dept. chemistry, 1984—91, 2003—. Cons., expert witness in field. Author: (textbooks) Chemistry: An Environmental Perspective, 1994, Chemistry Fundamentals: An Environmental Perspective, 1994, 2d edit., 2003, Principles of Environmental Chemistry, 2005; contbr. articles to profl. jours. Recipient Sr. Scholar award The Am. U., 1986-87, Leo Schubert award for outstanding teaching of sci. in coll. Washington Acad. Scis., 1995. Mem.: Am. Chem. Soc. Home: 6328 Karmich St Fairfax Station VA 22039-1621 Office: Am U Dept Chemistry 4400 Massachusetts Ave NW Dept Washington DC 20016-8003

GIRARD, LOUIS JOSEPH, ophthalmologist, educator; b. Spokane, Wash., Mar. 29, 1919; s. Harry and Agnes (Cain) G.; m. Bonita Crossnay, Mar. 31, 1945; children: Hilaire Michelle Bryan, Suzanne Christina Ann, Michael Sanford (dec.), Hugh Ashley, Gabrielle Inez; m. Loraine McMurrey, June 30, 1967; 1 son, Louis McMurrey; m. Louise Bell, June 14, 1975. BA, Rice U., 1941; MD, U. Tex., 1944; postgrad., NYU, Med. Sch., 1947-48. Diplomate: Am. Bd. Ophthalmology. Intern Jersey City Med. Ctr., 1944-45; assoc. Dr. Conrad Berens, NYC, 1947—49; asst. attending St. Clare's Hosp., 1948—53; resident ophthalmology NY Eye and Ear Infirmary, 1949-51; asst. attending Willard Parker Hosp., 1949-53; dir. chronic infection project, 1949-52; asst. attending N. Country Community Hosp., 1951-53; assoc. Dr. Conrad Berens, 1951—53; asst. surgeon, 1951-53; founder dept. rsch., 1956; assoc. dir. dept. rsch., 1953—57; asst. attending Nassau Hosp., 1951-53; cons. ophthalmologist Southside Hosp., 1951-53; attending ophthalmologist Jefferson Davis Hosp., 1953-59, VA Hosp., Houston, 1954—98, Tex. Children's Hosp., 1954—98, St. Luke's Episcopal Hosp., 1954—98, Meth. Hosp., 1955—98; cons. Montgomery County Hosp., 1955—98, Tex. Children's Hosp., 1953—57; assoc. prof., assoc. chmn. dept. ophthalmology Baylor Coll. Medicine, Houston, 1957—70, prof., chmn. dept., 1953—70; cons. VA Hosp., Houston, 1958—98; sr. attending Ben Taub Gen. Hosp., 1959—98, Meth. Hosp., 1959—98; cons. St. Luke's Episcopal Hosp., 1961—98, St. Joseph's Hosp., 1965—98; chief ophthalmology, co-chief surgery Ctr. Pavilion Hosp., 1970-76; clin. prof. Baylor Coll. Medicine, Houston, 1971—. Coord. grad. course ophthalmology NYU Postgrad. Med. Sch., 1948-49, instr., 1951-53; clin. asst. prof. U. Tex. Postgrad. Sch. Medicine, 1953-57, lectr., 1946; assoc. mng. dir. Ophthal. Found., N.Y., 1951-55, cons., 1957; founder Tex. Med. Ctr.-Lions Eye Bank, 1953; exec. dir. Girard Ophthal. Found., 1971—; cons. Meth. Hosp., St. Luke's Hosp.; founder, exec. dir. Inst. Ophthalmology, Tex. Med. Ctr., 1958—70; founder opthal. tissue culture lab. Baylor U., 1954; mem. Am. Orthoptic Coun., 1962-72; pres. Internat. Eye Film Library, 1967-71; med. adv. bd. Internat. Eye Bank, 1965-70; Pres. IX Pan Am. Congress Ophthalmology, 1972; presenter in field. Author: Advanced Techniques in Ophthalmic Microsurgery, Vol. I: Ultrasonic Fragmentation for Intraocular Surgery, 1979, Vol. II: Corneal Surgery, 1981; author, editor. over 8 books; prodr. 70 films.; editor: Corneal Contact Lenses, 1964, 2d edit., 1971, Corneal Scleral Contact Lenses, 1967, Proceedings of XI Pan Am Congress of Ophthalmology, 1974; mem. editl. bd. Ophthalmologia, 1965-72, Annals of Ophthalmology, 1968-74; contbr. articles to profl. jours.; cons. Highlights Ophthalmology, 1972; founded the Lions Ey Bank; founded the just Tissue laboratory devoted to ophthalmology in the world, 1959; established the first institute of ophthalmology in southwestern USA at Baylor College of Medicine, 1961. Recipient Alfred H. Bond award for rsch. in ophthalmology, 1950, Prof. Ignacio Barraquer Meml. award Inst. Barraquer, 1965, 2d prize Internat. Eye Film Festival, 1966, 1st prize, 1970, 1st prize, 1972, Golden Eagle award Internat. Film Festival Nantes, France, 1970, 71, Alumnus award Baylor U., 1984, First Disting. Alumnus award NY Eye and Ear Infirmary, 1984, Disting. Alumnus award Rice U., 1985, Disting. Alumnus award U. Tex. Med. Br. at Galveston, 1991; named to Hall of Fame, Alcon Labs., 1990. Fellow ACS (bd. gov. 1966-72); mem. Am. Acad. Ophthalmology (2d pl. award sci. exhibits 1960, Honor award, Sr. Honor award), Pan Am. Assn. Ophthalmology (1st pl. award sci. exhibits 1960, 62, vis. prof. 1967, v.p. 1972), Assn. Research Ophthalmology, N.Y. Acad. Medicine, NY Acad. Sci., Nassau, Houston ophthal. socs., French Soc. Ophthalmology, Houston Neurol. Soc., Jules Gonin Club, Tex. Opthal. Assn., Alumni Assn. NY Eye and Ear Infirmary, AMA (certificate of merit sci. exhibit 1961), So. Med. Assn., Nat. Med. Found. Eye Care, Assn. Am. Physicians and Surgeons, Am. Assn. Ophthalomologists, Nat. Med. Found. Eye Care, Tex. Rehab. Assn., Harris County Med. Soc., Am. U. Prof. Ophthalmologists (founder, chmn. com. on ophthalmic asst.), Med. Rsch. Found. Tex., Contact Lens Soc. Ophthalmologists (Exceptional Merit award 1968), Inst. Horacio Ferrer (corr., lectr. 1959), Am. Eye Study Club (pres.) Achievements include inventing several instruments; originator numerous surg. techniques. Home: 20126 Indigo Lake Dr Magnolia TX 77355-3163 Personal E-mail: louisgirard.md@sbcglobal.net.

GIRARD, NETTABELL, lawyer; b. Pocatello, Idaho, Feb. 24, 1938; d. George and Arranetta (Bell) Girard. Student, Idaho State U., 1957—58; BS, U. Wyo., 1959, JD, 1961. Bar: Wyo. 1961, D.C. 1969, U.S. Supreme Ct. 1969. Practiced in, Riverton, Wyo., 1963-69; atty.-adviser on gen. counsel's staff HUD; assigned Office Interstate Land Sales Registration, Washington, 1969-70; sect. chief interstate land sales Office Gen. Counsel, 1970-73; ptnr. Larson & Larson, Riverton, 1973-85; pvt. practice Riverton, 1985—. Condr. course on women and law; lectr. in field. Editor Wyoming Clubwoman, 1966-68; bd. editors Wyo. Law Jour., 1959-61; writer Obiter Dictum column Women Lawyers Jour., Dear Legal Advisor column Solutions for Seniors, 1988-94; featured in Riverton Ranger, 1994; also articles in legal jours. Chmn. fund dr. Wind River chpt., ARC, 1965; chmn. Citizens Com. for Better Hosp. Improvement, 1965; chmn. subcom. on polit. legal rights and responsibilities Gov.'s Commn. on Status Women, 1965—69, mem. adv. com., 1973—93; local chmn. Law Day, 1966, 1967, county chmn., 1994—97; mem. state bd. Wyo Girl Scouts USA, sec., 1974—89, bd. dirs., 2001—04; state vol. adv. Nat. Found. March of Dimes, 1967—69; legal counsel Wyo. Women's Conf., 1977; gov. apptd. State Wyo. Indsl. Siting Coun., 1995—2001; rep. Nat. Conf. Govs. Commn., Washington, 1966. Recipient Spl. Achievement award HUD, 1972, Disting. Leadership award Girl Scouts USA, 1973, Franklin D. Roosevelt award Wyo. chpt. March of Dimes, 1985, Thanks Badge award Girl Scout Coun., 1987, Women Helping Women award Riverton Club Soroptimist Internat., 1990, Spl. award 27 yrs. svc. Wyo. Commn. for Women, 1964-92, Appreciation award Wyo. Sr. Citizens and Solutions for Srs., 1994, Arts in Action Pierrot award for outstanding musician, 1998, Disting. Svc. award Wyo. Music Edn. Assn., 2003. Mem. AAUW (br. pres., condr. seminar on law for layman Riverton br. 1965), Wyo. Bar Assn., Fremont County Bar Assn. (Spl. Recognition cert. 1997), DC Bar Assn., Women's Bar Assn. DC, Wyo. Trial Lawyers Assn., Nat. Assn. Women Lawyers (del. Wyo., nat. sec. 1969-70, v.p. 1970-71, pres. 1972-73), Wyo. Fedn. Women's Clubs (state editor, pres.-elect 1968-69, treas. 1974-76), Prog. Women's Club (pres.-elect. 1994-95), Riverton Chautaqua Club (pres. 1965-67, 2000-01), Riverton Civic League (pres. 1987-89), Kappa Delta, Delta Kappa Gamma (state chpt. hon.). Home: PO Box 687 Riverton WY 82501-0687 Office: 513 E Main St Riverton WY 82501-4440 Office Phone: 307-856-9339. Business E-Mail: ngirard@tcinc.net. *I believe first and foremost in the freedom of the individual: the right of the individual to be different, to be unique, and to pursue his or her particular heart's desire so long as that pursuit does not endanger the life or freedom of another. Perhaps because as a woman lawyer in predominately a man's profession, I have experienced the bitterness and dissolutionment of discrimination, I have actively worked through the equal rights movement toward the realization of individual freedom for all people. I support equality, not in the sense of "sameness," but in the realization of greater opportunities for individual development and differentiation.*

GIRARD, RENÉ NOEL, author, educator; b. Avignon, France, Dec. 25, 1923; came to U.S., 1947; s. Joseph and Thérèse (Fabre) G.; m. Martha McCullough, June 18, 1951; children: Martin, Daniel, Mary. Archiviste-paléographe, Ecole des chartes, Paris, 1947; PhD, Ind. U., 1950. Tchr. Romance langs. Ind. U., 1947-52, Duke U., 1952-53, Bryn Mawr Coll., 1953-57; faculty Johns Hopkins U., 1957-68, prof. French lit., 1961-68, chmn. dept. Romance langs., 1966-68, James M. Beall prof. French and humanities, 1977-80; disting. faculty prof. arts and letters SUNY, Buffalo, 1971-77; Andrew B. Hammond prof. French and Comparative Lit., Stanford U., 1981-95. Hon. chair Colloquium on Violence and Religion. Author: Mensonge romantique et vérité romanesque, 1961, 78, Marcel Proust: A Collection of Critical Essays, 1962, 77, Deceit, Desire and the Novel, 1967, 76, La Violence et le Sacré, 1972, English transl., 1977, Critique dans un souterrain, 1976, Des Choses cachées depuis la fondation du monde, 1978, To Double Business Bound, 1978, Le Bouc émissaire, 1982, La Route antique des hommes pervers, 1985, Things Hidden since the Foundation of the World, 1987, Job: the Victim of his People, 1987, Shakespeare: Les feux de l'envie, 1990, A Theater of Envy. William Shakespeare, 1991, Quand ces choses commenceront, 1994, The Girard Reader (ed. James Williams), 1996, Resurrection from the Underground: Feodor Dostoevsky (ed. James Williams), 1997, Je Vois Satan Tomber Comme L'Éclair, 1999, I see Satan fall like Lightning, 2001, Celui par qui le scandale arrive, 2001, La voix méconnue du réel, 2002, Les origines de la culture, 2004; contbr. articles to profl. jours. Guggenheim fellow, 1960, 67; recipient Prix Médicis Essai, 1990, Premio Nonino, 1998. Mem. Acad. Arts and Scis., French Legion Honor, Acad. Francaise (Grand prix de philosophie 1996). Home: 705 Frenchmans Rd Stanford CA 94305-1004 also: 17 Av la Bourdonnais 75007 Paris France

GIRARD, ROBERT DAVID, lawyer; b. Pitts., Aug. 2, 1946; s. Oscar L. and Ruth (Alpern) G. AB, UCLA, 1967; LLB, Yale U., 1970. Bar: Calif. 1971, U.S. Dist. Ct. (ctrl. dist.) Calif. 1971. Ptnr. Musick, Peeler & Garrett, L.A., 1970-85, Girard, Ellingsen, Christensen & West, L.A., 1985-88, Jones, Day, Reavis & Pogue, L.A., 1988-92, Musick Peeler & Garrett, L.A., 1992—97; with Sonnenschein Nath & Rosenthal, L.A., 1997—. Bd. dirs. Eisner Pediatric and Family Med. Ctr., L.A., 1980—, chmn., 1998-2002. Mem. ABA, L.A. County Bar Assn., Am. Health Lawyers Assn., Calif. Health Care Lawyers Assn. (bd. dirs. 1982-85), Phi Beta Kappa. Office: Sonnenschein Nath & Rosenthal 601 S Figueroa St Ste 1500 Los Angeles CA 90017-5720 Office Phone: 213-623-9300.

GIRARD, THERESA MARY, language educator; b. Mount Clemens, Mich., Oct. 13, 1947; d. William Michael and Jeannette Marie Girard. AA, Macomb CC, Warren, Mich., 1976; BA, Wayne State U., Detroit, 1983, MA, 1988, PhD in English, 2001. Adj. prof. Oakland U., Rochester, Mich., 1993—95, U. Detroit-Mercy, Detroit, 1997, Wayne State U., 1989—, Ctrl. Mich. U., Troy, Mich., 1998—, Lawrence Tech. U., Southfield, Mich., 1998—. Presenter in field. Contbg. editor: (book chpt.) Short Stories for Students, 1998. Judge Nat. Hist. Day Lawrence Tech. U., 2002—04. Recipient Excellence in Teaching award, Wayne State U., 1990—91. Mem.: AAUP, AAUW, Planetary Soc. Democrat. Avocations: reading, exercise, astronomy, theater. E-mail: docterphd@aol.com.

GIRARD-DICARLO, DAVID FRANKLIN, lawyer; b. Bryn Mawr, Pa., Jan. 20, 1943; s. John J. Girard-DiCarlo and Elizabeth Ward; m. Constance Jean Bricker, Apr. 5, 1973. BS, St. Joseph's U., 1970; JD, Villanova U., 1973. Bar: Pa. 1973, US Dist. Ct., Ea. Dist., Pa. 1973, US Ct. Appeals, Third Circuit 1973, US Supreme Ct. 1978. Assoc. Wolf, Block, Schorr & Solis-Cohen, Phila., 1973—74, Dilworth, Paxson, Kalish, Levy & Kauffman, Phila., 1974—78, ptnr., 1979, Fell, Spalding, Goff & Rubin, Phila., 1979—82, Blank, Rome, Comisky & McCauley, Phila., 1982—, chmn., labor and employment law section, 1982—86, adminstrv. ptnr., 1986—87, mng. ptnr. & CEO, 1987—99; co-chmn., CEO & mng. ptnr. Blank Rome LLP (formerly Blank, Rome, Comisky & McCauley), Phila., 2000—02, chmn., 2003—. Mem. hearing com. Disciplinary Bd. of Supreme Ct. of Pa., Phila., 1981-84, chmn. hearing com., 1984-87; faculty mem. Workshop on Urban Mass Transp., Practicing Law Inst., San Francisco and Washington, 1978; bd. dirs. Midlantic Corp.; trustee Phila. Belt Line R.R. Co., 1992; lectr. in field; Editor-in-chief Villanova Law Rev., 1972, Transit Law Rev., 1977-81; contbr. articles to legal jours. Mem. Phila. Cmty. Leadership Seminar Program, 1978-79; chmn. bd. Southeastern Pa. Transp. Authority, 1979-82; mem. transp. taxation task force Tax Commn. of Commonwealth of Pa., 1981-82; chmn. N.E. Corridor Commuter Rail Authorities Com., 1981-83; mem. Pa. Rep. State Fin. Com., 1982—. Bd. dirs. Greater Phila. Partnership, 1981-83, Urban Affairs Partnership, 1983-85, Hermitage Homeowners Assn., 1982-86; mem. World Affairs Coun., Phila., bd. dirs., 1993; trustee Walnut St. Theatre, 1986-93, Harcum Jr. Coll., 1987-92, Drexel U., 1988-92, Phila. Acad. Music and Phila. Orch., 1988-95, mem. exec. com., 1988-95, vice chmn., 1991-94; mem. sch. of law bd. of consultors Villanova U., 1992; chmn. transition team Pa. Gov. Elect Tom Ridge, 1994; bd. mgrs. The Phila. Found., 1994; trustee St. Joseph's U., 1994. Fellow Am. Bar Found.; mem. ABA, Pa. Bar Assn., Phila. Bar Assn., Am. Pub. Transit Assn. (bd. dirs. 1979-82, chmn. bd. dirs. 1982, chmn. legis. com. 1980-81, mem. exec. com. 1980-82, v.p. govt. affairs 1981-82, mem. various coms.), Greater Phila. C. of C. (bd. dirs., sec., mem. exec. com. 1990). Office: Blank Rome LLP One Logan Sq Philadelphia PA 19103-6998 Office Phone: 215-569-5500. Office Fax: 215-569-5555. Business E-Mail: girarddicarlo@BlankRome.com.

GIRARDEAU, MARVIN DENHAM, physics professor; b. Lakewood, Ohio, Oct. 3, 1930; s. Marvin Denham and Maude Irene (Miller) G.; m. Susan Jessica Brown, June 30, 1956; children: Ellen, Catherine, Laura. BS, Case Inst. Tech., 1952; MS, U. Ill., 1954; PhD, Syracuse U., 1958. NSF postdoctoral fellow Inst. Advanced Study, Princeton, NJ, 1958—59; rsch. assoc. Brandeis U., 1959—60; staff mem. Boeing Sci. Rsch. Labs., 1960—61; rsch. assoc. Enrico Fermi Inst. Nuc. Studies, U. Chgo., 1961—63; assoc. prof. physics, rsch. assoc. Inst. Theoretical Sci., U. Oreg., Eugene, 1963—67, prof. physics, rsch. assoc., 1967—95, dir., 1967—69, chmn. dept. physics, 1974—76, prof. emeritus, 1995—; rsch. prof. optical scis. U. Ariz., 2000—. Contbr. articles to profl. jours. Recipient Humboldt Sr. U.S. Scientist award, 1984-85. NSF rsch. grantee, 1965-79; ONR rsch. grantee, 1981-87, 99—. Fellow Am. Phys. Soc.; mem. AAUP. Achievements include research on quantum-mech. many-body problems, statis. mechanics, atomic, molecular and chem. physics; Bose-Einstein condensation of atomic vapors, coherent control of quantum systems. Home: 288 N Bent Ridge Dr Green Valley AZ 85614-5949 Office: Optical Scis Ctr Univ Arizona Tucson AZ 85721-0001 E-mail: girardeau@optics.arizona.edu.

GIRARDI, FEDERICO PABLO, surgeon, educator; b. Rosario, Santa Fe, Argentina, Dec. 20, 1967; came to U.S., 1996; s. Hector Francisco Girardi and Martha Sylvia Malano; m. Maria Florencia Ferrero, May 4, 1996; children: Federico, Emilia. MD, 1991. Resident Hosp. de Clinicas Jose de San Martin, Buenos Aires U.; orthop. fellow Hosp. Spl. Surgery, N.Y.C., 1996-99, asst. attending orthop. surgeon, asst. scientist, 2000—; instr. Weill Coll. Medicine Cornell U., N.Y.C., 2000—. Dir. rsch. and edn. SpineCare Inst., Hosp. Spl. Surgery, N.Y.C., 2000—. Mem. AMA, N.Am. Spine Soc., Scoliosis Rsch. Soc., European Spine Soc., Med. Soc. State N.Y., N.Y. County Med. Soc. Office: Hosp Spl Surgery 535 E 70 St New York NY 10021 Fax: 212-472-1486. E-mail: GirardiF@hss.edu.

GIRARDI, THOMAS VINCENT, lawyer; b. Denver, June 3, 1939; s. Albert Girardi; married, Sept. 11, 1993; children: Jacqueline, Matthew, Jennifer. BS, Loyola U., L.A., 1961, LLB, 1964; LLM, NYU, 1965. Bar: Calif. 1964. Sr. ptnr. Girardi & Keese, L.A., 1965—. Assoc. prof. law Loyola U., L.A., 1976-. Contbr. over 50 articles to profl. jours. Fellow Internat. Acad. Trial Lawyers (bd. dirs.); mem. The Am. Bd. Trial Advocates (pres. L.A. chpt. 1998, nat. v.p.), The Inner Circle of Advocates, The Am. Bd. Profl. Liability Lawyers, The Internat. Soc. Barristers, The Consumer Attys. Assn. L.A., The L.A. Trial Lawyers (Trial Lawyer of Yr. 1995-96). Democrat. Roman Catholic. Avocations: golf, aviation. Home: 100 Los Altos Dr Pasadena CA 91105-1240 Office: Girardi & Keese 1126 Wilshire Blvd Los Angeles CA 90017-1904

GIRAUD, RAYMOND DORNER, retired language professional; b. N.Y.C., Aug. 26, 1920; s. Gabriel and Mabel (Dorner) G.; m. Lise Kurzmann, Feb. 1, 1948. BA, Coll. City N.Y., 1941; MA, U. Chgo., 1949; PhD, Yale, 1954. Instr. English and French Ill. Inst. Tech., 1946-49; instr., then asst. prof. French Yale, 1952-58; mem. faculty Stanford, 1958—, prof. French, 1962—, chmn. dept. French and Italian, 1968-72; prof. emeritus, 1986. Author: The Unheroic Hero, 1957, Flaubert, A Collection of Critical Essays, 1964. Served with AUS, 1942-45. Decorated Chevalier, Ordre des Palmes Acadèmique, 1967; Guggenheim fellow, 1961-62. Home: 2200 Byron St Palo Alto CA 94301-4007 E-mail: giraud2200@webtv.net.

GIRDHAR, SARVA PRIYA, surgeon; b. Ferozepur, India, 1941; MB BS, Med. Coll. Gauhati U., 1965. Diplomate Am. Bd. Surgery. Intern Gauhati Med. Coll., 1965-66; resident in surgery Church Home Hosp., Balt., 1971-72, Deaconess Hosp., St. Louis, 1972-74, Altoona (Pa.) Hosp., 1974-75; fellow in cardiovasc. disease St. Paul Hosp., Dallas, 1975-77; staff Carroll County Gen. Hosp., Westminster, Md. Mem. AMA. Home: 7 Valley Gate Way Baltimore MD 21208-1369 Office Phone: 410-848-1464.

GIRDLER, SUSAN SCOTT, psychologist, educator, researcher; b. Rockledge, Fla., Mar. 18, 1960; d. Harry Bell and Nancy Jackson Girdler; m. Charles Edward Pettee, Aug. 6, 1957; children: Jackson Charles Pettee, Noah Scott Pettee. BS in Psychology, U. Fla., 1982; MS in Counseling Psychology, Nova U., Fla., 1986; PhD, U. N.C., 1991. Asst. clin. prof. U. Calif., Fresno, 1992—93; assoc. prof. U. N.C., Chapel Hill, 1993—. Cons. NIH, Bethesda, Md., 2001—. Assoc. editor: Biol. Psychology, 2000—, guest editor:, 2005. Sunday Sch. tchr. U. Bapt. Ch., Chapel Hill, 2002—, tchr. Vacation Bible Sch., 2002—. Grantee, NIMH, 1995—, Nat. Heart, Lung and Blood Inst., 1997—2002, Nat. Inst. Drug Abuse, 2001—. Mem.: Soc. for Psychophysiological Rsch., Internat. Orgn. Psychophysiology, Soc. Behavioral Medicine (Young Investigator award 1996), Am. Psychosomatic Soc. (Early Career Contributions to Psychosomatic Rsch. award 2001). Democrat. Baptist. Avocations: swimming, hiking, backpacking. Office: U NC CB7175 Dept Psychiatry Chapel Hill NC 27599 Personal E-mail: sgirdler@med.unc.edu.

GIRDWOOD, DERIK RENARD, lawyer; b. Cliftonville, Mich., England, Feb. 14, 1952; s. George Renard and Else M. G.; m. Biserka Girdwood; children: John, Laura, Christopher, David. BS in Bus., Wayne State U., Detroit, 1974; JD, Detroit Coll. Law, 1992. Bar: Mich. 1992; U.S. Fed. Ct. (ea. dist.) 1998. Atty. pvt. practice, Sterling Heights, Mich., 1992—. Author: Law Review, 1990, 92. Mem. Macomb County Bar, Oakland County Bar. Office: 75 N Main St Mount Clemens MI 48043-5616

GIRGIS, SUZETTE, clinical pharmacologist, researcher; d. Fawzy and Narges Tawfeek Rashed; m. Ihab Girgis, June 4, 1995; children: Abigail Mary, Sarah Marie. BSc in Pharmacy with honors, Cairo U., 1992; MSc in Applied Pharm. Scis., U. R.I., 1997, PhD in Pharm. Scis., 1999. Postdoctoral fellow in clin. pharmacokinetics Janssen Rsch. Found. Johnson & Johnson, Titusville, NJ, 2000; sr. scientist in pharmacokinetics Schering-Plough Corp., Kenilworth, NJ, 2000—03, assoc. prin. scientist in pharmacokinetics, 2003; sr. rsch. investigator in clin. discovery/oncology-immunology Bristol-Myers Squibb Co., Princeton, NJ, 2003—05, assoc. dir. clin. discovery, 2005—. Sunday sch. tchr. St. Mary and St. Mena Coptic, Cranston, RI, 1996—2000, St. Mary Coptic Orthodox Ch., East Brunswick, 2000—. Mem.: Am. Coll. Clin. Pharmacology, Am. Soc. Clin. Pharmacology and Therapeutics, Am. Assn. Pharm. Scientists. Avocations: reading, drawing, painting, crafts. Home: 21 Brookside Dr Princeton NJ 08540 Office: Bristol-Myers Squibb Co US Hwy 206 & Province Line Rd Princeton NJ 08543-4000 Office Phone: 609-252-6053.

GIRGIS-HANNA, MARY FAHIM, music educator; b. Assiut, Egypt, Mar. 6, 1935; arrived in U.S., 1989; d. Fahim Girgis and Emily Matta Boctor; m. Fadel M. Hanna, Nov. 25, 1954; children: Baher, Farid, Wagih. BA in Edn., Am. U., Cairo, 1958, MA in Sociology, 1978; ATCL in Piano Tchg., Trinity Coll. London, 1972; PhD in Spl. Edn., U. Toledo, 1997. Tchr. Manor House H.S., Cairo, 1967—69; pvt. piano tchr. Cairo, 1972—88; tchr. family sociology Prebyn. Sem., Cairo, 1984—88; cons. gerontology Egyptian Ministry of Health, Cairo, 1980—83; instr. sociology U. Toledo, 1989—2000; dir., founder Rhapsody Sch. Music, Toledo, 1994—. Founder, bd. dirs. Ctr. for Geriatric Svcs., Cairo, 1976—88. Author: The Gerontologist, 1983. Bd. dirs. Lucas County Bd. Mental Retardation, Toledo, 1998—2000; Ohio rep. Trinity Coll. London, 1995—; chmn. internat. com. World Day of Prayer, 1978—82; active Christian Med. Commn., World Coun. Chs., Geneva, 1980—83; organist Judson Bapt. Ch., Toledo, 1992—, deacon of missions, 1997—2002. Named Model Mother, Presbyn. Women's Assn., 1980. Mem.: Toledo Piano Tchr. Assn. (pres. 2001—03), Nat. Piano Tchr. Assn. Avocations: piano, organ, accordion, singing, reading. Home: 3006 E Lincolnshire Blvd Toledo OH 43606 Office Phone: 419-866-4640.

GIRGUS, JOAN STERN, psychologist, educator, director; b. Albany, N.Y., Mar. 21, 1942; d. William Barnet and Louise (Mayer) Stern; m. Alan Chimacoff, Jan. 2, 1981; 1 child, Katherine Louise Stern. BA, Sarah Lawrence Coll., 1963; MA, The Grad. Faculty New Sch. for Social Research, 1965, PhD, 1969. Asst. prof. dept. psychology CCNY, N.Y.C., 1969-72, assoc. prof., 1972-77, assoc. dean div. social sci., 1972-75, dean, 1975-77; prof. psychology Princeton U., 1977—, dir. Pew Sci. Program Undergrad. Edn., 1987—2002, chair dept. psychology, 1996—2002, spl. asst. to dean of faculty, 2003—. Contbr. articles and chpts. to profl. jours. and books. NSF fellow, NIH fellow; Research grantee CUNY, 1971-74; Nat. Inst. Child Health and Human Devel. research grantee, 1972-74; NSF grantee, 1975-79; NIMH grantee, 1985-91. Fellow APA, Am. Psychol. Soc.; mem. Eastern Psychol. Assn., Soc. Rsch. in Child Devel. Home: 306 Ridgeview Rd Princeton NJ 08540 Office: Princeton U Green Hall Princeton NJ 08544

GIRGUS, SAM B., English literature educator; b. Dec. 30, 1941; m. Judith Scot-Smith; children: Katya Roberts, Meighan St. John, Jennifer Scot-Smith. BA in American Studies, Syracuse U., 1962; MA in English, State U. Iowa, 1963; PhD in American Studies, U. N.Mex., 1972. Reporter, critic Providence (R.I.) Jour., 1967-69; asst. prof. in Am. studies and English U. Ala., 1972-75, dir., 1973-75; assoc. prof., chmn. dept. Am. studies U. N.Mex., 1975-84, prof. English and Am. studies, 1980-87; prof. English, dir. Am. studies U. Oreg., Eugene, 1987-90; prof. English Vanderbilt U., Nashville, 1990—, dir. Am. studies, 1990-92, chair, dir., film studies, 2003—04. Chmn. disciplinary adv. com. Fulbright Scholars Awards in Am. Culture, 1989-93; cons. USIA visit at Sofia U., Bulgaria, 1985, Los Andes U., Bogota, Columbia, 1992, Hankuk U.,

Seoul, Korea, 1993, Aarhus U., Odense U., Denmark, 1995; lectr. in field; Uppsala chair in Am. studies Uppsala U., Sweden, 1996. Author: The Law of the Heart: Individualism and the Modern Self in American Literature, 1979, The New Covenant: Jewish Writers and the American Idea, 1984, Desire and the Political Unconscious in American Literature, 1990, The Films of Woody Allen, 1993, 2d edit., 2002, Hollywood Renaissance: The Cinema of Democracy in the Era of Ford, Capra and Kazan, 1998, America on Film: Modernism, Documentary, and a Changing America, 2002; editor: The American Self: Myth, Ideology and Popular Culture, 1981, The New Eden: Consensus and Regeneration in America, 1988, The Outsider: Dissent and Alienation in America, 1988; guest editor: Am. Literary Realism 1870-1910, 1977; prodr., writer: (film) In Loco Amicis: The New Vanderbilt Story, 2001; contbr. articles to profl. jours. With USN, 1963-67. Rockefeller Humanities fellow, 1980-81; Sr. Fulbright lectr. U. Heidelberg, Germany, 1984. Mem. MLA, Cinema Studies Assn., Am. Studies Assn., Modernist Studies Assn. Home: 402 Lynwood Blvd Nashville TN 37205-3435 Office: Vanderbilt U Dept English PO Box 1654 Sta B 318 Benson Hall Nashville TN 37235 Office Phone: 615-322-2271. Business E-Mail: sam.b.girgus@vanderbilt.edu.

GIRLING, ROBERT GEORGE WILLIAM, III, business owner; b. Eldorado, Ark., July 28, 1929; s. Robert George William Jr. and Mildred Addie (Massey) G.; m. Bettie J. Moore, Sept. 2, 1960. BA, Miss. Coll., 1950; BD, New Orleans Bapt. Theol. Sem., 1954; MS in Social Work, U. Tex., 1961. Pastor Bapt. chs., Miss., 1949-58; tchr. high sch. Miss., 1958-59; dir. social work Lena Pope Childrens Home, Ft. Worth, 1961-62, exec. dir., 1962-66; pres., CEO Girling Health Care, Inc., Austin, Tex., 1967—. Dir. social work. Austin State Sch., 1966-69, dir. profl. svcs 1970-71; clin. instr. U. Tex. Sch. Social Work, Austin, 1972-75. Capt. USAFR, 1955-65. Named Lord Chancellor, Knights of the Symphony, 1994; recipient Ida Mae Herbert Meritorious award Tex. Home Health Care. Mem. Acad. Cert. Social Workers, Tex. Assn. Home Health Agys. (treas. 1978-82, pres. 1984-86), Nat. Assn. Home Care (chmn. nominating com. 1978), Rotary (chmn. nominating com. 1976), Austin Country Club, Headliners Club, Austin Club. Baptist. Avocations: fishing, ranching, photography, swimming. Office: Girling Health Care Inc PO Box 4294 Austin TX 78765-4294

GIRMAN, DEE-MARIE, artist, singer; b. Duquesne, Pa., Apr. 10, 1919; d. Michael Girman and Marie Schuster. Student, Pitts. Musical Inst., Fillion Ballet Sch.; studied dress design with Louise Salinger; student, Barry U. Singer, Pitts.; iconographer, artist Barry U., Miami Shores, Fla. Author: Sandtrap, The Mathematical Genius Dog, 2003; one-woman shows include Chase Showing, 1974, Barrry U., 1983, Miami Art Ctr. Entertainer specialist Spl. Svc., USAAC, 1942—45. Named to Hall of Fame, Barry U., 1995, Meml. Hist. Roll of Honor, Am. Meml. Found., 1997. Republican. Roman Catholic. Achievements include design of icons of mother and child, 174 Keyhole mini-icon. Avocation: golf. Home: 1779 San Silvestro Dr Venice FL 34285 Personal E-mail: sansydee@msn.com.

GIROD, BERNARD A., electronics executive; BS, Univ. Ill.; MBA, Univ. Mich. With Harman Internat. Industries, Washington, 1986-93, exec. v.p., CFO, 1993-96, COO, 1993—98, pres., 1994—98, CEO, 1998—, vice chmn., 2000—. Office: Harman International Industries Ste 1010 1101 Pennsylvania Ave NW Washington DC 20004 also: Harman International Industries 8500 Balboa Blvd Northridge CA 91329*

GIROIR, LEO JEAN JR., accountant; b. New Orleans, Nov. 5, 1941; s. Leo Jean and Evelyn Gerhardt G.; children from previous marriage: Lisa Marie, Wendy Ann Giroir-Colson; m. Louise Moore. BBA, Loyola U., 1963. CPA, Calif., La. Staff acct. Haskins & Sells CPAs, New Orleans, 1966-71; ptnr. Ross Landis & Pauw CPAs, Riverside, Calif., 1971-79, Easley & Giroir CPAs, Colton, Calif., 1979-81, McGladrey Hendrickson CPAs, Colton, 1981-84; shareholder Leo J. Giroir Jr. CPA, APC, Riverside, 1984—. Chair bd. dirs. Riverside Arts Found., 1991-97, Riverside County ARC, 1997—; treas. Riverside Ballet Theatre, 1991-92; bd. dirs. BBB, So. Calif., 1981—. Served in U.S. Army, 1964-66. Republican. Roman Catholic. Avocations: cooking, fishing. Home and Office: PO Box 20257 Riverside CA 92516-0257

GIROLAMI, GREGORY SCOTT, chemistry educator; b. Honolulu, Oct. 16, 1956; s. Guido and Kristine Merle (White) G.; m. Vera Virginia Mainz, July 14, 1979. BS in Chemistry, BS in Physics, U. Tex., 1977; MS in Chemistry, U. Calif.-Berkeley, 1979, PhD in Chemistry, 1981. NATO postdoctoral fellow Imperial Coll. Sci. and Tech., London, 1982-83; asst. prof. chemistry U. Ill. at Urbana-Champaign, 1983-89, assoc. prof. chemistry, 1989-93, prof. chemistry, 1993—, head dept., 2000—. Vis. scientist AT&T Bell Labs., Murray Hill, N.J., 1991; cons. Exxon, 1991-95; vis. prof. U. Pierre et Marie Curie, Paris, 1998. Bd. editors Inorganic Chemistry, 1989-91, Organometallics, 1998-00; N.Am. editor Jour. Chem. Soc. Dalton Trans., 1995-98; contbr. over 130 articles to sci. jours. Recipient Young Investigator award in Chemistry, Office of Naval Rsch., 1986, Sloan Rsch. award A.P. Sloan Found., 1988, Dreyfus Tchr.-Scholar award Dreyfus Found., 1988; Univ. scholar U. Ill., 1990. Mem. Am. Chem. Soc. (treas. inorganic divsn. 1997-99), Royal Soc. Chemistry, Materials Rsch. Soc. Home: 2709 Holcomb Dr Urbana IL 61802-7724 Office: U Ill at Urbana-Champaign 600 S Mathews Ave Urbana IL 61801-3617 E-mail: girolami@scs.uiuc.edu.

GIRONE, JOAN CHRISTINE CRUSE, realtor, former county official; b. Kingston, Ont., Can., Aug. 30, 1927; d. Arthur William and Helen Wilson Cruse; m. Joseph MIchael Girone, June 26, 1954; children: Susan, Richard, William. Buyer Franklin Simon, Inc., N.Y.C., 1946-54; supr. Midlothian dist. Chesterfield County (Va.) Bd. Suprs., 1976-88, vice chmn., 1976-82; Founding mem. Capitol Area Agy. on Aging, 1973-89, Med. Coll. Va. Women's Health Adv. Coun., 1990-97, Chesterfield County Citizens for Responsible Govt., 1991—; comml. real estate agent Long and Foster Realtors, Richmond. Bd. dirs. Cen. Va. Ednl. TV Corp., 1989-94; commr., chmn. Richmond (Va.) Regional Planning Dist. Commn., 1976-88; Va. Power Consumer adv. bd.; chmn. cmty. edn. adv. com. Va. Bd. of Edn., 1972-79; mem. Va. Gov.'s Adv. Bd. on Aging, 1980-82; chmn. Richmond Met. Transp. Planning Orgn., 1981-88; bd. visitors Va. State U., 1980-84. Vice chmn., exec. com. Gateway Bus. Assn.; mem. Ctrl. Va. River Basin Com., 1985; mem. evaluation task force United Way of Greater Richmond, 1985; adv. bd. Chesapeake Bay Local Assistance Bd. Adv. Com. Midlothian YMCA, 2000; chmn. steering com. Bon Air Village Preservation, 1995—; mem. Coun. Advocates Va. Supportive Housing, 2001—; chmn. Chesterfield County Com. to elect John Warner and Paul Trible to U.S. Senate, 1979, 1982, 1984; Chesterfield chmn. Marshall Coleman for Gov., 1981—; chmn. Women for Reagen-Bush, 1984; vice chair Rt. 288 Freeway Comm., 1996, exec. com.; mem. candidate recruitment com. Va. Fedn. Rep. Women, 1995; bd. dirs. Maymount Found., 1982—89, YMCA Greater Richmond Metro, ARC Va. Capital chpt.; bd. mgrs. Chesapeake Bay Local Assistance Bd. Adv. Com. Midlothian YMCA, 1999, bd. dirs., 1994—, Caucus Future Ctrl. Va., 1994—, Coalition for Greater Richmond. Named Joan C. Girone Libr., Chesterfield Bus. County, 1995; recipient Good Govt. award, Richmond First Club, 1965. Mem. Va. Assn. Counties (exec. bd. 1982-87), Richmond Metro C. of C. (bd. dirs. Chesterfield Bus. Coun. 1989—), Chesterfield County C. of C. (mem. gov. rels. com. 2004), Hugeunot Rep. Woman's Club (Rep. Woman of Yr. 1983), Virginians for High Speed Rail (bd. dirs. 2004). Home: 2609 Dovershire Rd Richmond VA 23235-2815 Office Phone: 804-560-7625. Business E-Mail: joan.girone@longandfoster.com.

GIRON VIVES, ANA, language educator; b. Ponce, PR, Mar. 4, 1965; d. Antonio Vives Corretjer and Ana Cruz Lugo; m. John Glenn Giron, Jan. 4, 1986; children: Ana Nicole, Jorge Antonio, Gabriel David, Alejandra Francheska. MA in Spanish Lit., U. Tenn., Knoxville, 1993; BA, Lee U., 1987. Writer Editl. Evangelica, Cleveland, Tenn., 1986—88, translator, 1986—91, copy editor, computer art designer, mng. editor, 1988—91; grad. tchg. asst. U. Tenn., Knoxville, 1991—93; spanish instr. Eastfield Coll., Richland Coll., Dallas, 1994—99; spanish prof. Collin County CC, Plano, Tex., 1999. Spanish program coord. Collin County CC, Plano, 1999—2001. Active PTA, Dallas, 2000. Mem.: MLA, TCCTA. Democrat. Avocations: travel, reading, gourmet cooking. Home: 1309 Devonshire Mesquite TX 75150 Office: Collin County Cmty Coll 2800 Spring Creek Pkwy Plano TX 75228 Office Phone: 972-881-5724. Business E-Mail: agiron@ccccd.edu.

GIROUARD, MARVIN J., retail executive; B in Mktg., Tex. A&M U., 1961. Various mktg. positions Pier 1 Imports Inc., Ft. Worth, 1975—85, sr. v.p. merchandising, 1985—98, chmn., 1998—, CEO, 1999—; also bd. dirs. Bd. dirs. Brinker Internat., Tandy Brands Accessories, Inc. Mem. exec. com. U.S. Com. for UNICEF; mem. devel. coun. Coll. Bus. Adminstrn. Tex. A&M U.; bd. visitors M.J. Neeley Sch. Bus. Tex. Christian U. Commd. ensign USNR, 1963, advanced though grades to comdr. USNR, 1983, ret. USNR, 1983, served with USN, Vietnam. Recipient Hugh Downs award, U.S. Com. for UNICEF, 1994, Outstanding Alumni award, Coll. Bus. Adminstrn. and Grad Sch., Tex. A&M U., 1995. Office: 301 Commerce St Fort Worth TX 76102*

GIROUARD, PEGGY JO FULCHER, ballet educator; b. Corpus Christi, Tex., Oct. 25, 1933; d. J.B. and Zora Alice (Jackson) Fulcher; m. Richard Ernest Girouard, Apr. 16, 1954 (div. Mar. 1963); children: Jo Linne, Richard Ernest; m. James C. Boles, May 4, 1996. BS in Elem. Edn., U. Houston, 1970. Ballet instr. Emmamae Horn Studio, Houston, 1951-81; owner, dir. Allegro Acad. Dance, Houston, 1981—. Artistic dir. Allegro Ballet Houston, 1976—; asst. mgr. Sugar Creek Homes Assn., Sugar Land, Tex., 1979-90; coord. 1st Regional Dance Am. Nat. Festival, Houston, 1997. Choreographer (with Glenda W. Brown) Masquerade Suite, 1983, Sebelius Suite, 1983, Shannan, 1984, Papa Shamus, 1986, Silhouettes, 1987, Aspirations, 1989, Here Come the Clowns, 1990. Mem. Cultural Arts Coun. Houston; founding officer Regional Dance Am., 1988, bd. dirs., 1988—, sec., 1996-2001. Mem. Dance Masters Am. (dir. 1977-80), S.W. Regional Ballet Assn. (chmn. craft of choreography 1983-85, coord. to nat. assn. 1983-2003, Stream award 1986). Democrat. Home: 9945 Warwana Rd Houston TX 77080-7609 Office Phone: 281-496-4670. Personal E-mail: pgirouard77080@yahoo.com.

GIROUARD, TINA, artist, curator; b. De Quincy, La., May 26, 1946; BFA, U. La. Established studio, N.Y.C., 1968—85, Cecilia, La., 1980—, Port-au-Prince, Haiti, 1991—. One-woman shows include Univ. Gallery, Lafayette, La., 1968, 1973, 1974, 112 Greene St. Gallery, N.Y.C., 1971—73, 1975, Vehicule, Montreal, 1975, Alfred (N.Y.) U. Gallery, 1975, Memphis Acad., 1975, Holly Solomon Gallery, N.Y.C., 1976, 1978, 1980, Alexandra Monet Gallery, Brussels, 1979, Forum Stadtpark Mus., Graz, Austria, 1979, Elmhurst Park Gallery, Lafayette, 1981, De Vleeshal, Middelburg, Holland, 1982, Zeeuws Kuntenaarscentrum, 1982, Arthur Roger Gallery, New Orleans, 1983, Museo Tamayo, Mexico City, 1983, Fabric Workshop, N.Y.C., 1984, World's Fair, New Orleans, 1984, PS 1, L.I., 1985, Arthur Roger Gallery, New Orleans, 1985, Artist's Alliance, Lafayette, 1986, Contemporary Art Ctr., New Orleans, 1987, Quebec Delegation Gallery, Lafayette, 1987, C.A.C., New Orleans, 1989, Mus. Art, Alexandria, La., 1989, one-man shows include Atlantic Ctr. Arts, 1990, one-woman shows include Lafayette Regional Airport, 1990, Contemporary Arts Ctr., New Orleans, 1990, exhibited in group shows at 112 Green St. Gallery, N.Y.C., 1972, Leo Castelli Gallery, 1974, UCLA Gallery, 1976, Cin. Art Mus., 1978, Mus. Modern Art, Oxford, Eng., 1980, Holly Solomon Gallery, N.Y.C., 1982, Arthur Roger Gallery, New Orleans, 1984, Inst. Contemporary Art, 1987, Contemporary Art Ctr., La., 1990, numerous others, commns. include, Contemporary Art Ctr., New Orleans, 1989, Lafayette Regional Airport, 1990, videography includes, Maintenance I, 1971, Maintenance II, 1972, Maintenance III, 1973, Maintenance IV, 1975, Six of Hearts, 1976, Maintenance V, 1976, WAWA, 1979, 2 C 3 T S, 1981, others. CAPS grantee, Art Matters, Inc. grantee, Nat. Endowment Arts grantee, La. Divsn. Arts fellow, Nat. Endowment Arts fellow, Creative Artists Pub. Svc. fellow, 1973, Internat. Comm. Agy. fellow, 1979, Lila Wallace Arts Internat. fellow, 1993, Gottlieb Fatn fellow, 1997. Office: Tina Girouard Art Projects PO Box 64 Cecilia LA 70521-0064

GIRSHICK, FREDERICK WEIN, chemist; b. Bklyn., Aug. 31, 1954; s. Max and Hilda (Kahn) G.; m. Erica Wein, Jan. 3, 1993. BS in Chemistry and Math, Bklyn. Coll., 1975; MA in Chemistry, Princeton U., 1977, PhD in Chemistry, 1980; MS in Stats., Rutgers U., 1983. Rsch. chemist Exxon Rsch. and Engring., Linden, N.J., 1980-82, sr. chemist, 1982-85, staff chemist, 1987-90, group leader, 1990-95; sr. staff chemist Exxon Chem. Co., Linden, 1995-98; prin. scientist Esso Petroleum, Inc., Abingdon, Eng., 1985-87; formulation leader Infineum USA L.P., Linden, N.J., 1998—. Contbr. articles to profl. jours. V.p. Westfield (N.J.) Cmty. Band, 1988—; musicial dir. Westfield (N.J.) Dixie All-Stars, 1990—. Mem. ASTM, Am. Chem. Soc., Am. Phys. Soc., Am. Statis. Assn., Sigma Xi. Office: Infineum USA LP 1900 E Linden Ave Linden NJ 07036-1111

GIRSHIN, MARK DANILOVICH, writer, historian; b. Odessa, USSR, July 12, 1923; s. Daniel Romanovich Girshin and Anna Markovna Rudova; 1 child, Daniel. B, Odessa U., USSR, 1946—51. History tchr. H.S., Ukraine, 1951—53, Coll., Ukraine, 1953—74; waiter Workman's Circle, NY, 1974—75; trans. Russian newspapers, 1975—88; writer various pub. houses. Author: (book) Brighton Beach, 1984, The Death of the Emigrant, 1982, Mozaic et. al., 1980—2003, At Stalin's in Sochi, 1996. Mem.: Pen Club. Home: 24 Park St #3K Richfield Springs NY 13439

GIRTH, MARJORIE LOUISA, lawyer, educator; b. Trenton, N.J., Apr. 21, 1939; d. Harold Brookman and Marjorie Mathilda (Simonson) G. AB, Mt. Holyoke Coll., 1959; LLB, Harvard U., 1962. Bar: N.J. 1963, U.S. Supreme Ct. 1969, N.Y. 1976. Pvt. practice, Trenton, 1963-65; rsch. assoc. Brookings Instn., 1965-70; assoc. prof. law SUNY Law Sch., Buffalo, 1971-79, prof., 1979-91, assoc. dean, 1986-87; dean Ga. State U. Coll. Law, Atlanta, 1992-96, prof., 1992—. Vis. prof. U. Va. Law Sch., 1979-80; Southeastern Bankruptcy Law Inst. vis. prof. Emory Law Sch., spring 1991, vis. scholar, 1996; vis. legal educator W.Va. U. Coll. of Law Vis. Com., 1994-95; chancellor's search adv. com. Bd. of Regents, 1993-94; mem. com. on standards of the profession State Bar Ga., 1996-2005; mem. commn. on racial and ethnic bias in ct. sys. Ga. Supreme Ct, 1993-95, mem. commn. on equality, 1995-2004, sec., 1998-2000, mem. commn. on access and fairness in the cts., 2004-. Author: Poor People's Lawyers, 1976, Bankruptcy Options for the Consumer Debtor, 1981, (co-author) Bankruptcy: Problem, Process, Reform, 1971. Bd. dirs. Buffalo and Erie County YWCA, 1972-76, Buffalo Unitarian-Universalist Ch., 1981-84, Feminist Women's Health Ctr., 1993-94, ACLU, Ga., 1995-2001, Unitarian-Universalist Congregation of Atlanta, 1999—2003; mem. commn. on peace, justice and human rights Internat. Assn. Religious Freedom, 1976-79; mem. Found. Freedom Commn., 2005-. Ga. ct. appeals Centennial Celebration, 2005-; chmn. Erie County Task Force on Status of Women, 1985-87 Recipient award for pioneering achievements N.Y. State 8th Jud. Dist. Splty. Bar Assn. and Com. on Women in the Cts., 2000. Fellow Lawyers Found. Ga.; mem. ABA (mem. coun. bus. law sect. 1985-89, chmn. consumer bankruptcy com. 1983-86), Am. Arbitration Assn. (comml. arbitration panel 1997—), Assn. Am. Law Schs. (profl. devel. com. 2002—, nominations com. 1996), Am. Law Inst., N.Y. State Bar Assn. (mem. exec. com. bus. law sect. 1980-91, chmn. bankruptcy law com. 1980-82, chmn. banking corp. bus. law sect. 1986-87, mem. ho. of dels. 1990-91), Ga. Assn. Women Lawyers, Law Sch. Admissions Coun. (audit com. 1995-97, 1999—, fin. and legal affairs com., 1997-99), Mt. Holyoke Alumnae Assn. (Centennial award 1972). Unitarian Universalist. Office: Ga State U Coll Law PO Box 4037 Atlanta GA 30302-4037 Office Phone: 404-651-4916. E-mail: mgirth@gsu.edu.

GIRTMON, PAXTON M, music educator; s. Johnnye Rose and James Richard Girtmon; children: Lauren Paige, Calvin Haynes, Georgia Ann-Marie Rose. MusB with honors, Northwestern State U., 1985—90; MusM with honors, Northwestern State U., 1993—95; PhD in conducting, U. of So. Miss., 1995—97. Certificate for Music Education US Army, 1997, Certificate in Music Education State of Ga., 1995, La., 1993, Miss., 1997, Lern-On-Line Teaching LERN, 2001, Certified OJ2; Music Education; U.S. Army N.G., 1988, Certified LJ5; Specialist in Food Design U.S. Army N.G., 1985. Dir. of bands SE H.S., Macon, Ga., 1996—97; assoc. dir. of bands/asst. prof. of music Ft. Valley State U., Ga., 1997—98; assoc. dir. of bands/asst. prof. of music/music edn. specialist Tex. So. U., 1998—2002; asst. prof. of music, coord. of music edn. Grambling State U., La., 2001—05; assoc. dir. of bands, coord. of music edn., asst. prof. of music Jackson State U., Miss., 2005—. Min. of music Blooming Grove Bapt. Ch., Famerville, La., 2005—, Mt. Olive Bapt. Ch., Ruston, La., 2003—04, Redland Bapt. Ch., Negreet, La., 2002—00; advisor MENC, Jackson, La., 2005—, MENC-Grambling State U., Grambling, La., 1999—2000; advisor-student placement for field based experiences Dept. of Edn.-Jackson State U., 2005—, Dept. of Edn.-Grambling State U., Grambling, La., 1999—2000, Dept. of Edn.-Tex. Soutern U., 1997—99. Lecture-presentation, The Music of Julian C. Work: America's Lost Musical Heritage.; dir.: (guest conductor) Jackson Public School District All City Band Festival; monograph, Twentieth-Century African-American Wind Band Literature: Do You Hear What I Hear?, essay, Ulysses Kay: The Man and his Musical Craft: 1917-1995., Autumn Walk: A Musical Portrait, article, We Shall Not Be Moved, Portraits of the Bible: Shadrach, Meshach, and Abednego, by Julian Cassander Work: One of America's Forgotten Twentieth-Century African-American Impressionist Composers of Wind Band Literature., essay, Julian Cassander Work: One of the Few, the Proud, the Twentieth-Century, African-American, Impressionist Composers of Wind Band Literature., A Biographical And Analytical Study on Julian C. Work and his Compositions., magazie article, Innovative and Creative Techniques in Music Education.; dir.: (guest conductor) Los Alamos Wind Ensemble, Symphonic Bands, and Community Winds; Los Alamos, NM, All-Port Arthur Band Clinic; contbr. articles to profl. jours. Chmn. Coun. on Religious Music, Monore, La., 2005; v.p. Dept. of Gospel Activities, Shreveport, La., 2002—04. Recipient Silver award, Am. Assn. of Webmasters, 2004, Silver Award, 2002, Good Conduct award, U. S. Nat. Guard, 1990, Longetivity award, 1995. Mem.: Tex. Black Music Educators (licentiate), Sabine Parish Fatherhood Incentive Program (licentiate; v.p. 2000, Cetitificate for Appreciation 2002), Tex. Bandmasters Assn. (licentiate), Tex. Music Educators Assn. (licentiate), Coll. Music Soc.-South Regional (licentiate), Nat. Assn. for the Study and Performance of African-American Music (NASPAAM) (licentiate), Nat. Assn. of African-American Studies (licentiate; tex. chmn. 1998—2000, la. chmn. 2000—02), Music Educators Nat. Conf. (licentiate; advisor for grambling state u. 2002—03), Music Educators Nat. Conf. (licentiate), Miss. Bandmasters Assn. (licentiate). Office: Jackson State University/Dept of Music Po Box 17055 Jackson MS 39217 Office Phone: 832-236-7193. Personal E-mail: p.girtmon@att.net. E-mail: paxton.girtmon@jsums.edu.

GIRVIGIAN, RAYMOND, architect; b. Detroit, Nov. 27, 1926; s. Manoug and Margaret G.; m. Beverly Rae Bennett, Sept. 23, 1967; 1 son, Michael Raymond. AA, UCLA, 1947; BA with honors, U. Calif., Berkeley, 1950; MA in Architecture, U. Calif.-Berkeley, 1951. With Hutchason Architects, LA, 1952-57; owner, prin. Raymond Girvigian, LA, 1957-68, South Pasadena, Calif., 1968—. Co-founder, advisor LA Cultural Heritage Bd., 1961—; vice chmn. Hist. Am. Bldgs. Survey, Nat. Park Svc., Washington, 1966-70; co-founder, mem. Calif. Hist. Resources Commn., 1970-78; co-founder, chmn. governing bd. Calif. Hist. Bldgs. Code, 1976-91, chmn. adminstrv. law, 1992—, chmn. emeritus, 1993—; chmn. Calif. State Capitol Commn., 1985-98, chmn. emeritus, 1998—. Co-editor, producer: film Architecture of Southern California for Los Angeles City Sch., 1965; hist. monographs of HABS Landmarks, Los Angeles, 1958-80; historical monographs of Calif. State Capitol, 1974, Pan Pacific Auditorium, 1980, LA Meml. Coliseum, 1984, Powell Meml. Libr., UCLA, 1989; designed: city halls for Pico Rivera, 1963, LaPuente, 1966, Rosemead, 1968, Lawndale, 1970 (all Calif.); hist. architect for restoration of Calif. State Capitol, 1975-82, Workman/Temple Hist. Complex, City of Industry, Calif., 1974-81, Robinson Gardens Landmarks, Beverly Hills, Calif., 1983-92, Pasadena (Calif.) Ctrl. Libr., 1982-92, 95—, Mt. Pleasant House Mus., Heritage Sq., LA, 1972-95. With US Army, 1944-46. Recipient Outstanding Achievement in Architecture award City of Pico Rivera, Calif., 1968, Preservationist of Yr. award Calif. Preservation Found., 1987, LA Mayor's award for archtl. preservation, 1987, Gold Crown award Pasadena Arts Coun., 1990, Golden Palm award Hollywood Heritage, 1990; named Hist. Architect Emeritus, Calif. Legislature, 1998, commendation for state and national career achievemtns hist. preservation, Calif. Legislature, 1998; co-recipient honor award for rehab. Los Altos Apts., Calif. Preservation Found., 1999, co-recipient Calif. Preservation Found., 2003 Design award for Oaklawn Bridge Rehabilitation, Merit award Heritage Coalition of So. Calif., 2003. Fellow AIA, 1972 (Calif. state preservation chmn. 1970-75, state preservation coord. 1970-89, co-recipient nat. honor award for restoration Calif. State Capitol 1983, co-recipient honor award for restoration Pasadena Cen. Libr., Pasadena chpt. 1988); mem. Soc. Archtl. Historians, Nat. Trust for Historic Preservation, Calif. Preservation Found., Calif. Hist. Soc. (Neasham award 1982), Xi Alpha Kappa. Office: PO Box 220 South Pasadena CA 91031-0220 *I believe that we must all serve society in whatever way that we are best able; and if a worthy cause I have undertaken appears to have failed, I should ignore that possibility and press on with even greater determination and vigor to succeed. I would hope by that example to encourage others to join the cause and thereby futher the likelihood of a successful effort for the good of all.*

GIRVIN, EB CARL, retired biology professor; b. Georgetown, Tex., Dec. 27, 1917; s. Fitzhugh Bryson and Meta (Perlitz) G.; m. Virginia Lessor, Aug. 29, 1944; chilren: John Lessor, Eric Reed, Stacey Virginia. BA, U. Tex., 1940, MA, 1941, PhD, 1948. Prof. biology Millsaps Coll., 1948-53; prof. biology, head dept. Southwestern U., Georgetown, 1953-88; ret., 1988. Mem. Tex. Bd. Examiners Basic Sci., 1960-79; Mem. div. coll. work Episcopal Diocese Tex., 1962-65 Contbr. articles to profl. jours. Mem. Georgetown City Coun., 1981-87. Lt. comdr. USNR, 1941-45. Mem.: Sigma Xi. Home: 1703 E 16th St Georgetown TX 78626-7303

GIRVIN, STEVEN MARK, physicist, researcher; b. Austin, Tex., Apr. 5, 1950; s. Allen Fitzhugh and Margaret (Trowbridge) G.; m. Diane Desjardins, Jan. 1, 1972; children: Andrew T., Joshua M. BS magna cum laude, Bates Coll., 1971; MS, U. Maine, 1973, Princeton U., 1974, PhD, 1977. Postdoctoral rsch. assoc. Ind. U., Bloomington, 1977-79; staff scientist Nat. Inst. Stds. and Tech., Gaithersburg, Md., 1979-87; prof. Ind. U., Bloomington, 1987-92, disting. prof., 1992—2001; prof. physics Yale U., 2001—. Mem. Aspen (Colo.) Ctr. for Physics, 1990-94, NRC Panel on Condensed Matter and Materials Physics, Washington, 1996—; pres. adv. bd. Inst. Theoretical Physics, Santa Barbara, Calif., 1997-98. Editor: The Quantum Hall Effect, 1990. Fellow Am. Phys. Soc., Am. Acad. Arts & Sci. Avocation: amateur astronomy. Office: Yale U Dept Physics PO Box 208120 New Haven CT 06520-8120*

GISLASON, ERIC ARNI, chemistry professor; b. Oak Park, Ill., Sept. 9, 1940; s. Raymond Spencer and Jane Ann (Clifford) G.; m. Nancy Brown, Sept. 11, 1962 (dec. June 1994); children: Kristina Elizabeth, John Harrison; m. Sharon McKevitt Fetzer, Apr. 25, 1998. BA summa cum laude, Oberlin Coll., 1962; PhD, Harvard U., 1967. Postdoctoral fellow U. Calif-Berkeley, 1967-69; asst. prof. chemistry U. Ill., Chgo., 1969-73; assoc. prof. U. Ill.-Chgo., 1973-77, prof., 1977—; acting head chemistry dept. U. Ill., Chgo., 1993-94, head chemistry dept., 1994-99, interim dean Coll. Liberal Arts and Scis., 1997-98, interim vice chancellor rsch., 1999-2001, vice chancellor rsch., 2001—. Vis. scientist FOM Inst. Atomic and Molecular Physics, Amsterdam, 1977-78; prof. associé U. Paris South, 1985. Contbr. articles to profl. jours. Recipient Silver Circle Teaching award U. Ill., 1982, Excellence in Teaching award U. Ill., 1990. Mem. Am. Chem. Soc. (vis. assocs. program), Am. Phys. Soc., Phi Beta Kappa, Sigma Xi, Phi Kappa Phi. Congregationalist. Achievements include rsch. in theoretical studies of ion-molecule reactions, collision-induced dissociation, nonadiabatic transitions, molecular energy transfer, thermodynamics and isotope effects. Home: 7227 Oak Ave River Forest IL 60305-1935 Office: U Ill Chgo OVCR M/C 672 Rm 310 1737 W Polk St Chicago IL 60612-7727 Office Phone: 312-996-9450. Business E-Mail: gislason@uic.edu.

GISO, FRANK, III, lawyer; b. Haverhill, Mass., Feb. 14, 1949; s. Frank and Clementina Paula (Foresta) G; m. Deborah Jean Kracht, May 5, 1979; children: Christopher Anderson, Benjamin Hilding. BA Econs. magna cum laude, Brown U., 1971; JD magna cum laude, Cornell U., 1975. Bar: Mass. 1975, U.S. Dist. Ct. Mass. 1976, U.S. Ct. Appeals (1st cir.) 1976. Law clerk Mass. Superior Ct., Boston, 1975-76; assoc. Peabody & Brown, Boston, 1976-83, ptnr., 1983-88, Choate, Hall & Stewart, Boston, 1988—, chmn. real estate dept., 1988-98. Bd. dirs. Melrose (Mass.) Coop. Bank; pres. Melrose (Mass.) Affordable Housing Corp., 2003—. Vice chmn. Melrose Housing Authority, 1986-98, chmn. 1998—. Mem. ABA, Mass. Bar Assn., Boston Bar Assn., Phi Beta Kappa, Order of Coif. Avocations: tennis, golf. Office: Exchange Pl 53 State St Boston MA 02109-2804 Office Phone: 617-248-5117. Business E-Mail: fgiso@choate.com.

GISOLFI, DIANA (DIANA GISOLFI PECHUKAS), art history educator; b. NYC, Sept. 12, 1940; d. Anthony M. and Eleanor (Hayes) Gisolfi; m. Philip Pechukas, June 15, 1963 (div. Sept. 1991); children: Rolf, Maria, Sarah, Fiona (dec.), Amy. Student, Manhattanville Coll., 1958-60; BA magna cum laude, Radcliffe Coll., 1962; postgrad., Yale U., 1962-63; MA, U. Chgo., 1964, PhD, 1976. Instr. CUNY, 1967-68, Marymount Manhattan Coll., N.Y.C., 1977-79; asst. prof. art history Pratt Inst., Bklyn., 1979-84, assoc. prof., 1984-90, prof., 1990—, chmn. dept., 1981—99. Vis. asst. prof. Pratt Inst., 1976-79; dir. Pratt in Venice, Italy, 1984—; spkr. Conv. on Veronese, Venice, 1988, Conv. on Tintoretto, Venice, 1994, Symposium on Italian Art in Am., Fordham U., 1993, Mass. Coll. Art, 1998, AM Berger lecture, Manhattanville Coll., 2001; invited participant Veronese Reconsidered, CASVA, Washington, 1988; invited spkr. Coll. Art. Assn. 1990, 93, 95, 2002, discussant session Benedictine patronage, Medieval Conf., Kalamazoo, Mich., 2003; invited spkr. Medievel Conf. Kalamazoo, Mich., 2004; chmn. two Renaissance Art sessions, Renaissance Soc. Meeting, NYC, 2004. Illustrator (book) On Classic Ground, 1982; designer (book) Caudine Country, 1987; author: (with S. Sinding-Larsen) The Rule, the Bible, and the Council: The Library of the Benedictine Abbey at Praglia, 1998; contbr. articles on Veronese, Tintoretto and other sixteenth-century artists in North Italy and Venice to Art Bull., 1982, Artibus et Historiae 1987, 96, Art Veneta 1989-90, 2005, Nuovi Studi su Paolo Veronese, 1990, Burlington Mag., 1995, Dictionary of Art, 1996, Tintoretto Convegno Acts, 1996, Renaissance Quar., 1997, 2000, 01, Encyclopedia of Italian Renaissance and Mannerist Art, 2000, and others. Coord. Park Slope Freeze, Bklyn., 1984-86, Peace and Justice Com., St. Francis Xavier, 1984-86. Am. Philos. Soc. grantee, 1989, Delmas Found. grantee, 1995-96. Mem. Italian Art Soc., Renaissance Soc., Coll. Art Assn., Caucus for Design History, Phi Beta Kappa. Democrat. Roman Catholic. Home: 843 President St Brooklyn NY 11215-1405 Office: Pratt Inst Dept Art History East 250 Brooklyn NY 11205 Office Phone: 718-636-3600 ext 2300. E-mail: dgisolfi@pratt.edu, Dianagisolfi@aol.com.

GISSEL, L. HENRY, JR., lawyer; b. Houston, Oct. 20, 1936; m. Jo Claire Jones (div.); 3 children. BA, Rice U., 1958; LLB, So. Meth. U., 1961; postgrad., Georgetown U. Bar: Tex. 1961. Of counsel Fulbright & Jaworski, Houston. Trustee, sec. St. John's Sch., Houston, pres. Alumni Assn., dir. Alumni Assn.; exec. bd. mem., pres. Assn. Rice Alumni; dir. Retina Rsch. Found., Houston Alzheimer's Assn. Fellow Internat. Acad. Estate Trust Law (academician 1986-87, exec. coun.), Am. Coll. Trust and Estate Counsel (pres. 1995-96, regent 1981-87, 91-97, regent emeritus 1997—), Am. Bar Found. (bd. cert. estate planning and probate lab, Tex. bd. legal specialization); mem. Houston Bar Assn. (chmn. probate trust sect. 1982-83), coun. 1981-90, 94-97), ABA (sect. real property probate and trust law, chair 1988-89, Am. Bar Assn. (sect. del. 1994-97), River Oaks Country Club, The Forest Club (pres.). Office: Fulbright & Jaworski 1301 Mckinney St Ste 5100 Houston TX 77010-3031 Office Phone: 713-651-5214. Business E-Mail: hgissel@fulbright.com.

GISSER, MICHAEL VICTOR, lawyer; b. Bronxville, N.Y., Mar. 6, 1957; s. Philip and Norma Jean (Parcell) G.; m. Cynthia Ann Torres, Mar. 11, 1989; child, Spencer Williams, David. AB, Harvard U., 1977; JD, Stanford U., 1982. Bar: N.Y. 1985, Calif. 1987. Assoc. Wachtell, Lipton, Rosen & Katz, N.Y.C., 1984-86, Skadden, Arps, Slate, Meagher & Flom, L.A., 1986-90, 98—, ptnr., corp. internat., mergers and acquisitions, 1990-93, ptnr. Hong Kong, 1990-98. Mem. State Bar of Calif. (corps. com. 1992—). Office: Skadden Arps Slate et al 300 S Grand Ave Ste 3400 Los Angeles CA 90071 E-mail: mgisser@skadden.com.

GISSLER, SIGVARD GUNNAR, JR., journalist, educator, retired editor; b. Chgo., July 2, 1935; s. Sigvard Gunnar Sr. and Louisa (Anderson) Gissler; m. Mary Catherine Engman, Oct. 23, 1954; children: Gary, Glenn, Gregory. BA in Am. Civilization, Lake Forest Coll., 1956, LLD (hon.), 1991; student, Northwestern U., 1958-61. News editor Ind. Register, Libertyville, Ill., 1958-59; exec. editor News-Sun, Waukegan, Ill., 1963-67; editl. writer Milw. Jour., 1967-77, editl. page editor, 1977-84, assoc. editor, 1984-85, editor, 1985-93; v.p. Jour. Comm., Milw., 1987-93, also bd. dirs.; sr. v.p. Jour./Sentinel Inc., Milw., 1987-93, also bd. dirs.; assoc. prof. grad. sch. journalism Columbia U., N.Y.C., 1994—, acting assoc. dean, 1997, founder, dir. workshops on journalism, race and ethnicity, 1998-2000, sr. advisor, 2000—, adminstr. Pulitzer Prizes, 2002—. Vis. prof. dept. comm. Stanford U., 1993; mem. jury Pulitzer Prize. Recipient Disting. Svc. citation, Lake Forest Coll., 1977, Pub. of the Yr. award, Wis. Newspaper Assn., 1987, 1991, 1992; Journalism fellow, Stanford U., 1976, Sr. fellow, Freedom Forum Media Studies Ctr. Columbia U., 1993—94. Mem.: Soc. Profl. Journalists (Tchr. of the Yr. award 1998), Internat. Press Inst., Am. Soc. Newspaper Editors, Phi Beta Kappa. Home: 101 W 79th St Apt 6D New York NY 10024-6475 Office Phone: 212-854-7327. E-mail: sg138@columbia.edu.

GIST, HOWARD BATTLE, JR., lawyer; b. Alexandria, La., Sept. 17, 1919; s. Howard Battle and Marcie (Luckett) G.; m. Rosemary Flynn, Sept. 30, 1950; children: Howard Battle III, Marcie, Stephanie, Robert C., Ellen K., William M. Student, Washington and Lee U., 1936—38; BA, Tulane U., 1941, JD, 1943. Bar: La. 1943. Of counsel Gist Firm, Alexandria, La. Bd. dirs. Security First Nat. Bank, Alexandria, chmn. bd., 1983-93, dir. emeritus, 1993. Named 2000 Disting. Atty., La. Bar Found., 2000. Fellow Am. Coll. Trial Lawyers; mem. La. State Bar Assn. (pres. 1977-78), Alexandria Bar Assn. (pres. 1967), La. City Attys. Assn. (past pres.), La. Def. Attys. (pres. 1972-73), La. State Law Inst. (mem. coun. 1964—, past v.p.). Office: Gist Methvin 4615 Parliament Dr Ste 101 Alexandria LA 71309-1871 Office Phone: 318-448-1632.

GITELSON, JONATHAN STUART, artist, educator; b. Mount Kisco, N.Y., June 7, 1975; s. David Aaron and Diane Gitelson. MFA, Columbia Coll., 2004. Adj. faculty Columbia Coll., Chgo., 2002—; artist Benito Juarez Acad., Chgo., Beethoven Elem. Sch., Chgo., 2004—; artist in residence Snow City Arts, Chgo., 2005. Exhibitions, San Diego (Calif.) Art Inst., 2004, exhibitions include Cmty. Arts Assistance Program, Chgo., Ill., 2005, Projekt 30 Online Gallery (Juror's award, 2004), The Friend Project. Grantee, Geraldine R. Dodge Found., 2003, Chgo. (Ill.) Union League Civic and Arts Found., 2004, Puffin Found.; Albert P. Weisman Meml. fellowship, 2002. Personal E-mail: jon@thegit.net.

GITELSON, SUSAN AURELIA, finance company executive, consultant, volunteer; b. N.Y.C. d. Moses Leo and Miriam Evelyn (Silverman) G. BA, Barnard Coll.; MIA, Columbia Sch. Internat. Affairs; PhD, Columbia U.; student, Univ. Calif., Berkeley; degree (hon.), Hebrew U., 2004. Trainee Rockefeller Found.; asst. prof. internat. rels. Hebrew U., Jerusalem; rsch. assoc. Columbia U., N.Y.C.; dir. internat. affairs and third world World Jewish Congress, N.Y.C.; pres. Internat. Cons., Inc., N.Y.C., Magic Touch Icewares Internat. Corp., N.Y.C. Author: Multilateral Aid for National Development and Self-Reliance; editor, author: Israel in the Third World; contbr. articles to profl. jours.; mem. editl. com. Jerusalem Papers on Peace Problems. Mem. nat. adv. coun., sponsor Gitelson Essay awards Ctr. for Study of Presidency, Washington; co-chair dean's coun. Columbia Sch. Internat. and Pub. Affairs, sponsor Dr. Susan Aurelia Gitelson Fund for Innovative Programs; pres. Dr. Susan Aurelia Gitelson Found. Inc.; sponsor Gitelson Lecture on Human Rights and U.S. Fgn. Policy Columbia U.; sponsor Gitelson award for human values in internat. affairs Columbia Sch. Internat. and Pub. Affairs; sponsor Gitelson-Meyerowitz Human Rights essay award Columbia Ctr. for Study of Human Rights; sponsor Gitelson Peace prize Truman Inst.; sponsor Gitelson Peace Papers and Publs.; mem. bd. overseers Truman Inst. Hebrew U., Jerusalem; v.p. bd. dirs. Am. Friends of Hebrew U.; mem. Columbia U. seminars; trustee Nat. Com. Am. Fgn. Policy; sponsor Dr. Susan Aurelia Gitelson Fund Innovate Programs Columbia U. Faculty Arts and Scis.; sponsor Gitelson Policy Forum Columbia Sch. Internat. and Pub. Affairs; trustee Sutton Pl. Synagogue, sponsor Gitelson-Meyerowitz Disting. Svc. award. Recipient Outstanding Service award, Columbia Sch. Internat. and Public Affairs, Alumni medal for conspicuous svc., Columbia U. Mem. Nat. Inst. Social Scis., Columbia Sch. Internat. and Pub. Affairs Alumni Assn. (pres. 1980-84), Columbia U. Alumni Fedn. (mem. exec. com.), Nat. Com. on Am. Fgn. Policy (mem. bd. trustees), Carnegie Coun. on Ethics and Fgn. Affairs, Fgn. Policy Assn., Am. Jewish Com. Office: 1201 Broadway New York NY 10001-7504 Office Phone: 212-679-5260. E-mail: susangitel@aol.com.

GITENSTEIN, DONNA M., academic administrator; b. Florala, Fla. m. Donald Hart; children: Pauline, Samuel. BA in English, Duke U.; PhD in English and Am. Lit., U. N.C., Chapel Hill. Asst. prof. English Ctrl. Mo. State U.; prof. English SUNY, Oswego, chair English dept., assoc. provost; provost Drake U., 1992—98, exec. v.p., 1997—98; pres. Coll. of N.J., Ewing, 1998—. Commr. Mid. States Commn. on Higher Edn. Author: (book) Apocalyptic Messianism and Contemporary Jewish-Am. Poetry; contbr. articles and reviews on Jewish and Am. Lit. Named Salute to Policy Makers, Exec. Women of N.J., 2002, Tribute to Women, YWCA of Princeton, N.J., 2003; recipient Woman of Distinction award, Girl Scouts of Del.-Raritan Coun., 2002. Mem.: Am. Coun. on Edn. (mem. commn. on minorities in higher edn., pres. sponsor (N.J. chapt.) network of women leaders in higher edn.). Office: Office of the Pres Coll of NJ PO Box 7718 Ewing NJ 08628

GITLER, BERNARD, cardiologist, critical care specialist; b. Munich, Aug. 14, 1950; arrived in U.S., 1953, naturalized, 1957; s. Abe and Lola (Greenberg) G.; m. Ellen Spielman, Aug. 4, 1974; children: Stefanie, Cynthia, Bryan. BS in Chemistry, BS in Life Scis., MIT, 1972; MD, Cornell U., 1976. Diplomate Nat. Bd. Med. Examiners, Am. Bd. Internal Medicine, Am. Bd. Internal Medicine-Cardiovascular Diseases, Am. Bd. Internal Medicine-Critical Care Medicine, Nat. Bd. Echocardiography; cert. Bd. Nuclear Cardiology. Resident in internal medicine Bronx Mcpl. Hosp. Ctr., Albert Einstein Coll. Medicine, Bronx, NY, 1976—79; cardiology fellow Montefiore Med. Ctr., Albert Einstein Coll. Medicine, Bronx, 1979—81, chief fellow, 1980—81; clin. instr. Albert Einstein Coll. Medicine, Bronx, 1981—84, asst. clin. prof. medicine, 1984—92, assoc. clin. prof. medicine, 1992—; attending cardiologist Sound Shore Med Ctr. Westchester, New Rochelle, NY, 1991—; chief divsn. cardiology Sound Shore Med. Ctr. Westchester, New Rochelle, NY, 2002—; assoc. attending cardiologist Montefiore Med. Ctr., Bronx, 1993—; pvt. practice cardiology Westchester Heart Specialists, New Rochelle, 1981—; asst. attending cardiologist Columbia-New York. Presbyn. Med. Ctr., N.Y.C., 1992—; asst. prof. clin. medicine Columbia U., N.Y.C., 1992—. Physician cons. Island Peer Rev. Orgn., N.Y., 1985-88; faculty senator Albert Einstein Coll. Medicine, 1987-89, co-dir. cardiology curriculum New Rochelle Hosp. Housestaff, 1985-92; attending cardiologist dept. electrocardiography Montefiore Med. Ctr., Bronx, 1983—; attending cardiologist dept. medicine Westchester Med. Ctr., 2002—; pres. med. staff Sound Shore Med. Ctr. Westchester, 1996-99, bd. govs., 1993-99; clin. cardiology rschr. SSMC of Westchester, 1985—. Referee Am. Heart Jour., 1983-95, Jour. Am. Coll. Cardiology, 1987-89, N.Y. State Jour. of Medicine, 1990-91, Chest, 1998—; contbr. articles to profl. jours. Recipient Attending of the Yr. award Montefiore Hosp. Med. House Staff, 1985, Tchr. of the Yr. award New Rochelle Hosp. and Med. Ctr., 1986, William C. Schraft Jr. Meml. Tchg. award New Rochelle Hosp., 1996. Fellow ACP (Preceptorship award for outstanding tchg. 1996, Cmty. Based Excellence in Tchg. award 2004), Am. Soc. Echocardiography, Am. Coll. Cardiology, Am. Coll. Chest Physicians, Am. Heart Assn., N.Y. Cardioil. Soc.; mem. AMA, Soc. Critical Care Medicine, Am. Med. Athletic Assn., Am. Fedn. Med. Rsch., Am. Soc. Nuclear Cardiology, Soc. Chest Pain Ctrs., Phi Beta Kappa, Phi Lambda Upsilon, Mensa. Democrat. Jewish. Avocations: Okinowan Goju-ryu karate (black belt), marathon running. Office: Westchester Heart Specialists 150 Lockwood Ave New Rochelle NY 10801-4916 Office Phone: 914-633-7870. E-mail: bgmd@aol.com.

GITLOW, ABRAHAM LEO, retired dean; b. N.Y.C., Oct. 10, 1918; s. Samuel and Esther (Boolhack) G.; m. Beatrice Alpert, Dec. 12, 1940; children: Allan Michael, Howard Seth. BA, U. Pa., 1939; MA, Columbia U., 1940, PhD, 1947. Substitute instr. Bklyn. Coll., 1946-47; instr. NYU, N.Y.C., 1947-50, asst. prof., 1950-54, assoc. prof., 1954-59, prof. econs., 1959-89, prof. emeritus, 1989—; acting dean NYU Coll. Bus. and Pub. Adminstrn., 1965-66, dean, 1966-85, dean emeritus, 1989—. Hon. dir. Bank Leumi USA; pres. bd. edn. Ramapo (N.Y.) Ctrl. Sch. Dist. 2, 1963-66; pres., sec. Samuel and Esther Gitlow Found., Miami Beach, Fla. Author: Economics of the Mt. Hagen Tribes, New Guinea, 1947, Economics, 1962, Labor and Manpower Economics, 1971, Being the Boss: The Importance of Leadership and Power, 1992, NYU's Stern School: A Centennial Retrospective, 1995, Reflections on Higher Education: A Dean's View, 1995, Corruption in Corporate America, 2005; co-editor: General Economics: A Book of Readings, 1963; contbr. articles to profl. jours. Served to 1st lt. USAAF, 1943-46, PTO. Recipient Univ. medal Luigi Bocconi U., 1983. Mem. Am. Econ. Assn. Home and Office: 9 Island Ave Apt T3 Miami Beach FL 33139-1349

GITNER, FRED JAY, library administrator; b. N.Y.C., Nov. 28, 1951; s. Stanley and Sonia (Auerbach) G. AB, Hamilton Coll., 1973; MA, Middlebury Coll., 1976; MLS, Rutgers U., 1975. Asst. mgr. Christopher P. Stephens Bookseller, N.Y.C., 1975-76; libr. French Inst./Alliance Française, N.Y.C., 1976-84, libr. dir., 1984-94; spl. collections libr. N.Y. Acad. Medicine, N.Y.C., 1995; asst. head New Ams. Program Queens Borough Pub. Libr., Jamaica, NY, 1996—2004, coord., 2004—. Editor: Med. Trade Catalogs at the N.Y. Acad. of Medicine Libr., 1995; joint editor, contbr.: Bridging Cultures: Ethnic Services in the Libraries of New York State., 2001; contbr. articles to profl. jours. Decorated chevalier Ordre des Palmes Académiques (France). Mem. ALA, Pub. Libr. Assn., Internat. Rels. Round Table, N.Y. Libr. Assn., Am. Assn. Tchrs. French. Democrat. Jewish. Avocations: breweriana collecting, theater going, reading, travel. Home: 382 Central Park W New York NY 10025-6054 Office: Queens Borough Pub Libr 89-11 Merrick Blvd Jamaica NY 11432 Office Phone: 718-990-0892. E-mail: fred.j.gitner@queenslibrary.org.

GITNER, GERALD L., air transportation executive, investment banker; b. Boston, Apr. 10, 1945; s. Samuel and Sylvia (Berkovitz) Gitner; m. Deanne Gebell, June 24, 1968; children: Daniel Mark, Seth Michael. BA cum laude, Boston U., 1966. Staff v.p. TransWorld Airlines, N.Y.C., 1972-74; sr. v.p. mktg. and planning Tex. Internat. Airlines, Houston, 1974-80; pres., founder People Express Airlines, Newark, 1980-82; chmn. Pan Am. World Svcs. Inc., N.Y.C., 1982-85, exec. v.p., chief fin. officer, 1983-85; vice chmn. Pan Am. World Airways, N.Y.C., 1982-85, Pan Am Corp., 1984-85; pres. Tex. Air Corp., Houston, 1985-86; CEO, pres. ATASCO USA, Inc., aircraft trading firm, N.Y.C., 1986-89; chmn. D. G. Assocs. Inc., 1986—, Avalon Group, Ltd., N.Y.C., 1990-98; co-chmn. Global Aircraft Leasing Ltd., 1991-98; dir. TWA, Inc., 1993—2002, CEO, 1996-99, chmn., 1997—2002; chmn. bd. Kitty Hawk, Inc., 2002—; dir. Tricom, S.A., 2004—. Bd. advisers econs. dept. Boston U.; mem. chancellors coun. U. Mo., St. Louis, 1997—2000. Trustee, mem. exec. com. Boston U., 1984—96; trustee Rochester (N.Y.) Inst. Tech., 1999—2004. Recipient Disting. Alumni award, Boston U., 1982, 1984. Mem.: Cornell Club N.Y., Phi Alpha Theta.

GITTELMAN, MARC JEFFREY, manufacturing and financial executive; b. N.Y.C., Nov. 26, 1947; s. Sidney and Trudy (Eidus) G.; m. Nanci V. Geiger, Apr. 9, 1988; 1 child, Brandon Michael. BBA, Hofstra U., 1969; MBA in Fin., Adelphi U., 1972; postgrad., U. Colo., Denver. Credit analyst Security Nat. Bank Long Island, Melville, N.Y., 1969-72; dir. adminstrn. Tiger Leasing Group Inc., Chgo., 1973-78; asst. treas. Storage Tech. Corp., Louisville, Colo., 1979-83; v.p., treas. Holnam Inc. (formerly Ideal Basic Industries), Dundee, Mich., 1984-91, Andrew Corp., Orland Park, Ill., 1992—. Bd. dirs. Food Bank of Rockies. Mem. Nat. Assn. Corp. Treas. Republican. Jewish. Office: Andrew Corp 10500 153rd St Orland Park IL 60462-3071 E-mail: jeffrey.gittelman@andrew.com.

GITTELSON, BERNARD, public relations consultant, author, lecturer; b. N.Y.C., June 13, 1918; s. Sam and Gussie (Lefand) G.; m. Rosalind Weinstein, Mar. 1, 1945; children: Louise Barbara, Steven Henry. BA, St. John's U., 1939. Cons. on race relations N.Y. State War Council, 1939-41, N.Y. Com. on Industry and Labor Relations, 1941-42; dir. N.Y. State Legis. Com. on Discrimination, 1943-45; asso. coordinator Com. on Community Inter-relations, 1945-46; pres. Roy Bernard Co., Inc., 1946-65; chmn. Roy Bernard Co. Ltd., London, 1955-65; pres. Biorhythm Computers, Inc., Med. News. Service, Formulated Health Products, Fairfield Mktg. Corp., Advanced Health Research Products Inc.; chmn. bd. Time Pattern Research Inst., N.Y.C., U.S. Commemoratives Inc., Bernard Gittelson Cons. Inc. Cons. to govts., corps., instns. Author: Gittelson Biorhythm Code Book, Biorhythm, A Personal Science, How to Make Your Own Luck, Intangible Evidence, Special Stories for Children, Our America, Notre America, Nuestra America, Nossa America; syndicated writer column on biorhythm, 1987—; pub. Med. Hot Line. Mem. Am. Journalists and Authors, Authors Guild. Address: Mote Ranch 6808 Corral Cir Sarasota FL 34243-3858 Office Phone: 941-351-7903. E-mail: gittelsonb@aol.com.

GITTER, ALLAN REINHOLD, lawyer; b. Yonkers, N.Y., Aug. 26, 1936; s. George Reinhold and Katherine (Allan) G.; divorced; children: Alison, Ryne, Kent; m. Sandra Case Gitter, Apr. 2, 1988. BA, Washington & Lee U., 1958; LLB, U. Mich., 1961. Bar: N.C. 1963, U.S. Dist. Ct. (mid., ea. and we. dists.) N.C. 1964, U.S. Ct. Appeals (4th cir.) 1964, U.S. Dist. Ct. (mid. dist.) Pa. 1998. From assoc. to ptnr. Womble, Carlyle, Sandridge & Rice, Winston-Salem, N.C., 1969—. Fellow: Am. Coll. Trial Lawyers; mem.: Am. Bd. Trial Advs. Home: 1077 E Kent Rd Winston Salem NC 27104-1113 Office: Womble Carlyle Sandridge & Rice One W 4th St Winston Salem NC 27101 Office Phone: 336-721-3615. Personal E-mail: agitter@wcsr.com.

GITTER, MAX, lawyer; b. Samarkand, Uzbekistan, Nov. 17, 1943; came to U.S., 1950; s. Wolf and Paula (Nissenbaum) G.; m. Elisabeth Karla Gesmer, June 22, 1969; children: Emily F., Michael A. AB, Harvard U., 1965; LLB, Yale U., 1968. Bar: N.Y., D.C., U.S. Dist. Ct. (so. and ea. dists.) N.Y., U.S. Ct. Appeals (2d, D.C., 4th and 9th cirs.), U.S. Supreme Ct. Instr. U. Chgo. Law Sch., 1968-69; assoc. Paul, Weiss, Rifkind, Wharton & Garrison, N.Y.C., 1969-76, ptnr., 1976-99, Cleary, Gottlieb, Steen & Hamilton, N.Y.C., 1999—. Vis. lectr. law Yale U., 1986-88; mem. Internat. Steering Com. on Free Trade with Israel; vice-chmn., Yivo Inst. for Jewish Rsch. Spl. counsel Mayor of N.Y.C. to Investigate Office of Chief Medical Examiner, 1985. Mem. Fed. Bar Coun., Assn. Bar City of N.Y. (vice chmn. com. on profl. and jud. ethics 1985-86), Am. Law Inst. (spkr., panelist 1985-89), Practicing Law Inst. (spkr., panelist 1983-92), N.Y. State Bar Assn. (exec. com. sect. on comml. and fed. litigation 1994-99), Internat. Arbitration Inst. Office: Cleary Gottlieb Steen & Hamilton Rm 200 One Liberty Plz Ste 4300 New York NY 10006-1470 Office Phone: 212-225-2610. Business E-Mail: mgitter@cgsh.com.

GITTERMAN, ALEX, social work educator; b. Kolomea, Poland; came to U.S., 1948; s. Paul and Fay (Hirsch) G.; m. Naomi Janet Pines, Sept. 1963; children: Daniel Paul, Sharon Lynn. BA, Rutgers U., 1960; MSW, Hunter Coll., 1962; EdD, Columbia U., 1972. Div. dir. Bronx River Settlement, 1962-65; dir. East Side House Millbrook Ctr., Bronx, 1965-66; mem. faculty Columbia U., N.Y.C., 1966—, prof., 1972—, assoc. dean, 1981-85; mem. faculty U. Conn. Sch. Social Work, 2000—. Cons. Manhattan VA, N.Y.C., 1974-80, Family Service of Westchester (White Plains), N.Y., 1978-80, Bur. Child Welfare, 1977-80, Drug Abuse Prevention Program, Archdiocese of N.Y., 1985—, Keio Acad.; vis. prof. U. Conn. Sch. Social Work, 2000--. Author: (with C.B. Germain) The Life Model of Social Work Practice, 1980, (with L. Shulman) Mutual Aid Groups and The Life Cycle, 1986, Handbook of Social Work Practice with Vulnerable Populations, 1991, Mutual Aid Groups, Vulnerable Populations and the Life Cycle, 1994, (with C.B. Germain) The Life Model of Social Work Practice: Advances in Theory and Practice, 1996, Handbook of Social Work Practice with Vulnerable and Resilient Populations, 2001, Mutual Aid Groups, Vulnerable and Resilient Populations and the Life Cycle, 2005; contbr. articles to profl. jours. Recipient Hexter award Hunter Coll., 1981 Mem. Con. on Social Work Edn., Nat. Assn. Social Workers Democrat. Jewish. Office: U Conn Sch Social Work 1798 Asylum Ave West Hartford CT 06117-2001 Office Phone: 860-570-9016. Business E-Mail: Alex.Gitterman@uconn.edu.

GITTES, FRANKLIN M., lawyer; b. Newark, 1947; BSChE, Lehigh U., 1969; JD, Georgetown U., 1973. Bar: DC 1973, NY 1975. Law clk. to Hon. John Biggs, Jr. US Ct. Appeals (3d cir.), 1973-74; ptnr., corp. mergers and acquisitions Skadden, Arps, Slate Meagher & Flom, NYC. Editor: Georgetown Law Jour., 1972-73; contbr. articles to jours. Office: Skadden Arps Slate Meagher & Flom 4 Times Sq New York NY 10036 Office Phone: 212-735-3760. Office Fax: 917-777-3760. Business E-Mail: fgittes@skadden.com.

GITTINGER, D. WAYNE, lawyer; b. Kellogg, Jan. 22, 1933; s. Daniel Reese and Evelyn Caroline (Knudson) G.; 1 child, Marni; m. Anne Elizabeth Nordstrom, Dec. 17, 1984; stepchildren: John Hopen, Susan Dunn. BA, U. Wash., 1955, JD, 1957. Bar: Wash. 1957, U.S. Ct. Appeals (9th cir.) 1957, Tax Ct. of U.S., U.S. Supreme Ct. Teaching assoc. Northwestern U. Law Sch., Chgo., 1957-58; ptnr. Lane Powell PC, Seattle, 1959—. Bd. dirs. Nordstrom, Inc. Active U. Wash. Alumni Assn., 1965—. Lt. USCGR, 1958-67. Mem. Vintage Club, Seattle Golf Club, Seattle Yacht Club, 101 Club, Overlake Golf and Country Club (past pres. 1978-79). Republican. Avocations: golf, yachting. Office: Lane Powell PC 1420 5th Ave Ste 4100 Seattle WA 98101-2338 Office Phone: 206-223-7053. E-mail: gittingerw@lanepowell.com.

GITTINGER, LAURIE ELLEN, music educator, elementary school educator; b. Berea, Ohio, May 17, 1964; d. William Alfred and Patricia Ann Gittinger. MusB in Instrumental Music Edn., Bowling Green State U., 1986; MA in Adminstrn., Furman U., 1997. Cert. Music Education K-12 SC. State Dept. Edn., 1987, Educational Leadership K-8 SC. State Dept. Edn., 1997. Asst. dir. bands, instr. strings Bowling Green City Schs., Ohio, 1986—87; dir. bands D.W. Daniel H.S., Clemson, 1987—89; dir. strings program Travelers Rest High/Blue Ridge Mid./NW Mid./Gateway Elem., Greer, 1989—97; supervising coop. tchr. Furman U. and Bob Jones U., Greenville, 1991—97; lead tchr. strings Sch. Dist. Greenville County, 1992—97; state pres., pres.-elect, and festival chmn. S.C. Music Educators Assn., 1993—2001; program coord., adminstrv. asst. Beck Acad. Mid. Sch., 1997—2002; program dir. The 21st Century Cmty. Learning Ctr. After Sch. Program, 1999—2002; program coord. Bob Jones U., 1999—2002; dir. bands, program coord., adminstrv. asst. J.L. Mann H.S., 2002—03; dir. bands LaGrange H.S. and Gardner Newman Mid. Sch., 2003—05, Westside Fine Arts Magnet Sch., La Grange, Ga., 2005—. Percussion instr. Travelers Rest H.S., Travelers Rest, 1990—98; strings coach Carolina Youth Symphony Repertory Orchestra, Greenville, 1997—2000; guest condr. full orch. Florence City Sch. Dist., 1999—2000; accompanist St. Giles Presbyn. Ch., Greenville, 2001—02; program dir. Mathematics Policy Rsch. Program, Washington, 2000—02; accompaniest St. Giles Presiterian Ch., Greenville; rep. Greenville County Schools Tchr. Yr. Luncheon, 2000—01; coord. United Way Beck Mid. Sch., 1999—2000; mentor Greenville Sch. Dist. ADEPT Program, 1997—98; participant Ohio State U. Midwest Summer String Conf., 1997—98; sponsor Mid. Sch. Beta Club, 2000—02; participant Master Scheduling Com. Greenville Schs., 2001—02; guest condr. Florence City Sch. Dist., 2000—00; guest spkr. Anderson County Sch. Dist. Adminstrn. Students, 1996—99; adjudicator S.C. Music Educators Assn., Greenville, 1997—2000. Musician (performer): (orchestra performance in carniege hall) Lexington County School District (Invitation/Cert., 1992); percussion director (south carolina upper state marching fest) Performance (Third in Upper State of SC., 1993). Ch. accompaniest adult/elem. chior program St. Giles Presbyn. Ch., Greenville, 2001—02. Fellow: Ga. Music Educators Assn., Nat. Residence Hall

Hon. (life Outstanding Performance in Residence Hall); mem.: Music Educators Nat. Conf. Achievements include Superior Drumline/Marching Percussion Travelers Rest High School; South Carolina OUtstanding Performance Award for Bands Daniel High School; The National Residence Hall Honorary for Bowling Green State University; Winner of Bowling Green State University Music Department Organ Competition; Keith Montgomery Outstanding Musician Performance Award Port Clinton High School; Invitation/Performance to Washington D.C. for Band Program of Daniel High School, Clemson, South Carolina; Invitation of Blue Ridge High School Orchestra to University of Mississippi's Tenth Annual American Honor Orchestra Conference; Invitation for LaGrange High Marching Band perform for 65th Celebration of Pearl Harbor Honorary Parade, Hawaii. Office: Westside Fine Arts Magnet Middle Sch 301 Forrest Ave Lagrange GA 30240 Office Phone: 706-883-1550. Home Fax: 706-812-7976. Personal E-mail: gittingerle@troup.org.

GITTLEMAN, RICHARD M., lawyer; b. Providence; BA, Brown Univ., 1977; JD cum laude, Am. Univ., Washington, 1982. Bar: DC 1983. Ptnr., head project devel. and fin. practice group and chair info. tech. com. Akin Gump Strauss Hauer & Feld LLP, Washington. Scholar T. Morton McDonald Scholarship and Dean's Fellow, Am. Univ. Fluent in French. Office: Akin Gump Strauss Hauer & Feld LLP Robert S Strauss Bldg 1333 New Hampshire Ave NW Washington DC 20036-1564 Office Phone: 202-887-4444. Office Fax: 202-887-4288. E-mail: rgittleman@akingump.com.

GITTLER, JOSEPH BERTRAM, sociology educator; b. N.Y.C., Sept. 21, 1912; s. Morris and Toby (Rose) G.; m. Lami Shapiro, June 28, 1934 (dec. 1966); 1 child, Josephine; m. Susan Wolters, Sept. 15, 1968. BS, U. Ga., 1934, MA, 1936; PhD, U. Chgo., 1941. From instr. to assoc. prof. sociology U. Ga., 1936-43; research assoc. Va. Planning Bd., 1942-43, U. Chgo., 1944; prof. Iowa State U., 1945-54; prof. sociology, chmn. dept. Ctr. Study Group Relations, U. Rochester, 1954-61; dean faculty, prof. social scis. Queensborough Coll., CUNY, 1961-66; prof. sociology, dean Grad. Sch. Humanities and Social Scis., CUNY, N.Y.C., 1966-78; disting. vis. prof. sociology George Mason U. of State U. Va., Fairfax, 1978-79, disting. vis. prof., 1980-90, dir. Ctr. for Study of Race and Ethnic Relations, 1987-90, emeritus prof. sociology, 1990—. Mem. George Peabody award com. U. Ga., 1937; fellow Rockefeller Found./U. Chgo., 1938-41; vis. prof. Cardoza Law Sch., 1978-79, Hiroshima (Japan) U., 1979-80; lectr. various univs., U.S., Japan, Spain, Germany, Eng., The Netherlands, France, Italy, Mex., Israel, Finland, Taiwan, Ireland, Austria; cons. in field, 1940—; mem. Rochester cmty. coun. N.Y. State Commn. Against Discrimination, 1955-60; chmn. regional selection com. Woodrow Wilson Fellowship Found., 1955-58; co-chmn. Brotherhood Week edn. com. NCCJ, 1950; coun. fellows Upland Inst., 1965-72; disting. vis. prof. dept. sociology Duke U., 1990-94, Disting. Scholar-in-residence, 1994-99; Fulbright scholar, vis. prof. Ben Gurion U., Israel, 1990-91. Author: Social Thought Among the Early Greeks, 1941, Virginia's People, 1944, Social Dynamics, 1952, Your Neighbor Near and Far: A Study of Racial and Ethnic Relations in Rural Iowa, 1955, Review of Sociology, 1957, Understanding Minority Groups, 1964, Ethnic Minorities in the U.S.: Perspectives from the Social Sciences, 1977, Jewish Life in the United States, 1977, Jewish Life in the United States, 1981; co-editor: Internat. Jour. Group Tensions, 1986-94; editor, contbg. author: Ann. Rev. Conflict Knowledge and Conflict Resolution, vol. 1, 1989, vol. 2, 1990, vol. 3, 1991, Research in Human Social Conflict Series, Racial and Ethnic Conflict: Perspectives from the Social Disciplines, 1995; editor in chief: Internat. Encyclopedia of Racial and Ethnic Relations, 2000, Ideas of Concord and Discord in Religion, 1999; contbr. numerous articles to profl. jours. Fulbright scholar, Hiroshima (Japan) U. scholar, 1979-80, Ben Gurion U. scholar, Israel, 1990-91; recipient Walter B. Hill prize philosophy U. Ga., 1934, poetry award, best tchr. award, Disting. Faculty award George Mason U., 1984. Fellow Am. Sociol. Assn., N.Y. Acad. Scis.; mem. PEN, Internat. Sociol. Soc., Inst. Internat. Sociology, So. Sociol. Soc., Assn. for Higher Edn., Am. Assn. Acad. Deans, Phi Beta Kappa, Phi Kappa Phi, Pi Mu Epsilon. Home: 5 Glenmore Dr Durham NC 27707-3923

GITTLER, JOSEPHINE, law educator; b. Richmond, Va., May 13, 1943; d. Joseph and Lamie G. BA, Barnard Coll.; JD, Northwestern Coll., 1968. Bar: Conn. 1969. Law clk. U.S. Dist. Ct., New Haven, 1969-70, Conn. Supreme Ct., Hartford, 1970-71, U.S. Dist. Ct. Conn., 1971-72; from assoc. prof. Coll. Law to prof. Coll. Pub. Health U. Iowa, Iowa City, 1973—2002, prof. Coll. Pub. Health, 2002—. Chief counsel subcom. investigate juvenile deliquency jud. com. U.S. Senate, Washington, 1977-78; coord. U.S. Surgeon Gen.'s Conf., Washington, 1988; mem. exec. com. Consortium Ctrs. on Children Families & Law, 1989—2000; legis. cons. Nat. Assn. State and Territorial Maternal and Child Health and Crippled Children's Programs, 1982-86, recipient Pub. Svc. award 1982, 84; counsel interim study com. juvenile justice Iowa Gen. Assembly, Des Moines, 1975-77; vis. scholar Justice Ctr. of Atlanta, 1999; cons. in field. Contbr. articles to profl. jours. Chair Iowa Maternal and Child Health Adv. Coun., Des Moines, 1983-88; mem. Iowa Juvenile Justice Adv. Com., Des Moines, 1975—83, Iowa Crime Commn., Des Moines, 1974-75, interim com. Penal Reform and Correction, Des Moines, 1973-74. Office: U Iowa Coll Law Iowa City IA 52242

GIUFFRÉ, JOHN JOSEPH, lawyer; b. Bklyn., Nov. 30, 1963; s. John B. and Marilyn N. G.; m. Lauren P. Dippel, Sept. 1, 1990; children: John Paul, Danielle Emily. BA, Columbia Coll., 1984; JD cum laude, U. Pa., 1987. Bar: N.J. 1987, N.Y. 1988, Conn. 1988, Pa. 1988, U.S. Dist. Ct. (so. and ea. dists.) N.Y. 1989. Assoc. labor and employment law sect. Morgan, Lewis & Bockius, N.Y.C., 1987-88; assoc. McLaughlin & McLaughlin, Bklyn., 1988-93; founding ptnr. Giuffré & Kaplan, PC, Hicksville, N.Y., 1994—. Editor: U. Pa. Jour. Comparative Bus. and Capital Market Law, 1985-86; sr. editor: U. Pa. Jour. Internat. Bus. Law, 1986-87. Vol. lawyer Bklyn. Bar Assn. Vol. Lawyer Project, 1992-93; trustee 1st Presbyn. Ch., Flushing, N.Y., 1991-92, pres. bd. trustees, 1993, elder, 1996—, Sunday Sch. tchr., 1989—; trustee Flushing Christian Sch., 1994-2002, pres. bd. trustees 2004—; mem. Nassau County Rep. Com., 2002—. Mem. Nassau County Bar Assn., Phi Beta Kappa. Office: Giuffré & Kaplan PC 28 E Old Country Rd Hicksville NY 11801-4207 Office Phone: 516-935-4350.

GIUFFRIDA, TOM A., publisher; b. Glendale, Calif., Feb. 24, 1946; s. Alfred and Anna (LiPera) G.; m. Judith Lynn Price, Aug. 22, 1970; children: Jeffrey, Gregory, Christopher. BA in Journalism, Calif. State U., Northridge, 1967. Copy editor Santa Barbara (Calif.) News-Press, 1967, 69-70; copywriter to asst. dir., promotion and pub. relations L.A. Times (Times Mirror), 1971-79; from promotion dir. to v.p. and gen. mgr. Atlanta Jour. & Constitution (Cox Enterprises), 1979-85; publisher Palm Beach (Fla.) Post, 1985—. Bd. dirs. Palm Beach County Cmty. Found. Lt. (j.g.) USNR, 1967-69. Mem. Am. Newspaper Pubs. Assn., Fla. Press Assn. (pres. 1995-96), Soc. Profl. Journalists, Palm Beach Yacht Club. Home: 6325 S Flagler Dr West Palm Beach FL 33405

GIULIANI, MICHAEL J., medical educator; b. Cin., June 16, 1954; s. Edward and Churchill Giuliani; m. Anita Sandhu. BS in Biology, Tulane U., 1978; MD in Medicine, Ohio State U., 1982. Diplomate in neurology and clin. neurophysiology Am. Bd. Psychiatry and Neurology. From asst. prof. to assoc. prof. U. Pitts., 1987-93, prof., 1999—; dir. clin. rsch. devel. Wyeth-Ayerst Rsch., 2001—03; dir. clin. R&D Wyeth Rsch., Collegeville, Pa., 2001—03; sr. dir., clin. neurosci. Merck Rsch. Labs., West Point, Pa., 2003—. Dir. multidisciplinary clinic and neuromuscular program U. Pitts. Med. Ctr., 1990-2001, co-dir. EMG lab., 1989-2001; assoc. med. dir. Pitts. Clin. Rsch. Network, 1998-99; mem. internat. adv. bd. Genentech, Inc., 1996-99; lectr. in field. Mem. editl. bd.: Challenging Cases in Neuromuscular Disease, 1996-98; reviewer Muscle & Nerve, 1999; contbr. chpt. to book, numerous articles and abstracts to profl. pubs. Mem. Am. Acad. Neurology (mem. expert panel 1996-99), Am. Bd. Electrodiagnostic Medicine (cert.). Home: 904 Artis Rd Plymouth Meeting PA 19462 Office: Merck Rsch Labs PO Box 4 West Point PA 19486 Office Phone: 484-344-4048. E-mail: michael_giuliani@merck.com.

GIULIANI, RUDY (RUDOLPH WILLIAM LOUIS GIULIANI III), consultant, lawyer, former mayor; b. Brooklyn, NY, May 28, 1944; s. Harold A. and Helen (D'Avanzo) Giuliani; m. Regina Peruggi, Oct. 26, 1968 (annulled 1982); m. Donna Hanover, Apr. 15, 1984 (div. July 10, 2002); children: Andrew, Caroline; m. Judith Nathan, May 24, 2003. AB, Manhattan Coll., 1965; JD magna cum laude, NYU, 1968. Law clk. to Hon. Lloyd F. McMahon US Dist. Ct. (So. dist.) NY, NYC, 1968-70; asst. U.S. atty. (So. dist.) N.Y. US Dept. Justice, 1970-73, exec. asst. U.S. atty., chief narcotics sect., and chief spl. prosecutions sect., 1973-75, assoc. dep. atty. gen., 1975-77, assoc. atty. gen., 1981-83, U.S. atty. (So. dist.) N.Y., 1983-89; atty. Patterson, Belknap, Webb and Tyler, NYC, 1977-81, White & Case, NYC, 1989-90, Anderson Kill Olick & Oshinsky PC, NYC, 1990-93; mayor N.Y.C., 1994—2001; chmn., CEO Giuliani Partners LLC, NYC, 2002—; ptnr. Bracewell & Giuliani, NYC, 2005—. Rep. candidate for mayor N.Y.C., 1989, 93; speaker Rep. Nat. Convention, NYC, 2004. Author (with Ken Kurson): Leadership, 2002. Decorated Knight Commander of the British Empire; named Person of the Year, Time Mag., 2001, Consultant of the Year, Consultant mag., 2002. Republican. Office: Giuliani Partners 5 Times Sq New York NY 10036*

GIULIANO, LOUIS J., former industrial manufacturing company executive; BS in Chemistry, Syracuse U., 1968, MBA in Mktg., 1969. Various mgmt. positions Bendix, v.p., gen. mgr. Gen. Aviation Avionics divsn., v.p., group exec. Avionics Sys. Group Arlington, Va.; pres. Avionics Sys. Group Allied-Signal Aerospace Co.; v.p. def. ops. ITT Def., 1988; v.p. ITT Corp., 1988; sr. v.p. ITT Industries, Inc., pres., chief exec. def. and electronics White Plains, NY, 1991-98, pres., COO, 1998—2001, chmn., 2001—04, pres., CEO, 2001—04, non-exec. chmn., 2004. Mem. bd. govs. US Postal Service, Washington, 2005—. Mem. Nat. Def. Indsl. Assn. (vice chmn., bd. dirs.), Aerospace Industries Assn. (bd. govs.). Office: US Postal Svc 475 L Enfant Plz SW Rm 10300 Washington DC 20260

GIULIANO, ROBERT PAUL, pharmacist; b. N.Y.C., Mar. 7, 1943; s. Salvatore Anthony and Marie Rita (LoScalzo) G.; m. Maja Hreljanovic, July 2, 1966; children: Christopher Robert, Kenneth Paul. BS in Pharmacy, Fordham U., 1965; MS in Hosp. Pharmacy Adminstrn., L.I. U., 1970. Diplomate Am. Bd. Pharmacy, Nat. Registy Emergency Med. Technicians. Clin. pharmacist Columbia-Presbyn. Med. Ctr., N.Y.C., 1965—70; dir. pharmacy dept. St. Barnabas Hosp., N.Y.C., 1970—71; dir. dept. pharm. scis. Misericordia Hosp. Med. Ctr., N.Y.C., 1971—78, adminstrv. dir. material mgmt., 1978—79, asst. adminstrv. dir., 1979—81; pres. Apotheke Assos. Ltd., N.Y.C., 1980—81; pres., dir., CEO U.S. Home Health Care Corp. and Steri-Pharm subs., 1981—91; also chmn. bd.; mem. Tech. Adv. Svc. for Attys., 1988—. Pres. RPG Assoc., 1991—, pres. dir.; chmn. bd. Bryce Rx Labs Inc., 1995—; pres., dir. Red Rock Labs, Inc., 1997-99; exec. v.p. Red Rock Rsch., Inc., 2001-; cons. Weleda Internat., 1991-92; affil. clin. instr. St. John's U., 1971-81; cons. Healix Health Care, 1992-96, Rye Beach Pharmacy, 1992-96, Champlain Valley Physicians Hosp., 1993-94, Columbia Presbyn. Med. Ctr., 1984-97, Transworld Home Health Corp., 1991-93, N.Y. Med. Coll., 1992-95, ROR Group, 1992-93, Geneva Gen. RegionalHosp., 1994-95; home health care cons. Alternative Care Svcs., Inc., 1988-90, Robert Wood Johnson Found., 1985; mem. clin. pharmacy adv. bd., 1971-81; mem. exec. com. Bronx Emergency Med. Svcs. Coun., 1975-80; sr. emergency med. technician instr./coord. N.Y. State Dept. Health, Bur. Emergency Med. Svcs., 1975-81; spkr.'s bur., CPR instr. AHA, 1975-81; CPR instr. Westchester Heart Assn., 1977-80; mem. spkrs. bur. Misericordia Hosp. Med. Ctr., Westchester County Soc. Hosp. Pharmacists. Author: (with others) RX Technician Manual, 1994; editor: Misericordia Hosp. Pharmacy Newsletter, 1971-78. Asst. master Cub Scouts, Eastchester, N.Y., 1976-78; coach youth baseball T.Y.A., Eastchester, 1975-83. Mem. Am. Pharm. Assn., Italian Pharm Assn., Am. Soc. Cons. Pharmacists, Am. Soc. Healthcare Pharmacists, N.Y. State Coun. Hosp. Pharmacists, Nat. Assn. Sr. Emergency Med. Technician Instrs., Nat. Assn. Emergency Technicians (founding), Am. Soc. Parenteral-Enteral Nutrition, League IV Therapists, Nat. IV Therapy Assn., Nat. Assn. Retail Druggists, Pharmacy Compounding Ctrs. Am., Internat. Acad. Compounding Pharmacists, Fordham U. Pharmacy Alumni Assn. (dir. 1982-98, 1st v.p. 1990-91, pres. 1992-95), N.Y. Athletic Club. Republican. Roman Catholic. Home: 157 Oakland Ave Eastchester NY 10709-5403 Office: PO Box 1 Eastchester NY 10709-1403 Office Phone: 800-798-7279. E-mail: rx@brycerx.com, bobgrx@optonline.net.

GIULIANTI, MARA SELENA, mayor; b. N.Y.C., June 3, 1944; d. Leon and Bertha (Jablonky) Berman; m. Donald Giulianti, May 29, 1966; children: Stacey Alexander, Michael Alan. BA, Tulane U., 1966. Social worker L.A. County Social Svcs., 1966-68; adminstrv. asst. neurosurg. cons. D. Giulianti, MD, Hollywood, Fla., 1980-83; campaign mgr. City Commr. Suzanne Gunzburger, Hollywood, 1982; mayor City of Hollywood, 1986-90, 92—. Vice chmn. Broward Employment and Tng. Adminstrn., 1987-89, 92-94, 96-2000, 01-02, chmn., 1989-90, 94-96, 2000-01, Work Force One chmn., 2002-04, chmn. pro tem, 2004-05, vice chair 2005—; mem. exec. bd. Fla. League Cities, Tallahassee, 1986-90, 92-94, bd. dirs., 1990-91, 94—; mem. econ. devel. pol. com. Nat. League Cities, Washington, 1987-90, human devel. policy com., 1992-94, fin., adminstrn. and intergovtl. rels. steering com., 1994-2002; mem. Broward County Met. Planning Orgn., 1986-90. Columnist The Digest, Hallandale, Fla., 2001-02, South Fla. Sun-Times, 2002—, Beach Digest, 2002-03; contbr. articles to local newspapers. Pres. Women in Distress, Broward County, 1982-83, bd. dirs., 1983-90, trustee, 1994-97; mem. exec. bd. Nat. Jewish Cmty. Rels. Adv. Coun., 1985-87; v.p. CHARLEE Family Care Homes, Broward County, 1986-88, bd. dirs., 1988-92; mem. Broward County Commn. on Status Women, 1984-86, Fla. Commn. on Drug and Alcohol Concerns, Tallahassee, 1984-85, Broward County Dem. Exec. Com., 1984-88; pres. Hills Dem. Club, 1991-94; trustee Graves Mus. of Archeol. and Nat. History, Dania, Fla., 1993-97; bd. dirs. Hollywood Econ. Growth Corp., 1994-95, 98-99; chmn. Hollywood Cmty. Redevel. Agy., 1992—; v.p. South Broward unit Am. Cancer Soc., 1992-93, bd. dirs., 1993-99. Recipient Hannah G. Solomon award, 1983, Giraffe Stick Your Neck Out award Women's Advocacy--the Majority/Minority, 1986, Leadership award Leadership Hollywood Alumni, 1987, City of Peace award Israel Bonds, Broward County, 1987, Menorah award Histadrut, 1990, Juliette Gordon Low award Girl Scouts Broward County, 1997, Govt. Leadership award, ArtServe, 2002, Gracias award Hispanic Unity, 2000, Cmty. Covenant award, Broward Outreach Ctr., 2001, Breaking the Glass Ceiling award, Ziff Jewish Mus. of Fla., 2002, Spirit of Excellence award Am Bus. Women's Assn., 2003, Woman of Valor award Broward County Jewish Cmty. Ctr., 2003, Founders award Chaminade-Madonna Coll. Prep., 2004; named Broward County Woman of Yr., Am. Jewish Congress, 1988, Woman of Yr. Women in Comms., Inc., 1990, Crystal Vision award Hollywood Art and Culture Ctr., 2000; Honoree Boys & Girls Clubs of Broward, 2001, honoree Holocaust Documentation and Edn. Ctr., 2005; inducted Broward County Women's Hall of Fame, 1996. Mem. Nat. Coun. Jewish Women (nat. bd. dirs. 1985-89), Jewish Fedn. So. Broward (chair community rels. com. 1981-82, bd. dirs. 1982-90), Broward County Med. Aux. (br. pres. 1977-78), Rotary. Democrat. Avocations: writing, volunteer work, travel. Office: PO Box 229045 Hollywood FL 33022-9045 Office Phone: 954-921-3321. Business E-mail: mgiulianti@hollywoodfl.org.

GIUNTA, AGATINO JOHN, economics educator; b. Messina, Italy, Sept. 6, 1925; came to U.S., 1947, naturalized, 1963; s. Carmelo and Josephine (Savoca) G.; m. Santa Maria Molino, July 4, 1960; children— Carmen Joseph, Josephine-Ann, Lucia Catherine, Mary-Louise. B.S., SUNY-Binghamton, 1952; M.A., Syracuse U., 1954, Ph.D., 1956. Asst. prof. Western Md. Coll., Westminster, 1956-60; assoc. prof. U. Scranton, Pa., 1960-67, prof., 1967—1993, prof. emeritus, 1993. Author: Managerial Economics, 1966, An Introduction to Business Research, 1968. Mem. Scranton chpt. UNICO, 1966-72. Research grantee Schalkenback Found., 1982. Mem. Am. Econ. Assn. Democrat. Roman Catholic. Lodge: K.C. Avocations: home gardening, golf. Home: 1804 Monsey Ave Scranton PA 18509-1943 E-mail: giuntaal@teisprint.com.

GIURGOLA, ROMALDO, architect, educator; b. Rome, Sept. 2, 1920; s. Vincenzo and Maria Luigia (Petrin) Giurgola; m. Adelaide F. Bencivenga, Dec. 20, 1952; 1 child, Paola F. Laurea. BArch summa cum laude, Scuola Di Architettura Università' di Roma, 1948; MArch, Columbia U., 1951. Prof. architecture U. Pa., 1954; ptnr. Mitchell/Giurgola Archs., Phila., N.Y.C., from 1958; Ware prof. architecture Columbia U., 1966, chmn. dept. architecture, 1968-71. Fellow: AIA (gold medal 1982); mem.: AAAL, Academia Nazionale di San Luca (corr.). Office: 170 W 97th St New York NY 10025-6450*

GIUSTI, JOSEPH PAUL, retired academic administrator, consultant; b. Harrisburg, Pa., Mar. 4, 1935; s. Joseph and Ellen C. (Carletti) G.; m. Marie D. Mazza, Jan. 30, 1960; children: Jeannine Carolyn, Lynn Christine, Susan Marie. BA in English Lit., Villanova U., 1957; MSBA, Pa. State U., 1959, PhD in Higher Edn. Adminstrn., 1962; LHD (hon.), St. Vincent Coll., 1976. Instr. dept. commerce and fin. Pa. State U., 1958-60, grad. asst., 1961-62, asst. to v.p., 1963-65, mem. grad. faculty, 1963-79, assoc. prof. higher edn., 1965-79; campus dir., chief exec. officer Beaver campus, 1965-79; chancellor univ., prof. higher edn. Ind. U.-Purdue U., Fort Wayne, 1979-85; prof. edn. Ind. U., 1985-87; dir. global human resource devel. edn. programs/scholarships AMP, Inc., 1987-98; ret., 1998; cons. AMP, Inc., 1998-99. Cons. hemolytic disease study group divsn. blood diseases and resources Nat. Heart, Lung and Blood Inst., NIH, 1975-79; mem. adv. com. Edn. Mgmt. Info. Sys., Commonwealth of Pa., 1971-79; mem. joint adv. coun. Ft. Wayne Med. Edn. Program, 1979-85; mem. exec. com. Ft. Wayne Future, Inc., 1979-85, Ft. Wayne Ednl. Found., 1979-85, Allen County (Ind.) United Way, 1979-80; sec. Beaver Campus Adv. Bd., 1966-79, dir. emeritus, 1979—; mem. Corp. Coun., Ft. Wayne, 1981-85, also bd. dirs. Contbr. articles on fin. mgmt. and ednl. adminstrn. to profl. publs.; contbr. chpts. to books on fin. mgmt. and edn. Bd. dirs. Med. Ctr. Beaver County, Pa., 1966-79, chmn. bd. dirs., 1972-75, dir. emeritus, 1979—; bd. dirs. Parkview Meml. Hosp., 1982-85. Recipient Beaver Campus Disting. Service award, 1974; Trustee award Community Coll. of Beaver County, 1972; Civic Improvement League award, 1972; Benjamin Rush award Med. Soc. of Beaver County, 1976; resolutions in his honor for contbrs. to edn. and health care delivery in state Pa. State Senate and Ho. Reps., 1979; Beaver Campus Community Cultural Ctr.'s 1000 seat amphitheater named in his honor, 1980; lit. collection named in his honor Beaver Campus Library, 1980 Mem. Greater Fort Wayne C. of C. (dir. 1981-85), Ind. U. Ft. Wayne Alumni Assn. (life dir. 1982—), Purdue U. Ft. Wayne Alumni Assn. (life dir. 1982—). Roman Catholic.

GIUSTI, KATHY, foundation administrator; m. Paul Giusti; children: Nicole, David. BS in Biol. Sci., U. Vt., 1980; MBA in Gen. Mgmt., Harvard Bus. Sch., 1985. Asst. products mgr. Gilette Comp., Boston, 1985—88, sr. products mgr., 1988—93; assoc. dir., product mgmt. G.D. Searle & Co., 1993—94, dir., product mgmt., 1994—95, exe. dir., arthritis franchise worldwide, 1995—96; pres. Multiple Myeloma Rsch. Found., New Canaan, Conn., 1998—. Bd. dir. IMS Health. Recipient Women of Yr. award, Healthcare Businesswomen's Assn., 1998, Entrepreneurial award, Harvard Bus. Sch., 2001, Humanitarian award, McCarty Cancer Found., 2002, Joseph Michaeli award, Weill Med. Coll. of Cornell U., 2002, Angel award, Goldman Philanthropic Ptnrs., 2003. Mem.: Cancer Leadership Coun. Office: Multiple Myeloma Rsch Found 51 Locust Ave Ste 201 New Canaan CT 06840

GIUSTI, WILLIAM ROGER, lawyer; b. N.Y.C., Oct. 27, 1947; s. John Eletto and Rita Marie (Lucarini) G.; m. Ingrid Gerke, Dec. 12, 1980. AB, Columbia Coll., 1969; postgrad., Oxford U., 1969-71; JD, Yale U., 1974. Bar: N.Y. 1975. Law clk. to judge U.S. Ct. Appeals (2d cir.), N.Y.C., 1974-75; assoc. Cravath, Swaine & Moore, N.Y.C., 1975-80, Shearman & Sterling LLP, N.Y.C., 1980—82, ptnr., 1983. Mem.: Yale (N.Y.C.). Roman Catholic. E-mail: wgiusti@shearman.com.

GIUSTO, RICHARD J., lawyer; b. Bklyn., Dec. 15, 1959; BA with distinction, Univ. Va., 1982, JD, 1986. Bar: Fla. 1986. Shareholder, co-chair Miami Real Estate Dept. Greenberg Traurig LLP, Miami. Named one of Top Up and Comers in So. Fla, So. Fla. Legal Guide, 2004. Mem.: ABA, Fla. Bar Assn. Office: Greenberg Traurig 1221 Brickell Ave Miami FL 33131 Office Phone: 305-579-0500. Office Fax: 305-579-0717. Business E-Mail: giustor@gtlaw.com.

GIVAN, RICHARD MARTIN, retired judge; b. Indpls., June 7, 1921; s. Clinton Hodel and Glee (Bowen) G.; m. Pauline Marie Haggart, Feb. 28, 1945; children: Madalyn Givan Hesson, Sandra Givan Chenoweth, Patricia Givan Smith, Elizabeth Givan Whipple. LL.B., Ind. U., 1951. Bar: Ind. 1952. Ptnr. with Clinton H. Givan, 1952-59, Bowen, Myers, Northam & Givan, 1960-69; justice Ind. Supreme Ct., 1969-74, chief justice, 1974-87, assoc. justice, 1987-95, ret., 1995; dep. pub. defender Ind., 1952-53; dep. atty. gen., 1953—64; dep. pros. atty. Marion County, 1965-66, ret., 1995. Mem. Ind. Ho. Reps., 1967-68 Served to 2d lt. USAAF, 1942-45. Mem. Ind. Bar Assn., Indpls. Bar Assn., Ind. Soc. Chgo., Newcomen Soc. N.Am., Internat. Arabian Horse Assn. (past dir., chmn. ethical practices rev. bd.), Ind. Arabian Horse Club (pres. 1971-72), Indpls. 500 Oldtimers Club, Lions, Sigma Delta Kappa. Mem. Soc. Of Friends. Home: 6690 S County Road 1025 E Indianapolis IN 46231-2495

GIVANT, STEVEN ROGER, mathematician, computer scientist, educator; s. Paul and Irma Wilhemina Givant. BA, U. Calif., Berkeley, 1967, MA, 1969, PhD, 1975. Prof. math. and computer sci. Mills Coll., Oakland, Calif., 1975—. Contbr. articles to profl. jours. Founder, dir. Mills Summer Math. Inst., Oakland, 1991—95; dir. Project S.E.E.D., Oakland, Calif., 1966—73. Named Danforth Tchg. assoc., Danforth Found., 1978; fellow, German Academic Exch. Svc., 1967—68; grantee, IREX, 1991—92. Mem.: Assn. Symbolic Logic, Math. Assn. Am., Am. Math. Soc. Achievements include research in theory of relations. Office: Mills College Dept Math 5000 MacArthur Blvd Oakland CA 94613

GIVEN, KENNA SIDNEY, surgeon, educator; b. Charleston, W.Va., Nov. 22, 1938; s. Virgil and Chessie Given; m. Charlene K. Given; children: Kari, Patrick, Amy. BA, W.Va. U., 1960; MD, Duke U., 1964. Diplomate Am. Bd. Surgery, Am. Bd. Plastic Surgery (chairperson-elect 1996-97, bd. dirs. 1992—). Intern Ind. U. Med. Ctr., Indpls., 1964-65; resident, then chief resident gen. surgery Grady Meml. Hosp./Emory U. Hosp., Atlanta, 1965-69; asst. resident, then chief resident plastic surgery Duke U. Med. Ctr., Durham, N.C., 1975-77; clin. instr. surgery Emory U., Atlanta, 1972-74; chief surgery Lanier Meml. Hosp., Langdale, Ala., 1974; prof., chief divsn. plastic surgery Med. Coll. Ga., Augusta, 1977—2001, med. dir. oper. rm., 1989-90. Assoc. dir. burn unit Med. Coll. Ga. Hosp.; cons. Augusta Correctional and Med. Instrn.; plastic surgery dir. Children's Med. Svc., 1981—; mem. Residency Rev. Commn. for Plastic Surgery, 1991-2001, chmn., 1994-96; chair Am. Bd. Plastic Surgery, Inc., 1997-99; chmn. residency rev. com. Accreditation Coun. for Grad. Med. Edn., 1994-96; lectr. in field. Contbr. articles to profl. jours. Pres. Med. Rsch. Found. Ga., 1985-88; trustee Plastic Surgery Edn. Found., 1994-97, pres.-elect, 1997; bd. dirs. Augusta Country Day Sch.; bd. dirs. Augusta Prep. Day Sch., 1988, trustee, 1989-90. Fellow ACS; mem. AMA, Am. Assn. Plastic Surgeons (trustee 1994-97), Assn. Acad. Chmn. in Plastic Surgery (pres. 1996-97, bd. dirs. 1985-88, 93—), Southeastern Plastic and Reconstructive Surgery (chmn. continuing med. edn. com. 1987, bd. dirs. 1992-95), Am. Soc. Plastic and Reconstructive Surgery (bd. dirs. 1988), Am. Assn. Hand Surgery, Am. Cleft Palate Assn., Am. Soc. Aesthetic Plastic Surgeons, Internat. Soc. Clin. Plastic Surgeons, Ga. Plastic Surgery Soc. (pres. 1985), Med. Assn. Ga., Richmond County Med. Soc., Southeastern Surg. Congress., So. Med. Assn., Southeastern Soc. Plastic and Reconstructive Surgeons (pres. 1997), So. Surg. Soc. Baptist. Home: 748 Tripps Ct Augusta GA 30909-1816 Office: Med Coll Ga Divsn Plastic Surgery HB-5049 Augusta GA 30912

GIVEN, KERRY WADE, plastics industry executive; b. Ravenna, Ohio, Nov. 14, 1948; s. Earl Buren and Phyllis Virginia (Hamrick) G.; m. Charlotte Sue Brannon, Dec. 20, 1969; children: Duke Earl, Sean Bryan. BS, U. Fla., 1973; PhD, U. Minn., 1978. Rsch. chemist B.F. Goodrich, Brecksville, Ohio,

1978-80; from rsch. planning analyst to dir. rsch. planning Amoco Corp., Naperville, Ill., 1980-88, from mgr. sys. devel. to strategic planning Chgo., 1988-94; mgr. IT Amoco Chem., Lisle, Ill., 1994-99; dir. IT Cadillac Plastics, Troy, Mich., 1999—. Contbr. articles to profl. jours. Home: 2820 Parkwood Ln Aurora IL 60504-1348 Office: Cadillac Plastics 2855 Coolidge Hwy Troy MI 48084-3202

GIVENS, FLORENCE ROSIE, author, editor, publishing executive; b. Spotsylvania, Va., Apr. 2, 1948; d. Edward and Carrie Mae Camp; m. Anderson Jackson Sr., Aug. 31, 1963 (dec. Oct. 1967); children: Anderson Jackson Jr., Freda A. Jackson, Gregory T. Wright Sr., Mario D. Jackson; m. Josephus Givens Jr., Jan. 10, 2000; stepchildren: Alfreda, Roland, Dana, Deanna. Grad. high sch., Fredericksburg, Va. Acct., Stafford, Va., 1962—2003; legal clk. U.S. Fed. Govt., Washington, 1991—2001; author, editor, pub. Flo Bound Poems Pubs., Stafford, 1999—. Cons. Flobound Poems Pubs., 1999—. Author (editor): A Morning Without Coffee, 2000, Revisiting Friends: The Journey Home, 2001, The Ring of Friends: Forever, 2002, A Little More Cream Please, 2003. Recipient Highest Honor Spelling Bee, John J. Wright Consolidated Sch., Snell, Va., 1953, Pensmanship award, 1956. Democrat. Pentecostal Apostolic. Avocations: writing, reading, travel. Office: FloBound Poems Pubs PO Box 3101 Fredericksburg VA 22402-3101 Personal E-mail: morningpoemsflog@aol.com.

GIVENS, JOHN KENNETH, automotive executive; b. Highland Park, Mich., Aug. 21, 1940; s. John Hamilton and Marion Florence G.; children: Kevin John, Kirk David; m. Patricia Ann Bowlby, May 23, 1980. BA, Mich. State U., 1963. With Lincoln-Mercury divsn. Ford Motor Co., Cleve., 1963-71, sales promotion mgr. Lincoln-Mercury divsn. Dearborn, Mich., 1971-73; dir. sales and mktg. Ford South Africa, 1973-75; car advt. mgr. Ford Divsn., 1975-77; sr. v.p. Wells. Rich, Greene Advt., LA, 1977-79; v.p. mktg. Chrysler Corp., Highland Park, 1979-82; pres. Seal-Dry USA, Inc., Little Rock, 1982-92; chmn. Eastar, Inc. Holding Co., 1982-98, Spash Superpools, LLC, 1988—, SanduskyAthol Internat., 1992—, Deckrite, LLC, 1997—, Aqua Ventures, LLC, 2002—. Office: Splash LLC 3912 E Progress St North Little Rock AR 72114-5239 also: Eastar Inc 3130 W Monroe St Sandusky OH 44870-1811 Personal E-mail: jg82140@aol.com.

GIVENS, MARY ELIZABETH, librarian, gifted and talented educator; b. Monticello, Ark., Nov. 23, 1953; d. Audley Wayne and Winnie Claire (Smith) G. BS in Edn., Henderson State U., Arkadelphia, Ark., 1975; MEd, U. Ark., Little Rock, 1990. 6th grade tchr. Fouke (Ark.) Pub. Schs., 1975-77; 1st grade tchr. Vandervoort Elem. Sch., Cove, Ark., 1977-79; libr. Thornton (Ark.) Sch. Dist., 1979-85; tchr., coord. gifted and talented Bearden (Ark.) Sch. Dist., 1985—. Troop leader Girl Scouts Am., Fordyce, Ark., 1988-91. Mem. Arkansans for Gifted and Talented Edn., Nat. Assn. for Gifted Children, ALA, Bus. and Profl. Women's Orgn., Lions Club, Delta Kappa Gamma Soc. Baptist. Avocations: reading, crafts, travel, needlecrafts. Home: 427 Overstreet Dr Fordyce AR 71742-1715 Office: Bearden Elem Sch 100 Oak St PO Box 195 Bearden AR 71720 Office Phone: 870-687-2237. E-mail: beardengt@yahoo.com.

GIVENS, RANDAL JACK, communications educator; b. Borger, Tex., Mar. 17, 1951; s. Fred Frank and Doris Mae (Bley) Givens; m. Carol Marie Griffin, May 21, 1973; children: Mary Leanna, Anna Elizabeth. BA in Speech, Lubbock Christian Coll., 1973; MA in Speech Comm., Tex. Tech. U., 1974; MAR in Counseling Psychology, Harding U., Memphis, 1977, MAR in Missiology, 1978, MTh in Philosophy, 1978; diploma in French, IFCAD, Brussels, 1982; MA in Philanthropic Studies, Ind. U., 2004. Missionary (in French) Eglise du Christ, Brussels, 1979-82; dir. Internat. Sch. Conversational English, Brussels, 1982-89; acad. dean Internat. Christian U., Vienna, 1989-94; chmn. dept. comm., dir. forensics York (Nebr.) Coll., 1994-97, dir. grants and program devel., 1997—. Counselor Memphis Mental Health Ctr., 1976—78; group therapy coord. Memphis Rehab. Svc., 1976—78; chief coord. translating internat. confs., Strasbourg, France, 1983, Metz, France, 87; bd. dirs. Grant Profls. Cert. Inst., 2003—. Author: Induced Feedback, 1974; translator: Johnson's Notes, 1989; editor: Vienna Views newsletter, 1989—94. Bd. dirs. Blue Valley Cmty. Action Agy., 2001—. Recipient Svc. award, Lubbock Christian Schs., 1992. Mem.: Am. Assn. Grant Profls. (founding pres. 1998, pres. 1999, 2000—), L'Association de l'Ordinateur (mem. tech. panel Grant and Program Devel. Inst. 1999—), Speech Comm. Assn., Nebr. Speech Comm. Assn. (liaison for univ. affairs 1994), Speech Comm. Assn. Am., Nat. Soc. Fundraising Execs., Martial Arts Black Belt Assn. Republican. Mem. Ch. Of Christ. Avocations: martial arts, drums, woodworking, computers. Home: 1315 Blackburn Ave York NE 68467-2011 Office: York Coll 1125 E 8th St York NE 68467-2699 Office Phone: 402-363-5620. Business E-Mail: rjgivens@york.edu.

GIVHAN, EDGAR GILMORE, physician, writer; b. Montevallo, Ala., Aug. 6, 1935; AB in German Lit., Washington and Lee U., 1956; MD, Washington U., St. Louis, 1960. Diplomate Am. Bd. Internal Medicine. Intern Vanderbilt U., 1960, resident in internal medicine, 1965, instr. in hematology, 1965-66, Auburn U. Sch. Lab. Tech., 1967-85; co-owner Commercial Garden Design, Montgomery, Ala., 1982—. Pres. med. staff Montgomery Bapt. Hosp., 1974-75; cons. physician Ala. Medicaid Program, 1982-86; bd. dirs., cons. Humana Hosp. East Montgomery; med. dir. Humana Ins. Co. Ala.; chmn. bd. Direct Care, 1995—; horticulture lectr. Author: (guide and video) How to Grow Great Southern Gardens, 1992, Flowers for South Alabama Gardens, 1980, Conversations with a Southern Gardener, 1999, (with others) Heritage Gardens, 1992, Alabama Gardens Great and Small, 2002; contbr. articles to profl. jours. Chmn. bd. South Montgomery YMCA, 1973; bd. dirs. ARC, Montgomery, 1970-73, med. dir. blood processing ctr., Montgomery, 1973-80; bd. dirs. Montgomery Symphony Orch., Blue Cross and Blue Shield Ala., 1979-85, Montgomery C. of C., 1980-84; bd. vis. for the humanities Auburn U. Capt. USAF, 1962-64. Vanderbilt U. fellow, 1965-66. Fellow ACP; mem. AMA, Ala. Soc. Internal Medicine, Montgomery Soc. Internal Medicine (pres. 1970), Montgomery County Med. Soc. (pres. 1976), Ala. Soc. Clin. Oncology (v.p. 1982), Am. Soc. Hematology, So. Garden History Soc. (pres., bd. dirs.), Phi Beta Kappa. Office: 300 Taylor Rd Ste 600 Montgomery AL 36117-3555

GIVHAN, ROBERT MARCUS, lawyer; b. Mineral Wells, Tex., May 10, 1959; s. Walter Houston Givhan and Marion Blackwell Callen Stothart; m. Janet Lee Dothard, May 6, 1989; children: Vivian Lee, Charlotte Ann, Virginia Mae. BA, U. Ala., Tuscaloosa, 1981; JD, Cumberland Sch. Law, Birmingham, Ala., 1986. Bar: Ala. 1987, D.C. 1989, U.S. Supreme Ct. 1989, U.S. Ct. Appeals (D.C. and 11th cirs.), U.S. Dist. Ct. (so., mid. and no. dists.) Ala. 1987. Assoc. Perry and Russell, Montgomery, Ala., 1987-88; dep. dist. atty. 15th Jud. Cir. of Ala., Montgomery, 1988-91; dep. atty. gen. Office of Atty. Gen. of Ala., Montgomery, 1991-95; ptnr. Johnston Barton Proctor & Powell LLP, Birmingham, 1995—. Contbr. articles. Fellow: Am. Coll. Pros. Attys.; mem.: Am. Health Lawyers Assn., Birmingham Bar Assn. (co-chmn. econs. law practice com. 1998, chmn. 1999, co-chmn. jud. and legal reform com. 2002, chmn. 2003, chmn. cts. and legis. com. 2004), Ala. State Bar Assn., ABA (vice chmn. antitrust competition and trade regulation com. adminstrv. 1994—2000). Episcopalian. Avocations: whitewater rafting, hiking, music collecting, book collecting. Office: 2900 AmSouth/Harbert Plz 1901 6th Ave N Birmingham AL 35203-2618 Home: 1601 Shades Park Cove Birmingham AL 35209 Office Phone: 205-458-9444. Business E-Mail: rmg@jbpp.com.

GIZON, LAURENT, physicist; b. Grenoble, France, Jan. 26, 1970; s. Jean and Andree Gizon; m. Yekaterina Shabanova, Sept. 6, 2002; 1 child, Sophie. MSc in Astrophysics, U. Paul Sabatier, Toulouse, France, 1994; M.Eng. in Aerospace Engring., SupAero, Toulouse, 1994; PhD in Physics, Stanford U., 2003. Rsch. assoc. Stanford U., Calif., 2003—. Mem.: Am. Astron. Soc. Office: Hansen Exptl Physics Lab 455 Via Palou Stanford U Stanford CA 94305 Office Phone: +1 650 725 8858. Business E-Mail: lgizon@solar.stanford.edu.

GIZZI, MARTIN SHERMAN, neurologist, neurophysiologist; b. Yonkers, N.Y., Jan. 1, 1957; s. Vincent George and Laura (Cronkhite) G.; m. Barbara Buono, Mar. 15, 2002. PhD, NYU, 1983; MD, U. Miami, Fla., 1985. Diplomate Am. Bd. Psychiatry and Neurology. Med. intern New Rochelle (N.Y.) Hosp., 1985-86; resident in neurology Mt. Sinai Hosp., N.Y.C., 1986-89; asst. prof. neurology Mt. Sinai Sch. Medicine, N.Y.C., 1989-92; assoc. prof. neurosci. Seton Hall U. Sch. Grad. Med. Edn., 1992-96, prof., assoc. chair, 1996—2002, chair, 2002—. Mem. editl. bd. Vision Rsch.; bd. examiner Am. Bd. Psychiatry Neurology; sci. cons., co-investigator Microgravity Vestibular Investigations Group, NASA, Johnson Space Ctr., 1990—99; program dir. neurology residency Seton Hall U., JFK Med. Ctr., 1995—99. Pres. med. adv. bd. Music for all Seasons, NJ; grants officer JFK Med. Ctr., 2004—. Recipient Physician Scientist award, Nat. Eye Inst., 1989, Best doctor in the NY, NY Magazine, 1990, 2002—04, Best doctor in the NY met., Castle-Colloly Medical. Ltd., 1994—2004, Best Doctors in NJ, NJ Monthly, Life, 2001—05, Joint Legislative Resolution, NJ Senate and Gen. Assembly, 2004, Am. Top Physicians, Consumers' Rsch Coun. Am., 2004—05. Fellow Am. Acad. Neurology, N.Am. Neuro-Ophthalmol. Soc., Barany Soc. Democrat. Achievements include research in The Analysis of Moving Visual Patterns, Reprinted in SM Kosslyn and RA Andersen (Eds) Frontiers in Cognitive Neuroscience, 1995 MIT Press, Cambridge, MA; The familial incidence of benign paroxysmal positional vertigo. Acta Otolaryngologica (Stockh) 118:774-777,1998; Vestibular dysfunction does not directly cause cognitive or psychological symptoms. Journal of Head Trauma Rehabilitation, 18:398-407, 2003. Office: JFK Med Ctr PO Box 3059 Edison NJ 08818-3059 Office Phone: 732-321-7010. Business E-Mail: mgizzi@solarishs.org.

GJERDINGEN, ROBERT OWEN, music educator; b. Crookston, Minn., June 13, 1952; s. Owen Paul and Loretta Skalicky Gjerdingen; m. Catherine Shaffer, Dec. 30, 1978; 1 child, Owen Robert. PhD, U. Pa., Phila., 1980—84. Assoc. prof. Northwestern U., Evanston, Ill., 1995—. Sp5 U.S. Army, 1975—78, Hawaii.

GJERSET, RUTH ANNE, research scientist, educator; d. Oswald Seymour and Stefani Konrad Gjerset; m. Joseph Parello, Sept. 15, 1981; 1 child, Emmanuel Parello. BA in Biology with highest honors, U. Calif., San Diego, 1971; PhD, U. Calif., San Francisco, 1977. Postdoctoral fellow and chercheur associe Pasteur Inst., Paris, 1977—80; postdoctoral fellow U. Calif., San Francisco, 1980—82, assoc. specialist San Diego, 1986—91; rsch. assoc. Sidney Kimmel Cancer Ctr., San Diego, 1991—94, asst. prof., 1994—99, assoc. prof., 1999—. Contbr. articles to profl. jours. Recipient Gold Std. award, Dept. of Def. Breast Cancer Rsch. Program, 1996; grantee, Calif. Tobacco-Related Disease Rsch. Program, 1993—96, Calif. Tobacco-Related Disease rsch. Program, 2002—, U.S. Army Med. rsch. Command Breast Cancer Rsch. Program, 1996—2000, NIH/NCI, 1997—2002, Calif. Cancer Rsch. Program, 1999—2000, Calif. Breast Cancer Rsch. Program, 2000—02; Post doctoral fellow, Am. Cancer Soc., 1977—79, Muscular Dystrophy Assn., 1980—82. Mem.: AAAS, Am. Assn. for Cancer Rsch. Achievements include patents for Cancer Therapies based on p53 and DNA repair; patents pending for Cancer Therapies based on p14ARF and p53. E-mail: rgjerset@skcc.org.

GJERTSEN, O. GERARD, lawyer; b. Bklyn., June 24, 1932; s. Ole Gerhard and Hilma (Jorgensen) G.; m. Carol Ann Jurkops, June 2, 1962; children: Gerard, Gary, Krista, Karen. BA, Columbia Coll., 1954; JD, NYU, 1958. Bar: N.Y. 1958, U.S. Dist. Ct. (so. dist.) N.Y. 1960. Ptnr., counsel Thacher Proffitt & Wood, N.Y.C., 1964—. Vice chmn. Tuckahoe (N.Y.) Urban Renewal Agy. With U.S. Army, 1954-55. Mem. ABA, N.Y. State Bar Assn., Assn. of Bar of City of N.Y., Westchester County Bar Assn., White Plains Bar Assn., Scarsdale Golf Club. Avocations: music, sports. Home: 262 Dante Ave Tuckahoe NY 10707-3015 Office: Thacher Proffitt & Wood 50 Main St White Plains NY 10606-1934

GJOVIG, BRUCE QUENTIN, entrepreneur, consultant; b. Crosby, N.D., Mar. 24, 1951; s. Ronald Daniel and Agnes (Smedberg) G.; children: Mike Mohn, Todd Chaffee. BA, BS, U. N.D., 1974. Rsch. chemist Man-in-the-Sea Project, Grand Forks, N.D., 1975-76; campaign advisor Elkin for Gov. Com., Bismarck, N.D., 1976; exec. officer Grand Forks Bd. Realtors, 1977-81; devel. officer U. N.D. Found., 1981-84; founder, dir. Ctr. for Innovation, Grand Forks, 1984—. Bd. dirs. 1st Seed Capital Co., Grand Forks, SBIR Project West, Phoenix; founder, chmn. N.D. Entrepreneur Hall of Fame, 1985—; founder Skalicky Tech. Incubator, 1994—, N.D. Angel Capital Network, 1998—, Ina Mae Rude Entrepreneur Ctr., 2005—. Editor: The Business Plan: Step-by-Step, 1988, The Marketing Plan: Step-by-Step, 1990; author, editor: Boxcar of Peaches: Nash Finch Co., 1990, Pardon Me, Your Manners are Showing!, 1992; contbr. articles to profl. jours. Founder, sponsor 67th Patent & Trademark Depository Libr., 1991-2003; chair N.D. Mus. Art; chair U. N.D. Nordic Initiative, 1997—. Named Friend of Small Bus., Fargo C. of C., 1988, U. ND Outstanding Greek Alumnus, 1990, ANSA Norseman of Yr., 2001, Rsch. Adv. of Yr. for N.D. and Six States in Regiona VIII, SBA, 2003; recipient Outstanding Svc. award U. N.D. Alumni Assn., 1984, Western U.S. SBIR Support Person award, 1997, Tibbetts award SBA, 1998, Kauffamn Leadership award 1998, SBA Nat. Vision 2000 award, 1999, Rsch. Advocate of Yr., 2003, Entrepreneur Spirit award Greater ND Assn., 2004, Hon. Innovator, Sarpsborg, Norway, 2004, others; named to ND Entrepreneur Hall of Fame, 2001. Mem. Assn. Univ. Tech. Mgrs., Assn. Univ. Related Rsch. Pks., Univ. Small Bus. Tech. Consortium (state dir. 1986-90), Alumni Inter-Fraternity Coun. (chmn. 1982-86, 90-95, Outstanding Alumnus 1990), Rotary, Delta Tau Delta. Republican. Episcopalian. Avocations: reading, politics, art collector, fund raising, entrepreneur history collector. Home: Condo # 31 2501 26th Ave S Grand Forks ND 58201-6454 Office: Ctr for Innovation PO Box 8372 Ina Mae Rude Entrepreneur Ctr Grand Forks ND 58202-8372 Office Phone: 701-777-3134. Business E-Mail: bruce@innovators.net.

GLAAB, CHARLES NELSON, historian, educator; b. Williston, ND, Dec. 19, 1927; s. Reuben and Betty (Nelson) G.; m. Mary Ellen Anderson, Nov. 5, 1949; children— Martha Ann, John Reuben. BPh, U. N.D., 1951, MA, 1952; PhD, U. Mo., 1958. Rsch. assoc. history Kansas City project U. Chgo., 1956-58; from instr. to asst. prof. history Kans. State U., 1958-60; from assoc. prof. to prof. history U. Wis., Milw., 1960-68; dir. urban history sect. Wis. Hist. Soc., 1960-63; prof. history U. Toledo, 1968—. Dir. Fox Valley research project Wis. Hist. Soc., 1963-64; mem. Milw. Landmarks Commn., 1965-68, Toledo Landmark Com., 1968-70, Ohio Hist. Site Preservation Bd., 1979-81 Author: Kansas City and the Railroads, 1962, The American City: A Documentary History, 1963, (with A.T. Brown) A History of Urban America, 1967, (with L.H. Larsen) Factories in the Valley, 1969, (with Morgan A. Barclay) Toledo: Gateway to the Great Lakes, 1983; editor: Urban History Group Newsletter, 1962-68; co-editor, 1968-70, N.W. Ohio Quar., 1994-99; mem bd. editors Urban Affairs Quar, 1966-74, Soc. Press Wis, 1966-7 Jour. Urban History, 1973-88, Urban Affairs Ann. Rev, 1978-82, Frederick Law Olmsted Papers, 1985-90, Hayes Hist. Jour., 1987-91. Served with AUS, 1946-48. Mem. Orgn. Am. Historians, Am. Hist. Assn., Urban History Assn., VFW, Am. Legion, Phi Beta Kappa. Home: 2662 Densmore Dr Toledo OH 43606 Office Phone: 419-530-2296. E-mail: cglaab@accesstoledo.com.

GLACEL, ROBERT ALLAN, retired military career officer; b. Frankfurt, Germany, Oct. 31, 1947; (parents Am. citizens); m. Barbara Pate; children: Jennifer, Sarah, Ashley. Grad., U.S. Mil. Acad., 1969; M in Civil and Mech. Engring., MIT, 1977; MBA, Boston U., 1977; grad., Command and Gen. Staff Coll., 1982, Indsl. Coll. Armed Forces, 1990. Commd. 2d lt. U.S. Army, 1969, advanced through grades to brig. gen., 1995, FO, fire dir. officer 3d bn., 319th field arty., 1970-71, comdr. B battery, 1st Bn., 10th Field Arty., 3rd Inf. Divsn., 1971-72, S-2 (Intelligence) Divsn. Arty., 1972-74, asst. prof. engring. U.S. Mil. Acad. W. Point, N.Y., 1977-81, ops. officer, exec. officer 1st Bn., 37th Field Arty. Ft. Richardson, Alaska, 1982-85, with office Dep. Chief of Staff Pers. Hdqrs., Pentagon Washintgon, 1985-87, comdr. 1st Bn., 4th Field Arty., 2d Inf. Divsn. Republic of Korea, 1987-89, polit. mil. planner J-5 (Plans), the Joint Staff, Pentagon Washington, 1990-92, divsn. arty. comdr. 7th Inf. Divsn. (Light) Ft. Ord, Calif., 1992-93, exec. officer to the Under Sec. of the Army, Pentagon Washington, 1993-95; chief requirements and programs br. Office of Asst. Chief of Staff for Policy in SHAPE, Belgium, 1995-97; comdr. U.S. Army Test and Experimentation Command, Ft. Hood, Tex., 1997-99; ret. from active duty, 1999; v.p. America Online, Inc., Herndon, VA, 1999—. Decorated Legion of Merit, Bronz Star, Def. Meritorious Svc. medal, Meritorious Svc. medal, Disting. Svc. medal, Def. Superior Svc. medal. Office: America Online Inc 22020 Broderick Dr Dulles VA 20166-9323

GLAD, SUZANNE LOCKLEY, retired museum director; b. Rochester, N.Y., Oct. 2, 1929; d. Alfred Allen and Lucille A. (Watson) Lockley; m. Edward Newman Glad, Nov. 7, 1953; children: Amy, Lisanne Glad Lantz, William E. BA, Sweet Briar Coll., 1951; MA, Columbia U., 1952. Exec. dir. New York State Young Reps., N.Y.C., 1951-57; mem. pub. rels. staff Dolphin Group, L.A., 1974-83; scheduling sec. Gov.'s Office, Sacramento, 1983-87; dep. dir. Calif. Mus. Sci. and Industry, L.A., 1987-94; ret. Mem. Calif. Rep. League, Pasadena, 1969—; mem. Assistance League of Flintridge, 1970—, Flintridge Guild Children's Hosp., 1969-89. Mem. Sweet Briar Alumnae of So. Calif. (pres. 1972), Phi Beta Kappa, Tau Phi. Episcopalian. Avocations: reading, gardening.

GLADDEN, DEAN ROBERT, arts administrator, educator, consultant; b. Columbus, Ohio, Dec. 27, 1953; s. Cyril Robert and Eileen (Faulkner) G.; m. Jane Frances Tellers, Aug. 27, 1953; children: John Dean, Catherine Eileen. B in Music Edn., Miami U., Oxford, Ohio, 1976; MS in Urban Arts Mgmt., Drexel U., 1978; postgrad., Harvard U., 1998. Exec. dir. Council for Arts of Greater Lima, Ohio, 1977-80, Arts Comm. Greater Toledo, 1980-82; dir. devel. and adminstrn. Great Lakes Theater Festival, Cleve., 1982-86; assoc. mng. dir. The Cleve. Play House, 1986, mng. dir., 1987—. Cons. Ohio Arts Coun., Cleve., 1977—, chmn. sponsor/touring panel, 1981-83; adj. assoc. prof. U. Akron, Ohio, 1984-87; mem. adv. com. Mandel Sch. of Non-Profit Mgmt., Case Western Res. U., Cleve. Author booklets on the econs. of arts in Ohio, 1981, 83, 85, 87, 89, 91, 93. Mem. League Resident Theatres (exec. com.), Ohio Citizens for Arts (v.p.), Rotary (pres.). Episcopalian. Avocations: piano, drums. Home: 2687 Rocklyn Rd Cleveland OH 44122-2112 Office: The Cleve Play House 8500 Euclid Ave Cleveland OH 44106-2032

GLADDEN, GARNETT LEE, healthcare educator, psychologist, consultant; b. May 8, 1922; s. Martin L. and Beatrice G. (Palmer) Gladden; m. Vivianne C. Gladden, 1958; children: Mark L., Jeanne Sue. AB, U. Calif., 1943; MA, Claremont Coll., 1948; PhD, Honolulu U., 1989. Prof. emeritus Riverside (Calif.) City Coll., 1946-77; dir. Anza Human Rels. Ctr., Riverside, 1948—78; v.p. Golden State U., LA, 1978-82; dean Grad. Studies and provost Honolulu U., 1982-98; scientific cons. Japan Life Ltd., LA & Tokyo, 1986-98. Adj. prof. San Bernardino Valley Coll., 2002; faculty Osher Lifelong Learning Inst. U. Calif., Riverside, 2003—05; adj. prof. Riverside C.C., 2005. Author (with Vivianne Cervantes Gladden): How to Win the Aging Game, 1958. Fellow, Internat. Acad. Edn., 1983. Home: 6148 Turnberry Dr Banning CA 92220 Personal E-mail: gordront24@cs.com.

GLADDEN, JAMES WALTER, JR., lawyer; b. Pitts., Feb. 23, 1940; s. James Walter and Cynthia Unice (Hales) G.; m. Patricia T. Kuehn, Aug. 21, 1993; children: James, Thomas, Robert. AB, DePauw U., 1961; JD, Harvard U., 1964. Bar: Ill. 1964, U.S. Sup. Ct. 1978. Ptnr. Mayer, Brown, Rowe & Maw, Chgo., 1964—. Mem. ABA. Home: 1426 Chicago Ave Apt 5N Evanston IL 60201 Office: Mayer Brown Rowe & Maw 190 S La Salle St Ste 3900 Chicago IL 60603-3441 E-mail: jgladden@mayerbrownrowe.com.

GLADDEN, JOSEPH RHEA, JR., lawyer; b. Atlanta, Oct. 5, 1942; s. Joseph Rhea I and Frances (Baker) G.; m. Sarah Elizabeth (Bynum), Aug. 21, 1965; children: Joseph III, Elizabeth. BA, Emory U., 1964; LLB, U. Va., 1967. Bar: Ga., 1968; U.S. Dist. Ct. (no. dist.) Ga., 1968; U.S. Ct. Appeals (5th cir.), 1968; U.S. Ct. Appeals (11th cir.), 1985. Assoc. King and Spalding, Atlanta, 1967-73, ptnr., 1973-85; v.p., sr. staff counsel The Coca Cola Co., Atlanta, 1985-87, v.p., dep. gen. counsel, 1987-90, v.p., gen. counsel, 1990-91, sr. v.p., gen. counsel, 1991—99, exec. v.p., gen. counsel, 1999—2000; ret. Atlanta, 2001. Bd. dirs. Coca Cola Enterprises, Emory Healthcare; chmn. bd. dir. Wesley Woods Inc., Coca Cola Amatil. Chmn. bd. trustees Agnes Scott Coll.; bd. dir. Atlanta Ballet; trustee Lovett Sch.; Acad. Search Cons. Svc. Mem. ABA (com. corp. law, gen. counsel); Am. Corp. Counsel Assn.; Ga. Bar Assn.; State Bar Ga.; Assn. Gen. Counsel; Atlanta Bar Assn.; Commerce Club; Piedmont Driving Club. E-mail: sjgladden@mindspring.com.

GLADDEN, VIVIANNE CERVANTES, healthcare consultant, writer; b. Brookhaven, Miss., Oct. 8, 1927; d. Thomas James Guillory and Edna Beatrice Torry; m. Garnett Lee Gladden; children: Mark Lee, Jeanne Sue Wood. Grad., Edwin Lester Sch. Musical Theater, 1976; LittD (hon.), Union U., 1979; BA, Golden State U., 1980, PhD, DHL, Honolulu U., 1993. Ordained to ministry Cmty. Ch. of the Bay, 1985. Stage, film and TV actress, N.Y.C., Hollywood, 1950—64; model Harry Conover, N.Y.C., 1951; mannequin Jacques Heim, Paris, 1951; featured singer La Vien Rose, N.Y.C., 1951—52, Copa City, Fla., 1951—52; nutritional cons. Ctr. Holistic Health Cedars-Sinai Hosp., L.A., 1975—77; health and lifestyle counselor Beverly Hills and Newport, Calif., 1977—; lectr., cons. health sci. and products All Natural Products, Honolulu, Japan Life Inc., Tokyo. Radio ministry Sta. KIEV, Glendale, Calif., 1985—86; mem. adv. bd. Nat. Acad. Sports Medicine, Chgo., 1993—2002. Author (with Lee Gladden): (book) Heirs of the Gods, 1978 (Bronze Halo award So. Calif. Motion Picture Coun., 1982); author: (with Lee Gladden and Gary Couture) How to Win the Aging Game, 1979; author: Archeolinguistics, 1984. Chmn. Eco World, Hollywood, Calif., 1971; master of ceremonies Opening Ahmanson Theatre, L.A., 1976. Named to Hall of Fame, Oakwood Coll., Huntsville, Ala., 1956; recipient Gold award of merit, Martin Luther King Jr. Campaign Ctr., Port Arthur, Tex., 1988. Avocations: singing, piano, yoga, running. Office Phone: 951-769-0392. Personal E-mail: gordont24@cs.com.

GLADE, WILLIAM PATTON, JR., economics professor; b. Wichita Falls, Tex., July 29, 1929; s. William Patton and Billie (Hatcher) G.; m. Marlene Louise Joseph, July 10, 1954; children: Anita, Genie, Patton, John. BBA, U. Tex., 1950, MA, 1951, PhD, 1955. Instr., asst. prof. econs. U. Md., 1957-60; asst., assoc. prof. U. Wis., Madison, 1960-65, prof. Sch. Bus. and dept. econs., 1966-71; prof. econs. U. Tex., Austin, 1970—, dir. Inst. L.Am. Studies, 1971-86, dir. Mex. Ctr., 1997-2001; sr. program assoc. Smithsonian Instn. Wilson Ctr., 1987-88, acting sec. L.Am. program, 1989, sr. scholar, 1990-2000; assoc. dir. USIA, 1989-92; mem. rsch. adv. coun. Ctr. for Arts and Culture, 1998—. Mem. Mex.-U.S. Comm. Ednl. and Cultural Exch./Fulbright Commn., 2002—, Am. co-pres., 2002—04. Author: Las empresas gubernamentales descentralizadas, 1959, The Political Economy of Mexico, 1963, The Latin American Economies, 1969, Marketing in a Developing Economy - The Case of Peru, 1970; co-editor (with Charles A. Reilly) Inquiry at the Grassroots, 1993; contbr., editor Privatization of Public Enterprises in Latin America, 1991; author, editor: Bigger Economies, Smaller Governments: The Role of Privatization in Latin America, 1996. Mem. Latin Am. Studies Assn. (v.p. 1978, pres. 1979), S.W. Coun. Latin Am. Studies Assn. (v.p. 1995, pres. 1996), Assn. for Cultural Econs., Cosmos Club. Office: U Tex Dept Econs Austin TX 78712

GLADFELTER, WILBERT EUGENE, physiology educator; b. York, Pa., Apr. 29, 1928; s. Paul John and Marea Bernadette (Miller) G.; m. Ruth Isabelle Ballantyne, Jan. 26, 1952; children: James W., Charles D., Mary A. AB magna cum laude, Gettysburg (Pa.) Coll., 1952; PhD, U. Pa., 1960. NSF fellow U. Pa., Phila., 1956-58, NIH fellow, 1958-59, asst. instr., 1954-56; instr. physiology W.Va. U., Morgantown, 1959-61, asst. prof., 1961-69, assoc. prof., 1969-96, prof. emeritus, 1996—. Contbr. articles to profl. jours. Treas., Monongalia County chpt. W. Va. Heart Assn., 1976-95. With USN, 1946-48. NSF fellow, 1956-58. Mem. Am. Physiol. Soc., Soc. Neurosci., Soc. for

Integrative and Comparative Biology, Sigma Xi, Phi Beta Kappa, Beta Beta Beta. Lutheran. Home: 70 Pine Tree Ln Morgantown WV 26508-2929 Office: WVa U Health Sci Ctr Dept Physiology Morgantown WV 26506

GLADISH, DAVID STEPHEN, lawyer; b. Cedar Rapids, Iowa, Apr. 20, 1969; s. Allen and Michelle Gladish. BA in Criminal Justice cum laude, Calumet Coll. of St. Joseph, Hammond, Ind., 1991; JD, Valparaiso U., 1995. Bar: Ind. 1995, Ill. 1995, U.S. Dist. Ct. (no. and so. dists.) Ind. 1998, U.S. Dist. Ct. (no. dist.) Ill. 1998, U.S. Ct. Appeals (7th cir.) 1998, bd. cert. civil trial specialist, Nat. Bd Trial Advocacy, 2002. Probation officer Hammond City Ct., 1992-96; ptnr. Smith & DeBonis, Highland, Ind., 1995—. Office: Smith & DeBonis 9696 Gordon Dr Highland IN 46322

GLADSTONE, ARTHUR M., artist, writer, aerospace engineer; b. N.Y.C., Sept. 22, 1921; m. Margaret SeBastian, July 14, 1948 (dec. Mar. 1972); m. Helen Worth, Feb. 3, 1980 (dec. Aug. 2002); m. June Doris Bailey, Mar. 11, 2004. BA cum laude, NYU, 1942, MS in Chemistry, 1947. Cert. propulsion engr., U.S. Civil Svc. Rsch. chemist Am. Cyanamid, Bridgeville, Pa., 1947-48; rsch. supr. Pitts. Coke and Chem., 1978-53; product mgr. Nopco Chem., Harrison, N.J., 1953-59; v.p. Anchor Serum, St. Joseph, Mo., 1959-61; engr. advanced propulsion Hercules Powder, Rocket City, W.Va., 1961-68. Author (under pseudonym Margaret SeBastian): (novels) Miss Letty, My Lord, Rakehell, The Courtship of Colonel Crown, The Fortunate Belle, A Lesson in Love, Dilemma in Duet, A Keeper for Lord Linford; author: (as Maggie Gladstone) The Love Tangle, The Reluctant Debutante, The Impudent Widow, A Lesson in Love, others; author: (as Cilla Whitmore) His Lordship's Landlady; Represented in permanent collections Fed. Res., Richmond, Va. 1st lt. USAF, 1944—46, maj. USAF, ret. Decorated Meritorious Svc. medal USAF. Mem.: Va. Soc. Photographic Arts, Authors Guild. Avocations: theatre organ, 19th century literature, cooking, cosmology. Home: 323 Logtrac Rd Stanardsville VA 22973 Office Phone: 434-985-6211. Personal E-mail: amgladstone@hotmail.com.

GLADSTONE, HERBERT JACK, manufacturing executive; b. N.Y.C., May 12, 1924; s. Joseph D. and Ella (Shabman) G.; m. Sylvia Rosenberg, Dec. 28, 1946; children: Alan, Linda, Karen. Student, Hamilton Coll., 1944, Harvard U., 1945; BBA, CCNY, 1947. Mem. staff Gershon & Strell, CPAs, N.Y.C., 1947-51; budget dir. F.M.C., N.Y.C., 1951-55; v.p., treas. Condec Corp., Old Greenwich, Conn., 1955-85; treas., chief fin. officer Cober, 1985-92; ret., 1992. Prof. acctg. Sacred Heart U.; lectr. MBA program U. Conn.; bd. dirs. Consol. Controls Corp., Hammond Valve Corp. Pres. PTA, 1956-57; asst. scoutmaster Toquam coun. Boy Scouts Am., 1960-63. Served with USAAF, 1943-46. Mem. AICPA, Fin. Execs. Inst. (dir.), N.Y. State Soc. CPAs. Clubs: Roxbury Country (dir.), Roxbury Tennis and Swim (trustee). Home: 284 W Hill Rd Stamford CT 06902-1713 E-mail: shglad284@aol.com.

GLADSTONE, RICHARD WILTON, II, lawyer; b. Pitts., May 21, 1945; s. Richard Wilton and Doris (Whitehill) G.; m. Virginia Long Gladstone, Dec. 28, 1973; children: Chase Whitehill, Sheppard Heatherington. BS in Engring., Lehigh U., Bethlehem, Pa., 1967; JD, U. Pitts., 1970. Ptnr. Eckert, Seamans, Cherin & Mellott, Pitts., 1970—. Bd. mem. Animal Rescue League, Pitts., 1985-90, Sdopted Family Found., Pitts., 1990-98. Mem. Rolling Rock Club, Duquesne Club. Republican. Presbyterian. Avocations: tennis, squash. Office: Eckert Seamans Cherin & Mellott 42nd Fl 600 Grant St Pittsburgh PA 15219

GLADSTONE, ROBERT ALBERT, lawyer; b. Phila., June 2, 1942; s. Albert Frederick and Elizabeth (O'Neill) G.; m. Barbara M. Cranmer, June 21, 1964; children: Frederick Robert, Elizabeth Rose. BA, Ursinus Coll., Collegeville, Pa., 1964; JD, Rutgers U., Newark, 1968. Bar: N.J. 1968, U.S. Dist. Ct. N.J. 1968, U.S. Ct. Claims 1992. Assoc. Pellettieri & Rabstein, Trenton, NJ, 1968—71; ptnr. Brener & Gladstone, Trenton, 1971—74, Warren Goldberg & Berman, Princeton, NJ, 1975—82, Schaff, Motiuk, Gladstone & Reed, Flemington, NJ, 1982—90; city atty. City of Trenton, 1971—75; ptnr., shareholder Shanley & Fisher, P.C., Morristown, NJ, 1990—99, Drinker, Biddle & Shanley (merger Drinker, Biddle & Reath), Florham Park, NJ, 1999—2002; counsel Law Offices of Robert A. Gladstone, Belle Mead, NJ, 2002—. Twp. atty. Twp. of Lawrence, Lawrenceville, N.J., 1985-88; mem. com. on tax ct. N.J. Supreme Ct., 1982-86; chmn. D'Imperio Property Superfund Site Group, Hamilton Twp., N.J., 1994—; chmn. Lightman Yard Superfund Site Group, Winslow Twp., N.J., 2000—. Contbr. articles to law jours. Chmn. Mercer County Rep. Com., Trenton, 1977-80; chmn. bd. trustees Coll. of N.J., Ewing, 1977-2000; mem. devel. bd. Prevention Edn., Lawrenceville, 1992—, Greater Trenton Cmty. Mental Health Ctr., 1994—. Mem. ABA, N.J. Bar Assn. (chmn. local govt. law sect. 1981-84), Trial Attys. N.J. Avocations: golf, outdoor activities. Home: 297 Millstone River Rd Belle Mead NJ 08502-5607 Office: River House 297 River Rd Belle Mead NJ 08502 E-mail: gladlaw1@msn.com.

GLADSTONE, WILLIAM LOUIS, accountant; b. Bklyn., May 23, 1931; s. Archie C. and Bernice T. (Turk) G.; m. Mildred G. Rosenberg, June 21, 1953; children: Susan, Douglas. BS, Lehigh U., 1951; LLB, Bklyn. Law Sch., 1955; grad., Harvard U. Advanced Mgmt. Program, 1970; LLD (hon.), Lehigh U., 1992. CPA, N.Y. Staff acct. Arthur Young & Co., N.Y.C., from 1951, ptnr., 1963, mng. ptnr., 1981-88, chmn., 1985-89; co-chief exec. Ernst & Young, N.Y.C., 1989-91; pres. Tri-City ValleyCats, Inc. Baseball Club, 1992—. Lectr. acctg. Columbia U., N.Y.C., 1962-64; ptnr. N.Y.C. Partnership, 1989-91; bd. dirs. Nat. Baseball Hall of Fame and Mus., Inc. Contbr. articles to profl. jours. Mem. Corp. Congress N.Y. Pub. Libr., 1987-91, mem. conf. bd., 1987-93, trustee com. for econ. devel., 1988-94; bd. dirs. N.Y.-Pa. Baseball League, 1992—; trustee Nat. Asn. Profl. Baseball Leagues, 2000--. Lt. USAF, 1952-53. Mem. AICPA, N.Y. State Soc. CPAs, Lehigh Alumni Assn. (award 1976), Bklyn. Law Sch. Alumni Assn., Fin. Acctg. Found. (trustee 1988-91). Home: 30 Clubhouse Ln Scarsdale NY 10583-3146

GLADSTONE-GELMAN, RACHEL GWYN, poet, writer, language educator; d. Sanford Myron and Norma Gladstone; m. Jonathan Jay Gelman, Sept. 3, 1989; children: Grace, Isadora, Leo. BA, Queens Coll., Flushing, N.Y., 1986; MA, Sch. for Internat. Trng., Brattleboro, Vt., 1990. ESL instr. self employed, N.Y., 1985—86, Belitz of Am. and Japan, Fla., Japan, 1986—87, N.Y.C. Bus. Sch., Hong Kong; ESL instr. intern LaGuardia Cmty. Coll., Long Isl. City, NY, 1989; vis. prof. English Asia Univ., Toyko, Japan, 1990—91; poet, 1992—. Author: (short stories) Island of Bookends, 2000, In Public, 1997, Tear Hear, 1997, Gentle on the Heart, 1997; contbr. poems over 50 publ. to profl. jour. Avocation: voice.

GLADWELL, GRAHAM MAURICE LESLIE, mathematician, civil engineering educator; b. Otford, Kent, Eng., Feb. 21, 1934; emigrated to Can., 1969; s. Basil Maurice Edwin and Doris Alexandra (New) G.; m. Joyce Eugenie Nation, Mar. 29, 1958; children: Graham Hugh, Geoffrey Norman, Malcolm Timothy. B.Sc., U. London, 1954, PhD, 1957, D.Sc., 1969. Lectr. U. London, 1956-60, U. West Indies, Jamaica, 1960-62; sr. lectr. U. Southampton, Eng., 1962-69; prof. dept. civil engring. U. Waterloo, Ontario, Canada, 1969-99, prof. dept. applied math., 1979-99, Disting. prof. emeritus, 2001—. Author: Matrix Analysis of Vibration, 1965, Contact Problems in the Classical Theory of Elasticity, 1980, Inverse Problems in Vibration, 1986, 2d edit., 2004, Inverse Problems in Scattering, 1993, Functional Analysis: Applications to Mechanics and Inverse Problems, 1996; editor: Computer Aided Engineering, 1971, Contact Mechanics and Wear of Rail/Wheel Systems, 1983; series editor Solid mechanics and its Applications, 1989—. Fellow Am. Acad. Mechanics (dir. 1979-82), Inst. Math. and Its Applications, Royal Soc. Arts, Royal Soc. Can. Presbyterian. Office: Dept Civil Engring Univ Waterloo Waterloo ON Canada N2L 3G1 Business E-Mail: graham@gladwell.com.

GLADWELL, MALCOLM, writer; b. Fareham, Eng., 1963; s. Graham and Joyce Gladwell. BA in history, U. Toronto, 1984. Intern The Am. Spectator, Bloomington, Ind., 1984; freelance writer Washington, 1985—87; reporter The Washington Post, 1987—96, bus. reporter, science writer, NYC bureau chief, 1993—96; staff writer The New Yorker Mag., 1996—. Author: The Tipping Point: How Little Things Can Make a Big Difference, 2000 (NY Times bestseller), Blink: The Power of Thinking Without Thinking, 2005 (#1 NY Times bestseller). Named one of 100 Most Influential People of 2005, Time mag. Office: The New Yorker 4 Times Sq New York NY 10036*

GLAESEMANN, KURT R., chemist, researcher; m. Karen R. Brewer, Aug. 15, 1992; children: Lynnae, Erynn, John. BS, NE Mo. State U., 1993; PhD, Iowa State U., 1998. Postdoctoral fellow U. Utah, Salt Lake City, 1999—2000; chemist Lawrence Livermore (Calif.) Nat. Lab, 2000—. Office Phone: 925-423-1579. E-mail: glaesemann1@llnl.gov.

GLAESER, EDWARD LUDWIG, research economist, educator; b. N.Y.C., May 1, 1967; s. Ludwig and Elizabeth Abigail (Bayne) Glaeser; m. Nancy Schwartz, Oct. 2003. AB, Princeton U., 1988; PhD, U. Chgo., 1992. Asst. prof. Harvard U., Cambridge, Mass., 1992-96, prof. polit. econ., Paul Sack assoc., 1996-98, prof. econ., 1998—, provost ad interim, 2004—. Dir. Taubman Ctr., Kennedy Sch. Govt., Harvard U., Rappaport Inst. for Greater Boston Office: Harvard U 315 Littauer Ctr Cambridge MA 02138

GLANCY, DOROTHY JEAN, lawyer, educator; b. Glendale, Calif., Sept. 24, 1944; d. Walter Perry and Elva T. (Douglass) G.; m. Jon Tobias Anderson, June 8, 1979. BA, Wellesley Coll., 1967; JD, Harvard Law Sch., 1970. Bar: D.C. 1971, Calif. 1976, U.S. Dist. Ct. D.C. 1971, U.S. Ct. Appeals (D.C. cir.) 1972. Assoc. Hogan & Hartson, Wash., 1971-73; counsel U.S. Senate Judiciary Subcomm. on Constitutional Rights, Wash., 1973-74; fellow in Law & Humanities Harvard U., Cambridge, Mass., 1974-75; asst. to assoc. prof. law Santa Clara U., Calif., 1975-82, prof. law, 1984—; vis. prof. law U. Arizona, Tucson, 1979; asst. gen. counsel U.S. Dept. of Agr., 1982-83. Cons. Commn. Fed. Paperwork, Wash., 1976; dir. summer Law Study Program in Hong Kong, 1985-90; advisor Restatement, Third Property: Servitudes, 1986-97; mem. ct. tech. adv. com. Calif. Jud. Coun. Dir. legal rsch. project regarding privacy and intelligent trnsp. systems Fed. Hwy. Adminstrn., 1993-95; bd. dirs. Presidio Hts. Assn. Neighbors, 1990—. Fellow Wellesley Coll., Harvard U. Mem. ABA (chair ethics com. of sect. on natural resources, energy and environ. law, 1993-95, coun. mem. 1995-98), State Bar Calif. (mem. environ. law sect., adv. exec. com. 1993-96, advisor 1996—), Am. Assn. Law Schs. (chair environ. law sect. 1992-93, chair property sect. 1996-97), Am. Law Inst., Calif. Women Lawers, Soc. Am. Law Tchrs., Phi Beta Kappa. Democrat. Avocations: gardening, travel. Office: Santa Clara U Sch Law Santa Clara CA 95053-0001 Business E-Mail: dglancy@scu.edu.

GLANCY, HELEN DIANE, literature educator; b. Kansas City, Mo., Mar. 18, 1941; d. Lewis and Edith (Wood) Hall; m. Dwane Glancy, May 2, 1964 (div. Mar. 1983); children: David, Jennifer. MFA, U. Iowa. Prof. English Macalester Coll., St. Paul. Author: (novels) The Only Piece of Furniture in the House, 1996, Pushing the Bear, 1996, Flutie, 1998, Closets of Heaven, 1999, The Man Who Heard the Land, 2001, The Mask Maker, 2002, Designs of the Night Sky, 2002, Stone Heart: A Novel of Sacajawea, 2003, Dance Partner, 2005; contbr. short stories and essays to publs.; author: numerous poems. Named Edlestein-Keller Minn. Writer of Distinction, U. Minn., 1998; recipient Native Am. Prose award, 1991, Am. Book award, 1993, Prose-Playwriting award, Wordcraft Cir. Native Writers, 1997, Loft award of distinction, McKnight Fellowship, 1999, Cherokee medal of honor, Cherokee Honor Soc., 2001, Disting. Alumna award, U. Mo., 2003, NEA, 2003, Juniper Prize, U. of Mass. Press, 2003; fellow Many Voices, Playwrights Ctr., Mpls., 2001, Native Am. Screenwriter's fellow, UCLA, Sundance Inst., 1998, NEA, 2003. Office: Macalester Coll 1600 Grand Saint Paul MN 55105 Office Phone: 651-696-6516. E-mail: glancy@macalester.edu.

GLANCY, WALTER JOHN, lawyer; b. LA, Mar. 8, 1942; s. Walter Perry and Elva Thomasin (Douglass) Glancy; m. Jane Whetstone Schroeder, 1995; children from previous marriage: Jill Marie, Gregory Owens. AB, Princeton U., 1964; BA, Oxford (Eng.) U., 1966; LLB, Yale U., 1969. Bar: Tex. 1971. Law clk. to assoc. justice Byron R. White U.S. Supreme Ct., 1969-70; staff asst. NSC, 1970-71; staff asst. to Peter M. Flanigan, The White House, 1971; assoc. then ptnr. Jackson, Walker, Winstead, Cantwell & Miller, Dallas, 1972-76; ptnr. Hughes & Luce and predecessor, Dallas, 1976-85, Baker & Botts, Dallas, 1985-88, Hughes & Luce, Dallas, 1988-90; pvt. practice Dallas, 1991-95, 97-99; cons. Meyer, Hendricks, Victor, Osborn & Maledon, Phoenix, 1991-95; ptnr. Weil, Gotshal & Manges LLP, Dallas, 1995-96; sr. v.p., gen. counsel, dir Holly Corp., 1999—. Adj. lectr. corp. taxation So. Meth. U. Sch. Law, 1988. Note and comment editor Yale Law Jour., 1968-69. Bd. mgmt. Dallas YMCA Urban Svcs., 1975—84; bd. dirs. Dallas Family Guidance Ctr., 1982—96, pres. bd. dirs., 1985—86; bd. dirs. Child & Family Guidance Ctrs., Dallas, 1996—2003, pres. bd. dirs., 2001—02; bd. dirs. Dallas Opera, 1984—88, 1996—97; bd. trustees Hockaday Sch., Dallas, 1989—95; mem. adminstrv. bd. Lovers Ln. United Meth. Ch., Dallas, 1984—86, 1988—89; deacon Park Cities Bapt. Ch., Dallas, 1996—. Nat. Merit scholar, 1960-64, Marshall scholar, 1964-66. Mem.: ABA, State Bar Tex. (profl. ethics com. 1982—, chmn. tax sect. 1985—86, chmn. profl. ethics com. 1999—), Am. Law Inst., Dallas Bar Assn. (chmn. legal ethics com. 1980—81), Order of Coif, Park Cities Rotary Club (pres. 2003—04), Phi Beta Kappa. Republican. Home: 7420 Glenshannon Cir Dallas TX 75225 Office: 100 Crescent Ct Ste 1600 Dallas TX 75201-6915 Personal E-mail: johnglancy@mindspring.com.

GLANCZ, RONALD ROBERT, lawyer; b. Bay City, Mich., Jan. 29, 1943; s. Alexander and Ella (Josehart) Glancz; m. Margie Joan Pensler, Dec. 28, 1969. BA in Pre-Legal Studies, U. Mich., 1964, JD cum laude, 1968. Bar: Mich. 1968, U.S. Ct. of Appeals (D.C. cir.) 1969, U.S. Supreme Ct. 1972, D.C. 1974. Atty. civil divsn. Appellate Sec. U.S. Dept. Justice, Washington, 1968-75, asst. dir. civil divsn., 1975-79; dir. litigation divsn. Office of the Comptr. of the Currency, Washington, 1979-84; asst. gen. counsel Fed. Deposit Ins. Corp., Washington, 1984-88; ptnr. Venable LLP, Washington, 1991—. Contbr. Mem.: ABA (vice chair banking law com.), Jewish Found. for Group Homes (bd. dirs., past pres.), The Exchequer Club Washington, Order of Coif. Office: Venable LLP 575 7th St NW Washington DC 20004-1601 Office Phone: 202-344-4947. Business E-Mail: rglancz@venable.com.

GLANDEN, WILLIAM DONALD, pianist, music educator, composer; b. Wilmington, Del., Oct. 9, 1951; s. William Henry and Madalene Bell (Deputy) G.; m. JoLynn Thomas, Aug. 23, 1974; children: William Christian, Bradford Thomas. Student, West Chester State Coll., 1969-72; MusB, North Tex. State U., 1975; summer seminar student, Eastman Sch. Music, 1983; studied with, Bernard Peiffer, 1970-72, Sir Roland Hanna, 1980-82, Kenny Barron, 1991-93; MM, Rutgers U., 1997. Pianist Del. Symphony, Wilmington, 1979-84; chmn. jazz dept. Wilmington (Del.) Music Sch., 1984-86; mem. faculty Combs Coll. Music, Phila., 1987—, Univ. of Arts, Phila., 1996—. Faculty mem. jazz studies dept. Temple U., Phila., 1992-96; performed with Ernie Watts, 1995-96. Guest performer, lectr. Lincoln U., Oxford, Pa., 1979, Glassboro (N.J.) State Coll., 1983; pianist Henry Mancini in Concert, Wilmington, 1984; music dir., pianist Harrah's, Atlantic City, 1987; solo pianist Resorts Internat. Hotel Casino, Atlantic City, 1988; composer Original Compositions by Don Glanden, 1973, (piano preludes) The Four Elements, 1975, (jazz peices) Remembrance, 1982, A Waltz for Brad, 1983; recordings include Sudden Life, 1994; compact disc Only Believe, 1999; contbr. numerous articles for Downbeat Mag.; misc. studio and concert performances with: Donald Byrd, Terell Stafford, Eddie Gomez, Robin Eubanks, Patti Austin and Randy Brecker. NEA jazz fellow, 1980; Nicholas scholar for grad. work Rutgers U., 1991. Home: 2215 Coventry Dr Wilmington DE 19810-3921

GLANDT, EDUARDO DANIEL, chemical engineering educator; b. Buenos Aires, Mar. 4, 1945; arrived in US, 1973; s. Jacob and Matilde (Reidich) G. BS in chem. engring., U. Buenos Aires, 1968; M in chem. engring., U. Pa., 1975, PhD in chem. engring., 1977. Researcher Nat. Inst. Indsl. Technology, Buenos Aires, 1968-73; asst. prof. U. Pa., Phila., 1977-81, assoc. prof., 1981-85, prof., 1985—, chair dept. chem engring., 1990—94, Carl V.S. Patterson Prof., 1990—95, Russell P. and Elizabeth C. Heuer Prof., 1995—98, interim dean Sch. Engring. & Applied Sci., 1998—99, dean Sch. Engring & Applied Sci., 1999—, Robert D. Bent Prof. Chem. and Biomolecular Engring. Contbr. articles to profl. jours. Recipient S. Reid Warren Award for Disting. Tchg., Sch. Engring. and Applied Sci., U. Pa., 1977, Christian R. and Mary F. Lindback Award for Disting. Tchg., U. Pa., 1980. Mem. NAE, AAAS, AIChE, Am. Chem. Soc. (Viktor K. LaMer Award, Surface and Colloid Sci. Divsn., 1979), Am. Phys. Soc. Office: Dept of Chem Engring U Pa 220 S 33rd St, 311A Towne Bldg Philadelphia PA 19104-6393

GLANSTEIN, ELEANOR ELOVICH, lawyer; b. Bklyn., Feb. 23, 1944; d. Sol Herman and Fanny (Berglas) Elovich; m. Joel Charles Glanstein, July 2, 1966; children: David, Stacey. BA, Bklyn. Coll., 1964; MA, NYU, 1965; JD, Hofstra U., 1975. Bar: N.Y. 1976, U.S. Dist. Ct. (so. and ea. dists.) N.Y. 1976, U.S. Supreme Ct. 1978. Tchr. Lafayette High Sch., Bklyn., 1965-70; assoc. Markowitz & Glanstein, N.Y.C., 1975-80; pvt. practice N.Y.C., 1980—. Adj. faculty N.Y. Law Sch., 1989—. Mem. ABA, Indsl. Relations Rsch. Assn., N.Y. State Bar Assn., N.Y. County Lawyers Assn., Soc. Profls. in Dispute Resolution. Office: 880 3rd Ave New York NY 10022-4730

GLANTZ, GINA, consultant; b. N.Y.C., Apr. 3, 1943; d. Nathan L. and Lillian (Rosenbaum) Stritzler; m. Ronald A. Glantz, Oct. 17, 1968; children: Amy Samantha, Peter Samue. BA, U. Calif., Berkeley, 1965. Chief of staff to county exec. County of Essex, N.J., 1978-82; owner, mgr. Martin & Glantz LLC, Springfield, N.J., 1982-83; sr. cons. Mondale for Pres., Washington, 1984; nat. field dir. Mondale/Ferraro, Inc., Washington, 1984; ptnr. Martin & Glantz, Mill Valley, Calif., Rosslyn, Va., 1985—. Home: 96 Ave Del Norte San Anselmo CA 94960-2549

GLANVILLE, ROBERT EDWARD, lawyer; b. Binghamton, N.Y., Aug. 1, 1950; s. Robert S. and Betty J. (Garlick) G.; m. Susan Anne Kime, Sept. 3, 1970. BA magna cum laude, SUNY, Binghamton, 1972; JD magna cum laude, Cornell U., 1976. Bar: N.Y. 1977, U.S. Dist. Ct. (we. dist.) N.Y. 1978, U.S. Supreme Ct. 1981, U.S. Ct. Appeals (2d cir.) 1985, U.S. Ct. Appeals (D.C. cir.) 1991. Law clk. Appellate Divsn., 4th Dept., Rochester, 1976-78; from assoc. to ptnr. Phillips, Lytle, Hitchcock, et. al., Buffalo, N.Y., 1978-85, 88—; ptnr. Prahl & Glanville, Buffalo, 1986-88. Mem. ABA, N.Y. State Bar Assn., Erie County Bar Assn., Am. Gas Assn. Avocations: whitewater kayaking, sailing, mountain climbing, flying. Home: 9385 S Hill Rd Boston NY 14025-9667 Office: Phillips Lytle Hitchcock 3400 HSBC Ctr Buffalo NY 14203-2887 Office Phone: 716-847-7019. Business E-Mail: rglanville@phillipslytle.com.

GLANZER, MURRAY, psychology educator; b. N.Y.C., Nov. 18, 1922; s. Max and Norma (Reichenthal) G.; m. Mona Naomi Sorcher, Sept. 20, 1953; children: Michael, Marla, James. BA, City Coll., N.Y.C., 1943; MA, U. Mich., 1948, PhD, 1952. Instr. Bklyn. Coll., 1949-53; project dir. to program dir. Am. Inst. Rsch., 1954-58; lectr. U. Pitts., 1955-58; rsch. assoc. Walter Reed Army Inst. Rsch. U. Md. Sch. Medicine, 1958-63; prof. N.Y.U., 1963—. Numerous publications; contbr. articles to profl. jours. Fellow Ford Found. U. Chgo., 1953-54, Guggenheim, Hebrew U., Jeruslem, 1969-70. Mem. Am. Psychol. Assn., Psychonomic Soc., Soc. Exptl. Psychologists. Home: 17 Weston Pl Lawrence NY 11559-1524 Office: NYU 6 Washington Pl New York NY 10003-6634

GLAROS, ALAN G., psychologist, researcher; m. Eileen L. Spony, Jan. 26, 1974. PhD, SUNY, 1975. Lic. Psychologist Mo. Prof. U. Mo., Kansas City, 1988—2004; assoc. dean Kans. City U. Medicine and Bioscis., 2004—. Fellow: APA. Office: Kansas City U Med & Biosciss 1750 Independence Ave Kansas City MO 64106 Office Phone: 816-460-0507. Office Fax: 816-283-2357.

GLASBERG, H(ERBERT) MARK, psychiatrist, educator; b. N.Y.C., Oct. 11, 1939; s. Joesph and Elsa (Haber) G.; m. Paula Drillman, June 19, 1960; children: Scot Bradley, Hilary Jennifer. BA, Yeshiva U., 1953; MS, Columbia U., 1954; MD, SUNY, 1958. Diplomate Am. Bd. Psychiatry and Neurology. Intern Maimonides Hosp., N.Y.C., 1958-59; resident in psychiatry Kings County Hosp., N.Y.C., 1959-60; resident in internal medicine Kingbridge VA Hosp. of Columbia U. Coll. Med. Program, N.Y.C., 1960-61; resident Payne Whitney Psychiat. Clin., N.Y. Hosp., 1963-65; psychiatrist pvt. practice, N.Y.C., 1968—; attending physician dept. psychiatry Columbia U. Coll. Physicians & Surgeons; instr. Cornell U. Med. Sch., 1966-68; assoc. prof. psychiatry Mt. Sinai Sch. Medicine, 1968-80; dir. psychiat. outpatient svcs. Beth Israel Hosp., N.Y.C., 1968-74, assoc. attending physician, 1968-74, chief psychiat. emergency & cons. svcs., 1974-75; attending psychiatrist & clin. prof. psychiatry Coll. Physicians & Surgeons, Columbia U., 1986—; neurosurgery Coll. Physicians & Surgeons, N.Y. Presbyn. Med. Ctr., 1982, clin. prof. neurosurgery, 1995; clin. prof. neurosurgery, attending neurosurgeon N.Y. Presbyn. Med. Ctr., 1995. Examiner Am. Bd. Psychiatry & Neurology, 1988—; cons. mem. panel of ind. psychiatrists N.Y.C. Mental Health Info. Svc., 1968—. Mem. Manhattan physicians com. United Jewish Appeal, 1970—; mem. com. admission sel. Cornell U. Med. Coll., Ctr. Alumni Assn. N.Y. Hosp. Col. M.C. AUS, 1961-63. Fellow N.Y. Hosp., 1965-66, spl. rsch. fellow Nat. Inst. Mental Health, 1966-68, Cornell U. Med. Sch. Fellow ACP, Am. Soc. Neurosurgeons, Am. Psychiat. Assn. (internat. platform com. 1980—); mem. APA, AAAS, Am. Psychosomatic Soc., N.Y. Acad. Scis., N.Y. Acad. Medicine, Soc. Adolescent Psychiatry, Internat. Platform Assn. Office: 14 E 73rd St New York NY 10021-4128 Office Phone: 212-744-6600.

GLASBERG, LAURENCE BRIAN, investment company executive; b. NYC, Apr. 28, 1943; s. William and Tillie (Liebowitz) G.; m. Lana Lucille Pollack, Aug. 10, 1963; children: Jeffrey Scott, Glenn David. BBA, CUNY, 1964, MBA, 1968. Mgr. bus. affairs Sta. WCBS-TV, N.Y.C., 1970-72, dir. planning and adminstrn., 1972-74; gen. auditor Ea. ops. CBS Inc., N.Y.C., 1975-76; v.p. fin. and adminstrn. CBS Publs., 1976-82, v.p., gen. auditor, 1982-88; sr. v.p. fin. and adminstrn. N.Am. ops. AEG Corp., 1988-89; pres. Nat. Mgmt. Resources Group Inc., 1990—. Mng. dir. Future Resource Sys., Inc., 1994-96, exec. v.p. Future Bus. Ctr., Inc., 1995-96; sr. v.p., CFO MacDonald Comms. Corp., 1996-98; bus. and fin. mgr. Mus. Mags., 1998-2000; co-chmn. Media Resources Group, LLC, 2001-02. Fin. and tax com. Princeton Twp., NJ, 1991, elected committeeman, 1992, elected mayor, 1993; bd. dirs. AMAS Mus. Theatre, Inc., 1998-99. 1st lt. inf. U.S. Army, 1964-65. Mem. Fin. Execs. Inst. (nat. com. on govt. liaison, local bd. dirs. 1987-88, chpt. sec. 1989-92), Econ. Club (N.Y.C.). Avocations: physical fitness, outdoor and environmental activities, reading. E-mail: lglas2@yahoo.com.

GLASBERG, SCOT BRADLEY, plastic surgeon; b. NYC, June 30, 1964; s. H. Mark and Paula (Drillman) G.; m. Alisa Goldman, Oct. 17, 1999; 1 child, Alexander Zachary. BA cum laude, Columbia U., 1986; MD with honors, NYU, 1990. Diplomate Am. Bd. Plastic Surgery, Am. Bd. Surgery, Nat. Bd. Med. Examiners. Resident in surgery U. Conn./Hartford Hosp., 1990-95, chief resident, 1995-96; craniofacial rsch. fellow Inst. Reconstructive Plastic Surgery, NYU Med. Ctr., NYC, 1992-93; fellow SUNY Health Sci. Ctr., Bklyn., 1996-98, program dir., dir. plastic surgery edn., 1998—2000. Contbr. articles to profl. jours. Mem. young plastic surgeons com. Plastic Surgery Ednl. Found., Am. Soc. Plastic Surgeons, 1996—. NY State Regents scholar, 1982-86. Fellow ACS; mem. AMA (del. resident physician sect. 1990-93, 96—98, plastic surgery caucus 1996-97, 99—, del. young physicians sect. 1999-2004, young physicians sect. governing coun. 2002-2004), Am. Soc. Plastic Surgeons (vice chmn. govt. rels. com., chmn. govt. rels. com. 2005—, plastypac bd. govs. 2001—, Maliniac cir., parliamentary bd. dirs. 2005-), Am. Soc. Aesthetic Plastic Surgery (legis. com.), Northeastern Soc. Plastic Surgery (Resident/Fellows award 1997), Med. Soc. State NY (del. AMA resident physician sect. 1996-98, young physician sect. 1999—, mem. med. liability task force, legis./advocate steering com., Outstanding Svc. award 1990), NY County Med. Soc.(litigation com., managed care task force), NY Regional Soc. Plastic Surgeons (winner clin. paper competition 1997). Avocations: tennis, golf, swimming, card collecting. Office: Cosmetic & Reconstructive Plastic Surg 42A E 74th St New York NY 10021-2735 Address: 900 Park Ave Apt 19AB 10021 Office Phone: 212-717-8550. Business E-Mail: info@DrGlasberg.com. E-mail: scotbg@juno.com.

GLASBRENNER, KARL CHRISTIAN, federal agency administrator; s. Heinz Wilhelm Glasbrenner and Mariann Theresa Byrne; m. Brenda W. Wilkinson, Apr. 8, 1989; m. Irma Julia Monclova, Sept. 11, 1976 (div. Dec. 13, 1984); children: Jeromy Alan, Justin Tyler. BS, Pa. State U., 1976; MA, Pepperdine U., 1980. Cert. clin. hypnotist (Ericksonian hypnotherapy) Am. Hypnosis Tng. Acad., Inc., 2003; neurolinguistic programming practitioner Am. Neuro-Linguistic Programming Assn., 2000, pistol instr. NRA, 2002. Police officer Selfridge Air N.G. Base, Mt. Clemens, Mich., 1976—76; supervisory supply technician U.S. Army Garrison, Arlington Hall Station, Va., 1981—82; spl. agt. investigations br. Def. Intelligence Agy., Washington, 1982—86, spl. agt. overseas security ops., 1986—91, chief investigations br., 1991—96, chief force protection and tech. security br., 1996—2000, acting chief security ops. divsn., 1998, chief pers. security divsn., 2000—. Charter mem. East Coast chpt. Assn. of Threat Assessment Profls., Washington, 1995—; fellow Excellence in Govt. fellows program Coun. for Excellence in Govt., Washington, 1995—96, co-coach Excellence in Govt. fellows program, 1997—2000, vice chair sr. fellows bd. leaders, 1997—2001; mem. def. and intelligence coun. Am. Soc. for Indsl. Security, Alexandria, Va., 2003—. Singer: Alexandria Harmonizers (Internat. Chorus Champion, 1986); contr.: book The Colors of Poetry, 2003 (Best 100 Poets, 2003). Capt. U.S. Army, 1976—81. Recipient Res. Officer Tng. Corps scholarship, U.S. Army, 1974-1976, Achievement award, Coun. for Excellence In Govt., 2000, Def. Intelligence Dir.'s award, Def. Intelligence Agency, 2002. Master: Masons (25 Yr. Pin 2001); mem.: Fed. Exec. Inst. Alumni Assn., Am. Soc. for Indsl. Security (def. and intelligence coun. 2003). Avocations: singing, writing, swimming, traveling, genealogy. Office: Def Intelligence Agy Bldg 6000 Bolling AFB CLAR DAC-3 Washington DC 20340-5300 Office Phone: 703-907-1309. Business E-Mail: karl.glasbrenner@dia.mil.

GLASER, DAVID, painter, sculptor; b. Bklyn., Sept. 29, 1919; s. Samuel and Jennie (Oiffer) G.; m. Millie Sappol, Feb. 19, 1944; children: Susan, Sherry. Student, N.Y. Sch. Indsl. Art, 1937, N.Y. Sch. Contemporary Art, 1947-48, Bklyn. Mus. Art Sch., 1948-50. Illustrator, cartoonist comic books Popular Mechanics, Electronics Illustrated, Popular Sci., N.Y.C., 1939—42, 1946—50; pres., designer, inventor Mosamics Co., Bklyn., 1948—50; art dir., advt. mgr. Univ. Loudspeakers, White Plains, NY, 1951—60; owner, mgr., graphic designer Studio Concepts, Wantagh, NY, 1957—. Artist Civilian Conservation Corps, Adirondacks, 1936; tchr. art Ctr. Island Jewish Sch., Freeport, N.Y., 1959; newspaper artist Bering Breeze, Aleutian Islands, 1945-46; co-founder Northwest Pacific chpt. AVC Adak, 1945; worked with North Am. Philips (Amperex), Gen. Instruments, Gen. Signal (Cardion), Schweber Electronics, Singer-Telesignal; Veeco/Lambda Electronics, Plessey Inc.; Polytech. R&D, Univ. Loudspeakers, Harmon Kardon, Brit. Industries, Hohner Harmonicas; lectr. career guidance Mid. Sch. East students; presenter in field Author: (poetry) My Mother Died Dancing, 1960; designer, creator illuminated slide series L.I. Comty. chorus; contbr. poetry to anthologies; three-man show Heckscher Mus., Huntington, N.Y., 1964; exhibited in group shows Mcpl. Gallery, Jackson, Miss., 1943, Allied Artists of Am., 1957-85, Nat. Art Club, N.Y.C., 1959, Art Directions, 1959, ACA Galleries, 1960, Hofstra U., Adelphi U., Nassau C.C., 1980, L.I. Art Dirs. Exhbn. Firehouse Gallery, 1980, Nassau County Art Mus., 1980, Hempstead Harbor Art Assn., Glen Cove, L.I., 1982, Knickerbocker Artists, Islip Mus., 1983, Wantagh Libr., 1975, Levittown Libr., 1986, Freeport Libr., 1987, Plainview Libr., 2002, Brandeis U. Men's Club lecture series, 2002; illustrator: Planets (Willie Ley); author, creator: American Indian, Crime and Punishment, Superstition and Parapsychology, 1947-50; prodr. bicentennial pictorial chronological map of Entire Am. Revolution, Spirit of '76, 1975; inventor process for mass prodn. ceramic and transparent mosaics, silk screen sys. for printing inside compound curves; creator innovative 2 color graphics method; new age art: developer combining chemically colored copper (sculpture) plastic, resins and reflective integral elements with electronics, 1973—; prodr. crossover filming of painting, sculpture and poetry recitation as ongoing creative product of Bridges of Mind, 1993—, Career Forum, 1999—. Designer war posters visual aids for U.S. Army, 1942-44; creator comic character Giggy F. Useless, used in basic tng. and theatre dramatizations and for Army newspaper, 1943-46. Sgt. AUS, 1942-46. Art Student's League scholar, 1936-37; recipient grand prize for redesign Levitt Home, 1967, Printing Industries, N.Y., 1973, numerous graphics awards, 1973-84, graphic excellence award Monadnock Mills, 1975, Desi grand award, 1980-82, poetry award Nassau County Fine Arts Mus., 1981, award of excellence IEEE, World Trade Ctr., N.Y.C., 1984, Vets. Soc. Am. Artists, 1984, award of excellence Long Beach Art League, 1989. Mem. Internat. Soc. Poets, Freeport Arts Coun., Allied Artists Am. (pres. 1985-86), Huntington Twp. Art League, DAV, Comic Artist Guild (treas.), Nature Conservancy, various environ. groups. Achievements include development of process for mass-producing mosaics, both traditional and current for architecture as well as home decor; transparent (per-stained glass) and opaque. Home and Office: 33 Downhill Ln Wantagh NY 11793-1817 Office Phone: 516-785-5440.

GLASER, DONALD ARTHUR, physicist; b. Cleve., Sept. 21, 1926; s. William Joseph Glaser; m. Lynn Bercouitz, 1975. BS, Case Inst. Tech., 1946, ScD (hon.), 1959; PhD, Calif. Inst. Tech., 1949; ScD (hon.), U. Mich., 2002. Prof. physics U. Mich., 1949—59; prof. physics U. Calif., Berkeley, 1959—, prof. grad. sch., divsn. neurobiology, 1964—. Recipient Henry Russel award, U. Mich., 1955, Charles V. Boys prize, Phys. Soc., London, 1958, Nobel prize in Physics, 1960, Gold medal, Case Inst. Tech., 1967, Golden Plate award, Am. Acad. of Achievement, 1989; fellow NSF, 1961, Guggenheim, 1961—62, Smith-Kettlewell Inst. for Vision Rsch., 1983—84. Fellow: AAAS, Am. Physics Soc. (prize 1959), Neuroscis. Inst., Royal Swedish Acad. Sci., Royal Soc. Sci., Assn. Rsch. Vision and Ophthalmology, The Exploratorium (bd. dirs.), Fedn. Am. Scientists; mem.: NAS, Am. Philos. Soc., Internat. Acad. Sci., N.Y. Acad. Scis., Am. Assn. Artificial Intelligence, Sigma Xi, Theta Tau, Tau Kappa Alpha. Achievements include invention of the Bubble Chamber. Office: U Calif 221 Donner Lab Dept Physics and Neurobio 237 Hildebrand Hall #3206 Berkeley CA 94720-3206 Business E-Mail: glaser@berkeley.edu.

GLASER, GERARD R., science administrator; Acting exec. officer Nat. Sci. Bd., Arlington, Va., 2002—03, dir. divsn. grants and agreements, 2003—. Office: Nat Sci Found 4201 Wilson Blvd Arlington VA 22230

GLASER, GILBERT HERBERT, neuroscientist, educator; b. N.Y.C., Nov. 10, 1920; s. Burnard Richard and Sidelle (Rogers) G.; m. Morfydd Mai Pugh, Mar. 17, 1946; children: Gareth Evan, Sara Elizabeth. AB, Columbia, 1940, MD, 1943, Med. Sc.D., 1951; MA (hon.), Yale, 1963. Diplomate: Am. Bd. Psychiatry and Neurology. Intern Mt. Sinai Hosp., N.Y.C., 1943-44; resident neurology N.Y. Neurol. Inst., 1944-46; research asst. to assoc. neurology Columbia Coll. Physicians and Surgeons, 1948-52; research scientist N.Y. Psychiat. Inst., 1948-50; head. sect. neurology Sch. Medicine Yale U., 1952-71, chmn. dept. neurology Sch. Medicine, 1971-86, asst. prof. neurology Sch. Medicine, 1952-55, assoc. prof. Sch. Medicine, 1955-63, prof. neurology Sch. Medicine, 1963-91, prof. neurology emeritus, 1991—. Commonwealth Fund vis. prof. neurology U. London, Eng., 1965-66; cons. West Haven (Conn.) VA Hosp., 1955-91; vis. prof. neurology Nat. Hosp., London, 1972, Park Hosp., Oxford, Eng., 1973-86, Hunan Med. Coll., Peoples Republic of China, 1986, U. Niigata, Kyoto, Japan, 1989; Fulbright Disting. prof. neurology Zagreb U., Yugoslavia, 1981; vis. scholar Green Coll. Oxford U., Eng., 1987-88; mem. neurology research adv. com. USPHS, 1956-60, 68-72, spl. cons., 1973, epilepsy adv. com., 1974-77, chmn. basic sci. subcom., 1977-80; mem. neurobiology rev. com. VA, 1975-78, chmn., 1977-78. Author: EEG and Behavior, 1963; Editor: Epilepsia, 1958-76; adv. editor, 1976-86; editor: Recent Advances in Clinical Neurology, 1978, 81, 84, Antiepileptic Drugs: Mechanisms of Action, 1980; mem. editorial bd.: Jour. Nervous and Mental Diseases, Annats of Neurology, Jour. of Neurological Sci.; Contbr. articles to profl. jours. Capt. M.C. AUS, 1946-48. Recipient Janeway prize Columbia U., 1943, Bicentennial medal award, 1968, Book award Commonwealth Fund, 1975. Fellow Royal Soc. Medicine, ACP; mem. Am. Neurol. Assn. (hon., 1st v.p. 1977-78), Am. Acad. Neurology (pres. 1973-75 hon. mem. 1998), Am. Epilepsy Soc. (pres. 1963, Lennox lectr. 1985), Am. Electroencephalographic Soc. (council 1958-61, bd. qualifications), Eastern Assn. Electroencephalographers (pres. 1958), EEG Soc. (Gt. Britain), Assn. Brit. Neurologists, Soc. for Neurosci. (hon.), Epilepsy Found. Am. (med. adv. bd.), Myasthenia Gravis Foundation (med. adv. bd. chmn. 1964-65), Multiple Sclerosis Soc. (chmn. research programs com. 1973-74, med. adv. bd.). Clubs: Athenaeum (London). Home: 205 Millbrook Rd North Haven CT 06473-4334 Office: Yale U Sch Medicine 333 Cedar St New Haven CT 06510-3289

GLASER, LAURA MARIE, physician assistant; b. Dayton, Ohio, May 17, 1962; d. Charles Jerome Glaser and Darlene E. Miller; m. Lee K. Nicoloff, Oct. 31, 2004. BS in Health Professions magna cum laude, Kettering Coll. Med. Arts, 2000. Cert. physician asst. Nat. Commn. on Cert. of Physician Assts., 2005. Orthop. technologist Orthop. Inst. Dayton, Inc., Ohio, 1982—94; physician asst. TriHealth Bethesda Care, Sharonville, Ohio, 1998—2001; physician asst. Jean-Pierre Michaud MD Horizons Orthop. and Sports Medicine, Presque Isle, Maine, 2001—05; physician asst. Occupl. Health and Rehab., 2005—. Phys. asst. preceptor Kettering Coll. of Med. Arts, 2000. Career demonstrator TAMC Healthcare Survival Camp, Presque Isle, 2003, 2004; mission worker Hope for a Healthier Humanity, N.Y.C., 2000—. Alliance scholarship, Montgomery County Med. Soc., 1998, Julian and Marjorie Lange scholarship, Kettering Coll. of Med. Arts, 1997. Fellow: Physician Assts. of Orthop. Surgery (assoc.), Downeast Physican Assts. (assoc.), Am. Acad. of Physician Assistants (assoc.). Avocations: golf, motorcycling, travel. Home: 186 Coyle St Portland ME 04103 Office: 59 East Ave Lewiston ME 04240 Office Phone: 207-784-1680. Personal E-mail: palala99@msn.com.

GLASER, LUIS, biochemistry educator; b. Vienna, Mar. 30, 1932; came to U.S., 1953, naturalized, 1961; s. Hermann and Gisela (Kohn) G.; m. Ruth Walliser, May 18, 1961; children: Miriam, Nicole. BA, U. Toronto, Ont., Can., 1953; PhD, Washington U., St. Louis, 1956. Asst. prof. biol. chemistry Washington U., 1959-62, asso. prof., 1962-67, prof., 1967-75, chmn. dept. biol. chemistry, 1975-86; dir. Div. Biology and Biomed. Scis., 1980-86; exec. v.p., provost U. Miami, 1986—. Contbr. numerous articles on bacterial and mammalian metabolism to profl. jours.; editor Jour. Biol. Chemistry, 1969-74, 81-86, Jour. Supramolecular Structures, 1979-86, Jour. Cell Biology, 1981-92. Helen Hay Whitney fellow, 1956-59; NIH grantee; NSF grantee. Mem. Am. Soc. Biol. Chemists, Am. Chem. Soc., Am. Soc. Microbiology, Am. Soc. Neurochemists, AAAS. Democrat. Jewish. Office: PO Box 248033 Coral Gables FL 33124-8033 Office Phone: 305-284-3356. E-mail: lglaser@umiami.edu.

GLASER, PATRICIA L., lawyer; b. Charleston, W.Va., Sept. 15, 1947; d. Richard Stanley and Tilda Jane (Rosen) G.; m. Samuel Hunter Mudie, May 19, 1978; stepchildren: Heather and Jason Mudie. BA, Am. U., 1969; JD, Rutgers U., 1973. Bar: Calif. 1973, U.S. Dist. Ct. (no. and cen. dists.) Calif. 1973, U.S. Dist. Ct. (so. dist.) 1976, U.S. Ct. Appeals (9th cir.), U.S. Supreme Ct. Law clk. to presiding justice U.S. Dist. Ct.; from assoc. to ptnr. Wyman, Bautzer, Rothman, Kuchel & Silbert, Los Angeles, 1973—. Judge pro tem West br. Los Angeles Mcpl. Ct., panelist legal continuing edn. programs. Mem. fund-raising com. Deukmejian for Gov. of Calif.; participant Parole-Aide program. Mem. Los Angeles County Bar Assn. (fed. cts. and practices com.). Avocations: travel, skiing, tennis, reading.

GLASER, PETER EDWARD, retired mechanical engineer, consultant, educator; b. Zatec, Bohemia, Czechoslovakia, Sept. 5, 1923; came to U.S., 1948, naturalized July, 1954; s. Hugo and Helen (Weiss) G.; m. Eva F. Graf, Oct. 16, 1955; children: David, Steven, Susan. Diploma, Leeds Coll. Tech., Eng., 1943; 1st state exam, Czech Tech U., Prague, Czechoslovakia, 1948; MS, Columbia U., N.Y.C., 1951, PhD, 1955. Head design dept. Werner Mgmt. Co., N.Y.C., 1948-53; from mem. profl. staff to cons. Arthur D. Little, Inc., Cambridge, Mass., 1955—94, v.p., 1985, cons., 1994—99; pres. Power from Space Cons., Inc., Lexington, Mass., 1995—2005; ret., 2005. Cons. NASA, Washington, 1963-67, mem. adv. coun., 1986; mem. case study task force Lunar Energy Enterpise, 1988-89; mgmt. adv. bd. Ctr. for Space Power, Tex. A&M U. System, 1990-94; sr. adv. bd. mem. Space Studies Inst., 1990—; mem. bd. assessment NIST program NRC, 1993-96; cons. NRC, Washington, 1960-62, panel mem., 1994-95, Heritage Found., Washington, 1982-83; adv. panelist Office Tech. Assessment, Washington, 1980-81; mem. Awards Adv. Coun. of Space Found., 1988-96. Editor: The Lunar Surface Layer, 1964, Thermal Imaging Techniques, 1964, Solar Power Satellites-The Emerging Energy Option, 1993, Solar Power Satellites-A Space Energy System for Earth, 2d edit., 1998, Solar Power Systems in Space; contbr. Standard Handbook of Powerplant Engineering, 1998; assoc. editor Space Power Jour., 1980-86; editor-in-chief Jour. Solar Energy, 1972-85, mem. editl. bd., 1985-93; mem. editl. bd. Space Policy, Space Power, Jour. Practical Applications in Space, Solar Energy; patentee solar power satellite, 1973; guest editor spl. issue of "Space Policy" on Space Solar Power, 1999-2000. Mem. bd. overseers Combined Jewish Philanthropies, Boston, 1984-88; voting mem. engring. coun. Columbia U., N.Y.C., 1984; advisor Space Solar Power Rsch. Soc., Japan, 1998—. Recipient Carl F. Kayan medal Columbia U., 1974, Farrington Daniels award Internat. Solar Energy Soc., Australia, 1983; named to U.S. Space Found. Space Tech. Hall of Fame, 1996. Fellow AAAS, AIAA; mem. ASME, Internat. Astron. Fedn. (chmn. space power com. 1984-89), Internat. Acad. Astronautics, Internat. Solar Energy Soc. (pres. 1967-72), Am. Astron. Soc. (bd. dirs. 1977-84), Sunsat Energy Coun. (pres. 1978-94, chmn. 1994—2000), Nat. Space Soc. (bd. advisors 1990-94, dir. 1994-97, bd. govs. 1997—), United Socs. in Space (regent 1997—), Am. Soc. for Macro-Engring., Cosmos Club (Washington). Jewish. Avocation: archeology of Southern Arabia. Home: 62 Turning Mill Rd Lexington MA 02420-1010

GLASER, ROBERT, psychology educator; b. Providence, R.I., Jan. 18, 1921; 2 children. BS, City Coll., 1942; MA, Ind. U., 1947, PhD in Psychology Measurement and Learning Theory, 1949; DSc (hon.), U. Leuven, 1980, Ind. U., 1984, U. Goteborg, 1985, U. Trondheim, 1994. Instr. psychology Ind. U., 1948-49; asst. prof. U. Ky., 1949-50; rsch. asst. prof. U. Ill., 1950-52; sr. rsch. scientist Am. Inst. Rsch., 1952-56; prof. psychology U. Pitts., 1957-72, prof. edn., 1964-72, U. prof. psychology and edn., 1972—; dir. Learning R & D Ctr., Pitts., 1963—. Cons. project industry literacy Ford Found., 1981; vis. prof. Japan Soc. Prom. Sci., 1982; mem. com. rsch., math., sci. and tech. edn. NRC, 1983, mem. math. and sci. edn. bd., 1975-87, mem. com. on devels. in the sci. of learning, 1995—; mem. forum rsch. mgmt. com. Fedn. Behaviour Psychology and Cognitive Sci., 1987-89; mem. gov. bd. Lab. for Student Success, Temple U. Ctr. for Rsch. in Human Devel. and Edn., 1996—; mem. cognitive studies for ednl. practice adv. panel James S. McDonnell Found., 1994—; mem. GRE adv. com. Ednl. Testing Svcs., 1993—, mem. nat. adult literacy survey com., 1990—; mem. nat. com. on sci. edn. stds. and assessment NAS, 1992—; mem. nat. assessment of ednl. progress com. Nat. Acad. Edn., 1989—. Recipient Outstanding Rsch. Field Instructional Materials award Am. Edn. Rsch. Assn./Am. Edn. Publishers Inst., 1970, Disting. Sci. award Applied Psychol., 1987, Higher Edn. and Software and Curriculum Innovation award EDUCOM, 1992, Citation Classic award, 1993, James McKeen Cattell Fellow award Am. Psychol. Soc., 1993, Disting. Profl. Achievment award Nat. Soc. Performance and Instrn., 1995. Mem. AAAS, Am. Psychol. Assn. (bd. sci. affairs 1988, E.L. Thorndike award, Disting. Psychol. Contrbns. award 1981), Am. Edn. Rsch. Assn. (Disting. Rsch. Edn. award 1976), Nat. Assn. Edn. Publishers (design and analysis com. 1983), psychonomic Soc., Royal Norwegian Soc. Scis. and Letters. Office: U Pitts Learning R & D Ctr Pittsburgh PA 15260

GLASER, ROBERT, communications company executive; BA in Econ., MA in Econ., BS in Computer Sci., Yale U. CEO and chmn. Progressive Networks, Seattle; various pos. Microsoft Corp., 1983—93; founder, CEO RealNetworks, Seattle, 1995—. Adv. com. on pub. interest pres. Clinton. Editor: Yale Daily News. Office: Real Networks 2601 Elliott Ave Ste 1000 Seattle WA 98121-3307

GLASER, ROBERT EDWARD, lawyer; b. Cin., Jan. 12, 1935; s. Delbert Henry and Rita Elizabeth (Arlinghaus) G.; m. Kathleen Eileen Grannen, June 17, 1961; children— Petra M., Timothy X., Mark G., Bridget M., Christopher D., Jenny M., Michael F. BS in Bus. Adminstrn. cum laude, Xavier U., Cin., 1955; LLB, U. Cin., 1960; LLM, U. Chgo., 1962; postgrad., U. Tuebingen, Fed. Republic of Germany, 1961. Bar: Ohio 1960, U.S. Dist. Ct. (no. dist.) Ohio 1963, (so. dist.) Ohio 1964, U.S. Ct. Appeals (6th cir.) 1964, U.S. Tax Ct. 1970, U.S. Ct. Internat. Trade 1971, U.S. Ct. Fed. Claims 1992, U.S. Ct. Appeals (fed. cir.) 2000. Assoc. Arter & Hadden, Cleve., 1963-69, ptnr., 1970-2001, chmn., 1983-92; owner Law Office of Robert E. Glaser, 2001—. Arbitrator Cuyahoga County Ct. Common Pleas, Ohio, 1972—, Med. Malpractice Panel, 1985—, Mediator Settlement Week, 1990; lectr. Cleve. Tax Inst., 1966—2000, mem. exec. com., 1980—84, chmn., 1982; lectr. Can.-U.S. Law Inst., 1980, Res. Officers Assn., 1970—, Ret. Officers Assn., 1995—; mem. qualified list of neutrals IRS Rev. Proc., 2003—. Contbr. articles to legal jours. Sec. Bay View Hosp., 1972-81; trustee Mental Health Rehab. and Rsch., Inc., 1975-86, mem. exec. com., 1977-81, pres., 1979-81; trustee Cmty. Legal Svcs. Cleve., Inc., 2004—, legal counsel, 2004—; mem. men's com. Cleve. Play House, 1965-2003; mem. joint mental health and corrections com. Fedn. Cmty. Planning, 1978-81; mem. Cleve. Coun. on Fgn. Affairs, 1987-2002; mem. vis. com. Coll. Law Cleve. State U., 1987-97; mem. Soc. of Benchers, Case Western Res. Univ. Coll. Law, 1988—; trustee Univ. Circle, Inc., 1989-99, mem. exec. com., 1989-99. Col. U.S. Army, ret. Ford Found. grantee, 1960. Fellow Am. Bar Found. (life); mem. Ohio Bar Assn. (gen. tax com. 1998—, lawyer assistance com. 1999—), Nat. Bar Assn., Cleve. Bar Assn. (trustee 1983-87, chmn. bd. of com. grievance and discipline trial com. 1993, gen. tax com. 1983-2004, lawyer assistance com. 1999-2004), Legal Aid Soc. Cleve., Am. Judicature Soc., 8th Jud. Conf. (life), Am. Arbitration Assn. (nat. and internat. panel arbitrators 1969—), Citizens League Greater Cleve., Order of Coif, Union Club, Pentagon Officers Athletic Club, Serra Internat., Cleve. Club (exec. com. 1987-88, 90-91, 93-98, 2000-04, pres. 1994-96, 2002-04), KC. Roman Catholic. Office: Law Office of Robert E Glaser 1150 Huntington Bldg 925 Euclid Ave Cleveland OH 44115-1475 Home: 33750 Lorain Rd North Ridgeville OH 44039 Office Phone: 216-696-2938.

GLASER, ROBERT JOY, retired internist, foundation administrator; b. St. Louis, Sept. 11, 1918; s. Joseph and Regina Glaser; m. Helen Louise Hofsommer, Apr. 1, 1949 (dec. Oct. 1999); children: Sally Louise, Joseph II, Robert Joy. SB, Harvard U., 1940, MD magna cum laude, 1943; DS (hon.), U. Health Scis.-Chgo. Med. Sch., 1972; DS (hon.), Temple U., 1973; DS (hon.), U. N.H., 1979, U. Colo., 1979; LHD, Rush Med. Coll., 1973; DS, Mt. Sinai Med. Sch., 1984; DS (hon.), Washington U., 1988, Thomas Jefferson U., 1991; DHL, Johns Hopkins U., 2000; DS (hon.), Watson Sch. of Biol. Scis., 2001. Diplomate Am. Bd. Internal Medicine. Med. intern Barnes Hosp., St. Louis, 1944, asst. resident physician, 1945—46, resident physician, 1946—47, asst. physician, 1949—57; asst. resident physician Peter Bent Brigham Hosp., Boston, 1944—45; NRC fellow med. scis. Wash. U. Med. Sch., 1947—49, instr. medicine, 1949—50, asst. prof., 1950—56, assoc. dean., 1947, asst. dean, 1953—55, assoc. prof., 1956—57, assoc. dean, 1955—57; dean, prof. medicine Med. Sch. U. Colo., 1957—63, v.p. for med. affairs, 1959—63; vis. physician Washington U. Med. Service, St. Louis City Hosp., 1950; chief svc. Washington U. Med. Svc. St. Louis City Hosp., 1950—53; cons. Washington U. Med. Service, St. Louis City Hosp., 1953—57; attending physician Colo. Gen. Hosp., Denver, 1957—63; prof. social medicine Harvard U., Boston, 1963—65; pres. Affiliated Hosps. Ctr., Inc., 1963—65; v.p. med. affairs, dean Sch. Medicine, prof. medicine Stanford U., 1965—70, acting pres., 1968, cons. prof., 1972—97, prof. emeritus, 1997—; bd. dirs. Henry J. Kaiser Family Found., 1970—83, pres., chief exec. officer, 1972—83; attending physician Columbia-Presbyn. Med. Ctr., N.Y.C., 1971—72, clin. prof. medicine, 1971—72; dir. for med. sci. Lucille P. Markey Charitable Trust, 1984—97, trustee, 1989—97. Bd. dirs. Maxygen; cons. medicine VA Hosp., Denver, 1957—63, Fitzsimons Army Hosp., Aurora, Colo., 1957—63, Lowry AFB, Denver, 1957—63; mem. nat. adv. coun. NIMH, 1970—72, Harvard Fund Coun., 1953—56, Harvard Med. Alumni Coun., 1956—59, 1991—94, pres., 1993—94; assoc. mem. streptococcal commn. Armed Forces Epidemiologic Bd., 1958—61; chmn. com. study nat. needs biomed. and behavioral rsch. pers. NAS-NRC, 1974—77; mem. vis. com. Med. Sch. Harvard U., 1968—74, Sch. Pub. Health, 1971—77; bd. visitors Charles Drew Postgrad. Med. Sch., 1972—79; mem. com. on med. affairs Yale U., 1969—82, adv. bd. Sch. Orgn. and Mgmt., 1976—84; vis. com. Tufts Med. Sch., 1974—84. Editor: Pharos, 1962—97; editor emeritus:, 1997—; contbr. articles to sci. jours., chapters to books. Bd. regents Georgetown U., 1976—78; trustee Commonwealth Fund, 1969—88, v.p., 1970—72; trustee David and Lucile Packard Found., 1984—96, trustee emeritus, 1996—; trustee Pacific Sch. Religion, 1972—77, Washington U., St. Louis, 1979—87, 1988—, trustee emeritus, 1996—; trustee Albert and Mary Lasker Found., 1998—2003, Palo Alto Med. Found., 1974—, vice chmn., 1991—2000, trustee emeritus, 2000—; mem. Sloan Commn. on Govt. in Higher Edn., 1977—79; bd. dirs. Kaiser Found. Hosps., Kaiser Found. Health Plan, 1969—79, Coun. on Founds., 1974—79, Packard Humanities Inst., 1987—. Recipient William Greenleaf Eliot Soc. Search award, 1998, Hubert H. Humphrey Cancer Rsch. Ctr. award, Disting. Citizen award for outstanding leadership of med. edn. and rsch., Harvard Club of San Francisco, Harvard medal, 2003. Master: ACP; fellow: AAAS, Royal Coll. Physicians London, Am. Philos. Soc., Am. Acad. Arts and Scis. (exec. bd., v.p. 1972—76); mem.: N.Y. Acad. Medicine (John Stearns award for lifetime achievement in medicine 2000), Inst. Medicine NAS (acting pres. 1970—71, chmn. membership com. 1970—72, mem. exec. com. 1971—73), Nat. Inst. Allergy and Infectious Disease (tng. grant com. 1957—60), Am. Soc. Exptl. Pathology, Western Assn. Physicians (councillor 1960—63), Assn. Am. Physicians, Assn. Am. Med. Colls. (asst. sec. 1956—60, chmn. com. edn. and rsch. 1958—63, mem. exec. coun. 1959—63, v.p. 1963—64, chmn.exec. coun. and assembly 1968—69, mem. exec. coun. 1976—79, Abraham Flexner award, Disting. Svc. award), Am. Soc. Clin. Investigation, Ctrl. Soc. Clin. Rsch. (councillor 1955—58), Am. Fedn. Clin. Rsch. (chmn. midwestern sect. 1954—55), Am. Clin. and Climatological Assn. (pres. 1982—83), Century Club, Harvard Club (N.Y.C.), Alpha Omega Alpha (bd. dirs. 1963—77), Sigma Xi. Personal E-mail: robert.glaser@stanford.edu.

GLASER, RONALD, microbiologist, educator; b. N.Y.C., Feb. 27, 1939; s. Irving and Pauline G.; m. Janice Kiecolt, Jan. 17, 1980; children: Andrew, Erik. BA, U. Bridgeport, 1962; MS, U. R.I., 1964; PhD, U. Conn., 1968; postgrad., Baylor Coll. Medicine, 1968-69. Asst. prof. microbiology Pa. State U., Hershey, 1970-73, assoc. prof., 1973-77, prof., 1977-78; prof. chmn. dept. med. microbiology and immunology Coll. Medicine Ohio State U., Columbus, 1978—92; reviewer NIH and NASA study sects.; assoc. dean for rsch. and grad. edn. Med. Ctr. Ohio State U., Columbus, 1992-94, assoc. v.p. health sci. rsch. Med. Ctr., 1994-2001, assoc. v.p. rsch., 2001—03. Editor: (with T. Gottleib-Stematsky) Human Herpes Virus Infections: Clinical Aspects, 1982; (with others) Epstein-Barr Virus and Human Disease, 1987; (with J. Jones) Human Herpes Virus Infections, 1994; (with J. Kiecolt-Glaser) Handbook of Human Stress, 1994. NIH postdoc. fellow, 1968-69; Franco-Am. Exch. Program; Fogarty Internat. Ctr.; NIH and INSRM fellow, 1975, 77; Leukemia Soc. Am. scholar, 1974-79. Fellow: AAAS, Acad. Behavioral Medicine Rsch. (pres. psychoneuroimmunology rsch. soc. 2003); mem.: Am. Soc. Microbiology. Office: Ohio State U 2175 Graves Hall 333 W 10th Ave Columbus OH 43210-1239 Office Phone: 614-292-5526. E-mail: glaser.1@osu.edu.

GLASER, VERA ROMANS, journalist; b. St. Louis, Apr. 21, 1916; d. Aaron L. and Mollie (Romans); m. Herbert R. Glaser, Apr. 16, 1939; 1 dau., Carol Jane Barriger. Student, Washington U., St. Louis, George Washington U., Am. U., 1937-40. Reporter-writer Nat. Aero. mag., 1943-44; reporter

Washington Times Herald, 1944-46; pub. relations specialist Great Lakes-St. Lawrence Assn., 1950-51; promotion specialist, writer Congl. Quar. News Features, 1951-54; writer-commentator radio sta. WGMS, Washington, 1954-55; mem. Washington bur. N.Y. Herald Tribune, 1955-56; press officer U.S. Senator Charles E. Potter, 1956-59; dir. pub. relations, women's div. Rep. Nat. Com., 1959-62; press officer U.S. Senator Kenneth B. Keating, 1962-63; Washington corr. N.Am. Newspaper Alliance, 1963-69, bur. chief, 1965-69; columnist, nat. corr. Knight-Ridder Newspapers, Inc., 1969-81; assoc. editor Washingtonian Mag., 1981-88, contbg. editor, 1988—; columnist Maturity News Svc., 1988-94. Mem. Pres.'s Commn. on White House Fellows, 1969, Pres.'s Task Force on Women's Rights and Responsibilities, 1970; judge 1981 Robert Kennedy Journalism Awards. Free-lance writer nat publs., radio and TV appearances Stas. WTOP-TV, ABC, PBS, C-SPAN. Mem. nat. bd. Med. Coll. Pa., 1977-88; bd. dirs. Washington Press Club Found., 1986-88; bd. dirs. Internat. Women's Media Found., 1990-98. Mem. White House Corrs. Assn., Nat. Press Club (bd. govs. 1988, 89), Washington Press Club (pres. 1971-72), Cosmos Club. Unitarian Universalist. Home and Office: 5555 Friendship Blvd Apt 724 Chevy Chase MD 20815-7243

GLASERGREEN, LAWSON SCOTT, display designer; b. Owensboro, Ky., Aug. 16, 1959; s. Carlos Lee Green and Geraldine Beasley; m. Amy Elizabeth Glaser, June 19, 1993; children: Eve, Indra; m. Yvonne Adams, May 16, 1977 (div. Apr. 1983). AS, Ky. Wesleyan Coll., 1985, BA, 1991. Draftsperson Johnson, Depp & Quisenberry, Owensboro, Ky., 1977-78; draftsperson, quality control Modern Welding Inc., Owensboro, 1978-79; designer, on-site coord. David Hocker & Assocs., Owensboro, 1979-89; project mgr. Muller Assocs., Somerville, N.J., 1996-97; p.m. designer Wall Tech., Broomfield, Colo., 1997-98, Scott Coburn & Assocs., Boulder, Colo., 1998-99, Pear Interiors subsidiary U.S. Office Products, Denver, 1999, Gen. Svcs. Adminstrn., Lakewood, Colo., 1999—2000, Fluor Global Svcs. at IBM, Boulder, 2000—. Planner Fluor Global Svcs., IBM, Boulder, Colo.; art cons. Icshthus Studios, Owensboro, 1989-94; artist-in-residence Vista Vols. in Svc. to Am., 1991, Peace Corps, 1994. Prin. works include Ky. Wesleyan Coll., 1984, David Hocker & Assocs., 1985, J.B. Speed Mus., Ky., 1986, Dimensions 88 Nat., Kans., 1988, Brescia Coll., Ky., 1990, Owensboro Mus. Fine Art, 1993, The Capitol Arts Ctr., Ky., 1991, Trans Fin. Bank, 1991—93, Art Park, 1992—94, Louisville Artsfest, 1993—94, Centro de Promocion Cultural y Deportivo, Guatemala, 1995, El Atico, 1995—96, La Fuente, 1995—96, Taller Exptl. Pinturas y Escultura, 1996, Hunterdon Art Ctr. Stone Mill Shop, N.J., 1996—97, Scott Coburn and Assocs., Colo., 1998—99, Boulder County Aides Project, 1999, 2001, Rocky Mountain PBS, Colo., 2001, A Art House, 2001, The Mikaela Found., 2002. Tex. Gas scholar Tex. Gas Transmition Corp., Ky., 1989-91. Home: 104 Longs Peak Ave Longmont CO 80501 Office: Fluor Global Svcs at IBM PO Box 9275 6300 Diagonal Hwy Boulder CO 80301-9275

GLASGOW, CONSTANCE LENORE, pediatrician; b. N.Y.C., Jan. 31, 1934; d. Lester and Octavia Louisa Glasgow; m. Twitty Junius Styles, Aug. 11, 1962; children: Scott Peterson, Auria Octavia. BS, Hunter Coll., 1955; MD, SUNY Downstate, Bklyn., 1960. Intern Syracuse (N.Y.) Upstate Med. Ctr., 1960—61; resident Albert Einstein Bronx Mcpl. Hosp. Ctr., NY, 1961—63; rotating intern Upstate Med. Ctr., Syracuse, NY; pediat. resident Jacobi Hosp./Bronx Mcpl. Hosp. Ctr., Albert Einstein U., Bronx, NY; pvt. practice physician Clifton Park, NY, 1966—. Mem. ethics com. Ellis Hosp., Schenectady, NY, 1993—. Fellow: Am. Acad. Pediat.; mem.: Capital Dist. Links (co-chair nat. trends com. 1999—). Meth. Avocations: travel, music, walking. Office: Capital Care Pediat Clifton Park 942 Route 146 Clifton Park NY 12065 Office Phone: 518-371-8000.

GLASGOW, ROBERT E., mathematics professor; s. Robert E. and Marylou Glasgow; m. Betty N. Williams; children: Alyssa R., Melody E. PhD, U. Mo., 2000. Cert. math. tchr. grades 7-12 Mo. Math tchr. Barnsdall (Okla.) HS, 1985—89; assoc. prof. S.W. Bapt. U., Bolivar, Mo., 1989—. Cons. dept. elem. and secondary edn. Mo. Math. Acad., Jefferson City, 2000—. Contbr. articles to profl. jours. Mem.: Assn. Math. Tchr. Educators, Nat. Coun. Tchrs. Math. Southern Baptist. Home: 4435 S 88th Rd Bolivar MO 65613 Office: SW Bapt U 1600 University Ave Bolivar MO 65613 Office Phone: 417-328-1597. Personal E-mail: bglasgow@sbuniv.edu.

GLASGOW, ROBERT EFROM, lawyer; b. Portland, Oreg., Nov. 13, 1944; s. Joseph and Lee (Friedman) G.; m. Lesley G. Veltman, June 16, 1968; children: Jordan Robert, Emily Samantha. BA, George Washington U., 1966, JD with honors, 1969. Bar: Oreg. 1969. Assoc. Dusenbery, Martin, Beatty, Bischoff & Templeton, Portland, 1969-72; ptnr. Martin, Bischoff, Templeton & Biggs, Portland, 1973-76, Glasgow & Kelly, Portland, 1977-79, Glasgow & Kelly, PC, 1980-85, pres., 1982-85, Glasgow & Wight, PC, 1985-92; of counsel Black Helterline LLP, Portland, 1992—. Trustee Multnomah County Legal Aid Svc., 1974-76, chmn., 1976; trustee Mittleman Jewish Cmty. Ctr., 1975-76, 86-97, pres., 1991-93; trustee Oreg. Legal Svcs. Corp., 1980-82, Am. Jewish Com., Oreg., 1996—, treas., 1998-99, v.p., 1999-2000, pres., 2000-02; trustee, v.p. Oreg. Uniting, 2002-04; trustee Uniting To Understand Racism, 2004—; activities coun. Oreg. Art Inst., 1984-87; Dem. precinctman, 1986-87. Mem. ABA, Oreg. Bar Assn., Multnomah Bar Assn., West Hills Racquet Club (Portland). Office: 1900 Fox Tower 805 SW Broadway Portland OR 97205 Office Phone: 503-224-5560. Business E-Mail: reg@bhlaw.com.

GLASGOW, WILLIAM JACOB, lawyer, venture capitalist, business executive; b. Portland, Oreg., Sept. 29, 1946; s. Joseph Glasgow and Lena (Friedman) Schiff; m. Renée Vonfeld, Aug. 30, 1969; children: Joshua, Andrew. BS magna cum laude, U. Pa., 1968; JD magna cum laude, Harvard U., 1972. Bar: Oreg. 1972, U.S. Dist. Ct. Oreg. 1972, U.S. Ct. Appeals (9th cir.) 1978. Assoc. Rives, Bonyhadi & Drummond, Portland, 1972-76, ptnr., 1976-79; mng. ptnr. Perkins Coie, Portland, 1983-88; sr. v.p., gen. counsel PacifiCorp Fin. Svcs. Inc., Portland, 1988-89, chmn., CEO, 1989-95; sr. v.p. PacifiCorp, Portland, 1992-93, sr. v.p., CFO, 1993-95; pres. PacifiCorp Holdings Inc., Portland, 1992-95; pres., dir. NERCO, Inc., Portland, 1992-93; dir. Pacific-Telecom, Inc., 1992-93; co-chmn. Shaw, Glasgow & Co. LLC, 1995-96; pres., CEO BCN Data Sys. (a Bechtel/CellNet Data Sys. joint venture), Portland, 1996-2000, Madrona Venture Group LLP, Portland, 2000—; ret. PacifiCorp, Portland, 1996. Pres. bd. trustees Oreg. Mus. Sci. and Industry, Portland, 1981; pres. N.W. Fin. Symposium, Portland, 1985; trustee Oreg. Art Inst., 1990-92, 94—, Oreg. Grad. Inst. Sci. and Tech., 1991—, Discovery Inst., 1992—; pres. Portland Met. Sports Authority, 1992—; v.p. NIKE World Masters Games, 1994—; bd. dirs. Internat. World Masters Games, 1994—. Mem. Oreg. Bar Assn., Portland C. of C. (bd. dirs. 1983), Harvard Law Sch. Alumni Assn. (pres. Oreg. chpt. 1981). Democrat. Home: 3088 SW Fairmount Blvd Portland OR 97201-1439

GLASHOW, SHELDON LEE, physicist, researcher; b. NYC, Dec. 5, 1932; s. Lewis and Bella (Rubin) Glashow; m. Joan Glashow; children: Jason David, Jordan, Brian Lewis, Rebecca Lee. AB, Cornell U., 1954; AM, Harvard U., 1955, PhD, 1959; DSc (hon.), Yeshiva U., 1978, U. Marseille, 1982, Adelphi U., 1989, Bar Ilan U., 1989, Gustave Adolphus Coll., 1989, Case Western Res. U., 2001. NSF fellow U. Copenhagen, Denmark, 1958—60; rsch. fellow Calif. Inst. Tech., 1960—61; asst. prof. Stanford U., 1961—62; asst. prof., assoc. prof. U. Calif., Berkeley, 1962—66; prof. physics Harvard U., 1967—84, Higgins prof. physics, 1979—2000; disting. sci. Boston U., 1984—2000; Mellon prof. scis. Harvard U., 1988—93, Higgins prof. of physics emeritus, 2000—; Arthur G.B. Metcalf prof. sci. Boston U., 2000—. Cons. Brookhaven Nat. Lab., 1964, 1966—73; vis. prof. U. Marseille, 1970, MIT, 1974; cons. Brookhaven Nat. Lab., 1975; mem. sci. policy com. CERN, 1979—84; vis. prof. MIT, 1980, Boston U., 1983; affiliated sr. scientist U. Houston, 1983—96; univ. scholar Tex. A&M U., 1983—86; hon. prof. U. Nanjing, 1998—. Author (with Ben Bova): Interactions, 1988; author: Charm of Physics, 1990, From Alchemy to Quarks, 1994; contbr. articles to profl. jours. and popular mags.; founding editor Quantum mag., 1989—2000. Pres. Andrei Sakharov Inst., 1980—85, Nat. Com. for Excellence in Edn., 1985—88. Recipient J.R. Oppenheimer Meml. prize, 1977, George Ledlie prize, 1978, Nobel prize in Physics, 1979, Castiglione di Sicilia prize, 1983, Erice Sci. for Peace prize, 1991; fellow NSF, 1955—60, Sloan, 1962—66, CERN vis., 1968. Fellow: AAAS, Am. Phys. Soc.; mem.: NAS, Am. Philosophical Soc., Costa Rica Acad. Sci. (fgn.), Korean Acad. Sci. (fgn.), Russian Acad. Sci. (fgn.), Am. Acad. Arts and Scis., Sigma Xi, Phi Beta Kappa. Achievements include contbns. to theory of unified weak and electromagnetic interactions between elementary particles, including alia the prediction of the weak neutral current. E-mail: slg@bu.edu.*

GLASKOX, ANNA C, secondary school educator; b. Ackerman, Mo., June 16, 1965; d. Mayron Isaac and Fannie Mullen Cummins; m. John William Glaskox, Jan. 31, 1976; children: James, Rachael. BS in elem. edn., Mo. State U., 1990; BS in exceptional edn., 1995. Tchr. First Bapt. Ch., Gautier, Miss., 1980—85; asst. tchr. Gautier Elem., Miss., 1985—89, Weir Elem., Miss., 1990—91; tchr. Ethel H.S., Miss., 1991—. Cons. Mo. Wriing Inst., 1995—2003; transition coord. Attala County, 1990—. Office: Ethel HS P O Box 340 Ethel MS 39067 Personal E-mail: acglaskox@lycos.com.

GLASKY, ALVIN JERALD, retired medical research scientist; b. Chgo., June 16, 1933; s. Oscar and Bessie (Akwa) G.; m. Rosalie Anne Hanfling, Aug. 25, 1957; children: Michelle S., Karen R., Mark J., Ira D. BS in Pharmacy, U. Ill., Chgo., 1954, PhD in Biochemistry, 1958. Dir. biochem. research Michael Reese Hosp., Chgo., 1959-61; research pharmacologist Abbott Labs., North Chicago, Ill., 1961-66; v.p. research ICN, Burbank, Calif., 1966-68; pres., CEO Newport Pharms., Inc., Newport Beach, Calif., 1968—86, Neo Therapeutics, Inc., Irvine, Calif., 1987—2002; regents prof. U. Calif., Irvine, 1998—2000. Contbr. articles to profl. jours. Mem. AAAS, Am. Pharm. Assn., Calif. Pharm. Assn., Am. Soc. Microbiology, Am. Chem. Soc., Rho Chi. Jewish. Avocations: tennis, swimming, theater, wine. Home: 28872 Alanya Mission Viejo CA 92692-4965

GLASOFER, ERIC DAVID, allergist, immunologist, pediatrician, educator; b. Bklyn., May 23, 1950; BS, Lehigh U., 1971; PhD in Pharmacology, Thomas Jefferson U., 1975; MD, Jefferson Med. Coll., 1978. Resident pediat. Thomas Jefferson U. Hosp., Phila., 1978-81, fellow allergy and immunology, 1981-83; attending physician Our Lady of Lourdes Med. Ctr., Camden, NJ, West Jersey/Virtua Health Sys. Clin. asst. prof. pediat. Jefferson Med. Coll. Mem. AMA, Am. Acad. Allergy, Asthma and Immunology, Am. Coll. Allergy, Asthma and Immunology Office: 1000 White Horse Rd Ste 904 Voorhees NJ 08043-4415 Office Phone: 856-772-1200.

GLASRUD, CLARENCE ARTHUR, language educator; b. Cass County, N.D., Oct. 15, 1911; s. Claus Christian Glasrud and Anna Maren Skrove Haugan; m. Barbara Adams Crawford, June 19, 1948; 1 child, Charles Crawford. BS, Moorhead State Tchrs. Coll., 1933; MA, Harvard U., 1951, PhD, 1953. Tchr. Becker County (Minn.) Dist. 107, 1929-30, Jr. H.S., Pelican Rapids, Minn., 1935-36, H.S., Lake City, Minn., 1936-40, Mankato, Minn., 1940-42; prof. Moorhead (Minn.) State Tchrs. Coll., 1947-57, Moorhead State Coll., 1957-75, chmn. English dept., 1949-72; prof. Moorhead State U., 1975-77; ret. Editor: The Age of Anxiety, 1960, Hjalmar Hjorth Boyesen, 1963, A Heritage Deferred, 1981, Roy Johnson's Red River Valley, 1982, A Special Relationship, 1983, A Heritage Fulfilled, 1984, L'Heritage Tranquille, 1987, The Moorhead Normal School: A History, 1987, Moorhead State Teachers College: A History, 1989. Pres. Clay County Hist. Soc., Moorhead, 1960-78; rsch. dir. Red River Valley Hist. Soc., Moorhead, 1974-84; alderman City Coun., Moorhead, 1980-84. Tech. sgt. U.S. Army Air Corps, 1942-45, ETO. Named Disting. Alumnus, Moorhead State Coll., 1971, Century Alumnus, Moorhead State U., 1987. Mem. NEA (life), MLA (life), Norwegian Am. Hist. Assn. (life, bd. editors 1964-92), Studies in Am. Fiction (adv. editor 1974—), Rotary, Am. Legion. Avocations: tennis, gardening, travel. Home: 422 6th St S Moorhead MN 56560-2735

GLASS, ANDREW JAMES, newspaper editor; b. Warsaw, Nov. 30, 1935; came to U.S., 1941, naturalized, 1948; s. Martin Allan and Wanda (Mosewicka) G.; m. Eleanor Attianese Sorrentino, June 3, 1962; 1 child, Samuel Sorrentino. BA, Yale U., 1957. Fin. reporter N.Y. Herald Tribune, 1959-62, chief congl. corr., 1963-66; mem. nat. staff Washington Post, 1966-68; exec. asst. to Senator Charles Percy, U.S. Senate, Washington, 1968-70; sr. editor Nat. Jour., Washington, 1970-74; Washington corr. Cox Newspapers, 1974-77, chief Washington Bur., 1977-97, sr. corr., 1997—2001; mng. editor The Hill Newspaper, Washington, 2002—04, columnist, 2003—. Syndicated columnist N.Y. Times News Svc., 1980-2001. Chmn. Corr. Com. for Refugee Relief, 1975—78. With U.S. Army, 1958, mem. USAR, 1958—64. Fellow Shorenstein, J.F. Kennedy Sch. Govt., Harvard U., 2001. Mem.: Am. Soc. Newspaper Editors, Met. Club Washington. Office: The Hill 755 15th St NW Ste 1140 Washington DC 20005 Office Phone: 202-628-8500. E-mail: ajglass@cpcug.org, aglass@thehill.com.

GLASS, DAVID CARTER, psychologist, educator; b. N.Y.C., Sept. 17, 1930; s. Samuel and Dorothy (Braunstein) Glass; m. Kathleen Kehoe, May 15, 1982. AB, NYU, 1952, MA, 1954, PhD, 1959, postdoctoral fellow, 1959—62. Mem. staff social psychologist Russell Sage Found., N.Y.C., 1963—71; assoc. prof. psychology Rockefeller U., N.Y.C., 1966—68; prof. psychology NYU, N.Y.C., 1968—72; chmn., prof. dept. psychology U. Tex., Austin, Tex., 1972—75; vis. scholar Russell Sage Found., 1975—76; prof. psychology, dir. Lab. Biobehavior CUNY Grad. Ctr., N.Y.C., 1976—82; prof. psychology and psychiatry SUNY, Stony Brook, 1982—94, vice provost for rsch. and grad. studies, 1982—86, spl. advisor to provost, 1987—89, v.p. for rsch., 1990—93, prof. emeritus psychology, 1994—. Vis. prof. psychology Inst. Health Rutgers U., New Brunswick, NJ, 1994—96; interim dir. rsch. Kessler Inst., West Orange, NJ, 1997—98; cons. in field. Author: Behavior Patterns, Stress and Coronary Disease, 1977; co-author (with J.E. Singer): Urban Stress: Experiments in Noise and Social Stressors, 1972 (AAAS prize, 71); contbr. articles to profl. jours. Fellow: AAAS, APA; mem.: Acad. Behavioral Medicine Rsch. (pres. 1981—82), Soc. Expl. Social Psychology, Soc. Psychophysiol. Rsch., Am. Psychosomatic Soc., Phi Kappa Phi, Sigma Xi. Home: 330 E 33rd St Apt 11J New York NY 10016-9437

GLASS, DAVID D., retail executive, professional sports team executive; b. Liberty, Mo., 1935; m. Ruth Glass; 3 children. Gen. mgr. Crank Drug Co., 1957-67; v.p. Consumers Markets Inc., 1967-76; exec. v.p. fin. Wal-Mart Stores Inc., Bentonville, Ark., to 1976, vice chmn., CFO, 1976-84, pres., 1984-2000, COO, 1984-88, CEO, 1988-2000, also bd. dirs., chmn. exec. commn., 2000—; CEO, chmn. bd. dirs. Kansas City Royals, 1993—. Bd. dir. Nat. Baseball Hall of Fame, Cooperstown. Office: Wal-Mart Stores Inc 702 SW 8th St Bentonville AR 72716-6299 also: Kansas City Royals PO Box 419969 Kansas City MO 64141-6969*

GLASS, DENNIS ROBERT, insurance company executive; b. Milw., Oct. 4, 1949; s. Robert Joseph and Carmella (Bellart) Glass; m. Deborah Glass, 1984; 2 children. BBA, MBA, U. Wis.-Milw. Investment analyst Northwestern Mut. Life Ins. Co., Milw., 1973-77, v.p., treas., 1977-82, mgr. treasury ops., 1983; dir. fin., treas. Portman Cos., Atlanta, 1983, sr. v.p., chief fin. officer, 1983-91; exec. v.p., CFO Protective Life Corp., 1991-93; sr. v.p., CFO Jefferson-Pilot Corp., 1993, exec. v.p., CFO, pres. fin. operations, CFO, 1999—2001, pres., COO, 2001—04, pres., CEO, 2004—. Mem. academic staff U. Wis., Mliw., 1973-83; mem. adv. bd. Wachovia. Organizer United Way, Milw.; mem. Leadership Atlanta, 1985—86, Greensboro Partnership; bd. mem. Am. Coun. Life Insurers, Ins. Marketplace Stds. Assn., Life Office Mgmt. Assn., Wachovia Bank NC, Greensboro. Office: Jefferson Pilot Corp 100 N Greene St Greensboro NC 27401-2545 Office Phone: 336-691-3000.

GLASS, DONALD DAVID, anesthesiologist; b. Johnston, Pa., May 1, 1942; s. Donald S. and Meriel L. Glass; m. Bonnell W. Glass, Sept. 5, 1965 (div. Nov. 1992); children: David J., Jennifer J.; m. Alice M. Goldwine, June 27, 1998. Student, U. Pitts., 1960-62; MD, W.Va. U., 1966. Diplomate Am. Bd. Anesthesiology (chmn. CCM examination com. 1988—, asst. sec.-treas. 1991-94, chair com. on Americans and Disabilities Act 1991, chair credentials com. 1992, sec.-treas. 1994-96, pres. 1996-97); cert. spl. qualifications in critical care medicine, cert. continued demonstration of qualifications; lic. anesthesiologist Miss., N.H. Rsch. assoc. dept. surgery W.Va. U., 1965-66; intern in surgery U. Pitts., 1966-67, resident in surgery, 1969-70; asst. resident in anesthesia Mass. Gen. Hosp., Boston, 1970-71, chief resident in anesthesiology, 1971-72; clin. fellow Harvard U., 1972; dir. edn. dept. anesthesiology, dir. cardiovascu. anesthesia U. Miss. Med. Ctr., Jackson, 1972-77, asst. dir. inhalation therapy, 1972-77, asst. prof. anesthesia, 1972-76, med. dir. ICU, 1975-77, assoc. prof. anesthesiology and surgery, 1976-77; assoc. prof. surgery and medicine Med. Sch., Dartmouth Coll., Hanover, N.H., 1977-84, prof. surgery and medicine, 1984-88, prof. anesthesiology and medicine, 1988—; med. dir. adult unit ICU Dartmouth-Hitchcock Med. Ctr., Hanover, 1977-87, chief sect. anesthesiology, 1983-89, chmn. dept. anesthesiology, 1989. Mem nat. com. Accreditation Coun. for Grad. Med. edn., 1997—. Co-editor: (with M.P. Yeager) Anesthetic Management of the Vascular Surgical Patient, 1990; contbr. chpts. to books including Rhoads Textbook of Surgery, 1976, Intensive Care Therapeutics, 1980, Cardiac Anesthesia, 1987, Anesthesia in Vascular Surgery, 1989; contbr. numerous articles to med. jours. Elected rep. to ACGME Coun. Am. Bd. Med. Specialists. Recipient Lange Med. Publs. award, 1966. Fellow Am. Coll. Anesthesiology, Am. Coll. Chest Physicians, Faculty of Anesthesiologists of Royal Australian Coll. Surgeons; mem. Am. Soc. Anesthesiologists (U. Miss. preceptorship com. liaison 1974, coord. ICU workshop 1976, chmn. com. on sci. papers 1986, vice chmn. ann. meeting 1987, chmn. ann. meeting 1988, chair ABA-ASA joint select com. on recertification 1988), Internat. Anesthesia Rsch. Soc., Soc. Critical Care Medicine, Assn. Cardiac Anesthesiologists (elected), Assn. Univ. Anesthesiologists, Assn. Critical Care Anesthesiologists, N.H./Vt. Soc. Anesthsiologists, Soc. Acad. Anesthesia Chairmen, Alpha Omega Alpha. Home: 261 River Rd Lyme NH 03768-3008 Office: Dartmouth Hitchock Med Ctr Dept Anesthesiology Medical Center Dr Lebanon NH 03756

GLASS, DOROTHEA DANIELS, physiatrist, educator; b. NYC; d. Maurice B. and Anna S. (Kleegman) Daniels; m. Robert E. Glass, June 23, 1940; children: Anne Glass Roth, Deborah, Catherine Glass Barrett, Eugene. BA, Cornell U., 1940; MD, Woman's Med. Coll. Pa., 1954; postgrad., U. Pa., 1960—61; DMS (hon.), Med. Coll. Pa., 1987. Diplomate Am. Bd. Phys. Medicine and Rehab. (guest bd. examiner 1978, 89). Intern Albert Einstein Med. Ctr., Phila., 1954-55, clin. asst. dept. medicine, 1956-59, attending phys. medicine and rehab., 1968-70, chmn. dept. phys. medicine and rehab., sr. attending, 1971-85; chief rehab. medicine VA Med. Ctr., Miami, Fla., 1985-95; clin. prof. dept. orthop. and rehab. U. Miami Sch. Medicine, 1985—. Lois Mattox Miller fellow preventive medicine Woman's Med. Coll. Pa., 1955-56, instr. preventive medicine, 1956-59, instr. medicine, 1960-62; resident phys. medicine and rehab. VA Hosp., Phila., 1959-62, chief phys. medicine and rehab., 1966-68, cons., 1968-82; asst. clin. dir. Jefferson Med. Coll. Hosp., Phila., 1963-66, Camden County Stroke Program, Cooper Hosp., Camden, N.J., 1963-66; gen. practice medicine, Phila., 1956-59; asst. med. dir., chief phys. medicine and rehab. Moss Rehab. Hosp., Phila., 1968-70, med. dir., 1971-82, sr. cons., 1982-; mem. active staff Temple U., Phila., 1968-, asso. prof. rehab. medicine, 1968-73, prof., 1973-, dir. residency tng. rehab. medicine, 1968-82; program dir. Rehab. Rsch. and Tng. Ctr., 1977-80, chmn. dept. rehab. medicine, 1977-82; staff physician Hosp. Med. Coll. Pa., Phila., 1955-59, vis. assoc. prof. neurology, 1973-79, clin. prof., 1977-82, vis. prof., 1982-96; mem. cons. staff Frankford Hosp., Phila., 1968-82, Phila. Geriatric Center, 1975-82; mem. active staff Willowcrest-Bamberger Hosp., Phila., 1980-82; asso. phys. medicine and rehab. U. Pa. Sch. Medicine, Phila., 1962-66; asst. prof. clin. phys. medicine and rehab., 1966-68; asst. clin. dir. dept. phys. medicine and rehab. Jefferson Med. Coll., Phila., 1963-66; cons. Vols. in Medicine Clinic, Stuart, Fla., 1996—. Contbr. articles to profl. jours. Mem. profl. adv. com. Easter Seal Soc. Crippled Children and Adults Pa., 1975-82; active Goodwill Industries Phila., 1973-82, Cmty. Home Health Svcs. Phila., 1974-82, Ea. Pa. chpt. Arthritis Found., 1968-82. Recipient Humanitarian Svc. cert. Gov.'s Com. on Employment Handicapped, 1974, Outstanding Alumnae award Commonwealth of Pa. Bd., Hosp. Med. Coll. Pa., 1975, Humanitarian award Pa. Easter Seal Soc., 1981, John Eiselie Davis award Am. Kinesiotherapy Assn., 1988, Carl Haven Young Svc. award, 1994, Disting. Career award Moss Rehab. Hosp., 1997, Outstanding Svc. and Accomplishments award Fla. Soc. Phys. Medicine and Rehab., 2001, Susan B. Anthony award LWV of Martin County, 2002. Fellow Am. Congress Rehab. Medicine; mem. AMA, Am. Acad. Med. Dirs., Am. Acad. Phys. Medicine and Rehab. (Disting. Clinician award 1995, Krusen award 2000), Am. Assn. Electromyography and Electrodiagnosis (assoc.), Am. Assn. Sex Educators, Counselors and Therapists, Am. Burn Assn., Am. Coll. Angiology, Am. Coll. Utilization Rev., Am. Congress Rehab. Medicine (bd. govs. 1979-85, pres. 1986-87, gold Key award 1989), Am. Heart Assn. (coun. on cerebrovascular disease), Am. Lung Assn. Phila. and Montgomery County (bd. dirs. 1977-79), Am. Med. Women's Assn., Assn. Acad. Physiatrists, Assn. Med. Rehab. Dirs. and Coordinators, Coll. Physicians Phila., Emergency Care Rsch. Inst., Gerontol. Soc., Internat. Assn. Rehab. Facilities, Internat. Rehab. Medicine Assn., Pan Am. Med. Assn., Fla. Med. Assn., Fla. Soc. Phys. Medicine and Rehab. (pres. 1975-77, Award for Outstanding Svc. in Rehab. Medicine 2001), Pa. Med. Soc. (phys. medicine and rehab. adv. com. 1975-82), Pa. Thoracic Soc., Delaware Valley Hosp. Coun. Forum, Phila. Med. Soc., Phila. PSRO (bd. dirs. 1975-82), Phila. Soc. Phys. Medicine and Rehab. (pres. 1968-69), Laennec Soc. Phila., Royal Soc. Health, Alpha Omega Alpha. E-mail: glassrd@earthlink.net.

GLASS, J. KENNETH, bank executive; b. 1946; Grad., Harding U., 1969. With FedEx Corp., GTx, Inc., Arthur Andersen & Co., Memphis, 1970-74, First Horizon Nat. Corp., Memphis, 1974—, pres. Tenn. banking group, 1999; pres., retail fin. svc. First Horizon Nat. Bank, 1999—2001, First Horizon Nat. Corp., 2000—01, pres., COO, 2001—02, pres., CEO, 2002—, chmn., 2004—. Mem. Federal Reserve Advisory Council, 2005—; bd. dirs. FedEx Corp., GTx, Inc., Financial Services Roundtable, Tenn. Bankers Assn. Office: First Horizon Nat Corp 165 Madison Ave Memphis TN 38103-2723*

GLASS, JAMES ARTHUR, historian, educator; b. Goshen, NY, Sept. 19, 1952; s. Robert Leavitt and Marjory Brown Glass. BA in History and Spanish, Ind. Ctrl. Coll., Indpls., 1974; MA in Latin Am. History, Ind. U., Bloomington, 1975; MA in History of Urban Devel., Cornell U., Ithaca, 1984, PhD in History of Architecture and Urban Devel., 1987. Historian Indpls. Hist. Preservation Commn., 1975—82; project supr., hist. Am. bldgs. survey Nat. Pk. Svc., Washington, 1984—85; project mgr., hist. preservation Greenhorne & O'Mara, Inc., Greenbelt, Md., 1988—90; dir., Ind. divsn. hist. preservation & archaeology State of Ind., Indpls., 1990—94; dir., grad. program hist. preservation Ball State U., Muncie, Ind., 1994—, dir., ctr. hist. preservation, 2004—. Cons. Hist. Landmarks Found. Ind., Indpls., 1978, 81; mem. adv. bd. Nat. Trust Hist. Preservation, Washington, 1997—; bd. dirs. Del. County Hist. Alliance, Muncie, Ind., 1995—98, Hist. Landmarks Found. Ind., Indpls., 1995—. Author: (book) The Beginnings of A New National Historic Preservation Program, 1957-1969, 1990, (monthly newspaper column) Indpls. Star, 2003—; contbr. articles to profl. mag. Bd. dirs. You and the Year 2000, Inc., Muncie, Ind., 1998—2001; mem. millenium task force State of Ind., Indpls., 1998—2001. Named Sagamore of the Wabash, Gov. Evan Bagh of Ind., 1994; Cornell U. Grad. fellowship, 1986, Ronald F. Lee Rsch. fellowship, Ea. Nat. Pk. and Monument Assn., 1985. Mem.: Ind. Hist. Soc., Soc. Archtl. Historians, Am. Assn. State and Local History. Avocations: photography, travel, water-skiing, swimming, reading. Office: Divadgo Hist Preserv Dept Archit Ball State U Muncie IN 47306

GLASS, JERROLD A., air transportation executive; Grad., Boston U.; MPA in Mgmt. Sci., George Washington U. Various sr. positions Airline Indsl. Rels. Conf., 1980—89; pres., founder J. Glass and Assocs., 1989—2002; sr. v.p. employee rels. US Airways Inc., Arlington, Va., 2002—. Asst. econ. studies AAUP. Office: US Airways 2345 Crystal Dr Arlington VA 22227

GLASS, JOEL, lawyer; b. N.Y.C., Nov. 17, 1942; s. Sam and Ruth (Neselrod) G.; m. Sheila Zolenge, Apr. 30, 1983. BA, U. Buffalo, 1965; JD, Bklyn. Law Sch., 1968. Bar: N.Y. 1968. Assoc. Ackerman, Salwen & Linzer, N.Y.C., 1968—96; ptnr. Ackerman, Salwen & Glass, N.Y.C., 1996—, Saretsky, Katx, Dranoff & Glass, N.Y.C., 1997—. Lectr. Mt. Sinai Sch. Medicine, Emergency Care Inst., Sch. for Continuing Edn. Montefiore Hosp. and Med. Center, N.J. Hosp. Assn., Acad. Medicine, Hosp. Edn. and Research

Fund, United Hosp. Fund.; cons. N.Y. State Assembly Ins. Com.; vol. hosp. rep. McGill Commn. on Malpractice and other med. hearings; mem. med. malpractice task force Am. Hosp. Assn. Author: (with Gallet, Glass & Minkowitz) Rent Stabilization and Control Laws of New York, 1972. Served with USNG, 1970. N.Y. State Regents scholar, 1961, Nat. Merit scholar, 1961. Mem. ABA (med. legal com., health com.), N.Y. State Bar Assn., Assn. of Bar of City of N.Y. (liability ins. com., medicine and law com., med. malpractice com.), Greater N.Y. Hosp. Assn. (legal com. study of arbitration and mapractice), Non-Profit Coordinating Com. N.Y. (liability ins. com.). Office: Saretsky Katz Dranoff & Glass 331 Madison Ave New York NY 10017 E-mail: Joelg@skdglaw.com.

GLASS, JOHN DEREK See HOOPER, IAN

GLASS, KENNETH EDWARD, management consultant; b. Fort Thomas, Ky., Sept. 28, 1940; s. Clarence E. and Lucille (Garrison) Glass; m. Nancy Romanek, May 9, 1964; children: Ryan, Lara. ME, U. Cin., 1963, MS, 1965, grad. student, 1967. Registered profl. engr., Ohio; lic. Airline Transport Pilot. With Allis Chalmers Mfg. Co., Cin. and Eng., 1963—73; v.p. mfg. Fiat Allis Contrn. Machinery, Inc., Chgo., 1973—75; pres. Perkins Diesel Corp., Canton, Ohio, 1975—77; pres., CEO Massey-Ferguson, Inc., Des Moines, 1978; v.p., gen. mgr. N.Am. ops. Massey Ferguson Ltd., Des Moines, 1978; chmn., pres., CEO Union Metal Mfg. Co., Canton, Ohio, 1979—85; pres. Glass & Assocs. Inc. Glass & Assocs. Inc., 1985—2004, chmn., 1996—2005; pres. Stony Point Group, Inc., 1996—, also bd. dirs., chmn., 2005—. Chmn. Utica Corp., 2001—, UCA Holdings, 2001—, TECT Corp. Trustee U. Cin. Found.; dir. N.C. Outward Bound Sch., bd. dirs. Mem.: Young Presidents Orgn., Turnaround Mgmt. Assn. (bd. dirs.), Assn. Cert. Turnaround Profls. (bd. dirs., v.p. 1993—94, pres. 1995—96), Am. Bankrupcy Inst., Pi Tau Sigma. Achievements include patentee in field. Office Phone: 828-210-8120. Personal E-mail: keglass@attglobal.net.

GLASS, LAWRENCE, research scientist; Sr. v.p., dir. devel. SRA Technologies, Inc., Falls Church, Va.; pres., CEO SRA Life Sci., 1998—2000; exec. v.p. Corp. Develop. Virco Lab, Inc.; chief strategy officer, sr. cons. Panacea Pharmaceuticals, Inc., Gaithersburg, Md. Office: Panacea Pharms, Inc 207 Perry Pkw, Ste 2 Gaithersburg MD 20877 Office Phone: 240-243-8000. Office Fax: 240-465-0450. E-mail: LGlass@PanaceaPharma.com.*

GLASS, MARY JEAN, management executive; b. Urbana, Ill., Nov. 27, 1964; d. Sandra Kay and Bobby Dee Egner; 1 child, Jacob Steven. BS in Orgnl. Leadership, Mid-Continent U., 2001. Cert. quality auditor Am. Soc. Quality, 1995. Staff sgt. USAF, 1985, med. svc. specialist Belleville, Ill., 1985—89, med. svc. technician RAF Greenham Common, 1989—91; quality assurance technician North Star Steel Ky., Calvert City, Ky., 1991—99; quality assurance supr. Dura Automotive Sys., Inc., Fulton, Ky., 1999—2002; ISO coord. Jakel, Inc., Murray, Ky., 2002—04; with Newcomb Oil, Benton, Ky., 2004—. Internat. peace amb. Am. Biog. Soc.; capt. Dem. Nat. Party, Benton, Ky., 2003. Decorated Outstanding Unit with one oak leaf cluster USAF, Nat. Def. Svc. medal; named Woman of Yr., Am. Biog. Inst., 2002. Mem.: Am. Soc. Quality (publicity officer 1987—89). Democrat. Pentecostal. Avocations: reading, writing, internet. Home: 279 US Hwy 68E Benton KY 42025 Office: Newcomb Oil LLC 406 Main St Benton KY 42025 Office Phone: 270-527-3004. Personal E-mail: glaspane@bellsouth.net.

GLASS, PHILIP, composer, musician; b. Balt., Jan. 31, 1937; s. Benjamin C. and Ida (Gouline) Glass; m. JoAnne Akalaitas (div.); children: Juliet, Zachary; m. Luba Burtyk, 1980 (div.); m. Candy Jernigan (dec. 1991); m. Holly Critchlow, 2001; 1 child, Cameron. AB, U. Chgo., Ill., 1956; MS in Composition, Julliard Sch. Music, 1964; composition studies with, Vincent Persichetti, 1962, William Bergsma, Nadia Boulanger, Paris, 1964—66, Steve Reich, Darius Milhaud; studied flute, Peabody Conservatory. Began creating music for theatre while studying in Paris; composer in residence Pitts. Pub. Sch., 1962—64; worked and studied with Ravi Shankar, 1965—66; founder, dir. Philip Glass Ensemble, 1967—; owner Dunvagen Music Pubs.; founder Chatham Sq. Prodns., NYC, 1972. Composer of incidental music, film scores, chamber music, choral works and songs; various European concert tours, 1968—, US tours, 1972—; composer: Strung Out, 1967, In Again Out Again, 1967, Pieces in the Shape of a Square, 1968, How Now, 1968, Red Horse Animation, 1968, Two Pages, 1968, Music in Similar Motion, 1969, Music in Contrary Motion, 1969, Music in Eight Parts, 1969, Music in Fifths, 1969, Gradus, 1969, Music with Changing Parts, 1971, Music in Twelve Parts, 1971—74, Music for Voices, 1972, Another Look at Harmony, 1975, The Lost Ones, 1975, The St. and the Football Player, 1975, Einstein On The Beach, 1976, Modern Love Waltz, 1977, Dressed Like an Egg, 1977, Fourth Series Part I, 1978, Music for a Performance/Reading by C. DeJong: Fourth Series Part II, 1978, Cascando, 1979, Geometry of a Cir., 1979, Mercier and Camier, 1979, Dance No. 2, 1979, Dance No. 4, 1979, Mad Rush: Fourth Series Part III, 1979, Madrigal Opera: The Panther, 1980, Satyagraha, 1980, Facades, 1981, Vessels, 1981, Habeve Song, 1982, The Photographer, 1982, Hymn to the Sun, 1982, The Photographer, 1983, Akhnaten, 1983, The Civil Wars: A Tree is Best Measured When It Is Down, 1983, Pages from Cold Harbor, 1983, Floe, 1983, String Quartet No. 2: Co., 1983, Endgame, 1984, Glassworks, 1984, Dance from Akhnaten, 1984, String Quartet No. 3: Mishima, 1985, The Juniper Tree, 1985, Songs from Liquid Days, 1986, Three Songs, 1986, In the Upper Room, 1986, Dialogue, 1986, A Descent Into the Maelstrom, 1986, The Light for Orchestra, 1987, Itaipu, 1988, The Fall of the House of Usher, 1988, 1000 Airplanes on the Roof, 1988, The Making of the Representative for Planet 8, 1988, The Canyon, 1988, String Quartet No. 4: Boczak, 1989, Hydrogen Jukebox, 1989, The White Raven, 1991, The Voyage, 1992, Orphée, chamber opera after Couteau, 1993, Low Symphony, 1993, La Belle et la Bête, 1994, Symphony No. 2, 1994, The Marriages Between Zones Three, Four and Five, 1997, Aguas de Amazonia, 1999, Passage, 2001, The Man in the Bath, 2001, Dancissimo, 2001, Notes, 2001, Diaspora, 2001, Voices for Organ, Didgeridoo and Narrator, 2001, Philip on Film, 2001, The Elephant Man, 2002, Symphony No. 6 Plutonian Ode, 2002, Glasswork, 2003, (films) North Star: Mark Di Suvero, 1977, Koyaanisqatsi, 1983, Mishima, 1984, Dead End Kids, 1986, Hamburger Hill, 1987, Powaqqatsi, 1987, The Thin Blue Line, 1988, Mindwalk, 1990, A Brief History of Time, 1992, Candyman, 1992, Anima Mundi, 1992, Compassion in Exile, 1992, Candyman II: Farewell to the Flesh, 1995, Jenipapo, 1995, The Secret Agent, 1996, Bent, 1997, Kundun, 1997, Dracula, 1999, The Hours, 2002 (The Anthony Asquith Award for Achievement in Film Music, British Acad. Film Award (BAFTA), 2003), Naqoygatsi, 2002, The Fog of War, 2003, Secret Window, 2004, Taking Lives, 2004, Undertow, 2004, Naqoyqatsi; composer, keyboard artist (films) The Truman Show, 1998 (Golden Globe award, 1999); composer: (ballets) Witches of Venice, 1995, (dance opera) Les enfants terrible, 1996, (theatre) In the Penal Colony, 2000, (Operas) Monsters of Grace, 1999, Galileo Galilei, 2002; composer: (with Henry Hwang) The Sound of Voice, 2003; composer: (spl. events) Ceremonial Music at 1984 Olympics, original music for Atlanta Olympic Games, 1996, (benefit compact disc for Gehlek Rimpoche and Jewel Heart Orgn.) Dreaming Awake, Concerto for violin and orch., 1987, Concerto Fantasy for Two Timpanists and Orchestra, 2000, Tirol Concerto, piano and orchestra, 2000, Concerto for Cello and Orchestra, 2001, Concerto for Harpsichord and Orchestra, 2002, (Pandemic) Facing AIDS (documentary), 2002, (chamber and instrumental music) String Quartet, 1966, (vocal and choral music) Knee Play No. 3, 1976; Collaboration with David Bowie on Heros Symphony, 1997; author (with C. DeJong): Satyagraha: M.K. Gandhi in South Africa 1893-1914, 1980; author: Music by Philip Glass, 1987, Writings on Glass: Essays, Interviews, Criticism, 1997. Named composition grantee, Fulbright, 1966—67, Found. for Contemporary Performance Arts, 1970—71, Changes, Inc., 1971—72, Nat. Endowment for the Arts, 1974—75, Menil Found., 1974, Musician of Yr., Musical Am. mag., 1985; recipient Broadcast Music Industry award, 1960, Lado prize, 1961—67, Benjamin award, 1961—62, Young Composer's award, Ford Found., 1964—66. Mem.: PRS, ASCAP. Office: Dunvagen Music 632 Broadway Ste 902 New York NY 10012 Address: Orange Mountain Music 632 Broadway Rm 902 New York NY 10012-2614 also: Nonesuch Records 75 Rockefeller Plz 8th Fl New York NY 10019 Office Phone: 212-979-2080. Fax: 212-353-2007, 212-315-1124; Office Fax: 212-473-2842. E-mail: info@dunvagen.com.

GLASS, RENÉE, educational health foundation executive; b. Elizabeth, N.J., Jan. 27, 1928; d. Samuel and Helen Peritz m. Milton L. Glass, Feb. 5, 1950; children: Jill S., Mikel L. Student, Tufts U., 1952, Northeastern U., 1954, U. Mass., 1984-85. Bd. dirs. Inst. of Contemporary Art, Boston, 1979-83; pres. Connoisier Network, Boston, 1981; founder, pres. Jaw Joints Found., Boston, 1982—. Dir. Goldberg Ctr., Northeastern U., Boston, 1993—, exec.-in-residence, 1994—, mem. wellness com., 1994—, dir. Ctr. Health in Soc., 1999; participant, lectr. health forums, NIH, 1982—; bd. dirs. Health Practice and Policy Inst. Author numerous booklets and pamphlets on temporomandibular joint disorders, 1982—; mem. editl. bd. Bus. Ethics Resource. Mem. examining com. Boston Pub. Libr., 1983-84; bd. dirs. Boch Ctr. for the Performing Arts, Cape Cod. Mem. Internat. Catacomb Soc. (bd. dirs. 1987-97). Office: Jaw Joints/Musculo-Skeletal Disorders Found Forsyth Inst 140 Fenway Boston MA 02115-3782 Office Phone: 617-266-2550.

GLASS, ROBERT EDWARD, retired music educator; b. Cin., Jan. 13, 1943; s. Edward Boetler and Mildred M. Glass; m. Linda Morgan, June 6, 1981; 1 child, Bethany Lynn. BA, Morehead (Ky.) State U., 1966; MA, Miami U., Oxford, Ohio, 1980. Gen. music instr. Fairfield (Ohio) City Schs., 1966—2001. Dir. select elem. singing groups Fairfield City Schs., 1966—88, asst. band dir., 1966—70, elem. band dir., 1970—90; tuba player, 1966—95. Composer: Fairfield Alma Mater. V.p., sec. Fairfield Residents Assn., 1968—74; choir dir. Lindenwald Meth. Ch., Hamilton, Ohio, 1966—68, First United Meth. Ch., Hamilton, 1976, St. Marks United Meth. Ch., Fairfield, 1970—73. Achievements include design of the Fairfield City flag; teaching of 18,000 students and giving approx. 500 concerts in 35 years of teaching. Home: 6209 Morris Road Hamilton OH 45011

GLASS, ROGER I., virologist; b. Somerville, N.J., Jan. 10, 1946; MD, Harvard U., 1972. Intern Cambridge City Hosp., Mass., 1972—73; resident Mt. Sinai Hosp., N.Y.C., 1974—76; resident in microbiology U. Goteborg, 1984; chief viral gastroenteritis sect. Nat. Ctr. for Infectious Diseases, Ctrs. for Disease Control and Prevention, Atlanta; staff Grady Meml. Hosp., Atlanta. Co-recipient Pasteur award, Children's Vaccine Initiative, 1998. Mem.: Inst. Medicine, 2004 (life). Office: Nat Ctr for Infectious Diseases Ctrs for Disease Control/Prevention 1600 Clifton Rd NE Atlanta GA 30333 Office Phone: 404-639-3577. E-mail: rglass@cdc.gov.

GLASS, RONALD BERNHARD JACOB, radiologist; b. Salisbury, Rhodesia, Dec. 20, 1952; arrived in U.S., 1984; s. Joseph and Inge Selma Glass. MB BCh, U. Witwatersrand, 1976. Diplomate Am. Bd. Radiology. Fellow pediat. radiology Northwestern U., Chgo., 1984—86; radiologist U. Chgo., 1986—87, Loyola U., Maywood, Ill., 1987—88, Children's Nat. Med. Ctr., Washington, 1988—92, R.I. Hosp., Providence, 1992—93, U. Tex., Houston, 1993—95, Mt. Sinai Hosp. Med. Ctr., N.Y.C., 1995—. Reviewer Am. Jour. of Roentgenology, Radiology, Radiographics. Contbr. numerous articles to profl. jours.; editor (assoc. editor): Radiology, Examiner Am. Bd. of Radiology. Jewish. Office: Mt Sinai Med Ctr One Gustave L-Levy Pl New York NY 10029

GLASS, ROY LEONARD, lawyer; b. Littleton, N.H., Jan. 27, 1947; s. Jack Irving and Noreen (Leiuthwait) Kline; children: Shannon Renee, Ashley Leigh; m. Lauren Rachel Adams, Aug. 8, 1998. AA with honors, St. Petersburg Jr. Coll., Fla., 1971; BA, U. South Fla., 1972; JD, Fla. State U., 1975. Bar: Fla. 1976, U.S. Dist. Ct. (mid. dist.) Fla. 1977, U.S. Dist. Ct. (no. dist.) Fla. 1978, U.S. Supreme Ct. 1979, U.S. Ct. Appeals (11th cir.) 1983; cert. cir. ct. mediator, 2005. Assoc. Meyers, Mooney & Adler, Orlando, Fla., 1976-78, Barrett, Boyd & Bajoczky, Tallahassee, 1978-79; sole practice Tallahassee, 1979-81; ptnr. Deserio & Glass, St. Petersburg, Fla., 1981-82; assoc. Battaglia, Ross, Hastings, Dicus & Andrews, St. Petersburg, 1982-85; sole practice St. Petersburg, 1985—. Lectr. Floridians Against Constl. Tampering, Fla., 1984. Past mem. Roscoe Pound Inst., Capt. U.S. Army, 1966-70, Vietnam. Mem. ABA, ATLA, Am. Arbitration Assn., Fla. Acad. Trial Lawyers (mem. spkrs. bur.), Fla. Bar Assn. (health law com. 1984-85, chmn. health care profls. subcom. 1984-85, mem. exec. coun. health care sect. 1986-94, mem. spkrs. bur., Chair Client Security Fund Com. 2003-04), St. Petersburg Bar Assn. (legis. com. 1983-85, liaison med. soc., med. rels. com. 1985—, trial lawyers 1987—, mem. spkrs. bur.), Pinellas County Trial Lawyers Assn., St. Petersburg C. of C. (urban solutions task force 1983-84), Phi Delta Phi, Phi Kappa Phi, Beta Gamma Sigma. Clubs: Suncoast Tiger Bay (St. Petersburg, Fang & Claw award 1983), Breakfast Sertoma (Cert. of Appreciation 1984), Westgate High Twelve (Cert. of Appreciation 1987), Fla. Bar Health Law Sect. (client security fund com. Meritorious Svc. award 1994, Outstanding Leadership award 2003-04), Am. Coll. Barristers (sr. counsel). Office: 5501 Central Ave Saint Petersburg FL 33710-8050 Office Phone: 727-384-8888.

GLASSCOCK, LARRY CLABORN, health insurance company executive; b. Cullman, Ala., Apr. 4, 1948; s. Oscar Claborn and Betty Lou (Norman) G.; m. Lee Ann Roden, Sept. 13, 1969; children: Michael, Carrie BA, Cleve. State U., 1970; postgrad., Am. Inst. Banking, Columbia U. Vice pres. personnel and orgn. AmeriTrust Co., Cleve., 1974-75, v.p. nat. div., 1976-78, v.p., mgr. credit card ctr., 1978-79, sr. v.p. consumer fin., 1980-81, sr. v.p. nat. div., 1981-83, exec. v.p. corp. banking adminstr., 1983-87; group exec. v.p. AmeriTrust Corp. and AmeriTrust Co., Cleve., 1987-92; senior v.p., COO Anthem Ins., Indpls., 1998—99, pres., CEO, 1999—2004, chmn., 2003—04; pres., CEO WellPoint, Inc. (formerly Anthem Ins.), Indpls., 2004—. Chmn. Coun. for Affordable Quality Healthcare, Washington, DC, 2002-03; bd. dirs. Nat. Inst. Healthcare Mgmt., Zimmer Inc., 2001-, AT Fin. Corp., AT Capital Corp., AmeriTrust Internat. Banking, AmeriTrust Devel. Bank, CT Leasing Corp. Trustee Cleve. State U. Devel. Found.; campaign chmn. Geauga County United Way, 1989; mem. adv. bd. Northeast Ohio Employee Ownership Ctr. Kent State U., 1987—. Served with USMC, 1970-76. Co-recipient Ind. Entrepreneur of Yr. Award, Ernst & Young, 2003. Mem. Am. Inst. Banking, Am. Bankers Assn., Assn. Res. City Bankers, Greater Cleve. Growth Assn., Cleve. State U. Alumni Assn. (pres. 1987). Clubs: Union (Cleve.); Hillbrook (Chagrin Falls, Ohio); The Country (Pepper Pike, Ohio). Office: WellPoint Inc 120 Monument Cir Indianapolis IN 46204-4906

GLASSCOCK, SAMUEL TIMOTHY, music educator; s. Samuel Averitt Glasscock Hr. and Joyce Ann (Crouch) Glasscock. B in Music Edn., U. Louisville, 1991, M in Music Edn., 1998; DMA, U. Ky., 2005. Dir. choral activites Ind. U., New Albany, 1992—2000; choral conductor Campbellsville (Ky.) U., 2000—01; dir. vocal studies Youth Performing Arts Sch., Louisville, 2001—05. Artistic dir. Koutuokian Choral Union, New Albany, 2001—03, Louisville Chorus, 2002—05. Reviewer: Choral Jour., 2001—05. Mem.: Ky. Music Educators, Am. Choral Dir. Democrat. Roman Catholic. Avocations: poetry, history. Office: Youth Performing Arts Sch 1517 S 2nd St Louisville KY 40208

GLASSE, JOHN HOWELL, retired philosophy and theology educator; b. Buffalo, June 1, 1922; s. John Alfred and Jessie Elizabeth (Howell) G.; m. Wanda Lou Howard, June 16, 1950; children: Jeffrey Howell, Paulding Howard. BA, Williamette U., 1945; B.D., Yale U., 1948, PhD, 1961. Ordained to ministry Presbyn. Ch., 1948. Dir. field work Christian Activities Council, Hartford, Conn., 1948-50, exec. dir., 1950-52; dir. Danish program Scandinavian Seminar, Inc., 1952-53; mem. faculty Vassar Coll., Poughkeepsie, N.Y., 1956—, prof. religion, 1969-90, prof. emeritus, 1990—, Frederick Weyerhaeuser chair, 1971-90, chmn. dept. religion, 1965-67, 77-83, 87-90. Vis. prof. Harvard Div. Sch., 1970, vis. scholar, 1962, 69; vis. scholar Columbia U., Union Theol. Sem., 1980-81. Contbr. articles to profl. jours. Trustee Scandinavian Seminar, 1950— . Hon. fellow Am. Scandinavian Found., 1952; grantee Am. Philos. Soc., 1964; grantee Am. Council Learned Socs., 1965, 67 Mem. Am. Acad. Religion, Am. Philos. Assn., Metaphys. Soc. Am., Soc. Values in Higher Edn., AAUP. Address: Box 347 Vassar Coll 124 Raymond Ave Poughkeepsie NY 12604-0347

GLASSER, IRA SAUL, former civil liberties organization administrator; b. Bklyn., Apr. 18, 1938; s. Sidney and Anne (Goldstein) Glasser; m. Trude Maria Robinson, June 28, 1959; children: David, Andrew, Peter, Sally. BS in Math., Queens Coll., 1959; MA in Math., Ohio State U., 1960; LLD (hon.), N.Y. Law Sch., 2001. Instr. math. Queens Coll., N.Y.C., 1960—63; lectr. math. Sarah Lawrence Coll., Bronxville, NY, 1962—65; assoc. editor Current Mag., N.Y.C., 1962—64, editor, 1964—67; assoc. dir. N.Y. Civil Liberties Union, N.Y.C., 1967—70, exec. dir., 1970—78, ACLU, 1978—2001. Cons. U. Ill.-Champaign-Urbana, 1964—65; dir. Asian Am. Legal Def. and Edn. Fund, N.Y.C., 1974—2004; pres., bd. dirs. Drug Policy Alliance N.Y. (formerly Lindesmith Ctr./Drug Policy Found.), 1991—. Author: Visions of Liberty: The Bill of Rights for All Americans, 1991; co-author: Doing Good: The Limits of Benevolence, 1978; contbr. articles to profl. jours. Chmn. St. Vincents Hosp., N.Y.C., Cmty. Adv. Bd., N.Y.C., 1970—72. Recipient Martin Luther King, Jr. award, N.Y. Assn. Black Sch. Suprs., 1971, Gavel award, ABA, 1972, Allard K. Lowenstein award, Park River Ind. Dem., 1981, Malcolm, Martin, Mandela award, Greater Bapt. Trinity Ch., 1993, Justice in Action award, Asian Am. Legal Def. and Edn. Fund, 1999, Lifetime Achievement in Advocacy award, Correctional Assn. N.Y., 2005. Avocation: sports.

GLASSER, ISRAEL LEO, federal judge; b. N.Y.C., Apr. 6, 1924; s. David and Sadie (Krupp) G.; m. Grace Gribetz, Aug. 24, 1952; children— Dorothy, David, James, Marjorie. LL.B., Bklyn. Law Sch., 1948; BA, CUNY, 1976. Bar: N.Y. 1948. Fellow Bklyn. Law Sch., 1948-49, instr., 1950-52, asst. prof. law, 1952-53, asso. prof., 1953-55, prof., 1955-69, adj. prof., 1969-77, dean, 1977-81; judge U.S. Dist. Ct. N.Y., 1981—99, sr. judge, 1993—. Judge N.Y. State Family Ct., N.Y.C., 1969-77 Mem. ABA, Assn. of Bar of City of N.Y. Office: US Dist Ct 225 Cadman Plz E Brooklyn NY 11201-1818 E-mail: leo_glasser@nyed.uscourts.gov.*

GLASSER, JOSEPH, management consultant, educator; b. Phila., May 17, 1925; BS in Econs., U. Pa., 1947, MBA, 1948, postgrad., 1948-51. With NLRB, 1948-51; internal mgmt. cons., 1954-55; mem. faculty Sch. Bus. Adminstrn., U. Conn., 1955-81, prof. emeritus, 1981—; pres. Eljen Corp., 1971—. Arbitrator Fed. Mediation and Conciliation Service, VA, Nat. Mediation Bd., Soc. Security Adminstrn., Am. Arbitration Assn.; fact finder Mass. Bd. Mediation and Arbitration, Ct. Bd. Mediation and Arbitration, N.H. Pub. Employee Labor Relations Bd.; mediator Conn. Bd. Edn.; rev. officer FAA; mem. Nat. Def. Exec. Res.-Fed. Emergency Mgmt. Agy.; speaker seminars, also mgmt. groups in Eng., Austria and Hungary, Am. Mgmt. Assn. Author: Fundamentals of Applied Industrial Management; contbr. articles to profl. jours. Served to lt. col. USAF, ETO. Decorated Air medal with four oak leaf clusters, Air Force commendation medal. Mem. Soc. Profls. in Dispute Resolution, Indsl. Rels. Rsch. Assn., Nat. Assns. Mgmt. Educators (Innovative Mgmt. Edn. award 1976), Nat. Assn. Suggestion Systems (winner internat. papers competition 1975), Res. Officers Assn., Air Force Assn. Office: Eljen Corp 10 N Main St #216-217 West Hartford CT 06107-1968

GLASSER, LYNN SCHREIBER, publisher; b. Chgo., Sept. 19, 1943; d. Alexander Paul and Beatrice (Bollard) Schreiber; m. Stephen A. Glasser, Dec. 30, 1965; children: Susan, Laura, Jeffrey, Jennifer. BA, Chatham Coll., 1965. Publs. editor Inst. CLE U. Mich. Law Sch., Ann Arbor, 1966-68; asst. to dir. Practising Law Inst., N.Y.C., 1968-71; v.p., COO Law Jour. Press and Law Jour. Seminars, N.Y.C., 1971-78; exec. v.p., pub. Law & Bus./Harcourt Jovanovich, Inc., N.Y.C., 1978-86; co-pres. Prentice Hall Law & Bus., Englewood Cliffs, NJ, 1986-94; cons. Simon and Schuster, N.Y.C., 1994-95; pres. Glasser Publ. Inc., Little Falls, NJ, 1995—; co-pres. Glasser Legal Works, a Thomson Bus., 2003—04; pres. Sandpiper Ptnrs., LLC, Bloomfield, NJ, 2005—. Organizer, originator over 1000 CLE seminars, 1986—; organizer Woman Advt. Conf., N.Y.C., Chgo. and San Francisco, 1993-94; chmn. Woman Bus. Lawyer Conf., N.Y.C. and San Francisco, 1994. Trustee N.J. Chamber Music Soc., Montclair, 1989—, Montclair Art Mus., 1998—; Cmty. Found. of N.J., Morristown, 1995—; co-donor Lynn & Stephen Glasser Scholarship Fund, Colgate U., 1988—, Bloomfield Coll., 1993—. Office: 1515 Broad St Bldg B Bloomfield NJ 07003

GLASSER, MICHAEL A., lawyer; b. Norfolk, Va., Nov. 17, 1953; BA with distinction, U. Va., 1975; JD, U. Richmond, 1978. Bar: (Va.) 1978, U.S. Dist. Ct. Va. (ea. dist.) 1978, U.S. Ct. Appeals (4th cir.) 1978, U.S. Supreme Ct. 1997. Ptnr. Glasser & Glasser, Norfolk. Mem.: Va. State Bar (pres. 2001—02). Office: Glasser & Glasser Crown Ctr Bldg 580 E Main St Ste 600 Norfolk VA 23510

GLASSER, NORMA PENCHANSKY, sculptor; d. Oscar and Miriam Glasser; m. Nat Ehrlich; children: Seth, Lee. BS, Lesley Coll., 1962; MFA, Ea. Mich. U., 1973. Co-owner Washington St. Gallery, Ann Arbor, Mich., 1998—. Lectr. in field. Prin. works include Women Waiting, Waterford Complex, Okla. City, Okla., 1984, Summer Garden, Ind. U., 1991, Martha Graham, Las Sendas Devel., Tempe, Ariz., 1995, Represented in permanent collections Univ. Mich., Blue Cross/Blue Shield Mich., Ann Arbor (Mich.) Commerce Bank, Dennos Mus., Northwestern Mich. Coll., Marietta (Ohio) Coll., Hartland (Mich.) Coll., LaGrange (Ga.) Coll., Saginaw (Mich.) Valley State Coll., Samborn, Steketee, Otis and Evans Archtl. Firm, Toledo, Ohio, Boone Sculpture Garden, San Marino, Calif., Pacific Enterprises, L.A., Calif., St. Joseph's Hosp., Psychol. Counselling Svcs., Pasadena, Calif., The Dirs. Collection, one-woman shows include numerous including most recently, Washington St. Gallery, Ann Arbor, Mich., 1999, 2002, one-man shows include, 2005, one-woman shows include W.A.R.D. Gallery, Harbor Springs, Mich., 2002, exhibited in group shows at Washington St. Gallery, Ann Arbor, Mich., 1999, 2000, Ann Arbor (Mich.) Arts Ctr., 2002, Buckham Gallery, Flint, Mich., 2002, Pfizer Sculpture Exhibn., Ann Arbor, Mich., 2002, Saginaw Valley State Coll., Univ. Ctr., Mich., 2002, others, Art Roundtown, Saugatuck, Mich., 2005, Survey of Sculpture, Blissfield, Mich., 2005, Oakland (Mich.) C.C., 2005, U. Mich., Dearborn, 2005, numerous exhibitions, 1977—2000. Recipient Silver medal, Scarab Club, 1988, First Pl. award, Washtenaw Coun. Arts, 1991, Juror's Choice award, Ann Arbor (Mich.) Art Assn., 1994, Cleo Hartwig Meml. award, Nat. Assn. Women Artists, 1994, Purchase award, 2003, others.

GLASSER, PAMELA JEAN, musician, music educator; b. Livonia, Mich., June 26, 1953; d. Walter and Margaret Julia (Geersens) Glasser; m. Richard Barth Turner, Sept. 7, 1996. BEd in Music, Wayne State U., 1976; M of Music, Rice U., 1982. Prin. hornist Wyo. Symphony Orch., Casper, 1994—, Jackson Hole Symphony, 1999—2002; adj. prof. horn Casper Coll., 1998—2001; artistic dir. Casper Chamber Music Soc., 2001—; dir. music Fremont Sch. Dist. # 2, Dubois, Wyo., 2001—. Hornist music edn. programs Wyo. Arts Coun., 1993; hornist, solo performer Llangollen Eisteddfod North Wales, 1978. Mem.: SPLC, ACLU, NEA, Casper Chamber Music Soc. (ednl. liaison 1997—2001), Wyo. Edn. Assn., Am. Fedn. Musicians. Democrat. Episcopalian. Avocations: field and space science, organic gardening, cross country skiing, science fiction, crystal and mineral collecting, world music, religion. Home: PO Box 1357 Dubois WY 82513-1357 E-mail: pjglasser@yahoo.com.

GLASSER, PAUL HAROLD, sociologist, educator, social worker, university administrator; b. N.Y.C., Aug. 21, 1929; s. David and Rae (Startz) G.; m. Lois Hannah Naefach, Nov. 25, 1954 (div. June 1993); children: Heather Denys, Frederick Naefach. BS, CCNY, 1949; MS, Columbia U., 1951; PhD, U. N.C., 1961. Chief psychiat. social work sect. Mental Hygiene Clinic, Camp Chaffee Army Hosp., Ark., 1952-53; asst. dir. residence Child Guidance Home, Inc., 1953-55; instr. psychiat. group work, dept. psychiatry Med. Sch. U. Cin., 1953-55; asst. prof. U. Mich., Ann Arbor, 1958-63, assoc. prof., 1963-65, prof. Sch. Social Work, 1965-78; dean Grad. Sch. Social Work U. Tex., Arlington, 1978-88; dean Sch. Social Work Rutgers U., State U. of

N.J., New Brunswick, 1988-92, prof. II, 1988—. Vis. prof. Paul Baerwald Sch. Social Work, Hebrew U., Jerusalem, spring 1987, City U. Hong Kong, fall 1993, Bar-Ilan Sch. Social Work, spring 1997, Tel Aviv U., 2002-. Author: Small Groups in Hospital Community, 1967, Families in Crisis, 1970, Social Work Education for Family and Population Planning, 1973, Individual Change Through Small Groups, 1974, 2d edit., 1985, Social Work Roles and Functions in Family and Population Planning, 1974, Child Abuse and Neglect: A Challenge to the Caring Community, 1977, Group Workers at Work: Theory and Practice in the 80's, 1986, The First Helping Interview: Engaging the Client and Building Trust, 1996, in Russian, 2003, Il Primo Colloquio: Coinvolgimento e Relazione Nelle Professioni D'aruto, 1999; sr. editor: Ency. Social Work, 1971, LaRicerca Valutative, 1972; editor Jour. Health and Social Behavior, 1970-73, Jour. Social Work, 1965-69, Jour. Marriage and Family Counseling, 1974-82, Social Work with Groups, Hong Kong Jour. Social Work, 1998—, Jour. Social Work and Social Policy in Israel, 1988—. Bd. dirs. Washtenau County Family Svc., 1964-66, 69-70. Served to 1st lt. AUS, 1952-53. Fulbright Hays lectr. Italy, 1971; Fulbright Hays lectr. U. Philippines, 1966-67; Fulbright Hays lectr. Australia, 1973-74. Mem. NASW (chpt. chmn. 1962-63), Am. Sociol. Soc., Masons. Office: State U of NJ Rutgers U Sch Social Work 536 George St New Brunswick NJ 08901-1167 E-mail: pglasser@rci.rutgers.edu. *The generation and the dispersal of knowledge are the two primary ways in which the academician contributes to the society. He is an agent of change as he studies what is, in order to suggest what might be, and communicates this to his students. My career has been devoted to these principles and to stimulating others to follow them.*

GLASSER, STEPHEN ANDREW, publishing executive, lawyer; b. Memphis, July 27, 1943; s. Melvin A. and Esther (Kron) G.; m. Lynn Schreiber, Dec. 30, 1965; children: Susan, Laura, Jeffrey, Jennifer. BA cum laude, Colgate U., 1965; JD, U. Mich., 1968. Bar: D.C., 1968. Asst. dir. Practising Law Inst., N.Y.C., 1968-71; exec. v.p., exec. editor N.Y. Law Pub. Co., N.Y.C., 1971-77; pres. Law & Bus. Inc. div. Harcourt Brace Jovanovich, N.Y.C., 1977-86, Prentice Hall Law & Bus. div. Simon & Schuster Profl Info Group, Englewood Cliffs, NJ, 1986-94; chmn. Glasser Publs. Inc., Little Falls, NJ, 1995—2003; co-pres. Glasser Legal Works, a Thomson Bus., 2004; chmn. Sandpiper Ptnrs., LLC, Bloomfield, NJ, 2005—. Co-founder, editor, publisher Legal Times of Washington, 1978-86. Former trustee Mental Health Assn. of Essex County; trustee Bloomfield Coll., chmn. bd., 1999—2000, former chmn. fin. and property com., 2000—01, 1st vice chair, 2001—; former trustee The Hospice Inc.; adv. bd. SUNY (Stony Brook) Coll. Bus. Mem. ABA, D.C. Bar Assn., Assn. Bar City N.Y., Phi Beta Kappa, Montclair Golf Club. Home: 86 Highland Ave Montclair NJ 07042-1910 Office: Sandpiper Partners LLC 1515 Broad St Bldg B Bloomfield NJ 07003 Business E-Mail: steveglasser@sandpiperpartners.com.

GLASSER, STEPHEN C., lawyer; b. Bklyn., Jan. 11, 1951; BS, Bklyn. Coll.; JD, Bklyn Law Sch., 1976. Bar: NY 1977, Calif. 1983, US Dist. Ct. (so., ea. dist. NY) 1977, US Ct. Appeals (2d cir.) 1982. Law asst. Justices of NY State Supreme Ct. Appellate Div. 2d Compartment, 1976—80; of counsel Sullivan Papain Block McGrath & Cannavo PC, NYC, 1984—97, chief appellate counsel, 1997—. Mem.: Assn. Trial Lawyers Am., NY State Bar Assn., NY State Trial Lawyers Assn., NY County Trial Lawyers Assn. Office: Sullivan Papain Block McGrath & Cannavo PC 120 Broadway New York NY 10271 Office Phone: 212-732-9000. Office Fax: 212-266-4141.

GLASSER, WOLFGANG GERHARD, chemical engineering wood science researcher, educator; b. Oct. 9, 1941; came to U.S., 1969, naturalized, 2001; s. Joachim and Charlotte (Syjatz) G.; m. Heidemarie Reinecke, Mar. 18, 1969; children: Christine Glasser Sutherland, Stephan A. Degree in wood tech., U. Hamburg, Germany, 1966; PhD in Wood Chemistry, U. Hamburg, 1969. Rsch. assoc. U. Wash., Seattle, 1969-70, rsch. asst. prof., 1970-71; asst. prof. Va. Poly. Inst. and State U., Blacksburg, 1972-75, assoc. prof., 1975-80, prof. wood chemistry, 1980—2002, assoc. dean rsch. and grad. studies Coll. Forestry and Wildlife Resources, 1993-98, prof. emeritus wood sci. and forest products, 2002—. Adj. prof. Inst. of Paper Sci. and Tech., Atlanta, 1999-2003; dir. Pulp and Paper Rsch. Inst., Sao Paulo, Brazil, 1976, Biobased Materials Ctr., 1988-91; vis. prof. U. Grenoble (France), Centre de Recherche sur Macromolecules Vegetales, Grenoble, 1985, Nat. U. Singapore, 1993, Kyoto (Japan) U., 1998, U. Toulouse, France, 2000, 03, Chalmers U. Tech., Gothenborg, Sweden, 2001-02, U. de Guadalajara, Jalisco, Mex., 2005; vis. scientist Weyerhaeuser Corp., 2004; chmn. panel NAS, 1974-76; cons. to industry and govt. Mem. editl. adv. group Holzforschung, Braunschweig, Germany, 1985—, Cellulose Chem. Tech., 1987—, Cellulose, 1994-99, Jour. Wood Sci. (Japan), 1998—, Jour. Applied Polymer Sci., 1989—; patentee in field; contbr. articles to profl. jours.; book editor; editor-in-chief Cellulose, 2000—. Co-recipient George Olmsted award Am. Paper Inst., 1974; recipient Sci. Achievement award Internat. Union Forest Rsch. Orgns., 1986, Anselme Payen award Cellulose, Papr and Textile divsn. Am Chem. Soc., 2000. Fellow Internat. Acad. Wood Sci. Tech.; mem. Am. Chem. Soc. (fellow divsn. cellulose and renewable materials, alt. councilor 1983-85, pub. chmn. 1985-88, chmn. 1990, councilor 1991-2000, program chmn. 1993-96, nominations chair, Divsn. Fellow award Cellulose and Renewable Materials Divsn. 2003), Soc. Wood Sci. Tech., Sigma Xi, Phi Beta Delta. Lutheran. Office: Va Tech 230 Julian Cheatham Hall Wood Sci Forest Products Blacksburg VA 24061 Office Phone: 540-231-4403. E-mail: wglasser@vt.edu.

GLASSHEIM, ELIOT ALAN, editor, state legislator; b. N.Y.C., Feb. 10, 1938; s. Raymond S. and Edith (Ruthizer) G.; m. Patricia Sanborn, July 20, 1969 (div. Feb. 1979); children: Eagle, Don; m. Dyan Rey, Feb. 14, 1996. BA, Wesleyan U., 1960; MA, U. N.Mex., 1966, PhD, 1972. Copy boy, book reviewer Wash. Post, 1960-61; editl. proofreader Wall St. Jour., N.Y.C., 1962-64; mgmt. trainee Accessory Fashions, N.Y.C., 1964-66; asst. prof. English, Augusta (Ga.) Coll., 1968-70; fellow U. N.D., Grand Forks, 1971-73; mem. N.D. Ho. of Reps., Grand Forks, 1975-76, 93—, house appropriations com., 2001—, asst. Dem. leader, 2003—05; grant writer, dir. oral history project of 97 flood N.D. Mus. Art, Grand Forks, 1993-99; owner used bookstore and Internet sales Dr. Eliot's Twice Sold Tales, Grand Forks, 1992—; policy analyst No. Great Plains, Inc., Fargo, ND, 1999—. Dir. Population/Food Fund, Grand Forks, 1977-79; housing coord., grantswriter N.D. Migrant Coun., Grand Forks, 1979-81. Editor: Population and Food Issues, 1977, 1978, Voices from the Flood, 1999, Behind the Scenes, 2002, Renewing the Countryside--North Dakota, 2004, Toward New Horizons: Moving the Northern Great Plains Region to a Stronger Economic Future, 2002, Traceability in Agriculture, 2003; author: The New Marketplace in European Agriculture: Environmental and Social Values Within the Ford Chain, 2005; author: (poems) The Restless Giant, 1968. Exec. dir. Quad County Cmty. Action Agy., Grand Forks, 1981—87; field rep., office mgr. U.S. Senator Quentin Burdick, Grand Forks, 1987—92; mem. Grand Forks City Coun., 1982—, Grand Forks Planning and Zoning Com., 1984—96, mem. flood response com., 1997—2000, chmn. population task force, 2001; chmn. interim legis. Commerce Commn., 1999—2000; founder, dir. Red River Valley Habitat for Humanity, Grand Forks, 1988—99; chmn. Dist. 17/18 Dems., Grand Forks, 1980—81; bd. dirs. Prairie Pub. TV, 1997—2000. Home: 619 N 3rd St Grand Forks ND 58203-3203 E-mail: eglass@infionline.net.

GLASSHEIM, JEFFREY WAYNE, allergist, immunologist, pediatrician; b. Far Rockaway, N.Y., Sept. 16, 1958; s. Ronald Alan and Elinda (Deitch) G.; m. Paulette Renée, Apr. 16, 1989; children: Elyssa Gwen, Brenna Chase. BA cum laude, Temple U., 1980; DO with honors in Osteo. Medicine, U. New. Eng. Coll. Osteo. Medicine, 1984. Diplomate Am. Bd. Allergy and Clin. Immunology, Am. Bd. Pediatrics. Commd. 2d lt. U.S. Army, 1980, advanced through grades to maj., 1989, resigned, 1992; intern Winthrop-Univ. Hosp., Mineola, N.Y., 1984-85; resident Madigan Army Med. Ctr., Tacoma, 1985-87; fellow Fitzsimons Army Med. Ctr. and Nat. Jewish Med. Ctr., Denver, 1990—92, chief fellow allergy-clin. immunology, 1990—92; chief allergy-clin. immunology and immunizations svcs. Silas B. Hays Army Community Hosp., Fort Ord, Calif., 1992—93; resigned commn. USAR, 1993; dir. allergy-immunology dept. Pediatric Med. Group of Fresno, Calif., 1994-95; dir. allergy-immunology Northwest Med. Group, Fresno, 1995-97; pvt. practice allergy and immunology, 1997—. Cons. numerous pharm. companies. Contbr. articles to profl. jours.; mem. editl. adv. bd. Unique Opportunites, 1998—, contbg. editor, 2004—. Bd. dirs. Am. Lung Assn. Ctrl. Calif., 1999—2002. Fellow Am. Acad. Pediatrics (allergy and immunology sect.), Am. Acad. Allergy Asthma and Immunology, Am. Coll. Allergy, Asthma and Immunology; mem. AMA, Am. Osteo. Assn., Am. Physicians Fellowship for Medicine in Israel, Calif. Soc. Allergy, Asthma and Clin. Immunology, Ctrl. Calif. Allergy Soc., Fresno-Madera Med. Soc., Calif. Med. Assn., Osteo. Physicians and Surgeons of Calif. Republican. Jewish. Avocations: meteorology, sports, reading/current events, gardening, walking. Personal E-mail: glasjw@juno.com.

GLASSICK, CHARLES ETZWEILER, academic foundation administrator; b. Wrightsville, Pa., Apr. 6, 1931; s. Gordon J. and Melva G. (Etzweiler) G.; m. Mary Williams, Feb. 27, 1952; children: Bruce, Judith, Jeffrey, Robert, Jonathan. BS with honors, Franklin and Marshall Coll., 1953; MA, PhD, Princeton U., 1957; D.Sc. (hon.), U. Richmond, 1977; L.L.D. (hon.), Dickinson Sch. Law, 1986; LLD, Pepperdine U., 1996, Adrian Coll., 1997; LHD (hon.), Franklin & Marshall Coll., 1997. Research chemist Rohm & Haas Co., Phila., 1957-62; instr. gen. chemistry Temple U., Phila., 1957-62; prof. chemistry Adrian (Mich.) Coll., 1962-68; v.p. Great Lakes Colls. Assn., Ann Arbor, Mich., 1968-69; asso. dean for acad. affairs Albion (Mich.) Coll., 1969-71, v.p. for acad. affairs, 1971-72; pres. Va. Inst. Scientific Research, Richmond, 1972-77; provost, v.p. for acad. affairs U. Richmond, Va., 1972-77; pres. Gettysburg (Pa.) Coll., 1977-89, Woodruff Arts Ctr., Atlanta, 1990-96; sr. scholar Carnegie Found. for Advancement of Tchg., Stanford, Calif., 1989-90, acting pres. Menlo Park, Calif., 1995, interim pres., 1996-97, sr. assoc., 1997-2001, sr. assoc. emeritus, 2001—; interim pres. N.C. Wesleyan Coll., 2000-01, Reinhardt Coll., 2001—02, Thomas U., 2005—. Cons. NEH, 1971-72, NSF, 1963-67, Va. Coun. High Edn., 1972-76; mem. exec. com. Luth. Ednl. Conf. of N.Am., 1983-86; mem. Pres.'s Commn. Nat. Collegiate Athletic Assn., 1988-89; interim pres. Converse Coll., 1998-99; interim dir. Scholars Press, 1999-2000; vis. fellow Cambridge U., 2002. Mem. editorial bd. Liberal Education, 1978-82, Educational Record, 1985-97; co-author: (book) Scholarship Assessed-Evaluations of the Professoriate. Mem. Mental Health and Mental Retardation Task Force Manpower Devel., Richmond, 1975—77, ACE Commn. on Minorities; bd. dirs. Hist. Gettysburg/Adams County, 1979—89, Meth. Conf. Homes Aging, 1985—89, Atlanta Cultural Olympiad, 1991—96, Midtown Alliance, 1991—97; bd. dirs, exec. com. Spartanburg Habitat for Humanity, 2002—; bd. dirs. Cmty. Campus Partnership Health, 2003—; trustee, vice-chmn. Eisenhower Soc., 1985—95, Carnegie Found. Advancement in Tchg., 1991—97, Ga. Found. Ind. Colls., 1992—, Literacy Action, Inc., 1994—97, Found. Hosp. Art, 1994—; bd. trustees Ga. Found. Ind. Colls., 1996—; bd. curators Ga. Hist. Soc., 1997—99; bd. regents Am. Arch. Fedn., 1998—; Fulbright sr. scholar specialist, 2002—. Mem. AAAS, AAUP, Am. Chem. Soc., N.Y. Acad. Scis., Danforth Assocs., Am. Chem. Soc., Phi Beta Kappa (hon.), Beta Gamma Sigma, Omicron Delta Kappa, Alpha Chi Omega. Methodist. Home: 216 Mills Ave Spartanburg SC 29302 Personal E-mail: CEGlassick@aol.com.

GLASSMAN, ALEXANDER HOWARD, psychiatrist, researcher; b. Chgo., Feb. 4, 1934; s. Morris and Mindelle (Sosna) G.; m. B. Judith Cohen, Mar. 28, 1958; children: Steven, Laura Glassman Hercher. BS, U. Ill., Chgo., 1956, MD, 1958. Diplomate Am. Bd. Neurology and Psychiatry. Resident in psychiatry Albert Einstein Med. Coll. Medicine, Yeshiva U., N.Y.C., 1954-62; USPH fellow, 1963-64; asst. prof. psychiatry Albert Einstein Coll. Medicine, Bronx, N.Y., 1964-65, cons. psychopharmacologist, 1972-78; dir. residency tng. Letterman Gen. Hosp., San Francisco, 1967-68, chief psychiatry svc., 1968-69; dir. affective diseases N.Y. State Psychiat. Inst., N.Y.C., 1973-78, chief clin. psychopharmacology, 1978—; prof. clin. psychiatry Coll. Physicians and Surgeons, Columbia U., N.Y.C., 1980—. Mem. merit rev. bd. VA, Washington, 1987-90. Editor: Treatment Strategies in Refractory Depression, 1990, also 5 other books; contbr. articles to jours. in field; patentee in field. Lt. col. U.S. Army, 1967-69. Recipient Established Investigator award Nat. Assn. for Rsch. Affective Diseases and Schizophrenia, 1990, N.Y. State Psychiat. Rsch. award, 1994; invited spkr. Nobel Com. Conf. of Depression, Stockholm, 1983; Plenery spkr. German Psychiat. Assn., Fed. Republic Germany, 1990, Plenery spkr. Japanese Neurosci. Soc., Nagoya, 1994. Fellow Am. Coll. Neuropsychopharmacology, Am. Psychiat. Assn. (Lifetime achievement prize 1989); mem. AAAS, Am. Psychopath. Assn. (trustee), N.Y. Acad. Sci. Achievements include patent for clonidine in smoking cessation; first to recognize unique treatment response of delusionally depressed patients, to demonstrate relationship between antidepressant drug treatment outcome and individual differences in drug metabolism, to describe the cardiac antiarrhythmic effects of antidepressant drugs, to describe relationship between depression and cigarette smoking. Office: Columbia U Dept Psychiatry 1051 Riverside Dr New York NY 10032-2695 E-mail: ahg1@columbia.edu.

GLASSMAN, ARMAND BARRY, physician, pathologist, scientist, educator, administrator; b. Paterson, NJ, Sept. 9, 1938; s. Paul and Rosa (Ackerman) G.; m. Alberta C. Macri, Aug. 30, 1958; children: Armand P., Steven B., Brian A. BA, Rutgers U., 1960; MD magna cum laude, Georgetown U., 1964. Diplomate Am. Bd. Pathology, Am. Bd. Nuc. Medicine. Intern Georgetown U. Hosp., Washington, 1964-65; resident Yale-New Haven Hosp., West Haven VA Hosp., 1965-69; asst. prof. pathology, Coll. Medicine U. Fla.; chief radioimmunoassary lab. Gainesville (Fla.) VA Hosp.; practice lab. and nuc. medicine, 1969-71; dir. clin. labs., assoc. prof., prof. pathology, cellular, molecular biology Med. Coll. Ga., Augusta, 1971-76; cons. physician in nuc. medicine Univ. Hosp., Augusta, 1973-76; med. dir. clin. labs. Med. U. SC Hosp., Charleston, 1976-87; attending physician in lab. and nuc. medicine Med. U. SC, Charleston, 1976-87, assoc. med. dir. Med. U. Hosp. and Clinics, 1982-86, prof., chmn. dept. lab. medicine, 1976-87, med. dir. MT and MLT programs, 1976-87, clin. prof. pathology, lab. medicine, and radiology, 1987—, acting chmn. dept. immunology and microbiology, 1985-87, assoc. dean Coll. Medicine, 1979-85, asst. and assoc. dean Coll. Allied Health Sci., 1984-87, chmn. hosp. exec. com., 1985-86, acting med. dir. Univ. Hosp. and Clinics, 1985-86; med. dir. clin. labs. Charleston Meml. Hosp., 1976-87; cons. VA Hosp., Charleston, 1976-87; sr. v.p. med. affairs, prof. lab. medicine and nuc. medicine Montefiore Med. Ctr. and Albert Einstein Coll. Medicine, Bronx, NY, 1987-89; v.p., lab. dir. Nat. Reference Lab., Nashville, 1989-92; from clin. prof. to prof. dept. pathology Vanderbilt U., Nashville, 1990-94; dir. Vanderbilt Pathology Lab. Svcs., 1992-94; dir. clin. labs. Vanderbilt U. Med. Ctr., 1993-94, O. Stribling chair, prof., 1994—; head and chair divsn./dept. lab. medicine U. Tex., M.D. Anderson Cancer Ctr., Houston, 1994-96, also med. dir. Med. Tech. & Cytogenetic Tech. programs, 1994-96, 2001—, also dir. sect. cytogenetics, 1994—, 2002—, chair ops. and improvement mgmt. com. dept. hematopathology, 1998—2002, prof. Grad. Sch. Biol. Scis., 1994—. Adj. prof. Grad. Sch. Biol. Scis. and U. Tex. Health Scis. Med. Sch., 1994-; adv. coun. Trident Tech. Coll., 1976-87; bd. dirs. Fetter Family Health Ctr.; mem. steering com. pathology and lab medicine U. Tex. M.D. Anderson Cancer Ctr., 1998-2000, mem. radiation safety com., 1998-, pharmacy and therapeutics com., 2000-, vice chmn., 2004—, credentials com., 2002—, radiation drug rsch. com., 2003—, chmn. task force on antiemetic drugs, 2003—, chmn. medication process com., 2004—, faculty senate representative, 2004—; founding dir. Sealite, Inc., 1987-99, chmn. bd. dirs., 1995-99; founding dir., bd. dirs. SynthRx, Inc., 2003-; med. adv. com. Nashville Red Cross Blood Ctr., 1991-94, acting med. dir., 1991-92; v.p., bd. sci. advisors Nat. Health Labs./Nat. Reference Lab., 1992-94; trustee, bd. dirs. Gulf Coast Cmty. Blood Ctr., 1994—; cons. in field. Editor, co-editor 4 books; bd. editors Annals of Clin. and Lab. Scis., 1981—; contbr. over 170 articles to profl. jours., 30 chpts. to books. Trustee Coll. Prep. Sch., 1979-84, chmn. bd., 1983-84; trustee, bd. dirs., v.p. Mason Prep. Sch., 1984-87; bd. dirs. United Way, 1983-87, Am. Cancer Soc., 1984-87; co-founder, bd. dirs. Glassman Family Fund, 1998—. With USMCR, 1956-64. Johnson and Avalon Found. scholar Georgetown U., 1961-64, State scholar Rutgers U., 1956-60. Fellow ACP, Coll. Am. Pathologists (numerous coms.), Assn. Clin. Scientists (Diploma of Honor 1987, pres. 1990-91, exec. com. 1990-95, Clin. Scientist of Yr. 1993, C.P. Brown lectr. 1995, numerous coms.), Am. Soc. Clin. Pathology (coun. immunohematology and blood banking 1983-89, coun. grad. med. edn. and rsch. 1998—, Commr.'s award for Continuing Edn. 1989, nat. contbg. editor to Resident In-Svc. Exam. 2000-04), Am. Coll. Nuc. Medicine, NY Acad. Medicine; mem. Am. Bd. Pathology (transfusion medicine/blood bank test com. 1984-88), Internat. Acad. Pathology, Am. Assn. Pathologists, Soc. Nuc. Medicine (chmn. edn. com. 1973-77, acad. coun. 1979-92), AMA (Physician's Recognition award, instnl. rep. to sect. on med. schs., 1987-94, 2003—), So. Med. Assn., Am. Geriat. Soc. (founding fellow So. divsn.), Am. Soc. Microbiology, Am. Assn. Blood Banks (chmn. cryobiology com. 1974-83, edn. com. 1978-85, sci. program com. 1981-84, autologous transfusion com. 1979-83, bd. dirs. 1984-87, transfusion practices com. 1992-96), Assn. Schs. Allied Health Professions (bd. editors jour. 1979-83), Soc. Cryobiology (treas., bd. dirs. 1978-80), AAAS, NY Acad. Scis., Acad. Clin. Lab. Physicians and Scientists (exec. coun. 1978-85, pres. 1982-83), S.E. Area Blood Bankers (pres. 1979-81, exec. coun. 1980-85), Tenn. Assn. Blood Banks (treas. 1993-94), Am. Coll. Physician Execs., Sigma Xi, Alpha Eta, Alpha Omega Alpha. Avocations: jogging, tennis, community service. Office: U Tex MD Anderson Cancer Ctr Hematopathology Unit 72 1515 Holcombe Blvd Houston TX 77030-4009 Office Phone: 713-794-1095. Business E-Mail: abglassma@aol.com.

GLASSMAN, BILL, literature educator, music educator; b. Boston, July 15, 1938; s. Charles and Rachel Glassman; m. Kathleen Mary O'Connor, Aug. 11, 1968; children: David, Lisa. AA in English, Santa Ana (Calif.) Coll., 1958; BA in English, San Francisco (Calif.) State Coll., 1960, MA in English, 1962. Prof. English, reading, music Fullerton (Calif.) Coll., 1962—. Lectr. in field. Avocation: opera. Home: 229 E Commonwealth Ave Fullerton CA 92832 Office: Fullerton Coll 321 E Chapman Ave Fullerton CA 92832

GLASSMAN, CAROLINE DUBY, state supreme court justice; b. Baker, Oreg., Sept. 13, 1922; d. Charles Ferdinand and Caroline Marie (Colton) Duby; m. Harry Paul Glassman, May 21, 1953; 1 son, Max Avon. LLB summa cum laude, Williamette U., 1944. Bar: Oreg. 1944, Calif. 1952, Maine 1969. Atty. Title Ins. & Trust Co., Salem, Oreg., 1944-46; assoc. Belli, Ashe, Pinney & Melvin Belli, San Francisco, 1952-58; ptnr. Glassman & Potter, Portland, Maine, 1973-78, Glassman, Beagle & Ridge, Portland, 1978-83; justice Maine Supreme Judicial Ct., Portland, 1983-97. Lectr. Sch. Law, U. Maine, 1967-68, 80 Author: Legal Status of Homemakers in State of Maine, 1977. Mem.: ATLA, Russian Am. Rule of Law Consortium, Maine Trial Law Assn., Maine Bar Assn., Calif. Bar Assn., Oreg. Bar Assn., Am. Law Inst., Supreme Ct. Hist. Soc. Roman Catholic. Home: 56 Thomas St Portland ME 04102-3639

GLASSMAN, DEBRA, dentist; m. Steven Glassman; 3 children. BA in dental hygiene, Columbia U.; DDS, NYU Col. Dentistry. Dentist Glassman Dental Care, NYC. Office: NYC Cosmetic Dentists Glassman Dental Care 160 West End Ave New York NY 10023 Office Phone: 212-787-4860. Office Fax: 212-787-9238.*

GLASSMAN, EDWARD, public relations executive, educator, journalist; b. N.Y.C., Mar. 18, 1929; s. Jacob S. and Riesa (Bronfman) F.; children: Lyn Judith, Susan Fiona, Ellen Ruth, Marjorie Riesa. AB, NYU, 1949, MS, 1951; PhD, Johns Hopkins U., 1955. Mem. staff City of Hope Med. Ctr., Duarte, Calif., 1959-60; prof., faculty biochemistry dept. med. sch. U. N.C., Chapel Hill, 1960-90, head program for team effectiveness and creativity, 1981-90; prof. emeritus, 1990—; pres. Leadership Cons. Svcs., Inc., Creativity Coll., Chapel Hill, 1990—. Mem. grants and rev. study sect. NIMH, 1966-69, U. Calif., Irvine, 1978; vis. fellow Ctr. Creative Leadership, Greensboro, N.C., 1983; vis. scientist Stanford Rsch. Inst., Menlo Park, Calif., 1986; pres. Creativity Coll. divsn. Leadership Consulting Svcs., Inc., Chapel Hill. Author: Molecular Approaches to Neurobiology, 1967, For Presidents Only: Unlocking the Creative Potential of Your Management Team, 1990, Creativity Handbook, 1991, The Creativity Factor: Unlocking the Potential of Your Team, 1991; columnist Creativity at Work, Chapel Hill Newspaper, 1991-92, Triangle Bus. Jour., 1992-95, Chapel Hill Herald, 1992-94, Moore County Citizens News Record, 1994-96; mem. editl. adv. bd. Behavioral Biology, 1971-78, Pharmacology, Biochemistry and Behavior, 1973-88; mem. bd. advisors Neurochem. Rsch., 1975-78; contbr. 95 articles to profl. jours. Pub. rels. specialist Lions Club, 1995—. Adam T. Bruce fellow, 1954-55; Am. Cancer Soc. fellow, 1955-57; NIH fellow, 1958-59; NIH Career Devel. award, 1961-71; Guggenheim fellow, 1968-69 Fellow AAAS, Royal Soc. Edinburgh; mem. Soc. Neurosci. (pres. N.C. chpt. 1974-75), Elisha Mitchell Sci. Soc. (v.p. 1965-66) Home and Office: 679 Cedar Pt Vass NC 28394-8686

GLASSMAN, GERALD SEYMOUR, metal products executive; b. Hartford, Conn., July 6, 1932; s. Abram and Lena (Rulnick)) G.; m. Edwina Wellins, Dec. 1, 1963; children: Cynthia Anne Heilweil, Barbara Diane Dell, Richard Philip Glassman. BS, U. Vt., 1954. Exec. Bland Co., Hartford, Conn., 1954-63, Coleco Industries, Hartford, 1963-75; pres. Stanley Plating Co., Forestville, Conn., 1977-82; chmn. CBR Industries, Plainville, Conn., 1977-82; pres. Plainville Plating Co., 1975-97, chmn., 1998—; pres. Internat. Metal Finishing, Inc., 1986—; mem. regional adv. bd. Bank of Boston Ct., Plainville, 1979-89; mem. adv. bd. 1st Nat. Bank of New Eng., 1991—99. Pres. Tunxis C.C. Found., 1978-88; trustee Wheeler Clinic, 1979-89, Plainville YMCA, 1980—; mem. Assocs. U. Hartford. Mem. Nat. Assn. Metal Finishers, Conn. Assn. Metal Finishers Assn. Conn. (pres.), NAM, Am. Electroplaters Soc., Plainville C. of C., Masons. Jewish. Home: 2 Abbottsford Avon CT 06001 Office: 21 Forestville Ave Plainville CT 06062-2159 E-mail: gsglassman@comcast.net.

GLASSMAN, JAMES KENNETH, editor, writer, publishing executive; b. Washington, Jan. 1, 1947; s. Stanley G. and Elaine Ruth (Schiff) Garfield; children: Zoe Ann, Kate Julia. BA, Harvard, 1969. Editor, pub. Provincetown (Mass.) Advocate, 1971-72; editor-in-chief, exec. pub. Figaro, New Orleans, 1972-78; exec. editor Washingtonian Mag., 1979-81; pub. New Republic mag., Washington, 1981-84; pres. Atlantic mag., Washington, 1984-86; exec. v.p. U.S. News & World Report, Washington, 1984-86; editor-in-chief Roll Call, Washington, 1987-93; fin. and polit. columnist Washington Post, 1993—; resident fellow Am. Enterprise Inst., Washington, 1996—. Host Capital Gang Sunday, CNN-TV, 1995-98, Techno Politics, PBS-TV, 1995-99. Co-author: Dow 36,000, 1999; host www.TechCentralStation.com, 2000—; author: The Secret Code of the Superior Investor, 2002; columnist: Scripps Howard News Svc., 2004—. Office: Am Enterprise Inst 1150 17th St NW Washington DC 20036-4603 Home: 15 Battle Hill Rd Falls Village CT 06031

GLASSMAN, JEROLD ERWIN, lawyer; b. Newark, Oct. 12, 1935; s. Morris and Leah (Katz) G.; m. Joan Kay, June 15, 1957; children: Sherri, Steven, Jill. BS, Rutgers U., 1957; JD, Seton Hall U., 1966. Bar: N.J. 1966, Calif. 1977. Dir. labor rels. El Al Israel Airlines, N.Y.C., 1967; assoc. Grotta & Oberwager, Newark, 1967-70; ptnr. Grotta, Oberwager & Glassman, Newark, 1970-75; mng. ptnr. Grotta, Glassman & Hoffman, Newark, 1975-77, Roseland, N.J., 1977-2000, chmn., 2000—. Bd. dirs. Essex Valley Healthcare, Inc., East Orange, N.J., Theresa Grotta Ctr., West Orange, N.J.; mem. ethics com. N.J. Supreme Ct. part V-C. Spl. labor counsel Gov. Christine Todd Whitman, 1992—, N.J. Sports Authority, 1981—, N.J. Transit, 1984. With USNR, 1953-61. Mem. ABA (labor and econs. sects.), N.J. Bar Assn. (labor and casino law sects.), Greenbrook Club, Boca West Club. Republican. Jewish. Avocation: golf. Office: Grotta Glassman & Hoffman PA 75 Livingston Ave Ste 13 Roseland NJ 07068-3701 E-mail: glassmanj@gghlaw.com.

GLASSMAN, JON DAVID, aerospace executive; b. N.Y.C., Jan. 8, 1944; s. J. and Dorothy (Witkin) G.; m. Ann Tracy Hoitz, Nov. 12, 2003; 1 child, Amanda Louise. B in Fgn. Svc., U. So. Calif., 1965; MA, cert. Russian Inst., Columbia U., 1968, PhD, 1976. Joined Fgn. Svc. Dept. State, 1968; officer Am. Embassy, Madrid, 1968-70, Moscow, 1971-73, Havana, Cuba, 1977-79, Mexico City, 1979-81, Dept. State, Washington, 1974-77, 81-87; charge d'affaires Am. Embassy, Kabul, Afghanistan, 1987-89; dep. asst. for nat. security affairs to V.p. The White House, 1989-90, asst. to V.p. of U.S.,

1990-91; amb. to Paraguay Asuncion, 1991-94; dept. state chair Indsl. Coll. of the Armed Forces, Washington, 1994-96; dep. for Balkan mil. stabilization Dept. State, Washington, 1996-97; v.p. internat. bus. devel. electronic sys. sector Northrop Grumman Corp., Balt., 1998—. Mem. bd. Bus. Coun. for Internat. Understanding, 1999—. Author: Arms for the Arabs, 1976. Bd. dirs. Bus. Coun. for Internat. Understanding. Recipient Presdl. Meritorious Svc. award, 1991. Office: Northrop Grumman Corp Elec Sys Sector PO Box 451 MS A275 Baltimore MD 21203 Office Phone: 410-765-9353.

GLASSMAN, M. MELISSA, lawyer; b. Fort Rucker, Ala., 1955; BS summa cum laude, U. Tex., Austin, 1976; JD magna cum laude, George Mason U., Arlington, Va., 1987. Bar: Va. 1987, DC 1988, Md. 1995. Assoc. McGuire-Woods LLP, Tysons Corner, Va., 1987—96, ptnr., comml. litig. dept., 1996—, mng. ptnr. Tysons Corner office, 2004—. Mem.: Va. Bar Assn. (bd. mem. comml. litig. sect., chmn. constrn. & pub. contracts sect.). Office: McGuire-Woods LLP Ste 1800 1750 Tysons Blvd Mc Lean VA 22102-4215 Office Phone: 703-712-5351. Office Fax: 703-712-5228. Business E-Mail: mglassman@mcguirewoods.com.

GLASSMAN, STEVEN, dentist; m. Debra Glassman; 3 children. BA cum laude, Brandeis U.; DDS, Columbia Col. Dentistry. Dentist Glassman Dental Care, NYC. Office: NYC Cosmetic Dentists Glassman Dental Care 160 West End Ave New York NY 10023 Office Phone: 212-787-4860. Office Fax: 212-787-9238.*

GLASSMAN, STEVEN J., lawyer; b. N.Y.C., 1944; BS, MIT, 1964; JD, Georgetown U., 1968. Bar: N.Y. 1970. Patent examiner U.S. Patent Office, 1964-65; asst. sect. chief, counsel tech. utilization Nat. Aeronautics and Space Adminstrn., 1966-71; asst. U.S. Atty. so. dist. N.Y. U.S. Atty's. Office, 1971-76, chief civil rights sect. so. dist. N.Y., 1974-75, chief civil appellate atty. so. dist. N.Y., 1975-76; ptnr. Kaye Scholer LLP, N.Y.C., 1979—. Editor Georgetown Law Jour., 1967-68. Mem. ABA, Assn. Bar City N.Y., Fed. Bar Coun., Phi Delta Phi. Office: Kaye Scholer LLP 425 Park Ave New York NY 10022-3506

GLASSON, LLOYD, sculptor, educator; b. Chgo. s. Albert and Fay G.; m. Cathleen Naso, 1968. BFA, Sch. Art Inst. Chgo., 1957; MFA, Tulane U., 1959. Mannequin sculptor, 1959-60; exhibits designer Newark Mus., 1961-62; prof. emeritus U. Hartford, (Conn.), 1964—. Co-founder Artists Tenants Assn., 1961— One-man shows Dorsky Gallery, N.Y.C., 1966, 74, Trinity Coll., Hartford, 1977, SaltBox Gallery, West Hartford, 1985, The Greene Art Gallery, Guilford, Conn., 1997, Sculpture Showcase, Ltd., New Hope, Pa., 1997; represented in permanent collections Wadsworth Atheneum, Hartford, Bushnell Auditorium, Hartford, Ch. of St. Helena, West Hartford, U. N.H., Karen Horney Inst., N.Y.C., Yale U., New Haven, Hartford Hosp., Forma Viva, Kostanjevica, Slovenia, ACMAT Corp., New Britain, Conn.; recreated the 2 bronze angels atop Soldiers and Sailors Meml. Arch, Hartford; designer, Albert Schweitzer Humanitarian award. Served with U.S. Army, 1952-54. Recipient Gold medal 52d ann. exhbn. Nat. Sculpture Soc., 1985, James E. and Frances W. Bent award for Creativity, 1989. Fellow Nat. Sculpture Soc.; mem. NAD (Thomas Proctor prize 1985, Gold medal 1986), Sculptors Guild. Office Phone: 212-431-3313.

GLASSROTH, JEFFREY, internist, educator; b. NYC, Oct. 28, 1948; s. Murray and Marie (Cheynoweth) G.; m. Carol Holton, July 22, 1972; children: Marley, Drew. AB, Columbia U., 1969; MD, U. Cin., 1973. Diplomate Am. Bd. Internal Medicine, Subspecialty Bd. Pulmonary Medicine. Intern U. Cin. Med. Ctr., 1973-74, intern, resident, 1973-75, 77-78, resident, 1974-75, 77-78; fellow in pulmonary and critical care medicine Boston U., 1978-81, instr. medicine, 1979-81; from asst. to assoc. prof. medicine Northwestern U., Evanston, Ill., 1981-90, prof. medicine, 1990—95; prof. medicine, chair dept. Allegheny U. Health Scis., Phila., 1995—98; pres. Am. Thoracic Soc., NYC, 1999—2000; chmn., dept. of med. Univ. Wisconsin, 1998—2005; vice dean, prof. medicine Tufts U. Sch. Medicine, 2005—. Cons. Astra N.Am., Westboro, Mass., 1993-99, Genentech/Novartis, San Francisco, 2000-02; mem. adv. coun. for elimination of Tb, CDC, Atlanta, 1993-97; mem. ad hoc study sect. NIH, Bethesda, Md., 1993, 97. Editor: Scientific Basis Respiratory Infection, 1993; co-editor: Baum's Textbook of Pulmonary Diseases, 7th edit., 2003; assoc. editor Am. Jour. Respiratory Critical Care Medicine, 1994-99; mem. editl. bd. Chest, 1988-93. Surgeon, USPHS, 1975-77, Atlanta. Rsch. grantee NIH, 1987-97, recipient Pulmonary Acad. awards, 1983-89. Fellow ACP, Am. Coll. Chest Physicians; mem. AAAS, Am. Thoracic Soc. (sec. 1996-97, v.p. 1997-98, pres.-elect 1998, pres. 1999-2000), Ctrl. Soc. for Clin. Rsch. (pres. 2002-03), European Respiratory Soc., Internat. Union Against TB and Lung Disease, Assn. Profs. Medicine (pres.-elect 2003, pres. 2004-05). Avocations: skiing, distance running. Office: Tufts Univ Sch Med 136 Harrison Ave Boston MA 02111 Office Phone: 617-636-2727. Business E-Mail: jg@medicine.wisc.edu, jeff.glassroth@tufts.edu.

GLATT, LINNEA ELIZABETH, artist; b. Bismarck, N.D., Sept. 8, 1949; d. Joe J. and Helen (Weigel) Glatt; m. James B. Cinquemani, Jr., Apr. 28, 1979; children: Dominic Bernardo Cinquemani, Julia Helena Cinquemani. BS, Moorhead State U., 1971; MA, U. Dallas, Irving, 1972. Mem. faculty dept. art and humanities Richland Coll., Dallas, 1974-84; mem. faculty dept. art and history So. Meth. U., Dallas, 1985-88; founding mem. D.W. Gallery, Dallas, 1975. Lectr. in field. Exhibited in shows including Ft. Worth Art Mus., 1975, U. Tex. at Arlington, 1976, 89, D.W. Gallery, Dallas, 1977, 79, 80, 83, N.D. Mus. Arts, 1984 (Waco (Tex.) Art Ctr., 1984, Amarillo (Tex.) Art Mus., 1986, U. Colo. Art Gallery, 1987, San Angelo (Tex.) Mus. Art, 1989, El Paso Mus. Art, 1989, Bridge Ctr. for Contemporary Art, El Paso, 1994; represented in permanent collections at Dallas Mus. Art, Ft. Worth Art Ctr.; permanent installations include Passage Inacheve, Buffalo Bayou, Houston, 1990, Mimi's Garden, Dallas Arboretum and Bot. Soc., 1988, Harrow, Lubben Plz., Dallas, 1992, 27th Ave Waste Mgmt. Facility, City of Phoenix, 1993; subject of numerous articles; represented by Gerald Peters Gallery, Dallas. Recipient individual artist grant Art Matters, 1989, Anne Giles Kimbrough Fund grant Dallas Mus. Art, 1992; Nat. Endowment Visual Artist fellowship grantee, 1986. Home and Office: 2412 Hardwick St Dallas TX 75208-2014

GLATT, MITCHELL STEVEN, consumer products company executive; b. N.Y.C., Sept. 2, 1957; s. Herbert and Gloria (Comita) G.; m. Randy Ginsburg, Oct., 1987. BA, NYU, 1978, MBA, 1980. Agt. trainee Internat. Creative Mgmt., N.Y.C., 1980-81; exec. asst. to chmn. bd. Bozell, Jacobs, Kenyon & Eckhardt, Inc., N.Y.C., 1981-87; chmn. of bd. Magla Products Inc., Chatham, 1987—. Pres. GiGi Products, Inc., pres. Am. Med. Acceptance Corp., 1998—. Cons. Statue of Liberty Ellis-Island Found., N.Y.C., 1983-87, Juvenile Diabetes Found., N.Y.C., 1987; adv. bd. NYU Sch. of the Arts; mem. Playwrights Theater N.J. Recipient Commendation Advt. Women of N.Y., N.Y.C., 1986. Mem. Am. Mgmt. Assn., Young Pres. Orgn. Office: Am Med Acceptance Corp 11 West 42nd St New York NY 10036-4011

GLATZ, LAWRENCE FRANCIS, German language educator, researcher; b. Pitts., May 3, 1961; s. Charles Lawrence and Dorothy Christina Glatz; m. Jacqueline Roundy. BA with honors, U. Pa., 1984; MA, Pa. State U., 1988, PhD in German, 1995. Asst. prof. German Met. State Coll. of Denver, 1996-2001, assoc. prof. German, 2001—. Webmaster, bd. dirs. Colo. Congress Fgn. Lang. Tchrs., Denver, 2000—. Author: Heinrich Boell as Moralist, 1999. German Acad. Exch. Svc. fellow U. Hamburg/Free U. Berlin, 1992-93. Roman Catholic. Office: Met State Coll of Denver PO Box 173362 Campus Box 26 Denver CO 80217-3362 E-mail: glatz@mscd.edu.

GLAUBER, ROBERT R., stock exchange executive; BA in econ., Harvard Coll.; D in fin., Harvard Bus. Sch. Joined faculty Harvard Bus. Sch., 1964, prof. fin., 1964—88; under sec. of treas. for fin. US Govt., 1989—92; lectr. Ctr. Bus. and Govt., Harvard's Kennedy Sch. Govt., 1992—2000; mem. bd. NASD, Washington, 1996—, pres., 2000—01, CEO, 2000—, chmn., 2001—. Dir. Moody's Corp., Bermuda, XL Capital, Ltd., Am. Stock Exchange. Achievements include apptd. by Pres. Reagan to exec. dir. task force on market mechanisms ("Brady Commn.") to study stock market crash, 1987. Office: NASD 1735 K St NW Washington DC 20006-1500 Office Phone: 202-728-8000. Office Fax: 202-293-6260.

GLAUBINGER, LAWRENCE DAVID, retired manufacturing company executive; b. Newark, Nov. 26, 1925; s. Samuel I. and Pauline (Sandler) G.; m. Lucienne Lefebvre, Nov. 11, 1967. BS with honors, Ind. U., 1949; MBA, Columbia U., 1977; LLD (hon.), Ind. U., 1993. Adminstrv. asst. to pres. Ronson, Inc., Newark, 1949-51; mdse. mgr. United Mchts., N.Y.C., 1951-65; v.p. Marietta Silk Mills, Pa., 1965-66; pres., CEO Channel Textile Co. Inc., Bradford, Vt., 1966-75; chmn. bd., CEO Stern & Stern Industries, Inc., N.Y.C., 1977-2000, also bd. dirs.; ret., 2000. Pres. Lawrence Econ. Cons. Inc., Hallandale, Fla., 1977—; mgr. Beegee Trading Co. LLC, 2000—; bd. dirs. Leucadia Nat. Corp. Bd. overseers Columbia U. Sch. Bus., chmn. ann. funds campaigns, 1980-82; bd. dirs. Ind. U. Found.; mem. Ind. U. Bus. Sch. Acad. Alumni Fellows; bd. dirs. Ind. U. Varsity Club. Served with USCGR, 1943-46. Recipient Disting. Alumni Svc. award, Ind. U. Mem. Hoosier Hundred, Ind. U. Dean's Assocs., Columbia U. Bus. Assocs., Campaign for Columbia (co-chmn. bus. sch.), Am. Arbitration Assn., Princeton Club (N.Y.), Green Brook Country Club, Beta Gamma Sigma. Republican. Jewish. Home: Sterling House # 253 6307 S Hwy AIA Melbourne Beach FL 32951 Office: Lawrence Econ Cons PO Box 4463 Grand Ctrl Station New York NY 10163-4463

GLAUS, TROY, professional baseball player; b. Newport Beach, Calif., Aug. 3, 1976; Player Anaheim (Calif.) Angels, 1998—2004, Arizona Diamondbacks, 2004—. Named World Series MVP, 2002; named to, Am. League All Star Team, 2000—03. Achievements include led American League in Home Runs (47), 2000; member of World Series Champion Anaheim Angeles, 2002. Office: Arizona Diamondbacks 401 E Jefferson St Phoenix AZ 85004

GLAUTHIER, T. J., management consultant; b. Durham, N.C., Jan. 3, 1944; s. Theodore and Martha May (Myers) G.; m. Carrie L. Bostrom, June 11, 1966 (div. 1973); children: Jeff, Paul, Tad; m. M. Brigid O'Farrell, July 9, 1977; 1 child, Patrick O. AB, Claremont (Calif.) Men's Coll., 1965; MBA, Harvard Bus. Sch., 1967. Cons. Peat, Marwick, Livingston, L.A., 1967-68; with Applied Computer Tech., L.A., 1968-70; cons. Applied Decision Systems, Cambridge, Mass., 1970-74; v.p. Temple, Barker & Sloane, Inc., Lexington, Mass., 1974-90; head Pub. Policy Practice, 1980-90; head Washington office, 1986-90; dir. energy and climate change World Wildlife Fund, Washington, 1990-93; assoc. dir. nat. resources, energy and sci. U.S. Office Mgmt. and Budget, Washington, 1993-98; dep. sec., COO U.S. Dept. Energy, 1999-2001; pres., CEO Electricity Innovation Inst., Palo Alto, Calif., 2001—04; pres. TJG Energy Assocs., LLC, Moss Beach, 2005—. Mng. public and private partnerships for electricity tech. R&D. Pres. Lake Barcroft Assn., 1989—94; assoc. Lake Barcroft Watershed Improvement Dist., 1989—2001; del. Va. State Dem. Conv., 1993, 1997. Democrat. Unitarian Universalist. Home: 1001 Ocean Blvd Moss Beach CA 94038 Office: 1001 Ocean Blvd Moss Beach CA 94038 Office Phone: 650-353-6061. E-mail: tj@eE2I.org, tjglauthier@aol.com.

GLAVIC, NANCY CAROL, business education educator; b. Cleve., Mar. 16, 1947; d. August Barbara; m. Gerald J. Glavic, May 3, 1969; children: Traci, Marceen. BS in Edn., Bowling Green (Ohio) U., 1968; MS in Edn., Robert Morris U., 1990. Bus. tchr. Brush High Sch., Lyndhurst, Ohio, 1969, Lima (Ohio) Sr. High Sch., 1969-70, Guernsey Noble Career Ctr., Buffalo, Ohio, 1978—2001, East Muskingum Schs., New Concord, Ohio, 1980—; acct. instr. Muskingum Tech. Coll., Zanesville, Ohio, 1990—2001; computer tchr. Northern Local Schs., Thornville, Ohio, 2001—. Wing. aux. mem. Guernsey Meml. Hosp.; sec. Cambridge Softball League. Jennings scholar 1988. Mem. Ohio Bus. Tchrs. Assn., Delta Kappa Gamma, Delta Pi Epsilon. Office Phone: 740-743-1335.

GLAVIN, A. RITA CHANDELLIER (MRS. JAMES HENRY GLAVIN III), lawyer; b. Schenectady, NY, May 11, 1937; d, Pierre Charles and Helen C. (Fox) Chandellier; m. James H. Glavin, III, June 1, 1963; children: Helene, James, Rita, Henry. AB cum laude, Middlebury Coll., 1958; JD, Union U. Albany Law Sch., 1961. Bar: N.Y. 1961, U.S. Dist. Ct. (no. dist.) N.Y. 1961, U.S. Tax Ct. 1965, U.S. Supreme Ct. 1978. Assoc. Eugene Steiner, Albany, N.Y., 1961-64, Helen Fox Chandellier, Schenectady, 1965-76; mem. Glavin and Glavin, Waterford, Schenectady, 1965-86, 87—, Albany, 1965-86, 87—. Del. 4th Jud. Dist. Nominating Conv., 1966—67; confidential law clk. justices N.Y. State Ct. Claims, 1968—71; surrogate judge Saratoga County, 1986; dir. assn. coun. mems. and coll. trustees SUNY, 1991—2002, sec., 1996—2002. Mem. editl. bd. Albany Law Rev., 1960-61. Sec. Bellevue Women's Med. Ctr., 2001—02; bd. dirs., chmn. fin. com. Schenectady YWCA, 1979—81; bd. dirs. Schenectady Jr. League, 1974, 1976; del. pub. affairs com. N.Y. State Jr. League, 1976; sec. Bellevue Maternity Hosp., Inc., 1966—2001, bd. dirs., 1966—83, bd. advisors, 1984—2001; bd. dirs. Bellevue Women's Med. Ctr., 2001—02; trustee Middlebury Coll., 1978—88, chmn. law com., 1982—88, vice chmn. bd. dirs., 1986—87; trustee Waterford Hist. Mus. and Cultural Ctr., Inc., 2000—, sec., 2002—; mem. univ. coun. SUNY, Albany, 1985—2002; tech. advisor HSA Northeastern N.Y. Maternity and Pediat. Com., 1976. Mem. N.Y. State Bar Assn. (mem. ho. of dels. 1987-88, nominating com. 1988-90), Saratoga County Bar Assn. (exec. com. 1981—, v.p. 1985, pres. 1986), Schenectady County Bar Assn., Phi Beta Kappa, Kappa Kappa Gamma. Office: Glavin & Glavin PO Box 40 69 2nd St Waterford NY 12188-2422 Personal E-mail: gglaw@mindspring.com.

GLAVIN, JAMES EDWARD, landscape architect; b. Syracuse, N.Y., Aug. 18, 1923; s. James Edward and Florence Ellen (Nelson) G.; m. Helen Catherine Hartnett, Aug. 24, 1946; children— Kathleen Glavin Kopitsky, Timothy, David, Matthew, Martin, Maureen. BS in Landscape Architecture, SUNY Coll. Environ. Sci. and Forestry, Syracuse, 1948. City planner Syracuse Planning Commn., 1948-49; chief land planning dept. Sargent Webster Crenshaw & Folley, Syracuse, 1951-56; partner Hueber Hares Glavin (architects, landscape architects, and engr., and predecessor), Syracuse, 1956-88, James E. Glavin & Assos. (landscape architects), Syracuse, 1956-88, Syracuse Scale Models, 1968-88, Glavin & Van Iderstine Landscape Architects, 1980-88; pvt. cons., 1988—. Vis. juror, lectr. State U. Coll. Environ. Sci. and Forestry, 1959, 65, 69, State U. Coll. Agr., Cornell U., 1970—; mem. faculty adv. coun. Sch. Landscape Architecture, N.Y. State U. Coll. Environ. Sci. and Forestry, 1990—; cons. N.Y. State Council Arts, 1971; mem. N.Y. State Bd. Landscape Architects, 1987-91. Contbr. articles to profl. publs.; contbg.; editor: Empire State Architect, 1957-60. Mem. Citizens Found., Syracuse, 1957-77, St. Thomas More Found, 1965-88; bd. dirs. Hiawatha coun. Boy Scouts Am., 1980-88, mem. adv. bd., 1988-2003; bd. dirs. Adirondack Archtl. Heritage, 1993-2000, Clifton-Fine Hosp., 1998-2000; trustee Clifton Cmty. Libr., 1994-2000. Recipient Design award Am. Assn. Nurserymen, 1969, 71; named Outstanding Alumni, SUNY Coll. Environ. Sci. and Forestry Alumni Assn., 1994. Fellow Am. Soc. Landscape Architects (past co-chmn. pvt. practice com., Design award 1968, 71); mem. ASCE (past v.p. Syracuse chpt.), Sigma Lambda Alpha. Home and Office: PO Box 491 Cranberry Lake NY 12927-0491

GLAVIN, JAMES HENRY, III, lawyer; b. Albany, N.Y., Oct. 6, 1931; s. James Henry, Jr. and Elizabeth Mary (Gibbons) Glavin; m. A. Rita Chandellier, June 1, 1963; children: Helene Elizabeth, James C., Rita Marie, James Henry IV. AB, Villanova U., 1953; JD, Albany Law Sch., 1956. Bar: N.Y. 1956, U.S. Dist. Ct. (no. dist.) N.Y. 1957, U.S. Dist. Ct. (mid. dist.) Tenn. 1959, U.S. Ct. Mil. Appeals 1959, U.S. Supreme Ct. 1959, U.S. Ct. Appeals (DC cir.) 1976. Mem. Glavin and Glavin, Waterford, NY, 1960—. Chmn. regional bd. Key Bank, N.A., 1968—93. Author: (book) The Tour Broker and the Interstate Commerce Commission, 1977; editor: Administrative Law Practice in New York, 1988. Bd. dirs. Waterford Ctrl. Cath. Sch., 1969—; county chmn. Saratoga County Dems., NY, 1964—68; trustee St. Mary's Ch., Waterford, 1974—, Waterford Rural Cemetery; bd. dirs. Bellevue Maternity Hosp., 1968—2001. Served to capt. JAGC USAF, 1957—60. Mem.: ATLA, ABA, Mystery Writers Am., Internat. Soc. Gen. Semantics, Rensselaer County Bar Assn., Albany County Bar Assn., Saratoga County Bar Assn., Estate Planning Coun. Ea. N.Y., N.Y. State Bar Assn., Fed. Bar Assn., Nat. Health Lawyers Assn., Transp. Lawyers Assn., Am. Acad. Hosp. Attys., N.Y. Trial Lawyers Assn., Am. Psychology-Law Soc., Am. Acad. Polit. and Social Sci., Am. Soc. Law and Medicine, Assn. Former Intelligence Officers, Soc. Am. Baseball Rsch., Air Force Assn., Nat. Lawyers Club, KC, Lions. Roman Catholic. Home: 66 Saratoga Ave Waterford NY 12188-0040 Office: Glavin and Glavin PO Box 40 Waterford NY 12188-0040 E-mail: gglaw@mindspring.com.

GLAVINE, TOM (THOMAS MICHAEL GLAVINE), professional baseball player; b. Concord, Mass., May 25, 1966; m. Carri Dobbins, Nov. 7, 1992. Grad. high sch., Mass. Pitcher Atlanta Braves, 1987—2002, N.Y. Mets, 2002—. Recipient Cy Young award Baseball Writers' Assn. Am., 1991, 98, Silver Slugger award, 1991, 95; named Nat. League Pitcher Yr., Sporting News, 1991, named to Nat. League All-Star Team, 1991-93, 96-98, 2000-2002, 2004. Tied as leader of Nat. League pitching victories, 1991-92. Office: NY Mets Shea Stadium 123 01 Roosevelt Ave Flushing NY 11368-1699

GLAZE, LYNN FERGUSON, development consultant; b. Oakland, Calif., May 24, 1933; d. Kenneth Loveland and Constance May (Pedder) Ferguson; m. Harry Smith Glaze, Jr., July 3, 1957; children: Catherine, Charles Richard. BA, Stanford U., 1955, MA, 1966. Devel. dir. Greenwich Acad., Conn., 1982-84, Am. Lung Assn. of Del., 1988—89; devel. cons. St. Michael's Sch. and Nursery, Brandywine Mus., Opera Del., others, 1990—99. Author: Seasons of the Trail, 2000. Pres. Darien-Norwalk YWCA, Conn., 1973-76; sec. Darien Republican Town com., 1974-76; dist. chmn. Darien Rep. Meeting, 1974-76, mem. Rep. Nat. Conv. Platform Com., 1988; vestry St. Luke's Ch., Darien, 1979-82; justice of the peace, Darien, 1981-84; bd. dirs. Ingleside Homes, Inc., 1986-92, Henrietta Johnson Med. Ctr., 1994-97; pres. Del. ProChoice Med. Fund, 1997-99; mem. Gov.'s Small Bus. Coun., 1987, EEOC, New Castle County, 1991-94, Del. Common Cause, 1999—. Coro Found. fellow.

GLAZE, RICHARD TROY, music educator; b. Pensacola, Fla., Apr. 28, 1957; s. Woodie Lee and Vinona Hope Glaze; m. Lorena Rose Hickman, June 16, 7979; children: Rachel, Benjamin, Sarah. AA in Music, Pensacola Jr. Coll., 1977; BA in Music, U. W. Fla., 1979; MusM, Cinn. Coll., 1982. Asst. dir. bands Ft. Walton Beach (Fla.) H.S., 1982—86; music specialist Cherokee Elem., Niceville, Fla., 1988—90; prof. music U. W. Fla., Pensacola, 1990—, chair music, 2001—. Prin. clarinet Pensacola Symphony, 1990—2004. Avocations: bicycling, model building, computers. Home: 2787 Glen Eden Dr Pensacola FL 32514 Office: Univ W Fla Dept Music 11000 University Pkwy Pensacola FL 32514

GLAZE, RYAN JOEL, assistant principal; s. John and Louise Quirk Glaze; m. Anita Hunt, Sept. 1, 2001; children: Gavin Jonathan, Gabriel Josiah. BS, Ball State U., 1992, MS, 2002. Cert. K-12 adminstr. Ind. Dir. bands Attica HS, Ind., 1992—93, Tri-County HS, Remington, Ind., 1993—98, Yorktown HS, Ind., 1998—2002; asst. prin. Northeastern Elem., Fountain City, 2002—. Bd. mem. Town of Selma, 1999—2004. Mem.: Ind. Music Educators Assn., Ind. Assn. Sch. Principals, Phi Mu Alpha Sinfonia. Democrat. United Meth. Avocations: camping, bicycling, jogging. Office: Northeastern Elem Sch 534 Wallace Rd Fountain City IN 47341

GLAZE, THOMAS A., state supreme court justice; b. Jan. 14, 1938; s. Phyllis Laser; children: Steve, Mike, Julie, Amy, Ashley. BSBA, U. Ark., 1960, JD, 1964. Exec. dir. Election Research Council Inc., 1964-65; legal advisor Winthrop Rockefeller, 1965-66; staff atty. Pulaski County Legal Aid, 1966-67, asst. then dep. atty. gen., 1967-70; pvt. practice law, 1970-79; chancellor Ark. Chancery Ct., 6th Jud. Cir., 1979-80; judge Ark. Ct. Appeals, 1981-86; assoc. justice Ark. Supreme Ct., 1987—. Lecturer U. Ark., Little Rock, 1971, 72, 79, 80; lecturer U. Ark. Sch. Law, 1981, 82, 85, 87; chmn. Election Laws Inst., 1970-78. Past bd. dirs. Vis. Nurses Corp., Youth Home Inc. Office: Ark Supreme Ct Justice Bldg 625 Marshall St, 120 Justice Bldg Little Rock AR 72201-1054*

GLAZER, BARRY DAVID, lawyer; b. Cleve., Oct. 10, 1948; s. Jacob J. and Constance (Schwartz) Glazer; m. Deborah Werbner, Sept. 28, 1984. AB, Miami U., Oxford, Ohio, 1970; JD, Mich. Law Sch., 1973. Bar: Minn. 1973, U.S. Dist. Ct. Minn. 1973, France Conseil Juridique 1981. Assoc. Dorsey & Whitney, Mpls., 1973—78, ptnr., 1979—80, resident ptnr. Paris, 1980—86, London, 1986—91, mng. ptnr. Brussels, 1991—2000, London, 2001—. Mem.: Union Internat. des Avocats, Internat. Bar Assn., ABA. Office: Dorsey & Whitney LLP 21 Wilson St London EC2 England Office Phone: 44 207 588 0800. E-mail: glazer.barry@dorsey.com.

GLAZER, DONALD WAYNE, lawyer, corporate financial executive, educator; b. Cleve., July 26, 1944; s. Julius and Ethel (Goldstein) G.; children: Elizabeth M., Mollie S. AB summa cum laude, Dartmouth Coll., 1966; JD magna cum laude, Harvard U., 1969; LLM, U. Pa., 1970. Bar: Mass. 1970. Assoc. Ropes & Gray, Boston, 1970-78, ptnr., 1978-92, counsel, 1992-96; ptnr. Am. Bus. Ptnrs. LLC, Boston, 1996-98; pres. Mugar/Glazer Holdings, Inc., Boston, 1992-95; vice chmn. fin. New Eng. TV Corp. and WHDH-TV, Inc., Boston, 1992-93; adv. counsel Goodwin Procter LLC, Boston, 1997—; co-founder, corp. sec. Provant, Inc., Boston, 1998—, vice-chmn., 2002. Instr. corp. fin. Boston U. Law Sch., 1975; lectr. law Harvard U., Cambridge, Mass., 1978-91; trustee GMO Trust, Boston, 2000—, lead trustee, 2004, chmn. bd., 2005. Co-author: Massachusetts Corporation Law and Practice, 1991, Glazer and FitzGibbon on Legal Opinions, 1992, 2d edit., 2001; co-editor First Ann. Inst. on Securities Regulation, 1970; contbr. articles to legal jours. Past chmn., trustee Cowen Slavin Found.; past trustee Santa Fe Neuroscis. Inst.; past dir. Newton Girls Soccer League, past co-chmn. intramural com.; past trustee, past treas. Hillel Founds. of Greater Boston Inc.; past trustee Program for Young Negotiators. Fellow Salzburg Seminar in Am. Studies, 1975. Mem.: ABA (past chmn. legal opinions com., co-reporter Legal Opinions Prins., past chmn. subcom. on employee benefits and exec. compensation, fed. securities law com., past co-chmn. task force on sect. 16 devels., coun. bus. law sect.), Tri-Bar Legal Opinions Com. (co-chmn., co-reporter Third-party Closing Opinions, editor-in-chief The Remedies Opinion), Am. Law Inst. (Members Consultative Group Restatement Law Governing Lawyers), Boston Bar Assn. (past chmn., corp. sec., past chmn. securities law com., past co-chmn. legal opinions com.). Jewish. Home: 225 Kenrick St Newton MA 02458-2731

GLAZER, GUILFORD, real estate developer; b. Knoxville, Tenn., July 17, 1921; s. Aaron Usher and Ida (Bressoff) G.; children: Emerson, Erika; m. Diane Pregerson, Jan. 29, 1967. Mech. Engr., George Wash. U., 1939; Metallurgy, U. Louisville, 1943. Bd. dirs. The Torrance (Calif.) Co., 1990, Del Amo Fashion Ctr., Torrance, Calif., 1990; partial owner Allegheny Ctr., Pitts. Bd. dirs. Rand Corp. Ctr. for Middle East Pub. Policy. Developer various shopping ctrs. and office bldgs. in U.S. Pres. Reagan Libr. Found., Nixon Libr. Foun.; trustee L.A. Holocaust Meml., Stop Cancer, Bell Shelter for Homeless, Tel Aviv U.; founder Ford's Theatre, Washington, Am. Friends of the Israel Def. Force, Sino Judaic Inst., Nanjing, China, Moshe Dayan Ctr., Tel Aviv U. for Ea. and African Studies, U. Tenn. Judaic Studies Dept.; mem. Wilshire Blvd. Temple, L.A.County Mus. Art, Unified Fund Music Ctr. With USN, 1942-45, WWII. Recipient Hon. Fellow U. Tel Aviv. Mem. World Affairs Coun., Hillcrest Country Club, Monterey Country Club. Jewish. Avocation: golf. Office: Ste 610 9440 Santa Monica Blvd Beverly Hills CA 90210

GLAZER, JACK HENRY, lawyer; b. Paterson, N.J., Jan. 14, 1928; s. Samuel and Martha (Merkin) G.; m. Zelda d'Angleterre, 1979. BA, Duke U., 1950; JD, Georgetown U., 1956; postgrad., U. Frankfurt, Germany, 1956-57; SJD, U. Calif., Berkeley, 1977. Bar: D.C. 1957, Calif. 1968. Atty. GAO and NASA, 1958-60; mem. maritime divsn. UN Internat. Labour Office, Geneva, Switzerland, 1960, spl. legal adv., 1960-62; atty. NASA, Washington, 1963-66; chief counsel NASA-Ames Rsch. Ctr., Moffett Field, Calif.,

1966-88; gov. Calif. Maritime Acad., 1975-78; asst. prof. Hastings Coll. Law, 1985-87; prof., assoc. dean bus. sch. San Francisco State U., 1988-92; dir. San Francisco Palace Fine Arts, 1995. Contbr. articles to profl. jours. Comdr. Calif. Naval Militia, ret. Capt. JAGC, USNR, ret. Mem. Calif. Bar Assn., D.C. Bar Assn., White's Inn (reader). Office: White's Inn 37 White St San Francisco CA 94109-2609 Office Phone: 415-441-0236. Personal E-mail: whitesinn@aol.com.

GLAZER, JOSEPH A., medical association administrator; b. Middletown, N.Y., Feb. 3, 1961; s. Richard B. and Patricia A. Glazer; 1 child, Jeremy. AA, Ulster County C.C., Stone Ridge, N.Y., 1981; BA, SUNY, Albany, 1983; JD, Albany Law Sch., 1989. Bar: N.Y. 1990. Legis. staff various legis. offices, Albany; counsel, legis. dir. N.Y. State Assn. Counties, Albany, 1989-92; outreach coord. Alliance for Consumer Rights, Albany, 1993-97; pres., CEO Mental Health Assn. N.Y. State, Inc., Albany, 1997—. Spokesperson in field. Legis. staff various state legislators, Albany, N.Y., 1980-89; campaign mgmt. and staff local, state and presdl. campaigns, N.Y., 1983-96; candidate N.Y. State Assembly 102nd Dist., Upper Hudson Valley, N.Y., 1992. Mem. Found. Advocacy for Mental Health, Inc. (founder, sec./treas. 1998-2001). Office: Mental Health Assn NYS Inc Ste 415 194 Washington Ave Albany NY 12210 Office Fax: 518-426-8676. E-mail: mhanys@mhanys.org.

GLAZER, MALCOLM, professional sports team executive; b. Rochester, N.Y., Aug. 25, 1928; m. Linda; children: Avram, Kevin, Bryan, Joel, Ed, Darcie. Owner, pres. Tampa Bay (Fla.) Buccaneers, 1995—; shareholder Manchester United, 2003—, owner, 2005—. Pres., CEO First Allied Corp.; chmn. of bd. Zapata Corp., Houston, 1994-2002; bd. dirs. Specialty Equipment Cos. Active Am. Cancer Soc., Sloan-Kettering Cancer Ctr., United Jewish Appeal, Jewish Guild for the Blind. Office: Tampa Bay Buccaneers One Buccaneer Pl Tampa FL 33607*

GLAZER, MICHAEL, lawyer; b. L.A., Oct. 10, 1940; BS, Stanford U., 1962; MBA, Harvard U., 1964; JD, U. Calif., L.A., 1967. Bar: Calif. 1967. Law clk. to Hon. Roger J. Traynor Calif. Supreme Ct., 1967-68; commr. L.A. Dept. of Water & Power, 1973-76; chmn. Calif. Water Commn., 1976-78; asst. adminstr. nat. oceanic and atmospheric adminstrn. U.S. Dept. of Commerce, 1978-80; dir. Met. Water Dist. of So. Calif., 1984-91; ptnr. Paul, Hastings, Janofsky & Walker LLP, L.A. Articles editor U. Calif. at L.A. Law Rev., 1966-67. Mem. State Bar Calif. (com. on corps. 1986-87), L.A. County Bar Assn. (chair fed. securities regulation com. 1988-90, chair exec. com. bus. and corp. law sect. 1995-96), Order of the Coif, Phi Beta Kappa. Office: Paul Hastings Janofsky & Walker LLP 515 S Flower St Los Angeles CA 90071-2300

GLAZER, REA HELENE See KIRK, REA

GLAZER, RICHARD BASIL, university program director; b. Boston, Dec. 20, 1933; s. Edward and Marie (Stearns) G. BS in Biol. Scis., Colo. State U., 1957; MS in Zoology and Forestry, Pa. State U., 1959; postgrad., Cornell U. Assoc. dir. Project Biotech Am. Inst. Biol. Scis., Washington, 1971-73; dir. environ. and energy programs Ulster County C.C., Stone Ridge, N.Y., 1974-81, chair divsn. bus. and human resources, 1981-86; dean divsn. math., phys. engring., computer sci. techs. Westchester C.C., Valhalla, N.Y., 1986-96; dir. corp. found. and govt. rels. Iona Coll., New Rochelle, N.Y., 1996—. Pres. SUNY Coun. 4-Yr. Coll. Bus. Faculty Adminstrs. Bus. Schs. and Colls.; mem. SUNY Chancellor's Articulation Task Force in Bus.; chair mini-course devel. project NSF-Purdue U.; mem. nat. task force 2-yr. coll. biologists; vis. lectr. Am. Inst. Biol. Scis.; mem. commn. higher edn. Mid. States Assn. Schs. and Colls. evaluation team; mem. evaluation team N.Y. State Dept. Edn.; chmn. nat. task force on assoc. degrees in higher edn. in bus.; mem. oversight com. Am. Assn. Environ. Engring. Profs. Author over 100 curriculum materials in field. Chmn. health svcs. coun. United Way, Ulster County, N.Y., 1969-71; supr. Town of Rosendale, N.Y., 1974-80; bd. dirs. Mid-Hudson Valley Tech. Devel. Ctr., Fishkill, N.Y., 1988-96; pres. Rosendale Pub. Libr., 1989-95; dist. chmn. Minnewaska Trail Boy Scouts Am.; chmn. shared med. computer facilities com. Kingston and Benedictine Hosp.; bd. dirs. Am. Lung Assn. Hudson Valley chpt.; chmn. bd. rev. Hudson Valley Health Systems Agy.; firefighter Bloomington Fire Dept. Recipient cert. Spl. Recognition, U.S. Congress, 1995, Soc. Mfg. Engrs. award; fellow U.S. Dept. Interior Fish and Wildlife Svc., NSF, Cornell U. Mem. Am. Assn. C.C.s., Phi Sigma Soc. (hon.), Tau Alpha Pi (hon.), Alpha Beta Gamma (hon.). Avocations: fishing, hiking, photography, jogging. Home: 69 Pond View Ln Chappaqua NY 10514-3728

GLAZIER, LYLE, writer, educator; b. Leverett, Mass., May 8, 1911; s. Harry Lee and Mertie Abby (Briggs) G.; m. Amy Louise Niles July 15, 1939 (dec. Mar. 1987); children: Laura, Susan, Alis. AB, Middlebury Coll., 1933, MA Bread Loaf Sch. of English, 1937; PhD, Harvard U., 1950; postgrad. in word processing, Vt. C.C., 1993-94. Prin. Northfield Mass. Ctr. Graded Sch., 1934-35; housemaster Mt. Hermon Sch. for Boys, Gill, Mass., 1935-37; instr. English, Bates Coll., Lewiston, Maine, 1937-42, Tufts Coll., Somerville, Mass., 1942-44; asst. in Shakespeare, Harvard U., Cambridge, Mass., 1944-45; tchg. fellow Harvard U. and Radcliffe Coll., Cambridge, Mass., 1945-47; asst. prof. English, U. Buffalo, 1947-52, assoc. prof., chmn. Am. studies, 1952-63; prof. English and Am. studies SUNY, Buffalo, 1965-72, prof. emeritus, 1972—. Fulbright chair Am. studies U. Istanbul, 1961-63, Fulbright Lectr. Hacettepe U., Ankara, Turkey, 1968-69, vis. prof., 1970, 71; lectr. U. Madras, India, 1970, 71; cons. thematic studies CUNY, 1973-75; vis. prof. Sana'a U., North Yemen, 1980; vol. adj. prof. So. Vt. Coll., Bennington, 1984-86; USIS vol. expert Am. lit., India, 1971; vol. prof. Miles Coll., Birmingham, 1967. Author: (novel) Summer for Joey, 1987, Stills from a Moving Picture, 1974, (poetry) Orchard Park and Istanbul, 1965, You Too, 1969, Voices of the Dead, 1971, The Dervishes, 1971, Two Continents, 1976, Azubah Nye, 1988, Recalls, 1986, Prefatory Lyrics, 1991, Searching for Amy, 1993, 2d edit. 2000 (criticism) American Decadence and Rebirth, 1971, Great Day Coming, 1988, Bennington Politics and Schools, 1986, Included in Reflections on a Gift of a Watermelon Pickle and Other Modern Verse (children's poetry anathology selected by children), 1966, 95, Contemporary Authors Autobiography Series, 1996; contbr. poems and articles to profl. and lit. jours.; contbr. to Festschrift for S.M. Pandeya, Banaras Hindu U., 1996. Exec. com. Friends of Bennington Free Libr., 1990-92; mem. sch. bd., vice chmn. Orchard Park (N.Y.) Sch. Dist., 1952-58; mem. Town Charter Commn., Bennington, 1987-89; mem. Gamaliel Painter's Cane Soc., Middlebury Coll., 1990—, mem. founders soc. Founders Soc., 1998—, mem. exec. com. Friends of Libr., Middlebury Coll., 1987-89, Abernethy Poetry/Rare Book Collection, Starr Libr., Middlebury, 2000; mem. Ret. Srs. Vol. Program, 1973—; mem. Bennington County Dem. Com., 1984-87; mem. exec. com. Bennington Area AIDS Project, 1990—; mem. nat. steering com. Clinton/Gore 1996, 1995-98, Gore 2000, 1999—; mem. Bennington Area Art Coun., 1990—; mem. Bennington Area Home Health Assn., 1990—, Bennington Counseling Svc., 1990; mem. Bennington County Chorus, 1973-79, patron, 1980—; mem. Grad. Students Middlebury Gay Lesbians, 1995, Vt. Mountain Pride Media, 1999; mem. Acad. of Am. Poets, ACLU, Bennington Mus. Found. Libr. of Congress Assocs., S.W. Vt. Regional Cancer Ctr., Rattlesnake Gutter Trust, Bread Loaf Writers' Conf. Fellow Am. Coun. Learned Socs., 1951-52. Mem. MLA, Bennington Robert Frost Soc., Vt. Coun. on Arts, League Vt. Writers, Poets and Writers, Am. Assn. Ret. Persons, Edmund Hayes Soc., North Bennington Artists Soc., Bennington County Humane Soc., Vt. Hist. Soc., Nat. Trust for Hist. Preservation, New England Artists Trust. Avocation: music. Home: 20 Bull Hill Rd Amherst MA 01002-9515 *Our social, religious, and political institutions are medieval and inconsistent with our knowledge of the physical and biological universe. Unless we rid ourselves of nationalism, militarism and economic imperialism and the notion of an anthropomorphic universe, we are doomed to self destruction.*

GLAZIER, ROBERT CARL, publishing executive; b. Brandsville, Mo., Mar. 26, 1927; s. Vernie A. and Mildred F. (Beu) G.; m. Harriette Hubbard, June 5, 1949; children: Gregory Kent, Jeffrey Robert. Student, Drury Coll., 1944-46; BA, U. Wichita, 1949. Reporter Springfield (Mo.) Daily News, 1944-46; asst. city editor Wichita Eagle, 1946-49; journalism instr. U. Wichita, 1949-53; dir. pub. relations Springfield (Mo.) Pub. Schs., 1953-59; asso. dir. dept. radio and TV The Methodist Ch., Nashville, 1959-61; gen. mgr. WDCN-TV (Channel 2), Nashville, 1961-65, KETC (Channel 9), St. Louis, 1965-76; also exec. dir. St. Louis Ednl. TV Commn.; pres. So. Ednl. Communications Assn., 1976-80; chmn. bd. Springfield Communications, Inc., Mo., 1980—. Bd. dirs. Systematic Savs. & Loan Assn., Cox Health Sys.; pres. Lester E. Cox Med. Ctrs., 1999-2000 Bd. dirs. Adult Edn. Council Greater St. Louis, 1965-76, United Meth. Communications, 1980-86, Springfield Area Council of Chs., 1980-86. Served with AUS, 1945-46. Named to, Writers Hall of Fame of Am., 2003; recipient Ozarks Heritage award, Mus. of the Ozarks, 1990, Silver Beaver award, Boy Scouts Am., 2003. Mem. Nat. Sch. Public Relations Assn. (past regional dir.), Nat. Acad. TV Arts and Scis. (gov.), Mo. Instructional TV Council, Ill. Instructional TV Commn., Nat. Assn. Ednl. Broadcasters. Clubs: Rotary Internat. Methodist. Home: 2305 E Meadow Dr Springfield MO 65804-4536 Office: 520 S Union Ave Springfield MO 65802-2660

GLEASON, ABBOTT, history professor; b. Cambridge, Mass., July 21, 1938; s. Sarell Everett and Mary Eleanor (Abbott) G.; m. Sarah Caperton Fischer, June 11, 1966; children: Nicholas Abbott, Margaret Holliday BA, Harvard U., 1961, PhD, 1969. Asst. prof. history Brown U., Providence, 1969-73, assoc. prof. history, 1973-78, prof. history, 1978—, Keeney prof. history, 1993—; sec. Kennan Inst. for Advanced Russian Studies, Woodrow Wilson Ctr., Washington, 1980-82, chmn. history, 1989-92; dir. Watson Inst., 1999-2000, dir. univ. rels., 2000—03. Mem. overseers com. to visit Davis Ctr. for Russian Studies, Harvard U., Cambridge, 1981-85, 91-97; bd. dirs. Fabergé Arts Found. Author: European and Muscovite, 1972, Young Russia, 1980, Totalitarianism, 1995 (with William Taubman and Sergei Khrushchev), Nikita Khrushchev, 2000; co-editor: Bolshevik Culture, 1985, Shared Destiny, 1985, Nineteen Eighty-Four: George Orwell and our Future, 2005. Fellow, Howard Found., 1973—74; Rockefeller fellow, Aspen Inst., 1977, Mellon fellow, Harvard U., 1985. Mem. Am. Hist. Assn., Am. Assn. Advancement Slavic Studies (del. to Am. Coun. Learned Socs. 1984-87, bd. dirs. 1991-97, exec. com. 1994-97, pres. 1995). Democrat. Home: 30 John St Providence RI 02906-1043 Office: Brown U Dept History 142 Angell St Providence RI 02912-9040 E-mail: abbott_gleason@brown.edu.

GLEASON, BRUCE PHILIP, education educator, writer; b. Princeton, Minn., Aug. 30, 1958; s. Lindahl Bert and Joanne Peterson Gleason, Helen Winterfield Gleason (Stepmother). BA, Crown Coll., St. Bonifacious, Minn., 1980; BS, U. Minn., Mpls., Minn., 1981, MA, 1988; PhD, U. Iowa, Iowa City, Iowa, 1995. Cert. music tchg. Dept. Edn., Minn., 1982. Music tchr. k-12 Kennedy Cmty. Sch., Kennedy, Minn., 1982—88; tchg. asst. U. Iowa, Iowa City, 1991—95; dir. choirs Glenbard South H.S., Glen Ellyn, Ill., 1996—97; asst. prof. Gordon Coll., Wenham, Mass., 1997—99, U. St. Thomas, St. Paul, 1999—. Author: (program liner notes for cds) Band Music Promotion; co-author (with Michael Swanson): (cookbook) The Renaissance Man's Guide to the Kitchen; composer: (songs) The Captain, Come Away with Me Jean, The Mist at Widow's Run, Bantry Bay, Across the Seven Seas; editor (founding editor): (on-line journal) Research and Issues in Music Education; contbg. editor: (magazine) Christianity and the Arts; contbr. articles pub. to profl. jour. Specialist U.S. Army, 1988—91, 298th Berlin Brigade. Decorated Nat. Def. Svc. Medal U.S. Army, Army of Occupation Medal, Army Svc. Ribbon, Deutsche Bundeswehr Schutzenschnur Deutsche Bundeswehr/U.S. Army; grantee U. St. Thomas Faculty Rsch. Assistance Grant, 2002, German Am. Heritage Found. Grant, 2003. Mem.: Army Hist. Found., Am. Hist. Assn., Internat. Mil. Music Soc., MENC: The Nat. Assn. for Music Edn., Co. of Mil. Historians, U.S. Cav. Assn. (life). Achievements include research in Tracing the History of Horse-Mounted Bands. Avocations: travel, classic automobiles, home refurbishing, gardening, landscaping. Home: 1828 Carl St Saint Paul MN 55113 Office: Univ St Thomas Loras Hall 103 2115 Summit Ave Saint Paul MN 55105 Office Phone: 651-962-5729. Personal E-mail: brucegleason@comcast.net. Business E-Mail: bpgleason@stthomas.edu.

GLEASON, DALE LAWRENCE, music educator; b. Kirkland, Wash., July 27, 1942; s. John Truman Gleason, Jr. and Marie Mildred (Williamson) Gleason; m. Ann Carolyn Gleason, June 22, 1968; children: Joanne Lee, Jennifer Ann, Julie Lynn. BA in Music, U. Wash., 1965; MEd in Music, Western Wash. State U., 1968. Cert. tchr. 1972. Tchr. music Cascade Jr. H.S., Sedro-Woolley, Wash., 1965—66; instr. instrumental and vocal Western Wash. State Coll., Bellingham, Wash., 1966—68, Hazen H.S., Renton, Wash., 1968—77; instr. instrumental music and theory Bellevue C.C., Wash., 1977—2003; pub. Gleaside Music, Bonney Lake, Wash., 2002—. Chmn. music program Bellevue (Wash.) C.C., 1978—2002. Author: A Process Approach to Diatenic Harmony, 1988, A Process Approach to Chromatic Harmony, 1989; composer (songs) Sing to the World, 1981, Waverly Way Concert March, 1998. Sec. Hydrophonic and Racebout Mus., 1994—2002, bd. dirs., 1994—2002. Mem.: Wash. Music Edn. Assn. (bd. dirs. 1994—98, C.C. rep. 1994—98, v.p. 2000—02, 4 Outstanding Svc. awards 2002, Hall of Fame 2000), Seattle Composers Alliance. Avocations: boating, golf, restorations, composition. Home: 10408 Meadowlark Ct East Bonney Lake WA 98390 Office: Bellavue CC 3000 Landerholm Cir SE Bellevue WA 98007 Office Phone: 888-296-2094.

GLEASON, DANIEL J., lawyer; b. New Haven, Conn., Sept. 22, 1944; BA magna cum laude, Harvard Coll., 1967; JD cum laude, Harvard U., 1970. Bar: Mass. 1971, N.H. 1992. Ptnr., co-chmn. intellectual property litig. group Nutter, McClennen & Fish, Boston. Arbitrator, Am. Arbitration Assn. Mem. exec. com. Boston Lawyers Com. for Civil Rights Under Law; dir. Wide Horizons for Children. Named Mass. Super Lawyer, Boston mag., 2004 Fellow Am. Coll. Trial Lawyers; mem. ABA (chmn. subcom. intellectual property litig.), Mass. Bar Assn., Boston Bar Assn., Phi Beta Kappa. Office: Nutter McClennen & Fish World Trade Ctr West 155 Seaport Blvd Boston MA 02210-2604 Office Phone: 617-439-2233. Office Fax: 617-310-9233. Business E-Mail: dgleason@nutter.com.

GLEASON, JAMES D., lawyer; b. 1953; BS, No. Mich. Univ.; JD, Thomas M. Cooley Law Sch. Mem. Gleason Law Offices, Henniker, NH. Divsn. One Football official. Mem.: N.H. Bar Assn. (pres. 2004). Office: Gleason Law Office 24 Main St PO Box 4300 Henniker NH 03242-4300 Business E-Mail: gleasonlaw@conknet.com.

GLEASON, JAMES MULLANEY, lawyer, insurance company executive; b. Sept. 27, 1948; s. Harry H. and Dorothy (Mullaney) Gleason; m. Margaret McGuire; children: Matthew, Katherine. BA, Briar Cliff Coll., 1973; JD, Creighton U., 1976. Bar: (Iowa) 1976, Nebr. 1976. From asst. counsel to asst. v.p. Woodmen of the World, Omaha, 1976—93, asst. v.p., 1993—. With U.S. Army, 1968—69. Fellow: Life Mgmt. Inst. (master), Life Office Mgmt. Assn.; mem.: Assn. Life and Health Claims, Nebr. Fraternal Congress (pres. 1993—94), Internat. Claim Assn. (pres. 2002—03, exec. com.), Assn. Fraternal Benefit Counsel. Democrat. Roman Catholic. Office: Woodmen of World Life Ins Soc 1700 Farnam St Ste 2200 Omaha NE 68102-2007 E-mail: jgleason2@cox.net.

GLEASON, JEAN BERKO, psychology professor; b. Cleve., Dec. 19, 1931; d. Arthur E. and Alice (Gelberger) Berko; m. Andrew Mattei Gleason, Jan. 26, 1959; children: Katherine, Pamela, Cynthia. AB, Radcliffe Coll., 1953, AM, 1955, PhD, 1958. USPHS fellow MIT, 1958—59; research assoc. VA Med. Ctr., Boston, 1961—2000; vis. asst. prof. psychology Boston U., 1972—73, assoc. prof., 1973—76, prof., 1976—, chairperson dept. psychology, 1985—89, acting chair dept. psychology, 1997, dir. grad program devel. psychology, 1975—78, 1982—85, dir. grad. program human devel., 1997—2002; research assoc. edn. Harvard U., Cambridge, Mass., 1968—70, prin. research assoc. psychiatry, 1970—72. Rsch. scholar in residence Inst. Linguistics, Hungarian Acad. Sci., 1981, 83; mem. mental retardation rsch. com. Nat. Inst. Child Health and Human Devel., 1981-85; trustee Ctr. for Applied Linguistics, Washington, 1989-94. Author: The Development of Language, 1983, 6th edit., 2005, You Can Take It with You, 1989, Psycholinguistics, 1993, 2nd edit., 1998; mem. editl. bd. Child Development, 1971—77, Discourse Processes, 1982—2002, assoc. editor Language, 1997—2000; contbr. articles. Recipient Editors award Jour. Speech and Hearing Research, 1970. Fellow: APA, AAAS (coun. del. 2002—05); mem.: ACLU, Internat. Assn. for Study of Child Lang. (pres. 1990—93), Soc. for Rsch. Child Devel., Linguistic Soc. Am. (chmn. program com. 1980—81, resolutions com. 2004), Radcliffe Alumni Assn. (bd. dirs. 1969—72), Radcliffe Grad. Soc. (past pres.), Gypsy Lore Soc. (exec. bd. 1983—87, 1992—2002, pres. 1996—99, exec. bd. 2003—), Acad. Aphasia, Phi Beta Kappa (pres. Radcliffe chpt. 1965—68). Home: 110 Larchwood Dr Cambridge MA 02138-4639 Office: Boston U Dept Psychology 64 Cummington St Boston MA 02215-2407 Business E-Mail: gleason@bu.edu.

GLEASON, JOHN F., lawyer; b. Springfield, Ill., Aug. 28, 1950; AB, St. Louis U., 1972, JD, 1975; LLM in Taxation, Washington U., St. Louis, 1981. Bar: Ill. 1975., Mo. 1978, Ky. 1980. Atty. IRS, St. Louis, 1977-79; assoc. Wyatt, Tarrant & Combs, Louisville, 1981-84; sec., gen. counsel Courier-Jour. and Louisville Times Co., WHAS Inc., Standard Gravure Corp., Louisville, 1984-86; assoc. Woodward, Hobson & Fulton, Louisville, 1986-88, ptnr., 1988—. Mem. Phi Beta Kappa. Office: Woodward Hobson & Fulton 2500 National City Tower Louisville KY 40202

GLEASON, JOHN PATRICK, JR., trade association executive; b. N.Y.C., Nov. 11, 1941; s. John Patrick Sr. and Ruth T. (Madigan) G.; m. Judith Peper (dec. 1980); children: John P. III, Megan K.; m. Susan Leigh Collier, Mar. 31, 1984; children: Kevin M., Colin P. BS in Fgn. Service, Georgetown U., 1963; PMD, Harvard Bus. Sch., 1972. Gen. mgr. Pappagallo, Inc., Washington, 1964-67; export project mgr. U.S. Dept. Commerce, Washington, 1967-68; investment banker Blyth, Eastman Dillon, Inc., Washington, 1968-70; with U.S. Dept. Commerce, Washington, 1970-77, chief staff domestic and internat. bus. adminstrn., 1970-77, dep. asst. sec. commerce, 1970-77; pres. Brick Inst. Am., Reston, Va., 1977-86, Portland Cement Assn., Skokie, Ill., 1986—. Bd. dirs., chmn. Coun. Masonry Rsch., Reston, 1985—, Masonry Industry Com., Washington, 1984—. Recipient Silver medal U.S. Dept. Commerce, Washington, 1978. Mem. Am. Soc. Assn. Execs., Chgo. Soc. Assn. Execs., River Bend Country Club (Great Falls, Va.), Carlton Club (Washington), Skokie Country Club (Glencoe, Ill.). Republican. Office: Portland Cement Assn 5420 Old Orchard Rd Skokie IL 60077-1053

GLEASON, KATE, writer, educator, editor; b. Keene, N.H., Oct. 22, 1956; d. Allison Archie and Bertha Eleanor Sophie (Tonseth) Gleason. BA in Edn., U. Mass., 1981, postgrad., 1986; student, Amherst Writers and Artists, 1980-87. Editor, poetry editor Peregrine Lit. Jour., Amherst, Mass., 1985-91; proofreader Stratford Pub. Co., Brattleboro, Vt., 1994-95; poet-in-the-schs. Narragansett HS, Mass., 1994, Northfield Mt. Hermon, Mass.; creative writing workshop tchr. Writing From Your Inner Voice Workshops, Keene, 1992—; freelance editor Keene, 1994—. Author: (poems) Making As If to Sing, 1989, The Brighter the Deeper, 1995; contbr. poetry to anthologies and jours. Fellow, NEA/Ragdale, 1999. Mem.: N.H. Writers Project (Outstanding Emerging Writer award 1998).

GLEASON, KEN BELL, historian, educator, journalist; b. Manhattan, NY, Mar. 4, 1941; s. Arthur H. Kesten and Eleanor M. (Bell) Gleason, Woodrow W. Gleason; m. Carole Ann Horchler, July 20, 1963 (div. Dec. 3, 1976); children: Tara Ann, Darren Kenneth, Colin Alexis. BA in History Honors, Univ. Calif., Berkeley, 1989; MA in History, San Francisco State U., 1992. Editl. asst. Long Island Press, 1961—62; reporter Dover NJ Advance, 1963—65; copy editor Bergen NJ Record, 1965; reporter Newsday, Long Island, NY, 1965—66; wire news editor Suffolk LI Sun, 1966—69; asst. editor The Baltimore Sun, Md., 1969—77; copy editor San Jose Mercury News, Calif., 1983—84; instr. history Chabot Coll., Hayward, Calif., 1992—, Evergreen Valley Coll., San Jose, Calif., 1992—96, Santa Rosa Jr. Coll., Calif., 1994—, Coll. of Alameda, Calif., 1995—. Exec. coun. mem. All Faculty Assoc., Santa Rosa, Calif., 1998—2001; del. Bay Faculty Assoc., Oakland, Calif., 1998—2001; exec. coun. mem. AFT (Am. Fedn. Tchr) Local 1603, 1999—2001. Mem. Peralta Cmty. Coll. Dist. Save Our Cmty. Coll. Comm., Oakland, Calif., 1998; polit. action comm. mem. Faculty Assoc. Calif. Cmty. Coll., Sacramento, 1999—2000. Grantee, Nat. Endowment for Humanities, 1993. Democrat. Avocations: reading, jazz listening, baseball viewing. Home: Box 7302 Berkeley CA 94707-0302 Office: Chabot Coll 25555 Hesperian Blvd Hayward CA 94545 E-mail: kgleason@chabotcollege.edu.

GLEASON, STEPHEN CHARLES, physician; b. Leon, Iowa, June 30, 1946; s. Charles Gerald and Ferne Louise (Pollard) Gleason; m. Lisa Ann Corcoran, Aug. 22, 1981; children: Julia K., Alex K., Michael John, Timothy Charles, Christian Kelly, Sean Patrick, Keriann Louise, Julia, Alex. BS, Iowa State U., 1971; DO summa cum laude, Coll. Osteo. Medicine and Surgery, 1974; PhD, Washington U., 1999. Diplomate Am. Bd. Family Practice, Bd Cert. Addiction, Medicine, Toxicology. Resident in family practice Meml. Med. Ctr., Corpus Christi, Tex., 1974—75; family practice medicine Des Moines, 1975-93; chief of staff Iowa Gov. Tom Vilsack, 2002—05. Chmn. dept. family practice Mercy Hosp. Med. Center, Des Moines, 1979-82; pres., CEO chief med. officer Mercy Clinic System, 1984-97; mem. papal med. security team Pope John Paul's Am. Pilgrimage, 1979; asst. prof. Mayo Grad. Sch. Medicine, 1996—. Chmn. Iowa CARES Med. Found., 1987, Nat. Health Policy Coun., 1989-98; bd. dirs. Family Health Plan, HMO, 1985, Securecare PSD, Inc., 1990-99; White House health advisor, 1992-94; v.p. med. ops. Cath. Health Initiatives, 1997-98; sr. health adv. Pres. Clinton Campaign, 1996; sr. med. advisor Health Care Financing Adminstrn., 1998-99; dir. Dept. Pub. Health, State of Iowa, 1999-2002; pres. deligate World Health Orgn., 2000; active med. mission in El Salvador during earthquake disaster, 2001. Recipient Outstanding Young Iowan, 1982, Iowa Physician of Yr., 1990. Mem. AMA, Am. Acad. Family Physicians, Sigma Alpha Epsilon, Sigma Sigma Phi. Democrat. Office Phone: 515-281-0150.

GLEASON, SUSAN WHEELER, art educator, department chairman; b. Detroit, Oct. 26, 1955; d. Jean Shaughnessy Wheeler; m. James N. Gleason, June 30, 1979. BFA, U. Ill., Champaign, 1978, MA, 1987. Cert. tchr. Nat. Bd. Profl. Tchg. Stds., 2002. Tchr. Urbana (Ill.) Sch. Dist. #116, Urbana, Ill., 1979—. Art dept. chair Urbana H.S., 1994—2004, humanities divsn. chair, 2004—. Home: 803 W Washington St Champaign IL 61820 Office: Urbana HS 1002 S Race St Urbana IL 61801 Office Phone: 217-384-3505. Office Fax: 217-384-3539. Personal E-mail: swgleason@insightbb.com.

GLEAVES, LEON ROGERS, marketing and sales executive; b. Louisville, May 4, 1939; s. Leon Rogers and Fain Mae (King) G.; m. Hallie Virginia Dumke, Apr. 9, 1966 (dec. Dec. 20, 1990); 1 child, Keith Browning; m. Elizabeth Ann Smith, June 25, 2000 BS, U. Louisville, 1961, MBA, 1966. Sales mgmt. trainee GM, Louisville, 1965-67; advt. rep. The Christian Sci. Monitor, N.Y.C., 1967-72; mktg. and sales coord. White Lily Foods Co., Knoxville, Tenn., 1972-75; v.p. mktg. and sales Wilkins-Rogers, Inc., Ellicott City, Md., 1975—2002; pres., CEO, LRG, Ltd., 2002—. Spkr. in field. Bd. dirs. Bucknell U. Parents Assn., Lewisburg, Pa., 1992-95; adv. com. Md. Agrl. Edn. Found., Balt., 1993-96, Md. Food Bank, Inc., Balt.; home econ. adv. bd. Howard County Schs., Columbia, Md., 1993-2003, Balt. City Schs., 1994-97; mem. fin. com. So. Assn. State Depts. Agr., 1997, Md. Agrl. Commn., 2002-03; Md. Agrl. Commn., 2002-2003; spkr. Future Bus. Leaders Am., 1997-99. Mem. Balt./Washington Grocery Mfr. Rep., Md. Food Exporters Assn., Am. Mktg. Assn., Home Baking Assn. (dir. 1990-92), So. Assn. State Dept. Agr. (fin. com. 1997), Md. Agriculture Commn., 2002-2003. Avocations: tennis, classical and vintage jazz music, English mystery books and movies.

GLEESON, JOHN, judge, educator; b. 1953; BA, Georgetown U., 1975; JD, U. Va., 1980. Bar: N.Y. Law clk. to Hon. Boyce F. Martin Jr. U.S. Cir. Ct., 1980-81; assoc. Cravath, Swaine & Moore, N.Y.C., 1981-85; asst. U.S. atty. for ea. dist. N.Y. Dept. Justice, N.Y.C., 1985-94; judge U.S. Dist. Ct. (ea. dist.)

N.Y., Bklyn., 1994—. Adj. prof. law Bklyn. Sch. Law, 1990-97, NYU Law Sch., 1995—; vis. prof. law U. Va. Sch. Law, 1994. Office: US Dist Ct 225 Cadman Plz W Brooklyn NY 11201-2741*

GLEESON, THOMAS ALEXANDER, retired meteorologist; b. NYC, Aug. 11, 1920; s. John and Bertha Alexander Gleeson; m. Jeanette Lucas, Nov. 21, 1942; children: Vicki, Keith Thomas. BS, Harvard U., 1946; MS, NYU, 1947, PhD, 1950. Professional Member Am. Meteorol. Soc., Mass., 1945. Asst. prof. Fla. State U., Tallahassee, 1949—54, assoc. prof., 1954—59, full prof., 1959—94. Cons. USN, Norfolk, Va., 1962—67, NASA, Huntsville, Ala., 1964—73; state climatologist U.S. Weather Svc., Tallahassee, 1984—94. Contbr. articles to profl. jours. First lt. U.S. Army, 1942—45, U.S. and Middle East. Fellow: Am. Meteorol. Soc. (hon.; com. chmn. 1974—75); mem.: Sigma Xi (corr.). Home: 2106 Old Bainbridge Rd Tallahassee FL 32303 Office: Univ Dept Meteorology Fla State Tallahassee FL 32306

GLEICH, CAROL S., health professions education executive; b. Kewanee, Ill., Jan. 18, 1935; d. Carl and Edna (Krause) Gleich. BA, U. Iowa, 1958, MS, 1967, PhD in Health Sci. Edn., 1972. Cert. clin. chemistry technologist, Nat. Registry Clin. Chemistry. From instr. to asst. prof. pathology U. Iowa Sch. Medicine, Iowa City, 1972-77, edn. specialist divsn. allied health, 1977-88, chief resource devel. sec., 1988-90, health manpower edn. officer, physician manpower and credentialing, chief spl. projects and data analysis br. divsn. medicine, 1991-95, exec. sec. coun. grad. med. edn., 1996-99; dir. area health edn. ctr. nat. program Bur. Health Professions, Health Resources & Svcs. Adminstrn., Rockville, Md., 1977—. Allied health cons. to Egypt; gov. cons. in internat. health profl. ed., Russia, 1993-99; dir. Geriatric Edn. Ctrs. PHS; adj. assoc. prof. U. Md. Sch. Medicine; meme. Iowa Health Manpower Com., 1972—; cons. U. Wis. System Acad. Affairs, 1974; panelist and participant workshops; presenter and U.S. chief del. internat. congress. Assoc. editor Am. Jour. Med. Tech., 1974-83, Jour. Allied Health, 1982-85; contbr. articles to profl. jours. Mem. Am. Soc. Clin. Pathologists (assoc., cert. med. technologist, sec. ASCP Bd. Registry 1975-77), Am. Soc. Clin. Lab. Sci., D.C. Soc. Med. Tech. (Outstanding Med. Technologist of Yr. 1975), Beta Beta Beta (Pub. Health Svc. award 1995), Alpha Mu Tau. Home: 14800 Rocking Spring Dr Rockville MD 20853-3635 E-mail: carolgleich@mindspring.com.

GLEICHMAN, JOHN ALAN, state agency administrator; b. Anthony, Kans., Feb. 11, 1944; s. Charles William and Caroline Elizabeth (Emch) G.; m. Martha Jean Cannon, July 1, 1966; 1 son, John Alan Jr. BS in Bus. Mgmt., Kans. State Tchrs. Coll., 1966. Cert. hazard control mgr.; cert. safety profl. with a speciality in constrn. safety; cert. safety exec. Office mgr. to asst. supt. Barton-Malow Co., Detroit, 1967—72, coord. safety, 1972—76, corp. mgr. safety and security, 1976—89, dir. corp. safety and loss control, 1989—. Instr. U. Mich., Wayne State U., 1977-81, Lawrence Tech. U., 1994-96; mem. constrn. safety stds. commn. adv. com. for concrete constrn. and steel erection Bur. of Safety and Regulations, Mich. Dept. Labor, 1977—; rep. constrn. stds. com. Am. Nat. Stds. Inst., 1984—. Author: (with others) You, The National Safety Council, and Voluntary Standards, 1981, Construction Accident Analysis: The Inductive Learning Approach, 1991; mem. editl. bd. Safety and Health: Internat. Safety, Health and Environ. Mag., 1989—; contbr. chpts. to books. Instr. multimedia first aid ARC, 1976-89; past trustee Apostolic Christian Ch., Livonia, Mich. Recipient Safety Achievement awards Mich. Mut. Ins. Co., 1979-83; Cameron award Constrn. sect. Indsl. divsn. Nat. Safety Coun., 1982, 87. Mem. Mich. Safety Conf. (pres. 1984-85), Am. Soc. Safety Engrs. (pres. Detroit chpt. 1982, nat. adminstr. constrn. divsn. 1988-89, bd. dirs. 1988-90, Safety Profl. of Yr. 1984), Nat. Safety Coun. (chmn. tech. rev. constrn. sect. indsl. divsn. 1980-84, chmn. stds. com. indsl. divsn. 1983-85, chmn. assn. com. indsl. divsn. 1986-87, dir. sects. group indsl. divsn. 1987-89, chmn. elect indsl. divsn. 1989-90, chmn. 1990-91, bd. dirs. 1987-92, Disting. Svcs. to Safety award 1993), Am. Arbitration Assn. (panel arbitrators 1985). Office: Barton Malow Co 26500 American Dr Southfield MI 48034 Office Phone: 248-436-5402. Business E-Mail: john.gleichman@bartonmalow.com.

GLEICHMANN, FRANCES EVANGELINE, retired elementary school educator; b. Marion, N.C., Sept. 24, 1920; d. Alexander Rudolph and Margaret Katherine (McNeely) McCulloch; m. August O. Gleichmann, Dec. 1, 1945. Diploma, Pfeiffer Jr. Coll., 1940; BS in Edn., Asheville Coll., 1942; postgrad., Mount St. Agnes Coll., Johns Hopkins U., U. Md., U. R.I. Elem. tchr. Balt. City Pub. Schs., 1942-85. Cooperating tchr. for student tchrs. from Towson State U. Balt. City Pub. Schs., 1957-59. Co-author: Tales of the Smokies and Blue Ridge Mountains1, 1997; contbr. poetry to poetry.com, poetry to Internat. Libr. Poetry. Recipient Econ. Edn. Tchr, award Econ. Edn. Program Com., 1985, Disting. Alumni award Pfeiffer Coll., 1973, Tate award Balt. C. of C. and Tate Industries, 1975, Salute 13 award Sta. WJZ TV, 1980, Golden Poet award World of Poetry, 1985-88. Mem. NEA, Md. State Ret. Tchrs. Assn., Balt. City Ret. Tchrs. Assn., Alpha Delta Kappa (Md. state publicity chmn. 1988-90, Alpha Delta Kappa week chmn. 1986-88). Home: 10 Dungarrie Rd Baltimore MD 21228-3401

GLEIJESES, MARIO, holding company executive; b. Italy, Feb. 27, 1955; came to U.S., 1985; s. Luigi Gleijeses and Rosalba Catanoso; m. Betsy L. Miller, Mar. 14, 1992; children: Rosalba, Caterina. Student, U. Naples, 1973-77. Chartering mgr. Itex subs. Italgrani, Zurich, 1977-82; asst. to pres. Italgrani Spa, Naples, Italy, 1982-85; exec. v.p., bd. dirs. Italgrani USA Inc. and Italgrani Elevator Co., St. Louis, 1985-89; v.p., bd. dirs. New Eng. Milling Co., Ayer, Mass., 1987-89; bd. dirs. Green Bay Elevator Co., Burlington, Iowa; v.p., bd. dirs. Mayco Export, Inc., Mpls., 1988-89; pres., bd. dirs. McLean Elevator Co., Benedict, N.D., 1989; founder, pres., bd. dirs. Agricorp Holding Inc., 1989-92; pres.; bd. dirs. Granicorp Inc., 1989-92, Granicorp Export, Inc., U.S. Virgin Islands, 1989-92; chmn., CEO, bd. dirs. Granicorp France, S.A., Paris, 1991-92; founder, pres., bd. dirs. Gleijeses, Inc., 1993—; founder, chmn. bd. dirs. Lithoflex Corp., 1994—; pres. Hoky-Contico, LLC, 1995-96.

GLEIN, RICHARD JERIEL, SR., lawyer; b. L.A., Aug. 20, 1929; s. Henry Carl Glein and Elsie B. (Drummond) Glein Schurman; m. Rosalind Bell; children: Valerie, Kimberly, Richard Jr., Stacy (dec.); 1 stepchild, Steven Anders Bell. Student, U. Wash., 1953-58. Bar: Wash. 1963, U.S. Dist. Ct. (ea. and we. dists.) Wash. 1963, U.S. Ct. Appeals (9th cir.) 1963. Police officer, Seattle, 1952-63; dep. pros. atty. King County, Wash., 1963-65; from assoc. to ptnr. Clinton, Fleck & Glein, Seattle, 1965-92; pvt. practice Seattle, 1992—; pro-tem judge, arbitrator Dist and Superior Ct.; owner Legal Alternatives, LLC, Anacortes, Wash. Sgt. 1st class USAF, 1946-49, U.S. Army, 1950-51. Mem. FBA, Wash. State Bar Assn., Snohomish County Bar Assn., Internat. Footprint Assn. (pres. Seattle chpt. 1969-70, grand pres. 1982-83), Masons (master 1973). Republican. Home and Office: 5301 Sterling Dr Anacortes WA 98221-3037 E-mail: rnrlegalt@aol.com.

GLEKEL, JEFFREY IVES, lawyer; b. NYC, Apr. 8, 1947; s. Newton and Gertrude (Burr) G.; m. Cynthia R. Leder, June 18, 1988; 1 child, David L. AB magna cum laude, Columbia U., 1969; JD, Yale U., 1972. Bar: NY 1973, US Supreme Ct. 1981, US Ct. Appeals (2d cir.) 1974, US Dist. Ct. (So. Dist.) NY 1974. Law clk. to Hon. Edward Weinfeld US Dist. Ct. (So. Dist.) NY, 1972-73; asst. US atty. So. Dist. NY, 1973-77; law clk. to Hon. Byron R. White US Supreme Ct., Washington, 1977-78; ptnr., criminal and constitutional law and bus. fraud matters Skadden, Arps, Slate, Meagher & Flom, LLP, NYC, 1980—. Co-chmn., Civil Litigation Seminar, NY Law Jour., 1982—90; spkr. 2nd Cir. Jud. Conf., 1983. Editor, contbr., Civil Litigation Practice, 1990; Business Crimes: A Guide for Corporate and Defense Counsel, 1982; note and comment editor Yale Law Jour., 1971-72; contbr. articles to law jours. Mem. Assn. Bar City of NY (chmn. com. fed. legislation 1984-87), ABA. Office: Skadden Arps Slate Meagher & Flom 4 Times Sq New York NY 10036 Office Phone: 212-735-3460. Office Fax: 917-777-3460. Business E-Mail: jglekel@skadden.com.

GLEKLEN, DONALD MORSE, investment company executive; b. Providence, Oct. 16, 1936; s. Leo and Gertrude (Ketover) G.; m. Carol Ann Platzker, May 24, 1964; children: Jonathan, Adam, Rachel. BA, Cornell U., 1958; JD, Columbia U., 1963. Bar: N.Y. 1954. Assoc. Demov & Morris, N.Y.C., 1963-65; corp. counsel C.F. Childs & Co., N.Y.C., 1965-67; U.S. rep. Rea Bros. Ltd. Merchant Bankers, London, 1967-68; exec. v.p. Indsl. Valley Bank, Phila., 1968-84; sr. v.p. MEDIQ, Inc., Pennsauken, N.J., 1984-94; pres. Jocard Fin. Svcs., Inc., 1994; chmn., CEO InteliHealth, Inc., 1996—99; CEO The Maine Mcht. Bank, 1997-98, vice chair, 1998—. Bd. dirs. New West EyeWorks, Inc., Tempe, Ariz., 1988-93, Nutramax Products, Inc., Gloucester, Mass., Lason Sys. Holdings, Inc., Livonia, Mich., Kinetics Tech. Internat., The Hague, Netherlands, 1982-86. Trustee Pa. Coll. Optometry, Phila., 1979-98, chmn. bd., 1991-98, trustee emeritus, 2004-; trustee Walnut St. Theatre, Phila., 1983-96, Coriell Inst. Med. Rsch., Camden, N.J., 1994-96; dir. FirstTrust Bank, Phila., 2003-, Northwestern Human Svcs., Lafayette Hill, 2003-04. Served to lt. (j.g.) USNR, 1958-60. Home: 212 Jeffrey Ln Newtown Square PA 19073-2506 Office: 10 Presidential Blvd Ste 124 Bala Cynwyd PA 19004

GLEN, NIKI, artist, sculptor; b. Milw., Nov. 14, 1950; d. Alan and Janet (Marx) G.; children: Dana Alan Knops, Laramie Ann Glen. BS in Art Edn., U. Wis., 1973. Cert. in art edn. K-12. Pub. artist, muralist numerous orgns., various locations, 1973—; co-founder Madison (Wis.) Graphics, 1973-76; art educator various schs. various locations, 1973—; dir. S.W. Pub. Art Group, Phoenix, Ariz., 1996—. Exhibited in group shows Corcoran Gallery, Washington, 1986, Williams Ratliff Gallery, Sedona, Ariz., 1988, Veneble Neslage Galleries, Washington, 1989-92, Spirit of N.Mex. Art Exhbn., Washington, 1990, Marin-Price Galleries, Bethesda/Chevy Chase, Md., 1992, Am. Bank Gallery, Chevy Chase, 1994, Artisimo Gallery, Scottsdale, Ariz., 1995, Nat. Soc. Mural Painters Centennial Exhibit, N.Y.C., 1996, Exit Gallery, NYC, 1996, 2002, 1st Internat. Pub. Art and Mural Congress, Mexico City, 1998, Sietz Gallery, Harrisburg, Pa., 2003 (art installation) Phoenix Coll., Ariz. Ctr. Blind and Visually Impaired, Phoenix Childrens Hosp.; featured in publs. including Community Murals, 1984, Street Murals: The Most Exciting Cities of America, Britain and Western Europe, 1982, The Art of Handmade Tile, also numerous covers and illustrations for textbooks and periodicals; works featured in Mosaic: Techniques and Traditions. Pres. Arts and Creativity in Early Childhood, 1993-96; bd. dirs. Gaynor Mus. and Found., 1993-95, Cmty. Built Assn., 2000-; mem. Ariz. Alliance for Art Edn., 1990-95. Recipient Orchid award City of Madison, 1975, Tempe Diablo award of excellence in edn., 1996, 97, Livable Cities award, 2001, Beautification award Art in Pvt. Devel.; Ariz. Artist Project grantee Ariz. Commn. on Arts, 1994, Phoenix Children's Hosp.; grantee numerous orgns. including Atlantic Richfield, City of Whitewater, The Mills Corp., Phoenix Arts Commn., Medtronics Inc., Phoenix (Ariz.) Coll., NEA, YMCA, City of Tempe, IKEA Corp., Desert Bot. Garden, Phoenix Coll. Mem. Nat. Soc. Mural Painters. Avocations: swimming, reading, sailing, dance. Office Phone: 602-690-9399. Personal E-mail: publicartdesign@aol.com.

GLENDENING, EVERETT AUSTIN, architect; b. White Plains, N.Y., May 20, 1929; s. Gilbert Leslie and Elsie Jane (Fanjoy) G.; m. Wilhelmina Louise Hanley, Nov. 26, 1949; children: Nancy, James, Thomas, Terry, Susan. B.Arch., U. Cin., 1953; M.Arch., M.I.T., 1954. With Duffy Constrn. Co., Cleve., 1951-55, SIS Architects, Cin., 1956-58, T.J. Moore (architect), Denver, 1959; prof. architecture U. Cin., 1960-67; pvt. practice architecture Cin., 1959—. Prin. works include Queen's Towers, Cin., 1964, Summit Chase, Columbus, Ohio, 1966, Norwood High Sch., Cin., 1972, W.Va. State Mus., 1978, Douglass Montessori Sch., Cin., 1979, Christie Lane Workshop, Norwalk, Ohio, 1980, Coll. Law U. Cin., 1981, Elks Lodge, Columbus, Ind., 1981, Geology/Physics Sci. Ctr. U. Cin., 1983, U. Rio Grande Dormitory, 1989, U. Rio Grande Student Ctr., 1994, U. Rio Grande Math-Sci.-Nursing Bldg., 1995, Planetarium, Shawnee State U., 1998, Sch. for Creative and Performing Arts Auditorium, Cin. Pub. Schs., 1997, U. Rio Grande Student Conf. Ctr. Served as 1st lt. USAF, 1954-56. Fellow AIA (honor awards Ohio chpt. 1966-70, 74, 82, 90, 91, Cin. chpt. 1966-68, 70, 76, Bronze medal 1969, Apple award for arch. 1995, mem. U.S. delegation of architects to People's Republic China and Hong Kong 1990); mem. Architect's Soc. Ohio, Scarab. Methodist. Office: 8050 Montgomery Rd Cincinnati OH 45236-2950 Fax: (513) 791-2794. *A consistently positive point of view has perhaps been the single, most important factor in making possible what has been accomplished in my lifetime. I have always felt that anything was possible as long as I was willing to make the effort and, in fact, I can recall telling myself as a new college freshman that "while I may not be the most intelligent man in the class, there was no reason why I should not be the hardest working member of that class".*

GLENDENING, PARRIS NELSON, former governor, political science educator; b. Bronx, N.Y., June 11, 1942; m. Jennifer Elizabeth Crawford; 1 child, Raymond Hughes. AA, Broward County Jr. Coll., 1962; BA, Fla. State U., Tallahassee, 1964, MA, 1965, PhD, 1967. Asst. prof. U. Md., College Park, 1967-72, assoc. prof., 1972-94; coun. mem. Hyattsville City Coun., Md., 1973-74, Prince George's County Coun., Upper Marlboro, Md., 1974-82, coun. chmn., 1980, 81, county exec., 1982-95; gov. State of Md., 1995—2003; pres. Smart Growth Leadership Inst., Washington, 2004—. Vice chair state of Md.'s Chesapeake Bay Critical Area Commn., 1984-94; vice chair bd. dirs. World Trade Ctr., 1990-97; mem. bd. visitors U. Md. Sch. Pub. Affairs, 1990-97; trustee Ptnrs. for Livable Places, 1990-97. Author: (with Mavis Mann Reeves) Controversies of State and Local Political Systems, 1972, Pragmatic Federalism, 1977, 2d edit., 1984; contbr. numerous articles to profl. jours. Del. to Dem. Nat. Conv., San Francisco, 1984, Atlanta, 1988, N.Y.C., 1992; bd. govs., steering com. Am.'s Clean Water Found. Recipient numerous awards, including City and State mag., Prince George's County, Prince George's High Sch. Prins. Assn., State Assn. Retarded Citizens, Nat. Bus. League So. Md., Spanish Speaking Communities Md., Inc., Rotary Internat., Md. Assn. Psychol. Svcs., Elizabeth and David Scull award for disting. leadership to Washington met. region Coun. Govts., 1995, Dr. Nathan Davis award The Am. Med. Assn., 1991; Disting. Alumni award Fla. State U. Coll. Social Svcs., 1993, Outstanding Alumni The Am. Assn. of Com. Coll., 1997. Mem. AAUP, AAAS (profl. ethics group 1988—), Nat. Assn. Counties (bd. dirs. 1992—, chair large urban county caucus 1992—), Am. Polit. Sci. Assn., ASPA (profl. ethics com. mem. 1989—, chmn. 1991-92, SIAM mem. 1991—), Nat. Coun. Elected County Execs. (1st v.p. 1989-90, pres. 1991-92), Md. Assn. Counties (pres. 1987-88), Nat. Assn. Counties (bd. dirs. 1992—, vice chmn. intergovtl. rels. policy steering com. 1987-90, chair 1990—, taxation and fin. steering com. 1984-87), Nat. Govs. Assn. (chair 2000-01). Democrat. Office: Smart Growth America Ste 1050 1707 L St NW Washington DC 20036 Fax: (410) 974-3275. E-mail: governor@gov.state.md.us.*

GLENDENING, TERRY SKY, psychologist; b. Cin., Apr. 19, 1961; BA, Cornell U., 1983; MA, U. Cin., 1986, PhD, 1995. Lic. psychologist Ohio, Ky., cert. corrective thinking practitioner 1999. Dir. recreation Indian Hill Cmty. Edn., Cin., 1986—92; pvt. practice in clin. psychologist, psychotherapist, 1982—. Tchg. asst. Cornell U., Ithaca, NY, 1982—83; cons. IHHS Peer Counseling Program, Indian Hill, Ohio, 1987—96; lectr. in field. Author: (book) Thought Patterns in Depression and Somatization, 1986, Cognitive Specificity in Non-Clinical Depressive Manifestations of Distress, 1995, Timeless Parenting Techniques: Fair, Firm and Functional, 2002; author: (workshop series) Coping Skills for a New Millenium, 2000. Vol. recreation for disabled Camp Stepping Stones, Cin., 1997—98; vol. Spl. Olympics, Cin., 1997—98. Named Outstanding Young Woman of Am., 1986, Diplomate, Nat. Inst. Sports, 2004; recipient Sons and Daughters Am. Revolution award, 1974. Mem.: APA, Nat. Inst. Sports (diplomate 2004), Ohio Psychol. Assn., Psi Chi. Avocations: hiking, camping, art, sports, rock collecting.

GLENDENNING, DON MARK, lawyer; b. Dallas, Dec. 24, 1953; s. Don Thomas and Nancy (Malloy) G.; m. Carol Peterson, Dec. 30, 1979. BA, Rice U., 1976; JD, Stanford U., 1979. Bar: Tex. 1979. Assoc. Rain Harrell Emery Young & Doke, Dallas, 1979-85; ptnr. Rain, Harrell, Emery, Young & Doke, Dallas, 1985-87; shareholder Locke Liddell & Sapp (formerly Locke Purnell Rain Harrell, P.C.), Dallas, 1987-98; ptnr. Locke Liddell & Sapp LLP, Dallas, 1999—. Past pres. Human Rights Initiative North Tex., Tex.; pres. Scenic Dallas, Scenic Tex.; chair-elect Dallas Zool. Soc.; bd. dirs. Nat. Tree Trust, Tex. Trees Found.; chmn. Thanks-Giving Found. Republican. Presbyterian. Office: Locke Liddell & Sapp LLP 2200 Ross Ave Ste 2200 Dallas TX 75201-6776 Office Phone: 214-740-8623. E-mail: dglendenning@lockeliddell.com.

GLENDINNING, CHELLIS, writer, psychologist; b. Cleve., June 18, 1947; d. Paul and Mary Hooker (Daoust) G. BA in Social Scis., U. Calif., Berkeley, 1969; PhD in Psychology, Columbia Pacific U., 1984. Lic. profl. clin. counselor. Mem. adv. bd. Earth Island Inst., San Francisco, 1988-99, Earth Ways Found., Malibu, Calif., 1996—; Dept. Peace and Conflict Studies, U. Calif.-Berkeley, 1984-90, Loka Inst., Amherst, Mass., 1992-2000 Author: Waking Up in the Nuclear Age, 1987, When Technology Wounds, 1990 (nomination for Pulitzer prize 1991), My Name is Chellis and I'm in Recovery From Western Civilizations, 1994, Off the Map (An Expedition Deep into Imperialism, The Global Economy, and Other Earthly Whereabouts), 1999, Off the Map: An Expedition Deep into Empire and the Global Economy, 2002, Chiva: A Village Takes on the Global Heroin Trade, 2005. Bd. dirs. Elmwood Inst., Berkeley, 1986-93. Recipient Billy award San Francisco Examiner, 1983, First Times award N.Mex. Coun. for Humanities, Albuquerque, 1989, Zero Injustice award Rio Arriba County Commn., 1997, Book award Nat. Fedn. Press Women, 2000. Avocations: sustainable living, gardening, fishing, herb gathering. Home: PO Box 130 Chimayo NM 87522-0130

GLENDON, MARY ANN, law educator; b. Pittsfield, Mass., Oct. 7, 1938; m. Edward R. Lev; 3 children. BA, U. Chgo., 1959, JD, 1961, M of Comparative Law, 1963, LLD (hon.), 1992; DHL (hon.), Brigham Young U., 1990. Bar: Ill. 1964, Mass. 1980. Legal intern EEC, Brussels, 1963; assoc. Mayer, Brown & Platt, Chgo., 1963-68; asst. prof. Boston Coll. Law Sch., 1968—71, assoc. prof., 1971—73, prof., 1973—86; prof. law Harvard Law Sch., Cambridge, Mass., 1986—, Learned Hand prof. law, 1993—. Vis. prof. Harvard Law Sch., 1974, U. Chgo. Law Sch., 1983, 84, 86, Gregorian U., Rome. Author: Abortion and Divorce in Western Law, 1987 (Scribes Book Award, Am. Soc. Writeres on Legal Subjects, 1988), The Transformation of Family Law, 1989 (Order of the Coif Triennial Book Award, 1993), Rights Talk: The Impoverishment of Political Discourse, 1991, A Nation Under Lawyers, 1994, A World Made New: Eleanor Roosevelt and the Universal Declaration of Human Rights, 2001; co-author: Comparative Legal Traditions, 1994; editor: Intergenerational Solidarity, Welfare, and Human Ecology, 2004; co-editor: Seedbeds of Virtue: Sources of Competence, Character, and Citizenship in Am. Soc., 1995. Foreign Law Fellow U. Libre de Bruxelles, 1962-63, Ford Found. Fellow, 1975-76, Fellow Radcliffe Inst., 1975-76. Mem. Am. Acad. Arts & Sciences, Pres.'s Coun. Bioethics, Pontificial Acad. Social Sci. (pres. 2002-). Office: Harvard Law Sch 1563 Massachusetts Ave Cambridge MA 02138 Office Phone: 617-495-4769. Office Fax: 617-496-4913.

GLENN, CONSTANCE WHITE, art museum director, educator, consultant; b. Topeka, Oct. 4, 1933; d. Henry A. and Madeline (Stewart) White; m. Jack W. Glenn, June 19, 1955; children: Laurie Glenn Buckle, Caroline Glenn Galey, John Christopher. BFA, U. Kans., 1955; grad., U. Mo., 1969; MA, Calif. State U., 1974. Dir. U. Art Mus. & Mus. Studies program, from lectr. to prof. Calif. State U., Long Beach, 1973—2004, prof. and dir. emeritus, U. Art Mus. and Mus. Studies program, 2004—. Art cons. Archtl. Digest, LA, 1980-89. Author: Jim Dine Drawings, 1984, Roy Lichtenstein: Landscape Sketches, 1986, Wayne Thiebaud: Private Drawings, 1988, Robert Motherwell: The Dedalus Sketches, 1988, James Rosenquist: Time Dust: The Complete Graphics 1962-92, 1993, The Great American Pop Art Store: Multiples of the Sixties, 1997, The Artist Observed: Photographs by Sidney B. Felsen, 2003, Candida Höfer: Architecture of Absence, 2004; contbg. author: Encyclopedia Americana, 1995-, The Grove Dictionary of Art, 1989-, Double Vision: Photographs from the Strauss Collection, 2001, Carrie Mae Weems: The Hampton Project, 2000. Vice-chair Adv. Com. for Pub. Art, Long Beach, 1990-95; chair So. Calif. adv. bd. Archives Am. Art, LA, 1980-90; mem. adv. bd. ART/LA, 1986-94, chair, 1992. Recipient Outstanding Contbn. to Profession award Calif. Mus. Photography, 1986, Women of Distinction award Soroptimist Internat., 1999. Mem. Am. Assn. Mus., Assn. Art Mus. Dirs. (trustee 2000-02, emeritus 2004—), Coll. Art Assn., Art Table, Long Beach Pub. Corp. for the Arts (Arts Adminstr. of Yr. 1989), Kappa Alpha Theta. Office: Calif State Univ Art Dept 1250 Bellflower Blvd Long Beach CA 90840-3501 Office Phone: 562-985-5761. Business E-Mail: cglenn@csulb.edu.

GLENN, DANIEL O., lawyer; b. Elma, Wash., Aug. 1, 1942; m. Carleen Glenn. BA, Cen. Wash. U., 1963; JD, U. Wash., 1972. Bar: Wash., 1972, U.S. Dist. Ct. (W. dist.) Wash., 1972, U.S. Supreme Ct., 1974. Instr. Olympia (Wash.) Schs., 1963-69; ptnr. Buzzard, Brown & Glenn, Olympia, 1972-74, Buzzard & Glenn, Olympia, 1974-76, Buzzard, Glenn & Henderson, Olympia, 1976-77, 85-89, Buzzard, Glenn, Henderson & Morris, Olympia, 1977-85, Glenn, Henderson & Hoffman, Olympia, 1989-92, Glenn & Hoffman, Olympia, 1992-2000, Glenn & Assocs., Olympia, 2001—. Mem. ABA, Wash. State Trial Lawyers Assn., Wash. State Assn. Mcpl. Attys., Wash. State Bar Assn., Am. Trial Lawyers Assn. Office: 2424 Evergreen Park Dr SW Olympia WA 98502-6041

GLENN, EDWARD VERNON FERRELL, lawyer, consultant; b. Winston-Salem, N.C., Jan. 10, 1950; s. Douglas (Stepfather) and Rosena Ferrell Dillard, Joseph Henry Glenn; m. Andrea Leigh Hilsman, Apr. 8, 1985; children: Catherine Courtney Hilsman, Douglas Tyree Tinsley, Rosena Ferrell. BA in Polit. sci., U. N.C., Chapel Hill, 1972; JD, Wake Forest Sch. of Law, Winston-Salem, N.C., 1975. Cert.: Nat. Bd. of Trial Advs. (civil trial lawyer) 1994, advocate: Nat. Trial Coll. - Harvard Law 1998, cert.: S.C. Bd. of Arbitrators (cir. ct. mediator) 2004, bar: N.C. 1976, S.C. 1985, (U.S. Ct. Appeals (4th dist.)), (U.S. Supreme Ct.). Trial atty. Glenn & Crumpler, Winston-Salem, NC, 1977—84, Few & Glenn, Greenville, SC, 1984—87, McCoy, Taylor & Glenn, Charleston, SC, 1987—98, Law Office of E.Vernon F. Glenn, Mount Pleasant, SC, 1998—. Author: (articles) The Charlotte Observer, The Post & Courier, SCTLA Bulletin, ABA The Jour., S.C. Trial Lawyers Jour. Bd. dirs. U. N.C. Ednl. Found., 1977—99, Life Mgmt. Ctrs., Charleston, SC, 1999—2002, Carolina Low Country Girl Scout Coun., Charleston, SC, 1990—93, USO Coun., Charleston, SC; bd. trustees Charleston Day Sch., SC, 1999—2002. Fellow: Delta Kappa Epsilon (life; pres. collegiate chpt. 1971—72); mem.: ATLA (assoc.), ABA (assoc.), Am. Bd. of Trial Advs., N.C. Acad. of Trial Lawyers (assoc.), SC. Trial Lawyers Assn. (assoc.; chair ethics com. 1990—92), N.C. Bar Assoc. (assoc.), SC. Bar Assoc. (assoc.; medico-legal affairs 1985—86), So. Trial Lawyers Assn. (assoc.). Independent. Methodist. Achievements include Testified before Senate special committes on legal issues; Lobbyist - Republican Caucus of ATLA. Avocations: college athletics, travel, radio sports commentary, sports handicapper, hiking and biking. Office: Law Offices of Vernon Glenn 211 Scott St Mount Pleasant SC 29464 Office Phone: 843-971-1999. Home Fax: 843-971-0194. Office Fax: 843-971-0194. Personal E-mail: evfg@lowcountrylawyer.com.

GLENN, GERALD MARVIN, marketing, engineering and construction executive; b. Greenville, S.C., Aug. 20, 1942; s. Oscar Marvin and Lorene (Ashmore) G.; m. Candice Wilson, Oct. 24, 1986; children: Regina Lynn, Gerald Marvin II, Charles Wilson. BSCE, Clemson U., 1964. With Daniel Constrn. Co., Greenville, S.C., 1964-77, Fluor Corp., Santa Ana, Calif., 1977-94, sr. v.p. mktg., 1982-85, pres. U.S. ops., 1985-86, exec. v.p., 1986, group pres., dir. Irvine, Calif., 1986-94; owner, prin. The Glenn Group LLC, Cimarron, Colo., 1994—, Eagle Glen Ranch LLC, Cimarron, Colo., 1994—; chmn., pres., CEO, mng. dir. Chgo. Bridge & Iron Co. NV, The Woodlands, Tex., 1996—. Bd. dir. Woodforest Fin. Group, The Woodlands, Tex. Chmn. bd. dirs. Chgo. chpt. Am. Heart Assn., 1999—2001; bd. dirs. John Cooper Sch., The Woodlands, Tex., Jr. Achievement Southeast Tex. Mem.: AIChE, Gas Tech. Inst. (dir.), Am. Petroleum Inst., Chgo. Soc., Chgo. Coun. Fgn. Rels. (mem. Chgo. com.), Econ. Club Chgo., 25 Yr. Club Petroleum Industry,

Club at Carlton Woods, Woodlands Country Club, Ruth Lake Country Club, Univ. Club Houston, Execs. Club Chgo., Olympia Fields Country Club, Fairway Pines Golf Club. Republican. Methodist. Home: 3 Grand Regency Cir The Woodlands TX 77382 Office: CB&I 2103 Research Forest Dr The Woodlands TX 77380 Office Phone: 832-513-1777.

GLENN, GUY CHARLES, pathologist; b. Parma, Ohio, May 13, 1930; s. Joseph Frank and Helen (Rupple) G.; m. Lucia Ann Howarth, June 13, 1953; children: Kathryn Holly, Carolyn Helen, Cynthia Marie. BS, Denison U., 1953; MD, U. Cin., 1957. Diplomate Am. Bd. Pathology, Am. Bd. Radioisotopic Pathology. Intern Walter Reed Army Med. Ctr., Washington, 1957-58; resident in pathology Fitzsimons Army Med. Ctr., Denver, 1959-63; commd. 2d lt. U.S. Army, 1956; advanced through grades to col., 1972; demonstrator pathology Royal Army Med. Coll., London, 1970-72; chief dept. pathology Fitzsimons Army Med. Ctr., Denver, 1972-77. Past pres. med. staff St. Vincent Hosp., Billings, Mont.; past mem. governing bd. Mont. Health Sys. Agy. Contbr. articles to profl. jours. Fellow: Coll. Am. Pathologists (chmn. chemistry resources com., chmn. commn. sci. resources, mem. budget com., coun. on quality assurance, chmn. practice guidelines com., bd. govs., chmn. nominating com.); mem.: Midland Empire Health Assn. (past pres.), Soc. Med. Cons. to Armed Forces, Am. Registry Pathology (bd. dirs., exec. com., search com., planning com.), Am. Soc. Clin. Pathology, Rotary (bd. dirs. emeritus local chpt.). Home: 3225 Jack Burke Ln Billings MT 59106-1113 Personal E-mail: gcandlhglenn@earthlink.net.

GLENN, J. THOMAS, consumer products company executive; b. Mar. 1959; Degree in acctg., U. Ga., 1981; MBA, Duke U., 1984. Cert. CPA. Cons. Arthur Andersen, 1984—87; bd. mem. Ace Hardware, Chattanooga, 1987; bd. chmn. Ace Hardware Corp., Chattanooga, 1996; pres. Ace Hardware Chattanooga, 1997; chmn. Ace Hardware, Oak Brook, Ill., 2003—. Mem.: Brainerd Bapt. Ch. (deacon), Nat. Ctr. for Youth Issues (bd. mem.), Chattanooga United Way (tres., pres.). Office: Ace Hardware 2200 Kensington Ct Oak Brook IL 60523-2100

GLENN, JERRY HOSMER, JR., retired language educator; b. Little Rock, Sept. 5, 1938; s. Jerry Hosmer and Anne (Matthews) G.; m. Renate Drexl, July 29, 1978. BA, Yale U., 1960; MA, U. Tex., 1962; postgrad., Free U. Berlin, 1962-63; PhD, U. Tex., 1964. Asst. prof. German U. Wis., Milw., 1964-67; asst. prof. German U. Cin., 1967-69, assoc. prof., 1969-72, prof., 1972—2003, dir. honors program, 1977-79, head dept., 1980-83, prof. emeritus, 2003—. Author: Deutsches Schrifttum der Gegenwart (ab 1945), 1971, Paul Celan, 1973, Paul Celan: Eine Bibliographie, 1989, Paul Celan: A Bibliography of English Lang. Secondary Lit. 1955-1996, 1996; (with Jeffrey Todd) Paul Celan: Die zweite Bibliographie, 1998; mng. editor: Lessing Yearbook, 1969-74; editor: (with Uwe Faulhaber and others) Exile and Enlightenment, 1987; (with Joachim Herrmann and Rebecca Rodgers) Alfred Gong, Early Poems, 1987, Max Kade Occasional Papers, 2001—; translator (with Jennifer Kelley) On the Wrong Track, 1993, International Zone, 1999, Too-Late, Too-Early, 2000, (with Clarise Samuels) Landing Attempts, 2000, (with Aine Zimmerman) StadtFluchten/City Escapes, 2004. Mem. Lessing Soc. (sec-treas. 1968-74), Mideast Honors Assn. (exec. sec. 1977-78, pres. 1979-80), Am. Assn. Tchr. German, Soc. German-Am. Studies (v.p. 1987-89). Republican. Home: 54 Fairway Dr Southgate KY 41071-3025 Personal E-mail: jerry.glenn@uc.edu.

GLENN, JOHN HERSCHEL, JR., former senator, former astronaut; b. Cambridge, Ohio, July 18, 1921; s. John Herschel and Clara (Sproat) G.; m. Anna Margaret Castor, Apr. 1943; children: Carolyn Ann, John David. Student, Muskingum Coll., 1939-42, B.Sc., 1962; naval aviation cadet, U. Iowa, 1942; grad. flight sch., Naval Air Tng. Center, Corpus Christi, Tex., 1943, Navy Test Pilot Tng. Sch., Patuxent River, Md., 1954. Commd. 2d lt. USMC, 1943, assigned 4th Marine Aircraft Wing, Marshall Islands campaign, 1944, assigned 9th Marine Aircraft Wing, 1945-46; with 1st Marine Aircraft Wing, North China Patrol, also Guam, 1947-48; flight instr. advanced flight tng. Corpus Christi, 1949-51; asst. G-2/G-3 Amphibious Warfare Sch., Quantico, Va., 1951; with Marine Fighter Squadron 311, exchange pilot 25th Fighter Interceptor Squadron USAF, Korea, 1953; project officer fighter design br. Navy Bur. Aero. Washington, 1956-58; astronaut Project Mercury, Manned Spacecraft Center NASA, 1959-65; pilot Mercury-Atlas 6, 1st orbital space flight launched from Cape Canaveral, Fla., Feb. 1962; ret. as col., 1965; v.p. corp. devel. and dir. Royal Crown Cola Co., 1966-74; pres. Royal Crown Internat.; U.S. senator from Ohio, 1975-99; mem.-at-large Ohio State Dem. Com., 1999—. Mem. Spl. Com. on Aging, Armed Svcs. Com., Senate Dem. Tech. and Comm. Com., Intelligence Com.; ranking minority mem. Govtl. Affairs Com.; vice-chmn. Senate Dem. Policy Com. Co-author: We Seven, 1962; author: P.S., I Listened to Your Heart Beat. Made first supersonic transcontinental flight, July 16, 1957; trustee Muskingum Coll. Decorated D.F.C. (six), Air medal (18); recipient Astronaut medal USMC, Navy unit commendation, Korean Presdl. unit citation, Disting. Merit award Muskingum Coll., Medal of Honor N.Y.C., Congl. Space Medal of Honor, 1978, Centennial awd., Nat. Geographic Soc., 1988, other decorations, awards and hon. degrees. Mem. Soc. Exptl. Test Pilots, Internat. Acad. of Astronautics (hon.) Democrat. Presbyterian. Office: Ohio State U John Glenn Inst 100 Bricker Hall 190 N Oval Mall Columbus OH 43210-1321*

GLENN, MARSHALL ANDREW, psychologist; b. Wynnewood, Okla., Feb. 12, 1952; s. Marshall Neal Glenn and Reba Pauline Flippen; 1 stepchild, Jason Travis Seoy. BSE, East Ctrl. State U., 1974; MEd, U. Okla., 1975, PhD, 1995; post grad. program, Fielding Inst., 2002. Recreational aide Pauls Valley State Sch. for the Mentally Retarded, 1972—74; grad. rsch. asst./test libr. U. Okla., 1974—76; sch. psychologist Okla. State Dept. Edn., Okla. City, 1976—88, Western Heights Sch., 1988—93, Norman Schools, 1993—2004, Frisco Ind. Sch. Dist., 2004—. Delegate for Okla. Nat. Assn. of Sch. Psychologist, Bethesda, Md., 2001—05; exec. bd. Okla. Sch. Psychol. Assn., 1991—2004, vol., 1991—96. Psychologist Okla. Cmty. Children and Youth, 1999; bd. dirs. Okla. Inst. for Child Advocacy, 1998. Mem.: Tex. Assn. of Sch. Psychology, Nat. Assn. of Sch. Psychologists, Okla. Sch. Psychol. Assn., Phi Kappa Phi. Avocation: fly fishing. Home: 8513 Forest Highlands Dr Plano TX 75024 Office Phone: 469-633-6916.

GLENN, NORVAL DWIGHT, sociologist, educator; b. Roswell, N.Mex. Aug. 13, 1933; s. William N. and Mary E. (Cochrain) Glenn. BA, N.Mex. State U., 1954; PhD, U. Tex., 1962. Instr. Miami U., Oxford, Ohio, 1960—61, U. Ill., 1961—63, asst. prof., 1963—64; asst. prof. to assoc. prof. sociology U. Tex., Austin, 1964—70, prof., 1970—84, Ashbel Smith prof. sociology, 1984—, Raymond Dickson, Alton C. Allen and Dillon Anderson centennial prof., 1990—91, Stiles prof. Am. studies, 1991—. Author (with Leonard Broom): Tranformation of the Negro American, 1965, Cohort Analysis, 1977, 2004; author: (with Elizabeth Marguardt) Hooking Up, Hanging Out, and Looking for Mr. Right; editor (with Charles Bonjean): Blacks in the United States, 1969; editor: (with Marion Coleman) Family Relations, 1989; editor: Contemporary Sociology, 1977—80, Jour. Family Issues, 1984—89; compiler (with John Alston and David Weiner) Social Stratification: A Research Bibliography, 1969; contbr. articles to profl. jours. Mem. coun. Inter-Univ. Consortium Polit. and Social Rsch., 1980—84, assoc. dir., 1984—2000. Served to 1st lt. U.S. Army, 1954—56. Mem.: Population Assn. Am., Nat. Coun. Family Rels., Am. Assn. Pub. Opinion Rsch., Am. Sociol. Assn. Home: 13309 Villa Park Dr Austin TX 78729-3733 Office Phone: 512-232-6320. Business E-Mail: ndglenn@mail.la.utexas.edu.

GLENN, ROBERT EASTWOOD, lawyer; b. Catlettsburg, Ky., Dec. 24, 1929; s. Albert Sidney and Pauline Elizabeth (Eastwood) G.; m. Clydenne Reinhard, Mar. 16, 1956; children: Pauline Glenn O'Brien, Robert Eastwood Jr. BS cum laude, Washington and Lee U., 1951, JD cum laude, 1953. Bar: Va. 1952, U.S. Dist. Ct. (we. dist.) Va. 1958, U.S. Ct. Appeals (4th cir.) 1974, U.S. Supreme Ct. 1975, U.S. Tax Ct. 1994. Assoc. Eggleston & Holton, Roanoke, Va., 1957-60; ptnr. Glenn, Feldmann, Darby & Goodlatte, Roanoke, 1960—2003, of counsel, 2003—. Mem. Va. Bd. Bar Examiners, Richmond, 1982—, pres., 1993—. Mem. State Coun. for Higher Edn. for Va., 1980-84; rector Radford (Va.) U., 1975-79, bd. visitors, 1972-79; chmn. Roanoke City Rep. Com., 1968-70, Roanoke Valley ARC, 1974-76; mem. Va. Found. for Humanities, 1995-01. Lt. col. (ret.) USAF. Fellow: Va. Bar Found., ABA Found.; mem.: ABA, Roanoke Bar Assn. (pres. 1980—81), Va. Bar Assn., Roanoke Regional C. of C. (pres. 1988), Shenandoah Club (pres. 2001—03), Roanoke Country Club, Order of Coif, Beta Gamma Sigma. Roman Catholic. Home: 3101 Allendale St SW Roanoke VA 24014-3118 Office: Glenn Feldmann Darby & Goodlatte 210 1st St SW Ste 200 Roanoke VA 24011-1607 E-mail: rglenn@gfdg.com.

GLENN, ROLAND DOUGLAS, chemical engineer; b. Somerville, Mass., Mar. 22, 1912; s. Charles Rathford and Anna Amanda (Card) G.; m. Eleanor Norwood Greene, June 19, 1939; children: Meg Mary Eleanor Glenn-Albiez, Nancy Anne Hansen, Sara Elisabeth Baker, Rolene Douglas Ramsey. BSChemE, MIT, 1933, MSChemE, 1934, postgrad. Registered profl. engr., N.Y., Conn., Va. Prodn. supr. Union Carbide Corp., South Charleston, W.Va., devel. group leader, plant mgr., 1934-56, div. v.p. N.Y.C., 1957-68; v.p. Pope, Evans & Robbins, N.Y.C., Alexandria, Va., 1969-71; pres. Combustion Processes, Inc., N.Y.C., 1972-90, Darien, Conn., 1991-93. Editor: (directory) Consulting Services, 1978-88; contbr. numerous reports and papers to profl. jours. Sloan fellow MIT, 1939. Mem. Am. Inst. Chem. Engrs., Am. Chem. Soc., Assn. Cons. Chemists & Chem. Engrs. (dir. 1974-92).

GLENN, RUTH ESTHER MURPHY, psychologist; b. Havana, Ala., Apr. 14, 1928; d. Willie and Olivia (Brown) Murphy; m. Ephriam Martin, Sr., Apr. 7, 1947 (div. Nov. 1960); children: Ruth Taylor, Joyce Strickland; m. James Calvin Glenn, Mar. 29, 1962; children: Adrian Rozia, Andre Garnett. BA, Chgo. State U., 1974; MA, Govs.' State U., 1976. Diplomate Am. Psychotherapy Assn. Ammunition insp. Joliet Arsenal Ammunition Plant, Ill., 1951—53; mental health technician I, II, III, to supr. I Manteno Mental Health Ctr., Ill., 1954—64, social svc. aide II, 1971—74, social worker II, mental health specialist I, II, 1974—81, psychologist II, III, 1981—85; social caseworker Dist. 259 Elem. Sch., Hopkins Park, Ill., 1966—67; psychologist III Tinley Park Mental Health Ctr., Ill., 1985—92. Mem. libr. rev. bd., mem. med. record rev. bd. Manteno Mental Health Ctr., 1972—83; mem. reorganization and planning com. Tinley Park Mental Health Ctr., 1985—86. Founder, editor: Cmty. Voice newsletter, 1955; co-author: Psychiatric Treatment Manual, 1983. Mem. adv. bd. Pembroke Voters Civic League, Ill., 1964—72; vol. group counselor Thresholds Drug Abuse Program, Kanakee, Ill., 1974; class room vol. Dist. #259 Elem. Sch., Hopkins Park, 1991; trustee AFSCME, 1995; mem. exec. bd. dirs. #57/Retirees, Kanakee, 1999; establisher, dir. Money Find for Coll., St. Anne, Ill., 1993; bd. dirs. Pembroke Voters Civic League, 1964; dir. youth programs St. Anne Woods Chapel Cmty. Ch., 1970—81. Named Key Lay Leader of the Yr., Internat. Coun. Cmty. Chs., Frankfort, Ill., 1993; recipient Ill. Woman of Achievement award, 2000, others. Mem.: ACA, AAUW, NAACP (life), Ill. Mental Health Counselors Assn., Ill. Assn. for Assessment in Counseling, Ill. Counseling Assn., Govs. State U. Alumni Assn., Nat. Coun. Negro Women, Chgo. State U. Alumni Assn. (life). Democrat. Avocations: reading, travel, gardening, writing. Home: 13334 E 6000 S Rd Saint Anne IL 60964-4562

GLENN, T. MICHAEL, delivery/messenger service executive; b. Memphis; Bachelor's, U. Miss.; MBA, U. Memphis. With sales div. Dover Elevator Co.; with dept. corp. sales Fed. Express Corp. (now FedEx Corp.), 1981-83, mgr., 1983-84, mng. dir. dept. mktg., 1984-85, v.p. mktg. N.Am., 1985-92, sr. v.p. Catalog and Remail Svcs. div., 1992-93, sr. v.p. worldwide mktg., customer svc., corp. comm., 1993-98; exec. v.p. market devel. and corp. comm. FedEx Corp., Memphis, 1993—, overseer FedEx Custom Critical, 1993—. Bd. dirs. Make-A-Wish Found., United Way. Office: Fed Ex Corp 942 S Shady Grove Rd Memphis TN 38120-4117*

GLENNEN, ROBERT EUGENE, JR., retired university president; b. Omaha, Mar. 31, 1933; s. Robert E. and La Verda (Elledge) G.; m. Mary C. O'Brien, Apr. 17, 1958; children: Maureen, Bobby, Colleen, Billy, Barry, Katie, Molly, Kerry AB, U. Portland, 1955, M.Ed., 1957; PhD, U. Notre Dame, 1962. Asst. prof. U. Portland, 1956-60; asst. prof., assoc. prof. Eastern Mont. Coll., Billings, 1962-65; assoc. dean U. Notre Dame, South Bend, Ind., 1965-72; dean, v.p. U. Nev.-Las Vegas, 1972-80; pres. Western N.Mex. U., Silver City, 1980-84, Emporia (Kans.) State U., 1984-97; acting vice-chancellor U. Ark., Montecello, 1999; interim provost U. So. Colo., 1999-2000, interim pres., 2001—02. Bd. dirs. Emporia Enterprises; cons. HEW, Washington, 1964-84 Author: Guidance: An Orientation, 1966. Contbr. articles to profl. jours. Pres. PTA, South Bend, Ind., 1970-71; bd. trustees Am. Coll. Testing Corp., Iowa City, 1977-80; chmn. Kans. Regents Coun. of Pres., 1986-87, 92-93, 95-96. Recipient award of excellence Nat. Acad. Advising Assn., Disting. Alumnus award U. Portland, 1993, Kans. Master Tchr. award, 1994; named Coach of Yr., Coach and Athletic mag., 1958, Pub. Adminstr. of Yr., 1994, Athletic Hall of Fame, Portland, 1995; Rotary Paul Harris fellow, 1995, Ford Found. fellow, 1961-62. Mem. Kans. C. of C. (bd. dirs.), Emporia C. of C. Regional Devel. Assn. (bd. dirs., Bank IV), Am. Personnel and Guidance Assn., Am. Assn. State Colls. and Univs. (chair pres's. commn. on tchr. edn.), Am. Assn. Higher Edn., Nev. Personnel and Guidance Assn., Assn. Counselor Educators and Suprs., Am. Assn. Counseling and Devel., Nat. Assn. Student Personnel Adminstrs. Republican. Roman Catholic. Avocations: racquetball, walking, reading, hiking. Home: 1591 Meadow Hills Dr Richland WA 99352

GLENNER, RICHARD ALLEN, dentist, dental historian; b. Chgo., Apr. 14, 1934; s. Robert Joseph and Vivian (Prosk) G.; m. Dorothy Chapman, July 13, 1957; children: Mark Steven, Alison, Scott Jay. BS, Roosevelt U., 1955; BS in Dentistry, U. Ill., 1958, DDS, 1959; student, Army Med. Svc. Sch., 1960. Pvt. practice, Chgo., 1962—. Cons. on dental history to Smithsonian Instn., ADA, various corps., librs., univs., museums, dental jours, Dr. Samuel D. Harris Nat. Mus. Dentistry; dental and anthropol. rschr. Nat. Park Svc., Nat. Mus. Health and Medicine, 1993—; lectr. to various orgns. Author: The Dental Office: A Pictorial History, 1984, How it Evolved: Dentistry's Pursuit for Excellence, 1997; co-author: The American Dentist, 1990, A Visit to the Dentist: Then & Now, 1996; appeared in PBS video Sci. Am. Frontiers: The Wild West, 1995; cons. editor A Bicentennial Salute to Am. Dentistry, 1976; contbr. articles to profl. and popular jours.; film maker The Dental Office, 1994; reviewer Jour. ADA, 1999—. Served to capt. AUS, 1960—68. Mem. ADA (life), Ill. Dental Assn., Chgo. Dental Soc., Acad. Gen. Dentistry, Assn. Mil. Surgeons U.S., Am. Acad. History of Dentistry (historian 1984, chmn. smithsonian Instn. adv. group 1987, Hayden-Harris award 1983, columnist Jour. History of Dentistry 1989—, mem. editl. bd. 1993—, hist. display com. 1993—, pub. com. 1993—, Hayden-Harris award com. 1995-99), Fedn. Dentaire Internat., Lindsay Soc. G.B., Ill. Dental Soc. (history com.), Pierre Fauchard Acad., Am. Med. Writers Assn., Sci. Instrument Soc., Jewish War Vets. U.S., Westerners, Titanic Hist. Soc., Titanic Internat. Soc. (rschr.), Alpha Omega. Home: 6715 N Lawndale Ave Lincolnwood IL 60712-3711 Office: 3414 W Peterson Ave Chicago IL 60659-3447

GLENNON, CHARLES EDWARD, retired judge, lawyer; b. Monticello, Ill., Apr. 5, 1942; s. William Edward and Beatrice Jane (Pierson) G.; m. Sylvia Ann McClintock, Aug. 24, 1965 (div. Aug. 1972); children: David, Caroline; m. Victoria Louise Pearre, Oct. 26, 1974 (div. May 2001); 1 child, Andrew; m. Bonnie Jane Krueger, July 5, 2003. BA, U. Ill., 1964, JD, 1966. Bar: Ill. 1966, U.S. Supreme Ct. 1974. Assoc. Fellheimer & Fellheimer, Pontiac, Ill., 1968-73; ptnr. Gomien & Glennon Ltd., Dwight, Ill., 1973-75; cir. judge State of Ill., Pontiac, 1976-98; temporarily recalled to bench, 1999, 2003; chief judge 11th cir., 1991-95. Lectr., author criminal law Ill. Village atty., Dwight, 1973-75; chmn. Salvation Army Adv. Bd., Pontiac, 1976; chmn. criminal law com. Ill. Jud. Conf., 1989-99, del., mem. exec. com., 1993-98; former mem. Regional Youth Planning Commn., Livingston County Commn. on Children and Youth; mng. dir. Nat. Arts Found., 1998—. With U.S. Army, 1966-68. Fellow Ill. Bar Found.; mem. Livingston County Bar Assn. (pres. 1991-93), Ill. Bar Assn., Ill. Judges Assn., Am. Assn. Juvenile and Family Ct. Judges, Lions, Rotary, Elks. Republican. Episcopalian. Personal E-mail: chasness@aol.com.

GLENNY, BRUCE WILLIAM, music educator; b. Holyoke, Mass., Mar. 17, 1959; s. William H. Glenny and Claire Marie Yvon. MusB, Boston U., 1981; MusM, DMA, Eastman Sch. Music, 1988. Dir. music St. Michael Ch., Orland Park, Ill., 1989—98, St. Anastasia Ch., Troy, Mich., 1998—2001; music tchr. Radnor (Pa.) H.S., 2001, Garnet Valley H.S., Glen Mills, Pa., 2003—. Asst. organist, choir master St. Peter in the Gt. Valley Episcopal Ch., Paoli, Pa., 2003—; asst. organist St. David Episcopal Ch., Wayne, Pa., 2003—; spkr. in field; concert soloist on organ, harpsichord, clavichord, U.S., Italy, U.K. Contbr. articles to profl. publs. Mem.: Assn. Anglican Musicians, Am. Guild Organists, Midwest Hist. Keyboard Soc. (bd. dirs. 1999—2003, pres. 2003—05).

GLENZER, SIEGFRIED HEINZ, physicist, educator, researcher; b. Essen, Germany, June 27, 1966; came to U.S., 1994; s. Heinz and Hannelore (Reimers) G.; m. Anja Berkel, July 13, 1994; 1 child, Helena Ashley. Diploma, Ruhr-U. Bochum, Germany, 1990, D in Natural Scis., 1994. Tchg. asst. Ruhr-U. Bochum, 1987-90, sci. asst., 1990-94, sci. assoc., 1994; postdoctoral physicist Lawrence Livermore (Calif.) Nat. Lab., 1995-96, staff physicist, 1996—. Vis. scientist U. Provence, Marseille, France, 1994; vis. lectr. U. Calif., Berkeley, 1997-98, Ecole Polytechnique, Paris, 1998, U. Oxford, Eng., 1999, 2000, 01, 04. Contbr. more than 100 articles to profl. jours. Recipient Humboldt prize, 2004. Fellow: Am. Phys. Soc. (Excellence in Plasma Physics Rsch. award 2003, Humboldt prize 2004); mem.: Deutsche Physikalische Gesellschaft. Achievements include the demonstration of x-ray scattering and the introduction of Thomson scattering to measure temperatures in high-density inertial confinement fusion plasmas; contributions to plasma spectroscopy, short-wave length lasers, and fusion research. Office: Lawrence Livermore Nat Lab 7000 East Ave L-399 Livermore CA 94550-9516

GLESBY, MARSHALL JAY, physician, educator; b. Winnipeg, Manitoba, Canada, Sept. 27, 1963; U.S., 1985; MD, Johns Hopkins U., 1989, PhD, 1997; BSc, McGill U., 1985. Diplomate Am. Bd. Internal Medicine, Am. Bd. Infectious Diseases. Intern, resident Johns Hopkins Hosp., 1989—92; assoc. prof. medicine and pub. health Weill Med. Coll. Cornell U., N.Y., 2005—. Office: Weill Medical College of Cornell Univ 525 E 68th St Box 566 New York NY 10021 Office Phone: 212-746-4177.

GLESMANN, SYLVIA-MARIA, artist; b. Spardorf, Erlangen, Germany, June 8, 1923; arrived in the US, 1925; d. Rolf-Joseph and Auguste (Schultheiss) Hoffmann; m. John Brainerd Glesmann, Apr. 30, 1948; children: Glenn M., Eric B., Jonathan M. Degree, Acad. Fine Arts, Nurnberg, Germany, 1940, Acad. Fine Arts, Munich, 1944. Instr. Somerville Adult Edn. Exhibited in group shows at Carrier Clinic, 1993, Bergen Mus., 1993, Morris Mus., 1993, Nabisco Brands, 1993, Cultural and Heritage Gallery, Somerville, N.J., 1993-95, Salmagundi Club, 1994, Garden State Water Color Assn., Princeton, N.J., 1994, Barrons Art Ctr., 1993, Art on the Ave. Group Show of Flowers, 1991, Nat. Assn. Women Artists, N.Y.C., 1991, 94, SoHo, 1994, Bridgewater N.J. County Libr., 1996, 2001-02, Nat. Assn. Women Artists New World Art Ctr., Soho, N.Y., 1999, Children's Specialized Hosp., Westfield, N.J., 2002, Barrons Art Ctr, Woodbridge, 2002; one-woman shows include Childrens Specialized Hosp., Mountainside, N.J., 2002, N.U.I. Corp., Bridgewater, 1987, Salmagundi Club, N.Y.C., 1995, 2000, Am. Artists Profl. League, 1995-97, Somerset County Libr., Bridgewater, 1996, 2001-02, Barrons Art Ctr., Woodbridge, 1997, Barrons Art Ctr., Bridgewater Mcpl. Bldg, 1999-2001, Nat. Assn. Women Artists, Balt. Conv. Ctr., 2000, Bridgewater Libr., 2001, Nat. Assn. Women Artists, UN Visitors Lobby, 2002, Georgio Zikos Gallery, New Hope, Pa., 2002-03, over 25 one woman shows; author numerous poems. Recipient over 50 awards in water color, Editor's Choice award, 1998, Poetry Editors Choice award, 2002, Poetry award, Intenat. Libr. Poetry, 2003. Mem. Am. Artists Profl. League (pres. N.J. chpt. 1988-91, 2001, Bridgewater NJ Artists shows, 2002-2003), Nat. Assn. Woman Artists, Raritan Valley Arts Assn. (pres. 1976-78), Somerset Art Assn. (chairwoman 10th outdoor art show), Salmagundi Club, Nat. Mus. for Women in Arts (charter). Lutheran. Avocations: sports, music, reading, poetry. Home and Office: 36 Twin Oaks Rd Bridgewater NJ 08807-2343 *To be of cultural stamina in the arts - to help and influence the American public. To see the world through art-music poetry painting also Philosophy. To make people see and feel. And to look at nature as a miracle.*

GLIATTA, STEPHEN, lawyer; BS, Fordham U., 1980; JD, NYU, 1983. Bar: NY 1984. Ptnr., co-chair Real Estate Dept., mem. exec. com. Kaye Scholer LLP, NYC. Mem.: Nat. Assn. Real Estate Investment Trusts. Office: Kaye Scholer LLP 425 Park Ave New York NY 10022 Office Phone: 212-836-8618. E-mail: sgliatta@kayescholer.com.

GLICK, CYNTHIA SUSAN, lawyer; b. Sturgis, Mich., Aug. 6, 1950; d. Elmer Joseph and Ruth Edna (McCally) G.; m. Paul Allen, (dec. 2004). AB, Ind. U., 1972; JD, Ind. U.-Indpls., 1978. Bar: Ind. 1978, U.S. Dist. Ct. (so. dist.) Ind. 1978, U.S. Dist. Ct. (no. dist.) Ind. 1981, U.S. Supreme Ct. 2000. Adminstrv. asst. Gov. Otis R. Bowen of Ind., 1973-76; dep. pros. atty. 35th Jud. Cir., LaGrange County, Ind., 1980-82, pros. atty., 1983—90; pvt. practice LaGrange, Ind., 1979—. Campaign aide Ind. Rep. State Ctr. Com., Indpls., 1972-73; chmn. La Grange County Rep. Ctrl. com. Named Hon. Spkr., Ind. Ho. of Reps., 1972, Sagamore of the Wabash, Gov. of Ind., 1974. Fellow Ind. Bar Found.; mem. ABA, Ind. State Bar Assn., LaGrange County Bar Assn., DAR, Order Eastern Star, Phi Delta Phi, Delta Zeta. Methodist. Home and Office: 113 W Spring St Lagrange IN 46761-1843 Office Phone: 260-463-7414. Business E-Mail: sueglick@ligtel.com.

GLICK, EARL A., lawyer; b. Chgo., Feb. 20, 1930; s. Simon and Eva (Cohen) G.; m. Janet Esther Klein, Aug. 22, 1953; children: Michael J., Daniel H., Linda J. Richardson, Steven B. BS, U. Ill., 1951; JD, Northwestern U., 1953. Bar: Ill. 1953, Calif. 1962. Asst. atty. gen. State of Ill., Chgo., 1953-57; ptnr. Gerwin & Glick, Chgo., 1957-61; gen. counsel S & S Corp., Beverly Hills, Calif., 1961-62; ptnr. Gendel, Raskoff, Shapiro & Quittner, LA, 1962-90, Orrick, Herrington & Sutcliffe, LA, 1990-2000; of counsel Murphy & Assocs. Capital, LLC, Westlake Village, Calif., 2000—04, 2004—. Bd. govs. Fin. Lawyers Conf., LA, 1965—2000. Fellow Am. Coll. Comml. Fin. Lawyers; mem. ABA (chair program com. fin. svcs. subcom., 1993-96). Republican. Jewish. Avocations: travel, walking, reading. Home: 5560 Ostin Ave Woodland Hills CA 91367-3976 Office Phone: 818-716-1180. E-mail: eglick@socal.rr.com.

GLICK, GARLAND WAYNE, retired theological seminary president; b. Bridgewater, Va., Jan. 27, 1921; s. John T. and Effie (Evers) G.; m. Barbara Roller Zigler, Jan. 1, 1943; children— Martha (Mrs. Carl Barlett), Ted, Mary. B.D., Bethany Bibl. Sem., Chgo., 1946; MA in N.T, U. Chgo., 1949, PhD in Ch. History, 1957; LL.D., Bridgewater Coll., 1969. Ordained to ministry Ch. of Brethren, 1942, United Ch. Christ, 1978. Pastor, Lombard, Ill., 1945-48; instr., then asst. prof. Bibl. studies Juniata Coll., Huntingdon, Pa., 1948-53; mem. faculty Franklin and Marshall Coll., 1955-65, assoc. prof. religion, 1958-65, prof., 1965, v.p., 1962-65, acting pres., 1962-63, dir. rsch. and long-range planning, 1960, asst. to dean, 1960-61, dean coll., 1961-65; pres. Keuka Coll., Keuka Park, N.Y., 1966-74; dir. Moton Center Ind. Studies, Gloucester, Va., 1975-78; pres. Bangor (Maine) Theol. Sem., 1978-86. Vis. prof. Lancaster (Pa.) Theol. Sem., 1958-60, 64; coord. cons. Knox Seminars Ednl. Mgmt., 1963-65; seminar dir. Nat. Cath. Assn. Long-Range Planning Seminars, 1968; bd. dirs. Empire State Found. Ind. Liberal Arts Colls., Fund for Theol. Edn. (pres. 1988-92), Lancaster Guidance Ctr. Author: Maker of Modern Theology: Adolf von Harnack, 1967, Songs for my God, 1998; contbr. to Ency. Brit. Mem. Nat. Assn. Bibl. Instrs., Am. Soc. Ch. History, Lancaster Cliosophic Soc. (pres. 1995-97), Am. Conf. Acad. Deans (treas. 1965-66), Societas Orphea, Pi Gamma Mu, Tau Kappa Alpha. Mem. United Ch. Of Christ. Home: 1834 Ridgeview Ave Lancaster PA 17603-4316 *Clearly, a revolution has taken place in the last generation. The meaning of that revolution is not yet clear. I believe the name of the revolution is "longing" and Augustine's "God and the soul I want to know, nothing more," demarks its direction.*

GLICK, GINA PHILLIPS MORAN, retired physician; b. Chgo., Dec. 6, 1931; d. Edward Langan Moran and Virginia Louise Phillips; m. L. Michael Glick, Feb. 9, 1957; children: Mark Michael, Celeste Michele, Felicia Michele, Matthew Michael. Student, Mundelein Coll., Chgo., 1949-52; MD, Loyola U., Chgo., 1956. Diplomate Am. Bd. Anesthesiology. Intern Mercy Hosp., Chgo., 1956-57; resident in anesthesia Chgo. Wesley Mem. Hosp., 1957-59; pvt. practice anesthesia Cumberland, M.D., 1959-83; clin. instr. anesthesia U. Md., Balt.; chmn. dept. anesthesia Sacred Heart Hosp., Cumberland, 1967-83; asst. prof. anesthesia U. Tex. S.W. Med. Ctr., 1985—99; ret., 1999. Dir. Jenkins Anesthesiology Libr. Recipient gold, silver and bronze medals Md. chpt. Am. Heart Assn., Community Achievement award Sta. WCBC, 1981, St. Benedict medal St. Scholastica High Sch., Chgo., 1978. Mem. Am. Soc. Anesthesiologists, Tex. Soc. Anesthesiologists, Dallas County Soc. Anesthesiologists, Dallas County Med. Soc. Roman Catholic. Office: U Tex Sci Med Ctr Dept Anesthesiology 5323 Harry Hines Blvd Dallas TX 75390-7208

GLICK, J. LESLIE, entrepreneur; b. NYC, Mar. 2, 1940; s. Arthur Harvey and Hilda Lillian (Lichtenfeld) G.; m. Judith Sumiye Mihara; children: Geoffrey Michael, Jessica Michele. AB, Columbia U., 1961, PhD, 1964. Nat. Cancer Inst. postdoctoral fellow Princeton U., 1964-65; sr., then asso. cancer research scientist Roswell Park Meml. Inst., Buffalo, 1965-69; assoc. rsch. prof. physiology, physiology chmn. Roswell Park div. SUNY, Buffalo, 1968-70; from exec. v.p. to chmn. bd. Asso. Biomedic Systems, Inc., Buffalo, 1969-77; pres. Inst. Sci. and Social Accountability, Washington, 1975-79; pres., chief exec. officer Genex Corp., Gaithersburg, Md., 1977-87; chmn., CEO Bionix Corp., Potomac, Md., 1987-93. Chmn. HTI Corp., Buffalo, 1972-75; dir. Nat. Assn. Life Sci. Industries, 1975-77; rsch. prof. biology Niagara (N.Y.) U., Canisius Coll., Buffalo, 1968-70; mem. exec. com. SUNY Grad. Sch., Buffalo, 1968-70; vis. lectr. NATO Adv. Study Inst., Brussels, 1970; mem. biotech. tech. adv. com. U.S. Dept. Commerce, 1985-87; adj. prof. tech. mgmt. Grad. Sch., U. Md. Univ. Coll., 1988—, mem. adv. panel, 1988-2000, mem. grad. coun., 1992-94; professorial cons. NTU Satellite Network, Nat. Tech. U., 1989-90; vis. lectr. tech. mgmt. Johns Hopkins U., 1993-97; external examiner doctoral program Sch. Mgmt. Asian Inst. Tech., 1998-99; mng. dir. Cooper Alport Prodns., 1998—; chmn. bd. Marco Polo Techs., Inc., 1998-03; bd. dirs. Advanced Processing and Imaging, Inc., vice chmn. bd., 1999—; vice chmn. bd. Advanced Tracking Svcs., Inc., 2000-01, chmn. bd., 2001-03. Author: Fundamentals of Human Lymphoid Cell Culture, 1980; also articles; patentee in field; mem. editorial advisors bd. Strategic Direction, 1984-87; mem. adv. coun. High Tech. Mktg. Rev., 1986-87; mem. indsl. adv. bd. Biotech. Process Engring. Ctr., MIT, 1986-87; mem. editorial bd. Accountability in Rsch.: Policies and Quality Assurance, 1989—; editor-in-chief Tech. Mgmt., 1992-2001. Bd. overseers Simon's Rock of Bard Coll., 1984-85; trustee Nat. Faculty Humanities, Arts and Scis., 1985-87. Mem. Internat. Assn. for Mgmt. Tech., Am. Physiol. Soc., Indsl. Biotech. Assn. (pres. 1981-83, bd. dirs.1981-84), N.Y. Acad. Scis., Sigma Xi. E-mail: jlglick@ix.netcom.com.

GLICK, JANE MILLS, biomedical researcher, educator; b. Memphis, Nov. 26, 1943; d. Albert Axtell Jr. and Mary Louise (Baynes) Mills; m. John Harrison Glick, May 25, 1968; children: Katherine Anne, Sarah Stewart. AB, Randolph-Macon Woman's Coll., 1965; PhD, Columbia U., 1971. Postdoctoral trainee NIH, Bethesda, Md., 1971-73; postdoctoral fellow Sch. of Medicine Stanford (Calif.) U., 1973-74; rsch. asst. prof. biochemistry Sch. Dental Medicine U. Pa., Phila., 1974-77; asst. prof. biochemistry Med. Coll. Pa., Phila., 1977-82, assoc. prof. biochemistry, 1982-90, prof. biochemistry, 1990-94; sr. rsch. investigator Inst. Human Gene Therapy Sch. Medicine U. Pa., 1994—2002, faculty adminstr. cell and molecular biology group. Mem. metabolism study sect. NIH, 1993—97; adj. assoc. prof. Sch. Medicine U. Pa., 1996—. Assoc. editor: Jour. Lipid Rsch., 1985-86, mem. editorial bd., 1987-99; contbr. articles to profl. jours. Trustee Episcopal Acad., Merion, Pa., 1989-95, Swarthmore Presbyn. Ch., 1995-97, pres. 1997. Recipient Rsch. Svc. award NIH, 1975-77, Young Investigator award, 1980-83, Teaching award Lindback Found., 1985. Mem. AAAS, AAUP (sec. 1990-92), Arteriosclerosis Coun. Am. Heart Assn. (program com. 1990-93), Am. Soc. for Biochemistry and Molecular Biology, Am. Soc. for Human Genetics, Phi Beta Kappa, Sigma Xi. Presbyterian. Office: U Pa Sch Medicine 652 BRB II/III 421 Curie Blvd Philadelphia PA 19104 Business E-Mail: glickj@mail.med.upenn.edu.

GLICK, JOHN H., oncologist, medical educator; b. NYC, May 9, 1943; s. Arthur W. and Sybil (Goldman) Glick; m. Jane Mills, May 25, 1968; children: Katherine, Sarah. AB magna cum laude, Princeton U., 1965; MD, Columbia U., 1969. Diplomate Am. Bd. Med. Oncology, (sec. subsplty. com. med. oncology 1976-83, mem. subsplty. bd. med. oncology 1983-87, chmn. 1987-89, cert. exam. com. 1986-88, mem. bd. govs. 1987-89) Am. Bd. Internal Medicine. Intern in medicine Presbyn. Hosp., N.Y.C., 1969-70, asst. resident in medicine, 1970-71; commd. surgeon, clin. assoc. medicine br. Nat. Cancer Inst., USPHS, Bethesda, Md., 1971-73; postdoctoral fellow in med. oncology Stanford (Calif.) U., 1973-74; asst. prof. medicine U. Pa., Phila., 1974-79, Ann B. Young asst. prof. cancer rsch., 1974, assoc. prof., 1979-83, prof., 1983—, Madlyn and Leonard Abramson prof. clin. oncology, 1988—; dir. clin. trials U. Pa. Cancer Ctr., Phila., 1977-79, assoc. dir. for clin. rsch., 1980-85, dir. Cancer Ctr., 1985—, mem. numerous acad. coms., dept. medicine coms., hosp. coms., 1974—; pres. Abramson Family Cancer Rsch. Inst., Phila., 1998—, also bd. dirs. Attending physician Hosp. U. Pa., 1974—, dir. Hematology-Oncology Clinic, 1974—76; cons. Phila. VA Hosp., 1974—; mem. clin. trials rev. com. NIH, 1980—83, mem. radiosensitizer /radioprotector working group, radiotheraphy devel. br., 1980—85, chmn. consensus devel. panel conf. adjuvant therapy for breast cancer, 1985; mem. com. accreditation med. oncology tng. programs Accreditation Coun. Grad. Med. Edn., 1983—, mem. appeals panel, 1984—94; prin. investigator Ea. Coop. Oncology Group, U. Pa.; pres., dir. Abramson Family Cancer Rsch. Inst., 1987—; dir. Pa. Cancer Ctr., 1985—. Mem. editl. bd.: Am. Jour. Clin. Oncology, 1983—89, Blood, 1983—86, Jour. Clin. Oncology, 1987—93, mem. bd. editors: Internat. Jour. Radiation Oncology, Biology and Physics; editor (assoc. editor): Cancer Rsch., 1984—88; contbr. articles to profl. jours. Recipient Faculty Rsch. award, Am. Cancer Soc., 1982—86; Rsch. grantee, Nat. Cancer Inst., Ea. Coop. Oncology Group, Am. Cancer Soc., others. Master: ACP (mem. various splty. coms. 1983—84); fellow: Coll. Physicians and Surgeons; mem.: John Morgan Soc. U. Pa., Am. Fedn. Clin. Rsch., Am. Soc. Hematology, Am. Radium Soc. (mem. exec. com. 1986—87), Am. Assn. Cancer Rsch., Am. Assn. Cancer Edn., Am. Soc. Clin. Oncology (chmn. program com. 1983—84, nominating com. 1983—84, mem. pub. issue com. 1984—85, bd. dirs., pres. 1995—96), Alpha Omega Alpha, Phi Beta Kappa. Office: Abramson Cancer Ctr of Univ Pa 3400 Spruce St Philadelphia PA 19104-4283 Office Phone: 215-662-6065. Business E-Mail: glickjh@mail.med.upenn.edu.

GLICK, KAREN LYNNE, college administrator; b. Bucyrus, Ohio, Sept. 2, 1945; d. Phillip Dole and Bernice Grace Glick; children: M. Todd, K. Christine. BSJ, Bowling Green State U., 1967, MA, 1979. Editor Bowling Green (Ohio) State U., 1972-74; account exec. Howard E. Mitchell, Jr., Advt., Findlay, Ohio, 1974-77; asst. to dir. student devel. program Bowling Green State U., 1977-79; dir. pub. info. Bluffton (Ohio) Coll., 1980-83; asst. to v.p. for instl. advancement Findlay (Ohio) Coll., 1983-85; assoc. dir. devel. Bluffton Coll., 1985-90; assoc. dir. divsnl. support Miami U. Ohio, Oxford, 1990-93; sr. regional dir. devel. U. Ill. Found., Urbana, 1993—2003, assoc. campaign dir., 2003—. Bd. dirs. Mental Health Ctr. Champaign County. Mem.: Fla. Sea Kayaking Assn., Bowling Green U. Press Club (charter 1983). Anglican. Office: U Ill Found Harker Hall MC-386 1305 W Green St Urbana IL 61801-2945 Business E-Mail: glick@uif.uillinois.edu.

GLICK, LESLIE ALAN, lawyer; b. N.Y.C., May 22, 1946; s. Leo S. and Sylvia (Hall) G. BS, Cornell U., 1967, JD, 1970. Bar: N.Y. 1971, D.C. 1971, Md. 1974, U.S. Ct. Internat. Trade 1971, U.S. Supreme Ct. 1974. Ptnr. Porter Wright Morris & Arthur, Washington, 1987—. Author: Multilateral Trade Negotiations, 1984, Trading with Saudi Arabia, 1980, Guide to U.S. Customs and Trade Laws, 1991, 2d edit., 1996, Understanding the North American Free Trade Agreement, 1993, 2d edit., 1995; author, co-editor, contbr. Manual for the Practice of U.S. International Trade Law, 2001. Active Dem. State Cen. com., Md., 1982-84; chmn. adv. com. on Consumer Affairs, Montgomery County, Md., 1982-84. Mem. Fed. Bar Assn. (chmn. internat. law sect. 1986-88); Am. Bar Assn. Internat. Trade and Customs Law Com. (chmn. sect. Admin. Law and Regulatory Practice 2004-05). Office: Porter Wright Morris & Arthur 1919 Pennsylvania Ave NW Washington DC 20006 Office Phone: 202-778-3022. Business E-Mail: lglick@porterwright.com.

GLICK, MILTON DON, chemist, academic administrator; b. Memphis, July 30, 1937; s. Lewis S. and Sylvia (Kleinman) G.; m. Peggy M., June 22, 1965; children: David, Sander. AB cum laude, Augustana Coll., 1959; PhD, U. Wis., 1965. Asst. prof. chemistry Wayne State U., Detroit, 1966-70, assoc. prof., 1970-74, prof., 1974-83, chmn. dept., 1978-83; dean arts & scis. U. Mo., Columbia, 1983-88; provost Iowa State U., Ames, 1988-91, interim pres., 1990-91; sr. v.p., provost Ariz. State U., Tempe, 1991—2002, exec. v.p., provost of the univ., 2002—. Contbr. articles to profl. jours. Fellow dept. chemistry Cornell U., Ithaca, N.Y., 1964-66. Office: Ariz State Univ Exec VP and Provost 303 E University Dr PO Box 877805 Tempe AZ 85287-7805 Office Phone: 480-965-1224. Business E-Mail: glick@asu.edu.

GLICK, RUTH BURTNICK, literature educator, writer; b. Lexington, Ky., Apr. 27, 1942; d. Lester Leon and Beverly (Miller) Burtnick; m. Norman Stanley Glick, June 30, 1963; children: Elissa, Ethan. BA, The George Washington U., 1964; MA, U. Md., 1967. Lectr. S.W. Writers Conf., Houston, 1984, Nebr. Writers' Guild, Omaha, 1985, Bouchercon, Balt., 1986, Triangle Romance and Fiction Writers' Conf., Raleigh, 1988, Romantic Times Booklovers Conf., San Antonio, 1990, Orlando, 2001, Kansas City, 2003, St. Louis, 2005, Malice Domestic, Bethesda, 1993, Howard C.C., 1995—, World Fantasy Conv., 2003, Desert Dreams Conf., Phoenix, 2004, Writers Weekend, Seattle, 2004. Author: (with Nancy Baggett) Dollhouse Furniture You Can Make, 1977, Dollhouse Lamps and Chandeliers, 1979, Soup's On, 1985, Oat Bran Baking, 1989, Skinny Soups, 1992, 100 Percent Pleasure, 1994 (US Today list of 12 best cookbooks of 1994), Skinny Italian, 1996, One-Pot Meals for People with Diabetes, 2002; (with Eileen Buckholtz, Carolyn Males and Louise Titchener) Love Is Elected, 1982 (named one of best romances 1982), Southern Persuasion, 1983, (with Titchener) In the Arms of Love, 1983 (Romance best seller list), Brian's Captive, 1983 (Romance best seller list), Reluctant Merger, 1983 (Romance best seller list), Summer Wine, 1984, Beginner's Luck, 1984, Mistaken Image, 1985, Hopelessly Devoted, 1985, Summer Stars, 1985, Stolen Passion, 1986, Indiscreet, 1988, (with Baggett and Gloria Kaufer Greene) Don't Tell 'Em It's Good for 'Em, 1984, Eat Your Vegetables!, 1985, (with Buckholtz) End of Illusion, 1984, Space Attack, 1984, Mission of the Secret Spy Squad, 1984, Mindbenders, 1984, Doom Stalker, 1985, Captain Kid and the Pirates, 1985, The Cats of Castle Mountain, 1985, Logical Choice, 1986, Great Expectations, 1987, A Place in Your Heart, 1988, Saber Dance, 1988, Postmark, 1988, Roller Coaster, 1989 (Young Adult Best Seller List), Silver Creek Challenge, 1989, Needlepoint, 1989, Life Line, 1990, Shattered Vows, 1991, Whispers in the Night, 1991, Only Skin Deep, 1992, Trial By Fire, 1992, Hopscotch, 1993, Cradle and All, 1993, What Child is This, 1993, Midnight Kiss, 1994, Tangled Vows, 1994, Till Death Us Do Part, 1995, Prince of Time, 1995, Face to Face, 1996, For Your Eyes Only, 1997, Father and Child, 1997 (Peregrine Connection series) Talons of the Falcon, 1986, Flight of the Raven, 1986, In Search of the Dove, 1986 (Lifetime Achievement award for romantic suspense series 1987), (with Kathryn Jensen) The Big Score, 1989 (Young Adult Best Seller List), Night Stalker, 1989 (Young Adult Best Seller List), (sole author) Dollhouse Kitchen and Dining Room Accessories, 1979, Invasion of the Blue Lights, 1982, More Than Promises, 1985, The Closer We Get, 1989, Make Me a Miracle, 1992, Bayou Moon, 1992, Skinny One Pot Meals, 1994, The Diabetes Snack, Munch, Nibble, Nosh Book, 1998, Simply Italian, 1998, Nowhere Man, 1998, Shattered Lullaby, 1999, Midnight Caller, 1999, Never Too Late, 2000, Amanda's Child, 2000, Fabulous Lo-Carb Cuisine, 2001, The Man from Texas, 2001, Never Alone, 2001, Lassiter's Law, 2001, Body Contact, 2002 (Waldenbooks Series Best Seller List), From the Shadows, 2002, Phantom Lover, 2003, Killing Moon, 2003 (Berkley Sensation Launch Book), Intimate Strangers, 2003, Edge of the Moon, 2003, Witching Moon, 2003, Bedroom Therapy, 2004, Out of Nowhere, 2004, Undercover Encounter, 2004, Crimson Moon, 2005, Spellbound, 2005, Beyond Control, 2005, Riley's Retribution, 2005, others; contbr. articles to profl. jours. U. Md. Am. studies fellow, 1964-65; recipient Career Achievement award for series Romantic Mystery, 1994, Romantic Times Career Achievement award for series Romantic Suspense, 2000, Golden Leaf award for Best Long Contemporary novel and Best Novella, N.J. Romance Writers, 2001, Golden Leaf award for Best Paranormal novel N.J. Romance Writers, 2003, 04, Best Selling Author, NY Times, USA Today, 2003, Barclay Gold award for Best Futuristic, Fantasy and Paranormal novel Lake Country Romance Writers, 2004; nominee Best Series Romance Book of the Yr. 1993-94 Romantic Times, 1995, 99, 2001, nominee Series Storyteller of Yr., 1996, nominee Best Harlequin Intrigue of Yr., 1998, nominee Best Series Romantic Suspense Writer of Yr., 2000. Mem. Author's Guild, Romance Writers Am. (lectr. Detroit, 1984, Atlanta 1985, Dallas 1987, 96, 2004, Boston 1989, San Francisco 1990, New Orleans 1991, 2001, Denver 2002, N.Y.C. 2003, Reno, 2005), Washington Romance Writers (bd. dirs.), Sisters in Crime, Novelists Inc., Md. Romance Writers, Internat. Thriller Writers. E-mail: rglick@capaccess.org.

GLICKMAN, ALBERT SEYMOUR, psychologist, educator; b. Bklyn., Feb. 7, 1923; s. Irving and Molly Glickman; m. Blanche Buller, July 14, 1945; children: Ralph, Marc, Judith, Debra. BA summa cum laude, Ohio State U., 1943, MA, 1947, PhD, 1952. Asst. prof. psychology Ga. Inst. Tech., Atlanta, 1947-52; project dir. Am. Insts. Rsch., Newport, RI, Pitts., 1952-55; dir. psychol. rsch. dept. U.S. Naval Pers. Rsch. Activity, Washington, 1955-62; chief pers. rsch. staff U.S. Dept. Agr., Washington, 1962-67; dir. Inst. Rsch. Orgnl. Behavior, 1967—70; dep. dir. Washington office Am. Insts. Rsch., 1970—76; v.p. Advanced Rsch. Resources Orgn., Washington, 1976-78; eminent prof. psychology Old Dominion U., Norfolk, Va., 1979-90, eminent prof. emeritus, 1991—; pres. Orgn. Rsch. Group Tidewater, Inc., 1979-91; chmn. bd. Third Quarter: Inst. Retirement Rsch., 1985-91. Vis. prof. Tel Aviv U., 1986, Tulane U., 1994. Cons., editor: Jour. Applied Psychology, 1971—81; co-author: (book) Top Management Development and Succession, 1968, Police-Community Action: A Program for Change in Police-Community Behavior Patterns, 1973, Changing Schedules of Work: Patterns and Implications, 1974; editor: Changing Composition of Workforce: Implications for Future Research and Its Applications, 1982. Recipient Louis Brownlow Meml. Fund prize, Internat. Pub. Pers. Assn., 1965, Author award, Tng. and Devel. Jour., ASTD, 1967. Fellow: AAAS, Soc. Indsl. and Orgnl. Psychology, Internat. Assn. Applied Psychology, Am. Psychol. Assn., Am. Psychol. Soc.; mem.: Soc. Psychol. Study Social Issues, Phi Beta Kappa. Jewish. Home: 1801 E Jefferson St Apt 331 Rockville MD 20852 *Old enough to appreciate tradition. Young enough to facilitate change.*

GLICKMAN, ARTHUR, sculptor; b. NYC, Apr. 29, 1923; s. Alexander E. and Minnie S. Glickman; children: Alan Robert, Mindy Ellen. Studied with, Isaac Soyer, Nat. Acad. Design, Jean DMarco, 1964—68, Evangelo Frudakis, 1964—68, Bruno Luccesi, New Sch. Social Rsch., 1969. Commns., IBM, N.J., Washington Gas Light, New Synagogue of Ft. Lee, N.J. Bd. dirs. Adoptive Parents Com. N.Y.; pres. bd. Holly Ctr. N.J.; co-founder Family Focus Adoption Svcs. N.Y.; advocate for children in foster care. Cpl. U.S. Army, 1943—46, South Pacific. Recipient 1st prize in scupture, Bergen County Artists Assn., 1966, 2d prize in sculpture, Washington Sq., 1970, C-Span Presdl. Life Portraits award for relief of Pres. Thomas Jefferson, 2000. Mem.: Allied Artists of Am. (assoc. In Memoriam award 1987, 1993, 1994). Democrat. Jewish. Home: 538 Rutland Ave Teaneck NJ 07666 E-mail: minsartal@aol.com.

GLICKMAN, BENITA, language educator, writer, poet; b. Bronx, N.Y., Oct. 21, 1952; d. Marcus and Esther Glickman. BA in Spanish magna cum laude, CCNY, 1973; MA in Spanish, Lehman Coll., 1976; postgrad., Manhattan Coll., 1980—84. Cert. tchr. Spanish 7-12 N.Y., tchr. ESL, tchr. jr. h.s. Spanish, bilingual common brs. grades 1-6. Tchr. Spanish and reading Gilbert Sch., Bklyn., 1973—74; adult edn tchr. Spanish and ESL William Howard Taft H.S., Bronx, 1974—75; bilingual tchr. P.S. 91, Bronx, 1975—78; tchr. ESL John F. Kennedy H.S., Bronx, 1978—91, Christopher Columbus H.S., Bronx, 1991—, Internat. House coord., 2003—; poet, writer, 2001—. Cons. Brown U.-The Edn. Alliance, N.Y.C., 2003. Contbr. short story Chicken Soup for the Sister's Soul, 2002 (Alice Minnie Hertz Heniger award for Children's Lit., 2001), poetry Wedding Blessings: Prayers and Poems Celebrating Love, Marriage and Anniversaries, 2003, poetry to 41 jours. Mem.: Tchrs. English to Students of Other Langs., Acad. Am. Poets, N.Y. State Writing Project, N.Y.C. Writing Project, Phi Beta Kappa. Avocations: reading, cooking, gardening, yoga, nature walking. Home: 55 Knolls Crescent Bronx NY 10463 Office: Christopher Columbus HS 925 Astor Ave Bronx NY 10469 E-mail: bgcchs@yahoo.com.

GLICKMAN, CARL DAVID, banker; b. Cleve., July 29, 1926; s. Jack I. and Dora R. (Rubinowitz) G.; m. Barbara H. Schulman, Oct. 16, 1960; children: Lindsay Dale, David Craig, Robert Todd. Student, U. Minn., 1944, Inst. Fin. Mgmt., Harvard U., 1970. Pres. Glickman Orgn., Cleve., 1953—; chmn. bd., chief exec. officer Computer Research, Inc., Pitts., 1964-67, Am. Steel & Pump Corp., N.Y.C., 1968-71, Shelter Resources Corp., Cleve., 1971-75; pres. Leader Bldg., Inc., Cleve., 1959—, Capital Bancorp., Cleve., 1971-75, Real Property Corp., Cleve., 1975—; spl. ltd. ptnr. Bear Stearns & Co., 1978-85, dir., 1985—. Chmn. exec. com. Franklin Corp., N.Y.C., 1986-98, Cook United Inc., Cleve., 1986-87, Capital Nat. Bank Cleve., 1970-75; chmn. bd. dirs. Univ. Nat. Bank, Chgo., 1968-70; ltd. ptnr. S.B. Lewis & Co., N.Y.C., 1980-89; gen. ptnr. Millbrook Assocs., Chester Union Assocs.; founding gen. ptnr. Park Ctrl. Assocs.; pres. LGT Industries, Durham, N.C., 1987-95; bd. dirs. Royal Petroleum Properties Corp., Jerusalem Econ. Corp., Israel, Custodial Trust Co., Alliance Tyre and Rubber Co., Tel Aviv,Tnuport Ltd., Tel Aviv, Indsl. Structures, Inc., Tel Aviv, Office Max, Inc., InfoTech, Englewood Cliff, NJ, Lexington Corp. Properties, NYC, presiding trustee, chmn. exec. com. Active Mayor's Com. Urban Renewal, 1965-67, Mayors Task Force on Higher Edn., 1967-69; trustee Cleve. Growth Assn., 1972-75; co-chmn. Herzog Loan Fund Cleve. State U., 1970-76; chmn. Med. Arts Hosp., Houston, 1976-86; bd. visitors Case Western Res. Sch. Law; trustee Montefiore Home Aged, Mt. Sinai Hosp., Cath. Diocese Found., Cleve.; grievance com. Cleve. Bar Assn., 1982-85; foreman Cuyahoga County Grand Jury, Cleve., 1984-85; trustee Cleve. State U., 2000—, Cleve. Cath. Diocese Found.; disting. fellow, hon. trustee Cleve. Clinic; nat. co-chmn. Glickman Urol. Inst. Cleve. Clinic. With USAAF, 1944-46. Mem. Am. Bankers Assn., Am. Arbitration Assn. (arbitrator), Beechmont Country Club, Shaker Heights Country Club, Union Club, Standard Club, Harmonie Club, Town Club, Friars Club, Palm Beach Club, Yacht Club, High Ridge Country Club, Masons, Phi Sigma Delta, Phi Eta Sigma. Office: 1140 Leader Bldg Cleveland OH 44114 also: 383 Madison Ave New York NY 10167-0002 also: 1 N Breakers Row Palm Beach FL 33480-4021 Office Phone: 216-696-2650. E-mail: cdglickman@hotline.com.

GLICKMAN, DANIEL ROBERT, motion picture association executive, former congressman; b. Wichita, Kans., Nov. 24, 1944; s. Milton and Gladys Anne (Kopelman) G.; m. Rhoda Joyce Yura, Aug. 21, 1966; children: Jonathan, Amy. BA, U. Mich., Ann Arbor, 1966; JD, George Washington U., Washington, 1969. Bar: Kans. 1969, Mich. 1970. Trial atty. SEC, 1969-70; assoc. Sargent, Klenda & Glickman, Wichita, 1971—73, ptnr., 1973—76; mem. 95th-103rd Congresses from 4th Kans. Dist., 1977-95, mem. agrl. com., mem. judiciary, sci., space and tech. coms.; chmn. permanent select com. on intelligence 103d Congress; sec. USDA, Washington, 1995-2001; sr. advisor pub. law and policy group Akin Gump Strauss Hauer & Feld LLP, Washington, 2001—04; dir. Inst. Politics, John F. Kennedy Sch. Govt. Harvard U., 2002—04; pres. Motion Picture Assoc. Am., Encino, Calif., 2004—. Mem. Wichita Bd. Edn., 1973-76, pres., 1975-76. Mem. Order of Coif, Phi Delta Phi, Sigma Alpha Mu. Democrat. Jewish. Office: Motion Picture Assn Amer 15503 Ventura Blvd Encino CA 91436

GLICKMAN, FRANKLIN SHELDON, dermatologist, educator; b. Bklyn., Dec. 14, 1929; s. Arthur Zachary and Hilda (Kurtz) G.; m. Leatrice Sallie Alter, Mar. 29, 1953; children: Todd Scott, Jeff Bret. BA cum laude, Hofstra Coll., 1950; MD, SUNY-Bklyn., 1954; MS in Health Care Mgmt., NYU, 1990. Diplomate: Am. Bd. Dermatology. Intern Flushing (N.Y.) Hosp., 1954-55; resident in dermatology Kings County Hosp., Bklyn., 1957-58, Bronx VA Hosp., 1958-60; practice medicine specializing in dermatology Bklyn., 1960-94; mem. faculty dermatology dept. SUNY-Bklyn., 1960—82, clin. prof., 1982-93, adj. clin. prof., 1993—96; dir. med. edn. Wyckoff Heights Med. Ctr., Bklyn., 1990-96, chmn. dept. grad. med. edn., 1992-96. Author: General Dermatology, 1978, Fundamentals of Dermatology: A Study Guide, 1990; contbr. articles to profl. jours. Served to capt. M.C. USAF, 1955-57. Fellow N.Y. Acad. Medicine, ACP; mem. Am. Acad. Dermatology, Bklyn. Dermatol. Soc. (pres. 1970-72), N.Y. State Med. Soc., Kings County Med. Soc., AMA, N.Y. State Soc. Dermatology (pres. 1983-85), Phi Beta Kappa. Home: 6841 Treves Way Boynton Beach FL 33437-6485

GLICKMAN, HARVEY, retired social sciences educator; b. Bklyn., June 16, 1930; s. Herman Glickman and Helen Kramer; m. Sylvia Roberta Foodim, Sept. 2, 1956; children: Lisa McDonough, Nina Nathani, Peter Louis. BA, Princeton U., 1952; postgrad., Oxford U., 1953; MA, Harvard U., 1955, PhD, 1958; postgrad., London Sch. Econs., 1955—56. Cert. tchr. Mass. Prof. polit. sci. Haverford (Pa.) Coll., 1960—2003, prof. emeritus, 2003—, dean of faculty, 1976—77. Prof. African studies Hebrew U., Jerusalem, 1967—68; vis. lectr. U. Cape Town, South Africa, 1971—72, U. Calif., Berkeley, 1982—83; rsch. assoc. Fgn. Policy Rsch. Inst., Phila., 1985—; pres. AAUP Haverford br., 1970—72. Editor: Ethnic Conflict and Democratization in Africa; author: Problem of Internal Security in Britain, Toward Solving the Puzzle, Community Resources, Crisis and Challenge of African Development, Toward Peace and Security in Southern Africa, Political Leaders of Africa South of the Sahara (Outstanding Acad. Reference Book,Choice Mag., 1993), Political Science in The African World. Mem. World Affairs Coun., Phila., 1967—70; bd. dirs. Wynnewood (Pa.) Civic Assn., 1972—74; mem. Ams. for Dem. Action, Pa., 1982—89; chmn. Dem. Party, Lower Merion, Pa., 1972—75; trustee Main Line Reform Temple, Wynnewood, 1973—76; mem. Jewish Campus Activities Bd. -Hillel, Phila., 1985—88. Fellow, Woodrow Wilson Found., 1952—53, Fgn. Policy Assn., N.Y.C., 2002—; grantee, U.S. Dept. Edn., 1991—92, U.S. Inst. Peace, 1993; African Area Studies fellow, Ford Found., 1962—63, Fulbright fellow, USIA, 1967—68, 1972—73. Mem.: African Studies Assn. (editor Issue mag. 1987—93), Am. Polit. Sci. Assn. (sec. 1962—63), Princeton Club of Phila., Harvard Club of Phila., Phi Beta Kappa (sec. Haverford chpt. 1995—99). Jewish. Avocations: painting, travel. Home: 191 Presidential Blvd # 930 Bala Cynwyd PA 19004 Office: Haverford Coll 370 Lancaster Ave Haverford PA 19041

GLICKMAN, MARLENE, non-profit organization administrator; b. Evansville, Ind., May 13, 1936; d. Morris Jack and Sarah (Krawll) Foreman; m. Marshall Levi Glickman, Jan. 9, 1956 (dec. 2002); children: Cynthia Anne, Joseph Leonard. Student, Ohio State U., 1954-56. Area dir. Am. Jewish Com., Buffalo, 1981-2000; v.p. adminstrn. and fin. Network of Religious Cmtys., 2000—. Pres. Meals on Wheels of Buffalo and Erie County, 1981—83, N.E. Lakes Coun. and UAHC, Coun. Congl. Pres. Erie County, 1979—81; vice chair gen. campaign United Jewish Appeal, 1980, chair woman's divsn., 1979; pres. N.E. Lakes coun. Union Am. Hebrew Congregations, 1982—86; pres. Temple Beth Am, 1978—80, 2002—03, chair 50th anniversary, 2005; pres. Sisterhood Temple Beth Am, 1969—71, 1976—77; agy. allocations com. United Way, chair Towns and Villages divsn., 1981; pres. Human Rights Adv. Coun. Western N.Y., 1988—96; bd. dirs. YWCA, Buffalo and Erie County, 1990—96, Buffalo Fedn. Neighborhood Ctrs., Inc., 1994—98; exec. com., sec. Sheehan Meml. Hosp., Inc., 1994—98; pres., bd. dirs. Western N.Y. Martin Luther King Jr. Commn., 1991—97; active Western N.Y. Vision for Tomorrow 2000 C. of C./Buffalo Partnership. Recipient Abraham Pugash Cmty. Rels. award for establishing Kosher Meals on Wheels, Jewish Family Svc., Buffalo and Erie County, N.Y., 1975, NAACP Human Rels. award, 1997, Cmty. Rels. award Am. Jewish Com. Western N.Y., 2001; Marlene Glickman H.S. Human Rels. Award of Western N.Y. named in her honor for

Am. Jewish Com., 2004; Am.-Pol Eagle Citizen of Yr., 1995. Mem. NAACP (life), Union Am. Hebrew Congregations (exec., bd. dirs. 1982-99, exec. com.), Commn. on Synagogue Music, Joint Cantorial Placement Commn., FRJ Admin. (budget and finance), New Congregations, Maintenance of Union Membership, Hadassah (life), Assn. Reform Zionists Am. (del. to Israel 1987), Brandeis Women's Com. (life), Nat. Coun. Jewish Women (life, Hannah G. Solomon award 1985), Assn. Jewish Comty. Rels. Workers, Jewish Communal Svc. Assn., Arza/World Union (bd. dirs. 1992-2000). Avocation: singing. Home: 94 Broadmoor Dr Tonawanda NY 14150-5532 Office: M&M Connections 94 Broadmoor Dr Tonawanda NY 14150-5532 also: PMB 361 425 Carr 693 Dorado PR 00646 Personal E-mail: mglickman5@cs.com.

GLICKMAN, MICHAEL RICHARD, social studies educator; b. N.Y.C., Nov. 15, 1946; s. George Osiris Glickman and Hilda Ann Milmed; m. Irma S. Glickman, June 10, 1990; stepchildren: Scott D., Shari E. BA, Franklin (Ind.) Coll., 1969; MS, Coll. of S.I., 1997. Cert. tchr. social studies, N.Y. Paraprofl. N.Y.C. Bd. Edn., Bklyn., 1974—82, tchr. social studies, 1992—. Adj. prof. sociology Kings Borough Coll., Bklyn., 1998—; lectr. Housatonic C.C., Bridgeport, Conn., 2004—; tutor Williamsburg Settlement House, Bklyn., 1966-67, computer svcs. for children John Jay H.S., 1990-91. Head Young Dems., Dem. Party, Franklin Coll., Ind., 1968; vol. VISTA, 1969-70; tchr. Literacy Program John Jay H.S. Mem. United Fedn. of Tchrs., Am. Fedn. of Tchrs. Republican. Jewish. Avocations: reading, astronomy, computers, painting, music. Home: 22 H Lincoln Pl North Brunswick NJ 08902 Office: Murray Bergtraum HS 411 Pearl St New York NY 10002 E-mail: glickmoid@optonline.net.

GLICKMAN, NORMAN JAY, economist, urban policy analyst; b. Bklyn., July 27, 1942; s. Harry and Beatrice (Frankel) G.; m. Elyse M. Pivnick, May 8, 1983; children: Katy Rose, Madeline Claire. BA, U. Pa., 1963, MA, 1967, PhD, 1969. Prof. urban and regional planning U. Pa., Phila., 1980-82; Hogg prof. urban policy U. Tex., Austin, 1983-89; State of N.J. prof. urban planning Rutgers U., New Brunswick, 1989, dir. Ctr. for Urban Policy Rsch. State of N.J., 1989—, Disting. Univ. prof., 2000—. Vis. scholar U.S. HUD, Washington, 1978-79; fellow Netherland Inst. Advanced Studies, Wassenaar, 1981-82; sr. rsch. scholar Internat. Inst. Applied Systems Analysis, Laxenburg, Austria, 1977; appointee N.J. Coun. on Job Opportunities, N.J., 1992—. Co-author: The New Competitors, 1989 (Top 10 Bus. Week 1989). Chmn. Econ. Devel. Commn., Austin, 1985-89. Recipient Lindback award U. Pa., 1976, named Disting. Fulbright Prof., Monterrey (Mex.) Inst. of Tech., 1985; fellow Japan Found., 1976. Mem. EEFMS (charter), Regional Sci. Assn. (v.p. 1988-89), Am. Econ. Assn. Office: Rutgers U Ctr Urban Pol Rsch 33 Livingston Ave Ste 400 New Brunswick NJ 08901-1982 Office Phone: 732-932-3133.

GLICKMAN, ROBERT JEFFREY, bank executive; b. Mpls., Feb. 10, 1947; s. Joseph Charles and Beverly (Willis) G.; m. Hardye Simons Moel (div. 1983); children: Kate, Adam; m. Caryn Chernick, June 26, 1988. BA, Cornell U., 1969. Pres. River Forest Bancorp, Inc., Chgo., 1969—. Mem. Young Presidents Orgn. Jewish. Office: Corus Bancshares Inc 3959 N Lincoln Ave Chicago IL 60613-2431

GLICKMAN, ROBERT MORRIS, internist, educator, health facility administrator; b. Bklyn., June 23, 1939; s. David B. and Sally G.; m. Mary Holahan, June 20, 1961; children; Jonathan, Michael. BA magna cum laude, Amherst Coll., 1960; MD cum laude, Harvard U., 1964. Diplomate Am. Bd. Internal Medicine. Resident in medicine Harvard U. Med. Services, Boston City Hosp., 1965-66; research fellow in medicine Med. Sch., Harvard U., Boston, 1966-68; from instr. medicine to assoc. prof. Harvard U. Med. Sch., Boston, 1970-77; clin. and rsch. fellow in medicine Mass. Gen. Hosp., Boston, 1966-68, asst. in medicine, 1970-74, asst. physician, 1974-75; intern Harvard U. Med. Services, Boston City Hosp., 1964-65; chief divsn. gastroenterology, asst. physician Beth Israel Hosp., Boston, 1975-77, physician-in-chief, 1990—96; from assoc. prof. to prof. Coll. Physicians and Surgeons, Columbia U., N.Y.C., 1977-82, Samuel Bard prof. medicine, chmn. dept. medicine, 1982-90, chief divsn. gastroenterology, 1977-84, chmn. gastrointestinal sect. abnormal biology, 1978-84; attending physician Presbyn. Hosp., N.Y.C., 1981—90, dir. med. svc., 1982—90; Herrman L. Blumgart prof. medicine Harvard Med. Sch., Boston, 1990—98, chmn. exec. com. dept. medicine, 1996—98; physician-in-chief Beth Israel Deaconess Med. Ctr., 1996—98, sr. v.p. acad. and clin. strategies, 1996; dean NYU Sch. Medicine, N.Y.C., 1998—; CEO NYU Hosps. Ctr., N.Y.C., 2002—. Mem. Nat. Digestive Diseases Adv. Bd., 1985—. Mem. editorial bd. Jour. Lipid Research, 1978-79, Jour. Clin. Investigation, 1979-84, Am. Jour. Medicine, 1981—; contbr. articles to med. jours. Maj. M.C. U.S. Army, 1968-70. Fellow ACP; mem. AMA (pres. 1997-98), Am. Fedn. Clin. Rsch. (councillor Eastern sect. 1975-79, sec.-treas. 1976-79), Am. Gastroent. Assn. (v.p. 1985-87, pres. elect 1987, pres. 1988), Nat. Acad. Medicine, Inst. Medicine NAS, Harvey Soc., Interurban Clin. Club, Assn. Am. Physicians (councillor 1992, v.p. 1997), Nat. Found. Ileitis and Colitis (mem. sci. adv. bd. 1978), Am. Soc. Clin. Investigation (councillor 1981-84, pres. elect 1983, pres. 1984-85), Assn. Profs. Medicine (councillor 1989-94, pres. 1992-93), Am. Bd. Internal Medicine (sub-splty. bd. on gastroenterology 1988-93), Harvard Soc., Phi Beta Kappa, Sigma Xi, Alpha Omega Alpha. Office: NYU Sch Med 550 First Ave New York NY 10016

GLICKMAN, STEPHEN H., judge; AB, Cornell U., 1969; JD, Yale U., 1973. Ptnr. Zuckerman Spaede LLP, 1980-99, mng. ptnr., 1991—98; assoc. judge D.C. Ct. Appeals, 1999—. Office: DC Ct Appeals 500 Indiana Ave NW 6th Fl Washington DC 20001-2131

GLICKSMAN, ARVIN S(IGMUND), radiation oncologist; b. Bklyn., Mar. 14, 1924; s. Charles and Myrtle (Fetner) G.; m. Bernice R. Grobstein, Jan. 30, 1956; children: Jonathan, Jane Ellen, Merrylee, Caroline, Jeanette. MB, MD, Chgo. Med. Sch., 1949. Intern Kings County Hosp., Bklyn., 1948-50; AEC postdoctoral research fellow Duke U., 1950-51; postgrad. rsch. fellow Brookhaven Nat. Labs., Upton, N.Y., 1951-52; resident in medicine Meml. Hosp., N.Y.C., 1952-54, clin. asst. physician in medicine, 1955-64, asst. attending radiation therapist, 1964-65; rsch. fellow Sloan-Kettering Inst., N.Y.C., 1954-60, assoc., 1960-65; mem. med. rsch. inst. Michael Reese Hosp., Chgo., 1964-65, assoc. chmn. dept. radiation therapy, 1965-67; dep. dir. radiotherapy Mount Sinai Hosp., N.Y.C., 1967-73; prof. radiotherapy Mount Sinai Sch. Medicine, 1971-73; dir. radiation oncology R.I. Hosp., Providence, 1973-84, chmn. dept. radiol. medicine and biol. rsch., 1984-89; prof. med. scis., founding chair dept. radiation medicine Brown U., 1973-95, prof. emeritus, 1995—; chmn. dept. radiation oncology Roger Williams Med. Ctr., 1989-95; practice medicine specializing in radiation oncology. Hon. med. cons. NIH, Royal Marsden Hosp.; mem. cancer clinic, investigation rev. com. Nat. Cancer Inst., 1975-79, mem. radiation oncology com., 1976-86, mem. cancer intervention study sect., 1991-94; founding chair Brown U. Dept. of Radiadion, 1973-1995. Editor: (with others) Computers in Radiotherapy, 1970, 73; contbr.: numerous articles to profl. jours. Mem. exec. com. Am. Cancer Soc., R.I., 1987-96—, pres., 1987-89, nat. bd. dirs., 190-93; chmn. radiotherapy com. Cancer and Leukemia Group B.; dir. Quality Assurance Rev. Ctr., R.I. Cancer Control Bd., 1980-98, chmn. task force info. sys., mem. exec. com.; co-chmn. exec. com. ASSIST Program Nat. Cancer Inst./Am. Cancer Soc., 1991-98; exec. dir. R.I. Cancer Coun., 1999—. Dillon fellow Royal Marsden Hosp., Surrey, Eng., 1961-62; Rsch. Career Devel. awardee NIH, 1962-64; Fulbright sr. scholar, 1986-87; recipient St. George medal Am. Cancer Soc., 1991, Disting. Svc. award Am. Cancer Soc., 2003. Fellow Am. Coll. Radiology; mem. New England Soc. Radiation Oncologists (pres. 1975-76), N.Y. Roentgen Ray Soc. (chmn. sect. therapeutic radiology 1972-73), Am. Soc. Clin. Oncology, Am. Assn. Cancer Edn., Am. Assn. Cancer Rsch., Am. Radium Soc., Am. Soc. Therapeutic Radiologists, Brit. Inst. Radiology. Home: 15 Brown Ter Uxbridge MA 01569 Office: RI Cancer Coun Inc 249 Roosevelt Ave Ste 201 Pawtucket RI 02860-2134 Office Phone: 401-728-4835. Office Fax: 401-728-4816. Business E-Mail: glicksman@ricancercouncil.org.

GLICKSMAN, EUGENE JAY, lawyer; b. N.Y.C., Aug. 10, 1954; s. David and Elsie (Lerner) G.; m. Patricia Cardoso, Sept. 23, 1984; 1 child, Elizabeth Ann. BA in Polit. Sci., CUNY, 1975, JD, 1978. Bar: N.Y. 1980, U.S. Dist. Ct. (so. and ea. dists.) N.Y. 1980, U.S. Supreme Ct. 1992. Immigration inspector U.S. Dept. Justice, Immigration and Naturalization Svc., N.Y.C., 1976-80; assoc. Antonio C. Martinez, N.Y.C., 1980-81, Harry Spar, N.Y.C., 1981-83; pvt. practice pvt. practice, N.Y.C., 1983-93; ptnr. Glicksman & Cardoso, N.Y.C., 1993—. Arbitrator N.Y.C. Civil Cts., 1982-91; adminstrv. law judge N.Y.C. Taxi & Limousine Commn., 1991-98, N.Y.C. Environ. Control Bd., 1999-2000; aux. police officer N.Y.C. Police Dept., 1972-75. Mem. Am. Immigration Lawyers Assn. (N.Y. chpt. treas. 1993-94), N.Y. State Bar Assn., N.Y. County Lawyers Assn. (chair com. immigration and nationality law 1994-97, 2002—) Office: Glicksman & Cardoso 150 Broadway Rm 1115 New York NY 10038-4302 Office Phone: 212-406-2886. E-mail: glicardlaw@earthlink.net.

GLICKSMAN, MARTIN EDEN, materials engineering educator; b. N.Y.C., Apr. 4, 1937; s. Nathan Henry and Ruth Elaine (Rosensaft) G.; m. Lucinda Jeanette Mulder, May 7, 1967 B in Metall. Engring., Rensselaer Poly. Inst., 1957, PhD, 1961. Metall. engr. Procter & Gamble Co., Cin., 1957-58; research metallurgist Naval Research Lab., Washington, 1961-75, assoc. supt. materials sci. divsn., 1974-75; chmn. materials engr. dept. Rensselaer Poly. Inst., Troy, N.Y., 1975-86, prof., 1986—; prof. materials engring., chmn. dept. materials engring. Rensselaer Poly. Inst., Troy, N.Y., 1975-86, John Tod Horton prof. materials engring., 1986—. Van Horn lectr. Case Western Res. U., 1984; cons. in field. Author: Diffusion in Solids, 2000; contbr. in articles to profl. jours. Recipient Pure Sci. Rsch. award Rsch. Soc. of Am., 1968, Arthur Flemming award Washington Jr. C. of C., Space Processing medal AIAA, 1998; Minerals Metals and Materials Soc. fellow AIME, 1994. Fellow AAAS, ASM (M.E. Grossman award 1971), AIAA; mem. AIME (Bruce Chalmers award 1992), Am. Soc. Metals Internat. (Gold medal 2003), Univ. Space Rsch. Assn. (chmn. bd. trustees 1986, dir. microgravity divsn. 1986—), Nat. Acad. Engring. (Alexander von Humboldt Rsch. prize, 2001). Office: Rensselaer Poly Inst CII-9111 Troy NY 12180-3590 Business E-Mail: glickm@rpi.edu.

GLICKSMAN, MAURICE, engineering educator, retired dean, retired provost; b. Toronto, Oct. 16, 1928; came to U.S., 1949, naturalized, 1961; s. Robert Maxwell and Fanny Bella (Lachowitz) G.; m. Yetta Leich, Dec. 18, 1949; children: Howard David, Roslynn Sue, Marcie Ann. Student, Queen's U., 1946—49; MSc, U. Chgo., 1952, PhD, 1954; ScD (hon.), Brown U., 1997. Rsch. assoc. Inst. Nuc. Studies, U. Chgo., 1954; mem. tech. staff RCA Labs., Princeton, NJ, 1954-61, head Plasma Physics Group, 1961-63; dir. rsch. RCA Rsch. Labs., Tokyo, 1963-67; head Gen. Rsch. Group, Princeton, 1967-69; Univ. prof., prof. engring. Brown U., 1969-94, dean Grad. Sch., 1974-76, dean faculty and acad. affairs, 1976-78, provost, dean faculty, 1978-86, provost, 1986-90, prof. physics, 1990-94, prof. engring. rsch., 1994—2002, provost emeritus, 1990—, univ. prof. emeritus, 1994—, prof. engring. and physics emeritus, 1994—. Cons. RCA Corp., 1969-77; vis. scientist MIT, 1983-84; chmn. com. materials for radiation detection devices NAS, 1971-74; chmn. vis. com. U. Pa., 1977-83, Vanderbilt U., 1977-81; mem. vis. com. Emory U., 1981, U. Miami, 1990, Northwestern U., 1991, U. N.C., Greensboro, 1992; bd. dirs. Ctr. Rsch. Librs., 1981-87, chmn., 1983-84; mem. bd. overseers Fermilab, 1983-99, chmn., 1989-94; trustee OCLC, Dublin, Ohio, 1993-2004, vice chmn., 2002-04; dir. Manisses Comm. Group, Providence, 1993-2004; dir. Lifespan Corp., Providence, 1994-2000. Contbr. rsch. articles to profl. jours.; patentee frequency multipliers, hall-effect devices, semiconductor devices and circuits. Pres. Jewish Ctr., Princeton, 1962-63; v.p. cultural and ednl. affairs Jewish Cmty. Ctr., Tokyo, 1965-67; mem. Bur. Jewish Edn., R.I., 1974—, v.p., 1975-80; v.p. Jewish Fedn. R.I., 1980-83; trustee Miriam Hosp., 1979-85, 87-2003, chmn., 1993-97; v.p. Jewish Srs. Agy. R.I., 1998-2000, pres., 2000-03; chmn. World Affairs Coun. R.I., 1999—; pres. Tamarisk, Inc., 2003—. Recipient Outstanding Achievement award RCA, 1956, 62. Fellow IEEE, Am. Phys. Soc.; mem. AAAS, Am. Soc. Engring. Edn., N.Y. Acad. Scis., Phi Beta Kappa (pres. R.I. Alpha chpt. 1993-96), Sigma Xi. Home: 10 Westwood Ln Barrington RI 02806-2614 Office: Brown U Box D 79 Waterman St Providence RI 02912-9079 E-mail: maurice_glicksman@brown.edu.

GLICKSTEIN, STEVEN, lawyer; b. Bklyn., Jan. 3, 1952; s. Alexander and Esther (Camhi) G. BA, Lehigh U., 1973; JD, Columbia U., 1976. Assoc. Kaye Scholer, LLP, NYC, 1976-84, ptnr., 1985—, co-chair Product Liability Dept. Mem. ABA, DC Bar Assn., Fla. Bar Assn., NY State Bar Assn. Home: 144 Walnut St Englewood NJ 07631 Office: Kaye Scholer LLP 425 Park Ave New York NY 10022-3506

GLICK-WEIL, KATHY, library director; b. Milw., Jan. 11, 1950; d. Irving Robert and Janice Esther (Rosner) Glick; m. Gordon Weil, June 20, 1971; children: Jeffrey, Aaron. BA, Tulane U., 1971; MLS, U. Calif., Berkeley, 1972. Children's libr. Thayer Pub. Libr., Braintree, Mass., 1972-73; reference libr. Stoughton (Mass.) Pub. Libr., 1973-77; br. libr. Brockton (Mass.) Pub. Libr., 1977-78; asst. dir. Medford (Mass.) Pub. Libr., 1978-84; dir. Lincoln (Mass.) Pub. Libr., 1984-93, Newton (Mass.) Free Libr., 1993—. Mem. ALA, Mass. Libr. Assn. (v.p. 2005, pres-elect 2005—). Home: 46 Acacia Ave Chestnut Hill MA 02467-1351 Office: Newton Free Library 330 Homer St Newton MA 02459-1429 Office Phone: 617-796-1400. Business E-Mail: kglickweil@mlnlib.net.

GLIDDEN, JOHN REDMOND, lawyer; b. Sanford, Maine, July 24, 1936; s. Kenneth Eugene and Kathryn (Gilpatrick) G.; m. Jacqueline R. Scales, Aug. 6, 1964; children— Ian, Claire, Jason Student, U. Wis., 1954-55; BS, Coe Coll., 1958; LL.B., U. Iowa, 1961. Bar: Iowa 1961, Ill. 1965. Assoc. firm Williams & Hartzell, Carthage, Ill., 1965-67; ptnr. Hartzell, Glidden, Tucker & Hartzell and predecessor firms, Carthage, 1969—. City atty. City of Carthage, 1969— Capt., judge advocate USAF, 1961-65. Mem. ABA, VFW, Fed. Bar Assn., Ill. Bar Assn., Iowa Bar Assn., Hancock County Bar Assn., Am. Trial Lawyers Assn., Ill. Trial Lawyers Assn. (governing bd. 1973-80), Am. Legion, Carthage Golf Club (bd. dirs. 1967—), Phi Delta Phi, Sigma Nu. Home: PO Box 70 1625 N Highway 94 Carthage IL 62321-3435 Office: PO Box 70 Carthage IL 62321-0070 Office Phone: 217-357-3121. E-mail: jrglaw@adams.net.

GLIDDEN, REGINALD PRESTIN, JR., psychologist, writer; b. Cooperstown, N.Y., 1964; s. Reginald Prestin and Viola Louise Glidden; m. Ame Sloan Heller, Feb. 24, 1987; 1 child, Chelsey Hope. BA in Psychology, State U. Coll., 1986. Caseworker Schenectady (N.Y.) County Social Svcs., 1993—. Contbr. poetry to website. Democrat. Baptist. Avocations: science fiction, ghost hunter. Home: 1351 Ruffner Rd Schenectady NY 12309 Office: Schenectady County Adult Svcs 107 Nott Terrace Ste 206 Schenectady NY 12308 Office Phone: 518-386-2258 x232.

GLIDDEN, ROBERT BURR, academic administrator, music educator; b. Rippey, Iowa, Nov. 29, 1936; s. Burr Harold and Lora Elsie (Groves) Glidden; m. Rene Colete Siefken, Apr. 26, 1964; children: Melissa, Michele, Briana. BA, U. Iowa, 1958, MA, 1960, PhD, 1966; D of higher edn. adminstrn. (hon.), Bowling Green State U., 2004. Tchr. instrumental music Morrison Community High Sch., Ill., 1958-63, Univ. Schs., Iowa City, 1963-66; asst. prof. music Wright State U., Dayton, Ohio, 1966-67, Ind. U., Bloomington, 1967-69; also asst. dir. bands, 1969-72; assoc. prof. music U. Okla., Norman; dir. grad. studies in music, exec. dir. Nat. Assn. Schs. Music, Washington, 1972-75, treas., 1977-82, v.p., 1982-85, pres., 1985-88; dean Coll. Musical Arts, Bowling Green State U., Ohio, 1975-79; dean Sch. Music Fla. State U., Tallahassee, 1979-91, provost, v.p. for acad. affairs, 1991-94; pres. Ohio U., Athens, 1994—2004, pres. emeritus, cons. for devel., 2004—. Cons., higher edn., condr.; chmn. Coun. Specialized Accrediting Agys., 1976—77; chair Am. Coun. Edn. Commn. Leadership and Instnl. Effectiveness, 1998—2000; chair coun. pres. Mid-Am. Conf., 1997—99. Bd. dirs. Coun. on Postsecondary Accreditation, 1977—84, exec. com., 1979—84, chmn., 1981—83; bd. dirs. Arts, Edn. and Ams., Inc., 1978—81; chmn. advanced placement music com. Coll. Bd., 1977—79; active Coun. on Arts Task Force on Edn. Tng. and Devel. Profl. Artists and Art Educators, 1977—78; adv. coun. on accreditation Nat. League for Nursing, 1977—81; edn. adv. com. Nat. Endowment for Arts, 1987, adv. com. for arts in edn., 1989—90; chmn. bd. dirs. Coun. for Higher Edn. Accreditation, 1996—98. Recipient Disting. Alumni award, U. Iowa, 1997. Mem.: Ohio Inter-Univ. Coun. (chair 2001—02), Ohio Campus Compact (exec. com. 2000—04), Ohio Aerospace Inst. (exec. com. 1995—2004, chair 1998—2000), Ohio Supercomputer Ctr. (governing bd. 1996—2004), Ohio Sci. and Tech. Coun. (biotech. com. 1996—2004), So. Assn. Colls. and Schs. (commn. on coll. 1993—94), Assn. Specialized and Profl. Accreditors (bd. dirs. 1994—96), Coll. Music Soc. (chmn. govt. rels. com. 1976—78, task force on edn. coll. music tchrs. 1987), Mortar Bd., Pi Kappa Lamdba (nat. v.p. 1979—81, pres. 1981—85), Omicron Delta Kappa, Phi Kappa Phi, Phi Beta Kappa. Episcopalian. Home: PO Box 88 140 Gibraltar Forge Dr Rockbridge Baths VA 24473 Office Phone: 540-348-6360. Business E-Mail: gliddenr@ohio.edu.

GLIEBERMAN, HERBERT ALLEN, lawyer; b. Chgo., Dec. 6, 1930; s. Elmer and Jean (Gerber) G.; m. Evelyn Eraci; children— Ronald, Gale, Joel Student, U. Ill., 1947, Roosevelt U., 1948-50; JD, Chgo. Kent Coll. Law, 1953. Bar: Ill. 1954, D.C. 1987. Pvt. practice, Chgo., 1954—; lectr. Chgo. Kent. Coll. Law, Ill. Inst. Continuing Legal Edn. Lectr. in field numerous instns. including ABA, ATLA, Am. Acad Matrimonial Lawyers, Inst. Law Inst., others. Author: Some Syndromes of Love, 1965, Know Your Legal Rights, 1974, Confessions of A Divorce Lawyer, 1975, Closed Marriage, 1978, Four Weekends to an Ideal Marriage, 1981; former host 2 radio shows for NBC Sta. WMAQ: Ask the Lawyer, Law and Controversy; contbr. articles to profl. jours. Former trustee Chgo. Kent. Coll. Law; former bd. dirs. Chgo. Coun. on Alcoholism. Mem. Am. Acad. Matrimonial Lawyers (cert. of appreciation 1967), Decologue Soc. Lawyers (cert. of appreciation 1965, 66, 68), Assn. Trial Lawyers Am. (cert. of appreciation 1973), Ill. Trial Lawyers Assn. (cert. of appreciation 1974), ABA, Ill. State Bar Assn., Chgo. Bar Assn., N.C. Bar Assn., Idaho Bar Assn., Internat. Law Inst., Wash., D.C. Jewish (bd. dirs., pres. Temple) Office: 19 S La Salle St Chicago IL 60603-1401 Office Phone: 312-236-2879. Office Fax: 312-236-3417. Personal E-mail: hglieber@aol.com.

GLIER, INGEBORG JOHANNA, German language and literature educator; b. Dresden, Germany, June 22, 1934; came to U.S., 1972; d. Erich Oskar and Gertrud Johanne (Niese) G. Student, Mt. Holyoke Coll., 1955-56; Dr. phil. (Studienstiftung des deutschen Volkes), U. Munich, Germany, 1958; Dr. phil., Habilitation, 1969; MA (hon.), Yale U., 1973. Asst., lectr. U. Munich, 1958-69, universitätsdozentin, 1969-72; vis. prof. Yale U., 1972-73, prof. German, 1973—2004, chmn. dept., 1979-82, chmn. Medieval Studies New Haven, 1986-93, chmn. Women's Studies, 1995-96, sr. faculty fellow, 1974-75; vis. prof. U. Cologne, Germany, 1970-71, U. Colo., Boulder, spring 1983, U. Tubingen, summer 1984. Author: Struktur und Gestaltungsprinzipien in den Dramen John Websters, 1958, Deutsche Metrik, 1961, Artes amandi, Untersuchung zu Geschichte, Uberlieferung und Typologie der deutschen Minnereden, 1971; contbr. articles, book reviews to profl. jours. Mem.: Wolfram von Eschenbach Gesellschaft, Internat. Courtly Lit. Soc., Am. Assn. Tchrs. German, Medieval Acad. Am., MLA, Internat. Germanisten-Verband. Home: 111 Park St Apt 12T New Haven CT 06511-5421 Office: Yale Univ Dept Germanic Langs PO Box 208210 New Haven CT 06520-8210 Office Phone: 203-432-0788. E-mail: ingeborg.glier@yale.edu.

GLIKLICH, JERRY, physician, educator; b. Jelenia Góra, Poland, May 6, 1948; came to U.S., 1958; s. Henry and Henia (Gotajner) G.; m. Jane Salmon, Sept. 12, 1976; children: David, Benjamin. AB, Columbia U., 1969, MD, 1975. Intern N.Y. Hosp., N.Y.C., 1975-76, resident, 1977-78; fellow in cardiology Presbyn. Hosp., N.Y.C., 1978-81, attending physician, 1981—; asst. prof. medicine Columbia U., N.Y.C., 1981-91; assoc. clin. prof. Presbyn. Hosp., N.Y.C., 1991-97, clin. prof., 1997—2001, David A. Gardner prof. medicine, 2001—. Cons. in field. Contbr. articles to profl. jours. Mem. ACP, Am. Coll. Cardiology, Phi Beta Kappa. Office: Presbyn Hosp 161 Fort Washington Ave New York NY 10032-3713

GLIMCHER, ARNOLD B., art gallery executive; b. Duluth, Minn., Mar. 12, 1938; s. Paul and Eva (Fishman) G.; m. Mildred Louise Cooper, Dec. 20, 1959; children: Paul William, Marc Cooper. BA, Mass. Coll. Art., 1969; postgrad., NYU Sch. Psychology, Boston U. Founder, owner Pace Gallery, Boston, 1961-63; founder, chmn. Pace Wildenstein, N.Y.C., 1963—; founder Pace Editions, 1968—. Author: Louise Nevelson, 1972, paperback edit., 1976; (with Paul Vitz) Modern Art and Modern Science: The Parallel Analysis of Vision; contbr. articles to art jours.; prodr.: (films) Gorillas in the Mist, The Good Mother; prodr., dir.: (film) The Mambo Kings, Just Cause; editor, cataloger, text writer for various art vols. selector, installer various mus. exhibits and retrospectives. Named Chevalier de la Légion d'honneur. Fellow Israel Mus. (chmn. devel. com. 1976-77); mem. Am. Acad. Arts and Letters, Officier des Arts and Lettres, Art Dealers Assn. Am. (bd. dirs.). Office: Pace Wildenstein 32 E 57th St New York NY 10022-2513 Office Phone: 212-421-3292.

GLIMCHER, MELVIN JACOB, orthopedic surgeon; b. Brookline, Mass., June 2, 1925; s. Aaron and Clara (Fink) Glimcher; m. Karin Wetmore, Mar. 8, 2000; children from previous marriage: Susan Deborah, Laurie Hollis, Nancy Blair. Student, Duke U., 1943-44; BS in Mech. Engring. with highest distinction; BS in Physics with highest distinction, Purdue U., 1946; MD magna cum laude, Harvard, 1950; postgrad., Mass. Inst. Tech., 1956-59; PhD in Engring. (hon.), Purdue U., 2004. Intern surgery Strong Meml. Hosp., Rochester, N.Y., 1950-51; 3d asst. resident surgery Mass. Gen. Hosp., Boston, 1951-52, 2d asst. resident, 1952-53, asst. resident orthopedic surgery, 1954-55, chief resident, 1956, chief orthopedic service, 1965-71, chmn. dept. orthopedic surgery, 1968-71; asst. resident orthopedic surgery Children's Med. Center, Boston, 1953-54, jr. resident, 1955-56; mem. faculty Harvard Med. Sch., 1956—, Edith M. Ashley prof. orphopedic surgery, 1965-71, Harriet M. Peabody prof., 1971—; also chmn. dept.; orthopedic surgeon-in-chief Children's Hosp. Med. Center, Boston, 1971-81, dir. Lab. for Study of Skeletal Disorders and Rehab., 1980—. Trustee Forsyth Dental Infirmary, New England Sinai Hosp. With USMCR, World War II. Recipient Soma Weiss award Harvard Med. Sch., 1950, Borden Research award, 1950; Kappa Delta award, 1959; Internat. Assn. Dental Research award, 1964; Ralph Pemberton award Am. Rheumatism Soc., 1969; Bristol-Meyers/Zimmer instl. grant for excellence; Disting. Achievement in Orthopaedic Research award Orthopaedic Research Edn. Found.; William Neuman award Am. Soc. Bone and Mineral Rsch., 1996; Physician Achievement award Arthritis Found., 1996. Fellow Am. Acad. Arts and Scis., Am. Acad. Orthopaedic Surgeons (Silver anniversary Kappa Delta prize 1974, Alfred Shands award jointly awarded with Orthop. Rsch. Soc 1997), Am. Orthopedic Assn.; mem. Orthopedic Research Soc. (past pres.), Assn. Bone and Joint Surgeons (Nicholas Andry award 1978), Internat. Soc. for Study Lumbar Spine (Volvo award 1983), Societe Internationale de Chirurgie Orthopedique et de Traumatologie. Office: 300 Longwood Ave Boston MA 02115-5724

GLIMM, JAMES GILBERT, mathematician, educator; b. Peoria, Ill., Mar. 24, 1934; s. William Frederick and Barbara Gilbert (Hooper) G.; m. Adele Strauss, June 30, 1957; 1 dau., Alison. AB in engring. (hon.), Columbia U., 1956, AM (hon.) in math., 1956, PhD (hon.) in math., 1959. From asst. prof. to prof. math. MIT, 1960-69; prof. Courant Inst., NYU, 1969-74; prof. math. Rockefeller U., N.Y.C., 1974-82; prof. Courant Inst., NYU, N.Y.C., 1982-89; disting. prof., chair dept. applied math. and statis. SUNY, Stony Brook, 1989—; dir. Ctr. for Data Intensive Computing Brookhaven Nat. Labs., 1999—2004. Co-author: Quantum Physics, 1981; Collected Papers, Vols. I and II, 1985; mem. editorial bds. profl. jours.; contbr. articles to sci. publs. Guggenheim fellow, 1963, 65; recipient Dannie Heineman prize in math. physics, 1980, Nat. Medal Sci. award, 2002. Mem. NAS, Internat. Assn. Math. Physicists, Am. Phys. Soc., Am. Math. Soc. (Leroy P. Steele prize 1992), Soc. Indsl. and Applied Math., Math. Assn. Am., Am. Acad. Arts and

Scis., Soc. Petroleum Engrs., NY Acad. Scis. (award in phys. and math. scis. 1979) Office: Stony Brook U Dept Applied Math and Stats Math Bldg Rm P-138A Stony Brook NY 11794-3600 Business E-Mail: glimm@ams.sunysb.edu.

GLINDEMAN, HENRY PETER, JR., real estate developer; b. Coeur d'Alene, Idaho, Sept. 26, 1924; s. Henry Peter and Laura Mae (Buchanan) Glindeman; children: Pamela, Henry Peter III, John. BS, U.S. Naval Acad., 1945; postgrad., U.S. Naval War Coll., 1959-60. Commd. ensign U.S. Navy, 1945, advanced through grades to rear adm., 1973; exec. officer, comdg. officer Fighter Squadron 154, 1962-63; comdr. Attack Carrier Air Wing 15 Attack Carrier Air Wing 15, 1964-65; tng. officer attack carrier air wing, staff, comdr. U.S. Naval Air Forces, U.S. Pacific Fleet, 1965-66; readiness officer, staff comdr. U.S. First Fleet, 1966-68; comdg. officer U.S.S. Passumpsic, 1968-69; head Attack Carrier Weapons Requirements br. Office Chief Naval Ops., 1970-71; comdg. officer U.S.S. Ranger, 1971-73; chief Fleet Coordinating Group Nakhon Phanom, Thailand, 1973-74; dir. Office Program Appraisal, Office Sec. Navy, 1974-75; comdr. Carrier Group 7, 1975-76; comdr. Carrier Group 3, 1976; comdr. Carrier Group 5, Carrier Strike Force, 7th Fleet, 1976-77; comdr. Naval Safety Center, 1977-78; pres. Mr. Quick Lube Inc., Clearwater, Fla., 1978-81; v.p. Fla. Light and Save Inc., 1981-83; real estate developer, 1983-85; pres. GBS Devel. Inc., Redwood City, Calif., 1985-87; chmn., CEO Stormy Weather Guard, Inc., Clearwater, Fla., 1988-94. Bd. dirs., sec.-treas. Guardian Marine Corp., 1990—91; pres. Fiber Am. Inc., Clearwater, 1991—96. V.p. Edgar Allan Poe Jr. HS PTA, Annandale, Va., 1960—61, Annandale Am. Little League, 1961—62; sec. exec. com. Troop 674 Boy Scouts Am., Annandale, 1961—62; chmn. bd. dirs. USS Ranger Mus. Found., 2001—. Decorated Legion of Merit with 4 gold stars, DFC, Air medal with gold star. Mem.: Tailhook Assn., Mil. Officer Assn. Am., Assn. Naval Aviation, Mil. Order World Wars, U.S. Naval Acad. Alumni Assn., Navy League, Breakfast Club (San Francisco), Golden Gate Club. Episcopalian. Home: 3976 Long Leaf Dr Melbourne FL 32940-1464 Personal E-mail: radmu@earthlink.net.

GLINES, CARROLL VANE, JR., magazine editor; b. Balt., Dec. 2, 1920; s. Carroll Vane and Elizabeth Marion (Cross) G.; m. Mary Ellen Edwards, Oct. 1, 1943; children: Karen Ann, David Edwards, Valerie Jean. Student, Drexel Inst. Tech., 1938-40, Canal Zone Jr. Coll., 1946-48, U. Munich, 1948; BBA, U. Okla., 1952, MBA, 1954; MA, Am. U., 1969. Commd. 2d lt. USAF, 1942, advanced through grades to col., 1965; military service, 1941-68; mgr. publs. Nat. Bus. Aircraft Assn., Washington, 1968; assoc. editor Armed Forces Mgmt. mag., Washington, 1969-70; editor Air Cargo mag., Washington, 1970-71, Air Line Pilot mag., Washington, 1971-85, cons. editor, 1985-86, contbg. editor, 1989—; sr. editor Aviation Space mag., 1982-85; editor Profl. Pilot Mag., Alexandria, Va., 1986-88, sr. contbg. editor, 1988—, Aviation History mag. (formerly Aviation Heritage mag.), Leesburg, Va., 1990—. Mgr. publs. Air Line Pilots Assn., 1971-85, dir. comms., 1983-85; lectr. U. Dayton, U. Alaska, Am. U. Author 36 books; contbr. articles to mags.; gen. editor MacMillan, Air Force Acad. series, 1970-74; editl. cons. Van Nostrand Reinhold, 1980-85; contbg. editor Nation's Bus., 1981-86; mem. adv. bd. Hist. of Aviation Collection, U. Tex., Dallas, 1981-90, 95—, Alaska Aviation Heritage Mus., Anchorage, 1993-99; curator Doolittle Libr., U. Tex., Dallas, 1995—. Asst. to v.p. for spl. projects Evergreen Internat. Aviation, 1988-93; active Frontiers of Flight Mus., Dallas. Recipient numerous awards from press assns. Freedoms Found., Pres. award Air Force Pub. Affairs Alumni Assn., 2003; inducted into Interboro Hall of Fame, 2003, Glen-Ner Hall of Fame, 2005. Mem. Aviation-Space Writers Assn. (Lauren D. Lyman award), Air Force Assn., Air Force Hist. Found., Soc. Aerospace Communicators, Quiet Birdmen, Soc. Profl. Journalists, Order of Daedalians. Home: 1531 San Rafael Dr Dallas TX 75218-4444 Personal E-mail: ceevee1531@sbcglobal.net.

GLISMANN, CLEMENTINE, retired elementary school educator; b. Oakland, Nebr., Aug. 4, 1917; d. Louis Martin Larson, Edvinna Josephine Young; m. Leonard William Glismann, Feb. 24, 1940 (dec. Feb. 1997). BA, Midland Luth. Coll., Fremont, Nebr., 1939; postgrad., U. Nebr., 1942—43, Weber Coll., Ogden, Utah, 1945—47, U. Utah, 1963—78. Tchr. 1st grade Bd. Edn., Norfolk, Nebr., 1939—40, secondary tchr. Madrid, Nebr., 1941—42, 3d grade tchr. Ogden, Utah, 1945—56, 4th grade tchr., 1957—63, Salt Lake City, 1964—79; ret., 1979. Traveling dealer Lenswood, 1977—91. Author, prodr. (TV program) Wheels, KSL-TV Salt Lake City, Utah, 1951, Paper, 1952, Rubber, 1953, Clothes, 1954, Historical Masquerade (Great Americans), 1955, Mother Earth's Rock Family, Ogden City Schs. TV, 1962—63, There's More to Say to Your Story. State chmn. Luth. Ch. Women, Utah, 1963. Mem.: Golden Spike Gem and Mineral Soc., Delta Kappa Gamma. Republican. Lutheran. Achievements include having a 50-year collection of fossils, petrified wood, minerals and butterflies on permanent display at Midland Lutheran College in Fremont, Nebraska. Avocations: faceting gemstones, poetry.

GLOBERMAN, STEVEN, finance educator; s. Marvin Globerman and Belle Robinson; m. Daryl J. Madill, Oct. 12, 1992; children: Evan Madill, Martine Madill. BA, Bklyn. Coll., 1966; MA, UCLA, 1967; PhD, NYU, 1971. Asst. prof. York U., Toronto, Canada, 1972—80; assoc. prof. to full prof. Simon Fraser U., Vancouver, 1981—93; Ross Disting. prof. Western Wash. U., Bellingham, 1994—2002, Kaiser prof., 2003—. Adj. scholar The Fraser Inst., Vancouver, 1993—96; prin. Steven Globerman Assocs., Bellingham, 1994—. Author: Cure or Disease?, 1996; editor: Canadian-Based Multinationals, 1994, Assessing NAFTA, 1993. Sponsor Whatcom County Boys and Girls Club, Bellingham, 1996—; staff mem. Royal Comm. on Corp. Concentration; adv. bd. Friends of Fairhaven Libr., Bellingham, 1998—. Recipient Founders Day award, NYU, 1971. Mem.: Acad. of Mgmt., Acad. of Internat. Bus., Beta Gamma Sigma (life). Avocations: swimming, tennis, jazz. Home: 716 Fieldston Rd Bellingham WA 98225 Office: Western Washington Univ 566 High St Bellingham WA 98225 Office Phone: 360-650-7708. Business E-Mail: steven.globerman@wwv.edu.

GLOBUS, DOROTHY TWINING, museum director; b. Singapore, Aug. 31, 1947; d. Kinsley and Cynthia (Thébaud) T.; m. Stephen F. Globus, Sept. 9, 1973; children: Samuel Twining, Dorothy Schermerhorn. BA in Art History magna cum laude, Swarthmore Coll., 1969. Asst. to dir. Wilcox Gallery Swarthmore (Pa.) Coll., 1967-69; summer intern Smithsonian Instn., Washington, 1966-69, exhibits specialist Nat. Mus. Natural History, 1970-73, curator of exhbns. Cooper-Hewitt Nat. Mus. Design N.Y.C., 1973-92; mus. dir. Mus. at Fashion Inst. of Tech., N.Y.C., 1993—; curator of exhbns. Mus. Arts & Design, N.Y.C., 2004—. Mem. trustees coun. Preservation N.Y. State, 1989—. Mem. Fashion Group, Artable. Office: Fashion Inst of Tech Seventh Ave at 27th St New York NY 10001-5992*

GLOCER, THOMAS HENRY, publishing executive; b. NYC, Oct. 8, 1959; s. Walter W. and Ursula (Goodman) G.; m. Maarit Hanelle Leso, Aug. 5, 1988. BA, Columbia Coll., 1981; JD, Yale U., 1984. Atty. Davis, Polk & Warswell, NYC, 1985-93; corp. counsel Reuters Am. Inc., NYC, 1993-94; exec. v.p., gen. counsel Reuters Am. Holdings Inc., NYC, 1995-98; CEO Reuters L. Am., 1996—98; pres. Reuters Am., NYC, 1998—2001; CEO Reuters Info., 2000—01, Reuters Group PLC, 2001—. Dir. TVT Records, N.Y.C., 1985-93. Author computer software. Mem. Coney Island Assn. (founder, ptnr.); bd. dirs., Reuters, 2000-. Avocations: windsurfing, skiing, running. Office: Reuters Group PLC, Corporate Headquarters 85 Fleet Street London EC4P 4AJ England

GLOCK, CHARLES YOUNG, sociologist, writer; b. NYC, Oct. 17, 1919; s. Charles and Philippine (Young) G.; m. Margaret Schleef, Sept. 12, 1950; children: Susan Young, James William. BS, N.Y. U., 1940; MBA, Boston U., 1941; PhD, Columbia U., 1952. Research asst. Bur. Applied Social Research, Columbia U., 1946-51, dir., 1951-58, lectr., then prof. sociology, 1956-58; prof. sociology U. Calif. at Berkeley, 1958-79, prof. emeritus, 1979—, chmn., 1967-68, 69-71; dir. Survey Research Center, 1958-67; adj. prof. Grad. Theol. Union, 1971-79; Luther Weigle vis. lectr. Yale U., 1968. Co-author: American Piety, 1968, Waward Shepherds, 1971, Anti-Semitism in America, 1979, The Anatomy of Racial Attitudes, 1983; author (sr.): Religion and Society in Tension, 1965, Christian Beliefs and Anti-Semitism, 1966, To Comfort and To Challenge, 1967, Adolescent Prejudice, 1968, The Apathetic Majority, 1975; contbg. editor: Rev. Religious Rsch. Sociol. Analysis; editor: Survey Research in the Social Sciences, 1967, Prejudice U.S.A., 1969, Beyond the Classics, 1973, Religion in Sociological Perspective, 1973, The New Religious Consciousness, 1975, Unison-Newsletter of One Voice, 1990—96; contbr. numerous articles on social scis. Active parish edn. Luth. Ch. Am., 1970-72; mem. mgmt. com. Office Rsch. and Planning, 1973-80; bd. dirs. Pacific Luth. Theol. Sem., 1962-74, 80-86, Inst. Rsch. in Social Behavior, 1962-90, Interplayers, 1990-92, Sandpoint Christian Connection, 1995-97; pres. Cornerhouse Fund, 1982-92, One Voice, 1994-95, bd. dirs., 1995-97; mem. adv. com. Office Rsch. and Evaluation Evang. Luth. Ch. Am., 1988-94; mem. history com. Soc. Study of Religion, 1993-94; v.p. Sandpoint chpt. Idaho Writers' League, 2003—. Capt. USAAF, 1942-46. Decorated Bronze Star, Legion of Merit; recipient Roots of Freedom award Pacific bd. Anti-Defamation League, 1977, Garman-Hidy award for Disting. Contbn. to Life of Luth. Ch. in the West, 1999; Berkeley citation U. Calif., Berkeley, 1979; Rockefeller fellow, 1941-42; fellow Center Advanced Study Behavioral Scis., 1957-58; fellow Soc. for Religion in Higher Edn., 1968-69 Fellow Soc. Sci. Study Religion (Western rep., pres. 1968-69); mem. Am. Assn. Pub. Opinion Research (v.p., pres. 1962-64, pres. Pacific chpt. 1959-60), Am. Sociol. Assn. (v.p. 1978-79), Religious Research Assn., Sociol. Research Assn. Home: 319 S 4th Ave Sandpoint ID 83864-1219 Personal E-mail: cyg@netw.com.

GLOCKNER, PETER G., civil and mechanical engineering educator; b. Moragy, Hungary, Jan. 26, 1929; emigrated to Can., 1949; BSc in Civil Engring., McGill U., Montreal, Que., Can., 1955; MSc in Civil Engring., MIT, 1956; PhD in Civil Engring., U. Mich., 1964. Asst. prof. applied mechanics U. Alta., Can., 1958-60; from asst. prof. to prof. emeritus U. Calgary, Alta., 1960-94, prof. emeritus, 1994—, chmn. dept. mech. engring., 1976-87. Author: A Place of Ingenuity, 1994, more than 300 articles on shell theory, stability and non-linear behavior of thin-walled structures, dielectrics and non-linear constitutive theory. Whitney fellow, 1955-56, Ford Found. fellow, 1962-64; recipient CANCAM medal, 1993. Fellow ASCE (Moisseiff award and medal 1983), Can. Soc. Mech. Engring., Engring. Inst. Can. (Gzowski Gold medal 1971), Am. Acad. Mechanics (pres. 1995-96); mem. Can. Soc. Civil Engring., Assn. Profl. Engrs., Geologists and Geophysicists Alta., Order of U. Calgary. Home: 2536 Charlebois Dr Calgary AB Canada T2L OT6 E-mail: glockner@ucalgary.ca.

GLODAVA, MILA GARCIA, entrepreneur, educator, consultant; b. Bauan, Batangas, Philippines, May 27, 1945; d. Francisco Ramos Coronel and Rosalia Manalo (Coronel) Garcia; m. Mark Jeffrey Glodava, Jan. 29, 1972; children: Kirsten Angela, Kevin Marc. BS in Edn., St. Paul Coll., Manila, 1969. Tchr. Mt. Carmel H.S., Polillo, Philippines, 1969—72; bookkeeper First Nat. State Bank of NJ, Newark, 1974—74; owner Glodava, Inc., 2000—. Founding pres. Metro Infanta Found., Inc., 1996—. Co-author: Mail-Order Brides: Women for Sale, 1994, Labond ng Kawayan: Waling Through the Pathways and Streets of Infanta, 2002. Rep. First White House Briefing on Asian/Pacific Women, 1985; bd. dirs. Asian Pacific Ctr. for Human Devel., 1987—91; co-chair Festival Asian Arts and Culture, 1990; comm. dir. St. Joan of Arc Ch., 1987—89. Recipient Minoru Yasui Cmty. Vol. award, 1989, Peacemaker award, Archdiocese of Denver, 2000, Mile Hi Woman of Distinction, Girl Scouts USA, 2003, Quezon Medal of Honor, 2004. Fellow: Asian Pacific Am. Women's Leadership Inst.; mem.: Nat. Network of Asian and Pacific Women. Home and Office: 7350 Braun Way Arvada CO 80005-2843 Office Phone: 303-770-1155.

GLOGOWER, MICHAEL HOWARD, real estate company executive, consultant; b. Louisville, Jan. 6, 1944; s. Louis R. and Elaine R. (Switow) G. Student, Louisville Country Day Sch., 1958—61; BA in Polit. Sci., Kenyon Coll., 1965. Cert. lic. real estate broker Ky., Fla. Asst. gen. mgr. Mail Photo Svc. Inc., Louisville, 1966-69; pres. Mi-Glo Corp., Louisville, 1969-70; v.p. ops. Cherokee Coal Co. Inc., Louisville, 1970-71; area mgr. Owens/Corning Fiberglas Corp., Toledo, 1971-73; gen. mgr. Redd's Auto Parts Inc., Louisville, 1973-74; dist. mgr. Hackney Corp., Birmingham, Ala., 1974-75; area sales rep. J&W Fence Supply Co. Inc., Indpls., 1975-76; broker, salesman comml./investment divsn. Bass & Weisberg Realtors, Louisville, 1976-79; owner Michael H. Glogower Investment Realtor & Bus. Consulting, 1979—; housing programs specialist office pub. and Indian housing HUD, Washington, 1991-96, sr. functional specialist Honolulu, 1996-98, Miami, Fla., 1998—. Former mem. edn. com. Bd. Realtors, Louisville; former subs. instr. Jefferson C.C., Louisville; former moderator, ace designee, counselor Acad. Network II-Nat. Real Estate Exch. Former pres. bd. dirs. Waterford House Condo Assn., Arlington, Va., 1993—96; bd. dirs. Palace Condominium Assn., Miami, 1999—2002; pres. Am. Fedn. Govt. Employees HUD Union Local 1516, 1999—2001; pres. bd. dirs. Costa Brava Condo. Assn., Miami Beach, Fla., 2003—04, v.p., bd. dirs., 2004—05. Avocations: photography, real estate investment, antique and art collection, design work. Home: Apt 1012 11 Island Ave Miami Beach FL 33139-1325 Office: US Dept HUD 909 SE 1st Ave Ste 500 Miami FL 33131-3042 Office Phone: 305-536-5678 X 2274. E-mail: michael_h._glogower@hud.gov. *Living different places, doing different things, I have never ceased to be impressed by the resiliance and humanity of my fellow human beings. We should never sell our fellow man short.*

GLOGOWSKI, JEFFREY RONALD, director, music educator; b. Chgo., Jan. 17, 1973; s. Ron and Dee Glogowski; m. Tori Hicks, Oct. 14, 2000. BME in Vocal Music Edn., Ill. State U., Normal, 1997. Cert. music tchr. Ill. Choral dir., music tchr. Sherrard H.S., Ill., 1997—. Master tchr. Aurgus Quad Cities, 2004. Composer: (songs) choral music. Tchr., Ill. Mem.: Ill. Music Educators Assn. (assoc.). Democrat. Office Phone: 630-301-5066. Personal E-mail: glogowskije@hotmail.com.

GLOMSKI, EDWARD EARL, sales executive; b. Royal Oak, Mich., July 21, 1955; s. Edward James and Lorraine Anne Glomski; 1 child from previous marriage, Hannah Michelle; m. Shellee Anita Habig. Grad. with honors, Nat. Inst. of Tech., 1983. Owner Book Nook, Akron, Ohio, 1999; purchasing mgr. Stellar Pvt. Cable, Akron, 1997—2002; sales assoc. H.H. Gregg Co., 2002—. With USN, 1974-76. Mem.: Intertel (jour. editor 1998—, area coord. Ohio 1997—, pres. 2004—), East Ctrl. Ohio Mensa (exec. bd. 1997—99). Home: 300 Malacca St Akron OH 44305-3652

GLOSBAND, DANIEL MARTIN, lawyer; b. Salem, Mass., July 3, 1944; s. Leon Glosband and Ruth Pauline (Wentworth) Glosband School; m. Merrily Cotton, Dec. 23, 1967; children: Alexander, Gabriel, Oliver. BA, U. Mass., 1966; JD, Cornell, U., 1969. Bar: Mass. 1969, US Dist. Ct. Mass. 1970, US Dist. Ct. Conn. 1971, US Ct. Appeals (1st cir.) 1971, US Dist. Ct. Vt. 1974, US Supreme Ct. 1982, NY 2005. From assoc. to ptnr. firm Widett & Widett, Boston, 1969-75; ptnr. Goldstein & Manello, Boston, 1976-87, Goodwin, Procter LLP, Boston, 1988—. Advisor Am. Law Inst. Transnat. Insolvency Project, 1994—2000, Am. Law Inst. Transnational Insolvency Project, 1994—2000. Contbr. articles to profl. jours. Fellow: Mass. Bar Found., Am. Bar Found., Am. Coll. Bankruptcy (v.p. 2005—, sec. 2001—05); mem.: ABA (sect. on corps., chmn. internat. bankruptcy com. 1990—95), Conf., Nat. Bankruptcy Conf., Boston Bar Assn. (chmn. bankruptcy com. 1977—80), Mass. Bar Assn. (chmn. bankruptcy com. 1980—83), Internat. Bar Assn. (sect. bus. law, vice chmn. insolvency and creditors rights com. 1997—2000, del. UN Commn. Internat. Trade Law 2004—). Democrat. Jewish. Home: 34 Atlantic Ave Swampscott MA 01907-2404 Office: Goodwin Procter LLP Exchange Pl Boston MA 02109-2803 Office Phone: 617-570-1930. Business E-Mail: dglosband@goodwinprocter.com.

GLOSS, LAWRENCE ROBERT, fundraising executive; b. Colorado Springs, Colo., Oct. 31, 1948; s. Kenneth Edwin and Clara U. Gloss; children: Alexander Edwin, Carolyn Claire. BA, U. Denver, 1970. Vol. Peace Corps, Colombia and Peru, 1970-75; dir. natl. congress on volunteerism and citizenship NCVA, Washington, 1975-76; dir. devel. Vis. Nurses Assn., Washington, 1976-77; devel. cons. Am. Lung Assn., Washington and N.Y.C., 1977-78; exec. dir. Colo. Conservation Fund, Denver, Colo., 1978-79; dir. devel. Rose Med. Ctr., Denver, 1985-86; exec. dir. Rose Found., Denver, 1979-86; sr. campaign dir. J. Panas, Young and Ptnrs., San Francisco, 1986-88; pres. Gloss and Co., Denver, 1988—. Adv. coun. non-profit mgmt. Metro State Coll., Denver, 1994; cons. Native Am. Rights Fund, Boulder, Colo., Arts at the Sta., Denver, 1994, Up With People, 1995-96, Emily Griffith Ctr. Found., 1995-96, Colo. CASA, 1998-99, Women of the West Mus., 1998, 2000, Sister Cities-Denver and Kumming, China, 1999, sec. bd. Ctr. for Tax Policy. Guest spkr. Tech. Assistance Ctr., Denver, 1992—94; bd. dirs. Alzheimer's and Related Disorders Assn., Denver, 1985—86, Woman's Sch. Network, Denver, 1984—85, Colo. PTA, Englewood, 1991—92; active Emily Griffith Ctr. Found., 1997, U. Denver; active Episc. Ministries U. Colo., Boulder, 1996—2001; active Ctr. for Tax Policy, 1998—, Columbine H.S. Permanent Meml., Srs. Resource Ctr., 1998—99, Am. Humane Assn., 1998—99, Colo. Mil. History Mus., 2001—, Noah's Ark Pk., 2001—, Humane Soc. Pagosa Springs, 2001—02; mem. Prairie Wine Aninal Refuge, 2004; active Colorado Springs Soc. CPA Ednl. Found., 2004—05, Boulder Cmty. Hosp. Found.; mem. BMH-BJ Congregation, 1999—2003, sec., 2001. Mem.: Boulder Cmty. Hosp. Found. (active KUVO Radio Jazz 89), Colo. Soc. CPAs (mem. ednl. found. 2004—), Acad. Charter Schs., Assn. Profl. Rschrs. Advancement, Assn. Healthcare Philanthropy (region XII 1993—94), Am. Prospect Rsch. Assn., Nat. Com. on Planned Giving, Assn. Fund-Raising Profls., Assn. Profl. Fundraisers (Colo. chpt. 1992—94, bd. dirs.), Am. Lung Assn. of Colo., Nat. Assn. Mus. Exhibitors, Women of the West Mus., Arapahoe Ho., Englewood Hist. Soc., Colo. Planned Giving Roundtable, Soccer Ofcls. Assn. Colo., Colo. State Youth Soccer Assn., U.S. Soccer Assn., Rotary Club of Denver. Lutheran. Avocations: dressage, art, soccer. Office: Gloss and Co 2755 S Locust St Ste 113 Denver CO 80222-7131 E-mail: larrygloss@msn.com.

GLOSS, WENDY, principal; d. William Cyril and Carol Ann Wood; m. Scott Michael Gloss, June 24, 1995; children: Cole Joseph, Samantha Elizabeth, Chad William. BS, Buffalo State Coll., 1989; MS, SUNY, Buffalo, 1994; sch. dist. adminstrs. cert., Canisius Coll., 2003. Tchr. Orchard Park (NY) Ctrl. Sch., 1989—2003, asst. prin. mid. sch., 2003—04, prin. Windom Elem. Sch., 2004—. Mem. Orchard Park Youth Bd., 2002—, Orchard Park Cmty. Youth Orgn., 2003—. Mem.: ASCD, NY State Adminstrs. Assn., NY State Elem. Prins. Assn. Office: Orchard Park Ctrl Sch 3870 Sheldon Orchard Park NY 14127

GLOSSER, HARRY JOHN, JR., lawyer; b. Pottsville, Pa., Jan. 13, 1946; s. Harry Joseph and Anne (Rosenberger) G.; m. Lorraine D. Wanner, Jan. 28, 1995. BS in Acctg., Rider U., 1967; JD, Dickinson Sch. Law, 1970. Bar: Pa. 1970, U.S. Dist. Ct. (ea. dist.) Pa. 1974. Law clk., assoc. Curtin and Heefner, Morrisville, Pa., 1970-71; assoc. Timby & Godwin, Newton, Pa., 1970-74; ptnr. Godwin & Glosser, Newton, 1975; pvt. practice Morrisville, Pa., 1975-81, 85—; ptnr. Donahue & Glosser, Morrisville, 1981-85. Solicitor Bristol-Bensalem Human Svcs. Ctr., Bristol Twp., Pa., 1978-87, Morrisville Sch. Dist., 1985-88. Mem. sch. bd. Morrisville Sch. Dist., 1974; pres. Morrisville Sch. Bd. Dirs., 1975-78; sec. Palmer Farm Homeowners Assn., Inc. Mem. Pa. Bar Assn., Bucks County Bar Assn. (chmn. Orphans Ct. sect.). Home: 1988 Satter Ct Yardley PA 19067-7218 Office: 331 W Bridge St Morrisville PA 19067-2342

GLOSSER, JEFFREY MARK, lawyer; b. 1936; married; 1 child. BS in Econs. with distinction, U. Pa., 1958; LLB, Harvard U., 1961. Bar: D.C. 1962. Law clk. U.S. Ct. Claims, 1963-64; assoc. Emery & Wood, Washington, 1965-69; ptnr. Jeffrey M. Glosser, P.C., Washington, 1969-86, Whiteford, Taylor & Preston, Washington, 1987-95. Instr. CLE courses sponsored by D.C. Bar, 1976-95. Mem. ABA (adminstrv. law sect., various coms.), D.C. Bar Assn. (numerous coms.), Fed. Bar Assn. (U.S. Claims Ct. com.), Fed. Cir. Bar Assn. (rules com. 1985-95). Personal E-mail: glosser@mac.com.

GLOSSER, WILLIAM LOUIS, lawyer; b. Johnstown, Pa., Aug. 30, 1929; s. Saul I. and Eva (Hurwitz) G.; m. Patricia Freeman, Feb. 5, 1932; children: Alix Paul, Jill P., Jonathan. BS, Temple U., 1951; LLB, U. Pa., 1954. Bar: Pa. 1954, Fla. 1956, U.S. Dist. Ct. (we. dist.) Pa. 1956, U.S. Dist. Ct. (so. dist.) Fla. 1957. Assoc. Broad and Cassel, Miami Beach, Fla., 1956-57; sole practice Coral Gables, Fla., 1957-61, Johnstown, 1962—. Magistrate judge U.S. Dist. Ct. (we. dist.) Pa., 1972-93; corp. sec., dir. Glosser Bros., Inc., Johnstown, 1969-85; of counsel Smorto, Persio, Webb & McGill, Johnstown, 1988—. Bd. dirs. Lee Hosp., Johnstown, Greater Johnstown (Pa.) Cmty. Found., ret.; mem. Johnstown adv. coun. Pa. Human Rels. Commn.; pres. United Jewish Fedn. Johnstown, 1970-75, 2000—; chmn. fund drive United Way, 1985, pres., 1987-88; bd. dirs. Mt. Aloysius Coll., 1980-84, Cmty. Found. Greater Johnstown, Pa., 1990—. With U.S. Army, 1954-56. Mem. Pa. Bar Assn., Fla. Bar Assn., Cambria County Bar Assn., Greater Johnstown C. of C. (pres. 1985), Rotary (pres. 1990), B'nai B'rith (pres. lodge 1965-67, 83-84). Jewish. Home: 521 Luzerne St Johnstown PA 15905-2324 Office: Smorto Persio Webb & McGill 430 Main St Johnstown PA 15901-1823 Office Phone: 814-539-2839.

GLOSSINGER, DONALD LEO, library director; s. Marshall Hamilton and Betty Jean Vanderpool Glossinger; m. Caryn V. Tolchinsky, Nov. 28, 1981; 1 child, Micah Lee. B in Gen. studies, Ind. U., Gary, 1990; MLS, Ind. U., Bloomington, 1993. Cert. profl. mgr., adminstrv. mgr., Libr. I Ind. State Libr., Indpls. Congl. aide U.S. Rep. Katie Hall, Gary, Ind., 1983—85; employer rep. Kankakee Valley Job Tng. Program, LaPorte, Ind., 1985—90; supr. Michigan City Pub. Libr., 1990—93, dept. head, 1993—96, asst. dir., 1996—2000, dir., 2001—. Co-prodr.: (video) Internet Predators: Preventing the Attck Against Our Kids. Mem.: DFC Soc. (assoc.). Home: 7255 W Peppel Pky Michigan City IN 46360-9171 Office: Michigan City Pub Libr 100 E 4th St Michigan City IN 46360-9171 E-mail: dgloss@mclib.org.

GLOTH, F. MICHAEL, III, geriatrician; b. Balt., May 20, 1956; s. Fred M. and Mary Jane Gloth; m. Maybian P. Gloth; 4 children. MD, Wayne State U. Diplomate Am. Bd. Internal Medicine. Chief of geriatrics Union Meml. Hosp., Balt., 1996—2002. Panel mem. Nat. Osteoporosis Found., Washington, 1996—98; mem. com. Am. Geriat. Soc., N.Y.C., 2001—02; dir. geriatrics fellowship program Union Meml. Hosp., Balt., 1998—2002; assoc. prof. Johns Hopkins U. Sch. Medicine, Balt., 1998—; pres. Victory Springs Sr. Health Assoc., Reisterstown, Md., 1997—, Victory Springs Smart E-records (TM), Inc., Reisterstown, 2002—; mem. nat. adv. coun. on aging NIH, 2002—; mem. Md. Bd. Physicians, 2003—. U.S. sen. candidate, 1998; adv. com. White House Conf. on Aging, 2005. Recipient Outstanding Svc. award, Hospice Network of Md., 2001; fellow, Internat. Life Sci. Inst. Rsch. Found. fellow, 1991;, Am. Fedn. for Aging Rsch. fellow, 1990, Internat. Life Sci. Inst. Rsch. Found. fellow, 1990, John A. Hartford Found. scholar, 1991, NIH grantee, 1996. Fellow: ACP (C. Lockhard Conley award Md. chpt. 1999), Am. Soc. Internal Medicine, Am. Geriatrics Soc. (New Investigator award 1993); mem.: Md. State Med. Soc. (del. Balt. chpt. 1999, Rising Star of Md. Medicine award 1999), Alzheimer's Assn. Ctrl. Md. (bd. dir. 2001), Hospice Network of Md. (pres. 1999—2001, Outstanding Svc. award 2001). Avocations: sailing, golf. Office: Victory Springs Sr Health Assocs 210 Business Center Dr Reisterstown MD 21136 Office Phone: 410-526-1490.

GLOTZBACH, PHILIP A., academic administrator, philosopher, educator; m. Marie B Glotzbach; children: Jason, Elizabeth. BA summa cum laude, U. Notre Dame, 1972; PhD, Yale U., 1979. Assoc. prof. to chair of Philosophy dept. to chair of the faculty sen. Denison U., Granville, Ohio, 1977—92; dean of coll. of arts and scis., v.p. for academic affairs U. of Redlands, 1992—2003; pres. Skidmore Coll., 2003—. Mem.: Phi Beta Kappa. Office: Skidmore Coll 815 N Broadway Saratoga Springs NY 12866

GLOVER, CLIFFORD CLARKE, retired construction company executive; b. Newnan, Ga., May 15, 1913; s. Howard Clarke and Fannie Virginia (Jones) G.; m. Louise Liles, Jan. 16, 1937; children: Edmund Cook, Nancy Liles Glover Kennedy, Virginia Johnston Glover Lee, Laura Clarke Glover Thatcher. BCE, U. N.C., 1934. With Batson-Cook Co., West Point, Ga.,

1934-94; ret., 1994. Mem. West Point Sch. Bd., 1951-69, chmn., 1964-68; chmn. West Point Planning Bd., 1964-2000; trustee LaGrange Coll.; pres. George H. Lanier council Boy Scouts Am., 1977-78, dir. Southeast regional bd., 1987, recipient Silver Antelope award, 1992; bd. dirs. Joint Tech. Ga. Devel. Fund, 1987. Served with USNR, 1945-46. Recipient Silver Beaver award Boy Scouts Am., Silver Antelope award Boy Scouts Am.; Presdl. award George H. Lanier Coun. Boy Scouts Am., Disting. Citizen's award, 1988; Award of Merit Greater Valley C. of C., 1984; Golden Hammer award Profl. Constrn. Estimators Assn. Am., 1988; fellow La Grange Coll. Mem. Assoc. Gen. Contractors (past pres. Ga. br., Skill, Integrity and Responsibility award 1991) Methodist (ofcl. bd.). Clubs: Rotary (Paul Harris fellow); Capital City (Atlanta); Riverside (West Point). Office: Batson-Cook Co PO Box 151 West Point GA 31833-0151 Business E-Mail: cglover@batson-cook-wp.com.

GLOVER, CRISPIN HELLION, actor; b. N.Y.C., Apr. 20, 1964; s. Bruce Herbert and Betty Lillian Marie (Koerber) G. Stage debut The Sound of Music, L.A., 1977; appeared in My Tutor, 1982, Racing With the Moon, 1983, The Orkly Kid, 1983, Friday 13th-The Final Chapter, 1983, Teachers, 1984, Back To The Future, 1984, At Close Range, 1984, Rivers Edge, 1985, Twister, 1987, Where the Heart Is, 1989, Wild At Heart, 1989, The Doors, 1991, Ferdydurke, 1991, Little Noises, 1992, Rubin and Ed, 1992, Crime and Punishment, 1994, What's Eating Gilbert Grape, 1993, Chasers, 1994, Even Cowgirls Get the Blues, 1994, Dead Man, 1995, The People Vs. Larry Flynt, 1996, Nurse Betty, 1999, Charlie's Angels, 2000, Bartleby, 2000, Crime and Punishment, 2002, Like Mike, 2002, Willard, 2003, Charlie's Angels Full Throttle, 2003, What is it?, 2003 (dir. too); (TV film) High School U.S.A., 1983; author, pub.: (books) Rat Catching, 1987, Oak Mot, 1990, Concrete Inspection, 1992, What It Is and How It Is Done, 1995; dir., screenwriter, actor, prodr. What is It?, 1997, 98, 99.

GLOVER, DOUGLAS DENNIS, obstetrics, gynecology and pharmacology educator; b. Rowlesburg, W.Va., Feb. 7, 1929; s. Douglas and Iva (Hughes) G.; m. Barbara Anne Brady, Sept. 6, 1958; children: Joseph, William, Donald, Geoffrey, Robert. BS in Pharmacy, W.Va. U., 1951, BS in Medicine, 1959; MD, Emory U., 1961. Diplomate Am. Bd. Ob-gyn. Intern Grady Meml. Hosp., Atlanta, 1961-62, resident, 1962-65; pvt. practice, Marietta, 1965-82; prof. ob/gyn. Marshall U. Sch. Medicine, Huntington, W.Va., 1982-87, W.Va. U., Morgantown, 1987—2004, prof. Sch. Pharmacy, 1987—2004, prof. emeritus, 2004—. Vis. prof. Zhejiang Med. U., Hangzhou, People's Republic of China, 1993; past operator of 4 rural outreach clinics for disadvantaged pregnant women. Editor: Current Therapy in Obstetrics, 1988; contbr. articles to profl. jours.; rschr. in placental metabolism and pharmacokinetics of drugs during pregnancy; patentee in field. Mem. U.S. Pharmacopeial Conv., Inc., 1990-2005, mem. gen. com. of revision, 1990-2000, chmn. ob-gyn adv. panel, 1990-2000, mem. expert com. on nomenclature and labeling, 1990-2005. Served to 1st lt. AUS, 1952-53, Korea Decorated Bronze Star, Purple Heart; recipient Outstanding Svc. award W.Va. U., 1972, 87, Outstanding Alumnus award W.Va. U. Sch. Pharmacy, 1982, Disting. Alumnus award, 1999, Dr. James H. Beal award W.Va. Pharmacists Assn., 1989, W.Va.Gov.'s Meritorious Svc. award, 2004, W.Va. U. Most Loyal Mountaineer, 2004; W.Va. Sch. Medicine award Excellence Svc. to Sch., 2005, Faculty Recognition award, 2005 Fellow Am. Coll. Ob-Gyn., Am. Soc. Reproductive Medicine (co-chair sessions mgmt. com. 1990-2003, chair registrations com. 1992-98), Internat. Infectious Diseases Soc. for Ob-Gyn. (mem. nat. steering com.), Masons (32d deg.), Sigma Xi, Phi Delta Theta (chpt. advisor 1988-2000), Phi Chi, Phi Lambda Sigma. Republican. Presbyterian. Avocation: military history. Home: 5 Maple Ave Morgantown WV 26501-6542 Office: Dept Ob/Gyn WVa U Morgantown WV 26506 Office Phone: 304-293-5631. Business E-Mail: dglover2@wvu.edu.

GLOVER, ERYN M., music educator; b. Olney, Ill., Apr. 27, 1975; d. David Kent and Paula Jean Glover. MusB, Ill. State U., 1998; postgrad., So. Ill. U., 2002—. Cert. cert. music therapist. Music therapist Tenet Hosps., St. Louis, 1998—99, Cedar Ridge Healthcare Ctr., Lebanon, Ill., 1999—2001; Ill. Outreach coord. Alzheimer's Assn., St. Louis, 2001—02; prof. McKendree Coll., Lebanon, Ill.; grad. asst., keyboard devel. instr. So. Ill. U., Edwardsville, 2002—. Pvt. piano instr., Edwardsville, 1998—. Com. chair Memory Walk Alzheimer's Assn., Collinsville, Ill., 2000—02. Mem.: Music Tchrs. Nat. Assn., Gateway Arch (East chpt.). Republican. Roman Catholic. Avocations: playing board games, music, gardening, softball, sports.

GLOVER, FRED WILLIAM, information scientist, director; b. Kansas City, Mo., Mar. 8, 1937; s. William Cain and Mary Ruth (Baxter) G.; m. Diane Tatham, June 4, 1988; 1 child, Lauren Glover; children from previous marriage: Dana Reynolds, Paul Glover. BBA, U. Mo., 1960; PhD, Carnegie-Mellon U., 1965. Asst. prof. U. Calif., Berkeley, 1965-66; assoc. prof. U. Tex., Austin, 1966-69; prof. U. Minn., Mpls., 1969-70; John King prof. U. Colo., Boulder, 1970-87, US West chair in sys. sci., 1987-98, Media One chair in sys. sci., 1998—; rsch. dir. Artificial Intelligence Ctr., Boulder, 1984-90; disting. rschr. Hearing Ctr. Enterprise Sci., U. Miss., 2000—. Invited disting. lectr. Swiss Fed. Inst. Tech., Lausaunne, 1990-91, 2002-03, IMAG Labs., U. Grenoble, France, 1991, U. Canterbury, New Zealand, 1997, U. Paris, 1998; vis. Regents Chair in Engring., U. Tex., Austin, 1989; cons. U.S. Congress, 1984, Nat. Bur. Stds., 1986, also over 70 U.S. corps. and govt. agys., 1965—; lectr. NATO, France, Italy, Germany, Denmark, 1970, 78, 80, 82, 89, Inst. Decision Scis., 1984; bd. dirs. Heuristec, Boulder, OptTek, Boulder, Decision Analysis, Rsch. & Computation, Austin, 1971-83; head, rsch. assoc. Global Optimization Space Contrn. Ctr., Boulder, 1988—; rsch. prin. U. Colo.-U.S. West Joint Rsch. Initiative, 1990—; prin. investigator Air Force Office Sci. Rsch., Office Naval Rsch., 1990—; invited rsch. scholar U. B.C., 1994. Author: Netform Decision Models, 1983 (DIS award 1984), Tabu Search I, 1989, Tabu Search II, 1990, Tabu Search (book and special vols.) 1993, 97, 98, 2003, Ghost Image Processes for Neural Networks, 1993, Linkages with Artificial Intelligence, 1990, Network Models in Optimization and Their Application in Practice, 1992, Handbook of Metaheuristics, 2003, others; contbr. over 340 articles on math. optimization and artificial intelligence to profl. jours. Participant Host Vis. Exchange, Nat. Acad. Scis., 1981; mem. grants com. Queen Elizabeth II fellowships, Australia and US, 1984; mem. US nat. adv. bd. Univ. Rsch. Initiative on Combinatorial Optimization. Recipient Internat. Achievement award Inst. Mgmt. Scis., 1982, Energy Rsch. award Energy Rsch. Inst., 1983, Univ. Disting. Rsch. Lectr. award U. Colo., 1988, Rsch. Excellence prize Ops. Rsch. Soc., 1989, Nat. Best Theoretical/Empirical Rsch. Paper award Decision Scis. Inst., 1993, Computer Sci. Rsch. Excellence award Ops. Rsch. Soc. Am., 1994, Nat. Rsch. Excellence award Comp. Sci. Ops. Rsch. Soc., 1994, John Von Neumann Theory award Inst. for Operations Rsch. Mgmt. Sci., 1998, Spl. Recognition award INFORMS, 2004; named first U.S. West Disting. fellow, 1987. Fellow: AAAS, ICC Inst., Am. Assn. Collegiate Schs. Bus., Am. Inst. Decision Scis. (lectr. 1984, Outstanding Achievement award 1984); mem.: NAE, Alpha Iota Delta. Achievements include design of software systems used throughout the U.S. and abroad. Office: U Colo Coll Bus Box 419 Boulder CO 80309-0419 Office Phone: 303-492-8589. Business E-Mail: fred.glover@colorado.edu.

GLOVER, HARRY ALLEN, JR., lawyer; b. Chgo., Mar. 9, 1949; s. Harry Allen and Charlotte (Ley) G.; m. Mary Kathryn Burnette, July 18, 1986; children: Bryan Timothy, Ashley Marie, Kyle Ley. BA, U. Va., 1971, JD, 1975. Bar: Va. 1975, U.S. Ct. Appeals (6th cir.) 1975, U.S. Ct. Appeals (4th cir.) 1978. Law clk. U.S. Ct. Appeals (6th cir.), Danville, Ky., 1975—76; assoc. Woods Rogers PLC, Roanoke, Va., 1976—81, ptnr., 1982—. Mem. editl. bd. Va. Law Rev., 1973-75. Mem. ABA, Va. Bar Assn., Va. State Bar (bd. govs. adminstrv. law sect. 1985-89, 99-2003), Order of Coif, Phi Beta Kappa. Office: Woods Rogers PLC PO Box 14125 Roanoke VA 24038-4125 Office Phone: 540-983-7636. Business E-Mail: glover@woodsrogers.com.

GLOVER, JAMES TODD, manufacturing executive; b. Aberdeen, S.D., Apr. 30, 1939; s. Fay and Vi (Bruns) G.; m. Joann Elizabeth House; children: Jason, Jeffrey, Jamie. Student, S.D. State U.; BS in Math., No. State Coll., Aberdeen, 1961. Inside sales engr. Aberdeen Ops. Safeguard, 1961-64, asst. sales engr., 1965-67, mktg. mgr., 1968-72, gen. mgr., 1973-77; v.p. ops. Safeguard PowerTech Systems, Aberdeen, 1978-83, exec. v.p., 1984-85, pres., 1986-89; pres., chief exec. officer, chief ops. officer, dir. Hub City, Inc., Aberdeen, 1989—. Officer Safeguard Sci. Co., Inc.; v.p. corp. devel. Regal-Beloit (Wis.) Corp., 1990-93; v.p. HQ Cos., Mpls., 1993-98, gen. mgr. Pixall Ltd. Partnership, Clear Lake, Wis., 1993-98; pres. JTG Solutions, Inc., Peoria, Ariz., 1998--. Bd. mem. S.D. Swimming Assn.; S.D. Dist. Export Council. Export Devel. Authority; bd. dirs. No. State Found., James River Water Devel.; bd. mem., chmn. James River Water Devel. Dist. Recipient Ernie Gunderson award S.D. Swimming Assn. Mem. Power Transmission Distbrs. Assn. (past bd. dirs., past chmn. allied adv. bd.), Power Transmission Rep. Assn. (past bd. dirs., past chmn. allied adv. bd.), Aberdeen C. of C., S.D. Mfrs. Assn. (past dir.). Republican. Roman Catholic. Avocations: hunting, fishing, music.

GLOVER, JANET BRIGGS, artist; b. Allahabad, India, June 22, 1919; came to U.S., 1924; d. George Weston and Mary Ames (Hart) Briggs; m. Alan Marsh Glover, Feb. 5, 1949; children: Keith Terrot, John Carroll, Beth Marsh Glover Wittig. BA, Bennington Coll., 1943; postgrad., New Sch. Social Rsch., 1969-70. Artist, draftsman Chartmakers, Inc., N.Y.C., 1943-45; apprentice to Oscar Ogg Book of Month Club, N.Y.C., 1946; 2d grade tchr. Hartridge Sch., Plainfield, N.J., 1947-48, Country Day Sch., Lancaster, Pa., 1948-49; chmn. art dept. Women's Club Chatham, N.J., 1964-65, lectr. art, 1981-86; publicity chmn. N.J. Ctr. Visual Arts, Summit, 1980-81. One-man shows include Present Day Club, Princeton, N.J., 1967, Gallery 9 Upstairs, Chatham, 1978; group shows include Key Gallery, N.Y.C., 1980; contbg. editor N.J. Music and Arts Mag., 1970-71; art critic Madison Eagle, 1975-78. Recipient 1st prize Morris County Art Assn., 1966, Princeton Art Assn., 1969, Cmty. Art Assn., 1980. Mem. Chatham Twp. Art League (co-founder, 1st pres. 1988-90, editor Artist's Album 1993—, editor newsletter, 1996—), Drew U. Art Assn. (membership chmn. 1990-94, mem. directory illustrated 2000—). Democrat. Unitarian Universalist. Avocations: poetry, music.

GLOVER, JERE WALTON, lawyer; b. Brownsville, Tenn., June 20, 1944; s. William Lloyd and Betty Ruth (Shropshire) G.; m. Doris Ann Henderson, Mar. 30, 1968. BS, Memphis State U., 1966, JD, 1969; LLM, George Washington U., 1972. Bar: Tenn. 1969, Md. 1981, D.C. 1970. Trial atty. FTC, Washington, 1968-75; dir. legal div. Consumer Product Safety Commn., Washington, 1975-77; counsel small bus. com. Ho. of Reps., Washington, 1978; dep. chief counsel SBA, Washington, 1981, chief counsel advocacy, 1994-2001; pvt. practice Washington, 1981-94; counsel Senate Small Bus. Com., Washington, 2002—, Brand and Frulla, 2001—. Pres. Met. Lithotripsy Ctr., Inc., Washington, 1987-94; v.p. Scan Am., Inc., Washington, 1986-94. Mem. Md. Bar Assn., D.C. Bar Assn., Tenn. Bar Assn. Democrat. Avocation: sailing. Home: 1005 York Ln Annapolis MD 21403-4222 Office: 923 Fifteenth St NW Washington DC 20005 Office Phone: 202-662-9700. Business E-Mail: jereglover@brand-frulla.com.

GLOVER, JOHN, actor; b. Salisbury, Md., Aug. 7, 1944; s. John S. and Cade (Mullins) G. Student, Towson State Coll. Appeared in plays Look Homeward Angel, 1963, A Scent of Flowers, 1969, Subject to Fit, 1971, House of Blue Leaves, 1971, The Great God Brown, 1972, Don Juan, 1972, The Selling of the President, 1972, The Visit, 1973, Chemin de Fer, 1973, Holiday, 1973, Rebel Women, 1976, The Importance of Being Earnest, 1977, Treats, 1977, A Man for All Seasons, 1979, Frankenstein, 1981, Hedda Gabler, 1981, Booth, 1982, The Doctor's Delemma, 1982, A Doll's House, 1982, Whodonnit, 1982-83, Criminal Minds, 1984, Design for Living, 1984, Linda Her and the Fairy Garden, 1984, Digby, 1985, Henceforward, 1991, Love! Valour! Compassion!, 1994 (Tony award Featured Actor in a Play, 1995), The Paris Letter, 2005; films include Shamus, 1972, Annie Hall, 1977, Julia, 1977, Somebody Killed Her Husband, 1978, The Last Embrace, 1979, American Success Company, 1979, Mountain Men, 1980, Melvin and Howard, 1980, Brubaker, 1980, The Incredible Shrinking Woman, 1981, A Little Sex, 1982, The Evil That Men Do, 1984, A Flash of Green, 1985, White Nights, 1985, Willy/Milly, 1985, My Sister's Keeper, 1986, 52 Pick-up, 1986, Masquerade, 1988, A Killing Affair, 1988, Rocket Gibraltar, 1988, The Chocolate War, 1988, Scrooged, 1988, Meet the Hollowheads, 1989, Gremlins 2: The New Batch, 1990, Robocop 2, 1990, Dora Was Dysfunctional, 1993, Ed and His Dead Mother, 1993; TV movies include The Face of Rage, 1983, Ernie Kovacs: Between the Laughter, 1984, An Early Frost, 1985, Moving Target, 1988, Hot Paint, 1988, David, 1988, The Traveling Man, 1989, Twist of Fate, 1989, Breaking Point, 1989, El Diablo, 1990, What Ever Happened to Baby Jane?, 1991, Dead on the Money, 1991, Drug Wars: The Cocaine Cartel, 1992, Majority Rule, 1992, Assault at West Point, 1994, Night of The Running Man, 1995, In the Mouth of Madness, 1995, Schemes, 1995, Batman & Robin, 1997, Love! Valour! Compassion!, 1997, The Broken Giant, 1998, Dead Broke, 1999, Payback, 1999; mini-series include Kennedy, 1983, Rage of Angels, 1983, George Washington, 1984, Nutcracker: Money, Madness and Murder, 1987, Grass Roots, 1992; TV series appearances include (voice) The Adventures of Batman and Robin, 1992, South Beach, 1993, (voice) Batman: Gotham Knights, 1997, Dead Man's Gun, 1997, The Tempest, 1998, Brimstone, 1998, Macbeth in Manhattan, 1999, Dead Broke, 1999, On Edge, 2001, Sex & Violence, 2002, Mid-Century, 2002, Sweet Union, 2003, Tricks, 2003; (TV series) Smallville, 2001. Office: The Gersh Agy care Ken Kaplan 232 N Canon Dr Beverly Hills CA 90210-5302*

GLOVER, KAREN E., lawyer; b. Nampa, Idaho, Apr. 14, 1950; d. Gordon Ellsworth and Cora (Frazier) G.; m. Thaddas L. Alston, Aug. 17, 1979; children: Samantha Glover Alston, Evan Glover Alston. AB magna cum laude, Whitman Coll., 1972; JD cum laude, Harvard U., 1975. Bar: Wash. 1975, U.S. Dist. Ct. (we. dist.) Wash. 1975. Assoc. Preston, Thorgrimson Ellis & Holman, Seattle, 1975-80; ptnr. Preston Gates & Ellis LLP, Seattle, 1981—2005, mng. ptnr., 2005—. Bd. dirs. Adaptis, Inc., 2001—. Chmn. bd. dirs. United Way King County, Seattle, 1993-94; chmn. trustees Whitman Coll., Walla Walla, Wash., 2004—; bd. trustees King County Libr. Sys., Seattle, 1992-2001. Mem. Wash. State Bar Assn. (corp. and health sects.), Columbia Tower Club, Rainier Club. Episcopalian. Office: Preston Gates & Ellis 925 4th Ave Ste 2900 Seattle WA 98104-1158 Office Phone: 206-370-7624. Business E-Mail: karig@prestongates.com.

GLOVER, MICHAEL CONRAD, retired music educator, musician; b. Rochester, N.Y., July 2, 1937; s. Myron Theodore and Audrey Haynes Glover; m. Katherine Somogyi (div.). MusB, Eastman Sch. Music, 1959, MusM, 1963. Music tchr. Albany (N.Y.) City Sch. Dist., 1959—2003; organist, choir dir. Emmaus United Meth. Ch., Albany, 1964—; violinist Albany Symphony Orch., 1969—; music dir. Village Singers, Colonie, NY, 2003—. Violinist Symphony String Quartet. With U.S. Army, 1962—64, Korea. Mem.: Music Educators Nat. Conf. Methodist. Avocations: travel, bicycling. Home: 39 Fountain Ave Albany NY 12203-2613

GLOVER, SAVION, actor, dancer; b. Newark, N.J., Nov. 19, 1973; Head dance co. TiDii. Appeared in Broadway plays including The Tap Dance Kid, Black and Blue (Tony award nominee), Jelly's Last Jam (Jefferson award for supporting role in nat. tour) Bring In Da Noise, Bring In Da Funk, 1995 (Tony award, Drama Desk award, Outer Critics Cir. award, Obie awards (2), Fred Astaire awards (2), 1996); appeared in films including Tap, Savion Glover's Nu York (exec. prodr., choreographer), Bamboozled, 2000; TV appearances include Dance in America: Tap!, The Acad. Awards, Black Filmmakers's Hall of Fame, The Kennedy Ctr. Honors, (series regular) Sesame Street; appeared with nat. tour: Footnotes: The Concert; appeared in TV films: The Wall, 1998, Bojangles, 2001; choreographer Washington Soc. for Performing Arts, The Rat Pack (TV), 1998, Nike Free Style commls. Recipient Dance Mag.'s Choreographer of Yr. award, 1996, endowment grant for choreography NEA, Martin Luther King Jr. Outstanding Youth award, 1991. Office: William Morris Agy 151 El Camino Dr Beverly Hills CA 90212

GLOVER, SHEENA, academic administrator; BS, U. So. Miss., 1995, MEd, 1996, specialist in edn., 1998. Instr., chmn. dept. Antonelli Coll., Hattiesburg, Miss., 1996—97; coord. univ. programming and Greek affairs Edinboro (Pa.) U. Pa., 1998—2000; asst. dir. minority student svcs. Ctrl. Mich. U., Mt. Pleasant, 2000—01; dir. student activities ctr. Ga. So. U., Statesboro, 2001—. Grantee, Mich. Career Devel. Ctr., 2000. Mem.: Nat. Assn. Student Pers. Adminstrs., Delta Sigma Theta (mem. cons./advisement adv. bd., pres. 2002—03). Avocations: shopping, travel, reading, music. Office: Ga So U PO Box 8094 Statesboro GA 30460-8094 E-mail: sheenalglover@hotmail.com.

GLOVICZKI, PETER, surgeon; b. Nyiregyhaza, Hungary, May 5, 1948; m. Marta Matray; children: Peter Jr., Julia. Diploma, Benedictine Abbey, Pannonhalma, Hungary, 1966; MD, Semmelweis Med. U., Budapest, Hungary, 1972; postgrad., Mayo Grad. Sch. Medicine, 1981—83. Cert. vascular surgery Am. Bd. Surgery, gen. surgery Am. Bd. Surgery. Intern dept. pathology Semmelweis Med. U., Budapest, 1970—72, resident surg. clinic, 1972—75, resident Inst. Vascular Surgery, 1976—77, fellow vascular surgery Inst. Vascular Surgery, 1977—79, staff mem., 1979—81; resident cardiovasc. surgery Hosp. St. Michel and Hosp. St. Joseph, Paris, 1975—76; sr. assoc. cons. in vascular surgery Mayo Clinic, Rochester, Minn., 1987—89, vice chair divsn. vascular surgery, 1995—2000, chair divsn. vascular surgery, 2000—, dir. Gonda Vascular Ctr., 2002—. Rsch. dir. Mayo Clinic Vascular Surgery, Rochester, 1987—2002; mem., Cheselden vis. prof. St. Thomas's Hosp., London, 1999. Editor: Handbook of Venous Disorders, 1996, Atlas of Endoscopic Perforator Vein Surgery, 1997, Handbook of Venous Disorders, 2001; course dir., editor: CD-ROM Advances and Controversies in the Multidisciplinary Management of Vascular Disease, 1997, editor-in-chief: Perspectives in Vascular Surgery and Endovascular Therapy, 2000—, Outlook in Vascular Surgery and Endovascular Therapy, 2000—, assoc. editor: Internat. Angiology, 1998—, Vascular Surgery, 1998—, mem. editl. bd.: Jour. Vascular Surgery, Annals Vascular Surgery, Jour. Phlebology, Angiology News, Jour. Cardiovasc. Surgery, Giornale Italiano di Chirurgia Vascolare, Clinica Chirurgica e Microchirurgia, Linfologia, Brazilian Vascular Jour., guest editor: Seminars in Vascular Surgery. Fellow: ACS; mem.: Vascular Disease Found. (pres. 2003—), Midwest Vascular Surgery Soc. (treas., mem. exec. coun. 2000—, pres. 2004—), Soc. for Clin. Vascular Surgery (mem. program com. 1995, chair constn. and by-laws com. 1996—, pres.-elect 1998—99, pres. 1999—2000, Allastair Karmody Essay award 1994), Internat. Union Angiology (sec. N.Am. chpt. 1989—94, v.p. N.Am. chpt. 1994—97, pres.-elect 2000—02, v.p. N.Am. chpt. 2000—, pres. 2002—), Am. Venous Forum (chmn. membership com. 1994, chmn. com. on issues 1995, councillor at large 1996—, mem. internat. rels. com. 1997, mem. Sigvaris traveling fellowship com. 1997, councillor exec. com. 1997—, chmn. internat. rels. com. 1998, pres. elect 2001—02, pres. 2002—, mem. ad hoc com.), Soc. for Vascular Surgery (treas., Edwin Jack Wylie Traveling Fellowship award 1987). Avocation: magic. Office: Mayo Clinic 200 First St SW Rochester MN 55905

GLOVSKY, MYRON MICHAEL, medical educator; b. Boston, Aug. 15, 1936; m. Carole Irene Parks; five children. BS magna cum laude, Tufts U., 1957, MD, 1962. Bd. cert. Nat. Bd. Med. Examiners, Am. Bd. Allergy & Immunology, Am. Bd. Diagnostic Lab. Immunology. Intern Balt. (Md.) City Hosp., 1962-63; resident New Eng. Med. Ctr., Boston, 1965-66; spl. NIH fellow allergy and immunology Walter Reed Army Inst. Rsch., Washington, 1966-68; fellow hematology and immunology U. Calif., San Francisco, 1968-69; staff physician dept. internal medicine So. Calif. Permanente Med. Group, L.A., 1969-72, dir. allergy & immunology lab., 1970-84, chief dept. allergy and clin. immunology, co-dir. residency program in allergy & clin. immunology, 1974-84, dir. pheresis unit, 1978-80; dir. L.A. County Gen. Hosp./U. So. Calif. Asthma Clinic; prof. medicine, head allergy and immunology labs. pulmonary divsn., head allergy and clin. immunology divsn. pulmonary medicine. U. So. Calif., Sch. Medicine, 1984-89, prof. pathology, 1986-89; clin. prof. medicine, clin. prof. pathology U. So. Calif., 1989—2003; dir. asthma and allergy referral ctr. Huntington Meml. Hosp., Pasadena, 1989—2003. Head fellowship and career devel. program Nat. Heart Inst., NIH, Bethesda, Md., 1963-65, fellowship bd. mem., 1964-65; vis. assoc. in chemistry Calif. Inst. Tech., Pasadena, 1977—; acad. assoc. complement and allergy Nichols Inst., San Juan Capistrano, Calif., 1980-2003, med. dir. immunology, 1980-89, 2003—; clin. prof. medicine UCLA, 1983-84; vis. prof. clin. scholars program Eli Lilly & Co., Indpls., 1988; mem. steering com. Aspen Allergy Conf., 1988—. With USPHS, 1963-65. Fellow Am. Acad. Allergy; mem. AAAS, Am. Assn. Immunologists, Am. Thoracic Soc., Am. Fedn. for Clin. Rsch., Am. Coll. Allergy, Reticuloendothelial Soc., L.A. Soc. Allergy and Clin. Immunology (pres. 1979-80), Collegium Internat. Allergolicum. Home: 1961 Oak St South Pasadena CA 91030-4957 Office: Huntington Asthma & Allergy Ctr 960 E Green St Pasadena CA 91106 Office Phone: 626-793-6680. Business E-Mail: yksvolg@caltech.edu.

GLOWINSKI, ROLAND, mathematics professor; b. Paris, Mar. 9, 1937; s. Nathan and Anna (Cukiernik) G.; m. Angela Rimok, Nov. 3, 1963; children: Anne, Tania. B, Ecole Polytechnique, Paris, 1960; M, Ecole Nationale Supérieure des Télécommunications, Paris, 1963; PhD, U. Paris, 1971; D (hon.), U. Jyvaskyla, Finland, 2004. Registered profl. engineer; cert. prof. math. Rsch. engr. Office de Radio et Télévision Françaises, Paris, 1963-68, Institut National de Recherches en Informatique et Automatique, Paris, 1968-70; prof. U. Paris VI, 1970—98, chmn. math dept., 1981-85; Disting. prof. U. Houston, 1985—. Adj. prof. Rice U., Houston, 1986—; Sherman Fairchild Disting. visitor Calif. Inst. Tech., 1988-89; cons. CNET, Paris, 1968-85, Sci. Rsch. Coun., London, 1978-81; bd. dirs. Electricite de France, Paris, 1990-96, U. Leonardo da Vinci, Paris; dir. Centre Européen de Recherches et de Formation Avancée en Calcul Scientifique, Toulouse, France, 1992-94; docent prof. U. Jyvaskyla, Finland, 2001—; sci. bd. French Petroleum Inst., 2005— Lt. France Signal Corps, 1958-61. Decorated officer Nat. Merit, knight Order of Acad. Palms, knight Order Legion of Honor, France; recipient Cray prize Selected Jury, Paris, 1988, Marcel Dassault prize French Nat. Acad. Scis., 1996, Zienkiewicz Disting. lectureship, 1999, IMA, 1999, others. Mem. Soc. for Indsl. and Applied Math. (Theodore von Kármán Prize, 2004, selected jury), Am. Math. Soc., French Acad. Scis. (correspondent 1987), Academia Europea (London), French Nat. Acad. Tech. Office: U Houston Dept Math 651 Philip G Hoffman Hall Houston TX 77204-3008 Office Phone: 713-743-3473. Business E-Mail: roland@math.uh.edu.

GLUBE, CONSTANCE RACHELLE, retired judge; b. Ottawa, Ont., Can., Nov. 23, 1931; d. Samuel and Pearl (Slonemsky) Lepofsky; m. Richard Hillard Glube, July 6, 1952 (dec.); children: John B., Erica D. Glube Kolatch, Harry S., B. Joseph. BA, McGill U., Montreal, Can., 1952; LLB, Dalhousie U., Halifax, Can., 1955, LLD (hon.), 1983, Mount St. Vincent U., 1998, St. Mary's U., 2000. Bar: N.S. 1956, created queen's counsel, 1974. Assoc. Kitz, Matheson, Halifax, 1964-66; ptnr. Fitzgerald & Glube, Halifax, 1966-68; sr. solicitor City of Halifax, 1969-74, city mgr., 1974-77; puisne judge Supreme Ct. of N.S., Halifax, 1977-82, chief justice, 1982-98, N.S. Ct. Appeals, 1998—2004; ret., 2004. Vice chair Can. Judges Conf.; interim bd. dirs. Nat. Jud. Ctr., 1987; bd. dirs. Can. Inst. Adminstrs. Justice. Contbr. articles to profl. jours. Co-chair Can. Coun. Christians and Jews; bd. dirs. Halifax Heritage Found., 1984—95, Internat. Commn. Jurists, Can. br., 2003—; chmn. bd. N.S. Archives, 1998—2004; bd. mem. Queen Elizabeth II Found., 2005, Can. Civil Liberties Assn., 2005—, Halifax Cmty. Learning Network, 2005; chair (hon.) N.S. divsn. Can. Mental Health Assn., 1984—98; mem. adv. coun. Order N.S., 2001—04. Recipient award of merit City of Halifax, 1977, Frances Fish award, 1997, N.S. Women Lawyers Achievement award, Confedn. Can. medal (1867-1992), 1992, Commemorative medal Golden Jubilee of Her Majesty Queen Elizabeth II (1952-2002), 2002, Justice award Can. Inst. for Adminstrn. of Justice, 2003. Mem.: Nat. Jud. Inst. (bd. dirs. 1998—2004), Can. Jud. Coun. (chmn. edn. com. 1986—88, adminstrn. of justice com. 1992—94, equality com. 1994—99, jud. benefits com. 1994—99, fin. com. 1999—2002, chmn. edn. com. 2000—04, exec. com. 2001—04, vice chair jud. conduct com. 2001—04), Internat. Assn. Women Judges (hon.), Can. Bar Assn. (hon.; fellow Law of the Future Fund), Golden Key Internat. Honor Soc. (hon.). Jewish. Avocations: swimming, gardening. Home: 5920 Inglewood Dr Halifax NS Canada B3H 1B1 E-mail: cglube@judicom.ca.

GLUCK, CAROL, history professor; b. Newark, Nov. 12, 1941; d. David E. and Doris S. Newman; m. Peter L. Gluck, May 1, 1966; children: Thomas Edward, William Francis. Student, U. Munich, 1960-61, U. Tokyo, 1972-74;

BA, Wellesley Coll., 1962; MA, Columbia U., 1970, PhD, 1977. Asst. prof. Columbia U., N.Y.C., 1975-83, assoc. prof., 1983-86, prof., 1986-88, George Sansom prof. history, 1988—. Vis. rsch. assoc. faculty law Tokyo U., 1978-79, 85-86, 92; vis. prof. Harvard U., Cambridge, Mass., 1991, Inst. Social Sci. Tokyo U., 1993, Ecole des Hautes Etudes en Scis. Sociales, Paris, 1995, 98; fellow Inst. for Advanced Studies in the Behavioral Scis., 1999-2000; publs. bd. Columbia U. Press, N.Y.C., 1991-96; co-dir. project on Asia in the core Curriuculm NEH, N.Y.C., 1987—; Am. adv. com. Japan Found., 1986-96, chair, 1991-96; disting. lectr. N.E. Area Coun., 1988, Japan Soc. for Promotion of Sci., 1989. Author: Japan's Modern Myths, 1985 (Fairbank prize 1986, Trilling award 1987); co-editor: Showa: The Japan of Hirohito, 1992, Asia in Western and World History, 1997; contbr. numerous articles to profl. publs. Mem. Coun. on Fgn. Rels., U.S.-Japan Friendship Commn., 1994—2001; mem. com. on rsch. librs. N.Y. Pub. Libr., 1987—, mem. humanities adv. coun., 1996—. Recipient Fulbright 50th Anniversary Disting. Fellow award, 2002; fellow, Woodrow Wilson Found., Fgn. Area fellow; grantee Fulbright grantee, 1985—86, Japan Found. grantee. Fellow: Am. Acad. Arts and Scis.; mem.: Am. Philos. Soc., Asia Soc. (trustee 1992—98, 2002—), Japan Soc. (bd. dirs. 1990—), Assn. Asian Studies (coun. 1981—84, nominating com. 1985—86, pres. 1996—97, bd. dirs. 1995—99), Am. Hist. Assn. (coun. 1987—90), Phi Beta Kappa. Home: 440 Riverside Dr New York NY 10027-6828 Office: Columbia U East Asian Inst 420 W 118th St New York NY 10027-7213

GLÜCK, LOUISE ELISABETH, poet, educator; b. N.Y.C., Apr. 22, 1943; d. Daniel and Beatrice (Grosby) G.; m. Charles Hertz (div.); 1 child, Noah Benjamin; m. John Dranow, 1977 (div.). Student, Sarah Lawrence Coll., 1962, Columbia U., 1963-65; LLD, Williams Coll., 1993, Skidmore Coll., 1995, Middlebury, 1996. Vis. poet Goddard Coll., U. N.C., U. Va., U. Iowa; Elliston prof. U. Cin., 1978; vis. faculty Columbia U., 1979; faculty M.F.A. program Goddard Coll., also Warren Wilson Coll., Swannanoa, N.C.; Holloway lectr. U. Calif., Berkeley, 1982; vis. prof. U. Calif.-Davis, 1983; Scott prof. poetry Williams Coll., 1983; Regents prof. poetry UCLA, 1985-88; faculty Williams Coll., 1984—, Preston Parrish 3d century prof., 1997—2003, Margaret Scott Bundy lectr., 2003—04; Rosenkranz writer-in-residence Yale U., New Haven, 2004—. Vis. prof. Harvard U., 1995; Hurst prof. poetry Brandeis U., 1996; delivered Phi Beta Kappa poem Harvard U. commencement, 1990; baccalaureate spkr. Williams Coll.; Hopwood lectr. U. Mich.; spl. cons. Libr. of Congress, 2000; judge younger poets competition Yale U. Press, 2003—. Author: Firstborn, 1968, The House on Marshland, 1975, Descending Figure, 1980, The Triumph of Achilles, 1985, Ararat, 1990, The Wild Iris, 1992 (Pulitzer Prize for poetry 1993), Proofs and Theories (collected essays), 1994, Meadowlands, 1996, Vita Nova, 1999, The Seven Ages, 2001, October (chapbook), 2004. Grantee Rockefeller Found., Nat. Endowment for Arts, 1969-70, 79-80, 88-89, Guggenheim Found., 1975-76, 87-88, NEA, 1988-89; recipient lit. award Am. Acad. and Inst. Arts and Letters, 1981, award in poetry Nat. Book Critics Cir., 1985, Melville Cane award Poetry Soc. Am., 1986, Sara Teasdale Meml. prize Wellesley Coll., 1986, Bobbitt Natl prize Libr. Congress, 1992, Pulitzer prize, 1993, William Carlos Williams award, 1993, PEN/Martha Albrand award Non-Fiction, 1995, Lannan Found. award in poetry, 1999, New Yorker mag. award, 1999, Ambs. award English Spkg. Union, 1999, 50th Anniversary medal MIT, 2000, Bollingen prize, 2001, Medal for lifetime distinction Barnard Coll., 2004; named Poet Laureate of Vt., 1994, U.S. Poet Laureate, 2003. Fellow Am. Acad. Arts and Scis.; mem. Am. Acad. Arts & Letters, Am. Acad. Poets (chancellor 1999—), Phi Beta Kappa (hon.).

GLUCK, MICHELLE H., lawyer; b. Apr. 1959; m. Robert J. Gluck. BA, JD, U. Mich. Bar: Va. 1983. Assoc. Hunton & Williams, 1983—89; legal cons. Am. Household Inc., 1996—99, Office Depot, 1996—99; v.p., assoc. gen. counsel, asst. sec. The Sports Authority Inc., Ft. Lauderdale, Fla., 1999—2001, Kmart Corp., Troy, Mich., 2001—03; exec. v.p., gen. counsel, corp. sec. LandAmerica Fin. Group Inc., Richmond, Va., 2004—. Mem.: Am. Corp. Counsel Assn. (sec., bd. mem. South Fla. Chpt. 2001). Office: LandAmerica Fin Group Inc 101 Gateway Centre Pkwy Richmond VA 23235-5153 Office Phone: 804-267-8383. Business E-Mail: mgluck@landam.com.

GLUCKSBERG, SAM, psychologist, educator; b. Montreal, Que., Can., Feb. 6, 1933; came to U.S., 1945; s. Murray and Sonia (Afrin) G.; children: Matthew, Kenneth, Nadia Glucksberg. BS, CCNY, 1956; PhD, NYU, 1960. Instr. NYU, N.Y.C., 1958-60; chair psychology dept. Princeton (N.J.) U., 1974-80, from instr. to prof., 1963—. Cons., Princeton, 1980—. Author: Psychology, 5th edit., 1991; editor Jour. Exptl. Psychology: Gen., 1984-89, Psychological Science, 2000-04; author 100 sci. articles, book chpts., 3 books. Capt. U.S. Army, 1958-63. Fellow APA (pres. div. exptl. psychology 1988-89), AAAS, Soc. Exptl. Psychologists (sec.-treas. 1987-90), Am. Psychol. Soc. Avocations: music, theater, cooking. Home: 29 Bainbridge St Princeton NJ 08540-3901 Office: Princeton U Dept Psychology Princeton NJ 08544-0001 Business E-Mail: samg@princeton.edu.

GLUCKSMAN, MYRON LAWRENCE, psychiatrist; b. Vancouver, BC, Canada, Feb. 26, 1935; arrived in U.S., 1956; s. Maurice Glucksman and Julia Brown; m. Leslie Korn, July 7, 1963; children: Julie, Jane, Tina. BA, U. B.C., 1956; MD, U. Wash., 1959. Diplomate Am. Bd. Psychiatry and Neurology, 1966. Intern Kings County Hosp., Bklyn., 1959—60; resident NY Hosp./Cornell U., N.Y.C., 1960—63; rsch. investigator Rockefeller U., N.Y.C., 1963—67, Psychoanalytic Inst., N.Y. Med. Coll., 1968; chief consultation-liaison svc. NY Hosp./Cornell U., N.Y.C., 1967—68, Pa. Hosp., Phila., 1970—71; chief mental health clinic Danbury (Conn.) Hosp., 1971—73; pvt. practice psychiatry and psychoanalysis Danbury, 1973—, Redding, Conn., 1973—, N.Y.C., 1993—. Clin. prof. psychiatry NY Med. Coll., Valhalla, 1978—, dir. Psychoanalytic Inst., 1992—2002; lectr. in psychiatry Yale U. Sch. Medicine, New Haven, 1995—. Co-editor: Affect: Theory and Technique, 1983, Dreams in New Perspective, 1987; contbr. articles to profl. jours., chpts. to books. Lt. col. U.S. Army, 1968—70. Fellow: Am. Psychiat. Assn. (disting. life), Am. Coll. Psychoanalysis, Am. Acad. Psychoanalysis (pres. 1988—89). Jewish. Avocations: tennis, piano, sailing. Home: 68 Marchant Rd West Redding CT 06896 Office: 449 E 68th St New York NY 10021 also: 68 Marchant Rd West Redding CT 06896 Office Phone: 203-938-1188.

GLUCKSTEIN, FRITZ PAUL, veterinarian, biomedical information specialist; b. Berlin, Jan. 24, 1927; came to U.S., 1948; s. Georg Jakob and Hedwig Emilie (Heinrich) G.; m. Ethel Gold, July 31, 1955 (dec. Nov. 1993); 1 child, Ruth; m. Maran Ostchega, Nov. 29, 1996. BS, U. Minn., 1953, DVM, 1955; MLS, U. Md., 1984. Diplomate Am. Coll. Vet. Preventive Medicine. Vet. meat insp. U.S. Dept. Agr., South St. Paul, Minn., 1955-56, asst. vet. pathologist Ames, Iowa, 1958-59, vet. analyst Washington, 1959-63; chief microbiology br. Sci. Info. Exchange Smithsonian Instn., Washington, 1963-66; coordinator for vet. affairs Nat. Library of Medicine, Bethesda, Md., 1966-93; biomed. info. cons., 1993—. Mem. coordinating com. for research animal resources NIH, 1982-93; adv. sci. bd. Gorgas Meml. Inst. Tropical Preventive Medicine, Washington, 1967-70; chmn. continuing edn. com. 1989-90. Author: (annotated bibliography) Laboratory Animal Welfare, 1984-93; contbr. chpts. to books. Served to 1st lt. U.S. Army, 1956-58; commd. officer USPHS, 1966-93. Recipient cert. merit U.S. Dept. Agr., 1962 Fellow Royal Soc. Health (London); mem. AVMA, APHA, Assn. Mil. Surgeons of U.S., Am. Assn. Lab. Animal Sci., Am. Soc. Lab. Animal Practitioners, Med. Libr. Assn., Beta Phi Mu. Avocation: music. Home: 11801 Rockville Pike Apt 812 Rockville MD 20852-2723 Personal E-mail: opera.buff@verizon.net.

GLUCKSTERN, ROBERT LEONARD, physics professor; b. Atlantic City, July 31, 1924; BEE, CCNY, 1944; PhD, MIT, 1948. Asst. prof. physics Yale U., New Haven, 1950-57, assoc. prof., 1957-64; prof. physics U. Mass., Amherst, 1964-75, head dept., 1964-69, asso. provost, 1969-70, provost, vice chancellor for acad. affairs, 1970-75; prof. physics U. Md., College Park, 1975-97, chancellor, 1975-82, sr. rsch. scientist, 1997—2005; ret., 2005. Vis. prof. U. Tokyo, Japan, 1969; cons. on theory of high energy particle accelerators Brookhaven Nat. Lab., Fermi Nat. Accelerator Lab., Lawrence Berkeley Nat. Lab., Los Alamos Nat. Lab., Stanford Linear Accelerator Ctr. With USNR, 1944-46. AEC fellow U. Calif., Berkeley, 1948-49, Cornell U., Ithaca, N.Y., 1949-50, Yale fellow, 1961-62. Fellow AAAS, Am. Phys. Soc.; mem. SSC (bd. overseers 1990-93), SURA (trustee 1982-98, chmn. bd. trustees 1994-96, high energy physics adv. panel 1990-93), Fedn. Am. Scientists, Am. Assn. Physics Tchrs. Business E-Mail: RLG@physics.umd.edu.

GLUECKAUF, ROBERT LEWIS, psychologist, educator; b. Miami Beach, Fla., Oct. 8, 1949; s. Lewis Gustave and Josephine Lily (Simon) G.; m. Alexandra Louise Quittner, Aug. 27, 1981; children: Rachelle Leila, Jordanna Alexandra, Aaron Michael. BA, U. Fla., 1975; MS, Fla. State U., 1979, PhD, 1981. Lic. clin. psychologist. Rehab. psychologist Royal Ottawa (Ont., Can.) Regional Rehab. Ctr., 1981-83; clin. lectr. Sch. of Medicine U. Ottawa, 1981-83, U. Hosp., London, Ont., 1983-88, clin. health psychologist, 1983-88; assoc. prof. Sch. of Sci., dir. clin. and rehab. psychology PhD program Purdue U., Indpls., 1988-98; prof. dept. clin. and health psychology U. Fla., Gainesville, 1998—2003, dir. Ctr. Rsch. Telehealth and Healthcare Comms., 1998—2003; prof. humanities and social sci. Coll. Medicine, Fla. State U., Tallahassee, 2003—. Psychol. cons. Epilepsy Ont., London, 1983-88, Midwest AIDs Tng. and Edn. Ctr., ind. U. Sch. of Medicine, Indpls., 1988-91; adj. asst. prof. U. Western Ont., London, 1983-88. Cons. editor Rehab. Psychology, 1981—, book rev. editor, 1988-97, assoc. editor, 1999-2004; cons. editor Jour. of Sexuality and Disability, 1982-90; cons. reviewer Jour. of Strategic and Systemic Therapies, 1988-92; contbr. articles to profl. jours. Grantee Can. Ministry Health and Welfare, 1983—, Ont. Ministry Health, 1983—, NIDRR, 1992—, NIH, 2000—, U.S. Dept. Vet. Affairs, 1999—, Robert Wood Johnson Found., 2001, Bryd Alzheimer's Inst., 2004—. Fellow APA (mem.-at-large div. 22 1989-91, pres. divsn. 22 1993-94); mem. Phi Kappa Phi Avocations: hiking, birdwatching, canoeing. Home: 1767 Hermatage Blvd Apt 12106 Tallahassee FL 32308 Office: Coll Medicine Fla State Univ Dept Med Humanities & Social Sci 1115 W Call St Ste 1310-L Tallahassee FL 32306-4300 Business E-Mail: robert.glueckauf@med.fsu.edu.

GLUSBAND, STEVEN JOSEPH, lawyer; b. Berlin, Jan. 15, 1947; came to U.S., 1949; s. Morris and Docia (Waitman) G.; m. Roberta Gail Jacobs, Nov. 22, 1981; children: Ilana, Jonathan. BBA, CCNY, 1969; JD, Fordham U., 1973; LLM, NYU, 1978. Bar: N.Y. 1974, U.S. Dist. Ct. (so. dist.) N.Y. 1974, U.S. Ct. Appeals (2nd cir.) 1974. Trial atty. SEC, N.Y.C., 1974-75, spl. trial counsel, 1976-77; assoc. Sage Gray Todd & Sims, N.Y.C., 1977-80, ptnr., 1981-87; mem. exec. com. Carter, Ledyard & Milburn, N.Y.C., 1987—. Dir. MER Telemanagement Solutions Ltd. Mem. ABA (com. fed. regulation of securities, securities litigation), Assn. of Bar of N.Y.C. (com. on futures regulation 1986-88). Home: 343 E 30th St New York NY 10016-6417 Office: Carter Ledyard & Milburn 2 Wall St Fl 13 New York NY 10005-2072

GLUSHCHENKO, ANATOLIY V., physicist, educator, researcher, consultant; b. Malyn, Ukraine, Aug. 27, 1971; s. Volodymyr P. and Olga M. Glushchenko; m. Oksana V. Klyonts, Sept. 19, 1998; 1 child, Iryna A. BS in physics and math. (hon.), Zhytomyr State Pedagogical U., 1988—91, MS (hon.) in physics and math., 1991—93; PhD in physics, Inst. of Physics, 1993—96. Rsch. fellow Inst. of Physics, Kyiv, Ukraine, 1996—97; rschr. LG Electronics Inc., Anyang, Republic of Korea, 1998—99; vis. scientist Martin-Luther U., Halle, Germany, 1998; rschr., group leader Inst. of Physics, 1998—2000; postdoctoral fellow Liquid Crystal Inst., Kent, Ohio, 2000—01, rsch. assoc., 2001—02, WestLab mgr., 2003—; adj. prof. Kent State U., 2004—. Cons. LG Electronics Inc., Anyang, Korea (South), 1997—98. V.p. of the US office K2 Labs LLC, Kent, Ohio, 2003. Recipient Inventor Recognition award, Kent State U., 2004, Award of the Pres. of Ukraine, 1999, Gold Edn. medal, 1988, Honors diploma of Zhytomyr U., 1993; Spl. stipend of Zhytomyr U., 1988, 1989, 1990, 1991. Mem.: Soc. for Info. Displays, Am. Phys. Soc., Internat. Liquid Crystal Soc. Achievements include discovery of anchoring cumulative effect in liquid crystals; magnetically-mediated surface driven effect; multi-stable liquid crystal alignment using colloidal networks; controllable memory effect in filled liquid crystals; invention of stressed liquid crystal (SLC) materials; control of anchoring parameters of liquid crystals with boundary surfaces by photoalignment technique; emulsion liquid crystal - isotropic liquid; liquid crystals between polymer walls; suspension of ultrafine ferro-magnetic particles in liquid crystals; suspension of ultrafine ferro-electric particles in liquid crystals; surface phenomena in liquid crystals; alignment methods for nematic liquid crystals electro-optical devices; diffractive and beam steering devices; in liquid crystal displays; optical recording, processing and storage of information; heterogeneous systems on the liquid crystal base; nano-composite liquid crystal systems; development of new college courses liquid crystals, liquid crystal displays; innovative photopolymer materials for liquid crystal alignment; liquid crystal based optical phase arrays for steering lasers; novel advanced liquid crystal display modes: (I) in-plane sliding mode; (II) vertical alignment mode with a finite pretilt. Office: Liquid Crystal Inst Kent State Univ Kent OH 44242 Office Phone: 330-672-1559. Office Fax: 330-672-2796. Business E-Mail: anatoliy@lci.kent.edu.

GLUSKER, JENNY PICKWORTH, chemist; b. Birmingham, Eng., June 28, 1931; came to U.S., 1955, naturalized, 1977; d. Frederick Alfred and Jane Wylie (Stocks) P.; m. Donald Leonard Glusker, Dec. 18, 1955; children: Ann, Mark John, Katharine. BA in Chemistry, Oxford (Eng.) U., 1953, MA, DPhil, Oxford (Eng.) U., 1957; DSc (hon.), Coll. of Wooster, Ohio, 1985. Postdoctoral rsch. fellow Calif. Inst. Tech., Pasadena, 1955-56; rsch. fellow Inst. Cancer Rsch., Phila., 1956, rsch. assoc., 1957-67, asst. mem., 1967, assoc. mem., 1967-79, sr. mem., 1979—. Adj. prof. U. Pa., 1969—; mem. U.S. Nat. Com. for Crystallography, 1974—90, sec.-treas., 1977—79, chmn., 1982—84; vis. fellow Oriel Coll., Oxford, England, 1994—95; vis. prof. Internat. Union Crystallography, Egypt, 1997, Nat. Inst. Health, Biophysicis/Biochemistry A Study Sect., 1972—76; mem. Biotech. Rsch. Rev. Com., 1977—80, chmn., 1979—80; mem. Metallo Biochem. Study Sect., 1983—87, Divsn. Rsch. Grants Adv. Com., 1989—92, Rsch. Coun., 1995—99; mem. gov. bd. Cambridge Structural Database, England, 1988—2001, vice chmn., England, 1998—2001; mem. computer graphics lab. adv. com. U. Calif., San Francisco, 1985—, chmn., 1988—; cons., lectr. in field; dir.-at-large, mem. gov. bd. Am. Inst. Physics, 1980—83, exec. com., 1981—82; chmn. selection com. Rhodes Scholarship, Pa., 1984—89. Co-author (with K.N. Trueblood): (book) Crystal Structure Analysis: A Primer, 1972, Crystal Structure Analysis: A Primer, 2d edit., 1985; co-author: (with Dodson, Ramaseshan and Venkatesan) The Collected Works of Dorothy Crowfoot Hodgkin; editor: Structural Crystallography in Chemistry and Biology, Structures of Molecules of Biological Interest, 1981; co-editor (with McLachlan): Crystallography in North America, 1982; co-editor: (with S. Parthasarathy) Aspects of Crystallography in Molecular Biology, 1997; editor: Acta Crystallographcia sect. Biological Crystallography; co-editor (with M. Lewis, M. Rossi): Crystal Structure Analysis for Chemists and Biologists, 1994; co-editor: (with Patterson and Rossi) Patterson and Pattersons, 1987; mem. adv. bd. Molecular Structures in Biology, 1991, mem. editl. bd. Biophys. Jour., 1981—86; contbr. articles to profl. jours. Hon. fellow Somerville Coll., Oxford (Eng.) U., 2001. Fellow AAAS; mem. Am. Assn. Cancer Rsch., The Chem. Soc., Am. Soc. Biol. Chemists, Biophys. Soc., Am. Crystallog. Assn. (pres. 1979, Pub. Svc. award 1991, Fankuchen Meml. award 1995), Am. Chem. Soc. (Phila. sect. award 1978, Garvan medal 1979), Am. Phys. Soc., Sigma Xi. Office: Inst Cancer Rsch Fox Chase Cancer Ctr Philadelphia PA 19111 Office Phone: 215-728-2220. E-mail: jp_glusker@fccc.edu.

GLUSS, BRIAN, mathematician, statistician; b. London, Eng., Aug. 23, 1930; s. Joseph and Otilie (Tenenhaus) Gluss; m. Joan Marie Chodorow (div.); 1 stepchild, Lori Kim Smallwood. BA in Math., Cambridge (Eng.) U., 1952; MA, Cambridge U., Eng., 1957; diploma in Stats, Cambridge U., 1953; DEng, U. Calif., Berkeley, 1965. Rsch. asst. London Sch. Econs., 1953—54; actuarial clk. Prudential Assurance Co., London, 1954—55; statistician jury project U. Chgo., 1955—56; asst. to sr. rschr. bur. of stats. Canadian Govt., Ottawa, 1956—58; staff mem. Ill. Inst. Tech. Rsch Inst., Chgo., 1958—62; mathematician Rand Corp., Santa Monica, Calif., 1964—66; prof. U. Ill., Chgo., 1968—83, emeritus prof., 1983—. Cons. Ill. Inst. Tech. Rsch. Inst., Chgo., 1962—64; reviewer Math. Rev., 1966—74. Author: (Book) Introduction to Dynamic Programming, 1972; contbr. articles to profl. jours. and newspapers. Vol. performer for hosps., retirement homes etc., Berkeley, Calif., 2000—; polit. and human rights activism. With RAF, 1949, England. Scholar State scholarship to Cambridge U., Brit. Govt., 1948, Found. scholar, Pembroke Coll., 1952. Fellow: Royal Stats Soc. (London). Democrat. Avocations: acting, singing, dance, volunteering. Home: 3242 Idaho St Berkeley CA 94702

GLYNN, CARLIN (CARLIN MASTERSON), actress; b. Cleve., Feb. 19, 1940; d. Guilford Cresse and Lois Carlin (Wilks) G.; m. Peter Masterson, Dec. 29, 1960; children: Carlin Alexandra, Mary Stuart, Peter C.B. Student, Sophie Newcomb Coll., 1957-58. Prof. Columbia U. Grad. Film Sch., N.Y.C.; prof. MFA program Actors Studio at New Sch. U. Creative advisor Sundance Inst. Film Lab. Appeared in N.Y. as Miss Mona in: The Best Little Whorehouse in Tex., 1978-80; in London, 1981; starred in Pal Joey, Goodman Theatre, Chgo., 1988 (Joseph Jefferson award 1988), Cover of Life, Am. Place Theatre, N.Y., 1994, The Young Man from Atlanta, Signature Theatre Co., 1995 (Pulitzer prize for drama 1995), Amazing Grace, 1998, The Chemistry of Change, 1999, Frame 312, 2002, Safe, 2003, Spring Storm, 2004, The Oldest Profession, 2004; films include Three Days of the Condor, 1974, Resurrection, 1978, Continental Divide, 1981, Sixteen Candles, 1984, The Trip to Bountiful, 1985, Blood Red, Night Game, Convicts, 1989, Blessing, 1992, Judy Berlin, 1997, West of Here, 2001, Lost Junction, 2001, Intervention (now Whiskey Sch.), 2004; TV series Mr. President, 1987; dir. short film Love Divided By, 1993; dir. contemporary opera Cheri at Actors Studio, 2005. Recipient Theatre World award, 1978, Antoinette Perry award, 1979, best actress award in musical Soc. West End Theatres, Lawrence Olivier award, London, 1981 Mem. SAG, AFTRA, Actor's Studio (bd. dirs., co-artistic dir.), Actors' Equity Assn. Episcopalian.

GLYNN, EDWARD, retired academic administrator; b. Clarks Summit, Pa., Oct. 6, 1935; s. John J. G. AB, Fordham U., 1960, PhL, 1961, MAT, 1962; STB, Woodstock Coll., 1967; STM, Yale Divinity Sch., 1968; ThD, Grad. Theol. Union, 1971; LLD (hon.), Monmouth Coll., 1984, U. Scranton, 1990; LHD (hon.), Seton Hall U., 1989, St. Peter's Coll., 1990, Loyola Coll., 1993. Entered Soc. Jesus 1955; ordained 1967. Instr. Gonzaga H.S., 1961—64; asst. prof. Georgetown U., 1971-77; acad. v.p. Gonzaga U., Spokane, 1977-78, pres., 1996—97, St. Peter's Coll., Jersey City, 1978-90; provincial Md. Province Soc. of Jesus, Balt., 1990-96; interim provost U. Mass., Boston, 1997—98; pres. John Carroll U., Cleve., 1998—2005. Acting dir., mem., bd. dir. Churches' Ctr. for Theology and Pub. Policy, 1976-77; exec. dir. Woodstock Theol. Ctr., Washington, 1974-76, bd. dirs., 1974-76. Contbr. articles to profl. jours. Bd. dirs. U. Scranton, 1973-78, Fordham U., 1981-87, Canisius Coll., 1982-88, 2001—, LeMoyne Coll., 1983-89, 2000—04, St. Louis U., 1986-91, John Carroll U., 1987-90, 98—, Seton Hall U., 1990-96, St. Mary's Sem. and U., 1991-96, Weston Sch. Theology, 1990-96, NCAA's Pres. Commn., 1984-88, Commn. on Higher Edn., Mid. States Assn., 1988-90, Fairfield U., 1997-, Marquette U., 1998-, U. Detroit Mercy, 1999-, Wheeling Jesuit U., 2004-, Am. Coun. of Edn., 2001-2004, U.S. Dept. of Edn. (nat. adv. bd. 1999-2001), Fund for Improvement of Post Secondary Edn. Mem.: FIPSE. Office Phone: 216-397-4209. Business E-Mail: eglynn@jcu.edu.

GLYNN, EDWARD F., JR., lawyer; b. Boston, Mass., May 5, 1947; BA, McGill U., 1968; JD, Cornell Law Sch., 1971. Bar: NY 1972, DC 1975, Md. 1981, US Ct. of Appeals, Second, Ninth & DC Circuits, US Dist. Ct., NY (No., So. & Ea. Dist.), US Dist. Ct., Md., US Dist. Ct., DC. Various positions including trial atty. and asst. dir., internat. antitrust Federal Trade Commn., 1976—81, assoc. dir., bureau of competition, 1981—90; assoc. then ptnr., antitrust, consumer protection and trade regulation Venable LLP, Washington, 1991—. Mem.: ABA (former chmn., consumer protection com., antitrust section), DC Bar Assn., Md. Bar Assn., NYC Bar Assn. Office: Venable LLP 575 7th St NW Washington DC 20004 Office Phone: 202-344-4805. Office Fax: 202-344-8300. Business E-Mail: efglynn@venable.com.

GLYNN, ERNEST B., civil engineer, environmental engineer; b. Cambridge, Mass., Dec. 19, 1911; s. Frederick Stanley G. and Maude Lillian Landers; m. Beatrice Beverly Bakerink, Jan 27, 1951; children: Nancy Belva, Priscilla Beverly. Diploma Structural Design, MIT, 1939; BS, U. Md., 1956. Registered profl. engr., Washington. Archtl. engr. Office Chief of Engrs. U.S. Army, Washington, 1942, 45-47, archtl. engr. Hq. 2nd Army Balt., 1947-48, ports engr. bd. engr. river and harbors Washington, 1948-51, engr., intelligence specialist, asst. chief of staff G-2, 1951-63; sr. engr. rsch. specialist Def. Intelligence Agy., Washington, 1963-73; pvt. practice Washington, 1973-85, Alexandria, Va., 1985—; prof. engring. George Washington U., Washington, 1982-85. Presenter, lectr. in field. Contbr. over 30 articles to profl. jours. Mem. Mt. Vernon dist. Fairfax (Va.) Falls Ch., 1959-65; mem. citizen adv. com. Met Wash COG, Washington, 1965-96. Served in U.S. Army, 1942-45. Decorated Croix de Guerre with palm, France; recipient two presdl. citations. Fellow Am. Soc. Civil Engrs. (chair solid waste com. 1950, 51); mem. Am. Acad. Environ. Engr. (diplomate), Va. Soc. Profl. Engrs., Nat. Soc. Profl. Engr. (pres. George Washington chpt. 1976, outstanding engr. 1976, engr. of yr. award 1984), Solid Waste and Environ. Protection, Masons (master lodge 4 Washington). Home and Office: 4306 Ferry Landing Rd Alexandria VA 22309-3025

GLYNN, JAMES A., sociology educator, author; b. Bklyn., Sept. 10, 1941; s. James A. and Muriel M. (Lewis) G.; m. Marie J. Gates, Dec. 17, 1966 (div. Apr. 1995); 1 child, David S. AA, Foothill Coll., 1961; BA in Sociology, San Jose (Calif.) State U., 1964, MA in Sociology, 1966; PhD, U. Calif. at Riverside, 1972. Instr. in sociology Bakersfield Coll., Calif., 1966-98, prof. sociology, 1972—98; prof. sociology State Ctr. Cmty. Coll. Dist. Clovis Ctr. and Madera Ctr., 1998—2002, prof. emeritus State Ctr. Cmty. Coll. Dist., 2003. Adj. prof. Fresno (Calif.) State U., 1971-72, Chapman Coll., Orange, Calif., 1972, Calif. State U., Bakersfield, 1989-98, Chapman U., Visalia, Calif., 1997-98; del. acad. senate Calif. C.C., Sacramento, 1980-89; mem. coun. Faculty Assn. Calif. C.Cs., 1981—; columnist Madera Tribune, 1999-2001, 2004—. Author: Studying Sociology, 1979, Writing Across the Curriculum Using Sociological Concepts, 1983, Hands On: User's Manual for Data Processing, 1986; (with Elbert W. Stewart) Introduction to Sociology, 1972, 4th edit., 1985; (with Crystal Dea Moore) Guide to Social Psychology, 1992, Understanding Racial and Ethnic Groups, 1992, 98, 2001, Guide to Human Services, 1994, Focus on Sociology, 1994, 98; (with Charles F. Hohm and Elbert W. Stewart) Global Social Problems, 1996; contbg. editor Introduction to Sociology, 1996; contbg. author: California's Social Problems, 1997; editor, contbg. author (with Charles F. Hohm) California's Social Problems, 2d edit., 2001 Mem. Madera County Arts Coun., 2000—, co-chair fin. com., 2001—02, pub. rels. chmn., exec. bd., 2001—, v.p., 2002—03, pres., 2003—04; bd. dirs. San Joaquin Paleontology Found., 2003—. Recipient Innovator Yr. award League Innovations C.C., 1989, Innovator Yr. award Kern C.C. Dist., 1992. Mem. Calif. Sociol. Assn. (founder, treas. 1990-92, editor newsletter 1991-92, pres. 1992-93, exec. dir. 1993-2001), Commn. on Tchg., Pacific Sociol. Assn. (mem. editl. bd. Sociol. Perspectives 1996-99, awards com. 2000-03, Disting. Prof. award for Contbn. to Edn. 1997,), Population Reference Bur., World Watch Inst., World Future Soc., Kiwanis (editor newsletter 2001—, pres. 2001-02, bd. dirs. 2004—). Democrat. Home: 135 N Park Dr Madera CA 93637-3041 Office Phone: 559-674-4490. Personal E-mail: j_glynn@sbcglobal.net.

GLYNN, PETER ALEXANDER RICHARD, health facility administrator, consultant; b. Toronto, Ont., Can., Oct. 14, 1944; s. John Richard Lewis and Jessie Mackenzie Glynn; m. Arlene Dawne Whalen, Aug. 13, 1966; children: Jennifer Dawne, Jeffrey Alexander. B Engring., Royal Mil. Coll., Kingston, Ont., 1965; MASc, U. Waterloo, Ont., 1967, PhD, 1972. Dir. dept. continuing edn. Province of Sask., Regina, Can., 1975-80, exec. dir. prescription drug plan, 1980-81; assoc. dep. min. Sask. Ministry Health, Regina, 1981-84; asst. dep. min. Can. Health and Welfare, Ottawa, Ont., 1984-91; pres., CEO,

Kingston (Ont.) Gen. Hosp., 1991-2000. Bd. dirs. Inst. for Clin. Evaluative Scis., Toronto. Capt. Can. Army, 1961-69. Recipient Special Recognition award Can. Cancer Soc., 1991, Alumni Achievement medal U. Waterloo, 1998, Dedicated Svc. award Heart and Stroke Found. Can., 2002. Avocations: bicycling, hiking, kayaking.

GLYNN, ROBERT D., JR., electric power and gas industry executive; b. Orange, N.J., 1942; BSME, Manhattan Coll.; MS in Nuclear Engring., L.I. U.; postgrad., U. Mich., Harvard U. With L.I. Lighting Co., 1964-72; exec. v.p., prin., dir. Woodward Clyde Cons., 1972-84; with PG&E Corp., San Francisco, 1984—, pres., COO, 1997, CEO, 1997—, chmn. bd., 1998—, Pacific Gas and Electric Co. (subsidiary of PG&E Corp.), 2005—. Mem. Bus. Council, Calif. Commn. for Jobs and Economic Growth. Bd. govs. San Francisco Symphony. Office: PG&E Corp One Market St Spear Tower Ste 2400 San Francisco CA 94105*

GNANA ASIR, VIJI, plant pathologist; b. Trinelvelli, Tamil Nadu, India, Jan. 8, 1967; d. Samuel Gnana Asir and Florence Leelavathy; m. John Vijayaraj Sitther, Jan. 25, 1993. BS, Madras U., 1987, MS, 1989, PhD, 1997, MPhil, 1991; BEd, Annamalai U., Tamilnadu, India, 1992. Lectr. Women's Christian Coll., Madras, 1992; sr. rsch. fellow Madras U., 1993-97, project fellow, 1997-98; lectr. Loyola Coll., Madras, 1998; postdoctoral assoc. Pa. State U., University Park, 1998—. Coop. rschr. AgBio Devel., Inc., Westminster, Colo., 2000, U. Mass., Amherst, 2000—; Rockefeller Found. vis. rsch. scholar IRRI, Philippines, 1995. Contbr. articles to profl. jours. Sunday Sch. tchr. St. Thomas Ch., Madras, 1987-98, Calvary Bapt. Ch., State College, Pa., 1999—. Recipient Gate '92 fellowship, New Delhi, 1991, Outstanding Rsch. award Indian Coun. of Agrl. Rsch., New Delhi, 1992. Mem. Am. Phytopathol. Soc., Am. Soc. for Advancement of Sci., Pa. Turf Grass Coun., Sigma Xi. Avocations: music, fishing, gardening, sewing. Office: Pa State Univ 107 Buckhout Lab University Park PA 16802

GNANADESIKAN, RAMANATHAN, retired statistics educator, researcher; b. Madras, India, Nov. 2, 1932; came to U.S., 1953; s. Ambalavanan and Jegathambal Ramanathan; m. Mrudulla G., Feb. 18, 1965; children: Anand, Mukund. BSc with honors, U. Madras, 1952, MA, 1953; PhD, U. N.C., 1957. Sr. rsch. statistician Procter & Gamble Co., Cin., 1957-59; tech. staff Bell Telephone Labs., Murray Hill, N.J., 1959-68, dept. head, 1968-83; divsn. mgr. Bellcore, Morristown, N.J., 1983-86, asst. v.p., 1986-91; prof. stats. Rutgers U., Piscataway, N.J., 1991-98; prof. emeritus, 1998—. Adv. com. U.S. Bur. Census, Washington; math. scis. edn. bd. NAS, Washington; adv. com. NSF, Washington; panel chmn., NRC; various other coms. Author: Methods for Statistical Data Analysis of Multivariate Observations, 1977, 2d edit., 1997. Vol. Mended Hearts, N.J., 1995-99, Tucson, Ariz., 2000-, Northwest Interfaith Ctr., Tucson, 1999—, Elder Svcs., Edgartown, 2000—; v.p. Down Harbor Assn., Martha's Vineyard, Mass., 1979-81, pres., 1999-2002; bd. dirs. Katama Assn., Martha's Vineyard, 1997-2001. Recipient Ann. Recognition award Asian Indian Assn., 1989, Founders award, Am. Statis. Assn., 1997; cited for contbns. to State of N.J., N.J. State Legis., Trenton, 1989. Mem. Internat. Statis. Inst. (elected, v.p. 1997-2001). Avocations: world travel, gourmet foods, boating, fishing, photography. E-mail: RG@stat.rutgers.edu.

GNAT, RAYMOND EARL, librarian; b. Milw., Jan. 15, 1932; s. John and Emily (Syperek) Gnat; m. Jean Helen Monday, June 19, 1954; children: Barbara, Richard, Cynthia. BBA, U. Wis., 1954, postgrad., 1959; MS, U. Ill., 1958; MPA, Ind. U., Indpls., 1981. Page Milw. Pub. Libr., 1950-53, jr. libr., 1954, librarian, 1958-63; circulation asst. U. Ill., 1956-57, serials cataloger, 1957-58; asst. dir. Indpls.-Marion County Pub. Libr., 1963-71, dir., 1972-94. Exec. dir. Ind. Nat. Libr. Week, 1965. With AUS, 1954—56. Mem.: ALA, Bibliog. Soc. Am., Ind. Libr. Assn. (pres. 1980), Portfolio Club, Lit. Club. Home: 8246 Shadow Cir Indianapolis IN 46260-2761

GNEHM, EDWARD W., JR., ambassador; b. Nov. 10, 1944; s. Edward Sr. and Beverly (Thomasson) G.; m. Margaret Scott, June 13, 1970; children: Cheryl Lynn, Edward William III. BA, George Washington U., 1966, MA, 1968; postgrad., Am. U., Cairo, 1966—67; LLD, Thiel Coll., 2000. Head U.S. liaison office Dept. of State, Riyadh, Saudi Arabia, 1976-78, dep. chief of mission Am. Embassy Sanaa, Yemen, 1978-81, dir. jr. officer divsn. pers. Washington, 1982-83, dir. secretariat staff, 1983-84, dep. chief mission Am. Embassy Amman, Jordan, 1984-87; dep. asst. sec. def. for Near East and South Asia Dept. of Def., 1987-89, dep. asst. sec. state Bur. Near East and South Asian Affairs, 1989-90, U.S. amb. to Kuwait, 1990-94, dep. U.S. Permanent Rep. to UN, 1994-97; dir.-gen. of fgn. svc., dir. pers. U.S. Dept. of State, Washington; US amb. to Australia, 2000-2001; US amb. to Jordan, 2001—04; Shapiro prof. internat. affairs Elliot Sch. Internat. Affairs George Washington U., 2004—. Shapiro vis. prof. Elliott Sch. Internat. Affairs Geol. Washington U. Recipient Presdl. Disting. Honor award, 2000. Mem. Am. Philatelic Soc., Middle East Inst., Am. Svc. Assn., Am. Acad. Diplomacy, Omicron Delta Kappa, Sigma Chi. Presbyterian. Avocations: history, bicycling, stamps, hiking. Office: Elliott Sch Internat Affairs George Washington U 1957 E St NW Ste 401 Washington DC 20052 Personal E-mail: ambgnehm@gwu.edu.

GNICHTEL, WILLIAM VAN ORDEN, lawyer; b. Summit, N.J., Jan. 11, 1934; s. William Stone and Edith Parrot (Van Orden) G.; m. Emily Hopkins Martenet, July 11, 1959 (dec.); children: William Van Orden Jr., Edwin Martenet; m. Mary B. Gayley, June 7, 1996. BA, Trinity Coll., 1956; LLB, Columbia U., 1959. Bar: N.Y. 1961, Mass. 1997. Ptnr. Whitman & Ransom, N.Y.C., 1968-88, Chadbourne & Parke, N.Y.C., 1988-92; spl. counsel Law Firm of Salah Al-Hejailan, Riyadh, Saudi Arabia, 1986-95. Lectr. in field. Contbr. articles to profl. jours. Mem. Assn. Bar City N.Y. (mem. com. internat. security affairs 2001-04), Boston Bar Assn. (chmn. pub. policy com. bus. steering com. 1999-2004), Union Club, Knickerbocker Club (N.Y.C.), Onteora Club (Tannersville, N.Y.; exec. vp. 1974-75, pres. 1976-77, bd. dirs. 1970-77), Masons, Phi Delta Phi. Episcopalian. Address: PO Box 431 Lincoln MA 01773-0431 Personal E-mail: WVOGLAW@mindspring.com.

GNIEWEK, RAYMOND LOUIS, newspaper editor; b. Freeport, N.Y., Sept. 3, 1947; s. Edward and Jane (Park) G.; m. Noreen Ann Kopenhaver; 1 child, Edmond Louis; children by previous marriage: Brett Elizabeth, Jared Michael. BA, NYU, 1969; BS, SUNY, Brockport, 1979. Page one editor USA Today, 1982—89, sr. editor, 1989—. Theatre, dance photographer. Author computer pagination programs, 1985—. With U.S. Army, 1970-73, Vietnam. Decorated Bronze Star. Office: USA Today 7950 Jones Branch Dr Mc Lean VA 22102 E-mail: rgniewek@usatoday.com.

GO, BENEDICT ANTHONY, internist; b. Sept. 28, 1964; s. Fernando and Elsa (Lim) Go. MD, U. of the Philippines Coll of Medicine, Manila, 1990; JD, U. of Detroit Mercy Sch. of Law, 2001. Bar: Mich. 2001; diplomate Am. Bd. Internal Medicine, lic. Mich., 1991. Med. dir. Oakwood Healthcare-Brownstown, Brownstown, Mich., 1997—98; asst. med. dir. Oakwood Healthcare-Southgate, Southgate, Mich., 1998—2002. Contbr. articles to profl. jours. Mem. Assn. of Chinese Ams., Detroit, 2001—. Recipient Excellent Achievement in the Study of Health Law, CALI Excellence for the Future Award Program, 2001. Mem.: Am. Soc. Internal Medicine, Detroit Met.Bar Assn., ABA, ACP, Phi Kappa Phi. Home: 9970 Hawthorn Glen Grosse Ile MI 48138 Office: 1700 King Rd Trenton MI 48183 Business E-Mail: drbenesq@hotmail.com.

GO, MARILYN DOLAN, federal judge; b. 1950; BA, Radcliffe Coll., 1973; JD, Harvard U., 1977. Bar: N.Y. 1978, Hawaii 1990. Law clk. to Hon. William M. Marutani, Pa. Ct. Common Pleas, Phila., 1977-78; asst. U.S. atty. for ea. dist. N.Y., U.S. Dept. Justice, Bklyn., 1978-82; ptnr. Baden Kramer Huffman Brodsky & Go, N.Y.C., 1982-92; magistrate judge U.S. Dist. Ct. (ea. dist.) N.Y., Bklyn., 1993—. Mem.: Fed. Bar Coun. (trustee 1993—2000), ABA (vice chair, assn. standing com. minorities in the judiciary). Office: US Magistrate Ct 225 Cadman Plz E Brooklyn NY 11201-1818

GO, ROBERT A., management consultant; b. July 29, 1955; s. Michael and Sabina (Tan) G. BS, U Detriot, 1977; MBA, U. Santa Clara, 1981. Ptnr. Deloitte & Touche (formerly Touche Ross & Co.), Detroit, 1977—. Contbr. articles to profl. jours. Mem. Health Care Fin. Mgt. Assn., Am. Hosp. Assn., Renaissance Club. Office: Deloitte & Touche 600 Renaissance Ctr Fl 10 Detroit MI 48243-1804

GOAD, DANNY HARLAN, mechanical engineer; b. July 15, 1961; BS in Mech. Engring., Va. Tech. U., 1989; MBA, Coll. William and Mary, 1993. Engr. Newport News (Va.) Shipbuilding, 1989-96, Hoechst Celanese, Narrows, Va., 1996-98; prodn. supt. Indsl. Mfg., Albany, Ga., 1998-2000; engr. Aerofin Corp., Lynchburg, Va., 2000—01; realtor Owens and Co., 2001—. Address: 5075 Cove Rd NW Roanoke VA 24019-3503 E-mail: dhgoadpe@msn.com.

GOBAR, ALFRED JULIAN, retired economic consultant, educator; b. Lucerne Valley, Calif., July 12, 1932; s. Julian Smith and Hilda (Millbank) G.; m. Sally Ann Randall, June 17, 1957; children: Wendy Lee, Curtis Julian, Joseph Julian. BA in Econs., Whittier Coll., 1953, MA in History, 1955; postgrad., Claremont Grad. Sch., 1953-54; PhD in Econs., U. So. Calif., 1963; DHL (hon.), Whitter Coll., 2005. Asst. pres. Microdot Inc., Pasadena, Calif., 1953—57; regional sales mgr. Sutorbilt Corp., L.A., 1957—59; mktg. rsch. assoc. Beckman Instrument Inc., Fullerton, Calif., 1959—64; sr. mktg. cons. We. Mgmt. Consultants Inc., San Diego, 1964—66; ptnr., prin., chmn. bd. Darley/Gobar Assocs., Inc., San Diego, 1966—73; pres., chmn. bd. Alfred Gobar Assocs., Inc., Placentia, Calif., 1973—. Asst. prof. finance U. So. Calif., L.A., 1963-64; assoc. prof. bus. Calif. State U., L.A., 1963-68, 70-79, assoc. prof. Calif. State U.-Fullerton, 1968-69; mktg., fin. adviser 1957—; pub. spkr. seminars and convs. Contbr. articles to profl. publs. Trustee Whittier Coll., 1992—. Home: 1100 W Valencia Mesa Dr Fullerton CA 92833-2219 Office: 300 S Harbor Blvd Ste 900 Anaheim CA 92805-3721 Office Phone: 714-772-8900 x309. Business E-Mail: al@gobar.com. *I try not to be too quick to cast aside the social protocol that has taken centuries to evolve and test in order to define effective behavior.*

GOBBELL, RONALD VANCE, architect; b. Lawrenceburg, Tenn., Sept. 29, 1948; s. Dave Edward and Georgie Alice (Melton) G.; m. Phyllis Carol Gallaher, June 12, 1969; children: Dominique Marie, Caroline Megan. BArch, U. Tenn., 1971. Archtl. designer The Architects Collaborative, Cambridge, Mass., 1970; city planner U.S. Peace Corps, Karadj, Iran, 1971; archtl. designer Martin & Ortega Assocs., San Antonio, 1972-73; assoc. architect Taylor & Crabtree, Nashville, 1974-77; architect, pres. Gobbell Hays Ptnrs., Nashville, 1977—. Mem. Tenn. Archtl. and Engrig. Lic. Bd., 1988-96, chmn., 1990-91. Author: Indoor Air Quality: Solutions and Strategies, 1994; contbr. articles to profl. jours. Mem. bd. advisors Sta. WPLN, Nashville, 1979-83; mem. adv. panel for Home Living Guide, Nashville, 1985-86; mem. Nashville Mayor's Adv. Com. for Handicapped, 1985-87, Nashville Metro Hist. Zoning Commn., 1987—; bd. dirs. Hist. Nashville Inc., 1986-88. Recipient Hist. Preservation award Hist. Com. of Met. NAshville/Davidson County, 1984, 87, 89, 90, 93. Mem. AIA (grantee 1970), Mid. Tenn. AIA (chmn. conv. 1981, pres. 1985), Tenn. Soc. Architects (chmn. memberships 1979-80, treas. polit. action com. 1980-81, bd. dirs. 1984-85), Tenn. Archtl. and Engrig.Lic. Bd. (chmn. 1990-91), Nat. Coun. Archtl. Registration Bds., Nashville Area C. of C. (ctrl. cities devel. com. 1979). Democrat. Avocations: tennis, sailing. Home: 6633 Jocelyn Hollow Rd Nashville TN 37205-3910 Office: Gobbell Hays Ptnrs 217 5th Ave N Nashville TN 37219-1901

GOBEL, JOHN HENRY, lawyer; b. Oak Park, Ill., Oct. 21, 1926; s. Henry Andrew and Mary Ann (Coughlan) G.; m. Carol Zvara, Mar. 8, 1969; children: Kristina, Gregory. BA cum laude, DePaul U., 1950, JD cum laude, 1952. Bar: Ill. 1951, Md. 1975, Ohio 1976. Various positions law dept. Chgo. and North Western R.R. Co., Chgo., 1952-60, Balt. and Ohio R.R. Co., Balt., 1960-75; asst. gen. counsel Chesapeake and Ohio Ry. Co., Cleve., 1975-77, gen. solicitor, 1977-80, gen. counsel, 1980-82; v.p. govt. relations CSX Corp., Cleve., 1982-86; v.p., regional trial counsel CSX Transp., 1987. Served with U.S. Army, 1945-46. Fellow Internat. Soc. Barristers; mem. ABA (spl. com. on rules 1967-71), Ill. Bar Assn. (chmn. profl. ethics com., mem. assembly 1973-74), Nat. Assn. R.R. Trial Counsel (nat. sec. 1971-75), Soc. Trial Lawyers Ill. (dir. 1968-70), Ohio C. of C. (bd. dirs.), Ohio Pub. Expenditures Council (v.p. 1979-88), Ohio R.R. Assn. (chmn. 1979-87), W.Va. R.R. Assn. (chmn. 1975-87). Clubs: Union League (Chgo.), Law (Chgo.). E-mail: gobel-john@webtv.net.

GOBLE, PAUL, writer, illustrator, artist; b. Haslemere, Eng., Sept. 27, 1933; s. Robert John and Elizabeth Marian (Brown) G.; m. Janet A. Tiller, June 2, 1978; 1 son, Robert George; children by previous marriage: Richard, Julia. Nat. Diploma in Design with distinction, Central Sch. Art and Design, London, 1959; LHD (hon.), S.D. State U. Vis. lectr. indsl. design Central Sch. Art and Design, London, 1960-68; sr. lectr. indsl. design Ravensbourne Coll. Art and Design, London, 1968-77. Author, illustrator numerous children's books including: Custer's Last Battle, 1969, The Fetterman Fight, 1972, Lone Bull's Horse Raid, 1973, The Friendly Wolf, 1974, The Girl Who Loved Wild Horses, 1978 (Caldecott medal), The Gift of the Sacred Dog, 1980, Star Boy, 1983, Buffalo Woman, 1984, The Great Race, 1985, Death of the Iron Horse, 1987, Her Seven Brothers, 1988, Iktomi and the Boulder, 1988, Beyond the Ridge, 1989, Iktomi and the Berries, 1989, Dream Wolf, 1990, Iktomi and the Ducks, 1990, Iktomi and the Buffalo Skull, 1991, I Sing for the Animals, 1991, Crow Chief, 1992, Love Flute, 1992, The Lost Children, 1993, Iktomi and the Buzzard, 1994, Adopted by the Eagles, 1994, Hau Kola—Hello Friend, 1994, The Return of the Buffaloes, 1996, Remaking the Earth, 1996, The Legend of the White Buffalo Woman, 1998, Iktomi and the Coyote, 1998, Iktomi Loses His Eyes, Paul Goble Gallery: Three Native American Stories, 1999, Storm Makers Tipi, 2001, Mystic Horse, 2003, A Song of Creation, 2004, All Our Relatives, 2005. Fellow Royal Soc. Arts, Soc. Indsl. Artists and Designers, Grey Owl Soc. (hon.), Eagle Cir. Soc. (hon.). *I have felt the pull of the Native American tradition as long as I can remember, probably since the time my mother read to me stories of Grey Owl and Ernest Thompson Seton. As I grew up in England, I read everything I could lay my hands on about Indians. It was the books concerning the wisdom of Black Elk which finally determined my life's orientation.*

GOCHBERG, THOMAS, real estate investor, investment banker; b. Boston, Jan. 18, 1939; s. Hyman and Lee (Goredetsky) G.; m. Leatrice Eckber, Mar. 28, 1965; children: John, Sarah. AB, Columbia U., 1961. Pres., CEO Smith Barney Real Estate Corp., N.Y.C., 1969-84; dir. Smith Barney, Inc., N.Y.C., 1980-84; pres., CEO Security Capital Corp., N.Y.C., 1978—90, dir., 1978—2000. Chmn. Benjamin Franklin Savs. Assn. 1985-89, dir. 1981-89; chmn. Foster Mortgage Co., 1985-89, dir. 1981-89; pres., sole shareholder TJG Holdings Inc., 1991—; ptnr. TGM Assocs. L.P., 1991—; pres., dir. TGM Realty Corp. I, II, III, IV, V, VI, VII, X, XX, XXX, XL, 1993—. V.p. Rep. County Com. of N.Y., 1985—95, 2001—; trustee, treas. Nat. Maritime Hist. Soc., 1990—92; bd. dirs. Am. Sail Tng. Assn., 1994—2003, exec. com., chmn. devel. com., 1996—98, vice chair, 1999—2003; trustee Birch Wathan Sch., N.Y.C., 1980—88, South Street Seaport Mus., N.Y.C., 1992—, co-chair waterfront com., 1995—98, co-chair devel. com., exec. com.; bd. assocs. The Whitehead Inst. Biomed. Rsch., 1995—. With U.S. Army, 1960—63. Mem.: Pension Real Estate Assn. (pres. 1982—84, chmn. 1984—85), Ocean Cruising Club, Cruising Club of Am. (treas. NY sta. 1996—2000, rear commodore NY sta. 2000—02), Royal Western Yacht Club Eng., Univ. Club (N.Y.C.), NY Yacht Club (seamanship com. 1995—, membership com. 1998—2001). Jewish. Office: TGM Assocs 650 5th Ave Fl 28 New York NY 10019-6108 Business E-Mail: tgochberg@tgmassociates.com.

GOCHNAUER, RICHARD WALLIS, consumer products company executive; b. Kansas City, Mo., Dec. 3, 1949; s. Harry Wallis and Janet Elizabeth (Huff) G.; m. Beth Andrea Splinter, Dec. 18, 1971; children: Grant D., Mary E. BS in Indsl. Engring., Northwestern U., 1972; MBA, Harvard U., 1974. From shift supr. to pres. Schreiber Internat., Schreiber Foods, Green Bay, Wis., 1974-82; exec. v.p., gen. mgr. Dial Corp., Phoenix, 1989—93; pres. cheese div. Universal Foods, Milw., 1982-89; pres. Golden State Foods, 1993—2002; COO United Stationers Inc., Des Plaines, Ill., 2002, pres., CEO, 2002—. V.p. Nat. Cheese Inst., Washington, 1988-89. Chmn. bd. dirs. YMCA, Green Bay, 1981, Milw., 1988; mem. met. bd. dirs. YMCA, Phoenix, 1990. Mem. Soap and Detergent Assn. Office: United Stationers Inc 2200 E Golf Rd Des Plaines IL 60016*

GOCHNOUR, BEVERLY SHACIKOSKI, secondary school educator; b. Salina, Pa., Dec. 29, 1931; d. Anthony and Agnes (Petrosky) Shacikoski; m. Dwane F. Gochnour, June 11, 1960; children: Lori, Michael, Andrea. BS in Health and Phys. Edn., BS in Biol. Sci., Slippery Rock (Pa.) U., 1953; BS in Home Econs., Indiana U. Pa., 1984. Cert. tchr., Pa. High sch. tchr. Elderton (Pa.) Area Schs., 1953-55, Everett (Pa.) Area Schs., 1955-66; gymnastic sch. dir., program devel. Bedford (Pa.) Gym Scamps, 1973-84; elem. phys. edn. tchr. No. Bedford Schs., Loysburg, Pa., 1984—. Gymnastics judge U.S. Gymnastics Fedn., Pa., 1980-82; cons. in devel. phys. edn., Pa., 1984-92. Dir., choreographer Bedford County Jr. Miss Pageants, Bedford, 1964-68. Recipient Elk's award Bedford County, 1992, Citizen of Yr. award, Citation for Dedication and Svc. to Children and Community, Ho. Reps., Pa., 1993, Gatorade Sports Illustrated Game of Yr. award, 1999. Mem. AAHPERD, NEA, Pa. State Edn. Assn., Teaching Elem. Phys. Edn. Democrat. Roman Catholic. Avocations: creating and designing costumes, clothing, children's toys and games, cooking, writing. Home: 157 Maplewood Dr Everett PA 15537-6609

GOCKLEY, DAVID (RICHARD DAVID GOCKLEY), opera director; b. Phila., July 13, 1943; s. Warren and Elizabeth S. Gockley; children: Meredith, Lauren, Adam. BA, Brown U., 1965; MBA, Columbia U., 1970; DHL (hon.), U. Houston, 1992; DFA (hon.), Brown U., 1993. Dir. music Newark Acad., 1965-67; dir. drama Buckley Sch., N.Y.C., 1967-69; mgr. box office Santa Fe Opera, 1969-70; bus. mgr. Houston Grand Opera, 1970-71, assoc. dir., 1971-72, gen. dir., 1972—2005, San Francisco (Calif.) Opera, 2005—. Co-founder Houston Opera Studio, 1977. Prodr. (operas): Nixon in China (Emmy award 1988), Harvey Milk, Florencia en el Amazonas, Porgy and Bess (Tony award, Grammy award 1977), Treemonisha, A Quiet Place, Willie Stark, Resurrection, Carmen. Bd. dirs. Tex. Inst. Arts in Edn.; past pres. OPERA Am.; past chmn. Houston Theater Dist. Recipient Tony award League of N.Y Theaters and Producers, 1977, Dean's award Columbia Bus. Sch., 1982, Music Theater award Nat. Inst. Music Theater, 1985, William Rogers award, Brown U., 1995; named one of Outstanding Men Am., Nat. Jr. C. of C., 1976. Mem. OPERA Am. Avocation: tennis. Office: San Francisco Opera War Meml Open House 301 Van Ness Ave San Francisco CA 94102 Business E-Mail: dgockley@sfopera.com.

GODAGER, JANE ANN, retired social worker; b. Blue River, Wis., Nov. 29, 1943; d. Roy and Elmyra Marie (Hood) G. BA, U. Wis., 1965; MSW, Fla. State U., 1969. LCSW. Social worker III State of Wis. Dept Corrections, Wales, 1965—71; supervising psychiat. social worker I State of Calif., San Bernardino, 1972—75, La Mesa, 1975—77, psychiat. social worker San Bernardino, 1978—85; supr. mental health services Riverside (Calif.) County Dept. Mental Health, 1985—86; mental health counselor Superior Ct. San Bernardino County, 1986—2001; staff asst. to dist. dir. Calif. State Assembly, Calif., 2002, ret., 2002. Former mem. adv. bd. Grad. Sch. Social Work Calif. State U., San Bernardino, Mental Health Assn.; mem. County Hosp. Re-Use Com. Mem. commn. on sr. affairs City of San Bernardino, Calif.; mem. County Mental Health Commn.; sr. assemblyman Calif. Sr.Legislature. Mem. Nat. Assn. Social Workers, Acad. Cert. Social Workers (diplomate), Kappa Kappa Gamma Alumnae Assn. Avocations: travel, reading, music.

GODARD, JERRY HOLTON CARIS, dean, psychology professor; b. Durham, N.C., May 13, 1936; s. James McFate and Aura Holton Godard; m. Jane Godard Caris, Apr. 1977; children: Ginger Elise, Renée Denise, Michelle Leigh. BS, Auburn U., 1958; EdD, Columbia U., 1966. Asst. dean, instr. Auburn U., Ala., 1958-62; adminstrv. asst., instr. Columbia U., N.Y.C., 1962-64; dean students, asst. prof. Earlham Coll., Richmond, Ind., 1964-66; exec. dean, assoc. prof. Guilford Coll., Greensboro, NC, 1966-73, Dana prof. psychology and lit., 1975—2004, exec. v.p., dean, 2000—02; dean coll., prof. Warren Wilson Coll., Asheville, NC, 1973-75. Author: Color Them Motley, 1967, Mental forms Creating: William Blake Anticipates Freud, Jung and Rank, 1984, Eros Plays: Parts and Pieces from a Left-Handed Psychology, 1990; contbr. articles to profl. jours. Fellow NEH, Yale U., 1986. Avocations: canoeing, kayaking, running, hiking. Home: 43 Moores Pond Rd Fairview NC 28730 E-mail: jgodard@guilford.edu.

GODBEE, GARY RUSSELL, artist; b. Miami, Fla., Jan. 20, 1952; s. Jack O. and Phyllis Godbee; m. Irene C. Burtyk, Sept. 17, 1988; children: Nina, Julia. BFA, Boston U., 1974. Gallery artist First St. Gallery, N.Y.C., 1981-89; rep. artist Cudahy's Gallery, N.Y.C., 1990-92, J. Cacciola Gallery, N.Y.C., 2003—; artist Gary Godbee Fine Arts, Westfield, N.J., 1993—; painting/drawing instr. Acad. Realist Art, Workshop Program, Santa Fe, 1994, 95; painting instr. Montclair (N.J.) Art Mus. Sch., 1993—; artist Gary Godbee Portraits, Westfield, 1990—; illustrator Gary Godbee Illustration, Westfield, 1997—; commd. artist State of N.J., Dept. of Labor, Trenton, 1999-00; painting instr. Somerset Art Assn., NJ, 2000—. Guest instr. Art Student's League, N.Y.C., 1992-93; guest lectr. DuCret Sch. Arts, Plainfield, N.J., 1993; instr. painting Somerset (N.J.) Art Assn., 2000— Exhibited in group shows at Montclair Art Mus., 2005. Recipient Painting fellowship N.J. State Coun. on Arts, 1993, 2004; Merit award The Portrait Inst., 1996, Cert. of Merit, Soc. of Illustrators, 1998 Office Phone: 908-347-9653. E-mail: godbeeartwork@comcast.net.

GODBEY, ROBERT CARSON, lawyer; b. Houston, June 7, 1953; s. Charles Perry and Bobbye Lee Godbey; m. Ellen Carson, June 2, 1979. BS, BSEE magna cum laude, So. Meth. U., 1975; JD cum laude, Harvard U., 1980. Bar: U.S. Patent Office, 1981, Hawaii 1988. Telecommunications engr. Southwestern Bell, Dallas, 1975—76, Tex. Instruments, Dallas, 1976—77; assoc. Peabody, Lambert & Meyers, Washington, 1980—84; asst. U.S. atty. U.S. Dept. of Justice, Washington, 1984—87, Honolulu, 1987—91; ptnr. Godbey Griffiths Reiss Chong, 1991—. Mem. ABA, IEEE, Hawaii State Bar Assn. (past chmn. intellectual property sect. 1994-96, past chmn. tech. com., 1995-97), Phi Beta Kappa, Tau Beta Pi. Office: 2300 Pauahi Tower 1001 Bishop St Honolulu HI 96813-3429 Office Phone: 808-523-8894.

GODBOLD, CHRISTOPHER BOURKE, curator; s. Ferd and Penny Godbold. BA in history, Trinity U., 1994—98; MA in mus. sci., Tex. Tech U., 1998—2000. Student asst. Mus. of Tex. Tech U., 1998—2000; intern Heritage Farmstead Mus., Plano, Tex., 1999, Shelburne Mus., Shelburne, Vt., 2000; asst. curator Heritage Farmstead Mus., Plano, Tex., 2001—03, curator of collections, 2003—. Collections vol. Dallas Mus. of Natural History, 2001—. Co-missions chair CUMC Single LIFE class, Plano, Tex., 2004. Presdl. scholarship, Trinity U., 1994. Mem.: Am. Assn. for State and Local History, Mountain-Plains Mus. Assn., Tex. Assn. of Mus., Am. Assn. of Mus. Avocations: reading, travel, sports. Office: Heritage Farmstead Mus 1900 W 15th St Plano TX 75075 Office Phone: 972-881-0140. Office Fax: 972-422-6481. E-mail: cgodbold@heritagefarmstead.org.

GODBOLD, FRANCIS STANLEY, investment banker, security firm executive; b. Charleston, SC, Mar. 4, 1943; s. Francis Stanley and Ula Leigh (Waddey) G.; m. Lelia Elizabeth Harman, Sept. 24, 1966; children: John A., Laura H. Blair. BS in Indsl. Engring. with honors, Ga. Inst. Tech., 1965; MBA, Harvard U., 1969. V.p. Raymond, James & Assocs., Inc., St. Petersburg, Fla., 1969-74, sr. v.p., 1974-78, exec. v.p., 1978—; pres. Raymond James Fin., Inc., 1987—2002, vice chmn., 2002—. Regional firms adv. com. NY Stock Exch., 1990-93; bd. dirs. Raymond James Bank, Raymond James Fin. Pres. Baypoint Mid. Sch. Parent Action Com., 1982-83, Bay Vista Parent Action Com., 1979-80; mem. Leadership St. Petersburg, 1974—; mem. Lakewood H.S. Parent Action Com., 1984-90, pres., 1987-88, trustee Ga. Tech. Found., Inc., 2003-; dir. Ga. Tech. Indsl. and Sys. Engring. Alumni award, 1997, mem. Tampa Bay area regional devel. coun., 1995; bd. dirs.

Acad. Prep., 1999-, Elk River Properties Owners Assn. (chmn. fin. com., 2003-04, pres., 2004-), Banner Elk Heritage Found.(dir.). Capt. AUS U.S. Army, 1965—67. Mem. Securities Industry Assn. (vice chmn. so. dist. 1980, chmn. 1987, treas. 1986, exec. com. 1988-96, nat. dir. 1995-97, regional firms com. 1995-99, chmn. regional firms com. 1998, tax policy com. 1995-97, nominating com. 1997), Ga. Tech. Alumni Assn. (trustee 2002—), Harvard Club of West Coast Fla. (sec.-treas 1971-72, v.p. 1972-73, pres. 1973-74), Harvard Bus. Sch. Club (treas. 1984), St. Petersburg Country Club, Elk River Club, Diamond Creek Golf Club, Tau Beta Pi, Phi Kappa Phi, Alpha Pi Mu, Phi Delta Theta. Republican. Office: Raymond James Fin Inc 880 Carillon Pkwy Saint Petersburg FL 33716-1100 Office Phone: 727-567-5003.

GODBOLD, JOHN COOPER, federal judge; b. Coy, Ala., Mar. 24, 1920; s. Edwin Condie and Elsie (Williamson) Godbold; m. Elizabeth Showalter, July 18, 1942; children: Susan, Richard, John C., Cornelia. BS, Auburn U., 1940; JD, Harvard U., 1948; LLD (hon.), Samford U., 1981, Auburn U., 1988, Stetson U., 1994. Bar: Ala. 1948. With firm Richard T. Rives, Montgomery, Ala., 1948-49; ptnr. Rives & Godbold, 1949-51, Godbold & Hobbs and successor firms, 1951-66; cir. judge U.S. Ct. Appeals (5th cir.), 1966-81, chief judge, 1981, U.S. Ct. Appeals (11th cir.), 1981-86, sr. judge, 1987—; dir. Fed. Jud. Ctr., Washington, 1987-90. Mem. Fed. Jud. Ctr. Bd., 1976—81. With field arty. U.S. Army, 1941—46. Mem.: FBA, ABA, Montgomery County Bar Assn., Ala. Bar Assn., Phi Kappa Phi, Omicron Delta Kappa, Alpha Tau Omega. Episcopalian. Office: US Ct Appeals 11th Circuit One Church Street Montgomery AL 36104 Office Phone: 334-954-3920.

GODDARD, BRYAN LANCE, physician, director; b. July 13, 1954; s. Charles William and Alice Lance Goddard; m. Nancy Baumback, June 24, 1978; children: David, Jonathan. MD, NY Med. Coll., 1980. Diplomate Am. Bd. of Family Practice, 1983. Pvt. practice Self-employed, Gloversville, NY, 1983—87; residency faculty Wilson Family Practice Residency, Johnson City, NY, 1987—; med. dir. Johnson City Family Care Ctr., NY, 1983—91; med. dir. info. technologies United Health Services, Johnson City, NY, 1998—. Domestic cons. Lockheed-Martin Healthcare Systems, Owego, NY, 1999—2000; chmn., aids policy group NY Penn Health Systems Agy., Binghamton, 1988—89; med. cons. Broome County Child Protective Services, Binghamton, 1989—98; bd. mem. Rural Health Network of South Ctrl. NY, Whitney Point, NY, 2001—. Contbr. articles to profl. jours. Recipient Recognition for Outstanding Svc., Broome County Child Abuse Coun., 1989—97. Fellow: Am. Acad. of Family Physicians; mem.: Am. Med. Informatics Assn., Soc. of Teachers of Family Medicine. Christian, United Methodist. Office: United Health Services 40 Arch St Johnson City NY 13790

GODDARD, DONALD LETCHER, writer, editor; b. Cortland, N.Y., Apr. 16, 1934; s. Donald Gay and Adele Fournier (Letcher) G.; m. Hannah Wilke (dec. 1993), m. Helen Oppenheimer, 2000; children: Kathlyn Adele, Cornelia Marion AB, Princeton U., 1956; postgrad., Columbia U., 1958-60, NYU, 1966-68. Admitting clk. St. Vincent's Hosp., N.Y.C., 1956-58, St. Luke's Hosp., N.Y.C., 1958-59; with picture rsch. dept. Reader's Digest, N.Y.C., 1959-60; editor Am. Archives World Art, N.Y.C., 1960-65, McGraw-Hill Book Co., N.Y.C., 1966-68; dir. Editorial Photocolor Archives, N.Y.C., 1968-74; mng. editor Art News, N.Y.C., 1974-78, contbr. editor, 1978—90; editor Harry N Abrams, Inc., 1979—82; sr. editor Wildlife Conservation Soc., Bronx, 1981-96; art reviewer N.Y. Art World, 2000—. Adv. bd. art gallery Lehman Coll., Bronx, 1985-96. Author: Mark di Suvero: An Epic Reach, 1976, Harry Jackson, 1981, The Fashion Photographer, 1981, Sound/Art, 1983, American Painting, 1990, Saving Wildlife, 1995. Mem.: Internat. Assn. Art Critics. Office: 463 West St New York NY 10014-2010 Business E-Mail: goddard@wai.com.

GODDARD, EDWARD DEAN, stockbroker, accountant; b. Danville, Ill., Oct. 13, 1929; s. Oscar E. and Dorothea Goddard; m. Mary Lenny, Jan. 29, 1955; children: James, Daniel, Steven, Mark. BS in Acctg., U. Ill., 1955. CPA, Ill. Auditor Ernst & Ernst, Chgo., 1955-58; comptr., treas. various small/large corps., Chgo./Grand Rapids, Mich., 1958-69; stockbroker Kenower McArthur/The Ohio Co., Grand Rapids, 1969-80, Morgan Stanley Dean Witter, Orlando, Fla., 1980—. Writer, prodr. host TV shows: Relax It's Income Tax 13 Weeks, 1981, 89, Corporate Profile Weekly, 1982-87, Ballroom Dance Class, 13 weeks series, 1989. Candidate U.S. Congress, Dist. 7, 1994. With U.S. Army, 1946-48, Korea. Mem. Maitland Toastmasters Club (pres. 1997-98, gov. area 49 1998-99, Disting. Toastmaster 1999). Democrat. Episcopalian. Avocations: ballroom dance instructing, stamp collecting/philately. Home: 1316 Classic Dr Longwood FL 32779-5817 E-mail: edgoddard1@juno.com.

GODDARD, FRANCES BYRD, clinical social worker; b. Greensboro, N.C., Aug. 11, 1939; d. Henry Davis and Blanche Leavell Blake; m. Anthony Edward Goddard, Oct. 10, 1964; 1 child, Caroline Stuart. BA in Sociology with honors, Converse Coll., 1961; MSW, U. N.C., 1963. Lic. social worker; diplomate Am. Bd. Social Work Examiners. Social worker Children's Home Soc., Richmond, Va., 1964-71; supr. of svcs. Coun. of Culpeper, Va., 1971-74; dir. Culpeper Mental Health, 1974-76, Culpeper Family Counseling, 1976—; exec. dir. Am. Assn. State Social Work Bds., Culpeper, 1989-94. Bd. dirs. Va. Mental Health Assn. Author: 5 books in field, studies in field. Grantee, NIMH. Mem. Holloway-Amiss-Leavell Soc. (sec./treas. 1990—), Nat. Clearinghouse on Licensure, Enforcements and Regulations, Nat. Orgn. of Competency Assurance, am. Soc. Assn. Exec., Va. Commonwealth U. Social Work Adv. Bd. (past chmn.), numerous others. Episcopalian. Avocations: reading, travel, art, needlecrafts. Office: Culpeper Family Counseling Ste A 400 South Ridge Pkwy Culpeper VA 22713

GODDARD, HAZEL BRYAN, religious organization administrator; b. Mineral, Ill., Aug. 17, 1912; d. Thomas Benton and Maude Carrie (Riley) B.; m. John Howard Goddard; children: David Bryan, Joan Kathryn. BA, Judson Coll., 1966; MS, No. Ill. U., 1973; LittD (hon.), Calif. Grad. Sch. Theology, 1981. Lic. Marriage and family therapist, Fla., Colo. Clin. counselor Warrenville (Ill.) Med. Clinic, 1958-78; pres. Christian Counseling Ministries, Buena Vista, Colo., 1978-99, lectr., cons., 1978—, founder, pres. emeritus, 1999. Auhtor: Can I Hope Again, 1971, Mama, Are You There?, 1996, Somebody Else's Girl, Connie, Bob Bronson; contbr. articles to jours. Mem. Am. Pychotherapy Assn. (diplomat), Am. Assn. Marriage and Family Therapists (clin.), Nat. Assn. Social Workers, Am. Assn. Counseling and Devel. Republican. Baptist. Avocations: writing, music, hiking, fishing, travel. Office: Christian Counseling Ministries 12105 Ambassador Dr #132 Colorado Springs CO 80921 Office Phone: 719-395-6423, 719-481-8097. Business E-Mail: icmo@rockymountain.net, icmco@rockymountains.net.

GODDARD, LISA, meteorologist; b. Sacramento, Calif., Sept. 23, 1966; d. Glenn Kenneth Goddard and Marie Eleanor Betts; m. David Jeffrey Cooperberg, May 2, 1998; 1 child, Samuel Jonathan Cooperberg. PhD, Princeton U., 1995. Project scientist, Internat. Rsch. Inst. Climate Prediction, Forecasting Group, climate rsch. divsn. Scripps Inst. Oceanography, La Jolla, Calif., 1995—99; rsch. scientist, Internat. Rsch. Inst. Climate Prediction, The Earth Inst. Columbia U., Palisades, NY, 2000—. Contbr. articles and revs. to profl. jours. Global Change fellow, NASA, 1993—95. Mem.: AAAS, American Geophys. Union, Am. Meteorol. Soc. Office: IRI Earth Inst of Columbia U 61 Route 9W Palisades NY 10964 E-mail: goddard@iri.columbia.edu.

GODDARD, PETER, academic administrator, mathematical physicist; b. Woking, Surrey, U.K., Sept. 3, 1945; s. Herbert Charles and Rosina Sarah (Waite) G.; m. Helen Barbara Ross, Aug. 24, 1968; children: Linda Jane, Michael Alan Edward. BA, U. Cambridge, 1966, PhD, 1970, Sc.D, 1996. Rsch. fellow Trinity Coll., Cambridge U., 1969-73; vis. scientist CERN, Geneva, 1970-72; lectr. applied math. U. Durham, U.K., 1972-74; univ. asst. lectr. in math. U. Cambridge, 1975-76; tutor St. John's Coll., U. Cambridge, 1980-87, sr. tutor, 1983-87; univ. lectr. math. U. Cambridge, 1976-89, reader in math. physics, 1989—92, prof. theoretical physics, 1992—2004; dep. dir. Isaac Newton Inst. for Mathematical Sciences, Cambridge, England, 1991—94; master St. John's Coll., U. Cambridge, 1994—2004; chmn. local exam. syndicate U. Cambridge, 1998—2003; dir. Inst. of Advanced Study, Princeton, NJ, 2004—. Vis. prof. U. Va., Charlottesville, 1983; mem. Inst. Advanced Study, Princeton, N.J., 1974, 88, Inst. for Theoretical Physics, 1986, 90. Contbr. articles to profl. jours. Decorated comdr. Order Brit. Empire; recipient Dirac prize and medal, Internat. Ctr. for Theoretical Physics, Trieste, 1997. Fellow: Royal Soc., Trinity Coll. Dublin (hon.); mem.: London Math. Soc. (pres. 2002—03). Office: Inst for Advanced Study Einstein Dr Princeton NJ 08540 Office Phone: 609-734-8200. Business E-Mail: pgoddard@ias.edu.

GODDARD, RICHARD PATRICK, lawyer; b. South Bend, Ind., Sept. 29, 1952; s. Melvin and Barbara Louise (Dosmann) G.; m. Anne Unverzagt, Nov. 24, 1979; children: Timothy, Kathryn, Elizabeth, Margaret. BA, Oberlin Coll., 1974; JD magna cum laude, Washington and Lee U., 1979. Bar: Ohio 1979, U.S. Dist. Ct. (no. dist.) Ohio 1979, U.S. Ct. Appeals (6th cir.) 1981, U.S. Supreme Ct. 1983, U.S. Dist. Ct. (so. dist.) Ohio 1999. Assoc. Calfee, Halter & Griswold, Cleve., 1979-87, ptnr., 1987—. Mem. ABA, Ohio Bar Assn., Cleve. Bar Assn., Cleve. Athletic Club, Shaker Heights Country Club, Omicron Delta Kappa. Home: 3065 Fairfax Rd Cleveland OH 44118-4057 Office: Calfee Halter Griswold LLP 800 Superior Ave E Ste 1400 Cleveland OH 44114-2601 E-mail: rgoddard@calfee.com.

GODDARD, ROGER, education educator; s. Ralph and Charlene Goddard; m. Yvonne Goddard; 1 child, Bradley. BSBA, Ohio State U., 1989, MA, PhD, Ohio State U., 1998; MA in Tchg., U. Pitts., 1991. Cert. asst. supt. schs. Ohio, secondary sch. prin. Ohio. Acct. Deloitte, Haskins, and Sells, London, 1989, Deloitte and Touche, Pitts., 1989—90; math. tchr. Wicomico County Pub. Schs., Salisbury, Md., 1991—95; dir. of planning and rsch. Westerville (Ohio) City Schs., 1998—99; assoc. prof. of edn. U. Mich., Ann Arbor, 1999—. Recipient Culbertson award for Early Career Achievement, Univ. Coun. Ednl. Adminstrn., 2002; Postdoctoral fellow, Nat. Acad. of Edn., 2002—04. Office: U Mich 610 E University Ave Ann Arbor MI 48109-1259

GODDARD, STEVE, computer engineer, educator; b. Mpls., Minn., Nov. 28, 1963; BA, U. Minn., 1985; MS, U. NC at Chapel Hill, 1995, PhD, 1998. Sci. programmer Unisys Corp, Eagan, Minn., 1985—89; pres. S.M. Goddard & Co., Inc., Durham, NC, 1989—2000; assoc. prof. U. Nebr., Lincoln, 1998—. Contbr. articles various scientific papers. Recipient Layman award, Nebr. U. Found., 2000, J.D. Edwards Professorship, J.D. Edwards Honors Program, 2000—06; grantee Improving Aviation Safety through Real-Time Spatio-Temporal Resource Allocation, NASA, 2001-2002, A Geospatial Decision Support Sys. for Drought Risk Mgmt., NSF, 2001—05, Next Generation Enterprise Resource Planning Systems, 2001-2004, Collaborative Rsch.: Rate-Based Resource Allocation Methods for Real-Time Embedded Systems, 2002-2005, Risk Assessment and Exposure Analysis on the Agrl. Landscape, U.S. Dept. of Agr., 2002—05. Fellow: UNL Grad. Faculty; mem.: IEEE, Discrete, Exptl. and Applied Math. Achievements include patents pending for fault-tolerant firewall sandwiches; assured quality-of-service request scheduling; computer server having non-client-specific persistent connections; controlled server loading using L4/3 dispatching; controlled server loading; system and method for an application-space server cluster. Office: U Nebr 357 Avery Hall Lincoln NE 68588-0115 Office Phone: 402-472-9968. Business E-Mail: goddard@cse.unl.edu.

GODDARD, TERRY, state attorney general; BA, Harvard U., 1969; JD, Ariz. State U., 1976. Bar: Ariz. 1976, U.S. Ct. Appeals (9th cir.) 1980, U.S. Supreme Ct. 2003. Mayor City of Phoenix, 1983-90; of counsel Bryan Cave, Phoenix, 1990-94; atty. gen. State of Ariz., 2003—. Bd. dirs. Ariz Theatre Co.; former pres. Nat. League of Cities, 1989; former chmn. Ariz Mcpl. Water Users Assn., Maricopa Assn. Govts., Regional Pub. Transp. Authority, Rebuild Am. Coalition; adv. bd. State and Local Legal Ctr. With USNR, 1970—98. Mem.: ABA, Maricopa County Bar Assn., Ariz. State Bar Assn. Democrat. Office: Atty Gen 1275 W Washington St Phoenix AZ 85007 Office Phone: 602-542-4266. E-mail: ag.inquiries@azag.gov.

GODDESS, LYNN BARBARA, real estate investor; b. N.Y.C., Mar. 3, 1942; d. Eugene Daniel and Hazel Cecile (Kinzler) G.; divorced. BS, Columbia U., 1963, postgrad., 1964—66. Coord. John M. Burns Assembly Campaign, N.Y.C., 1963; dir. spl. events, projects Kenneth B. Keating Senatorial Campaign, N.Y.C., 1964; dist. dir. fund raising Muscular Dystrophy Assn. Am. Inc., N.Y.C., 1965-66; exec. acct. fund raising, pub. relations Victor Weingarten Co., N.Y.C., 1966-67, Oram Group (formerly Harold L. Oram Inc.), N.Y.C., 1967-70; dir. devel. City Ctr. Music Drama Inc., N.Y.C., 1970; sales person Whitbread-Nolan, N.Y.C., 1971-73; from asst. v.p. to sr. v.p. Cross and Brown Co., N.Y.C., 1973-1985; sr. dir., commercial real estate Cushman & Wakefield, Inc., N.Y.C., 1985—2004; chmn./CEO LYNN LLC, 2004—. Trustee Young Adult Inst.; founder, chmn. The Hazel K. Goddess Fund for Stroke Rsch. in Women., 2000—; mem. external adv. bd. Ga. Brain and Spinal Injury Rsch. Ctr., 2004—. Mem. Nat. Soc. Fund Raisers, Assn. Fund Dirs., Real Estate Bd. N.Y. (named Most Ingenious Broker Yr. 1975), Women's Forum (bd. dirs.). Personal E-mail: lbg22@earthlink.net.

GODDU, KEVIN ALBERT, secondary school educator; b. Lowell, Mass., Mar. 13, 1962; s. Albert Peter and Rita Theresa Goddu; m. Lorraine Ann Dolat, Oct. 4, 1997; children: Matthew Thomas, Alan Kevin. BA, U. of Lowell, Mass., 1989; MEd, U. of Mass., 1993; MA, Salem State Coll., Mass., 1999. Long-term substitute tchr. Nashua Sr. H.S., Nashua, NH, 1993—94, spl. edn. tchr. asst., 1994—95; social studies tchr. Timberlane Regional H.S., Plaistow, NH, 1995—. Author: (book) Monday's Mourning: A Retrospective of the 1915 Strike at the Nashua Manufacturing Company; contbr. articles to profl. jours. Bd. dirs. Nashua Hist. Soc., NH, 1991—92, 2d v.p., 1992—95; town meeting rep. Chelmsford, Mass., 2005—; mem. Chelmsford Hist. Commn., 2005—. Mem.: Am. Polit. Sci. Assn., The Omohondro Inst. of Early Am. History and Culture, The Soc. for Historians of the Early Am. Republic, New Eng. Hist. Assn., Am. Hist. Assn., Phi Theta Kappa, Pi Lambda Theta. Avocations: golf, travel. Home: 402 Wellman Ave North Chelmsford MA 01863-1364 Office: Timberlane Regional High School 36 Greenough Rd Plaistow NH 03865 Office Phone: 603-382-6541 482. Personal E-mail: kagoddu@comcast.net. E-mail: kgoddu@timberlanehs.com.

GODEKE, RAYMOND DWIGHT COOK, insurance company executive, accountant; b. San Diego, Nov. 26, 1947; s. Robert Carroll and Julia Mae (Caeser) G.; m. Norma Dean Rhodes, Oct. 31, 1966(div. 1970); 1 child, Melyssa Dawn; m. Vicki Lorraine Coleman, Feb. 19, 1972; 1 child, Kristin Francine. AA, Fullerton Coll., 1976; BA, Calif. State U.-Fullerton, 1978; MBA, Pepperdine U., 1980. Acct. Robert Johnston & Assocs., Lynwood, Calif., 1974-75; mem. acctg. staff Denny's, Inc., La Mirada, Calif., 1975-82, div. contr., 1982-87, Foster Farms, Livingston, Calif., 1987-90; indsl. health-care exec. TriCare, Irvine, Calif., 1990-92; produce distbn. exec. J.C. Produce, L.A., 1992-94; contr. Zacky Farms, South El Monte, Calif., 1994-98, Word & Brown Ins. Adminstrs. Inc., Orange, Calif., 1998—. Chmn. Arrowhead dist. Boy Scouts Am., 1986. With USMC, 1970-74. Mem. NRA, Nat. Assn. Accts. (bd. dirs. 1982-83), Inst. Internal Auditors (cert.), Inst. Mgmt. Accts. (cert.), Cert. Mgmt. Acct. Soc. So. Calif. (pres. 1999-2000), Masons (past master, 33d degree Scottish Rite), Shriners Republican. Presbyterian. Avocations: golf, reading. Office: Word & Brown 721 S Parker St Ste 300 Orange CA 92868-4732 E-mail: rgodeke@wordandbrown.com.

GODENNE, GHISLAINE DUDLEY, physician, psychotherapist, educator; b. Brussels; came to U.S., 1951; d. Pierre and Olive Dudley (Short) G. BS, Universite Catholique de Louvain, Belgium, 1948, MD, 1952. Intern Providence Hosp., Washington, 1951-52; resident in pediatrics, 1952-54; fellow in pediatrics Mayo Clinic, Rochester, Minn., 1954-57; fellow in pediatric research Johns Hopkins U., 1957-58, assoc. prof. mental hygiene, 1966-82, assoc. prof. psychiatry and pediatrics, 1966-82, psychoanalyst, 1972—, prof. psychology, 1973-90, prof. psychiatry, pediatrics, and mental hygiene, 1982—; resident in psychiatry Johns Hopkins Hosp., Balt., 1958-62, chief adolescent psychiat. service, 1964-73, dir. counseling and psychiat. services, 1973-90, dir. health svcs., 1978-88, dir. emeritus, 1990—; mem. staff various hosps. Balt., 1978-88; clin. prof. psychiatry U. Md., Balt., 1986—. Cons. psychiatrist Cylburn Children's Home, Balt., 1960-81, Catonsville (Md.) C.C., 1968-75, Good Shepherd Ctr., Balt., 1970-74, Assoc. Cath. Charity, Balt., 1970-77, Jewish Family of Children's Svcs., Balt., 1972-77, Mt. Washington Pediat. Hosp., Balt., 1974-81, Sheppard and Enoch Pratt Hosp., Balt., 1973-80, Loyola Coll., Balt., 1990-92. Mem. editorial bd.: Adolescent Psychiatry, 1978-83, Clinical Update Adolescent Psychiatry, 1982-85; contbr. articles to profl. jours. Bd. dirs. Balt. Girl Scouts Assn., 1958-60, 81-82, Met. Balt. Assn. Mental Health, 1965-69, Florence Crittendon Home, 1966-68; trustee McDonough Sch., 1975-83; pres. bd. Trustees Richmond Fellowship Md., 1975-77. Decorated Knight and Officer Order of Leopold (Belgium); recipient Christophe Plantin prize, Belgium, 1989; awarded Nobility Concession with the title of Baroness (Belgium) 1991; recipient Career Teaching award NIMH, 1963-65, Schonfeld award Am. Soc. Adolescent Psychiatry, 1995; grantee Fulbright Found., 1951-52, Parke Davis Co., 1957-58, NIMH, 1961-63. Fellow ACP, Am. Psychiat. Assn. (life), APHA (life), Am. Orthopsychiat. Assn. (life), Am. Soc. Adolescent Psychiatry (life, pres. 1981-82); mem. AAUP, Am. Psychoanalytic Soc., Md. Soc. Adolescent Psychiatry (pres. 1968-69), Md. Psychiat. Soc. (past chmn. program com., co-chmn. women's com. 1991-96), Md. State Conf. Social Welfare (past mem. child welfare com.), Am. Soc. Adolescent Medicine (charter), Am. U. and Coll. Counseling Ctr. Dirs., Internat. Soc. Adolescent Psychiatry (v.p. 1989-92, sec.-gen. 1992-95, v.p. 1995-99, co-editor monograph 2000-05), Women's Club of Johns Hopkins U. (pres. 1999-2000). Home: 15 Edgevale Rd Baltimore MD 21210-2215 Personal E-mail: g_godenne@comcast.net. Business E-Mail: gigodenn@jhmi.edu.

GODFREY, ALINE LUCILLE, music specialist, church organist; b. Providence, R.I., Dec. 4, 1943; d. Bernard Almasse and Rita Linda (Laramee) Brindamour; m. George Ruben Godfrey, Aug. 22, 1981; 1 child, Murray Aaron. BA, Rivier Coll., 1970; cert. of attendance, Am. Conservatory of Music, Fontainebleau, France, 1972; M of Music, U. Notre Dame, 1975. Cert. tchr. profl. all level music, provisional elem.-gen., Tex. Choir dir. Scituate (R.I.) High Sch., 1970-74; tchr. grade 4 McDowell Intermediate Sch., Hondo, Tex., 1974-75; tchr. grade 5 Wilson Elem. Sch., Harlingen, Tex., 1975-76; organist St. Albans Episcopal Ch., Harlingen, 1977-80; music specialist St. Mary's Sch. and Immaculate Conception Sch., Brownsville, Tex., 1977-79; choral accompanist Harlingen H.S., 1979-80; tchr. grade 6 Sam Houston Sch., Harlingen, 1980-81; music dir. St. Alban's Episcopal Sch., Harlingen, 1987-90; choral accompanist Marine Military Acad., Harlingen, 1988-90; tchr. Stuart Place Elem. Sch., Harlingen, 1990-91; msic specialist Harlingen Ind. Sch. Dist., 1991—. Organist St. James Ch., Manville, R.I., 1972-74, First United Meth. Ch., Mercedes, Tex., 1987-93; pianist, accompanist Cardinal Chorale, Harlingen, 1979-80. Composer: Songs for Tots, 1983; playwright: (musical) Why the Bells Rang, 1988, American Tribute, 1995; arranger, dir. (musicals) Across the U.S.A., 1988, Around the World at Wilson School, 1992; dir. Under the Big Top, 1989, United We Stand, 1991; music dir.: Together, 1995, Christmas in the West, 1995, Every Day is Earth Day, 1996. Vol. Hosts Program, Harlingen, 1981, Riofest, 1983, Dishman Spring Festival, Combes, Tex., 1993, 94, Wilson Spring Fest, 1996; dir. Crockett Sch. dedication, 1993. Mem.: Am. Assn. Ret. Persons, Smithsonian Instn., Tex. Music Educators Assn., PEO Sisterhood (pres. 1999—2001, v.p. 2001—). Avocations: travel, reading, sewing, aerobics, swimming. Home: PO Box 875 Combes TX 78535-0875 Office: Primera Rd PO Box 240 Harlingen TX 78551-0240 E-mail: aligod@harlingen.isd.tenet.edu.

GODFREY, CULLEN MICHAEL, lawyer, academic administrator; b. Ft. Worth, Apr. 8, 1945; s. Cullen Aubrey and Agnes (Eiland) Godfrey; m. Melinda McDonald, Aug. 29, 1970. BA, U. Tex., 1968, JD, 1970. Bar: Tex. 1969, U.S. Dist. Ct. (we. dist.) Tex. 1971, U.S. Ct. Appeals (5th cir.) 1979, U.S. Supreme Ct. 2004. Ptnr. Sloan, Muller & Godfrey, Austin, Tex., 1969-72; staff atty. Hunt Oil Co., Dallas, 1972-74, Tesoro Petroleum Corp., San Antonio, 1974-75, sr. atty., 1975-78, asst. gen. counsel, 1978-82, FINA, Inc., Dallas, 1982—88, gen. counsel, 1988-90, v.p., sec., gen. counsel, 1990-95, sr. v.p., sec., gen. counsel, 1995-2000; vice chancellor, gen. counsel U. Tex. Sys., Austin, 2000—04; ptnr. Jackson Walter LLP, 2004—. Bd. dirs. Finmar Reinsurance Co., 1991—95. Author: Legal Aspects of the Purchase and Sale of Oil and Gas Properties, 1992; contbr. articles to profl. jours. Bd. dirs. Finmar Reinsurance Co., 1991—95, Dallas County Heritage Soc., 1998—2000, United Way Met. Dallas, Inc., 1999—2000; trustee Dallas Mus. Art, 1993—95, 1998—2000; gen. campaign chmn. United Way Met. Dallas, Inc., 1999; bd. dirs. Cir. 10 Boy Scouts Am., 1999—2000; bd. dir. Greater Austin Crime Commn., 2003—; bd. dirs. United Way Capital Area, 2005—. Recipient Excellence in Corp. Practice award, Am. Corp. Counsel Assn., 1998, Jurisprudence award, Anti-Defamation League, 1999. Fellow: Travis County Bar Found. (founder), Dallas Bar Found. (sustaining life fellow), Tex. Bar Found. (sustaining life fellow); mem.: ABA (chmn. subcom. on fgn. investment reporting, internat. law sect. 1984—87), Nat. Conf. Commr. on Uniform State Laws, Greater Austin Crime Commn. (bd. dirs. 2001—, v.p. 2004—), Am. Law Inst., Ctr. Am. and Internat. Law (rsch. fellow), Greater Dallas Crime Commn. (bd. dirs. 1991—2000, chmn. bd. dirs. 1997—99), Tex. Bus. Law Found. (bd. dirs. 1990—, chmn. bd. dirs. 1995—98), Tex. Bd. Legal Specialization (bd. cert. oil, gas and mineral law), State Bar Tex. (coll. mem. 1989—, coun. oil, gas and mineral law sect. 1992—95, coun. bus. law sect. 1998—2004, chmn. bus. law sect. 2002—03, Cert. Merit 1999, 2003, Friends of CLE award 2004). Office: Jackson Walker LLP 100 Congress Ave Ste 1100 Austin TX 78701 Office Phone: 512-236-2366. Business E-Mail: mgodfrey@jw.com.

GODFREY, DONAL CHARLES, priest; b. Liverpool, Eng., Jan. 8, 1959; s. Robin Patrick Godfrey and Mary Frances McCambridge. BCL, Univ. Coll., Cork, Ireland, 1980; BL, The Hon. Soc. of King's Inns, Dublin, 1982; BPhil, Milltown Inst. of Theology and Philosophy, Dublin, 1986; MDiv/STB, U. Toronto, 1991; STL, Jesuit Sch. of Theology, Berkeley, Calif., 1993; D in Ministry, Ch. Divinity Sch. of Pacific, Berkeley, Calif., 2003. Bar: Dublin (Mem. Irish Bar) 1982; cert. Mem. Soc. of Jesus (Jesuits) Dublin, 1984. Tchr. Clongowes Wood Coll., Ireland, 1986—88; assoc. dir. campus ministry U. San Francisco, 1993—95, resident min., 1999—2003; reconciliation worker Jesuits, Belfast, Ireland, 1994—98, sabbatical Sydney, Australia, 1998—99; coord. Magis program Loyola U., Chgo., 2003—04, chaplain, 2004—. Deacon Most Holy Redeemer Ch., San Francisco, 1991—92; adj. prof. theology dept. U. San Francisco, 1993—94. Contbr. articles to profl. jours. and publs. Sec. interchurch fellowship Clergy Network, Belfast, 1997—99. Recipient Gold medal, Philos. Soc., Cork, Ireland, 1979, Law Soc., Cork, 1980; grantee grant to run ecumenical retreats, No. Ireland Govt., 1997—99. Mem.: Amnesty Internat. Avocation: hiking, novels, films, Bonsai. Home: Arrupe House 6525 N Sheridan Rd Chicago IL 60626 E-mail: donalgodfrey@yahoo.com.

GODFREY, HENRY GEORGE, surgeon; b. May Pen, Clerendon, Jamaica, Feb. 10, 1945; came to U.S., 1974. MB, BS, U. W.I., Jamaica, 1973. Diplomate Am. Bd. Surgery. Intern Columbia Coll. Phys. and Surg./Harlem Hosp. Ctr., N.Y.C., 1974-75, resident in gen. surgery, 1975-79, fellow in gastrointestinal endoscopy, 1979-80; dir. surgery North Gen. Hosp., N.Y.C., 1989-98, now attending surgeon; cons. Ralph Lauren Ctr. For Cancer Care, N.Y.C., NY. Cons. Breast Exam. Ctr. Harlem, N.Y.C., 1984—. Recipient cert. of appreciation Nat. Black Leadership Initiative on Cancer, 1992. Fellow ACS. Avocations: gardening, photography. Office: North Gen Hosp 1879 Madison Ave New York NY 10035-2709 Office Phone: 212-423-4050. E-mail: henry.godfrey@ngsc.org.

GODFREY, JOHN CARL, medicinal chemist; b. Cornelius, Oreg., Mar. 11, 1929; s. Carl H. and Ruth Emma (James) G.; m. Nancy Jane Williams, June 12, 1954; children: Laura Alexis, Helen Rebecca, Sabrina Lee. BA in Chemistry, Pomona Coll., Claremont, Calif., 1951; PhD in Organic Chemistry, U. Rochester, 1954. Rsch. chemist Shell Devel. Co., Emeryville, Calif., 1954-55; instr. chemistry Rutgers U., New Brunswick, N.J., 1955-59; asst. dir. clin. rsch. Bristol Labs., Syracuse, N.Y., 1959-79, Revlon Health Care, Tuckahoe, N.Y., 1979-86; assoc. dir. clin. rsch. Rorer Pharm. Corp., Horsham,

Pa., 1986-90; pres. Godfrey Sci. & Design, Inc., Huntingdon Valley, Pa., 1979—, cons., 1990—. Mem. sci. adv. bd. Quigley Corp., Doylestown, Pa., 1992—. Contbr. more than 60 articles to profl. jours. NSF fellow, 1951; DuPont fellow, 1952-53. Fellow Am. Inst. Chemists; mem. AAAS, Am. Soc. Microbiology, Am. Chem. Soc. Achievements include patents for formulation to deliver active zinc in treatment of common cold (U.S., U.K., Can., Europe), 57 total in U.S; elucidation of mechanism of action of zinc against common cold in humans; invention of original and enhanced formulations of major common cold intervention lozenges; Godfrey Stereomodels which uniquely demonstrate mechanisms of formation, properties and reactions. Office: Godfrey Sci & Design 1649 Old Welsh Rd Huntingdon Valley PA 19006-5835 Office Phone: 215-947-1861. Personal E-mail: jcandnj@aol.com.

GODFREY, JOHN MUNRO, economic consultant; b. San Antonio, Mar. 20, 1941; s. George Phillips and Frieda (Allen) G.; m. Nancy Porter, June 4, 1966 (div. 1976); 1 son, John Munro, Jr.; m. Flavel Mcmichael, July 30, 1994. AA, Armstrong State Coll., 1964; BBA, U. Ga., 1964, PhD, 1976. Rsch. officer, sr. fin. economist Fed. Res. Bank, Atlanta, 1969-81; sr. v.p., chief economist Barnett Banks Inc., Jacksonville, 1981-95; prin. Fla. Econ. Assocs., Jacksonville. Adj. prof. econs. and fin. Davis Coll. Bus., Jacksonville (Fla.) U., 1995-97; mem. Gov.'s Econ. Adv. Com.; mem. econ. adv. com. Am. Bankers Assn. Author: Monetary Expansion in the Confederacy, 1977. Mem. econ. adv. com. U.S. C. of C.; bd. dirs. Fla. Ballet at Jacksonville, Jacksonville Symphony Orch., Cummer Mus. of Art and Gardens; chmn. St. Vincent's (Hosp.) Found.; trustee St. Johns Country Day Sch.; vestryman St. Marks Episcopal Ch., Jacksonville; trustee, treas. St. Marks Episcopal Ch. Found. Recipient Disting. Alumnus award Terry Coll. of Bus., U. Ga., 1994. Mem. Econ. Roundtable of Jacksonville (pres. 1982-89), Nat. Assn. Bus. Economists (dir.), Am. Econ. Assn., So. Econ. Assn., U. Ga. Coll. Bus. Alumni Assn. (bd. dirs., pres.), Ponte Vedra Club, Fla. Yacht Club (bd. dirs.), Meninak Club (bd. dirs. Jacksonville chpt.), Timuquana Country Club, Epping Forest Yacht Club. Episcopalian. Office: Fla Econ Assocs 4168 Oxford Ave Jacksonville FL 32210-4464 Home: 4849 Ortega Blvd Jacksonville FL 32210-7637 E-mail: godfreyjon@aol.com.

GODFREY, MANDY JANE, psychologist; d. Alva Michael and Jane Bowers Godfrey; m. Paul Fredrick Condit, Apr. 2, 2005. BS Psychology, Valdosta State U., Valdosta, Ga., 1999, MS Clin. Counseling Psychology, 2001; PhD in Sch. Psychology, Auburn U., Auburn, Ala., 2005. Cert. Sch. Psychologist Ga., 2004. Sch. psychology inter Fla. State U., Tallahassee, 2003—04; sch. psychologist Clayton County Pub. Schs., Jonesboro, Ga., 2004—. Cons. Pvt. Clin. Psychologist, Auburn, Ala., 2002—03. Presenter (presentation) The impact of sleep on learning and behavior in school-aged children, We're people first: A celebration of diversity, (poster presentation) School violence: Assessing perceived severity and intervention strategies. Recipient Counseling and Counseling Psychology Outstanding Grad. Student, Auburn U., 2003, Clin. Counseling Psychology Student of the Yr., Valdosta State U., 2001, Phi Delta Kappa Honoree in Sch. Psychology, Phi Delta Kappa, 2003; scholar Ga. HOPE Scholarship Recipient, State of Ga., 1996-1999. Mem.: NASP (assoc.), Ga. Assn. of Sch. Psychologists (assoc.; exec. coun.: vsu rep. 1999—2001), Zeta Tau Alpha (life; membership chmn. 1998—99). Home: 306 Breezy Hill Walk Stockbridge GA 30281

GODFREY, NORMAN V., plastic surgeon; BS, Yale U., 1979; MD, Harvard U., 1973. Lic. physician N.Y., diplomate Am. Bd. Plastic Surgery. Resident in gen. surgery NYU-Bellevue Hosp. Med. Ctr., 1973—78, resident in plastic surgery, 1978—80; fellow in microvascular surgery Bellevue Hosp., 1978—80; pvt. practice plastic surgery N.Y.C., 1980—. Chief divsn. plastic surgery N.Y. VA Hosp., 1980—81; clin. instr. plastic surgery NYU-Bellevue Med. Ctr., 1980—; attending surgeon N.Y. Hosp. Med. Ctr. of Queens, 1982—, St. Vincent's Hosp. Med. Ctr., 1982—, Manhattan Eye, Ear and Throat Hosp., 1982—, N.Y. Flushing Hosp., 1997—; asst. clin. prof. surgery N.Y. Med. Coll., 1995—98, Cornell U. Med. Coll., 1998—; dir. divsn. plastic surgery N.Y. Hosp. Med. Ctr. of Queens, 1982—. Contbr. articles to profl. jours. Mem.: AMA, Am. Soc. Plastic and Reconstructive Surgeons, N.Y. State Med. Soc.

GODFREY, PHILIP M., plastic surgeon; BS, Yale U., 1974; MD, Med. Coll. Pa., 1981; DDS, U. Pa., 1981. Lic. physician N.Y., diplomate Am. Bd. Plastic Surgery. Resident in surgery Hartford Hosp., Conn.; resident in plastic surgery NY Hosp./Cornell Med. Ctr.; fellow in plastic surgery of the breast Meml. Sloan-Kettering Cancer Ctr.; pvt. practice plastic surgery Fresh Meadows, NY. Co-dir. divsn. plastic surgery N.Y. Hosp. Med. Ctr. of Queens, 1982—, attending surgeon, 1986—, St. Vincent's Hosp. and Med. Ctr., 1987—, Manhattan Eye, Ear and Throat Hosp., 1994—, N.Y. Flushing Hosp., 1997—; asst. clin. prof. surgery N.Y. Med. Coll., 1995—98, Cornell U. Med. Coll., 1998—. Contbr. articles to profl. jours. Mem.: AMA, Am. . Soc. Plastic and Reconstructive Surgeons, N.Y. State Med. Soc. Office: 16303 Horace Harding Hwy Fresh Meadows NY 11365

GODFREY, RAYMOND MICHAEL, information systems educator; b. Washington, Sept. 10, 1946; s. Raymond Godfrey and Agnes Watt; m. Nancy Roberts, Sept. 11, 1982; 1 child, Brenton. BA in Physics, Amherst Coll., 1968; MPA in Gen. Mgmt., U. So. Calif., L.A., 1975, PhD in Pub. Adminstrn., 1984. Cert. CDP Inst. for Certification of Computer Profls., N.Y. Physicist Assoc. Aero Sci. Labs., Ridgecrest, Calif., 1968—69; gen. mgr. Entropy Minus Mining & Milling, Johannesburg, Calif., 1969—72; software engr., test analyst Control Data Corp., China Lake, 1969—72; software engring. project mgr. Computer Scis. Corp., China Lake, 1973—75; pres. EM Sys. Assocs., Irvine, Calif., 1975—2002; prof. info. sys. Antioch U., Santa Monica, Calif., 1983—85, Calif. State U., Long Beach, 1995—2001. Sr. cons. RMG Assocs., L.A., 1975—90; editl. reviewer info. sys. textbooks and jours. Mem. supr.'s forum Long Beach Unified Sch. Dist., Long Beach, 1993—95; acad. program reviewer Irvine Unified Sch. Dist., Irvine, 1996—2003; co-developer U./K-12 Comty. Svc. Learning Partnerships, Long Beach, 1999—2002; Bd. dirs. Vision for Long Beach, Long Beach, 1991—93. Named univ. del. Nat. Forum on Tchg. Excellence, AAHE, 1994; fellow, UN (UNIDO), 1992, vis. scholar fellow, Claremont (Calif.) Grad. Sch. & Sch. of Theology, 1990—91. Mem.: IEEE, Ctr. for Process Studies (Claremont), Acad. Mgmt., Assn. for Computing Machinery, S.Am. Explorers Club. Office: EM Sys Assocs 2 Sandpiper Irvine CA 92604

GODFREY, RICHARD CARTIER, lawyer; b. Harvey, Ill., Sept. 25, 1954; s. Richard L. and Rosemary (Cartier) G.; m. Alice Bacon Woolsey, Aug. 27, 1983; children: John Cartier, Polly Woolsey. BA magna cum laude, Augustana Coll., 1976; JD magna cum laude, Boston U., 1979. Bar: Ill. 1979, US Dist.Ct. (no. dist.) Ill. 1979, US Dist. Ct. (ctrl. dist.) Ill. 1988, US Dist. Ct. (we. dist.) Mich. 1990, US Dist. Ct. (no. dist.) Ind. 1999, US Dist. Ct. Colo. 2002, US Ct. Appeals (7th cir.) 1983, US Ct. Appeals (6th cir.) 1988, US Ct. Appeals (8th cir.) 1994, US Ct. Appeals (10th cir.) 1996, US Ct. Appeals (11th cir.) 1997, US Ct. Appeals (5th and 9th cirs.) 1999, US Ct. Appeals (2d. cir.) 2002, US Ct. Appeals (1st cir.) 2003, US Ct. Appeals (3d cir.) 2003, US Ct. Appeals (4th cir.) 2005, US Claims Ct. 1990, US Supreme Ct. 2000. Assoc. Kirkland & Ellis, Chgo., 1979-85, ptnr., 1985—. Named one of Am. Leading. Bus. Lawyers Litig./Gen. Comml., Chambers USA, 2004—05. Mem. ABA, Ill. Bar Assn., Chgo. Bar Assn., Bd. Visitors Boston U. Sch. Law, Bd. Trustees Augustana Coll., Lawyers' Com. Nat. Ctr. State Cts., Office: Kirkland & Ellis Ste 6048 200 E Randolph Dr Chicago IL 60601 Office Phone: 312-861-2391. Office Fax: 312-861-2200. Business E-Mail: rgodfrey@kirkland.com.

GODFREY, ROBERT DOUGLAS, lawyer; b. Danbury, Conn., Sept. 11, 1948; s. Douglas and Rita (Cardinale) G. BA, Fordham U., 1970; JD, U. Conn., 1985. Bar: Conn. 1985. Com. clk. Conn. Gen. Assembly, Hartford, 1977-78; v.p. pub. affairs Greater Danbury C. of C., 1978-82; law clk. to presiding judge Probate Ct., City of Danbury, 1983; atty. Conn. Bank & Trust Co., Hartford, 1986-90; justice of the peace State of Conn., 1977—. Councilman Common Coun. of Danbury, 1985-89; mem. Charter Rev. Commn., Danbury, 1988; with Conn. Ho. of Reps., 1989—, dep. maj. leader, 1995-2005, dep. spkr., 2005—; mem. exec. com. Coun. State Govts., 1997-99; mem. exec. com. Ea. Regional Coun., Coun. State Govts., 2000—, vice chair, 2004, chair, 2005; bd. dirs. AIDS Project Greater Danbury, 2003—. With USNR, 1970-77. Recipient reproductive rights award Conn. Coalition for Choice, 1990, environ. energy award Peoples Action for Clean Energy, 1992, legis. leadership award Housing Authority Danbury, 1995, legis. svc. award Conn. Med. Assn., 1996, cmty. svc. award Midwestern Conn. Coun. on Alcoholism, 1998, Outstanding State Legislator award AFL-CIO, 2000, Apple Pie award Million Mom March, 2001, leadership award, Conn. After Sch. Svc., 2003, disting. svc. award, Conn., Freedom of Info. Commn., 2003, Disting. Svc. award Conn. Found. for Environmentally Safe Schs, 2004, legislative award, Am. Legion of Conn., 2005; recognized Conn. Coalition Against Gun Violence, 1993, spl. recognition award Danbury Dept. Elderly Svcs., 1995, sponsor youth and govt. Conn. YMCA; named Champion for Children, Conn. Coalition for Children, 1990, Legislator of Yr., Conn. Police Chiefs Assn., 1993. Cath. War Vets. (judge advocate 1978—) Home: 13 Stillman Ave Danbury CT 06810-8007 Office: Conn Ho of Reps Legis Office Bldg Rm 4107 Hartford CT 06106 Office Phone: 860-240-8500. E-mail: bob.godfrey@cga.ct.gov, robert.godfrey@snet.net.

GODFREY, ROBERT GORDON, physician; b. Wichita, Kans., June 11, 1927; s. Henry Robert and Pearl Madeline (Gaston) G.; m. Margaret Scott Ingling, June 24, 1951; children: Timothy, Katherine, Gwendolyn, Melissa. BA, U. Wichita, 1952; MD, U. Kans., 1958. Intern Boston City Hosp., 1958-59; resident in internal medicine Peter Bent Brigham Hosp., Boston, 1959-60, Colo. Gen. Hosp., Denver, 1961-63; asst. in medicine Peter Bent and Robert Brigham Hosp.-Harvard Med. Sch., 1959-61; fellow in rheumatology Robert B. Brigham Hosp., 1960-61, U. Colo., Denver, 1963-64; instr. medicine U. Kans. Med. Ctr., Kansas City, 1964-65, asst. prof. med., 1965-95, staff physician, chief arthritis sect., 1965-75; ret., 1995; assoc. chief of staff for ambulatory care VA Med Ctr., Kansas City, Mo., 1978-80; staff physician, sr. rheumatologist VA Med. Ctr., Kansas City, Mo., 1980-84; chief rheumatology sect., assoc. chief med. service ambulatory care Leavenworth VA Med. Ctr., Kans., 1984-88; cons. rheumatology Physicians Associated, Overland Park, Kans., 1988-93; pvt. cons. rheumatology, 1995—. Served with M.C., U.S. Army, 1945-47. Recipient Disting. Service award Kans. Arthritis Found., 1975 Fellow ACP, Am. Coll. Rheumatology (founding fellow original Am. Rheumatism Assn.); mem. Am. Soc. Clin. Rheumatology, Sigma Xi, Alpha Omega Alpha. Republican. Office: U Kans Med Ctr Divsn Allergy Clin Immunol Rheumatol 3901 Rainbow Blvd Kansas City KS 66160-0001 E-mail: rgodfrey@sound.net.

GODFREY, TERRI CELESTE, music educator; b. Henderson, Tex., Jan. 2, 1959; d. Francis L. and Patsy A. Wilson; m. William Timothy Godfrey, Dec. 27, 1980; children: Sarah Caroline, Zachary Wilson. MusB, Hardin Simmons U., 1982; MusM, Ariz. State U., 1989. Asst. choral dir. Perryton Jr. High/High Sch., Tex., 1984—86; instr. elem. music Iles Elem., Lubbock, 1986—87; tchr. elem. music Memphis City Schs., 1987—89; choral dir. Jefferson Mid. Sch., Abilene, Tex., 1990—92, Lincoln Mid. Sch., 1992—93, Abilene H.S., 1993—. Bd. trustees Abilene Philharm. Orch., 2000—05. Mem.: Tex. Music Educators Assn., Tex. Choral Dirs. Assn., Am. Choral Dirs. Assn. Office: Abilene High Sch 2800 North Sixth St Abilene TX 79603 Office Phone: 325-671-4232. E-mail: godfreyt@aisd.org.

GODFREY, WILLIAM ASHLEY, ophthalmologist; b. Arkansas City, Kans., May 19, 1938; BA, U. Kans., Lawrence, 1960; MD, U. Kans., Kansas City, 1965. Diplomate Am. Bd. Ophthalmology. Intern Tulane U., New Orleans, 1965-66; resident U. Kans. Sch. Medicine, 1968-71; rsch. fellow U. Calif., San Francisco, 1971-73; asst. prof., then assoc. prof. U. Kans. Sch. Medicine, 1973-84, prof. ophthalmology, 1984—. Mem. staff St. Luke's Hosp., Kansas City, Mo., 1973—, Kansas U. Med. Ctr., Kansas City, 1973—; cons. Kansas City Vets Hosp., Mo., 1973-89. Contbr. articles to profl. publs. With USAF, 1966-68. NIH fellow, 1971-73. Fellow ACP, Am. Acad. Ophthalmology (honor ward 1983), Am. Uveitis Soc.; mem. Am. COll. Physicians, AMA, Am. Fedn. Clin. Rsch., Am. Rheumatism Assn., Assn. Rsch. in Vision and Ophthalmology, Am. Math. Soc., Ocular Immunology and Microbiology Soc., Kansas City Soc. Ophthalmology, Kans. Med. Soc., Mo. Ophthalmology Soc., Jackson County Med. Soc., Am. Ophthal. Soc., Wyandotte County Med. Soc., Johnson County Med. Soc., Soc. Heed Fellows, Assn. Proctor Fellows, Kans. Ophthal. Soc., Alpha Omega Alpha. Office: U Kansas 3901 Rainbow Blvd Kansas City KS 66160-7379

GODINE, DAVID RICHARD, publishing company executive; b. Cambridge, Mass., Sept. 4, 1944; s. Morton Robert and Bernice (Beckwith) G.; m. Sara Eisenman, 1987; children: Addison Reuben, Madeline Sangree. BA (Sr. fellow), Dartmouth Coll., 1966; Ed.M., Harvard U., 1968. Founder David R. Godine, Pub., Inc., Boston, 1969, pres., 1969—, pub., editor, 1969—. Author: Renaissance Books of Science, 1970. Trustee Mass. Hort. Soc. Served with AUS, 1967. Fellow Pierpont Morgan Libr.; mem. Mass. Hist. Soc., Am. Antiquarian Soc., Soc. Printers, St. Botolph Club (Boston), Grolier Club (N.Y.C.). Office: David R Godine Pub Inc 9 Hamilton Pl Boston MA 02108-4715

GODINER, DONALD LEONARD, lawyer; b. Bronx, Feb. 21, 1933; s. Israel and Edith (Rubenstein) G.; m. Caryl Mignon Nussbaum, Sept. 7, 1958; children: Clifford, Kenneth. AB, NYU, 1953; JD, Columbia U., 1956. Bar: N.Y. 1956, Mo. 1972. Gen. counsel Stromberg-Carlson, Rochester, N.Y., 1965-71; assoc. gen. counsel Gen. Dynamics Corp., St. Louis, 1971-73; v.p., gen. counsel Permaneer Corp., St. Louis, 1973-75; ptnr. Gallop, Johnson, Godiner, Morganstern & Crebs, St. Louis, 1975-80; sr. v.p., gen. counsel, sec. Laclede Gas Co., St. Louis, 1980-98; of counsel Stone, Leyton and Gershman, P.C., St. Louis, 1999—. Editor Columbia U. Law Rev., 1955-56. Served with U.S. Army, 1956-58. Mem.: ABA, Bar Assn. of Metropolitan St. Louis. Office: Stone Leyton & Gershman PC 7733 Forsyth Blvd Ste 500 Saint Louis MO 63105-2122 Office Phone: 314-721-7011.

GODINEZ, JOSHUA RAY, social sciences educator; b. Palm Springs, Calif., June 18, 1979; s. Richard and Debra Susan Godinez. BA, U. Calif., Riverside, 2001; MA, Claremont (Calif.) Grad. U., 2002. Clear credential in single subject social sci. Calif. Outreach specialist Comty. Settlement, Riverside, Calif., 1997—2001; mktg. specialist Desert Sun Pub. Co., Palm Springs, Calif., 2000—01; tchr. social sci. AB Miller H.S., Fontana, Calif., 2001—; CSET instr. Claremont Grad. U., 2002—. Mem. adv. bd. Claremont Grad. Sch., 2002—. Recipient Tchr. Recognition award, UCSD. Mem.: Civil Rights Ctr., Social Studies Educators, Pi Lambda Theta.

GODINEZ FLORES, RAMON, bishop; b. Jamay, Jalisco, Mexico, Apr. 18, 1936; s. Ortega J. Cleofas G. and Maria del Refugio (Flores). Lic. in Philosophy, Sem. Guadalajara, (Jalisco, Mexico); theology degree, postgrad. in canon law, U. Gregoriana, Rome. Ordained priest Roman Catholic Ch., 1959. Prof., superior Diocesan Sem., Guadalajara; chaplain religious communities, Templo de San Jorge, Vallarta-San Jorge, Guadalajara; pastor Parroco de Nuestra Senora de la Luz, Guadalajara; sec. Archdiocese of Guadalajara, 1972—80, aux. bishop, 1980—. Sec. gen. Conferencia del Episcopado Mexicano, 1991—98; bishop of Aguascalientes, Mex., 1998. Contbr. articles to religious jours. Home and Office: Galeana 105 Norte Apartado Postal 167 CP 20000 Aguascalientes Mexico Office Phone: 01-449-9153261.

GODOFF, ANN, book editor; b. N.Y.C., July 22, 1949; d. Boris and Marilyn (Rosenstock) G. BFA, NYU, 1972. Sr. editor Simon & Schuster, N.Y.C., 1980-86; editor in chief Atlantic Monthly Press, N.Y.C., 1986-91; exec. editor Random House Inc., N.Y.C., 1991-96, pres., editor-in-chief, 1997—2003.

GODOFSKY, LAWRENCE, lawyer; b. Yonkers, N.Y., Mar. 30, 1938; s. Eli and Lily (Deutsch) G.; m. Thea Grace Schimel, June 11, 1961; children: Randee Felicia, Howard Charles. BA, Columbia U., N.Y.C., 1960, LLB, 1965. Bar: N.Y. 1965, Fla. 1974. Asst. counsel Mut. Life Ins. Co. of N.Y., N.Y.C., 1964-73; mem. Swann and Glass and predecessor firm, Miami, Fla., 1973-74; v.p., gen. counsel Diversified Mortgage Investors (formerly Diversified Advisors, Inc.), Miami, 1974-76; mem. Greenberg, Traurig P.A., Miami, 1976—. Mem. bd. dirs. Infants in Need, Inc., Miami, 1991—. Mem. ABA, Fla. Bar Assn., Am. Coll. Real Estate Lawyers, Am. Land Title Assn. (assoc.). Office: Greenberg Traurig PA 1221 Brickell Ave Miami FL 33131-3224

GODOFSKY, STANLEY, lawyer; b. NYC, May 24, 1928; s. Eli and Lily (Deutsch) G.; m. Elaine Gloria Weiss, Dec. 15, 1951 (dec. Feb. 1994); m. Phyllis A. Schaevitz, Jan. 16, 2000. AB, Columbia U., 1949, JD, 1951. Bar: N.Y. 1951, U.S. Supreme Ct. 1961. Assoc. Rogers & Wells, and predecessors, N.Y.C., 1951-64, ptnr., 1965-89. Co-adj. lectr. Rutgers Law Sch., 1990-91, adj. prof., 1992-93; adj. prof. Nova U. Law Sch., 1991-93; spl. asst. counsel N.Y. State Crime Commn., 1952. Bd. editors Columbia Law Rev., 1950, bd. revising editors, 1951. Trustee Jewish Cmty. Ctr. White Plains, N.Y., 1983-89; commn. on law and social action Am. Jewish Congress, 1986-98; mem. bd. advisors Lifelong Learning Soc. Fla. Atlantic U., 2004—. Mem. ABA, Am. Law Inst., N.Y. State Bar Assn., Assn. Bar City N.Y., Internat. Assn. Jewish Lawyers and Jurists (bd. govs. Am. sect. 1990-98, exec. com. and coun. 1999—), World Jurist Assn. Home: 17858 Deauville Ln Boca Raton FL 33496-2457 Personal E-mail: jenice45@bellsouth.net.

GODRIDGE, LESLIE V., bank executive; AB in History, Smith Coll.; MBA, NYU. Sr. exec. v.p. pvt. client svcs. Bank of NY, N.Y.C. Named one of 25 Women to Watch, US Banker Mag., 2003. Office: The Bank of NY One Wall Street New York NY 10286

GODSCHALK, DAVID ROBINSON, architect, urban development planner, educator; b. Enid, Okla., May 14, 1931; s. Harold J. and Helen Faye (Robinson) G.; m. Lallie Moore Kain, June 27, 1959; 1 child, David Kennedy. BA, Dartmouth Coll., 1953; B.Arch., U. Fla., 1959; M.Regional Planning, U. N.C., 1964, PhD, 1971. Vice pres. Milo Smith Assos., Tampa, Fla., 1959-61; planning dir. City of Gainesville, Fla., 1964-65; asst. prof. Fla. State U., Tallahassee, 1965-67; editor AIP Jour., Chapel Hill, N.C., 1968-71; assoc. prof. U. N.C., Chapel Hill, 1972-77, prof., 1977-94, Stephen Baxter prof. planning, 1994—2004, chmn. dept. city and regional planning, 1978-83. Cons. and expert witness in field. Author: (with others) Constitutional Issues of Growth Management, 1979, Land Supply Monitoring, 1986, Planning in America: Learning from Turbulence, 1974, Catastrophic Coastal Storms: Hazard Mitigation and Development Management, 1989, Urban Land Use Planning, 1995, Pulling Together: A Planning and Development Consensus Building Manual, 1994, Cooperating with Nature: Confronting Natural Hazards with Land Use for Planning Sustainable Communities, 1998. Natural Hazard Mitigation: Recasting Disaster Policy and Planning, 1999, Monitoring Land Supply with Geographic Information Systems, 2000; editor: (with others) Understanding Growth Management, 1989, The Planner as Dispute Resolver, 1989; editor Am. Inst. Planners Jour., 1968-71; mem. editl. bd. Jour. Planning Edn. and Rsch., 1983-89, 93-97, Jour. Am. Planning Assn., 1983-96, Jour. Archtl. Planning Rsch., 1991—, Australian Planner, 1997—. Active Town Coun., Chapel Hill, 1985-89, NC Legis. Rsch. Commn. on Statewide Comprehensive Planning, 1991-93, NC Legis. Commn. on Smart Growth, 1999-2001. With USNR, 1953-56, 61-62; comdr. Res.; ret., 1980. Recipient Disting. Alumnus award Dept. City and Regional Planning, U. N.C., 1996; Disting. Grad. Tchg. awd., U.N.C., 1999. Fellow AICP; mem. Am. Planning Assn. (bd. govs. 1978-79, Profl. Achievement award 1983, Elected Ofcl. award N.C. chpt. 1990), Am. Soc. Planning Ofcls. (bd. dir. 1974-77), Am. Inst. Cert. Planners (Svc. medal 1971), Assn. Collegiate Schs. Planning (Disting. Educator award 2002). Office: Univ NC Dept City & Regional Planning Chapel Hill NC 27599-3140 Business E-Mail: dgod@email.unc.edu.

GODSELL, RICHARD VERNON, elementary school educator; b. Detroit, June 18, 1949; s. Roy John and Bernadene Rosella Godsell; m. Marion Jures-Godsell, June 4, 1999. BS, U. Ctrl. Fla., 1997, MEd, 2004. Plumber Plumbers Union Local #98, Detroit, 1968—78; master plumber Wayne County Plumber Union Local #98, 1978—92; tchr. Orange County Pub. Schs., Ocoee, Fla., 1997—. With USN, 1966—67. Decorated Purple Heart Silver Star USN. Mem.: ASCD, Orange County Classroom Tchrs. Assn., Nat. Coun. Tchrs. Math. Democrat. Avocations: reading, swimming, walking. Home: 1030 Barons Ct Winter Garden FL 34787 Office: Ocoee Elem Sch 400 S Lakewood Ave Ocoee FL 34761 Office Phone: 407-877-5027. E-mail: godselr@ocps.net.

GODSEY, JOHN DREW, retired minister, theology educator emeritus; b. Bristol, Tenn., Oct. 10, 1922; s. William Clinton and Mary Lynn (Corns) G.; m. Emalee Caldwell, June 26, 1943 (dec. Oct. 1993); children: Emalee Lynn Godsey Murphy, John Drew Jr., Suzanne Godsey Douglas, Gretchen Godsey Brownley; m. Cozette Hapney Barker, Sept. 23, 1995. BS, Va. Poly. Inst. and State U., 1947; BD, Drew U., 1953; D.Theol., U. Basel, Switzerland, 1960. Ordained to ministry United Methodist Ch., 1952. Instr. systematic theology, asst. dean Drew U., Madison, N.J., 1956-59, asst. prof., 1959-64, assoc. prof., 1964-66, prof., 1966-68; prof., assoc. dean Wesley Theol. Sem., Washington, 1968-71, prof. systematic theology, 1971-88, emeritus prof., 1988—. Fulbright scholar U. Goettingen, W. Germany, 1964-65 Author: The Theology of Dietrich Bonhoeffer, 1960, Karl Barth's Table Talk, 1963, Preface to Bonhoeffer, 1965, Introduction and Epilogue to Karl Barth's How I Changed My Mind, 1966, The Promise of H. Richard Niebuhr, 1970; co-editor: Ethical Responsibility: Bonhoeffer's Legacy to the Churches, 1981, Dietrich Bonhoeffer, Discipleship, 2000. Mem. Montgomery County Fair Housing Assn., Md. Served with AUS, 1943-46. Recipient Disting. Svc. Alumni award, Drew U. Theol. Alumni Assn., 1995; Faculty fellow, Am. Assn. Theol. Schs., 1964—65. Mem. Am. Acad. Religion, Am. Theol. Soc. (pres. 1985-86), Bibl. Theologians, Internat. Bonhoeffer Soc. (editor newsletter 1989-92), Karl Barth Soc. N.Am., New Haven Theol. Discussion Group, Am.'s Registry of Outstanding Profls., Common Cause, Omicron Delta Kappa, Phi Kappa Phi, Alpha Zeta Democrat. Home: 8306 Bryant Dr Bethesda MD 20817-3137 Office: Wesley Theol Sem 4500 Massachusetts Ave NW Washington DC 20016-5690 *My goal has been to serve others with integrity, to do every job to the best of my ability, and to respect and further the rights and welfare of my fellow creatures on planet earth. Thus should my life be a testimony to my faith.*

GODSOE, PETER COWPERTHWAITE, retired banker; b. Toronto, Can., May 2, 1938; s. J. Gerald and Margaret (Cowperthwaite) G.; m. Shelagh Cathleen Reburn, Nov. 30, 1963; children: Craig, Cynthia, Eden. BSc in Math. and Physics, U. Toronto, 1961; MBA, Harvard U., 1966. Chartered acct., Can. Joined The Bank of N.S., various locations, 1966-71, various positions with internat., corp. banking divsn., 1971-82, vice chmn. bd., bd. dirs., 1982-92, pres., COO, vice chmn. bd., 1992—93, pres., CEO, 1993—2003, dep. chmn. bd., 1993—95, chmn. bd., 1995—2004. Chmn. Fairmont Hotels & Resorts, Sobeys Inc.; bd. dirs. Lonmin Plc, Ingersoll-Rand Co., Barrick Gold Corp., Rogers Comms. Inc., Templeton Emerging Markets Investment Trust, Onex Corp. Bd. dirs. Can. Coun. of Christians and Jews, Toronto, 1972—, Mt. Sinai Hosp., 1986; past pres. Bd. of Trade, Toronto, 1984-85; mem. adv. com. Western Bus. Sch., Richard Ivey Sch. Bus.; assoc. mem. bd. govs. Dalhousie U.; mem. chancellor's coun. Victoria U.; mem. adv. bd. Ctr. Rsch. Neurodegenerative Diseases; dir. (hon.) Sheena's Pl. Fellow Inst. Chartered Accts.; mem. Can. Bankers Assn. (past chmn.), Jr. Achievement of Met. Toronto and York Region (bd. govs.), Can. Club (past pres. 1982-83). Office: Scotia Plz 40 King St W Toronto ON Canada M5H 1H1

GODSON, GODFREY NIGEL, molecular geneticist, educator; b. London, June 20, 1936; s. Godfrey Edward and Elsie Louise (Harrington) G.; m. Barbara Cohen, Aug. 9, 1969; children: Rebecca Charlotte, Vanessa Alexandra. BS, London U., 1957, PhD, 1961, D.Sc. (hon.), 1984. Research fellow Calif. Inst. Tech., 1964-67; staff scientist Nat. Insts. Med. Research, Med. Research Council, Mill Hill, London, 1968-69; asst. prof., assoc. prof. radiobiology Yale Med. Sch., New Haven, 1969-74, 1974-80; prof./chmn. dept. biochemistry NYU Med. Sch., N.Y.C., 1980—. Mem. biochemistry sect. Nat. Bd. Med. Examiners, 1985-89; chmn. NIH, 1988-89; mem. tropical medicine and parasitology study sect. NIAID, 1985-90. Editor: Gene jour.,

1984-96, Jour. Cell and Molecular Biology, 1984-86; contbr. chpts. to books, articles to profl. jours. Mem. Am. Soc. for Biochemistry and Molecular Biology, N.Y. Acad. Scis. Office: NYU Med Sch 550 1st Ave New York NY 10016-6402

GODWIN, BENJAMIN BRAXTON, financial executive; b. Daytona Beach, Fla., Oct. 23, 1951; s. Braxton Olie and Ann (Bass) G.; m. Phyllis Hitchcock, Sept. 5, 1970; children— Allison Meredith, Lauren Elizabeth. B.B.A., Ga. State U., 1973. Asst. adminstr. Win Corp., Atlanta, 1971-73; adminstrv. officer First Atlanta Corp., 1973-78; v.p. Sun Bank-Suncoast, St. Petersburg, Fla., 1978-81, NCNB Nat. Bank, St. Petersburg, 1981-84, Home Fed. Bank, St. Petersburg, 1984-85, fin. Aanco Underwriters, Inc., St. Petersburg, 1985-86, also dir.; pres./cons. Halifax Fin. Services, Inc., 1985—; v.p., bd. dirs. Corson-Godwin & Assocs. Inc. (formerly Southeast Capital Appraisal Services, Inc.), St. Petersburg, 1986—; v.p., bd. dirs. Corwin Realty Inc., 1987—. Bd. dirs. Fla. Orch., St. Petersburg, 1983-86, St. Petersburg Neighborhood Housing Services, 1983-86; grad. Leadership St. Petersburg, 1983. Paul Harris fellow, 1985. Mem. Com. of 100. Republican. Episcopalian. Lodge: Rotary (pres. 1984-85). Office: Corson-Godwin and Assocs Inc 2201 4th St N Saint Petersburg FL 33704-4300

GODWIN, GAIL KATHLEEN, writer; b. Birmingham, Ala., June 18, 1937; d. Mose Winston and Kathleen (Krahenbuhl) G.; m. Douglas Kennedy, 1960 (div. 1961), m. Ian Marshall, 1965 (div. 1966). Student, Peace Jr. Coll., Raleigh, N.C., 1955-57; BA in Journalism, U. N.C., 1959; MA in English, U. Iowa, 1968, PhD, 1971; PhD (hon.), U. N.C., 1987, U. So.-Sewanee, 1994, SUNY, 1996. News reporter Miami Herald, 1959-60; rep., cons. U.S. Travel Service, London, 1961-65; editorial asst. Saturday Evening Post, 1966; instr. Univ. Iowa, Iowa City, 1967-71; lectr. Iowa Writer's Workshop, 1972-73, Vassar Coll., 1977, Columbia U. Writing Program, 1978, 81. Author: (novels) The Perfectionists, 1970, Glass People, 1972, The Odd Woman, 1974 (Nat. Book award nomination 1974), Violet Clay, 1978 (Am. Book award nomination 1980), A Mother and Two Daughters, 1982 (Am. Book award nomination 1982), The Finishing School, 1985, A Southern Family, 1987, Father Melancholy's Daughter, 1991, The Good Husband, 1994, Evensong, 1999, Evenings at Five, 2003; (short stories) Dream Children, 1976, Mr. Bedford and The Muses, 1983; editor: (with Shannon Ravenel) The Best American Short Stories 1985, 1985, Heart: A Personal Journey Through Its Myths & Meanings, 2001; librettist: (with Robert Starer) The Last Lover, 1975, Journals of a Songmaker, 1976, Apollonia, 1979, Anna Margarita's Will, 1981, Remembering Felix, 1987, Gregory The Great, 1996, The Other Voice: A Portrait of Hilda of Whitby in Words and Music, 1998, Magdalene At The Tomb, 1999, Abraham Remembers, 2000. Recipient Thomas Wolfe Meml. award Lipinsky Endowment of Western N.C. Hist. Assn., 1988, Janet Heidinger Kafka award U. Rochester, 1988; fellow Center for Advanced Study, U. Ill., Urbana, 1971-72; Am. specialist USIS, 1976; Nat. Endowment Arts grantee, 1974-75; Guggenheim fellow, 1975-76; recipient award in lit. Am. Acad. and Inst. of Arts and Letters, 1981 Mem. ASCAP, Authors Guild, Authors League. Home: PO Box 946 Woodstock NY 12498-0946

GODWIN, HAROLD NORMAN, pharmacist, educator; b. Ransom, Kans., Oct. 9, 1941; s. Harold Joseph and Nora Elva (Welsh) G.; m. Judy Rae Ricketts, June 9, 1963; children: Paula Lynn, Jennifer Joy. BS in Pharmacy, U. Kans., 1964; MS in Hosp. Pharmacy, Ohio State U., 1966. Lic. pharmacist, Kans., Ohio. Instr. Ohio State U. Coll. Pharmacy, Columbus, 1966-69; asst. dir. pharmacy Ohio State U., Columbus, 1966-69; dir. pharmacy U. Kans. Med. Ctr., Kansas City, 1969—2004; asst. prof. U. Kans. Sch. Pharmacy, Kansas City, 1969-74, assoc. prof., 1974-80, prof. pharmacy, 1980—, asst. dean pharmacy, 1975-89, assoc. dean pharmacy, 1989—, chmn. pharmacy practice, 1984—. John W. Webb lectr., vis. prof. Northeastern U., 1999; chmn. pharmacy exec. com. U. HealthSys. Consortium, 2001—04, exec. com., 2004—; mem. exec. com. Novation Pharmacy, 2003—05. Author: Implementation Guide to IV Admixtures, 1977; (with others) Remington's Pharmaceutical Sciences, 1980, 85, 90, 95, 2000; contbr. over 100 articles to profl. jours. Recipient Clifton J. Latiolais award Ohio State U. Residents Alumni, 1986, Disting. Alumni award Ohio State U. Coll. Pharmacy, 1995; named Tchr. of the Yr., U. Kans. Sch. Pharmacy, 2001, Harold N. Godwin Leadership Legacy award U. Kans. Med. Ctr., 2004. Fellow: Am. Soc. Health System Pharmacists (bd. dir. 1978—81, pres. 1982—83, bd. dir. rsch. and edn. found. 2002—, Harvey A.K. Whitney award 1991); mem.: Kans. Pharmacy Found. (v.p. 2004—), Am. Coun. Pharm. Edn. (bd. dir. 1988—2000, pres. 1992—96), Greater Kansas City Soc. Hosp. Pharmacists (pres. 1972), Kans. Soc. Hosp. Pharmacists (Kans. Hosp. Pharmacist of Yr. 1982, Harold N. Godwin award 1984), Kans. Pharmacists Assn. (pres 1977, Kans. Pharmacist of Yr. 1982), Am. Pharm. Assn. (Disting. Achievement award 2000). Republican. Methodist. Avocations: tennis, biking, cooking, wine tasting. Home: 10112 W 98th St Shawnee Mission KS 66212-5238 Office: U Kans Med Ctr MS4047 Rainbow Blvd At 39th St Kansas City KS 66106-7231 E-mail: HGodwin@kumc.edu.

GODWIN, HILARY A., chemistry professor, research scientist; BS in chemistry with honors, Univ. Chgo., 1989; PhD in phys. chemistry, Stanford Univ., 1994; NIH post doctoral fellow, Johns Hopkins Univ. Sch. Medicine, 1994—96. Preceptor Interdepartmental Biol. Sci. Program Northwestern Univ., 1996—, asst. prof. Dept. Chemistry and Dept. Biochemistry, Molecular Biology & Cell Biology, 1996—2001, assoc. prof., 2001—. Mem. Lurie Cancer Ctr. Northwestern Univ., 1997—, Dow Chem. Co. Rsch. Prof. in Chemistry, 2002—; prof. Howard Hughes Med. Inst., 2002—. Recipient Stanford Centennial Tchg. Asst. Award, Stanford Univ., 1992, Toxicology New Investigator Award, Burroughs Wellcome Fund, 1998, CAREER Award, Nat. Sci. Found., 1999, Camille Dreyfus Tchr.-Scholar Award, 2000, Paul Saltman Award, 2001; grantee Grad. Rsch. Fellowship, Nat. Sci. Found., 1989—92, Postdoctoral Rsch. Fellowship, Nat. Inst. Health, 1994—96. Mem.: Am. Assoc. Women in Sci., Am. Assoc. for Advancement of Sci., Biophysical Soc., Soc. for Neuroscience, Am. Chem. Soc., Iota Sigma Pi, Phi Beta Kappa. Office: Dept Chemistry Northwestern Univ 2145 Sheridan Rd Evanston IL 60208-3113 Office Phone: 847-467-3543. Office Fax: 847-491-5937. E-mail: h-godwin@northwestern.edu.

GODWIN, JOHN E., hematologist; b. Mobile, Ala., Dec. 28, 1951; married; 3 children. BS summa cum laude, U. Montevallo, Ala., 1970—74; MD, U. Ala. Sch. Medicine, Birmingham, 1974—78; MS in Epidemiology, U. Tex. Sch. Pub. Health, Houston, 1981—83. Cert. Nat. Bd. Med. Examiners, 1979, Am. Bd. Internal Medicine, 1981, in Hematology 1986. Intern, internal medicine Baylor Coll. Medicine, Houston, 1978—79, resident, internal medicine, 1979—81, fellow, internal medicine, 1981—82, fellow, hematology and oncology, 1982—83; instr., dept. medicine Ben Taub Hosp., Houston, 1981—83; fellow, hematology and oncology U. N.C., Chapel Hill, 1983—85; instr., dept. medicine N.C. Meml. Hosp., Chapel Hill, 1983—85; cons. Hines Veterans Hosp., Va., 1985—; attending physician Foster G. McGaw Hosp., 1985—, assoc. dir., spl. hematology clin. coagulation lab., dept. pathology, 1996—; asst. prof., dept. medicine and pathology Loyola U., Maywood, Ill., 1985—96, assoc. prof., dept. medicine and pathology, 1996—2002, prof., dept. medicine and pathology, 2002—. Chmn., blood utilization com. Loyola U. Med. Ctr., 1990—, dir., dept. medicine, bone marrow lab., 1993—, asst. dir., hematology and oncology fellowship program, 1995—98, mem., pharmacy & therapeutics com., 2001—; mem. Ctr. for Excellence in Molecular Hematology. Reviewer for various jours. Fellow, Coun. on Arteriosclerosis, Thrombosis and Vascular Biology, 1997. Fellow: Am. Heart Assn.; mem.: AAAS, Am. Soc. Hematology. Achievements include research in leukemia, its biology and treatment, and in clinical thrombosis. Office: Loyola Univ Chgo Cardinal Bernardin Cancer Ctr Divsn Hematology & Oncology 2160 S First Ave Maywood IL 60153 Office Phone: 708-327-3180.

GODWIN, LARRY A., protective services official; m. Nina Elizabeth Barlow; children: Anthony, Lucian, Angelina. BS in sci., Liberty U. Joined as Metro Narcotics officer Memphis Police Dept., 1973, numerous assignments as patrolman and sgt., instr., homicide investigator, fraud and document investigator, lt. crime response/bomb unit shift supervisor, 1992—98, major, comdr. crime response/bomb unit, 1998—2001, inspector, comdr. spl. svcs., 2001—03, dir. spl. ops., 2003—04; interim dir. police svcs. City of Memphis, 2004, dir. police svcs., 2004—. Mem.: Tenn. Assn. Chiefs of Police (1st v.p.). Office Phone: 901-545-5700. Office Fax: 901-545-3877.

GODWIN, MARY JO, editor, librarian, consultant; b. Tarboro, N.C., Jan. 31, 1949; d. Herman Esthol and Mamie Winifred (Felton) Pittman; m. Charles Benjamin Godwin, May 2, 1970. BA, N.C. Wesleyan Coll., 1971; MLS, East Carolina U., 1973. Cert. libr., N.C. From libr. asst. to asst. dir. Edgecombe County Meml. Library, Tarboro, 1970-76, dir., 1977-85; asst. editor Wilson Library Bull., Bronx, N.Y., 1985-89, editor, 1989-92; dir. govt. sales The Oryx Press, Phoenix, 1993-95, dir. mktg. svc., 1995-96, dir. mktg., sales and promotional svcs., 1996-2000; sr. mktg. mgr. Oryx, Greenwood Pub. Group, Westport, 2000—02; dir. mktg. Scarecrow Press and Scarecrow Edn., Rowman & Littlefield Pub. Group, Lanham, Md., 2002—. Mem. White House Conf. on Libr. and Info. Svcs. Task Force; bd. dirs. Libr. Pub. Rels. Coun., 1992-95. Bd. dirs. Friends of Calvert County Pub. Libr., 1994, Osborn Edn. Found., sec., 1997-98; mem. Ariz. Ctr. for the Book. Recipient Robert Downs award for intellectual freedom U. Ill. Grad. Sch. of Libr. Sci., 1992. Mem. ALA (bd. dirs. exhibitor roundtable 2004—, 3M/Jr. Mem. Roundtable Profl. Devel. award 1981), N.C. Libr. Assn. (sec. 1981-83), Info. Futures Inst., Ind. Librs. Exchange Roundtable (v.p., pres. elect 1994, pres. 1995-96). Democrat. Episcopalian. Office: Scarecrow Press 4501 Forbes Blvd Ste 200 Lanham MD 20706 Office Phone: 301-459-3366.

GODWIN, PAMELA JUNE, financial services executive; b. Council Bluffs, Iowa, Mar. 29, 1949; d. Fred Norman and Carol Ethel (Hatfield) Humphrey; m. Wallace Gill Godwin, Dec. 20, 1970; 1 child, Christopher Humphrey. BA in French, Pa. State U., 1970; postgrad., West Chester (Pa.) State U., 1971-74. Tchr. various schs., Phila., 1971-74; various underwriting/tng. positions Colonial Penn Ins. Co., Phila., 1974-77, mgr., 1977-81, dir., 1981-84, v.p., 1984-86, Colonial Penn Group, Inc., Phila., 1986-87, sr. v.p., 1987-88; sr. v.p. customer mgmt. Nat. Liberty Corp., Valley Forge, Pa., 1988-93; pres., COO, Acad. Ins. Group, Frazer, Pa., 1993-95, Nat. Home Life Assurance Co., Frazer, Pa., 1993-95; pres. Change Ptnrs., Inc., Havertown, Pa., 1995—96, 2002—; acting pres. Womens Way, Phila., 1998-99; pres., COO agy. divsn. GMAC Ins. Personal Lines (formerly Integon Corp.), Winston-Salem, NC, 1999—2001; pres. Change Ptnrs., Inc., Havertown, 2001—. Bd. dirs. Wheels, Inc., J.F. Kennedy Vocat. Tech. Sch., Phila., 1987-88; bd. dirs. Gt. Valley Cmty. Edn. Found., 1991-95, past pres.; mem. Westgate Hills Civic Assn., Havertown, 1974-; mem. Wharton Exec. Edn. adv. bd.; chmn. adv. bd. Pa. State Great Valley, 1996-2000, 2002-; bd. dirs. Winston-Salem C. of C., 1996-2001, Phila. Found., 2003-; mem. Com. of 200, 2000-. Named to Pa. Honor Roll of Women, 1996. Mem. Phila. Forum of Exec. Women (pres. 1998-99), Soc. Property and Casualty Underwriters (past pres. Phila. chpt. 1987-88), Phi Beta Kappa, Phi Sigma Iota. Democrat. Lutheran. Avocations: skiing, walking, reading. E-mail: changepartners@comcast.net.

GODWIN, RALPH EDWARD, retired computer operator; b. Wilmington, Del., Sept. 6, 1952; s. Ralph Winfield and Margaret Suzanne (Phillips) G. Diploma, U.S. Army S.E. Signal Sch., Fort Gordon, Ga., 1971, Armed Forces Air Intelligence, Lowry AFB, Colo., 1977, Control Data Inst., 1979; AAS, Del. Tech. & C.C., 1987. File clk. FBI, Washington, 1973-76, coding clk., 1978-79; data technician Carter/Mondale Presdl. Com., Inc., Washington, 1979-80; computer operator I Beneficial Nat. Bank (USA), Wilmington, Del., 1984-87; page Del. State Senate, Dover, Del., 1991; computer operator I New Castle County, Wilmington, 1988—2001. Dem. dist. committee person 22nd Del. State Rep. Dist. Dem. Com., Newark, Del., 1983-90; political strategist Dem. Nominee Richard A. DiLiberto, Jr., Del. State Ho. of Reps., 14th State Rep. Dist., Newark, 1992; co-campaign mgr. Dem. Nominee Barbara L. Erskine, Del. State Ho. of Reps., 27th State Rep. Dist., 1994; mem. nat. steering com. Clinton/Gore '96, 1995-96. Airman 1st class USAF, 1976-78. Named Un-sung Hero-1994 Polit. Campaign, Del. Dem. Women's Club, 1995. Mem.: William J. Clinton Presdl. Found. (founding), Am. Legion (sgt.-at-arms Newark chpt. 1994—97), Colonial Williamsburg Found. (hon. citizen 1993—), Carter Ctr., Concord Coalition, Woodrow Wilson Internat. Ctr. for Scholars, Nat. Trust for Hist. Preservation, John F. Kennedy Libr. Found. (founding mem. hon. fellows), Smithsonian Assocs. Democrat. Episcopalian. Avocations: politics, photography, travel, reading. Home: 7 Wedgewood Rd Newark DE 19711-2055

GODWIN, REBECCA T., writer, educator, editor; b. Charleston, S.C., July 9, 1950; d. Louis Bryan Thompson and Frances Carolyn Douglass; m. John K. Godwin, Oct. 28, 1968 (div. 1988); children: Melissa G. Buffington, Caroline K. Godwin; m. Deane O. Bogardus, Aug. 24, 1988. BA in English, Coastal Carolina Coll., Conway, S.C., 1977; MA in English, Middlebury Coll., 1988. Editor, writer Bennington (Vt.) Coll., 1992—2002; faculty mem. Bennington Coll., 2003—. Mem. faculty Bennington Writing Workshop, 1995, Wildacres Writing Workshops, Little Switzerland, NC, 1996, Bennington July Program, 1999, Bennington MFA in Writing Program, 2002. Author: (novels) Private Parts, 1992, Keeper of the House, 1994; contbr. fiction to Paris Rev., S.C. Rev. Epoch. Named winner, S.C. Fiction Project, 1988; fellow in lit., Nat. Endowment for Arts, 1994—95, MacDowell Colony, 2001. Mem Assoc. Writing Programs. Office: Bennington Coll Rte 67A Bennington VT 05201 Business E-Mail: rgodwin@bennington.edu.

GODWIN, SARA, writer; b. St. Louis, Feb. 18, 1944; d. Robert Franklin, Jr. and Annabelle Godwin; m. Charles D. James, May 1, 1990; children: Jane, Josh. BA, Calif. State U., 1967; postgrad., UCLA, 1968-70, U. Calif., Berkeley, 1970-71, W.I. Inst. Fairleigh Dickinson U., St. Croix, V.I., 1971-72; MA, Dominican Coll., 1974. Writer, editor Ortho Books, Std. Oil Calif., San Francisco, 1975-77; writer, editor Gannett Corp., San Rafael, Calif., 1977-79; sr. writer Shaklee Corp., San Francisco, 1979-88; freelance writer Marin County, Calif., 1988—. Featured spkr. Ask the Gardener Sta. KSFO, San Francisco, 1980—81; contbr., prodr. Raw Radio Travel, 1998—. Author: (book) Seals, 1990, Gorillas, 1990, The Angler's Companion, 1992, Hummingbirds, 1991, The Gardener's Companion, 1992 (N.Y. Times Rev., Garden Book Club selection), Landscaping Decks and Patios, 1994, Scott's See and Do: Lawns and Groundcovers, 1995; contbr. book Last Puff, 1990 (Lit. Guild selection), book The Sea, 1993; author (with others): (book) Smith and Hawken Book of Outdoor Gardening, 1996; author: (screenplays) Discover Canada, Discovering The USA; manuscript editor: All About Perennials, 1992, prin. lexicographer: Nat. Gardening Assn. Dictionary of Horticulture, 1994; scriptwriter, prodr.: China: The Middle Kingdom; contbr. CD ROM Microsoft Complete Gardening, 1996, CD ROM Frommer's Boston, 1996, articles to numerous U.S. and fgn. mags. Recipient 1st prize for personal column, Calif. Press Women, 1984. Mem.: PEN, Garden Writers Assn., Am. Soc. Journalists and Authors, Authors Guild. Avocations: reading, travel, gardening, fly fishing. Home: PO Box 1503 Ross CA 94957-1503

GOEBEL, JOHN J., lawyer; b. St. Charles, Mo., Feb. 3, 1930; s. Francis Joseph and Elizabeth (Lawler) G.; m. Margaret Mary Rooney, May 10, 1958; children— Laura, Margaret, John, Matthew BS, LL.B., St. Louis U., 1953. Bar: Mo. 1953, U.S. Dist. Ct. (ea. dist.) Mo. 1957. Jr. exec. Constrn. Escrow Service Inc., St. Louis, 1955-56; jr. ptnr. Bryan Cave LLP, St. Louis, 1956-66, ptnr., 1966-98, sr. counsel, 1998—. Served to 1st lt. USAF, 1953—55. Mem.: ABA, Mo. Bar Assn., St. Louis Bar Assn., Port Royal Club, St. Louis Club, Bellerive Country Club. Roman Catholic. Home: 245 Little Harbour Ln Naples FL 34102-7606 Office: Bryan Cave 1 Metropolitan Sq Ste 3600 Saint Louis MO 63102-2750 Business E-Mail: jjgoebel@bryancave.com.

GOEBEL, WILLIAM MATHERS, lawyer; b. Jacksonville, Ill., Nov. 5, 1922; s. William George and Elizabeth (Mathers) G.; m. Barbara Leeper, Mar. 10, 1944; children: William Mathers, Helen Elizabeth. AB, Ill. Coll., 1946; JD, U. Mich., 1948. Bar: Ill. 1949. Practice in, Carmi, 1949-59; partner Conger, Elliott, Goebel & Elliott, 1949-59; asst. gen. counsel Ill. Agrl. Assn. (and affiliated cos.), 1959-64; partner Dunn, Goebel, Ulbrich, Morel & Hundman, 1964-89, of counsel, 1989-96; lectr. dept. ednl. adminstrn. Ill. State U. Instr. Ill. Wesleyan U. Contbr. to: U. Ill. Law Forum, 1962. Mem. Ill. Citizens Com. for Uniform Comml. Code; mem. Ill. Sch. Problems Commn., 1965-69; bd. dirs. Bloomington-Normal Symphony Soc., 1967-73; trustee Brokaw Hosp., Normal, Ill., 1964-69; sec. bd. trustees, mem. exec. com. Ill. Wesleyan U., Bloomington, 1964-94. Served with AUS, World War II. Fellow Am. Bar Found., Ill. Bar Found.; mem. Am. Judicature Soc., ABA, Ill. Bar Assn. (past council chmn. comml. banking and bankruptcy law sect., mem. fed. judiciary appointments com. 1976-80), McLean County Bar Assn. (pres. 1983-84) Clubs: Bloomington Country. Lodges: Rotary. Democrat. Presbyterian. Home: 15 Arbor Ct Bloomington IL 61704

GOEHRING, KENNETH, artist; b. Evansville, Wis., Jan. 8, 1919; s. Walter A. and Ruth I. (Rossman) G.; m. Margretta M. MacNicol, Dec. 1, 1945. Student, Cass Tech. Inst., 1933-35, Meinzinger Sch. Applied Art, 1945-46, Colorado Springs Fine Arts Ctr., 1947-50. Works have appeared in over 100 exhibitions in 17 states and 20 museums; 17 one-man shows; exhibitor, Terry Inst., Miami, Symphony Hall, Boston, de Cordova Mus., Fitchburg Mus., Mass., Farnsworth Mus., Maine, Corcoran, Washington, Joslyn Meml. Mus., Nebr., Detroit Inst. Arts, Nebr. Galleries, Stanford U. Galleries, Calif, De Young Mus., San Francisco, Denver Art Mus., Okla. Art Ctr., La Jolla Art Ctr., Calif., Colorado Springs Fine Arts Ctr., 1998, 99, Boulder Mus. Avant Garde Art, 1999, others; represented in permanent collections, Sheldon Art Ctr., Lincoln, Nebr., Colorado Springs Fine Arts Ctr., Foothills Gallery, Golden Colo., Canon City Fine Arts Ctr., Colo., Washburn U. Gallery, Wichita, Kans., Swedish Consulate, Washington, El Pomar Found., Colo. Springs, in many pvt. collections Purchase awards include Colorado Springs Fine Arts Ctr., 1958; Washburn U., 1957; Am. Acad. Design, 1977. Address: 2017 W Platte Ave Colorado Springs CO 80904-3429

GOEHRING, MAUDE COPE, retired business educator; b. Persia, Tenn., Jan. 5, 1915; d. James Lawrence and Bobbie C. (Ross) Cope; m. Harvey John Goehring Jr., Aug. 12, 1950 (dec. Mar. 1992). Student, Lebanon Valley Coll., 1944-45; grad., Am. Inst. Banking, 1945; BS in Edn., Indiana U. of Pa., 1948; MEd, U. Pitts., 1950. Tchr. Penn Hills Sr. High Sch., Pitts., 1948-68, U. Pitts., 1959-60, ret., 1968; vol. chmn. ICU, operating rm. info. desk Margaret R. Pardee Meml. Hosp., Hendersonville, N.C., 1989-95; vol. Carolina Village Health Ctr., 1994-99. Coord. Henderson County Ct. House Vols., Hendersonville, 1983-89; cons., counselor tax aid program Am. Assn. Ret. Persons, Hendersonville, 1981-96. Neighborhood chmn. Girl Scouts U.S., Butler County Pa., 1976-79; bd. dirs. ARC, Hendersonville, 1986-91; sec.-treas., bd. dirs. Crime Stoppers of Henderson County, 1991-96; nat. bd. dirs. Second Wind Hall of Fame, 1991-95. Mem. AAUW (officer 1975-76), Gideon Internat. Aux. (pres., sec. 1969-70), Delta Pi Epsilon (life, Gamma chpt., pres., sec. 1956-59, nat. del. 1957). Republican. Lutheran. Avocations: gardening, crafts, sewing, reading.

GOEI, BERNARD THWAN-POO (BERT GOEI), architectural and engineering firm executive; b. Semarang, Indonesia, Jan. 27, 1938; came to U.S., 1969; naturalized, 1976; s. Ignatius Ing-Khien Goei and Nicolette Giok-Nio Tjioe; m. Sioe-Tien Liem, May 26, 1966; children: Kimberley Hendrika, Gregory Fitzgerald. BA in Fine Arts, Bandung Inst. Tech. State U. Indonesia, 1961, MA in Archtl. Space Planning, 1964; postgrad., U. Heidelberg, Germany, 1967-68. Co-owner, chief designer Pondok Mungil Interiors Inc., Bandung, 1962-64; dept. mgr., fin. advisor Gumarna Architects, Engrs. and Planners, Inc., Bandung, Jakarta, Indonesia, 1964-67; shop supr., model maker Davan Scale Models, Toronto, Ont., Can., 1968-69; chief archtl. designer George T. Nowak Architects and Assocs., Westchester, Calif., 1969-72; sr. archtl. designer Krisel & Shapiro Architects and Assocs., L.A., 1972-74; sr. supervising archtl. designer The Ralph M. Parsons A/E Co. (now Parsons Infrastructure and Tech. Group Inc.), Pasadena, Calif., 1974—. V.p. United Gruno U.S.A. Corp. Import/Export, Monterey Park, Calif., 1980-89. Mem. Rep. Presdl. Task Force, Washington, 1982—, Nat. Rep. Senatorial Com., Washington, 1983—, Nat. Rep. Congrl. Com., Washington, 1981—, Rep. Nat. Com., Washington, 1982—; active Am. Indonesian Cath. Soc. Recipient Excellent Design Achievement commendation Magneto-Hydro-Dynamics Program, 1976, Strategic Def. Initiative "Star Wars" Program, 1988, USAF Space Shuttle Program, West Coast Space-Port, 1984; scholar U. Heidelberg, 1967-68. Mem. NRA, Am. Air Gunner Assn., Tech. Comm. Soc., Indonesian Am. Soc., Dutch Am. Soc., Second Amendment Found., The Right to Keep and Bear Arms Com. Republican. Roman Catholic. Avocations: fire arms and daggers, photography, hi-tech electronics, stamps and coins, world travel. Home: 154 Ladera St Monterey Park CA 91754-2125 Office: Parsons Infrastructure & Tech Group Inc 100 W Walnut St Pasadena CA 91124-0001

GOELET, ROBERT G., investment company executive; b. Sandricourt, France, Sept. 28, 1923; s. Robert Walton and Anne Marie (Guestier) G.; m. Alexandra Gardiner Creel, Sept. 9, 1976. AB, Harvard U., 1945. Trustee Am. Mus. Natural History, 1958—, pres., 1975-88, chmn., 1988-89; trustee Boscobel Restoration Inc., 1976—, French Inst.-Alliance Francaise N.Y., 1951—, pres., 1967-93; trustee N.Y. Zool. Soc., 1951—, pres., 1971-75; trustee Carnegie Instn. of Washington, 1980—, Mus. Comparative Zoology, 1980—, N.Y. Geneal. & Biographical Soc., 1998—. Office: 540 Madison Ave Ste 21A New York NY 10022-3244

GOELL, JAMES EMANUEL, electronics company executive; b. N.Y.C., Oct. 13, 1939; s. Milton Jacob and Amy (Jacob) G.; m. Tamara Greenberg, Sept. 11, 1960; children: Lisa Sue, Fredric Scott. BEE, Cornell U., 1962, MS, 1963, PhD, 1965. Tech. staff Bell Labs., Holmdel, N.J., 1965-74; v.p., dir. engring., dir. fiber optics lab. Electro-Optical Products div. ITT, Roanoke, Va., 1974-81; pres. Lightwave Technologies, Inc., Van Nuys, Calif., 1981-85; v.p. mktg. PCO, Chatsworth, Calif., 1985-91; program mgr. HBT Ericsson Components, L.A., 1991-92; dir. engring. end-user bus. AMP, Harrisburg, Pa., 1992-97; dir. Netconnect Engring. Amp, Harrisburg, Pa., 1997-2000; mng. dir. program mgmt. TyCom, Eatontown, NJ, 2000—02; v.p. engring. Omni Guide, Cambridge, Mass., 2002—05, cons., 2005—. V.p. Middletown Twp. (N.J.) Bd. Edn. Fellow IEEE; mem. Optical Soc. Am., Am. Phys. Soc., Sigma Xi, Eta Kappa Nu, Tau Beta Pi, Phi Kappa Phi. Home: 6 Boxwood Ln Lexington MA 02420 Office Phone: 781-274-8151. E-mail: jim.goell@ieee.org.

GOELTZ, RICHARD KARL, finance company executive; b. Chgo., Sept. 11, 1942; s. Karl George and Adeline Caroline (Hoffeins) G. AB, Brown U., 1964; MBA, Columbia U., 1966; student, London Sch. Econs., 1962-63. Fin. analyst, Office Treas. Exxon Corp., N.Y.C., 1966—70; asst. treas. Joseph E. Seagram & Sons, Inc., N.Y.C., 1970—73, treas., 1973—76, v.p., fin., 1976—86, exec. v.p. fin., 1986—92; bd. dirs., CFO Nat. Westminster Bank, London, 1992—96; vice chmn., CFO Am. Express Co., N.Y.C., 1996—2000; ret., 2000. Bd. dirs. The New Germany Fund, Warnaco Group, Fed. Home Loan Mortgage Corp. (Freddie Mac), Aviva plc; trustee 59 Wall Street Fund, N.Y.C., 1984—92; bd. overseers Columbia Bus. Sch.; mem. ct. of govs. London Sch. Econs., dep. chmn., fin. and gen. purposes com. Bd. dirs., past pres. Opera Orch. of N.Y., 1980—. With USAR, 1966-72. Mem. Beta Gamma Sigma, Sleepy Hollow Country Club, Met. Opera Club, Racquet & Tennis Club, Brook Club. Republican. Episcopalian.

GOELZER, DANIEL LEE, lawyer; b. Milw., Feb. 14, 1947; s. Gerald Howard and Roberta (Hart) G.; m. Angela C. Carcone, Jan. 9, 1988; children: Christina H., Mary E., Michael W. BBA, U. Wis., 1969, JD, 1973; LLM, George Washington U., 1979. Bar: Wis. 1973, D.C. 1979, U.S. Dist. Ct. (we. dist.) Wis. 1973, U.S. Ct. Appeals (7th cir.) 1974, U.S. Ct. Appeals (2d, 9th and D.C. cirs.) 1975, U.S. Supreme Ct. 1976. Auditor Touche, Ross & Co., Milw., 1969-70; law clk. U.S. Ct. Appeals, Chgo., 1973-74; atty. SEC, Washington, 1974-78, exec. asst. to chmn., 1978-83, gen. counsel, 1983-90; ptnr. Baker and McKenzie, Washington, 1990—2002; bd. mem. Pub. Co. Acctg. Oversight Bd., Washington, 2003—. Adj. prof. Georgetown U. Law Ctr., Washington, 1986-92. Contbr. articles to profl. jours. With USAR, 1969-75. Mem. ABA, AICPA, Fed. Bar Assn. Republican. Congregationalist. Avocation: amateur radio. Home: 5941 Searl Ter Bethesda MD 20816-2022 Office: Pub Co Acctg Oversight Bd 1666 K St NW Washington DC 20006 Office Phone: 202-207-9070. Personal E-mail: dgoelzer@aol.com.

GOEMANNE, NOEL, choral director, composer; b. Poperinge, Belgium, Dec. 10, 1926; m. Janine Marloye; 3 children. Diploma, Lemmens Inst., 1948; degree in music, DMus, Madonna U.; degree, DMus, St. Joseph Coll. Organist, choirmaster Notre Dame, Rochefort, Belgium, 1949—52; recitalist Sta. NAMUR, Belgian Nat. Radio Broadcast, 1950—51; organist, choirmaster St. Mary's and Our Lady of Lourdes Chs., Victoria, Tex., 1952—55, St. Rita's Ch., Detroit, 1955—60; dir. The Croation Choir, 1956—59, Our Lady, Queen of Martrs Ch., Birmingham, 1960—68; tchr. piano, organ, harmony Palestrina Inst., Detroit, 1955—68. Instr. St. John's U., Collegeville, Minn., 1956, St. Joseph's Coll., Rensselaer, Ind., 1960—61, World Libr. Sacred Music, Cin., 1964—70, Gregorgian Inst. Chgo., 1964—70; organist, choirmaster St. Monica Ch., Dallas, 1968—71; faculty mem. Tarrant County Jr. Coll., Ft. Worth, 1972—79; organist, choirmaster Christ the King Cath. Ch., Dallas, 1972—. Recipient Pro Ecclesia award and medal, Vatican, 1977. Mem.: ASCAP, Am. Guild Organists, Am. Choral Dirs.

GOEN, BOB, television show host; b. Long Beach, Calif., Dec. 1, 1954; Grad., San Diego State U., 1976. DJ Stint Sta. KPRO-FM, Riverside, Calif., 1977-81; anchor, reporter, prodr., writer, editor Sta. KESQ-TV, Palm Springs, Calif., 1981—86; game show host Perfect Match, 1986, The Home Shopping Game, Blackout; daytime host Wheel of Fortune, 1989-92; game show host The Hollywood Game, 1992; corr., weekend anchor Entertainment Tonight, 1993—96, co-host, 1996—2004. Host Miss Universe, Miss USA, Miss Teen USA, 1993-96. Named to, Long Beach City Coll. Hall of Fame.

GOERGEN, ROBERT B., consumer products company executive; BA in Physics cum laude, Univ. Rochester, NY, 1960; MBA in Fin., Univ. Pa., 1962. With Procter & Gamble, Donaldson, Lufkin & Jenrette, McCann-Erickson; ptnr. McKinsey & Co.; founder, chmn. Blythe Inc., Greenwich, Conn., 1977—, CEO, 1978—. Chmn. Ropart Group, private equity investments, 1979—, XTRA Corp. trailer leasing, 1990—; bd. dir. Bionutrics Inc., 1999—, Protein Sciences Corp. Bd. trustees Univ. Rochester, 1982—; bd. overseers Wharton Sch., Univ. Pa., 1997—. Office: Blythe Inc 1 E Weaver St Greenwich CT 06831 Office Phone: 203-661-1926.*

GOERGER, TAMMY J., music educator; b. Grand Forks, N.D., Oct. 14, 1964; d. Stanley Hugh and JoAnne Marie Whicker; m. Edmund David Goerger, June 27, 1987; children: David, Marie, Samatha. BS in Music Edn., Moorhead State U., 1987. Music educator Lisbon (N.D.) Pub. Sch., 1988—90, St. John's Elem., Wahpeton, ND, 1990—94, Lidgerwood (N.D.) Pub. Sch., 1990—97, Wyndmere (N.D.) Pub. Sch., 1997—, Richland Sch. Dist., Colfax, ND, 2001—. Musician (flautist): FM Symphony, 1990—2001, FM Opera Co., 1990—95; guest conductor: Jamestown (N.D.) Coll., 1997. Mem.: Music Educators Assn. Avocation: reading.

GOERIG, MARIANNE, elementary school educator; b. Englewood, NJ, Mar. 26, 1945; d. Hans Scherf Franz and Margaret Louise Scherf; children: Heidi Young, Michelle Thibault. BS in edn., Wagner Coll., 1967. Cert. EMT NJ; tchr. of elem. edn. NJ, tchr. of secondary edn. NJ. Tchr. Fairlawn BOE, Fairlawn, NJ, 1967—69, US Army Dependent Sch., Zweibruchen, Germany, 1969—70, West Milford BOE, West Milford, NJ, 1970—72, 1978—. Tchr., medic Camp Hope, West Milford, NJ, 1996—. Emergency medical tech., crew chief West Milford First Aid Squad, West Milford, NJ, 1989—. Recipient 15 Yr. Svc. award, West Milford First Aid Squad, 2005, First Aid Rescue Squad award, State of NJ First Aid Coun., 2005. Mem.: Humane Soc. of U.S., Maple Rd PTO, NJ State First Aid Coun. Republican. Cath. Avocations: reading, classical music, low carb cooking. Home: 20 Lou Ann Blvd West Milford NJ 07480 Office: Maple Rd Sch 36 Maple Rd West Milford NJ 07480 Office Phone: 973-697-3606.

GOERING, JANEAL FAYE, mathematics educator; b. Newton, Kans., Dec. 14, 1962; d. Verne Maynard and Ruth Ella (Entz) Goering. Student, Grace Coll. of Bible, Omaha, 1981-82; BA in Math., Tabor Coll., 1985; MEd in Secondary Guidance and counseling, Northwestern Okla. State U., 1994. Asst. dir. South-Cen. Region Assn. Christian Schs. Internat., 1997—. Mennonite.

GOERING, KEVIN W., lawyer; b. Neodesha, Kans., July 3, 1956; BA, Univ. Kans., 1977; JD, Cornell Univ., 1981. Bar: NY 1982. Law clk. Judge Richard J. Cardamone, US Ct. Appeals 2d cir., 1983—84; ptnr., Global Litigation practice, head NY Litigation group Coudert Bros. LLP, NYC. Editor (mng.): Cornell Internat. Law Jour. Internat. law com. Media Law Resource Ctr.; dir. Volunteer Lawyers for the Arts, 2001—. Mem.: ABA (mem. Forum on Comm. Law), NY State Bar Assn. (chmn. Com. Media Law 1999—2002), Assn. Bar City of NY (mem. Com. Comm. & Media Law), Copyright Soc. USA, Phi Beta Kappa. Office: Coudert Bros LLP 1114 Ave of the Americas New York NY 10036 Office Phone: 212-626-4512. Office Fax: 212-626-4120. Business E-Mail: goeringk@coudert.com.

GOERINGER, STEVEN JOHN, telecommunications industry executive; b. Longmont, Colo., July 29, 1965; s. Ruben and Nina Goeringer; m. Kristi Lee Snell, Dec. 23, 1966; children: Heidi Lynn, Ian Scott. BS in Computer and Info. Sci., U. Md., 1999. Master intelligence analyst Nat. Security Agy., 1996. Technician telecom. sys. Nat. Security Agy., Ft. Meade, Md., 1987—89, intelligence analyst, 1989—2000; staff engr. Qwest Comm., Inc, Denver, 2000—04, tech. dir. engring., 2004—. Amateur radio operator FCC, 1988—2005; presenter in field. Contbr. articles to profl. jours. Specialist U.S. Army, 1983—87. Recipient Cryptologic Literature award, Nat. Security Agy., 1992. Mem.: IEEE, The Boulder Go Club. Conservative. Achievements include research in testing hybrid optical transport system. Avocations: violin, painting, Go, golf. Office: Qwest Communications Inc 1801 California St Suite 2620/2630 Denver CO 80202 Office Phone: 303-707-7482. Personal E-mail: clearforaction@msn.com. Business E-Mail: steven.goeringer@qwest.com.

GOERLICH, SHIRLEY ALICE BOYCE, publishing executive, educator, media consultant; b. Oneonta, NY, May 17, 1937; d. John Orlo and Nella Virginia (Bartow) Boyce; m. Robert Frank Goerlich, Aug. 19, 1967; children: Robert John, Daniel Lee. AAS, SUNY, Cobleskill, 1957; BA, Parsons Coll., 1962. Cert. tchr. N.Y., bus. owner N.Y. Tchr. Milw. Pub. Schs., 1962-64, Huntington (N.Y.) Pub. Schs., 1964-67, Fairfax (Va.) County Adult Edn., 1970-76; pvt. practice Greene, NY, 1979-83; prin., owner RSG Pub., Sidney, NY, 1984—. Cons. Cemetery Bds. Trustees, Chenango, Delaware and Otsego counties. Author: Genealogy: A Practical Research Guide, 1984 (CSG award, 1987), 2d edit., 1995, At Rest in Unadilla, Otsego Co., N.Y., 1987 (CSG award, 1988, Otsego County Local History award, 1993), Etched in Stone in Sidney, Delaware County N.Y., 1997, East Guilford Cemetery, 1997, History of Unadilla, 4 vols., 1998, History of West Unadilla, 1999, Town of Guilford, Chenango County, N.Y., Book 2 (Guilford, Chenango County, N.Y.) Cemeteries and Burial Grounds, 2000, History of East Unadilla, 2000; pub.: Author Unknown, 2001, transcribed and pub.: N.Y. State Censuses for Guilford, Chenango County, N.Y., 1855, 1865, 1875, 1905, Sidney (Delaware County, N.Y.) 1850, Masonville (Delaware County, N.Y.) 1845 along with the Civil War Roster for this town, transcriber, pub.: N.Y. State censuses for Unadilla, N.Y., 1855, 1865, 1875, 1892, Civil War roster town of Franklin, Delaware County, N.Y. Historian Town of Unadilla, NY, 1989—98; trustee Evergreen Hill Cemetery Assoc., Unadilla, 1996—2000, advisor, 2001—05; bd. dirs. Prospect Hill Cemetery Assn., Sidney, NY, 2001—04, v.p. bd. dirs., 2001, pres., 2002—03, sexton, 2003—04, area cemetery historian, 2004—, area cemetery cons., 2005—; transcriber, locator gravestones Chenango, Delaware and Otsego counties, 2004. Recipient Nat. award, Nat. Soc. New Eng. Women, 1989, award for Excellence, Otsego County Local History Adv. Com., 1995, Civil War Re-enactors award, Bainbridge Hist. Soc., 2002, Service Above Self award, Rotary Club of Greene, N.Y., 1981, Cmty. Pride award, Cmty. Found. Rotary, Sidney, NY, 2004. Mem.: Nat. Soc. New Eng. Women, N.Y. State Hist. Assn., Conn. Soc. Genealogists (Spl. Outstanding award 1989), Nat. Soc. Daus. Union Vets., Nat. Soc. DAR (chmn. 1989—91, organizing regent Gen. John Paterson chpt. 1978, Nat. Lineage Rsch. award 1987, 1988, 1989), Sidney Hist. Assn. (life). Republican. Presbyterian. Avocations: cooking, painting. Office: RSG Publishing 217 County Highway 1 Bainbridge NY 13733-3399: PO Box 441 Sidney NY 13838-0441

GOERTZ, ROGER LAMAR, retired education counselor; b. Freer, Tex., Apr. 24, 1938; s. Albert F. and Dorothy N. Goertz; m. Jean L. Humphrey, Mar. 29, 1980. BA, S.W. Tex. State U., 1964; MEd, Sul Ross State U., 1974. Cert. vocat. and spl. edn. counselor. Tchr., coach Knippa Schs., Tex., 1964—65, Sanderson Schs., Tex., 1965—69, Big Spring Schs., Tex., 1969—76, vocat. counselor, 1981—91, coord. career svcs., 1994—98; plan a counselor Plainview Schs., Tex., 1976—78; vocat. counselor Svc. Ctr. XV, San Angelo, Tex., 1978—81; ret., 1998. Mem. goals com. Future Goals City of Big Spring, 1995. Mem.: Big Spring Optimist Club (pres. 2000—02, 2004—05). Lutheran. Avocations: plays, jazz concerts, athletic events.

GOERZ, MARY ELIZABETH LARSEN, civic worker; b. Mpls., Apr. 1, 1935; d. David Paul and Myrtle Mary (Grunnet) Larsen; m. David J. Goerz, Jr., Jan. 26, 1962; children: David J. III, Karen Goerz Preston, Julie Goerz Mulvaney. BA, Stanford U., 1957. Mem. pers. staff Hewlett-Packard Corp., Palo Alto, Calif., 1960—62. Bd. dirs. Packard Children's Hosp., Stanford, Calif., 1985-96, chair art display com., 1989—; bd. dirs. Ch. of the Pioneers Found., Menlo Park, 1991—, pres., 1999-2003; bd. dirs. Lucile Packard Found. for Children's Health, Stanford, 1996-2001; chair art and display com. Packard Children's Hosp., Stanford, Calif., 1989—, founder Roth Aux., 1989, pres. Assn. of Auxs., 1986-89; pres. of corp. Menlo Park Presbyn. Ch., 1989-91, moderator women's ministries, 1989-91, elder, 1983—; pres. PTA, La Entrada Sch., Menlo Park, 1976-77; sec. Mid-Peninsula Access Corp., 1986-87. Mem. Stanford Alumni Assn., Stanford Club of Palo Alto (dir. 1971-73). E-mail: margrz@aol.com.

GOESTENKORS, GAIL, basketball coach; b. Waterford, Mich., Feb. 26, 1963; m. Mark Simons. BA, Saginaw Valley State U., 1985. Grad. asst. Iowa State U., 1985-86; asst. coach basketball Purdue U., West Lafayette, Ind., 1986-92; head basketball coach Duke U., Durham, N.C., 1992—. Coach U.S. Jones Cup Team, taiwan; head coach Festival Trials, 1991, 95; coach 1994 ACC All-Star Team, Latvia, Lithuania. Named ACC Coach of the Yr., 1995-96, 97-98, 98-99, Nat. Coach of Yr. 1999. Office: Duke University Cameron Indoor Stadium PO Box 90555 Durham NC 27708-0555

GOETHE, JOHN W., psychiatrist; b. Ridgeland, S.C. MD, Med. Coll. S.C., 1972. Diplomate Am. Bd. Psychiatry and Neurology. Resident in psychiatry Tulane Sch. Medicine, 1973—76, chief resident in psychiatry, 1975—76, instructor, 1976, asst. prof., psychiatry, 1976—81, dir. residency training, dept. psychiatry, 1977—83, assoc. dir., Adult Psychotherapy Clinic, 1979—83, assoc. prof., psychiatry, 1981—83; dir., Tulane Inpatient Psychiat. Svcs. Charity Hosp. of New Orleans, 1976—78, visiting physician in psychiatry, 1976—83; dir. Tulane Sleep Disorders Ctr., 1977—81; consulting psychiatrist V.A. Hosp., New Orleans, 1980—83; psychiat. cons. Tulane Sexual Dysfunction Clinic, 1981—83; assoc. dir. Tulane U. Hosp. Psychiatry Svc., 1981—83; supervising analyst Tulane Sch. Psychoanalytic Medicine, 1981—83; staff psychiatrist Inst. of Living, Hartford, Conn., 1983—, dir., Burlingame Ctr. for Psychiat. Rsch. and Edn., 1984—; adj. clin. assoc. prof., psychiatry Divsn. Psychoanalytic Training, N.Y. Med. Coll., 1985—, training and supervising analyst, 1986—; assoc. clin. prof., psychiatry Yale U. Sch. Medicine, 1985—; adj. prof., engring. and computer sci. Trinity Coll., Hartford, Conn., 1987—; assoc. clin. prof., psychiatry U. Conn. Sch. Medicine, 1991—; med. dir. quality mgmt. Hartford (Conn.) Hosp., 1997—; chief profl. svcs. Capital Region Mental Health Ctr., State of Conn. Dept. Mental Health and Addiction Svcs., 1997—2003; med. dir. Continuing Edn., 1999—. Contbr. articles to profl. jours., chpt. to book. Fellow: Am. Psychiat. Assn.; mem.: Am. Acad. Psychoanalysis. Office: Inst Living 200 Retreat Ave Hartford CT 06106

GOETSCH, HALEY MELISSA, psychologist; b. San Francisco, Dec. 21, 1970; d. Gerald Edward and Janet Gale Goetsch; 1 child, Sonja Anne Goetsch Avila. BA in Psychology, Humboldt State U., 1994, MA in Psychology, 2000. Cert. sch. psychology and counseling; tchr. Intern sch. psychologist Middletown (Calif.) Unified Sch. Dist., 2000—01; sch. psychologist, program specialist Calaveras County Office Edn., Angels Camp, Calif., 2001—. Mem. Student Attendance Rev. Bd., Angels Camp, 2001—03. Mem. Sierra Club, Murphys, Calif., 2003—04. Mem.: Am. Assn. Sch. Counselors, Nat. Assn. Sch. Psychologists, Calif. Assn. Sch. Psychology, Nat. Honor Soc. Green Party. Lutheran. Avocations: kayaking, yoga, hiking, camping. Home: PO Box 2154 Murphys CA 95247 Office: Calaveras County Office Edn 760 Main St Angels Camp CA 95221

GOETZ, ABRAHAM, retired mathematics professor; b. Grybów, Poland, Apr. 8, 1926; arrived in U.S., 1965; s. David and Regina Goetz; m. Janina Kupperman, July 28, 1955; children: George S., Victor S. MS, U. Wroclaw, Poland, 1949; PhD, Polish Acad. Scis., Warsaw, 1957. With U. Wroclaw, 1960—64; assoc. prof. U. Notre Dame, Ind., 1965—2000, prof. emeritus, 2000—. Vis. prof. U. Notre Dame, 1962, Technion U., Haifa, Israel, 1973—74. Mem.: Math. Assn. Am., Am. Math. Soc. Home: 17913 Ashmont Pl South Bend IN 46635 Office: U Notre Dame 255 Hurley Notre Dame IN 46556 Business E-Mail: goetz.2@nd.edu.

GOETZ, CHARLES JOHN, law and economics educator; b. NYC, 1939; AB, Providence Coll., 1961; PhD, U. Va., 1965. Asst. prof. U. Ill., 1965-67; assoc. prof. Va. Poly. Inst. & State U., 1967-72, prof. economics, dir. grad. program economics, 1972-75; vis. prof. U. Va. Sch. Law, Charlottesville, 1975-76, prof., 1976-83, Joseph M. Hartfield prof. law, 1983—. Co-author: Social Security Hearings and Appeals: A Study of the Social Security Administration Hearing System, 1978, Using Experts: Pretrial Preparation, Trial Testimony and Settling Cases, 1985, Antitrust Law: Interpretation and Implementation, 1998, 2002; author: Cases and Materials on Law and Economics, 1984, Uncommon Common-Sense vs. Conventional Wisdom: The Virginia School of Economics, 1991. NATO postdoctoral fellow, 1964-65. Mem. Phi Beta Kappa. Office: U Va Sch Law 580 Massie Rd Charlottesville VA 22903-1789 Office Phone: 434-924-3456. E-mail: cjg4t@virginia.edu.*

GOETZ, JACK RALPH, dean; b. LA, Mar. 4, 1955; s. Theodore Arthur G. and Jane Small; m. Reva Garfunkel, Aug. 1, 1982; children: Rachelle Elisabeth, Jason Randall. BA, San Diego State U., 1976; JD, Boston U., 1979; MBA, Pepperdine U., 1990. 2d v.p. Harcourt, Brace & Jovanovich Legal & Profl. Pubs., Inc., Chgo., 1979-89; CEO Am. Profl. Testing Svcs., Inc., Santa Monica, Calif., 1989-95; v.p. West Profl. Tng. Programs, Inc., Mpls., 1995-97, Kaplan Ednl. Svcs., Inc., N.Y.C., 1997—; pres., dean Concord U. Sch. Law, LA, 1998—2004, dean emeritus, 2004—. Trustee Distance Edn. and Tng. Coun., 2000-2002; mem. Law Sch. Coun., 2001—. Mem. State Bar Calif., Cheviot Hills Pony Baseball Assn. (bd. dirs. 1996-2001). Avocations: historian, sports.

GOETZ, KENNETH LEE, cardiovascular physiologist, research consultant, writer; b. Java, S.D., Jan. 7, 1932; m. Shirley Anne Caldwell, July 14, 1962 (div. 2003); children: Gregory Earl, Anne Katherine. PhD, U. Wis., 1963; MD, U. Kans., 1967. Instr., asst. prof. dept. physiology U. Kans. Med. Ctr., Kansas City, 1963-69; med. intern St. Luke's Hosp., Kansas City, 1969, head, div. of exptl. medicine, 1970-91, dir. rsch., 1980-91. Adj. prof. dept. physiology U. Kans. Med. Ctr., 1976-92; vis. prof. U. Kuopio, Finland, 1985, 91, U. Munich, 1992; vis. scientist German Inst. Aerospace Medicine, Cologne, 1993-94. Author (memoir): Bending the Twig, 2002. Recipient Alexander von Humboldt award, 1992. Fellow Am. Phys. Soc. (circulation sect.); mem. Am. Physiol. Soc., Alexander von Humboldt Assn. of Am. Achievements include research in Neurohumoral control of body fluid balance; influence of vasoctive peptides on hemodynamics; Vasopressin, atriopeptin, renal natriuretic peptide, endothelin; reflex control of the circulation. Home: 9535 Ash St # 211 Overland Park KS 66207 Personal E-mail: klg101@sbcglobal.net.

GOETZ, MAURICE HAROLD, lawyer; b. N.Y.C., Mar. 29, 1924; s. Morton M. and Elsie (Klein) G.; m. Pearl Goldberg, Sept. 12, 1948; children: Susan Goetz Zwirn, Janet L., Jill K. B Social Scis. in Econs. and History, CCNY, 1947; JD, Harvard U., 1950. Bar: N.Y. 1951. Assoc. Bandler Haas & Kass, N.Y.C., 1951-57; ptnr. Bandler Kass & Goetz, N.Y.C., 1957-66, Friedlander, Gaines, Ruttenberg & Goetz, N.Y.C., 1966-74, Rosenman & Colin, N.Y.C., 1974-92; of counsel KMZ Rosenman, N.Y.C., 1993—. Lectr. on labor law Contbr. articles to Nat. Law Jour., Fed. Publs., Inc., others. Office: KMZ Rosenman 575 Madison Ave New York NY 10022-2585

GOETZ, ROGER MELVIN, minister; b. Chgo., May 17, 1940; s. Charles Albert and Sidonia Helene (Heck) G.; m. Betty Jean Bokelheide, Nov. 22, 1969; 1 child, Anne Katharine. BS in Chemistry, Iowa State U., Ames, 1962, BS in Math., 1967; MDiv, Concordia Theol. Sem., 1967; STM, Luth. Theol. Sem., 1972. Ordained minister Luth. Ch., 1968. Asst. pastor, dir. music Gethsemane Luth. Ch., St. Paul, 1968-80; assoc. pastor, kantor St. John's Luth. Ch., Topeka, 1980—; instr. Walther Luth. Jr. H.S., St. Paul, 1968-80; archivist Kans. Dist. Luth. Ch.-Mo. Synod, Topeka, 1985-89, chmn. worship com., 1985-94, chair floor com. edn., 2000; instr. organ Luth. Ch. - Mo. Synod, 2000—02. Organ recitalist various Luth. chs., 1970—. Author: The Descendants of Johann Georg Götz, 1976, Double Cousins by the Dozens, 1982; editor: A Century of Grace: Centennial History of the Kansas District, 1888-1988, 1988; contbr. articles to profl. jours. including Luth. Witness and Concordia Hist. Inst. Quarterly; composer work for double mixed chorus. Bd. edn. Topeka Luth. Sch., 1996-2004; Rep. precinct committeeman Ward 11/Precinct 3, Topeka, 1996-98, 2002—. Mem.: Am. Guild Organists (chpt. pres. 1983—84, chpt. chaplain 1994—2001, v.p. 2001—02, chpt. pres. 2004—), Cosmopolitan Internat. (chpt. pres. 2005—), Alpha Chi Sigma, Phi Mu Alpha. Office: St Johns Luth Ch 901 SW Fillmore St Topeka KS 66606-1445 *In my life I have found that the less I try to control things and people and rather leave things in the hands of my loving God, the more God brings gifts and joy into my life.*

GOETZ, THOMAS E., musician, educator; b. Marshfield, Wis., Aug. 31, 1953; s. Ray Carlton and Beatrice Elnor Goetz; m. Paulette D. Hazelton, July 10, 1976; children: Matthew, Alison. BA, Fla. Internat. U., 1979; MusM, Northwestern U., 1980, MusD, 1990. Dir. music 1st Presbyn. Ch., Miami Springs, Fla., 1976—81; prof. music Miami Christian Coll., 1980—87; organ scholar Northwestern U., Evanston, Ill., 1987—89; dir. music 1st Presbyn. Ch., Arlington Heights, Ill., 1989—93; organist, dir. music St. Paul United Meth. Ch., Louisville, 1994—2005; sem. choir dir., adj. prof. music Louisville Sem., 1996—. Chmn. music in worship Ill. Choral Dirs. Assn., Chgo., 1992—93, Ky. Choral Dirs. Assn., Louisville, 2003—05. Mem.: Presbyn. Assn. Musicians, Am. Choral Dirs. Assn., Am. Guild Organists (colleague cert., dean Louisville chpt. 2000—02). Home: 97 Valley Rd Louisville KY 40204 Office: Louisville Presbyn Theol Sem 1044 Alta Vista Rd Louisville KY 40205 E-mail: goetzt@bellsouth.net.

GOETZ, THOMAS HENRY PAUL, literature educator; b. Phila., Feb. 9, 1936; s. John Thomas and Anna Marie (O'Neill) G.; m. Joanne E. Smith, June 27, 1970; 1 son, Justin Paul. BA, LaSalle U., Phila., 1961; MA, Syracuse U., 1963, PhD, 1967. Asst. prof. Ill. Wesleyan U., Bloomington, 1966-67; faculty mem. SUNY, Fredonia, 1967—, prof. French lit., 1978—, chmn. fgn. lang. dept., 1979—89, 2000—02, disting. svc. prof., 1991. Cons. La. Bd. Regents, Baton Rouge, 1982. Author: Taine and the Fine Arts, 1973; editor: Nineteenth Century French Studies jour., 1972-99; contbr. articles to profl. jours. With AUS, 1954-57. Syracuse U. Coll. tchg. fellow in humanities, 1964-66, SUNY Rsch. Found. fellow, 1969, 75, 80, Nat. Endowment for Humanities Coll. fellow, 1977, 79, 84, 87, 88; recipient N.Y. State UUP Excellence award 1990. Mem. Assn. des Membres de l'Ordre des Palmes Academiques (officer), MLA (del. 1979-81, 19th Century French studies colloquia com., 1978-99, exec. com. divsn. on 19th Century French lit. 1984-88). Democrat. Roman Catholic. Home: 6 Pine Dr Fredonia NY 14063-2218 Office: SUNY Dept Modern Langs and Lits Fenton Hall Fredonia NY 14063 Office Phone: 716-673-3387. E-mail: goetz@fredonia.edu.

GOETZMAN, BRUCE EDGAR, architecture educator; b. Rochester, June 6, 1931; s. Benjamin Byron and Ila Flowers G.; m. Jane Grady McRae,June 25, 1955; children: Adam Brit, Ben Evan. BArch, Carnegie Mellon U., 1954; MS in Architecture, Columbia U., 1956; M in Cmty. Planning, U. Cin., 1965; postgrad., U. London, 1968. Asst. prof. Univ. Cin., 1956-66; prin. Bruce Goetzman & Assocs., Cin., 1965-77; acting chmn. grad. div. Univ. Cin., 1966-67, assoc. prof., 1967-99; prof. emeritus, 1999; ptnr. Goetzman & Follmer Architects, Cin., 1977-85; prin. Bruce Goetzman, Restoration Architect, 1985-. Trustee Miami Purchase Assn. Hist. Preservation, Cin., 1972-91, Ohio Hist. Sites Preservation Adv. Bd., 1980-92; pres. Better Housing League of Cin., 1979-81; trustee Ohio Hist. Soc., 1986-96, pres., 1995-96; pres. Ohio Preservation Alliance, 1986-88; trustee Cin. Preservation Assn., 1993-2000. Mem.: AIA, Assn. Preservation Tech., Architects Soc. Ohio, Cincinnatus Assn. Democrat. Home: 187 Greendale Ave Cincinnati OH 45220-1223 Office Phone: 513-281-7244. Business E-Mail: bg@pastarc.com.

GOEWEY, DAVID W., lawyer; b. Andrews AFB, Md., Aug. 22, 1962; BA in Economics & Am. Govt., U. Va., 1984; JD, Coll. William & Mary, 1987. Bar: Va. 1987, DC 1988, Md. 2000, US Ct. of Appeals, Federal, DC & Fourth Circuit. Ptnr., civil litigation Venable LLP, Washington, 1987—. Prof., intensive trial advocacy program & deposition skills program Nat. Inst. for Trial Advocacy, Georgetown U. Office: Venable LLP 575 7th St NW Washington DC 20004 Office Phone: 202-344-4853. Office Fax: 202-344-8300. Business E-Mail: dwgoewey@venable.com.

GOFF, HARRY RUSSELL, retired manufacturing company executive; b. San Francisco, May 24, 1915; s. Harry Roy and Ethel S. (Ludwigsen) Goff; m. Kathleen K. Kloster, Feb. 10, 1940 (dec. Jan. 10, 1995); children: Kathi, Karen, Betsi; m. Mollie Sinclair, May 14, 2005. BA, Stanford U., 1937; MBA, Harvard U., 1939. With Nat. Lead Co., San Francisco, 1939—41; ptnr. James D. Dole & Assocs., San Francisco, 1946—60; pres. James Dole Corp., San Francisco, 1955—79; chmn. bd., dir. emeritus Pacific Sci. Co., Newport Beach, Calif., 1979—91. Mem. adv. coun. Stanford U. Libr. Assn., 1979—; mem. Nat. Pub. Adv. Com. on Regional Econs. Devel., 1974—76; trustee Am. Sch. Oriental Rsch., 1978—82, Calif. Hist. Soc., 1993—. Lt. comdr. USNR, 1941—46. Mem.: Inst. Food Technologists, Book Club Calif. (past pres.), Roxbourghe Club Calif., Univ. Club San Francisco, Bohemian Club. Republican. Home: 868 Southampton Dr Palo Alto CA 94303-3439 Personal E-mail: mollie-hrg@sbcglobal.net.

GOFF, MICHAEL HARPER, retired lawyer; b. Hartford, Conn., Aug. 4, 1927; s. Charles Weer and Fern (Harper) G.; m. Katharine Lyman Bliss, Feb. 11, 1949 (div.); children— Carlin Weer, Peter Lyman; m. Patricia Darilyn King, Apr. 20, 1984 Student, Loomis Sch., Conn., 1942-45, Bethany Coll., 1945, Trinity Coll., Conn., 1949; BA, Swarthmore Coll., 1950; LL.B., Columbia U., 1953. Bar: N.Y. 1953. Assoc. Debevoise & Plimpton, 1953-60, ptnr., 1961-91; asst. to dir. Legis. Drafting Rsch. fund, 1951-53. Lectr. Banking Law Inst., 1966; cons. Atty. Gen. State of N.Y., 1977; spl. cons. Temp. Commn. to Study Orgnl. Structure City N.Y., 1953-54 Served with USNR, 1945-46; to 2d lt. F.A., AUS, 1946-48 Harlan Fiske Stone Scholar, Columbia U., 1951-52; Robert Noxon Toppan prize, Columbia U., 1952; E. B. Convers Prize, Columbia U., 1953 Mem. ABA, N.Y. State Bar Assn., Assn. Bar City of N.Y., Moorings Club (Fla.), Phi Delta Phi, Kappa Sigma. Democrat. Episcopalian. Home: 151 Anchor Dr Vero Beach FL 32963-2957

GOFF, RENEE ROSENSTOCK, gifted and talented educator; b. Chgo., May 15, 1956; d. Alfred and Alice (Bronstein) Rosenstock; m. Gerald M. Goff; children: Gregory Scott, Carly Michelle. BA, Northeastern Ill. U., 1978; MEd, Nat. Louis U., 2001. Tchr. 5th and 6th grades Talala Elem. Sch., Park Forest, Ill., 1978—88; tchr. lang. arts and social studies West Oak Mid. Sch., Diamond Lake, Ill., 1989—2003; tchr. gifted grades 2-5 Mount Prospect Sch. Dist., Ill., 2003—. Leader 4-H Clubs, Park Forest and Diamond Lake,

1978—; Washington trip sponsor/assembly chairperson. Recipient Disney Am. Tchr. award nominee, 2001, Golden Apple nominee, 2003. Mem. Nat. Mid. Sch. Assn., Nat. Assn. Gifted Children, Ill. Assn. Gifted Children E-mail: renegoff@hotmail.com.

GOFF, ROBERT BURNSIDE, retired food company executive; b. Arcadia, La., Aug. 8, 1924; s. Carl and Ruth (Capers) G.; m. Mary Jane Ellis, June 14, 1947; children— Gayle M., Robert B. BS, Rice U., 1947. Engr. Tex. Pipe Line Co., Tulsa, 1947-48; v.p., dir. Comet Rice Mills, Inc., Houston, 1948-58; sr. v.p., dir. Riviana Foods, Inc., Houston, 1958-75; pres., dir. Food Corp. Internat., Houston, 1975-86. Trustee Found. for Retarded, 1982-90. Served to lt. (j.g.) USNR, 1942-46. Mem. Rice U. Alumni Assn. (exec. bd. 1985-88), River Oaks Country Club. Presbyterian. Home: 2710 Essex Ter Houston TX 77027-5212

GOFF, ROBERT EDWARD, healthcare executive, insurance company executive; b. Worcester, Mass., Nov. 19, 1952; s. Julius Lewis and Doris (Katz) G.; m. Jinny Sue Yaver, June 30, 1985; 1 child, Blake Adam. BSBA with honors, Northeastern U., Boston, 1976; MBA with honors, Babson Coll., 1978; cert., Cornell U., 1981. Adminstrv. dir. Adirondack PSRO Inc., Glens Falls, N.Y., 1977-80; v.p. No. Met. Hosp. Assn., Newburgh, N.Y., 1980-83, Good Samaritian Hosp., Suffern, N.Y., 1983-85; exec. dir., chief exec. dir. WellCare N.Y., Inc., Newburgh, 1985-97; pres. Wellcare Leasing Corp., Newburgh, N.Y., 1990-96, Well Care Med. Mgmt. Inc., 1992-96; exec. v.p. Well Care Mgmt. Group, Inc., 1992-97; prin. The ABER Group, 1997-98; exec. dir., CEO Univ. Physicians Network, 1998—. Pres., CEO, UPT Trust, mng. dir.; bd. dirs. Wellcare Mgmt. Group Inc.; pres. Wellcare Med. Mgmt.; mem. adj. prof. New Sch. Univ., N.Y.; cons. in field. Bd. dirs. Hospice Care, Inc., Hospice of Orange Inc. Recipient Vigil Honor award Order Arrow, 1969, Eagle Scout award Boy Scouts Am., 1970. Mem. Hudson Valley Hosp. Exec. Assn. (pres., bd. dirs. 1982-85), Healthcare Fin. Mgmt. Assn., Am. Coll. Hosp. Adminstrs., Beta Gamma Soc. Office: 1 Park Ave Fl 11 New York NY 10016-5802 Office Phone: 212-404-3515. Business E-Mail: robert.goff@nyumc.org.

GOFFART, WALTER ANDRÉ, history professor; b. Berlin, Feb. 22, 1934; emigrated to U.S., 1943, naturalized, 1959; s. Francis Leo and Andrée Juliette (Steinberg) G.; m. Ellen Horvath, May 19, 1961; children: Vivian, Andrea Judith; m. Roberta Frank, Dec. 31, 1977. AB, Harvard U., 1955, AM, 1956, PhD, 1961; postgrad., École pratique des Hautes-Études, Paris, France, 1957-58. Lectr. history U. Toronto, Ont., Can., 1961-63, asst. prof., 1963-66, assoc. prof., 1966-71, prof., 1971-99, acting dir. Ctr. for Medieval Studies, 1971-72, prof. emeritus, 1999; sr. rsch. scholar and lectr. history Yale U., 2000—. Vis. asst. prof. U. Calif. at Berkeley, 1965—66; vis. fellow Inst. Advanced Study, Princeton, NJ, 1967—68, Dumbarton Oaks Ctr. Byzantine Studies, Washington, 1973—74; residency Rockefeller Found. Study and Conf. Ctr., Bellagio, Italy, 2001. Author: The Le Mans Forgeries, 1966, Caput and Colonate, 1974, Barbarians and Romans, A.D. 418-584, 1981; The Narrators of Barbarian History: Jordanes, Gregory of Tours, Bede, and Paul the Deacon, 1988, Rome's Fall and After, 1989, Historical Atlases: The First Three Hundred Years, 1570-1870, 2003; translator: The Origin of the Idea of Crusade (C. Erdmann), 1978. Fellow Berkeley Coll. (Yale). Recipient Haskins medal Medieval Acad. Am., 1991; Can. Coun. fellow, 1967-68; Am. Coun. Learned Socs. fellow, 1973-74; Guggenheim fellow, 1979-80; Connaught sr. fellow in humanities U. Toronto, 1983-84; Newberry Libr. fellow, 1989. Fellow Medieval Acad. Am. (councillor 1977-80), Royal Hist. Soc., Royal Soc. Can.; mem. Internat. Soc. Anglo-Saxonists, Phi Beta Kappa. Office: Yale U Dept History PO Box 208324 New Haven CT 06520-8324

GOFFIGAN, CHRISTOPHER WAYNE, research associate; b. Norfolk, Va., June 10, 1960; s. James Edward and Lillie Pearl (Jones) G. AAS in Mgmt., AAS in Merchandising, Tidewater C.C., 1982. Cert. in profl. communication; cert. profl. cons. Libr. aide Tidewater C.C., Virginia Beach, Va., 1980-82; inventory taker Miller Rhodes, Virginia Beach, Va., 1984, 88; telephone sales rep. Energy Savs. Exterior Inc., Virginia Beach, Va., 1985, Sears Svc. Ctr., Virginia Beach, Va., 1985-86; credit clerical Sears Credit Ctrl., Virginia Beach, Va., 1986-87; telephone interviewer Issues Answers, Norfolk, Va., 1988; rsch. assoc. Leading Nat. Advertisers/Competitive Media Reporting/TNS Media Intelligence, Virginia Beach, 1990—. New mem. adv. panel Am. Mktg. Assn., Chgo., 1992-93. Vol. City of Virginia Beach, 1989. Recipient Cert. of Appreciation, Mil. Mail Call, 1984, Editors Choice award Nat. Libr. Poetry, 1996, 97; named Knight Chevalier Venerable Order of the Knights of Michael the Archangel, 1992, Hon. Sgt. At Arms, Nat. Assn. Chiefs of Police, 1993, named to Internat. Poetry Hall of Fame, 1997. Mem. Am. Fedn. Police and Concerned Citizens, Am. Police Hall of Fame & Mus., U.S. Marshals and Peace Officers Assn. Am., Nat. Assn. Chiefs of Police (hon. chief 1995, Good Samaritan award 1995, Gold Seal award 1995), Internat. Soc. Poets (Internat. Poet of Merit award 1996), Soc. for Human Resource Mgmt., Internat. Guild Profl. Cons. (cert.), Nat. Geographic Soc., Am. Biog. Inst. Rsch. Assn., Va. Employment Law Inst., Va. Crime Prevention Assn., Air Force Assn., History Channel Club. Avocations: bowling, pool, travel, reading, shopping. Home: 740 Cason Ln Virginia Beach VA 23462-1197

GOFFMAN, THOMAS EDWARD, radiobiologist, oncologist; b. Chgo., Apr. 16, 1953; s. E. and A. (Choate) G.; divorced; 1 child, James Edward. BA, Yale U., 1975; MD, Hahnemann U., 1979. Diplomate Am. Bd. Radiology, Am. Bd. Internal Medicine, Am. Coll. Radiation Oncology. Intern, resident Georgetown U. Hosp., Washington, 1979-82; med. staff fellow, epidemiology tng. program Nat. Cancer Inst., NIH, Bethesda, Md., 1982-83; resident in radiotherapy, Joint Ctr. for Radiation Therapy Harvard U. Med. Sch., Boston, 1983-86; instr. in radiation oncology Columbia U., N.Y.C., 1986-87, asst. prof. of radiation oncology, 1987; attending in radiation oncology Washington Hosp. Ctr., 1987-89, vice chmn. dept. radiation oncology, 1988-89; asst. dir. radiation oncology Sibley Meml. Hosp., 1989; asst. clin. prof. radiation medicine Georgetown U., 1989—; assoc. prof. dept. radiation oncology/biophysics, med. dir. Sentora Norfolk (Va.) Gen. Hosp., 1997—, chief radiation oncology, 1997—99. Head clin. therapy sect., radiation oncology br., Nat. Cancer Inst., Bethesda, 1989—; asst. prof. radiology USUHS, Bethesda, 1989-91, dir. radiation oncology tng., 1989-92, assoc. prof. radiology, 1991-92; dir. radiation oncology tng. Nat. Cancer Inst. USUHS, Bethesda, 1990-92; dir. radiation oncology St. Agnes Hosp., Balt., 1992-93; rschr. internat. epidemiology nat. radiation NIH, 1983-84; med. dir. radiol. oncology Sentara Norfolk Gen. Hosp., 1999-2000; adj. prof. microbiology and molecular cell biology, Eastern Va. Med. Sch. Contbr. articles to numerous profl. jours. Bd. dirs. Lee's Friends, 2000—. Mosby scholar, 1979, Excellence in Medicine award, 1979, Blue Ribbon award, 1979, Nat. Rsch. Svc. award, 1983, Epidemiology Tng. fellow Nat. Cancer Inst.-NIH, 1983; Named one of 2003 Top Physicians in Am Fellow ACP; mem. AAAS, ACS (oncology com. 2001—, bd. dirs.), Am. Soc. Clin. Oncology, Am. Soc. Therapeutic Radiology and Oncology (CMS com. 2003—), N.Y. Acad. Scis., Com. on Physicians Assn., D.C. Med. Soc. (legis. com.), Nat. Cancer Inst. (internal rev. bd. 1989-90, biol. operating com. 1991-), Astro Govt Rel. Subcom. 2003-, Va. Med. Soc. (grant reviewer several jour.). Office Phone: 757-363-9885. Personal E-mail: tomeg2@juno.com.

GOFFMAN, WILLIAM, mathematician, educator; b. Cleve., Jan. 28, 1924; s. Sam and Mollie (Stein) G.; m. Patricia McLoughlin, Feb. 7, 1964. BS, U. Mich., 1950, PhD, 1954. Math. cons., 1954-59; research asso. prof. Case Western Res. U., Cleve., 1959-71; dean Case Western Res. U. (Sch. Library Sci.), 1971-77; dir. Case Western Res. U. (Complex Systems Inst.), 1972-75. Contbr. numerous publs. to sci. jours. Served with USAAF, 1943-46. Recipient research grants NSF, research grants NIH, research grants USAF, research grants others. Fellow AAAS Home: 2 Bratenahl Pl Bratenahl OH 44108-1183 Office: Case Western Res Univ Cleveland OH 44106

GOFORTH, HAROLD W., physician, psychiatrist; MD, Wright State U., Dayton, Ohio, 1998. Lic. Physician Ill. Asst. prof. Duke U. Med. Ctr., Durham, NC, 2005—, fellow, geriatric psychiatry, 2004—05. Mem.: Am. Assn. for Geriatric Psychiatry. Achievements include research in elderly and sleep. Office: Duke Univ Med Ctr Box 3903 Durham NC 27710 Office Phone: 919-681-8742. Business E-Mail: gofor003@mc.duke.edu.

GOFORTH, JILL HASTINGS, assistant principal; b. Gainesville, Ga., Feb. 19, 1952; d. John Clifton and Enid McKinley Hastings; m. Charles Butler Goforth, July 9, 1977; children: Elizabeth Key, Charles Preston. AA, Gainesville Jr. Coll., 1972; BS in edn., U. Ga., 1974, MEd, 1978; EdS, Brenau U., 2001. Tchr. Oakwood Elem., Oakwood, Ga., 1975—82; dir. First Bapt. Preschool, Gainesville, Ga., 1985—87; tchr. Enota and Centennial Elem. Sch., Gainesville, Ga., 1987—2001; lit. coach Enota Elem., Gainesville, Ga., 2001—03; asst. prin. New Holland Elem., Gainesville, Ga., 2003—. Cons. Core Knowledge Found., Charlottsville, 2005. Mem. Gainesville Hall County Jr. League, 1994—2000. Recipient Tchr. of the Yr., Enota Elem., 1997—98, Gainesville City Schools, 1997—98. Mem.: Assn. for Supervision and Curriculum Develop., Profl. Assn. Ga. Educators, Kappa Delta Pi Internat. Honor Sci. Bapt.

GOFORTH, WILLIAM H., lawyer; b. Norfolk, Va., Nov. 28, 1947; s. Solomon Frank and Thelma Goforth; m. Glenna K. Ford, Nov. 24, 1972; 1 child, Jeff. BS, Troy State U., Fort Benning, GA, 1977; JD, La. State U., Baton Rouge, LA, 1982. Cert.: Nat. Bd. Trial Advocacy (Civil Trial Advocate). Pvt. practice, Lafayette, La., 1984—2000; shareholder Goforth & Lilley PLC, Lafayette, La., 2000—02. Bd. directors La. Trial Lawyers, Baton Rouge, 1993—93, Lafayette Vol. Lawyers, Lafayette, La., 2002—. Del. La. Rep. Conv., Baton Rouge, La., 2002—02. Sp5 US Army Security Agy., 1965—69, Southeast Asia. Mem.: Lafayette Parish Bar Assn. (bd. directors 2002—02), LTLA, ATLA, Million Dollar Advocates Forum, Lafayette Barrister's Club, Vietnam Veterans Am. Avocations: fishing, boating. Home: 160 Acacia Lafayette LA 70508 Office: Goforth & Lilley PLC 109 Stewart Street Lafayette LA 70501

GOGEL, RAYMOND E., information technology executive; M in Philosophy, Drew Univ., M in Philosophy, PhD with distinction, Drew Univ., Madison, NJ; doctoral rsch, Univ. Freiburg, Germany. Various positions Public Svc. Elec & Gas Co. of NJ; with bus. process mgmt. group IBM Corp., v.p. global client services, exec. in charge of info. tech. for Xcel Energy; now v.p. & chief info. officer Xcel Energy Inc., Mpls. Adj. prof., philosophy Drew Univ. and Upsala Coll.; bd. dir. MedicAlert Found, Seren Innovations (subs. of Xcel Energy); adv. bd. IBM on Demand; bd. trustees, Denver Chapter Mile High United Way. Author: (books) Quest for Measure. Office: VP & CIO Xcel Energy Inc 800 Nicollet Mall Minneapolis MN 55402

GOGGANS, DANA, paralegal, private investigator; b. Birmingham, Ala., Jan. 23, 1972; d. James and Sharron Starnes; children: Tyler, Kiana. Grad., Sch. Paralegal Studies, 1996. Paralegal Haskell Slaughter Young & Rediker, LLC, Birmingham, Ala., 1996—; legal asst. Gordon, Silberman, Wiggins & Childs, P.C., 1996—99. Mem.: Gulf Coast Paralegal Assn. (assoc.). Avocations: swimming, walking. Home: 824 Riverhaven Cir Birmingham AL 35244 Office: Haskell Slaughter Young & Rediker LLC 2001 Park Pl North Ste 1400 Birmingham AL 35203 Office Phone: 205-251-1000. Office Fax: 205-324-1133. Personal E-mail: dmg@hsy.com.

GOGGIN, DAN CHARLES, playwright, composer, theater director; b. Alma, Mich., May 31, 1943; s. Edward Ralph Goggin and Gretchen (Harris) Wilson. Student, Manhattan Sch. Music, 1961—62, U. Mich., 1962. Singer: (Broadway plays) Luther, 1963—64, Saxons, 1965—72; singer, composer: (plays) Hark, 1972; writer, composer: revues, trade shows, others, 1972—83; composer: (Broadway plays) Legend, 1976; writer, composer, dir.: (plays) Nunsense, 1983 (Outer Critic's Cir. Best Musical award, 1986, Outer Critic's Cir. Best Music award, 1986, Outer Critic's Cir. Best Book award, 1986); Balancing Act, 1992; writer, composer, dir. (plays) Nunsense II: The Second Coming, 1993, Sister Amnesia's Country Western Nunsense Jamboree, 1995; writer, composer, dir.: (plays) Nunsense A-Men!, 1998; Nuncrackers: The Nunsense Christmas Musical, 1998; Meshuggah-Nuns: The Ecumenical Nunsense, 2002; Nunsensations: The Nunsense Vegas Revue, 2005; (TV spl.) Nuncrackers (Emmy nomination for Best Musical Score); Nunsense; Nunsense II; Nunsense Jamboree; (recordings) Love Minus Zero; The Saxons in Concert; Dan Goggin is the Lunch-Counter-Tenor. Mem.: Players Club. Independent. Roman Catholic. Home: 680 W End Ave New York NY 10025 Office: Nunsense Inc 1130 Rt 9 D Garrison NY 10524 Office Phone: 845-424-4086. Home Fax: 212-666-0493.

GOGGIN, JOHN R., software engineer; b. Lynwood, Calif., June 26, 1951; s. John R. and Pauline Ruth (Robinson). BA in Math. and Computer Sci., U. Tex., 1974. Programmer, analyst Potomac Electric Power Co., Washington, 1974-75; assoc. Analytics, Inc., McLean, Va., 1975-79; sr. analyst Pattern Analysis & Recognition, Colorado Springs, 1979-80; research assoc. Colo. State U., Ft. Collins, 1980-81; software engr. Ford Aerospace, Colorado Springs, 1982-84; software design engr. Hewlett Packard Co., Colorado Springs, 1985-88; sr. software engr. Kentek Info. Systems, Boulder, Colo., 1988—89, Array Tech. Corp., Boulder, Colo., 1990-93; adv. software quality engr. StorageTek Corp. Mem.: Am. Soc. for Quality, Mensa. Avocations: skiing, high altitude mountaineering, bicycling, rock and ice climbing, fishing.

GOGGIN, MARGARET ENID (KNOX), librarian, educator; b. Nyack, N.Y., Feb. 24, 1919; d. Henry Julian and Eleanor (Green) Knox; m. John Mann Goggin, Nov. 22, 1962. AB, Maryville Coll., 1940; BS, Peabody Coll., 1942; MS, U. Ill., 1948, PhD, 1957. Tchr., librarian Flintville (Tenn.) High Sch., 1940-42; reference asst. Joint U. Library, Nashville, 1942-43, acting reference librarian, 1943-45; vis. instr. Peabody Library Sch., Nashville, 1943-45; readers adviser Youngstown (Ohio) Pub. Library, 1945-46; bibliographer, reference librarian Office Tech. Services Dept. Commerce, Washington, 1946-47; reference asst. U. Ill., 1948-49; asst. to dir. U. Fla. Libraries, asst. prof. library sci., 1949-50, head dept. reference and bibliography, asso. prof. library sci., 1950-62; asst. dir. U. Fla. Libraries (Readers Services), asso. prof. library sci., 1965-66, asst. dir. libraries, prof. library sci., 1966, acting dir. libraries, 1967-68; dean Grad. Sch. Librarianship, U. Denver, 1968-79, prof., 1979-84, prof. emeritus, 1984—. Vis. lectr. U. Okla. Libr. Sch., summer 1959, Emory U. Sch. Librarianship, 1965; dir. Satellite Libr. Info. Network, 1974-76; prin. investigator Telefax Libr. Info. Network, 1978-79; cons. U.S. Office Edn. divsn. Libr. Programs, 1968-69, 87, Aims C.C., Greeley, Colo., 1973, Wash. State Libr., 1978-79, Loretto Heights Coll., Denver, 1981; co-owner Book Seminars, Inc., 1986-95; interim dir. Collection Mgmt., Emory U., 1986-88; owner Margaret K. Goggin Books, 1994—. Recipient Colo. Libr. of Yr. award, 1979, Outstanding Svc. award U. Denver, 1985, Alumni citation Maryville Coll., 1987, Disting. Alumnus award Peabody Coll., 1987; Rockefeller Found. grantee, Haiti and Paris, 1958, 61-62, Fulbright grantee, 1972, OAS grantee for multi-nat. libr. edn. program, 1974-75 Mem. ALA (past div. pres.), Colo. Libr. Assn. (dir. 1978-79), Mountain Plains Libr. Assn. (dir. 1978-79), Assn. For Library and Info. Sci. Edn. (pres. 1977), Nat. League Am. Pen Women, Fla. Ctr. for the Book (mem. exec. bd. 1988—), Delta Kappa Gamma, Beta Phi Mu (past dir.), PEO. Clubs: Altrusa (bd. dirs. Denver 1974-76, 80-82, pres. 1983-84). Home: 1108 Camellia Rd Birmingham AL 35215-7208 E-mail: gog@gnv.fdt.net.

GOGLIA, CHARLES A., JR., lawyer; b. Phila., Aug. 29, 1931; s. Charles and Marie A. (Beckman) G.; m. Patricia A. Morrissey, July 26, 1958; children: Philip L., Catherine A. BS, St. Joseph's U., Phila., 1953; LLB, Boston Coll., 1958. Bar: Mass. 1958, U.S. Dist. Ct. Mass. 1959, U.S. Ct. Appeals (1st cir.) 1964, U.S. Tax Ct. 1977, U.S. Supreme Ct. 1993. Atty. Sheff & Gens, Boston, 1958-61, Foley, Hoag & Eliot, Boston, 1961-68, ptnr., 1968-74; pvt. practice Sherborn, Mass., 1974—. Corporator, trustee, mem. bd. investment, exec. com. Bank Five for Savs., Burlington, Mass., 1974-92; mem. hearing com. Bd. Bar Overseers, Boston, 1984-86; arbitrator Nat. Assn. Dispute Resolution, Inc., 2002—. Counsel Town of Nantucket, Mass., 1970-82, spl. counsel, 1982-85, Town of Weston, Mass., 1974-85, town counsel, 1986-92, spl. counsel, 1992—, mem. zoning bd. appeals, 1964-66, 74-85, mem. planning bd., 1973-74; spl. counsel Mass. Cable TV Commn., Boston, 1973-74. With USNAR, 1951-59. Mem. Wellesley Country Club (past pres.). Avocations: golf, travel. Home and Office: 43 Kendall Ave G-07 Sherborn MA 01770 Office Phone: 508-655-6292.

GOGO, GREGORY, lawyer; b. Varos, Lemnos, Greece, Oct. 6, 1943; s. Soterio and Christina (Choleva) G.; m. Paraskevi Vivi Batzaka, July 15, 1989; 1 child, Chloe. BA, U. Chgo., 1966; MA, Rutgers U., 1972; JD, Seton Hall U., 1980. Bar: N.J. 1980, U.S. Dist. Ct. N.J. 1980. Reporter The Trentonian, Trenton, N.J., 1968-69; asst. project dir. Trenton Health Ctr., 1969-71; dir. planning UPI, Trenton, 1973-77; instr. sociology Trenton State Coll., 1973-77; assoc. Merlino, Rottkamp, Trenton, 1980-83; pvt. practice Trenton, 1983—. Corp. counsel Coronis Bldg. Sys. Mem. parish coun. St. George Orthodox Ch., Hamilton Twp., NJ, 1984—88, atty. for St. George, 1995; exec. bd. dirs. ARC, Trenton, 1972—77; spl. advisor to Pres. NAACP, Trenton, 1973—74. Recipient Archon Politis award Am. Hellenic Ednl. Prog. Assn., 1981, Cert. Merit, ARC, Trenton, 1977. Mem. N.J. Bar Assn. (mem. mass disaster response team 1996—), Mercer County Bar Assn., N.J. Assn. Trial Lawyers, Hellenic Vision (founding mem. 1992, pres. 1999-2002). Democrat. Home: 14 Carla Way Lawrenceville NJ 08648-1500 Office: 1542 Kuser Rd Ste 1B Trenton NJ 08619-3829 E-mail: gogolaw@juno.com.

GOGOTSI, YURY, materials science educator; b. Kiev, Ukraine, Dec. 16, 1961; s. George A. and Svetlana (Potarykina) G.; m. Larissa Ganzha, Mar. 18, 1989; children: Pavel, Natalie. MS, Kiev Poly., 1984, PhD, 1986; DSc, Ukrainian Acad. Sci., Kiev, 1996. Rsch. assoc. Ukrainian Acad. Sci., 1986-90; Alexander von Humboldt fellow U. Karlsruhe, Germany, 1990-92; Japan Soc. Promotion of Sci. fellow Tokyo Inst. Tech., 1992-93; NATO rsch. fellow U. Oslo, 1993-95; rsch. assoc. U. Tübingen, Germany, 1995-96; asst. prof. U. Ill., Chgo., 1996-99, assoc. prof., asst. dir. Rsch. Resources Ctr., 1999-2000; assoc. dean, dir. A.J. Drexel Nanotech. Inst., 2003—; assoc. dean Coll. Engring., prof. materials engring., mech. engring. and chemistry Drexel U., Phila., 2000—. Author: Corrosion of Structural Ceramics, 1989, Corrosion of High-Performance Ceramics, 1992 (I.N. Frantsevich prize, 1993); editor: Materials Science of Carbides, Nitrides and Borides, 1999, Nanostructured Materials and Coatings for Biomedical and Sensor Applications, 2003, High Pressure Surface Science and Engineering, 2003; issue editor Jour. Materials Mfg. and Processing Sci., 1998—2004. Grantee, NSF, DARPA, DOE, 1999. Mem. AAAS, Am. Ceramic Soc., Materials Rsch. Soc., Electrochem. Soc., World Acad. Ceramis (academician 2004). Avocations: travel, reading. Office: Drexel U Dept Materials Engring 3141 Chestnut St Philadelphia PA 19104 Office Fax: 215-895-6760. Business E-Mail: gogotsi@drexel.edu.

GOH, CHAN HON, prima ballerina; b. Beijing, Feb. 1, 1969; arrived in Can, 1977; d. Choo Chiat and Lin Yee Goh. Attended Goh Ballet Academy, Vancouver. Corp de ballet dancer Nat. Ballet of Can., Toronto, 1988-90, second soloist, 1990-92, first soloist, 1992-93, prin. dancer, 1994—, The Suzanne Farrell Ballet, 1999—. Guest artist various ballet companies in Europe, Australia, N. Am., Asia; entrepreneur, owner Principal by Chan Hon Goh Inc., TM Dance Supplies and Dance Shoes, 1996—. Dancer (prin. roles) The Sleeping Beauty, La Fille Mal Gardée, Don Quixote, Romeo & Juliet, The Nutcracker, Taming of the Shrew, Swan Lake, Giselle, Cinderella, La Boutique Fantasque, La Sylphide, The Dream, Paquita, La Ronde, Desir, Mozartiana, La Bayadere, Apollo, Jewels, Afternoon of a Faun, Forgotten Land, others; author: Beyond the Dance: A Ballerina's Life, 2002; prodr., star and lead: The Stars of N.Am. Ballet, 2002; Dance at the Main Stage, 2003; An Evening with Dancers of the Nat. Ballet of Can, 2004. Recipient Prix de Lausanne, 1986, Solo Seal award, Royal Acad Dancing, 1987, Silver Medal, Adelene Genee Comp, London, 1988, New Pioneers Arts award, 2005, ACCE Entrepreneurial award for the innovation of prin. shoes; Can. Coun. grantee, 1987. Office: Nat Ballet of Canada 470 Queens Quay W Toronto ON Canada M5E 3K4 Office Phone: 416-345-9686.

GOHEEN, DEBRA ELAINE, secondary school educator; b. Beaumont, Tex., Apr. 11, 1962; d. Kenneth Charles and Doris Elaine (Berry) Cloud; m. Norman Ray Goheen, June 3, 1994. BA, Tex. A&M U., Commerce, 1986. Cert. tchr. English and History, Tex. English tchr. South Garland H.S., Garland, Tex., 1986-94, history tchr., 1994—2005, freshman cheerleader coach, 1987—90, junior varsity/varsity cheerleader coach, 1990—94; lbr. Webb Middle Sch., Garland, 2005—. Active various coms. Heather Glen Elem. PTA, Garland, pres., 1997-99; dir. Pee Vee Drill Team, Garland Cheerleader Drill Team Assn., 1996-98, dir. Bison Pep Club; mem. Fisrt Christian Ch. (Disciples of Christ). Avocations: reading, archaeology, travel, dance. Office: Webb Middle Sch 1610 Spring Creek Garland TX 75040

GOHEEN, ELLEN ROZANNE, art historian; BA in French and Art Hist., U. Kans., 1965, MA in art hist., 1967. Asst. curator Nelson-Atkins Mus. of Art, Kans. City, Mo., 1967—73, assoc. curator, 1973—75, curator of 20th century art, 1975—81, various posts, 1981—89, dir. collections and spl. exhibitions, 1989—99; ret., 1999. Adv. com. Mo. Arts Coun., 1977—83; adv. coun. Kans. Arts Commn., 1986—91; adv. panel Nebr. Arts Coun., 1984—86. Author: (book) Christo: Wrapped Walk Ways, 1978, The Collection of the Nelson-Atkins Mus. of Art, 1988; art critic Kans. City Bus. Jour., 1984—85. Bd. mem. Jr. League of Kans. City, 1975—; commr. Tax Increment Fin. Com., 1982—84; bd. mem. Sister Cities Commn., Kans. City, 2002—; pres. Kans. City Young Audiences, 2000—03, Historic Kans. City Found., 1989—91; vice chmn. Kans. City Redevelopment Authority, 1979—84. Recipient Getty Mus. Mgmt. Inst., UC Berkeley, 1990. Mem.: Jr. League of Kans. City, Soc. of Archtl. Historians. Home: 6135 Overhill Rd Prairie Village KS 66208

GOHEEN, JANET MOORE, counseling administrator, sales executive; b. Everett, Mass., Sept. 29, 1945; d. Franklin Pierce and Virginia Louise (Murphy) Moore; m. Peter Arthur Goheen, Apr. 2, 1967; children: Kevin Murphy Moore, Andrew Hudson Moore. BA, Ohio Wesleyan U., 1967; MS, U. Bridgeport, 1979. Cert. profl. guidance counselor Ohio. Tchr. English Nordinia Hills HS, Macedonia, Ohio, 1967-69, White Plains (N.Y.) HS, 1969-71, Hudson (Ohio) HS, 1982-83; tchr. emotionally disturbed Palisades Learning Ctr., Paramus, NJ, 1986-87; sales cons. Longaberger Co., Dresden, Ohio, 1983-84, br. advisor, 1984-90, regional advisor, 1990—2004, nat. sales leader, 2004—; counselor Hudson Mid. Sch., 1988—. Tchr. ESL Hitchcock Presbyn. Ch., Scarsdale, NY, 1976—79, Aurora (Ohio) City Schs., 1979—81, Hudson Local Schs., 1980—82. Mem. Jr. League Scarsdale, 1976—79, Jr. League Akron, 1979—82, Jr. League No. N.J., Ridgewood, 1983—85; trustee Am. Found. Suicide Prevention N.E. Ohio, 1997—; founder Anna Lee chpt. Questers, Hudson, 1981, Hudson Presbyn. Ch., 1980; mem. alumni bd. dirs. Ohio Wesleyan U., Delaware, 1990—93. Mem.: Ohio Sch. Counselors Assn., Am. Sch. Counselors Assn., Kappa Delta Pi, Kappa Kappa Gamma. Home: 97 Manor Dr Hudson OH 44236-3406 Office: Hudson Middle Sch 77 N Oviatt St Hudson OH 44236-3043 Office Phone: 330-653-1320.

GOHEEN, ROBERT FRANCIS, classicist, educator, former ambassador; b. Vengurla, India, Aug. 15, 1919; s. Robert H.H. and Anne (Ewing) G.; m. Margaret M. Skelly, June 21, 1941; children: Anne Goheen Crane, Gertrude Goheen Swain, Stephen, Margaret Goheen Lower, Elizabeth, Charles. BA, Princeton U., 1940, MA (Woodrow Wilson fellow), 1947, PhD (Procter fellow), 1948; hon. degrees from 26 univs. and colls. Instr. classics Princeton U., 1948-50, asst. prof., 1950-57, prof., 1957, pres., 1957-72, emeritus, 1972—; chmn. Coun. on Founds., 1972-77; pres. Edna McConnell Clark Found., 1977; amb. to India, 1977-80; sr. fellow Woodrow Wilson Sch., 1981—. Dir. Mellon Fellowships in the Humanities, 1981-92; mem. adv. com. Nat. Fgn. Lang. Ctr., Ctr. for Advanced Study of India. Author: The Imagery of Sophocles' Antigone, 1951, The Human Nature of a University, 1969. Trustee Bharatiya Vidya Bhavan (USA), Nat. Humanities Ctr., Village Charter Sch., Trenton, N.J., Woodrow Wilson Nat. Fellowship Found. Decorated Legion of Merit, Bronze Star. Mem. Am. Philos. Soc., Coun. Fgn. Rels., Am. Acad. Arts and Scis., Am. Acad. Diplomacy, Phi Beta Kappa, Princeton Club (N.Y.C.), Century Assn. (N.Y.C.), Cosmos Club (Washington), Nassau Club (Princeton), Springdale Club (Princeton), Eastward Ho Club (Mass.), Gymkhana and Delhi Golf Club (India). Address: 1 Orchard Cir Princeton NJ 08540-3025 E-mail: rfgoheen@princeton.edu.

GOHMERT, LOUIS BULLER, JR., congressman, former judge, lawyer; b. Pittsburg, Tex., Aug. 18, 1953; s. Louis B. and E. Sue (Brooks) G.; m. Kathryn Ann Bledsoe, June 24, 1978; children: Kathryn Blair, Caroline Sue, Sarah Louise. Student, Sch. for Internat. Tng., Putney, Vt., 1973; BA, Tex. A&M U., 1975; JD, Baylor U., 1977; postgrad., U.S. Army Judge Advocate Gen. Sch., 1978. Bar: Tex. 1978, U.S. Dist. Ct. (ea. and so. dists.) Tex. 1978, U.S. Ct. Appeals (5th cir.) 1986, U.S. Supreme Ct. 1986. Asst. dist. atty. 76th Judicial Dist., Mt. Pleasant, Tex., 1978; assoc. Potter Guinn Law Firm, Tyler, Tex., 1982-86; ptnr. Freeman, Smithson & Gohmert, Tyler, 1986; pvt. practice law Tyler, 1986—92; judge Smith County Dist. Ct., Tex., 1992—2002, 12th Cir. Appeals Ct. Tex., 2002—03; mem. U.S. Ho. Reps., 109th Congress, 1st Dist. Tex., 2005—, Ho. Judiciary com. Deacon, Green Acres Bapt. Ch., Tyler; mem. E. Tex. Coun. on World Affairs, Tyler. Capt. U.S. Army JAGC, 1978-82. Mem. Smith County Bar Assn. (treas. 1989), State Bar Tex. (litigation sect.), Tex. A&M Alumni Assn. (pres. Smith County chpt. 1988), Rotary (pres. local chpt. 1990-91). Republican. Baptist. Avocations: sports, creative writing. Office: 508 Cannon House Office Bldg Washington DC 20515-4301 Office Phone: 202-225-3035.*

GOIN, PETER JACKSON, art educator; b. Madison, Wis., Nov. 26, 1951; children: Kari, Dana. BA, Hamline U., 1973; MA, U. Iowa, 1975, MFA, 1976. Found. prof. art U. Nev., Reno, 1984—. Author: Tracing the Line: A Photographic Survey of the Mexican-American Border, 1987, Nuclear Landscapes, 1991, Arid Waters: Photographs from the Water in the West Project, 1992, Stopping Time: A Rephotographic Survey of Lake Tahoe, 1992, Humanature, 1996, Atlas of the New West, 1997, A Doubtful River, 2000, Changing Mines in America, 2004, Black Rock, 2005; one-man shows include Duke U. Mus. Art, Durham, N.C., 1992, Phoenix Mus. Art, 1992, Indpls. Mus. Art, 1992, Savannah (Ga.) Coll. Art and Design, 1992, Nev. Humanities Com. Traveling Exhibit, 1992, NICA, Las Vegas, Nev., 1997, Mus. for Photographie, Braunschweig, Germany, 1997, U. Oreg. Mus. of Art, Eugene, 1997, Nev. Mus. Art, Reno, 1996, 99, Princeton (N.J.) U. Art Mus., 1996, Whitney Mus. Am. Art, N.Y.C., 1996, Museet for Fotographie, Denmark, 1999, Recipient Millennium award for Excellence in Arts, Nev., 1999; grantee NEA, 1982, 90. Office: Univ Nev Dept Art Reno NV 89557-0007 Office Phone: 775-748-4974. Business E-Mail: pgoin@unr.edu.

GOINES, LEONARD, music educator, consultant; b. Jacksonville, Fla., Apr. 22, 1934; s. Buford and Willie Mae (Lamar) G.; m. Margaretta Bobo (div.); 1 child, Lisan Lynette. BMus, Manhattan Sch. Music, 1955, MMus, 1956; Cert., Fontainebleau Sch. Music, France, 1959; MA, Columbia U., 1960, profl. diploma, 1961, EdD, 1963; BA, New Sch. Social Rsch., 1980; MA, NYU, 1980; cert. in clin. counseling, Postgrad. Ctr. for Mental Health, N.Y.C., 1983; CAS, Harvard U., 1984. Lectr. music Queens Coll. CUNY, 1969, York Coll. CUNY, 1969, NYU, 1970—; trumpeter Symphony New World, N.Y.C., 1965-76; assoc. prof. music Morgan State Coll., Balt., 1966-68, Howard U., Washington, 1970-72; prof. Manhattan C. C. CUNY, N.Y.C., 1970—; freelance musician Broadway shows, theatre, orchestras, recording ensembles, jazz groups, 1959—. Vis. prof. Williams Coll., Williamstown, Mass., 1984, Vassar Coll., Poughkeepsie, N.Y., 1985; co-exec. prodr., Bklyn. Acad. Music Majestic Theatre, 1988-96; dist. vis. prof. Lafayette Coll., Easton, Pa., 1986; postdoctoral fellow Harvard U., Cambridge, Mass., 1982-85; ptnr. Shepard & Goines Organizational and Ednl Art. cons., Jazz rsch. cons. Nat. Endowment Arts, 1983; appointee U.S. Dept. Interior, Smithsonian Inst.; mem. Preservation Jazz Adv. Commn., 1992-93; cons. in field. Contbr. articles to profl. jours. Folklore cons., field rschr., African Diaspora, Smithsonian Instn., 1972-76; trustee Nat. Assn. Community Schs. of Arts, N.Y.C., 1982-85; chmn. spl. arts section panel N.Y. State Council on Arts, N.Y.C., 1982-85; music panelist Arts Connection, N.Y.C., 1985. Recipient Pub. Svc. award U.S. Dept. Labor, 1980, Scholar Incentive award CUNY, 1983-84; named Hon. Citizen City of Winnipeg, Can., 1958; Coll. Tchrs. fell NEH, 1982-83; Faculty Rsch. grantee Howard U., CUNY, NYU, 1971-73. Mem. Local 802 of Am. Fedn. Musicians, AAUP, Nat. Acad. Rec. Arts and Scis., Phi Delta Kappa, Phi Mu Alpha. Democrat. Episcopalian. Avocations: running, photography, travel. Home: 221 W 131st St New York NY 10027-2030 Office: CUNY Manhattan Community Coll 199 Chambers St New York NY 10007-1044

GOINES, PATRICK L., historian, educator; b. Austin, Tex., Aug. 17, 1955; s. William Henry Goines and Ruth Lentsch; m. JoAnna Benico, May 19, 1985. BS in Edn., U. Tex., 1978, MA in History, 1985, MA in Libr. and Info. sci., 1992. Assoc. prof. Austin C.C., 1986—. Contbr. articles, revs. to profl. publs. Mem.: Orgn. Am. Historians. Office: Austin CC 1212 Rio Grande Austin TX 78701 E-mail: pgoines@anstincc.edu.

GOING, WILLIAM THORNBURY, language educator; b. Birmingham, Ala., June 3, 1915; s. Clarence Johnston and Louise (Thornbury) G.; m. Margaret Moorer, Dec. 15, 1951. AB with honors, U. Ala., 1936; MA (scholar, fellow English), Duke U., 1938; Ed.D., U. Mich., 1954; LHD, So. Ill. U., 2000. Tchr. English West End High Sch., Birmingham, 1938-39; asst. prof. edn. Samford U., Birmingham, summer 1939; instr. to asso. prof. English U. Ala., 1939-57; teaching fellow U. Mich., 1952-53; prof. English So. Ill. U., Edwardsville, 1957-80, prof. emeritus, 1980—, dean instruction, 1958-63, dean acad. affairs, 1963-65, dean emeritus, 2004—. Mem. faculty com. Ill. Bd. Higher Edn.; mem. Ill. Fulbright com. Author: Wilfrid Scawen Blunt and the Tradition of the English Sonnet Sequence in the 19th Century, 1953; editor: 99 Fables by William March, 1960, Regional Perspective: Essays on Alabama Literature, 1975, Scanty Plot of Ground: Studies in the Victorian Sonnet, 1976; contbg. author: (casebook) A Rose for Emily, 1970, Victorian Britain: An Encyclopedia, 1987, Scribner Novel Guide: To Kill a Mockingbird, 1990, Gale Contemporary Literary Criticism, 1990, World Literature Criticism, 1500 to the Present, 1992, DISCovering Authors—British, 1994, Modern American Literature, Vol. II, 5th edit., 1998, Bloom's Guide: To Kill a Mockingbird, 2004; contbr. articles on lang. and lit. to profl. jours. including Victorian Poetry, Ga. Rev., Ala. Rev., Jour. Modern Lit., Jour. Pre-Raphaelite Studies, Papers on Lang. and Lit. Organist 2d Presbyn. Ch., Birmingham, Ala., 1939-42, 1st Meth. Ch., Tuscaloosa, Ala., 1943-50; mem. adv. bd. Alton Meml. Hosp. Nursing Sch. Recipient Pres'. award of Merit So. Ill. Univ., 1992; named Outstanding Educator of Am., 1973; Rhodes scholar-elect from Ala., 1938. Mem. NEA, Midwest MLA., Nat. Coun. Tchrs. English, MLA Am. Ill. Edn. Assn., Phi Beta Kappa, Phi Delta Kappa, Phi Kappa Phi, Phi Eta Sigma, Sigma Alpha Epsilon. Democrat. Presbyterian. Home: 1 Hickory Knoll Edwardsville IL 62025-3802

GOINGS, AUSTIN NELSON, sales executive; b. Brookhaven, Miss., Jan. 28, 1954; s. Nelson Porter and Mary Elizabeth Goings. Student, La. State U., 1972-77. Pvt. practice oil and gas landman, New Orleans, 1978-83; sales mgr. Telescan, Houston, 1983-88, Paradigm Techs., Houston, 1988-94, Landmark Graphics, Houston, 1995—98; regional mgr. Vignette Corp., Houston, 2001—; dir. sales Centical region Softface, Inc., 2001—. Founder, bd. dirs. Texchange, Houston, 2000—; spkr. in field. Bd. dirs. Houston Sigma Chi Alumni Assn., Houston, 1986-88; mem. leadership com. Cystic Fibrosis, 2002-; pres. Montgomery Mcpl. Utility Dist., 2001-. Mem. Coastal Conservation Assn. (bd. dirs. 1993-2001, pres. Houston chpt. 1994-96, state bd. dirs. 1996—, state exec. com. mem. 1996—, nat. bd. dirs. 2002-. Man of Yr. 1997), U. Club Houston, La. State U. Alumni Assn., Sigma Chi Alumni Assn. Office: Vignette Corp Ste 500 2603 Augusta Houston TX 77057 E-mail: agoings@sunbelt.net.

GOINGS, RALPH, artist; b. Corning, Calif., May 9, 1928; Student, Calif. Coll. Arts and Crafts, 1953; MA, Calif. State U., Sacramento, 1966. Solo. exhbns. Artists Coop. Gallery, Sacramento, 1960, 62, Artists Contemporary Gallery, Sacramento, 1968, O.K. Harris Works of Art, N.Y.C., 1970, 73, 77, 80, 83, 96, Solomon Dubnik Gallery, Sacramento, 1997, Bernarducci Meisel Gallery, N.Y.C., 2003; group shows include U. Oshkosh, Wis., 1983, Contemporary Art Ctr., New Orleans, 1982, Pa. Acad. Fine Arts European tour, 1982-83, Brainerd Art Gallery, SUNY-Potsdam, 1982, Stockholm Internat. Art Expo., Sweden, 1982, O.K. Harris West, Scottsdale, Ariz., 1982, Butler Inst. Am. Art, Youngstown, Ohio, 1982, Mus. Contemporary Art, L.A., 1984-85, Boise (Idaho) Gallery Art, 1985, Mus. of Art-R.I. Sch. Design, Providence, 1985, Isetan Mus., Tokyo, 1985, San Francisco Mus. Modern Art, 1985-87, Norton Ctr. for Arts, Danville, Ky., 1985, Wichita (Kans.) Art Mus., 1985-86, Mus. of Fine Arts, Boston, 1986-87, Tucson Mus. Art, 1986-87, Tucso Mus. ARt, 2002, Chiostro del Bramante, Rome, 2003, others; represented in permanent collections, Mus. Modern Art, Guggenheim Mus., N.Y.C., Whitney Mus. Am. Art, N.Y.C., Mus. Contemporary Art, Chgo.; contbg. author chpts. in books; contbr. numerous articles in field. Office: OK Harris Works of Art 383 W Broadway New York NY 10012-4398

GOIN-HARDING, CECILIA MARGARET, poet; b. Mansfield, Ohio, June 30, 1957; d. Cecil Eugene and Sara Jane Goin; 1 child, Flora Emma Beatrix Cessna. BA in English, Case Western Res. U., 1984; grad., Cleve. Sch. Ballet, 1984; postgrad., U. Geneva, 1984, postgrad., 1999—2000, Cornell U., 1985; student, Cleve. Inst. Music, 1980, Cleve. Inst. Art, 1992; diplôme de Langue, Alliance Francaise, 2000; student, Miami Conservatory Ballet, 2001, Coconut Grove Ballet Sch., Miami, Fla., 2001—, Martha Mahr Sch. Ballet, 2003—, Miami-Dade Equestrian Ctr., Homestead, Fla., 2003, Ballet Acad. Miami, 2003. Governess pvt. family, Woody Creek, Colo., 1975; legis. aid Annapolis (Md.) Legislature, 1977; swimming instr. YMCA/YWCA, Mansfield, Ohio, 1979; proof reader Sun Press, Cleve., 1979; tchr. Am.-Nicaraguan Sch., Managua, Nicaragua, 1986, Cuyahoga C.C., Cleve., 1992, Cleve. State U., 1992. Model Parson's Sch. Design, N.Y.C., NY, 1975, Cleve. Inst. Art, 1988—92; translator Adriana Schaked LLC, Miami, Fla., 2000—, ALS Translations. Exhibitions include The Art Ctr., Mansfield, Ohio, 1977; author (poetry): Figures Of A Voyage: Collected Poems (1984-2000), 2002, numerous poems. Vol. Kingwood Ctr., Mansfield, 1981, NAMI, Miami, 1995. Named on Wall of Tolerance, So. Poverty Law Ctr. Montgomery Ala., 2003; recipient divisional medalist, U.S. Ski Assn., 1970. Mem.: Broadcast Music Inc., End Abuse Family Violence Prevention Fund, Fairchild Tropical Garden, Nat. Tropical Bot. Garden. Avocations: ice skating, soccer, learning to play new instruments, mathematics, prose writing. Home: 4060 Battersea Rd Miami FL 33133 also: Compass Inn Tormarton North Badminton South Gloucestershire GL91JB England Office Phone: 305-667-8641.

GOINS, FRANCES FLORIANO, lawyer; b. Buffalo, Jan. 30, 1950; d. William and Anita (Graziano) Floriano; m. Gary Mitchell Goins; children: Matthew W., Mark W. MusB, Cleve. Inst. Music, 1971; MusM, Case Western Res. U., 1973, JD, 1977. Bar: Ohio 1977, U.S. Dist. Ct. Ohio 1978, U.S. Ct. Appeals (6th cir.) 1979, N.Y. 1984, U.S. Dist. Ct. NY 1984, U.S. Supreme Ct. 2002. Law clk to Hon. Frank J. Battisti U.S. Dist. Ct. (no. dist.) Ohio, Cleve., 1977-78; ptnr. Squire, Sanders & Dempsey, Cleve., 1986—2003, Ulmer & Berne LLP, Cleve., 2004—. Mem. vis. com. bd. overseers Case Western Res. U., Cleve., 1984-2000; faculty Nat. Inst. Trial Advocacy, Cleve.; faculty, lectr. trial advocacy seminar Cleve. State U. Sch. Law, 1989-90. Editor-in-chief law rev. Case Western Res. Sch. Law, 1976-77. Trustee, chairperson devel. com. Lyric Opera Cleve., 1985-92, 2003—; founding trustee Shoreby Club Cleve.; v.p. bd. trustees Bay Village Montessori Sch., 1994-96; chmn. bd. trustees No. Ohio Breast Cancer Coalition, 2003—. Mem. ABA (bus. law sect., bus. lit. com., governance com. 1995—, fed. regulation of securities com., subcom. on civil litigation and SEC enforcement 1992—), Ohio Women's Bar Assn. (founding mem.), Ohio State Bar Assn. (ad hoc com. on bus. cts. 1994-99), Cleve. Bar Assn. (com. on women and the law 1987-2000, ethics com. 1988-90, securities law inst., jud. selection com. 1996-2001). Democrat. Roman Catholic. Office: Squire Sanders & Dempsey 4900 Key Tower 127 Public Sq Ste 4900 Cleveland OH 44114-1304

GOINS, RICHARD ANTHONY, lawyer, educator; b. New Orleans, Mar. 1, 1950; s. James Milton and Vivian (Wiltz) G.; m. Jane Parker, Aug. 18, 1973 (div. Sept. 1987); m. Nannette Smith, Mar. 3, 1990. BA in History cum laude, Yale U., 1968—72; JD, Stanford U., 1972—75. Bar: La. 1975, Calif. 1977. Dep. dir. New Orleans Legal Asst. Corp., 1977-78, exec. dir., 1978-81; law clk. to Hon. A. Duplantier U.S. Fed. Dist. Ct., New Orleans, 1982; asst. prof. Loyola U. Law Sch., New Orleans, 1981-84; ptnr. Adams and Reese, New Orleans, 1987-96, The Goins Law Firm, New Orleans, 1997-99; shareholder Goins Aaron, PLC, 2000—. Asst. bar examiner torts La. Bar Exam., 1991-96, bar examiner civil procedure, 1996-2004; sec., dir. character and fitness La. Com. on Bar Admissions, 2004—; mem. merit selection panel for selection and appt. of U.S. Magistrate for Ea. Dist. La., 1992-95, 2000; mem. host com. jud. conf. Fed. 5th Cir. Ct. Appeals, 1995; mem. civic justice reform act adv. com. Ea. Dist. La., 2000-; adj. prof. Loyola U. Law Sch., New Orleans, 1984-92, 2003—. Co-author: Practical Issues in Class Action Litigation, 1995. Mem. Mayor of New Orleans Overall Econ. Devel. Plan Com., 1991, Orleans Intercmty. Coun., 1992; mem. spl. gifts. com. Yale Alumni Fund, 1991-92; bd. dirs. New Orleans Home Mortgage Authority, 1991-94, City Trust, New Orleans, 1983-94, State Mental Health Advocacy Sys., New Orleans, 1983-84, New Orleans Legal Assistance Corp., 1982-83, Milne Asylum for Destitute Orphan Boys, Inc., 1994-97. Fellow: La. Bar Found; mem.: ABA (conf. minority ptnrs. 1990—96), Calif. State Bar Assn., 5th Cir. Bar Assn., Fed. Bar Assn. (bd. dir. New Orleans chpt. 1992—99), Nat. Bar Assn. (comml. law sect. 1989—), La. State Bar Assn. (legal aid com. 1978—81, uniform fed. rules com. 1991—92, fed. ct. bench-bar liason com. 1993—99), Master Thomas Moore Inn of Ct. Democrat. Roman Catholic. Avocations: reading, computers. Home: 4412 Mandeville St New Orleans LA 70122-4928 Office Phone: 504-569-1800. Business E-Mail: rgoins@goinsaaron.com.

GOINS, WILLIAM MICHAEL, writer; b. Houston, June 2, 1949; s. Bill Charles and Rose Mildred G.; m. Karen Lee Marie Faust, June 3, 1995; children from a previous marriage: James Michael, Kristen Alyse; stepchildren: Alexander, Melissa. Student, U. Houston, 1967-71; MA, Antioch U., Yellow Springs, Colo., 2001. Ind. bus. cons., Houston, Atlanta, Miami, Phoenix, San Francisco, 1984-93; columnist Fort Bend Herald Coaster Hartman Newspapers, 1984-93; freelance writer, editor Houston, 1990—; owner BlueStockings profl. writing/editing svc., Houston, 1996—; creative writing instr. W. Tex. A&M U., U. Houston, West Houston Inst., 1996—; copy editor, designer Tex. Rev. Press Sam Houston State U., 1996—. Author: (young adult series) Angus McMouse, short stories; editor: Wing Walking, 1999, Into That Good Night, 2000; contbr. articles, revs. to mags. Recipient New Tex. New Writers award, 2000. Mem. Tex. Assn. Creative Writing Instrs., Houston League of Writers, Austin Writer's League, Bay Area Writer's League (award 1999), Panhandle Profl. Writers (award 1999, overall winner Frontiers in Writing Conf. 1999), Mensa. Address: 1413 Pony Ln Wallis TX 77485 E-mail: mgoins@usa.net.

GOKCEN, IBRAHIM, computer science researcher; b. Ankara, Turkey, Jan. 17, 1978; s. Hazim and Serra Gokcen. BS, Mid. East Tech. U., 1999; MS, Tulane U., 2003, PhD, 2004. Computer cons. Can A.s, Ankara, Turkey, 1996—96; network programmer Mid. East Tech. U. Computer Ctr., 1997—97; software engr. Mid. East Tech. U. Informatics Inst., 1998—98; rsch. asst. Tulane U., New Orleans, 1999—, tchg. asst., 2000—00; computer scientist Gen. Elec. Global Rsch. Ctr., Niskayuna, 2004—. Pres. Turkish Am. Assn. La., New Orleans, 2002—03. Named Grad. Rsch. Excellence Computer Sci., Tulane U., 2003; scholar, 1999. Mem.: Engring. Grad. Student Assn., ACM. Home: 709 London Square Dr Clifton Park NY 12065 Office: One Research Cir Niskayuna NY 12309 Personal E-mail: gokcen@eecs.tulane.edu.

GOKEL, GEORGE WILLIAM, organic chemist, educator; b. June 27, 1946; s. George William and Ruth Mildred G.; m. Kathryn Smiegocki, June 2, 1978; children: Michael Robert, Matthew George, Mark Arlington. BS in Chemistry, Tulane U., 1968; PhD in Organic Chemistry, U. So. Calif., 1971. Postdoctoral fellow UCLA, 1972-74; chemist cen. rsch. dept. E.I. Du Pont de Nemours & Co., Wilmington, Del., summer 1974; asst. prof. chemistry Pa. State U., University, 1974-78; assoc. prof. chemistry U. Md., College Park, 1978-82, prof. chemistry, 1982-85, U. Miami, Coral Gables, Fla., 1985-93, prof. dept. molecular biology and pharmacology Sch. Medicine, 1993—; dir. bioorganic chemistry program Washington U., 1993—. Cons. W.R. Grace Co., 1977-86, Lion Detergent Co., Tokyo, 1985—, Seal Sands Chem. Co., Stockton-on-Tees, Eng., 1983-88, Monsanto Co., St. Louis, 1989-91, A.H. Marks, Eng., 1990-99; dean's adv. com. Tulane U., 1997—; lectr. in field. Editor Supramolecular Chemistry jour., 1992-2000, Advances in Supramolecular Chemistry, 1990—, Jour. Supramolecular Chemistry, 2001—; mem. editl. adv. bd. Chemical Communications, 1998—; mem. editl. bd. New Jour. Chemistry, 2001—; author: Phase Transfer. Recipient Allan C. Davis medal Md. Acad. Sci., 1979; Leo Schubert award Washington Acad. Scis., 1980, Macrocycle Chemistry award Izatt-Christensen, 1996, Tomen Agro award excellence, 2000; Petroleum Rsch. Fund grantee, 1976-78; grantee NIH, 1979—, NSF, 1998—. Fellow AAAS; mem. Biophys. Soc., Protein Soc., Am. Chem. Soc., Chem. Soc. (London), Sigma Xi, Alpha Chi Sigma. Republican. Methodist. Home: 1817 Stenton Path Chesterfield MO 63005-4733 Office: Washington U Sch Medicine Dept Molecular Biology & Pharmacology Saint Louis MO 63110

GOLAN, STEPHEN LEONARD, lawyer; b. Chgo., Oct. 22, 1951; s. Leonard Walter and Carol (Pepper) G.; m. Sharon D. Robson, Aug. 16, 1980; children: Brianna, Jenna, Melissa. BA, Claremont (Calif.) Men's Coll., 1974; MBA, JD, Northwestern U., 1978. Bar: Ill. 1978, U.S. Dist. Ct. (no. dist.) Ill. 1978, U.S. Ct. Appeals (7th cir.) 1993. Ptnr. Seyfarth, Shaw, Fairweather & Geraldson, Chgo., 1978-93; founding ptnr. Field & Golan LLP, Chgo., 1993—. Mem. ABA, AICPA, Nat. Assn. JD-MBA Profls. (bd. dirs. 1984-86), Ill. Bar Assn., Chgo. Bar Assn., Tavern Club (mem. jr. com. 1984-86), Exmoor Country Club (Highland Park, Ill.), Lake Forest Caucus. Republican. Episcopalian. Office: Field & Golan LLP 70 W Madison St 15th Fl Chicago IL 60602 E-mail: slgolan@fieldgolan.com.

GOLANSKI, ALANI, lawyer; b. Hartford, Conn., May 29, 1954; s. Solomon and Etta Golanski; m. Gina Gabriella Schmeling, Oct. 30, 1999; 1 child, Creeley Leon Schmeling. BA in Philosophy, Trinity Coll., Hartford, Conn., 1983; JD, U. Conn., Hartford, 1986; LLM, Columbia U., 2003; MA in Philosophy, CUNY, 2004. Bar: Conn. 1986, N.Y. 1988, N.J. 1990, U.S. Dist. Ct. (ea. and so. dists.) N.Y. 1990, U.S. Dist. Ct. N.J. 1990, U.S. Ct. Appeals (2d cir.) 1990, U.S. Ct. Appeals (5th cir.) 1993, U.S. Ct. Appeals (8th and 10th cirs.) 1996. Law clk. Conn. Supreme Ct., Hartford, 1986—87; appellate counsel Criminal Appeals Bur., Legal Aid Soc., NYC, 1987—90, Levy Phillips & Konigsberg, NYC, 1990—2003; solo appellate practitioner Alani Golanski, Esq., Bklyn., 2003—. Articles editor Conn. Law Rev., 1985-86; contbr. articles to profl. jours. James Kent scholar, Columbia U. Sch. of Law, 2003. Mem. Assn. Bar City N.Y., Phi Beta Kappa. Avocations: philosophy of science, jazz history, Afro-Cuban drumming, swimming, poetry. Office: Alani Golanski Esq 138 Court Street #260 Brooklyn NY 11201 Office Phone: 718-406-4488. Office Fax: 718-260-0842. Personal E-mail: alanigolanski@earthlink.net.

GOLBE, LAWRENCE INGRAM, neurologist; b. N.Y.C., Oct. 1, 1952; s. Alvin Victor and Cynthia (Boyars) G.; m. Devra Lifshitz; children: Jonathan, Susan. AB, Brown U., 1974; MD, NYU Sch. Medicine, 1978. Diplomate Am. Bd. Psychiatry and Neurology. Resident, then chief resident in neurology NYU-Bellevue Med. Ctr., N.Y.C., 1980-83; instr. neurology Robert Wood Johnson Med. Sch., New Brunswick, NJ, 1983-89, assoc. prof., 1989-97, prof., 1997—. Mem. editl. bd. Movement Disorders, 1997-2000. Mem. Am. Neurol. Assn., Soc. for Progressive Supranuclear Palsy (chairperson sci. adv. bd. 1990—). Office: Robert Wood Johnson Med Sch Dept Neurology 97 Paterson St New Brunswick NJ 08901-2160 Office Phone: 732-235-7729. Business E-Mail: golbe@umdnj.edu.

GOLBERT, SANDRA, artist; b. San Juan, PR, Nov. 9, 1937; d. Leonard and Hortensia (Portilla) G.; div.; children: Michelle, Jeanette, Pedro. Student, Haystack Sch. Workshops, Parsons Sch. Design. One-woman shows include Curacao Mus., Netherlands, Antilles, 1974, La Fortaleza Gov.'s Mansion, San Juan, 1984, Origenes Origins, 1990, John Harms Ctr., Englewood, N.J., 1994, Art for Body and Wall, St. Thomas, VI, Curacao, San Juan, 1994, Paper, Silk and Shadow, N.Y.C., 1998, Art From My First 1000 Years, Franklin Lakes, N.J., 1999, exhibited in group shows at Centro de Amistad, Guadalajara, Mex., 1972, Art Ventures Gallery, Princeton, N.J., 1985, Citibank Gallery, Ateneo, San Juan, 1989, Women's Art Works II, Rochester, N.Y., 1992, Convergence '92, Washington, 1992, The Farrell Collection, 1992, Paramount Ctr. for Arts, Peekskill, N.Y., 1992, Lever House, N.Y.C., 1992, America House, Piermont, N.Y., 1992, Barbara Gibson Gallery, Nyack, N.Y., 1993, Nat. Arts Club, N.Y.C., 1993, Jacob K. Javits Fed. Bldg., 1994, West Broadway Gallery, Soho, N.Y., 1994, Johnson & Johnson HQ, New Brunswick, N.J., 1995, Old Ch. Cultural Ctr., Demerest, N.J., 1995, NAWA, Athens, 1996, Am. Craft Mus. Group Exhibit, N.Y.C., Represented in permanent collections Jane Voorhees Zemmerli Mus., Rutger U., New Brunswick. Recipient fashion designs published, Vogue Mag., 1959, residency, Millay Colony for Arts, 1993; fellow, Weir Farm Trust, 2000; grantee NEA, 1991, grant, Pollock-Krasner Found., 1991, Empire State Craft, 1997. Mem.: Arts Coun. Rockland, Nat. Assn. Women Artists, Salute to Women in Arts. Achievements include fashion designs published, Vogue Mag., 1959. Home: 12 Washington Ln Tappan NY 10983-2512 Office Phone: 845-365-6093. E-mail: sandra@fiberarte.com.

GOLD, ALAN H., plastic surgeon; b. Bronx, N.Y., 1946; MD, SUNY-Downstate Med. Ctr., 1971. Diplomate Am. Bd. Plastic Surgery. Intern North Shore U. Hosp., Manhasset, NY, 1971—72, resident in gen. surgery, 1972—75; resident in plastic surgery Kings County-SUNY Med. Ctr., Bklyn., 1976—78; fellow in hand surgery Nassau County Med. Ctr., East Meadow, NY, 1975—76; pvt. practice plastic surgery Great Neck, NY, 1979—. Attending plastic surgeon North Shore U. Hosp., Manhassett; clin. assoc. prof. surgery Weill Med. Coll. of Cornell U. Mem.: Am. Soc. Plastic Surgeons, Am. Soc. for Aesthetic Plastic Surgery. Office: 833 Northern Blvd Ste 240 Great Neck NY 11021-5308 Office Phone: 516-498-2800.

GOLD, ALBERT MARK (BERT GOLD), molecular biologist; b. N.Y.C., May 20, 1954; s. Bernard G. and Doris (Bauman) G. A.B., Washington U., St. Louis, 1976; Ph.D., Tufts U., 1981. Research technician Jewish Hosp. of St. Louis, 1977; grad. fellow Tufts U., Medford, Mass., 1977-81; research fellow dept. pathology Harvard Med. Sch., Boston, 1982; postdoctoral fellow Biol. Labs. Harvard U., Cambridge, 1983-85, teaching fellow, 1984-86; instr. Harvard U. Extension, Cambridge, 1986—; research scientist BioTechnica Internat., Inc., Cambridge, 1986-87; founder, chief scientist Organic Biotech. Inc., 1987—; sr. scientist, Am. Bio-Techs. Inc., 1988—; cons. Recipient Individual Nat. Research award NIH, 1982-85. Mem. AAAS, Genetic Soc. Am., Soc. Devel. Biology, Boston Gene Expression Group, Sigma Xi. Democrat. Jewish.

GOLD, ALLAN HAROLD, architect, structural engineer, educator; b. Chgo., Jan. 12, 1942; s. Melvin King and Estelle M. (Zucker) G.; m. Barbara Gail Edelstein, June 20, 1967 (div. Feb. 1989); children: Grant, Ross, Susan; m. Susan Carlucci, Dec. 30, 1989. BArch, U. Ill., Urbana, 1966, MS, 1967. Registered architect, Conn., Colo., Ill., Ind., La., Okla., Wis.; registered structural engr., Ill; registered profl. engr., Ind., La., Okla., Wis., Tex., Mich.; cert. Nat. Coun. Archtl. Registration Bds. (juror registration exam. 1985), Nat. Coun. Examiners Engrin. and Surveying Certification. Architect, project engr. various archtl., engring. cos., Chgo. area, 1963—68; project structural engr. Perkins & Will Archs., Chgo., 1968—70; structural engr. Chgo. Dept. Bldgs., 1970—73; owner, operator Allan H. Gold Arch./Structural Engr., Hazel Crest, Ill., 1973—81; project mgr., sr. structural engr. HKS/Structures, Dallas, 1981—84; dir. architecture and structural engring. URS Engrs., Dallas, 1984; owner, operator Allan H. Gold, Architect/Structural Engr., Dallas, 1985—88; project mgr. Hoffmann Architects, North Haven, Conn., 1988—90; prin. Allan H. Gold, Archt. & Structural Engr., Chgo., 1990—93; v.p. Salse Engrs., Northbrook, Ill., 1993—96; assoc. Thornton-Tomasetti Engrs./LZA Tech., Chgo., 1996—2001; prin. AHG Structural Engring. PC, Chgo., 2001—; asst. prof. archtl. tech. dept. constrn. tech. Purdue U., Hammond, Ind., 1976—80; assoc. prof. architecture U. Okla., Norman, 1980—81. Adj. assoc. prof. architecture U. Tex., Arlington, 1983-85; guest lectr. U. Wis. Ext., 1981.

Structural engr. Century Shopping Ctr., Chgo., 1973, Phoenix Tower, Houston, 1983, Xerox II, Irving, Tex., 1984. Mem. Village of Hazel Crest Plan Commn., 1979-81. Fellow: ASCE (tall bldgs. com. 1983—86, std. com. design loads on structure during constrn. 1989—, std. com. design engineered wood constrn. 1989—, editl. bd. Jour. Archtl. Engring. 1995—); mem.: AIA, Structural Engrs. Polit. Action Com. (chmn. 2004—), Am. Inst. Steel Constrn., Am. Arbitration Assn., Structural Engrs. Assn. Ill. (chmn. structural engrs. polit. action com. 2004—), Am. Concrete Inst., Shriners, Scottish Rite, Masons. Jewish. Home: 360 E Randolph St # 4204 Chicago IL 60601-7341 Office: AHG Structural Engring PC 120 W Madison St Ste 702 Chicago IL 60602 Office Phone: 312-782-2600. Business E-Mail: ahgold@ahgse.com.

GOLD, ARNOLD HENRY, judge; b. Santa Monica, Calif., Apr. 12, 1932; s. Louis and Rose (Shalat) G.; m. Gloria Victor; children: Jeffrey Alan, Kenneth Clarke, Susan Elizabeth. AB with distinction, Stanford U., 1953, JD, 1955. Bar: Calif. 1955, U.S. Dist. Ct. (so., ctrl. and no. dists.) Calif. 1955, U.S. Ct. Appeals (9th cir.) 1955, U.S. Supreme Ct. 1955. Law clk. to Hon. John W. Shenk Supreme Ct. of Calif., San Francisco, 1955-56; assoc. atty. Loeb & Loeb, L.A., 1956-61; pvt. practice Beverly Hills, Calif., 1961-70; ptnr. Pachter, Gold & Schaffer, and predecessors, L.A., 1970-88; judge Calif. Superior Ct. for County of L.A., 1988-2001, supervising judge probate dept., 1993-94. Mem. Calif. Atty. Gen.'s Com. on Charitable Reporting Stds., 1970—71; mem. exec. com. Stanford Law Soc. So. Calif., 1973—77; mem. Calif. Atty. Gen.'s Task Force on Charitable Solicitation Legis., 1975—78; chmn. probate and mental health com. Calif. Judges Assn., 1995—96; pres. bd. trustees Los Angeles County Law Libr., 1998—2000; Calif. rep. Nat. Coll. Probate Judges, 2003—; bd. dirs. Dispute Resolution Svcs., 2003—04; mem. adv. com. Calif. Jud. Coun. Probate and Mental Health, 1997—, 2004—05; lectr. in field. Co-author: Probate Module, California Civil Practice, 1993-; contbg. author: California Family Law Handbook, California Nonprofit Corporations Handbooks; mng. editor, bd. editors Stanford Law Rev., 1954-55. Mem. ABA, State Bar Calif. (vice chmn. conf. dels. 1986-87), L.A. County Bar Assn. (trustee 1981-83), Los Angeles County Bar Found. (bd. dirs. 1985-91), Mulholland Tennis Club, Phi Beta Kappa, Alpha Epsilon Pi, Phi Alpha Delta, Delta Sigma Rho. Office: 10842 Alta View Dr Studio City CA 91604-3901 Home: 10842 Alta View Dr Studio City CA 91604-3901 Office Phone: 323-312-6002. Personal E-mail: judgeagold@aol.com.

GOLD, ARNOLD P., neurologist; b. N.Y.C., Aug. 8, 1925; s. Michael and Rebecca (Perlman) Gold; m. Sandra Orenberg, Nov. 17, 1969; children: Jeffrey, Stephen, Jennifer, Amelia, Margaret. BA, U. Tex., 1947; MS, U. Fla., 1949; MD, U. Lausanne, 1954; D (hon.), U. Medicine & Dentistry N.J., 2001; DSc (hon.), Sacred Heart U., 2003. Diplomate Am. Bd. Pediatrics, in child neurology Am. Bd. Psychiatry and Neurology. Intern Charity Hosp of La., New Orleans, 1954—55; resident, chief resident in pediat. Children's Hosp, Cin., 1955—58; NIH fellow in pediatric neurology Columbia Presbyn. Med. Ctr., N.Y.C., 1958—; prof. clin. neurology Columbia U., N.Y.C., 1976—, prof. clin. pediat., 1976—, attending neurologist, 1958—, attending pediatrician, 1958—; advisory bd. Winston Sch., Short Hills, NJ, 2004—. Cons. Cmty. Sch., Teaneck, NJ, 1975—; mem. interdisciplinary coun. Devel. and Learning Disabilities, Bethesda, Md., 1997—; attending neurologist and pediatrician N.Y. Presbyn. Hosp., 1999—; attending pediatrician Childrens Hosp., N.Y.C., 1999. Editor, author: Neurology of Infancy and Childhood, 1974, Pediatric Therapy, 1963—80, Pediatrics, 1968, 1996; author: Merritt's Textbook of Neurology, 1984—2005. Chmn. bd. Arnold G. Gold Found., 2005—; bd. dirs. Homes for Developmentally Disabled, NJ, 1984—; pres. Myoclonus Rsch. Found., 1992—2004; trustee, sec. AMA Found., 1999—2004; mem. adv. coun. Naomi Berrie Diabetes Ctr., N.Y.C., 1997—; mem. adv. bd. Winston Sch., Short Hills, NJ; pres. Arnold G. Gold Found., Engelwood Cliffs, NJ, 1989—2005; mem. admissions com. Ben Guron U., Beer-Sheeva, Israel, 1997—98; trustee, bd. advisors N.J. Med. Sch., 2001—. Named Best Dr. in Am., Am. Health Mar. issue, 1996, Best Dr. in N.Y., 1997, 1998, 1999, 2000, 2001; recipient Brennerman award in pediat., 1968, Man of Yr. award, Assn. Brain Injured Children, 1968, Disting. Svc. award, Speech-Lang.-Hearing Assn., 1993, Miracle Maker of N.Y., Children's Miracle Network, 1994, Practitioner of Yr. award, Columbia Presbn. Med. Ctr., 1992, Disting. Svc. award, Columbia U., 1999, Lifetime Cmty. Svc. award, Autism Soc. Am., 2000, Humanitarian award, Sinai Inst., 2002, Humanitarian award multiple sclerosis rsch., U. Medicine and Dentistry N.J., 2003, Humanitarian award, N.J. Coun. for the Humanities, 2004, Disting. Citizen award, NJ Med. Sch., 2005. Fellow: Internat. Child Neurology Soc., Child Neurology Soc. (Lifetime Achievement award 2005), Am. Acad. Neurology, Am. Pediatric Soc., Am. Acad. Pediat. Avocations: gardening, stamp collecting/philately, coin collecting/numismatics. Office: Neurol Inst NY 710 W 168th St New York NY 10032-2603 Office Phone: 212-305-5483. Business E-Mail: apg1@columbia.edu.

GOLD, BELA, economist, educator; b. Kolozsvar, Hungary, Jan. 30, 1915; came to U.S., 1920, naturalized, 1927; s. Leo and Esther (Ludwig) G.; m. Sonia Steinman, July 5, 1938; 1 son, Robert. BS in Mech. Engring, NYU, 1934; PhD (Univ. fellow 1936-37), Columbia U., 1948. Research cons. Life Ins. Sales Research Bur., Hartford, Conn., 1938-39; asst. head div. program surveys Bur. Agr. Econs., 1939-42; econ. cons. subcom. war mblzn. U.S. Senate, 1943-44; econ. adviser FEA and Dept. Commerce, 1944-46; prof. indsl. econs. U. Pitts. Grad. Sch. Bus., 1947-66; Timken prof. and William E. Umstattd prof. indsl. econs., dir. research program indsl. econs. Case Western Res. U., 1966-83, chmn. dept. econs., 1967-73; Fletcher Jones prof. tech. and mgmt. Claremont Grad. Sch. (Calif.), 1983-2000; pres. Indsl. Econs. and Mgmt. Assocs., 1980-2000. Vis. professorial fellow Nuffield Coll., Oxford (Eng.) U., 1964; vis. prof. Imperial Coll. Scis. and Tech., London, 1967, 73; Disting. Internat. Sr. Rsch. fellow Centre Internat. Rsch. on Computer and Info. Tech., Melbourne, Australia, 1989, Adminstrv. Staff. Coll. India, Hyderabad, 1992, Rand Afrikaans U., South Africa, 1995; cons. to industry and ednl. instns., 1950—; mem. com. on steel industry Nat. Acad. Scis.-Nat. Materials Adv. Bd., 1977-78; mem. assembly of engring. com. on computer-aided mfg. NRC, 1978-82, mem. mfg. studies bd., 1982-86, mem. com. on machine tool industry, 1982-84; mem. Interdepartmental Adv. Com. on Fed. Policy on Indsl. Innovation, 1978-79; mem. ferrous metals panel Nat. Acad. Engring., 1980-84, panel on improving the competitiveness of U.S. Industries, 1985. Author: Wartime Economic Planning in Agriculture, 2d edit., 1969, How is Higher Education Financed, 1959, Foundations of Productivity Analysis, 1955, Explorations in Managerial Economics, 1971, Japanese edit., 1977, Technological Change: Economics Management and Environment, 1975, 80, Applied Productivity Analysis for Industry, U.K. edit., 1976, Russian edit., 1981, Chinese edit., 1982, Research, Technological Change and Economic Analysis, 1977, Productivity, Technology and Capital, 1979, 2d edit., 1982, Evaluating the Effects of Technological Innovations, 1980, Appraising and Stimulating Technological Advances in Industry, 1980, Improving Managerial Evaluations of Computer-Aided Manufacturing, 1981, Technological Progress and Industrial Leadership, 1984, 85, On the Increasing Role of Technology in Corporate Policy, 1991, Strengthening Corporate and National Competitiveness Through Technology, 1992, New Technological Foundations of Strategic Management: Some International Perspectives, 1993, Needed Technological Responses to International Competition, 1994, Emerging Technological Frontiers in International Competition, 1995, Changing the Technological Determinants of International Competitiveness, 1996, Advancing the International Competitiveness of U.S. Manufacturing, 1999; mem. editl. bd. Acad. Mgmt. Jour., 1962-73, Omega: Internat. Jour. Mgmt. Scis., 1972-99, Jour. Product Innovation Mgmt., 1983-99, Internat. Jour. Tech. Mgmt., 1989-99; corr. mem. editl. bd. Revue d'Économie Industrielle, 1978-90; mem. adv. editl. bd. Jour. Computer Integrated Mfg., 1985—, Transactions in Engring. Mgmt., 1986—, Jour. Engring. and Tech. Mgmt., 1988—, Mfg. Rev., 1989—, Prodn. and Ops. Mgmt., 1991—, Mng. Tech. Today, 1992—; contbr. numerous articles to profl. jours., chpts. in books. Social Sci. Research Council fellow, 1937-38, 77, 83; Ford Found. fellow, 1961-62, 66-67, 72 Mem. Am. Econ. Assn., Inst. Mgmt. Scis. (chmn. Coll. on Mgmt. of Technol. Change 1970-85), Nat. Assn. Accts. (subcom. on productivity measurement 1977-79), AAUP. Home: 130 Wellington G West Palm Beach FL 33417-2562

GOLD, CAROL SAPIN, international management consultant, speaker, writer; b. N.Y.C. d. Cerf Saul and Muriel Louise (Fudin) Rosenberg; children: Kevin Bart Sapin, Craig Paul Sapin, Courtney Byrens Sapin. BA, U. Calif., Berkeley, 1955. Asst. credit mgr. Union Oil Co., 1956; with U.S. Dept. State, 1964-66; mem. dept. pub. rels. Braun & Co., L.A., 1964-66; corp. dir. pers. tng. Gt. Western Fin. Corp., L.A., 1967-71; pres. Carol Sapin Gold & Assocs., L.A., 1971—. Bd. dirs. Marathon Nat. Bank, L.A.; cons., profl. spkr., Bath, Eng., 1987-90; cons., Can., Mex., India, Australia, New Zealand; host radio program The Competitive Edge; mem. expdn. to Syria and Jordan, 1994, to Morocco, 1995; mem. WORID Bus. Acad.; instr. Learning Annex; presenter Expertise Forum Presentations, Malaysia, Bangkok, 1997, others; instr. Asian program U. So. Calif., 1998. Author: Solid Gold Customer Relations and Success Secrets, Travel for Scholars, Paris, 1999; featured in tng. films Power of Words; author: Cassette Libraries, How to Present Seminars, Sound Selling. Bd. dirs. Ctr. Theatre Group, Town Hall, Music Ctr., Odyssey Theater; asst. dir. Burnhill Prodns., 1992—, asst. dir.Cabaret, Palisades Theatre; dir. Improv Corp.; vol. Exec. Svc. Corp., 1996—, CEO Leadership Forum. Mem. ASTD, Am. Film Inst. Assn., Sales and Mktg. Execs., Nat. Spkrs. Assn., Nat. Platform Assn., Women in Bus., KCET Women's Coun., Exec. Svc. Corps, World Affairs Coun., Blue Ribbon, Women in Arts, Women in Film, Manuscript Soc. Forum Scotland, Plato Soc., Brandeis Univ. Women, Sierra Club (Toure de Mt. Blanc), Supreme Ct. Hist. Soc., Dispute Resolution Svcs., Women of L.A., Marina Del Rey C. of C., Internat. CEO Exec. Forum, Manuscript Soc. Avocations: collecting famous manuscripts, coaching public speakers, music, theater, writing. Office: PO Box 11447 Marina Del Rey CA 90295 Office Phone: 310-823-0202. Personal E-mail: cconsult@aol.com.

GOLD, CHRISTINA A., cosmetics company executive; Grad., Carleton U., Ottawa; degree (hon.), U. Montreal, 1991. With human resources, sales, mktg., fin. and mgmt. depts. Avon Can., 1970-89, pres., CEO, 1989-93, head oper. bus. unit, 1993; sr. v.p., pres. Avon North Am., N.Y.C., 1993-98; exec. v.p. Global Direct Selling Devel., N.Y.C., 1997-98; co-CEO Teleglobe, Inc.; pres. Beaconsfield Group; chmn., pres., CEO Excel Comm., Inc., Dallas, Western Union Fin. Svcs. (subsidiary of First Data Corp.). Bd. dirs. Meredith Corp., 1999—2001, The Torstar Corp., The Conf. Bd., ITT Industries, N.Y. Life Investment Mgmt. LLC. Mem.: Direct selling Assn. (bd. dirs.), Conf. Bd. N.Y. and Can. (bd. dirs). Office: Western Union Financial Svcs 100 North Central Expwy Ste 600 Dallas TX 75201

GOLD, DANIEL HOWARD, ophthalmologist, educator; b. N.Y.C., Sept. 21, 1942; s. Isadore and Leona (Cotton) G.; m. Joann Aaron, Oct. 22, 1966 (div. Sept. 1985); m. Barbara Wood, June 19, 1988; children: David, Abigail, Michael. Student, U. Mich., 1959-66. Diplomate Am. Bd. Ophthalmology. Asst. chief dept. ophthalmology Walter Reed Army Med. Ctr., Washington, 1972-74; asst. prof. dept. ophthalmology Montefiore Hosp. Med. Ctr., Bronx, N.Y., 1974-76; asst. clin. prof. med. br. U. Tex., Galveston, 1977-85, assoc. clin. prof. med. br., 1986-91; physician, ophthalmologist Eye Clinic of Tex., Galveston, 1977—; clin. prof. ophthalmology med. br. U. Tex., Galveston, 1991—. Mem. med. staff exec. com. St. Mary's Hosp., Galveston, 1989-90, 95-96, chmn. dept. surgery, 1995-96. Editor: (textbook) The Eye in Systemic Disease, 1990, Color Atlas of the Eye in Systemic Disease, 2001, Clinical Eye Atlas, 2002; contbr. articles to profl. jours. Pres. United Orthodox Synagogues, Houston, 1997-2000. Maj. U.S. Army, 1972-74. Fellow: N.Y. Acad. Medicine, Royal Coll. Ophthalmologist Gr. Britain, Am. Acad. Ophthalmology (self-assessment com. 1989—92, editl. adv. bd. EyeNet 1996—2002, Honor award 1985, Sr. Honor award 2001); mem.: Tex. Med. Assn. (coun. on pub. health 1995—97), Galveston Physicians Svc. Assn. (bd. dirs. 1985—2000, pres. 1993—2000), Pan Am. Assn. Ophthalmology, Assn. Rsch. Vision and Ophthalmology, Macula Soc. Jewish. Office: Eye Clinic Tex 2302 Avenue P Galveston TX 77550-7992

GOLD, DEIDRA D., lawyer; b. Jan. 1955; m. Stephen A. Gold. BA, Wellesley Coll.; JD, Columbia U., 1979. Assoc. Jones Day Reavis & Pogue, Cleve., 1983—88, ptnr., 1988—91; v.p., gen. counsel Premier Industrial Corp., Cleve., 1991—97; ptnr. Goldberg Kohn Bell Black Rosenbloom & Mortiz, Chgo., 1998; counsel, corp. sec. Ameritech Corp., 1998—99; v.p., gen. counsel eLoyalty Corp., 2000—01; sr. v.p., gen. counsel, sec. United Stationers Inc., Des Plaines, Ill., 2001—. Office: United Stationers Inc 2200 E Golf Rd Des Plaines IL 60016-1267

GOLD, EDWARD DAVID, lawyer; b. Detroit, Jan. 17, 1941; s. Morris and Hilda (Robinson) Gold; m. Francine Sheila Kamin, Jan. 8, 1967; children: Lorne Brian, Karen Beth. Student, Wayne State U., 1958-61; JD, Detroit Coll. Law, 1964. Bar: Mich. 1965, U.S. Dist. Ct. (ea. dist.) Mich. 1965, U.S. Ct. Appeals (6th cir.) 1965, D.C. 1966. Atty. gen. counsel FCC, Washington, 1965-66; ptnr. Conn, Conn & Gold, Detroit, 1966-67, May, Conn, Conn & Gold, Livonia, Mich., 1967-69, Hyman, Gurwin, Nachman, Gold & Alterman, Southfield, Mich., 1971-88, Butzel Long, Bloomfield Hills, Mich., 1988—. Mem. Oakland County Criminal Justice Coordinating Coun., 1976—77; chmn. Friend of the Ct. Adv. Com., Lansing, Mich., 1982—88; contbr. lectr. Inst. Continuing Legal Edn., Ann Arbor, Mich., 1981—, Mich. Trial Lawyers Assn.; adj. prof. U. Detroit Mercy Sch. Law, 2001—. Author: (book) Michigan Family Law, 1988; contbr. articles to legal jours. Mem. Southfield Transp. Commn., 1975—77; chairperson atty. disp. bd. Tri-County Hearin Panel 71, 1994—2004; chmn. attys.' divsn. Jewish Welfare Fedn., Detroit; mem. nat. young leadership cabinet United Jewish Appeal, N.Y.C., 1978—80; pres. Jewish Family Svc., Detroit, 1988—90; bd. dirs. Oakland County Legal Aid Soc., 1979—84. Scholar Tau Epsilon Rho, 1963. Fellow: Am. Acad. Matrimonial Lawyers (bd. dirs. 1988—93, pres. Mich. chpt. 1992—93, nat. bd. govs. 1988—2001, nat. v.p. 2001—), Am. Coll. Family Trial Lawyers; mem.: Am. Arbitration Assn., Bar Assn. D.C., Southfield Bar Assn. (pres. 1975—76), Oakland County Bar Assn. (bd. dirs. 1984—93, pres. 1992—93), Mich. Bar Assn. (coun. real property law sect. 1973—81, coun. family law sect. 1974—75, 1977—82, chmn. family law sect. 1981—82, rep. assembly 1978—82, Lifetime Achievement award), Alpha Epsilon Pi (nat. pres. 1976—77, Order of Lion award 1986). Avocation: golf. Office: Butzel Long Ste 200 100 Bloomfield Hills Pkwy Bloomfield Hills MI 48304 E-mail: Gold@Butzel.com.

GOLD, GERALD SEYMOUR, lawyer; b. Cleve., Feb. 2, 1931; s. David N. and Geraldine (Bloch) G.; 1 child, Anne; m. Rosemary Grdina, 1994. AB, Case-Western Res. U., 1951, LLB, 1954. Bar: Ohio 1954, U.S. Supreme Ct. 1961. Practiced in, Cleve., 1954-60; chief asst. legal aid defender Cuyahoga County, Cleve., 1960-61, chief legal aid defender, 1961-65; assoc. Ulmer, Byrne, Laronge, Glickman & Curtis, Cleve., 1965-66; ptnr. Gold, Rotatori, Schwartz & Gibbons, Cleve., 1966—. Instr. in law Case-Western Res. U., 1965-66, Cleve. State Law Sch., 1968-69, Case-Western Res. Law-Medicine Center, 1961-77; lectr. to bar assns. commr. Cuyahoga County Pub. Defender, 1977-81. Contbg. author: American Jurisprudence Trials, 1966; Contbr. articles to profl. jours. Fellow Am. Coll. Trial Lawyers, Am. Bd. Criminal Lawyers, Ohio State Bar Found., Internat. Soc. Barristers; mem. ABA (criminal justice coun.), Cuyahoga County Criminal Ct. Bar Assn. (chmn., Lifetime Achievement award 1995), Ohio Bar Assn. (chmn. criminal law sect. 1974-78, ho. of dels. 1986—), Greater Cleve. Bar Assn. (Merit award 1974, trustee 1978—, pres. 1982-83), Nat. Assn. Criminal Def. Lawyers (pres. 1977, Merit award 1975), Ohio Acad. Trial Lawyers (chmn. criminal law sect. 1970-75), Ohio Assn. Criminal Def. Lawyers (bd. dirs. 1990), Case-Western Res. U. Law Alumni Assn. (pres. 1974-75, Outstanding Alumnus award 1991), Soc. Benchers, Court of Nisi Prius Club, Cleve. Skating Club. Home: 33000 Pinetree Rd Pepper Pike OH 44124-5514 Office: 526 Superior Ave E Ste 1140 Cleveland OH 44114-1497 Office Phone: 216-696-6122. Personal E-mail: goldjero@aol.com.

GOLD, HAROLD, lawyer, accountant; b. N.Y.C., Jan. 14, 1916; s. Samuel and Freida (Swedlow) G.; m. Ellen Facundus, June 18, 1946; children: Sandra L. Gold Brasier, Fred L. Gold. BS in Acctg., UCLA, 1938; JD, U. Minn., 1948. CPA, Minn., Calif. Lectr. income taxation U. Minn., Mpls., 1946-48; pvt. practice Mpls., L.A., 1946-51; regional counsel Western Regional Renegotiation Bd., L.A., 1951-57; mem. adv. bd. federal contracts reports Bur. Nat. Affairs, Washington, 1969-81. Contbr. articles to profl. jours. Capt. U.S. Army Engrs., 1942-46. Fellow ABA (chmn. Pub. Contract Law sect. 1973-74, mem. coun. sect. on Pub. Contract Law (hon.), Nat. Contracts Mgmt. Assn. E-mail: efgh1@verizon.net.

GOLD, HAROLD ARTHUR, lawyer; b. Pitts., Jan. 13, 1929; m. Anita Hubert, Aug. 18, 1937; children: Howard, Bradley. BBA, U. Pitts., 1952; JD, Georgetown U., 1956. Bar: Pa. 1956, D.C. 1956. Sole practice law, Pitts., 1956-64; atty. City of Pitts., 1960-69; ptnr. Baskin and Sears, Pitts., 1965-84, Reed, Smith, Shaw & McClay, Pitts., 1985-93; pres., chief exec. officer Coventry Care, Inc., Monongahela, Pa., 1970-86, chmn. bd., chief exec. officer, 1986-87. Adj. prof. law Duquesne U. Pres. Young Dem. Club of Pitts., 1960-66; presdl. elector Pa., 1960; chmn. bd. Mayview State Hosp., Pitts., 1971-75. Served to lt. U.S. Army, 1948-49, 52-53. Mem. ABA, Pa. Bar Assn., Allegheny County Bar Assn. (real property council 1983-86).

GOLD, HAZEL, Spanish language educator; b. Bklyn., May 5, 1953; d. Robert Murray and Thelma (Steinberg) Gold. BA, Mt. Holyoke Coll., 1973; MA, U. Pa., 1974, PhD, 1980. Asst. prof. Columbia U., N.Y.C., 1980-85, Northwestern U., Evanston, Ill., 1985-92; assoc. prof. Emory U., Atlanta, 1992—, chair, 2000—03. Cons. and reader Spanish advanced placement exams Ednl. Testing Svc., Princeton, N.J., 1989—; rev. panelist NEH, Washington, 1990, 2005; vis. prof. U. Calif., Berkeley, 1998, mem. adv. bd. Pa. State U., Pa. State Romance Studies Series. Author: The Reframing of Realism: Galdo's and the Discourses of the 19th Century Spanish Novel; mem. editorial bd. Jour. for Interdisciplinary Lit. Studies, Anales Galdosianos; contbr. articles to profl. jours. Grantee U.S.-Spain Joint Com. Cultural and Ednl. Cooperation, 1986, Am. Coun. Learned Socs., 1990, fellow 1988. Mem. AAUP, MLA (divsn. exec. com. Spanish lit. 1991-95, Katherine Singer Kovacs prize selection com. 1996-99), Soc. Study Narrative Lit., Asociacion Internacional de Galdosistas (v.p. 1993-95, pres. 1996-99), Asociacion Internacional de Hispanistas, Midwest Modern Lang. Assn., Pa. Modern Lang. Assn. (Am. Assn. Tchrs. Spanish and Portuguese, Soc. Lit. Española del Siglo XIX. Office: Emory Univ Dept Spanish Atlanta GA 30322-0001

GOLD, JAMES PAUL, museum director; b. Seattle, Sept. 26, 1944; s. William J. and Madlyn (Hunsberger) G.; m. Cheryl Magruder, Apr. 6, 1968. BA, Hiram Coll., 1966; MA, Cooperstown Sch. SUNY, 1967. Tchr., curator Elwood Mus., Amsterdam, N.Y., 1968-71; dir. New Eng. Fire and History Mus., Brewster, Mass., 1972-74; site mgr. Senate House, N.Y. State Parks Recreation and Hist. Preservation, Kingston, 1974-77; regional historic sites supr. Bear Mountain, 1977-79; dir. N.Y. State Bur. Historic Sites and Resource Ctr., Waterford, 1979—. Chair Design Rev. commn. Saratoga springs, 1992-2002; mem. N.Y. State Document Conservation Adv. Coun., 1984-87. Recipient Lifetime Achievement award, Saratoga Springs Preservation Found., 2003. Mem. Cooperstown Grad. Assn. (bd. dirs. 1983-93), N.Y. State Assn. Museums (bd. dirs. 1985-92), Am. Assn. Museums (bd. dirs. 1988-93), Am. Assn. State and Local History, Assn. Preservation Tech., Mid-Atlantic Assn. Mus. (bd. dirs. 1988-93, 94-98, pres. 1994-97, Katherine Coffey award for disting. svc. to mus. profession 2003). Democrat. Unitarian Universalist. Avocations: photography, architecture, gardening. Home: 199 Woodlawn Ave Saratoga Springs NY 12866-1507 Office: NY State Parks Recreation and Historic Preservation Peebles Island Waterford NY 12188

GOLD, JANET NOWAKOWSKI, Spanish language educator; b. Torrington, Conn., Oct. 24, 1948; d. Peter S. and Virginia (Eseppi) Nowakowski; m. Hector Zamora, Dec. 1974 (div. Sept. 1978); m. Stephen Gold, June 28, 1981. BA, Albertus Magnus Coll., 1971; MEd, Worcester State Coll., 1981; PhD, U. Mass., 1990. Elem. sch. tchr., Tegucigalpa, Honduras, 1971-72; instr. English Centro Internat. de Idiomas, Cuernavaca, Mexico, instr. ESL, 1973; tchr. Spanish-English bilingual program Worcester (Mass.) Elem. Sch., 1974-82; tchg. asst. U. Mass., Amherst, 1984-88; instr. Spanish lang. and lit. Bates Coll., Lewiston, Mass., 1989-91; asst. prof. Spanish La. State U., Baton Rouge, 1991-95; assoc. prof. Spanish U. N.H., Durham, 1995—. Author: Clementina Suarez: Her Life and Poetry, 1995; contbr. books Reinterpreting the Spanish American Essay: Studies in Nineteenth and Twentieth Century Women's Essays, 1994, A Dream of Light and Shadow: Portraits of Latin American Women Writers, 1995; contbr. articles and revs. to Hispanic studies jours. Fulbright grantee, Honduras, 1988-89. Mem. MLA, Am. Assn. Tchrs. Spanish and Portuguese,Latin Am. Studies Assn., Millay Soc., Asociacion de Literatura Femenina Hispanica, Maine Writers and Publ. Alliance. Home: PO Box 357 Eliot ME 03903-0357 Office: U NH Dept Spanish Murkland 209 Durham NH 03824

GOLD, JEFFREY MARK, brokerage house executive, financial analyst; b. Bronx, N.Y., Jan. 7, 1945; s. Samuel L. and Sylvia E. Gold; m. Lenore N. Gold, May 29, 1966; children: Brian, Steven, Samuel. BBA in Acctg, Pace U., 1967. Sr. acct. KPMG Peat, Marwick, N.Y.C., 1967-71; v.p., corp. controller Nat. Patent Devel. Corp., N.Y.C., 1971-78; exec. v.p. fin. and adminstrn., chief fin. officer Esquire, Inc., N.Y.C., 1978-84; exec. v.p. strategic planning and corp. devel. Simon & Schuster div. of Paramount Communications, N.Y.C., 1984; pres. Goldmark Advisers, Inc., N.Y.C., 1985—; chmn. Quarto Holdings, Inc., 1994—; dir. Vision Fund Am., 2002—. Home: 515 E 72nd St New York NY 10021-4032 Office: Goldmark Advisers Inc 276 5th Ave Rm 205 New York NY 10001-4509 Office Phone: 212-779-6059. Personal E-mail: jmg@goldmarkadvisers.com.

GOLD, JOSEPH, medical researcher; b. Binghamton, N.Y., Jan. 17, 1930; s. Leon and Gertrude J. G.; m. Judith Barbara Taylor, June 12, 1955; children: Shannon Gabriel, Skye Raphael. AB, Cornell U., 1952; MD, Upstate Med. Univ., Syracuse, 1956. Diplomate Nat. Bd. Med. Examiners. USPHS postdoctoral rsch. fellow U. Calif. Sch. Medicine, 1956—58; fellow dept. pharmacology Upstate Med. Univ., Syracuse, 1961—62, rsch. asst. prof., 1962—64, asst. prof. pathology, 1964—65; dir. Syracuse Cancer Rsch. Inst., 1965—, trustee, 1965—. Editor: Monsters and Madonnas, The Roots of Christian Antisemitism, 1999; contbr. numerous articles on cancer research and therapy; contbr. chpts. to books. Served with USAF, 1958-61. Recipient Presdl. citation for work in Mercury Astronaut Selection Program, 1960; named Disting. Grad. Binghamton Sch. Dist., 1994. Mem. Am. Assn. Cancer Rsch., Am. Assn. for Lab. Animal Sci., N.Y. Acad. Scis., Onondaga County Med. Soc., Med. Soc. State N.Y. Achievements include pioneering work in proposing gluconeogenesis as a biochemical mechanism of cancer cachexia, 1968; development of hydrazine sulfate, 1st specific anti-cachexia drug to be used in human cancer; invention of process for the synthesis and prodn. of DL-Glyceraldehyde-3-phosphate in a pure and stable form; patentee in field. Home: 127 Edgemont Dr Syracuse NY 13214-2010 Office: 600 E Genesee St Syracuse NY 13202-3111 Office Phone: 315-472-6616.

GOLD, JUDITH HAMMERLING, psychiatrist; b. NYC, June 24, 1941; d. James S. and Anne (Linder) Hammerling; m. Edgar Gold, June 27, 1965. MD, Dalhousie U., 1965; DHumL (hon.), Mt. St. Vincent U., 2002. Intern Victoria Gen. Hosp., Halifax, N.S., Can., 1964-65; resident Dalhousie U., Halifax, 1967-71; practice medicine specializing in psychiatry Halifax, 1971—2002; staff psychiatrist Dalhousie U. Student Health Clinic, 1971-73; vis. colleague U. Wales Med. Sch., 1973-75; asst. prof. dept. psychiatry Dalhousie U., Halifax, 1975-78, assoc. prof., 1978-80, part-time, 1980-87; pvt. practice Brisbane, 1998—. Vis. prof., reader in psychotherapy studies U. Queensland Dept. of Psychiatry, Brisbane, 1998-99. Editor: Clinical Practice Series, 1987-2001, 5 books; contbr. articles to profl. jours. Bd. govs. Mt. St. Vincent U., 1981-87, chmn., 1986-87. Med. Research Council Can. fellow, 1973-75; Health and Welfare Bd. Can. grantee, 1976-78 Fellow Am. Psychiat. Assn., Am. Coll. Psychiatrists (1st v.p. 1990-91, pres.-elect 1991-92, pres. 1992-93); mem. Can. Psychiat. Assn. (pres. 1981-82), Royal Coll. Phys. Surgeons Can. (exec. mem. 1992-94, coun. 1991-98), Order Can., Alpha Omega Alpha. Office Phone: (61) (7) 3839-4788.

GOLD, KEITH DEAN, advertising and design executive; b. Pique, Ohio, Mar. 7, 1956; Student, Ringling Sch. Art, 1974—74, U. Fla., 1975—76; BA, U. No. Fla., 1977. Art dir. Market Assocs., Jacksonville, Fla., 1975-76, Ambrose Design, Jacksonville, 1976-77; prin. Interpublic, WJT, Atlanta,

1977—78; exec. art dir., assoc. creative dir. Bates Worldwide Lewis, Clark and Graham, Atlanta, 1978-81; assoc. creative dir. Price/McNabb, Asheville, NC, 1981—83; sr. v.p., dir. creative svcs., ptnr. Earle, Palmer, Brown, Tampa, Fla., 1983—86; exec. v.p., ptnr., dir. creative svcs. Omnicom, Ann Arbor, Mich., 1986—88; pres., CEO, creative dir. GOLD & Assocs, Ponte Vedra Beach, Fla., 1989—; exec. creative dir, mng. dir. DMB&B/Gold, Atlanta, 1993-94. Prof. Kennesaw Coll., Atlanta, 1977-80; bd. dirs., ptnr. Package Material Sales, Inc., Tampa, Fla.; owner GOLD Investments, Inc., Ponte Vedra Beach, Fla.; lectr. in field. Author: Setting the Course of Excellence, 1986, Controlling The Weather, 1999; featured in Kodansha Pubs. World Graphic Design; designer U.S. postage stamp, Olympic posters, numerous books and CD covers; exhibited in shows at Mus. Modern Art, N.Y.C., Ringling Mus. Art, Sarasota, Fla.; work represented in Libr. of Congress, Ringling Mus. Art, Mus. TV and Radio, N.Y.C. Recipient over 850 awards including 1st pl. awards from Advt. Club N.Y., AIGA, Am. Graphic Design, Clio awards, Vision awards, Communications Arts, Graphis, Zurich Internat. Advt. Festival of N.Y., Internat. Poster Festival, N.Y. Soc. Illustrators, Pub. Broadcasting Sys., Print Mag., Telly awards, Internat. Film and TV Festival N.Y., London Internat. Advt., Global Creative awards, N.Y. Art Dirs. Club, The One Show, Global Mktg. awards, Internat. Festivals, N.Y. Advt. Festival, N.Y. Film Festival, Graphic Design: U.S.A., Creativity, Print Mags. Design Annual, Photo Design; named one of Fla.'s Top All Time Coll. Grads. Fla. Bd. Regents, 1989, U. North Fla. Outstanding Alumnus of Yr., 1999; named one of Top 10 Ad Execs. of the 1980's Wall St. Jour., 50 Comm. Execs. to Watch in the New Millenium Graphic Design: USA. Mem.: Am. Inst. Graphic Arts. Presbyterian. Avocations: painting, writing, golf, duck hunting. Office: Gold & Assocs Gold Bldg 6000C Sawgrass Village Cir Ponte Vedra Beach FL 32082-5026 Home: 204 Clearwater Dr Ponte Vedra Beach FL 32082

GOLD, KENNETH R., international business development executive; b. Providence, Ky., Aug. 9, 1934; s. R. Vernon Gold and Irene Frances Mitchell; m. Olga Ann Szakacs, Aug. 23, 1958; children: Victoria, Rebecca, Jennifer. AB, Wayne State U., 1960; MBA, Fla. State Christian U., 1971. Mktg. mgr. IBM Corp., 1960-70; dir. product devel. GTE Data Svcs., Tampa, Fla., 1970—73; internat. dir. Cincom Systems, Cin., 1973—79; internat. v.p. Mathematica, Princeton, NJ, 1980—88; founder, CEO 4 GL Inc., Miami, Fla., 1989—96, Seaplane Tech., West Palm Beach, Fla., 1996. Instr. I.T., U. Toledo, 1968-70. Contbr. articles to I.T. jours. With USN Seaplane Squadron VP-45, 1952-56. Republican. Presbyterian. Avocations: flying, travel. Home: 8005 Wren Ave Hobe Sound FL 33455 Office Phone: 772-263-6890. E-mail: goldkr@aol.com.

GOLD, LEONARD SINGER, librarian, translator, curator; b. Bklyn., July 3, 1934; s. Hyman B. and Gertrude (Singer) G.; m. Stella Schmidt, June 5, 1960; children: Yael, Dalia. BA, McGill U., 1956; MS in Libr. Service, Columbia U., 1966; MA, NYU, 1967, PhD, 1975; student, C. Redmond Art Students League, 1998—2001. Cert. profl. librarian, N.Y. Tchr. high sch., Kiryat Hayim, Israel, 1960-61; tchr. Hugim High Sch., Haifa, Israel, 1961-63; tech. asst. N.Y. Pub. Libr., N.Y.C., 1963-66, chief Jewish div., 1971-98, Dorot chief libr. Jewish div., bibliographer Jewish studies, 1987-98, asst. dir. Jewish, Oriental and Slavonic studies, 1980-88. Chmn. Jewish and Middle East studies program com. Rsch. Librs. Group, Inc., 1989-91; curator hist. exhbns. A Sign and A Witness: 2000 Years of Hebrew Books and Illuminated Manuscripts, N.Y. Pub. Libr., 1988-89, The Dead Sea Scrolls: Ancient Civilization, Modern Scholarship, N.Y. Pub. Libr., 1993-94. Translator (Nathan Shaham): The Other Side of the Wall, 3 novellas, 1983; editor: A Sign and A Witness: 2000 Years of Hebrew Books and Illuminated Manuscripts, 1988; exhibitions include Bob Laurie Gallery, N.Y.C., 2000, Broome St. Gallery, 2001, 2002; assoc. editor: Jewish Book Annual, 1979—94; contbr. to bibliog publs. Astor fellow, 1986-87. Mem. Assn. Jewish Librs. (pres. 1974-76, lifetime mem. award 1998), Coun. Archives and Rsch. Librs. in Jewish Studies (pres. 1978-80, disting. svc. award 1998), Jewish Book Coun. (v.p. 1980-90, pres. 1990-94), Assn. Jewish Studies, Rsch. Librs. Group (chmn. Jewish and Mid. East studies program com. 1989-91, mem. programs adv. group 1991-92), Jewish Publ. Soc. (editl. com. 1986-2002, nat. coun. 2002—). Personal E-mail: LGold10545@aol.com.

GOLD, LORNE W., Canadian government official; b. Saskatoon, Sask., Can., June 7, 1928; s. Alexander Stewart and Grace Dora (Davis) G.; m. Elizabeth Joan L'Ami, Sept. 8, 1951; children: Catherine Anne, Patricia Ellen, Judith Sharon, Kenneth Robert. BSc, U. Sask., 1950; MSc in Physics, McGill U., 1952, PhD, 1970. Research officer div. bldg. research Nat. Research Coucil Can., Ottawa, Ont., 1950-52, head snow and ice sect., 1953-69, head geotech. sect., 1969-74, asst. dir. div., 1974-79, assoc. dir. div., 1979-86, chmn., assoc. com. geotech. research, 1976-83, guest worker inst. research on constrn., 1987; rschr. emeritus Nat. Rsch. Coun. of Can., Ottawa, Ont., 1988—. Canadian del. to Intern. Union of Testing and Research Labs. for Materials and Structures, 1982-87, bd. dirs. Coun. Internat. du Batiment, 1983-86; sr. visiting scientist Ctr. for Cold Oceans Resources Engring., Meml. U. of Newfoundland, 1987-88; vis. rschr. Inst. for Marine dynamics, NRC of Can., 1990-91. Author: The Canadian Habbakuk Project, 1993. Chair coun. Rideau Park United Ch., Ottawa, 2003—05. Fellow Royal Soc. Can. (sec. Acad. Sci. 1997-2001), Can. Acad. Engring., Engring. Inst. Can., Can. Soc. Civil Engrs. (Horst Leipholz medal 1991); mem. Internat. Glaciol. Soc. (pres. 1978-81), Assn. Profl. Engrs. Ont., Engring. Inst. Can. (hon. treas. 1991-96), Can. Geotech. Soc. (Roger Brown Meml. award 2003). Mem. United Ch. Of Canada. Home: 1903 Illinois Ave Ottawa ON Canada K1H 6W5 Office: Nat Rsch Coun of Can Inst for Rsch in Constrn Ottawa ON Canada K1A 0R6

GOLD, MARI S., public relations executive; b. N.Y.C., June 17, 1940; d. George B. and Natalie (Machol) Sour; m. Joel S. Ullman, May 27, 1983. BA, Vassar Coll., 1962. Coord. Family Book Svc., Meredith Pub. Co., N.Y.C., 1962-64; assoc. producer Tanglewood Theatre, Lords Valley, Pa., 1966-68; producer CasperCitron Program, N.Y.C., 1968-70; free-lance publicist N.Y.C., 1970-74; with Lobsenz-Stevens Inc., N.Y.C., 1974—, exec. v.p., 1981—, assoc. gen. mgr., 1985-92; dep. press sec. N.Y.C. Health & Hosps. Corp., 1992-93, dr. mktg. and comm., 1993-95; dir. comm. MetroPlus Health Plan, N.Y.C., 1995—. Office: MetroPlus Health Plan 160 Water St New York NY 10038 E-mail: goldm@nychc.org.

GOLD, MARTIN ELLIOTT, lawyer, educator; b. NYC, Jan. 6, 1946; s. Herman and Rose (Zippin) G.; m. Mary Byrne. BA, Cornell U., 1967; JD, Harvard U., 1970, MPA, 1971. Bar: N.Y. 1972, U.S. Dist. Ct. (so. and ea. dists.) N.Y. 1974, U.S. Ct. Appeals (2d cir.) 1974. With Operation Crossroads Africa, The Gambia, 1965; cons. U.S. Dept. Justice, 1968; assoc. Freshfields, London, 1969; rsch. fellow Ctr. Law and Devel. Sri Lanka, Cambridge, Mass., 1971-73; assoc. Debevoise & Plimpton, N.Y.C., 1973-78; chief econ. devel. divsn. N.Y.C. Law Dept., 1978-85, N.Y.C. dir. corp. law, 1980-85; ptnr. Sidley Austin Brown & Wood, N.Y.C., 1985—. Adj. prof. Columbia U., 1987—; guest lectr. Fordham U., Yale U., Cornell U., U.S. Conf. of Mayors, U.S. Justice Dept., others. Author: Law and Social Change: A Study of Land Reform in Sri Lanka, 1977; contbr. articles to profl. jours. Mem. Legal Aid Soc., 1975-81, Cornell Real Estate Coun., 1988—; bd. dirs. Environ. Action Coalition, 1988-2002, INFORM, 1989—, J.F. Kennedy Sch., Tri State Coun., 1991-97; chmn. Ridgefield Coun. Lake Assns. Recipient awards, Rockefeller Bros. Fund, 1979, 1980, Fund for City N.Y., 1981, Leadership award, J.F. Kennedy Sch. Mem. ABA, Internat. Assn. Attys. and Execs. in Corp. Real Estate, Nat. Coun. for Pub. and Pvt. Partnerships, Natural Resources Def. Coun., Assn. Bar City N.Y. (environ., mcpl., energy and real property and housing law coms.), Urban Land Inst., Common Cause, Cornell Club. Home: 140 Riverside Dr Apt 12H New York NY 10024 Office Phone: 212-839-5481. Business E-Mail: megold@sidley.com.

GOLD, MICHAEL EVAN, law educator; b. Oakland, Calif., Apr. 14, 1943; s. Ellis and Ruth Lorraine Gold; m. Sarah Dogbe, Apr. 20, 1971; children: Elijah Laoba, Kebbeh Calypso. BA, U. Calif., Berkeley, 1965; LLB, Stanford U., 1967. Bar: Calif. 72, NY 78, U.S. Supreme Ct. 78. Vol. Peace Corps, Liberia, 1968—70; atty. Schwartz, Steinsapir & Dohrmann, LA, 1972—75; assoc. prof. San Fernando Valley Coll. Law, LA, 1975—77, Cornell U., Ithaca, NY, 1977—. Author: A Dialogue on Comparable Worth, 1983; contbr. articles to profl. jours. Home: 102 Oxford Pl Ithaca NY 14850-4720 Office: Cornell U Ives Hall Ithaca NY 14853-3901 Business E-Mail: meg3@cornell.edu.

GOLD, PAUL ERNEST, psychology and behavioral neuroscience educator; b. Detroit, Jan. 7, 1945; s. Hyman and Sylvia Gold; children: Scott David Gold, Zachary Alexander Korol-Gold. BA, U. Mich., 1966; MS, U. N.C., 1968; PhD, 1971. NIH postdoctoral fellow, lectr. psychobiology U. Calif., Irvine, 1972-76; asst. prof. U. Va., Charlottesville, 1976-78, assoc. prof., 1978-81, prof., 1981-97, Commonwealth prof., 1997—99, dir. neurosci. grad. program, 1991-95; prof. Binghamton (N.Y.) U., 1999-2000, U. Ill., Urbana-Champaign, 2000—. Dir. Med. Scholars Program U. Ill. Coll. Medicine, Urbana-Champaign, 2000—02, exec. com. Inst. Aging, 2001—, interim dir. neurosci. program, 2004—05. Editor Psychobiology, 1990-97, Neurobiology of Learning and Memory, 1998—; contbr. numerous articles to sci. publs. Mem. Commonwealth of Va. Alzheimer's and Related Disorders Commn., 1998-99. Recipient James McKeen Cattell award, 1983, Sesquicentennial Assn. award, U. Va., 1983, 90-93, Disting. Alumni award U. N.C., Chapel Hill, 2000; named APA Master Lectr., 2000; NIH fellow, 1967. Fellow APA (com. animal rsch. & ethics), AAAS, Am. Psychol. Soc. (mem. com. 1990-91, program com. 1991); mem. Soc. for Neurosci. (com. on animals in rsch. 1993-98), NSF Adv. Panel for Behavioral and Computational Neurosci., 1993-96. Office: U Ill at Urbana-Champaign Dept Psychology Champaign IL 61820 Business E-Mail: pgold@uiuc.edu.

GOLD, PETER FREDERICK, lawyer; b. N.Y.C., Nov. 10, 1945; s. John and Dolores (Soyer) G.; children: Joshua, Katharine. BA, Cornell U., 1967; MSc, London Sch. Econs., 1968; JD, NYU, 1971. Bar: D.C. 1988, N.Y. 1972, U.S. Dist. Ct. (so. dist.) N.Y. 1972, U.S. Dist. Ct. (ea. dist.) N.Y. 1972. Assoc. atty. Paul, Weiss, Rifkind, Wharton & Garrison, N.Y.C., 1971-75; legis. dir. Senator Gary Hart, Washington, 1975-81; ptnr. Wellford, Wegman, Krulwich, Gold & Hoff, Washington, 1981-84, Winthrop, Stimson, Putnam & Roberts, Washington, 1984-94; pres. The Gold Group, Chartered, Washington, 1994—, C.G. Sloan & Co., Inc., 1995-97. Editor in chief Review of Law and Social Change, 1970. Nat. policy dir. Hart for Pres. Campaign, Washington, 1984; chmn., founder First Book, Washington, 1992—; dir. Share Our Strength, Washington, 1990—; mem. Clinton-Gore Transition Team, Washington, 1992. Recipient Disting. Visitor Program European Econ. Community, Brussels, Belgium, 1982. Mem. D.C. Bar Assn., Fed. Bar Assn., N.Y.C. Bar Assn., Kenwood Golf & Country Club, Four Streams Golf Club (dir.). Democrat. Jewish. Avocations: tennis, golf. Home: 13640 Glenhurst Rd North Potomac MD 20878-3921 Office: The Gold Group Chartered 1319 F St NW Ste 1000 Washington DC 20004-1106 Office Phone: 202-347-5542.

GOLD, PHIL, immunologist, educator, researcher; b. Montreal, Sept. 17, 1936; m. Evelyn Katz; 3 children. BSc in Physiology with honors, McGill U., Montreal, 1957, MSc, MD, 1961, PhD in Physiology, 1965; DSc (hon.), McMaster U., 1986. Licentiate Med. Coun. Can. Jr. rotating intern Montreal Gen. Hosp., 1961—62, jr. asst. resident in medicine, 1962—63, sr. resident in medicine, 1965—66, jr. asst. physician, asst. and assoc. physician, 1967—73, sr. physician, 1973—2003, physician-in-chief, 1980-95, dir. divsn. clin. immunology and allergy, 1977—80, dir. McGill U. Med. Clinic, 1980—95, also sr. investigator Research Inst.; faculty dept. physiology McGill U., 1964—, mem. faculty of medicine, 1965—, prof. medicine and clin. medicine, 1973—, chmn. dept. medicine and clin. medicine, 1985—90, prof. physiology, 1974—, prof. oncology, 1989—, mem. faculty of medicine exec. com. representing clin. depts., 1985—, D. G. Cameron prof. medicine (inaugural), 1987—; exec. dir. Clin. Rsch. Ctr. Mont. Gen. Hosp. and McGill U. Hosp. Ctr., 1995—. Vis. scientist Pub. Health Research Inst. N.Y.C., 1967-68; Chester M. Jones Meml. lectr. Mass. Gen. Hosp., 1974; vis. prof. U. Caracas, Venezuela, 1974; Squires Club vis. prof. Wellesley Hosp., Toronto, 1983; Cecil H. and Ida Green vis. prof., 1984 autumn lectures U. Brit. Columbia; cons. in allergy and immunology Mt. Sinai Hosp., St. Agathe des Monts, Quebec, 1975—; hon. cons. dept. medicine Royal Victoria Hosp., Montreal; cons. dept. internal medicine Douglas Hosp. Ctr., Montreal; vice chmn. med. adv. com. Council of Physicians, Dentists and Pharmacists, 1985-90; mem. Conseil d'Adminstrn., Found. Quebecoise du Cancer, 1986-88, adv. com. Burroughs Wellcome fellowship fund, 1998—; health com. mem. Centre d'Entreprises et d'Innovation de Montreal, 1996—; Sir Arthur Sims travelling prof., 1998. Mem. editorial bd. Clin. Immunology and Immunopathology, 1972—, Immunopharmacology, 1978—, Diagnostic Gynecology and Obstetrics, 1978-83, Oncodevelopmental Biology and Medicine, 1979—, Modern Medicine of Can., 1984-90, Jour. Internal Medicine, 1988—, Canadians for Health Rsch., 1989—, Current Therapeutic Rsch., 1992—, Nutrition Quar., 1992—; editorial cons. Jour. Chronic Diseases, 1981-84; mem. editorial adv. bd. Cancer Research, 1971-73, assoc. editor 1973-80; contbg. editor Practical Allergy and Immunology, 1991—; editl. bd. Can. Jour. Allergy & Clin. Immunology, 1996—; contbr. over 140 articles to med. jours. External referee Can. Red Cross Soc. Decorated companion Order of Can., officer L'ordre nat. du Quebec, Great Montrealer, knight comdr. Sovereign Order St. John Jerusalem, Knights of Malta; named Most Outstanding Can. Med. Personality of the past 25 years, MacLean's Mag., 1986; recipient Hiram Mills Gold medal, Mosby Scholarship Book award, Wood Gold medal, E.W.R. Steacie prize, Nat. Rsch. Coun. Can., 1973, Can. Silver Jubilee medal, 1977, Johann-Georg-Zemmerman prize for cancer rsch., Medizinische Hochschule, Hannover, Germany, 1978, Gold medal award of merit, Internat. award, Gardner Found., Ernest C. Manning prize, F.N.G. Starr award Izzak Walton Killam prize, Can. Coun., 1985, Tower of Hope award, Israel Cancer Rsch. Fund, 1985, Sci. Achievement medal, Govt. of Italy, 1990, Agora trophy, Ambassador's Club, 1991, Internat. Soc. Oncodevel. Biol. Medicine Internat. Abbott award, 1992, Commemorative medal 125th Anniversary of Can. Confedn., Govt. of Can., 1992, Carl Goresky Meml. award, 1999, Christie award, Can. Assn. of Profs. of Medicine, 1999, 20th Anniversary of L'Actualité Medicale award for outstanding contbns. to medicine, 2000, Queen Elizabeth II Golden Jubilee medal, 2002, Edwin F. Ullman award, Am. Assn. for Clin. Chemistry, 2004, Alpha Omega Achievement medal, 2005; MacDonald scholar, J. Francis Williams scholar, Univ. scholar. Fellow: AAAS; mem.: Internat. Assn. Health Profls. (chmn. 1998). Achievements include discovery of Carcinoembryonic Antigen (CEA). Office: Clin Rsch Ctr Montreal Gen Hosp 1650 Cedar Ave Montreal PQ Canada H3G 1A4 Office Phone: 514-934-1934 x430. E-mail: phil.gold@mcgill.ca.

GOLD, PHRADIE KLING See KLING, PHRADIE

GOLD, RICHARD L., lawyer; b. N.Y.C., Feb. 23, 1950; s. Murray and Ruth Lillian (Nesselson) G.; m. Mary Laroe, Mar. 15, 1975; 1 child, Scott. BA, SUNY, Binghamton, 1972; student, Columbia U., 1972-73; JD, NYU, 1976. Bar: N.Y. 1976. From assoc. to ptnr. Bandler & Kass, N.Y.C., 1976-85; ptnr. Sylvor, Schneer, Gold & Morelli, N.Y.C., 1985—, Morelli & Gold, LLP, N.Y.C., 1996—. Contbr: You and the Law, 1984. Coach baseball Stamford (Conn.) Am. Little League, 1994-97, Stamford Babe Ruth, 1998. Mem. ABA, N.Y. State Bar Assn., Bar Assn. City of N.Y., Phi Beta Kappa. Avocation: sports. Office: 605 Third Ave New York NY 10158 Office Phone: 212-972-1100 237. E-mail: rlgold1977@aol.com.

GOLD, RICHARD N., management consultant; b. Chgo., May 27, 1945; s. Irving Louis and Victoria (Saltzman) G.; m. Renee Bonnie Rein, Nov. 3, 1968; children: Jedd Steven, Amanda Caryn. BSI, U. Wis., 1967; MBA with honors, Columbia U., 1971; MA with honors, NYU, 1971. Tchr., supr. Ocean-Hill Brownsville, NYC Pub. Schs., 1968—71; brand mgr. packaged soap and detergent divsn. Procter & Gamble Co., Cin., 1971—76; exec. v.p. Glendinning Assocs., Westport, Conn., 1976—81; pres. R.N. Gold & Co., 1981—; prodr., ptnr. Enterplan, NYC, 1983—85; dir. mktg. Downtown Coun., Cin., 1975—77. Bd. dirs. Hampton Products Internat. Corp., Soft-Lock.com Inc., Luminary Graphics Inc., Autolink.com Data Nat. Corp.; bd. advs. LA Brewing Co., Designer Fragrances Internat., Evolve Products Inc., CursorMate.com. Mem.: Am. Mgmt. Assn., Pres. Assn. Avocations: sports, theater, collecting antique electronic musical devices. Office: RN Gold & Co 19 Rowayton Ave Norwalk CT 06853-1627 Office Phone: 203-831-0001. E-mail: rngoldco@aol.com.

GOLD, SARAE R., art educator; b. Mpls., Mar. 26, 1950; d. Samuel N. and Lillian Himmelfarb; m. Gary L. Nagel, Dec. 26, 1971 (div. Feb. 1991); children: Jill S. Nagel, Marcy B. Nagel; m. Herbert Arnold Gold, Feb. 18, 1996. BA in Art Edn., Northeastern Ill. U., 1970; MS in Art Edn., No. Ill. U., 1999; postgrad., Grand Valley State U., 2002, U. Nev. Las Vegas, 2003. Cert. tchr. Ill., Nev. Tchr. Chgo. Pub. Schs., 1970—74; sales rep. ARA Serve, Chgo., 1981—83; mgr. area ADIA Pers. Svcs., Chgo., 1983—84, NJ, 1984—86; pres. Photo Promotions Plus, NY and NJ, 1986—90; v.p. Olsten Profl. Acctg. Svcs., Chgo., 1990—93; pres. Photo Promotions Plus, Chgo., 1993—95; tchr. Chgo. Pub. Sch., 1995—99; dir. Fine Arts Grand Rapids Pub. Schs., Mich., 1999—2002; tchr. art Clark County Sch. Dist., Las Vegas, 2002—. Adj. art edn. prof. U. Nev., Las Vegas, 2004. Art Peoples Park, UNLV, 2003, Something Fishy in Grand Rapids, 2000, Santa Training School, N.J., 1987. Recipient Educator of Yr., Grand Rapids, 2002. Mem.: Nat. Art Edn. Assn., Art Educators So. Nev. (co-chair state conf. 2003, dir.-elect 2003—). Avocations: woodcarving, pastels.

GOLD, SHARON CECILE, artist, educator; b. N.Y.C., Feb. 28, 1949; d. Henry Joseph and Betty (Kopan) G.; m. William McKay Watson III, July 12, 1992; 1 child, Miranda Cecile. Student, CUNY, 1967-68, Columbia U., 1968-70; BFA, Pratt Inst., 1976. Adj. prof. Art NYU, 1983; vis. artist SUNY, Purchase, 1985; assoc. prof. painting and critical theory Syracuse (N.Y.) U., 1986—; vis. artist The Art Inst. Chgo., Chgo., 1990. Lectr. in field; guest critic Sch. Visual Arts, N.Y.C., 1987, N.Y. Studio Sch., 1988. Solo exhibits include Stephen Rosenberg Gallery, N.Y.C., 1987, 89, 91, 55 Mercer St., N.Y.C., 1986, John Davis Gallery, Akron, Ohio, 1986, Pam Adler Gallery, N.Y.C., 1986; group exhibits include IRIS House, N.Y.C., 1992, Everson Mus. of Art, Syracuse, 1991, ARTSTAR, L.A., 1991, Stephen Rosenberg Gallery, N.Y., 1991, Rose Art Mus. Brandeis U., 1990, Robert Pardo Gallery, N.Y.C., 2001; performance/video works include A Video Tape 1990-1991 Stephen Rosenberg Gallery, 1991, North South Consonance St. Stephen's Ch., N.Y.C., 1984. Pratt Inst. Acad. fellow, 1974-76, NEA grantee, 1981, Penny McCall Found. grantee, 1988. Home: 10 Leonard St New York NY 10013-2929 Office Phone: 212-925-6885. Business E-Mail: sharon@watsongold.com.

GOLD, SIMEON, lawyer; b. Hartford, Conn., Jan. 3, 1949; s. Charles and Claire (Goldschein) G.; m. Heide Aline Turkel, Aug. 30, 1970; children: Jana, Craig. BS, Cornell U., 1970; JD, Harvard U., 1973. Bar: N.Y., U.S. Dist. Ct. (so. dist.) N.Y., U.S. Ct. Appeals (2d cir.). Assoc. Weil, Gotshal & Manges LLP, N.Y.C., 1973-81, ptnr., 1981—. Bd. dirs. Lawyers Alliance for N.Y. Contbr. articles to profl. jours. Mem. Coun. of Bus. Exec. Assn. for Help of Retarded Children, N.Y.C., Legal Aid Soc., N.Y.C.; bd. trustees Dalton Sch., 1997-2000. Mem. ABA, N.Y. State Bar Assn. (chair bus. law sect. 2000-01, chair corp. law com. 1993-97), Assn. of Bar of City of N.Y., N.Y. County Lawyers Assn., Harmonie Club, Old Oaks Country Club. Avocations: skiing, tennis, golf, travel. Office: Weil Gotshal & Manges LLP 767 5th Ave Fl Concl New York NY 10153-0119 Office Phone: 212-310-8226. Business E-Mail: simeon.gold@weil.com.

GOLD, STANLEY PHILLIP, diversified investments executive; b. 1942; AB, U. Calif., 1964; JD, U. So. Calif., 1967. Ptnr. Gang Tyre and Brown, 1967-85, Shamrock Holdings Inc., Burbank, Calif., 1985—; pres., CEO, Shamrock Holdings, Burbank. Bd. trustees, chmn. U. So. Calif. Office: Shamrock Holdings Inc 4444 W Lakeside Dr Burbank CA 91505-4054 Office Phone: 818-845-4444. E-mail: sgold@shamrock.com.

GOLD, STEVEN DOUGLAS, lawyer; b. Madisonville, Ky., Aug. 26, 1951; s. Marvin L. and Martha Jonell (Harvey) G.; m. Elaine Strehle, Nov. 26, 1971; children: Steven Richard, Francine Jonell. BA, Eastern Ky. U., 1973; JD, U. Ky., 1976. Bar: Ky. 1976, U.S. Ct. Mil. Appeals 1977, U.S. Dist. Ct. (we. dist.) Ky. 1979, U.S. Tax Ct. 1981. Pub. defender Commonwealth of Ky., Henderson, 1979-83, commonwealth atty., 1988-93; domestic rels. commr. Henderson Cir. Ct., 1999—2002, master commr., 1999—; assoc. L.B. Lawton, Attorney, Henderson, 1979-82; ptnr. Sheffer & Hoffman, Henderson, 1982-85; pvt. practice Henderson, 1985-98; sr. ptnr. Gold & Gold, Henderson, 1998—. Comments editor, UK Law Jour., 1975-76. Adv. bd. Salvation Army, Henderson, 1987—; bd. dir. Henderson County Tourism Corp., 1990-2003; elder 1st Christian Church. Capt. US Army, 1973-79, Okinawa. Named to Honorable Order of Ky. Colonels, 1987. Mem. Henderson County Bar Assn., Ky. Bar Assn., Am. Legion (post 40, judge advocate 1988-97), Moose Lodge. Democrat. Avocation: tennis. Office: 134 N Main St Henderson KY 42420-3102 Office Phone: 270-826-1188. E-mail: goldlaw@insightbb.com.

GOLD, STEVEN MICHAEL, lawyer; b. Bklyn., Sept. 19, 1953; s. Joseph and Gladys (Goss) G.; m. Susan Schwartz, Jan. 9, 1977; children: Rachel, David, Hannah. BA, Hobart Coll., 1975; JD, Cornell U., 1978. Bar: Conn. 1979, N.Y. 1979, U.S. Dist. Ct. Conn. 1979, U.S. Dist. Ct. (no. dist.) N.Y. 1979. Confidential law asst. 3d dept. appellate div. N.Y. Supreme Ct., Albany, 1978-79; assoc. Schatz & Schatz, Ribicoff & Kotkin, Hartford & Stamford, Conn., 1979-86, ptnr. Stamford, 1987-96, Shipman & Goodwin, LLP, Stamford, 1996—. Treas. Cmty. Coun. Westport/Weston, Conn., 1985, 1st v.p., 1987, bd. dirs., 1985-87; bd. dirs., counsel Urban League Greater Bridgeport, 1987-92; bd. dirs., v.p. Stamford Symphony Soc., 1990-95, counsel, 1994-95; bd. dirs. Nursing and Home Care, 1996-97, Women's Bus. Devel. Ctr., 2001-. Mem. ABA, N.Y. State Bar Assn., Conn. Bar Assn., Fairfield County Bar Assn. (dir. 2002—), Assn. Comml. Fin. Attys., Assn. Corporate Growth, Nat. Assn. Transp. Practitioners (treas. Conn. chpt. 1983-85), Entrepreneurship Inst. (adv. bd. 1989-91), Phi Delta Phi, Pi Gamma Mu. Democrat. Jewish. Avocation: squash. Office: Shipman & Goodwin LLP 300 Atlantic St Stamford CT 06902-3522 Office Phone: 203-324-8102. Business E-Mail: sgold@goodwin.com.

GOLD, STUART WALTER, lawyer; b. N.Y.C., Mar. 3, 1949; s. Morris I. and Barbara (Walters) G.; m. Michele M. Cardella, June 26, 1983. BA in Polit. Sci., Bklyn. Coll., 1969; JD, NYU, 1972. Bar: N.Y. 1973, U.S. Supreme Ct. 1983, U.S. Ct. Appeals (2d, 3d, 7th, 8th, 9th and D.C. cirs.). Law clk. to judge U.S. Dist. Ct. (so. dist.) N.Y., 1972-73; assoc. Cravath, Swaine & Moore LLP, N.Y.C., 1973-80, ptnr., 1980—. Mem. ABA, N.Y. State Bar Assn., Assn. of Bar City of N.Y. Democrat. Avocations: scuba diving, travel. Office: Cravath Swaine & Moore LLP 825 8th Ave Fl 40 New York NY 10019-7475 Office Phone: 212-474-1394. Office Fax: 212-474-3700. E-mail: sgold@cravath.com.

GOLD, WILLIAM ELLIOTT, health care management consultant, educator; b. Bklyn., Oct. 21, 1948; s. Theodore David and Debra (Fridovich) G.; m. Nili Rachel Scharf, June 1, 1972; children: Avitai, Doria Michelle. BA, SUNY, Stony Brook, 1970; MSS, Hebrew U. of Jerusalem, Israel, 1972; PhD, U. Minn., 1982. Rsch. asst. Hebrew U. of Jerusalem, 1971-72; cons. Dept. Health, Mpls., 1973-74; researcher Mt. Sinai Hosp., Mpls., 1973-74; hosp. adminstrn. instr. U. Minn., Mpls., 1974-75; coord., dir. Blue Cross/Blue Shield Greater N.Y. HMO, N.Y.C., 1975-85; pres. ANCHOR, Chgo.; v.p. Rush-Presbyn. St. Luke's Med. Ctr., Chgo., 1985-88; pres. Gold Health Strategies Inc., N.Y.C., 1988—. Bd. dirs. N.Y. Bus. Group on Health, chmn. managed care task force, 1989—; vice chmn. The HMO Group, 1987-88; steering com. U. Mo.-KC Nat. Ctr. for Managed Care Adminstrn., Kansas City, 1986-98; asst. adj. prof. Columbia U., N.Y.C., 1989-99, clin. prof., 1999—. Founding editor Managing Employee Health Benefits. Fellowship Caldwell B. Esselstyn Found., 1991-92; mem. task force pub. health and managed care PEW Charitable Trust, 1995-96; mem. task force improving cardiovascular health Am. Heart Assn., N.Y.C., 1995-96. Avocations: clarinet, music, sports, photography. Home: 322 W 72nd St # 14B New York NY 10023-2676 Office: Gold Health Strategies Inc 250 Park Ave St 1300 New York NY 10177-0001 Office Phone: 212-953-1504. E-mail: bgold@goldhealthstrategies.com.

GOLDBACH, JENNIFER DEBERDINE, bank executive; b. Quarryville, Pa. married; 1 child. BA in Computer Scis., Dickinson Coll., 1984. Mgmt. trainee to v.p. residential mortgage mgr. Fulton Bank, Lancaster, Pa., 1984—95; from v.p. and mgr. mortgage lending to sr. v.p. retail lending Sterlin Fin. Corp., Lancaster, 1995—2000, sr. v.p. retail lending, 2000—02; pres., CEO First Nat. Bank North East, Md., 2002—. Past pres. Child Abuse Prevention Com. Ctrl. Pa.; mem. Union Hosp. Found., Elkton, Md., Cecil CC Found., North East, Md., North East C. of C., pres.; mem. mission outreach com. Salem United Ch. Christ; bd. dir. Am. Heart Assn. Named One of 25 Women to Watch, U.S. Banker Mag., 2003. Mem.: Mortgage Bankers Assn. Ctrl. Pa. (chmn. conf. 2000, 2001, past pres., past gov.). Avocation: golf. Office: First National Bank North East 14 South Main St North East MD 21901 Office Phone: 410-287-5000 ext. 114.

GOLDBARD, LAURA E., lawyer; b. NYC, June 14, 1956; BA, Emory Univ., Atlanta, 1978; JD, Univ. Miami, 1981. Bar: NY 1983. Adminstrv. ptnr., intellectual property practice area Stroock & Stroock & Lavan LLP, NYC. Contbr. articles to profl. journals. Mem.: ABA, Copyright Soc. USA, Internat. Trademark Assn. Office: Stroock & Stroock & Lavan LLP 180 Maiden Ln New York NY 10038-4982 Office Phone: 212-806-6675. Office Fax: 212-806-6006. Business E-Mail: lgoldbard@stroock.com.

GOLDBERG, ALAN MARVIN, toxicologist, educator; b. Bklyn., Nov. 20, 1939; s. William and Celia Ida (Rudman) G.; m. Helene Schoenbach, Aug. 14, 1960; children: Michael David, Naomi Jill BS, Bklyn. Coll. Pharmacy, 1961; PhD in Pharmacology, U. Minn., 1966; DSc (hon.), L.I. U, 1995. Rsch. asst. U. Wis., 1961-62, U. Minn., 1962-66; rsch. assoc. Inst. Psychiat. Rsch. Ind. U., 1966-67, asst. prof. dept. pharmacology, 1967-69; asst. prof. environ. medicine Johns Hopkins U., Balt., 1969-71, assoc. prof., 1971-78, prof. dept. environ. health scis., 1978—, assoc. chmn. dept., 1978-80, acting dir. div. toxicology, 1979-80, dir. div. toxicology, 1980-82, dir. Ctr. Alternatives to Animal Testing, 1981—, chmn. Ctr. Alternatives to Animal Testing, 2005—, assoc. dean rsch., 1984-94; assoc. dean corp. affairs Sch. Pub. Health, Balt., 1994-99; adminstrv. head health edn. program Johns Hopkins U./Nat. Basketball Player Assn., 1990-95; cons. OECD, Paris, 1998—. Prin. rsch. scientist Chesapeake Bay Inst., 1979-84; mem. health hazard evaluation team of chem. waste dumps State of Tenn., 1980; mem. rev. panel EPA, 1980-82; mem. working group on harmonization of in vitro methods Orgn. Econ. and Cmty. Devel., 1995—; organizer 1st World Congress on Alternative and Animal Use in Life Scis., 1993; sci. adv. bd. subcom. on toxicology U.S. FDA, 1996-2001; mem. interagy. coord. com. for validation of alternative method HHS, 1998-2002; bd. sci. advisors Xenogen, Inc.; mem. sci. adv. com. Alternative Tchg. Methods, NIEHS, 2002— vis. prof. U. Utrecht Ctr. Animals and Society, 2002, chmn. bd. Ctr. Alternatives to Animal Testing, John Hopkins u., 2005-. Mem. editorial bd. Jour. Am. Coll. Toxicology, assoc. editor In Vitro Toxicology; contbr. articles to profl. jours. Trustee Hildergard Doerenkamp-Gerhard Zbinden Found., 1985-2001, hon. mem., 2002-. Recipient award Ind. Neurol. Soc., 1967, Russell and Burch award Human Soc. of U.S., 1991; named Disting. Alumnus, L.I. Univ., 1992. Mem. AAAS, Am. Soc. Pharmacology and Exptl. Therapeutics, Soc. Neurosci. (pres. Balt. chpt. 1971-73), Am. Soc. Neurochemistry, Am. Epilepsy Soc., Assn. Univ. Tech. Mgrs., Internat. Soc. Neurochemistry, Soc. Toxicology (Ambassador Mid-Atlantic sect. 1998), Soc. Toxicology (Enhancement of Animal Welfare award 2001, Hildergard Doerenkamp-Gerhard Zbinden award 2001), Internat. Study Group on Memory Disorders, Internat. Union Pharmacology, Office of Tech. Assessment Panel on Alternatives to Animal Use in Rsch. Testing and Edn. and Frontiers in Neuroscience, Nat. Acad. Sci., Inst. for Lab. Animal Resources. Office: 111 Market Pl Ste 840 Baltimore MD 21202-7113 Office Phone: 410-223-1692. Business E-Mail: goldberg@jhsph.edu.

GOLDBERG, ANNE CAROL, physician, educator; b. Balt., June 12, 1951; d. Stanley Barry and Selma Ray (Freiman) G.; m. Ronald M. Levin, July 29, 1989. AB, Harvard U., 1973; MD, U. Md., 1977. Diplomate Am. Bd. Internal Medicine, Am. Bd. Endocrinolgy and Metabolism. Intern in medicine Michael Reese Hosp., Chgo., 1977-78, resident in medicine, 1978-80; fellow in endocrinology Washington U., St. Louis, 1980-83, instr. medicine, 1983-85, asst. prof. medicine, 1985-94, assoc. prof. medicine, 1994—. Fellow ACP, Am. Heart Assn.; mem. AMA, Am. Diabetes Assn., Am. Med. Women's Assn., Endocrine Soc., Alpha Omega Alpha. Democrat. Jewish. Avocation: needlepoint. Office: Washington U Med Sch Box 8127 660 S Euclid Ave Saint Louis MO 63110-1010

GOLDBERG, ARTHUR ABBA, merchant banker, financial consultant; b. Jersey City, Nov. 25, 1940; s. Jack Geddy and Ida (Steinberg) G.; m. Jane Elizabeth Gottlieb, Aug. 10, 1968; children: Ari Matthew, Shoshana Eve, Benjamin Saul, Talia Akiva. AB with honors, Am. U., 1962; JD, Cornell U., 1965; PhD (hon.), HHD (hon.), Natchez Coll., 1992. Intern, staff mem. to senator, 1962; law clk. DeSevo & Cerutti, Jersey City, 1964; pvt. practice Jersey City, 1965-89; asst. prof. law U. Conn. Sch. Law., 1965-67; cooperating atty. NAACP Legal Def. Fund, 1965-72; adminstrv. asst. to congressman Ohio, 1966-67; dep. atty. gen. N.J., counsel Dept. Community Affairs and Housing Finance Agy., 1967-70; exec. v.p., dir., mgr. mcpl. fin. dept. Matthews & Wright, Inc., N.Y.C., 1970-88; exec. v.p., dir. Landamatic Systems Corp., N.Y.C., 1982-85; vice chmn. Matthews & Wright Realty, N.Y.C., 1986-88, Matthews & Wright Pacific, N.Y.C., 1986-88; pres. New Am. Fed. Credit Union, 1981-87; dir., treas. Fedn. Community Devel. Credit Unions, 1985-88; v.p. Alfus Corp., 1958-85, Basow Corp., 1965-86; ptnr. Shayna Enterprises, York Builders, Hudson Mgmt. Svcs., 1978-87; dir. investment strategies FAB Capital Corp., 1998-99. Mng. ptnr. Bank Bldg. Assocs., 1974—86, Inst. Profl. and Exec. Devel.; vis. lectr. Rutgers U., 1971—80, Practising Law Inst., 1969—76; mem. exec. com. N.J. Commn. Discrimination in Housing, 1975—80; mem. urban adv. coun. Anti-Defamation League, 1965—72; spl. cons. Exclusionary Zoning Nat. Com. Discrimination in Housing, 1965—70; cons. scholarship edn. Def. Fund for Racial Equality, 1965—72; gen. counsel N.J. chpt. Mcpl. Fin. Officers Assn., N.J. chpt. Nat. Assn. Housing and Redevel. Ofcls., 1966—74; chmn. Com. for Absorption of Soviet Emigrees (CASE), 1973—; pres. CASE-UNA Cmty. Devel. Corp., 1976; co-dir. Jews Offering New Alternatives to Homosexuality (JONAH), 1999—; v.p. Ophthalmic Mission Trust, India, 1988—91; fin. advisor Nat. Found. Manufactured Home Owners, 1994—, Ednl. Video Conference, Inc. (EVCI) Career Colls., 1997—; adv. bd. Parents and Friends of Ex-gays and Gays, 2001—, Internat. Healing Found., 2000—; chmn. monitoring of rsch. com. Nat. Assn. Rsch. Therapy Homosexuality, 2001—02, exec. sec., 2003—; pres. Positive Alternative to Homosexuality, 2003. Author: Financing Housing and Urban Development, 1975, Zoning and Land Use, 1972; adv. bd. Housing and Devel. Reporter, 1975-89; contbr. articles to law revs. Co-pres. New Synagogue, Jersey City, 1974-80; bd. dirs. Jersey City Hebrew Free Loan Assn., 1976-77; pres. Met. N.Y. Coord. Com. for Resettlement of Soviet Jewry, 1978-80; treas. Hebrew Free Loan N.J., 1977-90, pres., 1995—; bd. dirs. Hillel Acad., 1985-87; dir. Bayonne Jewish Cmty. Ctr., 1987-88, Jersey City United Jewish Appeal, 1984—, chmn. allocation com., 1994, chmn. nominating com., 1996; bd. dirs. South Bronx Cmty. Housing, Inc., 1977-81; chmn. Novy Americanitz, 1980-84; bd. dirs. Citizens Housing and Planning Coun., 1980-84, Boys Club of Jersey City, 1975-92; pres. CASE Mus. Contemporary Russian Art, 1980—; pres. Freedom Synagogue, 1982—85; mem. Settlement House Fund; treas. Coun. Jewish Orgns., Jersey City, 1977; mem. bd. edn. Yeshiva of Hudson County, 1977-85; pres. Hudson Yeshiva Parents Orgn., 1980-88. Mem. Conn. Assn. Mcpl. Attys. (exec. com., editor newsletter 1965-68), Nat. Housing Conf., Am. Polit. Sci. Assn., Nat. Acad. Polit. and Social Sci., Nat. Leased Housing Assn. (nat. pres. 1972-74, chmn. emeritus 1975—), Public Securities Assn. (legis. com. 1978), Nat. Housing Rehab. Assn. (dir. 1982-89, v.p. 1985), Omicron Delta Kappa, Pi Gamma Mu, Pi Sigma Alpha, Pi Delta Epsilon, Phi Alpha Delta. Home: 83 Montgomery St Jersey City NJ 07302-3723 Office: 80 Grand St Jersey City NJ 07302-4522 Office Phone: 917-929-0087. E-mail: agoldberg@evcinc.com.

GOLDBERG, BERTRAM J., social agency administrator; b. Bklyn., Oct. 23, 1942; s. Ralph Goldberg and Geraldine Janith (Herzog) Gerber; m. Lorri Ann Schwartz, Oct. 19, 1980; children: Ilissa, Andrea, Joshua, Randi. BA, Fairleigh Dickinson U., 1964; MSW, U. Pa., 1966. Diplomate Acad. of Cert. Social Workers. Tween worker Bernard Horwich Jewish Community Ctr., Chgo., 1966-68; dir. group svcs. Seattle Jewish Community Ctr., 1968-70; chief centralized intake Eastside Mental Health Ctr., Bellevue, Wash., 1970-73; coord. coll. age youth svcs. Jewish Fedn., Chgo., 1973-74; exec. dir. Jewish Family Svc., Allentown, Pa., 1974-77, Orange County, Calif., 1977-86; pres., CEO, Assn. Jewish Family and Children's Agys., East Brunswick, N.J., 1986—. Mem. NASW, Jewish Social Svc. Profls. Assn. (bd. dirs. 1977-97), Jewish Communal Svc. Assn. N.Am. (bd. dirs. 1979, pres. 1994-96), World Coun. Jewish Communal Svc. (bd. dirs. 1989—, treas. 1998—). Democrat. Jewish. Avocations: computers, reading. Office: Assn Jewish Family/Childrens Agys 620 Cranbury Rd East Brunswick NJ 08816 Office Phone: 732-432-7120. Business E-Mail: bgoldberg@ajfca.org.

GOLDBERG, BURTON DAVID, pathologist, researcher, educator; b. Milw., Jan. 6, 1927; s. Esrael and Martha Goldberg; m. Geraldine Anne Yencha, Dec. 15, 1984. BS, Northwestern U., 1948, MD, 1950. Internship Cin. Gen. Hosp., 1951-52; residency in pathology Mallory Inst. Boston City Hosp., 1952-55; rsch. fellow in biochemistry MIT, Cambridge, 1955-57; asst. prof. pathology NYU Med. Sch., 1957-59, assoc. prof. pathology, 1959-71, prof. pathology, 1971-84; prof., chmn. dept. pathology U. Wis. Med. Sch., Madison, 1985-93, prof. emeritus, 1993—. Vis. scientist Inst. Pasteur, Paris, 1993-94. Contbr. articles to profl. jours.; contbr. chpt. to Connective Tissue in Histology, 1988. With USN, 1944-45. NIH grantee, 1959—; recipient Career Devel. award USPHS, 1960-70. Mem. Am. Soc. Experimental Pathology, Am. Soc. Biol. Chemistry and Molecular Biology, Am. Soc. Cell Biology. E-mail: bgberg@adelphia.net.

GOLDBERG, CATHERINE T., lawyer; b. Devils Lake, ND, June 28, 1950; AB summa cum laude, U. ND, 1971; JD magna cum laude, U. N. Mex., 1975. Bar: N. Mex. 1975. Law clk. to Hon. Howard C. Bratton U.S. Dist. Ct., Dist. N. Mex., 1975—76; ptnr. Rodey, Dickason, Sloan, Akin & Robb PA, Albuquerque. Named one of best lawyers in Am., 2003—04. Mem.: Albuquerque Mus. Art, History & Sci. (bd. trustees 2000—, art adv. com. 1996—, found. bd. 1987—93, 1994—2000), Albuquerque Econ. Devel. Forum, Albuquerque Bar Assn. (former pres.), ABA (real property probate & trust law sect., bus. law sect.), Am. Coll. Mortgage Attys. (trustee, opinions com.), Am. Coll. Real Estate Lawyers (sec. opinions com., new mem.'s com.), Phi Beta Kappa, Order Coif. Office: Rodey Dickason Sloan Akin & Robb PA 201 Third St NW Ste 2200 PO Box 1888 Albuquerque NM 87103 Office Phone: 505-768-7318. Business E-Mail: ctgoldbe@rodey.com.

GOLDBERG, DANNY, recording industry executive; b. N.Y.C., July 4, 1950; s. Victor and Mimi (Paul) G.; m. Rosemary Carroll, Feb. 25, 1988; children: Kathryn G., Max. Diploma, Fieldston Sch., 1967. Freelance journalist, reviewed Woodstock Billboard Mag., 1969; freelance journalist, editor N.Y.C., 1969-72; dir. pub. rels. rock music div. Solters & Roskin, N.Y.C., 1973-74; v.p. Swan Song Records, U.S.A., L.A., 1974-76; pres. Danny Goldberg, Inc., N.Y.C., 1978-79; co-founder Modern Records, L.A., 1979-83; music cons. 20th Century Fox, L.A., 1983-84; pres. Gold Mountain Entertainment, L.A., 1984-92; sr. v.p. Atlantic Records, L.A., 1992-94, pres., 1994; chmn., CEO Warner Bros. Records, Inc., Burbank, Calif., 1995; co-publisher (with father Victor Goldberg) Tikkun mag., 1997—2001; founder, CEO Artemis Records, 1999—2005; CEO Air America Radio Network, 2005—. Author: Dispatches From the Culture War - How the Left Lost Teen Spirit. Bd. dirs. Children Now, 1990, Show Coalition, 1990, New York Civil Liberties Union; pres. ACLU Found. Southern Calif. Recipient 1st Amendment award in Arts and Entertainment. Mem. ACLU (chair so. Calif. found. 1988-90). Democrat. Jewish. Office: Air America Radio 3 Park Ave New York NY 10016*

GOLDBERG, DAVID, lawyer, law educator; b. N.Y.C., Dec. 31, 1934; s. Philip and Esther (Dobbs) G.; m. Emily Ruth Messing, Aug. 17, 1958; children: Sara, Ari. BA, CUNY, 1956; LLB, Yale U., 1959. Bar: N.Y. 1960. Law clerk to judge U.S. Dist. Ct., N.Y.C., 1960-62; assoc. Kaye, Scholer, Fierman, Hays and Handler, N.Y.C., 1962-68, ptnr., 1969-83, Cowan, Liebowitz and Latman, N.Y.C., 1983—. Adj. prof. law NYU, 1976-96. Contbr. articles on copyright and trademark law to N.Y. Law Jour., other profl. jours. Pres. Hillcrest Jewish Ctr., Jamaica Estates, N.Y., 1987-89. Served as sgt. U.S. Army, 1959-60. Mem. ABA (fin. officer sect. intellectual property law 1986-89, spkr. on copyright devels. 1984, 85, 87, 90, 2000), Copright Soc. USA (pres. 1978-80, hon. trustee 1980—, spkr. on copyright devels. annually 1984-2003), U.S. Trademark Assn. (spkr. on trademarks and copyright overlap 1987). Democrat. Avocation: fishing. Office: Cowan Liebowitz and Latman 1133 Avenue of the Americas New York NY 10036-6710 Business E-Mail: dxg@cll.com.

GOLDBERG, DAVID ALAN, investment banker, lawyer; b. N.Y.C., Oct. 31, 1933; s. Joseph R. and Rose (Trutt) G.; m. Victoria Liebson, July 7, 1957 (div. Mar. 1976); children: Eric S., Jeremy P. AB magna cum laude, Harvard U., 1954, JD, 1957, postgrad. in bus. adminstrn, 1956-57. Bar: N.Y. 1958. Counsel firm R.W. Pressprich & Co., Inc., N.Y.C., 1958-64, gen. partner, 1965-68, exec. v.p., 1968-78, also chmn. exec. com. Bd. dirs. Gen. Atomics, Gen. Atomics Techs. Corp., Newbridge, Inc Trustee Beth Israel Med. Center, N.Y.C., Continuum Health Ptnrs. Inc., St. Luke's-Roosevelt Hosp. Ctr.; trustee, bd. regents The L.I. Coll. Hosp. Served with AUS, 1957-58. Mem. Harvard Club (N.Y.C.), Phi Beta Kappa. Office Phone: 212-765-1164.

GOLDBERG, DAVID MEYER, retired biochemist; b. Glasgow, Scotland, Aug. 30, 1933; arrived in Can., 1975; s. Samuel Simon and Ethel (Elyan) G.; m. Pearl Gertrude Goldberg; children: Susan Simone, Tanya Marion. BSc with honors in Biochemistry, MB, ChB, U. Glasgow, 1959, PhD, 1966, MD, 1974. Intern Stobhill Hosp., Glasgow, 1960, So. Gen. Hosp., Glasgow, 1961; resident Western Infirmary, Glasgow, 1962-66; prof. dept. clin. biochemistry U. Toronto, Canada, 1975—2002, chmn., 1977-88, prof. emeritus, 2002—; biochemist-in-chief dept. biochemistry Hosp. for Sick Children, Toronto, 1975-88. Cons. chem. pathology and hon. lectr. United Sheffield Hosp., U. Sheffield, Eng., 1967-75 Joint editor-in-chief Clin. Biochemistry, 1982-94, Critical Revs. Clin. Lab. Scis., 1992—; mem. editl. bd. Enzyme, 1978-89, Clin. Chimica Acta, 1981-2004, Clin. Biochem. Physiology, 1982-96, Clin. Chemistry, 1986-88, Jour. Clin. Lab. Analysis, 1987—, European Jour. Lab. Medicine, 1993-2001, Am. Jour. Enology Viticulture, 1995-2001, Jour. Agrl. Food Chemistry, 1999-2004. Recipient Van Slyke award Am. Assn. Clin. Chemistry, 1982, Roman award Australian Assn. Clin. Chemists, 1983, Nova Idea prize Italian Soc. Clin. Pathologists, 1985, Norman Kubasick award Am. Assn. Clin. Chemistry, 1996. Mem. Can. Soc. Clin. Chemists (Ames award 1990, Beckman award 1999), Can. Assn. Med. Biochemists, Can. Soc. Clin. Investigation, Internat. Soc. Clin. Enzymology (pres. 1995-2000), Can. Atherosclerosis Soc. (chmn. edn. com. 1994-97). Jewish. Home: 9 Harrison Rd Willowdale ON Canada M2L 1V3 Personal E-mail: david.goldberg@utoronto.ca.

GOLDBERG, DAVID THEO, law educator, writer; b. Pretoria, South Africa, Jan. 8, 1952; came to U.S., 1978; s. Isidore and Florence (Lief) G.; m. Alena Luter, June 25, 1984; 1 child, Gabriel Dylan. BA in Econs. and Philosophy, U. Cape Town, South Africa, 1973, BA in Philosophy with honors, 1975, MA in Philosophy, 1978; PhD in Philosophy, CUNY, 1985. Adj. asst. prof. NYU, N.Y.C., 1984-87, Hunter Coll., CUNY, 1984-87; co-pres. Metafilms, N.Y.C., 1982-88; asst. prof. Drexel U., Phila., 1987-90; asst. prof. justice studies Ariz. State U., Tempe, 1990-92, assoc. prof., 1992-94, prof., dir., chair Sch. Justice Studies, 1995-2000; dir. Humanities Rsch. Inst. U. Calif., 2000—, prof. African Am. studies and criminology, law and soc. Irvine, 2000—. Author: Ethical Theory and Social Issues, 1989, Racist Culture: Philosophy and the Politics of Meaning, 1993, Racial Subjects: Writing on Race in America, 1997, The Racial State, 2001; editor: Anatomy of Racism, 1990, Multiculturalism: A Critical Reader, 1994; co-editor: Social Identities: A Journal of Race, Nation and Culture, Jewish Identity, 1993, Race Critical Themes, 2001, Blackwell Companion to Racial and Ethnic Studies, 2001, Between Law and Culture, 2001; co-dir. film The Island, 1982. Grantee N.Y. State Coun. on Arts, 1981, NSF, 1991, ACLS, 1988. Mem. Am. Philos. Assn. (mem. com. on Blacks 1992—), Law and Soc. Assn., Greater Phila. Philosophy Consortium (colloquia com. 1989-90), Soc. for Philosophy and Pub. Affairs (exec. com. 1987-88). Avocations: reading, swimming, surfing.

GOLDBERG, EDWIN, rehabilitation specialist, consultant, Interfaith Clergyman; b. Jan. 12, 1937; D Chiropractic magna cum laude, Columbia Inst. Chiropractic, 1960; postgrad. edn. of blindTchr's. Coll., Columbia U., 1965-67; postgrad., C.G. Jung Found., N.Y.C., 1972-73; postgrad. in edn. of blind, NYU, 1973-74; postgrad. Am. Inst. Psychoanalysis, Karen Horney Clinic, Moreno Inst. Psychodrama; postgrad. in spl. edn.; cert. of study, Alfred Adler Inst., 1970; postgrad. in spl. edn., Fordham U., 1971; MA in Edn., Hebrew Union Coll. Jewish Inst. Religion, 1971; cert. in crisis mgmt., Cornell U., 1972; postgrad. in tng. and devel., NYU, 1972; profl. diploma rehab. mgmt., Cornell U., 1973; cert. assessment in aging, U. Pa., 1987; cert. in addictions counseling, Mercer County Coll., 1996; cert. in microcounseling, U. Buffalo, 1999; grad., All Faiths Sem., 1999-2000. Cert. med. rehab. coord., rehab. therapist in mobility tng. of the blind Am. Assn. Med. Rehab. Therapists and Specialists, rehab. counselor, master therapeutic recreation specialist, Nat. Bd. Cert. Counselor; registered recreation adminstr., N.J.; cert. mobility instr., rehab. tchr., N.Y.; nat. cert. profl. rehab. tchr. of the blind AER.; cert. Rehab. dir. OVR accredited facilities, lic. rehab. counselor, N.J.; profl. disability examiner; ordained clergy, registered N.Y.C.; qualified mental retardation profl., N.J.; lic. health edn. tchr. N.J. Dept. Edn. State Bd. Examiners, cert. group psychotherapist, Am. Assn. Group Psychotherapy, 2005, . Mem. staff Dr. Samuel Losner staff coagulation lab. Isaac Albert Rsch. Inst., Jewish Chronic Disease Hosp., Bklyn., 1957-60; tech. eye bank and clin. Lab. Bklyn. Eye & Ear Hosp. Isaac Albert Rsch. Inst., Bklyn., N.Y., 1958-59; exec. Greater N.Y. couns. Boy Scouts Am., 1961—63; supr. blood products divsn. Knickerbocker Biologicals, Charles Pfizer & Co., N.Y.C., 1963-64; assoc. dir. Western Mediterranean ops. USO, Nice, France, Naples, Italy, 1964-65; coord. rehab. skills Jewish Guild Blind, N.Y.C., 1965-68, asst. dir., 1968-77; sect. chief Trenton (N.J.) Psychiat. Hosp., 1977-78; mobility cons. Elm & Maple Halls, Ancora Hosp., 1977-82; dir. Work Adjustment Ctr. Jewish Employment and Vocat. Svc., Phila., 1979-80; dir. Mary Campbell Ellis Vocat. Rehab. Ctr. S.I. (N.Y.) Aid for Retarded Children, 1980-86; sr. rehab. counselor/acting dir. Vocat. Rehab. dept. Ancora Hosp., Hammonton, N.J., 1982-87; rehab. cons. Dominican Coll. of Blauvet, ind. Jewish religion tchr., 1986—; tchr. mobility Ministry of Health, State of Israel Armed Forces, 1969—71; program chmn. NY Fed. of Workers for the Blind, 1972; rehab. cons. Shield Inst., Flushing, NY, 2003—04, FEGS, N.Y.C., 2003—04; rehab. cons., dir. Seamark Ctr., project of Goodwill Industries NY and No. NJ, Bklyn., 2003—. Habilitation plan coord. State of N.J. Div. Devel. Disabilities, Hammonton, 1988-91, New Lisbon Devel. Ctr., 1991-93; sr. rehab. counselor N.J. State Commn. for the Blind, 1992-2002; rehab. cons. Beth Israel Hosp., N.Y.C., Goldwater Meml. Hosp., N.Y.C., Montefirore Med. Ctr., Bronx, N.Y., Harlem Med. Ctr., Bklyn., Jewish Home and Hosp. for Aged, N.Y.C., Inst. Rehab. Medicine, NYU, Hillside Med. Ctr., Bklyn. Devel. Ctr., Manhattan (N.Y.) Psychiat. Hosp., Keener Unit of Gov. Hosp., Albert Einstein Coll. Medicine, Bronx, Downstate Med. Ctr., Bklyn., Manhattanville Coll., Westchester, N.Y., L.I. U., Bklyn., State of Israel Dept. of Def. and Ministry of Health, Yonkers (N.Y.) Home for the Aged Blind, Trenton State Coll., Bank Street Coll. of Edn., Staten Island C.C., Zeman Ctr. for Instrn., N.Y.C. Kingsbrook C.C., Exxon Homes, Morris Hall Rehab. Ctr., Jewish Geriatric Ctr., Phila., Nat. Rehab. Assocs.; mobility specialist for severely disabled blind State of N.Y., 1968-2003; coord. corrective therapy, internship program rehab dept. Manhattan Vets. Hosp., 1970-77; rehab. tng. specialist multiple disabled blind in N.Y. area, 1970-77; instr. group rels. ongoing workshops; sr. vocat. counselor, summer vocat. coord. for blind adolescents program Joseph Kohn Rehab. Ctr., New Brunswick, N.J.; coord. vocat. counselors monthly meeting Trenton; vocat. sr. counselor Bus. Enterprise Program State of N.J., Trenton, 1998-2002, sr. counselor coll. unit N.J. Commn. for Blind and Visually Impaired, Newark, 2002—; cons. rehab. Shield Inst., NY, 2002-03; adj. asst. prof. health and phys. edn. and adapted phys. edn. Hunter Coll., N.Y.C., 1971-76; adj. field supr. art psychotherapy Trenton (N.J.) State Coll.in conjuction with C.G. Jung Inst., N.Y.C. and Trenton Psychiat. Hosp., 1977-78; lectr. N.Am. Indian myth and medicine Found. Faith Sem., N.Y.C., 1976-77; lectr. in field, 1970—; mobiligy cons. Yonkers Home for Aged Blind, 1968-71; contbr. to developing tchr. tng. on phys. edn. Chung Yuan U., Republic of China, 1973-77p presenter in field. Author: Mobilitiy Training Manual for Teachers of Visually Impaired Children, 1969, Isolation From the Human Scene: The Meaning and Direction of Loneness, 1972, Adapted and Corrective Physical Education Curriculum Handicapped, 1972, Rehabilitation Assessment in Psychiatric Facilities, 1984, Overcoming Feelings of Inferiority: The Role of Mobility Training for the Blind An Adlerian Viewpoint, 1986; TV appearances include Am. Speaks, 1960-62. Legis rep. N.Y. State Fedn. Workers for Blind, 1973-76, program chmn., 1974; cons. legis. U.S. Senate and Congl. Subcoms., 1972-77; lectr. rehab. skills tng. of vision impaired Geriatrics Ctr. for Instrn., 1968-77; mem. Nat. Eagle Scout Assn. Boy Scouts Am.; mem. Workmen's Cir., Arbeiter Ring; leg. com. mem. NY Federation for the Blind. Recipient Silver award Nat. Coun. Boy Scouts Am., 1958, Recognition citation Rotary Club N.Y.C., 1959, Dr. Frank E. Dean Meml. award for outstanding contbns. to sci. edn., 1976, Thomas E. Watson Silver citation Citizenship in Action medal SAR, Lydia Hayes Disting. Svc. award N.J. Commn. for Blind and Visually Impaired, 2000. Fellow: World Med. Assn., Am. Inst. Sci., World Assn. Social Psychiatry, N.Y. Hist. Soc., N.Y. Acad. Scis., Royal Soc. Promotion Health; mem.: APA, APA, Internat. Assn. Pastoral Counselors, Nat. Assn. Wedding Officiants, Am. Assn. Jewish Chaplains (affiliate mem. 2005), Assn. Med. Rehab. Dirs. Coords., Am. Assn. Rehab. Therapy, Royal Inst. Pub. Health and Hygiene, Royal Soc. Health, Am. Congress Rehab. Medicine, Assn. Edn. and Visually Handicapped and Blind, Royal Soc. Medicine (affiliate), Am. Assn. Med. Rehab. Specialists and Therapists, Nat. Therapeutic Recreation Assn., Am. Orthopsychiat. Assn. for Applied Psychoanalysis, N.Y. Counseling Assn., N.Am. Soc. Adlerian Psychology, Am. Rehab. Counseling Assn., Am. Group Psychotherapy Assn. (elected clin. mem., cert. grop therapist), John Burroughs Meml. Assn. (life).

GOLDBERG, EVGUENI, computer scientist; b. Minsk, Russia, July 8, 1960; s. Isaac Lvovich Goldberg. MS, Belorussian State U., Minsk, Russia, 1982; PhD, Belorussian Acad. Scis., Minsk, Russia. Rschr. Inst. of Engring. Cybernetics, Belorussian Acad. of Scis., Minsk, Belarus, 1983—96; vis. rschr. U. Calif., Berkeley, 1996—97; rsch. scientist Cadence Design Systems, Berkeley Labs., Calif., 1997—. Mem.: IEEE. Achievements include research in Best paper award at DATE-2002 conference (Design Automation in Europe); co-authored development of the SAT-solver, BerkMin that was a winner of SAT-2002 and SAT-2003 international competitions; Developed The Theory Of Testing Satisfiability By Building A Stable Set Of Points; Developed a method of logic synthesis and equivalence checking of circuits with a common specification; patents for Have 3 pending patents on testing satisfiability, equivalence checking and logic synthesis. Office: Cadence Design Systems 1995 University Ave Ste 460 Berkeley CA 94704 Office Phone: 510-647-2825. Business E-Mail: egold@cadence.com.

GOLDBERG, FRED T., JR., lawyer; b. St. Louis, Oct. 15, 1947; m. Wendy Meyer; 5 children. BA in Econs., Yale U., 1969, JD, 1973. Instr. polit. sci. and econs., Yale Coll., asst. dean Calhoun Coll. Yale U., New Haven, 1971-73; assoc. then ptnr. Latham, Watkins & Hills, Washington, 1973-81; asst. to commr. IRS, Washington, 1981-82, chief counsel, prin. legal advisor to commr., 1984-86, commr., 1989-92; asst. sec. for tax policy US Dept. of Treas., Washington, 1992; ptnr. Skadden, Arps, Slate, Meagher & Flom, LLP, Washington, 1986—89, ptnr., tax, 1993—. Mem. Nat. Commn. on Restructuring the IRS, Ctr. for Strategic and Internat. Studies Nat. Commn. on Retirement Policy; exec. dir. Bi-Partisan Congressional Commn. on Entitlement and Tax Reform. Editorial bd. Yale Law Jour.; Author, "Filling the Void: Can the IRS Restructuring Bring Purpose and Meaning to the Random World of Tax Litigation?," TAXES Mag. 1999; Co-Author (with Michael Graetz) "Reforming Social Security: A Practical and Workable System of Personal Retirement Accounts," Administrative Aspects of Investment-Based Social

Security Reform, 2000. Office: Skadden Arps Slate Meagher & Flom LLP 1440 New York Ave NW Ste 600 Washington DC 20005 Office Phone: 202-371-7110. Office Fax: 202-661-8216. Business E-Mail: fgolder@skadden.com.

GOLDBERG, GARY DAVID, producer, writer; b. Bklyn., June 25, 1944; s. George and Anne (Prossman) G.; m. Diana Meehan; children: Shana Goldberg-Meehan, Cailin Elizabeth Goldberg-Meehan. Student, Brandeis U., 1962-64; BA, San Diego State U., 1975. Founder UBU Productions. Writer: Bob Newhart Show, CBS-TV, 1976, (films) Dad, 1989, Total Recall, 1990, Navy Seals, 1990; writer, prodr., dir.: Dad, 1989, Must Love Dogs, 2005; story editor: (TV series) Tony Randall Show, 1976-77, prodr., 1977-78; prodr.: Lou Grant, 1978-79; creator, prodr.: The Last Resort, CBS, 1979; exec. prodr., writer, dir: Making the Grade, CBS, 1982; creator, exec. prodr: Family Ties, NBC, 1982-89, Day By Day, 1988, The Bronx Zoo, 1987, Spin City, 1996—02, Battery Park, 2000; exec. prodr.: American Dreamer, 1990, Brooklyn Bridge, 1991-93, Sugar Hill, 1999. Recipient Peabody award U. Ga., 1979, Emmy award, 1979, five Humanities awards; inducted to Broadcasting mag. Hall of Fame, 1992; named Prodr. of Yr. Producer's Guild, 1991. Mem. Writers Guild Am. (Best Episodic Comedy TV Script award 1978), Actors Equity, AFTRA. Address: c/o Warner Bros Entertainment 4000 Warner Blvd Burbank CA 91522*

GOLDBERG, HARRY FINCK, lawyer, business consultant; b. Boston, May 5, 1936; s. Benjamin and Helen Sonia (Finck) G.; m. Vicki Lou Katz, Oct. 9, 1971 (div. Aprl. 1985); children: Andrew Seth, Ross Charles. BA magna cum laude, Yale U., 1958; JD cum laude, Harvard U., 1961. Bar: Mass. 1961, N.Y. 1966, Pa. 1973. Assoc. Cowan, Liebowitz & Latman, N.Y.C., 1965-68, Powers and McNiff, N.Y.C., 1969-70, Austrian, Lance & Stuart, N.Y.C., 1970-71; assoc. Blank, Rome, Comisky & McCauley, Phila., 1971-76, ptnr. 1976-84; ptnr. Wiener, Zuckerbrot & Weiss, N.Y.C., 1984-89; mem. firm Sills Cummis Zuckerman Radin Tischman Epstein & Gross, P.A., Newark, 1989-94; of counsel Law Office of Robert M. Becker, Newark, 1995-96; lectr. Pa. Bar Inst., 1981, 82, 83, N.Y. State Bar Assn., 1983, 84, 86. Bd. dirs. Soc. Hill Civic Assn., Phila., 1977-80, pres., 1978-79. Capt. U.S. Army, 1962-65. Mem. Fort Lee Hist. Soc. Co-author: Real Estate Limited Partnerships, 3d edit., 1991. Home and Office: 4 Horizon Rd Fort Lee NJ 07024-6743 E-mail: hfgoldberg@hotmail.com.

GOLDBERG, HOMER BERYL, language educator; b. Chgo., Feb. 4, 1924; married, 1956; 2 children. AB, U. Chgo., 1947, AM, 1948, PhD in English, 1961. Instr. English U. Chgo., 1950-54, asst. prof., 1954-60, Haverford (Pa.) Coll., 1960-61; assoc. prof. SUNY, Stony Brook, 1961-70, prof. English, 1970-88, Disting. teaching prof., 1988—, emeritus, 1991—. Fulbright lectr., Italy, 1956-57; dir. NDEA English Inst., 1965-66; editl. cons. L.I. Rsch. Inst., 1992-97. Author: The Art of Joseph Andrews, 1969; editor: Norton Critical Edition of Joseph Andrews and Shamela, 1987; contbr. articles to profl. jours. Mem. Suffolk County Campaign Fin. Bd., 1999—2005. Recipient Chancellor's award for Excellence in Teaching SUNY, 1973, Pres.'s award for Excellence in Teaching SUNY, 1987, others; faculty rsch. fellow SUNY, 1962, 67, 69. Mem. MLA. Office: SUNY Dept English Stony Brook NY 11794-5350

GOLDBERG, IRVING HYMAN, molecular pharmacology and biochemistry educator; b. Hartford, Conn., Sept. 2, 1926; s. Morris Wolfe and Rose (Krechevsky) Goldberg; m. Margaret Field Ziskin, Apr. 15, 1956; children: Daniel Eliot, Nancy Elizabeth. BS, Trinity Coll., 1949; MD, Yale U., 1953; PhD, Rockefeller U., 1960; AM (hon.), Harvard U., 1964. Intern Columbia-Presbyn. Med. Ctr., N.Y.C., 1953—54; asst. resident, chief resident, instr. medicine Columbia-Presbyn. Med. Ctr. (Coll. Phys. and Surgs.), 1954—57; asst. prof. medicine, biochemistry U. Chgo., 1960—64, assoc. prof., 1964; assoc. prof. medicine Med. Sch. Harvard, 1964—68; prof. medicine Med. Sch. Harvard U., 1968—, chmn. divsn. med. scis. Faculty Arts and Scis., 1968—70, Gustavus Adolphus Pfeiffer prof. pharmacology, 1972—83, chmn. dept. pharm., 1972—86, Otto Krayer prof. pharmacology, 1983—86, Otto Krayer prof. biol. chemistry and molecular pharmacology, 1986—; chief endocrinology-metabolism unit Beth Israel Hosp., 1964—68, physician, 1964—72, mem. bd. consultation in medicine, 1972—; cons. in pharmacology Dana-Farber Cancer Inst., Boston, 1980—87. Mem. rev. panel internat. program Howard Hughes Med. Inst., 1994; cons. in clin. pharmacology Children's Hosp. Med. Ctr., Boston, 1972—91; mem. rsch. com. Med. Found., Boston, 1968—77; mem. exptl. therapeutics study sect. NIH, 1974—77; mem. com. proposed legis. to restructure FDA Assembly Life Scis. NAS-NRC, Inst. Medicine, 1976; mem. sci. adv. com. Damon Runyon-Walter Winchell Cancer Fund, 1982—86; mem. life scis. panel NRC, 1992—93. Mem. editl. bd. Endocrinology, 1964—68, Antimicrobial Agents and Chemotherapy, 1974—88, Jour. Biochem. Pharmacology, 1973—84, Biochemistry, 1986—97. Rev. panel Internat. Program Howard Hughes Med. Inst., 1994. Served with USNR, 1945—46. Recipient Faculty Rsch. award, Am. Cancer Soc., 1960—71; fellow Guggenheim, dept. genetics, Oxford (Eng.) U., 1970—71, sr., Trinity Coll., 1974—76. Mem.: Brit. Pharm. Soc., Am. Soc. Microbiology, Am. Soc. Pharmacology and Therapeutics (Otto Krayer award 1994), Am. Chem. Soc., Assn. Am. Physicians, Am. Acad. Arts and Scis., Am. Soc. Clin. Investigation, Am. Soc. Biochemistry and Molecular Biology, Inst. Medicine NAS, Alpha Omega Alpha, Sigma Xi, Phi Beta Kappa. Home: 987 Memorial Dr Apt 472 Cambridge MA 02138-5737 Office: Harvard U Med Sch 45 Shattuck St Boston MA 02115-6091 Office Phone: 617-432-1787. Business E-Mail: irving_goldberg@hms.harvard.edu.

GOLDBERG, ITZHAK D., radiation oncologist; b. Haifa, Israel, Oct. 5, 1948; MD, Albert Einstein Coll. Med., 1976. Cert. Therapeutic Radiology 1982. Intern Brookdale Med. Ctr., Bklyn., 1976—77; resident Harvard Joint Ctr. Radiation Therapy, Boston, 1979—82; fellow Harvard Med. Sch., Boston, 1977—78, Beth Israel Deaconess Med. Ctr., Boston, 1978—79; chmn. radiation oncology Long Island Jewish Med. Ctr., New Hyde Park, NY, 1985—; physician North Shore U. Health Sys., Manhassett, NY; prof. radiation oncology Albert Einstein Coll. Medicine, 1990—. Office: Long Island Jewish Med Ctr 27005 76th Ave New Hyde Park NY 11040-1433

GOLDBERG, JACK, hematologist; b. Ulm, Germany, Feb. 7, 1948; came to U.S., 1952; s. Isaac and Mary (Selitska) G.; m. Doreen, July 28, 1970; children: Joshua, Alexis. BA, Boston U., 1969; MD, SUNY, 1973. From asst. prof. medicine to prof. medicine SUNY Health Sci. Ctr., Syracuse, 1977-89; prof. medicine Robert Wood Johnson Med. Sch., Camden, NJ, 1989—, Am. Cancer Soc. prof. clin. oncology, 1992—; head divsn. hematology-oncology U. Pa. Presbyn. Med. Ctr., 2003—; vice chmn. Abramson Cancer Ctr. U. Pa. Network. Prof. medicine Coriell Inst. for Med. Rsch., Camden, 1990-2002; med. dir. blood bank Cooper Hosp., Camden, 1990-2002, head divsn. hematology/oncology, 1989-2002; med. dir. CorCell, Camden, 1996—; head Cooper Cancer Inst., 1998-2002. V.p. N.J. divsn. Am. Cancer Soc., 1989-99; vol. Leukemia Soc., Camden, 1990—. Fellow Am. Coll. Medicine. Jewish. Avocations: exercise, travel. Office: Penn Medicine at Cherry Hill 409 Rte 70 East Cherry Hill NJ 08034 Office Phone: 856-429-1519. Business E-Mail: Jack.Goldberg@uphs.upenn.edu.

GOLDBERG, JAY, lawyer; b. N.Y.C., Jan. 2, 1933; s. Joseph and Lillian (Adler) G.; m. Rema, Dec. 27, 1959; children: Justin, Julie. BA, Bklyn. Coll., 1954; JD, Harvard U., 1957. Bar: N.Y. 1957, U.S. Ct. Appeals (2d, 4th and 9th cirs.) 1971, U.S. Supreme Ct. 1961. Asst. dist. atty. N.Y. County Dist. Atty. Office, N.Y.C., 1957-61; spl. asst. to atty. gen. Washington, 1961-63; spl. asst. to U.S. Atty. NJ Hammond, Ind., 1961-67; lawyer, sole practice N.Y.C., 1963—. Lectr. trial practice Harvard Law Sch., 1976-88; com. on grievances U.S. Dist. Ct. (so. dist.) N.Y., 1989—. Editorial mgr. White Collar Crime Law Reporter, 1989—; contbr. articles to profl. jours. Recipient Merit award for Advocacy of Individual Rights for Persons Advised, N.Y. Criminal Bar Assn., 1989. Mem. Friars Club (gov. 1988-92). Home: 200 E 65th St New York NY 10021-4451 Office: 250 Park Ave New York NY 10177-0001

GOLDBERG, JEROLD S., dean; b. NJ, 1945; m. Michele Goldberg; children: Megan, Abby. BS, Case Western Res. U., 1968, DDS, 1970. Mem. faculty Sch. Dentistry, Case Western Res. U., 1974, chmn. oral and maxillofacial surgery dept., 1985—96, dean, 1997—; interim dean Sch. Medicine, Case Western Res. U., 2002—03. Rschr. in field; co-founder Partnership in Hope Case Western Res. U. and City Hosp. of Klapeda, Lithuania, 1995—. Bd. mem. Ohio Dental Assn. Found. Recipient Cross of the Knight of the Order of the Lithuanian Grand Duke Gediminas, Govt. Lithuania, 2002. Mem.: Ohio Dental Assn. (mem. Ohio Dental Assn. Coun. on Dental Edn. and Licensure, del. and alt., House of Dels.). Office: Case Western Res U 10900 Euclid Ave Cleveland OH 44106-4920 Office Phone: 216-368-3266. Business E-Mail: jsg@case.edu.

GOLDBERG, JONAH JACOB, poltical columnist; b. N.Y.C., Mar. 21, 1969; s. Sid and Lucianne (Steinberger) Goldberg; m. Jessica Gavora; 1 child. BA, Goucher Coll., 1991. V.p. Lucianne Goldberg Lit. Agy., N.Y.C., 1991—; tchr. Prague, Czech Republic, 1991-92; rschr. Am. Enterprise Inst., Washington, 1993-94; prodr. New River Media, Washington, 1994; contributing ed. Nat. Review Online, Washington, 1998—, columnist Goldberg File, 1998—, editor. Prodr. Think Tank with Ben Wattenberg, Washington, 1996; writer, prodr. (documentary) Gargoyles: Guardians of the Gate, 1995, Notre Dame: Witness to History, 1996; contbr. articles to mags. and jours. Trustee Goucher Coll., Balt., 1992-95. Conservative. Jewish. Avocations: reading junk mail, international intrigue. Office: National Review 221 Pennsylvania Ave SE Washington DC 20003 Office Phone: 202-543-9226.

GOLDBERG, JOSEPH, lawyer; b. Washington, Aug. 21, 1950; s. Morris and Rose (Levin) G.; m. Christine Marie Riggott, Mar. 29, 1980; children: Benjamin R., Louis E. BS, Ohio U., 1972; JD, U. Pa., 1975. Bar: Pa. 1975, N.J. 1981, D.C. 1980, U.S. Ct. Appeals (3d cir.) 1980, U.S. Dist. Ct. (mid. dist.) Pa. 1987, U.S. Supreme Ct. 1989. Assoc. Margolis, Edelstein & Scherlis, Phila., 1975-81; ptnr. Margolis Edelstein, Phila., 1982—. Author: State and Local Government Immunity to Tort Claims, 1992, 2d edit., 1997. Mem. ABA, Pa. Def. Rsch. Inst., Pa. Jud. Rules Com., Phila. Assn. Def. Counsel, Phila. Bar Assn. Avocation: scuba diving. Office: Margolis Edelstein The Curtis Ctr 4th Fl Independence Sq West Philadelphia PA 19106 Office Phone: 215-931-5808. Business E-Mail: jgoldberg@margolisedelstein.com.

GOLDBERG, KENNETH YIGAEL, computer engineering educator, artist; b. Ibadan, Nigeria, Oct. 6, 1961; came to U.S., 1962; m. Melvin Morris and Ann Natalie (Glickman) G. BSEE, BS in Econs., U. Pa., 1984; MS in Computer Sci., Carnegie Mellon U., 1988, PhD in Computer Sci., 1990. Asst. prof. computer sci. U. Southern Calif., 1991—95, assoc. dir. Inst. Robotics and Intelligent Systems, 1991—95; asst. prof. U. of Calif. Berkeley, 1995—97, asst. prof. Industrial Engring. and Operations Rsch. (IEOR) dept., 1995—97; visiting prof. San Francisco Arts Inst., 1999, MIT Media Lab., 2000; assoc. prof. IEOR dept. U. of Calif. Berkeley, 1997—2002, prof. IEOR dept. with secondary appt. in Electrical Engineering and Computer Sci., 2002—. Exhbns. include Siggraph Art Show, 1991, 92, 93, 95, 96, Ars Electronica, Austria, Dutch Electronic Art Festival, 1996; inventor low friction gripper. Co-founder Melvin M. Goldberg fellowship U. Pa. Recipient Kobe prize 1995; finalist Nat. Info. Infrastructure awards 1995, 96; recipient rsch. grants NSF 1992, 93, 95, 96, 97; named Nat. Young Investigator 1994, Presdl. Faculty fellow 1995. Fellow: World Technol. Network. Office: U Calif 4139 Etcheverry Hall Berkeley CA 94720-1731

GOLDBERG, LEE DRESDEN, endocrinologist, educator; b. Point Pleasant, N.J., July 29, 1937; s. Milton J. and Maude (Dresden) G.; m. Lana Ditchek, July 23, 1967 (dec. 1991); children: Marissa Julie, Sara Amy, Rachel Sherry; m. Rhoda Kuperman, Mar. 10, 1994. BS summa cum laude, Yale U., 1959, MD, 1963. Diplomate Am. Bd. Internal Medicine, Am. Bd. Endocrinology, Nat. Bd. Med. Examiners. Rotating intern Mt. Sinai Hosp., N.Y.C., 1963—64; resident in internal medicine Montefiore Hosp., Bronx, NY, 1964, 1966—68; clin. rsch. fellow in endocrinology Albert Einstein Coll. Medicine, Bronx, 1968—69; fellow in endocrinology Bellevue Hosp.-NYU Med. Ctr., N.Y.C., 1969—70; pvt. practice Miami, Fla., 1970—. Co-chief endocrinology Mt. Sinai Hosp., Miami Beach, Fla., 1974-91, chief endocrinology, 1991—; tchg. asst. NYU Sch. Medicine, 1969-70; clin. instr. medicine U. Miami Sch. Medicine, 1970-71, clin. asst. prof., 1971-80, clin. assoc. prof., 1980-99, vol. prof. medicine, 1999—; chief internal medicine South Shore Hosp., Miami Beach, 1975-79; assoc. chmn. med. svcs. St. Francis Hosp., Miami Beach, 1977-78. Author: (with Goldberg) The Jewish Student's Guide to American Colleges, 1989; contbr. articles on endocrinology to med. jours. Bd. dirs. Hebrew Acad. Greater Miami, 1975-79. Lt. M.C., USNR, 1964-66. Fellow ACP, Am. Coll. Endocrinology; mem. Endocrine Soc., Am. Diabetes Assn. (past dir. Miami chpt.), Am. Assn. Clin. Endocrinologists, Yale Club, B'nai B'rith, Phi Beta Kappa, Sigma Xi. Office: 4302 Alton Rd Ste 830 Miami FL 33140-2876 Office Phone: 305-672-2244.

GOLDBERG, LEE WINICKI, furniture company executive; b. Laredo, Tex., Nov. 20, 1932; d. Frank and Goldie (Ostrowiak) Winicki; m. Frank M. Goldberg, Aug. 17, 1952; children: Susan, Arlene, Edward Lewis, Anne Carri. Student, San Diego State U., 1951—52. With United Furniture Co., Inc., San Diego, 1953—83, corp. sec., dir., 1963—83, dir. environ. interiors, 1970—83; founder Drexel-Heritage store Edwards Interiors subs. United Furniture, 1975; founding ptnr., v.p. FLJB Corp., 1976—86; 1980founding ptnr., sec., treas. Sea Fin., Inc., 1980; founding ptnr. First Nat. Bank San Diego, 1982. Den mother Boy Scouts Am., San Diego, 1965; vol. Am. Cancer Soc., San Diego, 1964-69; chmn. jr. matrons United Jewish Fedn., San Diego, 1958; del. So. Pacific Coast region Hadassah Conv., 1960, pres. Galilee group San Diego chpt., 1960-61; supporter Marc Chagall Nat. Mus., Nice France, U. Calif. at San Diego Cancer Ctr. Foun., Smithsonian Instn., L.A. (Calif.) County Mus., San Diego (Calif.) Mus. Contemporary Art, San Diego (Calif.) Mus. Art; pres. San Diego (Calif.) Opera, 1992-94; bd. dirs. The Old Globe, 2002-05 Recipient Hadassah Service award San Diego chpt., 1958-59; named Woman of Dedication by Salvation Army Women's Aux., 1992, Patron of Arts by Rancho Santa Fe Country Friends, 1993. Republican. Jewish.

GOLDBERG, LEONARD MARVIN, lawyer; b. Jersey City, Mar. 21, 1937; s. Jack Geddy and Ida Reva (Steinberg) G.; m. Susan Lee Horstein, Aug. 7, 1960; children: Mark Jay, Philip Seth. AB magna cum laude, Tufts U., 1957; JD magna cum laude, Harvard U., 1960. 010Bar: N.J. 1960, U.S. Tax Ct. 1964, N.Y. 1966. Trial atty. tax divsn. Dept. Justice, Washington, 1960-64; assoc. Roberts & Holland, N.Y.C/, 1964-70; ptnr. Clapp & Eisenberg, Newark, 1970-79; sr. ptnr. Goldberg, Mufson & Spar (formerly Goldberg & Stark), West Orange, NJ, 1979—. Lectr. Practicing Law Inst., ABA Taxation Soc., ABA Ctr. for Continuing Edn., N.J. Inst. CLE, Tenn. Fed. Tax Inst., Fairleigh Dickinson U. Tax Inst., Seton Hall U. Tax Inst., Estate Planning Couns.; N.J. del. to lawyers' liaison com. Mid-Atlantic region IRS, 1973-76. chmn. West Orange pub. edn. com., 1976-77, mem. Am. Jewish Com.; co-chmn. lawyers div., trustee Met. N.J. State of Israel Bonds, 1989-92; v.p., trustee Congl. Oheb Shalom, So. Orange, N.J., 1990-92; trustee Cong. Agudath Israel, Caldwell, N.J., 2000—; treas. Jewish Edn. Assn., 2003—; pres. Oheb Shalom Hebrew Free Loan Soc., 1990-96. Fellow Am. Coll. Trust and Estate Counsel; mem. (exec. counc., 1969—) ABA, N.J. Bar Assn. (chmn. taxation sect. 1973-75, chmn. small law firms comm. taxation sect.), N.Y. State Bar Assn., Essex County Bar Assn. (chmn. tax com. 1988-89), Estate Planning Coun. No. N.J., Internat. Assn. Jewish Lawyers and Jurists. Contbr. articles to profl. jours. Contbr. articles to profl. jours. Home: 6 Huntington Rd Livingston NJ 07039-5112 Office: 200 Executive Dr West Orange NJ 07052-3388 Office Phone: 201-736-0100.

GOLDBERG, LUCIANNE, literary agent; b. Apr. 1935; m. Sidney Goldberg. Gen. clerk promotion dept. Washington Post, 1957—65; press aide Lyndon Johnson's presdl. campaign; lit. agent, publicist Washington, DC, NYC, 1963—; columnist Lucianne.com. Author: Madame Cleo's Girls, 1992. E-mail: Lucianneg@aol.com.*

GOLDBERG, LUELLA GROSS, diversified financial services company executive; b. Mpls., Feb. 26, 1937; d. Louis and Beatrice (Rosenthal) Gross; m. Stanley M. Goldberg, June 23, 1958; chldrn: Ellen Goldberg Luger, Fredric, Martha Goldberg Aronson. BA, Wellesley Coll., 1958; postgrad. in philosophy, U. Minn., 1958-59. Dir. Reliastar Fin. Corp., 1978-2000, NRG Energy, Inc., Mpls., 2001—04. Bd. dirs. Northwestern Nat. Life Ins. Co., Mpls. TCF Fin. Corp., Mpls., Hormel Foods Corp., Austin, Minn., Personnel Decisions Internatl., dir. Communications System, Inc., ING Group, Amsterdam, 2001—. Pres. Minn. Orch. Women's Assn., Mpls., 1972-74; bd. dirs. Minn. Orch. Assn., 1972—, chmn., 1980-83, Mpls. chpt. United Way, 1978-88, Ind. Sector, Washington, 1984-90; regent St. John's U., Collegeville, Minn., 1974-83; trustee U. Minn. Found., Mpls., 1978—, chmn. bd. trustees, 1996-98; mem. bd. overseers Sch. Mgmt., U. Minn., Mpls., 1980—; chmn. bd. trustees Wellesley (Mass.) Coll., 1985-93, acting pres., 1993; trustee Wellesley Coll., 1978-96, emerita, 1996—, Northwest Area Found., 1994—. Recipient Disting. Svc. award, Minn. Orch. Assn., 1983, Community Svc. Leadership award, Mpls. YWCA, 1986, Disting. Svc. to Higher Edn. award, Minn. Pvt. Coll. Coun., 1992, Humanitarian award, NCCJ, 1992, Regents award, U. Minn., 2000, Alumnae Achievement award, Wellesley Coll., 2002, Disting. Women's award, Northwoods U., 2001, Lifetime Achievement award as Outstanding Dir., Twin Cities Bus. Monthly, 2001. Mem. Minn. Women's Econ. Round Table, Mpls. Club, Phi Beta Kappa. Avocations: water-skiing, wind surfing, travel. Home: 7019 Tupa Dr Minneapolis MN 55439-1643 Office Phone: 952-941-2624.

GOLDBERG, MARK ARTHUR, neurologist; b. N.Y.C., Sept. 4, 1934; s. Jacob and Bertha (Grushlawska) G.; 1 child, Jonathan. BS, Columbia U., 1955; PhD, U. Chgo., 1959, MD, 1962. Resident neurology N.Y. Neurol. Inst., N.Y.C., 1963-66; asst. prof. neurology Columbia U. Coll. Phys. and Surgs., N.Y.C., 1968-71; assoc. prof. neurology and pharmacology UCLA, 1971-77, prof. neurology and pharmacology, 1977—; chair dept. neurology Harbor UCLA Med. Ctr., Torrance, 1977—. Contbr. articles to profl. jours., chpts. to books. Capt. U.S. Army, 1966-68. Fellow Am. Neurol. Assn., Am. Acad. Neurology; Am. Soc. Neurochemistry, Assn. Univ. Profs. Neurology. Avocation: oriental cusine. E-mail: mrkgldbrg@yahoo.com.

GOLDBERG, MARK JOEL, lawyer; b. Pitts., June 2, 1941; s. Charles J. and Eleanore (Letwin) Goldberg; m. Wendy Witt, Dec. 23, 1988; children: Michael, Wendy, Josh, Jamie. BA, Washington and Jefferson Coll., 1963; JD, Case Western Res. U., 1966. Bar: Pa. 1966, Ohio 1966, U.S. Tax Ct. 1969, U.S. Supreme Ct. 1972. Assoc. Jerome Silver, Cleve., 1966-67; pvt. practice, Pitts., 1967-69; ptnr. Goldberg & Wedner, Pitts., 1969-80; ptnr., shareholder Gillotti Goldberg & Capristo, Pitts., 1981-91, Goldberg Gentile & Voelker, Pitts., 1991-92, Goldberg, Gruener, Gentile, Horoho & Avalli, P.C., Pitts., 1992—. Mem. drafting com. Pa. Divorce Code, 1978—80, 1988; lectr. Pa. Bar Inst., Pa. Trial Lawyers Assn. Contbr. articles to profl. jours. Pres. bd. dirs. Parent and Child Guidance Ctr., Pitts., 1984—86; committeeman Dem. Party, Pitts., 1970. Fellow: Am. Acad. Matrimonial Lawyers (lectr., pres. Pa. chpt. 1988—90, nat. bd. govs. 1991—95); mem.: Pa. Bar Assn. (family law sect. chmn. 1986—88), Allegheny County Bar Assn. (coun. mem. family law sect. 1972—, chmn. 1982—84), Am. Coll. Family Trial Lawyers (diplomate, officer), Westmoreland Country Club. Jewish. Avocations: golf, travel. Home: 1137 Frick Lane Pittsburgh PA 15217-3618 Office: Goldberg Gruener Et Al 230 Grant Bldg Pittsburgh PA 15219-2200 Office Phone: 412-261-9900. Business E-Mail: mgoldberg@gggha.com.

GOLDBERG, MARTIN, internist, educator; b. Phila., Sept. 15, 1930; s. Samuel and Esther (Shreibman) Goldberg; m. Lynn Taksey, June 17, 1951 (dec. Aug. 31, 1976); children: Meryl I, Karen L, Dara S; m. Marion Lindblad, May 26, 1978. BA, Temple U., 1951, MD, 1955; MA (hon.), U. Pa., 1971. Diplomate Am Bd Internal Med (chmn nephrology comt 1976-79, bd govs 1976-79), Nat Bd Med Examiners. Intern Phila. Gen. Hosp., 1955-56, resident, 1957-59, sr. attending physician, 1970-76; resident Cleve. Clinic, 1956-57; fellow nephrology Hosp. U. Pa., Phila., 1959-61, sr. attending physician, 1962-79; mem. faculty U. Pa. Sch. Medicine, 1960-79, prof. medicine, 1970-79, chief renal electrolyte sect., 1966-79, acting chmn. dept. medicine, 1975-76; sr. attending physician Phila. VA Hosp., 1968-79; Gordon and Helen Hughes Taylor prof. medicine U. Cin., 1979-86; chmn. internal medicine U. Cin. Coll. Med. and Hosp., 1979-86; prof. medicine Temple U. Sch. Medicine, Phila., 1986-96, dean, vice pres., 1986-89, prof. emeritus, 1997—, asst. to dean for computer assisted instrn., 1997-2000; chmn. sci. adv. com. Gen. Clin. Rsch. Ctr. Temple U. Hosp., 1993—. Study consult NIH, 1968—72, 1982—85; mem sci adv bd Nat Kidney Found, 1970—76; chmn kidney coun Am Heart Asn, 1973—74; bd mgrs St Christopher's Hosp Children, 1986—89. Mem. editl. bd.: Jour Clin Investigation, 1969—70, Kidney Int, 1972—74, Jour Mineral and Electrolyte Metabolism, 1977—91, Am Jour Hypertension, 1990—97, First Consult, 2000—; editor (physician-ed): Nephrology MKSAP Am Col Physicians, 1991—94; editor: (assoc ed) MKSAP 11, MKSAP 12, MACP, 1996—2000; mem. editl. adv. bd.: PDxMD, 2000—. Recipient Alumni Prize, Temple Univ Sch Med, 1955, Research Career Develop Award, NIH, 1963—70, Lindback Award for Distinguished Teaching, Univ Pa, 1972, Distinguished Med Scientist of the Yr Award, Med Alumni Temple Univ Sch Med, 1985, Honoree of the Yr Award, Greater Del Valley Kidney Found, 1997, A N Richards Award for Distinguished Contbns to Nephrology, Univ Pa, 1998, Centennial Award, Asn Chmn Depts Physiology, 1989; grantee Research, NIH, 1962—89, John Hartford Found, 1970—73. Master: ACP (nat sci program comt 1976—81); fellow: Royal Soc Med, Am Col Clin Pharmacology; mem.: Physicians for Social Responsibility (adv bd Philadelphia chpt 1988—98), Col Physicians Philadelphia, Am Med Informatics Asn, Int Soc Nephrology (coun 1975—84), Am Soc Nephrology (secy-treas 1975—78), Am Fedn Clin Research (chmn eastern sect 1967), Am Physiological Soc, Am Soc Clin Investigation, Asn Am Physicians, Asn Am Med Cols (coun deans 1986—89), Interurban Clin Club, Alpha Omega Alpha. Achievements include research in renal physiology and disease; electrolyte and acid-base metabolism, computer assisted instruction and diagnosis. Office: Temple Univ Hosp Nephrology Parkinson Pavilion Philadelphia PA 19140

GOLDBERG, MAUREEN MCKENNA, state supreme court justice; b. Pawtucket, RI, Feb. 11, 1951; m. Robert D. Goldberg. Grad., St. Mary's Acad., 1969; AB cum laude, Providence Coll., 1973; JD cum laude, Suffolk U., 1978, LLD (hon.), 1999. Bar: R.I. 1978, Mass. 1978, U.S. Ct. of Appeals (1st cir.) 1979. Asst. atty. gen. Adminstr. of the Criminal Divsn., 1978-84; town solicitor South Kingstown, 1985-87, Town of Westerly, 1987-90, acting town mgr., 1990; spl. legal counsel RI State Police; apptd. assoc. justice Superior Ct., 1990-96; assoc. justice RI Supreme Ct., 1997—. Mem. Com. to Study Proposed Amendments to R.I. Rules of Evidence, 1998—99; co-chair R.I. Supreme Ct. Law Day Com., 2001—, Advisory Com. on Code of Jud. Conduct, 2002; chair Indigent Defense Task Force, 2003, Jud. Performance Evaluation Com., 2003. Mem. ABA, R.I. Bar Assn., R.I. Trial Judges Assn., Pawtucket Bar Assn., R.I. Bar Found., Nat. Assn. of Women Judges, Mass. Bar Assn. Office: Rhode Island Supreme Ct 250 Benefit St 7th Fl Providence RI 02903-2719

GOLDBERG, MELVIN ARTHUR, communications executive; b. N.Y.C., Feb. 5, 1923; s. Louis and Anna (Bergman) G.; m. Norma N. Nertz, Oct. 18, 1956; children: Ronald, Richard, Joan Sandra. BS, CCNY, 1942; AM, Columbia U., 1950. Mem. staff Bur. Applied Social Rsch., Columbia, 1946-47; news editor, rsch. dir. TV mag., 1947-49; dir. sales planning and rsch. DuMont TV Network, 1949-52; dep. dir. Office Rsch. and Evaluation, U.S. Info. Agy., 1952-53; exec. sec. Ultra-High Frequency TV Assn., 1953-54; cons., chief of rsch. M-G Rsch., 1954-56; dir. rsch. Westinghouse Broadcasting Co., 1956-62; v.p., dir. rsch. Nat. Assn. Broadcasters, 1962-64; v.p. planning and rsch. John Blair & Co., 1964-69; pres. Melvin A. Goldberg Inc., N.Y.C., 1969-77; v.p. primary and social rsch. ABC-TV, 1977-80, v.p. news, social and tech. rsch., 1980-85; v.p. market planning, tech. and social rsch. ABC Inc.; exec. dir. Electronic Media Rating Coun., 1985-93; pres. Melvin A. Goldberg Inc., N.Y.C., 1993—. Former mem. ABA Commn. on Pub. Understanding About the Law. Mem. editorial bd. TV Quar.; Contbr. articles to profl. publs. Mem. Great Neck/North Shore Cable Commn., chmn.

long range planning com. Decorated D.F.C., Air medal with clusters. Mem. Am. Assn. Pub. Opinion Rsch., Radio-TV Rsch. Coun., Nat. Acad. TV Arts and Scis. Home: 17 North Dr Great Neck NY 11021-1337 Office: Melvin A Goldberg Inc Comm 17 North Dr Great Neck NY 11021-1337

GOLDBERG, MICHAEL IRA, obstetrician, gynecologist; b. Bklyn., June 8, 1944; MD, U. Rome, 1970. Diplomate Am. Bd. Ob-Gyn., Am. Bd. Gynecol. Oncology. Intern Maimonedes Med. Ctr., Bklyn., 1971, resident in ob-gyn., 1972-75; fellow in gynecol. oncology Miami (Fla.)-Jackson Meml. Hosp., 1975-77; pvt. practice New Brunswick, N.J. Mem. staff RW Johnson U. Hosp., New Brunswick; clin. prof. ob-gyn. U. Medicine and Dentistry of N.J., RW Johnson Med. Sch.; chief gynecol. oncology St. Peter's U. Hosp., New Brunswick. Fellow ACS, ACOG; mem. Soc. Gynecol. Oncology. Office: 78 Easton Ave New Brunswick NJ 08901-1865 Office Phone: 732-828-3300. Fax: 723-937-5739.

GOLDBERG, MORTON EDWARD, pharmacologist; b. Phila., July 11, 1932; s. Herman and Ethel (Shill) G.; m. Janet Louise Werlin, Aug. 15, 1954; children— Shellie, Ellen, David. BS, Phila. Coll. Pharmacy and Sci., 1954, MS in Pharmacology, 1955, DSc in Pharmacology, 1958. Sr. pharmacologist Abbott Labs., North Chicago, Ill., 1958-60; asst. dir. pharmacology Union Carbide Corp., Tuxedo, N.Y., 1960-69; dir. pharmacodynamics Warner Lambert Research Inst., Morris Plains, N.J., 1969-73; dir. pharmacology Squibb Inst. Med. Research, Princeton, N.J., 1973-77; v.p. biomed. research Stuart Pharms. div. ICI Americas, Wilmington, Del., 1977-84; v.p. rsch., devel., and regulatory affairs ICI Pharm. Group divsn. ICI Ams. (now Astra Zeneca Pharm.), Wilmington, Del., 1984-92; clin. prof. pharmacology and exptl. therapeutics Dept. Pharmacology U. Pa. Sch. Medicine, Phila., 1992-96. Vis. prof. toxicology Phila. Coll. Pharmacy and Sci.; vis. prof. pharmacology, Allegheny U. Med. Sch., Phila., 1978-2001, U. Pa. Sch. Med., Phila., 1996-2001; cons. to pharm. industry in drug discovery and devel., 1992—; mem. extramural sci. adv. bd. NIDA, 1993-95, mem. nat. adv. bd. 1996-2000. Editor-in-chief: series Pharmacological and Biochemical Properties of Drug Substances; contbr. articles to profl. jours. Asst. scoutmaster Boy Scouts Am., Glen Rock, N.J., 1968-72. NIH grantee, 1961-64 Fellow Acad. Pharm. Sci., AAAS, N.Y. Acad. Sci.; mem. Am. Soc. Pharmacology and Exptl. Therapeutics, Behavioral Pharmacology Soc., Internat. Soc. Biochem. Pharmacology, Soc. Toxicology (charter), Sigma Xi, Rho Chi. Home: 715 Severn Rd Wilmington DE 19803-1725 E-mail: mortjan@comcast.net.

GOLDBERG, MORTON FALK, ophthalmologist, educator; b. Lawrence, Mass., June 8, 1937; s. Maurice and Helen Janet (Falk) G.; m. Myrna Davidov, Apr. 6, 1968; children— Matthew Falk, Michael Falk AB magna cum laude, Harvard U., 1958, MD cum laude, 1962; Doctoris honoris causa, U. Coimbra, Portugal, 1995. Diplomate Am. Bd. Ophthalmology. Intern Peter Bent Brigham Hosp., Boston, 1962-63; resident Wilmer Inst. John Hopkins Hosp., Balt., 1963-67, head dept., dir. Wilmer Inst., 1989—2003; prof. and head ophthalmology Eye and Ear Infirmary U. Ill. Hosp., Chgo., 1970-89; Joseph Green prof. ophthalmology Johns Hopkins Med. Sch., 2003—. Author: (with D. Paton) Injuries of the Eye, the Lids and the Orbit: Diagnosis and Management, 1968, Management of Ocular Injuries, 1976; editor: Genetic and Metabolic Eye Disease, 1974, (with G.A. Peyman and D.R. Sanders) Principles and Practice of Ophthalmology (3 vols.), 1980; editor-in-chief Archives of Ophthalmology, Chgo., 1984-94; contbr. articles to profl. jours. Lt. comdr. USPHS, 1967-69 Recipient award for outstanding contbns. in the field of vision rsch. Alcon Research Inst., 1987, Univ. Scholar award U. Ill.-Chgo., 1986, Michaelson medal Isreal Acad. Scis. and Humanities, 2000, Greatest Living Ophthalmologists award Ophthalmology Times, 1999, Mildred Weisenfeld Lifetime Achievement award Fight for Sight, Inc., 2001, Pryor award Am. Soc. Retinal Specialists, 2004. Fellow: Am. Acad. Ophthalmology (sr. honor award 1985), Royal Australian Coll. Ophthalmologists (hon.); mem.: Internat. Academia Ophthalmologica, Academia Ophthalmologica Internationalis, Macula Soc. (pres. 1980—82, Patz medal 1999, David Paton medal 2002), Assn. Univ. Profs. Ophthalmology (trustee 1985—91, pres. 1990—91), Assn. Rsch. in Vision and Ophthalmology (trustee 1985—90, pres. 1989—90, Weisenfeld award 2000), Chgo. Ophthal. Soc. (pres. 1985—86), Am. Ophthal. Soc., Inst. Medicine-NAS. Avocation: snorkelling. Office: Johns Hopkins Med Insts Wilmer Eye Inst 600 N Wolfe St Baltimore MD 21287-0005 E-mail: mgoldberg@jhmi.edu.

GOLDBERG, NEIL ALAN, lawyer; b. NYC, Dec. 24, 1947; s. Bernard G. Goldberg; children: Jane Hana, Robert Saul. BA cum laude, SUNY, Stony Brook, 1969; JD cum laude, SUNY, Buffalo, 1973. Bar: N.Y. 1974, U.S. Dist. Ct. (we. dist.) N.Y. 1974. Sr. ptnr. Saperston & Day P.C., Buffalo, 1974—2001; founding ptnr. Goldberg Segalla LLP, Buffalo, 2001—. Editor-in-chief, contbg. author: Products Liability in New York Strategy and Practice, 1997; co-editor in chief: Preparing for and Trying the Civil Lawsuit, 2d edit., 2004. Mem.: ABA, Fedn. Ins. and Corp. Counsel, Fedn. Def. Corp. Counsel, Lawyers Civil Justice (pres. 2004—05, bd. chmn.), Erie County Bar Assn., NY State Bar Assn. (past chmn. torts ins. and compensation law sect. product liability com, past chmn. product liability com. torts), Am. Arbitration Assn. (bd. dirs. 1985—91, product liability adv. coun.), Def. Rsch. Inst. (pres. 2000—01, editor-in-chief Daubert compendium, editor, contbg. author 7 books def. complex personal injury cases), Internat. Assn. Def. Counsel. Office: Goldberg Segalla LLP Ste 400 665 Main St Buffalo NY 14203 Office Phone: 716-566-5475. Business E-Mail: ngoldberg@goldbergsegalla.com.

GOLDBERG, NIECA, cardiologist, educator; b. Bklyn., Oct. 21, 1957; BA, Barnard Coll., 1979; MD, SUNY, Bklyn., 1984. Diplomate Am. Bd. Internal Medicine. Resident in internal medicine St. Lukes-Roosevelt Hosp., N.Y.C., 1985-87; fellow in cardiology SUNY Health Sci. Ctr., Bklyn.; chief women's cardiac care Lenox Hill Hosp., N.Y.C.; asst. clin. prof. of medicine NYU Sch. Medicine. Nat. spokesperson Am. Heart Assn, adv. bd. Women's Day mag. Author: (book) Women Are Not Small Men: Life-Saving Strategies for Preventing and Healing Heart Disease in Women, 2003. Named to New York mag. Best Doctors issue, 1999, 2000, 2001, 2004, 2005. Mem. ACP, Am. Coll. Cardiology, Am. Heart. Assn., Am. Soc. Echocardiography, Am. Coll. Physicians. Office: Total Heart Care PC 177 E 87th St #503 New York NY 10128 Office Phone: 212-289-2045.

GOLDBERG, NOEL, psychologist, consultant; BA in Psychology, SUNY, Albany; MEd in Ednl. Psychology, U. N.C.; D in Psychology, Va. Consortium Program in Clin. Psychology, 2002. Lic. Clin. Psychologist Va., 2002. Clin. psychologist Vet. Affairs Med. Ctr., Washington, 2002, Pvt. Practice, Alexandria, Va., 2003. Author www.drgoldberg.org, Alexandria, Va., 2004. Author: (manuscript) The ABC's of Mental Health. Mem.: APA. Achievements include research in How Marriages Change over time. Home: 5021 Seminary Rd Ste 229 Alexandria VA 22311 Office: Private Practice 5021 Seminary Rd Ste 229 Alexandria VA 22311 Office Phone: 703-550-4848. Office Fax: 703-931-1931.

GOLDBERG, NORMAN ALBERT, music publisher, writer; b. Belleville, Ill., Mar. 11, 1918; s. Charles S. and Bessie (Tenenbaum) G.; m. Ruth E. Rodenberg, Dec. 29, 1940; children: Marcia Lee, Marc Edwin (dec.). BS, U. Ill., 1939, M in Music, 1942. Instr. U. Ill., Urbana, 1939-41; mem. faculty U. Iowa, Iowa City, 1941-42, Mo. High Sch., Univ. City, 1944-48; owner Baton Music Co., St. Louis, 1948-73; pres. Magnamusic-Baton Inc. (name now MMB Music), St. Louis, 1964—, G. Henle, USA, 1981-86, Norruth Music, Inc., 1985—; pub. Internat. Jour. Arts Medicine; pres. Contemporary Arts Corp., St. Louis, 1993—. Edn. com. St. Louis Symphony. Composer various works for alto and bass clarinets; arranger various symphony orchs. and bands. Bd. dirs. Internat. Assn. Music for Handicapped, Provo, Utah, St. Louis Conservatory and Sch. for the Arts (now Webster U. Cmty. Music Sch.), 1991—94, Rhythm for Life, 1992—96, Music Brain Info. Ctr., 1992—; mem. adv. coun. Webster U. Coll. Fine Arts, 2002—. With U.S. Army, 1943. Recipient Presdl. award Nat. Assn. Music Therapy, 1993, Constituent Leadership award U. Ill. Alumni Assn., 1997, Lifetime Achievement in the Arts award St. Louis Arts and Edn. Coun., 1999. Mem. Music Industry Conf. (bd. dirs. 1972-84, pres. 1982-84, Outstanding Svc. award 1986), Univ. City C. of C. (pres. 1971), Am. Assn. Music Therapy (bd. dirs. 1988-98, Joint Presdl. award with Nat. Assn. Music Therapy 1995, Lifetime Achievement award 1996), Jewish War Vets. (dep. comdr. 1953), Univ. Ill. Alumni Assn. (bd. dirs. 1990-96, chair constituents com. 1994-96, Constituent Leadership award 1997), Am. Orff-Schulwerk Assn. (life, bd. dirs. 1970-75, First Industry Svc. award 1998), St. Louis chpt. AOSA (life), Music Educators Nat. Conf. (exec. bd. 1982-84), Internat. Soc. for Music in Medicine, Internat. Arts Medicine Assn. (bd. dirs. 1990-99, v.p. 1997-2000, Bridge Builder award 1997), Am. Music Therapy Assn. Norman Goldberg Libr., B'nai El Cong. (life, past pres., First Eternal Light award with Ruth Goldberg 1999), Internat. Arts Med. Assn. (v.p. (1997-99), Soc. for the Arts in Healthcare (bd. dirs. 2000-01), Phi Mu Alpha, Rotary (past pres. 1967-78), Masons, Shriners. Democrat. Jewish. Avocations: woodworking, metalsmithing, reading. Office: MMB Music Inc Contemporary Arts Bldg 3526 Washington Ave Saint Louis MO 63103-1019 Home: 1 McKnight Pl # 251 Saint Louis MO 63124 Office Phone: 314-531-9635. Personal E-mail: goldbergnorm@yahoo.com.

GOLDBERG, PAMELA WINER, entrepreneur, educator; b. Boston, Oct. 14, 1955; d. Arthur Leonard and Marilyn (Miller) Winer; children from previous marriage: Frederick Warren, Alyssa Rachel, Meredith Hayley. BA, Tufts U., 1977; MBA, Stanford U., 1981. Day care dir. Cmty. Action Inc., Haverhill, Mass., 1977-79; lending assoc. Bankers Trust Co., N.Y.C., 1980-81; mgr., bank officer, corp. fin. dept. Citicorp, N.Y.C., 1981-82; assoc. dir., mergers and acquisitions group State St. Bank, Boston, 1983-85; ind. strategic cons. Wellesley, Mass., 1986-97; dir. bus. rels. Babson Coll., Wellesley, 1998—2002; prof., dir. Ctr. for Entrepreneurial Leadership Tufts U., 2002—. Exec. bd. friends Beth Israel Hosp., Boston, 1987—96; trustee Recuperative Ctr., Boston, 1988—95; exec. bd. trustees Temple Beth Elohim, Wellesley, 1992—2000, treas., 1997—2000, Synagogue 2000 nat. com., 2000—04; bd. dirs. Hunnewell Sch. PTO, 1991—96, Wellesley LWV, 1995—98. Avocations: swimming, tennis, singing. Home: 34 Ivy Rd Wellesley MA 02482-4554 Office: Tufts University 4 Colby St Medford MA 02155 Office Phone: 617-627-2153. Personal E-mail: pwg14@aol.com. Business E-Mail: pamela.goldberg@tufts.edu.

GOLDBERG, PAUL BERNARD, gastroenterologist, clinical researcher; b. Bklyn., Apr. 11, 1950; s. Samuel and Eva (Turkenitz) G.; m. Harriet Ruth Ferrer, July 8, 1973 (div. 1987); children: Deborah Lynn, Susan Michelle; m. Mary Alice Denaro, June 23, 1990; 1 child, Laura Alicia. BA in Chemistry summa cum laude, Cornell U., 1967-71, MD, 1971-75. Diplomate Am. Bd. Internal Medicine, Am. Bd. Gastroenterology. Intern in medicine Hosp. of U. of Pa., Phila., 1975-76, resident in medicine, 1976-78, fellow in gastroenterology, 1978-80, fellow in nutritional support svc., 1979-80; med. coord. and founder nutritional support svc. Lakeland (Fla.) Gen. Hosp., 1980-81; attending physician Halifax Med. Ctr., 1980—, Ormond Meml. Hosp., 1980—, Atlantic Med. Ctr., 1980-2000, Fish Meml. Hosp., New Smyrna Beach, Fla., 1989-99, Peninsula Med. Ctr., 1989-94. Pres. Sunshine Health Care Plan, Inc., 1983-86, v.p., 1986-87; chief staff Humana Hosp., Daytona Beach, 1986-88, trustee, 1986-89, mem. exec. com., 1984-91; mem. rev. bd. Coastal Instnl. Rev., 1990-93, chmn. rev. bd., 1993-96; expert reviewer Fla. Dept. Profl. Regulation, 1990—; pres. med. staff Halifax Hosp., 1996-97; clin. asst. prof. medicine dept. family medicine U. South Fla. Rschr. and author in field. Physician adv. Daytona chpt. Crohn's and Colitis Found., 1991-95. Recipient Nat. award Ford Future Scientists of Am., 1967, Westinghouse Sci. Talent Search finalist, 1967. Fellow ACP, Am. Coll. Gastroenterology; mem. Am. Gastroent. Soc., Am. Soc. Gastrointestinal Endoscopy, Am. Soc. for Parenteral and Enteral Nutrition (pres. Fla. chpt. 1991-92), Volusia County Med. Soc. (exec. com. 1991-94, co-chmn. mini internship program 1992-94, 2000-01), Fla. Gastrointestinal Soc., Fla. Med. Assn. (alt. del. to ho. of dels. 1990-95), Fla. Assn. Nutritional Support (1st pres.), Rotary, Phi Beta Kappa, Alpha Omega Alpha. Office: 1070 N Stone St Ste D Deland FL 32720 Office Phone: 386-822-9410. E-mail: pbgoldberg@aol.com.

GOLDBERG, RAY ALLAN, agriculturist, educator; b. Fargo, ND, Oct. 19, 1926; s. Max and Anne G.; m. Thelma R. Englander, May 20, 1956; children: Marc E., Jennifer E., Jeffrey L. AB, Harvard U., 1948, MBA, 1950; PhD, U. Minn., 1952; D of Pol. Sci. (hon.), U. Buenos Aires, Argentina, 2000. Officer, dir. Moorhead (Minn.) Seed & Grain Co., 1952-62; dir. Experience, Inc., Mpls., 1963-78, Arbor Acres Farm, Inc., N.Y.C., H.K. Webster Co.; mem. faculty Harvard U. Grad. Bus. Sch., 1955—, Moffett prof. agr. and bus., 1970-97; Moffett prof. agr. and bus. emeritus, 1997—; also dir. continuing edn. programs, participant seminars Harvard U. Grad. Bus. Sch. Bd. dirs. Daymon Assn., Smithfield Foods, Gold Kist, Inc.; hon. prof. Royal Agrl. Coll., Cirencester, England, 1996; vis. prof. U. Minn. Grad. Sch., 1960; adv. coun. Foods Multinat., Inc., 1972-77; agrl. investment com. John Hancock Ins. Co., 1971-95; cons. in field; adviser Instituto Centroamericano de Administracion de Empresa, Managua, Nicaragua, 1973—, Inst. Panamericano de Alta Direccion de Empressa, Mexico City, 1973—, U.S. Comptroller of Currency, 1975—, Food and Agr. Policy Project, Ctr. Nat. Policy, 1984—; study team, subgroup chmn. world food and nutrition study NRC, 1975—; com. tech. factor contbg. to nation's fgn. trade positions Nat. Acad. Engring., 1976—; chmn. agribus. adv. com. on Caribbean Basin USDA, 1982—; com. on indsl. policy for developing countries Commn. on Engring. and Tech. Systems, NRC, 1982—; task force on agr. Fowler-McCracken Commn., 1984—; adv. bd. The First Mercantile Currency Fund Inc., 1985—; internat. adv. bd. Atlantic Exchange Program, 1987—; mem. V.I. Lenin All-Union Acad. of Agrl. Scis., 1988—; mem. U.S. Presdl. Econ. Del. to Poland, Nov., 1989; scientific adv. bd. Sepragen Corp., 1993—, Inst. Food Technologists, 1999—; chmn. joint bus. scientific pub. policy consumer policy tech. com. U.S. Food System and Seminar, 1994—; internat. bd. vis. Zamorano, 1995—; adv. com. Foodfit.com., 1999—, sci. adv. bd., IFT/FDA Rsch. Contract, 1999, chmn. adv. panel for World Bank Guide to Developing Agrl. Markets and Agro-Enterprises, 1999, chmn. of suncommittee on Econ. and Social Devel. in a Global Context, Nat. Rsch. Coun., 2002; chmn. Task Force to utilize Tobacco Funds for Econ. Devel., Ky., Long Term Plan for Agricultural and Rural Development for the state of Kentucky, 2001, chmn. sub. com. on Econ. and Social Devel. in a Global Context for com. on opportunities in Agr.- NRC Bd. on Agr.; and Natural Resources, 2001 Author: Agribusiness Management for Developing Countries-Latin America, 1974, (with Lee F. Schrader) Farmers' Cooperative and Federal Income Taxes, 1974, (with John T. Dunlop et al) The Lessons of Wage and Price Controls-The Food Sector, 1977, (with Richard C. McGinity et al), Agribusiness Management for Devloping Countries-Southeast Asia Corn Study, 1979; editor: Research in Domestic and International Agribusiness Management, Vol. 1, 1980, Vol. 2, 1981, Vol. 3, 1982, Vol. 4, 1983, Vol. 5, 1984, Vol. 6, 1986, Vol. 7, 1987, Vol. 8, 1988, Vol. 9, 1989, Vol. 10, 1981, Vol. 11, 1995, Vol. 12, 1996; co-editor: (with Gerald E. Gaul) New Technologies and the Future of Food and Nutrition, 1991, The Emerging Global Food System: Public and Private Sector Issues, 1993; contbr. numerous articles to profl. jours.; chmn. editl. adv. bd. Agribus.: An Internat. Jour., 1983—. Bd. govs. Internat. Devel. Rsch. Ctr., Govt. of Can., 1978—; trustee Roxbury Latin Sch., Boston, 1973-76, Beth Israel Hosp., Boston, 1978—, mem. com. on patents and tech. transfer, 1982—, chmn. gerontology com., 1991—; mem. adv. com. to prep. sch. New Eng. Conservatory Music, 1974—, assoc. trustee, 1978—; vice chmn. bd. Spoleto Festival U.S.A., 1993; adv. mem. Polish Investment Fund, 1994—; chmn. adv. com. Sonoma Internat. Capital Assocs., 1994—; trustee Global Conservation Trust, Rome, 2002. Recipient Outstanding Alumni award, Dept. Agrl. Econs. U. Minn., 1992, 2d pl. McKinsey award, Harvard Bus. Rev., 2000, Disting. Svc. award, Harvard Grad. Sch. Bus. Adminstrn., 2001. Fellow Internat. Agribusiness Mgmt. Assn. (pres. 1990-92, bd. dirs. 1990—, chmn. Russian food mgmt. program sponsored rsch. project 1994—, coord. non-partisan ednl., govt., pvt., sci., med. and consumer group for food, safety, nutrition and environ. 1994—, chmn. subcom. econ. and social devel.), Agribus. Inst. Cambridge (chmn. bd., treas. 1991-93), Am. Agrl. Econ. Assn.(editl. coun. 1974-78, nat. agribus. edn. commn. 1988—), Am. Econ. Assn.; mem. Royal Agrl. Coll. Eng. (hon. prof. 1996—), V.I. Lenin All-Union Acad. Agrl. Scis. (fgn.), Am. Mktg. Assn., Am. Dairy Sci. Assn., Food Distbn. Rsch. Soc., Harvard Club (Boston and N.Y.C.), Bus. Coun. for Sustainable Devel. (adv. group for sustainable paper cycle project 1994—) Address: 975 Memorial Dr Apt 701 Cambridge MA 02138-5803 Office Phone: 617-495-6496. Business E-Mail: rgoldberg@hbs.edu.

GOLDBERG, RICHARD MILES, physician, medical oncologist; b. Utica, N.Y., Mar. 23, 1953; s. Bernard Wilcox and Miriam Ellen (Roth) G.; m. Lynda Punch,Mar. 13, 1983; children: Julia Rebecca, Samuel Aaron. AB cum laude, Harvard U., 1975; MD, SUNY, Syracuse, 1979. Diplomate in internal medicine and med. oncology Am. Bd. Internal Medicine. Assoc., vice chmn. medicine Geisinger Clinic, Danville, Pa., 1984-94; cons. Mayo Clinic, Rochester, Minn., 1994—. Assoc. editor PDQ Svc. of Nat. Cancer Inst., 1996—; cntbr. articles to profl. jours. V.p., pres. Am. Cancer Soc., Danville, Pa., 1985-94; v.p., pres.-elect Am. Cancer Soc., Rochester, 1994—, pres. 1997—. Grantee Nat. Cancer Inst., 1994—, also various pharm. cos., 1992—. Fellow ACP; mem. Am. Soc. Clin. Oncology, Am. Assn. Cancer Rsch. Avocation: fly tying and fly fishing. Office: Mayo Clinic E 12 200 1st St SW Rochester MN 55905-0002 Home: 111 Burnwood Ct Chapel Hill NC 27514-9514

GOLDBERG, RITA MARIA, foreign language educator; b. N.Y.C., Oct. 1, 1933; d. Abraham Morris and Hilda (Weinman) G. BA, Queens Coll., 1954; MA, Middlebury Coll., 1955; PhD, Brown U., 1968. Mem. faculty Queens Coll., N.Y.C., 1956, Oberlin (Ohio) Coll., 1957; mem. faculty St. Lawrence U., Canton, NY, 1957—2001, Dana prof. modern langs., 1975—2000, emerita, 2001—, chmn. dept., 1972—75, 1983—91, 2000—01. Chmn. Regional Conf. Am. Programs in Spain, 1979-81; mem. Nat. Fulbright Selection Com., 1990-92; mem. advanced placement devel. com. for Spanish, Ednl. Testing Svc., 1993-2000, chair, 1996-99, chief reader AP Spanish 2000-04. Spanish Ministry of Fgn. Affairs scholar, 1954-56; Danforth grantee, 1960-62, 63-64; N.Y. State Regents scholar, 1950-54, Brown U. scholar, 1960-62. Mem. Am. Assn. Tchrs. Spanish and Portuguese, AAUP, MLA, Am. Council Teaching of Fgn. Langs., N.E. Modern Lang. Assn., N.Y. State Assn. Fgn. Lang. Tchrs., Phi Beta Kappa, Sigma Delta Pi. Roman Catholic. Office: St Lawrence U Dept Modern Langs Lits Canton NY 13617 Business E-Mail: ritagoldberg@stlawu.edu.

GOLDBERG, ROBERT ALAN, history educator; b. N.Y.C., Aug. 16, 1949; s. Philip J. and Ruth (Dickler) Goldberg; m. Anne Freed, Jan. 14, 2001; children: David, Joshua, Stephen, Peter. BA, Ariz. State U., Tempe, 1971; MA, U. Wis., Madison, 1972, PhD, 1977. Prof. Dept. History, U. Tex., San Antonio, 1977—80, Dept. History, U. Utah, Salt Lake City, 1980—. Author: Barry Goldwater, 1995, Grassroots Resistance, 1996, Enemies Within, 2001. Mem.: We. History Assn., Orgn. Am. Historians, Am. Hist. Assn. Avocation: backpacking. Office: Univ Utah - Dept History 380 S 1400 E Salt Lake City UT 84112 Office Phone: 801-581-8311. Business E-Mail: bob.goldberg@utah.edu.

GOLDBERG, ROBERT B., molecular biologist, biology professor; b. Cleve., May 28, 1944; BS in botany, Ohio Univ., Athens, OH, 1966; MS in genetics, Univ. Ariz., Tucson, 1969, PhD in genetics, 1971. Asst. prof. Wayne State U., Detroit, 1973—76, UCLA, 1976—78, assoc. prof., 1978—83, prof., 1983—96, Disting. Prof. Molecular, Cell, and Devel. Biology, 1996—. Program dir. Genetic Mechanisms for Crop Improvement USDA, 1983, program dir. Plant Genetics and Molecular Biology, 84; chmn. Divsn. Cell, Molecular and Plant Biology UCLA, 1983, dir. Plant Molecular Biology Program, 1991—96, dir. Multicampus Seed Inst., 1986—; chair Edn. Found. Am. Soc. Plant Biologists, 1998—2002; co-founder and dir. Ceres Inc., Malibu, Calif., 1996—. Edtl. bd. (jour.) Developmental Genetics, 1981—84, Plant Molecular Biology, 1982—87, Molecular and General Genetics, 1982—87, Science, 1986—89, Sexual Plant Reproduction, 1998—, founding editor and editor-in-chief The Plant Cell, 1988—93. Named to NAS, 2001; recipient Recognition Disting. Tchg. and Rsch., Ohio House Rep., 1991, Disting. Svc. Award, Am. Soc. Plant Physiologists, 1993, Nat. Order Sci. Merit, Pres. of Brazil, 1998, Gold Shield Award, UCLA, 1998; grantee Professorship, Howard Hughes Med. Inst., 2002—. Office: UCLA Life Sciences Building 2835 Los Angeles CA 90095 Office Phone: 310-825-9093, 310-825-3270. E-mail: bobg@ucla.edu.

GOLDBERG, ROY J., geriatrician; BA, U. Pa., 1978; MD, Albert Einstein Coll. Of Medicine, Bronx, N.Y., 1982. Diplomate Med. Internal Medicine/geriat. Med. dir. Kings Harbor Multicare Ctr., Bronx, NY, 2003—; clin. asst. prof. medicine Albert Einstein Coll. Of Medicine, Bronx, NY, 2003—. Office Phone: 718-405-3535.

GOLDBERG, SAMUEL, retired mathematician, foundation administrator; b. N.Y.C., Mar. 14, 1925; s. Gedalia and Fannie (Lieberman) G.; m. Marcia Chinitz, June 21, 1953; 1 son, David. BS, CCNY, 1944; PhD, Cornell U., 1950. Instr., then asst. prof. math. Lehigh U., Bethlehem, Pa., 1950-53; mem. faculty Oberlin (Ohio) Coll., 1953—, prof. math., 1961-85, emeritus prof., 1985—; program officer Alfred P. Sloan Found., N.Y.C., 1985-90, cons., 1990—. Vis. assoc. prof. Harvard U. Grad. Sch. Bus. Adminstrn., 1959-60; vis. prof. U. W.Australia, 1976; mem. com. math. in social scis. Social Sci. Research Council, 1979; participant African Math. Project, Mombasa, Kenya, 1965, 68 Author: Probability: An Introduction, 1960 (translated into Greek, German and Spanish, paperback edit.), Introduction to Difference Equations, 1958 (translated into Spanish, German and Japanese, also paperback edit.), Some Illustrative Examples of the Use of Undergraduate Mathematics in the Social Sciences, 1977, Probability in Social Science, 1983. Bd. dirs. Allen Meml. Hosp., Oberlin, 1980-85, 92-2000. Served with AUS, 1944-46. NSF sci. faculty fellow, 1960-61, 67-68. Mem. Math. Assn. Am., Am. Math. Soc., Phi Beta Kappa, Sigma Xi.

GOLDBERG, SCOTT, recording industry executive, educator; s. Marvin Albert and Harriet Goldberg; m. Julie Ann Ward, May 5, 1996; 1 child, Jonathan Samuel. BS in Mgmt., San Diego State U., 1979—84. Cert. Pro Tools Instr. Digidesign Rec. Corp., 2002. Owner Jazzical Music Prodns., Milpitas, Calif. Composer: (soundtrack) Full Clip; author: (book) Guitar Fretrboard Theory and Harmony. Co-recipient Best Collegiate A Capella CD, A Capella Awards, 2004. Home: 251 W Capitol Ave Milpitas CA 95035 Office: Jazzical Music Prodns 251 W Capitol Ave Milpitas CA 95035 Office Phone: 408-946-7600. E-mail: snjgold@aol.com.

GOLDBERG, SETH A., lawyer; b. N.Y.C., Aug. 20, 1953; s. Seymour I. and Florence (Rovensky) Goldberg; m. Joan E. Shapiro, July 29, 1978; children: David, Emily. BA in History, SUNY, Binghamton, 1975; JD, Stanford U., 1978. Bar: D.C. 1978, Calif. 1991. Assoc. Steptoe & Johnson, Washington, 1978-86, ptnr., 1986—. Mem.: ABA, Environ. Law Inst. (pres.), Prettyman-Levanthal Am. Inn Ct. Home: 8303 Whittier Blvd Bethesda MD 20817-3124 Office: 1330 Connecticut Ave NW Washington DC 20036-1704 Office Phone: 202-429-6213. Personal E-mail: sgoldberg@steptoe.com.

GOLDBERG, STANLEY IRWIN, real estate company executive; b. Newport News, Va., May 13, 1934; s. David and Sara (Levy) G.; m. Marilyn Levin, Nov. 22, 1963 (dec. Oct. 1970); 1 child, Andrew Garfield. Student, Coll. William and Mary, 1952—54, U. Va., 1954—55. Lic. real estate broker, Va. V.p. Bedding Supply Co., Inc., Newport News, 1956-59, exec. v.p., 1960-61, pres., 1962-70; mng. ptnr. Goldkress Investment Co., Newport News, 1970—, also bd. dirs.; pres. Mut. Realty Corp., Newport News, 1973—. Trustee Temple Sinai, Newport News. Served with USAF, 1957-58. Mem. Nat. Assn. Realtors, Va. Assn. Realtors, Va. Peninsula Assn. Realtors, Elks. Home: 19 Hopemont Dr Newport News VA 23606-2146 Office: 11116 Jefferson Ave Newport News VA 23601-2551

GOLDBERG, STANLEY JOSHUA, federal judge; b. Balt., Feb. 16, 1939; s. Isidore and Lillian Frances (Kravatz) G.; m. Susan Jane Coplin, July 1, 1962; Rachel Hilary, David Mark. BS, U. Md., 1960, LLB, 1964; postgrad., NYU, 1966-69. Bar: Md. 1964, U.S. Dist. Ct. Md. 1964, N.J. 1967, U.S. Dist. Ct. N.J. 1967, U.S. Tax Ct. 1968. Tax trial atty. Office of Chief Counsel IRS, N.Y.C., 1965-69, 1971-76; assoc. Buckmaster, White, Mindel & Clarke, Balt., 1970; spl. trial atty. IRS, N.Y.C., 1976-84, asst. dist. counsel, 1984-85; spl. trial judge U.S. Tax Ct., Washington, 1985—. Mem.: D.C. Bar Assn. (hon.), Am. Coll. Tax Counsel (hon.). Office: US Tax Ct 400 2nd St NW Washington DC 20217-0002

GOLDBERG, SUSAN, editor; b. 1959; m. Gary Blonston (dec. Apr. 1999). Reporter Seattle Post-Intelligencer; asst. city editor Detroit Free Press, San Jose Mercury News, 1987—89, acting city editor, mng. editor, 1999—2003, v.p., 2001—, exec. editor, 2003—; dep. mng. editor USA Today, 1989—99. Chair mng. editors leadership and mgmt. com. AP. Mem. bd. visitors Northwestern U. Medill Sch. Journalism; bd. mem. Silicon Valley chpt. Am. Cancer Soc., 2003—. Mem.: Downtown San Jose Rotary Club. Office: San Jose Mercury News 750 Ridder Park Dr San Jose CA 95190-0001

GOLDBERG, VICTOR JOEL, retired data processing company executive; b. Chgo., Oct. 19, 1933; s. Albert J. and Ruth R. (Rosenberg) Goldbert; m. Harriet A. David, June 1, 1958 (dec. Apr. 1998); children: Susan A., Alan J.; m. Patricia A. Waldeck, Aug. 11, 2001. BS, Northwestern U., 1955, MBA, 1956. With IBM Corp., Armonk, N.Y., 1959-93, corp. dir. bus. plans, 1977-78, v.p. communications, 1979-81, corp. v.p., pres. communication products div., 1981-83, pres. nat. distbn. div., 1983-86, v.p. asst. group exec. marketing, 1986-88, v.p. mgmt. systems, 1988-93; dir. Edn. Through Music, 1998—. Mem. Forum for World Affairs, 1988-97; mem. planning bd. Village of Scarsdale, 1999—, chmn., 2002-05; bd. govs. Am. Jewish Com., 1998—; trustee Inst. Internat. Edn., 1978—, mem. exec. com., 1984—, vice chmn., 1988-2004; trustee Mental Health Assn., Westchester, 1984-99, exec. v.p., 1997-99; trustee Westchester Reform Temple, 1995-98, Scarsdale Found., 1998—, treas. 1999—2004; dir. Actors Shakespeare Co., 1995-98; chmn. adv. com. Long Term Care Ombudsmen Program, Westchester County, 1995-98; trustee New Alternatives for Children, 1997-2001, treas., 1998-2001; v.p. Thanks to Scandavia, Inc., 2001—; trustee Ford Found. Internat. Fellowships program, 2001—. With U.S. Army, 1956—59. Mem. Beta Gamma Sigma.

GOLDBERG, VICTOR PAUL, law educator; b. 1941; BA, Oberlin (Ohio) Coll., 1963, MA, 1964; PhD, Yale U., 1970. From asst. to full prof. U. Calif., Davis, 1967-83; prof. Northwestern U., Evanston, Ill., 1983-88; prof., co-dir. Ctr. Law and Econ. Studies Columbia U., NYC, 1988—, Thomas Macioce prof. law. Assoc. prof. U. Calif., Berkeley, 1977; prof. U. Va., Charlottesville, 1981; mem. Inst. for Advanced Study, Princeton, N.J., 1978-79. Fellow Ctr. for Study of Pub. Choice, Blacksburg, Va., 1975-76. Office: Columbia U Sch Law JG810 435 W 116th St New York NY 10027-7297 Office Phone: 212-854-8380. E-mail: vpgol@yahoo.com, vpg@law.columbia.edu.*

GOLDBERG, WHOOPI (CARYN ELAINE JOHNSON), actress; b. N.Y.C., Nov. 13, 1955; d. Robert and Emma (Harris) Johnson; m. Alvin Martin, 1973 (div. 1979); 1 child, Alexandrea Martin; m. David Claessen, 1986 (div. 1988); m. Lyle Trachtenberg, 1994 (div. 1995). Mem. San Diego Repertory Theatre, 1975—80, Blake St. Hawkeyes, Berkeley, Calif., 1980—84. Author: Alice, 1992, Book, 1997; actor: (plays) Living on the Edge of Chaos, 1988 (Calif. theatre award outstanding achievement, 1988); (Broadway plays) A Funny Thing Happened on the Way to the Forum, 1996—98, Funny Girl, 2002; (films) Citizen, 1982, The Color Purple, 1985 (Golden Globe for best actress motion picture drama, 1986), Jumpin' Jack Flash, 1986, Burglar, 1986, Fatal Beauty, 1987, The Telephone, 1987, Clara's Heart, 1988, Homer and Eddie, 1989, Comicitis, 1989, The Long Walk Home, 1990, Ghost, 1990 (Acad. award for best supporting actress, 1991, Golden Globe for best supporting actress motion picture, 1991), Soapdish, 1991, Blackbird Fly, 1991, The Player, 1992, Sister Act, 1992, Sarafina!, 1992, Made in America, 1993, National Lampoon's Loaded Weapon 1, 1993, Sister Act 2: Back in the Habit, 1993, Naked in New York, 1993, (voice) The Lion King, 1994, The Little Rascals, 1994, Corrina, Corrina, 1994, Star Trek: Generations, 1994, (voice) The Pagemaster, 1994, Boys on the Side, 1995, Moonlight and Valentino, 1995, Theodore Rex, 1995, Bogus, 1996, The Ghost of Mississippi, 1996, Eddie, 1996, Tales from the Crypt Presents: Bordello of Blood, 1996, The Associate, 1996, (voice) A Christmas Carol, 1997, How Stella Got Her Groove Back, 1998, (voice) The Rugrats Movie, 1998, Alegria, 1998, Deep End of the Ocean, 1999, Jackie's Back!, 1999, Girl, Interrupted, 1999, (narrator) A Second Chance at Life, 2000, More Dogs Than Bones, 2000, Kingdom Come, 2001, Monkeybone, 2001, Rat Race, 2001, (narrator) Golden Dreams, 2001, Star Trek: Nemesis, 2002, Blizzard, 2003, Jiminy Glick in La La Wood, 2004, (voice) Pinocchio 3000, 2004, Racing Stripes, 2005; (films, cameo) Beverly Hills Brats, 1989, House Party 2, 1992, Naked in New York, 1994; (TV films) My Past Is My Own, 1989, Kiss Shot, 1989, Defenders of Dynatron City, 1992, (voice) Yuletide in the 'hood, 1993, In the Gloaming, 1997, (voice) Mother Goose: A Rappin' and Rhymin' Special, 1997, Cinderella, 1997, A Knight in Camelot, 1998, Jackie's Back!, 1999, The Magical Land of the Leprechauns, 1999, Alice in Wonderland, 1999, (voice) Madeline: My Fair Madeline, 2002, It's a Very Muppet Christmas Movie, 2002, Littleburg, 2004; (TV series) Star Trek: The Next Generation, 1988—94, (voice) Captain Planet and the Planeteers, 1990, Bagdad Cafe, CBS, 1990, (voice) Happily Ever After: Fairy Tales for Every Child, 1997, (voice) Foxbusters, 1999, (voice) Liberty's Kids, 2002, (TV specials) Circus of the Stars #15, 1990, Tales from the Whoop: Hot Rod Brown, Class Clown, 1990; host: (TV series, talk show) The Whoopie Goldberg Show, 1992—93; actor, exec. prodr. (TV films) Call Me Claus, 2001, What Makes a Family, 2001, (TV series) Whoopi, 2003, actor, prodr. (TV films) Good Fences, 2003, (Broadway plays) Ma Rainey's Black Bottom, 2003; exec. prodr.: (TV films) Ruby's Bucket of Blood, 2001; (TV series) Strong Medicine, 2000; prodr.: Hollywood Squares, 1998—2002; (TV miniseries) Oh What A Time It Was, 1999; (Broadway plays) Thoroughly Modern Millie (Tony award for best musical, 2002); co-prodr.: (films) The Mao Game, 1999; dir., writer, performer (TV specials) Comic Relief, 1986, actor, writer (one-person show Broadway plays) Whoopi Goldberg on Broadway, 1984—85. Named Entertainer of the Yr., NAACP, 1990; recipient Grammy award for album of Broadway show, 1985, Hans Christian Andersen award for outstanding achievement by a dyslexic, 1987, Humanitarian of Yr. award, Starlight Found., 1989, Star on Hollywood Walk of Fame, 2001.

GOLDBERG, WILLIAM B., composer, musician; b. N.Y.C., Jan. 24, 1917; s. Harry B. and Frances B. Goldberg; 1 child, Mark. BSS, CCNY; postgrad. studies, Julliard Sch. of Music, N.Y.C. Tchr., composer, publisher of Music.

GOLDBERGER, ARTHUR EARL, JR., information technology executive; BS in Systems Engring., U. Ariz., 1974, BS in Indsl. Engring., 1975; MS in Indsl. Engring., Tex. A&M U., 1977; MBA, U. Denver, 2005. Cert. Novell engr.; cert. Microsoft sys. engr.; registered profl. engr., Ky., Tex., Mo., Ariz., Fla. Gen. engr. DARCOM/RRAD, Texarkana, Tex., 1975-77; mgr. DARCOM/AVSCOM, St. Louis, 1977-81; div. dir. prodn. improvement McDonnell Douglas, St. Louis, 1981-90; pres. Spectrum Techs., Inc., St. Louis, 1990—. Founder Salientinfo Inc., 2001; chmn. CAD/Expert System Tool Design, Seattle, 1991; cons. in field. Author: Real Leadership, 1993, Radical Leadership, 1997; contbr. articles to profl. jours. Bd. dirs. Engrs. Club St. Louis, 1978, Nat. Com. on U.S. Competitiveness, Washington, 1989—; judge, coach Scientific Olympiad, Mo., 1989. Recipient Quality Leadership award McDonnell Douglas Corp., 1988; named expert in inventory and prodn. mgmt. Am. Prodn. and Inventory Control Soc. Mem. IEEE (chmn. 1987-88, vice chmn. vehicle tech. soc. conf. 1991, bd. dirs. nat. com. on U.S. competitiveness, Leadership award 1988), Inst. Indsl. Engrs., Soc. Mfrg. Engrs., Data Mgmt. Assn. (bd. dirs. 1999—), Alpha Pi Mu. Achievements include rsch. in strategic marketing, business strategy, radio frequency identification, information systems, and supply chain execution, mfg. technology, process engring., healthcare operations and mgmt., RF and Network Comm., info. sys., ops. analysis, integration, and six sigma quality/process improvement.

GOLDBERGER, ARTHUR STANLEY, economics professor; b. N.Y.C., Nov. 20, 1930; s. David M. and Martha (Greenwald) G.; m. Iefke Engelsman, Aug. 19, 1957; children: Nina Judith, Nicholas Bernard. BS, N.Y.U., 1951; MA, U. Mich., 1952, PhD, 1958. Acting asst. prof. econs. Stanford U., 1956-59; assoc. prof. econs. U. Wis., 1960- 63, prof., 1963-70, H.M. Groves prof., 1970-79, Vilas research prof., 1979-98, prof. emeritus, 1998—. Vis. prof. Center Planning and Econ. Rsch., Athens, Greece, 1964-65, U. Hawaii, 1969, 71, Stanford U., 1990, 96, 2000; Keynes vis. prof. U. Essex, 1968-69. Author: (with L.R. Klein) An Econometric Model of the United States, 1929-52, 1955, Impact Multipliers and Dynamic Properties, 1959, Econometric Theory, 1964, Topics in Regression Analysis, 1968, Functional Form and Utility, 1987, A Course in Econometrics, 1991, Introductory Econometrics, 1998; editor: (with O.D. Duncan) Structural Equation Models in the Social Sciences, 1973, (with D.J. Aigner) Latent Variables in Socioeconomic Models, 1976; Assoc. editor: Jour. Econometrics, 1973-77; bd. editors: Am. Econ. Rev, 1964-66, Jour. Econ. Lit, 1975-77. Fulbright fellow Netherlands Sch. Econs., 1955-56, 59-60; fellow Ctr. for Advanced Study in Behavioral Scis., Stanford, 1976-77, 80-81; Guggenheim fellow Stanford U., 1972-73, 85. Fellow Am. Statis. Assn., Econometric Soc. (council 1975-80, 82-87), Am. Acad. Arts and Scis., AAAS; mem. Am. Econ. Assn. (Disting. fellow 1988), Nat. Acad. Scis., Royal Netherlands Acad. Scis. Home: 2828 Sylvan Ave Madison WI 53705-5228 Office: U Wis Dept Econs 1180 Observatory Dr Madison WI 53706-1320 Business E-Mail: asgoldbe@wisc.edu.

GOLDBERGER, GEORGE STEFAN, finance company executive; b. Oradea, Romania, July 3, 1947; arrived in U.S., 1962; s. Ladislau and Margareta (Schwartz) Goldberger; 1 child, David Michael. BS in Systems Engring., Bklyn. Poly. U., 1969; MBA in Fin., U. Pa., 1975. Sys. analyst Grumman Corp., Bethpage, NY, 1969-73; ops. analyst Internat. Paper Co., N.Y.C., 1973—74; mgmt. cons. Booz, Allen & Hamilton, 1975; asst. to chmn. W.R. Grace & Co., 1977—85; pres. Citizens Against Govt. Waste, Washington, 1986-89; COO Pres.'s Pvt. Sector Survey on Cost Control (Grace Commn.), 1986—89; dir. mergers and acquisitions Figgie Internat., Inc., Willoughby, Ohio, 1989-90; pres. Goldberger & Assoc., Inc., N.Y.C., 1991—98; chief bus. officer, CFO Progenitor Cell Therapy, LLC, Hackensack, NJ, 1999—. Contbr. articles to publs. Avocation: skiing. Personal E-mail: georgegoldberger@aol.com.

GOLDBERGER, MELVIN TOBIAS, bank executive; b. Knoxville, Tenn., June 6, 1919; s. Harry and Grace (Reich) G.; m. Betty Knox, June 4, 1944; children: Diane, Susan, Margy. BSBA, Ohio State U., 1940; postgrad., U. Tenn., 1940—41. Pres. Sq. Supply Co., Knoxville, 1946-64; chmn. Vector Co., 1965-72; pres. Seventh Investment Bancing Corp., Boca Raton, Fla., 1973—, Regency Highland Corp., Boca Raton, 1973—81. Treas. Fla. Philharm. Orch., Ft. Lauderdale, Fla., 1985-94, life bd. dirs., hon. life treas. emeritus, 1992-. Shrine mem. Kerbela Temple, 1947—; vice chmn. bd. dirs. Mae Volen Sr. Ctr., Boca Raton, 1989-2000, chmn. bd. dirs., 2001-02. Capt. Med. Adminstrn. Corps, U.S. Army, 1943-46. Mem. Elks Club. Avocations: golf, tennis, sports. Home: # 501 3001 Deer Creek CC Blvd Deerfield Beach FL 33442-8473 Office: Seventh Investment Bancing Corps 1599 NW 9th Ave Boca Raton FL 33486 Office Phone: 561-417-4100. E-mail: bocagrove6@comcast.net.

GOLDBERGER, PAUL JESSE, dean, architecture critic, writer; b. Passaic, NJ, Dec. 4, 1950; s. Morris and Edna (Kronman) G.; m. Susan Lynn Solomon, Feb. 17, 1980; children: Adam Hirsh, Benjamin James Solomon, Alexander David Solomon. BA, Yale U., 1972; LHD (hon.), Pratt Inst., 1992; LHD (hon.), Ctr. Creative Studies; doctoral degree (hon.), NY Sch. Interior Design. Staff editor The New York Times Mag., NYC, 1972-73; architecture critic The New York Times, NYC, 1973—, editor cultural news, 1990-94, chief cultural corr., 1994-95, freelance contbr., 1995—; architecture critic-Sly Line Column The New Yorker, NYC, 1997—; dean Parsons Sch. Design, NYC, 2004—. Vis. lectr. architecture Yale U., 1984— Author: The City Observed: New York, An Architectural Guide to Manhattan, 1978, The Skyscraper, 1981, On the Rise: Architecture and Design in a Post-Modern Age, 1983, House of the Hamptons, 1986, Above New York, 1988, The World Trade Ctr. Remembered, 2001, Up From Ground Zero, 2004; contbr. articles and essays to profl. publs. Mem. bd. overseers Parsons Sch. Design, 1986-90, 94—; bd. dirs. Jewish Found. for Christian Rescuers, 1994—, Guild Hall, East Hampton, N.Y., 1986-90. Recipient Pres. medal Mcpl. Art Soc., NYC, 1984, Pulitzer prize for Disting. Criticism, 1984, Roger Starr Journalism award Citizens Housing and Planning Coun., 1987, medal of honor NY Landmarks Preservation Found., 1991, Lit. Lion award NY Pub. Libr., 1993, Preservation Achievement Award, NYC Landmarks Preservation Commn, 1996. Mem. AIA (hon., medal 1981), Soc. Archtl. Historians (bd. dirs. 1977-79), Century Assn. Office: NY Times 229 W 43rd St New York NY 10036-3959*

GOLDBERG-SCHAIBLE, JOCELYN HOPE SCHNIER, market research professional; b. NYC, Mar. 29, 1953; d. Alex and Eileen Rosalie (Firstenberg) Schnier. AB, Princeton U., 1974; MBA, Harvard U., 1977. Statis. technician John Hancock Inc., Boston, 1974-75; product mgr. Gen. Foods Corp., White Plains, N.Y., 1977-78; strategic and tactical bus. planning analyst Bausch & Lomb Corp., Rochester, N.Y., 1979-81; mgmt. assoc. Gordon S. Black Corp. Harris Interactive, Rochester, 1981-84; pres. Rochester Rsch. Group, 1985—. Dirs. adv. coun. M&T Bank. Bd. dirs. U. Rochester Med. Ctr., 1991-98; life mem. JCC Greater Rochester, 1998-2004; trustee Geva Theater, 1992-99; v.p. class of '74, Princeton U., 1999—. Recipient achievement award Wall Street Jour., 1977; nominee Athena award, 2001. Mem. Profl. Ski Instrs. Am. (cert.), Harvard U. Bus. Sch. Club (bd. dirs.), Princeton Club Rocheater (v.p. 2005—). Home: 1666 Strong Rd Victor NY 14564-9133 Office: PO Box 22954 Rochester NY 14692-2954 Office Phone: 585-924-3620. Business E-Mail: Jocelyn@RochesterResearchGroup.com.

GOLD-BIKIN, LYNNE Z., lawyer; b. N.Y.C., Apr. 23, 1938; d. Herbert Benjamin Zapoleon and Muriel Claire (Wimpfheimer) Sarnoff; m. Roy E. Gold, Aug. 20, 1956 (div. July 1976); children: Russell, Sheryl, Lisa, Michael; m. Martin H. Feldman, June 28, 1987. BA summa cum laude, Albright Coll., 1973; JD, Villanova Law Sch., 1976; hon., 1996. Bar: Pa. 1976, U.S. Dist. Ct. (ea. dist.) Pa. 1976, U.S. Supreme Ct. 1979. Assoc. Pechner, Dorfman, Wolffe, Rounick & Cabot, Norristown, Pa., 1976-81; ptnr. Olin, Neil, Frock & Gold-Bikin, Norristown, 1981-82; pres. Gold-Bikin, Welsh & Assocs., Norristown, 1982-96, Wolf, Block, Schorr & Solis-Cohen, Norristown, 1996—. Course planner for 12 manuals on continuing legal edn., 1978—; pres. coun. Albright Coll., Reading, Pa., 1982-87. Author: Pennsylvania Marital Agreements, 1984, Divorce Practice Handbook, 1994, The Divorce Trial Manual, 2003; contbg. editor, Fairshare Mag., 1987—. Bd. trustees Albright Coll., 2000—. Named Pa. Honor Roll of Women, 1996, Pa. Super Lawyers, 2004. Fellow Am. Acad. Matrimonial Lawyers, Internat. Acad. Matrimonial Lawyers, Am. Coll. Matrimonial Trial Lawyers, Am. Bar Found., Am. Law Inst., Pa. Bar Found.; mem. ABA (family law sect. chair 1994-95, ho. of dels. 1995-2001, 2002—, bd. govs. 1998-2001), Pa. Bar Assn. (family law sect. coun. mem. 1980-89), Montgomery County Bar Assn. (chmn. family law com. 1984-86), Pa. Trial Lawyers Assn. (chmn. family law sect. 1988-90). Office: Wolf Block Schorr & Solis-Cohen One West Main St Norristown PA 19401-0869 Office Phone: 610-278-1511. Business E-Mail: lgold-bikin@wolfblock.com.

GOLDBLATT, BARRY LANCE, manufacturing executive; b. Palo Alto, Calif., July 29, 1945; s. Samuel and Joan Charlotte (Morton) Goldblatt. BS, U. So. Calif., 1967, MBA, 1968. Supr. market rsch. for brands Procter & Gamble Co., Cin., 1968-71; mgr. market rsch. Personal Products Co. subs. Johnson & Johnson, 1971-74; assoc. dir. consumer rsch. Johnson & Johnson Baby Products Co., Skillman, N.J., 1974-87; dir. market rsch. Johnson & Johnson Dental Care Co., New Brunswick, N.J., 1987-89, Johnson & Johnson Consumer Products Inc., Skillman, 1989-93; exec. dir. mktg. rsch. Johnson & Johnson Consumer Products Worldwide, 1994—2002; dir. market rsch. Church & Dwight Co., Inc., Princeton, NJ, 2002—. Bd. dirs. New Brunswick Hot Line, 1973; vol. Urban Cons. Group, 1977—. Recipient Cert. of Recognition Nat. Symposium Hispanic Bus. and Economy, Chgo., 1981, Cert. of Appreciation U. So. Calif., 1981. Mem. Am. Assn. Pub. Opinion Rschrs., U. So. Calif. MBAs, U. So. Calif. Commerce Assocs., Advt. Rsch. Found., Am. Mktg. Assn., Assn. MBA Execs., Mktg. Rsch. Coun.-The Conf. Bd., Am. Philat. Soc., U. So. Calif. Assocs., U. So. Calif. Alumni Club, Skull and Dagger, U. So. Calif. Alumni of N.J. (pres.), Zeta Beta Tau (asst. chpt. advisor Princeton U.). Republican. Home: 20 Andrews Ln Princeton NJ 08540-7633 Office: Church & Dwignt Co Inc 469 N Harrison St Princeton NJ 08543

GOLDBLATT, HAL MICHAEL, photographer, accountant; b. Long Beach, Calif., Feb. 6, 1952; s. Arnold Phillip and Molly (Stearns) G.; m. Shawn Naomi Doherty, Aug. 27, 1974; children: Eliyahu Yonah, Tova Devorah, Raizel, Shoshana, Reuven Lev, Eliezer Noach, Esther Bayla, Rochel Leah, Zalman Ber, Perle Sara. BA in Math., Calif. State U., Long Beach, 1975; MBA, Trinity U., 2003. Owner Star Publs., Las Vegas, 1975—; treas. Goldblatt, Inc., Las Vegas, 1980—; pres. SDG Computer Svc., Las Vegas, 1985—; chief fin. officer Martin & Mills Ltd., Las Vegas, 1992-93; controller Amland Devel., Las Vegas, 1993-95; CFO Stewart Constrn., Las Vegas, 1995-96; CEO Goldblatt, Inc., Las Vegas, 1996-97; cost acct. Ameristar Casinos, Inc., Las Vegas, 1997-99; dir. spl. projects Chabad So. Nev., Las Vegas, 1999-2000; dir. photography Lightons Creations, Las Vegas, 2000—; contr. Nev. Hand, Las Vegas, 2001—04; exec. MBA Trinity So. Univ., 2003; budget mgr. Rhodes Homes, 2004—. Photographer: (photo essays) Mikveh Yisroel, 1978, Chassidic Fabrengen, 1979, A Day at Disneyland, 1985, Shavous Trek, 1997, Garth Brooks World Tour, 1998, Care for Kids Telethon, 1998, 99, Chanukah - Festival of Lights, 1998-2004; prodr., engr.: (audio cassettes) From the Heart of My Dreams, 1980, Middle Class Dreams, 1981, Uforatzta Trio, 1982. Founder, pres. Jews for Judaism, Long Beach, 1975-82, v.p., 1983—; fundraising chmn. Friends of Lubavitch, Long Beach, 1977; bd. dirs. Congregation Lubavitch, Long Beach, 1987, 91-92; treas. Actor's Repertory Theatre, 1995-98, adv. bd., 1998-2003. Recipient Gold Press Card award, Forty Niner Newspaper, 1973, 1974, Floyd Durham Meml. award for outstanding cmty. svc., 1973, Georgie award, Actor's Repertory Theatre, 1995, ART Disting. Svc. award, 1996. Office: Rhodes Homes 4730 S Ft Apache Ste 300 Las Vegas NV 89147 Office Phone: 702-730-4388. E-mail: halgoldblatt@cox.net.

GOLDBLATT, LAWRENCE I., dean, educator, researcher; Undergrad., Georgetown U., DDS cum laude, 1968; grad. oral pathology residency program, Ind. U., 1971, MSD, 1973. Diplomate Am. Bd. Oral and Maxillofacial Pathology . Rotating dental intern U.S. Naval Hosp., St. Albans, NY; lt. to comdr. U.S. Naval Res. U.S. Navy Dental Corps., 1971—89, ret., 1989; asst. prof. oral pathology Ind. U. Sch. Dentistry, 1973—77, assoc. prof. oral pathology, 1977—82, prof. oral pathology, 1982—93, 1997—, named assoc. dean grad. and postgrad. edn., 1988, named assoc. dean acad. affairs, 1990, dean, 1997—; prof. oral pathology, dean Case Western Res. U. Sch. Dentistry, 1994—96. Tchr., rschr. in field; commr. ADA Commn. Dental Accreditation, 1998—2002. Contbr. scientific papers, articles to peer-reviewed jours. Fellow: Internat. Coll. Dentists, Am. Coll. Dentists; mem.: Internat. Assn. Dental Rsch., ADA, Am. Dental Edn. Assn. (v.p. deans), Am. Assn. Dental Rsch., Am. Acad. Oral and Maxillofacial Pathology, Ind. U. Sch. Dentistry Alumni Assn. (ad hoc mem. assn.'s bd. dirs.), Omicron Kappa Upsilon (past pres. Supreme chpt.). Office: 1121 West Michigan St Indianapolis IN 46202

GOLDBLATT, PHILLIP B., psychiatrist; b. Phila., Dec. 6, 1939; s. Samuel and Ida Goldblatt; children: Lisa, Dana. BA, U. Pa., 1961, MD, 1965. Intern Michael Reese Hosp., Chgo., 1965—66; resident in psychiatry Med. Sch. Yale U., New Haven, 1966—71, rsch. assoc. dept. psychiatry, 1970—73, asst. clin. prof. psychiatry Sch. Medicine, 1973—; chief Hosp. W. Haven, New Haven, 1973—77; pvt. practice New Haven, 1970—; attending psychiatrist St. Raphael's Hosp., New Haven, 1977—; cons. psychiatrist Bridgeport Cmty. Mental Health Corp., Conn., 1993—97, Conn. Mental Health Ctr., New Haven, 1997—. Bd. dirs. New Haven Pvt. Practice Com., 1996—. Bd. dirs. Jewish Family Svc., New Haven, 1985—91. Mem.: APA, AMA, Phi Beta Kappa. Office: 79 Trumbull St New Haven CT 06511 Office Phone: 203-624-1624.

GOLDBLATT, SAMUEL, lawyer; b. NYC, 1952; BS, SUNY, Brockport, 1974; JD, SUNY, Buffalo, 1977. Bar: NY 1978, US Dist. Ct. (We. and So. Dist. NY), US Dist Ct. (No. Dist. Ill.) 1979. Ptnr., practice group leader Products Liability, Toxic and Complex Tort Nixon Peabody LLP, Buffalo. Mem.: ABA, Defense Rsch. Inst. (mem. Drug & Medical Device Steering Com.), Product Liability Adv. Coun. Office: Nixon Peabody LLP 1600 Main Place Tower Buffalo NY 14202-3716

GOLDBLATT, STANFORD JAY, lawyer; b. Chgo., Feb. 25, 1939; s. Maurice and Bernice (Mendelson) G.; m. Ann Dudley Cronkhite, June 17, 1968; children: Alexandra, Nathaniel, Jeremy. BA magna cum laude, Harvard U., 1960, LLB magna cum laude, 1963. Bar: Ill. 1963. Law clk. U.S. Ct. Appeals, 5th Jud. Circuit, New Orleans, 1963-64; mem. firm Winston & Strawn, Chgo., 1964-67; v.p. Goldblatt Bros., Inc., Chgo., 1967-76, pres., chief exec. officer, 1976-77, chmn. exec. com., 1977-78; ptnr. Hopkins & Sutter, 1978-97, Winston & Strawn, Chgo., 1997—. Bd. dirs. MacLean-Fogg Co., Divergence, Inc. Trustee U. Chgo., Cancer Rsch. Found., U. Chgo. Hosps. Mem. Econ. Club, Racquet Club, Comml. Club. Office: Winston & Strawn 35 W Wacker Dr Ste 4200 Chicago IL 60601-9703

GOLDBLATT, STEVEN HARRIS, law educator; b. Bklyn., Apr. 30, 1947; s. J. Irving and Ethel (Epstein) G.; m. Irene P. Burns, June 12, 1981; children: Sarah P., Elizabeth G.B. BA, Franklin & Marshall Coll., 1967; JD, Georgetown U., 1970. Bar: Pa. 1970, D.C. 1981. With Phila. Dist. Atty.'s Office, 1970-81; dir. Appellate Litigation Program Georgetown U. Law Ctr., Washington, 1981-83, prof. law, dir. Appellate Litigation Progam, 1983—. Chair rules adv. com. U.S. Ct. Appeals for Armed Forces, 1998—; dir. Supreme Ct. Inst., 2005—. Co-author: Analysis and Commentary to the Pennsylvania Crime Code, 1973, Three Prosecutors Look at the Crimes Code, 1974, Ineffective Assistance of Counsel: Attempts to Establish Minimum Standards for Criminal Cases, 1983; reporter Criminal Justice in Crisis, 1988, Achieving Justice in a Diverse America, 1992, An Agenda for Justice: ABA Perspectives on Criminal and Civil Justice Issues, 1996. Mem. ABA (criminal justice sect. chmn. amicus curiae briefs com. 1981-99, crisis in criminal justice com. 1990-91, criminal justice standards com. 2002-04) Office: Georgetown U Law Ctr 600 New Jersey Ave NW Washington DC 20001-2075 E-mail: goldblat@law.georgetown.edu.

GOLDBLOOM, VICTOR CHARLES, pediatrician; b. Montreal, Que., Can., July 31, 1923; s. Alton and Annie (Ballon) G.; m. Sheila Barshay, June 15, 1948; children: Susan, Michael, Jonathan. MD, McGill U., Montreal, 1945; LLD (hon.), U. Toronto, Ont., Can., 1980, Concordia U., Montreal, 1993, St. Anne's U., N.S., Can., 1996; LittD, McGill U., Montreal, 1992; Dr. of Univ., U. Ottawa, Ont., 1994. Intern Montreal Children's Hosp., 1945-47, 1949-50; resident Babies Hosp., N.Y.C., 1947-48; pvt. practice, 1950-80; min. environment and mcpl. affairs Govt. of Province Que., Quebec, 1970-76; pres., CEO Can. Coun. Christians and Jews, Toronto, 1979-87; pres. Internat. Coun. Christians and Jews, 1982-90, Que. Environ. Pub. Hearings Bd., Quebec, 1987-90; exec. dir. Fonds de la recherche en santé du Qué., Montreal, 1990-91; commr. Official Langs., Ottawa, 1991—99. Can. del. UN Environment Conf., Stockholm, 1972, UN Habitat, Vancouver, B.C., 1976; tchr. McGill U., 1950—66; chair Montreal Regional Health and Social Svc. Bd., 2002—. Pres. (hon.) Jules and Paul-Emile Léger Found., Montreal. Decorated Companion Order of Can., officier Ordre Nat. du Que.; recipient Govt. of Can. award, 1990, James H. Graham award, Royal Coll. Pysicians and Surgeons of Can., 1996, Centennial medal, Assn. médecins langue française du Can. Mem.: Can. Jewish Congress (chair nat. exec. 2004—, Samuel Bronfman medal 2004), Allied Jewish Cmty. Svcs. Montreal (Samuel Bronfman medal 1989), Alliance Israelite Universelle (Rene Cassin medal 1987). Avocations: opera, lieder singing. Home: 5 Grove Pk Montreal PQ Canada H3Y 3E6 Office Phone: 514-949-5043.

GOLDBLUM, JEFF, actor; b. Pitts., Oct. 22, 1952; m. Patricia Gaul (div.), m. Geena Davis (div.) Nov. 1, 1993. Studied at, Neighborhood Playhouse, N.Y.C. Broadway theater debut in Two Gentlemen of Verona, 1971, also appeared in The Mooney Shapiro Songbook, 1981; off-Broadway appearances in Our Late Night, El Grande de Coca-Cola, City Sugar, 1978, The Pillowman, 2005 (Outer Critics Cir. award, oustanding featured actor in a play, 2005); films include California Split, 1974, Death Wish, 1974, Nashville, 1975, Next Stop Greenwich Village, 1976, Annie Hall, Between the Lines, 1977, Invasion of the Body Snatchers, 1978, Remember My Name, 1978, Thank God It's Friday, 1978, The Big Chill, 1983, The Right Stuff,

1983, Threshold, 1983, The Adventures of Buckaroo Banzai, 1984, Silverado, 1985, Into the Night, 1985, Transylvania 6-5000, 1985, The Fly, 1986 (Saturn award), Beyond Therapy, 1987, Vibes, 1988, Earth Girls Are Easy, 1989, The Tall Guy, 1990, The Bad Monkey, 1990, Mr. Frost, 1990, Deep Cover, 1992, The Favor, the Watch and the Very Big Fish, 1992, Fathers and Sons, 1992, Jurassic Park, 1993, Hideaway, 1995, Nine Months, 1995, Mad Dog Time, 1996, Independence Day, 1996, The Great White Hype, 1996, Lost World: The Jurassic Park, 1997, Hideaway, 1995, Nine Months, 1995, Mad Dog Time, 1996, The Great White Hype, 1996, Independence Day, 1996, Welcome to Hollywood, 1998, The Prince of Egypt (voice), 1998, Holy Man, 1998, Popcorn, 1999, Chain of Fools, 2000, Auggie Rose, 2000, One of the Hollywood Ten, 2000, Perfume, 2001, Cats & Dogs, 2001, Igby Goes Down, 2002, Dallas 362, 2003, Spinning Boris, 2003, Supermarket, 2004; TV movies include The Legend of Sleepy Hollow, 1980, Rehearsal for Murder, 1982, Ernie Kovacs: Between the Laughter, 1984, Lush Life, 1994, One of the Hollywood Ten, 2000, Legend of the Lost Tribe (voice), 2002, War Stories, 2003, The Life Aquatic with Steve Zissou, 2004; TV series Tenspeed and Brownshoe, 1980, Future Quest, 1994, Crank Yankers (voice), 2002; prodr. short action film: Little Surprises, 1995 (Acad. award nominee for best live short action film 1996); TV guest appearences Will & Grace, 2005.*

GOLDEN, ARTHUR F., lawyer; b. Bklyn., Apr. 14, 1946; s. Isadore and Dorothy (Schisel) G.; m. Elisabeth Lee Smith, Aug. 28, 1971; children: Frederick Tucker, James Alexander, Eliza Emerson. BS, Rensselaer Poly. Inst., 1966; JD, NYU, 1969. Bar: N.Y. 1970, U.S. Ct. Appeals (2d cir.) 1970, U.S. Dist. Ct. (so. dist.) N.Y. 1972, U.S. Supreme 1975, U.S. Ct. Appeals (D.C. cir.) 1979, D.C. 1980, U.S. Dist. Ct. D.C. 1980, U.S. Dist. Ct. (ea. dist.) N.Y. 1972, U.S. Dist. Ct. (no. dist.) Ohio 1985, U.S. Ct. Appeals (6th cir.) 1985, U.S. Ct. Appeals (7th cir.) 1996. With Davis Polk & Wardwell, N.Y.C., 1969—, ptnr., 1978—; co-founder Washington office Davis Polk, 1980-82. Bd. dirs. Emerson Electric Co., 2000-; mem. pension and governance com., ESCO Electronics Corp.; mem. exec. com., chmn. compensation com., 1990-96, Burns Internat. Svcs. Corp.; mem. exec. and audit and fin. coms., 1996-2000, Allegiance Corp., mem. audit and pub. policy com., 1996-99; trustee Rensselaer Poly. Inst. Trustee Rensselaer Poly. Inst., 2005—. With USAR, 1968—74. Mem. ABA, Assn. of Bar of City of N.Y., N.Y. State Bar Assn., N.Y. State Cmtys. Aid Assn. (bd. mgrs. 1986-89), New Canaan Winter Club (pres. 1988-91, bd. govs. 1987-93), Country Club New Canaan, River Club N.Y.C. Office: Davis Polk & Wardwell 450 Lexington Ave Fl 29 New York NY 10017-3911 Office Phone: 212-450-4388. Office Fax: 212-450-3388. Business E-Mail: arthur.golden@dpw.com.

GOLDEN, BRUCE PAUL, lawyer; b. Chgo., Dec. 4, 1943; s. Irving R. and Anne K. (Eisenberg) G. SB in Elec. Sci. and Engring., MIT, 1965, SM in Elec. Engring., 1966; JD, Harvard U., 1969. Bar: Ill. 1969, U.S. Dist. Ct. (no. dist.) Ill. 1970, U.S. Ct. Appeals (7th cir.) 1994, U.S. Supreme Ct. 1995, cert.: (arbitrator); lic. real estate broker. Assoc. McDermott, Will & Emery, Chgo., 1970-75, ptnr., 1976-91; of counsel Fishman & Merrick, P.C., Chgo., 1991-92, Coffield, Ungaretti & Harris, Chgo., 1992-96; Bruce P. Golden and Assocs., Chgo., 1996—; gen. counsel Piranha, Inc., 2000—02. Officer, dir. various corps.; speaker bank law, securities law, venture capital seminars Contbr. articles to Banking Law Jour., contbg. editor, 1979-90. Chmn. MIT Enterprise Forum Chgo.; bd. dirs. Entrepreneurship Inst. Chgo., Chgo. chpt. U.S. Entrepreneurs Network, Ill. Small Bus. Devel. Ctr., Kellogg Sch. Bus. community services com. Mem. MIT Alumni of Chgo. (dir. 1993—), Union League. Home and Office: 4137 N Hermitage Ave Chicago IL 60613-1820 Business E-Mail: bpgolden@lstcounsel.com.

GOLDEN, BRYAN, management consultant, writer; s. Samuel and Rachelle Golden; life ptnr. Sally Delmerico. BA with honors, SUNY, Purchase, 1978. Syndicated columnist various newspapers, Hopewell Junction, NY; mgmt. cons., owner Power Point Group, 1983—. Curriculum adv. com. mem. Dutchess C.C., Poughkeepsie, NY, 1984—; lead cons. N.Y. State Dept. Econ. Devel., Marist Coll., 1989—90; adj. prof. Marist Coll., 1983—98, Dutchess C.C., 1983—, Culinary Inst. Am., Hyde Park, NY, 1999. Author: Dare to Live Without Limits; editor: (newspaper) Common Sense Monthly; contbr. columns in newspapers. Founder People Beekman, NY, 1986—89. Regents scholar, N.Y. State, 1974. Mem.: Nat. Soc. Newspaper Columnists. Office Phone: 845-223-7223. E-mail: bryan@columnist.com, egolden@columnist.com.

GOLDEN, CHARLES EDWARD, pharmaceutical company executive; b. Ft. Wayne, Ind. BA in Econ., Lafayette Coll., 1968; MBA, Lehigh U., 1970. From treas. to corp. v.p. GM, 1970—96; exec. v.p., CFO Eli Lilly and Co., Indpls., 1996—. Office: Eli Lilly and Co Lily Corp Ctr Indianapolis IN 46285-0001

GOLDEN, CORNELIUS JOSEPH, JR., lawyer; b. Montreal, Que., Can., July 7, 1948; parents Am. citizens; s. Cornelius Joseph and Anna May (Gohlke) G.; m. Maureen Kay Schrader, Oct. 14, 1973; 1 child, Brendan Christopher. BA in Econs., Stanford U., 1970, JD, 1973. Bar: Calif. 1973, D.C. 1975, N.Y. 1988, U.S. Dist. Ct. D.C. 1976, U.S. Ct. Appeals (9th cir.) 1974, U.S. Ct. Appeals (D.C. cir.) 1975, U.S. Dist. Ct. (5th cir.) 1981, U.S Dist. Ct. (4th cir.) 1990, U.S. Supreme Ct. 1979. Rsch. fellow in comml. law Centre National de la Recherche Scientifique, Paris, 1974; assoc. Wilmer, Cutler & Pickering, Washington, 1974-79, Foreman & Dyess, Washington, 1980-81, ptnr., 1981-84, D'Amico, Luedtke, Demarest & Golden, Washington, 1984-86, Chadbourne & Parke, Washington, 1986—. Contbr. articles to profl. jours. Mem. Univ. Club Wash., Lowes Island Club (Sterling, Va.). Episcopalian. Home: 971 Saigon Rd Mc Lean VA 22102-2137 Office: Chadbourne & Parke Ste 300 1200 New Hampshire Ave NW Washington DC 20036-6812 Office Phone: 202-974-5630.

GOLDEN, DANIEL, journalist; b. Toledo, Ohio; BA magna cum laude, Harvard U. Staff reporter Springfield Daily News, Mass., 1978—81; regional corr. Boston Globe, 1981, gen. assignment reporter and investigative reporter, writer, Sunday "Focus" section, 1986—93, med. investigative reporter, 1993—94, projects reporter, 1994—98; reporter Wall St. Jour., 1999—2000, sr. special writer, 2000—. Recipient George Polk award for bus. reporting, 1985, George Polk award for edn. reporting, 2004, Nat. Headliner award, feature writing category, 1989, Nat. Headliner award, beat reporting category, 1999, First Place award for mag. reporting, Sigma Delta Chi, 1989, First Place award for investigative reporting, Sunday Mag. Editors, 1990, award for mag. reporting, Soc. Profl. Journalism, 1990, First Place award for investigative reporting, AP Sports Edit., 1993, Edn. Writers Assn., 1995, Nat. award for edn. reporting, 2002, 2004, Nat. award for edn. reporting special citation award, 1999, 2000, Pulitzer Prize for beat reporting, 2004; John S. Knight fellowship, Stanford U., 1998—99. Office: Wall Street Jour 200 Liberty St New York NY 10281

GOLDEN, DANIEL H., lawyer; b. NYC; BA, Univ. Wis., Madison, 1974; JD, SUNY, Buffalo, 1977. Bar: NY 1978, US Dist. Ct. (so., ea. dist.) NY. Sr. ptnr. Akin Gump Strauss Hauer & Feld LLP, NYC, ptnr., head financial restructuring practice group and mem. mgmt. com. Mem. SUNY Buffalo Law Rev. Mem.: ABA. Office: Akin Gump Strauss Hauer & Feld LLP 590 Madison Ave New York NY 10022-2524 Office Phone: 212-872-8010. Office Fax: 212-872-1002. Business E-Mail: dgolden@akingump.com.

GOLDEN, DAVID EDWARD, physicist; b. NYC, May 27, 1932; s. Barnet Dade and Rose (Rosenbaum) G.; m. Paula Englander, July 18, 1962; children: Richard, Jeffrey Bertram, Leila Justine. AB, NYU, 1954, PhD in Physics, 1960. Asst. prof. NYU, 1960-61, Adelphi U., Garden City, N.Y., 1961-62; engring. specialist GTE Lab., Palo Alto, Calif., 1962-63; staff scientist Lockheed Lab., Palo Alto, 1963-68; vis. prof. U. Bari, Italy, 1968-69; sr. scientist Sylvania Electric Products, Danvers, Mass., 1969-70; prof. U. Nebr., Lincoln, 1970-75; George Lynn Gross rsch. prof., chmn. U. Okla., Norman, 1975-85; provost, v.p. acad. affairs, prof. physics U. North Tex., Denton, 1985-89, prof., dir. ctr. for materials characterization, 1989-94, regents prof., 1993—2004; pres. Say It Straight Found., Carlsbad, Calif., 2004—. Cons. autometric divsn. Paramount Pictures, N.Y.C., 1961-62, Tracor, Austin, Tex., 1969-74, Lawrence Radiation Lab., Livermore, Calif., 1975-78, Minn. Mining and Mftg., Mpls., 1984-86, Motorola, 1997-2000, Charles Evans & Assocs., 1998—; hon. lectr. Mid-Am. State U. Assn., 1982-83; chmn. Tex. Higher Edn. Coordinating Bd. Com. on Satellite Ednl. Delivery Systems, 1986; lectr. in field. Contbr. articles to profl. jours., chpts. to books. Sr. cons. Say It Straight Found. Grantee various orgns.; fellow Centennial Edn. Program U. Nebr., 1974-75. Fellow Am. Phys. Soc. (com. mem.); mem. AAAS, Materials Rsch. Soc., Sigma Xi. Lodges: Kiwanis. Avocations: jogging, tennis. Business E-Mail: sayitstraight-info@sayitstraight.org. E-mail: golden@unt.edu.

GOLDEN, DONA LEE, artist; b. Waterford, Minn., Mar. 13, 1931; d. Eugene and Marjorie (McCorkell) Bolin; m. Darrell Richard Golden, Feb. 21, 1959; three children. BFA, Mpls. Sch. Art & Design, 1957, U. Iowa, 1959; MEd, U. Nebr., 1980. Art tchr. K-12 Waterloo (Nebr.) Pub. Sch., 1975-89; mem. Artist Coop. Gallery, Omaha, 1989—, Nebr. Women's Caucus for Art, Period Gallery, Omaha, 1999—. Exhibited in group shows Octagon Ctr. for the Arts, Ames, Iowa, 1998, 99, McCook C.C., 1998, Shafer Gallery, Great Bend, Kans., 1998, 99, Art Guild of Burlington, Iowa, 1995-99, Cheyenne (Wyo.) Juried Show, 1989-99; 2-person shows include St. Paul's Luth. Ch., Millard, Nebr.; group shows include Fremont, Nebr., 1998, Omaha, Nebr. Women's Caucus, 1995—. Mem. DAR, Kans. Watercolor Soc. (Wichita, signature mem.). Republican. Presbyterian. Avocations: golf, genealogy, hiking, canoeing, reading. Home: 2142 S 108th St Omaha NE 68144-3101

GOLDEN, EDWIN HAROLD, insurance company executive; b. Corsicana, Tex., Dec. 14, 1931; s. Mace Benjamin and Sarah (Alterman) G.; m. Dolly Moskowitz, Aug. 3, 1952; children: Jeffrey L., Beth Golden Marsh. BBA, U. Tex., 1953. Agt. N.Y. Life Ins. Co., Austin, Tex., 1955-80; ptnr. Hodges, Golden & Duckworth, Austin, 1967-77; owner Ed Golden & Assocs., Austin, Tex., 1977—. Pres. Golden World Travel, Austin, 1993. Chmn. bd. trustees City of Austin Retirement Sys., 1975—; bd. dirs. James Dick Found. for Performing Arts, Round Top, Tex., 1979—. With U.S. Army, 1953-54. Mem. CLU (Austin chpt., certs. in pension planning and estate planning), Nat. Assn. Life Underwriters, Million Dollar Round Table (life), Top of the Table (charter), Am. Soc. Pension Actuaries, Internat. Found. Employee Benefit Plans, Shriners, Masons, Travelers' Century Club. Jewish. Avocation: travel. Office: Ed Golden & Assocs PO Box 9448 Austin TX 78766-9448 E-mail: ed_g31@yahoo.com.

GOLDEN, ELLIOTT, judge; b. Bklyn., June 28, 1926; s. Barnet David and Rose (Fistel) G.; m. Ana Valbuena, July 8, 1990; children: Jeffrey Stephen, Marjorie Ruth, Peter Michael (dec.); stepchildren: Robert, Elizabeth, William, John. Student, Maritime Acad., 1944-46, NYU, 1947-48; LLB, Bklyn. Law Sch., 1951. Bar: N.Y. 1952, U.S. Dist. Ct. (ea. dist.) N.Y. 1953, U.S. Tax Ct., U.S. Dist. Ct. (so. dist.) N.Y. 1953, U.S. Supreme Ct. 1961. Assoc. Golden & Golden, 1952-64; asst. dist. atty. Kings County, N.Y., 1956-64, chief asst. dist. atty., 1964-76, acting dist. atty., 1968; judge Civil Ct. of City of N.Y., 1977-78; justice Supreme Ct. State of N.Y., 1979-98, jud. hearing officer, 1998-2000. Adj. assoc. prof. N.Y.C. Tech. Coll., 1987-93; arbitrator, mediator Nat. Arbitration & Mediation, 1998—; cons. in field. Contbr. articles to profl. jours. Bd. trustees Greater N.Y. coun. Boy Scouts Am.; hon. vice chmn. March of Dimes; bd. dirs. Bklyn. Philharmonia; mem. adv. bd. Bklyn. PAL; chmn. Bklyn. Lawyers div. Fedn. Jewish Philanthropies; co-chmn. Bklyn. Lawyers div. State of Israel Bonds; assoc. trustee Temple Beth Emeth of Flatbush; mem. exec. com. Lawyers div. United Jewish Appeal; past pres. counsel Hosp. Relief Assn.; bd. dirs. Kings Bay YM-YMHA of Bklyn.; bd. dirs. Bklyn. ARC, Archway Sch. for Spl. Children, Bklyn. Sch. for Spl. Children. Recipient Cert. of Merit, Hosp. Relief Assn., numerous plaques, awards and certs. of appreciation various civic orgns. Mem. Nat. Dist. Attys. Assn. (dir. 1976-77, Disting. Svc. award), Combined Coun. Law Enforcement Ofcls. State N.Y., N.Y. State Dist. Attys. Assn. (sec. 1965-77), K.P. (supreme coun.). Avocations: golf, fishing, computers. Home and Office: 49 E Glenwild Dr PO Box 762 Smallwood NY 12778-0762 Personal E-mail: egolden@hvc.rr.com.

GOLDEN, GERALD SAMUEL, retired national medical board executive; b. Newark, N.J., June 8, 1935; s. Clement Harold and Jeanette (Bellat) G.; m. Deborah Ann Berlatsky, March 22, 1959 (dec. 1984); children: Leah Rachel, Ruth Naomi; m. Constance Reisa Abramson, Jan. 26, 1985. AB, Princeton U., 1957; MD, Columbia U., 1961. Diplomate Am. Bd. Pediat., Am. Bd. Psychiatry and Neurology. Asst. prof. of neurology and pediatrics Albert Einstein Coll. of Medicine, Bronx, N.Y., 1967-73, assoc. prof., 1973-77; prof. pediatrics and neurology U. Tex., Galveston, 1977-84; prof. pediatrics and neurology, dir. ctr. for devel. disabl. U. Tenn., Memphis, 1984-92; v.p. Nat. Bd. Med. Examiners, Phila., 1993—2002, con., 2002—. Adj. prof. neurology U. Pa., 1993—98. Author: Textbook of Pediatric Neurology; assoc. editor: Pediatric Neurology Jour., 1987-92, Jour. of Devel. and Behavioral Pediatrics, 1987-2000, Jour. Epilepsy, 1987-92; contbr. numerous articles to profl. jours. Bd. dirs. Harwood Day Tng. Ctr., Memphis, 1987-92 Memphis-Shelby County Assn. for Retarded Citizens, 1987-92, Memphis Oral Sch. for Deaf, 1987-92, Temple Israel Memphis, 1989-92. Recipient fed. grant Adminstrn. on Devel. Disabilities, 1990, Dept. of Human Svcs., 1990. Fellow Am. Acad. Pediat. (neurology sect. head 1981-83), Am. Assn. Mental Deficiency (v.p. for medicine, 1984-86); mem. Am. Assn. U. Affiliated Programs (bd. dirs. 1987-92, pres. elect 1988-89, pres. 1989-90). Democrat. Jewish. Avocations: amateur radio, travel, bird watching.

GOLDEN, HAL, artist, consultant; b. Bklyn., Dec. 10, 1925; s. Benjamin and Dora Golden; m. Catherine Jane Hanson, Apr. 27, 1957; children: Cynthia, Deborah. Student, Art Students League, N.Y.C., 1945—46, CUNY, 1946. Dir. advt. and promotion Swivelier Lighting Corp., N.Y.C., 1951—53; dir. nat. advt. pub. rels. Fred Astaire Corp., N.Y.C., 1953—55; dir. pub. rels. Gimbel's, N.Y.C., 1956—57; v.p. and dir. pub. rels. United Fund N.Y., N.Y.C., 1957—79; faculty New Sch. U., N.Y.C, 1970; exec. v.p., COO United Way Tri-State, N.Y.C., 1979—80; pres. Hal Golden Assocs. Pub. Rels. Cons. and Svcs., N.Y.C., 1981—83, Huntington's Disease Found. Am., N.Y.C., 1983—85; artist, conservator Hal Golden Studios, Patterson, NY, 1985—92, N.Y.C., 1992—99, Providence, 2000—. Cons. in field. Author: How to Plan, Produce and Publicize Special Events, 1960, Working with the Working Press, 1962, The Grant Seekers, 1972; creator: mag. Telefare Weekly, 1946; two-person show, Providence Art Club, 2000, 2005, exhibitions include Gracie Square Art Show, N.Y.C., 1997, Am. Artists Profl. League 74th Grand Nat. Exhbn., 2002, Oil Painters Am. S.E. Regional Exhbn., Richmond, Va., 2002, Salmagundi Club, N.Y.C., 2003, 2004, Attleboro (Mass.) Mus. Ctr. for the Arts, 2003, Cmty. Arts Assn., Ridgewood, NJ, 2003, 2005. Pvt. USMC, 1943—44. Recipient Silver Anvil award, Pub. Rels. Soc. Am., 1959, Cert. of Excellence internat. poster contest, Latham Found., 1951, Louis Kuriansky Found. award, 1999. Mem.: Am. Inst. for Conservation Historic and Artistic Work, Oil Painters Am., Am. Artists Profl. League, Providence Art Club (exhibiting artist). Democrat. Episcopalian.

GOLDEN, HERBERT HERSHEL, retired Romance languages educator; b. Boston, Nov. 1, 1919; s. Max and Minnie (Turetzky) G.; m. Hilda Rachel Lazerow, June 13, 1943 (dec. May 1964); children: Robert Sherman, Barry Allen (dec. Aug. 2003), Steven Eliot; m. Evelyn Pauline Sowa, Oct. 7, 1965. BA, Boston U., 1941, MA, 1942, Harvard U., 1947, PhD, 1951. Lectr. Spanish and French, Boston U., 1945-49, instr. Romance langs., 1949-53, asst. prof., 1953-57, assoc. prof., 1957-63, prof., 1963-85, prof. emeritus, 1985—. Cons. for NDEA lang. insts. U.S. Office Edn., HEW, Washington, 1955-56; asst. to mng. editor Modern Lang. Jour., Nat. Fedn. Modern Lang. Tchrs. Assns., Boston, 1955-58; instr. French and Italian, Harvard U. Ext., Cambridge, Mass, 1960-79; mem., editor, mem. adv. com. on fgn. langs. Mass. Dept. Edn., Boston, 1960-69; Fulbright lectr. U. Rome, 1962-63. Co-author: Modern French Literature and Language: A Bibliography of Homage Studies, 1953, reprinted 1971, Modern Iberian Language and Literature: A Bibliography of Homage Studies, 1958, reprinted 1971, Modern Italian Language and Literature: A Bibliography of Homage Studies, 1959, reprinted 1971, Histoire de France à Travers les Journaux du Temps Passé (1715-1789). Lumières et Lueurs du XVIII Siècle, 1986; editor: Studies in Honor of Samuel Montefiore Waxman, 1969, Giulio Bertoni and the Aesthetic Factor in Linguistics, 1969; contbr. articles and revs. to profl. jours. With U.S. Army, 1942-45, ETO. Decorated Purple Heart, Bronze Star, Gold medal of cultural merit (Italy); recipient diploma of merit Internat. Assn. for Study Italian Lang. and Lit., 1973, diploma of appreciation, France, 2001; Rsch. fellow Marion and Jasper Whiting Found., 1979-80. Mem. MLA (steering com. fgn. lang. program 1956-59), Am. Soc. for 18th Century Studies (editor Festschriften: 18th Century Bibliography), Am. Assn. Tchrs. Italian (sec.-treas. 1959-64, pres. 1964-66), French Soc. 18th Century Studies, Masons, Phi Beta Kappa (pres. Mass. Epsilon chpt. 1970-72, cert. disting. merit 1985). Avocations: classical music, collecting French films on video, reading. Home: 29 Thorndike St Brookline MA 02446-2405 Personal E-mail: evieherb@earthlink.net.

GOLDEN, HOWARD IRA, lawyer, financial consultant; b. Chgo., Mar. 7, 1946; s. Alex and Mollie Ann (Brod) G.; m. Emily Weiss, Sept. 12, 1976; children: Molly Iris, Dani Rachel, Benjamin Abraham. BA in Econs., U. Wis., 1968, JD, MBA in Internat. Mktg., U. Wis., 1972. Bar: Wis. 1972, Ill. 1972, Israel 1976, N.Y. 1981. Assoc. Berger, Newmark & Fenchel, Chgo., 1972-74; asst. city atty. Municipality of Jerusalem, 1977-79; ptnr. Daniel Laitman, P.C., N.Y.C., 1980-85, Dimas, Golden & Johnston, N.Y.C., 1985-86; exec. v.p. Guaranty Acceptance Credit Corp., N.Y.C., 1986-87; ptnr. Eisenberger & Golden, N.Y.C., 1987-89, Howard I. Golden, P.C., N.Y.C., 1989—. Mng. dir. Brookdale Equity Ptnrs., L.P., Scarsdale, N.Y., 1991—, Brookdale Internat. Ptnrs. and Ctrl. European Pvt. Fund; mem. supervisory bd. Restitution Investment Fund of the Czech Republic, Restitution Investment Fund Slovak Republic; chmn. bd. dirs. Khazakstan Investment Fund, Romanian Growth Fund; bd. dirs. Romanian Investment Fund. Contbr. to profl. publs. Mem. Am. Jewish Congress (com. on law and social action 1983—). Jewish. Avocation: collecting antique maps. Office: 305 Madison Ave Fl 46 New York NY 10165-0006 Home: 63 Malvern Ln Scarsdale NY 10583-6808 E-mail: hgolden@brookdalefunds.com.

GOLDEN, JAMES LESLIE, information technology executive; b. Balt., Aug. 5, 1944; s. Leslie Logan and Gladys (Kinser) G.; m. Patsy Ann Creech, June 4, 1966; children: James Brett, Courtney Leigh. BA in Math. and Edn., U. Ky., 1966; MS in Tech. of Mgmt., Am. U., Washington, 1973. Cert. info. sys. security profl. (CISSP), profl. sys. analyst, info. security mgr. (CISM). Bus. sys. planning exec. U.S. Postal Svc. Hdqs., Washington, 1980—83, dir. planning and devel., 1983—86, dir. data mgmt., 1986—89, dir. info. svcs., 1989—92, mgr. office and exec. info., 1992—94, mgr., strategic initiatives, 1994—97, exec. program dir. Yr. 2000 Initiative, 1997—2000, exec. dir. info. security, chief info. security officer, 2000—03, exec. program dir., info. tech. governance, 2003—. Adj. faculty math. No. Va. C.C., 1976-77; adj. faculty Nat. Cryptologic Sch., 1993-99; mem. U.S. pres.'s Y2K coun. U.S. Postal Svc. Hdqs., Washington, 1998-2000; mem. govt. adv. bd. Cyber Security, 2003—. Coach Sterling (Va.) Youth Soccer Assn., 1980-86; pres. exec. exch. program Mobile Corp., 1979-80. Capt. cryptology USNR, 1969—99, ret. Recipient Fed. 100 award, 2000, V.P.'s Info. Tech. Leadership award, 2000, 02, USPS CTO Tech. Plus award, 2000; named Ky. col., 1995—; grantee NSF, 1968. Home: 117 Peyton Rd Sterling VA 20165-5605 Office: US Postal Svc SW Rm 2801 475 Lenfant Plz Washington DC 20260-2801 Office Phone: 202-268-2800. Business E-Mail: jgolden@usps.gov.

GOLDEN, JOHN DENNIS, lawyer; b. Providence, May 18, 1954; s. Edward J. and Ann V. (Cahill) G.; m. Olga Iglesias, Aug. 2, 1980; children: Jennifer, Jackelyn, John. BA, Providence Coll., 1976; JD, Thomas M. Cooley, 1980. Bar: Mich. 1980, Fla. 1981. Assoc. Harvey Kruse & Weston, Detroit, 1980-82, Blackwell & Walker, Miami, Fla., 1982-83; ptnr. Rumburger Kirk et al, Miami, 1983-89; mng. ptnr. Roth, Edwards & Smith, Miami, 1989-91; shareholder, dir. Popham, Haik, Schnobrich & Kaufman, Ltd., Miami, 1991-95; shareholder Carlton, Fields, Ward, Emmanuel, Smith & Cutler, Miami, 1996—. Sustaining mem. Product Liability Adv. Coun. Mem. ABA (sustaining, mem. products liability adv. coun.), Mich. Bar Assn., Fla. Bar Assn., Dade County Bar Assn. Republican. Roman Catholic. Avocations: golf, skiing. Office: Carlton Fields Ward Emmanuel Smith & Cutler PO Box 01901 4000 International Pl Miami FL 33131-9101

GOLDEN, JOHN F., packaging company executive; b. N.Y.C., Feb. 5, 1949; s. David and Sylvia G.; m. Marguerite Ann Sellars, May 30, 1981; 1 child, Rachel Jeanne. Student, Bowling Green State U., 1967-69; BA, U. Colo., 1971. Exec. v.p. Stephen Gould Paper Co., Inc., Whippany, N.J., 1973—. Office: Stephen Gould Paper Co Inc 35 S Jefferson Rd Whippany NJ 07981-1043

GOLDEN, JOHN JOSEPH, JR., information technology executive; b. New Milford, Conn., Jan. 13, 1943; s. John Joseph and Anne Munroe (Hope) Golden; m. Carolyn Joan Pachesa, May 29, 1965 (div. July 1984); children: Elizabeth Susan, Jennifer Leigh, John Joseph III, Matthew Benjamin; m. Ethel M. Piercy, July 8, 1991; 1 stepchild, Michael Joseph O'Neill. BS, MIT, 1966. V.p. systems devel. Quantum Computing Corp., Newton, Mass., 1968-70; mgr. computer ops. Polaroid Corp., Cambridge, Mass., 1970-75; dir. info. processing Schering-Plough Corp., Kenilworth, N.J., 1975-78; dir. info. systems Compugraphic Corp., Wilmington, Mass., 1978-80; dir. info. systems electro-optics div. Honeywell, Lexington, Mass., 1981-83, dir. adminstrn. electro-optics div. Wilmington, Mass., 1983-87, dir. materials electo-optics div. Marlboro, Mass., 1987-90; dir. ops. Micracor, Acton, Mass., 1990-96; dir. info. sys. Fresenius Med. Care, Lexington, Mass., 1996-97; mgr. computing and telecom. U.S. Postal Svc., Washington, 1997-2000; sr. v.p. ops. Ethentica, Lake Forest, Calif., 2000—01; dir. bus. devel. Legato, Inc., Mountain View, Calif., 2001—03, TKC Comm., Fairfax, Va., 2003—. With USAR, 1964—70. Mem.: IEEE, Assn. Computing Machinery, MIT Alumni Orgn., Sigma Alpha Epsilon, Mass. Iota Tau Assn. (treas. 1970—). Roman Catholic. Home: 5013 Ox Rd Fairfax VA 22030-4561 Office: TKCC Fairfax VA 22030 Office Phone: 703-766-6209.

GOLDEN, JOSEPH AARON, lawyer; b. Detroit, Oct. 27, 1940; s. Milton and Sally (Schweitzer) G.; m. Frances Miriam Rubenstein, Aug. 16, 1965 (div. Apr. 1973); children: Manine Rosa, Jay Dylan, Nicholas Michael Estuardo, Samuel Marcos, Jennifer Rose Mead, Natalie Elizabeth Mead; m. Cynthia Sisson Mead, June 24, 1979. BBA, Wayne State U., 1962; JD, U. Detroit, 1967. Bar: Mich. 1968, U.S. Ct. Appeals (6th cir.) 1974, U.S. Ct. Appeals (3d cir.) 1995, U.S. Supreme Ct. 2004. Supervising atty. Wayne County Neighborhood Legal Services, Ecorse, Mich., 1968-70; ptnr. Craig, Fieger & Golden, Southfield, Mich., 1970-73, Fieger, Golden & Cousens, Southfield, 1973-78; pvt. practice, Southfield, 1978-85; prin. Sommers, Schwartz, Silver & Schwartz, P.C., Southfield, 1985—. Adj. prof. labor law U. Detroit, 1987—. Co-author: Wrongful Termination Litigation in Mich., 1986; contbrg. author: Employee Dismissal Law: Forms and Procedures, 1986. Founder, pres. Coalition for Fairness in Workplace, 1993. Fellow Coll of Labor and Employment Lawyers; mem. ABA (pub. co-chmn. employee rights and responsibilities com. labor and employment law sect., sect. coun. 1988-92), ATLA, Mich. Trial Lawyers Assn., Nat. Employment Lawyers Assn. (nat. exec. bd. 1984-95, pres. 1991-93), Mich. Employment Lawyers Assn. (founder, v.p.). Office Phone: 248-355-0300. Personal E-mail: jgolden@s4online.com.

GOLDEN, JOSEPH DAVID, music educator; b. McKinney, Tex., Aug. 26, 1951; s. Joseph Tyler and Jo W. Golden. B in music, U. No. Tex., 1976, M in music, 1980. Assoc. organist, choirmaster Ch. of St. John the Divine, Houston, 1979—83; organist, choirmaster Hist. Trinity Espis. Ch., Columbus, Ga., 1983—95; prof. of music Schwab Sch. of Music, Columbus State U., Columbus, Ga., 1989—. Adv. Metropolitan Opera, N.Y.C., NY, 2000—; coun. on creating original opera Lincoln Ctr., N.Y.C. Editor: RILM Jour., 1986—89. Mem.: Nat. Convention Steering Com., Music Tchr's Nat. Assn., Nat. Assn. Tchrs. of Singing, Am. Guild of Organists. Episcopal. Achievements include development of James H. Thompson Scholarships @ U. of No.

Tex; The Jordan Internat. Organ Competition at River Ctr. for the Performing Arts. Avocation: gourmet cooking. Office: Schwab Sch of Music Columbus State U 4225 U Ave Columbus GA 31907 Office Phone: 706-649-7246. E-mail: golden_joseph@colstate.edu.

GOLDEN, JUDITH GREENE, artist, educator; b. Chgo., Nov. 29, 1934; d. Walter Cornell and Dorothie (Cissell) Greene; m. David T. Golden, Oct. 10, 1955 (div.); children: David T. Golden III, Lucinda Golden Rizzo. BFA, Art Inst. Chgo., 1973; MFA, U. Calif., Davis, 1975; PhD Art (hon.), Moore Coll. Art, 1990. Assoc. prof. art U. Ariz., Tucson, 1981-88, prof. art, 1989-96, prof. emerita, 1996—. NEA forum pub. grants panelist, 1987; project dir. U. Calif. L.A. NEA Lecture series, 1979, 84. One woman shows include Women's Bldg., LA, 1977, G. Ray Hawkins Gallery, LA, 1977, Quay Gallery, San Francisco, 1979, 81, A. Nagel Galerie, Berlin, 1981, Ctr. Creative Photography, U. Ariz., 1983, Colburg Gallery, Vancouver, Can., 1985, Etherton Gallery, Tucson, 1985, 89, 91, 95, Mus. Photog. Arts, San Diego, 1986, Friends of Photography, Carmel, Calif., 1987, Tucson Mus. Art, 1987, Mus. Contemporary Photography, Chgo., 1988, Visual Arts Ctr., Anchorage, Alaska, 1990, Temple Music and Art, Tucson, 1992, 97, 2005, Scottsdale (Ariz.) Ctr. Arts, 1993, Arte de Oaxaca, Mex., 1995, Etherton Gallery, Tucson, 1995, Columbia Art Ctr., Dallas, 1997, U. Arts, Phila., 2002, Temple Music & Art, Tucson, 2005; exhibited in group shows at Centre Georges Pompidou, Paris, 1981, Security Pacific Bank, LA, 1985, Phoenix Mus. Art, 1985, LA County Mus. Art, 1987, 2003, Tokyo Met. Mus. Photography, 1991, Laguna Art Mus., 1992, U. N.Mex. Mus. Art, Albuquerque, 1993, LA County Mus., 1994, Hara contemporary Mus., Tokyo, 1995, Mus. Women in Arts, Washington, 1997, Santa Barbara Mus. Art, Calif., 1997, Mus. Cont. Photography, 1998, Tucson Mus. Art, 1999, Calif. Mus. Photography, 1999, Ctr. for Creative Photography, 1999, 2004, Santa Barbara Mus. Art, 1999, Mus. Fine Arts, Santa Fe, N.Mex., 2002, U. Ariz. Mus. Art, 2003, Akron (Ohio) Mus. Art, others; represented in permanent collections at Art Inst. Chgo., Calif. Mus. Photography, Ctr. Creative Photography U. Ariz., Denver Art Mus., Fed. Reserve Bank San Francisco, Fogg Mus. Art, Grunwald Ctr. Graphic Arts, Internat. Mus. Photography George Eastman House, LA County Mus. Art, Mpls. Inst. Arts, Mus. Photographic Arts, San Diego, Calif., Mus. Fine Arts, Santa Fe, N.Mex., Newport Harbor Mus. Art, Oakland Mus. Art, Photography Mus. Osaka, Polaroid Corp., San Francisco Mus. Modern Art, Security Pacific Bank, Tokyo Met. Mus. Photography, Tucson Mus. Art, Weisman Found., LA, Mus. Cont. Photography, Chgo., Seattle Art Mus., Wash., Akron (Ohio) Art Mus., Avon Collection, N.Y.C. Individual artist grantee Tucson Pima Arts Coun., 1987; faculty rsch. grantee U. Ariz., 1986-87, 93-94; Ariz. Found. grantee U. Ariz., 1984; fellow Ariz. Commn. Arts, 1984; individual photography fellow NEA, 1979; Regent's faculty fellow Creative Rsch. U.Calif. L.A., 1977. Achievements include archive of artists' works and other material established at Center for Creative Photography. Personal E-mail: judithgolden@earthlink.net.

GOLDEN, LEON, classicist, educator; b. Jersey City, Dec. 25, 1930; s. Nathan and Regina (Okun) G. BA, U. Chgo., 1950, MA, 1953, PhD, 1958. Instr. ancient langs. Coll. William and Mary, 1958-60, asst. prof. ancient langs., 1960-65; assoc. prof. classical langs. Fla. State U., Tallahassee, 1965-68, prof., 1968—, dir. program in humanities, 1976—, chmn. dept. classics, 1986-95. Bd. dirs. Fla. Endowment for Humanities, 1983-87. Author: In Praise of Prometheus: Humanism and Rationalism in Aeschylean Thought, 1966, (with O.B. Hardison Jr.) Aristotle's Poetics, 1968, Aristotle: On Tragic and Comic Mimesis, 1992, Horace for Students of Literature, 1995, Understanding the Iliad, 2004. With AUS, 1953-55. Fellow coop. program humanities U.N.C. and Duke, 1964-65; fellow coop. program humanities Soc. for Religion in Higher Edn., 1971-72 Mem. Am. Philol. Assn., Archeol. Inst. Am., Classical Assn. Mid. West and South (pres. So. sect. 1972-74), Phi Beta Kappa. Address: 1526 Parchment Cove Tallahassee FL 32308 E-mail: lgolden352@msn.com.

GOLDEN, LOREN S., lawyer; b. 1943; State atty. Carroll County; pvt. practice Elgin, Ill. Mem.: Ill. State Bar (treas. 1994—95, 3d v.p., bd. govs., pres. 2003). Office: Ste 201A 2400 Big Timber Rd Elgin IL 60123

GOLDEN, LOUIS JOSEPH, retired editor, publishing executive; b. Hartford, Conn., Oct. 19, 1952; s. Merrill S. and Marjorie (Louis) G.; m. Christine Palm, June 27, 1981 (div. Dec. 1988); children: James Joseph, Daniel Louis. BA, U. Conn., 1975. Copy editor Hartford Courant, 1974-77, night city editor, 1977-79, editor Bus. Weekly, 1987-89, bus. editor, 1989-94, v.p. mktg. and bus. developer, 1994-98; v.p. external rels., dep. publ., 1998—; asst. editor Weekly World News, Lantana, Fla., 1979-80, editor, 1980-81; v.p. Greater Hartford C. of C., 1981-85, Decker Guertin Cheyne, Hartford, 1985-87.

GOLDEN, MARITA, English language educator, foundation executive; b. Washington, Apr. 28, 1950; d. Francis Sherman and Beatrice Lee Golden; m. Joseph Butlar Murray, Aug. 23, 1991; 1 child, Akintunde Michael Kayode. BA, Am. U., 1972; MSc, Columbia U., 1973; LittD (hon.), U. Richmond, 1998. Lectr. U. Lagos, Nigeria, 1975-79; asst. prof. Roxbury C.C., Boston, 1979-81, Emerson Coll., Boston, 1981-83; assoc. prof. George Mason U., Fairfax, Va., 1989-94; prof. English, Va. Commonwealth U., Richmond, 1994—2001. Author: Migrations of the Heart, 1983, A Woman's Place, 1986, Long Distance Life, 1989, And Do Remember Me, 1992, Wild Women Don't Wear No Blues, 1993, Saving Our Sons, 1995, Skin Deep, 1997, The Edge of Heaven, 1998, A Miracle Everyday, 1999, Gumbo, An Anthology of African American Writing, 2003, Don't Play in the Sun: One Woman's Journey Through the Color Complex, 2004. Pres. Hurston Wright Found., Hyattsville, Md., 1990—. Recipient Disting. Alumni award Am. U., 1994, Woman of Yr. award Zeta Phi Beta, 1997, Writers for Writers award Poets and Writers mag., 2001, Authors Guild Disting. Svc. award, 2002; named to Literary Hall of Fame, Chgo. State U., 2000. Mem. African Am. Writers Guild (pres. Washington 1986-90). Office: Hurston Wright Found Ste 531 6525 Belcrest Rd Hyattsville MD 20782

GOLDEN, OLIVIA ANN, human services administrator; b. N.Y.C., May 23, 1955; BA in Philosophy and Govt., MPP, PhD, Harvard U. Budget dir. office human svcs. State of Mass., 1983-85; lectr. in pub. policy J.F. Kennedy Sch. Govt. Harvard U., Cambridge, Mass., 1987-91; dir. programs and policy Children's Def. Fund, Washington, 1991-93; commr. on children, youth and families HHS, Washington, 1993-97, prin. dep. asst. sec. for children and families, 1997, asst. sec. for children and families, 1997—2001; dir. D.C. Child and Family Svcs. Agy., 2001—04; sr. fellow Urban Inst., Washington, 2004—. Mem. adv. com. children and youth City of Cambridge. Author: Poor Children and Welfare Reform, 1992. Candidate for state senator, Mass. Office: Urban Inst 2100 M St NW Washington DC 20037 Business E-Mail: ogolden@ui.urban.org.

GOLDEN, RAYMOND LEE, retired theology studies educator, retired minister; b. Canton, TX, Dec. 11, 1920; s. Eddie Lloyd and Annie Mae (Phillips) Golden. Diploma jr. coll., E Ctrl. Clark Memorial, Newton, Miss., 1946—48; BA sr. coll., Miss. Coll., Clinton, Miss., 1950; Theology, New Orleans Theology, New Orleans, La., 1950—53. Cert. locksmith home bus./ Pixley, CA, 2002. Salesman Book and Bible sales, student aid, Charleston, NC, 1950; tchr. Scott County Sch. Dist., Sabastopool, Miss., 1952—53; air craft repairman Hayes Aircraft Corp., Birmingham, Ala., 1953—55; mission pastor so. Bapt., Plainview, Calif., 1955—57; sr. case worker county welfare, Visalia, Calif., 1957—59; tchr. Tulare County Sch., Tulare, Calif., 1959—69; kennel care Kennel Farm, Pixley, Calif., 2002. Family hist.: family tree Genealogy, 1982—86; author (correspondance): (letters) letters; author: (novels) (autobiography) This Happened to Me. Comdt. of cadets Civil Air Patrol, Visalia, Calif., 1957—59. Corp. USAAF, 1942—45, Pacific. Republican. Southern Baptist. Avocations: pilot, photography, bicycling, hiking, travel, reading. Home: 11260 Rd 144 general delivery Pixley CA 93256-9999

GOLDEN, REYNOLD STEPHEN, geriatrician, educator; b. Herkimer, N.Y., Jan. 11, 1937; s. Harold Theodore and Ethel Anne (Myers) G.; m. Gale Holtz, Nov. 26, 1959 (div. May 1978); children: Nathan Myers, Jennifer Lynn (dec.), Laura Beth (Lieba); m. Ellen Jeanne Moore, Sept. 9, 1978; children: Melissa Nan, Benjamin Harold. AB cum laude, Harvard Coll., 1958; MD, SUNY, Syracuse, 1962. Diplomate Am. Bd. Family Practice, Am. Bd. Internal Medicine; cert. added qualifications in geriatrics. Intern Lankenau Hosp., Phila., 1962-63; resident in internal medicine SUNY, Syracuse, 1963-66; pvt. practice Utica, N.Y., 1966-78; dir. family practice residency St. Elizabeth Hosp., Utica, 1978-92, St. Francis Hosp., Poughkeepsie, N.Y., 1992-95; clin. assoc. prof. dept. family medicine SUNY, Syracuse, 1991-96; chief of geriatrics Unity Med. Group (formerly Rochester Park Med. Group), 1995—; med. dir. continuing care svcs. Park Ridge Health Sys. (now Unity Health Sys.), Rochester, 1995—; clin. asst. prof. dept. internal medicine U. Rochester, 1999—. Cons. residency assistance program, Kansas City, Mo., 1988-96; pres. med. staff St. Elizabeth Hosp., Utica, N.Y., 1978-80, Pk. Ridge Hosp., Rochester, N.Y., 2004; charter mem. N.Y. State Coun. on Grad. Med. Edn., N.Y.C., 1987-89. Editor: N.Y. Family Physician, 1987—92. Recipient Vincentian Award, Unity Health Sys., 2000. Jewish. Avocations: travel, computers, music, theater, wine. Office: Ste 216 1561 Long Pond Rd Rochester NY 14626 Personal E-mail: GoldenREN@aol.com.

GOLDEN, RICHARD MARK, cognitive scientist, educator, consulting engineer; b. N.Y.C., Apr. 17, 1959; s. Ralph and Sandra (Feller) G.; m. Karen, Aug. 6, 1989. BSEE, U. Calif. at San Diego, 1982; MSEE, PhD in Exptl. Psychology, Brown U., 1986. Assoc. engr. Aerospace Corp., El Segundo, Calif., 1982; grad. rsch. asst. psychology dept. Brown U., Providence, 1982-86; Andrew Mellon rsch. fellow U. Pitts., 1986-87; NIH rsch. fellow Stanford (Calif.) U., 1987-90; asst. prof. Sch. Human Devel. U. Tex. at Dallas, Richardson, 1990—. Reviewer for various jours. in field; speaker in field. Contbr. numerous articles to profl. jours. Recipient Brown U. fellowship, 1982-83, Connectionist Summer Sch. fellowship Carnegie-Mellon U., 1986, Andrew Mellon fellowship U. Pitts., 1986-87, Sigma Xi award for Outstanding Rsch., Brown U., 1987, NIH Rsch. Svc. Postdoctoral fellowship, 1987-90. Mem. Cognitive Sci. Soc., Soc. for Math. Psychology, Soc. for Text and Discourse, Behavioral and Brain Scis. Soc. Office: U Tex Dallas Sch Behavioral and Brain Scis GR41 PO Box 830688 Richardson TX 75083-0688 E-mail: golden@utdallas.edu.

GOLDEN, ROBERT CHARLES, finance company executive; b. Bklyn., July 12, 1946; s. Charles Joseph and Audrey (Griffin) Golden. BS in Acctg., Fordham U., 1968, MBA in Fin., 1978. V.p. internal audit Walston & Co., Inc., N.Y.C., 1969-73; v.p.-fin. Acan X-Ray Co., Inc., Detroit, 1973-76; exec. v.p. Prudential Securities Inc., N.Y.C., 1976-97, Prudential Ins. Co. Am., Inc., Roseland, NJ, 1997—. Bd. dirs. HeartShare Human Svcs. N.Y., 1985—; trustee Xaverian HS, Bklyn., 1987—93; v.p. Ireland-U.S. Coun. on Commerce and Industry. Named Educator of Yr., Assn. of Tchrs. of N.Y., 1986, Cath. Guardian Soc. Humanitarian of Yr., 1985, Chief Brehon of the Great Irish Fair, 1992, Knight of the Sovereign Mil. Order of Malta, 1995, Man of Yr., Cath. Big Bros. and Big Sisters, 2002; named to Diocesan Ct. of Honor, Diocese of Bklyn., Assembly of Stewarts, Diocese of N.Y., 1995, Knights of the Equestrian Order of the Holy Sepulchre, 1998; recipient citation, Coun. of the City of N.Y., Franciscan Heritage award, Franciscan Sisters of the Poor at Pla. Hotel, 1987, Apple award, Prudential Pacesetters, 1989, St. Francis Xavier Soc. award, Xaverian Bros., 1990, Thomas J. Cuite award, Irish Am. Heritage Wk. Com. of N.Y.C. Hall, 1991, Crystal Shield award, Salvation Army, 1992, Disting. Alumni award, Xaverian High Sch., 1993, Constance O. Garreson award, Minority Interchange, Inc., 1999, Ellis Island medal of honor, 2000, Bishop's Humanitarian award, Cath. Charities Diocese, Bklyn., 2001, Bus. 100 award, Irish Am. Mag., 2001, 2002, Disting. Leadership award, N.Y. Aquarium, 2001, Caritas award, Catholic Tchr. Assn, Diocese of Brooklyn, 2003, Outstanding Vol. award, OPUS, 2005. Mem.: Ft. Hamilton Hist. Soc., Securities Industry Assn., Friendly Sons St. Patrick City of N.Y., Acad. Magical Arts, St. Patrick Soc. Bklyn., Emerald Assn. L.I. (past pres.), Bishop's Coat of Arms Club, Fordham U. Pres. Club, Bay Ridge Men's Club, Cathedral Club Bklyn. (past pres., Man of the Yr. 1994), Mcpl. Club Bklyn., Bayfort Benevolent Assocs., KC, Ancient Order Hiberians (divsn. 22). Roman Catholic. Home: 33 Columbia Ave Staten Island NY 10305-3739 Office: Prudential Fin Inc 80 Livingston Ave Roseland NJ 07068-1798

GOLDEN, STEPHEN L., lawyer; b. San Antonio, Tex. BA, Tulane Univ., 1975; JD, St. Mary's Univ., 1978. Bar: Tex. 1978. Various exec. positions in real estate sales and devel. and utilities, 1984—90; now. ptnr., head, real estate practice group San Antonio Akin Gump Strauss Hauer & Feld LLP. Assoc. editor St. Mary's Law Jour., 1977—78. Mem.: ABA, San Antonio Bar Assn., State Bar of Texas (real estate and probate & truste sections), Phi Delta Phi. Office: Akin Gump Strauss Hauer & Feld LLP Ste 1500 300 Convent St San Antonio TX 78205-3732 Office Phone: 210-281-7077. Office Fax: 210-224-2035. Business E-Mail: sgolden@akingump.com.

GOLDEN, T. MICHAEL, state supreme court justice; b. 1942; BA in History, U. Wyo., 1964, JD, 1967; LLM, U. Va., 1992. Bar: Wyo. 1967, U.S. Dist. Ct. 1967, U.S. Ct. Appeals (10th cir.) 1967, U.S. Supreme Ct. 1970. Mem. firm Brimmer, MacPherson & Golden, Rawlins, Wyo., 1971-83, Williams, Porter, Day & Neville, Casper, Wyo., 1983-88; chief justice Wyo. Supreme Ct., Cheyenne, 1994—96, justice, 1988—. Mem. Wyo. State Bd. Law Examiners, 1977-82, 86-88. Capt. U.S. Army, 1967—71. Mem.: Wyo. State Bar Assn. Office: Wyo Supreme Ct Bldg 2301 Capitol Ave Cheyenne WY 82001

GOLDEN, THOMAS M., lawyer; b. Nov. 1947; Grad., Pa. State U., 1969, Dickinson U. Mng. ptnr. Golden Masano Bradley. Mem. adv. bd. Nat. Penn Bank. Mem. adv. bd. Jesuit Ctr. for Spirtual Growth. Fellow: Pa. Bar Found.; mem.: Pa. Bar Assn. (Ho. of Dels., zone 2 gov., vice chair editl. com., chair client and cmty. rels. com., task force for quality of life/balance, task force on entities and ops., pres.-elect, pres. 2003—, Spl. Achievement award 2000), Berks County Bar Assn. (dir. 1990—93, pres. 1992), Berks County Golf Assn. (past pres.). Office: Pa Bar Assn PO Box 186 100 South St Harrisburg PA 17108-0186

GOLDEN, WILLIAM EDWARD, physician; b. Brooklyn, N.Y., Dec. 26, 1953; s. Morton M. and Margaret (Polusky) G.; m. Kimberly Ann Johnson, Feb. 27, 1982; children: Emily Jane, Abigail Anne. AB, Brown U., 1975, Baylor Coll. of Med., 1978; attended, Wharton Business Sch., 1982. Resident Presbyterian-St. Luke's Med. Ctr., Chicago, Il., 1978-79 1980-82, chief resident, 1982, Morris Fishbein fellow, 1979-80; RWJ clin. scholar U. Pa., Philadelphia, Pa., 1982; asst. prof. U. Arkansas for med. sci., Little Rock, Ar., 1984-90, assoc. prof., 1990—; dir. gen. internal med. U. Ark.for Med. Scis., Little Rock, Ark., 1984—. Prin. clin. coord. Ark. Found. for Med. Care, 1992—; trustee Am. Soc. Internat. Med., Washington, 1986-95, pres., 1995-96; mem. Ctr. for Clin. Quality Evaluation, Washington, 1990—, chair, 1995-97; mem. Am. Med. Assn. coun. on med. edn., Chgo., 1989-96, chair, 1995-96. Fellow ACP (gov. 1998—); mem. AMA (accreditation coun. continuing med. edn. 1990-92, liaison com. for med. edn. 1992-97, chair 1997), Am. Assn. Med. Colls., Am. Soc. Internal Medicine, Soc. of Gen. Internal Medicine, Fed. Coun. Internal Medicine (chair 1996-97), Am. Health Quality Assn. (pres. 1997—). Office: Univ Arkansas for Medical Science 4301 W Markham St # 641 Little Rock AR 72205-7101

GOLDEN, WILLIAM THEODORE, retired diversified financial services company executive; b. N.Y.C., Oct. 25, 1909; s. S. Herbert and Rebecca (Harris) G.; m. Sibyl Levy, May 2, 1938 (dec. 1983); children: Sibyl Rebecca, Pamela Prudence. AB, U. Pa., 1930, LLD (hon.), 1979; postgrad. bus. adminstrn., Harvard U., 1930-31; DSc (hon.), Poly. Inst. N.Y., 1975, Bard Coll., 1988; MA, Columbia U., 1979, LLD (hon.), 1986, Hamilton Coll., 1987; DHL (hon.), CUNY, 1997, Mt. Sinai Sch. Medicine, NYU, 2000. Lic. amateur radio operator, 1922—, station 2AEN. Asst. to pres. Cornell, Linder & Co., N.Y.C., 1931-34; with Carl M. Loeb & Co., Carl M. Loeb, Rhoades & Co., 1934-41; dir. Woodward Iron Co., 1940-68; asst. to commr. AEC, Washington, 1946-50, cons., 1950-58; chmn. bd. Nat. U.S. Radiator Co. (and successor cos.), 1952-74; dir. Pitts. Railways Co., 1952-63, United Carbon Co., 1957-63, Crowell-Collier and Macmillan, Inc., 1964-71, Paribas Corp., 1965-69; trustee Mitre Corp., 1958-72, 76-85, System Devel. Corp., 1957-66, chmn. bd. trustees, 1961-66. Spl. cons. on rev. govt. sci. activities Pres. Truman, Washington, 1950-51; advisor on NSF to dir. Bur. Budget, 1950-51; mem. mil. procurement task force Commn. on Orgn. Exec. Br. Govt., Hoover Commn., 1954-55; mem. adv. com. on pvt. enterprise in fgn. aid, U.S. State Dept., 1964-65; pub. mem. Hudson Inst., 1964-94; mem. commn. on delivery personal health services Mayor's Piel Commn., 1966-68; mem. adv. council Sch. Gen. Studies, Columbia U., N.Y.C., 1966—; mem. vis. com. on astronomy Princeton (N.J.) U., 1969—, chmn., 1976-89; mem. vis. com. on engrng. and applied physics and on medicine and dental medicine Harvard U., Cambridge, Mass., 1969-77, mem. vis. com. on astronomy, 1976-90; mem. vis. com. Assn. Univs. for Research in Astronomy, 1973-76, dir. at large, 1988-91, Disting. advisor, 1991—; mem. vis. com. Space Telescope Sci. Inst., 1982-87; mem. adv. panel on space transp. ops. NASA, 1976-77; mem. adv. panel U.S. Postal Service, 1981-83; vice chmn. Mayor's Commn. on Sci. and Tech., 1983-91, hon. chair, 1992—, Commn. Coll. Retirement, 1984-88, Scientists Inst. Pub. Info., 1985-94; co-chmn. Carnegie Commn. on Sci., Tech. and Govt., 1988-96; bd. dirs. Verde Exploration, Ltd., Inc., Block Drug Co., Inc.; bd. dirs. emeritus Gen. Am. Investors Co.; founder Carnegie Group of Ministers of Sci. and Sci. Advisors to Heads of G8 countries, Russia and European Union, 1991—. Editor, co-author: Science Advice to the President, 1980, 2d rev. edit., 1993, Science and Technology Advice to the President, Congress and Judiciary, 1988, 2d rev. edit., 1993, Worldwide Science and Technology Advice to the Highest Levels of Governments, 1991; contbr. articles on govt. and sci. to various publs. Trustee Hebrew Free Loan Soc., 1935—, treas., 1985—, United Neighborhood Houses, 1952-61, Associated Hosp. Service N.Y., 1959-74, Univ. Corp. for Atmospheric Research, 1965-74, Riverside Research Inst., 1967-76, N.Y.C.-Rand Inst., 1969-75, Ctr. for Advanced Study Behavioral Scis., 1970-76, Bennington Coll., 1971-76, Haskins Labs., 1971-92, SIAM Inst. Math. and Soc., 1973-91, Columbia U. Press, 1974-77, John Simon Guggenheim Meml. Found., 1976-81, Nat. Humanities Ctr., 1978-90, emeritus, 1990—; trustee The Population Council, 1979-89, Catskill Ctr. for Conservation and Devel., 1981—, U. Pa. Press, 1985—; mem. Marine Biology Lab., Woods Hole, Mass., 1968—, trustee, 1968-87, trustee emeritus, 1987; trustee Mt. Sinai Hosp., N.Y.C., 1955—, vice chmn., 1977—; mem. governing council Courant Inst. Math. Scis., NYU, 1962-91, vice chmn., 1962-86, chmn., 1986-91; trustee Mt. Sinai Med. Sch., 1963—, vice chmn., 1977—; trustee N.Y. Found., 1963-84, treas., 1974-78; chmn. bd. trustees City Univ. Constrn. Fund, 1967-71; mem. exec. com. Health Research Council, City of N.Y., 1968-75; trustee Am. Mus. Natural History, 1968—, v.p., 1971-88, vice chmn., 1988-89, chmn., 1989-94, chmn. emeritus, 1994—; trustee Carnegie Instn. Washington, 1969—, sec., 1971-99, sr. trustee, 2000—; trustee Barnard Coll., 1973—, vice chmn., 1975-79, 86-92, treas. 1980-83, hon. vice chmn., 1992-98, emeritus, 1998—; trustee N.Y. Council for Humanities, 1975-78, chmn., 1976-78; bd. overseers Sch. Arts and Scis., U. Pa., Phila., 1976-97, emeritus, 1997—; mem. council Rockefeller U., 1978—; mem. bd. visitors Grad. Sch. and Univ. Ctr., CUNY, 1979-96, mem. bd. Grad. Ctr. Found., 1996—; trustee Am. Trust for Brit. Library, 1980-92, 98—, vice chmn., 1985-92, co-chmn., treas., 1998—; trustee Neurosci. Research Found., 1981-99, chmn., 1981-87; bd. dirs. Grad. Sch. of Arts and Sci. Alumni Assn., Columbia U., 1984-93, vice chmn. 1984-91; chmn. Black Rock Forest Consortium, 1988—; mem. adv. bd. Johns Hopkins Sch. Hygiene and Pub. Health, 1995-98; bd. dirs. Internat. Univ. Exch., Inc., 1996—; trustee, The After School Corp., 1999—. Served to lt. comdr. USNR, 1941—. Recipient Letters of Commendation with ribbon Sec. of Navy and chief Bur. Ordnance for invention of naval gunfire device used in WWII, Pub. Svc. award Mus. City of N.Y., 1981, Disting. Pub. Svc. award NSF, 1982, Tribute of Appreciation, Nat. Sci. Bd., 1991, Pub. Welfare medal NAS, 1996, medal of distinction Barnard Coll., Columbia U., 1999, Dean's award for disting. achievement Grad. Sch. A&S, Conservation Citizen award Ctr. Environ. Rsch. and Conservation, 2003. Fellow AAAS (treas., bd. dirs. 1969-2000, treas. emeritus 2000, Lifetime Achievement award 2001), N.Y. Acad. Scis. (hon. life; mem. bd. govs. 1977—, pres. 1988, chmn. 1989, life gov. 1991), Am. Acad. Arts and Scis. (Scholar-Patriot award 2001), Assn. Women in Sci., N.Y. Acad. Medicine; mem. Nat. Acad. Pub. Adminstrn., Am. Philos. Soc. (mem. coun. 1985-91, v.p. 1992—, Benjamin Franklin award for disting. pub. svc. 1995), History of Sci. Soc., Coun. Fgn. Rels., Army and Navy Club, Cosmos Club (Washington), Century Assn. Office: 500 Fifth Ave 50th Fl New York NY 10110-5099

GOLDEN, WILSON, lawyer; b. Holly Springs, Miss., Feb. 15, 1948; s. Woodrow Wilson and Constance Annette (Harris) G.; m. Krista Nix, July 10, 1999; children from previous marriage: Wilson Harris, Lewis Hamilton, Pamela Camille. BPA, U. Miss., 1970, JD, 1977. Bar: Miss. 1977, U.S. Dist. Ct. (no. and so. dists.) Miss. 1977, U.S. Ct. Appeals (5th cir.) 1977. Pub. affairs journalist PBS/Miss. Authority for Ednl. TV, Jackson, 1970-72; asst. sec. Miss. State Senate, Jackson, 1972-76; ptnr. Lane & Henderson, Greenville, Miss., 1977-80, Watkins Ludlam & Stennis, Jackson, 1980-89; pvt. practice Jackson, Washington, 1990-96; v.p. govt. rels. ICF Kaiser Internat., Inc., Fairfax, Va., 1996—99; sr. congl. liaison U.S. Dept. Transp., Washington, 1999-2001; v.p. Jefferson Govt. Rels., Washington, 2001—. Mem. Dem. State Exec. Com., 1976-84, 88-96; mem. Miss. Gov.'s Constl. Study Commn., 1986; mem. Dem. Nat. Com., 1990-92; charter mem. Dem. Leadership Coun. NETWORK, 1988; USDOT rep. Miss. Spl. Task Force for Econ. Devel. Planning, 2000—. Major USAR, 1970-90. Recipient Disting. Reporting award Am. Polit. Sci. Assn. 1971, U.S. Law Week award Bur. Nat. Affairs, Inc., Washington, 1978. Mem.: Miss. Bar Assn. Democrat. Presbyterian. Home: 7037 E Haycock Rd Falls Church VA 22043-2319 Office Phone: 202-626-8500. E-mail: Wilsongolden@aol.com.

GOLDENBERG, CHARLES LAWRENCE, real estate company executive; b. N.Y.C., Sept. 4, 1933; BS, NYU, 1955, JD, 1958. Associated with Brown, Harris, Stevens, Inc., 1955-75, officer, 1960-75, sr. v.p., dir. fin. dist. office; pres., CEO Sylan Lawrence Co., Inc., N.Y.C., 1975—. Former adj. prof. real estate NYU; cons., lectr. in field. Contbr. articles to N.Y. Times, Real Estate Weekly, and other profl. jours. Mem. Nat. Assn. Real Estate Bds., Internat. Real Estate Fedn., Real Estate Bd. N.Y. Inc. (gov.). Office: Sylvan Lawrence Co Inc 1350 Ave of the Americas New York NY 10019-4801 Office Phone: 212-344-0044 x300. E-mail: clg_ny@yahoo.com.

GOLDENBERG, DAVID MILTON, experimental pathologist, oncologist; b. N.Y.C., Aug. 2, 1938; s. Leo and Lillie (Spivak) G.; m. Hildegard Gruenbaum, Apr. 28, 1961 (div. 1996); children: Eva, Deborah, Marc, Denis, Neil, Lee; m. Cynthia Sullivan, Aug. 13, 1997. Student, Shimer Coll., 1954-56; BS, U. Chgo., 1958; ScD, U. Erlangen-Nuremberg, Fed. Republic of Germany, 1965; MD, U. Heidelberg, Fed. Republic of Germany, 1966. Assoc. rsch. prof. pathology U. Pitts. Med. Sch., 1968-70; assoc. prof. pathology Temple U. Med. Sch., Phila., 1970-72, U. Ky. Med. Ctr., Lexington, 1972-73; prof., dir. div. exptl. pathology U. Ky., Lexington, 1973-83; pres. Ctr. for Molecular Medicine and Immunology, Belleville, NJ, 1983—, Garden State Cancer Ctr., Belleville, N.J., 1992—; adj. prof. surgery N.J. Med. Sch., U. of Medicine and Dentistry of N.J., Newark, 1983—93. Adj. prof. microbiology immunology N.Y. Med. Coll., Valhalla, 1993—2000; mem. VA Merit Rev. Bd. for Oncology, Washington, 1974-77; exec. dir. Ephraim McDowell Cmty. Cancer Network, Lexington, 1975-80; pres. Ephraim McDowell Cancer Rsch. Foun., 1978-80; sec., treas. Ky. Cancer Commn., Frankfort, 1978-80; mem. sci. adv. bd. German Fund for Cancer Rsch., Bonn, 1980-90; mem. exptl. immunology study sect. NIH, Bethesda, Md., 1980-83; chmn bd. Immunomedics inc., Morris Plains, NJ, 1983-; bd. trustees, Ctr. Molecular Medicine and immunology, Belleville, NJ, 1983-. Author more than 1500 articles, book chpts., abstracts, 1962—; mem. editl. bd. Tumor Biology, Antibody, Immunoconjugates and Radiopharms., Jour. Nuclear Medicine, Cancer, Qtly. Jour. Nuclear Medicine, Tumor Targeting. Outstanding Investigator grantee Nat. Cancer Inst., 1985, 92; recipient Rsch. Found. award U. Ky., 1978, N.J. Pride award in sci. and tech. N.J. Monthly, 1986, Excellence in Cancer Rsch. award N.J. Legis., 1986, Herz Meml. lectureship Tel Aviv U., 1991, 3M/Mayneord Meml. lectureship Brit. Inst. Radiology, 1991, Abbott prize Internat. Soc. Oncodevelopmental Biol.

Medicine, 1994, Vikram Sarabhai Meml. Oration award, Soc. Nuclear Medicine, India, 1994, Ted Bloch Meml. lectr. Southwestern chpt. Soc. Nuc. Medicine, 1999, Elis Bervin lecture and medal, Swedish Oncology Soc., 2002, Garden State Cancer Ctr. Special Sci. award, 2003, Dist. Scientist award, Clinical Ligand Assay Soc., 2004, Paul Aebersold award, Soc. Nuclear Medicine, 2005; named Inventor of Yr., N.J. RCD Coun., 2005 Hon. mem. Argentine Cancer Assn. Jewish. Achievements include more than 100 patents in field. Office: Immunomedics Inc 300 American Rd Morris Plains NJ 07950 also: CMMI 520 Belleville Ave Belleville NJ 07109 Office Phone: 973-605-8200 ext. 128. Personal E-mail: dmg.gscancer@att.net.

GOLDENBERG, GEORGE, retired pharmaceutical company executive; b. N.Y.C., Mar. 12, 1929; s. Gersh and Rose (Kolpacci) G.; m. Arlene Sandra Yudell, May 22, 1955; children: Steven Alan, Heidi Michele Goldenberg Handelsman, Jeffrey Evan. Student, Bklyn. Coll., 1946-47; BS, Bklyn. Coll. Pharmacy L.I. U., 1951. Pharmacist Dolcorts Pharmacy, N.Y.C., 1951-56; export mgr. Chem. Specialties Co., Inc., N.Y.C., 1956-58; sales mgr. Syntex Chem. Co., Inc., N.Y.C., 1958-60; asst. to pres. Syntex Labs., Inc., N.Y.C., 1960-61; gen. sales mgr. Panray-Parlam Corp., Englewood, N.J., 1961-63; v.p. Ormont Drug & Chem. Co., Inc., Englewood, 1963-64, exec. v.p., dir., 1964-66, pres., dir., 1966-81; sec., dir. Goldleaf Pharmacal Co., Inc., Englewood, 1966-81; pres., dir. Moleculon, Inc., 1982-88; pres., CEO, dir. Argus Pharms. Inc., The Woodlands, Tex., 1988-92. Bd. dirs. Fed. Pharmacal Co., Ft. Lauderdale, Fla., Bedford Acme Surg. Co., Inc., Bklyn., Lawton Labs., Inc., Englewood, Ormont Diagnostics Ltd., London. Trustee L.I. U., Bklyn. Coll. Pharmacy. Mem. Bklyn. Coll. Pharmacy Alumni Assn. (pres.), Fedn. Alumni Assns. L.I. U. (pres.), Am. Pharm. Assn., Englewood Jr. C. of C., Young Pres. Orgn., Am. Mgmt. Assn., Drug and Allied Trades Assn., Delta Sigma Theta. Clubs: B'nai B'rith, The Polo Club of Boca Raton (past pres. bd. govs.), Jewish Fedn. of S. Palm Beach County (chmn.). Home: 16730 Colchester Ct Delray Beach FL 33484-6946 E-mail: aggpolo@aol.com.

GOLDENBERG, KIM, academic administrator, internist; BS, SUNY, Stonybrook, 1968; MS, Polytech. Inst. N.Y., 1972; MD, Albany (N.Y.) Med. Coll., 1979. Test engr. lunar lander and naval jets, Grumman, NY, 1968—75; resident internal medicine Western Res. Care Sys., Youngstown, Ohio, 1979—82; dir. gen. internal medicine Wright State U. Sch. Medicine, Dayton, Ohio, 1983—89, vice chair medicine, 1988—89, assoc. dean for students and curriculum, 1989—90, dean, 1990—98, pres., 1998—. Office: Wright State U Office of Pres Dayton OH 45435

GOLDENBERG, MYRNA GALLANT, English language/literature and Holocaust educator; b. Bklyn., Mar. 8, 1937; d. Harry and Fay (Solomon) Gallant; m. Neal Goldenberg, Jan. 27, 1957; children: Elizabeth, David Brian, Eve Lisa. BS cum laude, CCNY, 1957; MA, U. Ark., 1961; PhD, U. Md., 1987. Prof. emerita dept. English Montgomery Coll., Rockville, Md., 1971—2003, chair dept., 1979-81, coord. gen. edn., 1981-90, coord. women's studies program, 1990-94, dir. Paul Peck Humanities Inst., 1997—2003; Ida E. King disting. vis. scholar holocaust studies Richard Stockton Coll., NJ, 2005—. Lectr. Sch. Arts and Scis., Johns Hopkins U.; lectr. Holocaust and genocide studies, women's studies, Jewish women's studies, honors coll. English U. Md.; dir. project to integrate scholarship on women and minorities into the curriculum Ford Found., 1993-94; co-dir. project integrating scholarship of women in curricula of selected Md. C.C.s, FIPSE, 1988-90; chmn. Montgomery County Commn. on Humanities, 1984-91; chmn. Title IX adv. com. Montgomery County Pub. Schs., 1985-89; Ida E. King disting. vis. scholar Holocaust studies Richard Stockton Coll. N.J., 2005-2006. lectr. in field. Contbg. author/author: Common and Uncommon Concerns: The Complex Role of Community College Department Chairpersons/Enhancing Department Leadership, 1990, Different Horrors/Same Hell: Women Remembering the Holocaust, Thinking the Unthinkable: Human Meanings of the Holocaust, 1990, Writing Everybody In: Two-Year College English: Essays for a New Century, 1994, Testimony, Narrative and Nightmare: Experience of Jewish Women in the Holocaust: Active Voices/Women and Jewish Culture, 1995, Lessons Learned from Gentle Heroism: Women's Holocaust Narratives, 1995; The Beautiful Days of My Youth, 1997, Memoirs of Auschwitz Survivors: The Burden of Gender, 1998; editor: Experience and Expression: Women, the Nazis, and the Holocaust, 2003, Community College Guide to Curriculum Change, 1990; contbg. editor: Belles Lettres, 1989-98; editor C.C. Humanities Rev., 1990—; contbr. articles to profl. jours. Bd. dirs. Jewish Cmty. Coun., 1997-2002, Md. Humanities Coun., 1997-2003, Jewish Hist. Soc. Greater Washington, 1997—, Arts and Humanities Coun., 2000-02. Named Comcast Excellence in the Humanities award, 2002; recipient Disting. Humanities Educator award, C.C. Humanities Assn., 1989, Outstanding Faculty Mem. award, Montgomery Coll., 1990, Tchg. award, Md. Assn. for Higher Edn., 1991, William H. Meardy Faculty award, Assn. Cmty. Coll. Trustees, 1996; Acad. Adminstrn. fellow, Am. Coun. on Edn., 1981—82, Lowenstein Wiener fellow, Am. Jewish Archives, 1983. Mem. MLA (sec.), Nat. Women's Studies Assn. (sec.), Assn. Jewish Studies, Nat. Coun. Tchrs. English, Jewish Hist. Soc. Greater Wash. (bd. dirs. 1997—2002, Phi Kappa Phi. Avocations: walking, travel, writing, reading, knitting. Personal E-mail: myrnagoldenberg@hotmail.com.

GOLDENBERG, WILLIAM BRUCE, music educator, musician; b. Cleve., Nov. 1, 1950; s. David and Helen Goldenberg. BA, Oberlin Coll., 1972; MusM, SUNY, Stony Brook, 1974, Juilliard Sch., 1976; MusD, Ind. U., 1991. Head tchg. asst. SUNY, Stony Brook, 1972—74; piano tchg. fellow and accompanist Juilliard Sch., N.Y.C., 1974—76; personal asst. to Menahem Pressler Ind. U. Sch. of Music, Bloomington, 1976—80; disting. prof. piano and chamber music No. Ill. U., DeKalb, 1980—; chair dept. piano and collaborative piano No. Ill. U. Sch. Music, DeKalb, 1996—. Concert pianist Idyllwild (Calif.) Arts Music Festival, 1995—, Grand Teton Music Festival, Jackson Hole, Wyo., 1983—84; guest prof. Ind. U., 1995; adjudicator Joanna Hodges Piano Competition, Palm Springs, Calif., 1983, Grace Welsh Internat. Piano Competition, Chgo., 2002, Music Tchrs. Nat. Assn., Decatur, Ill., 2003, St. Charles (Ill.) Internat. Art and Music Festival Piano Competition, 1987—88; masterclass tchr. Shanghai Conservatory of Music, 2001; masterclasses tchr. Liszt Acad., Budapest, 2003. Musician: (CDs) Violin Sonatas with Vermeer Quartet Violinist Pierre Menard, Contemporary Chamber Music, Door County Suite, Petite Suite for my Grandchildren, (concert tours) Asia, 2001, 2004, Europe, 2003—, 2004, Scandanavia, 2005; contbr. articles to profl. publs. Named winner Concerto Competition, Oberlin Coll., 1971, Ind. U., 1978; Piano fellow, Tanglewood Music Festival, 1975. Mem.: East Meets West Music Arts- Chgo. (adv. bd. 1993—), Pi Kappa Lambda, Phi Beta Kappa. Achievements include grants for research in non-traditional repertoire from diverse cultures (Asian, Hispanic, Black) and contemporary music. Home: PO Box 165 Dekalb IL 60115 Office: No Ill U Dekalb IL 60115 Business E-Mail: goldenberg@niu.edu.

GOLDENFARB, PAUL BENNETT, internist, oncologist; b. Medford, Mass., Jan. 11, 1941; MD, Boston U., 1966. Diplomate Am. Bd. Internal Medicine, Am. Bd. Oncology. Intern Boston City Hosp., 1966-67, resident medicine, 1967-68, Duke U. Med. Ctr., 1970-71; fellow hematology/oncology Yale U., 1971-73; mem. staff Morton F. Plant Hosp., Clearwater, Fla., 1973—; pvt. practice Clearwater, 1973—. Mem. ACP, AMA, Am. Soc. Hematology, Am. Soc. Clin. Oncology, Fla. Med. Assn. Address: 55 Pelican Pl Belleair FL 33756-1512

GOLDENSHTEYN, VLADIMIR LEV, civil engineer; b. Kiev, Jan. 30, 1937; came to U.S., 1979; s. Lev Abram and Tanya Lev (Tsymberg) G.; m. Klara Shlema Sigal, Sept. 30, 1961; 1 child, Lena. Technician, Bldg. Technicum, Kiev, USSR, 1959; Civil Engr., Civil Enging. Inst., Voronezh, USSR, 1967. Technician, engr., dept. chief, chief specialist State Inst. Design of Installations for Transport and Purification of Water for Indsl. Enterprises; technician, engr., project coord., city planner, engr.-in-charge divsn. sewers City of N.Y. Dept. Environ. Protection, 1980—. Author computer programs hydraulic etc. calculations for water/sewer sys. Life mem. Rep. Presdl. Task Force. Mem. Profl. Engrs. Soc. Avocation: fishing. Office: City NY Dept Environ Protection Permit Control Office Cross Connection 59-17 Junction Blvd Flushing NY 11373 Office Phone: 718-595-5442.

GOLDER, HERBERT ALAN, classics educator; b. Oct. 29, 1952; BA, Boston U., 1975; MA, Yale U., 1977, MPhil, 1979, PhD, 1984; postgrad., Oxford U., 1982. Tchg. fellow, instr. in classics Yale U., New Haven, 1977-80; asst. prof. of classics Syracuse (N.Y.) U., 1982-85, Emory U., Atlanta, 1985-87, Boston U., 1988-93, assoc. prof. classics, 1993—2004, prof. classics, 2004—. Vis. asst. prof. classics Emory U., Atlanta, 1984-85; archival rschr. The White Diamond, 2004, The Wild Blue Yonder, 2005. Asst. dir.: (documentary) Little Dieter Needs to Fly, 1997 (Emmy nomination 1999, Disting. Achievement award Internat. Documentary Assn. 1998, Spl. Jury prize Amsterdam Internat. Documentary Film Festival 1997), Wings of Hope, 1999, My Best Fiend, 1999, The Lord and the Laden, 2000; asst. dir., co-writer, actor (film) Invincible, 2002; gen. editor: (with William Arrowsmith) The Greek Tragedy in New Translations, 1985-96, editor-in-chief: Arion, A Jour. Humanities and the Classics, 1990— (CELJ Phoenix award for significant editl. achievement 1992, APA Inaugural Scholarly Outreach award 2004); author: Sophocles' Aias, 1999, Euripides' Bacchae, 2001. Office: 621 Commonwealth Ave Boston MA 02215 Office Phone: 617-353-6480. Business E-Mail: redlog@bu.edu.

GOLDEY, JAMES MEARNS, retired physicist; b. Wilmington, Del., July 3, 1926; s. Robert Perkins and Ellen (Mearns) G.; m. Jeanne Calvert Potts, June 29, 1951; children: James P., Kristina. BS with honors, U. Del., 1950; PhD in Physics, M.I.T., 1955. Mem. tech. staff Bell Labs. (now Lucent Techs.), Murray Hill, N.J., 1954-56, supr., 1956-59, head integrated cir. and silicon transistor dept., 1959-60; dir. integrated cir. customer svc. lab. Bell Labs., Allentown, Pa., 1981-84, dir. linear and high voltage integrated cir. lab Reading, Pa., 1984-89; devel. v.p. high performance integrated cir. devel. AT&T Microelectronics, Reading, 1988-89, ret., 1989. Contbr. articles in field to profl. jours.; patentee in field. Served with U.S. Army, 1944-46. Fellow IEEE. Republican. Presbyterian. Home: 6770 Hawaii Kai Dr Honolulu HI 96825 E-mail: mosgolfi@aol.com.

GOLDFARB, BARRY JOSEPH, education educator; b. Rochester, NY, Nov. 21, 1946; s. Louis and Julia Gordon Goldfarb; m. Judith Ableman, Mar. 19, 1977; children: Adam, Joel. BS in bus. admin., Rochester Inst. Tech., 1968; MS in speech and broadcasting, SUNY Coll. at Geneseo, 1970. Various positions WXXI-TV/FM, 1971—78; asst. prof. SUNY Coll. at Brockport, 1979—87; assoc. prof. and chmn. visual and performing arts Monroe Cmty. Coll., 1987—. Freelance media prodr./writer/cons., 1977—. Cmty. adv. bd. Pub. Broadcasting Coun., Rochester, 1994—98; founding adv. bd. mem. Rochester Jewish Film Festival, 2001—02; cable TV commr. Brighton Cable TV, NY, 1992—96. Recipient Del. -Faculty Seminar, Acad. of TV Arts and Sci., 1997, Perkins III Equipment Grant, Monroe Cmty. Coll., 2000, 2001, 2002; Summer Faculty grant, Nat. Assn. of TV Program Exec., 1998. Mem.: Am. Film Inst., Acad. of TV Arts and Sci., Broadcast Ednl. Assn. Avocation: golf. Home: 88 Southwood Lane Rochester NY 14618 Office: Monroe Cmty Coll 1000 E Henrietta Rd Rochester NY 14623 Office Phone: 585-292-3127. Business E-Mail: bgoldfarb@monroecc.edu.

GOLDFARB, BERNARD SANFORD, lawyer; b. Cleve., Apr. 15, 1917; s. Harry and Esther (Lenson) Goldfarb; m. Barbara Brofman Goldfarb, Jan. 4, 1966; children: Meredith Stacy, Lauren Beth. AB, Case Western Res. U., 1938, JD, 1940. Bar: Ohio 1940. Since practiced in, Cleve.; sr. ptnr. firm Goldfarb & Reznick, 1967-95; pvt. practice Cleve., 1997—. Spl. counsel to atty. gen. Ohio, 1950, 1971—74; mem. Ohio Commn. Uniform Traffic Rules, 1973—80. Contbr. legal jours. Served with USAAF, 1942—45. Mem.: ABA, Cuyahoga County Bar Assn., Greater Cleve. Bar Assn., Ohio Bar Assn. Home: 39 Pepper Creek Dr Pepper Pike OH 44124-5279 Office: 55 Public Sq Ste 1500 Cleveland OH 44113-1998 Office Phone: 216-696-0606. Personal E-mail: bunnysgoldfarb@aol.com.

GOLDFARB, DAVID, investment banking executive; Grad., Robert H. Smith Sch. Bus., U. of Md., 1979. Various positions to sr. ptnr. Ernst & Young, 1979—93; joined Lehman Bros. Inc., 1993, controller, 1995—2000, CFO, 1998—; exec. v.p., CFO Lehman Bros. Holdings Inc., 2000—. Mem. Lehman Bros. Operating com. Recipient Dist. Alumnus award, Robert H. Smith Sch. Bus., U. Md., 2004. Mem.: SIA Fin. Mgmt. and Internal Audit divisions, AICPA Stock Brokerage Com. Office: Lehman Bros Holdings Inc 745 7th Ave 31st Fl New York NY 10019-6801

GOLDFARB, DAVID S., nephrologist, researcher; s. Edward and Norma Goldfarb. BA, Yale Coll., Conn., 1977; MD, Yale Sch. Medicine, Conn., 1981. Chief, nephrology sect. NY Harbor VA Med. Ctr., NYC, 2005—. Prof. of medicine and physiology NYU Sch. of Medicine, NYC, 2004—. Mem.: NY Soc. of Nephrology (pres. 1999—2000). Office: NY Harbor VA Medl Ctr 111G 423 E 23rd St New York NY 10010 Office Phone: 212-263-0744. Office Fax: 212-951-6842. Personal E-mail: dsgold@verizon.net. E-mail: goldfd01@popmail.med.nyu.edu.

GOLDFARB, ERIC DANIEL, information technology executive; b. Kalamazoo, Mich., Apr. 29, 1964; s. Russell Marshall and Clare Sara (Rosett) Goldfarb; m. Gwen Julia Oberman, Aug. 20, 1989; children: Adam, David. Bachelors, U. Mich., 1986. Project leader Domino's Pizza, Inc., Ann Arbor, Mich., 1986—90; mgr. info. sys. Interpublic Group (Lintas), Warren, Mich., 1990-91; mgr. bus. sys. The Limited Inc. (Express), Columbus, Ohio, 1991-94; CIO Elder-Beerman Stores Corp., Dayton, Ohio, 1994—96; CIO/CTO Pearson plc (Viacom-Macmillan), Indpls., 1996—2001; CIO Global Knowledge Inc., Cary, NC, 2001—02; CIO/exec. v.p. PRG-Schultz Internat., Inc., Atlanta, 2002—. Spkr. at nat. seminars for sr. corp. exec. Co-author: Ways to Reduce IT Spending, 2004; contbr. articles profl. jours., books. Named Premier 100 IT Leader, IDG ComputerWorld, 2003; recipient nat. Arthur D. Little "Best of the Best" award. Republican. Achievements include patents in field. Avocations: sailing, golf. Office: 600 Galleria Pkwy Atlanta GA 30339

GOLDFARB, IRENE DALE, retired financial planner; b. Newark, N.J., Jan. 13, 1929; d. Philip and Lucie (Mintz) Dale; m. Samuel Goldfarb, Jan. 28, 1951; children: Ruth Goldfarb Koizim, David Alan, Sally Fay, Judith Valerie. BS in Chemistry, Rutgers U., 1950; MBA, U. Pa., 1979. CFP. Asst. to assoc. provost Princeton (N.J.) U., 1968-70, asst. to provost, 1970-72, tech. staff, 1972-74, mgr. pers. svcs., 1974-75, asst. dir. pers. svcs., 1975-84; fin. planner, mgr. A.L. Herst Assocs., Inc., Princeton, 1984-86; pvt. practice Princeton, 1986-90; v.p. A.L. Herst Assocs., Inc., Princeton, 1990-92; fin. planner Glenmede Trust Co. N.J., Princeton, 1992—2001; ret., 2002. Cons. in field. Mem. Fin. Planning Assn. (founding officer Princeton-Western N.J. chpt. 1986-98, pres. 1988-89, chmn. 1989-90), Assn. Alumnae Douglass Coll. (chmn. ann. fund 1982-84, v.p. adminstrn. 1988-94), Phi Beta Kappa. Avocations: music, gardening, travel. Home and Office: 69 Balsam Ln Princeton NJ 08540-5326

GOLDFARB, JAMES MORRIS, physician, obstetrician-gynecologist; b. Cleve., Jan. 18, 1948; s. Morris B. and Marguerite (Schwartz) G.; m. Ronda Weiss, Dec. 17, 1972; children: Murray, Alan, Neil. BA, Miami U., Oxford, Ohio, 1970; MD, Ohio State U., 1973; postgrad., Case Western Res. U., 1990—. Intern U. Hosps. Cleve., 1973-74, resident, 1974-78; dir. reproductive endocrinology and infertility Univ. Hosps. and Case Western Res. U., Cleve., 1990—; dir. gynecology and in vitro fertilization Mt. Sinai Med. Ctr., Cleve., 1980-89; dir. in vitro fertilization Univ. Hosps. and Case Western Res. U., Cleve., 1990—. Asst. prof. reproductive biology Case Western Res. U., 1978-92, assoc. prof., 1992—. Contbr. articles to profl. jours. Pres. Orange (Ohio) Cmty. Athletic Assn., 1989-90. U. Hosps. Cleve. fellow, 1978-80. Fellow Am. Coll. Ob-Gyn., Soc. Reproductive Endocrinology, Soc. Reproductive Surgeons; mem. Soc. for Assisted Reproductive Techs. Achievements include first in vitro fertilization birth in Ohio, first in vitro fertilization/surrogate birth in world. Office: Univ Hosps of Cleve 11100 Euclid Ave Cleveland OH 44106-1736

GOLDFARB, JOEL PETER, internist, gastroenterologist; b. Fitchburg, Mass., Jan. 17, 1949; s. Abraham and Eunice (Caplan) G.; m. Elizabeth Weinshel, Dec. 5, 1954. BA, Yale U., 1971; MD, NYU, 1975. Diplomate Am. Bd. Internal Medicine, Am. Bd. Gastroenterology. Resident NYU Bellevue, N.Y.C., 1975-78; fellow (liver) Yale, New Haven, Conn., 1978-79; fellow (G.I.) Columbia, N.Y.C., 1979-81; asst. prof. medicine Yeshiva U., Bronx, N.Y., 1981-84; ptnr. D. Penn MD, J. Patrowitz MD, J. Goldfarb MD, PA., Fort Lee, N.J., 1984—. Asst. clin. prof. medicine Mt. Sinai. Named one of Best Doctors of N.J., N.J. Monthly Mag., 1996, 2001, N.Y. Mag., 2001, 2002, N.J. Life Mag., 2005. Fellow Am. Coll. Physicians, Am. Coll. Gastroenterology. Avocations: cross country skiing, swimming, hiking, scuba diving, opera. Home: 2621 Palisade Ave Apt 5B Bronx NY 10463-6108 Office: 1600 Parker Ave Fort Lee NJ 07024-7050 E-mail: jpgoldfarb@cs.com.

GOLDFARB, LISA MICHELE, psychiatrist; b. N.Y.C., Oct. 2, 1963; d. Herbert Allen and Beverly Susan (Rozman) G.; m. Steve Martin Chaiken, Jan. 8, 1994; 1 child, Jackson Archer. BS in life scis., MIT, 1985; MD, Columbia U., 1989. Diplomate Am. Bd. Psychiatry and Neurology. Intern St. Luke's-Roosevelt Med. Ctr., N.Y.C., 1989-90; resident in psychiatry N.Y. State Psychiat. Inst., Columbia-Presbyn. Hosp., N.Y.C., 1990-93; fellow in divsn. alcoholism and drug abuse, dept. psychiatry NYU Sch. Medicine, N.Y.C., 1993-95; clin. instr. NYU Med. Ctr., N.Y.C., 1994-96, clin. asst. prof. psychiatry, 1997—; doctoral candidate Columbia U., Ctr. for Psychoanalytic Tng. & Rsch., N.Y.C., 1995—. Med. staff Bellevue Hosp., N.Y.C., 1994—; med. staff with admitting privileges Tisch Hosp., NYU Med. Ctr., 1996—; homebound elderly program of Columbia-Presbyn. Hosp., 1993; assoc. med. staff Regent Hosp., 1991-93. Contbr. articles to profl. jours. Mem. Am. Psychiat. Assn. (com. on treatment svcs. for addicted patients 1996—), Am. Acad. Psychiatrists in Alcoholism and Addiction, Am. Med. Women's Assn. Office: 3 E 65th St New York NY 10021-6527

GOLDFARB, MARTIN, sociologist, researcher; b. Toronto, Ont., Can., May 6, 1938; s. David and Sonia (Silverstein) G.; m. Joan Freedman, June 7, 1961; children— Alonna, Baila, Rebecca, Daniel, Avi BA, U. Toronto, 1961, MA, 1965. Tchr. North York Bd. Edn., Toronto, 1965-67; chmn., pres. Can. Offices, CEO The Goldfarb Corp., Toronto, 1987—; CEO Goldfarb Cons., 1967—2000; counsel Goldfarb Intelligence Mktg., 2002—. Past bd. govs. York U., Toronto; bd. dirs. CLC Downsview Inc., Fleming Packaging Corp., chmn. SMK Speedy Internat., Inc., Altamira Workbrain. Author: The Goldfarb Report, 1981-99, Marching to a Different Drummer, 1988; contbr. articles to profl. jours. Past bd. dirs. Toronto Symphony Orch., Shaw Festival, Niagara-on-the-Lake, Can. Coun. Christians and Jews, Can. Opera Co., Toronto, Coun. for Can. Unity; trustee The Martin Goodman Trust for Canadian Nieman Fellows. Avocations: skiing, tennis. Office: Goldfarb Intelligence Mktg 18 Spadina Rd Ste 100 Toronto ON Canada M5R 2S7 E-mail: m.goldfarb@goldfarbmarketing.com.

GOLDFARB, MURIEL BERNICE, marketing consultant, advertising consultant; b. Bklyn., Mar. 29, 1920; d. Barnett and May (Steinberg) Goldfarb. BA, U. Miami, Coral Gables, Fla., 1942; postgrad., CCNY, 1950. Pub. info. asst. UNESCO, Paris, 1946—47; advt. mgr. Majestic Specialties Co., NYC, 1947—50; retail promotion mgr. Glamour Mag., 1955—61; advt. dir. County Tweeds Co., NYC, 1961—65, S. Augstein & Co., NYC, 1966—72, Feature Ring Co., Inc., Gotham Ring Co., Inc., Fidco Inc., NYC, 1972—77; dir. advt. promotion Wasko Gold Products Corp., NYC, 1977—81; advt. mktg. cons. specializing promotions sale vintage jewelry Bric-a-Brac. Lt. WAVES, 1943—46. Mem.: Women's Jewelry Assn. (corr. sec. 1983—85). Jewish.

GOLDFARB, RONALD LAWRENCE, lawyer, writer, literary agent; b. Jersey City, N.J., Oct. 16, 1933; s. Robert S. and Aida J. (Weintraub) G.; m. Joanne Jacob, June 9, 1957; children: Jody, Nicholas, Maximilian Goldfarb. AB, Syracuse U., 1954, LLB, 1956; LLM, Yale, 1960, JSD, 1962. Bar: N.Y. 1956, Calif. 1959, D.C. 1962, U.S. Supreme Ct. 1965. Spl. asst. to U.S. atty. gen. (organized crime sect.), 1961-64; ptnr. Goldfarb and Assocs. and predecessor law firms, 1966—. Dir. Brookings Instn. program on cts. and adminstrn. Justice, 1966-67; mem. staff counsel com. on law and social action Am. Jewish Congress, 1960-61; cons. Pres.'s Poverty Program, 1964, Riots Commn., 1967-68 Author: The Contempt Power, 1963, Ransom: A Critique of the American Bail System, 1965, (with Alfred Friendly) Crime and Publicity, 1967, (with Linda Singer) After Conviction--A Review of the American Correction System, 1973, Jails: The Ultimate Ghetto, 1975, Migrant Farm Workers: A Caste of Despair, 1981, (with James Raymond) Clear Understandings: A Guide to Legal Writing, 1983, (with Gail Ross) The Writer's Lawyer: Essential Legal Advice for Writers and Editors in All Media, 1989, Perfect Villains, Imperfect Heroes: Robert F. Kennedy's War Against Organized Crime, 1995, TV or Not TV: Television, Justice and Courts, 1998. Bd. dir. Va. Ctr. for the Creative Arts, The Alliance for Justice. Capt. JAG Corp. USAF, 1957—60. Arthur Garfield Hays fellow N.Y.U., 1960-61; Woodrow Wilson fellow. Mem. ACLU, D.C. Bar Assn., N.Y. Bar Assn., Calif. Bar Assn., Cosmos Club, Sigma Alpha Mu., Phi Delta Phi. Office: 721 Gibbon St Alexandria VA 22314 Office Phone: 202-466-3030.

GOLDFARB, RUTH, poet, educator; b. Bklyn., Aug. 13, 1936; d. Nathan Alter and Florence Goldfarb. BA in Psychology, L.I. Univ., 1980; MA in Edn., NYU, 1984. Tchr. kindergarten N.Y.C. Bd. Edn., 1963-64, early childhood tchr., 1993-94, N.Y.C., Bklyn., 1970-84; tchr. common br. Bklyn. Bd. Edn., 1986-93; clk. Primary Health Care Ctr. North Broward Med. Ctr., Pompano Beach, Fla., 1998—. Author (poetry) Whispers and Chants, 1997; CD recs. include Christmas Memories, 1999, The Miracle of Christmas, 2000, Songs of Praise, 2000. Mem.: AARP, Gold Coast Poetry Group, Acad. Am. Poets, Internat. Soc. Poets. Avocations: poetry, music, sculpture, writing stories.

GOLDFEIN, SHEPARD, lawyer; b. Englewood, NJ, 1948; AB, Rutgers U., 1970, JD, 1975; MA, U. Chgo., 1977. Bar: NY 1976, NJ 1977. Practice leader for antitrust Skadden, Arps, Slate, Meagher & Flom LLP, NYC. Editor: Rutgers Law Rev., 1974-75; contbr. articles to profl. jours.; co-author, monthly trade regulation column, NY Law Jour., 1983-. Mem.: Pi Sigma Alpha, Assn. of the Bar of the City of NY (chmn., sports law com. 1996—99), NY State Bar Assn. (chmn., civil practice and procedure com., antitrust sect. 1982—84), Phi Beta Kappa. Office: Skadden Arps Slate Meagher & Flom LLP 4 Times Sq 34th Fl New York NY 10036-6595 Office Phone: 212-735-3610. Business E-Mail: sgoldfei@skadden.com.

GOLDFIELD, EDWIN DAVID, statistician; b. N.Y.C., Oct. 26, 1918; s. Maurice and Sarah (Spears) G. BS, CUNY, 1939; MA, Columbia U., 1940; postgrad., Am. U., 1940-46. Rsch. assoc. dept. investigation, N.Y.C., 1938-39; statis. adviser Ct. Spl. Sessions, N.Y.C., 1939; with Bur. Census, Washington, 1940-75, asst. dir., 1967-71, chief internat. programs, 1971-75; with NAS, Washington, 1975—, study dir., 1975-78, exec. dir. com. on nat. statis., 1978-87, sr. assoc., 1987—. Cons. in field, 1951—; staff dir. subcom. census and statistics Ho. of Reps., 1959-60, 67. Contbr. articles. Editor: Papers on Labor Force Statistics in the United States, 1952. Recipient Meritorious Svc. award Dept. Commerce, 1954. Fellow Am. Statis. Assn.; mem. Washington Statis. Soc. (past pres.), Am. Econ. Assn., Population Assn. Am., Inter-Am. Statis. Inst., Internat. Assn. Survey Statisticians, Internat. Statis. Inst., Phi Beta Kappa. Home: 4311 23rd Pkwy Apt 1102 Temple Hills MD 20748-4462 Office: NAS 2101 Constitution Ave NW Washington DC 20418-0007 Office Phone: 202-334-3096.

GOLDFIELD, EMILY DAWSON, finance company executive, artist; b. Bklyn., May 31, 1947; d. Martin and Renee (Solow) Dawson; m. Stephen Gary Goldfield, June 17, 1973; children: Stacy Rose, Daniel James. BS, U. Mich., 1969; MEd, Pa. State U., 1971; PhD, U. So. Calif., 1977. Chmn. bd. Union Home Loan, Inc. Author: The Value of Creative Dance, 1971; Development of Creative Dance, 1977. U. Mich. scholar, 1969; Pa. State U.

fellow, 1970, U. So. Calif. fellow, 1972. Mem.: Pastel Soc. San Diego, Allied Artists of the Santa Monica Mountains, Pastel Soc. of the West Coast, Calif. Art Club, Calif. Mortgage Assn. Office: 23586 Calabasas Rd Ste 201 Calabasas CA 91302-1322

GOLDFRANK, LEWIS ROBERT, physician; b. N.Y.C., Sept. 8, 1941; s. Herbert John and Helen (Colodny) G.; m. Susan M. Harrington, Aug. 29, 1964; children: Michelle, Andrew, Jennifer, Rebecca. BA, Clark U., 1963; MD, U. Brussels, Belgium, 1970. Diplomate Am. Bd. Med. Toxicology (dir., chmn. 1985-90). Resident Montefiore Hosp., Bronx, N.Y., 1971-73; dir. emergency medicine Morrisania Hosp., Bronx, 1973-76, North Cen. Bronx Hosp., 1976-79, Montefiore Hosp., 1976-79, Bellevue Hosp., N.Y.C., 1979—, NYU Med. Ctr., N.Y.C., 1979—; dir. N.Y.C. Poison Ctr., 1979—; prof. and chmn. dept. emergency medicine Sch. Medicine NYU, N.Y.C., 2003—. Author, editor: Goldfrank's Toxicologic Emergencies, 1978, 7th edit., 2002, Emergency Doctor, 1987, Diagnostic Testing in the Emergency Department, 1984, 2d edit., 1995; editor: Preparing for Terrorism, 2002, Preparing for Psychological Consequences of Terrorisn, 2003. Recipient hon. mention Am. Med. Writers Assn., 1988, Disting. Tchr. award NYU, 2003; faculty scholar NYU, 1999. Fellow: ACP, Am. Acad. Clin. Toxicology, Am. Coll. Emergency Physician; mem.: NAS (Inst. Medicine), Soc. for Acad. Emergency Medicine (Hal Jayne Acad. Excellence award 1990, Leadership award 1999). Avocation: gardening. Home: 55 Grace Ln Ossining NY 10562-2129 Office: Bellevue Hosp Ctr 1st Ave and 27th St New York NY 10016 Fax: 212-562-3001. Office Phone: 212-562-3346. Business E-Mail: goldfl03@popmail.med.nyu.edu.

GOLDGAR, BERTRAND ALVIN, historian, educator; b. Macon, Ga., Nov. 17, 1927; s. Benjamin Meyer and Annie (Shapiro) G.; m. Corinne Cohn Hartman, Apr. 6, 1950; children: Arnold Benjamin, Anne Hartman. BA, Vanderbilt U., 1948, MA, 1949, Princeton U., 1957, PhD, 1958. Instr. in English Clemson (S.C.) U., 1948-50, asst. prof., 1951-52; instr. English Lawrence U., Appleton, Wis., 1957-61, asst. prof., 1961-65, assoc. prof., 1965-71, prof. English, 1971—, John N. Bergstrom prof. humanities, 1980—. Mem. fellowship panel NEH, 1979 Author: The Curse of Party: Swift's Relations with Addison and Steele, 1961, Walpole and the Wits: The Relation of Politics to Literature, 1722-1742, 1976; editor: The Literary Criticism of Alexander Pope, 1965, Henry Fielding's The Covent-Garden Jour., 1988, Henry Fielding's Miscellanies, Vol. 2, 1993, Jonathan Wild, 1997, The Grub Street Jour. 1730-1733, 2002; adv. editor: 18th Century Studies, 1977-82. With AUS, 1952-54. Fellow, Am. Coun. Learned Socs, 1973-74, NEH, 1980-81. Mem. Am. Soc. 18th Century Studies, Johnson Soc. Cen. Region. Home: 914 E Eldorado St Appleton WI 54911-5536 Office: Lawrence U Dept English Appleton WI 54912 Office Phone: 920-832-6694. Business E-Mail: bertrand.a.goldgar@lawrence.edu.

GOLDHABER, GERSON, astrophysicist, researcher; b. Chemnitz, Germany, Feb. 20, 1924; came to U.S., 1948, naturalized, 1953; s. Charles and Ethel (Frisch) G.; m. Judith Margoshes, May 30, 1969; children: Amos Nathaniel, Michaela Shally, Shaya Alexandra M.Sc., Hebrew U., Jerusalem, 1947; PhD, U. Wis., 1950; PhD honoris causus, U. Stockholm, 1986. Instr. Columbia U., N.Y.C., 1950-53; acting asst. prof. physics U. Calif., Berkeley, 1953-54, asst. prof., 1954-58, assoc. prof., 1958-63, prof. physics, 1963-92, prof. physics emeritus, 1992—; Miller research prof. Miller Inst. Basic Sci. U. Calif.-Berkeley, 1958-59, 75-76, 84-85, prof. Grad. Sch., 1994—; Morris Loeb lectr. in physics Harvard U., 1976-77. Named Calif. Scientist of Yr., 1977, Sci. Assoc., CERN, 1986; Ford Found. fellow CERN, 1960-61; Guggenheim fellow CERN, 1972-73 Fellow Am. Phys. Soc. (Panofsky prize 1991), Sigma Xi; mem. Am. Astron. Soc., Royal Swedish Acad. Sci. (fgn.), Nat. Acad. Sci. Office: Lawrence Berkeley Nat Lab Physics Ms 50 R5008 Berkeley CA 94720-0001 Office Phone: 510-486-6210. Business E-Mail: gerson@lbl.gov.

GOLDHABER, MAURICE, physicist, researcher; b. Lemberg, Austria, Apr. 18, 1911; arrived in U.S., 1938, naturalized, 1944; s. Charles and Ethel (Frisch) Goldhaber; m. Gertrude Scharff, May 24, 1939; children: Alfred S., Michael H. PhD, Cambridge U., Eng., 1936; PhD (hon.), Tel Aviv U., 1974; D (hon.), U. Louvain-La-Neuve, Belgium, 1982; DSc (hon.), SUNY, Stony Brook, 1983, U. Notre Dame, 1992. Bye fellow Magdalene Coll., Cambridge, 1936—38; asst. prof. physics U. Ill., 1938—43, assoc. prof., 1943—45, prof., 1945—50; sr. scientist Brookhaven Nat. Lab., 1950—60, chmn. dept. physics, 1960—61, dir., 1961—73, disting. scientist emeritus, 1973—. Cons. labs. AEC; Morris Loeb lectr. Harvard U., 1955, 93, Rabi Scholar lectr., 55; adj. prof. physics SUNY, Stony Brook, 1965—; Royal Soc. Rutherford Meml. lectr., Canada, 1987; nuc. sci. com. NRC. Assoc. editor Phys. Rev., 1951—53; contbr. articles on nuc. physics and elem. particles to sci. jours. Bd. govs. Weizmann Inst. Sci., Rehovoth, Israel, Tel Aviv U.; trustee Univs. Rsch. Assn. Co-recipient Rossi prize, Am. Astron. Soc., hign energy physics divsn., 1989; recipient citation for meritorious contbns., U.S. AEC, 1973, J. Robert Oppenheimer Meml. prize, 1982, Nat. medal of Sci., 1983, Am. Acad. Achievement award, 1985, Wolf Found. prize in physics, Jerusalem, 1991, Enrico Fermi award in physics, 1998. Fellow: AAAS, Am. Acad. Arts and Scis., Am. Phys. Soc. (pres. 1982); mem.: NAS, Am. Philos. Soc. (Lanutti Meml. lectr. 2003, Tom W. Bonner prize in nuc. physics 1971). Office: Brookhaven Nat Lab Bldg 510 Upton NY 11973

GOLDHAGEN, JEFFREY LEE, city health department administrator; m. Diana Goldhagen; children: Mia, Alanna, Tess, Eva, Julian. MD, U. Pitts.; MPH, U. Minn. Dir., med. programs for surg. aid Children of the World; co-dir., med. anthropology program Case Western Reserve U., Cleve.; med. dir. Cleve. Pub. Health Dept.; assoc. prof., pediat. U. Fla.; dir. Duval Co. Health Dept., Jacksonville, Fla., 1993—. Fellow: Am. Acad. Pediat. Office: Duval County Pub Health 515 W Sixth St MC #24 Jacksonville FL 32206

GOLDHAMER, DAVID J., medical educator, researcher; BS in Biology, Purdue U., 1979; PhD in Devel. Biology, Ohio State U., 1988; postgrad., Marine Biol. Lab., Woods Hole, Mass., 1984. Rsch. assoc. lab. renewable resources engring. Purdue U., 1979-82; grad. tchg. asst. Ohio State U., 1982-87; asst. instr. embryology Marine Biol. Lab., Woods Hole, Mass., 1985; postdoctoral fellow U. Va., 1988-91; rsch. assoc. Inst. for Cancer Rsch. Fox Chase Cancer Ctr., 1991-92; asst. prof. dept. cell and devel. biology U. Pa. Sch. Medicine, 1993—. Contbr. articles to profl. jours.; reviewer: Biochimica and Biophysica Acta, Devel., Devel. Biology, Differentiation, DNA and Cell Biology, Molecular and Cellular Biology, Trends in Cardiovasc. Rsch.; lectr. in field. Recipient Grad. Student Alumni Rsch. award, 1987, Established Investigatorship award Am. Heart Assn., 1996—; NIH Tng. grantee, 1984, Sigma Xi grantee, 1986; Presdl. fellowship Ohio State U., 1987-88, MDA Postdoctoral fellowship, 1988-89, MDA Jere Thompson Neuromuscular Rsch. fellowship, 1989-91. Mem. AAAS, Soc. for Devel. Biology, John Morgan Soc., Pa. Muscle Inst. (co-organizer seminar series on muscle devel. 1994, co-organizer ann. retreat 1995). Office: U Pa Sch Medicine Dept Cell & Developmental Biology 219 Anat/Chem 3620 Hamilton Walk Philadelphia PA 19104-6058

GOLDIN, DANIEL S., former federal agency administrator; b. N.Y.C., July 23, 1940; m. Judith Linda Kramer; children: Ariel, Laura. BS in Mech. Engring., CCNY, 1962; PhD (hon.), Case Western Res. U., Cen. State U., CCNY, Fla. Inst. of Tech., Framingham State U., Poly. U. of N.Y., U. Ariz., U. Md., U. Mich. Rsch. scientist Lewis Rsch. Ctr., NASA, Cleve., 1962-67; with TRW, from 1967, mem. tech. staff, 1967; v.p., gen. mgr. Space & Tech. Group, TRW, Redondo, Calif., 1987-92; adminstr. NASA, Washington, 1992—2001; speaker Leading Authorities, Inc., Washington, 2002; sr. fellow Council on Competitiveness, 2002—. Recipient 1996 Chmn. award Am. Assn. Engring. Societies, 1997, Civilian Kitty Hawk Sands of Time award, Goddard Quality award, Heald award Ill. Inst. of Tech., Nelson P. Jackson Aerospace award Nat. Space Club, Internat. Von Karman Wings award Aerospace Hist. Soc., Meritorious award (2) Nat. Assn. of Small and Disadvantaged Businesses, President's medal N.Y. Inst. of Tech., Nat. award for Space Achievement, Rotary, Space Pioneer award Nat. Space Soc.; named one of 100 Most Influential in Govt. Nat. Jour., One of 40 Most Influential Def. Industry Leaders, Def. Bus. mag. Fellow AIAA (Piper Gen. Aviation award), Am. Astronom. Soc. (John F. Kennedy Astronautics award), Inst. for Advancement of Engring. Achievements during his tenure at TRW include the building of 13 spacecraft, the launch and operation of NASA tracking and Data Relay Satellite-5 and the Compton Gamma Ray Observatory. The group also has worked on other NASA programs including the successfull grinding and testing of the worlds two largest X-ray mirrors fot the Advanced X-ray Astrophysics Facility. Office: Council on Competitiveness 1500 K St NW Ste 850 Washington DC 20005

GOLDIN, LEON, artist; b. Chgo., Jan. 16, 1923; s. Joseph P. and Bertha (Metz) G.; m. Meta Solotaroff, July 30, 1949; children: Joshua, Daniel. BFA, Art Inst. Chgo., 1948; MFA, U. Iowa, 1950. From instr. to assoc. prof. Columbia U., N.Y.C., 1964-82, prof., 1982-92, prof. emeritus, 1992—. Former tchr. Calif. Coll. Arts and Crafts, Phila. Coll. Art, Queen's Coll., Cooper Union; vis. prof. painting Stanford, summer 1973 One-man shows Oakland Art Mus., 1955, Felix Landau Gallery, L.A., 1956, 57, 59, Galleria L'Attico, Rome, 1958, Kraushaar Galleries, N.Y.C., 1960, 64, 68, 72, 84, 88, 90, 93, 96, 98, 2001, 04 U. Houston, 1981, Binghamton U. Art Mus., 2000, Ctr. for Maine Contemporary Art, 2000; represented in permanent collections Bklyn. Mus., City Mus. St. Louis, Worcester Mus., Addison Gallery Am. Art, Pa. Acad. Fine Arts, L.A. County Mus., Santa Barbara Mus., Oakland Art Mus., Munson Proctor Inst., Va. Mus. Fine Arts, Portland (Maine) Mus., Everson Mus., U. Ark., Okla. Art Ctr., Cleve. Mus. Fine Art. Served with AUS, 1943-46, ETO. Fulbright scholar to France, 1952, Prix de Rome Am. Acad. Rome, 1955-58, Jennie Sesnan Gold medal Pa. Acad. Fine Arts, 1966; Tiffany grantee, 1951; Guggenheim fellow, 1959, Nat. Endowment for Arts grantee, 1967, 80; Nat. Inst. Arts and Letters grantee, 1968, N.Y. Caps grantee, 1981. Mem. NAD (Benjamin Altman Landscape prize 1993, 1999, Adolph and Clara Obrig prize, 2003). Office Phone: 212-666-5559.

GOLDING, BRAGE, university president; b. Chgo., Apr. 28, 1920; s. Leon M. and Viola B. (Brage) G.; m. Hinda F. Wolf, Dec. 21, 1941; children: Brage, Susan, Julie. BS, Purdue U., 1941, PhD, 1948; LLD, Wright State U., 1975. Assoc. dir. research Lilly Varnish Co., Indpls.; also research assoc. Purdue U., 1948-57; vis. prof. engring. Purdue U., dir. research Lilly Varnish Co., 1957-59; head Sch. Chem. Engring. Purdue U., 1959-66; v.p. Ohio State U. and; Miami U., 1966-67; pres. Wright State U., Dayton, Ohio, 1967-72, San Diego State U., 1972-77, Kent State U., 1977-82, Met. State Coll., Denver, 1984-85; acting pres. Western State Coll., Gunnison, Colo., 1985, ret. Cons. Dept. Higher Edn., Pa. and N.J. Author: Polymers and Resins, 1959; Contbr. articles to profl. jours. Fellow AAAS; mem. Am. Chem. Soc., Phi Beta Kappa (hon.) Address: 3990 Foothill Ave Carlsbad CA 92008-7053 Personal E-mail: bgolding@mail.sdsu.edu.

GOLDING, CAROLYN MAY, former government senior executive, consultant; b. Essex County, N.J., July 1, 1941; d. Wesley Irwin and Florence Grace (Smith) G.; m. Gary Anthony Derosa, Oct. 18, 1975 (div. Sept. 1982). BA, Duke U., 1963, postgrad., 1965-66. English tchr. Parkersburg (W.Va.) H.S., 1963; asst. to registrar Duke U., Durham, N.C., 1963-65; mgmt. intern Dept. Labor, Washington, 1966-67, various other positions, 1967-72; dep. assoc. regional adminstr. Employment and Tng. Adminstrn., San Francisco, 1972-77, comptroller Washington, 1977-78, regional adminstr. San Francisco, 1979-82, dir. Unemployment Ins. Svc. Washington, 1982-87, adminstr. employment security, 1987-88, dep. asst. sec. employment and tng., 1988-96. Cons. on mgmt., labor force, long-range planning, workforce edn. issues and exec. coaching, 1996—. Recipient Disting. Career Svc. award Dept. Labor, 1979, Fed. Women's Career award Sec. Labor, 1983, Presdl. Meritorious rank, 1987, 95, Philip Arnow award Dept. Labor, 1988. Mem. Internat. Women's Forum, Women's Forum of Washington, Coun. for Excellence in Govt. (prin.), Women Mean Business (co-chair) Episcopalian.

GOLDING, SUSAN G., former mayor; b. Muskogee, Okla., Aug. 18, 1945; d. Brage and Hinda Fay (Wolf) G.; children: Samuel, Vanessa. Cert. Pratique de Langue Francaise, U. Paris, 1965; BA in Govt. and Internat. Rels., Carleton Coll., 1966; MA in Romance Philology, Columbia U., 1974. Assoc. editor Columbia U. Jour. of Internat. Affairs, N.Y.C., 1968-69; teaching fellow Emory U., Atlanta, 1973-74; instr. San Diego Community Coll. Dist., 1978; assoc. pub., gen. mgr. The News Press Group, San Diego, 1978-80; city council mem. City of San Diego, 1981-83; dep. sec. bus., transp., housing State of Calif., Sacramento, 1983-84; county supr. dist. 3 County of San Diego, 1984-92; mayor City of San Diego, 1992—2000; pres. & CEO The Golding Group, Inc., San Diego, 2000—; head Homeland Security Office, Titan Corp., San Diego, 2000—. Chmn. San Diego Drug Strike Force, 1987-88, Calif. Housing Fin. Agy., Calif. Coastal Commn.; bd. dirs. San Diego County Water Authority; trustee So. Calif. Water Com., Inc.; founder Mid City Comml. Revitalization Task Force, Strategic Trade Alliance, 1993, Calif. Big 10 City Mayors, 1993; mem. Gov. Calif. Mil. Base Reuse Task Force, 1994; established San Diego World Trade Ctr., 1993, San Diego City/State/County Regional Permit Assistance Ctr., 1994; mem. adv. bd. U.S. Conf. of Mayors, 1994; chair Gov. Wilson's Commn. on Local Governance for 21st Century. Bd. dirs. Child Abuse Prevention Found., San Diego Conv. and Vis. Bur., Crime Victims Fund, United Cerebral Palsy, San Diego Air Quality Bd., San Diego March of Dimes, Rep. Assocs.; adv. bd. Girl Scouts U.S.; trustee So. Calif. Water Comm.; mem. Rep. State Cen. Com.; co-chair com. Presidency George Bush Media Fund, Calif.; chair San Diego County Regional Criminal Justice Coun., race rels. com. Citizens Adv. Com. on Racial Intergration, San Diego Unified Sch. Dist.; hon. chair Am. Cancer Soc's. Residential Crusade, 1988. Recipient Alice Paul award Nat. Women's Polit. Caucus, 1987, Calif. Women in Govt. Achievement award, 1988, Willie Velasquez Polit. award Mex. Am. Bus. and Profl. Assn., 1988, Catalyst of Chance award Greater San Diego C. of C., 1994, Woman Who Means Bus. award San Diego Bus. Jour., 1994, Internat. Citizen award World Affairs Coun., 1994; named One of San Diego's Ten Outstanding Young Citizens, 1981, One of Ten Outstanding Rep. County Ofcls. in U.S.A., Rep. Nat. Com., 1987, San Diego Woman of Achievement Soroptimists Internat., 1988. Mem. Nat. Assn. of Counties (chair Op. Fair Share, mem. taxation and fin. com.), Nat. Women's Forum. Republican. Jewish. Office: The Golding Group Inc 9276 Scranton Rd Ste 600 San Diego CA 92121 E-mail: commerce@golding.org.

GOLDING, TERRY DAVID, engineering educator, researcher; b. Watford, Eng., Aug. 28, 1963; s. Ian David and Gillian Golding; m. Kathryn Smith, Dec. 12, 2001; m. Lisa Taratooty, Aug. 11, 1989 (div. Feb. 3, 1994); children: Alexander David, Myles David, Tarah-Rose. BS in Physics, U. of Leicester, Eng., 1985; PhD in Semiconductor Physics, Cambridge U., Eng., 1989. Rsch. scientist U.S. Army Night Vision Labs., Alexandria, Va., 1986—88; asst. prof. physics U. of Houston, 1989—93, assoc. prof. physics, 1993—2000; prof. physics and materials sci. and engring. U. of North Tex., Denton, 2000—. Pres. GEM Rsch. Inc, Houston, 1996—, Sigma Xi North Tex. Chpt., Dallas, 2002. Recipient Sci. and Engring. award, UK Rsch. Coun., 1985, 1986, 1987, Collaborative Award in Sci. and Engring., GE, 1985, 1986, 1987, 1988. Mem.: Sigma Xi (pres. 2002), Materials Rsch. Soc. (assoc.). Achievements include research in Properties of semiconductors, nanostructures, and novel electro-optical materials. Personal E-mail: golding@unt.edu.

GOLDMAN, ALAN IRA, brokerage house executive; b. N.Y.C., July 29, 1937; s. Julius and Florence (Blum) G.; m. Joanne T. Marren. AB, Cornell U., 1958; MBA, NYU, 1962; grad., Stonier Grad. Sch. Banking, 1967. Methods analyst, personnel-researcher Fed. Res. Bank of N.Y., N.Y.C., 1958-62; platform asst. Bankers Trust Co., N.Y.C., 1962-63, asst. mgr., 1963-64, mgr., 1964-65, asst. treas., 1965-66, asst. v.p., 1967-69; assoc. investment banking dept. Lehman Bros., N.Y.C., 1969-70; v.p. fin., chief fin. officer, treas. Interway Corp., N.Y.C., 1970-74; mgmt. cons. Montclair, N.J., 1974-75; v.p. fin. Mgmt. Assistance Inc., N.Y.C., 1975-80, sr. v.p. fin., 1980-85; ind. investment banker, bus. cons., 1985—; pres. Goldmark Capital, 1987-88. Lectr., adv., examiner Stonier Grad. Sch. Banking, 1968-71; lectr. Am. Inst. Banking, 1968-69; chair SGA Interactive Corp.; chair SGA Interactive, Inc. Co-chmn. Montclair chpt. campaign ARC, 1970-73; chmn. Cornell Funds' N.Y. Area Phonathons, 1972-74, UN Week, Montclair, 1973; trustee, treas., co-chair Cocteau Repertory Theatre, 1985-2000; bd. dirs. Planned Parenthood Fedn. Am., 1986-88; bd. dirs., treas. Planned Parenthood Met. N.J.; bd. dirs., chair, treas. Montclair ARC; adv. coun., vice chair Columbia U. Mailman Sch. Pub. Health; cochair Class of 1958 reunion com. Cornell U. Mem. Orange Lawn Tennis Club, Univ. Club (N.Y.C.), Aspatuck Tennis Club, Surf Club of Quogue, Phi Beta Kappa, Phi Kappa Phi, Zeta Beta Tau. E-mail: alangoldman@comcast.net.

GOLDMAN, ALLAN BAILEY, lawyer; b. Auburn, N.Y., Jan. 1, 1937; s. Charles and Rose Hortense (Abrahams) G.; m. Eleanor Ruth Levy, May 26, 1963; children: Jennifer Brooke Horwitz, Andrea Allison Gellert. AB magna cum laude, Harvard U., 1958, JD, 1963; LHD (hon.), Hebrew Union Coll.-Jewish Inst. Religion, 1992. Bar: Calif. 1964, D.C. 1977, U.S. Supreme Ct. 1977. Assoc. Wyman, Bautzer, Kuchel & Silbert, Beverly Hills, Calif., 1963-67, ptnr. L.A., 1967-91, Katten Muchin Rosenman, LLP, L.A., 1991—. Judge pro-tem Calif. Mcpl. and Small Claims Cts.; arbitrator Calif. Superior Ct. Contbr. articles to profl. jours. Chmn. Attys. for Brown for Gov., officer Brown for Pres., 1976; founder L.A. Com. for Civil Rights Under Law, Mus. Contemporary Art., L.A., Fraternity of Friends of L.A. Music Ctr.; trustee Calif. Mus. Sci. and Industry, 1981-89, St. John's Hosp. and Health Ctr. Found., 1978—, exec. com., 1979-89, bd. dirs., 1989-95, treas., 1990-94, chmn., 1994-95; chmn. nat. bd. trustees Union of Am. Hebrew Congregations, 1987-91; bd. govs. Hebrew Union Coll.-Jewish Inst. Religion, 1988—, bd. overseers L.A. campus, 1981-85, 88—; trustee SKirball Cultural Ctr., 1997—; pres. Leo Baeck Temple, L.A., 1975-77; mem. Conf. Pres.'s Major Jewish Orgns., 1987-91; mem. synagogue funding com. Jewish Fedn. Coun. of Greater L.A., 1979, chmn., 1985-88; Calif. Commn. Jud. Nominees Evaluation, 1999-2002. Lt. USNR, 1958-60. Mem. Calif. Bar Assn., D.C. Bar Assn. Democrat. Jewish. Avocations: trekking, running, tennis. Home: 347 Conway Ave Los Angeles CA 90024-2603 Office: Katten Muchin Rosenman LLP 2029 Century Park E Ste 2600 Los Angeles CA 90067 Office Phone: 310-788-4520. Business E-Mail: allan.goldman@kattenlaw.com.

GOLDMAN, ALLEN MARSHALL, physics professor; b. NYC, Oct. 18, 1937; s. Louis and Mildred (Kohn) G.; m. Katherine Virginia Darnell, July 31, 1960; children: Matthew, Rachel, Benjamin AB, Harvard U., 1958; PhD, Stanford U., 1965. Rsch. asst. Stanford U., Calif., 1960-65, rsch. assoc., 1965; asst. prof. physics U. Minn., Mpls., 1965-67, assoc. prof., 1967-73, prof., 1974—, inst. tech. prof., 1992—, dir. Ctr. for Sci. and Application of Superconductivity, 1989—, head Sch. of Physics and Astronomy, 1996—. Co-chmn. Gordon Conf. on Quantum Liquids and Solids, 1981; dir. NATO Advanced Study Inst., 1983; mem. materials rsch. adv. com. NSF, 1985-88; mem. vis. com. Francis Butter Nat. Magnet Lab., 1986-89, chmn., 1987-89; mem. vis. com. Nat. Nanofabrication Facility at Cornell, 1988-90, mem. user com., 1997-99; mem. vis. com. U. Chgo. Materials Program of Argonne Nat. Lab., 1992-98, chmn. 1995; mem. Buckley prize com., 1994-95, London prize com., 1994-98; mem. Helium Res. com. NAS/NRC, 1998-99. Mem. publs. oversight com. Am. Phys. Soc., 1996-99, chair 1997; mem. pub. policy com. Am. Inst. Physics, 1999-2005, assoc. editor Revs. of Modern Physics, 1999-2005; contbr. articles to profl. jours. Com. of vis. divsn. materials rsch. NSF, 1999. Alfred P. Sloan Found. fellow, 1966-70. Fellow AAAS, Am. Phys. Soc. (divisional councilor divsn. condensed matter physics 1994-96, 99-2003, mem. exec. com. 2001-03, Fritz London Meml. prize 2002). Jewish. Home: 1015 James Ct Mendota Heights MN 55118-3640 Office: U Minn Sch Physics and Astronomy 116 Church St SE Minneapolis MN 55455-0149 Office Phone: 612-624-6062. Personal E-mail: allen.goldman@comcast.net. Business E-Mail: goldman@umn.edu.

GOLDMAN, ALVIN IRA, philosopher, educator; b. Bklyn., Oct. 1, 1938; s. Nathan and Frances (Krugman) G.; m. Holly Martin Smith, June 15, 1969; children: Raphael, Sidra. BA, Columbia U., 1960; MA, Princeton U., 1962, PhD, 1965. From asst. prof. to prof. U. Mich., Ann Arbor, 1963-80; prof. U. Ill., Chgo., 1980-83, U. Ariz., Tucson, 1983-94, Regents' prof. philosophy, 1994—2002; Bd. Govs. Prof. Philosophy Rutgers U., New Brunswick, NJ, 2002—. Author: A Theory of Human Action, 1970, Epistemology and Cognition, 1986, Liaisons: Philosophy Meets..., 1992, Philosophical Applications of Cognitive Science, 1993, Knowledge in a Social World, 1999, Pathways to Knowledge, 2002. Guggenheim fellow, 1975-76, Ctr. for Advanced Study in Behavioral Scis. fellow, 1975-76, Nat. Humanities Ctr. fellow, 1981-82. Fellow: Am. Acad. Arts and Scis.; mem.: Soc. for Philosophy and Psychology (pres. 1987—88), Am. Philos. Assn. (Pacific divsn. pres. 1991—92). Avocations: music, athletics. Office: Rutgers U 26 Nichol Ave New Brunswick NJ 08901-1411 E-mail: goldman@philosophy.rutgers.edu.

GOLDMAN, ALVIN LEE, lawyer, educator, arbitrator; b. N.Y.C., Feb. 27, 1938; s. Joseph I. and Emma (Berger) G.; m. Elisabeth C. Paris, Nov. 23, 1956; children— Paula, Douglas AB, Columbia U., 1959; LL.B., NYU, 1962. Bar: Ky. 1969. Assoc. Parker, Chapin & Flattau, N.Y.C., 1962-65; mem. faculty U. Ky., Lexington, 1965—, prof. law, 1972—. Prof. in residence NLRB Zagoria staff, 1967-68; vis. scholar Inst. for Labor Law, U. Lueven, 1973; vis. prof. U. Calif., Davis, 1976-77. Author: Processes for Conflict Resolution, 1972, The Supreme Court and Labor-Management Relations Law, 1975, Labor Law and Industrial Relations in the USA, 2d edit., 1983, (with R. Covington) Legislation Protecting the Individual Employee, 1982, (with M. Finkin, C. Summers and K. Dau-Schmidt) Legal Protection for the Individual Employee, 1989, 2d edit., 1995, 3d edit., 2002, Settling for More: Mastering Negotiating Strategies and Techniques, 1991, Labor and Employment Law in the United States, 1996, (with J. Rojot) Negotiation: Theory and Practice, 2003. Bd. dirs. Central Ky. Jewish Assn., 1978-80, 81-84 Mem. ABA, Ky. Bar Assn., Nat. Acad. Arbitrators (bd. govs. 1994-97), Labor Law Group Trust (chmn. 1988-94), Internat. Soc. Labor Law (internat. v.p. 2000-03, exec. bd. U.S. br. 1982-85, 88—, vice-chair 1995-2001, chair 2001—), Internat. Indsl. Rels. Assn. Democrat. Office: U Ky Coll of Law Lexington KY 40506-0048 Office Phone: 859-257-3325. E-mail: agold00@email.uky.edu.

GOLDMAN, BENJAMIN EDWARD, lawyer; b. N.Y.C., Feb. 25, 1940; s. William Wolfe and Blanche (Kallenburg) G.; m. Lynda Ann Schwartz, July 27, 1950; children: Brian Edward, Victoria Beth, Adam Edward BS, NYU, 1965; JD, Fordham U., 1968; LLM, Georgetown U., 1970. Bar: N.Y. 1968, D.C. 1972, U.S. Dist. D.C., U.S. Ct. Appeals (D.C., 4th, 5th and 9th cirs.), Calif. 1986, U.S. Dist. Ct. (cen. dist.) Calif. 1986. Atty., advisor to chmn. NLRB, Washington, 1968-72; assoc. Arent, Fox, Kitner, Plotkin, Kahn, Washington, 1972-75; ptnr. Feldman, Krieger, Goldman, Tisch, Washington, 1976-83, Memel, Jacobs, Pierno, Gersh & Ellsworth, L.A., 1984-87, Graham and James, L.A., 1987-2001, Squire, Sanders & Dempsey LLP, L.A., 2001—. Mem. com. on devel. law under NLRB Act, 1968—; speaker Healthcare Fin. Mgmt. Assn., Calif., 1987, Nat. Health Edn. Conf. on AIDS, 1987, Inst. Corp. Counsel, 1986, Hosp. Coun. N. Calif., 1985, others. Contbr. articles to profl. jours. Mem. ABA (forum com. on health law 1983, mem. labor and employment law sect. 1968—), Nat. Health Lawyers Assn. (speaker ann. healthlaw update 1985), Calif. Bar Assn., N.Y. Bar Assn., D.C. Bar Assn., Am. Acad. Hosp. Attys. Office: Squire Sanders & Dempsey LLP 801 S Figueroa St Fl 14 Los Angeles CA 90017-2573 E-mail: bgoldman@ssd.com.

GOLDMAN, BERT ARTHUR, psychologist, educator; b. NYC, Apr. 4, 1929; children: Lisa, Linda. BA, U. Md., 1951; M.Ed., U. N.C., 1956; Ed.D., U. Va., 1960. Mem. faculty U. N.C., Greensboro, 1965—, prof. ednl. psychology, 1971-85, dean acad. advising, 1970-85, prof. higher ednl. adminstrn., 1985—86, acting chair dept. ednl. adminstrn., higher edn. and ednl. rsch., 1987-88, dept. coord. of higher edn., 1991—. Served with U.S. Army, 1951-53. Mem. APA. Office: U NC at Greensboro Dept Curriculum and Instrn PO Box 26170 Greensboro NC 27402-6170

GOLDMAN, BRIAN ARTHUR, lawyer, accountant; b. Balt., June 30, 1946; s. Marvin L. and Edythe R. Goldman; m. Eileen G. Safro, Aug. 22, 1970; children: Jonathan S., Evan M. BS in Real Estate Planning, Am.U., 1968; JD, U. Md., 1971. Bar: Md. 1972, U.S. Dist. Ct. Md. 1972, U.S. Tax Ct. 1977, U.S. Supreme Ct. 1977. Acct., Balt., 1974—; mem. Burke, Gerber & Wilen, 1972-77, Sapero & Sapero, 1977-78; pvt. practice, 1978-83; ptnr.

Goldman and Fedder, P.A., Balt., 1983—85, Fedder & Garten, P.A., Balt., 1986—88, Goldman & Vetter, P.A., Balt., 1989—2004, Goldman & Goldman, PA, Balt., 2004—. Asst. prof. income taxation U. Balt., 1974-75. Mem. ABA, Md. Bar Assn., Balt. City Bar Assn., Md. Assn. CPAs, Ctr. Club, Woodholme. Office: Goldman & Goldman PA 36 S Charles St Ste 2401 Baltimore MD 21201-3108 Office Phone: 410-547-1400. Business E-Mail: bgoldman@goldmangoldman.com.

GOLDMAN, CHARLES A., science administrator; b. Jamaica, N.Y., Sept. 20, 1964; s. Eric A. Goldman and Joyce E. Schulman; life ptnr. Gary L. Reisch. SB, MIT, 1986; PhD, Stanford U., 1993. Assoc. dir. edn. RAND Corp., Santa Monica, Calif., 2004—, sr. economist, 1993—. Prof. econs. Pardee RAND Grad. Sch., Santa Monica, 1996—. Author: (book) In Pursuit of Prestige, PhD Factory, Paying for University Research Facilities and Administration. Office: RAND Corp 1776 Main St Santa Monica CA 90401 Office Phone: 310-393-0411.

GOLDMAN, CHARLES NORTON, retired corporate lawyer; b. N.Y.C., Feb. 15, 1932; s. Morris and Mary Celia (Tames) G.; m. Jane Barbara Webbink, July 21, 1968; children: Alexander Daniel, Jeffrey David. AB with honors, Columbia U., 1953, LLB, 1955. Bar: N.Y. 1956. Practiced in, N.Y.C., 1955-60; atty.-advisor AID, Washington, 1960-62; regional legal advisor for India, Nepal and Ceylon AID mission to India, New Delhi, 1962-64; asst. gen. counsel for Latin Am. AID, 1965-68, dep. gen. counsel, 1968-69; staff counsel for Latin Am. ITT, N.Y.C., 1969-72, sr. counsel, asst. to gen. counsel, 1972-74, sr. counsel for Latin Am., 1974-75; v.p., gen. counsel ITT Europe Inc., Brussels, 1975-81; v.p. ITT, 1976-95, assoc. gen. counsel, 1981-95. Mem. Overseas Devel. Coun., 1988-95, Bretton Woods Com., 1992-95. Dir. Jewish Repertory Theater Inc., 1999—2001; bd. dirs. The Internat. Shakespeare Globe Ctr. Ltd., 2003—, Alliance of Resident Theatres, N.Y.C., 1996—98, The Shakespeare Globe Ctr. (USA) Inc., 1996—, pres., 2001—. Mem. Coun. on Fgn. Rels., Mid-Atlantic Club N.Y. Inc. (pres. 1996-2001), Univ. Club, Phi Beta Kappa. Home: 139 E 94th St New York NY 10128-1761 E-mail: chgoldman@aol.com.

GOLDMAN, DONALD AARON, lawyer; b. N.Y.C., Sept. 11, 1947; BA, UCLA, 1969, JD, 1972. Bar: Calif. 1972. Dep. atty. gen. Calif. Dept. Justice, L.A., 1972-79; ptnr. Memel, Jacobs & Ellsworth, L.A., 1979-87; ptnr., mem. firm exec. mgmt. com., chmn. firm compensation com., co-chmn. firm gender diversity com., co-chmn. firm radical & ethnic diversity com. McDermott, Will & Emery LLP, L.A., 1987—. Mem. exec. com. Children's Bur., L.A., 1990—, Pres.'s Invitational Golf Tournament, L.A., 1990-2000. Mem. Nat. Health Lawyers. Avocations: golf, woodworking. Office: McDermott Will & Emery LLP 2049 Century Park E Los Angeles CA 90067-3101 Office Phone: 310-551-9319. Office Fax: 310-277-4730. Business E-Mail: dogoldman@mwe.com.

GOLDMAN, ETHAN HARRIS, finance executive; b. Boston, Jan. 2, 1956; s. Marshall Irwin and Merle Dorothy (Rosenblatt) G.; m. Julie Ellen Hurwitz, Sept. 11, 1982; children: Jessica, Todd, David, Lauren. BA, BS in Econs., U. Pa., 1978; MBA, Harvard Coll., 1982. CPA, Md. 1st lt. U.S. Army, 1978—79; maj. USAR, 1979—2003; pub. acct. Touche Ross, Balt., 1979-80, Coopers and Lybrand, Boston, 1982-84; mgr. fin. planning Hit or Miss Stores subs. Zayre Corp., Stoughton, Mass., 1984-86; asst. v.p. ops. planning/new bus. ventures Zayre Stores subs. Zayre Corp., Framingham, Mass., 1986-88, asst. v.p. mdse. logistics, 1988-89; housewares buyer Ames Stores, Rocky Hill, Conn., 1989-90, dir. mdse. planning and adminstrn., 1990-91, dir. pull replenishment, 1991-93, divisional mdse. mgr., 1993-95; dir. fin. analysis ADVO, Inc., Windsor, Conn., 1995-98, v.p. strategic bus. devel., 1999—2001, v.p. network planning (strategic planning), 2001—02; CFO Flexcon, Inc., Spencer, Mass., 2002—. Jachal lectr., 2000—. Treas. West Hartford Youth Soccer, 2004—. Mem.: No. Conn. Harvard Bus. Sch. Club (bd. dirs.-at-large 1992—2003). Jewish. Avocations: distance running, soccer, stamp collecting/philately, tennis, history. Home: 9 Vardon Rd West Hartford CT 06117-2848 Office: One Flexcon Industrial Park Spencer MA 01562-2642 E-mail: ethangoldman@comcast.net.

GOLDMAN, GARY STEVEN, computer scientist, consultant; b. LA, Apr. 7, 1954; s. Fred and Claire Goldman; m. Rusty Lynn Goldman, May 7, 1983; children: Stephanie Lynn, Casondra Claire, Dora Nicole. BS in Computer Sci., BS in Engring., Calif. State U., 1976; PhD in Computer Sci., Pacific Western U., 1982. Lic. gen. contractor Calif. State Lic. Bd., 1989. Rsch. analyst L.A. Dept. Health Svcs., Lancaster, Calif., 1995—2002; dir. Pearblossom Pvt. Sch., Inc., Pearblossom, 1988—. V.p. systems devel. Cascade Graphics Devel., Irvine, Calif., 1980—84. Editor-in-chief: Medical Veritas: Journal of Medical Truth; author: Rashes of Controversy, numerous medical journal publications concerning MMR vaccination and autism, varicella vaccination, and impact on herpes-zoster epidemiology and capture-recapture methodology. Dir. Pearblossom Pvt. Sch. Inc., 1988—2004. Mem.: Phi Kappa Phi. Achievements include invention of First microcomputer-based computer aided drafting (CAD) system; patents for Power Wheel-efficient microprogrammed electric motor for vehicular transportation. Home: PO Box 847 Pearblossom CA 93553 Office: Pearblossom Pvt Sch Inc PO Box 847 Pearblossom CA 93553 Office Phone: 800-309-3569. Home Fax: 661-944-4483; Office Fax: 661-944-4483. E-mail: pearblossominc@aol.com.

GOLDMAN, GEORGE DAVID, psychologist; b. N.Y.C., Jan. 8, 1923; s. Irving Israel and Hattie Anna (Bennett) G.; m. Belle Hans, Sept. 11, 1948; children: Ira Stephen, Carol Marcia Goldman Reife, Deberah Sue Goldman Cohen. BS in Social Sci., CCNY, 1943; MA, NYU, 1946, PhD, 1950; cert. in psychoanalysis, William A. White Inst., N.Y.C., 1958. Diplomate Am. Bd. Profl. Psychology. Fellow CCNY, 1946-47, instr. psychology, 1947-53, NYU, 1948-51; pvt. practice psychology N.Y.C., 1952—; pvt. practice Jericho, N.Y., 1956-95; clin. psychologist Bronx VA Hosp., Montrose VA Hosp., 1947-52; staff psychotherapist Low Cost Psychoanalytic Svc. William Alanson White Inst., N.Y.C., 1952-58; clin. prof., supr., dir. clin. svcs. Postdoctoral Psychotherapy Ctr., Derner Inst., Adelphi U., Garden City, N.Y., 1958-94; supr. psychotherapy grad. div. Ferkauf Sch., Yeshiva U., Bronx, 1976-80. Cons. to supt. Manhasset (N.Y.) Pub. Schs., 1956-61; cons. psychotherapy VA, N.Y. area, 1959-79; mem. arbitration panel on marital conflicts Am. Arbitration Assn., 1968—. Co-editor: (with D.S. Milman) Modern Woman: Her Psychology and Sexuality, 1969, Psychoanalytic Contributions to Community Psychology, 1970, Innovations in Psychotherapy, 1971, The Neurosis of Our Time: Acting Out, 1973, Group Process Today, 1974, Man and Woman in Transition, 1978, Psychoanalytic Perspectives on Aggression, 1978, Modern Man: The Psychology and Sexuality of the Contemporary Male, 1979, Parameters in Psychoanalytic Psychotherapy, 1979, Therapists at Work: A Demonstration of Theory and Technique, 1979, Addiction—Theory and Treatment, 1980, Techniques of Working with Resistance, 1987; (with G. Stricker) Practical Problems of a Private Psychotherapy Practice, 1972, 2d edit., 1981; (with L. Saretsky) Integrating Ego Psychology and Object Relations Theory: Psychoanalytic Perspectives on Psychopathology, 1979; contbr. articles to profl. jours. Mem. profl. adv. bd. Nassau County chpt. Parents Without Ptnrs., 1970-95; pres. psychology divsn., bd. dirs. Am. Friends of Hebrew U. of Jerusalem, N.Y.C., 1975—. With U.S. Army, 1943-45. Decorated Bronze Star, Purple Heart with oak leaf cluster; named Disting. Practitioner in Psychology, Nat. Acads. of Practice, 1983; recipient Outstanding Contbn. to Psychology award CCNY, 1989, Disting. Svc. to Profession of Psychology award Am. Bd. Profl. Psychology, Inc., 1999. Fellow APA (pres. divsn. psychologists in ind. practice 1987, psychotherapy, clinic psych., pres. divsn. psychoanalysis, 1982, Disting. Contbn. award 1988, Disting. Psychologist award divsn. 42 1989, divsn. 39 award 1990, Disting. Lifetime Svc. award divsn. 39 2000), N.Y. State Psychol. Assn. (past bd. dirs. clin. div.), Nassau County Psychol. Assn. (past bd. dirs.), N.Y. Soc. Clin. Psychologists (pres. 1979), Am. Acad. Psychotherapists (past bd. dirs. and sec.). Democrat. Jewish. Avocations: swimming, travel. Office: 305 E 86th St Apt 22aw New York NY 10028-4702 Office Phone: 212-722-6515. Personal E-mail: drgdgoldman@aol.com.

GOLDMAN, IRA STEVEN, gastroenterologist; b. Bronx, NY, May 19, 1951; s. George David and Belle (Hans) G.; children: Zachary, Joshua. BA, U. Rochester, 1973; student, Oxford U., 1972; MD, Columbia U., 1977. Diplomate Am. Bd. Internal Medicine, Am. Bd. Gastroenterology. Intern Columbia Presbyn. Med. Ctr., N.Y.C., 1977-78, resident in internal medicine, 1978-80; fellow in gastroenterology and liver diseases U. Calif. Sch. Medicine, San Francisco, 1980-83; instr. in anatomy Columbia U., N.Y.C., 1978; asst. prof. medicine U. Calif., San Francisco, 1983-85, Cornell U. Med. Coll., N.Y.C., 1985-91, assoc. prof. clin. medicine, 1991-96; attending physician North Shore Univ. Hosp., Manhasset, N.Y., 1985—; assoc. prof. clin. medicine NYU Sch. Medicine, 1996—. Attending physician St. Francis Hosp., Roslyn, N.Y.; physicians adv. bd. Am. Liver Found., Greater N.Y. chpt., 1985—; sci. adv. commn. L.I. chpt. Nat. Found. for Ileitis and Colitis, 1985-91; vice chair clin. practice sec. Am. Gastroent. Assn., 1995-97, chmn., 1997-2000. Reviewer jours. Gastroenterology; contbr. articles to profl. jours., chpts. to books. Rsch. fellow Am. Liver Found., 1982, Clin. Investigator award NIH, 1983. Fellow ACP, Am. Coll. Gastroenterology; mem. Am. Assn. for Study of Liver Diseases, Med. Soc. State of N.Y., Nassau County Med. Soc., Nassau County. Acad. Medicine, N.Y. Soc. for Gastrointestinal Endoscopy (pres. 1996-97), Am. Gastroenterological Assn., Alpha Omega Alpha. Avocations: sailing, tennis. Office: 310 E Shore Rd Great Neck NY 11023-2432 Office Phone: 516-487-7677. Personal E-mail: isgoldman@aol.com.

GOLDMAN, ISRAEL DAVID, medical oncoggist, educator; b. Jersey City, N.J., Nov. 17, 1936; married; 3 children. BA, NYU, 1958; MD, U. Chgo., 1962. Diplomate Am. Bd. Internal Medicine; lic. physician, N.C., Va., N.Y. Internal medicine intern U. Chgo. Hosps., 1962-63, jr. and sr. asst. resident internal medicine, 1963-65; fellow biophysics biophys. lab. Harvard Med. Sch., Boston, 1965—66; from rsch. assoc. to sr. investigator Nat. Cancer Inst., Bethesda, Md., 1966—69; asst. prof. medicine U. N.C., Chapel Hill, 1969-72, assoc. prof. medicine and pharmacology, 1972-74; assoc. prof. medicine, vice-chmn. dept. medicine Med. Coll. Va., Richmond, 1974-83, prof. medicine and pharmacology, 1979—95, prof. medicine and pharmacology, chmn. divsn. hematology/oncology, 1982—95, dir. Massey Cancer Ctr., 1988—95; prof. medicine and molecular pharmacology, dir. cancer rsch. ctr. Albert Einstein Coll. Medicine, 1995—. Mem. exptl. therapeutics study sect. Nat. Cancer Inst., 1976-80, bd. sci. counselors divsn. cancer treatment, 1982-86; sci. adv. com. Damon Runyon-Walter Winchell Cancer Fund, 1986-90; mem. tobacco related disease study sect. U. Calif., 1992-94. Mem. editl. bd. Biochem. Pharmacology, 1984—2004, Jour. Biol. Chemistry, 1996—2001, Clin. Cancer Rsch., 1999—, Molecular Cancer Therapeutics, 2002—. With USPHS, Nat. Cancer Inst., NIH, Bethesda, Md., 1966-69. Recipient Rsch. Career Devel. award Nat. Cancer Inst., 1973-78, Outstanding Investigator award Nat. Cancer Inst., 1985-92, 92-99. Fellow ACP; mem. Am. Soc. Clin. Investigation, Assn. Am. Physicians. Home: 231 Loring Ave Pelham NY 10803-2254 Office: Albert Einstein Coll Med Cancer Ctr 1300 Morris Park Ave Bronx NY 10461-1926

GOLDMAN, JAY, industrial engineer, educator, dean emeritus; b. Norfolk, Va., Apr. 15, 1930; s. Louis H. and Rose O. Goldman; m. Renitta Librach, Dec. 20, 1959 BSME, Duke U., 1950; MSME, Mich. State U., 1951; DSc in Indsl. Engring., Washington U., St. Louis, 1955. Registered profl. engr., Mo. Lectr. indsl. engring. Washington U., 1952-56, asst. prof., 1956-64, acting chmn. human and orgn. factors, 1963-64; dir. dept. indsl. engring. Jewish Hosp., St. Louis, 1960-64; research assoc. dept. hosp. adminstr. U. N.C., Chapel Hill, 1964-68; prof., grad. adminstr. dept. indsl. engring. N.C. State U., Raleigh, 1964-68; prof., chmn. dept. indsl. engring. U. Mo., Columbia, 1968-84, prof. bioengring., 1969-75, prof. bioengring. and advanced automation, 1975-84; Disting. Svc. prof. and dean emeritus U. Ala., Birmingham, 1984—, dean, 1984-96. Cons. to fed., state agys., pvt. industry Contbr. to textbooks, profl. jours.; producer 6 tech. motion pictures; patentee in field V.p. Boone County Cmty. Svcs. Coun., 1973-76; v.p., exec. com., treas. Cmty. Rels. Coun.; bd. dirs. Birmingham Jewish Fedn.; vice-chmn., bd. dirs. Sloss Furnaces Nat. Hist. Landmark, bd. dirs., treas. Jewish Family Svcs. Named Ala. Engr. of Yr., ASPE; recipient Editl. award, Hosp. Mgmt. mag., 1969, U. Mo. Faculty Alumni award, 1981, Outstanding Engr. Educator in State award, ASPE. Fellow Inst. Indsl. Engrs. (trustee, exec. v.p., regional v.p., chpt. pres., v.p. edn. and profl. devel., editl. bd. Trans., Health Svcs. Devel. award 1981, Fred C. Crane award 1999, Medallion award, 2004), Accreditation Bd. Engring. and Tech. (dir., treas., fellow); mem. NSPE, Soc. Health Sys. (bd. dirs., pres.), Nat. Coun. Indsl. Engrs. Acad. Dept. Heads (chmn.), Ala. Soc. Profl. Engrs., Am. Soc. Engring. Edn., Sigma Xi, Alpha Pi Mu, Tau Beta Pi, Phi Kappa Phi, Omicron Delta Kappa. Home: 6068 Brookhill Cir Birmingham AL 35242 Office: U Ala-Birmingham Sch Engring 1075 13th St S Ste 310 Birmingham AL 35205-3430 Office Phone: 205-934-8400. Business E-Mail: jgoldman@uab.edu.

GOLDMAN, JEFFREY E., lawyer; b. Ft. Worth, Tex., Feb. 11, 1962; s. Murry Mores and Fran Ethel (Eddy) G. BS in Pharmacy, Phila. Coll Pharmacy & Sci., 1985; JD, Temple U., 1992. Assoc. Parker, McCauer, Criscoulu, Marlton, N.J., 1991-93; lawyer pvt. practice, Phila. and Cherry Hill, Pa., N.J., 1993—. Contbg. author National Employment Lawyers Annua., 1998. Bd. dirs. Phila. Gay and Lesbian Comty Ctr. 1996—, chmn. 1996-98. Mem. Nat. Employment Lawyers Assn. (v.p.). Democrat. Jewish. Office: 100 S Broad St Ste 1430 Philadelphia PA 19110

GOLDMAN, JOEL J., retired lawyer; b. N.Y.C., Sept. 7, 1940; s. Myron and Pearl (Jacobs) G.; m. Jane I. Stalker, July 23, 1973; children: Elizabeth Ann, Rebecca Lynn. BS, U. Va., 1962; JD, Syracuse U., 1965. Bar: N.Y. 1966, U.S. Dist. Ct. (we. dist.) N.Y. 1966. Law clk. Myron Goldman, N.Y.C., 1965; staff atty., chief trial counsel Legal Aid Soc., Rochester, N.Y., 1966-73; ptnr. Kaman, Berlove, Marafioti, Jacobstein & Goldman, Rochester, 1973-97; ret., 1997. Lectr. family law; spl. investigator N.Y. State Spl. Commn. on Attica, 1972; mem. panel arbitrators Am. Arbitration Assn.; mem. faculty Nat. Bus. Inst., 1985-97. Author continuing edn. materials; contbg. editor Bender's Forms for Civil Practice, 1986, Medina's Bostwick, 1986. Referee Ea. Assn. Inter-Collegiate Football Ofcsls., 1974-95, v.p. Empire chpt., 1988, pres., 1989, Observer, Ea. Coll. Athletic Conf., 1996—. Inductee Jewish Athletes Sports Hall of Fame, 1996. Fellow Am. Acad. Matrimonial Lawyers (ret.); mem. ABA, N.Y. State Bar Assn. (exec. com. family law sect. 1982, mem. exec. com. 1981-97), Monroe County Bar Assn. (chmn. family law sect. 1982, exec. com. 1981-86), Assn. Trial Lawyers Am. Jewish. Home: 67 Mountain Rd Rochester NY 14625-1816 also: 21 Bluebill Ave Apt 1005B Naples FL 34108-1765 Personal E-mail: jjgesq@att.net.

GOLDMAN, JOHN ABNER, rheumatologist, immunologist, educator; b. June 9, 1940; s. Leon and Belle (Hurwitz) G.; children from previous marriage: Joey, Beth; m. Deborah J. Staples, Aug. 1, 1993; children: Shelley, Michael. BS, U. Wis., 1962; MD, U. Cin., 1966. Diplomate Am. Bd. Internal Medicine, subspecialty in rheumatology, allergy-immunology, advanced achievement in internal medicine, 1987. Intern U. Oreg. Med. Sch., Portland, 1966-67; resident U. Cin. Med. Ctr., 1967-69, postdoctoral fellow in rheumatology and immunology, 1969-71; clin. prof. medicine Emory U. Sch. Medicine, Atlanta, 1973—. Contbr. numerous articles to sci. jours. Bd. dirs. Atlanta Arthritis Found.; med. adv. com. Lupus Erythematosus Found., Inc. Maj. U.S. Army, 1971-73. Fellow ACP, Am. Soc. Lasers in Medicine and Surgery, Am. Coll. Rheumatology (chair CORC SE network); mem. Ga. Soc. Rheumatology (pres. 1974-75), Med. Assn. Atlanta, Med. Assn. Ga. (coun. of splty. socs. ho. of dels., chmn. 3d party payers com., 2004), Met. Atlanta Rheumatology Soc. (co-pres.), Am. Soc. Clin. Densitometry (cert.), Ga. Medicare Carrier Adv. Com. (rheumatology rep.), Lupus Rsch. Inst. (adv. physician adv. coun.), Atlanta Bone Club (co-pres.). Office: Med Quarters Ste 293 5555 Peachtree Dunwoody Rd NE 293 Atlanta GA 30342-1711

GOLDMAN, JOSEPH ELIAS, retired advertising executive; b. N.Y.C., Nov. 26, 1923; s. A. Milton and Caroline (Elias) G.; m. Barbara Van Gelderen, Mar. 22, 1947; children: Carlee Georgette Goldman Paddock, Richard Jonathan. Student, Pratt Inst. Sch. Fine Art, 1941-42, 47-48. Gen. artist, designer Maxon, Inc., N.Y.C., 1948-50; officer, creative dir. Gamut, Inc., Garden City, N.Y., 1952-64; pres., chmn. bd. Adways, Inc., Jericho, N.Y., 1965-74; pres. Goldman Van Gelderen, Inc., Greenville, S.C., 1974-80; also bd. dirs.; pres. Gamut Agy., Inc., Hempstead, N.Y., 1975-77; v.p. Graphics Plus, Inc., Greenville, 1983-86; ret., 1986. Bd. dirs. Urban League L.I., 1976-77. With USMCR, 1942-46. Mem. League Advt. Agys. (pres. 1964-65), Art Dirs. Club L.I. (co-founder, pres. 1971-72, 72-73), Greenville Artists Guild (pres. 1986, bd. dirs. 1987), Upstate Visual Artists, Plein Air Artists Soc., Nat. Caricaturists Network, Alpha Delta Sigma.

GOLDMAN, L. BARTON, physician; b. Uniontown, Pa., Dec. 5, 1954; s. Mark Howard Goldman and Ann Louise Roman; m. Karen Jane Houser, Nov. 1, 1982; children: Elysa Brett, Eric Mitchell. BA with high distinction, Pa. State U., 1977; MD, Hahnemann U., 1984. Diplomate Am. Bd. Phys. Medicine and Rehab., Nat. Bd. Med. Examiners, Am. Bd. Ind. Med. Examiners. Intern, resident in phys. medicine and rehab. Temple U. Hosp., 1984-87; med. dir. Ctr. for Spine and Orthopedic Rehab., Englewood, Colo., 1987-96, CRPS Svc., Colo. Neurol. Inst., Englewood, 1991-96, R-Vision Corp., Denver, 1993-99; pres. Rehab. Assocs. Colo., P.C., Englewood, 1993-96, 2003—; med. dir. HealthOne Occupl. Medicine, Denver, 1996—99, HealthOne Clinic Svcs., 2000—03. Bd. mem. Colo. Health Care Rsch. Corp., Denver; chmn. Colo. Divsn. Workers Compensation Low Back Pain Guidelines Task Force, 1990-2000, Colo. Divsn. Workers Compensation Med. Care Adv. Com., Denver, 1991—. Sr. editor (newsletter) Neuropractice, 1994-2000; contbr. articles to profl. jours. Fundraiser Nat. MS Soc., 1989-92, Rocky Mountain Stroke Assn., Littleton, Colo., 1999; bd. mem. Colo. Neurol. Inst., Englewood, 1990-97, Spalding Rehab. Hosp., Denver, 1991-96. Fellow Am. Acad. Phys. Medicine and Rehab., Physiatric Assn. for Sports, Spine and Occupl. Rehab.; mem. Am. Acad. Med. Acupuncture, Am. Coll. Occupl. and Environ. Medicine, Am. Coll. Physician Execs., Rocky Mountain Rehab. Soc. (pres. 1995-99). Avocations: bicycling, skiing, hiking, yoga. Office: 1776 South Jackson St Ste 840 Denver CO 80210 Office Phone: 303-914-0065. E-mail: lawrencebarton@msn.com.

GOLDMAN, LAWRENCE SAUL, lawyer; b. Phila., Mar. 25, 1942; s. Ephraim Lederer and Belle Joan (Finkelstein) G.; m. Kathi Sue Schleifer, June 20, 1965; children: Carolyn, Jonathan. BA, Brandeis U., 1963; JD, Harvard U., 1966. Bar: N.Y. 1966. Asst. dist. atty. New York County, N.Y.C., 1966-71; asst. gen. counsel N.Y. State Commn. To Investigate N.Y.C., 1971-72; pvt. practice N.Y.C., 1972—2004; principal Law Offices of Lawrence S. Goldman, 2001—. Cons. N.Y.C. Commn. on Police Corruption, 1972. Contbg. author: Criminal Trial Advocacy, 1980-99. Trustee Congregation Rodeph Sholom, N.Y.C., 1983-92; bd. dirs. William F. Ryan Comty. Health Ctr., N.Y.C., 1986-88, Bronx Defenders, 1997-2004, chmn. 2004—; mem. N.Y. State Commn. on Jud. Conduct, 1990—, mem. adv. com. on the criminal law, 1992—, mem. N.Y. State Commn. on Future of Indigent Def. Svcs., 2003—. Recipient Man of Yr. award Hogan Assocs., 1984. Mem. NACDL (chmn. ethics adv. com. 1988-92, white collar com. 1992-97, 2004—, Robert C. Heeney award 1998, pres. 2001-2002), N.Y. State Assn. Criminal Def. Lawyers (pres. 1987-89, Thurgood Marshall award 1999), N.Y. Criminal Bar Assn. (pres. 1982-85, Outstanding Practitioner award 1994), N.Y. State Bar Assn. (Outstanding Practitioner award criminal justice sect. 1996), Harvard Club. Democrat. Office: 500 Fifth Ave 29th Flr New York NY 10110-0002 Office Phone: 212-997-7499. E-mail: LSG@lsgoldmanlaw.com.

GOLDMAN, LOUIS BUDWIG, lawyer; b. Chgo., Apr. 11, 1948; s. Jack Sydney and Lorraine (Budwig) G.; m. Barbara Marcia Berg, Oct. 2, 1983; children: Jacqueline Ilyse, Annie Dara, Michael Louis. BA magna cum laude, U. Calif., Berkeley, 1970; JD cum laude, U. Chgo., 1974. Bar: Calif. 1975, U.S. Dist. Ct. (no. dist.) Calif. 1975, U.S. Ct. Appeals (9th cir.) 1975, N.Y. 1976, U.S. Dist. Ct. (so. and ea. dists.) N.Y. 1976, U.S. Ct. Appeals (2nd cir.) 1976, Ill. 1991, Czech Republic, 1997; registered fgn. lawyer, Eng. 1999, Wales 1999. Law clk. U.S. Dist. Ct., San Francisco, 1974-75; assoc. Cleary, Gottlieb, Steen & Hamilton, N.Y.C. and Paris, 1975-81, Edwards & Angell, N.Y.C., 1981-83, ptnr., 1986-88, Wald, Harkrader & Ross, N.Y.C., 1983-86, Altheimer & Gray, Chgo., 1989—2003, co-chmn., 1999—2003; ptnr., mem. global bd. Salans, N.Y.C., 2003—. Mng. dir. Abacus & Assocs. Inc., N.Y.C.; supervisory bd. Pudliszki S.A. Mem. U. Chgo. Law Rev.; contbr. articles to profl. jours. Mem. Chgo.-Prague Sister Cities Com., Chgo.-China Sister Cities Com.; bd. dirs. Lyric Opera Ctr. for Am. Artists, New Trier Swim Club; sec. class of 1970, U. Calif., Berkeley; bd. trustees The Ravinia Festival. Mem. ABA (com. on privatization), Calif. Bar Assn., N.Y. State Bar Assn. (com. on internat. banking, securities and fin. transactions), Assn. of the Bar of City of N.Y., N.Y. County Lawyers Assn., Chgo. Bar Assn., Ill. State Bar Assn., Internat. Bar Assn., Order of Coif, Northwestern Assocs., Chgo. China Sister Cities Comm., Old Willow Club, The Law Club, Phi Beta Kappa. Home: 465 Grove St Glencoe IL 60022-1844 Office: Salans Rockefeller Ctr 620 Fifth Ave New York NY 10020 Office Phone: 212-632-8448. E-mail: lgoldman@salans.com.

GOLDMAN, LYNN ROSE, medical educator; b. Galveston, Tex., Apr. 24, 1951; d. Armond Samuel and Barbara Jean (Bangert) G.; m. Douglas George Hayward. BS, U. Calif., 1976; MPH, Johns Hopkins U., 1981; MS, U. Calif., Berkeley, 1979; MD, U. Calif., San Francisco, 1981. Diplomate Am. Bd. Pediatrics; lic. physician, Calif. Resident in pediatrics Children's Hosp. Med. Ctr., Oakland, Calif., 1985; resident in preventive medicine U. Calif., Berkeley, 1985; pub. health med. officer Calif. Dept. Health Svcs., Berkeley, 1985-91, pub. health med. adminstr., 1991-93; asst. adminstr. Office of Prevention, Pesticides and Toxic Substances, EPA, Washington, 1993-98; prof. Sch. Hygiene and Pub. Health, Johns Hopkins U., Balt., 1999—. Democrat. Office: Johns Hopkins U Bloomberg Sch Pub Health 615 N Wolfe St Rm W8511 Baltimore MD 21205-1900 E-mail: lgoldman@jhsph.edu.

GOLDMAN, MARVIN GERALD, lawyer; b. L.A., June 1, 1939; s. Harry Eli Goldman and Esther Cynthia Brodsky; m. Marilynn Sue Cohen, Oct. 11, 1964; children: Daniel, Sharon, Haviva. AB, UCLA, 1960, JD, 1963; LLM in Comparative Law, NYU, 1964. Bar: Calif. 1964, N.Y. 1966. Assoc. Reid & Priest, N.Y.C., 1965—73; ptnr. Thelen Reid & Priest, N.Y.C., 1974—2004, of counsel, 2004—. Author: El Al: Star in the Sky, 1990; editor Thelen Reid & Priest Doing Business the U.S. Manual, 1999-2004. Ford Found. grantee NYU Sch. Law, 1963-64; Fulbright grantee U.S. Govt. Mexico, 1964-65; UCLA Law Rev. award 1963. Mem. ABA (sect. internat. law, chmn. internat. coml. arbitration com. 1979-83), U.S. Coun. for Internat. Bus. (arbitration com.), World Airline Hist. Soc. Avocations: civil aviation history, antique airline postcards, javanese gamelan, fluorescent minerals. Office: Thelen Reid & Priest LLP 875 3d Ave New York NY 10022-6225 Business E-Mail: mgoldman@thelenreid.com.

GOLDMAN, MICHAEL P., lawyer; b. Chgo., June 10, 1960; s. William J. and Judith Ann (Holleb) G.; m. Karla Sue Berman, June 26, 1983; children: Joshua, Adam, David. BS in Accountancy, U. Ill., 1982; JD cum laude, Loyola U. Chgo., 1985. Bar: Ill. 1985, U.S. Dist. Ct. (no. dist.) Ill. 1985; CPA, Ill. Acct. L. Karp & Sons Inc., Elk Grove Vill., Ill., 1979-81; tax analyst Beatrice Foods Corp., Chgo., 1981-84; ptnr. Katten Muchin & Zavis, Chgo., 1984-2000, Sidley Austin Brown & Wood, Chgo., 2000—. Lectr. in field. Contbr. articles to profl. jours. Bd. dirs. K.I.D.S.S. for Kids (auxiliary of Children's Meml. Hosp., Chgo.), 1993—. Mem. ABA (tort and ins. and bus. law sects.), Chgo. Bar Assn.(ins. and corp. lawcoms.), Ill. CPA Soc. (chmn ins. co. com.), Soc. Fin. Ins. Examiners. Republican. Jewish. Avocations: skiing, handball. Fax: 312-853-7036. E-mail: mgoldman@sidley.com.

GOLDMAN, MICHAEL S., lawyer; b. NYC, Nov. 4, 1962; BA cum laude, Univ. Pa., 1984; JD cum laude, Fordham Univ., 1987. Bar: NY 1988. Assoc. Cravath Swaine & Moore LLP, NYC, 1987—95, ptnr., corp., 1995—. Mem.: ABA, Assn. of Bar of City of NY, NY State Bar Assn. Office: Cravath Swaine & Moore LLP Worldwide Plz 825 Eighth Ave New York NY 10019-7475 Office Phone: 212-474-1929. Office Fax: 212-474-3700. Business E-Mail: mgoldman@cravath.com.

GOLDMAN, NEIL, association administrator; b. St. Louis; married; 3 children. Student, Washington U., St. Louis. Pres. Nat. Mus. Am. Jewish Mil. History, Washington, 1999—2002, nat. ins. chmn., nat. outreach chmn., vice chmn. nat. centennial com.; buyer, merchandiser Mays, St. Louis; sr. buyer, merchandiser Dallas; owner bus. Mem. Dallas Holocaust Ctr., Yad V'Shem Holocaust Mus., Jerusalem. Mem.: Jewish War Vets. U.S.A. (nat. comdr. 1995—96), Disabled Am. Vets. Office: Nat Mus Am Jewish Mil History 1811 R St NW Washington DC 20009-1603

GOLDMAN, NORMAN LEWIS, chemistry professor; b. Bklyn., Aug. 11, 1933; s. Sam and Rose (Schrager) G. BS, CCNY, 1954; AM, Harvard U., 1956; PhD, Columbia U., 1959, Postdoctoral NSF fellow, 1959-60; NIH postdoctoral fellow, Columbia U., N.Y.C., 1960-61. Mem. faculty Queens Coll., CUNY, 1961—, prof. chemistry and biochemistry, 1976-98; prof. chemistry emeritus Queens Coll., 1998—; chmn. dept. Queens Coll., CUNY, 1972-77, acting assoc. dean faculty, 1977-78, acting dean faculty, div. math. and natural scis., 1978-79, dean faculty, div. math. and natural scis., 1979-98. Contbr. articles to profl. jours. Mem. Am. Chem. Soc., Y. Acad. Sci. (vice chair chem. sci. sect. 1998-99, chair 1999-2000), Sigma Xi, Phi Beta Kappa. Home: 75-10 Grand Central Pky Forest Hills NY 11375-5562 Office: CUNY Queens Coll 120 Remsen Hall Flushing NY 11367-1597 Office Phone: 718-997-4196. E-mail: norman_goldman@qc.edu.

GOLDMAN, PATRICIA BAIRD, academic administrator, educator; b. Charleston, W.Va., Sept. 10, 1938; d. William Albert and Genevieve Mary (Lowpine) Baird; m. Richard M. Goldman, June 24, 1979; children: Bruce, Leigh, Crissy, John. BA in English, U. Charleston, 1961; MA in Counseling, W.Va. Grad. Coll., Institute, 1994. Asst. editor W.Va. Edn. Assn., Charleston, 1959-60; tchr. Kanawha County Schs., Charleston, 1961-62, Norfolk (Va.) City Schs., 1963-64, Fairfax County Schs., 1964-78, Tucker County Schs., Parsons, W.Va., 1984-86; tchr., coll. lectr. Davis & Elkins (W.Va.) Coll., 1987-90; exec. dir. Act II Retreat Ctr., St. George, W.Va., 1993—. Mem. adj. faculty dept. counseling W.Va. Grad. Coll. Inst., 1995. Contbr. articles to profl. jours. Chair pub. awareness and edn. com. Tucker County Devel. Authority, Parsons, W.Va., 1986-90; pres., founder. Tucker County Literacy Vols. Am., Parsons, 1987-89. Ogden Meml. scholar, 1957-58. Mem. AAUW (state pres. and v.p. 1990—, grantee 1990-91), ACA, Am. Mental Health Counselors Assn., Internat. Assn. Marriage and Family Counselors, Assn. for Humanistic Edn. and Devel., Alpha Delta Kappa, Phi Mu Gamma. Avocations: writing, clothing design, piano, gardening, reading. Home and Office: 1 Dogwood Ln Saint George WV 26287-9400

GOLDMAN, PETER LOUIS, writer; b. Phila., Feb. 8, 1933; s. Walter and Dorothy (Semple) G.; m. Helen Dudar, July 16, 1961. BA, Williams Coll., 1954; MS, Columbia U., 1955. Staff writer St. Louis Globe Democrat, 1955-62; assoc. editor Newsweek, N.Y.C., 1962-64, gen. editor, 1965-68, sr. editor, 1968-88, contbg. editor, 1988—. Field dir. Spl. Election Unit, 1984—2004. Author: Civil Rights: The Challenge of the Fourteenth Amendment, 1965, Report from Black America, 1970, The Death and Life of Malcolm X, 1973, rev. 2d edit., 1979; co-author: Charlie Company: What Vietnam Did to Us, 1983, The Quest for the Presidency 1984, 1985, The Quest for the Presidency 1988, 1989, Quest for the Presidency 1992, 1994, The End of the World That Was, 1986, Brothers, 1988; editor: The Attentive Eye: Selected Journalism by Helen Dudar, 2002. Nieman fellow, Harvard U., 1961; recipient Sigma Delta Chi award 1962, Robert F. Kennedy Journalism award 1972, ABA Silver Gavel award 1972, Page One awards N.Y. Newspaper Guild, 1967, 72, 86, 88, 89, Nat. Mag. award, 1982, 92, Freedom Found. award, 1982, Am. Legion Fourth Estate award 1982, N.Y. Bar Media award, 1984. Home: 36 Gramercy Park E New York NY 10003-1741 Office: Newsweek 251 W 57th St New York NY 10019 Office Phone: 212-974-3288. E-mail: petergoldman@msn.com.

GOLDMAN, RALPH FREDERICK, research physiologist, educator; b. Boston, Mar. 3, 1928; s. Harry and May (Field) G.; m. Joan R. Krinsky, May 27, 1957; children: Harry, Ellen. BS in Chemistry, U. Denver, 1949; MA in Physiology, Boston U., 1951, PhD in Physiology, 1954; MS in Engring., Northeastern U., Boston, 1962. Rsch. physiologist Natick Labs. U.S. Army, Mass., 1955—61; dir. div. environ. medicine U.S. Army Rsch. Inst., Natick, 1961—82; prin. cons. Dept. of Army for Environ. Physiology, Natick, 1971—82; chief scientist Multi-Tech Corp., Natick, 1982—88; chief scientist, R&D, clothing and human comfort Comfort Tech., Inc., Framingham, Mass., 1989—; sr. cons. tech. and product devel. Arthur D. Little, Inc., Cambridge, Mass., 1993—97. Adj. prof. Boston U., 1970—, N.C. State U., 1989—; lectr. MIT, Cambridge, 1974-94; vis. scientist Peoples Rep. of China, 1981—; vis. scholar lectr. Springfield (Mass.) Coll., 1977, Ohio State U., 1977, 88; chmn. rsch. group biomed. effects of clothing, NATO, 1981-86. Author: 2 books; contbr. over 500 articles, abstracts and tech. reports to profl. jours., 22 chpts. to books. Scoutmaster Boy Scouts Am., Framingham, Mass., 1956-90, exec. bd., 1991-2002; mem. town meeting Town of Framingham, 1983-88. Recipient Meritorious Civilian Svc. award U.S. Army R&D Command, 1963, Exceptional Civilian Svc. award Sec. of Army, 1976, Sr. Exec. Svc. award U.S. Civil Svc., 1979, Silver Beaver award Boy Scouts Am., 1981. Fellow: ASHRAE (life; bd. dirs. 1982—85, assoc. editor HVAC&R Rsch. 1995—2001, Disting. Fellow award 1992), Am. Coll. Sports Medicine (editl. bd. 1979—85), Ergonomics Soc. (hon.); mem.: ASTM, IEEE (life; AEMB Coun. 1978—84), Assn. Mil. Surgeons U.S., Am. Physiol. Soc. (editl. bd. 1972—78), Framingham Amateur Radio Assn. (treas. 1970—84), Tarpon Cove Yacht and Racquet Club, Naples, Fla. Jewish. Avocations: piano, gardening, duplicate bridge, tennis. Office: Comfort Tech 7 W Trevor Hill Plymouth MA 02360 E-mail: ralphgoldman@cs.com.

GOLDMAN, RALPH MORRIS, political science professor; b. Bklyn., May 14, 1920; s. Benjamin and Rose (Smotritski) G.; m. Joan Alicia Walsh, Oct. 20, 1953 (div. Feb. 1990); children: Peter Timothy, Marjorie Edythe; m. Barbara Elizabeth Alban, Mar. 24, 1990. BA, NYU, 1947; MA, U. Chgo., 1948, PhD, 1951. Rsch. assoc. Brookings Instn., Washington, 1953-56; asst. prof., then assoc. prof. Mich. State U., East Lansing, 1956-62; prof. San Francisco State U., 1962-86, prof. emeritus, 1987—, dir. Inst. for Rsch. on Internat. Behavior, 1964-67, dean faculty rsch., 1965-67, chmn. dept. polit. sci., 1971-74. Pres. Ctr. for Party Devel., Washington and Seattle, 1992-2003; dir. Congrl. Studies Program Cath. U., Washington, 1992-96; vis. prof. Am. U., Washington, 1955, 85, 90, U. Chgo., 1961-62, U. Calif., Berkeley, 1963, Stanford (Calif.) U., 1966, U. Calif., San Diego, 1979; cons. rsch. divsn. Dem. Nat. Com., Washington, 1952, 86; cons. Ednl. Testing Svc., Princeton, N.J., 1976-77, CEELI ABA, 1993-96; commentator on pub. affairs Voice of Am., Washington, 1985-86; sr. cons. Nat. Dem. Inst. for Internat. Affairs, Washington, 1986-89. Author: Contemporary Perspectives on Politics, 1972, Behavioral Perspectives on American Politics, 1973, Search for Consensus: The Story of the Democratic Party, 1979, Arms Control and Peacekeeping: Feeling Safe in This World, 1982, Dilemma and Destiny: The Democratic Party in America, 1986, The National Party Chairmen and Committees: Factionalism at the Top, 1990, From Warfare to Party Politics: The Critical Transition to Civilian Control, 1990, How to Build and Maintain a Democratic Party System, 1993, The United Nation in the Beginning: Conflict Processes, Colligation, Cases, 2001, The Future Catches Up: Selected Writings of Ralph M. Goldman, 4 vols., 2002, The Mentor and the Protege: The Story of Presidents Calles and Cardenas, 2003, From DNA to Culture: The Synthesis Principle in Human Development, 2003; co-author: The Politics of National Party Conventions, 1960, Political Science Concept Inventory, 1979, Building Trust: An Introduction to Peace Keeping and Arms Control, 1997; also contbr. chpts. to books and encys.; editor: Transnational Parties; Organizing the World's Precincts, 1983; co-editor: Presidential Nominating Politics in 1952, 1954, Promoting Democracy: Opportunities and Issues, 1988; contbg. editor: Encyclopedia of American Political Parties and Elections, 1991; mem. editorial com. Background jour., 1963-66; mem. editorial bd. Ctr. for Study of Armament and Disarmament, 1984—; founding editor Party Devels., 1993-99. Bd. dirs. Frederic Burk Found. for Edn., San Francisco, 1967-78, chmn. bd., 1968-71; coord. Peace Force Proposition Campaign, San Francisco, 1972-73. Capt. U.S. Army, 1946. Edward Hillman fellow U. Chgo., 1948-49, Social Sci. Rsch. Coun. fellow, 1949-50, Air Force Office of Sci. Rsch., 1958; grantee U.S. Office of Naval Rsch., 1968, NSF, 1968-69. Mem. Am. Polit. Sci. Assn. (life), Internat. Polit. Sci. Assn., Internat. Studies Assn., Assn. to Unite the Democracies (bd. dirs. 1989-95). Democrat. Avocation: ballroom dancing. Home: 6825 117th Ave NE Kirkland WA 98033-8451 E-mail: rmgoldman@aol.com.

GOLDMAN, RICHARD HARRIS, lawyer, director; b. Boston, June 17, 1936; s. Charles M. and Irene M. (Marks) Goldman; m. Patricia Grollman, June 21, 1959; children: Elaine, Stephen. BA, Wesleyan U., 1958; LLB, NYU, 1961. Bar: Mass. 1961, U.S. Dist. Ct. Mass. 1961. Mem. Slater & Goldman, Boston, 1961—76, Widett, Slater & Goldman, PC, Boston, 1976—93, Sullivan & Worcester LLP, Boston, 1993—. Past trustee, chmn. audit com. and clk. Grove Bank. Co-author: The Ritual Dance Between Lessee and Lender; contbr. articles to profl. jours. Former chmn. Newton (Mass.) Human Rights Commn.; hon. trustee, former v.p. Temple Israel. Recipient Cmty. Svc. award, Am. Jewish Cmty., 2003. Mem.: ABA, Mass. Conveyancers Assn., Boston Bar Assn. (chmn. leasing com. 1996—97, lectr., chmn. seminar comml. real estate fin. 1997, real estate steering com. 1997—, co-chair real estate sect. 1999—2002, co-chair sr. lawyer sect. 2003—), Mass. Bar Assn., Belmont Country Club (v.p., sec.). Home: 47 Vaughn Ave Newton MA 02461-1038 Office: Sullivan & Worcester LLP 1 Post Office Sq Ste 2300 Boston MA 02109-2129 Office Phone: 617-338-2942. E-mail: rgoldman@sandw.com.

GOLDMAN, RICHARD N., foundation administrator; b. San Francisco, Apr. 16, 1920; s. Richard and Alice Goldman; m. Rhoda Haas (dec.); children: Richard (dec.), John, Douglas, Susan. BA, U. Calif., Berkeley, 1941, postgrad. Chmn. Goldman Ins. Svcs.; pres. Richard and Rhoda Goldman Fund. Former mem. port commn., pub. utilities commn., chief of protocol City and County of San Francisco. Trustee World Fine Arts Mus. San Francisco, Nat. Symphony, U. Calif.-Berkeley Berkeley Found., Washington Inst. for Near East Policy, World Affairs Coun. No. Calif.; bd. dirs. Am. Jewish History Soc., Internat. House, Berkeley, Jerusalem Found., League to Save Lake Tahoe, San Francisco Ballet; mem. coun. Yosemite Fund; mem. exec. com. Bay Area Internat. Forum; mem. dv. com. Bus. Execs. for Nat. Security; bd. visitors Inst. for Internat. Studies, Stanford U.; bd. dirs., former pres. Jewish Cmty. Fedn., San Francisco; mem. adv. coun. Pacific Grad. Sch. Psychology; mem. governing coun. Save-the-Redwoods League; mem. pres.' adv. coun. San Francisco State U. With U.S. Army, 1942-46. Recipient The Chairman's Medal, Heinz Awards, 2005. Mem. San Francisco Planning and Urban Renewal Assn. (mem. adv. coun.), Concordia-Argonaut Club, The Family, Villa Taverna, Calif. Tennis Club. Office: Richard and Rhoda Goldman Fund 1 Lombard St Ste 303 San Francisco CA 94111-1130

GOLDMAN, ROBERT W., retired gas and oil industry executive; Mgmt. DuPont, 1965-88; v.p., controller Conoco, 1988-98, sr. v.p., CFO, 1998—. Mem. Am. Petroleum Inst. (gen. com.), Fin. Execs. Inst. Office: Conoco 600 N Dairy Ashford Rd Houston TX 77079

GOLDMAN, STANFORD MILTON, medical educator; b. Salt Lake City, Nov. 28, 1940; s. Osher and Miriam (Solomon) G.; m. Harriet Kaplow, Apr. 2, 1965; children: Etan, Nava. BA, BRE, Yeshiva U., 1961; MD, Einstein Coll. Medicine, 1965. Intern Jefferson U. Sch. Medicine, Phila., 1965-66; resident Einstein Coll. Medicine, Bronx, 1966-69; chmn. dept. radiology USPHS Phoenix Indian Med. Ctr., 1969-71; asst. prof. radiology Einstein Coll. Medicine, Bronx, 1971-72; from instr. to asst. prof. radiology Johns Hopkins U. Sch. Medicine, Balt., 1972-79; from asst. prof. to assoc. prof. U. Md., Balt., 1975-81; assoc. prof. Johns Hopkins U., 1979-86; clin. prof. Uniformed Svcs. U., Bethesda, Md., 1981-94; prof. radiology Johns Hopkins U., 1986-94, prof. urology, 1988-93; prof., chmn. radiology U. Tex. Med. Sch., Houston, 1993—2000, prof. urology, 1995—, prof. radiology, 1993—. Adj. prof. radiology and urology Baylor Coll. Medicine, Houston, 1994—; med. dir. radiol. sch. tech. Houston C.C., 1994, ultrasound sch. tech., 1999-2001; prof. radiology M.D. Anderson Cancer Ctr., Houston, 1995—. Editor: Computed Tomography of Kidneys & Adrenals, 1983, CT & MRI of the Genitourinary Tract, 1990, Tc E Rm Del Trattos Genito-Urinario, 1994; assoc. editor: Urologic Radiology, 1982-85, Radiology, 1986-94; cons. editor Urology, 1998—. Mem. Radiation Control Adv. Bd., Md., 1989—93. Lt. comdr. USPHS, 1969—71. Recipient Albert Einstein Disting. Alumni award, 1996. Mem.: AMA (CPT adv. bd. 1995—2000), Johns Hopkins Med. and Surg. Assn., Assn. Univ. Radiologists (rep. AMA CPT adv. bd. 1995—2000, ethics com. 1997, nominating com. 1997—98), European Soc. Urogenital Radiology, Houston Radiol. Soc. (treas. 2000—, pres.-elect 2001, pres. 2002, past pres. 2003, chmn. nominating com. 2003, chmn. bd. trustees 2005—, bd. trustees 2005—, chmn. judicial affairs com. 2005—, chmn. nominating com. 2005—, bd. govs. 2005—, chmn. bylaws com. 2005—), Houston Med. Soc., Tex. Radiol. Soc. (program com. 1994—96, chmn. long range planning com. 1996—97, bd. dirs. 1996—, fellowship nominating com. 1998—2000, 2d v.p. 2001, 1st v.p. 2002, chmn. program com. 2002—03, exec. com. 2002—, pres.-elect 2003, chmn. legis. com. 2003—04, pres. 2004—05, chair orgnl. structure coun. 2005—, chair nominating com. 2005—, chair jud. affairs com. 2005—, bd. govs. 2005—, bd. trustees 2005—, chair bd. trustees 2005—, chmn. Bit245), Tex. Med. Soc. (chmn. bylaws com. 2005—), Soc. Uroradiology (bd. dirs. 1992—98, med. equipment com. 2000—01, ethics com.), Radiol. Soc. N.Am. (chmn. sci. exhibits awards com. 1988—90, chmn. program coms. subcom. on gu radiology 1996—99), Am. Urol. Assn. (hematuria guidelines panel 1998—99), Am. Soc. Emergency Medicine (bd. dirs. 1994—, indsl. com. 1994—, abstract com. 1995—97, chmn. audit com. 1995—99, chmn. sci. program com. 1996—97, vice chair program com. 1996—97, fin. com. 1996—98, site com. 1996—98, ad hoc audit com. 1996—, sec.-treas. 1998—2000, exec. com. 1998—, mem. exec. com. 1998—, sec.-treas. 2001, pres.-elect 2001—02, pres. 2002—04, nominating com. 2002—, chair site selection com. 2002—, past pres. 2004—, chmn. by laws com. 2004—, mem. edn. and rsch. com 2004—, past pres. 2004—, site selection com., mem. edn. and rsch. com.,), Am. Roentgen Ray Soc., Am. Coll. Radiology (alt.-counselor from Tex. 1995—96, counselor from Tex. 1996—2002, mem. com. on coding and nomenclature of commn. on econs. 1996—2002, nominating com. 1999, co-chmn. nominating comm. 2000—01, alt. counselor 2002—05, alt. counselor from Tex. 2002—, ACR liaison to com. on Trauma, Am. Coll. Surgeons 2004—), U.S.-Israel Bi-Nat. Sci. Found., Albert Einstein Alumni Assn. (bd. dirs. 1991—2002, Disting. Alumni award 1996), U. Md. Alumni Assn. (assoc.). Jewish. Avocations: swimming, music. Office: U Tex Med Sch Dept Radiology 6431 Fannin St Ste 2100 Houston TX 77030-1501 Office Phone: 713-704-1714. Business E-Mail: stanford.m.goldman@uth-tmc.edu.

GOLDMAN, STANLEY A., law educator; BA magna cum laude, U. Calif.; JD cum laude, Loyola Law Sch. Dep. public defender LA County; prof. Loyola Law Sch., LA; spl. correspondent CBS; host numerous TV programs CNBC; legal correspondent, legal affairs editor Fox News Network. Legal columnist NY Daily News; appeared on over 1,500 TV programs and 500 radio shows. Contbr. articles to profl. jours. Office: 919 Albany St Los Angeles CA 90015-1211 Office Phone: 213-736-1092. Office Fax: 213-380-3769. E-mail: stanley.goldman@lls.edu.

GOLDMAN, STUART MILES, podiatrist; b. Phila., Pa., May 26, 1955; s. Albert and Minnie Goldman; m. Debbie Schlecker, Sept. 4, 1988; children: Nechama, Aryeh, Goldie, Shoshana, Avraham. BA, Dickenson Coll., 1976; Doctorate in podiatric medicine, PA Coll. of Podiatric Medicine, 1980. Cert. Foot and Ankle Surgery Am. Bd. of Podiatric Surgery, 1984. Author: Neurogenic Positional Pedal Neuritis: Pedal Manifestations of Spinal Stenosis, Value of a Grocery Cart and Wheeled Walker in Identification and Management of Symptomatic Spinal Stenosis in Patients presenting with Neuropathy or Claudication., Diabetic Peripheral Neuropathy or Spinal Stenosis: Prevalence of Overlap or Misdiagnosis, Spinal Stenosis: Positional History, Positional Testing, Positional Therapy Facilitate Identification and Management of Lower Extremity Symptoms, Nocturnal Neuropathic Pain in Diabetics: It may be Caused by Spinal Stenosis; contbr. articles various profl. jours. Mohel, Fla. Fellow: Am. Coll. of Foot and Ankle Surgeons. Jewish. Achievements include research in spinal stenosis: A common cause of podiatric symptoms; diabetic peripheral neuropathy or spinal stenosis: Prevelance of overlap of misdiagnosis. Avocations: story teller, teacher, guitar. Home: 7539 London Ln Boca Raton FL 33433 Office: South Fla Foot Ctr 1905 Clint Moore Rd Ste 310 Boca Raton FL 33496 Office Phone: 561-995-0229. Personal E-mail: podmohel@aol.com.

GOLDMAN, WILLIAM, writer, scriptwriter; b. Chgo., Aug. 12, 1931; s. M. Clarence and Marion (Well) Goldman; m. Ilene Jones, Apr. 15, 1961; children: Jenny, Susanna. BA, Oberlin Coll., 1952; MA, Columbia U., 1956. Author: (novels) The Temple of Gold, 1957, Your Turn to Curtsy, My Turn to Bow, 1958, Soldier in the Rain, 1960, Boys and Girls Together, 1964, No Way to Treat a Lady, 1964, The Thing of It Is, 1967, Father's Day, 1971, The Princess Bride, 1973, Marathon Man, 1974, Wigger, 1974, Magic, 1976, Tinsel, 1979, Control, 1982, The Silent Gondoliers, 1983, The Color of Light, 1984, Heat, 1985, Brothers, 1987, (non-fiction) The Season: A Candid Look at Broadway, 1969, Adventures in the Screen Trade, 1983; author: (with Mike Lupica) Wait Until Next year, 1988, Hype and Glory, 1990, Four Screenplays, 1995, Five Screenplays, 1997, Which Lie Did I Tell, 2000; author: (essays) The Big Picture, 1999; author: (with James Goldman) (plays) Blood Sweat and Stanley Poole, 1961; author: (with James Goldman and John Kander) (musical) A Family Affair, 1962; author: (films) Masquerade, 1965, Harper, 1966, Butch Cassidy and the Sundance Kid, 1969 (Acad. award Best Original Screenplay, 1970), The Hot Rock, 1972, The Stepford Wives, 1974, The Great Waldo Pepper, 1975, Marathon Man, 1976, All the President's Men, 1976 (Acad. award Best Screenplay Adaptation, 1977), A Bridge Too Far, 1977, Magic, 1978, The Princess Bride, 1987, Heat, 1987, Misery, 1990, The Year of the Comet, 1992, Memoirs of an Invisible Man, 1992, Chaplin, 1992, Maverick, 1994, Ghost and the Darkness, 1996, Absolute Power, 1997, Hearts in Atlantis, 2001, Dreamcatcher, 2003. Recipient Laurel award for Lifetime Achievement in Screenwriting, 1983. Office: c/o William Morris 151 El Camino Dr Beverly Hills CA 90212-1804

GOLDMANN, JAMES ALLEN, healthcare consultant; b. Milw., Feb. 26, 1952; s. Allen Abraham and Ruth Lois (Kolbur) G.; m. Pamela Anne McCole, June 6, 1980; children: Michael, Elissa, Kerry. AB, Harvard Coll., 1974; MHA, Washington U., St. Louis, 1979. V.p. Riverside Meth. Hosp., Columbus, Ohio, 1980—85; COO Children's Med. Ctr., Dallas, 1986—92; cons. APM, Inc., N.Y.C., 1993—96; ptnr. Arthur Andersen, Dallas, 1996—2000, IBM, Dallas, 2001—03, JHD Group, Dallas, 2004—. Bd. dirs. Hope Cottage, Dallas, 1989-93; scout leader Boy Scouts Am., Columbus and Grapevine, Tex., 1980-84, 92, 93. Fellow Am. Coll. Healthcare Execs. Office: JHD Group 5001 Spring Valley Rd Ste 400E Dallas TX 75244 Office Phone: 972-383-1255. E-mail: jgoldmann@jhdgroup.com.

GOLDMANN, MORTON AARON, cardiologist, educator; b. Chgo., July 11, 1924; s. Harry Ascher and Frieda (Cohon) G.; m. Doris-Jane Tumpeer, July 18, 1951; children: Deborah, Jory, Erica, Leslie BS, U. Ill., 1943, MD, 1946. Diplomate Am. Bd. Internal Medicine. Intern Cook County Hosp., Chgo., 1946-47, resident physician, 1949-52, practice medicine specializing in internal medicine and cardiology Skokie, Ill., 1952—2003, trustee emeritus, 2003—; chief of medicine Rush North Shore Med. Ctr. (formerly Skokie Valley Hosp.), 1964-65, also trustee, 1968—2002, trustee emeritus, 2002—, pres. med. staff, 1968-69, attending physician, med. dir. heart sta. and cardiac rehab. unit, 1973-96, bd. dirs., 1970—; former attending physician Ill. Rsch. Hosp.; former assoc. prof. Abraham Lincoln Sch. Medicine, U. Ill., Chgo.; prof. Cook County Grad. Sch. Medicine. Pres. Heart Assn. North Cook County, 1978-81, North Suburban Assn. Health Resources, 1974-77 Contbr. numerous articles to profl. jours. Capt. M.C., AUS, 1947-49, PTO Fellow ACP, Inst. Medicine Chgo., Am. Coll. Cardiology; mem. AMA, Am. Soc. Internal Medicine, Am. Heart Assn., Ill. Med. Soc., Chgo. Med. Soc., Chgo. Heart Assn. (bd. govs., bd. dirs. 1978-87, bd. trustees 1979-83).

GOLDNER, BRIAN, toy company executive; V.p., mgmt. dir. J. Walter Thompson, 1994—95, sr. ptnr., mgmt. dir., 1995—97; sr. ptnr., worldwide dir. JWT Entertainment, J. Walter Thompson, 1997; exec. v.p., sales and mktg. Bandai America Inc., 1997—99, exec. v.p., COO, 1999—2000; sr. exec. v.p., COO, Tiger Electronics Ltd. (subs. Hasbro Inc.), 2000; sr. v.p., gen. mgr., U.S. Toys Hasbro Inc., 2000—01, pres., U.S. Toy Segment, 2001—. Office: Hasbro Inc 1027 Newport Ave Pawtucket RI 02862

GOLDNER, JANET, artist; b. Washington, June 6, 1952; d. Lester and Claire (Weiner) G. BA, Antioch Coll., 1974; MA, NYU, 1981; travels in West Africa, Experiment in Internat. Living, 1973; studies with Nancy Graves, Mac Adams, N.Y.C., 1980. Artist in residence U. Georgia Studies Abroad, Cortona, Italy, 1987. Dir. art workshop series Until That Last Breath: Women With AIDS, Beth Israel Hosp., N.Y.C., 1988-89; dir., curator South African Women Artists in Resistance Exhbn., catalogue, panel, 1988-90. One woman show Stamford Mus., 1977, 80, Washington Square East Galleries, 1978, 80, Phoenix Gallery, N.Y.C., 1983, Elmira Coll., 1984, Soho 20 Gallery, 1989; exhibited in group shows at Bell Gallery, 1977, Phoenix Gallery, 1981-82, Langman Gallery, 1983, 4x27 Women Collaborate Gallery, 345, 1983, BFM Gallery, 1984, 55 Mercer Gallery, N.Y.C., 1985, Cornell Coll., Mt. Vernon, Ia., 1985, Women's Studio Workshop, Rosendale, N.Y., 1985, Zeus Trabia Gallery, N.Y.C., 1986, Bronx Mus., 1987, AIR Gallery, N.Y.C., 1988, Cortona, Italy, 1988, Air Gallery, N.Y.C., 1987, New Mus., N.Y.C., 1989, Women's Bldg., L.A., 1989, Pyramid Art Ctr., Rochester, N.Y., 1988, Kulturforum, Monchengladbach, Fed. Republic Germany, 1989; represented in numerous pub. and pvt. collections; works include Fiber Forest, 1976-80, Prehistoric Sites, 1981—, site specific sculptures, Auslerlitz, N.Y., 1981, Bethesda, Md., 1981, 82, Wilton, Conn., 1982. Participant Forum '85, United Nations Women's Conf., Nairobi, Kenya. Fellow Millay Colony for the Arts, 1981, Va. Ctr. for Creative Arts, 1982, 88, Yaddo, Saratoga Springs, N.Y., 1982; recipient award Visual Artists Exchange, N.Y. Feminist Art Inst., 1983. Mem. Coll. Art Assn., Nat. Women's Studies Assn., Women's Caucus for Art (nat. adv. bd. 1986—). Office: 52 Warren St New York NY 10007-1035

GOLDNER, SHELDON HERBERT, retired import/export company executive; b. Bklyn., Aug. 3, 1928; s. David and Esther (Maskowsky) G.; m. Lila Diane Silber, Aug. 14, 1954; children: Jonathan Shepard, Jeffrey Scott, Barbara Jill. BS in acctg., L.I. U., 1950. C.P.A., N.Y. Acct. S.H. Goldner & Co., N.Y.C., 1950-59; v.p. fin. Connell Rice & Sugar Co., Inc., Westfield, N.J., 1959-89, ret., 1989. Pres., trustee Temple Israel, Union, N.J. Served with U.S. Army Signal Corps, 1946-47, PTO. Mem. AICPA, N.Y. State Soc. CPAs, Halloween Yacht Club (Stamford, Conn.), Royal Veere (Netherlands) Yacht Club, Dartmouth Yacht Club (Devon, Eng.), Miles River Yacht Club (St. Michaels, Md.).

GOLDPAUGH BROWN, BETHANY J. (BEVERLY), theater educator, writer, costume designer; b. Columbus, Ohio, Aug. 25, 1951; d. Francis Duane Brown and Jerrene Chambers Hartshorn; m. Thomas Walter Goldpaugh, Aug. 24, 1974 (div. Apr. 1, 1985); 1 child, Matthew Ambrose Goldpaugh. B cum laude, Ohio U., 1973; MS in Edn., SUNY, New Paltz, 1976, MA in Eng., 1999. Lic. tchr. N.Y. State Bd. Regents, 1977, cert. tchr. Alexander technique Alexander Found. of Phila., 1991. Pub. sch. tchr. Ulster and Dutchess County Sch. Dists., NY, 1976—2002; tchr. Alexander Alliance, Rosendale, NY, 1991—2003. Playwright Three Women of Paris, 2003; contbr. short story; dancer Tara Senwerville Dancers, 1998—2005; author: (novel) Charity Begins at Home, 2004; costume designer Sylvia, Much Ado About Nothing, Comedy of Errors, Conference of the Birds, 2002—04, Toulouse!, 2002—04; actor: Much Ado About Nothing, Comedy of Errors, Conference of the Birds, Twelth Night, Madwoman of Chaillot; playwright Three New Lives, 2002, Three Women, Three Lives, Amelia Earhart Speaks After 50 Years, 2000, Methodist Church Activity, 1999—2005. Worship com., choir mem. United Meth. Ch., New Paltz, 1999—2003. Fellow, SUNY, Eng. Dept., New Paltz, 1973—74; grantee, SUNY, New Paltz, 1975—76. Methodist. Avocations: set design, ballet, travel, baking, interior design. Home: 1012 Creek Locks Rd Rosendale NY 12472 Office Phone: 845-338-4759. Personal E-mail: highpeke@aol.com.

GOLDREICH, PETER MARTIN, astrophysics and planetary physics educator; b. N.Y.C., July 14, 1939; s. Paul and Edith (Rosenfield) Goldreich; m. Susan Kroll, June 14, 1960; children: Eric, Daniel. BS in Physics, Cornell U., 1960, PhD in Physics, 1963. Instr. Cornell U., summers, 1961—63; post-doctoral fellow Cambridge U., 1963—64; asst. prof. astronomy and geophysics UCLA, 1964—66, assoc. prof., 1966; assoc. prof. planetary sci. and astronomy Calif. Inst. Tech., 1966—69, prof. planetary sci. and astronomy, 1969—, Lee DuBridge prof. astrophysics and planetary science physics, 1981—, emeritus. Named Calif. Scientist of Yr., 1981; recipient Chapman medal, Royal Astron. Soc., 1985, Gold medal, 1990, Nat. medal of Sci., 1995; fellow Woodrow Wilson hon., 1960—61, NSF, 1961—63, Sloan Found., 1968—70. Fellow: NAS, Am. Acad. Arts and Scis.; mem.: Royal Soc. (foreign mem. 2003—), Am. Astron. Soc. (Henry Norris Russell lectr., Dick Brouwer award 1986, George P. Kuiper prize divsn. planetary sci. 1992). Office: Calif Inst Tech Msc 150-21 1200 E California Blvd Pasadena CA 91125-0001

GOLDRICK, HEIDI ELIZABETH, language educator; b. New Bedford, Mass., Sept. 22, 1976; d. Everett Anthony and Pamela Ann Goldrick. BA in English, Bridgewater State Coll., 1998, MA in English, 2002. English tchr. Taunton (Mass.) H.S., 1998; ELA curriculum supr. Taunton Pub. Sch., 2002—. Profl. devel. instr. Taunton Pub. Sch., 2000—. Mem. adv. bd. Greater New Bedford (Mass.) Regional Vocat. H.S., New Bedford, Mass., 1993. Achievements include research in treatment of language in adolescent fantasy literature. Office: Taunton Pub Sch 50 Williams St Taunton MA 02780 Office Phone: 508-821-1126.

GOLDRING, ELIZABETH, environmental media artist, poet; b. Forest City, Iowa, Feb. 13, 1945; d. James C. and Vera (Farrington) Olson; m: Otto Piene, 1 child, Jessica Tova Farrington Goldring. BA cum laude, Smith Coll., 1967; MEd, Harvard U., 1978. Art tchr. St. Louis Pub. Schs.; exhibits developer The Children's Mus., Boston, 1973-76; fellow Ctr. for Advanced Visual Studies MIT, Cambridge, Mass., 1977—96, exhibits and projects dir. Ctr. for Advanced Visual Studies, 1977—97, lectr. Dept. of Architecture, 1989—94; sr. fellow CAVS/MIT, 1996—. Co-dir. Sky Art Conf., CAVS, MIT, 1981—; mem. adv. coun. on art-sci. tech. MIT, 1994—; corr. mem. European Acad. Arts, Scis., Humanities; project dir. Desert Sun/Desert Moon, Lone Pine, Calif., 1986. Prin. works include with CAVS/MIT ICA, Boston, 1976, Documenta 6, Kassel, 1977, Smithsonian Institution, Washington, 1978, Secession, Vienna, 1979, Musee de l'art Moderne del la Ville de Paris, 1985, Eye/Sight interactive installations Lights/Orot, prin. works include Yeshiva U. Mus., N.Y.C., 1988, Kunstverein Karlsruhe, Fed. Republic Germany, 1988, Celebration of light, Savolinna, Finland, 1989, Washington Project for the Arts, 1989, MIT Mus., 1994, A Visual Language for the Blind and Retina Prints, 1991—; artist/producer (tapes with Vin Grabill) The Inner Eye-From the Inside Out, 1985, A Visual Language for the Blind, 1991, Interactive Cybervision Environments for the Blind, 1996, Eye Dance, 2000, (audiotapes) International Alarm, 1982, Der Hahnenschrei, 1983, Coyote, 1986, Kikeriki, 1989; co-author: (book) Sky Art Manifesto, 1996, (poetry books include) Laser Treatment, 1983, Without Warning, 1985, A Prairie Schooner Portfolio, 2001, EY-, 2002, Groliers Poetry Reading Series, 2003; exhibitions include Compton Gallery, MIT, 2003, Groton Sch., 2003, Adams House, Harvard U., 2003; contbr. various pubs. Named one of Best and Brightest, Tech. Rev., 1998; named to Prix Arts Electronics honorable mention, 1996; recipient article New Eng. Jour. Optometry, 1990, Smith Coll. medalist, 2004; fellow Charlotte Moorman, MIT, 1997; grantee NEA InterArts, 1985, Diabetes Rsch. and Edn., 1986, NASA, 2002, MIT Coun. for the Arts, 2002. Office: MIT Ctr Adv Visual Studies MIT N 52 265 Mass Ave Cambridge MA 02139-4312 Office Phone: 617-253-4517. Business E-Mail: goldring@mit.edu.

GOLDRING, NANCY DEBORAH, artist, educator; b. Oak Ridge, Jan. 25, 1945; d. David and Evelyn (Lasky) G. BA, Smith Coll., 1967; MFA, NYU, 1969-70. Instr. English lit. U. Pisa, Italy, 1967-68; lectr. sculpture Sch. Visual Arts, N.Y.C., 1970-71; lectr. art history Fashion Inst. Tech., N.Y.C., 1971; vis. lectr./critic RISD, Providence, 1974-75; artist-in-residence Haverford Coll., Pa., 1978; prof. dept. art Montclair (N.J.) State U., 1972—. Lectr., cons. in field. One-woman shows include Carlsson Meml. Gallery, Bridgeport, Conn., 1979, Gladstone-Villani Gallery, N.Y.C., 1979, Monique Knowlton Gallery, N.Y.C., 1979, Nassau County Mus., 1980-81, Inst. for Architecture and Urban Studies, N.Y.C., 1980-81, Am. Cultural Ctrs. Jerusalem and Tel Aviv and Gallery Haifa U., 1982, Miss. Mus. Art, Open Gallery, Jackson, Miss., 1983, Herzliya Mus., A&M Artworks, N.Y.C., 1984-85, Michael Bennett Gallery, N.Y.C., 1986, Galleria S.Fedele, Milan, Italy, 1986, Inst. d'Arte, Dossa Dossi, Ferrara, Italy, 1986, Drury Coll., Mo., 1988, Jayne H. Baum, N.Y.C., 1988, 90, 93, Meridian Gallery, San Francisco, 1991, Istituto d'Arte, Dosso Dossi, Ferrara, Italy, 1991, Eliot Smith Gallery, St. Louis, 1992, Grand Cen. Sta., N.Y.C., 1992, Jayne H. Baum Gallery, N.Y.C., 1993, Hampshire Coll. Amherst Coll., 1993, Elliot Smith Gallery, St. Louis, 1994, Duane Reed Gallery, 1996, ACTA Internat., Rome, 1996, Nat. Ctr. Performing Arts, Bombay, 1997, DIF Web Gallery, U. Houston, 2000, Alva Gallery, New London, Conn., 2000, S.E. Mus. Photography, Daytona Beach, 2000, Baruch Coll., N.Y.C., 2001, Houston Ctr. for Photography, 2002, Lyman Allen Mus., New London, Conn., 2002, Comune di Parma, San Vitale, Italy, 2003, Palazzo Pigorini Parma, 2005, Fotofo, Bratislava, Czech Republic, 2003; exhibited in group shows at Muse Gallery, Phila., 1980, Rabinovitch Gallery, 1981, Ohio State Galleries, Columbus, 1982, Gallery North, Setauket, N.Y., 1982, Mus. Modern Art, 1983, Galleria D'Arte E Architettura Moderna, Rome, 1983-84, A.I.R. Gallery, N.Y.C., 1984, 86, Allen/Wincor Gallery, N.Y.C., 1985, Jayne H. Baum Gallery U. Calif., Berkeley, 1987-90, SSC&B, Lintas Internat., N.Y.C., 1987, Alternative Mus. N.Y.C., 1987-88, Copley Soc., Boston, 1987, R.H. Love Gallery, Chgo., 1988, Haggerty Mus., Milw., 1988, White Columns, 1989, Squibb Corp., Princeton, 1989, Bard Coll., 1989, Nat. Mus. Am. Art, 1989, Nat. Mus. Am. Art, Washington, 1989, Jayne H. Baum Gallery, N.Y., 1989, Burden Gallery, N.Y., 1990, Photographic Resource Ctr. with Boston Archtl. Ctr., 1990, West Collection Traveling exhbn., 1990-91, Andrea Ruggieri Gallery, Washington, 1990, Ellis Island, N.Y., 1990-92, Polaroid at Fotokine, Cologne, Germany, 1990, Art Mus. Fla. Internat. U., 1991, Montclair State U., 1991, Pacific Security, L.A., 1992, Campion Corp., 1992, Palazzo Cini, Ferrera, Italy, 1993, Elliot Smith Gallery, St. Louis, 1993, Caldwell Coll., N.J., 1994, Southeast Mus., Daytona, Fla., 1995, NYU, 1995, Duane Reed Gallery, St. Louis, 1995, Ctr. Photography, Tokyo, 1996, Katonah Mus., N.Y., 1996, SOHO, N.Y., 1996, Trinity Coll., 1997, Pitts. Ctr. Arts, 1997, Internat. Ctr. Photography, 1997, S.E. Mus. Photography, 1998, Alva Gallery, 1999-2000, 03, Contemporary Mus., Balt., 2000, William Benton Mus., U. Conn., 2002, Gallery Showcase, Sothebys, N.Y.C., 2002, Santa Fe Art Inst., 2002, Gallery 138, N.Y.C., 2004, Smith Coll., Mass., 2005, Bayley Mus., Va., 2005, others; represented in permanent collections at Bibliotheque Nationale, Paris, Herzlyia Mus., Israel, Eastman House Kodak Mus., I.T.T. of N.J., Padiglione d'Arte Contemporanea, Milan, IBM, Polaroid Corp., Citybank, NYNEX Corp., others; contbr. articles to profl. jours Grantee Montclair State U. Art Dept., 1982-87, N.Y. State Coun. Arts, 1978-79, 86—; NDEA fellow, 1967; Fulbright fellow, 1967-68, Fulbright S.E. Asia fellow, 1994-95; NYU grad. teaching fellow, 1969-70, others; Disting. scholar Montclair State U., 2003. Mem. Interarts. Office: Montclair State Univ Art Dept Calcia Hall Upper Montclair NJ 07043

GOLDRING, NORMAN MAX, advertising executive; b. Chgo., June 22, 1937; s. Jack and Carolyn (Wolf) G.; m. Cynthia Lois Garland, Dec. 20, 1959; children: Jay Marshall, Diane. BS in Bus., Miami (Ohio) U., 1959; MBA, U. Chgo., 1963. Advt. account mgr. Edward H. Weiss & Co., Chgo., 1959-61; sr. v.p., dir. mktg. svcs. Stern, Walters & Simmons, Inc., Chgo., 1961-68; chmn. Goldring & Co., Inc., Chgo., 1968-89; pres., CEO CPM, Inc., 1969-93, chmn., 1994-99; pres. CPO Inc., 1994—. Dir. Creative Works, Inc., 1994-97, MediaSmith, Inc., 2004—; instr. mktg. and advt. mgmt. Roosevelt U., 1965-68. Mem. editl. bd. Jour. Media Planning; mem. editl. bd. advisors Response Mag., 2001—. Commr. Ridgeville Park Dist., Evanston, Ill., 1971-75, pres. 1974-75; bd. dirs., v.p. Mus. Broadcast Comm., 1983-92; bd. dirs. Chgo. Chamber Musicians 1988—, Chgo. Metro History Fair, 1990; bd. dirs. Lake Forest Grad. Sch. Mgmt., 2000—, mem. exec. com., 2002—; trustee Chgo. Assn. Dirs. Mktg. Ednl. Found., 2001-2005. Mem. Am. Mktg. Assn. (speaker), Advt. Coun. Inc. (Midwest adv. bd. 1983-90), Am. Mgmt. Assn., Direct Mktg. Assn. (mem. chmn., broadcast coun.), Chgo. Assn. Dirs. Mktg., Elec. Ret. Assn. Home: 855 Beverly Pl Lake Forest IL 60045-3901 Office: CPO Inc 505 N LaSalle St Ste 500 Chicago IL 60610 Office Phone: 312-645-7700 x202. Business E-Mail: ngoldring@cpodirect.com.

GOLDSBOROUGH, ROBERT GERALD, publishing executive, author; b. Chgo., Oct. 3, 1937; s. Robert Vincent and Wilma (Janak) G.; m. Janet Elizabeth Moore, Jan. 15, 1966; children: Suzanne Joy, Robert Michael, Colleen Marie, Bonnie Laura. BS, Northwestern U., 1959, MS with honors, 1960. Reporter A.P., 1959, City News Bur., Chgo., 1959; with Chgo. Tribune, 1960-82, reporter neighborhood news sect., asst. editor Sunday mag. and TV sect., 1963-66, editor TV Week mag., 1966-67, asst. to features editor, 1967-71, asst. to editor, 1971-72, Sunday editor, 1972-75, editor Sunday mag., 1975-82; exec. editor Advt. Age Mag., Chgo., 1982-88, spl. projects dir., 1988-91; corp. projects editor Crain Comm., Chgo., 1991-96, spl. projects dir., 1997—2004, spl. projects cons., 2005—. Author: Great Railroad Paintings, 1976, Nero Wolfe Mysteries: Murder in E-Minor, 1986, Death on Deadline, 1987, The Bloodied Ivy, 1988, The Last Coincidence, 1989, Fade to Black, 1990, The Crain Adventure, 1992, Silver Spire, 1994, The Missing Chapter, 1994, The Year Diz Came to Town, 2003, Three Strikes You're Dead, 2005. Served with AUS, 1961. Recipient Svc. award, Northwestern U. Alumni, 2001. Mem. Arts Club. Presbyterian. Office Phone: 312-280-3134. Personal E-mail: rgoldsborough@crain.com.

GOLDSCHEIDER, FRANCES K., sociologist, educator; b. Balt., June 12, 1942; d. George Hyde and Ida Thomas (Sledge) Engeman; m. David R. Kobrin, Sept. 23, 1961 (div. 1978); children: Sarah, Janet; m. Calvin Goldscheider, Aug. 18, 1983. BA, U. Pa., 1965, MA, 1967, PhD, 1971. Asst. prof. sociology Skidmore Coll., 1969-74, Brown U., Providence, 1974-86, prof., 1986—, chair dept. sociology, 1984-87, dir. Social Sci. Data Ctr., 1984-85, dir. Population Studies and Tng. Ctr., 1989-92, 94-95, 2003—04; rsch. assoc. RAND Corp., 1980—, Inst. Social Rsch., U. Mich., Ann Arbor, 1989—. Vis. assoc. prof. demography The Hebrew U., 1983—84; vis. prof. sociology Stockholm U. Author: (with C. Goldscheider) The Ethnic Factor in Family Structure and Mobility, 1978, Ethnicity and the New Family Economy, 1989, (with Linda Waite) New Families, No Families: The Transformation of the American Home, 1991, (with C. Goldscheider) Leaving Home Before Marriage, 1993, (with C. Goldscheider) The Changing Transition to Adulthood: Leaving and Returning Home, 1999; editor: Demography, 1994-95; assoc. editor: Jours. of Gerontology, 1992-94, Am. Sociol. Rev., 1990-92, 2005—, Jour. Marriage and Family, 1987—, Demographic Research, 2002-; contbr. articles to profl. jours. NEH grantee, 1973-74; Fulbright fellow, 1983-84, 2001-02. Mem. Am. Sociol. Assn. (chair population sect. 1988-89), Internat. Union for Sci. Study of Population, Population Assn. Am. (bd. dirs. 1987-90, 2nd v.p. 1991-92, chair Dorothy Swaine Thomas Award com. 1985-86, chmn. pubs. com. 2002-03). Home: 15 Fones Alley Providence RI 02906-3338 Office: Brown U Dept Sociology Providence RI 02912-0001 Office Phone: 401-863-2535. Business E-Mail: frances_goldscheider@brown.edu.

GOLDSCHMID, HARVEY JEROME, law educator, commissioner; b. NYC, May 6, 1940; s. Bernard and Rose (Braiker) G.; m. Mary Tait Seibert, Dec. 22, 1973; children: Charles Maxwell, Paul MacNeil, Joseph Tait. AB, Columbia U., 1962, JD, 1965. Bar: N.Y. 1965, U.S. Supreme Ct. 1970. Law clk. to judge 2d Circuit Ct. Appeals, NYC, 1965-66; assoc. firm Debevoise & Plimpton, NYC, 1966-70; asst. prof. law Columbia U., 1970-71, assoc. prof., 1971-73, prof., 1973-84, Dwight prof. law, 1984—, founding dir. Ctr. for Law and Econ. Studies, 1975-78; gen. counsel SEC, 1998-99, adv. to chmn. Washington, 2000, commr., 2002—05; of counsel Weil, Gotshal & Manges, NYC, 2000—02, 2005—. Cons. in field to pub. and pvt. orgns.; mem. planning and program com. 2d Cir. Jud. Conf., 1982-85; reporter 2d Cir. Jud. Conf. Evaluation Com., 1980-82, 88-89; mem. legal adv. com. N.Y.S.E., 1997-98, chmn. subcom. on corp. governance. Author: (with others) Cases and Materials on Trade Regulation, 1975, 5th edit., 2003; editor: (with others) Industrial Concentration: The New Learning, 1974, Business Disclosure: Government's Need to Know, 1979, The Impact of the Modern Corporation, 1984. Chmn. bd. advisors program on philanthropy and the law NYU Sch. Law, 1992-94; bd. dirs. Nat. Ctr. on Philanthropy and the Law, 1996—; nat. coun. Washington U. Sch. of Law, 1999—; bd. dirs. Greenwall Found., 1996—, vice chair, 1999-2002. Fellow Am. Bar Found.; mem. ABA (task force on lawyers polit. contbrns. 1997-98), Am. Law Inst. (reporter part IV, duty of care and the bus. judgment rule, corp. governance project 1980-93), N.Y. State Bar Assn., Assn. Bar City N.Y. (v.p. 1985-86, chmn. exec. com. 1984-85, chmn. com. on antitrust and trade regulation 1971-74, com. on the 2d century, chmn. com. on securities regulation 1992-95, chmn. audit com. 1988-96, chmn. com. on corp. takeover legislation 1985-86, 88-92, treas., mem. exec. com. 1996-98, chmn. nominating com. 2000-01), Assn. Am. Law Schs. (chmn. sect. antitrust and econ. regulation 1976-78), Am. Assn. Internat. Commn. Jurists (sec.-treas., bd. dirs. 1969-2002, 05—), Century Assn., Riverdale Yacht Club (bd. dirs. 1987-90), Phi Beta Kappa. Office: Jerome L Green Hall Rm 520 435 W 116th St New York NY 10027 Office Phone: 212-854-2654. Business E-Mail: goldschmidh@sec.gov. E-mail: goldschm@law.columbia.edu.

GOLDSCHMIDT, ARTHUR EDUARD, JR., historian, educator, writer; b. Washington, Mar. 17, 1938; s. Arthur Eduard and Elizabeth (Wickenden) G.; m. Louise Robb, June 17, 1961; children: Stephen Robb, Paul William. AB, Colby Coll., Waterville, Maine, 1959; AM, Harvard U., 1961, PhD, 1968. Asst. prof. history Pa. State U., University Park, 1965-73, assoc. prof., 1974-89, prof. Mid. East History, 1989-2000, prof. emeritus, 2000—. Vis. assoc. prof. mid. east history Haifa U., Israel, 1973-74; vis. prof. Semester at Sea, 1987, 2001, vis. rsch. fellow Durham U., 1989, 90; acad. dean N.J. Scholars, Lawrenceville, 1985. Author: Concise History of the Middle East, 1979, Modern Egypt, 1988, 2d edit., 2004, The Memoirs and Diaries of Muhammad Farid: An Egyptian Nationalist Leader (1868-1919), 1992, Historical Dictionary of Egypt, 3d edit., 2003, Biographical Dictionary of Modern Egypt, 2000; contbr. AHA Guide to Historical Literature, 3d edit., 1995, American National Biography, 1999, Understanding the Contemporary Middle East, 2000, 2d edit., 2003, Literature of Exploration and Travel, Encyclopedia of African History, History in Dispute: The Middle East; cons., contbr. The Encyclopedia of the Modern Middle East, 1996, 2d edit., 2004, Encarta On-Line Encyclopedia, 2000, 2d edit., 2005; editor: Articles on the Middle East, 1947-71, 1980; editor, contbr.: Re-Envisioning Egypt, 1919-1952, 2005. Trustee Unitarian-Universalist Fellowship, State College, Pa., 1977-80, 85-87, 2000-04. Recipient AMOCO Tchg. award Pa. State U., 1981, Mentoring award Mid. East Studies Assn., 2000; Fulbright rsch. fellow, 1981-82; faculty fellow Am. Rsch. Ctr. Egypt, 1998. Mem. Mid. East Studies Assn., Am. Rsch. Ctr. Egypt (bd. govs. 1989-92), Am. Hist. Assn., Ctrl. Pa. Torch Club (pres. 1993), Voices Ctrl. Pa. (founding pres. 1993-97, v.p. 2002-04, pres. 2004—). Democrat. Avocations: cooking, reading. Home: 1173 Oneida St State College PA 16801-5938 Business E-Mail: axg2@psu.edu.

GOLDSCHMIDT, CHARLES, advertising agency executive; b. N.Y.C., June 15, 1921; s. Harry and Adele (Safir) G.; m. Patricia Nevins, Jan. 17, 1951; children: Richard Walter, Jane, Peter. BA, NYU, 1941. Advt. copywriter Warner Bros. Pictures Co., 1946-48, Buchanan & Co., N.Y.C., 1948-49, Ray Austrian Assocs., N.Y.C., 1949-52; founder, ptnr. Daniel & Charles Inc., N.Y.C., 1952; chmn. bd. dirs. LCF&L, Inc., 1980—. Author fiction, play, articles. Served to lt. USNR, 1941-46. Mem. Beach Point Club (Mamaroneck, N.Y.), Phoenix Country Club. Democrat. Home: 710 The Cres Mamaroneck NY 10543-4531 Office: LCF&L Inc 260 Madison Ave New York NY 10016-2401

GOLDSCHMIDT, LYNN HARVEY, lawyer; b. Chgo., June 14, 1951; d. Arthur and Ida (Shirman) H.; m. Robert Allen Goldschmidt, Aug. 27, 1972; children: Elizabeth Anne, Carolyn Helene. BS with honors, U. Ill., 1973; JD magna cum laude, Northwestern U., 1976. Bar: Ill. 1976. Ptnr. Hopkins & Sutter, Chgo., 1976-2001, Foley & Lardner, Chgo., 2001—02; prin. D and G Cons. Group, 2002—. Articles editor Northwestern U. Law Rev. Mem. Airport Coun. Internat., N. Am., Order of Coif. Personal E-mail: lhg@dg-cg.com.

GOLDSCHMIDT, MATTHEW JOEL, maxillofacial surgeon; b. Hartford, Conn., Oct. 28, 1970; s. Paul Richard and Janice Linda Goldschmidt; m. Lauren Melissa Davis, Sept. 27, 1998; 1 child, Abigail Ilyse. BA, Trinity Coll., 1992; DMD, U. Conn., 1996, MD, 1999. ACLS, ATLS, BLS. Maxillofacial surgery resident U. Conn., Farmington, 1996—99, gen. surgery resident, 1999—2001, chief resident, maxillofacial surgery, 2001—02; fellow Cosmetic Surgery Ctr., Little Rock, 2002—03; attending surgeon Western Res. Ctr. Facial Surgery, Lakewood, Ohio, 2003—. Honor bd. chmn. U. Conn., 1992—96, didactic inst., 1998—99. Contbr. articles various profl. jours., 1995—2003. Vol. South Pk. Homeless Shelter, Hartford, Conn., 1992—95, Spl. Olympics, New London, Conn., 1996. Recipient Rsch. award, NASA Space Grant, Trinity Coll., 1995, Undergraduate achievement, Am. Assn. Oral Maxillofacial Surgeons, 1996. Fellow: Am. Dental Soc. Anesthesiology, Am. Coll. Surgeons (assoc.); mem.: Am. Assn. Oral Maxillofacial Surgeons. Avocation: golf. Office: Western Res Facial Surgery Ctr 14700 Detroit Ave Lakewood OH 44107 Office Phone: 216-227-3333. E-mail: matthewgoldschmidt@hotmail.com.

GOLDSCHMIDT, WALTER ROCHS, anthropologist; b. San Antonio, Feb. 24, 1913; s. Hermann and Gretchen (Rochs) G.; m. Beatrice Lucia Gale, May 27, 1937 (dec.); children: Karl Gale (dec.), Mark Stefan. BA, U. Tex., 1933, MA, 1935; PhD, U. Calif. at Berkeley, 1942. Social scientist Bur. Agrl. Econs., 1940-46; mem. faculty UCLA, 1946—, prof. anthropology, 1956—, chmn. dept., 1964-69, prof. anthropology and psychiatry, 1970-83, prof. emeritus, 1983—. Vis. lectr. Stanford, 1945, U. Calif., Berkeley, 1949, Harvard, 1950 Dir. radio program: Ways of Mankind, 1951- 53, Culture and Ecology in E. Africa, 1960-68. Spl. editor: World of Man Series, Aldine Pub. Co., 1966-75. Author: Small Business and the Community, 1946, As You Sow, 1947, 2nd edit., 1978, Nomlaki Ethnography, 1951, Ways to Justice, 1953, Man's Way, 1959, Exploring the Ways of Mankind, 1960, 3rd edit., 1977, Comparative Functionalism, 1966, Sebei Law, 1967, Kambuya's Cattle, The Legacy of an African Herdsman, 1968, On Being an Anthropologist, 1970, Culture and Behavior of the Sebei, 1976, The Sebei: A Study in Cultural Adaptation, 1986; The Human Career: The Self in The Symbolic World, 1990, The Bridge to Humanity, 2005, The Bridte to Humanity: How Affect Hunger Trumps The Selfish Gene; co-author: Haa Aaní, Our Land: Tlingit and Haida Land Rights and Use, 1998; editor: The U.S. and Africa, rev. 1963, French edit., 1965, The Anthropology of Franz Boas, 1959, (with H. Hoijer) The Social Anthropology of Latin America, 1970, The Uses of Anthropology, 1979, Anthropology and Public Policy: A Dialogue, 1986, Am. Anthropologist, 1956-59; founding editor: Ethos, 1972-79 Fulbright scholar U.K., 1953; grantee Social Sci. Rsch. Coun., 1953; grantee Wenner-Gren. Found., 1953; NSF postdoctoral fellow, 1964-65; fellow Center Advanced Study Behavioral Scis., 1964-65; sr. sci. fellow NIMH, 1970-75; disting. lectr. U. Indonesia, 1993. Fellow Am. Anthrop. Assn. (pres. 1975-76, Dist. Svc. award 1994), African Studies Assn. (founding, bd. dirs. 1957-60); mem. Southwestern Anthrop. Assn. (pres. 1950-51), Am. Ethnol. Soc. (pres. 1969-70), Phi Beta Kappa, Sigma Xi. Home: 978 N Norman Pl Los Angeles CA 90049-1535 Business E-Mail: walterg@ucla.edu.

GOLDSLEGER, CHERYL, artist, educator; b. Phila., Dec. 16, 1951; d. Abraham and Ruth Edith (Richman) G.; m. Larry Wayne Millard; 1 child, David Richman. Student, Tyler Sch. Art, Temple U., Rome, Italy, 1971; BFA, Phila. Coll. Art, Pa., 1973; MFA, Washington U., St. Louis, Mo., 1975. Asst. prof. Western Carolina U., Cullowhee, N.C., 1975-77, Piedmont Coll., Demorest, Ga., 1988—2001, Ga. State U., Atlanta, 2001—. Vis. lectr. Ga. Southern Coll., Statesboro, Ga., 1981; artist in residence East Carolina U., Greenville, N.C., 1986. One woman shows include Miss. Mus. Art, Jackson, 1983, Southeastern Ctr. for Contemporary Art, Winston-Salem, N.C., 1985, High Mus. Art, Atlanta, 1985, Heath Gallery, Atlanta, 1980, 83, 89, Arden Gallery, Boston, 1988, 90, 92, Jessica Berwind Gallery, Phila., 1992, Bertha Urdang Gallery, N.Y.C., 1982, 84, 87, 89, 91, 93, Rosenberg & Kaufman Fine Art, N.Y.C., 1996, 98, 99, 2001, 02, 05, Halsey Gallery, Coll. Charleston, S.C., 2002, Greenville (S.C.) County Mus. Art, 2002, Macon (Ga.) Mus., 2002, Kidder Smith Gallery, Boston, 2003, Mus. Contemporary Art Ga., 2003; exhibited in group shows at The Inst. Contemporary Art, Phila., 1983, Islip (NY) Art Mus., 1984, Va. Mus. Fine Arts, 1985, Alternative Mus., N.Y.C., 1985, Greenville Mus., S.C., 1985, Mint Mus. Charlotte, 1986, New Orleans Mus., 1986, 87, Ivan Dougherty Gallery/City Art Inst., Australia, 1986, Bklyn. Mus., 1986, Am. Acad. and Inst. of Arts and Letters, N.Y.C., 1987, Ga. Mus. Art, Athens, Ga., 1987, Norton Gallery, Palm Beach, Fla., 1987, Corcoran Gallery, Washington, D.C., 1989, Israel Mus., Jerusalem, 1989, Perugia, Italy, 1991, Stephen Rosenberg Gallery, N.Y.C., 1994, U. Tenn., Knoxville, 1999, Montclair (N.J.) Mus., 2000, N.C. Mus. Art, Raleigh, 2000, Krannert Mus., Champaign, Ill., 2002, Cin. Art Mus., 2002, Bowdoin (Maine) Coll. Mus. Art, 2002; permanent collections include Albright Knox Art Gallery, Buffalo, Bklyn. Mus., High Mus., Atlanta, Israel Mus., Jerusalem, Mus. Modern Art, N.Y.C., Tel Aviv Mus., Israel, R.I. Sch. Design Mus. Artist fellow Pa. Coun. on the Arts, 1981, Sr. Artists fellow Ohio Arts Coun., 1982, Sr. Artist's fellow Nat. Endowment for the Arts, 1982, 91, RJR fellow Southeastern Ctr. for Contempory Art, 1986, Artist's fellow Ga. Coun. for the Art's, 1991, U.S./France fellow Nat. Endowment for the Arts, 1993, La Napoule Found. fellow, France, 1994; 5th Fl. Found. grantee, 1999. Mem. Coll. Art Assn. Home: 170 Greenwood Dr Athens GA 30606-4704 Office: Ga State U Sch Art & Design Atlanta GA 30303 E-mail: cgold@gsu.edu.

GOLDSMITH, BILLY JOE, real estate broker, rancher; b. Blum, Tex., Nov. 6, 1933; s. John T. and Gladys Aileen (Curlee) G.; m. Jean Elizabeth Wendel, Oct. 20, 1962; 1 child, Anne. BS, Tex. A&M U., 1955. Asst., county agrl. agt. Harris County Tex. Extension Svc., Houston, 1957-64; mgr. Rice Coun., Houston, 1964-75, exec. v.p., 1975-95, ret., 1995; owner, broker real estate co. Houston, 1995—; owner Goldsmith Realty, Houston, Bill Goldsmith Agrl. Consulting. Arena dir. Houston Livestock Show and Rodeo, 1966-73; bd. dirs. Tex. Soc. to Prevent Blindness. With U.S. Army, 1955-57. Internat. Rice Festival honoree, 1992. Mem. Tex. Cattle Raisers Assn., Southwestern Cattle Raisers Assn., Nat. Cattlemen's Assn., Houston Livestock Show and Rodeo Rancher, Res. Officer Assn., Harris County Ext. Bd. Advisors. Home: 5826 Cheena Dr Houston TX 77096-5928

GOLDSMITH, BRAM, banker; b. Chgo., Feb. 22, 1923; s. Max L. and Bertha (Gittelsohn) G.; m. Elaine Maltz; children: Bruce, Russell. Student, Herzl Jr. Coll., 1940, U. Ill., 1941—42. Asst. v.p. Pioneer-Atlas Liquor Co., Chgo., 1945-47; pres. Winston Lumber and Supply Co., East Chicago, Ind., 1947-50; v.p. Medal Distilled Products, Inc., Beverly Hills, Calif., 1950-75; pres. Buckeye Realty and Mgmt. Corp., Beverly Hills, 1952-75; exec. v.p. Buckeye Constrn. Co., Inc., Beverly Hills, 1952-75; chmn. bd., CEO City Nat. Corp., Beverly Hills, 1975-95; CEO City Nat. Bank, 1975-96, chmn., 1975-95, City Nat. Corp., 1995—. Mem., bd. dirs. L.A. Philharm. Assn.; bd. dirs. Cedars/Sinai Med. Ctr.; pres. Jewish Fedn. Coun. Greater L.A., 1969-70; nat. chmn. United Jewish Appeal, 1970-74; regional chmn. United Crusade, 1976; co-chmn. bd. dirs. NCCJ; chmn. Am. com. Weizman Inst. Sci. With signal corps U.S. Army, 1942-45. Mem. Masons, Hillcrest Country Club, Balboa Bay Club. Office: City Nat Corp 400 N Roxbury Dr Beverly Hills CA 90210 Business E-Mail: bram.goldmith@cnb.com.

GOLDSMITH, CLIFFORD HENRY, former tobacco company executive; b. Leipzig, Germany, Sept. 6, 1919; came to U.S., 1940, naturalized, 1943; s. Conrad and Elise (Stahl) G.; m. Katherine W. Kaynis; children: Corinne Elizabeth Goldsmith Dickinson (dec.), Audrey Jane Goldsmith Kubie, Alexandra Eve Goldsmith Fallon. Grad., Bradford (Eng.) U., 1939. Technologist, Glenside Mills Corp., Skaneateles, NY, 1940-41; supt. Falls Yarn Mills, Woonsocket, RI, 1941-42, Aldon Spinning Mills, Talcotville, Conn., 1942-43; with Benson & Hedges Co., 1945-53, plant mgr., 1945-53; with Philip Morris, Inc., 1954-84, pres., 1978-83, vice chmn., 1983-84; chmn. Prendel Co., LLC, 2005—. Chmn. emeritus Nat. Multiple Sclerosis Soc., FOJP Svc. Corp.;

trustee Mr. Sinai Sch. Medicine, Mt. Sinai Hosp. and Med. Ctr. With inf. U.S. Army, 1943—45. Mem. Textile Inst. (Manchester, Eng., assoc.), Commonwealth Club (Richmond), Univ. Club (N.Y.), Century Club (N.Y. Office: 900 Park Ave New York NY 10021-0231

GOLDSMITH, DAVID L., health facility administrator; BA, Occidental Coll.; MBA, Columbia Univ. Chmn. Apria Healthcare Group. Office: Apria Healthcare Group 26220 Enterprise Ct Lake Forest CA 92630-8405 Office Phone: 949-639-2000. Office Fax: 949-587-9363.*

GOLDSMITH, DONNA, sports association executive; b. Long Island; Degree in comm., SUNY, Oswego. Worked at Swatch Watch USA, Revlon Inc.; v.p. licensing NBA; sr. v.p. consumer products World Wrestling Fedn. Entertainment Inc., Stamford, Conn., 2000—. Mem.: NY Women in Comm. Office: World Wrestling Fedn Entertainment Inc 1241 E Main St Stamford CT 06902 E-mail: donna.goldsmith@wwfent.com.

GOLDSMITH, ETHEL FRANK, medical social worker; b. Chgo., May 31, 1919; d. Theodore and Rose (Falk) Frank; m. Julian Royce Goldsmith, Sept. 4, 1940; children: Richard, Susan, John. BA, U. Chgo., 1940. Lic. social worker, Ill. Liaison worker psychiat. consultation svc. U. Chgo. Hosp., 1964—68; med. social worker Wyler Children's Hosp., Chgo., 1968—98. Treas. U. Chgo. Svc. League, 1958-62, bd. dirs.; chmn. camp Brueckner Farr Aux., 1966-72; pres. Bobs Roberts Hosp. Svc. Commn., 1962; bd. dirs. Richardson Wildlife Sanctuary, 1988-2000; mem. Field Mus. Women's Bd., 1966—; bd. dirs. Hyde Park Art Ctr., 1964-82, Chgo. Commons Assn., 1967-77, Alumni Assn. Sch. Social Svc. Adminstrn., 1976-80, Self Help Home for Aged, 1985-2000; vol. Chgo. Found. for Edn.; mem. womens bd. U. Chgo., 1999—. Recipient Alumni Citation Pub. Service, U. Chgo., 1972. Mem. Phi Beta Kappa. Home: 5550 S Shore Dr Apt 1313 Chicago IL 60637

GOLDSMITH, GARY NORMAN, psychiatrist, psychoanalyst; b. N.Y.C., Oct. 30, 1948; s. Walter J. and Mildred (Cohen) G. BA, Brandeis U., Waltham, Mass., 1969; MD, Georgetown U., 1973. Intern Evanston (Ill.) Hosp., 1973-74; clin. fellow in psychiatry Med. Sch. Harvard U., Boston, 1974-77; resident in psychiatry Mass. Mental Health Ctr., Boston, 1974-77; pvt. practice psychiatry Brookline, Mass., 1977—; faculty Psychoanalytic Inst. New Eng., Needham, Mass., 1988—; mem. faculty, supervising analyst Mass. Inst. for Psychoanalysis, 1994—. Cons. in psychiatr. R.I. Inst. Mental Health, Cranston, 1977-78; staff psychiatrist VA Med. Ctr., Brockton, mass., 1978-82; med. dir. Brockton Area Multi-Svcs., Inc., 1982-84; staff psychiatrist Tufts-New Eng. Med. Ctr., 1984-86; assoc. in psychiatry Beth Israel Hosp., Boston, dir. Russian lang. psychiat. svcs., 1994—; clin. instr. psychiatry Harvard U., 1977-82, 89—; faculty mem., Psychoanalytic Inst. of Eastern Europe, 2002-. Mem. Am. Psychiat. Assn., Am. Psychoanalytic Assn. (chair com. on Russian ednl. exch. 2000—), Assn. for Russian-Spkg. Profls. in Health Care. Office: 1419 Beacon St Brookline MA 02446-4808 E-mail: G6676@aol.com.

GOLDSMITH, HARRY LOUIS, lawyer; b. Memphis, Sept. 4, 1951; s. Robert Tobias and Elvis (Ginsberg) G. Student, Washington and Lee U., 1969-71; BBS, U. Tex., 1973; JD, Memphis State U., 1977. Bar: Tenn. 1977. With firm Goodman, Glazer, Greener, Schneider & McQuiston, Memphis, 1977-82, Brown, Reese & Goldsmith, Memphis, 1984-89; with Fed. Express Corp., Memphis, 1982-84; v.p., gen. counsel, sec. AutoZone, Inc., 1993—96, sr. v.p., gen. counsel, sec., 1996—. Trustee Goldsmith Found. Mem. Bata Alpha Psi, Beta Gamma Sigma. Office: Autozone Inc 123 S Front St Memphis TN 38103 Office Phone: 901-495-6500. Office Fax: 901-495-8300.

GOLDSMITH, HARRY SAWYER, surgeon, educator; b. Newton, Mass., Sept. 30, 1929; s. Leo and Dorothy Amy (Appleton) G.; m. Linda Perry, Dec. 8, 1961; children: John, Robert, Lynne. AB, Dartmouth, 1952; MD, Boston U., 1956; degree in medicine (hon.), Shanghai Second Med. U., 1988, Xuzhou (China) Med. Coll., 1995. Intern Boston City Hosp., 1956-57, resident in surgery, 1957-61, Meml. Sloan Kettering Inst., N.Y.C., 1963-65, chief gastric and mixed tumor svc., 1965-70; Samuel D. Gross prof. surgery, chmn. dept. Jefferson Med. Coll., Phila., 1970-77; surgeon-in-chief Jefferson U. Hosp., 1970-77; disting. prof. surgery Jefferson Med. Coll., Phila., 1977; prof. surgery Dartmouth Coll. Med. Sch., Hanover, N.H., 1977-83; prof. surgery, adj. prof. neurosurgery Boston U. Sch. Medicine, 1983-95; clin. prof. surgery U. Nev., Reno, 1996—. Editor-in-chief: Goldsmith's Practice of Surgery, 1976-89; editor: The Omentum: Research and Clinical Applications, 1990, The Omentum: Application to Brain and Spinal Cord, 2000; contbr. articles to profl. jours. Capt. U.S. Army, 1961-63. Mem. ACS, Soc. Vascular Surgery, Brit. Assn. Surg. Oncology, Soc. for Surgery of Alimentary Tract, Internat. Surg. Soc., Ctrl. Surg. Assn., New England Surg. Soc. Address: PO Box 493 Glenbrook NV 89413-0493 Office Phone: 775-749-5801. Office Fax: 775-749-5861. Personal E-mail: hlgldsmith@aol.com.

GOLDSMITH, HOWARD, writer, consultant; b. N.Y.C., Aug. 24, 1945; s. Philip and Sophie (Feldman) G. BA with honors, CUNY, 1965; MA with honors, U. Mich., Ann Arbor, 1966. Research psychologist Mental Hygiene Clinic, Detroit, 1966-70; freelance writer Ency. Britannica Ednl. Corp., Chgo., 1970; writer, pvt. practice editorial cons. Flushing, N.Y., 1970—. Editorial cons. Mountain View Ctr. for Environ. Edn., U. Colo., Boulder, 1970-85. Author poetry, videos, plays, numerous short stories, books, novels including: The Whispering Sea, 1976, What Makes a Grumble Smile?, 1977, The Shadow and Other Strange Tales, 1977, Terror by Night, 1977, Spine-Chillers, 1978, Sooner Round the Corner, 1979, Invasion: 2200 A.D., 1979, The Ivy Plot, 1981, Three-Ring Inferno, 1982, Plaf Le Paresseux, 1982, Ninon, Miss Vison, 1982, Toufou Le Hibou, 1982, Fourtou Le Kangourou, 1982, The Tooth chicken, 1982, Mireille l'Abeille, 1982, Little Dog Lost, 1983, Stormy Day Together, 1983, The Sinister Circle, 1983, Shadow of Fear, 1983, Treasure Hunt, 1983, The Square, 1983, The Circle, 1983, The Contest, 1983, Welcome, Makoto!, 1983, Helpful Julio, 1984, The Secret of Success, 1984, Pedro's Puzzling Birthday, 1984, Rosa's Prank, 1984, A Day of Fun, 1984, The Rectangle, 1984, Kirby the Kangaroo, 1985, Ollie the Owl, 1985, The Twiddle Twins' Haunted House, 1985, Young Ghosts, 1985, Von Geistern Besessen, 1987, The Further Adventures of Batman, 1989, Visions of Fantasy, 1989, The Pig and the Witch, 1990, The Mind-Stalkers, 1990, Spooky Stories, 1990, Little Quack and Baby Duckling, 1991, The Proust Syndrome, 1992, The President's Train, 1993, Thomas Edison Had A Bright Idea, 1993, The Day My Dad and I Got Mugged, 1993, Evil Tales of Evil Things, 1993, The Christmas Star, 1994, The Curiosity Kid, 1994, Tales of the Batman, 1995, Dream Weavers, 1996, The Gooey Chewy Contest, 1997, The Twiddle Twins' Music Box Mystery, 1997, The Twiddle Twins' Amusement Park Mystery, 1998, Science Through Stories (series), 1998-99, The Twiddle Twins' Single Footprint Mystery, 1999, The Tooth Fairy Mystery, 1999, Roundabout the Rain, 2000, Three Bags of Chips, 2000, See It Fly!, 2000, Strike up the Band, 2000, Danger Zone, 2000, Thomas Edison to the Rescue!, 2003, Mark Twain at Work, 2003, John F. Kennedy and the Stormy Sea, 2005. Fellow U.S. Pub. Health Svc., 1965; Rackham predoctoral fellow U. Mich., 1966; recipient Phi Sigma Sci. award, 1966. Mem. Poets and Writers, Sci. Fiction Writers of Am., Soc. Children's Book Writers and Illustrators, Phi Beta Kappa, Psi Chi, Sigma Xi, Phi Kappa Phi. Avocations: classical music, book collecting, chess, old movies. Home: 41-07 Bowne St Apt 6B Flushing NY 11355-5629

GOLDSMITH, JACK LANDMAN, III, law educator, former federal agency administrator; BA summa cum laude, Washington & Lee U., 1984; BA, Oxford (England) U., 1986, MA with hons., 1991; JD, Yale U., 1989; diploma in Pvt. Internat. Law, Hague Acad. Internat. Law, 1992. Bar: D.C. Law clk. to hon. J. Harvie Wilkinson U.S. Ct. Appeals (4th cir.), 1989—90; law clk. to Hon. Anthony M. Kennedy U.S. Supreme Ct., 1990—91; legal asst. to Hon. George Aldrich Iran-U.S. Claims Tribunal, Netherlands, 1991—92; assoc. Covington & Burling, Washington, 1992—94; assoc. prof. law U. Va., 1994—97; prof. law U. Chgo., 1997—2003, U. Va., 2003—04; spl. counsel to gen. counsel US Dept. Def., Washington, 2003; asst. atty. gen. Office Legal Counsel US Dept. Justice, 2003—04; prof. law Harvard U., Cambridge, 2004—. Visiting scholar Am. Enterprise Inst., 2004—. Mem.: ABA, Am. Soc. Internat. Law. Office: Harvard Law Sch 1563 Massachusetts Ave Cambridge MA 02138 E-mail: jgoldsmith@law.harvard.edu.

GOLDSMITH, JEFF CHARLES, management consultant; b. Portland, Oreg., Oct. 31, 1948; children: Jason, Trevor, Amelia. BA, Reed Coll., 1970; PhD, U. Chgo., 1973. Dir. health planning, regulatory affairs U. Chgo. Med. Ctr., 1975-82; nat. advisor Ernst & Young, 1982-94; pres. Health Futures, Inc., 1982—; dir. Cerner Corp., 1999—, Essent Healthcare, 2000—; assoc. prof. med. edn. Sch. Medicine U. Va., 1997—. Lectr. U. Chgo. Grad. Sch. Bus., 1979—90, Wharton Sch., U. Pa., 1994—; adv. Burrill Biotech. Capital Fund. Author: Can Hospitals Survive?, 1981; mem. editl. bd. Health Affairs, 1990--; contbr. articles to profl. jours. including Harvard Bus. Rev., Jour. AMA, Health Affairs. Recipient Woodrow Wilson Nat. Fellowship, 1971. Avocations: skiing, audiophile, native american art, whitewater. E-mail: hfutures@healthfutures.net.

GOLDSMITH, JEFFREY H., lawyer; b. New Brunswick, N.J., Aug. 15, 1969; s. Sanford Leon and Myrna Beth (Nomberg) G. BA, Seton Hall U., 1991, JD, 1994. Bar: N.J. 1994, Pa. 1995, U.S. Dist. Ct. N.J., 1994, U.S. Dist. Ct. (ea. and so. dists.) N.Y. 1997, U.S. Ct. Appeals (2d and 3d cirs.) 2000, U.S. Ct. Appeals (2d cir.) 2001. Judicial law clk. Hon. Martin L. Greenberg, Newark, 1994-95; assoc. Bumgardner, Hardin & Ellis, Springfield, N.J., 1995-97, Hardin, Kundla, McKeon & Poletto, Springfield, 1997—. Leader Boy Scouts Am., Brick, N.J., 1987—. Recipient Congl. award U.S. Congress, Washington, 1991/92. Jewish. Avocations: camping, sports, running, swimming. Home: 6 Club House Rd Brick NJ 08723-6711 Office: Hardin Kundla McKeon & Poletto 673 Morris Ave Springfield NJ 07081-1512 Office Phone: 973-912-5222. E-mail: jgoldsmith@hkmpp.com.

GOLDSMITH, LEE SELIG, lawyer, physician; b. N.Y.C., Nov. 18, 1939; s. Isidore L. and Elsie (Friedman) G.; m. Arlene F. Applebaum, June 10, 1962; children: Ian Lance, Helena Ayn, Jordan Seth. BS with honors, N.Y. U., 1960, MD, 1964, LL.B., 1967. Bar: N.Y. 1968, N.J. 1974; cert. civil trial atty. 2000. Assoc. clk. Speiser, Shumate, Geoghan Krause & Rheingold, 1965-70; individual practice law, 1970-72; mem. firm Lea, Goldberg, Goldsmith & Spellen, N.Y.C., 1972-74; of counsel Newark, 1974-77; mem. firm Goldsmith, Cohen & Simon, 1976-77, Goldsmith & Cohen, 1977-80, Greenstone, Greenstone, Naishuler & Goldsmith, Newark, 1981, Goldsmith & Richman, P.C., N.Y.C., 1981-2000, Goldsmith & Richman, P.A., Englewood, N.J., 1981-2000. Adj. prof. law Fordham U., 1976-88; spl. counsel N.Y. State Senate health com., 1971; lectr. Practicing Law Inst.; chmn. Am. Bd. Law in Medicine, 1984-85. Author: Malpractice Made Easy, 1976, Hospital Liability Law, 1972, 2d edit. 1979; editor: Jour. Legal Medicine, 1978-81, Legal Aspects of Med. Practice, 1981—, Medical Malpractice, Guide to Medical Issues, 7 vols., 1986; contbr. articles to various publs. Fellow: NY Acad. Medicine, Am. Coll. Legal Medicine (bd. govs. 1982, pres.-elect 1986—87, pres. 1987—88, chmn. com. legis. rev.); mem.: ATLA (sec. NJ chpt. 1988—89, treas. 1989—89, 2d v.p. 1990—91, 1st v.p. 1991—92, pres. 1993—94, PAC bd. govs. 1996—2000, treas. NJ PAC 1996—97, bd. govs. 2000—), AMA, NY Trial Lawyers Assn., Assn. Bar City NY (sec. sci. and law com. 1985—87), NY County Med. Soc., NY Med. Soc. Home: 1 Kelwynne Rd Scarsdale NY 10583-4507 Office: Goldsmith Richman & Harz LLP 747 3rd Ave New York NY 10017-2803 also: 140 Sylvan Ave Englewood Cliffs NJ 07632-2502 Office Phone: 201-363-1122.

GOLDSMITH, LOWELL ALAN, medical educator; b. Bklyn., Mar. 29, 1938; s. Isidore Alexander and Ida (Kaplan) G.; m. Carol Amreich, June 11, 1960; children: Meredith, Eileen. AB, Columbia Coll., 1959; MD, SUNY, Bklyn., 1963; MPH, U. Rochester Sch. Medicine & Dentistry, 2002. Diplomate Am. Bd. Dermatology. Intern, then resident in medicine UCLA Med. Ctr., 1963-65; resident in dermatology Harvard U. Med. Sch., Boston, 1967-69, asst. prof. dermatology, 1970-73; asst. in dermatology Mass. Gen. Hosp., Boston, 1970-71, asst. dermatologist, 1971-73; assoc. prof. medicine Duke U. Med. Ctr., Durham, NC, 1973-78, prof., 1978-81; James H. Sterner prof. dermatology Sch. Medicine and Dentistry, U. Rochester (NY), 1981-96, chief dermatology unit, 1981-87, acting chmn. dept. medicine, 1985-87, chmn. dept. dermatology, 1987-96; dean Sch. Medicine and Dentistry U. Rochester, 1996-2000, dean emeritus, 2000—; prof. dermatology U. NC, Chapel Hill, 2002—, clin. prof. epidemiology Sch. Pub. Health, 2002—. Mem. dermatology adv. com. FDA, 1983-87; chmn. Gordon Rsch. Cong. on Epithelial Differentiation and Keratiniazation, 1987, AAD-CDC Conf. on skin cancer prevention and edn., Washington, 1995; mem. gen. medicine A study sect. USPHS, NIH, 1988-92, chmn., 1990-92; mem. coun. NIAMS, NIH, 1996-99; chmn. med. adv. bd. Nat. Alopecia Areata Found., 1981-87, 90-2002, bd. dirs.; bd. dirs. Monroe Cmty. Hosp., Rochester, Ctr. for Alternatives in Animal Testing, Balt.; chmn. NIH Consensus Conf. on Diagnosis and Treatment of Early Melanoma, Bethesda, Md., 1992. Author, editor: Biochemistry and Physiology of the Skin, 1983, 2d edit., 1991, Physiology, Biochemistry and Molecular Biology of the Skin, 1991, Differential Diagnosis of Skin Disease, 2d edit., 1996; mem. editl. bd. Archives Dermatology, 1981-92, Clinics in Dermatology, 1982-96, Seminars in Dermatology, 1991-96, Jour. Dermatological Sci., 1994-2002; mem. editl. bd. Jour. Investigative Dermatology, 1987-95, editor, 2002-, also numerous articles. With USPHS, 1965-67. Recipient Rsch. Career Devel. award USPHS, 1975-80; Macy Found. fellow, 1978-79. Mem. Assn. Am. Physicians, Am. Soc. Clin. Investigation, Am. Acad. Dermatology (bd. dirs., Presdl. citation 2003), Soc. Investigative Dermatology (bd. dirs., pres. 1994-95, Rothman Gold medal), Nat. Ichthyosis Found. (chmn. adv. bd. 1981-85), Assn. Profs. Dermatology (bd. dirs. 1984-87, pres. 1992-94), Am. Bd. Dermatology (bd. dirs. 1993-96), NY State Soc. Dermatology (pres. 1985-89), Am. Dermatol. Assn. (bd. dirs. 1996-2001, pres. 2002—2003, Buffalo-Rochester Dermatology Soc. (pres. 1987), Rochester Dermatology Soc., Rochester Acad. Medicine, Polish Dermatol. Assn. (hon.), Brit. Dermatology Assn. (hon.), Japanese Dermatology Assn. (hon., DOHI lectr. 2003), Berlin Dermatology Soc. (hon.), Alpha Omega Alpha. Office: U NC Dept Dermatology 3100 Thurston-Bowles Bldg CB #7287 Chapel Hill NC 27599 Office Phone: 919-843-3097. Business E-Mail: Lowell_Goldsmith@med.unc.edu.

GOLDSMITH, MERWIN, actor, theater director; b. Detroit, Aug. 7, 1937; s. Max Harold and Alice Flora (Singer) Goldsmith; m. Susan Leigh Benson, Mar. 1966 (div. 1969); m. Barbara Parry, July 1996. BA in Theater, UCLA, 1960; student, Bristol Old Vic Theatre Sch., Bristol. Actor: (plays) Aunti Mame, 1958, License to Murder, 1964, The Tempest, Trap for a Lonely Man, Phaedra, Gentlemen Prefer Blondes, 1965, Billy Budd, 1967, Fiddler on the Roof, 1968—69, Minnie's Boys, 1970, Much Ado About Nothing, Pal Joey, 1973, Last of the Red Hot Lovers, 1974, Hedda Gabler, 1975, Dirty Linen, 1977, Oklahoma!, 1978, Death of a Salesman, The Importance of Being Ernest, 1982, Hello Dolly!, 1983, La Boheme, 1984, The Taming of the Shrew, 1985, Hamlet, 1986, Me & My Girl, 1988, 1989, Grand Hotel, The Musical, 1991, Merry Widow, 1991, Learned Ladies, 1991, Ain't Broadway Grand, 1993, The Little Prince, 1993, An Imaginary Life, 1993, Beau Jest, 1994, After-Play, 1995, By Jeeves, 1996, Loot, 2000, The Investigation, 2001, Bloomer Girl, 2001, The Pajama Game, 2001, Franklin of Philadelphia, 2002; (films) Shamus, 1972, Boardwalk, 1979, So Fine, 1981, Blue Heaven, 1984, Making Mr. Right, 1986, Cadillac Man, 1991, It Could Happen to You, 1993, Quiz Show, 1993, Rounders, 1998, The Hurricane, 1998, Company Man, 1999, Joe Gould's Secret, 1999, Au Plus Pres du Paradis, 2001, Unholy, 2005; (TV series) All My Children, Ryan's Hope, The Guiding Light, Search for Tomorrow, As the World Turns, Another World, Wide World of Mystery, The Connection, Law & Order; dir.: (theatre) Vanities, 1980. With USAFR. Nominee Best Actor in a Musical, Variety Critics Poll, 1972, Best Supporting Actor in a Musical, 1973, Best Actor in a Musical, Joseph Jefferson Awards, 1972. Mem.: NARAS (Grammy awards voter), SAG, AFTRA, Actors Equity Assn., The Century Assn., The Players Club. Avocations: photography, studying French and Hebrew. Office: Leading Artists Inc 145 W 45th St New York NY 10036-4008 Office Phone: 212-391-4545.

GOLDSMITH, MICHAEL ALLEN, oncologist, educator; b. Bronx, Jan. 28, 1946; s. Walter and Bertha (Tannenberg) G.; m. Judith Harriet Plaut, June 6, 1971; children: Sharon, Esther, Eva, Steven. BA, Yeshiva U., 1967; MD, Albert Einstein Coll. Medicine, 1971. Diplomate Am. Bd. Internal Medicine. Intern Bronx Mcpl. Hosp. Ctr., 1971-72; staff assoc. Nat. Cancer Inst., Bethesda, Md., 1972-74; resident in medicine Mt. Sinai Hosp., N.Y.C., 1974-75, fellow in neoplastic diseases, 1975-77, asst. clin. prof. medicine and neoplastic diseases, 1977—; attending physician Oncology Consultants, P.C., N.Y.C., 1977—. Assoc. editor Cancer Investigation. 2001—; reviewer Jour. AMA, 1988-90, New Eng. Jour. Medicine, 1995—. Contbr. articles to med. jours. Vice-pres. Congregation Orach Chaim, N.Y.C., 1978-83. Lt. comdr. USPHS, 1972-74. Fellow ACP; mem. Am. Soc. Clin. Oncology, Am. Assn. Cancer Rsch. Achievements include research in new anticancer drugs. Office: Oncology Cons PC 1045 5th Ave New York NY 10028-0138 Office Phone: 212-628-6500.

GOLDSMITH, OWEN L., composer; b. Borger, Tex., Oct. 8, 1932; s. Harold L. and Mary C. Goldsmith; m. Ann Morrill Lopes (div.); children: Karen, Stephanie. BA in Music magna cum laude, San Francisco State U., 1959, MA in Music, 1965. Cert. tchr. Calif. Tchr. choir and orch. Livermore High Sch., Calif., 1960—69, Clayton Valley High Sch, Concord, 1969—79; tchr. music Los Medanos Coll., Pittsburg, 1979—81; composer, arranger Mountain Ranch, 1981—. Composer: Warner Bros. Pubs.; feature writer: Keyboard Mag., 1975—81. Staff sgt. USAF, 1951—55. Recipient 3d prize, Ams. Vocal Ensemble Contest, NYC, 1999, winner vocal ensemble contest, Am. String Tchrs. Assn. and Nat. Sch. Orch. Assn., N.Y.C., 1999. Mem.: ACLU, Calif. Music Educators Assn. (pres. Bay sect. 1970—72, newsletter editor 1972—74, adjudicator-music festivals 1965—98), Am. Choral Dirs. Assn., Music Educators Nat. Conf., Air Force Vets. Assn. Avocations: mountain climbing, travel. Home: PO Box 198 Mountain Ranch CA 95246

GOLDSMITH, PAUL FELIX, physics professor, astronomy professor; b. Washington, Nov. 5, 1948; s. Raymond William and Selma Evelyn (Fine) G.; m. Sheryl E. Reiss, June 5, 1988. AB, U. Calif., Berkeley, 1969, PhD., 1975. Mem. tech. staff AT&T Bell Labs., Holmdel, N.J., 1975-77; asst. prof. U. Mass., Amherst, 1977-82, assoc. prof., 1982-85, prof. physics and astronomy, 1985-92; prof. astronomy, dir. Nat. Astronomy and Ionosphere Ctr. Cornell U., Ithaca, NY, 1993—2002, James A. Weeks prof. phys. sci., 1999—. Cons. MIT Lincoln Lab., Lexington, Mass., 1977-80; v.p. R & D Millitech Corp., South Deerfield, Mass., 1983-92. Author: Quasioptical Systems, 1998; editor: Instrumentation and Techniques for Radio Astronomy, 1988; contbr. articles on radio astronomy and millimeter and submillimeter wavelength tech. to profl. jours. Fellow IEEE; mem. Microwave Theory Tech. Soc. of IEEE (mem. spkr.'s bur. 1989-90, Disting. lectr. 1992-93), Am. Astron. Soc. Office: Dept Astronomy Cornell University Space Sciences Building Ithaca NY 14853 Office Phone: 607-255-0606. Business E-Mail: pfg@astro.cornell.edu.

GOLDSMITH, ROBERT LEWIS, youth association magazine executive; b. N.Y.C., Jan. 9, 1928; s. Arthur and Elizabeth (Kohn) G.; m. Joan M. Hartman, 1976. BS, NYU, 1950. Advt. promotion mgr. Esquire, Inc., N.Y.C., 1952-53; advt. dir. Schine Hotels, N.Y.C., 1953; promotion dir. Dell Pub. Co., N.Y.C., 1953-58, Outdoor Life Mag., N.Y.C., 1958-65; assoc. dir. mag. div. Boy Scouts Am., N.Y.C., 1965-89, ret., 1989. N.Am. rep. Ea. Art Report, London, 1991—. Bd. dirs. Inst. Asian Studies, N.Y.C., 1981—, assoc. dir., 1989—, pres., 1995-99; mem. Friends of Asian Art, Met. Mus. Art, Oriental Art Coun. Bklyn. Mus., Indpls Mus. Art, life trustee. Mem. N.Y. Sales Execs. Club, Mktg. Comms. Execs. Assn., Am. Mktg. Assn., Asia Soc., Japan Soc., China Inst. Am., NYU Club (bd. govs., v.p. exec. com.). Office: 141 E 44th St New York NY 10017-4006 *The general purpose I have had in mind is to leave the world no worse a place than I found it, and to try in my own way to make improvements wherever possible. To help people, to teach them to help themselves, to combat ignorance, to give material and emotional support to those who need, to the extent that is possible... are all factors of great importance. I have tried to learn about a wide variety of subjects and to use that knowledge to make both my business life and my personal life more satisfying and more productive.*

GOLDSMITH, STANLEY JOSEPH, nuclear medicine physician, educator; b. Bklyn., Aug. 17, 1937; s. Jack and Mae (Greenzweig) G.; m. Miriam Schulman, June 6, 1959; children: Ira, Arthur, Beth, Mark. BA, Columbia U., 1958; MD, SUNY, Bklyn., 1962. Diplomate Am. Bd. Internal Medicine, Am. Bd. Nuclear Medicine (bd. dirs. 1990-96, treas. 1995-96). Intern SUNY-Kings County Med. Ctr., Bklyn., 1962-63, resident, 1965-66, chief resident, 1966-67; fellow in endocrinology Mt. Sinai Hosp., N.Y.C., 1967-68, dir. physics nuclear medicine, 1973-92; clin. dir. nuclear medicine Meml. Sloan-Kettering Cancer Ctr., N.Y.C., 1992-95; dir. nuclear medicine N.Y. Hosp.-Cornell Med. Ctr., N.Y.C., 1995—. Rsch. assoc. radioisotope svc. Bronx (NY) VA Hosp., 1968-69; dir. nuclear medicine, asst. dir. endocrine dept. Nassau County Med. Ctr., East Meadow, NY, 1969-73; asst. prof. medicine radiology SUNY-Stony Brook Health Sci. Ctr., 1971-73; asst. prof. medicine Mt. Sinai Sch. Medicine, 1973-76, assoc. prof., 1976-84, prof. clin. medicine, 1985-91, prof. radiology and medicine, 1991-92, Cornell U. Med. Coll., 1993—, prof. radiology, medicine; bd. dirs. Capintec, Inc., Ramsey, NJ; rsch. collaborator Brookhaven Nat. Labs., Upton, NY, 1971-75; cons. nuclear medicine; cons. dept. health State of N.Y., 1973-77, Health Svcs. Adminstrn., NYC, 1976; radiopharm. adv. com. FDA, 1987-90, low level radioactive waste disposal site commn., N.Y., 1987-95. Assoc. editor Newline, 1984-93, Jour. Nuclear Medicine, editor-in-chief, 1993-98; mem. editl. bd. Am. Jour. Cardiology, 1978-82, European Jour. Nuclear Medicine, 1993-98, Cancer Biotherapy and Radiopharm., 1998—; reviewer Israeli Jour. Med. Scis., 1979, JAMA, 1983-92, Jour. Am. Coll. Cardiology, 1984-94, Jour. Nuclear Medicine, 1989-93, 99—, Cancer, 2003—, Kidney Internat., 2004— Capt. U.S. Army, 1963-65. Recipient Radiology Educator award, SUNY Downstate Alumni, 2001. Fellow ACP, Am. Coll. Cardiology, Am. Coll. Nuclear Physicians (chmn. nuclear med. tech. affairs, chmn. Washington oversight com.), N.Y. Acad. Sci.; mem. AAAS, Am. Fedn. Clin. Rsch., Am. Coll. Radiology, Endocrine Soc., N.Y. Acad. Medicine (pres sect. on nuclear medicine 2004—), Radiol. Soc. N.Am. (program com. 2002—), Soc. Nuclear Medicine (trustee 1982-84, pres.-elect 1984-85, prse. 1985-86, chmn. govt. rels. com. 1991-93, sec. Greater N.Y. chpt. 1975-78, pres. 1979-80, pres. therapy coun. 2001-2003, named Outstanding Educator, 2000). Home: 72 Ivy Way Port Washington NY 11050-3817 Office: NY Presbyn Hosp Weill Cornell Med Ctr 525 E 68th St New York NY 10021-4885 Office Phone: 212-746-4580. Business E-Mail: sjg2002@med.cornell.edu.

GOLDSMITH, WILLIS JAY, lawyer; b. Paris, Feb. 21, 1947; arrived in U.S., 1949; s. Irving and Alice (Rosenfeld) Goldsmith; m. Marilynn Jacobson, Aug. 12, 1973; children: Andrew Edward, Helene Sara. AB, Brown U., 1969; JD, NYU, 1972. Bar: N.Y. 1973, U.S. Ct. Appeals (2d cir.) 1975, D.C. 1978, U.S. Ct. Appeals (4th cir.) 1979, U.S. Ct. Appeals (D.C. cir.) 1979, U.S. Supreme Ct. 1980, U.S. Ct. Appeals (6th cir.) 1985, U.S. Ct. Appeals (7th cir.) 1989, U.S. Ct. Appeals (3d cir.) 1991, U.S. Ct. Appeals (5th cir.) 1998. Atty. Dept. Labor, Washington, 1972-74; assoc. Guggenheimer & Untermyer, NYC, 1974-77, Seyfarth, Shaw, Fairweather & Geraldson, Washington, 1977-79, ptnr., 1979-83, Jones Day, Washington, 1983—, and chmn. labor and employment law practice, 1991—. Adj. prof. law Georgetown U., 1988—91; mem. Nat. Adv. Com. on Ergonomics; adv. Am. Law Inst., 2004—. Editor (contbg.): Employee Rels. Law Jour., 1983—91; editor: (assoc.) Occupl. Safety and Health Law; mem. editl. adv. bd. Benefits Law Jour., 1991—2002. Fellow, Coll. Labor and Employment Law, 1997—. Mem.: ABA (sec. labor and employment law com. on employee benefits, com. on occupl. safety and health), D.C. Bar Assn., NYU Ctr. for Labor and Employment Law (bd. dirs.), Kenwood Golf and Country Club Bethesda, Met. Club Washington. Democrat. Jewish. Office: Jones Day 51 Louisiana Ave NW Washington DC 20001-2113 Office Phone: 202-879-3920. Business E-Mail: wgoldsmith@jonesday.com.

GOLDSTEIN, ALFRED GEORGE, consumer products company executive; b. N.Y.C., Sept. 22, 1932; s. Milton and Pauline M. G.; m. Hope D. Perry, July 5, 1959; children: Mark, Robert. AB, CCNY, 1953; MS, Columbia

U., 1954. With Sears, Roebuck & Co., Chgo., 1957—79, v.p. mdse, group nat. mdse. mgr., 1976-79; sr. v.p. consumer bus. Am. Can Co., Greenwich, Conn., 1979-81, sr. v.p. waste recovery bus., 1981-82, exec. v.p. plastics packaging bus., 1982-83, pres. splty. retailing sector, 1983-87; pres. splty. merchandising and direct mktg. group, Sears Logistics Svc. Sears, Roebuck & Co., Chgo., 1987-93; pres., CEO AG Assocs., Chgo., 1993 —; bd. dirs. Sears Mdse. Group, Sears Can., Ltd. Former vice chmn., CEO, bd. dirs. Fingerhut Corp.; chmn. bd. dirs. Pickwick Internat.; chmn., CEO, Musicland Group; bd. dirs. Gander Mountain Corp., 1994; adv. bd. in bus. ethics Kellogg Grad. Sch. Bus. Northwestern U., 1995-2004 Exec. editor: Internat. Jour. Addictions, 1975-80. Trustee Archaeus Found., 1978—90; bd. dirs. United Negro Coll. Fund, 1991—, mem. exec. com., 1996, vice chmn., 2001—, trustee com. econ. devel., 1999—; mem. mktg. com. bd. trustees Art Inst. Chgo., 1988—2002; mem. adv. bd. Goizueta Bus. Sch. Ctr. Leadership and Career Studies, Emory U., 1990—97; mem. exec. com. Columbia U. Grad. Sch. Bus. Alumni Assn., 1980—86, Am. Can Co. Found.; bd. dirs. Art Americana, 1996; mem. adv. bd. chief exec. leadership inst. Yale U., 2000—. Mem. Am. Arbitration Assn. (arbitrator), Bus. Execs. Nat. Security.

GOLDSTEIN, ALLAN LEONARD, biochemist, educator; b. Bronx, N.Y., Nov. 8, 1937; s. Morris and Miriam (Siegel) G.; m. Linda Jo Tish, Dec. 23, 1975; children: Jennifer Joy, Dawn Eden, Adam Lee. BS, Wagner Coll., 1959, DSc (hon.), 1997; MS, Rutgers U., 1961, PhD, 1964. Tchg. asst. Rutgers U., New Brunswick, NJ, 1959-61, asst. instr. biology, 1961-63, instr. physiology, 1963-64; rsch. fellow Albert Einstein Coll. Medicine, 1964-66, instr. biochemistry, 1966-67, asst. prof., 1967-71, asso. prof., 1971-72; prof., dir. divsn. biochemistry U. Tex. Med. Br., Galveston, 1972-78, acting dir. multidisciplinary rsch. program in mental health, 1973-78; prof., chmn. dept. biochemistry and molecular biology George Washington U. Sch. Medicine, Washington, 1978—, pres., sci. dir. Inst. for Advanced Studies in Immunology and Aging, 1985-95; chmn. bd. Alpha 1 Biomeds., 1982-2000, RegeneRX Biopharms., Inc., 2000—. Cons. Syntex Rsch., 1972-74, Hoffmann-LaRoche, 1974-82; spl. cons. bd. sci. counselors Nat. Inst. Allergy and Infectious Diseases, 1975; mem. med. rsch. svc. rev. bd. in oncology VA, 1977-80; cons. mem. decisive network com. Biol. Response Modifiers program Divsn. Cancer Treatment, Nat. Cancer Inst., 1982-84; mem. sci. adv. com. to pres. Papanicolaou Cancer Rsch. Inst. Miami, Inc., 1981-84; mem. AIDS task force adv. com. Nat. Cancer Inst., 1983-84; mem. sci. bd. Alliance for Aging Rsch., 1986—; trustee Albert Sabin Vaccine Inst., 2000—. Discoverer (with Abraham White) Thymosins, hormones of thymus gland and HGP-30 a "core" based p17 AIDS Vaccine. Decorated chevalier des Palmes Academiques (France), comdr. Order Vasco Nuñez de Balboa, 2003; recipient Career Scientist award NYC Health Rsch. Coun., 1967, Alumni Achievement award Wagner Coll., 1974, Gordon Wilson medal Am. Clin. and Climatol Soc., 1976, Disting. Faculty Rsch. award U. Tex. Sch. Biomed. Scis., 1976, Van Dyke award in pharmacology Columbia Coll. Physicians and Surgeons, 1984, award Burroughs Wellcome Found., FASEB, 1986, Fernandez-Cruz award, 1989, Martin Rubin award Am. Coll. Advancement in Medicine, 1990, Michele Fodera Internat. prize for Biomed. Rsch., Italy, 1990, Disting. Rsch. award George Washington U. Med. Sch., 2003, Catherine Birch McCormick medal Group, Wash. U. Med. Sch.,2005. Mem. AAAS, Endocrine Soc., Am. Soc. Biol. Chemists and Molecular Biologists, Am. Assn. Immunologists, Internat. Soc. Immunopharmacology (coun. mem. 1985-94), Assn. Med. Sch. Chm. of Depts. Biochemistry, AAUP, Acad. Medicine of Washington, Toastmasters Internat. (pres. NY chpt. 1971), Sigma Xi. Home: 800 25th St NW Apt 1005 Washington DC 20037-2207 Office: George Washington U Med Ctr Dept Biochemistry/Molecular Biology 2300 I St NW Washington DC 20037-2336 Business E-Mail: bcmalg@gwumc.edu.

GOLDSTEIN, ALVIN, lawyer; b. N.Y.C., Nov. 21, 1929; s. Abraham and Florence (Bruckner) G.; m. Eleanor Kronish, Dec. 27, 1959; children— Eric, Michael, Eileen. BSS., Coll. City N.Y., 1950; LL.B., Bklyn. Law Sch., 1953, S.JD magna cum laude, 1960. Bar: N.Y. State 1953, U.S. Supreme Ct. Asso. firm Levine & Berman, N.Y.C., 1955-59, partner, 1963; practiced in N.Y.C., 1960-62; partner firm Berman, Paley, Goldstein, Kannry, N.Y.C., 1964—. Contbr. articles to profl. publs. Served with AUS, 1953-55. Mem.: ABA, Assn. Bar City of N.Y., N.Y. State Bar Assn. Home: 1 Chester Ter Hastings On Hudson NY 10706-3907 Office: Berman Paley Goldstein & Kannry 500 5th Ave Fl 43 New York NY 10110-0375 Office Phone: 212-354-9600. Business E-Mail: agoldstein@bpgk-law.com.

GOLDSTEIN, ARTHUR LOUIS, retired utilities executive; s. David and Henrietta (Frankfort) Goldstein; m. Vida F. Fishbach; children: Jonathan M., Susanne B., James A. BSChemE, Rensselaer Poly. Inst., 1957; MSChemE, U. Del., 1959; MBA, Harvard U., 1960. Pres., CEO Ionics, Inc., Watertown, Mass., 1971—2003, chmn., 1991—2004; ret., 2004. Bd. dirs. State St. Corp., State St. Bank and Trust Co., Cabot Corp., Ptnrs. Healthcare Sys. Inc. Trustee Calif. Inst. Tech., Mass. Gen. Physicians Orgn., Inc., Dana-Farber/Ptnrs. Cancer Care; co-chmn. Indsl. Rels. and Ventures com. Ptnrs. Healthcare Sys. Inc.; mem. NAE and its industry adv. bd.; exec. com. CEOs for Fundamental Change in Edn., Inner-City Scholarship Fund; chmn. Mass. High Tech. Coun., 1985—87, bd. dirs., mem. exec. com.; past pres. Rensselaer Coun.; former bd. dirs. Jobs for Mass., Inc.; former mem. vis. com. Harvard Bus. sch., Harvard Sch. Pub. Health; cardiovasc. adv. coun. Harvard Environ. Health Coun. Achievements include patents for purification and processing of liquids. Office: 24 Hubbard Rd Weston MA 02493

GOLDSTEIN, AVRAM, pharmacology educator; b. N.Y.C., July 3, 1919; s. Israel and Bertha (Markowitz) Goldstein; m. Dora Benedict, Aug. 29, 1947; children: Margaret, Daniel, Joshua, Michael. AB, Harvard, 1940, MD, 1943. Intern Mt. Sinai Hosp., N.Y.C., 1944; successively instr., assoc., asst. prof. pharmacology Harvard U., 1947—55; prof. dept. pharmacology Stanford U., Palo Alto, Calif., 1955—89, exec. head dept., 1955—70, prof. emeritus, 1989—. Dir. Addiction Rsch. Found., Palo Alto, Calif., 1973—87. Author: Biostatistics, Principles of Drug Action, 1965, ADDICTION: From Biology to Drug Policy, 2001. Served from 1st lt. to capt., Med. Corps U.S. Army, 1944—46. Mem.: AAAS, Am. Soc. Biol. Chemists, Am. Soc. Pharmacology and Exptl. Therapeutics, Am. Acad. Arts and Scis., Inst. Medicine NAS.

GOLDSTEIN, BERNARD, transportation executive, hotel executive; b. Rock Island, Ill., Feb. 5, 1929; s. Morris and Fannie (Borenstein) G.; m. Irene Alter, Dec. 18, 1949; children: Jeffrey, Robert, Kathy, Richard. BA, U. Ill., 1949, LLB, 1951. Bar: Iowa 1951. With Alter Co., Bettendorf, Iowa, 1951—, chmn. bd., 1979—, Isle of Capri Casinos, Inc., Biloxi, Miss., 1992—, chmn. CEO, 1997—. Bd. visitors U. Ill. Coll. Law, 2004—. Pres. Quad City Jewish Fedn., 1975. Named Top Performing Gaming CEO of the Yr., Am. Gaming Assn., 2001; recipient Ernst and Young Entrepreneur of the Yr. award, 1999, Rivers Hall of Fame Achievement award, 1999, Simon Wiesenthal Disting. Cmty. award, Compass award, Passenger Vessel Assn., Outstanding Bus. Leader award, Jewish Fedn. South Palm Beach County, Jerusalem medal, State of Israel Bonds, Disting. Alumnus award, U. Ill. Coll. Law, 2004—05. Jewish.

GOLDSTEIN, BERNARD DAVID, public health service officer, educator; b. Bronx, N.Y., Feb. 28, 1939; m. Russellyn Carruth, May 6, 1995; children: Lara, Ross. BS, U. Wis., 1958; MD, NYU, 1962. Diplomate Am. Bd. Toxicology, Am. Bd. Internal Medicine, Am. Bd. Hematology. Faculty depts. environ. medicine and medicine NYU Med. Ctr., N.Y.C., 1968—80; attending physician Bellevue and Univ. Hosps., N.Y.C., 1968—80; prof., chmn. dept. environ. and cmty. medicine U. Medicine and Dentistry, N.J.-Robert Wood Johnson Med. Sch., Piscataway, 1980—, dir. grad. program in pub. health, 1982—89, dir. environ. and occupl. health scis. inst., 1985—; asst. adminstr. for R & D EPA, Washington, 1983—85; acting dean Sch. Pub. Health of N.J., Piscataway, 1998—99; dir. Nat. Inst. Environ. Health Scis. Ctr. of Excellence, 1988—94. Chmn. clean air sci. adv. com. EPA, 1982—83; toxicology study sect. NIH, 1980—84, chmn., 1982—84; bd. sci. dirs. Risk Sci. Inst., 1986—, nat. adv. environ. health effects coun., 1987—91; chmn. ad hoc com. on dioxin EPA, 1988—89, vice-chmn., chmn. sci. group on methodology for sci. evaluation chems., 1989—, chmn. working group on Air Quality Guidelines for Major Urban Air Pollutants, 1985; health rev. com., chmn. health rsch. com. Health Effects Inst., 1987—2000; bd. dirs. Internat. Life Sci. Inst., Roy F. Weston, Inc.; pres. Soc. for Risk Analysis, 2002. Recipient Solomon Berson Med. Alumni Achievement award, NYU, 1989, Kehoe award, Am. Coll. Occupl. Environ. Medicine, 1993, Stuagis award, Am. Coll. Preventive Medicine, 1995, Sullivan award, N.J. Pub. Health Assn., 1998, Disting. Achievement award, Soc. for Risk Analysis, 1999, Sen. Frank Lautenberg award, UMDNV Sch. Pub. Health, 2005. Fellow: ACP, Am. Coll. Preventive Medicine; mem.: Am. Soc. Clin. Investigation, Inst. Medicine NAS. Achievements include research in in concept of biological markers in the field of risk assessment. Office: Deans Office Univ Pitts Grad Sch Pub Health 130 Desoto St Pittsburgh PA 15261 Business E-Mail: bdgold@pitt.edu.

GOLDSTEIN, BRAM H., medical researcher; b. Honolulu, Sept. 6, 1969; s. Gerald B. and Arleen Danor Goldstein. PhD, U. Ariz., 1998. Post doctoral fellow U. Pa., Phila., 1998—2000; post doctoral rschr. UCLA, L.A., 2000—01; clin. rschr. Hoag Meml. Hosp. Presbyn. and Ob-Gyn. Assocs., Newport Beach, Calif., 2002—. Office Phone: 949-642-1361. Office Fax: 949-646-7157. E-mail: bram@gynoncology.com.

GOLDSTEIN, BRUCE I., lawyer; b. Newark, Nov. 4, 1942; s. Samuel C. and Gertrude A. Goldstein; m. Marjorie R. Goldstein, Aug. 21, 1969; children: Jed, Geoffrey. JD, Cornell U., 1967. Exec. asst., U.S. atty., chief spl. prosecutions U.S. Atty.'s Office Dist. N.J., Newark, 1971-77; mng. ptnr., trial lawyer Saiber Schlesinger Satz & Goldstein LLC, Newark, 1977—. Adj. prof. Rutgers U. Law Sch., N.J., 1975-78; mediator U.S. Dist. Ct. N.J., 1989—, mem. lawyer's adv. com., 1993; chmn. fee arbitration com. N.J. Supreme Ct., 1989—; pres. comml. subtrack adv. com. Supreme Ct. Complex. Fellow Am. Bar Found., Am. Coll. Trail Lawyers; mem. Assn. Fed. Bar State N.J. (pres. 1988-89, mem. adv. bd.). Home: 15 Deerwood Trail Warren NJ 07059 Office: Saiber Schlesinger Satz and Goldstein 1 Gateway Ctr Newark NJ 07102-5311 E-mail: big@saiber.com.

GOLDSTEIN, BURTON JACK, psychiatrist; b. Balt., Sept. 23, 1930; s. Hyman and Roz (Levin) C.; m. Linda Feuer, June 16, 1989; children: Howard, Herbert, Brian, Esther, Leonard, Mark. BS in Pharmacy, U. Md., 1953, MD, 1960. Diplomate Am. Bd. Psychiatry and Neurology (bd. examiner). Intern Jackson Meml. Hosp., Miami, Fla., 1960-61, NIMH fellow in psychiatry, 1961-63, chief resident, 1963; dir. div. clin. psychopharmacology, dept. psychiatry U. Miami, 1964-92, chief div. research, 1964-71, prof. pharmacology, 1973—, prof. psychiatry, 1973—, acting chmn. dept. psychiatry, 1983-85; prof. epidemiology, pub. health Sch. Medicine, 1999; sr. cons. in psychopharmacology Mt. Sinai Med. Ctr., Miami Beach, 1993—; dir. psychiat. consultation liaison svc. Mt. Sinai Hosp., Miami Beach, 1993—. Bd. advs. Fla. Mental Health Inst. U. South Fla.; cons. in psychiat. rsch. South Fla. State Hosp., West Hollywood; cons. indsl. security program Dept. Def.; cons. VA Psychiatry Svc., Miami; chmn. panel on neuropharmacologic drugs U.S. Pharmacopeial Conv., Inc., mem. exec. com.; mem. faculty Health Svcs. Ctr., U. Miami, 1996; med. rev. officer Dept. Athletics U. Miami, 1996—. Mem. editorial bd. Miami Medicine, Clin. Advancement in Treatment of Depression; contbr. chpts. to books, articles to profl. publs. Served to maj. AUS, 1953-62. Fellow Am. Psychiat. Assn. (life), Am. Coll. Psychiatrists, Am. Coll. Clin. Pharmacology, Am. Coll. Neuropsychopharmacology (life); mem. Royal Soc. Health, Am. Assn. Clin. Pharmacology and Chemotherapy, Am. Soc. Addiction Medicine, Collegium Internationale Neuropsychopharmacologium. Office: 1150 NW 14th St Ste 501 Miami FL 33136-1131 Office Phone: 305-243-3485. Business E-Mail: bgoldste@med.miami.edu. E-mail: bhls@earthlink.net.

GOLDSTEIN, CHARLES ARTHUR, lawyer; b. N.Y.C., Nov. 20, 1936; s. Murray and Evelyn V. Goldstein; m. Judith Stein, Sept. 29, 1962 (div. 1982); 1 child, Deborah Ruth; m. Carol Sager, Nov. 10, 1990 (div. 1995). AB, Columbia U., 1958; JD cum laude, Harvard U., 1961. Bar: N.Y. 1962. Law clk. U.S. Ct. Appeals (2d cir.), 1961-62; assoc. Fried, Frank, Harris, Shriver & Jacobson, N.Y.C., 1962-69; ptnr. Schulte Roth & Zabel, N.Y.C., 1969-79, Weil, Gotshal & Manges, N.Y.C., 1979-83, counsel, 1983-85; ptnr. Shea & Gould, N.Y.C., 1985-94, Sutherland, Asbill & Brennan, N.Y.C., 1994-95; counsel Squire, Sanders & Dempsey, N.Y.C., 1996-01; counsel to amb. Ronald S. Lauder, 2001—. Lectr. Columbia U. Law Sch. Gen. counsel to Citizens Budget Commn., 1980-87; mem. Temp. Commn. on City Fins., 1975-77; mem. Gov.'s Task Force on World Trade Ctr. Mem. Am. Coll. Real Estate Lawyers. Republican. Home: 220 E 65th St New York NY 10021-6620 Office: 767 Fifth Ave Ste 4200 New York NY 10153 Office Phone: 212-572-4092. Business E-Mail: cgoldstein@rslmgmt.com.

GOLDSTEIN, CHARLES HENRY, architect, consultant; b. Winthrop, Mass., Mar. 23, 1938; s. Daniel and Rose (Shulman) G.; children: Brent R., Scott H., Nathan H., Lindsay H., Vanessa H. Cert., Boston Archtl. Ctr., 1965. Registered architect, Mass., N.H., Conn. Chief designer Milo Hart Assocs., Lynnfield, Mass., 1970-72; prin. C.H. Goldstein Assocs., Methuen, Mass., 1972-73; ptnr. Sarver & Goldstein, Saugus, Mass., 1973-75; chief architect A.D. Maclaren Assocs., Andover, Mass., 1975-80, Allen & Demurjian, Boston, Mass., 1980-83; prin. Archtl. Energies, North Hampton, N.H., 1983—, North Andover, Mass., 1983—. Guest lectr. Wentworth Inst., Boston, 1982—, Merrimack Coll., North Andover, Mass.1978—, U. Debrecen, Hungary, 1992. Mem. bd. selectmen, bd. of health Town of Tewksbury (Mass.), 1969-72; mem. sch. coms., Merrimac and West Newbury, Mass., 1977-87. Recipient Honorable Mention award Interval Internat., 1982, N.H. Sam awards (5) for design, 1989-91; Boston Soc. Architects scholar, 1960; John Worthington Ames scholar, 1964; Rotch scholar finalist, 1964. Mem. Nat. Council Archtl. Registration Bds., Boston Soc. Office: Archtl Energies 200 Sutton St North Andover MA 01845-1656 E-mail: aearchitect@rcn.com.

GOLDSTEIN, DARRA JANE, language educator, editor; b. Lakewood, N.J., Apr. 28, 1951; d. Irving S. and Helen Haft Goldstein; m. Dean Adams Crawford, Aug. 23, 1980; 1 child, Leila Adams Crawford. BA, Vassar Coll., 1973; MA, Stanford U., 1976, PhD, 1983. Prof. Russian Williams Coll., Williamstown, Mass., 1983—; founding editor Gastronomica: The Jour. of Food and Culture, Berkeley, Calif., 2000—. Mem. acad. adv. coun. The Am. Coll. in Georgia; restaurant cons. Firebird, N.Y.C., 1996, Russian Tea Rm., N.Y.C., 1999—2000. Author: A la Russe: A Cookbook of Russian Hospitality, 1983, reissued as A Taste of Russia, 1985, 1991, 2d rev. edit., 1999, All About Love, 1985, Art for the Masses, 1985; author: (with Elizabeth Gaynor and Kari Haavisto) Russian Houses, 1991; author: The Georgian Feast: The Vibrant Culture and Savory Food of the Republic of Georgia, 1993, reprinted, 1999, Nikolai Zabolotsky: Play for Mortal Stakes, 1993, The Vegetarian Hearth: Recipes and Reflections for the Cold Season, 1996, reprinted as The Winter Vegetarian, 2000; author: (with Deborah Rothschild and Ellen Lupton) Graphic Design in the Mechanical Age, 1998; contbr. articles to profl. jours.; editor (with Jill Meredith): The World Opened Wide: 20th Century Russian Women Artists from the Collection of Thomas P. Whitney, 2001; series editor California Studies in Food and Culture, food editor Russian Life mag., mem. adv. bd. Finalist M.F.K. Fisher award, Les Dames d'Escoffier, 2002; recipient Sophie Coe Subsidiary prize in food history, The Oxford Symposium on Food History, 1997; Nat. Def. Fgn. Lang. fellow, 1975—77, Fulbright-Hays Doctoral Dissertation Abroad grantee, Slavic Inst., Stockholm U., 1980—81, rsch. grantee, Internat. Rsch. and Exchs. Bd., 1980—81, 1982—83, 1987, 1994, Mellon Found., 1984, 1997, Kennan Inst. for Advanced Russian Studies Rsch. fellow, 1986, rsch. fellow, Am. Coun. Learned Socs., 1987, coll. tchrs. fellow, NEH, 1999. Mem.: Internat. Assn. Culinary Profls., Am. Assn. for Advancement of Slavic Studies, Culinary Historians of Boston. Office: Williams Coll Weston Hall 995 Main St Williamstown MA 01267 Business E-Mail: darra.goldstein@williams.edu.

GOLDSTEIN, DAVID ARTHUR, biophysicist, educator; b. Rochester, NY, Nov. 8, 1934; s. Jacob David and Elizabeth Maude (Brown) G.; m. Marie Elaine Nardone, May 25, 1969; 1 child, David James. AB in Physics, Harvard U., 1956, MD, 1960. Rsch. fellow biophys. lab Harvard Med. Sch., Cambridge, Mass., 1960-62, rsch. assoc. biophys. lab., 1964-65; asst. prof. radiation biology and biophysics Rochester Sch. Med. and Dentistry, 1965-68, assoc. prof. biophysics, 1968—, assoc. prof. biomath., 1969-74, assoc. prof. med. informatics, 1988—. Dir. Med. Ctr. Computing, U. Rochester Med. Sch., 1975-77, assoc. chmn. dept. radiation biology and biophysics, 1980-85, dir. divsn. med. informatics, 1988-98; cons. mathematician NIMH, Bethesda, Md., 1963-64. Contbr. articles to profl. jours. Treas. Stormers Soccer Club, Rochester, 1983-93; bd. dirs. Monroe County Girls Soccer League, Rochester, 1988-93. Surgeon, USPHS, 1963-64. Grantee AEC, NIH, NSF, ERDA, DOE, 1965-96. Mem. Biophys. Soc., N.Y. Acad. Scis. Home: 75 Deer Creek Rd Pittsford NY 14534-4147 E-mail: dgoldst2@frontiernet.net.

GOLDSTEIN, DAVID BAIRD, energy executive, physicist; b. Cleve., June 29, 1951; s. Laurence and Gloria Reta (Baumgarten) G.; m. Julia Beth Vetromile, May 17, 1980; children: Elianna Louise, Abraham Micah. AB in Physics, U. Calif., Berkeley, 1973; PhD in Physics, U. Calif., 1978. Rsch. asst. Lawrence Berkeley (Calif.) Lab., 1975-78, staff scientist, 1978-80; sr. scientist, dir. energy program Natural Resources Def. Coun., San Francisco, 1980—. Sub-com. chair standing standards project com. 90.1 ASHRAE, Atlanta, 1983-96; vice-chmn. bd. Consortium for Energy Efficiency, Inc., Sacramento, 1991-93, 99-02, bd. dirs., 2002—, advisor, 1993-96; initiator and advisor Super Efficient Refrigerator Program, Inc., 1991-96. Contbr. articles to profl. jours. Recipient Champion of Energy Efficiency award Am. Coun. for an Energy Efficient Economy, 1988, 94, Excellence in Achievement award Calif. Alumni Assn., 2003; MacArthur Found. fellow, 2002. Fellow: Am. Phys. Soc. (Leo Szilard award 1998); mem.: Residential Energy Svcs. Network (v.p. 2004—), Inst. Location Efficiency (treas. 1999—, bd. dirs.), New Bldgs. Inst. (pres. 2000—, co-initiator), Inst. Market Transformation (chmn. 1995—, initiator, bd. dirs.), Sigma Xi, Phi Beta Kappa. Jewish. Avocations: travel, hiking, music, photography. Home: 1240 Washington St San Francisco CA 94108-1041 Office: Natural Resources Def Coun 111 Sutter 20th Fl San Francisco CA 94104 Office Phone: 415-875-6100. Business E-Mail: dgoldstein@nrdc.org.

GOLDSTEIN, DONALD MAURICE, historian, educator; b. Dec. 15, 1932; s. Max A. and Jean M. Goldstein; m. Mariann Norma Zinck, Aug. 5, 1961; children: Tammie, Timmie, Tommie, Teri. BA, U. Md., 1954, MA, 1962; MS, Georgetown U., 1963; MPA, George Washington U., 1965; PhD, U. Denver, 1970; grad., War Coll., 1973, Air Command and Staff Coll., 1965. Commd. 2d. lt. USAF, 1955, advanced through grades to lt. col., 1972, comdr. missile site, 1958-59; staff officer US Strike Command, 1961-64; rsch. assoc. Airstaff Pentagon; assoc. prof. history USAF Acad., 1965-71, asst. track coach, 1965-71; ret., 1977; assoc. prof. history Troy State U., Ala., 1971-74; prof. aerospace studies U. Pitts., 1975-77, assoc. prof. pub. and internat. affairs, 1975-92, prof., 1993, dir. placement and alumni, 1977-85, assoc. dean, 1985-88. Author: Ennis C. Whithead Aerospace Commander, 1970, Adolph Hitler in the Perspective of the Am. Press, 1961, Adolph Hitler Administr. of a Society, 1965, (with others) Miracle at Midway, 1982, 2001, 3d edit., 2002, Target Tokyo: The Story of the Surge Spy Ring in Japan, 1984, 3d edit., 2001; collaborator: At Dawn We Slept: The Untold Story of Pearl Harbor, 1981, 3d edit., 2001, Pearl Harbor: The Verdict of History, 1985, 3d edit., 2001, December 7, 1941: The Day the Japanese Attacked Pearl Harbor, 1990, Fading Victory: The Diary of Matome Ugaki, 1991, The Way It Was: A Pictorial Hist.of Pearl Harbor, 1991, The Williwar War: The Arkansas Nat. Guard in World War II, 1992, The Pearl Harbor Paper, 1993, Classics in Internat. Affairs with Others, 1993, 3d edit., 2005, D Day: A Pictorial Hist., 1994, Nuts: The Battle of the Bulge, 1994, Security in Korea: War, Stalemate and Negotiation, 1994, Rain of Ruin: A Photographic Hist. of Hiroshima and Nagasaki, 1995, Amelia Earhart: A Biography, 1997, Vietnam: A Pictorial History, 1997, The Spanish American War: A Centennial Hist., 1998, The Korean War: The Story and Photographs, 2000, World War I: The Story and Photographs, 2002, God's Samurai: Lead Pilot at Pearl Harbor, 2003, The Pacific War Paper, 2004, Classics in International Affairs, 3d edit., 2005; asst. editor papers on fgn. policy for House Com. on Internat. Affairs, 1947-54; contbr. articles on def. policy and nat. security affairs to profl. jour. Decorated Soldiers medal, Meritorious Svc. medal with 2 oak leaf clusters, Joint Svc. Commendation medal, Air Force Commendation medal with oak leaf cluster; recipient Peabody award, 1991, Univ. Pitts. Tchr. of Yr., 2003, Chancellor Disting. Tchr. award, 2003. Mem. Nat. Assn. Soc. Pub. Adminstrs. (Tchr. of Yr. award 2001), Am. Hist. Assn., Internat. Studies Assn., Am. Soc. Pub. Adminstr., Am. Polit. Sci. Assn., Air Force Assn., Toastmasters, Omicron Delta Kappa, Phi Kappa Phi, Phi Alpha Theta, Sigma Nu. Roman Catholic. Home: 2146 Meadowmont Dr Upper St Clair Pittsburgh PA 15241 Office: U Pitts Grad Sch Pub Int Affairs Dean's Office 3N25 Posvar Hall Pittsburgh PA 15260 Office Phone: 412-648-1026. Business E-Mail: goldy@pitt.edu, dmgh@aol.com.

GOLDSTEIN, DORA BENEDICT, pharmacologist, educator; b. Milton, Mass., Apr. 25, 1922; d. George Wheeler and Marjory (Pierce) Benedict; m. Avram Goldstein, Aug. 29, 1947; children: Margaret E. Wallace, Daniel P., Joshua S., Michael B. Student, Bryn Mawr Coll., 1940-42, Stanford U., 1945. Research assoc. Stanford U., 1955-70, sr. research assoc., 1970-74, adj. prof., 1974-78, prof. pharmacology, 1978-92, prof. pharmacology emerita, 1992—, co-dir. faculty mentoring program sch. medicine, 1994—2001. Author: Pharmacology of Alcohol, 1983; contbr. articles to sci. jours. Bd. dirs. Parents, Families and Friends of Lesbians and Gays, 2000—. Mem.: Intersex Soc. N.Am. (med. adv. bd. 2003—05). E-mail: dody@stanford.edu.

GOLDSTEIN, E. ERNEST, lawyer, consultant; b. Pitts., Oct. 9, 1918; s. Nathan E. and Annie (Ginsberg) G.; m. Peggy Janet Rosenfeld, June 22, 1941 (dec. Aug. 2003); children: Susan M. Goldstein Lipsitch, Daniel F. AB cum laude, Amherst Coll., 1939; student, U. Chgo. Law Sch., 1940-42; LL.B., Georgetown U., 1947; S.JD, U. Wis., 1956. Bar: D.C. 1947, Tex. 1958, U.S. Supreme Ct. 1967, conseil juridique, France 1973-79. Pvt. practice, Washington, 1947; with Dept. Justice, also War Claims Commn., 1947-50; assoc. counsel crime com. U.S. Senate, 1950-51; gen. counsel antitrust subcom. jud. Ho. of Reps., 1951-52; restrictive trade practices specialist Office U.S. Spl. Rep., Paris; also U.S. rep. productivity and applied research com. OEEC, 1952-54; prof. law U. Tex., 1955-65; spl. asst. to Pres. U.S. Lyndon B. Johnson, 1967-69; counsel Coudert Freres, Paris, 1966-67, ptnr., 1969-79; cons. CBS, Inc., 1980-85; advisor Ransom Humanities Rsch. Ctr. U. Tex., 1995—2003; ret. Cons. on antitrust European coal and steel cmty., Luxembourg, 1956, on trade regulation Justice Sec., P.R., 1962; internat. law cons. Naval War Coll., 1962, 64; lectr. Inst. Advanced European Studies, U. Nice, France, 1967, Free U. Brussels, 1967, Europa Inst., Amsterdam, 1970; vis. prof. U. P.R. Law Sch., 1962; prof. Am. sem., Salzburg, Austria, 1963, 79; adj. prof. law U. Tex., 1993-95; chmn. Internat. Lawyers Ann. Conf. Mgmt. Ctr., Europe, 1971-79. Author: Patent, Trademark and Copyright Law, 1959, American Enterprise and Scandinavian Antitrust Law, 1962; contbr. author: LBJ: To Know Him Better, 1995, procs. of The Conference on Global Responsibility of Law Librarians, 1990; founder Tex. Internat. Law Jour., 1963, adv. bd., 1983—. Membership chair Am. Vets. Com., Washington, 1946-47; chmn. S.W. regional adv. bd. Anti-Defamation League, 1964-65; bd. dirs. Am. C. of C. in France, 1970-79, Ctr. Internat. Formation Européene, 1971—; trustee Leadership Enrichment Arts Program, 1996—; dir. Bus. Alliance for Vietnamese Edn., 1996—, chmn. adv. bd., 1994, co-chmn. adv. bd., 1995—; bd. govs. Am. Hosp. Paris, 1972-79, sec., 1974-79; chmn. fund raising Dem. Party Com. in France, 1973-77; nat. com. Lyndon B. Johnson Meml. Grove, 1972-74; nat. fin. coun. Dem. Nat. Com., 1975-77. With AUS, 1942-46. Decorated Legion of Merit; chevalier Légion d'Honneur, chevalier Ordre des Arts et des Lettres; recipient Carl Fulda Internat. Law award U. Tex., 1978, medal of Honor, Am. C. of C., Paris, 1984; Carnegie Found. fellow, 1954-55, Ford. Found. Internat. Studies fellow, 1959-60. Mem. Am. Club Paris (pres. 1976-78), Philos Soc. of Tex., Tex. Internat. Law Soc. (founder), Headliners Club, Austin Town and Gown Club, Order of Coif, Phi Delta Phi. Home: Cambridge Tower 1801 Lavaca St Apt 15F Austin TX 78701-1333

GOLDSTEIN, EDWARD DAVID, lawyer, former glass company executive; b. N.Y.C., July 12, 1927; s. Michael and Leah (Kirsh) G.; m. Rhoda Gordon, Apr. 18, 1950; children: Linda, Ellen, Ruth, Michael. BA, U. Mich., 1950, JD with distinction, 1952. Bar: Calif. 1952. Assoc. Orrick, Dahlquist, Herrington & Sutcliffe, San Francisco, 1952-54, Johnston & Johnston, San Francisco,

1954-56; with legal dept. Ohio Match Co., Hunt Foods & Industries, 1956-58; asst. gen. mgr., sales mgr. Glass Containers Corp., Fullerton, Calif., 1958-62, v.p., gen. mgr., 1962-68, pres., CEO, 1968-83. Chmn. bd. Knox Glass Co., Fairmount Glass Cos., 1967-68; gen. counsel FHP, Internat., FHP, Inc., 1985-87. Chmn. bd. trustees St. Jude Hosp., Fullerton, 1984-88. Served with USNR, 1945-46. Mem. ABA, State Bar Calif., Orange County Bar Assn., Nat. Health Lawyers Assn., Am. Arbitration Assn., Calif. Soc. Healthcare Attys. Home: 2230 Yucca Ave Fullerton CA 92835-3320 Office: 110 E Wilshire Ave STe 305 Fullerton CA 92832-1900 Office Phone: 714-525-5055. Personal E-mail: edgatty@aol.com.

GOLDSTEIN, ELLIOTT, lawyer, director; b. Atlanta, Oct. 23, 1915; s. Max Fullmore and Sarah Ray (London) G.; m. Harriet Weinberg, Oct. 24, 1942; children: Lillian, Ellen. Student, Ga. Sch. Tech., 1932-33; BS, U. Ga., 1936; LL.B., Yale U., 1939. Bar: Ga. 1938, D.C. 1977. Asso. firm Little, Powell, Reid & Goldstein, Atlanta, 1939-40; partner firm Powell, Goldstein, Frazer & Murphy, Atlanta, 1946-77, 80—, Washington, 1977-80. Spl. counsel com. on standards ofcl. conduct U.S. Ho. of Reps., 1978; mem. legal adv. com. N.Y. Stock Exchange, 1982-85. Author: Counselling the Board of Directors in its Structure, Functions and Compensation, 1985, Georgia Corporation Law and Practice, 1989; contbr. articles to profl. jours. Hon. v.p. Am. Jewish Com.; chmn. Atlanta Hist. Soc., 1990-94. Lt. col. F.A., U.S. Army, 1941-46, ETO. Decorated Bronze Star. Fellow ABA Found.; mem. ABA (chmn. com. corp. laws 1979-84, chmn. ad hoc com. ALI Corp. governance project 1982-86, mem. coun. sect. corp. banking and bus. law 1983-86, sr. del. ho. of dels. 1986-94), Am. Law Inst., Ga. Bar Assn., Atlanta Bar Assn., Lawyers Club Atlanta, Commerce Club, Standard Club. Democrat. Home: 2660 Peachtree Rd NW Atlanta GA 30305-3673 Office: Powell Goldstein LLP One Atlantic Center 1201 West Peachtree St NW 14th Fl Atlanta GA 30305 Office Phone: 404-572-6605. Business E-Mail: egoldste@pogolw.com.

GOLDSTEIN, FRANK ROBERT, lawyer; b. July 31, 1943; s. Morris Herman and Maxine (Herzfeld) G.; m. Phyllis Ellen Levy, Jan. 26, 1967; children: Matthew Alexander, Andrew Stephen. AB, Duke U., 1964; LLB, U. Md., 1967. Bar: Md. 1967, D.C. 1981, Mass. 1985. Clk. to chief justice U.S. Dist. Ct. Md., Balt., 1967—68; assoc. Piper & Marbury, Balt. and Washington, 1968—74, ptnr. Washington, 1974—88, Morgan, Lewis & Bockius LLP, Washington, 1989—96, Sidley Austin Brown & Wood LLP, Washington, 1997—. Bd. govs. Reconstructionist Rabbincal Coll., Wyncote, Pa. 1992-94; bd. dirs. Washington-Balt. Regional Assn., 1984-93, Al Marah Neighborhood Assn., Bethesda, Md., 1982-85, Paine Webber Mortgage Fin. Inc., Columbia, Md., 1987-93 Author: Mournful Numbers, 1995; co-author: District of Columbia Limited Liability Company Forms and Practice Manual, 1995. Pres. Meadowbrook Neighborhood Assn., Potomac, Md., 1990—93, Tidesfall Neighborhood Assn., Columbia, Md., 1972; bd. visitors U. Md. Sch. Law, Balt., 1992—2001; pres. Adat Shalom Reconstructionist Congregation, Bethesda, Md., 1982—85. Fellow Am. Bar Found.; mem. ABA, D.C. Bar Assn. (chmn. ptnr. com. 1985-86, treas. 1988-89), Mass. Bar Assn., Md. State Bar Assn. (chmn. ptnr. com. 1980-82, chmn. sect. legal edn. and admission to bar com. 1975, chmn. D.C. corp. code rev. project 1989-93), Order of Coif. Jewish. Home: 100301 Strathmore Hall St Apt 306 North Bethesda MD 20852 Office: Sidley Austin Brown & Wood LLP 1501 K St NW Washington DC 20005 Business E-Mail: fgoldstein@sidley.com.

GOLDSTEIN, GARY SANFORD, executive recruiter; b. Rochester, N.Y., Nov. 29, 1954; s. Perry Leon and Joyce Lorraine (Hoffman) G.; m. Lisa Ann Bernstein, Sept. 24, 1977 (div. 1980); m. Alicia de la Caridad Lazaro, Jan. 3, 1983 (div. 1992); children: Jessica Leigh, Vanessa Kyle; m. Jill Allyson Brooke, June 11, 1995; 1 child, Parker Leon. BS in Acctg., Canisius Coll., 1976; OPM, Harvard U. Acct. Arthur Andersen & Co., N.Y.C., 1976-79; mng. dir. A-L Assocs., N.Y.C., 1979-84; chmn., pres. The Whitney Group, N.Y.C., 1984—; chmn., CEO Headway Corp. Resources, 1992—2003; CEO Whitney Group LLC, N.Y.C., 2003—. Coun. mem. The Brookings Instn., Washington, 1990—; mem. bd. dirs. Rippowam Cisqa Sch., 1992—2000. Mem. Young Pres. Orgn. Avocations: horseback riding, tennis, collecting photorealistic art, basketball. Home: 161 Buxton Rd Bedford Hills NY 10507-2310 Office: Whitney Group LLC 850 3rd Ave New York NY 10022-6222 E-mail: ggoldstein@whitneygroup.com.

GOLDSTEIN, HOWARD BERNARD, investment banker; b. Bronx, N.Y., Dec. 4, 1943; s. Maurice and Matilda Goldstein; m. Susan Nadine Goldberg, June 25, 1967; children: Jill Alecya, Brett Adam. Student, Bernard Baruch/CCNY, 1962-63; BFA, Pratt Inst., 1970. Lic. ins. agt., N.Y., spl. tng. radiation detection, chemical, electrical and fire disaster, damage assessment specialist; lic. health and life ins. agt.; cert. for 1st responder hazardous materials ops., N.J. State Police/Bergen County Law and Pub. Safety Inst.; registered security broker, spl. training with Ft. Lee Police Dept. SWAT Team, 2005. Art dir. Fairfax Advt. divsn. Ogilvy & Mather, Inc., N.Y.C., 1968—72; creative dir. Hoffman Advt., N.Y.C., 1972—80, Miller, Addison, Steele, Inc., N.Y.C., 1980—82; pres. Gould Advt., Cliffside Park, NJ, 1969—; br. officer, tax shelter coord. E.F. Hutton & Co., Inc., N.Y.C., 1983—85; security broker, sr. v.p., mem. chmn.'s coun., dir.'s coun. Lehman Bros., 1985—94, mem. guided portfolio mgmt. program, 1985—94; securities broker, sr. v.p. Gruntal & Co., N.Y.C., 1994—2002; securities broker, sr. v.p., health and life ins. agt. Ryan Beck & Co., Ft. Lee, NJ, 2003—. V.p. bd. dirs. Winston Tower 200, Condominium Assn.; mem. Internat. Assn. Fin. Planning, Inst. Cert. Fin. Planners, Coll. Cert. Fin. Planners, Denver Grad. Police & Fire Acad. of Bergen County, N.J., 1986; capt., team leader Dept. Justice Emergency Response to Terrorism, 2000; trainee Nat. Fire Acad., Fed. Emergency Mgmt. Agy.; spl. trainee radiation detection, chm., elec. and fire disaster; damage assessment specialist ARC, Bergen Crossroads chpt., 1998; terrorism cons. Ft. Lee Office of Emergency Mgmt., 2002—; mem. Bergen County Weapons of Mass Destruction, Terrorism Task Force, 2003--. Designed Seal for art svcs. for ARC, 1961; exhibited photo show Bronx Hist. Soc., N.Y.C., 1970, paintings Soc. of Illustrators show, 1971-72, numerous other shows; represented in permanent collection Smithsonian Inst. Fin. officer N.J. State Police Office of Emergency Mgmt., Cliffside Park, 1986; spl. police officer Cliffside Park Police Dept., N.J. State Police Benevolent Assn., 1986—, Montclair State Coll. World of Computers, 1981; mem. steering com. Coalition Bus., Labor and Cmty. Orgns. N.Y., 1992, mem. exec. com., chmn. fin., 1992—; bd. advisor to UN Nat. Com. for Habitat, 1993—; first Am. investment banker to coord. pvt. bus. coun. meeting N.Y.C. with His Excellency Saparmurad A. Niyazov (1st elected pres. The Rep. of Turkismanistan, previously part of USSR) and cabinet of ministers, 1993; mem. Rep. Senatorial Inner Circle, 1992; mem. Graphic Artists Guild, 1976-80, Bronx County Hist. Soc., 1968-71, Cliffside Park Baseball Assn., 1979—, coach, 1981, 83; sponsor Project High Frontier, U.S. Govt., 1986, sustaining mem. Rep. Nat. Com., 1981—; preferred mem. U.S. Senatorial Club, 1984—; majority mem. Nat. Rep. Senatorial Com., 1984—; mem. Heritage Found., 1990—, Nat. Rep. Congrl. Com., 1984—, N.J. Rep. State Com., 1994—; capt., team leader emergency response to terrorism Dept. Justice, 2000; terrorism cons. Ft. Lee Office of Emergency Mgmt., 2002—, emergency man. first response team task forse exercise, Fort Lee, Bergen County 2003. Sachs Art scholar, 1955; recipient medal for art svc. Youth Friends Assn., 1961, Ga. Pacific award, 1978, Scholastic Mixed media award Scholastic Mag., 1961. Mem. Citizens Against Govt. Waste, The City Club N.Y. (govt. ops. com.), Tenafly Rifle and Pistol Club Inc., Nat. Rifle Assn. Clubs: Fort Lee Racquetball. Lodges: Bnai Brith. Jewish. Achievements include being first responder to World Trade Center Disaster, Sept. 11, 2001. Address: 200 Winston Dr Cliffside Park NJ 07010-3235 Office Phone: 201-585-6183. E-mail: howard.goldstein@ryanbeck.com.

GOLDSTEIN, HOWARD WARREN, lawyer; b. N.Y.C., Mar. 29, 1949; s. Murray and Claire (Millrod) G.; m. Wendy Jo Zacharius, Sept. 9, 1973; children: Lindsay Rebecca, Amanda Mikael, Justin Zacharius. BA, Northwestern U., 1970; JD, NYU, 1973. Bar: N.Y. 1974, U.S. Dist. Ct. (so. and ea. dists.) N.Y. 1974, U.S. Ct. Appeals (2d cir.) 1975, U.S. Ct. Appeals (10th cir.) 1984, U.S. Ct. Appeals (6th cir.) 1985, U.S. Ct. Appeals (3d cir.) 1997, U.S. Supreme Ct. 1984, U.S. Claims Ct. 1988. Law clk. to judge U.S. Dist. Ct. (ea. dist.) N.Y., 1973-74; assoc. Cravath, Swaine & Moore, N.Y.C., 1974-76; asst. U.S. atty. Office of U.S. Atty. (so. dist.) N.Y., N.Y.C., 1976-80; assoc. Mudge, Rose, Guthrie, Alexander & Ferdon, N.Y.C., 1980-81, ptnr., 1982-90, Fried, Frank, Harris, Shriver & Jacobson, N.Y.C., 1990—. Author: Grand Jury Practice, 1998; co-author: The Rights of Crime Victims, 1985, RICO: Civil and Criminal, Law and Strategy, 1989, Corporate Sentencing Guidelines, 1993. Mem. Fed. Bar Coun., Assn. of Bar of City of N.Y., Nat. Assn. Criminal Def. Lawyers, N.Y. Coun. Def. Lawyers, Order of Coif, Phi Beta Kappa. Jewish. Office: Fried Frank Harris Shriver & Jacobson One New York Plz New York NY 10004

GOLDSTEIN, IRVIN L., elementary school educator; b. Louisville, Aug. 12, 1929; s. Henry S. and Dorothy (Zillman) G.; m. Daisy Baker, Aug. 21, 1955; children: Steven, Alan, Sara, Lynne. BA in Edn., U. Ky., 1951; MEd in Supervision and Adminstrn., U. Louisville, 1961. Camp dir. Jewish Community Ctr., Louisville; elem. tchr. Louisville Pub. Schs.; elem. tchr., coord. camping New Albany (Ind.) Floyd County Schs. Speaker profl. confs.; prin. religious sch. The Temple, Louisville, 1957-98, life mem. bd. trustees, 1998; exch. tchr., Vancouver, B.C., Can., 1955-56; mem. leadership edn. adv. bd. Bellarmine Coll., 1987-96. Contbr. articles to profl. mags; author Teacher's Hanbook for Creative Learning, 2004. Mem. Floyd County Comprehensive Health Planning Coun., South Ind. Comprehensive Health Plan; active numerous community orgns. Named Valley Forge Classroom Tchr. of Yr., 1963, Floyd County Conservation Classroom Tchr. of Yr., 1973, 88, Reform Jewish Educator, 1986; recipient Tchr. of Yr. award Floyd County Schs., 1990; finalist Ind. Tchr. Yr., 1990; Ind. Coun. on Econ. Edn. grantee, 1989, 90, 91, 92, 93, Olin Davis award, Tchr. Creativity award Lilly Found., 1992. Mem. NEA, Nat. Assn. Temple Educators (nat. bd. dirs. 1994-98), Ind. Tchrs. Assn., Environ. Edn. Assn. Ind., NAFCEA (pres. 1968-69), Leadership Edn. Alumni Assn. (pres. 1990-91), Phi Delta Kappa. Home: 3430 Bryan Way Louisville KY 40220-1930

GOLDSTEIN, IRVING SOLOMON, chemistry professor, consultant; b. Bronx, N.Y., Aug. 20, 1921; s. Jacob and Jennie (Rathsprecher) G.; m. Helen Haft, Dec. 16, 1945; children: Ardath Ann, Darra Jane, Jared. BS in Chemistry, Rensselaer Poly. Inst., 1941; MS in Chemistry, Ill. Inst. Tech., 1944; PhD in Organic Chemistry, Harvard U., 1948. Teaching asst. Ill. Inst. Tech., Chgo., 1941-42; teaching fellow Harvard U., Cambridge, Mass., 1946-48; rsch. chemist N.Am. Rayon Corp., Elizabethton, Tenn., 1948-51; mgr. wood chemistry rsch. Koppers Co., Inc., Pitts., 1951-63; sr. rsch. scientist Nalco Chem. Co., Chgo., 1963-66; mgr. paper rsch. Continental Can Co., Chgo., 1966-68; prof. forest sci. Texas A&M U., College Station, 1968-71; prof., head wood and paper sci. dept. N.C. State U., Raleigh, 1971-78, prof. wood chemistry, 1978-92; prof. emeritus, 1992—. Editor: Wood Technology: Chemical Aspects, 1977, Organic Chemicals From Biomass, 1981, Composition and Structure of Wood, 1991; contbr. articles to profl. jours.; 15 inventions in field. Lt. USNR, 1942—46, ATO, PTO. Fellow Internat. Acad. Wood Sci.; mem. AAAS, Am. Chem. Soc. (chmn. cellulose div. 1982), Tech. Assn. Pulp and Paper Industry, Forest Products Rsch. Soc., Soc. Wood Sci. and Tech. E-mail: isgold@unity.ncsu.edu.

GOLDSTEIN, JACK, biopharmaceutical executive, microbiologist; b. N.Y.C., June 7, 1947; s. Arnold L. and Rachel (Vogel) G.; m. Laurie Ann Sacks, Aug. 28, 1969; 1 child, Justin T. BA, Rider U., Trenton, N.J., 1969; MS, St. John's U., Jamaica, N.Y., 1974, PhD, 1976. Diplomate Am. Bd. Med. Microbiology. Asst. dir. microbiology Queens Hosp. Ctr., Jamaica, 1976-81; dir. diagnostic labs. API div. Sherwood Med. Co., Plainview, N.Y., 1981-83; v.p. research and devel. MicroScan div. Baxter, Sacramento, 1983-86; group v.p. Ortho Diagnostic Systems Inc. div. Johnson & Johnson Co., Raritan, N.J., 1986-88; group v.p., gen. mgr. infectious disease bus. Ortho Diagnostic Systems, Inc. div. Johnson & Johnson Co., Raritan, N.J., 1988-92; exec. v.p. worldwide Ortho Diagnostic Sys. Inc. divsn. Johnson & Johnson Co., Raritan, N.J., 1992-93, pres. Ortho Diagnostic Sys. Inc. divsn., 1993-97; pres., CEO Applied Imaging Corp., Santa Clara, Calif., 1997-2001, chmn. bd., 2001—02; gen. ptnr. Windamere Venture Ptnrs., San Diego, 2001—02; pres. blood testing divsn. Chiron Corp., Emeryville, Calif., 2002—04, interim COO, 2004—05, pres., COO, 2005—. Mem. exam. com. Am. Bd. Med. Microbiology, Washington, 1984-91. Mem. editl. bd. Jour. Clin. Microbiology, Wasington, 1983-91; contbr. articles to profl. jours. Mem. Am. Soc. Microbiology, Am. Soc. Clin. Chemistry, Beta Beta Beta. Avocations: reading, skiing. Office: Chiron Corp 4560 Horton St Emeryville CA 94608-2916 Office Phone: 510-923-3850. E-mail: jack_goldstein@chiron.com.

GOLDSTEIN, JANE D., lawyer; b. Oct. 21, 1960; BA magna cum laude, Boston Univ., 1982, JD magna cum laude, 1989. Bar: Mass. 1989. Assoc. Ropes & Gray, Boston, 1989—98, ptnr. corp. dept., 1998—, head, retail & consumer branded products practice group. Mem.: Mad River Ski Club (bd. dir.). Office: Ropes & Gray 1 International Pl Boston MA 02110-2624 Office Phone: 617-951-7431. Office Fax: 617-951-7050. Business E-Mail: jane.goldstein@ropesgray.com.

GOLDSTEIN, JEFFREY A., corporate financial executive; b. Dec. 2, 1955; m. Nancy Coles Goldstein; 3 children. Student, London Sch. Econs., 1976; BA in Econs. with honors, Vassar Coll., 1977; MA in Econs., Yale U., 1980, PhD in Econs., 1983, MPhil in Econs., 1989. With Brookings Instn., Washington, 1977—78; instr. econs. Princeton U., NJ, 1982—83; with BT Wolfensohn, N.Y.C., 1984—99, co-chmn., 1982—99; mng. dir., CFO World Bank Group, Washington, 1999—2004; mng. dir. Hellman & Friedman, NYC, 2004. Guest lectr. fin. Grad. Sch. Orgn. and Mgmt. Yale U., 1982; cons. in field; bd. dirs. Internat. Ctr. Rsch. Women. Contbr. chapters to books. Bd. trustees Vassar Coll., German Marshall Fund U.S.; pres., bd. trustees Big Brothers/Big Sisters N.Y.C., 1997—99; fin. com. Rockefeller Family Fund, 1997—99; photography coun. Mus. Modern Art; bus. persons adv. panel Am. Friends Svc. Com., 1985. Fellow, Yale U. Grad. Sch.; Wells fellow for grad. study in econ., Vassar Coll. Mem.: Coun. Fgn. Rels., Social Sci. Rsch. Coun. (mem. investment com. 1989—98), Fgn. Policy Assn., Omicron Delta Epsilon, Phi Beta Kappa. Office: Hellman & Friedman 375 Park Ave 20th Fl New York NY 10022 Office Phone: 212-871-6680. Business E-Mail: goldstein@hf.com.

GOLDSTEIN, JEROME ARTHUR, mathematics professor; b. Pitts., Aug. 5, 1941; s. Morris and Henrietta (Vogel) G.; children: Maurice Roland, David Jonathan, Devra. BS, Carnegie-Mellon U., 1963, MS, 1964, PhD, 1967; S.MD (hon.), Internat. Boswell Inst., Loyola U., New Orleans, 1973. Mem. Inst. Advanced Study, Princeton, N.J., 1967-68; asst. prof. math. Tulane U., New Orleans, 1968-71, assoc. prof., 1971-75, prof., 1975-91; prof. Math. Sci. Rsch. Inst. U. Calif., Berkeley, 1990-91; prof. math. La. State U., Baton Rouge, 1992-96, U. Memphis, 1996—. Author: Semigroups of Linear Operators and Applications, 1985; editor: P.D.E. and Related Topics, 1975, Mathematics Applied to Science, 1988, Differential Equations in Biology, Physics and Engineering, 1991, Semigroups of Operators and Applications, 1993, Stochastic Processes and Functional Analysis, 1997, Applied Analysis, 1999, Semigroup Forum, 1982—, Applied and Computational Mathematics, 1983—, Differential and Integral Equations, 1988—, Electronic Jour. Differential Equations, 1992—, Advances in Differential Equations, 1995—, Communications in Applied Analysis, 1995—, Positivity, 1996—, Jour. Math. Analysis and Applications, 1998—, Jour. of Computational Analysis and Applications, 1998—, Internat. Jour. Differential Equations and Applications, 1999—, Jour. Evolution Equations, 2000—, Electronic Jour. Math. Phys. Sci., 2002-, others; contbr. articles to profl. jours. Recipient Faculty Excellence in Research award Coll. Arts and Scis., Tulane U., 1985; NSF grantee, 1968-96. Mem. Am. Math. Soc., Math. Assn. Am., Soc. Indsl. Applied Math., London Math. Soc. Soc. Math. Brazil, Edinburgh Math. Soc., Assn. Women in Math., Sigma Xi (Rsch. award 1972). Jewish.

GOLDSTEIN, JEROME CHARLES, retired professional society administrator, otolaryngologist, surgeon; b. Glens Falls, N.Y., Nov. 4, 1935; s. Morris and Estelle (Ginsburg) G.; m. Rochelle Jacobs; children: Harry Glenn, Bradley John, Brian Louis. AB, U. Rochester, 1957; MD, SUNY, Syracuse, 1963. Diplomate Am. Bd. Otolaryngology (bd. dirs. 1982-2000). Intern Phila. Gen. Hosp., 1963-64; resident in gen. surgery Bronx Mcpl. Hosp. Ctr., N.Y.C., 1964-65; resident in otolaryngology SUNY, Syracuse, 1965-68; asst. prof. Northwestern U. Med. Sch., Chgo., 1968-71; pvt. practice Glens Falls, NY, 1971-74; prof. surgery, head divsn. otolaryngology Albany (N.Y.) Med. Coll., 1974-83; exec. v.p. Am. Acad. Otolaryngology-Head and Neck Surgery, Washington, 1984-94, sr. exec. v.p., 1995-96, exec. v.p. emeritus, 1997-99. Otolaryngologist-in-chief Albany Med. Ctr. Hosp., 1974-83; prof. dept. otolaryngology, head and neck surgery Johns Hopkins Med. Sch., 1986—, Georgetown Med. Sch., 1990; pres. Centurions of Deafness Rsch. Found., N.Y.C., 1987-88. With USAFR, 1965-70. Fellow ACS, Royal Coll. Surgeons Edinburgh, Am. Acad. Facial, Plastic and Reconstructive Surgery, Triologic Soc., Am. Laryngol. Assn., Am. Soc. for Head and Neck Surgery (pres. 1982-83), Soc. Head and Neck Surgeons, Am. Neurotol. Soc. (hon.), Am. Bronchoesoph. Soc., Am. Head and Neck Soc., Nat. Assn. Physicians for the Environment (founding pres. 1993-95, pres. 1999-2000); mem. AMA, Am. Otol. Soc. (hon.), Internat. Fedn. Otorhino-Laryngol. Socs. (regional sec. for N.Am. 1985-2000), Coun. of Med. Specialty Socs. (pres. 1996), Pan Pacific Surg. Assn. (pres. 2004—06). Home and Office: 4119 Manchester Lake Dr Lake Worth FL 33467-8175 Office Phone: 561-432-7220. Office Fax: 561-649-9412. Personal E-mail: JCGMD@aol.com.

GOLDSTEIN, JEROME ERIC, emergency physician surgeon, lawyer; b. Bronx, Feb. 21, 1952; s. Stanley Irving and Hortense (Silverstein) Goldstein; m. Cheryl Lynn Goldstein; children: Tikva Aliza, Kikira Laila, Nitzana Kfira. BSc with honors, Tulane U., 1973; MD summa cum laude, U. Bologna, Italy, 1982; JD with hon., U. Pitts., 2001. Bar: Pa., U.S. Dist. Ct. (we. dist.) Pa., Fla.; diplomate Am. Bd. Internal Medicine. Intern St. Orsula Hosp. U., Bologna, Italy, 1982; resident in gen. surgery Booth Meml. Med. Ctr., NYU Sch. Medicine, 1983; resident in pediatrics Morristown Meml. Hosp., Columbia U. Sch. Medicine, 1984; resident in gen. surgery Easton Hosp., Hahnaman U. Sch. Medicine, 1985-86; cardiology fellow Grad. Hosp. Phila., Phila., 1989—91; resident in internal medicine Easton Hosp., Hahnaman U. Sch. Medicine, 1987-88; emergency physician Albert Einstein Med. Ctr., Phila., 1989-94, Parkview Hosp., Phila., 1991-92, Chester (Pa.) Cmty. Hosp., 1992-94; med. dir. Holmsburg Prison, Phila., 1994-95; asst. dir. emergency medicine Clearfield (Pa.) Hosp., 1995-96; emergency physician Lewistown (Pa.) Hosp., 1996-98; CEO, pres. Med. Malpractice Experts, Pitts., 1998—; assoc. atty. Law Offices of Sheller, Ludwig & Badey, Phila., 2002—03; CEO, pres. Jerry Eric Goldstein Law Firm, Phila., 2003—. Adj. faculty prof. medicine Temple U. Sch. Podiatric Medicine, 2003—. Mem.: ACP, Pa. Trial Lawyers Assn., Assn. Emergency Physicians. Republican. Jewish. Avocations: horology, gourmet cooking, international travel, camping, photography. Home and Office: 548 Hunter St Woodbury NJ 08096-2524 Office Phone: 856-686-1931. E-mail: jegmdjd@yahoo.com.

GOLDSTEIN, JONATHAN, lawyer; b. NYC, Nov. 20, 1943; BA, Yale U., 1965; LLB, Harvard U., 1968. Bar: NY, 1969. Assoc. to mng. ptnr. Winston & Strawn LLP, NYC, 1968—. Mem.: NY State Bar Assn., Phi Beta Kappa. Office: Winston & Strawn 200 Park Ave Rm 4100 New York NY 10166-0005

GOLDSTEIN, JORDAN, lawyer; m. Victoria Lesser; children: Jonah, Eli. BA, U. Pa., 1989; JD, Hofstra U., 1994. In-house counsel Prudential Securities Inc.; assoc. Rivkin Radler & Kremer, Uniondale, NY, Proskauer Rose, NYC, 1997—99; assoc. gen. counsel TheStreet.com, 1999—2000, v.p. & gen. counsel, 2000—. Office: TheStreet.com 15 Wall St 15th Fl New York NY 10005 Office Phone: 212-321-5000.

GOLDSTEIN, JOSEPH IRWIN, materials scientist, educator; b. Syracuse, N.Y., Jan. 6, 1939; s. Louis and Sylvia (Scharfeld) G.; m. Barbara Hammond, June 30, 1963; children: Steven (dec.), Anne. BS in Metallurgy, MIT, 1960, MS, 1962, ScD in Metallurgy, 1964. Instr. metallurgy dept. MIT, 1960-63; phys. metallurgist Smithsonian Astron. Obs., Cambridge, Mass., 1963-64; aerospace technologist NASA-Goddard Space Ctr., Greenbelt, Md., 1966-68; lectr. chem. engring. U. Md., 1966-68; asst. prof. metall. and materials sci. Lehigh U., Bethlehem, Pa., 1968-70, assoc. prof., 1970-75, prof., 1975-93, T.L. Diamond Disting. prof., 1976-79, assoc. v.p. rsch., 1979-83, v.p. rsch., 1983-90, R.D. Stout prof. materials sci. and engring., 1990-93; dean engring. U. Mass., Amherst, 1993—2004, disting. prof., 2003—. Author, editor 8 books; contbr. more than 200 articles to profl. jours. Recipient Nat. Environ. Rsch. Coun. award, Britain, 1974. Fellow Am. Soc. for Metals; mem. Microbeam Analysis Soc. (pres. 1977-78, Sci. award 1991, Svc. award 1984), Meteoritical Soc. (mem. coun. 1979-81, treas. 1995-99, v.p. 2005-). Democrat. Jewish. Home: 49 Sheerman Ln Amherst MA 01002-1584 Office: U Mass Coll Mech and Indsl Engring Amherst MA 01003 Business E-Mail: JIG0@ecs.umass.edu.

GOLDSTEIN, JOSEPH LEONARD, molecular biologist, educator; b. Sumter, SC, Apr. 18, 1940; s. Isadore E. and Fannie A. Goldstein. BS, Washington and Lee U., 1962, DSc, 1986; MD, U. Tex., Dallas, 1966; DSc (hon.), U. Chgo., 1982, Rensselaer Poly. Inst., 1982, U. Paris, 1988, U. Buenos Aires, 1990; DSc (hon.), So. Meth. U., 1993, U. Miami, 1996; DSc (hon.), Rockefeller U., 2001. Intern, then resident in medicine Mass. Gen. Hosp., Boston, 1966—68; clin. assoc. NIH, 1968—70; fellow U. Wash., Seattle, 1970—72; faculty U. Tex. Southwestern Med. Ctr., Dallas, 1972—77, Paul J. Thomas prof. medicine, chmn. dept. molecular genetics, 1977—85, regental prof., 1985—. Harvey Soc. lectr., 1977; mem. sci. rev. bd. Howard Hughes Med. Inst., 1978—84, med. adv. bd., 1985—90, chmn. med. adv. bd., 1995—2002, trustee, 2002—, non-resident fellow Salk Inst., 1983—94; chmn. award jury Albert Lasker Med. Rsch., 1996—; mem. bd. sci. govs. Scripps Rsch. Inst., 1996—. Co-author: The Metabolic Basis of Inherited Disease, 5th edit., 1983. Trustee Rockefeller U., 1994—; mem. sci. adv. bd. Welch Found., 1986—; bd. dirs. Passano Found., 1985—. Recipient Heinrich-Wieland prize, 1974, Pfizer award in enzyme chemistry, ACS, 1976, Passano award, Johns Hopkins U., 1978, Gairdner Found. award, 1981, award in biol. and med. scis., NY Acad. Sci., 1981, Lita Annenberg Hazen award, 1982, Rsch. Achievement award, Am. Heart Assn., 1984, Louisa Gross Horwitz award, 1984, 3M Life Sci. award, 1984, Albert Lasker award in basic med. rsch., 1985, Nobel Prize in physiology or medicine, 1985, Trustees's medal, Mass. Gen. Hosp., 1986, US Nat. medal of sci., 1988, prize, Warren Alpert Found., 2000, prize in Medicine and Biomed. Rsch., Albany Med. Ctr., 2003. Mem.: Tex. Philos. Soc., Royal Soc. London (fgn. mem.), Inst. Medicine, Am. Philos. Soc., Am. Fedn. Clin. Rsch., Am. Soc. Biol. Chemists, Am. Acad. Arts and Scis., Am. Soc. Human Genetics (William Allan award 1985), Am. Soc. Clin. Investigation (pres. 1985—86), Assn. Am. Physicians, ACP (award 1986), NAS (coun. 1991—94, Lounsbery award 1979), Alpha Omega Alpha, Phi Beta Kappa. Home: 3831 Turtle Creek Blvd Apt 22B Dallas TX 75219-4538 Office: U Tex Southwestern Med Ctr 5323 Harry Hines Blvd Dallas TX 75390-9046 E-mail: jgolds@mednet.swmed.edu.

GOLDSTEIN, JULIA SONIA, librarian; b. Balt., Mar. 20, 1923; d. Fred Soloman and Etta (Marburg) Deutsch; m. Harold Goldstein, Nov. 4, 1943 (dec.); children: William M., Richard H. BS, U. Ill., 1963, MLS, 1968. Tchr. Thomas Paine Sch., Urbana, Ill., 1963-65; libr. Flossie Wiley Sch., Urbana, 1965-67; interlibr. loan libr. State Libr. Fla., Tallahassee, 1968-71, children's libr. cons., 1971-72; interlibrary libr. State Library of Fla., 1972—76; libr. Fla. Dept. Commerce, Tallahassee, 1976-78, Fla. Dept. Labor, Tallahassee, 1978-80, labor and employment and tng. specialist, 1980-85, labor, employment and tng. rep., 1989. Mem. Fla. State U. summer program Oxford (Eng.) U., 1988, 90, libr. Florence (Italy) summer program 1992; mem. U. Okla. summer libr. seminar Oxford U., 1992. Bd. dirs. Tallahassee Opera Guild, 1988-94,Tallahassee Theatre Guild, 1997-99, pres. 1997—, Mus. Associated, Sch. Music Fla. State U., 1993—. Mem. Internat. Torch Club (pres. Tallahassee chpt. 1988-89), Univ. Club Fla. State U. (pres. 1989-90), Assn. Ret. Faculty (bd. dirs. 1994—, pres. 1998-99), Toastmasters Internat. (pres. Fla. Dept. Transp. chpt. 1983). Home: 1911 Angel Hollow Rd Tallahassee FL 32308-6189

GOLDSTEIN, JULIUS LESTER, biomedical engineer, consultant; b. Bklyn., July 9, 1935; s. Benjamin and Dorothy (Steinberg) G.; m. Batya Abramson, June 17, 1962; children: Hillel N., Miriam D., Naama L., Avi D. BEE, Cooper Union, 1957; MEE, Poly. Inst. Bklyn., 1960; PhD, U.

Rochester, 1965. Postdoctoral fellow Inst. for Perception Rsch., Eindhoven, Netherlands, 1965-66; rsch. assoc., Lab. Psychophysics Harvard U., Cambridge, Mass., 1966-68; asst. prof. elec. engring. MIT, Cambridge, Mass., 1968-71, assoc. prof. elec. engring., 1971-73; dir. biomed. engring. Tel Aviv U., Israel, 1973-76, chmn. dept. electronics, 1976-78, assoc. prof., 1973-82, prof. elec. engring., 1982-90; vis. prof. Johns Hopkins U., Balt., 1986-88; rsch. prof. Ctrl. Inst. for the Deaf, St. Louis, 1988-96; adj. prof. elec. engring. Washington U., St. Louis, 1996—, adj. prof. biomed. engring., 2001—. Pres. Israel Soc. for Med. and Biomed. Engrs., Tel Aviv, 1975-77; dir. biomed. engring. program Tel Aviv U., 1973-76; cons. Digital Speech Systems, Tel Aviv, 1984-86, Models of Human Hearing, AT&T Bell Labs., Murray Hill, NJ, 1991-96; co-founder, pres. Hearing Emulations, LLC, 2000. Contbr. articles profl. jour. Achievements include the discovery and formulation of math models of basic principles of auditory signal processing, including nonlinear cochlear sound analysis, detection of signal peaks and intervals, central processing in pitch perception, hearing aids based on auditory models. Bd. dir. Epstein Hebrew Acad., Block Yeshiva HS, St. Louis, 1991-94, 98-2003; organizer, symposium chmn. Assn. for Rsch. in Otolaryngology 17th Midwinter meeting, 1994. NIH grantee MIT, 1972, Johns Hopkins U., 1986-88, U.S./Israel Binational Fund grantee, 1977-80, NIH-NIDCD grantee Ctrl. Inst. for the Deaf, 1990-95, NSF-IBN grantee Washington U., 1998-00, NIH-NIDCD SBIR grantee BECS Tech., 1999-2004. Fellow Acoustical Soc. Am., Collegium Oto-Rhino-Laryngologicum Amicitae Sacrum, 1980; mem. IEEE (sr.). Achievements include invention of hearing aids with instantaneous gain compression and adaptive nonlinear waveform compression. Office: Hearing Emulations LLC 9479 Dielman Rock Island Dr Saint Louis MO 63132

GOLDSTEIN, KENNETH F., entertainment company executive; b. Detroit, Mar. 10, 1962; s. Earl Goldstein and Sarita (Bow) Snow. BA in Philosophy and Theater, Yale U., 1984. Freelance writer, TV and film producer, L.A., 1984-89; writer, producer Cinemaware Corp., Westlake Village, Calif., 1989-91; designer, producer Philips Interactive Media, L.A., 1991-92; exec. publisher Carmen Sandiego series Broderbund Software, Inc., Novato, Calif., 1992-96, v.p. entertainment, gen. mgr. divsn. Red Orb Entertainment Myst, Riven Series, 1996-98, Journeyman Project series, Warlords series, 1996-98; sr. v.p., gen. mgr. Disney Online, 1998-2000; exec. v.p., mng. dir. Walt Disney Internet Group, 2000—. Author: (screenplays) 8; designer (software programs) Carmen Sandiego: Jr. Detective Edition, 1994 (Software Publs. Assn. award 1995), Reading Galaxy, 1994 (Family PC, Mac World awards 1996), In the 1st Degree, 1995 (Software Publs. Assn. award 1996); pub. Disney's Toontown Online, 2002-05, Playhouse Disney Preschool Time Online, 2005, Blast, 1998-2005, FamilyFun website, 1999-2005, Movies website, 2002-05. Vol. Olive Crest Treatment Ctr., 1986, Free Arts for Abused Children, 1988; sec. bd. trustees Full Circle Programs, Marin County, Calif., 1992-98; vice chmn. bd. trustees Hathaway Children & Family Svcs, 2002—; bd. advs. Mediascope, 2002-04; bd. dirs. L.A. Make-A-Wish Found., 2005—. Recipient Pub. Svc. awards, Olive Crest Treatment Ctrs., 1986, Free Arts for Abused Children, 1988; named one of Top 100 Multimedia Producers, Multimedia Producer Mag., 1995, Best of What's New in Computers, Electronics, Popular Sci. Mag., 1995, Upside Mag. Elite 100, Honorable Mention Digital Entertainment, 1998, Best of Festival award Internat. Web Awards, 2000, Web Mktg. Assn. Web Awards Best Game, Family, Movie, Entertainment Sites award 2001, Modalis Rsch. Excellence award, 2001, Outstanding Achievement award Web Mktg. Assn., 2002, 03, Web Internet Visionary award, Best of the Web, 2001, All Star Software award Software Rev., 2003, People's Voice award kids' category Webby Awards, 2003, Internet Safety award WiredKids website, 2005. Mem. Writers Guild of Am. West, Acad. Interactive Arts and Scis (founding mem., bd. govs. L.A.), Yale Univ. Alumni (schs. com. 1988—), Internat. Game Developers Assn. Office: Disney Online 500 S Buena Vista St Burbank CA 91521-0001

GOLDSTEIN, LEONARD BARRY, dentist; b. Seaford, N.Y., Feb. 6, 1944; s. Jacob Martin and Adele (Pelzner) G.; m. Phyllis Lynn Kerwin, June 25, 1967; children: Marcie Ilene, Sherri Elysse. Student, Ind. U., 1961-63; DDS, Case Western Reserve U., 1967; Cert. in Orthodontics, Dewey Sch. Orthodontics, N.Y.C., 1969; PhD in Electro-Medicine, City U., LA, 1988. Diplomate Am. Acad. of Pain Mgmt., Am. Bd. Forensic Medicine, Am. Bd. Forensic Dentistry. Gen. practice dentistry, Smithtown, 1969—; attending orthodontist Abe Stark Philanthropies Dental Clinic, Bklyn., 1970-77; med. dir. TMJ Facial Pain Ctr. Southside Hosp., Bay Shore. Guest prof. Dept. Phys. Edn. Queens Coll., N.Y., 1979—; guest lectr. Dept. Phys. Edn. Queensboro (N.Y.) C.C., 1980—; dir. dental svcs. Good Samaritan Profl. Svcs., St. James, N.Y., 1979—, v.p. med. bd., 1979—; attending dental staff St. John's Episc. Hosp., 1980—, Cmty. Hosp. Western Suffolk, 1980—; bd. dirs. L.I. Ctr. for Cranio-Facial Pain, Smithtown; med. dir. TMJ/Facial Pain Ctr., Southside Hosp.; dir. grad. program in forensic exam. Touro Coll. Sch. Health Scis., Bay Shore; chmn. Instnl. Review Bd., Touro Coll.; vice chmn. com. on scholarly rsch., Touro Coll. Sch. Health Scis.; asst. dean grad. program devel., Touro Coll. Sch. Health Scis. Contbr. articles to profl. jours. Served to capt. Dental Corps, U.S. Army, 1967-69. Fellowship in removeable prosthetics, U.S. Army Dental Corps, 1967. Fellow Acad. Stress and Chronic Disease, Acad. Gen. Dentistry, Am. Endodontic Soc., Internat. Coll. Dentists; mem. Am. Equilibration Soc., Am. Coll. Sports Medicine, Internat. Acad. Preventive Medicine, Cranial Acad. of Am. Osteopathic Soc., Am. Orthodontic Soc., Internat. Soc. Orthodontists, Am. Dental Soc., Cronio-Mandibular Study Club of N.Y., L.I. Gnathological Study Club, Northeastern Gnathological Soc. Business E-Mail: leonardg@touro.edu. E-mail: ddsphd@aol.com.

GOLDSTEIN, MANFRED, retired consultant; b. Vienna, Jan. 30, 1927; arrived in US, 1939, naturalized, 1945; s. Isidore and Anna (Hahn) G.; m. Shirley Marie Lavine, Aug. 27, 1950 (dec. Feb. 2001); children: Cindy Marie, Lynn Alyse; m. Rhonda J. Demarsh, Mar. 23, 2005 Student, Manhattan Trade Ctr., 1947; E.E., Capitol Radio Engring. Inst., 1963; student, L.I. U., 1961, Indsl. Coll. Armed Forces, 1967-68; postgrad., SUNY at Delhi, 2003. Sr. technician Bklyn. Radio, 1953-55, Budd Stanley, Inc., Long Island City, N.Y., 1955; lead engr. telephone equipment Precision Indsl. Design Newark, 1955-57; project engr., contract adminstr., sales mgr. Leico, Inc., Syossett, NY, 1957-65, v.p., 1964-65; mgmt. and engring. cons., 1965-91; ret. Pres. Positive Cons. Inc., Bellmore, N.Y., 1967-86, Lake Luzerne, N.Y., 1986-91, 95—; owner Lake Luzerne Seaplane Base, 1969-2005; tchr. intermediate computer courses Hadley-Luzerne Pub. Libr., Lake Luzerne, 2003—. Mem. small bus. adv. com. to Congressman Thomas J. Downey, 1977-91; mem. small bus. adv. council L.I. Assn. Commerce; founder NCMA L.I. Scholarship Fund; mem. Town of Lake Luzerne Zoning Bd. of Appeals, 2002--. Served with AUS, 1945-46. Fellow Nat. Contract Mgmt. Assn. (bd. dirs. L.I. chpt., v.p. 1983-85); mem. IEEE (sr.), Soc. Plastics Engrs., Am. Indsl. Preparedness Assn. (exec. bd. mgmt. div.), ABA (assoc.), Air Force Assn., Capitol Radio Engring. Inst. Alumni (sr.), Nat. Pilots Assn., Aircraft Owners and Pilots Assn., Internat. Platform Assn., Am. Legion, VFW. Inventor torpedo fire control cable and connector for Polaris, high pressure seals for Polaris submarine antennae. Home: 18 Bay Rd PO Box 11 Lake Luzerne NY 12846-0011

GOLDSTEIN, MARC, surgeon, urologist, educator, health facility administrator; b. N.Y.C., Mar. 22, 1948; BS cum laude, CUNY, Bklyn., 1968; MD summa cum laude, SUNY, Bklyn., 1972. Diplomate Nat. Bd. Med. Examiners, Am. Bd. Urology. Surgical intern Columbia-Presbyn. Med. Ctr., N.Y.C., 1972-73, surgical resident, 1973-74; asst. instr., resident, chief resident dept. urology Downstate Med. Ctr. SUNY, Bklyn., 1977-80, asst. prof. urology dept. urology Downstate Med. Ctr., 1980-82; asst. attending surgeon Univ. Hosp., SUNY Downstate Med. Ctr., and Kings County Hosp. Ctr., Bklyn., 1980-82; fellow-in-residence Population Coun. Rockefeller U., N.Y.C., 1980-82, rsch. assoc., 1980-83; assoc. physician Rockefeller U. Hosp., N.Y.C., 1980-86, vis. assoc. physician, 1986-87; asst. attending surgeon urology N.Y. Hosp., N.Y.C., 1982-88; asst. prof. surgery Cornell U. Med. Ctr., N.Y.C., 1982-88; staff scientist Population Coun. Ctr. Biomed. Rsch., N.Y.C., 1982—2002, sr. scientist, 2002—; dir. divsn. male reproductive medicine and microsurgery, dept. urology N.Y. Hops.-Cornell Med. Ctr., N.Y.C., 1982—; assoc. attending surgeon N.Y. Hosp., N.Y.C., 1988-94; assoc. prof. surgery Cornell U. Med. Coll., N.Y.C., 1988-94; attending surgeon N.Y. Hosp., 1994—; prof. urology Cornell U. Med. Coll., N.Y.C., 1994—, prof. urology and reproductive medicine, 1999—, dir. ctr. for male reproductive medicine and microsurgery, 1982—, co-exec. dir. Cornell Inst. Reproductive Medicine, 1999—; surgeon-in-chief Inst. Reproductive Medicine Cornell Ctr., 2001—. Mem. adv. com. Assn. Voluntary Surgical Contraception, 1984—; participant concept clearance meeting NIH, 1989; mem. editorial bd. Microsugery, 1983—, Jour. of Andrology, 1991-93, Andrology Report, 1992—. Author: (with M. Feldberg) The Vasectomy Book: A Complete Guide to Decision Making, 1982, 2nd edit., 1985, (with G. Berger, M. Fuerst) The Couples Guide to Fertility, 1989, 2nd edit., 1995, 3rd edit., 2001, (with Doubleday Co.) Surgery of Male Infertility, 1995, Atlas of the Urology Clinics: Surgery for Male Infertility, 1999; contbr. chpts. to books, articles to profl. jours.; patentee in field. Maj. USAF, 1974-77, USAFR, 1977-90. Honor scholar Downstate Med. Ctr., 1969; Summer Rsch. fellow Downstate Med. Ctr., 1969-70, Ferdinand C. Valentine fellow N.Y. Acad. Medicine, 1980-82; recipient Ferdinand C. Valentine Urology prize N.Y. Acad. Medicine and N.Y. sect. Am. Urological Assn., 1981, Best Movie award Am. Fertility Soc. and Can. Fertility and Andrology Soc., 1986, 96, Excellence in Video Prodn. award Video Urology, 1987, 90; commd. Ky. Col., Commonwealth of Ky., 1988. Fellow ACS; mem. AMA, Am. Soc. Andrology (mem. various coms.), Am. Fertility Soc., Am. Urological Assn. (scholar 1980-82, mem. various coms., Best Movie award vasectomy reversal 2004), N.Y. County Med. Soc., Internat. Microsurgical Soc., Soc. Study Reproduction, Soc. Reproductive Surgeons (fellowship com. 1989—), Soc. for Male Reproduction and Urology (pres. 1996), Alpha Omega Alpha, N.Y. Rd. Runners Club (completed 19 N.Y.C. marathons), Brit. Mountaineering Coun. Office: NY Hosp-Cornell Med Ctr Dept Urology 525 E 68th St Dept Urology New York NY 10021-4885 Office Phone: 212-746-5470. Business E-Mail: mgoldst@med.cornell.edu.

GOLDSTEIN, MARCIA LANDWEBER, lawyer; b. Bklyn., Aug. 7, 1952; d. Jacob and Sarah Ann (Danovitz) Landweber; m. Mark Lewis Goldstein, June 3, 1973. AB magna cum laude, Cornell U., 1973, JD cum laude, 1975. Bar: NY 1976, US Dist. Ct. (So. and Ea. dists.) NY, US Ct. Appeals (2nd, 3rd, 5th, 7th and 9th cirs.); cert. mediator, So. Dist. NY. Assoc. Weil, Gotshal & Manges LLP, NYC, 1975-83, ptnr. to mng. ptnr., 1983—, co-chair, bus. fin. & restructuring devel. Adv. bd. Colliers on Bankruptcy, 15th edit., editor (15th edit. revised); vis. lectr. Yale Law Sch., 1986-88; lectr. Columbia Law Sch., Practicing Law Inst. ALI-ABA, Southeastern Bankruptcy Law Inst., NYU bankruptcy workshop; served as mediator for several Chapter 11 cases; trustee Chapter 11; serves on the Law Sch. Adv. Coun.; mem. Cornell Law Sch. Dean's Spl. Leadership Com. Articles editor Cornell Law Review, 1974—75. Mem. ABA (com. on creditors' rights, corp. counse. com.), Assn. of Bar of City of NY (chair bankruptcy and reorgn. com.), Nat. Bankruptcy Conf. (chair misc. com.), Am. Coll. Bankruptcy, Internat. Insolvency Inst. Office: Weil Gotshal & Manges LLP 767 5th Ave New York NY 10153 Office Phone: 212-310-8214. Office Fax: 212-310-8007. Business E-Mail: marcia.goldstein@weil.com.

GOLDSTEIN, MARK KINGSTON LEVIN, information technology executive, researcher; b. Burlington, Vt., Aug. 22, 1941; s. Harold Meyer Levin and Roberta (Butterfield) Goldstein; m. Kyoko Matsubara, Mar. 8, 1984; 1 child, Amanda Kellie. BS in Chemistry, U. Vt., 1964; PhD, U. Miami, Coral Gables, 1971. Pres. IBR, Inc., Coral Gables, Fla., 1970-74; group leader Brookhaven Nat. Lab., Upton, NY, 1974-77; sr. rschr. East-West Ctr., Honolulu, 1977-79; sr. tech. advisor JGC Corp., Tokyo, 1979-81; pres., chmn. bd. Quantum Group, Inc., La Jolla, Calif., 1981—; exec. dir. Magnatek, Inc., Brotas, Brazil, 1982—. Project leader proliferation and waste mgmt. policy study for Pres. Ford's sci. advisor. Fellow NSF, 1964, 1965. Mem.: AAAS, Am. Chem. Soc., Hawaii Yacht Club (Honolulu). Achievements include patents for biomimetic carbon monoxide sensors, carbon monoxide catalyst, fuel cell reform catalyst and sensors; thaser co-generators; supermitters; thermphotovolaics self powered gas appliance; photon control systems; gas safety valve; eyesafe laser radar; photon wedding; fuel cell reformer catalyst; superemissive light pipe. Home: 2248 Del Mar Heights Rd Del Mar CA 92014-3022 Office: Quantum Group Inc 7737 Kenamar Ct San Diego CA 92121-2425 E-mail: mklgoldstein@aol.com.

GOLDSTEIN, MARTIN S., obstetrician/gynecologist, educator; b. N.Y.C., Aug. 21, 1940; MD, SUNY Syracuse, 1966. Diplomate Am. Bd. Ob-Gyn. Intern Bronx Mcpl. Hosp. Ctr., N.Y.C., 1966-67; resident Mt. Sinai Hosp., N.Y.C., 1967-71; ob-gyn N.Y.C., 1971—. Assoc. clin. prof. ob-gyn Mt. Sinai Sch. Medicine, N.Y.C. Fellow Am. Coll. Ob-Gyn; mem. N.Y. Ob-Gyn Soc. Office: 40 E 84th St New York NY 10028-1115

GOLDSTEIN, MARVIN MARK, lawyer; b. Bklyn., Jan. 24, 1944; s. Abraham and Regina (Winkler) G.; m. Linda Ann Sinkoff, Aug. 4, 1969; 1 child, Randal Ian. BS, Cornell U., 1966; JD, Boston U., 1969. Bar: N.Y. 1969, N.J. 1972. Corp. labor counsel Gen. Cable Corp., N.Y.C., 1970-72; assoc. Grotta, Oberwager & Glassman, Newark, N.J., 1972-76; ptnr. Grotta, Glassman & Hoffman P.A., Roseland, N.J., 1976-99; resident, ptnr. Proskauer Rose LLP, Newark, N.J., 1999—. Asst. sec. Hackensack (N.J.) Univ. Med. Ctr., 1987-93, mem. exec. com., 1987-96; bd. trustees United Jewish Community Bergen County, N.J., 1984-90; bd. visitors Sch. Law Boston U., 1998—. Mem. ABA (chmn. subcom. fair labor standards act labor law sect.), N.J. Bar Assn. (chmn. adminstrv. law sect. 1987-89, co-chair NLRB subcom. 1999—). Office: Proskauer Rose LLP 1 Newark Ctr Fl 18 Newark NJ 07102-5211 Office Phone: 973-274-3210, 973-274-3200. Business E-Mail: mmgoldstein@proskauer.com.

GOLDSTEIN, MARVIN NORMAN, physician; b. Balt., Aug. 10, 1940; s. Manuel Quezon and Sylvia (Wagenheim) G.; m. Athene Schiffmann, July 1, 1962; children: Joshua, Claire. AB summa cum laude, Western Md. Coll., 1960; MD, U. Md., 1964. Diplomate Am. Bd. Psychiatry and Neurology. Intern in internal medicine U. Chgo. Hosp., 1964-65; resident in neurology Strong Meml. Hosp., U. Rochester, N.Y., 1965-68, chief resident in neurology, 1967-68; asst. attending neurologist, instr. U. Md. Hosp., Balt., 1968-69, Johns Hopkins Hosp., Balt., 1969-70; asst. prof. neurology and anatomy U. Rochester Sch. Medicine and Dentistry, 1970-74, clin. asst. prof. neurology and anatomy, 1974-78, clin. assoc. prof. neurology and anatomy, 1978-97; sr. attending neurology The Genesee Hosp., Rochester, 1978—, dir. neurology unit, 1996—2001; clin. prof. neurology U. Rochester Sch. Medicine, 1997—. Instr. in neurology and anatomy U. Rochester Sch. Medicine and Dentistry, 1965-68, Sch. Medicine, Georgetown U., Washington, 1968-70; staff neurologist U.S. Naval Hosp., Bethesda, 1968-70; med. staff exec. com. The Genesee Hosp., Rochester, 1989-90. Contbr. articles to profl. jours. Bd. dirs. Rochester Area Multiple Sclerosis, Rochester, 1972-78: adult edn. com. Temple Beth El, Rochester, 1985-90. Lt. comdr. USNR, 1968-70. Grantee NIH, 1972-74; recipient Merit award Rochester Acad. Medicine, 2002. Fellow Am. Acad. Neurology, Royal Soc. Medicine; mem. AMA, Am. Epilepsy Soc., Am. Acad. Clin. Neurophysiology, Sigma Xi. Avocations: gardening, canoeing, model shipbuilding, fishing. Home: 20 Varinna Dr Rochester NY 14618-1508 Office: 2101 Lac de Ville Blvd Rochester NY 14618-

GOLDSTEIN, MATTHEW, academic administrator; BA in Stats. and Math., City Coll. CUNY, 1963; PhD, U. Conn., 1970. Asst. prof. math. Polytech. Inst. N.Y., 1971-75; assoc. prof., assoc. provost CUNY, 1976-78, prof. stats., mem. doctoral faculty, 1978-98, pres. Rsch. Found., 1982-90, acting vice chancellor acad. affairs, 1990-91, pres. Bernard M. Baruch Coll., 1991-98, apptd. chancellor, 1999—; pres. Adelphi U., 1998-99; mem. commn. leadership devel. Am. Coun. Edn., 1996—; mem. bd. overseers Albert Einstein Sch. Medicine, 1998—; mem. bd. dirs. Lincoln Ctr. Inst. Arts in Edn., 1999—, New Plan Excel Realty Trust, Inc., 2000—; mem. Jewish Cmty. Relations Coun. of NY, 2000—, United Way of NY, 2002—. With JP Morgan Funds, 2003—, Nat. Financial Ptnrs., 2003-04; trustee Bronx-Lebanon Hosp. Ctr., 1992—, chmn. strategic planning com., 1992-04; ex-officio trustee Jean Cocteau Repertory, 1990—; mem. NY adminstrv. com. Fleet Nat. Bank. Co-author: Discrete Discriminant Analysis, 1978, Intermediate Statistical Methods and Applications, 1983, Multivariate Analysis, 1984; contbr. articles for leading scholarly publs. in math. and stats. Bd. dirs. Lincoln Ctr. Inst. Arts in Edn.; bd. trustees Albert Einstein Sch. Medicine, 1998. Recipient Jewish Nat. Fund Tree Life award, Townsend Harris medal, Liberty award for Disting. Accomplishments in Field Edn., Lower East Side Multicultural Fest., 2001, Leadership in Edn. and Pub. Svc. award Italo-Am. Assn., 2002, Ellis Island medal of honor, 2002, Max Rowe Ednl. Leadership award Am. Friends Open U. Israel, 2003, Pres.'s award NY Found. Arch., 2004. Fellow NY Acad. Scis.; mem. Am. Coun. Edn.'s Commn. Leadership Devel., Gov. George E. Pataki's Adv. Com. Rivers Inst., Senator Charles Schumer's Group of 35 Blue-Ribbon Task Force on Comml. Space, Am. Assn. State Colls. and Univs. (com. on policies and purposes), NY State Senate Higher Edn. Com.'s Adv. Com., Am. Statis. Assn. (pres. NY chpt. 1981-83, nat. coun. 1981-83), Golden Key, Beta Gamma Sigma. Achievements include being the first graduate of City Collegeto lead the nation's most prominent urban public university in 1963. Office: CUNY 535 E 80th St New York NY 10021-0795

GOLDSTEIN, MICHAEL, retail executive; b. Brooklyn, New York, 1941; Exec. v.p., treas., CFO Toys R Us, Inc., Rochelle Pk., NJ, exec. v.p. fin. and adminstrn., vice chmn., CEO, chmn. bd., 1998—2001, dir, 2001—. Chmn. Toys R Us Children's Fund, Rochelle Pk., NJ, 2001; dir. United Retail Group, Inc., Finlay Enterprises, Inc., Houghton Mifflin Co., Nat. Retail Fedn.

GOLDSTEIN, MICHAEL B., lawyer; b. NYC, Sept. 29, 1943; s. Isaac and Betty (Friedman) G.; m. Jinny M. Loewenthal, Dec. 18, 1966; 1 child, Eric Loren. BA in Govt., Cornell U., 1964; JD, NYU, 1967. Bar: N.Y. 1967, Ill. 1974, D.C 1978. Spl. asst. to the dep. mayor Office of Mayor, N.Y.C., 1965-66, asst. city adminstr., dir. univ. rels., 1969-72; dir. N.Y.C. Urban Corps, 1966-69; assoc. vice chancellor for urban and govtl. affairs, assoc. prof. urban sci. U. Ill., Chgo., 1972-78; mem. Dow, Lohnes & Albertson PLLC, Washington, 1978—. Practice leader Higher Edn.; chmn. task force on pub. policy Commn.on Higher Edn. and Adult Learner Am. Coun. on Edn. Contbr. articles to profl. texts and jours. Pres. Nat. Ctr. Pub. Svc. Internship Programs, 1975-77; bd. dirs. Washington Ctr. Internships and Acad. Seminars, 1977—; bd. dirs. and gen. counsel Washington Ballet, 1978—; bd. dirs. Greater Washington Rsch. Ctr., 1982-96, Chgo. Urban Corps, 1972-75, Am. Assoc. Higher Edn., 1998-05; trustee, chmn. acad. affairs com. Fielding Inst., 1989-94, 98—; trustee, chmn. fin. com. Mt. Vernon Coll., 1991-96; dir. Am.-Russian Cultural Cooperation Found., 1995—; bd. visitors Mt. Vernon Coll., 1996-98; bd. dirs. Sta. WETA, 1997-99; mem., pres. Friendship Fire Assocs., DC Fire Dept., 1985-, pres., 2004-. Wall St. Jour. Newspaper Fund fellow, 1963, Loeb fellow Harvard U., 1972. Mem. ABA (chmn. edn. law com. 1991-92), D.C. Bar Assn. (vice chair edn. task force 1999—2003), FBA (co-chmn. edn. grants com. 1985-86, 91-92), Nat. Assn. Coll. and Univ. Attys. (mem. ctrl. office com. 1986-88, vice chmn. pvt. bar com. 1989-90, chair continuing legal edn. com. 2001-2004, mem. fin. com. 2004—), Nat. Soc. Internships and Exptl. Edn. (pres. 1972), Am. Assn. Higher Edn. (bd. dirs. 1997—). Democrat. Jewish. Office: Dow Lohnes & Albertson 1200 New Hampshire Ave NW Washington DC 20036-6802

GOLDSTEIN, MICHAEL GERALD, lawyer, director; b. St. Louis, Sept. 21, 1946; s. Joseph and Sara G. (Finkelstein) G.; m. Ilene Marcia Ballin, July 19, 1970; children: Stephen Eric, Rebecca Leigh. BA, Tulane U., 1968; JD, U. Mo., 1971; LLM in Taxation, Washington U., 1972. Bar: Mo. 1971, U.S. Dist. Ct. (ea. dist.) Mo. 1972, U.S. Tax Ct. 1972, U.S. Ct. Appeals (8th cir.) 1974, U.S. Supreme Ct. 1976. Atty. Morris A. Shenker, St. Louis, 1972-78; ptnr. Lashly, Caruthers, Baer & Hamel and predecessor, St. Louis, 1979-84, Suelthaus & Kaplan, P.C. and predecessors, St. Louis, 1974-91; ptnr., chmn. dept. tax & estate planning Husch & Eppenberger, 1991-99; pres., CEO 1st Fin. Resources, 1999—2001; sr. v.p. EPS Fin. Solutions Corp., 1999-2000; sr. v.p., gen. counsel The Benefits Group, Inc., 2001—03; pres., COO Benefits Group Worldwide, 2003—. Adj. prof. tax law Washington U. Sch. Law, 1986-97; planning com. Mid-Am. Tax Confs., chmn. ALI/ABA Tax Seminar; lectr., author taxation field. Author: BNA Tax Mgmt. Portfolios, ABA The Insurance Counselor Books; contbr. articles to profl. jours. Bd. dirs. Jewish Family and Children's Svc. St. Louis, 1980—, pres., 1986-88; bd. dirs. Jewish Fedn. of St. Louis; trustee United Hebrew Temple, 1986-88; grad. Jewish Fedn. St. Louis Leadership Devel. Coun.; co-chmn. lawyers divsn. Jewish Fedn. St. Louis Campaign, 1981-82, Leadership St. Louis, 1988-89. Capt. USAR, 1970-78. Fellow Am. Coll. Tax Counsel, Am. Coll. Trust and Estate Counsel; mem. ABA (chmn. tax seminar, group editor newsletter for taxation sect.), Am. Law Inst., Mo. Bar Assn., Bar Assn. Met. St. Louis, St. Louis County Bar Assn. Home: 2011 Yacht Mischief Newport Beach CA 92660-6713 Office: 1875 Century Park East Ste 2100 Los Angeles CA 90067 Office Phone: 949-760-9098. Business E-Mail: mgoldstein@benefitsgroup.com.

GOLDSTEIN, MICHAEL L., neurologist; b. Chgo., June 14, 1945; s. Charles and Dorothy (Mack) G.; m. Barbara Joan Kaplan, June 18, 1967; children: Rachel, Elizabeth, Adam. AB, Princeton, 1966; MD, U. of Chgo., 1970. Intern Stanford U., 1970-71; resident in neurology Beth Israel Hosp., Boston, 1971-74; fellow in neurology Harvard U. Med. Sch., 1971-74; chief resident in neurology Children's Hosp., Boston, 1973-74; with Western Neurol. Assoc., Salt Lake City. Cons. Soc. Sec., Balt., 1990-91; bd. dirs., edn. comm. chmn. Rowland Hall, St. Marks Sch., Salt Lake City, 1986-92; examiner Am. Bd. Psychiatry and Neurology, 1987—; clin. assoc. prof. U. Utah Med. Sch., Salt Lake City, 1977—. Co-author: Managing Attention Disorders, 1990, Parent's Guide to ADD, 1993; co-producer: Educating Inattentive Children, 1992, It's Just Attention Disorder, 1993. Pres. synagogue, Salt Lake City, 1985-86. Fellow Am. Acad. Pediat., Am. Acad. Neurology (chair practice com, 1995-2000, treas. 2001—). Office: Western Neurol Assn 1151 E 3900 S Salt Lake City UT 84124-1216

GOLDSTEIN, MICHAEL SAUL, sociologist; b. NYC, Aug. 1, 1944; s. Abraham J. and Rose G.; m. Laura Geller, Dec. 23, 1979 (div. May 1992); children: Joshua, Adam, Elana. BA, Queens Coll., Flushing, N.Y., 1965; MA, Brown U., Providence, 1967, PhD, 1971. Lectr. Brown U., Providence, 1970-71; asst. prof. Sch. Pub. Health, UCLA, 1971-78, assoc. prof., 1978-88, prof., 1988—, chair dept. community health, 1988-91. Author: The Health Movement, 1992, Alternative Health Care: Medicine, Miracle or Mirage?, 1999; author, editor: 50 Simple Things You Can Do to Save Your Life, 1992. Mem. APHA, Am. Sociol. Assn. Soc. for Study Social Problems, Hastings Inst. Soc. Ethics and the Life Scis. Office: UCLA Sch Pub Health PO Box 95177 Los Angeles CA 90095

GOLDSTEIN, MORRIS, retired consumer products company executive; b. Pitts., Feb. 2, 1945; s. Irving and Clara (Caplan) G.; m. Diane Donna Davis, Aug. 21, 1966 (div. Nov. 1985); children: Jonathan, Julie; m. Kathy Evelyn Niemeier, July 7, 1990. BS, Carnegie Inst. Tech., 1967; MBA, U. Pa., 1979. Sales rep. computer divsn. RCA, Cherry Hill, N.J., 1968-70; sales mgr. Sedgwick Printout Sys., Princeton, N.J., 1970-76, pres., 1976-80; v.p. Courier-Jour. Louisville Times, 1980-81; mgr. bus. devel. Ziff-Davis Pub., N.Y.C., 1982-2000; pres. Information Access Corp. divsn., Foster City, Calif., 1982-2000; pres., COO Imagination Network Inc., Oakhurst, Calif., 1994; sr. v.p. Ziff-Davis Pub., Foster City, Calif., 1994; CEO Info. Access Co., A Thomson Corp. Co., Foster City, Calif., 1995-96, Thomson Tech. Ventures, San Mateo, Calif., 1997; pres., CEO Alliance Gaming Inc, Las Vegas, Nev., 1997-99; pres. entertainment bus. divsn. InnoVentry LLC, Las Vegas, 1999-2000; ret., 2000; exec. v.p. Global Cash Access, Las Vegas, 2001—03; prin., owner Nev. Slots and Supplies. Founder Nev. Slots and Supplies, Las Vegas, 2002. Dep mayor Mt. Laurel Twp., N.J., 1974-78. Home: 3581 E Maule Ave Las Vegas NV 89120-2918 Office: Nevada Slots and Supplies 2245 N Green Valley Pkwy Ste 283 Henderson NV 89120 Office Phone: 702-596-8609.

GOLDSTEIN, MURRAY, medical research administrator; b. N.Y.C., Oct. 13, 1925; s. Israel and Yetta (Zeigen) G.; m. Sue Mary Michael, June 13, 1957; children: Patricia Sue Robertson, Barbara Jean Warner. BA, NYU, 1947; DO, Des Moines U., 1950; MPH, U. Calif., 1959; DSc (hon.), Kirksville Coll. Osteo. Medicine, 1970, U. New Eng., 1984, Ohio U., 1986,

U. Osteo. Medicine and Health Scis., 1990, Mich. State U., 2000; LLD (hon.), N.Y. Inst. Tech., 1982; Dr. honoris causa, Med. Univ. Pecs, Hungary, 1985; LHD (hon.), Coll. Osteo. Medicine Pacific, 1988; Dr. honoris causa, Med. Sch. U. Lund, Sweden, 1994. Diplomate Am. Osteo. Bd. Preventive Medicine (sec.-treas. 1987-88, vice chmn. 1988-92). Rotating intern Still Coll. Osteo. Hosp., Des Moines, 1950-51, resident internal medicine, 1951-53; commd. corps USPHS, 1953, advanced through grades to asst. surgeon gen., 1980, ret., 1993; asst. to chief, then asst. chief, grants and tng. br., Nat. Heart Inst. NIH, Bethesda, Md., 1953-58, dir. epidemiology and biometry tng. grant program, divsn. rsch. grants, 1956-58, asst. chief rsch. grants rev. br., divsn. rsch. grants, 1959-60; exec. sec. joint coun. subcom. cerebrovascular disease Nat. Inst. Neurol. Diseases and Stroke and Nat. Heart and Lung Inst., NIH, Bethesda, Md., 1961-67, 69-75; dir. extramural programs Nat. Inst. Neurol. and Communicative Disorders and Stroke, NIH, Bethesda, Md., 1961-76, dir. stroke and trauma program, 1976-78, dep. dir., 1978-81, acting dir., 1981-82, dir., 1982-93; pub. health trainee epidemiology Calif. State Dept. Pub. Health, Berkeley, 1958, acting chief sect. virus diseases ctrl. nervous system, Bur. Acute Communicable Disease, 1958; med. dir., COO, United Cerebral Palsy Rsch. and Edn. Found., Washington, 1993—, bd. dirs., 1972-93; clin. prof. neurol. medicine N.Y. Coll. Osteo. Medicine, 1977—; sr. lectr. dept. neurology Uniformed Svcs. U. Health Scis., 1986—; osteo. pioneer Des Moines U., 2000. Bd. dirs. Nat. Stroke Assn., Burke Rsch. Inst., Robarts Rsch. Inst.; adj. prof. pub. health Nova-Southeastern U., 1995—; chmn. Commd. Corps Adv. Com. to NIH dir., 1990-93, WHO Task Force on stroke and other vascular cerebral disorders, 1986-89; dir. WHO Neurosci. Collaborating Ctr., Bethesda, 1981-93; liaison, mem. sci. adv. bd. Kent Waldrep Nat. Paralysis Found., 1989-94; vis. prof. med. rsch. Semmelweis Med. U., Budapest, Hungary, 1975; vis. sci. sect. neurology Mayo Clinic and grad. sch., Rochester, Minn., 1967-68; vis. scholar Henry Ford Hosp., 1979-80; v.p. Eisenhower Inst. Stroke Rsch., 1975-88; cons. bur. rsch. Am. Osteo. Assn., 1990-99; mem. nat. adv. coun. Nat. Ctr. Complimentary and Alternative Medicine/NIH, 2000-05; pres. Acad. Medicine, Washington, DC, 2004—; mem. nat. adv. bd. rehab. rsch. NICHD/NIH, 2004—; lectr., cons. in field. Assoc. editor Stroke: A Journal of Cerebral Circulation, 1976-91, consulting editor, 1992—; mem. editl. bd. Osteo. Annals, 1973-85, 87-88, Internat. Jour. Neurology, 1980-04, Jour. Neuroepidemiology, 1981-90, Hosp. and Community Psychiatry, 1980—, Alzheimer Disease: An Internat. Jour., 1985-93, Cerebralvascular and Brain Metabolism Revs., 1985-93; contbr. articles to profl. jours. Bd. dirs. Bapt. Home for Children and Adults, 1999-2001. With U.S. Army, 1943-45. Decorated DSM, Silver Star, Purple Heart; recipient USPHS Disting. Svc. medal with oak leaf cluster, Surgeon Gen.'s Exemplary Svc. medal, Surgeon Gen.'s medallion, Founders Day medal U. Osteo. Medicine and Health Scis., 1983, Patenge Pub. Svc. medal Mich. State U., 1987, Marjorie Guthrie award The Huntington's Disease Soc. Am., 1988, Burke award Buke Found., 1988, Spl. Leadership award United Cerebral Palsy Rsch. & Ednl. Found., 1989, Phillips Pubs. Svc. medal Ohio U., 1990, others; named Pioneer in Osteo. Medicine, Des Moines U., 2000. Fellow: Am. Acad. Neurology (mem. long range planning com. 1972—75, mem. manpower com. 1979—85, mem. neurology in govtl. svcs. and insts. com. 1979—85, chmn. 1981—83, 1981—83, mem. internat. affairs com. 1981—90, mem. com. govt. rels. 1983—85, ANA-AAN del. to World Fedn. Neurology 1983—85, mem. AAN com. on pub. comm. and legislation 1983—85, mem. ad hoc com. for soc. neurology liaison 1987—89, sr. advisor uniformed svcs. orgn. neurologists com. 1987—93, chmn. 1993—95, bd. dirs. 1993—95); mem.: Acad. of Medicine of Washington (pres. 2004—), NIH Alumni Assn. (v.p. bd. dirs. 1999—2004), Am. Acad. Cerebral Palsy and Devel. Medicine (liaison mem., bd. dirs.), United Cerebral Palsy Assn. (interim dir. 1998). Avocations: gardening, golf, swimming. Home: 6210 Swords Way Bethesda MD 20817-3349 Office: United Cerebral Palsy Rsch & Ednl Found 1660 L St NW Ste 700 Washington DC 20036-5616

GOLDSTEIN, NAOMI, retired psychiatrist; b. N.Y.C., Apr. 24, 1932; d. Eli and Caroline (Kleppner) G.; m. Franklin Feldman, June 3, 1956; children: Sarah, Eve, Jacob. AB, Vassar Coll., 1952; MD, N.Y. Med. Coll., 1956. Diplomate in psychiatry Am. Bd. Psychiatry and Neurology. Pvt. practice, N.Y.C., 1960-98; staff psychiatrist Criminal Ct. Psychiat. Clinic, 1961-68; psychiat. adminstr. N.Y.C. Probation Methadone Clinic, Bernstein Inst., 1970-72; dir. Supreme and Criminal Ct. Psychiat. Clinics, 1968-72; staff psychiatrist Liaison Svc. Bellevue Hosp., 1972-74; chief psychiatry Met. Correction Ctr. Fed. Bur. Prisons, N.Y.C., 1974-78; attending psychiatrist Bellevue Hosp., 1978-90; clin. prof. psychiatry NYU Med. Sch., N.Y.C., 1990—. Pres. Am. Bd. Forensic Psychiatry, Balt., 1988-89; mem. N.Y. State Bd. Profl. Med. Conduct, Albany, 1978—, chmn., 1982-84; lectr. law Columbia U., N.Y.C., 1988; bd. advisors Fed. Correctional Instn., Otisville, N.Y., 1980-85. Contbr. articles to profl. jours. Fellow AMA, Am. Psychiat. Assn. (life, trustee-at-large 1982-85, pres. N.Y. County dist. br. 1985-86), N.Y. Acad. Medicine (chmn. psychiatry sect. 1993-94), Am. Acad. Psychiatry and the Law, Assn. Women Psychiatrists, Am. Med. Women's Assn., Acad. Hon. Soc. N.Y. Med. Coll., Phi Beta Kappa. Jewish.

GOLDSTEIN, NATHAN, artist, writer; b. Chgo., Mar. 26, 1927; s. Joseph and Sarah (Kommisarov) G.; m. divorced; 1 child, Sarah; m. Harriet Joan Fishman, Feb. 20, 1947; 1 child, Jessica. MFA, Sch. of Art Inst. Chgo., 1952. Instr. in drawing and painting New Eng. Sch. Art, Boston, 1957-61; inst. De Cordova Mus. Sch., Lincoln, Mass., 1959-63; asst. prof. Sch. Visual Arts Boston U., 1962-63, assoc. prof., 1973-77; instr. Northeastern U., Boston, 1973-75; assoc. prof. Mount Ida Coll., Newton, Mass., 1966-71; prof., chmn. Found. Program Art Inst. Boston, Lesley U., 1972—2001. Author: The Art of Responsive Drawing, 6th edit., 2005, Figure Drawing: The Structure, Anatomy, and Expressive Design of Human Form, 6th edit., 2005, A Drawing Handbook: Themes, Tools, and Techniques, 1986, Painting: Visual and Technical Fundamentals, 1979, 100 American and European Drawings: A Portfolio, 1982, Design and Composition, 1989; co-author: (with Harriet Fishman) Drawing To See, 2004. With USN, 1945-47. Inducted into Nat. Acad. Design, 1996. Office: Art Inst Boston 700 Beacon St Boston MA 02215-2598 Personal E-mail: ngoldste@comcast.net.

GOLDSTEIN, SIR NORMAN, dermatologist; b. Bklyn., July 14, 1934; s. Joseph H. and Bertha (Docteroff) Goldstein; m. Ramsay Goldstein, Feb. 14, 1980; children: Richard, Heidi. BA, Columbia Coll., 1955; MD, SUNY, 1959. Intern Maimonides Hosp., N.Y.C., 1959—60; resident Skin and Cancer Hosp., 1960—61, Bellevue Hosp., 1961—62, N.Y.U. Postgrad. Ctr., 1962—63; ptnr. Honolulu Med. Group, 1967—72; pvt. practice dermatology Honolulu, 1972—; clin. prof. dermatology U. Hawaii Sch. Medicine, 1973—. Bd. dir. Pacific Laser, Skin Cancer Found.; trustee Dermatol. Found., 1979—82; pres. Hawaii Med. Libr., 1987. Editor: Hawaii Med. Jour.; contbr. articles to profl. jours. Pres. Hawaii Theater Ctr., 1985—89; mem. Oahu Heritage Council, 1986—94, Hawaii Govs. Blue Ribbon Panel on Living and Dying with Dignity. With U.S. Army, 1960—67. Named Physician of Yr., Hawaii Med. Assn., 1993, 2003, Physcians Adv. Coun., 2003, Businessman of Yr., Bus. Adv. Coun., 2003; recipient Henry Silver award, Dermatol. Soc. Greater N.Y., 1963, Husik award, NYU, 1963, Spl. award, Acad. Dermatologia Hawaiiana, 1971, Outstanding Scientific Exhibit award, Calif. Med. Assn., 1979, Spl. Exhibit award, Am. Urologic Assn., 1980, Svc. to Hawaii's Youth award, Adult Friends for Youth, 1991, Nat. Cosmetic Tattoo Assn. award, 1993, Cmty. Svc. award, Am. Acad. Dermatology, 1993, Nat. Leadership award and hon., Physians Adv. Bd., Washington, 2003. Fellow: ACP (Laureate award 2005, Laureate award 2005), Royal Soc. Medicine, Am. Soc. Lasers Medicine & Surgery, Am. Acad. Dermatology (Silver award 1972); mem.: AAAS, Internat. Soc. Dermatology (bd. dirs.), Hawaii Public Health Assn., Hawaii Dermatol. Soc. (sec.-pres.), Am. Coll. Sports Medicine, Honolulu County Med. Soc. (gov.), Pacific Health Research Inst., Pacific Dermatol. Assn., Hawaii State Med. Assn. (mem. public affairs com.), Am. Soc. Preventive Oncology, Internat. Soc. Dermatol. Surgery, Am. Coll. Cryosurgery, Physicians Exchange of Hawaii (bd. dir.), Am. Med. Writers Assn., Am. Soc. Micropigmentation Surgery, Internat. Soc. Cryosurgery, Am. Soc. Photobiology, Soc. Investigative Dermatologists, Internat. Soc. Tropical Dermatologists (Hist. and Culture award), C. of C., Pacific Telecom Council, Am. Assn. for Med. Systems and Info., Health Sci. Communication Assn., Pacific and Asian Affairs Council, Soc. for Computer Medicine, Biol. Photog. Assn., Assn. Hawaii Artists, Oahu Country Club, Chancellor's Club, Plaza Club, Outrigger Canoe Club (pres. bd. dir. 1990—92), Ancient Gaelic Nobility Soc. (named Knight of the Niadh Nask 1995), Hemlock Soc. USA (mem. bd.), Rotary, Preservation Action, Nat. Wildlife Fedn., Japan Am. Soc. Hawaii (bd. dir.), Navy League. Office: Tan Sing Bldg 1128 Smith St Honolulu HI 96817-5197 also: Puuone Plz 1063 E Main St C-225 Wailuku HI 96793 Office Phone: 808-538-7044. Personal E-mail: skinyouluv@aol.com.

GOLDSTEIN, NORMAN RAY, international trading company executive, consultant; b. Chgo., Nov. 20, 1944; s. Max and Rose (Weiner) G.; m. Bonnie A. Brod, Aug. 31, 1969; children: Russell, Matthew, Jamie. AA, Wright Jr. Coll., 1965; BS in Fin., No. Ill. U., DeKalb, 1967; MS in Acctg. cum laude, Roosevelt U., 1986. Cert. treasury profl., Assn. Fin. Profls. Gen. bus. mgr. Greenstreet Corp., Whiting, Ind., 1967; wholesale credit mgr. Atlantic Richfield Co., Chgo., 1968-74; v.p. fin., treas. Barton Inc. (Barton Brands, Ltd.), Chgo., 1974-96; chmn., CEO Gold Internat., 1996—. Spl. master U.S. Dist. Ct., 1998; chmn. ABC Fin. Comm. Forum, Chgo., 1987-88; v.p. Consort Corp., Chgo., 1971-80; spl. master U.S. Dist. Ct., 1998; adj. prof. fin. No. Ill. U., 2000--, mem. adv. bd. dept. fin., 2003-; instr. Ctr. Profl. Edn., 1997—; bd. mgrs. No. Ill. Angels LLC, 2004—; spkr. in field. Contbg. author: Handbook of Cash Flow and Treasury Management, 1987; contbr. articles to profl. publs. Bd. dirs. Maine Twp. Jewish Congregation Shaare Emet, Des Plaines, 1986—, pres. 1989-91. Named Outstanding Credit Exec. of Yr., Nat. Assn. Credit Mgmt., 1987, Disting. Alumnus Coll. Bus. No. Ill. U., 1998, Outstanding Alumnus Dept. Fin., No. Ill. U., 2001. Fellow Nat. Inst. Credit; mem. Fin. Mgrs. Assn. Chgo. (treas. 1991-92), Treasury Mgmt. Assn. Chgo. (chmn. ednl. scholarship com. 1995-99, chmn. Windy City Summit Treasury Conf. 1999-2000, 2003-04, bd. dirs. 2003—), Distillers Imports and Vintners (chmn. 1980-82), N.Y. Credit and Fin. Mgmt. Assn., Chgo. Midwest Credit Mgmt. Assn. (bd. dirs. 1984-87), Dept. Fin. Advisors Bd. No. Ill. U 2003-, No. Ill. U. Exec. Club (bd. dirs., v.p. 2003—).

GOLDSTEIN, PAUL, lawyer, educator; b. Mount Vernon, N.Y., Jan. 14, 1943; s. Martin and Nan Goldstein; m. Jan Thompson, Aug. 28, 1977. BA, Brandeis U., 1964; LLB Columbia U., 1967. Bar: NY 1968, Calif. 1978. Asst. prof. law SUNY-Buffalo, 1967-69, assoc. prof., 1969-71, prof., 1972-75; vis. assoc. prof. Stanford U., Calif., 1972-73, prof. law, 1975—, Stella W. and Ira S. Lillick prof. law, 1985—; of counsel Morrison and Foerster, San Francisco, 1988—. Author: Changing the American Schoolbook--Law, Politics and Technology, 1978, Real Estate Transactions--Cases and Materials on Land Transfer, Development and Finance, 1980, 3d edit. (with G. Korngold), 1993, Real Property, 1984, Copyright, 4 vols., 3d edit., 2005, Copyright, Patent, Trademark and Related State Doctrines--Cases and Materials on the Law of Intellectual Property, revised 5th edit., 2002, Copyright's Highway: From Gutenberg to the Celestial Jukebox, 1995, revised edit., 2003, International Copyright Law, 2001, International Intellectual Property Law, 2001. Mem. Assn. Litteraire et Artistique Internationale, Copyright Soc. U.S.A. Office: Stanford U Law Sch Nathan Abbott Way Stanford CA 94305 Office Phone: 650-723-0313. E-mail: paulgold@stanford.edu.

GOLDSTEIN, PAUL ROBERT, management company executive, consultant; b. Indpls., May 13, 1928; s. Harry and Belle Witcovski Goldstein; m. Nancy L. Fink, Dec., 18, 1955 (div. May 1969); children: Lynne G. Throop, James H. BS, Ind. U., 1948; postgrad., NYU, 1948, Purdue U., 1954. Registered money mgr. SEC. Rsch. corr. Merrill, Lynch, Pierce, Fenner & Smith, N.Y.C., 1950, account exec. trainee, 1953; account exec. Merrill, Lynch, Pierce, Fenner & Reaves, Indpls., 1954—61, DuPont, Glore, Forgan, Indpls., 1961-73, Paine, Webber, Jackson & Curtis, Indpls., 1973-78; dep. assessor Marion County, Indpls., 1978-83; mgr. margin dept. C.L. McKinney & Co., L.A., 1985-86; CEO PRG Mgmt. Co., Indpls., 1987—. Columnist I.U. Daily Student, 1945-46. Commdr. post #114 Jewish War Vets., Indpls., 1994; regional adv. bd. Anti-Defamation League, Indpls., 1962-66; ward chairperson Dem. Cen. Com., Indpls., 1978-82; mem. vet. adv. bd. Roude Bush VA Hosp., 1996-98. Sgt. Corps. of Engrs., 1950-52, Korea. Recipient 50 Yr. Gold Cir., Sigma Alpha Mu, 1995. Mem. Am. Legion, Greater Indpls. Progress Com. (sec., profl. sports sub-com. 1966-68), B'nai B'rith (pres. lodge # 58 1961-62). Democrat. Jewish. Avocations: collecting art and rare books, tennis, golf. Home: 226 E 45th St Indianapolis IN 46205 Office: PRG Mgmt Co 226 E 45th St Indianapolis IN 46205

GOLDSTEIN, PETER DOBKIN, lawyer; b. Bklyn., Apr. 12, 1953; s. Louis B. and Martha (Dobkin) G.; m. Marge W. Lilienthal, Aug. 28, 1982; children: Jenna Lilienthal, Daniel Reid. BA cum laude, Brandeis U., 1974; MS, Harvard U., 1977; JD magna cum laude, Boston Coll., 1980. Bar: Conn. 1980, N.Y. 1981, U.S. Dist. Ct. Conn. 1981, U.S. Dist. Ct. (so. and ea. dists.) N.Y. 1983, U.S. Ct. Appeals (2d cir.) 1982, U.S. Ct. Appeals (3d cir.) 1990, U.S. Supreme Ct. 1990. Assoc. Cummings & Lockwood, Stamford, Conn., 1980-82, Bond and Camhi, N.Y.C., 1982-84; ptnr. Dorsey & Whitney, N.Y.C., 1988-92; br. chief divsn. enforcement SEC, N.Y.C., 1992-97; dep. gen. counsel Gabelli Asset Mgmt. Inc., Rye, 1997-2000; v.p. Goldman Sachs Asset Mgmt., N.Y.C., 2000—04; dir. regulatory affairs Gabelli Asset Mgmt. Inc., 2004—. Editor Am. Jour. Law and Medicine, 1979-80. Office: One Corp Ctr Rye NY 10580 Office Phone: 941-921-7732. E-mail: pgoldstein@gabelli.com.

GOLDSTEIN, RICHARD A., consumer products company executive; b. 1942; married. BBA, U. Mass.; LLB, Boston U.; LLM, Harvard U. Atty. Choate Hall & Stewart, 1968-70; spl. asst. to cabinet mem. U.S. Govt., Washington, 1970-73; assoc. Arnold & Porter, Washington, 1973-75; staff atty., asst. gen. counsel Lever Bros. Co., 1975-80, v.p. asst. to chmn., 1980-84; pres., CEO Unilever Can. Ltd., 1984; exec. v.p., COO Unilever U.S., N.Y.C., 1988, pres., CEO, 1989; chmn., CEO Unilever Can. Ltd., 1989-97; pres., CEO Unilever N.Am. Foods, 1996-00; pres. and CEO Unilever U.S. Inc., 1989—2000; chmn., chief exec. ofcr. Intl. Flavors & Fragrances, N.Y.C., 2000—. Office: IFF 521 W 57th St New York NY 10019 Office Phone: 212-765-5500.*

GOLDSTEIN, ROBERT MICHAEL, surgeon; b. Elizabethton, Tenn., Mar. 21, 1953; s. Buford Jack and Mary Jane Goldstein; m. Amanda Elizabeth Goldstein, May 16, 1992. BA, U. Tenn., 1975; MD, U. Tenn., Memphis, 1981. Diplomate Am. Bd. Gen. Surgery, Am. Bd. Surg. Care. Pediatric intern Ohio State U., Columbus, 1981-82; surgery resident W.Va. U., Morgantown, 1982-84, 85-87; rsch. fellow Johns Hopkins, Balt., 1984-85; transplant fellow U. Pitts., 1987-88, Baylor U. Med. Ctr., Dallas, 1987-88, asst. dir. transplant svcs., 1988—, dir. transplant intensive care, 1990—. Fellow: ACS; mem.: Am. Bd. Surg. Critical Care. Office: Baylor U Dept Transplantation Dallas TX 75246

GOLDSTEIN, SANDRA CARA, lawyer; b. Bklyn., May 12, 1964; BA, Barnard Coll., 1984; JD, NYU, 1987. Bar: N.Y. 1988. Assoc. Cravath Swaine and Moore LLP, NYC, 1987—94, ptnr., 1994—. Office: Cravath Swaine & Moore LLP Worldwide Plz 825 8th Ave Fl 38 New York NY 10019-7475 Office Phone: 212-474-1000. Office Fax: 212-474-3700. Business E-Mail: sgoldstein@cravath.com.

GOLDSTEIN, SCOTT M., ophthalmologist, surgeon; b. Buffalo, Nov. 28, 1969; s. James A. Goldstein and Karen J. Tabor; m. Suzy G. Grossman, Aug. 13, 1994; children: Joshua A., Allison J. Diploma, BS, Cornell U., 1992; MD, Boston U., 1996. Diplomate Am. Bd. Ophthalmology, 2001. Intern internal medicine Thomas Jefferson U. Hosp., Phila., 1996—97; resident ophthalmology U. Pa., 1997—2000; fellow oculoplastic surgery Children's Hosp. Phila., 2000—02; oculoplastic surgeon U. Pa., Phila., 2002—03, Tri County Eye Physicians and Surgeons, Southampton, Pa., 2003—. Dir. of med. edn. Dept Of Ophthalmology, U. of Pa, Philadelphia, Pa., 2002—03; clin. asst. prof. ophthalmology U. Pa.; staff physician Wills Eye Hosp. Fellow: Am. Soc. Ophthalmic Plastic and Reconstructive Surgeons, Am. Acad. Ophthalmology. Home: 8 Viburnum Ct Lafayette Hill PA 19444 Office: Tri County Eye Physicians & Surgeons 319 Second St Pike Southampton PA 18966 Office Phone: 215-355-4428. E-mail: goldstein@tricountyeye.com.

GOLDSTEIN, SIDNEY, sociologist, educator, demographer; b. New London, Conn., Aug. 4, 1927; s. Max and Bella (Hoffman) G.; m. Alice Dreifuss, June 21, 1953; children: Beth Leah, David Louis, Brenda Ruth. BA, U. Conn., 1949, MA, 1951; PhD, U. Pa., 1953. Instr. sociology U. Pa., 1953-55; mem. faculty Brown U., Providence, 1955—, prof. sociology, 1960—, George Hazard Crooker prof., 1977—, prof. emeritus, 1993—, rsch. prof. population studies, 1997—, chmn. dept. sociology and anthropology, 1963-70, dir. Population Studies & Tng. Ctr., 1965-89. Demographic advisor Chulalongkorn U., Bangkok, 1968-69; cons. UN Econ. and Social Commn. for Asia and Pacific, 1971-72, 77-82, Nat. Ctr. Health Stats., 1970-77, Internat. Program Population Analysis, Smithsonian Instn., 1971-76; mem. U.S. Bur. Census Adv. Com., 1965-71, Rand Corp., 1975-83; mem. nat. com. rsch. 1980 census Social Sci. Rsch. Coun., 1981-88; mem. governing bur. Com. Internat. Cooperation in Nat. Rsch. Demography, 1981-98, treas., 1994-98; mem. com. on population Nat. Rsch. Coun., Nat. Acad. Scis., 1983-87; chmn. nat. tech. adv. com. Jewish population studies Coun. Jewish Fedns., 1984-95; co-chmn. internat. sci. com. 1990 census surveys world Jewry, Jerusalem, 1988-92. Author: Patterns of Mobility, 1910-1950, 1958, Consumption Patterns of the Aged, 1960, The Norristown Study: An Experiment in Interdisciplinary Research Training, 1961, (with K.B. Mayer) The First Two Years: Problems of Small Business Growth and Survival, 1961, Migration and Economic Development in Rhode Island, 1958, (with Calvin Goldscheider) Jewish Americans, 1968, Urbanization in Thailand, 1947-1960, 1970, The Demography of Bangkok, 1972, (with V. Prachuabmoh and A. Goldstein) Urban-Rural Migration Differentials in Thailand, 1974, (with A. Speare and W. Frey) Residential Mobility, Migration and Metropolitan Change, 1975, Circulation in the Context of Total Mobility in Southeast Asia, 1978; editor: (with D.F. Sly) Basic Data Needed for the Study of Urbanization, 1975, The Measurement of Urbanization and the Projection of Urban Population, 1975, Patterns of Urbanization: Comparative Country Studies, 1977, (with wife) A Test of the Potential Use of Mulltiplicity in Research on Population Movement, 1979, Population Mobility in the People's Republic of China, 1985, Surveys of Migration in Developing Countries: A Methodological Review, 1981, Migration and Fertility in Peninsular Malaysia, 1983, Urbanization in China, 1985, (with wife) Migration in Thailand: A Twenty-Five Year Review, 1986, (with C. Goldscheider) The Jewish Community of Rhode Island: A Social and Demographic Survey, 1988, Comparative Migration Patterns to Shanghai and Bangkok, 1989, Urbanization in China, 1982-1987, The Role of Migration and Reclassification, 1990, (with wife and Zai Liang) Migration, Gender, and Labor Force in Hubei Province, 1985-90, (with wife) Permanent and Temporary Migration Differentials in China, 1991, Demographic Issues and Data Needs for Mega-City Research, 1994, The Impact of Temporary Migration on Urban Places, 1993, (with R. Neupert) Urbanization and Population Redistribution in Mongolia, 1994, (with wife) Jews on the Move, 1996, (with Gang Liu) Migrant-Non Migrant Fertility in Anhui China, 1996, (with Dang Anh) Internal Migration and Development in Vietnam, 1997, (with wife and Michael White) Migration Fertility and State Policy in Hubei Province, China, 1997, (with wife) Lithuanian Jewry, 1993: A Demographic and Sociocultural Profile, 1997, (with wife) Conservative Jewry in the United States: A Sociodemographic Profile, 1998,(with wife and Yanyi Djamba) Permanent and Temporary Migration During Periods of Economic Change: Vietnam and China Compared, 1999. Bd. dirs. Jewish Fedn. R.I., 1964-68, 78-82, 85—, area v.p., 1997—; bd. dirs. Bur. Jewish Edn., Providence, 1959-82, 94—, bd. dirs.; bd. dirs. Coun. Jewish Fedns., 1987-94 Recipient Disting. Svc. medal Chilalongkorn U., 1969, Disting. Svc. medal Mahidol U., 1992; Disting. Leadership award Coun. Jewish. Fedns., 1992, Tribute award, 1998; Lifetime Achievement award Assn. Social Sci. Study of Jewry, 1992, sr. rsch. award CSC-PRC, NAS, 1983, Jewish Cultural Achievement award Nat. Found. Juewish Culture, 2002, Lauredale award Internat. Union for Sci. Study of Population, 2005; Harrison fellow, 1953, Social Sci. Rsch. Coun. fellow, 1961-62, Guggenheom fellow, 1961-63, rsch. fellow Inst. Contemporary Jewry, Hebrew U. Jerusalem, 1969—, sr. fellow East-West Population Inst., Honolulu, 1976, 82, 90, fellow Inst. Advanced Study, Ind. U., 1995, vis. fellow Australian Nat. U., Canberra, 1977; scholar-in-residence Rockefeller Study Ctr., Bellagio, 1990, sr. vis. scholar Hebrew U., 1990 Mem. Am. Sociol. Assn., Population Assn. Am. (pres. 1975-76), Assn. Jewish Demography and Stats. (dir.), Internat. Union Sci. Study Population (chair com. urbanization and population distbn. 1971-76), Assn. Sociol. Study Jewry, Phi Beta Kappa. Home: 95 Kiwanee Rd Warwick RI 02888-4040 Office: Brown U Sociology Dept 79 Waterman St Providence RI 02912-9079

GOLDSTEIN, SIDNEY, pharmacist; b. Phila., Mar. 27, 1932; s. Israel and Gertrude (Stein) G.; m. Janice Levy, June 19, 1955; children: Rhonda, David, Nina. BSc in Pharmacy, Phila. Coll. Pharmacy & Sci., 1954, MSc in Pharmacy, 1955, DSc in Pharmacy, 1958. Cardiovascular unit head Eaton Labs, Norwich, NY, 1958—59; anti-inflammatory unit head Lederle Labs, Pearl River, N.Y., 1959-61; with Merrell Dow Rsch. Inst., Cin., 1961-93; v.p. global pharm. and analytical scis. Marion Merrell Dow Inc., Kansas City, Mo., 1991-93; v.p. sci. and tech. Duramed Pharm., Inc., Cin., 1994-98, v.p. bus. devel., sci. and tech., 1998—2002; chief sci. officer Prasco, Cin., 2002—. Adj. assoc. prof. U. Cin. Coll. Pharmacy, 1984-98, dean's adv. coun., 1998—; lectr. pharmacology Phila. Coll. Pharmacy, 1967-70, chair PQRI-drug product tech. com., 1997—, mem. steering com., 2003-05; mem. So. Ohio Life Sci. Task Force, 1999-2001, GPhA sci. com., 2001—; mem. tech. validation adv. bd. Cinn. Children's Hosp., 2003—. Contbr. articles to profl. jours. Bd. trustees Glen Manor Home for Aged, Cin., 1983-89. Recipient Award for Nicoderm, R&D Mag., 1992. Mem. Am. Assn. Pharm. Scientists, Am. Soc. Clin. Pharmacology and Therapeutics, Soc. Exptl. Biology and Medicine, Am. Soc. Pharmacology and Exptl. Therapeutics, B'nai B'rith (chpt. v.p. 1978). Home: 1125 Fort View Pl Cincinnati OH 45202-1713 Office: Prasco 7155 Kemper Rd Cincinnati OH 45249 Office Phone: 513-618-3333. E-mail: s.goldstein@prasco.com.

GOLDSTEIN, STANLEY PHILIP, engineering educator; b. Bklyn., Feb. 3, 1923; s. Max and Rose (Ahrenstein) G.; m. Wanda Rouse, June 6, 1949; children— Bruce, Richard. BS, U. Okla., 1949; MS, NYU, 1956; PhD in Astronautics, Poly. Inst. Bklyn., 1969. Engr. Vapor Recovery Systems Corp., Compton, Calif., 1950-52; project engr. Alderson Research Labs., N.Y.C., 1952-54; mem. faculty Hofstra U., Hempstead, N.Y., 1954—, prof. engring., 1957-84, prof. emeritus, 1984—, chmn. engring. sci. dept., 1956-68, 70-72, 80-83, dir. acad. computer center, 1970-72; assoc. dean Hofstra U. (Coll. Arts and Scis.), 1973-74, 77, assoc. provost for planning, budgeting and instl. research, 1974-76. Pres. Techmark Enterprises, Inc.; Alcorn Combustion Co., N.Y.C. Transit Authority, Hofstra Internat. Trade & Devel. Corp.; dir. Collegiate Sci. and Tech. Entry Program Hofstra U., 1987-89 Served to 1st lt. USAAF, 1942-45, ETO. Decorated DFC, Air medal with four oak leaf clusters, French Normandy medal. Mem. Sigma Xi. Home: 18 Millers Ln Kingston NY 12401-4426 Office: Hofstra U Engring Dept Hempstead NY 11550 Personal E-mail: stanwand@aol.com.

GOLDSTEIN, STEVE, corporate financial executive; Grad, U. Ariz. Asst. to sec., dir. of the office of pub. affairs U.S. Dept. of Interior, Bush Adminstrn.; sr. v.p. Ins. Info. Inst., NYC; v.p. corp. comm. Dow Jones & Co./The Wall St. Jour.; exec. v.p., pub. affairs and mktg. TIAA-CREF, 2003—. Office: TIAA-CREF 730 3rd Ave New York NY 10017

GOLDSTEIN, STEVEN, lawyer; b. St. Louis, Sept. 8, 1950; s. Alexander Julius and Dorothy Lea (Matier) G.; m. Laura Lou Staley, July 20, 1980. BS in Speech, Northwestern U., Evanston, Ill., 1972; JD, U. Mich., 1975. Bar: Mo. 1975. Prin. Goldstein & Pressman, P.C., St. Louis, 1993—. Mem. ABA, Mo. Bar Assn. (chmn. bankruptcy com. 1983-85), Bar Assn. of Met. St. Louis. Home: 712 Swarthmore Ln Saint Louis MO 63130-3618 Office: Goldstein & Pressman PC 121 Hunter Ave Ste 101 Saint Louis MO 63124-2082 Office Phone: 314-727-1717. Business E-Mail: stg@goldsteinpressman.com.

GOLDSTEIN, STEVEN EDWARD, psychologist; b. Bronx, NY, Nov. 25, 1948; s. Maurice and Matilda (Weiss) Goldstein. BS in Psychology, CCNY, 1970, MS in Sch. Psychology, 1971; EdD in Sch. Psychology, U. No. Colo., 1977. Lic. psychologist Nev., cert. sch. psychologist N.Y., Calif. Tchr. N.Y.C.

Pub. Schs., 1970-71, 72-73, tchr., counselor, 1974; extern in sch. psychology N. Shore Child Guidance, 1972; sch. psychologist Denver Pub. Schs., 1975; asst. prof. psychology Northeastern Okla. State U., Tahlequah, 1976-78; coord. inpatient, emergency svcs. Winnemucca (Nev.) Mental Health Ctr., 1978-80; residential dir. Desert Devel. Ctr., Las Vegas, Nev., 1980-82; sr. psychologist Las Vegas Mental Health Ctr., 1982-92; pvt. practice psychology Las Vegas, 1983—; sr. psychologist Desert Regional Ctr., 1992—2004. Participant NSF biofeedback seminar, 1977; presenter papers to profl. confs. Sec. grad. coun. CUNY, 1971; pres. grad. coun. CCNY, 1971. Mem.: APA (Nev. coord. office profl. practice 1987—88), So. Nev. Soc. Cert. Psychologists (pres. 1984—86), Nev. Soc. Tng. and Devel. (dir. 1982—83), Biofeedback Soc. Nev. (membership dir. 1982—90), CCNY Alumni Assn. (bd. dirs. So. Nev. chpt. 2003—), Jewish Fedn. Las Vegas (bus. and profl. com. 1995—2003). Office: 3180 W Sahara Ave Ste C-25 Las Vegas NV 89102-6073 Office Phone: 702-525-9170. Personal E-mail: goldsteinse@aol.com.

GOLDSTEIN, STUART N., lawyer; b. Rochester, NY, May 26, 1967; BS, Cornell Univ., 1989; JD, Boalt Hall Sch. Law, Univ. Calif., 1992. Bar: Calif. 1992, NY 1996. Ptnr. Cadwalader Wickersham & Taft LLP, Charlotte, NC. With CDO group, Cadwalader, CMBS group, Cadwalader. Office: Cadwalader, Wickersham & Taft LLP 227 W Trade St Ste 2400 Charlotte NC 28202*

GOLDSTEIN, STUART WOLF, lawyer; b. Buffalo, N.Y., Sept. 9, 1931; s. Joseph and Esther (Wolf) G.; m. Myra Saft Stuart, June 1960 (dec. Aug. 1981); children: Jeffrey, Jonathan, Meryl; m. Nancy Baynes Lux, 1993. Student, U. Buffalo, 1949-52, JD, 1955; postgrad., U. Va., 1956. Bar: N.Y. 1956, Fla. 1974, Ariz. 1977, U.S. Supreme Ct. 1960, U.S Dist. Ct. (we. dist.) N.Y. 1956, U.S. Ct. Mil. Appeals 1957, U.S. Ct. Appeals (2d cir.) N.Y., 1978, U.S. Dist. Ct. Ariz. 1981. Sole practice, Buffalo, 1960-79, 82-85, Phoenix, 1980-82, 85—. Pres., founder Cystic Fibrosis Found., Buffalo, 1960; fund-raiser United Fund, United Jewish Appeal; pres. Boys League; active Erie County Spl. Task Force on Energy, Buffalo, 1978. 1st lt. JAG, U.S. Army, 1956-60. Fellow Ariz. Bar Found.; mem. ATLA, Ariz. State Bar Assn., N.Y. Trial Lawyers Assn., Erie County Trial Lawyers, Ariz. Trial Lawyers Assn. (Ariz. real property sect.), N.Y. State Bar Assn., Fla. Bar Assn., Am. Arbitration Assn., Maricopa County Bar Assn., Buffalo Skating Club, Curling Skating Club (legal counsel). Avocations: astronomy, breeding boston terriers. Office: 2700 N 3rd St Ste 2010 Phoenix AZ 85004-4602 Office Phone: 602-279-1666. Business E-Mail: stuart@stuartgoldsteinlaw.com.

GOLDSTEIN, SYDNEY RACHEL, photographer, writer, radio producer; b. San Francisco, Oct. 13, 1944; d. Edward William and Dorian Claire G.; m. Charles R. Breyer, Jan. 18, 1976; children: Katherine, Joseph. Grad. h.s., San Francisco. Photographer, writer, 1970—; prodr., founding exec. dir. City Arts & Lectures, Inc., San Francisco, 1981—; exec. prodr. City Arts & Lecturs, Radio Broadcasts, 1997—. Author: Earned Income, 2001. Adv. bd. Grants for the Arts, San Francisco Hotel Tax Fund, 1979-82. Recipient Koret Israel prize Koret Found., 1990. Democrat. Office: City Arts & Lectures Inc 1955 Sutter St San Francisco CA 94115

GOLDSTEIN, TAMARA BETH, musician; b. Tenafly, N.J., Dec. 20, 1961; d. Nathan and Beatrice Goldstein. MusB, Ind. U, 1984; MusM, Juilliard Sch., 1987; Mus D, U Colo., 1996. Accompanist faculty Aspen Music Festival, Aspen, Colo.; asst. prof./artist-in-residence Metro State Coll. of Denver, 2002—. Bd. dirs. Denver Philharm. Orch.; founder, dir. www.pianocelebration.com. Mem.: Suzuki Assn. Am., Denver Musicians Assn./Am. Fedn. Musicians, Music Tchr. Nat. Assn., Pi Kappa Lambda. Office Phone: 303-556-3391. Business E-Mail: goldstet@mscd.edu.

GOLDSTEIN, WALTER ELLIOTT, biotechnology executive; m. Paula G. Copen. BS in Chem. Engring., Ill. Inst. Tech., 1961; MBA, Mich. State U., 1968; MSChemE, U. Notre Dame, 1971, PhDChemE, 1973. Registered profl. engr., Ind. Process devel. engr. Linde div. Union Carbide, Tonawanda, N.Y., 1961-64; assoc. project engr. Miles Labs., Elkhart, Ind., 1964-67, assoc. rsch. scientist, 1967-72, rsch. scientist, 1972-73, rsch. supr., 1973-76; mgr. chem. engring. rsch. & pilot svcs. Chem. Engring. Rsch. & Pilot Svcs., Elkhart, Ind., 1976-78, dir., 1978-82; chem. engring. rsch. v.p. Biotech. Group, Elkhart, 1982-87; v.p. R&D ESCAgenetics Corp., San Carlos, Calif., 1987-94; pres. Goldstein Cons. Co., Foster City, Calif., 1994—; co-founder Transcyte Corp., Inc., 1996—, Phytonic Corp., 2001—; coord. Biotech. Ctr., Shadowlane Campus, U. Nev., Las Vegas, 2003—. Adj. prof. chem. engring. U. Notre Dame, 1974-75, San Jose State U., 1995—; cons. Bernard Wolnak, Chgo., 1987 Contbr. chpts. to books; inventions and publs. in chem. engring., pharm., food, diagnostics and biotech. field. Vice-pres. B'nai B'rith, South Bend., Ind., 1978-89. Mem. AAAS, Am. Chem. Soc., Am. Soc. Pharmocognosy, Soc. for Competitive Intelligence Profls., Am. Inst. Chem. Engrs., N.Y. Acad. Scis., Inst. Food Technologists, Sigma Xi. Avocations: reading, computers, outdoor sports, social/charitable causes. Office Phone: 702-774-2325, 702-804-5952. E-mail: goldconsul@aol.com, walter.goldstein@ccmail.nevada.edu.

GOLDSTEIN, WILLIAM A., investment counsel; b. Chgo., June 24, 1939; s. Jacob E. and Marion B. G.; m. Anne B. Goldstein, Aug. 19, 1962; chidlren: Deborah, Catherine. BS, Purdue U., 1962. Registered rep. Hornblower & Weeks-Hemphill Noyes, Chgo., 1962-70; exec. v.p. Burton J. Vincent-Chesley & Co., Chgo., 1970-83; chmn. Prescott Asset Mgmt., Prescott, Ball & Turben, Chgo., 1983-89; pres. Lodestar Investment Counsel LLC, Chgo., 1989—; dir. The Pvt. Bank, Chgo. Trustee Chgo. Symphony Orch., chmn. governing mems., 1997-99, vice chmn., treas.; bd. dirs. Grant Park Concert Soc., Chgo., 1995-97. Mem. Standard Club, Chgo. Yacht Club. Avocations: sailing, bicycling, golf, reading. Office: Lodestar Investment Counsel LLC 208 S Lasalle St Chicago IL 60604-1000 Office Phone: 312-630-9666.

GOLDSTEIN, WILLIAM MARKS, lawyer; b. Phila., Aug. 28, 1935; s. David and Estelle (Marks) Goldstein; m. Lillia E. Demchuck; 1 child, Laura;children from previous marriage: Adam, Benjamin, Daniel. AB, Princeton U., 1957; JD magna cum laude, Harvard U., 1960. Bar: Pa. 1961, DC 1977. Law clk. to judge U.S. Ct. Appeals, Phila., 1960-61; assoc. firm Morgan Lewis & Bockius, Phila., 1961-66, ptnr., 1967-75, 77-82, Drinker, Biddle & Reath LLP, Phila., 1982—; dep. asst. sec. tax policy Dept. Treasury, Washington, 1975-76. Contbr. articles to profl. jours. Mem. Lower Merion (Pa.) Dem. Com., 1965—68; candidate Sch. Bd. Lower Merion, 1965, state legis., 1966. Mem.: ABA, Am. Coll. Tax Counsel, Am. Law Inst., DC Bar Assn., Phila. Bar Assn., Pa. Bar Assn. Jewish. Home: 787 Trephanny Ln Wayne PA 19087-1931 Office: Drinker Biddle & Reath LLP l Logan Sq 18th & Cherry St Philadelphia PA 19103-6996 Office Phone: 215-988-2982. Business E-Mail: Goldstwm@dbr.com.

GOLDSTEIN-ERICKSON, ELLIE, school librarian; b. Chattanooga, Tenn., Dec. 22, 1948; d. Louis Goldstein and Lillian Amlin; m. Clifton Carl Erickson, July 13, 1975; children: Jacob, Jonathan. BA, U. Conn., 1970; MLS, U. Calif., 1973. Cert. life tchg., Crosscultural Lang. and Academic Devel. credential. Head libr. Richmond (Calif.) H.S., 1973—83; libr. Piedmont (Calif.) Unified Sch. Dist., 1991—92, West Contra Costa Unified Sch. Dist., Richmond, 1992—96; libr. media tchr. Berkeley Unified Sch. Dist., 1996—. Contbr. articles to profl. jours. Bd. dirs. Congregation Beth El, Berkeley, 1991—98. Named Outstanding Educator, Berkeley Pub. Edn. Found., 2003. Mem.: Am. Assn. Sch. Libr., Am. Libr. Assn., Calif. Sch. Libr. Assn. (v.p./legis. 2002—). Jewish. Office: Berkeley High Sch Libr 1980 Allston Way Berkeley CA 94704 Office Phone: 510-644-6857. Business E-Mail: ellie@berkeley.k12.ca.us.

GOLDSTEN, ROBERT EMANUEL, lawyer, investor; b. Charlottesville, Va., Oct. 8, 1916; s. Joseph and Rebecca S. (Shapero) B.; m. Janice F. Wasserman, Nov. 30, 1979; children by previous marriage: Douglas Kahn, Ina Lee. BS in Commerce, U. Va., 1937, LLB, 1940. Bar: Va. 1939, D.C. 1941. Ptnr. Goldsten Bros. Developers & Builders, Washington, 1941-72; pres. Gen. Mortgage Corp., Washington, 1948-66, Vero Beach (Fla.) Yacht Basin, Inc., 1957-71, Devel. Funding Corp., Washington, 1972-74; v.p. Allied Fin. Corp., Silver Spring, Md., 1950-58, World Wide Airlines, Burbank, Calif., 1960-62; pres., CEO McLean (Va.) Savs. & Loan Assn., 1977-80; dir. McLean Fin. Corp., 1981-87; chmn. U.S. Mortgage Credit Corp., 1983-87, Allied Protective Sys. Inc., 1981-88; pres. Gen. Funding Corp., Washington, 1998—. Vis. lectr. real estate mgmt. Am. U., 1950-57. Pres., Brotherhood, Washington Hebrew Congregation, 1955-56; treas., bd. dirs. Washington Area Coun. on Alcoholism and Drug Abuse, 1971-77, Carl G. Jung Fund of Washington, 1976-79; co-founder Washington Inst. Natural Medicine, 1998; mem. D.C. governing bd. Anti-Defamation League, 1997—. Recipient award for outstanding contbn. to success of Home Builders Met. Washington, 1966, Spl. Beautification award City of Alexandria, Va., Disting. Svc. award Washington Area Coun. Alcoholism and Drug Abuse, 1977. Mem. U. Va. Alumni Club Washington, Indian Spring Club, Woodmont Country Club, Tower Club, Boca Rio Golf Club, Univ. Club, B'nai B'rith, Georgetown Club. Democrat. Mailing: 3134 Ellicott St NW Washington DC 20008-2025

GOLDSTICK, THOMAS KARL, biomedical engineering educator; b. Toronto, Ont., Can., Aug. 21, 1934; came to U.S., 1955, naturalized. s. David and Iva Sarah (Kaplan) G.; m. Marcia Adrienne Jenkins, July 4, 1982. BS, MIT, 1957, MS, 1959; PhD, U. Calif., Berkeley, 1966, U. Calif., San Francisco, 1966-67. Asst. prof. Northwestern U., Evanston, Ill., 1967-71, assoc. prof. chem. engring. and biol. sci., 1971-81, prof. chem. engring., neurobiology and physiology, 1981-85, prof. chem. engring., biomed. engring., neurobiology and physiology, 1985-99, prof. emeritus, 1999—. Adj. prof. ophthalmology U. Ill., Chgo., 1981-91. Editor: Oxygen Transport to Tissue V, 1983, VII, 1985, X, 1988, XI, 1989, XII, 1990, XIII, 1992. Rsch. grantee NIH, 1968—; Spl. Rsch. fellow U. Calif., San Diego, LaJolla, 1971-73. Mem. Internat. Soc. Oxygen Transport to Tissue (sec. 1980-86, exec. com. 1986-93), Biomed. Engring. Soc. (bd. dirs. 1983-86, chmn. publs. bd. 1985-86). Home: 2025 Sherman Ave Apt 504 Evanston IL 60201-3269 Office: Biomed Engring Dept Northwestern U Evanston IL 60208-3107 Office Phone: 847-491-5518. Business E-Mail: t-goldstick@northwestern.edu.

GOLDSTINE, STEPHEN JOSEPH, academic administrator; b. San Francisco, Nov. 16, 1937; s. Edgar Nathan and Regina Thelma (Benno) G.; m. Emily Raechel Miller Keeler, Apr. 12, 1981; children: Rachel, Bettina, Simone Massimiliana Student, Calif. Sch. Fine Arts, 1951, 58; BA, U. Calif., Berkeley, 1961, postgrad. in philosophy, 1962-67. Teaching asst. rhetoric dept. U. Calif., Berkeley, 1963-66; asst. prof. St. Mary's Coll., Moraga, Calif., 1964-70, chmn. art dept., 1969-70; cons. Freeman & Gossage, San Francisco, 1967-69; dir. neighborhood arts program Art Commn. City and County San Francisco, 1970-77; exec. sec. Mayor's Interagency Com. for Arts, San Francisco, 1971-75; founding dir. Performing Arts for the Third Age, San Francisco, 1973; co-dir. Rockefeller Tng. Fellowships in Mus. Edn., San Francisco, 1975; pres. San Francisco Art Inst., 1977-86; dir. grad. programs Calif. Coll. Arts and Crafts, 1986—; visiting faculty San Francisco State U.; Dennis Leon prof. grad. studies Calif. Coll. Arts and Crafts, 2002—. Sr. cons. Daniel Solomon Architects and Planners, 1988; mem. chancellor's adv. bd. Univ. Art Mus., U. Calif., Berkeley, 1979—; exec. com., trustee San Francisco Arts Edn. Found., 1985—; mem. Oakland Cultural Affairs Commn., 2002—; mem. prominent orgns. panel Calif. Arts Coun., 1981, vice chmn., 1983, chmn., 1985-87; chmn. invited session Am. Philos. Assn. (Pacific divsn.), 1986, lectr. UCLA, 1976, Stanford U., 1966, Harvard U., 1976, 71; docent Lycee Internat. Franco-Am., 1993—. Editor: Western Round Table on Modern Art, 1993; co-prodr., co-dir. (film) Walz um die Wände hoch zu gehen, 1999. Condr. The Art Orch., Calif. Palace of the Legion of Honor, 1997. Democrat. Jewish. Home: 1331 Green St San Francisco CA 94109-1926 Office: Calif Coll Arts Crafts 1111 Eighth St San Francisco CA 94107-2206 Office Phone: 415-551-9212. E-mail: mrgoldstine@earthlink.net.

GOLDSTON, JAMES, television producer; Grad., Oxford U. Sr. prodr.: (current affairs news series) Tonight with Trevor McDonald, ITV1 network, England, 1999—2001 (Nominee BAFTA TV award for Best News and Current Affairs Journalism, 2000); exec. prodr.: Tonight with Trevor McDonald, 2002—04 (Three-time award winner of Royal TV Soc. Program of Yr. award), ABC News Nightline, Washington and NYC, 2004—. Office: ABC 77 W 66th St New York NY 10023

GOLDSTON, ROBERT J., research scientist; BS magna cum laude, Harvard U., 1972; PhD in Astrophysical Sci., Princeton U., 1977. Rsch. asst. Princeton Plasma Physics Lab. Princeton U., NJ, 1972—77, assoc. dir. rsch., 1995—97, dir., 1997—, head Tokamak Fusion Test Reactor physics program divsn. Prof. astrophysical sci. Princeton U., 1992—. Co-author: (textbook) Introduction to Plasma Physics. Achievements include research in high temperature plasmas required for thermonuclear fusion leading to the National Spherical Torus Experiment (NSTX), an experimental nuclear reactor promoting plasma efficiency. Office: Plasma Physics Lab Princeton U MS37 C-Site B333 PPL Princeton NJ 08540 Office Phone: 609-243-3553. Office Fax: 609-243-2749. E-mail: rjg@princeton.edu.

GOLDSTON, STEPHEN EUGENE, community psychologist, educator, consultant; b. N.Y.C., Apr. 19, 1931; s. Michael Louis and Molly Ruth (Rothenberg) G.; children: Beth Karen, Lisa Robin BA, NYU, 1952; MSPH, Columbia U., 1953, MA, 1957, EdD, 1958. Lectr., instr. Columbia U., N.Y.C., 1956-58; asst. to dir. Westchester County Cmty. Mental Health Bd., White Plains, N.Y., 1958-60; chief mental health edn. unit, dir. mental health consultation program N.Y.C. Cmty. Mental Health Bd., 1960-62; staff asst. to assoc. dir. extramural programs NIMH, Rockville, Md., 1962-63, tng. specialist pilot and spl. grants sect. Tng. and Manpower Resources br., 1963-65, tng. specialist exptl. and spl. tng. br., 1966-67, chief pub. health sect. exptl. and spl. tng. br., 1967-69, spl. asst. to dir. for preventive programs, 1967-71, coord. primary prevention program, 1972-80, chief primary prevention service programs, Div. Mental Health Service Program, 1980-81, dir. office of prevention, 1981-85; cons. in preventive psychiatry Neuropsychiat. Inst., UCLA, 1985-87; assoc. dir. UCLA Preventive Psychiatry Ctr., 1987-89, chair ann. nat. conf., 1987, 88; staff dir. Mayor's Citizen's Task Force on Cen. City East, Los Angeles, 1986-88; pres. Goldston & Assocs., Chgo., 1986—. Chmn. nat. conf. UCLA Preventive Psychiatry Ctr., 1987-88; coord. nat. conf. Mental Health in Pub. Health Tng., 1967-68; lectr. Bar-Ilan U. Sch. Social Work, Ramat Gan, Israel, 1996-98, 2000—03, The Hebrew U. Sch. Social Work, Jerusalem, Israel, 1997-2000, 03; sr. editor NIMH Prevention Publ. Series, 1976-85; assoc. editor coun. Am. Assn. Applied and Preventive Psychology, 1991—. Mem. editl. bd. Jour. Preventive Psychiatry, Jour. Primary Prevention; contbr. articles to profl. jours. With U.S. Army, 1953-55, USPHS, 1957-85. Recipient Sustained High Quality Peformance award HEW, 1968, 72, 76; Superior Work Performance award HEW, 1970; Outstanding Contbn. to Prevention in Mental Health award Nat. Council Community Mental Health Ctrs., Washington, 1985 Fellow Am. Psychol. Assn. (Disting. Profl. Contbns. award 1984), Am Psychol. Soc. (charter mem.), Am. Pub. Health Assn. (chmn. com. on prevention, mental health sect. 1974-77, Am. Assn. Applied and Preventive Psychology (founding). E-mail: goldston@netvision.net.il.

GOLDSTONE, JEFFREY, physicist, educator; b. Manchester, Eng., Sept. 3, 1933; arrived in U.S., 1977; m. Roberta Gordon; 1 child, Andrew. BA, Cambridge (Eng.) U., 1954, PhD, 1958. Fellow Trinity Coll., Cambridge, 1956-60, 62-82, hon. fellow, 2000; lectr., reader U. Cambridge, England, 1961-76, MIT, Cambridge, Mass., 1977—2004, Cecil and Ida Green prof. physics, 1983—2004, prof. emeritus, 2004. Recipient Dannie Heineman prize, Am. Phys. Soc., 1981, Guthrie medal, Inst. Physics, 1983, Dirac prize, Internat. Ctr. Theoretical Physics, 1991. Mem.: Am. Acad. Arts and Scis., Royal Soc. Office: MIT 77 Massachusetts Ave NE 25 4041 Cambridge MA 02139-4307 Business E-Mail: goldston@mit.edu.

GOLDSTONE, SANFORD, psychologist, educator; b. N.Y.C., July 17, 1926; s. Albert and Anna (Steckel) G.; children: Susan Beth, Arthur Craig, Nancy Lynn; stepchildren: Peter B., Anthony A., Jane P., Elisabeth W.; m. Lois Adams. BS, CCNY, 1947; PhD, Duke U., 1953. Intern Duke Sch. Medicine, 1949-51; chief clin. psychologist Duke Sch. Medicine (Psychiat. Out-Patient Clinic), 1951-54, lectr. psychology, 1953-54, asso. dept. psychiatry, 1953-54; asst. prof. to prof. psychiatry, chief psychologist, program dir. Baylor U. Coll. Medicine, 1955-67; prof., head div. psychology dept. psychiatry Cornell U. Med. Coll., 1967-79; prof. psychology field neurobiology Cornell U. Med. Coll. (Grad. Sch. Med. Scis.), 1969-79; prof., dir. clin. tng., dept. psychology U. Maine, Orono, 1979-86, prof. psychology emeritus, 1986—. Cons. VA Hosps., Durham, N.C., 1953-54, Houston, 1959-67, Temple, Tex., 1964-67, Montrose, N.Y., 1968-79, Togus, Maine, 1979-88; mem. profl. staff Eastern Maine Med. Center and; Bangor Mental Health Inst., 1980-86; trustee Miles Meml. Hosp., Damariscotta, Maine, 1990-99; cons. criminal law sect. Am. Bar Assn., 1967-69, Westchester County Probation Dept., 1968-71, Community Service Bur., N.Y. State Tng. Schs., 1969-75; head div. psychology Houston State Psychiat. Inst., 1958-67, acting bus. mgr., 1959-60, head div. crime and delinquency, 1966-67; clin. asso. prof. to clin. prof. U. Houston, 1958-67; dir. mental health services Harris County Probation Dept., Houston, 1963-67; cons. Silver Hill Found., 1974-81; psychologist-in-chief Payne Whitney Psychiat. Clinic, 1967-74, Westchester div. N.Y. Hosp., 1967-74; attending psychologist N.Y. Hosp., 1967-79; head, community cons. services outpatient dept. Payne Whitney Psychiat. Clinic, 1970-73; head community cons. services Westchester div. N.Y. Hosp.-Cornell Med. Center, 1973-75 Contbr. numerous articles to profl. jours. Served with USAAF, 1945. USPHS grantee, 1955-65, 79-86. Fellow APA (life); mem. Am. Psychopath. Assn. (life). Home: PO Box 282 East Boothbay ME 04544-0282 Office: U Maine Psychology Little Hall Orono ME 04469 Business E-Mail: sanfordg@maine.edu. E-mail: sanfordg@wiscasset.net.

GOLDSTONE, STEVEN F., former consumer products company executive; b. N.Y.C., Jan. 30, 1946; s. Milton Harold and Beatrice (Chase) G.; m. Elizabeth Caravella; children: Elissa Eve, Margaret Chase, Douglas. BA, U. Pa., 1967; JD, NYU, 1970. Bar: N.Y. 1971, U.S. Dist. Ct. (so. dist.) N.Y. 1972, U.S. Ct. Appeals (2d cir.) 1971). Assoc. Davis, Polk & Wardwell, N.Y.C., 1970-78, ptnr., 1978-95; gen. counsel RJR Nabisco, Inc., 1995; chmn., CEO, bd. dirs. RJR Nabisco Inc., 1995-2000; also bd. dirs. Nabisco Holdings, Inc., 1997-2000; pvt. exec. Silver Spring Group, N.Y.C., 2000—. Bd. dirs. ConAgra Foods, Inc., Am. Standard Co., Greenhill & Co. Chmn. Ridgefield Sr. Ctr. Found., Roundabout Theatre Co., NY. Office: Silver Spring Group 570 Lexington Ave Fl 37 New York NY 10022-6837

GOLDTHWAIT, CHRISTOPHER E., ambassador; b. Atlanta; s. John and Betty Goldthwait. BA, Am. U.; MPA, Harvard U. Joined U.S. Fgn. Agrl. Svc., agrl. attaché, 1978-82, agrl. counselor Lagos, Nigeria, 1982-86, various positions, then Gen. Sales Mgr., 1993-99; U.S. ambassador to Republic of Chad, 1999—. Author: (books) Salvation is a Homecoming, 2001. Achievements include first Fgn. Agrl. administr. to become a chief of mission. Office: US Embassy Ave Felix Ebou Box 413 N'Djamena Chad E-mail: goldthwaitce@state.gov.

GOLDWASSER, SHAFRIRA, computer scientist; b. NYC, 1958; BS in math., Carnegie Mellon U., 1979; MS in computer sci., PhD in computer sci., U. Calif., Berkeley. RSA prof. elec. engring. and computer sci.; co-leader cryptology and info. security group Lab. Computer Sci. Prof. math. scis. Weitzmann Inst. Sci., Israel. Recipient Göbel prize, Theoretical Computer Sci., 1993, 2001, ACM Gracy Murray Hopper award, 1996, RSA award in math., 1998. Mem.: Am. Acad. Arts and Scis., Nat. Acad. Scis. Office: MIT Dept Elec Engring and Computer Sci 77 Massachusetts Ave Cambridge MA 02139 Business E-Mail: shafi@csail.mit.edu.

GOLDWATER, MARILYN R(UBIN), medical/surgical nurse, state legislator; b. Boston, Jan. 29, 1927; d. Frederick and Rebecca (Geller) Rubin; m. William H. Goldwater, Aug. 8, 1948; children: Charles Alan, Diane Louise. Diploma, Mt. Sinai Hosp. Sch. Nursing, N.Y.C., 1948. RN, Md. Legislator State of Md., Annapolis, 1975-86; dir. Office Fed. Rels. Md. Dept. Health and Mental Hygiene, 1987-90; exec. asst. for health issue Gov.' Office, 1990—; mem. Md. Ho. of Dels., 1995—. Speaker on econs. and politics of health care; faculty assoc. U. Md., George Mason U. and Johns Hopkins U. schs. nursing. Author: (with Mary Jane Lloyd Zusy) Prescription for Nurses: Effective Political Action, 1990; mem. editl. adv. bd. Policy, Politics, and Nursing Practice, 2000; contbr. articles to profl. jours. Recipient Ann London Scott Legis. Excellence award, 1979, Legislator of Yr. award Md. Pub. Health Assn., 1982, Legis. Contbns. to Home Health Care award Upjohn Co., 1982, Disting. Alumna award Mt. Sinai Hosp. Sch. of Nursing, 1993; honored MedStar Health Vis. Nurse Assn., 2000. Fellow: Am. Acad. Nursing (hon.); mem.: ANA (bd. dirs. Hon. Recognition award 1980), Nat. Assn. Jewish Legislators, Order Women Legislators, Sigma Theta Tau. Office: Md Gen Assembly Lowe House Office Bldg Rm 221 Annapolis MD 21401-1691 Home: Apt 1927 5801 Nicholson Ln Rockville MD 20852-5738*

GOLDWAY, RUTH Y., federal agency administrator; b. N.Y., Sept. 17, 1945; d. David and Mahilda G.; chldren: Casey, Anthony, Julie. BA, U. Mich., 1965; MA, Wayne State U., 1968; postgrad., UCLA, 1970-71. Asst. dir. Dept. Consumer Affairs, L.A., 1975-78; mayor City Santa Monica, Calif., 1979-83; dir. pub. affairs Calif. State U., L.A., 1984-91; mgr. pub. affairs Getty Trust, L.A., 1991-94; commr. postal rate commn., Washington, 1998—. Chair and founder Santa Monica Pier Restoration Corp., 1981-94; founding mem. Consumer Adv. Panel, GTE, San Francisco, 1974-76. Author: Letters From Finland, 1998; contbr. articles to profl. jours., 1994-97; actress in film Dave, 1992. Bd. dirs. So. Calif. Consumer Affairs Profls., 1986-92. Recipient Best Diplomatic Role Model, Helsinik City Mag., 1996. Avocations: biking, cooking, travel. Office: Postal Rate Commn 1333 H St NW Ste 300 Washington DC 20268-0002 Office Phone: 202-789-6810. Business E-Mail: goldwayr@prc.gov.

GOLDWEIT, RICHARD SCOTT, cardiologist; b. N.Y.C., 1956; MD, Cornell U., 1982. Diplomate Am. Bd. Internal Medicine. Asst. attending physician N.Y. Hosp., 1987—; intern NYU-Bellevue Med. Ctr., N.Y.C., 1982—83; resident in internal medicine N.Y. Hosp., N.Y.C., 1983—85, fellow in cardiology, 1985; attending physician Englewood (N.J.) Hosp., 1988—, Hackensack (N.J.) Med. Ctr., 1988—, Holy Name Hosp., Teaneck, NJ, 1988—. Named one of Top Drs. in N.Y. Metro Area, Castle Connolly, Top Drs. 2003, N.J. Monthly Mag. Office: Cardiology Consultants 200 Grand Ave Ste 202 Englewood NJ 07631-4363

GOLEC, MARK JOSEPH, music educator; b. Putnam, Conn., Dec. 23, 1957; s. Joseph Golec and Helen Tyburski; m. Colleen Carrie Duffy, July 12, 1987; children: Kathryn) Carrie, Elizabeth Therese. MusB in Edn., Berklee Coll. Music, 1979; M in Elem. Edn. Adminstrn., R.I. Coll., 1993. Cert. music tcrh. Dept. of Edn. R.I., 1986. Co-owner Oasis Music, Johnston, RI, 1981—87; music tchr. Providence Pub. Sch., 1987—90; tchr. elem. instrumental music Warwick (R.I.) Pub. Sch., 1990—. Composer: (soundtracks) Voices and Visions. Mem.: Am. Fedn. Tchrs. Roman Catholic. Avocations: golf, bicycling, tennis, gardening, photography. Home: 152 Youngs Ave Coventry RI 02816 Office: Warwick Pub Sch Warwick RI 02888

GOLEMBE, CARLA DRU, artist; b. Boston, June 20, 1951; d. Stanley Norman and Thelma (Levowich) G.; m. Joseph H. Eudovich, July 12, 1981. BA, Bennington Coll., 1972; MFA, U. Guanajuato, Mex., 1979. Instr. Newbury Coll., Brookline, Mass., 1981-96, Md. Coll. Art and Design, Silver Spring, 1998—. Author, illustrator: Annabelle's Big Move, 1999, Dog Magic, 1997; illustrator children's books: Why the Sky Is Far Away, 1992, the Creation, 1993, How Night Came from the Sea, 1994, People of Corn, 1995, the Woman in the Moon, 1996; one-woman shows at Cove Gallery, Wellfleet, Mass., 1988, 90-95, 98, 99, Kolbo, Brookline, 1988, 93, Wheelock Coll., Boston, 1991, Galeria Prin. Altos de Chavon, Dominican Republic, 1994, Designs for Living, Boston, 1995, Spirit Echoes Gallery, Austin, Tex., 1996, Soho Gallery, Pensacola, Fla., 1996, Golden Pacific Gallery, San Diego, 1997; exhibited in group shows at Fuller Art Mus., Brockton, Mass., 1988, Artists Found. Gallery at Cityplace, Boston, 1989, Boston Ctr. for Arts, 1989, Estampe du Rhin, Strasbourg, France, 1990, U. Mass. Med. Ctr. Gallery,

Worcester, 1990, Galeria Mesa, Ariz., 1990, Zenith Gallery, Washington, 1990, 91, 93, 94, 98, Stamford (Conn.) Mus., 1990, boston Pub. Libr., 1992, soc. Illustrators, N.Y.C., 1992, Saga Graphics, N.Y.C., 1993, Fletcher Priest Gallery, Worcester, 1994, Muse Gallery, Kansas City, Mo., 1995, Soho Gallery, 1996, Cove Gallery, 1996, Stoughton (Mass.) JCC Gallery, 1997, Boston U. Art Gallery, 1997, Starr Gallery, Newton, Mass., 1998, Steven Scott Gallery, Balt., 2000; represented in numerous permanent collections at Bessamer Venture Ptnrs., Goldstein and Monello, Boston Pub. Libr., Hyatt Corp., Med. Coll. Va. Hosps., McCormack and Dodge, Peabody and Brown, others. Recipient Jones award Faber Birren Color Show, 1990, Best Illustrated Children's Book award N.Y. Times, 1992, Picture Book honor Parents Choice, 1995, Aesop Accolade Am. Folklore Soc., 1996. Mem. Lee Art Ctr. Printmaking Studio, Wash. Children's Book Guild. Avocations: dance, drumming, travel. Home: Apt K43 2020 Baltimore Rd Rockville MD 20851-1226 E-mail: cyber2lip@aol.com.

GOLEMBESKI, JEROME JOHN, manufacturing executive; b. Nanticoke, Pa., Mar. 16, 1931; s. Edward and Mary Ellen (Grozio) G.; m. June Beverly Chadwick, Aug. 9, 1958; children— Dale, Gary, Gregg, Cheryl, Kim. BS, U. Conn., 1957. Auditor Price Waterhouse & Co., Hartford, Conn., 1957-59; mem. controller's staff Insilco Corp., Meriden, Conn., 1959-86; Times Fiber Comm. Inc. Times Wire & Cable Co., Wallingford, Conn., 1959-86; contr., treas. Uniset Inc., Wallingford, 1986—. Served with USNR, 1949-53. Mem. Nat. Assn. Accountants (Cost Accounting award Hartford chpt.) Office: Uniset Inc 258 Legend Hill Rd Madison CT 06443-1879

GOLEMON, RONALD KINNAN, lawyer; b. Atlanta, Tex., Nov. 22, 1938; s. William Layton and Avis (Bogle) G.; m. Jacqueline Alice Burst, Sept. 2, 1966; children: Donald Brent, Jennifer Alice. BS in Indsl. Mgmt. Engring., U. Okla., 1961; LLB, U. Tex., 1967. Bar: Tex. 1967, U.S. Ct. Appeals (5th cir.) 1970, U.S. Dist. Ct. (so. dist.) Tex. 1968, U.S. Dist. Ct. (we. dist.) Tex. 1981, U.S. Dist. Ct. (no. dist.) 1986. Engr. asst. Tex. Water Pollution Control Bd., Austin, 1964-67; assoc. Keys, Russell, Watson & Seaman, Corpus Christi, Tex., 1967-71, ptnr., 1971-73, Brown McCarroll, LLP (formerly Brown McCarroll & Oaks Hartline), Austin, 1973—; mng. ptnr. Brown McCarroll & Oaks Hartline, 1989-94. Contbg. author The Southwestern Legal Foundation, 40th Annual Institute on Oil and Gas Law and Taxation, 1989, The Southwestern Legal Foundation, 43rd Annual Institute on Oil and Gas Law and Taxation, 1992; contbr articles to profl. jours. Alt. mem. RCRA permit adv. com. U.S. EPA, 1983; mem. Gov.'s Hazardous Waste Task Force, 1984-85; v.p. St. Stephen's Sch. PTA, 1985-86, pres., 1986-87; mem. cmty. adv. bd. Ronald McDonald House, Austin, 1990—. Fellow Am. Bar Found.; mem. ABA (mem. ho. dels. 2000—, standing com. on membership, 1997-2000, constnl. and by-laws 2000-03, environl. law 2004—, chmn. standing com. environ. law 2004—, constnl. and by-laws, 2001-03, market rsch. task force 1995-96, chmn. sect. natural resources, energy and environ. law 1994-95, chmn.-elect 1993-94, vice-chmn. 1992-93, coun. liaison environ. group 1989-91, chmn. air quality com. 1986-89, vice-chmn. 1982-86), State Bar Tex. (chmn. environ. law sect. 1971-72), Tex. Mining and Reclamation Assn. (dir. 1988-00), Travis County Bar Assn., U. Tex. Law Alumni Assn. (pres. 1984-85, exec. bd. 1984-86), N.Am. Corriente Assn (bd. dirs. 2004—, pres. 2005—), Tex. Corriente Cattle Assn. (bd. dirs. 2002-05). Avocations: ranching, hunting, skiing, golf. Office: Brown McCarroll LLP 111 Congress Ave Ste 1400 Austin TX 78701-4043 Office Phone: 512-479-9707. Personal E-mail: kgolemon@mailbmc.com.

GOLER, MICHAEL DAVID, lawyer; b. Cleve., June 29, 1952; s. George and Harriet G.; children: Jonathan A. Jennifer S. BA with honors in Classics (Greek), Union Coll., 1974; JD, Case Western Res. U., 1977. Bar: Ohio 1977, U.S. Dist. Ct. Ohio 1977, U.S. Ct. Appeals (6th cir.) 1982. Assoc. Persky, Marken, Konigsberg & Shapiro, Cleve., 1977-81; assoc. counsel Cardinal Fed. Savings Bank, Cleve., 1981-84; assoc. Arter & Hadden, Cleve., 1984-86, Kohrman, Jackson & Krantz, Cleve., 1986—94, ptnr., 1988-94, Goodman Weiss Miller LLP, Cleve., 1994—. Fellow Am. Coll. Mortgage Attys., Cleve. Bar Assn. (founder, chmn. environ. law sect. 1991-95, chmn. real estate sect. 1989-90, real estate inst. com. 1989—); mem. ABA (sect. real property probate and trust law, chmn. com. enforcement of creditors rights and bankruptcy, 1991-95, vice chair, 1995-97, chair, 1997-2001, com. on econs., tech. and practice methods, mng. editor EDirt electronic newsletter 1999—, mem. coun. 2001—, mem. tech standing com., civic chair, 2005—, mem. planning com., liaison to ABA sect. law practice mgmt. sect. 1999—, CLE com. 1999—, liaison to ABA soc. tech. com. 2003—, mem. law practice mgmt. sect., vice chmn. membership and mktg., 2004—, mem. soc. joint membership com., mem. nominating com. 2005—, named Ohio Super Lawyer 2004, 05). Avocations: music, golf, bicycling, skiing. Office: Goodman Weiss Miller LLP 100 Erieview Plz Fl 27 Cleveland OH 44114-1824 Home: 12931 Shaker Blvd #301 Cleveland OH 44120 Office Phone: 216-696-3366. E-mail: goler@goodmanweissmiller.com.

GOLER, WENDELL, political correspondent; Student, Univ. Mich. Reporter WRC TV, Washington, WJLA TV, Washington; White House corr. Associated Press Broadcast Svcs., Fox News Channel, 1996—. Office: Fox News Channel 400 N Capitol St NW Ste 550 Washington DC 20001*

GOLIAN-LUI, LINDA MARIE, librarian; b. Woodbridge, N.J., Mar. 27, 1962; d. Joseph John Golian and Mary Grace (Juba) Rodriguez; m. Gary S. Lui, Oct. 6, 1988; 1 child, Katherine Jana Lui-Golian. BA, U. Miami, 1986; MLIS, Fla. State, 1988; EdS, Fla. Atlantic U., 1995, EdD, 1998; postgrad., Fla. Gulf Coast U., 1999—2002. Libr. tech. asst. U. Miami, 1981-86; serials control libr. U. Miami Law Sch., 1986-89; serials dept. head Fla. Atlantic U., Boca Raton, 1990-97; univ. libr. Fla. Gulf Coast U., Ft. Myers, 1997—2002, adj. instr. Coll. Arts and Scis., 1999—2002; dir. U. Hawaii, Hilo, 2002—. Adj. instr. Fla. Atlantic U. Coll. Continuing & Distance Edn., 1993-97, U. So. Fla. Coll. Libr. Sci., 1995-2002; program specialist Marriott Statford Ctr. Sr. Living Cmty., Boca Raton, 1994-96. Vol. storyteller Aid to Victims of Domestic Assault, Delray Beach, Fla., 1994—96. Mem. NOW, AAUW, NAFE, ALA, Hawaii Libr. Assn. (state chpt. councilor 2003-), Spl. Libr. Assn., N.Am. Serials Interest Group (co-chair mentoring com. 1996-97), ASCD, Southeastern Libr. Assn., Assn. Libr. and Info. Sci. Educators, Am. Libr. Assn., Am. Assn. Higher Edn., Assn. Libr. Collection & Tech. Svcs., Libr., Adminstrn. & Mgmt. Assn., Reference & User Svcs. Assn. (continuing libr. edn. network & exch. round table, intellectual freedom round table, libr. instruction round table, new members round table, staff orgn. round table, women's studies sect. comm. com. 1994—, serials nomination com. 1993, Miami local arrangements com. 1994, chair libr. sch. outreach 1994—, pres. 1998-99, 3M profl. devel. grantee 1995), Assn. Coll. Rsch. Libr. (Lazerow rsch. fellow 1997), Laubach Literary Vols. of Am., Am. Assn. Adult and Continuing Edn., Fla. Libr. Assn. (serials libr. or yr. 1994, grantee 1987), Am. Coun. Edn. Hilo Chpt. Women in Edn. Roman Catholic. Avocations: reading, fishing, ceramics, tennis. Office: U HI Hilo Edwin H Mookini Lib & Graphic Ser 200 W Kawili St Hilo HI 96720-4091 Office Phone: 808-933-3132. Business E-Mail: golianlu@hawaii.edu.

GOLICK, TOBY, law educator, legal services administrator; b. Boston, Apr. 9, 1945; d. Albert David and Sara (Sharaf) G.; children: Benjamin Taylor, Samuel Taylor. BA, Columbia U., 1966, JD, 1969. Bar: N.Y. 1969. Mng. atty. Queens (N.Y.) Legal Svcs., 1969-70; atty. Columbia Ctr. on Social Welfare Policy, N.Y.C., 1970-71; sr. atty. Legal Svcs. for Elderly, N.Y.C., 1972-74, 76-85; clin. prof. Yeshiva U. Cardozo Law Sch., N.Y.C., 1985—; dir. Cardozo Bet Tzedek Legal Svcs., N.Y.C., 1985—, Southside Guitars. Recipient Eleanor Roosevelt award State of N.Y., 1986, Disting. Svc. award Brookdale Ctr. on Aging, N.Y.C., 1998. Mem. N.Y. State Bar Assn., Assn. Bar City N.Y. Home: 54 Morningside Dr New York NY 10025-1740 Office: Yeshiva U Cardozo Law Sch 55 5th Ave New York NY 10003-4301 Office Phone: 212-790-0240. Business E-Mail: tgolick@yu.edu.

GOLINKIN, WEBSTER FOWLER, healthcare executive, media consultant; b. NYC, Aug. 3, 1951; s. Joseph Webster and Ruth Forman (Fowler) G.; m. Allison Ann Willeford, Apr. 19, 1985; children: Joseph Webster, George Willeford. BA, Harvard U., 1973. Comms. project adminstr. IBM Corp., Armonk, N.Y., 1974-76; v.p. Geer, DuBois Advtg., N.Y.C., 1976-79, Reeves Comm. Corp., 1979-88; sr. v.p. Reeves Entertainment Group, 1986-88; pres. Reeves Corp. Svcs., N.Y.C., 1979-88; co-chmn., CEO, Am. Med. Comms., Inc., Houston, 1988-93; chmn., CEO, America's Health Network, Inc., Orlando, Fla., 1993-99; vice chmn., chief mktg. and sales officer Norwood Promotional Products Inc., Austin, Tex., 1999—2001; pres., CEO Interfit Health, Houston, 2001—. Mem. World Presidents' Orgn. Home: 806 Briar Ridge Dr Houston TX 77057-1116 Office: Nine Greenway Plz Houston TX 77046 Office Phone: 713-935-0333. E-mail: w.golinkin@worldnet.att.net.

GOLISANO, B. THOMAS, finance company director, human resources director; b. Irondequoit, N.Y., 1941; BS, SUNY, Alfred, 1961. Founder, chmn., CEO Paychex, Inc., Rochester, N.Y., 1971—. Mem. exec. com. Prevention Ptnrs; founder B. Thomas Golisano Found; chmn. capital campaign for Sch. of the Holy Childhood; trustee Rochester Inst. Tech., past mem. bd. dirs. Rochester Gen. Hosp. and St. John Fisher Coll.; founding mem. Independence Party. Named to INC mag.'s Dream Team of the Eighties list, Entrepreneur of the Decade, Rochester Bus.; Paychex listed with 200 Best Growth Cos. by Fin. World, among the 1000 Most Valuable in Am. by Forbes; recipient Herbert W. VanderBrul Entreprenurial award, 1987, Humanitarian of Yr. award, Boy's Town of Italy, 1993, Commerce and Industry award, Rochester C. of C., 1993, Shumway Disting. Svc. award, 1995. Office: Paychex Inc 911 Panorama Trl S Rochester NY 14625-2396

GOLITZ, LOREN EUGENE, dermatologist, medical association administrator, pathologist; b. Apr. 7, 1941; s. Ross Winston and Helen Francis (Schupp) G.; m. Deborah Burd Frazier, June 18, 1966; children: Carrie Campbell, Matthew Ross. MD, U. Mo., Columbia, 1966. Diplomate Am. Bd. Dermatology, Nat. Bd. Med. Examiners. Intern USPHS Hosp., San Francisco, 1966-67, med. resident, 1967-69, resident in dermatology S.I., N.Y., 1969-71, dep. chief dermatology, 1972-73; vis. fellow dermatology Columbia-Presbyn. Med. Ctr., N.Y.C., 1971-72; asst. in dermatology Coll. Physicians Surgeons, Columbia, N.Y.C., 1972-73; vice-chmn. Residency Rev. Com. for Dermatology, 1983-85; assoc. prof. dermatology, pathology Med. Sch. U. Colo., Denver, 1974-88, prof., 1988-97, clin. prof. pathology, dermatology, 1997—. Chief dermatology Denver Gen. Hosp., 1974-97; med. dir. Ambulatory Care Ctr., Denver Gen. Hosp., 1991-97. Mem. editl. bd. Jour. Cutaneous Pathology, Jour. Am. Acad. Dermatology, Advances in Dermatology (editl. bd. Current Opinion in Dermatology); contbr. articles to med. jours. Fellow Royal Soc. Medicine; mem. AMA (residency rev. com. for dermatology 1982-89, dermatopathology test com. 1979-85), AAAS, Am. Soc. Dermatopathology (sec., treas. 1985-89, pres.-elect 1989, pres. 1990), Am. Acad. Dermatology (chmn. coun. on clin. and lab. svcs., coun. sci. assembly 1987-91, bd. dirs. 1987-91, chmn. joint dermatopathology com.), Soc. Pediat. Dermatology (pres. 1981), Soc. Investigative Dermatology, Pacific Dermatol. Assn. (exec. com. 1979-89, sec.-treas. 1984-87, pres. 1988), Noah Worcester Dermatol. Soc. (publs. com. 1980, membership com. 1989-90), Colo. Dermatol. Soc. (pres. 1978), Am. Bd. Dermatology Inc. (chmn. part II test com. 1989—, exec. com. 1993—, v.p. 1994, pres.-elect 1995, pres. 1996, dir. Emeritus, cons. to bd. 1997—), Colo. Med. Soc., Denver Med. Soc., Denver Soc. Dermatopathology, Am. Dermatol. Assn., Women's Dermatologic Soc., So. Med. Assn., Internat. Soc. Pediat. Dermatology, Am. Contact Dermatitis Soc., Am. Soc. Dermatologic Surgery, Physicians Who Care, Am. Bd. Med. Specialties (del.), N.Y. Acad. Scis., Brit. Assn. Dermatologists (hon.), Brazilian Soc. Dermatology (hon.), U. Mo. Med. Alumni Orgn. (bd. govs. 1993—). Home: 130 S Elm St Denver CO 80246-1131 Office: Dermatopathology Svc PO Box 6218 Denver CO 80206-0218

GOLKIEWICZ, GARY J., federal official; b. Corning, NY, June 15, 1955; m. Cindy Golkiewicz; children: Keli Lynn, Kate Marie. BS in Acctg., Canisius Coll., 1977; JD, Catholic U., 1980. Law clk. SEC, 1980; staff atty., Grant Appeals Bd. US Dept. HHS, Washington, 1980—84; sr. atty. US Ct. Fed. Claims, 1984—87, chief of staff to Chief Judge Loren A. Smith, 1987—88, chief spl. master, 1988—. Mem.: DC Bar, Ct. Fed. Claims Bar Assn., Fed. Bar Assn., DC Bar Assn. Office: US Ct Fed Claims Office of Spl Masters 717 Madison Pl NW Washington DC 20005 Office Phone: 202-219-9657.

GOLL, GEOFFREY STEVEN, lawyer; b. Columbus, Ohio, Feb. 2, 1944; s. Carl F. and Dru R. Goll; m. Kim Shauck; children: Megan E., Yvonne M. B.A., Denison U., 1966; J.D., Ohio State U., 1973. Bar: Ohio 1973, U.S. Dist. Ct. (no. dist.) Ohio 1974, U.S. Supreme Ct. 1980. Ptnr. Law Offices of Geoffrey S. Goll L.P.A., Salem, Ohio, 1982— . Mem. exec. bd. Columbiana coun. Boy Scouts Am., 1978, mem. nat. coun., 1981-92, pres., 1984-85; mem. exec. bd. Mobile Meals of Salem, Inc., 1976—; mem. adv. bd. Salem Salvation Army, 1979-81, chmn., 1981; mem. exec. bd. Salem Area Indsl. Devel. Corp., 1980—, Columbiana County Port Authority, 1981-96, Columbiana Bd. Elections, 1984-91; vice chmn. Columbiana County Republican Central Com., 1977-84; elder Presbyn. Ch.; trustee Salem Cmty. Found., 1995—2005, Salem Rotary Club Found., 1995—, Saxon Scholarship Found., 1988—; mem. Salem Ohio Utilities Com., 1993—, chair, 1995—. Served to lt. col. USAFR, 1966-93. Recipient District Merit award Boy Scouts Am., 1980, Silver Beaver award, 1984. Mem. ABA, Columbiana County Bar Assn. (sec.-treas. 1979—2004), Ohio State Bar Assn. (local com. 1980—), Columbiana County Mental Health Assn., Ohio State U. Alumni Assn. (trustee Columbiana County 1979-81, pres. 1984-86), Salem C. of C. (bd. dirs. 1979, 81-85, pres. 1984-85). Clubs: Saxon. Lodges: Elks, Rotary (v.p. Salem club 1984, pres. 1985). Avocations: golf; travel. Home: 1989 Quaker Ln Salem OH 44460-1875 Office: PO Box 92 Salem OH 44460-0092 Office Phone: 330-337-9529.

GOLL, PAULETTE SUSAN, education educator; b. Cleve., June 5, 1947; d. Ferdinand Paul and Lillian Clarice (Mehalko) Goll. BA in English, Cleve. State U., 1969, MEd, 1974; MA in English, U. Bridgeport, Conn., 1979; PhD in English, Case Western Res. U., 1987. Cert. secondary tchr. Ohio, English tchr. Ohio, asst. supr. Ohio, secondary prin. Ohio. Part-time instr. U. Bridgeport, 1978-79, Case Western Res. U., Cleve., 1985-87, lectr., 2002—; tchr. English, Cleve. Pub. Schs., 1969—99, chmn. dept., coord. Ohio Proficiency Test, 1991—96; regional dir. Summer Inst. Gifted Midwest Region, Granville, Ohio, 2000—02. Adj. instr. English Case Western Res. U., Cleve. State U., 1999—2000; vis. assoc. prof. edn. Dickinson Coll., Carlisle, Pa., 2000; advisor Students Against Drunk Drivers, 1985—86; coord. project success Lincoln West HS, Cleve., 1987—90; ACT vis. tchr., 1999; external reviewer Bedford/St. Martins, Reading Critically, Writing Well, 2003, Wadsworth, the Informal Reader, 2004. Co-author: Shakespearean Comedies, 1985; textbook cons. McDougal Littel, 1999—2000. Mem. com. human rels. Cleve. Partnerships, 1989—92; co-chmn. High Schs. for Future, 1985—86; liaison Metrohealth/Lincoln-West Partnership, 1989—92. Named Master Tchr., Martha Holden Jennings Found., 1988; recipient Congl. Commendation Mary Rose Oaker, 1988, award of Excellence, Rotary, 1989, Tchr. of the Yr., Brit. Petroleum, 1997; NEH fellow, 1985, NEH Ind. Studies Humanities fellow, 1993, Jennings scholar, 1985, 1988. Mem.: ASCD (presenter), North Ctrl. Assn. (chair vis. team 1991, 1993), Nat. Assn. Gifted (presenter 2001), Phi Delta Kappa (v.p. programs 1993). Republican. Roman Catholic. Avocations: travel, music, needlepoint, writing, camping. Home: 11366 Clarke Rd Columbia Station OH 44028-9626 Personal E-mail: gollp@earthlink.net.

GOLL, STEPHEN E., telecommuncations executive; b. Independence, Kans., Oct. 11, 1948; s. Robert L. and Frances M. (Forslund) Goll.; m. Stella L. Adamson, Aug. 6, 1978; children: Sondra Goll Knaus, Stacy Aaron Goll. AA, Independence (Kans.) C.C., 1968; BA, Pitts. State U., 1974; attended, U.S. Navy Schs., 1974—77, U.S. Army Schs., 1981—82; BS, DeVry Inst. Tech., 1989. Faculty asst., computer lab. monitor DeVry Inst. Tech., Kansas City, Mo., 1988-89; comms. specialist RDA/Logicon, Ft. Leavenworth, Kans., 1989-92; retail sales rep. Comp-USA, Overland Park, Kans., 1993; computer product specialist Best Buy, Lenexa, Kans., 1993-94; writer, photographer, columnist The Fog-Line, Bonner Springs, Kans., 1994-95. Tchr. Bonner Springs Elem. Sch. Contbr. to World's Best Short Stories; with Better Than Fair Players, Bonner Springs, Kans. RM2 USN, 1975-81, sgt. U.S. Army, 1981-85. Mem. DAV (life), VFW (life), Soc. for Creative Anachronisms, Internat. Soc. Poets (Disting. mem., Cert. of Achievemnt), Bardic Cir., Am. Legion, Delta Psi Omega, Beta Phi Gamma, Kappa Alpha Mu. Libertarinan. Avocations: computers, reading. Personal E-mail: scavenger13@earthlink.net.

GOLLADAY, MARY JEAN, statistician; b. Spokane, Wash., Oct. 12, 1942; d. James T. Albertson and Gladys I. Graves; m. Frederick L. Golladay Aug. 22, 1965; children: Addison, Kendall, Ann, Catherine. BA with honors, U. Puget Sound, 1964; MAT, Northwestern U., 1965, PhD, 1970. Tchr. secondary sch. Evanston Twp. (Ill.) H.S., 1965-68; instr. edn. adminstrn. U. Wis., Madison, 1969, project assoc., 1969-74; statistician U.S. Dept. Edn., Washington, D.C., 1975-84, NSF, Arlington, Va., 1984—. Cons. Nat. Acad. Science, Washington, 1984—, U.S. Dept. Edn., Washington, 1984—. Editor: (book) Women, Minorities and Persons With Disabilities in Science and Engineering, 1994, (statistical report) Condition of Education, 1975, 76, 77, 78. Named Disting. Lectr. The MITRE Corp., 1993. Mem. Am. Statistical Assn., Am. Ednl. Rsch. Assn., Assn. for Institutional Rsch., Math. Assn. Am. Office: National Science Foundation Social Behavioral & Economc Sci 4201 Wilson Blvd Arlington VA 22230-0002

GOLLAHALLI, SUBRAMANYAM RAMAPPA, engineering educator; b. Sadali, Karnataka, India, Nov. 26, 1942; came to U.S., 1976; s. Bagepalli Ramappa and Nagalakshamma Rao Ramappa; m. Rangamani Nadig Gollahalli, Dec. 25, 1967; children: Suma, Anil. BE in Mech. Engring., U. Mysore, Karnataka, India, 1963; ME in Mech. Engring., Indian Inst. Sci., Bangalore, 1965; MASc in Mech. Engring., U. Waterloo, Ont., Can., 1970, PhD in Mech. Engring., 1973. Registered profl. engr., Okla. Lectr. Indian Inst. Sci., Bangalore, 1965-68; asst. prof. U. Waterloo, 1973-76; from asst. prof. to full prof. U. Okla., Norman, 1976-92, Lesch Centennial prof., 1992—, Lesch Centennial chair, 1998—, dir. Aerospace and Mech. Engring. Rsch. Ctr., 2001—. Cons. in field. Editor: ASME Conf. Proc., 1990, 91, 92; assoc. editor Jour. Energy Resources Tech., 1994—, Jour. Equipment Gas Turbines and Power, 1999-2005. Advance com. chair Boy Scouts Am., Norman, 1988-90. Recipient Ralph Angus medal Inst. Engrs., Can., 1978, Ralph Teetor award Soc. Automotive Engrs., 1978, George Westinghouse Gold medal, 2005. Fellow ASME (Ralph James award 1993, chair emerging energy tech. com. 1990-93), AIAA (assoc.; mem. tech. com., Energy Sys.award 2001); mem. Pi Tau Sigma. Achievements include research in spray combustion, particularly for delineating the structure of droplet wake flames, and turbulent flames in cross-flows. Office: Univ of Oklahoma 865 Asp Ave Norman OK 73019-1050 Office Phone: 405-325-1728. E-mail: gollahal@ou.edu.

GOLLANCE, ROBERT BARNETT, ophthalmologist; b. NYC, Oct. 25, 1937; s. Harvey and Sarah (Chinitz) G.; m. Carmen Côté Gollance, Nov. 8, 1969; 1 child, Stephen Andrew. BA cum laude, Harvard Coll., 1958; MD, Columbia Coll., 1962. Diplomate Am. Bd. Ophthalmology, Nat. Bd. Med. Examiners. Intern in medicine NYU-Bellevue, 1962-63, resident and chief resident in ophthalmology, 1963-66; fellowship NIH, 1964-69; sec.-treas. Ophthalmology Assocs., Wayne, N.J., 1970-93; pres. Eye Assocs. of Wayne, 1993—; lectr. in ophthalmology Columbia U., N.Y.C., 1998-2001; adv. bd. for devel. UMDNJ, 2002—. Chmn. ophthalmology Chilton Meml. Hosp., Pompton Plains, N.J., 1987-89, pres. med. staff, 1991; great hands adv. com. Becton Dickinson Corp., Franklin Lakes, N.J., 1990—; adv. com. Bausch & Lomb Corp., Rochester, N.Y., 1980-83; mem. found. bd. Eye Inst. of the N.J. Med.-Dental Sch.; faculty on cataract surgery and lens implantation; cons. Pharmacia Corp. Clin. Rsch. Glaucoma Medications, 2002—. Contbr. articles to profl. jours. Chmn. parents fund raising Loomis Chaffee Sch., Windsor, Conn., 1989-90. Capt. U.S. Army, 1966-68. Recipient Letter of Appreciation Korean Opthalomology Soc., 1967, Cath. Med. Ctr., 1967. Fellow ACS, Am. Soc. Cataract and Refractive Surgery, Am. Acad. Ophthalmology, European Soc. Cataract and Refractice Surgery. Office: Eye Assocs of Wayne 968 Hamburg Tpke Wayne NJ 07470-3225 Office Phone: 973-696-0300. E-mail: rbgollance@yahoo.com, rbgollance@njeyeinstitute.com.

GOLLEHER, GEORGE, food company executive; b. Bethesda, Md., Mar. 16, 1948; s. George M. and Ruby Louise (Beecher) Golleher; 1 child, Carly Lynn. BA, Calif. State U., Fullerton, 1970. Supr. acctg. J.C. Penney, Buena Park, Calif., 1970-72; sys. auditor Mayfair Markets, Los Angeles, 1973, v.p., CFO, 1982-83; contr. Fazio's, Los Angeles, 1974-78; group contr. Fisher Foods, Ohio, 1978-79; v.p. fin. Stater Bros. Markets, Colton, Calif., 1979-82; sr. v.p., CFO Boys Markets Inc., Los Angeles, 1983-95; CEO Ralph Grocery Co., Compton, Calif., 1995-99; pres., COO Fred Meyer Inc., Portland, Oreg., 1997-99; chmn. Farrs Supermarkets, Albuquerque, 2001—. Office: Farrs Supermarkets PO Box 1037 Placitas NM 87043-1037 also: Ste 240 3 Corporate Plaza Dr Newport Beach CA 92660-7973

GOLLER, GLORIA JANET HILLESTAD, librarian; b. Mauston, Wis., Oct. 7, 1945; d. Gilbert and Janet Alicia (Cattle) Hillestad; m. Erwin Goller, May 18, 1974. BA, U. Wis., Oshkosh, 1967; MLS, U. Wis., Milw., 1988. Ref. librarian bus. services Wauwatosa (Wis.) Pub. Library, 1967—. Mem. Wis. Library Assn. Lutheran. Office: Wauwatosa Pub Libr 7635 W North Ave Milwaukee WI 53213-1718 Office Phone: 414-471-8485.

GOLLIN, MICHAEL A., lawyer; b. Rochester, NY, July 3, 1957; AB, Princeton U., 1978; MS, U. Zurich, 1981; JD, Boston U., 1984. Bar: NY 1985, Mass. 1985, DC 1991, Md. 1991, US Patent and Trademark Office. Ptnr., intellectual property, patent law, environmental law Venable LLP, Washington. Adjunct prof. McDonough Sch. of Bus., Georgetown U., 2001—. Founder Public Interest Intellectual Property Advocates; trustee Rene Dubos Ctr. for Human Environments, Inc., 1994—. Recipient Young Lawyer's Chair award, 1994, Benjamin R. Civiletti Pro Bono Lawyer of the Yr. award, 2004. Mem.: ABA (vice chair, emerging tech. com., nat. resources & environ. law section 1992—2000). Office: Venable LLP 575 7th St NW Washington DC 20004 Office Phone: 202-344-4072. Office Fax: 202-344-8300. Business E-Mail: magollin@venable.com.

GOLLIN, STUART ALLEN, accountant; b. Bronx, N.Y., Aug. 7, 1941; s. Samuel and Suggie (Schreiber) G.; m. Harriet Joy Friedlander, Aug. 16, 1964; children: Deborah Lynn, Mark David, Adam Douglas, Seth Craig. BBA, CCNY, 1963. CPA, N.Y., N.J. Ptnr., nat. dir. retailing Touche Ross & Co., Newark, 1963-80; ptnr., nat. dir. retailing, nat. dir. bankruptcy and insolvency, dir. litigation and ins. cons. svcs. Laventhol & Horwath, N.Y.C., 1980-90; ptnr. in charge bankrupty litig. support and ins. cons. David Berdon & Co., N.Y.C., 1990-92; v.p. insolvency Buccino & Assocs., N.Y.C., 1993-94; dir. litig. and appraisal svcs. J.H. Cohn & Co., N.Y.C., 1994-96; mng. dir. corp. transactions KPMG Peat Marwick, N.Y.C., 1996-97, Morrison & Gollin LLP, N.Y.C., 1998—. Bd. dirs. Dad's Club of Hartsdale, Mid-Westchester YM/YMHA; treas. Am. Liver Found.; bd. dirs. The Transplant Living Ctr.; pres. Scarsdale Sports Assn. Mem. AICPA, N.Y. State Soc. CPAs, Am. Bankruptcy Inst., Nat. Cert. Insolvency & Reorgn. Acct., N.J. Soc. CPAs (acctg. and auditing stds., rels. with bankers, rels. with fin. writers coms., rels. with credit unions, chmn. bankruptcy and involvency com., litig. support com.), Nat. Assn. Accts. (dir. Westchester chpt.), Turnaround Mgmt. Assocs., Nat. Retail Mchts. Assn., Nat. Mass Retailers Inst., N.J. Retail Mchts. Assn., Met. Retail Fin. Execs. Assn., White Plains Jaycees, Bergen County C. of C., Ardsley Swim Club (dir.), Ridgeway Country Club, Beta Alpha Psi. Home: 34 Benedict Rd Scarsdale NY 10583-7340

GOLLIN, SUSANNE MERLE, cytogeneticist, cell biologist; b. Chgo., Sept. 22, 1953; d. Harvey A. and Pearl (Reiffel) G.; m. Lazar M. Palnick; 1 child, Jacob Hillel . BA in Biology, Northwestern U., 1974, MS, 1975, PhD, 1980. Diplomate Am. Bd. Med. Genetics with cert. in clin. cytogenetics; cert. food protection specialist, 2002. Postdoctoral fellow U. Rochester (N.Y.) Med. Ctr., 1979-81; rsch. assoc. in cell biology Baylor Coll. Medicine, Houston, 1981-83, rsch. assoc. in genetics, 1983-84; asst. prof. dept. pathology and pediat. U. Ark. for Med. Sci., Little Rock, 1984-87; dir. cytogenetics lab. Ark. Children's Hosp., Little Rock, 1984-87; assoc. mem. Pitts. Cancer Inst., 1987-95, mem., 1995—; dir. U. Pitts. Cancer Inst. Cytogenetics Facility, 1989—; asst. prof. human genetics U. Pitts., Grad. Sch.

Pub. Health, 1987-95, dir. clin. cytogenetics lab., 1988-99, assoc. prof., 1995—2003, prof., 2003—, prof. human genetics, otolaryngology, pathology, 2003; dir. rsch., clin. cons. Pitts. Cytogenetics Lab., 1999—. Mem. pediat. oncology group, mem. exec. com. Ark. Genetics Program, 1984-87; mem. organizing com. Am. Cytogenetics Conf., 1990-2002; mem. Allegheny County Bd. Health, 1992-2004, vice chmn., 1997, 2000-04; bd. dirs. Tobacco-Free Allegheny; mem. clin. lab. improvement adv. com. Ctrs. Disease Control and Prevention, HHS, 1994-2000, mem. genetic testing subcom., 1997-2000; vis. sci. German Cancer Rsch. Ctr., Heidelberg, 1995; cons. med. devices adv. com. FDA, 1996—; mem. oral biol. med. I study sect. NIH, 1997; master gardener, 2000; mem. spl. emphasis panel Nat. Cancer Inst., 2000; mem. genetics spl. emphasis panel ZRG1-GEN-01S, NIH Ctr. for Sci. Rev., 2000, spl. emphasis panel Nat. Cancer Inst., Minority Instn./Cancer Ctr. Partnerships, 2000, 05, mem. mammalian genetics study sect., 2002; lectr. U.S.-Japanese Cancer Rsch. Collaborative Conf., Tokyo, 2001; mem. immunol. devices panel FDA, 2004—. Contbr. articles to profl. jours. and encys. Mem. deans' adv. com. Pa. Sch. Excellence for Healthcare Profls., 1991-95; v.p. faculty senate U. Pitts. Grad. Sch. Pub. Health, 1994-95, senate anti-discriminatory policies com., 1999-2002, faculty senate athletics com., 2004—, search com. dean Grad. Sch. Pub. Health and chair human genetics, 2004—; vol. Lighthouse for Blind, Houston, 1983; vol. hort. dept. Pitts. Zoo, 2000-2001; chmn. med. ethics and civil liberties com. ACLU, Pitts., 1989-91; alt. del. Dem. Nat. Conv., 1992, 96, 2000, mem. rules com., 2004. Fellow Am. Coll. Med. Genetics (founder); mem AAAS, Am. Assn. Cancer Rsch., Am. Soc. Human Genetics, Am. Soc. Cell Biology, Soc. Analytical Cytology, Pitts. Cancer Inst., Pitts. Cytogenetics Club (founder, coord. 1989-95), Phipps/Pitts. Garden Place, Western Pa. Conservancy, Rivers Club, Carnegie Museums, Pitts. Zoo, Sigma Xi. Avocations: mountain dulcimer, gardening, photography, pulled thread embroidery. Office: U Pitts Dept Human Genetics Grad Sch Pub Health 130 Desoto St Pittsburgh PA 15213-2535 Business E-Mail: sgollin@hgen.pitt.edu.

GÖLLNER, MARIE LOUISE, musicologist, retired educator; b. Ft. Collins, Colo., June 27, 1932; d. Francis Gilbert and Gertrude Valentine (Steele) Martinez; m. Theodor W. Göllner, Sept. 30, 1959; children: Katharina, Philipp. BA, Vassar Coll., 1953; postgrad., Eastman Sch. Music, 1953-54, U. Heidelberg, Germany, 1954-56; PhD summa cum laude, U. Munich, 1962, Dr. phil. habil., 1975. Research asst. Bavarian State Library, Munich, 1964-67; lectr. Coll. Creative Studies, U. Calif., Santa Barbara, 1968; asst. prof. UCLA, 1970-74, assoc. prof., 1974-78, prof. musicology, 1978-2000, chmn. dept. music, 1976-80, chmn. dept. musicology, 1985-89; ret., 2000. Author: Die Musik des frühen Trecento, 1963, Katalog der Musikhandschriften der Bayerischen Staatsbibliothek München, vol. 2, 1979, vol. 1, 1989, Joseph Haydn, Symphonie 94, 1979, Orlando di Lasso: Sämtliche Werke, Neue Reihe, Das Hymnarium, (1580-82), 1980, Eine neue Quelle zur italienischen Orgelmusik des Cinquecento, 1982, The Manuscript Cod. lat. 5539 of the Bavarian State Library (Musicological Studies & Documents 43), 1993, Essays on Music and Poetry in the Late Middle Ages, 2003, The Early Symphony: 18th-Century Views on Composition and Analysis, 2004; contbr. articles to profl. jours. NEH grantee, 1983, Fulbright grantee, 1954-56; Gordon Anderson Meml. lectr. U. New Eng., Armidale, Australia, 1984 Mem. Internat. Assn. Music Libraries, Am. Musicol. Soc., Internat. Musicol. Soc., Medieval Acad. Am. Episcopalian. Home: 817 Knapp Dr Santa Barbara CA 93108-1941 Business E-Mail: gollner@ucla.edu.

GOLLOB, HERMAN COHEN, retired publishing executive; b. Waco, Tex., July 7, 1930; s. Abe and Ruybe (Cohen) G.; m. Barbara Kowal, Apr. 9, 1961; children: Emily, Jared. BA, Tex. A & M U., 1951. Lit. agt. MCA, Beverly Hills, Calif., 1956-58, William Morris, N.Y.C., 1958-59; editor Little, Brown & Co., Boston, 1959-64, Atheneum Pubs., N.Y.C., 1964-68, v.p., editor-in-chief, 1971—; editor-in-chief Harper's Mag. Press, N.Y.C., 1968-71; v.p., editorial dir. The Literary Guild, N.Y.C., 1979-81; v.p., sr. editor Simon & Schuster, N.Y.C., 1981-86; sr. v.p., editor-in-chief Doubleday Pub. Co., 1986-90, editor-at-large, 1990-95; ret., 1995. Author: Me and Shakespeare, 2002. Served to lt. USAF, 1951-53. Home: 40 Frederick St Montclair NJ 07042-4106

GOLLOBIN, LEONARD PAUL, chemical engineer; b. NYC, July 2, 1928; s. Morris and Jennie (Levine) G.; m. Charlotte Weissman, Jan. 21, 1951; children: Michael L., Susan D. Brown. BSChemE, CUNY, 1951; MS, Kans. State U., 1952; grad. mgmt. program, Harvard U., 1975. Design engr. Foster Wheeler Corp., N.Y.C., 1952-55; mfg. engr. Gen. Electric Co., Waterford, N.Y., 1955-58; program dir. ORI, Inc., Silver Spring, Md., 1958-63; chmn, chief exec. Presearch, Inc., Fairfax, Va., 1963—2004; dir. Level II Sys., Longboat Key, Fla., 2004—. U.S. del. NATO Indsl. Avd. Group, 1989, chmn., 1992-93, chmn. emeritus, 1994-95; bd. visitors Nat. Def. U., Washington, 1989-98. Bd. dirs. Cultural Alliance Greater Washington, 1980-88, northern Va. bd. Va. Opera, 2000-01; trustee Washington Opera, 1988-90. Recipient NSIA Adrm. Charles Weakley award, 1986, Meritorious Pub. Svc. award U.S. Dept. Navy, 1987, U.S. Marine Corps, 1989. Mem. Nat. Security Indsl. Assn. (exec. com. 1986—, chmn. antisubmarine warfare com. 1981-84, chmn. amphibious warfare com. 1986-89, chmn. environ. com. 1990-92, chmn. internat. com. 1991-93, vice chmn. exec. com. 1993, chmn. 1994, chmn. bd. trustees 1994-95), Nat. Def. Indsl. Assn. (chmn. fin. com. 1998—, mem. exec. com.), Am. Chem. Soc., Naval Undersea Warfare Found. Mus., Loudon Golf and Country Club (Purcellville, Va.), Lougboat Key Club. Home: 3010 Grand Bay Blvd #425 Longboat Key FL 34228

GOLOBY, GEORGE WILLIAM, JR., environmental scientist, editor; b. Franklin, Ky., Mar. 21, 1949; s. George William Sr. and Katherine Jacqueline (Panchot) G.; m. Diane Grayson, Dec. 29, 1974; children: Amy Vanessa, George William III. BS in Wildlife Sci., Tex. A&M U., 1971. Zookeeper of birds Houston Zool. Gardens, 1971—72; warehouseman, driver Houston Ind. Sch. Dist., 1972—76; lab. mgr. Empak Inc., Houston, 1976—80; asst. sect. chief City of Houston Dept. Pub. Works, 1980—90; environ. quality specialist III City of Houston Dept. Pub. Works & Engring., 1990—. Founder, owner Penfeathers Tours, Houston, 1984—; instr. Houston Arboretum and Nature Ctr., 1999; instr. Tex. birding cert. Armand Bayou Nature Ctr., U. Houston, 1999-2003. Editor (newsletters) Water Environment Assn. Tex. (WEAT) Pipeline 1984-2001, Tex. Ornithol. Soc. Newsletter, 1989-99, Penfeathers Newsletter, 1986—, Panchot Paper, 1989-93, Houston Audubon Soc., 1977-80, The Naturalist, 1986-89; asst. editor (books) Houston, 1978, Encyclopedia of American Cities, 1979; advt. mgr. Tex. WET Mag., 2002—. Mem. Houston Proud, 1986, Cy-Fair Houston C. of C., 1986, Greater Houston Conv. and Vis. Bur., 1986-88. Mem. Water Environ. Assn. Tex. (com. chmn. 1984—), Tex. Water Utilites Assn., Houston Audubon Soc. (v.p. adminstrv. affairs 1986-89), Am. Birding Assn., Outdoor Nature Club, Parrot People Club (v.p. Houston chpt. 1985-86), Purple Martin Conservation Assn., Whooping Crane Conservation Assn., Tex. Nature Conservancy. Office: City Houston 4545 Groveway Dr Houston TX 77087-1122 Office Phone: 713-641-9169. E-mail: pfcompany@aol.com.

GOLODNER, JACK, labor association official; b. NYC, Nov. 2, 1931; s. Maurice S. and Regina (Gaber) G.; m. Linda Louise Fowler, June 14, 1964; children: Dean Dovid, Daniel Dimmick, Jonathan Wilmot. BS, Cornell U., 1953; JD, Yale U., 1958. Labor arbitrator, Washington, 1958-60; exec. asst. to U.S. Congressman Giaimo, 1960-62; cons. pub. affairs, 1962-80; exec. sec. Coun. AFL-CIO Unions for Profl. Employees, 1967-77; dir. dept. for profl. employees AFL-CIO, 1977-89, pres., 1989—2001. V.p. bd. trustees Ford's Theater, Washington, 1973-79, Actors Studio, NY, 1982-87; bd. dir. Nat. Theatre, 1978—; mem. gen. bd. Am. Coun. for the Arts, 1981-96; presdl. appointee Nat. Info. Infrastructure adv. coun., 1994-96; mem. adv. coun. nat. orgns. Corp. Pub. Broadcasting, 1973-79; mem. Labor Adv. Com. for Multilateral Trade Negotiations of Dept. of Labor, 1975-2002; mem. arts and humanities com. Pres.'s Commn. on Internat. Women's Year, 1975-76; mem. US del. UNESCO govtl. experts meeting, Paris, 1980; US del. to adv. com. on salaried and profl. workers Internat. Labor Orgn., 1981, 85, 94, US labor del. Plenary Internat. Labor Orgn. Conf., 1981, 82; chmn. labor del. tripartit meeting on salaried authors and inventors, 1987, Internat. Labor Orgn.; mem. coun. Cornell U., 1987-93; chmn., mem. adv. coun. Cornell Sch. of Indsl. and Labor Rels., 1980-88, 90-94, mem. outside rev. com., 1986-87; mem. US govt. del. Diplomatic Conf. on Certain Copyright and Neighboring Rights Questions, World Intellectual Property Orgn., Geneva, 1996. Capt. USAF, 1953-55. Recipient William B. Groat award Cornell U., 1979 Mem. Indsl. Rels. Rsch. Assn. (exec. bd. 1993-96), Internat. Secretariat Arts, Mass Media and Entertainment Trade Unions (world v.p. 1987-93), Media and Entertainment Internat. (1st v.p. 1993-97), Nat. Policy Assn. (exec. com. New Am. Realities Program 1987-2003, co-chair nat. digital econ. opportunity com. 2000-2002), Phi Kappa Phi. Home: 1739 Q St NW Washington DC 20009-2407 Office: 1140 Conn Ave NW Washington DC 20036

GOLOMB, FREDERICK MARTIN, surgeon, educator; b. NYC, Dec. 18, 1924; s. Jacob J. and Hannah (Loewy) G.; m. Joan E. Schneider, Nov. 28, 1954; children: James Bradley, Susan Lynn. BS, Yale U., 1945; MD, U. Rochester, 1949. Diplomate: Am. Bd. Surgery. Intern Johns Hopkins Hosp., 1949-50; resident NYU Hosp., 1950-56; mem. staff NYU Med. Center, 1950—, dir. chemoimmunotherapy divsn. tumor svc. dept. surgery, 1967-96; attending surgeon Tisch Hosp.; vis. surgeon Bellevue Hosp.; mem. faculty NYU Sch. Medicine, 1956—, prof., clin. surgery, 1977—. Cons. N.Y.C. div. Am. Cancer Soc., 1968—; mem. clin. trials rev. com. Nat. Cancer Inst., 1976-79; chmn. melanoma com. Eastern Coop. Oncology Group, 1978-80; prin. investigator Central Oncology Group, 1969-77, exec. com., 1976-77; mem. met. med. com. Chemotherapy Found.; co-prin. investigator Ea. Coop. Oncology Group NYU, 1978-95. Contbr. articles to profl. jours. Served with M.C. AUS, 1953-54, Korea. Recipient John E. Sullivan award Beth Israel Med. Ctr., 1993. Fellow ACS; mem. AMA, Soc. Head and Neck Surgeons, Am. Assn. Cancer Rsch., Am. Soc. Clin. Oncology, N.Y. Cancer Soc. (pres. 1974-75), N.Y. Surg. Soc., N.Y. State Med. Soc., N.Y. County Med. Soc., Soc. Surg. Oncology, George Hoyt Whipple Soc., Brit. Assn. Surg. Oncology (editl. adv. panel 1980-85), Am. Alpine Club, Explorers Club, Sigma Xi. Office: Frederick M Golomb MD 59 Churchill Rd Tenafly NJ 07670-3123 Business E-Mail: frederick.golomb@med.nyu.edu.

GOLOMB, HARVEY MORRIS, hematologist, oncologist, educator; b. Pitts., Feb. 13, 1943; s. Russell Austin and Dorothy (Simon) G.; m. Lynne Rooth, Dec. 28, 1965; children: Adam, Sara. BA, U. Chgo., 1964; MD, U. Pitts., 1968. Diplomate Am. Bd. Internal Medicine, Am. Bd. Med. Oncology. Intern Boston City Hosp., 1968-69; resident Johns Hopkins U., Balt., 1971-72, fellow, 1972-73, U. Chgo., 1973-75, asst. prof. dept. medicine, 1975-79, assoc. prof., 1979-83, prof., 1983—, chief sect. hematology/oncology, 1981-98, chmn. dept. medicine, 1998—2005, dean clin. affairs divsn. biol. scis., 2005—. Chmn. subspecialty bd. med. oncology Am. Bd. Internal Medicine, 1991-95. Contbr. over 300 articles, papers to profl. publs.; co-editor: Lung Cancer, 1988. Capt. U.S. Army, 1971-73. Mem. Am. Soc. Hematology (bd. dirs. 1987-91), Am. Soc. Oncology (pres. elect 1989-90, pres. 1990-91). Office: U Chgo MC 1000 5841 S Maryland Ave Chicago IL 60637-1463 Business E-Mail: hgolomb@medicine.bsd.uchicago.edu.

GOLOMB, SOLOMON WOLF, mathematician, educator, director, electrical engineer; b. Balt., May 31, 1932; s. Elhanan Hirsh and Minna (Nadel) G. AB, Johns Hopkins U., 1951; MA, Harvard U., 1953, PhD, 1957; postgrad., U. Oslo, 1955—56; DSc (hon.), Dubna Internat. U., Russia, 1995; DHL (hon.), Hebrew Union Coll., LA, 1996. Mem. faculty Boston U., 1954-55, Harvard U., 1954-55, UCLA, 1957-61, Calif. Inst. Tech., 1960-62; sr. rsch. engr. Jet Propulsion Lab., Pasadena, Calif., 1956-58, rsch. group supr., 1958-60, asst. chief telecom. rsch. sect., 1960-63; assoc. prof. U. So. Calif., LA, 1963-64, prof. elec. engring. and math., 1964—, vice provost for rsch., 1986-89, univ. prof., 1993—, dir. tech. Annenberg Ctr. for Comm., 1995-98, Viterbi prof. comm., 1997—. Cons. to govt. and industry. Author: Digital Communications with Space Applications, 1964, 81, Polyominoes, 1965, rev. edit., 1994, Shift Register Sequences, 1967, 82, Basic Concepts in Information Theory and Coding, 1994; contbr. articles to profl. jours. Recipient Lomonosov medal Russian Acad. Sci., 1994, Disting. Alumnus award Johns Hopkins U., 2002. Fellow IEEE (Shannon award Info. Theory Soc. 1995, Hamming medal 2000), AAAS, Am. Acad. Arts and Scis.; mem. NAS, NAE, Internat. Sci. Radio Union, Russian Acad. Natural Scis. (fgn., Kapistsa medal 1995), Am. Math. Soc., Math. Assn. Am., Soc. Indsl. and Applied Math., Golden Key, Phi Beta Kappa, Sigma Xi, Pi Delta Epsilon, Eta Kappa Nu, Phi Kappa Phi. Office: U So Calif Univ Park Dept Elec Engring Eeb 504A Los Angeles CA 90089-0001 Office Phone: 213-740-7333. E-mail: milly@usc.edu.

GOLOMB, SUSAN L., literary agent; b. N.Y.C., Feb. 17, 1960; d. Frederick Martin and Joan Ellen Golomb; m. Gregory Thomas Martin, July 17, 1999; 1 child, Jacob Gabriel Golomb Martin. BA, U. Pa., 1982. Prodn. coord. WNET-TV Great Performances, N.Y.C., 1982; asst. agt. Harold Ober Assocs., N.Y.C., 1982—83; reader Samuel Goldwyn Prodns., N.Y.C., 1984; agt. Rosenstone/Wender, N.Y.C., 1984—88; story editor Mirage Prodns., N.Y.C., 1988—89, Hearst Entertainment, N.Y.C., 1989—91; owner Susan Golomb Lit. Agy., N.Y.C., 1991—. Mem.: Women's Media Group. Avocations: rock climbing, hiking, theater. Office: The Susan Golomb Literary Agy 875 6th Ave #2302 New York NY 10001 E-mail: susan@sgolombagency.com.

GOLOMBEK, MATTHEW PHILIP, planetary geologist; b. New Haven, Sept. 20, 1954; s. Martin I. and Sonia G.; m. Connie M. Morgan, Apr. 26, 1980; children: Sydney Morgan, Benjamin Clayton. AB in Geology with honors, Rutgers Coll., 1976; MS in Geology, U. Mass., 1978, PhD in Geology, 1981. Rsch. asst. in sedimentology Rutgers U., New Brunswick, NJ, 1976; tchg. asst. U. Mass., 1979, rsch. asst. in structural and planetary geology, 1976-81; vis. postdoctoral fellow Lunar and Planetary Inst., Houston, 1981-82, vis. scientist, 1982-83; sr. scientist Jet Propulsion Lab. Calif. Inst. Tech., Pasadena, 1983-84, rsch. scientist Jet Propulsion Lab., prin. scientist, 1984—, Mars Pathfinder project scientist Jet Propulsion Lab., 1994-98, chair sci. ops. working group. Lectr. U. Houston, Clear Lake City, 1983, Calif. State Poly. U., Pomona, 1986; Viking guest investigator Jet Propulsion Lab., 1977, US Geol. Survey, Astrogeology Br., Flagstaff, Ariz., 1978; mem. Mars Sci. Working Group, 1989-96, Mars Exploration Edn. Outreach Adv. Bd., 1994-98; chmn. Mars Pathfinder Project Sci. Group, 1994-98; mem. Am. Geophys. Union, Planetology Exec. Com., 1994-97; mem. assessment group Mars Exploration Program, 1999—, landing site scientist, 2000—, Mars Exploration Rover sci. ops. working group chair, 2002—; spkr., lectr. in field. Planetology editor EOS, Transactions Am. Geophy. Union; assoc. editor Tectonophysics, 1986; contbr. articles to profl. jour. Recipient Schlumberger scholarship Rutgers U., 1975-76, Vinton Gwinn Meml. prize Rutgers U., 1976, numerous grants, 1983—, Laurels award for Outstanding Achievement in Space, Aviation Week and Space Technology, 1997, award for excellence Jet Propulsion Lab./Project Scientist for Mars Pathfinder Mission, 1998, Disting. Alumni award for Profl. Svc. U. Mass., 1988, Hall of Disting. Alumni award Rutgers U. Alumni Fedn., 1998, NASA Exceptional Sci. Achievement medal, 1998, others; Dr. Matt Golombek Day named in his honor City of Hackensack, NJ, Feb. 12, 1998; asteroid named Golombek in his honor, 1992. Fellow Geol. Soc. Am.; mem. Am. Geophy. Union. Office: Jet Propulsion Lab MS 183-501 4800 Oak Grove Dr Pasadena CA 91109-8001 E-mail: mgolombek@jpl.nasa.gov.

GOLOMSKI, WILLIAM ARTHUR JOSEPH, consulting company executive; b. Custer, Wis. s. John Frank and Margaret Sophie (Glisczinski) G.; m. Joan Ellen Hagen; children: Gretchen E., William A. Jr. MS, Marquette U.; MBA, U. Chgo; MS in Engring. Mgmt., Milw. Sch. Engring; MA, Roosevelt U. Registered profl. engr., Calif. Prin. W.A. Golomski & Assocs., Algoma, Wis., 1949—, pres., 1971—. Judge Malcolm Baldridge Nat. Quality award, 1988; sr. lectr. Grad. Sch. Bus., U. Chgo., 1990-95. Author chpts. in books; co-editor A Quality Revolution in Manufacturing, 1989; founding editor Quality Mgmt. Jour., 1993. Mem. Avoca Sch. Bd., Wilmette, Ill.; adv. bd. Milw. Sch. Engring., 1967-72, 83-87, indsl. engring. com. Hon. mem. Philippine Soc. Quality Control, 1992. Fellow AAAS, Am. Soc. Quality Control (Eugene L. Grant award 1991, Edwards medal, William A. Golomski rsch. award named in his honor 1986, Am. Deming medal met. sect., hon. mem. 1993), N.Y. Acad. Scis., Royal Soc. Health, Am. Statis. Assn., Inst. Indsl. Engrs. (Frank and Lillian Gilbreth Indsl. Engring. award 1999), World Assn Productivity Sciences; mem. NAE. Achievements include devel. of world class orgns.; first jour. for quality mgmt. and quality in higher edn. Office: N9690 County Road U Algoma WI 54201-9528

GOLON, MARYANNE, photojournalist; Picture editor Time Mag., NY, NY, 1983—99; coord. photographic coverage of the Olympic Games for Time mag., 1984—; photography editor of the Gulf War for Time and Life mag., Dhahran and Saudi Arabia, 1991—92; dir. of Photog. US News and World Report, 1999—2002; picture editor Time Mag., NY, NY, 2002—. Recipient Afred Eisenstaedt Award, Mag. Photgraphy; fellow On the Jury of Visa Pour L'Image, Pepignand. Mem.: Eddie Adams Workshop (Bd. of dir.).

GOLOVE, DAVID M., law educator; b. 1959; BA, U. Calif., Berkeley, 1979, JD, 1982; LLM, Yale U., 1993. Bar: Calif. 1982, NY 1991. Law clk. to Hon. Marilyn Hall Patel US Dist. Ct. No. Dist. Calif., San Francisco, 1982—83; assoc. Law Office of Thomas Steel, San Francisco, 1985—87, Rabinowitz, Boudin, Standard, Krinsky & Lieberman, NYC, 1987—91, ptnr., 1992—93; assoc. prof. U. Ariz. Coll. Law, 1994—98, Benjamin N. Cardozo Sch. Law, Yeshiva U., NYC, 1998—2001; prof. law NYU Sch. Law, 2001—, dir. JD/LLM program in internat. law. Vis. prof. NYU Sch. Law, 2000—01; mem. faculty exec. com. NYU Inst. Internat. Law and Justice. Office: NYU Sch Law Vanderbilt Hall Rm 411H 40 Washington Sq S New York NY 10012-1099 Office Phone: 212-998-6220. E-mail: goloved@juris.law.nyu.edu.

GOLPER, JOHN BRUCE, lawyer; b. El Paso, Tex., Sept. 6, 1950; s. Marvin Norman and Jean Rose (Becker) Golper; m. Leslie Ann Lawry, Mar. 21, 1981; children: Matthew Brent, Brian Yale, Todd Nicholas. BA with honors, Ind. U., 1972; JD, UCLA, 1975. Bar: Calif. 1975, U.S. Dist. Ct. (ctrl. dist.) Calif. 1975, U.S. Ct. Appeals (9th cir.) 1977, U.S. Dist. Ct. (no. and so. dists.) Calif. 1981, U.S. Supreme Ct. 1981, U.S. Ct. Appeals (3d cir.) 1982, U.S. Dist. Ct. (ea. dist.) Calif. 1986. Extern law clk. Calif. Ct. Appeals, 1st Dist., San Francisco, 1974; assoc. Bodkin, McCarthy, Sargent & Smith, L.A., 1975—78; ptnr. Parker Milliken, Clark, O'Hara & Samuelian, L.A., 1978—86, Ballard, Rosenberg, Golper & Savitt, LP, University City, Calif., 1986—. Mem. Calif. Comparable Worth Task Force, Sacramento, 1984—86. Named among Top 25 Attys. of San Fernando Valley, San Fernando Bus. Jour., 2002; recipient Cert. of Recognition, Compensation Practices Assn., San Diego County, 1983—84; scholar Grable Meml. scholar, Ind. U., 1968, Ind. State scholar, 1968, Honors Divsn. Merit Scholar, 1971—72. Mem.: ABA, Indsl. Rels. Rsch. Assn., So. Calif. Def. Counsel, Def. Rsch. and Trial Lawyers Assn., Assn. Bus. Trial Lawyers, L.A. County Bar Assn., Fed. Bar Assn., Calif. Bar Assn., Jonathan Club. Republican. Jewish. Office: Ballard Rosenberg Golper & Savitt LLP 10 Universal City Plz 16th Fl Universal City CA 91608-1097 Office Phone: 818-508-3700. E-mail: jgolper@brgslaw.com.

GOLPHIN, ELOUISE, writer, educator; b. Augusta, Ga., Aug. 4, 1950; d. Lewis R. Golphin and Ruby M. Adderley; life ptnr. Descombe Wells Gray; children: Lanita Brinson, Tarveia Williams-Dunson, John Williams, Sabrina Cater, Timothy Yarbrough(dec.), Romanieo, Rutherford Wilson. A in Gen. Studies, Ga. Mil. Jr. Coll., Ft. Gordon, 1984; BS, Brenau Profl. Coll., Gainesville, Ga., 1990. Author: Poetry for All Reasons, 1994, Poetry for All Reasons Book II, 1999, CHEMO: My Son's Struggle With Cancer, 1999, Read, It's Fun!, Poetry for All Reasons Book III, 2003, Please Stop Hitting Me!, 2003, A-B-C's, 1-2-3's and Things, 2003, Ruddy's Room, 2003. Mem.: NAACP. Baptist. Avocations: writing, travel, reading. Home: 2686 Crosscreek Rd Hephzibah GA 30815-7600 Office: Poetry for All Reasons 2686 Crosscreek Rd Hephzibah GA 30815-7600 E-mail: weezyg4@bellsouth.net.

GOLTZ, ROBERT WILLIAM, dermatologist, educator; b. St. Paul, Sept. 21, 1923; s. Edward Victor and Clare (O'Neill) G.; m. Patricia Ann Sweeney, Sept. 27, 1945; children: Leni, Paul Robert. BS, U. Minn., 1943, MD, 1945. Diplomate: Am. Bd. Dermatology (pres. 1975-76). Intern Ancker Hosp., St. Paul, 1944-45; resident in dermatology Mpls. Gen. Hosp., 1945-46, 48-49, U. Minn. Hosp., 1949-50; practice medicine specializing in dermatology Mpls., 1950-65; clin. instr. U. Minn. Grad. Sch., 1950-58, clin. asst. prof., 1958-60, clin. assoc. prof., 1960-65, prof., head dept. dermatology, 1971-85; prof. medicine and dermatology U. Calif., San Diego, 1985—2004, emeritus prof., 2004—, acting chair divsn. dermatology, 1995-97; prof. dermatology, head div. dermatology U. Colo. Med. Sch., Denver, 1965-71. Former mem. editl. bd. Archives of Dermatology; editor Dermatology Digest. Served from 1st lt. to capt., M.C. U.S. Army, 1946-48. Mem. Assn. Am. Physicians, Am. Dermatol. Assn. (dir. 1976-79, pres. 1985-86), Am. Soc. Dermatopathology (pres. 1981), Am. Dermatologic Soc. Allergy and Immunology (pres. 1981), AMA (chmn. sect. on dermatology 1973-75), Dermatology Found. (past dir.), Minn. Dermatol. Soc., Soc. Investigative Dermatology (pres. 1972-73, hon. 1988), Histochem. Soc., Am. Acad. Dermatology (pres. 1978-79, past dir.) (hon.), Brit. Assn. Dermatology (hon.), Chilean Dermatology Soc. (hon.), Colombian Dermatol. Soc. (corr. mem.), Can. Dermatol. Soc. (hon. mem.), German Dermatol. Soc. (hon.), Pacific Dermatol. Soc. (hon.-mem.), S. African Dermatol. Soc. (hon. mem.), N.Am. Clin. Dermatol. Soc., Assn. Profs. Dermatology (sec.-treas. 1970-72, pres. 1973-74), West Assn. Physicians. Home: 6097 Avenida Chamnez La Jolla CA 92037-7404 Office: U Calif San Diego Med Ctr Divsn Dermatology H-8420 200 W Arbor Dr San Diego CA 92103-1911

GOLTZMAN, DAVID, endocrinologist, educator, researcher; s. Jack and Lily (Roth) G.; m. Naomi Lyon, Dec. 29, 1968; children: Jonathan, Rebecca, Daniel. BSc, McGill U., 1966, MD, 1968. Diplomate Am. Bd. Internal Medicine, Am. Bd. Endocrinology and Metabolism. Med. intern Royal Victoria Hosp., Montreal, 1968-69; med. resident Columbia U. Coll. Physicians and Surgeons, N.Y.C., 1969-71; clin. and rsch. fellow in endocrinology Mass. Gen. Hosp., Boston, 1971-75; instr. medicine Harvard Med. Sch., Boston, 1974-75; asst. prof. medicine McGill U., Montreal, 1976-78, assoc. prof., 1978-83, prof., 1983—, chmn. physiology, 1988-93, dir. calcium rsch. lab., 1981—, hosmer prof. physiology, 1992-93, Massabki prof. medicine, 1994—, chmn. medicine, 1994—2004; dir. Ctr. Bone and Periodontal Rsch., 2002—. Sr. physician dept. medicine Royal Victoria Hosp., 1987-94, physician-in-chief, 1994-98; physician-in chief, McGill U. Hlth. Ctr., 1998-2004; chmn. exptl. medicine com. Med. Rsch. Coun. Can., Ottawa, Ont., 1984-88; mem. gen. medicine B study sect., NIH, Bethesda, Md., 1987-91; active Exec. Med. Rsch. Coun. Can., 1993-99. Author: (with others) Principles of Bone Biology, 2001, Primer of Metabolic Bone Disease and Disorders of Mineral Metabolism, 1996, 1989, Primer of Osteoporosis, 2000, Principles and Practice of Endocrinology and Metabolism, 2001; editl. bd. Endocrinology Jour., 1985-90, Jour. Bone Mineral rsch., 1985-90, Bone and Mineral, 1991-94, Osteoporosis Internat., 1991-94, Assoc. Edn. Bone, 1989-94; assoc. editor: Jur. Bone Mineral research, 1995-2002; contbr. numerous articles to profl. jours. Recipient Chercheur Boursier award Que. Med. Rsch. Coun., 1980-83, Scientist award Med. Rsch. Coun. Can., 1983-88, Andre Lichtwitz prize Nat. Inst. for Med. Rsch., France, 1987; named officer Order of Can., 2000—, John G. Haddad Meml. Lectr. Penn. U, 2004 Fellow Royal Coll. Physicians and Surgeons, Royal Soc. Canada; mem. Can. Soc. Endocrinology and Metabolism (pres. 1990-92), Am. Soc. for Bone and Mineral Rsch. (chmn. program com. 1989-90, pres. 1999-00), Am. Assn. Physicians, Endocrine Soc. (program com. 1989-91), Can. Soc. Clin. Investigation (councillor 1986-89, pres. 1998-99) Am. Soc. Clin. Investigation, Canadian Assn. Profs. of Medicine (pres. 1998-99). Avocations: classical music, gardening, tennis. Office: Royal Victoria Hosp 687 Pine Ave W Montreal PQ Canada H3A 1A1 Business E-Mail: david.goltzman@mcgill.ca.

GOLUB, HARVEY, food products executive, former financial services company executive; b. N.Y.C., Apr. 16, 1939; Student, Cornell U., 1956-58; BS, NYU, 1961. Jr. ptnr. McKinsey & Co. Inc., N.Y.C., 1967-74, sr. ptnr., 1977-83; pres. Shulman Air Freight, N.Y.C., 1974-77; pres., CEO IDS Fin. Svc., Mpls., 1984-90; chmn., CEO IDS Fin. Svcs. (name changed to Am. Express Fin. Advisors), Mpls., 1990—2001; vice chmn., dir. Am. Express Co., N.Y.C., 1990-91, pres., 1991-93, chmn., CEO, 1993-2001, Am. Express Travel Related Svcs. Co. Inc., N.Y.C., 1991; chmn. AirClic, Blue Bell, Pa.,

2001—04, Campbell Soup Co., Camden, NJ, 2004—. Bd. dir. Campbell Soup Co., 1996—, Dow Jones & Co. Inc. Bd. dirs. Am. Enterprise Inst., Columbia Presbyn. Hosp., Carnegie Hall, N.Y.C. Partnership, N.Y. C. of C. and Industry, United Way of N.Y.C.; mem. Bus. Roundtable, Bretton Woods Com.; apptd. mem. Pres.'s Com. for Arts and Humanities, Pres.'s Adv. Trade and Policy Negotiations. Mem. World Travel and Tourism Coun. (exec. com., chmn.-elect). Office: Campbell Soup Co 1 Campbell Pl Camden NJ 08103*

GOLUB, LEWIS, supermarket company executive; b. 1931; BS, Mich. State U., 1953; LHD (hon.), SUNY--Empire State Coll., 1998. With Golub Corp., 1953—, v.p., 1963-71, exec. v.p., 1971-72, pres., treas., 1972-82, chmn. bd., 1982—, also chief exec. officer, dir. Schenectady. Bd. dirs. Taylor Made Co., Racemark Internat., Dot Foods Inc., Paradigm Value Fund, CIES; mem. regional adv. bd. Chase Bank. Advisor MBA program Russell Sage Coll.; mem. adv. coun. grad. mgmt. inst. Union Coll.; bd. dirs. Empire State Coll. Found., Saratoga Performing Arts Ctr., Proctor's Theatre, Food Mktg. Inst., N.Y. State Bus. Coun.; active Found. SUNY. Served with U.S. Army. Recipient Marketer Exec.-Citizen award Sales and Mktg. Execs. Ea. N.Y., 1988, Disting. Citizen award SUNY, 1989, Dr. Norman D. Kathan Cmty. Svc. award YMCA, 1990, Tree of Life award Jewish Nat. Fund, 1992, Disting. Cmty. Svc. award Chinese Cmty., 1993, Cmty. Svc. award Inter-Faith Cmty. of Schenectady, 1993, Cmty. Svc. accolate Northeastern N.Y. chpt. Arthritis Found., 1993, Achievement award Am. Diabetes Assn., 1994, Disting. Citizen Laureate award U. Albany Found., 1994, John J. O'Connor Excellence in Leadership award United Way, 1995, Disting. Citizen award Boy Scouts Am., 1995, N.Y. State Chiefs of Police, 1995, Cmty. Svc. awar Office of Aging, 1996, Legends of the Industry award N.Y. State Food Mchts. Assn., 1996, Corning award N.Y. State Bus. Coun., 2003; named Man of Yr., Am. Jewish Com., 1981, Exec. of Yr., The Capital Dist. Bus. Rev., 1989, Humanitarian of Yr., Ctr. for Disabled, 1999; named to Hall of Fame, Capital Region Bus., 1997, Jr. Achievement, 1997; Paul Harris hon. fellow Rotary Internat., 1992. Office: Golub Corp 501 Duanesburg Rd Schenectady NY 12306-1092*

GOLUB, SHARON BRAMSON, retired psychologist, educator; b. N.Y.C., Mar. 25, 1937; m. Leon M. Golub, June 1, 1958; children: Lawrence E., David B. Diploma, Mt. Sinai Hosp. Sch. Nursing, 1957; BS, Columbia U., 1959, MA, 1966; PhD, Fordham U., 1974. Head nurse Mt. Sinai Hosp., N.Y.C., 1957—59; contbg. editor RN Mag., Oradell, NJ, 1967—74; asst. prof. psychology Coll. New Rochelle, NY, 1974—79, assoc. prof., 1979—86, prof., 1986—98, prof. emeritus, 1998—. Pvt. practice individual and group psychotherapy, 1976—; dir. women's studies Coll. New Rochelle, 1978—79, chmn. dept. psychology, 1979—82; adj. prof. psychiatry N.Y. Med. Coll., Valhalla, 1980—94. Editor: Menarche, 1983 (Assn. Women in Psychology Disting. Pub. award 1984, Book of Yr. award Am. Jour. Nursing 1984), Lifting the Curse of Menstruation, 1983, Health Care of the Female Adolescent, 1984, Health Needs of Women as They Age, 1984, PERIODS from Menarche to Menopause, 1992; (with Rita Jackaway Freedman) Psychology of Women: Resources for a Core Curriculum, 1987; editor Women and Health, 1982-86, mem. editorial bd., 1986—; mem. editorial bd. Psychology of Women Quar., 1989-2000. Grantee Nat. Libr. Medicine, 1983-84; NIH rsch. fellow, 1971-74. Fellow Am. Psychol. Assn. (chmn. task force on teaching psychology of women 1980-83), Am. Psychol. Soc.; mem. Soc. for Menstrual Cycle Rsch. (pres. 1981-83, bd. dirs. 1981-93), Assn. Women in Psychology, Westchester County Psychol. Assn. (pres. acad. divsn., Disting. Svc. award 2003), Phi Beta Kappa, Sigma Xi, Psi Chi. E-mail: sgolubny@aol.com.

GOLUB, TODD R., research scientist; BS, Carleton Coll.; MD, U. Chgo., 1989; postdoctoral tng., Children's Hosp., Boston, Dana-Farber Cancer Inst., Brigham and Women's Hosp., Harvard Med. Sch. Charles A. Dana investigator human genetics Dana-Farber Cancer Inst.; assoc. prof. pediat. Harvard Med. Sch.; investigator Howard Hughes Med. Inst.; dir. cancer genomics program Whitehead Inst. Biomedical Rsch. Named Inventor Yr., Health Category, Discover mag., 2000; recipient Judson Daland prize, Am. Philosophical Soc., 2001, Cornelius Rhoads award for Outstanding Achievement in Cancer Rsch., AACR, 2002; Freedom to Discover grant, Bristol-Myers Squibb, 2004. Office: Dana Farber Cancer Inst Dana bldg Rm 640C 44 Binney St Boston MA 02115

GOLUSIN, MILLARD R., obstetrician, gynecologist; b. Detroit, Feb. 14, 1947; s. Raddie and Joan (Lalich) G.; m. Yvonne Marie Cronovich, Sept. 29, 1974 (dec.); children: Milan, Marko, Matthew; m. Cvetana Cindy Pavlovich, June 4, 2005. BS with honors, Wayne State U., 1968, MS, 1970, MD, 1975. Diplomate Am. Bd. Obstetrics and Gynecology. Intern, then resident William Beaumont Hosp., Royal Oak, Mich., 1975-78; practice medicine specializing in obstetrics and gynecology Village Gynecologic and Obstetric Assocs., P.C., Southfield and Troy, Mich., 1978-92; pvt. practice specializing in obstetrics and gynecology Troy, Mich., 1992-98; assoc. Wilshire Obstetrics-Gynecol. Assocs. PC, Troy, 1998—. Mem. quality assurance com. William Beaumont Hosp., Royal Oak, Mich., 1979—, mem. gynecol. quality assurance com., 1993—; charter mem., pres. Preferred Ob-Gyn. Mgmt. Group L.L.C.; bd. dirs. ptnr. Unasource Health, Troy, Mich., 2000-. Trustee, mem. credentials com. Preferred Provider Network, 2000; trustee United Beaumont Physicians Group, 1993—. Served with U.S. Army, 1969-71. Fellow ACOG; mem. Am. Soc. Reproductive Medicine, Mich. State Med. Soc., Am. Inst. Ultrasound Medicine, Serbian Singing Soc., Ravanica (musical dir. 1967—, pres. 1981-82). Republican. Serbian Eastern Orthodox. Avocations: music, golf. Office: Wilshire Obstetrics-Gynecol Assocs PC 4550 Investment Dr Ste 200 Troy MI 48098-6369

GOMBERG, SYDELLE, dancer educator; m. Ralph Gomberg. Student, Met. Opera Ballet Sch.; studies with Pierre Vladimiroff, Anatale Oboukoff, Edward Caton, Anatole Vilzak, Vincenzo Celli, Margaret Craske; student, Sch. Am. Ballet. Dir. Boston Ballet Sch., until 1993; faculty mem. Boston Converatory of Music; resident master teacher Walnut Hill School, Natick, Mass., 1993-96; guest tchr., mem. adv. bd. Walnut Hill Sch., Natick, Mass., 1996—. Performed with Met. Opera Ballet, Radio City Ballet; soloist (Broadway play) Lute Song starring Mary Martin and the Late Yul Brynner. Founder dance dept. All Newton Music Sch., Walnut Hill Sch., 1971-85, apptd. dean arts, trustee, adv. bd. mem.; regional sec. Royal Acad. Dancing; mem. dance panel Mass. Coun. on the Arts and Humanities; chmn. spl. com. Dance Edn. Home: 93 Pilgrim Rd Concord MA 01742

GOMBOCZ, ERICH ALFRED, biochemist; b. Vienna, Aug. 29, 1951; came to U.S., 1990; s. Erich and Maria (Mayer) G.; m. Gisela M. Dorner, June 12, 1973 (div. Apr. 1992); 1 child, Manfred Alexander (dec.). Cert., T.U., Vienna, 1970-75. With Fed. Inst. for Food Analysis and Rsch., Vienna, 1975-90, head of sect. dept. biochem. analysis, 1980-90, contbr. Cen. Lab. Info. Mgmt. System, 1987-90; chmn. scientific adv. bd. LabIntelligence, Inc., Menlo Park, Calif., 1989-99, COO, v.p. R & D, 1989-99; chief sci. officer NucleoTech Corp., San Mateo, Calif., 1999-2000; chief sci. officer, chief tech. officer Biosentients, Inc., Emeryville, Calif., 2000—03; v.p., chief sci. officer IO Informatics, Inc., Emeryville, 2003—. Speaker and lectr. in field. Editor: Computers in Electrophoresis, Jour. Proteome Rsch.; contbr. articles to profl. jours.; patentee in field. Postdoctoral Rsch. award NIH, Bethesda, Md., 1985-86, 88. Mem. Internat. Assn. for Cereal Chemistry, Internat. Electrophoresis Soc., Am. Electrophoresis Soc., Am. Chem. Soc., N.Y. Acad. Scis., Microsoft Developers Network, Silicon Valley Computer Soc. Roman Catholic. Avocation: photography. Office: IO Informatics Inc 2000 Powell St Ste 50 Emeryville CA 94608 Office Phone: 510-420-8400. E-mail: egombocz@ix.netcom.com.

GOMER, ROBERT, chemistry professor; b. Vienna, Mar. 24, 1924; m. Anne Olah, 1955; children: Richard, Maria. BA, Pomona Coll., 1944; PhD in Chemistry, U. Rochester, 1949; AEC fellow chemistry, Harvard, 1949-50. Instr. dept. chemistry James Franck Inst. U. Chgo., 1950-51, asst. prof., 1951-54, assoc. prof., 1954-58, prof., 1958-96, Carl William Eisendrath Disting. Service prof., 1984-96, prof. emeritus, 1996—. Dir. James Franck Inst. U. Chgo., 1977-83 Bd. dirs. Bull. Atomic Scientists, 1960-84. Served with AUS, 1944-46. Recipient Kendall award in surface chemistry Am. Chem. Soc., 1975, Davisson Germer prize Am. Phys. Soc., 1981, Medard W. Welch award Am. Vacuum Soc., 1989, Arthur W. Adamson award Am. Chem. Soc., 1996; Sloan fellow, 1958-62, Guggenheinm fellow, 1969-70; Bourke lectr. Eng., 1959. Mem. Leopoldina Acad. Scis., Nat. Acad. Scis., Am. Acad. Arts and Sci. Home: 4824 S Kimbark Ave Chicago IL 60615-1916 Office: 5640 S Ellis Ave Chicago IL 60637-1433 Office Phone: 773-702-7191. Business E-Mail: r-gomer@uchicago.edu.

GOMERY, DOUGLAS, communications educator, writer; b. NYC, Apr. 5, 1945; s. John Edgar and Julia G.; m. Marilyn L. Moon, Jan. 13, 1973. BS, Lehigh U., 1967; MA, U. Wis., 1970, PhD, 1975. Asst. prof. mass communication U. Wis., Milw., 1974-79, assoc. prof., 1980, U. Md., College Park, 1981-87, prof., 1987—. Sr. rschr. media studies project Woodrow Wilson Ctr. for Internat. Scholarship, Washington, 1988-92; vis. prof. Northwestern U., Evanston, Ill., 1980, U. Iowa, Iowa City, 1982, U. Utrecht, The Netherlands, 1990, 92; cons. Am. Film Inst., Washington, 1982-90; resident scholar Libr. Am. Broadcasting, 2004-. Author: High Sierra, 1979, The Hollywood Studio System, 1986, Movie History: A Survey, 1991, Shared Pleasures, 1992 (Am. Theater Libr. Assn. Book award, 1992), The FCC's Newspaper-Broadcast Cross-Ownership Rule: An Analysis, 2002, The Coming of Sound, 2005—, The Hollywood Studio System: A History; co-author (with Robert C. Allen): Film History: Theory and Practice, 1985; co-author: (with Phil Cook and L.W. Lichty) American Media, 1988; co-author: (with Annette Michelson) The Art of Moving Shadows, 1989; co-author: (with Ben Compaine) Who Owns the Media, 2000 (Picard prize award Assn. for Edn. in Journalism and Mass Comm., 2001); editor: The Will Hays Papers, 1987, Marquee, 1991, The Future of News, 1992;: Media in America, 1998; mem. editl. bd.: Cinema Jour., 1983—92, Jour. Film and Video, 1983—, Jour. Media Econs., 1989—, contbg. editor: Iris, 1983—89, Screen, 1984—89, Jour. of Comm., 1995—, columnist: Am. Journalism Rev., 1995—; contbr. articles to profl. jours. Cons. Joint Com. on Landmarks Washington, 1983, 85, 86, 90, NEH, 1980—, Nat. Endowment Arts, 1980—, Md. State Hist. Preservation Office, 1988, Voice of Am., Nat. Gallery Art., Wis. Dept. Revenue, 1978; trustee Am. Film Inst., 1986-89. Mem. Theatre Hist. Soc. (chmn. Weiss award com. 1984-87, bd. dirs. 1987-89, Weiss prize 1988), Soc. Cinema Studies, Univ. Film and Video Assn. (editorial bd. jours. 1983-92), Broadcast Edn. Assn., Assn. for Edn. in Journalism and Mass Comm., Internat. Comm. Assn. Avocation: economics. Home: 4817 Drummond Ave Chevy Chase MD 20815-5428 Office: U Md Coll Journalism College Park MD 20742-0001 Office Phone: 301-405-9160. Business E-Mail: dgomery@umd.edu.

GOMES, NORMAN VINCENT, retired industrial engineer; b. New Bedford, Mass., Nov. 7, 1914; s. John Vincent and Georgianna (Sylvia) G.; m. Carolyn Moore, June 6, 1942 (dec. Apr. 1983); m. Helen Groesbeck Kurzawa, Apr. 22, 1995. BS in Indsl. Engring. and Mgmt., Okla. State U., 1950; MBA in Mgmt., Xavier U., 1955. Asst. chief engr. Leschen divsn. H.K. Porter Co., St. Louis, 1950-52; staff mfg. cons. GE Co., Cin., 1952-57; lectr. indsl. mgmt. U. Cin., 1955-56; staff indsl. engr. Gen. Dynamics, Ft. Worth, 1957-60; chief ops. analysis Ryan Elecs., San Diego, 1960-64; sr. engr. Jet Propulsion Lab. Calif. Inst. Tech., Pasadena, 1964-67, mem. tech. staff, 1967, mgr. mgmt. sys., 1967-71; industry rep. and cons. U.S. Commn. Govt. Procurement, Washington, 1970-72; adminstrv. officer GSA, Washington, 1973-78, program dir., 1979. Vis. lectr. indsl. mgmt. Xavier U. Grad. Sch. Bus. Adminstrn., 1956-57; vis. lectr. mgmt. San Antonio Coll., 1982-85. Active Sierra Internat., v.p. membership San Antonio chpt., 1991-92, mem. Drug and Alcohol Adv. Coun., N.E. Ind. Sch. Dist., San Antonio, 1989-95. Maj. C.E. AUS, 1941-46. Decorated Army Commendation medal, Armed Svcs. Res. medal; recipient Apollo Achievement award, 1969, Outstanding Performance award GSA, 1974-75, 76, 77, 79. Mem. Am. Inst. Indsl. Engrs. (nat. chmn. prodn. control rsch. com. 1951-57, bd. dirs. Cin., Fort Worth, San Diego, L.A., San Antonio chpts. 1954-84, pres. Cin. chpt. 1956-57, pres. L.A. chpt. 1970-71, nat. dir. cmty. svcs. 1969-73), Ret. Officers Assn. U.S. (chpt. pres. 1968-69, recipient Nat. Pres. cert. Merit 1969), Nat. Security Indsl. Assn. (mgmt. systems subcom. 1967-69), Vis. Nurse Assn. San Antonio (mem. adv. coun. 1988-95), Freedoms Found. at Valley Forge (v.p. edn. and youth leadership programs San Antonio chpt. 1987-89), Pillars San Fernando Cathedral, Old Dartmouth Hist. Soc., Equestrian Order of Holy Sepulchre Jerusalem (knight comdr. with star), KC (4th deg.). Republican. Roman Catholic. Home: c/o Cravey 2103 A La Casa Dr Austin TX 78704 E-mail: h.k.gomes@aol.com.

GOMES, PETER JOHN, clergyman, educator; b. Boston, May 22, 1942; s. Peter L. and Orissa Josephine (White) G. AB, Bates Coll., Lewiston, Maine, 1965; STB (Rockefeller fellow 1967-68), Harvard U., 1968; DD (hon.), New Eng. Coll., 1974; LHD (hon.), Waynesburg Coll., 1978; HumD (hon.), Gordon Coll., 1985; LittD (hon.), Knox Coll., 1987; DD (hon.), U. South, 1989, Bates U., 1997; LHD (hon.), Duke U., 1997, U. Nebr., 1997, Wooster Coll., Trinity Coll., Bowdoin Coll., Colby Coll., Olivet Coll., Mount Holyoke Coll., Furman U., Baker U., Mount Ida Coll., Willamette U., SUNY at Geneseo, Ursinus Coll., Wagner Coll., Lesley U., Williams Coll., Morris Coll., Ursinus Coll., U. NC, Chapel Hill, Hamilton Coll., Hebrew Union Coll. Ordained to ministry Am. Bapt. Ch., Mass., 1968. Instr. history, dir. freshmen exptl. program Tuskegee (Ala.) Inst., 1968-70; asst. minister, then acting minister Meml. Ch. Harvard U., 1970-74, Pusey minister Meml. Ch., 1974—, Plummer prof. Christian morals, 1974—. Nat. chaplain Am. Guild Organists, 1978-82; hon. fellow Emmanuel Coll., U. Cambridge, Eng.; vis. prof. Duke U., Durham, N.C., 1993-94; presenter numerous sermons, addresses and lectures throughout the US and British Isles. Author: Proclamation Series Commentaries, Lent, 1985, Proclamation Series Lent, 1995, History of Harvard Divinity School, 1992, The Good Book: Reading the Bible With Mind and Heart, 1996, Sermons: Biblical Wisdom for Daily Living, 1998, Sundays at Harvard, 1995, 96, 97, 98, The Good Life: Truths That Last in Times of Need, 2002, Strength for the Journey: Biblical Wisdom for Daily Living, 2003, The Backward Glance, 2005, Forward Look, 2005; co-author: Books of the Pilgrims; editor: Parnassus, 1970, History of the Pilgrim Society, 1970; editor: Harvard Divinity School History, 1992; contbr. articles and papers to profl. jours.; mem. edtl. bd. Pulpit Digest; mem. adv. bd. The Living Pulpit; profiled in The New Yorker, 60 Minutes, Talk mag. article Best Talkers in Am.: Fifty Big Mouths We Hope Will Never Shut Up, 1999. Trustee Bates Coll., 1973-78, 80-94, Pilgrim Soc., 1970—, pres. 1989, 93, Charity of Edward Hopkins, 1974—, Donation to Liberia, 1973—, Plimoth Plantation, 1977—, Roxbury Latin Sch., 1982—, Wellesley Coll., 1985—, Boston Found., 1985—, Plymouth Pub. Libr., 1985—, Harvard U. trustee Mus. Fine Arts; acting dir. W.E.B. DuBois Inst. for Afro-Am. History Harvard U., 1990—. Named Clergy of Yr., Religion in Am. Life, 1998; recipient Phi Beta Kappa tchg. award, Harvard U., 2001. Fellow Royal Soc. Arts; mem. Royal Soc. Ch. Music, Colonial Soc. Mass., Mass. Hist. Soc., Handel and Hayden Soc. (trustee), New Eng. Conservatory (trustee), Signet Soc. (former pres.), Country Day Sch. Headmasters Assn. (hon.), Phi Beta Kappa. Clubs: Tavern. Office: Harvard U Meml Ch Cambridge MA 02138 E-mail: jan_randolph@harvard.edu.

GOMES, WAYNE REGINALD, academic administrator; b. Modesto, Calif., Nov. 15, 1938; s. Frank C. and Mary (Rogers) G.; m. Carol L. Gerlach, Sept. 2, 1964 (deceased); children: John Charles, Regina Carol; m. Anne Freitas, Nov. 27, 2004. BS, Calif. Poly. State U., 1960; MS, Wash. State U., 1962; PhD, Purdue U., 1965. Asst. prof. dairy sci. Ohio State U., Columbus, 1965-69, assoc. prof. dairy sci., 1969-72, prof. dairy sci., 1972-81; prof., head dept. dairy sci. U. Ill., Urbana, 1981-85, prof., head dept. animal scis., 1985-89, acting dean Coll. Agr., 1988-89, dean, 1989-95; v.p. agr. and natural resources U. Calif. System, Oakland, 1995—. Fulbright prof. Zagreb U., Yugoslavia, 1974; vis. scholar Kyoto U., Japan, 1980; mem. bd. on agr. and natural resources NRC. Editor: The Testis, Vols. 1-4, 1970—77; contbr. over 100 articles to jours., chapters to books. Mem. Coun. for Agrl. Sci. and Tech., Am. Soc. of Animal Sci., Am. Dairy Sci. Assn., Soc. for Study of Reprodn., Endocrine Soc., others. Lodges: Rotary. Office: U Calif 1111 Franklin St Oakland CA 94607-5201 Office Phone: 510-986-0060. E-mail: wr.gomes@ucop.edu.

GOMEZ, CURTIS V., district judge; b. St. Croix, V.I., Mar. 26, 1962; Transfer, Dickinson Coll., 1981—84; BA, George Washington U., 1983—84; JD, Harvard U. Law Sch., 1986—89. Bar: V.I. 1989, DC 1990. Assoc. Patton, Boggs & Blow, 1989—93; atty. US Attorney's Office, 1997—2001, asst. US Atty., Ea. Dist. Va., 2001—02, asst. US Atty., Dist. V.I., 2002—05; US dist. judge US Dist., V.I., 2005—. Office: US Dist Judge US Courthouse and Federal Bldg 5500 Veterans Dr Ste 260 St Thomas VI 00801*

GOMEZ, DAVID FREDERICK, lawyer; b. L.A., Nov. 19, 1940; s. Fred and Jennie (Fujier) G.; m. Kathleen Holt, Oct. 18, 1977. BA in Philosophy, St. Paul's Coll., Washington, 1965, MA in Theology, 1968; JD, U. So. Calif., 1974. Bar: Calif. 1975, US Dist. Ct. (cen. dist.) Calif. 1975, US Dist. Ct. (ea. dist.) Calif. 1977, Ariz. 1981, US Dist. Ct. Ariz. 1981, US Ct. Claims 1981, US Ct. Appeals (9th cir.) 1981, US Supreme Ct. 1981; ordained priest Roman Cath. Ch., 1969; law clk. Law clk./field atty. Nat. Labor Rels. Bd., L.A., 1974-75; ptnr. Gomez, Paz, Rodriguez & Sanora, L.A., 1975-77, Garrett, Bourdette & Williams, San Francisco, 1977-80, Van O'Steen & Partners, Phoenix, 1981-85; pres. Gomez & Petitti, PC, Phoenix, 1985—. Faculty Practicing Law Inst., 1989; instr. contracts law Nat. Lawyers Guild, Peoples Coll. Law, 1975-76; mem. Missionary Soc. St. Paul the Apostle (Paulist Fathers), 1963-75; jud. oversight coun. ltd. jurisdiction Cts. Maricopa County, 2002—. Author: Somos Chicanos: Strangers in Our Own Land, 1973; co-author: Advanced Strategies in Employment Law, 1988, Arizona Employment Law Handbook, Vol. 2, 1995, 2000. Fellow: Ariz. Bar Found.; mem.: ABA, Ariz. State Bar Assn. (com. on rules of profl. conduct 1991—97, civil jury instrns. com. 1992—94, peer rev. com. 1992—2000, task force on future of the legal profession 1998—2001), Ariz. Employment Lawyers Assn. (bd. dirs. 1996—), Calif. State Bar Assn., Nat. Employment Lawyer's Assn., Los Abogados Hispanic Bar Assn., Maricopa County Bar Assn. Democrat. Office: 2525 E Camelback Rd Ste 860 Phoenix AZ 85016-4279 Office Phone: 602-957-8686. E-mail: dfg@gomezlaw.net.

GOMEZ, FRANCIS DEAN, consumer products company executive, former foreign service official; b. Belle Fourche, SD, July 24, 1941; s. Frank Garcia and Mae Elizabeth (Larive) G.; m. Esperanza Narino, Sept. 30, 1966; children: Frank T., Laura E. BA, U. Wash., 1964; MS in Adminstrn., George Washington U., 1982; cert. in translation, NYU, 1995. With US Info. Agy, 1965; asst. cultural affairs officer Bogotá, Colombia, 1965-67, San José, Costa Rica, 1968-71; Caribbean desk officer, 1971-72; writer, editor West Hemisphere Newswire, 1972-73; mid-career fellow USIA, Princeton, NJ, 1973-74; pub. affairs officer Am. Embassy, Bamako, Mali, 1974-76, pub. affairs Haiti, 1976-78; chief fgn. service personnel USIA, Washington, 1978-80; dep. asst. sec. pub. affairs Dept. State, Washington, 1980-82; dir. fgn. press centers USIA, Washington, 1984—88; cons. pub. affairs Washington, 1986—2001; dir. pub. affairs Philip Morris Mgmt. Corp., NYC, 1988—; dir. media rels. and exec. outreach Altria Corp. Svcs., Inc., 2001—. Adj. faculty NYU, 1995—. Founder, pres. Hispanic Employees Coun., Dept. State, 1979-81; trustee WETA TV, Washington, 1983-86; bd. dir. Nat. Hispanic Scholarship Fund, 1991-94; pres. bd. dir. Pan Am. Devel. Found. Recipient Superior Honor award USIA, 1967, Meritorious Honor awards 1976, 78, Annual Agy. EEO award, 1980; named Outstanding Young Men Am. US Jaycees, 1968, NYU Outstanding Svc. award, 2000. Mem. Am. Fgn. Svc. Assn., Nat. Assn. Hispanic Journalists, Nat. Press Club, Hispanic Coun. Internat. Rels., Princeton Club NY, Pi Alpha Alpha. Office: Altria Corp Svcs Inc 120 Park Ave 25th Flr New York NY 10017-5592

GOMEZ, JOSE HORACIO, archbishop; b. Monterrey, Mex, Dec. 26, 1951; arrived in US, 1987, naturalized, 1995; s. Jose H and Esperanza (Velasco) Gomez. Degrees in acctg. and philosophy, Nat. U., Mex., 1975; BA in theology, U. Navarre, Rome, 1978; PhD in theology, U. Navarre, Pamplona, Spain, 1980. Ordained as priest, Prelature of Opus Dei by Cardinal Franz Konig, Shrine of Torreciudad, Spain, 1978; in residence Our Lady of Grace, San Antonio, 1987—99; ministered St. Bartholomew Parish, Katy, Tex.; vicar Del. of Tex. Prelature of Opus Dei, 1999—2001; auxiliary bishop Archdiocese of Denver, 2001—05, moderator of the curia, 2003—05, vicar gen.; pastor Cathedral of the Immaculate Conception, Denver, 2001—03, Mother of God Ch., Denver, 2004—05; archbishop Archdiocese of San Antonio, 2005—. Mem. at large bd. dirs. Nat. Cath. Coun. Hispanic Ministry, 1997—98, treas., 1999; steering com. Encuentro 2000, LA, 1998—2000. Named one of 25 Most Influential Hispanics, Time Mag., 2005. Mem.: US Conf. Cath. Bishops (Com. on Doctrine 2002—, Com.on Priestly Formation 2002—, Com. on Hispanic Affairs 2002—, Com. for Priestly Life & Ministry 2003—, Ad Hoc Com. on the Span. Lang. Bible for the Ch. in Am. 2003—), Nat. Assn. Hispanic Priests (regional rep. 1991, pres. 1995, exec. dir. 1999—2001, El Buen Pastor Award 2003). Office: Archdiocese of San Antonio 2718 W Woodlawn San Antonio TX 78228-5195*

GOMEZ, LUIS OSCAR, Asian and religious studies educator, clinical psychology educator; b. Guayanilla, P.R., Apr. 7, 1943; s. Manuel Gomez and Lucila Rodriguez; m. Ruth Cedenia Maldonado, Dec. 24, 1963; children: Luis Oscar, Jr., Miran Ruth. BA, U. P.R., 1963; PhD Asian Langs. and Lit., Yale U., 1967; MA in Clin. Psychology, U. Mich., 1991, PhD, 1998. Lic. clin. psychologist. Vis. asst. prof. U. P.R., Rio Piedras, 1967, lectr., 1969-70, assoc. prof., 1970-73; assoc. prof. dept. Asian langs. and cultures U. Mich., Ann Arbor, 1973-80, prof. Buddhist studies, prof. religious studies dept. Asian langs. and cultures, 1980—, chmn. dept., 1981-89, 2002—, prof. psychology dept. psychology, 1999—. Vis. asst. prof. U. Wash., Seattle, 1967-68; Evans-Wentz Disting. lectr. Stanford (Calif.) U., 1983, vis. prof., 1985; vis. prof. Otani U. Kyoto, Japan, 1991-94. Author: The Land of Bliss, 1996; co-editor: Barabudur, Problemas de Filosofia, Studies in the Literature of the Great Vehicle, 1989. Mem. Am. Psychol. Assn., Soc. for Sci. Study Religion, Am. Acad. Religion, Internat. Assn. Buddhist Studies (gen. sec. 1986-89), Assn. Asian Studies. Home: 3204 Lockridge Dr Ann Arbor MI 48108-1722 Office: U Mich Dept Asian Langs & Cultures 105 S State St Ann Arbor MI 48109-1285

GOMEZ, MANUEL RODRIGUEZ, physician; b. Minaya, Spain, July 4, 1928; came to U.S., 1952, naturalized, 1961; s. Argimiro Rodriguez Herguedas and Isabel Gomez Torrente; m. Joan A. Stormer, Sept. 25, 1954; children: Christopher, Gregory, Douglas, Timothy. MD, U. Havana, Cuba, 1952; MS in Anatomy, U. Mich., 1956. Intern Michael Reese Hosp., 1952-53, asst. resident in pediatrics, 1953-54; resident in neurology U. Mich., 1954-56; fellow in pediatric neurology U. Chgo. Med. Sch., 1956-57; instr. neurology U. Buffalo Med. Sch., 1957-58, 59-60; clin. clk. neurology Inst. Neurology, U. London, 1958-59; asst. prof., then assoc. prof. neurology Wayne State U. Med. Sch., 1960-64; mem. faculty Mayo Med. Sch., Rochester, Minn., 1964—, prof. pediatric neurology, 1975—, emeritus prof. pediatric neurology Rochester, Minn., 1994—. Cons. pediatric neurology, head sect. Mayo Clinic, 1964-84, sr. cons. 1992—; vis. prof. King Faisal Hosp., Riyjadh, Saudia Arabia, 1994, Children's Hosp. Miami, 1995, Seville, Spain, 1995. Author: Tuberous Sclerosis, 1979, 2nd edit., 1988, 3d edit., 1999, Neurocutaneous Diseases, 1987; co-editor: Tuberous Sclerosis and Allied Disorders, 1991, Neurologia y Neuropsicologia Pediatrica, 1996; adv. bd. Brain and Devel., Pedriatrika. Recipient Ramón y Cajal award Academia Iberoamericana de Neuropediatría, 1995. Mem. Am. Acad. Neurology, Am. Neurol. Assn., Child Neurology Assn. (founder, former pres., Hower award 1989), N.Y. Acad. Scis., Philippine Pediatric Soc. (hon.), Sociedad Española de Neurologia (hon.), Sociedad Española de Neuropediatria (hon.), Assn. Research Nervous and Mental Disease, Orton-Dyslexia Soc. (adv. bd.), Am. Epilepsy Soc., Internat. Child Neurology Soc. (founder), Cen. Soc. Neurol. Research, Nat. Tuberous Sclerosis Assn. (hon. profl. advisor, Leadership award 1994), Sociedad Centroamericana de Neurologia y Neurociugia, Colombian Neurologic Soc. (hon.), Soc. Psiquiatría y Neurologia de Infancia y Adolescencia Chile (hon.), Costarican Neurol. Sci. Soc. (hon.), soc. Argentina de Neurologia Infantil (hon.). Home: 4225 Meadow Ridge Dr SW Rochester MN 55902-6640 Office: Mayo Clinic 200 1st St SW Rochester MN 55905-0001

GOMEZ, MIRTA, musician, educator; b. Cuba, May 17, 1965; arrived in US, 1969; d. E. Guillermo and Mirta (Tamayo) Gomez. Grad., Juilliard Sch., 1985. Lectr. in field; lectr. Conf. on Cuban Composers of the 19th and 20th

Centuries, Guadeloupe. Pianist: tours Grand Theatre de Geneve, Switzerland, Hochschule fur Musik Hanns Eisler, Berlin, Germany, Civic Ctr. Auditorium, Monterey, Calif., UN Concert Hall, N.Y.C., Town Hall, N.Y.C., Carnegie Recital Hall, N.Y.C., Merkin Hall, N.Y.C., private recital for Mayor and Mrs. Guiliani at Gracie Mansion, N.Y.C., television performance Concervatorio Nacional Lopez Buchardo, Buenos Aires, Argentina, recitals Leo S. Bing Auditorium, L.A. County Mus., Metropolitan Mus. of Art, N.Y.C., four city tour throughout Spain, 2004—05, pvt. lectr./recital Fundacion Esperanza of Mex. on TV program Espectaculos, TV Azteca, Mex., lectr./recitals standard repertoire of 19th and 20th century Cuban composers on four month tour of the Americas, film documentary by Ivan Acosta How to create a Rumba (shown at 2001 Internat. Film Festival in N.Y.C., performed at Grand Bay Club, Key Biscayne, Fla.).

GOMEZ, SYLVIA, newscaster; m. Jon Duncanson. BS in Mass Comm., U. Md., 1985. Field prodr. WRC-TV, Washington, 1983—88; weekend anchor KTSM-TV, El Paso, Tex., 1988—90; reporter and fill-in anchor KTVT-TV, Dallas, 1990—92, WMAQ-TV, Chgo., 1992—94, WBBM-TV, Chgo., 1994—96; weekend anchor WFLD-TV, Chgo., 1996—97; weekend evening anchor and reporter WBBM-TV, Chgo., 1998—. Office: WBBM-TV 630 McClurg Ct Chicago IL 60601

GOMEZ, WILLIAM, orthopedist; b. N.Y.C., Apr. 29, 1955; Degree, NYU/Poly. Inst. N.Y.; MD, Columbia U., 1982. Diplomate Am. Bd. Orthop. Surgeons. Intern in gen. surgery St. Vincent's Hosp., N.Y.C., 1982—84; resident in orthop. Columbia-Presbyn. Med. Ctr., N.Y.C., 1984—87; fellow in sports medicine U. Pitts., 1987—88; pvt. practice Trenton, NJ. Orthop. team physician Trenton Titans, Trenton Thunder; affiliated physician St. Francis Med. Ctr., Trenton, Robert Wood Johnson Univ. Hosp., Hamilton, NJ, Capital Health Sys., Trenton. Named one of Top Drs. N.Y. Metro Area, Castle Connolly, Top Drs. 2003, N.J. Monthly Mag. Fellow: Am. Acad. Orthop. Surgeons; mem.: N.J. Orthop. Soc., Mercer County Med. Soc., N.J. Med. Soc., Am. Orthop. Soc. Sports Medicine. Office: Orthop Surgery Bldg D Ste 220 1225 Whitehorse Mercerville Rd Trenton NJ 08619-3882 Office Phone: 609-581-2200.

GOMEZ-JIMÉNEZ, CARLOS, science educator, microbiologist, geneticist; s. Carlos Gómez-Vázquez, Sr. and Emma Jiménez-Gómez BS in Biology with honors, U. PR, 1986, MS in Microbiology and Genetics, 1992; postgrad., Alliance Theol. Sem. Tchr. asst. U. PR, Mayagüez, 1986-88, 91, biochemistry lab. technician, 1988, full prof. Aguadilla, 1992—; quality assurance analyst Microbiology and Cell Culture Lab. Ortho Biologics, Inc., Manatí, PR, 1989-90; prof. Inter Am. U., Aguadilla, PR, 1991-92, San Germán, 1992—; MCAT, PCAT, and DAT invited prof. Kaplan PR Ctr., 1997—; prof. Pontifica Cath. U. PR, 2000—. Acad. counselor sci. rsch. adad. teachers and gifted students, Am. U., San Germán, PR, 1992-; sci. advisor Young Scholars Program-NSF-Inter Am. U., San Germán, 1992-; cons. drugs, alcohol, violence & HIV/AIDS Prevention programs U. PR, Aguadilla, 1992-; curriculum & course dir., U. PR-Aguadilla, 1992-; mem. over 40 coms. U. PR pres. office & U. PR-Aguadilla, 1992-; dir. honor program, 1996-98, mem. exec. com. Superior Edn. Council, 1996, 2001; acad. sen. 2002-05, adminstrv. bd. 2003-05; mem. Nat. Collegiate Honors Coun., 1996-; bd. dirs. Assn. Hon. Programs; mentor prof. NSF & U. PR Program, 2001- Editor (newsletters) The Probe-Caribbean Soc. Biotech., Inc., 1994-, Biosfera-U. PR-Aguadilla, 1994-; contbr. articles to profl. jours.; author acad. manuals and modules in Microbiology, Genetics, Human Genetic, and General Biology Co-founder Leguísamo First Baptist Ch., Mayagüez, 1977-; first tenor Mayagüez Municipal Choir, 1994-, ROMANTIEZER Interdenominational Singing Ministry, 1996-; judge,advisor HS and Undergrad. Sci. Competitions, 1987-; liaison U. PR-Aguadilla & Am. Red Cross Assn. Communitarian Svc., 1994-. Mem.: AAAS, Assn. U. Honor Programs (bd. dirs. 1997—), Biostudy I (counselor, bd. dirs. 1997—), Assn. Food Sci, Tech., P.R. Sci. Tchr. Assn., Soc. Mycology (bd. dirs. 2002, pres. 2003—04, bd. dirs. 1995—97), Caribbean Soc. Biotech. (bd. dirs. 1995—2005), Am. Soc. Microbiology, Bapt. Student Union, Beta Beta Beta. Baptist. Avocations: singing, book collecting, French cooking. Office: U PR Aguadilla Dept Nat Scis PO Box 250160 Aguadilla PR 00604-0160 Office Phone: 787-890-2681 ext. 230, 226. E-mail: cgj_upra@yahoo.com.

GOMEZ MARTINEZ, JUAN CARLOS, advertising executive; b. Caracas, Venezuela, Sept. 20, 1965; arrived in U.S., 1997; s. Nicolas Gomez Dosantos and Elsa Martinez Rosales; m. Pauline Gaspard Morell, Nov. 30, 1996; 1 child, Nicolas Antonio Gomez Gaspard. BA in Pub. Acctg., Universidad Catolica Andres Bello, Caracas, Venezuela, 1990; MBA with Specialization in Internat. Bus., U. Miami, Miami, Fla., 2000. Auditor i Price Waterhouse, Caracas, Venezuela, 1988—91; contr. Reckitt & Colman de Venezuela, Caracas, Venezuela, 1991—94; andean region corp. contr. Motorola de los Andes y el Caribe, Caracas, Venezuela, 1994—97; sr. ops. contr. l. Am. north, south & Mex. Motorola Inc, Ft. Lauderdale, Fla., 1997—2000; sr. divsn. contr., mfg. ops. Motorola Do Brasil, Campinas, Brazil, 2000—01; dir. fin. americas supply chain orgn. Motorola Inc, Harvard, Ill., 2001—02, dir. fin. l.am. Ft. Lauderdale, Fla., 2003—03; sr. v.p., CFO Foote Cone and Belding L.Am., Miami, 2003—. Mem.: Beta Gamma Sigma. Roman Catholic. Office: Foote Cone and Belding Latin America 1401 Brickell Ave Miami FL 33131 Office Phone: 305-372-8235. Personal E-mail: juancarlosgomez@bellsouth.net. Business E-Mail: jgomez@fcb.com.

GOMOLL, MATILDE I., multi-media specialist; b. Caye Caulker, Belize, Nov. 16, 1947; d. Antonio Lorenzo Vega, Sr. and Lidia Barbara Alamina de Vega; m. Kip Douglas Gomoll, July 28, 1978; children: Kevin T., Ben C., Alexander S. BA in Art Edn., Viterbo U., 1973. Tchr. Pallotti H.S., Belize, Belize, 1973—78, 1968—70; sch. asst. Lansing Sch. Dist., Immaculate Heart of Mary Sch., St. Casimir Cath. Schs., Mich., 1989—2000; asst. media tech. Lansing Sch. Dist., 2001—; v.p. Henry H. North Elem. Sch., Lansing, 1989—92. Art cons. for office newsletter SJ Mission Bur., St. Louis, 1970—78. Author: (non-fiction book) Caye to Success. Fin. support United Way, Lansing, 1995—2004, Habitat for Humanity, Lansing, 1990—2004; vol. works, fin. support Immaculate Heart of Mary Ch., Lansing. Democrat-Npl. Roman Catholic. Avocations: writing, reading on natural history issues, listening to classical music, computer related activities, visiting the elderly. Home: 5835 Annapolis Dr Lansing MI 48911

GOMORY, RALPH EDWARD, mathematician, manufacturing company executive, foundation executive; b. N.Y.C., N.Y., May 7, 1929; s. Andrew L. and Marian (Schellenberg) Gomory; m. Laura Dumper, 1954 (div. 1968); children: Andrew C., Susan S., Stephen H. BA, Williams Coll., 1950, ScD (hon.), 1973; postgrad., Kings Coll., 1950—51, Cambridge U., Eng., 1950—51; PhD in Math., Princeton U., 1954; LHD (hon.), Pace U., 1986; DSc (hon.), Poly. U., 1987, Syracuse U., 1989, Worcester Poly. U., 1989, Carnegie-Mellon U., 1989. Rsch. assoc. Princeton U., 1951—54, asst. prof. math., Higgins lectr., 1957—59; with IBM, Yorktown Heights, NY, 1959—86, dir. math. scis., rsch. div., 1965—67, dir. rsch., 1970—86, v.p., 1973—84, sr. v.p., 1985—89, sr. v.p. for sci. and tech., 1986—89, mem. corp. mgmt. bd., 1983—89, dir. Asia Pacific Group, 1982—88; pres. Alfred P. Sloan Found., NYC, 1989—. Served President's Coun. Advisors on Sci. and Tech., 1984—92; mem. President's Coun. Advisors on Sci. and Tech. and Committee on Science, Engineering, and Pubic Policy. Co-author (with William J. Baumol): MIT Press book. Mem. governing bd. NRC, 1980—83, 1980—, chmn. com. on mandatory retirement in higher edn., 1989—91; trustee Hampshire Coll., 1977—86, Alfred P. Sloan Found., 1988—, Princeton U., 1985—89; bd. dir. Washington Post Co., Lexmark Internat. Inc. With USN, 1954—57. Recipient Lanchester prize, Ops. Rsch. Soc. Am., 1963, Harry Goode Meml. award, Am. Fedn. Info. Processing Socs., 1984, John Von Neumann Theory prize, Ops. Rschl. Soc. Am. and Inst. Mgmt. Scis., 1984, IRI medal, Indsl. Rsch. Inst., 1985, Engring. Leadership Recognition award, IEEE, 1988, Arthur M. Bueche award, NAE, 1993, Heinz award for Tech., the Economy and Employment, 1998; fellow IBM, 1964; Sheffield Fellowship award, Yale U. Faculty Engring., 2000. Fellow: NAS (coun. 1977—78, 1980—83, 1997—, com. sci. engring. and pub. policy 1985—), Am. Acad. Arts and Scis., Econometric Soc.; mem.: IEEE (hon.), Am. Philos. Soc. (coun. 1986—92), Nat. Acad. Engring. (coun. 1986—92). Home: 260 Douglas Rd Chappaqua NY 10514-3100 Office: Alfred P Sloan Found 630 5th Ave Ste 2550 New York NY 10111-0100

GOMPF, HENRY L. (HANK), lawyer; b. 1947; BME with distinction, Cornell Univ., 1969; JD magna cum laude, Univ. Mich., 1976. Bar: Ohio 1977, Tex. 1981. Coord. bus. practice group Jones Day, Dallas, now adminstrv. ptnr. Assoc. editor Law Rev., 1976. Mem.: ABA, Dallas Bar Assn., State Bar of Tex., Order of Coif. Office: Jones Day 2727 N Harwood St Dallas TX 75201-1515 Office Phone: 214-969-3707. Office Fax: 214-969-5100. Business E-Mail: hlgompf@jonesday.com.

GONCHARKO, EVELYN MARIE, writer, school librarian, educator; b. Youngstown, Ohio, Aug. 15, 1927; d. John and Mary Kolos; m. Alexander Goncharko, May 15, 1948; children: Michael, Alexandra. BA in Tchg. and Libr. Sci., Kean U., Union, N.J., 1974. 2d grade tchr. Holy Family Sch., Hazlet, NJ, 1972—77; libr. Pt. Pleasant (NJ) Schs., 1977—86, Sandhills Cmty. Coll., Pinehurst, NC, 1988; head libr. Farm Life Sch., Carthage, 1988—89. Author: Pick Your Own Strawberries, 1983, Daniel Scott and the Monster, 1989, My Tree, 1987, Hugo the Squirrel, 1991, The Halloween Monster, 1992, The Catbird, the Catfish and the Cat, 1993, Sticky Ricky, 1994, Oatmeal, 1997, Sasha, That's Me, 1999, Grandma from Manhattan, 2001, short stories. Mem.: NEA.

GONDEK, DIANA STASIA, lawyer; b. Waltham, Mass., Jan. 27, 1948; d. Adolph Joseph and Stasia (Czekanski) G. BA, Duke U., 1970; JD, Boston U., 1973. Bar: Mass. 1973, N.Y. 1974, U.S. Dist. Ct. Mass. 1976, U.S. Supreme Ct. 1978, U.S. Ct. Appeals (1st cir.) 1979. Staff atty. Mass. Dept. Edn., Boston, 1973-75; pvt. practice Boston, 1975—. Author: General Laws of Education Relating to School Committees as of January 1, 1984, Issues and Concerns of Importance to Public School Officials, Vol. 1, 1986, Vol. 2, 1988, Legal Status of Professional Personnel in the Public Schools, 1986; writer The Mass. School Law Digest, 1993—. Mem.: ABA, Mass. Bar Assn. Home: 46 Falconer Ave Brockton MA 02301-5831 Office: 121 Mount Vernon St Boston MA 02108-1104

GONDOLESI, GABRIEL EDUARDO, transplant surgeon; b. Tandil, Buenos Aires, Argentina, Nov. 6, 1968; s. Carlos Eduardo Gondolesi and Marta Esther Bahi; m. Carolina Rumbo, May 15, 1998; children: Manuel children: Ignacio. MD, Facultad de Ciencias Medicas, Universidad Nacional de La Plata, La Plata, Buenos Aires, Argentina, 1987—92. Diplomate Buenos Aires, 1993. Chief resident on gen. surgery Surgery Svc., pavilion Finochietto of the Hosp. Interzonal de Agudos, La Plata, Argentina, 1993—97; fellow hepatobiliary surgery and liver transplantation. Liver and Liver Transplant Unit at Fundación Favaloro, Buenos Aires, 1997—99; fellow multi-organ transplantation Recanati/Miller Transplantation Inst., N.Y.C., 1999—2001, asst. prof. pediatric and adult liver transplant, surgical dir. intestinal transplant, 2002. Contbr. chapters to books, scientific papers, articles to profl. jours. including Jour. Gastrointestinal Surgery, Annals Surgery. Recipient Gold Medal, Best med. student (9, 9/10 pints average qualifications at the end of the 6 years of med. sch.). Facultad de Ciencias Medicas. UNLP., 1986-1992, Rotary Club prize for performance in the med. field, La Plata's Rotary Club. Argentina, 1996, 2004. Mem.: Soc. Surgery of Alimentary Track, Transplantation Soc., Miembro de la Asociacion Argentina de Cirugia (assoc.), Am. Assn. of Transplant Surgeons (assoc.), Internat. Hepato-Bilio-Pancreatic Assn. (assoc.). Office: Recanati/Miller Transplantation Inst 1425 Madison Ave 3d Fl New York NY 10029 Office Phone: 212-659-9300. Personal E-mail: gegondolesi@yahoo.com. Business E-Mail: gegondolesi@msnyuhealth.org.

GONDRY, MICHEL, film director; b. Versailles, France, May 8, 1963; Dir.: (films) Vingt p'tites tours, 1989, Human Nature, 2001; writer, dir., actor (films) The Letter, 1998, writer, dir. One Day, 2001, Pecan Pie, 2003, Eternal Sunshine of Spotless Mind, 2004 (Best Dir., Washington, DC Film Critic award, 2004, Academy award for best original screenplay, 2005); dir.: (music video for Björk: Volumen) (Human Behavior, Army of Me, Isobel, Hyperballad, Jóga, Bachelorette), 1998, (music videofor Clip Cult Vol. 1: Exploding Cinema) Sugar Water, 1999, (video) Massive Attack: Eleven Promos, 2001, The Chemical Brothers: Singles 93-03, 2003, The Work of Director Michel Gondry, 2003, I've Been Twelve Forever, 2003, (commercials) for Gap, Smirnoff, Air France, Nike, Coca Cola, Adidas, Polaroid, & Levi. Address: Commerical/Music Video Partizan Entertainment 7083 Hollywood Blvd Ste 401 Los Angeles CA 90028 Office Phone: 323-468-0123.*

GONEN, MITHAT, statistician, researcher; b. Ankara, Turkey, Feb. 2, 1968; s. Soner and Turkan Gonen; m. Elza Erkip; children: Deniz, Selin. PhD, Tex. Tech U., Lubbock, 1991—96. Assoc. attending biostatistician Meml. Sloan-Kettering Cancer Ctr., N.Y.C., 1999—. Contbr. articles to profl. jours. Mem.: Am. Statis. Assn. (v.p., N.Y. chpt. 2004—). Office: Meml Sloan-Kettering Cancer Ctr 1275 York Ave New York NY 10021 Office Phone: 646-735-8100. Office Fax: 646-735-0010.

GONG, EDMOND JOSEPH, lawyer; b. Miami, Fla., Oct. 7, 1930; s. Joe Fred and Fayline G.; m. Sophie Vlachos, July 25, 1957 (dec.); children: Frances Fayline, Peter Joseph (dec.), Madeleine, Joseph Fred, II, Edmond Joseph; m. Dana Leigh Clay, Dec. 7, 1988. AB cum laude, Harvard U., 1952, postgrad. in law, 1954-55; JD, U. Miami, 1960. Bar: Fla. 1960. Spl. writer Hong Kong Tiger Standard, 1955-56; staff writer Miami Herald, 1958-59; assoc. firm Helliwell, Melrose and DeWolf, 1960-61; asst. U.S. atty. So. Dist. Fla., 1961-62; mem. Fla. Ho. of Reps., 1963-66, Fla. Senate, 1966-72; trustee Fla. Gulf Realty Trust, 1974-80; pres. Inflahedge Resources Fund, Edmond Gong and Co., Inc., 1969—, Pub. Policy Cons. Inc., 1988—. Sr. pub. policy analyst and legal counsel Everett Clay Assocs., Inc., 1988—; chmn. Fla. Land Sales Advisory Council, 1974-76; vice chmn. Bd. Bus. Regulation, State of Fla., 1976-77; fellow Inst. Politics John Fitzgerald Kennedy Sch. Govt., Harvard U., 1969-70, assoc. dir., 1971-72 Mem. Harvard 350th Commn., 1984-86; mem. com. on univ. resources, bd. overseers and pres. and fellows Harvard Coll., 1984-86; mem. North Key Largo Habitat Conservation Planning Study Com., 1984-88; regional chmn. Selection Com. for Anglo-Am. Conf., Johns Hopkins Sch. Advanced Internat. Studies, 1985; mem. Fairbanks Ctr. Com., Fairbank Ctr. for East Asian Research, Harvard U., 1987-90. Mem. ABA, Fla. Bar, Harvard U. Alumni Assn. (dir.-at-large), Miami City Club, Fla. Audubon Soc. (bd. dirs. 1990-93). Episcopalian. Office: Pub Policy Cons 6161 Blue Lagoon Dr #270 Miami FL 33126

GONG, HENRY, JR., internist, researcher, educator; b. Tulare, Calif., May 23, 1947; s. Henry and Choy (Low) G.; m. Janice Wong; children: Gregory, Jaimee. BA, U. of the Pacific, 1969; MD, U. Calif., Davis, 1973. Diplomate Am. Bd. Internal Medicine, 1977, Pulmonary Disease subspecialty bd., 1980. Resident in medicine Boston U., 1973-75; fellow in pulmonary medicine UCLA Med. Ctr., 1975-77; asst. prof., then assoc. prof. Sch. Medicine UCLA, 1977-89, prof. medicine, 1989-93; assoc. chief pulmonary div. UCLA Med. Ctr., 1985-92; chief Environ. Health Svc. Rancho Los Amigos Med. Ctr., 1993—; prof. medicine U. So. Calif., 1993—, prof. preventive medicine, 1997—. Dir. Environ. Exposure Lab., UCLA, 1988-93; chmn. dept. medicine Rancho Los Amigos Med. Ctr., 1996—; mem. pub. health and socio-econs. task force South Coast Air Quality Mgmt. Dist., El Monte, Calif., 1989-90, Calif. Air Resources Bd., 2004—. Contbr. over 300 articles to rsch. publs., chpts. to books; editorial bd. Jour. Clin. Pharmacology, 1983-02, Am. Jour. Critical Care, 1992-2001, Arch Environ. Health, 2000—, Inhalation Toxicology, 2005—. Elder on session Pacific Palisades Presbyn. Ch., 1984-86, 89-91, 2003. Fellow Am. Coll. Chest Physicians (pres. Calif. chpt. 1991-92), Am. Coll. Clin. Pharmacology; mem. Am. Thoracic Soc., Am. Fedn. Clin. Rsch., Western Soc. Clin. Investigation, Phi Eta Sigma. Avocation: travel. Office: Environ Health Svc Rancho Los Amigos Med Ctr 7601 Imperial Hwy Downey CA 90242-3456 Office Phone: 562-401-7561. Business E-Mail: hgong@ladhs.org.

GONG, NANCY YEE, glass artist, small business owner; b. Rochester, N.Y., June 8, 1957; d. Don S. and Sue H. Gong; m. Peter W. Fisk, July 10, 1983. Student Sch. for Am. Craftsmen, Rochester Inst. Tech., 1973—78; student, Champlain Coll., 1975—76, Empire State Coll., 1976—77, Naples Mills Sch. Arts & Craft, 1976. Propr., artist Gong Glass Works, Rochester, NY, 1979—; presenter glass art tech. workshops and confs. Rochester Mus. & Sci Ctr., 1979—83; coord. spl. projects Pyramid Art Gallery, Allofus Art Workshop, Inc., Rochester, 1979—86. Educator ALLOFUS Art Workshop, Inc., Rochester, 1976-80, PORTCON "82 Art Glass Conf., San Diego, 1982, Environ. Art Glass Conf., Oklahoma City, 1989, Profl. Art Glass Sem., San Antonio, 1990, Pub. Art Politics and Processes Symposium, Arts for Greater Rochester, 1990, Glass Art Soc. Conf., Monterey, Calif., Corning, N.Y., 1993, Huntington, W.Va., Toronto, Ont., Can., 1978—; instr. Rochester Mus. and Sci. Ctr., 1979-86, ALLOFUS Art Workshop, 1979-86, Jewish Community Ctr., 1979-86, Norman Howard Sch., 1979-86, cons. Edge Pub. Group, 1989-93, Profl. Stained Glass Guild, Brewster, N.Y., 1989-93, Arts for Gtr. Rochester, 1990; presenter numerous seminars; speaker numerous orgns. Exhibited at Lincoln First Plaza Gallery, Rochester, Meml. Art Gallery U. Rochester (Excellence award 1981), Glassmasters Guild Finalist N.Y.C., 1981, First Place, San Francisco, 1982, Oakland County Cultural Offices, Southfield, Mich., 1987 (Best Stained Glass), Glass Growers Gallery, Erie, Pa., Kunst Art & Form Internat., Vienna, Austria, Galerie, NY, 1988-89, Greater Rochester Internat. Airport, 1991, Crafts Nat. 27, 1993, Women's Art Works 4, 1994, 6, 1996, Kraft Lieberman Gallery, 2002, Glass Gallery, 2002, Kane Marie Gallery, 2002, Galleria of Sculpture, 2002, Lockhart Gallery, 2002, Swanson Reed Gallery, Glass Now, 2003, 04, Maitlins, 2003, Artform Internat., 2003, The Glass Gallery, 2003, 04, Kraft Lieborman Gallery, 2003, Mattlins, 2003, Collectors Fine Art, 2004, Pritam and Eames, 2004, Pritam & James, 2004, Crafts Nat. 38 Zoller Gallery, 2004, 05, Sofa Chgo., 2004, Port of Rochester Pub. Art Competition, 2004; represented in permanent collections Blue Cross & Blue Shield, Meml. Art Gallery Rochester, Women's Coun. Room, Cornell U. Ithaca Faculty Club, Paychex, Inc., GM, Genesee Region Home Care Assn. Hospice Unit, Eastman Kodak Co., Lodge at Woodcliff, Monroe C.C., Duke U. Fuqua Sch. Bus. Conf. Ctr., Genesee Hosp., Rochester Gen. Hosp., Kemper, Virgin Vacations, Virgin Atlantic, Time Warner, Corning Tropel Corp., Graham Mfg., Strong Meml. Hosp., St. John Fisher Coll., U. Rochester, N.Y. State Appellate Ct. House, Rochester Yacht Club, Oak Hill Country Club, Key Bank, Ferry Terminal Port of Rochester, Rochester Inst. Tech., St. Ann's Cmty., Constellation Key Bank; appeared in numerous mags.; contbr. articles to profl. jours. Past bd. dirs. Arts for Greater Rochester, 1991; trustee Sta. WXXI Pub. Broadcasting Svc.; mem. Meml. Art Gallery Univ. Rochester, hon. adv. Arts for Greater Rochester Mem. Glass Art Soc., Am. Crafts Coun., Toastmasters Internat., Rochester Women's Network, Women and Minority Bus. Enterprise. Studio: Gong Glass Works 42 Parkview Dr Rochester NY 14625-1034 Office Phone: 585-288-5520.

GONG, SU, computer engineer; s. Shaoquan Su and Hanqiao Shi. PhD, Columbia U., 1994—2003. Chief software engr. NeXtorage Inc., N.Y.C., 2000—03. Recipient Best Paper Award, Elsevier Sci. Pub., 2001. Mem.: ACM. Office: Columbia University Dept of Computer Sci New York NY 10027 E-mail: gongsu@cs.columbia.edu.

GONG, XIAOYI, engineer; b. Beijing, Dec. 6, 1958; arrived in US, 1998; d. Run-Gang Gong and Jun-Shu Lin; m. Yuqing Justin Yang, Apr. 2, 1986; 1 child, Guan Yang. BSc, Northwestern Poly. U., Xian, China, 1982; MSc, Chengdu (China) U. Sci. and Tech., 1985, PhD, 1988. Rsch. fellow Chinese Acad. Scis., Guangzhou, China, 1988—91, U. Leeds, England, 1991—92; prof. Guangdong U. Tech., Guangzhou, 1995; rsch. scientist CSIRO Molecular Sci., Melbourne, Australia, 1995—98; rsch. assoc. Pacific N.W. Nat. Lab., Richland, Wash., 1998—2000; sr. staff engr. Conoco, Inc., Ponca City, Okla., 2000—. Contbr. articles to profl. jours. Named Youth Chemist, Chinese Chem. Soc., Beijing, 1990; named one of Ten Most Outstanding Women, Guangdong Province Govt., 1995; fellow, Brit. Coun., London, 1991. Mem.: AAAS, Am. Chem. Soc. Achievements include materials research and device development in electronic, biomedical and environmental applications; research in surface chemistry to develop new materials and new products. Avocations: travel, reading. Home: 2908 Rice St Ponca City OK 74604 Office: ConocoPhillips 1000 S Pine Ponca City OK 74602

GONGORA, EDUARDO, plastic surgeon; b. Baja, Calif., July 9, 1963; MD, U. Autonoma, Baja, Calif. Owner Clinica Genesis, Rosarito Baja, Calif. Office: PO Box 148 Chula Vista CA 91912-0148

GONICK, HARVEY CRAIG, nephrologist, educator; b. Winnipeg, Man., Can., Apr. 10, 1930; s. Joseph Wolfe and Rose (Chernick) G.; m. Gloria Granz, Dec. 16, 1967; children: Stefan, Teri, Julie, Suzanne. BS in Chemistry, UCLA, 1951; MD, U. Calif., San Francisco, 1955. Diplomate Am. Bd. Internal Medicine, Am. Bd. Nephrology. Intern Peter Bent Brigham Hosp., 1955-56; fellow in nephrology Mass. Meml. Hosp., 1956-57; fellow in nephrology, resident in internal medicine Wadsworth VA Hosp., Los Angeles, 1959-61, clin. investigator, 1961-64, chief metabolic balance unit, 1964-67, rsch. assoc. L.A., 2002—; instr. medicine Sch. Medicine, UCLA, 1961-64, asst. prof., 1964-69, assoc. prof., 1969-72, adj. assoc. prof., 1972-76, adj. prof., 1976—2003, clin. prof., 2003—, assoc. chief div. nephrology, 1965-72, co-dir. Bone and Stone Clinic, 1972-76, coordinator postgrad. nephrology edn., 1975-78; mem. staff St. John's Hosp., Santa Monica, Calif., Century City Hosp., L.A., med. dir. dialysis unit, 1972-79, chief medicine, 1978-79; mem. staff Cedars-Sinai Med. Ctr., L.A., dir. trace element lab., 1979-96, clin. chief nephrology, 1983-85, coord. renal tng., dir. hypertension rsch., 1996—2003; practice medicine specializing in nephrology Los Angeles, 1972-94. Co-founder, med. dir. Berkeley East Dialysis Unit, Santa Monica, 1971-75; co-founder, cons. Kidney Dialysis Care Units Inc., Lynwood, Calif., 1971-78; co-dir. Osteoporosis Prevention and Treatment Ctr., Santa Monica, 1987-93; mem. numerous adv. coms. to state and fed. agys., 1969-83. Contbr. articles to profl. jours.; editor: Current Nephrology, 1977-96. Served to capt. M.C., USAF, 1957-59. Fellow Charles Nelson Fund, Kaiser Found., NIH; recipient Oliver P. Douglas Meml. award Los Angeles County Heart Assn., 1959, Vis. Scientist award Deutscher Academischer Austauschendienst, 1978. Fellow ACP; mem. AMA, AAAS, Internat. Soc. Nephrology (organizing com. internat. cong. 1984), Am. Soc. Nephrology, European Dialysis and Transplant Assn., Soc. Exptl. Biology and Medicine, Calif. Med. Assn., Los Angeles County Med. Assn., Nat. Kidney Found. (active ann. conf. 1963-65, sec. nat. med. adv. coun. 1969-70, regional rep. and legis. com. nat. med. adv. coun. 1970-73, grantee 1963), So. Calif. Kidney Found. (chmn. sci. adv. coun. 1968-70, co-chmn. legis. com. 1970-73, bd. dirs. 1974-83, honoree 1979), Am. Soc. Bone and Mineral Rsch., Am. Coll. Toxicology, Soc. Toxicology, Am. Heart Assn. (renal sect. of coun. on circulation), Am. Fedn. Clin. Rsch., Western Soc. Clin. Rsch., Western Assn. Physicians, Phi Beta Kappa, Sigma Xi, Alpha Omega Alpha, Phi Eta Sigma, Alpha Mu Gamma, Phi Lambda Upsilon. Avocation: tennis. Office: West LA VA Hosp Rsch Svc 11301 Wilshire Blvd Los Angeles CA 90073 Office Phone: 310-268-3053. Business E-Mail: hgonick@ucla.edu.

GONNELLI, PATRICK M., finance company executive; BS in Econs., U. Pa. CPA, Pa. Various exec. positions KPMG Peat Marwick, Revlon Corp.; CFO, Simon & Schuster, Towers Perrin, Phila., 1991-2000. Office: Towers Perrin 1 Stanford Plaza 263 Tresser Blvd Stamford CT 06901-3226

GONNERING, RUSSELL STEPHEN, ophthalmic plastic surgeon; b. Milw., Nov. 21, 1949; s. Russell Richard and Virginia Mary (Mlinar) G.; m. Sandra Lynne Brubaker, Aug. 6, 1971; children: Julie Kathleen, Stephen Russell, Scott Duncan. Student, U. Vienna, Austria, 1969—70; AB in History cum laude, Boston Coll., 1971; MD, Med. Coll. Wis., 1975. Diplomate Am. Bd. Ophthalmology; lic. physician, Wis. Intern St. Luke's Hosp., Milw., 1975-76; resident in ophthalmology Med. Coll. Wis., Milw., 1977-80, asst. clin. prof. dept. ophthalmology, 1985-2000, prof. ophthalmology, 2000—; fellow in ophthalmic plastic and reconstructive surgery U. Wis., Madison, 1980-81, asst. clin. prof. dept. ophthalmology, 1981-92, assoc. clin. prof. dept. ophthalmology, 1992-96, clin. prof. dept. ophthalmology, 1996—, Kambara lectr., 1997; ophthalmologist Children's Hosp. Wis., Milw., St.

Luke's Hosp., Milw., chief ophthalmologist, 1983-94, 97-99, vice chief staff, 2000; pvt. practice Ophthalmic Plastic & Reconstructive Surgery, 1981-2000. Full-time acad. practice, 2000—; rsch. assoc. in corneal physiology Med. Coll. Wis., 1976-77; rsch. advisor to fellowship in ophthalmic plastic and reconstructive surgery U. Wis., Madison, 1983-2002; presenter in field. Author: (with others) Infections of the Eye and Ocular Adnexa, 1986, Oculoplastic, Orbital and Reconstructive Surgery, 1988, Oculoplastic and Orbital Emergencies, 1990, Ophthalmic Plastic, reconstructive and Orbital Surgery, 1997, Ophthalmic Surgery: Principles and Techniques, 1999; sect. editor: Principles and Practice of Ophthalmic Plastic and Reconstructive Surgery, 1995; contbr. numerous articles to profl. jours. Recipient Wisdom Soc. Honor award, 1999. Fellow: ACS (coun. Wis. chpt. 1996—2000), Am. Soc. Ophthalmic Plastic and Reconstructive Surgery (editl. bd. 1987—99, edn. com. 1988—99, vice chmn. edn. com. 1995—97, chmn. edn. com. 1997—99, Marvin H. Quickert award 1982, Rsch. award 1982, Reeh Pathology award 1999), Am. Acad. Ophthalmology (basic and clin. sci. course com. 1986—92, chmn. 1988—92, Honor award 1990, Ruedemann lectr. 1994, Sr. Achievement award 2001); mem.: Nat. Assn. for Healthcare Quality, Project Mgmt. Inst., Christian Med. and Dental Assn., Am. Soc. Quality, Milw. Surg. Soc., Nat. Soc. to Prevent Blindness (mem. adv. bd. Wis. chpt. 1987—88), Am. Soc. Ocularists (med. adv. bd. 1987—2001), Milw. Ophthalmol. Soc. (treas. 1989—90, sec. 1990—91, v.p. 1991—92, pres. 1992—93), Milw. Acad. Surgery, Milw. Acad. Medicine, Milw. County Med. Soc. (del. to state med. soc. 1987—90, bd. dirs. 1989—94, Dirs. citation 1994), Med. Soc. Wis., Assn. for Rsch. in Vision and Ophthalmology, Internat. Dacryology Soc., European Soc. Ophthalmic Plastic and Reconstructive Surgery, Internat. Soc. Orbital Disorders, Black Belt Six Sigma (Villanova Univ.), Mensa. Avocations: sailing, skiing, tai kwon do, bicycling. Office: Med Coll Wisconsin Dept Ophthalmology 925 N 87th St Milwaukee WI 53226 Office Phone: 414-456-2020. Personal E-mail: rsgonnering@hotmail.com.

GONNERMAN, JENNIFER, writer, journalist; b. Jan. 24, 1971; Attended, Oxford U.; BA, Columbia U., 1994. Staff writer The Village Voice, 1997—. Author: Life on the Outside: The Prison Odyssey of Elaine Bartlett, 2004 (Nat. Book Award finalist, 2004). Finalist Livingston Award, Nat. Mag. Award; recipient Gold Typewriter Award, N.Y. Press Club, Meyer Berger Award, Columbia U. Sch. Journalism, Front Page Award, Newswomen's Club N.Y. Office: Village Voice 36 Cooper Square New York NY 10003

GONSALVES, MARGARET LEBOY, elementary school educator; b. Paia, Maui, Hawaii, Feb. 10, 1935; d. John Algarin and Antonia (Leboy) G. BS in Edn., Marylhurst U., 1959; elem. tchr. cert., U. Hawaii, 1971. Cert. elem. tchr., Hawaii. Nurses' aide St. Vincent Hosp., Portland, Oreg., 1956; office clk. Bur. Med. Econs., Honolulu, 1959; tchr. State of Hawaii Dept. Edn., Honolulu, 1959—, Benjamin Park Sch., Kaneohe, Hawaii, 1966-92. Tchr. ESEA-Title I Chpt. I reading and math. fed. program, 1979-92, coord. Parker Sch. Chpt. 1 reading and math. program. Vol. Am. Cancer Soc., Honolulu, 1979, Am. Diabetes Assn., Honolulu, 1992; reporter Nat. Data Corp.-Price Waterhouse, Springfield, Va., 1991-2002. Mem. NEA, Internat. Reading Assn., Hawaii State Tchrs. Assn. (faculty rep. 1960-62, 87-89, Golden Heart cert., 2003), Sigma Delta Pi. Roman Catholic. Avocations: reading, sweepstakes, fishing, gardening, travel. Home: 1328 Maalahi St Honolulu HI 96819-1727

GONSHAK, ISABELLE LEE, nurse, civic worker; b. Newark, Apr. 4, 1932; d. Robert John and Clara Kate (Cooperman) McClelland; m. David M. Gonshak, Aug. 8, 1953; children: Evan J., Brett A., Kathryn Susan. RN, N.J. Nurse Newark City Hosp., 1953; tchr. Ideal Sch. for Nurse's Aides, Miami, Fla., 1972-74. Vocal soloist numerous TV and social affairs; photographer multiple media, multi-faceted subjects. Bd. dirs. Miami Beach Symphony, 1971—, pres., 1978-79; bd. dirs. South Fla. Symphony; life mem. Opera Guild Soc. Ft. Lauderdale; active Statue of Liberty Refinishing Com. Mem. Greater Miami Opera Assn., Hadassah (life). Jewish. Home: 1700 SW 72d Ave Plantation FL 33317-5037

GONSON, S. DONALD, lawyer; b. Buffalo, June 13, 1936; s. Samuel and Laura Rose (Greenspan) G.; m. Dorothy Rose, Aug. 28, 1960; children: Julia, Claudia AB, Columbia U., 1958; JD, Harvard U., 1961; postgrad., U. Bombay, India, 1961-62; cert., London (Eng.) Sch. Econs., 1957. Bar: Mass. 1962, N.Y. 1983. With Hale and Dorr, Boston, 1962—, sr. ptnr., 1972-2000; of counsel Wilmer, Cutler, Pickering, Hale and Dorr LLP, Boston, 2000—. Co-chmn. Speech-Tech., NYC, 1987; instr. in law Boston U., 1963-65, bd. trustees Boston Five Cents Savs. Bank, 1978-83, bd. advisors, 1983-88; adj. prof. internat. law Tufts U. Fletcher Sch. Law and Diplomacy, 1999—; lectr. Fin. Times (UK), Instnl. Investors, New Eng. Law Inst., Mass. Soc. CPAs; vis. scholar Green Coll., Oxford U., 2004— Chmn. Mass. Comty. Devel. Fin. Corp., 1976-82; pres. Cambridge Ctr. for Adult Edn., 1985-88; bd. dirs. Boston Psychoanalytic Soc. and Inst., 1994—. Fulbright scholar, 1961-62. Fellow Am. Bar Found.; mem. ABA, Internat. Bar Assn., Mass. Bar Assn., Boston Bar Assn. (chmn. internat. law sect. 1998-2001), Harvard Faculty Club, Mount Auburn Club. Home: 32 Hubbard Park Rd Cambridge MA 02138-4731 Office: Wilmer Cutler Pickering Hale & Dorr LLP 60 State St Boston MA 02109-1816 Office Phone: 617-526-6735. Business E-Mail: donald.gonson@wilmerhale.com.

GONTHIER, CHARLES DOHERTY, retired judge; b. Montreal, Que., Can., Aug. 1, 1928; m. Mariette Morin; children: Georges, François, Pierre, Jean-Charles, Yves. BA, Paris Coll. Stanislas, Montreal, 1947; BCL, McGill U., Montreal, 1951, LLD (hon.), 1990; DHC (hon.), U. Montreal, 2002; DU (hon.), U. Ottawa, 2003. Queen's counsel, 1971. Atty. Hackett, Mulvena and Laverty, Montreal, 1952-57, Laing, Weldon, Courtois, Clarkson, Parsons, Gonthier & Tetrault (now McCarthy & Tetrault), Montreal, 1957-74; judge Superior Ct. Que., Montreal, 1974-88, Que. Ct. Appeal, Montreal, 1988-89, Supreme Ct. Can., Ottawa, 1989—2003; ret., 2003; of counsel McCarthy Tetrault LLP, 2004. Sec. Montreal br. Can. Inst. Internat. Affairs, 1957-58; bd. dirs. Montreal Legal Aid Bur., 1959-69; pres. Jr. Bar Montreal, 1960-61; pres. jr. bar sect. Can. Bar Assn., 1961-62, sec. Que. div., 1963-64; bd. dirs. Montreal Bar, 1961-62; mem. Com. on Bldg. Contracts Que. Civil Code Rev., 1969-72; mem. com. on discipline Bar Que., 1973-74; chmn. Commn. for Nat. Judges, 1st World Conf. on Independence of Justice, Montreal, 1983; pres. Can. Inst. for Adminstrn. Justice, 1986-87; pres. Can. Judges Conf., 1988-89. Chmn. Assn. Anciens Coll. Stanislas, Montreal, 1954-55; hon. sec. Montreal Mus. Fine Arts, 1961-76; bd. dirs. McCord Mus. Can. History, Montreal, 1976-89; chmn. bd. Coll. Stanislas, Montreal, 1984-90; mem. Internat. Commn. Jurists. Decorated knight L'Ordre des Palmes académiques (France). Fellow Am. Coll. Trial Lawyers (hon.); mem. Univ. Club (Montreal), Can. Bar Assn. (pres. jr. bar sect. 1961-62, sec. Que. divsn. 1963-64), Can. Inst. Adminstrn. Justice (pres. 1986-87), Assn. Henri Capitant, Que. Assn. Comparative Law. Roman Catholic. Office: McCarthy Tetrault LLp 1170 Peel St 5th Fl Montreal PQ Canada H3B 4S8 Office Phone: 514-397-4165. E-mail: cdgonthier@mccarthy.com.

GONTHIER, MISTY, psychologist; b. San Bernandino, Calif., Oct. 1, 1977; d. Hugh Eugene and Patricia Anne Gonthier. BA in Psychology, Calif. State U., 1999; EdS, U. Denver, 2004. Lic. spl. svcs. CDE, CO. Victim advocate San Bernendino Sexual Assault Svcs., 1998—2000; tchr. Fisher Early Learning Ctr., Denver, 2000—03; sch. psychologist Centennial BOCES, Greeley, Colo., 2004—. Mem.: Nat. Assn. Sch. Psychologists.

GONTIER, JEAN ROGER, medicine and physiology educator; b. Lens, France, Mar. 8, 1927; s. Paul Maurice and Marie Jeanne (Tricoche) G.; m. Sylviane Prevost, Dec. 8, 1968; children: Sylviane, Yannick, Jean-Yves, Yann. BA magna cum laude, Arras Coll., France, 1944; BS summa cum laude, Etampes Coll., Paris, 1946; MS magna cum laude, Coll. Scis., Paris, 1948; MD summa cum laude, Sch. Medicine, Paris, 1965. Prof., chair dept. physiology UGSEL, Paris, 1957-62; instr. in medicine Sch. Medicine, Paris, 1960-65; resident Hop Cochin, Paris, 1964; assoc. prof. medicine Hop Bicetre, Paris, 1966; dir. physiology Sch. Medicine, Reims, 1966-68; prof. physiology U. Montreal, 1970-78; cons. in internal medicine Paris, 1979—. Prof. physiology Bicetre U. Hosp., Paris, 1967-68; cons. editor various pubs., N.Y.C., 1975-78, Paris, 1969-73, Montreal, 1986-89; rsch. in diving physiology in man. Author: (textbooks) Hormones, Nervous System and Digestion, 1968, Respiration, 1977, Digestion, 1969, Textbook of Medical Physiology, 1980, Human Physiology, 1989, Biochemistry For Medical Students, 2000, Physiology for Medical Students, 2001, Human Genetics, 2001, Biochemistry, 2004, Organic Chemistry, 2004. Recipient Silver medal Sch. Medicine, Paris, 1965. Mem. AAAS, Am. Physiol. Soc. (teaching physiology/respiration/cardiovascular/history sects.), Can. Physiol. Soc., N.Y. Acad. Scis., French Physiol. Soc., Cercle de l'Etrier Club, La Baule Country Club. Roman Catholic. Achievements include research in diving physiology in man. Avocation: sailing. Home and Office: 133 Rue Michel Ange F75016 Paris France Office Phone: 0146512505. Personal E-mail: jean.gontier@wanadoo.fr.

GONWA, THOMAS ARTHUR, nephrologist, educator; b. Chgo., Sept. 2, 1949; s. George Joseph and Darline (Sears) G.; m. Mary Alice Westrick, Sept. 28, 1974; children: Claire, Charlotte. BS, St. Joseph's Coll., 1971; MD, U. Ill., 1975. Diplomate Am. Bd. Internal Medicine, Am. Bd. Nephrology, Am. Bd. Critical Care Medicine. Resident Bowman Gray, Winston-Salem, N.C., 1975-78, renal fellow, 1978-80; postdoctoral rsch. fellow U. Calif., San Francisco, 1980-82, instr., 1982-83; asst. prof. U. Iowa, Iowa City, 1983-86; pvt. practice, Dallas, 1986-2001; assoc. dir. transplant Baylor U. Med. Ctr., Dallas, 1987-2001; med. dir. renal and pancreas transplant Mayo Clinic, Jacksonville, Fla., 2001—; prof. medicine Mayo Med. Sch., 2001—. Clin. assoc. prof. medicine U. Tex. Southwestern Med. Sch., 1993-2001. Assoc. editor Jour. Immunology, 1985-86; editl. bd. Transplantation, Graft, Clin. Transplantation; contbr. more than 150 articles to profl. jours. Recipient rsch. award VA, 1984. Fellow ACP; mem. Am. Soc. Transplant Physicians (sec., treas. 1990-93, pres. 1994-95, Upjohn award 1983, Sr. Achievement award, 2005), Am. Soc. Nephrology, Am. Assn. Immunologists, Transplantation Soc., Nat. Kidney Found. (head coun. transplantation 1998-99, bd. dirs. 1998-99, chm. pub. policy com. 1999-2001).

GONYA, JEFFREY KEENAN, lawyer; b. Manchester, N.H., Mar. 15, 1961; m. Ann Martin; 1 child, Caroline P. BA with high honors, U. Va., 1983, JD, 1986. Bar: Ga. 1986, Md. 1988. Assoc. O'Callaghan, Saunders and Stumm, Atlanta, 1986-87; assoc. then ptnr., taxation, trusts & estates Venable LLP (formerly Venable, Baetjer and Howard), Balt., 1987—. Trustee Balt. Bar Found., 1993—. Trustee Mpala Wildlife Found., Inc., Balt., 1992—, mem. Reading, Runs & Ripken Com., Balt. Reads, Inc., Fund Mgmt. Com., Ctr. Health & Population Rsch. Mem. ABA (mem. tax section com. on estate & gift taxes), Md. Bar Assn., Bar Assn. Balt. City (sec.-treas. young lawyers sect. 1991-92, chmn.-elect 1992-93, chmn. 1993-94). Office: Venable LLP 1800 Two Hopkins Plz Baltimore MD 21201-2930 Office Phone: 410-244-7507. Office Fax: 410-821-0147. Business E-Mail: jkgonya@venable.com.

GONZALES, ALBERTO R., United States attorney general, former state supreme court justice; b. San Antonio, Tex., Aug. 4, 1955; s. Pablo and Maria Gonzales; m. Rebecca Turner; 3 children. Student, U.S. Air Force Acad., 1975-77; BA, Rice U., 1979; JD, Harvard U., 1982. Bar: Tex. Ptnr. Vinson & Elkins, LLP, Houston, 1982-95; gen. counsel Gov. George W. Bush, 1995-97; sec. state State of Tex., 1997—99; justice Supreme Ct of Texas, Austin, Tex., 1999—2000; asst. to Pres. & gen. counsel The White House, Washington, 2001—05; atty. gen. US Dept. Justice, Washington, 2005—. Adj. prof. U. Houston Law Ctr. Trustee Tex. Bar Found., 1996-99; mem. Tex. Jud. Dists. Bd., 1996-97; bd. dirs. United Way of Tex. Gulf Coast, 1993-94; pres. Leadership Houston, 1993-94; chair Commn. for Dist. Decentralization of Houston Ind. Sch. Dist., 1994; mem. com. on undergrad. admissions Rice U., 1994; chair Rep. Nat. Hispanic Assembly of Houston, 1992-94; pres. Houston Hispanic Forum, 1990-92; chair adv. com. Tex. Real Estate Ctr., 1989-90; bd. dirs. Big Bros. and Sisters, Houston, 1985-91, Cath. Charities, Houston, 1989-93, others. With USAF, 1973—75. Recipient Commitment to Leadership award United Way, 1993, Hispanic Salute award Houston Metro Ford Dealers, 1989, Presdntl. Citiation, State Bar of Tex., 1997, Latino Lawyer of the Year, Hispanics Nat. Bar Assn, 1999, Harvard Law Sch. Assn. award, 2002, Good Neighbor award, US-Mex. C.of C., 2003, Presdntl. award, US Hispanic CofC and League of United Latin Am. Citizens; named one of Five Outstanding Young Texans, Tex. Jaycess, 1994, Outstanding Young Lawyer of Tex., Tex. Young Lawyers Assn., 1992; inducted into the Hispanics Scholarship Fund Alumni Hall of Fame, 2003; named Disting. Alumnus of Rice U., Assn. of Rice Alumni; named one of 25 Most Influential Hispanics, Time Mag., 2005. Mem. Houston Bar Assn., Houston Hispanic Bar Assn. (pres., 1990-91), State Bar Tex. (bd. dirs. 1991-94), Am. Law Inst. Republican. Office: US Dept Justice Robert F Kennedy Bldg 10th St & Constitution Ave NW Rm 5111 Washington DC 20530*

GONZALES, GREGORY, music educator; s. Federico and Ann Gonzales. Mus M, U. of Tex., 1997. Jazz and blues saxophonist, vocalist The Mighty Houserockers et. al., San Antonio, 1965—; woodwind instr. Judson Sch. Dist., Converse, Tex., 1993—2000; music instr. St. Philip's Coll., San Antonio, 2000—. Composer (musician): (saxophone quartet) D Sonata; composer: (song cycle for soprano, flute, and piano) Canciónes de Jiménez, (electronic composition) At the Weasel Jamboree. Mem.: Am. Fedn. of Musicians. Avocations: hiking, nature photography.

GONZALES, RICHARD JOSEPH, lawyer; b. Tucson, Mar. 5, 1950; s. Diego D. and Helen O. (Olivas) G.; children: Adrianne, Laura. BA, U. Ariz., 1972, JD, 1975. Bar: Ariz. 1976, U.S. Dist. Ct. Ariz. 1976, U.S. Ct. Appeals 1977, U.S. Supreme Ct. 1993. Asst. pub. defender Pima County Pub. Defenders Office, Tucson, 1976-77; dep. atty. criminal div. Pima County Atty.'s Office, Tucson, 1977-80; ptnr. Gonzales & Villarreal, P.C., Tucson, 1980-96, The Gonzales Law Firm, Tucson, 1997—. Assoc. instr. bus. law Pima Community Coll.,Tucson, 1977, criminal law, 1978-80; judge pro tem Pima County Superior Ct., 1983—; magistrate City of South Tucson, 1982-85; spl. magistrate City of Tucson, 1982-85; comn. appellate ct. appointments, 1991-95; sr. coun. Coll. Master Advocates and Barristers, 2002. Mem. Tucson Tomorrow, 1984-89, Citizen's adv. coun. Sunnyside Sch. Dist., 1986-88; chmn. com. Udall for Congress 2d Congl. Dist., United Way Hispanic Leadership Devel. Program, 1984-86, vice-chmn., 1983-84, chmn., 1984-85; bd. dirs. Girls Club of Tucson, Inc., 1980-81, Teatro Carmen, Inc., 1981-84, Sunnyside Devilaides, Inc., 1982-83, Alcoholism Coun. Tucson, 1982-83, Crime Resisters, 1984-85, La Frontera Ctr., Inc., 1985-96, Crime Prevention League, 1985-87; gen. counsel U. Ariz. Hispanic Alumni; bd. dirs. U. Ariz. Law Coll. Assn., 1984-95, Am.-Israel Friendship League, 1990—, Tucson Internat. Mariachi Conf., 1990—. Named one of Outstanding Young Men of Am. U.S. Jaycee's, 1980; recipient Vol. of Yr. award United Way Greater Tucson, 1985, Cmty. Svc. award Ariz. Minority Bar Assn., 1992, Citizen Svc. award U. Ariz. Hispanic Alumni, 1995, League United Latin Am. Citizen's F.B.I. Community Svcs. Award, 1996, human betterment award Roots & Wings, Inc., 1996, Centennial Achievement award U. Arizona Alumni Assn., 1998, Noche De Las Estrellas Award, Sunnyside High Sch., 2000; honoree State Bar Arizona One Hundred Women & Minority Lawyers, 2001. Fellow Ariz. Bar Found.; mem. ABA, Ariz. Bar Assn., Pima County Bar Assn., Assn. Trial Lawyers Am., Ariz. Trial Lawyers Assn. (bd. dirs.), Nat. Orgn. on Legal Problems of Edn., Supreme Ct. Hist. Soc., Univ. Ariz. Alumni Assn. (bd. dirs. 1988-91), Tucson 30, Phi Delta Phi. Lodges: Optimists (Optimist of Yr. 1981). Democrat. Roman Catholic. Office: The Gonzales Law Firm 3501 N Campbell Ave Ste 104 Tucson AZ 85719-2032 Office Phone: 520-327-1121. Business E-Mail: rick@gonzaleslaw.com.

GONZALES, RICHARD ROBERT, counselor; b. Palo Alto, Calif., Jan. 12, 1945; s. Pedro and Virginia (Ramos) G.; m. Jennifer Ayres; children: Lisa Dianne, Jeffrey Ayres. AA, Foothill Coll., 1966; BA, San Jose (Calif.) State U., 1969; MA, Calif. Poly. State U., San Luis Obispo, 1971; grad., Def. Info. Sch., Def. Equal Opportunity Mgmt. Inst. Lic. marriage family child counselor, Calif.; cert. counselor Nat. Bd. Cert. Counselors. Counselor student activities Calif. Poly. State U., San Luis Obispo, 1969-71, instr. ethnic studies, 1970-71; counselor Ohlone Coll., Fremont, Calif., 1971-72, coord. coll. readiness, 1971; counselor De Anza Coll., Cupertino, Calif., 1972-78, mem. cmty. spkrs. bur., 1975-78; counselor Foothill Coll., Los Altos Hills, Calif., 1978—, mem. cmty. spkrs. bur., 1978—. Instr. Def. Equal Opportunity Mgmt. Inst., 1984-96; mem. U. Calif. C.C. Counselor Adv. Com., 1998—. Mem. master plan com. Los Altos (Calif.) Sch. Dist., 1975-76; vol. worker, Chicano cmtys., Calif.; active mem. Woodside (Calif.) Recreation Commn. Commd. officer Calif. Army N.G., now ret. Adj. Gen. Corps, USAR. Masters and Johnson fellow. Mem. ACA, Am. Coll. Counseling Assn., Calif. Assn. Marriage and Family Therapists, Calif. C.C. Counselor Assn. (former pres.), Calif. Assn. Counseling and Devel. (former pres. Hispanic Caucus, former pres.), Calif. Assn. for Humanistic Edn. and Devel. (former pres.), Calif. Assn. for Multi-Cultural Counseling, Res. Officers Assn., La Raza Faculty Assn. Calif. C.C., Nat. Career Devel. Assn., Phi Delta Kappa, Chi Sigma Iota. Republican. E-mail: rrgincal@aol.com.

GONZALES, RON, mayor, former county supervisor; b. San Francisco; m. Alvina Gonzales; 3 children: Miranda, Rachel, Alejandra. BA in Community Studies, U. Calif., Santa Cruz. Formerly with Sunnyvale (Calif.) Sch. Dist., City of Santa Clara, Calif.; then human resource mgr. Hewlett-Packard Co.; market program mgmt. cons. state and local govts.; mem. city coun. City of Sunnyvale, 1979-87, mayor, 1982, 87; mem. bd. suprs. Santa Clara County, 1989-96; edn. program mgr. Hewlett Packard Co., 1996-98; mayor San Jose, Calif., 1999—. Bd. chair, 1993; bd. transit suprs. Santa Clara County, 1989—; bd. dirs. Joint Venture: Silicon Valley, The Role Model Program, Bay Area Biosci. Ctr., Am. Leadership Forum, Santa Clara County. Office: City Hall Office Mayor 801 N 1st St Rm 600 San Jose CA 95110-1704*

GONZALES-DAY, KENNETH ROBERT, artist, educator; b. Santa Clara, Calif., Nov. 11, 1964; s. Peter Jose and Nancy Dea (Mabbitt) Gonzales. BFA, Pratt Inst., 1987; MA, CUNY, N.Y.C., 1990; postgrad., Whitney Mus. Am. Art, 1993; MFA, U. Calif., Irvine, 1995. Preparator New Mus. Contemporary Art, N.Y.C., 1985-90, Am. Craft Mus., N.Y.C., 1985-90; asst. curator Bklyn. Mus., 1987-88; personal asst. Charles Cowles Gallery, N.Y.C., 1990-92; devel. officer Alternative Mus., N.Y.C., 1991-92, Pub. Art Fund, N.Y.C., 1993; assoc. prof. and art and art history dept. chmn. Scripps Coll., Claremont, Calif., 1995—. Mem. adv. bd. L.A. Freewaves, 1997-1998; mem. artist adv. bd. Mcpl. Art Gallery, Barnsdall Art Park, L.A., 1998-2000, residency, Latino Iniatives Program, Smithsonian Inst., 2003, Rockefeller Found. Bellagio Study Ctr., 2002. Author: St. James Press Gay and Lesbian Almanac, 1998; contbr. articles to profl. jours.; works exhibited at Christine Rose Gallery, N.Y.C., 1996, White Columns, N.Y.C., 1996, Post, L.A., 1997, Barnsdall Art Park-Mcpl. Gallery, L.A., 1998, L.A. County Mus. of Art, Head Mus. Phoenix, Artists Space N.Y.C., Laguna Art Mus. Laguna, Calif., San Fransico Camerwork, San Fransico, Calif. Recipient New Genre Individual Artist award NEA Western States Art Fedn., 1996; faculty rsch. grantee Scripps Coll., Claremont, 1992-2002; Graves award in the Humanities, 2002. Mem. Soc. for Photographic Edn. (co-chair), Coll. Art Assn. Office: Scripps Coll 1030 Columbia Ave Claremont CA 91711-3986

GONZALEZ, ANTONIO, academic administrator, title company executive; b. Edinburg, Tex., Mar. 14, 1943; s. Manuel Gonzalez and Natalia Torres; m. Elma De Luna, Oct. 10, 1975; 1 child, Julissa Priscilla. BA, U. Md., Balt., 1971; MA, U. Tenn., 1973; JD, Miles Coll., 1979. Law clk. Crain Caton James & Oberwetter, Houston, 1979-81; instr. U. Houston, 1981-83, asst. dir., 1983-86; instr. Houston C.C., 1982—85, 1995, 2001—02; assoc. dir. No. Ill. U., Dekalb, 1986-88; adminstr. Prairie View (Tex.) A&M U., 1988—96; instr. Houston Internat. U., 1988-89, pres., CEO, 1989-90, Am. Fidelity Mortgage & Title Co., Houston, 1992-95; instr. North Harris Coll., Houston, 1994-95, Wharton County Jr. Coll., 1996—2002, Tomball Coll., 2001—02, Montgomery Coll., 2002—03, Tex. So. U., 2003. Mem. adv. com. Houston C.C., 1994-95. Editor: Mexican-American Musicians, 1987; mem. editl. bd. Jour. Minority Issues, 1993-94. Chair tng. and devel. LULAC Dist. 18, Houston, 1994-96; dir. Inst. Chicano Culture, Houston, 1995; mem. SER Jobs for Progress, Houston, 1994-96; Dem. candidate Tex. Ho. Reps. Dist. 130, 1994; mem. Tejano Ctr. for Cmty. Concerns. With USAF, 1966-70, Vietnam. Named Man of Yr. LULAC, Ill., 1987. Mem.: VFW, AAUP, Tex. Assn. Coll. and Univ. Student Pers. Adminstrs., Nat. Bar Assn., Tex. Fgn. Lang. Assn., Tex. Assn. Mortgage Brokers, Tex. C.C. Tchrs. Assn., Tex. Assn. Coll. Admissions Counselors, Tex. Assn. Chicanos in Higher Edn., Am. Hist. Assn., Air Force Assn., Am. Legion, Vietnam Vets. Assn., Delta Theta Phi, Phi Delta Kappa. Roman Catholic. Avocations: writing, research. Home: 16614 Dounreay Dr Houston TX 77084-3410 Office: 3100 Cleburne St Houston TX 77004 Office Phone: 713-313-7665. Business E-Mail: Amerfideli@aol.com.

GONZALEZ, ANTONIO, voter registration project executive; Undergraduate study, Univ. Calif., San Diego, 1975—77; BA, Univ. Tex., San Antonio, 1981; graduate study, Univ. Calif., Berkeley, 1981—82. Organizer Southwest Voter Registration Edn. Project, San Antonio, 1984—90, pres., 1994—; policy prog. dir. William C. Velasquez Inst., 1990—94, pres., 1994—. Bd. dir. Ctr. for Voting & Democracy. Commentator Tavis Smiley Show, Nat. Public Radio, host weekly radio show, Strategy Session, KPFK radio, LA. Office: Southwest Voter Registration Edn Project 2d Fl 206 Lombard St San Antonio TX 78226*

GONZALEZ, APRIL LEE, literature and language educator; b. Somerville, N.J., Mar. 18, 1964; d. Robert Lewis Krase and Arleen Frances Brady; m. Jose Ignacio Gonzalez, Apr. 26, 1987; children: Christian Lee, Justin Evan, Cody Shane, Jordan Ryan. BA, Montclair State Coll., 1987; MA in Tchg., Marygrove Coll., 2004. Advisor freshman class South Brunswick High Sch., Monmouth Junction, NJ, 1987—88, tutor SAT, 1990, adv. lit. mag., 1991—94, mentor and coop. tchr., 1996—; mentor tchg. coord. South Brunswick Bd. Edn., 2004—; tchr. English South Brunswick High Sch, 1987—88, 1990—. Mem. task force quality tchg. N.J. State Dept. Edn., Trenton, 2005—, mem. task force mentoring, 2003—. Contbr.: Differentiated Instruction in the English Classroom, 2003, When Text Meets Text, 2005. Mem. Am. Diabetes Assn., Alexandria, Va., 2003—; vol. Providence Presbyn. Ch., Burlington, NJ, 2004—. Recipient Outstanding Tchr. award, U. Phila., 1999. Mem.: NEA, ASCD, Southwest Brunswick Edn. Assn. (rep. 1998—2001), Nat. Coun. Tchrs. English, Phi Kappa Phi, Kappa Delta Pi, Psi Chi (pres.). Independent. Avocations: reading, aerobics, cross stitch, card stamping, crocheting. Home: 37 Canidae St Burlington NJ 08016 Office: South Brunswick High Sch 750 Ridge Rd Monmouth Junction NJ 08852

GONZALEZ, ARTHUR PADILLA, artist, educator; b. Sacramento, July 22, 1954; s. John and Rita (Padilla) G.; m. Christine Carol Ciavarella, Feb. 11, 1988; stepchild, Nick Port. BA, Calif. State U., Sacramento, 1977, MA, 1979; MFA, U. Calif., Davis, 1981. Vis. artist La. State U., Baton Rouge, 1982-83, U. Ga., Athens, summer 1984, R.I. Sch. Design, Providence, 1985; asst. prof. U. Calif., Davis, 1985-86, Berkeley, 1987-88; vis. artist, instr. San Francisco Art Inst., 1990-91; assoc. prof. art Calif. Coll. Arts, Oakland, 1991—. Juror Sacramento Met. Arts Commn., 1994-95. One-person shows include Sharpe Gallery, N.Y.C., 1984, 85, 86, 88, Phyllis Kind Gallery, N.Y.C., 1995, John Elder Gallery, N.Y.C., 1999, 2002. Recipient awards Nat. Endowment for Arts, 1982, 84, 86, 90, Virginia Groot award, 1997. Democrat. Avocation: polynesian dance. Home: 1713 Versailles Ave Alameda CA 94501-1650 Office: Calif Coll Arts & Crafts 5212 Broadway Oakland CA 94618-1426 Office Phone: 510-594-3617. Business E-Mail: art@arthurgonzalez.com. E-mail: windeater@alamedanet.net.

GONZALEZ, CALEB, ophthalmologist, educator; b. Humacao, P.R., May 1, 1929; s. Carlos Pilar and Julia (Mercado) Gonzalez; m. Flora Caroline Harrison, June 29, 1956; children: Lisa Gay, Patricia Jo, Sandra Pilar, Erica Irene, Kristie Juliana. BA, Inter Am. U., San German, P.R., 1949; MD, U. P.R., 1954; MA, Yale U., 1981. Intern Wayne County Gen. Hosp., Eloise, Mich., 1954—55; resident in ophthalmology Kings County Hosp., Bklyn., 1959—62; fellow pediat. ophthalmology Bellevue Hosp., NYC, 1962—64; assoc. prof. ophthalmology U. P.R., San Juan, PR, 1971—76; chmn. dept. ophthalmology, chief ophthalmology Yale U., New Haven, 1977—96, prof. ophthalmology, 1981—. Mem. editl. bd.: Jour. Pediat. Opthalmology, 1977—85; author: Strabismus and Ocular Motility, 1983. Pres. local chpt. Exch. Club, San Juan, 1974; active Congregational Ch., Woodsridge, Conn.,

1976—. Lt. comdr. USNR. Recipient Disting. Alumnus award, Inter Am. U., 1983. Fellow: Am. Bd. Ophthalmologists, Am. Assn. Pediat. Ophthalmology (Honor award 1997), Am. Acad. Ophthalmology (Honor award 1992); mem.: Alpha Omega Alpha. Republican. Avocation: tennis. Office: Yale Sch Medicine 330 Cedar St New Haven CT 06520

GONZALEZ, CARMEN GRACIA, law educator; b. Havana, Cuba, Jan. 6, 1962; d. Francisco and Carmen (Bonachea) Gonzalez. BA, Yale U., New Haven, Conn., 1985; JD, Harvard Law Sch., Cambridge, Mass., 1988. Bar: Calif. 1988, DC 1989. Law clerk to Judge Thelton E. Henderson U.S. Dist. Ct. (no. dist.) Calif., San Francisco, 1988-89; atty. Pillsbury, Madison & Sutro, San Francisco, 1989-91, Pacific Gas & Electric Co., San Francisco, 1991-94; asst. regional counsel U.S. EPA, San Francisco, 1994—98; with ABA Ctrl. and East European Law Initiative, Ukraine, 1996-97; prof. Sch. Law Seattle U., 1999—. Fellow, Supreme Ct., 2004—05; Fulbright scholar, Argentina, 1998. Mem.: ABA, Am. Soc. Internat. Law, Hispanic Nat. Bar Assn. Office: Seattle Univ School Law 900 Broadway Seattle WA 98122 Office Phone: 206-398-4067. E-mail: gonzalez@seattleu.edu.

GONZALEZ, CHARLES A., congressman; b. San Antonio, Tex., May 5, 1945; s. Henry B. and Bertha G.; m. Becky Whetstone; children: Leo Gonzalez, Benjamin and Casey Schmidt. BA in Govt., U. Tex., Austin, 1969; JD, St. Mary's Sch. Law, San Antonio, 1972. 5th grade tchr. Kindred Elem. Sch. So. San Antonio Sch. Dist.; pvt. practice San Antonio, 1972-82; mcpl. ct. judge; county ct. at law judge, 1983-87; dist. judge, 1989-97; mem. U.S. Congress from 20th Tex. dist., Washington, 1999—; mem. banking and fin. svcs. com, small bus. com. Appointed regional whip for the Dem. Caucus; elected v.p. freshman class for 106th Congress; as mem. of Congl. Hispanic Caucus, named chair of Census Task Force; co-chair Census Task Force for Dem. Caucus Bd. dirs. Arthritis Found., Literacy Coun., YMCA Metroboard, Camp Fire Girls, March of Dimes, Easter Seals. Democrat. Achievements include being recognized as one of the highest rated trial judges; responsible for introducing the latest in tech. into the courtroom and streamlining the dockets; earned reputation as ardent mediator. Office: 327 Cannon Ho Office Bldg Washington DC 20515-4320*

GONZALEZ, EDUARDO, language educator, interpreter, translator; s. Mario S. Gonzalez and Rosa D. Muñiz; m. Janet R. Meyer; children: Sandra, Edward J., Jane Marie, Margaret Rose. Lic. summa cum laude, Havana U., 1977; PhD, Linguistic U., Moscow, 1986. Cert. tchr. English for speakers of ther langs. Havana, 1970, fed. US interpreter Adminstrv. Office of Cts., 1999. Lang. prof. and interpreter-translator Fgn. Lang. Coll., Havana, Cuba, 1970—88; nat. and internat. interpreter, 1972—87; ct. and med. interpreter Miami-Dade County, Fla., 1992—99; prof. langs., transl. and interpreting U. Nebr., Kearney, 2001—, dir. transl.-interpreting program, 2001—05; guest prof. U. Guyana, Georgetown, 1987. Contbr. tching. manuals and dictionary. Blood donor ARC, Kearney, 2001—05. Mem.: Nat. Assn. Judiciary Interpreters. Office: U Nebr Thomas Hall 215 Kearney NE 68849-1310 Office Phone: 308-865-8536. Business E-Mail: gonzalezel@unk.edu.

GONZALEZ, EDWARD CHARLES, principal; b. San Francisco, Nov. 24, 1957; s. Alfonso Sanchez and Mercedes Baeza Gonzalez; m. Barbara G. Council, Mar. 25, 1995; children: Phillip Edward Miller, Amy Denise Byrne, Miranda Mercedes, Alana Marie, Selena Angelica. BA in Polit. Sci., Calif. State U., Fresno, 1981, MA in Ednl. Adminstrn., 2000. Tchr. 6th & 8th grades Dixieland Sch., Madera, Calif., 1982—95; tchr. 6th grade Ripperdan Sch., 1995—97; vice prin. Martin Luther King Jr. Mid. Sch., 1997—98, prin., 1998—2004, John Adams Elem. Sch., 2004—. Mem. Madera Adminstrv. Team. Composer: Saudade, Ages and Ages Ago, Song Without Words; contbr. articles to profl. jours.; author: several poems and short stories. Mem. Second Take Choral Ensemble, Madera, 1991—. Recipient Nat. Adminstr. of Yr. award, Sch. Libr. Jour., 2003. Office: John Adams Elem Sch 1822 National Ave Madera CA Office Phone: 559-674-4631. Office Fax: 559-674-3867. E-mail: gonzalez_e@madera.k12.ca.us.

GONZALEZ, EUGENE ROBERT, investment banker; s. Eugenio Tomas and Alice Marie (Macdonald) Gonzalez-Mandiola. BA in Internat. Rels., Yale U., 1952; postgrad., Georgetown U., 1954; postgrad. sem. in advanced mgmt., Internat. Mgmt. Devel. Inst., Lausanne, Switzerland, 1967. Econ. officer Dept. Defense, Washington, 1954-57; project fin. officer Devel. Loan Fund (now AID), Washington, 1957-58; fin. mgr. RCA Internat., N.Y.C., 1958-61; fin. instns. specialist Interam. Devel. Bank, Washington, 1961-62, fin. officer, 1962-63, dep. regional rep. for Europe Paris, 1964; exec. v.p. Adela Investment Co., Luxembourg, 1964-74; pres., chief exec. officer Adelatec Mgmt. Cons. Co., 1969-72; mng. dir. Adela Investment Co., 1974-75, pres., chief exec. officer, 1975-76; adviser, regional coordinator Ibero Am. Morgan Stanley Internat., N.Y.C., 1977-89; sr. v.p., head internat. pvt. banking Barclays Bank, N.Y.C., 1989-91; mng. dir. Kidder, Peabody & Co., N.Y.C., 1992-94; pres. Quasar Capital Corp., S.A., 1995—. Author: International Sources of Financing, 1961. Served with U.S. Army, 1952-54. Mem. Nat. Com. on Am. Fgn. Policy, Internat. Assn. Fin. Planners, Am. Soc. Profl. Cons., Presidents Assn., Americas Soc., Spanish Inst., Met. Club (Washington), City Tavern Club (Washington), Brook Club (N.Y.C.), Racquet and Tennis Club (N.Y.C.), Yale Club (N.Y.C.), Pacific Union Club (San Francisco), Zeta Psi Soc. N.Am. Home: 165 E 66th St # 9K New York NY 10021-6132 Personal E-mail: egonz88888@aol.com.

GONZALEZ, GEORGE G., pastor; b. Miami, Nov. 21, 1939; s. David and Anna G. BS in Philosopy, Loyola U., 1963, MDiv in Theology, 1968. Assoc. pastor Cath. Ch., Miami, 1967-70, San Antonio, 1970-75; chaplain U.S. Army, various locations, 1976-96; pastor Our Lady of Lourdes, Columbus, Ga., 1996-98, St. Mary's Americus, Midland, Ga., 1998—. Recipient medal of honor U.S. Army, 1996. Republican. Roman Catholic. Avocations: tennis, swimming, soccer, reading, jogging. Office: St Mary's Americus 332 S Lee St Americus GA 31709-3916 Home: 4707 Winged Foot Way Columbus GA 31909-8006

GONZALEZ, GUILLERMO ENRIQUE, diplomat; b. Córdoba, Argentina, Dec. 30, 1942; m. Adriana Posse; six children. Degree in Polit. and Social Scis. Joined Fgn. Svc. Argentine Republic, 1965, promoted to rank amb. extraordinary and plenipotentiary, 1993; from mem. office dir. gen. policy to amb. Ministry Fgn. Affairs, Buenos Aires, 1965—99; amb. Argentina to Switzerland Ministry of Fgn. Affairs, Bern, Switzerland, 2002—. Office: Embassy of Argentine Rep Jungfraustrasse 1 3005 Bern Switzerland Fax: 202-332-3171.

GONZALEZ, HECTOR HUGO, nursing educator; b. Roma, Tex., Mar. 9, 1937; s. Amadeo Lorenzo and Carlotta (Trevino) G. BSN, Incarnate Word Coll., 1963; MSN, Cath. U. Am., 1966; PhD in Edn., U. Tex., 1974. RN, Tex. Staff nurse Santa Rosa Med. Ctr., San Antonio, 1962-65; asst. dir. nursing divsn. Incarnate Word Coll., San Antonio, 1968-72; prof., chmn. dept. nursing San Antonio Coll., 1972-92, dir. Ctr. for Assoc. Degree Edn. Rsch. and Svc., 1987-92, prof. and chmn. emeritus, 1993—. Cons. NIMH, 1973, FDA, 1989-93, mem. anesthesiology and respiratory devices panel, mem. dispute resolution panel, 2000—01; numerous ednl. instns. and hosps. in U.S., Mex., P.R., Kuwait; mem. Nat. Adv. Coun. on Alcohol Abuse and Alcoholism, 1976-80; mem. nat. adv. coun. nurses edn. and practice, 1992-96; mem. panel on nursing practice U.S. Pharmacopeia, 1985-2000. Contbr. articles to profl. jours.; peer reviewer Nursing Outlook, 1983, Advancing Clinical Care. Mem. legis. affairs adv. com. State Senator Glen Kothman, San Antonio, 1983; bd. dirs. Family Svcs. Assn. San Antonio; mem. multidisciplinary academic external com. U. Autonoma de Nuevo Leon, Mex., 1986-88. Capt. nurse corps U.S. Army, 1966-68. Recipient cert. of appreciation Citizens of Bexar County, San Antonio, 1970, Nat. Student Nurses Assn., 1977. Mem. ANA (mem. adv. bd. minority fellowship program 1976-80), Nat. Assn. Hispanic Nurses (pres. 1982-84, bd. dirs. 1995-97, CEO San Antonio chpt. 1998—, project dir. breast cancer tng. grant Am. Cancer Soc. and Nat. Assn. Hispanic Nurses 1992-96, historian 2000—), Nat. League for Nursing (bd. dirs. 1973-81). Democrat. Roman Catholic. Home: 114 Magnolia Dr San Antonio TX 78212-3115 Office Phone: 210-733-7460. Personal E-mail: hhgzz@cs.com.

GONZALEZ, IRMA ELSA, federal judge; b. Palo Alto, Calif., 1948; BA, Stanford U., 1970; JD, U. Ariz., 1973. Law clk. to Hon. William C. Frey US Dist. Ct. (Ariz. dist.), 1973-75; asst. U.S. atty. US Attys. Office Ariz., 1975-79, US Attys. Office (ctrl. dist.) Calif., 1979-81; trial atty. antitrust divsn. US Dept. Justice, 1979; assoc. Seltzer Caplan Wilkins & McMahon, San Diego, 1981-84; judge US Magistrate Ct. (so. dist.) Calif., 1984-91; ct. judge San Diego County Superior Ct., 1991-92; judge US Dist. Ct. (so. dist.) Calif., San Diego, 1992—, chief judge, 2005—. Adj. prof. U. San Diego, 1992; trustee Calif. Western Sch. Law; bd. visitors Sch. Law U. Ariz. Mem. Girl Scout Women's Adv. Cabinet. Mem. Lawyers' Club San Diego, Inns of Ct. Office: Edward J Schwartz US Courthouse 940 Front St Ste 5135 San Diego CA 92101-8911*

GONZALEZ, JOE FRED, JR., mathematical statistician, educator; b. San Antonio, Tex., Jan. 16, 1947; s. Joe Fred Gonzalez, Sr. and Gloria Rodriquez Gonzalez; m. Patricia Vaive Gonzalez, July 15, 1987; children: Joe Fred III, Jennifer Melanie Wasko, Michele Yvette Frates, Francesca Joelle. BS in Math., St. Mary's U., 1965—70; MS in Stats., The George Wash. U., 1979—81. Math. statistician Office of Rsch. and Methodology, Nat. Ctr. for Health Stats., Hyattsville, Md., 1972—. Adj. asst. prof. Montgomery Coll., Rockville, Md., 1985—99, U. of Md. U. Coll., Coll. Pk., Md., 1990—; presenter Nat. Acad. Scis., Washington, 2002—03; lead organizer, chair Discrete Math. and Theoretical Computer Sci. Working Group Rutgers U. Co-author (with Lester R. Curtin): (math. computer graph) The Bivariate Normal Distbn. (Rho=0.8) (Most Creative Use of Software, First Place-monochrome, 1986); co-author: (online modules) Modules for UMUC Online BMGT 230 Bus. Stats. Class; contbr. articles to profl. jours., papers to conf. procs. Pres. Richard Montgomery H.S. Band Parents Orgn., Rockville, Md., 1984—85; swim team rep. Hungerford Stoneridge Swim Club, Rockville, pres., 1984—86. Recipient Cited with biosketch and photo in a textbook Advanced Math., Precalculus with Discrete Math. and Data Analysis, Houghton Mifflin Co., 1992, U. Md. Univ. Coll. Tchg. Recognition award, 2005; scholar LULAC Scholarship Award, League of United Latin Am. Citizens, 1965. Mem.: Wash. Statis. Soc. (assoc.), Am. Statis. Assn. (assoc.; chair, com. on minorities in stats. 1992—95), Math. Assn. of Am. (assoc.), Am. Statis. Assn. (assoc.; mem. asa adv. com. on continuing edn. 1999—2002). Office: Nat Ctr for Health Statistics 3311 Toledo Rd Rm 3121 Hyattsville MD 20782 Office Phone: 301-458-4239. E-mail: jgonzalez@cdc.gov.

GONZALEZ, JOE MANUEL, lawyer; b. N.Y.C., Aug. 18, 1950; s. Reinaldo Fabregas and Mary Louise (Cermeno) G.; m. Ruia Jane Whiteside, Dec. 30, 1977; children: Matthew Ray, Jane Marie, Jeffrey Joseph, Joseph Manuel. BA, U. South Fla., 1972; JD, Gonzaga U., 1980; LLM in Taxation, Georgetown U., 1981. Bar: Fla. 1981, U.S. Tax Ct. 1983, U.S. Dist. Ct. (mid. dist.) Fla. 1984, U.S. Ct. Appeals (11th cir.) 1984, U.S. Supreme Ct. 1985. Atty. Gonzaga U. Legal Services, Spokane, Wash., 1980; mng. ptnr. Cotterill, Gonzalez, Hayes & Grantham, Fla., 1981-88, Cotterill & Grantham, Pa., 1982-92, Cotterill, Gonzalez & Grantham, Pa., Pa., 1992-93; prin. Joe M. Gonzalez, P.A., 1993—; atty. Hispanic Def. League, Tampa, Fla., 1982-90. Assoc. editor Gonzaga Law Rev. Spl. Report: Pub. Sector Labor Law, 1980. Mem. Sheriff's Hispanic Adv. Coun., Hillsborough County, Fla., 1982-93, City of Tampa Hispanic Adv. Coun., 1983—, chmn. 1993—, U. So. Fla. Hispanic Adv. Bd., 1999-2001; chmn. citizens adv. com. Hillsborough County Planning Commn., 1988-90; pres. Tampa Hispanic Heritage, Inc., 1985-93; founder Carnavale En Tampa, Inc., 1986-90; master of ceremonies Gasparilla Sidewalk Art Festival, 1988; mem. police chief's adv. com., 1988-93; sec. Hispanic Bus. Inst. Fla., Inc., 1988-93; dir. Housing and Edn. Alliance, 2001— . Mem. ABA, Fla. Bar Assn. (jud. nominating prodedures com. 1988-89), Hillsborough County Bar Assn., Assn. Trial Lawyers Am., Nat. Inst. for Trial Advocacy, Complete Census Count Com., Rotary, Phi Delta Phi. Democrat. Presbyterian. Home: 5801 Mariner St Tampa FL 33609-3411 Office: 304 S Willow Ave Tampa FL 33606-2147 Office Phone: 813-254-0797. E-mail: joegonzalez@aol.com.

GONZALEZ, JOSE ALEJANDRO, JR., federal judge; b. Tampa, Fla., Nov. 26, 1931; s. Jose A. and Luisa Secundina (Collia) G.; m. Frances Frierson, Aug. 22, 1956 (dec. Aug. 1981); children— Margaret Ann, Mary Frances; m. Mary Sue Copeland, Sept. 24, 1983 BA, U. Fla., 1952, JD, 1957; LLD, Nova Southeastern U., 1998. Bar: Fla. 1958, U.S. Dist. Ct. (so. dist.) Fla. 1959, U.S. Ct. Appeals 1959, U.S. Supreme Ct. 1963. Practice in, Ft. Lauderdale, 1958-64; claim rep. State Farm Mut., Lakeland, Fla., 1957-58; assoc. firm Watson, Hubert and Sousley, 1958-61, ptnr., 1961-64; asst. state atty. 15th Cir. Fla., 1961-64; cir. judge 17th Cir. Ft. Lauderdale, 1964-78, chief judge, 1969-70; assoc. judge 4th Dist. Ct. Appeals, West Palm Beach; U.S. dist. judge So. Dist. Fla., 1978—, sr. judge, 1996—. Bd. dirs. Arthritis Found., 1962-72; bd. dirs. Henderson Clinic Broward County, 1964-68, v.p., 1967-68. Served to 1st lt. AUS, 1952-54. Recipient Kupferman award Laymen's Nat. Bible Assn., 1991; named Broward County Outstanding Young Man, 1967, one of Fla.'s Five Outstanding Young Men, Fla. Jaycees, 1967, Broward Legal Exec. of Yr., 1978. Mem.: ABA, Broward County Bar, Fla. Bar Assn., Fed. Bar Assn., Am. Judicature Soc., Pittsfield Country Club, Fla. Blue Key, Kiwanian Club (pres. 1971—72), Lauderdale Yacht Club, Ft. Lauderdale Jaycees (dir. 1960—61), Phi Alpha Delta, Sigma Chi (Significant Sig). Democrat. Office: US Dist Ct 205 US Courthouse 299 E Broward Blvd Fort Lauderdale FL 33301-1944

GONZALEZ, MARY LOU, elementary school educator; b. Alice, Tex., Oct. 17, 1955; d. Jose Maria and Guadalupe Martinez; children: Christina Marie, Andrea Denise. AA, Del Mar Jr. Coll., 1976; BS, U. Tex., 1978; MS, Corpus Christi State U., 1986. Cert. reading specialist Tex. State Bd. Edn., 1989, elem. (grades 1-8) Tex. State Bd. Edn., 1978, elem. reading Tex. State Bd. Edn., 1978, Bilingual/ESL Tex. State Bd. Edn., 1979, elem. grades 1-8 Mo. State Bd. Edn., 1983, reading specialist k-12 Mo. State Bd. Edn., 1983. Tchr. 3d grade Gibson Elem. - Corpus Christi Ind. Sch. Dist., Tex., 1978—79; tchr. 6th grade Rogers Mid. Sch. - San Antonio Ind. Sch. Dist., 1980—81; tchr. 4th grade Fairview Elem. - Sch. Dist. Jennings, St. Louis, 1981—83; tchr. 1st and 2d grade Antilles Elem. - Antilles Consol. Sch. Sys., Fort Buchanan (San Juan), 1983—88; tchr. 1st and 4th grade Alvarez Elem. - McAllen Ind. Sch. Dist., Tex., 1988—91; tchr. kindergarten and 1st grade Hampton Oaks Elem. - Stafford County Pub. Schls., Va., 1992—94; tchr. 2d grade Howsman Elem. - Northside Ind. Sch. Dist., San Antonio, 1994—99, reading specialist, 1999—. Facilitator lang. arts Northside Ind. Sch. Dist. Howsman Elem., 1999—; coord. parent literacy Howsman Elem., 1999—; state trainer 3d grade reading acads. Svc. Ctr. - Region 20, 2002—03; curriculum adv. bd. Antilles Elem., 1983—88; primary early learning framework curriculum com. Northside Ind. Sch. Dist., San Antonio, 1995—97. Mem. Clark High Band Booster, San Antonio. Recipient Nat. Blue Ribbon Sch. Employee, Dept. Edn., Washington, 1999—2000. Mem.: Alamo Reading Coun., Tex. State Reading Assn., Internat. Reading Assn., Parent Tchr. Assn. Democrat. Roman Catholic. Avocations: reading, travel, scrapbooks, photography, gardening. Home: 6227 Stable Point San Antonio TX 78249 Office: Shirley J Howsman Elem Sch 11431 Vance Jackson San Antonio TX 78230 Office Phone: 210-397-2350. Personal E-mail: marylougonzalez@satx.rr.com. Business E-Mail: marylougonzalez@nisd.net.

GONZALEZ, NOEL H., investment company executive, small business owner; b. Arecibo, PR, Jan. 19, 1970; s. Willie H. Gonzalez Riviera and Maria Gonzalez Crespo. Student, Ridge Vocat. Tech. Sch., 1989, Tom Hen Ry Elec. Sch., 2000. CEO NG Elec. Co., Kissimmee, Fla., 1997—2003; pres. U-Save Repair Svc., Inc., Kissimmee, Fla., 2003—. Mem.: Am. Radio Relay League. Republican. Roman Catholic. Office: U-Save Repair Svc Inc 210 Capps Rd Lake Wales FL 33898

GONZALEZ, RAQUEL MARIA, pharmacist; b. Veguitas, Oriente, Cuba, June 1, 1952; d. Ernesto Esteban and Evora Cristina (Ramirez) G. BS in Biology, Ga. Coll., 1974; BS in Pharmacy, Mercer U., 1977. Registered pharmacist, Ga., Fla., Tenn.; registered pharmacist cons., Fla. Staff pharmacist Cobb Gen. Hosp., Austell, Ga., 1978, VA Hosp., Nashville, 1978-79, Decatur, Ga., 1979-81, Lewisburg (Tenn.) Community Hosp., 1981-89; pharmacist Pharmacy Staffing Svcs. Inc., Brentwood, Tenn., 1989—; chief pharmacist Super D Drug Store # 50, Fayetteville, Tenn., 1989-93; chief of pharmacy Fred's Discount Pharmacy, Lewisburg, Tenn., 1993—. Relief pharmacist Farmer's Market Pharmacy (Kroger), Nashville, 1989—. Mem. Tenn. Pharmacist Assn., Ducks Unltd., Atlanta Ski Club. Republican. Roman Catholic. Avocations: piano, white water rafting, skiing, snorkeling, gardening. Home: RR 1 Box 35 Belfast TN 37019-9801 Office: Fred's Discount Pharmacy 1800 Mooresville Hwy Lewisburg TN 37091-2010 Office Phone: 931-270-6775.

GONZALEZ, RICARDO, surgeon, educator; b. Buenos Aires, June 26, 1943; s. Salvador Maria and Clyde Alcira (Prevettoni) G.; children: Diego Andres, Carlos Ricardo. BA, Coll. Nat. San Isidro, 1959; MD, U. Buenos Aires, 1965. Diplomate Am. Bd. Urology. Resident in surgery Hosp. Mil. Ctr., Buenos Aires, 1966—68; intern in surgery U. Minn., Mpls., 1969—70, resident, med. fellow in urologic surgery, 1970—74, from instr. to prof. urology, 1974—85, prof. urology, 1985—94, prof. pediat., 1993—94; chief, pediat. urology Children's Hosp. of Mich., Detroit, 1994; prof. urology Wayne State U., Detroit, 1995—99; prof. urology and pediat., chief pediat. urology divsn. U. Miami /Jackson Meml. Hosp., Fla., 1999—2002; dir. pediat. urology fellowship A.I. du Pont Hosp. for Children, Wilmington, Del., 2002—; prof. urology Thomas Jefferson U., Phila., 2002—, pres., 2002. Pres. Pediat. Urology P.C., Detroit, 1995-2000; vis. prof. Harvard U., Cambridge, Mass., 1994, John Hopkins U., Balt., 1995, U. Washington, Seattle, 1995, U. Calif., San Francisco, 1996, Cornell U., N.Y., 1998, U. Montreal, 2000, McGill U., 2000, U. Vienna, Austria, 2003, Chinese U. Hong Kong, 2003, SUNY Upstate Med. Coll., Syracuse, 2003, U. Zurich, Switzerland, 2005, U. Belgrade, 2005; presenter in field. Contbr. over 300 articles to profl. jours., over 50 chpts. to books; editor 2 books. Am. Acad. Pediat. fellow, 1981, Nat. Kidney Found. rsch. fellow 1974-76; co-prin. investigator USPHS cancer grant 1976-78. Fellow Am. Acad. Pediat. (exec. sect. on urology com. 1995-98); mem. Am. Urol. Assn., Mex. Coll. Urology (hon.), Venezuelan Soc. for Spina Bifida, Argentine Confedn. Urology, Societé Internat. d'Urologie, Ibero-Am. Soc. Pediat. Urology (pres. 1995-98, Medal of Merit 2000), Soc. for Pediat. Urol. Surgeons (by invitation), European Soc. Paediat. Urology (hon.). Avocations: opera, music, language, reading, writing. Office: AI duPont Hosp for Children Dept Urology 1600 Rockland Rd Wilmington DE 19899 Office Phone: 302-651-5107. Business E-Mail: rgonzale@nemours.org.

GONZALEZ, RICHARD A., pharmaceutical executive; b. Jan. 21, 1954; B in BioChemistry, U. Houston; M in BioChemistry, U. Miami. Rsch. biochemist U. Miami Sch. Medicine; numerous positions in divsn. diagnostics Abbott Labs., Abbott Park, Ill., 1977—92, divisional v.p., gen. mgr., 1992—95, v.p. HealthSystems divsn., 1995—98, sr. v.p. hosp. products, 1998—2001, pres., COO med. products, 2001—. Mem. bd. dirs. Abbott Labs. Mem. bd. dirs. Lyric Opera Chgo., Shed Aquarium. Office: Abbott Labs 100 Abbott Park Rd Abbott Park IL 60064-6400

GONZALEZ, ROSE A-NAVARRO, artist; b. Granada, Nicaragua, May 22, 1936; d. Manuel Navarro and Candelaria (Guerrero) Martinez; m. Simeon Gonzalez, Oct. 15, 1959. Diploma, Nat. Inst. Orient, Granada, Nicaragua, 1956, Sch. Art and Design, N.Y.C., 1964, Abbey Sch. N.Y., 1972; postgrad., Art Student's League, N.Y.C., 1972-73. Group exhbns. include Empire Savs. Bank, N.Y.C., 1973, Mus. City of N.Y., 1977, 82, Cayman Gallery, 1977, New Rochelle Gallery, 1978, Los Sures Gallery, 1978, Bklyn. Mus. Gallery, 1979, Louis Aborns Arts for Living Ctr., 1979, Studio 54, 1983, Keanne Mason Gallery, N.Y.C., 1983, Queen's Coll., 1984, St. Sabastian Parish Ctr., 1991, Latino Open-Air and Cultural Festival, N.Y.C., 1992, SUNY, 1992, Agora Gallery, N.Y.C., 1993, Progress Gallery, N.Y.C., 1993-94, 98, Dist. Coun. 37, N.Y.C., 1994, 95, New Rochelle Pub. Libr., 1996, Goya Gallery, N.Y.C., 1997, Colombian Consulate, N.Y.C., 1997, Aguilar Libr., N.Y.C., 1997, Oller Campeche Gallery, 1997, N.Y.C., Taller Romano Gallery, Madrid, 1998, N.E. Hispanic Cath. Ctr., N.Y.C., 1999, Dic St. Coun. 37, N.Y.C., 1999, Hispanic Cath. Ctr., N.Y.C., 2000, Consulate Domican Republic, 2000, Ctrl. Pk. Gallery, N.Y.C., 2001, Fundtion Gallery, N.Y.C., 2001, Consulate Ecuador, N.Y.C., 2001, Hostus Cool, N.Y.C., 2001, Sant Peter's Ch., N.Y.C., 2001, Golden Ctr., N.Y.C., 2001, Golden Ctr., N.Y.C., 2001, Centro Cutural Latino, N.Y.C., 2001, Mus. Paterson N.J., 2001. Mem. coun. Eisenhower Commn., Rep. Nat. Com., Washington, 1995. Recipient spl. prize Friends of Puerto Rico; Comision awarded Hispana Pro-Obra Ruben Dario, 1999; recipient Medal of Freedom, 1999, Outstanding Artist and Designer of the 20th Century medal, award Nicaraguan Consultate, N.Y.C., named Rep. N.Y. as Republican of Yr., 2001, Cuidad de Ange Les award N.Y., 2001. Mem. Lions Club Internat. (v.p. 1995—, Melvin Jones award 1993-94). Republican. Roman Catholic. Home: 1121 Morrison Ave Bronx NY 10472-4235

GONZALEZ, RUBEN RENE, biochemist, researcher; s. Rafael Angel Gonzalez-Carabia and Maria del Rosario Perez-Rivera; m. Margarita Perla Ramos-Garcia, Dec. 2, 1996; children: Ruben Gonzalez-Ramos, Rene Gonzalez-Ramos, Frank Angel Gonzalez-Ramos. Biochemist, U. Havana, 1974, PhD, 1985. Scientist Nat. Inst. Endocrinology, Havana, Cuba, 1989—96; vis. scientist Boston Biomed. Rsch. Inst., Watertown, Mass., 2000—02, instr., 2002—; assoc. scientist Vincent Ctr. for Reproductive Biology Mass. Gen. Hosp., Boston, 2003—. Rschr. fellow in enzymology-microbiology Moscow Rsch. Inst. Food Sci., 1978—79; rsch. fellow enzymology-microbiology INSA, Toulouse, 1983—84; rsch. fellow immunoassay-reproductive hormones Karolinska Inst., Stockholm, 1989, U. Oulu, Finland, 1989—90; fellow in vitro fertilization technologies IVI-Madrid, 1999; rsch. fellow embryo implantation Inst. of Mother and Child Rsch. U. Chile, Santiago, 1996—2000; rsch. fellow embryo implantation U. Geneva, 1998; rsch. fellow embryo implantation IVI-Valencia U. Valencia, Spain, 1998; rsch. fellow embryo implantation U. Geneva, 1999; rsch. fellow embryo implantation IVI-Valencia U. Valencia, 1999; invited spkr. Internat. Symposium Contraceptive Rsch. IOM, NAS, 2003. Author: (sci. paper) Extracellular Matrix, ISSN 0268-1617, 17 (23), 1999 (Current Awareness Biomedicine, 1999), Revista IberoAmericana de Fertilidad XVII (4): 59-79, 2000 (Sci. Prize, 2000); contbr. articles to profl. jours. Sci. adviser, rev. com. WHO-Rockefeller Found. Initiative on Embryo Implantation Rsch., 2000—04; sci. reviewer CONRAD Twinning Program, 2003. CONRAD Grant, Leptin Peptide Antagonists, 2002—04. Mem.: Spanish Soc. Fertility (assoc. Serono Sci. prize XIII Nat. Congress 2000), Am. Soc. Reproductive Medicine (assoc.). Achievements include patents for Preimplantation Factor (Infertin Appln., No PCT/US02/20599); development of Novel inhibitors of leptin function (leptin peptide antagonists); discovery of Expression of leptin and leptin receptor by human and rabbit endometrium; research in Leptin role in embryo implantation. Office: Boston Biomed Rsch Inst 64 Grove St Watertown MA 02472 E-mail: gonzalezr@bbri.org.

GONZALEZ, TYWAN, professional basketball player; s. Brenda Joyce Simpson; m. Khush Issursing, Aug. 6, 2004. BBA, Savannah (Ga.) State U., 2001; MEd, Bowling Green (Ohio) State U., 2004; student, U. Mich., 2005—. Corp. staff human resources intern Weyerhaeuser Corp., Federal Way, Wash., 1997; intern field mgmt. Kmart Corp., Savannah, 1999; scholar Dr. Ronald E. McNair Achievement Program U. Tenn., Knoxville, Tenn., 2000; archivist asst. intern Ops. Support Command U.S. Army, Rock Island, Ill., 2002; grad. asst. Bowling Green (Ohio) State U., 2002—03; skill devel. specialist Wood County Bd. of Mental Retardation and Devel. Disabilities, Bowling Green, 2003—04; profl. player Atleticos de San German Profl. Basketball Team, San German, PR, 2004; rsch. assoc. Campus Diversity Initiative James Irvine Found., Claremont, Calif., 2004—, grad. asst. Dr. Ronald McNair Achievement Program, 2004—. Mem. minority mentor program Claremont (Calif.) Grad. U., 2004—05, mem. grad. student coun., 2004—05. Actor: (plays) That's Just My Baby's Daddy. Named Most Valuabe Player Men's Basketball, Savannah (Ga.) State U., 2000; recipient Computer Info. Sys. cert.,

Savannah (Ga.) State U. Coll. of Bus. Adminstrn., 2001, Men's BasketballSr. Academic award, Savannah (Ga.) State U., 2001; Presdl. scholar, 2000, Douglas and Ethel Pearce Endowed fellowship, Claremont Grad. U., 2004—05. Fellow: Epsilon Pi Tau; mem.: Assn. Info. Tech. Profls., Internat. Tech. Edn. Assn., Toledo Indsl. Recreation and Employee Svcs. Coun., Grad. Christian Fellowship Claremont Colleges, Black Grad. Student Assn. Personal E-mail: tywangonzalez@yahoo.com.

GONZALEZ, WILLIAM G., healthcare advisor; s. William G. and Blanche Irene; m. Shirley Ann Mos, Aug. 15, 1964; children: Dana Lynn, Liane Renee. BA, Rutgers U., 1964; MBA, Cornell U., 1966; cert., Sloan Inst. Hosp. Adminstrn., 1966; MPA, NYU, 1980. Bus. adminstr. U. Calif.-San Francisco Med. Ctr., 1966-68, asst. dir., various positions, 1968-74; dep. dir. Capital Dist. Psychiat. Ctr., Albany, N.Y., 1974-79; instr. Albany Med. Coll., 1974-79; adj. asst. prof. SUNY-Albany, 1978-79; dir. U. Calif.-Irvine Med. Ctr., Orange, 1979-85; sr. lectr. Grad. Sch. Mgmt. and Calif. Coll. Medicine, U. Calif., Irvine, 1980-85; bd. dirs. Hosp. Coun. So. Calif., 1983-85; pres., chief exec. officer Butterworth Health Corp. and Butterworth Hosp., Grand Rapids, Mich., 1985-99; pres., CEO Spectrum Health, Grand Rapids, 1999-2000; healthcare advisor Wm. Gonzalez & Assocs., Chgo., 2000—. Adj. prof. health svcs. adminstrn. Mich. State U. Coll. Human Medicine, 1985—; mem. gov.'s Task Force on Access to Health Care, 1987-89; mem. nursing task force Joint Commn. on Accreditation Health Care Orgns., 1988-90; trustee Mich. Hosp. Assn., 1990-96; chmn. M in Mgmt. adv. coun. Aquinas Coll., Grand Rapids, 1992-95; bd. dirs. Grand Rapids Area Med. Edn. Ctr., chmn., 1995-97; mem. accreditation coun. grad. med. edn., 1994-98, Am. Hosp. Assn., coordinating Com. on Med. Edn.; regent ACHE Area B., Mich., 1994-98. Bd. dirs. Grand Rapids Pub. Edn. Fund, 1993-99; bd. dirs. Old Kent Fin. Corp., 1994-2000; active Health Professions Coun., San Francisco, 1971-74; active Planned Parenthood-World Population, Alameda Calif. and San Francisco, 1972-74; mem. coun. of dels. sect. on met. hosps. Gov.'s Coun., 1989-92; mem. regional policy bd. AHA, 1990-93. Served with M.C. U.S. Army, 1961-64. William Stout scholar, 1964; Alfred P. Sloan scholar, 1964-65; N.Y. State Regents scholar, 1964-65; Rotary Internat. exchange fellow in hosp. adminstrn. Australia, summer 1982 Fellow: Accreditation Commn. on Ed. for Health Svc. Adminstrn., (staff cons. 2004—). Office: Wm Gonzalez & Assocs 500 N Michigan Ave Ste 300 Chicago IL 60611 Office Phone: 312-396-4088.

GONZALEZ-DEL-VALLE, LUIS TOMAS, Spanish language educator; b. Nov. 19, 1946; BA in Spanish cum laude, Wilmington Coll.-U. N.C., Wilmington, 1968; MA in Spanish and Spanish-Am. Lits., U. Mass., 1972; Phd in Spanish and Spanish-Am. Lits. five coll. coop. program, Amherst Coll., Hampshire Coll., Mt. Holyoke Coll., Smith Coll., U. Mass., 1972. Asst. prof. modern langs. Kans. State U., 1972-75, assoc. prof. modern langs., 1975-77; assoc. prof. modern langs. and lits. U. Nebr., Lincoln, 1977-79, prof. modern langs. and lits., 1979-86; prof. Spanish and Portuguese U. Colo., Boulder, 1986—, chmn. dept. Spanish and Portuguese, 1986-98, assoc. chair for grad. studies, 2003—04. Reading cons. South-Western Pub. Co., Inc., 1974, Eliseo Torres & Sons, 1974; dir. Ibero-Latin Am. Studies Ctr., 1987—; lectr. in field. Author: La nueva ficcion hispanoamericana a traves de M.A. Asturias y G. Garcia Marquez, 1972, La ficcion breve de Valle Inclán, 1990, El Canon: Reflexiones Sobre la Recepcion Literaria-Teatral, 1993, La canonización del Diablo: Baudelaire y la estética moderna en España, 2002, Quiroga's Viages, 2005; co-author: Luis Romero, 1979; gen. editor Anales de la literatura española contemporánea, 1975—, Siglo XX/20th Century, 1985—; editor: Jour. Spanish Studies: 20th Century, 1972—80, Studies in 20th Century Lit., 1975—79, Annual Bibliography of Post-Civil War Spanish Fiction, 1977—82, Ecos de Cuba, 1997; co-editor: La generacion de 1898 ante España, 1997; contbr. articles to profl. jours. Recipient Postdoctoral Rsch. award Coun. for Internat. Exch. Scholars, 1984, 500th Rsch. award Spanish Fgn. Ministry, 1992, Silver Medal of Honor Galician Govt., 2000; grantee Coun. on Rsch. and Creative Work, U. Colo., 1986-87, Com. for Ednl. & Cultural Affairs, U. Nebr.-Lincoln, Chancellor's Rsch. Initiation Fund, U. Nebr.-Lincoln, 1980-81, Rsch. Coun., U. Nebr.-Lincoln, 1978-79; Sr. Faculty Summer Rsch. fellow Rsch. Coun., U. Nebr.-Lincoln, 1978, Woodrow Wilson Dissertation fellow, 1971-72, Univ. fellow U. Mass., 1968-72, Grad. fellow, 1969-70. Mem.: MLA, Nebr. Fgn. Lang. Assn., Cervantes Soc. Am., Cir. de Cultura Panamericano (exec. coun. 1972), 20th Century Spanish Assn. (exec. sec. 1982—), Soc. Spanish and Spanish-Am. Studies (bd. dirs. 1975—), Am. Assn. Tchrs. Spanish and Portuguese (Excellence in Tchg. award Colo. chpt. 1996), Assn. Europea de Profesores de Espanol, Fgn. Lang. Adminstrs. of Colo., Assn. de Escritores y Artistas Espanoles (U.S. rep.), Assn. Colegial de Escritores (spl. rep. to U.S., v.p.), Spain's Pen Club (founding 1984), Conf. Editors of Learned Jours. (bd. dirs. 1987—), N.Am. Acad. Spanish Lang. (corr.), Castilian Assn. Writers (hon.), others, Phi Kappa Phi. Home: 1875 Del Rosa Ct Boulder CO 80304-1800 Office: U Colo Dept Spanish Portuguese Boulder CO 80309-0001 Office Phone: 303-492-5900. Business E-Mail: gonzalel@colorado.edu.

GONZALEZ ECHEVARRIA, AMELIA L., librarian, counselor; b. Santurce, P.R., June 22, 1950; d. Raul A. and Arminda (Echevarria) Gonzalez; m. Angel Sepulveda, Sept. 11, 1980 (div. 1982). BA, U. P.R., Rio Piedras, 1967, MLS, 1975, MA, 1989; EdD, Interam. U., San Juan, 1992—. Tchr. spl. edn. Colegio Bautista Carolina (P.R.), 1972-73; dist. supr. Youth Program of P.R., Carolina, 1973-75; libr. dir. New Hampshire Coll., San Juan, P.R., 1985-89, Municipality of San Juan, 1975—. Counselor Fundacion Sida P.R., San Juan, 1987—; mem. Asegrab, San Juan, 1984—, Pracde, San Juan, 1985—. Mem. coun. Mcpl. Assembly, Municipality of Carolina, 1972-75; sec. Democrat. Com. of Carolina, 1969-72; mem. Consejo Vecinal Seguridad, Isla Verde, Carolina, 1989—; asst. treas. Salon de la Fama Deporte, Carolina, 1984-86; bd. dirs. Condominium St. Tropez, pres. 1989—, sec. 1987-88; sec. Asociación Condominios de Isla Verde, P.R., 1989-92; mem. Vecinal Coun. for Security, 1989—; vol. AIDS Found. of P.R., 1987—, counselor, 1987—. Mem. ALA, Sociedad de Bibliotecarios, Federación Nacional Puertorriqueña de Análisis Transaccional Inc., Assn. de Ex-Alumnos de la Escuela Graduada de Bibliotecología (sec. 1984-86), P.R. Assn. for Counselling and Devel. Baptist. Avocations: reading, theater and arts, travel, sewing. Home: PO Box 29700 San Juan PR 00929-0700

GONZALEZ-FALLA, SONDRA GILMAN, art collector; Trustee Whitney Mus. Am. Art, NYC; chmn. bd. Am. Theatre Wing. Avocation: collector of Am. photography. Mailing: c/o Whitney Mus Am Art 945 Madison Ave New York NY 10021 also: c/o American Theatre Wing 570 Seventh Ave Ste 501 New York NY 10018*

GONZALEZ-LICEA, AUGUSTIN, pathologist, public health service officer; b. Mexico City, Sept. 27, 1936; arrived in U.S., 1981; s. Benjamin and Guadalupe (Licea) Gonzalez; m. Virginia Marcela Hernandez, Jan. 5, 1981; children: Monica Rosanne, Karla Gabriella. BS, Ctr. U. Mex., Mexico City, 1953; MD, Nat. Autonomous U. Mex. (UNAM), Mexico City, 1960. Diplomate Mex. Bd. Pathology. Intern in pathology UNAM Gen. Hosp., Mexico City, 1960-61, resident in pathology, 1961-64; fellow in pathology Johns Hopkins U., Balt., 1964-67; rschr., dept. scientific investigation Nat. Med. Ctr., Mexico City, 1969-80, head evaluation and control, Rsch. Programs Office, 1974-77, dir. Biomed. Rsch. Unit, 1978-80; med. dir., blood chemistry Miles Labs., Inc., Elkhart, Ind., 1981-89; dir. med. affairs Technicon Instruments, Inc., Tarrytown, N.Y., 1990-92; med. officer FDA, Rockville, Md., 1992—. Republican. Roman Catholic. Avocation: tennis. Office: FDA/ODE OIVD HFZ-440 2098 Gaither Rd Rockville MD 20850-4009 Office Phone: 224-276-0443. E-mail: alg@cdrh.fda.gov.

GONZALEZ-MARTINEZ, JULIO C., education educator; b. San Juan, P.R., July 7, 1970; s. Julio C. Gonzalez-Andino and Heyda M. Martinez-Tirado; life ptnr. Mary Elisabeth Motz. BA, Loyola U., New Orleans, 1993; M.Spl. Edn., U. of Mass., 1996, EdD, 2004. Cert. spl. needs instr. Mass. Dept. of Edn., 1996, neonatal neurobehavioral examiner The Brazelton Inst. at the Boston's Children's Hosp., 1999. Tchg. assoc. U. of Mass., Amherst, 1998—2002; spl. edn. tchr. Gerald Adams Elem. Sch., Key West, Fla., 1994—96; adult literacy program instr. Literacy Vols. of Am., Key West, Fla., 1996—98; project and tchg. asst. Learning Resources Ctr. at the U. of Mass., Amherst, 1995—96; family cons. Cmty. Resources for People with Autism, Easthampton, Mass., 1995—96; spl. edn. instrnl. asst. Amherst and Pelham Regional Sch. Sys., Amherst, Mass., 1993—95; asst. prof. in edn. Southampton Coll. of LI U., Southampton, NY. Internat. svc. learning in spl. edn. Coun. for Exceptional Children, Belize City, Belize, 2003—; cons. Hampton Bays Union Free Schs., Hampton Bays, NY, 2002—, Pollock-Krasner Ho., East Hampton, NY, 2004—04, Anti-Bias Task Force, Southampton, NY, 2002—; rsch. cons. Latin Am. Outreach Ctr. Inc., Sag Harbor, NY, 2002—; vis. faculty edn. and psychology Mount Holyoke Coll., South Hadley, Mass., 1999—2002. Author: (monograph) Meeting the Educational Needs of the Hispanic and Latino Community on Eastern Long Island, New York; panelist (panel of experts) Recognizing the Latino Community on Eastern Long Island: Creating Community Awareness of Unmet Needs; contbr. articles to profl. jours., chapters to books. Advisor Orgn. Latino Americana (OLA), Watermill, NY, 2004; advisor to the county exec. Suffolk County Hispanic Adv. Bd., Hauppauge, NY, 2004; sch. adv. bd. mem. Children's Sch., Southampton, NY, 2003—04; adv. bd. mem. Nuestra Prensa/Southampton Press, Southampton, NY, 2003—04. Recipient Sallie Mae Tchr. of the Yr. award, Monroe County, Fla., 1996—97; fellow Opportunities fellow, U. of Mass. at Amherst, 1998—99. Mem.: Internat. Soc. of Early Intervention, Puerto Rican Studies Assn., ASCD, Assn. of Integrative Studies, Nat. Assn. of Hispanic and Latino Studies, Nat. Assn. for the Edn. of Young Children, Am. Ednl. Rsch. Assn., Coun. for Exceptional Children, Phi Delta Kappa. Catholic And Buddhist. Avocations: sailing, travel, cooking, reading, outdoor activities. Office: Long Island University 239 Montauk Hwy Southampton NY 11968 Office Phone: 631-287-8201. E-mail: julio.gonzalez@liu.edu.

GONZALEZ NIEVES, ROBERTO OCTAVIO, archbishop; b. Elizabeth, N.J., June 2, 1950; Student, St. Joseph Seraphic Sem., Sienna Coll., Washington Theol. Union, Fordham U. Joined Franciscan Order, 1976, ordained priest Roman Cath. Ch., 1977. Titular bishop Ursona and aux. bishop, Boston, 1988-95; coadjutor bishop Diocese of Corpus Christi, 1995-97, bishop, 1997-2000; archbishop Archdiocese of San Juan, 1999—. Roman Catholic. Office: PO Box 9021967 San Juan PR 00902-1967

GONZALEZ-PITA, J. ALBERTO, lawyer; b. Havana, Cuba, Aug. 20, 1954; came to U.S., 1960; s. Benigno Jesus and Maria Modesta (Diaz) G.P.; m. Suzanne J. Martin, Apr. 7, 1984; children: Roberto Martin, Antonio Martin. AA, Miami-Dade Community Coll., 1973; BA, U. Miami, 1974; JD, Boston U., 1977. Bar: Fla. 1977, U.S. Dist. Ct. (so. dist.) Fla. 1977, U.S. Ct. Appeals (5th cir.) 1977, U.S. Ct. Appeals (11th cir.) 1981. Assoc. Walton, Lantaff, Schroeder & Carson, Miami, Fla., 1977-80, Patton & Kanner, Miami, 1980-82, ptnr., 1982-86, mng. ptnr., 1986-89; ptnr. McDermott, Will & Emery, Miami, 1989-91, White & Case, Miami, 1991-99; v.p. group counsel, International BellSouth Corp, 1999—2001; v.p. International Legal, Regulatory and External Affairs BellSouth Corp., 2001—04; exec. v.p., gen. counsel Tyson Foods, Inc., Springdale, Ark., 2004—. Chair Worldwide Privatization Practice Group; co-chair Latin Am. Practice Group. Mem. Acad. for Community Edn., Miami, 1980-90; bd. dirs. Inst. Innovative Intervention, Miami, 1980-90; trustee St. Thomas U., Miami, 1991-96. Mem. ABA, Internat. Bar Assn. (co-chair corp. coun. com. 2002-2004), Inter-Am. Bar Assn., Cuban-Am. Bar Assn., Maritime Law Assn. U.S. Roman Catholic. Office: Tyson Foods Inc 2310 West Oakburn Springdale AR 72762-6999

GONZALEZ-SANCHEZ, ENRIQUE, economist; b. Concepcion del Oro, Zacatecas, Mex., May 28, 1959; s. Pablo and M. de la Luz (Sanchez) Gonzalez. B in Econs., U. Nuevo Leon, Monterrey, Mex., 1981; MA in Econs., U. Chgo., 1986; diploma, Studien Centrum Gerzensee, Switzerland, 1991, Internat. Monetary Fund, Washington, 1992, EU-Rio Group, Montevideo, Uruguay, 1994. Analyst Bank of Mex., Mexico City, 1982-84, specialist, 1986-88, chief economist, 1988-93, vice mgr. internat. economy, 1993-98, vice mgr., 2002—; asst. to exec. dir. Internat. Monetary Fund, Washington, 1998—2002. Contbr. articles to profl. publs. Recipient Disting. Pl. award Internat. Essay Contest Ludming von Mises, Mexico City, 1990. Fellow U. Chgo. Ex-Students in Mexico Soc. (founder). Avocation: swimming. Home: Lirios 232 Col La Florida 53160 Naucalpan, Edo. de Mexico Mexico Office: Banco de Mexico 5 de Mayo 20 4 piso 06059 Mexico City Mexico E-mail: enrique20037@hotmail.com.

GONZALEZ-SCARANO, FRANCISCO ANTONIO, neurologist, virologist; b. Ponce, P.R., Mar. 23, 1950; s. Francisco and Genoveva (Scarano) Gonzalez-Hernandez; m. Barbara Jean Turner, June 23, 1979; children: Genevieve Carre, Stephanie Katharine, Lisa Frances. BA, Yale U., 1971; MD, Northwestern U., Chgo., 1975; MA (hon.), U. Pa., Phila., 1988. Diplomate Am. Bd. Neurology. Intern Hosp. U. Pa., 1975-76, resident in neurology, 1976-79; fellow U. Pa., Phila., 1979-82, NIMR, London, 1981-82; asst. prof. depts. neurology and microbiology U. Pa., Phila., 1982-88, assoc. prof., 1988-94, prof., 1994—. Vice-chair for rsch. neurology dept. U. Pa, 1998-99, chair 1999—; co-dir. Pa. Ctr. for HIV and AIDS, 1998—; chmn. bd. sci. counselors Nat. Inst. Neurol. Diseases and Stroke, Bethesda, Md., 1993-97, Nat. Adv. Neurol. Diseases and Stroke Coun., 2004-2008. Assoc. editor Viral Pathogenesis, 1997; editl. bd. Jour. Neurovirology, 1996—, Virus Rsch., 1997—, AIDS, 1995-2002, GLIA, 1999—, Jour. Virology, 2000—, Virology, 2003--. Trustee Swarthmore Presbyn. Ch., 1997-2000, session 2004-. Harry Weaver scholar Multiple Sclerosis Soc., N.Y.C., 1982-87. Mem.: Am. Soc. Clin. Investigation, Am. Acad. Neurology (mem. sci. issues com. 1985—89, profl. and pub. issues com. 1987—93), Am. Neurol. Assn. (exec. coun. 2001—03), Scroll & Key, John Morgan Soc, Penn Club, Alpha Omega Alpha. Presbyterian. Avocation: photography. Office: U Pa Dept Neurology Hosp U Pa 3 W Gates Bldg Philadelphia PA 19104-4283 Office Phone: 215-662-3360. E-mail: francisco.gonzalez@uphs.upenn.edu.

GONZALEZ-TORNERO, SERGIO, artist; b. Santiago, Chile, May 22, 1927; came to the U.S., 1962; s. Higinio and Rebecca (Tornero) Gonzalez; m. Maxine Adrienne Cullom, 1962; children: Katya, Alicia, Savina. Studies in, Chile, Brasil, U.S., France and Eng., 1959-62; student under S.W. Hayter, Atelier 17, Paris, 1959-62. Exhibitions include Mus. Fine Arts, Santiago, Chile, 1993; one-man exhbns. paintings Haida Gwaii Mus., Qay'Llnagaay, Skidegate, B.C., 1996, Gallery of Tribal Art, Vancouver, 1996, Mus. No. B.C. at Prince Rupert, 1997, Putnam Arts Coun., Mahopac, NY, 1999, Greenhill Invitationals, Yorktown, NY, 2000, Silvermine Galleries, New Canaan, Conn., 2001, 04, Shelnutt Gallery, Rensselaer Polytechnic Inst., Troy, NY, 2001, 04, The Studio, Armonk, NY, 2002, Chappaqua (NY) Libr. Gallery, 2004, Solon Dorblum Gallery, New Canaan, Conn., 2004; retrospective of 218 prints at Antiguo Asilo de Beneficencia, San Juan, 1998; numerous pub. and pvt. collections. Recipient UNESCO prize Internat. Bienial of Prints, Krakow, 1966, 1st prize X Bienial of Prints, L.Am. and the Caribbean, San Juan, P.R., 1993, 26 other prizes, 1960—; NY State Coun. for the Arts fellow, 1987; grantee Adolph and Esther Gottlieb Found., NY, 1990. Mem. Soc. Am. Graphic Artists. Home and Office: 30 Highridge Rd Mahopac NY 10541-2165 Office Phone: 845-628-6571. E-mail: alicia2mil@aol.com.

GONZALEZ-VELASCO, ENRIQUE ALBERTO, mathematics professor; b. Madrid, July 28, 1940; came to U.S., 1964; s. Enrique Gonzalez-Garrido and Alberta Velasco-Martinez; m. Donna M., Jan. 22, 1971. MSEE, Brown U., 1966, PhD in Applied Math., 1969; PhD in Telecom. Engring., Poly. U. Madrid, 1971. Asst. prof. math. Boston Coll., 1968-74; prof. math. Poly. U. Barcelona (Spain), 1974—76; asst. prof. math. U. Lowell (Mass.), 1976-81, assoc. prof. math., 1981-87; prof. U. Mass., Lowell, 1987—. Author: Fourier Analysis and Boundary Value Problems, 1996; contbr. articles to profl. jours. Office: Univ Mass One Univ Ave Lowell MA 01854 Office Phone: 978-934-2713. Business E-Mail: enrique_gonzalez@uml.edu.

GONZOL, DAVID J, music educator; b. Somerville, NJ, June 17, 1955; s. Andrew John and June Carmina Gonzol; m. Karen Faye Lehman, July 28, 1979; children: April Elizabeth, Darren John. BS, Messiah Coll., 1977; M in Music Edn., Temple U., 1979; PhD in music edn., U. Md. at Coll. Pk., 1995. Orff-Schulwerk Mastery Cert. U. St. Thomas, St. Paul, Minn., 2002, Kodály Mastery cert. U. St. Thomas, St. Paul, Minn., 2002. Music instr. Phila. Pub. Schools, 1979—82; adj. lectr. in music Messiah Coll., Grantham, Pa., 1982—96; grad. asst. U. Md. at Coll. Pk., 1988—89; music instr. Shippensburg U., Pa., 1989—95, West Shore Cumberland and Mechanisburg Pub. Schools, 1995—97; asst. prof. music Minn. State U. Moorhead, 1997—2000; adj. lectr. in music Wilson Coll., 1992; assoc. prof. music Idaho State U., 2000—05; asst. prof. music edn. Shepherd U., 2005—. Chancel choir dir. First Presbyn. Ch., Pocatello, Idaho, 2001—04. Mem.: Orgn. Am. Kodály Educators, Am. Orff-Schulwerk Assn. (pres. Idaho chpt. 2004—05), Music Educators Nat. Conf. Avocation: reading. Address: 112 Veterans Way Martinsburg WV 25401 Office Phone: 304-876-5555. Business E-Mail: dgonzol@shepherd.edu.

GOO, ABRAHAM MEU SEN, retired manufacturing executive; b. Honolulu, May 21, 1925; s. Tai Chong and Lily En Wui (Dai) Goo; m. Shin Quon Wong, June 12, 1950; children: Marilynn, Steven, Beverly Cardinal. BSEE, U. Ill., 1951; postgrad., MIT, 1975. With Boeing Co., Seattle, 1951—73; mgr. B-1 avionics program, v.p., gen. mgr. aircraft armament divsn. Boeing Aerospace Co., Seattle, 1974—77; v.p. mil. sys., exec. v.p., pres. Boeing Mil. Airplane Co., Wichita, Kans., 1977—87; pres. Boeing Advanced Sys., Seattle, 1987—89. With USAAF, 1946—47. Recipient Chinese-Am. Engrs. and Scientists of So. Calif. Achievement award, Sci. and Engring., 1989, Pioneer award, Unmanned Vehicle Sys., 1989. Home: 18909 SE 282nd Ct Kent WA 98042-5458 Personal E-mail: amssgg@msn.com.

GOO, JUNG-SUK, semiconductor company research engineer; b. Seoul, Republic of Korea, June 4, 1966; arrived in U.S., 1995; s. Jae-Gyu Goo and Kee-Joon Kim; m. Inseong Kim; children: Philip children: Timothy. BS, Yonsei U., Seoul, 1988; MS, Stanford U., 1997, PhD, 2001. Sr. engr. LG Semicon, Seoul, Republic of Korea, 1988—95; analog design and modeling engr. Atheros Comm., Inc., Sunnyvale, Calif., 2001—01; sr. mem. tech. staff Advanced Micro Devices, Sunnyvale, 2001—. Contbr. articles to profl. jours. Mem.: IEEE. Achievements include research in the field of the hot carrier effect and high frequency MOSFET noise; invention of world-record CMOS low-noise amplifier; patents in field. Home: 1485 Oakhurst Ave Los Altos CA 94024 Office: Advanced Micro Devices One AMD Place PO Box 3453 MS 79 Sunnyvale CA 94088-3453 Personal E-mail: goojs@stanfordalumni.org. Business E-Mail: Jung-Suk.Goo@amd.com.

GOOCH, ANTHONY CUSHING, retired lawyer; b. Amarillo, Tex., Dec. 3, 1937; s. Cornelius Skinner and Sidney Seale (Crawford) G.; m. Elizabeth Melissa Ivanoff, May 27, 1963 (div. Nov. 1983); children: Katherine C., Jennifer C. Gooch Avery, Melissa G., Andrew E.; m. Linda B. Klein, Nov. 7, 1987 (dec. Apr. 25, 2004). BA, U. of South, 1959; diploma, Coll. of Europe, 1960; JD, NYU, 1963, M in Comparative Law, 1964. Bar: N.Y. 1963. Assoc. Cleary, Gottlieb, Steen & Hamilton, N.Y.C., Paris, Brussels, 1963-72, ptnr. Rio de Janeiro, 1973-78, N.Y.C., 1978-99, sr. counsel, 2000—03, ret. ptnr., 2004—; gen. counsel Internat. Inst. Rural Reconstruction, 2000—02, bd. trustees, 2002—. Co-author: Loan Agreement Documentation, 1982, 2d edit., 1991, Swap Apreement Documentation, 1987, 2d edit., 1988, Documentation for Derivatives, 1993, Credit Support Supplement, 1995, Cross-Product Risk Mgmt. Supplement, 2000, 4th edit., 2002, Master Agreement Supplement, 2003, Documentation for Loans, Assignments and Participations, 1996, ISDA Master Agreement Supplement, 2004, Supplement on the Cross-Product Master Agreement, 2004; articles editor NYU Law Rev., 1962-63. V.p. planned giving Assoc. Alumni, U. of the South, Sewanee, Tenn. Mem. ABA, N.Y. State Bar Assn., Assn. Bar City N.Y. Episcopalian. Home: 7 Mine Hill Rd Redding CT 06896-2701 E-mail: tonygooch@aol.com.

GOOCH, WARREN PETER, composer, music educator; b. Duluth, Minn. s. Warner Ritzman and Charlotte Emma (Doty) G.; m. Colleen Ann Fitzgerald, Aug. 16, 1975; 1 child, Jonathan. B of Music Edn., Coll. St. Scholastica, Duluth, 1975; MEd, U. Minn., Duluth, 1984; DMus, U. Wis., 1988. Dir. choral activities Ind. Sch. Dist. #709, Duluth, 1975—82; music instr. U. Minn., Duluth, 1983—84, U. Wis., Madison, 1986—88; music prof. Truman State U., Kirksville, Md., 1988—. Coord. MACRO Internat. Composition Competition Truman State U., 1998—; cons. McGraw-Hill Pub. Co., 1996—; adjudicator various regional and nat. composition competitions, 1990—. Composer: (choir) Let the Nations Tremble, 2004, Very Long Ago, 1984, Lullabye for the Infant King, 1990, A Song of Night, 1995, Teach Me the Way of Thy Word, 1996, Hosannah in the Highest, 2002, The Harvest Moon, 2003, (percussion ensemble) Out of the Primordial Ocean, 1995, (piano) Dragon Music, 1995, (saxophone) Romanza and Galop, 2000, (brass ensemble) And Grant Us Peace, 2001, (clarinet and piano) Sonata: 1990, 2002, Soliloquy for Oboe and Piano, 2002, Sonata for Soprano Saxophone and Piano, 2002, Rhapsody for Saxophone and Piano, 2003. Chair music com., mus. dir. Grace Cmty. Bible Ch., Kirksville, Mo., 1995—, Duluth Gospel Tabernacle, 1973—84. Mem.: Music Tchrs. Nat. Assn. (mem. composers commissioning adv. bd. 2000—03). Avocations: natural history, speleology, travel. Home: 3009 E Illinois St Kirksville MO 63501 Office: Truman U Divn Fine Arts Kirksville MO 63501

GOOD, CONNIE J., artist, venture capitalist; b. Nov. 27, 1953; Student, UCLA, 1972-76, Santa Monica Coll. Artist; pvt. venture capital investor, 1997—. Mem. organizing com. Brushes, Beads, Collage & Camera, Three Arts Club, Chgo.; spl. guest artist, lectr., demonstrator Studio Two Ten Gallery, Seaside, Fla., 1999; featured artist Jay Mendolsohn Gallery, Chgo., 1999. Exhibited in group shows Peter Jones Gallery, 1998, Sulzer Pub. Libr., 1999, One Illinois Ctr., 1999, Barrington (Ill.) Libr., 2000; commd. art installation CB Richard Ellis, Chgo., 1999-2000. Mem. benefit com. River North Dance Com., Chgo.; co-chmn. River North Dance Co., 2000. Mem. Chgo. Artist Coalition., Investment Analysts Soc. Home: 360 E Randolph St Chicago IL 60601-5069 Studio: Peter Jones Gallery 1806 W Cuyler Ave Chicago IL 60613-2402 Fax: 312-616-3612. E-mail: afgood@earthlink.net.

GOOD, EDITH ELISSA (PEARL WILLIAMS), writer; b. Hollywood, Calif., Jan. 10, 1945; d. Jack Brian and Rose Marie (Miller) Good; m. Michael Lawrence Black, Dec. 18, 1966 (dec.). Student, UCLA and U. Calif., Berkeley, 1962-92, Ballet Folklorico, Mex., 1963; BA in English, Calif. State U., Northridge, 1974. Explorer Mayan ruins, Mex., 1963; author, pub. Gull Press, L.A., 1990—. Participant numerous dance, art, music, lit., math. and sci. classes; dancer Hajde Dance Troop, Berkeley, Calif., 1962-66. One-woman shows, L.A., 1962-95; singer, various venues, L.A., 1986; author: (pseudonym Pearl Williams) The Trickster of Tarzana, 1992, Short Stories, 1995, Mad in Craft, 1995, Missives, 1995, others; contbr. numerous poems to lit. publs.; CDs, radio and internet broadcasts. Fundraiser, del. to local convs. Dem. clubs, Calif. and Mex., 1962—; supporter mental health orgns., 1962—; participant Consciousness raising groups, del. local convs., fundraiser, canvasser, office worker, driver, participant W.E.B. DuBois Club, Congress Racial Equality, San Francisco, Berkeley, L.A., and Oakland, 1965, Peace in Alliance for Survival, Berkeley, Oakland, L.A., 1964-80, women's rights Westside Women's Ctr., Woman's Bldg., L.A., 1974-80, Environment in Earth Day, L.A., 1977, phys. and mental health VA, cons. book reviewer, tutor, Mental Health Assn., L.A., 1962—; supporter residential collectives, 1985— Recipient Leonardo DaVinci prize Internat. Biographical Ctr., Cambridge, Eng., 2004. Mem. Mensa, Am. Soc. Composers, Authors, and Pubs., Plummer Park Writers, Westside Writers. Achievements include writing chosen by a jury of experts for inclusion in the permanent collecton of the Library of Congress. Home: 1470 S Robertson Blvd Apt B Los Angeles CA 90035-3402 Office Phone: 310-276-8933.

GOOD, ESTELLE M., minister; b. Charleston, S.C., Oct. 5, 1927; d. John Wesley and Minnie Estelle Hilton; divorced; children: Raymond L., Lee Good Sanders. BTh, Clarksville Sch. Theology, 1972, ThM, 1975, ThD, 1976, ThD, 1978, B in Sacred Music, 1980; PhD of Christian Psychology, Cornerstone U., 1992. Ordained to preach 1955; cert. hypnotherapist Internat. Assn. Counselors and Therapists, 1994. Organizer, pastor Covenant Life Cathedral, Macon, Ga., 1962—. Pres. Lighthouse Bible Tng. Ctr., 1976—88. Fellow: Nat. Christian Counselors Assn. (diplomate 1993, lic. temperament therapist 1991, Christian counselor and therapist 1992); mem.: Women Preachers Coun. Am., Full Gospel Fellowship of Churches and Ministers Internat. Office: Covenant Life Cathedral 4543 Bloomfield Rd Macon GA 31203

GOOD, HAROLD KENNETH, music educator, singer; b. Vineland, N.J., May 19, 1979; s. Harold Kenneth and Cathy Gayle Good. B in Music Edn., Westminster Choir Coll., 2001; MEd, Am. Intercontinental U., 2005. Cert. tchr. music N.J., 2001. Tchr. music Atlantic City Bd. Edn., 2001—. Pvt. voice tchr. Youth Opera Co., Ocean City, NJ, 2005—. Personal E-mail: haroldkgood@aol.com.

GOOD, HELEN MARIE, writer; b. Elkhart County, Ind., Mar. 15, 1939; d. Irven Glen and Mary Esther Good; 1 child, Timothy Alexander. AA Liberal Arts, Goshen Coll., 1961; BA Foods & Nutrition, Geshen Coll., 1988. Sr. lab. tech. Miles Lab. (not Bayer), Elkhart, Ind., 1968—88; writer, 1999—. Republican. Presbyterian. Avocations: violin, reading, knitting, gardening. Home: 1725 Roys Ave Elkhart IN 46516

GOOD, IRVING JOHN, statistician, educator, philosopher; b. London, Dec. 9, 1916; arrived in US, 1967; s. Morris Edward and Sophia (Polikoff) Good. ScD, Cambridge (Eng.) U., 1963; DSc, Oxford (Eng.) U., 1964. Scientific officer Fgn. Office, Bletchley, Eng., 1941-45; lectr. math. and electronic computing Manchester (Eng.) U., 1945-48; sr. prin. sci. officer Govt. Communications Hdqrs., Cheltenham, Eng., 1948-59; spl. merit dep. chief sci. officer Admiralty Rsch. Lab., Teddington, Middlesex, Eng., 1959-62; sr. rsch. fellow Trinity Coll., Oxford U. and Atlas Computer Lab., Didcot, Berkshire, Eng., 1964-67; Univ. disting. prof. stats, adj. prof. philosophy Va. Poly. Inst. and State U., Blacksburg, 1967—; prof. emeritus. Adj. prof. Ctr. Study of Sci. in Society; mem. comm. theory com. Ministry Supply, London, 1953-56; mem. com. com. electronics rsch. com. Ministry Aviation, London, 1960-62; mem. rsch. sect. com. Royal Statis. Soc., London, 1965-67. *Irving John Good's work cannot be summarized briefly. He showed Tukey a Fast Fourier Transform in 1957. Good used Empirical Bayes (1953), the EM method (1956), the log-linear model, penalized likelihood, maximum entropy, generalized linear models, and hierarchical Bayes, in some cases before they were named. He invented "necessitude and sufficitude" for legal philosophy. Since 1990 he has refuted many attempts to prove the inconsistency of the kinematics of special relativity. This work included a "Swings and Roundabouts" theorem in relation to clock paradoxes. Good early speculated about hierarchical universes, and about our universe as a rotating black hole in a maternal universe.* Author: Probability and the Weighing of Evidence, 1950, The Estimation of Probabilities, 1965, Good Thinking, 1983; co-author (with Donald Michie and Geoffrey Timms): General Report on Tunny with Emphasis on Statistical Methods, 1945; co-author: (with David B. Osteyee) Information, Weight of Evidence, the Singularity between Probability Measures and Signal Detection, 1974; gen. editor: The Scientist Speculates, 1962, (also French and German translations); contbr. chpt. to The Codebreakers, 1994, also 5 chpts. in Festschriften, over 1000 articles to profl. jours. Recipient Smith's prize, Cambridge, Eng., 1940, Internat. Order of Merit, 1993, Congl. medal of excellence, 2004; grantee NIH, 1970—89. Fellow Royal Stats. Soc. (hon.), Am. Acad. Arts and Scis., Va. Acad. Scis., Inst. Math. Stats., Am. Statis. Assn.; mem. IEEE Computer Soc. (Pioneer award 1998), Internat. Statis. Inst. (hon.). Home: 1309 Lynn Dr Blacksburg VA 24060-3001 Office: Va Poly Inst and State U Dept Stats Blacksburg VA 24061-0439 E-mail: ijgood@vt.edu.

GOOD, LARRY IRWIN, gastroenterologist, educator; b. N.Y.C., Feb. 8, 1948; s. Samuel and Lillie (Sternlight) G.; m. Judy Chafetz, Aug. 16, 1969; children: Adam Eric, Lauren Elyse, Bryan Scott, Allison Jill. BA, Colgate U., 1969; MD, Med. U. of SC, 1973. Diplomate Am. Bd. Internal Medicine, Am. Bd. Gastroenterology. Intern in medicine Tchg. Hosp. Med. U. of SC, 1973-74, resident in medicine Tchg. Hosp., 1974-75, chief resident in medicine Tchg. Hosp., 1975-76; fellow in gastroenterology U. Pa., 1976-78; with Hempstead (NY) Gen. Hosp., 1978—, Nassau County Med. Ctr., East Meadow, NY, 1978—, South Nassau Cmtys. Hosp., Oceanside, NY, 1978—, chief divsn. gastroenterology dept. medicine, 1989. Asst. prof. Sch. of Medicine, SUNY, Stony Brook, 1978; mem. health adv. bd. Hofstra Health Dome Uniondale, NY, 1983; with Lydia E. Hall Hosp., Freeport, NY, 1978-86, Mercy Hosp., Rockville Centre, NY, 1978-80. Contbr. articles to Am. Jour. Gastroenterology, The Papilla Vateri and its Diseases, Med. Times, New Eng. Jour. Medicine., Gastroenterology, Alpha Omega Alpha. Trustee, dir. Little Village Sch. & House, Garden City, NY, 1985—. Recipient Rsch. Svc. award NIH, 1977. Fellow Am. Coll. Gastroenterology; mem. AMA, ACP, L.I. Gastroenterologic Assn., Am. Gastroenterologic Assn. Jewish. Office: 229 7th St Ste 307 Garden City NY 11530-2913 Office Phone: 516-766-0300. Personal E-mail: goodlb@verizon.net.

GOOD, LAURANCE FREDERIC, hospital administrator; b. Wheeling, W.Va., Sept. 26, 1932; s. Sidney Samuel and Jeannette (Berg) G.; m. Barbara S. Mayer, Oct. 18, 1959; children: Philip (dec.), Jay, Paul, Jenny, Heidi. BA, Brown U., 1954; postgrad., U. Va., 1955. CLU, ChFC, cert. employee benefits specialist, health ins. assoc.; registered health underwriter, LUTCF. V.p., gen. mdse. mgr. L.S. Good & Co., Wheeling, 1961-80, exec. v.p., 1969-80, vice chmn., sec. bd., 1961-80, Good's of Wheeling, W.Va., Starkeville, Ohio, St. Clairsville, Ohio, Gables, Altoona, Pa., Knapps, Lansing, Miss., Jackson, Miss., Fowler's, Binghamton, NY, Kann's, Wash., Arlington, Va., Purcell's, Lexington, Ky., D.M. Christian Co., Owasso, Mich., Smith-Bridgeman, Flint, Mich., Grand Blanc, Mich., Robinson's Battle Creek, Mich.; pres. Personal History Systems, Inc.; life underwriter Equitable Life Assurance Soc. Am., 1983-89; health and welfare cons. Mockenhaupt, Mockenhaupt, Cowden & Parks, 1989; employee benefit specialist, life underwriter Lincoln Fin. Svcs., Inc., Pitts., 1990; exec. dir. Wheeling Works, Inc., Wheeling, W.Va., 1993-95; dir. Office of Gift Planning Med. Park Found., Wheeling, W.Va., 1995—; dir. devel. Wheeling Hosp. Mem. Million Dollar Roundtable, 1985-86; pres. Personal History Systems. Producer: Wheeling Rediscovered; Author: My Lifetime Book. Bd. dirs. Wheeling Symphony Soc., 1964-67, 68-73; with Ohio Valley Indsl. and Bus. Devel. Corp., Wheeling, 1971; chmn. Brown U. Alumni Program, 1954-88, W.Va.; Christmas seals chmn. Tb Assn. Ohio Valley, 1973; co-chmn. United Jewish Appeal, 1971-73; v.p., chmn. fin. com. Temple Shalom, 1986-89; co-founder Good Zoo in memory of eldest son, Philip; co-founder, pres. Good Zoo Friends, 1974-78; chmn. establishment com. Wheeling Devel. Conf.; bd. found. W. Liberty State Coll., 1971; creator Kraft-Good Archives; bd. dirs. Wheeling Hosp., 1972-87, hon. bd. dirs., 1988-96; bd. visitors Bethany Coll., 1972-77; trustee Oglebay Inst., 1972-90; mem. Estate Planning Coun. of Ohio Valley and Pitts.; co-chair Greater Wheeling/Bel-o-Mar Empowerment Zone/Enterprise Community Initiative, 1994; campaign dir. Toward the Next Century, Wheeling Hosp., 1998, dir. capital funds campaign, 2004. With USN, 1955-57. Charter recipient Disting. West Virginian award, 1976. Mem. Nat. Retail Mchts. Assn. (dir. merchandising div. 1966-71, del. conf. 1969), Ohio Valley Assn. Life Underwriters (pres. 1987), W.Va. Assn. Life Underwriters (regional dir. 1988). Office: Med Park Found Office Gift Planning One Medical Pk Wheeling WV 26003 Office Phone: 304-243-4438. Personal E-mail: goodforyou@earthlink.net. Business E-Mail: lgood@wheelinghospital.com.

GOOD, MARK, retail executive; BA, U. Calif. at Berkeley; MBA, San Francisco State U. Planning engr. The Gap, Inc., 1980—83, tech. services mgr., 1983—85, dir. distbn. planning, 1985—87, dir. internat. expansion, 1987—89; mgr. distbn. centers and transp. centers Cost Plus Imports, Inc., 1989—90; dir. logistics and info. systems A Pea in the Pod, Inc., 1990—94; dir. distbn. Westinghouse Elec. Supply co., 1994—97; v.p., gen. mgr. parts Sears Roebuck and Co., 1997—98, v.p., gen. mgr. parts and carry in svc., 1998—99, exec. v.p., product repair services, 1999—. Mem. Coun. of Logistics Mgmt. Office: Sears Roebuck and Co 3333 Beverly Rd Hoffman Estates IL 60179

GOOD, MARY LOWE (MRS. BILLY JEWEL GOOD), investment company executive, educator; b. Grapevine, Tex., June 20, 1931; d. John W. and Winnie (Mercer) Lowe; m. Billy Jewel Good, May 17, 1952; children: Billy, James. BS, Ark. State Tchrs. Coll., 1950; MS, U. Ark., 1953, PhD, 1955, LLD (hon.), 1979; DSc (hon.), U. Ill., Chgo., 1983, Clarkson U., 1984, Ea. Mich. U., 1986, Duke U., 1987; hon. degree, St. Mary's Coll., 1987, Kenyon Coll., 1988, Stevens Inst. Tech., 1989, Lehigh U., 1989, Northeastern Ill. U., 1989, U. S.C., 1989, N.J. Inst. Tech., 1989; hon. law degree, Newcomb Coll. of Tulane U., 1991; LLD (hon.), Coll. of William and Mary, 1992; DSc (hon.), Manhattan Coll., 1992, Ind. U., 1992, SUNY, Binghamton, 1994, Rensselaer Polytechnic Inst., 1994, Monmouth U., 1995, La. State U., 1995, Ill. Inst. Tech., 1997, Mich. State U., 1997, U. Mich., 1998; DEng (hon.), Colo. Sch. Mines, 2000. Instr. Ark. State Tchrs. Coll., Conway, summer 1949; from instr. to prof. La. State U., Baton Rouge, 1954—63, prof. New Orleans, 1963—80; v.p., dir. rsch. UOP, Inc., Des Plaines, Ill., 1980-84; pres. Signal Rsch. Ctr. Inc., 1985-87; pres. engineered materials rsch. divsn Allied-Signal Inc., Des Plaines, Ill., 1986-88, sr. v.p.-tech. Morristown, N.J., 1988-93; under sec. of commerce for technology Dept. of Commerce, Washington, 1993-97; mng. mem. Venture Capital Investors LLC, Little Rock, 1997—2005, Fund for Ark., 2005—; Donaghey Univ. prof., dean Coll. Info. Sci. & Systems Engr U. Ark., Little Rock, 1998—. Chmn. Pres.'s Com. for Nat. Medal Sci., 1979-82; adv. bd. NSF Chemistry Sect., 1972-76; com. medicinal chemistry NIH, 1972-76, Office of USAF Rsch., 1974-78, chemist divsn. Brookhaven and Oak Ridge Nat. Labs., 1973-83, chem. tech. divsn. Oak Ridge Nat. Lab., catalysis program Lawrence-Berkeley Lab.; catalysis program coll. engring. La. State U.; bd. dirs. BiogenIdec, Inc., Acxiom, Delta Bank and Trust, Acxiom Inc.; bd. chem. sci. and tech., Nat. Rsch. Council, 2003-04, Govt. U., industry roundtable, NRC, 2000-, Ark. Sci and Tech. Authority, 1998-2003, Dialoge Com, Am. Chem. Coun., 2002-. Contbr. articles to profl. jours. Mem. Nat. Sci. Bd., 1980-91, vice chair, 1984-88, chair, 1988-91; mem. Pres.' Coun. Advisors for Sci. and Tech., 1991-93. Recipient Agnes Faye Morgan rsch. award, 1969, Disting. Alumni citation U. Ark., 1973, Scientist of Yr. award Indsl. R&D mag., 1983, Delmer S. Fahrney medal Franklin Inst., 1988, N.J. Women of Achievement award Douglass Coll., Rutgers U., 1990, Indsl. Rsch. Inst. medal, 1991, Disting. Svc. award NSF, 1992, Roe award ASME, 1993, Gold medal SME, 1995, Earle Barnes award ACS, 1996, Priestley medal, 1997, UCLA Glenn T. Seaborg medal, 1996, Nat. Materials Advancement award Fedn. Materials Socs., 1996, Othmer medal award Chem. Heritage Found., 1998, Henry Michel award, Civil Engring. Rsch. Found., 1998, Heinz award for tech. The Economy and Employment, 2000, Vannevar Bush award NSF, 2004; AEC tng. grantee, 1967, NSF Internat. travel grantee, 1968, NSF rsch. grantee, 1969-80, Albert Fox Demers award, 1992. Fellow AAAS (Abelson award 1999, pres. 2000, chmn. bd. dirs. 2001), Am. Inst. Chemistry (Gold medal 1983), Chem. Soc. London, Royal Soc. Chemistry (hon.); mem. NAE, Acad. Arts and Scis, Am. Philos. Soc., Swedish Acad. Engring., Am. Chem. Soc. (1st woman dir. 1971-74, regional dir. 1972-80, chmn. bd. 1978, 80, bd. publs., pres. 1987, Garvan medal 1973, Herty medal 1975, award Fla. sect. 1979, Charles Lathrop Parsons award 1991), Internat. Union Pure and Applied Chmistry (pres. inorganic div. 1980-85),Alliance for Sci. and Tech. Rsch. in Am. (chmn. bd. dirs. 2000—), Zonta (past pres. New Orleans club, chmn. dist. status of women com. and nominating com., chmn. internat. Amelia Earhart scholarship com. 1978-88, pres. internat. Found. 1988-93, mem. internat. bd. 1988-90), Rotary Internat., Phi Beta Kappa, Sigma Xi, Iota Sigma Pi (regional dir. 1967-93, hon. mem. 1983), Ark. Women's Forum. Home: 13824 Rivercrest Dr Little Rock AR 72212-1521 Office: U Ark at Little Rock Coll Info Sci/Sys Engring 2801 S University Ave Little Rock AR 72204-1000 Office Phone: 501-569-8189. Personal E-mail: thegoods@aristotle.net. Business E-Mail: mlgood@ualr.edu.

GOOD, RICHARD STANDISH, geologist; b. West Chester, Pa., Sept. 18, 1928; s. Bernard Stafford Good and Marjorie Payne Johnson; m. Edith Read Brodhead, Oct. 15, 1966 (div. Aug. 1982); m. Marsha Wallace, Apr. 29, 2000. BS in Geology and Mineralogy, Pa. State U., 1950, MS in Geology, 1955. Cert. profl. geologist, Va. Chem. analyst Foote Mineral Co., Malvern, Pa., 1951; project engr. Aeroprojects, Inc., West Chester, Pa., 1952-53; rsch. asst. Pa. State U., State College, 1953-55; geologist Geo-Tech Devel. Co., Ltd., Toronto, Ont., Can., 1955-56, Hunting Tech Svcs., Ltd., London, 1957-58; cons., geologist San Francisco, 1958-60; chem. analyst Kawecki Chem. Co., Boyertown, Pa., 1960. Tchg. asst. Bryn Mawr Coll., Pa., 1962-64; geologist, head Geol. Lab. Va. Divsn. of Mineral Resources, Charlottesville, Va., 1966-91; collection mgr. rocks/fossil, Va. Museumont Naturaly History, 1992. Vol. Hospice, Charlottesville, 2001. Fellow NSF, Bryn Mawr, 1963-64. Fellow Assn. Exploration Geochemists; mem. Geol. Soc. Am., Soc. Mining Engrs., Va. Acad. Sci., AAAS, Sigma Xi. Avocations: writing, tennis, hiking, reading. Home: 63 Woodlake Dr Charlottesville VA 22901

GOOD, STEVEN LOREN, real estate consultant; b. Tokyo, Nov. 16, 1956; came to U.S., 1957; s. Sheldon F. and Lois (Kroll) G. Student, Oxford U., 1975; BS in Fin., Syracuse U., 1978; JD, DePaul U., 1981. Bar: Ill. 1981, U.S. Dist. Ct. (no. dist.) Ill. 1982, Fla. 1983, U.S. Ct. Appeals (7th cir.) 1983. Assoc. Sheldon Good & Co., Internat., Chgo., 1978-82; v.p., gen. counsel Sheldon Good & Co., Chgo., 1982-87, pres., 1987—2000, chmn., CEO, 2001—. Lectr., instr. FDIC, Washington, 1985, Mo. Auction Sch., Kansas City, 1981-97; instr. Reppert's Sch. of Auctioneering, 1998-; speaker Crittenden Rsch., Novato, Calif., 1985-91; lectr., speaker numerous confs., colls. and univs. Author: Churches, Jails, and Gold Mines: Mega-Deals from a Real Estate Maverick, 2003; columnist: Auction World mag., 2004—; contbr. articles. Mem. men's coun. Mus. Contemporary Art, Chgo., 1985-91; vice chmn. real estate divsn. Jewish United Fund, Chgo., 1986, 88, 91; bd. dirs. United Cerebral Palsy, Chgo., 1987-97, chmn. telethon for Chgo., 1996; trustee Robert Morris Coll., Chgo., 1989-92; assoc. trustee U. Chgo. Cancer Rsch. Found., 1989-93. Recipient Alumni Service Award for Outstanding Service to the Business Community, DePaul U. Coll. Law, 2001, Infinitec Corporate Leadership award, United Cerebral Palsy Assn., Community Svc. award, Easter Seals, 2003. Mem. ABA, Ill. Bar Assn., Fla. Bar Assn., Chgo. Bar Assn., Nat. Assn. Realtors (dir., chmn. Real Estate Auction Forum, 2004), Ill. Assn. of Realtors (dir. 2000-), Chgo. Assn. Realtors (pres. 2003-2004, lectr., instr. 1981—), Young Pres. Orgn., Standard Club, Lamda Alpha. Avocations: tennis, skiing, shooting skeet, music, theater. Office: Sheldon Good & Co 333 W Wacker Dr Ste 400 Chicago IL 60606-1284 Office Fax: 312-373-4350. E-mail: slevenmgood@sheldongood.com.

GOOD, VIRGINIA JOHNSON, real estate executive; b. Onancock, Va., Mar. 1, 1919; d. Obed Wilbur and Sallie Mildred (Deyerle) Johnson; m. William Dennis Good, Jan. 14, 1941 (dec. Apr. 1970). Bus. cert., Elon College, N.C., 1937; real estate cert., U. Miami, 1973; student, Montgomery County Jr. Coll., 1974. Acct. Carolina Biol. Supply Co., Elon College, N.C., 1935-39, Sears Roebuck, Richmond, Va., 1939-40, Ritchie Electric, Charlottesville, Va., 1940-41; mgmt. investor Dr. & Mrs. William D. Good Real Estate, Washington and Gaithersburg, Md., 1941-70, Good Properties, Washington and Miami Beach, Fla., 1970-94, Dennis Apts., Miami Beach, Fla., 1972-94; owner Good Properties, Orlando, Fla., 1994—. Mem. D.C. Apt. Owners/Mgmt. Assn., Washington, 1970-84, Miami Beach Apt. Owners Assn., 1970-86, North Shore Apt. Owners Assn., Miami Beach, 1986-88. Exec. com. Anti Rock Quarry, Dawsonville, Md., 1959, Save Our Coast, Miami Beach, 1982-86; mem. Montgomery County Hist. and Geneal. Soc., Rockville, Md., 1977—, Nat. Geneal. Soc., 1980-95, Greater Miami Geneal. Soc., Miami, 1982-96, Va. Hist./Geneal. Soc., Richmond, 1988—, Bradley Blvd. Civic Assn., Bethesda, Md., 1989. Mem. La Gorce Country Club, Miami Beach, Columbia Country Club (Chevy Chase, Md.), DAR, Nat. Soc. So. Dames, United Daus. of Confederacy, Nat. Soc. Colonial Dames of XVII Century, Nat. Huguenot Soc. Mem. United Church of Christ. Avocation: genealogy. Home and Office: 3607 Lake Sarah Dr Orlando FL 32804-3425

GOOD, WALTER RAYMOND, investment company executive; b. Oak Park, Ill., Sept. 9, 1924; s. Walter William and Elsie Sophia (Lussow) G.; m. Jean W. Stockman, Feb. 5, 1949; children: Elizabeth, Deborah, William. Ph.B., U. Chgo., 1947, MBA, 1949. Buyer fats and oils Procter and Gamble, Cin., 1949-52; security analyst, dir. research Brown Bros. Harriman, N.Y.C., 1952-70; exec. v.p., dir. Lionel D. Edie, N.Y.C., 1970-80; v.p. Continental Group Inc., Stamford, Conn., 1980-85; mng. ptnr. Actively Managed Universes, Darien, Conn., 1985-86; pres. Mellon Universe Mgmt. Group, Stamford, 1986-90; mng. ptnr. Capital Market Systems, Darien, 1990-98. Mem. investment adv. panel Pension Benefit Guaranty Corp., Washington, 1980-83; dir., mem. exec. com. Retirement Systems for Savs. Instns., N.Y.C., 1985-86; mem. investment adv. council N.Y.C. Retirement Funds, 1980-85; mem. Pension Execs. Conf., 1981-85, chmn., 1983, mem. fin. adv. panel The Aerospace Corp., 1986—. Author: (with D. Love) Managing Pension Assets: Pension Finance and Corporate Financial Goals, 1990, (with R. Hermansen and J. Meyer) Active Asset Allocation: Gaining Advantage in a Highly Efficient Stock Market, 1993, (with R. Hermansen) Index Your Way to Investment Success, 1998; mem. editl. bd. Fin. Analysts Jour., 1972-97. Served with USAAF, 1943-46. Recipient Graham and Dodd Scroll Fin. Analysts Fedn., 1979. Mem. Inst. Chartered Fin. Analysts (council examiners 1980-86), Stamford CFA Soc. Personal E-mail: walter_r_good@sbcglobal.net.

GOOD, WILLIAM ALLEN, professional society executive; b. Oak Park, Ill., May 29, 1949; s. Fred Clifton and Dorothy Helen (Stockdale) G.; m. Julianne Doggett, Jan. 8, 1972 (div. Apr. 1980); m. Paulette Edith Gordon, Apr. 23, 1983 (div. Apr. 1991); m. Laura Elizabeth Wellbank, Sept. 25, 1993. MBA, U. Chgo., 1992. Supr. Dun & Bradstreet, Inc., Chgo., 1972-73; gen. mgr. Nat. Roofing Contractors Assn., Chgo., 1973-85, exec. v.p., Rosemont, Ill., 1987—; dir. mktg. Rand Devel. Corp., San Antonio, 1985-86; co-owner GT Communications, Inc., Dallas, 1985-87. Mem. Am. Soc. Assn. Execs. (cert.), Inst. for Orgn. Mgmt. (chmn. 1990-91), Chgo. Soc. Assn. Execs. (pres. 1996-97). Republican. Roman Catholic. Avocations: tennis, photography. Office: Nat Roofing Contractors Assn 10255 W Higgins Rd Rosemont IL 60018-5606 Office Phone: 847-299-9070. E-mail: bgood@nrca.net.

GOODACRE, CHARLES J., academic administrator; b. 1946; m. Ruth E. Goodacre. DDS, Loma Linda U., 1971; MSD, Ind. U., Indpls., 1974. Prof. Loma Linda U., dean, Sch. Dentistry. Contbr. articles to profl. jours. Mem.: Acad. Prosthodontics, Am. Coll. Prosthodontics. Avocations: woodworking, sports, Lionel trains, off-road motorcycling. Office: Loma Linda Univ Loma Linda CA 92350

GOODACRE, GLENNA, sculptor; b. 1939; m. CL Mike Schmidt. Vietnam Women's Meml., 1993, statue of Ronald Reagan, Reagan Library, Calif., 1998, Crossing the Prairie, 2002, Sacagawea (appears on dollar coin issued by US Mint), 2000, Irish Meml., 2002, statue of West Point Coach Col. Earl 'Red' Blaik, 2003, & many others. Named to Cowgirl Hall of Fame, 2003; recipient Tex. Medal Arts, 2003. Fellow: Nat. Sculpture Soc.; mem.: Nat. Acad. Design (academician 1994—). Mailing: c/o Galleria Silecchia 12 S Palm Ave Sarasota FL 34236 E-mail: goodacre@glennagoodacre.com.*

GOODACRE, JILL, model; b. Lubbock, Texas, Mar. 29, 1965; m. Harry Connick, Jr., Apr. 16, 1994, 3 children. Model Elite Model Mgmt. Corp. Appearances include Victoria's Secret catalogues; (TV Series) Friends, 1994, Duckman, 1997, (films) Odd Jobs, 1984, Ladybird Ladybird, 1994, The Uninvited, 1997.

GOODALE, ARTHUR WORTHINGTON, civil engineer, researcher; b. Dover, N.J., Aug. 19, 1912; s. Arthur Huston and Caroline W. (Worthington) G.; m. Winifred Bryant, Jan. 1, 1946; children: Sondra, Alan. BSCE, Newark Coll. Engring., 1937. Civil engr. Frederick Snare Corp., N.Y.C., 1946-49, Hardaway Contracting, Columbus, Ga., 1950-58; pvt. practice Dunedin, Fla., 1960-80; civil estimator Inter-Bay Marine Constrn., Largo, Fla., 1980—. Rsch. and structural cons., St. Petersburg, Fla., 1980—. Lt. USN, 1943-46, PTO. Mem. ASCE (life). Republican. Presbyterian. Achievements include investigations of various Fla. bridges and structures of poor construction; research in construction materials used in bridges. Home: 1753 San Mateo Dr Dunedin FL 34698-3718

GOODALE, JAMES CAMPBELL, law professor, television producer, media consultant; b. Cambridge, Mass., July 27, 1933; s. Robert Leonard and Eunice (Campbell) G.; m. Toni Krissel, May 3, 1964; children: Timothy Fuller, Ashley Krissel; foster child: Joseph Clayton Akiwenzie. Grad., Pomfret Sch., 1951; BA, Yale U., 1955; JD, U. Chgo., 1958. Bar: N.Y. 1960. Assoc. Lord, Day and Lord, N.Y.C., 1959-63; gen. atty. N.Y. Times Co., 1963-67, gen. counsel, 1967-72, sr. v.p., 1972-73, exec. v.p., 1973-79, vice-chmn., 1979-80; ptnr. Debevoise and Plimpton, 1980-93, founder, head media-comm. and intellectual property sect., 1980—96, mem. exec. com., 1981-84, of counsel, 1994-96; co-prodr., host Digital Age (formerly The Telecom. and Info. Revolution), 25 WYNE, N.Y.C., 1995—. With Cmty. Law Office, East Harlem, 1968-70; vis. lectr. Yale U. Law Sch., 1977-80; adj. prof. NYU Sch. Law, 1983-86, Fordham Law Sch., 1986—; affiliated scholar N.Y. Law Sch., 1995—; mem. N.Y. State Privacy and Security Com., 1976-79; 2nd cir. Commn. Reduction of Burdens and Costs in Civil Litigation, 1977-80; vice chmn. N.Y. State Jud. Commn. on Minorities, 1987-90, chmn., 1990-91, bd. dirs. com. to protect journalists, 1989—, chmn., 1989-94; mem. adv. bd. Comm. and the Law, 1980—; pres., owner Midtown Skating Corp., 1981-90; chmn. bd. Cable TV Law and Fin., 1981—; trustee N.Y.C. Citizens Budget Commn., 1990-98; advisor U.S. Supreme Ct. Jud. Conf. Com. on the Judiciary, 1980-89; chmn., founder PLI Comm. Law Seminar, 1972—; sec. N.Y. Observer, 1988-92, Paris Rev. Found., 2001-. Author: All About Cable, 1987; compilor, editor: The New York Times Company vs. U.S., 1971; bd. editors: Media Law Reporter (co-founder), Nat. Law Jour., 1983—; columnist nat. and N.Y. law jours.; contbr. articles on comms. law to profl. jours. Mem. rules com. Dem. Nat. Conv., 1988; chmn. N.Y. lawyer com. for Dukakis, 1988; former bd. dirs. N.Y. Times, N.Y. Times Neediest Cases Fund, N.Y. Times Found.; former trustee Pomfret Sch., Gunnery Sch., St. Bernard's Sch., Boys' Club N.Y., Salzburg Seminar, Fed. Bar Coun.; mem. vis. com. U. Chgo. Law Sch., 1977-80; bd. dirs. Human Rights Watch, 1994-96, Sky Rink Scholarship Fund, Inc., 1990-99, Citizens Pub. Utilities, 1996-99, Ice Theatre of N.Y., 1999—. Internat. Ctr. Journalists, 1998—, Paris (France) Rev. Found., 2003—. With AUS, 1958-59, Res., 1959-64. Named one of 200 Rising Leaders in U.S., Time mag., 1974, with 100 Most Influential Lawyers in U.S., Nat. Law Jour., 1991-97, one of Best Lawyers in Am., 1991-99; William Brinckerhoff Jackson scholar, 1954-55, Nat. Honor scholar U. Chgo. Law Sch., 1955-58. Fellow Inst. Judicial Adminstrn., N.Y. State Bar Assn. (chmn. spl. com. on pub. access to info. and proc. 1979-84, spl. com. on media law 1985-92); mem. N.Y.C. Bar Assn. (chmn. comm. law com. 1978-83, mem. corp. law com. 1977-81), ABA (governing bd. comm. law forum, commn. on pub. understanding about law 1979-82), Fed. Bar Coun. (trustee 1980-84), Columbia U. Seminars on Media and Society. Clubs: Yale (gov. 1964-67), Century Assn, Economic, St. Elmo, Elihu (gov. 1966-70), Washington Conn. (gov. 1972-78). Office: Debevoise & Plimpton 919 3rd Ave Fl 30 New York NY 10022-6225 Office Phone: 212-909-6253.

GOODALE, RALPH E., Canadian government official; b. Regina, Sask., Can., Oct. 5, 1949; s. Thomas Henry and Winnifred Claire (Myers) G.; m. Pamela Jean Kendel, Feb. 8, 1986. BA, U. Regina, 1971; LLB, U. Sask., 1972. M.P. from Assiniboia, Sask. Ho. of Commons, Ottawa, 1974-79; leader Sask. Liberal Party, 1981-88; mem. Legis. Assembly from provincial riding Assiniboia-Gravelbourg, Sask., 1986-88; corp. sec. Pioneer Life Ins. Co., 1989-90, Soveriegn Life Ins. Co., 1990-93; M.P. from Wascana Ho. of Commons, Ottawa, 1993—; also min. Agr. and Agri-Food Can., Ottawa, 1993-97; min. Nat. Resources Can., Can. Wheat Bd., 1997—2002; fed. interlocutor for Metis and Non-States Indians Govt. of Canada, 1997—2003, min. of state, leader of the govt. Ottawa, 2002—03, min. pub. works and govt. svcs., 2002—03, min. finance, 2003—. Parliamentary sec. to Min. Transport, Min. Wheat Bd., Pres. Privy Coun., 1974-79. Active polit. coms. Mem. Law Soc. Sask. Lutheran. Office: L Esplanade Laurier 21st Fl East Tower 140 O Connor St Ottawa ON K1A 0A6 Canada

GOODALE, TONI KRISSEL, research and development company executive; b. N.Y.C., May 26, 1941; d. Walter DuPont and Ricka Krissel; m. James Campbell Goodale, May 3, 1964; children: Timothy Fuller, Ashley Krissel, Clayton A. (Ward). AB cum laude, Smith Coll., 1963; student, U. Geneva, 1962-63; postgrad., Hunter Coll., 1964-65. Congl. intern Senator Keating U.S. Senate, Washington, 1963; broadcast analyst FCC, Washington, 1963-

64; adminstrv. asst., dir. grant rsch. dept. Ford Found., N.Y.C., 1964-67, cons. pub. edn. dept., 1968-69; N.Y. rep. Smith Coll., N.Y.C., 1975-78, asst. dir. devel., 1978-79; pres. Goodale Assocs., N.Y.C., 1979-92, chmn., CEO, 1992—. Mem. NYC 2000 Millennium Coun.; vis. com. continuing edn. New Sch. Social; mem. bd. advs. First Women's Bank; bd. dirs. N.Y. Outward Bound., mem. exec. com., chmn. alumni com.; lectr., writer in field. Columnist Fund Raising Mgmt. Bd. dirs. N.Y. Pub. Libr.; bd. dirs., mem. exec. com. Pen Am. Ctr., chmn.; mem. Women's Fgn. Policy Group; mem. UNA Chmn. Coun.; lectr. U.S. Naval Acad.; mem. alumnae fund com. Smith Coll., v.p. class, chmn. 25th reunion, Women's Forum; univ. chmn.'s coun., trustee, alumnae fund chmn., mem. alumnae coun.; bd. dirs. Brearley Sch.; mem. exec. com. Parents' Assn., St. Bernard's Sch.; mem. benefit com. N.Y. Philharmonic; trustee, bd. govs. Churchill Sch.; co-chmn. spl. events com. Carnegie Hall, The Joffrey Ballet Opening Gala; chmn. Coro Benefit Dinners; trustee N.Y. Inst. Child Devel.; mem. women's divsn. Legal Aid Soc.; mem. N.Y. com. Joffrey Ballet; mem. benefit com. Grosvenor House; vice chmn. N.Y.C. Opera Benefit, Peir Ctr. Benefit; mem. com. Sch. Am. Ballet; active Women's Forum. Mem. Am. Coun. Arts (vice-chmn. bd., exec. com., chmn. nat. patrons commn., chair long range planning com.), Nat. Cultural Alliance (bd. dirs.), Am. Assn. Fund-Raising Counsel (bd. dirs. trust for philanthropy), Nat. Assn. Fund Raising Execs., Assn. Healthcare Philanthropy, Brearley Sch. Alumnae Assn., Smith Coll. Alumnae Assn., Cosmopolitan Club, Smith Club, Washington Club, Seventh Regiment Armory Club, Doubles Internat. Club, Women's Forum (Women's Leadership Forum select cir., transition team, NYC pub. adv.). Office Phone: 212-759-2999. Personal E-mail: riowoman@aol.com.

GOODALL, JANE, zoologist; b. London, Apr. 3, 1934; d. Mortimer Herbert and Vanne (née Joseph) Morris-Goodall; m. Hugo Van Lawick, 1964 (div. 1974); one child, Hugo Eric Louis; m. Derek Bryceson, 1975 (dec. 1980). PhD, Cambridge U., 1965. Asst., sec. to Dr. Louis S. B. Leakey Coryndon Meml. Mus. Nat. History, Olduvai Gorge, Tanzania; rschr. in animal behavior, sci. dir. Gombe Stream Rsch. Ctr., Tanzania, 1960—2003. Vis. prof. psychiatry, human biology Stanford U., 1971-75; hon. vis. prof. zoology U. Dar Es Salaam, Tanzania, 1973—; lectr. Yale U., 1973; disting. adj. prof. occupl. therapy and anthropology U. So. Calif., 1990; Andrew D. White prof.-at-large Cornell U., 1996-2002; messenger of peace UN, 2002; spkr. 20/20, Nightline, Good Morning America. Author: My Friends the Wild Chimpanzees, 1967, In the Shadow of Man, 1971, The Chimpanzees of Gombe, 1986, The Chimpanzee Family Book, 1989, Through a Window, 1990, Visions of Caliban, 1993, Jane Goodall: With Love, 1994; author: (with Philip Berman) Reason for Hope, 1999; author: Dr. White, 1999, 40 Years at Gombe, 1999, The Eagle and the Wren, 2000, Africa in My Blood: An Autobiography in Letters, 2000, Chimpanzees I Love: Saving Their World and Ours, 2001, Beyond Innocence: An Autobiography in Letters, 2001; author: (with Marc Bekoff) The Ten Trusts: What We Must Do To Care for the Animals We Love, 2002; contbr. Primate Behavior, 1965, Primate Ethology, 1967, Am. Handbook of Psychiatry, 1976, Understanding Chimpanzees, 1990; author: Brutal Kinship, 1999. Founder Jane Goodall Inst. Wildlife Rsch., 1977—. Named Dame of Brit. Empire, 2003; recipient Franklin Burr award, Nat. Geographic Soc., 1963, 1964, Centennial award, 1988, Hubbard medal, 1995, Conservation award, Women's Br. N.Y. Zool. Soc., 1974, Albert Schweitzer award, Internat. Women's Inst., 1987, Kyoto prize, Inamori Found., 1990, Tanzanian Kilimanjaro medal for Contbn. to Wildlife Conservation, Pres. Mwinyi, 1996, Mt. Kilimanjaro award, 1996, Pub. Svc. award, Nat. Sci. Bd., 1998, John Hay award, Orion Soc., 1998, Huxley Meml. medal, Royal Anthrop. Inst. Gt. Britain and Ireland, 2001, 2002, Gandhi/King award for Non-Violence, 2001, Benjamin Franklin medal in Life Sci., 2003, Prince of Asturias award, 2003, Gandhi/King award, Nierenberg Prize for Sci. in the Pub. Interest, 2004, European Heroes award, Time Mag., 2004, President's Medal for Exemplary Achievement, Westminster Coll., 2005, Natura award, Pax, 2005. Mem. Am. Acad. Arts. and Scis. (hon. fgn.). Office Phone: 240-645-4000. Business E-Mail: jginformation@janegoodall.org.

GOODALL, LEONARD EDWIN, public administration educator; b. Warrensburg, Mo., Mar. 16, 1937; s. Leonard Burton and Eula (Johnson) G.; m. Lois Marie Stubblefield, Aug. 16, 1959; children: Karla, Karen, Greg. BA, Ctrl. Mo. State U., 1958; MA, U. Mo., 1960; PhD, U. Ill., 1962; AA (hon.), Schoolcraft Coll., 1977. Asst. prof. polit. sci., asst. dir. Bur. Govt. Rsch., Ariz. State U., Tempe, 1962-65, bur. dir., 1965-67; assoc. prof. polit. sci., assoc. dean faculties U. Ill. at Chgo. Circle, 1968-69, vice chancellor, 1969-71; chancellor U. Mich., Dearborn, 1971-79; pres. U. Nev., Las Vegas, 1979-85, prof. mgmt. and pub. administrn., 1985—2000. Cons. Ariz. Acad., Phoenix, 1964-67; dir. Peace Corps tng. program for Chile, 1965; vice chmn. bd. Comml. Bank of Nev., 1993-98; chmn. bd. Colonial Bank Nev., 1998—. Contbg. editor: Can. Moneysaver, 1997—; Author: The American Metropolis: Its Governments and Politics, 1968, rev. edit., 1975, Gearing Arizona's Communities to Orderly Growth, 1965, State Politics and Higher Education, 1976, When Colleges Lobby States, 1987, Managing Your TIAA-CREF Retirement Accounts, 1990, The World Wide Investor, 1991, Nevada Government and Politics, 1996, Reinventing the System, 2001; editor: Urban Politics in the Southwest, 1967. Mem. univ. exec. com. United Fund, 1966-67; v.p. Met. Fund, Inc.; mem. Mich. Gov.'s Commn. Long Range Planning, 1973-75, Tempe Planning and Zoning Commn., 1965-67, New Detroit Com., 1972-79; mem. Wayne County (Mich.) Planning Commn., 1973-79, vice chmn., 1976-79; mem. exec. bd. Clark County chpt. NCCJ, 1979-86; bd. dirs. Nev. Devel. Authority, 1980-86, Boulder Dam coun. Boy Scouts Am., 1980-89; bd. dirs. Nev. Power Co. Consumer Adv. Coun., 1984-90, chmn., 1986-89. Served with AUS, 1959. Kendrick C. Babcock fellow, 1961—62. Mem. Am. Polit. Sci. Assn., Am. Soc. Pub. Adminstrn. (chpt. pres. 1989-90), Western Govtl. Rsch. Assn. (exec. coun. 1966-68), Dearborn C. of C. (dir. 1974-79), Rotary, Phi Sigma Epsilon, Phi Kappa Phi Found. (bd. dirs. 1994-96). Home: 6530 Darby Ave Las Vegas NV 89146-6518 Office: U Nev Dept Pub Adminstrn Las Vegas NV 89154 E-mail: patgoodall@aol.com.

GOODART, NAN L., lawyer, educator; b. San Francisco, Apr. 4, 1938; BA, San Jose State U., 1959, MA, 1965; JD, U. of the Pacific, 1980. Bar: Calif. 1980, U.S. Dist. Ct. (ea. dist.) Calif. 1981. Tchr. Eastside Union High Sch., San Jose, Calif., 1960-65; counselor San Jose City Coll., 1965-75; atty. Sacramento, 1981—. Speaker numerous seminars throughout no. Calif. and other western states, 1988—. Author: Who Will It Hurt When I Die? A Primer on the Living Trust, 1992 (Nat. Mature Media award 1993), The Truth About Living Trusts, 1995 (Nat. Mature Media award 1996). Judge pro tem Sacramento County Small Claims Ct., 1988-96; instr. continuing edn. of bar Am.'s Legal Ctr., Sacramento, 1992—. Mem. Nat. Acad. Elder Law Attys., Calif. State Bar Assn., Sacramento County Bar Assn. Office: 7230 S Land Park Dr Ste 121 Sacramento CA 95831-3658

GOODE, B. ERICH, sociologist, educator, retired criminologist; b. Austin, Tex., Sept. 21, 1938; s. William Josiah and Josephine Mary (Cannizzo) Goode; m. Alice N. Neufeld, Dec. 23, 1968 (div.); m. Barbara S. Weinstein, Mar. 23, 1984; children: Sarah Rachel, Lawrence Daniel. BA, Oberlin Coll., 1960; PhD, Columbia U., 1966. Asst. prof. NYU, N.Y.C., 1965—67; asst. prof. sociology SUNY, Stony Brook, 1967—70, assoc. prof., 1970—81, prof., 1981—2000; vis. prof. U. Md., College Park, 2000—03; ret., 2003. Vis. assoc. prof. U. N.C., Chapel Hill, 1977; Lady Davis vis. prof. Hebrew U., Jerusalem, 1993. Author: The Marijuana Smokers, 1970, Drugs in American Society, 1972, 2005, Deviant Behavior, 1978, 2005, Paranormal Beliefs, 2000, Deviance in Everyday Life, 2002. Recipient Chancellors award for excellence in tchg., SUNY, 1997; grantee, NIMH, 1968; Guggenheim fellow, 1975—76. Office: U Md Dept Criminal and Criminal Justice Le Frak Hall College Park MD 20742 Personal E-mail: egoode2001@comcast.net.

GOODE, BOBBY CLAUDE, retired secondary school educator; b. Celeste, Tex., Dec. 10, 1940; s. Claude Elmer and Clarice Edna G.; m. Jean Helen Ames, June 9, 1963; children: James Lonnie, Joel Dietrich, John Shalom. BS, MIT, 1963; MA, Andover Newton Sem., Newton Centre, Mass., 1968; MS, Rensselaer Poly. Inst., 1972. Cert. tchr. sci. and math. Tchr. math. Lawrence D. Bell High Sch., Hurst, Tex., 1966-67; tchr. physics and chemistry Grapevine (Tex.) High Sch., 1967-70; tchr. advanced physics, advanced chemistry, advanced biology South Plainfield (N.J.) High Sch., 1970-96, ret., 1996. Sci. tchr. Princeton (N.J.) U., 1983. Disting. Secondary Sch. Tchg. finalist, 1983. Author: (booklets) Lap Physics, 1973, Stars, Planets, People, 1980, Atoms and Molecules, 1980, Physics Problem Solutions, 1980. Mem. Civil Rights Commn., Piscataway, N.J., 1977, Sr. Citizens Housing Com., Piscataway, 1975; ch. sch. tchr. First Bapt. Ch. of New Market, 1970-96. Named Outstanding Sci. Tchr., Sigma Xi, 1986. Mem. NEA, N.J. Edn. Assn., Am. Assn. Physics Tchrs., Nat. Sci. Tchrs. Assn. (recipient Exemplary Secondary Sci. Tchr. Nat. award 1980). Democrat. Avocations: family, travel, writing, sports. Home: 129 Stonegate S Boerne TX 78006-3411 Personal E-mail: bobgoode@gvtc.com.

GOODE, CLEMENT TYSON, retired English language educator; b. Richmond, Va., July 10, 1929; s. Clement Tyson and Bessie Mae (Trimble) G.; m. Jane Anderson, Aug. 19, 1952; children: Sara Elizabeth, Robert Clement. BA, Hendrix Coll., 1951; MA, Vanderbilt U., 1953, PhD, 1959. Instr. English Vanderbilt U., Nashville, 1954-56; instr. English, Baylor U., Waco, Tex., 1957-58; asst. prof., 1958-60; asso. prof., 1960-63; prof., 1963-97; prof. emeritus Baylor U., Waco, Tex., 1997—; Exchange prof. Seinan Gakuin U. Fukuoka, Japan, 1972-73. Author: (with Oscar Santucho) A Comprehensive Bibliography of Secondary Materials in English: George Gordon, Lord Byron with a Review of Research, 1976, George Gordon, Lord Byron: A Comprehensive, Annotated Research Bibliography of Secondary Materials in English 1973-1994, 1997. Mem. adv. bd. Salvation Army, Waco, 1968-69; deacon First Bapt. Ch., 1970— . So. Fellowship Fund grantee, 1956-57; named Outstanding Tchr., Student Congress, Baylor U., 1971; recipient Outstanding Tchr. award Baylor U., 1985. Mem. MLA, South Central MLA, Coll. Conf. Tchrs. English, Byron Soc. (Dangerfield prize 1997), Keats Shelley Assn., Nat. Council Tchrs. English. Democrat. Home: 2720 Braemar St Waco TX 76710-2119

GOODE, CORALYN, lawyer; b. New Brunswick, NJ, 1956; AB, Georgetown U., 1978; JD, Coll. William & Mary U., 1981. Bar: DC 1981, US Dist. Ct., DC 1993. Ptnr., energy, project finance Squire, Sanders & Dempsey, LLP, Houston, mem. mgmt. com., mng. ptnr.-Houston Office. Fluent in Spanish. Office: Squire Sanders & Dempsey LLP 6250 Chase Tower 600 Travis St Houston TX 77002-3000 Office Phone: 713-546-3355. Office Fax: 713-546-5830. Business E-Mail: cgoode@ssd.com.

GOODE, DAVID RONALD, transportation company executive; b. Vinton, Va., Jan. 13, 1941; s. Otto and Hessie M. (Maxey) G.; m. Susan Skiles, June 22, 1963; children: Christina, Martha. AB, Duke U., 1962; JD, Harvard U., 1965; LHD (hon.), Old Dominion U., 2003. With Norfolk & Western Ry., Roanoke, Va., 1965—82; chmn., pres., CEO Norfolk So. Corp., Va., 1982—2004, chmn., CEO, 2004—. Bd. dirs. Caterpillar, Inc., Delta Air Lines, Ga.-Pacific Corp., Tex. Instruments, Inc., Assn. Am. R.R., Bus. Comm. for Arts, Ctr. for Energy and Econ. Devel. Bd. trustees Gen. Douglas MacArthur Meml. Found., Va. Found. Ind. Colls.; Duke U.; mem. Am. Soc. Corp. Execs., The Bus. Coun., Bus. Roundtable, Coal Industry Adv. Bd., Com. to Encourage Corp. Philanthropy, Kennedy Ctr. Corp. Fund Bd., Nat. Freight Transp. Assn. Mem. ABA, Va. State Bar Assn. Democrat. Presbyterian. Avocation: golf. Home: 7301 Woodway Ln Norfolk VA 23505-3149 Office: Norfolk So Corp 3 Commercial Pl Norfolk VA 23510-2191

GOODE, JANET WEISS, elementary school educator; b. Chattanooga, Sept. 3, 1935; d. Albert H. and Dorothy E. (Crandall) Weiss; m. Gene G. Goode, June 11, 1961; children: Jennifer E., Amy V. BS in Biology, Carson-Newman Coll., 1957; MA in Botany, Vanderbilt U., 1959; MEd, Lynchburg Coll., 1980. Cert. postgrad. profl. tchr., Va. Instr. gen. biology, botany, zoology, animal ecology Carson-Newman Coll., Tenn., 1959-61; tchr. biology, chemistry Salem Acad., Winston-Salem, N.C., 1961-64; tchr. chemistry Wade Hampton High Sch., Greenville, S.C., 1964-65; tchr. sci. Va. Treatment Ctr. for Children, Richmond, 1966; tchr. biology Quantico (Va.) H.S., 1969-70; pvt. tutor Madison Heights, Va., 1980-85, James River Day Sch. and Seven Hills Sch., Lynchburg, Va., 1980-85; reading specialist Title I reading program Monelison Mid. Sch., Madison Heights, 1985-93; reading specialist Amherst County Adult Basic Edn. Program, 1992—94, 1995—2004; reading specialist Title I reading and Reading Recovery Pleasant View Elem. Sch., Monroe, Va., 1993-96, Madison Heights (Va.) Elem. Sch., 1996—. Vis. instr. U. Chattanooga, summer 1960; mem. learning disabilities del. to Russia and Lithuania, Citizen Amb. Program, 1993; mem. mentor tchr. program Amherst County Pub. Schs., 1999-2000. Author: Can You Read a Baseball Card?; co-author: Transitional Intervention Program. Sponsor sch. lit. mag. Monelison Mid. Sch., Pleasant View Elem. Sch.; organist, past newsletter editor for Ptnr. Ch. com. First Unitarian Ch.; mem. Friends of Libr., Madison Heights Br. Libr., helper ann. book sale. Recipient Reading Tchr. of the Year Piedmont Va. Area Reading Coun., 1993-94. Mem. NEA, Nat. Coun. Tchrs. of English, Va. Edn. Assn., Amherst Edn. Assn., Internat. Dyslexia Assn., Piedmont Area Reading Coun. (past newletter editor, past treas.), Va. State Reading Assn., Internat. Reading Assn., Lynchburg Stamp Club. Personal E-mail: chidog04@aol.com.

GOODE, JOHN MARTIN, manufacturing executive; b. Chgo., Sept. 24, 1934; s. Robert C. and Alyce (Belz) G.; children: John Martin, Sue Ellen, James Edward, Leslie Maureen. B Commerce, DePaul U., 1960; MBA, U. Chgo., 1966; EdD, No. Ill. U., 1984. CPA, Ill.; CMA, Ill. Contr. farm equipment div. Allis Chalmers, Milw., 1966-69; v.p., contr. Maremont Corp., Chgo., 1969-73; sr. v.p. Whittakers Corp., Chgo., 1973-75; assoc. dean DePaul U., Chgo., 1976-78, asst. prof., 1975-80; sr. v.p. fin. and corp. planning J.I. Case Co., Racine, Wis., 1980-85; chmn. bd., chief exec. officer Prestolite Electric Inc., Toledo, 1986-91; dean Sch. Mgmt. and Bus. Nat. U., San Diego, 1991-93; investor, 1993—; chmn. bd. dirs., CEO K&W Products, LLC, Bloomington, Ind., 1996-2000. Chmn. bd. dirs., CEO, A.P. Labs, Inc., San Diego, Am. Innotek Inc., San Diego. Mem. San Diego Yacht club, Univ. Club, Del Mar Country Club. Home: PO Box 170 Genoa NV 89411-0170

GOODE, RICHARD BENJAMIN, economist, educator; b. Ft. Worth, July 31, 1916; s. Flavius M. and Laura Nell (Carson) G.; m. Liesel Gottschalk, June 23, 1943 (dec. May 2002). AB, Baylor U., 1937; MA, U. Ky., 1939; PhD, U. Wis., 1947. Economist U.S. Bur. Budget, 1941-45, Treasury Dept., 1945-47; asst. prof. econs. U. Chgo., 1947-51; with IMF, Washington, 1951-59, 65-81, dir. fiscal affairs dept., 1965-81; mem. staff Brookings Instn., Washington, 1959-65, guest scholar, 1981-87; professorial lectr. Sch. Advanced Internat. Studies, Johns Hopkins U., 1981-88. Cons. Treasury Dept., 1947-51, UN, 1950, World Bank, 1964. Author: The Corporation Income Tax, 1951; The Individual Income Tax, 1964, rev. edit., 1976; Government Finance in Developing Countries, 1984; Economic Assistance to Developing Countries through the IMF, 1985. Editor Nat. Tax Jour., 1948-51. Mem. Am. Econ. Assn., Royal Econ. Soc., Nat. Tax Assn. (Holland medal for contbns. to study and practice of pub. fin. 1997), Internat. Inst. Pub. Fin., Cosmos Club. Home: 5420 Connecticut Ave NW Washington DC 20015-2813

GOODE, STEPHEN HOGUE, publishing company executive; b. Charlotte, N.C., Dec. 25, 1924; s. Henry Grady and Marie Louella (Creamer) G.; m. Jean Cameron Advena, Oct. 16, 1953; children: Elizabeth Whitston Joane Downe, Polly Turpin Dulcinea Hogue. BA, U. Md., 1948; MA, U. Pa., 1954, PhD, 1958. Asst. prof. English Rensselaer Poly. Inst., 1958-59; asst. prof. Fairleigh Dickinson U., 1960-65; dir. libraries, asso. prof. English Russell Sage Coll., 1965-78; pres., chmn. bd. Whitston Pub. Co., Troy, N.Y., 1968-81, Turpin Book Corp., Troy, 1973-80; pres. Penkevill Pub. Co., Greenwood, Fla., 1982—. Dir. Trenowyth Pub. Co., Penkivil Book Co. Author: Index to Little Magazines, 1943-47, 1965, Index to Little Magazines, 1940-42, 1967, Index to Commonwealth Little Magazines, 1966-67, 68, plus, biennial, Index to American Little Magazines, 1920-39, 1969, 1900-1919, 1974; editor: Studies in 20th Century, 1968-75; founding editor Am. Humanities Index, 1978-82. Served with AUS, 1943-46, 49-52. Decorated Purple Heart, Bronze Star with oak leaf cluster. Mem. MLA, Am. Hist. Assn., Bibliog. Soc. (London), Bibliog. Soc. Am., Bibliog. Soc. U. Va., Index Soc. (London). Clubs: Grolier (N.Y.C.).

GOODE, VIRGIL H., JR., congressman; b. Richmond, Va., Oct. 17, 1946; m. Lucy D. Dodson; 1 child, Catherine S. BA, U. Richmond, 1969; JD, U. Va., 1973. Mem. Va. Senate, 1973-97, U.S. Congress from 5th Va. dist., 1997—; mem. appropriations com., subcoms. on military contruction, agr. and vet. admin. Recipient Outstanding Legis. Svc. award Va. State Sheriffs' Assn., Outstanding Svc. award Vol. Rescue Squads, 1994. Mem. Phi Beta Kappa, Omicron Delta Kappa, Lambda Chi Alpha, Phi Alpha Delta. Republican. Baptist. Office: Ho of Reps 1520 Longworth Ho Office Bldg Washington DC 20515-4605*

GOODELL, GARY LLOYD, minister, educator; b. Portland, Maine, Nov. 12, 1937; s. George Lloyd and Doris Elizabeth Goodell; m. Janice Elaine Bailey, July 2, 1965; children: Miriam Elizabeth Goodell1, Sharon Elaine Eygabroad. BA, Ea. Nazarene Coll., Quincy, Mass., 1969; MA, Ea. Nazarene Coll., 1970; MA in Religion, Ea. Bapt. Theol. Sem., Phila., 1981; DMin, Ea. Bapt. Theol. Sem., 1983; ThD, U. South Africa, 1996. Ordained Ch. of the Nazarene, 1969. Pastor Ch. of the Nazarene, Berwick, Maine, 1967—68, Boston, 1968—71, Ch. of the Nazarene, Balt., 1971—74, New Egypt, NJ, 1974—81, Alloway, NJ, 1981—89, Ch. of the Nazarne, Burlington, NJ, 1989—94; acad. dean Swaziland Nazarene Bible Coll., 1994—96; dean Faculty of Arts Africa Nazarene U., Nairobi, Kenya, 1996—99; pastor Ch. of the Nazarene, Rochester, NY, 2000—. Author: Heavenly Tongues or Earthly Languages?, 1989. Served with U.S. Army, 1954—57. Mem.: Wesleyan Theol. Soc. Avocations: fishing, travel. Home: 228 Dean Rd Spencerport NY 14559-9541 Office: Ch of the Nazarene 855 Long Pond Rd Rochester NY 14612 Office Phone: 585-225-1690. Personal E-mail: GGoodell@netscape.com.

GOODELL, GEORGE SIDNEY, retired finance educator; b. Sheboygan, Wis., Nov. 29, 1921; s. George Sidney and Emma (Kreuter) G.; m. Anne Stubenrauch, June 16, 1951; children: Margaret Anne, John Winfield. BA, Carroll Coll., 1943; MBA, U. Chgo., 1947; JD, Marquette U., 1949; PhD, Northwestern U., 1959. Bar: Wis. 1949; chartered fin. analyst. Pvt. practice, Sheboygan, 1949-52; credit analyst U.S. Steel Corp., Chgo., 1952-53; asst. sec. Ill. Bankers Assn., Chgo., 1953-56; tech. writer Bank Rsch. Inst., Chgo., 1956-57; from asst. to assoc. prof. fin. Ohio State U., Columbus, 1957-66; prof. Kent State U., Ohio, 1966-71; dean Coll. Bus. Adminstrn. Roosevelt U., Chgo., 1971-75; prof., chmn. dept. fin. Loyola U., Chgo., 1975-80, Miami U., Oxford, Ohio, 1980-92, prof. emeritus, 1992—; ret., 1992. Served to lt. (j.g.) USN, 1943-46, PTO. Mem. Inst. Chartered Fin. Analysts, Fin. Mgmt. Assn., Midwest Fin. Assn., Wis. Bar Assn. Methodist. Home: 124 Country Club Dr Oxford OH 45056-9049

GOODELL, JOSEPH EDWARD, manufacturing executive; b. El Paso, Tex., Aug. 18, 1937; s. Joseph Edward and Grace Louise (Beck) g.; m. Margaret Rives, Aug. 12, 1961 (di. June 1978); children: Marian, Margaret Trout, MarthaLamanna, Maryellen Olszyk; m. Mary Ellen Hager, Sept. 17, 1993. BSME, MIT, 1959; MBA, Harvard U., 1961. Project engr. Bechtel Corp., San Francisco, 1961-65; mfg. engr. Chase Brass and Copper Co., Cleve., 1965-67; adminstrv. mgr. Montpelier, Ohio, 1967-69, Waterbury, Conn., 1969-71; v.p., gen. mgr. Montpelier, 1971-76; group v.p. Chase Brass and Copper Co., Cleve., 1976-79, Pangborn div. Carborundum, Hagerstown, Md., 1979-81; v.p. planning Standard Oil Ind. Products, Cleve., 1981—85, sr. v.p., 1982-85; pres., CEO Am. Brass Co., Buffalo, 1985—90; chmn. bd. Empire Steel Co., 1999—2001, West Tex. and Buffalo Steam Ship & Rwy. Co., 2001—. Bd. dirs. WNED Pub. Broadcasting Sta., Buffalo, Tech. Devel. Corp., Buffalo, Tech. Bldg. Corp., Boston; owner, operator pvt. railroad car Daguy Taggart. Active Boy Scouts Am., Waterbury, Conn.; past chmn. Buffalo Health Care Coalition; vice chmn. Greater Buffalo Partnership; chmn. Horizons Waterfront Commn.; dir. Downtown Devel., Inc.; dir. Buffalo State Coll. Found.; trustee, past pres., past exec. dir. Buffalo Philharm. Orch.; chmn. planning com. Buffalo Expo Pan Am. 2001; past bd. adv. Symphony Orch. Inst.; past v.p. Sheas Preservation Soc.; past bd. dirs. Kenmore Mercy Hosp.; bd. dirs. Kleinmans Music Hall, Erie County Who Does What Commn., Erie County Exec. Transition Com., Erie County Stabilization Project, 2005. Recipient Spl. award Buffalo Philharm. Orch., 1999; named Citizen of Yr. Buffalo, 1996. Mem. Buffalo Club, Wanakah Country Club. Home: 6746 Lake Shore Rd Derby NY 14047-9739

GOODELL, ROSEMARY WILSON, artist, educator; d. Virgil Elwood and Estelle Fletcher Wilson; m. Richard Henry Goodell, June 12, 1974; children: Heather Lee, Richard Henry, Nelson Wilson. BA, U. Calif., Berkeley, 1968, MA, 1970. Instr. Baton Rouge C.C., 1999—, chair art dept., 2000—03. Reviewer Wadsworth Pub., Belmont, Calif.; panelist La. Divsn. Art, Baton Rouge; artist mem. Baton Rouge Gallery; painting resident Skidmore Coll., 1996, Vt. Studio Ctr., 2001. Exhibitions include Seasons of the Mind, New Work, The Landscape of Sleep. Visual Art fellow, La. Divsn. Arts, 2003, Fullbright Meml. fellow, Japan, 1998, Artist Mini-grantee, La. Divsn. Arts, 1998, 2000. Mem.: Coll. Art Assn. (assoc.), Phi Beta Kappa (life). Home: 16720 Caesar Ave Baton Rouge LA 70816 Office: Baton Rouge CC 5310 Florida Blvd Baton Rouge LA 70806 Office Phone: 225-216-8039.

GOODEN, BENNY L., school system administrator; Supt. Ft. Smith (Ark.) Pub. Schs. State finalist Nat. Supt. Yr. award, 1993; recipient Phoebe Apperson Hearst Outstanding Educator award Nat. PTA, 1999. Office: Ft Smith Pub Schs 3205 Jenny Lind Rd Fort Smith AR 72901-7101 Office Phone: 479-785-2501.

GOODEN, ERIC, government agency administrator, real estate agent; b. Balt., Apr. 20, 1974; s. Esau Gooden, Jr. and Shirley May Spell. BA Polit. Sci., Morgan State U., 1997, MA Internat. Studies, 2003. Cert. realtor Long and Foster Real Estate Inst., Md., 1998. Contact rep. IRS, Balt., 1998—2001; summer intern Diplomatic Security, Washington, 2001; dist. adjudicators officer INS, Balt., 2001—; real estate agt. Von Realty, Inc., Balt., 2001—. Fellow Morris Goldseker fellowship, Morgan State U., 1998—99; scholar Dacosta scholarship, 2000. Mem.: Balt. Coun. Fgn. Affairs, Psi Sigma Alpha. Avocations: studying Mandarin Chinese, travel. Home: 2901 Presbury St Baltimore MD 21216-3522 Personal E-mail: eincognito4life@aol.com.

GOODEN, GREGORY ALLEN, music educator; s. Edward and Elsie Gooden. MusB in Edn., Kans. State U., 1981, MusM, 1996; postgrad., U. Memphis, 1986—91. Orff Schulwerk Cert. levels 1-3 and Masters class. Elem. gen. music tchr. Buhler (Kans.) Sch. Dist., 1981—2002; lectr. music Sterling (Kans.) Coll., 1998—2005; dir. McPherson (Kans.) Arts Coun. Children's Choir, 2003—05; substitute tchr. Salina (Kans.) Sch. Dist., 2002—. Orff clinician Suzuki String Festival Parsons (Kans.) Suzuki Orgn., 1997—2005; level 1 recorder instr./workshop coord. Orff-Schulwerk Kans. State U., 1997, Baker U., 2002; Orff clinician Suzuki String Festival Heart of Am. Suzuki Orgn., Independance, Mo., 2003; recorder instr./workshop coord. Orff-Schulwerk level 2 cert. Baker U., Baldwin City, Kans., 2002—04; Kans. music propel trainer KSDE, mem. music stds. writing team, Kans.; bd. dirs. Kans. Alliance For Arts Edn.; presenter in field. Composer: (Orff-Schulwerk arrangement) Bill of Rights Rap, 1993. Mem.: Am. Choral Dirs. Assn., NEA (mem. Ark valley adminstrv. bd. Kans. chpt. 1999—2002, pres. Buhler chpt. 2001—02, mem. coord. com. Kans. chpt., mem. negotiations team Buhler chpt.), Music Educators Nat. Conf., Am. Orff-Schulwerk Assn., Kans. Orff Chpt. (pres. 1992—94, bd. dirs.), Kans. Music Educators Assn. (state elem. chmn. 1989—91, bd. dirs. 1991—2001, guest dir. elem. honor choir 1994—96, 1999—2000), Kans. State U. Alumni Assn., Kappa Delta Pi. Personal E-mail: ggooden7401@aol.com.

GOODENBERGER, DANIEL MARVIN, medical educator; b. McCook, Nebr., Apr. 24, 1948; s. Marvin Eugene and Mary Ellen (Marshall) G.; m. Janet Ann King, July 30, 1979; children: James Michael, Katherine Elizabeth. BS, U. Nebr., 1970; MD, Duke U., 1974. Diplomate Am. Bd. Internal Medicine, Am. Bd. Emergency Medicine (examiner 1983-95), Am. Bd. Pulmonary Disease, Am. Bd. Critical Care Medicine. Intern Peter Bent Brigham Hosp., Boston, 1974-75, resident in internal medicine, 1975-76; clin. assoc. Nat. Cancer Inst., Bethesda, Md., 1976-78; fellow pulmonary and critical care medicine Boston U. Med. Ctr., 1985-88; assoc. dir. emergency dept. Arlington (Va.) Hosp., 1979-82; edn. dir. emergency dept. Georgetown U. Hosp., Washington, 1982-85; dir. emergency svcs. U. Hosp., Boston, 1986-87; dir. pulmonary and critical care fellowship Washington U. Med. Schs., St. Louis, 1989-93; dir. pulmonary cons. svcs. Barnes Hosp., St. Louis, 1990-93, dir. internal medicine residency program, 1992—; assoc. prof. medicine Washington U., St. Louis, 1995-99; dir. divsn. med. edn. Washington U. Sch. Medicine, St. Louis, 1998—, prof. medicine, 1999—. Chief Wood-Moore Firm, Barnes-Jewish Hosp., 1996-2001. Editor Careers, 1996-98. Lt. comdr. USPHS, 1973-78. Winthrop Breon and Am. Coll. Chest Physicians scholar, 1987. Fellow ACP, Am. Coll. Chest Physicians; mem. AMA, Am. Thoracic Soc., Am. Clin. and Climatological Assn., Assn. Program Dirs. Internal Medicine (nominating and publs. com. 1991-98, councillor 2004—), St. Louis Met. Med. Soc. (councilor 1997-2000), St. Louis Club, Harbor Point Yacht Club, Phi Beta Kappa, Alpha Omega Alpha. Methodist. Avocations: theater, symphony music, travel, sailing. Home: 4355 Maryland Ave Saint Louis MO 63108-2737 Office: Washington U Sch Medicine Box 8121 660 S Euclid Ave Saint Louis MO 63110-1010 Office Phone: 314-362-8065. Personal E-mail: goodenberger@sbcglobal.net.

GOODENDAY, LUCY SHERMAN, internist, educator; b. N.Y.C., Oct. 2, 1937; d. Leo Daniel and Winnie Victoria (Bornstein) Sherman; m. Kenneth Benjamin Goodenday, Aug. 31, 1958. AB, Bryn Mawr Coll., 1959; MD, N.Y. Med. Coll., 1963. Diplomate cardiovasc. disease Am. Bd. Internal Medicine; cert. nuclear cardiology. Clin. instr. U. Calif., San Francisco, 1969-71, asst. clin. prof., 1971-75; asst. prof. medicine U. Mich., Ann Arbor, 1975-78; assoc. prof. med. Med. Coll. Ohio, Toledo, 1979—2002, prof. medicine, 2003—. Editor: Hypertension in the Community, 1971; author: (movie, booklet) Current Approach to the Hypertensive Patient, 1970, (tape) Pro and Con Views on Routine Exercise Testing, 1977, Nuclear Cardiology Interactive Learning System, 1996—; editor-in-chief Studies in Nuclear Cardiology, 2001—; contbr. articles to profl. jours. Trustee N.W. Ohio AHA, 1983—, mem. rsch. rev. bd., 1988—; trustee Ohio Valley affil. AHA, mem. exec. com., 1996—99. Fellow NIH, 1965-68, AAUW, 1968-69, Med. Coll. Ohio Tchg. Scholars Fellow, 2000; grantee VA, 1973-78, Am. Heart Assn., 1977-84, Warner Lambert, 1976, Nycomed Amersham, 2000-01. Mem. Am. Fedn. for Clin. Rsch., Am. Soc. Nuclear Medicine, Am. Soc. Nuclear Cardiology (founding mem.), Med. Rsch. Soc., Am. Coll. Cardiology. Mem. Soc. Of Friends. Avocation: horse breeding and training. Office: Med Coll Ohio PO Box 10008 Toledo OH 43699-0008 E-mail: lgoodenday@mco.edu.

GOODENOUGH, ELIZABETH NOBLE, literature educator, child advocate; b. Detroit, May 12, 1947; d. Daniel Webster Goodenough and Margaret Brooks Van Dusen; m. James Gillespie Leaf, Aug. 14, 1976; children: James Munro Leaf, William Goodnough Leaf. BA, Smith Coll., 1969; MAT, Harvard U., 1971, PhD, 1982. Tchr., admissions officer Phillips Acad., Andover, Mass., 1972—74; asst. sr. tutor Eliot House, Harvard U., Cambridge, Mass., 1975—82, Allston Burr sr. tutor, 1982—88; lectr. English Harvard U., Cambridge, Mass., 1982—88; asst. prof. English Claremont (Calif.) McKenna Coll., 1988—93; vis. prof. English U. Mich., Ann Arbor, 1993—95; lectr., adj. prof. English U. Mich. Residential Coll., Sch. Edn., Ann Arbor, 1995—. Bd. dirs. Alliance for Childhood, College Park, Md., 2001—; adv. bd. Skillman Ctr. for Children, Detroit, 2000—; asst. editor Mich. Quar. Rev., Ann Arbor, 2000—; series editor Landscapes of Childhood Wayne State U. Press. Editor: Secret Spaces of Childhood, 2003; co-editor: (jour.) Lion and the Unicorn, 2000, Infant Tongues: Voice of the Child in Literature, 1994. Exhbn. curator Garden Club of Mich., Grosse Pointe, 1999; hunger kitchen vol. St. Clare's Episc. Hunger Coalition, Ann Arbor, 1993—. Fellow: Soc. for Values in Higher Edn.; mem.: U. Mich. Com. for Children, Children's Literature Assn. Democrat. Episcopalian. Avocations: yoga, squash, tennis, hiking. Office: U Mich Residential Coll East Quad Ann Arbor MI 98109-1245 Home: 2260 Pinegrove Ct Ann Arbor MI 48103 Business E-Mail: lizgoode@umich.edu.

GOODENOUGH, JOHN BANNISTER, engineering educator, research physicist; b. Jena, Germany, July 25, 1922; came to U.S., 1922; parents Am. citizens. s. Erwin Ramsdell and Helen Meriam (Lewis) G.; m. Irene Johnston Wiseman, June 16, 1951. AB, Yale U., 1943; MS, U. Chgo., 1951, PhD, 1952; DHC (hon.), U. Bordeaux, France, 1967; MA (hon.), Oxford (Eng.) U., 1976; DHC U. Santiago de Compostela (hon.), 2002. Rsch. engr. Westinghouse Rsch. Corp., 1951-52; rsch. scientist, group leader Lincoln Lab., MIT, 1952-76; prof., head inorganic chem. lab. U. Oxford, England, 1976-86; Virginia H. Cockrell Centennial Chair and prof. engring. U. Tex., Austin, 1986—. Cons. numerous firms in U.K. and U.S.; trustee, fellow Neuroscis. Rsch. Program, 1962-76; Centenary lectr. Royal Soc. Chemistry, 1976; vis. Raman prof. Indian Inst. Sci., 1983; hon. prof. Northwestern U., Changchun, China, 1996, Jilin U., Shenyang, China, 1996. Author: Magnetism and the Chemical Bond, 1963, Les Oxydes des métaux de transition, 1973; assoc. editor Materials Rsch. Bull., 1966—, Jour. Solid State Chemistry, 1968—, Structure and Bonding, 1977—, Solid State Ionics, 1980—, Superconductor Sci. and Tech., 1987, Jour. Materials Chem., 1991—, Chem. of Materials, 1989-92; mem. exec. editorial bd. Jour. Applied Electrochemistry, 1982-89, European Jour. Solid State and Inorganic chemistry, 1992—, contbr. over 550 articles to profl. jours., 85 revs., chpts. to books. Capt. USAAF, 1942-48. Recipient Solid State Chemistry prize Chem. Soc. U.K., 1980, Sr. Rsch. award Am.Soc. for Engring. Edn., 1990; professorial fellow St. Catherine's Coll., Oxford U., 1976; recipient medal for disting. achievement U. Pa., 1996, John Bardeen award Minerals, Metals and Materials Soc., 1997, Olin Palladium award Electrochem. Soc., 1999, Japan prize, 2001. Fellow AAAS, Royal Soc. Chemistry, Am. Phys. Soc. (profl.), Indian Acad. Scis. (fgn. assoc.), Nat. Acad. Engring., Academie des Scis. L'Institut de France (fgn. assoc.), Materials Rsch. Soc. (hon.), Academia de Cienias Exactas, Fisicas y Naturales (fgn. assoc.); mem. Am. Chem. Soc., Materials Rsch. Soc. (Von Hippel award 1989), Japanese Phys. Soc., Ashmolean Club (Oxford), Skull and Bones, Phi Beta Kappa, Sigma Xi, registered Profl. Engr. Episcopalian. Achievements include discovery of lithium cobalt oxide. Office: Mechanical Engineering Dept U Tex ETC 9 102 1 Univ Sta C2200 Austin TX 78712-0292 Office Phone: 512-471-1646. Business E-Mail: jgoodenough@mail.utexas.edu.

GOODENOUGH, OLIVER RAMSDELL, lawyer, educator; b. Phila., Dec. 18, 1952; s. Ward Hunt and Ruth (Gallagher) G.; m. Alison Hudnut Clarkson, Apr. 26, 1955; children: Ward Hunt, William Hudnut Clarkson. BA, Harvard U., 1975; JD, U. Pa., 1978. Bar: Pa. 1978, N.Y. 1980, U.S. Dist. Ct. (so. and ea. dists.) N.Y. 1980. Assoc. Cleary Gottlieb Steen & Hamilton, N.Y.C., 1978-81, Fulop & Hardee, N.Y.C., 1981-82, Kay Collyer & Boose, N.Y.C., 1983-86, ptnr., 1986-90, of counsel, 1991—2003; prof. law Vt. Law Sch., South Royalton, 1991—. Lectr. law U. Pa., Phila., 1988-90; vis. scholar Cambridge (Eng.) U., 1991, 99-2000; bd. dirs. Vt. Film Commn., Montpelier, 1996-2003; vis. prof. Charité, Humboldt U., Berlin, 2003—. Author: Privacy and Publicity, 1996; co-author: This Business of Television, 1991, 2d. edit. 1998. Gruter Inst. rsch. fellow, 1994—. Democrat. Episcopalian. Avocation: music. Office: Vt Law Sch Chealsea St South Royalton VT 05068 Office Phone: 802-831-1231. Business E-Mail: ogoodenough@vermontlaw.edu.

GOODENOUGH, WARD HUNT, anthropologist, educator; b. Cambridge, Mass., May 30, 1919; s. Erwin Ramsdell and Helen Miriam (Lewis) G.; m. Ruth Gallagher, Feb. 8, 1941, (dec. March 6, 2001); children: Hester G. Goodenough Gelber, Deborah L. Goodenough Gordon, Oliver R., Garrick G. Grad., Groton (Mass.) Sch., 1937; AB, Cornell U., 1940; PhD, Yale U., 1949. Instr. anthropology U. Wis., 1948-49; mem. faculty U. Pa., Phila., 1949—, prof. anthropology, 1962-89, university prof., 1980-89, emeritus univ. prof., 1989—, chmn. dept. anthropology, 1976-82. Vis. prof. Cornell U., Ithaca, N.Y., 1961-62, vis. lectr., summer 1950; vis. lectr. Swarthmore Coll., spring 1955, Bryn Mawr Coll., fall 1955, U. Hawaii, summer 1959, 75-77; vis. prof. U. Wis., Milw., summer 1967, Yale U., New Haven, spring 1969, Colo. Coll., spring 1979, U. Hawaii, 1982-83; anthrop. studies in Truk, 1947, 64-65, Gilbert Islands, 1951, New Guinea, 1951, 54; Pacific Sci. bd. Nat. Acad. Scis.-NRC, 1962-66; standing com. anthropology and social scis. Pacific Sci. Assn., 1962-66; cons. Office Sci. and Tech., 1961-62. Author: Property, Kin and Community on Truk, 1951, Cooperation in Change, 1963, Explorations in Cultural Anthropology, 1964, Description and Comparison in Cultural Anthropology, 1970, Culture, Language and Society, 1971, Trukese-English Dictionary, 1980, 90, Prehistoric Settlement of the Pacific, 1996, Under Heaven's Brow, 2002. Bd. dirs. Human Rels. Area Files, Inc., 1964-86, chmn., 1971-81; bd. dirs. East Rock Inst., 1986-98, sec., 1995-98. With AUS, 1941-45. Fellow Center Advanced Study Behavioral Scis., 1957-58; Guggenheim fellow, 1979-80; Fulbright lectr. St. Patrick's Coll., Ireland, 1987. Mem. NAS, AAAS (v.p., chmn. sect. H 1971, bd. dirs. 1972-75), Am. Philos. Soc., Am. Acad. Arts and Scis., Royal Anthrop. Inst., Am. Anthrop. Assn. (editor 1966-70, Disting. Svc. award 1986), Am. Ethnol. Soc. (pres. 1962), Soc. Applied Anthropology (pres. 1963, Malinowski award 1997), Linguistics Soc. Am., Inst. on Religion in an Age of Sci. (pres. 1987-89), Polynesian Soc., Assn. Social Anthropology in Oceania, Phi Beta Kappa, Sigma Xi, Phi Kappa Phi. Office: Univ Penn Univ Museum Philadelphia PA 19104-6398 Business E-Mail: whgooden@sas.upenn.edu.

GOODENOW, ROBERT W., lawyer, former sports association administrator; b. Dearborn, Mich., Oct. 29, 1952; BA, Harvard U., 1974; JD, U. Detroit, 1979. Atty., Detroit; dep. exec. dir. NHL Player's Assn., Toronto, Canada, 1990—92, exec. dir., gen. counsel, 1992—2005.*

GOODFELLOW, ROBIN IRENE, surgeon; b. Xenia, Ohio, Apr. 14, 1945; d. Willis Douglas and Irene Linna (Kirkland) G. BA summa cum laude, Western Res. U., Cleve., 1967; MD cum laude, Harvard U., 1971. Diplomate Am. Bd. Surgery. Intern, resident Peter Bent Brigham Hosp., Boston, 1971-76; staff surgeon Boston U., 1976-80, asst. prof. surgery, 1977-80; pvt. practice medicine specializing in surgery Jonesboro, La., 1980-81; practice medicine specializing in surgery Albion, Mich., 1984-87, Coldwater, Mich., 1987—. Bd. Overseers Case Western Res. U., 1977-82. AAUW fellow, 1970. Fellow ACS; mem. AMA, Phi Beta Kappa. Republican. Methodist.

GOODFRIEND, HERBERT JAY, lawyer; b. N.Y.C., Sept. 9, 1926; s. Sidney and Blanche (Prager) G.; m. Barbara Gottlieb, Oct. 12, 1952; children: Sandra, Beth Ann. AB, NYU, 1947, LLB, 1950, LLM in Taxation, 1953. Bar: N.Y. 1950, U.S. Dist. Ct. (so. dist.) N.Y. 1951, U.S. Dist. Ct. (ea. dist.) N.Y. 1952, U.S. Ct. Appeals (2nd cir.) 1953, U.S. Tax Ct. 1954. Assoc. Otterbourg, Steindler Houston & Rosen, N.Y.C., 1950—55, ptnr., 1955—86; counsel Summit, Solomon & Feldesman, 1986-93, N.Y.C., Philips, Nizer, 1993—. Counsel N.Y. Bd. Trade, N.Y.C., 1981-87, bd. dirs., 1982-88; spl. master Supreme Ct. New York County, N.Y.C., 1977-79; vice chmn., bd. dirs. Jones Apparel Group, Inc., 1990-98., sec., 1990-2001. Columnist N.Y. Law Jour., 1977-79, treas. 2001-04. Treas., dir. N.Y.C. Alliance Against Sexual Abuse, 2001—; dir. Cmty. Health Charities N.Y., 2004—. With U.S. Army, 1945-46. Fellow Am. Bar Found., Coll. Law Practice Mgmt.; mem. ABA (chmn. econs. law practice sect. 1984-85, ho. of dels. 1994-97), N.Y. State Bar Assn. (chmn. com. on law office econ. and mgmt. 1983-85), N.Y. County Lawyers Assn. (com. on arbitration 1974-87), NYU Club (v.p. exec. com. 1976-80), Adelphi U. Inst. for Paralegal Tng. (adv. bd. 1976-96), Am. Apparel Mfg. Assn. (fin. mgmt. com. 1980-2001), Tau Delta Phi (nat. pres. 1952-57). Avocations: golf, computers. Home: 176 E 71st St New York NY 10021-5159 Office: Phillips Nizer 666 Fifth Ave New York NY 10103 Office Phone: 212-841-0720. Business E-Mail: hgoodfriend@phillipsnizer.com.

GOODHARTZ, GERALD, law librarian; b. N.Y.C., Oct. 23, 1938; s. Jack and Anna (Sperling) G.; m. Carol Scialli, Aug. 18, 1969; children: Joanna, Allison. BSCE, CCNY, 1961; MLS, U. So. Calif., 1970. Night reference asst. Assn. Bar of City of N.Y., 1956—61; libr. asst. Cravath, Swaine & Moore, N.Y.C., 1961—65; head libr. Rosenman, Colin, Freund, Lewis & Cohen, N.Y.C., 1965—69, Keatinge & Sterling, L.A., 1969—70, Kaye, Scholer, Fierman, Hays & Handler, N.Y.C., 1970—98; mgr. info. svcs. Broad and Cassel, Orlando, 1998—99; dir. libr. svcs. Brown Raysman Millstein Felder & Steiner LLP, N.Y.C., 1999—. Libr. planning cons. Olympic Towers, N.Y.C., 1975; lectr. in field. Mem.: ABA, Mem. ABA, ALA, Am. Assn. Law Librs. (cert.), Law Libr. Assn. Greater NY, Assn. Law Librs. of Upstate NY, Spl. Librs. Assn., Am. Soc. Info. Scientists, Am. Mgmt. Assn., Assn. Info. Mgrs., Nat. Micrographics Assn. Office: Brown Raysman Millstein Felder & Steiner LLP 900 3rd Ave New York NY 10022 Business E-Mail: ggoodhartz@brownraysman.com.

GOODHEART, EUGENE, language educator; b. Bklyn., June 26, 1931; s. Samuel and Miriam G.; m. Patricia Somer, Aug. 13, 1960 (div. July 1973); children: Eric, Jessica; m. Joan Bamberger, July 8, 1977. BA, Columbia U., 1953, PhD in English and Comparative Lit., 1961; MA in English, U. Va., 1954; postgrad. (Fulbright fellow), Sorbonne, U. Paris, 1956-57. From instr. to asst. prof. English Bard Coll., 1958-62; asst. prof. U. Chgo., 1962-66; assoc. prof. Mt. Holyoke Coll., 1966-67; from assoc. prof. to prof. MIT, 1967-74; prof., chmn. dept. English Boston U., 1974-83; Edytha Macy Gross prof. emeritus humanities Brandeis U., 1983—2001, emeritus, 2001—. Vis. prof. Wesleyan U. Summer Sch., 1963-64, 66, 69; Gauss seminarist Princeton U., 1972. Author: The Utopian Vision of D.H. Lawrence, 1963, The Cult of the Ego, 1968, Culture and the Radical Conscience, 1973, The Failure of Criticism, 1978, The Skeptic Disposition in Contemporary Criticism, 1984, Pieces of Resistance, 1987, Desire and Its Discontents, 1991, The Reign of Ideology, 1996, Does Literary Studies Have a Future, 1999, Confessions of a Secular Jew, 2001, Novel Practices: Classic Modern Fiction, 2004. Fellow Am. Coun. Learned Socs., 1965-66, Guggenheim Found., 1970-71, NEH, 1980-81, Nat. Humanities Ctr., 1987—; resident Rockefeller Found., Bellagio. Mem. MLA, PEN. Home: 25 Barnard Ave Watertown MA 02472-3412 Office: Brandeis Univ Dept English Waltham MA 02454 E-mail: goodheart@brandeis.edu.

GOODHUE, PETER AMES, obstetrician and gynecologist, educator; b. Ft. Fairfield, Maine, Feb. 26, 1931; s. Lawrence and Zylpha (Ames) G.; m. Edith Ann Helfenstein, June 21, 1958; children: Lisa Grace, Scott Ames. BA, Amherst Coll., 1954; MD, U. Vt., 1958. Diplomate Am. Bd. Ob-Gyn. Intern Bellevue Hosp., N.Y.C., 1958-59; resident Yale-New Haven Med. Ctr., 1959-62; practice medicine specializing in ob-gyn. Stamford, Conn., 1964—. Assoc. clin. prof. ob-gyn. N.Y. Med. Coll., 1984—98; asst. clin. prof. ob-gyn. Columbia Presbyn. Hosp., 1999—. Contbr. articles to profl. jours. Served to capt. USAF, 1962-64. Recipient Carbee prize U. Vt., 1958. Fellow ACOG (chmn. Conn. sect. 1976, pres. Conn. sect. 1973-76), ACS, Am. Fertility Soc., Am. Soc. for Colposcopy and Cervical Pathology, Am. Assn. Gynecologic Laproscopists; mem. Conn. Med. Soc., Conn. Soc. Am. Bd. Obstetricians and Gynecologists (pres. 1973-76), Fairfield County Med. Soc., Fairfield County Gynecol. and Obstet. Soc., Stamford Med. Soc. (pres. 1989-90). Republican. Episcopalian. Office: Stamford Gynecology PC 70 Mill River St Stamford CT 06902-3725 Office Phone: 203-359-3340.

GOODHUE, WILLIAM WALTER, JR., pathologist, military officer, educator; b. St. Louis, Feb. 5, 1945; s. William W. and Rose Marie (Vahousek) Goodhue. BS cum laude, Georgetown U., 1966; MD, Cornell U., 1970. Diplomate Am. Bd. Pathology. Anat. pathology intern N.Y. Hosp.-Cornell Med Ctr., N.Y.C., 1970-71, resident anat. pathology, 1971-74; chief resident pediatric pathology Columbia-Presbyn. Med. Ctr., N.Y.C., 1974-75; resident clin. pathology Tripler Army Med. Ctr., Honolulu, 1976-78, chief pathology grad. med. edn., dir. electron microscopy, 1994-97, asst. chief dept. pathology and area lab. svcs., 1997-2001; first dep. med. examiner, de facto mayoral cabinet mem. City and County of Honolulu, 2001—. Chief dept. pathology U.S. Army Hosp., Ft. Campbell, Ky., 1978—80; chief dept. pathology, med. dir. Sch. Med. Tech., dir. pathology residency tng. Gorgas Army Hosp.; C.Z. and assoc. prof. med. tech. Panama Canal Coll., 1980—82; resident officer U.S. Army Command and Gen. Staff Coll., Ft. Leavenworth, Kans., 1982—83; divsn. surgeon 2d Inf. Divsn., 1983—84; dep. comdr. clin. svcs., chief dept. primary care and cmty. medicine, staff pathologist, acting comdr. Bayne-Jones Army Hosp., Ft. Polk, La., 1984—85; chief dept. pathology and are lab. svcs., dir. pathology residency tng. Dwight David Eisenhower Army Med. Ctr., Ft. Gordon, Ga., 1985—94; clin. assoc. prof. pathology Med. Coll. Ga., Augusta, 1986—94, Sch. Medicine U. Hawaii, Honolulu, 1997—; cons. in pathology Eisenhower Health Svc. Region to Comdg. Gen.; cons. ARC, 1978—80; rep. Alt. Army Med. Dept. Coll. Am. Pathologists Ho. of Dels., Am. Soc. Clin. Pathologist Adv. Coun., 1990—2001; mem. profl. adv. bd. Med. Lab. Observer, 1993—95; Army councillor-at-large Armed Forces Med. Lab. Scientists, 1993—2001; v.p. Land Bd. R.W. Meyer, Ltd. Assoc. editor: Hawaii Med. Jour., 2003—04; contbr. articles to profl. jours. Col. M.C. U.S. Army, 1975—2001. Decorated Order Mil. Med. Merit; recipient Surgeon Gen.'s "A" designator med. splty. excellence, 1997; fellow Rsch., USPHS, 1971—74. Fellow: Coll. Am. Pathologists, Am. Soc. Investigative Pathology, Nat. Assn. Med. Examiners, Am. Soc. Clin. Pathologists (lab. accreditation insp. & accreditation program 1988—), Am. Acad. Forensic Scis.; mem.: AMA (Physicians Recognition award 1976, 1978, 1980, 1982, 1986, 1989, 1992, 1995, 1998, 2001, 2004), U.S.-Can. Acad. Pathology, Clin. Lab. Mgrs. Assn. (bd. dir. 1989—92), Alliance Française, Assn. U.S. Army, Soc. Armed Forces Med. Lab. Scientists, NY Acad. Sci., Hawaii Soc. Pathologists, Soc. Ultrastructural Pathology, Am. Assn. Blood Banks, Assn. Mil. Surgeons U.S., Med. Assn. Isthmian Canal Zone (v.p. 1980—81), Soc. Pediat. Pathology, Makani Kai Yacht Club, Outrigger Canoe Club, Cornell Club NY. Republican. Roman Catholic. Home: 45-995 Wailele Rd # 52 Kaneohe HI 96744-3040 Office: Dept Med Examiner 835 Iwilei Rd Honolulu HI 96817 Office Phone: 808-527-6777.

GOODING, CHARLES ARTHUR, radiologist, physician, educator; b. Cleve., Feb. 28, 1936; s. Joseph J. and Florence G. (Pitt) G.; m. Gretchen Wagner, June 19, 1961; children: Gunnar, Justin, Britta. BA, Western Res. U., 1957; MD, Ohio State U., 1961. Intern Ohio State U. Hosp., 1961-62; resident in radiology Peter Bent Brigham Hosp., Children's Hosp. Med. Center, both Boston, 1963-65; rsch. fellow radiology Harvard Med. Sch., Boston, 1962, tchg. fellow, 1965-66; Harvard Med. Sch. fellow Hosp. for Sick Children, London, Karolinska Hosp., Stockholm, 1966; faculty U. Calif. Med. Center, San Francisco, 1967—, prof. radiology and pediatrics, 1976—, exec. vice-chmn. dept. radiology, 1974—2001. Pres. Radiology Rsch. and Edn. Found., 1973-96, Radiology Outreach Found., 1988-2002, pres. emeritus 2002—; hon. mem. faculty Francesco Maroquin U. Sch. Medicine, Guatemala City. Contbr. chpts. to books.; Editor: Pediatric Radiology, 1973—96; editor: Diagnostic Radiology, 1972-92; contbr. articles to profl. jours. Capt. M.C. USAR, 1967-68. Recipient Outstanding Alumni award Brigham Women's Hosp. Harvard Med. Sch., 1994, Disting. Alumnus award Ohio State U., 1986, Case Western Res. U., 1999, Beclere medal Internat. Soc. Radiology, 1998; named to Disting. Alumni Hall of Fame Cleve. Heights H.S., 1999, Top Pediat. Radiologist San Francisco mag., 2001. Fellow Am. Coll. Radiology, Coll. Radiologists (hon.), Royal Coll. Radiologists London (hon.), Armenian Radiol. Soc. (hon.); mem. Am. Roentgen Ray Soc., Assn. Univ. Radiologists, European Soc. Pediat. Radiologists (hon.), Pacific Coast Pediat. Radiologists Assn., Radiol. Soc. N.Am., Polish Radiology Soc. (hon.), Hungarian Radiology Soc. (hon.), San Francisco Med. Soc., Soc. Pediat. Radiology (v.p. 1994, pres. 1997 pres. SPR rsch. and edn. found. 1993-96, chmn., bd. dirs. 1998), Rocky Mountain Mountain Radiol. Soc. (hon.), Australian Soc. for Pediatric Imaging (hon.), Chinese Radiol. Soc. (hon.), Swiss Radiol. Soc. (hon.), Malaysian Radiol. Soc. (hon.), Vietnamese Radiol. Soc. (hon.), Thailand Radiology Soc. (hon.), French Soc. Radiology (hon.), Indian Radiol. and Imaging Soc. (hon.), Radiol. Soc. Pakistan (hon.), Indonesian Radiol. Soc. (hon.), Mongolian Nat. Radiol. Assn. (hon.), Nepal Radiol. Soc. (hon.), Armenian Med. Diagnostic Assn. (hon.), Brazilian Coll. Radiology (hon.), Cuban Radiol. Soc. (hon.), Indonesian Pediatric Radiol. Soc. (hon.), Asian and Oceanean Radiol. Soc. (gold medal 2004). Office: U Calif Med Ctr Dept Radiology San Francisco CA 94143-0628 E-mail: charles.gooding@radiology.ucsf.edu.

GOODING, CHARLES THOMAS, psychologist, educator, retired academic administrator; b. Tampa, Fla., Nov. 18, 1931; s. Charles T. and Gladys (Bingman) G.; m. Shirley Ann Puckett, June 7, 1953; children: Steven Thomas, Carol Ann, David Lee, Mark Charles. BA, U. Fla., 1954, M.Ed., 1962, Ed.D., 1964; postgrad., U. Tampa, 1956-58. Tchr. Meml. Sch., Tampa, 1956-58; asst. prin., then prin. St. Mary's Sch., Tampa, 1958-62; grad. fellow U. Fla., Gainesville, 1962-63, instr., 1963-64; assoc. prof., then prof. SUNY, Oswego, 1964-79, prof. psychology, 1980-98, assoc. dean grad. studies, 1982-89, dean grad. studies and rsch., 1989-95, provost, v.p. for acad. affairs, 1995-98, emeritus, 1998—. Vis. prof. U. Liverpool, Eng., 1979-80; mem. SUNY Chancellor's Task Force on Tchr. Edn., 1984. Author: Learning Theories in Educational Practice, 1971; contbg. author: Florida Studies in the Helping Professions, 1969, Questioning and Discussion: A Multidisciplinary Study, 1988, Research Matters to the Science Teacher, 1992; contbr. articles to profl. jours. Trustee U. of South, 2002—; bd. dirs. Oswego Coll. Found., 1996—. Served to 1st lt. USAR, 1954-56. SUNY Rsch. Found. grantee, 1966, 69-70, NY State Dept. Edn. grantee, 1971-72, 88-94, NSF grantee, 1980-81, 85-88, 90-95. Mem. APA, Ea. Ednl. Rsch. Assn. (v.p. 1979-81, treas., dir. 1983-85, pres.-elect 1987-88, pres. 1989-91, editl. bd. 1991-2000), Am. Ednl. Rsch. Assn. (chair ednl. enterprises SIG, 1994-96). Avocations: antique and classic automobiles, Jaguar sports cars specialist. Home: 603 Wild Pine Way Venice FL 34292-4618 E-mail: tgooding@comcast.net.

GOODING, CUBA, JR., actor; b. Bronx, N.Y., Jan. 2, 1968; s. Cuba, Sr. and Shirley Gooding; m. Sara Gooding, 1994; 2 children. Films include: Coming to America, 1988, Sing, 1989, Boyz N the Hood, 1991, Gladiator, 1992, A Few Good Men, 1992, Hitz, 1992, Judgement Night, 1993, Lightning Jack, 1994, Losing Isaiah, 1995, Outbreak, 1995, Jerry Maguire, 1996 (Golden Globe nomination, Academy award for Best Supporting Actor, 1997), The Audition, 1996, As Good As It Gets, 1997, What Dreams May Come, 1998, A Murder of Crows, 1999, Instinct, 1999, Menof Honor, 2000 (NAACP Image award nominee), Pearl Harbor, 2001, Rat Race, 2001, In the Shadows, 2001, Snow Dogs, 2002, Boat Trip, 2002, Psychic, 2003, The Fighting Temptations, 2003, Radio, 2003, Home on the Range (voice), 2004; TV movies include: Kill or Be Killed, 1990, Murder with Motive: The Edmund Perry Story, 1992, Daybreak, 1993, Tuskegee Airmen, 1995 (NAACP Image award nominee); (TV appearances) MacGyver, Hill Street Blues, The Untouchables. Office: Rogers & Cowan 1888 Century Park E Ste 500 Los Angeles CA 90067-1709 also: Endeavor Talent Agy 9701 Wilshire Blvd Fl 10 Beverly Hills CA 90210

GOODING, DIANE CAROL, psychology educator, researcher; b. N.Y.C., July 27, 1963; d. Conrad Lynwood and Anne Danforth Gooding. AB, Harvard U., 1985; PhD, U. Minn., 1996. Sr. rsch. asst. Murray Rsch. Ctr., Cambridge, Mass., 1985—87; asst. prof. U. Wis., Madison, 1996—2002, assoc. prof., 2002—. Bd. dirs. Nat. Alliance for Mentally Ill, 1999-2005 Recipient Young Investigator award Internat. Congress Schizophrenia Rsch., 1999; dissertation fellow Ford Found., Nat. Rsch. Coun., 1992. Mem. N.Y. Acad. Sci., Sigma Xi. Office: U Wis-Madison 1202 W Johnson St Madison WI 53706 Office Phone: 608-262-3918. E-mail: dgooding@wisc.edu.

GOODING, GRETCHEN ANN WAGNER, physician, educator; b. Columbus, Ohio, July 2, 1935; d. Edward Frederick and Margaret (List) Wagner; m. Charles A. Gooding, June 19, 1961; children: Gunnar Blaise, Justin Mathias, Britta Meghan. BA magna cum laude, Ohio Dominican U., 1957; MD cum laude, Ohio State U., 1961. Diplomate Am. Bd. Diagnostic Radiology. Intern Univ. Hosps., Columbus, 1961-62; rsch. fellow Boston City Hosp., 1962-63, Boston U., 1963-65; with dept. radiology U. Calif., San Francisco, 1975—, assoc. prof. in radiology, 1981-85, prof., vice chmn., 1986—2003; asst. chief radiology VA Med. Ctr., San Francisco, 1978-87, chief radiology, 1987—2003, chief ultrasonography, 1975—. Chair com. acad. pers. U. Calif., San Francisco, 1993-94, bd. dirs. commn. accreditation vascular labs., 1993-96. Co-editor Radiologic Clinics of N.Am., 1993—; mem. editl. bd. San Francisco Medicine, 1986—, Applied Radiology, 1987-89, Current Opinion in Radiology, 1992-93, The Radiologist, 1993—, Emergency Radiology, 1993-2003, Jour. Clin. Ultrasound, 1997—; guest editor Emergency Radiology, 1999; contbr. articles to profl. jours. Recipient Recognition award Inter Societal Commn. for Accreditation of Vascular Labs., 1997, Disting. Alumna award, Ohio State U. Coll. Medicine and Pub. Health, 2001. Fellow Am. Coll. Radiology (mem. commn. on ultrasound 1984-2000, chair stds. com. commn. on ultrasound 2004-05, chmn. com. practice guidelines and tech. standards 2004-05), Am. Inst. Ultrasound in Medicine (bd. govs. 1981-84, chair conv.

program 1986-88, Presdl. Recognition award 1984), Am. Soc. Emergency Radiology, Soc. Radiologists U.S.; mem. AMA, San Francisco Med. Soc. (chmn. membership com. 1992-94, bd. dirs. 1996—), RSNA (course com. 1984-88, tech. exhibit com. 1992-96), Bay Area Ultrasound Soc. (pres. 1979-80), Soc. Radiologists Ultrasound (chair membership com. 1991-93, chair corp. com. 1996-97), ARRS, AUR, CRS, Calif. Med. Assn., Am. Assn. Women Radiologists (pres. 1984-85, trustee 1991-94, Alice Ettinger Disting. Achievement award 2003), VA Chiefs of Radiology Assn. (pres.-elect, pres. 1994-95), San Francisco Radiol. Soc. (pres. 1990-91), Hungarian Radiol. Soc. (hon.), Pakistan Radiol. Soc. (hon.), Cuba Radiol. Soc. (hon.). Office: VA Med Ctr Radiology Svc 4150 Clement St San Francisco CA 94121-1545 E-mail: gretchen.gooding@radiology.ucsf.edu.

GOODING, JUDSON, writer; b. Rochester, Minn., Oct. 12, 1926; s. Arthur Faitoute and Frances (Judson) G.; m. Françoise Ridoux, June 21, 1952; children: Amélie, Timothy. Grad. with honors, Yale U., 1948; diplome d'Études Françaises, U. Paris, 1950. Staff writer Dept. Army, Hdqrs. EUCOM, Germany, 1950-52; script writer Affiliated Film Producers, N.Y.C., 1952-53; news writer WCCO-CBS, Mpls., 1953; reporter Mpls. Tribune, 1953-57, Life mag., N.Y.C., 1957-60, fgn. corr. Paris, 1960-62, Time mag., Paris, 1962-65; chief of bur. Time-Life News Service, San Francisco, 1966-68; edn. editor Time mag., N.Y.C., 1968-69; assoc. editor Fortune mag., 1969-73; v.p. Urban Research Corp.; also editor Trend Report, Chgo., 1973-75; mng. partner Trend Analysis Assocs., 1975—; exec. editor Next Mag., N.Y.C., 1979-81, contbg. editor, 1981-82; counselor for pub. affairs U.S. Permanent Del. to UNESCO, 1982-84. Vis. lectr. in journalism U. Paris, Ecole Nationale d'Administration, also Togo, Kenya, Zaire, Senegal and Nigeria; writing cons. UN, Ford Found., Am. Assembly, also corps.; vis. lectr. in journalism, Barbados, Grenada, Dominica, Haiti and Martinique Author: The Job Revolution, 1972; contbr. to: American Dreams, The Environment, The Hippies, The Survival Equation, The Failure of Success; Contbr. articles to popular mags. and profl. jours. Bd. patrons Wilson Ctr., Faribault, Minn.; mem. program com. Internat. Found. for Cultural Cooperation, Courchevel, France; trustee Friends of John Jay Homestead, Walpole Hist. Soc., Walpole Pub. Libr. Served with USNR, 1944-46. Recipient 1st place award U. Mo. Sch. Journalism Penney-Mo., 1980, hon. certificate Program Mgmt. Devel. Harvard U. Grad. Sch., Disting. Alumnus award Middlesex Sch., 1994. Mem. Inst. Current World Affairs (elected), Common Cause, World Future Soc., Nat. Trust Hist. Preservation, Am. Soc. Journalists and Authors, Mensa. Clubs: Elizabethan (New Haven); Century Assn. (N.Y.C.), Yale (N.Y.C.); Bedford Bicycle Polo (founder, co-capt.); Polo de Paris, The Travellers (Paris). Home: 21 Mountain View Dr Keene NH 03431

GOODKIN, MICHAEL JON, publishing company executive; b. N.Y.C., June 10, 1941; s. Harold and Rose (Mostkoff) G.; m. Helen Graham Fairbank, Oct. 1, 1971; children: Graham Laird, Nathalie Fairbank Emami. BA, Harvard U., 1963; postgrad., U. Chgo., 1964. Trainee Random House, N.Y.C., 1964-65; asst. dir. Simulmatics, N.Y.C., 1966-67; account exec. World Book Ency., Inc., Chgo., 1967-70, rsch. dir., 1970-73, v.p. mktg., 1973-76, v.p., gen. mgr. mail order div., 1976-78, pres., chief operating officer, 1978-86, chmn., chief exec. officer, pres., dir., 1983; exec. v.p. World Book Inc., 1978-84, pres., 1984-86, sr. v.p., 1979-80; exec. v.p., corp. dir. mktg., dir. World Book Internat. Inc., 1983-84; dep. dir. World Book Pty. Ltd., Australia, 1983-86; pres. World Book Life Ins. Co., 1983; prin. Chgo. City Capital Group, 1987-91; chmn. Med. Holdings, Inc., Chgo., 1987-91; sr. v.p. mktg. internat. P.F. Collier, N.Y.C., 1992—94, pres., 1994—96; dir. KT holdings, 1996—99; mng. mem. Arlington Haven Partners LLC, 2000—. Bd. dirs. Chgo. Area Project; pres. aux. bd. Art Inst. Chgo., 1975-77, trustee, 1974-99; trustee Modern Poetry Assn., Latin Sch. Chgo., 1983-92, chmn. ednl. policy com., pres., 1990-92, mem. long range com., chmn. mktg. com., 1979-99; trustee DMA Edn. Found., 1983-94, mem. exec. com., 1988-94; mem. vis. com. visual arts U. Chgo., 1990-2002. With Army N.G., 1963-69. Mem. Direct Mktg. Assn. (internat. coun. steering com. 1983), Direct Selling Assn. (internat. com. 1982-86), Racquet Club, Harvard Club (N.Y.C.), Harvard Club (Boston). Business E-Mail: hmgoodkin@worldnet.alt.net.

GOODKIN, RICHARD ELLIOT, French educator, writer; b. Chgo., Sept. 15, 1953; s. Ben Goodkin and Minnie (Becker) Green. BA, Swarthmore Coll., 1975; MA, Princeton U., 1979, PhD, 1981. Asst. prof. French Yale U., New Haven, Conn., 1980-86, assoc. prof. French, 1986-89, U. Wis., Madison, 1989-92, prof. French, 1992—. Cons. in field. Author: The Symbolist Home and The Tragic Home, 1984, The Tragic Middle, 1991, Around Proust, 1991, Birth Marks, 2000; editor: Autour de Racine, 1989; translator: Proust Between Two Centuries, 1992; contbr. articles to profl. jours. Recipient Whiting Humanities fellowship, 1979-80, Ind. Rsch. fellowship NEH, 1984-85, Sidonie Miskimin Clauss prize for tchg. excellence Yale Coll., 1987; John Simon Guggenheim fellow, 2005—. Mem. MLA, N.Am. Soc. for French Seventeenth Century Lit., Phi Beta Kappa. Avocations: swimming, bicycling, photography. Office: U Wis Dept French Italian 618 Van Hise Hall 1220 Linden Dr Madison WI 53706-1525

GOODKIN, ROBERT, neurosurgeon, educator; Diploma, Coll. William and Mary, 1958, NYU, 1960; MD, Chgo. Med. Sch., 1964. Diplomate Nat. Bd. Med. Examiners, 1965, Am. Bd. Neurol. Surgeons, 1973. Intern Bellevue Hosp. Ctr. NYU, N.Y., 1964—65, resident in neurology Bellevue Hosp. Ctr., 1965—66, resident in neurol. surgery Bellevue Hosp. Ctr., 1966—71; attending staff Barrow Neurol. Inst., Phoenix, 1971—76; adj. assoc. prof. divsn. neurol. surgery U. Fla., Gainesville, 1976—78; assoc. prof. and chief divsn. neurol. surgery Jacksonville (Fla.) Hosps. Ednl. Program, U. Fla., 1976—78; chief dept. neurol. surgery U. Hosp. Jacksonville, 1976—78; pvt. practice neurosurgery Hollywood, Fla., 1978—81; clin. assoc. prof. dept. neurol. surgery U. Miami, Fla., 1978—82; clin. prof. dept. neurol. surgery U. So. Calif., L.A., 1981—2000; dir. dept. neurol. surgery City of Hope Nat. Med. Ctr., Duarte, Calif., 1981—86; assoc. prof. neurol. surgery U. Wash. Med. Sch., Seattle, 1987—2003; chief neurosurgery Madigan Army Med. Ctr., Tacoma, 1987—89; chief neurosurgery sect. VA Puget Sound Health Care Sys., Seattle, 1989—2003; prof. neurol. surgery U. Wash. Med. Sch., Seattle, 2003—. Faculty U. Wash. Med. Sch., Seattle, 1987—; mem. Neurosurgical Consultants Com. Surg. Svc., VA Ctrl. Office-Hdqrs., Washington, 2000—, chmn., 2000—03; co-dir. gamma knife radiosurgery ctr. Harborview Med. Ctr., 2004—. Mem. editl. bd.: Surg. Neurology, 2004—. Mem.: Soc. for Neuro-Oncology, Internat. Spinal Cord Soc., Movement Disorder Soc., N.Am. Skull Base Soc., Am. Assn. Stereotactic and Functional Neurosurgery, N.Y. Acad. Scis., Am. Spinal Injury Assn., Congress Neurol. Surgeons, Neurosurg. Soc. Am. (pres. 1997—98), Am. Paraplegic Soc., World Soc. Stereotactic and Functional Neurosurgery, Am. Assn. Neurol. Surgeons. Office: UWMC-Harborview Medical Center Box 359766 325 9th Ave Seattle WA 98104 Office Phone: 206-744-9300.

GOODKIND, CONRAD GEORGE, lawyer; b. Arlington, Va., Aug. 8, 1944; s. Bernard Arthur and Sylvia (Lieber) G.; m. Sandra Timme, Aug. 27, 1966; children: Carley M., Adam B., Erica L., Anne G. BS, U. Wis., 1966, JD, 1969. Bar: Wis. 1969, U.S. Dist. Ct. (ea. and we. dists.) Wis. 1969. Assoc. Kivett & Kasdorf, Milw., 1969-71; counsel Citizens' Study Com. on Jud. Orgn., Madison, Wis., 1971-73; dep. commr. securities State of Wis., Madison, 1973-79; assoc. Quarles & Brady, Milw., 1979-81, ptnr., 1981—, mem. exec. com., 1983—. Adj. prof. securities law U. Wis. Law Sch., Madison, 1975-79, Marquette U. Law Sch., Milw., 1981-83; mem. Gov.'s Bus. Cts. Task Force, 1994-98, state regulation com. Nat. Assn. Securities Dealers, Inc., Washington, 1986-92; bd. dirs. Able Distbg. Corp., 1995-; bd. dirs., sec. Cade Industries, Inc., 1989-99; sec. Brady Corp., 1999—. Bd. dirs. Milw. Repertory Theatre, 1995-2001, exec. com. mem., 1997-2001. Mem. ABA (vice chmn. state regulation securities com. 1986-89, chmn. 1989-92, vice chmn. bus. law sect. com. on insts. and seminars 2001—2003)chmn. 2003—, Wis. Bar Assn. (chmn. securities com., 1981-95, bd. dirs. sect. bus. law 1991-2001, vice chair sect. bus. law 1996-98, chair 1998-2000). Office: Quarles & Brady LLP 411 E Wisconsin Ave Ste 2550 Milwaukee WI 53202-4497 Office Phone: 414-277-5305. Business E-Mail: cgg@quarles.com.

GOODLAD, JOHN INKSTER, education educator, writer; b. North Vancouver, BC, Can., 1920; s. William James and Mary Goodlad; m. Evalene M. Pearson, 1945; children: Stephen John, Mary Paula. BA, U. B.C., 1945, MA, 1946; PhD, U. Chgo., 1949; DPS (hon.), Brigham Young U., 1995; LHD (hon.), Nat. Coll. Edn., 1967, U. Louisville, 1968, So. Ill. U., 1982, Bank Street Coll. Edn., 1984, Niagara U., 1989, SUNY Coll. Brockport, 1991, Miami U., 1991, Linfield Coll., 1993, W.Va. U., 1998; LLD (hon.), Kent State U., 1974, Pepperdine U., 1976, Simon Fraser U., 1983, U. Man., 1992; DEd (hon.), Eastern Mich. U., 1982, U. Victoria, 1998; LittD (hon.), Montclair State U., 1992; PedD (hon.), Doane Coll., 1995; LHD (hon.), U. Nebr., Lincoln, 1999, U. So. Maine, 2001. Cert. tchr. Vancouver Normal Sch., 1939. Tchr. Surrey Schs., B.C., 1939-41, prin., 1941-42; dir. edn. Provincial Sch. For Boys, B.C., 1942-46; cons. curriculum Atlanta Area Tchr. Edn. Service, 1947-49; assoc. prof. Emory U., 1949-50; prof., dir. div. tchr. edn. Agnes Scott Coll. and Emory U., 1950-56; prof., dir. U. Chgo. Center Tchr. Edn., 1956-60; prof., dir. Univ. Elem. Sch. UCLA, 1960-85, dean Grad. Sch. Edn., 1967-83; prof. U. Wash., Seattle, 1985-91; prof. emeritus, 1991—; dir. Ctr. for Ednl. Renewal U. Wash., Seattle, 1986-2000; pres. Inst. for Ednl. Inquiry, Seattle, 1992—. Chmn. Coun. on Coop. Tchr. Edn., Am. Coun. Edn., 1959-62; dir. rsch. Inst. for Devel. of Ednl. Activities, 1966-82; mem. governing bd. UNESCO Inst. for Edn., 1971-79. Author: (with others) The Elementary School, 1956, Educational Leadership and the Elementary School Principal, 1956, (with Robert H. Anderson) The Nongraded Elementary School, 1959, rev. edit., 1963, reprinted, 1987, (with others) Computers and Information Systems in Education, 1966, Looking Behind the Classroom Door, 1970, rev. edit., 1974, Toward a Mankind School, 1974, The Conventional and the Alternative in Education, 1975, Curriculum Inquiry: The Study of Curriculum Practice, 1979, Planning and Organizing for Teaching, 1963, School Curriculum Reform, 1964, The Changing School Curriculum, 1966, School, Curriculum and the Individual, 1966, The Dynamics of Educational Change, 1975, Facing the Future, 1976, What Schools Are For, 1979, A Place Called School, 1983, Teachers for Our Nation's Schools, 1990, Educational Renewal: Better Teachers, Better Schools, 1994, In Praise of Education, 1997, (with others) Education for Everyone: Agenda for Education in a Democracy, 2004, Romances with Schools: A Life of Education, 2004; author, editor: The Changing American School, 1966, (with Harold S. Shane) The Elementary School in the United States, 1973, (with M. Frances Klein and Jerrold M. Novotney) Early Schooling in the United States, 1973, (with Norma Feshback and Alvima Lombard) Early Schooling in England and Israel, 1973, (with Gary Fenstermacher) Individual Differences and the Common Curriculum, 1983, The Ecology of School Renewal, 1987, (with Kenneth A. Sirotnik) School-University Partnerships in Action, 1988, (with Pamela Keating) Access to Knowledge, 1990, (with others) The Moral Dimensions of Teaching, 1990, Places Where Teachers Are Taught, 1990, (with Thomas C. Lovitt) Integrating General and Special Education, 1992, (with Timothy J. McMannon) The Public Purpose of Education and Schooling, 1997, (with others) Developing Democratic Character in the Young, 2001, (with Timothy J. McMannon) The Teaching Career, 2004; mem. bd. editors Sch. Rev, 1956-58, Jour. Tchr. Edn, 1958-60; contbg. editor: Progressive Edn, 1955-58; mem. editorial adv. bd. Child's World, 1952-80; chmn. editorial adv. bd. New Standard Ency, 1953-; chmn. ednl. adv. bd. Ency. Brit. Ednl. Corp, 1966-69; contbr. chpts. to books, articles to profl. jours. Recipient Disting. Svc. medal Tchrs. Coll., Columbia U., 1983, Outstanding Book award Am. Ednl. Rsch. Assn., 1985, Disting. Contbns. to Ednl. Rsch. award 1993; named Faculty Rsch. Lectr. U. Wash., 1987-88, faculty of High Distinction, UCLA, 1987, Edward C. Pomeroy award, Am. Assn. Coll. Tchr. Edn., 1995, Disting. Svc. award Coun. Chief State Sch. Officials, 1997, Harold W. McGraw, Jr. Prize in Edn., 1999, Edn. Commn. State James Bryant Conant award, 2000, Brock Internat. prize in edn., 2002, NY Acad. Edn. medal, 2003, Am. Edn. award Am. Assn. Sch. Adminstrs., 2004, Disting. Educator award ATE, 2005. Fellow Internat. Inst. Arts and Letters; mem. Nat. Acad. Edn. (charter; sec.-treas.), Am. Ednl. Rsch. Assn. (past pres., award for Disting. Contbns. to Ednl. Rsch. 1993), Nat. Soc. Coll. Tchrs. Edn. (past pres.), Nat. Soc. for Study of Edn. (dir.), Am. Assn. Colls. for Tchr. Edn. (pres. 1989-90). Office: Inst for Ednl Inquiry 124 E Edgar St Seattle WA 98102

GOODLATTE, ROBERT WILLIAM (BOB GOODLATTE), congressman, lawyer; b. Holyoke, Mass., Sept. 22, 1952; m. Maryellen Flaherty; children: Jennifer, Robert. BA, Bates Coll., 1974; JD, Washington & Lee U., 1977. Bar: Mass. 1977, Va. 1978, U.S. Ct. Appeals (4th cir.) 1981. Dist. mgr. Congressman M. Caldwell Butler U.S. Ho. of Reps., Washington, 1977-79; pvt. practice Roanoke, Va., 1979-81; ptnr. Bird, Kinder & Huffman, Roanoke, 1981-93; mem. 103d-108th Congresses from 6th Va. dist., Washington, 1993—, dep. majority whip, chmn. agriculture com., jud. com., co-chair of Congl. Internet Caucus, Rep. policy com., chmn. Ho. Rep. high tech working group, ho. Rep. cybersecurity task force, vice chmn. the cts., the Internet. and intellectual property subcom. Mem. bldg. better bds. adv. com. United Way of Roanoke Valley, Roanoke, 1988-92; chmn. Roanoke City Rep. Com., 1980-83, 6th Cong. Dist. Rep. Com., Va., 1983-88. Mem. Civitan (pres. Roanoke chpt. 1989-90). Republican. Avocations: tennis, travel, swimming, hiking, reading. Office: US Ho of Reps 2240 Rayburn Hob Washington DC 20515-4606 Business E-Mail: talk2bob@mail.house.gov.

GOODLET, MICHAEL J, music educator; b. Washburn, Wisc., Feb. 10, 1969; s. Victor Robert and Marian Celina Goodlet; children: Grant Christopher, Alexander Michael. BA in music edn., Northland Coll., 1987—91; MA in edn., St. Mary's U., 1997. Music specialist Maple Sch. Dist., Wis., 1999—2001, dir. of choral activities, 2001—. Vol. Dem. Nat. Convention, Superior, Wis., 2000—; dir. of music Chester Pk. United Meth. Ch., Duluth, Minn., 1998—. Recipient Tchr. of the Yr., Maple Sch. Dist., 1997; Tchg. fellowship, Herb Kohl Found., 1999. Mem.: Music Educators Nat. Conf., Am.Choral Dir. Assn. Democrat. United Meth. Avocations: interior decorating, bicycling, travel.

GOODMAN, ALLEN CHARLES, economist, educator; b. Cleve., Oct. 28, 1947; s. Nathan and Pearl (Dorfman) Goodman; m. Janet Hankin, July 22, 1984; 1 child, Sara. AB, U. Mich., 1969; PhD, Yale U., 1976. Asst. prof. Lawrence U., Appleton, Wis., 1975-78; rsch. scientist Johns Hopkins U., Balt., 1978-86; economist HUD, Washington, 1985-86; assoc. prof. Wayne State U., Detroit, 1986-88, prof. econs., 1988—, chmn. dept., 1988-96. Author: Changing Downtown, 1987, Economics of Housing Markets, 1989, Economics of Health and Health Care, 4th edit., 2004. Mem. Mayor's Coord. Coun. Criminal Justice, Balt., 1984—86. Fellow, Homer Hoyt Advanced Studies Inst., 2002—. Mem.: Am. Real Estate and Urban Econs. Assn., Am. Econs. Assn., Internat. Health Econs. Assn. Office: Wayne State U Dept Econs Detroit MI 48202 Business E-Mail: allen.goodman@wayne.edu.

GOODMAN, ALVIN IRWIN, internist, nephrologist, educator; b. N.Y.C., July 12, 1929; s. Morris and Fanny (Rifkin) G.; m. Suzanna Elizabeth Gebhard; children: Nadine, Derek, Danielle, Leslie, Reva. BA, NYU, 1949; MD, U. Geneva, 1955. Diplomate Am. Bd. Internal Medicine, Am. Bd. Nephrology. Intern Jewish Hosp. Bklyn., 1956, resident in medicine, 1957—58; fellow in medicine Yale U. Sch. Medicine, New Haven, 1960—62, resident in medicine, 1962—63; dir. nephrology and renal ctr. Westchester County Med. Ctr., Valhalla, 1963—2000; prof. medicine, dir. nephrology N.Y. Med. Coll., Valhalla, 1975—2000, prof. med., 1963—2005, prof. med. emeritus, 2005. Dir. endstage renal disease program Bur. Quality Assurance, USPHS, Rockville, Md., 1974-75. Contbr. numerous articles to medl jours. Capt. M.C., U.S. Army, 1958-60. Recipient President's award Nat. Kidney Found., 1977, Cardinal Cook award N.Y. Med. Coll., 1986, Disting. Svc. award N.Y. Med. Coll., 2002. Fellow ACP; mem. Am. Soc. Nephrology, Internat. Soc. Nephrology, Am. Soc. Transplant Physicians, N.Y. Soc. Nephrology (pres. 1980-81), Beta Lambda Sigma. Avocation: travel. Office: Westchester Med Ctr NY Med Coll Valhalla NY 10595 Office Phone: 914-493-7703. Personal E-mail: dralvingoodman@aol.com.

GOODMAN, ALVIN S., engineering educator, consultant; b. N.Y.C., Mar. 14, 1925; s. Solomon and Dora Goodman; m. Nettie Leef Gilson, Sept. 9, 1951; children: Sandra, Lynn, Nancy, Sally. B of Civil Engring., CCNY, 1944; MSCE, Columbia U., 1948; PhD, NYU, 1966. Registered profl. engr. N.Y., Mass., Conn., N.C.; profl. hydrologist, AIH. Engr. Interstate Sanitation Commn., N.Y.C., 1950-51; project engr. Tippets-Abbett-McCarthy-Stratton, N.Y.C., 1951-62, staff cons. water resources, 1962-85; prof. civil engring. Northeastern U., Boston, 1962-69, NYU, N.Y.C., 1969-73, Poly. U., Bklyn., 1973—, head dept., 1985—90. Cons. engring. firms, ednl. instns., 1970—. Author: Principles of Water Resources Planning, 1984, Infrastructure Planning, 2005; contbr. articles to profl. jours., papers and reports to confs. 1st lt. C.E., U.S. Army, 1944-47; ETO. Fellow ASCE; mem. Am. Water Resources Assn., Am. Geophys. Union, Water Environ. Fedn., Am. Soc. Engring. Edn., Sigma Xi, Tau Beta Pi, Chi Epsilon. Office: Poly U Dept Civil Engring 6 Metrotech Ctr Brooklyn NY 11201-3840 E-mail: asgpoly@aol.com, agoodman@poly.edu.

GOODMAN, BARRY JOEL, lawyer; b. N.Y.C., May 28, 1953; s. Walter Louis and Shirley (Lenzer) G.; m. Nicole Goodman; children: Aaron, Rebecca, Noah, Jacob. BA, Bradley U., 1974; JD with honors, Stetson U., 1977. Bar: Fla. 1977, U.S. Ct. Appeals 1978, Mich. 1979, U.S. Dist. Ct. (we. dist.) Fla., U.S. Dist. Ct. (ea. dist.) Mich. With Diecidue, Ferlita & Prieto, Tampa, Fla., 1977-78; assoc. Provizer, Eisenberg et al, Southfield, Mich., 1979-82, Thurswell, Chayet & Weiner, Southfield, 1982-87, ptnr., 1987-93; owner Gordon, Goodman & Acker, Southfield, 1993-98, Goodman Acker, Southfield, 1998—. Lectr. Inst. Continuing Legal Edn., Ann Arbor, Mich., Mich. Trial Lawyer's Assn., State Bar of Mich. Officer-at-large Mich. Dem. Party; v.p. Anti-Defamation League, 1983—; bd. dirs. B'nai B'rith Youth Orgn., Mich., 1995—97, West Bloomfield (Mich.) Woods Homeowners Assn., 1980—83. Mem.: State Bar of Mich. (vice chair bd. negligence sect.), Oakland County Trial Lawyers Assn., Oakland County Bar Assn., Mich. Trial Lawyers Assn. (bd. dirs. 1985—, treas. 1995, sec. 1996, v.p. 1997, pres.-elect 1998, pres. 1999—2000), ATLA. Democrat. Jewish. Avocations: tennis, golf, reading, theater. Office: Goodman Acker PC 17000 W 10 Mile Rd 2nd flr Southfield MI 48075-2945 Office Phone: 248-483-5000. Business E-Mail: bgoodman@goodmanacker.com.

GOODMAN, BARRY MICHAEL, lawyer; b. L.A., Nov. 22, 1946; s. Ralph Arthur and Natalie Bell (Hamburger) G.; BA in History, Calif. State U., 1967; JD, U. So. Calif., 1970; m. Susan Lynn Reigrod, June 18, 1969; children: Gregory, Alison. Bar: Calif. 1971, D.C. 1972. Sr. atty. Office of Chief Counsel, Urban Mass Transp. Adminstrn., Washington, 1971-74; dir. Office Pub. Transp., City of Houston, 1974-78; exec. dir. Met. Transit Authority, Houston, 1978-79; pres. Goodman Corp., Houston, 1979— . Mem. ABA, Calif. Bar Assn., D.C. Bar Assn., Urban Land Inst., Transp. Research Bd. Jewish. Home: 11223 Claymore Rd Houston TX 77024-6704 Office: Goodman Corp 3200 TravisSt Ste 200 Houston TX 77006 Office Phone: 713-951-7951. E-mail: Barry@thegoodmancorp.com.

GOODMAN, BENNETT J., hedge fund founder; b. Apr. 4, 1957; BA in engring., Lafayette Coll., 1979; MBA, Harvard Bus. Sch., 1984. With Drexel Burnham Lambert, 1984—88, Donaldson, Lufkin & Jenrette Inc., 1988—2000, mng. dir. capital markets, 1995—96; mng. dir. high yield bonds Donaldson, Lufkin & Jenrette Inc. (merged with Credit Suisse First Boston in 2000), 1997—2000; mgr. dir. global leveraged fin. Credit Suisse First Boston LLC, 2000—03, chmn. merchant banking and leveraged fin., 2003—04; head, alternative capital div. Credit Suisse First Boston, N.Y.C., 2004; co-founder GSO Capital Partners, 2005—.*

GOODMAN, BERNARD, physics professor; b. Phila., June 14, 1923; s. Louis and Fannie (Solomon) G.; m. Joyce Janet Willoughby, Mar. 3, 1950; children— David Nathan, Jonathan Bernard, Mark William AB, U. Pa., 1943, PhD, 1955. Stress analyst Internat. Harvester Co., Chgo., 1947-52; research assoc. U. Mo., 1952, asst. prof. physics, 1954-58, assoc. prof., 1958-64, prof., 1964—; prof. physics U. Cin., 1965-93, prof. emeritus, 1993—. Vis. sci. Argonne Nat. Lab., 1956-57, 61-62, 65-66, 70, Brookhaven Nat. Lab., 1960, Bell Telephone Lab., 1967, Ohio U., 1969; Nordita guest prof. Inst. Theoretical Physics, Uppsala, Sweden, 1962-63, Gothenberg, Sweden, 1971-72; vis. prof. Inst. Theoretical Physics, Gothenberg, 1985. Guggenheim fellow, 1962-63, Gordon Godfrey fellow U. NSW, Sydney, Australia, 1990; Fulbright scholar Inst. Theoretical Physics, Trieste, Italy, 1979-80 Fellow: Am. Phys. Soc.; mem.: AAAS, Phi Beta Kappa, Sigma Xi. Achievements include research in condensed matter theory. Home: 3411 Cornell Pl Cincinnati OH 45220-1501 Office: U Cin Dept Physics Cincinnati OH 45221-0011 Office Phone: 513-556-0537. Business E-Mail: goodman@physics.uc.edu.

GOODMAN, BRUCE, managed health care company executive; Degree in elec. engring., NYU; postgrad., Stanford U. CLU, chartered fin. cons. Former CEO Prudential Svc. Co., C2K Tech. Ptnrs., Inc., Livingston, NJ; sr. v.p., chief info. officer Humana, Inc., 1999—2002, sr. v.p., chief svc. and info. officer, 2002—. Office: Humana Inc 500 W Main St Louisville KY 40202

GOODMAN, CAROL HOCKENBURY, retired elementary school educator, consultant; b. Chgo., Nov. 12, 1943; d. Norman J. and Margaret Griffith Hockenbury; children: Kellie S., Krista L., Kirk A. BS, Lock Haven U., Pa., 1965; MEd, Shippensburg U., 1968. Cert. permanent tchg. cert. Pa. Elem. tchr. Wyalusing (Pa.) Area Sch. Dist., 1965—69, N.E. Bradford Sch. Dist., Rome, Pa., 1988—2004; adj. prof. Pa. State U., State College, 2001—, ret., 2004. Dir. Goodwriting Assocs., Wyalusing, 2002—. Dir., author, choreographer: elem. sch. musicals Broadway Dreams, American Pride, The Great American Vacation, others. Mem.: NEA (assoc.), Delta Kappa Gamma (state com. chair 2001—03). Avocations: writing, reading, travel, grandchildren. Home: PO Box 254 Wyalusing PA 18853 Personal E-mail: cgoodman@epix.net.

GOODMAN, CHARLES DAVID, physicist, researcher; b. N.Y.C., May 9, 1928; s. Jacob and Libby (Freed) G.; m. Joan Louise Wright, June 11, 1952; children: Henry N., Diana R. AB, Clark U., 1949; PhD, U. Rochester, 1955. Rsch. scientist Oak Ridge Nat. Lab., Tenn., 1955—80; prof. physics Ind. U., Bloomington, 1980—98, prof. emeritus, 1999—. Vis. scientist Weizmann Inst. Sci., Rehovot, Israel, 1966; vis. prof. U. Colo., Boulder, 1972-73; guest scientist Los Alamos (N.Mex.) Nat. Lab., 1979-94, Lawrence Berkeley (Calif.) Lab., 1980—, Lawrence Livermore (Calif.) Lab., 1980—, Laboratoire Nat Saturne, Saclay, France, 1982-91; originator, organizer internat. nuc. physics confs., Telluride, Colo., 1979, 82, 85, 88, 91. Contbr. articles to profl. jours. Recipient Humboldt Found. Rsch. award, Germany, 1991. Fellow AAAS, Am. Phys. Soc. (Tom W. Bonner Prize 1983); mem. IEEE, Sigma Xi. Achievements include mapping of Gamow-Teller strength function; patent on neutron detector. Office: Ind U Milo Sampson Ln Bloomington IN 47408 Business E-Mail: goodmanc@indiana.edu.

GOODMAN, COREY SCOTT, neuroscientist, educator, biotechnologist; b. Chgo., June 29, 1951; s. Arnold Harold (dec.) and Florence (Friedman) G.; m. Marcia M. Barinaga, Dec. 8, 1984. BS, Stanford (Calif.) U., 1972; PhD, U. Calif., Berkeley, 1977. Postdoctoral fellow U. Calif., San Diego, 1979; asst. prof. dept. biol. scis. Stanford U., 1979-82, assoc. prof., 1982-87; prof. neurobiology and genetics U. Calif., Berkeley, 1987—2005, Evan Rauch prof. neurosci., 1999—2001, adj. prof. neurobiology, 2005—; co-founder Renovis Inc., 2000—, CEO, pres., bd. dirs., 2001—; co-founder Exelixis, Inc., 1995. Investigator Howard Hughes Med. Inst., 1988—2001; dir. Helen Wills Neurosci. Inst., 1999—2001; chair bd. life sci. NRC, 2001—. Contbr. more than 200 articles to profl. jours. Pres. McKnight Found. Endowment Fund Neurosci., 2000—05, v.p., 2005—. Recipient Charles Judson Herrick award, 1982, Alan T. Waterman award Nat. Sci. Bd., 1983, Javits Neurosci. Investigator award NIH, 1985, 92, NIH Merit award, 1985, Found. IPSEN Neuronal Plasticity prize, 1996, J. Allyn Taylor Internat. prize in medicine, 1996, Gairdner Found. Internat. award for achievement in med. sci., 1997, Ameritec Found. Basic Rsch. Toward Cure Paralysis prize, 1997, Wakeman award for rsch. in neurosci., 1998, March-Of-Dimes prize in Devel. Biology, 2001. Fellow Am. Acad. Arts and Scis.; mem. NAS, Am. Philos. Soc. Office: Renovis Inc Two Corporate Dr South San Francisco CA 94080 Office Phone: 650-266-1476. E-mail: goodman@renovis.com.

GOODMAN, DAVID S., lawyer; b. Cleve., 1952; BA, Oberlin Coll., 1974; JD, Harvard U., 1977. Bar: Ohio 1977. Ptnr. Squire, Sanders & Dempsey LLP, Cleve., chmn., Pub. Securities Practice Group. Mem.: Nat. Assn. Bond Lawyers, Ohio Bar Assn., Cleve. Bar Assn. Fluent in German. Office: Squire Sanders & Dempsey LLP 4900 Key Tower 127 Public Sq Cleveland OH 44114-1304 Office Phone: 216-479-8649. Office Fax: 216-479-8780. Business E-Mail: dgoodman@ssd.com.

GOODMAN, DAVID WAYNE, research chemist, educator; b. Dec. 14, 1945; s. Henry G. and Anniebelle G.; m. Sandra Faye Hewitt, June 9, 1967; 1 child, Jac Hewitt. BS, Miss. Coll., 1968; PhD, U. Tex., 1974. NATO postdoctoral fellow Tech. Hochschule, Darmstadt, Fed. Republic of Germany, 1974-75; NRC postdoctoral fellow NBS, Washington, 1975-76, mem. rsch. staff, 1976-80, Sandia Labs., Albuquerque, 1980-85, head surface sci. divsn., 1985-88; prof. chemistry Tex. A&M U., College Station, 1988-94, head phys. and nuc. divsn., 1991-94, Welch prof., 1994—, Welch chair, 1998—, disting. prof., 2000—. Lectr. Tex. A&M U., 1987, U. Tex., 1990, Northwestern U., 1993. Named Disting. Alumnus, Miss. Coll., 1992, Robert Burwell lectr., N.Am. Catalysis Soc., 1997, Langmuir Disting. lectr., 1991; recipient Yarwood medal, 1994, Humboldt Rsch. award, 1995, Giuseppe Parravano award, 2001, Disting. Rsch. Visitor award, U. Auckland, 2003; Fulbright Disting. scholar, 2002. Mem.: Am. Vacuum Soc. (mem. exec. coun. 1981, 1985—87), Am. Chem. Soc. (treas. divsn. colloid and surf. sci. 1980—83, vice chair 1983, chmn. 1984, Ipatieff award 1983, Surface Chem. award 1993, Arthur W. Adamson award 2002, Gabor A. Somorjai award 2005). Office: Tex A&M U Dept Chem PO Box 30012 College Station TX 77842-3012 Office Phone: 979-845-0214. Business E-Mail: goodman@mail.chem.tamu.edu.

GOODMAN, DONALD JOSEPH, dentist; b. Cleve., Aug. 14, 1922; s. Joseph Henry and Henrietta Inez (Mandel) G.; BS, Adelbert Coll., 1943; DMD, Case-Western Reserve U., 1945; m. Dora May Hirsh, Sept. 18, 1947; children: Lynda (Mrs. Barry Allen Levin), Keith, Bruce; m. Ruth Jeanette Weber, May 1, 1974. Pvt. practice dentistry, Cleve., 1949-86; lectr. in field. With Dental Corps, USNR, 1946-48. Mem. Am. Acad. Gen. Dentistry, ADA Ohio State Dental Assn., Cleve. Dental Soc., Fedn. Dentaire Internationale, Cleve. Council on World Affairs, Greater Cleve. Growth Assn., Council of Smaller Enterprises, Phi Sigma Delta, Zeta Beta Tau, Alpha Omega. Clubs: Masons (32 deg.), Shriners, Travelers' Century (Gold award, special award), Circumnavigators. Home: 29099 Shaker Blvd Pepper Pike OH 44124-5022

GOODMAN, EDWIN A., venture capitalist; s. Andrew and Nena Goodman; m. Lorna Goodman. BA, Yale U., 1962; MS, Columbia U. Bus. Sch., 1979. With Patricof & Co., 1974—81; CEO U.S. ops. Hambros Bank, 1985—99; co-founder, gen. ptnr. Milestone Venture Ptnrs., 1999—. Chair Ann. Venture Investing Conf. Internat. Bus. Forum, 1986—95; team mem. Isabella Capital, LLC; chmn. bd. Fashion Inst. Tech., NY. Mem. Nat. Coun. Trustees Nat. Jewish Med. and Rsch. Ctr. Office: Milestone Venture Ptnrs 551 Madision Ave 7th Fl New York NY 10022

GOODMAN, ELIZABETH ANN, retired lawyer; b. Marquette, Mich., Aug. 11, 1950; d. Paul William and Pearl Marie Goodman; m. Herbert Charles Gardner, Sept. 24, 1977. Student, U. Munich, 1970-71; BA cum laude, Alma (Mich.) Coll., 1972; JD cum laude, U. Mich., 1977. Bar: Minn. 1978, Mich. 1978, U.S. Dist. Ct. Minn. 1979. Cert. real property law specialist, real property sect. Minn. Bar Assn. High sch. tchr. Onaway (Mich.) High Sch., 1973-74; assoc. Dorsey & Whitney LLP, Mpls., 1978-82; ptnr. Dorsey & Whitney, Mpls., 1983-99; v .p., chief gen. counsel Ryan Cos., 2000—03; ret., 2003.

GOODMAN, ELLEN HOLTZ, journalist; b. Newton, Mass., Apr. 11, 1941; d. Jackson Jacob and Edith (Weinstein) Holtz; m. Robert Levey; 1 dau., Katherine Anne. BA cum laude, Radcliffe Coll., 1963; hon. degrees, Mt. Holyoke Coll., Amherst Coll., U. Pa., U. N.H. Researcher, reporter Newsweek Mag., 1963-65; feature writer Detroit Free Press, 1965-67; feature writer columnist Boston Globe, 1967-74, assoc. editor, 1986—2001; syndicated columnist Washington Post Writers Group, 1976—; radio commentator Spectrum, CBS, 1978-80, NBC, 1979-80; commentator NBC Today Show, 1979-81. Vis. prof. Stanford U., 1995. Author: Close to Home, 1979, Turning Points, 1979, At Large, 1981, Keeping in Touch, 1985, Making Sense, 1989, Value Judgments, 1993, (with Patricia O'Brien) I Know Just What You Mean, 2000, Paper Trail, 2004. Trustee Radcliffe Coll.; judge Livingston Awards for Young Journalists, 1986—. Nieman fellow Harvard U., 1974, Lyndhurst fellow, 2000; named New Eng. Newspaper Woman of Year New Eng. Press Assn., 1968; recipient Catherine O'Brien award Stanley Home Products, 1971, Media award Mass. Commn. Status Women, 1974, Columnist of Year award New Eng. Women's Press Assn., 1975, Pulitzer Prize for Commentary, 1980, prize for column writing Am. Soc. Newspaper Editors, 1980, Hubert H. Humphrey Civil Rights award, 1988, William Allen White award 1995. Office: 5 JFK St Cambridge MA 02138 E-mail: ellengoodman@globe.com.

GOODMAN, ELLIOT RAYMOND, political scientist, educator; b. Indpls., Sept. 3, 1923; s. Lazure L. and Esther (Miller) G.; m. Norma B., Mar. 1, 1947; children— Laura Goodman Humphrey, Jordan, Roger. AB, Dartmouth Coll., 1948; MA and cert. Russian Inst., Columbia U., 1951, PhD, 1957; MA (hon.), Brown U., 1960. Ford teaching intern Brown U., Providence, 1955-56, instr., 1956-58, asst. prof., 1958-60, asso. prof., 1960-70, prof. polit. sci., 1970-87, prof. emeritus, 1987—. Author: The Soviet Design for a World State, 1960, The Fate of the Atlantic Community, 1975; contbr. numerous articles to profl. jours. Served with U.S. Army, 1943-46. Guggenheim fellow, 1962-63; NATO research fellow, 1962-63 Mem. Internat. Inst. Strategic Studies (London), Atlantic Council U.S. (politico-mil. com. 1971-74, acad. assoc. 1985—), New Eng. Polit. Sci. Assn., Am. Polit. Sci. Assn., Am. Assn. Advancement of Slavic Studies, Com. Atlantic Studies (N. Am. sect.) Home: 45 Amherst Rd Cranston RI 02920-6010 Office: Brown U Dept Polit Sci Providence RI 02912-0001

GOODMAN, ELLIOTT I(RVIN), retired lawyer; b. Mar. 28, 1934; s. Sidney W. and Jean (Strauss) G.; m. Sybil J. Shapiro, Dec. 25, 1957; children: Jessica, Paul, Jonathan. BS, Northwestern U., 1955, JD, 1958. Bar: Ill. 1958, U.S. Dist. Ct. (no. dist.) Ill. 1959; CPA, Ill. With Gottlieb & Schwartz, Chgo., 1959-90, ptnr., 1966-90, mng. ptnr., 1981-88; ptnr. D'Ancona and Pflaum, Chgo., 1990-95; exec. v.p. ATI Carriage House, Inc., Lombard, Ill., 1995-99. Permanent arbitrator Amalgamated Social Benefit Ins. Plan. Sec., bd. dirs. Ind. Basketball Players Assn., 1971-74, Abe Saperstein Found., Athletes for Better Edn. Found., 1975-79 Mem. Highland Park Housing Commn. (Ill.), 1980-87. Mem. ABA (labor law com. 1977-97, environ. law com. 1988-97), Chgo. Bar Assn. (past chmn. Am. citizenship com. 1967-69, mem. labor law com. 1971—, environ. law com. 1988-97), Human Resource Mgmt. Assn. Chgo., Lake Geneva Yacht Club. Home: 211 Rivershire Ln Apt 201 Lincolnshire IL 60069-3817 Office: ATI Carriage House Inc 1111 N Ridge Ave Lombard IL 60148-1212

GOODMAN, ERIK DAVID, engineering educator; b. Palo Alto, Calif., Feb. 14, 1944; s. Harold Orbeck and Shirley Mae (Lillie) G.; m. Denise Rowand Dyktor, Aug. 10, 1968 (div. 1976); m. Cheryl Diane Barris, Aug. 27, 1978; 1 child, David Richard. BS in Math., Mich. State U., 1966, MS in Systems Sci., 1968; PhD in Computer Communication Sci., U. Mich., 1972; Hon. Doctorate, Dneprodzerzhinsk State Tech U., Ukraine, 1996. Asst. prof. elec. engring. Mich. State U., East Lansing, 1972-77, assoc. prof. elec. engring., 1977-84, dir. case ctr. for computer aided engring. and mfg., 1983—2002, prof. elec. engring., dir., 1984—, prof. mech. engring., 1992—. Dir. Mich. State U. Mfg. Rsch. Consortium, 1993—2003; v.p. Red Cedar Tech., Inc., East Lansing, Mich., 1999-; pres. Tech. Gateway, Inc., East Lansing; cons. Chinese Computer Comms., Inc., Lansing, 1988—; gen. chair First Internat. Conf. on Evolutionary Computation and its Applications, Moscow, 1996, Seventh Internat Conf. on Genetic Algorithms, 1997, Genetic and Evolutionary Computation Conf., 2001; gen. co-chmn. Internat. Computer Graphics Conf., Detroit, 1986; adv. prof. Tongji U., Shanghai, China, 2002-; mem. ACM SIGEVO (Generic Evolutionary Computation), founded, 2005. Author: (with others) SYSKIT: Linear Systems Toolkit, 1986; patentee in field. Academician, Internat. Informatization Acad. (Russia), 1993—. Fellow Internat. Soc. Genetic and Evolutionary Computation (sr., exec. com. 2001-04, chair 2001-04); mem. AIAA (chair rsch. and future dirs., subcom. CAD/CAM tech. com. 1987-89, Outstanding Svc. 1990), IEEE Computer Soc., Assn. Computing Machinery (chair spl. interest group genetic and evolutionary computation 2005—), Soc. Mfg. Engrs., Aircraft Owners and Pilots Assn., Acad. Engring. Scis. Ukraine. Avocations: musician, tennis, studying Chinese. Office: Mich State U Dept Elec & Computer Engring 2308M Engineering Bldg East Lansing MI 48824 Business E-Mail: goodman@egr.msu.edu. E-mail: e.goodman@redcedartech.com. *Evolutionary computation is now allowing huge advances in engineering design optimization and design automation of complex structures.*

GOODMAN, ERIKA, dancer, actress; b. Phila. d. A. Allan and Laura (Baylin) G. Student, Sch. of Am. Ballet, 1961-63; BA in Theatre and Dance, Empire State Coll., 1993; master classes, Princeton Ballet, 1994, Hartford Ballet Co., 1995, Va. Intermont Coll., 1995—. Mem. faculty Actors and Dirs. Lab., N.Y.C., 1979—; founding mem. ensemble theater co. The Barrow Group, N.Y.C., 1986—; mem. dance faculty CCNY, 1990. Mem. dance faculty CCNY, 1990; guest tchr. ballet Balettakademein, Stockholm, 1986, 89; instr. master classes Rutgers U., East Carolina U., 1989, Hofstra U., U. Kans., 1990, Harvard U., summer 1993, Cornell U., Skidmore Coll., Vassar Coll., 1992—, Conn. Coll.; vis. prof. ballet, head ballet dept. CCNY, 1992—, lectr. world arts, 1993—. Dancer N.Y.C. Ballet Co., 1964-65, prin. dancer Joffrey Ballet, N.Y.C., 1966-75; performer (with Barrow Group) Seymour in the Heart of Winter, Perry St. Theatre, N.Y.C., 1986, When You Comin' Back Red Rider, 1987, Father Hat, Three Sisters, 1989; casting dir. (films) Hazing in Hell, Neon Red; dir. ballet rehearsal Ballet Hispanico. Richard Porter Leach fellow, 1992-93. *In my life as with my art, I have strived to achieve purity, truth and beauty— to preserve my integrity when it was challenged, and never to compromise the dictates of my heart.*

GOODMAN, GARY A., lawyer; b. N.Y.C., Mar. 8, 1948; s. Nathaniel and Edith (Rosen) G.; m. Susan Schachter, Aug. 13, 1972; children: Max, Jonah, William, Zachary, Holden. AB in History summa cum laude, Economics with honors, U. Rochester, 1970; JD, NYU, 1973. Bar: N.Y. 1974, U.S. Dist. Ct. (so. dist. and ea. dists.) N.Y. 1974, U.S. Dist. Ct. Guam, 1975, U.S. Ct. Appeals (2d cir.) 1975, Calif. 1996, Tex. 1996. Ptnr. Sonnenschein Nath & Rosenthal LLP, N.Y.C., 2002—. Contbr. numerous articles to profl. jours. Mem. bd. edn. Locust Valley (N.Y.) Ctrl. Sch. Dist., 1995-96, v.p., 1996-97, pres., 1997-98. Mem.: ABA (vice chmn. internat. investment in real estate com. 1983—90, chmn. Pacific Rim trans. subcom. real estate financing com. 1987—88), Mortgage Bankers Assn. Am., Comml. Mortgage Securities Assn., Assn. Fgn. Investors in Real Estate, Real Estate Bd., Internat. Coun. Shopping Ctrs. (task force environ. issues 1987—90, law com. 1991—94), Assn. Bar of City of N.Y. (uniform state laws com. 1978—80, real property law com. 1991—94, land use com. 1994—97, real property law com. 1997—2000), N.Y. State Bar Assn. (chmn. fgn. investment in U.S. real estate com. 1987—88). Office: Sonnenschein Nath & Rosenthal LLP 1221 Ave of the Americas New York NY 10020 Office Phone: 212-768-6916. E-mail: ggoodman@sonnenschein.com.

GOODMAN, GEORGE JEROME WALDO (ADAM SMITH), writer, television journalist, consultant; b. St. Louis, Aug. 10, 1930; s. Alexander Mark and Viola (Cremer) G.; m. Sallie Cullen Brophy, Oct. 6, 1961; children: Alexander Mark, Susannah Blake. AB magna cum laude, Harvard U., 1952; AB Rhodes scholar, Oxford (Eng.) U., 1952-54. Reporter Barron's, 1957; contbg. editor, assoc. editor Time and Fortune mags., 1958—60; portfolio mgr., v.p. Lincoln Fund, 1960—62; co-founder New York mag., 1967, contbg. editor, v.p., 1967—77; exec. editor, then cons. Esquire, 1978—81; 1st editor, exec. v.p., bd. dirs. Instl. Investor, 1967—72; chmn. Continental Fidelity Group, 1980—98, also dir. Exec. v.p., dir. Instl. Investor Systems, 1969-72; dir. USAIR, Inc., 1978-99, Hyatt Hotels, 1977-81, Cambrex, Inc., 1981-2003, Providentia Ltd., Sweden, 1984-86; mem. dirs. adv. bd. MetLife, 2003—; lectr. Harvard Bus. Sch., Princeton; commentator NBC News, 1974, PBS, 1981—; creator, host, editor-in-chief Adam Smith's Money World, PBS, 1984-97; 1st U.S. pub. affairs TV broadcast in Russia, 1990—; host, editor-in-chief Adam Smith's Money Game, PBS, 1998-99; editl. chmn. N.J. Monthly, 1976-79; adv. com. publs. U.S. Tennis Assn., 1978-83; chmn. Adam Smith Global TV, 1997—; lectr. media and global affairs Princeton U., 2003—. Screenwriter, L.A., 1962-65, screenplay The Wheeler Dealers; author: The Bubble Makers, 1955, A Time for Paris, 1957, Bascombe, The Fastest Hound Alive, 1958, A Killing in the Market, 1958, The Wheeler Dealers, 1959; under pseudonym Adam Smith: The Money Game, 1968 (#1 bestseller), Supermoney, 1971 (#1 bestseller), Powers of Mind, 1975, Paper Money, 1981, The Roaring 80's, 1988; mem. editl. bd. N.Y. Times, 1977; contbr. articles to profl. jours. Trustee Glassboro (N.J.) State Coll., 1967-71, co-chmn. presdl. selection com., 1968; trustee C.G. Jung Found., 1981-88; mem. adv. council econs. dept. Princeton U., 1970-89, chmn., 1975-77; rep. com. on shareholder responsibility Harvard U., 1971-74, mem. vis. com. psychology and social relations dept., 1974-80—, mem. vis. com. Middle East Inst.; mem. adv. council Sloan Fellowships, Princeton U., 1976-79, Ctr. for Internat. Studies, Princeton U., 1990—; trustee The Urban Inst., 1986-96, Found. for Child Devel., 1986-88. Served with AUS, 1954-56. Recipient G.M. Loeb award for disting. achievement bus. and fin. writing U. Conn., 1969, Media award for econ. understanding with TV documentary Amos Tuck Sch., Dartmouth Coll., 1978, Overseas Press award, 1996; Ind. award Brown U., 1993; nominee 8 Emmy awards, 1985-97, winner Best Interview 1995, winner 3 Emmys, graphics, 1985-94, Adam Smith Internat. PBS Documentaries gold medal Houston Internat. Film Festival, 2001, 02. Mem.: Assn. Harvard Alumni (bd. dirs. 1972—75), Authors Guild (bd. dirs. 1975—), Authors League Fund (v.p.), Coun. Fgn. Rels., Knickerbocker Club, Century Assn., Harvard Club. Office: Adam Smith Global TV 26 E 63rd St New York NY 10021-8030

GOODMAN, GERTRUDE AMELIA, civic worker; b. El Paso, Tex., Oct. 24, 1924; d. Karl Perry and Helen Sylvia (Pinkiert) G. BA, Mills Coll., 1945. Pres. El Paso chpt. Tex. Social Welfare Assn., 1963-65, bd. dirs. 1965-70, state bd. dirs., 1965-70; state bd. dirs. Pan-Am. Round Table, El Paso, 1966—, bd. dirs. 1970-71, sec., 1973-74, life mem.; founder, 1st chmn. El Paso Mus. Art Mem. Guild, 1962-68; bd. dirs. Mus. Art Assn., 1962-69, also v.p.; chmn. dir. El Paso C. of C. women's Dept., 1976-77; bd. dirs. Rio Grande Food Bank, 1988-94; bd. dirs. El Paso Pub. Libr., 1972-80, pres. bd. dirs., 1978-80; pres. El Paso County Hist. Soc., 1981-82, bd. dirs., 1986-92; mem. planning com. El Paso United Way, 1953—; mem. El Paso Mus. Art Bd. Coun.; pres. Las Comadres, 2000-01. Recipient Hall of Honor award El Paso County Hist. Soc., Nat. Human Rels. award NCCJ, 1981, numerous awards for civic vol. work. Avocations: tennis, travel, art, books. Home: 905 Cincinnati Ave El Paso TX 79902-2435

GOODMAN, HERBERT IRWIN, petroleum company executive; b. Pitts., Mar. 11, 1923; s. Meyer Irwin and Bessie (Crossof) G.; m. Mary Katherine Schilken, Aug. 12, 1978; children: Michael Christopher, Anne Katheryn, Nancy Hjortshoj, Sara Elizabeth, Mary Elien. BS, U. Pitts., 1943; cert., U. Besancon, 1945; MBA, Harvard U., 1949, AM, 1950. Commd. officer U.S. Fgn. Svc., 1951; served in U.S. Embassy, Copenhagen, 1951-53, Vietnam, 1953-54, U.S. Fgn. Service, Kampuchea, 1954-55; intelligence rsch. officer Dept. State, 1956-57; with Gulf Oil Corp., 1957-84, coord. European sales London, 1957-59; gen. mgr. Pacific Gulf Oil, Tokyo, 1960-64, coord. crude oil dept. Pitts., 1964-66, coord. Far East, 1966-70; pres. Gulf Oil Co. South Asia, Singapore, 1970-72, Gulf Oil Trading Co., Pitts., 1972-80, Gulf Trading and Transp. Co., Houston, 1980-84, GOTCO USA, Inc., Houston, 1984-87, SARMAR Corp., Houston, 1987—; chmn. bd. Applied Trading Sys., Houston, 1988-96, IQ Holdings, Inc., Houston, 1996—2004, pepex.net LLC, 2000—05. Bd. dirs. Houston Livestock Show and Rodeo, Genesis Energy L.P.; adv. bd. Pacific Inst. Bd. dirs., chmn. internat. adv. bd. Tex. A&M U.; bd. dirs. U. Houston Coll. Bus., U. St. Thomas Sch. Bus., AA Grapevine, Inc.; trustee gen. svc. bd. Alcoholics Anonymous. 1st lt. U.S. Army, 1943-46. Decorated Bronze Star; médaille de la Réconnaissance (France). Mem. Am. Petroleum Inst., Am. Mgmt. Assn., Coun. on Fgn. Rels., Assn. Asian Studies, Mid East Inst., Asia Soc. N.Y. (corp. coun.), Assn. Internat. Petroleum Negotiators, Harvard Club (N.Y.C.), Racquet Club, Univ. Club, Petroleum Club. Office: SARMAR Corp One Riverway Ste 1700 Houston TX 77056 Office Phone: 713-840-6499. Personal E-mail: herbg@pepex.net. Business E-Mail: hgoodman@houston.rr.com.

GOODMAN, JEROME DANIEL, lawyer; b. Annapolis, Md., June 1, 1913; s. Aaron Lee and Jeanette Clarice (Isaacson) G.; m. Margery Isobel Rose; children: Jane Loise Quinn, Carol Sue Comras. AB, St. John's Coll., Annapolis, 1934; LLB, Harvard U., 1937. Bar: Mass. 1938, U.S. Dist. Ct. Mass. 1939, U.S. Tax Ct. 1954. Lawyer in pvt. practice, Boston, 1938-43, 46-77; ptnr. Goodman & Goodman, Boston, 1977—. Asst. dist. atty. Norfolk County, Mass., Dedham, 1958-62; spl. town counsel Town of Brookline, Mass., 1960-65. Mem. town meeting Town of Brookline, 1948-69; mem. Rep. Town Com. of Brookline, 1950—; pres. Jewish Big Brother Assn., Boston, 1960-61; chmn. lawyers div. Combined Jewish Philanthropies, Greater Boston, 1970; pres. Brookline Citizens Com., 1973; life trustee Temple Israel, Boston. Sgt. U.S. Army, 1943-46. Recipient Citizens award Combined Jewish Philanthropies. Mem. Mass. Bar Assn. (Sr. Mem. award), Boston Bar Assn. (Sr. Mem. award), Norfolk Bar Assn., Am. Legion, Jewish War Vets. Republican. Office: Goodman & Goodman 462 Washington St Wellesley MA 02482-5908 Home: 250 Hammond Pond Pkwy Apt 980N Chestnut Hill MA 02467-1527 E-mail: goodman-mi@msn.com, csgoodmanesq@juno.com.

GOODMAN, JEROME DAVID, psychiatrist; b. Chester, Pa., Oct. 23, 1933; s. William Henry and Amelia (Kopl) G.; m. Gail Ann Theis, Feb. 10, 1961; children: David Hammond, Douglas Andrew. BA, Swarthmore Coll., 1955; MD, U. Pa., 1959. Diplomate Am. Bd. Psychiatry and Neurology with subspecialty in child psychiatry. Asst. clin. prof. psychiatry Coll. Physicians and Surgeons Columbia U., N.Y.C., 1964—75; pvt. practice Saddle River, NJ, 1968—. Author: Child Mental Status Examination, 1967, 2d edit., 1998; composer: Sonata for Violin and Piano, 1990, Six Cryptic Rhythms for Chamber Orch., 1992, Montségur Suite, 1993, Symphony # 2, 1994, Violin Concerto, 1995, Concerto for Clarinet, Violoncello and Orch., 1996, Dance Patterns: A Choreographic Poem for Orch., 1997, Stockbridge Overtones: Tone Poem for Orch., 1998, Saddle River Almanac: A Tone Poem for Orchestra, 2002, Saxophone Quartet, 2002, Two Elizabethan Lyrics for Soprano and Piano, 2003, Concert Piece for Piano Trio and Percussion, 2003, Three Preludes for Band, 2004, American Vigil for Accompanied Chorus, 2005 Capt. U.S. Army, 1966-68. Recipient Margaret Fairbanks Jory award, 1992. Jewish. Office: 45 W Saddle River Rd Saddle River NJ 07458-3016 Office Phone: 201-825-0384.

GOODMAN, JERRY L(YNN), judge; b. Mangum, Okla., Apr. 17, 1939; s. A.O. and Viola Louise (Bogart) G.; m. Donna L. Rudy, Dec. 16, 1961; children: Courtney L., Polly K., Mallory E., Benjamin R. BA, U. Tulsa, 1961; JD, Georgetown U., 1964. Bar: Okla. 1964. Law clk. antitrust divsn. Dept. Justice, 1962-63; legis. asst. to U.S. Senator J. Howard Edmondson, 1963-64; assoc. David M. Thornton Atty.-at-Law, 1964-65; asst. city atty. City of Tulsa, Okla., 1965-68; ptnr. Owens & Goodman, Tulsa, 1968-70; gen. counsel OTASCO Stores, Tulsa, 1970-74, v.p., gen. counsel, 1974-85, chmn., CEO, 1985-89; spl. counsel Bank of Okla., 1989-90; pres., gen. counsel The Sigma Asset Mgmt. Group, Inc., 1991-92; sec. policy and mgmt., COO Office of Gov., State of Okla., Tulsa, 1992-94; judge Okla. Ct. Civil Appeals, Tulsa, 1994—. Bd. dirs. United Way, 1984—87; chmn., bd. trustees Univ. Ctr. at Tulsa, 1992. Lt. USNR, 1964—70. Mem.: ABA, Tulsa County Bar Assn. (v.p. 1971), Okla. Bar Assn., Okla. Jud. Conf. (pres. 2001), Tulsa C. of C. (chmn. 1988). Presbyterian. Home: 3417 E 87th St Tulsa OK 74137-2628 Office: Okla Ct Civil Appeals 601 State Office Bldg 440 S Houston Ave Tulsa OK 74127-8922 Office Phone: 918-581-2711. E-mail: jerry.goodman@oscn.net.

GOODMAN, JESSE, physician, director, public health facility administrator, research scientist; BS, Harvard U.; MD, Albert Einstein Coll. of Medicine; MPH, U. Minn. Prof. medicine, dir. US Govt. Interagency Task Force Antimicrobial Resistance, 1998—2000; dep. dir. medicine Ctr. Biologics, Evaluation, and Rsch. FDA, 1999—2000, dir. medicine Ctr. Biologics, Evaluation, and Rsch., 2003—; dir. divsn. infectious diseases U. Minn. Med. Sch., 1998—2001. Adj. prof. medicine U. Minn., Howard U.; attending physician NIH Clin. Ctr. and Walter Reed Army Med. Ctr. Mem.: Am. Soc. for Clin. Investigation. Office: Ctr Biologics Evaluation and Rsch FDA 1401 Rockville Pike Ste 200N Rockville MD 20852-1448

GOODMAN, JOE READ, utilities executive; b. Corsicana, Tex., Dec. 28, 1952; s. Joe Read and Betty Lane Goodman; m. Patricia Norman, June 1, 1996; children: Aaron Daniel Risinger, Rachel Marie Risinger. BS, U. Houston, 1988. Cert. pub. mgr. Tex., 2000. Gen. mgr. Galveston County Mcpl. Utility Dist. # 1, 1984—89; tech. cons. Cmty. Resources Group, Nashville, 1989—90; waste treatment supt. City of Galveston, Tex., 1990—93; city adminstr. City of Kountze, Tex., 1993; dir. pub. works City of Harker Heights, Tex., 1994; pub. works maintenance mgr. City of Houston, 1995—. Pres. Rice Belt Water Utility assn., Tex., 1985, Gulf Area Water Utility Dist., Tex., 2001. Disaster chmn. ARC, Galveston, Tex., 1986—87. Mem.: Tex. Water Utilities Assn. Baptist. Office: City of Houston 611 Walker Houston TX 77002 Office Phone: 713-837-0054. Personal E-mail: pjgoodman@houston.rr.com. E-mail: joe.goodman@cityofhouston.net.

GOODMAN, JOHN, actor; b. St. Louis, June 20, 1952; m. Annabeth Hartzog, 1989; 1 daughter. Student, Meramac Community Coll.; BFA in Theater, S.W. Mo. State U., 1975. Performer dinner and children's theater prodns., off-Broadway plays; appeared on Broadway in Loose Ends, 1979, Big River, 1985; TV credits include Mystery of the Moro Castle, Face of Rage, Heart of Steel, 1983, Moonlighting, Chiefs, 1983, The Paper Chase, Murder Ordained, The Equalizer; series regular, Roseanne, 1988-96 (Emmy award nominations outstanding lead actor in comedy series, 1989, 90, 93, 94), Father of the Pride (voice), 2004, Center of the Universe, 2004-; actor (films) The Survivors, 1983, Eddie Macon's Run, 1983, Revenge of the Nerds, 1984, C.H.U.D., 1984, Maria's Lovers, 1985, Sweet Dreams, 1985, True Stories, 1986, The Big Easy, 1987, Burglar, 1987, Raising Arizona, 1987, The Wrong Guys, 1988, Everybody's All-American, 1988, Punchline, 1988, Sea of Love, 1989, Always, 1989, Stella, 1990, Arachnophobia, 1990, King Ralph, 1990, Barton Fink, 1991, The Babe, 1992, Matinee, 1993, Born Yesterday, 1993, The Flintstones, 1994, Kingfish: A Story of Huey P. Long, 1995, Mother Night, 1996, Fallen, 1997, Combat!, 1997, The Borrowers, 1997, The Big Lebowski, 1998, Blues Brothers 2000, 1998, Dirty Work, 1998, The Runner, 1999, Bringing Out the Dead, 1999, Coyote Ugly, 2000, O Brother, Where Art Thou?, 2000, What Planet Are You From, 2000, Hitting the Wall, 2000, My First Mister, 2000, One Night at McCool's, 2000, Emperor's New Groove (voice), 2000, Monsters, Inc. (voice), 2001, Dirty Deeds, 2002, Masked and Anonymous, 2003, The Jungle Book 2 (voice), 2003, Clifford's Really Big Movie (voice), 2004, Beyond the Sea, 2004; actor (TV movies) The Jack Bull, 1999; prodr. (TV movies) Kingfish: A Story of Huey P. Long, 1995; guest star (TV series) The West Wing, 1999; appeared in numerous commls. Office: Creative Artists Agency c/o Fred Specktor 9830 Wilshire Blvd Beverly Hills CA 90212-1825

GOODMAN, JOHN B., heating/air conditioning manufacturing executive; CEO Goodman Mfg., Houston, 1999—. Office: Goodman Mfg 2550 N Loop W Ste 400 Houston TX 77092-8908 Office Fax: (713) 861-2176.

GOODMAN, JOHN C., think-tank executive; PhD in Econs., Columbia U. Pres. Nat. Ctr. Policy Analysis, Dallas, 1983—, CEO, 1983—. Contbr. articles to profl. jours. Recipient Duncan Black award, 1988. Office: National Ctr Policy Analysis 12770 Coit Rd Ste 800 Dallas TX 75251-1339 also: National Ctr Policy Analysis 601 Pennsylvania Ave NW Ste 900 So Bldg Washington DC 20004

GOODMAN, JOHN M., construction executive; b. Omaha, Apr. 5, 1947; BS in Acctg., Calif. State U., Long Beach, 1970; JD, Pepperdine U., 1974. CPA, Calif.; cert. real estate broker, Calif.; cert. ins. agt., Calif.; lic. contractor, Calif. CFO Lewis Homes Mgmt. Corp., Upland, Calif., 1978—92, sr. v.p., CEO, dir., 1992—. Office: Lewis Operating Corp 1156 N Mountain Ave PO Box 670 Upland CA 91785-0670

GOODMAN, JONATHAN EDWARD, web applications manager; b. Queens, N.Y., Nov. 7, 1970; s. Susan Jill Goodman; life ptnr. Duc Trinh, July 12, 2004. BFA, Ringling Sch. of Art and Design, Sarasota, Fla., 1993; MS, Coll. of New Rochelle, 2001; MBA, Fairleigh Dickinson U., 2004. E-commerce prodr. Earthweb, N.Y.C., 1998—2000; mgr. web applications Suburban Propane, Whippany, NJ, 2000—. Bd. dirs. First Unitarian Soc. of Rockland County, Pomona, NY, 1998—99. Recipient Photo of the Yr. award, Photograpy Bd. of Sarasota, 1993. Mem.: Internet Soc. (assoc.), Am. Inst. for Graphic Design (assoc.). Conservative. Unitarian Universalist-Jewish. Office: Suburban Propane 240 Rte 10 W Whippany NJ 07981 Office Phone: 973-503-9967. Home Fax: 973-503-9273; Office Fax: 973-503-9273. Personal E-mail: jgoodman@suburbanpropane.com.

GOODMAN, JORDAN ELLIOT, journalist; b. N.Y.C., Sept. 13, 1954; s. Elliot Raymond and Norma (Bromberg) G.; m. Suzanne Kay Koblentz, June 20, 1981; 1 child, Jason Koblentz. Student, London Sch. Econ., 1974-75; BA, Amherst Coll., 1976; MA, Columbia U., 1977. Editor in chief Info Mag., N.Y.C., 1977-79; sr. reporter Money Mag., N.Y.C., 1979-92, Wall St. corr., 1992-97. Commentator Fin. News Network, N.Y.C., 1985—91, Mut. Broadcasting Sys., Washington, 1988—97, Marketplace Pub. Radio Internat., 1988—, Cable News Network, N.Y.C., 1989—90; regional dir. Soc. Profl. Journalists, Chgo., 1989—90; columnist onmoney.com, 2000—02, Moneyanswers.com, 2000—. Author: Dictionary of Finance and Investment Terms, 1986;: 6th edit., 2003, Barron's Finance and Investment Handbook, 1987, rev., 1991;: 6th edit., 2003, Dictionary of Business Terms, 1989, 1998, Everyone's Money Book, 1993, rev. edit., 1997, 3rd edit., 2001, Reading Between the Lies, 2003, Everyone's Money Book Series, 2002. Mem. Common Cause, N.Y.C., 1985—. Mem. Mid-Atlantic Club, N.Y.C. Fin. Writers Assn., N.Y. Deadline Club (pres. 1986-87). Democrat. Jewish. Avocation: sailing. Home and Office: 84 Walworth Ave Scarsdale NY 10583-1139 Office Phone: 914-722-0032. Personal E-mail: jordan.goodman@verizon.net.

GOODMAN, JOSEPH WILFRED, electrical engineering educator; b. Boston, Feb. 8, 1936; s. Joseph and Doris (Ryan) G.; m. Hon Mai Lam, Dec. 5, 1962; 1 dau., Michele Ann. BA, Harvard U., 1958; MS in E.E., Stanford U., 1960, PhD, 1963; DSc (hon.), U. Ala., 1996. Postdoctoral fellow Norwegian Def. Rsch. Establishment, Oslo, 1962-63; rsch. assoc. Stanford U., 1963-67, asst. prof., 1967-69, assoc. prof., 1969-72, prof. elec. engring., 1972-99; vis. prof. Univ. Paris XI, Orsay, France, 1973-74; dir. Info. Sys. Lab. Elec. Engring. Stanford U., 1981-83, chmn. dept. of elec. engring., 1988-96, William E. Ayer prof. elec. engring., 1988-99, sr. assoc. dean engring., 1996-98, acting dean engring., 1999, prof. emeritus, 2000—. Cons. to govt. and industry, 1965—; v.p. Internat. Comm. for Optics, 1985-87, pres., 1988-90, past pres., 1991-93; founding chmn. bd. ONI Systems, Inc.; chmn. bd. Nanoprecision Products Inc.; former bd. mem. E-TEK Dynamcis. Author: Introduction to Fourier Optics, 1968, 3d edit., 2005, Statistical Optics, 1985, (with R. Gray) Fourier Transforms: An Introduction for Engineers; editor: International Trends in Optics, 1991; contbr. articles to profl. jours. Recipient F.E. Terman award Am. Soc. Engring. Edn., 1971, Frederic Ives Medal, 1990, Optical Soc. Am., Ester Hoffman Beller award Optical Soc. of Am., 1995. Fellow AAAS, Optical Soc. Am. (dir. 1977-83, editor jour. 1978-83, Max Born award 1983, Frederick Ives award 1990, Esther Hoffman Beller medal 1995, v.p. 1990, pres.-elect 1991, pres. 1992, past pres. 1993), IEEE (edn. medal 1987), Soc. Photo-optical Instrumentation Engrs. (bd. govs. 1979-82, 88-90, Dennis Gabor award 1987), Am. Acad. Arts & Scis.; mem. NAE, Electromagnetics Acad. Home: 570 University Ter Los Altos CA 94022-3523 Office: Stanford U Dept Elec Engring Stanford CA 94305 Business E-Mail: goodman@ee.stanford.edu.

GOODMAN, KIM, marketing professional, computer company executive; B in Polit. Sci., M in Indsl. Engring., Stanford U.; MBA, Harvard U., 1992. V.p. Bain & Co., Inc.; v.p. bus. devel., exec. asst. to the CEO Dell Inc., 2000, v.p., gen. mgr. for networking product group; v.p. mktg. Dell Americas Public Sector, Round Rock, Tex., 2003—. Office: Dell Inc One Dell Way Round Rock TX 78682

GOODMAN, LARRY J., health facility administrator; b. Detroit, 1950; Undergrad. degree with distinction, U. Mich., MD, 1976. Diplomate Am. Bd. Internal Medicine, Am. Bd. Infectious Disease. Intern Rush Presbyn.-St. Luke's Med. Ctr., Chgo., 1976—77; resident in internal medicine Rush U. Med. Ctr., Chgo., 1977—79, chief resident, 1979, fellow in infectious disease, 1979—81, mem. faculty and staff, 1981—87, former prof., assoc. dean med. student programs, former dir. divsn. specialized tng. programs, dir. interinstnl. affairs, sr. v.p. for med. affairs, 1998—2002; Henry R. Russe dean, prof. Rush Med. Coll., Chgo., 2000—02; pres., CEO Rush U. Med. Ctr., 2002—; med. dir. Cook County Hosp., Chgo., 1996—98. Pres. Rush U., Chgo.; prin. officer Rush Bd. Trustees; CEO, chmn. bd. dirs. Rush Sys. for Health; mem. site survey team Liaison Com. on Med. Edn. Contbr. articles to profl. jours. Office: Rush U Med Ctr 1650 W Harrison St Chicago IL 60612

GOODMAN, LEONARD S., healthcare product manufacturing company executive; b. Phila., Mar. 8, 1944; BSME, Pa. State U., 1964; JD, Temple U., 1968. Bar: Pa. 1968, N.J. 1980, U.S. Dist. Ct. N.J. 1985. CFO, v.p., treas. Datascope Corp., Montvale, N.J. Co-author: A Bankers Guide to Consumer Bankruptcy;, 1979; assoc. editor Temple Law Quar., 1967-68. Mem. ABA, Pa. Bar Assn., N.J. State Bar Assn., Phila. Bar Assn. (chmn. consumer fin. svcs. com., corp., banking and bus. law sect. 1988-89), Camden County Bar Assn., Tau Epsilon Rho. Office: Datascope Corp 14 Philips Pkwy Montvale NJ 07645

GOODMAN, LILA VIDA, retired secondary school educator; b. Bklyn., Nov. 15, 1934; d. Abraham John and Martha (LeWinter) Silverman; m. Harold Ralph Sandler (div. 1977); children: Elisa Sandler Shafran, Pamela Sandler Greenbaum, Adam; m. Gerald Goodman, 1984. BA, Bklyn. Coll., 1955; MA, L.I. U., 1976. Cert. tchr., N.Y. Tchr. English John Dewey High Sch., 1975—94; ret., 1994. Home: 89 Lotus Oval N Valley Stream NY 11581-2327

GOODMAN, LOUIS ALLAN, lawyer; b. Providence, Nov. 13, 1943; s. Jacob and Frieda (Feldman) G.; m. Phebe Silver, June 9, 1968; children: Jonathan J., Rebecca A. AB, Columbia U., 1965; MA, Harvard U., 1966, JD, 1969. Bar: N.Y. 1970, Mass. 1973. Assoc. Skadden, Arps, Slate, Meagher & Flom LLP, 1970—77, ptnr., 1978—. Home: 59 North St Newton MA 02460-1065 Office: Skadden, Arps, Slate, Meagher & Flom LLP 1 Beacon St Boston MA 02108-3107

GOODMAN, MAJOR MERLIN, botanical sciences educator; b. Iowa, Sept. 13, 1938; s. Jarrett Wilson and Mable Ollie (Michael) G.; m. Sheila Balfour Dail; children: Sean Balfour Dail, Andrew Scot Dail. BS, Iowa State U., 1960; MS, N.C. State U., 1963, PhD, 1965. Rsch. asst. N.C. State U., Raleigh, 1960-61, NSF coop. fellow, 1961-65; NSF postdoctoral fellow Inst. de Genetica Escola Superior de Agricultura, Piracicaba, Sao Paulo, Brazil, 1965-67; vis. asst. prof. N.C. State U., Raleigh, 1967-68, asst. prof., 1968-70, assoc. prof., 1970-76, prof. crop sci., statistics, genetics, botany, 1976-88, W.N. Reynolds disting. univ. prof., 1988—. Co-author: Races of Maize in Brazil and Adjacent Areas, 1977; author numerous tech. artilces. Recipient research awards Sigma Xi, 1973, N.C. State U. Alumni Assn., 1982, O.M.Gardner award, 1987, Meyer medal, 2000, Holladay medal, 2003, Holladay medal, 2003; named Outstanding PhD Phi Sigma and Phi Kappa Phi, 1965. Mem. Crop Sci. Soc. Am., Soc. for Econ. Botany, Nat. Acad. Scis. Achievements include clarification of genetics of numerous isozyme loci in maize including chromosomal localizations; devel. of several commercially used parental inbred lines of corn. Office: NC State Univ Crop Sci Dept PO Box 7620 Raleigh NC 27695-0001 Office Phone: 919-515-7039. Business E-Mail: major_goodman@nesu.edu.

GOODMAN, MARK, journalist, educator; B in Journalism with honors, U. Mo., 1982; JD, Duke U., 1985. Lectr. U. Md. Univ. Coll., College Park, 1987-88; exec. dir. Student Press Law Ctr., Washington, 1985—. Mem. faculty Inst. Study Ednl. Policy, U. Wash., Seattle, 1987; instr. summer journalism workshops Ball State U., Muncie, Ind., 1988, U. Iowa, Iowa City, 1991, 92, 93, 94, Mich. State U., East Lansing, 1991, 93; adj. guest lectr. Sch. Mass Comm., Bowling Green (Ohio) State U., 1990; mem. faculty coll. newspaper advisers seminar Poynter Inst. Media Studies, St. Petersburg, Fla., 1989, 90, 92; media law com. Coll. Media Advisers, Inc.; panelist Danforth Found., 1988, 89, Assn. Edn. in Journalism and Mass Comm., 1987, 88; guest lectr. Sch. Comm. Am. U., Washington, 1989, 90, 94. Contbr. articles to profl. jours. Recipient Golden Quill award Garden State Scholastic Press Assn., 1987, Disting. Svc. award Mich. Interscholastic Press Assn., 1987, Ind. Scholastic Journalism award Ball State U., 1988, Disting. Svc. award So. Interscholastic Press Assn., 1988, Presdl. citations Coll. Media Advisers, Inc., 1987, 88, 89, Disting. Svc. award Fla. C.C. Press Assn., 1989, Knight award, Earl English Scholastic Journalism award Mo. Interscholastic Press Assn./Mo. Journalism Edn. Assn., 1992, Cert. of Merit, Soc. Collegiate Journalists, 1989, Gold Key award Columbia U. Scholastic Press Assn., 1988, Carl Towley award Journalism Edn. Assn., 1992. Mem. Kappa Tau Alpha. Office: Student Press Law Ctr Inc 1101 Wilson Blvd Ste 1100 Arlington VA 22209-2275 Business E-Mail: director@splc.org.

GOODMAN, MAX A., lawyer, educator; b. Chgo., May 24, 1924; s. Sam and Nettie (Abramowitz) G.; m. Marlyene Monkarsh, June 2, 1946; children: Jan M., Lauren A. Packard, Melanie Murez. AA, Herzl Jr. Coll., 1943; student, Northwestern U., 1946-47; JD, Loyola U., 1948; LLD (hon.), Southwestern U. Sch. Law, 2000. Bar: Calif. 1948; cert. family law specialist, 1980, 85, 90. Pvt. practice, L.A., 1948-53; ptnr. Goodman, Hirschberg & King, L.A., 1953-81; prof. Southwestern U. Sch. Law, L.A., 1966—. Lectr. Calif. Continuing Edn. of the Bar, 1971—90. Contbr. articles to profl. jours. Served to cpl. U.S. Army, 1943-45. Mem. ABA (chmn. law sch. curriculum com. family law sect. 1987-88, family law sect. 1987-88, 97-98), State Bar Calif. (del. conf. dels. 1972, 80-87, 91, exec. com. family law sect. 1981-85), Los Angeles County Bar Assn. (chmn. family law sect. 1971-72, editor family law handbook 1974-89). Avocation: contract bridge. Office: Southwestern U Sch Law 675 S Westmoreland Ave Los Angeles CA 90005-3905 Office Phone: 213-738-6823. Business E-Mail: mgoodman@swlaw.edu.

GOODMAN, MICHAEL B(ARRY), communications educator; b. Dallas, July 10, 1949; s. Harold A. and Dora (Einhorn) G.; m. Karen E. Kailenta, June 4, 1977; children: 1 stepchild, Craig Cook, 1 child, John David. BA, U. Tex., 1971; MA, SUNY, Stony Brook, 1972, PhD, 1979. Adj. instr. SUNY, Old Westbury, 1976-79; adj. asst. prof. N.Y. Inst. Tech., N.Y.C., 1976-82, N.Y.U., 1979-81; asst. prof. SUNY, Stony Brook, 1979-81, Northea. U., Boston, 1982-86; prof., corp. comm. Fairleigh Dickinson U., Madison, NJ, 1986—, dir. MA in Corp. Comm. program, 1996—2002, founder, dir. Corp. Comm. Inst., 1999—. Cons. in corp. comms. to numerous orgns. in U.S.; condr. seminars and workshops on corp. comm., 1979—; conf. chmn. Internat. Profl. Comm. Conf., Phila., 1993, New Orleans, 1999; founder Ann. Conf. on Corp. Comm., 1988-98, 2002—; adj. prof. Baruch Coll., CUNY, 2004—; lectr. in field. V.p. Friends Sem. PTA, N.Y.C., 1990-91; mem. adv. bd. Bus. Diplomatic Action, 2003—. Named to Resident Faculty Nat. Faculty Excellence in Teaching English Program, Vassar Coll., 1984. Fellow Royal Soc. Encouragement Arts, Mfrs. and Commerce (London), Soc. Tech. Comm.; mem. Profl. Comm. Soc. of IEEE (sr., mem. adminstrv. com., Alfred Goldsmith award 1994), MLA, Nat. Coun. Tchrs. of English, Am. Mgmt. Assn., Assn. for Bus. Comm. (v.p. 2005—, bd. dirs. 2005—), Authors Guild, Authors League, Arthur W. Page Soc., Assn. Bus. Comm. (v.p. ea. region U.S., bd. dirs. 2005—), Nat. Investors Rels. Inst. Avocations: hiking, skiing, bicycling. Home: 28 W 38th St Apt 11W New York NY 10018-6287 Office: Fairleigh Dickinson U 285 Madison Ave Madison NJ 07940-1099 Office Phone: 973-443-8709. Business E-Mail: cci@corporatecomm.org. E-mail: goodman@fdu.edu.

GOODMAN, NAOMI ASCHER, writer; b. N.Y.C., Aug. 26, 1920; d. Moses and Helen M. Ascher; m. Percival Goodman, Sept. 28, 1944 (dec. Oct. 1989); children: Rachel, Joel. BA, Wellesley Coll., 1942; postgrad., Columbia U., 1943-44, Art Students League, 1945-46. Assoc. Women and Soc. Sem. Columbia U., 1993—; co-chair Berkshire Conf. of Women Historians, mem. book award com., 1987-91, mem. com., 1986, 92-2001; pres. Jewish Peace Fellowship, 1972-87, sec., 1987—. Co-author: (with Marcus and Woodlandler) The Goodbook Cook Book, 1986, rev. edit., 1995; co-editor: (with Murray Polnar) The Challenge of Shalom: The Jewish Tradition of Peace and Justice, 1994, On Borrowed Time: Poems of Two Centuries, 2005. Coord. Peace Portolios I and II, 1970-76; interior designer religious instns. Goodman Interiors Ltd., 1955-70; mem. nat. coun. Fellowship of Reconciliation, 1970-87, hon. vice-chair, 1988—; mem. exec. com. Internat. Fellowship of Reconciliation, 1974-84. Democrat. Jewish. Home: 40 W 77th St New York NY 10024-5128

GOODMAN, OSCAR BAYLIN, mayor, lawyer; b. Phila., July 26, 1939; s. A. Allan and Laura (Baylin) G.; m. Carolyn Goldmark, June 6, 1962; children: Oscar B. Jr., Ross C., Eric A., Cara Lee. BA, Haverford Coll., 1961; JD, U. Pa., 1964. Bar: Nev., U.S. Ct. Appeals. Ptnr. Goodman, Chesnoff and Keach, Las Vegas, 1965—; mayor City of Las Vegas, 1999—. Adv. bd. Us. Conf. of Mayors. Mem. Nat. Assn. Criminal Def. Lawyers (pres. 1983). Jewish. Office: Off of the Mayor 400 Stewart Ave Las Vegas NV 89101-2927 also: Goodman Chesnoff & Keach 520 S 4th St Las Vegas NV 89101-6524*

GOODMAN, PHYLLIS L., public relations executive; b. N.Y.C., Sept. 7, 1946; d. Bernard Jacob and Claire (Rosenberg) Goodman. BS, Cornell U., 1967. Ext. home economist Nassau County Ext. Svc., Mineola, N.Y., 1967-68; editl. asst. Funk & Wagnalls, N.Y.C., 1968-69; sr. v.p. Glick & Lorwin, Inc., N.Y.C., 1969-80, Sci. and Medicine, N.Y.C., 1980-82; v.p. Hill and Knowlton, Inc., N.Y.C., 1982-85; assoc. v.p. comm. and pub. affairs St. Luke's-Roosevelt Hosp. Ctr., N.Y.C., 1985-92; owner Goodman Pub. Rels., Albuquerque, 1993-95; v.p. corp. comm. Sun Healthcare Group, Inc., Albuquerque, 1995-2000; v.p. mktg. and comms. St. Vincent Hosp., Santa Fe, 2000-01; v.p. mktg. and comm. Cin. Children's Hosp. Med. Ctr., 2001—. Mem. com. pub. affairs Greater N.Y. Hosp. Assn., 1988-92. Bd. dirs. Chamber Music Albuquerque, 1998-2001. Mem. Am. Soc. Health Care Mktg. and Pub. Rels. (treas. N.Mex. chpt. 1993-94), Pub. Rels. Soc. Am. (accredited, pres. N.Mex. chpt. 1996), Healthcare Pub. Rels. and Mktg. Soc. Greater N.Y. (pres. 1990-91), Westside C. of C. N.Y.C. (bd. dirs. 1986-92), Pi Lambda Theta. Office: Cin Childrens Hosp MLC 9102 3333 Burnet Ave Cincinnati OH 45229

GOODMAN, REBECCA GRUVER, education educator, writer; b. St. Joseph, Mo., Nov. 3, 1931; d. Arthur Lester Gruver and Dana Theodore Brooks; m. Phil P. Goodman, June 17, 1972 (dec. June 1986). BA, Stanford U., 1954; MA, U. Calif., Berkeley, 1956, PhD, 1964. Full time lectr./prof. Hunter Coll., CUNY, 1961—73, part time adj. prof., 1973—97. Author: (history) Am. Nationalism 1783-1830, (history textbook) An Am. History, 1972—85, (book chapters) Ency. of U.S. Fgn. Rels., 1997. Mem.: Soc. for Historians of Am. Fgn. Rels., Orgn. of Am. Historians, Am. Hist. Assn. Avocations: baseball, theater.

GOODMAN, RICHARD, writer; b. Dayton, Ohio, July 11, 1945; BA, U. Mich., Ann Arbor, Mich., 1967; MA, Wayne State U., Detroit, Mich., 1970. Creative nonfiction faculty Spalding U., Louisville, 2003—. Author: French Dirt: The Story of a Garden in the South of France, 1991. Recipient Hopwood Award, U. Mich., 1966; scholar Joseph N. Whitten Meml. Scholarship, Palmer Sch., LI U., 1996; Fellowship, MacDowell Colony, 1993, 1995, Va. Ctr. for the Creative Arts, 2003.

GOODMAN, RICHARD SHALEM, lawyer, orthopedic surgeon; m. Jemi Horn; children: Lorraine, Carolyn Pianin, Deborah Lieb, Keith London, Evan London. BA, Alfred (N.Y.) U., 1955; MD, N.Y. U., 1960; JD, Touro Coll., 1987. Bar: N.Y. 1991, U.S. Ct. Claims 1995, U.S. Ct. Mil. Appeals 1995, U.S. Ct. Appeals 1995, U.S. Supreme Ct. 1995; lic. physician, N.Y., Calif.; diplomate Am. Bd. Orthopedic Surgery. Intern Ind. U. Med. Ctr., Indianapolis, 1960—61; asst. resident in gen. surgery Bronx Mcpl. Hosp. Ctr., 1961—62; resident in orthopedics N.Y.C. Med. Ctr. and various others, 1964—67; attending physician St. Catherine of Sienna Hosp. (formerly St. John's Episcopal Hosp.), Smithtown, NY, 1967—, pres. med. staff, 1978; attending physician Cmty. Hosp. Suffolk, Smithtown, 1967—96; cons. in orthop. LIJ Hosp., New Hyde Park, NY, 1996—; adjunct staff dept. Orthop. Surgery North Shore U. Med. Ctr., 2001—. Asst. prof. dept. anatomy SUNY, Stony Brook, 1971-88, Stonybrook Found. Pres. Marine Scis. Rsch. Ctr., 1984-87; pres. staff Community Hosp. of We. Suffolk, 1977-78; policy advisor Inst. Advancement Health Care Mgmt., U. Albany, SUNY, 1992—; cons. to numerous bus., govt. agys., and ins. cos.; presenter, speaker, and panelist in fields. Co-author: American Jurisprudence Proof of Facts, 3d series, vol. 2 Pelvic Injuries, 1988, Handling Soft Tissue Injury Cases: Medical Aspects, 1988, 2d edit., 1993, Preparing and Winning Medical Negligence Cases, 1989, 2d edit., 1994, Legal Medicine: Legal Dynamics of Medical Encounters, 2d edit., 1990; contbr. articles to med. and lega. jours., chapters to books; mem. editl. bd.: Orthopedics and Orthopedics Today, 1984—87, Med. Malpractice Prevention, bd. editl. cons.: Trustee Alfred U., 1978-84; policy adv. Inst. Advancement Health Care Mgmt. U. Albany; nat. chmn. U. Albany Parents Fund, 1991-94; nat. chmn. U. Albany Parent's Fund, 1991-92; active Arthritis Found. Fellow: Am. Coll. Legal Med. (mem. policy and planning com., program chmn. annual meeting 1988—), Am. Acad. Orthoped. Surgeons; mem.: Pitts. Inst. Legal Med., Nat. Health Lawyers Assn., Assn. Bar City N.Y., Suffolk County Bar Assn., N.Y. Bar Assn., Am. Acad. Legal and Industrial Med. (bd. govs.), N.Y. State. Soc. Orthoped. Surgeons, Arthritis Found., PanAm. Med. Assn., Internat. Coll. Surgeons, N.Y. State Med. Soc., Suffolk County Med. Soc., Am. Rheumatism Assn., Am. Coll. Sports Med., Am. Soc. Law and Med., Ea. Orthoped. Assn., Am. Coll. Legal Medicine (chmn. exhibits com. ann. meeting 1989—90, mem. policy and planning com., mem. program com. ann. meeting 1989—90, co-chmn. exhibitor's com. 1993, mem. rsch. com. 1993, mem. com. to confer with com. Med. Soc. State N.Y. 1991—, mem. student awards com. 1993, chmn. computer bull. bd. sys. 1995, assoc. editor Communique and newsbriefs), Bach Aria Group (bd. dirs. 1970—88), NYU Bellevue Alumni Assn., Stony Brook Yacht Club, Mutton Town Golf Club, Univ. Club. Office: 285 E Main St Smithtown NY 11787 also: 70 Glen Cove Rd Roslyn Heights NY 11577 also: 743 Columbia Tpke East Greenbush NY 12061 Office Phone: 631-724-2727. Personal E-mail: RSGMDESQ@aol.com.

GOODMAN, ROBERT LEE, nursing administrator; b. Sumter, SC, July 30, 1962; s. Helen Ragin Goodman; m. Deborah Jean Clark, Oct. 16, 1999; children: Janeen Goodman Malloy, Bionca Anne. Cert. nursing asst., Bremerton Tech. Sch., 1989; cert. in med. assistance, Eton Coll., 1999. Cert. med. asst., nursing asst. Nursing asst. Bremerton (Wash.) Convalescent Home, 1989—92, Harrison Meml. Hosp., Bremerton, 1993—95, Port Orchard (Wash.) Convalescent Home, Port Orchard, 1996—98; med. asst. Kitsap Pain Clinic, Bremerton, 1998—99; staff coord. Kindred Health Care Corp., Winston-Salem, NC, 1999—. Author: Born of Rage, 2002. With USN, 1980—85. Scholar, Eton Coll. Found., 1998. Avocations: bowling, singing, song writing, bird breeding, fish breeding.

GOODMAN, ROBERT STANLEY, management educator; s. Irwin Aaron and Virginia Rose Goodman; m. Roberta Lynn Louis, June 28, 1987; children: Shoshana Hannah, Evan Simcha. BS, U. Wis.; MA, U. Iowa; MBA, PHD, U. Minn., 1988. Exec. trainee, asst. cashier, asst. v.p. Nat. Bank Albany Park, Chgo., 1974—78; v.p. Deerbrook State Bank, Deerfield, Ill., 1978—80; v.p., sr. lending officer First Nat. Bank Waukegan, Ill., 1980—82; asst. prof. orgn. and mgmt. Syracuse (N.Y.) U., 1986—89; asst. prof. strategic mgmt. York U., Toronto, Canada, 1988—91; asst. prof. mgmt. U. Wis., Madison, 1991—95; asoc. prof. mgmt. Bentley Coll., Waltham, Mass., 1995—98; assoc. prof. mgmt. Northeastern Ill. U., Chgo., 1998—2000; assoc. prof. strategic mgmt. and internat. bus. Niagara (N.Y.) U., 2000—02; program dir., assoc. prof. bus. adminstrn. divsn. East-West U., Chgo., 2002—. Presenter in field. Co-author: Managing for Global Competitiveness: A Study Guide for BGS 3-004, 1998; editor: International Research in the Business Disciplines, Vol. 4, 2003; contbr. articles to profl. jours. Bd. dirs., mem. exec. com. Hist. Keyboard Soc., Milw., 1994—97. Fellow, U. Minn., Mpls., 1983—84; grantee, U. Minn. Strategic Mgmt. Rsch. Ctr., 1985, 1994, U. Minn. Grad. Sch., 1986, Syracuse U. Senate, 1987, Office Info. and Econ. Rsch., Fed. Home Loan Bank Bd., 1989, Ont. Ctr. for Internat. Bus./The Estonian Bus. Sch., 1990, York U., Toronto, 1991, U. Wis. Sch. Bus., 1992—93, U.S. Dept. Edn., Washington, 1996—99. Mem.: Internat. Assn. for Bus. and Soc. (charter), Strategic Mgmt. Soc., Acad. Mgmt., Internat. Cantorial Found., Univ. Club Chgo., Beta Gamma Sigma. Avocations: swimming, racquetball, reading, travel. Office: East-West Univ 816 S Michigan Ave Chicago IL 60605

GOODMAN, ROBERT UHLE, lawyer; b. Shreveport, La., Apr. 18, 1929; s. Uhle Slater and Edith (Caskey) Goodman; m. Martha Knox McGuffin, Mar. 22, 1957. BA, Washington and Lee U., 1950; LLB, La. State U., 1953. Bar: La. 1953. Ptnr. Naff, Goodman, and Johns and successor firms, Shreveport, 1956—89; pvt. practice Robert U. Goodman, P.C., Shreveport, 1989—. Former asst. city atty. City of Shreveport; former asst. atty. gen. State of La.; bd. dirs. Pioneer Bank, Aeropres Corp., Sound Fighter Sys., Inc. Gen. counsel Housing Authority City of Shreveport; bd. dirs., former pres. North La. Goodwill Industries Rehab. Ctr., Inc.; former bd. dirs. Salvation Army; chancellor, former vestry mem. St. Mark's Cathedral, 1965—; past pres. Holiday in Dixie. Capt. USAF, 1953—55. Recipient Runner-up Outstanding Man of Yr. Mem.: Housing and Devel. Law Inst., 5th Cir. Bar Assn., Garden of the Gods Club, Ambassadors Club (past chmn.), Cambridge Club, Shreveport Club. Republican. Episcopalian. Office: 416 Travis St Ste 1105 Shreveport LA 71101-5504 Office Phone: 318-221-1601. E-mail: rugus@bellsouth.net.

GOODMAN, ROY MATZ, corporate financial executive, former state senator; b. NYC, Mar. 5, 1930; s. Bernard A. and Alice (Matz) G.; m. Barbara Christine Furrer, June 28, 1955; children: Claire Goodman Pellegrini Cloud, Leslie Alice, Randolph Bernard. BA cum laude, Harvard U., 1951, MBA with distinction, 1953; DHL (hon.), Pratt Inst., 1994; LLD (hon.), Baruch Coll. CUNY, 2002. Assoc. buying and new bus. dept. Kuhn, Loeb & Co. Investment Bankers, 1955-60; pres., dir. Drug Devel. Corp., Ex-Lax, Inc., Roycemore, Inc., 1962-71; mem. N.Y. State Senate, 1969—2002; pres., CEO UN Devel. Corp., N.Y.C., 2002—. Dep. majority leader for policy, chmn. investigations, taxation and govt. ops. com.; chmn. Senate spl. com. on arts and cultural affairs; mem. Senate task forces on def. spending, AIDS, vandalism, religious desecration and bigotry, and econ. recovery and devel.; fin., rules, cities, edn., crime and correction and transp. coms., subcom. on libraries chmn. legis. com. on pub. pvt., coop., 1985-88; chmn. housing and urban devel. com., 1968-76; pres. Goodman Family Found.; bd. dirs. 1st Empire State Corp., 1984-2000; adv. bd. M & T Bank Corp., 2000-, commr. fin., fin. adminstr. City of N.Y., 1966-68; mem. N.Y.C. Banking Commn., 1966-68; past trustee N.Y.C. Police Pension Fund, N.Y.C. Fire Dept. Pension Fund, 1966-68; mem. Mayor's Cabinet and Supercabinet, 1966-68, N.Y.C. Treasurer, 1966-68; Chmn. State Charter Revision Commn. for N.Y.C., 1972-76; adj. prof. pub. admin. Baruch Coll. CUNY, 1975; mem. Mayor Guiliani Transition Team, 1993; mem. Gov. Pataki Transition Team, 1994. Bd. dirs. Citizens Com. N.Y.C.; past mem. bd. Brotherhood-In-Action; trustee Heart Rsch. Found.; exec. asst. to chmn. N.Y. State Assembly Jud. Com., 1963-64; asst. to atty. gen. State N.Y., 1960; pres. 9th A.D. Rep. Club, 1963-64; del. N.Y. State Rep. Convs., 1966-2000, del. Rep. Nat. Conv., 1968,

72, 76, 80, 84, 88, 92, 96, 2000, 2004, Presdl. Elector, 1984; chmn. N.Y. County Rep. Com., 1981-2002, treas., 1965; mem. N.Y. Rep. State Com., exec. com.; N.Y. State co-chmn. Bush-for-Pres. campaigns, 1988, 92, Bush-Quayle Nat. Fin. Com., 1988, 92; candidate for Mayor of N.Y.C., 1977; trustee Carnegie Hall Soc., Inc., Carnegie Hall Corp., past trustee Columbia Coll. Pharm. Scis., L.I. Coll. Hosp., N.Y. Com. Young Audiences, United Jewish Appeal, Tel Aviv U., Freedom House, Dalton Schs. Brotherhood-In-Action, Heart Rsch. Found.; presdl. appointee to Nat. Commn. Fine Arts, 1985-89, Nat. Endowment Arts Coun., 1989-96, trustee John F. Kennedy Ctr. for Performing Arts, 2002-; amb. arts NEA, 2000; fellow Met. Mus. Art; patron Met. Opera; sponsor N.Y. Philharm. Soc.; mem. Regents vis. com. N.Y. State Mus.; trustee Temple Emanu-El; past bd. dirs. Freedom House; mem. N.Y. Com. for Young Audiences, Harvard Com. on Univ. Resources,; mem. bd. overseers John F. Kennedy Sch. Govt./Harvard U. Lt. USNR, 1953-56. Decorated Adm.'s Meritorious Svc. citation; recipient Disting. Service award Jaycees, 1966, Mt. Scopus citation Hebrew U., Jerusalem, 1968, Scroll of Honor United Jewish Appeal, 1970, Kennedy Ctr. award for Disting. Leadership in Arts-in Edn., Nat. Arts Club Citation of Merit, City U., Medal of Merit, 1972, Man of Yr. award Brotherhood-in-Action, 1972, Humanitarian award Soc. for Prevention Cruelty to Children, 1976, citation for cmty. service Odyssey House, 1976, Our Town newspaper award for leadership in City Charter revision, 1976, Fiorello H. LaGuardia Meml. award, 1979-80, citation for outstanding service N.Y. Young Rep. Club, 1982, Disting. Alumni award Hunter Coll. Elem. Sch. Parents Assn., 1985, Service awards N.Y. Police Found. and N.Y. Fire Safety Found., 1986, Patriotic Service award U.S. Treasury Dept., N.Y. Gov.'s Arts Medal, 2002, Sutton Area Cmty. Svc. Award, 2002, WNYC Radio Arts Award, 2002, U.N. Delegations' Citizen of the World Award, 2002, Alliance of N.Y. Arts Org. Arts Advocate Award, 2002, City Club of N.Y. Disting. New Yorker Award, 2002, Internat. Coun. for Caring Communities Caring Citizen of the Humanities Award, 2003; named to honor scroll Columbia Assn. of N.Y.C. Police Dept., 1979, N.Y. State Rep. of Yr. Ripon Soc., 1972, Cmty. Activist award Lenox Hill Neighborhood Assn., Inc., 1995, Artists fellowship award, John LaFarge Meml. award for interracial justice, Local Hero award Stanley Isaacs Assn., Playwrights Horizon award, 1995, Gari Melchers Meml. medal, 1995, South Street Seaport Mus. award, 1995, Friend of the Arts award Town Hall Found., 1995, Legacy of Hope award N.Y. Foundling Home, Carnegie Hall, 1996, Margaret Sanger award Family Advs. N.Y., 1997; Statesman Father of Yr. award, 1984, named to Econ. Hon. Soc. St. John's U., 1991. Mem. Anti-Defamation League (bd. govs. N.Y.), Am. Young Pres.'s Orgn., Fin. Analysts Fedn., N.Y. Soc. Security Analysts, Council Fgn. Rels., Woodrow Wilson Internat. Ctr. Scholars (mem. adv. group), Assn. Harvard Alumni (past dir.), Harvard Club (gov.), Century Assn., Century Country Club, Dutch Treat Club, Senate Club (pres.), Harvard Bus. Sch., City Club, Omicron Delta Epsilon (hon.). Home: 1035 5th Ave New York NY 10028-0135 Office: 2 UN Plaza 27th Fl New York NY 10017

GOODMAN, SAM RICHARD, electronics company executive; b. N.Y.C., May 23, 1930; s. Morris and Virginia (Gross) G.; m. Beatrice Bettencourt, Sept. 15, 1957; children: Mark Stuart, Stephen Manuel, Christopher Bettencourt. BBA, CCNY, 1951; MBA, NYU, 1957, PhD, 1968. Chief acct. John C. Valentine Co., N.Y.C., 1957-60; mgr. budgets and analysis Gen. Foods. Corp., White Plains, N.Y., 1960-63; budget dir. Crowell Collier Pub. Co., N.Y.C., 1963-64; v.p., chief fin. officer Nestle Co., Inc., White Plains, 1964; chief fin. officer Aileen, Inc., N.Y.C., 1973-74, Ampex Corp., 1974-76; exec. v.p. fin. and adminstrn. Baker & Taylor Co. div. W.R. Grace Co., N.Y.C., 1976-79, Magnuson Computer Systems, Inc., San Jose, Calif., 1979-81; v.p., chief fin. officer Datamac Computer Systems, Sunnyvale, Calif., 1981; pres. Nutritional Foods Inc., San Francisco, 1983-84; chmn., chief exec. officer CMX Corp., Santa Clara, Calif., 1984-88; dir., sr. v.p. Masstor Systems Corp., Santa Clara, 1988—; pvt. cons. Atherton, Calif., 1990—; sr. mgmt. cons. Durkee/Sharlit, 1991—; pres. Mayfair Packing Co., 1991—; mng. dir. Quincy Pacific Ptnrs., L.P., 1992—; pres., CEO Mayfair Packing Co., San Jose, Calif., 1991-94; pvt. cons. BMG Assocs., 1994—. Lectr. NYU Inst. Mgmt., 1965-67; asst. prof. mktg. Iona Coll. Grad. Sch. Adminstrn., 1967-69; prof. Golden Gate U., 1974—; prof. fin. and mktg. Pace U. Grad. Sch. Bus. Adminstrn., 1969-79. Author 7 books, including Controller's Handbook; contbr. articles to jours. Lt. (j.g.) USNR, 1951—55. Decorated Korean Occupation Svc. medal Armed Forces Svc., Nat. Def. Svc. medal. Mem. Fin. Execs. Inst., Nat. Assn. Accts., Am. Statis. Assn., Am. Econs. Assn., Planning Execs. Inst., Am. Arbitration Assn., Turnaround Mgmt. Assn. Home and Office: 60 Shearer Dr Atherton CA 94027-3957 E-mail: bgoodman@cbnorcal.com.

GOODMAN, SEYMOUR EVAN, computer science and international studies educator, researcher, consultant; b. Chgo., June 19, 1943; s. Paul S. and Shirley (Young) G.; m. Diane Margit Samuel, Dec. 18, 1966; children: Richard Michael, Steven Neal. BS, Columbia U., 1965, MS, 1966; PhD, Calif. Inst. Tech., 1970. Asst. prof. applied math. U. Va., Charlottesville, 1970-75, assoc. prof. applied math. and computer sci., 1975-81; prof. mgmt. info. sys. U. Ariz., Tucson, 1981—; prof. Sam Nunn Sch. Internat. Affairs Coll. of Computing, Ga. Inst. of Tech., Atlanta, 1999—; co-dir. Ctr. Internat. Strategy Tech. and Policy, 2000—, Ga. Tech. Info. Security Ctr., 2000—. Vis. prof. pub. and internat. affairs, Princeton (N.J.) U., 1977-79, rsch. fellow, 1978-79; vis. scholar U. Chgo., 1979; mem. Mid. Ea. Ctr., 1992—; Carnegie Sci. fellow Ctr. Internat. Security and Arms Control, Stanford U., 1994-97; dir. program info. tech. and nat. security, 1996-98, dir. Consortium for Rsch. on Info. Security and Policy, Stanford U., 1998—, vis. prof. dept. engring. econ. sys. and ops. rsch., 1998-99; mem. adv. com. Internat. Trade Adminstrn., Dept. Commerce, 1979-82; mem. adv. com. Def. Sci. Bd., Dept. Def., 1981-84, Def. Intelligence Agy., 1983-87, NRC coms., 1985-92, Dept. State, 1987-89; chmn. NRC com. Internat. Devel. in Computer Sci. and Tech., 1987-88; chmn. computer tech.-subpanel NRC panel on Future Design and Implementation of U.S. Nat. Security Export Controls, 1989-91; cons. govtl. agys. Danforth Assoc., 1977-82; Sesquicentennial Assoc. State of Va., 1977; mem. telecom study panel U.S. Dept. Def., 2003-04. Editor: Technology and Transnational Political Issues, International Information Systems, 1991-93; adv. bd. PRIISM, 1995-97; adv. editor Jour. Global Info. Tech. Mgmt., 1997—; contbr. numerous articles to profl. jours. NSF grantee, 1978-79, 83, 2001-; numerous grant and rsch. contracts Office Tech. Assessment, U.S. Congress, MacArthur Found., 2003-, Los Alamos Nat. Lab., USAF, Battelle Meml. Labs., IBM, Nat. Coun. for Soviet and East European Rsch., Dept. Commerce, Dept. Def., NSF; U.S. participant U.S.-USSR IREX program, 1988-89. Mem. Assn. for Computing Machinery (nat. lectr. 1981-82, com. computing and pub. policy 1981-83, 93—, contbg. editor Internat. Perspectives, Comms. 1991—), Am. Assn. for Advancement of Slavic Studies, Computer Soc. of IEEE (com. on pub. policy 1987-95), Highlands Forum. Office: Sam Nunn Sch Internat Affairs Coll Computing Ga Inst Tech 781 Marietta Ave NW Atlanta GA 30332-0610 Office Phone: 404-385-1461. E-mail: goodman@cc.gatech.edu.

GOODMAN, SIDNEY, artist; b. Phila., 1936; Degree in Illustration, Phila. Coll. Art, 1958. Prof. Phila. Coll. Art., 1960—79, Pa. Acad. Fine Arts, 1979—. Exhibitions include Artist's Retrospective, Phila. Mus. Art, 1996. Recipient Visual Art award, Southeastern Ctr. Contemporary Art, 1991, Ford Found. Purchase award, 1991; grantee Guggenheim Fellowship, 1991, NEA Fellowship, 1991, Yale-Norfolk Fellowship, 1991. Mailing: c/o Pa Acad Fine Arts 118 North Broad St Philadelphia PA 19102*

GOODMAN, STANLEY, lawyer; b. Cin., June 16, 1931; s. Sol and Ethel (Barsman) G.; m. Diane Elaine Kassel, Apr. 15, 1956; children: Julie Lerner, Jeffrey Stephen, Richard Paul. BA, U. Cin., 1953, JD, 1955. Bar: Ohio 1955, Ky. 1976. Ptnr. Goodman & Goodman, Cin., 1955—. Dir. Winbco Tank Co., Ottumwa, Iowa; lectr. Ohio Bar Continuing Legal Edn. Series; mediator Am. Health Lawyers Alternative Dispute Resolution Svc.; mediator/arbitrator Thomas H. Crush Dispute Resolution Svc. Mem. ABA, Am. Health Lawyers Assn., Ohio State Bar Assn. (chair eminent domain com. 1997-2000), Ky. Bar Assn., Cin. Bar Assn., Bankers Club, Ridge Club. Jewish. Office: 123 E 4th St Cincinnati OH 45202-4003 Office Phone: 513-621-1505. E-mail: sgoodman@goodlaw.com.

GOODMAN, STANLEY ERWIN, surgeon; b. Norwalk, Conn., May 4, 1926; s. Robert M. and Francine (Cotler) G.; m. Alice Marie Vanderbecq, June 20, 1962; m. ed. Francine Joan. BS, Trinity Coll., Hartford, 1947; MA, U. Pa., 1949; MD, Cornell U., 1953. Diplomate Am. Bd. Surgery. Intern Strong Meml. Hosp., Rochester, N.Y., 1953-54; asst. resident surgery Kings County Hosp., Bklyn., 1955-58; asst. resident Mt. Sinai Hosp., N.Y.C., 1954—55; chief resident surgery Kings County Hosp., Bklyn., 1958-59, attending surgeon vascular service and breast tumor bd., 1959—. Research asst. State U. N.Y. Med. Sch., Bklyn., 1956-57; gen. surgery practice, Norwalk, 1959-88; sr. attending surg. staff Norwalk Hosp., former chief sect. neoplastic diseases; asst. instr. SUNY Med. Sch., 1956-57, instr. clin. surgery, 1959-87; bd. regional advisors People's Bank Bridgeport, Conn. Bd. dirs. So. Fairfield County unit Am. Cancer Soc.; bd. regional advs. Norwalk Tech. Coll.; bd. dirs. Greater Norwalk Community Council. Served with USNR, 1944-46. Fellow ACS; mem. AAAS, Royal Soc. Health, Pan Am. Med. Assn., Norwalk Med. Soc. (past pres.), N.Y. Acad. Medicine, Am. Heart Assn. Home: 40 Pequot Trl Westport CT 06880-2931

GOODMAN, STANLEY LEONARD, advertising executive; b. N.Y.C., Jan. 21, 1920; s. Abraham and Leah (Fellman) G.; m. Anita Davis, Aug. 30, 1960; children— Patricia, Laurence; stepchildren— Marilyn Rice, Stuart Rice. BS in Econs, Wharton Sch. U. Pa., 1941; certificate electronics, U. Richmond, 1943. Asst. to pres. Decca Records, Inc., N.Y.C., 1941-56; v.p., mktg. dir. Grayson Robinson Stores, N.Y.C., 1956-61; club plan creative dir. Popular Mdse. Co., Inc., Passaic, N.J., 1961-62, dir. mktg., 1962-64; pres. Elliot, Goodman & Russell, Inc., advt., N.Y.C., 1964, EGR Travel Promotion, Inc., N.Y.C., 1969-80, EGR Mktg., Inc., N.Y.C., 1968-80, EGR Communications, Inc., Detroit, 1969-80; chmn. Consol. Tech. Industries, Northvale, N.J., 1987—. Pres., dir. EGR Communications, Inc., N.Y.C., 1968—; dir. Pub. Service Mut. Ins. Co., N.Y.C.; Lectr. Am. Mgmt. Assn., 1964-82; instr. mktg. dept. Pace Coll.; chmn. Consolidated Tech. Industries, Inc., 1988—. Contbr. articles to sales mags. Bd. trustees Westchester Philharmonic Orch., 1996—, Union Am. Hebrew Congs., 1996—. Mem. Sales Promotion Execs. Assn. (Sales Promotion Man of Year N.Y. 1959, internat. pres. 1960-62, honored Stanley Goodman grant 1954—), Direct Mail Advt. Assn., Council Sales Promotion Agys. (pres. 1969-71), Am. Mktg. Assn., Hundred Million Club, Westchester Alumni Assn. U. Pa. (v.p. 1966—) Home: 46 Crosshill Rd Hartsdale NY 10530-3013 Personal E-mail: stanlgee@aol.com.

GOODMAN, STEPHEN MURRY, lawyer; b. Phila., Oct. 8, 1940; s. Edward and Jean (Landau) G.; m. Janis Freeman, Jan. 8, 1983; children: Carl, Rachel. BS cum laude, U. Pa., 1962, LLB magna cum laude, 1965. Bar: D.C. 1967, Pa. 1969. Law clerk to Hon. David Bazelon U.S. Ct. Appeals (D.C. cir.), Washington, 1965-66; law clk. to Hon. William J. Brennan Jr. U.S. Supreme Ct., Washington, 1966-67; ptnr. Goodman & Ewing, Phila., 1970-83, Wolf, Block, Schorr & Solis-Cohen, Phila., 1983-94, Morgan, Lewis & Bockius LLP, Phila., 1995—. Mem. Order of Coif. Democrat. Jewish. Avocation: profl. jazz pianist. Office: Morgan Lewis & Bockius LLP 1701 Market St Philadelphia PA 19103-2903 Office Phone: 215-963-5086. Business E-Mail: sgoodman@morganlewis.com.

GOODMAN, SUSAN, literature educator; b. Boston, Mar. 20, 1951; d. Ralph and Rhoda (Cohen) R.; m. Carl Dawson, July 28, 1995. BA, U. N.H., 1972, MEd, 1974, MA, 1985, PhD, 1988. English tchr. various sch. dists., Maine, N.H., 1972-83; asst. to assoc. prof. English Calif. State U., Fresno, 1989-94, U. Del., Newark, 1994—, now HF Brown Prof. Author: Edith Wharton's Women: Friends and Rivals, 1990, Edith Wharton's Women, 1994, Ellen Glasgow: A Biography, 1998, Civil Wars: American Novels of Manner, 1880-1940, 2003, (with Carl Dawson) William Dean Howells: A Writer's Life, 2005. Resident fellow Va. Ctr. for the Humanities, 1991. Mem. MLA, Ellen Glasgow Soc., Edith Wharton Soc., Soc. Study of So. Lit., William Dean Hawell Soc Business E-Mail: sgoodman@udel.edu.

GOODMAN, SYLVIA KLUMOK, film center executive; b. Moorhead, Miss., June 19, 1940; d. Sol Harry and Fannie Ida (Davidson) Klumok; m. Carl Gerald Goodman, June 5, 1960; children: Lisa Wynne Goodman Stone, Gary Steven, Jeffry David. BS in Zoology with honors, Newcomb Coll., 1962; M in Zoology, Tulane U., 1963; postgrad., Harvard U., summer 1990. Tchr. Midway Jr. H.S., Shreveport, La., 1963-68; instr. biology La. State U., Shreveport, 1967-68; instr. physiology, asst. coord. plans La. State U. Med. Ctr., Shreveport, 1970-74; chmn. bd. dir. Goldring Woldenberg Inst. So. Jewish Life, 2000—03; pres., CEO Robinson Film Ctr., Shreveport, La., 2004—. Pres. Shreveport Jewish Fedn., 1982—83; mem. C. of C. 100 Women of the Century; chmn. Food Project, Shreveport, 1990—92; chair beautification com. Shreveport Regional Airport, 1990—94, So. Jewish Inst., 2000—; pres. Sci-Port Discovery Ctr., 1993—95; trustee Shreveport-Bossier Cmty. Fedn., chmn., 1993—; vice chmn. Meadows Art Mus., 1995; mem. Shreveport Mayor's Women's Commn., 1986—90; vice-chair La. State Mineral Bd., Baton Rouge, 1988—92; bd. dir. Sci-Port Discovery Ctr., Shreveport, 1990—. Meadows Art Mus., 1991—97, La. Endowment Humanities, 1996—99, La. Film Theater, 2003—, chair capital campaign, 2003; mem. chancellor's adv. com. LSU-S, 1996—; chmn. bd. dir. Goldring/Woldenberg Inst. So. Jewish Life, 2000—. Recipient Humanitarian award NCCJ, Humanitarian award Caddo Commn., 1991, Vol. Fundraiser award Nat. Fedn. Fundraising Execs., 1996, Angel award Blue Cross Blue Shield, 1998, award Point of Light Found., 1999, Friend of Edn. award Caddo Assn. Educators, 2001; named Women Who Made a Difference Shreveport Celebration of Women Week, 1996, Best-Dressed Woman of No. La. Shreveport Times, 1998, Women of Century, Shreveport C.of C. Mem. Jr. League Shreveport (Sustainer of Yr. award 1995, Daily Point of Light 1999), Mensa, Phi Beta Kappa, Alpha Epsilon Phi. Jewish. Avocations: theater, piano, dance, taking courses, movies. Home: 409 Southfield Rd Shreveport LA 71106-2213 Office Phone: 318-424-9090. E-mail: sgoodman@lapilmcenter.org.

GOODMAN, TOBY RAY, lawyer; b. Wichita Falls, Tex., Nov. 2, 1948; s. Johnnie U. and Opal E. (Johnson) G.; m. Lisa C. Schrader, Sept. 14, 1967 (div. 1982); children; Brian Scott, Lauri Ann; m. Gloria Jean Majors, June 14, 1983; 1 child, Christie Louise. BBA, Tex. Christian U., 1971; JD, Baylor U., 1974. Bar: Tex. 1974, U.S. Dist. Ct. (no. dist.) Tex. 1974, U.S. Ct. Appeals (5th cir.) 1977. Asst. city atty. City of Arlington, Tex., 1974-76; ptnr. Remington & Goodman, Arlington, 1976-84, Goodman & Clark, Arlington, 1984—; state rep. State of Tex. Dist. 93, 1990—. Chair Rep. Party, Arlington, 1987; chair Tarrant 2000 Civil Justice, 1989-90; mem. Rep. Caucus Tex. Ho. of Reps. Fellow Tex. Bar Found.; mem. Arlington Bar Assn. (dir.), Tarrant County Bar Assn. (dir.); mem.chair house comm. Juvinal & Family Issues. Baptist. Home: 2801 Knotted Oaks Trl Arlington TX 76006-2759 Office: Goodman & Clark 1600 E Lamar Blvd Ste 250 Arlington TX 76011-4588

GOODMAN, VALERIE DAWSON, psychiatric social worker; b. Bluefield, W.Va., Feb. 2, 1948; d. Francis Carl and Lesly (Collett) Dawson; m. David William Goodman, June 9, 1985; 1 child, Amanda Lynn. BS, W.Va. U., 1970, MS, 1972; MSW, U. Md., 1980. Lic. clin. social worker, Md. Social worker Md. Children's Aide Family Svcs. Soc., Balt., 1972-78; social worker III Montgomery County Dept. Social Svcs., Rockville, Md., 1980-81; clin. social worker Johns Hopkins Hosp., Balt., 1981-83; pvt. practice Suburban Psychiat. Assoc. Hopkins at Greenspring Station, Balt., 1986—. Supr. Johns Hopkins Hosp., 1983-86, chair Brogden com., 1984-85, spl. events com. depression and related affective disorders dept. psychiatry, 1994; spkr. in field. Parent vol. Park Sch. Mem. Kappa Delta. Avocations: reading, piano, gourmet cooking, weightlifting. Home: 54 Bellchase Ct Pikesville MD 21208-1300 Office: Suburban Psychiat Svc Md Adult Ctr ADD Johns Hopkins at Greenspring Sta Falls Concourse Falls Rd Ste 306 Lutherville MD 21093 Office Phone: 410-583-2724.

GOODMAN, WILLIAM BEEHLER, editor, literary agent; b. Bklyn., July 1, 1923; s. Philip Howard and Anne Louise (Landersman) G.; m. Lorraine Rappaport, Nov. 24, 1948; children: Jonas Robert, Sara Emily. BA, Washington Sq. Coll., NYU, 1948; MA, U. Mich., 1952. Editor coll. and trade Harcourt Brace Jovanovich Inc., N.Y.C., 1956-76; gen. editor Harvard Univ. Press, Cambridge, Mass., 1976-79; editorial dir. David R. Godine Pub., Inc., Boston, 1979-90, editor, lit. agt., 1990—. Tutor history and lit. Harvard U., 1953-54, lectr. in English, 1982-83, 84-85. Contbr.: essay Reading in the 1980's, 1983. Trustee Warner Library, Tarrytown, N.Y., 1973-75. Served with U.S. Army, 1943-44. Mem.: Harvard (N.Y.C.). Home: 26 Pickman Dr Bedford MA 01730-1005 Office Phone: 781-275-3419. Personal E-mail: goodbill@comcast.net.

GOODMAN, WILLIAM RICHARD, insurance adjusting company executive; b. Staunton, Va., Sept. 19, 1930; s. Harry and Ruth (Meyer) G.; m. Alice Helene Katzenstein, June 13, 1954; children: Harvey, Laurie, Barry. BS, U. Md., 1952; JD, U. Balt., 1955. Cert. fellow profl. pub. adjuster, sr. profl. pub. adjuster. Pub. ins. adjuster, lawyer Goodman-Gable-Gould Co., Balt., 1952-73, v.p., 1973-85, pres., 1985-97, CEO, 1985—, chmn. bd., 1989—. Chmn. Baltimore County Indsl. Devel. Commn., 1967-69; mem. Met. Transit Authority, Balt., 1969-71, bd. rev. Dept. Transp., Md., 1971-76, Md. Racing Commn., 1984. Mem. Nat. Assn. Pub. Ins. Adjusters (dir., v.p., pres., chmn. bd. dirs., Disting. Svc. award 1987, Man of Yr. 1995, fellow in profession of pub. adjusting), B'nai B'rith (v.p. Menorah Lodge 1992-94, pres. 1996-98). Democrat. Jewish. Avocation: collecting toy trains and antique cars. Home: 7811 Park Heights Ave Baltimore MD 21208-4322 Office: Goodman-Gable-Gould Co Adjusters Internat 6 Reservoir Cir Ste 202 Baltimore MD 21208-7310 Office Phone: 410-602-0800.

GOODMAN-MILONE, CONSTANCE B., writer; b. Phila., Sept. 3, 1963; d. Marvin Joshua and Linda S. Goodman; m. David C. Milone, May 5, 2002. BA in Psychology, George Washington U., 1985; MSW, Barry U., Miami Shores, Fla., 1999. Freelance writer, Phila., 1987—88, N.Y.C., 1989—96; social work intern Vets. Adminstrn. Med. Ctr., Miami, 1999; case mgr. Health South Drs. Hosp., Skilled Nursing, Coral Gables, Fla., 2000; freelance writer Miami, 2001—. Author: (poetry, photo) Medicinal Purposes Lit. Rev., 1995—2003, (poem, article, photos) Vitas Vital Signs, 2001—03, (poem) Today's Caregiver, 2002; contbr. poetry and articles to newspapers and jours. Mem. Dem. Nat. Com., Washington, 1996—; hospice vol. Vitas Healthcare, Miami, 2000—; leadership coun. So. Poverty Law Ctr., Montgomery, Ala., 2002—; charter mem. women's action coun. Amnesty Internat., N.Y.C., 2004—; chair creative writing contest Jr. Orange Bowl Com., Coral Gables, Fla., 2003—; mem. Dem. Congl. Campaign Com., Washington, 2003—. Mem.: Acad. Am. Poets, Acad. Am. Poetry, Amnesty Internat., Assn. for Death Edn. and Counseling South Fla. chpt. (cmty. outreach chair 2002—), Nat. Writers Union, South Fla. Writers Assn. (v.p. mktg. 2003—05, dir. cmty. rels. 2005—, Bill Katzker Mem. of Yr. award 2003, Bereavement Vol. of Yr. Vitas Dade Program 2001), Soc. Social Work Leaders in Health Care (Fla. Chpt.), Nat. Assn. Social Workers, Nat. Assn. Poetry Therapy, Phi Eta Sigma, Psi Chi, Delta Epsilon Sigma. Democrat. Jewish. Avocations: volunteering, photography, tennis, walking, books. Home and Office: 12920 SW 95 Ave Miami FL 33176-5792 E-mail: cgmilone@bellsouth.net.

GOODNER, NORMAN WESLEY, governmental relations specialist; b. Fort Smith, Ark., Apr. 16, 1969; s. Charles E. and Sharron A. (Langston) G. BS in Pub. Adminstrn., U. Ark., 1990, student, 1991-92. Govt. rels. Auditor of State's Office, Little Rock, 1992—. Mem. Ark. State Dem. Com., 2002—. Bd. dirs. Scott County Friends of Libr., Waldron, Ark., 1988; asst. coord. Little Rock Town Hall Meeting On Africa, 1997; constituent liaison Ark. Senate Adv. Com., Waldron, 1983-2000; vol. Victims Svcs. Program, 2001. Recipient Capitol citation Ark. Sec. of State, 1986, Jeffrey Ledbetter Meml. award, 2003. Democrat. Methodist. Avocations: hiking, reading. Home: Apt A-108 2501 Riverfront Dr Little Rock AR 72202-1772

GOODNICK, PAUL JOEL, psychiatrist; b. Phila., Sept. 29, 1950; BA magna cum laude, U. Pa.; MD with honors, SUNY Downstate Med. Ctr., Bklyn. Diplomate Am. Bd. Psychiatry and Neurology. Resident Washington U., St. Louis, Columbia U., N.Y.C.; fellow Mt. Sinai Hosp., N.Y.C.; asst. prof. psychiatry Wayne State U., Detroit, 1980-81, U. Chgo., 1981-84, Columbia U., N.Y.C., 1984-87, U. Miami, Fla., 1987-89, clin. assoc. prof. psychiatry, 1989-90, assoc. prof., 1990-93, prof., 1993—2002, clin. prof. of psychiatry, dir. mood disorders program, dept. psychiatry, 1989—2003; dir. clin. svc. Carrier Clinic, Belle Mead, NJ, 2003—; clin. prof. psychiatry U. Medicine and Dentristry, NJ, 2004—. Dir. outpatient svcs. and affective disorders program Fair Oaks Hosp., Boca/Delray, Fla., 1987-90; cons. APA, 1991. Assoc. editor jour. Lithium, 1989-94; editor: Chronic Fatigue and Related Immune Deficiency Syndromes, 1993, Predictors of Response in Mood Disorders, 1996, Mania, 1998; editor Expert Opinion on Pharmacotherapy, 1999—, Annals of Clinical Psychiatry, 2000—, Expert Opinion on Drug Safety, 2001—. Mem. nat. adv. bd. Jerusalem Health Ctr. Recipient Clin. Excellence award N.Y. Alliance for Mentally Ill, 1987, SUNY Downstate award, 2001. Fellow Am. Psychopathol. Assn., Am. Psychiat. Assn., Internat. Soc. Affective Disorders; mem. AAAS, Soc. Biol. Psychiatry, N.Y. Acad. Sci., Am. Acad. Clin. Psychiatry, KP. Office: Carrier Clinic 252 Rte 601 POB 147 Belle Mead NJ 08502 Office Phone: 908-281-1484. Personal E-mail: pgoodnick@aol.com.

GOODNIGHT, JAMES H., software company executive; b. Wilmington, N.C., Jan. 6, 1943; B, M, PhD in Statistics, NC State U., 1972—76. Faculty N.C. State U., 1972-76; co-founder, chmn. SAS Inst. Inc., pres. & CEO Cary, NC, 1976—. Adj. prof. N.C. State U., 1976—. Fellow Am. Statis. Assn. Office: SAS Inst Inc Attn Miranda Drake-Shaw Corp Commn Dept SAS Campus Dr Cary NC 27513 E-mail: software@sas.com.

GOODNOUGH, ROBERT ARTHUR, artist; b. Cortland, NY, Oct. 23, 1917; s. Leo J. and Hariett (Summers) G. BFA, Syracuse U., 1940; MA, NYU, 1950; student, New Sch. for Social Research, 1949, Ozenfant Sch. Art, 1950-51, Hoffman Sch. Art, 1951. Instr. painting NYU, 1953, Fieldston Sch., Riverdale, NY, 1953-60, Cornell U., 1960. Instr. painting NYU, 1953, Fieldston Sch., Riverdale, NY, 1953-60, Cornell U., 1960 Contbr. articles to nat. mags.; one-man shows: Tibor de Nagy Gallery, NYC, Andre Emmerich Gallery, NYC, Nina Freudenheim Gallery, Bklyn.; work exhibited in permanent collections: Albright Art Gallery, Buffalo, Art Inst. Chgo., Mus. Modern Art, NYC, Whitney Mus., NYC, NYU Mus., R.I. Sch. Design Mus., NC Mus. Art, also pvt. collections. Served with US Army, 1941-45. Recipient award Art Inst. Chgo., 1962; Guggenheim fellow, 1972 Office: Gallery at Lincoln Ctr Concourse Shippee Gallery New York NY 10023*

GOODPASTER, JOHN VINCENT, chemist; b. South Bend, Ind., Aug. 12, 1973; s. Kenneth Edwin and Harriet Catherine Goodpaster; m. Mindi Cecile Kensinger, Sept. 27, 2003. BA in Chemistry, Gustavus Adolphus Coll., St. Peter, Minn., 1991—95; MS in Criminal Justice, PhD in Chemistry, Mich. State U., East Lansing, 1995—2000. Rsch. chemist Nat. Inst. Standards and Tech., Gaithersburg, Md., 2001—03; forensic chemist ATF Forensic Sci. Lab., Ammendale, Md., 2003—. Contbr. articles to profl. jours. Recipient Kenan Analytical Award, Union Carbide, 1998; fellow, NSF, 1996—99; Nat. Merit Scholar, 1991—95. Mem.: Am. Acad. Forensic Scis., Am. Chem. Soc. (assoc.). Democrat. Office: ATF Forensic Sci Lab 6000 Ammendale Rd Ammendale MD 20705-1250 Office Phone: 240-264-1412.

GOODPASTURE, PHILIP HENRY, lawyer; b. Lisbon, Portugal, Sept. 16, 1960; s. Henry McKennie and Ellen Ingabor (Moller) G.; m. Paige Everett Hargroves, June 25, 1994. BA with high distinction, U. Va., 1982, JD, 1985. Bar: Va. 1985, U.S. Dist. Ct. (ea. dist.) Va. 1985. Assoc. Christian & Barton and predecessor firm, Richmond, Va., 1985-92, ptnr., 1993—2004, vice-chmn. corp. team, 1994-97, mem. exec. com., 1998; ptnr. Williams, Mullen, P.C., 2004—. Dir. Downtown Presents Inc., Richmond, 1993-2001, Va. League for Planned Parenthood, Richmond, 1989-95, Vol. Emergency Families for Children, Richmond, 1998-2000; dir. Parliament City of Richmond, 1997-98; mem. Leadership Metro Richmond, 1994; mem. Leadership Devel. Coun. ARC, 1995. Mem. Va. Bar Assn., Richmond Bar Assn. Office: Williams Mullen 1021 E Cary St Ste 1700 Richmond VA 23219 Office Phone: 804-783-6904. Business E-Mail: pgoodpasture@williamsmullen.com.

GOODREAU, ROBERT CHARLES, surgeon; b. Wellsboro, Pa., Aug. 10, 1934; s. Charles William and Nellie Marie Goodreau; m. Stephanie Lynne Hauser, Sept. 10, 1958; 7 children. M in Psychiatry, Harvard U., 1958, PhD in Neuropsychiat. Surgery, 1969. Physician FBI, 1956—75, VA, 1975—. Inventor automatic gear shift, ball point and felt tip pens. Col. U.S. Army, 1953—56, Korea. Methodist. Achievements include design of Creator of the original blue prints for television camera and receiver. Avocation: reading.

GOODRICH, GEORGE HERBERT, judge; b. Charleston, W.Va., June 19, 1925; s. Edgar Jennings and Beulah Etta (Lenfest) G.; m. Nancy Ann Needham, Sept. 3, 1949; children: George Herbert, Craig N., Thomas A. BA, Williams Coll., 1949; LL.B., U. Va., 1952. Bar: D.C. 1953, Md. 1958. Gen. practice law, Washington, also, Md., 1953-69; asso. judge D.C. Superior Ct., 1969-91, sr. judge, 1991—; lectr. law Am. U., 1969-74. Pres. Homemakers Service, 1962-63; v.p. Hillcrest Children's Center, 1963-69; mem. community adv. com. Jr. League D.C., 1969-73; bd. dirs. ARC. Served with USNR, 1943-46. Mem. D.C. Bar Assn., Delta Psi. Clubs: Chevy Chase. Republican. Presbyterian. Home: 6003 Corbin Rd Bethesda MD 20816-3402 Office: DC Superior Ct 500 Indiana Ave NW Ste 1 Washington DC 20001-2131

GOODRICH, HERBERT FUNK, JR., lawyer; b. Phila., Dec. 14, 1942; s. Herbert Funk and Mary (Dern) G.; m. Virginia Page, Sept. 10, 1966; children: Cynthia Dern, Matthew Page, Steven Withington. AB, Dartmouth Coll., 1964; LLB, Harvard U., 1967. Bar: Pa. 1967, U.S. Dist. Ct. (ea. dist.) Pa. 1967. Assoc. Dechert Price & Rhoads, Phila., 1967-74, resident ptnr. Brussels, 1974-78, ptnr. Phila., 1978—. Vis. lectr. Villanova (Pa.) U., 1985—; faculty participant Pa. Bar Inst., Harrisburg, 1980—. Bd. dirs. Episc. Cmty. Svcs., Phila., 1988—; trustee Chestnut Hill Healthcare Corp., Phila., 1993—, vice chmn., 1995-2000, chmn., 2001—. Mem. ABA, Phila. Bar Assn., Pa. Bar Assn., Am. Law Inst. Republican. Office: Dechert Price & Rhoads 4000 Bell Atlantic Tower 1717 Arch St Philadelphia PA 19103-2793 E-mail: herbert.goodrich@dechert.com.

GOODRICH, ISAAC, neurosurgeon, educator; b. Milledgeville, Ga., Sept. 19, 1939; s. Ellis and Frieda (Bergman) G.; m. Dianne L. Brittain, Aug. 28, 1965; children: Mindy Anne, Scott David, Jennifer Gale. AA, Ga. Mil. Coll., 1959; BS, U. Ga., 1961; MD, Med. Coll. Ga., 1964. Cert. Am. Bd. Neurol. Surgery. Intern Columbia-Presbyn. Med. Ctr., N.Y.C., 1964-65; resident in neurosurgery Yale-New Haven Med. Ctr., 1967-71; practice medicine specializing in neurosurgery New Haven, 1971—. Instr. neurosurgery, Yale U. Med. Sch., 1970-71, asst. clin. prof., 1978-86; assoc. clin. prof., 1986—; attending neurosurgeon Yale-New Haven Hosp., 1973—, Hosp. St. Raphael, 1971—; mem. courtesy staff Milford Hosp., 1986—; cons. staff Midstate Med. Ctr., 1986—, VA Hosp., West Haven, 1990—, Griffin Hosp., 1992-99, St. Mary's Hosp., 1995-99, courtesy staff, 1999—. Contbr. articles to profl. jours. Capt. U.S. Army, 1965-67. Decorated Bronze Star, Air Medal; recipient Disting. Alumni award Ga. Mil. Coll., 1980; named Hon. Citizen, Boys Town, Nebr., 1971. Fellow: ACS, Royal Soc. Medicine, Internat. Coll. Surgeons; mem.: AAAS, AMA (Physicians Recognition awards for Continuing Med. Edn.), N.Y. Acad. Scis., New Haven County Med. Assn. (pres. 1998—99), Conn. State Med. Soc. (v.p. 2000—01, pres.-elect 2001—02, pres. 2002—03), Conn. State Neurosurg. Soc. (pres. 2001—03), Am. Assn. Neurol. Surgeons, Soc. Med. Cons. to Armed Forces, Pan Pacific Surg. Assn., New Eng. Neurosurg. Soc. (pres. 1997—99), Congress Neurol. Surgeons, Veterans of Fgn. Wars, New Haven City Med. Assn. (pres. 1989—90), 28th Inf. Assn., Soc. 1st Inf. Divsn., Am. Legion. Jewish. Home: 330 Orchard St Ste 316 New Haven CT 06511 Office: 330 Orchard St Ste 316 New Haven CT 06511-4430 Office Phone: 203-781-3400.

GOODRICH, JAMES A., veterinarian, researcher; BS, U. Conn., 1983; DVM, Tufts U., 1988. Diplomate Am. Coll. Lab. Animal Medicine. Assoc. prof. Med. U. SC, Charleston, 1995—. Contbr. articles to profl. jours. Grantee, NIH, 1999, 2000, 2002—. Mem.: AVMA, SC. Assn. Veterinarians, N.Am. Menopause Soc. (Young Investigator award 2000), Am. Soc. Reproductive Medicine, Am. Heart Assn. Office: Med Univ SC 114 Doughty St Charleston SC 29425 Office Phone: 843-876-5202. Office Fax: 843-876-5210. E-mail: goodrija@musc.edu.

GOODRICH, JAMES TAIT, neuroscientist, neurosurgeon; b. Portland, Oreg., Apr. 16, 1946; s. Richard and Gail (Josselyn) Goodrich; m. Judy Loudin, Dec. 27, 1970. Student, Golden West Coll., 1971—72; AA, Orange Coast Coll., 1972; BS cum laude, U. Calif., Irvine, 1974; PhD, Columbia U., 1970, MPhil, 1979, MD, 1980. Diplomate Am. Bd. Neurol. Surgery. Intern Columbia-Presbyn. Med. Ctr., N.Y.C., 1980—81; resident in neurol. surgery N.Y. Neurol. Inst., N.Y.C., 1981—86; assoc. Montefiore Med. Ctr., Bronx, NY, 1986—; mem. staff Jacobi Med. Ctr., 1986—; assoc. Weiler Hosp. Albert Einstein Coll. Medicine, N.Y.C., 1986—, prof. nuerosurgery, 1998—. Prof. neurosurgery U. Palermo, Sicily, Italy, 1992—. Editor: Jour. Child Nervous Sys., Neurosurgery; contbr. scientific papers to profl. jours. Named one of Best Med. Drs. in N.Y., N.Y. Mag.; named to Guide to Am.'s Top Surgeons, Consumers Coun. Am., 2002, Best Drs. in Am., 2003; recipient Roche Labs. award in Nuersci., 1978, Mead-Johnson award, 1978, Bronze medal, Alumni Assn. Coll. Physicians and Surgeons, 1980, Sandoz award for Outstanding Rsch., 1980; Willamette Industries scholar, NIH grantee. Fellow: Royal Soc. Medicine (London); mem.: AMA, AAAS, Dionysius Coun. Presbyn. Hosp. N.Y.C., Les Amis du Vin, Am. Osler Soc., Soc. Ancient Medicine, Colubain Presbyn. Med. Soc., Soc. Bibliography Natural History (London), ISIS History Sci. Soc., Med. History Soc. N.J., Congress Neurol. Surgeons, Am. Assn. Neurol. Surgery (chmn. sect. history neurol. surgery), N.Y. Acad. Scis., Brit. Brain Rsch. Assn., Am. Assn. History Medicine (Sir William Osler medal 1977—78), N.Y. Acad. Medicine (Melicow award 1980), Internat. Soc. Pediat. Neurosurgeons, European Brain Rsch. Assn., Am. Soc. Pediat. Neurosurgeons, Am. Epilepsy Soc., Am. Assn. Neurol. Surgeons, U. Calif. Alumni Assn., Friends Columbia U. Librs., Worshipful Soc. Apothecaries (London), S. Coast Wine Explorers Club (past chmn.), Sigma Xi, Alpha Gamma Sigma. Achievements include research in neuronal regeneration, brain reconstruction and craniofacial reconstruction. Home: 125 Tweed Blvd Nyack NY 10960-4913 Office: Albert Einstein Coll Medicine Montefiore Med Ctr Div Pediat Neurosurg 111 E 210th St Bronx NY 10467-2401 Office Phone: 718-920-4197. Business E-Mail: goodrich@aecom.yu.edu.

GOODRICH, JAMES WILLIAM, retired historian, retired historian executive; b. Burlington, Iowa, Oct. 31, 1939; s. Martin Glenn and Marion Elizabeth (Prasse) G.; m. Linda Marlyse Andreoli, Aug. 31, 1963 (div. Aug. 1989); children: Anne Marlyse, Kimberly Ann. BS in Edn., Cen. Mo. State U., 1962; MA, U. Mo., 1964, PhD, 1974. Archivist Sec. of State, Mo., 1966; asst. then assoc. editor State Hist. Soc. Mo., Columbia, 1967-78, assoc. dir., 1978-85, dir., 1985—, ret., 2004. Cons. USDA Soil Conservation Svc., Columbia, 1976, Mus. History and Sci., Kansas City, Mo., 1978, Mo. State Mus., 1989, Mo. Dept. Conservation, 1990, 91, 95, 97; mem. Mo. Hist. Records Adv. Bd., Jefferson City, 1985—, State Records Commn., Jefferson City, 1984—, Mo. Bd. Geographic Names, 1995--; dir. Western Hist. Manuscript Collection, 1985—; adj. prof. history U. Mo., Columbia, 1988—. Co-author: Historic Missouri, 1988; editor: Report on a Journey to North America, 1980; assoc. editor Mo. Hist. Rev., 1967-85, editor 1985—; co-editor: German-American Experience in Missouri, 1986; co-editor, contbr. Marking Missouri History, 1998; contbr. articles to profl. jours. Mem. Planning and Zoning Commn., Columbia, 1975-77; councilman City of Columbia, 1977-79, 79-81; chmn. city audit com., Columbia, 1981-88; v.p. Friends of Mo. St. Archives, 1989-94; mem. 13th Jud. Cir. Bar Rev. Com., 1991-97; bd. dirs. Mo. Mansion Preservation Inc., 1991—; bd. dirs. Boone County Cmty. Trust, 1992—; mem. exec. com. Mo. State U. Alumni Assn., 1988-92, pres. 1991; mem. 6th Regional Disciplinary Com. Mo. Judiciary, 1997—; mem. Mo. Lewis and Clark Bicentennial Com., 1997—. Mem. Orgn. Am. Historians, Western History Assn., Am. Assn. for State & Local History, Conservation Fedn. Mo., Ducks Unlimited, Mo. Mus. Assn., Mo. Press Assn., Wild Canid Survival and Rsch. Ctr. Avocations: decoy collecting, waterfowl hunting, orinthoscopy. Office: State Hist Soc Mo 1020 Lowry St Columbia MO 65201-7207

GOODRICH, JOHN BERNARD, lawyer, consultant; b. Spokane, Wash., Jan. 4, 1928; s. John Casey and Dorothy (Koll) G.; m. Therese H. Vollmer, June 14, 1952; children— Joseph B., Bernadette M., Andrew J., Philip M., Thomas A., Mary Elizabeth, Jennifer H., Rosanne M. JD, Gonzaga U., 1954. Bar: Wash, 1954, Ill. 1955. Indsl. traffic mgr. Pacific N.W. Alloys, Spokane, 1950-54; asst. to gen. counsel Cromium Mining & Smelting Corp., Chgo., 1954-56; with Monon R.R., 1956-69, atty., gen. solicitor, 1956-66, sec., 1957-69, treas., 1959-66, v.p. law, 1966-69; also dir.; sec.-treas. I.C.G.R.R., Chgo., 1970-79, sec., gen. atty., 1979-85; gen. counsel Ill. Devel. Fin. Authority, Chgo., 1985-92, spl. counsel, 1993; atty., cons. pvt. practice, Park Forest, Ill., 1994—. Mem. Park Forest Traffic and Safety Commn., 1963-66; mem. Park Forest Recreation Bd., 1966-77, chmn., 1969-70; trustee Village of Park Forest, 1977-80; mem. bd. Sch. Dist. 163, 1984-89; pres. South Cook Orgn. for Pub. Edn., 1988-89; conf. and meeting planner The Compassionate Friends, Inc., Oak Brook, Ill., 1991-94; bd. dirs. Park Forest Art Ctr., 1993-95, Ill. Philharm. Orch., 1994-98, treas., 1995-98; mem. adv. bd. Chgo. Self Help Ctr., 1993-94; bd. dirs. Ill Self Help Coalition, 1994-96; treas. Bereaved Parents of the U.S.A., 1995-2000, bd. dirs. 2000-03, Tall Grass Arts Assn., 1999-2003; trustee Chgo. South Suburban Mass Transit Dist., 1996—, treas., 2000-04, vice chmn., 2004—. Inducted into Park Forest Hall of Fame, 1998. Mem. KC, The Parkforesters, Inc. (pres. 1998-2004, dir.), Kiwanis. Roman Catholic. Home and Office: 35 Cunningham Ln Park Forest IL 60466-2094

GOODRICH, KENNETH PAUL, retired college dean; b. Elkhorn, Wis., 1933; s. Kenneth Potter and Helene (Keller) G.; m. Elaine L. Ashby, June 12, 1954; children— Laurel Lynn, David Kenneth, Paul Ashby, Karen Elaine. AB Oberlin Coll, 1955; MA, U. Ia., 1958, PhD, 1959. Mem. faculty U. Pa. Phila., 1959-63; lectr., project assoc. U. Wis., Madison, 1963-65; mem. faculty psychology Macalester Coll., St. Paul, 1965-73, chmn. dept. psychology, 1965-67, dean coll., 1967-69, dean and dir. ednl. resources, 1969-71, v.p. for acad. affairs and provost, 1971-73; dean Coll. Arts and Scis., prof. psychology Syracuse (N.Y.) U., 1973-78; provost Ohio Wesleyan U., Delaware, 1978-83; v.p. acad. affairs, dean of faculty Linfield Coll., McMinnville, Oreg., 1983-94, spl. asst. to pres. for instnl. rsch. and planning, 1994-95. Bd. dirs. Group Health Plan, Inc., St. Paul, 1970-73, Yamhill County (Oreg.) United Way, 1991-95, McMinnville Area Habitat for Humanity, 1993-95; vol. carpenter Greater Columbus Habitat for Humanity, 1995-2004. Personal E-mail: kgoodric@world.oberlin.edu.

GOODRICH, THOMAS MICHAEL, engineering and construction executive, lawyer; b. Milan, Tenn., Apr. 28, 1945; s. Henry Calvin and Billie Grace (Walker) Goodrich; m. Gillian Comer White, Dec. 28, 1968; children: Michael, Braxton, Charles, Grace. BSCE, Tulane U., 1968; JD, U. Ala., 1971. Bar: Ala. 1971. Adminstrv. asst. Supreme Ct. Ala., Montgomery, 1971—72; from various mgmt. positions to CEO BE & K, Inc., Birmingham, Ala., 1989—95, pres., CEO, 1995—, chmn., 2003, also bd. dirs. Bd. dirs. First Comml. Bank, Energen Corp., Birmingham, Synovus Fin. Corp., Columbus, Ga. Trustee Nat. Bldg. Mus., Elsenhowen Exchg. Fellow. Capt. U.S. Army, 1970—72. Mem.: Constrn. Industry Roundtable, Assn. Builders and Contractors (pres. 1990), Ala. State Bar Assn., ABA, TAPPI. Office: B E & K Inc 2000 Internat Park Dr Birmingham AL 35243

GOODRIDGE, ALLAN D., lawyer; b. Bucharest, Romania, June 12, 1936; s. Benjamin F. and Fanny M. (Weissman) G.; m. Lora, Sept. 12, 1965; children: Jeremy P., Andrew P. BA, Harvard U., 1957; JD, Columbia U., 1960. Bar: N.Y., U.S. Dist. Ct. (so. dist., ea. dist. N.Y.), U.S. Ct. Appeals (2d circuit). Assoc. Wickes, Riddell, Bloomer, Jacobi & McGuire, N.Y.C., 1960-64, Spitzer & Feldman, N.Y.C., 1965, Demov, Morris & Hammerling, N.Y.C., 1965-70, ptnr., 1970-85, Schnader, Harrison, Segal & Lewis, N.Y.C., 1985—. Mem. ABA, N.Y. Bar Assn. Clubs: Harvard (N.Y.C.). Home: 336 Central Park W New York NY 10025-7111 Office: Schnader Harrison Ste 3100 140 Broadway New York NY 10005 Office Phone: 212-973-8145. Business E-Mail: agoodridge@schnader.com.

GOODSELL, CHARLES TRUE, public administration educator, researcher; b. July 23, 1932; BA, Kalamazoo Coll., 1954; MPA, Harvard U., 1958, MA, 1959, PhD, 1961. Asst. prof. U. P.R., Rio Piedras, 1961-64; prof. So. Ill. U., Carbondale, 1966-78; prof. pub. adminstrn. Va. Tech., Blacksburg, 1978—2002, prof. emeritus, 2002—. Author: Administration of A Revolution, 1965, American Corporations and Peruvian Politics, 1974, The Social Meaning of Public Space, 1988, The American Statehouse, 2001, The Case for Bureaucracy, 4th edit., 2004. Recipient Waldo award for lifetime contbn. to lit. in pub. adminstrn., 2003. E-mail: goodsell@vt.edu.

GOODSELL, G. VERNE, lawyer; b. Watertown, S.D., Jan. 22, 1943; AA, Miltonvale Wesleyan Coll., 1964; BS, No. State Coll., 1967, MS, 1970; JD, Washburn U. Topeka, 1973. Bar: S.D. 1974. Atty. Gunderson, Palmer, Goodsell & Nelson, LLP, Rapid City, SD. Mem.: ABA (vice chair litigation com. gen. practice sect. 1990), Black Hills Claims Assn. (pres. 1984—85), Pennington County Bar Assn. (pres. 1981), Am. Jurisprudence Assn., Assn. Trial Lawyers Am., S.D. Trial Lawyers Assn., State Bar S.D. (commr. 1984—87, professionalism com. 1989, mem. disciplinary bd. 1990—95, co-chair disciplinary bd. 1995—96, chair advt. com. 1999—2000, chair ethics com. 2000, pres.-elect 2002, mulit-jurisdictional/internet com., pres. 2003). Office: Gunderson Palmer Goodsell and Nelson LLP 3d and 4th Fls PO box 8045 Rapid City SD 57709-8045

GOODSON, CAROL FAYE, librarian; b. Detroit, Mar. 28, 1947; d. Norman Elwood and Wilma Mary (Harmon) G.; m. Lawrence J. Price, May 10, 1974 (div. 1977). BA, SUNY, Buffalo, 1970, MLS, 1972; MA, State U. West Ga., 1996. Libr. SUNY, Buffalo, 1970-72, St. Louis Pub. Libr., 1973-77; community sch. dir. St. Louis Bd. Edn., 1977-80; reference libr. Ga. Dept. Edn., Atlanta, 1981-84; head pub. svcs. Atlanta campus Mercer U., Chamblee, Ga., 1985; mem. Dominican Sisters of Nashville, 1985-90; asst. dir. Clayton County Libr. System, Jonesboro, Ga., 1990-91; coord. off-campus libr. svcs. State U. West Ga., Carrollton, 1991-96, head libr. access svcs., 1996—. State coord. Ga. Summer Reading Club, 1991; owner and moderator, ALA-PLAN listserv., FISC-L listserv and WOODY-L listserv. Author: The Complete Guide to Performance Standards for Library Personnel, 1997, Providing Library Services for Distance Education Students, 2001; editor: Ga. conf. AAUP Summary, 1996—98, Jour. Libr. Svcs. Distance Edn., 1997—; contbr. articles to profl. jours. Pres. Tower/Literacy Vols. Am., Clayton County, 1991; with Leadership Clayton, 1990-91. Mem. ALA, Ga. Libr. Assn., Libr. Info. Tech. Assn. (program planning com. 1992-97, sec. 1993-95), Assn. Coll. Rsch. Librs. (clip notes com. 1992-96, extended campus libr. svcs. sect., comm. com. 1994-98), Libr. Adminstrn. and Mgmt. Assn., Beta Phi Mu, Phi Kappa Phi, Omicron Delta Kappa, Sigma Tau Delta. Avocations: genealogy, computers. Home: 210 Oak Ave Carrollton GA 30117-3726 Office: State U West Ga Ingram Libr 1500 Maple St Carrollton GA 30117-4233 Office Phone: 678-839-6507. Business E-Mail: cgoodson@westga.edu.

GOODSON, RICHARD CARLE, JR., chemist; b. Toledo, June 22, 1945; s. Richard Carle Goodson Sr. and Norma (Buehler) Robinson; m. Deborah Ann Hart, Mar. 29, 1969 (div. Feb. 1978); 1 child, Geoffrey Carle; m. Thelma Agnes Matthews, Nov. 22, 1978. BS in Chemistry, Union Coll., 1967; MS in Inorganic Chemistry, U. Conn., 1970. Dist. engr. Drew Chem. Corp., Boonton, N.J., 1972-74, product supr., 1974-75, regional tech. supr., 1975-76; chief chemist, tech. dir. Environ. Waste Removal, Waterbury, Conn., 1976-79; gen. mgr., dir. tech. lab. Conn. Treatment Corp., Bristol, 1978—82; dir. ops., corp. dir. waste mgmt. and regulatory compliance Hampden Mathieu Chem. Co., Springfield, 1990—2000; pres., owner Goodson Assoc., Farmington, Conn., 1982—. Mem. Am. Chem. Soc. Republican. Avocations: boating, hiking, skiing, bicycling. Home and Office: 2 Azalea Ct Farmington CT 06032-2037 Personal E-mail: richardgoodson@m.com.

GOODSPEED, KATHRYN ANN, pre-school educator; b. Elgin, Ill., Oct. 2, 1939; d. Earle Muller and Ruby Vera Curtiss; m. Robert Harrison Goodspeed, Feb. 4, 1961; children: Julie, Jill, Jerry, Jeff, Jennifer. BS, No. Ill. U., 1961. Tchr. spl. edn. Sch. of Hope, Rockford, Ill., 1962—65; home day care provider, 1971—78; tchr. presch., dir. Melrose DayCare Ctr., Iowa City, 1978—89; tchr. Blind Children's Learning Ctr., Santa Ana, Calif., 1989—92, dir. early childhood ctr., 1992—2001, asst. exec. dir., 2001—, interim exec. dir., 2004—05. Bd. pres. So. Calif. Network Serving Infants and Preschool Children with Visual Impairments, 1998—. Co-treas. Joint Action Com. Visually Impaired, Calif., 1997—; co-chair Infant Vendor Com., Santa Ana, 2000; edn. commn. head Yorba Linda United Meth. Ch., 1998—2002. Named Laywoman of Yr., Yorba Linda United Meth. Ch., 2000. Mem.: Family Support Ntetwork Bd., Assn. for Edn. and Rehab. Blind and Visually Impaired, Coun. Exceptional Children, Calif. Transcribers & Educators Multihandicapped Specialist, Calif. First Chance Consortium (co-chair, bd. dir., family support network com., mem. camp TLC). Avocations: reading, cooking, travel. Home: 856 Amber Ln Anaheim CA 92807 Office Phone: 714-573-8888.

GOODSPEED, LINDA A., manufacturing executive; BSME, Mich. State U., 1984, MA in Bus. Adminstrn., 1989. Engr. Ford Motor Co., 1984—89; with R&D dept. Nissan, 1989—96; with GE, 1996—2001, range product devel. mgr., 1997, gen. mgr. Six Sigma divsn., 1999, product gen. mgr. GE Appliances, 1999—2001; pres., COO Partminer, Inc., 2001; chief tech. officer Lennox Internat., Richardson, Tex., 2001—. Office: Lennox Internat 2140 Lake Park Blvd Richardson TX 75080

GOODSTADT, RANDEE BRENNER, educational administrator, educator; b. Elyria, Ohio, Nov. 24, 1951; s. Nathan Rich and Beatrice Halpern Brenner; m. Allan Goodstadt, Aug. 25, 1981 (div.); children: Daniel Joseph, Julie Susannah. BA, Kent State U., 1975; MA, Harvard U., 1977, ABD, 1981. Instr. Asheville-Buncombe Tech. C.C., N.C., 1993-2001, chair social and behavioral scis., 2000—. Contbr. to lit. mags. Mem. Hist. Resources Commn., Asheville, 1991-95; bd. dirs. Quality Forward, 2000-02, Ctr. for Jewish Studies, UNCA, 2001—. Recipient Horizon award Phi Theta Kappa; Bourguiba Inst. fellow, 1977; Radcliffe grantee for grad. women, 1979. Mem.: The Hist. Soc., Am. Hist. Assn. Home: 167 Brucemont Cir Asheville NC 28806 Office: Asheville Buncombe Tech C C 340 Victoria Rd Asheville NC 28801 Fax: 828 252 5848; Office Fax: 828 251 6355. E-mail: rgoodstadt@abtech.edu.

GOODSTEIN, AARON E., federal magistrate judge; b. Sheboygan, Wis., Apr. 28, 1942; BA, U. Wis. Madison, 1964; JD, U. Wis., 1967. Bar: Wis. 1967, U.S. Dist. Ct. (ea. and we. dists.) Wis. 1967, U.S. Ct. Appeals (7th crct.) 1968. Law clk. to Hon. Myron L. Gordon U.S. Dist. Ct., Ea. Dist. Wis., 1967-68; shareholder Chernov, Croen & Goodstein, S.C., Milw., 1968-79; U.S. magistrate judge Ea. Dist. Wis., Milw., 1979-87, reapptd., 1987—. Panelist Current Issues Relating to the Fourth, Fifth and Sixth Amendments, Jud. Conf. of 7th Cir., 1991; speaker fed. ct.'s class Marquette Law Sch., 1992; moderator probation and pretrial svcs. divsn. U.S. Cts., 1992; chair magistrate judges edn. com. Fed. Jud. Ctr., 1990-98, mem. magistrate judges com. of Jud. Conf. of U.S., 1993-99; adv. com. local rules and practice Ea. Dist. Wis., mem. adv. panel under Civil Justice Reform Act 1990; faculty mem. in field. Prodr: (video) Complaints, Warrants for Arrest and Search Warrants, 1992, Administrative Matters Pertaining to Magistrate Judges and Their Staff, 1993, Social Security: Process and Problems, Parts One and Two, 2000; mem. editl. adv. panel Handbook of Federal Civil Discovery and Disclosure, 1998; contbr. articles to profl. jours. Bd. dirs. Milw. Legal Aid Soc., 1974-79, Milw. Jewish Coun., 1977-79; pres. Milw. Forum, 1979-80, alumni mem.; pres. Congregation Shalom, 1990-92. Recipient Pro Bono award Gene and Ruth Posner Found., 1988. Mem. ABA (former chair magistrate judges com. Nat. Conf. Fed. Trial Judges), Fed. Magistrate Judges Assn. (pres. 2004-05, mem. adv. com. 2004-05), State Bar Wis. (pres. young lawyers divsn. 1975-76, bd. govs. 1975-77), Milw. Bar Assn. (exec. bd. 1978-79, sec. 1979-82), U. Wis. Law Sch. Alumni Assn. (bd. dirs. 1989-98), Order of Coif, Phi Kappa Phi. Office: US Magistrate Judge 258 US Courthouse 517 E Wisconsin Ave Milwaukee WI 53202-4500 Office Phone: 414-297-3963.

GOODSTEIN, BARNETT MAURICE, lawyer; b. Dallas, Oct. 1, 1921; s. Arthur Louis and Viola Esther (Levy) G.; m. Mira Brodsky, Jan. 26, 1947; children: Pamela Renee, Heather Ann, Robin Leslie. Student, Rice Inst., 1938—40; BA, MA, U. Tex., 1942; postgrad., U. Wis., 1949—51; JD, So. Meth. U., 1957. Bar: Tex. 1957, U.S. Dist. Ct. (no. dist.) Tex. 1963, U.S. Supreme Ct. Acting dir. case analysis Wage Stblzn. Bd., Dallas, 1951-53; practice of law Dallas, 1957—; pres. Goodstein & Starr, P.C., 1977-91, Goodstein, Starr & Pascoe, P.C., 1991—95; adminstrv. law judge City of Dallas, 1994—95; pvt. practice, 1995—. Lectr. econs. So. Meth. U., Dallas, 1946-48, 51-60; lectr. Massey Realty Coll., Real Estate Inst., Dallas; labor arbitrator, 1953—; former permanent arbitrator City of San Antonio, Police Officers' Assn.; mem. permanent arbitration panel Tinker AFB, Okla., 1984-88, Am. Fedn. Govt. Employees, 1984-90, SW Bell Tel., AT&T, CWA, IBEW, 1988—, FAA, 1993—, Nat. Assn. Air Traffic Specialists, 1994—, Ga. Pacific, 1994—, UPIU, 1994—, U.S. Customs and INS, 2001--, also various VA Med. Facilities, paper and copper industries, others; mem. permanent panel Dallas Area Rapid Transit Sys., 1988-90, 94-96; adminstrv. law judge City of Dallas, 1994-96. Hearing officer work suspensions appeals bd. City of Dallas, 1981-83; trustee Dallas County Sch. Bd., 1980-2005, v.p., 1990-91, 2003-2005; past trustee Temple Emanu-El; mem. legal representation com. Nat. Acad. Arbitrators, 1992-96, chmn. legal affairs com. 1997-99. Served with USAAF, 1942-46, China, 1945-46 Mem.: ABA, Am. Arbitration Assn. (Southwestern adv. coun. 1985—92), Indsl. Rels. Rsch. Assn. (pres. North Tex. chpt. 1985—86, neutral mem. bd. dirs. North Tex. chpt. 1990—92), Nat. Acad. Arbitrators (chmn. S.W. region 1987—88), Tex. Bar Assn. Home: 6427 Forest Creek Dr Dallas TX 75230-2814 Office: Law Offices of Barnett M Goodstein Ste 215J 4230 Lyndon B Johnson Fwy Dallas TX 75244-5816 Office Phone: 972-387-4303. Personal E-mail: bgoodsteinb@aol.com.

GOODSTEIN, DAVID LOUIS, physics professor; b. Bklyn., Apr. 5, 1939; s. Sam and Claire (Axel) G.; m. Judith R. Koral, June 30, 1960; children: Marcia, Mark. BS, Bklyn. Coll., 1960; PhD, U. Wash., 1965. Research instr. U. Wash., Seattle, 1965-66; research fellow Calif. Inst. Tech., Pasadena, 1966-67, asst. prof., 1968-71, asso. prof., 1971-76, prof., 1976—, vice-provost, 1987—, Frank J. Gilloon disting. teaching and svc. prof., 1995—. Vis. scientist Frascati Nat. Lab., Italy, 1971— . Author: States of Matter, 1975, (with J. Goodstein) Feynman's Lost Lecture, 1996, Out of Gas, 2004; mem. editl. bd. Il Nuovo Cimento, 1987—; contbr. articles to profl. jours.; project dir., host physics TV course The Mechanical Universe. Bd. dirs. Calif. Coun. Sci. and Tech., 1989—, Sierra Monolithics; sci. adv. com. David and Lucille Packard Found., 1988—. NSF postdoctoral fellow, 1967-68; Sloan Found. fellow, 1969-71; recipient Oersted medal, 1999, John P. McGovern Sci. and Soc. award, 2000. Fellow AAAS; mem. Am. Phys. Soc., Am. Inst. Physics. Office: Calif Inst Tech Dept Physics Pasadena CA 91125-0001 E-mail: dg@caltech.edu.

GOODWICK, DAVID LEE, advertising executive; b. Beloit, Wis., Oct. 20, 1954; s. James Lee and Helen Maude (Alton) G.; m. Christie Wren Spencer, Apr. 18, 1981; children: Jesse David, Lindsey Leah, Jamie Christopher. BA in Polit. Sci., BA in Journalism, U. Wis., Whitewater, 1976. Intern J. Walter Thompson, Chgo., 1975; advt. mgr. LRP, Inc., Lake Geneva, Wis., 1976; mktg. svcs. mgr. Mercury Marine, Fond du lac, Wis., 1976—77; advt. mgr. Johnson Outboards, Waukegan, Wis., 1977—79; advt. account mgr. GE, Fairfield, Conn., 1979—82; ptnr. Profl. Svcs. Assocs., Inc., Newtown, Conn., 1986—91, Hist. Property Preservations, Ltd., Newtown, 1986—91; pres., owner Typ-Hi Printers, Newtown, 1989—92; v.p., ptnr. Best Homes Constrn. Co., Janesville, Wis., 1993—96; pres., owner Goodwick Assocs., Inc., Newtown, 1982—99, Bandwick Prodns., Newtown, 1998—2004; CEO, creative dir. The Leverage Mktg. Svcs., Newtown, 1999—; chmn. Goodwick/Liazon Co., Newtown, 1999—. Advisor Insight Assocs., Westport, Conn., 1984-89; press sec. to Gov. Patrick Lucey of Wis., Madison, 1974. Pub.: newspaper The Alternative, 1974—76. Co-prodr. Ox Ridge Charity Horse Show, Darien, Conn., 1984-86; chmn. comms. com. United Way, Danbury, Conn., 1987-88; bus. mem. Newtown H.S. Alliance, Ancell Sch. Bus., Western Conn. State U.; bd. mem. NHS Blue and Gold Booster Club,

Newton HS Recipient numerous readership-based and creative competition awards various mags. including Most Significant Ads of the 20th Century award Indsl. Equipment News. Mem. Am. Entreprenurial Assn., Internat. Platform Assn. Avocations: musician, fishing. Home: 201 Hattertown Rd Newtown CT 06470-2451 Office: Leverage Mktg Group 117-119 S Main St Newtown CT 06470-2380 Business E-Mail: david@leverage-marketing.com.

GOODWIN, ALFRED THEODORE, federal judge; b. Bellingham, Wash., June 29, 1923; s. Alonzo Theodore and Miriam Hazel (Williams) G.; m. Marjorie Elizabeth Major, Dec. 23, 1943 (div. 1948); 1 child, Michael Theodore; m. Mary Ellin Handelin, Dec. 23, 1949; children: Karl Alfred, Margaret Ellen, Sara Jane, James Paul. BA, U. Oreg., 1947; JD, 1951. Bar: Oreg. 1951. Newspaper reporter Eugene (Oreg.) Register-Guard, 1947—50; practiced in Eugene until, 1955; circuit judge Oreg. 2d. Jud. Dist., 1955—60; assoc. justice Oreg. Supreme Ct., 1960—69; judge U.S. Dist. Ct. Oreg., 1969—71, U.S. Ct. Appeals for (9th cir.), Pasadena, Calif., 1971—88, chief judge, 1988—91, sr. judge, 1991—. Editor: Oreg. Law Rev., 1950—51. Adv. bd. Eugene Salvation Army, 1956—60; chmn., 1959; Bd. dirs. Central Lane YMCA, Eugene, 1956—60, Salem (Oreg.) Art Assn., 1960—69. Capt., inf. AUS, 1942—46, ETO. Mem.: ABA (ho. of dels. 1986—87), Am. Law Inst., Am. Judicature Soc., Order of Coif, Alpha Tau Omega, Sigma Delta Chi, Phi Delta Phi. Republican. Office: US Ct Appeals 9th Cir PO Box 91510 125 S Grand Ave Pasadena CA 91105-1621 Office Phone: 626-229-7100. E-mail: alfred_goodwin@ca9.uscourts.gov.

GOODWIN, ANDREW WIRT, II, radiologist; b. Oil City, Pa., Feb. 4, 1932; s. Frank Bert and Florence Bickford (Green) G.; m. Anita Faye Adkins, May 27, 1987; children: Andrew, Victoria, Mary Elizabeth, Mark H., Martha J., Lisa R. BA, Colgate U., 1953; MD, U. Mich., 1957. Diplomate Am. Bd. Radiology, Am. Bd. Nuclear Medicine. Intern Mary Hitchcock Meml. Hosp., Hanover, N.H., 1957-58; resident in radiology Mayo Clinic, Rochester, Minn., 1958-61, resident, 1958-61; radiologist Associated Radiologists, Inc., Charleston, W.Va., 1961-86, Radiol. Physicians Assn., Fairmont, W.Va., 1988—; pvt. practice. Republican. Episcopalian. Fax: 304-926-0851; Home Fax: 304-926-0851. E-mail: agoodwinii@aol.com.

GOODWIN, BECKY K., educational technology resource educator; Sci. tchr. USD 233 Sch. Dist., Olathe, Kans. Christa McAuliffe fellowship grantee State of Kans., 1992, 94, 97; named Kans. Tchr. of Yr., 1995; recipient Presdl. award for Excellence in Sci. and Math. Secondary Sci. for Kans., 1992, Outstanding Biology Tchr. award Nat. Assn. Biology Tchrs., 1992, Sci. Teaching Achievement Recognition Star award NSTA, 1993, Milken Nat. Educator award, 1995, Tandy Tech. Tchr. award, 1998. Office: USD 233 14090 Black Bob Rd Olathe KS 66063

GOODWIN, BRUCE KESSELI, retired geology educator, researcher; b. Providence, Oct. 14, 1931; s. Thomas William and Lizetta Christina (Kesseli) G.; m. Joan Marilyn Horton, June 9, 1956; children: Stephen Bruce, Susan Joan, Jennifer Anne. AB, U. Pa., 1953; MS, Lehigh U., 1957, PhD, 1959. Grad. asst. Lehigh U., Bethlehem, Pa., 1956-59; geologist Vt. Geol. Survey, Burlington, 1956-58; instr. U. Pa., Phila., 1959-63; asst. prof. geology Coll. William and Mary, Williamsburg, Va., 1963-66, assoc. prof. geology, 1966-71, prof. geology, 1971-96, chmn. dept. geology, 1970-76, 82-88, 92-96; tchr. geology Math.-Sci. Ctr., Richmond, Va., 1968-70. With Va. Bd. Geology, 1982-88, chair, 1983; mem. Va. Geologic Mapping Adv. Com., 1993-2003. Contbr. articles to profl. jours. Pres. Lafayette Ednl. Fund, Inc., Williamsburg, Va., 1976-79, Lafayette H.S. PTA, Williamsburg, Bruton Heights PTA, Williamsburg; mem. com. Va. Jr. Acad. Sci., 1971-73. Recipient Thomas Jefferson Tchg. award Coll. William and Mary, 1971; cert. of merit Math.-Sci. Ctr. Fellow Geol. Soc. Am. (edn. com. 1994-96); mem. AAAS, Nat. Assn. Geology Tchrs. (pres. ea. sect. 1982), Va. Acad. Sci. (chmn. geology sect. 1970, 98), Am. Inst. Profl. Geologists (sec., treas. Va. sect. 1989, pres. Va. sect. 1990), St. Andrews Soc., Coun. on Undergrad. Rsch (geology councilor 1988-94), Delta Upsilon. Republican. Presbyterian. Avocations: fishing, sailing, geology, travel, ballroom dancing. Home: 103 Wakerobin Rd Williamsburg VA 23185-4441

GOODWIN, BRUCE T., engineer; BS in physics, City Coll. NY; MS in aeronautical and astronautical engring., PhD in aeronautical and astronautical engring., U. Ill. Staff mem. Los Alamos Nat. Lab.; with Lawrence Livermore Nat. Lab., 1985—, B Program/B Divsn. leader def. and nuclear tech., 1996—2001, assoc. dir. def. and nuclear tech., 2001—. Recipient Aerospace Laurels Honor, Aviation Week & Space Tech. Mag., 2000, Ernest Orlando Lawrence award, US Dept. Energy, 2002. Office: Lawrence Livermore Nat Lab 7000 E Ave Livermore CA 94550

GOODWIN, CRAUFURD DAVID, economics professor; b. Montreal, Que., Can., May 23, 1934; came to U.S., 1962; s. George G. and Roma (Stewart) G.; m. Nancy Virginia Sanders, June 7, 1958. BA, McGill U., 1955; PhD, Duke U., 1958. Econ. research asst. Courtauld's Can., Ltd., 1955; lectr. econs. U. Windsor, Ont., 1958-59; exec. sec. Commonwealth Studies Center, Duke U., also; vis. asst. prof., 1959-60; hon. research fellow Australian Nat. U., 1960-61; asst. prof. econs. York U., Toronto, 1961-62; asst. prof. econs., asst. to provost Duke U., Durham, N.C., 1962-63, assoc. prof. econs., sec. to Univ., asst. to provost, 1963-64, assoc. prof. econs., sec. Univ., asst. provost, 1964- 66, assoc. prof. econs., asst. provost, dir. internat. studies, 1966-68, prof. econs., vice provost for internat. studies, 1968-69, prof. econs., vice provost, dir. internat., 1969-72, prof. econs., 1971-74, James B. Duke prof. econs., 1974—, dean Grad. Sch., vice provost for research, 1980-86, interim chair Dept. Econs., 2002—03. Smuts vis. prof. Cambridge U., 1967-68; officer in charge European and internat. affairs Ford Found., 1971-76. Author: Canadian Economic Thought: The Political Economy of a Developing Nation 1814-1914, 1961, Economic Enquiry in Australia, 1966, The Image of Australia, 1974, (with M. Nacht) Absence of Decision, 1983, Fondness and Frustration, 1984, Decline and Renewal, 1986, Abroad and Beyond, 1988, Missing the Boat, 1991; editor: (with W.B. Hamilton and Kenneth Robinson) A Decade of the Commonwealth 1955-64, 1966, (with I.B. Holley) The Transfer of Ideas, 1968, (with R.D.C. Black and A.W. Coats) The Marginal Revolution in Economics, 1973, Exhortation and Controls, 1975, Energy Policy in Perspective, 1981, Economics and National Security, 1991, International Investment in Human Capital, 1993, (with Alan Smith, Ulrich Teichler, and Peggy Blumenthal) Academic Mobility in a Changing World: Regional and Global Trends, 1996, (with M. Nacht) Beyond Government, 1995, Talking to Themselves, 1995, Art and the Market, 1998, (with N. Demarchi) Economic Engagements with Art, 2000; editor: (jour.) History of Political Economy, 1969—, (series) Historical Perspectives on Modern Economics, 1981—. Guggenheim fellow, 1967-68 Home: PO Box 957 Hillsborough NC 27278-0957 E-mail: goodwin@econ.duke.edu.

GOODWIN, DAVID B., lawyer; AB, U. Calif., Santa Cruz, 1974; BA, Oxford Univ., 1976, MA, 1979; JD, Stanford Univ., 1982. Bar: Calif. Atty., shareholder Heller Ehrman LLP, San Francisco, 1986—, co-chair appeals and strategy. Office: Heller Ehrman LLP 333 Bush St San Francisco CA 94104 Fax: 415-772-6268. Office Phone: 415-775-6319. Business E-Mail: david.goodwin@hellerehrman.com.

GOODWIN, DORIS HELEN KEARNS, historian; b. Rockville Centre, NY, Jan. 4, 1943; d. Michael Alouisius and Helen Witt (Miller) Kearns; m. Richard N. Goodwin, 1975; children: Richard, Michael, Joseph. BA magna cum laude, Colby Coll., 1964; PhD, Harvard U., 1968. Intern US Dept. State, Washington, 1963, Ho. of Reps., 1965; rsch. assoc. U.S. Dept. Health, Edn., & Welfare, 1966; spl. asst. to Willard Wirtz U.S. Dept. Labor, 1967; staff asst. to President Lyndon B. Johnson The White House, 1968; prof. govt. Harvard U., Cambridge, Mass., 1969—79. Spl. cons. to Pres. Lyndon Johnson, 1969-73; hostess "What's the Big Idea", WGBH-TV, Boston, 1972; polit. analyst news desk, WBZ-TV, Boston, 1972; mem. Women's Polit. Caucus, Mass., 1972, Dem. Party Platform Com., 1972; reg. panelist News Hour with Jim Lehrer; commentator NBC, MSNBC. Author: Lyndon Johnson and the American Dream, 1976, The Fitzgeralds and the Kennedys: An American Saga, 1987, No Ordinary Time: Franklin and Eleanor Roosevelt: The Homefront in World War II, 1994 (Harold Washington Lit. award, New England Bookseller Assn. award, Ambassador Book award, Wash. Monthly Book award, Pulitzer Prize for History, 1995), Wait Till Next Year: A Memoir, 1997, numerous articles on politics and baseball; contbr.: Telling Lives: The Biographer's Art, 1979; forward: Mortal Friends: A Novel, 1992, Kennedy Weddings: A Family Album, 1999. Trustee Wesleyan U., Colby Coll., Robert F. Kennedy Found. Named Fulbright fellow, 1966, White House fellow, 1967. Mem. Am. Polit. Sci. Assn., Coun. Fgn. Relations, Women Involved, Group for Applied Psychoanalysis, Signet Soc., Soc. Am. Historians, Am. Acad. Arts & Scis., Harvard U. Bd. Overseers, Phi Beta Kappa (outstanding young women of yr. award 1966), Phi Sigma Iota. Roman Catholic. Office: c/o Dori Lawson Soldier Creek Assoc PO Box 477 Rockport ME 04856*

GOODWIN, FRANK ERIK, materials engineer; b. Bethlehem, Pa., Jan. 6, 1954; s. Francis Black and Grethe Julie (Andresen) G.; m. Rosalind Ann Volpe, May 30, 1987; children: Adrian Edmond, Marianna Rose. BS, Cornell U., 1975; ScD, MIT, 1979. Plant engr. Chambersburg (Pa.) Engring. Co., 1979-80; devel. dir. Chromalloy Rsch. & Tech., Orangeburg, N.Y., 1980-82; mgr. devel. Internat. Lead Zinc Rsch. Orgn., Research Triangle Park, N.C., 1982-84, mgr. metallurgy, 1984-86, v.p. materials sci., 1986—2004, exec. v.p., 2004—. Mem. peer review com. on lead Dept. Energy, Washington, 1987-89. Author: Galfan Galvanizing Alloy & Technology, 1984; editor: Stress Calculations for Zinc Die Castings, 1988, Engineering Properties of Zinc Alloys, 1988; contbr. articles to profl. jours., chpts. to books. Mem. ASM, N.Am. Die Casting Assn. (rsch. com.), N.Y. Acad. Scis. Republican. Episcopalian. Achievements include patents (with other) for new aluminum alloy, new lead alloy for batteries. Office: Internat Lead Zinc Rsch Org 2525 Meridian Pky Ste 100 Durham NC 27713-2261

GOODWIN, FREDERICK KING, psychiatrist; b. Cin., Apr. 21, 1936; s. Robert Clifford and Marion Cronin (Schmadel) G.; m. Rosemary Powers, Oct. 19, 1963; children: Kathleen Kelly, Frederick King, Daniel Clifford. BS, Georgetown U., 1958; philosophy fellow, St. Louis U., 1958—59, MD, 1963. Intern medicine and psychiatry SUNY, Syracuse, 1963-64; resident in psychiatry U. N.C., Chapel Hill, 1964-65; commd. med. officer USPHS, 1965; clin. assoc. adult psychiatry br. NIMH, 1965-67; rsch. fellow Lab. Biochemistry, Nat. Heart Inst., NIH, Bethesda, Md., 1967-68; chief sect. on psychiatry NIMH, Bethesda, 1968-73, chief clin. psychobiology br., 1977-81, sci. dir., 1981-88; apptd. by Pres. adminstr. Alcohol, Drug Abuse and Mental Health Adminstrn., Washington, 1988-92; pvt. practice Chevy Chase, Md., 1967—; dir. NIMH, Rockville, Md., 1992-94; dir. Ctr. on Neurosci. Med. Progress and Soc. George Washington U. Med. Ctr., Washington, 1994—. Faculty George Washington U. Sch. Medicine, Washington Sch. Psychiatry, Uniformed U. Sch. Health Scis.; vis. prof. U. Calif., Irvine, U. Wis., Boston U., U. So. Calif., Duke U.; cons. AMA Coun. on Drugs; AIDS coord. Alcohol, Drug Abuse and Mental Health Adminstrn., 1986-90; participant pub. edn. programs on local and network TV and radio. Author: (with K.R. Jamison) Manic-Depressive Illness, 1990 (Best Med. Book award 1990 Assn. Am. Pubsd.); editor-in-chief Psychiatry Research, 1979-97; mem. editl. bd. Archives of Gen. Psychiatry, 1978—, Psychopharmacology, 1976-79; contbr. articles to med. jours.; host (pub. radio program) The Infinite Mind, 1998— (EDI award for excellence in media Easter Seal Soc., 1999). Mem. adv. bd. Max Planck Inst., Munich. Recipient Psychopharmacology Rsch. prize Am. Psychol. Assn., 1970, Internat. Anna-Monika prize for rsch. in depression, 1971, Taylor Manor award, 1976, Adminstrs. award HEW, 1977, Superior Svc. award USPHS, 1980, Strecker award, 1983, Sr. Exec. Svc. Presdl. Meritorious Rank award, 1982, Disting. Rank award, 1986, Disting. Exec. Svc. award Sr. Exec. Assn. Profl. Devel. League, 1986, Best Tchr. in Am. Psychiatry award CME Inc., 1989, Svc. to Sci. award Nat. Assn. for Biomed. Rsch., 1990, Pub. Svc. award. Fed. Am. Socs. for Exptl. Biology, 1990, 1st recipient of Fawcett Humanitarian award NDMDA, 1990, McAlpin award NMHA, 1991, EDI award Easter Seal Soc., 1999, Nola Maddox Falcone prize, 1999; NIMH Spl. fellow, 1967-68. Fellow Am. Psychiat. Assn. (chmn. com. on protection of human subjects, task force on rsch. tng., Hofheimer prize for rsch. 1971, chmn. task force on future of psychiat. rsch.), Am. Coll. Neuropsychopharmacology (chmn. com. on problems of pub. concern); mem. Inst. Medicine, NAS, AAAS, Am. Psychosomatic Soc., Soc. Biol. Psychiatry (A.E. Bennett award 1970), Am. Acad. Psychoanalysis, Soc. for Neurosci., Psychiat. Rsch. Soc. (pres. 1998-2000), Washington Psychiat. Soc. Home: 5712 Warwick Pl Chevy Chase MD 20815-5502 Office: Ctr Neuroscience Med Progress Soc 2500 Old Georgetown Rd Ste 601 Bethesda MD 20814 Business E-Mail: fred@drgoodwin.com. *Many aspects of one's innerself contribute to shaping a career, most, I suspect, evolving and changing along the way. For me, one characteristic stands out as unchanging - the capacity to derive genuine pleasure and a special sense of satisfaction from the successes and the growth of those whose careers you have helped - in a sense, your professional "children".*

GOODWIN, GEORGE EVANS, public relations executive; b. Atlanta, June 20, 1917; s. George and Carrie (Clark) G.; m. Lois Milstead, Nov. 2, 1940; children: Clark, Allen. AB with cert. in journalism, Washington and Lee U., 1939, HDL, 1997. Reporter Atlanta Georgian, 1939, Charleston (S.C.) News and Courier, 1940, Washington Times-Herald, 1940-41, Miami Daily News, 1941-42; staff writer Atlanta Jour., 1945-52; exec. dir. Central Atlanta Improvement Assn., 1952-54; v.p. First Nat. Bank of Atlanta, 1954-64; exec. v.p. Bell & Stanton, Inc., 1965-76; mng. dir. Manning, Selvage & Lee, Atlanta, 1976-85, sr. counselor, 1985—. Exec. sec. Ga. Senatorial Transit Study Com., 1954 Chmn. Atlanta Bicentennial Commn., 1974-76; trustee emeritus Oglethorpe U.; life dir. Alliance Theater; elder Presbyn. Ch.; mem. Ga. Citizens Y2K Task Force, 1999-2000. Decorated Purple Heart, Navy Unit Commendation; recipient Pulitzer prize for local reporting, 1948, Sigma Delta Chi award for gen. reporting, 1948, Pall Mall Big Story award, 1949. Mem. SAR, Pub. Rels. Soc. Am., Rotary Internat., Delta Tau Delta, Soc. Profl. Journalists/Sigma Delta Chi (award for gen. reporting on vote fraud 1948), Omicron Delta Kappa. Home: 3302 Ivanhoe Dr NW Atlanta GA 30327-1528 Office: Manning Selvage & Lee Ste 400 1170 Peachtree St NE Atlanta GA 30309 Office Phone: 404-875-1444. Business E-Mail: george.goodwin@mslpr.com.

GOODWIN, HEATHER MARIE, educational consultant; b. Houston, May 19, 1968; d. Ron and Cynthia Coffman. BA in Humanities, Trinity U., San Antonio, 1990, MA in Tchg., 1991. Cert. tchr. spl. edn. pre-sch.-12, elem. self-contained 1-6, elem. English 1-6, elem. history 1-6, English as 2d lang. pre-K-12. Life skills tchr. for students with mild-moderate disabilities Alief Ind. Sch. Dist., Houston, 1991—94, tchr. spl. edn. and literacy, 1994—96, dist.-wide behavior/inclusion specialist, 1996—99; ednl. cons. Stetson & Assocs., Houston, 1999—2001; dir. behavior programs Sopris West Ednl. Svcs., Longmont, Tex., 2001—04; owner HMG Ednl. Svcs., Inc., 2004—. Mentor gifted/talented students Saturday Morning Experience, San Antonio, 1989—90; mentor, tutor h.s. students Upward Bound, San Antonio, 1990—94; adult literacy instr. Neuhaus Ctr., Houston, 1994—96; presenter in field. Author, cons.: sci. textbook McGraw-Hill Science 2000, 1998. Recipient Tchr.-Rschr. grant, NICHD. Mem.: CEC, Coun. for Children with Behavior Disorders, Assn. for Curriculum and Devel. Avocations: reading, running, hiking, water-skiing, bicycling. Home: 1423 Ashland St Houston TX 77708

GOODWIN, IRWIN, journalist, writer; b. Chgo., Aug. 19, 1929; s. Albert and Sarah Esther (Wallen) Goodwin; m. Mary Margaret Revell, Apr. 21, 1966 (div. 1986). AB, Roosevelt U., Chgo., 1948; MA, U. Mich., 1949. Reporter City News Bur., Chgo., 1949-50; reporter, asst. editor Newsweek, Chgo. and NYC, 1952-58; dir. pub. info. Sci. Rsch. Assocs., Chgo., 1958-60; corr. Newsweek, London, 1960-70; Caribbean corr. Washington Post, San Juan, PR, 1970-72; corr. NBC News, 1970—72; spl. asst. to dir. Smithsonian Instn., Washington, 1972-73; sr. editor NAS, Washington, 1973-82; editor Washington bur. Physics Today, Washington, 1983-93, sr. editor Washington bur., 1993-2000; corr. Nature, 2000—. Co-author: Physics and Nuclear Arms Today, 1991; editor: Paying for America's Health Care, 1973, Energy and Environment: Collision of Crises, 1974; contbr. articles to profl. jours. Sgt. maj. U.S. Army, 1950-52. Recipient News Writing award Overseas Press Club, 1971, 72, Pub. Svc. Group Achievement award NASA, 1981. Mem. AAAS, Nat. Assn. Sci. Writers, Fedn. Am. Scientists, Fgn. Affairs Coun., DC Sci. Writers Assn., Nat. Press Club, Phi Beta Kappa. Business E-Mail: goodwin@aip.org. E-mail: irwingoodwin@aol.com.

GOODWIN, JAMES E., retired air transportation executive; BBA, Salem Coll. With United Airlines, 1967, sr. v.p. internat., 1992, sr. v.p. N.Am., 1992—98, pres., COO, 1998—99; chmn., CEO UAL Corp., Elk Grove Twp., Ill., 1999—2001; mem. bd. of dir. AAR Corp., Wood Dale, Ill., 2002—. Bd. dir. AAR Corp., Wood Dale, Ill., 2001—, Labe Bank, DBS Commn. Inc. Trustee Lewis U.; bd. dirs. Chgo. Coun. Fgn. Rels. Mem. Exec. Club Chgo. (bd. dirs.), Comml. Club Chgo. (civic com.). Office: AAR Corp One AAR Place 1100 Wood Dale Rd Wood Dale IL 60191*

GOODWIN, JANE AYERS, pediatric anesthesiologist; b. Providence, R.I., July 27, 1968; d. Robert and Carole Ayers; m. Salvatore Robert Goodwin, Mar. 12, 1994; 1 child, Casey. MD, U. of Fla., Gainesville, 1994. Diplomate anesthesiology Am. Bd. of Anesthesiology. Clin. asst. prof. dept. anesthesiology U. of Fla., Gainesville, 1999—2000; asst. prof., cons. dept. anesthesiology Nemours Children's Clinic, Jacksonville, Fla., 2000—. Contbr. articles to rsch. publs. Mem.: Internat. Anesthesia Rsch. Soc., Soc. for Pediat. Anesthesiology, Am. Soc. of Anesthesiology, Alpha Omega Alpha. Achievements include research in Collaborative research efforts with bioengineering colleagues in Portugal regarding development of fetal, neonatal, and infant simulation software and models which may be used for education; Model for Educational Simulation of Infant Cardiovascular Physiology. Office: Nemours Children's Clinic 807 Children's Way Jacksonville FL 32207 Office Phone: 904-202-8332. Office Fax: 904-396-1630.

GOODWIN, JEAN MCCLUNG, psychiatrist; b. Pueblo, Colo., Mar. 28, 1946; d. Paul Stanley and Geraldine (Smart) McClung; m. James Simeon Goodwin, Aug. 8, 1970; children: Laura (dec.), Amanda Harding Goodwin, Robert Caleb, Paul Joshua, Elizabeth Cronin Goodwin. BA in Anthropology summa cum laude, Radcliffe Coll., 1967; MD, Harvard U., 1971; MPH, UCLA, 1972. Diplomate Am. Bd. Psychiatry and Neurology, Am. Bd. Forensic Psychiatry, added qualifications in forensic psychiatry, psychoanalytic tng. Resident in psychiatry Georgetown U. Hosp., Washington, 1972-74, U. N.Mex. Sch. Medicine, 1974-76, asst. dir., dir. psychiat. residents tng., 1979-85; prof. Med. Coll. Wis., 1985-92, U. Tex. Med. Br., Galveston, 1992-98, prof. clin. psychiatry, 1998—; pvt. practice in gen. psychiatry, psychoanalysis. From instr. to assoc. prof. dept. psychiatry U. N.Mex. Sch. Medicine, 1976-85; cons. protective services Dept. Human Services, N.Mex., 1976-84; faculty Houston-Galveston Psychoanalytic Inst., 1999—; founding bd. dirs. Houston-Galveston Trauma Inst.; lectr. in field Author: Effects of High Altitude on Human Birth, 1969, Sexual Abuse: Incest Victims and Their Families, 1982, 2d edit., 1989, Rediscovering Childhood Trauma: Historical Casebook and Clinical Applications, 1993, Mischief and Mercy, 1993; co-author (with Reina Attias) Splintered Reflections: Images of the Body in Trauma, 1999; mem. editl. bd. Jour. Traumatic Stress, 1985-93, Dissociation, 1988-98, Psychotherapy Rev., 1998-2000, Trauma and Dissociation, 2000—; contbr. articles to profl. jours. Chmn. work group on child sexual abuse Surgeon Gen.'s Conf. on Violence and Pub. Health, Leesburg, Va., 1985; mem. adv. bd. Nat. Resource Ctr. on Child Sexual Abuse, 1989-96. Recipient Esther Haar award Am. Acad. Psychoanalysis, 1990, Cornelia Wilbur award Internat. Soc. for Study of Dissociation, 1994; Nat. Cen. Child Abuse and Neglect grantee, 1979-82, Nat. Inst. Aging grantee, 1980-85. Fellow Internat. Soc. Study Dissociation (exec. com. 1991-96), Am. Psychiat. Assn. (dist. br. treas., sec. N.Mex. br. 1980-82, exhibits and programs subcoms. 1985-91). Democrat. Roman Catholic. Office: 4925 Fort Crockett Blvd Apt 510 Galveston TX 77551-5949 Office Phone: 409-762-1101. Personal E-mail: jmgoodwin@aol.com.

GOODWIN, JOHN ALAN, chemistry professor, inorganic chemist; b. Russellville, Ky., May 9, 1958; s. Dan Frey and Shirley Faye Goodwin; m. Catherine Anne Chase, Sept. 28, 1985; children: John Andrew, Samuel Chase, Catherine Faye. PhD, Rice U., 1988. Asst. prof. Eckerd Coll., St. Petersburg, Fla., 1991—96; assoc. prof. Coastal Carolina U., Conway, SC, 1996—. Contbr. articles to profl. jours. Mem.: Project Kaleidoscope F21, Am. Chem. Soc. Presbyterian. Achievements include design of Cafeteria Grading; discovery of Catalytic Oxygen Activation By Pentacoordinate (Nitro)Cobalt Porphyrins. Avocation: musician. Home: 146 Citadel Dr Conway SC 29526 Office: Coastal Carolina University PO Box 261954 Conway SC 29528-6054 Office Phone: 843-349-2295. Personal E-mail: jgoodwin@coastal.edu.

GOODWIN, JOSEPH ROBERT, judge; b. 1942; BS, W.Va. U., 1965, JD, 1970. Bar: W.Va. 1970. Ptnr. Goodwin & Goodwin, 1970-95; judge U.S. Dist. Ct. (so. dist.) W.Va., Charleston, 1995—. Editor W.Va. Law Rev. Mem. W.Va. U. Bd. Advisors, 1981-86; bd. visitors W.Va. U. Coll. Law, 1995-98, chmn., 1998. With USAR, 1965-67. Mem. ABA, W.Va. State Bar Assn., Jackson County Bar Assn., 4th Cir. Jud. Conf. Office: US Dist Ct So Dist WVa 300 Virginia St Charleston WV 25301 Office Phone: 304-347-3192.

GOODWIN, MARK B., transportation services executive, lawyer; b. 1949; BA, Thomas More Coll.; JD, Washington Coll. Law, Am. U., 1977. Bar: DC 1977. Atty. Steptoe & Johnson, Washington; asst. gen. solicitor Union Pacific Railroad Co., Omaha, 1983—92; v.p. Overnite Corp., Richmond, Va., 1992—98, gen. counsel, 1992—, sr. v.p., 1998—, sec., 2003—. Bd. commissioners Va. Port Authority. Mem.: Va. Trucking Assn. (1st v.p. 2002, pres. 2004—). Office: Overnite Corp 1000 Semmes Ave Richmond VA 23224 Office Phone: 804-231-8000. Office Fax: 804-231-8504.

GOODWIN, MARTIN BRUNE, retired radiologist; b. Vancouver, B.C., Can., Aug. 8, 1921; came to U.S., 1948; m. Cathy Dennison, Mar. 7, 1980; 1 child, Suzanne; stepchildren: Chuck Glikas, Dianna; 1 child from previous marriage, Nancijane Goodwin Hilling. BSA in Agriculture, U. B.C., 1943, postgrad., 1943-44; MD, CM, McGill U. Med. Sch., Montreal, Can., 1948. Diplomate Am. Bd. Med. Examiners, lic. Med. Coun. Can.; cert. diagnostic and therapeutic radiology Am. Bd. Radiology; cert. Am. Bd. Nuclear Medicine. Intern Scott & White Hosp., Temple, Tex., 1948-49; fellow radiology Scott & White Clinic, 1949-52, mem. staff, 1952-53; instr. U. Tex., Galveston, 1952-53; radiologist Plains Regional Med. Ctr., Clovis, N.Mex., Portales, N.Mex., pres. med. staff; chief radiology De Baca Gen. Hosp., Ft. Sumner, N.Mex.; cons. Cannon AFB Hosp., Clovis; pvt. practice radiology Clovis, Portales, Ft. Sumner and Tucumcari, 1955—2005; ret., 2005. Adj. prof. health scis. Ea. N.Mex. U., 1976-77; adj. clin. prof. health scis. We. Mich. U., 1976-78 Apptd. N.Mex. Radiation Tech. Adv. Coun., N.Mex. Bd. Pub. Health; former chmn. N.Mex. Health and Social Svcs. Bd.; mem. Regional Health Planning Coun.; treas. Roosevelt County Rep. Ctrl. Com. Capt. U.S. Army M.C., 1953-55; Col. USAF M.C., 1975-79. Fellow AAAS, Am. Coll. Radiology, Am. Coll. Radiology (past councillor); mem. Am. Soc. Thoracic Radiologists (founder), Radiol. Soc. of N.Am. (past councillor), N.Mex. Med. Soc. (various coms., chmn. joint practice com., councillor bd. dirs.), N.Mex. Radiol. Soc. (past pres.), N.Mex. Thoracic Soc. (past pres.), N.Mex. Med. Review Assn. (bd. dirs. 1970-93), N.Mex. Med. Soc. Found. for Med. Care (bd. dirs. 1975—, former v.p., former treas.), County Med. Soc. (past pres., past v.p., past sec.), Clovis C. of C. (chmn. civic affairs com., bd. dirs.), Clovis Elks Lodge (past exalted ruler), Clovis Noonday Lions Club (past sec.). Republican. Presbyterian. Home: 505 E 18th St Portales NM 88130-9201 Fax: 505-356-5035.

GOODWIN, MICHAEL, labor union administrator; V.p. Office and Profl. Employees Internat. Union, 1985—97, pres., 1997—. Mem. exec. council AFL-CIO. Office: Office/Profl Employees Internat Union 265 W 14th St 6th Fl New York NY 10011-5300 Office Phone: 800-346-7348.

GOODWIN, NANCY LEE, computer company executive; b. Peoria, Ill., Aug. 11, 1940; d. Raymond Darrell and Mildred Louise (Brown) G. BA (Nat. Meth. scholar, Nat. Merit scholar), MacMurray Coll., 1961; MA, U. Colo.,

1963; PhD, U. Ill., 1971. Tchr. Roosevelt Jr. High Sch., Peoria, 1961-62; counselor U. Ill., Urbana, 1963-66, staff assoc., asst. prof. edn. measurement Chgo., 1967-71; asst. v.p., assoc. prof. stats. Fla. Internat. U., Miami, 1971-78; pres. Greenfield (Mass.) Community Coll., 1978-82, Arapahoe Community Coll., Colo., from 1982; corp. owner MTF Enterprises; prof. Nat. U.; owner C.A.T.S. Inc., 1987—; corp. mgr. DRM Enterprises. Dir. Cons. Mid-Am. Computer Corp., First Chance Network U.S. Office Edn., 1972-78 Mem. Com. on Ill. Govt., Higher Edn. Task Force; mem. Vol. Action Center, Miami, 1972-78; active Girl Scouts U.S.A.; mem. Franklin/Hampshire Area Service Planning Team, 1978; incorporator Franklin County (Mass.) United Way, Farren Meml. Hosp.; adv. Franklin County Public Hosp.; bd. dirs. Women's Inst. Fla., Franklin County Arts Council, Franklin County Devel. Corp., Western Welcome Week, Inc.; bd. dirs., mem. fin. monitoring com. New Eng. Soy Dairy, 1980. Recipient Merit award Chgo. Tchrs. Assn., 1969; citation Girl Scouts U.S.A., 1973 Mem. NEA, Am. Assn. Higher Edn., Am. Ednl. Research Assn., Assn. Instl. Research, Centennial C. of C. (dir. 1983) Home: 5228 Del Rey Ave Las Vegas NV 89146-1414

GOODWIN, RICHARD HALE, botany educator; b. Brookline, Mass., Dec. 14, 1910; s. Harry Manley and Mary Blanchard (Linder) G.; m. Esther Bemis, Oct. 12, 1936; children: Mary G. Wetzel, Richard H. Jr. AB, Harvard U., 1933, MA, 1934, PhD, 1937. Fellow Am.-Scandinavian Found., U. Copenhagen, 1937-38; instr. botany U. Rochester, NY, 1938-41, asst. prof., 1941-44; prof. Conn. Coll., New London, 1944-76, prof. emeritus, 1976—. Dir. Conn. Arboretum, New London, 1944-65, 67-68; pres. Conservation and Rsch. Found., Boston, 1953-94; treas. Inst. Ecology, Washington, 1975-77. Co-author: Inland Wetlands of the U.S. Fellow AAAS, Am. Acad. Arts and Scis.; mem. Nat. Com. Plant Sci. Socs. (coord. 1961-62), Am. Inst. Biol. Scis. (governing bd. 1967-71), Nature Conservancy (pres. 1956-58, 64-66), Conservation and Rsch. Found. (pres. 1953-94), Am. Soc. Plant Biology, Ecol. Soc. Am., New Eng. Bot. Soc., Bot. Soc. Am., Torrey Bot. Club. Democrat. Unitarian-Universalist. Achievements include research in plant morphogenesis, growth inhibitors, fluorescent constituents of plants, long range vegetation studies, effects of prescribed burning.

GOODWIN, SCOTT CRAIG, interventional radiologist; b. Gardena, Calif., July 15, 1957; s. Alfred Boree Goodwin and Dorothy Tena Curtis; m. Suzie May El-Saden, Aug. 7, 1993; children: Alexander Boree, Adam El-Saden. BS magna cum laude with dept. honors, UCLA, 1979; MD, Harvard U., 1984. Intern in internal medicine St. Luke's Hosps./Wash. U., St. Louis, 1984-85; resident in diagnostic radiology UCLA Med. Ctr., 1985-88, fellowship in cardiovascular and interventional radiology, 1988-89, vis. asst. prof. radiology, 1989, from asst. prof. to assoc. prof., 1989—2001, prof. radiology, 2001—, chief vascular, interventional radiology, 1994-2001, vice chmn. radiology, 2003—; chief angiography and interventional radiology Daniel Freeman Hosp., Inglewood, Calif., 1989-91; vice chmn. imaging svcs. Irvine (Calif.) Med. Ctr., 1991-92; chmn., prof. radiology Wayne State U., Detroit, 2001—02; chmn. radiology Greater L.A. VA Med. Ctr., 2002—. Lectr. in field. Author (with others): Uterine Artery Embolization for the Treatment of Uterine Leiomyomata, 1997; contbr. articles to profl. jours. Recipient numerous rsch. grants. Office: Greater LA VA Med Ctr 11301 Wilshire Blvd 500-0608 Los Angeles CA 90073 Office Phone: 310-268-3778. Business E-Mail: scott.goodwin@med.va.gov, sgoodwin@mednet.ucla.edu.

GOODWIN, W. JARRARD, otolaryngologist, educator; MD, Albany Med. Coll., 1972. Prof. dept. otolaryngology U. Miami, Fla., 1989—; dir. Sylvester Comprehensive Cancer Ctr. U. Miami Hosp. and Clinic, 1993—. Mem. Am. Acad. Otolaryngology/Head and Neck Surgery (Disting. Svc. award 1996), Am. Head and Neck Soc., Triologic Soc., Am. Soc. for Clin. Oncology, Am. Assn. for Cancer Rsch. Office: 1611 NW 12th Ave Miami FL 33136-1005 Office Phone: 305-243-4387. Business E-Mail: jgoodwin@miami.edu.

GOODWIN, WILLIAM MAXWELL, financial executive; b. Muncie, Ind., Oct. 13, 1939; s. Donald Dunkin and Beth Virginia (Maxwell) G.; m. LaDonna Sherry Erickson, June 9, 1962; children: Lauri Michelle, Lisa Dianne. AB, Ind. U., 1961, MBA, 1966. CPA, Ind. Staff acct., supr. Ernst & Whinney (now Ernst Whinney & Young), Indpls., 1966-72; contbr. Lilly Endowment, Inc., Indpls., 1972-82, treas., sec., 1983-95, v.p. cmty. devel., 1996—. Advisor Sch. Bus., Ind. U., Bloomington, Ind., 1980-95; fin. advisor U.S. Gymnastic Fedn., Indpls., 1983-89; treas., dir. Nat. Gymnastics Found. Inc., Indpls., 1988-89. Contbr. articles to profl. jours. Treas., dir. Ind. Sports Corp., Indpls., 1979-88; dir. Youth Works, Inc., Indpls., 1977-85, Greater Indpls. Progress Com., 1996—; treas. Nat. Sports Festival, Indpls., 1982; treas., mem. exec. com. 1987 Pan Am. Games, Indpls.; chmn. AAU Sullivan Award Dinner, Indpls., 1983-94, mem. award selection com., 1993—. Capt. U.S. Army, 1962-64. Mem. AICPA, Ind. Assn. CPAs, Beta Gamma Sigma, Delta Phi Alpha. Republican. Methodist. Home: 3586 Inverness Blvd Carmel IN 46032-9380 Office: Lilly Endowment Inc PO Box 88068 Indianapolis IN 46208-0068 Office Phone: 317-924-5471. Business E-Mail: goodwinb@lei.org.

GOODY, JOAN EDELMAN, architect; d. Beril and Sylvia (Feldman) Edelman; m. Marvin E. Goody, Dec. 18, 1960 (dec. 1980); m. Peter H. Davison, Aug. 11, 1984 (dec. 2004). BA, Cornell U., 1956; MArch, Harvard U., 1960. Prin. Goody, Clancy & Assocs., Inc., Boston. Asst. prof., design critic Harvard U., Cambridge, Mass., 1973-80, Eliot Noyes vis. critic, 1985; faculty Mayors Inst. for Design, 1989—; lectr. in field. Mem. Boston Landmarks Commn., 1976-87; chair Boston Civic Design Commn., 1994-2005; bd. dirs. Historic Boston. Fellow AIA (design awards 1980), Boston Soc. Architects (award of honor 2005), Boston Archtl. Ctr. (hon.), Saturday Club, Tavern Club. Office: Goody Clancy & Assocs Inc 334 Boylston St Boston MA 02116-3866

GOODY, RICHARD MEAD, geophysicist; b. Welwyn-Garden-City, Eng., June 19, 1921; came to U.S., 1958, naturalized, 1966; s. Harold Earnest and Lilian (Rankine) G.; m. Elfriede Koch, Sept. 11, 1946; 1 dau., Brigid. PhD, Cambridge U., 1949; MA (hon.), Harvard U., 1958. With Brit. Civil Service, 1942-46; fellow St. John's Coll., Cambridge, 1950-53; reader London U., 1953-58; prof. div. applied scis. Harvard U., 1958-91; dir. Blue Hill Obs., 1958-70, Center for Earth and Planetary Physics, 1970-71. Disting. vis. scientist Jet Propulsion Lab., 1977—. Author: Physics of the Stratosphere, 1947, Atmospheric Radiation, 1964, rev. edit., 1989, Atmospheres, 1974, The Principles of Atmospheric Physics and Chemistry, 1995. Fellow Am. Geophys. Union (William Bowie medal 1998), Am. Meteorol. Soc. (hon., 50th Anniversary medal 1970, Cleveland Abbé award 1977); mem. Royal Meteorol. Soc. (Buchan prize 1955), Nat. Acad. Scis., Am. Philos. Soc., Internat. Radiation Commn. (hon., Gold medal 2004). Home: 101 Cumloden Dr Falmouth MA 02540-1609 Business E-Mail: goody@huarp.harvard.edu.

GOOGASIAN, GEORGE ARA, lawyer; b. Pontiac, Mich., Feb. 22, 1936; s. Peter and Lucy (Chobanian) G.; m. Phyllis Elaine Law, June 27, 1959; children— Karen Ann, Steven George, Dean Michael BA, U. Mich., 1958; JD, Northwestern U., 1961. Bar: Mich. 1961. Assoc. Marentay, Rouse, Selby, Fischer & Webber, Detroit, 1961-62; asst. U.S. Atty. U.S. Dept. Justice, Detroit, 1962-64; assoc. Howlett, Hartman & Beier, Pontiac and Bloomfield Hills, Mich., 1964-81; ptnr. Googasian Hopkins Hohauser & Forhan, Bloomfield Hills, Mich., 1981-96, The Googasian Firm, Bloomfield Hills, 1996—. Mem. bd. law examiners State of Mich., 1997—2002, pres., 2001—02. Author: Trial Advocacy Manual, 1984, West Groups Michigan Practice Torts, vols. 14 and 15, 2001. Pres. Oakland Parks Found., Pontiac, 1984-89; chmn. Oakland County Dem. party, Pontiac, 1964-70; state campaign chmn. U.S. Senator Philip A. Hart, Detroit, 1970; bd. dirs. Big Bros. Oakland County. 1968-73 Fellow Am. Bar Found., Am. Coll. Trial Lawyers, Internat. Acad. Trial Lawyers; mem. ABA (del. 1992-93, exec. coun. nat. conf. bar pres. 1993-96), ATLA, Am. Bd. Trial Advocates, State Bar Mich. (pres. elect 1991-92, pres. 1992—), Internat. Soc. Barristers, Oakland County Bar Assn. (pres. 1985-86), Oakland Bar Found. (pres. 1990-92). Clubs: U. Mich. Club Greater Detroit. Presbyterian. Home: 3750 Orion Rd Oakland MI 48363-3029 Office: 6895 Telegraph Rd Bloomfield Hills MI 48301-3138 Office Phone: 248-540-3333.

GOOGINS, SONYA FORBES, state legislator, retired banker; b. New Haven, Nov. 9, 1936; d. Edward and Madeline Forbes; m. Robert Reville Googins, June 21, 1958; children: Shawn W. and Glen. R. BE, U. Conn., 1958. Tchr. Manchester (Conn.) High Sch., 1958-61; pres. Colonial Printing Co., Glastonbury, 1971-76; bank officer Conn. Nat. Bank, Hartford, 1982-89; mem. Conn. Ho. of Reps., 1994—. Mem. employment and tng. commn. Greater Hartford United Way, Conn., 1995; vice-chair commerce Nat. Conf. State Legislatures; mayor Town of Glastonbury, 1983—85, 1987—91, 1993—95; mem. Town Coun., 1979—94, Rep. Town Com., Capitol Region Coun. Govts., 1983—94, chmn., 1989—94; chair Conn. Adv. Commn. Intergovtl. Rels., 1992—; chair fin. svc. com. Nat. Conf. of State Legislators, 2002—; advocacy com. Am. Diabetes Assn.; bd. dirs. Conn. Capitol Region Growth Coun., 1994—96, Conn. Audubon Soc., 1997—99, Hartford Symphony Orch., 1997—. Recipient Outstanding Svc. award Friends of Glastonbury Youth, 1990, Disting. Svc. award Capitol Region Coun., 1994, Svc. award Women's Campaign School, 2004; named Glastonbury Rep. of Yr., 1992. Mem. Auto Assn. Am. Allied Group Inc. (bd. dirs. 1994—), Glastonbury Bus. and Profl. Women (past pres. and founder, Woman of Yr. 1988), Glastonbury C. of C. (bd. dirs. 1994—), Glastonbury Jr. Woman's Club (past pres.). Roman Catholic. Avocations: golf, tennis, sailing. Home: 74 Forest Ln Glastonbury CT 06033-3918 Personal E-mail: sonya.googins@cga.ct.gov.

GOOKIN, THOMAS ALLEN JAUDON, civil engineer; b. Tulsa, Aug. 5, 1951; s. William Scudder and Mildred (Hartman) G.; m. Sandra Jean Andrews, July 23, 1983. BS with distinction, Ariz. State U., 1975. Registered profl. engr., Calif., Ariz., Nev., land surveyor Ariz., hydrologist. Civil engr., treas. Gookin Engrs. Ltd, Scottsdale, Ariz., 1968—. Chmn. adv. com. Ariz. State Bd. Tech. Registration Engring., 1984—. Recipient Spl. Recognition award Ariz. State Bd. Tech. Registration Engring., 1990. Mem. NSPE, ASCE, Ariz. Soc. Profl. Engrs. (sec. Papago chpt. 1979-81, v.p. 1981-84, pres. 1984-85, named Young Engr. of Yr. 1979, Outstanding Engring. Project award 1988), Order Engr., Ariz. Congress on Surveying and Mapping, Ariz. Water Works Assn., Tau Beta Pi, Delta Chi (Tempe chpt. treas. 1970-71, sec. 1970, v.p. 1971), Phi Kappa Delta (pres. 1971-73). Republican. Episcopalian. Achievements include co-author Globe Equity # 59 Call System. Avocations: disneyana, science fiction, computer gaming. Home: 10760 E Becker Ln Scottsdale AZ 85259-3868 Office: Gookin Engrs Ltd 4203 N Brown Ave Ste A Scottsdale AZ 85251-3946 Office Phone: 480-947-3741.

GOOLD, DOUGLAS, think-tank executive; BA, McMaster U.; MA, U. Alta.; PhD in Modern History, Cambridge U. Investment editor, columnist The Globe and Mail newspaper, 1992—97, editor Report on Bus. sect., 1997—2000; editor Report on Bus. Mag., 2000—04; pres., CEO Can. Inst. Internat. Affairs, Toronto, Canada, 2004—. Author (with Andrew Willis): The Bre-X Fraud; author: Peace Without Promise. Killam Postdoctoral fellow, U. B.C. Office: Can Inst Internat Affairs Ste 302 205 Richmond St West Toronto ON Canada M5V 1V3

GOOLDY, PATRICIA ALICE, retired elementary school educator; b. Indpls., Nov. 23, 1937; d. Harold Emanuel and Emma Irene (Wade) VanTreese; m. Walter Raymond Gooldy, May 4, 1968. BS, U. Indpls., 1959; MS, Butler U., 1963. Tchr. Franklin Twp. Cmty. Schs., Indpls., 1959-68, 72-99, USA Dep. Schs., Bad Kreuznach, Germany, 1969-72; ret., 1999. Owner Ye Olde Genealogie Shoppe, Indpls., 1972—; lectr. in field. Author: 21 Things I Wish I'd Found, 1984; editor: Indiana Wills to 1880: Index to Indiana Wills, 1987; co-editor: Indiana Manual For Gen, 1991, Illinois Manual For Gen, 1994. Named Ky. Col., 1995; named one of Outstanding Elem. Tchrs. of Am., 1974. Mem. Franklin Twp. Hist. Soc. (founder), Ind. Geneal. Soc. (chartered). Office: Ye Olde Genealogie Shoppe PO Box 39128 Indianapolis IN 46239-0128 Office Phone: 317-862-3330, 800-419-0200. Personal E-mail: yogs@iquest.net.

GOOLKASIAN, PAULA A., psychologist, educator; b. Methuen, Mass., Aug. 9, 1948; d. Paul K. and Sadie T. (Touma) G.; m. Francis C. Martin, July 29, 1978; 1 child, Christopher. BA, Emmanuel Coll., 1970; MS, Iowa State U., 1972, PhD, 1974. Asst. prof. U. N.C., Charlotte, 1974-79, assoc. prof., 1979-85, prof. psychology, 1985—, pres. faculty, 1989—. Cons. in field. Exec. editor: Jour. Gen. Psychology. NDEA fellow, 1971-74; grantee NSF, NIH, numerous others. Fellow APA; mem. Am. Psychol. Soc., Psychonomics Soc., Soc. for Computers in Psychology (sec.-treas. 1989-91, pres. 1994), Sigma Xi, Phi Kappa Phi. Office: U NC Dept Psychology 9201 University City Blvd Charlotte NC 28223 Office Phone: 704-687-4749. Business E-Mail: pagoolka@uncc.edu.

GOOLKASIAN RAHBEE, DIANNE, musician, composer, music educator; b. Somerville, Mass., Feb. 9, 1938; d. Peter Aharon Goolkasian and Isabelle Yeshilian; m. Alfred Rahbee, Apr. 28, 1973; children: David, Adam. Degree, Julliard Sch. Music, 1960, Mozarteum, Salzburg, Austria, 1966. Piano tchr. pvt. practice; lectr. various internat. workshops and concerts. Musician: Carnegie Hall, Weill, various locations; composer: (albums) Seda 333, 1994, Concertino No. 1 Op.82, Preludes and Toccatinas, Three Preludes Op.68, Celebration, MMC 2009, 1994. Pres. Am. Women Composer. Mem.: European Piano Tchr. Assn., New England Piano Tchr. Assn. Home: 45 Common St Belmont MA 02478-3022 Office: SEDA Productions 45 Common St Belmont MA 02478-3022 Personal E-mail: grdianne@aol.com.

GOOLRICK, JOHN COLE, congressional staff member, writer, consultant; b. Fredericksburg, Va., July 7, 1935; s. John Tackett and Olive Elizabeth (Jones) G.; m. Alice Solone Rock, Mar. 26, 1960 (div. June 1992); 1 child, Lisa Cole. Student, U. Richmond, 1953-58. Polit. reporter, columnist Star, Fredericksburg, 1957-87; dist. rep. U.S. Congressman French Slaughter, Washington, 1987-91, U.S. Congressman George Allen, Washington, 1991-92, U.S. Congressman Herbert Bateman, Washington, 1993-2000, U.S. Congressman Jo Ann Davis, Washington, 2001—. Polit. columnist Va. newspapers. Mem. Va. Bd. Hist. Resources, Va. Bd. Mil. Affairs, Richmond, Mil. Adv. Coun., Richmond, Va. Charitable Gaming Bd. Mem. Nat. Assn. Uniformed Svcs., Va. Capital Corr. Assn. (co-founder), Elks, Pythians, Eagles, Am. Legion, Gen. Meade Soc. Phila., Three Stooges Fan Club. Republican. Avocations: history, travel. Home: Box 8283 Fredericksburg VA 22404 Office: 4500 Plank Rd Fredericksburg VA 22407 E-mail: JohnCGoolrick@aol.com.

GOOLSBY, ALLEN CUNNINGHAM, III, lawyer; b. Richmond, Va., Oct. 19, 1939; s. Allen C. Goolsby Jr. and Adelaide Rawles; m. Louanna Godwin. BA, Yale U., 1961; LLB, U. Va., 1968. Bar: Va., U.S. Dist. Ct. (ea. dist.) Va. Ptnr. Hunton & Williams, Richmond, Va., 1975—. Bd. dirs. Noland Co. Author: Virginia Corporation Law Practice, 1990, Goolsby on Virginia Corporations, 2002. Fellow Am. Bar Found., Va. Bar Found. Office: Hunton & Williams Riverfront Plz East Tower PO Box 1535 Richmond VA 23218-1535

GOOLSBY, MICHELLE, lawyer, food products executive; b. 1958; BBA, JD, U. Tex. Various positions Trammel Crow Co., Winstead Sechrest & Minick, 1988-98; ptnr., chair bus. sect., mem. compensation com.; exec. v.p., gen. counsel, chief adminstrv. officer, sec. Dean Foods Co. (formerly Suiza Foods Corp.), Dallas, 1998—. Mem. ABA. Office: 2515 Mckinney Ave Ste 1200 Dallas TX 75201-1945

GOOLSBY, O. B., JR., food products executive; Former exec. v.p. prepared food ops. Pilgrim's Pride Corp., Pittsburg, Tex., pres., COO, 2002—. Office: Pilgrims Pride Corp 110 S Texas St Pittsburg TX 75686-0093

GOONATILAKE, ROHITHA, mathematician, educator; s. Don Charles and Leedha Waidyaratne Gunathilake; m. Chandrika Gunadasa, Feb. 11, 1956; 1 child, Ruchi(tha). BSc in Math., U. Peradeniya, Sri Lanka, 1979, Postgrad. Diploma in Math., 1981, MSc in Math., 1982; MA in Applied Math., Kent State U., 1993, PhD in Applied Math., 1999; MA in Actuarial Sci., Ball State U., 1999. Asst. prof. of math. Tex. A&M Internat. U., Laredo, 2000—03, assoc. prof. of math., 2003—. Mem.: Inst. Math. Stats., Math. Assn. Am., Am. Math. Soc. Office: Texas A&M Internat Univ 5201 University Blvd Laredo TX 78041-1900 Office Phone: 956-326-2588. Home Fax: 956-326-2439; Office Fax: 956-326-2439. Business E-Mail: harag@tamiu.edu.

GOORLEY, JOHN THEODORE, consulting chemist; b. Mar. 12, 1907; s. William H. and Emma (Ness) G.; m. Ethel L. Coleman, Nov. 27, 1935; children: John. ALice (Mrs. Harold A. Bread, Jr.), Robert, Richard. BS in Pharmacy, Ohio State U., 1930; MS in Pharm. Chemistry, Purdue U., 1932, PhD in Pharm. Chemistry, 1934. Chief control chemist Burroughs Wellcome & Co., Tuckahoe, NY, 1933-38; rsch. dir. Labs. Lex, Havana, Cuba, 1939-42, Ben Venue Labs., Bedford, Ohio, 1946-48, Johnson & Johnson de Argentina, Buenos Aires, 1948-50; owner, dir. Labs. Goorley, Buenos Aires, 1950-55; prof. pharm. chemistry Ohio No. U., Ada, 1956-57; v.p., gen. mgr. Inland Alkaloid Co., Tipton, Ind., 1957-58; prof. pharm. chemistry N.E. La. U., Monroe, 1957-68, prof. pharmacognosy, 1968-72; chemist Labs. Finlay, S.A., San Pedro Sula, Honduras, 1974-76; prof. chemistry and pharmacy U. Nacional Autonoma de Honduras, Tegucigalpa, 1976; Fulbright prof. U. Honduras, 1966-67; cons. chemist, 1967—; exec. v.p. Enviro-Med. Labs., Ruston, La., 1978-82. Vis. prof. U. El Salvador, 1968. Active Little Theater, Monroe; rsch. in pharm. chemistry and biochemistry; contbr. articles to profl. jours.; patentee in field. Chief staff govts. Ky., La. Served to capt. AUS, 1942-46; lt. col. AUS, 1956-63. Mem. AAAS, Am. Pharm. Assn., Am. Chem. Soc., NY Acad. Scis., Sigma Xi, Rho Chi, Phi Delta Chi, Tau Kappa Epsilon. Achievements include being the first to isolate the antibiotic Bacitracin in pure form. Home: 7110 University Dr Ste 117 Shreveport LA 71105

GOORLEY, JOHN TIMOTHY, nuclear engineer; b. Ft. Campbell, Ky., Apr. 13, 1974; s. John Thomas and Sherrie Goorley. BS in nuc. engring., Tex. A&M U., 1992—96; BS in radiol. health engring., Tex.A&M U., 1992—96; MS in nuc. engring., PhD in nuc. engring., MIT, 1996—2002. Technical staff Los Alamos Nat. Lab., N.Mex., 2002—. Scholar President's Endowed scholarship, Tex. A&M U., 1992—96. Mem.: Am. Nuc. Soc., Sigma Xi, Alpha Nu Sigma. Avocations: medieval studies, travel, fencing. Home: 601 West San Mateo #80 Santa Fe NM 87505 Personal E-mail: jgoorley@alum.mit.edu.

GOOS, ROGER DELMON, retired mycologist; b. Beaman, Iowa, Oct. 29, 1924; s. Gus and Georgiana Bertha (Witt) G.; m. Mary Lee Engel, Sept. 21, 1946; children: Marinda Lee, Suzanne Maurine. BA, U. Iowa, 1950, PhD, 1958. Mycologist United Fruit Co., Norwood, Mass., 1958-62; scientist USPHS, NIH, Bethesda, Md., 1962-64; curator of fungi Am. Type Culture Collection, Rockville, Md., 1964-68; assoc. researcher, vis. assoc. prof. botany U. Hawaii, Honolulu, 1968-70; assoc. prof. botany U. R.I., Kingston, 1970-72, chair dept. of botany, 1971-86, prof. botany, 1972-95, prof. emeritus, 1995—. Trustee Am. Type Culture Collection, Rockville, Md., 1977-82; vis. rschr. U. B.C., 1977, U. Hawaii, 1977, U. Exeter, U.K., 1984, Bishop Mus., 1990. Served with U.S. Army, 1944-46, 50-51. Decorated Bronze Star, Purple Heart, Combat Infantry badge; Indo-Am. fellow, U. Madras, India, 1981; Fulbright scholar U. Lisbon, 1993. Mem. Mycol. Soc. Am. (sec.-treas. 1980-83, v.p. 1983-84, pres.-elect 1984-85, pres. 1985-86), Bot. Soc. Am., Am. Soc. Microbiology, Am. Phytopath. Soc., Mycol. Soc. Japan, Brit. Mycol. Soc. Home: 4 Tanglewood Trl Narragansett RI 02882-1034 Business E-Mail: rgoos@uri.edu.

GOOSEN, RETIEF, professional golfer; b. Pietersburg, S. Africa, Feb. 3, 1969; m. Tracy Goosen; children: Leo, Ella. Profl. golfer PGA European Tour, PGA Tour. Mem. Pres. Cup Team, 2000, 03, World Cup Team, 1993, 95, 2000, 01, Dunhill Cup Team, 1995—2000. Achievements include winner US Open, PGA Tour, 2001, 04; 4 career PGA Tour victories incouding US Open; 12 PGA European Tour victories. Office: McCormack Ho Hooper Bus Pk Burlington Ln London W4 2TH England Office Phone: +44 208 233 5300.

GOOSSEN, DWIGHT PAUL, music educator; b. Warsaw, Ind., Oct. 14, 1953; s. Paul Franz and Hildegard Marie Goossen; m. Ruth Ann Nichols, June 15, 1974; children: Glen Isaac, Paul Allan, Luke Aaron. B in sacred music, Grace U., 1971—76; M in music edn., U. Nebr.-Lincoln, 1977—80. Band dir. Mead Pub. Schools, Mead, Nebr., 1978—80, Berean Acad., Elbing, Kans., 1980—84, Sutton Pub. Schools, Nebr., 1989—92, Emmanuel Bapt. Sch., Toledo, 1992—93, Springfield Local Schools, 1994—96, Pike-Delta York Local Schools, Delta, Ohio, 1996—. Dir. Delta Cmty. Band, 2002—. Mem.: Ohio Edn. Assn., Music Educators Nat. Conf., Phi Delta Kappa. Republican. Christian Missionary And Alliance. Avocations: woodworking, model cars. Home: 4508 Talmadge Green Rd Toledo OH 43623 Personal E-mail: goossen@buckeye-express.com.

GOOTNICK, MARGERY FISCHBEIN, lawyer; b. Rochester, N.Y., Oct. 24, 1927; d. Morris R. and Regina (Kroll) Fischbein; m. Lester T. Gootnick, Mar. 1, 1952; children— Jonathon, David, Amy. B.A., Harvard U., 1949; J.D., Cornell U., 1952. Bar: N.Y. 1952. Assoc. Stone & Hoffenberg, Rochester, N.Y., 1952-55; sole practice, Rochester, 1968—; permanent arbitrator Am. Airlines and Assn. Profl. Flight Attendants, NW Airlines and Teamsters Local 2000, Presbyn. Hosp.-N.Y. State Nurses Assn., U. Rochester and U. Rochester Security Guards Union, numerous others; chmn. Fgn. Service Impasse Disputes Panel, Washington, 1983-97; apptd. fgn. svc. grievance bd. U.S. State Dept., 1997; mem. exec. com. N.Y. State Bar, 1998. Mem. Rep. Jud. Screening Com., Rochester, 1976—. Mem. ABA, Fed. Bar Assn., Nat. Acad. Arbitrators (v.p. 1992-94, chair membership com. 1988-91, exec. com. 1987, bd. govs. 1983-86), N.Y. State Bar Assn. (labor and employment sect. chair elect 1994—, exec. com. 1982—), Soc. Fed. Labor Rels. Profls. (1st v.p. 1993—), Am. Arbitration Assn. (upstate N.Y. labor adv. panel). Office e-mail: mornings@ix.netcom.com. Home and Office: 46 Knollwood Dr Rochester NY 14618-3513 E-mail: mgootnich@ix.netcom.com.

GOOTT, ALAN F(RANKLIN), lawyer; b. Washington, Aug. 6, 1947; BA, George Washington U., 1969; JD cum laude, Harvard U., 1973. Bar: N.Y., 1974, U.S. Dist. Ct. (so., ea. dists.) N.Y. 1974, U.S. Ct. Appeals (2d cir) 1974. Assoc. Kaye Scholer LLP, N.Y.C., 1973-82, ptnr., 1982—. Office: Kaye Scholer LLP 425 Park Ave New York NY 10022-3598 Office Phone: 212-836-8157. Business E-Mail: agoott@kayescholer.com.

GOOTT, DANIEL, government official, consultant; b. N.Y.C., Apr. 23, 1919; s. Hyman and Min (Novak) G.; m. Sylvia Blousman, Aug. 29, 1940; children: Alan F., Eugene M. BSS, CCNY, 1940; postgrad., Columbia U., 1940-41; diploma, Grad. Sch. Internat. Studies, Geneva, 1946. Assoc. chief labor rels. br. War Prodn. Bd., 1942-43; spl. asst. internat. labor affairs to under sec. state US Dept. State, Washington, 1955—60; dep. coord. internat. labor affairs Office Sec. State, Washington, 1961-62; 1st sec., labor attache Am. Embassy, Paris, 1962-65; chief spl. profl. affairs Office Dep. Undersec. of State for Adminstrn., Washington, 1965—. Labor and UN advisor Bur. European Affairs; mem. U.S. del. 7th spl. and 30th regular sessions UN Gen. Assembly, 1975; mem. U.S. delegations to ann. confs. of UN Spl. Agy., ILO, Geneva, 1955-60; pvt. cons. internat. labor and bus. affairs, 1980. With AUS, 1943-46. Decorated Bronze Star. Mem. Am. Econ. Assn., Indsl. Rels. Rsch. Assn., Am. Fgn. Svc. Assn., Am. Acad. Polit. and Social Sci., Am. Club. Home: 15101 Interlachen Dr Apt 917 Silver Spring MD 20906-5620

GOPALAKRISHNAN, CHENNAT, economics professor; b. Ernakulam, India, Oct. 9, 1936; came to U.S., 1963; d. Palliyil Narayana Menon and Chennat (Sarada) Amma; m. Malini Varma Gopalakrishnan, Sept. 15, 1962; 1 child, Shalini. BA, Kerala U., 1955, MA, 1957; PhD, Mont. State U., 1967. Asst. prof. of nat. resource econ. Mont. State U., Bozeman, 1967-69; assoc. prof. U. Hawaii, Honolulu, 1969-74; visiting prof. U. So. Calif., Los Angeles, 1976-77, U. Wyo., Laramie, 1982-83; prof. U. Hawaii, 1974—. Reviewer NSF, Washington, 1981; cons. Argonne (Ill.) Nat. Lab., 1986—, Gas Rsch. Inst., Chgo., 1983-84. Author: Natural Resource and Energy: Theory and Policy, 1980; editor: The Emerging Marine Economy of the Pacific, 1984; contbr. over 50 articles to profl. jours. Named Outstanding Researcher

Gamma Sigma Delta, 1980; recipient Outstanding Service award Marine Tech. Soc., 1981; Law Inst. for Economists national fellow, 1986, Summer Inst. for Univ. Faculty national fellow, 1988, Carnegie Coun. Faculty Inst. on Ethics fellow, 1990. Mem. Internat. Assn. Energy Econs., Am. Agrl. Econs. Assn. (assoc., governing bd. 1988—, com. on econ. edn. 1988-89), Western Agrl. Econs. Assn. (coun. 1990-92), Am. Water Resources Assn., Western Regional Sci. Assn., Internat. Agrl. Econs. Assn., Gamma Sigma Delta (Internat. award for disting. svc. 1989). Avocations: reading, hiking, movie and theater patron. Home: 2916 Date St Apt 10C Honolulu HI 96816-1186 Office: U Hawaii Dept Agrl and Resource Econ 3050 Maile Way # 115 Honolulu HI 96822-2231

GOPALAKRISHNAN, J, mathematician; b. Calicut, India; PhD, Tex. A&M U., 1995—99. Asst. prof. U. of Fla., Gainesville, Fla., 2001—. Mem.: SIAM. Office: U Fla 358 Little Hall Gainesville FL 32611-8105

GOPHEN, MOSHE, research scientist; b. Kibbutz Afikim, Israel, Dec. 18, 1936; s. Itzchak and Sara (Sheinberger) G.; m. Eva Gophen, May 5, 1998; children from previous marriage: Michal, Yair, Ruth, Rachel. BSc, Hebrew U., Jerusalem, 1963, MSc, 1967, PhD, 1976. H.S. tchr., Beit-Yerach, Israel, 1963-69; sr. scientist Kinneret Limnological Lab., Tiberias, Israel, 1968—; lectr. Hebrew U., 1972-73, Haifa U., Oranim, Israel, 1973-78; sr. scientist Kinneret Limnological Lab., Tiberias, Israel, 1968—2001, dir., 1980-86; rsch. prof. U. Okla., Norman, 1992-94; ret., 2001. Sci. coord. Hula (Israel) Project, 1995—, chmn. Hula com., 1997--; sr. coord. Hula Project MIGAL Galilee Tech. Ctr., 2001--; prof. Tel-Hai (Israel) Coll., 1995—; cons. Ilopango Assn., San-Salvador, El-Salvador, 1995—, Lake Amatitlan Assn., Guatemala City, Guatamela, 1995-96. Author: Lake Kinneret, 1992 (Kinneret Authority award 1989); co-author: Scientific Basis for Water Resurces Management, 1985, Large Lakes-Ecological Structure and Function, 1990 (Minerva award 1990), Guidelines of Lake Management, 1995 (Kinneret Lab. award 1995); contbr. articles to profl. jours. Edn. com. Karmiel mcplty., 1979; chmn. Ctrl. Com. for Labor Party, Karmiel, 1987-88; vol. Ecological Com., Karmiel, 1995—. Sgt. Israel mil., 1955-58. Eshkol Found. Water Rsch. fellow Israel Kinneret Inst., 1973, DAAD fellow, Germany, 1982, Minerva fellow, Germany, 1987-88. Mem. Internat. Assn. Limnology, Am. Soc. Limnology and Oceanography, Freshwater Biol. Assn. (life). Avocations: classical music, art, astronomy and universe sciences, nature. Home: Hativat Iftach St 73/1 20100 Karmiel Israel Office: MIGAL POB 90000 12100 Rosh-Pina Israel

GOPIKRISHNAN, PARAMESWARAN, investment company executive; s. R. Parameswaran Nair and M. Indira Devi; married. PhD, Boston U., 2001. Rsch. asst. Boston U., 1994—2001; v.p. Goldman Sachs & Co., N.Y.C., 2001—. Contbr. articles to profl. jours. STATPHYS 20 Conf. scholar, NSF, 1998. Achievements include discovery of first to report the inverse cubic power-law distribution of stock return distribution. Personal E-mail: gopi@bu.edu.

GOPINATH, GITA, economics professor; PhD, Princeton U., 2001. Asst. prof. econs. U. Chgo., 2001—, Harvard U., Cambridge, Mass., 2005—. Office Phone: 617-495-8161.

GOPLERUD, C. PETER, III, dean, law educator; m. Mariette Brodeur; children: Zoe, Ava. BA in English, JD, U. Kan. Law clk. to Justice David Prager, Supreme Ct., Kans.; prof. U. Akron Sch. Law, So. Ill. U. Sch. Law, dean, assoc. dean; prof., dean U. Okla. Coll. Law; dean Drake Law Sch., Des Moines, 1997—2003, prof. law, 1997—2004; dean, prof. law Fla. Coastal Sch. Law, 2004—. Vis. prof. U. Auvergne, Clermont-Ferrand, France, U. Nantes, France, St. Louis U. Sch. Law. Mem.: Sports Lawyers Assn. (bd. mem.). Office: Fla Coastal Sch Law 7555 Beach Blvd Jacksonville FL 32216-3000 Office Phone: 904-680-7707. Business E-Mail: pgoplerud@fcsl.edu.

GOPNIK, BLAKE, art critic; Chief art critic Washington Post, Washington, 2003—; art critic ArtWatch with Blake Gopnik, Washington Post. Office: Washington Post 1150 15th St NW Washington DC 20071 Office Phone: 202-334-6000.*

GOPPELT, JOHN WALTER, physician, psychiatrist; b. Saginaw, Mich., Jan. 20, 1924; s. Paul Gustave and Marion LeRoy (Payne) G.; m. Martha Keller Rowland, Mar. 31, 1956; 1 child, Edmund H. S.B., MIT, 1949; MD, U. Pa., 1955. Diplomate Am. Bd. Psychiatry and Neurology. Intern Bryn Mawr Hosp., Pa., 1955—56; resident in psychiatry Inst. of Pa. Hosp., Phila., 1956-59; practice medicine, specializing in psychiatry Haverford, Pa., 1959—. Contbr. articles to profl. jours. Chmn. Drug and Alcohol Coun. Del. County, Media, Pa., 1979—83; committeeman Rep. Party, Haverford Twp., Pa., 1980. With U.S. Army, 1943—46. Recipient Legion of Honor award Chapel of Four Chaplains. Mem. AMA, Am. Psychiat. Assn., N.Y. Acad. Scis., Math. Assn. Am., Sigma Xi. Avocation: mathematics. Address: 369 Exeter Rd Haverford PA 19041-1084 Office Phone: 610-649-2047. Personal E-mail: mgoppelt@yahoo.com.

GORA, JOANN M., academic administrator; BA, Vassar Coll.; M in Sociology, D in Sociology, Rutgers U. Dean Coll. Arts and Scis., sr. dean Madison campus Fairleigh Dickinson U., 1985—92; provost, v.p. for acad. affairs, prof. sociology Old Dominion U., Norfolk, Va., 1992-01; chancellor U. Mass., Boston, 2001—04; pres. Ball State U., Muncie, Ind., 2004—. Author: The New Female Criminal: Empirical Reality or Social Myth?; co-author: Emergency Squad Volunteers: Professionalism in Unpaid Work; contbr. numerous articles to profl. jours. Office: Ball State U Office Pres AD Bldg 101 Muncie IN 47306 Office Phone: 765-285-5555. Business E-Mail: president@bsu.edu.

GORA, SUSANNAH PORTER MARTIN, journalist, poet; b. NYC, Sept. 4, 1977; d. Joel Mark and Ann Ray Martin Gora. BA in English cum laude with high distinction, Duke U., 1999. Intern NY1 News, NYC, 1994, CBS News, NYC, 1996, Brillstein-Grey Entertainment, Beverly Hills, Calif., 1998; prodn. asst. ABC TV, NYC, 1999—2000; asst. to the editor Premiere Mag., NYC, 2000—01, assoc. editor, 2001—04; entertainment journalist publs. including Elle, Variety and Woman's Day, 2004—; host, writer Classics on Film, 2005—. Contbr. of entertainment coverage AP Radio, NYC, 2002—. Author: (poetry) Where Home Is, numerous poems. The E. Blake Byrne scholarship for creative writing, Duke U., 1997. Mem.: NY Women in Comm., Inc., Phi Eta Sigma, Kappa Kappa Gamma (life; dir. of pub. rels. 1998—99). Personal E-mail: susannahgora1@aol.com.

GORALSKI, DONALD JOHN, public relations executive, counselor; b. Buffalo, Apr. 21, 1957; s. John Bernard and Irene (Kazmierczak) G. BA, Canisius Coll., 1980. Cmty. svc. rep. western N.Y. chpt. March of Dimes Birth Defects Found., Buffalo, 1981-82, pub. rels. dir. western N.Y. chpt., 1982-83, pub. rels. dir. no. Jersey chpt. Fairfield, N.J., 1983-84; pub. rels. dir. Ellis Singer, Greve, St. Paul, Minn., 1984-87, Buffalo, 1984-87; sr. pub. rels. officer Multidisciplinary Ctr. for Earthquake Engring. Rsch., Buffalo, 1987—. Guest lectr. U. Buffalo, Buffalo State Coll., Medaille Coll., 1984-88, 95, Canisius Coll., 1990, 95, 97, 99, 2000, 01, 05. Mem. spl. events com. Am. Cancer Soc., Western N.Y. chpt., 1985—86; mem. mktg. subcom. St. Mary's Sch. for the Deaf, 1987; mentor Pub. Rels. Student Soc. of Am., Buffalo, 1989—91; mem. Allied Comm. Talent for Literacy, Buffalo, 1990—91; mem. meeting and event planners coun. Univ. at Buffalo, 1992; mem. comm. com. World Assn. Vet. Athletes 1995 Games, 1994—95; mem. Ad Coun. Western N.Y., 1995; mem. comm. com. Buffalo Alliance for Edn., 1993; mem. Mayor's Adv. Com. for a City Vision, Buffalo, 1994—95; trustee Turner/Carroll H.S., 1996—97; mem. Dr. Marilyn G.S. Watt scholarship com. Canisius Coll., 1997—, mem. May C. Randazzo Meml. scholarship com., 1997—; liaison State Employees Federated Appeal/United Way, 1998—; mem. comm. com. ARC Greater Buffalo chpt., 2000—. Mem. Pub. Rels. Soc. Am. (bd. dirs. Buffalo-Niagara chpt. 1987-91, pres.-elect 1992, pres. 1993, past pres. 1994-95, accredited, 1995, assembly del. 1997-2001, N.E. dist. sec./treas. 1999, N.E. dist. chair elect 2000, N.E. dist. chair 2001, N.E. dist. immediate past chair 2002, nat. nominating com. 2001, Cert. Recognition 1993, Nat. Chpt. Banner award Buffalo/Niagara chpt. 1993), Pub. Rels. Assn. Western N.Y. (treas. 1986-87, v.p. 1987-88, pres. 1989), Western N.Y. Pub. Rels. and Comm. (exec. steering com. 1987-90, 92-94, chmn. 1994). Avocations: golf, football, reading, current events, on-line computer networks/services. Office: Multidisciplinary Ctr Quake Engring Rsch U Buffalo Red Jacket Quad Buffalo NY 14261 Home: 50 Kemp Ave Cheektowaga NY 14225-4535 E-mail: goralski@buffalo.edu.

GORAN, MARK H., lawyer; BA, Washington U., St. Louis, 1971, JD, 1974; MS, U. Wis., 1973. Bar: Mo. 1975. Ptnr., group leader Health Care Bryan Cave LLP, St. Louis. Office: Bryan Cave LLP One Metropolitan Square 211 N Broadway, Ste 3600 Saint Louis MO 63102 Office Phone: 314-259-2686. E-mail: mhgoran@bryancave.com.

GORAY, GERALD ALLEN, real estate company executive, lawyer; b. Detroit, Aug. 22, 1939; s. James A. and Lucille (Rankin) G.; m. Donna Marie Belian, Apr. 26, 1958; children: Brian M., Gregory D. BBA magna cum laude, U. Detroit, 1963; JD, U. Mich., 1965. Bar: Mich. Atty. Parsons, Tennant et al, Birmingham, Mich., 1966-70, U.S. Dept. of Housing, Detroit, 1970-71, Rodgers & Goray, Southfield, Mich., 1971-75; pres. Goray Devel. Co., Boca Raton, Fla., 1975—. Pres. Stonemark Devel. Co., Boca Raton, 1988—. Vice-chmn. Lathrup Village (Mich.) Zoning Bd. Appeals, 1981. Mem. Village Athletic Club (pres. 1975-76). Office: Goray Devel Co 621 NW 53rd St Ste 255 Boca Raton FL 33487-8281

GORBATY, MARTIN LEO, chemist, researcher; b. Bklyn., Nov. 17, 1942; s. Julius and Florence (Birnbach) G.; m. Dianne Morse, June 30, 1968; children: Howard M., Matthew J., Lisa R. BS in Chemistry with honors, CCNY, 1964; PhD in Organic Chemistry, Purdue U., 1969. Rsch. chemist Esso Agrl. Products Lab. Esso Rsch. and Engring. Co., Linden, NJ, 1969-70; sr. rsch. chemist Corp. Rsch. Lab., Exxon Rsch. and Engring. Co., Linden, 1970-73, sr. rsch. chemist Baytown (Tex.) R & D divsn., 1973-75, group head Corp. Rsch. Labs. Linden, 1975-78, lab. dir. corp. rsch., 1978-84; disting. rsch. assoc. Corp. Rsch.-Resource Chemistry Lab., ExxonMobil Rsch. and Engring. Co., Annandale, NJ, 1984—. Mem. internat. editorial bd. Fuel, 1983—; chmn. Gordon Conf. Fuel Sci., 1988. Editor 5 books on synthetic crudes and coal sci.; contbr. some 70 articles to profl. jours.; holder more than 50 patents. Recipient R.A. Glenn award Bituminous Coal Rsch., Inc., 1990, Disting. Alumnus award Sch. of Sci. Purdue U., 1993, Disting. Svc. award, Petroleum Chemistry, 2003. Mem. AAAS, Am. Chem. Soc. (chmn. divsn. petroleum chemistry 1983-84, program com. 1978—, councilor 1988-99, 2001—, divsn. fuel chemistry, adv. bd. ACS books 1984-87, editl. bd. Chemtech 1986-99, Henry H. Storch award 1993), N.Y. Acad. Scis., Soc. Sigma Xi, Phi Lambda Upsilon. Achievements include patents in field of of coal and petroleum processing. Office: ExxonMobil Rsch & Engring Co 1545 Route 22 East Annandale NJ 08801-0998 Office Phone: 908-730-3012.

GORBELL, MICHAEL RANDALL, management consultant, director; b. L.A., Oct. 23, 1953; s. Frederick John and Elsie Klemm; m. Deborah Kay Rasberry, Oct. 15, 1988. BS, U. So. Calif., 1974, MS, 1980; postgrad., Oxford (Eng.) U., 1998. CIA support officer, San Salvador, El Salvador, Cairo, Beirut, 1982-88; chmn. AEEA London, 1991-93; dir. fin. and adminstrn. Ogden Allied Facility Mgmt., Inc., N.Y.C., 1988-89; dir. travel and relocation svcs. CIA, Washington, 1989-91, chief adminstrv. officer external, 1994-99; CFO Calif. Space Authority Inc., Santa Maria, 2000—03; dir. client svcs. Your People Profls., 2003—; v.p. fin. and adminstrn. Space Island Group, Inc., Santa Maria, 2003—. Bus. mgmt. cons., 1988—. Capt. USMC, 1974-82. Mem. Nat. Eagle Scout Assn., Spl. Forces Club. Avocations: travel, aviation, auto racing. Office Phone: 805-878-2845. E-mail: gorbell@msn.com.

GORBERG, DAVID J., lawyer; BL, U. Wis., 1985; JD, Southwestern Sch. Law, 1988. Bar: Pa. Mng. atty. David J. Gorberg and Assoc., PC, Phila. Mem.: Phila. Bar Assn., Phila. Trial Lawyers Assn., Pa. Trial Lawyers Assn. Achievements include design of a website which was named as one of the Best Legal Websites in the nation by Law Office Computing Magazine in 2003. Office: David J Gorberg and Assoc PC 1234 Market St Ste 2040 Philadelphia PA 19107 Office Phone: 215-563-7210. E-mail: david@myleman.com.

GORBIEN, MARTIN JOHN, medical educator, geriatrician; b. Chgo., Dec. 24, 1955; MD, Autonomous U., Guadalajara, Mexico, 1983. Cert. internal medicine 1996, geriatric medicine 1998. Intern to resident, geriatric medicine Mercy Hosp. and Med. Ctr., Chgo., 1984—87; fellowship, geriatric medicine UCLA, 1987—89; asst. prof. medicine U. Chgo. Pritzer Sch. Medicine, Chgo., 1994—98; assoc. prof., dir. Rush Med. Coll., St. Lukes Med. Ctr., Geriatric Dept., Chgo., 1998—. Office: Rush U Med Ctr 1725 W Harrison St Ste 955 Chicago IL 60612 Office Phone: 312-942-3362. Business E-Mail: mgorbien@rush.edu.

GORBOLD, ROBERT REESE, lawyer; b. St. Charles, Ill., May 30, 1952; s. Robert S. and Janis (Bevan) G.; m. Dianne Carol Block, Aug. 18, 1973; children: Stephanie Ann, Robert Clifford, Scott Thomas. BA, Wheaton (Ill.) Coll., 1974; JD with distinction, John Marshall Law Sch., Chgo., 1979. Bar: Ill. 1979, U.S. Dist. Ct. (no. dist.) Ill., 1979. Assoc. Wennlund, Condon & Bruggeman, New Lenox, Ill., 1979-80, Thomas, Wallace, Feehan, Baron & Kaplan, Joliet, Ill., 1980-87, Rooks, Pitts & Poust, Joliet, Ill., 1987-91, ptnr., 1991—. Treas. Christian Layman's Assn. of Will County, Joliet, 1988-89, pres., 1989-92. Mem. Ill. Bar Assn. Avocations: racquetball, skiing, golf. Office: Rooks Pitts & Poust 111 N Ottawa St Joliet IL 60432-4222

GORBY-SCHMIDT, MARTHA LOUISE, pharmacologist, researcher; d. Charles and Louise Gorby. BS in Nursing, Villanova U., 1983. RN Pa., 1983; cert. paralegal. Clin. rsch. asst. Scirex, Blue Bell, Pa., 1996—97; mgr. data quality compliance Aventis Pharma/Rhone Poulenc Rorer, Bridgewater, NJ, 1998—2001; mgr. clin. data rev. Premier Rsch. Worldwide, Phila., 1997—98; assoc. dir. Yamanouchi Pharma Am., Paramus, NJ, 2001—04; global project data mgr. Merck Rsch. Labs., Blue Bell, 2004—. Meddra blue ribbon panel Northrup Grumman, Alexandria, Va., 2003; spkr. in field. Editor: Pen and Ink Mag. (Svc. Award, 1979). Office vol. adminstr. Ch. Good Samaritan, Paoli, Pa., 1990—94, 12 step group facilitator, 1990—94, music dir. sch. com., advt. chmn., 1990—94. Mem.: NAFE, Am. Assn. Critical Care Nurses, ANA, N.Y. Acad. Scis., Oncology Nurse Soc., Am. Chem. Soc., Am. Heart Assn., Assn. Clin. Rsch. Profls., Soc. Clin. Data Mgmt., Regulatory Affairs Profl. Soc., Am. Soc. Clin. Oncology (assoc.), Drug Info. Assn. (assoc.; spl. interest action com. 2003—). Episcopalian. Achievements include research in oncology-early to late stage development. Avocations: music, travel, reading, comedy, hiking. Home: 660 Hampshire Dr Sellersville PA 18960 Office: Merck Rsch Labs 785 Jolly Rd UNC-221 Blue Bell PA 19422 Office Phone: 484-344-2148. Personal E-mail: mlgs2327@aol.com. Business E-Mail: martha_schmidt@merck.com.

GORCHELS, LINDA MARIE, marketing director, consultant; b. Antigo, Wis., Mar. 24, 1955; d. John Joseph and Ann Stacia (Drozdik) Galarowicz; m. Charles Ronald Gorchels, Aug. 21, 1982; children: Elise, Kimberly. BBA, U. Wis., Oshkosh, 1976; MBA, Mich. State U., 1979. Mktg. rschr. Lear-Siegler, Inc., Zeeland, Mich., 1977; adj. instr. U. Wis., Eau Claire, 1979-83; dir. mktg. rsch. William C. Brown Pubs., Dubuque, Iowa, 1983-84, acquisitions editor, 1984-87; mktg. mgr. Verex Assurance, Madison, Wis., 1987-88; dir. exec. sales program U. Wis. Mgmt. Inst., Madison, 1988-90; dir. exec. mktg. program U. Wis. Exec. Edn. Ctr., Madison, 1990—. Author: The Product Manager's Handbook, 1996, 2000, The Product Manager's Field Guide, 2003, The Manager's Guide to Distribution Channels, 2004; contbr. articles to profl. publs. Bd. dirs., officer Cath. Charities, Madison, 1989-95; trainer USAID/U. Wis.-Madison, Poland and Hungary, 1992. Mem. Am. Mktg. Assn. (exec. mem.), World Future Soc., Product Devel. and Mgmt. Assn. Avocations: biking, trend watching. Office: UW-Madison Sch of Business Fluno Ctr for Exec Ed 601 University Ave Madison WI 53715

GORCHOV, RON, artist; b. Chgo., Apr. 5, 1930; s. Herman and Grace (Bloomfield) G.; children: Michael, Jolie. Exhibited in pub. collections Mus. Modern Art, N.Y.C., Met. Mus. Art, N.Y.C., Whitney Mus. Am. Art, N.Y.C., Guggenheim Mus., N.Y.C., Art Inst. Chgo., Denver Art Mus., Detroit Art Mus. Recipient Ingram Merrill Found. award, 1959, NEA award for painting, 1975; John Simon Guggenheim fellow for painting, 1994. Address: 113 Nelson St Brooklyn NY 11231 Office Phone: 847-461-1871. E-mail: ron@nosuchsite.net.

GORCHOW, BRUCE D., investment company executive; b. Mpls., Mar. 13, 1958; s. Neil Gorchow, Roslyn Gorchow; m. Marie L. Fioramonti; children: Grace Fioramonti-Gorchow, Sophia Fioramonti-Gorchow, Gabriel Fioramonti-Gorchow. BA, Haverford Coll., 1980; MBA, U. Pa., 1982. Investment mgr. TIAA/CREF, New York, NY, 1982—86; v.p. Equitable Capital Mgmt., Inc., 1987—91; exec. v.p. PPM Am., Inc., Chgo., 1991—2000; pres. PPM Am. Capital Ptnrs., LLC, 2000—. Bd. dirs. PPM Am., Inc.; bd. dir. Global Imaging Systems, Inc., Tampa, Fla., 1996—2002; bd. dirs. Elizabeth Arden Salon and Spa Holdings, Inc, Phoenix, Examination Mgmt. Svcs., Inc, Dallas; Director Tomah Products, Inc, Tomah, WI, 1997—99, Applied Process Solutions, Inc., Tulsa, OK, 1998—2000, Corvest Promotional Products, Miami, FL, 1999—. Mem.: U. Club Chgo., Phi Beta Kappa. Office: PPM Am Capital Ptnrs LLC 225 West Wacker Dr Ste 1200 Chicago IL 60606 Office Phone: 312 634-2512.

GORDEN, PATRICIA ANN, social services administrator, artist; b. Oak Park, Ill., May 16, 1955; d. Herbert E. Stafford and Nelda M. Bouvier, Delbert G. and Noma A. Hey; m. Paul D. Gorden, Oct. 17, 1992; children: Jeremiah J. Cassell, Justin R. Cassell, Jeffrey A., April M. AA, Mendocino C.C., Ukiah, Calif., 1981. Honor Certificate/Structural Mechanic USN, 1974. Dog groomer/dog handler Hey's Kennel, Addison, Ill., 1969—72; veteran's svcs. asst. Mendocino C.C., Ukiah, 1978—81; dog groomer Hartlip's 101 Kennel, Ukiah, 1980—83; self employed - dog groomer Pat Cassell's Grooming, Ukiah, 1983—88; child care worker, ctrl. office mgr. Trinity Sch. for Cildren, Ukiah, 1989—92; tchrs. aide Ukiah Unified Sch. Dist., 1991—91; direct care worker, ho. mgr. CRF for the Developmentally Disabled, Panama City, Fla., 1992—96; composing artist Ukiah Daily Jour., 1997—2001; transitional housing placement program adminstrv. mgr. Redwood Children's Services, Ukiah, 2000—04, spl. projects, 2004—. Teen counselor Redwood Children's Services, Ukiah, 2000—04. Design, Bus & Vehicle Logo for Local Transit Company (Monetary/Cmty. Acknowledgement, 1984), painting, Mural for America's 200th Birthday, community fundraising event, Pastel Mural for 'Pastels on the Plaza'. Vol. Plowshares Cmty. Dining & Services Facility, Ukiah, 2004—04, Ukiah Players Theatre, 1986—86. With USN, 1973—77. Avocations: graphic arts, reading, writing, walking.

GORDENKER, LEON, political science professor; b. Detroit, Oct. 7, 1923; s. Samuel and Anna (Posalsky) G.; m. Belia Emilie Strootman, Aug. 16, 1956 (dec. Apr. 1984); children: Robert Jan Mario, Hendrik Willem Paul, Emilie Elise Saskia. AB, U. Mich., 1943; student, Inst. d'Etudes Politiques, Paris, 1951-52; MA, Columbia U., 1954, PhD, 1958; postgrad., Acad. Internat. Law, Hague, The Netherlands, 1958. Journalist AP, 1943, Detroit Free Press, 1944-45; info. officer Nat. War Labor Bd., 1945; pub. info. officer UN, 1945-53; instr. Dartmouth Coll., 1956-58; mem. faculty Princeton U., 1958—, prof. politics, 1966-86, faculty assoc. Ctr. Internat. Studies, 1963—, prof. emeritus, 1986—, sr. rsch. polit. scientist, 1990-94; prof. Institut Universitaire de Hautes Internationales, Geneva, 1986-89, vis. prof., 1979-80; dir. Centre de Recherches sur les Institutions Internationales, Geneva, 1986-89. Vis. prof. Columbia U., 1961, 67, Makerere U., Uganda, 1969-70, U. Pa., 1971, 74, U. Witwatersrand, South Africa, 1976, Leiden U., 1984-85, 93, Erasmus U., 1985, CUNY, 1989, 90, 92, 95, Inst. Social Studies, The Hague, 1993-97. Author: The United Nations and the Peaceful Unification of Korea, 1959, The UN Secretary-General and the Maintenance of Peace, 1967, The United Nations in the International System, 1971, International Aid and National Decisions, 1976, The International Executive, 1978, (with W.P. Davison) Resolving Nationality Conflicts, 1980, (with P.R. Baehr) The United Nations: Reality and Ideal, 1984, 2d edit., 2005, Refugees in International Politics, 1987, (with T.G. Weiss) Soldiers, Peacekeepers and Disasters, 1991, (with P.R. Baehr) The United Nations: Reality & Ideal, 1991, 4th edit., 2005, De Verenigde Naties: Werkelijkheid en Ideaal, 1992, 94, 96, (with Benjamin Rivlin) The Challenging Role of the UN Secretary-General, 1993, (with others) International Cooperation in Response to AIDS, 1995, (with T.G. Weiss) NGOs, The UN and Global Governance, 1996, (with P.R. Baehr) The United Nations: Reality and Ideals, 1991, 4th edit., 2005, The UN Secretary-General and Secretariat, 2005; mem. editl. bd. Acta Politica, Global Governance. Fellow The Netherlands Inst. Advanced Study, 1972-73, 96-97. Mem. Acad. Coun. on UN, Princeton Club of N.Y. Office: Princeton U Inst Internat Studies Princeton NJ 08544-0001 Business E-Mail: gordenke@princeton.edu.

GORDER, JOE, energy executive; BBA, U. Mo., St. Louis; MBA, Our Lady of the Lake U. Various pos., including dir. info. systems, asst. treas., dir. comml./indsl. sales, and v.p. bus. devel. Ultramar Diamond Shamrock (later merged with Valero Corp.); sr. v.p. corp. devel. Valero Corp., San Antonio, 2003—. Office: Valero Corp Hdqrs One Valero Place San Antonio TX 78212-3186*

GORDIMER, NADINE, author; b. Springs, Republic of South Africa, Nov. 20, 1923; d. Isidore and Nan (Myers) Gordimer; m. Reinhold Cassirer, Jan. 29, 1954; children: Oriane, Hugo. Ed., Convent Sch., Springs, Republic of South Africa; honorary degree, Yale U., Harvard U., Columbia U., New Sch. for Social Rsch., USA, U. Leuven, Belgium, U. York, Eng., U. Cape Town and Witwaterstrand, South Africa, Cambridge U., Eng. Author: (story collections) Face to Face, 1949, The Soft Voice of the Serpent, 1952, Six Feet of the Country, 1956, Friday's Footprint, 1960 (W.H. Smith and Son Literary award 1961), Not for Publication, 1965, Livingstone's Companions, 1971, Selected Stories, 1975, Some Monday for Sure, 1976, A Soldier's Embrace, 1980, Something Out There, 1984, Crimes of Conscience, 1991, Jump, 1991, Why Haven't You Written: Selected Stories 1950-1972, 1992; (polit. and lit. essays) The Essential Gesture, 1988, Three in a Bed, 1991, Living in Hope and History: Notes From Our Century, 1999; (literary criticism) The Black Interpreters, 1973, Writing & Being: Charles Eliot Norton Lectures, 1995; (essays) Living in Hope and History: Notes from Our Century, 1999; (novels) The Lying Days, 1953, A World of Strangers, 1958, Occasion for Loving, 1963, The Late Bourgeois World, 1966, A Guest of Honour, 1970 (James Tait Black Meml. prize 1973), The Conservationist, 1974 (Booker prize for fiction Eng. 1974), Burger's Daughter, 1979, July's People, 1981, A Sport of Nature, 1987, My Son's Story, 1991, None to Accompany Me, 1994, The House Gun, 1998, The Pickup, 2001, Loot, 2003; (other) On the Mines, 1973, Lifetimes Under Apartheid, 1986; editor: (with Lionel Abrahams) Southern African Writing Today, 1967; edited Telling Tales, 2004. Decorated comdr. de l'Ordre des Arts et des Lettres (France), 1986; recipient Thomas Pringle award English Acad. South Africa, 1969, CNA award, 1974, 79, 81, 91, Grand Aigle d'Or, 1975, Disting. Svc. in Lit. Commonwealth award, 1981, MLA award, 1982, Nelly Sachs prize (Germany), 1985, Malaparte award (Italy), 1986, Bennett award, 1986, Internat. Premo Leui award, 2002, Mary McCarthy award, 2003; Benson medal, 1990, Nobel Prize for Literature, 1991; Neil Gunn fellow Scottish Arts Coun., 1981. Fellow Royal Soc. Lit.; mem. AAAS, Com. European Authors, Am. Acad. (hon.), Inst. Arts and Letters (hon.), Internat. PEN (v.p.).*

GORDIS, DAVID MOSES, academic administrator, rabbi; b. N.Y.C., June 4, 1940; s. Robert and Fannie (Jacobson) G.; m. Felice Witztum, Sept. 3, 1962; children: Lisa, Elana. BA, Columbia U., 1960, MA, 1966; MHL, Jewish Theol. Sem., 1962, PhD, 1980. Ordained rabbi, 1964. Dean of students Tchrs. Inst., Jewish Theol. Sem., N.Y.C., 1966-72; exec. dir. Found. for Conservative Judaism, 1981-84; assoc. prof., v.p. U. of Judaism, L.A., 1972-84; v.p. Jewish Theol. Sem., N.Y.C., 1981-84; exec. v.p. Am. Jewish Com., N.Y.C., 1984-87; v.p. U. Judaism, L.A., 1988-92, dir. Wilstein Inst. of Jewish Policy Studies, 1988—, adj. assoc. prof. Talmud, 1988-92, dir. inst. rsch.; pres. Hebrew Coll., 1993—. Mem. editl. bd.: Tikkun. Pres., prof. rabbinics Hebrew Coll., 1993—;

exec. com. Am. Found. for Polish-Jewish Studies, 1988—; trustee Am. Jewish Hist. Soc., 1993—, vice-chair Archives for Hist. Documentation, 1995—; chair United Synagogue Coun. on Jewish Edn., 1973-82. Mem. Rabbinical Assembly Am., Assn. Colls. of Jewish Studies. Avocation: cello. Office Phone: 617-559-8772. Business E-Mail: dgordis@hebrewcollege.edu.

GORDIS, LEON, physician; b. N.Y.C., July 19, 1934; s. Robert and Fannie (Jacobson) Gordis; m. Hadassah Cohen, June 14, 1955; children: Daniel, Elihu, Jonathan. BA, Columbia, 1954; BHL, Jewish Theol. Sem., 1954; MD, SUNY, 1958; MPH, Johns Hopkins U., 1966, DPH, 1968. Intern, then resident in pediat. Jewish Hosp., Bklyn., 1958—61; fellow in pediat. Sch. Medicine Johns Hopkins U., 1962—66, instr. Sch. Medicine, 1966—68, assoc. prof. epidemiology, Sch. Hygiene and Pub. Health, 1971—73; asst. med. dir. ambulatory care Sinai Hosp., Balt., 1966—68, chief dept. community medicine, 1968—69; prof. epidemiology Johns Hopkins, 1973—, chmn. dept. epidemiology, 1975—93; prof. pediat., 1992—; assoc. dean admissions & Acad. affairs Johns Hopkins Sch. Medicine, 1993—99. Vis. prof. med. ecology Hebrew U., Jerusalem, 1969—71. Served with USPHS, 1961—65. Fellow: AAAS, Am. Acad. Pediat.; mem.: APHA, Assn. Tchrs. Preventive Medicine, Am. Heart Assn., Soc. Pediatric Rsch., Am. Pediatric Soc., Am. Epidemiol. Soc. (pres. 1983—84), Soc. Epidemiologic Rsch. (pres. 1979—80), Inst. Medicine NAS. Home: 105 Swanhill Ct Baltimore MD 21208-1608 Office: 615 N Wolfe St Baltimore MD 21205-2103

GORDLEY, JAMES RUSSELL, law educator; b. 1946; BA, U. Chgo., 1967, MBA, 1968; JD, Harvard U., 1970. Fellow U. Florence Inst. Law, Italy, 1970-71; assoc. Foley, Hoag & Eliot, Boston, 1971-72; fellow comparative law Harvard U., Cambridge, Mass., 1973-78; acting prof. U. Calif., Berkeley, 1978-81, prof., 1981—, Shannon Cecil Turner prof. jurisprudence, 1995—. Fellow Deutsche Forschungsgemeinschaft, 1983, sr. NATO fellow, 1991, Guggenheim fellow, 1995-96, Fulbright fellow, 1996. Fellow Am. Acad. Arts and Scis. Office: U Calif Sch Law Boalt Hall Berkeley CA 94720

GORDLY, AVEL LOUISE, state legislator, political organization worker; b. Portland, Oreg., Feb. 13, 1947; d. Fay Lee and Beatrice Bernice (Coleman) G.; 1 child, Tyrone Wayne Waters. BS in Adminstrn. of Justice, Portland State U., 1974; Grad. John F. Kennedy Sch. Govt., Harvard U., 1995; grad., U. Oreg. Pacific Program, 1998. Phone co. clk. Pacific West Bell, Portland, 1966-70, mgmt. trainee, 1969-70; work release counselor Oreg. Corrections Divsn., Portland, 1974-78, parole and probation officer, 1974-78; dir. youth svcs. Urban League of Portland, 1979-83; dir. So. Africa program Am. Friends Svc. Com., Portland, 1983-89, assoc. exec. sec., dir. Pacific N.W. region, 1987-90; freelance writer Portland Observer, Portland, 1988-90; program dir. Portland House of Umoja, 1991; mem. Oreg. Ho. of Reps., Portland, 1991-96, mem. joint ways and means com., adv. mem. appropriations com., rules and reorgn. com., low income housing com., energy policy rev. com., others; mem. Oreg. Senate from 10th dist., Salem, 1997—; mem. crime and corrections com., trades econ. devel. com. Oreg. Senate, 1997, mem. joint ways and means com. on pub. safety, 1997, mem. joint ways and means com. on edn., 1999, chair, joint ways and means pub. safety com., 2005—, chair, joint ways and measn edn. com., 2005—, chair, joint ways and means, full com., 2005, emergency bd., co-chair, interim task force on parental and family abductions, 2003—04. Mem. joint ways and means com. on edn., mem. gov. drug and violent crime policy bd., mem. Oreg. liquor control commn. task force, mem. sexual harrassement task force, mem. Hanford waste bd., mem. Gov.'s Commn. for Women, Gov.'s Drug and Violent Crime Policy Bd.; originator, producer, host Black Women's Forum, 1983-88; co-producer, rotating host N.E. Spectrum, 1983-88. Mem. corrections adv. com. Multnomah Cmty.; mem. adv. com. Oregonians Against Gun Violence; mem. Black Leadership Conf.; treas., bd. dirs. Black United Fund; co-founder, facilitator Unity Breakfast Com.; co-founder Sisterhood Luncheon; past project adv. bd. dirs. Nat. Orgn. Victims Assistance; past citizen chmn. Portland Police Bur.; past mem. coordinating com. Portland Future Focus Policy Com.; past coord. Cmty. Rescue Plan; past vice chmn. internat. affairs Black United Front; past sec. Urban League Portland, past vice chmn. and exec. com.; past adv. com. Black Ednl. Ctr.; past vice chmn. Desegregation Monitoring; also past adv. com., past chmn. curriculum com., founder African Am. Leg. Issues Roundtable; founder Black Women Gathering; other past orgn. coms.; elected state senate First African Am. Woman, 1996. Recipient Outstanding Cmty. Svc. award NAACP, 1986, Outstanding Women in Govt. award YWCA, 1991, Girl Scout-Cmty. Svc. award, 1991, N.W. Conf. of Black Studies-Outstanding Progressive Leadership in the African-Am. Cmty. award, 1986, Cmty. Svc. award Delta Sigma Theta, 1981, Joint Action in Cmty. Svc.-Vol. and Cmty. Svc. award, 1981, Quality of Life Photography award Pacific Power & Light Co., 1986, Am. Leadership Forum Sr. fellow, 1988, Equal Opportunity award, Urban League, 1996, Outstanding Alumni, 1996, PSU, Causa '98 En Defensa de la Comunidad award, 1997, Matrix award Assn. for Women in Comm., 1999, Pres.'s award Portland Oreg. Visitors Assn., 1999, Legacy award Black United Fund, 2000, Leadership award Albina Ministerial Alliance, 2000 Mem. NAACP. Avocations: reading group, mentoring, photography, walking. Home: 6805 NE Bradway St Portland OR 97213-5304

GORDON, ALAN LEE, psychiatrist; b. NYC, Nov. 26, 1936; s. Abe and Fan Gordon; m. Lois Goldfein; 1 child, Robert Michael. AB, Columbia Coll., 1957; MD, U. Wis., 1963. Resident Albert Einstein Coll. Medicine, N.Y.C., 1964-66, 68-69; dir. of aftercare Riverdale Mental Health Clinic, N.Y.C., 1969-78; clin. instr. Mt. Sinai Sch. Medicine, N.Y.C., 1982-90; psychiatrist divsn. of post-institutional svcs. Human Resources Adminstrn.-City of N.Y., 1986—; psychiatrist Bowery Residence Com., CSS Program, N.Y.C., 1990—. Lectr. in field; TV, radio interviewer; spkr. in field. Author: American Chronicle: Six Decades in American Life, 1920-79, 1987, American Chronicle: Seven Decades of American Life 1920-89, 1990, Columbia Chronicles of America Life, 1960-92, 1995, American Chronicle: Year by Year through the Twentieth Century, 1999; contbr. poetry to various jours. Capt. U.S. Army, 1966—68. Mem.: Alpha Omega Alpha. Democrat. Jewish. Avocations: history, literature, sports. Office: 300 Central Park W New York NY 10024-1513 Office Phone: 212-362-4011.

GORDON, ALLEN BARRY, musician, composer; b. L.A., Mar. 12, 1950; s. Rubin and Florence Irene G.; m. Susan Sutwarti, Jan. 2, 1976. Studied piano with Antonio Iturioz; student, Santa Monica Coll., 1998. Master jazz pianist. Head pianist Filmex, 1979-81, Jonathan Club, 1989-91; freelance pianist. Instr. piano. Played televised banquet, Biltmore Hotel, Ted Kennedy (US senator), 1981, concert for Mikhail Gorbachev (former Russian Premier), Pheonix Hall Anaheim, 2000, jazz and musical compositions played in 25 countries worldwide. Played concerts for sr. citizens; played concert at VA Hosp. Recipient Pub. Citation award, City of L.A. Mem. ASCAP. Democrat. Jewish. Avocations: playing and listening to music, reading biographies, teaching, coin collecting/numismatics, baseball art. Home: 4140 Grand View Blvd Los Angeles CA 90066-5258 Office Phone: 310-398-1180.

GORDON, ANNE KATHLEEN, editor; m. Phillip L. Berman; 1 child, Aaron. BA speech pathology and audiology, U. Denver, 1979; postgrad., Columbia Grad. Sch. Journalism, 1983. Fin. writer Rocky Mountain Bus. Jour., Denver, 1981, Sun-Tattler, Hollywood, Fla., 1982-83, fin. editor, 1983; asst. bus. editor Ft. Lauderdale (Fla.) News, 1983-85; bus. editor The Denver Post, 1985-88, asst. mng. editor, 1988; news cons. Sta. KCNC-TV, Denver, 1988-89, assignment mgr., 1989-90; editor Jackson Hole News, 1990-92; editor Sunday Mag. The Plain Dealer, Cleve., 1993-99; arts and entertainment editor The Phila. Inquirer, 1999—2000, from assoc. mng. editor to dep. mng. editor arts and features, 2000—02, mng. editor, 2002—. Comm. dir. Colo. Dem. Party, Clinton presdl. campaign, 1992. Author: A Book of Saints, 1994. Recipient Best of Show award Colo. Press Assn., 1981, 86, Woman of Yr. award Broward County Bus. and Profl. Women's Assn., 1983, 1st Pl. Spot News award Colo. Associated Press, 1986, 1st Pl. Breaking News award Colo. Press Assn., 1986, Gen. Excellence award Wyo. Press Assn., 1991, Gen. Excellence award Nat. Newspaper Assn., 1992; Eisenhower fellow, 2000. Home: 149 Fairview Rd Narberth PA 19072-1330 Office: The Philadelphia Inquirer 400 N Broad St Philadelphia PA 19130-4015 E-mail: agordon@phillynews.com.

GORDON, BARON JACK, stockbroker; b. 1926; m. Ellin Bachrach, Aug. 20, 1954; children: Jonathan Ross, Rose Patricia, Alison. Midshipman, U.S. Naval Acad., 1946; BS, Lynchburg Coll., 1953. Asst. treas. Henry Montor Assocs., Inc., N.Y.C., 1956; v.p., sec. Propp & Co., Inc., N.Y.C., 1957-58; ptnr. Koerner, Gordon & Co., N.Y.C., 1959-62; sr. ptnr. Gordon, Kulman Perry, and predecessor firm, N.Y.C., 1962-71, pres., chmn. bd., 1971-74, Palison, Inc., White Plains, N.Y., 1974—; chmn. bd. Rojon, Inc., Williamsburg, Va., 1979—. Mem. N.Y. Stock Exch., White Plains, N.Y., 1974—. Mem. Harrison (N.Y.) Archtl. Rev. Bd., 1970-72, Harrison Planning Bd., 1975-77; bd. dirs. Montefiore Hosp. Assn., YM-YWHA, Lafayette Ednl. Fund, Inc., 1986-92; internat. adv. coun. Mus. of Am. Folk Art, 1990—. Lt. USNR, 1953—55, U.S.S. Midway, naval aide-de-camp to gov. (rank of capt.), 1989—98, Va. Recipient Wisdom award of honor and eminent wisdom; fellow Wisdom Hall of Fame. Mem. Folk Art Soc. (bd. dirs. 1987-95, mem. nat. adv. bd. 1996—), U.S. Naval Acad. Alumni Assn. (life), Stock Exch. Luncheon Club (N.Y.C.), Buttonwood Club. Home: 113 Elizabeth Meriwether Williamsburg VA 23185-5107 Office: Drawer JG Williamsburg VA 23187

GORDON, BARTON JENNINGS (BART GORDON), congressman, lawyer; b. Murfreesboro, Tenn., Jan. 24, 1949; s. Robert Jennings and Margaret Louise (Barton) G.; m. Leslie Peyton, 1998. BS, Middle Tenn. State U., 1971; JD, U. Tenn., 1973. Bar: Tenn. 1974. Mem. U.S. Congress from 6th Tenn. dist., Washington, 1985—; mem. energy and commerce com.; mem. sci. com., mem. energy and air quality, telecom, trade and consumer protection subcoms.; ranking mem. space and aeronautics subcom. Mem. Tenn. Democratic Exec. Com., 1974-83, exec. dir., 1979-81, chmn., 1981-83; bd. dirs. Middle Tenn. State U. Found.; chmn. Rutherford County United Givers Fund, Rutherford County Cancer Crusade Mem. Rutherford County C. of C. (bd. dirs.) Democrat. Methodist. Office: US Ho of Reps 2304 Rayburn Ho Office Bldg Washington DC 20515-0001*

GORDON, BASIL, retired mathematics professor; b. Balt., Dec. 23, 1932; s. Basil and Helen (Williams) G. MA, Johns Hopkins, 1953; PhD, Calif. Inst. Tech., 1956. Instr. Calif. Inst. Tech., 1956-57; asst. prof. math. U. Calif. at Los Angeles, 1959-63, assoc. prof., 1963-67, prof., 1967-93; prof. emeritus, 1993—. Editor: Pacific Jour. Mathematics, 1969-70, 72-73, Jour. Combinatorial Theory, 1970-2002, Ramanujan Jour., 1997—; contbr. articles to profl. jours. Served with AUS, 1957-59. Alfred P. Sloan fellow, 1962-64 Mem. Math. Assn. Am., Pi Mu Epsilon. Achievements include rsch. on number theory, combinatorics, group theory, and function theory. Home: 526 Palisades Ave Santa Monica CA 90402-2722 Office: 405 Hilgard Ave Los Angeles CA 90095-9000 Business E-Mail: bg@math.ucla.edu.

GORDON, BENJAMIN DICHTER, pediatrician, educator, health facility administrator; b. Bklyn., Mar. 4, 1927; s. Abraham S. and Selma F. (Dichter) G.; m. Ellen M. Nimaroff, June 10, 1951; children: Wendy, Marcy, Amanda. AB, Amherst Coll., 1947; MD, U. Md., 1951. Diplomate Am. Bd. of Pediatrics. Rotating intern Kings County Hosp., Bklyn., 1951-52, asst. resident in pediatrics, 1953-54, Maimonides Hosp., Bklyn., 1952-53; research fellow Irvington House, Irvington-on-Hudson, N.Y., 1954-55; practice medicine specializing in pediatrics Stratford & Bridgeport, Conn., 1955-73; assoc. attendant, emergency dept. Bridgeport Hosp., 1973-78; asst. dir. emergency dept. Danbury (Conn.) Hosp., 1978-82; clin. dir. Union Carbide Corp., Danbury, 1982-87; med. dir Chesebrough-Ponds, Inc., Trumbull, Conn., 1987-90. Asst. prof. occupational medicine Yale U.; chmn. Rheumatic Fever com. Conn. State Heart Assn.; cons. to cosmetic industry and product-testing labs.; attending occupl. med. clinic Milton (Mass.) Hosp., Jordan Hosp., Plymouth, Mass. Author: Practical Guide for New Parents, 1970; contbr. articles to profl. jours. Chmn., Bd. Health, Town of Yarmouth, Mass.; mem. Regional Emergency Planning Com. for Barnstable County. Served with USNR, 1945-46. Fellow: Am. Coll. Occupl. and Environ. Medicine, Am. Acad. Pediats.; mem.: Barnstable Dist. Med. Soc. (com. on violence), Mass. Med. Soc., Occupl. Med. Assn. Conn. (pres. 1987—88), Fairfield County Med. Soc. (past chmn. pub. health com.), Conn. State Med. Soc. (past chmn. comty. pub. health), Williams Club (N.Y.C.). Jewish. Avocations: music, dance, skiing, reading, history, golf. Home: 14 Hillsea Rd Yarmouth Port MA 02675-1111 Fax: 508-375-0559. E-mail: b.gordonmd@comcast.net.

GORDON, BERNARD M., computer company executive; b. 1927; B.E.E., MIT, 1948, M.E.E., 1949. Co-founder EPSCO, Inc., 1953—64; founder Gordon Engring. (became Analogic Corp.), 1964—69; founder, pres., CEO, chmn. Analogic Corp., Peabody, Mass., 1969—94, CEO, 1969—2003, chmn., 1969—2004, chmn. emeritus, 2004—; co-founder, pres. Neuro-Logica Corp., Danvers, Mass., 2004—. Founder Gordon Inst. Tufts U., 1984—. Bd. trustees Tufts U., 1996—. Recipient Nat. Medal Tech., 1986, John Fulke Sr. Meml. award, 1993, Benjamin Franklin award for Innovation in Engineering and Technology, Franklin Inst, Walker prize, Museum of Science, 2004. Fellow IEEE (Leadership Recognition award 1992); mem. Nat. Acad. Engrs, 1991. Achievements include pioneer in high-speed analog-to-digital conversion; patents for over 200 inventions including the first solid state x-ray generator, the first baseband quadrature-detecting ultrasound scanner, the first fetal monitor, and the first instant imaging CT system. Office: Analogic Corp 8 Centennial Dr # B-1 Peabody MA 01960-7987*

GORDON, BRUCE S., civil rights organization executive, former telecommunications company executive; b. Camden, N.J., Feb. 15, 1946; s. Walter and Violet Gordon; m. Genie Alston, Feb. 20, 1970 (div.); 1 child, Taurin; m. Tawana Gordon. BA, Gettysburg Coll., 1968; MS, MIT, 1988. With Bell Atlantic Corp., Arlington, Va., 1968—70, bus. office mgr., 1970—72, sales mgr. mktg., 1972—74, personnel supr., 1974—76, market mgmt. supr., 1976—78, mktg. mgr., 1978—80, divsn. staff mgr., 1980—81, divsn. ops. mgr., 1981, divsn. mgr. phone ctr., 1981—83, mktg. mgr., 1983—84, gen. mgr., mktg./sales, 1985—88, v.p. mktg., 1988—93; group pres. bus. unit Bell Atlantic Corp. (mergered with GTE), 1993—2000; pres. retail markets group Verizon Communications Inc., N.Y.C., NY, 2000—03; pres., CEO NAACP, Balt., 2005—. Bd. dirs. Southern Co., Tyco Internat. Ltd., Office Depot, Bartech Personnel Svcs., Urban League, 1984—86, Innroads of Phila., 1985—88; bd. trustees Gettywburg Coll., Alvin Ailey Dance Found., Lincoln Ctr. Named Exec. of Yr., Black Enterprise Mag., 1998; fellow Alfred P. Sloan, MIT. Office: NAACP National HQ 4805 Mt Hope Dr Baltimore MD 21215*

GORDON, COREY LEE, lawyer; b. Mpls., Aug. 22, 1956; s. Jack I. and LaVerne (Shedlov) G.; m. Ciel Schaeffer, Aug. 29, 1982; children: Jared Isaac, Lian Miriam. BA, Macalester Coll., 1976; JD cum laude, U. Minn., 1980. Bar: Minn. 1980, U.S. Dist. Ct. Minn. 1981, U.S. Ct. Appeals (8th cir.) 1983, U.S. Supreme Ct. 1983, Wis. 1987, U.S. Dist. Ct. (ea. and we. dists.) Wis. 1987, N.Y. 1991, U.S. Dist. Ct. (so. dist.) N.Y. 1991, U.S. Ct. Appeals (3d cir.) 1992, Ill. 1993, U.S. Dist. Ct. (no. dist.) Ill. 1995, Fla. 1995, U.S. Dist. Ct. (we., ea., and no. dists.) N.Y. 1999, U.S. Ct. Appeals (11th cir.) 1999, U.S. Ct. Appeals (7th cir.) 1999, U.S. Dist. Ct. (so. and ctrl. dists.) Ill. 1999, U.S. Ct. Appeals (2d cir.) 1999, U.S. Dist. Ct. (so. and no. dists.) Fla. 2000, U.S. Dist. Ct. (mid. dist.) Fla. 2003. Assoc. Fried, Frank, Harris, Shriver & Jacobson, N.Y.C., 1980-81; ptnr. Shapiro, Lavintman & Gordon P.A., Mpls., 1982-85; assoc. Robins, Zelle, Larson & Kaplan, St. Paul, 1986-88; ptnr. Robins, Kaplan, Miller & Ciresi, Mpls., 1989—2000; dep. atty. gen. State of Minn., St. Paul, 2001—02; special counsel Blackwell & Igbanugo, P.A., Mpls., 2002—03; ptnr. Shapiro Gordon LLC, Mpls., 2003—. Bd. dirs. Jewish Family and Children's Svc. of Mpls., 1992-96, Mpls. Fedn. for Jewish Svc., 1994-99, chair bd. dirs. Circus Juventas, 2002—, bd. dirs. Jewish Vocational Svc., 2002—. Treas. The H.H.H. Fund, Minn., 1984—89; bd. dirs., sec.-treas. Minn. Humane Soc., 1985—86; active Dem. Farm Labor Party; trustee Bet Shalom Synagogue, 1992—93, v.p., 1993—97, pres., 1997—99. Mem.: ATLA (co-chair inadequate security litigation group 1992—95), Rape and Incest Nat. Network (RAINN) (legal adv. bd. 2004—), Nat. Crime Victim Bar Assn. (adv. bd. 2004—). Jewish. Avocations: folk music, scuba diving, photography. Home: 2640 Glenhurst Pl Minneapolis MN 55416-3957 Office: Shapiro Gordon LLC 340 Parkdale Plz 1660 Hwy 100 South Minneapolis MN 55416 E-mail: cgordon@shapirogordon.com.

GORDON, CRAIG JEFFREY, oncologist, educator; b. Detroit, Feb. 10, 1953; s. Maury Allen and Shirley Phoebe (Jacoby) G.; m. Susan Ann Blase, Aug. 3, 1980; children: Sari, Scott, Brittany. BS, Oakland U., 1978; DO, U. Osteo. Med. and Health Scis, Des Moines, 1983. Diplomate Am. Bd. Internal Medicine, Am. Bd. Med. Oncology. Intern-chief Botsford Gen. Hosp., Farmington Hills, Mich., 1983-84, resident, 1984-87; fellow in hematology and oncology Wayne State Univ. (affiliated Hosp.'s Prog.), Detroit, 1987-90, fellow-chief, 1989-90; clin. asst. prof. dept. medicine Wayne State U., Detroit, 1990—; dir. divsn. hematology and oncology Botsford Hosp., Livonia, Mich., 1992—; med. dir. Angela Hospice, 1993—98, Weisberg Cancer Ctr., Karmanos Cancer Inst., 2000—. Mem. extrarenal transplantation com. Mich. Dept. Pub. Health; physician advisor Gilda's Club Mich., 1993—2001; mem. Greater Detroit Area Health Care Coun. on Cancer Care. Contbr. articles to profl. jours. Named Intern of the Yr. Botsford Hosp. Staff, 1984, Resident of the Yr., 1985-87; clin. fellow Am. Cancer Soc., 1987-90. Fellow Am. Coll. Osteo. Internists; mem. Am. Osteo. Assn., Mich. Assn. Osteo. Physicians and Surgeons, Mich. Soc. Hematology and Oncology, Assn. Cancer Execs., S.W. Oncology Group, Am. Soc. Clin. Oncologists, Oakland County Osteo. Assn. Avocations: sports, popular music, astronomy, electronics. Office: 31995 Northwestern Hwy Farmington MI 48334-1625 Personal E-mail: gordondo@comcast.net.

GORDON, DANE REX, philosophy educator, minister; b. London, June 15, 1925; came to US, 1954; s. Leonard and Heather (Gibson) G.; m. Elizabeth May Marshall, Aug. 16, 1952 (dec. Apr. 1987); m. Judith Fisher Ward, July 6, 1991. BA, U. Cambridge, 1951, MA, 1958; BD, U. London, 1956; MA in Philosophy, U. Rochester, 1960. Ordained to ministry Presbyn. Ch., 1958. Profl. actor, Eng., 1938-43; bookseller Hatchards, London, 1946-48; assoc. minister Cen. Presbyn. Ch., Rochester, N.Y., 1958-61; asst. prof. Rochester Inst. Tech., 1962-71, Danforth assoc., 1967-69, assoc. prof., then prof., chmn. dept., asst. dean, acting dean, 1976-77, assoc. dean Coll. Liberal Arts, 1976-87, prof. philosophy, 1976—2000, chmn. dept. philosophy, 1994, prof. emeritus, 2000. Vis. lectr. in philosophy and religion Adam Mickiewicz U., Poznan, Poland, 1993; Provost fellow for internat. partnerships and vis. disting. lectr., Am. U. in Bulgaria, 1996; Balkan scholar in philosophy Am. U., Bulgaria, 1999-2000. Author: New Way Eng., 1964, Philosophy of Religion Study Guide, 1973, Rochester Instit. of Tech.: Industrial Develop. and Ed. Innovation in an Am. City, 1982: The Old Testament: A Beginning Survey, 1985, Thinking and Reading in Philosophy of Religion, 1994, Philosophy and Vision, (Eng. and Polish translation), 1994, The Old Testament in its Cultural, Hist. and Religious Context, 1994; co-author: (with Milford Fargo) A Family Christ Mass, 1973, Away He Run, 1976; editor: Philosophy in Post Communist Europe, 1998, (with Jozef Niznik) Criticism and Defense of Rationality in Contemporary Philosophy, 1998, (with David Durst) Civil Soc. in Southeast Europe, 2004, A Feeling Intellect and a Thinking Heart, 2002, (with David Suits) Epicurus: His Continuing Influence and Contemporary Relevance, 2003. Served with Royal Navy, 1943-46 Recipient Eisenhart award Outstanding Teaching, 1996-97. Mem. AAUP, Am. Philos. Assn., Am. Soc. Composers, Authors, Producers, Presbytery of Genesee Valley. Office: Rochester Inst Tech Coll Liberal Arts Dept of Philosophy Rochester NY 14623 Office Phone: 585-475-7182. Fax: 585-475-7120. Business E-Mail: drggla@rit.edu. *As we get older, we understand less and trust more.*

GORDON, DAVID, playwright, theater director, choreographer; b. N.Y.C., July 14, 1936; m. Valda Setterfield; 1 child, Ain. Founder, dir. Pick Up Performance Co., Inc., N.Y.C., 1978—. Playwright, dir. dance, theater, music prodn. The Mysteries and What's So Funny?, 1991; writer, dir. TV program (1992-93) and theatrical work (1996) Punch and Judy Get Divorced; co-writer, dir.: (with Ain Gordon) The Family Business, 1994-95; dir. Shlemiel The First, Am. Repertory Theater, 1994-95; dir., choreographer: The Firebugs, The Guthrie Theater, 1995; co-writer, dir. (with Ain Gordon) First Picture Show, 1999; dir.: Past/Forward with Mikhail Baryshnikov, 2000-01, Autobiography of a Liar, 1999, Private Livees of Dancers, 2001-03, Dancing Henry Five, 2004, The Chairs, 2004. Guggenheim fellow, 1981, 87. Office: Pick Up Performance Co 520 8th Ave Ste 303 New York NY 10018 Office Phone: 212-244-7622. E-mail: pickupperformance@earthlink.net.

GORDON, DAVID, museum director; b. London; m. Maggi Gordon; 2 children. Grad., Balliol Coll., Oxford; studied at, London Sch. Econs., Harvard U. Financial journalist; asst. editor The Economist, CEO, 1981; sec. Royal Acad. Art, 1996—2002; dir. Milw. Art Mus., 2002—. Gov. British Film Inst., 1982—92; bd. mem. South Bank Centre, 1988—96; trustee Architecture Found., 1991—2001; chmn. Contemporary Art Soc., 1992—98; trustee Tate Gallery, 1993—98. Office: Milw Art Mus 700 N Art Mus Dr Milwaukee WI 53202

GORDON, DAVID A., lawyer; BA, Cornell Univ., 1982; JD, Syracuse Univ., 1986. Bar: Calif. 1986, NY 1995. Mng. ptnr. Latham & Watkins LLP, NYC. Named one of the 45 Elite Lawyers in the US under age 45, Am. Lawyer mag., 2003. Mem.: ABA. Office: Latham & Watkins LLP Ste 1000 885 Third Ave New York NY 10022-4834 Office Phone: 212-906-1251. Business E-Mail: david.gordon@lw.com.

GORDON, DAVID JAMIESON, tenor; b. Phila, Pa, Dec. 7, 1947; s. David William and Lois Irene (Lukens) G.; m. Ginna Bell Bragg, Feb. 14, 2004. Student, Coll. of Wooster, 1965-68, McGill U., Montreal, Que., Can., 1968-70; student of Dale Moore, 1965—. Mem. faculty Sonoma State U. Debut with Lyric Opera Chgo., 1973; leading tenor Landestheater Linz (Austria), 1975-79; prin. roles with San Francisco Opera, Houston Grand Opera, Met. Opera, Hamburg Staatsoper, Washington Opera, Mostly Mozart Festival, Salzburg Festival; concert soloist with Bach Festivals: Carmel, Calif., Bethlehem, Pa., Festival Casals, Stuttgart, Tokyo, Buenos Aires, Eugene, Oreg., Boston Symphony, Berlin Philharm., Czech Philharmonic, Vienna Symphony, St. Louis Symphony, San Francisco Symphony, LA Philharm., Seattle Symphony, Phila. Orch., Cleve. Orch., Nat. Symphony Washington, Baltimore Symphony; appears in opera, concerts, chamber music, recitals throughout US and Europe as performer, lectr., and tchr.; specialist in music of J.S. Bach; performing artist for Delos, Dorian, Telarc, London Records, Decca Records, Smithsonian Collection of Recs., RCA Red Seal, Nonesuch Records. Home: Po Box 4843 Carmel CA 93921-4843 E-mail: dgordon@spiritsound.com.

GORDON, DOUGLAS, artist; b. Glasgow, Scotland, 1966; Student, Glasgow Sch. Art, 1984—88, Slade Sch. Art, London, 1988—90. One-man shows include Mus. d'Art Moderne de la Ville de Paris, 1993, Tramway, Glasgow, 1993, Kunst-werke, Berlin, 1993, Lisson Gallery, London, 1994, Rooseum Espresso, Malmö, 1995, Ctr. Georges Pompidou, Paris, 1995, Van Abbe Mus., Eindhoven, 1995, The Agy., London, 1995, Kunstlerhaus, Stuttgart, 1995, Tate Gallery, London, 1996, Galerie Walchenturm, Zurich, 1996, Mus. Gegenwartskunst, 1996, Canberra Contemporary Art Space, 1996, Galleria Bonoma, Rome, 1996, Uppsala Konstmus, 1996, FRAC Languedoc-Roussillion, Montpelier, France, 1996, Deutsches Mus., Bonn, 1997, Kunstverein Hannover, 1997, Biennale de Lyon, 1997, Gandy Gallery, Prague, 1997, Gelerie Mot & Van den Boogaard, Brussels, 1997, Munster Skulptur Projekt, 1997, Galerie Micheline Swajcer, Antwerp, 1997, Bloom Gallery, Amsterdam, 1997, Galleri Nicolai Wallner, Copenhagen, 1997, others, exhibited in group shows at Hayward Gallery, London, 1996, Transmission Gallery, Glasgow, 1996, Soros Contemporary Art Gallery, Kiev, 1997, Southampton City Art Gallery, 1997, Ashiya City Mus. Art and History, 1998, Guggenheim Mus. SoHo, N.Y., 1998, numerous others. Recipient Turner prize, 1996, Premio 2000 award, Venice Biennale, 1997.

GORDON, EDGAR GEORGE, retired lawyer; b. Detroit, Feb. 27, 1924; s. Edgar George and Verna Florence (Hay) G.; m. Alice Irwin, Feb. 4, 1967; children: David A., J. Scott. AB, Princeton U., 1947; JD, Harvard U., 1950. Bar: Mich. 1951, U.S. Supreme Ct. 1953. Assoc. Poole, Warren & Littell, Detroit, 1950-54; ptnr. Poole, Warren, Littell & Gordon, Detroit, 1953-63; gen. counsel Hygrade Food Products Corp., Detroit, 1963-69, sec., 1966-69, v.p., 1968-69; v.p., sec. counsel City Nat. Bank of Detroit, 1969-81; v.p., sec., gen. counsel No. States Bancorp, 1970-81; v.p., sec., counsel First of Am. Bank Corp., Kalamazoo, 1981-84; also ptnr. Howard & Howard, Kalamazoo, 1981-2000; ret., 2000. Dir. First Citizens Bank, Troy, Mich., 1973-81, First Nat. Bank, Plymouth, Mich., 1974-81; pres., chmn. bd. First of Am. Mortgage Co., Kalamazoo, 1978-84. Commr. City of Kalamazoo, 1995-2001. Lt. (j.g.) USN, 1943-46. Mem. ABA, Mich. Bar Assn., Kalamazoo Bar Assn., Country Club of Detroit (Grosse Pointe, Mich.). Republican. Presbyterian. Home: 4339 Lakeside Dr Kalamazoo MI 49008-2802

GORDON, ELLEN RUBIN, candy company executive; d. William B. and Cele H. (Travis) Rubin; m. Melvin J. Gordon, June 25, 1950; children: Virginia, Karen, Wendy, Lisa. Student, Vassar Coll., 1948—50; BA, Brandeis U., 1965; postgrad., Harvard U., 1968. With Tootsie Roll Industries, Inc., Chgo., 1968—, corp. sec., 1970-74, v.p. product devel., 1974-76, sr. v.p., 1976-78, pres., COO, 1978—; v.p., dir. HDI Investment Corp. Mem. coun. on divsn. biol. scis. and Pritzker Sch. Medicine U. Chgo.; mem. med. sch. adv. coun. for cell biology and pathology Harvard U.; mem. bd. fellows Faculty of Medicine, Harvard Med. Sch. Mem. adv. coun. J.L. Kellogg Grad. Sch. Mgmt. at Northwestern U.; mem. univ. resources and overseers com. Harvard U.; mem. bd. advisors Women Inc. Recipient Kettle award, 1985. Mem. Nat. Confectioners Assn. (bd. dirs.). Office: Tootsie Roll Industries Inc 7401 S Cicero Ave Chicago IL 60629-5885

GORDON, EZRA, architect, educator; b. Detroit, Apr. 5, 1921; s. Abraham and Rebecca (Reimer) G.; m. Jeanette Greenberg, Oct. 8, 1942; children: Cheryl P. Gordon Van Ausdal, Rana Gordon Oremland, Judith Gordon Eichhorn.. Roosevelt Coll., 1946-48; BS in Architecture, U. Ill., 1951. Draftsman Pace Assos. Architects, 1951-53; sr. planner Chgo. Plan Commn., 1953-54; project architect Harry Weese & Assos., 1954-61; ptnr. Gordon-Levin & Assocs., Chgo., 1961-84, Gordon & Levin, Inc., Chgo., 1984-95; cons. Dept. Urban Renewal City Chgo., Council for Jewish Elderly, Chgo. Jewish Fedn. Prof. emeritus U. Ill.-Chgo. Sch. Architecture; former mem. Mayor's Adv. Coun. on Bldg. Code Amendments; master juror Nat. Coun. Archtl. Registration Bds. Works include Long-Kogan Office Bldg., 1957, 5401 Hyde Park Apt. Bldg., Chgo., 1962, South Commons, Chgo., 1968, The Commons Townhouse Devel., Chgo., 1968, Hyde Park West Apts., Chgo., 1969, IBM Office bldgs., Kalamazoo, 1969, Moline, Ill. 1970, Jefferson City, Mo., Omaha, 1971, Eastwood Tower Apts., Chgo., 1970, Wexler Pavilion and Siegel Inst.,U. Chgo. Stats Lab. Design Constrn., 1970, Cardiac Intensive Care Unit and Tumor Clinic, 1971, Michael Reese Hosp., Chgo., 1971, Arbor Trails Apts. and Townhouses, Park Forest, Ill., 1972, Kenmore Plaza Apts. Sr. Housing, Chgo., 1972, Kennaly Sq. Warehouse Apts., Chgo., 1972-74, Pontiac Office Bldg., Mich., 1972, Concourse Office Towers, Skokie, 1972, Belle Plaine Apts., Chgo., 1972, Newberry Plaza Apts., Chgo., 1973, Greenwood Park Apts., Chgo., 1974, River Plaza Apts., Chgo., 1976, Elm St. Plaza, Chgo., 1976, Dearborn Park, Twin Tower Apts., Chgo., 1979, Huron Plaza Apt., Chgo., 1981, 400 E. Ohio Condominiums, Streeterville, Chgo., 1983, East Bank Club, Chgo., 1983, U. (Champaign) Ill. Speech and Hearing Clinic, 1985, Dearborn-Elm Apts., Chgo., 1986-87; designer World Trade Ctr. Apts., Chgo., 1989, Lachman Montisorri Sch. for Hearing Impaired Children, Deerfield, Ill., 1990, Elm Street Apts., 1990, restoration of 1130 S. Michigan Ave., 1991, Chgo. Montessori Sch. for the Hearing Impaired, 1991, Love residence addition, Glencoe, Ill., 1991, Drs. Barak & Oremland offices, Skokie, Ill., 1991, Oral Rehab. Ctr., Skokie, 1992, residence addition, Glencoe, 1998. Former bd. dirs. Hyde Park-Kenwood Cmty. Conf., Astor St.-Lake Shore Dr. Assocs.; former v.p. Harper Ct. Found.; mem. Art Inst. Chgo., Mus. Sci. and Industry, Spertus Mus., Mus. Contemporary Art, Chgo. Hist. Soc.; mem. Landmarks Preservation Coun., Chgo. Archtl. Found.; former v.p. 1300 Lake Shore Drive Condo Assn. Decorated Croix de Guerre with palm; recipient Honor award Dept. Housing and Urban Devel., 1967, Honor award AIA-Chgo. C. of C., 1967, award AIA-House & Home Mag., 1967, Distinguished Bldg. award AIA, 1957, 63, 69, 71, 73, 75, award City of Chgo. Beautification, 1969, 75, award of excellence Concrete Post Tensioning Inst., 1984, Silver Circle award for excellence in teaching U. Ill., Chgo., 1985. Fellow AIA (bd. dirs Chgo. chpt.); mem. AIA, Labor Zionist Alliance, Am. Profs. for Peace in Middle East, Am. Jewish Congress, Chgo. Archtl. Found., Lambda Alpha. Clubs: Cliff Dwellers. Jewish.

GORDON, FLORENCE SHANFIELD, mathematics professor; b. Montreal, Que., Can., Mar. 11, 1942; came to U.S., 1968; d. Morris and Jean (Rubacha) Shanfield; m. Sheldon P. Gordon, June 27, 1965; children: Craig, Kenneth. BSc with honours in Math., McGill U., Montreal, 1963, MSc in Math. Stats., 1964, PhD in Math. Stats., 1968. Asst. prof. C.W. Post Coll., L.I. U., Greenvale, N.Y., 1968-71, Adelphi U., Garden City, N.Y., 1982-83; prof. math. N.Y. Inst. Tech., Old Westbury, 1983—. Precalculus reform project NSF, 1991—96. Author: (book and software) Contemporary Statistics: A Computer Approach, 1994; co-author: Functioning in the Real World: A Precalculus Experience, 2004; co-editor: Statistics for the Twenty First Century, 1986, A Fresh Start for Collegiate Mathematics: Rethinking the Courses Below Calculus, 2005; contbr. articles to profl. jours. Mem. Math. Assn. Am., Am. Statis. Assn., Am. Math. Assn. for Two Yr. Colls. Home: 61 Cedar Rd East Northport NY 11731-4128 Office: NY Inst Tech Dept Math Old Westbury NY 11568

GORDON, FRAN, writer; b. Bklyn., 1965; BSChemE, U. Va., 1986; MFA in Creative Writing, Vt. Coll., 1996. bd. govs. Nat. Arts Club, N.Y.C. Tchr. English dept. Rutgers U.; tchr. writing program New Sch. U. Vis. writer Am. Acad. Rome. Author: (novel) Paisley Girl, 1999. Recipient Award for Precocious Youth, Johns Hopkins, Gold medal Nat. Art Club; Yaddo fellow; fiction scholar Wesleyan U. Writers Conf. Mem. SAG, Writers Room (N.Y.C.).

GORDON, FRANCINE E., consultant, executive coach; b. Bklyn., Nov. 12, 1948; d. Emil and Sylvia (Packer) G. BA in Psychology, Vassar Coll., 1969; MA in Organizational Behavior, Yale U., 1971, PhD in Organizational Behavior, 1973. Asst. prof. Grad. Sch. Bus. Stanford U., 1972-77; gen. mgr. Calif. Actors Theatre, Los Gatos, 1977-80; assoc. dir. career planning and placement San Jose (Calif.) State U., 1981; dir. new bus. devel. Pacific Bell, San Ramon, Calif., 1981-87; recruiting mgr. Tandem Computers, Cupertino, Calif., 1987-89; dir. tng. and employment Ungermann-Bass, Santa Clara, Calif., 1989-95; mgr. Boston Cons. Group, 1995-2000; self employed cons., 2001—. Self employed, cons. 1973-81. Author: Bringing Women Into Management, 1974, Perspectives on Bringing Women Into Management, 1975; contbr. articles to profl. jours. Recipient Mervin Haskel award Textile Vets; 1970. Mem.: Internat. Enneagram Assn., Profl. Coach & Mentors Assn., Am. Psychol. Assn., Phi Beta Kappa. Avocations: bicycle riding, sailing, walking, guitar. E-mail: francine@fgordon.com.

GORDON, FRANK JEFFREY, medical educator; b. Washington, Dec. 5, 1948; married; 2 children. Attended, Case Western Reserve U., 1966-69; BS in Biology, N.Mex. State U., 1972, MA in Psychology, 1974; PhD in Biopsychology, U. Iowa, 1980. Interdisciplinary rsch. fellow U. Iowa, Iowa City, 1978-80, postdoctoral rsch. fellow Dept. Internal Medicine, 1980-81, rsch. scientist, 1981-82; asst. prof. dept. pharmacology Emory U. Sch. Medicine, Atlanta, 1982-88, assoc. prof., 1988—. Spkr. in field. Editl. bd. Am. Jour. Physiology, 1989-93. Mem. com. on risk factors Iowa Heart Assn., 1982. USPHS pre-doctoral fellow, 1978-80, post-doctoral fellow, 1980-82; rsch. starter grantee Pharm. Mfgs. Assn. Found., 1983-85. Fellow Coun. High Blood Pressure Rsch.; mem. Am. Physiol. Soc., Am. Soc. Pharmacology and Exptl. Therapeutics, Am. Heart Assn. (rsch. investigatorship Ga. affiliate 1987-88, AHA established investigator 1989-94), Soc. Neurosci., Sigma Xi. Achievements include research in brain and spinal cord regulation of peripheral cardiovascular systems in normal and pathological states. Office: Dept Pharmacology Rollins Rsch Ctr Rm 5011 Atlanta GA 30322-0001 Office Phone: 404-727-5893.

GORDON, GEORGE G., lawyer; b. Cheverly, Md., 1966; Student, London Sch. Econs., 1986—87; BA in Econs. cum laude, Brandeis U., 1988; UD, U. Pa., 1991. Bar: Pa. 1991, NJ 1991. Assoc. Dechert, Price & Rhoads, Phila.; ptnr. Dechert LLP (formerly Dechert, Price & Rhoads), Phila., 1999—. Spkr. in field. Former mem. editl. bd.: Ann. Rev. Antitrust Law Devel.; contbr. articles to profl. jours. Named one of Top 40 Lawyers Under 40, Nat. Law Jour., 2005. Mem.: ABA (litigation and antitrust sect., co-chair intellectual property com.). Office: Dechert LLP 4000 Bell Atlantic Tower 1717 Arch St Philadelphia PA 19103-2793 Office Phone: 215-994-2382. Business E-Mail: george.gordon@dechert.com.*

GORDON, GILBERT, chemist, educator; b. Chgo., Nov. 11, 1933; s. Walter and Catherine Gordon; m. Joyce Elaine Masura; children: Thomas, Lyndi. BS, Bradley U., 1955; PhD, Mich. State U., 1959. Postdoctoral rsch. assoc. U. Chgo., 1959-60; asst. prof. U. Md., College Park, 1960-64, assoc. prof., 1964-67, prof., 1967; prof. chemistry U. Iowa, Iowa City, 1967-73; prof., chmn. dept. Miami U., Oxford, Ohio, 1973-84, Volwiler Disting. Rsch. prof., 1984—2003, prof. emeritus, 2003—. Mem. editl. bd. synthesis inorganic metal, organic chemistry; contbr. articles to chem. jours. Named Cin. Chemist of Yr., 1981 Mem.: Faraday Soc., Chem. Soc. London, Am. Chem. Soc., Internat. Ozone Assn. (dir. 1995—, treas. 1998—2004, pres. 2002—04), Phi Kappa Phi, Sigma Xi. Home: 190 Shadowy Hills Dr Oxford OH 45056-1441 Office: Miami U Dept Chemistry Oxford OH 45056 Office Phone: 513-529-3336. Business E-Mail: gordong@muohio.edu. *My objectives have been to investigate meaningful areas of chemistry in an attempt to better understand chemical phenomena affecting our everyday lives (such as better and less expensive ways to purify drinking water), and to work diligently with the public while helping to educate them to be better citizens and aware of the exciting potential of science.*

GORDON, GLEN FRANK, lawyer; b. Wuerzburg, Germany, Apr. 7, 1965; s. Thomas Jon and Catherin Ann (Fillinger) G.; m. Christine Marie Johnson, Apr. 21, 1992. BA with honors, U. Mich., 1987; JD, U. Colo., 1990. Bar: Colo. 1990, U.S. Dist. Ct. Colo. 1990, U.S. Ct. Appeals (10th cir.) 1990. Summer assoc. Latham & Watkins, L.A., 1988; assoc. Buchanan, Gray, Purvis & Schuetze, Boulder, Colo., 1990-94; ptnr. Purvis, Gray & Gordon LLP, Boulder, 1994—, Schuetze & Gordon LLP, Boulder, 2002—. Mem. Boulder Bar Assn. (chmn. civil litigation sect., med.-legal sect.), Am. Inns. of Ct. Office: Schuetze & Gordon LLP 1327 Spruce St Ste 300 Boulder CO 80302 also: 370 17th St Ste 3590 Denver CO 80202 Fax: 393 444-5932. E-mail: glen@schuetze-gordon.com.

GORDON, GRANVILLE HOLLIS, church official; b. Picayune, Miss., Oct. 12, 1922; s. Thomas and Eugenia (Landrum) G.; m. Miriam C. Culpepper, Sept. 6, 1942; children: Tessa Eileen, Gerald Keith, Cathy Annette, Connie Jean, Donna Lynn. Student, Jacksonville Bapt. Coll. & Sem., 1950-52. Ordained to ministry Bapt. Ch., 1950. Pastor Friendship Bapt. Ch., Jewett, Tex., 1950-51, Little Flock Bapt. Ch., Jewett, 1950-51, Rural Shade Bapt., Kerens, Tex., 1951-52, Ogden Ave. Bapt., Mobile, Ala., 1952-54, Stanton Way Bapt., Mobile, 1954-58, Creston Hills Bapt., Jackson, Miss., 1958-65, 1st Bapt. Shady Grove, Laurel, Miss., 1965-74, Creston Hills Bapt., Jackson, Miss., 1974-84, Rolling Hills Bapt., Jacksonville, Fla., 1984-86, Temple Bapt. Ch., Lucedale, Miss., 1986-89, Highland Pk. Bapt., Hattiesburg, Miss., 1990-96, Shiloh Bapt. Church, Mt. Olive, Miss., 1996-98; Pastor Pear Orchard Bapt. Ch., Jackson, Miss., 1998—. With USAF, ETO. Mem. Miss. Bapt. Assn. (rec. clk. 1961-70), Bapt. Missionary Assn. (rec. clk. 1975-94). Baptist. Office: Baptist Missionary Assoc of Am 193 Old Canton Hills Dr Jackson MS 39211-3337 Office Phone: 601-957-2086.

GORDON, HAROLD SONNY, bank executive; b. Montreal, 1937; BA, Sir George Williams U., 1961; BCL, McGill U., 1964, BComm, 1958. Apptd.: Queen's Counsel 1985. Atty. Stikeman Elliott, Montreal, 1967-75, ptnr., 1975-95; vice-chmn. Hasbro, Inc., Pawtucket, RI, 1995—2002; chmn. Dundee Corp., Toronto, 2001—. Bd. dirs. Alliance Atlantis Comms. Inc., Dorel Industries Inc., Dundee Corp., Transcontinental Inc., Madaly Entertainment. Office: Dundee Bancorp Inc 40 Kings St W 55th Fl Toronto ON Canada M5H 4A9 Office Phone: 416-365-8766.

GORDON, HAROLD W., psychologist; b. Chgo., Ill., May 7, 1945; m. Karen DeGroot, July 21, 1946; children: Shefa, Shira. BS with honors in physics, Case Inst. of Tech., 1967; PhD in psychobiology, Calif. Inst. of Tech., 1973. Sr. lectr. Technion, Haifa, Israel, 1973—79; assoc. prof., psychiatry U. Pitts., Sch. of Medicine, Pitts., 1979—91; psychologist, program official Nat. Inst. on Drug Abuse, Bethesda, Md., 1991—. Contbr. articles various profl. jours., chapters to books. Various rsch grants. Mem.: AAAS, NY Acad. of Sci., Soc. for Neuroscience. Office: Nat Inst on Drug Abuse 6001 Exec Blvd Bethesda MD 20892-9551 Office Phone: 301-443-4877. Office Fax: 301-443-6814. E-mail: hg23r@nih.gov.

GORDON, HEATHER MARIE, artist, painter; b. Ft. Lauderdale, Fla., Apr. 30, 1967; d. Frank Gordon and Patricia Reynolds. BA, St. Lawrence U., 1989. Author: Travelers' Tales, 2000; exhibitions include in galleries, N.Y., San Francisco, Seattle, Santa Fe. Mem. Marin Arts Coun., 1998-99. Named Best Emerging Bay Area Artist, 1998. Avocations: travel, reading, swimming, writing, photography. Home: 23 Camino De Herrera San Anselmo CA 94960-1501

GORDON, J. HOUSTON, lawyer, political organization worker; b. Camden, Tenn., Sept. 16, 1946; s. Houston Darnal and Florence Jane (Culvahouse) G.; m. Deborah Watridge; children: Nathan, Baker, Blake. BS in Liberal Arts cum laude, U. Tenn., Martin, 1968; JD, U. Tenn., Knoxville, 1970; LLM in Taxation, George Washington U., 1973. Bar: Tenn. 1970, D.C. 1978. Asst. dist. atty. 16th Jud. Cir. Tenn., 1974-75; county atty. Tipton County, Tenn., 1981-84, delinquent tax atty.; atty. pvt. practice. Mem. dean's alumni adv. council Coll. Law U. Tenn., 1974-87, trustee, 1990-96, vice chair, 1994-95, vis. lectr.; instr. Dyersburg State C.C.; vis. lectr. U. S.C., Memphis State U., U. Ala., Valdosta State Coll. Contbr. articles to profl. jours. Alt. del. Nat. Dem. Conv., 1978 96; Dem. nominee U.S. Senate, Tenn., 1996; chair Tenn. Dem. Party, 1997—. 2d lt. Mil. Police Corps U.S. Army, 1970, capt. JAGC, 1970-74. Named Tenn. Outstanding Young Man, 1978. Fellow Am. Bar Found., Am. Coll. Trial Lawyers; mem. ABA, ATLA, Am. Bd. Trial Advocates (adv.), Tenn. Bar Assn. (advisor young lawyers divsn.), Tenn. Bar Found., Tenn. Trial Lawyers Assn. (bd. govs. 1976-78, 80-96, pres. 1989-90), D.C. Bar Assn., Memphis-Shelby County Bar Assn., Tipton County Bar Assn., U. Tenn. Alumni Assn. (bd. govs. 1976-78). Office: 114 W Liberty Ave PO Box 865 Covington TN 38019-0865

GORDON, JACK DAVID, foundation administrator, real estate company officer; b. Detroit, June 3, 1922; s. A. Louis and Henrietta (Rodgers) G.; m. Myra L. MacPherson; children: Andrew Louis, Deborah Mary, Jonathan Henry; stepchildren: Leah Siegel, Michael Siegel. BA, U. Mich., 1942. Engaged in real estate and ins. businesses, Miami Beach, Fla., 1946-52; founding dir., pres., chief mng. officer Washington Savs. & Loan Assn., Miami Beach, 1952-80, vice chmn. bd., 1980-81; founding dir. Jefferson Nat. Bank of Miami Beach, 1962-77, past chmn. exec. com.; dir. Inst. Pub. Policy and Citizenship Studies Fla. Internat. U., now the Jack D. Gordon Inst.; pres. The Hospice Found. of Am., Miami. Mem. Fla. Senate, 1972-92; housing fin. cons. Dept. State and; expert cons. UN Tech. Assistance Program in Costa Rica, Nicaragua, Panama, Ethiopia, Somali Republic, Nigeria, 1959-63; cons. to ROCAP, 1962-64, Eastern Nigerian Housing Corp., 1963; contract supr. AID Housing Guaranty Program in Latin Am., 1966-69; chmn. Miami Beach Housing Authority. 1947-56. Author: (with others) A Survey of New Home Financing Institutions in Latin America, 1969. Mem. Dade County Bd. Pub. Instrn., 1961-68. Served with AUS, 1943-46. Mem. Am. Jewish Congress, Am. Friends of Hebrew U., ACLU. Democrat. Office: 12000 Biscayne Blvd # 505 North Miami FL 33181 E-mail: senatorjack@att.net.

GORDON, JAMES A., investment company executive; B summa cum laude, Northwestern U. With Gordon's Wholesale, 1971—86; founder, mng. ptnr. Edgewater Growth Capital Ptnrs. Treasurer Whitney Mus. Am. Art, trustee; bd. dir. Des Moines Ballet; mem. bd. Grinnell Coll., chmn. investment com.; bd. dir. Chgo. Mus. Am. Art, Northwestern Meml. Found., John F. Kennnedy Ctr. Performing Arts, Chgo. Cares Inc., Bankers Trust Co., Methodist Med. Adv.; bd. dir. & former pres. Des Moines Art Ctr.; bd. dir. Iowa Soc. to Prevent Blindness, Des Moines Opera. Office: Edgewater Funds Growth Capital Ptnrs 900 N Michigan Ave Ste 1800 Chicago IL 60611 Mailing: c/o Whitney Mus Am Art 945 Madison Ave New York NY 10021 Office Fax: 312-664-8649. Business E-Mail: jim@edgewaterfunds.com.*

GORDON, JAMES S., lawyer, director; b. N.Y.C., Feb. 15, 1941; s. George S. and Sylvia A. (Wolfson) Gordon; m. Marcia G. Gordon, Dec. 22, 1968 (dec.); children: Daniel, Sarah; m. Debbie S. Pase, June 15, 1996. BA with high honors, U. Fla., 1962; LLB, Yale U., 1965. Bar: Ill. 1965, Fla. 1966, U.S. Supreme Ct. 1974. Asst. prof. Ind. U. Sch. Law, Bloomington, 1967-68, assoc. prof., 1969; ptnr. Feiwell, Galper & Gordon, Chgo., 1970-72; pvt. practice Chgo., 1972-80; pres. James S. Gordon, Ltd., Chgo., 1981-93; chmn. Gordon, Glickman, Flesch, & Rosenwein, Chgo., 1994—; dir. Mo. Metals, LLC. Editor: Yale Law Jour., 1963—65; contbr. articles to profl. jours. Ford Found. grantee, 1965—66. Mem.: Order of the Coif, Fla. Blue Key, Birchwood Club (Highland Park, Ill.), Lawyers Club Chgo., Phi Beta Kappa, Phi Alpha Delta. Office: 140 S Dearborn St Ste 404 Chicago IL 60603-5202 Office Phone: 312-346-1080. Business E-Mail: jgordon@lawggf.com.

GORDON, JAMES SAMUEL, psychiatrist; b. N.Y.C., Oct. 12, 1941; s. Jules David and Cynthia (Hymanson) G. AB magna cum laude, Harvard U., 1962, MD, 1967. Diplomate Am. Bd. Psychiatry and Neurology. Tchg. fellow gen. edn. Harvard U., Cambridge, Mass., 1963-67; NIH rsch. fellow, tchg. asst. dept. pathology Cornell Med. Coll., N.Y.C., 1964-65; intern Mt. Zion Hosp., San Francisco, 1967-68; resident in psychiatry Albert Einstein Coll. Medicine, Bronx, N.Y., 1968-70, chief resident, clin. instr. psychiatry, 1970-71; research psychiatrist NIMH, Rockville, Md., 1971-82, cons. alternative forms of svc., 1974-82, dir. spl. study Pres.'s Commn. Mental Health, 1977-78; chief adolescent svcs. St. Elizabeth's Hosp., Washington, 1980-82; clin. prof. Georgetown U. Med. Sch., Washington, 1980—; founder dir. Ctr. for Mind-Body Medicine, Washington, 1991—. Chair program adv. coun. Office of Alternative Medicine NIH, 1994-97; sr. cons. L.Am. Youth Ctr., Washington, 1984—; mem. cancer adv. panel NIH, 1998—; chair White House Commn. on Complimentary and Alternative Medicine Policy, 2000-02; vis. scholar Aurora Assocs., Washington, 1982-84; rsch. psychiatrist divsn. spl. mental health programs NIMH, 1980-82; med. cons. wellness program Walter Reed Army Med. Ctr., Washington, 1980-82; sr. cons. on adolescence divsn. child and adolescent svcs. St. Elizabeth's Hosp., Washington, 1979-80; Blanche Ittleson cons. Group for Advancement of Psychiatry, 1979; dir. spl. study on alternative svcs. Pres.' Commn. on Mental Health, 1977-78; vis. lectr. Cmty. Therapy Tng. Ctr., Washington, 1975, Cath. U. Am., Washington, 1974; lectr. in field. Author: The Golden Guru, 1987, Holistic Medicine, 1988, Transforming Medicine, 1996, Manifesto for a New Medicine, 1996, Comprehensive Cancer Care, 2000; editor: Health for the Whole Person (Med. Self Care Book award 1980), Mind, Body and Health: Towards and Integral Medicine, 1984; contbr. articles to profl. jours. Commdr. USPHS, 1971-82. Recipient award Ford Found., 1982, O. Spurgeon English Humanitarian award, 2002. Fellow Am. Assn. Social Psychiatry; mem. Am. Psychiat. Assn., Am. Holistic Med. Assn. (founding mem. 1980, trustee 1980-86), Am. Assn. Med. Acupuncture (founding mem. 1987), Physicians for Social Responsibility (exec. com. 1984-86). Office: Ctr Mind Body Medicine Ste 414 5225 Connecticut Ave NW Washington DC 20015-1845 Office Phone: 202-537-6837.

GORDON, JEFF, race car driver; b. Pittsboro, Ind., Aug. 4, 1971; m. Brooke Sealy. Stock race car driver DuPont Chevrolet, 1993—. Named Maxx Race Cards Rookie of Yr., 1993, winner, NASCAR Winston Cup, 1994, 1997, 1998, 2001, Busch Clash, 1994, The Winston, 1995, 1997, 2001, Brickyard 400, 1994, 1998, 2001, 2004, Goodwrench 500, 1995, Purolator 500, 1995, Ford City 500, 1995, 1997, 1998, Pepsi 400, 1995, Slick 50 300, 1995, Mountain Dew So. 500, 1995—98, 2002, MNBA 500, 1995, Daytona 500, 1997, 1999, 2005, CMT 300, 1997, Bud at the Glen, 1997, 1998, Calif. 500, 1997, 1999, Pocono 500, 1997, Coca-Cola 600, 1997, 1998, Goody's 500, 1997, Goodwrench 400, 1997, 1998, Pa. 500, 1998, Pepsi 400, Daytona, 1998, AC Delco 500, 1998, NAPA 500, 1998, Cracker Barrel 500, 1999, Save Mart/Kragen 350, 1998, 1999, Frontier at the Glen, 1999, NAPA Autocave 500, 1999, UAW-GM 500, 1999, Die Hard 500, 2000, Chevrolet Monte Carlo 400, 2000, UAW Daimler Chrysler 400, 2001, MBNA Platinum 400, 2001, Kmart 400, 2001, Global Crossing at the Glen, 2001, Protection One 400, 2001, 2002, Va. 500, 2003, Subway 500, 2003, Bass Pro Shops MBNA 500, 2003; named to McDonald's All-Star Team, 1994, 1995. Achievements include 2d youngest Winston Cup Champion NASCAR ever at age 24. Office: NASCAR PO Box 2875 Daytona Beach FL 32120-2875 E-mail: JGFAN@Primenet.com.

GORDON, JEFFREY IVAN, gastroenterologist, educator, molecular biologist, researcher; BA in Biology, Oberlin Coll.; MD, U. Chicago. Intern & junior asst. resident Barnes Hospital, St. Louis, 1973—75; rsch. assoc. biochemistry lab Nat. Cancer Ins., NIH, 1975—78; sr. asst. resident Wash. U. Medical Service, John Cochran VA Hospital, 1978—79; fellow Wash. U. Sch. of Medicine, St. Louis, 1979—81; asst. prof. medicine Wash. U., St. Louis, 1981—84, assoc. prof. medicine, 1985—87, prof. medicine, 1987—90, head molecular biology, pharmacology dept., 1991—, Robert J. Glaser disting. prof., 2002—, dir. Ctr. Genome Sciences, 2004—. Named Morton I. Grossman Disting. Lecturer, Am. Gastroenterologic Assn., 1999, Horace W. Davenport Disting. Lecturer, Am. Physiological Assn., 2003, Sir Arthur Hurst Lecturer, British Soc. Gastroenterology, 2004; recipient Young Investigator award, Am. Federation Clinical Rsch., 1990, NIDDK Young Scientist award, 1990, Marion Merrell Dow Disting. prize in Gastrointestinal Physiology, 1994, Janssen Sustained Achievement award in Digestive Sciences, 2003, Sr. Scholar award in Global Infectious Diseases, Ellison Medical Found., 2003; grantee John A. & George L. Hartford Found. Fellowship, 1981—84, Established Investigatorship, Am. Heart Assoc., 1985—90. Fellow: AAAS, Am. Acad. Arts and Scis., Am. Acad. Microbiology; mem.: NAS, Am. Gastroenterology Assn. (Disting. Achievement award 1992), Assn. Am. Physicians. Office: Wash U Campus Box 8510 4444 Forest Park Saint Louis MO 63108*

GORDON, JEFFREY NEIL, law educator; b. Richmond, Va., June 18, 1949; s. Irving Leonard and Viola Anne (Clayman) G. BA, Yale U., 1971; JD, Harvard U., 1975. Bar: N.Y. 1977, U.S. Dist. Ct. (so. and ea. dists.) N.Y. 1978, U.S. Ct. Appeals (2nd cir.) 1979, D.C. 1981. Reporter Rocky Mount News, Denver, 1971-72; law clk. to judge U.S. Ct. Appeals (10th cir.), Denver, 1975-76; assoc. Cleary, Gottlieb, Steen & Hamilton, N.Y.C., 1976-78; spl. asst. to gen. counsel, atty. advisor U.S. Treasury, Washington, 1978-81; prof. law NYU, NYC, 1982-88, Columbia U., NYC, 1988—, Alfred W. Bressler prof., 1998—. Co-dir. Ctr. Law and Econ. Studies, Columbia U. Contbr. articles to profl. jours. Recipient Exceptional Svc. award U.S. Dept. Energy, 1982. Mem. ABA, Am. Law Inst., Assn. of Bar of City of N.Y., Harvard Club, Phi Beta Kappa. Democrat. Jewish. Home: 410 Riverside Dr Apt 81 New York NY 10025-7923 Office: Columbia Law Sch Ctr Law Econ Studies 435 W 116th St New York NY 10027-7297 Office Phone: 212-854-2316.

GORDON, JOHN CHARLES, forestry educator; b. Nampa, Idaho, June 10, 1939; s. John Nicholas and Ada Elizabeth (Scheuermann) G.; m. Helka Lehtinen, Aug. 6, 1964; 1 child, Sean Nicholas. BS, Iowa State U., Ames, 1961, PhD, 1966; postgrad., U. Helsinki, Finland, 1961-62; MA (hon.), Yale U., New Haven, 1984; LHD (hon.), Unity Coll., 2000. Instr. forestry Iowa State U., Ames, 1965-66; plant physiologist U.S. Forest Service, Rhinelander,

Wis., 1966-70; prof. forestry Iowa State U., Ames, 1970-77; prof., head dept. forest sci. Oreg. State U., Corvallis, 1977-83; prof., dean forestry and environ. studies Yale U., New Haven, 1983-92, 97-98, Pinchot prof. forestry and environ. studies, 1991—2001, acting dir. Inst. for Biospheric Studies, 1994-95, 96; founding ptnr. Interforest LLC, 1996—; chmn., mem. exec. com. Candlewood Timber Group, 1999—; Pinchot prof. emeritus Yale U., New Haven, 2001—. Chmn. Commn. on Rsch. and Resources Mgmt. in Nat. Pks., 1988—89, Nat. Commn. on Sci. and Sustainable Forestry, 2000—02, bd. dirs., 2000—; chmn. com. on forestry rsch. NAS, 1989—92; lectr. Syracuse U., 1990, Oreg. State U., 1993, U. Fla., 1994, U. Mont., 1998. Editor: Symbiotic Nitrogen Fixation, 1983; author (books) Agroforestry Research, 1991, Environmental Leadership, 1993, Ecosystems, 1998, Forests to Fight Poverty, 1999, Forest Certification, 1999, Buy on the Upside: Stock Investing, 2005; contbr. articles to profl. jours. Bd. dirs. Friends of Gray Towers, Milford, Pa., 1983-87, Yale U. Alumni Fund, 1985-92, Tropical Forest Found., 1991-94, Wintock Internat., 1993-95, Soc. for Protection N.H. Forests, 2001—; vis. com. Harvard U., 1985-92; pres. C.V. Riley Found., N.Y.C., 1985, 92-94, Conn. Fund for Environ., 1986-92; mem. rsch. adv. com. U.S. AID, 1988-92; co-chmn. 7th Am. Forest Congress, 1994-97. Fulbright scholar, 1961, 84; hon. sr. fellow U. Glasgow, Scotland, 1975-76; Green vis. prof. U. B.C., Vancouver, 1985; named Conservationist of the Yr., Pacific Rivers Coun., 1992; fellow Timothy Dwight Coll., Yale U.; disting. svc. award Am. Forests, 1996. Mem. Soc. Am. Foresters, Am. Forestry Assn. (Disting. Svc. award 1996), Sigma Xi (hon.), Phi Kappa Phi (hon.). Clubs: Yale (N.Y.C.), Morys (New Haven), Cosmos (Washington). Presbyterian. Avocations: hiking, fishing, writing short stories. Home: 27 Evans Rd Holderness NH 03245 Office Phone: 603-536-7571. Business E-Mail: johngordon@fcgnetworks.net.

GORDON, JOHN L., JR., historian, educator; b. Elizabethtown, Ky., July 14, 1942; s. John L. and Rose (Kemph) G.; m. Susan L. Cooper, Sept. 1963; 1 child, Sarah Elizabeth. AB History and Mathematics, Western Ky. U., 1963; MA, Vanderbilt U., 1965, PhD, 1972. From instr. to assoc. prof. history U. Richmond, Va., 1967-90, prof. history, 1990—, interim v.p., provost, 1983, interim dean faculty arts and scis., 1981-82, assoc. dean faculty arts and scis., 1980-87, dean grad. studies, 1980-87, chair dept. history, 1989—. Spkr. in field; rschr. in field, England, Ireland, Can. Contbr. numerous articles to profl. jours. Grantee Can. Studies Faculty Enrichment Program, 1987; Duke Alberta Rsch. fellow, 1984; faculty summer rsch. fellow, grantee U. Richmond, 1977, 88, 95. Mem. Am. Hist. Assn., Assn. Can. Studies in U.S., Can. Hist. Assn., Carolinas Symposium Brit. Studies, N.Am. Conf. Brit. Studies, S.E. Coun. Can. Studies (exec. com., pres. 1993-96), So. Conf. Brit. Studies (exec. coun., program chair 1993, 94), So. Hist. Assn., Omicron Delta Kappa, Phi Alpha Theta. Home: 4 Bostwick Ln Richmond VA 23226-3107 Office: U Richmond Ryland Hall Richmond VA 23173

GORDON, JOHN STEELE, writer, columnist; b. N.Y.C., May 7, 1944; s. Richard Haden Gordon and Mary Alricks Steele. BA, Vanderbilt U., 1966. Prodn. editor Harper & Row, N.Y.C., 1966—72; press. sec. to Congressman Herman Badillo, N.Y.C., 1976—77; columnist Am. Heritage Mag., N.Y.C., 1989—. Author: Hamilton's Blessing, The Great Game, The Business of America, A Thread Across the Ocean, An Empire of Wealth, The Scarlet Woman of Wall Street. Mem.: Union Club. Home and Office: 8 Bogtown Rd North Salem NY 10560 Business E-Mail: jsg@johnsteelegordon.com.

GORDON, JONATHAN DAVID, psychologist, lawyer; b. Watertown, N.Y., Nov. 5, 1949; s. Morton Lawrence and Anna (Lesser) Gordon; m. Doris Susan Perkel, Jan. 16, 1972 (div.); 1 child, Pamela Michelle; m. Janet S Levick, Nov. 25, 1984 (div.); children: Lisa Danielle, Jaclyn Gabrielle. BA, Fairleigh Dickinson U., 1971, MA, 1973; PhD, Hofstra U., 1976; JD, Fordham U., 1998. Diplomate Child Custody Evaluation Am Col Forensic Examiners, Am Bd Med Psychotherapists, Int Acad Behavioral Med, Am Acad Pain Mgt, Nat Registry Neurofeedback Providers. Team supr., psychologist dept. ambulatory care Mt. Sinai Med. Ctr., N.Y.C., 1976-80; pvt. practice clin. psychology Teaneck, N.J., 1978-97; chief psychologist, coord. profl. svcs. Holley Child Care and Devel. Ctr. Youth Consultation Svc., Hackensack, N.J., 1980-85; staff psychologist div. psychol. svcs. Fairleigh Dickinson U., Hackensack, 1982-85, acting dir., 1989; dir. adult outpatient psychiatry Jersey City Med. Ctr., 1985-87; dir. Bergen Biofeedback and Psychotherapy Ctr., Teaneck, 1986—; dep. atty. gen. N.J. Div. Law, Newark, 1999—. Sch consult Leonia (NJ) High Sch, 1987—88. Mem.: APA, ATLA, ABA, Perineometer Research Inst (cert), Biofeedback Cert Inst Am (cert), Asn Applied Psychophysiology and Biofeedback, Bergen County Asn Lic Psychologists, NY State Psychol Asn, NJ Psychol Asn, NJ Bar Asn, NY State Bar Asn. Office: NJ Divsn Law 124 Halsey St PO Box 45029 Newark NJ 07101-8002 E-mail: gordojon@law.dol.lps.state.nj.us.

GORDON, JOSEPH ELWELL, university official, educator; b. Deatsville, Ala., July 2, 1921; s. Joseph Elwell and Martha (Berry) G.; m. Doris Elizabeth Smith, June 5, 1948; children— Cecile Lizabeth, Joseph Elwell, Melissa Innes. AB, Birmingham-So. Coll., 1942; MS, Auburn U., 1949; PhD, U. Chgo., 1951. Tchr. math., Montgomery, Ala., 1946-48; instr. math. Auburn U., 1948-49; research asst. North Central Assn. Colls. and Secondary Schs., Chgo., 1949-51; program analyst Air U., Maxwell AFB, 1951-54; mem. faculty Tulane U., 1954—, asst. prof. edn., 1958—, assoc. dir. admissions, 1957-63, dean Coll. Arts and Scis., 1964-84, dir. found. rels., 1984-86, spl. asst. to v.p. devel., 1986-90, univ. historian, 1990-96, vice provost, 1996-97. Author (with Clarence Mohr): Tulane: The Emergence of a Modern University 1945-1980, 2001. Served to lt. USNR, 1942-46. Mem. Omicron Delta Kappa, Phi Delta Kappa, Pi Kappa Alpha. Democrat. Presbyterian. Home: 1108 Lowerline St New Orleans LA 70118-5205

GORDON, JOSEPH HAROLD, lawyer; b. Tacoma, Mar. 31, 1909; s. Joseph H. and Mary (Obermiller) G.; m. Jane Wilson, Sept. 12, 1936 (dec.); children: Joseph H., Nancy Jane; m. Eileen (Rylander) Rademaker, Jan. 7, 1967 (dec. 2001). BA, Stanford, 1931; LLB, JD, U. Wash., 1935. Bar: Wash. 1935. Since practiced in, Tacoma; ptnr. Gordon & Gordon, Tacoma, 1935-50, Henderson, Carnahan, Thompson & Gordon, Tacoma, 1950-57, Carnahan, Gordon & Goodwin, Tacoma, 1957-70, Gordon, Thomas, Honeywell, Malanca, Peterson & Daheim, Tacoma, 1970—. Mem.: ABA (ho. dels. 1951—, bd. govs. 1962—72, treas. 1965—72), Tacoma Bar Assn. (past pres.), Wash. State Bar Assn., Tacoma Golf and Country Club, Tacoma Club, Rotary. Presbyterian (Elder). Home: 233 St Helens Ave Tacoma WA 98402 Office: Gordon Thomas Honeywell Malanca Peterson & Daheim PO Box 1157 2200 Wells Fargo Plz Tacoma WA 98401-1157 Office Phone: 253-620-6408. Business E-Mail: gordsr@gth-law.com.

GORDON, JUDITH, communications consultant, writer; b. Long Beach, Calif. d. Irwin Ernest and Susan (Perlman) G.; m. Lawrence Banka, May 1, 1977. BA, Oakland U., 1066; MS in Libr. Sci., Wayne State U., 1973. Researcher Detroit Inst. of Arts, 1968-69; libr. Detroit Pub. Libr., 1971-74; caseworker Wayne County Dept. Social Svcs., Detroit, 1974-77; advt. copywriter Hudson's Dept. Store, Detroit, 1979; mgr. The Poster Gallery, Detroit, 1980-81; mktg., corp. communications specialist Bank of Am., San Francisco, 1983-84, mgr., consumer pubs., 1984-86; prin. Active Voice, San Francisco, 1986—. Contbr. edit. The Artist's Mag., 1988-93; contbr. to book Flowers: Gary Bukovnik, Watercolors and Monotypes, Abrams, 1990. Vol. From the Heart, San Francisco, 1992, Bay Area Book Festival, San Francisco, 1990, 91, Aid & Comfort, San Francisco, 1987, Save Orch. Hall, Detroit, 1977-81, NOW sponsored abortion clinic project. Recipient Nat. award Merit. Soc. Consumer Affairs Profls. in Bus., 1986, Bay Area Best award Internat. Assn. Bus. Communicators, 1986, Internat. Galaxy awards, 1992, 95, 97, Internat. Mercury awards, 1995, Charles Schwab Excellence in Svc. award, 2000. Mem. AAUW, Nat. Writers Union, Editl. Freelancers Assn. Inc., Clarity, Achenbach Graphics Arts Coun., Women's Nat. Book Assn., Assn. Women in Comms., Fin. Women's Assn., Plain Lang. Assn., FIMA West (bd. dirs.), ZYZZYVA (bd. dirs.). Office: 899 Green St San Francisco CA 94133-3756 E-mail: activvduo@msn.com.

GORDON, JULIE PEYTON, foundation administrator; b. Jacksonville, Fla., June 21, 1940; d. Robert Benoist Shields and Bessie (Cavanaugh) Peyton; m. Robert James Gordon, June 22, 1963. BA, Boston U., 1963; MA, Harvard U., 1965, PhD, 1969. Asst. prof. English Ill. Inst. Tech., Chgo., 1968-75, assoc. prof., 1975-77, asst. dean students, 1975-78; asst. dean acad. affairs Northwestern U., Evanston, Ill., 1978-80, lectr. English, Univ. Coll., 1978—, assoc. dean Univ. Coll., 1980-85, sec. Econometric Soc., 1975—, exec. dir. Econometric Soc., 1985—. Mem. nat. adv. com. ALA, Chgo., 1983—86. Author: Seasons in the Contemporary American Family, 1984. Grantee NEH, 1971-73; project scholar NEH, 1983-86. Mem. Phi Beta Kappa. Avocation: writing fiction and poetry. Home: 202 Greenwood Evanston IL 60201-4714 Office: Northwestern U Dept Econs Econometric Soc Evanston IL 60208-2600 Office Phone: 847-491-3615. Business E-Mail: jpg@northwestern.edu.

GORDON, LANA G., state representative; b. Kansas City, Mo., Aug. 20, 1950; m. Arnold Gordon; children: Jennifer, Stacey, Jamie. BS in Edn., U. Kans., 1971. Subst. tchr., Mo., 1971—72; tchr. Lee's Summit (Mo.) Pub. Sch., 1972—73; test adminstr. State of Kans., 1978—80; sec., treas. Cardinal Bldg. Svcs., 1997—2001; office gen. Cardinal DBA/BG Svc. Solution, 2002—; mem. Kans. Ho. of Reps., 2001—. Bd. dirs. Kansas, Inc. Sec. citizens adv. coun. USD 501 Dist., 1982—85; bd. dirs. USD 501 Sch. Found., 1994—97, Vol. Ctr. Topeka, 1998—, Jr. League Topeka, 2002—04, Topeka Conv. and Visitors Bur., 2004—. Republican. Jewish. Office: 181-W State Capitol 281 W 10th Ave Topeka KS 66612 Address: 5820 SW 27th St Topeka KS 66614

GORDON, LARRY JEAN, environmental health educator; b. Tipton, Okla., Oct. 16, 1926; s. Andrew J. and Deweylee (Stewart) G.; m. Nedra Callender, Aug. 26. 1950; children: Debra Gordon Dunlap, Kent, Gary. Student, U. Okla., 1943-44; BS, U. N.Mex., 1949, MS, 1951; MPH, U. Mich., 1954. High sch. sci. tchr., N.Mex., 1949-50; various positions N.Mex. Dept. Health, 1950-55; commd. officer USPHS, 1957—, advanced through grades to Dir. Grade (Navy capt.), dir. Albuquerque Environ. Health Dept., 1955-68, 82-86; dir. Environ. Improvement Agy., Santa Fe, 1968-73; adminstr. for health and environ. programs N.Mex. HHS Dept., Santa Fe, 1976-78; dir. N.Mex. Sci. Lab. System, Albuquerque, 1973-76; dep. sec. N.Mex. Health and Environ. Dept., Santa Fe, 1978-82, sec., 1987-88; vis. prof. pub. adminstrn. U. N.Mex., Albuquerque, 1988—, adj. prof. polit. sci., 1997—, sr. fellow Inst. for Pub. Policy, 1997—. Chmn. N.Mex. Water Quality Commn., 1971-73. Asst. editor Jour. Environ. Health, 1975-78; cons. editor Environ. News Digest, 1970-82; editl. cons. Jour. Pub. Health Policy, 1980-96, Underwriters Labs., 1996; contbr. over 240 articles to profl. jours. Recipient Samuel J. Crumbine award for Outstanding Devel. of Comprehensive Program for Environ. Sanitation, 1959 and 65, Sanitarians Disting. Service award Internat. Assn. Milk, Food, and Environ. Sanitarians, 1962, Outstanding Contrbn. award N.Mex. Assn. Pub. Health Sanitarians, 1967, Boss of Yr. award Santa Fe chpt. Nat. Secs. Assn., 1970, Walter F. Snyder award For Achievement in Environ. Quality, 1978, Commendation for Leadership in Health Care N.Mex. Hosp. Assn., 1981, N.Mex. Outstanding Pub. Svc. award, 1988, Zimmerman award U. N.Mex. Alumni, 1993, L.A. County Breslow award L.A. County Dept. Health Svcs., 1994, Outstanding Leadership in Environ. Adminstrn. award Am. Soc. for Pub. Adminstrn., 1994. Mem. APHA (exec. bd. 1975-82, pres. 1980-81, John J. Sippy Meml. award 1962, other coms., Sedgwick award 1987), Am. Acad. Sanitarians (founder, David Calvin Wagner Excellence award 1984), N.Mex. Pub. Health Assn. (past pres., Disting. Svc. award 1970, Spl. award, 1978, D.A. Larrazola award 1989), N.Mex. Environ. Health Assn., (past pres.), Am. Lung Assn. N.Mex. (bd. dirs. 1982-94, Clinton P. Anderson award for Outstanding Contbn. to Lung Health 1987), Nat. Accreditation Coun. Environ. Health Curricula, Nat. Audubon Soc. (pres. coun. 1982-86), U. Mich. Sch. Pub. Health Alumni Assn. (bd. govs. 1985-88, Outstanding Alumnus award 1995), Royal Soc. Promotion of Health, London (hon.), N.Mex. Soc. Pub. Adminstrn. (Disting. Pub. Adminstr. award 1996), Delta Omega, Phi Kappa Phi, Phi Sigma. Republican. Avocations: fishing, boating, golf, genealogy. Home: 1674 Tierra Del Rio NW Albuquerque NM 87107-3259 Personal E-mail: 1016Larry@msn.com.

GORDON, LEE DIANE, school librarian, educator; b. Lafayette, Ind., Oct. 30, 1948; d. Henry Charles and Leonora (Brower) G.; m. James J. Thomas, Aug. 27, 1977 (div. Feb. 1994); m. Daniel L. Weber, July 10, 1999. BA, Calif. State U., Long Beach, 1970; MEd, U. Nev., Las Vegas, 1980. Cert. tchr., Nev., Calif.; cert. libr., Nev. Tchr. Carmenita Jr. High Sch., Cerritos, Calif., 1971-77, Jim Bridger Jr. High Sch., North Las Vegas, Nev., 1977-79, libr., 1979-84, Eldorado High Sch., Las Vegas, 1984—2001, Sierra Vista H.S., Las Vegas, 2001—. Adj. faculty U. Nev.-Las Vegas, 1997—. Co-author: The Overworked Teacher's Bulletin Board Book, 1981; filmstrips, 1983; author: World Historical Fiction Guide for Young Adults, 1996; contbr. articles to profl. jours. Mem. Am. Assn. Sch. Librs. (affiliate del., various coms. 1987—; dir. Region VII 1999-2001), Nev. Assn. Sch. Librs. (chair 1987), Clark County Sch. Librs. Assn. (pres. 1987-88), Delta Kappa Gamma (Iota chpt. pres. 1990-92). Office: Sierra Vista High Sch 8100 W Robindale Rd Las Vegas NV 89113

GORDON, LEO I., hematologist, oncologist, educator; b. Milw., Nov. 24, 1947; s. Abraham and Fira (Weinstein) G.; m. Linda Robinson; children: Elizabeth, Peter. BA, U. Chgo., 1969; MD, U. Cin., 1973. Diplomate Am. Bd. Internal Medicine, 1976, Am. Bd. Internal Medicine Hematology, 1978, Am. Bd. Internal Medicine Oncology, 1979. Intern in medicine U. Chgo. Hosps., 1973-74, resident in medicine, 1974-76, fellow in hematology/oncology, 1978-79; fellow in hematology U. Minn., Mpls., 1976-78; asst. prof. medicine Northwestern U., Evanston, Ill., 1979-85, assoc. prof., 1985-95, prof. medicine, 1995—. Chief divsn. hematology/oncology, Northwestern U. Med. Sch., Chgo., 1996—. Contbr. over 125 articles and abstracts to profl. jours.; author book. Office: Northwestern U Med Sch 303 E Chicago Ave Chicago IL 60611-3072 E-mail: l-gordon@northwestern.edu.

GORDON, LEONARD, retired sociology educator; b. Detroit, Dec. 6, 1935; s. Abraham and Sarah (Rosen) G.; m. Rena Joyce Feigelman, Dec. 25, 1955; children: Susan Melinda, Matthew Seth, Melissa Gail. BA, Wayne State U., 1957; MA, U. Mich., 1958; PhD, Wayne State U., 1966. Instr. Wayne State U., Detroit, 1960-62; research dir. Jewish Community Council, Detroit, 1962-64; dir. Mich. area Am. Jewish Com., N.Y.C., 1964-67; asst. prof. Ariz. State U., Tempe, 1967-70, assoc. prof., 1970-77, prof., 1977—, chmn. dept. sociology, 1981-90, assoc. dean for acad. programs Coll. Liberal Arts and Scis., 1990-2001, rsch. prof., 2001—02, prof. emeritus, 2002—, founding mem. emeritus coll. coun., 2005—. Cons. OEO, Maricopa County, Ariz., 1968 Author: A City in Racial Crisis, 1971, Sociology and American Social Issues, 1978, (with A. Mayer) Urban Life and the Struggle To Be Human, 1979, (with R. Hardert, M. Laner and M. Reader) Confronting Social Problems, 1984, (with J. Hall and R. Melnick) Harmonizing Arizona's Ethnic and Cultural Diversity, 1992. Sec. Conf. on Religion and Race, Detroit, 1962-67; mem. exec. bd. dirs. Am. Jewish Com., Phoenix chpt., 1969-70. Grantee NSF, 1962, Rockefeller found., 1970, 84. Fellow Am. Sociol. Assn. (chair task force on current knowledge on hate/bias acts on coll. and univ. campuses 2000—, mem. AAUP, Pacific Sociol. Assn. (v.p. 1978-79, pres. 1980-81), Soc. Study Social Problems (chair C. Wright Mills award com. 1988, treas. 1989-96), Ariz. State U. Alumni Assn. (faculty dir. 1981-82, founding mem. emeritus coll. coun., 2005-). Democrat. Jewish. Home: 13660 E Columbine Dr Scottsdale AZ 85259-3753 Office: Ariz State U Dept Sociology Tempe AZ 85287-4802 Business E-Mail: len.gordon@asu.edu.

GORDON, LEONARD H(ERMAN) D(AVID), history educator; b. N.Y.C., Aug. 8, 1928; s. Herman and Ray (Keidan) G.; m. Marjorie J(osephine) Hunt, June 11, 1951; children: Herman, David. *Wife, Marjorie, served in the WAVES during World War II (1944-46) and later graduated from Indiana University in 1949 with a BA, and in 1951 with a MA. Majoring in Government, her Master's Thesis was "Origins of the New Japanese Constitution, May 3, 1947." She later served as an Instructor in International Relations and Modern European History for the University of Maryland, Tokyo, in 1960. She taught English in Taiwan for the US AID program in 1959 and on Japan's national radio in 1965. Entering into politics, she was elected to the West Lafayette City Council, Indiana, 1975-79, and served on the Area Plan Commission of Tippecanoe County.* BA, Ind. U., 1950, MA, 1953; PhD, U. Mich., 1961. Far Eastern diplomatic historian U.S. Dept. State, Washington, 1961-63; asst. prof. East Asian history U. Wis., Madison, 1963-67; assoc. prof. Chinese history Purdue U., West Lafayette, Ind., 1967-94, chmn. Asian studies program, 1992-94, prof. emeritus Chinese history, 1994—. Mem. preliminary screening com. Am. Coun. Learned Socs., N.Y.C., 1971-72, nat. com., 1972-74, joint com. Social Scis. Rsch. Coun. Editor: Taiwan: Studies in Chinese Local History, 1970; co-editor: Doctoral Dissertations on China, A Bibliography of Studies in Western Languages, 1945-70, 1972, Bibliography of Sun Yat-Sen in China's Republican Revolution, 1985-1925, 1991, 2d edit., 1998; co-author: All Under Heaven: Sun Yat-Sen and His Revolutionary Thought, 1991. With U.S. Army, 1953-56. Faculty grantee U. Wis., 1963, 64, Faculty grantee Purdue U., 1968, grantee Am. Philos. Soc., 1963, 67, 80; Fulbright Rsch. fellow, Tokyo, 1959-60; Inter-Univ. fellow for Field Tng. in Chinese, Taipei, 1958-59. Mem. Assn. for Asian Studies (publs. com. 1968-71, editor newsletter). Office: Dept of History Purdue U West Lafayette IN 47907-1358 E-mail: lhdgordon@alumni.indiana.edu.

GORDON, LESLIE PEYTON, executive recruiting consultant; b. Asheville, N.C., July 15, 1962; d. William Madison and Grace Baker Peyton; m. Barton Jennings Gordon, June 27, 1998. BA in Econ. (with honors), U. N.C., 1984; MBA, U. Va., 1989. Assoc. Bankers Trust Co., N.Y.C., 1988-92; v.p. then sr. v.p. The Whitney Group, N.Y.C., 1992-96; mng. dir. Korn/Ferry Internat., N.Y.C., 1996—. Com. chair N.Y. Jr. League, N.Y.C., 1994-97. Recipient YWCA Acad. Women Achievers award, 1996. Mem. Congl. Club, Univ. Club (N.Y.C.). Democrat. Episcopalian. Office: Korn/Ferry Internat 200 Park Ave Fl 37 New York NY 10166-3702 Fax: 212-661-2547. E-mail: leslie.gordon@kornferry.com.

GORDON, LINCOLN, political economist; b. N.Y.C., Sept. 10, 1913; s. Bernard and Dorothy (Lerned) G.; m. Allison Wright, June 25, 1937 (dec.); children: Anne, Robert W., Hugh, Amy. AB, Harvard, 1933; D. Phil. (Rhodes scholar), Oxford (Eng.) U., 1936; LL.D., Fairleigh Dickinson U., 1965, Columbia, 1967, Rutgers U., 1967, U. Md., 1968, Wash. Coll., 1968, U. Del., 1969; L.H.D., Loyola Coll., Balt., 1968. Instr., faculty instr. govt. Harvard, 1936-41, William Ziegler prof. internat. econ. relations, 1955-61; research technician water, energy resources U.S. Nat. Resources Planning Bd., Washington, 1939-1940; mem. staff requirements com. W.P.B., 1942-45, program vice chmn., 1945; dir. bur. reconversion priorities Civilian Prodn. Adminstrn., 1945-46; assoc. prof. bus. Harvard, 1946-47, prof. govt. and adminstrn., 1947-50; cons. U.S. Rep. UN AEC, 1946, Army and Navy Munitions Bd., Dept. of State, 1947, ECA, 1948; North Atlantic Council Com. of Three on non-mil. aspects of NATO, 1956; dir. program div. Office ECA, spl. rep. in Europe, 1949-50; econ. adviser to spl. asst. to President, 1950-51; asst. dir. Office of Mut. Security, 1951-52; chief Marshall Aid mission and minister econ. affairs in Am. Embassy in London, 1952-55; U.S. amb. Brazil, 1961-66; asst. sec. state for inter-Am. affairs, 1966-67; pres. Johns Hopkins, Balt., 1967-71; vis. prof. polit. economy Sch. Advanced Internat. Studies, Washington, 1971-72; fellow Woodrow Wilson Internat. Center for Scholars, 1972-75; sr. fellow Resources for Future, Washington, 1975-80; mem. sr. rev. panel CIA, 1980-82, nat. intelligence officer-at-large, 1982-83; guest scholar Brookings Instn., 1984—. Author: The Public Corporation in Great Britain, 1938; author: (with M. Fainsod) Government and the American Economy, 1941; author: rev. edit., 1948, 1959, Fuel and Power in Industrial Location and National Policy, Nat. Resources Planning Bd., 1942, Representation of the U.S. Abroad (in part), 1956, rev. edit., 1964; author: (with Engelbert L. Grommers) United States Manufacturing Investment in Brazil, 1961; author: A New Deal for Latin America, 1963, Growth Policies and the International Order, 1979; author: (with Joy Dunkerley and others) Energy Strategies for Developing Nations, 1981; author: (with J.F. Brown and others) Eroding Empire: Western Relations with Eastern Europe, 1987; author: (with T. Stanley) Integrating Economic and Security Factors in East-West Relations, 1988; author: Brazil's Second Chance: #En Route toward the First World, 2001, Portuguese translation, 2002; editor: International Stability and Progress: U.S. Interests and Instruments, 1957, From Marshall Plan to Global Interdependence, 1978. Bd. dirs. Atlantic Council U.S.; hon. trustee Com. for Econ. Devel. Decorated Grand Cross Order Quetzal Guatemala; Grand Cross Order Cruzeiro do Sul Brazil). Fellow Am. Acad. Arts and Scis.; mem. Am. Polit. Sci. Assn., Coun. on Fgn. Rels., Internat. Inst. Strategic Studies, Royal Econ. Soc., Phi Beta Kappa, Cosmos Club Washington. Home: 3069 University Ter NW Washington DC 20016-3462 Office Phone: 202-797-6259. Business E-Mail: lgordon@brookings.edu.

GORDON, LINDA, history educator; b. Chgo., Jan. 19, 1940; d. Bill and Helen (Appelman) G.; m. Allen Hunter; 1 child, Rosa Gordon Hunter. BA in History magna cum laude, Swarthmore Coll., 1961; MA in History and Russian Studies, Yale U., 1963, PhD in History with distinction, 1970. Prof. history U. Mass., Boston, 1968-84, U. Wis., Madison, 1984-90, Florence Kelley prof. history, 1990—, Vilas disting. rsch. prof., 1993—2004; prof. history NYU, 1999—. Vis. prof. U. Amsterdam, 1984; cons. and lectr. in field. Author: Woman's Body, Woman's Right: A Social History of Birth Control in America, 1976, 1977, 1990, Cossack Rebellions: Social Turmoil in the Sixteenth Century Ukraine, 1983, Heroes of Their Own Lives: The Politics and History of Family Violence, Boston 1880-1960, 1988 (AHA Joan Kelly prize, Wis. Libr. Assn. award, 1988);: Heroes of Their Own Lives: The Politics and History of Family Violence, Boston 1880-1960, 1989, Pitied But Not Entitled: Single Mothers and the History of Welfare, 1994 (winner Berkshire prize, 1995, Gustavus Myers human rights award, 1995), The Great Arizona Orphan Abduction, 1999 (winner Bancroft and Beveridge prizes). NIMH rsch. grantee, 1979-82, Am. Coun. Learned Socs. travel grantee, 1980; Guggenheim fellow, 1983-84, Bunting Inst. fellow, 1983-84, Am. Coun. Learned Socs./Ford Found. fellow, 1985-86, Harry Frank Guggenheim Found. fellow, 1987, Russell Sage Found. fellow, 1997-98; recipient Antonovych prize, 1983, Bird Meml. Lectureship, U. Maine, 1986, Am. Philos. Soc. Rsch. award, 1988-89, Joan Kelly prize, 1988, Berkshire prize, 1994. Mem. Presdl. Adv. Coun. on violence against women, Am. Hist. Assn. (jour. editl. bd. 1990-93), Orgn. Am. Historians (exec. bd. 1991-94, mem. editl. bd. jour. 1994-97), Inst. for Rsch. on Povety (exec. com. 1990-95). Jewish. Office: NYU 53 Washington Sq S New York NY 10012 Office Phone: 212-998-8627. Business E-Mail: Linda.Gordon@nyu.edu.

GORDON, LOIS G., language educator; b. Englewood, N.J. d. Irving David and Betty (Davis) Goldfein; m. Alan Lee Gordon, Nov. 13, 1961; 1 son, Robert Michael. BA (Nat. Merit scholar, Barbour scholar), U. Mich., 1960; postgrad., Columbia U., 1960-61; MA, U. Wis., 1962, PhD (Dissertation Completion fellow), 1966. Teaching asst. U. Wis., 1962-64; lectr. CCNY, 1964-66; asst. prof. U. Mo., Kansas City, 1966-68; asst. prof. English Fairleigh Dickinson U., Teaneck, N.J., 1968-71, assoc. prof., 1971-75, prof., 1975—, chmn. dept. English and comparative lit., 1982-90. Vis. exch. prof. Rutgers U., 1994; cons. U. Mo. Press, 1968-69, Doubleday Inc., 1974, Fairleigh Dickinson U. Press, 1975—, Prentice Hall, 1977—, Duke U. Press, 1986—, U. Wis. Press, Rutgers U. Press, Cambridge U. Press, Harper Collins, The New Yorker. Author: Stratagems To Uncover Nakedness: The Dramas of Harold Pinter, 1969, Donald Barthelme, 1981, Robert Coover: The Universal Fiction-Making Process, 1983, American Chronicle: Six Decades in American Life, 1920-79, 1987, Seven Decades in American Life, 1920-89, 1990, Harold Pinter: A Casebook, 1990, The Columbia Chronicles of American Life, 1910-1992, 1995, The World of Samuel Beckett, 1906-1946, 1996, Chinese edit., 2001, American Chronicle: Year by Year Through the Twentieth Century, 1999, Pinter at 70, 2001, Reading Godot, 2002; asst. editor Lit. and Psychology, 1968-71; contbr. book revs. to profl. jours. and newspapers. Research grantee U. Mo., 1968, Fairleigh Dickinson U., 1985, 89, 97, 2001. Mem. MLA, PEN, Internat. Bach Soc., Internat. League Human Rights, Authors Guild, Acad. Am. Poets, Harold Pinter Soc., Samuel Beckett Soc., U.S. Hist. Landmarks Commn. Jewish. Home: 300 Central Park W New York NY 10024-1513 Office: Fairleigh Dickinson U Dept English Teaneck NJ 07666 Office Phone: 701-692-2263. Personal E-mail: loisgord@aol.com.

GORDON, MALCOLM STEPHEN, biology professor; b. Bklyn., Nov. 13, 1933; s. Abraham and Rose (Walters) G.; m. Diane M. Kestin, Apr. 16, 1959 (div. Sept. 1973); 1 child, Dana Malcolm; m. Marjorie J. Weinzweig, Jan. 28, 1976 (dec. Mar. 1990); m. Carol A. Cowen, July 19, 1992. BA with high honors, Cornell U., 1954; PhD, Yale U., 1958. Instr. UCLA, 1958-60, asst. prof., 1960-65, assoc. prof., 1965-68, prof. biology, 1968—, dir. Inst. Evolutionary and Environ. Biology, 1971-76, chmn. interdept. com. Environ. Sci. Engring. Program, 1984-88; asst. dir. rsch. Nat. Fisheries Ctr. and Aquarium, U.S. Dept. of Interior, Washington, 1968-69. Vis. prof. zoology Chinese U. Hong Kong, 1971-72; panel on marine biology, panel on oceanography Pres.'s Sci. Adv. Com., 1965-66; nat. adv com. R/V Alpha Helix, Scripps Inst. Oceanography, 1969-73; com. on Latimeria, NAS, 1969-72; mem. tech. adv. com. Santa Monica Bay Restoration Project, EPA, 1988—; tech. adv. group on milkfish reprodn. AID, 1984-92; chmn. Commn. on Comparative Physiology, Internat. Union Physiol. Sci., 1993—; co-founder Inst. of Environment, UCLA, 1997; vis. assoc. in bioengring. and aeronautics Calif. Inst. Tech., 2003— Author coll. textbooks, technical books; mem. editorial bd. Fish Physiol. Biochem. Jour., 1986—, Jour. Exptl. Zool., 1990-93; contbr. articles to profl. jours. Active cmty. orgns. on environ., civil liberties. NSF fellow Yale U., 1954-57, Fulbright fellow U.K., 1957-58, Guggenheim fellow Italy and Denmark, 1961-62; Sr. Queen's fellow in marine sci. Australia, 1976; Irving-Scholander Meml. lectr., U. Alaska-Fairbanks, 2000. Fellow AAAS; mem. Am. Physiol. Soc. (exec. com. pub. affairs 1989-92, internat. physiol. com. 2002-05), Am. Soc. Ichthyologists and Herpetologists, Soc. Integrative Comparative Biology (chmn. divsn. ecology 1979-80, chmn. divsn. comparative biochem. physiology 1988-89), Soc. Exptl. Biology, Internat. Union Physiol. Sci. (coun. mem. 2005—) Home: 2801 Glendower Ave Los Angeles CA 90027-1118 Office: UCLA Dept Ecology Evolutionary Biol PO Box 951606 Los Angeles CA 90095-1606 Office Phone: 310-825-4579. Business E-Mail: msgordon@ucla.edu.

GORDON, MARC STEWART, pharmacist, research scientist; b. Cleve., June 13, 1958; s. Eugene and Eileen (Israel) G.; m. Diane Southwell, Aug. 11, 1985; children: Evan, Emma. BS in Pharmacy, U. Mich., 1982. Registered pharmacist, Calif. Staff rschr. II, mgr. Syntex Rsch., Palo Alto, Calif., 1982—95; sr. scientist, new product planning rschr. Inhale Therapeutic Systems, Palo Alto, Calif., 1995—2002; dir. formulation devel. ARYx Therapeutics, Santa Clara, Calif., 2003—05; assoc. dir. formulation devel. Celera Genomics, San Francisco, 2005—. Contbr. numerous articles to profl. jours.; numerous patentee pharmaceuticals. Mem. Am. Assn. Pharm. Scientists, Am. Pharm. Assn., BioSci. Forum, Rho Chi. Avocations: reading, hiking. Home: 1474 Samedra St Sunnyvale CA 94087-4054

GORDON, MARCUS, judge; b. Union, Miss. s. Marcus Benton and Flossie C. Gordon; m. Polly Gordon; 4 children. Attended, East Central Community Coll.; BA, U. Miss., JD, 1959. Bar: 1959. Private practice with brother Rex Gordon, 1959—71; dist. atty. 8th Circuit Ct. Dist., 1971—77; circuit ct. judge Neshoba County, Miss., 1977—87; private practice with brother Rex and nephew Rex Jr., 1987—90; circuit ct. judge Neshoba County, Miss., 1990—. Served USAF, 1951—53. Achievements include presiding judge over Mississippi versus Ray Edgar Killen, convicted of the 1964 manslaughter of 3 civil rights workers, Andrew Goodman, James Chaney and Michael Schwerner in June 2005. Office: P O Box 220 Decatur MS 39327 Office Phone: 601-635-3540.*

GORDON, MARJORIE, soprano, vocalist, educator; b. N.Y.C. d. Theodore and Minnie (Glantz) Fishberg; m. Nathan Gordon; children: Maxine, Peter Jon. BA cum laude, Hunter Coll. Nat. cert. voice tchr. Prof. voice Duquesne U., 1957-59, Wayne State U., 1961-91, Nat. Music Camp, Interlochen, 1963-65, Meadowbrook Sch. Music, 1966-71, U. Mich., 1970, Mich. State U., 1971; soloist, tchr. Am. U.-Wolf Trap Program, Washington, 1973. Spl. edn. cons. Detroit Grand Opera Assn.; adj. prof. Oakland (Mich.) U.; pres., gen. dir. Piccolo Opera Co., Inc. *A lyric-coloratura soprano, she is an international star of opera, concerts, chamber music, radio, television, and theatre. She started piano lessons at age 5, voice lessons at age 17, and graduated cum laude at 18 from Hunter College. Her solo debut was with the New York Philharmonic and her operatic debut with the New York City Opera Company. She appeared with major symphonies and opera companies both domestically and internationally. She is the executive director of Piccolo Opera Company, and awarded a resolution by the Michigan Senate. She has been on the facilities of several universities, and established a voice scholarship with the National Opera Association.* Solo debut N.Y. Philharm. Symphony, 1950, soprano soloist, N.Y.C. Opera, 1955-57, Chautauqua Opera Co., 1949-61, Pitts. Opera, 1956; dir. Detroit Opera Theatre, 1960-72, Piccolo Opera Co., 1961—; soloist with Chgo. Symphony, Phila. Symphony, Pitts. Symphony, other orchs., opera cos., summer stock, on radio and TV; recitals U.S., Greece, Europe, Can., Israel; editor: Opera Study Guide, 1968—. Mem. music adv. panel Mich. Arts Coun., 1980-90; mem. Palm Beach County Cultural Coun., 1992—; opera producer Blue Lake Fine Arts Camp, 1993—. Recipient resolution honoring 25th Anniversary Piccolo Opera Co., Mich. Senate; established voice scholarship in perpetuity Nat. Opera Assn. Mem.: AFTRA, Nat. Assn. Tchrs. Singing, Met. Opera Guild, Ctrl. Opera Svc., Nat. Opera Assn., Music Tchrs. Nat. Assn., Am. Guild Mus. Artists, Mich. Music Tchrs. Assn. (voice chmn. 1970—76), Fla. Music Tchrs. Assn., Boca Delray Music Soc., Broward County Music Club, Mu Phi Epsilon. Avocations: handcrafts, swimming, reading, sketching. Fax: 561-394-0520. Office Phone: 800-282-3161. Business E-Mail: leejon51@msn.com.

GORDON, MARSHA L., dermatologist; b. Annapolis, Md., 1958; BA, Rutgers U., 1980; MD, U. Pa., 1984. Diplomate Am. Bd. Dermatology. Intern Cooper Med. Ctr., Camden, 1984—85; resident in dermatology Mt. Sinai Med. Ctr., N.Y.C., 1985—88, chief cons., 1988—, vice chair dermatology, 1996—. Asst. prof. Mt. Sinai Sch. Medicine, N.Y.C., 1988—97, assoc. clin. prof., 1997—. Office: Mount Sinai Med Ctr Box 1048 5 E 98th St New York NY 10029-6501 Office Phone: 212-241-9728.

GORDON, MARSHALL, former university president; b. LaCenter, Ky., Sept. 1, 1937; s. Ollie James and Dora Ellen (Everett) G; m. Annette Waters, Mar. 17, 1962; 1 child, Mary Ann. BA, Murray (Ky.) State U., 1959; PhD, Vanderbilt U., 1963. Instr. Murray State U., summer 1959; teaching asst. Vanderbilt U., Nashville, 1959-63; rsch. chemist E.I. duPont de Nemours & Co., Inc., Chattanooga, summer 1961; from asst. prof. to prof. chemistry Murray (Ky.) State U., 1963-75, dean, 1975-77, v.p. for univ. svcs., 1977-83, pres., 1981, S.W. Mo. State U., Springfield, 1983-92; mgmt. cons., 1992—. Cons. in field. Contbr. articles to profl. jours. Bd. dirs. Lester E. Cox Med. Ctr., Springfield, 1985—, Hammons Heart Inst. Reg. Adv. Bd., Springfield, 1983—. Mem. ACS (sec.-treas. 1968-70), Am. Assn. State Colls. and U. (com. on agr. and rural devel.), Springfield C. of C. (bd. dirs. 1983-86), Rotary. Avocation: various outdoor activities. Home: PO Box 3691 Springfield MO 65808-3691

GORDON, MARY CATHERINE, writer; b. L.I., N.Y., Dec. 8, 1949; d. David and Anna (Gagliano) G.; m. James Brain, 1974 (div.); m. Arthur Cash, 1979; children: Anna Gordon, David Dess Gordon. BA, Barnard Coll., 1971; MA, Syracuse U., 1973. Tchr. English Dutchess Community Coll., Poughkeepsie, N.Y., 1974-78, Amherst (Mass.) Coll., 1979-80, Barnard Coll., 1988—. Author: (novels) Final Payments, 1978, The Company of Women, 1981, Men and Angels,1985, The Other Side, 1989, The Rest of Life, 1993, Spending, 1998, (short stories) Temporary Shelter, 1987, Good Boys and Dead Girls and Other Essays, 1991, The Rest of Life: Three Novellas, 1993, The Shadow Man, 1996, Seeing Through Places, 2000, Joan of Arc, 2000. Guggenheim fellow; recipient Kafka prize for Fiction, 1979, 82, Lila Acheson Wallace Reader's digest award. Roman Catholic. Office: Barnard Coll Dept English 3009 Broadway New York NY 10027-6501 Agent: Sterling Lord Literistic 65 Bleecker St Fl 12 New York NY 10012-2420

GORDON, MELVIN JAY, food products executive; b. Boston, Nov. 26, 1919; s. Jacob S. and Sadye Z. (Lewis) G.; m. Ellen Rubin, June 25, 1950; children: Virginia Lynn, Karen Dale, Wendy Jean, Lisa Jo. BA, Harvard, 1941, MBA, 1943. V.p. Clear Weave Hosiery Stores, Inc., Boston, 1945-50, Tenn. Knitting Mills, Inc., Columbia, 1945-56; pres. P.R. Hosiery Mills, Inc., Arecibo, 1956-61; ptnr. Manchester (N.H.) Hosiery Mills, 1946-69; chmn. bd. Tootsie Roll Industries, Chgo., 1962—, pres., 1968-69, 75-78, Hampshire Designers Inc., 1969-77, HDI Investment Corp., 1977—, MJG Inc., 1981—, Ellen Gordon Inc., 1984-88, Lisa Gordon Inc., 1987—, Wendy Gordon Inc., 1989—. Adv. com. Mfrs. Hanover Bank, N.Y.C., 1967-88. Author: Better Than Communism, 1958. Mem. Pres.'s Citizens Adv. com. Fitness Am. Youth, 1957-60, exec. com. 1959-60; del. White House Conf. Youth Fitness, 1962; co-chmn. Com. Support Psychol. Offensive, 1961-63; bd. dirs. mem. exec. com. Coun. World Tensions, N.Y.C., 1960-65; chmn. Mass. Gov.'s Com. Youth Fitness, 1958-64; bd. dirs. New Eng. Econ. Edn. Coun., 1960-63, N.H. Coun. on World Affairs, 1962-65; bd. dirs., chmn. exec. com. Citizen Exchange Corps., N.Y.C., 1964-66, hon. chmn. adv. coun. 1966-67; del. Prime Minister's Econ. Conf., Israel, 1968, 73; bd. overseers Harvard Coll., mem. vis. com. behavioral scis., 1967-71, vis. com. psychology, 1972; vis. com. Russian Rsch. Ctr., 1972-76; dir. Rensselaerville Inst., N.Y., 1966—; chmn. N.E. region m. Com. for Weizmann Inst. Sci. Rehovot, Israel, 1972-73; dir. Am. com., 1973-75; nat. trustee Nat. Symphony Orch., Washington, 1993—. Recipient Dean's award Nat. Candy Wholesalers Assn., 1978 Mem. Chief Execs. Orgn., World Bus. Coun., World Affairs Coun. Boston (treas., bd. dirs. 1966-67, v.p., bd. dirs. 1968-74), New Eng. Soc. N.Y.C., Harvard Varsity Club, Harvard Club (Boston). Clubs: Harvard (Boston); Varsity (Harvard). Office: Tootsie Roll Industries Inc 7401 S Cicero Ave Chicago IL 60629-5885*

GORDON, MICHAEL MACKIN, lawyer; b. Boston, Apr. 15, 1950; s. Lawrence H. and Gladys (Mackin) G.; m. Linda Lowry, June 8, 1991; children: Alexandra, Harrison. AB, Vassar Coll., 1972; JD, Columbia U., 1976. Bar: N.Y. 1977, U.S. Dist. Ct. (so. and ea. dists. N.Y. 1977), D.C. 1980, U.S. Ct. Appeals (2d cir.) 1985, U.S. Supreme Ct. 1985, U.S. Claims Ct. 1991, U.S. Ct. Appeals (3d cir.), 1992, U.S. Dist. Ct. (no. dist.), Tex. 1993, U.S. Ct. Appeals (5th cir.) 1995, U.S. Dist. Ct. (ea. dist.) Tex. 1996, U.S. Dist. Ct. (no. dist. N.Y.) 1999. Assoc. Seward & Kissel, N.Y.C., 1977-79, Cadwalader, Wickersham & Taft, N.Y.C., 1979-85, ptnr., 1985—2005, King & Spalding, LLC, N.Y.C., 2005—. Mem.: ABA, N.Y. State Bar Assn., N.Y. County Lawyers Assn., Vassar (N.Y.C.). Home: 12 W 72nd St New York NY 10023-4163 Office: King & Spalding LLP 1185 Ave of the Americas New York NY 10036 Office Phone: 212-556-2190. Business E-Mail: mgordon@kslaw.com.

GORDON, MICHAEL WALLACE, law educator; b. May 4, 1935; s. Seery Clarence and Anne Catharine (Gregory) Gordon; m. Elsbeth Leimomi Kunzig, Mar. 15, 1958; children: Huntly Milne, Elsbeth Wallace. BS, U. Conn., 1957, JD, 1963; MA, Trinity Coll.; Diploma de Droit Compare, U. Strasbourg, France, 1973; Maestria en Derecho, Iberoamerica, Mex., 1982; auditor, L'Academie de Droit de la Haye, 1973, auditor, 1982. Bar: (Conn.) 1963. Assoc. Shipman & Goodwin, Hartford, Conn., 1963—66; asst. dean U. Conn. Law Sch. of Law, Hartford, 1966—68; prof. law U. Fla., Gainesville, 1968—94, Chesterfield Smith prof. law, 1994—2005, John and Mary Lou Dasburg prof. law, 2005—. Vis. prof. U. Costa Rica, 1970, Duke U., 1984; Lyle T. Alverson vis. prof. George Washington U., 1986—87, U. Konstanz, 1995; Fulbright prof. U. Mex., U. Guatemala, U. Frankfurt; Centennial prof. London Sch. Econs., 1992; John Stone prof. U. Ala., 1998; vis. lectr. U. Francisco Marroquin, Guatemala, Escuela Libre de Derecho, Mexico, U. Edinburgh, U. Aberdeen, U. Bombay, U. Brasilia, Leiden U., Leuven U., U. Nairobi, Zagreb U., U. Montpellier, U. Nicaragua, U. Regensburg, U. Tijuana, U. Peking, Hong Kong U., U. Tamaulipas, U. Cochin; external examiner U. Khartoum; of counsel Ogarrio y Diaz, Mex. City, 1976—; cons. govt. agys. Nigeria, Brazil, Honduras, India, Mex., Yugoslavia, Paraguay, Panama, Oman, Sudan, Costa Rica; contbg. editor Lawyer of the Am.; mem. editl. bd. Syracuse Jour. Internat. Law and Commerce, Fla. Jour. Internat. Law, UCLA Pacific Basin Jour.; lectr. Coun. Fgn. Rels., Brit. Inst. Internat. and Comparative Law. Author: Fla. Corp. Law (5 vols.), 1975, The Cuban Nationalizations-The Demise of Fgn. Pvt. Property, 1976, Multinat. Corps. Law-Mex., Ctrl. Am., Panama and the CACM (2 vols.), 1978, The Civil Code of Mex., 1978; author: (with Glendon and Osakwe) Comparative Legal Traditions, 1982, 1994, Comml., Bus. and Trade Laws of Mex., 1983, Fgn. State Immunity in Comml. Transactions., 1990; author: (with Folsom and Spanogle) Internat. Bus. Transactions, 1985, 1989, 1993, 1997, 2002, 2003, 2004, Handbook on NAFTA Dispute Settlement, 1999; author: (with Folsom and Lopez) Law of NAFTA, 2004; author: (with Baldwin, Brand and Epstein) Internat. Civil Litig., 2003. Lt. j.g. USNR, 1957—60. Presdl. scholar, U. Fla., 1977, scholar-in-residence, Bellagio Found., Italy. Mem.: Am. Assn. for Comparative Study of Law, Brit. Inst. Internat. and Comparative Law, Am. Fgn. Law Assn., Am. Soc. Internat. Law, Guatemala Bar Assn. (hon.), Mex. Acad. Pvt. Internat. and Comparative Law (hon.). Republican. Episcopalian. Office: Coll Law U Fla Gainesville FL 32611

GORDON, MORRIS AARON, microbiologist; b. Waterbury, Conn., Apr. 3, 1920; s. Samuel and Anna (Rubinstein) G.; m. Ruth Kathryn McKee, May 22, 1945 (div. 1970); children: Barbara Jean, David Spencer, Sarah Elizabeth. BS, City Coll. N.Y., N.Y.C., 1940; MS, U. Chgo., 1942; PhD, Duke U., 1949. Diplomate Am. Bd. Microbiology; cert. lab. dir., N.Y. Lab. officer Regional Hosp., U.S. Army, Camp Blanding, Fla., 1945-46; mycologist Communicable Disease Ctr., Atlanta, 1949-54; biol. warfare specialist Chem. Corps Training Command, Fort McClellan, Ala., 1954-55; assoc. prof. microbiology Med. Coll. S.C., Charleston, 1955-59; sr. to prin. rsch. scientist, dir. mycology labs. N.Y. State Dept. Health, Albany, 1959-87, dir. clin. microbiology & mycology labs., 1983-87, dir. emeritus clin. microbiology and mycology labs., 1987—. Study sect. NIH, Washington, 1971-75; adv. com. Brown-Hazen Awards, N.Y.C., 1974-78; cons. VA Hosp., Albany, 1959-96; rsch. prof. Albany Med. Coll., 1975-90. Author: Laboratory Identification of Pathogenic Fungi, 1970; founder/editor Bull. Med. Mycol. Soc. Ams., 1976-94; contbr. over 150 articles to numerous profl. jours. Lt. comdr. USPHS, 1949-54. Recipient various rsch. grants NIH, teaching fellowship Duke U., 1947-49; Fulbright professor, 1978, Inter-Am. fellow La. State U., 1959. Mem. Med. Mycol. Soc. Ams. (pres. 1978-79, Benham award 1988), Internat. Soc. Human and Animal Mycology (v.p. 1982-85, Georg award 1991), Am. Soc. Microbiology (pres. mycology sect.), Phi Beta Kappa, Sigma Xi (pres. Albany chpt. 1972). Achievements include invention of latex test for cryptococcosis; initiation of diagnostic immunofluorescence for human fungal diseases; cultured pathogenic lipophilic yeasts; establishment of first presence in North America and first presence in humans of Dermatophilus infection. Address: 251 Springmoor Dr Raleigh NC 27615 Personal E-mail: gordonmeyer@peoplepc.com.

GORDON, NANCY HERMAN, music educator; b. Cleve., Apr. 10, 1946; d. William Robert and Marjorie Helen (Ritterhoff) Herman; m. Seth Eldon Gordon, Dec. 27, 1971. BMus, Westminster Coll., New Wilmington, Pa., 1968; M.Music Edn., Duquesne U., Pitts., 1970; Orff Schulwerk level III, New Eng. Conservator, Boston, 1978. Cert. tchr. Pa., Mass. Choral dir. Duxbury Intermediate Sch., Mass., 1970—81; dir. choral activities Duxbury H.S., 1981—92; elem. music specialist Duxbury Elem. Sch., 1992—, Chandler Primary Sch., 1992—, Duxbury Mid. Sch., 1992—. Dir. Citrus Springs Cmty. Chorus, 2002—, Citrus Concert Band, 2004—. Contbr. articles to profl. jours. Tchr. rep. Chandler Sch. Improvement Coun., Duxbury, 1998—2001; artistic dir./coord. Pilgrim Progress Re-enactments, Plymouth, Mass., 1980—83; bd. dirs. Plymouth Philharm. Orch., 1989—92; bd. trustees, treas. Plymouth United Meth. Ch., 1992—95. Named VIP of the Wk., Old Colony Meml. Newspaper, 1984; grantee, Duxbury Edn. Found., 1996, 2001. Mem.: Duxbury Tchrs. Assn. (bldg. rep.), Mass. Music Educators Assn., Southeasternn Mass. Bandmasters Assn. (sec. 1977—79), Am. Orff Schulwerk Assn. (New Eng. chpt. mid. sch. liaison 1974—76), Persephone's Daughters (singer). Methodist. Avocations: bicycling, travel. Home: 1246 W Fan Dr Citrus Springs FL 34434-6639

GORDON, NICHOLAS, broadcast executive; b. Chgo., Apr. 12, 1928; s. Jacques and Ruth (Janeway) G.; m. Gladys Sack, Apr. 10, 1950 (div. 1976); children: Catherine, Christopher, Susan; m. Julie E. Miles, Aug. 12, 1977 (dec. May 2, 2005). Ph.B., U. Chgo., 1946. Reporter City News Bur., Chgo., 1948; radio-TV analyst William Weintraub Agy., N.Y.C., 1949-50; dir. rsch. and sales planning Keystone Broadcasting Sys., N.Y.C., 1951-52; with NBC, 1953-74, mgr. rates and program evaluation, 1956-58, mgr. sales devel. NBC-TV Sales, 1959-60, dir. sales devel. NBC-TV Sales, 1960-63, account exec. TV sales, 1964-68, v.p. Ea. sales, 1968-70, v.p. radio network sales N.Y.C., 1970-74; pres. Keystone Broadcasting Sys., N.Y.C., 1974-85, chmn., 1985—. Vice chmn. Riverdale Cmty. Coun., 1968-71; mem. N.Y.C. Planning Bd., Riverdale, 1969-75, vice chmn., 1972-74; pres. Riverdale Cmty. Planning Assn., 1972-76; mem. vol. corps N.Y.C. Dept. Commerce, 1968-70; bd. dirs. Wave Hill Ctr. Environ. Studies, 1969-80, exec. v.p., 1970-80; mem. Bronx Democratic County Com., 1968; bd. dirs. Music Mountain, Inc., Falls Village, Conn., 1970-, pres., 1974-; bd. dirs. Riverdale Neighborhood House, Bronx, N.Y., 1970-74, Bronx Coun. Arts, 1970-72, Phila. Orch. Media Inst., 1998—2003; trustee St. Hilda's and St. Hugh's Sch., 1965-76. Decorated chevalier l'Ordre des Arts et des Lettres (France) Mem. Century Assn., Univ. Club, Explorers Club (N.Y.C.), Tavern Club, Cliff Dwellers Club (Chgo.), East India Club (London). Office: Keystone Broadcasting Syst PO Box 1739 Sharon CT 06069-1739 Office Phone: 860-364-2080. Business E-Mail: ngordon@keystonebroadcasting.com.

GORDON, NORMAN BOTNICK, psychologist, educator; b. N.Y.C., Feb. 12, 1921; s. Moses and Molvine (Botnick) G.; m. Diana Jean Drews, July 27, 1974; children: Jane Ellen, Judith Ann, Marc Daniel, Aaron Drew. BA, Bklyn. Coll., 1942; MA, New Sch. Social Research, 1951; PhD, NYU, 1957. Research psychologist U.S. Naval Tng. Device Ctr., Port Washington, N.Y., 1951-58; assoc. prof. psychology Yeshiva U., N.Y.C., 1959-68, prof., 1968-74; guest investigator Rockefeller U., N.Y.C., 1964-77; prin. rsch. scientist N.Y. State Office of Drug Abuse Svcs., 1974-77; prof. SUNYCO-Oswego, 1977—, chmn. dept. psychology, 1977-86, prof. emeritus, 1988—. Adj. prof. SUNY-Oswego, 1988-97, rsch. assoc., 1997—. Served with U.S. Army, 1942-46. Grantee USPHS, 1966-74, 64-67 Mem. APA, Eastern Psychol. Assn., Sigma Xi. Home: 900 County Route 20 Oswego NY 13126-5672 Office: SUNY Coll Dept Psychology Oswego NY 13126 Business E-Mail: ngordon@oswego.edu.

GORDON, PAUL, retired dentist, artist; b. Phila., Jan. 22, 1936; s. Benjamin and Pearl (Kravitz) Gordon; m. Jeanette Epstein, Jan. 26, 1958 (dec. 1993). DDS, Temple U., 1960. Inventor dental device (Silver Circle award, 1971); Exhibited in group shows at Greater Del. Valley; author: (novels) Concrete Solution, 2001, (short stories) Van Gogh's Last Painting and Other Stories from the Edge; portraits of entertainment celebrities. Violinist Savannah (Ga.) Symphony Orch., 1960—62. Lt. USN, 1960—62. Mem.: Phila. Art Mus., Portrait Soc. of Am. Jewish. Avocations: painting, violin, writing, inventing, teaching. Home: 616 Grand Ave Moorestown NJ 08057 Office: PO Box 210 590 S Lenola Rd Maple Shade NJ 08052-1602

GORDON, PAUL JOHN, management educator; b. N.Y.C., Oct. 14, 1921; s. Arthur L. and Georgiana (McDonough) G.; m. Mary Brigid Keany, Jan. 28, 1950; children: Brian Joseph, Peter Christopher, Martha Ann, Hugh John, Paul John. BBA, CCNY, 1945; MBA, Cornell U., 1949; PhD, Syracuse U., 1958. With Brooks Bros., N.Y.C., 1941-43, Lago Oil & Transp. Co., Ltd., Netherlands W. Indies, also Bayway Refinery, Linden, N.J. and Standard Oil Co. N.J., 1943-48; asst. prof. Cornell U., Ithaca, N.Y., 1949-54; prof., chmn. dept. mgmt. Sch. Bus. Duquesne U., Pitts., 1954-55; rsch. cons. Sloan-Kettering Meml. Ctr. for Cancer, N.Y.C., 1955-56; assoc. prof. bus. adminstrn., planning dir. grad. program hosp. adminstrn. Sch. Bus. Adminstrn. Emory U., Atlanta, 1956—59; assoc. prof. Grad. Sch. Bus. Ind. U., 1959-63, prof., chmn. dept. mgmt. adminstrv. studies Grad. Sch. Bus., 1963-67, prof. mgmt. Grad. Sch. Bus., 1963-89, chmn. adminstrv. and behavioral studies Grad. Sch. Bus., 1980-83, prof. emeritus mgmt. Grad. Sch. Bus., 1989—; disting. prof. mgmt. St. John's U., N.Y.C., 1990-93. Fulbright/FLAD chair in strategic mgmt. Tech. U. Lisbon, Portugal, 1997; chief U.S. Dept. State-Ford Found. party Ljubljana U., Yugoslavia, 1967; vis. prof. Trinity Coll., Dublin, 1967; vis. prof., Fulbright lectr. Instituto Post-Universitario Per Lo Studio Dell Organizazzione Aziendale, Turin, Italy, 1963; Fulbright lectr., cons. Nat. U. Republic Uruguay, 1970; disting. guest Systems Rsch. Inst., Polish Acad. Scis., 1980; vis. Fulbright prof. Helsinki Sch. Econs. and Bus. Adminstrn., Finland, 1990; mem. U.S. AID Mgmt. Edn. Reconnaissance Survey, India, also Pakistan, 1971; cons. IRS, 1956-63, Am. Coll. Hosp. Adminstrs., 1957—; with Inst. Higher Studies of Adminstrn., Caracas, Venezuela, 1973-79. Editor Acad. Mgmt. Jour, 1964-66, mem. editorial bd., 1961-75; editorial cons. adv. bd.: Bus. Horizons, Hosp. Adminstrn, W.B. Saunders Co.; contbr. articles to profl. jours. Mem. Cath. Commn. on Intellectual and Cultural Affairs, 1973—, chmn., 1980-81; chmn. UNESCO multi-nat. bus. conf. Ind. U., 1972; chmn. adv. screening com. in bus. mgmt. Coun. for Internat. Exch. of Scholars, Fulbright-Hays Program, 1979-80, 90-93, chmn., 1991-93; bd. dirs. Ind. Newman Found., 1971-82; mem. adv. bd. Abbey Press, St. Meinrad, Ind., 1991-95. Fellow, IBM, 1964; grantee, Ford Found., 1963, 1966, 1970. Fellow Acad. Mgmt. (v.p. program 1967, pres. 1969, Disting. Svc. award 1992), Internat. Acad. Mgmt., Am. Acad. Med. Adminstrs. (hon.); mem. Fulbright Assn. (life). Home: 1422 S Winfield Rd Bloomington IN 47401-6152 E-mail: pauljgordon@aol.com.

GORDON, PHILIP BRUCE, mayor; b. Chgo., Apr. 18, 1951; s. Sid and Judy Gordon; m. Christa Severns; children: David, Jeff, Rachel, Jacob. BA in History Edn., U. Ariz.; JD cum laude, Ariz. State U. Chmn. Landiscor Aerial Photography Co.; atty. Pearlstein Law Firm; councilman Phoenix (Ariz.) City Coun., 1997—2003; mayor City of Phoenix, 2003—. Founder, chmn. Slumlord Task Force; chmn. Ariz. Child Occupant Protection Task Force, Men's Anti-Violence Network; bd. dir. Voice for Crime Victims; mem Madison Sch. Bd. Bd. dir. Orpheum Theatre Found., Downtown YMCA, Phoenix (Ariz.) Ballet Co., Roosevelt Action Assn. Office: City Hall 200 W Washington St 11th Fl Phoenix AZ 85003-1611*

GORDON, PHILLIP, lawyer; b. Potgietersrust, S. Africa, July 11, 1943; m. Norma. BA, U. Witwaterstrand, S. Africa, 1964, BA (hon.), 1965; BA, Oxford U., 1967, MA, 1973; JD, U. Chgo., 1969. Bar: Ill. 1969, N.Y. 1973. Acted as interim gen. counsel Strategic Hotel Capital, Chgo., 1997-98; ptnr. Perkins Cole LLC, 2003—. Tchg. assoc. Northwestern U. Sch. Law, Chgo., 1967-68. Author: Ill. Practice Consultant, Midwest Transactional Guide, 1981. Dir. Lyric Opera Chgo.; trustee Spertus Inst. Jewish Studies, Chgo.; advising fellow Oxford U. Ctr. Socio-Legal Studies, London. Mem. ABA, Chgo. Bar Assn., Hotel Devel. Coun., Urban land Inst. Office: Perkins Cole LLC Santa Fe Bldg 224 S Michigan Ave Ste 1300 Chicago IL 60604-2507

GORDON, REVA JO, retired librarian; b. Martinsville, Mo., Feb. 16, 1928; d. Earl G. and Claudia Olive (Goodwin) Kerns; m. Roland Gordon, Nov. 24, 1949; children: Gary Paul, Gloria Gay Gordon Zuber. BS, N.W. Mo. State U., 1949; postgrad., State U. Iowa, 1951; MA in Libr. Sci., U. Mich., 1970. Ordained elder and deacon Presbyn. Ch. Bus. tchr. LeRoy (Iowa) H.S., 1948; bus./English tchr. Malvern (Iowa) Consolidated Schs., 1949-51; English tchr. Flushing (Mich.) Cmty. Schs., 1959-64, libr., media dir., 1964-86, ret., 1986. Author: The Goodwins and Hensleys, 1990, Sammy's Red Shirt, 2003; contbr. articles to newspapers and mags. Mem. Mich. Assn. Retired Sch. Personnel (W. Genesee County chpt.), Flushing Hist. Soc., Flushing Book Club, Royal Quarter. Avocations: writing, lecturing. Home: PO Box 406 Flushing MI 48433-0406 Personal E-mail: revajg@aol.com.

GORDON, RICHARD M. ERIK, private investor, educator; b. Atlanta, 1949; s. David Albert and Harriet Sonya G. V.p. The Original Gt. Am. Chocolate Chip Cookie Co., Inc., Atlanta, 1984-85, sr. v.p., COO, 1985—, pres., 1990—; dir. Ctr. for Retailing Edn. and Rsch. U. Fla., Gainesville, 1996-2000, dir. MBA programs, 2000—, dir. Ctr. for Tech. and Sci. Commercialization Studies, 2001—; assoc. dean, dir. Grad. Divsn. Bus. and Mgmt., Johns Hopkins U., 2004—, interim assoc dean and prof. Balt., 2003—. Adj. prof. Ga. State U. Coll. Bus. Adminstrn., 1994-96 Mem. IEEE, AAAS, Am. Chem. Soc., Am. Fin. Assn., Am. Mgmt. Assn., Am. Mktg. Assn., Assn. for Consumer Rsch., Internat. Franchise Assn. (edn., internat. and legis. coms., bd. dirs.), Inst. for Ops. Rsch. and Mgmt. Sci., Assn. Computing Machinery,.

GORDON, ROBERT A., food products executive, lawyer; b. 1952; Grad., Yale U., 1973; JD, U. Va., 1976. Litig. ptnr. Pillsbury Madison & Sutro, 1984—99; dep. gen. counsel Safeway, Inc., Pleasanton, Calif., 1999—2000, sr. v.p., gen. counsel, 2000—. Office: Safeway Inc 5918 Stoneridge Mall Rd Pleasanton CA 94588-3229

GORDON, ROBERT EUGENE, lawyer; b. LA, Sept. 20, 1932; s. Harry Maurice and Minnie (Shaffer); 1 child, Victor Marten. BA, UCLA, 1954; LLB, U. Calif., Berkeley, 1959, JD, 1960; cert., U. Hamburg, Germany, 1960. Bar: Calif. 1960. Assoc. Lillick, Geary, McHose, Roethke & Myers, LA, 1960-64, Schoichet & Rifkind, Beverly Hills, Calif., 1964-67; ptnr. Baerwitz & Gordon, Beverly Hills, 1967-69, Ball, Hunt, Hart, Brown & Baerwitz, Beverly Hills, 1970-71; of counsel Jacobs, Sills & Coblentz, San Francisco, 1972-78; ptnr. Gordon & Hodge, San Francisco, 1978-81; pvt. practice San Francisco, 1981—89, Corte Madera, Calif., 1989—2002, Sausalito, Calif., 2002—. Adj. prof. entertainment law Hastings Coll. Law, San Francisco, 1990-91, U. Calif., Berkeley, 1992. Served to 1st lt. U.S. Army, 1954-56. Mem. ABA (forum com. on entertainment and sports law), LA Copyright Soc. (bd. trustees 1970-71), Copyright Soc. of USA. Avocations: bicycling, skiing. Home: 35 Elaine Ave Mill Valley CA 94941-1014 Office: One Harbor Dr Ste 106 Sausalito CA 94965 Office Phone: 415-331-0611. Personal E-mail: lawmuse@aol.com.

GORDON, ROBERT JAMES, economics professor; b. Boston, Sept. 3, 1940; s. Robert Aaron and Margaret (Shaughnessy) G.; m. Julie S. Peyton, June 22, 1963. AB, Harvard U., 1962; MA, Oxford U., Eng., 1969; PhD, MIT, 1967. Asst. prof. econs. Harvard U., 1967-68; asst. prof. U. Chgo., 1968-73; prof. econs. Northwestern U., Evanston, Ill., 1973—, Stanley G. Harris prof. social scis., 1987—, chair econs. dept., 1992-96. Rsch. assoc. Nat. Bur. Econ Rsch., 1968—; mem. Brookings Panel Econ. Activity, 1970—; co-chmn. Internat. Seminar Macroecons., 1978-94; mem. exec. com. Conf. Rsch., Income and Wealth, 1978-83; mem. panel rev. productivity measures NAS, 1977-79; cons. bd. govs. Fed. Res. Sys., 1973-83, U.S. Dept. Treasury, 1967-80, U.S. Congl. Budget Office, 1996—, U.S. Bur. Econ. Analysis, 1999—; mem. Nat. Commn. on Consumer Price Index, 1995-97. Author: Macroeconomics, 1978, 10th edit., 2006, Milton Friedman's Monetary Framework, 1974, Challenges to Interdependent Economies, 1979, The American Business Cycle: Continuity and Change, 1986, The Measurement of Durable Goods Prices, 1990, International Volatility and Economic Growth, 1991, The Economics of New Goods, 1997, Inflation, Unemployment and Productivity, 2003; editor Jour. Polit. Economy, 1970-73. Recipient Lustrum prize Erasmus U., 1999; Marshall fellow, 1962-64; fellow Ford Found., 1966-67; grantee NSF, 1971—; fellow Guggenheim Meml. Found., 1980-81; rsch. fellow German Marshall Fund, 1985-86. Fellow AAAS, Econometric Soc. (treas. 1975—); mem. Am. Econ. Assn. (bd. editors 1975-77, mem. exec. com. 1981-83), Phi Beta Kappa Office: Northwestern U Dept Econs Evanston IL 60208-2600 Office Phone: 847-491-3616. E-mail: rjg@northwestern.edu.

GORDON, ROBERT JAY, lawyer, educator; b. Miami, Fla., May 10, 1956; s. Jerome B. and Florence (Lipschitz) G.; m. Leslie C. Gottlieb, Sept. 5, 1982. B.A. with distinction, U. Mich., 1977; J.D. with honors, George Washington U., Washington, 1980. Bar: Pa. 1980, U.S. Dist. Ct. (ea. dist.) Pa. 1981, U.S. Ct. Appeals (3d cir.) 1984, N.J. 1985, U.S. Dist. Ct. N.J. 1985, U.S. Supreme Ct., 1986, N.Y. 1987, U.S. Dist. Ct. So. N.Y. 1987, U.S Dist Ct. Ea. N.Y. 1992. Asst. dist. atty. Phila. Dist. Atty.'s Office, 1980-84; assoc.& ptnr. Greitzer & Locks, Phila., 1984—1991; mem. & chief trial atty. Weitz & Luxenberg, N.Y.C. Adj. prof. Temple U., Phila., 1983-85. Contbr. articles to profl. jours. Mem. Assn. Trial Lawyers Am., ABA, Assn. Bar City of N.Y., N.Y.S. Trial Lawyers Assn., Trial Lawyers for Public justice, Pa. Trial Lawyers Assn., Pa. Bar Assn., Phila. Bar Assn. Named one of Top 40 Lawyers under 40 by Nat. Law Jour., 1995. Democrat. Jewish. Office: Weitz & Luxenberg 180 Maiden Lane New York NY 10038 Office Phone: 212-558-5505. Business E-Mail: rgordon@weitzlux.com.

GORDON, ROBERT W., law educator; b. 1941; AB, Harvard U., 1967, JD, 1971. Bar: Mass. 1971. Asst. prof. SUNY, Buffalo, 1971-74, assoc. prof., 1974-77, U. Wis., Madison, 1977-80, prof., 1980-83, Stanford U., Calif., 1983-95; prof. law Yale U., New Haven, 1995—, Johnston prof., 1996—, Chancellor Kent Prof. of Law and Legal History. Reporter Newsweek, 1966-67; asst. to dir. John F. Kennedy Sch. Govt., Harvard U., 1963; staff Ctr. for Study of Pub. Policy, 1970, Office of Atty. Gen., Mass., 1971; vis. prof. Harvard U., Cambridge, Mass., 1979-80, Stanford U., 1982-83; vis. lectr. Oxford U., 1988. Vis. fellow, European U. Inst., 1992. Fellow: Whitney Humanities Ctr.; mem.: ABA, Am. Soc. for Legal History (pres. 2001—03). Office: Yale Law Sch PO Box 208215 New Haven CT 06520 E-mail: robert.w.gordon@yale.edu.*

GORDON, SANDRA CAROL, lawyer; d. William Lee Gordon and Lucy Irma Jonet. BA, UCLA; JD, Loyola Marymount U., L.A., 1987. Bar: Fla. 1991, Calif. 1987. Atty. Lewis, D'Amato, Brisbois & Bisgaard, L.A., 1987—88, Barger & Wolen, Irvine, Calif., 1989—91, Broad & Cassel, Orlando, Fla., 1993—95, Greenberg Traurig, P.A., Orlando, Fla., 1995—. Bd. of advisors U. Cen. Fla. Tech. Incubator, Orlando, 2004—. Editor (author): (articles) Loyola Law Review; contbr. articles to law revs. Mem. Planned Parenthood of Greater Orlando, 2001—05, Leadership Orlando, 1997. Mem.: Calif. Bar Assn., Fla. Bar Assn. Avocations: skiing, travel, Western/Southwestern art. Office: Greenberg Traurig PA Ste 650 450 S Orange Ave Orlando FL 32801 Office Phone: 407-420-1000. Home Fax: 407-420-5909; Office Fax: 407-420-5909.

GORDON, SANDY GALE COMBS, medical/surgical nurse, community health nurse; b. Lafollette, Tenn., Sept. 8, 1950; d. Wise and Edna Leona (Boshears) Combs; m. Ralph William Gordon, Aug. 30, 1975 (dec. Feb. 1998). Diploma, Middletown Hosp., 1971. RN, Ohio. Staff nurse Middletown Hosp., Ohio, 1971—79; pub. health nurse Bur. Pub. Health, Middletown, Ohio, 1979-82. Named Internat. Women of Yr., 1994-95. Mem. Middletown Hosp. Alumni Assn. Home: 1107 Ellen Dr Middletown OH 45042-3341 Personal E-mail: sgordon@erinet.com.

GORDON, SANFORD DANIEL, economics professor; b. Newark, June 23, 1924; s. Harry Louis and Beatrice (Safris) G.; m. Alice Lillian Pressman, May 27, 1948; children— Ellen Ann, Eric Alan. Student, Tulane U., 1942; BS magna cum laude, NYU, 1947, MA, 1948, PhD, 1953. Instr. econ. NYU, 1948-50; mem. faculty State U. Coll., Oneonta, N.Y., 1950—, prof. econs., 1957—, chmn. dept., 1960—; asst. vice chancellor for policy and planning State U. N.Y. Central Adminstrn., 1972-76, provost for policy analysis, 1976-79; exec. dir. N.Y. State Coun. on Econ. Edn., 1979-89; prof. econs. Russell Sage Coll., 1979-89. Adj. prof. econs. U. So. Fla., 1989-99; lectr. to elder hostels; econ. editor Kennikat Press, Inc., Port Washington, N.Y., 1970—; cons. to govt., industry, banks, pub. schs., 1954—; vis. prof. State U. N.Y., Buffalo, 1965, U. Miami, 1967. Author: (with J. Witchel) An Introduction to the American Economy, 1967, A Visual Analysis of the American Economy, 1968, (with G. Dawson) The American Economy, 1969, Introductory Economics, 1972, 7th edit., 1991; (with Conover and Ramstadder) Business Dynamics, 1982, 2d edit., 1988, The Economy of New York State, 1987, Basic Economic Principles, 1988, Economics U$A: A Resource Guide for Teachers, 1988, (with A. Stafford) Applying Economic Principles, 1994; lectr., writer: pub. TV series The American Economy, Conversations on Economic Issues, 1970— . Mem. Parks Commn., also Charter Revision Commn., Oneonta, 1957—; v.p. Oneonta Brotherhood, 1958; Dem. candidate for 13th Congl. Dist., Fla., for U.S. Ho. of Reps. Served to sgt. USAAF, 1942-44. Recipient Kazajian Found. award, 1967, Bessie B. Moore Service award, 1987. Mem. N.Y. Econ. Assn. (past pres.), AAUP (past pres. N.Y. conf.) Home: 7127 Fairway Bend Ln Sarasota FL 34243-3608 E-mail: Budalice@aol.com. *Success has less to do with innate ability than with self-confidence, motivation, and perhaps most important, resiliancy.*

GORDON, SARAH BARRINGER, law educator; BA, Vassar Coll., 1982; JD, Yale U., 1986, MAR (Ethics) magna cum ladue, 1987; PhD in History, Princeton U., 1995. Law clk. to Hon. Arlin M. Adams US Third Cir. Ct. Appeals, 1986—87; assoc. Fine, Kaplan & Black, Phila., 1987—89; asst. prof. law U. Pa. Law Sch., Phila., 1994—98, prof. law and history, 1998—, assoc. dean, 2000—02. Author: The Mormon Question: Polygamy and Constitutional Conflict in Nineteenth-Century America, 2002; contbr. articles to law jours. Mem.: ABA, Utah State Hist. Soc., Libr. Co. of Pa., Hist. Soc. of Pa., Am. Assn. Univ. Profs., Mormon History Assn., Soc. Am. Law Tchrs., Law & Soc. Assn., Western History Assn., Am. Acad. of Religion, Am. Soc. for Legal History, Orgn. Am. Hist., Am. Hist. Assn. Office: U Pa Law Sch 3400 Chestnut St Philadelphia PA 19104 Office Phone: 215-898-3069. Office Fax: 215-573-2025. E-mail: sgordon@law.upenn.edu.*

GORDON, SCOTT (HARRY SCOTT BUEHLMEIER), entertainer, actor; b. Dumont, N.J., Oct. 12, 1949; s. Harry Gordon and Florence Victoria (Bielawski) B.; m. Dian Mary Kenlon, Nov. 10, 1973. Grad. high sch., Mahwah, N.J. Pres. Scott Gordon Enterprises, Inc., Paramus, N.J., 1974—; performer, writer The Uncle Floyd Show, West Orange, N.J., 1976—, Gordon and Rogue, 1993—; ptnr. WWW.PlanetShowbiz.com, 1999—2001, www-.GoofyPartyPeople.com; writer Burns and Hope at Madison Sq. Garden, N.Y.C., 1989. Audio cons. Playhouse on the Mall, Paramus, NJ, 1974; make-up cons. Ken's Costumes, Fair Lawn, NJ, 1976—94, SYSOP/Cons. Genie On-Line Svc., 1990—97; rec. artist Mercury Records; comedy team mem. Gordon and Rogue; mem. nominating com. MixMag. TEC Awards, 1998—. Author, editor (Profl. mag.) Psychicos, 1978-80; author (column) Vibrations, 1987; maker radio commls.; San Antonio Rose with Willie Nelson, B-52s, Labour of Lust, First Exposure; enbr. (radio programs) The Italian American Serenade, The Colavita Music Hall, Italian Melodies, Sunday Funnies; air personality Remember When, 1987-98, syndicates 1995; entertainer Nickelodeon Turkey TV; appeared on Broadway with Collinsport Players, 1995. Mem. AFTRA, Psychic Entertainers Assn. (bd. dirs. 1978-80, founder), Audio Engring. Soc., Circle Tri Corbies, The Radio Repertory Co. of Am. Avocations: musician (guitar, bass, drums), performing psychic. Office: Scott Gordon Enterprises Inc PO Box 791 Paramus NJ 07653-0791 Office Phone: 201-670-0054. E-mail: audio@sge-inc.com.

GORDON, STEPHEN LOUIS, lawyer; b. Syracuse, N.Y., Oct. 31, 1956; s. Richard E. and Carole (Silverstein) G.; m. Lorraine (Winheim) Gordon, Oct 24, 1999; children, Samantha and Dana; 2 stepchildren, Matthew Fenster and Emily Fenster. AB, Cornell U., 1978; JD, Harvard U., 1981. Bar: N.Y 1982. Ptnr., tax dept. Cravath, Swaine & Moore LLP, N.Y.C., 1981—. Mem. ABA (tax sect.), N.Y. State Bar Assn. (tax sect.), Assn. of Bar of City of N.Y. Office: Cravath Swaine & Moore 825 8th Ave Fl 38 New York NY 10019-7475 Office Phone: 212-474-1704. Office Fax: 212-474-3700. Business E-Mail: gordon@cravath.com.

GORDON, STEPHEN MAURICE, manufacturing company executive, rancher; b. Chgo., Aug. 20, 1942; s. Milton A. and Elinor (Loeff) G.; m. Helene Lindow, Feb. 11, 1978 (div. Mar. 1998); 2 children: Hallie Lindow, Lacey Edison; m. Marilee Ann Enright, Mar. 21, 1998. Student, Middlebury Coll., 1960-61; BA, U. Chgo., 1964; JD, N.Y. U., 1967; D.I.L., Cambridge (Eng.) U., 1968. Bar: N.Y. State 1968. Aide to Vice Pres. Hubert Humphrey, Democratic Nat. Com., Washington, 1968; assoc. firm Marshall, Bratter, Greene, Allison & Tucker, N.Y.C., 1968-70; sr. rsch. assoc. Halle & Stieglitz, Inc., N.Y.C., 1970-72, v.p., 1972-75, pres., 1975-79; pres., chief exec. officer Irvin Industries Inc., N.Y.C., 1979-89; pres. Diamond G Ranch Inc., Dubois, Wyo. Chmn. bd. dirs. Vincennes Steel Corp., 1989—97; dir. Minerva Health; mem. vis. com. U. Chgo. Mem. Nat. Wildlife Art Mus. (dir., treas.), MacLean-Fogg (dir.), Am. Red Angus Assn., Young Pres.' Orgn., Beta Gamma Sigma, Psi Upsilon. Home: Diamond G Ranch Dunoir Rd Dubois WY 82513 Office: PO Box 25009 Jackson WY 83001-7000

GORDON, STEVE, real estate company executive; b. Ottawa, Ont., Can., July 13, 1951; m. Laurie Gordon, 1973; children: Erin, Nina, Shanon, Alex, Aliza. BSc, U. Ottawa, 1973; D (hon.), Northwestern U. Cert. property mgr., residential appraiser, profl. land economist. Pres., CEO The Regional Group of Cos., Inc., Ottawa, Canada, 1982—. Chmn. Regional Capital Properties; pres. Regional Realty Ltd., Gemini Capital Corp.; bd. govs. Ottawa Boys & Girls Club; active Jr. Achievement Can.; co-chair Counsellors of Real Estate, Can.; past exec. mem. Ottawa-Carleton Econ. Devel. Corp. Bd.; past chmn. Ottawa-Carleton Bd. Trade; past pres. Real Estate Inst. Can., Ea. Ont. chpt., Inst. Real Estate Property Mgmt., Ottawa, Housing & Urban Devel. Assn. Can., Ottawa; past nat. dir. Real Estate Inst. Can. Recipient Man of Yr. award HUDAC. Fellow Real Estate Inst. Can.; mem. Internat. Real Estate Inst., Am. Soc. Real Estate Counsellors (counselor), Inst. Real Estate Mgmt., Appraisal Inst. Can., Can. Home Builders Assn. (Presdl. award of honour), Assn. Ont. Land Economists, AF&AM, Rideau Club, Can. Club, Lambda Alpha Internat. Avocations: walking, swimming, mountain hiking. Office: The Regional Group of Cos Inc 200 Catherine St 6th Fl Ottawa ON Canada K2P 2K9

GORDON, STEWART LYNELL, musician, educator; b. Olathe, Kans., Aug. 28, 1930; s. Lynell Frank and Guanetta (Stewart) Gordon. Diploma, State Conservatory Music, 1951; BA, U.Kans., 1954, MA, 1955; D of Musical Arts, Eastman Sch., Rochester, N.Y., 1965. Asst. prof. music Wilmington (Ohio) Coll., 1957—60; from asst. prof. to assoc. prof. to prof. U. Md., Coll. Park, 1960—86, music dept. chair, 1979—86; v.p. for acad. affairs, provost Queens Coll., Flushing, NY, 1986—89; prof. keyboard studies U. So. Calif., LA, 1989—, chair keyboard studies, dir undergrad. studies, 1996—2004. Adjudicator Gina Bachauer Internat. Piano competition, Canadian Music Competition finals, Gilmore Found. Nominating Com.; touring pianist Europe, 1955—60, N. Am., 1960—80, Middle East, 1968, Asia, 1977—79; founder, dir. Wm. Kapell Internat. Piano Competition, Md., 1970—85, Savannah On Stage Festival and Am. Trads. Competition, 1989—2002, Cultural Heritage and Great Gospel Competitions, Queens, NY, 1990—91. Author: (book) Etudes for Piano Teachers, Essays on the Teachers' Art, 1995, A History of Keyboard Music for the Piano and Its Forerunners, 1996, Mastering the Art of Performance, 2005; co-author (with others): The Well Tempered Keyboard Teacher 2d edit., 1999; composer several music theater works including: Spirit of the Navy, 1955. Lt. j.g. USN, 1954—57. Recipient Danforth Tchr. Study grant, Danforth Found., 1963—64, Lifetime Achievement award, Md. Music Tchrs. Assn., 1983, Ramo Music Faculty award, U. So. Calif., 2001. Mem.: Calif. Music Tchrs. Assn., Nat. Music Tchrs. Assn. (adjudicator nat.music competition finals), Phi Kappa Phi, Phi Kappa Lambda, Phi Beta Kappa. Avocations: gardening, bull terriers, tropical fish, languages. Home: 775 E Mel Ave Palm Springs CA 92262-4832

GORDON, STUART A., lawyer; BA, U. Pa., 1962; JD, NYU, 1965. Bar: NY 1965, US Dist. Ct. So. and Ea. Dists. NY 1966. Mng. ptnr., mem. ops. group Bryan Cave LLP, NYC. Office: Bryan Cave LLP 1290 Ave of the Americas New York NY 10104 Office Phone: 212-541-2060. E-mail: sagordon@bryancave.com.

GORDON, SUSAN J., writer; b. N.Y.C., Nov. 12, 1943; m. Kenneth Gordon, Nov. 21, 1965; children: Edward, Peter. BA in Am. Studies, Queens Coll., 1964; MA in Am. Studies, NYU, 1967. Vis. artist Westchester (N.Y.) Arts Coun., 1983—. Author: Wedding Days: When and How Great Marriages Began, 1998. Mem. Am. Soc. Journalists and Authors, Authors Guild. Home: 11 Avondale Rd White Plains NY 10605-4101

GORDON, SUSAN JOAN, physician, educator; b. Atlantic City, Aug. 14, 1942; Student, Goucher Coll., 1959-62; MD, Jefferson Med. Coll., 1966. Diplomate Am. Bd. Internal Medicine, Am. Bd. Gastroenterology. Intern in medicine Hahnemann Med. Coll. and Hosp., Phila., 1966-67; resident in medicine Jefferson Med. Coll. Hosp., Phila., 1967-69; instr. Thomas Jefferson U., Phila., 1971-73, asst. prof., 1973-78, assoc. prof., 1978-87, clin. prof. medicine, 1987-97; jr. coord. medicine Jefferson Med. Coll., Phila., 1971-82; prof. medicine MCP-Hahnemann U., Phila., 1997—. Contbr. articles to profl. jours. Fellow ACP; mem. Am. Gastroenterol. Assn. (biliary sect., abstract reviewer, chairperson clin. biliary sect.), Am. Assn. Study Liver Disease, Pa. Med. Soc., Phil. Gastrointestinal Rsch. Forum, Sigma Xi. Office: Grad Hosp 1800 Lombard St Philadelphia PA 19146-1497

GORDON, WALTER KELLY, retired academic administrator, retired language educator; b. Bklyn., Jan. 25, 1930; s. William Benjamin and Grace Adele (Kelly) G.; m. Lydia Caroline Fruchtman, Aug. 29, 1959; 1 child, Karyn Gay. AB, Clark U., 1950; MA, U. Pa., 1956, PhD, 1961. Instr. Cedar Crest Coll., 1959-61; faculty Rutgers U., Camden, 1961-97, prof., dean coll., 1974-81, acad. dean, provost Camden campus, 1981-97; ret., 1997. Cons. Campbells Soup Co., 1976-94. Author: (with J.L. Sanderson) Exposition and the English Language, 1963, 2d edit., 1968, Literature in Critical Perspectives, 1969. Bd. dirs. Walt Whitman Internat. Poetry Center, 1974-77. Served to lt. USNR, 1951-56. Recipient Lindback award for disting. teaching, 1970 Home: 2803 Salem Dr Riverton NJ 08077-4027 Office: Rutgers U Camden Coll Arts & Scis 379 Armitage Hall Camden NJ 08102

GORDON, WILLIAM CHARLES, college administrator; m. Kathryn Gordon; children: Jason, Scott, Kate, Jonathan. Bachelor's degree, Master's degree, Wake Forest U.; PhD in Exptl. Psychology, Rutgers U. Asst. prof. psychology SUNY, Binghamton, 1973-78; tchr. psychology dept. U. N.Mex., Albuquerque, 1978, chair psychology dept., 1990, interim dean Coll. Arts and Scis., 1992, dean, 1993, provost, v.p. for acad. affairs, 1996, interim pres., 1998—; pres., 1999—2002; provost Wake Forest U., 2002. Office: Office of the Provost Wake Forest U 1834 Wake Forest Rd Winston Salem NC 27106 Business E-Mail: gordonwc@wfu.edu.

GORDON, WILLIAM EDMUND, JR., lawyer; b. Bryn Mawr, Pa., Aug. 9, 1948; s. William Edmund and Margaret Elizabeth (Bernstiel) G.; m. Mary Jo DeMatteo; 1 son, William Edmund III. B.S., Parsons Coll., 1971; J.D., S. Tex. Coll. Law, 1976. Bar: Tex. 1976, U.S. Dist. Ct. (so. dist.) Tex. 1976, U.S. Dist. Ct. (ea. dist. Pa.) 1978, U.S. Ct. Appeals (5th cir.) 1976, U.S. Dist. Ct. (ea. dist.) Tex. 1977. Assoc. firm Ryan & Marshall, Houston, 1976-77; asst. U.S. atty. Dept. Justice, Tyler, Tex., 1977-78, Phila., 1978-81; assoc. firm Curtin & Heefner, Morrisville, Pa., 1981-83; atty. E.I. du Pont de Nemours & Co., Wilmington, Del., 1984—; instr. Atty. Gen.'s Advocacy Inst., Washington, 1979-80. Editor-in-chief S. Tex. Law Jour., 1975. E.E. Townes scholar S. Tex. Coll. Law, 1976. Mem. Pa. C. of C. (mem. truth and fairness in litigation com. 1984). Republican. Roman Catholic. Home: 20 Walnut Valley Rd Chadds Ford PA 19317-9434

GORDON, WILLIAM EDWIN, physicist, educator, electrical engineer, academic administrator; b. Paterson, NJ, Jan. 8, 1918; s. William and Mary (Scott) G.; m. Elva Freile, June 22, 1941 (dec. Feb. 2002); children: Larry Scott, Nancy Lynn; m. Elizabeth Bolgiano, Aug. 31, 2003. BA, Montclair (N.J.) State Coll., 1939, MA, 1942; MS, NYU, 1946; PhD, Cornell U., Ithaca, N.Y., 1953. Registered profl. engr., Tex. Assoc. prof. Cornell U., 1953-59, prof., 1959-65; Walter R. Read prof. engring. Arecibo Ionospheric Obs., PR, 1965; prof. elec. engring. and space physics and astronomy Rice U., Houston, 1966-86, dean engring. and sci., 1966-75, dean Sch. Natural Scis., 1975-80, provost, v.p., 1980-86; fgn. sec. NAS, 1986-90. Conceived, directed design and early operation of Arecibo Obs. and 1000 foot antenna, 1960-65 (named Milestone in Elec. Engring. and Landmark in Mech. Engring. 2001); chmn. bd. trustees Upper Atmosphere Rsch. Corp., 1971, 73-78, Univ. Corp. for Atmospheric Rsch., 1979-81, 86-89, 91-92; trustee Cornell U., 1976-80; mem. Arecibo Obs. Adv. Bd., 1977-80, 90-93. Bd. dirs. Taping for the Blind, Houston, 1994-2002. Capt. USAAF, 1942-46. Recipient Balth. Vander Pol award for disting. rsch. in radio sci., 1966; 50th Anniversary medal Am. Meteorol. Soc., 1969, Arktowski medal, 1984, Arecibo Telescope award, 2001; Guggenheim fellow, 1972-73. Fellow IEEE (chmn. profl. group on antennas and propagation 1964-65), Am. Geophys. Union; mem. AAAS, NAS, NAE, Am. Acad. Arts and Scis., Internat. Sci. Radio Union (v.p. 1975-81, pres. 1981-84, hon. pres. 1990—), Internat. Coun. Sci. Unions (v.p. 1988-93), Am. Meteorology Soc., Philos. Soc. Tex., Cosmos Club, Sigma Xi, Tau Beta Pi, Kappa Delta Pi, Sigma Kappa Nu, Phi Kappa Phi. Achievements include research in radio scattering.

GORDON-LARSEN, PENNY, nutritionist, educator, researcher; children: Isabella, Frederick. PhD, U. Pa., 1997. Instr. U. Pa., Phila., 1995—98; Dannon postdoctoral fellow U. N.C. Chapel Hill, 1998—2000, asst. prof. nutrition, 2000—. Rev. panels, obesity rsch. NIH, Bethesda, Md., 2003—; sci. meeting planning com. N.Am. Assn. for Study of Obesity, Silver Spring, Md., 2004—, mem. pediat. obesity interest group, 2004—; cluster head macro & built environment U. N.C. Chapel Hill, 2004—. Chair pers. com. Chapel Hill Day Care Ctr., 2002—03. Recipient Young Investigator Awards, N.Am. Assn. for Study of Obesity; Ind. Rsch. Grants, NIH, 2002—, Dannon Nutrition Inst. Postdoctoral Fellowship Interdiscplinary Rsch., Dannon, 1998—2000. Fellow: Ctr. for Regional and Urban Studies (assoc.), Carolina Population Ctr. (assoc. Fellow 2001-present). Achievements include research in obesity, pediatric and adolescent medicine, interdisiplinary studies, health disparities; development of population-based GIS methods for epidemiologic research. Avocations: running, swimming, cooking. Office: Univ NC-Chapel Hill Univ Sq CPC 123 W Franklin St Chapel Hill NC 27516 Office Phone: 919-843-9966. Office Fax: 919-966-1959. E-mail: pglarsen@unc.edu.

GORDON-REED, ANNETTE, historian, law educator; d. Alfred Gordon, Sr. and Bettye Jean Gordon; m. Robert Raymond Reed, June 8, 1984; children: Susan Jean Gordon Reed, Gordon Penn Reed. AB, Dartmouth Coll., 1981; JD, Harvard U., 1984. Bar: N.Y., U.S. Dist. Ct. (so. dist.) N.Y. Law assoc. Cahill Gordon & Reindel, N.Y.C., 1984—87; counsel N.Y.C. Bd. Correction, N.Y.C., 1987—91; prof. N.Y. Law Sch., N.Y.C., 1992—. Bd. mem. Internat. Ctr. for Jefferson Studies, Charlottesville, Va., The Papers of Thomas Jefferson, Princeton, NJ, Children for Children Found., N.Y.C., Frederick D. Patterson Rsch. Inst. (United Negro Coll. Fund), Fairfax, Va. Author: (work of history) Thomas Jefferson and Sally Hemings: An American Controversy, 1997; co-author (with Vernon Jordan): (memoir) Vernon Can Read, 2004 (Best Nonfiction Book, Black Caucus of the ALA, 2001, Anisfield-Wolf Book award, 2002); editor: (book of essays) Race on Trial: Law and Justice in American History, 2003. Participant TransAtlantic Forum, Dresden, Germany, 2003, Arizona, 2004, Aspen Inst. Exec. Seminar. Recipient Bridging the Gap award for Fostering Racial Reconciliation, Bridging the Gap Found., Achievement award, Am. History Roundtable, 1998, Attys. Achievement award, Assn. Black Woman, N.Y., 1998, Women of Power and Influence award, NOW, N.Y., 1999, Trailblazer award, Met. Black Bar Assn., 2002. Mem.: The Constn. Project, Soc. Historians of the Early Am. Republic, Am. Soc. for Legal History, Orgn. Am. Historians, Coun. on Fgn. Rels. Methodist. Avocation: bicycling. Office: New York Law School 57 Worth St New York NY 10013 Office Phone: 212-431-2110. Business E-Mail: agordon@nyls.edu.

GORDON-TENNANT, JENNIFER JAY, secondary school educator; b. N.Y.C., Nov. 6, 1949; d. Frank P. and Jayne (Charles) Jay; m. Walmer A. Gordon Tennant, Aug. 11, 1973; children: Michael, Courtney. BS, Fordham U., 1972, MS, 1976; PhD, Long Island U., 1985. Cert. English, reading, provisional supervision and instrn., N.Y. Tchr., reading St. Peter of Alcantara Sch., Port Washington, N.Y.; tchr., high sch. equivalency Roslyn (N.Y.) Adult Edn. Program; tchr., English Mount Alvernia High Sch., Montego Bay, Jamaica, West Indies, Sewanhaka Cen. High Sch. dist., Elmont, N.Y. Mem. NCTE, Sewanhaka Fedn. of Tchrs., Columbia Univ. Scholastic Press Assn., Jr. League of L.I., Phi Delta Kappa. Home: 83 Carlton Ave Port Washington NY 11050-3533

GORDY, BERRY, entrepreneur, film producer, recording industry executive; b. Detroit, Nov. 28, 1929; children from a previous marriage: Berry IV, Hazel Joy, Terry James, Kerry A., Sherry R., Kennedy W., Stefan K., Rhonda Ross-Kendrick. PhD of Music (hon.), Ea. Mich. U., 1971. Founder Motown Record Corp., 1961—; exec. prodr. motion pictures; chmn. bd. dirs. West Grand Media, 1998—; founder Jobete Music Co., Inc., 1997—. Dir.: (films) Mahogany, 1975; exec. prodr.: Lady Sings the Blues, 1972, Bingo Long

Traveling All-Stars and Motor Kings, 1975, Berry Gordy's the Last Dragon, 1984; author: To Be Loved: The Music, the Magic, the Memories of Motown, 1994. Named star, Hollywood Walk of Fame, 1996; named to Minority Hall of Fame, Atlanta U. Sch. Bus. Adminstrn., 1981, Leading Entrepreneurs of Nation, Babson Coll., 1978, Rock and Roll Hall of Fame, 1988, Nat. Bus. Hall of Fame, Jr. Achievement, 1998; recipient Bus. Achievement award, Interracial Coun. for Bus. Opportunity, 1967, Golden Mike and MLK, Jr.'s Leadership award, NATRA, 1969, 2d Ann. Am. Music award for outstanding contbn. to music industry, 1975, Whitney M. Young Jr. award, L.A. Urban League, 1980, Trustees award, NARAS, 1991, 20th Century award, Black Radio Exclusive, 1993, Abe Olman Pub. award, Songwriters Hall of Fame, 1993, Livetime Achievement award, Black Bus. Assn., 1993, Generation award, Congl. Black Caucus Found., 1993, Am. Legend award, ASCAP Pop Music Awards, 1998, Lifetime Achievement award, NABOB, 1998, Legend award, BESLA, 1998, A.G. Gaston Lifetime Achievement award, Black Ent./Bank of Am., 2001, Wall St. Project Millennium award, Rainbow/Push, 2000, Legend award, Rainbow/Push Coalition, 2001, Candle award for Lifetime Achievement in Arts and Entertainment, Morehouse Coll., 2005; Gordon Grand fellow, Yale U., 1985. Mem.: NAACP, Acad. Motion Picture Arts and Scis., BMI, Dirs. Guild Am. Office: West Grand Media LLC Ste 1110 6255 W Sunset Blvd Los Angeles CA 90028-7412

GORE, AL (ALBERT ARNOLD GORE JR.), former Vice President of the United States; b. Washington, Mar. 31, 1948; s. Albert and Pauline LaFon Gore; m. Mary Elizabeth Aitcheson, May 19, 1970; children: Karenna, Kristin, Sarah, Albert III. BA cum laude (Univ. scholar), Harvard U., 1969; student, Grad. Sch. of Religion, Vanderbilt U., 1971-72, Vanderbilt Law Sch., 1974-76. Investigative reporter, editorial writer The Tennessean, 1971-76; homebuilder and land developer Tanglewood Home Builders Co., 1971-76; livestock and tobacco farmer, 1973—; mem. 95th-98th Congresses from Tenn., 1977-85; U.S. senator from Tenn., 1985-93; v.p. U.S., 1993-2001; Dem. candidate for Pres., 2000; vice chmn. Metropolitan West Fin., Los Angeles, Calif., 2001—; sr. advisor Google, Inc., 2001—; chmn. Generational Investment Mgmt. Inc., London, 2004—; co-founder Current TV, San Francisco, 2005—. Bd. dirs. Apple Computer Inc., 2003—; vis. prof. Columbia U. Sch. Journalism, 2001, Fisk U., Middle Tenn. State U., UCLA, 2001—. Author: Earth in the Balance: Ecology and the Human Spirit, 1992, Let the Glory Out: My South and it's Politics, 2000; co-author: (with Joseph Kaufman)The World According to Al Gore: An A-To-Z Compilation of His Opinions, Positions, and Public Statements, The Spirit of Family, (with Tipper Gore) 2002, Joined at the Heart: The Transformation of the American Family, 2002. Served with U.S. Army, 1969-71, Army Journalist, Vietnam. Recipient Webby Lifetime Achievement award, Internat. Acad. of Digital Arts and Sciences, 2005. Mem. Farm Bur., Tenn. Jaycees. Clubs: Am. Legion, VFW. Democrat. Baptist.

GORE, ANDREW, editor-in-chief periodical; Contbg. editor early Mac pubs.; products editor Macintosh News; with Compyuter Reseller News; exec. editor, sr. new editos, exec. editor/news MacWeek; mgr. editl. dept. MacUser, 1996-97; editor-in-chief Mac World, San Francisco, 1997—. Co-author: Power Book, The digital Nomad's Guide, AT&T EO Personal Communicator, Newton's Law.

GORE, STEVEN LOWELL, state agency administrator; b. Paducah, Ky., June 22, 1953; *Sister, Marsha and brother-in-law Dale Lamphey, electrician, Paducah, Kentucky, have two children, Michael, air force militant, and Melissa Walker, sonographer, Paducah. Melissa has a son, Carson. Sister Sharon, married to brother-in-law Wally Brines, wildlife biologist, Cookeville, Tennessee. Also has a sister, Denise Bradford, Paducah. Brother, Jesse Gore is president and CEO Genetics Associates, Nashville. His wife is Gloria. They have five children: Jonathan, BS from FIT, Nashville; Benjamin, mattress store manager, Nashville; Steven, student at UT Knoxville; Kristen; and Zachary. Benjamin is married to wife Carolyn and they have a daughter, Aliyah.* BS in Acctg., David Lipscomb U., 1975. CPA Tenn., cert. treasury profl. Analyst fiscal svcs. King Faisal Hosp., Riyadh, Saudi Arabia, 1976—77; facility acct. Am. Retirement Corp., Nashville, 1983; staff auditor Hosp. Corp. Am., Nashville, 1984—87; contr. Sumner Regional Med. Ctr., Gallatin, Tenn., 1987—2003; devel. officer Genetics Assocs., Inc., Nashville, 2003—05; freelance cons. Nashville, 2005—; examiner Dept. Commerce and Ins., Nashville, 2005—. Vol. Margaret Maddox YMCA-East, Nashville, 1997—2000; active Friends of Warner Parks, Nashville, 1996—; poll ofcl. Metro-Davidson County Election Commn., Nashville, 1999. Recipient Appreciation Letter for Svc. United Way of Sumner County, 1997-2000. Mem.: AAAS, UN Assn. USA, Am. Math. Soc., Math Assn. Am., Nat. Space Soc., Population Reference Bur., World Future Soc., Planetary Soc., N.Y. Acad. of Sci., Am. Pub. Health Assn., Am. Chem. Soc., Cheekwood. Avocations: fishing, reading, jogging, golf. Office: Tenn Dept Commerce and Ins 500 James Robertson Pkwy Ste 750 Nashville TN 37243-1169 Home: 1413 Clifton Ln Nashville TN 37215-1615 Office Phone: 615-741-2677. Personal E-mail: stevengore@msn.com.

GORE, TIPPER (MARY ELIZABETH GORE), wife of the former vice president of the United States; b. Washington, Aug. 19, 1948; m. Albert Gore Jr., May 19, 1970; children: Karenna, Kristin, Sarah, Albert III. BA in Psychology, Boston U., 1970; MA in Psychology, Vanderbilt U., 1975. Freelance photographer. Mental health policy advisor to pres. Author: Raising PG Kids in an X-Rated Society, 1987, Picture This: A Visual Diary, 1996; co-author The Spirit of Family, 2002, Joined at the Heart: The Transformation of the American Family, 2002; co-prodr. (with Nat. Mental Health Assn.) Homeless in America: A Photographic Project. Co-founder Parents Music Resource Ctr., Arlington, Va., 1985; founder Tenn. Voices for Children, 1990; co-chair Am. Goes Back to Sch. Initiative, 1996—; chair Congl. Wives Task Force, 1978-79. Democrat. Office: 2100 West End Ave Nashville TN 37203

GORE, TUSHAR, marketing professional; s. Balkrishna and Anuradha Gore; m. Ramya Kumbale, June 10, 1996. BSChemE, Indian Inst. of Tech., Bombay, 1994; PhD in Chem. Engring., U. Minn., 2000. Assoc. cons. McKinsey and Co., Florham Park, NJ, 2000—02; assoc. dir. bus. analyst Novo Nordisk Pharm. Inc., Princeton, NJ, 2003—. Presenter in field. Contbr. articles to profl. publs. Project coord. Am. India Found., N.Y.C., 2001. Grantee, U. Minn. Mem.: NY Acad. Scis. Avocations: scuba diving, model railroad, guitar, photography.

GORE, WILLMA CLARICE, writer, educator; b. Big Pine, Calif., 1922; d. Roy Dunlap and Elva (Tate) Willis; m. Charles Frederic Gore, Nov. 10, 1968 (dec. 1991); stepchildren: Alan, Gillian, Janice, David, Andrew; m. John A. Simpson (div.); children: John Jr., James, Gregory. BA, U. Calif., L.A., 1947; postgrad., Calif. State U., 1968. Freelance writer, Fullerton, Calif., 1950—62; mgr. pub. Fullerton C. of C., 1963—64, mg. pub., 1969—72; writer, pub. Civic Pub., Buena Park, Calif., 1965—66; publicist Bazaar Sabado, Fullerton, 1966—67; asst. editor Nutrilite Products, Inc., Buena Park, 1968—69; freelance writer, 1973—. Publicist Orange County Philharmonic, Calif., 1955—57; spkr. in field. Author: (children's books) About News and How It Travels, 1961, About Pioneers, 1962, My Favorite City, 1963, Sand & Man, 1968; co-author (with M. Westover and D. Rhodes): The Very Important People series (12 books); author: (Holiday Books) Earth Day, Mother's Day, Independence Day, 1992—93, Just Pencil Me In-Your Guide to Moving and Getting Settled After 60, 2002, (novel) Something's Leaking Upstairs, 2005. Named Communicator of Achievement, Calif. Press Women, 1989; recipient, 1988, 1989, 1990. Mem.: Outdoor Writers Calif., Soc. S.W. Authors. Democrat. Unitarian Universalist. Avocations: hiking, photography. Address: PO Box 20135 Sedona AZ 86341 Personal E-mail: wgore@npgcable.com.

GOREA, LUCIA-IOSEFINA, language educator, poet; arrived in U.S., 1993; d. Joseph and Emilia Badea; m. Simion Liviu Gorea, Apr. 22, 1989; 1 child, Alex Raoul. MA in Philology, U. Bucharest, Romania, 1986; secondary degree, U. Bucharest, 1989; PhD in English, Atlantic Internat. U., Miami, Fla., 2002. Notary pub. Oreg. English tchr. Magherani H.S., Mures, Romania, 1986—89; English prof. U. Mures, Romania, 1989—92; 2d grade tchr. Columbia Acad., Portland, Oreg., 1998—2000; English instr. Marylhurst (Oreg.) U., 2000—01, Portland C.C., 2000—, tchr. ESL, 2000—, Mt. Hood C.C., Portland, 2000—. Founder, leader Poetry Around the World, Beaverton, Oreg. Author: Welcome to America: A Practical Guide to Life Survival Skills, 2004, numerous poems. Recipient Pres.'s award for lit. excellence, Nat. Authors Registry, 2000, Internat. Poet of Merit award, Internat. Soc. Poets, 2001, Silver award, 2002, Outstanding Achievement in Poetry Silver Cup award, 2003, Bronze Medallion Commemorative award, 2003, Cert. of Achievement in Poetry, 2004, Shakespeare Troph of Excellence, 2004. Mem.: NEA, Internat. Libr. Poetry (Poet of Merit 2000), Oreg. Edn. Assn. Avocations: reading, writing, philosophy, performing arts, classical music. Home: 18645 SW Farmington Rd PMB 310 Aloha OR 97007 Personal E-mail: luciag_esl@yahoo.com.

GOREAU, ANGELINE WILSON, writer; b. Sept. 12, 1951; d. Theodore Nelson and Eloise (Keaton) G.; m. Stephen Jones McGruder, Mar. 19, 1983; 1 child, Keaton Angeline. BA, Barnard Coll., 1973. Hodder fellow Princeton (N.J.) U., 1982-83; lectr. Vassar Coll., Poughkeepsie, N.Y., 1980's. Judge for various prizes. Author: Reconstructing Aphra, 1980, The Whole Duty of a Woman, 1984; contbr. articles to mags., newspapers, essays to books. Fellow NEH, 1976, Nat. Endowment for Arts, 1981, Belgian Ministry of Culture, Hodder fellow, 1982-83. Mem. PEN, Book Critics' Cir., Authors' Guild. Office: c/o Georges Borchardt 136 E 57th St New York NY 10022-2707 E-mail: Angelinegoreau@aol.com.

GORELICK, JAMIE SHONA, lawyer; b. N.Y.C., May 6, 1950; d. Leonard and Shirley (Fishman) G.; m. Richard E. Waldhorn, Sept. 28, 1975; children: Daniel H., Dana E. BA magna cum laude, Harvard U., 1972, JD cum laude, 1975. Bar: D.C. 1975, U.S. Dist. Ct. D.C. 1976, U.S. Tax Ct. 1976, U.S. Ct. Claims 1976, U.S. Ct. Appeals (D.C. cir.) 1976, U.S. Ct. Appeals (5th cir.) 1977, U.S. Supreme Ct. 1979, U.S. Ct. Appeals (Fed. cir.) 1982, U.S. Ct. Internat. Trade 1984, U.S. Dist. Ct. Md. 1985, U.S. Ct. Appeals (4th cir.) 1986, U.S. Ct. Appeals (3d. cir.) 1988. With Miller, Cassidy, Larroca & Lewin, Washington, 1975-79, 80-93; asst. to sec., counselor to dep. sec. U.S. Dept. Energy, 1979—80; gen. counsel Dept. Def., 1993—94; dep. atty. gen. Dept. Justice, Washington, 1994-97; vice chair Fannie Mae, Washington, 1997—2003; ptnr. litigation, co-chmn. Nat. Security & Govt. Contracts dept., co-chmn., Public Policy & Strategy group Wilmer Cutler Pickering Hale and Dorr LLP, Washington, 2003—. Mem. chmn.'s adv. coun. U.S. Senate Jud. Com., 1988-93; tchr. Trial Advocacy Workshop Harvard Law Sch., Cambridge, Mass., 1982, 84; vice chair task force evaluation of audit investigative inspection components Dept. Def., 1979-80; mem. sec.'s transition team Dept. Energy, 1979; bd. dirs. United Technologies Corp., Schlumberger Ltd., Fannie Mae Found., 1997-2005, 9/11 oyb, discover project John D. & Catherine T. MacArthur Found., Urban Inst., 1999-2003, Am.'s Promise-Alliance for Youth, 1997-2004, Nat. Park Found., 1997-2004, Carnegie Endowment, 1989-93, Nat. Women's Law Ctr., 1991-93, Washington Legal Clinic for Homeless; bd. overseers Harvard Coll., 1998-2004; mem. nat. security adv. panel CIA, 1997-2005; mem. Pres.'s Intelligence Rev. Panel, 2001-2002; mem. threat reduction adv. com. Dept. of Def.; mem. coun. Am. Law Inst., 1997-2000, D.C. Bar Found.; co-chair adv. com. Presdl. Commn. on Critical Infrastructure Protection, 1997-99; mem. Nat. Commn. Support Law Enforcement, Washington, 1995-97; mem. Supreme Ct. Judicial fellow. Selection Com.; commr., The Nat. Commn. on Terrorist Attacks Upon the U.S. (The 9-11 Commn.), 2002-04. mem. editl. bd. Corp. Criminal Liability Reporter, 1986-93, Destruction of Evidence, 1989; bd. Legal Affairs. Contbr. articles to profl. jours. Named one of Top 30 Lawyers in Washington, Washingtonian mag., 100 Most Powerful Women, 50 Most Powerful Women in Bus., Fortune mag., America's Top Businesswomen, forbes.com, 50 Smartest Women in Money Bus., Money Mag.; recipient Corp. Leadership award, DC C. of C., 2003, Aiming High award, NOW Legal Def. & Edn. Fund, 2002, Judge Learned Hand award, Am. Jewish Com., 1999, Wickersham award for exceptional pub. svc., 1998, Outstanding Advocate of the Year, Equal Justice Works, 1997. Fellow Am. Bar Found.; mem. ABA (chair complex crimes litigation com. litigation sect. 1984-87, vice-chair complex crimes litigation com. 1983-84, sec. litigation sect. 1988-90, coun. mem. 1990-93, com. on profl. discipline, ho. of dels. 1991-93, 97—, Margaret Brent award 1997), D.C. Bar (pres. 1992-93, bd. govs. 1982-88, sec. bd. govs. 1981-92, bar found. advisors 1985-93, legal ethics com.), Women's Bar Assn. (Lawyer of the Year award 1993, Star of the Bar award 2003), Am. Law Inst. (coun.), Coun. on Fgn. Rels. Office: Wilmer Cutler Pickering Hale and Dorr LLP 2445 M St NW Washington DC 20037 Office Phone: 202-663-6500. Office Fax: 202-663-6363. Business E-Mail: jamie.gorelick@wilmerhale.com.

GOREN, JOHN ALAN, lawyer; b. Houston, June 9, 1948; s. Jack and Leah Sakowitz (Nathan) G. BS in Econs., U. Pa., Phila., 1970; JD cum laude, U. Ga., 1974. Bar: Ga. 1974, Tex. 1977, U.S. Supreme Ct. 1979, U.S. Ct. Appeals (5th cir.) 1984, U. S. Ct. Appeals (fed. cir.) 1984, U.S. Dist. Ct. (no. dist.) Tex. 1983; bd. cert. Civil Appellate Law, Tex. Bd. Legal Specialization, 1987. Sole practitioner, Dallas. Developer For Kid's Sake Seminar, Collin County, Tex., 1992-99; mem. worship com. Temple Emanu-El, Dallas, 1990-96; former dir. Dallas chpt. Am. Jewish Com.; pres. Wharton Alumni Club Dallas, 1980; active worker Dallas County Rep. Party and numerous Rep. campaigns, including chmn. ballot security, senatorial spl. election, 1992, v.p. Metrocrest Rep. Club, 1997-98, treas., 1995-96, 93-94, mem. Dallas County Rep. Assembly, Dallas County Rep. Forum, other sustaining orgns.; del. Rep. Party State Conv., 1996, alternate, 1990, 92, 94. Mem. Dallas Bar Assn. (founder, chmn. appellate law sect. 1990-91, chmn. Dallas Ct. Appeals centennial celebration com. 1993, chair house com. 2001, Most Outstanding Sect. Chair award 1992), Plano (Tex.) Bar Assn. (pres. 1994-95), State Bar of Tex. (mandatory continuing legal edn. com. 1995-2001). Home: 11308 Park Central Pl Apt D Dallas TX 75230-3311 Office: 4627 N Central Expy Dallas TX 75205-4022

GORENBERG, CHARLES LLOYD, finance company executive; b. Phila., Mar. 1, 1938; s. Abraham and Esther (Freedman) G.; m. Roslyn Grobman, May 22, 1960; children: David M., Kenneth M. BA, Franklin & Marshall Coll., 1960; MS, The Am. Coll., Bryn Mawr, Pa., 1981. Cert. Employee Benefit Specialist, CLU, ChFC. Sales assoc. Landis & Co., Phila., 1960-62; agt. Phoenix Mut. Life, Phila., 1962-64, supr., 1964-67; dir. tng. Rittenhouse Assocs., Phila., 1967-75; exec. v.p. Corp. Pension Actuaries, Phila., 1975-91; pres. Delta Fin. Group, Phila., 1991-97, Chaslyn Fin. Group, Marlton, N.J., 1997—. Co-editor: (book) Planning for Business Owners and Professionals, 1988; contbr. over 35 articles to mags. Mem. Internat. Soc. Cert. Employee Benefit Specialists, Am. Soc. CLUs and ChFCs (various offices), Am. Soc. Pension Actuaries. Avocation: golf. Office: Chaslyn Fin Group 1002 Lincoln Dr W Ste C Marlton NJ 08053-1531 Office Phone: 856-988-0480. Business E-Mail: chuck@chaslynfinancialgroup.com.

GORENCE, PATRICIA JOSETTA, judge; b. Sheboygan, Wis., Mar. 6, 1943; d. Joseph and Antonia (Marinsheck) G.; m. John Michael Bach, July 11, 1969; children: Amy Jane, Mara Jo, J. Christopher Bach. BA, Marquette U., 1965, JD, 1977; MA, U. Wis., 1969. Bar: Wis. 1977, U.S. Dist. Ct. (ea. and we. dists.) Wis. 1977, U.S. Ct. Appeals (7th cir.) 1979, U.S. Supreme Ct. 1980. Asst. U.S. atty. U.S. Atty.'s Office, Milw., 1979-84, 1st asst. U.S. Atty., 1984-87, 89-91, U.S. Atty., 1987-88; dep. atty. gen. State of Wis. Dept. Justice, Madison, 1991-93; assoc. Ginbel, Reilly, Guerin & Brown, Milw., 1993-94; U.S. magistrate judge U.S. Dist. Ct. Wis., Milw., 1994—. Bd. dirs. U. Wis.-Milw. Slovenian Arts Coun., 1989—, treas., 1989—, Milw. Dance Theatre, 1993-98; bd. chair Bottomless Closet, 1999—. Recipient Spl. Commendation, U.S. Dept. Justice, 1986, IRS, 1988. Mem. ABA, Am. Law Inst., Nat. Assn. Women Judges, Fed. Magistrate Judges Assn. (cir. dir. 1997-2000), Milw. Bar Assn. (chair cmty. rels. com. 2000-03, Prosecutor of Yr. 1990, Disting. Svc. award 2003, Wis. Law Jour. Innovator of Yr. award 2003), State Bar Wis. (chair lawyer dispute resolution com. 1986—, chair professionalism com. 1988-2000, vice chair legal edn. commn. 1994-96, Pres. award 1995), 7th Cir. Bar Assn. (chair rules and practices com. 1991-95), Assn. for Women Lawyers, Profl. Dimensions (sec. 1998-2000, v.p. adminstrn. 2000-2002).

GORENSTEIN, CHARLES, lawyer; b. Phila., Nov. 25, 1950; s. Samuel and Ethel (Gershman) G.; m. Gail Barbara Newman, July 8, 1973; children: Jeremy L., Heather M. BS in Engring. Mechanics, Pa. State U., 1972; JD, Am. U., 1980. Bar: D.C. 1981, Va. 1988, U.S. Patent and Trademark Office 1979, U.S. Dist. Ct. (D.C. dist.) 1982, U.S. Dist. Ct. (ea. dist.) Va. 1989, U.S. Dist. Ct. (ea. dist.) Mich. 1995, U.S. Dist. Ct. (ea. dist.) Wis. 1995, U.S. Ct. Appeals (D.C. and fed. cirs.) 1982, U.S. Ct. Appeals (4th cir.) 1989, U.S. Dist. Ct. (Colo.) 2000. Examiner U.S. Patent & Trademark Office, Washington, 1972-79; patent advisor U.S. Army Electronics Rsch. & Devel. Command, Adelphi, Md., 1979-81; assoc. Finnegan, Henderson, Farabow, Garrett & Dunner, Washington, 1981; ptnr. Birch, Stewart, Kolasch & Birch, Falls Church, Va., 1982—. Indsl. and profl. adv. coun. Coll. Engring./Pa. State U., University Park, Pa., 1988-93, 2000—. Mem. ABA, Internat. Trademark Assn., Am. Intellectual Property Law Assn., Inter-Am. Soc. Indsl. Property. Avocations: skiing, golf. Home: 1718 Crestview Dr Potomac MD 20854-2630 Office: 8110 Gatehouse Rd Ste 500 E Falls Church VA 22042-1210

GORENSTEIN, DAVID G., chemistry and biochemistry professor; b. Oct. 6, 1945; s. Ben and Shirley (Adelberg) G.; m. Deborah H. Joseph, June 11, 1967; 1 child, Jennifer. BS in Chemistry, M.I.T., 1966; MA in Chemistry, Harvard U., 1967, PhD in Chemistry, 1969. Asst. prof. U. Ill., Chgo., 1969-73, assoc. prof., 1973-76, prof., 1976-85; prof. chemistry Purdue Univ., West Lafayette, Ind., 1985-94; dir. Purdue Biochem. MRI Lab., West Lafayette, Ind., 1985-94, NSF Nat. Biol. Facilities Ctr., West Lafayette, 1987-93, NMR and Structural Biology Cores, West Lafayette, 1988-94; dep. dir. NIH Designated AIDS Rsch. Ctr., West Lafayette, 1993-94; prof. human biol. chemistry and genetics U. Tex. Med. Sch., Galveston, 1994—; sr. investigator Sealy Ctr. Molecular Sci. U. Tex. Med. Br., Galveston, 1994—; dir. Nuclear Magnetic Resonance Ctr. U. Tex. Med. Br., Galveston, dir. Sealy Ctr. for Structural Biology, 1995—2002, dep. dir. NIEHS Ctr., 1996—2002, Charles Marc Pomerat Disting. Prof. of biology, 1997—, vice chmn. human biol. chem. genetics, 1999—2002, assoc. dean rsch., 2002—. Dir. Gulf Coast NMR Consortium; founder, chmn. AptaMed, Inc., 2003—; vis. assoc. prof. U. Wis., Madison, 1975; vis. prof. Oxford U., 1977-78, U. Calif., San Francisco, 1986; adj. prof. Biomed. Engring. U. Tex., Austin, 1996—; cons. Baxter Travenol, 1985-95, Merck and Co., 1988, Eli Lilly, 1987-89, Ill. Tool Works, 1973-85, Chronomatic Inc., 1973-85, U.S. Dept. of Labor, 1975, Continental Group, Inc., 1982-84, Abbott Corp., 2001- Abbott Diagnostics, 2002; active numerous univ. coms.; lectr. in field. Editor Bull. of Magnetic Resonance, 1982-99; mem. editorial bd. Magnetic Resonance Revs., 1983-93, Jour. Magnetic Resonance, 1992-99, Biophys. Jour., 1992-98; pub. abstracts; contbr. articles to profl. jours. Grantee: NSF, 1987-93, NIH, 1970—, Eli Lilly, 1988-94 and numerous others; tchg. fellow Harvard U., 1966-69, trainee summer fellow NSF, 1966, predoctoral fellow NIH, 1967-69, Alfred P. Sloan fellow 1975-79, Sr. Rsch. fellow Fulbright, 1977-78, Guggenheim fellow, 1986; recipient Internat. Lectr. award Fulbright, 1978. Fellow AAAS; mem. Am. Soc. for Biochemistry and Molecular Biology, Am. Chem. Soc. (program chmn. divsn. biol. chemistry 1985-87, vice chmn. Purdue sect. 1990-91, chmn. 1991-92), Biophys. Soc., Protein Soc., Sigma Xi, Phi Lambda Upsilon. Achievements include patents in process for Preparing Dithiophosphate Oligonucleotide Analogs via Nucleoside Thiophosphoramidite Intermediates and in vivo selection of aptamers; research in proteomics and applications of NMR spectroscopy and other physical techniques to biological systems, theoretical bio-organic chemistry, biomolecular design; cancer and anti-viral drugs development. Address: 3922 Crown Ridge Ct Houston TX 77059-3711 Office: U Tex Med Br Sch Medicine Galveston TX 77555-1157 Office Phone: 409-747-6800. Business E-Mail: david@nmr.utmb.com.

GORENSTEIN, SAMUEL, retired mathematician, educator; s. Isidore and Bessie Gorenstein; m. Shirley Slotkin, July 3, 1948; children: Ethan Ezra, Gabriel William. PhD, N.Y. U., 1968. Sr. mathematician Sys. Devel. Corp., Paramus, NJ, 1959—63; mathematician advisor IBM, Armonk, NY, 1963—89. Adj. prof. Poly. Inst. N.Y., N.Y. U., N.Y.C., 1968—83. Contbr. articles to profl. jours. Vol. math tutor Union Settlement Cmty. Ctr., N.Y.C., 1997—2000. 2nd lt. navigator Army AC, 1943—45, European Theatre of Operations. Fellow, NASA, 1966. Mem.: Ops. Rsch. Soc. (chair computer sci. sect. 1975—81). Achievements include development of constructed price index for total cost of computing systems. Personal E-mail: samgoren12@aol.com.

GORES, CHRISTOPHER MERREL, lawyer; b. N.Y.C., Aug. 27, 1943; s. Guido James and Mary (Callaway) G.; children: Ellen, Eugenia. AB, Princeton U., 1965; LLB, Columbia U., 1968. Bar: N.Y. 1968, Tex. 1973, U.S. Dist. Ct (no. dist.) Tex. 1977. Assoc. Akin, Gump, Strauss, Hauer & Feld, LLP, Dallas, 1973-79, ptnr., 1979—. Bd. dirs. Shakespeare Festival of Dallas, 1982-88. Lt. USNR, 1969-72. Office: Akin Gump Strauss Hauer & Feld LLP 1700 Pacific Ave Ste 4100 Dallas TX 75201-4675 Office Phone: 214-969-2716. Business E-Mail: cgores@akingump.com.

GORES, THOMAS C., lawyer; b. Milw., Sept. 24, 1948; s. Kenneth W. and Carolyn (Camblin) G.; m. Ann P. Pacelli, June 13, 1970; children: Lauren, Jake, Kathryn. BA, U. Notre Dame, 1970, JD, 1973; LLM, U. Miami, 1977. Bar: Wash. 1973, U.S. Tax Ct. 1973. Assoc., then ptnr. Bogle & Gates, Seattle, 1973-78, ptnr., 1978-93, Gores & Blais, Seattle, 1993-2001, Perkins Coie LLP, 2001—. Fellow Am. Coll. Trust and Estate Counsel; mem. Wash. State Bar Assn., Seattle Estate Planning Coun. (pres.). Office: Perkins Coie LLP 1201 3rd Ave Ste 4800 Seattle WA 98101-3099 Office Phone: 206-628-2828, 206-359-8555. Business E-Mail: tgores@perkinscole.com.

GOREY, THOMAS C., retail executive; B, Calif. State U.; MA, U. Minn. Retail mgmt. trainee Sears Roebuck and Co., 1968, variety mgmt. positions, 1969—79; store mgr. El Centro, Calif., 1979—81; retail group oper. mgr. Sears Roebuck and Co., Los Angeles, 1981—84, store ops. policy and procedure, 1984—87, dir. planning, 1987—88; nat. mgr. positions, logistics, retail systems, systems planning, 1988—93; v.p. stores, southwest region Sears Roebuck and Co., 1993—94, v.p. logistics ops. integration, 1994—99, v.p. supply chain mgmt., 1999—2001, v.p. performance improvement project, 2001—02, v.p. strat. initiatives, 2002—. Bd. govs. Uniform Code Coun. Mailing: Sears Roebuck and Co 3333 Beverly Rd Hoffman Estates IL 60179 Office Phone: 847-286-8400.

GORFINKEL, MARC PAUL, lawyer; b. Yonkers, N.Y., May 14, 1954; s. Samuel Lewis and Shirley (Ehrlich) G.; m. Phyllis Zimilover, Aug. 27, 1978; children: Raizy, Nechama, Yirmi. BA, Yeshiva U., 1975; JD, NYU, 1978. Bar: N.Y. 1979, U.S. Dist. Ct. (so., no. and ea. dists.) N.Y. 1979, U.S. Dist. Ct. (we. dist.) N.Y. 1980, U.S. Dist. Ct. (we. dist.) Mich. 1991, U.S. Dist. Ct. (ea. dist.) Wis. 1992, U.S. Dist. Ct. (ea. dist.) Mich. 1995, U.S. Ct. Appeals (6th cir.) 1993, U.S. Ct. Appeals (7th cir.) 1996, U.S. Dist. Ct. Colo. 1998. Editor Matthew Bender, N.Y.C., 1978-79; law clk. to judge N.Y. Appellate Ct., Bklyn., 1979-82; assoc. Rivkin Radler, Uniondale, NY, 1982-88, ptnr., 1989—. Pres. Congregation Toras Chaim, Hewlett, N.Y., 1992-94. Democrat. Avocations: talmud, hiking, classical music, american history, modern painting and sculpture. Home: 1012 S End Woodmere NY 11598-1027 Office: Rivkin Radler Eab Pla Uniondale NY 11556-0001 Office Phone: 516-357-3000. E-mail: paul.gorfinkel@rivkin.com.

GORHAM, BRADFORD, lawyer; b. Providence, Mar. 7, 1935; s. Sayles and Ruth C. (Campbell) G.; m. Diann Gebow, Aug. 1, 1959; children: Christopher, Nicholas, Joshua, Jane, Nancy. Degree, Dartmouth Coll., 1957, Harvard U., 1964. Bar: R.I. 1964. Ptnr. Gorham & Gorham, Scituate, R.I., 1964—. State rep. R.I. State Ho. of Reps., Providence, 1969-70, 77-90; state senator R.I. State Senate, Providence, 1991-97. Capt. USMC, 1957-60. Named Legislator of Yr. Nat. Conf. State Legislatures, 1985, Outstanding Legislator Am. Legis. Exch. Coun., 1986. Republican. Home: 11 Cucumber Hill Rd Foster RI 02825-1211 Office: Gorham & Gorham 25 Danielson Pike Scituate RI 02857-1801 Office Phone: 401-647-1400.

GORHAM, EVILLE, retired ecologist; b. Halifax, N.S., Can., Oct. 15, 1925; s. Ralph Arthur and Shirley Agatha (Eville) G.; m. Ada Verne MacLeod, Sept. 29, 1948; children: Kerstin, Vivien, Jocelyn, James. BSc in Biology with distinction, Dalhousie U., 1945, MSc in Zoology, 1947, LLD (hon.), 1991; PhD in Botany, U. London, Eng., 1951; DSc (hon.), McGill U., 1993, U. Minn., 1999. Lectr. botany U. Coll., London, Eng., 1951-54; sr. sci. officer Freshwater Biol. Assn., Ambleside, Eng., 1954-58; lectr., asst. prof. botany U. Toronto, 1958-62; assoc. prof. botany U. Minn., Mpls., 1962-65, prof., 1966-75, head dept., 1967-71, prof. ecology, 1975-84, Regents' prof. ecology and botany, 1984-98, Regents' prof. emeritus, 1999—; prof., head dept. biology U. Calgary, Alta., Can., 1965-66. Mem. for Can., Internat. Commn. on Atmospheric Chemistry and Radioactivity, 1959-62; mem. vis. panel to rev. toxicology program NAS-NRC, 1974-75, mem. com. on inland aquatic ecosys. Water Sci. and Tech. Bd., 1994-96, mem. com. to evaluate indicators for monitoring aquatic and terrestrial environments Water Sci. and Tech. Bd., 1997-99, mem. com. on hydrologic sci. bd. on Atmospheric Scis. and Climate, 1998-99; mem. coordinating com. for sci. and tech. assessment environ. pollutants Environ. Studies Bd., 1975-78; mem. com. on med. and biologic effects of environ. pollutants Assembly Life Scis., 1976-77; mem. com. to recommend nat. program for assessing problem of atmospheric deposition (acid rain) President's Coun. on Environ. Quality, 1978; mem. com. on atmosphere and biosphere Bd. Agr. and Renewable Resources, 1979-81; mem. panel on environ. impact diesel impact study com. NAE-NRC, 1980-81; mem. U.S.-Can.-Mex. joint sci. com. on acid precipitation Environ. Studies Bd., NAS-NRC, Royal Soc. Can., Mex. Acad. Scis., 1981-84; mem. health and environ. rsch. adv. com. U.S. Dept. Energy, 1992-94; mem. Water Sci. and Tech. Bd. NAS-NRC, 1996-99; mem. coun. sci. advisors Marine Biol. Lab., Woods Hole, Mass., 1996-99. Mem. editl. bd. Ecology, 1965-67, Limnology and Oceanography, 1970-72, Conservation Biology, 1987-88, Ecol. Applications, 1989-92, Environ. Revs., 1992-2004; contbr. articles on limnology, ecology, and biogeochemistry to profl. jours. Bd. dirs. Acid Rain Found., 1982-87, sec.-treas. 1982-84 Recipient Regents' medal U. Minn., 1984, Benjamin Franklin medal in earth sci. Franklin Inst., Phila., 2000; Royal Soc. Can. rsch. fellow State Forest Rsch. Inst., Stockholm, Sweden, 1950-51; grantee NSF, AEC, NIH, ERDA, NASA, Dept. of Energy, NRC Can., Ont. Rsch. Found., Environment Can., Office Water Resources Rsch., Dept. Interior, Andrew W. Mellon Found., N.Y.C. Fellow AAAS, Royal Soc. Can., Am. Acad. Arts and Scis.; mem. NAS, Am. Soc. Limnology and Oceanography (G. Evelyn Hutchinson medal 1986), Ecol. Soc. Am., Internat. Assn. Theoretical and Applied Limnology, Soc. Wetland Scientists (Lifetime Achievement award 2005), Swedish Phytogeog. Soc. (hon.), Gown in Town Club. Home: 1933 E River Ter Minneapolis MN 55414-3673

GORHAM, PETER WELLINGTON, physics professor; b. LA, Sept. 3, 1956; s. Frank Wellington and Esther Marian Gorham; m. Amy Keiko Arakaki, Mar. 4, 1995; children: Daniel Alexander, Rachel Madina. PhD in Physics, Univ. of Hawaii at Manoa, 1986. Rsch. fellow in physics Calif. Inst. of Tech., Pasadena, Calif., 1987—89, sr. rsch. fellow in physics, 1989—91; rsch. prof. of physics Univ. of Hawaii at Manoa, Honolulu, 1991—96; sr. mem. of the tech. staff Jet Propulsion Lab., Pasadena, 1996—2001; prof. of physics Univ. of Hawaii at Manoa, Honolulu, 2001—. Recipient Outstanding Jr. Investigator, Dept. of Energy, High Energy Physics Divsn., 2002; grantee Prin. Investigator, Antarctic Impulsive Transient Antenna (ANITA) Project, NASA, 2003—. Achievements include discovery of First Observation of Askaryan Effect, Coherent Radio Cherenkov Emission from High Energy Particle Cascades. Office: Univf Hawaii Dept of Physics 2505 Correa Rd Honolulu HI 96822 Office Phone: 808-956-9157.

GORHAM, WILLIAM, organization executive; b. N.Y.C., Dec. 14, 1930; s. Jack and Fay (Blank) G.; m. Gail Wiley Finsterbusch, 1973; children from previous marriage: Sarah, Nancy, Kim, Jennifer, Becky (dec.). Student, MIT, 1949-50; BA, Stanford U., 1952; LLD (hon.), Trinity Coll., 1996. Mem. rsch. staff RAND Corp., 1953-62; dep. asst. sec. def. U.S., 1962-65; asst. sec. health, edn. and welfare, 1965-68; co-chmn. (with Daniel Bell) Pres.'s Panel Social Indicators, 1967-68; chmn. Pres.'s Task Force on Child Devel., 1966; pres. Urban Inst., Washington, 1968-2000, pres. emeritus, life trustee, 2000—. Bd. dirs. Insituform Group Ltd., 1986-92, chmn., 1987-92; bd. dirs Insituform Techs., Inc., 1992-97; mem. Internat. Commn. on Edn. for 21st Century, Delors Commn., UNESCO, 1992-97; mem. U.S. adv. com. Internat. Inst. Applied Sys. Analysis, 1974-82; bd. dirs.-at-large Social Sci. Rsch. Coun. Editor: (with Nathan Glazer) The Urban Predicament, 1976; mem. bd. editors Policy Scis, 1969—, Jour. Policy Analysis and Mgmt., 1980—. Bd. dirs. Price Charities, 2000—, San Diego Revitalization Corp., 2002—. Recipient Disting. Civilian Svc. award U.S. Dept. Def., 1965. Mem. Nat. Acad. Pub. Admisntrn., Assn. Pub. Policy Analysis and Mgmt. (policy coun. 1979-85), Cosmos Club (Washington). Office: Urban Institute 2100 M St NW Washington DC 20037-1264 Office Phone: 202-261-5700.

GORIG BROOKLYN, MYRA L., artist; b. N.Y.C., Jan. 8, 1943; AAS, Fashion Inst. Tech.; MA, Acad. der Bildenden Kunste, Munich, Germany. One woman exhibitions include Brigitte March Gallery, Stuttgart, Germany, 1988, 91, Projuzenten Gallery, Munich, Germany, 1988; exhibited in group shows at Kunsthalle, Baden-Baden, Germany, 1971, Henry St. Settlement, N.Y.C., Bklyn. Mus., 1974, New Mus. Contemporary Art, N.Y.C., 1983, Sculptural Arts Mus., Atlanta, 1983, Gasteig, Munich, 1986, 50 West Gallery, N.Y.C., 1986, Goethe Haus, San Francisco, 1987, Kunstmesse, Frankfurt, Germany, Fodor Mus., Amsterdam, Holland, 1990, Seidelville, Munich, 1994, Wisteria Gallery, N.Y.C., 1994, Brigitte March Gallery, 1995, Spital, Wurtzburg, Germany, 1996, Art Fair, Frankfort, 1997, Winter and Winter, Munich, 2005; permanent collections include London, Eng., Fellbach, Germany, Artists Space grantee, 1991. Home: 82 Greene St New York NY 10012-4301

GORING, DAVID ARTHUR INGHAM, chemist, educator; b. Toronto, Ont., Can., Nov. 26, 1920; s. George Ingham and Susan Edna (Jones) G.; m. Elizabeth Dodds Haswell, Aug. 24, 1948; children— James, Rosemary, Christopher. B.Sc., U. London, 1942; PhD, McGill U., 1949, Cambridge U., 1953. Scientist NRC, Halifax, N.S., Can., 1951-55; with PAPRICAN, Pointe Claire, Que., Can., 1955-85, dir. research, 1971-77, v.p. sci., 1977-83, v.p. acad., 1983-85; prof. U. Toronto, 1986—2002, ret., 2002—. Research assoc. McGill U., 1955-69, sr. research assoc., 1969-86 Contbr. chpts. to books and articles to profl. jours. Patentee in field. Served as flying officer RAF, 1943-46 Recipient Le Sueur Meml. Lecture award Can. Sect. Soc. Chem. Industry, 1988, Notable Achievement award Internat. Symposium on Wood and Pulping Chemistry, 2001. Fellow Royal Soc. Can., Chem. Inst. Can., TAPPI (Gunnar Nicholson Gold medal 1986), Internat. Acad. Wood Sci.; mem. Can. Pulp and Paper Assn. (tech. sect., cert. appreciation 1986, John Bates Meml. Gold medal 1995), Am. Chem. Soc. (cellulose paper textile chemistry div., Anselm Payen award 1973). Anglican. Avocations: fishing, music. Home: 14 1/2 Ottawa St Toronto ON Canada M4T 2B6

GORKER, SUE ELLEN, secondary school educator; b. Bartlesville, Okla., May 17, 1954; d. John Grant and Edith Virginia (Padget) G.; 1 child, Nathan Daniel Butler. BA in Secondary English and Math. Edn., Graceland Coll., 1976; M in Secondary Curriculum and Instrn., Cen. Mo. State U., 1989. Cert. secondary math. and English tchr. Tchr. math. Ralston (Nebr.) Pub. Schs., 1976-77, Omaha Pub. Sch. System, 1977-80, Sperry (Okla.) Pub. Schs., 1981-84, Blue Springs (Mo.) Pub. Schs., 1984-87; math. and math. resource tchr. Kans. City (Mo.) Sch. Dist., 1987—. Exhibitor math. convs., 1984-93. Mem. Nat. Coun. Tchrs. of Math., Mo. Coun. Tchrs. of Math. (conf. speaker 1989, 90), Kansas City Assn. Tchrs. of Math., Phi Kappa Phi. Mem. RLDS Ch. Avocations: youth, voice. Office: Lincoln Mid Magnet 2012 E 23rd St Kansas City MO 64127-3702 Home: 2504 NW 9th St Blue Springs MO 64015-1510

GORLIN, ROBERT JAMES, medical educator; b. Hudson, N.Y., Jan. 11, 1923; s. James Alter and Gladys Gretchen (Hallenbeck) G.; m. Marilyn Alpern, Aug. 24, 1952; children: Cathy, Jed. AB, Columbia U., 1943, postgrad., 1947-50; DDS, Washington U., St. Louis, 1947; MS, State U. Iowa, 1956; DSc (hon.), U. Athens, Greece, 1982, U. Thessalonike, 1993, U. Md., 1999, U. Minn., 2002, U. Copenhagen, 2003. Oral pathologist VA Hosp., Bronx, N.Y., 1950-51; instr. dentistry Columbia U., N.Y.C., 1950-51; dental dir., pathologist Op. Blue Jay, Thule, Greenland, 1951-52; mem. exec. faculty, chmn. oral pathology and genetics Sch. Dentistry U. Minn., Mpls., 1956-90, assoc. prof. div. oral pathology Sch. Dentistry, 1956-58, prof. Sch. Dentistry, 1958-93, prof. pathology and dermatology Sch. Medicine, Sch. Dentistry, 1971-93, prof. pediatrics, ob-gyn, otolaryngology Sch. Medicine, 1973-93, Regents' prof. oral pathology Mpls., 1978-93; Fulbright exch. prof., Guggenheim fellow Royal Dental Coll., Copenhagen, 1961; 1st Lingamfelter lectr. dermatology U. Va., 1971; 1st Boyle lectr. Case Western Res. U. Med. Ctr., Cleve., 1972; vis. prof. UCLA-Harbor Gen. Hosp., 1972; asst. chief dental service Glenwood Hills Med. Ctr., 1959-61, chief, 1962-64, cons., 1969-73; Regents' prof. emeritus U of Minn. Sch. of Dentistry, Mpls, 1994—. Mem. Minn. Adv. Bd. Human Genetics, 1959—73; Minn. mem. U.S. Congl. Liaison Com. for Dentistry, 1963—80; mem. Ctr. Histologic Nomenclature and Classification of Odontogenic Tumors and Allied Lesions WHO, 1966—80; mem. adv. com. periodontal disease and soft tissue study NIH, 1967—78, mem. dental sect., 1970—73; mem. adv. com. Nat. Found. Clin. Rsch., 1974—; vis. prof. Tel Aviv U., 1980, Sch. Dentistry, Jerusalem, 1981; 2nd Edward Sheridan lectr., Dublin, 89; Windemere lectr. Brit. Paediatric Assn., 1990; founder, bd. dirs. Found. for Devel. and Med. Genetics, 1994; lectr. in field; cons. in field. Author: (with M. Cohen) Syndromes of the Head and Neck, 1964, 76, 90, 2001 (with R. Goodman) The Face in Genetic Disorders, 1970, 77, The Malformed Infant and Child, 1983, (with B. Konigsmark) Genetic and Metabolic Disorders, 1977, Hereditary Hearing Loss and Its Syndromes, 1995; co-contbr.: Computer Assisted Diagnosis in Pediatrics, 2d edit., 1971; editor: (with H. Goldman) Thoma's Oral Pathology, 1970, Chromosomes and Human Cancer (J. Cervenka and B. Koulischer), 1972; editorial cons. Jour. Dental Rsch., Geriatrics, Archives of Oral Biology, Jour. Pediats., Pediats., Am. Jour. Diseases of Children, Syndrome Identification, Radiology; editor oral pathology Oral Surgery, Oral Medicine, Oral Pathology, Clin. Pediats.; assoc. editor Am. Jour. Human Genetics, 1970-73, Jour. Oral Pathology, 1972-83, Jour. Maxillofacial Surgery, 1973—, Cleft Palate Jour., 1976—, Clin. Pediat., 1985—; mem. bd. Excerpta Medica, 1976-80, Jour. Craniofacial Genetic Devel. Biology, 1980—, Jour. Clin. Dysmorphology, 1982-86, Gerodontics, 1984-86, Birth Defects Ency., 1986—, Dysmorphology Clin. Genetics, 1987—; cons. editor Stedman's Med. Dictionary, 1959—; contbr. numerous articles to profl. jours. Bd. dirs. Minn. div. Am. Cancer Soc., 1959-60, mem. nat. clin. fellowship com., 1962-65. With U.S. Army, 1943-44; lt. USNR, 1953-55. Recipient Fredrick Birnberg Rsch. award, Columbia U., 1987, Lifetime Achievement award, March of Dimes, 1989, award, Am. Cleft Palate Assn., 1993, Disting. Alumni award, Washington U., 1997, Goldhaber award, Harvard U., 1997, Premio Anni Verdi award, Spoleto, Italy, 1997; fellow, Columbia U., 1947—48, NIH, 1948—49, Nat. Insts. Dental Rsch., 1949—50. Fellow: Royal Soc. Surgeons of Eng., Royal Soc. Surgeons of Ireland, Am. Bd. Oral Pathology, Am. Acad. Oral Pathology (v.p. 1957—58, sec. 1958—64, v.p. 1964—65, pres. 1966—67, award 1993, diplomate), Am. Coll. Med. Genetics (hon.); mem.: Inst. Medicine, ADA (Norton Ross prize 1995, Gold medal 2003), Internat. Soc. Craniofacial Biology (bd. dirs. 1966—67, v.p. 1967—68, pres. 1969—70), Skeletal Dysplasia Soc. (hon.), Nat. Inst. Medicine NAS (sr.), Internat. Assn. Oral Pathology (hon.), Hollywood Acad. Medicine (hon.), Internat. Skeletal Soc., Royal Soc. Medicine London (Burrough Wellcome fellow 1991, R. Abercrombie award in med. genetics 1994, Disting. lectr. 2001), Am. Soc. Human Genetics (Disting. lectr. 2001, Excellence in Human Edn. award 2004), Minn. Soc. Pathologists, Internat. Assn. Dental Rsch. (sec. Minn. divsn. 1958—59, pres. 1959—60, Crones Facial Biology Rsch. award 1997), Nat. Trust Medicine (sr.), Omicron Kappa Upsilon, Sigma Xi. Office: U Minn 16-206 Moos Tower 515 Delaware St SE Minneapolis MN 55455 E-mail: gorli002@tc.umn.edu.

GORMAN, CHARLOTTE A., business executive; b. Tuscaloosa, Ala., Apr. 12, 1945; d. Buster and Rosie Gorman; m. C. Curtis Trent, May 5, 1984. BS, Delta State U., 1970; MA, U. Tenn., 1973, Ball State U., 1977, EdD, 1978. Sci. tchr. West Boliver Elem. Sch., Rosedale, Miss., 1970—71; ext. home economist Miss. State U., Starkville, 1973—75; state ext. specialist U. Ark., Little Rock, 1978—84; pres. GT Assocs., Cleburne, Tex., 1985—; ext. agt. U. Ark., Little Rock, 1993—97, Tex. A&M U. Sys., College Station, 1997—2005. Author: The Frugal Mind, 1990 (Book Club selection), The Frugal Mind rev. edit., 1998, The Little Book of Living Frugal, 2001; co-author: Speak for Yourself, 2002. Recipient Charlotte Gorman Day named in her honor, County Judge, Miss. County, Ark., 1993. Mem.: Cleburne C. of C., Cleburne Toastmasters Club. Avocations: garage sales, piano. Home: 708 Meadowview Cleburne TX 76033

GORMAN, COLUM ALPHONSUS, retired endocrinologist; b. Mayobridge, No. Ireland, June 27, 1936; arrived in U.S., 1960; s. James and Mary (McCollum) Gorman; m. Una Elizabeth O'Neill, Feb. 9, 1961; children: Kevin, Paul, Fiona, Michael. MB, Bch, BAO, Queens U., Belfast, Ireland, 1959; PhD, U. Minn., 1968. Cons. endocrinology Mayo Clinic, Rochester, Minn., 1966—; from asst. prof. to assoc. prof. Mayo Grad. Sch. Medicine, Rochester, 1971—81, prof., 1981-89; chmn. div. endocrinology Mayo Clinic, Rochester, 1985-92, bd. govs., 1999—2000, acting chair dept. health scis. rsch., 2000—01; assoc. dir. for rsch. devel. Mayo Found., Rochester, 2003—. Cons. in field. Editor, author: book The Eye and Orbit in Thyroid Disease, 1984. Fellow: ACP; mem.: AAAS, Endocrine Soc., Am. Thyroid Assn. (sec. 1984—88, pres. 1995—96). Republican. Avocations: reading, cross country skiing, auto restoration. Home and Office: 2607 Merrihills Dr Rochester MN 55902-1168

GORMAN, GERALD WARNER, lawyer; b. North Kansas City, Mo., May 30, 1933; s. William Shelton and Bessie (Warner) G.; m. Anita Belle McPike, June 26, 1954; children: Guinevere Eve, Victoria Rose AB cum laude, Harvard U., 1954, LLB magna cum laude, 1956. Bar: Mo. 1956. Assoc. firm Dietrich, Tyler, Davis, Burrell & Dicus, Kansas City, 1956-62; ptnr. Dietrich, Davis, Dicus, Rowlands, Schmitt & Gorman, 1963-90; dir. Slagle, Bernard & Gorman, P.C., 1990—. Bd.dirs. Musser-Davis Land Co., Curry Investment Co. Bd. govs. Citizens Assn. Kansas City, 1962—; trustee Harvard/Radcliffe Club Kansas City Endowment Fund, chmn. bd. trustees, 1977-83; trustee Kansas City Mus., 1967-82; chmn. bd. trustees Avondale Meth. Ch., 1969-92, chmn endowment comn., 2001—; mem. Citizens Bond Com. of Kansas City, 1973-2000, chmn. 7th jud. cir. citizens com., 1982-84; chmn. Downtown Coun. Allis Plaza Reconstrn., 1983-85; bd. dirs. Spofford Home for Children, 1972-77, Clay County Econ. Devel. Commn., 1989-94, mem. exec. com., 1991-93, bd. dirs. Jackson County Hist. Soc. 2001-2004, Clay Co. Devel. Disabities Resources Bd., 2002-05. With U.S. Army, 1956-58; capt. USAR, 1958-64. Mem. Lawyers Assn. Kansas City (exec. com. 1968-71), ABA, Mo. Bar Assn., Kansas City Bar Assn., Clay County Bar Assn., Harvard Law Sch. Assn. Mo. (pres. 1973), Harvard Club (pres. 1966), Univ. Club (bd. dirs. 1983-86, 88-93, pres. 1990-91), Kansas City Club (bd. dirs. 1993-97), 611 Club (bd. dirs. 1987-91, pres. 1990), Kansas City Country Club, Old Pike Country Club, River Club., Nat. Golf Club of Kansas City. Republican. Home: 917 NE Vivion Rd Kansas City MO 64118-5317 Office: 4600 Madison Ave Ste 600 Kansas City MO 64112-3031 Office Phone: 816-410-4604. E-mail: ggorman@sbg-law.com.

GORMAN, JACK MATTHEW, psychiatrist, educator, neuroscientist; b. NYC, Sept. 16, 1951; s. Elliot and Kate Gorman; m. Lauren Kantor Kantor, May 22, 1977; children: Rachel Lisa, Sara Elizabeth. MD, Columbia U., NY, 1977. Prof. and chair, dept of psychiatry Mt. Sinai Sch. of Medicine, NYC, 2002—. Author: (non-fiction book) The Essential Guide to Psychiatric Drugs. Grantee Rsch. grants, NIMH, 1982—. Fellow: Am. Coll. of Neuropsychopharmacology. Jewish. Avocations: piano, tennis, skiing. Office: Mount Sinai Sch Medicine One Gustave L Levy Pl Box 1230 New York NY 10029 Office Phone: 212-659-8763. E-mail: jack.gorman@mssm.edu.

GORMAN, JAMES CARVILL, pump manufacturing company executive; b. Mansfield, Ohio, Apr. 16, 1924; s. James Carville and Ruth (Barnes) G.; m. Marjorie Newcomer, Apr. 10, 1950; children: Jeff, Gayle. BS, Ohio State U., 1949. Sales engr. Gorman Rupp Co., Mansfield, Ohio, 1949-58, sales mgr., 1958-64, pres., 1964-89, chmn., CEO, 1989-99, chmn., 1999—. Pres. Manairco, Inc., 1952-85, chmn. bd., 1985—; chmn. Mansfield Airport Commn., 1954-2000; treas. EAA Aviation Found., Oshkosh, Wis., 1973-2003. Capt. USAAF, 1942-46. Mem. Constrn. Industry Mfrs. Assn. Episcopalian. Home: PO Box 2599 Mansfield OH 44906-0599 Office: Gorman Rupp 305 Bowman St Mansfield OH 44903-1600 Office Phone: 419-755-1223. E-mail: mng19sl@aol.com.

GORMAN, JAMES P., finance company executive; b. Australia; m. Penny Gorman; 2 children. Bachelor's Degree, Law Degree, U. Melbourne; MBA, Columbia U. Atty. Phillips Fox & Masel, Melbourne, Australia, 1982—85; ptnr. McKinsey & Co., 1992—97, co-head personal fin. svcs. practice N.Am., 1992—96, chmn. N.Y. pers. oper. com., 1996—99, mem. ptnr. election com., 1997—99, sr. ptnr., 1997—99; chief mktg. officer Merrill Lynch & Co., Inc., 1999; exec. v.p. Merrill Lynch & Co., 1999; head USPC client relationship group Merrill Lynch & Co., Inc., 2000, pres. global pvt. client, 2001—05, exec. v.p. acquisitions, strategy and rsch., 2005—. Chmn. bd. dirs. Graham-Windham. Office: Merrill Lynch & Co Inc Four World Financial Center New York NY 10080*

GORMAN, JOSEPH GREGORY, JR., lawyer; b. Chgo., Sept. 27, 1939; s. Joseph Gregory Sr. and Genevieve C. (Smith) G.; m. Mary (Molly) O'Donovan, Mar. 23, 1968; children: Jennifer Ann Gorman Patton, Joseph Gregory III. BA, U. Calif., Berkeley, 1961; MBA, UCLA, 1963, JD, 1966. Bar: U.S. Dist. Ct. (cen. dist.) Calif. 1967, U.S. Ct. Appeals (9th cir.) 1967, U.S. Tax Ct. Assoc., ptnr. Sheppard, Mullin, Richter & Hampton LLP, L.A., 1966—. Chair death and gift tax com. LA County Bar Assn., chair probate & trust law sect., 1980-81; chair death and gift tax com. Calif. State Bar, 1976-77; co-founder U. So. Calif. Probate & Trust Conf., 1974—; adv. bd. U. Miami Heckerling Inst. Estate Planning, 1978—. Contbr. articles to profl. jours. Served with USAR, Calif. NG, 1962-68. Fellow Am. Coll. Trust and Estate Counsel, Academician, The Internat. Acad. of Estate and Trust Law. Clubs: Annandale Golf (Pasadena); Jonathan (Los Angeles). Republican. Roman Catholic. Office: Sheppard Mullin Richter & Hampton LLP 333 S Hope St Fl 48 Los Angeles CA 90071-1448 Office Phone: 213-617-4121. Business E-Mail: jgorman@sheppardmullin.com.

GORMAN, JOSEPH TOLLE, retired automotive parts manufacturing executive; b. Rising Sun, Ind., 1937; BA, Kent State U., 1959; LLB, Yale U., 1962. Assoc. Baker, Hostetler & Patterson, Cleve., 1962-67; with legal dept. TRW Inc., Cleve., 1968-69, asst. sec., 1969-70, sec., 1970-72, v.p. sr. counsel automotive worldwide ops., 1972-73, v.p., asst. gen. counsel, 1973-76, v.p., gen. counsel, 1976-80, acting head communications function, 1978, exec. v.p. indsl. and energy sector, 1980-84, exec. v.p., asst. pres., 1984-85, pres., CEO, 1985-88, chmn., CEO, 1988—2001, also bd. dirs. Bd. dirs. Aluminum Co. Am., Procter & Gamble Co.; mem. adv. bd. BP Am. Inc.; bd. dirs. U.S.-China Bus. Coun., bd. dirs.; mem. Bd. of The Prince of Wales Bus. Leaders Form; mem. hon. com. Fedn. Internat. des Soc. d'Ingenieurs des Tech. de l'Automobile; mem. Def. Industry Initiative Steering Com.; chmn. Internat. Trade and Investment Task Force; mem. strengthening of Am. Initiative Ctr. for Strategic and Internat. Studies; adv. com. Nat. Security Telecom.; mem. Conf. Bd., Bus. Coun., Trilateral Commn., Bus. Roundtable's Policy Com., Coun. on Fgn. Rels., Pres.'s Export Coun., Coun. on Competitiveness. Trustee New Ohio Inst., Cleve. Tomorrow, Mus. Arts Assn., Cleve. Inst. Art, United Way Svcs., Cleve. Clinic Found., Com. for Econ. Devel., com. for econ. devel. and the Malcolm Baldrige Nat. Quality Award Found.; mem. Ohio Gov.'s Edn. Mgmt. Coun., Kent State U. Found.; bd. mem. The New Am. Schs. Devel. Corp., The Bus.-Higher Edn. Forum, Civic Vision 2000 and Beyond. Recipient Japan Prime Minister's Trade award, 1994.

GORMAN, JOYCE J(OHANNA), lawyer; b. N.Y.C., Aug. 23, 1952; d. Peter J. and Jane M. (Kelly) G. Student, Williams Coll., 1972-73; BA, Smith Coll., 1974; JD with honors, U. Md., 1977. Bar: Md. 1977, D.C. 1988. Assoc. Miles & Stockbridge, Balt., 1977-84, ptnr., 1984-87, Washington, 1987-88, Ballard, Spahr, Andrews & Ingersoll, Washington, 1988-94, Piper & Marbury, Washington, 1994-98; spl. counsel Cadwalader, Wickersham & Taft LLP, Washington, 1998—. Bd. dirs. Va. Opera, 1994-98. Mem. Md. Bar Assn. (sec. corp. banking and bus. sect. 1983-84, vice chmn. 1984-85, chmn. 1985-86), Merchants Club (Balt. bd. dirs. 1980-87). Roman Catholic. Avocations: swimming, gourmet cooking, travel. Home: 9492 Lynnhall Pl Alexandria VA 22309-3064 Office: Cadwalader Wickersham & Taft LLP Ste 1100 1201 F St NW Washington DC 20004

GORMAN, LIZ, communications educator; d. Richard and Ruby Gorman; m. Joel Paisner, Aug. 5, 1984; children: Natalie, Noah. MA, U. Minn., Mpls., 1986. Account exec. Seattle Weekly, Seattle, Wash., 1986—88; dir. of mktg. comm. Jewish Fedn. of Gt. Seattle, Seattle, Wash., 1989—95. Pub. rels., cmty. rels. Eddie Bauer Corp., Redmond, Wash., 1995—2000; owner, cons. Liz Gorman Comm., www.GormanCommunications.com, Wash., 2000—. Editor: (published report) Starbucks 2004 Corporate Social Responsibility Report (Named as one of the top 50 Global Reports, 2004). Pres., chair JT News (formerly The Jewish Transcript), Seattle, 2002—04. Scholar Grad. sch. tuition scholarship, Dept. of Speech Comm., U. of Minn., 1985. D-Liberal. Jewish. Avocation: tennis, travel. Office: Liz Gorman Communications 17841 29th Ave NE Lake Forest Park WA 98155 Office Phone: 206-347-3578. Personal E-mail: www.gormancommunications.com. E-mail: liz@gormancommunications.com.

GORMAN, MARCIE SOTHERN, personal care industry executive; b. Feb. 25, 1949; d. Jerry R. and Carole Edith (Frendel) Sothern; m. N. Scott Gorman, June 14, 1969 (div.); children: Michael Stephen, Mark Jason; m. Stanley E. Althof, Jan. 24, 2004. AA, U. Fla., 1968; BS, Memphis State U., 1970. Tchr. Memphis City Sch. Sys., 1970-73; tng. dir. Weight Watchers Palm Beach County, Weight Watchers So. Ala., West Palm Beach, Fla., 1973-97; pres. Weight Watchers Franchise Assn., 1999—. Pres. Markel Enterprises, LLC (formerly Markel Ads, Inc.). Cubmaster Boy Scouts Am.; hon. lt. col. a.d.c. Ala. Militia; bd. dirs. Crossroads Program, Palm Beach C.C., 2001—, Cmtys. in Schs., West Palm Beach, 2003—. Named Woman of Distinction, March of Dimes, 2004; recipient Athena award, Nat. C. of C., 2004. Mem. NAFE, NOW, Women Am. ORT (program chmn. 1975), Weight Watchers Franchise Assn. (chair mktg. com., advt./mktg. coun., chairperson region IV bd. dirs., treas., 2d v.p. 1991, 1st v.p., region IV co-chair 1998-99, bd. dirs., nat. pres. 1999—), Exec. Women of Palm Beaches, Am. Bus. Women's Assn., Women's C. of C. (Giraffe award West Palm Beach chpt. 2004), Zonta. Office: Weight Watchers Office 2435 10th Ave N Lake Worth FL 33461-3128 Office Phone: 561-964-8100.

GORMAN, MARTHA LEE, mathematics educator; b. Hillsboro, Ohio, Mar. 4, 1954; d. Robert G. and Ruby M. Stevens; m. Charles Ray Gorman, Oct. 14, 1954; children: Charles Ray Jr., James Lee, Rochelle M. Sturgill. MEd, Cambridge Coll., Boston, 2000. Lic. tchr. Ohio. Day care owner, adminstr. Martha's Kiddie Kollege, West Union, Ohio; tchr. math. Peebles (Ohio) HS, 1994—. Cons. 8th grade Math Achievement Test Content Adv. Com., Columbus, Ohio, 2004—. Republican. Church Of Christ. Avocations: travel, reading, dogs. Office: Peebles HS 25719 State Rt 770 Peebles OH 45660 Office Phone: 937-587-2681.

GORMAN, MICHAEL JOSEPH, library director, educator; b. Witney, Oxfordshire, Eng., Mar. 6, 1941; came to U.S. 1977; s. Philip Denis and Alicia F. (Barrett) G.; m. Anne Gillett, Mar. 6, 1962 (div. 1992); children: Emma, Alice; m. Anne Christine Reuland, June 6, 2003. Student, Ealing Sch. Librarianship, 1964-66. Dir. gen. services dept. Univ. Library U. Ill., Urbana, 1977-88, acting univ. librarian, 1986-87; prof. library adminstrn. U. Ill., Urbana, 1977-88; vis. prof. U. Chgo. Library Sch., 1984, 86-88, U. Calif., Berkeley, 1989-91; dean libr. svcs. Calif. State U., Fresno, 1988—. Vis. lectr. U. Ill. Grad. Sch. Library Sci., Urbana, 1974-75; bibliog. cons. Brit. Library Planning Secretariat, 1972-74; head cataloguing Brit. Nat. Bibliography 1969-72. Author: A Study of the Rules for Entry and Headings in the

Anglo-American Cataloguing Rules, 1967, 68, Format for Machine Readable Cataloguing of Motion Pictures, 1973, Concise AACR2, 1980, 3d edit., 1999, Technical Services Today and Tomorrow,1990, 2nd edit., 1998, Future Libraries (with Walt Crawford) 1995, Our Singular Strengths: Meditations for Librarians, 1998, Our Enduring Values, 2000, The Enduring Library, 2002, Our Own Selves, 2005, others; editor: Anglo-American Cataloguing Rules, 2d edit., 1978, rev., 1988, Catalogue and Index, 1973, Non Solus, 1981, Crossroads, 1986, Convergence, 1990; contbr. articles to profl. jours., chpts. to books Recipient Blackwell scholarship award, 1997. Fellow: Libr. Assn. (Eng.), Brit. Libr. Assn., Chartered Inst. Libr. and Info. Profls. U.K. (hon.); mem.: ALA (mem. coun. 1991—95, 2002—, mem. exec. bd. 2003—, pres.-elect 2004—05, pres. 2005—, Margaret Mann citation 1979, Melvil Dewey medal 1992, Highsmith award 2001), Libr. Info. and Tech. Assn. (mem.-at-large exec. bd. 1982—85, pres. 1999—2000). Office: Calif State U Henry Madden Libr 5200 N Barton Ave Fresno CA 93740-8014 Office Phone: 559-278-2403. Business E-Mail: michaelg@csufresno.edu.

GORMAN, PATRICIA JANE, editor; b. Oak Ridge, Tenn., Feb. 28, 1950; d. Joseph Francis and Ruth (Kommedahl) G.; m. Adrian Thomas Higgins, Apr. 22, 1978; children: Mary Catherine, Patrick Edward. BJ, U. Mo., 1972. Feature writer, copy editor Northamptonshire Evening Telegraph, Eng., 1972-76; asst. editor Am. Tchr. newspaper Am. Fedn. Tchrs., AFL-CIO, Washington, 1976-82, editor, 1982-2000; exec. editor editl. dept. Am. Fedn. Tchrs., Washington, 2000—. Mem. delegation of labor editors to Israel, AFL-CIO, Washington, 1983 Author TV study guides for tchrs., 1979-83 Mem. Internat. Labor Communications Assn. Democrat. Roman Catholic. Office: Am Fedn Tchrs 555 New Jersey Ave NW Washington DC 20001-2029

GORMAN, ROBERT SAUL, architect; b. N.Y.C., June 28, 1933; s. Philip and Lillian (Weiss) G.; m. Judith Alice Albaum, July 2, 1965; children: Melissa, Sahsa William Shannon. BArch, MArch, Yale U., 1966. Apprentice to Frank Lloyd Wright, 1953-56; designer Eero Saarinen, Hamden, Conn., 1961-67; architect, planner Victor Gruen Assocs., N.Y.C., 1967-69; Juster/Pope, Architects, Shelburne Falls, Mass., 1977-78; arch. Robert Gorman Assocs., Architects, Planners, Solar Energy, Richmond, N.H., 1969-80; founder, prin. Rawson Place Architects, 1980-89, Green River Archs., 1989—. Cons. Bklyn. Coll., 1967-69. Served with AUS, 1956-58. Fellow Frank Lloyd Wright Found., 1953—. Mem. AIA (Design award 1972). Achievements include development of of many original solar applications in environmentally concerned architecture. Home: 48 Morningside Common Brattleboro VT 05301 Office: Green River Architects 93 Green River Rd Brattleboro VT 05301-9202 E-mail: robert@greenriverarchitects.com.

GORMAN, RUDOLPH CARL (R.C. GORMAN), artist; b. Chinle, Ariz., July 26, 1933; s. Carl Nelson and Adelle Katherine (Brown) G. Student, No. Ariz. U., U. of Ams., Mexico City; LHD (hon.), Ea. N.Mex. U., 1980. Practicing artist and model, San Francisco & Taos, N. Mex., 1960-70; owner Navajo Gallery, Taos, N.Mex., 1967—. One man shows include: Rosequist Galleries, Tucson, 1969, Artisan Gallery, Houston, 1969, Citizens First Nat. Bank, Tyler, Tex., 1970, Navajo Community Coll., Many Farms, Ariz., 1970, Gallery of Modern Art, Scottsdale, Ariz., 1971, Aspen (Colo.) Gallery Art, 1973, 74, Stables Gallery, Taos, 1973, Jamison Gallery, Santa Fe, N.Mex., 1973, Jamison Gallery, Houston, 1973, Art Wagon Gallery, Scottsdale, 1973, 74, Navajo Gallery, Taos, 1974, Pendulum Gallery, Ft. Worth, 1974, Baylor U., 1974, Western Art Gallery, Albuquerque, 1974, Mus. Am. Indian, N.Y.C., 1975, Mus. Navajo Ceremonial Art, Santa Fe. 1975, Gallery of N.Mex., Santa Fe, 1976, Freeman-Anacker Gallery, New Orleans, 1976, White Buffalo Gallery, Wichita, Kans., 1976; group shows include: Philbrook Art Ctr., Tulsa, Oreg. State U., San Francisco Civic Ctr. Art Festival, Scottsdale Nat. Indian Arts Exhbn., Am. Indian Heritage Art Exhbn., Oklahoma City, The Gallery, Seattle, The Gallery, Wilmington, Del., Heard Mus. Indian Arts and Crafts Show, Phoenix, N.Y.C. Ctr., Met. Mus. Art, N.Y.C., Mary Livingston's Gallery, Santa Ana, Calif., 1973, numerous others; represented in permanent collections at Met. Mus. Art, N.Y.C., Mus. Am. Indian/Heye Found., N.Y.C., Santa Fe Mus. Fine Arts, Heard Mus., Philbrook Art Ctr., Mus. Indian Arts/Am. Hist. Soc., San Francisco, Pacific N.W. Indian Ctr., Gonzaga U., Spokane, Wash.; father and son exhbns. include: Philbrook Art Ctr., Tulsa, 1964, Heard Mus., Phoenix, 1965, Am. Indian Hist. Soc., San Francisco, 1967, Navajo Tribal Mus., Window Rock, Ariz., 1981, Davis U., Davis, Calif., 1984; in numerous pvt. collections; author: American Indian Painters, 1968, Indians of Today, 1971, Arrow III, 1971, Great American Desert, 1972, Southwest Indian Painting, 1973, A Taos Mosaic, 1973, The Man Who Sent the Rain Clouds, 1974, Palette in the Kitchen, 1974, others. Fellow Kellogg Fellowship screening com. Navajo Health Authority, Window Rock, Ariz; mem. standards com., juror N.Mex. Arts and Crafts Fair, 1975; bd. dirs. Pacific N.W. Indian Ctr., Gonzaga U., Spokane, Wheelwright Mus., Santa Fe, Taos Festival of Music, Music at Angel Fire, N.Mex., Coll. of Ganado, N.Mex. Recipient hon. mention N.Mex. Fiesta Biennial, Santa Fe, 1969, 1st prize in drawing Tanner's All Indian Invitational Pottery and Painting Show, 1974, Key to City of El Paso, Tex., San Antonio, Houston, Scottsdale, Ariz., 1988; R.C. Gorman day named in his honor, State of N.Mex., 1979, San Francisco, 1986; recipient Humanitarian award in Fine Art Harvard U., 1986, deemed Picasso of Am. Indian Art, NY Times. Address: RC Gorman Gallery PO Box 1756 Taos NM 87571-1756 Office Phone: 505-758-3250. Business E-Mail: navajo@rcgormangallery.com.*

GORMAN, THOMAS JAMES, lawyer; b. Rockville Centre, N.Y., May 16, 1960; s. Gerard Gregory and Marilyn Agnes (Wurm) G.; m. Nannette Bernadette Wallace, Apr. 6, 1991; children: Patrick Gerard, Brendan James, Caroline Marie. BA, Boston Coll., 1982; JD, Duke U., 1985. Bar: Tex. 1985, U.S. Dist. Ct. (no. dist.) Tex. 1985, N.C. 1987, U.S. Dist. Ct. (we. dist.) N.C. 1987. Assoc. Baker, Smith & Mills, Dallas, 1985-87, Petree, Stockton & Robinson, Charlotte, N.C., 1987; pvt. practice Charlotte, 1988-2001; ptnr. Gorman & Dittner P.A., Pa., 2001—. Instr. real property law Inst. Fin. Edn., Charlotte, 1995; instr. real property seminar Nat. Bus. Inst., Milw., 1996; seminar leader estate planning Am. Express, Charlotte, 1996. Mem. Mecklenburg Attys.' Real Property Coun., N.C. Jaycees (state officer, state legal counsel 1989-90), Charlotte Jaycees (life, v.p. 1987-2000, Project Chmn. of the Yr. 1990), KC (adv. 1992-95, Knight of the Month 1992). Republican. Roman Catholic. Avocations: golf, boating, video editing. Home: 10616 Old Wayside Rd Charlotte NC 28277-2792 Office: Gorman & Dittner P A 13925 Ballantyne Corp Pl Ste 200 Charlotte NC 28277 Office Phone: 704-544-2500. E-mail: tgorman@gormlaw.com.

GORMLEY, BARBARA, psychologist, educator; d. John Robert and Nancy Marie Gormley. AB, U. Mich., 1984; PhD, Mich. State U., 2002. Lic. psychologist Fla., 2004. Postdoctoral psychology fellow U. of Calif., San Francisco, 2002—04; asst. prof. of counseling psychology U. of Miami, Coral Gables, Fla., 2004—. Contbr. articles to profl. jours. Grantee, NSF scholar, 2003. Mem.: APA (com. chair divsn. 17 sect. on advancement of women 1997—98). Business E-Mail: b.gormley@miami.edu.

GORMLEY, DENNIS MICHAEL, research scholar; b. Meriden, Conn., Feb. 1, 1943; s. Lawrence Edward and Anna (Seitz) G.; m. Elizabeth Carol Festa, Aug. 12, 1967 (div. Sept. 1984); children: Douglas Lawrence, Jennifer Marie; m. Janet Lee Johnson, Mar. 23, 1985 (div. Nov. 2004); m. Sonia Ben Onagrham, June 4, 2005 BA, U. Conn., 1965, MA, 1966. Advanced through grades to 1st lt. U.S. Army; rsch. specialist fed. civil svc. Army Materiel Command, Washington, 1969-72; chief fgn. intelligence U.S. Army Harry Diamond Labs, Washington, 1972-79; sr. v.p. Pacific-Sierra Rsch. Corp., Arlington, Va., 1979-99; pres. Blue Ridge Consulting Group, Inc., 1999—. Cons. Sci. Applications Internat. Corp., 1996—, Sandia Nat. Labs., Albuquerque, 1992—, Rand Corp., Santa Monica, Calif., 1987-90, 2000—, The Brookings Instn., Washington, 1973-75; govt. adv. com. chmn., mem. Dept. Def., Washington, 1983—; vis. scholar Geneva Ctr. for Security Policy, 1997—; sr. fellow Monterey Inst. for Internat. Studies, Ctr. for Nonproliferation Studies, 2003; sr. lectr. U. Pitts. Grad. Sch. Pub. and Internat. Affairs, 2005— Author: Double Zero and Soviet Military Strategy, 1988, rev. paperback, 1990, Dealing with the threat of Cruise Missiles, 2001; co-author: Controlling the Spread of Land-Attack Cruise Missiles, 1995; contbr. articles, book revs. to profl. jours. and newspapers. Vol. home hospice work. 1st lt. U.S. Army, 1966-69. Rsch. assoc. Internat. Inst. for Strategic Studies, London, 1984, sr. fellow, 2000-02. Mem. AAAS, Internat. Inst. for Strategic Studies, Arms Control Assn., Nat. Liberal Club, London, Phi Alpha Theta. Avocations: fly fishing, marathons, bicyling, volunteer work. Home: 3514 Valley Dr Alexandria VA 22302 Personal E-mail: dmgormley@comcast.net. Business E-Mail: dennis.gormley@miis.edu.

GORMLEY, KENNETH, lawyer; b. NYC, Mar. 8, 1969; BA, Fordham U., 1991, JD, 1994. Bar: NY 1995, NJ 1995, US Dist. Ct. So., Ea., & No. Districts NY, US Ct. Appeals 2nd Cir., US Supreme Ct. Ptnr. Wilson, Elser, Moskowitz, Edelman & Dicker LLP, NYC. Mem.: NY State Bar Assn. Office: Wilson Elser Moskowitz Edelman & Dicker LLP 23rd Fl 150 E 42nd St New York NY 10017-5639 Office Phone: 212-490-3000 ext. 2328. Office Fax: 212-490-3038. Business E-Mail: gormleyk@wemed.com.

GORMLEY, PAMELA D., controller; BBA, So. Methodist U., Dallas. With U.S. Bancorp, Portland, Oreg., 1980—93; CFO, Society Nat. Bank Keycorp, Cleveland, Ohio, 1994, CFO, Great Lakes Regional Bank; dir. fin. BankBoston, 1998—99; corp. contr. FleetBoston Fin. Corp. (BankBoston and Fleet Fin. Group merged), 1999—. Mem. Fleet's Leadership Adv. Group. Office: FleetBoston Fin Corp 100 Federal St Boston MA 02110

GORMLEY, ROBERT JOHN, retired publishing executive; b. Lynn, Mass., Oct. 14, 1939; s. Ernest Raymond and Catherine Louise (Maitl) G.; m. Beatrice LeCount, Sept. 4, 1966; children: Catherine, Jennifer. BA, Williams Coll., 1961; MA, U. Calif. at Berkeley, 1964. With Wadsworth Inc., 1964-85; pres., pub. PWS Pubs. (encompassing various divs. Wadsworth, Inc.), Boston, 1980-85; pres. Duxbury Press, Boston, 1971-80; corp. v.p. Wadsworth, Boston, 1981-83, Ea. group v.p., 1983-85; exec. dir. Orbis Books, Maryknoll, N.Y., 1986-98; pub. Chatham House, N.Y.C., 1998-2001; ptnr. Seven Bridges Press, N.Y.C., 1998-2001; pub. Wiley/Jossey Bass Edn., 2001—; editor-in-chief Northeastern U. Press, 2002—04. Bd. dirs. Mayflower Mental Health Assn.; trustee Duxbury Free Library; pres. Greater Boston Irish Children's Fund, Inc. Served with U.S. Army, 1964-69. Mem. Cath. Book Pubs. Assn. (pres.). Democrat. Roman Catholic. Home: PO Box 3922 1775 Drift Rd Westport MA 02790-0299

GORNBEIN, HENRY SEIDEL, lawyer; b. Detroit, May 27, 1943; s. Abe Siedel and Lillian (Westerman) G.; m. Debra Marilyn Gornbein, June 13, 1993; children: Jonathan David and Laurie Beth. B in Philosophy, Wayne State U., 1965; JD, U. Mich., 1968. Bar: Mich. 1968. Law clk. Wayne County Cir. Ct., Detroit, 1968-69; assoc. Gage & Brukoff, Southfield, Mich., 1969-70, Coleman, Goodman & Schifman, Southfield, 1970-71; ptnr. Bayer, Goren, Gornbein, Gropman & Kaplan, P.C., Southfield, 1979-81; sole practice and ptnr. in various entities, 1971-81; assoc. Baskin, Feldstein & Gornbein, Birmingham, Mich., 1982-85; pvt. practice Birmingham, 1985-95; ptnr. Bookholder, Bassett, Gornbein, Solomon & Cohen PLLC, 1995—98, Gornbein, Fletcher & Smith, PLLC, Bloomfield Hills, Mich., 2005—. Creator, host (cable TV show) Practical Law; pres. Am. Divorce Info. Network, Inc., pub. Divorce Online (internet). Recipient Professionalism award, Oakland County Bar Assn., 2004. Office: Gornbein Fletcher & Smith PLLC 40900 Woodward Ave Ste 111 Bloomfield Hills MI 48304-5116 Office Phone: 248-594-3444. E-mail: hgorbein@qfsfamilylaw.com, henrygornbein@earthlink.net.

GORNEY, MARK, plastic surgeon, medical director; b. Mexico City, Mex., Dec. 24, 1924; s. Adolfo and Adella Gorney; m. Elizabeth Majo, Oct. 6, 1950 (div. 1982); children: Cynthia, Douglas; m. Geraldine Thomas, June 14, 1983. BA, Harvard U., 1946; MD, U. Chgo., 1948. Intern U. Mich. Hosp., 1949-50; resident gen. surgery, 1952-55; resident plastic surgery, 1955-58; instr. surgery Tulane U., New Orleans, 1957-58; clin. prof. emeritus Stanford U., Palo Alto, Calif., 1963—; chief plastic surgeon St. Francis Hosp., San Francisco, 1968-98; mem. faculty Stanford U. Hosp., Palo Alto, Calif., 1970-98; founding mem. The Doctors Co., Napa, Calif., 1976, med. dir., exec. v.p., 1987—. Pres. Reconstructive Surgery Found., San Francisco, 1985—; sr. examiner Am. Bd. of Plastic Surgery, chmn. 1977-97. Contbr. articles to profl. jours. and profl. texts. Comdr. USN, 1950-60. Fellow Am. Assn. of Plastic Surgeons (sr.); mem. Calif. Soc. Plastic Surgeons (pres. 1976-77), Am. Soc. Plastic Surgeons (pres. 1982-83, Spl. Achievement award 1963, Recognition award 1996), Internat. Confedn. Plastic Surgery (exec. com., pres. 1995-99). Avocations: sculptures, model railroading, music. Home: 5200 Country Ln Napa CA 94558 Office: The Doctors Co 185 Greenwood Rd Napa CA 94558-6270

GORNEY, RODERIC, psychiatrist, educator; b. Grand Rapids, Mich., Aug. 13, 1924; s. Abraham Jacob Gorney and Edelaine (Roden) Harburg; m. Carol Ann Sobel, Apr. 13, 1986. BS, Stanford U., 1948, MD, 1949; PhD in Psychoanalysis, So. Calif. Psychoanalytic Inst., 1977. Diplomate Am. Bd. Psychiatry and Neurology. Pvt. practice psychiatry, San Francisco, 1952-62; asst. prof. UCLA, 1962-71, assoc. prof., 1971-73, prof. psychiatry, 1980—, dir. psychosocial adaptation and the future program, 1971—. Faculty So. Calif. Psychoanalytic Inst. Author: The Human Agenda, 1972. Served with USAF, 1943-46. Fellow AAAS, Acad. Psychoanalysis, Am. Psychoanalytic Assn., Internat. Psychoanalytic Assn., Am. Psychiatric Assn. (essay prize 1971), Group for Advancement of Psychiatry. Avocation: music. Office: Semel Inst Neurosci and Human Behavior 760 Westwood Plz Los Angeles CA 90095-8353 E-mail: preadapt@ucla.edu.

GORNIK, KATHY, electronics executive; Co-founder & pres. THIEL Audio, 1975—. Bd. dirs. Lexington Partnership for Workforce Devel., Econs. Am.-Ky. Named Top 40 Women in Bus., The Lane Report; recipient Ky. / So. Ind. Entrepreneur of Yr., Ernst and Young, Inc. Mag. and Merrill Lynch. Mem.: Electronics Industries Alliance (bd. govs.), Consumer Electronics Assn (co-vice chair, chair 2003, bd. dirs & exec. com., former chair, Audio Div. & Specialty Audio Sub-div.), Electronic Industries Found. Achievements include being the first women, the first executive of a small manufacturing company, and the first representative of the high-end audio cmty. to serve as Chair for the Consumer Electronics Assn. bd. dirs. Avocations: reading, skiing. Office: THEIL Audio 1026 Nandino Blvd Lexington KY 40511-1207

GORONKIN, HERBERT, physicist; b. Pitts., Jan. 9, 1936; s. Sander (Tammie) and Mae (Shulman) G.; children: David, Jeffrey, Michael; m. Pamela Louise Cooper, Oct. 4, 1980; children: Rebecca Louise, Theresa Louise, James David. BA, Temple U., 1961, MA, 1962, PhD, 1973. Physicist Internat. Resistance Co., Phila., 1963-65; sr. rsch. physicist Honeywell Inc., Ft. Washington, Pa., 1965-66; sect. head Am. Electronic Labs., Colmar, Pa., 1966-69; project engr. GE, Syracuse, NY, 1969-75; mgr. semiconductor ops. Varian Assocs., Beverly, Mass., 1975-77; from mgr. high speed devices to chief scientist Phoenix corp. rsch. labs. Motorola Inc., Phoenix, 1977-88, mgr. to dir. phys. rsch. lab., 1988-99; v.p. phys. rsch. labs. Phys. Scis. Rsch. Labs., Phoenix, 1999—2003, dir. rsch. activities in molecular electronics, spintronics, biotechnology and nanosci.; pres. Tech. Acceleration Assoc., 2003—. Chmn. Workshop on Compound Semiconductor Microwave Materials and Devices, 1984-86, Quantum Electronics, Quantum Functional Devices and Compound Semiconductor Devices, 1986, Advanced Hetrostructure Workshop, 1994; program chair Internat. Symposium on Compound Semiconductors, 1994, gen. chair, 1997; govering bd. Ctr. of Intergrated Nanosystems, 2003-, co-chmn. NanoBus. Alliance Tech. Adv. Bd. Guest editor MRS Bull. on Future Memories; contbr. articles to profl. jours., chpts. to books; patentee in field. Served with USAF, 1954-57. Recipient Motorola Disting. Innovator award, 1993, Motorola Master Innovator award, 1995, Motorola Dan Noble fellow, 1996; named IEEE Phoenix Sect. Sr. Engr. of Yr., 1993. Fellow IEEE (IEDM compound semiconductor tech. program com. 1983-86); mem. Am. Phys. Soc., Sigma Xi. Avocations: hiking, japanese, cooking. Home and Office: 8641 S Willow Dr Tempe AZ 85284-2473 E-mail: hgoronkin@cox.net.

GORONZY, JORG J., medical educator; Prof. medicine and immunology Mayo Med. and Grad. Sch., Rochester, Minn., 1990—2003; prof. medicine Emory U., Atlanta, 2004—. Office: Emory U 101 Woodruff Cir Ste 1003 Atlanta GA 30322 Office Phone: 404-727-7310.

GOROVITZ, AARON JAY, lawyer; b. Passaic, N.J., June 29, 1958; s. Joseph Lewis and Roslyn (Paul) G.; m. Elizabeth Shey, May 29, 1982; children: Marisa, Jeremy, Samuel. BA, Muhlenberg Col., 1980; JD, George Washington U., 1983. Bar: Fla. 1983, N.J. 1984. Partner Lowndes, Drosdick, Doster, Kantor & Reed, P.A., Orlando, Fla., 1983—. Bd. dirs. NAIOP Ctrl. Fla. Comml. Real Estate Soc., Downtown Athletic Club Found., Orlando, Fla., Orange County Sch. Bd. Bus. Advisory Com., Orlando, Jewish Fedn. Greater Orlando, Congregation Oheu Shalom, Orlando. Mem. Fla. Bar Assn., Orange County Bar Assn., Orange County Real Property Com., New Jersey Bar Assn. Avocations: charitable work, golf, tennis. Office: Lowndes Drosdick Doster Kantor Reed PA 215 N Eola Dr Orlando FL 32801-2095

GORRELL, CHRIS, investment company executive; s. David Gorrell and Lisa Raser. BA, Wash. U., St. Louis, 2001. Pres. Lit. Searches, LLC, St. Louis, 2000—; ptnr. Terry & Gorrell, LLC, St. Louis, 2004—. Neuro-oncology rsch. fellow Wash. U. Sch. of Medicine, St. Louis, 2002; health policy fellow Wash. Inst. for Health Policy Leadership, Washington, 2002; pediatric neurosurgery fellow NYU Sch. of Medicine, N.Y.C., 1996; young scholars program in medicine fellow Wright State U. Sch. of Medicine, Dayton, Ohio, 1995; journalism intern MTV, St. Louis, 1998—99. Author: (poetry) Too Close.Again, 1995 (2d pl. Libr. of Poetry Contest); global health logo, The Uninsured, 2003 (Global Health Design Contest award Am. Med. Student Assn.). Bd. mem. State of Mo. Coun. on the Uninsured, Jefferson City, 2004—05; mem. Court Appointed Special Advocate (CASA), 1999—2000; adminstr. Physicians for a Nat. Health Program, St. Louis, 1999—; mem. Am. Med. Student Assn., Reston, Va., 1999—, Wash. U. Eliot Soc. Fundraising Com., St. Louis, 1999—. Scholarship for Scholastic Excellence, Kodak, 1995, Ignation Scholarship for Excellence in Pub. Health, St. Louis U., 2003—05, Leadership Devel. Acad. scholarship, 2000, Acad. scholarship, Wash. U., 1995—99. Mem.: Phi Eta Sigma, Omicron Delta Kappa, Golden Key, Alpha Lambda Delta, Sigma Chi (life). Achievements include invention of Integrated winter glove and titanium watch, 1995. Fax: 314-997-0211. Personal E-mail: cmgorrel@hotmail.com. E-mail: admin@literature-searches.com.

GORRELL, J. WARREN, JR., lawyer; b. Lexington, Ky., Feb. 7, 1954; s. John Warren and Geraldine (Standiford) G. AB magna cum laude, Princeton U., 1976; JD, U. Va., 1979. Bar: D.C. 1979, N.Y. 1995. Assoc. Hogan & Hartson, Washington, 1979-85, ptnr., 1986—, chmn., 2001—, mem. exec. com., 1991—93, 1995—97, 1999—2001, dir. corp. and securities group, 1997—. Mem. ABA (bus. sect. 1979—), Nat. Assn. Real Estate Investment Trusts, City Club Washington. Office: Hogan & Hartson LLP 555 13th St NW Washington DC 20004-1161 Office Phone: 202-637-8618. Office Fax: 202-673-5910. Business E-Mail: jwgorrell@hhlaw.com.

GORRIE, MILLER, construction executive; b. Birmingham, Ala. m. Frances Gorrie. BS, Auburn U., 1957. Chmn., CEO Brasfield & Gorrie LLC, Birmingham, Ala. Trustee Colonial Properties Trust; bd. mem. Am. Cast Iron Pipe Co., Met. Develop. Bd., Econ. Develop. Partnership of Ala., Ala. Symphony Orchestra, U. of Ala. at Birmingham Civil Engineer Adv. Bd. Co-founder Cloister Creek Ednl. Ctr. Named to State of Ala. Engring. Hall of Fame; recipient Outstanding Corp. Citizen, Nat. Soc. Fund Raising Execs., Tree of Life award, Jewish Nat. Fund, Hope award, Multiple Sclerosis Soc. Office: Brasfield & Gorrie PO Box 10383 729 30th St S Birmingham AL 35233-2939 Office Fax: 205-251-1304.*

GORROW, TEENA RUARK, education educator; b. Cambridge, Md., Nov. 13, 1958; s. Paul Kenneth and Ellen Parks Ruark; m. Wayne Dennis Gorrow, June 21, 1987. Named Outstanding Faculty Mem. of Yr., Salisbury U. Student Govt. Assn., 2002—03, Tchr. of Yr., Talbot County Pub. Schs., 1989; recipient Excellence award, Md. State Dept. of Edn., Md. Student Svc. Alliance, 1998. Mem.: Assn. for Supr. And Curriculum Devel., Kappa Delta Pi Internat. Honor Soc. in Edn., Phi Delta Kappa. Avocations: reading, piano, basket collector. Office: Salisbury U 1101 Camden Ave Salisbury MD 21801 Business E-Mail: trgorrow@salisbury.edu.

GORRY, G. ANTHONY, medical educator; BSE, Yale U., 1962; MS, U. Calif., Berkeley, 1962; PhD in Computer Sci., MIT, 1967. From asst. prof. to assoc. prof. Sloan Sch. Mgmt., 1967—73, assoc. prof. computer sci., 1973—75; from assoc. prof. cmty. medicine to prof. health mgmt. Baylor Coll. Medicine, Houston, 1975—85, prof. divsn. neurosci., v.p. info. tech., 1986—89; dean tech., v.p. for info. tech. Rice U., Houston, 1989—, dir. Ctr. Tech. in Tchg. and Learning, dir. W.M. Keck Ctr. Computational Biology; adj. prof., dir. neurosci Baylor Coll. Medicine; prof. dept. computer sci. Rice U. Assoc. faculty Oper. Rsch. Ctr. MIT, 1971—75; lectr. dept. med. Tufts U. Sch. Medicine, 1971—75; adj. assoc. prof. math. sci. Rice U., 1975—78, adj. prof. dept. computer sci., 1985—; adj. prof. bus. and econ. Tex. Women's U., 1978—79; mem. com. Nat. Libr. Med., 1984—88; dir. W.M. Keck ctr. computer biology Baylor Coll. Med. and Rice U.; dir. evaluation rsch. group Nat. Heart and Blood Vessel Rsch. and Demonstration Ctr., 1975—82, dir. health mgmt. rsch., 1978—80; 1978-80; adj. prof. neurosci. and cmty. medicine Baylor Coll. Medicine. Fellow: Am. Coll. Med. Informatics; mem.: Inst. Med.-NAS. Office: Rice University PO Box 1892 Houston TX 77251-1892

GORRY, ROBERT W., jazz radio producer, engineering executive; b. New Haven, June 18, 1964; BSEE, U. Conn., 1987; MEE, Yale U., 1993. Chief engr. Madrigal Audio Labs., Middletown, Conn., 1997—2003; chief technologist founder AeVee Labs., North Haven, Conn., 2003—. Prodr., disk jockey WNHU 88.7 Jazz Radio, West Haven, Conn., 1996—; pres. New Haven Improvisers Collective, 2004—. Composer: (new music composition) Picasso in the Trenches. Mem.: IEEE, New Haven Improvisers Collective (pres. 2004—05), Audio Engring. Soc., Eta Kappa Nu (life). Democrat. Achievements include patents for a display for guitar fretboard. Avocations: kayaking, bicycling, travel, beer brewer, music. Office: AeVee Labs 605 Washington Ave North Haven CT 06473

GORSEN, ROBERT MARC, neurosurgeon; b. Phila., Mar. 10, 1953; s. Herman Irving Gorsen and Marilyn Joyce Freedman; m. Sharon Virginia Grant, May 13, 1989; children: Devin Marily, Dillon Robert. BA, Haverford Coll., 1975; PhD, Thomas Jefferson U., 1980, MD, 1982. Internship Lenox Hill Hosp., N.Y.C., 1982—83; neurosurgery resident Thomas Jefferson U. Hosp., Phila., 1983—88; pvt. practice Fairfax County, Va., 1988—. Named Top Drs., Washingtonian Mag., 1993, 1995, 1999, 2002, Top Spine Specialists, 2003. Achievements include patents for cervical traction collar; posture lumbar traction device. Office: Robert M Gorsen MD PHD PC 3301 Woodburn Rd Annandale VA 22003 Office Phone: 703-573-4700. Personal E-mail: neusur@aol.com.

GORSKE, ROBERT H., lawyer; b. Milw., 1932; m. Antonette Dujick; 1 child, Judith Mary (Mrs. Charles H. McMullen). Student, U. Wis., Milw., 1949-50; BA cum laude, Marquette U., 1953, JD magna cum laude, 1955, MS in Clin. Psychology, 1996; LLM (W.W. Cook fellow), U. Mich., 1959; student, Hague Acad. Internat. Law, The Netherlands, 1981. Bar: Wis. bar 1955, D.C. bar 1975, U.S. Supreme Ct. bar 1970; cert. Gerontology, Marquette U., 2002. Assoc. firm Quarles, Spence & Quarles, Milw., 1955-56; atty. Allis-Chalmers Mfg. Co., West Allis, Wis., 1956-62; instr. law U. Mich. Law Sch., Ann Arbor, Mich., 1958-59; lectr. law Marquette U. Law Sch., Milw., 1963; assoc. firm Quarles, Herriott & Clemons, Milw., 1962-64; atty. Wis. Electric Power Co., Milw., 1964-67, gen. counsel, 1967-94, v.p., 1970-72, 76-94, dir., 1991-94; mem. firm Quarles & Brady, Milw., 1972-76; gen. counsel Wis. Energy Corp., Milw., 1981-94. Tutor in psychiatry Med. Coll. Wis., 1995. Contbr. articles to profl. jours.; Editor-in-chief: Marquette Law Rev, 1954-55. Bd. dirs. Guadalupe Children's Med. Dental Clinic, Inc.,

Milw., 1976-86; bd. dirs. Milw. Urban League, 1991-94, treas., 1993-94; trustee Ronald McDonald House, Wauwatosa, Wis., 1987-94, St. Mary's Visitation Parish, Elm Grove, Wis., 2003-. Mem. State Bar Wis., Edison Electric Inst. (vice chmn. legal com. 1975-77, chmn. 1977-79), Am. Arbitration Assn. (panelist comml. arbitrators 1985—), Ctr. for Pub. Resources (com. on alt. dispute resolution 1985-94, exec. com. 1991-94, panel disting. neutrals 1991-94).

GORSKI, WALDEMAR, chemist, educator; MS in Chemistry, Warsaw U., 1980, PhD in Chemistry, 1990. Postdoctoral assoc. Miami U., Oxford, Ohio, 1990—94; vis. scholar U. Fla., Gainesville, 1994—96; asst. and assoc. prof. chemistry U. Tex., San Antonio, 1996—, Welch departmental rsch. grant adminstr., 2002—. Co-chmn. tech. session Electrochem. Soc., San Antonio, 1996. Author: (research papers) Published In Premier Scientific Journals; contbr. articles to profl. jours. Grantee NIH, Welch Found., Rsch. Corp. Mem.: Am. Chem. Soc. (organizer, chmn. tech. session 57th SW meeting 2001). Achievements include development of integration of enzymes and electrodes using a biopolymer chitosan; discovery of new synthetic route to catalytic films of mixed metal oxides; invention of new electrocatalytic systems for determination of insulin.

GORSLINE, STEPHEN PAUL, security specialist; b. Washington, Aug. 22, 1954; s. Robert William and Patricia Ann (Ketchum) G. AAS in Criminal Justice, Coll. of Lake County, 1987; BS in Criminal Justice, Madonna U., 1998. Dir. safety ops. Thielenhaus Corp., Novi, Mich., 1998-99; with US Dept. of Def. Vol. Nat. Rep. Com., Washington, 1992. Staff sgt. USAF, 1977-82. Mem. Safety/Security Mgmt. Assn. (exec. dir. 1996-99), Fraternal Order Police. Roman Catholic. Avocations: collecting stamps, old coins and postcards. E-mail: stevegorsline@yahoo.com.

GORSON, MATTHEW B., lawyer; b. Phila., Apr. 29, 1948; BA cum laude, Tulane Univ., 1970; JD, Univ. Chgo., 1973. Bar: Fla. 1973. Nat. operating shareholder, bd. dir. Greenberg Traurig LLP, Miami, Fla. Bd. mem. Tulane Univ. Adminstrs.; chmn. Downtown Miami Charter Sch.; bd. mem. Downtown Devel. Authority, Miami, Mt. Sinai Hosp. Office: Greenberg Traurig LLP 1221 Brickell Ave Miami FL 33131 Office Phone: 305-579-0777. Office Fax: 305-579-0717. Business E-Mail: gorsonm@gtlaw.com.

GORSUCH, EDWARD LEE, former chancellor; Degree in Econ. and Cmty. Devel., U. Mo. Dir. Inst. Social and Econ. Rsch., 1976-94; dean Sch. Pub. Affairs U. Alaska, Anchorage, 1988-94, chancellor, 1994—2004. Bd. dirs. Commonwealth North; mem. adv. bd. Alaska Airlines Anchorage Cmty.; mem. civilian adv. bd. ALCOM; mem. Fiscal Policy Coun. Alaska, U.S. Artic Rsch. Com., U.S. MAB; dir. High Latitude Ecosystems. Mem., pres. Alaska Assn. Sch. Bds. Mem.: AAAS (pres. Alaska chpt.). Office Phone: 360-647-5233. Business E-Mail: lee.gorsuch@uaa.alaska.edu.

GORT, MICHAEL, economics professor; b. Minsk, USSR, Sept. 30, 1923; came from China to U.S., 1937; m. Elizabeth Ann Mitchell, June 15, 1957; children: William Henry, Adam Michael. AB, Bklyn. Coll., CUNY, 1943; AM, Columbia U., 1951, PhD, 1954. Lectr. in econs. U. Calif., Berkeley, 1951-54; mem. research staff Nat. Bur. Econ. Research, N.Y.C., 1954-57; assoc. prof. fin. U. Chgo., 1957-62; cons. Dept. Commerce, Washington, 1962-63; prof. econs. SUNY, Buffalo, 1963—. Vis. prof. econs. Northwestern U., Evanston, Ill., 1967-68; sr. research staff mem. and dir. research program in indsl. orgn. Nat. Bur. Econ. Research, N.Y.C., 1971-75; pres. Michael Gort Assocs., Buffalo, 1977—. Author: Diversification and Integration in American Industry, 1962, Changes in the Size Standard of Business Firms, 1964; contbr. articles to profl. jours. Mem. adv. com. U.S. Bur. of the Census, 1994-2000. Social Sci. Rsch. Coun. fellow, 1950-51. Mem. Am. Econ. Assn. Home: 71 Smallwood Dr Buffalo NY 14226-4028 Office: SUNY Dept of Econs North Campus Buffalo NY 14260 Business E-Mail: gort@buffalo.edu.

GORTATOWSKI, MELVIN JEROME, retired chemist; b. Chgo., Oct. 30, 1925; s. Walter Harry and Anna Martha (Santowski) G. BS, U. Ill., 1950, PhD, 1956; MS, Wash. State U., 1952. Research instr. biochemistry U. Utah, Salt Lake City, 1955-58, research assoc. psychiatry, 1958-59, research instr. biochemistry, chemist VA Hosp., 1959-65; assoc. investigator, asst. rsch. prof. pediatrics, biochemistry U. So. Calif. Children's Hosp., Los Angeles, 1965-71; dir. bur. clin. chemistry Utah State Health Lab., Salt Lake City, 1971-87, safety officer, 1980-87. Contbr. articles to profl. jours. Served with U.S. Army, 1944-46. Eastman Kodak fellow U. Ill., 1954. Mem. Am. Chem. Soc., Mineral Collectors Utah, Utah Numismatic Soc. (bd. dirs. 1976-77), Sigma Xi, Phi Lambda Upsilon. Roman Catholic. Avocations: photography, philatelics, music, mineral collecting, swimming. Home: 4045 Foubert Ave Salt Lake City UT 84124-3410

GORTON, NATHANIEL M., federal judge; b. 1938; m. Jodi Linnell; 3 children. AB, Dartmouth Coll., 1960; LLB, Columbia U., 1966. Bar: Mass. 1966, U.S. Dist. Ct. Mass. 1967, U.S. Ct. Appeals (5th cir.) 1975, U.S. Ct. Appeals (9th cir.) 1977, U.S. Ct. Appeals (1st cir.) 1979, U.S. Ct. Appeals (11th cir.) 1990. Assoc. Nutter, McClennen & Fish, Boston, 1966-69, Powers & Hall, P.C., Boston, 1970-74, ptnr., dir., 1975-92; judge U.S. Dist. Ct., Mass., 1992—. Trustee Buckingham Browne & Nichols Sch., Cambridge, Mass., 1984-93, chmn., 1989-93; mem. corp. New Eng. Home for Little Wanderers; mem. Wellesley Town Meeting, 1971-86; sr. warden All Saints Episcopal Ch., Brookline, Mass., 1975-80; apptd. Mass. Citizens Commn. on Gen. Ct., 1976; mem. com. Modern Legis., 1967-69; coach Wellesley Little League and Youth Hockey, 1983-87; bd. dirs. Rep. Club Mass., 1991-92; mem. fin. com. Citizens for Joe Malone, 1989-90; mem. Weld/Cellucci Com., 1989-90. Lt. (j.g.) USNR, 1960-62. Mem. Boston Bar Assn. (law day classroom program, 1987-93, litigation, adminstrn. justice sect.). Avocations: hockey (member Boston Atoms Hockey North America national finalist 1988, 91), tennis, skiing, sailing. Office: US Dist Ct 1 Courthouse Way Ste 3110 Boston MA 02210

GORTON, SLADE (THOMAS SLADE GORTON III), lawyer, former senator; b. Chicago, Ill., Jan. 8, 1928; s. Thomas Slade and Ruth (Israel) Gorton; m. Sally Jean Clark, June 28, 1958; children: Tod, Sarah Jane, Rebecca Lynn. AB, Dartmouth Coll., 1950; LLB with honors, Columbia U., 1953. Bar: Wash. 1953. Assoc. law firm, Seattle, 1953—65; ptnr. law firm, 1965—69; atty. gen. State of Wash., Olympia, 1969—81; ptnr. Davis, Wright & Jones, Seattle, 1987—89; senator from Wash. U.S. Senate, 1981—87, 1989—2001; of counsel Preston, Gates & Ellis, Seattle and Washington, 2001—. Mem. Wash. Ho. of Reps., 1959—69, majority leader, 1967—69, nat. Rep. senatorial com., Indian affairs, budget com., appropriations com., commerce/sci. and transp. com., energy and natural resources com.; chmn. commerce, sci. and transp. subcom. on aviation, com. on appropriations subcom. on interior; commr. The Nat. Commn. on Terrorist Attacks Upon the U.S. (The 9-11 Commn.), 2002—04. Trustee, founding mem. Pacific Sci. Ctr., Seattle, 1977—78; mem. Pres.'s Consumer Adv. Coun., 1975—77, Wash. State Law and Justice Commn., 1969—80, chmn., 1969—76; mem. State Criminal Justice Tng. Commn., 1969—80, chmn., 1969—76. Served with U.S. Army, 1946—47, to 1st lt. USAF, 1953—56, col. (ret.) USAF. Mem.: ABA, Nat. Assn. Attys. Gen. (pres. 1976—77, Wyman award 1980), Wash. Bar Assn., Wash. Athletic Club (Seattle), Seattle Tennis Club, Phi Beta Kappa, Phi Delta Phi. Office: Preston Gates & Ellis 925 4th Ave Ste 2900 Seattle WA 98104-1158*

GORTON-HORAN, ANN HILBERT, vice principal; b. N.Y.C., Mar. 30, 1937; d. Clarence Webb and Irene Madden Hilbert; children: Gwynne Gorton Zisko, Melissa Gorton Sadin, Lara Leigh Gorton. BS in Elem. Edn., SUNY, 1959; MA in devel. reading, Coll. NJ, 1986. Cert. K-8 elem. sch. tchr., NJ tchr. of reading, reading specialist. Tchr. Mamaroneck Sch. Dist., NY, 1959—61, Bridgewater-Raritan Sch. Dist., NJ, 1961—63, Hillsborough Township Sch. Dist., NJ, 1965—76, Branchburg Twp. Sch. Dist., NJ, 1977—98; asst. prin. Whiton Sch., 1998—. Contbr. articles various profl. jours. Mem., v.p. BOE, Hillsborough Twp., NJ, 1972—89. Named Citizen of Yr., Rotary Club, 1974, Media Ctr. named after Ann Hilbert Gorton-Horan, Hillsborought BOE, 1990, Tchr. of Yr., Branchburg Twp. Sch. Dist., 1985, Reading Tchr. of Yr., NJRA Mary Filosa award, 1990. Mem.: Reading Recovery Coun. of N. Am., NJ Prin./Suprv. Assn., Assn. for Suprv. of Curriculum Devel., Nat. Coun. of Tchrs. of English, Ctrl. NJ Reading Coun., NJ Reading Assn., Internat. Reading Assn., Delta Kappa Gamma, Kappa Delta Phi. Avocations: knitting, crewel, reading, travel. Home: 10 Fairmont Ave Somerville NJ 08876 Office Phone: 908-371-0842. Office Fax: 908-369-1582. E-mail: aghoran@aol.com.

GORZYCKI, LOUISE JOAN, nurse, consultant; d. Thomas Frank and Judith Anne (Neitge) Gorzycki. BA, Coll. St. Scholastica, 1984; postgrad., Parish Nurse Inst., 1999; MS, Winona State U., 2002. RN Minn., Wis., cert. pub. health nurse, Minn., Wis. Float nurse Rochester (Minn.) Meth. Hosp., 1984—89; pub. health nurse, HIV educator Fillmore County Pub. Health, Preston, Minn., 1989—91; nurse outpatient surgery St. Mary's Hosp., Duluth, Minn., 1991—92; oper. rm. nurse Luth. Hosp., LaCrosse, Wis., 1992—93; house float staff nurse Mayo Found./St. Mary's Hosp., Rochester, 1993—96; pub. health nurse Dakata County, Apple Valley, Minn., 1996—98; clinical nurse specialist Fairview Ridges Hosp., Burnsville, Minn., 1998—2002; surg./bariatric clin. nurse specialist Bellin Health, Green Bay, Wis., 2004—. Cons. in field. Advocate United Way, Rochester, 2002—04; internat. med. mission Grace Ch., Lima, Peru, 2002; active quilt group Long Lake Conservation Ctr., Palisade, Minn., 1989—2002. Mem.: Nat. Assn. Clinical Nurse Specialists, Am. Assn. Legal Nurse Cons., Sigma Theta Tau. Avocations: quilting, reading, gardening. Office: Bellin Health 744 S Webster Ave Green Bay WI 54305-3400 Business E-Mail: ljgorz@bellin.org.

GOSAL, PARNEET, marketing executive; b. Chandigarh, India, Mar. 16, 1975; d. D.S. and Surinder Gosal. MBA in Mktg., William E. Simon Sch. Bus., U. Rochester, 1999. Dir., mktg. strategy, bus. devel. Elind, Inc., NYC, 2004; dir., mktg. strategy marketRx, Inc., Bridgewater, NJ, 2004—. Assoc. product mgr. Becton, Dickinson and Co., Franklin Lakes, NJ, 1999—2000; sr. mgr., strategy, bus. devel. iRail, LLC, Maplewood, 2000—04. Office Phone: 908-541-0045.

GOSCIEWSKI, ROBERT LOUIS, logistician; b. Bristol, Pa., Mar. 10, 1957; s. Victor Stanley and Palma Mary Gosciewski; m. Maria Luisa Capasso, May 26, 1984; children: Diana Dawn, Kathryn Kelly. BA, U. Pa., 1979; prof. cert. Italian, Def. Lang. Inst., Monterey, Calif., 1981; MSBA, Boston U., 1985; M of Strategic Studies, U.S. Army War Coll., 2004. Cert. profl. logistician Internat. Soc. Logistics Engrs., 3wizard 3com Corp., CTM Toastmasters Internat. Instr. Big Bend C.C., Vicenza, Italy, 1984-85; cons. engring. Ingegneria Info. S.p.A., Turin, Italy, 1985-86; prodn. mgr. L.F. Lambert Spawn Co., Coatesville, Pa., 1986-89; computer systems analyst Army Legal Svcs. Agy., Falls Church, Va., 1989-92; treas. Valley Ctr. Corp., Parkesburg, Pa., 1989-90; mktg. cons. Conemar, Manassas, Va., 1989-92; computer specialist, engr. Office Dep. Chief of Staff, U.S. Army, Heidelberg, Germany, 1992-93; info. mgmt. officer Office Provost Marshal, HQUSAREUR, Mannheim, Germany, 1993-96; logistics automation specialist Logistics Automation Divsn., Vicenza, Italy, 1996-98; chief Logistics Automation divsn. So. European Task Force, Vicenza, Italy, 1998—2000, 2002—; chief programs integration and execution, dir. combat devel. Combat Svc. Support, U.S. Army Combined Arms Support Commd., 2000—02. Cons. Engring. Ingegneria Informatica S.p.A., Torino, Italy, 1985—86; internet working computer cons., local wide area networking svcs. Army Mgmt. Staff Coll., 1993—98, 2001. Mem. West End Fire Co. No. 3, Coatesville, 1989. Capt. inf. U.S. Army, 1979—83. Mem.: Military Officers Assn. Am., Assn. U.S. Army, Internat. Soc. Logistics, Am. Econs. Assn., Beta Theta Pi. Roman Catholic. Avocations: community service, golf. E-mail: gosciews@alumni.upenn.edu.

GOSCINAK, VIRGINIA CASEY, lawyer; b. Boston, July 29, 1948; d. James D. and Virgina (Burke) Casey. BS in Biology, Simmons Coll., 1970; MAT, Suffolk U., 1975, JD, 1981. Bar: Mass. 1981, U.S. Dist. Ct. Mass. 1982, U.S. Ct. Appeals (1st cir.) 1982. Assoc. Bingham, Dana & Gould, Boston, 1982-85; ptnr. Kilburn, Casey Goscinak, P.C., Boston, 1985—2002. Arbitrator Am. Arbitration Assn., Boston, 1987—; apptd. mediator, master, arbitrator, guardian ad litem, Suffolk, Norfolk and Middlesex counties, 2000—. North Area Task Force mem. Charlestown (Mass.) Preservation Soc., 1983—; mediator Cambridge Mediation Group, Multidoor Mediation Group; mem. Friends of City Sq., 1998—. Mem. Internat. Assn. Def. Counsel, Mass. Bar Assn., Boston Bar Assn., Mass. Assn. Women Lawyers, Def. Rsch. Inst., Mass. Assn. Sch. Coms. Office: Labor Dept Boston Pub Schs 26 Court St Boston MA 02108 E-mail: vgoscinak@boston.k12.ma.us.

GOSECO, AMANDA S., pediatrician, endocrinologist; arrived in U.S., 1994; MD, U. of the East, Philippines, 1992. Diplomate Am. Bd. Pediat., 1997. Intern U. of the East, 1992—93; resident in pediat., 1994—97; chief resident in pediat. Westchester (NY) Med. Ctr., 1997—98; fellow in pediat. endocrinologiy N.Y. Presbyn. Hosp., N.Y.C., NY, 1998—2001; pediatric endocrinologist Driscoll Children's Hosp., Corpus Christi, Tex., 2002—05, U. Mass. Meml. Med. Ctr., Worcester, 2005—. Office: Univ Mass Meml Med Ctr 55 Lake Ave North Worcester MA 01655 Office Phone: 508-856-4280. Business E-Mail: gosecoa@ummhc.org.

GOSFIELD, MARGARET, secondary school educator, school system administrator, consultant, editor; b. Marshall County, Minn., Mar. 9, 1942; d. William Jay and Evelyn Pearl (Anderson) Wayne; m. Amor Gosfield, Aug. 21, 1964. BA in History, U. Calif., Santa Barbara, 1966, secondary tchrs. credential, 1968, MA in Edn., 1976. Cert. tchr. Calif. Tchr. Ventura (Calif.) Unified Sch. Dist., 1969-89, coord. gifted and talented edn. program, 1982-97; cons. gifted edn. Author: (book) History of the Anderson Family, 1981, History of the Wayne Family, 1983; editor: Meeting the Challenge: A Guidebook for Teaching Gifted Students, 1996, Gifted Edn. Communicator, 1998—. Named Calif. Outstanding Educator, Johns Hopkins U., 1994; recipient Ednl. Achievement award, Phi Delta Kappa, 1997. Mem.: Calif. Assn. for the Gifted (regional rep. 1990—94, v.p. 1994—96, pres. 1996—98, Tchr. of the Yr. 1985), Santa Barbara Mus. Art. Avocations: travel, writing, family historical research, gardening. Home: 3136 Calle Mariposa Santa Barbara CA 93105-2775 Office: Calif Assn for Gifted 15141 E Whittier Blvd Ste 510 Whittier CA 90603 Office Phone: 562-789-9933. Personal E-mail: gosfield@cox.net.

GOSHEN, ZOHAR, law educator; LLB, Hebrew U., 1987; LLM, Yale U., 1990, SJD, 1991. Law clk. to Hon. Meir Shamgar Supreme Ct. Israel, 1986—87; dir. Israel Securities Authority, 1995—97, Discount Bank, Israel, 1997—2002; vis. prof. Columbia Law Sch, NYC, 2001, 2002, 2003, prof. law, 2004—; Phillip P. Mizock and Estelle Mizock prof. law Hebrew U. of Jerusalem. Chairperson Disciplinary Ct. of Securities Advisers and Portfolio Mgrs., 1997—2000; vis. prof. Yale Law Sch., 1999, NYU Law Sch., 2000. Grantee Fulbright Fellowship, 1989, Rothschild Fellowship, 1989, Olin Found. Fellowship, Ctr. Law, Econs. and Pub. Policy, Yale Law Sch., 1990. Mem.: Israel's Democracy Inst. Office: Columbia Sch Law 435 W 116th St New York NY 10027 Office Phone: 212-854-9760. Office Fax: 212-854-7946. E-mail: zgoshen@law.columbia.edu.

GOSIN, BARRY M., real estate company executive; BA in Econs. and History, Ind. U. Prin. Newmark & Co. Real Estate Inc., N.Y.C., 1978—, CEO, 1979—. Bd. govs. Real Estate Bd. of NY. Bd. mem. Fed. Employment and Guidance Svcs. (FEGS); trustee Parker Jewish Inst., Pace U.; mem. Sen. Schumer's Group 35; bd. mem. Partnership of NYC, NYC and Co. Mem.: World Econ. Forum (former host com. mem.), Ave. of the Ams. Assn. (bd. dirs.), Young Men's/Women's Real Estate Assn. (past chmn.). Office: Newmark & Co Real Estate Inc 125 Park Ave New York NY 10017 Office Phone: 212-372-2000.

GOSLEE, DWIGHT J., agricultural products executive; BS in Acctg., U. Minn. CPA. Formerly with Touche Ross & Co.; asst. corp. controller to v.p./controller internat. divsn. ConAgra, Inc., Omaha, 1985—94, sr. v.p. mergers and acquisitions, CIO, 1994—. Office: ConAgra Inc 1 ConAgra Dr Omaha NE 68102

GOSLIN, GERALD HUGH, concert pianist, educator; b. Detroit, Jan. 7, 1947; s. Hugh Jennings and Helen Margaret (Senauit) Goslin. Student, Wayne State U., Detroit, 1966—69. Music tchr. Peralta Music, Farmington, Mich., 1965—80, Hammell Music, Livonia, 1980—83; prof. music Oakland CC, Farmington Hills, 1983—; host The Piano Hour Sta. WHND-AM, Oak Park, 1995; recitalist Allen, Rodgers and Baldwin Organs, Detroit, 1975—90; prof. voice, theory and piano Livonia Conservatory, 1998—. Judge Leontyne Price Vocal Competition, 1986—2005, Verdi Opera Assn. Vocal Competition, 1995—96. Block capt. Rogers Park Residents Assn., Redford, Mich., 1995—2002; choirmaster, organist Bushnell Congl. Ch., Detroit, 2000—. Mem.: Am. Guild Organists, Am. Choir Dir. Assn., Detroit Fedn. Musicians Local # 5. Home and Office: 22600 Middlebelt Rd C-10 Farmington Hills MI 48336-3672 Office Phone: 313-330-3529.

GOSLIN, THOMAS B., career officer; BA in Polit. Sci., La. State U., 1970; grad., Officer Tng. Sch., 1970; student pilot tng., Columbus AFB, Miss., 1971-72; student, Squadron Officer Sch., 1974; MA in Guidance and Counseling, La. Tech U., 1975; student, Air Command and Staff Coll., 1975, Air War Coll., 1980, Armed Forces Staff Coll., 1981, Can. Nat. Def. Coll., 1988, Duke U., 1995. Commd. 2d lt. USAF, 1970, advanced through grades to lt. gen., 2002; forward air controller Tan Son Nhut Air Base, S. Vietnam, 1972-73; pilot, instr. pilot 71st Air Refueling Squadron, Barksdale AFB, La., 1973-76; air staff tng. officer, intelligence threat assessment Pentagon, Washington, 1976-77, various positions, 1993-94; pilot, instr. pilot, flight comdr. 62d Bomb Squadron, Barksdale AFB, 1977-80; stationed at Hdqs. USAF, Pentagon, Washington, 1981-84, 94-95, now dep. dir. programs, dep. chief staff plans and programs; fighter lead-in tng. Holloman AFB, N.Mex., 1984; pilot 162d Tactical Fighter Group Air N.G., Tucson, 1984; various comdr. assignments, 1984-93; asst. dir. ops. Hdqs. Air Combat Command, Langley AFB, Va., 1995-96; comdr. 509th Bomb Wing, Whiteman AFB, Mo., 1996—98; dep. dir. prog., dep. chief of staff for plans and programs HQ USAF, Washington, 1998—99; dir., ops. HQ US Space Command, Peterson AFB, Colo., 1999—2001; commander Space Warfare Ctr., Schriever AFB, Colo., 2001—02; dep. commander US Strategic Command, Offutt AFB, Nebr., 2002—. Decorated Legion of Merit, D.F.C. with oak leaf cluster, Air medal with seven oak leaf clusters, Rep. Vietnam Gallantry Cross. Office: Dep Commander Strategic Command Offutt A F B NE 68113-6020

GOSLINE, NORMAN ABBOT, real estate appraiser, consultant; b. Gardiner, Maine, Nov. 6, 1935; s. Arthur N. and Katherine R. (Wadsworth) G.; m. Shirlene Heath Hoch; children: M. Lee (dec.), Jeffrey C., Mark A; stepchildren: Jolene Hoch Collins, Ellen M. Hoch, William K. Hoch Jr. BA, U. Maine, 1957. With Gosline & Co., Gardiner, 1960—. Mem. faculty (part-time) U. Maine, Augusta, 1973-81; cons. in real estate to various agys. and firms of No. New Eng., 1965—; mem. real estate team visit to People's Republic of China, Citizen Amb. Program of People to People, 1995. Past mem. Gardiner Planning Bd. ambulance adv. com. Mem. Am. Inst. Real Estate Appraisers (pres. N.E. chpt. 1985), Soc. of Real Estate Appraisers (pres. Maine chpt. 1975-76, 81-82), Appraisal Inst. (dir. 1993-96), Nat. Assn. Realtors (bd. dirs. 1967), Maine Assn. Realtors (pres. 1967), Am. Soc. Real Estate Counselors, Kennebec Valley Bd. Realtors (pres. 1963-64, Realtor of Yr. 1967), Rotary (Paul Harris fellow), Shrine. Home: 87 W Hill Rd Gardiner ME 04345-1931 Office: PO Box 247 Gardiner ME 04345-0247 Office Phone: 207-582-1100.

GOSLING, JOHN THOMAS, space plasma physicist, researcher; b. Akron, Ohio, July 10, 1938; s. Arthur Warrington and Wilhelmina (Bell) G.; m. Marie Ann Turner, Dec. 21, 1963; children: Mark Raymond, Steven Arthur; m. Margaret Judith Hughes, Jan. 8, 1994. BS in Physics, Ohio U., 1960; PhD in Physics, U. Calif., Berkeley, 1965; postdoctoral studies, Los Alamos (N.Mex.) Nat. Lab., 1965-67. Staff mem. Nat. Ctr. Atmospheric Research, Boulder, Colo., 1967-75; staff mem., Space Plasma Physics Team Los Alamos Nat. Lab., 1975—2005, fellow; sr. rsch. assoc. Lab. Atmospheric & Space Physics U. Colo., Boulder, 2005—. Mem. Nat. Rsch. Council Com. on Solar-Terrestrial Rsch, 1994-97. Contbr. more than 400 articles to profl. jours. Recipient Tech. Achievement award Nat. Ctr. Atmospheric Research, Boulder, 1974, several Achievement Awards from NASA. Fellow Am. Geophys. Union (pres. space physics and aeronomy sect. 2000-02, John Adam Fleming medal, 2000, Parker Lecture 2004); mem. AAAS, Internat. Astron. Union. Democrat. Avocations: sports, hiking, music. Home: 790 Niwot Ridge Ln Lafayette CO 80026 Office: LASP 1234 Innovation Dr Boulder CO 80303 Business E-Mail: jack.gosling@lasp.colorado.edu.

GOSLING, RYAN (RYAN THOMAS GOSLING), actor; b. Cornwall, Ont., Can., Nov. 12, 1980; s. Thomas and Donna. Actor: (TV series) The Mickey Mouse Club, 1993—94; (films) Frankenstein and Me, 1996, Remember the Titans, 2000, The Believer, 2001, The Slaughter Rule, 2002, Murder By Numbers, 2002, The United States of Leland, 2003, The Notebook, 2004; (TV films) Nothing Too Good for a Cowboy, 1998, The Unbelievables, 1999; (TV series) Breaker High, 1997—98, Young Hercules, 1998—99. Office: IFA Talent Agy 8730 Sunset Blvd Ste 490 Los Angeles CA 90069

GOSNELL, DAVINA J., dean, nursing educator; BSN, U. Pitts.; MS, PhD, Ohio State U. Dean Sch. Nursing, prof. Kent (Ohio) State U. Chair Ohio Pub. Health Coun. Recipient U. Pitts. Sch. Nursing Disting. Alumni award. Mem. ONA, NLN, STT, GSA, Delta Kappa Gamma. Office: Kent State U Sch Nursing PO Box 5190 Kent OH 44242-0001 E-mail: dgasnell@kent.edu.

GOSNELL, GUY R., lawyer; b. Kans. City, Mo., Oct. 29, 1965; BSEE, BS in Computer Engring., Univ. Mo., 1988; JD magna cum laude, St. Louis Univ., 1992. Bar: NC 1992, registered: Patent and Trademark Off. Ptnr., chmn., Intellectual Property - Electronics and Computer Tech. group Alston & Bird LLP, Charlotte, NC. Office: Alston & Bird LLP Ste 4000 Bank of Am Plz 101 S Tryon St Charlotte NC 28280-4000 Office Phone: 704-444-1029. Office Fax: 704-444-1111. Business E-Mail: ggosnell@alston.com.

GOSNELL, NANCI LITTLE, information technology executive, nurse; BS in Nursing, Old Dominion Univ., Norfolk, Va., 1978; MBA, Marymount Univ., Arlington, Va. Staff nurse, emergency dept. and operating room Sibley Mem. Hosp., Washington; mgr., clin. applications Inova Health Sys., Falls Church, Va., 1990—99, asst. v.p., info. svc., 1999—2002, and interim chief info. officer, 2000—02, v.p., info. svc. & chief info. officer, 2002—. Adj. prof. George mason Univ. Mem.: Coll. of Healthcare Info. Mgmt. Executives. Office: VP & CIO Inova Health Sys Ste 200 2990 Telestar Ct Falls Church VA 22042

GOSS, JAMES WILLIAM, lawyer; b. London, Ont., Can., Mar. 10, 1941; s. Joseph Allen and Virginia Ruth (Farrah) G.; m. Rita Meyer, Aug. 2, 1969; children: Anne Candace, Jennette Courtney. BBA, We. Mich. U., 1966; MS, U. Ill., 1972; JD, Georgetown U., 1974. Bar: Mich. 1974, U.S. Dist. Ct. (ea. dist.) Mich. 1974, U.S. Ct. Appeals (6th cir.) 1974. Sr. acct. Price Waterhouse & Co., Washington, 1969—71; assoc. Miller, Canfield, Paddock & Stone, Detroit, 1974—82, James W. Goss P.C., Southfield, Mich., 1982—88; ptnr. Dean & Fulkerson, Troy, Mich., 1988—95, James W. Goss P.C., Grosse Pointe Farms, Mich., 1995—. Adj. lectr. U. Mich. Law, Ann Arbor, 1978—82. Bd. dirs. Old Newsboys Goodfellow Fund of Detroit, 1990—96, Adrian Coll., 1991—96; bd. dirs., v.p. Svc. to Older Citizens Soc., Grosse Pointe, Mich., 1997—2001; assoc., bd. govs., mem. exec. com. William L. Clements Libr. U. Mich., 1998—. Named Outstanding Goodfellow, Old Newsboys Goodfellows of Detroit, 1991; recipient Disting. Alumni award Western Mich. U., 1995. Mem. Georgetown U. Law Alumni Assn., Grosse Pointe Yacht Club, Georgetown Club of Mich., Commanderie de Bordeaux, Hundred Club, Rotary (Grosse Pointe Rotarian of Yr. 2000-01), Masons. Presbyterian.

Avocations: wine collecting, cartographic collecting, book collecting. Home: 398 Rivard Blvd Grosse Pointe MI 48230-1629 Office: 230 Punch and Judy Bldg 21 Kercheval Ave Grosse Pointe MI 48236-3698 Office Phone: 313-885-7500. E-mail: jameswgoss@earthlink.net.

GOSS, JARED, curator; s. Richard and Michele Goss. Rsch. asst. Met. Mus. Art, NYC, asst. curator. Co-recipient Award for Best Architecture or Design Show, Internat. Assn. Art Critics/USA, 2005. Office: Met Mus Art 1000 5th Ave New York NY 10028-0198*

GOSS, JEROME ELDON, craftsman, retired cardiologist; b. Dodge City, Kans., Nov. 30, 1935; s. Horton Maurice and Mary Alice (Mountain) G.; m. Lorraine Ann Sanchez, Apr. 20, 1986. BA, U. Kans., 1957; MD, Northwestern U., 1961. Diplomate Am. Bd. Internal Medicine, Am. Bd. Cardiology (fellow, bd. govs. 1981-84), fine bookbinding Glasgow Met. Coll., 2005. Intern Met. Gen. Hosp., Cleve., 1961-62; resident in internal medicine Northwestern U. Med. Ctr., Chgo., 1962-64; fellow in cardiology U. Colo., Denver, 1964-66; asst. prof. medicine U. N.Mex., Albuquerque, 1968-70; pvt. practice N.Mex. Heart Clinic, Albuquerque, 1970—99, Presbyn. Med. Group, Albuquerque, 2000—02; with Presbyn. Heart Group, Albuquerque, 2003—05; propr. fine bookbinding and repair, 2005—. Bd. alumni counsellors Northwestern U. Med. Sch., 1977-89, nat. alumni bd., 1991-97; chief dept. medicine Presbyn. Hosp., Albuquerque, 1978-80, exec. com., 1980-82, dir. cardiac diagnostic svcs., 1970-96. Contbr. articles to profl. jours. Bd. dir. Presbyn. Heart Inst., Ballet West N.Mex., N.Mex. Symphony Orch.; pres. Albuquerque Mus. Found., Corrales Hist. Soc. (pres. 2002-05). Lt. comdr. USN, 1966-68. Nat. Heart Inst. research fellow, 1965-66; named one of Outstanding Young Men Am., Jaycees, 1970; recipient Alumni Service award Northwestern U. Med. Sch., 1986, Disting. Achievement award Albuquerque Mus. Found., 1997, Sr. Svc. award Presbyn. Healthcare Sys., 1999. Fellow ACP, ACC, Coun. Clin. Cardiology of Am. Heart Assn., Soc. Cardiac Angiography, Am. Soc. of Geriatric Cardiology; mem. Albuquerque-Bernalillo County Med. Soc. (sec. 1972, treas. 1975, v.p. 1980), Alpha Omega Alpha. Republican. Methodist. Office Phone: 505-462-8412, 505-792-1516. E-mail: jegoss@comcast.net.

GOSS, JOEL FRANCIS, writer; b. Pawnee, Okla., Nov. 15, 1955; s. William Richard and Mary Ann (Webb) G.; m. Cat Guthrie, 1992; 1 child, William Keaton Guthrie-Goss. BA, U. Tenn., 1985. Staff writer Sta. WDXB, Chattanooga, 1970-73, Sta. WGOW, Knoxville, Tenn., 1973-75; writer, dir. V.T. Films, Knoxville, 1974-76; writer Hi-Test Films, Knoxville, 1976; freelance writer N.Y.C., 1976-80; writer, mgr. Improvisation, Inc., N.Y.C., 1980-84; writer, producer CB Prodns., N.Y.C., 1984; mng. dir. Albuquerque '49, N.Y.C., 1983—; v.p. Buster Keaton Archive, N.Y.C., 1985—. Cons. Rohauer Films, London, 1985-88, Am. Theatre Wing, N.Y.C., 1987; film instr. Brown Sch., Knoxville, 1976; chmn. Film com., Knoxville, 1974-76. Author: Albuquerque '49, 1973; author: (with Michael Kaluta) The Shadow, 1992; author: Coils of Leviathan, 1993, (screenplays) The Prairie Traveler, 1986, Manhattan Underground, 1987, Bard of Broadway, 1988, Sandhogs, 1991, Battling Butler, 1991; author: (with Mike Rowe) Warm Toast, 1989; author: (with Eliot Camaren) Good Night Bassington, 2003; translator: (tng. manuals) Construzione Aeronauticle, 1973; co-screenwriter (with Raymond Rohauer), rschr. Buster Keaton-A Hard Act to Follow, 1987, writer Spectacular Days of Radio, 1990, (with Martin Connor) Madame Sherry, 1989, Cat Guthrie in Concert, 1992, The Rich Conaty Radio Show, 1992, (with others) The Rocketeer, The Shadow, 1994, The Shadow & the Mysterious 3, 1994, (with M. Kaluta and Gary Gianni) Hell's Heat Wave, 1994, Buster Keaton: Genius In Slapshoes, 1995, Cut To The Chase: Buster Keaton, 1995, The Sound of Buster Keaton, 1995, Complete Films of BK, A Satin Doll Christmas, 2000; restored dialog to film: with Bruce Goldstein The Donovan Affair (1929), 1992, Cliff Edwards--Fascinatin' Rhythm, 1996; author (with Cat Guthrie): A Day In The Life of a Mother & Wife, 2001. Vol. Nat. Music Theatre Network, N.Y.C., Washington, 1985, 87, Nat. Theatre Wing, N.Y.C., 1987, Muscular Dystrophy Assn., N.Y.C., 1987; signings for St. Jude's Children's Hosp., 1994. Grantee U. Tenn., 1975, CB Prodns., 1984. Mem. Buster Keaton Soc., CVPO Assn. Office Phone: 914-420-2339. E-mail: keatonguy@cs.com, joelgoss1@cs.com, joelgoss@compuserve.com.

GOSS, MARY E. WEBER, sociology educator; b. Chgo., May 8, 1926; m. Albert E. Goss, 1945; 1 son, Charles. BA in Sociology with distinction (Univ. Merit scholar 1946-47, Chi Omega Sociology prize 1947), U. Iowa, 1947, MA, 1948; PhD (Gilder fellow 1951-52), Columbia U., 1959. Rsch. asst. U. Iowa, 1947-48, Amherst Coll., 1949; instr. Smith Coll., 1949-50, U. Mass., 1950-51, 55-56, adj. mem. grad. faculty, 1961-66; rsch. assoc. Bur. Applied Social Rsch., Columbia U., 1952-53; cons. sociology, mem. rsch. staff, rsch. coord. N.Y. Hosp.-Cornell U. Med. Center, N.Y.C., 1957-66; mem. faculty dept. medicine Cornell U. Med. Coll., 1959-72, prof. sociology in pub. health, 1973-92, prof. emerita, 1992—. Author: Physicians in Bureaucracy, 1980; also numerous articles; editor: Jour. Health and Social Behavior, 1976-78; co-editor: Comprehensive Medical Care and Teaching: A Report on the N.Y. Hospital-Cornell Medical Center Program, 1967; mem. editorial bd. profl. jours. Fellow APHA, N.Y. Acad. Medicine; mem. AAAS, AAUP, Am. Sociol. Assn., Assn. Tchrs. Preventive Medicine, Acad. Health, Internat. Sociol. Assn., Ea. Sociol. Soc., Phi Beta Kappa, Sigma Xi. Home: 25 Hillcrest Drive Piscataway NJ 08854

GOSS, PORTER JOHNSTON, CIA director, former congressman; b. Waterbury, Conn., Nov. 26, 1938; m. Mariel Robinson; children: Leslie, Chauncey, Mason, Gerrit. BA, Yale U., 1960. Clandestine svcs. officer CIA, 1962-71; co-founder Island Reporter, Sanibel, Fla., 1973; mayor City of Sanibel, 1975—77, 1982, coun. mem., 1974—80, 1981—82; commr. County of Lee, Fla., 1983—88, chmn., 1985—86; mem. U.S. Congress from 14th Fla. dist., 1989—2004; chmn. Perm. Select Com. on Intelligence, 1997—2004; mem. rules com.; mem. Select Com. on Homeland Security; dir. CIA, Washington, 2004—. Port commr. S.W. Fla. Regional Airport. Dir. Lee County Mental Health Ctr., J.N. "Ding" Darling Found.; dir. chmn. Sanibel-Captiva Conservation Found.; chmn. bd. Canterbury Sch.; mem. S.W. Fla. Mental Health Dist. Bd. Intelligence officer U.S. Army, 1960-62. Republican. Presbyterian. Office: CIA Office of Dir Washington DC 20505*

GOSS, RICHARD HENRY, lawyer; b. Worcester, Mass., Oct. 24, 1935; s. George Lee and Marion Bernadine (Henry) G.; children: Margaret Elizabeth, Richard Henry Eric, Emily Charlotte; m. Eleanor Kirsten Berg, Nov. 27, 1971. Student, Mich. State U., 1952-54; BA in Econs., Clark U., 1956; JD, Northwestern U., 1959. Bar: Ill. 1959, U.S. Supreme Ct. 1970. Asst. cashier Nat. Blvd. Bank of Chgo., 1959-61; v.p. Paul D. Speer & Assocs. Inc., Mcpl. Fin. Cons., Chgo., 1962-68; mng. ptnr. Chapman and Cutler, Attys. at Law, Chgo., 1968-95. Bd. dirs. Japan Am. Soc. Chgo., 1987-96, v.p., chmn. mem. com., 1988-90; chmn. bd. dirs. Brays Island Plantation Colony, Inc., 1995-97. Mem. Black Diamond Golf Club. Republican. Episcopalian. Avocations: hunting, skeet, sporting clays and trap shooting, travel, oriental studies. Home: 3843 N Baltusrol Path Lecanto FL 34461

GOSS, SHERYL E., director; b. Kingston, Pa., Aug. 19, 1960; d. Sheron and Betty Whitesell; m. Kenneth Goss, Sept. 12, 1981; children: Megan A., Kevin B. AAS, Coll. Misericordia, 1980, BS in Radiography, 1998, MS, 2003. Supr. sonography Wyo. Valley Health Care, Wilkes-Barre, Pa., 1983—2003; program dir. Coll. Misericordia, Dallas, Pa., 2003—, Diagnostic Med. Sonography. Mem.: Am. Inst. Ultrasound Medicine, Soc. Diagnostic Med. Sonographers, Northeastern Pa. Soc. Ultrasound (v.p. 1990—2003), Soc. Vascular Ultrasound. Mem. Ch. Christ. Avocations: travel, reading. Home: 5678 Main Rd Hunlock Creek PA 18621 Office: Coll Misericordia 301 Lake St Dallas PA 18612 Personal E-mail: sgoss@misericordia.edu.

GOSSAGE, WAYNE, library director, management consultant, entrepreneur; b. Bellingham, Wash., June 13, 1926; s. Coy Dell and Sadie Fay (Campbell) G.; m. Grace Villella, July 3, 1950; children: Leslie Anne, Gordon; m. Muriel Regan, Sept. 8, 2003. BS, U. Wash., 1947; MS, Columbia U., 1951, MA, 1969. Asst. head adult svcs. East Orange Pub. Libr., East Orange, NJ, 1951—54; head adult svcs. Levittown Pub. Libr., Levittown, NY, 1954—55; dir. Warner Libr., Tarrytown, NY, 1956—63; asst. libr. Tchrs. Coll. Columbia U., N.Y.C., 1964—67; dir. Bank St. Coll. Edn. Libr., N.Y.C., 1967—80; pres. Gossage Regan Assocs., Inc., N.Y.C., 1980—2000; chmn. Gossage Sager Assocs. LLC, N.Y.C., 2000—03; ret., 2003. Libr. search cons. Gossage Regan Assocs., Inc., N.Y.C., 1980-2000, Gossage Sager Assocs., LLC, N.Y.C., 2000-; 1st exec. search cons. dirs. pub. libr. sys., u. deans librs., 1983. Contbr. articles to profl. jours. Vice pres. Hist. Soc. Tarrytown, 1960-61; trustee Harvard Libr., N.Y., 1978-2000; mem. alumni trustee nominating com. Columbia U., 1974-76; bd. advisors Pratt Inst. Sch. Info. and Libr. Sci., 1988-2001. With USNR, 1944-46. Coun. on Libr. Resources fellow, 1978-79; recipient Disting. Community Svc. award Tarrytown, 1962. Mem. ALA (notable books coun. 1961-62, ACRL bd. dirs. 1975-76, chmn. edn. and behavioral scis. sect. 1975-76, Ralph Shaw award for libr. lit. jury 1975-76, chmn. Wilson indexes com. 1978-81, Mudge citation com. 1985-87), N.Y. Libr. Assn. (v.p. resources and tech. svcs. sect. 1974-75, legis. com. 1974-75, pres. coll. and univ. librs. sect. 1978-79), N.Y. Libr. Club (pres. 1990-91), Spl. Libr. Assn. (chmn. div. social sci. 1975-76), Columbia U. Sch. Libr. Svcs. Alumni Assn. (sec.-treas. 1974-76, pres. 1977-78), Archons of Colophon (convenor 1989-90). Achievements include first personnel firm to provide library temporary services; first personnel firm to provide nationwide library executive search services. Avocations: reading, writing, walking, travel. Office: Gossage Sager Assocs LLC 25 W 43d St New York NY 10036-7406 E-mail: murielregan@zianet.com.

GOSSAN, BRIAN WESLEY, clergyman, educator, real estate broker; b. Escanaba, Mich., Feb. 18, 1954; s. Alfred Anthony and Virginia Anne (Abraham) G.; m. Janice Diane Phillips, Feb. 5, 1983; children: Brijan Kahla, Kristopher Ryan, Philip Jemayel. AA, Bay De Noc Community Coll., 1978; BS, Andrews U., 1980; postgrad., Grand Valley State U. Ordained to ministry United Pentecostal Ch. Internat., 1984. Lay worker and evangelist United Pentecostal Ch., Escanaba, 1975-77; youth minister Bethel Apostolic Tabernacle, Buchanan, Mich., 1978-80; sec. Mich. United Pentecostal Ch. Internat. Conquerors, Holland, Mich., 1979-80, pres., 1979-85; pastor Holland Abundant Life Fellowship, 1980—97; realtor Prudential Realty, Grand Rapids, Mich., 1997—2000, Five Star Real Estate Lakeshore L.L.C., 2000—04, Smith Diamond Realty, 2004—; pres. A.I. Residential Svcs., Inc., 1995—. Dir. Christian edn., youth leader sect. 6 Upper Peninsula of Mich., 1974-76; camp dir. jr. and sr. h.s. camps, Albion, Mich., 1980-91; tchr., evangelist Fishermen's Workshop; Bible tchr. Beirut, Seoul, Republic of Korea, 1973, 88, 94, Belize City, Belize, 1989, 91, Milan, Italy, 1990; athlete sponsor Holland Pub. High Sch., 2000-2005. Contbg. editor Mich. Dist. News, 1980-93; contbr. articles to Life, others. Leader Cub Scouts, 1992-93; bd. dirs. Ctrl. Ave. Group Home of the Mich. West Shore chpt., Mich. Soc. for Autistic Children; mem. Harrington Pub. Elem. Sch. Improvement Com., 1994-96; A.A.C.C. counselor, charter mem., 1995-96; pres. A.I. Residential Svcs. Ctrl. Ave. Home, Holland, 1995-96; pres. Ctrl. Ave. Group Home, 1995-99; sponsor parent varsity tennis Holland Pub. H.S., mem. comml. com. for Holland athletes, 2004-2005. Recipient Youth Leader Honor award sect. 4 S.W. Mich. United Pentecostal Ch. chs., 1980, sect. 5, 1982, Fishermen's Workshop award Christian Ch. Kingston, Jamaica, 1983, Camp Dir. Honors award Mich. dist. Christian Ch., 1983—, Outstanding Service award World Evangelism Ctr. United Pentecostal Ch. Internat., 1984. Mem. Nat. Fedn. Decency, Christian Action Coun., Non-Denominational Internat. Mins. Network, Travelers Protection Assn., The Attending Holland Hosp. Clergy Assn., Global Christian Mins. Avocations: fishing, boating, hunting, scuba diving, skiing. Home: PO Box 66 Macatawa MI 49434-0066 Office: 76 SRiver St Holland MI 49423 Office Phone: 888-538-6337 206. *To avail oneself to all of the Word's gifts and promises bestows to mankind the same Acts of the Apostles to our world.*

GOSSARD, ARTHUR CHARLES, physicist, researcher; b. Ottawa, Ill., June 18, 1935; s. Arthur Paul and Mary Catherine (Lineberger) G.; m. Marsha Jean Palmer, Jan. 8, 1965; children: Girard Christopher, Elinore Suzanne. BA, Harvard U., 1956; PhD, U. Calif., Berkeley, 1960. Solid state physicist, disting. mem. tech. staff AT&T Bell Labs., Murray Hill, N.J., 1960-87; prof. materials and electrical and computer engring. U. Calif., Santa Barbara, 1987—. Author tech. papers magnetic resonance, magnetism, transition metals, molecular beam epitaxy, quantum structures, semiconductors. Sr. fellow Humboldt Found. Fellow IEEE, Am. Phys. Soc. (Oliver Buckley condensed matter physics prize 1984, James McGroddy prize for New Materials 2001); mem. NAS, Nat. Acad. of Engring. Office: U Calif Materials Dept Santa Barbara CA 93106 Business E-Mail: gossard@engineering.ucsb.edu.

GOSSELIN, BENOIT JEAN, otolaryngologist, facial plastic surgeon, head and neck reconstructive surgeon; b. Quebec City, Can., Oct. 24, 1962; BSc, U. Ottawa, 1983, MD, 1988. Diplomate Am. Bd. Otolaryngology, Bd. of Facial Plastic & Reconstructive Surgery. Resident in otolaryngology U. Ottawa, Canada, 1989-93; fellow head and neck surgery U. Toronto, Canada, 1993-94; fellow in microvascular and facial plastic surgery Mercy Hosp. Pitts., 1994-95; asst. prof. surgery Dartmouth Coll., Hanover, NH, 1995—; staff otolaryngology sect. Dartmouth-Hitchcock Med. Ctr., Lebanon, NH, 1995—; staff otolaryngologist, head and neck surgeon VA Med. Ctr., White River Junction, Vt., 2002—; dir. comprehensive head and neck cancer program Norris Cotton Cancer Ctr., Lebanon, 2003—. Fellow ACS, Royal Coll. Surgeons (Can.), Am. Soc. Head and Neck Surgery; mem. AMA, Am. Acad. Otolaryngology, Head and Neck Surgery, Am. Acad. Facial Plastics and Reconstructive Surgery, Am. Rhinologic Soc., Am. Soc. Univ. Otolaryngologists, Can. Soc. Otolaryngology, Head and Neck Surgery, Can. Med. Assn. Office: Dartmouth-Hitchcock Med Ctr Sect Otolaryngology One Medical Ctr Dr Lebanon NH 03755 Office Phone: 603-650-8112.

GOSSELIN, EDWARD A., academic administrator, history professor; b. Rutland, Vt., Feb. 12, 1943; s. Alberic William and Marie (L'Ange) G.; m. Claudia Isabelle Hoffer, July 11, 1970; children: Elisabeth Anne, David Edward. BA, Yale U., 1965; MA, Columbia U., 1966, PhD, 1973. From asst. to assoc. prof. Calif. State U., Long Beach, 1969-79, prof., 1979—, chair history dept., 1986—. Author: King's Progress to Jerusalem, 1976; editor, translator: Giordano Bruno, The Ash Wednesday Supper, 1977; editor The History Teacher, 1985—. NEA grantee, 1973-74, NEH grantee, 1980. Mem. Am. Hist. Assn., Am. Assn. for Reformation Rsch., Soc. for History Edn. (bd. of govs. 1985—), History of Sci. Soc., Renaissance Soc. Am., Renaissance Conf. of So. Calif. (pres. San Marino, Calif. chpt. 1986-87). Office: Calif State U 1250 N Bellflower Blvd Long Beach CA 90840-0001

GOSSELS, CLAUS PETER ROLF, lawyer; b. Berlin, Aug. 11, 1930; came to US, 1941; s. Max and Charlotte (Lewy) G.; m. Nancy Lee Tuber, June 29, 1958; children: Lisa Rae, Amy Devra, Daniel Joshua. AB, Harvard U., 1951, LLB, 1954. Bar: Mass. 1955, US Dist. Ct. Mass. 1957, US Ct. Appeals (1st cir.) 1957, US Supreme Ct. 1965. Assoc. Sullivan & Worcester, Boston, 1956-65; mem. Zelman, Gossels & Alexander, Boston, 1965-72, Weston, Patrick, Willard & Redding, Boston, 1972—. Master Superior Ct. Mass., 1984—; guardian ad litem, conservator Mass. Probate Family Ct. Co-author, editor: Vetaher Libenu, 1980, Chadesh Yamenu, 1997, Canfey Hashachar, 2003; contbr. articles to profl. jours. Moderator Town of Wayland, Mass., 1982—. With US Army, 1954-56. Mem. Mass. Bar Assn., Boston Bar Assn., Mass. Moderators Assn., Mass. Acad. Trial Lawyers. Jewish. Avocations: reading, tennis, travel, gardening, theater. Home: 32 Hampshire Rd Wayland MA 01778-1021 Office: Weston Patrick Willard & Redding 84 State St Boston MA 02109-2299 Office Phone: 617-742-9310. Business E-Mail: pgossels@socialaw.com.

GOSSEN, EMMETT JOSEPH, JR., motel chain executive, lawyer; b. Kenosha, Wis., Aug. 23, 1942; s. Emmett J. and Julia (Tribur) G.; m. Patricia E. Zele, June 14, 1968; children: André, Nicole. BA, Case Western Res. U., 1965; PhD, Yale U., 1970; JD, Harvard U., 1974. Bar: Mass. 1974, D.C. 1975. Assoc. Hale and Dorr, Boston, 1974-77; counsel The Sheraton Corp., Boston, 1977-83, sr. v.p., dir. devel., 1983-86; exec. v.p. corp. devel. Inter-Continental Hotels, Montvale, N.J., 1988-90; sr. v.p., dir. devel. Motel 6, L.P., Santa Barbara, Calif., 1986-88, exec. v.p. corp. affairs and devel. Dallas, 1990—.

GOSSETT, JASON BRIAN, music educator; b. Lakenheath, Great Britain and Northern Ireland, Oct. 27, 1977; s. Donald Edward and Hilda Irene Gossett; m. Christine Eudelia Erdley, Dec. 29, 2001. MusB Edn., Murray State U., Murray, Ky., 2001. Percussion tchr. Grayson County H.S., Leitchfield, Ky., 1997—, Muhlenberg North H.S., Greenville, Ky., 1999—2001. Asst. band dir. Grayson County H.S., Leitchfield, Ky., 1999—, choir dir., 2001—. Composer: (musical composition for organ) Dreamscape, 1997. Mem.: Ky. Music Educators Assn., World Assn. of Symphonic Bands and Ensembles, Percussive Arts Soc., Music Educators Nat. Conv., Phi Mu Alpha Sinfonia (v.p. 1998—99). R-Consevative. Southern Baptist. Avocation: golf.

GOSSETT, KATHRYN MYERS, language professional, educator; b. Baltimore, Ohio; d. Charles Edgar and Vera Mae (Good) Myers; m. William Thomas Gossett, June 30, 1984. BA summa cum laude, Ohio U., 1931, MA, 1936. Cert. tchr., Ohio, Pa., Mich. Latin and English tchr. Beccaria Twp. High Sch., Coalport, Pa., 1931-32; French, Latin and English tchr. Buford (Ohio) High Sch., 1932-36; tchr. fgn. langs. Oak Hill (Ohio) High Sch., 1936-42; critic tchr. Ohio U. and Athens High Sch., 1942-43; English and Spanish tchr. Eastern High Sch., Lansing, Mich., 1943-45; French tchr. Kingswood/Cranbrook Pvt. Sch., Bloomfield Hills, Mich., 1945-55, chmn. fgn. lang., 1955-75. Fulbright tchr. Lycée de Jeunes Filles, Annecy, France, 1953-54. Contbr. articles to profl. jours. Decorated chevalier des Palmes Academiques (France); recipient Cranbrook Founders medal, 1976; U. Besancon (France) scholar. Mem. AAUW, Am. Assn. Ret. Persons, Eastern Star, Bloomfield Hills Country Club, The Ocean Club of Fla. (Ocean Ridge), The Little Club (Gulf Stream, Fla.), The Village Club (Bloomfield Hills), Phi Beta Kappa. Republican. Episcopalian. Avocations: art, music, history. Home: 1276 Covington Rd Bloomfield Hills MI 48301-2365

GOSSETT, LINDA KELLEY, retired secondary school educator; b. Maysville, Ky. d. Harvey Early and Nancy Kelley; m. Robert Lebus Gossett, June 3, 1968; children: Robert Kelley, Richard Lebus. BS, Morehead State U., 1966, MA, 1969. Bus. tchr. Harrison County H.S., Cynthiana, Ky., 1966—67, Ripley-Union-Lewis H.S., Ripley, Ky., 1967—75, Fleming County H.S., Flemingsburg, Ky., 1975—; founder Panther Bank, Flemingsburg, 1996; ret., 2004. Dept. head Fleming County H.S., 1987—, adv., 2000—; tax prep. Kelley Tax Svc., Flemingsburg, 1998—. Mem.: NEA, Ky. Bus. Edn. Assn., Ky. Edn. Assn., Fleming County Edn. Assn. (v.p.). Avocations: reading, travel, golf tournaments. Office: Kelley Tax Service 113 W Water Flemingsburg KY 41041

GOSSETT, PHILIP, musicologist; b. NYC, Sept. 27, 1941; s. Harold and Pearl (Lenkowsky) G.; m. Suzanne Solomon, Aug. 4, 1963; children: David, Jeffrey. BA summa cum laude, Amherst Coll., 1963; student, Columbia U., 1961-62; MFA, Princeton U., 1965, PhD, 1970; LHD, Amherst Coll., 1993. Asst. prof. music and humanities U. Chgo., 1968-73, assoc. prof., 1973-77, prof., 1977-84, Robert W. Reneker Disting. Svc. prof. music, 1984—, dean divsn. humanities, 1989-99. Vis. assoc. prof. Columbia U., 1975, Inst. de Musicologie Universite de Paris, 1988, Gauss seminars, Princeton U., 1991; Hambro prof. opera studies Oxford U., 2001; musicological cons. Verdi Festival, Parma, 2001; prof. U. Rome, 2004—. Gen. editor: The Works of Giuseppe Verdi, Edizione Critica della opere di Gioachino Rossini; mem. editorial bd. Am. Musicol. Soc., 1972-78; cons. editor: Critical Inquiry, 1974—, Ninteenth Century Music, 1976—, Cambridge Opera Jour., 1987-2002, Rivista Italiana di Musicologia, 2004—; translator Treatise on Harmony (Jean-Philippe Rameau), (with Charles Rosen) Early Romantic Opera, Anna Bolena and the Maturity of Gaetano Donizetti, 1985, Il Barbiere di Siviglia, 1993, Don Pasquale, 2000, also numerous critical edits.; prepared vocal ornamentation for operas in Milan, Rome, Bologna, Pesaro, Chgo., Miami, St. Louis, N.Y., Santa Fe, Paris. Trustee Chgo. Symphony Orch., 1991-2001, Ct. Theatre, Chgo., 1994—. Decorated Gold medal 1st class (Italy), 1985, Grande Ufficiale della Rep. (Italy), 1997, Order Rio Branca, Brazil, 1998, Cavaliere di Gran Croce (Italy), 1998; recipient Disting. Achievement award Mellon Found., 2004; Woodrow Wilson fellow, 1963-64, 66-67; Fulbright scholar Paris, 1965-66; Martha Baird Rockefeller fellow, 1967-68; Guggenheim fellow, 1971-72; NEH sr. scholar, 1982-83, Phi Beta Kappa Vis. scholar, 2002-03; Deems Taylor award of ASCAP, 1986. Fellow AAAS, Academia Filarmonica of Bologna (hon.), Ateneo Veneto, Accademia di Santa Cecilia Rom (accademico onorario); mem. Am. Musicol. Soc. (coun. 1972-74, bd. dirs. 1974-76, v.p. 1986-88, Albert Einstein award 1969, pres. 1994-96), Internat. Musicol. Soc., Am. Inst. Verdi Studies (bd. dirs.), Societa Italiana di Musicologia, Soc. Textual Scholarship (pres. 1993-95), Premio Paolo Borciani (pres. 1997, 2002). Office: U Chgo Dept Music Chicago IL 60637 Office Phone: 773-834-4181. Business E-Mail: phgs@uchicago.edu.

GOSSETT, ROBERT FRANCIS, JR., merchant banker; b. San Antonio, Tex., Nov. 19, 1943; s. Robert Francis and Anne Elizabeth (Donnell) G.; m. Pauline Washington Gillespie, June 27, 1964; children: Robert Francis III, Frank Morgan Gillespie. BA, U. Tex., 1964; JD, Georgetown U., 1967; MBA, U. Pa., 1969. Assoc., investment bank div. Merrill Lynche, Pierce, Fenner & Smith, N.Y.C., 1969-74; v.p. Oppenheimer Properties, Inc., N.Y.C., 1974-78; exec. v.p., dir. Loeb Rhoades Hornblower Capital Corp., N.Y.C., 1978-81; chmn. bd., pres. Vance Capital Corp., N.Y.C., 1981—. Gen. ptnr. First San Bernardio Assoc., Ltd., Long Beach, Calif., 1979-2004, First Riverside (Calif.) Assoc., 1980-2004, First Portland Assoc., Beaverton, Oreg., 1980—, Corp. Realty Income Fund I, Ltd., N.Y.C., 1986—, Vance, Teel & Co. Ltd., San Antonio, 1998—; chmn. bd. dirs. 1345 Realty Corp., N.Y.C., 1994—, Minn. Street Assoc., Inc., St. Paul, 1988—; gen. ptnr. Hoopes Assocs., Ltd., Rockport, Tex., 1989—, Teel Land and Cattle Co., LLC, Yancey, Tex., 1997—. Mem. bd. regents Georgetown U., 1993-99. Mem. Campfire Club, The Mashomack Preserve Club. Office: Vance Capital Corp 406 E 85th St New York NY 10028-6302 Office Phone: 212-751-3515. E-mail: rfgossett@aol.com.

GOSSICK, LEE VAN, rental company executive, consultant, retired military officer; b. Meadville, Mo., Jan. 23, 1920; s. Clark and Myrtle (Staats) G.; m. Ruth Matter, Apr. 29, 1942; children: Roger V., Cynthia L. BS in Aero. Engring, MS, Ohio State U., 1951; grad., Air War Coll., 1959, Advanced Mgmt. Program, Harvard, 1961. Aviation cadet, 1941-42; commd. 2d lt. USAAF, 1942; advanced through grades to maj. gen. USAF, 1968; fighter pilot (87th Fighter Squadron), North Africa, 1942- 43; various R & D posts, 1951-64; comdr. Arnold Engring. Devel. Center, 1964-67; dep. for F-111 Aero. Systems div., Wright-Patterson AFB, Ohio, 1967-68; vice comdr. Aero. Systems Div., 1968-69, comdr., 1969-70; dep. chief staff systems Hdqrs. Air Force Systems Command, Andrews AFB, Md., 1970-71, chief of staff, 1971-73, ret., 1973; asst. dir. regulation AEC, Washington, 1973-74; exec. dir. ops. Nuclear Regulatory Commn., Washington, 1975-79; v.p., dep. gen. mgr. Sverdrup Tech. Inc., Tullahoma, Tenn., 1980-89. Decorated D.S.M. with oak leaf cluster; Legion of Merit with oak leaf cluster; D.F.C.; Air medal with 9 oak leaf clusters; named Distinguished Alumnus Ohio State U., 1960, Centennial Achievement award, 1970; recipient Vandenberg trophy Arnold Air Soc., 1967, Distinguished Service award AEC, 1974; named to Tenn. Aviation Hall of Fame, 2004. Fellow AIAA, Arnold Engring. Devel. Ctr. Home: 106 Blantonwood Dr Tullahoma TN 37388-5801

GOSTIN, LAWRENCE O., lawyer, educator; b. Oct. 19, 1949; s. Joseph and Sylvia (Berkman) G.; m. Jean Catherine Allison, July 30, 1977; children: Bryn Gareth, Kieran Gavin. BA summa cum laude, SUNY, Brockport, 1971; LLD (hon.), SUNY; JD, Duke U., 1974. Bar: N.Y. 1981, Coun. Europe. Legal dir. Nat. Assn. Mental Health, London, 1975-82; vis. fellow U. Oxford Ctr. for Criminol. Rsch., 1982-83; gen. sec. Nat. Coun. Civil Liberties, London, 1983-85; sr. fellow in health law Harvard U. Sch. Pub. Health, 1985—. Vis. prof. social policy McMaster U., Hamilton, Ont., Can., 1978-79; exec. dir. Am. Soc. Law, Medicine, and Ethics, Boston, 1987-94; adj. assoc. prof. Sch. Pub. Health, Harvard U., 1988—, adj. prof., 1990—, lectr. Law Sch., 1990—; vis. prof. Georgetown U. Law Ctr., 1993-94, assoc. prof., 1994-95, prof.,

1996—, John Carroll rsch. prof., 2004-05, assoc. dean for rsch. and acad. programs, 2005—; prof. Johns Hopkins Sch. Hygiene and Pub. Health, 1994—; co-dir. Georgetown/Johns Hopkins Program on Law and Pub. Health; dir. CDC Collaborating Ctr. on Law and the Pub.'s Health; legis. coun. U.S. Senate Labor and Human Resources Com., Washington, 1987, 88; bd. dirs., nat. exec. com. Am. Civil Liberties Union, 1987—; assoc. dir. Harvard U. WHO Internat. Collaborating Ctr. on Health Legis., 1989— Western European editor Internat. Jour. Law and Psychiatry, London, 1978-81; editor in chief: Law Medicine & Health Care; exec. editor: Am. Jour. Law and Medicine; sect. editor Jour. AMA; editor: Secure Provision, 1985, AIDS and the Health Care System, 1990, Surrogate Motherhood: Politics and Privacy, 1990, Implementing the Americans with Disabilities Act, 1993; co-editor: Law, Science and Medicine, 2d edit., 1996; author: Human Rights and Public Health in the AIDS Pandemic, 1997, The Rights of Persons with HIV Disease, 1996, Mental Health Services: Law and Practice, 1986, Institutions Observed, 1986, Mental Health: Tribunal Procedure, 1984, 2d edit., 1992, A Human Condition, 1975, 2d vol., 1977, Civil Liberties in Conflict, 1988, Public Health Law: Power, Duty, Restraint, 2000, The AIDS Pandemic: Complacency, Injustice and Unfulfilled Expectations, 2004; editor Public Health law and Ethics: A Reader, 2002, The Human Rights of Persons with Intellectual Disabilities: Different But Equal, 2003. Legal affairs com. Internat. League Socs. for Mentally Handicapped, Brussels, 1980—; trustee Cobden Trust, London, 1983-85; chmn. Advocacy Alliance, London, 1981-84; sec. All Party Parliamentary Civil Liberties Group, London, 1984-85; bd. dirs. ACLU, 1986—, exec. com., 1988—; mem. com. experts drafting conventions on human experientation UN, Siracusa, Italy, 1980-82. Recipient Rosemary Deldridge Meml. award Nat. Consumer Coun. U.K., 1983; fellow Kennedy Inst. Ethics, 1994—, Fulbright fellow U. Oxford, 1974-75. Avocations: climbing, vegetable growing. Home: 10413 Masters Ter Potomac MD 20854-3862 Office: Georgetown U Law Ctr 600 New Jersey Ave NW Washington DC 20001-2075 Business E-Mail: gostin@law.georgetown.edu.

GOSWAMI, BISWENDU B., virologist; b. Calcutta, West Bengal, India, Aug. 31, 1948; arrived in U.S., 1977; s. Jnanendu B. and Jyotsna Goswami; m. Raka Goswami, Dec. 7, 1982; 1 child, Sashwata. BS in Chemisry with honors, U. Calcutta, 1968, M in Biochemistry, 1970, PhD, 1975. Rsch. assoc. Georgetown U., Washington, 1989—91; virologist FDA, Laurel, Md., 1991—. Recipient Secretary's award for Disting. Svc., US Dept. HHS, 1998; fellow, U. Calcutta, 1975—77. Mem.: Am. Soc. Virology. Achievements include research in role of Interferon in host response to virus infection. Office: FDA OARSA HFS-025 8301 Muirkirk Rd Laurel MD 20708 Office Phone: 301-827-8627. E-mail: bgoswami@cfsan.fda.gov.

GOTHARD, DONALD LEE, retired auto company executive; b. Madison, Wis., Dec. 2, 1934; s. William Henry and Lorraine Marie (Williams) G.; m. Doris Marie Lockhart, May 27, 1990; children from previous marriage: children: Donald Lee Jr., Ann Marie. BSEE, U. Notre Dame, 1956. Elec. engr. AC Spark Plug div. Milw. GM, 1956-62, systems engr. AC Electronics div. Wakefield, Mass., 1962-63, Oak Creek, Wis., 1963-67, sr. project engr., supr. Delco Electronics div. Bethpage, N.Y., 1967-71; systems engr., asst. mgr. engring. staff GM Tech. Ctr., Warren, Mich., 1971-75; asst. staff engr., then staff engr. Chevrolet Engring. div. Warren, 1975-82; chief engr. GM Truck & Bus. Engring., Pontiac, Mich., 1982-85, exec. engr. Auburn Hills and Troy, Mich., 1985-90; dir. rsch. and adminstrv. svcs. GM Rsch. and Environ. Activities Staff, Warren, 1990-92; exec. prototype, process engring. GM Design Ctr., GM Tech. Ctr., Warren, 1992-93; dir. quality and mfg. engrs. GM N.Am. Ops. N.Am. Tech. Ctr., Warren, 1993-96. Cons. United Technologies Automotive, 1996. Chmn. fin. com. adv. coun. Utica (Mich.) Cmty. Schs., 1975; mem. Shelby Twp (Mich.) Cable TV Coordinating Com., 1980; mem. engring. adv. coun. U. Notre Dame, 1988—, mem. minority engring. program adv. coun., 1994—; bd. dirs. Sci. Engring. Fair Met. Detroit, 1992-99; chmn. ch. fin. com., 1996-2003; judge, Internat. Sci. and Engring. Fair, 1996-2001. 1st lt. U.S. Army, 1956-58. Recipient Cert. of Commendation MIT, 1969, Apollo Achievement award NASA, 1969, Disting. Svc. award Utica Cmty. Schs., 1976, Cert. of Recognition Coun. of Engring. Deans of Historically Black Colls., Mobil Corp. and U.S. Black Engr. Mag., 1991; team leader, internat. land speed records with Pickup Truck, Internat. Motor Sports Assn./So. Calif. Timing Assn., 1989, U. Notre Dame Coll. of Engring. Honor award, 1994, Rev. Edward Williams Svc. award U. Notre Dame Black Alumni, 1994. Mem. Soc. Automotive Engrs. (excellence in oral presentation award 1987, Black Engr. of Yr. award for lifetime achievement-industry 1995), Black Alumni Assn. U. Notre Dame (coord.-at-large exec. bd. 1987-94). Avocations: photography, senior softball and volleyball, exercising. Home: 5510 Brookside Ln Washington MI 48094-2683

GOTHOLD, STUART EUGENE, school system administrator, education educator; b. L.A., Sept. 20, 1935; s. Hubert Eugene and Adelaide Louise (Erickson) G.; m. Jane Ruth Soderberg, July 15, 1955; children: Jon Ernest, Susan Louise, Eric Arthur, Ruth Ann. BA, Whittier Coll., 1956, MA in Edn., 1961, LLD (hon.), 1988; EdD, U. So. Calif., 1974. Tchr. grades 1-9 El Rancho Sch. Dist., Pico Rivera, Calif., 1956-61, prin. jr. h.s., 1961-66; curriculum cons. L.A. County Office Edn., 1966-70; asst. supt. South Whittier (Calif.) Sch. Dist., 1970-72, supt., 1972-77; asst. supt. L.A. County Office Edn., Downey, 1977-78, chief dep. supt., 1978-79, supt., 1979-94; clin. prof. U. So. Calif., L.A., 1994—. Charter mem. Edn. Insights, Detroit, 1990—; chmn., bd. dirs. Fedco Found.; co-chmn. LA (Calif.) Music Ctr. Edn. Coun. Author: (book) Inquiry, 1970, Decisions-A Health Edn. Curriculum, 1971. Recipient Alumni Merit award USC, 1993, Alumni Achievement award Whittier Coll., 1986; named Dist. Educator Calif. State U., 1993. Republican. Roman Catholic. Avocations: tennis, choral singing, photography, hiking. Home: 10121 Pounds Ave Whittier CA 90603-1649 Office: U So Calif WPH 902 C Los Angeles CA 90089-4039 Office Phone: 213-740-3451. Business E-Mail: gothold@usc.edu.

GOTLIEB, ALLAN E., former ambassador; b. Winnipeg, Man., Can., Feb. 28, 1928; s. David Phillip and Sarah (Schiller) G.; m. Sondra Kaufman, Dec. 20, 1955; children: Rebecca, Marcus, Rachel. BA, U. Calif., 1949; LLB, Harvard U., 1954; MA, BCL (Vinerian Law scholar), Oxford U., 1956; LLD (hon.), U. Toronto. Bar: Eng. 1956. Fellow Wadham Coll. and univ. lectr. in law Oxford U., 1954-56; joined Can. Dept. External Affairs, 1957; asst. under sec. for external affairs and legal adviser, 1967-68; dep. minister communications, 1968-73; dep. minister manpower and immigration, 1973-76; chmn. Can. Employment and Immigration Commn., 1976-77; under sec. Dept. External Affairs, 1977-81; Can. ambassador to U.S., Washington, 1981-89; chmn. Can. Coun., Ottawa, 1989-94. Vis. fellow All Souls Coll., Oxford, 1975-76; William Lyon Mackenzie King vis. prof. Harvard U., 1989, Claude Bissell vis. prof. U. Toronto, 1989; sr. fellow Massey Coll.; former gov. Internat. Devel. Rsch. Ctr., Nat. Film Bd.; former pub. Saturday Night Mag.; bd. dirs. Davis and Henderson Income Trust; mem. adv. bd. Nestle Canada, Inc.; N.Am. vice chmn. Trilateral Commn.; chmn. Donner Canadian Found., Sotheby's Can.; sr. advisor Stikeman Elliott, Toronto; trustee Art Gallery Ont. Author: Disarmament and International Law, 1965, Canadian Treaty-Making, 1968, Impact of Technology on the Development of International Law, 1982, I'll Be With You In A Minute, Mr. Ambassador, 1991; editor: Human Rights, Federalism and Minorities, 1979; editor: Harvard Law Rev., 1950-51. Decorated companion Order of Can.; recipient outstanding achievement award Govt. of Can., 1983, Haas internat. award U. Calif. Bd. Regents, 1985, Woodrow Wilson Pub. Svc. award, Woodrow Wilson Internat. Ctr. Scholars, 2002; hon. fellow Wadham Coll. Oxford. Office: Commerce Court West PO Box 85 Ste 5300 Toronto ON Canada M5L 1B9

GOTLIEB, CALVIN CARL, computer scientist, educator; b. Toronto, Ont., Mar. 27, 1921; s. Israel and Jennie G.; m. Phyllis Fay Bloom, June 12, 1949; children: Leo, Margaret, Jane. BA, U. Toronto, 1942, MA, 1944, PhD, 1947; D in Math. (hon.), U. Waterloo, Can., 1968; D in Engring. (hon.), N.S. Tech. U., 1985; LLD (hon.), U. Toronto, 1996. Faculty U. Toronto, 1949—; dir. Inst. Computer Sci., 1962-70, chmn. dept. computer sci., 1964-67, prof. computer sci., 1962—, emeritus, 1986—. Pres. C.C. Gotlieb Cons. Ltd., 1978—; cons. info. scis. to various govts., internat. orgns., indsl. cos., 1969—; McKay vis. prof. U. Calif., Berkeley, 1981; chmn. tech. com. 9 on relationship between computers and soc. Internat. Fedn. for Info. Processing, 1975-81 Author: (with J.N.P. Hume) High-Speed Data Processing, 1958, (with A. Borodin) Social Issues in Computing, 1973, (with L.R. Gotlieb) Data Types and Structures, 1978, Economics of Computers, 1985; editor, editor-in-chief, contbr. various Can., Netherlands, U.S. sci. jours. Recipient Silver Core award Internat. Fedn. of Info. Processing Socs., 1974, Auerbach award, 1994; rsch. grantee Nat. Sci. and Engring. Rsch. Coun. Can., 1955-90, C.M. Order of Can., 1996. Fellow: Assn. Computing Machinery (Pres.'s medal 2002), Brit. Computer Soc., Royal Soc. Can.; mem.: Can. Info. Processing Soc. (hon.), Nat. Yacht Club (Toronto), Faculty Club (U. Toronto). Jewish. Home: 19 Lower Village Gate PH 06 Toronto ON Canada M5P 3L9 Office: U Toronto Dept Computer Sci Toronto ON Canada M5S 3G4 Office Phone: 416-978-2980. Business E-Mail: ccg@cs.toronto.edu.

GOTLIEB, JAQUELIN SMITH, pediatrician; b. Washington, Oct. 20, 1946; d. Turner Taliaferro and Lois Barbara (Fisk) Smith; m. Edward Marvin Gotlieb, June 25, 1970; children: Sarah Ruth, Aaron Franklin, David Jacob. BS in Zoology, Duke U., 1968; MD, Med. Coll. Va., 1972. Diplomate Am. Bd. Pediat. Rotating intern Med. Coll. Va. Hosps.-Va. Commonwealth U., Richmond, 1972—73, resident in pediat., 1973—74; pvt. practice Richmond, 1974—75, Stone Mountain, Ga., 1976—86, 1987—; resident in pediat. U. Colo., Denver, 1975—76; med. dir., cons. CIGNA Healthplan Ga., Atlanta, 1986—87. Sch. physician Richmond City Schs., 1974-75. Bd. dirs. Ga. Health Found., Atlanta, 1985-95, vice chmn., 1995-99, chmn., 1999—. Fellow Am. Acad. Pediat. (Ga. chpt. bd. dirs. 1996-99); mem. Med. Assn. Ga., Ga. Perinatal Assn. (bd. dirs. 1994-2002, pres. 1999-2000), DeKalb Med. Soc. (chmn. com. 1976). Office: Pediatric Ctr 5405 Memorial Dr Ste D Stone Mountain GA 30083-3236 Office Phone: 404-296-3800.

GOTO, MIDORI, classical violinist; b. Osaka, Japan, Oct. 25, 1971; Attended, Juilliard Sch. Music; grad., Profl. Childrens Sch., 1990; BA in Psychology and Gender Studies, NYU, 2000. Performer worldwide, 1982—; founder Midori and Friends, 1992; faculty Manhattan Sch. Music, 2001—. Recordings on Philips, Sony Classical, Columbia Masterworks; performed with N.Y. Philharmonic Orch., Boston Symphony Orch.; worldwide performances include Berlin, Chgo., Cleve., Phila., Montreal, London; recordings include Encore, Live at Carnegie Hall; recordings (albums) Paganini: 24 Caprices, 1989, Encore!, 1992, Midori's 20th Anniversary CD, 2001. Named Best Artist of Yr. by Japanese Govt., 1988; recipient Dorothy B. Chandler Performing Arts award, L.A. Music Ctr., 1989, Crystal award Ashani Shimbun Newspaper contbn. arts, Suntory award, 1994. also: Midori and Friends 850 7th Ave Ste 1103 New York NY 10019-5230*

GOTSCHLICH, EMIL CLAUS, physician; b. Bangkok, Jan. 17, 1935; arrived in U.S., 1950, naturalized, 1955; s. Emil Clemens and Magdalene (Holst) Gotschlich; m. Kathleen-Anne Haines, May 24, 1975; children: Emil Christopher, Hilda Christina, Emil Chandler, Emily Claire. BA, NYU, 1955, MD, 1959. Intern Bellevue Hosp., N.Y.C., 1959—60; mem. faculty Rockefeller U., N.Y.C., 1960—, prof. microbiology, 1978—, sr. physician, 1978—, prof., v.p. med. sci. Capt. med. corps U.S. Army, 1966—68. Recipient Squibb award, Am. Soc. Infectious Disease, 0197, Lasker award, Albert and Mary Lasker Found., 1978. Mem.: NAS, Am. Soc. Clin. Investigation, Am. Assn. Immunologists, Peripatetic Club, Alpha Omega Alpha, Sigma Xi. Office: Rockefeller U Dept Bacterial Pathogenesis & Immunology 1230 York Ave New York NY 10021-6399*

GOTSDINER, MURRAY BENNETT, lawyer; b. Des Moines, Jan. 2, 1953; s. harold B. and Shirlee Ann (Gorshel) G.; m. Debora Zadina, Feb. 5, 1972; children: Alexander, Erik, Elizabeth. BA, Drake U., 1975, JD, 1979. Bar: Iowa 1980, Tex. 1989, U.S. Dist. Ct. Iowa, 1980, U.S. Ct. Appeals (8th cir.), 1982, U.S. Supreme Ct. 1983. Shareholder McEnroe, Gotsdiner, Brewer, Burdette and Steinbach, PC, Des Moines, 1980. Mem. Iowa Bar Assn., Tex. Bar Assn., Polk County (Iowa) Bar Assn., Des Moines Club. Republican. Jewish. Avocations: golf, deep sea fishing. Home: 13211 Sunset Cir Clive IA 50325-8805 Office: McEnroe Gotsdiner Brewer Burdette and Steinbach PC Westown Bus Ctr Ste 100 1701-48th St West Des Moines IA 50266-6723 Office Phone: 515-267-9000.

GOTT, WESLEY ATLAS, art educator; b. Buffalo, Mar. 6, 1942; s. Raymond and Rowena (Pettitt) Gott; m. Alice Blalock, May 26, 1972; children: Andrew, Deidre. BS, SW Mo. State U., 1965; M in Ch. Music, SW Theol. Sem., 1969; MFA, George Washington U., 1975; postgrad., Nova U. Tchr. ceramics Springfield Art Mus., Mo., 1964—66; min. music Terrace Acres Bapt. Ch., Ft. Worth, 1966—70; min. music and youth First Bapt. Ch., Wheaton, Md., 1970—75; asst. prof. art S.W. Bapt. U., Bolivar, Mo., 1975—79, assoc. prof., chmn. art dept., 1979—. Judge art contests H.S., Bolivar, 1978—. Christmas sculpture with lights, 1981—84. Recipient Parkway Disting. Prof. award, 2002—03. Mem.: Mid-Am. Coll. Art Assn., Coll. Art Assn. Am., Cmty. Concert Assn., Nat. Trust for Historic Preservation, Smithsonian Assocs., Phi Mu Alpha, Alpha Gamma Theta. Baptist. Avocations: hunting, fishing, boating, tennis, golf. Home: 127 W Maupin St Bolivar MO 65613-1946 Office: SW Bapt U 1600 University Ave Bolivar MO 65613-2597 Office Phone: 417-328-1650. Business E-Mail: wgott@sbuniv.edu.

GOTTA, ALEXANDER WALTER, anesthesiologist, educator; b. Bklyn., Apr. 10, 1935; s. A. Walter and Helen C. (Bruskewic) G.; m. Colleen A. Sullivan, July 17, 1965; 1 child, Nancy C. BS summa cum laude, St. John's U., 1956; MD, NYU, 1960. Diplomate Am. Bd. Anesthesiology, Am. Bd. Med. Examiners. Intern U. Chgo., 1960-61; resident in surgery Boston City Hosp., 1961-62; resident in anesthesiology N.Y. Hosp.-Cornell U., N.Y.C., 1962-64; instr. anesthesiology Cornell U., 1965-66; adj. prof. St. John's U., 1977—79; dir. anesthesia St. Mary's Hosp., Bklyn., 1968-78; from asst. prof. to prof. SUNY, Bklyn., 1968—97; prof. emeritus, 1997—; mem. dean's adv. bd. St. John's Coll., 2003—. Dir. anesthesia L.I. Coll. Hosp., Bklyn., 1983-90, Kings County Hosp. Ctr., 1990-97; spkr. in field. Editor: Anesthesiology Clinics Trauma, 1996; contbr. articles to profl. jours. Capt. U.S. Army, 1966-68, Vietnam. Fellow N.Y. Acad. Medicine (chmn. anesthesia sect. 1990, recognition for svc. to urban medicine 1997), Am. Coll. Anesthesiologists, Am. Soc. Anesthesiologists (ho. dels. 1986-97, chmn. refresher course com. 1995); mem. N.Y. Soc. Anesthesiologists (bd. dirs. 1983-97, chmn. sci. program com. 1991-93, chmn. PGA 1994-96, v.p. 1994, pres.-elect 1995, pres. 1996), N.Y. Soc. Critical Care Medicine (pres. 1985), Assn. Univ. Anesthesiologists, Acad. Anesthesia. Republican. Roman Catholic. Home: 29 Ascot Ridge Rd Great Neck NY 11021-2912 Office: Kings County Hosp Ctr 451 Clarkson Ave Brooklyn NY 11203-2097 E-mail: alexwg@optonline.net.

GOTTENGER, EMANUEL EZEQUIEL, physician; s. Andre and Amalia Gottenger; m. Patricia Margarita Babilonia, Mar. 2, 1996; children: Leonardo Issac, Deborah. BS, Coll. Moral y Luces Herzl Bialik, Caracas, Venezuela, 1980—85; MD, U. Ctrl. de Venezuela, Caracas, 1986—93. Cert. Fla., 2001, diplomate Am. Bd. Urology, 2003. Physician Ministry of Health and Social Assistance, Caracas, Venezuela, 1993—94; rsch. scholar Baylor Coll. Medicine, Houston, 1994—95; surg. intern Beth Israel Med. Ctr., N.Y.C., 1995—96, surg. resident, 1997—98, urology resident, 1998—2001; urologic oncology, laparoscopy fellowship Dept. Veterans Affairs Med. Ctr., West Palm Beach, Fla., 2001—02, attending urologist, physician-in-charge laparoscopic urology, 2002—05, Yone Urology P.A., 2005—. Contbr. articles to profl. jours., chapters to books. Recipient Scholars in Urology Award, Pfizer Corp., 1999, 2000. Mem.: Endourological Soc., Am. Urol. Assn. Avocations: computers, travel, bicycling. Office: Palm Ct Plz 5130 Linton Blvd Ste F-6 Delray Beach FL 33483 Office Phone: 561-496-4444. Business E-Mail: urologist40@adelphia.net.

GOTTESMAN, A(RTHUR) EDWARD, lawyer; b. Hillside, NJ, July 29, 1937; s. Joseph Jack Gottesman, Sadonia Herskowitz; m. Patricia Jo Matson; m. Allison Pierce Coudert (div.); children: Polly Moore, Catherine Coudert. BA, U.Chgo., 1954; LLB, Yale U., 1957. Bar: N.Y. 1959. Ptnr. Coudert Bros., London, 1963—70; sr. ptnr. Gottesman Jones & Partners, London, 1970—. Pres. Am. C. of C., London, 1981—83; chmn. Derby Internat. Corp., Luxembourg, 1986—98, Exeter Internat. Corp., Luxembourg, Prin. Healthcare Fin. Ltd., London. Author: Blueprint for Public Company Reform, Moral Economics, 2003. Dir. London Bach Orch., 1980—89; Member Yale University President's Council on International Activities, New Haven. Private US Army, 1960—61, Fort Dix, N.J. Mem.: Yale Club, Reform Club. Office: Centenary International Corporation 1120 Avenue of the Americas New York NY 10036 Personal E-mail: centenint@aol.com. Business E-Mail: gottesmanjones@aol.com.

GOTTESMAN, CHARLES R., music educator; b. Abington, Pa., Aug. 24, 1971; s. Charles and Beatrice Boston Gottesman; m. Lauren L Lopez, Dec. 22, 2001. MusB, Temple U., Philadelphia, PA. Cert. tchr. Pa., 1994. Music educator Sch. Dist. of Springfield Twp., Oreland, Pa., 1994—. Recipient Lloyd C. Clemmer PTA Citizenship award, Erdenheim Elem. Sch. PTA, 1999. Home: 500 Greenhill Rd Willow Grove PA 19090 Office: Springfield Twp HS 1801 E Paper Mill Rd Erdenheim PA 19038 Personal E-mail: chuck_gottesman@sdst.org.

GOTTESMAN, DAVID SANFORD, investment company executive; b. N.Y.C., Apr. 26, 1926; s. Benjamin and Esther (Garfunkel) G.; m. Ruth Levy, Aug. 17, 1950; children: Robert, Alice, William. BA, Trinity Coll., 1948; MBA, Harvard U., 1950; LHD (hon.), Yeshiva U., 1988. Sr. mng. dir. First Manhattan Co., N.Y.C., 1964—. Bd. dirs. Berkshire Hathaway, Inc. Vice-chmn., trustee Am. Mus. Natural History; trustee Mt. Sinai Hosp.; chmn. emeritus Yeshiva U., N.Y.C. Mem. The Century Assn., Econs. Club, Harmonie Club, Century Country Club. Office: First Manhattan Co 437 Madison Ave New York NY 10022-7001

GOTTESMAN, IRVING I., psychologist, educator; b. Cleve., Dec. 29, 1930; s. Bernard and Virginia (Weitzner) G.; m. Carol Applen, Dec. 23, 1970; children: Adam M., David B. BS, Ill. Inst. Tech., 1953; PhD, U. Minn., 1960. Diplomate in clin. psychology and psychol. assessment; lic. psychologist Calif., Va. Intern clin. psychology VA Hosp., Mpls., 1959-60; lectr. dept. social relations Harvard U., 1960-63; USPHS fellow in psychiat. genetics Inst. Psychiatry, London, 1963-64; assoc. prof. psychiat. & genetics, dept. psychiatry U. N.C., 1964-66; prof. dept. psychology, psychiatry and genetics U. Minn., 1966-80; prof. dept. psychiatry and genetics Washington U., St. Louis, 1980-85; Commonwealth prof. psychology U. Va., Charlottesville, 1985-94, Sherrell J. Aston prof. psychology, prof. clin. pediats., 1994-2001, prof. emeritus, 2001—; sr. fellow, Drs. Irving and Dorothy Bernstein prof. adult psychiatry U. Minn., 2001—. Cons. NIMH, Washington, 1975-79, 92-96, NIMH Nat. Plan for Schizophrenia, 1988-89; mem. Pres.'s Commn. on Huntington Disease, 1977; tng. cons. VA, Washington, 1968-85, 2001—; fellow Ctr. for Advanced Studies in the Behavioral Scis., Stanford, Calif., 1987-88; Inst. of Medicine Com. cons. Vietnam War Experience Study, 1987-88, Med. Follow-Up Agy., 2000—; NRC cons. Workshop on Schizophrenia, 1995-96; cons. human rights Equal Opportunities Commn., Hong Kong, 1999-2003, 05-06; mem. Inst. Medicine Follow-up Agy., 2000—; chair twins com. Inst. Medicine, 2000—, mem. com. on genomics and the public's health in the 21st century, 2004-05. Author: Schizophrenia and Genetics, 1972 (Hofheimer prize), Schizophrenia The Epigenetic Puzzle, 1982, Schizophrenia Genesis: The Origins of Madness, 1991 (transl. into Japanese and German, William James Book award, Phi Beta Kappa U. Va. Book award 1992), Schizophrenia and Genetic Risks, 1992, 3d edit., 1999, Schizophrenia and Manic Depressive Disorder: Biological Roots of Mental Illness Revealed by Study of Identical Twins, 1994, transl. into Japanese, 1998, Seminars in Psychiatric Genetics, 1994, 2d edit., 2004, Psychiatric Genetics and Genomics, 2002, revised, 2004; editor: Man, Mind and Heredity, 1971, Vital Statistics, Demography and Schizophrenia, 1989. Served with USNR, 1949-53, 56-61; USN, 1953-56. Guggenheim fellow U. Copenhagen, 1972; recipient R. Thornton Wilson prize Ea. Psychiat. Rsch. Assn., 1965, Stanley Dean award Am. Coll. Psychiatrists, 1988, Eric Stromgren medal Danish Psychiat. Soc., 1991, Kurt Schneider prize, Bonn, 1992, Alexander Gralnick prize Am. Assn. Suicidology, 1992, Jonathan Logan award Nat. Alliance for Mentally Ill, 1995; David C. Wilson lectr. U. Va. Sch. Medicine, 1967, Lifetime Achievement award Internat. Soc. for Psychiat. Genetics, 1997; Parker lectr. Ohio State U. Sch. Medicine, 1983, 93, others. Fellow APA (Disting. Scientist award divsn. 12, sect. 3 1994, Disting. Sci. Contbns. award 2001), AAAS, Am. Psychopathol. Assn., Royal Coll. Psychiatrists (hon.), Am. Psychol. Soc. (human capital initiative task force for psychopathology rsch. agenda 1993-96); mem. Minn. Human Genetics League (v.p. 1969-71), Soc. Study Social Biology (v.p. 1976-80), Behavior Genetics Assn. (pres. 1976-77, T. Dobzhansky award 1990), Am. Soc. Human Genetics (editl. bd. 1967-72), Soc. Rsch. in Psychopathology (pres. 1993, Joseph Zubin award 2001), Japanese Soc. Biol. Psychiatry (spl. lecture award 2001), Inst. of Psychiatry (14th Eliot Slater Lectr., 2002). Home: 5823 Vernon Ln Edina MN 55436 Business E-Mail: gotte003@umn.edu.

GOTTESMAN, MICHAEL MARC, biomedical researcher; b. Jersey City, N.J., Oct. 7, 1946; s. Jacob Joseph and Frieda (Shapiro) G.; m. Susan Kemelhor, Feb. 5, 1966; children: Daniel Eric, Rebecca Fran. AB, Harvard Coll., 1966; MD, Harvard Med. Sch., 1970. Diplomate Am. Bd. Internal Medicine. Med. intern then resident Peter Bent Brigham Hosp., Boston, 1970-71, 74-75; rsch. assoc. NIH, Bethesda, Md., 1971-74; asst. prof. Harvard Med. Sch., Boston, 1975-76; sr. investigator Nat. Cancer Inst., Bethesda, 1976-80, sect. head, 1980-90, lab. chief, 1990—. Acting dir. Nat. Ctr. for Human Genome Rsch., 1992-93, deputy dir. intramural rsch., 1994—. Author and editor: Molecular Cell Genetics, Molecular Genetics of Mammalian Cells, The Role of Proteases in Cancer. With USPHS, 1971—. Recipient Milken Family award for cancer rsch., 1990. Fellow AAAS; mem. Am. Soc. Biochemistry Molecular Biology, Genetics Soc. Am., Am. Soc. Cell Biology, Am. Assn. Cancer Rsch. (Richard and Hinda Rosenthal Found. award 1992), Inst. Medicine, 2004. Achievements include rsch. on molecular basis of resistance to anti-cancer drugs. Office: Nat Cancer Inst Lab Cell Biology Bdlg 37 Rm 1A09 37 Convent Dr MSC 4255 Bethesda MD 20892-0001

GOTTESMAN, STEPHEN THANCY, astronomy educator, researcher; b. N.Y.C., Feb. 23, 1939; s. Jacob Frank and Edna Beatrice (Goldner) G.; m. Celia F. Docherty, June 29, 1968 (div. Aug. 1990); children: Lorna Rachel, Ian Kenneth Jacob, Emily Caitlin; m. Mariou Barr, Oct. 20, 1990; children: Erika Barr(step), Alexander Barr (step). BA magna cum laude, Colgate U., 1960; PhD, Victoria U. Manchester Eng., 1967. Lectr. physics and astronomy U. Keele, England, 1968—69; rsch. fellow Calif. Inst. Tech., Pasadena, 1971; rsch. assoc. Nat. Radio Astron. Obs., Charlottesville, Va., 1969—71; asst. prof. astronomy U. Fla., Gainesville, 1972—76, assoc. prof. astronomy, 1976—81, prof. astronomy, 1981—, chmn. dept. astronomy, 1988—93. Visiting prof. Instituto de Astrofisica de Canaricas, 1995-96. Co-editor: Galactic Models, 1990, Nonlinear Astrophysical Fluid Dynamics, 1991, Nonlinear Dynamics and Chaos in Astrophysics, 1998, Nonlinear Dynamics in Astronomy and Physics: In Memory of Henry Kardrup, 2005; contbr. articles to scholarly and profl. astrophys. and astronomy jours. Treas. ACLU, Gainesville, 1988-92. Leverhulme fellow U. Manchester, Eng., 1961-64, Fulbright scholar, 1961. Mem. Am. Astron. Soc., Internat. Astron. Union (chmn. working group com. #28 1979-85), Internat. Union of Radio Sci., Astron. Soc. of Pacific, Phi Beta Kappa (v.p. 2004-05, pres. 2005—) Democrat. Achievements include research on measured properties of the interstellar medium and the structure, kinematics and dynamics of the galaxies; findings concerning limitations on "dark matter" in the universe and dynamics of barred spiral galaxies. Office Phone: 352-392-2052. Office Fax: 352-392-5089. Business E-Mail: gott@astro.ufl.edu.

GOTTFRIED, EUGENE LESLIE, physician, educator; b. Passaic, N.J., Feb. 26, 1929; s. David Robert and Rose (Chill) G.; m. Phyllis Doris Swain, Aug. 16, 1957. AB, Columbia U., 1950, MD, 1954. Cert. Nat. Bd. Med. Examiners, Am. Bd. Internal Medicine. Intern Presbyn. Hosp., N.Y.C., 1954-55, asst. resident in medicine, 1957-58; resident Bronx (N.Y.) Mcpl. Hosp. Ctr., 1958-59, fellow in medicine, 1959-60; asst. instr. medicine Albert Einstein Coll. Medicine Yeshiva U., N.Y.C., 1959-60, instr., 1960-61, assoc., 1961-65, asst. prof., 1965-69; assoc. prof. medicine Cornell U. Med. Coll.,

N.Y.C., 1969-81, assoc. prof. pathology, 1975-81; clin. prof. dept. lab. medicine U. Calif., San Francisco, 1981-93, prof., 1993-99, vice chmn. dept. lab. medicine, 1981-98, prof. emeritus, 1999—. Hosp. appointments include asst. vis. physician Bronx Mcpl. Hosp. Ctr., 1960-66, assoc. attending physician, 1966-69; assoc. attending physician N.Y. Hosp., N.Y.C., 1969-81, assoc. attending pathologist, 1975-81, dir. lab. clin. hematology, 1969-81; chief lab. medicine San Francisco Gen. Hosp. Med. Ctr., 1981-98, dir. clin. labs., 1981-98. Assoc. editor Jour. Lipid Research, 1971-72, 75-77; mem. editorial bd. Jour. Lipid Research, 1972-77. Dir. Rescue One Found., 1998—, Moraga-Orinda Fire Protection Dist., 2002—. Lt. comdr. USNR, 1955—57. Recipient Career Scientist award Health Research Council City of N.Y., 1964-72. Fellow ACP, Am. Soc. Hematology, Internat. Soc. Hematology, Acad. Clin. Lab. Physicians and Scientists; mem. Nat. Com. for Clin. Lab. Stds., Rotary (pres. Orinda club 2004-05), Phi Beta Kappa, Alpha Omega Alpha. Personal E-mail: gottfrie@labmed2.ucsf.edu.

GOTTFRIED, IRA SIDNEY, management consulting executive; b. Bronx, N.Y., Jan. 4, 1932; s. Louis and Augusta (Champagne) G.; m. Judith Claire Rosenberg, Sept. 19, 1954; children: Richard Alan, Glenn Steven, David Aaron. BBA, CCNY, 1953; MBA, U. So. Calif., 1959. Lic. airline transport pilot. Sales mgr. Kleerpak Plastics, North Hollywood, Calif., 1956-57; head sys. and procedures Hughes Aircraft Co., Culver City, Calif., 1957-60; mgr. corp. bus. sys. The Aerospace Corp., El Segundo, Calif., 1960-61; dir. adminstrn. Eldon Industries, Inc., Hawthorne, Calif., 1962; mgr. info. sys. Litton Industries, Inc., Woodland Hills, Calif., 1963-64; exec. v.p. Norris & Gottfried, Inc., L.A., 1964-69; pres. Gottfried Cons., Inc., L.A., 1970-85; exec. ptnr. PriceWaterhouseCoopers, LLP, L.A., 1985-88, ret., 1988. V.p. Cresap/Towers Perrin, 1988-90; pres., dir. Gottfried Cons. Internat. 1990—; vice chmn. ACME Inc., 1984-85; dir., mem. exec. com. Blue Cross of Calif., 1968-77. Contbr. articles to profl. jours. Bd. dirs. ARC, 1988-2003, Westside Amateur Radio Club, Univ. Synagogue, 1986-92. With USNR, 1953-56. Recipient Pres.'s award United Hosp. Assn. Mem. Inst. Mgmt. Cons. (life), Am. Arbitration Assn., Assn. Info. Tech. Profls. (life), Alpha Phi Omega (life), Brentwood Country Club. Jewish. Avocations: amateur radio K6IRA, flying, model railroading. Home: 12118 La Casa Ln Los Angeles CA 90049-1530 Office Phone: 310-476-2124.

GOTTFRIED, KURT, physicist, researcher; b. Vienna, May 17, 1929; came to U.S., 1952, naturalized, 1965; s. Salomon and Augusta (Werner) G.; m. Sorel B. Dickstein, June 26, 1955; children: David M., Laura S. B.Eng., McGill U., 1951, MS, 1952; PhD, MIT, 1955. Jr. fellow Soc. Fellows, Harvard, 1955-58; research fellow Inst. Theoretical Physics, Copenhagen, 1958-59, Harvard, 1959-60, asst. prof. physics, 1960-64; assoc. prof. physics Cornell U., Ithaca, N.Y., 1964-68, prof. physics, 1968—, chmn. dept., 1991-94, prof. physics emeritus. Staff mem. European Orgn. for Nuclear Research, Geneva, Switzerland, 1970-73 Author: Quantum Mechanics, 1966, Concepts of Particle Physics, Vol. 1, 1984, Vol. 2, 1986; co-editor: Crisis Stability and Nuclear War, 1988. Fellow AAAS, Am. Acad. Arts and Scis., Am. Phys. Soc. (chmn. div. particles and fields 1981, councillor 1990-94), Union Concerned Scientists (bd. dirs. 1978—, vice-chair 1997—, chair 1999—), Coun. on Fgn. Rels. Office: Newman Lab Nuclear Studies Cornell U Ithaca NY 14853

GOTTFRIED, MARK ELLIS, accountant, consultant; b. Toledo, Mar. 12, 1953; s. Max and Barbara Alice (Johnston) G.; m. Linda Jean Perkins, Aug. 7, 1976; children: Christopher Ellis, Katharine Powell. BA, Northwestern U., 1975; MBA, U. Chgo., 1980. CPA Ill., Ind., Va. Sr. acct. Deloitte Haskins & Sells, Chgo., 1980-84; corp. mktg. mgr. Micro Data Base Systems, Lafayette, Ind., 1984-85; sr. cons. Deloitte Haskins & Sells, Indpls., 1985-86, mgr., 1986-88; owner Gottfried & Assocs., Indpls., 1988-91; v.p. fin., sec. Trilithic, Inc., Indpls., 1989-92; pres. TriVox Corp., 1990-92, Performance Ptnrs., Inc., 1991-93; prin., owner Gottfried Cons., Va., 1995—; CFO Frontier Broadband LLC, Va., 2000—02. Bd. dirs., treas. Ptnrs. in Mktg. Inc., 1992-93; bd. dirs. ReproComm. Inc., 1992-95; instr., bus. cons. Premier FastTrac tng. program Va. Peninsula C. of C., 1996-99 Editorial bd. Computers in Acctg., 1984-89. Bd. dirs. Chgo. Theatre Group, 1984; bd. dirs. Ind. Repertory Theatre, mem. fin. com., 1987-92; cons. Jr. Achievement, Indpls., 1986-87. Mem. AICPA, Ind. Soc. CPAs, Va. Soc. CPAs, Inst. Mgmt. Acct., Indpls. C. of C. (govt. com. 1986-89), Ind. Electronics Mfrs. Assn. (v.p. fin. and legal 1989-91), Ind. Small Bus. Coun., U. Chgo. Grad. Sch. Bus. Alumni Assn. (pres. Ind. chpt. 1987-95), Columbia Club. Republican. Episcopalian. Home: 109 William Claiborne Williamsburg VA 23185-6536 E-mail: megottfried@yahoo.com.

GOTTFRIED, PAUL EDWARD, humanities educator, editor-in-chief; b. N.Y.C., Nov. 21, 1941; s. Andrew Gottfried and Ruth Weiser; m. Diane Zelcer, June 15, 1969 (dec. Feb. 1994); children: Barbara Hollander, Joseph, Jonathan, Beth, Sara; m. Mary Zwir, May 12, 2000. BA, Yeshiva U., 1963; MS, Yale U., 1965, PhD, 1967. Grad. fellow Yale U., New Haven, 1965-66; asst. prof. history Case Western Res. U., Cleve., 1968-71; vis. asst. prof. history NYU, N.Y.C., 1971-72; chmn. history dept. Rockford (Ill.) Coll., 1974-86; sr. editor The World and I, Washington, 1986-93; prof. humanities Elizabethtown (Pa.) Coll., 1989—; editor-in-chief This World, 1992—. Author: The Conservative Movement, 1993, After Liberalism, 1999; contbr. articles to profl. jours. Recipient award NEH, 1969; Earhart fellow, 1970, 73, 77, 83, 88, Guggenheim fellow, 1984; NEH tchg. fellow U.S. Naval Acad., 1993. Mem. Neoclassical Reform Jewish Movement (organizer), Società Libera (assoc.). Avocations: jogging, tennis, gardening. Home: 327 College Ave Elizabethtown PA 17022-2414 E-mail: gottfrpe@etown.edu.

GOTTHARDT, MARY JANE, religious studies educator; b. Davenport, Iowa, Sept. 22, 1940; d. Harry Claus and Roseanne (Beulah May) Stoltenberg; m. Lawrence John Gotthardt, July 8, 1967; children: Michael John, Paula Formold. BA, DeLourdes Coll., 1987; MAT, Nat. Louis U., 1999. RN Ill. Nurse Resurrection Hosp., Chgo., 1960—70; chmn. pub. rels. Mark Hopkins Sch., Elk Grove, Ill., 1975—78, Transfiguration Night Train, Wauconda, Ill., 1980; tchr. religious edn. Transfiguration Sch., Wauconda, 1979—2002, tchr. and libr. aid, 1979—2000, tchr., 2000—; tchr. religious edn. St. Peter Ch., Volo, Ill., 1998—2002, dir. religious edn., 2000—. Co-owner Mannheim Rental Equipment, Franklin Pk., Ill., 1968—. Sec. Homeowner's Assn., Wauconda. Mem.: AAAS, Nat. Mid. Sch. Assn., Pope John Paul II Cultural Ctr., Smithsonian Inst., Gallop Poll, Hist. Ill. Preservation Soc., Phi Delta Kappa. Roman Catholic. Avocation: travel. Office: Transfiguration Sch 316 W Mill St Wauconda IL 60084

GOTTHOFFER, LANCE, lawyer; b. N.Y.C., June 23, 1949; s. Joel Sidney and Muriel (Diamond) G. BA, Monmouth Coll., 1971; JD, Georgetown U., 1974. Bar: N.Y. 1975, U.S. Dist. Ct. (so. dist.) N.Y. 1975, U.S. Ct. Appeals (2nd, 3rd, 5th, 6th and 9th cirs.) 1981, U.S. Ct. Internat. Trade 1986, U.S. Supreme Ct. 1987. Legal asst. Office of N.Y.C. Coun. Pres., N.Y.C., 1970-73; assoc. Mudge, Rose, Guthrie & Alexander, N.Y.C., 1974-77; ptnr. Marks & Murase, N.Y.C., 1977-94, Oppenheimer, Wolff & Donnelly, N.Y.C., 1994—2002, Reed Smith, N.Y.C., 2003—. Guest lectr. Grad. Sch. Bus., Baruch Coll., N.Y.C.; speaker in field. Mem. ABA. Office: Reed Smith 599 Lexington Ave New York NY 10022 Home: 245 E 40th St New York NY 10016 Office Phone: 212-549-0289. Business E-Mail: lgotthoffer@reedsmith.com.

GOTTHOLD, WILLIAM EUGENE, emergency physician; b. Long Beach, Calif., Sept. 20, 1942; BA, Trinity U., 1964; MD, Tulane U., 1969. Cert. emergency medicine. Intern Letterman Army Med. Ctr., San Francisco, 1969-70, resident in gen. surgery, 1970-72; mem. staff Ctrl. Wash. Hosp., Wenatchee, 1978—; med. infomatics officers Wenatchee (Wash.) Valley Clinic. Mem. AMA, Am. Coll. Emergency Physicians, Wash. State Med. Assn., Am. Bd. Emergency Medicine (cert., sr. dir.). Office: Wenatchee Valley Med Ctr 820 N Chelan Ave Wenatchee WA 98801-2028 Office Phone: 509-663-8711. E-mail: wgotthold@wvclinic.com.

GOTTI, VICTORIA, columnist, writer, actress; b. Bklyn., 1963; d. John J. and Victoria (DiGiorgio) Gotti; m. Carmine Agnello, 1984 (div. Feb. 2002); children: John Gotti Agnello, Carmine Gotti Agnello, Frank Gotti Agnello. BA, St. John's U. Weekly features columnist NY Post; entertainment corr. EXTRA!, 2002; columnist Star mag., exec. editor-at-large; editor-in-chief Red Carpet mag. Actress & exec. prodr. (reality TV series) Growing Up Gotti, A & E, 2004—; author: Women & Mitral Valve Prolapse: A Comprehensive Guide to Living & Coping With MVP & Its Symptoms, 1995, The Senator's Daughter, 1997 (Mystery of Yr., Mystery Writers Assn.), I'll Be Watching You, 1998, Superstar, 2000, The Fifth Avenue Club, The Loyal Son; actor: (plays) We're Still Hot, 2005. Named Woman of Yr., Nat. Chpt. Am. Heart Assn., Writer of Yr., Women's Writer's Guild, Woman of Yr., Women's Coalition for Equal Rights; recipient Outstanding Humanitarian, St. Frances Guild Inc. Mailing: c/o Theatre at St Luke's 308 West 46 St New York NY 10019*

GOTTLANDER, ROBERT JAN LARS, dental company executive; b. Bohuslan, Sweden, Sept. 5, 1956; came to U.S., 1986; s. Jan H. K. and Ragnhild S.E. (Rutgerson) G.; m. Eva L.M. Svenson, July 4, 1987; children: Daniel J.R., Magdalena A.E., Linnea E.R. Student, Kongahalla Coll., Sweden, 1975; candidate of odontology, U. Gothenburg, Sweden, 1976, DDS, 1980. Dentist Swedish Health Care, Trollhattan, Sweden, 1980-82; asst. prof. dept. orthodontics Community Dentistry, Trollhattan, 1982-84; mgr. tng. and edn. Nobelpharma AB, Gothenburg, 1984-85, product mgr., 1985; v.p., mgr. edn. and product Nobelpharma USA Inc., Waltham, Mass., 1986-87, v.p. profl. affairs, 1987-88, v.p., gen. mgr. Chgo., 1988—; v.p. global mktg. Nobel Rnocare AB, Gothenburg, Sweden, 2002. Pres. V-Dal Union of Dentists, Trollhattan, Sweden, 1982-84; chmn. V-Dal Dental Soc., Sweden, 1983-84, sec. 1981-82; v.p. Global Mktg., Nobel Biocare AB, Sweden, 2002-. Lt. Swedish Royal Navy, 1976-79. Mem. AMA, Swedish Dental Soc., Swedish Orthodontic Soc.; affiliate mem. ADA, Acad. of Osseointegration. Lutheran. Avocations: sailing, skiing, tennis, reading. Business E-Mail: robert.gottlander@nobelbiocare.com.

GOTTLIEB, ALAN MERRIL, advertising, fundraising and broadcasting executive, writer; b. L.A., May 2, 1947; s. Seymour and Sherry (Schutz) G.; m. Julie Hoy Versnel, July 27, 1979; children: Amy Jean, Sarah Merril, Alexis Hope, Andrew Michael. Grad., Inst. on Comparative Political and Economic Sys. at Georgetown U., 1970; BS Nuc. Engring., U. Tenn., 1971. Press sec. Congressman John Duncan, Knoxville, Tenn., 1971; regional rep. Young Am. for Freedom, Seattle, 1972, nat. dir. Washington, 1971-72; nat. treas. Am. Conservative Union, Washington, 1971—, bd. dirs., 1974—; pres. Merril Assoc., 1974—. Chmn. Citizens Com. for Right to keep and Bear Arms, Bellevue, Wash., 1972—, exec. dir., 1973; pres. Ctr. Def. of Free Enterprise, Bellevue, 1976—. Second Amendment Found., Bellevue, 1974—, NoInternetTax.org, 2001—; pub. Gun Week, 1985—, The Gottlieb-Tartaro Report, 1995—; bd. dir. Nat. Pk. User Assn., 1988—; bd. dirs. Am. Polit. Action Com., 1988—; bd. dir. Com. Nat. Policy, bd. gov., 1985—, Svc. Bur. Assn., pres., dir., 1974—, Chancellor Broadcasting, Inc., Las Vegas, 1990—93; pres. Sta. KBNP Radio, Portland, 1990—, Sta. KITZ Radio, Evergreen Radio Network, Seattle, 1990—93, Westnet Broadcasting Inc., Bellevue, 1990, Sta. KSBN Radio, Spokane, 1995—, KGTK Radio, Olympia, Wash.; chmn. Talk Am. Radio Networks, 1994—2001, Univ. Talk Network, 2002. Author: The Gun Owners Political Action Manual, 1976, The Rights of Gun Owners, 1981, rev. edit., 1991, The Gun Grabbers, 1988, Gun Rights Fact Book, 1989, Guns for Women, 1988, The Wise Use Agenda, 1989, Trashing the Economy, 1993, Thinks You Can Do To Defend Your Gun Rights, 1993, Alan Gottlieb's Celebrity Address Book, 1994, 2d edit., 2001, More Things You Can Do To Defend Your Gun Rights, 1995, Politically Correct guns, 1996, She Took a Village, 1998, Double Trouble, 2001, Gun Rights Affirmed, 2001, George W. Bush Speaks to the Nation, 2004. With U.S. Army, 1968-74. Recipient Good Citizenship award Citizens Home Protective Assn., Honolulu, 1978, Cicero award Nat. Assn. Federally Licensed Firearms Dealers, Fla., 1982, Second Amendment award Scope, 1983, 91, Outstanding Am. Handgunner award, Am. Handgunners Award found., Milwaukee, Wisc., 1984, Roy Rogers award, Nat. Antique Arms Collectors Assn., Reno, Nev., 1987, Golden Eagle award, Am. Fedn. Police, Washington, 1990. Mem. NRA. Republican. Office Phone: 425-454-7012. Personal E-mail: alangottlieb@aol.com.

GOTTLIEB, ALICE B., dermatologist; PhD in Immunology, Rockefeller U., 1979; MD, Cornell U., 1980. Diplomate Am. Bd. Dermatology, bd. cert. rheumatology and internal medicine. Fellow in rheumatology Cornell U. Hosp. for Spl. Surgery, N.Y.C., 1982—84; resident in internal medicine N.Y. Hosp., N.Y.C., 1980—82, resident in dermatology, 1990—93; W. H. Conzen chair in clin. pharmacology, prof. medicine UMDNJ-Robert Wood Johnson Med. Sch., New Brunswick, NJ, 1995—. Office: Clin Rsch Ctr Robert Wood Johnson Med Sch One Robert Wood Johnson Pl PO Box 19 New Brunswick NJ 08903-0019 Office Phone: 732-418-8484.

GOTTLIEB, ALLAN, computer science educator; b. Queens, N.Y., Aug. 2, 1945; s. Irving and Frances (Caggiano) G.; m. Alice Bendix, Jan. 7, 1972; children: David, Michael. BS in Math., MIT, 1967; MA in Math., Brandeis U., 1968, PhD in Math., 1973. Acting instr. of math. U. Calif., Santa Cruz, Calif., 1971-72; instr. of math. State Coll. Mass., North Adams, Mass., 1972-73; asst. prof. math. York Coll. CUNY, N.Y.C., 1973-79, coord. computer math., 1976-81, assoc. prof. math., 1979-81; vis. mem. Courant Inst. NYU, N.Y.C., 1979-81, assoc. res. prof., 1981-85, assoc. prof. computer sci., 1985-90; prof. computer sci. NYU, N.Y.C., 1990—, dir. Ultracomputer Rsch. Lab., 1989—. Editorial mem. Cambridge Internat. Series on Parallel Computation, 1989; chmn. program com. 18th Ann. Symposium on Computer Architecture, 1992. Editor Jour. Parallel and Distbn. Computing, 1986—. Mem. IEEE Computer Soc., Assn. Computing Machinery, Am. Math. Soc., N.Y. Acad. Scis. Office: NYU Ultracomputer Rsch Lab 715 Broadway Fl 10 New York NY 10003-6860 Home: 4 Gunning Ln Gladwyne PA 19035-1135

GOTTLIEB, BEATRICE, historian; b. N.Y.C., June 6, 1925; d. Joseph and Anna (Slud) G. BA, Cornell U., 1945, MA, 1948, Columbia U., 1968, PhD, 1974. Copy chief Time Inc. (Sports Illustrated), N.Y.C., 1954-67; asst. prof. history Smith Coll., Northampton, Mass., 1976-77. Contbg. author: (book of essays): Family and Sexuality in French History, 1980, Women of the Medieval World, 1985; author: The Family in the Western World, 1994; translator: The Marquis of Keith, 1951, 62, The Problem of Unbelief in the 16th Century, 1982; contbr. dance revs. and essays to Dance Observer, Dance News, Kenyon Rev., Hudson Rev., Theatre Arts, 1948-54. NEH Translation grantee, 1979, 80. Mem. Am. Hist. Assn., Coordinating Coun. of Women in History, Berkshire Conf. of Women Historians, Soc. for Study of Women in the Renaissance. Home: 501 W 123rd St Apt 10H New York NY 10027-5057

GOTTLIEB, GARY L., hospital administrator; b. May 6, 1955; m. Derri Shtasel; 2 children. BS cum laude, Rensselaer Poly. Inst., 1975; MD, Albany Med. Coll., 1979; MBA Health Care Admin. with distinction, U. Pa., 1985. Diplomate in psychiatry and geriatric psychiatry Am. Bd. Psychiatry and Neurology; lic. physician, Pa., N.Y. Rotating intern NYU Med. Ctr., NYC, 1979-80, resident in psychiatry, 1980-82, chief resident in psychiatry, 1982-83; Robert Wood Johnson Found. clin. scholar U. Pa., Phila., 1983-85; from instr. to assoc. prof. dept. psychiatry U. Pa. Sch. Medicine, Phila., 1985-94, clin. prof. psychiatry, 1994—; assoc. dean for managed care U. Pa. Med. Ctr., Phila., 1992-94, interim chair dept. psychiatry, 1993-94; dir., CEO Friends Hosp., Phila., 1994—2002; prof. psychiatry Harvard Med. Sch., 1998—; pres. Brigham & Women's/Faulkner Hosp., 2002—. Ascher-Globus vis. prof., lectr. dept. psychiatry Cornell U. Sch. Medicine, N.Y.C., 1993. Mem. editorial bd. Internat. Jour. Geriatric Psychiatry, 1988—; asst. editor Am. Jour. Geriatric Psychiatry, 1992—; contbr. articles to profl. jours. Recipient Henry J. Kaiser prize Wharton Grad. Sch., U. Pa., 1985, Earl Bond award for teaching excellence U. Pa., 1989, Christian R. and Mary F. Lindback Found. award for Disting. Teaching, U. Pa., 1991. Mem. Am. Psychiat. Assn., Am. Geriatrics Soc., Am. Assn. Gen. Hosp. Psychiatrists, Alzheimer's Assn., Am. Assn. Geriatric Psychiatry (bd. dirs. 1987-90, pres. 1993-95), Assn. Acad. Psychiatry, Gerontol. Soc. Am., Pa. Psychiat. Soc., Phila. Psychiat. Soc., Soc. for Health and Human Values, Beta Gamma Sigma.

GOTTLIEB, GIDON ALAIN GUY, law educator; b. Paris, Dec. 9, 1932; m. Antoinette Rozoy Countess de Roussy de Sales, May 12, 1965. LLB with honors, London Sch. Econs., 1954, Cambridge (Eng.) U., 1956, diploma in comparative law, 1958; LLM, Harvard U., 1957, SJD, 1962. Bar: Called to bar Lincoln Inn, London 1958. Lectr. govt. Dartmouth Coll., 1960-61; assoc. firm Shearman & Sterling, N.Y.C., 1962-65; mem. faculty N.Y. U. Law Sch., 1965-76; Leo Spitz prof. internat. law and diplomacy emeritus U. Chgo. Law Sch., 1976—. UN rep. Amnesty Internat., 1966-72; mem. founding com. World Assembly Human Rights, 1968; adv. bd. Internat. League Rights of Man; disting. vis. fellow Hoover Instn., Stanford, Calif., 1991-94, 97—. Author: The Logic of Choice: An Investigation of the Concepts of Rule and Rationality, 1968, Nation Against State, 1993. Fellow N.Y. Coun. on Fgn. Rels. (sr. fellow, dir., Middle East Peace Project 1988-94); mem. Am. Soc. Internat. Law, Century Assn. (N.Y.C.). Office: U Chgo Law Sch 1111 E 60th St Chicago IL 60637-2776

GOTTLIEB, GILBERT, psychobiologist, educator; b. Bklyn., Oct. 22, 1929; s. Leo and Sylvia Sherman; m. Nora Lee Willis, Feb. 28, 1961; children: Jonathan Brian, David Herschel (dec.), Aaron Lee, Marc Sherman. AB, U. Miami, 1955, MS, 1956; PhD, Duke U., 1960. Clin. psychologist Dorothea Dix Hosp., Raleigh, N.C., 1959-61; rsch. scientist N.C. Divsn. Mental Health, Raleigh, 1961-82; head dept. psychology U. N.C., Greensboro, 1982-86, Excellence Found. prof., 1982-95, mem. faculty Carolina consortium human devel. Chapel Hill, 1988—; rsch. prof. psychology U. N.C. Ctr. Devel. Sci., Chapel Hill, 1995—. Guest Czechoslovak Acad. Scis., 1967, USSR Acad. Scis., 1989; advisor German NSF, 1977; U.S. del. Internat. Ethological Congress com., 1977-83; exec. com. Ctr. for Devel. Sci., U. N.C., 1993—; vis. lectr. Inst. Child Devel., U. Minn., 1975; vis. scholar Ctr. Interdisciplinary Rsch., U. Bielefeld, Germany, 1977; disting. vis. prof. psychology dept. U. Colo., Boulder, 1985; vis. fellow The Neuroscis. Inst., San Diego, 1996; disting. vis. lectr. dept. psychology U. Alta., 1996, Clark U., 1999; cons. in field. Author: Development of Species Identification in Birds, 1971, Individual Development and Evolution: The Genesis of Novel Behavior, 1992, reprinted, 2002, Synthesizing Nature-Nurture: Prenatal Roots of Instinctive Behavior, 1997 (Eleanor Maccoby Book award Am. Psychol. Assn., 1998), Probabilistic Epigenesis and Evolution, 1999; editor: Behavioral Embryology, 1973, Aspects of Neurogenesis, 1974, Neural and Behavioral Specificity, 1976, Early Influences, 1978, Measurement of Audition and Vision in the First Year of Postnatal Life, 1985; assoc. editor: Jour. Comparative and Physiol. Psychology, 1974—80. Recipient Disting. Sci. Contbn. award for child devel., Soc. Rsch. Child Devel., 1997, Eleanor Maccoby award devel. psychology divsn., APA, 1998; grantee, Nat. Inst. Child Health and Human Devel., 1963—84, 1989—95, NIMH, 1962—63, 1993—2003, NSF, 1963, 1985—88, 2001—. Fellow: AAAS; mem.: Animal Behavior Soc., Internat. Conf. Infant Studies, Internat. Soc. Devel. Psychobiology (pres. 1986—87). Home: 4908 Forestville Rd Raleigh NC 27616-9683 Office: U NC Ctr Devel Sci Chapel Hill NC 27599-8115

GOTTLIEB, JEFFREY PAUL, journalist; b. L.A., Oct. 15, 1953; s. Irvin Mathews and Zelda (Grossman) G. AB, Pitzer Coll., 1975; MS, Columbia U., 1980. Reporter Simi Valley (Calif.) Enterprise, 1979, Riverside (Calif.) Press-Enterprise, 1980-82; assoc. editor Ofcl. Olympic Souvenir Program, L.A., 1983-84; reporter L.A. Herald Examiner, 1985-88; staff writer/asst. city editor San Jose (Calif.) Mercury News, 1988-97, L.A. Times, 1997—. Mem. panel advisors George Polk Awards, Bklyn., 1992—. Contbr. articles to profl. jours. Recipient Spanish Lang. fellowship Nat. Press Club, 1982, George Polk award L.I. U., 1991. Mem. Investigative Reporters and Editors. Democrat. Jewish. Avocations: sports, music, movies, reading, bicycling. Home: 235 Belmont Ave Apt 7 Long Beach CA 90803-1521 Office: LA Times 1375 Sunflower Ave Costa Mesa CA 92626-1697 Office Phone: 714-966-7819. Business E-Mail: jeff.gottlieb@latimes.com.

GOTTLIEB, JERROLD HOWARD, advertising executive; b. N.Y.C., Aug. 25, 1946; s. Saul and Sylvia (Siegel) G.; m. June L. Brownstein, June 18, 1978; children: Steven Andrew, Melissa Eve. BA, Mich. State U., 1968; MBA, Am. U., 1969. Sales rep. Gen. Foods Corp., White Plains, NY, 1969-71, sr. product mgr., 1976-78; v.p., account mgr. J. Walter Thompson, N.Y.C., 1971-75, sr. v.p. N.Y. office, account dir., 1980-82, sr. v.p. U.S.A., mng. dir., 1982-84, sr. v.p. U.S.A., worldwide mng. dir., 1984-87, sr. v.p. worldwide, dir. account mgmt., 1987-90; v.p., account mgr. Batten, Barton, Durstein & Osborn, N.Y.C., 1978-80; exec. v.p. Backer Spielvogel Bates Inc., N.Y.C., 1991-92, exec. v.p., mng. dir. office of chmn., 1992-94; pres. Lane Gottlieb Advt., N.Y.C., 1994-96; chmn., CEO McCaffery Ratner Gottlieb & Lane LLC, N.Y.C., 1997—. Bd. dirs. Advt. Hall of Fame, N.Y.C., U.J.A. Fedn. N.Y. Founder Washington Saturday Coll., 1969; chmn. Am. U. campus, Washington, 1969; mem. adv. coun. ARC, Washington, 1981-86; vice chmn. mktg. UJA Fedn., N.Y.C., 1987-91, chmn., 1992-96, bd. dirs., 1994-2001. Mem.: Metropolis Club (bd. govs., v.p.). Home: 1095 Park Ave New York NY 10128-1154 Office: McCaffery Ratner Gottlieb & Lane 370 Lexington Ave New York NY 10017-6503

GOTTLIEB, JONATHAN W., lawyer; b. Washington, June 24, 1959; s. Julius Judah and Charlotte (Papernick) G.; m. Deborah Jo Levine, June 28, 1987; children: Maya Lane, Seth Joseph. BA with honors, DePaul U., 1982; student, Am. U., 1984-85; JD, N.Y. Law Sch., 1985. Bar: Pa. 1986, D.C. 1989, U.S. Ct. Appeals (D.C. cir.) 1990. Trial atty. Fed. Energy Regulatory Commn., Washington, 1987-88; assoc. Wickwire, Gavin & Gibbs, Washington, 1988-89, Ballard Spahr Andrews & Ingersoll, Washington, 1990-92, Reid & Priest, Washington, 1992-94, ptnr., 1995-98, Thelen Reid & Priest, Washington, 1998-99, Baker & McKenzie, Washington, 1999—. Chmn. legal affairs task force Nat. Hydropower Assn., 1992-95; counsel Mid-Atlantic Ind. Power Producers; gen. counsel Power Markets Devel. Co. (PPL Global), 1995-96; adv. bd. Bradley Energy Internat., 1997—; acting gen. counsel Packard Bell NEC, Inc., 1998. Contbg. editor Project Fin. Monthly; editor Competitive Utility, 1993—. Donor mem. Corning Mus. Glass. Mem. Fed. Energy Bar Assn., Pa. Bar Assn., D.C. Bar Assn., Southeastern Energy Soc. Republican. Avocations: glass collecting, stained glass making, gardening. Home: 9317 W Parkhill Dr Bethesda MD 20814-3966 E-mail: jonathan.w.gottlieb@bakernet.com.

GOTTLIEB, JULIUS JUDAH, podiatrist; b. Jersey City, May 27, 1919; s. Joseph Uziel and Gussie (Farber) G.; m. Charlotte Papernik, Oct. 18, 1942; children: Sheldon, Cynthia, Lorinda, David, Jonathan. Student, NYU, 1938-39, Ill. Coll. Podiatric Medicine, 1940-42; DPM, Ohio Coll. Podiatric Medicine, 1943. Diplomate Am. Podiatric Med. Specialties Bd. Pvt. practice podiatric medicine, Washington, 1943-92; pres. Chevy Chase Profl. Cons., 1993-96. Past cons. Army Footwear Clinic. Co-inventor fiberglass foot prosthetics and plastic shoe lasts. Podiatry dir. Greater Washington Hebrew Home for the Aged, 1963; pres. Franklin Knolls Citizens Assn., 1963, Ridgefield Citizens Inc., 1994-96, 97-2003; chmn. com. Nat. Capital Area coun. Boy Scouts Am., 1969-73; pres. Active Retirees of Kehilat Shalom, 1996-98. Recipient Shofar award Boy Scouts Am. Fellow Acad. Ambulatory Foot Surgeons (region 8 sci. chmn. 1987-88); mem. Am. Podiatric Med. Assn. (life), Am. Pub. Health Assn., Am. Podiatric Circulatory Soc., Am. Bd. Foot Surgeons (founding diplomate), D.C. Podiatric Med. Soc. (past pres.), Am. Assn. Foot Specialists (past pres., Foot Specialist of the Yr. 1973), Am. Assn. Individual Investors, Am. Physicians Fellowship Inc. for Medicine in Israel, Columbia Heights Bus. Men's Assn. (past pres., Man of Yr. 1964), Parents Assn. U. Md. (co v.p. parents fund 1980-81, co-recipient Outstanding Svc. Award), B'nai B'rith. Republican. Jewish. Home: 15812 Ancient Oak Dr Darnestown MD 20878-2110

GOTTLIEB, KATHERINE, health facility administrator; BA, Alaska Pacific U., 1990, MBA, 1995. Cmty. health aide, Seldovia, Alaska, 1987; pres., CEO Southcentral Found., Anchorage, 1987—. Named MacArthur Fellow, John D. and Catherine T. MacArthur Found., 2004. Achievements include development of over 75 medical, behavioral health and community programs that service Native Alaskans. Office: Southcentral Found 4501 Diplomacy Dr Anchorage AK 99508 Office Phone: 907-729-4955. Office Fax: 907-729-5000.*

GOTTLIEB, KRISTA, lawyer, arbitrator, mediator; b. Prague, Czechoslovakia, June 26, 1955; came to U.S., 1965; d. Paul and Krista (Podzimkova) G.; m. F. Joseph Coveney, Oct. 11, 1980; 1 child, David O. BA in Polit. Sci. cum laude, Barnard Coll., 1976; JD, Albany Law Sch., 1979. Bar: N.Y. 1980, U.S. Dist. Ct. (so., ea., we., no. dists.) N.Y. 1980, U.S. Ct. Appeals (2d cir.). Assoc. Fisher & Fisher, Bklyn., 1979-82, Reich, Rosen, Barrison & Felzen, N.Y.C., 1982-83, Moritt, Wolfeld & Resnick, Garden City, N.Y., 1983-85; ptnr. Mattar D'Agostino & Gottlieb, LLP, Buffalo, 1986—. Mem. mediation and arbitration panel BBB, AAA, Post Office, EEOC. Mem. NAFE, ABA, AAUW, Am. Arbitration Assn., Assn. Conflict Resolution, Women's Bar Assn., N.Y. State Bar Assn., Ask Women, Erie County Bar Assn. (co-chair ADR com.). Office: Mattar D'Agostino & Gottlieb LLP 17 Court St Ste 600 Buffalo NY 14202-3294 Office Phone: 716-856-4022.

GOTTLIEB, LEONARD SOLOMON, pathology educator; b. Boston, May 26, 1927; s. Julius and Jeanette (Miller) G.; m. Dorothy Helen Apt, Mar. 23, 1952; children: Julie Ann, William Apt, Andrew Richard. AB cum laude, Bowdoin Coll., 1946; MD, Tufts U., 1950; MPH, Harvard U., 1969. Diplomate Am. Bd. Anatomic Pathology. Intern in surgery Boston City Hosp., 1950-51, resident Mallory Inst. Pathology, 1951-55; assoc. pathologist Mallory Inst. Pathology, Boston, 1957-66, assoc. dir., 1966-72, dir., 1972—2003; asst. chief pathology U.S. Naval Hosp., Chelsea, Mass., 1955-57; chief pathology dept. Boston U. Med. Ctr. Hosp., 1973-96; prof. pathology Tufts U. Sch. Medicine, 1967—71; prof. pathology and lab. medicine Sch. Medicine Boston U., 1971—, chmn. dept., 1980—2003, chmn. emeritus, 2003—; dir. Mallory Inst. Pathology Found., 1980—2003; pathologist-in-chief divsn. pathology Boston City Hosp., 1994-96; pathologist-in-chief, divsn. pathology Boston Med. Ctr., 1996—2003. Lectr. Harvard Med. Sch., 1963-98; dir. student faculty exch. program Boston U. and Hebrew U., Hadassah Med. Sch., 1988—. Gen. editor Biopsy Pathology Series, Chapman and Hall, 1981-93, editor emeritus, 1993—; mem. editl. bd. Am. Jour. Surg. Pathology, 1981-2000, Judeo Med. Jour., 2002—; author or co-author approximately 180 publs. and abstracts and 14 book chpts. dealing primarily with exptl. and human diseases of the liver and gastrointestinal tract. Assoc. mem. bd. govs. Hebrew U. Jerusalem, 1991-95, mem. bd. govs., 1995—, mem. exec. com., 2001—; pres. New Eng. region Am. Friends of Hebrew U., 1989-97, 2000—, coun. trustees, 1992—, founder, 1991, trustee, 1994, guardian, 2000, mem. grants com., 1997—, mem. nat. bd. dirs., 2005—; mem. sci. adv. bd. Boston chpt. Israel Cancer Rsch. Fund, 1991-92; co-chair and chair Physicians divsn. Greater Boston chpt. State of Israel Bonds Cabinet, 1991-98; pres. Am. Physicians Fellowship for Medicine in Israel, 1990-93; class sec. 1977 Program for Health Sys. Mgmt., Harvard Bus. Sch., 1995-97. Lt. M.C. USNR, 1955-57, lt. comdr. res. ret. 1963. Recipient Stanley L. Robbins award for excellence in tchg. Boston U. Sch. Medicine Students, 1986, Jerusalem City of Peace award Boston chpt. State of Israel Bonds, 1992, Disting. Bowdoin Educator award, 1995, Torch of Learning award Am. Friends of The Hebrew U., 1997, Lion of Judah award State of Israel Bonds, 1998, Lifetime Achievement award The Hebrew U., 2000; named hon. mem. faculty medicine Hebrew U., 1987; James Bowdoin scholar, 1945, Bingham scholar, 1944-50; hon. fellow, Wall of Life, Hebrew U. Jerusalem, 2001. Mem. AAAS, Am. Soc. for Investigative Pathology, Am. Assn. for Study of Liver Diseases, U.S.-Can. Acad. Pathology, Coll. Am. Pathologists, Am. Soc. Cell Biology, Am. Gastroenterol. Assn., Am. Soc. for Clin. Pathology, Am. Coll. Physician Execs., Coll. Am. Pathologists, New Eng. Soc. Pathologists (pres. 1968-69), Mass. Med. Soc., Charles River Med. Soc., Assn. Pathology Chairs (Lifetime Achievement award 2003), N.Y. Acad. Sci., Chester S. Keefer Soc. (charter), Torch of Jerusalem Soc. (founding mem.), Am. Friends Hebrew U., Alpha Omega Alpha (faculty mem.). Office: Mallory Inst Pathology 784 Massachusetts Ave Boston MA 02118-4130 Office Phone: 617-638-4500. Business E-Mail: leonard.gottlieb@bmc.org.

GOTTLIEB, LESLIE, geneticist, educator; BA in English Lit., Cornell U., 1957; PhD in Botany, U. Mich., 1969. Prof. genetics dept. evolution and ecology U. Calif., Davis. Contbr. articles to profl. jours. Recipient Merit award Bot. Soc. Am., 2000. Achievements include research on molecular genetics and evolution of phosphoglucose isomerase in plants, particularly in the wildflower Clarkia; research on genetic basis for large morphological differences between closely related plant species and subspecies. Office: U Calif Davis 5310 Storer Hall One Sheilds Ave Davis CA 95616 E-mail: ldgottlieb@ucdavis.edu.

GOTTLIEB, LESTER M., entrepreneur; b. NYC, May 3, 1932; s. Samuel and Eva (Schoenfeld) G.; children: Cynthia, Curtis, Mark, Alyssa, Adine. BA, CCNY, 1954; postgrad., NYU, 1956. With IBM, 1956-69, mgr. bus. planning for systems devel. div., 1967-69; pres. Data Dimensions, Inc., 1969-84, vice chmn., 1984-90; pres. CAMAC Securities, Ltd., Greenwich, Conn., 1981-91, also chmn. bd. dirs., 1991—; pres. CAMAC Equities, Ltd., 1981—. Chmn. bd. dirs. Drain King, LLC, New Rochelle, NY, Elite Health, Peekskill, NY; adj. asst. prof. econs. U. Bridgeport; lectr. Assn. Computing Machinery; bd. dirs. Ctr. for Internat. Mgmt. Studies. Nat. Bd. YMCA's, 1972-90, Greater N.Y. YMCA; bd. dirs., treas. City Coll. Fund, 1990, v.p., 1996-99. With AUS, 1954-56. Recipient Leo Klauber award, Mark Asa Abbott award; named Vol. of Yr. Greater N.Y. YMCA, 1994. Mem. Am. Arbitration Assn. (comml. arbitrator 1981—), CCNY Alumni Assn. (bd. dirs. 1983, pres. alumni varsity assn. 1987-88, Alumni Svc. award, Athletic Hall of Fame). Republican. Home: 10 Stewart Pl Apt 7 BE White Plains NY 10603

GOTTLIEB, MARISE SUSS, epidemiologist, physician; b. N.Y.C., July 16, 1938; d. Lester J. and Fannie (Freeman) Suss; m. A. Arthur Gottlieb, June 8, 1958; children: Mindy Cheryl Davidson, Joanne Meredith. AB, Barnard Coll., 1958; MD, NYU, 1962; MPH, Harvard U., 1966. Intern, Mass. Meml. Hosp., 1962-63; resident preventative medicine dept. epidemiology Harvard U. Med. Sch., 1965-68, instr. dept. medicine, H.M., Boston, 1969-70, also fellow, asst. in Medicine Peter Bent Brigham Hosp.; dir. chronic disease control N.J. Dept. Health, Trenton, 1970-75; asst. prof. dept. community medicine Rutgers Med. Sch., Piscataway N.J., 1972-75; assoc. prof. dept. medicine Tulane U. Sch. Medicine, New Orleans, 1975-91; assoc. prof. dept. epidemiology Sch. Pub. Health, 1975-80; chief chronic disease control, La. Dept. Health and Human Resources, New Orleans, 1975-85; dir. clin. and regulatory affairs, v.p. med. affairs Imreg Inc., New Orleans, 1985-98; sec. treas. Pres. Endeaver Corp., 1998—; mem. epidemiology and disease control study sect. NIH, Bethesda, Md., 1982-85. NIH traineeship, 1965-66, spl research fellow Nat. Inst. Arthritis, Metabolism and Digestive Diseases, 1966-68. Diplomate Am. Bd. Preventive Medicine. Fellow Am. Coll. Preventive Medicine, Am. Coll. Epidemiology; mem. Am. Diabetes Assn., Soc. Epidemiol. Rsch., Am. Fedn. Med. Rsch., Am. Pub. Health Assn. Contbr. articles to profl jours Home: 215 Chestnut Hill Rd Chestnut Hill MA 02467-1313 Business E-Mail: marsgott@massmed.org.

GOTTLIEB, MICHAEL NORMAN, internist, educator, health facility administrator; b. Bklyn., July 26, 1943; s. Louis and Grace Gottlieb; m. Anne A. Appelman, Dec. 25, 1965; children: Brian, Elizabeth. BA, SUNY, Binghamton, 1964; MD, SUNY, Bklyn., 1968. Diplomate Am. Bd. Internal Medicine. Intern Univ. Hosp. U. Calif., San Diego, 1968-69, resident Univ Hosp., 1969-71, clin. fellow in nephrology, 1971-72, 1971-72; rsch. fellow in medicine Harvard Med. Sch., Boston, 1972-73; spl. fellow Peter Bent Brigham Hosp. NIH, Boston, 1972-73; instr. in medicine Peter Bent Brigham Hosp., Harvard Med. Sch., Boston, 1974-77; asst. clin. prof. medicine Harvard Med. Sch., Boston, 1976—; ptnr. Commonwealth Nephrology Assn., Boston, 1977—; assoc. chair dept. medicine Metrowest Med. Ctr., Framingham, Mass., 1992-95, chief med. officer, 1995—. Assoc. in medicine Peter Bent Brigham Hosp., Boston, 1975—82; med. dir. West Suburban Artificial Kidney Ctr., Framingham, Mass., 1980—, The Kidney Ctr., Boston, 2001—, MetroWest Artificial Kidney Ctr., Waltham, Mass., 1990—, active staff, 1992—; assoc. physician Brigham and Women's Hosp., Boston, 1982—; courtesy staff Norwood (Mass.) Hosp., 1994—; bd. dirs. End Stage Renal Disease Network #1. Contbr. to med. textbooks, numerous articles to profl. jours. Mem. AMA, ACP, Am. Soc. Nephrology, Am. Soc. Artificial Internal Organs, Mass. Med. Soc., Am. Soc. Enteral and Parenteral Nutrition, Am. Coll. Physician Execs., Internat. Soc. Artificial Organs. Avocations: boating, sailing. Office: Metrowest Med Ctr 67 Union St Natick MA 01760-6056 E-mail: michael.gottlieb@tenethealth.com.

GOTTLIEB, PAUL MITCHEL, corporate financial executive; b. N.Y.C., Mar. 30, 1954; s. Henry Gottlieb and Thelma Ethel (Friedman) Miller; m. Helene Manya Roiter, Apr. 3, 1982; children: Jordan Seth, Zachary Michael. BA, Hobart Coll., 1976; JD, MBA, Washington U., St. Louis, 1980. Bar: Ill. 1980, U.S. Dist. Ct. (no. dist. Ill.) 1980, N.Y. 1988; lic. securities series 7, 9, 10, 24 2002. Assoc. Rudnick & Wolfe, Chgo., 1980-81; ind. trader Chgo. Bd. of Trade, 1981—82; staff atty. Chgo. Merc. Exch., 1983-84, v.p. market regulation, 1984—87; commodity counsel Morgan Stanley and Co. Inc., N.Y.C., 1987-89; spl. counsel commodities, futures and derivative products Skadden, Arps, Slate, Meagher & Flom, N.Y.C., 1989-92; ptnr., chair derivative products practice group Seward & Kissel, N.Y.C., 1992-96; dir., sr. counsel structured products & commodities Union Bank of Switzerland, N.Y.C., 1996-98; sr. v.p., dep. gen. counsel PaineWebber Inc., N.Y.C., 1998—2000; exec. dir. UBS Warburg LLC, N.Y.C., 2000-01; mng. dir., COO RBC Capital Mkts. Corp., NYC, 2001—; sr. v.p. Royal Bank of Can., 2001—. Contbr. chpts. to books, articles to profl. jours. Mem.: Securities Industry Assn. (law and compliance divsn.), Chgo. Bd. Trade, Chgo. Mercantile Exch., N.Y. Stock Exch. Jewish. Avocations: coaching youth hockey and lacrosse, golf, skiing. Home: 11 Highpoint Pl West Windsor NJ 08550-5238 Office: RBC Capital Markets Corp 1 Liberty Plz 165 Broadway New York NY 10006-1404

GOTTLIEB, ROBERT, publishing executive; b. NYC; BA, Elmira Coll., NY, 1976. Agent-in-training William Morris Agy., NYC, 1976—77, dept. asst., literary dept., 1977—82, literary agent, 1982—89, sr. v.p., 1989—92, exec. v.p., bd. dir., 1992—2000; co-founder, chmn. Trident Media Group, NYC, 2000—. Exec. coun. The Quills. Office: Trident Media Group LLC Fl 36 41 Madison Ave New York NY 10010 Office Phone: 212-333-1500. Office Fax: 212-262-4849. Business E-Mail: gottlieb.assistant@tridentmediagroup.com.*

GOTTLIEB, ROBERT ADAMS, dance critic, writer; b. N.Y.C., Apr. 29, 1931; s. Charles and Martha (Keen) G.; m. Maria Tucci, Apr. 26, 1969; children— Roger, Elizabeth, Nicholas. BA, Columbia U., 1952; postgrad., Cambridge (Eng.) U., 1952-54. Editor-in-chief, v.p. Simon & Schuster, 1955-68; editor-in-chief Alfred A Knopf, Inc., N.Y.C., 1968-87, exec. v.p., 1968-73, pres., 1973-87; editor New Yorker mag., 1987-92. Author: Reading Jazz, 1996, George Balanchine: The Ballet Maker, 2004; co-author: Reading Lyrics, 2000; dance critic N.Y. Observer. Mem. Phi Beta Kappa.

GOTTLIEB, ROBERT GENE, lawyer; b. Newark, May 13, 1951; BA cum laude, Penn. State U., 1973; JD with honors, George Washington U., 1976. Bar: Va. 1976, DC 1978. Ptnr., real estate & taxation Venable LLP, Washington. Adjunct prof. George Washington U., 1985—95, Georgetown U., 1990—. Mem.: ABA (mem. tax section), Am. Coll. Real Estate Lawyers, Va. Bar Assn., DC Bar Assn. Office: Venable LLP 575 7th St NW Washington DC 20004 Office Phone: 202-344-8526. Office Fax: 202-344-8300. Business E-Mail: rggottlieb@venable.com.

GOTTLIEB, ROBERT W., lawyer; b. NYC, Jan. 28, 1942; BA cum laude, Alfred U., 1963; LLB magna cum laude, Columbia U., 1966. Bar: NY 1967, US Ct. Appeals, 2nd Cir., US Dist. Ct., Ea. and So. Dist. NY, US Supreme Ct. Ptnr. Katten Muchin Zavis Rosenman, NYC. Office: Katten Muchin Zavis Rosenman 575 Madison Ave New York NY 10022 Office Phone: 212-940-7090. Office Fax: 212-935-8405. E-mail: robert.gottlieb@kmzr.com.

GOTTO, ANTONIO MARION, JR., internist, educator; b. Nashville, Tenn., Oct. 10, 1935; s. Antonio M. and Reather (Gray) Gotto; m. Anita Louise Safford, July 21, 1959; children: Jennifer, Gillian, Teresa. BA magna cum laude, Vanderbilt U., 1957, MD, 1965; DPhil, Oxford (Eng.) U., 1961; LLD (hon.), Abilene Christian U., 1979; MD (hon.), U. Bologna, 1982. Diplomate Am. Bd. Internal Medicine. Intern Mass. Gen. Hosp., Boston, 1965—66, resident, 1966—67; practice medicine specializing in internal medicine, 1967—; head molecular disease br. Nat. Heart and Lung Inst. NIH, Bethesda, Md., 1969—71; dir. and prin. investigator Lipid Rsch. Clinic, Houston, 1971—77; prof. medicine, chief dir., arteriosclerosis and lipoprotein rsch. Baylor Coll. Medicine, Houston, 1971—96; dir., prin. investigator specialized ctr. rsch. in arteriosclerosis Nat. Heart, Lung and Blood Inst., 1971—96, dir., prin. investigator Spl. Ctr. Rsch. Arteriosclerosis, 1971—96; J.S. Abercrombie prof. Baylor Coll. Medicine, 1976—96, Disting. Svc. prof., 1985—96; sci. dir. Meth. Hosp. and Baylor Nat. Rsch. and Demonstration Ctr., 1974—83, 1987—90; Bob and Vivian Smith prof. and chmn. dept. medicine Baylor Coll. Medicine, 1977—96; chief internal medicine svcs. The Meth. Hosp., 1977—96; dean Weill Med. Coll., Cornell U., 1997—; provost med. affairs Cornell U., 1997—. Hon. guest lectr. various med. socs., schs. and hosps., 1972—; mem. nat. diabetes adv. bd. HEW (now HHS), 1977—84; mem. steering com. Italian-Am. com. on cardiovascular disease NIH, 1978—; mem. adv. coun. Nat. Heart, Lung and Blood Inst., 1987—91; hon. prof. U. Buenos Aires, 1985. Author (with Michael E. DeBakey): The Living Heart, 1977; author: The Living Heart Diet, 1984, The New Living Heart Diet, 1996, The New Living Heart, 1997; editor: Current Atherosclerosis Reports, 1998—, Current Practice of Medicine, 1999—; co-editor: Atherosclerosis Rev. Series, 1976—92, Jour. Cardiovasc. Risk, 1994—; mem. editl. bd.: Jour. Biol. Chemistry, 1976—81, Advanced in Lipid Rsch., 1973—78, Am. Heart Jour., 1981—, Arteriosclerosis, 1981—89, Circulation Rsch., 1974—79, Cardiovascular Rsch. Ctr. Bull., 1972—; contbr. articles on biochem. and cardiovascular rsch. to profl. publs. Mem. sci. adv. bd. Fondation Cardiologique Princesse Liliane, Brussels, 1976—, Lorenzini Found., Milan, Fritz Thyssen Found., Cologne, Germany; mem. Mission of Houston Econ. Devel. Coun., 1985; walkathon chmn. Juvenile Diabetes Found., 1986. With USPHS, 1967—69. Decorated knight Order of Merit, Italy, Order of the Lion Finland; named hon. cons., Adm. Bristol Hosp., Istanbul, Turkey, Houston Internat. Exec. Yr., 1987; recipient Albert Weinstein award, 1965, Laurea ad Honorem, U. Bologna, Seale Harris award, So. Med. Assn., 1995; grantee, John A. Hartford Found., 1971—75. Fellow: Am. Coll. Cardiology; mem.: Am. Longevity Assn., Am. Assn. Rhodes Scholars, Am. Bd. Internal Medicine, Am. Heart Assn. (pres. 1983—84, past pres. 1984—86, Paul Ledbetter award for disting. svc., Paul Dudley White award for outstanding contbns., Gold Heart award 1989), Am. Diabetes Assn., Am. Soc. Biol. Chemists, Am. Assn. Physicians, Internat. Soc. Atherosclerosis (pres. 1985—, Achievement award 1982), So. Soc. Clin. Investigation, Am. Soc. Clin. Investigation (v.p. 1980—81), Inst. Medicine of NAS, River Oaks Country Club, Alpha Omega Alpha. Presbyterian. Home: 435 E 70th St Apt 31 J K New York NY 10021-5351 Office: Weill Med Cornell U 1300 York Ave Rm F 105 New York NY 10021-4805 Office Phone: 212-746-6005. Business E-Mail: dean@med.cornell.edu.

GOTTRY, STEVEN ROGER, communications executive, scriptwriter; b. Mpls., Dec. 7, 1946; s. Roger Eugene and Helen Viola (Johnson) G.; m. Joanne Moritz (div. Nov. 1983); children: Jonathan, Michelle; m. Karla Mae Styer, Nov. 7, 1984; 1 child, Kalla Paige. BA in Advt. and Radio-TV Prodn., U. Minn., 1970. With promotion dept. Sta. WCCO-TV, Mpls., 1967-69; pres. Visual Communications, Inc., Mpls., 1970-87, The Gottry Comm. Group, Inc., Bloomington, Minn., 1987-96; pub. Priority Multimedia Group, Mesa, Ariz., 1995—. Writer in residence Grand Canyon U., Phoenix. Co-author: The Spirit of Tocayo, 1995, Options, 1996, The Screenwriter's Story Planning Guide, 1999, (with Ken Blanchard) The On-Time, On-Target Manager, 2004, (with Linda Jensvold Bauer) A Kick in the Career, 2005, Author: Common Sense Business, 2005; several scripts for cable TV movies; collaborator with Dr. Ken Blanchard on numerous book projects; contbr. articles to mags. amd newspapers. Recipient Internat. Advt. Festival N.Y. award, 1988, three Silver Microphone Nat. Radio awards, 1990, Internat. Travel Competition award, 1991. Mem. Rotary (bd. dirs., named New Rotarian of Yr. 1990). Avocations: boating, camping, biking, aviation. Office: 2339 W Lomita Cir Mesa AZ 85202-6458 Personal E-mail: gottry@mac.com.

GOTTS, ILENE KNABLE, lawyer; b. Phila., Nov. 25, 1959; d. Harry Lee and Ethel Beatrice (Teitelman) Knable; m. Michael D. Gotts, May 25, 1986; children: Isaac, Samuel. BA magna cum laude with hon., U. Md., 1980; JD cum laude, Georgetown U., 1984. Bar: D.C. 1984, N.Y., 1997, U.S. Dist. Ct. D.C. 1986, U.S. Ct. Appeals (D.C. cir.) 1985, U.S. Dist. Ct. Md. 1987, U.S. Ct. Appeals (fed. cir.) 1989, U.S. Supreme Ct. 1988. Staff atty. FTC, 1984-86; assoc. Foley & Lardner, Washington, 1986-92, ptnr., head legis./adminstrv. group, antitrust practice group, 1992-96; ptnr. Wachtell, Lipton, Rosen & Katz, N.Y.C., 1996—. Adj. prof. George Washington U. Law Ctr., 1995-96; bd. trustees U. Md. Found., 2003—, Nat. Law Alumni Bd., Georgetown U. Law Ctr. Mem. editl. bd. Practical Lawyer, 1994-2004, Antitrust Counselor, 1995—; mem. adv. bd. Antitrust Trade and Regulatory Report, 2003-; contbr. articles to profl. jours. Mem. legal adv. bd. Momentum, 2001—. Recipient Sklar award U. Md., 1980; Mary Elizabeth Robey scholar. Mem.: NOW (legal momentum adv. bd. 2001—), FBA (chair health care com. of antitrust sect. 1991—95, chair antitrust and trade regulation sec. 1995—97), ABA (antitrust sect. 1988—, consumer protection com. 1994—96, vice chair intellectual property com. 1994—97, vice chair Clayton Act com. 1997—98, chair 1998—2001, chair merger rev. task force 1998—2003, coun. 2001—04, program officer 2004—05, internat. officer 2005—, editor The Merger Rev. Process, 2d edit.), Internat. Bar Assn., N.Y. Women's Bar Assn., N.Y. State Bar Assn. (exec. com. antitrust law sect. 2000—, sec. 2003—04, vice-chair 2004—), Washington Coun. Lawyers (exec. com. and bd. dirs. 1988—97, pres. 1994—95), Am. Law Inst., D.C. Bar (steering com., antitrust and trade regulation com. 1994—95), Phi Beta Kappa, Mortar Board, Phi Alpha Theta, Pi Sigma Alpha, Phi Kappa Phi. Democrat. Jewish. Office: Wachtell Lipton Rosen & Katz 51 W 52d St New York NY 10019 Office Phone: 212-403-1247. Business E-Mail: ikgotts@wlrk.com.

GOTTS, LAWRENCE J., lawyer; b. Washington, Apr. 18, 1958; BS summa cum laude, Univ. Md., 1980; JD with high honors, George Washington Univ., 1985. Bar: Va. 1985, DC 1989, US Patent & Trademark Office, US Ct. Appeals (Fed. cir.). Patent examiner US Patent & Trademark Office, 1981—83; ptnr., chmn. Litigation group Pillsbury Winthrop Shaw Pittman, McLean, Va. Mem.: Am. Intellectual Property Law Assn., Am. Soc. Mech. Engineers, Order of the Coif. Office: Pillsbury Winthrop Shaw Pittman 1650 Tysons Blvd Mc Lean VA 22102-4859 Office Phone: 703-770-7604. Office Fax: 703-770-7901. Business E-Mail: larry.gotts@pillsburylaw.com.

GOTTSCHALK, ALEXANDER, radiologist, educator; b. Chgo., Mar. 23, 1932; s. Louis R. and Fruma (Kasden) G.; m. Jane Rosenbloom, Aug. 13, 1960; children: Rand, Karen, Amy. BA magna cum laude, Harvard U., 1954; MD, Washington U., St. Louis, 1958. Diplomate: Am. Bd. Radiology, Am. Bd. Nuclear Medicine. Intern U. Ill. Research and Edn. Hosps., Chgo., 1958-59; resident U. Chgo., 1959-62, asst. prof., 1964-66, assoc. prof., 1966-68, prof. radiology, 1968-74, chmn. dept. radiology, 1971-72; research assoc. Donner Lab., Lawrence Radiol. Lab., Calif., 1962-64; dir. Frinklin McLean Meml. Research Hosp., 1967-74; prof. and dir. nuclear medicine Sch. Medicine Yale U., New Haven, 1974-77, acting chmn. radiology, 1980-81, vice-chmn. radiology, 1977-89; prof. radiology Mich. State U., East Lansing, 1990—. Contbr. chpts. to books, articles to publs. in field. Fleischner lectr., 1983 Fellow Am. Coll. Radiology, Am. Coll. Chest Physicians; mem. Radiol. Soc. N.Am. (2d v.p. 1977, Gold medal 2004), Assn. Univ. Radiologists (pres. 1971, Gold medal 1987), Soc. Nuclear Medicine (pres. 1974-75), Am. Roentgen Ray Soc., Fleischner Soc. (treas. 1978-83, pres. 1989-90), Phi Beta Kappa, Alpha Omega Alpha. Home: 4246 Van Atta Rd Okemos MI 48864-3137 Office: Radiology Bldg Rm 120 Mich State U East Lansing MI 48824-1303 Business E-Mail: alg@rad.msu.edu.

GOTTSCHALK, ALFRED, retired academic administrator, museum administrator; b. Oberwesel, Germany, Mar. 7, 1930; came to U.S., 1939, naturalized, 1945; s. Max and Erna (Trum-Gerson) G.; m. Deanna Zeff, 1977; children by previous marriage: Marc Hillel, Rachel Lisa. AB, Bklyn. Coll., 1952; MA with honors, Hebrew Union Coll.-Jewish Inst. Religion, 1957; PhD, U. So. Calif., 1965, STD (hon.), 1968, LLD (hon.), 1976, U. Cin., 1976, Xavier U., 1981, Mt. St. Joseph Coll., 1995, No. Ky. U., 1996; DHL (hon.), U. Judaism, 1971, Jewish Theol. Sem., 1986, Bklyn. Coll., 1991, Trinity Coll., 1996; LittD (hon.), Dropsie U., 1974, St. Thomas Inst., 1982; D Religious Edn. (hon.), Loyola-Marymount U., 1977; DD (hon.), NYU, 1985. Ordained rabbi, 1957. Dir. Hebrew Union Coll., Jewish Inst. Religion, L.A., 1957-59, dean, 1959-71, prof. Bible and Jewish intellectual history, 1965—, pres., 1971-95, chancellor, 1996—2000, chancellor emeritus, disting. prof. emeritus of Jewish Intellectual History, 1995—; pres. Mus. of Jewish Heritage, N.Y.C., 1999—2001; sr. fellow Mus. Jewish Heritage, 2001—. Hon. fellow Hebrew U., Jerusalem, 1972, Oxford Ctr. for Hebrew and Jewish Studies, 1994. Author: Your Future as a Rabbi-A Calling that Counts, 1967, (translator) Hesed in the Bible, 1967, The Man Must be the Message, 1968, Jewish Ecumenism and Jewish Survival, 1968, Ahad Ha-Am, Maimonides and Spinoza, 1969, Ahad Ha-Am as Bible Critic, 1971, A Jubilee of the Spirit, 1972, Israel and the Diaspora: A New Look, 1974, Limits of Ecumenicity, 1979, Israel and Reform Judaism: A Zionist Perspective, 1979, Ahad Ha-Am and Leopold Zunz: Two Perspectives on the Wissenschaft Des Judentums, 1980, Hebrew Union College and Its Impact on World Progressive Judaism, 1980, Diaspora Zionism: Achievements and Problems, 1980, What Ecumenism Means to a Jew, 1981, Introduction: Religion in a Post-Holocaust World, 1982, Problematics in the Future of American Jewish Community, 1982, Introduction to the American Synagogue in the Nineteenth Century, 1982, A Strategy for Non-Orthodox Judaism in Israel, 1982, Our problems and Our Future: Jews and America, 1983, From the Kingdom of Night to the Kingdom of God: Jewish Christian Relations and the Search for Religious Authenticity after the Holocaust, 1983, The Making of a Contemporary Reform Rabbi, 1984, Is Yom Kippur Obsolete?, 1985, Ahad Ha-am: Confronting the Plight of Judaism, 1987, To Learn and To Teach, Your Future as a Rabbi, 1988, Preface to Gezer V: The Field I Caves, 1988, The American Reform Rabbinate Retrospect and Prospect, A Personal View, 1988, The German Pogrom of November 1938 and the Reaction of American Jewry, 1988, Building Unity in Diversity 1989, Ahad Ha'am and the Jewish National Spirit (Hebrew), 1992; contbr. to Studies in Jewish Bibliography, History, and Literature, 1971, The Yom Kippur War: Israel and the Jewish People, 1974, The Image of Man in Genesis and the Ancient Near East, 1976, The Public Function of the Jewish Scholar, 1978, The Reform Movement and Israel: A New Perspective, 1978, The Use of Reason in Maimonides--An Evaluation by Ahad Ha-Am, 1993, Reform Judaism of the New Millenium: A Challenge, 2001, Israel and America: Beyond Survival and Philanthropy, 2000, Life of Reason, Ahad Ha-Am and Her Work, 2003; also numerous articles to profl. jours. Mem. Pres. Johnson's Com. on EEO, 1964-66, Gov.'s Poverty Support Corps Program, 1964-66, Pres.'s Commn. on Holocaust, 1979, U.S. Holocaust Meml. Coun., 1980-92, 96-01 (exec. com., 1980-87, 96—, chmn. edn. com., 1986-88, chmn. acad. com., 1988-96, com. on conscience, 1996—); chmn. N.Am. Assoc. Internat. Ctr. Univ. Teaching of Jewish Civilization, 1982-93; bd. trustees Am. Sch. Oriental Rsch., Albright Inst. Archaeol. Rsch., 1972-95; sr. fellow Mus. of Jewish Heritage, N.Y.C., 2001—; bd. govs. Oxford Ctr. for Hebrew and Jewish Studies, 1995—; bd. trustees Mus. Jewish Heritage, N.Y.C., 2001-; exec. com. Nat. Underground Railroad Freedom Ctr., 1997-2000, Nat. Adv. Bd., Nat. Underground Freedom Ctr., 1996—; mem. coun. World Union Jewish Studies, 1997. Recipient award for contbns. to edn. L.A. City Coun., 1971, Human Relations award Am. Jewish Com., 1971, Tower of David award for cultural contbn. to Israel and Am., 1972, Gold medallion Jewish Nat. Fund, 1972, Alumnus of Yr. award Bklyn. Coll., 1972, Myrtle Wreath award Hadassah, 1977, Brandeis award Z.O.A., 1977, Nat. Brotherhood award NCCJ, 1979, Alfred Gottschalk Chair in Communal Svc. HUC, 1979, Jerusalem City of Peace award 1988, Defender of Jerusalem award honoree, 1990, Isaac M. Wise award, 1991, Heritage award Jewish Club of 1933, 1991, Nat. award NCCJ, 1994, Shanghai Acad. Social Scis. award, 1994, others, Xavier Medallion, Xavier U., 1996, Elie Wiesel Holocaust Rememerance award, State of Israel bonds, 2001; grantee State Dept./Smithsonian Instn., 1963, 67.; honoree Assn. Hebrew Union Coll., 1996; recipient Award Svc. to City, Cin. City Council, 2001. Mem. AAUP, NEA, Union Am. Hebrew Congregations and Ctrl. Conf. Am. Rabbis (exec. com., bd. govs. Hebrew Union Coll.), Soc. Study Religion, Am. Acad.

Religion, Soc. Bibl. Lit. and Exegesis, Internat. Conf. Jewish Communal Svc., Israel Exploration Soc., So. Calif. Assn. Liberal Rabbis (past pres.), So. Calif. Jewish Hist. Soc. (hon. pres.), World Union Jewish Studies (internat. coun.), World Union Progressive Judaism (gov. bd.), Coun. for Initiatives in Jewish Edn. (bd. dirs.). Office: Hebrew Union Coll Jewish Inst of Religion One W 4th St New York NY 10012-1186 Office Phone: 212-674-5300. *I value the need for the individual to feel unique and for the collective to remain hospitable to diversity. I believe in unity without uniformity and in humanity's capacity to redeem himself.*

GOTTSCHALK, ALLAN, anesthesiologist, educator, neuroscientist; b. Amityville, N.Y., May 16, 1956; s. Carl and Sally (Sikorski) G.; m. Barbara Bulik, Aug. 25, 1983; children: Lindsey, Laura Michelle, Chelsea Lynn. BS summa cum laude in Biomed. Engring., Boston U., 1978; MS in Sys. Engring., U. Pa., 1983, MS in Biomed. Engring., MD, 1984, PhD in Anatomy, 1992. Diplomate Am. Bd. Anesthesiology. Intern dept. medicine Presbyn. Hosp., Phila., 1984-85; resident dept. anesthesia U. Pa., Phila., 1985-87, fellow dept. anesthesia, 1988-89, instr. dept. anesthesia, 1988-90, asst. prof. dept. anesthesia, mem. Vision Ctr., 1990—. Mem. Inst. Neurol. Sci., U. Pa., 1994—; mem. Ctr. for Sleep and Respiratory Neurobiology, 1991—. Contbr. articles to Procs. Royal Soc., Archives Gen. Psychiatry, Am. Jour. Physiology, Neural Computation, Jour. AMA. Harold C. Case scholar Boston U., 1977; grantee Optimal Image Rep., 1993. Mem. IEEE, AAAS, ASTM, Internat. Anesthesia Rsch. Soc., Am. Soc. Anesthesiologists, Tau Beta Pi. Achievements include demonstration that many aspects of early visual processing can be explained in terms of well-established principles of information theory, and a clear demonstration that intraoperative anesthetic technique can have a long-term beneficial effect on postoperative pain and recovery of function. Office: Hosp Univ Pa Dept Anesthesia 3400 Spruce St Philadelphia PA 19104-4206 E-mail: ag@mail.med.upenn.edu.

GOTTSCHALK, FRANK KLAUS, real estate company executive; b. Berlin, Jan. 25, 1932; came to U.S. 1947, naturalized 1953; s. Richard and Grete Johanna (Singer) G.; m. Ellen Ruth Meinhardt, June 16, 1957. Student N.Y. Inst. Banking & Fin., N.Y.C., 1952-53, NYU, 1955-56. Lic. comml. real estate broker. Trainee, investment securities Newborg & Co. mem. N.Y. Stock Exchange, N.Y.C., 1951-52; fin. analyst Bendix Luitweiler & Co. Investment Bankers, N.Y.C., 1952-53; assoc. broker, v.p., dir. Peter F. Pasbjerg & Co., Inc., Mortgage Bankers, Newark, N.J., 1955-62; v.p., dir. Baldwin Bros., Inc. Real Estate Investors, Erie, Pa., 1962—; pres., treas., dir. The Baldwin-Gottschalk Group, Investment Real Estate, asset. mgmt. cons., Erie, Pa., Charleston, W.Va., 1994—; pres. Baldwin-Gottschalk, Inc. Real Estate and Mortgage Financing, N.Y.C., Erie, Charleston, 1962—; pres., treas., dir. Baldwin Gottschalk Properties, Erie, 1967—, Balgot Realty Corp., Erie, 1963—, Balgot Bldg. Corp., Erie, 1967—; pres. The Kanawha Realty Investment Group, Investment Real Estate, Charleston, Erie, 1990—; pres., treas., dir. Kanawha Realty & Devel. Corp., Charleston, 1959—, Associated Properties Holdings, Inc., Charleston, 1962—; pres. Assoc. Properties Holdings Pension Trust, Charleston, W. Va., 1982—; pres., dir. APH Securities, Charleston, W. Va., 1990—; trustee Assoc. Properties Holding Retirement Trust, Charleston, 1982—; mng. ptnr. Kanawha-Monarch Holdings, Erie, 1980—, Balgot-Kanawha Holdings, Erie, Pa., 1994—. Trustee, Erie Philharm., 1971-90; corporator Gannon U., 1980—. Served with U.S. Army, 1953-55, ETO. Mem. Internat. Real Estate Inst., Erie Club, Aviation Country Club Erie, Mizner Country Club, Delray Beach, Fla. Office: Baldwin Gottschalk Inc 5 W 10th St Erie PA 16501-1492

GOTTSCHALK, SISTER MARY THERESE, nun, hospital administrator; b. Doellwang, Germany, June 21, 1931; arrived in U.S., 1953, naturalized, 1959; d. John and Sabina (Dietz) G. BS in Pharmacy, Creighton U., 1960; M.H.A., St. Louis U., 1970; DHL (hon.), U. Okla., 2001. Joined Sisters of the Sorrowful Mother, Roman Catholic Ch, 1952. Dir. pharmacy St. Mary's Hosp., Roswell, N.Mex., 1960-68, chief exec. officer, 1972-74; asst. adminstr. St. John Med. Ctr., Tulsa, 1970-72, pres., CEO, 1974-99, St. John Health Sys., Tulsa, 1982—; pres. Marian Health Sys., Tulsa, 1989—. Vol. ARC, United Way. Fellow: Am. Coll. Hosp. Adminstrs.; mem.: Cath. Health Assn. (bd. dirs. 1995—2001), Tulsa C. of C., Okla. Conf. Cath. Hosps. (past pres.), Tulsa Hosp. Coun., Okla. Hosp. Assn. (pres. 1984), Am. Hosp. Assn. (ho. of dels., regional policy bd., governing coun.). Office: St John Med Ctr 1923 S Utica Ave Tulsa OK 74104-6502

GOTTSCHALK, STEPHEN ELMER, lawyer; b. Rochester, Minn., Oct. 9, 1947; s. Elmer H. and Ruth F. (Thurley) G.; m. Lorilyn J. Dopp, Feb. 14, 1970; children: Andrew Stephen, Stephanie Beth, Lorissa Christine, Michael Donald. BS, Valparaiso U., 1969, JD, 1972. Bar: Minn. 1972, U.S. Dist. Ct. (Minn.) 1972. Jud. clk. Minn. Supreme Ct., St. Paul, 1972-73; assoc. Dorsey & Whitney, Minn., 1973-78, ptnr., 1979—, co-chmn., employee benefits dept., 1986-91, 98—. Adj. prof. employee benefits Sch. Law U. Minn. Bd. dirs. Habitat for Humanity of Minn. Recipient Svc. award Valparaiso Alumni Assn., 1986. Mem. Midwest Pension Conf. Office: Dorsey & Whitney 50 S 6th St Ste 1500 Minneapolis MN 55402-1498 Office Phone: 612-340-2941. Office Fax: 612-340-2868. E-mail: gottschalk.steve@dorsey.com.

GOTTSCHALK, THOMAS A., lawyer; b. Decatur, Ind., July 5, 1942; s. John Simson and Edith (Liechty) G.; m. Barbara J. Risen, Aug. 28, 1965; children: Deborah, Diane. AB, Earlham Coll., 1964; JD, U. Chgo., 1967. Bar: Ill. 1967, D.C. 1986, U.S. Supreme Ct. Assoc. Kirkland & Ellis, Chgo., 1967-73, ptnr., 1973-94; sr. v.p., gen. counsel Gen. Motors Corp., Detroit, 1994—2001, exec. v.p., law and public policy, gen. counsel, 2001—. Trustee Earlham Coll., Richmond, Ind., 1972—, chmn., 1985-91. Mem. ABA (mem. litigation, antitrust and criminal law sects.), D.C. Bar Assn., Chgo. Coun. of Lawyers, Conf. Bd. Coun. of Chief Legal Officers; mem. bd. of trustees, Am. Univ., Wash., D.C. Office: Gen Motors Corp 300 Renaissance Ctr Detroit MI 48265-0001

GOTTSCHALL, EDWARD MAURICE, art director; b. N.Y.C., Dec. 28, 1915; s. Myer and Stephanie (Kraus) G.; m. Lee Beatrice Natale, Feb. 6, 1943 (dec. 1984); 1 child, Robert J.; m. Alice J. Wise, Jan. 20, 1985. BS, CCNY, 1937; MS, Columbia U. Sch. of Journalism, 1938. Mng. editor Graphic Arts Prodn. Yearbook, Colton Press, 1937-51; editor Art Direction, 1952-69; sr. editor Popular Merchandising Co., Passaic, N.J., 1964-67; co-pub., editorial dir. Advt. Trade Publs., Inc., 1967-69; exec. dir. Am. Inst. Graphic Arts, N.Y.C., 1969-75; exec. v.p. Internat. Typeface Corp., N.Y.C., 1975-86, vice chmn., 1986-90; editor U & lc, 1981-89, cons. editor, 1990—. V.p. Design Processing Internat., Inc., 1977-85; U.S. rep. Assn. Typographique Internat., 1978-89, chmn. world conf. on typographic communication, 1988; lectr. Pratt Inst. Evening Art Sch., 1947-64, N.Y. U., 1955-64 Author: (with F.C. Rodewald) Commercial Art as a Business, 3d edit., 1972; Author: Vision '80s, 1980, Graphic Communication '80s, 1981, Typographic Communications Today, 1988, reprinted 1992; co-editor: Advertising Directions, vols. 1-4, 1960-64, Editor Typographic i, 1969-79; cons. editor: Graphic Arts Manual, 1973-80; contbr. essay to Contemporary Masterworks, 1992. Served with Signal Corps. U.S. Army, 1943-44, USAAF, 1944-45, ETO. Mem. Type Dirs. Club (past pres., Spl. award 1963), N.Y. Club of Printing House Craftsmen (Fellowship award 1993), Masons, Wednesday Sr. Men's Club of Jewish Cmty. Ctr. of Mid-Westchester (pres. 1999, 2000, 04-05), Phi Delta Pi. Home: 63 Highland Ave Eastchester NY 10709-3627 *Knowledge is never enough. One must be able to evaluate, to judge, to have taste, and to make decisions.*

GOTTSCHALL, JOAN B., judge; b. Oak Ridge, Tenn., Apr. 23, 1947; d. Herbert A. and Elaine (Reichbaum) G. BA cum laude, Smith Coll., Mass., 1969; JD, Stanford Univ., Calif., 1973. Bar: Ill. 1973. Assoc. Jenner & Block, 1973-76, 78-81, ptnr., 1981-82; staff atty. Fed. Defender Program, 1976-78, Univ. of Chgo., Office of Legal Counsel, 1983-84; magistrate judge U.S. Dist. Ct. (no. dist.) Ill., Chgo., 1984—96, judge, 1996—2002. Mem. vis. com., past chair Divinity Sch., U. Chgo., 1984—97. Bd. dirs. Martin Marty Ctr., U. Chgo. Div. Sch., Ill. Humanities Coun. Mem.: Divinity Sch. (vis. com.), Women's Bar Assn. Ill., Chgo. Bar Assn., Am. Bar Assn. Office: Everett McKinley Dirksen Bldg 219 S Dearborn St Ste 1978 Chicago IL 60604-1877 Office Phone: 312-435-5640.

GOTTWALD, FLOYD DEWEY, JR., chemical company executive; b. Richmond, Va., July 29, 1922; s. Floyd Dewey and Anne (Cobb) G.; m. Elisabeth Morris Shelton, Mar. 22, 1947; children: William M., James T., John D. BS, Va. Mil. Inst., 1943; MS, U. Richmond, 1951. With Albemarle Paper Co., Richmond, 1943-62, sec., 1956-57, v.p., sec., 1957-62, pres., 1962; exec. v.p. Ethyl Corp., Richmond, 1962-64, vice chmn., 1964-68, chmn., 1968-94, CEO, 1970-92, chmn. exec. com., 1970-94, vice chmn., 1994-96. Bd. dirs. Tredegar Industries, Inc., 1994-2005; vice-chmn. Albemarle Corp. Past bd. dirs. Nat. Petroleum Coun.; trustee U. Richmond; mem. River Rd. Bapt. Ch.; past trustee V.M.I. Found., Inc.; mem. bd. visitors Coll. William and Mary, 1993-97; pres. bd. trustees Va. Mus. Fine Arts, 1994-96. Decorated Bronze Star, Purple Heart. Mem. NAM (former bd. dirs.), Am. Petroleum Inst. (bd. dirs.), Am. Chem. Coun. (bd. dirs.), Internat. Game Fish Assn. (trustee 1992—), Alfalfa Club, Country Club Va., Commonwealth Club. Office: Albemarle Corp PO Box 1335 Richmond VA 23218-1335 Office Phone: 804-788-5737.

GOTTWALD, WILLIAM M., chemicals executive; Pres., sr. vice-pres. Whitby Inc.; vice-pres. Albemarle Corp., 1996—2001, chmn. bd., 2001—. Office: Albemarle Corp 498 Albemarle Rd Charleston SC 29407 Office Phone: 843-769-2010.*

GOTZEN-BERG, CHRISTOPHER DAVID, musician, educator; b. Provo, Utah, Jan. 28, 1978; s. Ken and Ann Marie Gotzen-Berg; m. Shannon Mormile, Oct. 13, 1981. MusM in Performance, SUNY, Potsdam, NY, 2005. Prin., owner Studio Christopher Gotzen-Berg, Amsterdam, NY. Performer WEPA Records, Amsterdam, NY, 2001—05; adj. instr. SUNY, Potsdam, 2004—05. Composer: (albums) The Lingering Look, 2005 (New Artist award ASCAP, 2005). Bd. dirs. Kingsboro Assembly God, Gloversville, NY, 2003—04. Mem.: ASCAP (assoc.). Republican. Avocations: guitar, literature, poetry, composing. Office Phone: 518-866-1654. E-mail: chrisgotzenberg@yahoo.com.

GOU, JIHUA, engineering educator; b. Pengzhou, China, Sept. 29, 1970; s. Yilin Gou and Bangfen Qian; m. Weiwei Li, June 22, 1999; 1 child, Zachary Y. BS in Materials Engring., Chongqing (China) U., 1993, MS in Materials Engring., 1996; PhD in Materials Engring., Shanghai Jiao Tong U., 1999; PhD in Indsl. Engring., Fla. State U., 2002. Rsch. asst. Chongqing U., 1993—96, Shanghai Jiao Tong U., 1996—99, Fla. State U., Tallahassee, 1999—2002; asst. prof. U. South Ala., Mobile, 2002—. Session chair 10th Internat. conf. on Composites/Nano Engring., 2003. Contbr. articles to profl. jours. Recipient Best Poster prize in materials modeling methodologies at Internat. Conf. on Multiscale Materials Modeling at U. London, Engring. and Phys. Sci. and Rsch. Coun., 2002. Mem.: ASME, Soc. Mfg. Engrs., Soc. for Advancement of Material and Processing Engring. Achievements include patents pending for a method for fabricating nanocomposites with preformed carbon nanotube network and resin infusion techniques. Office Phone: 251-460-7457. E-mail: jgou@jaguar1.usouthal.edu.

GOUBEAUD, KARLEEN R., education educator; b. Pitts., Oct. 18, 1962; d. H. Leo and Janet E. Goubeaud. BS in biology, Bob Jones U., 1985; MEd in sci. edn., U. Pitts., 1993; EdD in Curriculum and Instrn., Ind. U. Pa., 2002. Rsch. asst., assoc. U. Pitts., 1985—91; tchr. North Hills Christian Sch., North Hills, Pa., 1993—98; asst. prof. edn. dept. curriculum and instrn. LI U., Brookville, NY, 2002—. Dir. of student tchg. LI U., C.W. Post Campus, Brookville, NY, 2003—. Contbr. articles various profl. jours. and chapters to books. Grant Award Tng., Am. Ednl. Rsch. Assn. Inst. for Statis. Analysis for Edn. Policy, 2001. Mem.: NSTA, Assn. for Sci. Tchr. Edn., Am. Ednl. Rsch. Assn. Achievements include research in ednl. rsch. of instructional practices of tchr. educators using nat. databases. Office: Long Island U CW Post Campus 720 Northern Blvd Brookville NY 11548 Office Phone: 516-299-3385. Office Fax: 516-299-3312. Business E-Mail: karleen.goubeaud@liu.edu.

GOUGAR, HANS DAVID, nuclear engineer, director; b. Joliet, Ill., Oct. 12, 1962; s. Harry William and Janet Mae Gougar; m. Mary Lou Dunzik, Oct. 17, 1992; children: Charles Dunzik, Elizabeth Dunzik. BS in Edn., U. Wis., 1985; MS in Nuc. Engring., Pa. State U., 1997, PhD in Nuc. Engring., 2004. Cert. secondary sci. edn. 1985. Engr. Idaho Nat. Lab., Idaho Falls, 1998—2003, mgr. fission and fusion sys. dept., 2003—. Sci. tchr. Parker H.S., Janesville, Wis., 1985—88, Am. Sch. in Switzerland, Eng. Am. Sch., Thorpe, Surrey, 1989—92, Upper Darby H.S., Pa., 1992—94; pres. Snake River Montessori Schs., Idaho Falls, 2001—04. Treas. cmty. theater Stage One, Inc., Janesville, Wis., 1985—88. Scholar, Pitts. sect. Am. Nuc. Soc., 1996. Mem.: Am. Nuc. Soc. (com. chair bylaws and rules, student sects. 1998—2003). Achievements include development of the first modern design technique for pebble-bed nuclear reactors. Office Phone: 208-526-2760.

GOUGH, CAROLYN HARLEY, library director; b. Paterson, N.J., Sept. 23, 1922; d. Frank Ellsworth and Mabel (Harrison) Harley; m. George Harrison Gough, Sept. 21, 1944; children: Deborah Ann Gough Bornholdt, Douglas Alan. BA, Coll. William and Mary, 1943; MLS, Drexel U., 1966. Rsch. asst. Young and Rubicam, Inc., N.Y.C., 1943-44; libr. dir., asst. prof. Cabrini Coll., Radnor, Pa., 1966-81; chmn. Palm Beach County Libr. Bd., 1984-86. Mem. resources study com. Tredyffrin Twp. Libr., 1964-65; docent Henry Morrison Flagler Mus., 1982-92. Mem. AAUP, DAR (Palm Beach chpt.), Tri-State Coll. Libr. Coop. (v.p. 1973-74, pres. 1974-75), Assn. Coll. and Rsch. Librs. (dir. 1978-81), Questers, Inc. (1st nat. v.p. 1964-66), Atlantis Golf Club, Atlantis Women's Club (co-pres. 1982-83), Sir Robert Boyle Soc., Beta Phi Mu, Kappa Delta. Republican. Episcopalian. Home: 3007 Willow Spring CT Williamsburg VA 23185-3772

GOUGH, CLARENCE RAY, retired designer, educator; b. Denton County, Tex, Dec. 7, 1919; s. Herman Lang and Gertrude (Page) G.; m. Georgia Belle Leach, Feb. 7, 1975. BS in Art, U. North Tex., Denton, 1940, MS in Art, 1941; BArch, Ill. Inst. Tech., 1950. Art tchr. Edinburg Ind. Sch. Dist., Tex., 1941; interior designer Contemporary House, Dallas, 1950; environ. designer Gough Assoc., Denton, 1951-90; prof. U. North Tex., Denton, 1951-88. Juror Nat. Coun. Interior Design Qualifications, 1983-88; chmn. accreditation com. Found. Interior Design Rsch., 1985-90. Illustrator Modern Dance for the Youth of Am., 1944, photographer (exhibitions) Visual Arts Ctr., Denton, 2001; exhibitions include photography No. Tex. area Art League Exhbn., 2003. Exhbn. chmn. U. North. Tex., Denton, 1950-63; curator exhbns. Greater Denton Arts Coun., 1997-98. Lt. USNR, 1942-46, PTO. Recipient Career Educator award Am. Soc. Interior Designers, 1993, Dallas, Svc. award Gov. Conf. on the Arts, Denton, 1990; Internat. Artist award, North Tex. Area Art League, 2003, Green Glory award, U. North Tex., 2004. Avocations: photography, collecting art. Home: 1813 Willowwood St Denton TX 76205-6992

GOUGH, DENIS IAN, geophysics educator; b. Port Elizabeth, Cape, South Africa, June 20, 1922; came to Can., 1966; s. Frederick William and Ivy Catherine (Hingle) G.; m. Winifred Irving Nelson, June 2, 1945; children—Catherine Veronica, Stephen William Cyprian B.Sc., Rhodes U., Grahamstown, Republic of South Africa, 1943, M.Sc., 1947, D.Sc. (hon.), 1990; PhD, U. Witwatersrand, Johannesburg, Republic of South Africa, 1953. Research officer Nat. Phys. Lab., Johannesburg, S. Africa, 1947, sr. research officer; lectr. Univ. Coll. Rhodesia, Salisbury, 1958, sr. lectr.; assoc. prof. geophysics Southwest Ctr. for Advanced Studies, Dallas, 1964-66; prof. geophysics U. Alta., Edmonton, Can., 1966-87, prof. emeritus, 1987—, dir. Inst. Earth and Planetary Physics, 1975-80. Contbr. numerous articles to profl. jours. Royal Soc. Can. fellow, 1972 Fellow Royal Astron. Soc. (Chapman medal 1988), Am. Geophys. Union; Geol. Assn. Can.; mem. Can. Geophys. Union (past pres., J. Tuzo Wilson medal 1983), Internat. Assn. Geomagnetism and Aeronomy (pres. 1983-87), S. African Geophys. Assn. (Rudolf Krahmann medal 1989). Avocations: reading, music, poetry. Office: Univ Alta Dept Physics Edmonton AB Canada T6G 2J1 E-mail: iangough@incentre.net.

GOUGH, JANET, writer, consultant; b. N.Y.C. BA in English, Montclair St U., 1982; MA in English, Seton Hall U., 1986. Cons. systems, documentation and tng. for biotech., device and pharm. cos.; dir. tech. comm. Cerus Corp., Concord, Calif., 2000—02; prof. English Seton Hall U., South Orange, NJ, Rutgers U., New Brunswick, NJ; course dir. tech. writing, process writing, ESL and electronic record keeping for profl. tng. orgns. Author: Write It Down: Guidance for Preparing Effective and Compliant Documentation, 2000, 2d edit., 2004, Hosting a Compliance Inspection; co-author: Electronic Record Keeping: Achieving and Maintaining Compliance with 21 CFR Part II and 45 CFR Parts 160,162, 164, The Internal Quality Audit, The External Quality Audit, The Clinical Trial Manual; contbr. articles to profl. jours. Mem.: Tchrs. of English to Spkrs. of Other Langs., Am. Med. Writers Assn., Regulatory Affairs Profl. Soc. Office Phone: 973-252-3731. E-mail: janetgough@optonline.net.

GOUGH, ROBERT ALAN, painter; b. Quebec City, Can., Aug. 13, 1931; arrived in US, 1937; s. John Bernard and Ethel Mary (Perrin) Gough; m. Jocelyn Ann Olcott, Aug. 23, 1952; children: Robert Perrin, Kathryn Ann Gough Boulger. Attended, Am. Acad. Art, Chgo., 1949—53. Trustee Ross County Hist. Soc., Chillicothe, Ohio, 1965—84, Ohioana Libr., Columbus, Ohio, 1981—91; bd. mem. Chillicothe Charter Commn., 1971—72. Pvt. first class U.S. Army, 1953—55, Norfold, Va. Recipient Henry Ward Ranger prize, Nat. Acad., NYC, 1961, Best of Show and Purchase award, Union League Club, Chgo., 1961, Purchase prize, Butler Inst. Art, Youngstown, Ohio, 1962, Statehood Achievement award, Kiwanis Club, 1971, Ohioana Citation, Ohioana Libr. Assn., 1981, Silver Arrow Humanitarian award, Scioto Soc., 1989. Presbyterian. Avocations: classical music, attending concerts, plays, and operas. Home: 220 Brookside Dr Chillicothe OH 45601

GOUGH, WILLIAM CABOT, engineer; b. Jersey City, Aug. 22, 1930; s. William Lincoln and Lillian May (Mansmann) G.; m. Marion Louise McConnell, Apr. 27, 1957; children: Barbara Louise, William Scott. BS in Engring., Priceton U., 1952, MA in Engring., 1953; postgrad., Harvard U., 1966-67. Registered prof. engr., Calif. Adminstr. engr. Civilian Power Program AEC, Washington, 1953-55, indsl. info. officer, 1958-60, tech. asst. for systems, plans and programs, div. controlled thermonuclear rsch., 1960-74; project engr. nuclear aircraft program USN, Washington, 1955-58; program mgr. fusion power Electric Power Rsch. Inst., Palo Alto, Calif., 1974-77; sr. DOE/EPRI energy porgram coord., tech. dir. Office Program Assessment and Integration U.S. Dept. of Energy, San Francisco and Palo Alto, 1977-81; dir. DOE Site Office Stanford Linear Accelerator Ctr. Stanford (Calif.) U., 1981-88; ret., 1988; co-founder, pres. Found. for Mind-Being Rsch., Los Altos, Calif., 1980, chmn. bd. dirs., 2001—. Bd. dirs. MERU Found., San Anselmo, Calif., 1988-93; bd. advisors Bonny Found., Salina, Kans., 1990—; mem. physics of humanity coun. Inst. Heart Math., Boulder Creek, Calif., 1993—. Contbr. chapters to books, articles to profl. jours. Lt. (j.g.) USN, 1955-58. Mem. AAAS, Am. Nuclear Soc., N.Y. Acad. Sci., Fedn. Am. Scientists, Soc. for Sci. Exploration, Internat. Soc. Study of Subtle Energies and Energy Medicine (jour. adv. bd. 1990—, program chair ann. conf. 1996), World Future Soc., Common Cause, UN Assn., Sci. and Med. Network. Achievements include being co-inventor of the Fusion Torch concept; initiated and directed independent program of fusion power research for utility industry; developed first organized effort to evaluate technoloty problems confronting fusion; research on the relationship between science and consciousness. Home and Office: 442 Knoll Dr Los Altos CA 94024-4731 Office Phone: 650-941-7462. Personal E-mail: wgough@pacbell.net.

GOUGHER, RONALD LEE, language educator; b. Allentown, Pa., July 27, 1939; s. Samuel Franklin and Beatrice Dorothy (Shanaberger) G.; 1 child, Robert. BA, Muhlenberg Coll., 1961; postgrad., Albright Coll., 1962, Stanford U., 1963; MA, Lehigh U., 1964; postgrad., Harvard U., 1964, U. Pa., 1964—75; advanced cert., Goethe Inst., Munich, 1969. Chmn. fgn. lang. dept. Parkland H.S., Allentown, 1961-65; tchr. German Moravian Sem. for Girls, 1965-69; instr. German Lehigh U., 1965-69; assoc. prof. German West Chester (Pa.) U., 1969—, coord. German studies, 1972—, dir. internat. edn., 1974-83, chmn. dept. fgn. langs., 1977-96, campus dir. Expt. in Internat. Living, 1972-92. Treas. Pa. Consortium Internat. Edn., 1978-83, pres., 1983-86, World Learning Inc., 1992—; coord.-chairperson Assn. Depts. Fgn. Langs., State Sys. Higher Edn., Pa., 1984-88, del. First Joint Conf. Chinese and Am. Edn. Great Hall of People, Beijing, 1992; citizen amb. Linguistics del. to China, 1991, 92, lectr. in field, cons. Franklin Mint, 1992—; cons., program dir. Chester County Intermediate Unit; guest lectr. Ufa, Ivanova, Russia, 1993, Czestochowa, Poland, Ufa, Russia, Sendai, Japan, Jurmala, Riga, Valmiera, Latvia, 1994-96, Kaunus, Lithuania, 1995; participant Hungarian Parliament Sessions, Budapest, 1994; dir. Am.-European studies program, West Chester U. and Soros Found., Latvia, Lithuania, Czech Republic, Slovakia, Hungary, Romania, Yugoslavia, Bulgaria, Croatia, Slovenia, Macedonia, 1994, Moldova, 1995, Estonia, 1996, Albania, Bosnia, Kyrgystan, Mongolia, 1997—, Kazakhstan, 1998—, Azerbaijan, 1999, Kosovo, 2001-02, Georgia, 2003; dir. Internat. Sch.-U. Partnership Program, West Chester U. and Chester County Intermediate Unit, 1988—. Co-editor, Individualization Fgn. Lang. Learning in Am., 1970-75; author numerous publs. in German lang. and lit., individualizing instrn. in fgn. langs. Bd. dirs. Peters Valley Crafts Ctr., U.S. Info. Agy., 1988-95; active Congress-Bundestag Youth Exch. Program, 1988-96, Citizen Amb. Program, China, 1991, 92. Fulbright travel grantee, 1963, 69, Soros Found., 1990-94; travel and study grantee, Finland and Leningrad, Russia, 1990; travel grantee to Poland, Slovakia, Romania, 1991-92, Russia, 1993, 95, Bulgaria, Slovenia, 1994, Kagoshima, Japan and Taipei, Taiwan, 1996, Croatia, Latvia, Lithuania, Slovenia, 1996, Hungary, Bulgaria, Macedonia, 1999, Mongolia, 1999; Fed. Fgn. Lang. Assistance Act grantee, 1992-96, dir. Internat. Sch.-U. Ptnrs. program Chester County Intermediate Unit and West Chester U., 1991-97, Soros Found. grantee internat. program devel. Latvia, Lithuania, Czech Republic, Slovakia, Hungary, Slovenia, Yugoslavia, Romania, Bulgaria, Macedonia, Moldova, Estonia, Mongolia, Kyrgystan, Bosnia, Albania, 1994—; Open Soc. grantee, 1994-2003, others; recipient Chapel of Four Chaplains award, 1981. Mem. Am. Assn. Tchrs. German, Am. Coun. Tchg. Fgn. Langs., N.E. Conf. Tchg. Fgn. Langs., Internat. Platform Assn., Smithsonian Instn., Ruffed Grouse Soc., Trout Unlimited, Ducks Unlimited. Republican. Lutheran. Home: 3309 Windsor Ln Thorndale PA 19372-1038 Office: West Chester U Dept Fgn Langs West Chester PA 19380 Business E-Mail: rgougher1@msn.com.

GOUGHNOUR, ROY ROBERT, civil engineer, educator; b. Canton, Ohio, May 10, 1928; s. Roy George and Doris Belle (Malone) G.; m. Marilynn Ruth Knoll, Sept. 20, 1948 (div. Mar. 1968); children: Robert Lee, Steven David, Mekyla Ann Goughnour Hart; m. Mary Rosetta Strahan, June 28, 1968. BS, Mich. State U., 1961, MS, 1965, PhD, 1967. Registered profl. engr., Mich. Vice pres. A.C. Aukerman Co., Jackson, Mich., 1958-64; assoc. prof. No. Ariz. U., Flagstaff, 1967-68, Mich. State U., East Lansing, 1968-72; v.p. Aukerman-Goughnour Co., Jackson, 1972-76; pres. Strahan Mfg. Co., Tampa, Fla., 1976-77; v.p. R & D, Vibroflotation Found. Co., Pitts., 1976-86; exec. v.p. GeoSystems, Inc., Sterling, Va., 1986-89; v.p. Geotechnics Am., Inc., Peachtree City, Ga., 1989—2000; mgr. engring. Nilex Corp., Centennial, Colo., 2000—. Cons. Hubbell, Roth & Clark, Bloomfield Hills, Mich., 1989-91, Tensar Corp., Morrow, Ga., 1989-91. Contbr. articles to profl. jours.; patentee slipform and ground improvement fields. Rsch. grantee NSF, 1969, Fed. Hwy. Assn., 1980. Mem. ASCE (assoc.), Internat. Soc. Soil Mechanics and Found. Engring., SE Asian Geotech. Soc. Republican. Avocations: hunting, target shooting. Home: 705 Duff Rd NE Leesburg VA 20176-4907 Office: Nilex Corp 15171 E Fremont Dr Centennial CO 80112 Business E-Mail: bgoughnour@potomaccrossing.net.

GOULART, RONALD JOSEPH, writer; b. Berkeley, Calif., Jan. 13, 1933; s. Joseph Silveira and Josephine (Macri) G.; m. Frances Ann Sheridan, June 13, 1964; children: Sean, Steffan. BA, U. Calif., Berkeley, 1955. Copywriter Guild, Bascom & Bonfigli, San Francisco, 1955-57, 58-60, Alan Alch, Inc., Los Angeles, 1960-63, Hoefer, Dietrich & Brown, San Francisco, 1966-68; freelance writer Weston, Conn., 1968—. Author: (sci. fiction) Brinkman, Brainz, Inc., 1985, Suicide, Inc., 1970, After Things Fell Apart; (sci. fiction story collection) Odd Job 101, Skyrocket Steele Conovers the Universe, 1990; (mystery novels) Ghosting, A Graveyard and My Own, 1985, The Wisemann Originals, 1989, The Tijuana Bible, 1990, Even the Butler Was Poor, 1990, Now He Thinks He's Dead, 1992, Groucho Marx, Secret Agent, 2002, Groucho Marx, King of the Jungle, 2005; (fiction) The Tremendous Adventures of Bernie Wine, Capricorn One; (sci. fiction) The Robot in the Closet, The Cyborg King, Big Bang, Daredevils Ltd., 1987, The Curse of the Obelisk, 1987, Everybody Comes to Cosmo's, 1988; (non-fiction): (TV) An American Family, The Great Comic Book Artists, 1986, The Dime Detectives, 1988 (nominated for Edgar award, 1989), The Funnies, 1995; editor: The Great British Detective, Ency. Am. Comics, 1990; cons. to Tek War novels by William Shatner, 1988—; pub. Ron Goulart's Weekly, 1994—. Recipient Edgar Allan Poe award Mystery Writers Am., 1971 Mem. Sci. Fiction Writers Am. (past v.p.), Mystery Writers Am. (bd. dirs. 1979-88, 89-91, 92-93). Democrat. Mailing: c/o Ivy F Stone Fifi Oscard Agy 16th Fl 110 W 40th St New York NY 10018*

GOULAZIAN, PETER ROBERT, retired broadcasting executive; b. N.Y.C., Apr. 17, 1939; s. G.B. and Alice Goulazian; m. Mary C. Holland, Dec. 19, 1965; children: Cindy Anne, Peter Robert. BA, Columbia U., 1962. With media and programming dept. Dancer-Fitzgerald-Sample, Inc., N.Y.C., 1963-67; v.p., mktg. dir. Katz Communications, Inc., N.Y.C., 1967-79, v.p. broadcasting, 1980-81; pres. Continental TV div., 1981-84, pres. TV group, 1985-91; pres., CEO Katz Media Corp., 1992-94. Bd. dirs. The TV Bur., Seltel Inc., Cable Media Corp., Katz Internat., Petry Media Corp. Mem. Varsity "C" Club, N.Y. Athletic Club, Nantucket Anglers Club, Columbia U. Club, Woodstock Rotary. Home: PO Box 404 Woodstock VT 05091 E-mail: longlake@valley.net.

GOULD, ALAN BRANT, academic administrator; b. Aug. 2, 1938; m. Mary Nell; children: Adam, Charles, Christopher. BA in History cum laude, Marshall U., 1961, MA in History, 1962; PhD in Am. History, W.Va. U., 1969. Grad. instr., dept. history W.Va. U., Morgantown, 1962-65; instr., dept. history D.C. Tchrs. Coll., 1965-66; asst. prof. history No. Va. Community Coll., 1966-69; prof., dept. history Marshall U., Huntington, W.Va., 1969—, sr. v.p., 1988-89, provost, 1989-92, interim pres., 1990-91, v.p. for acad. affairs, 1991-94, dean Coll. Liberal Arts, 1980-88, acting v.p. acad. affairs, 1984-86, asst. to pres. for spl. projects, 1986, chmn. dept. history, 1977-80, asst. to v.p. acad. affairs, 1976-77, coord. Regents BA degree program, 1976-80, 86-94; exec. dir. John Deaver Drinko Acad., 1994—. Adj. prof. history W.Va. Coll. Grad. Studies, 1976-86; lectr. Ohio U., Ironton, 1970-74; vis. lectr. for Project Newgate, Fed. Youth Correction Inst., Summit, Ky., fall 1970. Contbr. articles to hist. jours, also conf. papers. Chmn. Cabell County Hist. Landmark Commn., 1983-92; trustee Huntington Mus. Art, 1983-93, chmn. edn. com., mem. exec. com.; pres. River Cities Cultural Coun., 1985-91; bd. dirs. W.Va. Humanities Coun., 1986-90, v.p., 1989-91, pres., 1991-94, W.Va. Coalways, Inc., 1987—; mem. Mayor of Huntington's Main St. Project, 1987-92, Marshall U. Rsch. Corp., 1988, mem., 1982-86; mem. W.Va. Antiquities Commn., 1975-77, Cabell County Commn. on Crime, Delinquency and Corrections, 1982-86, statewide steering com. Ideas That Built Am., 1985-86, Carter G. Woodson Meml. Commn., 1986—; mem. steering com. Ethics W.Va. Program, 1983-84, chmn. Great Books Program; mem. affirmative action bd. City of Huntington, 1989-91, mem. Cabell County (W.Va.) hist. landmark commn., 1989-91, 94—; trustee W. Va. Ednl. Found., Inc., 1993-2001; mem. W.Va. Libr. Commn., 1997—. Inducted into Huntington East High Sch. Hall of Fame, Class of 1986, City of Huntington (W.Va.) Wall of Fame, 1997; recipient Charles Daugherty Humanities award W.Va. Humanities Coun., 1996. Mem. Am. Hist. Assn. (com. on status of history in schs. 1974-76), Orgn. Am. Historians (state rep.), W.Va. Hist. Assn. (sec. 1974, v.p. 1975, pres. 1976), W.Va. Assn. Acad. Deans (mem. exec. bd. 1982-86). W.Va. Bd. Regents (univ. rep., acad. affairs adv. com. 1984-86), Soc. Yeager Scholars (steering com. 1986-87), W.Va. Humanities Ctr. (exec. com. 1987—), Gamma Theta Upsilon, Omicron Delta Kappa, Phi Alpha Theta, Phi Eta Sigma, Pi Sigma Alpha. Avocations: tennis, travel. Office: Marshall U John Deaver Drinko Acad One John Marshall Dr Huntington WV 25755-0003 Office Phone: 304-696-2739. E-mail: gould@marshall.edu.

GOULD, ALAN I., lawyer; b. Phila., Jan. 4, 1940; s. Louis and Yvette (Balasny) G.; m. Joyce P. Feinstein, Sept. 19, 1965; 1 child, Traci Eve. BBA, U. Miami, Fla., 1961, JD, 1964. Bar: Fla. 1964, N.J. 1966, U.S. Dist. Ct. N.J. 1966, U.S. Supreme Ct. 1983, U.S. Ct. Appeals (3rd cir.) 1985. Assoc. George M. James Esq., Wildwood, N.J., 1966-70; pvt. practice Wildwood, 1970-75; ptnr. Gould & Neidig, Wildwood, 1975-80, Alan I. Gould, Wildwood, 1980-82, Valore, McAllister, Westmoreland, Gould, Vesper & Schwartz, Wildwood and Northfield, 1982-87, Mairone, Biel, Gould, Zlotnick, Feinberg & Griffith, Wildwood and Atlantic City, 1988, Cooper, Perskie, April, Niedelman, Wagenheim & Levenson, Wildwood, Northfield and Atlantic City, 1989-95; prin. Alan I. Gould, P.C., Wildwood, 1996—. Chmn. N.J. Lawyers Fund for Clients Protection, 1987-91, chmn. 1991; mem. N.J. Commn. on Professionalism in Law; lectr. in field. Mem. editl. bd. N.J. Lawyer, Weekly Newspaper. Solicitor Lower Twp. Pub. Schs., 1980-85, Wildwood Crest Pub. Schs., 1985-95, Cape May County Drug Abuse Coun., Parking Authority, City of Wildwood, 1973-87, Cape May County br. Am. Cancer Soc., Cape Ednl. Fund Inc.; trustee in bankruptcy U.S. Trustee of N.J.; mem. Supreme Ct. N.J. Task Force on Spl. Civil Part, 1986-88; Supreme Ct. apptd. trustee Interest on Lawyers Trust Accts. (IOLTA) Fund, 1993-97, chair, 1997; chmn. bd. govs. Burdette Tomlin Meml. Hosp., 1985-89, mem., 1976-79, pres., 1979-84. Recipient Profl. Lawyer of Yr. award N.J. Commn. on Professionalism in the Law and Cape May County Bar Assn., 1997, N.J. State Bar Found. medal of honor, 1998. Fellow Am. Bar Found.; mem. ABA, Cape May County Bar Assn. (pres. 1982), N.J. Bar Assn. (trustee 1982-89, chair jud. and prosecutor appts. com., mem. jud adminstrn. com.), N.J. Bar Found. (trustee), Fla. Bar Assn., Fed. Bar Assn., Assn. Trial Lawyers Am., Am. Judicature Soc., Assn. Criminal Def. Lawyers, Navy League of U.S., Lions (pres. 1974), N.J. Lawyer (editl. bd. weekly newspaper). Avocations: running, golf, tennis, basketball. Office: 3000 Pacific Ave Wildwood NJ 08260-4945 Fax: 609-729-2111. E-mail: Aigould@jerseycape.com.

GOULD, ALVIN R., manufacturing executive; b. Seattle, May 16, 1922; s. Charlie I. and Laura (Klos) G.; m. Ruth Nelson, May 25, 1946; children: Stephen Charles, Jon Patrick. Grad. pub. schs. Mem. engring. dept. Pacific Car & Foundry Co., Renton, Wash., 1943-45, asst. mgr. indsl. sales, 1945-48, mgr. indsl. sales, 1948-55, gen. sales mgr., 1956-60, Peterbilt Motors Co., Newark, Calif., 1961-64; v.p., dir., gen. sales mgr. Honolulu Iron Works Co., 1964-66, exec. v.p., dir., chief operating officer, 1966, pres., dir., chief exec. officer, 1968—71; group pres. Food Equipment Group Ward Foods Inc., N.Y.C., 1970-71; v.p. merchandising Dillingham Corp., Honolulu, 1972-73, v.p. mining and merchandising, 1973-75, group v.p., exec. mgmt. com. mining and merchandising; pres. Truck Center Corp., Seattle, 1976-90, co-owner, sec.-treas., 1991-95; pvt. practice in personal investments, 1996—. Mem. nat. export expansion Council Dept. Commerce, 1969-74, chmn. regional export expansion council, 1969-74; mem. Western Regional Export Council; chmn. Honolulu Export Council, 1975-77; Chmn. bd. trustees Hawaii Pacific Coll., 1973-77; bd. dirs. Center for Internat. Bus. Mem. Hawaii C. of C. (chmn. trade com. 1968-69), Hawaii World Trade Assn. (mem. exec. com. 1968-69), Hawaii Assn. Industries (v.p., dir. 1975-76), Navy League (dir.), Rotary Club, Outrigger Canoe Club, Rainier Club. Home: 8464 W Mercer Way Mercer Island WA 98040-5633

GOULD, BONNIE M., realtor; b. Cleve., Sept. 3, 1947; d. Edward Louis and Frances (Dee (Pavlovich) Marincic. Student, John Carroll U. Asst. prodn. mgr. Nelson Stern Advt., Cleve., 1966-73; sec. acctg. S. James Dubin & Assocs., Eastlake, Ohio, 1976-78; sec., atty. James Todoroff, Andrews & Todoroff, Eastlake, 1977-78; realtor sales Century 21-Baur, Euclid, Ohio, 1978-82; relocations dir., mgr. Century 21, Euclid, 1979-82; realtor assoc., relocation dir. Century 21-Malone, Inc., Willowick, Ohio, 1982-83, Century 21-William T. Byrne, Cleve., 1983—85, Smythe, Cramer Co., Euclid, 1984-86; sr. v.p., treas., corp. mgr. Acacia Realty Profls. Inc., 1986-98; pres., treas., interior design coord. Acacia Design and Trade Profls. Inc. Gen. Contractors, 1990—; pres., CEO Acacia Design Fine Homes and Properties, 1999—. Mem. Realtors Polit. Action Com., Cleve., 1981—; vice chmn. local taxation and legislation com. Cleve. Area Bd. Realtors, 1983-84, vice chmn. polit. affairs, 1987—, chmn. home and flower 1986, mem. enlarged legis. com., 1986-97, internat. rules and fin. com., 1993-95, chmn. 1995; sec., trustee Euclid Gateway Found., 1987—. Recipient Disting. Svc. award Cleve. Bd. Realtors, 1983-87, 96, Woman of Yr. award 1990. Mem. Cleve. Bd. Realtors (dir. 1984-86, 93—, 2d v.p. 1994, treas. 1995, gov. No. Ohio multiple listings svc. 1992-95, contract and fin. com., 1992—), Ohio Assn. Realtors (trustee 1981-97, dir. 2004—), Nat. Assn. Realtors Women's Coun. of Realtors (treas. Cleve. chpt. 1986-87, v.p. 1987-88, pres. 1989, chmn. nominating com. 1990, Woman of Yr. 1990), Lake and Geague Area Assn. Realtors (fin. com. 2001—, 2d v.p. 2004, pres.-elect 2005), North East Roundtable (sec. 1980, chair 1981) Republican. Roman Catholic. Office: Acacia Design Fine Homes & Properties 293 E 266th St Cleveland OH 44132-1552 E-mail: acaciadsgn@aol.com, acaciarelo@aol.com.

GOULD, BRUCE ELLIOTT, physician, medical educator, academic administrator; b. Queens, N.Y., 1954; BA, Cornell U.; MD, SUNY, Syracuse, 1979. Intern U. Mass. Med. Ctr., Worcester, resident in medicine, fellow in medicine; prof. gen. internal medicine U. Conn. Sch. Medicine, assoc. dean primary care; med. dir. St. Francis Hosp./U. Conn. Primary Care Ctr. Burgdorf /Fleet Health Ctr., Hartford. Dir. Conn. area health edn. ctr. program U. Conn. Sch. Medicine, 1997—, founder, participant Migrant Farm Workers program, 1998—; chair nat. adv. coun. migrant health U.S. Dept. HHS, 2004—. Mem.: AMA Found. (Pride in Profession award 2004). Office: Burgdorf Health Ctr 131 Coventry St Hartford CT 06112 Address: U Conn Health Ctr 263 Farmington Ave Farmington CT 06030-2926

GOULD, BURNHAM SYLVESTER, retired military analyst; b. Hartford, June 9, 1932; s. Burnham Sylvester and Edith Swendsen Gould; m. Vivian Anne Woods, Sept. 3, 1955; children: Burnham III, Eric, Dana. AB, Princeton U., 1954; MS, MIT, 1956. Cert. real estate broker N.J., N.Y., Va. Indsl. rsch. engr. Ea. Gas and Fuel Assn., Boston, 1956—59; mgmt. scientist Dunlap & Assocs., Stamford, Conn., 1959—62; mgr. ops. planning Gen. Mills, Inc., Wayzata, Minn., 1962—69; mgr. ops. rsch. CPC Internat., Englewood Cliffs, NJ, 1969—74; pvt. practice real estate broker Woodcliff Lake, NJ, 1974—78; chief analysis Dept. Def., 1978—94; ret. Adj. prof. Fairleigh Dickinson U., Teaneck, NJ, 1974—78, William Paterson Coll., Mahwah, NJ, 1977—78, Elizabeth City (N.C.) State U., 2002; spkr. in field. Contbr. articles to profl. jours. Pres. Chicahauk Property Owners Assn., Southern Shores, 1996—98; chmn. Rep. Party, Southern Shores, NC, 1998—2002, Dare County, NC, 2002—. Recipient Disting. Career award, Def. Logistics Agy., 1994. Mem.: Dare Squares (pres. 2002—). Unitarian-Universalist. Avocations: birdwatching, kayaking, bicycling, travel, running. Home: 71 Gravey Pond Ln Southern Shores NC 27949 Personal E-mail: bsgould@msn.com.

GOULD, CLAUDIA, museum director; BA in Art History, Boston Coll.; M in Mus. Studies, NYU. Curator, project dir., curator exhbns. Wexner Ctr. Arts, Ohio State U., 1989-91; ind. curator N.Y.C., 1992-94; exec. dir. Artists Space, N.Y.C., 1994-99, Inst. Contemporary Art, Phila., 1999—. Office: Inst Contemporary Art 118 S 36th St Philadelphia PA 19104-3289 Office Phone: 215-573-9973. E-mail: clgould@pobox.upenn.edu.*

GOULD, DAVID, lawyer; b. L.A., Feb. 19, 1940; s. Erwin and Beatrice (Altman) G.; m. Bonnie Becker, Feb. 12, 1967; children: Julie M., Michael. AB, U. Calif., L.A., 1962; LLB, U. Calif., Berkeley, 1965. Bar: Calif. 1965, U.S. Dist. Ct. (cen., so., ea. and no. dists.) Calif. 1966, U.S. Ct. Appeals (9th cir.) 1967, U.S. Supreme Ct. 1995. Dep. atty. gen. Calif. Dept. of Justice, L.A., 1965-68; assoc. Loeb & Loeb, L.A., 1968-73, Danning, Gill, Gould, Diamond & Spector, L.A., 1974-76, ptnr., 1976-92, McDermott, Will & Emery, L.A., 1992—. Adj. assoc. prof. Southwestern U. Sch. of Law, L.A., 1978-80; adj. prof. Pepperdine U. Sch. of Law, Malibu, Calif., 1982. Co-author: Local Bankruptcy Practice Manual for the Central District of California, 2d edit., 1990—. Fellow: Am. Coll. Bankruptcy; mem.: L.A. Bankruptcy Forum (bd. trustees 1989, sec. 1990—, pres. 1993—94, lawyer rep. ctrl. dist. Calif. to 9th cir. jud. conf.), Calif. Bankruptcy Forum, L.A. County Bar Assn. (fed. cts. com. 1987—, treas. 1998—99, sec. 1999—), Calif. Bar Assn. (debtor/creditor rels. and bankruptcy com. 1984—87, chair 1987—88, advisor 1988—89, uniform comml. code com. 1988—92, bankruptcy cons. gorup bd. legal specialization 1989—93), ABA (bus. bankruptcy com. sect. on bus. law 1982—, vice chair rules subcom. 1986—92, chair 1992—). Avocation: trap and skeet shooting. Office: McDermott Will & Emery LLP 2049 Century Park E Ste 3400 Los Angeles CA 90067-3208

GOULD, DONALD EVERETT, retired chemical company executive, consultant; b. Concord, NH, May 19, 1932; s. Everett Luther and Gladys (Wilcox) G.; m. Marilyn Bachelder, June 13, 1953; children: Barbara, Allen, Douglas. BS in Chem. Engring., U. N.H., 1954; postgrad., Rutgers U., 1955—59. Devel. chem. engr. plastics divsn. Union Carbide Co., Bound Brook, N.J., 1954-59, tech. svc. engr. Bound Brook and Wayne, N.J., 1959-64, mgr. tech. svc. indsl. bag dept. Wayne, 1964-66, mgr. tech. svcs. indsl. fabricated products dept., 1966-67, mktg. mgr. indsl. bags, 1967-69, sr. packaging engr., 1969-72, mgr. packaging, 1972-74, mgr. distbn. safegy and regulations, 1974-79, staff engr. packaging, 1980-85, sr. staff engr. packaging, labeling, 1985-91, prin. engr. packaging, labeling and regulations, 1991-94, cons., 1994—. Contbr. articles to profl. jours.; contbg. author Encyclopedia of Engineering Materials and Processes. Chmn. Andover (N.H.) Planning Bd., 2000—. Mem. Inst. Packaging Profls. (vice chmn. films, foils and laminations com. 1962-64, chmn. 1964-66, sect. leader bottle containers, chmn. bag com. 1975-78, 85-88, exec. com. chem. packaging 1985-94, hon. life mem. 1992), Am. Soc. Quality Control (hon., life), Chem. Mfrs. Assn. (chmn. distbn. work group), Am. Coun. Chem. Labeling, Andover Hist. Soc. (treas.), Andover Planning Bd. (chmn.), Alpha Chi Sigma, Alpha Gamma Rho. Home and Office: 21 Lawrence St PO Box 231 East Andover NH 03231-0231

GOULD, DOROTHY MAE, executive secretary, soprano; b. Bridgeport, Conn., Sept. 9, 1927; d. Clifford Alexander and Mary Irene Hedin; m. John Colquitt Gould, Nov. 26, 1958; children: Natalie Mary, Clifford Gardner, Andrew Woodhouse. BA in English Lit. and Creative Writing, U. Mont., 1997; studied voice with Estelle Liebling, Julliard, 1959—63, studied voice with Bernard Taylor, 1943; scholar, New Eng. Conservatory. Legal sec. Thompson Knight, Dallas, White, McElroy, Dallas, Gibbons, Tucker, Smith, McEwen, Coxer and Taub, Tampa, Fla., Curtis, Trevethan & Gerety, Bridgeport, Conn., Music Corp. Am., N.Y.C., NY; sec. GE Co., Bridgeport, Columbia Artists Mgmt., N.Y.C., AMF, Greenwich, Conn.; soprano USO, Conn., 1944—45, Tampa Opera, 2002—; oratorio singer, soloist soprano N.Y., Conn., Fla. Finalist Barnum Festival Jenny Lind contest, 1948, Stamford Advocate, Greenwich Times contest, 1985—86. Home: 13871 N 91st Ln Peoria AZ 85381 E-mail: colquitt3@msn.com.

GOULD, EDWIN SHELDON, chemist, educator; b. Los Angeles, Aug. 19, 1926; s. Ben and Margaret (Mandel) G.; m. Marjorie McFarlin, Jan. 25, 1952; children: Richard Forrest, Kirk Benson. BS, Calif. Inst. Tech., 1946; PhD, UCLA, 1950. Instr. Poly. Inst. Bklyn., 1950-52, asst. prof., 1952-56; asso. prof. chemistry Polytech. Inst. Bklyn., 1956-59; sr. inorganic chemist Stanford Research Inst., 1959-66; prof. San Francisco State U., 1966-67, Kent State U., 1967-82, Univ. Prof., 1982—. Author: Inorganic Reactions and Structure, 1962, Mechanism and Structure in Organic Chemistry, 1959. Mem. London Chem. Soc., Am. Chem. Soc., Amateur Chamber Music Players Assn. Rsch. inorganic chemistry. Home: 1583 Morris Rd Kent OH 44240-4529 Office: Kent State U Dept Chemistry Kent OH 44242-0001 Office Phone: 330-672-2267. Business E-Mail: esgould@kent.edu.

GOULD, ELIZABETH, neuroscientist, educator; BA in Psychology, St. John's U., 1984; MA in Behavioral Neuroscience, UCLA, 1986, PhD in Behavioral Neuroscience, 1988; post-Dal fellow in Neuroendocrinology, Rockefeller U., 1989—92. Asst. prof. Rockefeller U., 1993—96, adj. prof., 1997—; asst. prof. dept. psychology Princeton U., 1997—2000, prof., 2000—. Contbr. articles to profl. jours. Recipient Troland Rsch. award NAS, 2000. Office: Dept Psychology Princeton Univ Princeton NJ 08544-1010

GOULD, HARRY EDWARD, JR., paper company executive; b. NYC, Sept. 24, 1938; s. Harry Edward and Lucille (Quartucy) Gould; m. Barbara Clement, Apr. 26, 1975; children: Harry Edward III, Katharine Elizabeth. Student, Oxford U., 1958; BA cum laude, Colgate U., 1960; postgrad., Harvard Bus. Sch., 1960—61; MBA, Columbia U., 1964. Assoc. in corp. fin. dept. Goldman, Sachs & Co., NYC, 1961—62; exec. asst. to sr. v.p. ops. Universal Am., NYC, 1964—65; sec., treas. Young Spring & Wire Corp., Detroit, 1965—67, exec. v.p., COO, 1967—69, also bd. dirs.; v.p. adminstrn. and fin. Universal Am. Corp., 1968—69; mem. exec. com., v.p., sec.-treas. Daybrook-Ottawa Corp., Bowling Green, Ohio, 1967—69; dir., mem. exec. com. Am. Med. Ins. Co., NYC, 1966—74; chmn., pres., CEO Gould Paper Corp., NYC, 1969—, also chmn. bd. dirs.; chmn. bd., dir. Vrisimo Mfg., Inc., Ceres, Calif., 1974—99; chmn. bd. Lewis & Gould Paper Co., Inc., Northfield, Ill., 1975—78; chmn., pres., CEO Signature Comm. Ltd., LA and NYC, 1986—; chmn. bd. Legion Paper West Corp., Commerce, Calif., 1997—2003. Chmn. bd. dirs. Samuel Porritt & Co., East Peoria, Ill., 1970—86, Ingalls Mfg., Inc., Ceres, 1974—99, Hawthorne Paper Co., Kalamazoo, 1970—75, Weiss/McNair/Ramacher, Inc., Chico, 1974—; ltd. ptnr. Hardy & Co., NYC, 1973—78; chmn. exec. com., bd. dirs. Richard Lewis Paper Corp., Northfield, 1992—97; bd. dirs., mem. environ. and health and safety com. Domtar, Inc., Montreal, Canada, 1995—2003; chmn. Price & Pierce Internat. Inc., Stamford, Conn., 2004—, Price & Pierce Finland Oy, Helsinki, Finland, 2004—, Price & Pierce (Asia Pacific) Pte Ltd., Singapore, 2004—. Co-chmn. Pacesetters com. Boy Scouts Am., 1967—69; participant as U.S. Pres.'s rep. UN E-W Trade Devel. Commn., 1967; mem. nat. coun. Colgate U., 1973—76, trustee, mem. budget, devel., fin. and student affairs coms., 1976—82; mem. exec. com., chmn. export expansion subcom., mem. export promotion subcom. U.S. Pres.'s Export Coun., 1979—82; nat. trustee, mem. exec. com. Nat. Symphony Orch., Washington, 1978—99; mem. force NY State Cultural Life & Arts, 1975—78; pres. Harry E. Gould Found., NYC, 1971—; mem. bd. govs. Actors Studio Drama Sch. of New Sch. U., 1995—; mem. exec. br. Acad. Motion Picture Arts and Scis., 1985—; trustee Riverdale Country Sch., 1990—98; mem. Dem. Nat. Fin. Coun., 1974—78, vice chmn. exec. com., chmn. budget and audit coms.; treas. NY State Dem. Com., 1976—77; mem. mayor's citizens com. Dem. Nat. Conv., 1976; bd. dirs. United Cerebral Palsy Rsch. and Ednl. Found., 1976—97, Nat. Multiple Sclerosis Soc., 1977—, NYC Housing Devel. Corp., 1977—, USO of Met. NY, 1981—, Housing NY Corp., 1986—, vice chmn., 1987—; bd. dirs., chmn. exec. com. Cinema Group, Inc., LA, 1979—86, chmn., pres., 1982—86; bd. dirs. Residential Mortgage Ins. Corp., 1992—. Mem.: Fin. Execs. Inst., Am. Mgmt. Assn. (trustee, audit com. 1997—2000), Young Pres. Orgn., Paper Distbn. Coun. (chmn. 1993—94), Paper Mchts. Assn. NY (dir. 1972—84), Nat. Paper Trade Alliance (dir., mem. printing paper com. 1973—74), Les Ambassadeurs (London), Paper Club NY, Harvard Club, Friars Club, Pres.'s NY Club (co-chmn. assocs. divsn. 1964—68), Harvard Bus. Sch. Club, Phi Kappa Tau. Office: Gould Paper Corp 11 Madison Ave Fl 14 New York NY 10010-3629 Office Phone: 212-301-0000. *In business the most difficult problem to resolve is blending the profit goals with the dignity of human relations. In the long run, it is probably best to forego some of the profits in order to successfully meld the economic and human sides of business.*

GOULD, HARRY J., III, neurology educator; b. Columbus, Ohio, Mar. 1, 1947; s. Harry J. Jr. and Madeline (Folger) G.; m. Anne Marie Thompson, Jan. 30, 1971; children: Trevor Nicholas, Laura Nicole. BS, SUNY, Stony Brook, 1969; PhD, Brown U., 1974; MD, La. State U., 1990. Asst. prof. Med. Sch. U. Cin., 1974-80; asst. prof. Med. Sch., La. State U., New Orleans, 1980-86, assoc. prof., 1986, resident in neurology, 1990-94; asst. prof. med. sch. La. State U., New Orleans, 1994-98, assoc. prof. neurology, 1998—, Tom Benson prof. neurology, dir. Multidisciplinary Pain Ctr. Contbr. articles to profl. jours. With USAR, 1970-76. NSF grantee, 1986-89. Mem. Internat. Assn. for the Study Pain, Soc. for Neurosci., Am. Acad. Neurology, Am. Pain Soc., Am. Acad. Pain Medicine. Republican. Methodist. Avocations: songwriting, banjo, guitar. Home: 104 Paradise Pt Slidell LA 70461-3225 Office: La State U Med Ctr Dept of Neurology 533 Bolivar St New Orleans LA 70112-2825 Office Phone: 504-568-8171. Business E-Mail: hgould@lsuhsc.edu.

GOULD, JAMES L., biology professor; b. Tulsa, July 31, 1945; s. James L. and Doris Mae (Frazier) G.; m. Carol Holly Grant, June 6, 1970; children: Grant Frazier, Clare Holly. BS, Calif. Inst. Tech., 1970; PhD, Rockefeller U., 1975. Asst. prof. Princeton (N.J.) U., 1975-80, assoc. prof., 1980-84, prof. biology, 1984—. Author: Ethology, 1982, Biological Science, rev. edit., 1996, The Honey Bee, 1988, Sexual Selection, 1989, The Animal Mind, 1994, Biostats Basics, 2001; contbr. more than 100 articles to profl. jours. With U.S. Army, 1967-68. Guggenheim Found. fellow, 1987, AAAS fellow, 1988, Animal Behavior Soc. fellow, 1992; grantee NSF, 1976, 79, 82, 85, NIH, 1976, Nat. Geogrphic Soc., 1984; named Prof. of Yr. Carnegie Found. N.J., 1996, Tchr. of Yr. Animal Behavior Soc., 1997. Presbyterian. Achievements include research in animal behavior. Office: Princeton U Dept Ecol Evol Biology Princeton NJ 08544-0001 E-mail: gould@princeton.edu.

GOULD, JAY MARTIN, economist, consultant; b. Chgo., Aug. 19, 1915; s. Max and Ida (Dolger) G.; m. Paula Halpern, Nov. 10, 1942 (div.); children: Diana, Emily; m. Jane S. Auerbach, Nov. 17, 1970. BA, Bklyn. Coll., 1936; MA, Columbia U., 1938, PhD, 1946. Economist McGraw-Hill, N.Y.C., 1946-48; mng. dir. Market Statistics, N.Y.C., 1948-66; pres. Econ. Info. Systems, N.Y.C., 1966-81; cons. economist Winston and Strawn, Chgo., 1960-80; cons. Dept. Justice, Washington, 1954-55; exec. cons. Control Data Corp., Mpls., 1981—. Dir. Ctr. Internat. Mgmt. Studies, Chgo., 1978—, Feminist Press, Woodbury, N.Y., 1980—, Inst. Policy Studies, Washington, 1982— Author: Productivity Trends in U.S. Public Utilities, 1946, The Technical Elite, 1966, Input-Output Databases, 1979, Structure of U.S. Business, 1980, Quality of Life in American Neighborhoods, 1986, (with Benjamin Goldmay) Deadly Deceit: Low Level Radiation High Level Cover Up, 1990, The Enemy Within: The High cost of Living Near Nuclear Reactors, 1995. Dir. radiation and pub. health project. Home: 302 W 86th St New York NY 10024-3144 E-mail: jaymgould@aol.com.

GOULD, JOHN PHILIP, economist, educator; b. Chgo., Jan. 19, 1939; s. John Philip and Lillian Gould; children: John Philip III, Jeffrey Hayes; m. Kathleen A. Carpenter. BS with highest distinction, Northwestern U., 1960; MBA, U. Chgo., 1963, PhD, 1966. Faculty U. Chgo., 1965—, prof. econs., 1974—, disting. service prof. econs., 1984—, dean Grad. Sch. Bus., 1983-93, v.p. planning, 1988—91; Steven G. Rothmeier prof., disting. svc. prof. econs., 1996—; exec. v.p. Lexecon Inc., Chgo., 1994—2004; pres. Cardean, Chgo., 1999—2001. Vis. prof. Nat. Taiwan U., 1978; spl. asst. econ. affairs to sec. labor, 1969-70; spl. asst. to dir. Office Mgmt. and Budget, 1970; past chmn. econ. policy adv. com. Dept. Labor; bd. dirs. DFA Investment Dimensions Group, Harbor Capital Advisors, Chgo. bd. of Trade, 1986-89; chmn. Pegasus Funds, 1996-99, Milw. Mutual, 1997—, Unext.com, 1999—; adv. com. competitive markets Chgo. (Ill.) Merc. Exch., 2004—. Author: (with E. Lazear) Microeconomic Theory, 6th edit, 1989; contbg. author: Microeconomic Foundations of Employment and Inflation Theory, 1970; editor: Jour. of Bus., 1976-83, Jour. Fin. Econs., 1976-83, Jour. Accounting and Econs., 1978-81; contbr. articles to profl. jours. Bd. dirs. United Way/Crusade of Mercy, 1986-91, Lookingglass Theatre Co., 1994-96. Recipient Wall St. Jour. award, 1960, Am. Marketing Assn. award, 1960; Earhart Found. fellow. Mem. Am. Econs. Assn., Econometric Soc. (chmn. local arrangements 1968), Econ. Club of Chgo., Comml. Club of Chgo., Beta Gamma Sigma. Home: 100 E Huron St Apt 2105 Chicago IL 60611-5903 Office: U Chgo Grad Sch Bus 5807 S Woodlawn Chicago IL 60637-1511

GOULD, JON JUSTON, artist; b. Lake Arrowhead, Calif., Sept. 15, 1971; BS in Painting, BSA in Sculpture, Western Oreg. U., 1997, BS in Graphic Design, 1998. Lic. property mgr. Mont. Child care dir. YMCA of Portland, 1999; prodn. mgr., artist Precision Screen Printing, Missoula, Mont., 2000;

ope. mgr. The Apt. Store, Inc., Missoula, 2001—. Democrat. Avocations: skiing, mountain biking, music. Office: The Apt Store Inc 201 W Main Ste 100 Missoula MT 59802 E-mail: gould0330@yahoo.com.

GOULD, KEELY ANN, music educator, conductor; b. Newburgh, N.Y., May 9, 1973; d. William S. and Cheryl A. Gould. BS in Music Edn., The Coll. St. Rose, 1995; MS in Music Edn., Ctrl. Conn. State U., 2000. Cert. tchr. SUNY State Edn. Dept., 2000. Band dir. Warwick Valley Ctrl. Sch. Dist., NY, 1995—2000, orch. dir., 1998—; orch. condr. Skylands Youth Symphony, Vernon, NJ, 2002—. Elem. sch. planning com. Warwick Valley Ctrl. Sch. Dist., 1996—97, advisor all-county club, 1996—, advisor NYSSMA club, 1996—, interview com. new tchrs., 1996—2004, com. mem. beginning orch. program, 1996—98, music adv. com. mem., 1999—, mid. sch. new compact team mem., 2002—, mid. sch. adv. coun. rep., 2003—, mentor new tchrs., 2003—. Musician Greater Newburgh Symphony Orch., Newburgh, 1996—2000; worship team mem., class worship music leader Grace Cmty. Bapt. Ch., Washingtonville, NY, 1998—2004, h.s. youth leader, 1999—2001, wilderness trip leader, 1999—2003, coord., leader inner city Vacation Bible sch., 2001—01, summerquest Bible tchr., 1998—98. Mem.: Orange County Music Educators Assn. (chair orch. 1996—, musician 1996—2000), Am. String Tchr. Assn. with Nat. String Orch. Assn., Music Educators Nat. Conf., N.Y. State Sch. Music Assn. Achievements include NYSSMA Majors Festival Evaluation - Gold Rating for the Middle School Orchestra 2002. Avocations: gardening, quilting, passion for working with/mentor to/teaching youth and teens, outdoor activities. Home: 303 Buttermilk Falls Road Warwick NY 10990 Office: Warwick Valley Central School District PO Box 595 Warwick NY 10990

GOULD, KENNETH LANCE LANCE, physician, educator; b. Wilsonville, Ala., Oct. 28, 1938; s. Kenneth Newton and Elizabeth May (Barrett) G.; m. Helene Freiin von Eckardstein, Sept. 28, 1970; 1 son, Stefan Anton. BA in Physics, Oberlin Coll., 1960; MD, Western Res. U., 1964. Intern U. Wash. Hosps., Seattle, 1964-65, resident, 1965-67; instr. medicine U. Wash., Seattle, 1970-72, asst. prof., 1972-76, assoc. prof., 1976-79; prof. dept. internal medicine and cardiology U. Tex., Houston, 1979—, dir. div. cardiology, 1979-85, vice chmn. clin. affairs dept. medicine, 1980-84, dir. Positron Diagnostic and Research Ctr., 1979-87. Mem. editorial bds. Circulation, 1988-92, Circulation Res., 1982-87, Jour. Am. Coll. Cardiology, 1982-88, Am. Jour. Cardiology, 1978-86; assoc. editor Circulation, 1993—; contbr. articles to profl. jours. Recipient George von Hevesy prize, 1978, ACC Young Investigators award, 1983 Fellow Am. Coll. Cardiology (trustee 1984-89), Am. Heart Assn. (chmn. coun. on circulation, Brown Meml. lectr. 1990); mem. Am. Soc. Clin. Investigation, Soc. Nuclear Medicine, N.Am. Soc. Cardiac Radiology, Am. Physiologic Soc., Assn. Am. Physicians, Assn. Univ. Cardiologists, NIH diagnostic radiol. study sect., Houston Cardiol. Soc. (pres. 1983) Democrat. Achievements include first to Founding Leader In Cardiac Perfusion Imaging. Office: PO Box 20708 Houston TX 77225-0708 Office Phone: 713-500-6611. E-mail: k.lance.gould@uth.tmc.edu.

GOULD, LEWIS F., JR., lawyer; b. Brewer, Maine, June 4, 1940; BS, Temple U., 1962; JD, Dickinson Sch. Law, 1966. Bar: Pa. 1966, Fla. 1982, US Ct. Appeals 3rd Cir., US Ct. Appeals Fed. Cir., US Dist. Ct. Ea. Dist. Pa., US Patent & Trademark Office, US Supreme Ct., Supreme Ct. Pa., Supreme Ct. Fla. Patent atty. Warner Lambert Pharm. Co., Morris Plains, NJ, 1966—68; assoc. Howson & Howson, Phila., 1968—76, ptnr., 1976—78, Steele, Gould & Fried, Phila., 1978—90, Eckert Seamans Cherin & Mellott, LLC, Phila., 1990—99, Duane Morris LLP, Phila., 1999—, chair firm intellectual property practice group. Commr. Ward 11 Twp. Lower Merion, Pa., 1996—. Mem. Pa. Interest on Lawyers Trust Account Bd., 2002—; bd. trustees Temple U.; bd. dirs. Harriton House, Delaware Valley Regional Planning Commn. Mem.: Phila. Bar Assn., Pa. Bar Assn., Phila. Intellectual Property Law Assn., Am. Intellectual Property Law Assn., Internat. Trademark Assn., Rep. State Com. Pa. Office: Duane Morris LLP One Liberty Pl Philadelphia PA 19103-7396 Office Phone: 215-979-1282. Office Fax: 215-979-1020. Business E-Mail: lfgould@duanemorris.com.

GOULD, LEWIS LUDLOW, historian, educator; b. N.Y.C., Sept. 21, 1939; s. John Ludlow and Carmen L. (Lewis) G.; m. Karen D. Keel, Oct. 24, 1970. AB, Brown U., 1961; MA, Yale U., 1962, PhD, 1966. Instr., then asst. prof. history Yale U., 1965-67; mem. faculty U. Tex., Austin, 1967—, prof. history, 1976—, Eugene C. Barker centennial prof. Am. History, 1983-98, chmn. dept., 1980-84, prof. emeritus, 1998—. Author: Wyoming: A Political History, 1868-1896, 1968, Progressives and Prohibitionists: Texas Democrats in the Wilson Era, 1973, Reform and Regulation: American Politics, 1900-1916, 1978, The Presidency of William McKinley, 1980, The Spanish-American War and President McKinley, 1982, Reform and Regulation: American Politics from Roosevelt to Wilson, 1986, Lady Bird Johnson and the Environment, 1988, Wyoming: From Territory to Statehood, 1989, The Presidency of Theodore Roosevelt, 1991, 1968: The Election That Changed America, 1993, Lady Bird Johnson: Our Environmental First Lady, 1999, Grand Old Party, 2003; co-author: Photojournalist: The Career of Jimmy Hare, 1977, Texas, Her Texas: The Life and Times of Frances Goff, 1997, American Passages: A History of the United States, 1999; editor: The Progressive Era, 1974, American First Ladies: Their Lives and Their Legacy, 1996; co-editor: The Black Experience in America, 1970, Inside the Natchez Trace Collection, 1999. Recipient Carr P. Collins award Tex. Inst. Letters, 1973; Younger Humanist fellow NEH, 1974-75 Mem. Am. Hist. Assn., So. Hist. Assn., Tex. Hist. Assn., Phi Beta Kappa. Democrat. Address: 2602 La Ronde St Austin TX 78731-5924

GOULD, MARILYN A., writer, educator; b. Cleve., Feb. 12, 1928; d. Seymour Irving Amster and Edith (Eisner) Amster-Klein; m. Paul Irving Gould, Jan. 29, 1950; children: Sheri Sindell, Melanie Adams, George. AA, UCLA, 1948; student, Columbia U., 1948; BS, U. So. Calif., L.A., 1950; teaching credential, Calif. State U., Northridge, 1963. Elem. tchr. L.A. (Calif.) City Schs., 1963-75; elem. physiology tchr. Montclair Coll. Prep., L.A., 1974; freelance writer, speaker various cities, 1975—. Instr., lectr. So. Calif. Schs. and Librs. Author: Skateboards You Can Make, 1978, Playground Sports, 1979, Golden Daffodils, 1982, Cars Cars Cars, 1984, The Twelfth of June, 1986, Skateboarding, 1991, Graffiti Wipeout, 1992, Friends True and Periwinkle Blue, 1992. Docent Orange Co. Mus. Art, Newport Beach, Calif.; youth program Orange County Philharm., Newport Beach. Mem. PEN, Soc. Children's Bookwriters, So. Calif. Booksellers, So. Calif. Coun. Lit. for Children and Young People. Home: 726 Bison Ave Newport Beach CA 92660-3207

GOULD, MARTHA BERNICE, retired librarian; b. Claremont, NH, Oct. 8, 1931; d. Sigmund and Gertrude Heller; m. Arthur Gould, July 29, 1960; children: Leslie, Stephen. BA in Edn., U. Mich., 1953; MS in Libr. Sci., Simmons Coll., 1956; cert., U. Denver Libr. Sch., 1978. Childrens libr. N.Y. Pub. Libr., 1956-58; adminstr. libr. svcs. act demonstration regional libr. project Pawhuska, Okla., 1958-59; cons. N.Mex. State Libr., 1959-60; children's libr. then sr. children's libr. L.A. Pub. Libr., 1960-72; acctg. dir. pub. svcs., reference libr. Nev. State Libr., 1972-74; pub. svcs. libr. Washoe County (Nev.) Libr., 1974-79, asst. county libr., 1979-84, county libr., 1984-94; ret., 1994. Cons. Nev. State Libr. and Archives, 1996—2003; part-time lectr. libr. adminstrn. U. Nev.; acting dir. Nev. Ctr. for the Book; vice-chair Nat. Commn. in Librs. and Info. Sci., 1993—2000, chair, 2000—03; mem. adv. coun. Nev. Coun. on Librs. and Literacy, 2001—05; mem. adv. bd. Fleischmann Planetarium, 1999—2003. Co-editor: Nevada Women's History Project Annotated Bibliography, 1999; contbr. articles to jours. Exec. dir. Kids Voting/USA, Nev., 1996; treas. United Jewish Appeals, 1981; bd. dirs. Temple Sinai, Planned Parenthood, 1996-97, Truckee Meadows Habitat for Humanity, 1995-98; trustee RSVP, North Nevadans for ERA; No. Nev. chmn. Gov.'s Conf. on Libr., 1990; bd. dirs. Campaign for Choice, No. Nev. Food Bank, Nev. Women's Fund (Hall of Fame award 1989); mem. No. Nev. NCCJ, Washoe County Quality Life Task Force, 1992—, Washoe County Elections Taskforce, 1999—; bd. dirs. KUNR Pub. Radio, 1999-00, chair bd. dirs., 2000-04; chair Sierra Nevada Cmty. Access TV; adv. bd. Partnership Librs. Washoe County; co-chair social studies curriculum adv. task force Washoe County Sch. Dist.; mem. Nev. Women's History Project Bd.; chair Downtown River Corridor Com., 1995-97; vice chair Dem. Party Washoe County, 1998-00; v.p. Nev. Diabetes Assn. for Children and Adults, 1998-02, pres., 2002-04, mem. adv. bd., 2004—; chair devel. com. Planned Parenthood, 2002-; bd. dirs. Washoe Libr. Found., 2003-05; mem. adv. Adv. Coun. on Edn./to the Holocaust, 2000-; chair Washoe County Dem. Women's Club, 2003-05; coord. Chrone Disease Prevention Project Storytime, 2005—, Diabetes Edn. Prevention Program, Nev., 2005-; chair 2nd Century Endowment for Washoe Century Libr. Recipient Nev. State Libr. Letter of Commendation, 1973, Washoe County Bd. Commrs. Resolution of Appreciation, 1978, ACLU of Nev. Civil Libertarian of Yr. 1988, Freedom's Sake award AAUW, 1989, Leadership in Literacy award Sierra chpt. Internat. Reading Assn., 1992, Woman of Distinction award 1992, Cornerstone award Sierra chpt. Assn. Fundraising Profls., 2003. Mem. ALA (bd. dirs., intellectual freedom roundtable 1977-79, intellectual freedom com. 1979-83, coun. 1983-86), ACLU (bd. dirs. Civil Libertarian of Yr. Nev. chpt. 1988, chair gov.'s conf. for women 1989), Nev. Libr. Assn. (chmn. pub. info. com. 1972-73, intellectual freedom com. 1975-78, govt. rels. com. 1978-79, v.p., pres.-elect 1980, pres. 1981, Spl. Citation 1978, 87, Libr. of Yr. 1993). Personal E-mail: mgould@unr.edu.

GOULD, PHILLIP, engineer; b. N.Y.C., Feb. 19, 1940; s. Isaac and Blanche Gould; m. Elizabeth West Ratigan, Nov. 29, 1980; children: David Elliot, Jessica Ann. BSME, CCNY, 1961; MS, MIT, 1963, ScD, 1965. Asst. prof. mech. engring. MIT, Cambridge, 1965-67; mem. staff Inst. for Def. Analyses, Alexandria, Va., asst. dir., 1984—. Dir. Def. Sci. Study Group, 1998—. Fellow, Ford Found., 1965. Fellow: AAAS; mem.: Am. Soc. Engring. Edn., Inst. for Ops. Rsch. and Mgmt. Sci., N.Y. Acad. Scis., Washington Congregation for Secular Humanistic Judaism (past pres.), Soc. for Humanistic Judaism (pres.), Sigma Xi. Home: 4950 Indian Rock Ter NW Washington DC 20007-2567 Office: Inst Def Analyses 4850 Mark Ctr Dr Alexandria VA 22311-1882 E-mail: pgould@alum.mit.edu.

GOULD, PHILLIP LOUIS, engineering educator, department chairman; b. Chgo., May 24, 1937; m. Deborah Paula Rothholtz, Feb. 5, 1961; children: Elizabeth, Nathan, Rebecca, Joshua. BS, U. Ill., 1959, MS, 1960; PhD, Northwestern U., 1966. Structural designer Skidmore, Owings & Merrill, Chgo., 1960-63; prin. structural engr. Westenhoff & Novick, Chgo., 1963-64; NASA trainee Northwestern U., Evanston, Ill., 1964-66; asst. prof. civil engring. Washington U., St. Louis, 1966-68, assoc. prof., 1968-74, prof., 1974—, chmn. dept. civil engring., 1978-98, Harold D. Jolly prof. civil engring., 1981—. Vis. prof. Ruhr U., Fed. Republic Germany, 1974-75, U. Sydney, Australia, 1981, Shanghai Inst. Tech., Peoples Republic of China, 1986; dir. Earthquake Engring. Rsch. Inst., exec. coun. Internat. Assn. for Shell and Spatial Structures, pres. Great Lakes chpt. and New Madrid chpt. Earthquake Engring. Rsch. Inst. Author: Static Analysis of Shells: A Unified Development of Surface Structures, 1977, Introduction to Linear Elasticity, 1984, Finite Element Analysis of Shells of Revolution, 1985, Analysis of Shells and Plates, 1987, 2d edit., 1999; co-author: Dynamic Response of Structures to Wind and Earthquake Loading, 1980; co-editor: Environmental Forces on Engineering Structures, 1979, Natural Draught Cooling Towers, 1985; editor: Engineering Structures, 1979—. Dir. Earthquake Engring. Rsch. Inst., 1993—95; vice chmn. Mo. Seismic Safety Commn., 1998—99, chmn., 2000—01; St. Louis regional dir. Mid-Am. Earthquake Ctr. Recipient Sr. Scientist award Alexander von Humboldt Found., Fed. Republic Germany, 1974-75 Fellow ASCE (bd. dirs. St. Louis sect. 1985-87, Otto Nutli award, Profl. Recognition award); mem. Am. Soc. Engring. Edn., Internat. Assn. Shell Structures, Structural Engrs. Assn. Ill. (Outstanding Engr. in Edn. award), Civil Engring. Alumni Assn. U. Ill., Urbana-Champaign (Disting. Alumnus award). Home: 102 Lake Frst Saint Louis MO 63117-1303 Office: Washington U Dept Civil Engring PO Box 1130 Saint Louis MO 63188-1130 E-mail: pgoul@seas.wustl.edu.

GOULD, RONALD MURRAY, federal judge; b. St. Louis, Oct. 17, 1946; s. Harry H. and Sylvia C. (Sadofsky) Gould; m. Suzanne H. Goldblatt, Dec. 1, 1968; children: Daniel, Rebecca. BS in Econs., U. Pa., 1968; JD, U. Mich., 1973. Bar: Wash. 1975, U.S. Dist. Ct. (we. dist.) Wash. 1976, U.S. Ct. Appeals (9th cir.) 1980, U.S. Supreme Ct. 1981, U.S. Dist. Ct. (ea. dist.) Wash. 1982, U.S. Ct. Appeals (fed. cir.) 1986. Law clk. to hon. Wade H. McCree Jr. U.S. Ct. Appeals (6th cir.), Detroit, 1973—74; law clk. to hon. justice Potter Stewart U.S. Supreme Ct., Washington, 1974—75; assoc. Perkins Coie, Seattle, 1975—80, ptnr., 1981—99; judge U.S. Ct. Appeals (9th cir.), Seattle, 1999—. Adj. prof. U. Washington Law Sch., 1986—89. Editor-in-chief: Mich. Law Rev., 1972—73; editor: Washington Civil Procedure Deskbook, 1981. Exec. bd. chief Seattle coun. Boy Scouts Am., 1984—; bd. dirs. econ. devel. coun. Seattle and King County, 1991—94; citizens cabinet mem. Gov. Mike Lowry, Seattle, 1993—96; bd. trustees Bellevue CC, 1993—99; mem. cmty. rels. coun. Jewish Fedn. of Greater Seattle, 1985—88. Fellow: ABA (antitrust sect., litig. sect.); mem.: Am. Judicature Soc., King County Bar Assn. (Disting. Svc. award 1987), Wash. State Bar Assn. (bd. govs. 1988—91, pres. 1994—95), 9th Jud. Cir. Hist. Soc. (bd. dirs. 1994—), Supreme Ct. Hist. Soc. Jewish. Avocations: reading, chess. Office: US Courthouse 1200 6th Ave Fl 21 Seattle WA 98101-3123

GOULD, ROXANNE JEAN, history professor, researcher; b. Sioux Falls, S.D., June 15, 1958; d. Ronald Dean and Roberta Jean (Stevenson) Gould; children: Gabriel Siert, Ronelle Siert. BA, U. S.D., Vermillion, 1980, MA, 1990; EdD, U. Minn., Mpls., 2004. Program dir. Am. Indian Svcs. Program, Sioux City, Iowa, 1981—83; dir. Ednl. Equity, Indian Edn., Sioux City Schs., Iowa, 1983—96; adj. faculty Nebr. Indian CC, Sioux City, Iowa, 1993—95; dir. Am. Indian Learning Resource Ctr., U. Minn., Mpls., 1997—. Bd. dirs. Resource Ctr. Ams., Mpls., 1997—98; mem. Ptnrs. in Am. Indian Retention, Mpls., 1997—2001; bd. dirs. All Nations U., Mpls., 2004—. Contbr. articles to profl. jours. Co-founder Sharing the Dream, Guatemala, 1996—; fundraiser, organizer Caminos Juntos, Tlamarazapa, Mexico, 2002; co-founder Sobriety Coun., Sioux City, Iowa, 1990—91, Iowa Cuba Com., 1994—96. Recipient Sioux City Human Rights Award, Sioux City Human Rights Commn., 1984; fellow, Kellogg Found., 1993—96, Bush Found., 2003—04. Mem.: Am. Coll. Personnel Assn., Nat. Indian Edn. Assn., Am. Ednl. Rsch. Assn. Avocations: native dance, beadwork. Home: 4715 Xerxes Ave S Minneapolis MN 55410 Office: Am Indian Learning Resource Ctr 125 Fraser 106 Pleasant St Minneapolis MN 55455

GOULD, ROY WALTER, engineering educator; b. LA, Apr. 25, 1927; s. Roy Walter Gould and Rosamonde Belle (Stokes) Termain; m. Ethel Stratton, Aug. 23, 1952; children: Diana Stratton, Robert Clarke. BS, Calif. Inst. Tech., 1949, PhD, 1956; MS, Stanford U., 1950. With Calif. Inst. Tech., Pasadena, 1955—, exec. officer for applied physics, 1972-79, chmn. div. engring. and applied sci., 1979-84, Simon Ramo prof. engring., 1979-96, prof. emeritus, 1996—. Dir. div. controlled thermonuclear research U.S. Energy Research Devel. Agy., Washington, 1970-72. Contbr. articles to profl. jours. Served with USN, 1945-46. Fellow IEEE, Am. Phys. Soc. (James Clerk Maxwell prize in plasma physics 1994); mem. NAS, Am. Acad. Arts and Scis., Nat. Acad. Engring. Office: Calif Inst Tech Dept Engring Applied Sci Ms 128 95 Pasadena CA 91125-0001 Business E-Mail: rwgould@caltech.edu.

GOULD, W. SCOTT, financial administrator; b. Boston, July 19, 1957; m. Michèle A. Flournoy; 1 child, Alexander. AB, Cornell U., 1979; MBA, EdD, U. Rochester. Commd. ensign USN, advanced through grades; mgmt. cons. TB&A, 1988-90, mng. assoc., 1990-91; asst. receiver, dir. ops. City of Chelsea, Mass., 1991-93; spl. asst. to chmn. Export-Import Bank of U.S., Washington, 1993-94; spl. asst. White House Chief of Staff, Washington, 1993-94; dep. asst. sec. Dept. Treasury, Washington; CFO, asst. sec. adminstrn. Dept. Commerce, Washington, until 1999; CFO, Exoice Inc., Washington, 1999—. Mem. adv. bd. Simon Sch. Bus.; class agt. Roxbury Latin Sch. Ann. Fund; mentor Cornell U. Extern Program. Comdr. USNR. Mem. Inst. Mgmt. Consultants (assoc.), Kappa Delta Pi. Office: 6725 Honesty Dr Bethesda MD 20817-5516

GOULD, WILLIAM BENJAMIN, IV, lawyer, educator, federal agency administrator; b. 1936; AB, U. R.I., 1958; LLB, Cornell U., 1961; postgrad., London Sch. Econs., 1962—63; LLD (hon.), U. R.I., 1986, D.C. Sch. Law, 1995, Stetson U., 1996; LLD, Capital U., 1997, Rutgers U., 1998. Bar: Mich. 1962. Asst. gen. counsel UAW, AFL-CIO, Detroit, 1961—62; atty. NLRB, Washington, 1963—65; assoc. Battle, Fowler, Stokes & Kheel, N.Y.C., 1965—68; prof. Wayne State U., Detroit, 1968—71, Stanford U. Law Sch., 1972—, Charles A. Beardsley prof. law, 1984—2002, emeritus, 2002—; William M. Ramsey Disting. Prof. Law Willamette Coll. Law, 2002—04. Chmn. Nat. Labor Rels. Bd., Washington, 1994—98, Coun. Adminstrv. Conf. U.S., Washington, 1994—95; vis. prof. Harvard U., 1971—72; overseas fellow and vis. prof. Churchill Coll., Cambridge, England, 1975; vis. scholar U. Tokyo, 1975, 78; Fulbright-Hays Disting. lectr. Kyoto Am. Studies Summer Seminar; Charles A. Beardsley prof. Stanford Law Sch., 1984; vis. fellow Australian Nat. U. Faculty of Law, 1985; vis. prof. European U. Inst., Florence, Italy, 1988, U. Witwatersrand, Johannesburg, 1991; lectr. Am. and fgn. indsl. rels., labor law U.S., Europe, Japan, S.E. Asia, Africa, Eastern Europe. Author: Diary of a Contraband: The Civil War Passage of a Black Sailor, Labored Relations: Law, Politics and the NLRB- A Memoir, 2000, International Labor Standards: Globalization, trade and Public Policy, 2003, A Primer on American Labor Law, 2004. Fellow, Rockefeller Found., 1975, Guggenheim, 1978. Mem.: ABA (sec. labor and employment law sect.), Internat. Soc. for Labor Law and Social Security (exec. com. U.S. nat. br.), Nat. Acad. Arbitrators. Office: Stanford Law School Crown Quadrangle 559 Nathan Abbot Way Stanford CA 94305-8610*

GOULDEN, JOSEPH CHESLEY, author; b. Marshall, Tex., May 23, 1934; s. Joe C. and Lecta M. (Everitt) G.; m. Leslie Cantrell Smith, 1979; children by previous marriage: Joseph C., Jim Craig. Student, U. Tex., 1952-56. Reporter Marshall News Messenger, 1956, Dallas News, 1958-61, Phila. Inquirer, 1961-68. Dir. media analysis Accuracy in Media, 1989-98. Books include The Curtis Caper, 1965, Monopoly, 1968, Truth Is the First Casualty, 1969, The Money Givers, 1971, Meany, 1972, The Superlawyers, 1972, The Benchwarmers, 1974, The Best Years, 1976, The Million Dollar Lawyers, 1978, Korea: The Untold Story of the War, 1982, Jerry Wurf: Labor's Last Angry Man, 1982, The Death Merchant, 1984, (as Henry S.A. Becket) The Dictionary of Espionage, 1986, Fit to Print: A.M. Rosenthal and His Times, 1988; author: (with Paul Dickson) There Are Alligators in Our Sewers, 1983, (with Paul Dickson) Myth-Informed, 1993, (with Reed Irvine and Cliff Kincaid) The News Manipulators, 1993; editor: books include Mencken's Last Campaign, 1976. Served with U.S. Army, 1956-58. Mem.: Internat. Studies Program, Va. Mil. Inst. (bd.), Assn. Former Intelligence Officers, Washington Ind. Writers, Tex. Inst. Letters, H.L. Mencken Soc., Cosmos Club, Phi Kappa Tau. Home: 1534 29th St NW Washington DC 20007-3060 Office: Brandt & Hochman 1501 Broadway New York NY 10036-5601 Address: # 206 The Henlopen Rehoboth Beach DE 19971 E-mail: josephg894@aol.com.

GOULDER, GERALD POLSTER, retail executive, management consultant, lawyer; b. Columbus, Ohio, Apr. 30, 1953; s. Norman Ernest and Betty (Polster) G.; children: Gavrielle, Nathaniel. BA, Ohio State U., 1975; JD, Washington U., 1978. Bar: Ohio 1978, N.C. 1985; cert. mediator N.C. Superior Ct., N.C. Indsl. Commn. Spl. prosecutor office state atty. gen. Divsn. Medicaid Fraud Control, Columbus, 1979-80; spl. prosecutor Antitrust Divsn., Columbus, 1981-82; atty. James M. Schottenstein & Assocs., Columbus, 1982-84; chmn., CEO Carolina Drug Distbrs., Inc. and Emporium Stores, Ltd., Greensboro, NC, 1984-96. Mediator Mediation Practice N.C., Bus. Mediation Svc., 2001-03; prin. Equine Dispute Resolution Svc., N.C. Bus. Mediation Coun. Assoc. editor Washington U. Urban Law Ann., 1977-78; contbr. articles to profl. jours. Trustee Wexner Heritage Village, Columbus, 1983-84, bd. dirs. Eastern Music Festival, Greensboro, 1991-94, U. N.C.-Greensboro Spartan Club, 1991-95; v.p. Beth David Synagogue, Greensboro, 1992-95, pres., 1996; participant Leadership Greensboro, 1985, Triad Leadership, 1991; mem. Crime Study Commn., Greensboro, 1992, Greensboro Devel. Corp., 1993-95. Fellow, Inst. of Polit. Leadership, 2004. Mem. Am. Arbitration Assn., Am. Intellectual Property Lawyers Assn., N.C. Bar Assn., Greensboro Bar Assn., Columbus Bar Assn., Ohio Bar Assn., Leadership Greensboro Alumni Assn., Am. Immigration Lawyers Assn. Office: Goulder Immigration Law Firm 3200 Northline Ave Ste 130 Greensboro NC 27408 Home: 12 Wedgewood Ct Greensboro NC 27403-1074 E-mail: ggoulder@triad.rr.com.

GOULDEY, GLENN CHARLES, manufacturing executive; b. N.Y.C., July 28, 1952; s. George Howard and Jeannette Ruth Williamson; m. Leslie Jeanne Ruth, Oct. 2, 1982; children: Jeremy Charles, Nicholas Glenn, Alexander James George. BS in Bus., Coll. N.J., 1976; postgrad., Portland State U., 1980; MBA, Rider U., 1981; postgrad., Dartmouth Coll., 1994—95. Cert. in purchasing mgmt., cert. in prodn. and inventory control. Sr. planner Eaton Corp., Flemington, N.J., 1975-77, pricing mgr., distbn., 1977-79, inventory control mgr., 1979-80, materials mgr., purchasing Beaverton, Oreg., 1980-81, mfg. and materials mgr., 1981-83, mktg. and materials mgr., 1983-87, plant and gen. mgr., 1987-88, v.p. sales and mktg. Carol Stream, Ill., 1988-89, mgr. ops. divsn., 1989-93, gen. bus. mgr., 1993-95, pres., gen. mgr. Lectron Products divsn. Rochester Hills, Mich., 1995-99, v.p., gen. mgr. Actuator Sensor Divsn., 2000—01; v.p. technology, planning strategy IT Eaton Automotive Group Worldwide, Southfield, Mich., 2001—. Patentee in field. Mem. bd. advisors Oakland U. Bus. Sch., Mich. Colls. Found., Albion Coll.-Gerstacker Inst.; bd. dirs., chair Rochester Cmty. Schs. Found.; asst. coach lacrosse Rochester Hills United H.S. Mem. Am. Prodn. Inventory Control Soc., Nat. Youth Sports Coaches Assn. (cert.), Soc. Automotive Engrs. Internat. Republican. Lutheran. Office: Eaton Corp 26201 Northwestern Hwy Southfield MI 48076-3926 Office Phone: 248-226-6776. E-mail: GlennGouldey@eaton.com.

GOULDIN, DAVID MILLEN, lawyer; b. Binghamton, N.Y., Mar. 8, 1941; s. Paul C. and Virginia M. Gouldin; m. Deborah A. Gouldin, Aug. 20, 1966; children: Robert, Michael, Lauryn, Derek. AB, Princeton U., 1963; JD, Cornell U., 1966. Bar: N.Y., U.S. Dist. Ct. N.Y. Ptnr. Levene, Gouldin & Thompson, LLP, Binghamton, 1966—. Mem. N.Y. State Bd. Law Examiners, 1999—. Author: (with others) Commercial Litigation in New York Courts, 1995. Chmn. Broome County (N.Y.) Arena, 1981; chmn. Broome County Health Fair, 1986-87; gen. chmn. ministry endowment campaign Broome County Coun. Chs., 1986-87; pres. United Way Broome County, 1982-84; mem. United Way N.Y. State, 1985-99, chmn., 1991-92; chancellor Wyo. conf. United Meth. Ch., 1987—; bd. dirs. Roberson Ctr. for Arts, 1983-89, United Health Svcs. Hosps., 1990-2002; bd. dirs. Broome County Urban League, 1994-2000, sec., 1995-2000; trustee Wyo. Sem., 1973-88, Miller S. Gaffney and Adelaide S. Gaffney Found., 1996—; trustee Edwin A. Link and Marion C. Link Found., 1989—, chmn., 1993—, dir. Binghamton U. Found., 2003-, chair, Harpur Forum, 2003-. Recipient Sertoma Svc. to Mankind Dist. award, 1988, Disting. Citizens award Baden-Powell coun. Boy Scouts Am., 1996; named to Sect. Four Hall of Fame, 1978, Outstanding Young Men of Am., 1974, Sect. IV Hall of Fame, 1978; named Man of Yr. Post 80 Am. Legion Hall of Fame, 1989. Mem. N.Y. State Bar Assn. (chmn. TICL sect. 1992, Root-Stimson award 1987, John Leach award 1999), Broome County Bar Assn. (pres. 1989), Fedn. Bar 6th Dist. (pres. 1974), Rotary. Republican. Home: 85 Highland Ave Binghamton NY 13905-4039 Office: PO Box F1706 Binghamton NY 13902-0106 Office Phone: 607-584-5706. E-mail: dgouldin@binghamtonlaw.com.

GOULDING, NORA See CLARK, SUSAN

GOULDTHORPE, KENNETH ALFRED PERCIVAL, publisher, state official; b. Jan. 7, 1928; came to U.S., 1951, naturalized, 1956; s. Alfred Edward and Frances Elizabeth Finch (Callow) G.; m. Judith Marion Cutts, Aug. 9, 1975; children: Amanda Frances, Timothy Graham Cutts. Student, U. Westminster, 1948-49; diploma, City and Guilds of London, 1949; student, Washington, 1951-52. Staff photographer Kentish Mercury, London, 1949-50, St. Louis Post-Dispatch, 1951-55, picture editor, 1955-57; nat. and fgn. corr. Life mag., Time, Inc., N.Y.C., 1957-61, Paris Bur., 1961-65, regional editor

Australia-New Zealand, 1966-68, editl. dir. Latin Am., 1969-70; editor Signature mag., N.Y.C., 1970-73; mng. editor Penthouse mag., N.Y.C., 1973-76, pub. cons., 1976-79; editor, exec. pub. Adventure Travel mag., Seattle, 1979-80; sr. ptnr. Pacific Pub. Assocs., Seattle, 1979-80; editor, pub. Washington mag., 1984-89; vice-chmn. Evergreen Pub Co., 1984-89; dir. tourism State of Wash., 1989-91. Pub., cons., writer, 1991—; bd. dirs. Grand Fir Pub. Corp., Pacific Pub. Assocs., Seattle; tchr. design, editl. techniques Parsons Sch. Design, N.Y.C.; lectr., contbr. elem. schs. lit. progs. Author: Design for Music, 1998, Seafood Secrets of the Pacific Northwest, 2002; contbr. articles, photographs to nat. mags., books by Life mag. With Royal Navy Cadet Corps., 1943-45, Sea Service, 1946-48. Decorated Naval Medal and bar; recipient awards of excellence Nat. Press Photographers Assn., AP and UP, 1951-57, Pres.'s medal Ea. Wash. U., 1986; certs. excellence Am. Inst. Graphic Arts, 1971, 72, 73, Comm. Arts, 1980, 81, 84; Spl. award N.Y. Soc. Publs. Designers, 1980; nominated for Pulitzer Prize for coverage of Andrea Doria disaster, 1956. Mem. Regional Pubs. Assn. (v.p., pres., Best Typography award 1985, Best Spl. Issue 1989), Western Publs. Assn. (Best Consumer Mag. award, Best Travel Mag. awards 1980, Best Regional and State Mag. award 1985, 86, 88, Best New Publ. award 1985, Best Column award 1985, Best Signed Essay 1986, 87, Best Four-Color Layout 1985, Best Four Color Feature Design), City and Regional Mag. Assn. (William Allen White Bronze awards), Time/Life Alumni Soc., Assn. Washington Gens. (gen. of state 1995, bd. dirs.), Medieval Knights of London, Sigma Delta Chi. Episcopalian. Home: 3049 NW Esplanade Seattle WA 98117-2624 Office Phone: 206-782-6658. E-mail: kgouldthorpe@comcast.com.

GOULET, CHARLES RYAN, retired insurance company executive; b. Fond du Lac, Wis., Oct. 13, 1927; s. Charles N. and Irene (Ryan) G.; m. Jeanne Comfort, Aug. 18, 1951; 1 child, Christopher Robert. BA, Beloit Coll., 1951; MBA, U. Chgo., 1953. Adminstrv. resident Jefferson-Hillman Hosp., Birmingham, Ala., 1952-53; adminstrv. asst., asst. supt. Cleve. City Hosp., 1953-55; asst. prof. U. Pitts., 1955-58; asso. dir. Johns Hopkins Hosp., 1958-62; dir. U. Chgo. Hosps. and Clinics, 1962-69; prof. hosp. adminstrn. U. Chgo., 1962-69, assoc. dir. program in hosp. adminstrn., 1962-69; prin. Cresap, McCormick and Paget, Inc.; mgmt. cons., Chgo., 1969-71; v.p. Blue Cross-Blue Shield, Chgo., 1971-75, exec. v.p., 1975-88; vice chmn., dir. H.M.O. Ill. Inc., 1980-88; exec. sec. Assn. U. Programs in Hosp. Adminstrn., 1962-65, pres. Chgo. Hosp. Council, 1968; pres. HMO Ill., Inc., 1976-82. Treas. Ill. Hosp. Assn., 1969; mem. exec. com. Council Teaching Hosps., Assn. Am. Med. Colls., 1966-69 Mem. adv. coun. Kellogg Found., 1965-67; bd. dirs. Hyde Park Dept. YMCA, 1966-68, Coop. Blood Replacement Plan, Home for destitute Crippled Children, 1965-69, Chgo. Home for Incurables, 1966-69, Harvard-St. George Sch. Chgo., 1968-72, Hosp. Planning Coun. Met. Chgo., 1968-69, Comprehensive Health Planning, Chgo., 1968-71, Ill. Regional Med. Program, 1967-69, Am. Blood Commn., 1976-89, v.p., 1978-83, Geneva (Ill.) Cmty. Chest, 1990, 93-96, pres., 1975-76; mem. governing commn. Cook County Hosp., 1969-70; mem. Ill. Health Fin. Authority, 1979-82, Ill. Health Care Cost Containment Com., 1984-96; trustee Alexian Bros. Med. Ctr., Elk Grove Village, Ill., 1993-94; bd. govs. Alexian Bros. Health Sys., 1995—; dir. Alexian Bros. Health Providers, 1996—. 1st lt. Med. Adminstrn. Corps AUS, 1946-47. Recipient Bachmeyer award U. Chgo., 1953; Disting. Service award Beloit Coll., 1976 Fellow Am. Coll. Hosp. Adminstrs.; mem. Am. Hosp. Assn., Skyline Club (Chgo.), Big Foot Country Club (Fontana, Wis.), Quadrangle Club (Chgo.), Oasis Country Club (Palm Desert, Calif.), Marrakesh Country Club (Palm Desert), Phi Kappa Phi.

GOULET, DENIS ANDRÉ, writer; b. Fall River, Mass., May 27, 1931; s. Fernand Joseph and Lumena (Bouchard) G.; m. Ana Maria Reynaldo, Nov. 21, 1964; children: Andrea, Sinane. BA in Philosophy, St. Paul's Coll., Washington, 1954, MA in Philosophy, 1956; MA in Social Planning, Institut de Recherche et de Formation en Vue du Développement, Paris, 1960; PhD in Polit. Sci., U. São Paulo, Brazil, 1963. Laborer, France, Spain, Algeria, 1956-59; planning advisor AID, Recife, Brazil, 1964-65; vis. prof. U. Sask., Regina, Can., 1965-66; assoc. prof. Ind. U., Bloomington, 1966-68; vis. fellow Ctr. for Study of Dem. Instns., Santa Barbara, Calif., 1969; vis. prof. U. Calif., San Diego, 1969-70; sr. fellow Ctr. for Study Devel. and Social Change, Cambridge, Mass., 1970-74; vis. fellow Overseas Devel. Coun./OAS, Washington, 1974-76; sr. fellow Overseas Devel. Coun., Washington, 1976-79; O'Neill chair in edn. for justice, dept. econs. U. Notre Dame, Ind., 1979—2002, O'Neill chair emeritus, 2002—; faculty fellow Kellogg Inst. for Internat. Study, Kroc Inst. for Internat. Peace Studies. Vis. prof. U. Warsaw, Poland, 1989-90. Author: The Cruel Choice, 1971, The Uncertain Promise, 1977, Mexico: Development Strategies for the Future, 1983, Incentives for Development: The Key to Equity, 1989, Development Ethics: A Guide to Theory and Practice, 1995. Editl. bd. Jour. of Health and Population in Developing Countries; internat. adv. coun. TODA Inst. for Global Peace and Policy Rsch.; internat. adv. bd. Internat. Centre for Islamic Political Economy. Decorated chevalier Odre Nat. du Cèdre (Lebanon), 1960; OAS grantee, 1961-62, Fulbright grantee, 1986; recipient Reinhold Niebuhr award U. Notre Dame, 1988. Democrat. Roman Catholic. Avocation: piano. Home: 825 Ashland Ave South Bend IN 46616-1307 Office: U Notre Dame 519 Flanner Hall Notre Dame IN 46556-5677 Business E-Mail: dgoulet@nd.edu.

GOULET, LORRIE, sculptor; b. Riverdale, N.Y., Aug. 17, 1925; Student, Inwood Potteries Studios, N.Y.C., 1932-36, Black Mountain Coll., N.C., 1943-44. Tchr. Mus. Modern Art, 1957, 64, Scarsdale Studio Workshop, 1959, 61, New Sch., 1961—75, Art Students League, 1981—. One-woman shows include Clay Club Sculpture Ctr., N.Y.C., 1948, 1955, Cheney Libr., Hoosick Falls, N.Y., 1951, Contemporaries Gallery, N.Y.C., 1959, 1962, 1966, 1968, Rye (N.Y.) Art Ctr., 1966, New Sch. Assocs., N.Y.C., 1968, Temple Emeth, Teaneck, N.J., 1969, Kennedy Galleries, N.Y.C., 1971, 1973, 1975, 1978, 1980, 1982, 1986, Carolyn Hill Gallery, 1988, 1991, Caldwell (N.J.) Coll., 1989, Nat. Mus. Women in the Arts, Washington, 1998, Harmon-Meek Galleries, Naples, Fla., 2000, David Findlay Jr. Gallery, 2001, 2002, 2004, 2005, exhibited in group shows at Mus. Natural History, 1936, Whitney Mus. Am. Art, N.Y.C., 1948—50, 1953, 1955, Met. Mus. Art, 1951, Detroit Inst. Art, 1960, Pa. Acad., 1950—52, 1954, 1959, 1964, AD, N.Y.C., 1966, 1975, 1977, Corcoran Gallery, Washington, 1966, Hofstra Mus., N.Y.C., 1990, The McNey Mus., 1990, The Copley Soc., Boston, 1991, The Spanish Inst., 1992, Lehigh U. Art Gallery, 1992, Iowa State U. Brunne Gallery, 1992, Paine Art Ctr., Oshkosh, Wis., 1992, Mitchell Art Gallery, St. John's Coll., Annapolis, Md., 1992, Erie (Pa.) Art Mus., 1995, Nat. Sculpture Soc., 2001, Art Students League, N.Y.C., 2003, David Findlay Jr. Gallery, 2005, Represented in permanent collections Hunter Mus., Chattanooga, N.J. State Mus., Wichita Mus. Art, Hirschhorn Sculpture Mus., Washington, The Philharm. Ctr., Naples, Fla., Art Students League, N.Y.C., Savannah Coll. Arts. Recipient Malvina Hoffman award Nat. Acad. Design, 2001, others; grantee Fhorsheim Art Fund, 1997. Fellow: Nat. Sculpture Soc. (coun.); mem.: NAD (academician 1989, mem. coun. 1994), Fine Arts Fedn. (pres. 1998—2002, hon. v.p. 2003), N.Y. Artists Equity Inc. (pres. 1998—2002), Visual Artists and Galleries Assocs., Sculptors Guild.

GOULET, ROBERT GERARD, entertainer; b. Lawrence, Mass., Nov. 26, 1933; s. Joseph and Jeannette (Gauthier) G.; m. Louise Longmore, 1956 (div.); 1 child, Nicolette; m. Carol Lawrence, 1963 (div.); children: Christopher, Michael; m. Vera Chochrovska Novak, 1982. Student, Royal Conservatory Music, Toronto, Ont. Made Broadway debut in Camelot, 1960; numerous stage appearances including: Thunder Rock 1951, Sunshine Town 1951, Visit To a Small Planet 1951, Carousel, 1955, Finian's Rainbow, 1956, Gentlemen Prefer Blondes, 1956, Spring Thaw, 1955-57, The Pajama Game, 1957, The Optimist, 1957, The Beggar's Opera, 1958, Bell's Are Ringing, 1959, Meet Me in St. Louis, 1960, The Happy Time, 1968 (Tony award); (Broadway plays) I Do I Do, 1970, Carousel, 1979, On a Clear Day, 1980, Kiss Me Kate, 1981, South Pacific, 1986-88, Fantasticks, 1990, Camelot as King Arthur, 1990, 92-94; (nat. tour and Broadway) South Pacific, 1995, Moon Over Buffalo, 1996, Man of La Mancha, 1996-97, Camelot, 1998, 2004, South Pacific, 2002, La Cage aux Folles, 2005; numerous television specials and TV appearances series including Blue Light, 1966, The Big Valley, 1967, Police Story, 1970, Mission Impossible, 1972, Police Woman, 1975, Cannon, 1976, The Dream Merchants, 1980, Matt Houston, 1983, Glitter, 1984, Murder, She Wrote, 1985, Finder of Lost Love, 1985, Mr. Belvedere, 1986, 88, 89, 90, (CBS pilot) Make My Day, 1991, In the Heat of the Night, 1992, Based on a Untrue Story, 1992, Burke's Law, 1994, Get Smart, 1994, ESPN Coll. Basketball Commls., 1995-97, Recess 1998, George & Leo 1998, Just Shoot Me, 1998, Two Guys and a Girl, 1999; star films Honeymoon Hotel, 1964, I'd Rather Be Rich, 1964, I Deal in Danger, 1966, Underground, 1970, Atlantic City, 1981, Beetlejuice, 1988, Scrooged, 1989, Naked Gun II 1/2, 1991, Mr. Wrong, 1996, (voice) Toy Story 2, 1999, The Last Producer, 2000, G-Men From Hell, 2000; has recorded over 60 albums. Recipient numerous awards including World Theatre award, Tony award, Grammy award Best New Artist, 1962, Grammy award Gold Album for My Love Forgive Me, 1964. Fellow (hon.) Toronto Royal Conservatory Music. Fellow Royal Conservatory Music (hon.). Office: Rogo & Rove Inc 3110 Monte Rosa Ave Las Vegas NV 89120-3040

GOULI, VLADIMIR VASILIEVICH, entomologist; b. Troizk, Cheliabinsk, Russia, Oct. 20, 1938; arrived in U.S., 1995; s. Vasili Ivanovich Gouli and Maria Vladimirovna Taranova; m. Tamara Chadjieva (dec.); m. Svetlana Ribina, Feb. 16, 1993; children: Elena, Vasil, Vladislav. MS, U. Vladicaucasus, Russia, 1961; PhD, Inst. Cytology and Genetics, Novosibirsk, Russia, 1967, DSc, 1974. Lead biocontrol dept. Siberian Inst. Agr., Novosibirsk, 1971—80; lead microbial control dept. All-Union Inst. Biol. Plant Protection, Kishinev, Russia, 1980—85; lead entomol. dept. Agrouniversity Moldova, Kishinev, 1985—92; prodr. biopesticides Claveles Colombianos, Bogota, Colombia, 1993—95; rsch. assoc. U. Vt., Burlington, 1995—. Author: Viruses in Forest Protection, 1975, Microorganisms Useful for Biological Control, 1981, Microbial Control of Noxious Organisms, 1982, Dictionary for Biological Plant Protection, 1986, Virsuses of Insects and Their Diagnostics, 1988, Integrated Pest Management, 1992, Protectia Integrata a Plantelor, 1994, Biological Plant Protection, 2004; contbr. articles to profl. jours. Mem.: Soc. Invertebrate Pathology, Entomol. Soc. Am. Achievements include patents in field. Avocation: plant propagation in vitro. Home: 140 Van Patten Pky Burlington VT 05401 Office: U Vt 661 Spear St Burlington VT 05405 Office Phone: 802-656-5438. Office Fax: 802-658-7710. Personal E-mail: visgouli@adelphia.net. Business E-Mail: vgouli@uvm.edu.

GOULIANOS, KONSTANTIN, physicist, educator; b. Thessaloniki, Greece, Nov. 9, 1935; came to U.S., 1958, naturalized, 1967; s. Achilles and Olga (Nakopoulou) G. Student, Aristotelian U. Thessaloniki, 1953—58; PhD, Columbia U., 1963. Research assoc. Columbia U., N.Y.C., 1963-64; instr. physics Princeton U., N.J., 1964-67, asst. prof., 1967-71; assoc. prof. physics Rockefeller U., N.Y.C., 1971-81, prof., 1981—. Patentee electronic device of analysis of radioactivitively labeled gel electrophoretograms Fulbright scholar, 1958-59 Fellow: Am. Phys. Soc. Home: 11 W 69th St Apt 4A New York NY 10023-4700 Office: Rockefeller U Lab Expt High-Energy Physics 1230 York Ave New York NY 10021-6399 E-mail: dino@rockefeller.edu.

GOURAS, GUNNAR K., neurologist; b. Washington; s. Peter Gouras, Ute K. Gouras; m. Maria Holvoe. BA, Columbia Coll., 1985; MD, Columbia U., 1989. Diplomate Am. Bd. Psychiatry and Neurology. Postdoctoral rsch. fellow Johns Hopkins U. Sch. Med., Balt., 1989—91; neurology resident Harvard Med. Sch., Boston, 1992—95; postdoctoral fellow Cornell U. Med. Coll., N.Y.C., 1995—97, asst. prof., 1999—. Guest investigator Rockefeller U., N.Y.C., 1998—. Contbr. articles to profl. jours. (Beeson, 2000, Neurology Alzheimer award, 2001). Recipient Paul Beeson Physician Faculty in Aging award, Am. Fedn. Aging, Alliance for Aging Rsch., 2000—, Young Investigator award in Alzheimer's Disease, Am. Acad. Neurology, 2001—, Mentored Clin. Scientist Devel. award, NIH, 1999—2002. Mem.: Am. Acad. Neurology, Soc. Neurosci. Office: Weill Cornell Med Ctr Dept Neurology 525 E 68th St New York NY 10021 Office Phone: 212-746-6598. Business E-Mail: gkgouras@med.cornell.edu.

GOUREVITCH, PHILIP, editor; b. Phila. Student, Cornell Univ. Sr. fellow World Policy Inst. Contbg. editor Forward newspaper, staff writer New Yorker mag.; editor: Paris Review, 2005—; author: We Wish to Inform You that Tomorrow We Will Be Killed with Our Families: Stories from Rwanda, 1998 (Nat. Book Critics Cir. award for nonfiction, George Polk award for fgn. reporting), A Cold Case, 2001. Office: Paris Review 541 E 72nd St New York NY 10021

GOURLEY, DICK R., college dean; b. Franklin, Ky., Dec. 26, 1944; m. Greta Ann Kimbrough, Dec. 7, 1968; 1 child, Kristin Marie. BS in Pharmacy, U. Tenn., 1969, D of Pharmacy, 1970. Lic. pharmacist Tenn. Asst. prof. clin. pharmacy Mercer U., Atlanta, 1970-72, prof., dean., 1984-89, Coll. Pharmacy, U. Tenn., Memphis, 1989—; asst. prof., chmn. dept. pharmacy practice U. Nebr., Omaha, 1972-73, assoc. prof., chmn., 1973-81, prof. chmn., 1981-84. Vis. prof. U. Sydney, Australia, 1978; vis. tutor Ctrl. Inst. Tech., Upper Hutt, New Zealand, 1978; bd. dirs. Internat. Found. for Pharmacy Edn., MERTT, Accredo, Inc.; cons. Eli Lilly Co., 1983-85, Australian Nat. Health and Med. Rsch. Coun., 1982—, Lancaster County Bd. Lancaster Manor Nursing Home, 1981-82, Nebr. State Dept. Pub. Instns., 1976-84, Family Health Care, Inc., Omaha, 1975-84, Tri-County Meml. Hosp., Lexington, Nebr., 1975-76, Pharmacy and Therapeutics Com. Luth. Med. Ctr., Omaha, 1975, Henderson-Floyd Drugs and Shannondale Nursing Home, Knoxville, Tenn., 1971-72, Drs. Meml. Hosp. Atlanta, 1971-72, Ga. Narcotic Treatment Program, 1971-72, Grady Meml. Hosp., Atlanta, 1971-72, and numerous others; active Bd. Pharm Specialists, 1993—, vice chmn., 1994, chair 1995, 96, 97). Author: (with J. McHan) Laboratory Manual for Introductory Pharmacy, Physical Pharmacy and Pharmacy Technology, 1971; (with others) Practicing Pharmacist Handbook: Guidlines for the Establishment of High Blood Pressure Control Services by the Practicing Pharmacist, 1977, various chpts. in Pharmacy Technicians' Manual, 1988, Applied Therapeutics for Clinical Pharmacists, 1983, Clinical Pharmacy and Therapeutics, 1982, Pharmaceutics and Pharmacy Practice, 1981, Sourcebook on Clinical Pharmacy, 1980, Clinical Pharmacy and Therapeutics, 1979, Handbook of Non-Prescription Drugs, 1979, Handbook for Institutional Pharmacy Practice, 1979; editor: A Study Guide for the PCAT Examination, 1983, 3d edit., 1998, 4th edit., 1999, 5th edit., 2000, 6th edit, 2001, 7th edit., 2002, 8th edit., 2004, Comprehensive Review of Pharmacy, 2003, 2nd edit., 2004, 5th edit., 2005; co-editor: Clinical Pharmacy and Therapeutics, 4th edit., 1988, 5th edit., 1992, Textbook of Therapeutics: Drug and Disease Management, 6th edit., 1996, 7th edit., 2000; mem. editorial bds. Topics in Hosp. Mgmt., Clin. Rsch. Practices and Drug Regulatory Affairs, World Pharmacy Sci., Am. Jour. Managed Care; published audio-visual ednl. materials; contbr. articles to profl. jours. Chmn. UNMC Coll. Pharmacy United Way Campaign, 1979-81; judge Greater Nebr. Sci. and Engring. Fair, 1973-79. Grantee Eli Lilly and Co., 1996, 97, 98, U. Nebr-Lincoln, 1979, HEW, 1976-80, Area Health Edn. Ctr., 1974, 73, Robert Wood Johnson Found., 1973-76, Novartis, 1994, 95, 96, 97, 98, Schering Plough, 1997, SKB, 1997, Roche, 1997; fellow Internat. Ctr. for Pharmacy Edn. and Rsch., 1988, U. Nebr., 1978. Mem. Am. Coun. Pharm. Edn. (mem. site vis. team), Am. Soc. Hosp., Pharmacists (chmn., vice chmn. ASHP-ANA Joint Com., 1977-79, bd. dirs. 1981-84, del. Ho. Delegates, 1977, 78, 82, 83, 84, bd. liaison Coun. on Legal and Pub. Affairs, 1983-84, Coun. Edn. and Manpower 1982-83, Coun. Organizational Affairs, 1981-82, mem. several other coms.), Am. Assn. Colls. of Pharmacy (chmn. Sect. Teachers of Clin. Instrn. 1977-79, chmn. Coun. of Sects. 1995—, chmn. Standing Rules of Procedure Com., 1974-76, mem. several other coms.), Am. Pharm. Assn. (del. Ho. Delegates, 1977, 88-94), Nebr. Soc. Hosp. Pharmacists (chmn. Program Com. 1979-81, co-chmn. 1976-77, Spl. Svc. to Hosp. Pharmacy award 1984), Ga. Pharmaceutical Assn., Greater Omaha Pharmacists Assn. (bd. dirs. 1974-77), Nebr. Pharmacists Assn., Tenn. Pharmacists Assn., Internat. Found. for Pharmacy Edn. (pres. 1992—), Fedn. Internat. Pharm., Soc. Hosp. Pharmacists Australia, Pan Pacific Found. (program coord. II Conf. 1979-82, III Conf. 1982—, IV Conf. 1987, chmn. V Conf. exec. v.p. 1982-92), public mem. Commn. on Credentialing Pharmacy Residencies, 2003—, mem. bd. pharmacy specialties (chair 1995-97), Blue Lodge, Shriners, Phi Delta Chi (v.p. collegiate affairs 1973-78), Rho Chi (counselor region V 1976-78). Office: U Tenn Coll Pharmacy 847 Monroe Ave Memphis TN 38103-4901 Office Phone: 901-448-6036. Business E-Mail: dgourley@utmem.edu. E-mail: dgourley@bellsouth.net.

GOURLEY, GRETA ANN KIMBROUGH, pharmaceutical sciences educator; b. Oak Ridge, Tenn., July 23, 1946; m. Dick R. Gourley, Dec. 7, 1968; 1 child, Kristin Marie. RN, East Tenn. Bapt. Hosp. Sch. Nursing, 1967; BSN magna cum laude, U. Nebr., 1975, MSN in Cmty. Health Nursing summa cum laude, 1979, PhD in Adult Edn./Cmty. & Human Resources summa cum laude, 1983; postgrad., Mercer U., 1987-89; PharmD with highest honors, U. Tenn., 1993. Lic. nurse Tenn., Ga., Nebr.; lic. pharmacist Tenn. Staff nurse med. surg. unit East Tenn. Bapt. Hosp., Knoxville, 1967—68; staff nurse in med.-surg. and coronary care Bapt. Meml. Hosp., Memphis, 1968-70; instr. med. surg. nursing in cardiac and intensive care Ga. Bapt. Hosp. Sch. Nursing, Atlanta, 1971-72; drug studies unit nurse Nebr. Psychiat. Inst., Omaha, 1972-73; instr. cmty. health nursing Midland Luth. Sch. Nursing, Fremont, Nebr., 1979-81; rsch. asst. in health svcs. adminstrn. U. Nebr. Hosp. and Clinic, Omaha, 1981-82; asst. prof. cmty. health nursing U. Nebr. Coll. Nursing, Omaha, 1982-84; assoc. prof. cmty. health nursing Mercer U. Sch. Nursing, Atlanta, 1985—87; intern in pharmacy Germantown (Tenn.) Bapt. Hosp., 1990-91; resident in geriatric pharmacy VA Med. Ctr., Memphis, 1993-94; asst. prof. dept. pharmacy practice and pharmacoecons. U. Tenn. Coll. Pharmacy, Memphis, 1994—95, assoc. prof. dept. pharmacy practice and pharmacoecons., 1996—98, dir. ednl. experience program, 1998—2001, dir. grad. program in health sci. adminstrn., 2001—04. Bd. dirs., profl. adv. com. Vis. Nurses Assn., Inc., Memphis, 1996—; pub. edn. com., state coalition bd. Tenn. Diabetes Prevention and Control Program, 1996—; cons. panel on diabetes Bayer Pharm. Co., 1997—; diabetes panel Aventis Pharms., 2001—; lectr. in field. Contbr. chpts. to gooks, articles to profl. jours. Nursing scholar East Tenn. Bapt. Hosp., 1966 Mem. ANA, Am. Pharm. Assn., Am. Soc. Hosp. Pharmacists, Am. Coll. Clin. Pharmacists, Am. Assn. Colls. Pharmacy, Tenn. Pharmacists Assn. (profl. affairs com. 1996-97), MidSouth Coll. Clin. Pharmacy, Sigma Theta Tau, Rho Chi.

GOURLEY, JAMES LELAND, editor, publishing executive; b. Mounds, Okla., Jan. 29, 1919; s. Samuel O. and Lodema (Scott) G.; m. Vicki Graham Clark, Nov. 24, 1976; children: James Leland II, Janna Lynn Rousey, Kelly Clark, Brandon Clark. BA in Liberal Studies, U. Okla., 1963. Editor, pub., pres. Daily Free-Lance, Henryetta, Okla., 1946-73; editor, pub. Oklahoma City Friday, 1974—; CEO Nichols Hills Pub. Co., 1974—; pres. Suburban Graphics, Inc., 1991-93. Pres. Central Okla. Newspaper Group, 1987, 90, 93, 96, 98, 99, 2000—; pres. Sta. KHEN, KHEN-FM, Henryetta, 1955-63; pres. Hugo (Okla.) Daily News, 1953-63; chief of staff gov. Okla., 1959-63; chmn., pres. State Capitol Bank, 1962-69; v.p. sta. KXOJ Sapulpa, 1972-75; treas. Sta. KJEM-FM, Oklahoma City, 1962-67. Mem. Pres. Nat. Pub. Advisory Com. to U.S. Sec. Commerce, 1963-66; exec. dir. Gov's Comm. Higher Edn., 1960-61; Dem. candidate for gov. Okla., 1966. Dist. chmn. Boy Scouts Am., 1963-65; bd. dirs. So. Regional Edn. Bd., 1959-67, Okla. Symphony Soc., 1976-88, Oklahoma City Crimestoppers, 1982—, Salvation Army, Oklahoma City, 1985-87, Okla. Goodwill Industries, 1989-91; mem. Gov.'s Reform Com., 1984; bd. trustees Okla. City Univ., 1993—; bd. dirs. Okla. City Edn. Round Table, 1992—; mem. steering com. Ofcl. Maps for Kids, 2000-2003. Maj. AUS, 1942-46, ETO. Recipient Best Okla. Small Daily newspaper awards, 1949-58, 69-72, Best Large City Weekly newspaper awards, 1977-80, 83-85, 87-91, 94-95, 97, 98, 2004; inducted into Okla. Journalism Hall of Fame, 1980. Mem. UP Internat. Editors Okla. (pres. 1958-59), Okla. Disciples of Christ Laymen (pres. 1964-65), Suburban Newspapers Am. (dir. 1980-89), Nat. Newspaper Assn., Okla. Press Assn. (pres. 1988-89, treas. 1991-93), Oklahoma City C. of C. (dir. 1975—), Henryetta C. of C. (pres. 1955), Oklahoma City Golf and Country Club (bd. dirs. 1991-95), Econ. Club Okla., Oklahoma City Com. of 100, Rotary (pres. Oklahoma City club 1992-93), Mil. Order of World Wars, The Ret. Officers Assn., Pi Kappa Alpha. Republican. Home: 6435 Grandmark Dr Oklahoma City OK 73116-6535 Office: 10801 Quail Plaza Dr Oklahoma City OK 73120-3123 Office Phone: 405-755-3311. Business E-Mail: lgourley@okcfriday.com.

GOURLEY, PAULA MARIE, art educator, artist, designer bookbinder, writer, publisher; b. Carmel, Calif., Apr. 29, 1948; d. Raymond Serge Voronkoff and Frances Eliseyvna Gourley; m. David Clark Willard, Feb. 10, 1972 (div. Oct. 1973). AA, Monterey (Calif.) Peninsula Coll., 1971; BA, Goddard Coll., 1978; MFA, U. Ala., 1987; pvt. bookbinding study with, Donald Glaister, Roger Arnoult, Paule Ameline, Michelene de Bellefroid, Francoise Bausart, Sun Evrard, James Brockman. Radiologic technologist Cen. Med. Clinic, Pacific Grove, Calif., 1970-71, Community Hosp. of Monterey, 1972-75, Duke U. Med. Ctr., Durham, N.C., 1975-77; dept. head, ultrasound technologist Middlesex Meml. Hosp., Middletown, Conn., 1977-79; asst. prof. U. Ala., Tuscaloosa, 1985-93, assoc. prof., 1993-98. Established Pelegaya Press and Paperworks, 1978, Lilyhouse Studio Editions, 1999; asst. dir. Inst. for Book Arts U. Ala., 1985—88, coord., 1988—94, co-dir. MFA program in the book arts, 1994—97; U.S. rep. Les Amis de la Reliure d'Art, Toulouse, France, 1989—; founding dir. Southeastern chpt. Guild of BookWorkers, 1995—99; guest artist Marriott Libr. Book Arts Program U. Utah, 1999—2003; guest artist Ariz. State U., 2004, Jaffe Book Arts Collection, Fla. Atlantic U., 2002—04; contbr. journalist for U.S. to Art et Metiers du Livre Revue Internat., Paris; adj. faculty Lane Micro Bus./Lane C.C., resource and edn. coord., 2002—04; Saturday Market resource coord., Eugene, Oreg., 2001—; instr. Downtown Initiative for Visual Arts, 2004—; tchr. coord. Cultural Homestay Internat., 2004—; bd. dirs. Eugene (Oreg.) Saturday Mkt., Oreg. Micro Enterprise Network, Oreg. Coun. Bus. Edn.; small bus. counselor, lectr. Bus. Devel. Ctr., Lane CC; coord. life-enhancing activity programs Pearl Bull Ctr., Eugene, Oreg., 2005—. Editor First Impressions (newsletter), 1988-97; contbr. articles to profl. jours.; numerous nat. and internat. bookbinding exhbns., 1978—; contbr. editor Resource Corner, Saturday Market Newsletter. Vol. PLUS Literacy Program, Tuscaloosa, 1991-96. U. Ala. grantee, 1988, 89, 90, 92; recipient Diplome of honneur Atelier d'Arts Appliques, France, 1986, Craft fellowship Ala. State Coun. on Arts, 1993-94. Mem. Guild of Bookworkers (founder and bd. dirs. Southeastern regional chpt., editor, pub. newsletter True Grits, mem. exec. com.), Hand Bookbinders Calif., Bookbinders Internat. (v.p. U.S. 1989-92), Pacific Ctr. for the Book Arts, Am. Craft Coun., Ala. Craft Coun., Can. Bookbinders and Book Artists Guild, Nat. Mus. Women in Arts, Willamette Jazz Soc. (founding mem.), Artists Equity of the Ctrl. Coast, Downtown Initiative for the Visual Arts, Handcrafted Soapmakers Guild. Avocations: photography, quilting, reading, cuisine, travel. Studio: 1936 W 34th Ave Eugene OR 97405-1709 Office Phone: 541-686-0947. E-mail: lilyhousestudio@aol.com.

GOURLEY, SARA J., lawyer; b. 1955; AB cum laude with honors, Ripon Coll., 1977; JD, Univ. Ill., 1980. Bar: Ill. 1980, US Dist. Courts (no. dist. Ill. and dist. of Ariz.), US Ct. of Appeals (4th, 7th, 8th. and 11th circuits). Ptnr. product liability litig. Sidley Austin Brown & Wood LLP, Chgo., and mem. exec. com. Mem. Univ. Ill. Law Rev., 1978—80. Mem.: ABA, Def. Rsch. Inst. Office: Sidley Austin Brown & Wood llP Bank One Plz 10 S Dearborn St Chicago IL 60603 Office Phone: 312-853-7694. Office Fax: 312-853-7036. Business E-Mail: sgourley@sidley.com.

GOURLEY, VICKI CLARK, publishing executive; b. Lawton, Okla., Aug. 31, 1946; d. Tom L. Graham and Mary Helen McKenzie; m. Jerry Allan Clark, Aug. 23, 1965 (div. Sept. 1974); children: Kelly Brett, Brandon Graham; m. James Leland Gourley, Nov. 24, 1976. Student, Okla. State U., 1963-66, 71-73. Adminstrv. asst. Anaheim (Calif.) H.S. Dist., 1966-71; mng. editor Oklahoma City Friday, 1974-76, exec. editor, 1976—; pres. Nichols Hills Pub. Co., Oklahoma City, 1976-99, chmn., 1999—. Cons. Suburban Graphics, Inc., Oklahoma City, 1990-98, Ctrl. Okla. Newspaper Group, Oklahoma City, 1980—; com. chmn. Suburban Newspaper Am., Chgo., 1993-95. Photographer Crossing America, 1994. Pres. The Christmas Connection, 1986-90, Cmty. Literacy Ctr., Oklahoma City, 1991-94; commr. Govs. Literacy Commn., Oklahoma City, 1991-99, Nichols Hills (Okla.) Park Bd., 1995-99; bd. mem. Oklahoma Symphony Soc., Oklahoma City, 1990-92, The Village (Okla.) CrimeStoppers, 1990-98; co-chmn. Nichols Hills Employees Scholarship Fund Program, 1997—, Okla. State U. Bring Dreams to Life Drive, Stillwater, 1999-2000. Recipient Golden Rule award J.C. Penney Co., Oklahoma City, 1992, Humanitarian award Nat. Conf. Christians and Jews, Oklahoma City, 1997, Lt. Govs. Media awad Cmty. Literacy Ctr., Oklahoma City, 1992; named Exec. Woman of Yr., High Noon Club, Oklahoma City U., 2000, Woman Vol. Yr., Byliners Club, Oklahoma City, 1993, Woman Vol. Yr., Girl Scouts Am., Oklahoma City, 1997. Mem. Nat. Newspaper Assn., Okla. Press Assn. (conv. chmn. 1991-92), Soc. for Profl. Journalists, Rotary Anns Oklahoma City (pres. 1987-88), Delta Delta Delta. Republican. Methodist. Avocations: travel, reading, scuba diving. Home: 6435 Grandmark Dr Nichols Hills OK 73116 Office: Oklahoma City Friday PO Box 20340 Oklahoma City OK 73156 also: Nichols Hills Pub Co PO Box 20340 Oklahoma City OK 73156-0340 E-mail: vcgfriday@aol.com.

GOURVITZ, ELLIOT HOWARD, lawyer; b. Lewiston, Pa., Sept. 21, 1945; s. Louis and Irene (Brass) Gourvitz; m. Bonnie S. Hirsch; children: Evan, Amy, Ross, Ari. BA, Rutgers U., 1966, JD, 1969. Bar: N.J. 1969, N.Y. 1985, U.S. Dist. Ct. N.J. 1969, U.S. Dist. Ct. (ea. dist.) Wis. 1985, U.S. Ct. Appeals (3d cir.) 1972, U.S. Ct. Appeals (2d, 4th, 5th, 7th, 8th, 9th, 10th, and fed. cirs.) 1982, U.S. Tax Ct. 1970, U.S. Ct. Claims 1970, U.S. Ct. Internat. Trade 1985, U.S. Supreme Ct. 1973, cert.: N.J. (matrimonial atty.). Pvt. practice, Springfield, NJ. Chmn. Early Settlement Panel of Union County, NJ; panelist Essex and Middlesex Counties. Contbr. articles to profl. jours. Named Man of Yr., United Cerebral Palsy League Union County, 1980. Fellow: Internat. Acad. Matrimonial Lawyers, Am. Acad. Matrimonial Attys. (pres. N.J. chpt.); mem.: N.Y. State Bar Assn., N.J. Bar Assn., Am. Coll. Trial Lawyers (diplomate). Business E-Mail: ehg@gourvitz.com.

GOUSE, S. WILLIAM, JR., mechanical engineering executive, researcher; b. Utica, N.Y., Dec. 15, 1931; s. S. William and Charlotte G.; m. Jacqueline Ann McLaughlin, Aug. 6, 1955; children: Linda Ellen, S. William III. S.B., S.M., Mass. Inst. Tech., 1954, Sc.D., 1958. Instr. mech. engring. MIT, 1956-57, asst. prof., 1957-61, 62-65, assoc. prof., 1965-67, lectr., 1967-68; prof. mech. engring., prin. rsch. engr. Transp. Rsch. Inst., Carnegie-Mellon U., 1967-69; staff mem. Office Sci. and Tech. of Exec. Office of the Pres., Washington, 1969-70; assoc. dean Carnegie Inst. Tech. and Sch. Urban and Pub. Affairs Carnegie-Mellon U., 1971-73, dir. Environ. Studies Inst., 1971-73, adj. prof. engring. and pub. policy, 1980-90; dir. Office R&D, sci. advisor to sec. U.S. Dept. Interior, 1973-75; acting dir. Office Coal Rsch., 1974-75; dep. asst. adminstr. fossil energy ERDA, 1975-77; chief scientist MITRE Corp., 1977-79, v.p., 1979-80, v.p., gen. mgr. Ctr. for Civil Systems, 1980-84, sr. v.p., gen. mgr. Ctr. for Civil Systems, 1984-90, 1990-92, sr. v.p., 1992-94; mng. dir. Energy Sys. and Tech., 1994—. Cons. and mem. panels various industry and govt. agys. including U.S. Dept. Commerce, U.S. Office Sci. and Tech., NSF; mem. rsch. adv. com. Electric Power Rsch. Inst., 1973-76; chmn. rev. adv. bd. on coal liquefaction Internat. Energy Agy., Paris, 1981-82; mem. energy engring. bd. NRC, 1985-88; U.S. rep. to com. energy conservation in indsl. processes World Energy Conf., 1984-89; mem. com. on environ. and energy aspects of waste handling World Energy Coun., vice chmn. com. on efficient use of energy utilization using high tech.; mem. adv. bd. Aspen Inst. Humanistic Studies Com. Pub. Policy Issues Energy and Resources, 1982-95; internat. adv. bd. World Energy Coun.; dir. Colshire Group, 1997; tech. advisor AB Volvo, 1996-2000; tech. adv. bd. Earth First Techs., 2002-03; assoc. dir. Aspen Inst., 1996. Editorial bd. Internat. Jour. Environ. Studies, 1971-81; editor-in-chief Energy Systems and Policy, 1973-93; assoc. editor Energy Sources, 1994-2001; contbr. to books, profl. jours., and congl. testimony. Mem. vis. com. mech. engring. dept. MIT, 1978-85. Served with ordnance AUS, 1961-62. Visking Corp. fellow, 1954-55; GE W. Rice Jr. fellow, 1955-56; recipient Ralph Teetor award Soc. Automotive Engrs., 1966; Sir A.L. Mudslior lectr in tech. Al Alagappa Chettiar Coll. Tech., U. Madras, 1969; Disting lectr. mech. engring. Pa. State U., 1980; recipient Outstanding Svc. award No. Area Environ. Coun., Allegheny County, Pa., 1973, Meritorious Svc. award ERDA, 1976, 60th Lord Melchett Medal Lectr. Inst. Energy London, 1994. Fellow ASME, AIAA (assoc.); mem. AAAS, SAE, U.S. Energy Assn. (bd. dirs. 1987-88, 91-92, audit com. 1992—), Internat. Com. Coal Rsch., Cosmos Club, Explorers Club (steering com. Washington group 2001—), Tower Club. Office Phone: 540-399-9825. Personal E-mail: swgjmg@erols.com. Business E-Mail: swgjmg@alum.mit.edu.

GOUTERMAN, MARTIN PAUL, chemistry educator; b. Phila., Dec. 26, 1931; s. Bernard and Melba (Buxbaum) G.; 1 child, Mikaelin BlueSpruce. BA, U. Chgo., 1951, MS, 1955, PhD in Physics (NSF Predoctoral fellow), 1958. Faculty Harvard U., Cambridge, Mass., 1958-66, postdoctoral fellow to asst. prof. chemistry dept.; mem. faculty U. Wash., Seattle, 1966—, prof. chemistry, 1968-99, prof. emeritus, 2000—. Fellow Am. Inst. Physics; mem. Am. Chem. Soc., Sigma Xi. Achievements include research and publications in spectroscopy and quantum chemistry of porphyrins and their use as luminescence sensors for biomedical and aeronautical application, in particular pressure sensitive paint; developed BS degree program in biochemistry and a chemistry minors program. Office: U Wash Chemistry Box 351700 Seattle WA 98195-1700

GOUTI, SAMMY YASIN, psychologist, educator, television talk show host, psychotherapist, writer; b. Gaza, Jordan, June 19, 1963; arrived in U.S., 1981, naturalized, 1994; s. Yasin Ahmed and Helala Yossef (Abomarie) Gouti; m. Inna Annatolievna, 1998; 1 child, Chelsey Ann. AS, San Jacinto Coll., Pasadena, Tex., 1984; BS with honors, U. Houston-Ctrl., 1987; MA, U. Houston-Clear Lake, 1989, postgrad., 1993-95; Cert. Massage Therapy, Phoenix Sch. Massage, Houston, 1992; student, TVI Actors Studios, Hollywood, Calif., 1995; cert. in acting, The Mayo Hill Sch., 1994; postgrad., Sam Houston State U., 1995; cert. in filming and directing, Access Houston TV, 1998. Lic. profl. counselor-intern. Asst. tchr. presch. U. Houston Human Lab. Sch., 1986-87; social sci. instr. George I. Sanchez High Sch., Houston, 1989-90; psychotherapist Life Resource-A Mental Health Ctr., Beaumont, Tex., 1990-91; psychology instr. Lamar U., Orange, Tex., 1991; assoc. clin. psychologist Tex. Dept. Mental Health and Mental Retardation, Beaumont, 1991-92; counseling program Sam Houston State U., 1995; massage therapist The Houstonian Health Club, 1993-95; prof. psychology U. Houston System, 1992—2000; prof. Houston C.C. System, 1998—; pub., CEO Profiles & Portraits mag., 2000—02. Founder The Ctr. for Stress Release, Houston, 1992, The SHUMS World Magic Ctr., Houston, 1992; creator Psychotherapeutic Massage, and Psychobodynalysis, 1996, 97; adj. prof. psychology Kingwood Coll., 1996-98, San Jacinto Coll., 1996-98, U. Houston, Clear Lake, 1997-99; Dem. Nat. Com. rep. State of Tex., 1995—; CEO, founder Crescent Moon Entertainment TV & Film Prodns., 1998—. Trade Mark (TM) Super Human Universal Monkeys, 1992, The SHUMS, 1992, (screenplay, animated film) The SHUMS Adventures, 1992; appeared in music videos with Clay Walker, Clinton Gregory, 1995; appeared on John Bradshaw TV Talk Show, 1996; guest appearance on The Bradshaw Difference, 1996; featured in 6 Hollywood films including Tin Cup, Rocket Man, Killing the Badge, The Evening Star, Apollo 11, Cable TV, Rough Riders; featured on mag. cover AMOCO's; TV host Arab-Am. TV and TV Houston, 1996-98; founder, prodr., host of weekly show Arab Broadcasting Network (ABN), 1998-2000; prodr., host (weekly talk show) Profile and Portraits, 1998—, ABN with Sammy Gouti, 1998—, Excel TV programs special, 2002; spl. corr. Jordan TV, 1998—, ANA Radio and Satellite Net TV, 1998—; guest host: HCCTV: Author Showcase, 1999; host, prodr.: The Sammy Gouti Show, 1999— (AEGIS award for excellence in TV prodn., 2003, Top Hohors award for programming excellence, 2003), (TV program) Greetings with Love, 1998, Greetings with Love, Part II, 2000, (TV spl.) H.M. King Hussein of Jordan, First Memorial, 2000, King Abdullah II of Jordan, 2002; author: (poems) The Shums, 1993, The Encounter, 1994, Princess, 1995; co-writer, co-prodr., co-host: (TV programs) The Life Contentment Inventory: A Psychological Test, 1992, The Life Priority Questionnaire, 1992, Peace Talks The Palestinian Israeli & American Perspectives, 1997, Jordan: A Special Program, 2001; author: A Multidimensional Approach to the Treatment of Stress: Psychology, Psychiatry and Massage Therapy, 1997, Massage Methods, 1996, Psychotherapeutic Massage and Psychobodyanalysis, 1997; editor, writer Almaraya newspaper, 1998-99; freelance reporter El Dia newspaper, 1999-2002; contbr. articles to profl. jours. Rep. Dem. Nat. Com., 1995—; mem. The Carter Ctr., 1997-99, Juvenile Diabetes Found., 2000—. Recipient Editor's Choice award Nat. Libr. Poetry, 1993, 94, 95, Pres. Clinton's Leadership Recognition award, 1997, Letter of Appreciation, Pres. Clinton, 2000; U. Houston scholar, 1986-87, 88-89, Award of Appreciation Al Gore, 1998. Fellow Royal Soc. New Zealand; mem. AACC, Arab Am. Cultural Cmty. Ctr. (dir. media 1998-2000) Am. Screenwriters Assn., N.Am. Assn. Masters in Psychology, Royal Inst. Linguistics and Anthropology, New Zealand Stats. Assn., Stats. Soc. Australia, Sci. Fiction and Fantasy Writers Am., Am. Film Inst., Internat. Soc. Poets (life), Assn. for Humanistic Psychology, Jordanian Am. Assn. (media cons. 1999-2001), Inst. Noetic Scis., Nat. Guild Hypnotists, Nat. Geographic Soc., The Carter Center, Assn. for Body and Massage Profls., Am.-Palestinian C. of C. (dir. media 1998-2000), Nat. Scholars Honor Soc. (Award of Recognition 2001), Golden Key, Psi Chi, Alpha Epsilon Delta. Avocations: pencil drawing, poetry, photography, writing, calligraphy, pencil drawing, poetry, writing, photography, calligraphy. Mailing: PO Box 631693 Houston TX 77263 Office Phone: 713-712-1051. Personal E-mail: sammygouti@yahoo.com.

GOUVERNET, GERARD RAOUL, language educator; b. Aigues Vives, Gard, Sept. 19, 1939; s. Raoul Marius Gouvernet and Andrée Rose Pinol; m. Suzanne d'Autremont Gouvernet, Mar. 30, 1968; 1 child, Philippe. PhD, Harvard U., 1978. Prof. dept. fgn. lang. SUNY, Geneseo, 1982—. Author: (book) Le Valet chez Molière et ses successeurs, 1985; co-author: Homage to Paul Benichou, 1994, Dictionnaire Analytique du Théâtre, 1998. Avocations: reading, tennis, Pétanque. Home: 61 Pelham Rd Rochester NY 14610 Office: SUNY College Dept Fgn Lang 1 College Cir Geneseo NY 14454-1401 E-mail: gouverne@geneseo.edu.

GOUW, JULIA SURYAPRANATA, accountant; b. Surabaya, Indonesia, Aug. 22, 1959; came to U.S., 1978; d. Moertopo Suryapranata and Indira (Koelani) Suryapranata; m. Ken Keng-Hok Gouw, June 1, 1981. B.S. with highest honors, U. Ill., 1981. CPA, Ill. Acct., Texaco, Inc., Los Angeles, 1981-83; from asst. acct. to sr. audit mgr. KPMG Peat Marwick, LA, 1983-89; joined East West Bank as v.p., contr., San Marino, CA, 1989, exec. v.p., CFO, East West Bancorp Inc., 1994-, dir., 1997- . Bd. dirs. Huntington Meml. Hosp.; bd. visitors UCLA; bd. overseers LA Philharmonic; mem. Alexis de Tocqueville Soc. United Way. Named Philanthropist of Yr., United Way's Women Leaders for Giving and Nat. Assn. Bus. Owners, 2003, LA Bus. Jour. Women Making a Difference Awards, 2003; Named one of The Top 25 Most Powerful Women in Banking, US Banker mag., 2003. Mem. Chinese Am. CPA's, Nat. Assn. Female Execs., Beta Alpha Psi, Fin. Execs. Inst., Calif. Soc. CPA's . Office: East West Bank 415 Huntington Dr San Marino CA 91108 Office Phone: 626-583-3512. E-mail: jgouw@eastwestbank.com.

GOVAHN, BARBARA A., secondary school educator; b. Newark, May 31, 1948; d. Lenton Alfred and Maggie Carter; children from previous marriage: Jermaine, LeVar. BS, Winston Salem State U., 1969; MA in Bus. Edn., Rider U., 1987. Cert. comprehensive bus. edn. N.J. Tchr. Jersey City Bd. Edn., 1970—75, Linden (N.J.) Ada HS, 1975—80, Roselle (N.J.) Bd. Edn., 1990—; assoc. prof. Union County Coll., Cranford, NJ, 1982—90. Prin.'s mentor Roselle Bd. Edn., 2000—02. Mem.: ISIE, NAACP, N.J. Edn. Assn., Alpha Kappa Alpha. Baptist. Avocations: reading, travel, cooking. Office: Roselle Bd Edn 710 Locust St Roselle NJ 07203-1919

GOVAN, GLADYS VERNITA MOSLEY, retired critical care nurse, medical/surgical nurse; b. Tyler, Tex., July 24, 1918; d. Stacy Thomas and Lucy Victoria (Whitmill) Mosley; m. Osby David Govan, July 20, 1938; children Orbrenett K. (Govan) Carter, Diana Lynn (Govan) Gray. Student, East Los Angeles Coll., Montebello, Calif., 1951; lic. vocat. nurse, Calif. Hosp. Med. Ctr., L.A., 1953; cert., Western States IV Assn., L.A., 1978. Lic. vocat. nurse, Calif.; cert. in EKG. Intravenous therapist Calif. Hosp. Med. Ctr., cardiac monitor, nurse; ret. Past pres. PTA, also hon. mem., 1963-2000; charter mem. Nat. Rep. Presdl. Task Force.

GOVAN, MICHAEL, museum director; b. Washington; m. Kathryn Ross. BA in Art History and Studio Art, Williams Coll.; postgrad., U. Calif., San Diego. Acting curator and spl. assts. to the dir. Williams Coll. Mus. Art, Williamstown, Mass.; dep. dir. Solomon R. Guggenheim Mus., N.Y.C.; dir. Dia Art Found., N.Y.C., 1994—. Fundraiser for Dia Beacon (N.Y.) Mus., 1999—2003; bd. mem. Andy Warhol Mus and Triple Aught Found. Office: Dia Art Found 535 W 22nd St New York NY 10011

GOVANDE, VINAYAK PRABHAKAR, pediatrician; b. Pune, India, Sept. 8, 1971; arrived in U.S., 2002; s. Prabhakar Balkrishna and Usha Prabhakar Govande; m. Archana Vinayak Jahagirdar, Sept. 26, 1975; children: Janhavi, Soham. MBBS, Seth G.S. Med. Coll., Mumbai, India, 1995, MD in Pediats., 1998; diploma in child health, Coll. Physicians and Surgeons, Mumbai, 1998; diploma in hosp. mgmt., All India Inst. Mgmt. Studies, Chennai, 2001; MD, Brookdale Hosp. Med. Ctr., 2005. Attending and chief pediatrician Sanjivani Hosp., Surat, India, 1998—2002; resident pediatrician Brookdale Hosp. Med. Ctr., Bklyn., 2002—. Educator Hindu orgn., Khopoli, India, 1991—94. Mem.: AMA, Am. Assn. Pediats., Indian Acad. Pediats., Am. Acad. Pediats. Office: Brookdale Hosp Med Ctr 1 Brookdale Plz Brooklyn NY 11212 Home: 7 Hergeman Ave Apt 20C Brooklyn NY 11212 E-mail: drgovande@yahoo.co.in.

GOVE, SAMUEL KIMBALL, retired political science professor; b. Walpole, Mass., Dec. 27, 1923; Student, Mass. State Coll., 1941—43; BS in Econs, U. Mass., 1947; MA in Polit. Sci, Syracuse U., 1951. Research asst. govt. and pub. affairs U. Ill., 1950-51, research asso., 1951-54, mem. faculty, 1954—, prof. polit. sci., 1966-89, prof. emeritus, 1989—; dir. Inst. Govt. and Pub. Affairs, 1967-85, dir. emeritus, 1987—. Staff asst. Nat. Assn. Assessing Officers, 1949; mem. rsch. staff Ill. Commn. Study State Govt., 1950—51; staff fellow Nat. Mcpl. League, 1955—56; exec. asst. Ill. Auditor Pub. Accounts, 1957; program coord. Ill. Legis. Staff Intern Program, 1962—70; mem. com. financing higher edn. Ill. Master Plan Higher Edn., 1963; mem. Ill. Commn. Orgn. Gen. Assembly, 1965—69, 1970—73, Ill. Commn. State Govt., 1965—67; cons. elections ABC, 1964, 66, 68; chmn. Champaign (Ill.) County Econ. Opportunity Coun., 1966—67; state legis. rsch. fellow Am. Polit. Sci. Assn., 1966—68; cons. Am. Council Edn., 1966—67; sec. Local Govts. Commn., 1967—69; staff dir. Ill. Constn. Study Commn., 1968—69; exec. sec. Gov. Ill. Constn. Research Group, 1969—70; mem. Ill. Constn. Study Commn., 1969—70; chmn. Citizens Task Force on Constl. Implementation, 1970—71; mem. Gov. Elect's Task Force on Transition, 1972, 1991—92; adv. coun. Ill. Dept. Local Govt. Affairs, 1969—79, Gov.'s Human Resources, 1991—93, Ill. Commn. on Regulatory Rev., 1994—98, Ill. Bd. Higher Edn., 1998—, Ill. Issues Bd., 1974—2003, chmn. bd. dirs., 1974—93. Lt. j.g. USNR, 1943—46. Fellow Nat. Acad. Pub. Adminstrn.; mem. AAUP (past chpt. pres., mem. nat. com. R 1969-75, 78-84, nat. coun. 1978-80), Am. Polit Sci. Assn., Am. Soc. Pub. Adminstrn. (past chpt. chmn.; chmn. univs. govtl. rsch. conf. 1969-71), Govtl. Rsch. Assn. (dir. 1969-71), Ill. Hist. Soc., Midwest Polit. Sci. Assn. (v.p. 1978-80), Nat. Mcpl. League (council 1972-80, 81-84, 85), Nat Civic League (coun. advisors 1987-89), Cosmos Club. Home: 2006 Bruce Dr Urbana IL 61801-6419 Office: 1007 W Nevada St Urbana IL 61801-3812 Personal E-mail: s.gove@uiuc.edu.

GOVE, WALTER R., sociology educator; b. June 8, 1938; married; 2 children. BS, SUNY, Syracuse, 1960; MA in Sociology, U. Wash., 1967, PhD in Sociology, 1968. From asst. prof. to assoc. prof. Vanderbilt U., Nashville, 1968-75, prof. sociology, 1975—, dir. grad. studies, 1985-86. Dir. NIMH Grad. Tng. Program, 1972-76; organizer confs., symposia in field; participant profl. confs., presenter in field. Author: (with Michael Geerken) At Home and at Work: The Family's Allocation of Labor, 1983; (with Michael Hughes) Household Crowding: Social and Structural Determinants of Its Effects, 1983; editor: Deviance and Mental Illness, 1982, co-editor: Labelling Deviant Behavior: Evaluating a Perspective, 1975, 2 edit., 1980, The Fundamental Connection Between Nature and Nurture, 1982, A Feminist Perspective in the Academy, 1983; adv. editor Social Forces, 1971-74; cons. editor Am. Jour. Sociology, 1974-76, Women and Politics, 1978-86; assoc. editor Social Sci. Rsch., 1974—, Social Psychology Quarterly, 1978-80, Jour. Health and Social Behavior, 1981-83, 1997-2003, Jour. Family Issues, 1984-92; contbr. articles to profl., non-profl. jours., book revs. Recipient Reuben Hill award Nat. Coun. Family Rels., 1979, Outstanding Grad. Tchr. award Vanderbilt U., 2001; grantee PHS, 1963-65, 71-76, 79-82, NSF, 1973-77, 93, Dept. Justice, 1984-85, Okla. Dept. Corrections, 1993-94, Ethel Mae Wilson Found., 1980-81, Shell Found., 1974, others. Fellow: AAAS; mem.: So. Sociol. Soc. (pres.-elect 1992—93, pres. 1993—94, exec. coun., program com. 1986), Am. Sociol. Assn. (liaison com. to AAAS 1990—94, Leo Reeder award for disting. svc. to med. sociology 2003), Am. Soc. Criminology, Sociology Rsch. Assn., Soc. Study of Social Problems (Outstanding Scholarship and Svc. to Psychiat. Sociology award 1989). Avocation: numerous first ascents as mountaineer, primarily in Alaska. Home: PO Box 1399 Boulder UT 84716 Business E-Mail: walter.r.gove@vanderbilt.edu.

GOVEKAR, PAUL LOUIS, JR., marketing professor, consultant; b. Waukegan, Ill., Apr. 11, 1945; s. Paul Louis Sr. and Dorothy Leona (Bergstrom) G.; m. Michele Ann Canning, Nov. 4, 1967; children: Christopher Paul, Eileen Michele. Dr. of Bus. Adminstrn., Nova Southeastern U., Fr. Lauderdale, FL; MBA, De Paul U., Chicago, IL, 1967—71; BBA, Loyola U., Chicago, IL, 1963—67. Asst. prof. of mgmt. Ohio No. U., Ada, Ohio, 2004—; asst. prof. of bus. B luffton Coll., Bluffton, Ohio; commd. officer US Army, 1967—92. Cons. P & M Associates, Kenton, Ohio. Contbr. articles to profl. jours. Bd. mem. United Way of Hardin County, Kenton, Ohio, 2000. Lt. col. US Army, 1967—92. Decorated Bronze Star. Mem.: Assn. for Rsch. on Nonprofit Associations and Voluntary Action (assoc.), Soc. for the Advancement of Mgmt. (assoc.), Acad. of Mgmt. (assoc.; divsn. bd. mem. 2000—). Roman Catholic. Avocation: golf. Office: Ohio Northern University 525 N Main Street Ada OH 45810 Office Phone: 419-772-3124. Office Fax: 419-772-3125. Personal E-mail: govekarp@wcoil.com. E-mail: p-govekar@onu.edu.

GOVER, ALAN SHORE, lawyer; b. Lyons, N.Y., Sept. 5, 1948; s. Norman Marvin and Beatrice L. (Shore) Gover; m. Ellen Rae Ross, Dec. 4, 1976 (dec. Jan. 8, 2004); children: Maxwell Ross, Mary Trace. AB, Tufts U., 1970; JD, Georgetown U., 1973. Bar: Tex. 1973, U.S. Dist. Ct. (so. dist.) Tex. 1974, U.S. Ct. Appeals (5th cir.) 1974, U.S. Supreme Ct. 1976, U.S. Dist. Ct. Appeals (DC cir.) 1977, U.S. Ct. Appeals (2d cir.) 1979, DC 1980, U.S. Ct. Appeals (8th, 9th and 11th cirs.) 1981, U.S. Dist. Ct. (no. dist.) Tex. 1988, U.S. Dist. Ct. (ea. dist.) Tex. 1990. Assoc. Baker & Botts, Houston, 1973-80, ptnr., 1981-85, Weil, Gotshal & Manges, Houston, 1985—2001; ptnr., co-chmn. corp. reorganization & bankruptcy group. mem. mgmt. com. Dewey Ballantine LLP, Houston, 2001—. Co-author: (book) The Texas Nonjudicial Foreclosure Process, 1990; editor, chmn. editl. bd. P. L. I. Oil and Gas and Bankruptcy Laws, 1985. Trustee Houston Ballet, 1986—93, 2003—, v.p., 1993—96, 2005—; chmn. ann. fund St. John's Sch., Houston, 1993—95, trustee, 1996—2004, Retina Rsch. Found., Houston, 1996—; chmn. East Downtown Mgmt. Dist., Houston, 2000—03; Adv. trustee Salvation Army Houston Area Command, 2005—; v.p. Congregation Beth Israel, Houston, 1996—2001, pres., 2001—03; trustee Seven Acres Jewish Home for Aged, 2005—. Fellow: Tex. Bar Found.; mem.: D.C. Bar, State Bar Tex., Houston Bar Assn., ABA, Harmonie Club (N.Y.), Coronado Club Houston, The Argyle (San Antonio). Jewish. Office: Dewey Ballantine LLP Suite 1900 700 Louisiana St Houston TX 77002-2725 Office Phone: 713-445-1550. Office Fax: 713-445-1533. Business E-Mail: agover@dbllp.com.

GOVER, RAYMOND LEWIS, retired newspaper executive; b. Somerset, Ky., Dec. 5, 1927; s. Raymond Bolen and Leslie Fay (Silvers) G.; m. Frieda Jane McGill, July 27, 1957; children: Janine Gover Park, Mark H., Janet L., Matthew R. BA, U. Mich., 1951; PhD (hon.), Shippensburg U., 1996. Reporter Port Huron Times, Mich., 1951-54; reporter, asst. city editor, city editor The Jour., Flint, Mich., 1954-70, editor, 1976-78; editor, pub. The News, Saginaw, Mich., 1970-76, 78-81; pub. The Patriot News, Harrisburg, Pa., 1981-97; pres. Patriot News Co., Harrisburg, 1997-2001; ret., 2001. Bd. dirs. Hershey Trust Co. Bd. dirs. Ctrl. Pa. Hospice, 2000-01, YMCA, Harrisburg, 1984-90, Harrisburg Symphony Orch., Milton Hershey Sch.; v.p. Tri-County United Way, Harrisburg; bd. adv. Pa. State U., Harrisburg; trustee. v.p. Pa. Newspaper Pubs. Found., pres. 2004—05, Pine St. Presbyn. Ch., Harrisburg, Greater Harrisburg Found. Mem. Newspaper Assn. Am., Pa. Newspaper Assn. (bd. dirs. 1987—, pres. 1990-91), Am. Soc. Newspaper Editors, Mich. Press Assn. (bd. dirs. 1978-81), Soc. Profl. Journalists, West Shore Country Club (mem. bd. govs. 1991-95), Masons. Avocations: golf, fishing, hunting. Home: 905 Grandon Way Mechanicsburg PA 17050-9171 Office: Patriot-News Co PO Box 2265 812 Market St Harrisburg PA 17101-2827 Office Phone: 717-728-2711. Personal E-mail: r.gover@verizon.net.

GOVERN, FRANK STANLEY, health facility and research administrator, healthcare educator, writer; b. Plainfield, NJ, May 18, 1951; s. Fred John and Jane Louise (Schweitzer) Govern; m. Patricia Loretta Hermanns, Aug. 19, 1972; children: Jason, Heather. AAS, Middlesex County Coll., 1973; BA, Salem State Coll., 1979; MAS, Johns Hopkins U., 1981; PhD in law, policy, and soc., Northeastern U., 1997. Asst. adminstrn. Circle Terrace Hosp., Alexandria, Va., 1981-84; CEO Tyrone (Pa.) Hosp., 1984—85; pres., CEO Charles River Hosp., Wellesley, Mass., 1985—86; COO Joint Ctr. Radiation Therapy, Boston, 1986—98; dep. dir. radiation oncology scis. program, chief oncology outreach, radiation rsch. Nat. Cancer Inst., Bethesda, Md., 1998—. Sr. instr. Northeastern U., Boston, 1986—98; instr. Harvard Med. Sch., Boston, 1986—98. Author: U.S. Health Policy and Problem Definition: A Policy Process Adrift, 2000; contbr. chapters to books, articles to profl. jours. Founder, pres. Cmty. for Ednl. Excellence, Beverly, Mass., 1991. Capt. USAF, 1974—76. Avocations: bicycling, reading, writing, skiing. Home: 11908 Bristol Manor Ct North Bethesda MD 20852-5804 Office: NCI Exec Plz N 6130 Exec Blvd Ste 6020 Bethesda MD 20892

GOVERN, MAUREEN, information technology executive; B in Math., No. Ill. U.; M in operations rsch., Stanford U. Sr. positions Bell-Northern Rsch., NYNEX Sci. and Tech.; joined Bell Labs., 1978; v.p. network architecture and tech. network sys. group Motorola Inc., v.p. advanced tech. devel., global telecom., solutions sector; chief tech. officer Convergys Corp., 2002—. Named one of Premier 100 Info. Tech. Leaders, Computerworld mag., 2004. Office: Convergys Corp 201 E 4th St Cincinnati OH 45202

GOVIL, NARENDRA KUMAR, mathematics professor; b. Aligarh, India, Jan. 5, 1940; arrived in U.S., 1983; s. Panna Lal and Kamla Devi (Agrawal) G.; m. Urmila Agrawal, Feb. 1, 1964; children: Sanjay, Sandeep. BSc, Agra (India) U., 1957; MSc, Aligarh (India) U., 1959; PhD, U. Montreal, Que., Can., 1968. Lectr. Concordia U., Montreal, 1967-68, asst. prof., 1968-70, Indian Inst. Tech., New Delhi, 1970-78, assoc. prof., 1978-80, prof., 1980-85; assoc. prof. Auburn (Ala.) U., 1985-86, prof., 1986—. Vis. scientist Dalhousie U., Halifax, Canada, 1980; vis. prof. U. Alberta, Edmonton, Canada, 1981, Auburn U., 1983—85; mem. exec. com. Forum Interdisciplinary Math, Delhi, 1989—91; reviewer Math. Reviews; mem. editl. bd. Jour. of Inequalities and Applications, Internat. Jour. Math. and Math. Sci., Internat. Jour. of Pure and Applied Math, Scis., Global Jour. of Math. and Math. Sci., Pan-Am. Math. Jour., 1994—98, Archives of Inequalities and Applications, 2003—04. Editor: Jour. Inequalities in Pure and Applied Math., Australian Jour. Math. Analysis and Applications; contbr. articles to profl. jours.; co-editor: Fourier Analysis, Approximation Theory and Applications, 1997, Approximation Theory, 1998. Mem. exec. India Cultural Assn. East Ala., Auburn, 1986, 96-97. Fellow: Nat. Acad. Scis. India (life); mem.: Indian Math Soc. (life), India Cultural Assn. East Ala. (pres. Auburn 1991). Avocations: music, reading. Home: 523 Owens Rd Auburn AL 36830-2513 Office: Auburn Univ Dept Math Auburn AL 36849 Office Phone: 334-844-6558. Business E-Mail: govilnk@auburn.edu.

GOVINDARAJAN, VIJAY, finance educator; b. Madras, India, Nov. 18, 1949; s. Krishnamachari Vijayaraghavan and Deshikachari Padmasini; m. Kirthi Sundararajan, Feb. 6, 1980; children: Tarunya, Tapasya. BA in Commerce, Annamalai U., Tamil Nadu, India, 1969; Chartered Acct., Inst. of

Chartered Accts., Delhi, India, 1972; MBA, Harvard Bus. Sch., Boston, MA, 1976, PhD in Bus., 1978. Mgmt. trainee DCM, India, 1972—74; assoc. prof. Indian Inst. of Mgmt., Ahmedabad, India, 1974—80; vis. assoc. prof. Harvard Bus. Sch., Boston, 1980—81; assoc. prof. Ohio State U., Columbus, 1981—85; prof. Dartmouth Coll., Hanover, NH, 1985—. Author: (book) Strategic Cost Management, 1993 (Best Book, 1999), The Quest for Global Dominance, 2001, Management Control Systems, 2001; co-editor: The Many Facets of Leadership, 2002; author: Global Strategy and Organization, 2003, Management Control Systems, 2003, (article) Academy of Management Journal, 1984 (Best Paper, 1986). Named Best Bus. Sch. Prof., Bus. Week, 2001; named to Top 10 Prof., 1993. Mem.: Acad. of Internat. Bus., Strategic Mgmt. Soc., Acad. of Mgmt. Avocation: travel. Home: 13 Rope Ferry Rd Hanover NH 03755 Office: Dartmouth Coll Tuck Sch of Bus 100 Tuck Dr Hanover NH 03755 Business E-Mail: vijay.govindarajan@dartmouth.edu.*

GOVINDJEE, biophysics professor, biochemistry professor, biology professor; b. Allahabad, India, Oct. 24, 1933; arrived in U.S., 1956, naturalized, 1972; s. Vishveshwar Prasad and Savitri Devi Asthana; m. Rajni Varma, Oct. 24, 1957; children: Anita Govindjee, Sanjay Govindjee. BSc, U. Allahabad, 1952, MSc, 1954; PhD, U. Ill., 1960. Lectr. botany U. Allahabad, 1954-56; grad. fellow U. Ill., Urbana, 1956-58, rsch. asst., 1958-60, USPHS postdoctoral trainee biophysics, 1960-61, mem. faculty, 1961—, assoc. prof. botany and biophysics, 1965-69, prof. biophysics and plant biology, 1969-99, disting. lectr. Sch. Life Scis., 1978, emeritus prof. biophysics, plant biology and biochemistry, 1999—. Author (with E. Rabinowitch): Photosynthesis, 1969; editor: Bioenergetics of Photosynthesis, 1975, Photosynthesis: Energy Conversion by Plants and Bacteria Carbon Assimilation and Plant Productivity, 2 vols., 1982 (Russian transl. 1987); co-editor: The Oxygen Evolving System of Photosynthesis, 1983, Light Emission by Plants and Bacteria, 1986, Excitation Energy and Electron Transfer in Photosynthesis, 1989, Molecular Biology of Photosynthesis, 1989, Photosynthesis: From Photoreactions to Productivity, 1993, Concepts in Photobiology: Photosynthesis and Photomorphogenesis, 1999, Chlorophyll a Fluorescence: A Signature of Photosynthesis, 2004, Discoveries in Photosynthesis, 2005; editor Hist. Corner: Photosynthesis Rsch., 1989—; guest editor spl. issue Biophys. Jour., 1972, Photochemistry and Photobiology, 1978, Photosynthesis Research, 1993, 96, 2002-04; editor-in-chief Photosynthesis Rsch., 1985-88; series editor: Advances in Photosynthesis and Respiration, vol. 1, 1994, vol. 2, 1995, vols. 3, 4 and 5, 1996, vols. 6 and 7, 1998, vol. 8, 1999, vol. 9, 2000, vols. 10 and 11, 2001, vol. 12, 2002, vol. 13, vol. 14, 2003, vols. 15, 16, 17, 18 and 19, 2004, vols. 18, 20-23, 2005; contbr. articles to profl. jours., also Sci. Am. Fulbright scholar, 1956-61, 96-97. Fellow AAAS, NAS (India); mem. Am. Soc. Plant Biologists, Biophys. Soc. Am., Am. Soc. Photobiology (coun. 1976, pres. 1981), Internat. Photosynthesis Soc. (exec. com., publ. com. 1995-01, hon. pres. 13th Internat. Photosynthesis Congress 2004), Sigma Xi (emeritus). Business E-Mail: gov@life.uiuc.edu.

GOWA, ANDREW, investor, lawyer; b. NYC, Nov. 6, 1949; s. Everett M. and Louise (Friedman) G.; m. Robin P. Lincoln May 21, 1995; children: Catherine J., Jon T., Timothy M., Melissa Lincoln, Jennifer Lincoln. AB magna cum laude, Tufts U., 1971; JD, U. Pa., 1974. Bar: Pa. 1974, N.Y. 1982. From assoc. to ptnr. Blank, Rome, Comisky & McCauley, Phila., 1974-84; sr. v.p North Atlantic Investment Corp., Phila., 1984-85; pres., chief exec. officer First Equity Devel. Corp., West Chester, Pa., 1984-90; ptnr. Schnader Harrison Segal & Lewis LLP, Phila., 1990—2002; chmn. Gowa Lincoln, PC, Phila., 2002—. Bd. dirs. Equitrust Real Estate Corp., West Chester; developer Brampton Chase, Malvern, Pa., 1988-89; faculty Grad. Builders Inst. Pa. State U., State Coll., 1987-90; faculty Pa. Bar Inst., 1991—; chmn. Allegheny Cardiovascular Inst., 1997, Likoff Cardiovascular Inst., 1995-97. Mem. Tufts U. Alumni Coun., Medford, Mass., 1982-88; bd. overseers Tufts U., Medford, 1988-93; bd. dirs. Kaiserman Ctr. Jewish Cmty. Ctrs. Phila, 1982-88. Recipient Disting. Service medal Tufts U., 1982. Mem. Pa. Bar Assn. (ho. dels. 1983-87), Phila. Bar Assn. (bd. govs. 1985, chmn. real estate sect. 1985, exec. com. real estate sect. 1983-89), Am. Coll. Real Estate Laywers. Avocations: amateur radio, cooking. Office: Gowa Lincoln PC 1525 Locust St Ste 1000 Philadelphia PA 19102 E-mail: andy@gowalaw.com.

GOWANS, SIR JAMES LEARMONTH, science administrator, immunologist; b. Sheffield, Eng., May 7, 1924; s. John Gowans and Selma Ljung; m. Moyra Leatham, July 28, 1956; children: William, Jenny, Lucy. MB, BS, U. London, 1947; MA, DPhil, Oxford U., 1953; ScD (hon.), Yale U., 1966; DSc (hon.), U. Chgo., 1971, U. Birmingham, Eng., 1978, U. Rochester, 1987; MD (hon.), U. Edinburgh, Scotland, 1979, U. Sheffield, Eng.; DM (hon.), U. Southampton, Eng., 1987; LLD, U. Glasgow, Scotland, 1988. Rsch. prof. sch. pathology Oxford U., Eng., 1962-77, dir. med. rsch. coun. cellular immunology unit, 1963-77; sec., CEO U.K. Med. Rsch. Coun., 1977-87; cons. WHO Global Program on AIDS, Geneva, Switzerland, 1987-88; rsch. programs adv. com. Nat. Multiple Sclerosis Soc., N.Y.C., 1988-90; sec.-gen. Human Frontier Scis. Program, Strasbourg, France, 1989-93. Chmn. European Med. Rsch. Coun., 1985-87; mem. governing coun. Internat. Agy. for Rsch. on Cancer, Lyon, France, 1980-87; mem. awards assembly GM Cancer Rsch. Found., N.Y.C., 1988-92; dir. European Iniative for Communicators of Sci., Munich, Germany, 1995-99, Charing Cross Sunley Rsch. Ctr., London, 1989-91. Contbr. articles on cellular immunology to profl. jours. Recipient Gairdner Found. award, 1968, Paul Ehrlich prize, 1974, Feldberg award, 1979, Wolf prize in medicine, 1980, Medawar prize, 1990. Fellow Royal Soc. (Royal Medal 1976); mem. NAS (fgn. assoc.), Am. Assn. Immunologists (hon.), Am. Assn. Anatomists (hon.). Avocations: music, gardening, old books. Fax: (44) 1865-865548. Office Phone: (44) 1865-862304.

GOWDY, FRANKLIN BROCKWAY, lawyer; b. Burlington, Iowa, Dec. 27, 1945; s. Franklin Kamm and Dorothy Faye (Brockway) G.; m. Jennifer June McKenrick, Nov. 27, 1982; stepchildren: Jeffrey F. Hammond, Tracy Lawrence, Jonathan R. Hammond, Julie E. Rawls. BA in Polit. Sci., Stanford U., 1967; JD, U. Calif., Berkeley, 1970. Bar: U.S. Dist. Ct. (no. dist.) Calif. 1971, U.S. Ct. Appeals (9th cir.) 1971, U.S. Dist. Ct. (ea. dist.) Tex., 1971, U.S. Dist. Ct. (cen. dist.) Calif. 1984, U.S. Ct Appeals (fed. cir) 2003, U.S. Supreme Ct. 1979. Assoc. Brobeck, Phleger & Harrison, San Francisco, 1971-78, ptnr., 1978—2003; mng. ptnr.-San Francisco Office Morgan, Lewis & Brockius LLP. Named Calif. Lawyer of Yr. for civil litigation, Calif. Lawyer mag., 2003, Calif. Lawyer of Yr. for law practice, 2004. Fellow Am. Coll. Trial Lawyers; mem. ABA, Calif. Bar Assn., San Francisco Bar Assn., Assn. Bus. Trial Lawyers (bd. govs.). Office: Morgan Lewis Bockius LLP Spear St Tower 1 Market Plz San Francisco CA 94105-1420 Office Phone: 415-442-1525. Office Fax: 415-442-1001. Business E-Mail: fgowdy@morganlewis.com.*

GOWENS, WALTER, II, financial and business services executive; b. Tampa, Fla., Sept. 30, 1954; s. Walter and Bessie (Bridges) G. BS, Ariz. State U., 1975; MBA, Ind. U., 1977. CFP; registered investment advisor. Fin. analyst Am. Can Co., Greenwich, Conn., 1977-79; cons. Norman Jaspan Assocs., N.Y.C., 1979; pvt. cons. practice N.Y.C., 1979-80; mgr. fin. reporting YMCA Greater N.Y.C., 1980-81; sr. fin. analyst Met. Transp. Authority, N.Y.C., 1981-83; pres. Prudential Vanguard Cos., Inc., N.Y.C., 1983—. Portfolio mgr., lic. ins. broker, N.Y.C., 1986—; former contbg. pers. fin. advisor to online expert svcs. incl. Allexperts.com. and Infomarkets.com. Founder, editor Prudential Vanguard Tax & Investment newsletter, 1986-89. Recipient Entrepreneurial Skills award C.A. C. of C., 1987; Consortium Grad. Study fellow, 1975. Mem. Nat. Soc. Tax Profls., Fin. Planning Assn., Nat. Soc. Accts., Nat. Notary Assn., Am. Assn. Individual Investors. Avocations: theater, tennis. Office: Prudential Vanguard Cos Inc 1501 Broadway Ste 1607 New York NY 10036-5601 Office Phone: 212-749-9000. E-mail: wgowens@prudentialvanguard.net.

GOWER, JAMES M., biotechnology company executive; BS, MBA Ops. Rsch., U. Tenn. Chmn., CEO Rigel Pharms., San Francisco, 1997—; sr. v.p. Genentech, 1982—92; pres., CEO Tularik, Inc., 1992—96. Office: Rigel Inc 1180 Veterans Blvd South San Francisco CA 94080-1985

GOWLER, VICKI SUE, newspaper editor, journalist; b. Decatur, Ill., Apr. 16, 1951; d. Carroll Eugene and Audra Janet (Briggs) G. BS in Journalism, U. Ill., 1973. Reporter Iroquois County Daily Times, Watseka, Ill., 1973-75, Quincy (Ill.) Herald-Whig, 1975-78; from reporter to mng. editor Miami (Fla.) Herald, Stuart, Delray Beach, West Palm Beach, 1089-88; asst. news editor Knight-Ridder Washington Bur., 1988-93; exec. editor Duluth (Minn.) News-Tribune, Knight-Ridder newspaper, 1978—2001, editor and v.p., 1993—97, editor, 2001—; mng. editor Pioneer Press, Knight-Ridder newspaper, 1997—2001, editor, 2001—; sr. v.p. and editor St. Paul Pioneer Press, Knight-Ridder newspaper, 2001—. Recipient numerous awards for journalistic works, including RFK award, state AP awards in all categories. Mem. Am. Soc. Newspaper Editors. Methodist. Avocations: reading, tennis, playing clarinet, travel, visiting with her family.

GOYAK, ELIZABETH FAIRBAIRN, retired public relations executive; b. Chgo., Oct. 7, 1922; d. Lewis Howard and Berenice Marie (Bowers) Fairbairn; m. Edward Anthony Goyak, May 20, 1951. BEd, So. Ill. U., 1943; MA, No. Ill. U., 1979. Reporter Internat. News Svc., Chgo., 1945-49, Chgo. Tribune, 1949-52; writer Gardner & Jones, Chgo., 1954-59, Aaron Cushman & Assocs., Chgo., 1959-60; v.p. Daniel J. Edelman, Chgo., 1960-76; mgr. pub. rels. Stone Container Corp., Chgo., 1976-82; pres. pub. rels. Firm Chgo. Connection, Matteson, Ill., 1982-98. Dir. pub. rels. Ill. Dem. Women for Adlai Stevenson, 1952; founder, pres. bd. dirs. Matteson Pub. Libr., 1958-87; chmn. Matteson Bicentennial Commn., 1973-76. Mem. Pub. Rels. Soc. Am. (accredited, Silver anvil award 1975), Publicity Club Chgo. (sec., bd. dirs. 1964-76, Golden Trumpet award 1965, 66, 75), Chgo. Press Vets. Mem. United Ch. Christ. Home: 9200 Lalique Ln Apt 1503 Fort Myers FL 33919-7408

GOYAN, JERE EDWIN, pharmaceutical executive, dean; b. Oakland, Calif., Aug. 3, 1930; s. Gerald H. and Lucille (Johnson) G.; m. Patricia B. Mesirow, Aug. 24, 1952 (div.); children: Pamela, Terrence H., Andrea; m. Linda Lloyd Hart, Mar. 25, 1988. BS, U. Calif. Sch. Pharmacy, 1952, PhD, 1957. Asst. prof. pharmacy U. Mich., 1956-61, assoc. prof., 1961-63; assoc. prof. pharmacy and pharm. chemistry U. Calif. at San Francisco, 1963-65, prof., 1965-79, 81-92; assoc. dean Sch. Pharmacy, 1966-67, dean, 1967-79, 81-92; pres., COO Alteon, Inc., Ramsey, N.J., 1993-99; pres. Goyan & Hart Assocs., 1999—. Commr. FDA/HHS, 1979-81 Fellow AAAS; mem. Inst. Medicine of NAS, N.Y. Acad. Scis., Am. Pharm. Assn., Acad. Pharm. Scis., Am. Assn. Pharm. Scientists (pres. 1990), Calif. Pharm. Assn., Am. Assn. Colls. Pharmacy (pres. 1978-79), Sigma Xi, Rho Chi, Phi Lambda Upsilon. Office Phone: 281-360-6551. Personal E-mail: jgoyan@aol.com.

GOYER, ROBERT ANDREW, pathology educator; b. Hartford, Conn., June 2, 1927; s. Andrew R. and Cecelia P. (Castonquay) G.; m. Mary Ellen Wilke, Feb. 4, 1955; children: Barbara, John, Peter, Ellen. BS, Holy Cross Coll., 1950; MD, St. Louis U., 1955. Diplomate: Am. Bd. Pathology. Intern St. Francis Hosp., Hartford, 1955-56; resident in pathology St. Louis U. Hosps., 1956-60; practice medicine specializing in pathology St. Louis, 1956-65; instr. pathology St. Louis U., 1960-62, asst. prof., 1962-65, Sch. Medicine, U. NC, Chapel Hill, 1965-68, assoc. prof., 1968-71, prof. pathology, 1971-74, adj. prof. pathology, 1979-87; clin. pathologist Cardinal Glennon Meml. Hosp. for Children, St. Louis, 1961-62, dir. labs., 1962-64; staff pathologist NC Meml. Hosp., Chapel Hill, 1965-74; chief pathology U. Hosp., London, Canada, 1974-79; prof. pathology Health Scis. Centre, U. Western Ont., Canada, 1974-79, 87-92, prof. emeritus, 1992—; dept. dir. Nat. Inst. Environ. Health Scis., Research Triangle Park, NC, 1979-87; pvt. cons. health effects, toxic metals Chapel Hill, 1992—. Nat. assoc. Nat. Acads.; mem. com. WHO/IPCS, NAS, NRC. Contbr. articles to profl. jours.; mem. editl. bd. Yearbook Pathology, 1979-88, AMA Archives of Pathology, 1973-82. Served with USN, 1945-47. Recipient Merit award, Soc. Toxicology, 2004; Nat. Found. fellow, 1959—60. Mem. Coll. Am. Pathology, Am. Assn. Pathologists, Internat. Acad. Pathology, Soc. Exptl. Biology and Medicine, Soc. Toxicology (Merit award 2004). Roman Catholic. Achievements include research in experimental pathology and metal toxicology. Office: 6405 Huntingridge Rd Chapel Hill NC 27517 Office Phone: 919-419-1804. Personal E-mail: robert_goyer@msn.com.

GOYER, ROBERT STANTON, retired communications educator; b. Kokomo, Ind., Oct. 7, 1923; s. Clarence V. and Genevieve M. (Sober) G.; m. Patricia Ann Stutz, Aug. 12, 1950; children: Karen, Susan, Linda, Amy. BA, DePauw U., 1948; MA, Miami U., Oxford, Ohio, 1950; PhD, Ohio State U., 1955. Instr. Miami U., Oxford, 1949-51; instr., then asst. prof. Ohio State U., Columbus, 1955-58, rsch. assoc., cons. rsch. found., 1956-63; from asst. to assoc. to prof. Purdue U., West Lafayette, Ind., 1958-66; prof. Ohio U., Athens, 1966-81, dir. ctr. communication studies, 1966-74, 79-81, assoc. dean grad. coll., 1978, dean grad. coll., acting dir. rsch., 1979, acting assoc. provost grad. and rsch. programs, 1979, prof. emeritus, 1981—; prof., chmn. dept. communication Ariz. State U., Tempe, 1981-89, prof., 1989-94, prof. emeritus, 1994—. Cons. in field. Author books; contbr. articles to profl. jours. 1st lt. U.S. Army, 1943-46, 52-53. Decorated Bronze Star. Fellow AAAS, Internat. Comm. Assn.; mem. APA, Nat. Comm. Assn. Presbyterian. Home: 517 W Summit Pl Chandler AZ 85225-7799

GOYOL, APOLLOS BITRUS, education educator; b. Gindiri, Nigeria, June 30, 1960; s. Goyol Bitrus Bakkuk and Rhoda Bitrus Goyol; m. Jemima Apollos Phillip, June 5, 1993; children: Wadelnen Jane, Nenfot Samuel. PhD, Western Mich. U., 1997—2002. Asst. prof. and evaluator U. of Ark. for Med. Sciences, Little Rock, 2003—05; head of dept. Plateau State Poly., Barkin-Ladi, Nigeria, 1984—97; coord. sr. evaluation U. Ky., Lexington, Ky., 2005—. Dir. of planning and implementation Alternative Trade Network of Nigeria, Plateau State, Nigeria, 1995—2002. Author: Adjustment Problems of African Students at Public Universities in America, 2005. Pres. of African student union Western Mich. U., 1999—2001. Recipient Outstanding Cmty. Svc. award, Met. Kalamazoo Chpt. of Jack & Jill of Am., Inc, 1998. Mem.: Am. Ednl. Rsch. Assn., Am. Evaluation Assn. (assoc.). Home: 100 Lakeshore Dr Apt 94 Lexington KY 40502 Office: Univ of Ark for Med Sci 4301 W Markham St # 595 Little Rock AR 72205-7101 Office Phone: 859-257-0038. Home Fax: 501-686-7053; Office Fax: 501-686-7053. E-mail: apollos.goyol@uky.edu.

GOZANI, TSAHI, nuclear physicist; b. Tel Aviv, Nov. 25, 1934; came to U.S., 1965; s. Arieh and Rivcca Gozani; m. Adit Soffer, Oct. 14, 1958; children: Mor, Shai Nachum, Or Pinchas, Tal. BSc, Technion-Israel Inst. Tech., Haifa, 1956, MSc, 1958; DSc, Swiss Fed. Inst. Tech. (ETH), Zurich, Switzerland, 1962. Registered profl. nuclear engr., Calif.; accredited nuclear material mgr. Rsch. physicist Israel Atomic Energy Commn., Beer-Sheva, 1962-65; rsch. assoc. nuclear engring. dept. Rensselaer Poly. Inst., Troy, N.Y., 1965-66; sr. staff scientist General-Atomic & IRT, San Diego, 1966-70, 71-75; prof. applied physics Tel Aviv U., 1971; chief scientist, divsn. mgr. SAIC, Palo Alto and Sunnyvale, Calif., 1975-84, v.p., chief scientist Sunnyvale, 1984-87, corp. v.p Santa Clara, Calif., 1987-93, sr. v.p., 1993-97; pres., CEO Ancore Corp., Santa Clara, 1997—2002; pres. Ancore, Santa Clara, 2002—05, Rapiscan Sys. Neutronics and Advanced Tech. Corp., Santa Clara, 2005—. Lady Davis vis. prof. Technion-Israel Inst. Tech., 1983-84; bd. dirs. Radiation Sci. Inst., San Jose State U. Author: Active Non-Destructive Assay of Nuclear Materials, 1981; co-author: co-author: Handbook of Nuclear Safeguards Measurement Methods, 1983; contbr. chapters to books, articles to profl. jours. Recipient 1989 Laurel award Aviation Week Jour., R&D 100 award, 1988, Most Innovative New Products. Fellow Am. Nuclear Soc.; mem. Am. Phys. Soc., Inst. Nuclear Materials. Achievements include patents for explosive detection system, explosive detection system using an artificial neural system, multi sensor explosive detection system, composite cavity structure for an explosive detection system, apparatus and method for detecting contraband using fast neutron activation, contraband detection system using direct imaging pulsed fast neutrons; invention of method to measure nuclear reactor's reactivity. Office: Rapiscan Sys Neutronics and Advanced Tech Corp 2950 Patrick Henry Dr Santa Clara CA 95054-1813 Business E-Mail: tgozani@rapiscansystems.com.

GOZEMBA, PATRICA ANDREA, women's studies and English language educator, writer; b. Medford, Mass., Nov. 30, 1940; d. John Charles and Mary Margaret (Sampey) Curran; m. Gary M. Gozemba, Sept. 4, 1967 (div. Feb. 1975). BA, Emmanuel Coll., Boston, 1962; MA, U. Iowa, 1963; EdD, Boston U., 1975. Tchr. Waltham (Mass.) H.S., 1963-64; prof. Salem (Mass.) State Coll., 1964—. Vis. fellow East-West Ctr., 1995; vis. prof. U. Hawaii, 1997-98; co-chair The History Project, Boston, 2000—; bd. dirs. Healthlink, Salem Alliance for the Environment, 2001—. Editor: New England Women's Studies, 1977—87; mem. editl. bd.: Thought and Action, 1990—93; contbr. articles to profl. jours.; author: Pockets of Hope: How Students and Teachers Change the World, 2002. Bd. dirs. Salem Alliance for the Environment, 2003—. Mem. NEA (standing com. 1982-93), NOW, NAACP, Nat. Women's Studies Assn. (gov. bd. 1977-89), Nat. Coun. Tchrs. English, Nat. Gay and Lesbian Task Force, Mass. State Coll. Assn. (editor 1982-90, 92-97), Herb Soc. Am. Democrat. Avocations: walking, tennis, gardening, photography. Home and Office: 17 Sutton Ave Salem MA 01970-5728

GRAB, JOHN H., mathematics educator; b. Coatesville, Pa., Mar. 30, 1945; s. Luther Brooks and Edna Leese Grab; m. Susan C. Oldynski, July 31, 1976; 1 child, Jennifer S. BS in Math Edn., Millersville State U., 1967, MS in Math Edn., 1980. Cert. tchr. Pa., 1967. Educator Milton Hershey Sch., Pa., 1967—. Sch. bd. mem. Derry Twp. Sch. Dist., Hershey, Pa., 1995—2003, pres., 1993—94. Mem.: Hershey/Hummelstown Kiwanis Club. Home: 21 Tice Ave Hershey PA 17033-2151 Office: Milton Hershey Sch Box 830 Spartan Ln Hershey PA 17033-0830 Office Phone: 717-520-2738. Office Fax: 717-520-2644. Business E-Mail: grabj@mhs-pa.org.

GRABAR, ANDREW, art educator, artist; b. N.Y.C., June 22, 1947; 1 child, Koa A.G.S.L. Assoc. prof. art U. Hawaii, Hilo, 1997—. Masters abstracts, Primordial Beginnings. Sr. Scholar award, William J. Fulbright Fgn. Scholarship Bd., 2004. Mem.: Am. Coun. South Asian Art, Coll. Art Assn. Am., Fulbright Assn. (life). Office: Univ Hawaii Hilo Art Dept 200 West Kawili St Hilo HI 96720 Office Phone: 808-974-7793. Personal E-mail: grabar@hawaii.edu.

GRABAR, OLEG, retired art educator; b. Strasbourg, France, Nov. 3, 1929; arrived in U.S., 1948, naturalized, 1960; s. Andre and Julie (Ivanova) G.; m. Terry Ann Harris, June 9, 1951; children: Nicolas Howard, Anne Louise. BA magna cum laude, Harvard U., 1950; licence d'Histoire, U. Paris, 1950; PhD, Princeton U., 1955; D (hon.), U. Mich. Instr. U. Mich., 1954-55, asst. prof., 1955-59, assoc. prof., 1959-64, prof., 1964-69; dir. Am. Sch. of Oriental Rsch., Jerusalem, Jordan, 1960-61, v.p., 1968-75; prof. fine arts Harvard U., 1969-81, Aga Khan prof. Islamic art, 1981-90; with sch. hist. studies Inst. For Advanced Study, Princeton, NJ, 1990-99; ret., 1999. Dir. Mich.-Harvard U. excavations in Syria, 1964-71. Author: Coinage of Tulunide, 1957, Islamic Architecture and Its Decoration, 1967, Sasanian Silver, 1967, The Formation of Islamic Art, 1973, The Alhambra, 1978, City in the Desert, 1978, Epic Images, 1982, Illustrations of the Maqamat, 1984, Islamic Art, 1987, Great Mosque of Isfahan, 1989, The Mediation of Ornament, 1992, The Shape of the Holy, 1996, La Peinture Persane, 1999, Mostly Miniatures, 2000, Islamic Art and Architecture, 660-1250, 2001; editor: Ars Orientalis, 1957—71, Muqarnas, 1983—92; contbr. articles to profl. jours. Mem. Coll. Art Assn. (dir. 1968-72), Archeol. Inst. Am., Mediaeval Acad. Am., German Archeol. Inst., Mid. Ea. Studies Assn., Am. Acad. Arts and Scis., Am. Philosophy Soc., Brit. Acad. (hon.), Austrian Acad. (hon.), Acad. Inscriptions et Belles-Lettres (Paris). Home: 43 Maxwell Ln Princeton NJ 08540-4931 Office: Inst for Advanced Study Princeton NJ 08540 Office Phone: 609-734-8310. Business E-Mail: grabar@ias.edu.

GRABEEL, DENNIS CRAIG, management consultant, small business owner; b. Pennington Gap, Va., Dec. 4, 1946; s. Charles Lavoy and Virginia (Smith) G.; m. Deborah Kathryn Jodlowski, Sept. 27, 1980; children: Nathan Charles, Justin Adam. BS in Edn., U. Va., 1970; MPA, Fla.-Atlantic U., 1981; master's cert. in project mgmt., George Washington U., 1999; MDiv, Va. Union U., 2005. Cert. project mgmt. profl. Educator, head basketball coach M.N. Smith Jr. H.S., Accomac County, Va., 1970-71; mcpl. administr. City of Boynton Beach, Fla., 1978-92, asst. to city mgr.; dir. mgmt. svcs., 1986-92; cons., instr. Dept. of Navy, Sr. Leader Seminar-TQL, 1992-98; cons. Eagle Assocs. Internat., 1998—; v.p. Hampton Roads chpt. Project Mgmt. Inst., 1999-2001. Adult scouting vol. Boy Scouts Am., chaplain, 2003—, Tidewater coun., coun. relationships com., 2000—, internat. scouting rep., 2004—; lay spkr. Salem United Meth. Ch., 1993—, lay leader, 2000-02, lay del. to ann. conf., 2003—; vol. Virginia Beach City Schs., 1998-2000; scouting ministries coord. Norfolk dist. United Meth. Ch., 2001-02, leadership devel. inst. Va. conf., 2002—. Lt. USN, 1971-77, comdr. USNR, ret., 1992. Mem. World Affairs Coun., Project Mgmt. Inst., Nat. Eagle Scout Assn. (life), Fla.-Atlantic U. Alumni Assn. (life), U. Va. Alumni Assn. (life), Nat. Assn. United Meth. Scouters (life), Mil. Officers Assn. (life), Pi Alpha Alpha Nat. Hon. Soc., Palm Beach Rugby Football Club (co-founder, past pres.), Trout Unlimited (life). Avocations: fishing, swimming, scouting, golf. Home and Office: 1212 Eagle Way Virginia Beach VA 23456-5869 Personal E-mail: cgrabeel@aol.com.

GRABER, DORIS APPEL, political scientist, writer, editor; b. St. Louis, Nov. 11, 1923; d. Ernest and Martha (Insel) Appel; m. Thomas M. Graber, June 15, 1941; children: Lee Winston, Thomas Woodrow, Jack Douglas, Jim Murray, Susan Doris. AB, Washington U., St. Louis, 1941, MA, 1942; PhD, Columbia U., 1947. Feature writer St. Louis County Observer, Univ. City Tribune, St. Louis, 1939-41; civilian dir. U.S. Army Ednl. Reconditioning Program, Camp Maxey, Tex., 1943-45; editor legal mags. Commerce Clearing House, Chgo., 1945-46; lectr. polit. sci. Northwestern U., 1948-49, U. Chgo., 1950-51, rsch. assoc. Ctr. for Study Am. Fgn. and Mil. Policy, 1952-71; lectr. polit. sci. North Park Coll., 1952; mem. faculty U. Ill., Chgo., 1964—, assoc. prof. polit. sci., 1964-69, prof., 1970—; editor textbooks Harper & Row, Evanston, 1956-63. Vis. prof. Harvard U., 1996. Author: The Development of the Law of Belligerent Occupation, 1949, 68, Crisis Diplomacy: A History of U.S. Intervention Policies and Practices, 1959, Public Opinion, The President and Foreign Policy, 1968, Verbal Behavior and Politics, 1976, Mass Media and American Politics, 1980, 84, 89, 93, 96, 2001, 2005, Crime News and the Public, 1980, (with others) Media Agenda Setting in a Presidential Election, 1981, Processing the News: How People Tame the Information Tide, 1984, 88, 94, Public Sector Communication: How Organizations Manage Information, 1992; editor, contbr. The President and the Public, 1982; editor: Media Power in Politics, 1984, 90, 94, 2000, Political Comm., 1992-98, founding editor emeritus, 1998—, mem. editl. bd., 2001—; editor: (with others) The Politics of News: The News of Politics, 1998, Processing Politics: Learning from Television in the Internet Age, 2001 (Goldsmith Book prize 2003), The Power of Communication, 2003; book rev. editor Polit. Psychology, 1998—; mem. editl. bd. Polit. Sci. Quarterly, 1978—, Human Comm. Rsch., 1979-80, Pub. Opinion Quarterly, 1980-84, 93-98, Jour. Comm., 1985-91, 99—, Social Sci. Quarterly, 1989-2003, P.S.: Polit. Sci. and Politics, 1990-93, Discourse and Soc., 1990—, Orgnl. Comm: Emerging Perspectives, 1994—, Jour. Health Comm., 1995-98, Harvard Internat. Jour. Press/Politics, 1995—, Acta Politica: Internat. Jour. Polit. Sci., 1997—, Comm., Soc. and Politics Series, Cambridge U. Press, 1999—, Polit. Comm., 2001-, Media and Am. Politics Ency., 2003—; contbr. articles to profl. jours. Recipient Disting. Alumna award, Washington U., 2001, Univ. Scholar award, U. Ill., Chgo., 2003—. Mem. LWV, Am. Assn. Pub. Opinion Rsch., Midwest Assn. Pub. Opinion Rsch. (coun. mem. 1978-83, program chmn. 1978-79, pres. 1980-81, Career award 1988), Midwest Polit. Sci. Assn. (past pres. 1972-73, coun. 1973-74, program sect. chair 1979, Career award 1994), Am. Polit. Sci. Assn. (coun. 1978-79, v.p. 1980-81, program chmn. 1984, chmn. polit. comm. sect. 1989-91, chmn. editl. bd. P.S. 1992-94), Internat. Polit. Sci. Assn., Internat. Commn. Assn. (divsn. program chmn. 1978-80, divsn. chmn. 1980-82, chmn. program 1990, chmn. pre-program 2004, Career award 1996), Assn. Edn. for Journalism, Acad. Polit. Sci., Am. Acad. Polit. and Social Sci., Internat. Soc. Polit. Psychology (coun. 1992-93, 95-98, co-program chmn. 1993-94, pres. 1995-96), Phi Beta Kappa (pres. Iota of Ill. chpt. 1991-92), Pi Sigma Alpha, Pi Alpha Alpha. Home: 2895 Sheridan Pl Evanston IL 60201-1725 Office: U Ill 1007 W Harrison St Chicago IL 60607-7135 Office Phone: 312-996-3108. E-mail: dgraber@uic.edu.

GRABER, ELLEN MAUREEN, elementary school educator; b. Mpls., July 24, 1949; d. Raymond Leo and Gladys Emily Hayden; m. Kenneth Leu Graber, Apr. 16, 1971; children: Angie Marie Fanset, Christa Rae Teevan. BS, U. Minn., 1971; MS, Mankato State U., 1991. Cert. tchg. State of Minn., 2002. Tchr. Farmington (Minn.) Sch., 1979—. Chairperson leadership com. Ch. of St. John Neuman, Eagan, Minn., 2000—04. Named Dist. Tchr. of Year, 2000; recipient Award of Excellence, Mn Elem. Sch. Prin. Assn., 1999—2000. Independent. Roman Catholic. Avocations: reading, golf, tennis, gardening, travel. Home: 12855 Foliage Ave Apple Valley MN 55124 Office: Farmington Sch 421 Walnut St Farmington MN 55024 Office Phone: 651-460-1800.

GRABER, GLENN C., medical educator, educational consultant; b. Knoxville, Tenn., June 2, 1942; s. George Garnel and Virginia Fort Graber; m. M. Caroline Rigsby, Aug. 1, 1964; 1 child, Rosalie Caroline; 1 child, Janna Graber Werner. PhD, U. of Mich., Ann Arbor, MI, 1964—72; BA, U. of Ky., Lexington, KY, 1960—64. Prof. of philosophy U. of Tenn., Knoxville, Tenn., 1968—; prof. of medicine U. of Tenn. Grad. Sch. of Medicine, Knoxville, Tenn., 1978—. Author (principal author): (monograph) Ethical Analysis of Clin. Medicine; editor (co-editor): (textbook) Bioethics; author (principal author): (monograph) Theory and Practice in Med. Ethics; author: (secondary author) Euthanasia - Toward an Ethical Social Policy; author: (essays in prof. journals,) 42 essays; dir.: (26 PhD dissertations), (16 MA theses) applied ethics. Mem., ethics com. United Network for Organ Sharing, Richmond, Va., 1993—95; adv. com., code of med. ethics online curriculum (CMEOC) AMA, Chgo., 2000—01; adv. bd. Tenn. Donor Services, Knoxville, Tenn., 1987—2002; cons. to Hosp. ethics com. St. Mary's Med. Ctr., Knoxville, Tenn., 1984—2002. Recipient, Phi Beta Kappa, 1963, Lindsay Young Professorship, U. of Tenn., 1980-1981, Chancellor's Citation for Extraordinary Svc. to the U., 1979; fellow Woodrow Wilson Fellowship, Woodrow Wilson Fellowship Found., 1964-1965, fellowship for postdoctoral clin. residency at The U. of Tenn. Ctr. for the Health Sciences, Inst. for Human Values in Medicine, 1976. Mem.: Assn. for Practical and Profl. Ethics, Am. Soc. for Bioethics and Humanities, Am. Philos. Assn. Episcopal. Achievements include first to developed Graduate Concentration in Medical Ethics within graduate program in Philosophy at the University of Tennessee; established the Center for Applied and Professional Ethics at the University of Tennessee. Home: 7325 Toxaway Drive Knoxville TN 37909-3130 Office: The Univ of Tennessee 801 McClung Tower Knoxville TN 37996-0480 E-mail: ggraber@utk.edu.

GRABER, RICHARD WILLIAM, lawyer, political organization worker; b. Lakewood, Ohio, July 31, 1956; s. Richard Allen and Lynn Carol (Hurschman) G.; m. Alexandria Ahlquist Richardson, Apr. 28, 1984; children: Scott Bailey, Erik Richard. AB magna cum laude, Duke U., 1978; JD, Boston U., 1981. Bar: Wis. 1981. Mem. Reinhart Boerner Van Deuren Norris & Rieselbach, S.C., Milw., Wis., 1981—. Vice chmn. Fed. Home Loan Bank Chgo., Chgo.; bd. dirs. Crane Mfg. & Svc. Corp., Cudahy, Wis. Mem. bd. of governors, Wis. Patient Compensation Fund, 1988-97; chmn. fin. com. Wis. Rep. Party, 1993-97, chmn., 1999—; mem. exec. com. North Shore Rep. Club, Milw., 1988—, Reps. of Wis., 1991; mem. Am. Coun. Young Polit. Leaders, 1990; candidate for Wis. Assembly, 1990; chmn. Kasten for Senate com. 1993; mem. bd. of appeals, Village of Shorewood, 1991—, mem. bd. of trustees of the Medical College of Wis., 1997—. Mem. Rotary (pres. Milw. 1988-89, Paul Harris fellow 1990). Avocations: politics, softball, basketball. Home: 2726 E Shorewood Blvd Milwaukee WI 53211-2458 E-mail: rgraber@reinhartlaw.com, rgraber@wisgop.org.

GRABER, SAMUEL DAVID, environmental and water resources engineer, consultant; b. N.Y.C., Jan. 12, 1942; s. Sam Mandel Graber and Maud Alice Larson; m. Arlene Jenkins Graber, June 19, 1965; children: Steven David, Brian Earl, Keven Lee, Allen Eben. BSME, U. Miami, 1963; SMME, MIT, 1965, CE, 1966. Profl. engring., N.Y., 1970, Ma., 1975. Project engr. Camp Dresser & McKee Inc, Boston, 1966—67, dir. hydraulic svcs., 1969—74; wastewater tech. dir. Metcalf & Eddy Inc, Boston, 1974—77; cons. engr. Stoughton, Mass., 1977—. Contbr. articles to profl. jours. Scout leader Boy Scouts Am., Stoughton, 1976—, scoutmaster, 1980—94. Capt. U.S. Army, 1967—69, Panama. Recipient Eagle Scout, Boy Scouts Am., 1954. Mem.: ASME, ASCE (urban drainge stds. com. 1993—, Samuel A. Greeley award 1969, J.C. Stevens award 1972, Samuel A. Greeley award 2005), Water Environment Fedn., Tau Beta Pi. Independent. Unitarian Universalist. Avocations: reading, history, genealogy, fishing, travel. Home: 118 Larson Rd Stoughton MA 02072 Office Phone: 781-341-0390.

GRABER, SUSAN P., federal judge; b. Oklahoma City, July 5, 1949; d. Julius A. and Bertha (Fenyves) Graber; m. William June, May 3, 1981; 1 child, Rachel June-Graber. BA, Wellesley Coll., 1969; JD, Yale U., 1972. Bar: N.Mex. 1972, Ohio 1977, Oreg. 1978. Asst. atty. gen. Bur. of Revenue, Santa Fe, 1972—74; assoc. Jones Gallegos Snead & Wertheim, Santa Fe, 1974—75, Taft Stettinius & Hollister, Cin., 1975—78; assoc., then ptnr. Stoel Rives Boley Jones & Grey, Portland, Oreg., 1978—88; judge pro tem Multonomah County Dist. Ct., 1983—88; arbitrator Oreg. Circuit Ct., 4th Jud. Dist., 1985—88; mediator US Dist. Ct., Dist. Oreg., 1986—88; judge, then presiding judge Oreg. Ct. Appeals, Salem, 1988—90; assoc. justice Oreg. Supreme Ct., Salem, 1990—98; judge US Ct. Appeals (9th cir.), Portland, 1998—. Mem. Gov.'s Adv. Coun. on Legal Svcs., 1979—88; mem. bd. visitors Sch. Law, U. Oreg., 1986—93; bd. dirs. U.S. Dist. Ct. of Oreg. Hist. Soc., 1985—, Oreg. Law Found., 1990—91. Mem.: Am. Law Inst., ABA, Am. Inns of Ct. (master), Oreg. Appellate Judges Assn. (sec.-treas. 1990—91, vice chair 1991—92, chair 1992—93), Oreg. Jud. Conf. (edn. com. 1988—91, program chair 1990), Ninth Cir. Jud. Conf. (chair exec. com. 1987—88), Oreg. State Bar (jud. adminstrn. com. 1985—87, pro bono com. 1988—90), Phi Beta Kappa. Mailing: US Ct Appeals 9th Cir Pioneer Courthouse 555 SW Yamhill St Portland OR 97204*

GRABER, THOMAS M., orthodontist, researcher; b. St. Louis, May 27, 1917; Diplomate Am. Bd. Orthodontics. DMD, Washington U., St. Louis, 1940; MS in Dentistry, Northwestern U., 1946, PhD in Anatomy, 1950; Doctorate (hon.), U. Gothenberg, 1989; DSc (hon.), Washington U., 1991, U. Mich., 1994, U. Kunming, 1996. Diplomate Am. Bd. Orthodontics (Recognition award 1990, Dewel award, 1992). Mem. faculty Northwestern U. Dental Sch., 1946-58, assoc. prof. orthodontics, 1954-58; dir. research Northwestern U. Dental Sch. (cleft lip and palate Inst.), 1947-58; assoc. attending orthodontist Children's Meml. Hosp., Chgo., 1951-58; vis. lectr. U. Mich. Dental Sch., 1958-67; dir. Kenilworth Research Found., Ill., 1967—; prof. orthodontics Zoller Dental Clinic; pediatrics research assoc. prof. anthropology and anatomy U. Chgo., 1969-81, assoc. prof. plastic and reconstructive surgery, 1980-82; research scientist ADA Research Inst., Chgo., 1980-90; dir. G.V. Black Inst. for Continuing Edn., 1967—; vis. prof. U. Mich., 1984-94; clin. prof. orthodontics U. Ill. Coll. Dentistry, Chgo., 1994—. Northcroft lectr., Birmingham, Eng., 1989; cons. in field. Author textbooks, articles; editor-in-chief Am. Jour. Orthodontics, 1985-2000, World Jour Orthodontics, 2000—. Served as capt. Dental Corps AUS, 1941-45. Decorated Japanese Order of the Sacred Treasure; recipient Alumni Merit award Northwestern U., 1977; named Disting. Alumnus Washington U., 1980; NIH grantee, 1954, 56-60, 76, 77, 79, 80, 85, 86. Fellow Royal Coll. Surgeons (Eng.), Am. Coll. of Dentists, Internat. Coll. of Dentists; mem. Am. Dental Soc., Ill. Dental Soc., Am. Assn. Orthodontists (gen. chmn. 1960, 77, 80, founding mem., chmn. coun. on orthodontic edn. and audio visual com. 1962, 67, gen. chmn. jour. 1977, trustee, Grieve Meml. award 1964, 84, Disting. Service award 1970, Ketcham award 1975, Salzmann award 1979, 75th Anniversary citation 1990, Mershon award 1989, Horace Hayden award 1991, Jarabak Internat. Teaching and Rsch. award 1994, Heritage award 1998, 99), Internat. Assn. Research (chmn. Chgo. sect. 1973-74), Chgo. Orthodontists Assn. (pres. 1961-62), European Orthodontists Soc.(hon.life mem. 2002), Ill. Orthodontists Soc. (pres. 1969-70, Outstanding Tchg. award 1999), Angle Soc. (pres. 1968), Japan Orthodontists Soc., World Fedn. Orthodontists (hon., Millenium award 2000, hon. doctorate Thessalonipi, Greece, 2005), Ill. Soc. Orthodontists, SAR. Republican. Presbyterian. Home: 2895 Sheridan Pl Evanston IL 60201-1725 Office: U Ill Coll Dentistry MC842 801 S Paulina St # Mc842 Chicago IL 60612-7210 Office Phone: 312-996-2293. Personal E-mail: tmgraber@comcast.net. Business E-Mail: tgraber@uic.edu.

GRABER, THOMAS WOODROW, emergency physician; s. Doris A. and T. M. Graber; m. Ellen R. Rike, May 27, 1979; children: Melinda A., Gretchen L., Emily E. BA, U. Chgo., 1970; MD, Case Western Res. U., 1975. Med. dir. Team Health Inst. Edn. and Patient Safety, Ft. Lauderdale, Fla., 2002—; chmn., dept. emergency medicine St. Vincent Charity Hosp., Cleve., 2004. Clin. asst. prof. emer. medicine Case Western Res. U. Sch. Medicine. Med. exec. com. Team Health, Knoxville, Tenn., 1999. Fellow: Am. Coll. Emergency Physicians (hon.); mem.: Am. Bd. Emegency Medicine. Achievements include development of Medical Director Education Course; Multiple Publications related to Emergency Medicine. Avocations: skiing, wind surfing. Office: St Vincent Charity Hosp 2351 E 22nd St Cleveland OH 44115 Office Phone: 216-363-2786. Office Fax: 216-241-5804. Business E-Mail: twgraber@comcast.net.

GRABER, WILLIAM RAYMOND, former pharmaceutical executive; b. Vancouver, Wash., Apr. 10, 1943; s. R. Archie and Josephine N. (Martin) G.; m. Mary Lynn McArthur, June 19, 1965; children: Kristine, Kathleen, Timothy. BA in Math., Wash. State U., 1965. Fin. mgr. GE, 1965-91; contr. The Mead Corp., Dayton, Ohio, 1991—99; CFO, sr. v.p. McKesson HBOC, San Francisco, 2000—03. Avocations: golf, jogging.

GRABILL, JAMES R., JR., education educator, editor, writer; b. Bowling Green, Ohio, Nov. 29, 1949; s. James R. Sr. and Bette L. (Baker) G.; ptnr. Marilyn Burki. BFA, Bowling Green State U., 1974; MA, Colo. State U., 1984, MFA, 1988. Poet, writer, 1968—; instr. Colo. State U., Ft. Collins, Colo., 1985-87, CCC, PCC, OWW, Portland, Oreg., 1990—. Editor, pub. Leaping Mountain Press, Ft. Collins, 1985-86; editor: The Banyan, 2002—; author: (poems) Poem Rising Out of the Earth, 1995 (Oreg. Book Award), Listening to the Leaves Form, 1997, (poems and essays) Through the Green Fire, 1995, An Indigo Scent After the Rain, 2003; contbr. numerous poems and essays to lit. publs. Coord. readings Power Plant Arts Ctr., Ft. Collins, 1984-86. Grad. fellow Colo. State U., 1981-83, 87-88, Nat. Presbyn. fellow, 1967-70. Avocations: art, drawing, reading, running. E-mail: jimg@clackamas.edu.

GRABILL, TIM, band director, paramedic; s. LeRoy and Patricia Grabill; m. Mary Grabill, June 9, 1979; children: Joseph, Trish. MusM in Edn., U. So. Miss., 1990. Lic. paramedic Ala. Band dir. Greystone Christian Sch., Mobile, Ala., 1979—84, Millry (Ala.) H.S., 1984—92; paramedic Simmons Ambulance, Monroeville, Ala., 1992—2000; band dir. Monroe County H.S./Monroeville Jr. H.S., 1992—2000; paramedic Atmore (Ala.) Ambulance, 2000—; band dir. Bay Minette (Ala.) Mid. Sch., 2000—04; tchr. band Jeremiah A. Denton Middle Sch., Ala. Sch. Math and Sci., 2004—. Freelance profl. musician. Mem.: Music Educators Nat. Conf., Pi Gamma Delta. Baptist. Avocations: motorcycling, camping, scuba diving. Home: 46110 Dawn Cir Bay Minette AL 36507

GRABINER, SANDY, mathematics professor; b. N.Y.C., Dec. 15, 1939; s. Morris and Anna (Present) G.; m. Judith Victor, June 14, 1964; children: David, Rebecca. BA, Rice U., 1960; AM, Harvard U., 1961, PhD, 1967. Instr. MIT, Cambridge, 1967-69; asst. prof. Claremont Grad. Sch., Calif., 1969-74; assoc. prof. math. Pomona Coll., Claremont, 1974-82, prof., 1982—. Editl. bd. Carus Monographs, 1990-93; contbr. articles to profl. jours. Mem. Math. Assn. Am. (program chmn. 1984-85), Am. Math. Soc., London Math. Soc., AAAS. Office: Pomona Coll Dept Maths 610 N College Ave Claremont CA 91711-6398

GRABLE, MARIE DENISE, school psychologist; d. Joseph Patrick and Denise Marie Walsh; m. Michael P. Grable, June 26, 1999 (div.); 1 child, Kaitlyn Marie. BA in Psychology and Spl. Edn., Salve Regina U., Newport, RI, 1991; MA in Ednl. Psychology, RIC, Providence, 1997; C.A.G.S. in Sch. Psychology, U. Maso Boston, 1999. Nat. cert. sch. psychologist 2003. Edn. evaluator Old Colony Y DAC, Fall River, Mass., 1992—95; program coord. CHARMSS Collaborative Mid. Sch., Randolph, Mass., 1996—97; spl. edn. HS tchr. Mashpee Pub. Schs., Mass., 1997—98, sch. psychologist, 1998—. Presenter in field. Sys. wide coord. Mashpee Pub. Schs., behavior task force facilitator, chairperson tchr. assistance team, violence prevention team mem.; mem. Parent Adv. Coun. Sandwich Ind. Presch., 2004—; profl. devel. com. mem. Mashpee Pub. Schs.; mem. com. Molly Hirshberg Fund Grant, 2002—, sec., 2004—. Mem.: APA, NASP, RI Sch. Psychology Assn., New Eng. Ednl. Rsch. Orgn., Mass. Sch. Psychology Assn. Achievements include development of an administrative tool for professional evaluation of school psychologists; a system of referral for Teacher Assistance Teams; a process for the completion of Functional Behavioral Assessments; design for alternative programs for at-risk students. Avocations: exercise, travel. Office: Mashpee Pub Schs 500 Old Barnstable Rd Mashpee MA 02649 Office Phone: 508-539-3600 ext. 2272. Office Fax: 508-539-1511. Business E-Mail: mgrable@mashpee.k12.ma.us.

GRABOW, RAYMOND JOHN, mayor, lawyer; b. Cleve., Jan. 27, 1932; s. Joseph Stanley and Frances (Kalata) G.; m. Margaret Jean Knoll, Nov. 27, 1969; children: Rachel Jean, Ryan Joseph. BSBA, Kent State U., 1953; JD, Western Res. U., 1958. Bar: Ohio 1958. Counsel No. Ohio Petroleum Retailers Assn., Cleve., 1965-78; counsel, trustee Alliance of Poles Fed. Credit Union, 1972; also gen. counsel Alliance of Poles of Am., Parma Polish Am. League; councilman City of Warrensville Heights (Ohio), 1962-68, mayor, 1968-98. Sec. Space Comfort Co., S.S.K., Inc.; fed. panelist U.S. Dist. Ct.; active Dem. Exec. Com. Cuyahoga County, 1966—98, precinct com., 1966—80; trustee Brentwood Hosp., Nat. League Cities, Brentwood Found.; bd. govs. Meridia Southpoint Hosp., 1996—99. Mem. Ohio Jud. Conf. (life), Ohio State Bar Assn., Cuyahoga County Bar Assn., Cleve. Bar Assn., U.S. Conf. of Mayors, Am. Legion, PLAV Vets, Cleve. Soc., Warrensville Heights C. of C. (trustee 1989-98), Ohio Assn. Pub. Safety Dirs., Ohio Mcpl. League, Mcpl. Treas. Assn., Order of Alhambra, Fraternal Order of Eagles, West Harbor Lagoons Assn. (pres.); bd. dirs. Brentwood Ctr. Excellence, LLC Southpointe Hosp. Home: 10545 Cambridge Cir Cleveland OH 44133-Office: 5005 Rockside Rd Cleveland OH 44131-2194 Office Phone: 216-447-4496. Business E-Mail: rjggfl@juno.comm.

GRABOW, STEPHEN HARRIS, architecture educator; b. Bklyn., Jan. 15, 1943; s. Philip and Ida (England) G.; 1 child, Nicole Elizabeth. BArch., U. Mich., 1965; MArch., Pratt Inst., 1966; postgrad., U. Calif.-Berkeley, 1966-67; PhD, U. Wash., 1973. Architect-planner U.S. Peace Corps, Tunisia, 1967-69; regional planning cons. Teheran, Iran, 1969; asst. prof. architecture U. Ariz., 1969-70; teaching assoc. U. Wash., 1970-72; lectr. town and regional planning Duncan of Jordanstone Coll. Art, U. Dundee, Scotland, 1972-73; asst. prof. architecture and urban design U. Kans.-Lawrence, 1973-76, assoc. prof., 1976-82, prof., 1982—, dir. architecture, 1979-82, 83-86; vis. fellow U. Calif.-Berkeley, 1977; research and design cons. Design Build Architects, Lawrence; bd. dirs. Assn. Collegiate Schs. Architecture, 1982-87. Vis. lectr. Royal Danish Acad. Fine Arts, Copenhagen, 1987-88. Author: Christopher Alexander and the Search for a New Paradigm in Architecture, 1983; mem. editorial bd.: Jour. Archtl. Edn., 1982-84. Recipient award Nat. Endowment for Arts, 1974, citation for excellence in design rsch. NEA, 1980, Biennial Svc. award Denmark's Internat. Studies Program, 1997, Bradley Tchg. award in architecture U. Kans., 1998; Fulbright Scholar award, 1987-88; NEH fellow, 1976-77. Mem. Nat. Archtl. Research Council (appointee 1986-87). Home: 1518 Crossgate Dr Lawrence KS 66047-3504 Office: U Kans Sch Architecture & Urban Design 1465 Jayhawk Blvd Lawrence KS 66045-7614 Office Phone: 785-864-3186. Business E-Mail: sgrabow@ku.edu.

GRABOWSKI, RICHARD J., lawyer; b. LA, 1961; BA with great distinction, Calif. State Univ., Long Beach, 1983; JD, Univ. Calif., LA, 1986. Bar: Calif. 1986, admitted to practice: US Ct. of Appeals, Ninth Cir., US Dist. Courts, Northern, Southern, Eastern, Central Districts of Calif. Ptnr.-in-charge Irvine office Jones Day, Calif. Mem.: Orange County Bar Assn. (bd. dir. bus. litig. section), Fed. Bar Assn. (bd. dir.), Assn. of Bus. Trial Lawyers (bd. dir.), Order of Coif. Office: Jones Day Ste 1100 3 Park Plz Irvine CA 92614-8505 Office Phone: 949-553-7514. Office Fax: 949-553-7539. Business E-Mail: rgrabowski@jonesday.com.

GRACE, GEORGE H., not-for-profit fundraiser; m. Barbara Grace; 3 children. BS, Tuskegee U.; MS, U. Miami. Cert. Engring. Corp. regional svc. mgr. Bell South, Fla. Mem. Hialeah and Greater Miami C. of C., Dade County Sch. Ptnrs., Dade County Urban League, Dade County Role Models of Distinction, Achievers of Greater Miami, Sweet Home Missionary Bapt. Ch., Dade County Commrs. Round Table. Named one of Most Influential Black Americans, Ebony mag., 2004; recipient City of Miami Disting. Svc. Award, Dade Sch. Ptnrs. Award. Mem.: Nat. Emergency Network Assn., Dade County NAACP, Omega Psi Phi Fraternity, Inc. (Grand Basileus 2003—, Chap and Dist. Omega Man of Yr., Superior Svc. Award, Omega Eagle Award). Avocations: travel, golf. Office: Omega Psi Phi Fraternity 3951 Snapfinger Pkwy Decatur GA 30035 Office Phone: 404-284-5533. E-mail: omegagrace@oppf.com.*

GRACE, JAMES MARTIN, JR., lawyer; b. Columbus, Ohio, Sept. 6, 1967; s. James Martin and Letitia Jean (Stively) G.; m. Michèle Lee Sirna, June 22, 1991. BA, U. Notre Dame, 1989; JD cum laude, U. Houston, 1992. Bar: Tex. Law clk. to Hon. Samuel B. Kent U.S. Dist. Ct. (so. dist.) Tex., Galveston, 1992—93; assoc. Baker Botts, LLP, Houston, 1993—2000; sr. counsel Enron N.Am. Corp., Houston, 2000—01; mgr. Enron Wholesale Svcs., Houston, 2001—02; dir. Tex. state affairs Ctr. Point Energy Inc., Houston, 2002—05; shareholder Winstead, Sechrest & Minick PC, Houston, 2005—. Mem.: Houston Law Alumni Assn. (dir.), Greater Heights Area C. of C. (bd. dirs.), Houston Law Rev. Alumni Assn. (dir.), Houston Bar Assn., State Bar Tex., U. Notre Dame Alumni Assn. (pres. Class of '89), R Club PAC (pres. 1989—99, 2004, dir.), Notre Dame Club Houston (bd. dirs.), Order of the Barons, Phi Delta Phi. Republican. Roman Catholic. Avocations: soccer, football, reading. Office: Winstead Sechrest & Minick PC 910 Travis St Ste 2400 Houston TX 77002 Office Phone: 713-650-2769. Business E-Mail: jgrace@winstead.com.

GRACE, JOHN EUGENE, business forms company executive; b. Dundee, Ill., Nov. 22, 1931; s. Arnold Victor and Louise Joan (Boncosky) G.; m. Janice Rae Fohey, June 30, 1956; children: Gregory Alan, Michael Brian, Michele Marie. BS in Bus. Adminstrn. with high honors, U. Ill., 1958; MSBA in Fin., No. Ill. U., 1976. Gen. acctg. mgr. Elgin Watch Co., Ill., 1958-60; corp. controller Newell Cos., Freeport, Ill., 1960-68; controller jewelry div. Josten's, Inc., Owatonna, Minn., 1968-71; v.p. fin., chief fin. officer, asst. sec. Duplex Products Inc., Sycamore, Ill., 1971-87, cons., 1987-97. Cons. in field Active local United Fund, Little League, YMCA. Served with USAF, 1951-53. Mem. Fin. Execs. Inst. (past pres., dir. Fox-Rock chpt.), IMA (past dir.), Adminstrv. Mgmt. Soc. (past dir.), Jaycees, C. of C., Beta Alpha Psi. Clubs: Elks. Republican. Methodist. Home and Office: 405 Timber Ln Palm Harbor FL 34683-3737

GRACE, JOHN JOSEPH, retired priest; b. Chgo., Jan. 20, 1924; s. John Joseph and Mary Hamilton Grace. MA, St. Mary of Lake Sem., 1946, Licentiate of Sacred Theology, 1950. Ordained priest St. Mary of Lake Sem., 2000. Visitation asst. pastor, Chgo., 1950—60; asst. pastor St. Mary Ch., Des Plaines, Ill., 1960—65, Old St. Patrick Ch., Chgo., 1965—69; pastor St. Ludmilla, Chgo., 1969—83, St. Tarcissus, Chgo., 1983—2001; ret., 2001. Helper Cath. Charities, Chgo., 1970—. Home: St Benedict Home # 27 6930 W Touhy Ave Niles IL 60714

GRACE, JULIANNE ALICE, retired investment company executive; b. Riverdale, N.Y., Oct. 29, 1937; d. Arthur Edward and Julia May (McCarthy) Thompson; m. Daniel Vincent Grace, July 2, 1960; children: Daniel Vincent III, Deirdre Elizabeth Beck. BA, Marymount Manhattan Coll., 1959; MA, Fordham U., 1960. Dir. admissions Marymount Manhattan Coll., N.Y.C., 1966-72; mgr. human resources The Perkin-Elmer Corp., Norwalk, Conn., 1972-78, dir. human resources, 1978-81, asst. sr. v.p. semiconductor equipment, 1981-83, asst. pres., 1983-85, v.p., asst. to CEO, 1985-86, v.p. adminstrn., 1986-90, v.p. corp. rels., 1990-95; pres. The Jagcom Group, New Canaan, Conn., 1995—2004; ret., 2004. Bd. dirs. Norwalk and Wilton chpts. ARC, 1975—85, Metropool, 1991—98; pres., bd. dirs. Waveny (Conn.) Care Ctr., 1998—; bd. dirs. Waveny Network; trustee Norwalk YMCA, 1986—94; active Norwalk C.C. Found., 1986—90, Fairfield 2000; mem. corp. cabinet U. Conn. Downstate Initiative, 1995—98, mem. adv. com., lectr. exec. edn. program U. Conn., 1996—2001; bd. dirs. New Canaan Cmty. Found., Conn., 2004. Fellow Woodrow Wilson Nat. Found., 1959—60. Mem.: Fairfield Pub. Rels. Assn., Nat. Investor Rels. Inst. (sr. exec. roundtable), Econ. Soc. Conn., Saugatuck Harbor Yacht Club (bd. govs., flag officer fleet capt.), Wolfpit Running Club, Sports Car Club Am. Home and Office: 54 Louises Ln New Canaan CT 06840-2120

GRACE, MARCIA BELL, advertising executive; b. Pitts., July 29, 1937; d. Daniel Henry and Gertrude Margaret (Loew) Bell; m. Roy Grace, May 16, 1966; children: Jessica Bell, Nicholas Bell. AB, Harvard U., 1959. V.p., assoc. creative dir. Doyle Dane Bernbach, N.Y.C., 1964-77; sr. v.p., creative dir. Wells, Rich, Greene, Inc., N.Y.C., 1977-85, exec. v.p., creative dir., 1986-90; cons. Marcia Grace & Co., N.Y.C., 1990—. Represented in permanent collections Mus. Modern Art. Recipient 1st Pl. ANDY award Advt. Club N.Y., 1968, 70, 72, 75, 1st Pl. Gold award The One Show, 1973, 78, Hall of Fame award The Clio Show, N.Y.C., 1982, 86. Avocations: horseback riding, gardening.

GRACE, NANCY A., news correspondent; LLM, NYU; JD, Walter F. George Sch. Law, Mercer U. Bar: 1984. Law clk. to fed. ct. judge; practiced law with Fed. Trade Commn.; asst. dist. atty., Fulton County Atlanta, 1987—96; tv host Closing Arguments, Court TV; sub. host Larry King Live, CNN; radio show host Rapid Fire with Nancy A. Grace, Clear Channel's KNEW-AM, 2004—; host CNN Headline News. Lit. instr. Sch. Law, Ga. State U.; bus. law instr. Sch. Bus., Ga. State U.; appeared as legal commentator on ABC's The View, The Oprah Winfrey Show and numerous other cable and network programs. Contbr. articles to ABA Jour., various law reviews, and op-eds; author: Objection!: How High-Priced Defense Attorneys, Celebrity Defendants, and a 24/7 Media Have Hijacked Our Criminal Justice System, 2005 (Publishers Weekly Harcover bestseller list, 2005). Staff Atlanta Battered Women's Ctr. Hotline. Mem.: State Bar Ga. Achievements include while at Atlanta Fulton County Dist. Atty. Office, compiled a perfect record of nearly 100 felony convictions at trial and no losses. Office: Court TV 600 Third Ave 3rd Fl New York NY 10016 Office Phone: 212-973-7933.*

GRACE, PRISCILLA ANNE, labor union executive; b. Ft. Worth, Mar. 20, 1943; d. John Paul and Pauline (Greer) G.; children: K. C. Caldwell Jr., George E. Caldwell, Kristina Caldwell Henry. Grad. pvt. sch., Our Lady of Victory Sch., Ft. Worth. Telephone operator Southwestern Bell Telephone, Ft. Worth and Houston, 1968-70; letter carrier U.S. Postal Svc., Humble, Tex., 1973-85; officer local 283, Nat. Assn. Letter Carriers, Houston, 1984-98, pres., 1998—. Chmn. bd. dirs. Houston Postal Credit Union, 1990—; mem. exec. bd. Harris County AFL-CIO, Houston, 1988-98. Editor Houston Letter Carrier Newsletter, 1978-84. Mem. Tex. AFLCIO (v.p. 1997—), Nat. Assn. Letter Carriers. Lutheran. Avocations: geneaology research, needlecrafts, travel, reading. Office: Nat Assn Letter Carriers 2414 Broadway St Houston TX 77012-3812

GRACE, ROBERT J., JR., lawyer; b. Detroit, July 2, 1965; s. Robert J. and Corrine F. (Snyder) Grace; m. Jennifer A. Reese, July 15, 1995; children: Robert III, Caroline. BA, Ind. U., 1987; JD, U. Miss., 1990; LLM in Internat. Banking, Boston U., 1991. Bar: Fla. 1992, U.S. Dist. Ct. (mid. dist.) Fla. 1992, U.S. Ct. Appeals (11th cir.) 1992. Assoc. Stiles & Taylor, Tampa, Fla.,

1992-97; ptnr. Stiles, Taylor & Grace, Tampa, Fla., 1997—. Roman Catholic. Avocations: golf, photography, skiing, sailing. Office: Stiles Taylor & Grace 315 S Plant Ave Tampa FL 33606-2325 Home: 1001 Taray De Avila Tampa FL 33613-1045

GRACE, TOPHER, actor; b. NYC, July 19, 1978; Attended, Groundings Improvisation Sch., Neighborhood Playhouse, U. So. Calif. Actor: (plays) Our Town, Godspell, Lost in Yonkers, A Funny Thing Happened on the Way to the Forum, The Night Before Christmas, The King and I; (TV series) That 70s Show, 1998—; (films) Traffic, 2000, (voice) Pinocchio, 2002, Mona Lisa Smile, 2003, Win a Date with Tad Hamilton!, 2004, P.S., 2004, In Good Company, 2004 (Nat. Bd. Rev. award Best Breakthrough Performance by an Actor, 2004); TV appearances include King of the Hill, 2003. Office: co That 70s Show 4024 Radford Bldg 1 Ste 111 Studio City CA 91604*

GRACE, WILLIAM PERSHING, petroleum geologist, real estate developer; b. Mineral Point, Mo., Sept. 19, 1920; s. William Francis and Bertha Luciel (Nephew) Grace; m. Jeannette Marie Grace, Mar. 28, 1942 (dec.); children: Joyce Medaris, Pamela, Sonia Scott, Patricia Lawser. Student, Corpus Christi U., 1946-47; B in Geology, Tex. Tech. U., 1947-50; student (GRI), U. Colo. Extension, 1968-69. Capt. USAF, 1940-46; regional geologist Anderson-Prichard Oil Corp., San Antonio, Tex., 1950-62; real estate broker Grace Reality, Aurora, Colo., 1963-66; pres. Kimberley Homes, Construction, Aurora, 1966-72; pres., broker Grace-Scott-Cooper Corp., Aurora, 1972—. Pres. Friends of the Aurora Pub. Libr., 1967, trustee mem., 1978; chmn. Adams County Rep. Party, 1970—72; mem. vocat. edn. coun. Sch. Dist. 28J, 1989—; mem. of del. with Gov. Owens, Colo., 1996. Named Colorado of Yr., Colo. State Libr. Assn., 1988. Mem.: Sixty Five Roses Found., Aurora C. of C. (dir. 1966—68, Man of Yr. 1980), Aurora Bd. Realtors (treas. 1979, Realtor of Yr. 1980), Colo. State Friends and Trustees Assn., Colo. Assn. Realtors, Rocky Mountain Assn. Petroleum Geologists, Nat. Assn. Realtors, Am. Assn. Petroleum Geologists (del., House of Dels. 1961—62), Aurora Kiwainis (internat. del. in Nice, France 1993, lt. gov. Rocky Mountain divsn. 1992, sec. 1965, pres. 1972), Denver Petroleum PioneersClub, Sigma Gamma Epsilon. Lutheran. Avocations: geologic exploration, flying, golf, skiing, travel. Home: 13618 E Bethany Pl 204 Aurora CO 80014 Office Phone: 303-671-4426.

GRACEY, DOUGLAS ROBERT, internist, educator, physiologist; b. Fort Dodge, Iowa, Aug. 7, 1936; s. Warren Robert and Areta Mary (Thompson) G.; m. Edith Ann Haas, Dec. 23, 1961; children— Laura, Douglas Robert BA, Coe Coll., 1958; MD, Northwestern U., 1962; MS, U. Minn., 1968. Diplomate Am. Bd. Internal Medicine. Intern Cook County Hosp., Chgo., 1962-63; resident Mayo Grad. Sch. Medicine, 1963-66, 68-69; asst. prof. medicine Northwestern U. Med. Sch., 1969-75; assoc. prof. medicine Mayo Med. Sch., Rochester, Minn., 1975-83, prof., 1983—, vice chmn. pulmonary div., 1982-87; vice chmn. for practice dept. medicine Mayo Clinic, Rochester, 1983-93, dir. critical care medicine div., 1985-89, chmn. revenue systems com., chmn. divsn. pulmonary and critical care medicine. Author: (with W.W. Addington) Tuberculosis, 1972, Flying Lessons, Ambulances and other Air Force Vignettes, 2000; editor: Pulmonary Diseases in the Adult, 1981; contbr. articles to profl. jours. Trustee Coe Coll., 1976-92. Served to capt. M.C., USAF, 1966-68 Am. Thoracic Soc. tng. fellow, 1968-69 Fellow ACP, Am. Coll. Chest Physicians, AMA. Lodges: Masons, Shriners. Republican. Office: Mayo Clinic Chmn Div Pulmonary & Critical Care Med Rochester MN 55901 Business E-Mail: dgracey@mayo.edu.

GRACEY, JAMES STEELE, manufacturing executive, director; b. Newton, Mass., Aug. 24, 1927; s. Ernest James and Edna Alicia (Steele) G.; m. Dorcas Randall Neal, June 15, 1949; children: Kevin S., Cheryl A., Pamela R. BS, U.S. Coast Guard Acad., 1949; MBA, Harvard U., 1956. Commd. ensign USCG, 1949, advanced through grades to adm.; comptroller 2d Coast Guard Dist., St. Louis, 1962-65; dep. Governors' Island (N.Y.) project and Coast Guard Base, 1965-69; chief programs div. Chief of Staff's Office, Washington, 1969-74; chief of staff 5th Coast Guard Dist., Portsmouth, Va., 1974; comdr. 9th Coast Guard Dist., Cleve., 1974-77; chief of staff Coast Guard Hqtrs., Washington, 1977-78; comdr. Coast Guard Pacific Area and 12th Coast Guard Dist., San Francisco, 1978-81, Coast Guard Atlantic Area and 3d Coast Guard Dist., N.Y.C., 1981-82; commandant of USCG, Washington, 1982-86; sr. fellow Inst. for Higher Def. Studies, Capstone, 1986—2001. Chmn. Fed. Exec. Bd. Cleve., 1976-77; coord. regional emegency transp. Fed. Region IX, 1978-81; bd. dirs. Marine Spill Response Corp., chmn. audit com., 1991-2003; bd. dirs. Maguire Group, Inc., 1993—, Maguire Group Conn., Inc., chmn., 1993-98; advisor New Sulzer Diesel Group, 1991-95; cons. Mitre Corp., 1987-92; vis. lectr. Nat. Def. U., Navy, Air and Army war colls., Fgn. Svc. Inst., Presdl. Classroom, Sloane Fellows, MIT, Kennedy Sch. Govt., Harvard U., 1982-86; bd. mgrs. Am. Bur. Shipping, 1982-86; leader U.S. del. to Internat. Maritime Orgn., UN Assembly, 1983, 85; bd. vis. Mich. Maritime Acad. Mem. world bd. govs. USO, 1982-91; trustee, chmn. Calvary United Meth. Ch., 1988-2001, chmn. ch. coun. Decorated Legion of Merit with gold star, D.S.M. with gold star; named Bay Stater of Yr., Maritime Man of Yr., San Diego NL Man of the Yr.; recipient Michelob Schooner award, San Francisco Honor medal. Mem. Ret. Officers Assn./Mil. Officers Assn. Am. (bd. dirs. 1986-92), Coast Guard Found. (bd. dirs. 1982—), Navy League, Nat. Mil. Family Assn. (advisor 1986-2002), Assn. for Rescue at Sea (bd. dirs., vice chmn. 1988-97, chmn. 1997-2003), Army-Navy Country Club. Home and Office: 1411 21st St S Arlington VA 22202-1507

GRACEY, PAUL C., JR., lawyer, utilities executive; b. 1959; BBA, U. Mich., 1981; JD cum laude, U. Calif., 1985; diploma in Sr. Exec. Fin. Progam, Templeton Coll., Oxford, Eng., 1998. Bar: Calif., Ill. V.p., gen. counsel Edison Mission Energy Ltd., London, 1993—2000, Midwest Generation, Chgo., 2000—02; v.p. Nicor Inc. and Nicor Gas, Naperville, Ill., 2002—, gen. counsel, 2002—, sec., 2002—. Mem.: Calif. Bar Assn., Ill. Bar Assn. Office: Nicor Inc 1844 Ferry Rd Naperville IL 60563 Office Phone: 630-983-8676.

GRACEY, ROBERT WILLIAM, financial advisor, minister; b. Steubenville, Ohio, Aug. 11, 1941; s. Robert S. and Mary O. (Barnett) G.; m. Patricia J. Zapka, Aug. 29, 1964; children: R. Stephen, Jonathan B. BA, Davis & Elkins Coll., 1963; MDiv, Pitts. Theol. Sem., 1966, postgrad., 1968-70, Coll. Fin. Planning, 1991-93. CFP; cert. hotel adminstr.; registered rep.; registered investment advisor; lic. ins. agt.; ordained to ministry Presbyn. Ch. Pastor, dir. Clay County Larger Parish, Manchester, Ky., 1966-68; pastor Union First Presbyn. Ch., Cowansville, Pa., 1968-78; caseworker Family Counseling Ctr., Kittanning, Pa., 1970-78; gen. mgr. Quality Inn/Royle, Kittanning, 1978-84; mgr. Wheeling (W.Va.) Country Club, 1984-87; investment exec. Legg Mason Wood Walker, Inc., Wheeling, 1987-93, Fifth Third/The Ohio Co., Steubenville, Ohio, 1993-98; fin. advisor Legg Mason Wood Walker, Inc., 1998—. Supply preacher Presbytery of Upper Ohio Valley, Wheeling, 1985—; part time instr. WV Northern C.C. Trustee Presbyn. Homes, Inc., Camp Hill, Pa., 1992-96, Elmhurst, The Ho. of Friendship; chair ch. and cmty. com. Presbytery of Upper Ohio Valley, 1989-91, sec. com. on ministry, 1995-98, chair Mission Support and Adv. Coun., chair stewardship unit; chair Mark H. Kennedy Park, Community Home Care and Hospice; mem. Flood Relief Network of Upper Ohio Valley, Wheeling, 1990-91; bd. dirs., sec.-treas. B.O.L.T., Inc., Weirton, W.Va., 1990-94, Brancazio Free Clinic, Weirton. Named Mgr. of Yr. Aladdin Food Mgmt. Svcs., Inc., Wheeling, 1987. Mem. Brooke County Geneal. Soc., Cumberland Trail Geneal. Soc., Tuscarawas County Geneal. Soc., Geneal Soc. Southwestern Pa., Mining Your History Found., Rotary Internat. (pres. Weirton club 1994-95, dir.-at-large, asst. gove. dist. 7530 1997-98, dist. conf. com. chair, Rotarian of Yr. 1990, Paul Harris Fellow, Rotary Found. benefactor, distl conf. com. chair), Weirton C. of C., Elmhurst (bd. trustees). Republican. Avocations: genealogy, gourmet foods and wines, travel. Home: 12 Boxwood Cir Wheeling WV 26003-5602 Office: Legg Mason Wood Walker Inc Ste 1000 1233 Main St Wheeling WV 26003-2839 Office Phone: 304-232-7333. E-mail: rwgracey@leggmason.com, rwgracey@comcast.net.

GRACHEV, ANDREY A., physicist, researcher; b. Yuzhno-Sakhalinsk, Sakhalin Island, Russia, May 7, 1957; s. Anatoliy V Grachev and Tatiana A Gracheva; m. Elena L. Gordienko, May 7, 1983; children: Leonid A., Anna A. Gracheva. BS in Ocean and Atmosphere Physics, MS in Ocean and Atmosphere Physics, Moscow Inst. Physics and Tech., 1980; PhD in Physics and Math., A. M. Obukhov Inst. of Atmospheric Physics, Russian Acad. of Sciences, 1983. Sr. scientist A. M. Obukhov Inst. of Atmospheric Physics, Russian Acad. of Scis., Moscow, 1983—97; rsch. prof. Ariz. State U., Tempe, Ariz., 1997—99; rsch. assoc. Coop. Inst. for Rsch. in Environ. Scis., U. Colo. and NOAA, Environ. Tech. Lab., Boulder, Colo., 1999—. Recipient Medal and award for the best rsch. for young scientists in oceanography, atmospheric physics and geog., USSR Acad. of Sciences, 1990; grantee EU Project INTAS 94-2255 (Team Leader), INTAS (the Internat. Assn. for the promotion of co-operation with scientists from the New Ind. States of the former Soviet Union), 1994-1997, EU Project INTAS No. 96-1692 (Team Leader), 1997-1999, NSF award # OPP-00-84322 (Co-Principal Investigator), NSF, 2000-2003, NSF award # OPP-00-84323 (Prin. Investigator), 2000-2003. Mem.: Am. Geophys. Union, Am. Meteorol. Soc. Achievements include research in atmospheric and oceanic physics including physics of the atmospheric boundary layer and air-sea interaction. Office: NOAA Environ Tech Lab 325 Broadway Boulder CO 80305-3328 Office Phone: 303-497-6436. E-mail: andrey.grachev@noaa.gov.

GRACHEV, MIKHAIL VLADIMIROVICH, business educator, researcher; b. Moscow, Apr. 2, 1954; arrived in U.S., 2002; s. Vladimir Aleksandrovich Grachev and Maya Arkadievna Gracheva; m. Mariya Aleksandrovna Bobina; children: Anastasia, Aleksandra. MA in Econ., Moscow State U., 1976; PhD in Econ., Russian Acad. Scis., 1982, postdoctorate degree Econs. and Internat. Mgmt., 1998. Prof. mgmt. U. Tulsa, 1993—95, Case We. Res. U., Cleve., 1995—2000; sr. rsch. fellow, contbg. editor Wharton Sch. U. Pa., Phila., 1997—2001; prof. mgmt. Ecole Superieur de Commerce et Mgmt., France, 2001; dept. head., dean Russian Acad. Scis., Moscow, 2002; prof. mgmt. We. Ill. U., Moline, 2002—. Rsch. fellow Ritsumeikan U., Japan; adj. prof. mgmt. U. Iowa, 2005—, U. Md., 2005—. Author: 4 books; contbr. articles to profl. jours. Founding mem. Global Leadership and Orgnl. Behavior Effectiveness, 2002—. Fellow, Russian Acad. Scis., 1976—2002, Pitsumeikan U., Japan, 1989, Sahl U., Pa., 1998. Mem.: Acad. Mgmt. (strategic leadership forum 1990—96, bd. dirs., Internat. Leadership Assn. 2002—04). Avocation: music. Office: Western Ill Univ 3561 60th St Moline IL 61265

GRACIN, HANK, lawyer; b. Massapequa Park, N.Y., Jan. 27, 1957; s. Bernard Tobias and Ada (Rosenberg) G.; m. Marisol L. Perez, Sept. 9, 1990. BA with honors, SUNY, Binghamton, 1978; JD cum laude, NYU, 1981. Bar: N.Y. 1982, U.S. Dist. Ct. (so. dist.) N.Y. 1982. Assoc. Sullivan & Cromwell, N.Y.C., 1981-83, Schulte Roth & Zabel, N.Y.C., 1983-86, Fulbright Jaworski & Reavis McGrath, N.Y.C., 1986-90; corp. counsel Computer Assocs. Internat., Inc., 1990-94; ptnr. Lehman & Eilen, 1994—. Editor: Private Placements and Restricted Securities, 1981. Mem. South Palm Beach County Bar Assn., Order of Coif (NYU chpt.). Avocations: bicycling, reading, piano. Office: Lehman & Eilen LLP Ste 505 50 Charles Lindbergh Blvd Uniondale NY 11553-3612 Office Phone: 516-222-0888. Business E-Mail: HGracin@Lehmaneilen.com.

GRACY, DAVID BERGEN, II, archivist, information science educator, writer; b. Austin, Tex., Oct. 25, 1941; married; 3 children. BA, U. Tex., Austin, 1963, MA, 1966; PhD in History, Tex. Tech. U., 1971. Cert. archivist. Archivist S.W. Collection Tex. Tech. U., 1966-71; from asst. prof. to assoc. prof. urban life Ga. State U., 1971-77; archivist So. Labor Archives, 1971-77; dir. Tex. State Archives, 1977-86; Gov. Bill Daniel prof. in archival enterprise U. Tex., Austin, 1986—, assoc. dean Grad. Sch. of Libr. and Info. Sci., 1991-95; interim dir. preservation and conservation studies program U. Tex. Grad. Sch. Libr. and Info. Sci.; dir. Ctr. for the Cultural Record, 2000—. Gen. ptnr. David B. Gracy II & Assocs., 1989—; adj. prof. history De Kalb C.C., 1973—74; vis. prof. archival enterprise San Jose State U., 2001, U. Ariz., 2003; instr. Ga. Archives Inst., Grad. Sch. Libr. and Info. Sci. U. Tex., Austin, Modern Archives Inst. Nat. Archives of U.S., Rare Books Sch. Columbia U., Soc. Am. Archivists, S.W. Archivists, Spl. Librs. Assn., Tex. State Libr., Trinity U., U.S. Info. Agy. for U. Philippines, Presdl. Commn. on Culture and Arts, Univ. Republic, Uruguay, Utah State Archives, Western Archives Inst.; cons. N.Mex. State Archives and Libr. Bldg. project, 1994—98, Nat. Episc. Ch. Archives, 1978, Oral Roberts U., 1978, Archives Civil Rights, M.L. King Ctr., Atlanta, 1976—81, Am. Heritage Ctr. U. Wyo., 1988—89, San Antonio Pub. Libr., 1988, Nat. Assn. for Preservation and Perpetuation of Storytelling, Jonesborough, Tenn., 1988—89, King Ranch, Kingsville, Tex., 1987; coord. Tex. Hist. Records Adv. Bd., 1979—86; mem. Ga. Hist. Records Adv. Bd., 1976, Nat. Hist. Publs. and Rec. Commn., 1980—85; lectr. U. Tex., Austin, 1980—81, sr. lectr., 1982—86. Author: Littlefield Lands: Colonization on the Texas Plains, 1912-1920, 1968, Archives and Manuscripts: Arrangement and Description, 1977, It's Your Heritage: The Archives of Texas, 1977, An Introduction to Archives and Manuscripts, 1981, Moses Austin: His Life, 1987; co-author: Ships of the Texas Navy, 1979; bibliography advisor The New Handbook of Texas, 1988-94; mem. editl. bd. Libraries and Culture, 1985—, Am. Archivist, 1976-79; founder, editor Ga. Archive (subsequently Provenance), 1972-76; contbr. to Reflections of Western Historians, 1969; assoc. editor Tex. Mil. History, 1962-88; editl. asst. Southwestern Hist. Quar., 1963-66; contbr. articles to profl. jours. Bd. dirs. Nat. Archives Episcopal Ch., 1986—98, vice chair, 1995—98; bd. dirs. Task Force on Preservation Edn., Commn. on Preservation and Access, 1989—90, mem., 1991—97; chmn. task force on archives Summerlee Commn. on Tex. History, 1989—93, Tex. Preservation Task Force, 1988—90; sec. Coun. on Libr. and Info. Resources, 1997—2000. Named Disting. Alumnus Dept. History Tex. Tech. U., 1987; recipient award of merit Am. Assn. for State and Local History, 1969, Disting. Svc. award Organized Labor and Workmen's Circle, Atlanta, 1976, Cert. Merit Soc. Ga. Archivists, 1976, Soc. S.W. Archivists, 1978, Tex. Excellence in Teaching award Grad. Sch. Libr. and Info. Sci. U. Tex. at Austin, 1987, San Jacinto award, 1993. Fellow: Tex. State Hist. Assn., Tex. State Geneal. Soc., Soc. Am. Archivists (v.p., pres. 1982—84, award of merit 1975); mem.: Soc. Ga. Archivists (pres. 1972—74, cert. merit 1976), Acad. Cert. Archivists (bd. regents 1990—93, v.p., pres. 1999—2000), Pan Am. Inst. Geography and History (U.S. rep. archives com. 1982—97), Assn. Records Mgrs. and Adminstrs. (pres. Austin chpt. 1980—81, cert. award 1981), Internat. Coun. Archives (editor Edn. and Devel. News 1989—96, listmaster sect. archival edn. and tng. listserv. 1996—2002, v.p. sect. on archival edn. and tng.), Am. Assn. State and Local History (award of merit 1968), Tex. Bar Hist. Found. Office: U Tex Sch of Info Austin TX 78712-0390 E-mail: gracyiis@hotmail.com, gracy@ischool.utexas.edu.

GRACY, ROBERT, science educator; Assoc. v.p. rsch. alliance devel. U. North Tex. Health Sci. Ctr., Ft. Worth, 1993—97, dean rsch. and biotech., 1997—. Recipient Wilford I. Doherty award Am. Chem. Soc., 1995. Office: U North Tex Health Sci Ctr 3500 Camp Bowie Blvd Fort Worth TX 76107-2644

GRAD, FRANK PAUL, lawyer, educator; b. Vienna, May 2, 1924; came to U.S., 1939, naturalized, 1943; s. Morris and Clara Sophie (Scher) G.; m. Lisa Szilagyi, Dec. 6, 1946; children: David Anthony, Catharine Ann. BA magna cum laude, Bklyn. Coll., 1947; LLB, Columbia U., 1949. Bar: NY 1949. From assoc. in law to prof. emeritus Columbia U. Law Sch., N.Y.C., 1949—95, Joseph P. Chamberlain prof. emeritus legis. and spl. lectr., 1995—; assoc. House, Grossman, Vorhaus & Healey, 1950—53; legal adv. com. U.S. Council Environ. Quality, 1970-73; mem. N.Y. Deptl. Com. Ct. Adminstrn., Appellate Div., 1st Dept., 1970-74; counsel N.Y. State Spl. Adv. Panel Med. Malpractice, 1975; legal counsel Nat. Mcpl. League, 1967-88. Cons. in field; reporter U.S. Superfund Study group, 1981-82; dir. rsch. N.Y.C. Charter Revision Commn., 1982-83, N.Y. State-City Commn. on Integrity in Govt., 1986. Author: Public Health Law Manual, 1st edit., 1965, 2d rev. edit., 1990, 3d rev. edit., 2004, The Drafting of State Constitutions, 1963, Environmental law: Sources and Problems, 3d edit., 1985, 4th edit. (with Joel Mintz), 2000, Treatise on Environmental Law, 8 vols., 1973—; co-author other legal reports; contbr. articles to profl. jours.; draftsman mcpl. codes and state legislation. With AUS, 1943—46. 10th Horace E. Read Meml. lectr. Dalhousie Law Sch., 1984; Career Accomplishment award Pub. Health Law Assn., 2005. Mem. ABA, APHA, Assn. of Bar of City of N.Y., N.Y. Bar Assn., Am. Law Inst., Am. Soc. Law and Medicine, World Conservation Union (commn. on environ. law 1991—), Human Genome Orgn., Internat. Coun. Environ. Law, N.Y. Soc. Med. Jurisprudence. Office: Columbia U Sch Law 435 W 116th St New York NY 10027-7297 Office Phone: 212-854-2685. Business E-Mail: fgrad@law.columbia.edu.

GRADDICK, CHARLES ALLEN, judge; b. Mobile, Ala., Dec. 10, 1944; s. Julian and Elvera (Smith) G.; m. Corinne Whiting, Aug. 19, 1966; children: Charles Allen, Herndon Whiting, Corinne. JD, Cumberland Sch. Law, 1970. Bar: Ala. 1970. Clk. Ala. Supreme Ct., 1970; asst. dist. atty. County of Mobile, Ala., 1971-75, dist. atty., 1975-79; atty. gen. State of Ala., Montgomery, 1979-87; ptnr. Thorton, Farish and Gaunt, Montgomery, 1987-89, Anderson, Graddick and Nabors, P.C., Montgomery, 1989-90; dist. atty. Montgomery County, Montgomery County, Ala., 1991-93; ptnr. Graddick & Belser, P.C., Montgomery and Mobile, 1992-99, Sims, Graddick & Dodson, Mobile, 2000—04; cir. judge Mobile County, 2004—. Served with USNG, 1969-96. Named Outstanding Young Man of Mobile, Mobile Jaycees, 1976, State Conservationist of Yr., Ala. Wildlife Fedn.; recipient cert. appreciation Ala. Peace Officers, 1978, Appreciation award Optimists, 1978. Mem. Ala. Bar Assn., Mobile Bar Assn., Nat. Assn. Attys. Gen., Ala. Cir. Judges Assn. Republican. Office: Paul W Brock Inn of Ct Govt Plaza 205 Government St Ct Rm 6200 Mobile AL 36644 Office Phone: 251-574-5639. E-mail: charlie.graddick@alacourt.gov.

GRADDICK-WEIR, MIRIAN, human resources specialist; d. Sam Massenberg. BA, Hampton U.; MS, PhD, Penn State U. With AT&T, Bedminster, NJ, 1981—, various positions in human resources and customer svc., 1981—94, v.p. multimedia products group, exec. v.p. human resources. Bd. dirs. Harleysville Ins. Cos., Joint Ctr. Polit. and Econ. Studies, Human Resources Policy Assn. Named Human Resources Exec. of Yr., Human Resources Exec. mag., 2000; recipient Disting. Psychologist in Mgmt. award, Soc. Psychologists in Mgmt., 2003. Fellow: Nat. Acad. Human Resources. Office: AT&T Corp One AT&T Way Bedminster NJ 07921 Office Phone: 908-221-2000. Office Fax: 908-532-1673.*

GRADE, JEFFERY T., manufacturing executive; b. Chicago, 1943; BS, Ill. Inst. Tech., 1966; MBA, DePaul U., 1972. With Plasto Mfg. Corp., 1965-66, Motorola Inc., 1966-67, Bell and Howell, 1967-68, Ill. Cen. Gulf R.R., 1968-73; v.p. fin. IC Industries, 1973-83; with Harnischfeger Corp., Milw., 1983-99, pres., COO, bd. dirs., 1986—, CEO, 1991-99, also chmn., CEO. Served with USN, 1865-66. Office: Harnischfeger Industries Ste 2780 100 E Wisconsin Ave Milwaukee WI 53202-4127

GRADEL, JAMES D., lawyer; b. Toledo, Ohio, Sept. 1, 1954; BBA summa cum laude, U. Cin., 1975; JD with honors, Ohio State U., 1978. Bar: Wash. 1979. Ptnr., Fin. Inst. Practice Area Perkins Coie LLP, Seattle. Named a Wash. Super Lawyer, Washington Law & Politics. Mem.: King County Bar Assn., Wash. State Bar Assn., Beta Gamma Sigma. Office: Perkins Coie LLP 1201 Third Ave Ste 4800 Seattle WA 98101-3099 Office Phone: 206-359-8401. Office Fax: 206-359-9000. Business E-Mail: jgradel@perkinscoie.com.

GRADO, ANGELO JOHN, artist; b. N.Y.C., Feb. 17, 1922; s. Pasquale and Rose (Valenti) G.; m. Justine Barbara Johnson, June 26, 1943; children: Barbara, Paul, John, Frank, Richard. Student, Art Students League, Nat. Acad. Design, Frank Reilley Sch. Art. Comml. artist N.Y. Jour.-Am., N.Y.C., 1946-52; art dir. Harrison Publs., N.Y.C., 1952-55; art dir., owner advt. agy. Angelo John Assocs., N.Y.C., 1955-70; artist oils and pastels, 1970—. Tchr. Nat. Art League, N.Y., Naples Art League, Von Lebig Art Ctr., Naples, Fla.; lectr., Europe and U.S. Author: Mastering the Craft of Painting, 1985. Served with USAAF, 1943-46. Recipient 92 nat. awards, 1957—; recipient Best in Show-Newington award, 1980 Mem.: Degas Pastel Soc. (award 2003), Am. Watercolor Soc., Pastel Soc. Am. (elected master pastelist, $1000 Mrs. Pearl Kalikow award 2001, award 2003), Hudson Valley Art Assn. (Best Portrait award 1994), Am. Artists Profl. League (pres. N.Y. 1977—88, pres. emeritus 1988—), Salmagundi Club. Home: 641 46th St Brooklyn NY 11220-1410 Office Phone: 718-853-3244. Personal E-mail: angelograd0@aol.com.

GRADO-WOLYNIES, EVELYN (EVELYN WOLYNIES), nursing educator; b. N.Y.C., Apr. 2, 1944; d. Joseph Frederick and Evelyn Marie (Ronning) Grado; m. Jon Gordon Wolynies, July 12, 1964; children: Jon Andrew, Kristine Elisabeth; m. Brian Bereika, 1999. AAS, Burlington County Coll., 1990; AS, Camden C.C., 1990; BSN cum laude, Thomas Jefferson U., 1991, MSN summa cum laude, 1992; postgrad., Johns Hopkins U., 1993-95. RN N.J., Pa. Charge nurse Hampton Hosp., Westampton, N.J., 1990-92; adjunct clin. instr. psychiat. nursing Burlington County Coll., Pemberton, N.J., 1992-93; project leader Alzheimer's disease clin. drug study Olsten Health Care, Cherry Hill, N.J., 1992-95, psychiat. case mgr., 1992-94; CNS neuropsych in Huntingtons Disease Dr. Allen Rubin, Camden, N.J., 1992; psychiat. case mgr. Moorestown (N.J.) Vis. Nurses Assn., 1992; charge nurse, group therapist, rschr. Friends Hosp., Phila., 1994-99; clin. mgr. The Caring Link partial geriatric outpatient program Frankford Hosp., Phila., 1996-99; psychotherapist Penn Friends, Marlton, NJ, 2000—02. Pvt. practice hypnotherapy/psychotherapy; cons. psychiat. care, Alzheimer's Disease, RN/home health aide instr. Olsten-Kimberly Home Care; clin. preceptor U. Pa. Sch. NSG, MSN, GNP and Adult Mental CS Programs. Contbr. articles to nursing jours. Mem. Burlington County Coll. Alumni Bd.; founder, dir. Support Group for Adult Children with Aging Parents; Developed music therapy/exercise program for Geriatric Psych patients. Recipient Juanita Wilson award, 1991, Farber fellowship, 1991-92.; Nurse in Washington intern, 1992; named to Burlington County Coll. Hall of Fame, 1994 Mem. Am. Assn. of Neuroscience Nurses, Am. Psychiat. Nurses Assn., N.J. State Nurses Assn., Sigma Theta Tau (Delta Rho chpt.), Phi Theta Kappa. Home: PO Box 3604 Cherry Hill NJ 08034-0550

GRADY, JAMES MICHAEL, JR., art educator, theater director; b. Holyoke, Mass., May 5, 1965; s. James Michael and Johanna Elizabeth Grady; m. Susan Kelly Little, Oct. 8, 1995; 1 child, Kell Sullivan. BS in Bus. Mgmt., Bentley Coll., 1987; MS in Arts Adminstrn., Lesley U., 1993; cert. in Nonprofit Mgmt., Duke U., 1998. Dir. adminstrn. Pa. Stage Co., Allentown, 1994—95; mng. dir. Actor's Express, Atlanta, 1995—97, Hangar Theatre, Ithaca, NY, 1998—2000, Icarus Theatre Ensemble, Ithaca, 2000—; devel. dir. Little Theatre of Winston-Salem, NC, 1997—99; asst. prof. Ithaca Coll., 2000—. Cons. Independant Arts Consultants, Ithaca, 2000—. Mem. Tompkins County Strategic Tourism and Planning Bd., Ithaca. Mem.: Assn. Arts Adminstrs. Educators, Theatre Comm. Group. Avocations: photography, reading, travel, music. Office: Ithaca Coll 201 Dillingham Center Ithaca NY 14850 Business E-Mail: jgrady@ithaca.edu.

GRADY, JOYCE (MARIAN JOYCE GRADY), psychotherapist, consultant; b. Riverside, N.J., Sept. 27, 1930; d. David and Agnes Marian (Conroy) Lawber; children: Andrea, Christine; m. James F. Moller, June 11, 1983. BA in Clin. Psychology, U. Penna, 1951; M in Social Work, certificate in alcohol studies, Rutgers U., New Brunswick, N.J., 1968; certificate in psychotherapy, Inst. Psychoanalytic Psychotherapy, 1973. Lic. clin. social worker, N.J. Caseworker Upward Bound Program, Rutgers U., New Brunswick, summer 1966; psychiat. social work supr., chief psychiat. social worker Roosevelt Hosp., Edison, N.J., 1968-92, in-svc. educator in nursing and social work, 1972-92, support group caregiver, 1970-92; nursing home cons. Abbot Manor Nursing Home, Plainfield, N.J., 1984-92; pvt. practice psychotherapy, Highland Park, N.J., 1975—. Adj. prof., field instr. grad. sch. social work Rutgers U., New Brunswick, 1970-92; guest lectr. depression and geriatrics Rutgers Sch. Social Work, New Brunswick, 1975-92; cmty. lectr. dying, aging, loss, and depression in long term care; outreach cons. personal assistance and homebound elderly, Middlesex County, N.J., 1975-78; mem. adv. bd., chmn. Middlesex County Adv. Coun. Aging, North Brunswick, N.J., 1973-95.

Contbr. papers, panelist in field. Advocate, Middlesex County Adv. Coun. on Aging, North Brunswick, 1970-92; mem. Cmty. Outreach Adv. Coun.; participant seminars svc. providers, Middlesex County, N.J., 1995. Mem.: NASW (guest panel mem., guest spkr. psychotherapy confs.), Rutgers Club, Penn Club N.Y.C. Avocations: writing, decorating, music, computers, gardening. Office: 12 N 4th Ave Highland Park NJ 08904-2736

GRADY, KENNETH ALAN, lawyer, consumer products company executive; b. Detroit, Nov. 10, 1956; s. James Valentine and Ellen Hofman Grady; m. June Wojtowicz, May 25, 1985; children: Marie Elizabeth, Erin Margaret, Brendan Connor. BA, Drake U., 1978; M in M in Mgmt., JD, Northwestern U., 1984. Bar: Ill. 1984, U.S. Dist. Ct. (no. dist.) Ill. 1984, U.S. Ct. Appeals (7th cir.) 1985, Iowa 1996, Mass. 2004. Assoc. Levin & Funkhouser, Ltd., Chgo., 1984—88, McDermott, Will & Emery, Chgo., 1988—90, ptnr., 1991—94; sr. counsel HON INDUSTRIES Inc., Muscatine, Iowa, 1994—96; v.p., gen. mgr. The HON Co., Cedartown, Ga., 1996—98; group counsel, asst. sec. Payless ShoeSource, Inc., Topeka, 1999—2000, v.p., group counsel, asst. sec., 2000—01; v.p., gen. counsel, sec. KB Toys, Inc., Pittsfield, Mass., 2001—04, exec. v.p. adminstrn., gen. counsel, sec., 2004—05; v.p., gen. counsel, sec. PC Connection, Inc., Merrimack, NH, 2005—. Trustee, sec. Sunflower Soccer Assn., Topeka, 2000—01; commr. Pittsfied Mcpl. Airport Commn., 2003—04; dir. Polk Med. Ctr., Cedartown, 1997—98. F.C. Austin scholar, Northwestern U., J.L. Kellogg Grad. Sch. Mgmt., 1980—84. Mem.: ABA, Soc. Corp. Secs. and Governance Profls., Assn. Corp. Counsel. Office: PC Connection Inc 730 Milford Ave Merrimack NH 03054 Office Phone: 603-683-3696. Business E-Mail: kgrady@pcconnection.com.

GRADY, LEE TIMOTHY, pharmaceutical chemist; b. Chgo., Mar. 21, 1937; s. Thomas Aloysius and Lentella Kathryn (Eibel) G.; m. Ann Marie Gill, Aug. 8, 1964; children: Patricia Ann, Meghan Elizabeth. BS in Pharmacy with high honors, U. Ill., 1959, PhD in Chemistry, 1963. Registered pharmacist, Ill., Va., Md. Analyst CIA, Langley, Va., 1963—65; sr. rsch. pharmacologist Merck Inst. Therapeutic Rsch., West Point, Pa., 1965-68; dir. drug standards lab. Am. Pharm. Assn. Found., Washington, 1968-74; dir. drug rsch. and testing lab. U.S. Pharmacopeia, Rockville, Md., 1975-78, v.p., dir. stds. devel., dir. drug stds., 1979-99, v.p., dir. emeritus, 2000—. Mem. expert coms. WHO, Geneva, 1980-87; temp. advisor Pan Am. Health Orgn., Washington, 1984; observer Internat. Conf. Harmonization, 1990-2000; mem. Pharmacopeial Discussion group, U.S., Japan, Europe, 1989-2000. Contbr. articles to sci. jours.; sci. editor U.S. Pharmacopeia National Formulary, 1980-2000. Docent Nat. Mus. Am. History, 2000—; vol. Nat. Park Svc, Fairfax County Med. Res. Corp., 2004—. Recipient rsch. award Am. Soc. Hosp. Pharmacists, 1982. Fellow AAAS, Am. Assn. Pharm. Scientists; mem. Am. Pharm. Assn. (J.L. Powers rsch. achievement award 1990), Am. Chem. Soc., Cath. Acad. Scis. U.S. (sec.), Order of Holy Sepulchre, Rho Chi, Phi Kappa Phi, Sigma Chi. Roman Catholic. Avocations: swimming, hiking. Personal E-mail: ltgrady@cox.net.

GRADY, MARK F., law educator, former dean; b. 1948; AB, UCLA, 1970, JD, 1973. Bar: Pa. 1975. Dir. office of policy planning & evaluation FTC, Washington, 1975-77; project mgr. Am. Mgmt. Systems, Inc., Arlington, Va., 1978-79; prof. Northwestern U., Chgo., 1985—92; John M. Olin vis. prof. law and econs. Duke U., 1992—93; prof. law UCLA; dean and prof. law George Mason U., Arlington, Va., 1997—2004; prof. law UCLA Sch. Law, 2004—. Minority Counsel Senate Jud. Com., Washington, 1979; mem. Cons. Dept of Energy, Washington, 1978. Fellow U. Chgo. 1977, Civil Liability Yale, 1982. Mem. Phi Beta Kappa. Office: UCLA Sch Law Box 951476 Los Angeles CA 90095-1476 E-mail: grady@law.ucla.edu.

GRADY, PATRICIA A., health institute director, researcher; Diploma in nursing, St. Francis Hosp. Sch. Nursing, 1964; BSN, Georgetown U., 1967; MS, Sch. Nursing U. Md., 1968; PhD, Sch. Medicine U. Md., 1977; D of Pub. Svc. (hon.), U. Md., 1996; cert. in sr. mgrs. in govt., John F. Kennedy Sch. Govt., Cambridge, 1994. Instr. Sch. Nursing Washington Hosp. Ctr., 1966-67; from instr. to rsch. asst. prof. Sch. Nursing U. Md., Bethesda, 1968-88, rsch. assoc., 1976-77; health sci. administrator Nat. Inst. Neurol. Disorders and Stroke NIH, Bethesda, 1988-92, asst. dir. Nat. Inst. Neurol. Disorders and Stroke, 1992-93, acting dir., dep. dir. Nat. Inst. Neurol. Disorders and Stroke, 1993-94, dep. dir. Nat. Inst. Neurol. Disorders and Stroke, 1994-95, dir. Nat. Inst. Nursing Rsch., 1995—. Cons., spkr., presenter in field. Contbr. articles to profl. jours., chpts. to books.; ad hoc reviewer SCIENCE; mem. editl. bd. STROKE. NIH fellow, 1973-76; NIN(C)DS grantee, 1976-88; recipient Sol Greenberg award for leadership ability and clin. excellence St. Francis Hosp., 1964, Rozella M. Schlottfeld Disting. Lecture award Case Western Reserve U., 1996, Centennial Achievement Medal, Georgetown U. Fellow Am. Heart Assn. Stroke Coun. (excellence in nursing lectr. award 1995); Mem. AAAS, ANA, Am. Acad. Nursing, Am. Lung Assn., Am. Soc. Profl. and Exec. Women, Am. Acad. Neurology (lectr. 1993-95), Am. Neurol. Assn., Soc. Neuroci., N.Y. Acad. Scis., Neurotrauma Soc., Sigma Theta Tau (award 1966), Inst. Medicine, 1999-. Office: Nat Inst Nursing Rsch NIH 31 Center Dr Bldg 31 Bethesda MD 20892-0001 Fax: (301) 594-3405.

GRADY, SANDRA C., minister, counselor; b. Kinston, N.C., July 8, 1941; d. William Devereaux Cobb and Nora Cathleen Davenport; m. Sanders W. Grady; children: Daniel, Dean. BS in Bus. and Eng. Edn., East Carolina u., Greenville, N.C., 1963, MS in Counseling and Edn., 1971; ThD, Wagner Leadership Inst., Colo. Springs, Colo., 2000. School tchr. and counselor, 1965—94; owner and instr. Grady Studies, Fairfax, Va., 1975—; founder and dir. Va. Prayer Network, Fairfax, Va., 1990—, Master's Keys, Fairfax, Va., 2002—. Prayer coord. Well Builders, Aledo, Tex., 1991—; mid-Atlantic dir. and coord. U.S. Strategic Prayer Network, Washington, 1998—, intercessional counselor Eagles team, 1998—, mem. nat. adv. bd., 2003—; cons. Stefanu, Inc., Alexandria, Va., 2000—; mem. adv. bd. Nat. Coun. Govt. Intercessions, 2005—, Internat. Leadership Embassy, Washington, 2005—; instr. The Citadel, Washington, 2000—, Colombia; internat. spkr. and Biblical counselor, 1990—. Mem.: Nat. Fedn. Music Tchrs., Internat. Coalition of Apostles. Republican. Avocations: writing, composition.

GRADY, WAYNE J., retired government official; b. Halifax, NS, Can., Dec. 15, 1943; s. Joseph Myles and Helen Virginia (McNeil) G. B.Comm., St. Mary's U., Halifax, 1973; MHA, U. Alta., Edmonton, 1975. Cons. Health Commn., Halifax, 1975-78; asst. to dep. minister Dept. of Health, Halifax, 1978-87, dep. minister health, 1987-91; dep. minister Dept. of the Environment, Halifax, 1991-96, ret., 1996. Roman Catholic. Personal E-mail: wgrady@hfx.eastlink.ca.

GRAEBNER, CAROL F., lawyer; b. Ridgway, Pa., Dec. 15, 1954; BA in Internat. Rels. cum laude, Dickinson Coll., 1975; JD, Am. U., 1978. Bar: Pa. 1978, Tex. 1982, N.Mex. 2003. Assoc. Eckert Seamens Cheria & Mellott, Pitts., 1978—82; staff atty. through gen. counsel Global Power subsidiary Conoco Inc., 1982—98; sr. v.p., gen. counsel Duke Energy Internat., 1998—2003; exec. v.p., gen. counsel Dynegy Inc., 2003—. Editor (mng.): Am. Univ. Law Rev. Bd. dir., Houston div. Am. Heart Assn.; bd. dir. Internat. Inst. Edn. Mem.: ABA, Am. Corp. Counsel Assn., State Bar N.Mex., State Bar Tex. Office: Dynegy Inc 1000 Louisiana Ste 5800 Houston TX 77002 Business E-Mail: carol.f.graebner@dynegy.com.

GRAEBNER, JAMES HERBERT, transportation executive; b. New Castle, Pa., Aug. 5, 1940; s. Herbert Conrad and Mildred Elizabeth (Fessel) Graebner; children: Karla Elizabeth, Michael Conrad, James Conrad, David Fessel, Mildred Ann. BA, Valparaiso U., 1962; MBA, Case Western Res. U., 1970. Assoc. W. C. Gilman & Co., Inc., Cleve., 1967-71; with Regional Transp. Dist., Denver, 1971-75; gen. mgr. R.I. Pub. Transit Authority, Providence, 1975-78; dir. Santa Clara County Transp. Agy., Calif., 1978-84; dir. product devel. UTDC, 1984-86; pres. Lomarado Group, Denver, 1986—. Vis. prof. Northwestern U., 1979; COO Transit Constrn. Authority, Denver, 1987—89; v.p. San Jose Hist. Trolley Corp.; guest lectr. numerous univs. Bd. dirs. Denver Rail Heritage Soc. Mem.: Denver Union Station Adv. Commn. (co-chair 2003—), Regional Transit Assn. Bay Area LoDo Dist. Inc. (bd. dirs. 1999—, pres. 2002), Calif. Assn. Publicly Owned Transit Sys. (vice chmn. 1984), Am. Pub. Transit Assn. (pres. 1983—84). Lutheran. Office Phone: 303-628-5510. Personal E-mail: carbarn@aol.com.

GRAEBNER, NORMAN ARTHUR, historian, educator; b. Kingman, Kans., Oct. 19, 1915; s. Rudolph William and Helen (Brauer) G.; m. Laura Edna Baum, Aug. 30, 1941; m. Jane Shannon, Jan. 3, 1998 (dec. 2002); m. Mary Moon, July 2, 2004. BS, Milw. State Tchrs. Coll., 1939; MA, U. Okla., 1940; PhD, U. Chgo., 1949; Litt.D., Albright Coll., 1976; MA, Oxford (Eng.) U., 1978; D.H.L., U. Pitts., 1981, Valparaiso U., 1981, Eastern Ill. U., 1986, U. Wis., Milw., 1997, Averett U., 2003; D of Pedagogy, Marshall U., 1993. Asst. prof. Okla. Coll. for Women, 1942-43, 46-47; from asst. prof. to prof. Iowa State Coll., 1948-56; prof. history U. Ill., Urbana, 1956-67, chmn. dept. history, 1961-63; Edward R. Stettinius prof. modern Am. history U. Va., 1967-82, Randolph P. Compton prof., Miller Ctr. Pub. Affairs, 1982—. Vis. prof. Stanford U., 1952-53, summers 1959, 72, U. Colo., summer 1968, Concordia Tchrs. Coll., summer 1971, U.S. Mil. Acad., West Point, N.Y., 1981-82, Beloit Coll., spring 1987, Va. Mil. Inst., fall 1987, Coll. of William and Mary, spring 1988, Marshall U., spring 1989; Commonwealth Fund lectr. U. Coll., London, 1958; Fulbright lectr. U. Queensland, Brisbane, Australia, 1963, U. Sydney, Australia, 1983, U. Heidelberg, Germany, 1998-99; disting. vis. prof. history Pa. State U., 1975-76; Harmsworth prof. Am. history Oxford U., 1978-79; Phi Beta Kappa vis. scholar, 1981-82; Thomas Jefferson vis. scholar Downing Coll., Cambridge U., 1985; disting. vis. prof. Nat. War Coll., 1994-95. Author: Empire on the Pacific, 1955, The New Isolationism, 1956, Cold War Diplomacy, 1962, rev. edit., 1977, The Age of Global Power, 1979, America As a World Power: A Realist Appraisal from Wilson to Reagan, 1984, Foundations of American Foreign Policy: A Realist Appraisal from Franklin to McKinley, 1985, A Twentieth-Century Odyssey: Memoir of a Life in Academe, 2002; co-author: A History of the United States, 2 vols, 1970, A History of the American People, 1970, 2d edit., 1975, Recent United States History, 1972; Editor: The Enduring Lincoln, 1959, Politics and the Crisis of 1860, 1961, An Uncertain Tradition: American Secretaries of State in the Twentieth Century, 1961, The Cold War: A Conflict of Ideology and Power, 1963, rev. edit., 1976, Ideas and Diplomacy, 1964, Manifest Destiny, 1968, Nationalism and Communism in Asia: The American Response, 1977, Freedom in America: A 200-Year Perspective, 1977, American Diplomatic History before 1900, 1978; Traditions and Values: American Diplomacy, 1790-1865, 1985, 1865-1945, 1985; The National Security: Its Theory and Practice, 1945-1960, 1986; contbr. articles to hist. jours. Dir. bicentennial program Pa. State U., 1975-76. Served to 1st lt. U.S. Army, 1943-46. Recipient Thomas Jefferson award U. Va., 1985. Mem. Am., So. hist. assns., Orgn. Am. Historians, Soc. Am. Historians, Soc. Historians Am., Fgn. Rels. (pres. 1972), Am. Acad. Arts and Scis., Mass. Hist. Soc., Phi Beta Kappa. Home: 1135 Inglecress Dr Charlottesville VA 22901 *One should never demand more of society than society can grant to all without suffering chaos or disintegration.*

GRAEDEL, THOMAS ELDON, industrial ecology educator, researcher; b. Portland, Oreg., Aug. 23, 1938; s. Philip Edward and Helen Beatrice (Peterson) G.; m. Susannah Grace Ketchum, July 23, 1966; children: Laura, Martha. BSChemE, Wash. State U., 1960; MA in Physics, Kent State U., 1964; MS in Astronomy, U. Mich., 1967, PhD in Astronomy, 1969. Tech. staff Bell Labs., Murray Hill, N.J., 1969-84; disting. mem. tech. staff AT&T Bell Labs., Murray Hill, N.J., 1984-96; prof. indsl. ecology Yale U., 1997—. Bd. dirs. Am. Inst. Physics; exec. com. Bd. Atmospheric Scis. and Climate Nat. Rsch. Coun., 1989—93; convener Global Emission Inventory Project Internat. Global Atmospheric Chem. Programme; chmn. Chem. Rsch. Applied to World Needs Poster Session, NAS panel to rev. U.S. High Speed Civil Transport Rsch. Program, 1993; bd. advisors Bowers Medals of the Franklin Inst., Phila.; mem. NAS Panel to Rev. the FY 1991 U.S. Global Change Rsch. Program; commr. Commn. on Geoscis., Environment and Resources, NRC, 1997—2001; chmn. NAS commn. Grand Challenges in Environ. Scis., 2000, NAS Commn. Rev. U.S. Climate Change Sci. Program, 2002. Author: Chemical Compounds in the Atmosphere, 1978; co-author: Atmospheric Chemical Compounds: Sources, Occurrence and Bioassay, 1986, Atmospheric Change: An Earth System Perspective, 1993, Industrial Ecology, 1995, 2d edit., 2002, Atmosphere, Climate and Change, 1995, Design for Environment, 1996, Industrial Ecology and Automobile, 1997, Streamlined Life Cycle Assessment, 1998, Atmospheric Corrosion, 2000; assoc. editor Atmospheric Environment, 1979—82, Rev. of Geophysics, 1987—91, Jour. Geophys. Rsch., 1989—92; author/co-author: more than 250 tech. papers and articles for profl. jours. Chmn. Environ. Commn., Mendham, N.J., 1971-74; ruling elder First Presbyn. Ch., Mendham, 1989-91. Capt. Armed Svcs., 1960-62. Fellow: AAAS, Am. Geophys. Union; mem.: Am. Chem. Soc., Conn. Acad. of Sci. and Engring., Nat. Acad. Engring. (elected). Presbyterian. Achievements include patents for composition useful for detecting H2S and for protection of devices; research on sulfur chemistry in lower atmosphere, on trends in atmospheric "greenhouse" gases, on atmospheric compounds, on chemistry in atmospheric droplets, on effects of atmosphere on materials, on the formation of copper patinas in the atmosphere, on the implications of trends in atmospheric composition, and on theoretical and practical foundations of industrial ecology. Office: Yale U Sch Forestry Envir Studies 205 Prospect St New Haven CT 06511-2106

GRAEF, LUTHER WILLIAM, civil engineer; b. Milw., Aug. 14, 1931; s. John and Pearl (Luther) G.; m. Lorraine Linnerud, Sept. 18, 1954; children: Ronald, Sharon, Gerald. BCE, Marquette U., 1952; MCE, U. Wis., 1961. Registered profl. engr., Wis., Colo. Engr. C.W. Yoder & Assocs. cons. engrs., Milw., 1956—61; ptnr. Graef Anhalt Schloemer, cons. engrs., Milw., 1961—67; chmn. bd. Graef Anhalt Schloemer Assocs., Inc., Milw., 1978—96. Mem. accreditation bd. for engring. and tech., 1989-95. Active boy Scouts Am.; chmn. bd. assessment City of Milw., 1962-89; bd. dirs. Luther Manor. 1st lt. AUS, 1953-56. Named Disting. Marquette U. Alumnus, 1982, Wis. Profl. Engr. of Yr., 1983. Mem. ASCE (sect. pres. 1968, nat. bd. dirs. 1989-92, nat. v.p. 1993-95, nat. pres. 1997-98), NSPE, Am. Assn. Engring. Soc. (vice chmn. 2000, chmn. 2001), Wis. Soc. Profl. Engrs., Cons. Engrs. Coun. Wis. (pres. 1973-75), Engrs. Scientist Milw. (pres. 1975), World Fedn. Engr. Orgns. (exec. coun. 2001—), World Fedn. Engring. Socs. (U.S. rep. 2002—). Home: 8503 Country Club Dr Franklin WI 53132-2710 Office: Graef Anhalt Schloemer 125 S 84th St Ste 401 Milwaukee WI 53214-1470 Office Phone: 414-259-1500. Personal E-mail: graefl6@aol.com.

GRAEFE, FREDERICK H., lawyer; b. Des Moines, Iowa, Apr. 16, 1944; s. Harry B. and Harriet (Sargent) G.; m. Mary Pat Kelley, May 12, 1970; children: Erin, Caroline, Maureen, Mary Kate. AB, Loyola U., New Orleans, 1966; MA, Georgetown U., 1971, JD, 1973. Bar: Iowa 1973, D.C. 1974, U.S. Supreme Ct. 1976. Law clk. to Hon. Howard F. Corcoran U.S. Dist. Ct. Washington, 1973-75; assoc. Howrey & Simon, Washington, 1975-79; ptnr. Finley, Kumble, Wagner, Heine, Underberg, Manley, Myerson & Casey (formerly Perito, Duerk & Pinco, P.C.), Washington, 1980-87, Baker & Hostetler, Washington, 1988—. Meets sr. health care policymakers in Cong., White House, NIH, others; counsel health care trade assns., coalitions hosps., physicians, mfrs., others. Capt. USMC, 1967-70, Vietnam. Mem. Fed. Bar Assn. (chmn. health law com. 1984-85), Kenwood Country Club (Bethesda, Md.), Columbia Country Club. Democrat. Roman Catholic. Office: Baker & Hostetler 1050 Connecticut Ave NW Washington DC 20036-5304 E-mail: fgraefe@bakerlaw.com.

GRAEFF, ALAN S., health association executive; BS in Distributed Scis., Am. U. Biologist metabolism branch Nat. Cancer Inst., NIH, Bethesda, Md., 1977—81; researcher Nat. Inst. of Allergy and Infectious Diseases, NIH, Bethesda, Md., 1981—87, various IT positions, 1987—95; chief Clin. Ctr. info. sys. dept. NIH, 1995-98, CIO Bethesda, Md., 1998—. Office: NIH Ctr for Info Tech 10401 Fernwood Rd Bethesda MD 20817

GRAESSLEY, WILLIAM WALTER, retired chemical engineering professor; b. Muskegon, Mich., Sept. 10, 1933; s. William Walter and Mary Iva (Isler) G.; m. Helen Lorraine Carlsen, June 13, 1953; children: Kathryn Lorraine, William W., Laurie Jo. BS, BS in Engring, U. Mich., 1956, MS in Engring, 1957, PhD, 1960. With Air Reduction Co., 1959-63, group leader, 1962-63; mem. faculty Northwestern U., Evanston, Ill., 1963-82, assoc. prof. chem. engring. and materials sci., 1966-70, prof., 1970-81, Walter P. Murphy prof., 1981-82, asst. dir. Materials Research Ctr., 1968-69; sr. sci. advisor Exxon Research and Engring. Co., 1982-87; prof. chem. engring. Princeton U., 1987-98. Sr. vis. fellow Cambridge U., 1979-80; disting. lectr. various univs. Asst. editor Trans. Soc. Rheology, 1969-75; mem. editorial adv. bd. Jour. Polymer Sci., 1979-2000, Rubber Revs., 1981-85, Macromolecules, 1983-85; contbr. articles to profl. jours. NSF fellow, 1956-59; Bingham medalist Soc. Rheology. Fellow Am. Phys. Soc. (exec. com., div. high polymer physics 1975-78, high polymer physics prize awardee); mem. Soc. Rheology (exec. com. 1971-73), Am. Inst. Chem. Engrs., Am. Chem. Soc., Nat. Acad. of Engring. Achievements include rsch. in synthetic polymers. E-mail: graessle@princeton.edu.

GRAETZ, MICHAEL J., law educator; b. Atlanta, 1944; m. Brett Dignam; children: Lucas, Dylan, Jacob. BBA, Emory U., 1966; LLB, U. Va., 1969; LLD (hon.), Capital U., 1992. Bar: Va. 1969. Advisor tax policy Asst. Sec. Treas., Washington, 1969-72; asst. prof. U. Va., Charlottesville, 1972-74, assoc. prof., 1974-77, prof., 1977-79, U. So. Calif., Los Angeles, 1979-83, Yale U., New Haven, 1983—86, Justus S. Hotchkiss Prof. Law, 1986—; dep. asst. sec. tax policy Dept. Treasury, Washington, 1990-92, asst. to sec., spl. counsel, 1992. Author: Life Insurance Taxation, The Mutual vs. Stock Differential, 1986, Federal Income Taxation: Principles and Policies, 1988, Foundations of International Income Taxation, 2003; co-author: Death by a Thousand Cuts: The Fight Over Taxing Inherited Wealth, 2005; contbr. articles to legal and econs. jours. Recipient Exceptional Svc. award Dept. Treasury, 1972; Guggenheim fellow, 1989. Fellow: Am. Acad. Arts and Scis. Office: Yale Law Sch Box 208215 New Haven CT 06520-8215 E-mail: michael.graetz@yale.edu.*

GRAF, ARNOLD HAROLD, financial planner; b. Buffalo, Oct. 30, 1930; s. John Edward and Rose Ruth (Tyman) G.; m. Joan Nensel, Sept. 1, 1956 (div. Apr. 1980); children: Jenny, David, Laurie, Paul, Ellen, Amy; m. Rita Mary DiFlorio, Aug. 3, 1981; stepchildren: Patricia, William, Kathleen, Stephan. Student, Rutgers U., 1955-58; BS in Econs., U. Pa., Phila., 1968; postgrad., Command-Gen. Staff Coll., 1966; MA in Internat. Rels., Army War Coll., 1973-75; JD, Weidner U., 1985. CLU, CFP ChFC. Commd. 2d lt. U.S. Army, 1952, advanced through grades to col., 1975, served in Korea, served in Vietnam, ret., 1983; shift supr. Campbell Soup Co., Camden, N.J., 1956-57; pers. dir. Container Corp. of Am., Phila., Oaks, Pa., 1957-59; special agt. Provident Mut. Life Ins. Co., Phila., 1959-60; dist. and regional mgr. Franklin Life Ins. Co., Phila., 1960-68; field mktg. dir. Nat. Liberty Corp., Frazier, Pa., 1968-70; regional mgr. Southland Life Ins. Co., King of Prussia, Pa., 1970-72; sr. supt. agys. Ins. Co. N.Am., Phila., 1972-75; career gen. agt. Aetna Life Ins. Co., Phila., 1975-80; pres. Nebsco Fin. Svcs. Inc./Nebsco Mortgage Profls. Ltd., Newtown Square, Pa., 1980—. Mortgage banker, 1995—, HUD/FHA Mortgages, 2000—. Contbr. articles to profl. jours. Dir. sch. bd. Marple/Newtown Sch. Dist., 1995-2000, 2004—. Paul Harris fellow Rotary Found., 1988, fellow Guntaker Found., 1990; recipient Humanitarian award Chapel of Four Chaplains, 1996. Mem. Pa. Assn. Ins./Fin. Advisors (dir. 2000—), Rotary Internat. (pres. Newton Sq. club 1987-88, R.I. dist. gov. 1990-91, chair dist. 7450 Rotary found. 2000—), Masons (32 degree), Del. County Assn. Life Underwriters (pres.), Serra Internat. (gov. dist. 28 1996-98, trustee found. 1998-2000). Republican. Roman Catholic. Avocations: bowling, golf, walking, reading. Home: 4107 Meadow Ln Newtown Square PA 19073-1611 Personal E-mail: agraf@comcast.net.

GRAF, DOROTHY ANN, human resources specialist; b. Nashville, Mar. 21, 1935; d. Henry George and Martha Dunlap (Hill) Meek; m. Peter Louis Graf, Oct. 28, 1971; children: Sidney E. Pollard, Deborah Lynn Pollard, Robert George Pollard, Michelle Joy Graf. Student, Montgomery Coll., 1979—. Office mgr. Pa. Life Ins. Co., Miami and Dallas, 1957-72; exec. sec. to med. dir. Pitts. Children's Hosp., 1974; sec. GE/TEMPO, Washington, 1974-76; adminstrv. asst. to sr. v.p. Logistics Mgmt. Inst., Washington, 1976-81, dir. adminstrv. svc., 1981-97, dir. recruiting and tng., 1995-97, dir. human resources, 1997-99; cons. human resources specialist, 1999—2000. Dir. KHI Svcs., Inc. Mem. Washington Tech. Pers. Forum. Democrat. Baptist. Home: 1400 Newry Circle Ormond Beach FL 32174 Personal E-mail: dotsie123@earthlink.net.

GRAF, DOROTHY JO, elementary school educator; b. Ft. Campbell, Ky., June 12, 1954; d. Raymond Suarez, Jr. and Dorothy Olson; m. Christian William Graf Sr., June 19, 2001. BS in Elem. Edn., SW Tex. State U., 1976; M of Elem. Edn., Tex. A&M U., 1991. Texas Tchr. Cert. Elem. Edn. TEA/Tex., 1976. Elem. tchr. San Antonio Archdiocese, Selma, Tex., 1976—85; tchr. 5th grade math., sce., social studies, tech. Regency Pl. Elem. Sch. N.E. Ind. Sch. Dist., San Antonio, 1985—. Named Tchr. of Yr., Regency Pl. Eme. Sch., San Antonio N.E. Ind. Sch. Dist.; recipient N.E. Regency Place Tchr. of Yr., 2001—02; scholar NEISD Teachers Assn. Profl. Devel. Scholarship award, North East Tchrs. Assn., 1986. Mem.: NEA, PTA-Regency Pl. Elem., North East Tchrs. Assn., Tex. Classroom Tchrs. Assn. Avocation: an advocate for the protection and welfare of children. Office: Regency Place Elem Sch 2635 Bitters San Antonio TX 78217-4599 Office Phone: 210-650-1525. E-mail: dgraf120@neisd.net.

GRAF, HANS, conductor; b. Austria, Feb. 15, 1949; m. Margarita Graf; 1 child, Anna. Studied with Franco Ferrera and Arvid Jansons. Dir. Iraqi Nat. Symphony Orch., Baghdad, Iraq, 1975—76; music coach Vienna State Opera, Austria, 1977—84; music dir. Mozarteum Orch., Salzburg, Austria, 1984-94, Calgary Philharm. Orch., 1995—2003, Orch. Nat. de Bordeaux-Aquitaine and Opera de Bordeaux, France, 1998—, Houston Symphony, 2000—; artist-in-residence Shepard Sch. of Music, Rice Univ., Tex. Guest condr. Vienna Symphony, Vienna Philharm., Orchestre Nat. de France, Leningrad Philharm., Pitts. Symphony, Boston Symphony. Recipient Chevalier de l'Ordre de la Legion d'Honneur, French Govt., 2002. Avocation: fine wine. Office: Houston Symphony 615 Louisiana St Suite 102 Houston TX 77002*

GRAF, JOHN A., finance company executive; b. Chgo., 1959; BA in Econs., U. Ill., 1981. Sr. v.p. Conseco, Inc.; exec. v.p., chief mktg. officer Western Nat. Life Ins. Co., 1993—97, pres., CEO, 1997—98; vice chmn. We. Nat. Corp., 1996—98; pres., retirement svcs. Am. Gen. Fin. Group, Houston, 1998—2001; pres. We. Nat. Corp., 1998—; sr. vice chmn., asset accumulation Am. Gen. Fin. Group, 2000—01; exec. v.p., retirement savings Amer. Internat. Group Inc., 2002—; vice chmn. AIG SunAmerica Inc., 2001—. Bd. dirs. Jr. Achievement S.E. Tex., Inc., W. Univ. Parks Bd.; vol. St. Vincent de Paul Cath. Ch.; mem. devel. coun. Tex. Children's Hosp. Mem. Young Pres.'s Orgn. Office: Amer Internat Group Inc 70 Pine St New York NY 10270

GRAF, KARL ROCKWELL, nuclear engineer; b. San Diego, Apr. 19, 1940; s. Frederic August and Beatrice (Rockwell) G.; m. Nancy Ann Scott, June 9, 1962; children: Robin Elizabeth, Scott Frederic. BS, U. S. Naval Acad., 1962. Submarine officer USN, 1962-84; comdg. officer USS George Bancroft, 1978—82; dep. comdr. readiness and tng. officer Submarine Squadron One, USN, Pearl Harbor, Hawaii, 1982—84; sr. mgmt. cons. Advanced Sci. and Tech. Assn., Solana Beach, Calif., 1984; dir. nuclear support Ill. Power Co., Decatur, 1985, dir. ops. monitoring, 1986-89, dir. quality assurance, 1990-92, dir. engring. projects, 1992-94, leader life cycle mgmt., 1994-2000; dir. adminstrn. St. Paul's Luth. Ch., Decatur, Ill., 2000—. Founder life cycle mgmt. program Clinton Nuclear Power Sta. Author: Monitoring Manual, 1986. Exec. dir. St. John's Luth. Ch., 1995-97; chmn. zoning bd. Village of Forsyth, Ill., 1988-96, chmn. long-range plan com., 1989-92, mem. long range plan task force, 1999-2002. Mem. Am. Nuclear Soc., U.S. Submarine League, Ret. Officers Assn. Achievements include the development and implementation of an innovative monitoring program at Illinois Power Company's Clinton Nuclear Power Station to monitor, evaluate and trend such things as individual responsibility and professionalism and develop actions to improve performance standards relating to the nuclear reactor, steam turbine and electrical generating systems. Home: 736 Weaver Rd Forsyth IL 62535-9777 Office: St Pauls Luth Ch 352 W Wood St Decatur

IL 62522-3197 E-mail: k4n@insightbb.com. *To determine the right thing to do, and then to really do what is right is a formula that not only defines our integrity, but helps us to avoid many of the pitfalls that can be so destructive to success and meaningful relationships in all aspects of our lives.*

GRAF, PETER GUSTAV, accountant, lawyer; b. Vienna, June 19, 1936; came to U.S. 1940, naturalized, 1945; m. Rosalie Greenbaum, Apr. 6, 1963; 1 child, Paul Evan BS in Econs., U. Pa., 1957; LLB, NYU, 1960, LLM, 1962. Bar: N.Y. 1960; CPA, N.Y. Tax acct. J.K. Lasser & Co., N.Y.C., 1961-62; with Joseph Graf & Co., N.Y.C., 1962-66, ptnr., 1966—. V.p., founder, dir. AGS Computers Inc., N.J., 1967—; ptnr., founder, treas., dir. Nardin Gallery, Inc., Somers, N.Y.; founder Cable Sys. USA Assocs., W.Va., Pa., Ohio, USA Mobile Commn., Inc., Cellular USA Inc., USA Ventures Ltd., MDchoice-.com., 1999, Tongue Sys.; chmn. Phonetel Technologies, Inc., 1995-99. Mem. AICPA, N.Y. State Soc. CPA, N.Y. State Bar Assn. Home: 87 Holly Pl Briarcliff Manor NY 10510-2107 Office: Graf Repetti & Co 1114 Avenue Of The Americas New York NY 10036-7703 Business E-Mail: pggraf@grafrepetti.com.

GRAF, RUDY J., communications company executive; BA, St. Thomas U., Miami, Fla. Mgmt. AT&T; reg. v.p. Metromedia Telecomms.; pres., COO Centennial Cellular Corp., 1991-99; CEO, pres. and COO Citizens Communications, 1999—2004, chmn., 2004—. Office: c/o Citizens Communications 3 High Ridge Park Stamford CT 06905*

GRAF, TRUMAN FREDERICK, agricultural economist, educator; b. New Holstein, Wis., Sept. 18, 1922; s. Herbert and Rose (Sell) G.; m. Sylvia Ann Thompson, Sept. 6, 1947; children: Eric Kindley, Siri Lynne, Peter Truman. BS, U. Wis., 1947, MS, 1949, PhD, 1953. Mktg. specialist, coop. agt. USDA and U. Wis., 1948-50; instr. agrl. econs. U. Wis., Madison, 1951-53, asst. prof., 1953-56, assoc. prof., 1956-61, prof., 1961-85, prof. emeritus, 1985—. Expert witness, 1982—; mem. Gov.'s Com. on Wis. Dairy Mktg.; mem. 3-man team to make mktg. analysis in Nigeria, USDA, 1962, made U.S. milk mktg. study, 1971; made mktg. analyses in 13 Carribbean countries, 1964; made mktg. analysis U. Wis., Mex., 1965; made mktg. analyses U.S. Ednl. Found., Finland, 1970, Rumanian Ministry Edn., U.S. Dept. State, Rumania, USSR, 1976, France, 1981, Russia, 1992, Ukraine, 1992, 98, Bulgaria, 1992, 93, Hungary, 1993, Poland, 1993, Zimbabwe, Africa, 1994, Ukraine, 1998, Kazakhstan, 1999, Uganda, 2000, US Treasury Dept., Cuba, 2002, Amenia, 2003, Czech Republic, 2004, Honduras, 2005, others; rschr. in field. Contbr. articles to profl. jours. Active Cub Scouts; bd. dirs. Univ. Houses Assn., 1955-56, Univ. Hill Farm Assn., 1958-59, Univ. Hill Farm Swim Club, 1959-60, Oakwood Retirement Homes, 1992-2001. Recipient Uhlman award Chgo. Bd. Trade, 1952, recipient Man of Yr. award World Dairy Expn., 1976, Disting. Svc. award U. Wis. Extension, 1981, Coop. Builder award Fedn. Coops., 1982, Internat. Trade Spl. award Gov. Wis., 1983. Mem. AARP (econ. security adv. com.), Am. Agrl. Econs. Assn. (Published Rsch. award 1974), Am. Mktg. Assn., Madison Naval Res. Assn. (pres. 1968-72), Am. Econ. Assn., Hist. Soc., United Dairy Industries Assn. (adv. com.), Wis. Fedn. Coops., Lakeshore Federated Dairy Coop., Wis. Ret. Educators Assn. (bd. dirs.), Wis. Coalition of Annuitants (vice chair), Civil War Club, Kiwanis (pres. Golden K). Lutheran. Home: 405 Samuel Dr Madison WI 53717-2144 Office: U Wis Dept of Agr Dept Agriculture Madison WI 53706

GRAFF, ARTHUR STEVEN, educational consultant; b. Highland, Ill., June 15, 1946; s. William Arthur and Roberta Pauline (Partridge) Graff; m. Janet Marie Hall, Dec. 27, 1975; children: Geoffrey Hall, Hannah Marie. BA, Coll. Wooster, 1968; MA, Case Western Reserve U., 1972; EdD, Teachers Coll., Columbia U., 1981. Asst. dir. admissions Coll. Wooster, Ohio, 1971—73, assoc. dir. admissions, 1973—79, instr. freshman studies, 1974—81; dir. Westminster House, 1977—79; dir. admissions planning and rsch., 1979—81; dir. admissions and guidance svcs. Coll. Bd., Evanston, Ill., 1981—2000, sr. cons./dir. enrollment info. Reston, Va., 2000—; sr. dir., mem. staff bok/gardner commn. ATP New Possibilities Project, 1989—90. Served with U.S. Army, 1968—70. Mem.: Am. Assn. Coll. Registrars and Admissions Officers, Nat. Assn. Coll. Admissions Counselors. Presbyterian. Avocations: camping, singing.

GRAFF, GAVIN R., pediatrician, pulmonologist; s. Leon R. and Pauline Graff; m. Amy Jo Loser; children: Zoey Z., Julian R. MD, Temple Sch. Medicine. Board Certified Pediatric Pulmonogist Abp, Bd. Certified pediatric pulmonology Pa. State Coll. Medicine, Hershey, 2002—; asst prof. pediat. U. Mo., Columbia, 1997—2002. Mem.: Am. Acad. Pediat., Am. Thoracic Soc. (assoc.). Office: Pa State Childre's Hosp 500 University Dr Hershey PA 17033 Office Phone: 717-531-5338. Office Fax: 717-531-0761. E-mail: ggraff@psu.edu.

GRAFF, GEORGE LEONARD, lawyer; b. Bklyn., Sept. 6, 1940; s. Charles M. and Nettie (Starr) G.; m. Judith S. Udell, Apr. 20, 1963; children: David, Peter, Matthew. AB, Columbia U., 1962, LLB magna cum laude, 1967. Bar: N.Y. 1967, U.S. Dist. Ct. (so., ea. and no. dists.) N.Y. 1970, U.S. Ct. Appeals (2d, 3rd, 9th and Fed. cirs.) 1975, U.S. Ct. Claims, 1980, U.S. Supreme Ct. 1985. Law clk. to Hon. Stanley H. Fuld N.Y. Ct. Appeals, Albany, 1967-70; assoc. Nickerson, Kramer, Lowenstein, Nessen & Kamin, N.Y.C., 1970-74; member Milgrim, Thomajan & Lee, P.C., N.Y.C., 1974-92; ptnr. Paul, Hastings, Janofsky & Walker, N.Y.C., 1992—. Lt. comdr. USNR, 1962-64. Mem. ABA (advisor to drafting com. uniform computer info. transactions act 1994-2003, sci. and tech. sect. 1999-2003, mem. coun.), Assn. of Bar of City of N.Y. (chmn. state legislation com. 1973-75), Intellectual Property Owners Am. (vice chair amicus com.). Home: 112 Holly Pl Briarcliff Manor NY 10510-2107 Office: Paul Hastings Janofsky & Walker 75 E 55th St New York NY 10022

GRAFF, GEORGE STEPHEN, aerospace transportation executive; b. N.Y.C., Mar. 16, 1917; s. George Russell and Marjory Eleanor (Dolan) G.; m. Mary Rita Shaughnessy, Oct. 3, 1942 (dec.); children: Mary Ann, George Stephen, James Russell, Thomas Gerald, Maureen Rita; m. Marjory V. Kassabaum, Apr. 4, 1987; stepchildren: Douglas George, Ann Denise, Karen Jane. AB cum laude, DeSales Coll., Toledo, 1939; B.Aero. Engring., U. Detroit, 1942. Draftsman Continental Aviation & Engring. Corp., Detroit, 1940-42; with McDonnell Aircraft Co., 1942-82, dir. system tech., 1961-64, v.p. engring. tech., 1964-68, v.p. engring., 1968-70, exec. v.p., 1970-71, pres., 1971-82, also dir.; v.p. McDonnell Douglas Corp., 1971-82, mem. exec. com., 1974-87, also bd. dirs. Mem. subcom. stability and control NACA, 1951-56; mem. subcom. aerodynamic stability and control NASA, 1956-58, com. missile and spacecraft aerodynamics, 1959-61, com. aircraft aerodynamics, 1964-65, chmn. aircraft aerodynamics com., 1965-67, mem. research and tech. adv. com. on aeros., 1967-71 Mem. industry com. Parks Coll., St. Louis, 1950-58; chmn. bd. trustees Fontbonne Coll., 1977-87; bd. dirs. Jr. Achievement of Mississippi Valley, Inc. Recipient trophy for design excellence Continental Aviation and Engring. Corp., 1942; Outstanding Engring. Alumnus of Yr. award U. Detroit, 1973 Fellow AIAA (regional dir., chmn. com. aircraft design 1964-67, fellow grade com. 1975-76); mem. Nat. Acad. Engring., Tau Beta Pi. Home: 750 S Hanley Rd #38 Saint Louis MO 63105 E-mail: graffgsgxp67@sbcglobal.net.

GRAFF, HARVEY J., history and humanities educator; b. Pitts., June 19, 1949; BA in History with honors, Northwestern U., 1970; MA in History and History of Edn., U. Toronto, 1971, PhD in History and History of Edn., 1975; cert., Newberry Libr. Inst. Instr. summer sch. Northwestern U., 1973; extramural lectr. Ont. Inst. for Studies in Edn., 1974-75; asst. to assoc. to prof. history and humanities U. Tex., Dallas, 1975-98, dir. divsn. behavioral and cultural sci., prof. history San Antonio. Rsch. assoc. Newberry Libr., 1980-81; vis. adj. prof. history Loyola U., Chgo., 1980; vis. prof. English and Edn., English and history summer sch. Simon Fraser U., 1980, 81; cons., reviewer NEH, 1978—, Nat. Inst. Edn., 1980—, Tex. Com. for Humanitites, 1976—; cons.-advisor Tex. local and regional hist. socs. and groups, 1976—; mem. adv. bd. Dallas Jewish Hist. Soc., 1987—; resource person Collaborative Approach to Svcs. for Elderly, U. Tex. Coun. Pres., 1977—; advisor Sta. KERA-TV, Dallas; advisor Handbook on Tex. Women, 1983—, American Teenagers: A Documentary Film, 1997. Author: Children and Schools in Nineteenth-Century Canada/L'école Canadienne et L'enfant au Dix-Neuvieme Siecle, 1979, rev. edit., 1993, The Literacy Myth: Literacy and Social Structure in the Nineteenth Century, 1979, rev. edit., 1991, The Legacies of Literacy, 1987, The Labyrinths of Literacy, 1987, rev. edit., 1995, Conflicting Paths: Growing Up in America, 1995, also fgn. transls., others; editor Growing Up in America: Historical Experiences, 1987; mem. editl. bd. History Edn. Quar., 1975-79, Social Sci. History, 1994—; contbr. articles to profl. jours.; cons. editor Interchange: Quar. Rev. Edn., 1974-78, 94—. NEH fellow The Newberry Libr., 1979-80, Spencer fellow Nat. Acad. Edn., 1979-82, short-term fellow Newberry Libr., 1985-86, Am. Antiquarian Soc./NEH fellow, 1988-89; rsch. grantee U. Tex., Dallas, 1983-85, 87-89, Spencer Found., 1991, 92; recipient Critics Choice award Am. Ednl. Studies Assn., 1987. Mem. Can. Assn. Am. Studies (exec. com. 1972-75, program com. 1974), Am. Ednl. Rsch. Assn. (program com. div. F 1973), Can. Population Studies Group (steering and program coms. 1974-76), History of Edn. Soc. (nominating com. 1976, 79), Women in History Profession (coord. S.W. coordinating com. 1977-79), Social Sci. History Assn. (regional network coor. 1976-84, founding chmn. Allan Sharlin Meml. award com. 1984-85, exec. com. 1987-89), Am. Hist. Assn., Orgn. Am. Historians, Social History Soc. Office: Behavioral and Cultural Scis U Tex 6900 N Loop 1604 W San Antonio TX 78249-1130

GRAFF, HENRY FRANKLIN, historian, educator; b. NYC, Aug. 11, 1921; s. Samuel F. and Florence Babette (Morris) G.; m. Edith Krantz, June 16, 1946; children: Iris Joan (Mrs. Andrew R. Morse), Ellen Toby (Mrs. Martin A. Fox). BSS magna cum laude, Coll. City N.Y., 1941; MA, Columbia U., 1942, PhD, 1949, LittD, 2005. Fellow history Coll. City N.Y., 1941-42, tutor history, 1946; lectr. history Columbia U., N.Y.C., 1946-47, instr. to asso. prof., 1946-61, prof. history, 1961-91, prof. emeritus, 1991—, chmn. dept. history, 1961-64; sr. fellow Freedom Forum Media Studies Ctr., N.Y.C., 1991-92; disting. lectr. Med. Sch. Columbia U., N.Y.C., 1992. Lectr. Vassar Coll., 1953; chmn. advanced placement com. Am. History Coll. Entrance Exam. Bd., 1959-63; presdl. appointee Nat. Hist. Publs. Commn., 1965-71; mem. hist. adv. com. to sec. Air Force, 1972-80; acad. cons. Gen. Learning Corp., Time-Life Books; cons. editor Alfred A. Knopf, Inc.; hist. adviser to CBS for Bicentennial TV Series The American Parade, 1973-76, Presdl. Portraits, 1987-88; disting. spkr. U.S. Air Force Acad., 1980; hist. adviser to ABC for TV series Our World, 1986-87, 20th Century Project, 1993-99; presdl. appointee J.F.K. Assassination Records Rev. Bd., 1993-98; humanities lectr. Med. Sch. Yale U., 1993; Richard W. Cooper lectr. Phi Beta Kappa Assocs., 1996. Author: Bluejackets with Perry in Japan, 1952; author: (with Jacques Barzun) The Modern Researcher, 1957, 2004; author: (with Clifford Lord) American Themes, 1963; author: (with John A. Krout) The Adventure of the American People, 3d edit., 1973; author: The Free and the Brave, 4th edit., 1980, Thomas Jefferson, 1968, American Imperialism and the Philippine Insurrection, 1969, The Tuesday Cabinet, 1970; author: (with Paul J. Bohannan) The Call of Freedom, 1978, The Promise of Democracy, 1978; author: This Great Nation, 1983, The Presidents: A Reference History, 1984, 2d edit., 1996, paperback, 1997, 3d edit., 2002, America: The Glorious Republic, 1985, rev. edit., 1990, Grover Cleveland, 2002; cons. editor Life's History of the United States, 1963—64, Presidential Inaugurations, 2005; contbr. articles to profl. jours. 1st lt. AUS, 1942-46. Recipient citation War Dept., 1945, Townsend Harris medal CCNY, 1966, Mark Van Doren award Columbia U., 1981, Gt. Tchr. award Columbia U., 1982, Kidger award New Eng. History Tchrs. Assn., 1990; Am. Coun. Learned Socs. fellow, 1942, Presdl. medal George Washington U., 1997, James Madison award ALA, 1999, Disting. Author award Westchester C.C. Found., 2000, Kaul Found. Award of Excellence, 2001. Mem. Orgn. Am. Historians, Am. Hist. Assn., Coun. Fgn. Rels., Author's Guild, P.E.N., Soc. Am. Historians, Soc. Historians Am. Fgn. Rels., Mass. Hist. Soc. (corr.), Century Assn. (N.Y.C.), Sunningdale Country Club, Phi Beta Kappa (former pres. Gamma chpt.), Phi Beta Assocs. (hon.). Home: 47 Andrea Ln Scarsdale NY 10583-3115

GRAFF, JEFFREY G., emergency physician; b. Chgo., Aug. 25, 1949; MD, U. Ill. Coll. Medicine, 1975. Intern Evanston Hosp., 1975—76, resident in emergency medicine, 1976—78; asst. prof. emergency medicine Northwestern U.; head divsn. emergency medicine Evanston Northwestern Healthcare; assoc. prof. emergency medicine Northwestern U. Feinberg Sch. Medicine. Bd. mem. Am. Bd. Emergency Medicine, 1996—, pres., 2003—04. Office: 2100 Pfingsten Rd Glenview IL 60025-1301 Office Phone: 847-657-5632.

GRAFF, LOUIS GEORGE, emergency physician, researcher; s. Louis and Elizabeth Graff; m. Martha Radford, 1980. MD, Harvard U., 1976. Lic. emergency medicine Am. Bd. Emergency Medicine, internal medicine Am. Bd. Internal Medicine. Assoc. dir. emergency medicine New Britain (Conn.) Gen. Hosp., 1984—2005, med. dir. of quality, 2003—; prof. emergency medicine U. of Conn. Sch. of Medicine, Farmington, 2001—, prof. clin. medicine, 2001—. Editor: (textbook) Observation Medicine, Observation Units: Implementation and Management Strategies. Office: New Britain Gen Hosp 100 Grand St New Britain CT 06050 Office Phone: 860-224-5675. Office Fax: 860-224-5774. Personal E-mail: louisgraff4@aol.com. E-mail: lgraff@nbgh.org.

GRAFF, PAT STUEVER, secondary school educator; b. Tulsa, Mar. 24, 1955; d. Joseph H., Sr. and Joann (Schneider) Stuever; m. Mark A. Rumsey; children: Earl, Jr., Jeremy. BS in Secondary Edn., Okla. State U., 1976; postgrad., U. N.M., 1976-87. Cert. tchr. lang. arts, social studies, journalism, French, N.Mex. Substitute tchr. Albuquerque Pub. Schs., 1976-78; tchr. Cleveland Mid. Sch., Albuquerque, 1978-86, La Cueva H.S., Albuquerque, 1986—, co-chair English dept., 1996—, chair sch. restructuring coun., 1999-2001. Adviser award winning lit. mag. El Tesoro, sch. newspapers The Edition, Huellas del Oso; instr. journalism workshops, N.Mex. Press Assn., Ind. U., Bloomington, Nat. Scholastic Press, Mpls., Kans. State U., Manhattan, Interscholastic Press League, Austin, Tex., St. Mary's U., San Antonio, Ala. Scholastic Press Assn., Wash.; keynote spkr. at numerous confs. in Ohio, Ind., Kans., S.C., Utah, La., Okla., Ala., N.Mex., Tex., Wash., Idaho, and N.Y.; reviewer of lang. and textbooks for several cos.; instr. Dial-A-Tchr., N.Mex., 1991-05; texbook evaluator Holt Pub., Inc., 1991; nat. bd. cert. tchr. adolescent/young adult English lang. arts, 2001—; mem. N.Mex. Network of Nat. Bd. Cert. Tchrs., 2002—, 2d v.p., 2003-; state bd. dirs. N.Mex. Coun. for the Social Studies, 1998-, chair state conf., 2001, state pres., 2002-03, state treas., 2003-; comm. officer, sec. ABQ Tchrs. Fedn. 2003-05. Author: Journalism Text, 1983; contbg. author: Communication Skills Resource Text, 1987, Classroom Publishing/Literacy, 1992; contbr. articles to profl. jours. Troop leader Girl Scouts U.S., 1979—90, coord. various programs, asst. program com. chmn. Chaparral Coun., 1988—89, chmn. adult recognition task force, 1991—96, bd. dirs., 1991—98; active PTA Gov. Bent Elem. Sch., 1983—86, v.p., 1985—86, Osuna Elem. Sch., 1986—92, N.Mex. PTA, 1994—2000; pub. various children's lit. mags., 1987—; pub. parent's newsletter, 1986—; newsletter layout editor Albuquerque Youth Soccer Orgn., 1985—88; active YMCA youth and govt. model legis.; faculty advisor La Cueva del., 1986—2002, press corps advisor, 1987—2001, asst. state dir., 2001—; asst. den. leader Boy Scouts Am., 1987—88, den leader, 1988—91. Recipient Innovative Tchg. award Bus. Week mag., 1990, Svc. commendation Coll. Edn. Alumni Assn., Okla. State U., 1990, Alumni Recognition award, 1993, Mem. Yr. Svc. award Bernalillo County Coun. Internat. Reading Assn., Thanks to Tchrs. award Apple Computers, 1990, Spl. Recognition Albuquerque C. of C., 1992, Disting. Svc. award NCTE, 2002; Gov.'s Outstanding Women in N.Mex. honoree, 2004; named Spotlighted Mem. Phi Delta Kappa, 1990, Spl. Recognition Advisor Dow Jones Newspaper Fund, 1990, Nat. H.S. Journalism Tchr. of Yr., 1995, Disting. Advisor, 1991, U.S. West Tchr. Yr. finalist, 1991, N.Mex. Pubs. Adviser of Yr., 1991, N.Mex. State Tchr. of Yr., 1993, finalist Nat. Tchr. Yr., 1993, finalist Am. Tchr. Awards, Disney, 1998; named USA Today All-Am. Tchr., 1999; grantee Phi Delta Kappa 1989, 91, Geraldine R. Dodge Found., 1990, 92, 95-97, Learn and Serve Am., 1999. Mem.: AAUW (chpt. newsletter editor 1995—2001, local v.p. 1997—99, state program v.p. 1997—99, state media chair 2000—03), ASCD (editor newsletter 1991—92, focus on excellence awards com. 1992—94, state bd. dirs. 2002—. Focus on Excellence award 1990), Albuquerque (N.Mex.) Tchrs. Fedn. (PR and comms. officer 2003—, sec. 2003—), N Mex. Coun. for Social Studies (mem. bd. 1999—2002, state v.p. 2001—02, pres. 2002—03), N. Mex. World Class Tchr. Network (state vice-pres. 2002—), N.Mex. Goals 2000 (panel mem. 1994—97), Quill & Scroll (adv. La Cueva chpt. 1986—, judge nat. newspaper rating contest 1988—97), Albuquerque Press Women (v.p. 1994, pres. 1995, Communicator of Achievement award 1993), N.Mex. Press Women (state scholarship chair 1994, publicity chair 1995—96, state treas. 1996—98, state v.p. 1998—99), N.Mex. Scholastic Press Assn. (state v.p. 1985—89, coord. workshop 1986, editor newsletter 1986—89, asst. chair state conf. 1988, 1989, state bd. dirs. 1991—2000, state v.p. 1992—95), N.Mex. Coun. Tchrs. English (regional coord. Albuquerque 1983—86, chair state confs. 1985—87, editl. bd. N.Mex. English Jour. 1986—88, state pres. 1987—88, chair facilities for Fall conf. 1988—93, chair English Humanities expo com. 1988—99, adv. mgr. 1989—90, editor N.Mex. English Jour. 1999—2003, Svc. award 1989, Outstanding H.S. English Tchr. N.Mex. 1991), Journalism Edn. Assn. (judge nat. contests 1988—, mem. nat. cert. bd. 1989—99, presenter nat. convs. 1989—, cert. journalism educator 1990, nat. bd. 1991—2002, master 1991—), Nat. Fedn. Press Women, Nat. Sch. Pub. Rels. Assn. (issues seminar planning com. 1990, chair 1991, master journalism educator 1991—, nat. conf. chmn. 1997—99, Zia chpt., contest winner 1991—94, Pres.'s award 1993), Nat. Coun. Tchrs. English (nat. chair com. English Tchrs. and Pubs. 1988—91, chair English Humanities Expo com. 1990—99, standing com. affiliates 1991—94, nat. chair 1995—98, chair English Humanities Expo com. 2001—03, nat. exec. com. 2001—03, nat. chair assembly for advisors of student pubs., regional rep. Tex., La., N.Mex., Disting. Svc. award 2002), Nat. Alliance High Schs. (tchr. rep. 1997—2000), Nat. Assn. Secondary Sch. Prins. (Breaking Ranks tchr. rep.), Phi Delta Kappa (pres. U. N.Mex. br. 2002—), Delta Kappa Gamma (state profl. affairs com. chair 2003—), Pi Lambda Theta (Ethel Mary Moore award Outstanding Educator 1993, Gov.'s Outstanding Women in N.Mex. 2004). Roman Catholic. Avocations: soccer, running, hiking, travel, skiing. Home: 8101 Krim Dr NE Albuquerque NM 87109-5223 Office: La Cueva H S 7801 Wilshire Ave NE Albuquerque NM 87122-2807 Fax: 505-797-2250. Office Phone: 505-823-2327. Personal E-mail: pgraff@aol.com.

GRAFF, RANDY, actress; b. Bklyn., May 23, 1955; Grad., Wagner Coll. Profl. theater debut in Gypsy, Village Dinner Theater, Raleigh, N.C.; appeared in Godspell, Raleigh; other appearances include Pins and Needles, Roundabout Theatre, N.Y.C., 1978, Something Wonderful, Westchester Regional Theatre, Harrison, N.Y., 1979, Sarava, Mark Hellinger Theatre, N.Y.C., 1979, Coming Attractions, Playwrights Horizons, Mainstage Theatre, N.Y.C., 1980, Keystone, McCarter Theatre, Princeton, N.J., 1981, A...My Name is Alice, Village Gate Theatre, N.Y.C., 1984, Amateurs, Playhouse in the Park, Cin., 1985, Fiorello!, Goodspell Opera House, East Haddam, Conn., 1985, Absurd Person Singular, Phila. Drama Guild, Phila., 1986, Les Miserables, Broadway Theatre, N.Y.C., 1987, City of Angels, Va. Theatre, N.Y.C., 1989 (Drama Desk award Featured Actress in Musical 1989, Tony award Supporting of Featured Actress in Musical 1990), Falsettos, 1993, Laughter on the 23rd Floor, 1993, Moon Over Buffalo, Martin Beck Theatre, 1995-96, High Society, St. James Theatre, N.Y.C., 1998, A Class Act, Ambassador Theatre, N.Y.C., 2001, Fiddler on the Roof, Minskoff Theatre, 2004, The Lady with All the Answers, 2005; (TV shows) include Mad About You, Law & Order, Love & War, Pros & Cons; (films) Key's to Tulsa, 1995. Office: Peter Strain & Assoc Ste 2900 1501 Broadway New York NY 10036

GRAFF, STUART LESLIE, accounting executive; b. Bklyn., Nov. 5, 1945; s. Irving and Ruth Graff; m. June Hilda Mannheimer, Mar. 2, 1969; children: Ivan Henry, Rachel Caroline. BA in Chemistry and Edn., Queens Coll., 1968; MBA, Loyola U., Chgo., 1972. CPA, Md.; cert. mgmt. acct., cert. govt. fin. mgr. Chemist, then motor vehicle analyst Atlantic Richfield Co., Harvey, Ill., Chgo., Phila., 1967—72; cost acct. Nat. Freight, Inc., Vineland, NJ, 1972—75; transp. cost analyst ICC, 1976—80; assoc. A.T. Kearney, Inc., mgmt. cons., Alexandria, Va., 1980—82; sys. acct. Arlington County, Va., 1982—85, D.C., Washington, 1985—86; mgr. acctg. Arlington County, 1981—88; tech. mgr. AICPA, Washington, 1988—89; contr. D.C. Govt. Dept. Fin. and Revenue, Washington, 1989—91; dir. fin. reporting and tech. issues staff U.S. Dept. Edn., Washington, sr. tech. adv. for fin. reporting and sys. ops., 1991—98; sr. staff acct. Corp. for Nat. and Cmty. Svc., 1998—. Adj. instr. acctg. Montgomery Coll., Germantown, Md. Pres. Pavilion Tenants Assn., 1980; bd. dirs. governmentwide cost acctg. working group. Contbr. articles to Traffic World, Govt. Acct.'s Jour., Mgmt. Acctg.; patentee halide addition and distbn. Mem. AICPA (Elijah Watt Sells award 1980, govt. com.), Inst. Mgmt. Accts. (cert. mgmt. acct., pres. Washington chpt., Andrew Barr award for excellence in acctg. lit. Washington chpt. 1984-85, 94-95), Greater Washington Soc. CPA (chmn. govt. acctg. and auditing com. 1984-86), Md. Assn. CPA, Assn. Govt. Accts., Govt. Fin. Officers Assn. Jewish. Home: Apt 1241 198 Halpine Rd Rockville MD 20852-7613 Office Phone: 202-606-5000 230.

GRAFFAM, WARD IRVING, lawyer; b. Portland, Maine, Sept. 2, 1940; s. Irving Hall and Mary Earl (Williams) G.; m. Linda Lewsen, June 10, 1967; children: Ward Jr., Kristen, Jerome. Bar: Maine 1967, U.S. Dist. Ct. Maine 1967. Lawyer Unum Life Ins. Co., Portland, 1968-70, assoc. counsel, 1970-75, counsel, 1975-80, v.p. ltd. products, 1980-83, v.p. employee benefits mktg., 1983-85, v.p. reins ops., 1985-86, v.p. flexible benefits, 1986, v.p., counsel, 1986-88, v.p. internat. ops., 1988-90; chmn. NEL Britannica Life Assurance, 1990-92; pres., mng. dir. Unum European Holding Co. Ltd. (London), 1990-97; chmn. Unum, Ltd., 1990—95; sr. v.p. internat. ops. Unum European Holding Co. Ltd. (London), 1992-97; COO, Young Am. America's Cup Syndicate, 1997-98; co-owner Wayfarer Marine Corp., Camden, Maine, 1997-2000. Bd. dirs. Camden Nat. Corp., Acadia Trust, Montalvo Corp., J. Weston Walch; chmn. Me. Employers Mutual Ins. Co., Waldron Group, ACLI Internat. Life Ins. Coun.; sec. N.E. Health; chmn. bd. dirs. Maine Internat. Trade Ctr., 1995-99, Waldron Group of Cos., 2002—; vice chmn. bd. dirs. Maine World Trade, Internat. Ins. Coun., Found. for Blood Rsch.; bd. visitors U. Maine Law Sch.; vice-chmn., trustee Maine Maritime Acad. Author: (with others) The Mutual Company, 1971; editor-in-chief U. Maine Law Rev., 1966-67. Chmn. bd. South Portland HUD, 1973-75; mem. Gov.'s Coun. on Alcohol and Drug Abuse, Augusta, Maine, 1980-82; bd. dirs. Cumberland unit Am. Cancer Soc., Portland, 1976-78, Vis. Nurses Assn., Portland, 1971-72, YMCA, Portland, 1984-89; bd. dirs. Maine World Affairs Coun., Maine Maritime Mus.; mem. Gov.'s Internat. Adv. Bd., 1995-96; treas., bd. dirs. Maine Maritime Acad., 1997—. Recipient 1st Place award Moot Ct. Competition U. Maine Sch. Law, Dist. Alumni award. Mem. ABA, Am. Corp. Counsel Assn., Maine State Bar Assn., Cumberland Bar Assn. (award), Portland Country Club, Portland Yacht Club (commodore 1983-84), Masons. Home: 29 Orchard St Portland ME 04102-3613 Office: Graffam & Assocs 29 Orchard St Portland ME 04102

GRAFFEO, MARY THÉRÈSE, music educator, performer; b. Mineola, N.Y., Jan. 20, 1949; d. Michael Joseph and Florence Marie (Lonette) G. BA in Music Edn., Adelphi U., 1972; MusM in Vocal Performance, Kent State U., 1982. Cert. music tchr. NY. Tchr., therapist Nassau County Bd. Coop. Ednl. Svcs., Westbury, NY, 1972-85; tchr. music, developer curricula Great Neck (N.Y.) Pub. Schs., 1985-87; tchr. music Syosset (N.Y.) Pub. Schs., 1987-88, 89-90, Jericho (N.Y.) Pub. Schs., 1988-89; tchr. music, developer creative programs Lawrence (N.Y.) Pub. Schs., 1990-92; tchr. music Herricks Pub. Schs., New Hyde Park, N.Y., 1992-93, Hempstead (N.Y.) Pub. Schs., 1993—. Music dir. summer programs Friends Acad., Locust Valley, N.Y., 1989-95. Author: Creative Enrichment Programs/America: The First 300 Years in Song, 1990, (curriculum) Music for the Trainable Mentally Retarded, 1973, Music for the Early Childhood Center of Hempstead Public Schools, 2002, Composing with Kindergarten, 2004; co-author: The Remediation of Learning Discrepancies Through Music, 1980; composer: (mus. play) Red Riding Hood's Day, 1993, The Bell of Atri, The Children's Song, 1995. Cultural adv. bd. Lawrence Pub. Schs., 1990-92, Hempstead Pub. Schs., 1993—; founding mem. United We Stand Am., Dallas, 1992-93. Scholar Adelphi U., 1968-72, Blossom Festival Sch., Kent, Ohio, 1978-79. Mem. NEA, Am. Fedn. Tchrs., Music Educators Nat. Conf., N.Y. State United Tchrs., N.Y. State Sch. Music

Assn., Nassau Music Educators Assn. Democrat. Roman Catholic. Avocations: aviculture, needlecrafts, travel, photography, concerts. Home: 18 Osborne Ln Greenvale NY 11548-1140 Office: Early Childhood Ctr 436 Front St Hempstead NY 11550-4212 E-mail: mgraffeo@optonline.net.

GRAFFEO, VICTORIA A., state appeals court judge; b. Rockville Centre, NY, Apr. 13, 1952; m. Edward E. Winders. BA, State U. Coll., Oneonta, 1974; JD Albany Law Sch., Union U., 1977. Pvt. practice, 1978—82; asst. counsel NY State Divsn. Alcoholism and Alcohol Abuse, 1982—84; counsel to minority leader pro tempore Kemp Hannon NY State Assembly, 1984—89; chief counsel to minority leader Clarence D. Rappleyea Jr. N.Y. State Assembly, 1989—94; solicitor gen. State of NY, 1995—96; justice NY State Supreme Ct. (3rd Jud. Dist.), 1996—98; assoc. justice Appellate divsn., 3rd dept., 1998—2000; assoc. judge NY State Ct. Appeals, Albany, 2000—. Office: 20 Eagle St Albany NY 12207

GRAFFIS, LEISTER F., retired engineering executive; b. Pekin, Ill., May 7, 1909; s. Runnion Abraham and May (Perdue) Graffis; m. Marian Doris Graffis, Sept. 10, 1943 (dec.); children: Beverly Jean, Elaine Velma. AEE, N.D. State Coll. Sci., 1937; cert. in trade and internat. edn., Colo. State Coll., 1940; cert. in advanced radar and comm. equipment, Harvard U., MIT, 1943. Supt. State Tng. Sch., Mandan, ND, 1937—41; precision assembler Lockheed Aircraft, Burbank, Calif., 1941—42; radio engr. Civil Svc., San Francisco, 1942; staff engr. radio divsn. Bendix, Towson, Md., 1945—50, chief field engr., 1950—57, asst. mgr. field engring., 1957—59, mgr., 1959—62; pres. Bendix Field Engring. Corp., Towson, Md., 1962—70; exec. asst. to corp. v.p. Bendix, Washington, 1970—73; ret., 1973. Contbr. articles to profl. jours. Treas., bd. dirs. Md. Bapt. Children's Aid; mem. Balt. area coun. exec. bd. Boy Scouts Am.; exec. dir. Md. Found.; trustee Golden Gate Bapt. Theol. Sem. Lt. comdr. AC USN, 1942—45, PTO. Named Man of the Yr., Bendix, 1969, Alumnus of the Yr., N.D. State Coll. Sci., 1991; recipient Pub. Svc. award, NASA, 1969, Internat. Honors citation, Epsilon Pi Tau, 1997. Mem.: Masons, Iota Lambda Sigma. Republican. Avocations: science and technology, photography, music. Home: 211 Willow Valley Sq # B204 Lancaster PA 17602

GRAFFMAN, GARY, academic administrator, pianist, music educator; b. NYC, Oct. 14, 1928; s. Vladimir and Nadia (Margolin) G.; m. Naomi Helfman, Dec. 5, 1952. Student, Curtis Inst. Music, 1936-46, Columbia U., 1947-48; studied with Vladimir Horowitz, Rudolf Serkin, Isabelle Vengerova; MusD (hon.), Trinity Coll., 1986, Juilliard Sch., 1993; MusD, Moravian Coll., 1995; MusD (hon.), St. Josephs U., 1996, Univ. Pa., 1997, New Eng. Conservatory Music, 2003. Dir. Curtis Inst. Music, Phila., 1986-95, pres., dir., 1995—. Soloist debut, Phila. Orch, 1947; first tours U.S., 1951, S.Am., 1955, Europe, 1956, Asia-Australia, 1958, South Africa, 1961; solo appearances with N.Y. Philharmonic, Boston, Chgo., Cleve., San Francisco, Los Angeles, London, Cape Town symphony orchs., Philharmonia London, Halle Orch. of Manchester, Royal Liverpool, Berlin, Lisbon, Oslo, Warsaw philharmonic orchs., Johannesburg, Sydney, Melbourne orchs., others; rec. artist with N.Y., Phila., Boston, Cleve., Chgo., San Francisco orchs., also solo recs.; author: I Really Should Be Practicing, 1981. Fulbright scholar, 1950; Ford Found. fellow, 1962; recipient Rachmaninoff Fund. spl. award, 1948, Leventritt award, 1949, Pa. Gov. Excellence in Arts award, 1991. Office: Curtis Inst Music Office of Director 1726 Locust St Philadelphia PA 19103-6187 also: ICM Artists Ltd 40 W 57th St Fl 16 New York NY 10019-4001*

GRAFSTEIN, BERNICE, physiology and neuroscience educator, researcher; BA, U. Toronto, Ont., Can., 1951; PhD, McGill U., Montreal, Que., Can., 1954. Prof. physiology and biophysics Cornell U. Med. Coll., N.Y.C., disting. prof. neurosci. Office: Cornell U Weill Med Coll Dept Physiology New York NY 10021 Office Phone: 212-746-6364. E-mail: bgraf@med.cornell.edu.

GRAFTON, ANTHONY THOMAS, history professor; b. New Haven, May 21, 1950; s. Samuel and Edith (Kingstone) G.; m. Louise Erlich, May 13, 1972; children: Samuel David, Anna Temma Rachel. BA, U. Chgo., 1971, MA, 1972, PhD, 1975. Instr. Cornell U., Ithaca, N.Y., 1974-75; from asst. prof. to assoc. prof. Princeton (N.J.) U., 1975-85, prof., 1985—, Andrew Mellon prof., 1988-93, Dodge prof. of history, 1993-2000, Henry Putnam prof., 2000—. Meyer Schapiro lectr. Columbia U., 1996-97; exhibit curator N.Y. Pub. Libr., N.Y.C., 1992, Libr. of Congress, Washington, 1993. Author: Joseph Scaliger, 1983-93, Defenders of the Text, 1991, New Worlds, Ancient Texts, 1992, The Footnote: A Curious History, 1997, Commerce with the Classics, 1997, Cardano's Cosmos, 1999, Leon Battista Alberti, 2000, Bring Out Your Dead, 2001. Recipient L.A. Times prize for history, 1993, Balzan prize for History of Humanities, 2002, Mellon Disting. Achievement award, 2003; Danforth fellow, 1971-75, Guggenheim fellow, 1988-89, Fairchild fellow Calif. Tech. Inst., 1988-89, Behrman fellow Princeton U., 1994-95. Mem. Am. Philos. Soc., Brit. Acad., Berlin-Brandenburgische Akad. der Wissenschaften (corr.). Democrat. Jewish. Avocations: walking, reading. Office: Princeton U Dickinson Hall History Dept Hl Princeton NJ 08544-0001

GRAFTON, SUE, novelist; b. Louisville, Apr. 24, 1940; d. Cornelius Warren and Vivian Boisseau (Harnsberger) G.; children: Leslie, Jay, Jamie; m. Steven Humphrey, Oct. 1, 1978. BA, U. Louisville, 1961. Lectr. L.A. City Coll., Long Beach (Calif.) City Coll., U. Dayton (Ohio) Writers Conf., Midwest Writers Conf., Canton, Ohio, Calif. Luth. Coll., Thousand Oaks, Santa Barbara (Calif.) Writers Conf., L.A. Valley Coll., Antioch Writers Conf., Yellow Springs, Ohio, S.W. Writers Conf., Albuquerque, Smithsonian Campus on the Mall, Washington, and others. Author: (novels) Keziah Dane, 1967, The Lolly-Madonna War, 1969, "A" is for Alibi, 1982 (Mysterious Stranger award 1982-83), "B" is for Burglar, 1985 (Shamus award 1986, Anthony award 1987), "C" Is For Corpse, 1986, "D" is for Deadbeat, 1987, "E" is for Evidence, 1988 (Doubleday Mystery Guild award 1989), "F" is for Fugitive, 1989 (Doubleday Mystery Guild award 1990, The Falcon award 1990), "G" is for Gumshoe, 1990 (Doubleday Mystery Guild award 1991, Anthony award 1991, Shamus award 1991), "H" is for Homicide, 1991 (Doubleday Mystery Guild award 1992), "I" is for Innocent, 1992 (Doubleday Mystery Guild award 1992, Mystery Scene Am. Mystery award 1993), Kinsey and Me, 1992, "J" is for Judgement, 1994, "K" is for Killer, 1994 (Shamus award 1994), "L" is For Lawless, 1995, "M" is For Malice, 1996, "N" is for Noose, 1998, "O" is for Outlaw, 1999, "P" is for Peril, 2001, "Q" is for Quarry, 2002, "R" is for Ricochet, 2004; editor: Writing Mysteries, 1992; author short fiction, short stories, screenplay, teleplay TV episodes. Named to, Am. Acad. Achievement, 2000. Mem. Writers Guild Am. West, Mystery Writers Am. Inc. (pres. 1994), Private Eye Writers Assn. (pres. 1989-90, Life Achievement award 2003), Crime Writers Assn. Address: Penguin/Putnam 375 Hudson St New York NY 10014-3672

GRAGG, KARL LAWRENCE, lawyer; b. Watertown, NY, Sept. 25, 1946; s. Karl Lawrence and Pauline (Sykes) G.; m. Maureen Gilluly, Dec. 13, 1975; children: Meaghan Christina, Erika Lawrence, Jenny Camille. BS, Fla. State U., 1968; JD, U. Fla., 1974, LLM in Taxation, 1975. Bar: Fla. 1975, U.S Dist. Ct. (so. dist.) Fla., U.S. Tax Ct., U.S. Ct. Appeals (5th cir.). Assoc. Mershon, Sawyer, Johnson, Dunwoody & Cole, Miami, Fla., 1975-80, ptnr., 1980-82, Gunster, Yoakley, Criser & Stewart, Palm Beach, Fla., 1982-84, Walker Ellis Gragg & Deaktor, Miami, 1984-86, White & Case, LLP, Miami, 1987—. Adj. prof. law U. Miami, 1978-89; mem. tax com. Fla. Ho. of Reps., Tallahassee, 1983. Contbr. articles to U. Fla. Law Rev. Vol. Miami United Way, 1977-80; bd. dirs. New Word Sch. of the Arts Found., 1998—, Bapt. Health Sys. Found., 2004—; trustee U. Fla. Law Sch. Found., 2004—. Mem. ABA (taxation sect.), Nat. Assn. State Bar (chmn. 1986), Am. Coll. Tax Counsel, Fla. Bar Assn. (tax sect., chmn. tax sect. 1991, chmn. coun. of sect.), Nat. Assn. Indsl. and Office Parks (bd. dirs. 1989-91), Ctr. for Health Techs., Inc. (bd. dirs. 1992-98), Japan Soc. South Fla. (bd. dirs. 1990-98), Miami City Club (bd. dirs. 2004—). Office: White & Case LLP 200 S Biscayne Blvd Ste 4900 Miami FL 33131-2352 Office Phone: 305-371-2700. E-mail: LGragg@whitecase.com.

GRAGLIA, LINO ANTHONY, lawyer, educator; b. Bklyn., Jan. 22, 1930; s. Pasquale and Antoinette (Romeo) G.; m. F. Carolyn Pennington, July 17, 1954; children: Donna, Carol, Laura. BA, CCNY, 1952; LLB, Columbia U., 1954. Bar: N.Y. 1954, D.C. 1957, Tex. 1980. U.S. Supreme Ct. Atty. U.S. Dept. Justice, Washington, 1954-57; pvt. practice law Washington and N.Y.C., 1957-66; prof. law U. Tex., Austin, 1966—. Author: Disaster by Decree: The Supreme Court Decisions on Race and the Schools, 1976. Recipient George Washington medal Freedoms Foundation at Valley Forge, 1989. Republican. Avocations: tennis, biking, hiking, billiards. Office: U Tex Sch Law 727 E 26th St Austin TX 78705-3224 Office Phone: 512-232-1363. Business E-Mail: lgraglia@law.mail.utexas.edu.

GRAHAM, ALLISTER P., food products executive; b. Toronto, Can. With The Oshawa Group Ltd., Toronto, Canada, 1960—99, pres., COO, 1985—90, CEO, 1990—98, chmn., 1990—99; now chmn. Nash Finch Co., Mpls. Past chmn. Retail Coun., Canada, Food Distbr. Intern., Washington; dir. Manulife Fin. Corp.; trustee Associated Brands Income Fund. Office: 7600 France Ave S Minneapolis MN 55435-5924*

GRAHAM, ANITA LOUISE, correctional and legal nurse consultant, community health nurse; b. Casa Grande, Ariz., Sept. 17, 1959; d. Therman Louis (dec. 1995) and Annie Clessie (Dornan) Nichols; m. Richard Arthur Christy, Aug. 27, 1990; children: Amanda Sue Wells, Kristi Lynn Foster. AS in Practical Nursing, Ctrl. Ariz. Coll., 1982; AAS, RN, Gateway C.C., Phoenix, 1985, Degree in Health Svc. Mgmt., 1992; cert. legal nurse cons., Nat. Inst. Paralegal Art-Scis., Phoenix, 1999. RN, Ariz., Okla.; cert. BLS, ACLS, chemotherapy. CNA, Hoemako Hosp., Casa Grande, 1977-82; LPN, Mesa (Ariz.) Luth. Hosp., 1982-85; nurse Mesa Gen. Hosp., 1985-86, East Mesa Care Ctr., 1986-88; nurse, case mgr. Interim Healthcare, Phoenix, 1988-93; nurse, nurse clinician PDR Carum Care, Phoenix, 1991-97; correctional nurse Ariz. Dept. Corrections, Florence, 1993-95; IV nurse clinician Signature Home Care, 1994-97; nurse, unit mgr., home health IV specialist Select Care, Globe, Ariz., 1997-99; legal nurse cons., Chandler, Ariz., 1999—. Mem. RN adv. bd. Interim Healthcare, 1990-93. Mem. Ariz. Nurses Assn., Internat. Platform Assn. Republican. Avocations: stitchery, reading. Home: 1646 N Pennington Dr Chandler AZ 85224-5115 E-mail: www.ngraham803@yahoo.com.

GRAHAM, ANNA REGINA, pathologist, educator; b. Phila., Nov. 1, 1947; d. Eugene Nelson and Anna Beatrice (McGovern) Chadwick; m. Larry L. Graham, June 29, 1973; 1 child, Jason. BS in Chemistry, Ariz. State U., 1969, BS in Zoology, 1970; MD, U. Ariz., 1974. Diplomate Am. Bd. Pathology. With Coll. Medicine U. Ariz., Tucson, 1974—, asst. prof. pathology, 1978-84, assoc. prof. pathology, 1984-90, prof. pathology, 1990—. Fellow Am. Soc. Clin. Pathologists (bd. dirs. Chgo. chpt. 1993-2003, sec. 1995-99, v.p. 1999-2000, pres.-elect 2000-01, pres. 2001-02), Internat. Acad. Pathology, Am. Telemedicine Assn., Coll. Am. Pathologists; mem. AMA (alt. del. Chgo. chpt. 1992-99, del. Chgo. chpt. 1999-2004), Ariz. Soc. Pathologists (pres. Phoenix chpt. 1989-91), Ariz. Med. Assn. (treas. Phoenix chpt. 1995-97). Republican. Baptist. Avocations: motorcycles, piano, choir. Office: Ariz Health Scis Ctr Dept Pathology 1501 N Campbell Ave Tucson AZ 85724-5108 Office Phone: 520-626-6828. Business E-Mail: agraham@umcaz.edu.

GRAHAM, BARBARA MARY, music educator; b. Winniped, Manitoba, Canada, Aug. 9, 1946; arrived in U.S., 1999; d. Alexander Henry and Christine Drummond (Lorimer) Graham. BA, U. Manitoba, 1966; MMus, Ithaca Coll., 1970; MEd, U. Manitoba, 1985; PhD, Simon Fraser U., 1998. Tchr. Winnipeg Sch. Divsn., 1967—69; musician Nurnberg Symphoniker, Germany, 1970—71; tchr. St. Boniface, 1973—85, Seven Oaks Sch. Divsn., Winnipeg, 1985—89, prin., 1990—94; prof. Ball State U., Muncie, Ind., 1999—2001. Mem.: Am. Ednl. Rsch. Assn. Office: Ball State U Tchrs Coll Rm 813 Muncie IN 47406

GRAHAM, BARBARA S., retired electric power industry executive; Sr. v.p., treas., CFO Delmarva Power & Light Co. (now Connectiv), Wilmington, Del.; chief adminstrv. officer Connectiv, 1999—, ret. Office: Connectiv PO Box 231 800 King St Wilmington DE 19899

GRAHAM, BERTA, humanities educator, researcher; b. Beloit, Kans., Apr. 28, 1950; d. Paul and Virginia (McKelvey) Bohning; m. Gregory Graham, June 6, 1970; children: Della, Samuel. BA in Sociology, Drake U., 1978; MA in Selected Studies, U. S.D., 1994; AA in Journalism, Harper Coll., Palatine, Ill., 2004. Adj. faculty Dordt Coll., Sioux Center, Iowa, Morningside Coll., Sioux City, Iowa, Northwestern Coll., OrangeCity, Iowa, 1992—2002. Author: Democracy in Lebanon, Vol I: Reconstruction, Democracy in Lebanon, Vol II: Relativity. Office: Associated Arts 565 Carl Ave #102 Barrington IL 60010

GRAHAM, BILLY (WILLIAM FRANKLIN GRAHAM), evangelist; b. Charlotte, N.C., Nov. 7, 1918; s. William Franklin and Morrow (Coffey) G.; m. Ruth McCue Bell, Aug. 13, 1943; children: Virginia Leftwich, Anne Morrow, Ruth Bell, William Franklin, Nelson Edman. BA, Wheaton Coll. (Ill.), 1943; ThB, Fla. Bible Inst., Tampa, 1940; ThB numerous hon. degrees, including, Houghton (N.Y.) Coll., Baylor U., The Citadel, William Jewell Coll. Ordained to ministry So. Baptist Conv., 1939; minister First Bapt. Ch., Western Springs, Ill., 1943-45; 1st v.p. Youth for Christ, Internat., 1945-50; pres. Northwestern Coll., Mpls., 1947-52; founder World Wide Pictures, Inc., Burbank, Calif.; worldwide evangelistic campaigns, 1949—; speaker weekly Hour of Decision radio program, 1950—; also periodic Crusade Telecasts; founder Billy Graham Evangelistic Assn., 1950; hon. chmn. Lausanne Congress World Evangelization, 1974. Author: Peace with God, 1953, World Aflame, 1965, The Jesus Generation, 1971, Angels: God's Secret Agents, 1975, How To Be Born Again, 1977, The Holy Spirit, 1978, Till Armageddon, 1981, A Biblical Standard for Evangelists, 1984, Approaching Hoofbeats, 1983, Unto the Hills, 1986, Facing Death and The Life After, 1987, Answers to Life's Problems, 1988, Hope for the Troubled Heart, 1991, Storm Warning, 1992, (autobiography) Just As I Am, 1997, Hope for Each Day, 2002; also writer of daily newspaper column. Recipient numerous awards, including Bernard Baruch award, 1955, Humane Order of African Redemption, 1960, Gold award George Washington Carver Meml. Inst., 1964, Horatio Alger award, 1965, Internat. Brotherhood award NCCJ, 1971, Sylvanus Thayer award Assn. Grads. U.S. Mil. Acad., 1972, Franciscan Internat. award, 1972, Man of South award, 1975, Liberty Bell award, 1975, Templeton prize for Progress in Religion, 1982, Presdl. Medal of Freedom, 1983, William Booth award Salvation Army, 1989, Congl. Gold Medal, 1996; Freedom award Ronald Reagan Presdl. Found., 2000, Hon. Knight Comdr. Order British Empire, 2001; named to the Gospel Music Hall of Fame, Gospel Music Assn., 1999. Baptist. Office: Billy Graham Evangelistic Assn PO Box 1270 Charlotte NC 28201-1270 Address: Billy Graham Evangelistic Assn 1 Billy Graham Pkwy Charlotte NC 28201

GRAHAM, BOB (DANIEL ROBERT GRAHAM), former senator, former governor; b. Coral Gables, Fla., Nov. 9, 1936; s. Ernest R. and Hilda Simmons Graham; m. Adele Khoury, 1959; children: Gwendolyn Patricia, Glynn Adele, Arva Suzanne, Kendall Elizabeth. BA, U. Fla., 1959; LLB, Harvard U., 1962. Atty.; cattle and dairy farmer; real estate developer; mem. Fla. Ho. of Reps., 1966-70, Fla. Senate, 1970-78; gov. State of Fla., Tallahassee, 1978-86; U.S. senator from Fla., 1987—2005. Chmn. Edn. Commn. of the States, 1980-81, Caribbean/Central Am. Action, 1980-81, U.S. intergovtl. adv. council on edn.; mem. So. Growth Policies Bd., chmn., 1982-83; chmn. So. Govs.' Assn.; chmn. com. trade and fgn. affairs Nat. Govs.' Assn.; energy & natural resources, environ. & pub. works com., fin. com., VA affairs/intelligence com., senate Dem. steering & coord. com.; ranking mem. long-term growth, debt and deficit reduction com., com. on fin., 1997-2005; mem. com. environment and pub. works, ranking mem. clean air, wetlands, pvt. property and nuc. safety com., 1995-2005; mem. com. energy and natural resources, ranking mem. energy rsch., devel., prodn. and regulation subcom., 1997-2005 Co-author: (with Jeff Nussbaum) Intelligence Matters: The CIA, the FBI, Saudi Arabia, and the Failure of America's War on Terror, 2004. Active 4-H Youth Found., Nat. Commn. on Reform Secondary Edn., Nat. Found. Improvement Edn., Nat. Com. for Citizens in Edn., Sr. Centers of Dade County, Fla.; chmn. So. Regional Edn. Bd., 1979-81 Named one of 5 Most Outstanding Young Men in Fla. Fla. Jaycees, 1971; recipient Allen Morris award for outstanding 1st term mem. senate, 1972, Allen Morris award for most valuable mem. senate, 1973, Allen Morris award for 2d most effective senator, 1976, named to Fla. Housing Hall of Fame, 2005. Mem. Fla. Bar Assn. Democrat. Mem. United Ch. Of Christ.

GRAHAM, BRUCE S., dean, educator; b. Windsor, Ont., Can. naturalized, U.S. m. Linda Graham; children: Todd, Beth. Student, U. Windsor, 1966; DDS, U. Toronto, 1970; MS, cert. in prosthodontics, Ohio State U., 1974; MEd, Dalhousie U., 1989. Instr. Ohio State U. Coll. Dentistry, U. Toronto; asst. to assoc. dean acad. affairs Dalhousie U., Halifax, Canada; dean, prof. restorative dentistry U. Detroit-Mercy Sch. Dentistry, 1992—2000; dean U. Ill. Chgo. Coll. Dentistry, 2000—. Spkr. in field. Fellow: Am. Coll. Dentists; mem.: Internat. Assn. Dental Rsch., Am. Assn. Dental Rsch., ADA. Office: 801 South Paulina Chicago IL 60612

GRAHAM, CHARLES PASSMORE, retired army officer; b. Seward, Alaska, Dec. 19, 1927; s. Thomas Phillip and Lynnie Ethel (Passmore) G.; m. Alice Ann Chandler, Nov. 20, 1954; children: Susan Kay, Edwin C., Richard C. BS, U.S. Mil. Acad., 1950; MS in Engring, U. Mich., 1957. C. Commd. 2d lt. U.S. Army, 1950, advanced through grades to lt. gen., 1977; dir. force programs and structure, office of dep. chief of staff for ops. Hdqrs. Dept. Army Washington, 1975-77; comdg. gen. 2d Armored Div. Ft. Hood, Tex., 1977-80; dep. chief of staff for ops. Hdqrs. U.S. Army Forces Command Ft. McPherson, Ga., 1980-81; chief of staff Hdqrs. U.S. Army Forces Command, 1981-83; comdg. gen. 2d U.S. Army Ft. Gillem, Ga., 1983-85; mgmt. cons., 1985—. Mediator Justice Ctr. of Atlanta, 1993—. Exec. dir. Ga. Internat. Cultural Exch., Inc., prodr. of fine arts and cultural exhbns., 1994-95. Decorated D.S.M., Legion of Merit, Bronze Star, Purple Heart. Mem. Assn. U.S. Army, Armor Assn., Assn. Grads U.S. Mil. Acad., Assn. Grads Army War Coll., 2d Armored Divsn. Assn. Lodges: Kiwanis. Presbyterian. Home: 134 Warbler Way Georgetown TX 78628-4804 *Guided by the principle of "Duty, Honor, Country" learned as a cadet at West Point, my goal was to do my very best in every assignment I was given, remembering that what was best for the United States, best for the U.S. Army, and best for the American soldier was the proper solution to each problem. With that goal, success would come naturally.*

GRAHAM, CYNTHIA ARMSTRONG, banker; b. Charlotte, N.C., Jan. 3, 1950; d. Beverly Weller and Katherine (Anderson) Armstrong; m. Walter Raleigh Graham Jr., May 23, 1970. AB in Chemistry, Bryn Mawr Coll., 1971; MBA in Fin. with distinction, U. Pa., 1976. Computer programmer Philco-Ford, Ft. Washington, Pa., 1973-74; asst. dir. admissions Wharton Sch., U. Pa., Phila., 1974-76; asst. v.p. N.C. Nat. Bank, Charlotte, 1976-80; v.p. Barclays Am. Corp., Charlotte, 1980-86; sr. v.p. Barclays Bank Del., N.A., Wilmington, 1986-87, Barnett Banks, Inc., Jacksonville, Fla., 1987-97; chmn., pres. Barnett Mcht. Svcs., Inc., Jacksonville, 1987-89, TeleCheck Southcoast, 1987-89, Barnett Card Svcs. Corp., Jacksonville, 1989-97; exec. v.p. customer info. and segment mgmt. Nat. City Corp., Cleve., 1998-2000; sr. v.p. customer info. & programs J.P. Morgan Chase & Co., N.Y.C., 2000—. Bd. advisors Nat. DAta Corp., Atlanta, 1987-88; delivery sys. advisor VISA U.S.A., Inc., San Mateo, Calif., 1987-91; mcht. svcs. advisor MasterCard, Internat., N.Y.C., 1989-92; mem. U.S. regional bus. com. MasterCard, 1992-97, strategic adv. Bank Adminstr. Inst., 1999—, adv. com. Direct Mktg. Assn., 2000—; card products advisor VISA U.S.A., Inc., San Mateo, 1991-94, VISA Internat., 1994, mem. mktg. com., 1994-97; bd. dirs. Inst. for Servant Leadership. Mem. Jacksonville Women's Network, 1988-92, bd. dirs., 1991-92, treas., 1992; mem. bd. suprs. Spaceport Fla., 1990-92. Mem. Am. Bankers Assn. (exec. com. card divsn. 1991-94, vice chmn. 1993, chmn. 1994), Jacksonville C. of C.

GRAHAM, DAVID BOLDEN, food products executive; b. Miami Beach, Fla., Feb. 10, 1927; s. Robert Cabel and Bertha Eugenia (Hack) G.; m. Stuart Hill Smith, Sept. 1, 1956; children: Bird, Ellen, Darnall, Lamar, Lyle, Gerard, Barbara, David Bolden. Student, Colegio de san Bartolome, Bogota, Colombia, 1946; BS, Georgetown U., 1949; postgrad., Harvard Bus. Sch., 1950. Chmn. Graham Farms, Inc., Washington, Ind., 1950-99, Graham Cheese Corp., Washington, 1950-99; sec. Bal Harbour Square, Fla., 1956-57, Graham Bros., Inc., Washington, 1950-72. Contbr. articles on agr., transp., early fur traders to various publs. Past pres. Washington Planning Commn., Regional Planning Commn.; past bd. dirs. Hist. Landmarks Found., Ind.; mem. revolving fund com., mem. rural preservation com.; past mem. Ind. Agrl. Adv. Coun.; past mem. adv. coun. Bur. Water and Mineral Resources; past mem. Natural Resources Commn.; dir. Ind. Regional Hwy. Coalition; v.p. I-69 Mid-Continent Hwy. Coalition; past pres. Nat. Turkey Fedn.; mem. Olympic Yachting Staff, 1996; active Coast Guard Aux., Lic. Master Great Lakes or Inland Waters, FCC Marine Radio Lic. Lt. col. USAF Res., 1949-77. Mem. Columbia Club (Indpls.), Rotary (hon., past pres., Paul Harris fellow), Atlantic Cruising Club, Inland Yacht Club, Elks, Soc. of Children's Book Writers, N.Am. Fishing Club (life). Republican. Roman Catholic. Home and Office: Graham Farms PO Box 391 Washington IN 47501-0391

GRAHAM, DAVID BROWNING, lawyer; b. Wildwood, N.J., Dec. 20, 1942; s. William Browning and Mary Graham; m. Linda Lea Beasley, Feb. 20, 1971; children: Owen, Mary. BS, La. State U., 1966, JD, 1969. Bar: La. 1969, D.C. 1972, U.S. Ct. Appeals (D.C. cir.) 1974, Ill. 1980, Ohio 1999. Atty. U.S. EPA, Washington, 1972-73; corp. counsel Nat. Rural Elec. Coop. Assn., Washington, 1973-77; dir. office hearing and appeals U.S. Dept. Interior, Arlington, Va., 1977-79; dep. gen. counsel Velsicol Chem. Corp., Chgo., 1979-84; ptnr. Freedman, Levy, Kroll & Simonds, Washington, 1984-89, Kaye, Scholer, Fierman, Hays & Handler, Washington, 1989-92, Howrey & Simon, Washington, 1992-98, Baker & Hostetler, Cleve., 1998—2003, Kaufman & Canoles, Williamsburg, Va., 2003—. Mem. bd. advisors Toxics Law Reporter, Washington, 1987—, Chem. Waste Litigation Reporter, Washington, 1986—. Co-author: Emergency Response: Is Your Company Ready?, 2002, New Approaches to Environmental Law and Agency Regulation: The Daubert Litigation Approach, 2000; contbr. articles to profl. jours. Mem. ABA (former officer sect. environ., energy & environ. law), D.C. Bar Assn., Ohio Bar Assn., Cleve. Bar Assn. Presbyterian. Avocations: running, skiing. Home: 221 William Claiborne Williamsburg VA 23185

GRAHAM, DAVID F., lawyer; b. Chgo., Sept. 14, 1953; BA with high honors, Haverford Coll., 1975; JD, U. Chgo., 1978. Bar: Ill. 1978. Law clk. to Hon. Charles Levin Mich. Supreme Ct., 1978-79; Bigelow teaching fellow, lectr. on law U. Chgo., 1979-80; with Sidley Austin Brown & Wood LLP, Chgo., 1980—, ptnr. comml. litig., 1986—, and mem. exec. com. Past gen. counsel Chgo. Coun. of Lawyers. Adv. bd. Legal Aid Soc., Chgo. Mem.: Phi Beta Kappa. Office: Sidley Austin Brown & Wood LLP Bank One Plz 10 S Dearborn St Chicago IL 60603 Office Phone: 312-853-7596. Office Fax: 312-853-7036. Business E-Mail: dgraham@sidley.com.

GRAHAM, DAVID G., preventive medicine physician, psychiatrist; b. Nov. 17, 1949; s. Thomas and Catherine G.; m. Katherine A. Graham; children: Brigitte, John. BA magna cum laude, Walsh U., 1971; MD, U. Puerto Rico, 1980; MPH, Columbia U., 1985. Diplomate Am. Bd. Preventive Medicine, Am. Bd. Clin. Psychiatry. Intern, then resident in psychiatry SUNY, Stony Brook, 1980-84, resident in preventive medicine, 1984-86, asst. prof. preventive medicine, 1985—; attending physician VA Med. Ctr., Northport, N.Y., 1985—; dir. pub. health Suffolk County (N.Y.) Dept. Health Svcs., 1986—, chief dep. health commr., 2005—. Author: Medieval Minds, 1985, Profiles in Protest, 1987, Statistics, 1987, Mental Status Manual, 1989. Fellow Am. Coll. Preventive Medicine; mem. APHA, Am. Psychiatric Assn., Am. Assn. Pub. Health Physicians, Alumni Assn. Columbia U. Avocations: gardening, antiques, tennis, reading, outdoor recreation. Office Phone: 631-848-4732.

GRAHAM, DAVID RICHARD, orthopedic surgeon; b. Detroit, May 15, 1940; s. Lewis J. and Elberta Y. Graham; m. Dorothy T. Young, June 11, 1966; children: Rebecca, Jeffrey. BA cum laude, Harvard U., 1962; MD, U. Rochester, 1966. Diplomate Am. Bd. Orthop. Surgery. Intern Highland Hosp., Rochester, NY, 1966—67, resident in surgery, 1967—68; resident in orthopaedic surgery Henry Ford Hosp., Detroit, 1970—72; orthopaedic surgeon Elmira (N.Y.) Orthopaedic Assocs., P.C., 1972—2001, pres., 1992—2001. Pres. Arnot Ogden Med. Staff, Elmira, 1990; clin. assoc. Sch. Medicine & Dentistry U. Rochester, 1992—. Lt. comdr. U.S. Navy, 1968-70. Fellow Am. Coll. Surgeons, Am. Acad. Orthop. Surgeons; mem. AMA, Med. Soc. State N.Y., Ea. Orthop. Assn., Am. Coll. Sports Medicine, Chemung County Med. Soc. (pres. 1993-94), Elmira Torch Club (pres. 1990). Republican. Presbyterian. Home and Office: 690 W Clinton St Elmira NY 14905-2226

GRAHAM, DAVID YATES, gastroenterologist; b. Balboa, Panama, Dec. 24, 1940; came to U.S., 1941; s. Harry Edward and Helen Graham; m. Janet Susan Butel, Mar. 31, 1967; children: Kathleen, David. BS, U. Notre Dame, 1963; MD with honors, Baylor U., 1966. Diplomate Am. Bd. Internal Medicine, Am. Bd. Gastroenterology. Intern Ban Taub Gen. Hosp., VA Hosp., Houston, 1966-67; resident internal medicine Baylor Affiliated Hosps., Houston, 1969-71, fellow gastroenterology, 1972-73; from asst. prof. to prof. medicine Baylor Coll. Medicine, Houston, 1973—, chief gastroenterology sect. VA Med. Ctr., 1976—, from assoc. prof. to prof. virology, 1981-89, prof. molecular virology, 1989—; chief gastroenterology sect. Meth. Hosp., Houston, 1988—. Dir. gastroenterology fellowship program Ben Taub Gen. Hosp., Houston, 1975-80, 88—; chief div. digestive disease dept. medicine Baylor Coll. Medicine, Houston, 1988—; planning com. 10th World Congresses of Gastroenterology, 1991-94; advisor to Japanese Rsch. Soc. for Helicobacter pyloria Related Gastroduodenal Diseases, 1995; editor-in-chief of jour. Helicobacter. Contbr. 60 chpts. in 28 books, numerous articles to profl. jours. With U.S. Army, 1967-69. Recipient Joseph B. Kirsner award Am. Gastroenterology Assn., 1994, Michael E. DeBakey, M.D. award for Excellence in Rsch., 1994, Janssen award for Special Achievement in Gastroenterology, 1995, Frank Brown Berry prize in Fed. Medicine, 2000. Fellow AAAS, Am. Coll. Physicians, Am. Coll. Gastroenterology (Henry Baker Lecture award 1983, pres. 1990-91), Am. Acad. Microbiology, Infectious Diseases Soc. Am., World Innovation Found.; mem. Am. Gastroent. Assn., Am. Soc. Gastrointestinal Endoscopy, Tex. Soc. for Gastrointestinal Endoscopy, Houston Gastroent. Soc., Gastrointestinal Rsch. Group, Alpha Omega Alpha. Office: Vet Affairs Med Ctr 2002 Holcombe Blvd Houston TX 77030-4211 also: Baylor Coll of Medicine Dept of Medicine One Baylor Plaza Houston TX 77030-3498 E-mail: dgraham@bcm.tmc.edu.

GRAHAM, DEBORAH DENISE, minister, educator; b. Akron, Ohio, Dec. 15, 1961; d. Douglas Eugene Ward and Ruby Lucille (Head) Lockett; m. Curnell Graham, May 21, 1988; children: Shakira Denaé, Victoria Patrice. BA, U. Akron, 1984, PhD, 1998; MDiv, Duke U., 1987. Ordained elder East Ohio Conf. English tchr. Upward Bound Program, Akron, 1982—87, dormitory counselor, 1982—87; tchg. asst. Duke U., Durham, NC, 1984—87; rschr., tchr. U. Akron, 1987—94, adminstrv. asst. women's studies, 1987—94; sr. pastor Holy Trinity United Meth. Ch., Akron, 1987—. Bus. adminstr. Holy Trinity United Meth. Ch., Akron, 1987—; profl. counselor Juvenile Ct., Akron, 1987—; leadership trainer Akron Dist./Shirley Caesar, 1996—. Spkr. M. King Fed. Ctr., Battle Creek, 1999; expert in residence Kellog Found., Battle Creek, Mich., 1998; bd. mem. InterFaith Caregivers, Akron, 1999—2000. Named Most Loved Pastor, Gospel Today Mag., 2001; recipient Cmty. Leadership award, God First Ministries, 2002. Mem.: East Ohio Bd. Ordained Mins., Delta Sigma Theta. Democrat. Avocations: organ, reading, journaling, running, dining. Home: 1291 Morse St Akron OH 44320 Office: Holy Trinity UMC 1127 Copley Rd Akron OH 44320

GRAHAM, DIANE E., newspaper editor; b. Gary, Ind., June 29, 1953; d. William M. and Mary Jane (Shreve) Graham; m. Daniel Kevin Miller, Oct. 18, 1986. B, Drake U., 1974. Reporter Des Moines Tribune, 1974—78, Des Moines Register, 1978—84, bus. editor, 1984—86, dep. mng. editor, 1986—95, mng. editor, 1995—. Pres. Iowa Freedom of Info. Coun., Des Moines, 1992—93; chair adv. bd. Drake U. Sch. Journalism, Des Moines, 1995—. Recipient Davenport fellow for bus./econ. reporting, U. Mo., 1983. Avocations: playing pipe organ, gardening. Office: Des Moines Register 715 Locust St Des Moines IA 50309-3767

GRAHAM, DON BALLEW, literature educator, writer; b. Lucas, Tex., Jan. 30, 1940; s. Willie and Mrytle Joyce (Ballew) G.; m. Betsy Anne Berry, 1991. BA (high honors), North Tex. State U., Denton, 1962, MA, 1964; PhD, U. Tex., 1971. Asst. prof. U. Pa., Phila., 1971-76; instr. S.W. Tex. State U., San Marcos, 1965-1969; prof. U. Tex., 1976-1985, J. Frank Dobie Regents Prof.of Am. and English lit., 1985—. Author: No Name on the Bullet: A Biography of Audie Murphy, 1989; (criticism) Texas: A Literary Portrait, 1986, The Fiction of Frank Norris: The Aesthetic Context, 1978, Kings of Texas: The 150-year Saga of an American Ranching Empire, 2003; (cinema history) Cowboys and Cadillacs: How Hollywood Looks at Texas, 1983; editor: (anthology) South by Southwest: 24 Stories from Modern Texas, 1985; (criticism) The Texas Literary Tradition: Fiction Folklore History, 1983, Critical Essays on Frank Norris, 1978, Lone Star Literature; From the Red River to the Rio Grande, 2003; (film criticism) Western Movies, 1979. Mem. Tex. Inst. of Letters. Avocations: travel, writing. Office: University of Texas Calhoun Hall Austin TX 78712 Office Phone: 512-471-8387. Business E-Mail: dgbb@mail.utexas.edu.

GRAHAM, DONALD EDWARD, publishing company executive; b. Balt., Apr. 22, 1945; s. Philip L. and Katharine (Meyer) Graham; m. Mary L. Wissler, Jan. 7, 1967; 4 children. BA, Harvard U., 1966. Patrolman Washington Met. Police Dept., 1969—70; formerly with Newsweek mag.; with The Washington Post, 1971—, asst. mng. editor sports, 1974—75, asst. gen. mgr., 1975—76, exec. v.p., gen. mgr., 1976—79, pub., 1979—2000, chmn., 1993—; pres. The Washington Post Co., 1991—93, CEO, 1991—, chmn., 1993—, also dir., 1974—. Mem. Pulitzer Prize Bd., 1999—; dir. BrassRing, Inc. Trustee Fed. City Coun.; pres. DC Coll. Access Program; bd. dirs. The Summit Fund of Washington. Info. specialist 1st Cavalry Divsn. U.S. Army, 1967—68, Vietnam. Mem.: Am. Antiquarian Soc. Office: Washington Post 1150 15th St NW Washington DC 20071-0002*

GRAHAM, DONALD JAMES, food technologist, hygienic design consultant; b. York, N.Y., Sept. 24, 1932; s. Howard Alexander Graham and Naomi Irene (Fletcher) Graham Horgan; m. Dorothy Jane Schroeder, Jan. 1, 1965; children: Christopher Howard, Jonathan Edward. AAS, N.Y. State Agrl. Tech. Inst., 1952; BS with honors, Mich. State U., 1958, MS, 1959; postgrad., Oreg. State U., 1959-62. Cert. quality control sanitarian Am. Inst. Baking. Profit planning dir. Green Giant Co., LeSueur, Minn., 1962-67; dir. tech. svc. Green Giant of Can., Windsor, Ont., 1967-77; dir. quality assurance William Underwood Co., Westwood, Mass., 1977-83; internat. tech. dir. Pet, Inc., St. Louis, 1983-87; sr. food technologist, food sanitation cons., lectr., fellow Sverdrup Corp., St. Louis, 1988-99; pres. Graham Sanitary Design Consulting, Ltd., Chesterfield, Mo., 1999—. Faculty, com. mem. Food Processors Inst., Washington, 1980-92. Contbr. articles to tech. publs. Troop com. chmn. Boy Scouts Am., Medfield, Mass., 1979-82, treas., Chesterfield, Mo., 1984-89; mem. Minn. Rep. Com., 1965-67. Served U.S. Army, 1952—54, Med. and Veterinary Corp., Korea. Mem. Inst. Food Technologists, Internat. Assn. for Food Protection, Inst. Thermal Processing Specialists (bd. dirs. 1980-82), Mo. Food Processors Assn. (bd. dirs. 1992-2003, pres. 1994, 95, 96, exec. v.p. 1997-), Am. Soc. Quality Control, Alpha Zeta (chancellor Kedzie chpt. 1957-58). Avocations: photography, videotaping, genealogy. Home: 14318 Aitken Hill Ct Chesterfield MO 63017-2820 Office: Graham Sanitary Design Cons 14318 Aitken Hill Ct Chesterfield MO 63017-2820 Office Phone: 314-878-5333. Personal E-mail: grahamdj@prodigy.net.

GRAHAM, DONALD LYNN, federal judge; b. Salisbury, N.C., Dec. 15, 1948; s. Ernest Jethro and Mildred (Donald) G.; m. Brenda Joyce Savage, Sept. 27, 1969; 1 child, Sherrian Lynne. BA magna cum laude, W.Va. State Coll., 1971; JD, Ohio State U., 1974. Bar: Ohio 1974, U.S. Ct. Mil. Appeals, 1974, Fla. 1980, U.S. Dist. Ct. (so. dist.) Fla. 1980, Supreme Ct. 1980, U.S. Ct. Appeals (5th and 11th cirs.) 1981. Asst. U.S. atty. U.S. Dist. Ct. (so. dist.) Fla., Miami, 1979-84; ptnr. Raskin & Graham, Miami, 1984-91; judge U.S. Dist. Ct. (so. dist.) Fla., Miami, 1991—. Instr. U. Md., Hanau, Fed. Republic Germany, 1977-78, Embry Riddle U., Homestead, Fla., 1978-79. Maj., asst. staff judge adv. U.S. Army, 1974-79. Recipient Arthur S. Fleming award Washington Jaycees, 1982, Superior Performance award U.S. Dept. Justice; named one of Outstanding Young Men of Am., 1984. Mem. Assn. Trial Lawyers Am., Nat. Bar Assn., Fed. Bar Assn. (so. Fla. pres. 1984-85, treas. 1982-83), Fla. Bar Assn., N.Y. Bar Assn., Ohio Bar Assn., Wilkie D. Ferguson Jr. Bar Assn., NAACP, Alpha Phi Alpha. Democrat. Baptist. Avocations: fishing, reading. Office: US Courthouse 99 NE 4th St Rm 1155 Miami FL 33132-2138

GRAHAM, DOROTHY E., elementary school educator; b. Orangeburg County, S.C., Jan. 13, 1941; d. Benjamin Howard Easterlin and Charlie Belle Murray; m. Thomas Wayne Graham, Sept. 3, 1959; children: Janet Elizabeth, Katherine Elaine. BA with hon., McNeese State U., 1967; diploma in religious edn., New Orleans Bapt. Theol. Sem., 1963; diploma in Japanese lang. and culture, Kansai Gakuin U., 1971. Cert. tchr. State of Fla., 1996. Elem. sch. tchr. Lake Charles Sch. Dist., La., 1967—68; missionary, tchr. Japan Bapt. Conv., Kobe, 1968—94; min. children First Bapt. Ch., Ft. Myers, Fla., 1994—96; tchr. elem. sch. Lee Dist. Sch., 1996—. Dir., organizer 100 Voice Children's Chorus, Cape Coral, 2000—06, After Sch. Arts Programs Children, Cape Coral, Fla., 2000—04, Japanese Children's Chorus, Kobe, 1986—93; choral dir., organizer City Wide Cmty. Chorus, Kobe, 1980—94; dir., organizer. sr. chorus First Bapt. Ch., Ft. Myers, 1994—96. Recipient Mayor's award for Outstanding Cmty. Svc., City Kobe, Japan Mayor Miyazaki, 1992, Outstanding Tchr. award, C. of C., 2000—01, 2001—02, Sam's Club Outstanding Tchr. Yr., Sam's Club Stores, Ft. Myers, Fl, 2003. Mem.: Fla. Music Educator's Assn. Avocations: travel, reading, classical music. Home: 1230 Braman Avenue Fort Myers FL 33901 Office: Cape Elementary School 4519 Vincennes Blvd Cape Coral FL 33904 Personal E-mail: grahamprs@aol.com.

GRAHAM, FRANCES KEESLER (MRS. DAVID TREDWAY GRAHAM), psychologist, educator; b. Canastota, N.Y., Aug. 1, 1918; d. Clyde C. and Norma (Van Surdam) Keesler; m. David Tredway Graham, June 14, 1941; children: Norma, Andrew, Mary. BA, Pa. State U., 1938; PhD, Yale U., 1942; DSc (hon.), U. Wis., 1996. Acting dir. St. Louis Psychiat. Clinic, 1942-44; instr. Barnard Coll., 1948-51; research assoc. Sch. Medicine, Washington U., St. Louis, 1942-48, 53-57, U. Wis., Madison, 1957-64, asso. prof. pediatrics and psychology, 1964-68, prof., 1968-86, Hilldale research prof., 1980-86; prof. U. Del., Newark, 1986-89, prof. emerita, 1989—. Disting. faculty lectr., U. Del., Newark, 1989; cons. Nat. Inst. Neurol. Diseases and Blindness perinatal research br.; mem. exptl. psychology research review com. NIMH, 1970-74, NRC, 1971-74; mem. bd. sci. counselors NIMH, 1977-81, chmn., 1979-81; mem. Pres.'s Commn. for Study of Ethical Problems in Medicine and Biomed. and Behavioral Research, 1980-82 Mem. editorial bd. Jour. Exptl. Child Psychology, 1964-67, Child Devel., 1966-68, Jour. Exptl. Psychology, 1968-73, Psychophysiology, 1968-73; contbr. articles to profl. jours. Recipient Rsch. Scientist award NIMH, 1964-89, Disting. Alumna award Pa. State U., 1983, Wilbur L. Cross medal Yale U., 1992, Gold medal Am. Psychol. Found., 1995. Fellow AAAS (chmn. sect. psychology 1979, mem. nominations com. 1992-95), APA (coun. 1975-77, pres. div. physiol. and comparative psychology 1978-79, G. Stanley Hall award 1982, Disting. Scientist award 1990); mem. NAS, Am. Psychol. Soc. (William James fellow 1990), Soc. Rsch. Child Devel. (council 1965-71, pres. 1975-77, Disting. Sci. Contbns. award 1991), Soc. Psychophysiol. Rsch. (dir. 1968-71, 72-75, pres. 1973-74, Disting. Contbns. award 1981), Soc. Exptl. Psychologists, Soc. Neurosci., Fedn. Behavioral Psychol. and Cognitive Scis. (exec. com. 1991-94), Psychonomic Soc., Acoustical Soc. Am., Internat. Soc. Devel. Psychobiology, Phi Beta Kappa, Sigma Xi. Home: 311 Dove Dr Newark DE 19713-1211 E-mail: fkgraham@udel.edu.

GRAHAM, FRED PATTERSON, news correspondent, journalist; b. Little Rock, Oct. 6, 1931; s. Otis Livingstone and Lois (Patterson) G.; m. Lucile McCrea, Dec. 28, 1961 (div. March 1982); children— Grier, David Silliman, Alyse; m. 2d Skila Harris, Sept. 11, 1982. BA, Yale U., 1953; LL.B., Vanderbilt U., 1959; diploma in law, Oxford U., 1960. Bar: Tenn., 1959, D.C., 1974. Atty. Trabue, Sturdivant & Harbison, Nashville, 1960-63; chief counsel subcom. constl. amendments U.S. Senate, Washington, 1963; spl. asst. to sec. US Dept. Labor, Washington, 1964-65; Supreme Ct. corr. N.Y. Times, N.Y.C., 1965-72; law corr. CBS News, Washington, 1972-87; anchor, sr. editor Sta. WKRN-TV, Nashville, 1987-89; chief anchor, mng. editor Courtroom TV Network, N.Y.C., 1989—. Regents lectr. Boalt Sch. Law, U. Calif., Berkeley, 1982. Author: The Self Inflicted Wound, 1970, Press Freedom Under Pressure, 1972, The Alias Program, 1977, Happy Talk, 1990. Mem. bd. Boalt Hall Trust, 1985-90; bd. dirs. Nat. Constitution Ctr., 1987-90; trustee Reporters Com. for Freedom of Press, 1969-77, 87—. 1st lt. USMCR, 1953-56 Recipient George Foster Peabody award, 1975, 3 Emmy awards Am. Acad. TV Arts and Scis., 1974; Fulbright scholar, 1960; named Disting. Alumnus of the Year, Vanderbilt U., 1992 Office: Courtroom TV Network 600 3rd Ave New York NY 10016-1901*

GRAHAM, GEORGE ANDREW, JR., psychologist, consultant; b. Bakersfield, Calif., Dec. 7, 1930; s. George Andrew Graham and Mary Pearl Sandidge; m. Patricia Anne Phillips, June 19, 1953; children: G. Andrew III, Ronald Glen, Holly Anne Meikle. BA, U. Redlands, 1952; BD, Andover Newtown Theol. Sch., 1956; MA, Boston U., 1956; M in Sacred Theology, Union Theol. Sch., N.Y.C., 1957; postgrad., U. Chgo., 1957-60, 69-70; PhD, Marquette U., 1974. Lic. psychologist, Wis. Min. young adults Old S. Ch., Boston, 1952-55; min. youth 1st Bapt. Ch., Mt. Vernon, NY, 1955—57, min., chaplain Iowa City, 1960-63; lab sch. psychologist U. Chgo., 1957-60; chaplain U. Redlands, Calif., 1963-70; assoc. McGinley & Co., Milw., 1970-73; asst. v.p. personnel divsn. 1st Wis. (became Firstar, then US Bank), Milw., 1973-75, dir. employment and devel., 1975-77, v.p., 1977-81, 1st v.p., 1981-85, dir. employment, counseling, devel. and tng., 1985-88; 1st v.p. Firstar Corp., 1988-92; pres. Graham Consulting, Waukesha, Wis., 1992—. Adj. prof. U. Wis., Milw., 1978-88. Pres. Wis. chpt. Leukemia Soc. Am., Wis. Epilepsy Assn., Lad Lake; bd. dirs. Wis. Sch. Profl. Psychology, Wis. Conservatory Music, Wis. Coun. Econ. Edn.; personnel com. ARC; chmn. pers. com. United Way, Milw.; exec. com. Potawatomi Area coun. Boy Scouts Am. Recipient Silver Beaver award Boy Scouts Am., 1988. Mem. Am. Psychol. Assn., Soc. Indls. and Orgnl. Psychologists, Human Resource Planning Soc., Univ. Club Milw. Republican. Home and Office: N8W30095 Woodcrest Dr Waukesha WI 53188 Office Phone: 262-968-5814. E-mail: g1207@msn.com.

GRAHAM, GLORIA FLIPPIN, dermatologist; b. Durham, N.C., Mar. 3, 1935; d. James Meigs and Ida Mae (Boyd) F.; m. Douglas Graham (div.); 1 child, Wayne Meigs; m. James Herbert Graham, July 29, 1989. BS, Wake Forest U., 1957; MD, Bowman-Gray Sch. Medicine, 1961. Diplomate Am. Bd. Dermatology. Intern Sch. Medicine Vanderbilt U., 1961-62; resident, dermatology U. Va. Med. Ctr., Charlottesville, 1962-65; pvt. practice Columbia, S.C., 1965-66; attending physician Crystal Coast Dermatology Svcs., P.A., Morehead City, N.C., 2000; physician, owner Wilson (N.C.) Dermatology Clinic, 1966-94; physician, pres. Grahams' Dermatology Svcs., Morehead City, NC, 1992—2005; attending physician Crystal Coast Dermatology Svcs., P.A., Morehead City, NC, 2000—01; physician, pres. Down East Med. Assocs., Morehead City, 2005—. Cons. Carteret Gen. Hosp., Morehead City, 1986-2000; clin. attending prof. Bowman Gray Sch. Medicine, Winston-Salem, N.C., 1991-2000; adj. clin. prof. U. N.C. Sch. Medicine, Chapel Hill, 1995-2001; assoc. prof. dermatology Wake Forest U. Med. Sch., 2001-2004, bd. visitors, 2003— Co-exhibitor: Two Hereditary Osseocutaneous Syndromes, Acad. Dermatology, 1965 (Silver award), So. Med. Assn. Exhibit Hereditary Acrokeratotic Poikiloderma, 1970 (Third Place award). Named Woman of Yr., Women's Residence Coun. Wake Forest U., 1982, Practitioner of Yr., Dermatology Found., 1998. Mem.: Internat. Soc. Cryosurgery (v.p. 2001—05, honorary mem. 2005), Women's Dermatologic Soc. (pres. 1997—98, Rose Hirschler award 2001), Am. Dermatologic Assn. (elect), Am. Acad. Dermatology (bd. dirs. 1991—96, audit com. 1996—2000, ethics com. 1996—2001, nominating com. 2002—, chair nominating com. 2003, honorary mem. 2005, Fox award 2003), N.Am. Clin. Dermatologic Soc. (bd. dirs. 1995—2001), World Congress Dermatology (co-chmn. cryosurgical symposium 1997, 2001), Wake Forest U. Sch. Medicine Alumni Assn. (bd. dirs.). Avocations: travel, fishing. Home: 106 Cypress Dr Pine Knoll Shores NC 28513-6706 Personal E-mail: ggfgraham@aol.com. Business E-Mail: ggraham@wfubmc.edu.

GRAHAM, HARDY MOORE, lawyer; b. Meridian, Miss., Oct. 21, 1912; s. Sanford Martin and Mary Emma (Hardy) G.; Cora Lee Poindexter, Oct. 26, 1938; children: Hardy Poindexter, Richard Newell. Student, U. So. Calif., 1932; BA, LLB, U. Miss., 1934. Bar: Miss. 1934, Tenn. 1946, U.S. Ct. Appeals (D.C. cir.) 1943, U.S. Dist. Ct. Miss. 1934, U.S. Supreme Ct. 1943, U.S. Dist. Ct. (we. dist.) Tenn. 1952. Ptnr. Graham & Graham, Meridian, 1934-43; atty. FTC, Washington, 1943-44; pvt. practice Union City, Tenn., 1946—2000. City judge City of Union City, 1950-58; bd. dirs., 1st v.p. Meridian Coca-Cola Bottling Co., 1964-97; ptnr. Union City Coca-Cola Bottling Co.; v.p. Coca-Cola Coin Caterers Corp. 7-Up Bottler; pres. Tenn. Soft Drink Assn., 1963-65. Mayor City of Union City, 1950-58; pres. Union City C. of C., 1948-50, bd. dirs.; chmn. March of Dimes, Obion County Tenn., 1947; mem. Union City Sch. Bd., 1958-66, vice chmn., 1958-60, chmn., 1964-66; chmn. indsl. bd. Union City, 1968-97; bd. dirs. Tenn. Mcpl. League, 1950-58, pres., 1956-57; former trustee Union U., Jackson, Tenn., 1st Bapt. Ch., Union City; pres. U. Tenn. Martin Devel. Com., 1970-72; mem. U. Tenn., Knoxville Devel. Coun., 1970-75, 82-85, bd. dirs. U. Miss. Found., 1987-93. Lt. USNR, 1944-46, ETO. Named Law Alumnus of Yr., U. Miss. Law Sch., 1984, Young Man of Yr., Union City, 1948; recipient Disting. Svc. award U. Tenn., Martin, 1989, U. Miss. Hall of Fame Disting. Alumnus award, 1989; Union City named Graham Park in his honor, 1986. Mem. ABA, Tenn. Bar Assn., Miss. Bar Assn., Union City-Obion County Bar Assn., (pres. 1948-49, past. bd. dirs.), Meridian Country Club, Union City Country Club, Rotary (pres. Union City 1963-64, Paul Harris fellow). Republican. Baptist. Avocation: international travel. Home: 630 E Main St Union City TN 38261-3515 Office: 1915 E Reelfoot Ave Union City TN 38261-6007

GRAHAM, HEATHER, actress; b. Milw., Jan. 29, 1970; Motion picture actress. Films include License to Drive, 1988, Drugstore Cowboy, 1989, I Love You to Death, 1990, Guilty as Charged, 1991, Diggstown, 1992, 6 Degrees of Separation, 1993, Don't Do It, 1994, Swingers, 1996, Boogie Nights, 1997 (MTV movie award 1998), Scream 2, 1997, Austin Powers: The Spy Who Shagged Me, 1999, Bowfinger, 1999, Kiss & Tell, 2000, Sidewalks of New York, 2001, From Hell, 2001, Killing Me Softly, 2002, The Guru, 2002, Alien Love Triangle, 2002, Hope Springs, 2003, Blessed, 2004, Gray Matters, 2005; T.V. series include Twin Peaks, 1990, 92, Scrubs. Recipient ShoWest award for Female Star of Tomorrow, 1999. Office: Creative Artists Agency 9830 Wilshire Blvd Beverly Hills CA 90211*

GRAHAM, HOWARD BARRETT, publishing company executive; b. Boston, Dec. 7, 1929; s. Robert M. and Belle (Brown) G.; m. Rita J. Mahony; children: Ronni M., Erica. BA, Syracuse U., 1951. Gen. mgr. sch. supply div., sales mgr. ednl. div. Milton Bradley Co., Springfield, Mass., 1954-63; gen. mgr. jr. book div. McGraw-Hill Co., 1964-69; pres., dir. Franklin Watts Inc., N.Y.C., 1970-87; also chmn. bd. Franklin Watts Ltd.; sr. v.p. mktg/product devel., dir. Grolier, Inc., 1983-89, exec. v.p., 1988-89; pres. Grolier Internat., 1986-89; chmn., chief exec. officer Graham Internat. Pub. and Rsch., Inc., 1989—; ptnr. SMG Assocs., 1990; dir., v.p. The Millbrook Press, 1990-96, chmn. bd. dirs., 1997—; pres., CEO Chambers Kingfisher Graham, Publishers Inc., 1994-96. Mem. adv. bd. Internat. Exec. Svc., 1994-98. Served with USAF, 1951-53. Mem. Mensa, Save the Children (adv. bd. mem. 1994-98). Home: PO Box 77 Sagaponack NY 11962-0077 Office: 27 Main St # A Southampton NY 11968-4808 E-mail: gipr2@aol.com.

GRAHAM, HOWARD LEE, SR., finance company executive; b. Monroe, Mich., May 26, 1942; s. Carl Lee and Myrtle Leota (Manis) G.; m. Bobbie Jo Hamilton; children: Kimber Lee, Howard Lee Jr., Jacquelyn Leota, John-Nathan Howard. Grad., Dake Bible Sch., Atlanta, 1960-62; student, Cen. Bible Coll., Springfield, Mo., 1964-67; grad., Internat. Sem., 1993, DD, 1996. Debit agt. Met. Life Ins. Co., Colorado Springs, Colo., 1963-64, agt. Allen Park, Mich., 1964-67, 68; agy. mgr. Preferred Risk Life Ins. Co., Allen Park, 1968-72; agy. owner Howard Graham Ins. Agy., Taylor, Mich., 1972-85; spl. agt., rep. Prudential Ins. Co., Cleve., 1985-89; regional mgr. Primerica Fin. Svcs., Abingdon, Va., 1995—; pres. Graham & Graham Canvas Shoppe, Inc., 1976-95, CEO, 1995—. Pres. Graham Enterprises, Cleve., 1985—; CEO Graham & Graham Canvas Shoppe, Inc., 1976; nat. and regional sales leader Preferred Risk Ins. Co., Des Moines, 1969-72. Life mem. Full Gospel Bus. Men's Fellow, Detroit, 1963-85, officer, 1974-80, officer, Cleve., 1985—; active Gideons Internat., Cleve., 1963—; pres. Truth Alive, Inc., 1988—; Bible tchr., missionary. Named Central Region Agt. of Yr., 1985; admitted to Million Dollar Round Table, 1985, Hall of Honor, 1986. Mem. Indsl. Fabrics Assn. Internat., Am. Coll., Nat. Assn. Life Underwriters, Internat. Platform Assn. Republican. Mem. Pentecostal Ch. Avocations: sports, bible research.

GRAHAM, JAMES C., food service executive; m. Becky Graham; 3 children. BSBA, Kans. State U., 1972. With Mid-Ctrl. Fish & Frozen Foods, Inc., 1969—74, mktg. assoc., 1974—78, mgr. direct sales, 1978—80; v.p. mktg. Sysco Corp. (formerly Mid-Ctrl. Fish & Frozen Foods, Inc.), 1980—85; exec. v.p. Sysco Corp., 1986—88, pres., CEO, 1988—2000, sr. v.p. food svc. ops. Olathe, Kans., 2000—. Office: Sysco Corp 1915 Kansas City Rd Olathe KS 66061

GRAHAM, JAMES CHRISTOPHER, psychologist, consultant; s. J. Keith and Barbara Ann Graham; m. L. Jill Graham, Mar. 21, 1998; 1 child, Eben. BA magna cum laude, Wichita State U., 1980; MA, U. Tex., 1994, PhD, 1997. Rsch. specialist Tex. Dept. Protective and Regulatory Services, Austin, 1997—2000; statistician, rsch. supr. State of Wash. Dept. of Social and Health Svcs., Office Children's Adminstrn. Rsch., Seattle, 2000—. Contbr. articles to profl. jours.; author reports in field. Dir. Friends Along the Rd., Fort Myers, Fla., 2002. Fellow, U. Tex., Austin, 1982—84; Leader scholar, Wichita State U., 1976—80, Postdoctoral fellowship, NIH, 2001—03. Mem.: Soc. for Personality and Social Psychology, Puget Sound Mycol. Soc., Am. Psychol. Soc., Am. Statis. Assn., Phi Kappa Phi, Omicron Delta Kappa, Sigma Xi. Office: Office of Children's Admin Research Ste 400 4045 Delridge Way SW Seattle WA 98106 E-mail: gchr300@dshs.wa.gov.

GRAHAM, JANET LORRAINE, music educator; b. Halifax, NC, Jan. 15, 1947; d. Lloyd Cartez and Waline Wilkins; m. Aaron Richard Graham, June 21, 1969; children: Andrea Yvonne, Aaron Richard II. BA, NC Ctrl. U., 1969. Cert. music tchr. N.C., Ohio, N.J. 4th grade tchr., H.S. chorus dir. Scotland Neck (NC) Schs., 1969; elem./jr. high music tchr. Akron (Ohio) schs., 1969—71; gen. music tchr. grades K-6 Bergenfield (NJ) schs., 1971—. Composer: (songs) Lessons for Kindergarten, 2005. Bd. dirs. Bergen Philharm., Englewood, NJ, 1997—. Named Tchr. of Yr., State of NJ Dept. Edn., 1994. Mem.: NEA, No. NJ Orff Schulwerk Assn. (pres. 1999—2002), Bergenfield Edn. Assn., Tri-M Music Honor Soc. (life), Zeta Phi Beta. Achievements include featured in music textbooks on music methods. Avocations: travel, reading, dance. Home: 86 Church St Teaneck NJ 07666 Personal E-mail: Janyvo25@yahoo.com.

GRAHAM, JEWEL FREEMAN, social worker, lawyer, educator; b. Springfield, Ohio, May 3, 1925; d. Robert Lee and Lula Belle Freeman; m. Paul N. Graham, Aug. 8, 1953; children: Robert, Nathan. BA, Fisk U., 1946; student, Howard U., 1946-47; MS in Social Svc. Adminstrn., Case Western Res. U., 1953; JD, U. Dayton, 1979; LHD (hon.), Meadville-Lombard Theol. Sch., 1991. Bar: Ohio; cert. social worker. Assoc. dir. teenage program dept. YWCA, Grand Rapids, Mich., 1947-50, coord. met. teenage program Detroit, 1953-56; dir. program for interracial edn. Antioch Coll., Yellow Springs, Ohio, 1964-69, from asst. prof. to prof., 1969-92, prof. emeritus, 1992—.

Mem. Ohio Commn. on Dispute Resolution and Conflict Mgmt., 1990-92. Mem. exec. com. World YWCA, Geneva, 1975-83, 87—, pres., 1983; bd. dirs. YWCA of the U.S.A., 1970-89, pres., 1979-85; bd. dirs. Antioch U., 1994-96. Named to Greene County Women's Hall of Fame, 1982, Ohio Women's Hall of Fame, 1988; named 1 of 10 Outstanding Women of Miami Valley, 1987; recipient Ambassador award YWCA of the U.S.A., 1993. Mem. ABA, Nat. Assn. of Social Workers (charter), Nat. Coun. of Negro Women (life), Alpha Kappa Alpha. Democrat. Unitarian Universalist. Avocations: bicycling, swimming, walking, needlecrafts. Office: Antioch Coll Livermore 51 Yellow Springs OH 45387 E-mail: jewelg@aol.com.

GRAHAM, JOHN H., IV, health science association administrator; BA, Franklin and Marshall Coll., 1971. Mem. Valley Forge coun. Boy Scouts Am., 1971—79; exec. dir. Am. Diabetes Assn., Phila., 1979—83, dir. devel. divsn. N.Y.C., 1983—85, asst. exec. v.p. Alexandria, Va., 1985—88, dep. exec. v.p., 1988—90, CEO, 1990—2003; pres., CEO Am Soc. Assn. Executives, 2003—. Mem.: Combined Health Appeal, Independent Sector, Greater Washington Soc. Assn. Execs., Nat. Health Coun., Am. Soc. Assn. Execs. Office: Am Society of Assn Executives 1575 I St NW Washington DC 20005*

GRAHAM, JOHN HAMILTON, II, professional athletics manager; b. Waynesboro, Va., Mar. 30, 1960; s. John Hamilton and Joan (Clay) G. BA in Polit. Sci., Christopher Newport Coll., 1983; DD, Am. Fellowship, 1986. Notary pub.: Va., Ga. Dir. pub. rels. Peninsula Pilots (minor league affiliate Phila. Phillies), Hampton, Va., 1977-79, dir. broadcasting and pub. rels., 1979-81, asst. gen. mgr., 1981-85; v.p., gen. mgr. Peninsula White Sox (minor league affiliate Chgo. White Sox), Hampton, 1985-87; gen. mgr. Auburn (NY) Astros Baseball Club, 1988-92; pres. Sports of the Peninsula, Hampton, 1992-94; customer svc. specialist Airborne Express, Atlanta, 1994-96; sr. agt., night ops. mgr. Airborne Express Internat., College Park, Ga., 1996—2001; chmn. Peninsula Pro Baseball Hall of Fame, Hampton, 1993; pres. Graham Web Wizard; pres., CEO Field of Dreams Cmtys.; pres., gen. mgr. Blackstone Bomber Pilots. Vice-chmn. Rep. Nat. Com., 1981, Rep. Party Va., Hampton, 1982-92; election bd., election ofcl. Commonwealth of Va., Hampton, 1985-95; chmn. Field of Dreams Cmty.; notary pub. Commonwealth of Va., Richmond, 1988—; mem. Carolina League Champion Peninsula Pilots, 1977, 80, 97, Confederate Meml. Soc., Va. Air and Space Mus., Va. Living Mus., NRA, Va. Sheriffs Inst., Smithsonian Assn., Rep. Presdl. Task Force, Sons of Confederate Soldiers, Rep. Party Platform Planning Com., Spl. Olympics, Nat. Rep. Senatorial Com., Presdl. Trust; pres. Virtual U.S. Polit. Simulation; exec. v.p. Clay's Rest Home, Graham Retirement Ctr. Named Broadcaster of Yr. Carolina League, Hampton, 1980, 81, 85, 87, Exec. of Yr. NY Penn League, Auburn, 1991; named to Peninsula Pro Baseball Hall of Fame, 1992, Hampton Rds. Baseball Hall of Fame, 1994, Auburn Baseball Hall of Fame, 1993; recipient Bill Dancy award Phila. Phillies, 1987. Mem. NRA, Nat. Assn. Writers and Broadcasters, Assn. Profl. Ballplayers Am. (life), Probaseball Execs. Assn. (pres.), Baseball USA, Smithsonian Instn., Nature Conservancy, Mus. of the Confederacy, Va. Air and Space Ctr., Va. Living Mus., Vietnam Vets. Meml. Fund, Va. Sheriffs Inst., Pro Baseball Broadcasters USA (pres.), Major League Baseball Alumni Assn., Minor League Baseball Alumni Assn., Players Alumni Assn., Va. Retirement Assn. (chmn.), First Family of Va., USA Freedom Corps, Moose, Am. Legion, Baseball USA, Baseball Club, Va. League, Notary. Avocations: tennis, art. Personal E-mail: jhg@shgraham.net. E-mail: john@johngraham.net.

GRAHAM, JOHN ROBERT, JR., financial executive; b. Chgo., Oct. 11, 1930; s. John Robert and Grace Beatrice (Strangeman) G.; m. Bettina Abigail Hoffman, Sept. 6, 1958 (div. June 1975); children: Jonathan, Karl; m. Beverly Criley, Dec. 31, 1975. BS, U.S. Mcht. Marine Acad., 1952; MBA, Harvard U., 1959. Ship officer Moore-McCormack Lines, N.Y.C., 1952-53, 55-58; asst. v.p., loan officer Hartford (Conn.) Nat. Bank, 1959-67; asst. treas. Heublein, Inc., Hartford, 1967-68, treas., 1968-74; sr. v.p. fin. and adminstrn. Sikorsky Aircraft Co., Stratford, Conn., 1974-80; v.p. fin., CFO Planning Rsch. Corp., Washington, 1980-82; v.p., CFO Uniroyal Inc., Middlebury, Conn., 1982-88, Uniroyal Holding, Inc., Waterbury, Conn., 1982-88, also bd. dirs.; v.p. fin., CFO, treas., dir. Healthware Corp., Seattle, 1989-92. Bd. dirs. Uniroyal Goodrich Tire Co., Akron, Ohio, U.S. Mcht. Marine Acad. Found.; trustee CDU Holding, Inc. Liquidating Trust, N.Y.C., 1986—. Co-author: Nonwoven Textiles-An Unbiased Appraisal, 1959. Corporator Middlesex Hosp., Middletown, Conn., 1964-85; v.p., treas. Conn. Valley YMCA, Deep River, 1962-64; pres. Essex (Conn.) Bus. Assn., 1964-65; bd. dirs. U.S. Mcht. Marine Acad. Found., 1987—. Lt. (j.g.) USNR, 1953-55, PTO, Korea. Mem. Harvard Club (N.Y.C.), Masons. Avocations: sailing, skiing. Home: 1806 Bellevue Way NE Bellevue WA 98004 Office Phone: 203-720-1427. Personal E-mail: cascade82@aol.com.

GRAHAM, JORIE, writer, educator; b. N.Y.C., May 9, 1951; d. Curtis Bell and Beverly (Stoll) Pepper; m. James Galvin. BFA, NYU, 1973; MFA, U. Iowa, 1978. Asst. prof. Murray (Ky.) State U., 1978-79, Humboldt State U., Arcata, Calif., 1979-81; instr. Columbia U., N.Y.C., 1981-83; mem. staff U. Iowa, Iowa City, 1983—99, prof. English, dir. Writer's Workshop, 1999; Boylston Prof. of Oratory and Rhetoric Harvard U., 1999—. Poetry editor Crazy Horse, 1978-81; chancellor Acad. Am. Poets, 1997-2003. Author: Hybrids of Plants and of Ghosts, 1980 (Great Lakes Colls. Assn. award 1981), Erosion, 1983, The End of Beauty, 1987, Region of Unlikeness, 1991, Materialism, 1993, The Dream of the Unified Field: Selected Poems 1974-94, 1995, The Errancy, 1997, Swarm, 1999, Never, 2002, Overlord, 2005; editor: Earth Took of Earth: 100 Great Poems of the English Language, 1996; co-editor: The Best American Poetry 1990. Recipient Am. Acad. Poets award, 1977, Young Poet prize Poetry Northwest, 1980, Pushcart prize, 1980, 82, American Poetry Review prize, 1982, Pulitzer prize in poetry, 1996, Lavan award Acad. Am. Poets, 1991, Martin Zaubel award Acad. and Inst. of Arts and Letters, 1992; Bunting fellow Radcliff Inst., 1982, Guggenheim fellow, 1983, John D. and Catherine T. MacArthur Found. fellow, 1990; grantee Ingram-Merrill Found., 1981. Office: Harvard U English Dept Barker Cntr 12 Quincey St Cambridge MA 02138*

GRAHAM, K(ATHLEEN) M. (K. M. GRAHAM), artist; b. Hamilton, Ont., Can., Sept. 13, 1913; d. Charles and G. Blanche (Leitch) Howitt; m. J. Wallace Graham, Dec. 17, 1938; children: John Wallace, Janet Howitt. BA, U. Toronto, Ont., 1936. (one-woman shows) Carmen Lamanna Gallery, Toronto, 1967, Trinity Coll., U. Toronto, 1968, Founders Coll., York U., Toronto, 1970, Pollock Gallery, Toronto, 1971,73,75, Art Gallery Coburg, Ont., 1973, City Hall, Toronto, 1974, David Mirvish Gallery Gallery, Toronto, 1976, Klonaridis, Inc., Toronto, 1978, Watson-Willour Gallery, Houston, 1980, Downstairs Gallery, Edmonton, Alta., 1980, 82, Lillian Heidenberg Gallery, N.Y.C., 1981,86, Klonaridis, Inc., Toronto, 1981-85, 87, 88, 90, ELCA London Gallery, Montreal, Que., Can., 1983, MacDonald-Stewart Art Centre, Guelph, Ont., 1984, Glenbow Mus., Calgary, 1984, Concordia Gallery, Montreal, 1984, Hart House Gallery, Toronto, 1985, Lillian Heidenberg Gallery, N.Y.C., 1986, Klondaridis Inc., Toronto, 1985, 87, 88, 90, 91, Feheley Fine Arts, Toronto, 1989, Douglas Udell Gallery, Vancouver, 1993, Meml. Art Gallery, St. Johns, N.F., 1994, Beaverbrook Gallery, Fredericton, N.B., 1994, Costin and Klintworth, Toronto, Ont., 1994, 95, The Art Gallery of Ont., 1997, The Moore Gallery, Toronto, 2000, 2001, (group shows) Montreal Mus. Fine Arts, 1976, Hirshhorn Mus., Washington, 1977, Edmonton (Alta., Can.) Art Gallery, 1977, Norman MacKenzie Art Gallery, Regina, Sask., Can., 1977, David Mirvish Gallery, Toronto, Watson De Nagy Gallery, Houston, Galerie Wentzel, Hamburg, Fed. Republic Germany, Beaverbrook Gallery, Fredericton, N.B., Associated Am. Artists, N.Y.C., 1986, 88, Elca London, Montreal, 1987, Klondaris Inc., Toronto, 1987, 91, Douglas Udell Gallery, Vancouver, 1987, Associated Am. Artists, N.Y.C., 1988, Feheley Fine Art, Toronto, 1989, (other) (traveling shows) CanadaxTen, 1974, The Can. Canvas, 1975-76, Changing Visions, 1976-77, The Shell Canada Collection, 1977, The Fauve Heritage, 1997, 14 Canadians Hirschhorn Mus., Washington, 1977, Certain Traditions, 1978, 79, (travelling shows) Bolduc Fournier Graham, 1981, The Heritage of Jack Bush, 1981-82, Selections from the Westburne Collection, 1982-83, (permanent collections) Nat. Gallery Can., Ottawa, Edmonton Art Gallery, Art Gallery Ont., Art Gallery Hamilton, Ont., MacDonald-Stewart Art Gallery, Guelph, Ont., Toronto City Hall, The Brit. Mus., London, Art Gallery Vancouver, Agnes Etherington Art Centre, Kingston, Ont., Can., Musee d'Art Contemporarin Montreal, Beaverbrook Art Gallery, Fredericton, N.B., Art Gallery Nfld.and Labrador, Art Gallery, Peterborough, Ont., Robert McLaughlin Gallery, Oshawa, Ont., Kitchener Waterloo Art Gallery, McMichael Can. Art Gallery, Hart House Art Gallery, Toronto, also numerous corp. collections. Hon. fellow Trinity Coll., U. Toronto, 1988. Mem. Royal Can. Acad.

GRAHAM, KENNETH ROBERT, psychologist, educator; b. Phila., June 5, 1943; s. Edgar and Margit (Leafgreen) Graham; m. Michele Carolyn Monroe, Aug. 10, 1968; children: Mark Andrew, Richard Alan. BA, U. Pa., 1964; PhD, Stanford U., 1969. Lic. psychologist, Pa. Asst. prof. Muhlenberg Coll., Allentown, Pa., 1970-77, assoc. prof., 1977-84, prof., 1984-99, emeritus prof., 1999—, head psychology dept., 1984-93; rsch. psychologist Unit for Exptl. Psychiatry Inst. of Pa. Hosp., Phila., 1969-70; adj. asst. prof. U. Pa., Phila., 1969-70. Cons. smoking cessation various hosps., 1985-1999. Author: (text) Psychological Research, 1977; asst. editor Am. Jour. Clin. Hypnosis, 1974-95; contbr. over 30 articles to profl. and sci. jours. Bd. dirs., pres. Lehigh Valley Child Care, Allentown, 1979-85; advisor Pathways (Conf. of Chs.), Allentown, 1989-98, N.E. Pa. Synod Luth. Ch. in Am., Wescosville, Pa., 1989-93. Mem. APA (pres. divsn. psychol. hypnosis 1980-81), European Soc. Hypnosis in Psychotherapy and Psychosomatic Medicine, Kiwanis (pres. Allentown chpt. 1991-92, lt. gov. Pa. dist. 1994-95). Democrat. Avocations: swimming, collecting glass paperweights and signatures of 19th century explorers. Office: Muhlenberg Coll Psychology Dept Allentown PA 18104 E-mail: krg6543@aol.com.

GRAHAM, LANIER, art historian, curator; b. Shawnee, Okla., Mar. 6, 1940; s. Floyd and Martha Graham; m. Gloria K. Smith; 1 child, Jennifer R. Ulrich. BA in Internat. Polit. & Cultural Rels., Am. U., 1963; MA in Art History, Columbia U., 1966. Planner cultural instns., 1965—; assoc. curator architecture and design Mus. Modern Art, N.Y.C., 1965-70; curator of paintings and sculpture, renaissance to modern Fine Arts Mus., San Francisco, 1970-76; curator Cultural Resource Mgmt. Ctr., San Francisco, 1976-83; curator of prints and books Australian Nat. Gallery, Canberra, 1984-87; curator of paintings, sculpture and prints, renaissance to modern Norton Simon Mus. Art, Pasadena, Calif., 1987-91; dir. Art Info. Ctr. - An Info. Svc., Northbank, Calif., 1991-97, Univ. Art Gallery, Calif. State U., Hayward, 1998—. Art history lectr., religious studies, mus. studies educator U. Calif., Berkeley, John F. Kennedy U., Calif. Inst. Asian Studies, Naropa Inst., Boulder, Humboldt State U., Arcata, Calif. State U., Hayward, 1977—. Author: Leonardo's Book Illustrations, 1961, Botticelli's Dante, 1963, Mies van der Rohe Drawings, 1966, The Architecture of Louis I. Kahn, 1966, Chess Sets, 1968, Hector Guimard, 1970, Three Centuries of American Painting, 1971, Three Centuries of French Art, vol. 1, 1973, vol. 2, 1975, Claude Monet, 1974, Brother Sun & Sister Moon: Alchemical Symbols in Traditional and Modern Art, 1979, Illustrated Books of Henri Matisse, 1979, Leonardo & the Androgyne: Nonduality in World Art, 1980, Decades of Light: Early Modern French Painting, 1980, The Spontaneous Gesture: Prints and Books of the Abstract Expressionist Era, 1987, Vincent Van Gogh: Painter, Printmaker, Collector, 1990, The Prints of Willem de Kooning: A Catalogue Raisonné, vol. 1, 1991, Impossible Realities: Marcel Duchamp and the Surrealist Tradition, 1991, Sacred Visions: A Survey of World Art and Architecture, vol. 1, 1991, vol. 2, 1992, The Double Serpent: Symbol of Transformation in World Art, 1993, Rhythms and Reverberations: Multicultural Art in the United States and its Development from the Tribal World, 1993, Solidity and Infinity: The Symbolism of the Circle and Square in World Architecture, 1995, Goddesses in Art, 1997, Life, Death and Laughter: The Art of Masami Teraoka, 1998, The Art of the Book: The Modern Livre d'Artiste, 1999, Duchamp and Androgyny: Art, Gender, and Metaphysics, 2003; collections of poetry include Nature Poems, 1958, The Sin of 100 Debts, 1967, Heavy Light: Haiku on the Theme of Modern Physics & Ancient Wisdom, 1978, Electro-Magnetism: Poems on the Theme of Complementarity, 1982, Fragments of Feelings: Selected Poems, 1994, Undulations of Eternity: Collected Poems, 1994; gen. editor: The Rainbow Book: Color-...from Ancient to Modern Times, 1975, 76, rev. edit., 1979, Rodin Graphics: A Catalogue Raisonné, 1975, American Art from the Collection of Mr. and Mrs. John D. Rockefeller 3d, 1976, Giorgione & the Experts: A Documentary Exhibition of the Three Ages of Man & the Process of Authentication, 1993, 94, Leonardo's Light in the Last Supper and Christ among the Doctors, 1995; co-author Code of Ethics for Australian Assn. Mus., 1970-87; author studies in renaissance and modern art from Impressionism to Contemporary Art; rsch. in relationships between modern and traditional art, particularly symbols of the sacred; editor BOA: Bull. of Archives of Art Info. Ctr., 1960—, Renaissance Studies, 1963—, Muse: Newsletter of Visual Edn. and Cultural Planning, 1969—, Bi-Singularity: Double Images of Nonduality in World Art, 1979—, Leonardo Studies, 1980—, Sacred Spaces: World Architecture & Symbolism, 1976—, Poësis: A Rev. of Poetry by Artists, 1987-93, Iconography of Infinity: Essays on Art and Philosophy, 1992—; planner various cultural instns. including Internat. Study Ctr., N.Y.C., Mus. Modern Art, Greenwich Village Hist. Preservation Dist., N.Y.C., Fine Arts Mus., San Francisco, Urban Planning Think Tank, San Francisco, Exploratorium, San Francisco, Bay Area Conservation Ctr., San Francisco, Archives Am. Art, San Francisco, Ft. Mason Ctr., San Francisco, Headlands Ctr. Arts, Golden Gate Nat. Recreation Area, Nat. Pk. Svc., Sausalito, Yerba Buena Ctr. Arts, San Francisco, J. Paul Getty Mus., Malibu, Louvre Mus., Paris, Morris Graves Art Mus., Eureka, Calif. Indian Mus. and Cultural Ctr., Golden Gate Nat. Recreation Area, Nat. Park Svc., San Francisco. Mem. Soc. of Archtl. Historians, Nat. Soc. of Lit. and the Arts, World Print Coun. (adv. com. we. region), Archives of Am. Art, Smithsonian Instn., Internat. Soc. Poets., Inst. for Aesthetic Devel. Avocations: printmaking, poetry, publishing private press editions. Business E-Mail: lanier.graham@csueastbay.edu.

GRAHAM, LAUREN, actress; b. Honolulu, Mar. 16, 1967; d. Lawrence Graham and Donna Grant. BA in English, Barnard Coll., Columbia U.; MFA in acting, So. Meth. U., 1992. Founder Good Game prodn. co. Actor: (TV series) Good Company, 1996, Townies, 1996, Conrad Bloom, 1998, M.Y.O.B., 2000, Gilmore Girls, 2000—; (films) Nightwatch, 1997, Confessions of a Sexist Pig, 1998, One True Thing, 1998, Dill Scallion, 1999, Sweet November, 2001, Chasing Destiny, 2001, Bad Santa, 2003, Lucky 13, 2004; actor, actor: (films) Seeing Other People, 2004, The Moguls, 2005, The Pacifier, 2005; prodr.: Something More, 2003; actor(guest appearance): (TV series) Caroline in the City, 1995—96, 3rd Rock from the Sun, 1996, Law & Order, 1997, Seinfield, 1997, NewsRadio, 1997. Office: ICM 8943 Wilshire Blvd Beverly Hills CA 90211-1934*

GRAHAM, LAURIE, editor, writer; b. Evanston, Ill., Nov. 22, 1941; d. Thomas Harlin and Mary Elisabeth (Stoner) Graham; m. George McKay Schieffelin, Dec. 12, 1980 (dec. Jan. 1988); m. Robert Dale Shearer, Apr. 6, 1994 (dec. Nov. 2002). Student, Mt. Holyoke Coll., 1959-61; BA, U. Colo., 1963. Editor Charles Scribner's Sons, NYC, 1969-87. Originator, co-project dir. The Greater Pitts. Poem Chase, 2001; bd. dirs. Pitts. Arts and Lectures. Author: Rebuilding the House, 1990, Singing the City, 1998; mem. editl. bd. Creative Nonfiction, 1994—, (press series) Emerging Writers in Creative Nonfiction, Duquesne U., 1994—; contbg. author: Pittsburgh Sports, 2000, Creative Nonfiction, 2003, 05. Mem.: PEN, NY Jr. League, Colony Club. Personal E-mail: lauriegraham@comcast.net.

GRAHAM, LINDSEY O., senator; b. Pickens County, S.C., July 9, 1955; s. E. J. and Millie Graham. BA in Psychology, U. S.C., 1977, JD, 1981. Area def. counsel Shaw AFB, 1982-84; cir. trial counsel USAF Europe, 1984-88; asst. county atty. County of Oconee, S.C., 1988-92; pvt. practice, 1988-94; city atty. Central, S.C., 1990-94; mem. S.C. Ho. of Reps., 1992—95, U.S. Congress from 3d S.C. dist., 1995—2001, U.S. Senate, 2002—, mem. Judiciary Com. With SC Air N.G., 1989-95, Desert Shield/Desert Storm; col. USAF Res., 1995—. Republican. Office: US Senate 290 Russell Senate Ofc Bldg Washington DC 20510*

GRAHAM, LOREN RAYMOND, historian, educator; b. Hymera, Ind., June 29, 1933; s. Ross Raymond and Hazel Mae (McClanahan) G.; m. Patricia Parks Albjerg, Sept. 6, 1955; 1 child, Marguerite Elizabeth. BS, Purdue U., 1955, D.Letters (h.c.), 1986; MA, Columbia U., 1960, PhD, 1964; postgrad., Moscow U., 1960-61. Gandy-dancer Pa. R.R., 1950-51; research chem. engr. Dow Chem. Co., 1955; lectr. dept. history Ind. U., 1963-64, asst. prof., 1965-66; vis. asst. prof. dept. public law and govt. Columbia U., 1965-66, assoc. prof., dept. history, 1967-72, prof., 1972-78, adj. prof., 1978-89; mem. Russian Inst., 1966-78; assoc., mem. exec. com. Davis Ctr. for Russian and Eurasian Studies/Harvard U., 1980—; acting dir. Davis Ctr. for Russian Studies/Harvard U., 1995-96; vis. prof. dept. history of sci. Harvard U., 1985-99; prof. MIT, 1978—. Vis. scholar U. Chgo., 1991-92; mem. adv. bd. Internat. Sci. Found., 1992-96; mem. adv. coun. U.S. Civilian R&D Found., 2002--. Author: The Soviet Academy of Sciences and The Communist Party, 1967, Science and Philosophy in the Soviet Union, 1972, Between Science and Values, 1981, Sci. Philosophy and Human Behavior in the Soviet Union, 1987, Science in Russia and the Soviet Union: A Short History, 1993, The Ghost of the Executed Engineer: Technology and the Fall of the Soviet Union, 1993, A Face in the Rock: Tale of a Grand Island Chippewa, 1995, What Have We Learned About Science and Technology From the Russian Experience?, 1998, Moscow Stories, 2005; editor (with others) Functions and Uses of Disciplinary History, 1983, (with R. Stites) Red Star: The First Bolshevik Science Utopia, 1983, Science and the Soviet Social Order, 1990; contbr. numerous articles to profl. jours.; narrator, cons. Nova TV, 1987. Trustee European U., St. Petersburg, Russia, 2000—, Nat. Lighthouse Mus., 1997—. Served with USN, 1955-58, Coast Guard Aux., 1979—. Recipient Gross award Saginaw Valley State U., 2003; Woodrow Wilson fellow, 1958-59; Danforth fellow, 1958-63; Fulbright Hayes fellow, 1966; Guggenheim fellow, 1969-70; Rockefeller fellow, 1976-77; Smithsonian Instn. fellow, 1981-82. Fellow AAAS, Am. Acad. Arts and Scis., Am. Philos. Soc.; mem. Acad. Natural Scis. (fgn.; Moscow), Acad. Humanitarian Scis. (fgn.; Moscow), Am. Hist. Assn., Am. Assn. Advancement of Slavic Studies, History of Sci. Soc. (Sarton medal 1996), Soc. History of Tech., Soc. Social Study of Sci., Mich. Hist. Soc. (Follo award 2000). Home: 7 Francis Ave Cambridge MA 02138-2009 Office: MIT E51-163 77 Massachusetts Ave Cambridge MA 02139-4307 E-mail: lrg@mit.edu.

GRAHAM, MARJORIE GADARIAN, lawyer; b. San Antonio, Tex., Mar. 13, 1947; d. Ardzvig Vartan and Dorothy Marie Gadarian; m. Stuart M. Graham, Jr., Apr. 17, 1982. BA in German, Northwestern U., 1969; JD, U. Fla., 1972. Bar: Fla. 1972, U.S. Dist. Ct. (so. dist.) Fla. 1973, U.S. Ct. Appeals (11th cir.) 1974, U.S. Supreme Ct. 1978. Rsch. aide to Hon. James H. Walden Fourth Dist. Ct. of Appeal, 1972-73; shareholder Jones & Foster, P.A., 1974-87; sole practitioner Palm Beach Gardens, Fla., 1987—. Contbr. articles to profl. jours. Mem. citizens involvement roundtable Martin County Met. Planing Orgn., 1997-99 Mem. ABA, Palm Beach County Bar Assn., Def. Rsch. Inst., Fedn. Ins. and Corp. Counsel, Fla. Def. Lawyers (bd. dirs. 1982-83, 88-90), past chair Amicus Curiae com.), Am. Law Inst. Office: Ste D129 11211 Prosperity Farms Rd Palm Beach Gardens FL 33410-3449

GRAHAM, MARY J., elementary school educator; d. Joseph and Estelle Silsby; m. William M Graham, July 21, 1978; children: Renee Blackstone, Connie Roy, Adam, Amy LaRochelle. BS, U. of Maine at Presque Isle, 1973—78; MS in edn., U. of So. Maine, 1985—88. General Elementary K-8 Maine Dept. of Edn., 2004, Teacher Disabled Students Maine Dept. of Edn., 2004. Ld tchr. grades k-8 M.S.A.D.#45, Washburn, Maine, 1979—81; ld tchr. Msad #1, Presque Isle, Maine, 1982—88, grade 4 tchr., 1988—. Chairperson Young Authors' Inst., Aroostook County, Maine, 1985—; mentor tchr. U. of Maine, Presque Isle, Maine. Mem. Delta Kappa Gamma, Presque Isle, Maine, 1999, Beta Sigma Phi, Presque Isle, Maine, 1981—2001; covenant leader Presque Isle Wesleyan Ch., Presque Isle, Maine, 2002; com. mem. James Sch., Presque Isle, Maine, 2004. Recipient Time Warner Nat. Tchr., Time Warner Cable, 2001, Ednl. Unsung Hero award, No. Life, 1998, Local Walmart Tchr. of the Yr., Walmart Co., 2001, Literacy award, Walmart, 2001; SEED Adaptor, Mainecenter, 2001, MBNA grant, MBNA, 1999. Mem.: NEA, Maine Ednl. Assn., Internat. Reading Assn., Aroostook Right to Read (co-chair 2004). Wesleyan. Office: EH Zippel Elementary Sch 42 Griffin St Presque Isle ME 04769 Personal E-mail: mary.graham@sad1.org.

GRAHAM, PATRICIA, information technology executive; With Prudential; dir. info. sys. Prudential Fin., Roseland, NJ. Past officer Data Mgmt. Assn. N.J.; presenter in field. Named one of Premier 100 Info. Tech. Leaders, ComputerWorld, 2003. Office: Prudential Group and Fin Svcs 55 Livingston Ave Roseland NJ 07068

GRAHAM, PATRICIA ALBJERG, education educator; b. Lafayette, Ind., Feb. 9, 1935; d. Victor L. and Marguerite (Hall) Albjerg; m. Loren R. Graham, Sept. 6, 1955; 1 child, Marguerite Elizabeth. BS, Purdue U., 1955, MS, 1957, DLett (hon.), 1980; PhD, Columbia U., 1964; MA (hon.), Harvard U., 1974; DHL (hon.), Manhattanville Coll., 1976; LLD (hon.), Beloit Coll., 1977, Clark U., 1978; DPA (hon.), Suffolk U., 1978, Ind. U., 1980; DLitt (hon.), St. Norbert Coll., 1980; DH (hon.), Emmanuel Coll., 1983; DHL (hon.), No. Mich. U., 1987, York Coll. of Pa., 1989, Kenyon Coll., 1991, Bank St. Coll. Edn., 1993; LLD (hon.), Radcliffe Coll., 1994, Salem State Coll., 1998. Tchr. high sch., Norfolk, Va., 1955-56, 57-58, N.Y.C., 1958-60; lectr., asst. prof. Ind. U., 1964-66; asst. prof. history of edn. Barnard Coll. and Columbia Tchrs. Coll., N.Y.C., 1965-68, assoc. prof., 1968-72, prof., 1972-74; dean Radcliffe Inst., 1974-77; also v.p. Radcliffe Coll., Cambridge, Mass., 1976-77; prof. Harvard U., Cambridge, Mass., 1974-79, Warren prof., 1979—2001, Warren Rsch. prof., 2001—; dean Grad. Sch. Edn., 1982-91; pres. Spencer Found., Chgo., 1991-2000. Author: Progressive Education: From Arcady to Academe, 1967, Community and Class in American Education: 1865-1918, 1974, S.O.S. Sustain Our Schools, 1992, Schooling America, 2005. Bd. dirs. Dalton Sch., 1973-76, Josiah Macy, Jr. Found., 1976-77, 79—; trustee Beloit Coll., 1976-77, 79-82, Northwestern Mut. Life, 1980-2005, Found. for Teaching Econs., 1980-87; bd. dirs. Spencer Found., 1983-2000, Johnson Found., 1983-2001, Hitachi Found., 1985-2004, Carnegie Found. for Advancement of Tchg., 1984-92, Ctrl. European U., Budapest, 2002—, Apache, 2002—. Mem.: AAAS (coun. 1993—96, v.p. 1998—2001), Ctr. for Advanced Study in the Behavioral Scis. (bd. dirs. 2001—), Am. Philos. Soc., Am. Hist. Assn. (v.p. 1985—89), Nat. Acad. Edn. (pres. 1984—89), Sci. Rsch. Assocs. (dir. 1980—89), Phi Beta Kappa. Episcopalian. Office: Harvard U Grad Sch Edn Cambridge MA 02138

GRAHAM, PHILIP L., epidemiologist, physician; b. Seattle, June 18, 1969; s. Philip L. Graham and Burnley D. Dame; m. Dara K. Sicherman, Sept. 20, 2003; 1 child, Arla Marisol. BA, Trinity Coll., Hartford, Conn., 1989—93; MD, George Wash. U., Washington, D.C., 1994—98; MSc, Columbia U. Sch. Pub. Health, N.Y.C., 2001—03. Cert. N.Y., 1999. Pediatric resident Columbia U. Med. Ctr., N.Y.C., 1998—2001, pediatric infectious disease fellow, 2001—03, asst. prof., pediat., 2003—; attending physician, asst. hosp. epidemiologist Children's Hosp. N.Y., N.Y.C., 2003—. Office: Columbia Univ Med Ctr 622 W 168 St New York NY 10032 Office Phone: 212-305-2790.

GRAHAM, ROBERT, medical association executive; b. Pueblo, Colo., Feb. 15, 1943; married. AB, Earlham Coll., 1965; MD, U. Kans., 1970. Asst. adminstr. agy. goals Health Svc. & Mental Health Admn. Dept. Health Edn. & Welfare, Washington, 1970—73; resident in family practice Bapt. Meml. Hosp., 1974—75; asst. dir. divsn. edn. Am. Acad. Family Physicians, Kansas City, Mo., 1973—76; dep. dir. Bur. Health Manpower, Health Resources Adminstrn. Dept. Health Edn. & Welfare, 1976—78, dep. adminstr., 1978—79; profl. staff mem. subcom. health & sci. rsch. Comty. Labor & Human Resources, U.S. Senate, 1979—80; acting adminstr. health resources adminstrn. Dept. Health & Human Svc., 1981—82, adminstr., 1982—85; exec. v.p. Am. Acad. Family Physicians, Kansas City, Mo., 1985—2001; dir. Agency for Healthcare Research and Quality, Ctr. for Practice and Technology Assessment, 2001—. Mem. staff Program Health Mgmt. Baylor Coll. Medicine, 1976; exec. sec. Grad. Med. Edn. Nat. Adv. Com., 1978—79; bd. dirs. Alliance for Health Referendum, 1994—, Sun Valley Forum Nat. Health.

Contbr. articles to profl. jours. Mem.: AMA, Am. Soc. Assn. Execs., Am. Assn. Med. Soc. Execs., Am. Acad. Med. Dirs., Am. Acad. Family Physicians, Assn. Am. Med. Colls., Inst. Medicine of NAS (exec. v.p., CEO 1985—2000). Office: AHRQ 540 Gaither Rd Rockville MD 20850-6649

GRAHAM, ROBERT, sculptor; b. Mexico City, Aug. 1938; Study, San Jose (Calif) State Coll., 1961-63, San Francisco Art Inst., 1963-64. Prin. works include Whitney Mus. Am. Art & Mus. Modern Art, N.Y., Hirshhorn Mus. & Sculpture Garden, L.A. County Mus., Dallas Mus. Fine Art, Kunstmus., Cologne, Germany; commd. Fed. Res. Bank San Francisco, 1983, San Jose Fed. Bldg., 1984, L.A. Olympic Organizing Com., 1984, Joe Louis Meml., Detroit, Duke Ellington Meml., Central Park, N.Y., 1992, and others; exhbited in group shows at Galerie Neuendorf, Hamburg, Germany, 1979; one-man shows include Walker Art Ctr., 1981, L.A. County Mus. Art, 1988, Dorothy Rosenthal Gallery, 1981, Sch. Visual Arts, N.Y., 1981; Robert Miller Gallery, N.Y., 1982, 89, 90, 92, Whitney Mus. Am. Art, 1983, 84, 86, 88, 89, Mus. Fine Arts, Houston, 1987-89, Contemporary Arts Ctr., New Orleans, 1990; author: (bibliography) Maurice Tuchman, The Duke Ellington Meml. In Progress, L.A. County Mus. Art, 1989, John McEwen, Robert Graham Statues, Frankfurt, Galerie Neuendorf, Twenty-one Figures, N.Y., Robert Miller Gallery. Office: care Robert Miller Gallery 524 W 26th St New York NY 10001-5504*

GRAHAM, ROBERT ALBERT, research physicist; b. Dallas, Feb. 11, 1931; s. John Mark and Eleanor Ball (Evans) G.; m. Lettie Barbara Umphres, Sept. 1, 1951; children: Stephanie Ann Graham Farrow, Mark Lee, Stuart Russell; m. Nell Heard Griffin, Apr. 6, 1996. AA, Allen Jr. Coll., 1951; BS in Civil Engring., U. Tex., 1954, MS in Engring. Mechanics, 1958; DSc in Materials Sci. and Engring., Tokyo Inst. Tech., 1990. Rsch. engr. S.W. Rsch. Inst., San Antonio, 1956-57; staff mem. Sandia Labs., Albuquerque, 1958-83; disting. mem. tech. staff Sandia Nat. Labs., Albuquerque, 1983-96; dir. rsch. Tome Group, 1996—; curator Meteorite Crater S. Tex. exhibit, Uvalde, Tex., 2005—. Adviser NAS, Washington, 1982—, Ctr. for Explosives Tech. Rsch., Socorro, N.Mex., 1983-88, U. N.Mex., Albuquerque, 1988—. Editor: Proc. 1981 Shock Conference, Proc. 1983 Shock Conference, N.Mex. Genealogist, 1974—75, High Pressure Exptl. Processing of Ceramic Trans. Tech., 1987; co-editor: Shock Waves in Condensed Matter, 1982, 1983, 1984, High Pressure Explosive Processing of Ceramics, 1987; editor-in-chief Springer-Verlag book series on Shock Compression of Condensed Matter, 1988—96, mng. editor Shock Waves Internat. Jour., 1991—96; author: Solids Under High Pressure Shock Compression: Mechanics, Physics and Chemistry, 1993; contbr. articles to profl. jours. Vice pres. Amigos de las Ams., Albuquerque, 1968-70; host family Am. Field Service, Albuquerque, 1969. 1st lt. U.S. Army, 1954-56. Recipient Excellence award Dept. Energy, 1983, G.B. Sawyer Meml. award Sawyer Rsch. Products, 1984, Am. Phys. Soc. Shock Compression Sci. award, 1993. Fellow: AAAS, Am. Phys. Soc. (organizing com. 1979, 1983, topical conf. 1993); mem.: Am. Chem. Soc., Materials Rsch. Soc., IEEE (sr.; local arrangements chmn. 1975), Phi Theta Kappa, Chi Epsilon, Tau Beta Pi. Achievements include patents in field. Home and Office: 608 Cenizo Blvd Uvalde TX 78801-4009 Personal E-mail: tomecenizo@aol.com.

GRAHAM, ROGER JOHN, photography professor, journalism professor; b. Phila., Feb. 16; s. William K. and Peggy E. (Owens) G.; divorced; children: John Roger, Robb Curt; m. Debbie Kenyon, Dec. 28, 1991. AA, Los Angeles Valley Coll., 1961; BA, Calif. State U., Fresno, 1962, MA, 1967; postgrad, UCLA, 1976. Cert. in elem., jr. high, high sch., cmty. coll., counseling and adminstrn. Tchr. Riverdale (Calif.) Sch., 1963, Raisin City (Calif.) Sch., 1964; tchr., counselor Calif. State Prison, Jamestown, 1966; tchr. trainer UCLA's Western Ctr. War on Poverty, 1967; chmn. media arts dept. Los Angeles Valley Coll., Van Nuys, Calif., 1968—, prof. emeritus, 1999—. Vis. prof. Pepperdine U., Malibu, Calif., 1976, Calif. Luth. Coll., Thousand Oaks, 1973, South Africa, 1997; vis. prof. Chapman U., Orange, Calif., 1996, GAIN prof., 1998; del. Calif. Fedn. Tchrs. Conv., 1997; dir. Photography Seminar, Spain, summer 1990. Co-author: Observations on the Mass Media, 1976; author: Our Lives in Bits and Pieces, 1998, Patchwork of Life, 2001, L.A. to Philly - Looking Back, 2002, (jour.) Jr. Coll. Jour., 1972; co-author: We Remember WW II, 2003, L.A. Valley College History, 2005; photo illustrator: The San Fernando Valley, 1980, display advertiser: Turlock (Calif.) jour., 1962, Fresno Guide, 1963; contbr. articles to profl. jours.; author: L.A. to Philly - Looking Back: Again, 2005. Mem. Tom Hayden's Com. for Schs., Santa Monica, Calif., 1984; pres. Pacific Palisades Dem. Club, 1992; rep. to 41st assembly dist. Calif. Dem. Party State Ctrl. Com., 1993, sec. srs. caucus, 1993—. With USN, 1957. NEH scholar 1981; recipient Mayor's Outstanding Citizen award Los Angeles Mayor's Office, 1974, Extraordinary Service award UCLA, 1971; named one of Outstanding Young Men Am., 1971. Mem. C.C. Journalism Assn. (nat. pres. 1978—, Nat. Dedication Journalism award 1972-76), Journalism Assn. C.C. (pres. Calif. sect. 1972—), Calif. Srs. Caucus (state sec. 1993—), L.A. Profs. Club, Dem. Club Pacific Palisades (pres. 1992-93), Patrons Assn. (bd. dirs. 2000—), L.A. Valley Coll. Retirees Assn. (Outstanding Alumnus award 1999, pres. 1999), Am. Legion (sgt. at arms 1986—, Palisades chpt. adminstrv. officer 1996—), Patrons Assn. (bd. dirs. 2000), Sons of the Desert, Sons Revolution, Sigma Delta Xi, Phi Delta Kappa, Pi Lambda Theta. Avocation: scuba diving. Home: 7878 Naylor Ave Los Angeles CA 90045-2909 Office: LA Valley Coll 5800 Fulton Ave Van Nuys CA 91401-4096

GRAHAM, SELDON BAIN, JR., lawyer, engineer; b. Franklin, Tex., Apr. 14, 1926; s. Seldon Bain and Lillian Emma (Struwe) G.; m. Patricia Gene Noah, Feb. 14, 1953; children: Seldon Bain (dec.), Kyle, Laurie. BS, U.S. Mil. Acad., 1951; JD, U. Tex., 1970. Registered profl. engr., Tex. Bar: Tex. 1970, U.S. Dist. Ct. (so. dist.) Tex. 1980, U.S. Ct. Appeals (5th cir.) 1983; cert. in oil, gas and mineral law Tex. Bd. Legal Specialization, 1986-2001. With U.S. Army, 1944, advanced through grades to col., 1979; with Office of Dep. Chief of Staff for Pers., 1979, ret., 1979. Area reservoir engr. ARCO, Okla., 1954-60; div. regulatory engr. Mobil Oil Co., Corpus Christi, 1961-67; counsel Exxon Co. USA, Houston, 1970-85. Decorated Legion of Merit. Mem. Soc. Petroleum Engrs. Methodist. Home and Office: 4713 Palisade Dr Austin TX 78731-4516

GRAHAM, STEPHEN MICHAEL, lawyer; b. Houston, May 1, 1951; s. Frederick Mitchell and Lillian Louise (Miller) G.; m. Joanne Marie Sealock, Aug. 24, 1974; children: Aimee Elizabeth, Joseph Sealock, Jessica Anne. BS, Iowa State U., 1973; JD, Yale U., 1976. Bar: Wash. 1977. Assoc. Perkins Coie, Seattle, 1976-83, ptnr., 1983-2000, Orrick, Herrington & Sutcliffe LLP, Seattle, 2000—, practice leader corp. div. Bd. dirs. Wash. Spl. Olympics, Seattle, 1979—83, pres., 1982—83; trustee Friends of the Children of King County, 2002—; mem. Seattle Fair Campaign Practices Commn., 1982—88; trustee Cornish Coll. Arts, 1986—91, mem. exec. com., 1989—91; trustee Seattle Repertory Theatre, 1993—95, Seattle Children's Theatre, 1996—98, mem. exec. com., 1997—98; trustee Fred Hutchinson Cancer Rsch. Ctr., 1999—; bd. dirs., mem. exec. com. WSA, 2002—; trustee Arboretum Found., 1994—96; mem. Seattle Bd. Ethics, 1982—88, chmn., 1983—88; mem. exec. com. Sch. Law Yale U., 1988—92, 1993—97; bd. dirs. Wash. Biotech. and Biomed. Assn., 1996—, mem. exec. com., 1997—. Mem.: ABA, Wash. State Bar Assn., Rainier Club, Wash. Athletic Club. Episcopalian. Office: Orrick Herrington & Sutcliffe Ste 900 719 Second Ave Seattle WA 98104-7063 Office Phone: 206-839-4320. Business E-Mail: sgraham@orrick.com.

GRAHAM, STEVEN ANTHONY, writer; b. Portland, Oreg. M in Theol. Studies, George Fox U., 2002; postgrad., Portland State U., 2002—, Goethe Inst., 2000, Ark. Inst. Holy Land Studies, 2000, Hebrew U., Jerusalem, 2004. Pvt. profl. mime, ny, USSR, 1978—2002; martial arts instr. Portland, 1983—84; acting instr. Troutman Modeling Agy., Portland, 1984—86, ABC-Kids, Portland, 1984—86; profl. model Nike, Glamour, N.Y.C., 1984—89; profl. actor Pub. Theater, CBS, ABC, N.Y.C., 1984—90; acting instr. The Acting Co., Portland, 1985—86, The Weist-Barron Acting Sch., New York, NY, 1986—87; profl. actor Fox TV among others, L.A., 1990—97; tchg. asst. Bibl. Hebrew George Fox U., Portland, 2000—01, tchg. asst. Koine Greek, 2001—02, rsch. asst. Author: (novels) Tell of His Glory: Growing up Penguin-Style, 2004, Hit It Again, (screenplays) BT, The Odds are in my favor: An Adaptation of Elijah on Mount Carmel, (plays) Compromise, never!...well, probably. An Adaptation of the Gospel of Jude, The Wizard of Uz: An Adaptation of the Book of Job, Trials: An Adaptation of the Gospel to the Philippians, Manasseh in Scripture and Tradition: An Analysis of Ancient Sources and the Development of the Manasseh Tradition, 2002; contbr. articles to profl. publs. Developed and oversaw youth ministry Willamette Valley Weslyan Ch., Wilsonville, Oreg., 1998—99; youth counselor Kansas City (Kans.) Youth For Christ, 1996—97. Grantee Richter Rsch. grantee, George Fox U., 2001. Mem.: Soc. Bibl. Lit. (corr.). Personal E-mail: stevegrahamis@yahoo.com.

GRAHAM, STUART EDWARD, construction company executive; b. Wilkes Barre, Pa., Feb. 17, 1946; s. Stuart E. Graham; m. Kathryn Virginia; children— Cameron, Stuart E. Jr., Devon BS in Econs., Holy Cross Coll., 1967. Supt. Sordoni Constrn. Co., Parsippany, N.J., 1969-72, project mgr., 1972-75, v.p. ops., 1975-78, pres., 1978—. Mem. Young Pres. Orgn. Clubs: Westmoreland (Wilkes-Barre, Pa.), University (NYC). Republican. Roman Catholic. Office: Skanska Constrn Co 400 Interpace Pkwy Parsippany NJ 07054-1120

GRAHAM, SUSAN LOIS, computer science educator, consultant; b. Cleve., Nov. 16, 1942; m., 1971 AB in Math., Harvard U., 1964; MS, Stanford U., 1966, PhD in Computer Sci., 1971. Assoc. rsch. scientist, adj. asst. prof. computer sci. Courant Inst. Math. Sci., NYU, 1969-71; asst. prof. computer sci. U. Calif., Berkeley, 1971-76, assoc. prof., 1976-81, prof. computer sci., 1981—, Chancellor's prof., 1997—2000, Pehong Chen disting. prof., 2001—; chief computer scientist NSF Nat. Partnership for Advanced Computational Infrastructure, 1997—2005; sr. scientist Lawrence Berkeley Nat. Lab., Calif., 1999—. Vis. scientist Stanford U., 1981; mem. adv. com. div. computer and computation rsch. NSF, 1987-92, mem. program for sci. and tech. ctrs., 1987-91; mem. vis. com. for elec. engring. and computer sci. MIT, 1989—; mem. vis. com. for engring. and applied sci. Calif. Inst. Tech., 1994-99; mem. vis. com. for applied scis. Harvard U., 1995—; mem. commn. on phys. sci., math. and applications NRC, 1992-95; mem. Pres.'s Com. on Nat. Medal Sci., 1994-96; mem. Pres.'s Info. Tech. Adv. Com., 1997-2002; bd. dirs. Harvard Alumni Assn., 1997-2000; mem. bd. overseers Harvard U., 2001-. Co-editor: Comms. ACM, 1975—79; editor: ACM transactions on Programming Langs. and Systems, 1978—92. NSF grantee. Fellow AAAS, Assn. for Computing Machinery, Am. Acad. Arts and Sci.; mem. IEEE, NAE. Office: U Calif-Berkeley Computer Sci Div EECS 771 Soda Hall 1776 Berkeley CA 94720-1776 Office Phone: 510-642-2059. Business E-Mail: graham@CS.Berkeley.edu.

GRAHAM, SUSETTE RYAN, retired English educator; b. Plattsburgh, N.Y., Aug. 31, 1929; d. Andrew Warren Ryan and Lillian Grace MacDougall; m. James H. Graham, July 1, 1950; children: Marguerite, Andrea, James Jr., Martha, Amy, Matthew. BA, Wellesley Coll., 1950; MA, U. Rochester, 1967, PhD, 1987. Prof. English Nazareth Coll., Rochester, N.Y., 1963-93, prof. emerita, 1993; ret. Contbr. articles, revs. to profl. jours. Fulbright sr. lectr., Poland, 1992-93. Mem. AAUW, MLA, Am. Acad. Poets. Democrat. Avocations: travel, reading, genealogical research. Home: 10 Arbor Ct Fairport NY 14450-1602 also: 603 Pipers Ln Surfside Beach SC 29575-5846 E-mail: jamesgraham@sc.rr.com.

GRAHAM, THOMAS, JR., lawyer; b. Louisville, Oct. 9, 1933; s. Thomas and Charlotte (Henriques) G.; m. Clover Nicholas, Aug. 10, 1968 (div. Dec. 1982); children: Elizabeth Malcolm, Thomas Lawrence, Clover Chace; m. Christine Coffey Ryan, Sep. 26, 1983; stepchildren: Thomas Coffey Ryan, Mary Christine Ryan. AB, Princeton U., 1955; postgrad., L'institute des Sciences Politiques, 1955-56; JD, Harvard U., 1961. Bar: Ky. 1961, D.C. 1963, N.Y. 1966. Law clk. U.S. Cir. Ct. Appeals (D.C. cir.), 1961-62; chief counsel U.S. Ho. Reps. Com. on Banking and Currency, Washington, 1962-63; counsel to compt. of currency Treasury Dept., Washington, 1963-64; assoc. Wyatt, Grafton & Sloss, Louisville, 1964-66, Shearman & Sterling, N.Y.C., 1966-69; lawyer Office of Sec. USAF, Washington, 1969-70; asst. gen. counsel U.S. Arms Control and Disarmament Agy., Washington, 1970-73, dep. gen. counsel, 1973-77, gen. counsel, 1977-81, 83-94, dir. Congl. rels. and pub. affairs, 1981-83, acting dir., 1993, acting dep. dir., 1993-94; spl. rep. of Pres. (amb.) Arms Control, Non-Proliferation and Disarmament, 1994-97, ret., 1997. Legal advisor U.S. SALT II del., Geneva, 1974-79; legal advisor U.S. del. to rev. conf. Nonproliferation Treaty, Geneva, 1980; sr. arms control advisor U.S. del. to negotiations on Intermediate Range Nuclear Forces, 1981-82; legal advisor U.S. del. to Conf. Disarmament, Geneva, 1985; legal advisor U.S. del. to negotiation on nuc. and space arms, Geneva, 1985-88, U.S. del. to ABM Treaty Rev. Conf., Geneva, 1988; sr. arms control advisor, legal advisor U.S. del. Conventional Armed Forces in Europe negotiation, 1989-90; legal advisor U.S. del. START Negotiation, 1991, START II Negotiation, 1992; chmn. U.S. del. ABM Treaty rev. conf., 1993, U.S. rep. Nonproliferation Treaty Ext. Conf., 1993-95; chmn. U.S. Del. Conventional Armed Forces Europe rev. com., 1996; chmn. bd. dirs. Mex. Energy Corp., 1997—; lectr. U. Va. Law Sch., 1984-91; adj. prof. Georgetown U. Law Ctr., 1991-93, Georgetown Sch. Fgn. Svc., 1991-94, Stanford U., 1999-, U. Washington, 2002-; pres. Lawyers Alliance for World Security, Washington, 1997-2002, chmn. bd. dirs., 2002-, spl. counsel Morgan, Lewis and Bockius, Washington, 2002-04, sr. counsel, 2004; bd. dirs. Thorium Power Inc.; sr. cons. Eisenhower Inst., Washington, 2002-04, sr. cons., fellow, 2004-. Author: Disarmament Sketches, Thirty Years of Arms Control and International Law, 2002, Cornerstones of Security, Arms Control Treaties in the Modern Era, 2003, Common Sense on Weapons of Mass Destruction, 2004. Spl. asst. to chmn. United Citizens for Nixon-Agnew, Washington, 1968. With U.S. Army, 1956-58, 1st lt. U.S. Army Res., 1958-61. Mem. ABA (chmn. com. on arms control 1986-94), D.C. Bar Assn., N.Y. State Bar Assn., Ky. Bar Assn., Coun. on Fgn. Rels., Chevy Chase Club, Cosmos Club, Met. Club, Louisville Country Club, Ausable Club. Republican. Episcopalian. Avocations: tennis, golf, skiing, hiking. Home: 7609 Glenbrook Rd Bethesda MD 20814 Office: Morgan Lewis & Bockius 1111 Pennsylvania Ave NW Washington DC 20004 Office Phone: 202-739-5115. Business E-Mail: tgraham@morganlewis.com.

GRAHAM, THOMAS RICHARD, lawyer; b. Shelbyville, Ind., Nov. 23, 1942; s. Kermit A. and Esther L. (Thompson) G.; m. Rosemond Eve Toner, June 12, 1965; children: Rachel Graham Cody, Thomas Ian. BA, Ind. U., 1965; JD, Harvard U., 1968. Bar: DC 1970, US Supreme Ct. 1973. Exec. asst. to pres. Ford Motor de Venezuela, Caracas, 1968-70; vis. prof. law U. Catolica Andres Bello, Caracas, 1968-70; legal officer UN, Geneva, 1970-73; dep. gen. counsel Office U.S. Trade Rep., Washington, 1974-79; vis. prof. U. N.C., Chapel Hill, 1979-80; assoc. Patton, Boggs & Blow, Washington, 1980-81; counsel, ptnr. Kilpatrick & Cody, Washington, 1981-85; ptnr. Skadden, Arps, Slate, Meagher & Flom, Washington, 1985-2000, King & Spalding, Washington, 2000—05, of counsel, 2005—. Adj. prof. law Georgetown U., Washington, 1977-85, 95-98; vis. fellow Brookings Instn., Washington, 1978-79; sr. assoc. Carnegie Endowment, Washington, 1979-80. Co-editor: Managing Trade Relations in the 1980's, 1983, Trade and Environment, 1982; contbr. articles to profl. jours. Chief advisor on internat. trade John Glenn Presdl. Campaign, 1984. Mem. ABA (chmn. subcom. exports 1985-89), Am. Soc. Internat. Law (chmn. internat. econ. law sect. 1981-83). Avocations: history, sports. Home: 6115 33rd St NW Washington DC 20015-2403 Office: King & Spalding Ste 1000 1730 Pennsylvania Ave NW Washington DC 20006-4706 Office Phone: 202-626-5609. Business E-Mail: tgraham@kslaw.com.

GRAHAM, W. THOMAS, lawyer; b. Cleve., Nov. 9, 1950; s. William T. and Ilah K. (Kotts) Graham; m. Teresa M. Pillarelli, Oct. 7, 1984; children: Stephen T., Mallory M. BA, Johns Hopkins U., 1973; JD, U. Toledo, 1976. Bar: Mich. 1976, Ohio 1977, U.S. Dist. Ct. (ea. dist.) Mich. Ptnr. Lennard, Graham & Goldsmith, P.L.C., Monroe, Mich., 1980—. Office: Lennard Graham and Goldsmith PLC 222 Washington St Monroe MI 48161-2146 Office Phone: 734-242-9500.

GRAHAM, WALLACE KARL, chemical company executive; b. N.Y.C., Sept. 12, 1928; s. Samuel and Mildred G.;/ m. Ruth R. Winer, July 29, 1950; children: James (dec.), Steven L., Eric P. BSChemE, Columbia U., 1950; MS, NYU, 1954. With Nat. Starch and Chem. Corp., 1950-93, corp. v.p., gen. mgr. adhesive div. Bridgewater, N.J., 1972-77, group v.p., 1977-78, pres., chief operating officer, dir., 1978-83, pres., chief exec. officer, 1983-84, chmn., chief exec. officer, 1984-85; group head chems. Unilever PLC and Unilever NV, 1986-91, also bd. dirs., 1986-91. Bd. dirs. Jorin Ltd., U.K. Fellow Instn. Chem. Engrs. London; mem. Soc. Chem. Industry, Am. Inst. Chem. Engrs., Princeton Club, Sky Club, Mid-Ocean (Bermuda) Club, Wentworth Golf Club, Algonquin Club.

GRAHAM, WARREN KIRKLAND, dentist; b. Albuquerque, July 22, 1938; s. Warren Reno and Alice Barbara (Eller) G.; m. Nancy Lou White, Apr. 2, 1966; children: John Warren, Jason Kirkland. BS, U. N.Mex., 1960; DDS, Baylor U., 1964. Pvt. practice dentistry, Albuquerque, 1965-89; dental dir. Farmington Cmty. Health Ctr., 1989—; corp. dental dir. Presbyn. Med. Svcs., 1994—; adj. asst. prof. Coll. Dentistry, Baylor U., 1995—; adj. asst. prof. dental programs U. N.Mex., 1996-2000, U. Mo. Dental Sch., Kansas City, 2000—. Mem. N.Mex. Bd. Dental Health Care, 1997-2002, chmn., 2000-02; bd. dirs., examiner Western Regional Exam Bd., 1998—; founder Albuquerque (N.Mex.) sr. citizens' dental program, 1985. Bd. dirs. N.Mex. Coun. on Smoking and Health, 1969-71; mem. N.Mex. Medicaid Adv. Bd., 1972-77, Mid Rio Grande Health Planning Coun., 1972-76; chmn. N.Mex. Health Sys. Agy. Subarea Coun., Dist. II, 1977-78. Capt. USAF, 1964-65. Fellow Am. Coll. Dentists, Acad. Gen. Dentistry (pres. Albuquerque chpt. 1976), Pierre Fauchard Acad.; mem. ADA, N.Mex. Acad. Gen. Dentistry (pres. 1990-91), N.Mex. Dental Assn. (sec.-treas. 1982-86, v.p. 1986-87, pres. 1988-89), Albuquerque Dist. Dental Soc. (pres. 1976), Am. Assn. Pub. Health Dentistry, Nat. Network Oral Health Access, Am. Assn. Dental Examiners, Sigma Chi, Delta Sigma Delta. Republican. Mem. Lds Ch. Office: Presbyn Med Svcs Farmington Cmty Health Ctr PO Box 3239 Farmington NM 87499-3239

GRAHAM, WILLIAM B., pharmaceutical company executive; b. Chgo., July 14, 1911; s. William and Elizabeth (Burden) G.; m. Edna Kanaley, June 15, 1940 (dec.); children: William J., Elizabeth Anne, Margaret, Robert B.; m. Catherine Van Duzer, July 23, 1984. SB cum laude, U. Chgo., 1932, JD cum laude, 1936; LLD, Carthage Coll., 1974, Lake Forest Coll., 1983; LLD (hon.), U. Ill., 1988; LHD, St. Xavier Coll. and Nat. Coll. Edn., 1983; LHD (hon.), Barat Coll., 1997, DePaul U., 1998. Bar: Ill. 1936. Patent lawyer Dyrenforth, Lee, Chritton & Wiles, 1936-40; mem. Dawson & Ooms, 1940-45; v.p., mgr. Baxter Internat., Inc., Deerfield, Ill., 1945-53, pres., 1953-71, CEO, 1960-80, chmn. bd., 1980-85, sr. chmn., 1989-95, chmn. emeritus, 1995—. Prof., chair Weizmann Inst. Sci., Rehoboth, Israel, 1978; lectr. U. Chgo., 1981-82. Chmn. bd. dirs. Lyric Opera Chgo.; bd. dirs. Big Shoulders, Wendy Will Care Fedn., Chgo. Hort. Soc.; trustee Orchestral Assn., U. Chgo., Evanston (Ill.) Hosp.; past pres. Cmty. Fund of Chgo. Recipient V.I.P. award Lewis Found., 1963, Disting. Citizen award Ill. St. Andrew Soc., 1974, Decision Maker of Yr. award Am. Statis. Assn., 1974, Marketer of Yr. award AMA, 1976, Found. award Kidney Found., 1981, Chicagoan of Yr. award Chgo. Boys Club, 1981, Bus. Statesman of Yr. award Harvard Bus. Sch. Club Chgo., 1983, Achievement award Med. Tech. Svcs., 1983, Disting. Fellows award Internat. Ctr. for Artificial Organs and Transplantations, 1982, Chgo. Civic award DePaul U., 1986, Internat. Visitors Golden Medallion award U. Ill., 1988, Chgo. medal U. Chgo., 1992, Laureate award Lincoln Acad. Ill., 1992, Lyric Opera Carol Fox award, 1992, Good Scout award N.E. Coun. Boy Scouts Am., 1993, Making History award Chgo. Hist. Soc., 1996; recognized for pioneering work Health Industry Mfrs. Assn., 1981; inducted Jr. Achievement Chgo. Bus. Hall of Fame, 1986, Modern Healthcare Hall of Fame, 1994, Art Alliance Legend award Dreihaus Found., 2000. Mem. Am. Pharm. Mfrs. Assn. (past pres.), Ill. Mfrs. Assn. (past pres.), Pharm. Mfrs. Assn. (past chmn., award for spl. distinction leadership 1981), Chgo. Club (past pres.), Commonwealth Club, Comml. Club, Indian Hill Club, Casino Club, Old Elm Club, Seminole Club, Everglades Club, Bath and Tennis Club, Links Club, Phi Beta Kappa, Sigma Xi, Phi Delta Phi. Home: 40 Devonshire Ln Kenilworth IL 60043-1205 Office: Baxter Internat Inc 1 Baxter Pkwy Deerfield IL 60015-4625

GRAHAM, WILLIAM C., Canadian government official; b. Montreal, Can. m. Catherine Graham; children: Katherine, Patrick. BA, LLB, U. Toronto; LLD, U. Paris. Ptnr. Fasken & Calvin, Toronto, Canada, 1967-80; dir. Ctr. Internat. Studies U. Toronto, 1986-88, prof. law, 1988-93; parliamentarian House of Commons, Ottawa, Canada, 1993—; min. of fgn. affairs Govt. of Canada, 2002—04, min. nat. def., 2004—. Vis. lectr. law McGill U., U. Montreal; former dir. Ctr. Internat. Studies, U. Toronto; past pres. Alliance Française, Toronto. Author several books. V.p. Orgn. Security and Coop. in Europe, 1997—; treas. Liberal Internat., 1996-2000. Recipient Chevalier de Legion d'Honneur de la France, 1985, Jean-Baptiste Rousseau prize, City of Paris Silver medal, Gold medal of Alliance Française, Order of Merit, Assn. French-Speaking Jurists of Ont., Chevalier of Ordre de la Pléiade. Mem.: Can. Coun. Internat. Law (hon.; life). Office: House Commons Confederation Bldg Rm 261 Ottawa ON Canada K1A 0A6 Also: 365 Bloor St E Ste 1805 Ontario Toronto M4W 3L4 Canada Office: Dept Nat Def 101 Colonel By Dr Ottawa ON K1AOK2 Canada Office Phone: 613-996-3100.

GRAHAM, WILLIAM EDGAR, JR., lawyer, utilities executive; b. Jackson Springs, N.C., Dec. 31, 1929; s. William Edgar and Minnie Blanch (Autry) G.; children: William McLaurin, John McMillan, Sally Faircloth. AB, U. N.C., 1952, JD with honors, 1956. Bar: N.C. bar. Law clk. U.S. Ct. Appeals 4th Circuit, 1956-57; individual practice law Charlotte, N.C., 1957-69; judge N.C. Ct. Appeals, 1969-73; sr. v.p., gen. counsel Carolina Power & Light Co., Raleigh, N.C., 1973-81, exec. v.p., 1981-85, vice chmn., 1985-93; counsel Hunton & Williams, 1994—. Served with USAF, 1952-54. Mem. ABA, N.C. Bar Assn., Wake County Bar Assn. Presbyterian. Office: Hunton & Williams PO Box 109 Raleigh NC 27602-0109 E-mail: dgraham@hunton.com.

GRAHAM, WILLIAM HENRY, lawyer; b. Newark, Jan. 6, 1946; s. Robert and Ruth Ellen (McElroy) G.; m. Lorraine Majeski, Mar. 23, 1969; 1 child, Allison. BA, Ohio State U., 1968; JD, Rutgers U., 1973; LLM in Corp. Law, NYU, 1978, LLM in Trade Regulation Law, 1980. Law clk. Connell Foley & Geiser, Roseland, N.J., 1971-73, atty., 1973-77, Bethlehem (Pa.) Steel Corp., 1977-79, sr. atty., 1979-81, gen. atty., 1981-85, asst. gen. counsel, 1985-89, asst. gen. counsel, asst. sec., 1989-92, gen. counsel, 1992-95, v.p., gen. counsel, sec., 1995-2000, sr. v.p., gen. counsel, sec., 2000—. Bd. dirs. Atlantic Legal Found., N.Y.C., 1986—; bd. mem. Pa. Civil Justice Coalition, Harrisburg, Pa., 1987—; chmn. Pa. Task Force on Product Liability, Harrisburg, 1989—. 1st lt. U.S. Army, 1969-71, Vietnam. Mem. ABA, N.J. Bar Assn., Pa. Bar Assn., Trial Attys. N.J., Am. Iron and Steel Inst., Assn. Gen. Counsel. Lutheran. E-mail: william.graham@bethsteel.com.

GRAHAM, WILLIAM JAMES, packaging company executive; b. Johnstown, Pa., Sept. 20, 1923; s. John Ellis and Margaret (Euwer) G.; m. Natalie Joan Stolk, Feb. 17, 1951; children: Susan, Margaret, John, Elizabeth, Joan, Catherine. BA cum laude, Amherst Coll., 1948. Salesman, Owens-Ill., Inc., 1953-60, closure sales mgr., 1960-66, v.p. sales Pacific region, 1966-69, v.p., gen. mgr. Pacific region, 1969-72, v.p. sales and mktg., 1972-75, v.p., gen. mgr. plastic products div. Toledo, 1975-82, group v.p. plastics and closures, 1982-85, sr. v.p. West, 1985-88, ret., 1988. Bd. dirs. G.W. Plstics, Garden Grow Co., Inc. Trustee, pres. Filoli, 1990-96; trustee Strybing Arboretum, 1996—. Served to 1st lt. U.S. Army, 1943-46, 50-51. Mem. Soc. Plastics Industry (dir.-at-large, exec. com.), Plastic Bottle Inst. (chmn. 1983-86), Mgmt. Policy Council (exec. com.), Menlo Country, Foothills Tennis, Eastman (N.H.) Golf Club. Republican. Presbyterian. Home: 8 Hawk View St Portola Valley CA 94028 E-mail: wjgra@aol.com.

GRAHAM, WILLIAM PIERSON, investment banker, entrepreneur; b. East St. Louis, Ill., Feb. 19, 1935; s. William Schley and Opal Elizabeth (Gray) G.; m. Margaret Newton McDowell, Sept. 30, 1961; children: Lisa, Heather, Jennifer. BS, U. Ill., 1956. With IBM Corp., 1956-69, asst. to pres., 1967-68, dir. mktg. comml. industries data processing div., 1968-69; exec. v.p. EDP Tech., Inc., Washington, 1969-71, pres., CEO, 1971-73; pres. Washington

Profl. Group, 1973-81; pres. SRC Corps. Equisource Source Corps; mng. dir. Pierce Investment Banking, Inc. Dir., mem. exec. com. Cornerstone R.E.I.T., 1993-96; chmn. bd. Paradigm Integration Corp., Empowernet, Inc. Asst. for domestic programs White House, Washington, 1966-67; chmn. bd. dirs. Congl. Mgmt. Found.; mem. fgn. service profl. devel. rev. group Dept. State, 1976; mem. U.S. Adv. Com. Vocat. Edn., 1968-69, U.S. Fed. Adv. Com. Employment Security, 1968-71, Com. for Excellence in Govt.; panel cons. Edn. Profl. Devel. Act, HEW, 1969-71; del. German Am. Forum, Bonn, Berlin, 1975; chmn. parents assn. Sidwell Friends Sch., Washington, 1976-78; vice chmn. fin. adv. com. Nat. Com. for Effective Congress, 1976-77. Served with AUS, 1957. White House fellow, 1966-67. Mem. White House Fellows Assn. (pres. Assn. and Found. 1973-74). Home and Office: 3238 O St NW Washington DC 20007-2842

GRAHAM, WILLIAM THOMAS, lawyer; b. Waynesboro, Va., Oct. 24, 1933; s. James Monroe and Margaret Virginia (Goodwin) G.; m. Kent Hill, Feb. 1, 1958; children: Ashton Cannon, William Thomas Jr. AB in Econs., Duke U., 1956; JD, U. Va., 1962. Bar: N.C. 1962, Va. 1962, D.C. 1970, U.S. Supreme Ct. 1970. Assoc. Craige, Brawley and predecessor firms, Winston-Salem, NC, 1962-64; ptnr. Craige, Brawley, Horton & Graham, Winston-Salem, 1965-69; asst. gen. counsel HUD, Washington, 1969-70; ptnr. Billings & Graham, Winston-Salem, 1971-75; judge N.C. Superior Ct., 1975-79; pvt. practice Winston-Salem, 1981-87; commr. of banks State of N.C., Raleigh, 1987-95; counsel Patton Boggs, LLP, Raleigh, 1995-98; pvt. practice William T. Graham Law Office, Raleigh and WinstonSalem, 1999—. Chmn. N.C. Inst. for Constl. Law, 2003—. Chmn. Forsyth County Reps., Winston-Salem, 1966-69, 73-75, George Bush for Pres., N.C., 1988. With U.S. Army, 1957-58. Mem. Old Town Club. Methodist. Avocation: travel. Home: 465 Sheffield Dr Winston Salem NC 27104 Office Phone: 336-725-3884. E-mail: wtggtw@aol.com.

GRAHAME, HEATHER H., lawyer; b. 1955; BA in Human Biol., Stanford Univ., 1978; JD, Univ. Oreg., 1984. Bar: Alaska 1984. Atty. Bogle & Gates PLLC, Anchorage; ptnr., co-chair, telecom. practice group Dorsey & Whitney LLP, Anchorage. Editor-in-chief Oreg. Law Rev., 1983—84. Pres. Alaska Dance Theatre, 2002—. Named Assoc. Mem. Yr., Alaska Telephone Assn., 1993. Mem.: ABA, Alaska Bar Assn., Federal Comm. Bar Assn. (Pacific NW chapt.). Achievements include Sixth place, US Cycling Team Time Trial Championships, 1988; Seventh place, Women's World Championship Sled Dog Race, 2002. Avocation: dog sledding. Office: Dorsey & Whitney LLP Ste 600 1031 W Fourth Ave Anchorage AK 99501-5907 Office Phone: 907-257-7822. Office Fax: 907-276-4152. Business E-Mail: grahame.heather@dorsey.com.

GRAHMANN, CHARLES V., bishop; b. Halletsville, Tex., July 15, 1931; Student, Assumption-St. John's Sem., Tex. Ordained priest Roman Cath. Ch., 1956. Ordained titular bishop Equilium and aux., San Antonio, 1981—82; 1st bishop Victoria, Tex., 1982—89; coadjutor biship Dallas, 1990; bishop Diocese of Dallas, 1990—. Office: Diocese of Dallas Chancery Office PO Box 190507 Dallas TX 75219-0507*

GRAINGER, AMANDA R., lawyer; b. Little Rock, Ark., Sept. 2, 1973; BS, Cornell U., 1995; MBA, JD, Emory U., 1999. Bar: Tex. 1999. Assoc. Winstead, Sechrest & Minick, Dallas, 1999—2004; assoc., pub. law & policy strategies group Sonnenschein Nath & Rosenthal LLP, Washington, 2004—. Office: Sonnenschein Nath & Rosenthal LLP Ste 600, E Tower 1301 K St NW Washington DC 20005 Office Phone: 202-408-3223. Office Fax: 202-408-6399. Business E-Mail: agrainger@sonnenschein.com.

GRAINGER, JOHN R., medical association administrator; COO Laidlaw, 1997-99; pres., CEO Am. Med. Response, Aurora, Colo., 1999—. Office: Am Med Response Inc 6200 S Syracuse Way Ste 200 Greenwood Village CO 80111-4739

GRAJKOWSKI, MICHELLE A., literary agent; b. Janesville, Wis., July 8, 1973; d. William E. Jabs and Carla J. Guildner; m. Kurt E. Grajkowski, July 1, 1995; children: Kara L., Creighton A. BS in Family and Consumer Comm., U. Wis., 1995. Systems cons. Vanguard Computers, Inc., Madison, Wis., 1995—99; purchasing agt. U. Wis. Hosp. and Clinics, Madison, 1999—2000; owner and lit. agt. 3 Seas Lit. Agy., Madison, 2000—. Family readiness leader Co. B, 132 SB Family Readiness Group Leader, Mauston, Wis., 2004—05; daisy troop co-leader Girl Scouts Am., Madison, 2004—05; mem. at large Home and Sch. Bd. for St. Dennis Sch., Madison, 2004—05. Mem.: Chgo. Women in Pub., Romance Writers Am. Office: 3 Seas Literary Agency PO Box 8571 Madison WI Office Phone: 608-221-4306. Personal E-mail: threeseaslit@aol.com.

GRALA, JANE M., security firm executive; b. Phila. d. Stanley and Anna. BS, Rutgers U., Camden, 1976; MBA, Winthrop U., 1979; postgrad., Am. Mgmt. Assn., N.Y.C., 1980-82, Am. Inst. Real Estate Appraisers, Chgo., 1985. Mgr. acctg. dept. NDI Engring. Co., Pennsauken, N.J., 1968-72, project mgr., 1972-76; rep. sales Am. Cyanamid, Wayne, N.J., 1976-80; dist. mgr. Am. Appraisal Assocs., Phila., 1980-86; assoc. v.p. investments Wachovia Securities LLC, Clearwater, Fla., 1986—. Adj. prof. fin. area Tampa (Fla.) Coll., 1995. Mem. Nat. Assn. Accts. (dir. advt. So. Jersey chpt. 1983-86), Assn. MBA Execs., Bus and Profl. Women's Assn., Nat. Assn. for Female Execs., Chi Delta, Phi Chi Theta. Republican. Avocation: archeology. Office: Wachovia Securities Inc 28100 Us Highway 19 N Ste 100 Clearwater FL 33761-2660

GRALAPP, MARCELEE GAYL, librarian; b. Winfield, Kans., Nov. 2, 1931; d. Benjamin Harry and Lelia Iris (Compton) G. BA, Kans. State Tchrs. Coll., 1952; MA, U. Denver, 1963. Children's libr. Hutchinson (Kans.) Pub. Libr., 1952-57, Lawrence (Kans.) Pub. Libr., 1957-59; assoc. libr. Boulder (Colo.) Pub. Libr., 1959-66, libr. dir., 1966—. Vis. faculty U. Denver, 1965-66, 67, Kans. State Tchrs. Coll., Emporia, 1965. Chmn. state plan for libr. devel. Librs.-Colo., 1974; city staff liaison Boulder Arts Commn., 1979—; bd. dirs. Boulder Ctr. for Visual Arts, 1975-79. Named Woman of Yr., Boulder Bus. and Profl. Women, 1997; recipient Gov.'s award, Colo. Coun. on Arts and Humanities, 1981, Boulder Spunky Woman award, 2001, Pacetter award for arts and entertainment, Daily Camera, 2003. Mem. ALA, Colo. Libr. Assn. (Lifetime Achievement award 1992), Delta Kappa Gamma. Democrat. Home: 3080 15th St Boulder CO 80304-2614 Office: Boulder Pub Libr PO Drawer H 1000 Canyon Blvd Boulder CO 80302-5120 E-mail: gralappm@ci.boulder.co.us.

GRALLA, EUGENE, natural gas company executive; b. N.Y.C., May 3, 1924; s. Jacob and Anna Ruth (Kleiman) G.; m. Beverly Dorman, Apr. 7, 1946; children: Rhona Gralla Spilka, Steven Stuart. BS, U.S. Naval Acad., 1945; MBA, Harvard U., 1947. Commd. ensign USN, 1945, advanced through grades to comdr., 1961; served sea duty, 1947-49, 54-56; control officer (Naval Supply Depot, Guantanamo Bay), Cuba, 1959-61; with (Office Asst. Sec. Def. for Installations and Logistics), 1961-64; ret., 1966; dir. data systems planning Trans World Airlines, N.Y.C., 1966-68; corp. dir. mgmt. info. systems Internat. Paper Co., N.Y.C., 1968; v.p. electronic data processing Columbia Gas System Service Corp., Wilmington, Del., 1969-73; sr. v.p. Columbia Gas Distbn. Cos., Columbus, Ohio, 1973-86, pres., 1986-89, ret., 1989. Mem. Harvard Bus. Sch. Club, Palm Beach Club, Ret. Officers Assn., Masons. Home: 7641 La Corniche Cir Boca Raton FL 33433-6007 Personal E-mail: bevandgene@aol.com.

GRALLA, LAWRENCE, publishing company executive; b. Bronx, N.Y., June 24, 1930; s. Meyer and Julia (Barnett) G.; m. Yvette Glickenstein, Dec. 24, 1952; children— Adele, Heidi. BS, BCNY, 1951. V.p. Nationwide Trade News Service, N.Y.C., 1951-55; pres. Gralla Publs., N.Y.C., 1955-87, exec. cons., 1987-2001; founding pub. Kitchen Bus., 1955, Bank Systems & Equipment, 1964, Multi-Housing News, 1966, Meeting News, 1977, Comml. Property News, 1988. Pres. Woodlands Community Temple, White Plains, N.Y., 1979-81. Recipient Govt. Israel Spl. Trade award 1980, Townsend Harris medal CCNY, 2002; named to Comm. Alumni Hall of Fame C.C.N.Y., 2000. Jewish.

GRALLA, MILTON, publisher; b. Bklyn., Jan. 28, 1928; s. Meyer and Julia (Barnett) G.; m. Shirley Edelson, Aug. 31, 1950; children— Edward, Karen, Dennis. BA in Journalism, CCNY, 1948; LHD (hon.), Yeshiva U., 1991. News reporter, 1948-51; co-founder nat. bus. news agy. N.Y.C., 1951-55; co-founder, exec. v.p. Gralla Pubs., N.Y.C., 1955-93. Adj. prof. journalism NYU, Ramapo Coll., Yeshiva U., 1989—; del. leader Reawakening 1990-91, Moscow, 1990. Author: How Good Guys Grow Rich, 1995. Candidate for Congress, N.J., 1974; chmn. Israel Salute parade, 1993-94. Recipient major awards (trade) Govt. of Israel, (community service) Brandeis U., United Jewish Appeal, Orgn. Rehab. Through Tng., NCCJ, medal of honor Ellis Island. Mem. Friars Club, 24 Karat Club. Republican. Jewish.

GRALOW, JULIE R., physician; b. Sanford, Fla., Feb. 10, 1959; d. Richard Thomas and Ruth Haas Gralow; m. Hugh Willison Allen. BS, Stanford U., 1981; MD, U. So. Calif., 1988; residency, Brighman Women's, Harvard, 1991. Cert. internal medicine 1991, med. oncology 1995. Rsch. asst. Becton Dickinson Monoclonal Ctr., Mountain View, Calif., 1981—83, Stanford U. Sch. Medicine, 1983—84; rsch. fellow U. So. Calif. Sch. Medicine, 1985; acting instr. U. Wash., Fred Hutchinson Cancer Rsch. Ctr., Seattle, 1994—97, asst. prof., 1998—2002, assoc. prof. med. oncology, 2002—. Dir. breast cancer inst. U. Wash. and Fred Hutchinson Cancer Rsch. Inst., Seattle, 2003—; assoc. program head breast cancer Fred Hutchinson Cancer Rsch. Ctr., 2001—. Author: (jour. article) Jour. Immunology, 1984, New Eng. Jour. Medicine, 1984. Cons. program for appropriate tech. in health USAID Ukraine Breast Cancer Assistance Project, 1997—2000; mem. ASCO Pub. Issues Com., 1999—; co-chair breast cancer com. Southwest Oncology Group, 2000—; co-chair ASCO Pub. Issues Com., 2000—02; liaison ASCO Health Svcs. Rsch. Com., 2000—; del. U. Wash. Ctr. for Women and Democracy, 2003. Recipient Career Devel. award, Am. Soc. Clin. Oncology, 1995—98, Clin. Career Devel. award, Am. Cancer Soc., 1995—98, Irving I. Lasky award, 1988, Janet M. Glasgow Achievement award, Am. Med. Women's Assn., 1988; U.S.C. Rsch. Fellowship, 1984—85, 1985—86. Mem.: Wash. State Med. Oncology Soc., Am. Soc. Breast Disease, Susan G. Komen Found. Breast Cancer Rsch., Nat. Alliance Breast Cancer Orgn., Puget Sound Oncology Group, Am. Assn. Cancer Rsch., Am. Soc. Clin. Oncology, AMA. Office: Seattle Cancer Care Alliance 825 Eastlake Ave E G4-830 Seattle WA 98109-1023 Office Phone: 206-288-7722.

GRAMBS, JENNIFER, writer; d. Mary E. (Butler) Koser; m. Jeffrey Wood Grambs, Sept. 28, 1970; 1 child, Alison Rebecca. BA in English Lit., Hunter Coll., 1980, MA in English Lit., 1986. City editor The East Orange (N.J.) Record, 1965-67; asst. to fashion columnist Eugenia Sheppard, N.Y. Post Women's Wear Daily, 1967-73; bus. owner The Jennifer Grambs Collection, N.Y.C., 1985—. Author: Alaska, 1990, Texas, 1990, Florida, 1990; contbr. articles to profl. publs.; also theater, film and video work. Hotline vol., support group facilitator Self-Help for Women with Breast Cancer (S.H.A.R.E.), 1994—; project LEAD grad. Nat. Breast Cancer Coalition, Washington.

GRAMES-LYRA, JUDITH ELLEN, artist, educator, municipal official; b. Inglewood, Calif, Feb. 7, 1938; d. Glover Victor and Dorothy Margaret (Burton-Bellingham) Hendrickson and Carolyne Marie Carrick Hendrickson (stepmother); children: Nanséa Ellen Ryan, Amber Jeanne Shelley-Harris, Carolyn Jane Angel Longmire, Susan Elaine Gomez, Robert Derek Shallenberger; m. Jon Robert Lyra, Feb. 14, 1997. Cert in journalism, Newspaper Inst. Am., N.Y.C., 1960; AA, Santa Barbara City Coll., 1971; BA, U. Calif., Santa Barbara, 1978, cert. in teaching, 1979. Cert. bldg. inspector, plumbing inspector, Calif. Editor, reporter, photographer Goleta Valley Sun Newspaper, Santa Barbara, 1968-71; editor, team asst. Bur. of Ednl. Rsch. Devel., Santa Barbara, 1971; bus. writer, graphics cons. Santa Barbara, 1971-77; art and prodn. dir. Bedell Advt. Selling Improvement Corp., Santa Barbara, 1979-81; secondary sch. tchr. Coalinga Unified Sch. Dist., Calif., 1981-83; bldg. insp. aide Santa Barbara County, Lompoc, 1983-88, from bldg. engring. inspector I to III, 1988-99, asst. plans examiner, 1999—2003. Exhibited in group shows at Foley's Frameworks and Interiors, 1984, Grossman Gallery, 1984, 98, Lompoc Valley Art Assn., 1984— (Best of Show 1985, 1st pl. 1984, 94, 2002, 04, 05, 2d pl. 1984, 86, 88, 96-97, 99, 3d pl. 1987, 89, 97, 2003-05, Judge's Choice award 2004, others), Brushes and Blues Invitational, 1998; featured artist Harvest Arts Festival, 1989, Cypress Gallery, 1994, 2004; author numerous poems Mem. disaster response team Calif. Bldg. Ofcl., 1992-2003, cmty. emergency response team; exec. bd. dir. Lompoc Mural Soc., 1991-2003; planning commr. City of Lompoc Scholar, Delta Kappa Gamma. Mem. NOW, Nat. Abortion Rights Action League, Nat. Mus. of Women in the Arts (charter), Nat. Womens History Mus. (charter), Lompoc Valley Art Assn. (bd. dirs.), Toastmasters Internat. (Outstanding Speaker award 1991-93). Avocations: painting, stained glass, home improvement activities, illustrating note cards, writing children's stories.

GRAMLICH, EDWARD MARTIN, public policy and economics educator, former federal agency administrator; b. Rochester, N.Y., June 18, 1939; s. Jacob Edward and Harriet (Williams) G.; m. Ruth Brown, Aug. 29, 1964; children: Sarah and Robert. BA, MA, Williams Coll.; PhD, Yale U. Mem. research div. Fed. Res. Bd., 1965-70, office of edon. opportunity policy research div., 1970-73, dir., 1971-73; sr. fellow The Brookings Inst., 1973-76; prof. econs. and pub. policy U. Mich., 1976—97, 2005—, dir. Inst. Pub. Policy Studies, 1979-83, 1991—95, chmn. econs. dept., 1983—86, dean Sch. Public Policy, 1995—97, interim provost & exec. v.p. for acad. affairs, 2005—; mem. bd. gov. Fed. Res. Sys., 1997—2005. Vis. lectr. Monash U., Australia, 1970, Stockholm U., 1979; adj. prof. George Washington U., 1974-75; vis. prof. Cornell U., 1975-76; cons. Res. Bank of Australia, 1970, Nat. Inst. Edn., 1973-75, Dept. of Labor, 1973-75, HEW, 1974—, Congl. Budget Office, 1975-78, Senate of Puerto Rico, 1975, Collier's Encyclopedia, 1975-79, Indsl. Research Inst., Sweden, 1979-81, Abt Assocs., 1979-80, Minimum Wage Study Commn., 1981, Fed. Res. Bd. Acad. Cons., 1981. Author: Savings Deposits, Mortgages and Housing in the FRB-Mit-Penn Econometric Model, 1972, Educational Performance Contracting: An Evaluation of an Experiment, 1975, Setting National Priorities: The 1975 Budget, 1974, Setting National Priorities: The 1976 Budget, 1975, Benefit-Cost Analysis of Governmental Programs, 1981, Tax Reform: There Must Be A Better Way, 1982. Editorial bd. National Tax Jour., 1970-73, Jour. Policy Analysis and Mgmt., 1980, Evaluation Review, 1980-83, Jour. Econ. Lit., 1981—. Contbr. articles to profl. jours. Mem. Brookings Panel on Economic Activity, 1973—, Brookings Panel on Social Experimentation, 1973-74, White House Summit Conf., 1974, Econ. Adv. Panel Nat. Inst. of Edn., 1973-74, Edn. Grants Panel, Nat. Inst. Edn., 1973-74, Edn. and Human Resources Adv. Bd., Rand Corp., 1975-78, Com. on Evaluation Research, Social Sci. Research Council, 1977-79, N.Y. State Productivity Commn., 1977-79, Assn. for Pub. Policy and Mgmt. (policy council 1979-84, v.p. 1979-80, program chmn. 1981), Nat. Acad. of Scis. Edn. Research Found., 1980—, State of Mich. Com. on Prof. and Occupational Licensure, 1981-82, Sime-Dime Rev. Panel, Dept. of Health and Human Services, 1980-81, Vis. Com. Albion Coll. Pub. Policy Sch., 1981—, Truman Scholarship Selection Panel, Michigan-Ohio, 1982—, Review Com., Md. Econs. Dept., 1993—, Chmn., Nat. Inst. of Edn. Policy Study Group, 1983. Office: U Mich 3074 Fleming Bldg Ann Arbor MI 48109 E-mail: nedg@umich.edu.

GRAMLICH, LARRY E., lawyer; b. Independence, Mo., 1961; BA, Valparaiso Univ., 1983; JD, Duke Univ., 1986. Bar: Ga. 1986. Assoc. Troutman Sanders LLP, Atlanta, 1986—94, ptnr., real estate fin., 1995—, practice leader, comml. develop. and real estate investments, 1998—2000, hiring ptnr., 2000—01. Mem.: ABA, Nat. Assn. Office and Industrial Properties, Atlanta Bar Assn., State Bar Ga. Office: Troutman Sanders LLP One Logan Sq Ste 5200 600 Peachtree St NE Atlanta GA 30308-2216 Office Phone: 404-885-3607. Office Fax: 404-962-6573. Business E-Mail: larry.gramlich@troutmansanders.com.

GRAMM, WENDY LEE, economics professor, retired government agency administrator; b. Waialua, HI, Jan. 9, 1945; d. Joshua and Angeline (AnChin) Lee; m. Phil Gramm, Nov. 2, 1970; children: Marshall Kenneth, Jefferson Philip. BA in Econs., Wellesley Coll., 1966; PhD in Econs., Northwestern U., 1971. Staff dept. quantitive methods U. Ill., 1969; asst. prof. Tex. A&M U., 1970-74, assoc. prof. dept. econs., 1975-79; research staff Inst. Def. Analyses, 1979-82; asst. dir. Bur. Econs. FTC, 1982-83, dir., 1983-85; adminstr. Office Info. and Regulatory Affairs, OMB, 1985-87; chmn. Commodity Futures Trading Commn., 1988-93; prof. econs. and pub. adminstrn. U. Tex., Arlington, 1993; chmn., regulatory studies prog. & disting. sr. fellow, Mercatus Ctr. George Mason U. Bd. dirs. Enron Corp., 1993—2002, Tex. Pub. Policy Found.; legal adv. bd. Nat. Fedn. Ind. Bus. Contbr. articles to profl. jours. Mem.: Ind. Women's Forum (bd. dirs.). Office: GMU Mercatus Ctr 3301 N Fairfax Dr, Ste 450 Arlington VA 22201

GRAMMER, JEFFREY, wireless semiconductor company executive; BA in Internat. Econ., MA in Internat. Econ., Boston U. With Intel; joined Chips and Technolgies, Inc., 1985; pres., CEO Summit Sys., 1991—95, Databook Inc., 1995—96; co-founder, pres., CEO N*ABLE Technologies (acquired by Wave Sys. Corp.), Danvers, Mass., 1996—99; co-founder, mng. dir. TechFarm Ventures, 2000—02; pres., CEO Ember Corp., Boston, 2002—. Office: Ember Corp 343 Congress St 5th Fl Boston MA 02210 Office Phone: 617-951-0200. Office Fax: 617-951-0999.

GRAMMER, JOHN COLQUITTE, cardiologist; b. Brenham, Tex., June 20, 1925; Student, Tex. A&M U., 1942-44; MD, U. Tex., 1947. Diplomate Am. Bd. Internal Medicine, Am. Bd. Cardiovascular Diseases. Intern Ft. Worth City-County Hosp., 1947-48; resident internal medicine Kansas City (Mo.) Gen. Hosp., 1948-51, U. Pa. Hosp., Phila., 1953-54; fellow cardiology Scripps Clin. Rsch. Found., 1966-67; dir. cardiac care unit St. Paul Med. Ctr., Dallas, 1967-97; clin. assoc. prof. internal medicine U. Tex. S.W.; pvt. practice. Med. author, lectr., filmmaker. Lt. USNR, 1951—53. Fellow ACP, Am. Coll. Cardiology, Am. Coll. Chest Physicians. Office: 3602 N Versailles Ave Dallas TX 75209-6230 Office Phone: 214-521-5068.

GRAMMER, KELSEY, actor; b. St. Thomas, V.I., Feb. 21, 1955; s. Sally and Allen Grammer; m. Camille Donatacci, Aug. 2, 1997; children: Mason Olivia, Jude Gordon. Studied, Juilliard Sch., N.Y.C. Actor (films) Toy Story 2 (voice), 1999, 15 Minutes, 1999, New Jersey Turnpikes, 1999, Standing on Fishes, 1999, The Real Howard Spitz, 1998, Down Periscope, 1996, (voice) Anastasia, 1997, (TV series) Cheers, 1984-93, Frasier, 1993-2004 (Best New Comedy award Viewers Quality TV, Favorite Male in New TV Series award 20th Ann. People's Choice Awards, Lead Actor Emmy award - Comedy Series, 1994, 1995, 98, Best Actor in TV Series Golden Globe award 1996, 2000, Emmy award Outstanding Lead Actress in a Comedy Series, 2004, other awards), 15 Minutes, 2001; appeared in (Off-Broadway prodns.) Plenty, A Month in the Country, Sunday in the Park with George, Quartermaine's Terms, (Broadway prodns.) Macbeth, Othello, TV appearances include Kate and Allie (premiere episode), Wings, Tracy Ullman Show, The Simpsons, mini-series include Kennedy, 1983, George Washington, 1984, Crossings, 1986; TV movies include Dance 'til Dawn, 1988, Beyond Suspicion, 1993, (also exec. prodr.) The Innocent, 1994, London Suite, 1996, The Pentagon Wars, The Sports Pages, 2001; exec. prodr. (TV series) Fired Up, 1997; voice (video) Bartok the Magnificent, 1999, (TV) Animal Farm, 1999, The Hand Behind the Mouse: The Ub Iwerks Story, 1999; guest appearance Stark Raving Mad, 1999. Recipient SAG award, 2000. Office: The Artists Agency Ste 301 1180 S Beverly Dr Los Angeles CA 90035-1154

GRAMMIG, ROBERT (BOB) JAMES, lawyer; b. Oceanside, Calif., June 15, 1956; s. Richard Adolf and Mary Elizabeth (Spisak) G.; m. Laurel Jean Lenfestey, Aug. 10, 1996; children: Clare Marie, James Richard. BA summa cum laude, MA, U. Pa., 1978; JD, Harvard U., 1981. Bar: Fla. 1982, D.C. 1986, U.S. Dist. Ct. (mid. dist.) Fla. 1982, U.S. Ct. Appeals (11th and 5th cirs.) 1982, U.S. Supreme Ct. 1985. Law clk. to Hon. Thomas A. Clark U.S. Ct. Appeals (5th and 11th cirs.), Atlanta, 1981-82; assoc. Holland & Knight LLP, Tampa, Fla., 1982-88, ptnr., 1989—, mem. dir. com. Contbr. articles to profl. jours. Bd. dirs. Child Abuse Coun., Tampa, 1993-97; mem. Leadership Tampa, 1994-95; Sec. Tampa Bay Internat. Trade Coun., 1994, vice chmn., 1995. Mem. Hillsborough County Bar Assn., Tampa Bay Coun. on Fgn. Rels., German Am. C. of C., U.S.-Austrian C. of C., Phi Beta Kappa. Republican. Roman Catholic. Home: 21 Bahama Cir Tampa FL 33606-3317 Office: Holland & Knight LLP 100 N Tampa St Ste 4100 Tampa FL 33602-4322 Office Phone: 813-227-8500. Business E-Mail: rgrammig@hklaw.com.

GRAMSTORFF, JEANNE B., retired farmer; b. Floydada, Tex., June 23, 1930; d. David Stephen Battey and Ruth Asbury Pitts; m. John C. Gramstorff, Feb. 14, 1951 (dec. Feb. 1993); children: Susan G. Gramstorff Fetzer, John C. BA, Tex. Tech U., 1951. Cert. tchr. Tex. Tchr. Perryton (Tex.) Mid. and HS's, 1951-66; farmer Gramstorff & Son, Farnsworth, Tex., 1951-2000; ret., 2000. Bd. dirs. Perryton Nat. Bank. Trustee, officer Perry Meml. Libr., Perryton, 1956—, pres., 2000—03; officer Tex. Panhandle Libr. Sys. Coun., Amarillo, 1978—, chmn., 2001—02; bd. dirs. Lydia Patterson Inst., 1993—2000; sec. Accord Agr., Inc., Farnsworth, 1995—; historian, v.p., pres. N.W. Tex. United Meth. Women; chmn. religion and race com., chmn. dist. mission N.W. Tex. Conf. United Meth. Ch., 1996—2005, chmn. comm. religion and race, 2004—05, mem. ann. conf., 1976—2004, mem. conf. ministry team, 2004—05. Avocations: reading, needlepoint. Home: PO Box 250 Farnsworth TX 79033-0250 Personal E-mail: jgram@starband.net.

GRANADE, CALLIE VIRGINIA SMITH, federal judge; b. Lexington, Va., Mar. 7, 1950; d. Milton Hannibal and Callie Dougherty (Rives) Smith; m. Fred King Granade, Oct. 9, 1976; children: Taylor Rives, Milton Smith, Joseph Kee. BA, Hollins Coll., 1972; JD, U. Tex., 1975. Bar: Tex. 1975, Ala. 1976, U.S. Ct. Appeals (5th cir.) 1976, U.S. Dist. Ct. (so. dist.) Ala. 1977, U.S. Supreme Ct. 1980, U.S. Ct. Appeals (11th cir.) 1981. Law clk. to chief judge John Godbold US Ct. Appeals (5th cir.), Montgomery, Ala., 1975-76; asst. US atty. US Dept. Justice, Mobile, 1977, sr. litigation counsel, 1987-90; chief criminal sect. US Atty.'s Office, Mobile, 1990-97; 1st asst. US Atty. Southern Dist. of Ala., 1997—2001, interim US Atty., 2001—02, judge, 2002—, chief judge, 2003—. Mem. ABA, Fed. Bar Assn., Ala. State Bar Assn., Tex. State Bar Assn., Mobile Bar Assn., Am. Coll. Trial Lawyers. Presbyterian. Office: US Courthouse 113 St Joseph St Mobile AL 36602

GRANATH, HERBERT A., television industry executive; b. NYC, 1928; Grad., Fordham U., 1954. Pres. Capital Cities/ABC Video Enterprises, Inc., N.Y.C.; chmn. ESPN Cable Network, Arts & Entertainment Cable Network, Lifetime Cable Network, Biography Channel, History Channel; founding ptnr. Eurosport; vice-chmn. TV Acad. Trustee Am. Mus. Moving Image; bd. dirs. Ctrl. European Media, Crown Media, Intl. Radio and TV Soc., others. Named to Rose d'Or Hall of Fame, 2005; recipient Two Tony awards, Emmy award, Lifetime Achievement in Sports TV, Lifetime Achievement in Intl. TV. Mem.: League NY Theater Owners & Producers, Trans-Atlantic Dialogue European Comm. Office: Capital Cities/ABC Video Enterprises Inc 77 W 66th St New York NY 10023-6201*

GRANATO, CAROL ANNE, writer; b. Phila., May 2, 1946; d. Leo Joseph De Stephanis and Margaret McLean; m. Robert Natale Granato, June 20, 1964; children: Robert Anthony, Stephen. Clk. typist Reliance Ins., Phila., 1963-65; receptionist Phila. Coll. Art, 1984-85; nursing office asst. Meth. Hosp., Phila., 1987; freelance writer, editor Garnet Pub., Phila., 1999—. Author, editor: The Universe and Beyond, 1999; contbr. poems to lit. jours. Asst. dir. Edward Rendell for Mayor, Phila., 1988, 92. Democrat. Roman Catholic. Avocations: paranormal research, gardening, cooking, educational reading. Home: 2506 S 18th St Philadelphia PA 19145-3701 Office: Garnet Pub PO Box 11955 Philadelphia PA 19145 E-mail: garnet1945@aol.com.

GRANATO, CATHERINE (CAMMI GRANATO), Olympic athlete; b. Downers Grove, Ill., Mar. 25, 1971; d. Natalie and Don Granato. Student, Providence Coll., R.I., 1989-93, Concordia U., 1994-97. Hockey player U.S.

Nat. Team, 1992—. Recipient Gold Medal, Women's Ice Hockey, Nagano Olympic Games, 1998, Silver Medal, Salt Lake City Olympic Games, 2002. Office: USA Hockey Inc 1775 Bob Johnson Dr Colorado Springs CO 80906-4090

GRANATSTEIN, JACK LAWRENCE, historian; b. Toronto, May 21, 1939; s. S. Benjamin and Shirley (Geller) G.; m. Mary Elaine Hitchcock, 1961; children: Carole, Michael (dec.) BA, Royal Mil. Coll., Kingston, Ont., 1961; MA, U. Toronto, 1962; PhD, Duke U., 1966; DLitt (hon.), Meml. U., 1993; LLD (hon.), U. Calgary, 1994, Ryerson Polytech. U., 1999, U. We. Ont., 2000, McMaster U., 2000, Niagara U., 2004. Historian Dept. Nat. Def., Ottawa, Ont., 1965-66; prof. history York U., 1966-95, Disting. rsch. prof. history emeritus, 1995—; Rowell Jackman fellow Canadian Inst. of Internat. Affairs, 1995-98; commr. Spl. Commn. on the Restructuring of the Can. Forces Reserves, 1995; CEO, dir. Can. War Mus., 1998-2000; chair Coun. for Can. Security in 21st Century, 2001—05. Author: Politics of Survival, 1967, Canada's War, 1975, Broken Promises, 1977, Ties That Bind, 1977, American Dollars-Canadian Prosperity, 1978, A Man of Influence, 1981, The Ottawa Men, 1982, Twentieth Century Canada, 1983, The Great Brain Robbery, 1984, Canada 1957-67, 1986, Sacred Trust? Brian Mulroney and the Conservatives in Power, 1986, The Collins Dictionary of Canadian History, 1988, Marching to Armageddon, 1989, How Britain's Weakness Forced Canada into the Arms of the United States, 1989, A Nation Forged in Fire, 1989, Pirouette: Pierre Trudeau and Canadian Foreign Policy, 1990, Mutual Hostages: Canadians and Japanese in the Second World War, 1990, Spy Wars, Espionage and Canada from Gouzenko to Glasnost, 1990, For Better or Worse: Canada and the U.S. to the 1990's, War and Peacekeeping, 1991, English Canada Speaks Out, 1991, Oxford Dictionary of Canadian Military History, 1992, The Generals: The Canadian Army's Senior Commanders in the Second World War, 1993, Empire to Umpire: Canada and the World to the 1990's, 1994, The Good Fight: Canadians and World War II, 1995, Victory 1945: Canadians From War to Peace, 1995, Yankee Go Home? Canadians and Anti-Americanism, 1997, The Canadian 100, 1997, Petrified Campus: The Crisis of Canada's Universities, 1997, The Veterans Charter and Post World War II Canada, 1998, Who Killed Canadian History?, 1998, Trudeau's Shadow, 1998, Prime Ministers, 1999, Our Century, 2000, Canada's Army, 2002, First Drafts, 2002, Importance of Being Less Earnest, 2003, Who Killed the Canadian Military, 2004, Hell's Corner, 2004, Battle Lines, 2004, The Last Good War, 2005. Bd. govs. Royal Mil. Coll., 1996-2005, Can. Def. and Fgn. Affairs Inst., 2004—. Served to lt. Can. Army, 1956-66. Recipient Tyrrell medal for Can. history, 1992, J.W. Dafoe prize, 1993, medal for biography U. B.C., 1993, Vimy award Conf. Def. Assns. Inst., 1996, Pierre Berton prize 2004; Killam rsch. fellow Can. Coun., 1982-84, 91-93; rsch. grantee Can. Dept. External Affairs, 1978-80, Can. Dept. Nat. Def., 1987-88, Social Sci. and Humanities Rsch. Coun. Can., 1978-79, 82-84, 85-89, 91-97; named officer Order of Can., 1997. Fellow Royal Soc. Can. Home: 52 St Andrews Gardens Toronto ON Canada M4W 2E1 Personal E-mail: jgranatstein@bellnet.ca.

GRANATSTEIN, VICTOR LAWRENCE, electrical engineer, educator; b. Toronto, Feb. 8, 1935; s. Charles Samuel and Bella (Godfrey) G.; m. Bethie Mills, Sept. 4, 1955; children: Rebecca Miriam, Abraham Solomon, Annie Sara Khaya. BS, Columbia U., 1960, MS, 1961, PhD, 1963. Rsch. staff physicist Bell Tel. Labs., Murray Hill, NJ, 1964-72; head high power electromagnetic radiation br. Naval Rsch. Lab., Washington, 1972-83; prof. elec. engring. U. Md., College Park, 1983—, acting dir. Inst. for Plasma Rsch., 1986-88, dir., 1988-98. Vis. lectr. Hebrew U., Jerusalem, 1969—70; vis. prof. Tel Aviv U., 1994, 2003, Sackler prof. of spl. standing, 2004—; cons. BDM Corp., McLean, Va., 1981—83, Sci. Applications Corp., McLean, Va., 1983—, Omega-P Inc., New Haven, 1983—2000, Pulse Scis. Inc., San Leandro, Calif., 1985—88, Jet Propulsion Lab., Pasadena, Calif., 1987—91, Mission Res. Corp., Newington, Va., 2001—. Editor: Wave Heating and Current Drive in Magnetic Plasmas, 1985, High Power Microwaves, 1987, Applications of High Power Microwaves, 1994; contbr. articles to profl. jours.; patentee microwave devices. Pres. Bethesda-Chevy Chase Jewish Cmty. Group, 1983—84. Recipient R.D. Conrad award Sec. Navy, 1981, Superior Civilian Svc. award Office Naval Rsch., 1980, E.O. Hulbert award Naval Rsch. Lab., 1980, Robert L. Woods award Sec. Def., 1998; Fulbright sr. scholar, 1993-94, Fulbright sr. specialist, 2003, 2004-05. Fellow IEEE (life, vice chmn. plasma sci. com. 1984-85, Plasma Sci. and Applications award 1991), Am. Phys. Soc. Democrat. Avocations: folk dancing, swimming. Home: 13508 Rippling Brook Dr Silver Spring MD 20906-3177 Office: U Md Inst Rsch in Electronics and Applied Physics College Park MD 20742-3511 Business E-Mail: vlg@umd.edu.

GRANBERRY, EDWIN PHILLIPS, JR., safety engineer, consultant; b. Orange, N.J., Aug. 20, 1926; s. Edwin Phillips Sr. and Mabel (Leflar) G.; m. Joanne Park, June 15, 1991; children: Melissa, Edwin Phillips III, James, Jennifer, Claudia. BS, Rollins Coll., 1950; MBA, Embry Riddle Aero. U., 1985. Cert. profl. chemist. Weapons sys. engr. Martin Co., Orlando, Fla., 1958-62; supt. indsl. safety Guided Missiles Range divsn. Pan Am. World Airways, Cape Canaveral, Fla., 1962-72; mgr. indsl. hygiene/safety engring. Pratt & Whitney Aircraft, West Palm Beach, Fla., 1972-88; mgr. indsl. and sys. safety engring. Chem. Sys. divsn. United Tech. Corp., San Jose, Calif., 1988-89; pres. Granberry & Assocs. Inc., Winter Park, Fla., 1989—. Adj. faculty Valencia C.C., Orlando; mem. Fla. State Toxic Substances Adv. Coun., 1984-88, Fla. State Emergency Response Commn., 1988, Fla. Divsn. Safety Customer Adv. Coun.; mem. restoration adv. bd. U.S. Naval Tng. Sta., Orlando, 1996—. Scoutmaster Boy Scouts Am., 1946-74, dist. chmn. Wekiwa dist. Ctrl. Fla. coun., 1946-74, also coun. commr. Served with USNR, 1944-54, PTO. Recipient Silver Beaver award Boy Scouts Am., 1960. Fellow Am. Inst. Chemists; mem. ASTM, Welding Soc., Am. Chem. Soc., Am. Bd. Forensic Examiners, Am. Nat. Stds. Inst., Nat. Fire Protection Assn., Rollins Coll. Alumni Assn. (bd. dirs. 1958-61), Am. Soc. Safety Engrs. (chmn. Gold Coast chpt. 1979-90, pres. 1981-84, regional v.p. 1984-88, 94—, v.p. divsns. 1988-90, adminstr. environ. divsn. 1992—, nat. bd. dirs. 1984-90, 94—), Am. Soc. Safety Engrs. Found. (chmn. 1997—, Saftey Profl. of Yr. Fla., Ga., P.R. chpts., 1985, Saftey Profl of Yr. divs., 1991, Saftey Profl. of Yr. Environ. Divsn. 1995-96), Safety Coun. Palm Beach County (pres. 1981-82, chmn. bd. 1983, treas. 1984). Home: 521 Langholm Dr Winter Park FL 32789-5251 Office: Granberry & Assocs Inc 2431 Aloma Ave Ste 276 Winter Park FL 32792-2566

GRAND, MARCIA, civic worker; b. N.Y.C., Aug. 9, 1933; d. Irving and Dorothy (Miller) Kosta; m. Richard Grand, Jan. 27, 1952. Student, U. Ariz., 1950-52, 59-60. Docent, coord., docent trainer Tucson Mus. Art, 1965-71; bd. dirs., 1972-79; chmn. edn. com., 1975-79; v.p., sec. Richard Grand Found., 1966-80; pres., 1980—. Bd. dirs., sec. U. Ariz. Found., 1979-80, v.p., 1986-87, chmn. exec. com., 1986-87; mem. spl. com. office of chair U. Ariz., 1987-92; bd. dirs. Tucson Airport Authority, Greenfield Schs., 1977-82; bd. fellows Ctr. Creative Photography, 1984-98, chmn., 1993-98, mem.-at-large, bd. dirs. Tucson Mus. Art League, 1977-78; bd. trustees San Francisco Art Inst., 1995-2003. Nominated for YWCA Woman on the Move award, 1982; recipient Cmty. Svc. award Mortar Bd., 1978, Disting. Citizen award U. Ariz. Coll. Fine Arts, 1979. Office: 127 W Franklin St Tucson AZ 85701-1020 E-mail: rg@rgrand.com.

GRAND, RICHARD D., lawyer; b. Danzig, Feb. 20, 1930; came to U.S., 1939, naturalized, 1944; s. Morris and Rena Grand; m. Marcia Kosta, Jan. 27, 1952. BA, NYU, 1951; JD, U. Ariz., 1958. Bar: Ariz. 1958, Calif. 1973, U.S. Supreme Ct. 1973; cert. specialist in injury litigation Ariz. Bd. Legal Specialization. Dep. atty., Pima County, Ariz., 1958-59; pvt. practice trial law Tucson, 1959—; founder, 1st pres. Inner Circle Advocates, 1972-75; founder Richard Grand Found., 1966, now chmn.; hon. pres. Richard Grand Soc., 1997—. Contbr. articles to legal publs. Mem. bd. visitors law sch. Ariz. State U. Recipient citation of honor Lawyers Coop. Pub. Co., 1964, Profl. Achievement award U. Ariz., 2002. Fellow Am. Acad. Forensic Scis., Internat. Soc. Barristers; mem. Internat. Med. Soc. Paraplegia (assoc.), Am. Coll. Legal Medicine (assoc.), ABA, Pima County Bar Assn., Am. Bd. Trial Advs. (cert. in civil trial advocacy), Brit. Acad. Forensic Scis., Richard Grand Soc. (hon. pres.), Bohemian Club. Address: 127 W Franklin St Tucson AZ 85701-1020 Office Phone: 520-622-8855. Business E-Mail: RG@rgrand.com. *His thinking is his passport. Dream— there is no charge for alterations. The Jury grows a communal nose with which it smells out the strengths and weaknesses of a case.*

GRANDI, ATTILIO, engineering consultant; b. La Spezia, Italy, Sept. 24, 1929; s. Luigi and Egle (Canese) G.; m. Maria Teresa Berti, Apr. 23, 1962; 1 child, Giovanni. Maturita scientifica, Liceo Scientifico Pacinotti, La Spezia, 1949; univ. degree in aero. engring., U. Pisa (Italy), 1958. Project engr. S.p.A. Piaggio, Pontedera, Italy, 1959-60, Termomeccanica Italiana, La Spezia, 1960-71, tech. mgr., 1971-85, rsch. and mktg. mgr., 1985-88; cons. hydraulic machinery refrigeration and marine propulsive systems, 1988—. Patentee in field. Mem. Italian Standard Hydraulic Machinery Roman Catholic. Avocations: mathematics, old languages, fishing.

GRANDIN, TEMPLE, industrial designer; b. Boston, Aug. 29, 1947; d. Richard McCurdy and Eustacia (Cutler) G. BA in Psychology, Franklin Pierce Coll., 1970; MS in Animal Sci., Arizona State U., 1975; PhD in Animal Sci., U. Ill., Urbana, 1989; D (hon.), McGill U., 1999. Livestock editor Ariz. Farmer Ranchman, Phoenix, 1973-78; equipment designer Corral Industries, Phoenix, 1974-75; ind. cons. Grandin Livestock Systems, Urbana, 1975-90, Fort Collins, Colo., 1990—; lectr., assoc. prof. animal sci. dept. Colo. State U., Fort Collins, 1990—. Chmn. handing com. Livestock Conservation Inst., Madison, Wis., 1976—; surveyor USDA. Author: Emergence Labelled Autistic, 1986, Recommended Animal Handling Guidelines for Meat Packers, 1991, Livestock Handling and Transport, 1993, 2nd edit., 2000, Thinking in Pictures, 1995, Genetics and the Behavior of Domestic Animals, 1998, Beef Cattle Behavior Handling and Facilities Design, 2000, Animals in Translation, 2005; contbg. editor Meat and Poultry mag., 1987-98; contbr. articles to profl. jours.; patentee in field. Named One of Processing Stars of 1990 Nat. Provisioner, 1990, Woman of Yr. in Svc. to Agr. Progressive Farmer, 1999; recipient Meritorious Svcs. award Livestock Conservation, Madison, Wis., 1986, Disting. Alumni award Franklin Pierce Coll., 1989, Industry Innovators award Meat Mktg. and Tech. Mag., 1994, Brownlee award for internat. leadership in sci. publ. promoting respect for animals Animal Welfare Found. of Canada, 1995, Harry Roswell award Scientists Ctr. for Animal Welfare, 1995, Humane Ethics in Action award Geraldine R. Dodge Found., 1998, Forbes award Nat. Meat Assn., 1998, Founders award Am. Soc. Prevention Cruelty Animals, 1999, Humane award Am. Vet. Med. Assn., 1999, Joseph Wood Krutch award, Humane Soc. of U.S., 2001, Knowlton Innovation award in Meat Mktg. and Tech. Mag., 2001, 2002, Animal Welfare award, Brit. Soc. Animal Sci. and Royal Soc. Prevention Cruelty to Animals, 2002, Pres.'s award, Nat. Inst. Animal Agr., 2004. Mem. Autism Soc. Am. (bd. dirs. 1988-, Trammel Crow award 1989), Am. Soc. Animal Sci. (Animal Mgmt. award 1995, Disting. Svc. award We. sect. 2003), Am. Soc. Agrl. Cons. (bd. dirs. 1981-83), Am. Soc. Agrl. Engrs., Am. Meat Inst. (supplier mem., Industry Advancement award 1995), Am. Registry of Profl. Animal Scis. Republican. Episcopalian. Achievements include design of stockyards and humane restraint equipment for major meat packing companies in the U.S., Canada and Australia; development of an objective scoring system used for monitoring animal welfare in slaughter plants. Office: Colo State U Animal Sci Dept Fort Collins CO 80523-0001 Office Phone: 970-229-0703.

GRANDMAISON, J. JOSEPH, federal agency administrator; b. Nashua, N.H., May 19, 1943; s. Oscar N. and Irene P. (Bouchard) G. BA, Burdett Coll., 1963. Campaign dir. Dukakis for Gov., Boston, 1973-74; dir. fed. state relations Commonwealth of Mass., Washington, 1975—; Dem. candidate U.S. Ho. of Reps., 1976; fellow John F. Kennedy Inst. Politics Harvard U., 1976—; fed. co-chmn. New Eng. Regional Commn., Washington, 1977-81; econ. devel. and polit. cons. Augusta, Maine, 1981—93; v.p. Weil & Howe, Augusta, 1983—93; commentator, polit. analyst Sta. WMUR-TV, Manchester, 1986—; dir. U.S. Trade and Devel. Agy., Washington, 1993—2001. Adj. prof. Boston U. Coll. Communications; co-host Focus N.H., 1987-90; bd. dirs. U.S. Export-Import Bank. Mem. bd. aldermen, Nashua, NH, 1970—71; chair N.H. Dem. Party, 1987—90; dem. nominee Gov. of N.H., 1990. Democrat. Roman Catholic. Office: US Export Import Bank Bd of Dir 811 Vermont Ave NW Washington DC 20571-0001 Office Phone: 202-565-3530.

GRAND-MAITRE, JEAN, performing company executive; b. Hull, Quebec; Studied at, York U., Montreal's L'Ecole superieure de danse du Quebec, 1983—86. Ind. choreographer Can. and Europe, 1990—2002; artistic dir. Alberta Ballet, 2002—. Danced with Theatre Ballet of Can., 1987—89, Les Ballets de Montreal Eddy Toussaint, 1990, Ballet British Columbia, 1991; artist in residence Bayerisches Staatsballet, 1998—99, Nat. Norwegian Ballet, 1999—2000. Major commissions include La Veglia degli Angeli, Teatro all Scala, Milan, 1995, Exilium, Stuggart Ballet, 1997, Eja Mater, Paris Opera Ballet, 1997, Ecclesia and Emma B., Bavarian State Ballet, Munich, 1998, 1999, Liaisons Dangereuses, Nat. Ballet of Norway, 2000, Frames of Mind, Hartford Ballet, 1995, Ancient Airs and Uroboros, 1996, 1999, Romeo and Juliet, Dance Conneticut, 2000, The Winter Room, Ballet BC, 1995, Boy Wonder, 1996, Tema Celeste, 2000, La Memoire de l'eau, Les Grand Ballets Canadiens, 1997, Carmen, 2002, Cinderella, 2004, Alberta Ballet. Nominee Dora Mavor Moore award. Office: Alberta Ballet Nat Christie Ctr 141-18 Ave South West Calgary AB T2S 0B8 Canada Office Phone: 403-245-4222 ext. 523. Business E-Mail: jeang@albertaballet.com.

GRANDPRÉ, MARY, illustrator, pastel artist; Attended, Minn. Coll. Art & Design. Conceptual illustrator various local editl. clients; visionary, environ. & scenery dept. DreamWorks' prodn. Antz; illustrator Harry Potter Series, 1997—. Harry Potter & Sorcerer's Stone, 1997, Harry Potter & the Chamber of Secrets, 1998, Harry Potter & the Prisoner of Azkaban, 1999, Harry Potter & Goblet of Fire, 2000, Harry Potter & the Order of the Phoenix, 2003, Harry Potter & the Half-Blood Prince, 2005, children's books, The Snow Storm, 1983, The Vegetables Go to Bed, 1994, Curtain of Night, 1997, Pockets, 1998, The House of Wisdom, 1999, The Purple Snerd, 2000, Aunt Claire's Yellow Beehive Hair, 2001, The Sea Chest, 2002, Plum, 2003, The Thread of Life, 2003, Henry and Pawl, 2004, Sweep Dreams, 2004, Tales from Shakespeare, 2004. Mailing: c/o Scholastic Inc 555 Broadway New York NY 10001-3999 Business E-Mail: sabriel@wowway.com.*

GRANDY, FRED, foundation administrator, former congressman, former actor; b. Sioux City, Iowa, June 29, 1948; s. William Frederick and Bonnie Grandy; m. Catherine Mann, 1987; children: Marya, Charlie, Monica. BA in English, Harvard U., 1970. Founder improvisational group The Proposition, Harvard U.; mem. 100th-104th Congresses from 6th (now 5th) Iowa Dist., 1987-94; mem. standards of official conduct com.; mem. ways and means com.; CEO Goodwill Industries Internat. Inc., 1995—. Appeared in play Green Julia, N.Y.C., Joe Papp's In The Boom Boom Room, until 1974; collaborator rev.: in play Pretzels; film appearances include Close Encounters of the Third Kind; television films include The Girl Most Likely To, 1973, Blind Ambition, 1979, Love Boat II, Love Boat III; television series: The Monster Squad, 1976-77, The Love Boat, 1977-86; other television appearances include Welcome Back Kotter. Office: Goodwill Industries Intl 15810 Indianola Dr Rockville MD 20855

GRANDY, WALTER THOMAS, JR., physicist, researcher; b. Phila., June 1, 1933; s. Walter Thomas and Margaret Mary (Hayes) G.; m. Patricia Josephine Langan, Dec. 27, 1955; children: Christopher, Neal, Mary, Jeanne. BS, U. Colo., 1960, PhD, 1964. Physicist Nat. Bur. Standards, Boulder, Colo., 1958-63; mem. faculty U. Wyo., Laramie, 1963—, prof. physics, 1969-98, head dept., 1971-78; prof. emeritus, 1998—. Fulbright lectr. U. Sao Paulo, Brazil, 1966-67, vis. prof., 1982; vis. prof. U. Tubingen, W. Germany, 1978-79, U. Sydney, Australia, 1988. Author: Introduction to Electrodynamics and Radiation, 1970, Foundations of Statistical Mechanics: Volume I, Equilibrium Theory, 1987, Vol. II, Nonequilibrium Phenomena, 1988, Relativistic Quantum Mechanics of Leptons and Fields, 1991, Scattering of Waves from Spherical Targets, 2000. Served with USNR, 1953-57. Fellow AAAS; mem. Am. Phys. Soc., Brasilian Phys. Soc., Am. Assn. Physics Tchrs., Sigma Xi, Sigma Pi Sigma. Achievements include rsch. on statis. mechanics, electrodynamics, quantum theory. Home: 604 S 18th St Laramie WY 82070-4304 Business E-Mail: wtg@uwyo.edu.

GRANGER, CLIVE WILLIAM JOHN (SIR CLIVE GRANGER), retired economist; b. Swansea, Wales, Sept. 4, 1934; arrived in U.S., 1974; s. Edward John and Evelyn Agnes (Hessey) G.; m. Patricia Anne Loveland, May 14, 1960; children: Mark, Claire. BA, U. Nottingham, Eng., 1955, PhD in Stats., 1959, DSc, 1992; DSc (hon.), Carlos III, Madrid, 1997; D in Econs. (hon.), Stockholm Sch. Econs., 1998; DSc (hon.), Loughborough U., 2002. Lectr. in math. U. Nottingham, 1956—64, prof. stats., 1964—74; prof. econs. U. Calif., San Diego, 1976—2002, chancellor's assoc. chair, 1994—2002; ret., 2003. Author: Forecasting Stock Markets, 1970; editor: Commodity Markets, 1973. Decorated knight batchelor Royal Order, 2005; fellow Harkness Fund, 1959-60, Econometric Soc., 1973, Guggenheim Found., 1988, recipient Nobel Prize in Econs., 2003. Fellow: Am. Econ. Soc. (Disting.), Am. Acad. Arts and Scis., Brit. Acad. (corr.). Avocations: hiking, swimming, travel, reading. Office: U Calif San Diego Econs Dept D-008 La Jolla CA 92093 Office Phone: 858-534-3856. Business E-Mail: cgranger@ucsd.edu.

GRANGER, HARRIS JOSEPH, physiologist, educator; b. Erath, La., Aug. 26, 1944; s. Willis Gabriel and Edith Ann (Hebert) G.; m. Ramona Ann Vice; children: Ashley, Jarrod, Brent BS, U. S.W. La., Lafayette, 1966; PhD, U. Miss., Jackson, 1970. Asst. prof. physiology U. Miss. Med. Ctr., Jackson, 1970-74, assoc. prof. physiology, 1974-76; vis. assoc. prof. U. Calif.-San Diego, LaJolla, 1975-76; assoc. prof. dept. med. physiology Tex. A&M U., College Station, 1976-78, prof. med. physiology, 1978—, head dept. med. physiology, 1982—. Dir. Microcirculation Rsch. Inst., Tex. A&M U., 1981-99, dir. Cardiovascular Rsch. Inst., 1999—; mem. study sect. NIH Exptl. Cardiovascular Scis. Study Sect., 1981-86, 88-93; chmn. Gordon Conf., 1982. Co-author: Circulatory Physiology II, 1975; mem. editorial bd.: Circulation Research, 1982-89, Microvascular Research, 1978-85; mem. editorial bd. Am. Jour. Physiology, 1986—, assoc. editor, 1987-93, editor, 1993-99; contbr. chpts. to books, articles to profl. jours. Recipient Research Career Devel. award Nat. Heart Lung & Blood Inst., 1978-83; Disting. Achievement award in research Tex. A&M U., 1982, Merit award Nat. Heat, Lung and Blood Inst., 1987. Mem. Microcirculatory Soc. (coun. 1978-81, pres. 1989, Landis award 1992), Am. Physiol. Soc. (sec. cardiovascular sect. 1991, treas. 1992, chmn. 1993, Harold Lamport award 1978, RM Berne Disting. Lectr 1995). Home: Apt 1302 5217 Old Spicewood Springs Austin TX 78731 Office: Tex A&M U Sys Health Sci Ctr Cardiovascular Rsch Inst College Station TX 77843-1114 E-mail: granger@tamu.edu.

GRANGER, HARVEY, JR., retired manufacturing company executive; b. Savannah, Ga., Sept. 9, 1928; s. Harvey and Marion (Rauers) G.; m. Barbara Brandt, Sept. 8, 1951; children: Harvey, Matthew Brandt, Barbara James. B in Indsl. Engring., Ga. Inst. Tech, 1951. Indsl. engr. Union Camp Paper Co., Savannah, 1950-56, Great Dane Trailers, Savannah, 1956-61, plant mgr., 1961-71, v.p. mfg., 1971-78, exec. v.p., chief operating officer, 1978-84, pres., chief exec. officer, 1984-91; cons. Savannah, 1992-96; ret., 1996. City adv. bd. dirs. Nations Bank, Savannah, 1979-95. Mem. adv. bd. Sch. Engring. Ga. Inst. Tech., 1985-91; mem. bd. trustees St. Joseph's Hosp., Savannah, 1988-97, vice-chmn. 1995, chmn. 1996-97; chmn. bd. trustees St. Joseph's-Candler Health Sys., Savannah, 1997-2000, vice chmn., 2000—03; dir. vol. trustees Not-For-Profit Hosps., Washington, 1995—2003, mem. exec. com., 1997, sec., 1998, vice chmn., 1999—2003. With USN, 1945-47. Mem. Truck Trailer Mfrs. Assn. (chmn. 1986-87). Clubs: Oglethorpe (Savannah) (pres. 1984-85), Savannah Golf. Avocations: golf, fishing. Home: 405 Coveview Dr Savannah GA 31406-3204

GRANGER, KAY, congresswoman; b. Greenville, Tex., Jan. 18, 1943; children: John Dean, Chelsea, Brandon. BS, Tex. Wesleyan U., 1965, DHL, DHL, Tex. Wesleyan U.; PhD in Pub. Svc. (hon.), Tenn. Wesleyan Coll. Mem. zoning com. City of Ft. Worth, 1981—89; mem. pvt. industry coun., 1988-89; councilwoman City of Ft. Worth, 1989-91, mayor, 1991-95; elected to Ho. of Reps., 1996; mem. 105th-108th Congress from 12th Tex. dist., 1997—; prin., owner G&R Ins. Agy., Ft. Worth, Kay Granger & Assocs. Bd. visitors USAF Acad.; bd. trustees Southwestern U. Recipient Woman of Yr. award, 1987, Bus. and Profl. Woman award, 1987; named Exec. of Yr., Ft. Worth Bus. Hall of Fame, 1999; inductee Tex. Women's Hall of Fame, 1999. Mem. Am. Planning Assn., Internat. Sister Cities Assn., Women's Policy Forum (bd. dirs.), East Ft. Worth Bus. and Profl. Assn. (bd. dirs.), Ft. Worth Bus. and Estate Planning Coun., Meadowbrook Bus. and Profl. Womens Assn., East Ft. Worth C. of C. (vice chmn.). Republican. Methodist.*

GRANGER, LUC ANDRE, dean, psychologist; b. St. Jean, Que., Can., Apr. 8, 1944; s. Andrew and Georgette (Lacasse) G. BA, U. Montreal, 1962, B.Sc., 1964, L.P.S., 1966, PhD, 1969. Asst. prof. psychology U. Montreal, 1969-73, assoc. prof., 1973-79, prof., 1979—, head dept., 1979-83, 90—, assoc. dean, 1983-87. Author: Apprentissage et Therapie, 1972, La Therapie Behaviorale, 1976, La Communication dans le Couple, 1979. Postdoctoral fellow U. Lille, France, 1969 Mem. Can. Psychol. Assn. (sec.-treas. 1982-85, pres. 1992-95), Corp. des Psychologues (treas. 1974-78, pres. 1986-90). Office: U Montreal Dept Psychology CP 6128 Succa Centre Ville Montreal PQ Canada H3C 3J7 E-mail: luc.granger@umontreal.ca.

GRANGER, PHILIP RICHARD, minister; b. Detroit, June 19, 1943; s. Myrl Richard and Alvirta May (Kling) Granger; m. Karen Elizabeth Draper, Feb. 20, 1965 (div. 1972); children: Mark, Leslie; m. Susan Kay Alderfer, Mar. 4, 1973; children: Randall, Candace. AA, Jackson Jr. Coll., 1963; BA, MBA, Mich. State U., 1965, 67; MDiv, No. Bapt. Theol. Sem., Lombard, Ill., 1978; D in Ministry, Oral Roberts U., 1986. CPA Mich.; ordained deacon United Meth. Ch., 1977, odrained elder United Meth. Ch., 1980. Audit staff, cons. Ernst & Ernst, Detroit, 1967-71; mem. contrs. staff Assocs. Corp., South Bend, Ind., 1971-73; v.p., contr. 1st Fed. Savs. and Loan, Chgo., 1973-76; pastor Mokena (Ill.) United Meth. Ch., 1976-82; dir. fin. No. Ind. Conf. United Meth. Ch., Marion, 1982-86; sr. pastor St. Lukes United Meth. Ch., Kokomo, Ind., 1986-89, Trinity United Meth. Ch., Huntington, Ind., 1989-94; dist. supt. Kokomo (Ind.) Dist. United Meth. Ch., 1994-99; sr. pastor Coll. Ave. United Meth. Ch., Muncie, Ind., 1999—2001; pres., CEO Mission Soc. United Meths., 2001—. New life missioner Gen. Bd. Discipleship, Nashville, 1980—; mem. adj. faculty Huntington Coll., 1990—94; past chmn. bd. dirs. Good News, Wilmore, Ky., Samaritan Ctr., Inc., Huntington Found. Mission and Ministry, Inc., Marion; del. gen. conf. United Meth. Ch., 1988, 92, 96, 2000; bd. dirs. Ch. & Soc., Washington, 1996—2004. Author: Discerment Planning, 1986. Founding mem. Tri-Village Crisis Intervention Ctr., Mokena, 1978—81; bd. dirs. Mental Health Assn. Ill., Chgo., 1974—75; treas. Village of Mokena, 1978—82. Mem.: Am. Assn. Christian Counselors, Rotary, Beta Alpha Psi, Beta Gamma Sigma, Delta Sigma Pi. Avocations: reading, travel, computers. Office: Mission Soc United Meths 6234 Crooked Creek Rd Norcross GA 30092 Home: 228 Brookcliff Dr Sugar Hill GA 30518-8197 Office Phone: 770-446-1381. Business E-Mail: pgranger@msum.org. *To experience life requires more than experiencing the simple joys and pleasures that life provides. To really experience life is to experience the Christian community of caring and sharing that only occurs when we are truly one in Christ.*

GRANGER, RANDY WILLIAM, art educator, consultant; b. Point Pleasant, N.J., May 13, 1948; s. Charles William Granger and Dorothy Marie Wright; m. Irene Elizabeth McHenry, Oct. 4, 2003; children: Fletcher, Michael, Gordon, Willa. Cert. permanent art edn. N.J., Pa., early adolescence, young adulthood art Nat. Bd. Certification. Instr. visual arts dept. Summit Pub. Schs., 1972—73, founding chair dept. photography, 1974—75; instr. visual arts dept. William Penn Charter Sch., 1975—, chair visual arts dept., 1981—. Project dir. William Penn Charter Sch., Phila., 2000—; part-time instr. visual arts Phila. Parkway Program, 1969—70; instr. design, continuing edn. program Phila. U., 2003—; adj. asst. prof. grad. art edn. dept. U. of the Arts, 2004—. With USNR, 1966—72. Named to Nat. Tchrs. Hall of Fame, 2005; recipient Randy W. Granger Chair in Visual Arts endowed chair established in his name, Randy Granger endowed scholarship fundin art edn. established in his name, Nat. Disney Tchr. award, 2005, Pa. Outstanding Art Educator of Yr., 2005. Mem.: Nat. Art Edn. Assn., Am. Coun. for Internat. Studies, Pa. Assn. Ind. Schs. (mem. visual arts profl. devel. com. 2003—), Pa. Coun. on Arts, Pa. Art Edn. Assn. (pres.-elect 2002—04, pres. 2004—, mem. celebration steering com. 2003—). Office: William Penn Charter Sch 3000 W School House Ln Philadelphia PA 19144

GRANGER, ROBERT ALAN, mechanical and aerospace engineering educator; b. Evanston, Ill., Aug. 7, 1928; s. Robert Alan and Kathleen (Buehr) G.; m. Ruth Nickerson, Oct. 7, 1951; children: Eric Carl, Erin Alyson. BA, Pomona Coll., 1955; MS, Drexel Inst. Tech., 1959; PhD, U. Md., 1970. Sr. rsch. scientist Martin Co., Balt., 1955-60; prin. engr. Boeing Co., Renton, Wash., 1975; prof. mech. and aerospace engrng. U.S. Naval Acad., Annapolis, Md., 1960-98, discipline dir., 1972-75; ret., 1998. Prof. emeritus U.S. Naval Acad., Annapolis, 2001; adj. prof. LSC Coll., 1999, lectr., U. Cambridge (Eng.), 2000—; fellow (hon.) Cambridge (England) U., 1991; pub., CEO Sci. Archives, Inc., 1997; sci. contbr. editor Daily Sun newspaper, 1999; cons. NASA, Boeing Co.; vis. prof. U. Petroleum and Minerals, Saudi Arabia, 1977-79, U. Zurich, Switzerland, 1978, Yale U., 1989; dir. Vortex Dynamics Symposium von Karman Inst., Brussels, Belgium; dir., prin. lectr. Introduction to Wing Flutter Symposium, 1991. Author: Fluid Mechanics, 1985, Unified Method of Aeroelasticity, 1986, Experiments in Fluid Mechanics, 1986, Design of Spacecraft, 1988, Introduction to the Flutter of Winged Aircraft, 1992, Experiments in Heat Transfer and Thermodynamics, 1994, Fluid Mechanics, 1994, Life on Mars, 1997; contbr. over 700 articles to profl. publs. Served with U.S. Army, 1950-52, Korea. Ford Found. fellow, 1965; recipient USN Meritorious Civilian award, 1996, Euler Math. prize, 1999. Hon. mem. Inst. Modern Physics (Athens, Greece); mem. AIAA, Kappa Mu Epsilon, Alpha Gamma Sigma. Republican. Avocations: composing, mountain climbing, writing, tennis, swimming. Home: 31 Hickory Head Hammock Lady Lake FL 32159-8868 Personal E-mail: ragranger@thevillages.net.

GRANGER, ROD, public relations executive, consultant; BA, Vassar Coll.; MA in Cinema Studies, N.Y. U. Staff reporter and critic The Hollywood Reporter, 1984—86; U.S. corr. Screen Internat., 1988; editor and publicist Am. Zeotrope; staff reporter Broadcasting & Cable, 1988—90, Electronic Media, 1990—92; mktg. editor Multichannel News, 1992—95; v.p. corp. The Lippin Group, 1995—98; dir. corp. comm. VH1, 1998—2000; v.p. Trylon Comm., 2000—02; freelance pub. rels. cons. and writer, 2002; comm. editor Pearson Edn., 2003—. Book and film reviewer. Rschr.: Citizen Welles by Frank Brady, 1988; author: The Screenwriter's Guide, 1988; contbr. articles to profl. jours. Address: #3P 350 Bleeker St New York NY 10014

GRANGER, TERRY MARK, real estate appraiser; s. John Dean and Mary W. Granger; m. Terry K. Clark, July 23, 2003. BA Double Maj. Bus. & Psychology, Tex. Wesleyan U., Fort Worth, Tex., 1975. Cert. Ifa Nat. Assn. Of Ind. Fee Appraisers, 2002, Real Estate Appraiser State Of Tex., 1992, ASA Sr. Mem. Real Property Urban Am. Society Of Appraisers, 1986, Aga Assn. Of Govtl. Appraisers, 1984. Real estate appraiser Granger & Assoc, Fort Worth, Tex., 1982—. Web editor naifa ft. worth chpt. Nat. Assn. Of Ind. Fee Appraisers Ft. Worth Chpt., Fort Worth, Tex., 2003—, dir. of edn., 2004—. Mem.: Nat. Assn. Of Ind. Fee Appraisers (pres. of ft. worth chpt. naifa 2003—04). Home: P O Box 3 Fort Worth TX 76101 Office: Granger P O Box 3 Fort Worth TX 76101 Office Phone: 817-377-8333. Home Fax: 817-377-8333; Office Fax: 817-377-8333. Business E-Mail: terry@pob3.com.

GRANHOLM, JENNIFER MULHERN, governor; b. Vancouver, B.C., Can., Feb. 5, 1959; arrived in U.S., 1962; d. Civtor Ivar and Shirley Alfreda (Dowden) Granholm; m. Daniel Granholm Mulhern, May 23, 1986; children: Kathryn, Cecelia, Jack. BA, U. Calif., Berkeley, 1984; JD, Harvard U., 1987. Bar: Mich. 1987, U.S. Dist. Ct. (ea. dist.) Mich. 1987, U.S. Ct. Appeals (6th cir.) 1987. Jud. law clk. 6th Cir Ct. Appeals, Detroit, 1987—88; exec. asst. Wayne County Exec., Detroit, 1988—89; asst. U.S. atty. Dept. Justice, Detroit, 1990—94; corp. counsel Wayne County, Detroit, 1994—98; atty. gen. State of Mich., Lansing, 1999—2002, gov., 2003—. Gen. counsel Detroit/Wayne County Stadium Authority, 1996—98. Contbr. articles to profl. jours. Commr. Great Lakes Commn.; mem. bd. Cyberstate.org YWCA. Mem.: Inc. Soc. Irish Lawyers, Women's Law Assn., Detroit Bar Assn. Democrat. Roman Catholic. Avocations: running, family, laughing. Office: Gov Office PO Box 30013 Lansing MI 48909

GRANICK, MARK S, medical educator; b. New York, NY, July 7, 1951; m. Carol Singer, Feb. 17, 1994. MD, Harvard Med. Sch., 1977. Cert. Am. Bd. of Plastic Surgery, 1984. Prof. of surgery NJ. Med. School-UMDNJ, Newark, 2001—. Fellow: ACS. Office: NJ Med Sch UMDNJ 90 Bergen St Ste 7200 Newark NJ 07103 also: 290 South Livingston Ave Livingston NJ 07039 Office Phone: 973-972-8092.

GRANIELA-RODRIGUEZ, MAGDA, writer, educator; b. Cabo Rojo, P.R. BA, U. P.R., Mayaguez, 1977; AM, U. Ill., 1979, PhD, 1987. Instr. U. P.R., Mayaguez, 1985, asst. prof., 1987-90, assoc. prof., 1990-95, prof., 1995—. Dir. writing lab. U. P.R., 1987-92. Author: Como raiz dilatada a un sueno, Santo Domingo: Alfa y Omega, 1990, El papel del lector en la novela mexicana contemporanea, Washington, D.C.: Scripta Humanistica, 1991, Gramatica Ancestral Aguadilla: Mester, 1999; (with others) Conflictos Culturales en la Literatura Contemporanea, 1993; Mujeres 98 Antologia de poesia femenina puertorriquena, 1998; editor: Linea Plural, 1986-87; author poems; contbr. articles to profl. jours. Member Foster Parents Internat., Ecuador, 1985—, NARAL, 1983—; mem. disasters relief com. ARC, 1986-87, Foster Parent for World Vision, 1996—; bd. dirs. Clara Lair. NEH fellow, 1988; recipient Teaching award U. P.R., 1988. Mem. ASCD, MLA, Acad. Arts and Scis., Iberoamerican Inst., Union of Concerned Scientists, Pen Club of P.R., Phi Kappa Phi, Alpha Delta Kappa.

GRANIK, RUSSELL T., sports association executive; m. Joyce Granik; children: Daniel, Erynn. Grad. magna cum laude, Dartmouth Coll., 1969; law degree cum laude, Harvard U., 1973. With Breed, Abbott & Morgan, N.Y.C.; staff atty. NBA, 1976-78, asst. gen. counsel, 1978-80, gen. counsel, 1980-84, exec. v.p., 1984-90, dep. commr., 1990—. V.p. USA Basketball, 1989-96, pres. 1996-2000, mem. exec. com., 2000-; chairman, bd. trustees, Naismith meml. Basketball Hall of Fame, 2003-. Office: Nat Basketball Assn Olympic Tower 645 5th Ave Fl 15 New York NY 10022-5910*

GRANIK, VLADIMIR, mechanic engineering educator, researcher; b. May 16, 1934; arrived in US, 1991, naturalized, 1996; m. Galina Gaevskaya, Apr. 28, 1957; children: Yuri, Tanya. BS summa cum laude, Civil Engring. Inst., Odessa, USSR, 1957; PhD, Ctrl. Rsch. Inst. Concrete, Moscow, 1967; Assoc. Prof. Strength of Materials, Higher Exam. Bd. USSR, Moscow, 1970, D Tech. Scis., 1990. Rsch. engr. Ctrl. Rsch. Inst. Structural Mechanics, Moscow, 1957-66; assoc. prof. Civil Engring. Inst., Odessa, 1966-69; assoc. prof. structural mechanics Mil. Engring. Acad., Odessa, 1969-72, prof. continuum mechanics, 1972-88; prof. strength of materials Maritime Engring. Inst., Odessa, 1988-91; rsch. fellow in continuum mechanics U. Calif., Berkeley, 1991-93, rsch. assoc. continuum mechanics, 1993—98, prof. cons. strength of materials and structural mechanics, 1998—. Head optimization theory dept. Rsch. Inst. Automation, Odessa, 1985-88; founder Doublet Mechanics. Co-author, co-editor: Advances in Doublet Mechanics, 1997; contbr. articles to profl. jours.; assoc. mem., reviewer Jour. Structural Mechanics and Structure Design, 1981-91. Recipient First Prize Queueing Theory Application award Ministry Def., Moscow, 1976, Academician Gadolin medal Ministry Def., 1984. Achievements include rsch. in doublet mechanics; microstructural mechanics of granular media; stochastic dynamics of granular flows in tall shells (silos); reassessment of classical theory of plasticity and yield criteria; stochastic dynamics of supply and demand in a single market; a new theory of osmotic pressures in non-electrolytic solutions of any concentration. Home: 615 W 7th St Apt 205 Antioch CA 94509-1675

GRANIRER, EDMOND ERNEST, mathematician, educator; b. Constanza, Romania, 1935; s. Jacob G. MSc, Hebrew U., Jerusalem, 1959, PhD, 1962. Mem. faculty dept. math. U. Ill., 1962-64, Cornell U., 1964-65, U. B.C., Vancouver, Canada, 1965—66, 1967—, prof. math., 1970-97, prof. emeritus, 1997—; faculty U. Montreal, Canada, 1966-67. Contbr. articles to profl. jours. Grantee NSERC, 1996. Fellow Royal Soc. Can.; mem. Can. Math. Soc., Am. Math. Soc. Office: U BC Dept Math Vancouver BC Canada V6T 1Z2 Business E-Mail: granirer@math.ubc.ca.

GRANITO, FRANK H., III, lawyer; b. NYC, Jan. 25, 1959; s. Frank H. Jr. and Helen Elizabeth (Altieri) G.; m. Monica Ann Marino, July 8, 1989; 1 child, Frank H. IV. BA, Franklin & Marshall, 1981; JD, St. John's U., 1987. Bar: N.Y. 1987, N.J. 1988; U.S. Dist. Ct. (ea. and so. dists.) N.Y. 1988, U.S. Dist. Ct. N.J. 1988. Regional mgr. Pilgrim Airlines, NY, 1982-84; assoc. Bower & Gardner, NYC, 1987-88, Speiser, Krause & Madole, NYC, 1988; ptnr. Speiser Krause Nolan & Granito, NYC. Mem.: ABA (Com. on Aeronautics, Litig. Sect. 1991—, chmn., Com. on Aeronautics, Litig. Sect. 2000—01, co-chmn, Aviation Litig. Com.), Lawyer-Pilots Bar Assn., Assn. Trial Lawyers Am., NY State Trial Lawyers Assn., Assn. Bar City NY. Roman Catholic. Office: Speiser Krause Nolan & Granito 34th Fl Two Grand Central Tower 140 E 45th St New York NY 10017 Office Phone: 212-661-0011. Office Fax: 212-953-6483.

GRANLIE, DENNIS W., music educator, director; b. Williston, N.D., Dec. 10, 1947; m. Marianne L. Schwartz, Sept. 7, 1968; children: Carrie Lynn Barnhart, Diedri Dawn Durocher, Tyson Danin. AA, Dawson Coll., 1968; BS, Ea. Mont. Coll., 1971; MusM in Edn., VanderCook Coll. Music, 1982; cert. in Music Adminstrn. and Supr., U. Mont., 1994. Instr. music Lavina (Mont.) Pub. Schs., 1970—73; dir. bands Roundup (Mont.) H.S., 1973—74, Dawson County H.S., Glendive, Mont., 1974—79, Charles Russell H.S., Great Falls, Mont., 1979—94; supr. music Gt. Falls (Mont.) Pub. Schs., 1994—2005. Condr. Winds of Mont. Adult Band, Great Falls, Mont., 1994—, Mont. Statehood Centennial Band, Great Fall, Mont., 1989. Co-author: Teacher Success Kit; contbr.: films Music Adjudication Seminar. Musician Gt. Falls (Mont.) Symphony Orch., 1981—2000; dir. choir Redeemer Luth. Ch., Great Falls, 1987—93. Named Outstanding Band Alumnus, Ea. Mont. Coll., 1988, Tchr. of Yr., Charles Russell H.S., 1989, Outstanding Educator of Yr., Dufresne Found., 1994; fellow, Goethe Inst., 1974. Mem.: Mont. H.S. Assn. (chmn. music com. 2000—05), Nat. Fedn. Music Assn. (chmn. music adv. com. 2003—05, named Sect. 8 Outstanding Music Educator 2003), Mont. Bandmasters Assn. (pres. 1987—89), Mont. Music Educators Assn. (pres. 1993—95, Leadership award 1994), Am. Sch. Band Dirs. Assn. (state chair 1987—93), The Nat. Assn. for Music Edn. (nat. exec. bd. mem. 1997—99, pres. N.W. divsn. 1997—99, N.W. Divsn. Disting. Svc. award 2005), Great Falls (Mont.) Symphony Assn., Phi Delta Kappa, Phi Beta Mu (internat. bd. of directors mem. 1994—96). Avocations: performing music, boating, camping, travel. Office: Great Falls Public Schools 1100 4th St South Great Falls MT 59405

GRANN, PHYLLIS, former publisher, editor; b. London, Sept. 2, 1937; d. Solomon and Louisa (Bois-Smith) Eitingon; m. Victor Grann, Sept. 28, 1962; children: Allison, David, Edward. BA cum laude, Barnard Coll., 1958. Sec. Doubleday Pubs., N.Y.C., 1958-60; editor William Morrow Inc., N.Y.C., 1960-62, David McKay Co., N.Y.C., 1962-70; sr. editor Simon & Schuster Inc., N.Y.C., 1970—74, editor-in-chief, Pocket Books paperbacks divsn., 1974—76; editor-in-chief G.P. Putnam's & Sons, N.Y.C., 1976—79, editor-in-chief, pub., 1979—84, pub., pres., 1984—86; pres. Putnam Berkley Group, N.Y.C., 1986—87, pres., CEO, 1987—91, chmn., CEO, 1991—96; pres., CEO Penguin Putnam, Inc., 1996—2001; vice chmn. Random House, 2002, sr. editor, Doubleday Broadway Publishing Co., 2003—. Adj. asst. prof. fin. and economics Columbia Bus. Sch., N.Y.C., 2003—. Co-founder Victor & Phyllis Grann Family Found.

GRANNAN, KATY, photographer; b. Arlington, Mass., 1969; BA, U. Pa., 1991; MA, Harvard U., 1993; MFA, Yale U., 1999. One-woman shows include Dream Am., Kohn Turner Gallery, LA, 2000, 51 Fine Art, Antewerp Belgium, 2001, Morning Call, Salon 94, NYC, 2003, Sugar Camp Rd., Artemis Greenberg Van Doren Gallery, NYC, 2003, Arles Photography Festival. Arles, France, 2004, Emily Tsingou Gallery, London, 2005, Jackson Fine Art, Atlanta, Ga., 2005, exhibited in group shows, ArtSpace, New Haven, Conn., 1998, Another Girl, Another Planet, Lawrence Rubin Greenberg Van Doren Fine Art, NY, 1999, Reflections Through A Glass Eye, Internat. Ctr. Photography, NY, 2000, Smile, Here, NY, 2001, Boomerang: Collector's Choice II, Exit Art, NY, 2001, Women by Women, Cook Fine Art, NY, 2002, True Blue, Jackson Fine Art, Atlanta, 2002, Girls Night Out, Orange County Mus. Art, LA, 2003, Moving Pictures, Guggenheim Mus., Bilbao, Spain, 2003, Open House: Working in Bklyn., Bklyn. Mus. Art, 2004, Whitney Biennial, Whitney Mus. Am. Art, 2004, From NY with Love, Covivant Gallery, Tampa, Fla., 2004, Land of the Free, Jack Hanley Gallery, San Francisco, 2004. Recipient Bucksbaum Award, 2004; Rema Hort Mann Found. Grant, 1999. Mailing: c/o Artemis Greenberg Van Doran Gallery 730 Fifth Ave 7th Floor New York NY 10019*

GRANNE, REGINA, artist, educator; b. NYC, Jan. 16, 1939; d. Meyer and Mildred Biernoff; m. Martin Granne, Oct. 27, 1963; 1 child, Michael. Cert., Cooper Union, 1956—59; student, Hunter Coll., 1959—60; BFA, Yale U., 1961, MFA, 1963. Instr. painting and drawing Ridgewood (N.J.) Sch. Art, 1967—73; asst. prof. art Bard Coll., Annandale on Hudson, NY, 1973—74; lectr. art Queens Coll., Flushing, NY, 1973—84; faculty Parsons Sch. Design, N.Y.C., 1979—, 2001—05, coord. MFA program, 1993—2001; faculty Milton Avery Sch. of the Arts, Annandale on Hudson, 1983—2005. One-woman shows include Tatistcheff Gallery, N.Y.C., 1989, Genovese Sullivan Gallery, Boston, 1991, 1996, 1997, 1999, 2003, A.I.R. Gallery, N.Y.C., 1995, 1997, 1999, 2002, Lehman Wing Sch. Internat. Studies, Columbia U., 2000, Univ. Art Gallery, Sewanee, Tenn., 2001. Home: 237 Bleecker St New York NY 10014 Personal E-mail: rgranne@verizon.net.

GRANNER, DARYL KITLEY, physiology and medicine educator; b. Algona, Iowa, Dec. 12, 1936; married, 1958; 2 children. BA, U. Iowa, 1958, MS, MD, 1962. Asst. prof. medicine U. Wis., 1969-70; asst. prof. U. Iowa, 1970-72, assoc. prof., 1972-75, prof. medicine and biochemistry, dir. div. endocrinology and metabolism, 1975-84, dir. Diabetes and Endocrinology Rsch. Ctr., 1979-84; prof., chmn. molecular physiology and biophysics Vanderbilt U., Nashville, 1984—98, dir. med. sci. tng. program, 1986-93, dir. Diabetes Rsch. and Tng. Ctr., 1993—. Mem. bd. sci. counselors Nat. Inst. Diabetes, Digestive and Kidney Diseases, 1986-90, mem. adv. coun., 1992-96. Mem. Endocrine Soc., Am. Soc. Biol. Chemists, Am. Fedn. Clin. Rsch., Am. Soc. Clin. Investigation, Assn. Am. Physicians, Am. Diabetes Assn. Achievements include research in molecular endocrinology, insulin action and diabetes mellitus. Office: Vanderbilt U medical Ctr 1211 22nd Ave S Nashville TN 37232

GRANO, JOSEPH J., JR., securities industry executive; b. Hartford, Conn., Mar. 7, 1948; m. Kathleen Grano; children: Angela, Andrea, Joe. Attended Ctrl. Conn. Coll.; LLD (hon.), Pepperdine U.; LHD (hon.), CUNY. Investment exec. Merrill Lynch & Co., New Haven, 1972—76, v.p., 1976—84, sr. v.p., bus. unit dir. for affluent customers, 1984—85, sr. v.p., dir. nat. sales for consumer markets, 1985—88; pres., retail sales & mktg. PaineWebber Inc., N.Y.C., 1988—94, pres., 1994—2000; pres., CEO UBS Paine Webber, N.Y.C., 2000—01; CEO UBS Wealth Mgmt. USA, 2001—04, chmn., 2001—; group exec. bd. UBS, Switzerland, 2001—. Chair Pres.'s Homeland Security Adv. Coun., 2002—03, Homeland Security Adv. Coun., 2003—. Bd. dirs. Lennox Hill Hosp.; mem. Bus. Leadership Coun. CUNY. Capt. Special Forces U.S. Army, 1967—72. Named Bus. Leader of the Yr., Georgetown U. Sch. Bus., 2000; recipient Ellis Island Medal of Honor, 1996, Gold Medal Award for Disting. Svc., USO, 2000, Corp. Leadership Award, Thurgood Marshall Scholarship Fund, 2002. Mem.: Coun. for the US and Italy. Office: UBS Financial Services 1285 Avenue Of The Americas New York NY 10019-6028

GRANOF, MICHAEL H., finance educator, department chairman; b. N.Y.C., June 16, 1942; s. David H. and Diana (Simon) G.; m. Dena Gloria Hirsch, Aug. 27, 1972; children: Leah, Joshua AB, Hamilton Coll., 1963; MBA, Columbia U., 1965; PhD, U. Mich., 1972. CPA, Tex. Sr. acct. Coopers & Lybrand, N.Y.C., 1966-68; asst. prof. to prof. acctg. U. Tex., Austin, 1972-84, Ernst & Young disting. centennial prof., chmn. acctg. dept., 1984-88. Mem. Nat. Council on Govtl. Acctg., 1982-84, Govtl. Acctg. Standards Adv. Council, Norwalk, Conn., 1984-90; Fulbright prof. Council for Internat. Exchange Scholars, Hebrew U., Jerusalem, 1978-79; vis. prof. U. Tel Aviv, 1981. Author: How To Cost Your Labor Contract, 1973, Financial Accounting: Principles and Issues, 1977, 4th edit., 1990, Accounting for Managers and Investors, 1983, 2d edit., 1993, Government and Not-for-Profit Accounting, 1998, 3d edit., 2005, Core Concepts in Government and Not-for-Profit Accounting, 2003; co-editor: Government Accounting and Auditing Update, 1989-97. Co-pres. Congregation Agudas Achim; treas. Austin Area Urban League. With USCG, 1965-66 Erskine fellow U. Canterbury, Christchurch, N.Z., 1983 Mem. AICPAs (com. on govt. acctg. and auditing), Am. Acctg. Assn. (chmn. pub. sector sect. 1981-82), Tex. Soc. CPAs (chmn. govt. acctg. standards com.), Govt. Fin. Officers Assn., Assn. Govt. Accts. Jewish. Home: 7310 Valburn Dr Austin TX 78731-1146 Office: U Tex Dept Acctg CBA 4M 202 Austin TX 78712 Business E-Mail: michael.granof@mccombs.utexas.edu.

GRANOFF, GARY CHARLES, lawyer, investment company executive; b. N.Y.C., Feb. 2, 1948; s. N. Henry and Jeannette (Trum) G.; m. Leslie Barbara Resnick, Dec. 21, 1969; children: Stephen, Robert, Joshua. BBA in Acctg., George Washington U., 1970, JD with honors, 1973. Bar: N.Y. 1974, Fla. 1974, U.S. Dist. Ct. (so. dist.) N.Y. 1976. Assoc. Dreyer & Traub, N.Y.C., 1973-75; ptnr. Ezon, Langberg & Granoff, N.Y.C., 1975-78, Granoff & Walker, N.Y.C., 1982-92, Granoff, Walker & Forlenza PC, N.Y.C., 1993—; pvt. practice N.Y.C., 1978-81; pres., also bd. dirs. Elk Assocs. Funding Corp., N.Y.C., 1979—, GCG Assocs., Inc., N.Y.C., 1982—; pres., dir. Gemini Capital Corp., 1996—; pres., chmn. Ameritrans Capital Corp., 1999—. Atty. del. to U.S.-China Joint Session on Trade, Investment and Econ. Law, Beijing, 1987; dean's adv. bd. George Washington U. Law Sch., 1993—. Campaign vol. Mondale for Pres., N.Y.C., 1984; fundraiser Robert Garcia for Congress, Dem. Senatorial Campaign Com., N.Y.C., 1987—88; active N.Y. Lawyers for Dukakis Com., 1988; chmn. N.Y.C. chpt. George Washington U. Nat. Law Ctr. Leadership Gifts Com., 1998—; trustee George Washington U., 1998—2003, 2005—, chmn. fin. com., 2001—02, sr. advisor investment com. bd. trustees, 2003—; trustee Parker Jewish Inst. for Health Care and Rehab., 2001—, chmn. investment com., 2005—; fundraiser John F. Kerry for Pres., 2004. Recipient Jacob Burns award, George Washngton U. Law Sch., 1998. Mem. N.Y. State Bar Assn., Fla. Bar Assn., Assn. Bar City N.Y., People to People Internat., Nat. Assn. Investment Cos. (legis com.), George Washington U. Alumni Assn. (chmn. N.Y.C. chpt., bd. dirs. law sch. alumni assn., alumni com. 21 century, trustee), North Shore Country Club (chmn. legal com., bd. govs. 1994-96, 98-2001, chmn. admissions com. 1999-2001, chmn. nominating com. 2004). Avocations: golf, tennis, skiing. Office: Granoff Walker & Forlenza 747 3rd Ave Fl 4 New York NY 10017-2803

GRANOTT, NIRA, psychologist, researcher; b. Petah-Tikva, Israel; came to U.S., 1987; d. Jacob and Celia Granott; children: Guy A. Farber, Bali Farber. MA, Tel Aviv U., 1983; EdM, Harvard U., 1988; PhD, MIT, 1993. Dir. multi-media project Edn. TV, Tel-Aviv, 1974—80; sr. analyst, software developer Control data Corp., Tel-Aviv, 1983—86; asst. prof. psychology U. Tex. at Dallas, Richardson, 1993—95, dir. microdevel. lab., 1993—2002, asst. prof. psychology, 1997—2002; co-founder, pres. OORIM, LLC, 2000—. Vis. prof. psychology and lectr. edn. Harvard Grad. Sch. Edn., Cambridge, Mass., 1996-97; grant cons. Harvard U., 1995-96. Rsch. grantee NSF, 1999, Tex. Higher Edn. Bd., 2000, Timberlawn Rsch. Found., 1999; vis. scholar Tufts U., 2002-04. Mem. Am. Psychol. Soc., Soc. for Rsch. on Child Devel. Avocations: painting, photography, dance, yoga. Personal E-mail: ngranott@aol.com.

GRANSTAFF, WILLIAM BOYD, artist; b. Paducah, Ky., May 17, 1925; s. William Lawrence Granstaff and Belle Hunsaker Frankie; m. Joann McBride, June 17, 1948; children: William Frank, Ann Laurie. Grad., Kans. City Art Inst., Am. Acad. of Art, Chgo. Instr. Famous Artist Sch., Westport, Conn., 1963—65; illustrator Southern Bapt., Nashville, 1965—71; freelance, painting portraits and landscapes self employed, Princeton, Ky., 1971—. Home: 806 S Jefferson St Princeton KY 42445-2370

GRANSTROM, MARVIN LEROY, civil and sanitary engineering educator; b. Anaconda, Mont., Sept. 25, 1920; s. Carl August and Alida Sophia (Eckstrom) G.; m. Ruth Maybelle Olsen, Jan. 1, 1944; children— David Marvin, Kay Ruth, Chris Carl. BS, Morningside Coll., 1942; BS in Civil Engrng, Iowa State Coll., 1943; MS in San. Engrng, Harvard, 1947, PhD, 1955. Engrng. aide Soil Conservation Service, Whiting, Iowa, 1939; cons. engr. Sioux Falls, S.D., 1946; instr. civil and san. engrng. Case Inst. Tech., 1947-49; assoc. prof. san. engrng. U. N.C., 1949-58; prof. civil engrng. Rutgers U., New Brunswick, N.J., 1958-83, prof. emeritus, 1983; research participant Oak Ridge Nat. Labs., 1954; cons. Nat. Engrng. Sch., Lima, Peru, 1955-57, WHO, 1966—. Cons. in hydrology, 1970— Author articles in field. Served with USMCR, 1943-46 Research grantee N.C., 1953; Research grantee NIH, 1954-58; Research grantee NSF, 1954-63; Research grantee Army Chem. Center, 1961-64; Research grantee surgeon gen. U.S. Army, 1962; Research grantee Office Water Resources Research, Dept. Interior, 1965-76; Research grantee N.J. Dept. Environ. Protection, 1957—; fellow Nat. Found., 1946-47; fellow USPHS, 1952-53 Mem. Am. Chem. Soc., ASCE, Am. Water Works Assn., Am. Water Resources Assn., Am. Acad. Environ. Engrs., Tau Beta Pi, Sigma Xi, Delta Omega, Chi Epsilon. Home: Apt 347 620 Hwy 35 S Middletown NJ 07748

GRANT, ALEXANDER MARSHALL, retired ballet director; b. Wellington, New Zealand, Feb. 22, 1925; s. Alexander Gibb and Eleather May (Marshall) G. Ed., Wellington Coll.; scholarship student, Sadler's Wells Sch., London, 1946-46. Mem. Sadler's Wells Ballet (now Royal Ballet), London, 1946-76, prin. dancer, 1950-76, co-dir. Ballet for All touring co., 1970-71, dir., 1971-76; artistic dir. Nat. Ballet Can., 1976-83, ret. Judge internat. ballet competitions, Jackson, Miss., Moscow, Varna, Bulgaria, Helsinki, Paris, Budapest, Hungary. Prin. dancer London Festival Ballet (now English Nat. Ballet), 1985-91; guest artist Royal Ballet, Joffrey Ballet, English Nat. Ballet; numerous leading roles on stage, also in film Tales of Beatrice Potter, others; staged La Fille Mal Gardeé, Facade, various cities, 1965—. Decorated comdr. Brit. Empire; scholar Royal Acad. Dance.

GRANT, AMY, singer, songwriter; b. Augusta, Ga., Nov. 25, 1960; d. Burton and Gloria (Napier) Grant; m. Gary Chapman, 1983 (div. 1999); children: Matthew Garrison Chapman, Millie Chapman, Sarrah Cannon Chapman; m. Vince Gill, 2000; 1 child, Corinna. Student, Furman U., Vanderbilt U., Coll. Arts & Sci., 1982. Albums include Amy Grant, 1977, My Father's Eyes, 1979, Never Alone, 1980, Amy Grant in Concert, 1980, Amy Grant in Concert II, 1981, Age to Age (Grammy award), 1982, A Christmas Album, 1983, Straight Ahead, 1984, Unguarded (Grammy award), 1985, The Collection, 1986, Lead Me On, 1988, Heart in Motion, 1991, (with Vince Gill) House of Love, 1994, The Connection, 1993, Behind the Eyes, 1997, A Christmas to Remember, 1999, Legacy Hymns & Faith, 2002, Simple Things, 2003. Recipient 3 Dove awards Gospel Music Assn., Grammy award for contemporary gospel performance NARAS, 1982, for female gospel performance, 1983, 84, for female gospel vocal, 1985; Walk of Fame honoree, 2001. Office: Blanton Harrell Entertainment 25 Music Sq W Nashville TN 37203-3205

GRANT, BARBARA, venture capitalist; PhD in Organic Chemistry, Stanford U., 1974. Rsch. scientist rsch. divsn. IBM, 1975-86; product mgr. IBM Sys. Printer Products, 1986-91; dir. IBM Storage Divsn. Magnetic Recording Head Bus. Unit, 1991-94; v.p. bus. devel. IBM Storage Sys. Divsn., 1994-95, v.p., gen. mgr. Removable Media Storage Solutions Bus. Unit, 1995—96; pres., CEO Siros Technologies, 1996—2004; exec.-in-residence Amer. River Ventures, 2004—. NSF fellow. Office: Amer River Ventures 2270 Douglas Blvd Ste 212 Roseville CA 95661

GRANT, BARBARA HURWITZ, history educator; b. Ottawa, Ont., Can., Mar. 12, 1955; d. Jan Krosst and Helen Ruth Hurwitz; children: Reilly Morgan, Alexander Maxim. AB, Yale U., 1977, MA, 1978, MPhil, 1979, PhD, 1983. Post-doctoral fellow Wesleyan U., Middletown, Conn., 1983—84; asst. prof. RISD, Providence, 1984—88; rschr., editor Mid. English Dictionary U. Mich., Ann Arbor, 1991—93; vis. scholar dept. nr. ea. studies Cornell U., Ithaca, NY, 1994—96, curator law rare books Law Libr., 1995—96; faculty Commonwealth Sch., Boston, 1997—. Chmn. Yale Medieval Consortium, New Haven, 1980; chmn. Liberal Arts Lecture Series RISD, Providence, 1984—85, mem. com. on dyslexia policy, 1985, mem. admissions com., 86; mem. Yale Alumni Schs. Com., Boston, 1996—97; dir. Commonwealth Sch. Libr., Boston, 1999—2004. Robert C. Bates Traveling fellow, Yale U., 1976, Marshall Bidwell fellow, 1977—78, Yale U. fellow, 1978—80, Mary Miller fellow, 1981, Post-doctoral fellow, 1986—87, Hughes Faculty Project grantee, Commonwealth Sch., 2002—04. Mem.: Am. Hist. Assn., Medieval Acad. Am., Phi Beta Kappa. Avocations: swimming, bicycling, travel. Office: Commonwealth School 151 Commonwealth Ave Boston MA 02116 Office Phone: 617-266-7525. Business E-Mail: bgrant@commschool.org.

GRANT, CARL N., communications executive, sales executive; b. Sharon, Pa., July 10, 1939; s. Carl and Hedwig Theresa Nothhaft; m. Carol Ann Pasacic, June 12, 1965; children: Carl, Kevin, Heather Lee. BA, Kent State U., 1963, MA, 1966; PhD, Ohio State U., 1972. With various radio, TV stas., Ohio and Mich., 1962-67; asst. news dir. Sta. WLWC-TV, Columbus, Ohio, 1967-69; news and pub. affairs dir. Sta. WKBS-TV, Phila., 1969-72; exec. staff dir., nat. com. employer support and guard Dept. Def., Washington, 1972-73; dir. Pres. Com. on White House Fellows, Washington, 1973-74; dir. news and pub. affairs Kaiser Broadcasting Corp., Washington, 1974; assoc. dir. and editor Def. Manpower Commn., Washington, 1974-76; dir. pub. affairs Gen. Svcs. Adminstrn., Washington, 1976-77; sr. v.p., exec. counselor to pres. U.S. C. of C., Washington, 1977—. Brig. gen. Army Nat. Guard, ret. 1999. Recipient Investigative Reporting award AP, 1968, 69, Emmy award nomination NATAS, 1968, George Washington medal Freedoms Found., 1989, William Taylor Disting. Alumnus award Kent State U., 1991, Legion of Merit award, 1994. Avocations: running, weight training, golf, bicycling. Office: US C of C 1615 H St NW Washington DC 20062-0001

GRANT, CYNTHIA D., writer; b. Brockton, Mass., Nov. 23, 1950; d. Robert Cheyne and Jacqueline Ann (Ford) G.; m. Daniel Heatley; 1 child: Morgan; m. Erik Neel; 1 child, Forest. Author: Joshua Fortune, 1980 (Woodward Park Sch. annual book award 1981), Summer Home, 1981, Big Time, 1982, Hard Love, 1983, Kumquat May, I'll Always Love You, 1986, Phoenix Rising, 1989 (Mich. Libr. Assn. Young Adult Caucus best book of yr. 1990, PEN/Norma Klein award 1991, Detroit Pub. Libr. Author Day award 1992), Keep Laughing, 1991, Shadow Man, 1992, Uncle Vampire, 1993 (ALA best books for young adults list 1994), Mary Wolf, 1995, The White Horse, 1998, The Cannibals, Starring Tiffany Spratt, 2002. Recipient Book of Distinction award Hungry Mind Review, 1993, 94. Mem.: PEN (Norma Klein award 1991). Avocations: reading, volunteer work, Cloverstock. Home: PO Box 95 Cloverdale CA 95425-0095 Office: Writers House LLC 21 W 26th St New York NY 10010

GRANT, DANIEL GORDON, information technology executive; b. Taplow, Bucks, Eng., June 28, 1957; came to U.S., 1981; s. Victor Daniel and Annie (McKeown) G.; m. Gaynor Kerry Swainson, Aug. 8, 1981; children: Andrew Douglas, Alexander Daniel, Megan Louise. BS in Computer Sci. with commendation, Portsmouth (Eng.). Polytech., 1979; postgrad., Carnegie Mellon U., 1994-95. Chartered engr. info. scis.; cert. EMT, Nat. EMS registry. Cons. in computers, London, 1979-80; applications cons. Tymshare, U.K., London, 1980-81; from cons. to dep. pres. Tangent Internat., N.Y.C., 1981-90, pres., 1990—, pres., CEO, 1991-94, also bd. dirs.; owner, pres., COO DXI Inc., Pitts., 1994-95, also bd. dirs.; CEO, bd. dirs. Lecor Inc, Pitts., 1995-96; owner, pres., CEO Parallel Tech. Corp., Livingston, N.J., 1996—. Contbr. articles to profl. jours. V.p. Upper Saddle River Vol. Ambulance Corps. Named Chevalier, Conte de Poznan, 1986, Hon. Col. U.S. Army, 1986. Mem. Brit. Computer Soc., Knights of St. John of Jerusalem. Clubs: Franklin Lakes Rangers (N.J.) (capt. 1981). Roman Catholic. Avocations: basketball, soccer, scottish history, pittsburgh dynamos. Office: Parallel Tech Corp 443 Walnut St Sewickley PA 15143 E-mail: dgrant@2lines.com.

GRANT, DANIEL ROSS, retired academic administrator; b. Little Rock, Aug. 18, 1923; s. James Richard and Gracie (Sowers) Grant; m. Betty Jo Oliver, June 17, 1947; children: Carolyn, Shirley, Ross. BA, Ouachita Bapt. U., 1945; MA, U. Ala., 1946; PhD, Northwestern U., 1948. Asst. prof. polit. sci. Vanderbilt U., 1948-54, assoc. prof., 1954-63, prof., 1963-70, dir. Urban and Regional Devel. Ctr., 1968-70; pres. Ouachita Bapt. U., Akadelphia, Ark., 1970-88, pres. emeritus, 1988—. Assoc. dir. Harris County Home Rule Commn., Houston, 1957; vis. prof. mcpl. govt. and planning Thammasat U., Bangkok, 1958—59; cons. U.S. Adv. Commn. Intergovernmental Rels., 1962—67; mem. adv. com. federalism and met. govt. Nat. Com. Econ. Devel., 1969—73. Author (with others): (book) Plan of Metropolitan Government for Nashville and Davidson County, 1956, Metropolitan Surveys: A Digest, 1958, The States and Metropolis, 1968, Government and Politics: An Introduction to Political Science, rev. edit., 1971; author: The Christian and Politics, 1968; author: (with Lloyd Omdahl) State and Local Government in America, 6th edit., 1993. Chmn. Coop. Svcs. Internat. Edn. Consortium (name now Consortium Global Edn.), 1987—88, cons., 1988—90, pres., 1990—98; active So. Bapt. Found., 1959—60, Ark. Bapt. Found., 1991—97, vice chmn., 1995—96, chmn., 1996—97; mem. regional rev. panel Harry S Truman Scholarship Found., 1982—96, chmn., 1984—96; active Ark. Post-secondary Edn. Planning Commn., 1980—89; mem. Ark. Higher Edn. Coordinating Bd., 1997—, vice chmn., 2002—04; mem. commn. religious liberty and human rights Bapt. World Alliance, 1971—95, vice chmn., 1985—90; mem. edn. commn. So. Bapt. Conv., 1973—80, chmn., 1978—80; 1st v.p. Ark. Bapt. State Conv., 1989—91. Mem.: Am. Soc. Pub. Adminstrn., Ark. Polit. Sci. Assn., Am. Polit. Sci. Assn., Arkadelphia C. of C. (bd. dirs. 2000—02), Rotary (pres. 1986—87). Home: 4 Glendale Pl Arkadelphia AR 71923-3529 Office: Ouachita Bapt Univ PO Box 3636 Arkadelphia AR 71998-3636 E-mail: dangrant@iocc.com.

GRANT, DAVID JAMES WILLIAM, pharmacy educator; b. Walsall, Eng., Mar. 26, 1937; came to U.S., 1988; s. James and Attie Hilda May (Stringer) G. BA in Chemistry with 1st class honors, Oxford U., Eng., 1961, MA, DPhil in Phys. Chemistry, 1963, DSc in Phys. Sci., 1990. Lectr. chemistry U. Coll. of Sierra Leone, Freetown, 1963-65; lectr. then sr. lectr. pharm. chemistry U. Nottingham, Eng., 1965-81; prof. phys. pharmacy Sch. Pharmacy, U. Toronto, Ont., Can., 1981-88, assoc. dean grad. studies and rsch., 1984-87; endowed prof. pharmaceutics Coll. Pharmacy, U. Minn., Mpls., 1988—. Bd. dirs. Hosokawa Micron Internat., Inc., 1998-2001; mem. grants com. for pharm. sci. Med. Rsch. Coun. Can., Ottawa, 1983-87; mem. com. on health rsch. Ont. Univs., Toronto, 1985-87; vis. prof. Med. Rsch. Coun. Can.; mem. stds. expert com. for excipients: test methods for U.S. Pharmacopeia, 1991—; cons. to numerous chem. and pharm. cos. Co-author: Physical Chemistry for Students of Pharmacy and Biology, 1977, Solubility Behavior of Organic Compounds, 1990; mem. editl. bd. Jour. Pharm. Scis., 1990-93, assoc. editor, 1994—; mem. editl. adv. bd. Pharm. Devel. and Tech., 1995—, Kona, 1996—, AAPS Pharm. Sci., 1999—; contbr. more than 200 articles to sci. jours. Lt. Brit. Army, 1955-57. Recipient Rsch. award Leverhulme Found., U.K., 1969, Pharmaceutics award of excellence PhRMA Found., 1999, award European Soc. Applied Phys. Chemistry, 2004, Mettler Toledo award N. Am. Thermal Analysis Soc., 2005; grantee rsch. couns. and indsl. cos., U.K., Can., U.S. Fellow AAAS, Royal Soc. Chemistry, Am. Assn. Pharm. Scientists (sustaining charter mem. 1986—, Dale E. Wurster award 2004), Internat. Union Pure and Applied Chemistry; mem. Am. Inst. Chem. Engrs., Am. Crystallographic Assn., Am. Chem. Soc. Achievements include showing how small amounts of additives or impurities modify the physical properties of crystalline drugs and excipients; development of crystal engineering of pharmaceutical substances. Office: U Minn Dept Pharmaceutics Weaver-Densford Hall 308 Harvard St SE Minneapolis MN 55455-0343 Business E-Mail: grant001@umn.edu.

GRANT, DEANDRA MICHELLE, lawyer; b. Denton, Tex., July 28, 1968; d. Robert and Ginger Grant. BSBA, Trinity U., 1990; JD, So. Meth. U., 1993. Bar: Tex. 1993. Atty. Dallas County Dist. Atty.'s Office, Dallas, 1993-94; ptnr. Dueno & Grant, Dallas, 1995-2001; prin. Law Office of Deandra M. Grant, Dallas, 2001—. Bd. dirs. White Rock Rep. Women, Dallas, 1997-2000, pres. 2000—. Mem. Dallas Criminal Def. Lawyers Assn., Tex. Criminal Def. Lawyers Assn. Roman Catholic. Office: 5630 Yale Blvd Dallas TX 75206 E-mail: dgrant@mymail.net.

GRANT, EDWARD ROBERT, chemistry professor, science association executive; b. Tacoma, Sept. 23, 1947; s. Melven Edwin and Estelle Muriel (Glueck) G.; m. Catherine Janine Carey, Aug. 10, 1980; children: Alexander Edward, Janine Catherine. BA in Chemistry, Occidental Coll., 1969; PhD in Chemistry, U. Calif., Davis, 1974. Asst. prof. Cornell U., Ithaca, NY, 1977-83, assoc. prof., 1983-86; prof. chemistry Purdue U., West Lafayette, Ind., 1986—, assoc. head dept. chemistry, 1989-93; CEO SpectraCode, Inc., 1996—; head dept. chemistry U. B.C., Vancouver. Vis. prof. Laboratoire Photophysique Moleculaire, Universite de Paris-Sud, 1991; vis. prof. Technische Universitat Munchen, 1992-93; directeur de recherche associe (5 éme) échelon CNRS Laboratoire Aimé-Cotton, Paris; fellow, Joint Inst. for Lab. Astrophysics, U. Colo., 2000. Contbr. numerous articles to profl. jour. Recipient Nobel Laureate Signature award, 1986, Humbuldt Rsch. award for sr. US sci., 1992, R & D 100 award, 1998, Henry Ford Tech. award, 1999; Fulbright sr. scholar, 1988. Fellow Am. Phys. Soc. Office: U BC Dept Chemistry Vancouver Canada V6T 1Z3 Office Phone: 604-822-2471. E-mail: edgrant@chem.ubc.ca.

GRANT, EDWIN RANDOLPH, retail executive, manufacturing executive; b. Stoneham, Mass., Oct. 6, 1943; s. Lauris Levi and Dorothy Hall (Lewis) Grant; m. Ruth Louise Kennedy, June 24, 1967; children: Randolph T., George C. BFA, Denison U., 1966; MBA, Syracuse U., 1969. Trainee Sears, Roebuck & Co., Springfield, Mass., 1968—69; asst. to pres. Kennedy Bros., Inc., Vergennes, Vt., 1969—70, v.p., 1970—72, exec. v.p., 1972—74, pres., treas., 1974—; dir., corp. sec. Porter Med. Ctr., Inc., 1999—. Ptnr. Vergennes (Vt.) Shopping Ctr., 1974—82; exec. bd. Chittenden Trust Co., Vergennes, 1980—94; chmn. bd. Burlington Coll., Vt., 1983—85; commr. Commn. Status of Women, 1984—85; devel. founder Kennedy Bros. Factory Marketplace, Vergennes, 1987; bd. dirs. Middlebury Inn, 1989—; chair Porter Health Sys., Inc. subs. Porter Med. Ctr., Inc., Middlebury, Vt., 1996—2002. Com. chmn. Cub Scout Pack 539, 1987—96; mem. com. Boy Scout Troop 539, 1991—2000, chair, 1997—2000; active Boy Scouts Am., Vergennes; bd. dirs. Addison County (Vt.) Career Devel. Ctr., 1994—97, Friends of Vergennes Opera House, 1993—2004, pres., 2000—02, chmn., 2000—03. Mem.: Vt. Attractions Assn. (pres. 1978—80), Vt. Retail Assn., Lake Champlain C. of C. (bd. dirs. 1977—81), Addison C. of C. (bd. dirs. 1975—76, 1986—93, Bus. of the Yr. award 1990), Vt. State C. of C. (bd. dirs. 1977—78), Vergennes Area C. of C. (pres. 1976—81), Lake Champlain Yacht Club (bd. govs. 1989—94), Green Mountain Transp. Club (pres. 1976—77), Rotary. Home and Office: 11 N Main St Vergennes VT 05491

GRANT, FRANCES BETHEA, editor; b. Sumter, S.C., Jan. 25, 1932; d. Edward Samuel and Mildred (Ladson) Bethea; m. Victor Rastafari Grant, July 2, 1960 (div.); children: Christine Sharon, Pamela Ellen. BA, SUNY, Albany, 1954; postgrad., Temple U., summers 1955-59; MS, Coll. St. Rose, Albany, 1984. Cert. social studies tchr., N.Y. Tech. editor GE Knolls Atomic Power Lab., Schenectady, NY, 1976-89; tech. editor, writer Westinghouse Machinery Apparatus Operation, Schenectady, 1989-96. 1st black effective listening instr. GE Knolls Atomic Power Lab., Schenectady, 1988-89, Westinghouse Machinery Apparatus Operation, Schenectady, 1992; effective listening trainer Grant Enterprises, Albany, N.Y., 1988. Author, editor: Something to Believe In, 1973; author: (poetry) There's More to Tell, 1976, Waiting to Blossom, 2002; puppeteer, ventriloquist Puppet People, 1978-95; editor newsletter Jayncee, 1967-68. Founder, dir. Minority Women's Breast Cancer Network, Albany, 1992—; v.p. Empire State Black Arts and Cultural Festival Com., Albany, 1984-86; YWCA of Albany, 1986-92, YWCA of Schenectady, 1992-95; founder, 1st chairperson Diversity in Schenectady, AAUW Study Group, 1993-95; mem. nat. nominating com. YWCA/USA, Eastern states region, 1994-96; com. mem. Troy Conf. Ethnic Minority Scholarship Com., Latham, N.Y., 1990-96; vol. Reach to Recovery, Raleigh, 1997—, N.C. Assn. for Edn. of Young Children, 1998; bd. mem. Make a Joyful Noise, Raleigh, 1997-2002, Loaves and Fishes, Raleigh, 1998-2002, Nat. Coalition Bldg. Inst., Durham, N.C. Recipient Centennial award GE Knolls Atomic Power Lab., Schenectady, 1978, Scholar award First Reformed Ch., Albany, 1980, award of excellence Westinghouse Machinery Apparatus Operation Facility, Schenectady, 1994, Women of Note award, African Am. Cultural Complex, Raleigh, N.C., 2000, Disting. Alumni award, Coll St. Rose, Albany, NY, 2003. Mem. AAUW (life, chairperson internat. rels. 1973-74, chairperson vol. interpreters directory com. 2002, scholar award 1981, 83, cmty. action grant 1992, Edn. Found. grant honoree 1995), NAACP (life), Nat. Orgn. Black Chemists and Chem. Engrs. (copy editor newsletter 1995-97), Nat. Assn. Black Storytellers, Internat. Listening Assn. (life), Assn. Black Psychologists (life), Nat. Coun. Negro Women (life, co-founder Capital area sect. NC 1997), Nat. Story Telling Assn., N.Am. Assn. Ventriloquists, Puppeteers of Am., Fellowship of Christian Puppeteers, Nat. Women's History Mus. (charter mem.). Avocations: blues guitar, ventriloquist, poet, freelance writer, puppeteer.

GRANT, GRETCHEN GULLICKSEN, artist; b. Elmhurst, Ill., Dec. 5, 1958; d. Spencer Ole and Dorothy Margery (Bohmer) Gullicksen; m. Stephen Lawrence Grant, Sept. 6, 1980; children: Mason G., Claire M. Art instr. various pub. schs., Kenilworth, Ill., 1991-93, Barrington, Ill., 1993-97. One-woman shows include Friendsof the Arts,Chgo., Barrington Libr. Gallery, 1999; group shows include Barrington Area Arts Coun. Gallery, 1998, 99; muralist. Vol. PTO, Kenilworth, 1991-93, Barrington Hills, 1994—, Citizens Conservation, 1994—; mem. Barrington Hist. Soc., 1994—; assoc. dir. N. Cook County Soil and Water Conservation, 1998—. Mem. Art. Inst. Chgo., Barrington Area Arts Coun., Chgo. Area Lace Guild (editor corr. 1992). Avocation: making bobbin lace. Home: 800 Johnson St Healdsburg CA 95448 Personal E-mail: gretchen@gretchengrant.net.

GRANT, HUGH, actor; b. London, Sept. 9, 1960; BA in English Lit. with honors, Oxford (Eng.) U., Eng., 1982. Formed Simian Films. Debuted on stage at Nottingham Playhouse; formed revue group The Jockeys of Norfolk, 1985; appearences include (films) Privileged, 1982, Maurice, 1987, White Mischief, 1988, The Lair of White Worm, 1988, The Dawning, 1988, Remando al Viento, 1988, La Nuit Bengali, 1988, Impromptu, 1991, Crossing the Line, 1991, Bitter Moon, 1992, The Remains of the Day, 1993, Four Weddings and a Funeral, 1994 (Golden Globe award best actor, 1994, BAFTA award best actor, 1994), Sirens, 1994, Restoration, 1994, The Englishman Who Went Up a Hill But Came Down a Mountain, 1995, Nine Months, 1995, An Awfully Big Adventure, 1995, Sense and Sensibility, 1995, Extreme Measures, 1996, Notting Hill, 1999, Mickey Blue Eyes, 1999, Small Time Crooks, 2000, Bridget Jones's Diary, 2001, About a Boy, 2002, Two Weeks Notice, 2002, Love Actually, 2003, Bridget Jones: The Edge of Reason, 2004, Travaux on sait quand ça commence, 2005; guest appearances include A Very Peculiar Practice, 1986. Stanley Kubrick Britannia award for excellence in film, BAFTA, 2003. Office: Creative Artists Agency c/o Josh Lieberman 9830 Wilshire Blvd Beverly Hills CA 90212-1825 also: Simian Films 335 North Maple Dr Ste 350 Beverly Hills CA 90210

GRANT, HUGH, biotechnology company executive; b. Mar. 1958; BS in Molecular Biology and Agrl. Zoology, Glasgow U., Scotland; MS, Edinburgh U., Scotland; MBA, Internat. Mgmt. Ctr., Buckingham, Eng. Co-pres. agrl. sector Pharmacia Corp., 1998; v.p., COO Monsanto Co., 2000; pres., COO Monstanto Co., 2000, exec. v.p., COO, 2000—. Mem. exec. com. Microedit Summit Campaign; mem. internat. adv. bd. Scottish Enterprise. Bd. govs. United Way St. Louis. Mem.: Internat. Policy Coun. on Agr., Food and Trade. Address: 800 N Lindbergh Blvd Saint Louis MO 63167*

GRANT, ISABELLA HORTON, retired judge; b. L.A., Sept. 24, 1924; d. John Daniel and Hannabelle (Horton) Grant. BA, Swarthmore Coll., 1944; MA, UCLA, 1946; JD, Columbia U., 1950; LLD (hon.), Molloy Coll., 1976. Jr. profl. asst. OSS, Washington, 1944-45; economist Inst. Indsl. Rels., UCLA, 1946-47, Office Price Stblzn., L.A., 1951-52; ptnr. Livingston, Grant, Stone & Kay, San Francisco, 1953-79; judge Mcpl. Ct., San Francisco, 1979-82, Superior Ct., San Francisco, 1982-97; ret., 1997. Bd. dirs. Kid's Turn, Pocket Opera; mem. San Francisco Ethics Commn., 1997-2002, chair, 2001. Fellow ABA; mem. Am. Arbitration Assn. (action dispute resolution, resolution remedies), San Francisco Bar Assn. (bd. dirs. 1978-79), Acad. Matrimonial Lawyers (pres. No. Calif. chpt. 1976), Assn. Family and Conciliation Cts. (pres. Calif. chpt. 1987-89), Nat. Coll. Probate Judges (William W. Treat award 2000), Queen's Bench (pres. 1964), Calif. Tennis Club, Phi Beta Kappa. E-mail: ihortongrant@cs.com.

GRANT, J. KIRKLAND, lawyer, educator; b. Monroe, Mich., Feb. 14, 1943; s. Stanley Gordon and Neva Alene (Piper) G.; 1 child, Alexandra. BBA, U. Mich., 1965, JD cum laude, 1967. Bar: Mich. 1968, N.Y. 1970, S.C. 1975, U.S. Supreme Ct. 1979. Acct. Peat Marwick Mitchell, Detroit, 1964-65; asst. prof. Ga. State U., 1967-70, U. Toledo, 1970-71; assoc. coun. Sullivan & Cromwell, N.Y.C., 1970-72; prof. U. S.C., 1972-80; dean, prof. Del. Law Sch., Wilmington, 1980-83; assoc. counsel Bingham, Dana & Gould, Boston, 1983-84; prof. of law Touro Law Sch., Huntington, NY, 1984—; academic dean Touro Law Ctr., Huntington, N.Y., 1984-85; pvt. practice Charleston, SC, 1987—, Huntington, NY, 1984—. Vis. scholar Columbia U., 1980, Harvard U.,1982-83; chair com. on legal edn. N.Y. State Bar Assn, 1992-95; cons. in the field; comml. and securities arbitrator; arbitrator, mediator U.S. Dist. Ct. Author: Securities Arbitration, 1994; reporter Revision of S.C. Bus. Corp. Law, 1981; editor: Gold Corp. Law Handbook, 1980-; contbr. articles to profl. jours. Mem. ABA, Am. Law Inst., Scribes, Alexander Hamilton Inn of Ct. (pres. 1998-2000, 2002—), Harvard Club (N.Y.), Sand Dollar Club (Folly Beach). Office: Touro Law Ctr 300 Nassau Rd Huntington NY 11743-4342 Home (Summer): PO Box 1111 1550 E Ashley Ave Folly Beach SC 29439 Office Phone: 631-421-2244 ext. 407. Business E-Mail: grantlaw@usa.com.

GRANT, JOAN JULIEN, artist; b. Cornwall, Ont., Can., Apr. 15, 1934; d. John Duncan Julien and Winnifred Josephine McCormick; m. Douglas MacDougal Grant, Sept. 24, 1955; children: Stephen John, Ann Elizabeth, Abigail Jennifer, David King. AA, West L.A. C.C., 1975; BFA, Otis Art Inst., 1977, MFA, 1979. Instr. Plymouth (N.H.) State Coll., 1998; pvt. art instr. Represented in permanent collections; author, editor: Terrestis, 1995, Flight of the Muse, 2002. Active Citizens for a Livable Culver City, 1998—2000. Avocations: reading, book discussion groups, walking, hiking. Home: 4274 LeBourget Ave Culver City CA 90232 Office Phone: 310-839-6638. E-mail: joan.grant@earthlink.net.

GRANT, JOHN P., lawyer; b. Omaha, Nebr., June 24, 1951; BA, U. Nebr., 1973; JD, Creighton U., 1976. Bar: Nebr. 1976. Atty. Grant Law Offices, PC, Omaha. Mem.: Nebr. State Bar Assn. (Ho. Dels. 1990—, chair 1999, pres.-elect 2002—03). Office: Grant Law Offices PC 3717 Harney St Omaha NE 68131-3848

GRANT, JOSEPH MOORMAN, finance company executive; b. San Antonio, Oct. 30, 1938; s. George William and Mary Christian (Moorman) G.; m. Sheila Ann Peterson, Aug. 26, 1961; children: Mary Elizabeth, Steven Clay. BBA, So. Meth. U., 1960; MBA, U. Tex., 1961, PhD, 1970. Banking officer Citibank, N.Y.C., 1961-65; sr. v.p., economist Tex. Commerce Bank (N.A.) also Tex. Commerce Bancshares, Houston, 1970-73; pres., dir. Tex. Commerce Bank, Austin, 1974-75; chmn., CEO Tex. Am. Bankshares/Ft. Worth, 1986-89; pres. Tex. Am. Bank/Ft. Worth, 1976-89, chmn., CEO, 1983-89; exec. v.p., CFO Electronic Data Systems, Dallas, 1990-98; chmn., CEO Tex. Capital Bancshares, 1998—. Bd. dirs. Vignette Corp., Wingate Ptnrs. Author: (with Lawrence L. Crum) The Development of State-Chartered Banking in Texas, 1978, The Great Texas Banking Crash, 1996. Trustee Tex. Christian U., 1989-94, So. Meth. U., 1980-89; chmn. adv. coun. Coll. Bus. Adminstrn. Found., U. Tex., Austin; trustee Dallas County C.C.; bd. dirs. North Tex. Commn., 1976-86, chmn., 1981-82; trustee Paul Quinn Coll., 1995-98; bd. dirs. Communities Found. Tex., KERA. Recipient Man of Yr. award Anti-Defamation League B'nai B'rith, 1988, Banker of the Year award Am. Banker, 2001; named to Disting. Alumni, U. Tex. at Austin, Coll. Bus. Adminstrn., 1982, Hall of Fame U. Tex. Coll. Bus. Adminstrn., Austin, 1999, Am. Banker, 2001, Ernst & Young's Entrepeneur of Yr. fin. svs., 2002, Dallas Citizen's Coun., 2002. Mem. Ft. Worth C. of C. (past chmn.), Dallas C. of C., Young Pres. Orgn. (bd. dirs. 1980-89, internat. pres. 1987-88, exec. com.), Blue Key, World Presidents Ogrn., Exch. Club, Sigma Alpha Epsilon. Episcopalian. Home: 4305 Overhill Dallas TX 75205 Office Phone: 214-932-6610.

GRANT, LENA Y., retired librarian; b. Greensboro, N.C., Jan. 6, 1946; d. Carl Jay and Merle Briggs Yow; m. William Sawyer Grant, Sept. 14, 1968; children: William S. II, Robert Edward. BS, Radford Coll., 1968; MS in Edn., Old Dominion U., 1993. Asst. circulation libr. Radford (Va.) Coll. Libr., 1968-69; sch. libr. Truitt Jr. H.S., Chesapeake, Va., 1969-70, Handley H.S., Winchester, Va., 1970-72, Western Br. Mid. Sch., Chesapeake, 1973—2005. Recipient Dist. award of merit Merrimac Dist. Boy Scouts Am., 1989, Silver Beaver award Tidewater Coun., 1991. Mem. AAUW (pres. Portsmouth br. 2003-05), Va. Ednl. Media Assn., Chesapeake Edn. Assn. (bd. dirs. 1999-2003), Delta Kappa Gamma (sec. 1998-2000, v.p. 2002-04), Phi Kappa Phi, Kappa Delta Pi. Methodist. Home: 4211 Radcliffe Ln Chesapeake VA 23321-4525

GRANT, LEONARD TYDINGS, clergyman; b. Lakewood, NJ, May 8, 1930; s. Allaire Harrison and Edith Dorothy (MacEntee) Grant; m. Nancy Elisabeth MacKerell, June 21, 1958; children: Scott Alexander, Elisabeth Tydings, Constance Allaire. BA, Rutgers U., 1952; BD, Princeton Theol. Sem., 1955; STM, Temple U., 1958; PhD, U. Edinburgh, 1961; LHD (hon.), Elmira Coll., 1987. Ordained Presbyn. Ch. U.S.A., 1955. Pastor 4th Presbyn. Ch., Camden, N.J., 1955-58, Meml. Presbyn. Ch., Wenonah, N.J., 1961-65; instr. Rutgers U., 1956-58; lectr. Conwell Sch. Theology, Phila., 1962-65; prof. history Indpls. Univ., 1965-76; grad. dean Indpls. U., 1966-76, acad. dean, 1974-76; pres. Elmira (N.Y.) Coll., 1976-87; pres. emeritus, 1987—; pres. Independent Coll. Fund N.Y., 1987-95; interim assoc. pastor Presbyn. Ch., Westfield, NJ, 1995-97; assoc. pastor Ctrl. Presbyn. Ch., Summit, NJ, 1997—2002, dir. planned giving, 2003—. Author: Prayers and Devotions of Richard Baxter, 1965; contbr. articles on edn., history and religion to jours. Former mem. adv. com. Am. Inst. Banking, Arnot-Ogden Hosp., Coun. Ind. Coll., Ind. Coll. Fund N.Y.; former mem. adv. com. Sullivan Trail Coun. Boy Scouts Am.; former mem. adv. com. Coun. Elizabeth Presbytery, Found. for Ind. Higher Edn.; trustee mem. Permanent Jud. Com.; pres. Elizabeth Presbytery. Mem.: Princeton Club N.Y.C., Rotary, Phi Delta Kappa, Phi Alpha Theta, Alpha Sigma Lambda. Presbyterian. Office Phone: 908-273-0441 ext. 29. Business E-Mail: lgrant@centralpres.org.

GRANT, LEWIS O., agricultural products executive, meteorology educator; b. Washington, Pa., Mar. 29, 1923; s. Lewis F. and Rita J. (Jacqmain) G.; m. Patricia Jean Lovelock, July 23, 1949; children: Ann, Nancy, Brenda, Andrew, Laura. BS, U. Tulsa, Okla., 1947; MS, Calif. Inst. Tech., Pasadena, 1948. Meteorological cons. Water Resources Devel. Corp., Pasadena, Calif., 1948-54, Denver, 1948-54; rschr. and rsch. dir. Am. Inst. Aerological Rsch., Denver, 1954-59; asst. prof., assoc. prof., prof. atmospheric sci. dept. Colo. State U., Ft. Collins, 1959-93, emeritus prof., 1993—; pres. Piedmont Farms, Inc., Wellington, Colo., 1975-98; sr. cons. Grant Family Farms, Wellington, 1998—. Cons. Colo. Legis., Denver, 1971-73; bd. dirs. adv. com. Integrated

Pest Mgmt. Contb. to profl. jours. Scout master, com. chmn. Boy Scouts of Am.; pres. Partner Communities, Ft. Collins, Colo., 1988; elder Presbyn. Ch., 1980—; 1st lt. U.S. Field Artillery and USAF, 1943-46. Recipient Vincent J. Schaefer award Weather Modification Assn., 1991, Soil and Water Conservation award Ft. Collins Soil Conservation Dist., 1994. Fellow Am. Meterological Assn.; mem. NAS (sect. chmn. 1975-76, mem. climate com.), Organic Farming Rsch. Found. (bd. mem. 1995-2001). Republican. Presbyterian. Avocation: organic farm-scale gardening. Office: Grant Family Farms 1020 W County Road 72 Wellington CO 80549-1912 also: Colo State U Dept Atmospheric Sci Fort Collins CO 80523-0001 Personal E-mail: lgrant3309@aol.com.

GRANT, LINDA HESS, language educator; b. Cin., Aug. 17, 1949; d. Guy Cleveland and Mildred Moore Hess; m. James Benjamin Grant, Oct. 21, 1972; children: Mirrin Elizabeth, Lindsey Ann. BS in Speech Pathology, U. Cin., 1971, MA in Audiology, 1972. Clin. audiologist Mercy Hosp., Hamilton, Ohio, 1972-73; ednl. audiologist Davison Sch., Atlanta, 1973-77; ESL faculty Ga. Inst. Tech., Lang. Inst., Atlanta, 1979-96; asst. dir., faculty ESL program Emory U., Atlanta, 1998—2001. Adj. faculty applied linguistics grad. program Ga. State U., 1994—; cons. in field. Author: Well Said, 1993, 2d edit., 2000; contbr. chpts. to books. Chmn. bd. Bond Cmty. Fed. Credit Union, Atlanta, 1983—84; Olympic torchbearer, 2001; v.p. Candler Park Neighborhood Orgn., Atlanta, 1979—80; sec. Fernbank PTA, Atlanta, 1987—88; founding bd. dirs. Inman Park Parent Coop. Presch., Atlanta, 1974—84. Recipient Lee Foshay award, Cin. Speech and Hearing Ctr., 1971. Mem. Ga. Tchrs. English to Spkrs. of Other Langs. (newsletter editor 1986-87, v.p. 1987-89, Profl. Svc. award 1989, 92), Southeast Regional Tchrs. English to Spkrs. of Other Langs. (conf. chair 1991), Internat. Tchrs. English to Spkrs. of Other Langs. (chair interest sect. 2000), Phi Beta Kappa. Avocations: reading, writing, travel, gardening, pottery. Personal E-mail: lhgrant@bellsouth.net.

GRANT, LINDA KAY (LINDA KAY SCOTT), small business owner, sales executive; b. Galesburg, Ill., Oct. 15, 1949; d. Claire Arline Tabb and Addie Mae (Smith) Stedman; m. James G. Scott, Feb. 20, 1968 (div. Dec. 1977); children: Angela Christine, Aaron Christopher; m. Daryl Quinn Grant, Sept. 20, 1986; 1 child, Rachael Jane. Student, Balckhawk East Coll., 1984-86. Sec. Flynn Beverage, Inc., Rock Island, Ill., 1972-76, Lee's Place, Inc., Rock Island, 1976-81; merchandising rep. Polaroid Corp., Boston, 1981-84; sales rep. Drawing Bd. Greeting Cards, Dallas, 1984-86; owner Card Creations, Galva, Ill., 1986-90; mktg. rep. Q.C. Metall. Labs., Davenport, Iowa, 1989-94; contract pharmacy rep. PDI Corp./Johnson & Johnson, Mahwah, N.J., 1994-96, Innoves Inc./Novartis Corp., Parsippany, N.J., 1996-2000; owner Spiritwood Farms, Kewanee, Ill., 2001—. Mem. Henry County Rural Revolving Loan Bd., 1994—. Mem. Dem. Women for Henry County, Cambridge, Ill., 1985—; pres. Galva/UA C. of C., 1988; advisor Galva/UA Econ. Devel. Com., 1989. Mem. NOW, Nat. Assn. for Female Execs. Methodist. Achievements include patents for wound flush. Home: RR 1 Kewanee IL 61443-9801 Address: 10128 E 2300 St Kewanee IL 61443

GRANT, M. DUNCAN, lawyer; b. Madison, Wis., Apr. 22, 1950; s. David Evans and Margaret Jane (Bloomfield) G.; m. Marcia Joan Cox, Sept. 18, 1970 (div. Dec. 1975); 1 child, Thomas David; m. Margaret Ann MacDonald, Mar. 24, 1990 (div. Jan. 1995); m. Victoria Lynn Nichols, Oct. 14, 2000. AB, Princeton U., 1972; JD, U. Pa., 1975. Bar: Pa. 1975, Del. 1991, U.S. Dist. Ct. (ea. dist.) Pa. 1976, U.S. Ct. Appeals (3d cir.) 1977, U.S. Supreme Ct. 1980, U.S. Dist. Ct. (Del.) 1992, U.S. Ct. Appeals (10th cir.) 1986, U.S. Ct. Appeals (11th cir.) 1996, U.S. Ct. Appeals (fed. cir.) 2002. Law clk. to judge U.S. Ct. Appeals (3d cir.), Phila., 1975-76; assoc. Pepper Hamilton LLP, Phila., 1976-83, ptnr., 1983—. Ed. in chief U. Penn Law Review. Am. fellow, Salzburg Seminar, 1986. Mem. ABA, Pa. Bar Assn., Phila. Bar Assn., Del. State Bar Assn. Democrat. Avocations: baseball, wine, golf. Home: 415 Gate Ln Philadelphia PA 19119-2815 Office: Pepper Hamilton LLP 3000 Two Logan Sq 18th & Arch Sts Philadelphia PA 19103-1083 Office Phone: 215-981-4343. Business E-Mail: grantm@pepperlaw.com.

GRANT, MARK ANTONIO, organization administrator; b. Newark, June 16, 1954; s. Louis Wallace and Mary Louise (Bantum) G. Student, Glassboro State Coll., 1972—75; BA, William Paterson U., 1977; postgrad., UCLA, 1984. Film editor ABC, Hollywood, Calif., 1978—81, video engr., 1981—84; pub. info. specialist United Way L.A., 1984—85; blood cons. ARC, Santa Monica, Calif., 1985—86, dir., 1986—89; project coord., spokesman South Coast Air Quality Mgmt. Dist., 1989—91; coord. nat. youth Best Campaign for Drug Free Tomorrow, Sherman Oaks, Calif., 1991—; aide State Senator Ronald L. Rice, NJ, 1992—95; prodr. KLCS-TV L.A. Unified Sch. Dist., 1995—98, coord. spl. projects, 1998—; cmty. liaison The Children's Collective, Inc., L.A., 2001—03; internat. liaison Future Schs., Gosford City, Australia, 2003—05; dep. spl. projects City Councilman Bill Rosendahl, L.A., 2005—. Mem. Emergency Ops. Ctr., Santa Monica, 1986—; assoc. dir. Ednl. Ctr. Tchg. and Tng., Torrance, Calif., 2005— Bd. dirs. UN Assn., West Los Angeles, 1987—; mem. adv. bd. vol. ctr. West Los Angeles, 1988. Named Outstanding Young Man Am., 1982, 84, 88, Emmy award nominee, 1997. Mem.: Kiwanis. Democrat. Episcopalian. Avocations: running, bicycling, basketball, reading. Home: 4237 Inglewood Blvd Apt 206 Los Angeles CA 90066-2612 Office: 4237 Inglewood Blvd # 206 Los Angeles CA 90662 Office Phone: 310-568-8772. Personal E-mail: mgxnj@yahoo.com.

GRANT, MERRILL THEODORE, television producer; b. N.Y.C., July 9, 1932; s. Samuel and Rae (Renko) G.; m. Barbara Rosner, May 24, 1961; children: Andrea, Jonathan Samuel. BBA, CCNY, 1953; MS, Columbia U., 1954. V.p., dir. programming Benton & Bowles, N.Y.C., 1957-70; sr. v.p., dir. radio and TV Grey Advt., N.Y.C., 1970-72; v.p. Viacom Internat., N.Y.C., 1972-74; pres. Don Kirshner Prodns., N.Y.C., 1974-78, Grant Case McGrath, N.Y.C., 1978-79, Grant-Reeves Entertainment, N.Y.C., 1979-85; chmn., CEO Reeves Entertainment, N.Y.C., 1985-93. Served with AUS, 1954-56.

GRANT, MERWIN DARWIN, lawyer; b. Safford, Ariz., May 7, 1944; s. Darwin Dewey and Erma (Whiting) G.; m. Charlotte Richey, June 27, 1969; children: Brandon, Taggart, Christian, Brittany. BA in Econs., Brigham Young U., 1968; JD, Duke U., 1971. Bar: Ariz. 1971, U.S. Dist. Ct. Ariz., U.S. Dist. Ct. (we. dist.) Tex., U.S. Ct. Appeals (5th, 7th, 8th, 9th and 10th cirs.), U.S. Tax Ct., U.S. Supreme Ct. Pres. Merwin D. Grant, P.C., Phoenix, 1977—; ptnr. Beus, Gilbert & Morrill, Phoenix, 1984—93; pres. Grant Williams P.C., Phoenix, 1994—, Grant & Vaughen P.C. Guest condr. Phoenix Symphony Orch., 1989. Bd. dirs. Grand Canyon coun. Boy Scouts Am., Phoenix, 1974-76, Maricopa Hosp., Health Sys. Bd., 1997—, Ariz. Motorsports Charitable Found.; pres., bd. dirs. Golden Gate Settlement, Phoenix, 1975-80, 84-88, Phoenix Internat. Raceway Charities, Ariz. Acad. Decathalon Assn., exec. com., 1999-2002; charter mem. Rep. Presl. Task Force, Washington, 1984—; vice chmn. Ariz. Joint County Tobacco Revenue Use and Security Charitable Trust, 2000—; mem. Ariz. Joint House/Senate Ad Hoc Com. on Health Care Dists., 2001; chmn. Citizens' Task Force, Maricopa County Hosp., 2002—. Fellow Ariz. Bar Found.; mem. ABA (litigation sect.), Assn. Trial Lawyers Am., Kiwanis (bd. dirs. Phoenix chpt. 1972-79). Office: Grant & Vaughn PC 6225 N 24th St Ste 125 Phoenix AZ 85016 Office Phone: 602-393-4322. E-mail: grant@phxlaw.com.

GRANT, MICHAEL ERNEST, educational administrator, management educator; b. LA, June 6, 1952; s. Ernest Grant and Shirley Ruth (George) G. BA in Spanish, Calif. State U., Long Beach, 1974, MA in Edn. Adminstrn., 1978; EdD, Pepperdine U., 1984. Cert. elem., secondary, and cmty. coll. tchr., bilingual and cross-cultural edn., adminstr. Tchr. kindergarten through adult edn. Long Beach Unified Sch. Dist., 1975-83, tchr. 5th grade, 1975, tchr. 6th grade, 1975-76, bilingual multicultural specialist k-6, 1976-78, Spanish tchr. 6th, 7th and 8th grades, 1978-79, mgmt. program specialist, 1979-80, adminstr., program specialist, 1980-81, vice prin., 1981-83; asst. prof. tchr. edn. Calif. State U., San Bernardino, 1986-88, prin. dir. IMPACT/TEACH, assoc. prof. ednl. psychology and adminstrn. Long Beach, 1988-91; pres., founder Mykulphone-An Empowerment Through Edn. Project, Beverly Hills, Calif., 1991—; Spanish instr. Calif. Disting. Sch., Beverly Hills, 1993—; founder, pres. Dr. Michael Grant Enterprises, 2004—. Asst. instr. tchr. edn. Grad. Sch. Edn., Calif. State U., Long Beach, 1983-86; pres., CEO Mykulphone, Real Estate Developer, 1999—; lectr. in field. Exec. prodr., dancer, singer, songwriter (3D animated music video) The Flashy Dancer, 2004; contbr. articles to profl. jours. Pepperdine U. scholar, 1983-84; Calif. State U. grantee, 1988-89, 89-90, 89-91. Mem. NEA, Am. Coun. on Tchg. of Fgn. Langs., Assn. Calif. Sch. Adminstrs., Nat. Assn. Tchr. Educators, Nat. Coun. States In-Svc. Edn., Nat. Black Congress Faculty, Calif. Faculty Assn., Calif. State Intersegmental Coordination Coun., Calif. Black Faculty and Staff Assn., Calif. Assn. Tchr. Educators, Calif. Edn. Rsch. Assn., Calif. Lang. Tchrs. Assn., Intersegmental Coordinating Coun. Democrat. Baptist. Avocations: shotokon karate (black belt), acting, dance, singing, songwriting. Home and Office: No 911 9663 Santa Monica Blvd Beverly Hills CA 90210-9999 Office Phone: 310-850-5040. E-mail: drmichaelgrant@verizon.net.

GRANT, MICHAEL PETER, electrical engineer; b. Oshkosh, Wis., Feb. 26, 1936; s. Robert J. and Ione (Michelson) G.; m. Mary Susan Corcoran, Sept. 2, 1961; children: James, Steven, Laura. BS, Purdue U., 1957, MS, 1958, PhD, 1964. With Westinghouse Research Labs., Pitts., summers 1953-57; mem. tech. staff Aerospace Corp., El Segundo, Calif., 1961; instr. elec. engring. Purdue U., West Lafayette, Ind., 1958-64; sr. engr. Combustion Engring. Corp., Columbus, Ohio, 1964-67, mgr. advanced devel. and control systems, 1967-72, mgr. control and info. scis. div., 1972-74, asst. gen. mgr. indsl. systems div., 1974-76, mgr. system design, 1976-87; v.p., chief scientist SynGenics Corp., Columbus, 1987—; dir. Nat. Ctr. for Mfg. Scis., Ann Arbor, MIch., 1987-95. Contbr. articles to profl. jours.; holder 8 patents in field of automation. Mem. IEEE, Sigma Xi, Eta Kappa Nu, Pi Mu Epsilon, Tau Beta Pi Home: 4461 Sussex Dr Columbus OH 43220-3857 Office Phone: 614-451-8844. E-mail: mpgrant1@cs.com.

GRANT, NEWELL M., real estate investment manager; b. Denver, Nov. 2, 1941; s. Edwin Hendrie and Mary Belle (McIntyre) G.; m. Judith G. Wilson, June 19, 1971; children: Margaret, James, Newell, Caroline. BA, Dartmouth Coll., 1964; postgrad, U. Pa., 1967-68. Assoc. Kidder Peabody Realty, N.Y.C., 1969-74; ptnr. Borden, Danielson & Grant, Denver, 1975; cons. N.M. Grant & Co., Denver, 1976-78; ptnr. Grant Mgmt. Co., Denver, 1978—. Gen. ptnr. Grant Properties, Denver, 1977-93; chmn. bd. Colo. Nat. Bank Southwest, Littleton, 1983-89; Inc., 1991—. Pres. bd. trustees Denver Botanic Gardens, 1976—; pres. Denver Botanic Garden Endowment Inc., 1991—; active Gov.'s Task Force for Efficiency and Economy in Colo. State Govt., Denver, 1976; mem. Dartmouth Alumni Coun., 2002—; bd. dirs. Colo. World of Golf, 1990. Served to 1st lt. U.S. Army, 1965-66. Mem. Urban Land Inst. (assoc.)., Garden of the Gods (Colorado Springs). Democrat. Episcopalian. Avocations: hunting, gardening, reading. Home: 1325 Cherryville Rd Littleton CO 80121-1221

GRANT, PATRICK ALEXANDER, lawyer; b. Denver, Nov. 14, 1945; s. Edwin Hendrie and Mary Belle (McIntyre) G.; m. Carla Clyde Yancey, Aug. 16, 1975; children: Mary Cameron, Sara Mansur, Alexis Hendrie. BA with honors, Colgate U., 1967; MBA, Denver U., 1973; JD, Drake U., 1976. Bar: Colo. 1977. Law clk. to Judge Donald P. Smith, Jr. Colo. Ct. Appeals, Denver, 1976—77; assoc. Grant, McHendrie, Haines & Crouse, PC, Denver, 1977—83, ptnr., v.p., 1984—91, bd. dirs.; state rep. Colo. Gen. Assembly, Denver, 1984—92, vice-chmn. fin. com., 1987—88, chmn. audit com., 1989—90, chmn. judiciary com., 1988—92, chmn. legal svcs. com., 1988—89. Mem. Colo. Coun. Elected Ofcls. for Soviet Jewry, Denver, 1985-92, Colo. Spl. Task Force Tort Liability and Ins., Denver, 1985, Local U.S. Bank Bd., 2003—04; bd. dirs. Colo. Sports Hall of Fame, 1992-98, Colo. State U. Livestock Leader Coun. Kent Denver Leadership Fund, 1996-97, upper sch. chmn. parents divsn.; mem. Denver Cmty. Mental Health Commn., 1985-86; mem. exec. coun., planning com. St. Joseph Hosp., Denver, 1985-88; mem. Denver Bd. for Developmentally Disabled, 1987-88; vestryman, jr. warden St. Barnabas Parish, Denver, 1979-84; adv. com. Nat. Ctr. Preventive Law, 1987-90; bd. dirs. Colo. Jud. Inst., 1990-96, Denver Metro Conv. and Visitors Bur.,2001-, chmn. search com., 2004, chmn. Govt. Affairs com., 2004, exec. com. 2004; exec. bd. Parents Assn., Gettysburg (Pa.) Coll., 1997-2001, chmn. parents fund, 2000-01, nat. campaign steering com., 2000-01; mem. steering com. Colgate U. (NY) Soc. of Families, 2001-04; exec. bd. Denver coun. Boy Scouts Am., scout show chmn., 1997—; mem. Colo. Revised Statutes Adv. Group, 1999, Roundup Riders of Rockies, 1989—; mem. bd. govs. Colo. State U. Sys., 2001— (exec. com. 2003-05, sec. 2004, chmn. 2005-). Gates Found. fellow John F. Kennedy Sch. Govt. Harvard U., 1985, Toll Fellow Coun. of State Govts., 1987; recipient Outstanding Alumni award Kent Denver Country Day Sch., 1986, Colo. Wildlife Fedn. Appreciation award, 1987, Disting. Svc. to Higher Edn. award U. Denver, 1988, Bus. Legis. of Yr., award Colo. Pub. Affairs Coun., 1989, Outstanding Achievement award EPA, 1989, award of honor Hist. Denver, 1989, Stephen H. Hart award Colo. Hist. Soc., 1990, Spl. Recognition award AIA, Gen. Heritage award for Former Legislator, 1997; named one of Outstanding Young Men in Am., U.S. Jaycees, 1980, Legislator of Yr. Associated Builders and Contractors, 1991, Citizen of West, 2000, U. Col. Health Scis. Ctr. Chancellor Soc. Lunch honoree, 2003. Mem. Colo. Med. Soc. Found. (bd. dirs., pres. 1997-99, pres. emeritus 1999—), West Stock Show Assn. (exec. com., bd. dirs., exec. v.p., CEO 1990-91, pres., CEO 1991—), Metro Denver C. of C. (bd. dirs., chmn. econ. devel. coun. 1995-96, co-chmn. pub. affairs coun. 1999-2000, co-chmn. entrepeneurship coun. 2001-02), Assn. Rodeo Coms. (bd. dirs.). Republican. Episcopalian. Avocations: wood chopping, horseback riding. Home: 3777 S Dahlia St Englewood CO 80113-4215 Office: 4655 Humboldt St Denver CO 80216-2818

GRANT, PAUL, chemical engineer, real estate broker, lawyer; b. Patuxent River, Md., May 19, 1949; s. Ralph F. and Elizabeth (Payne) G. BS in Chem. Engring., Auburn U., Ala., 1971; MS in Chem. Engring., U. Md., College Park, 1975; Cert. Hungarian linguist, U.S. Army, 1972; JD U. Denver, 1995. Lic. real estate broker. Sales engr. Mixing Equipment Co., Rochester, N.Y., 1976-78; precious metals salesman James U. Blanchard & Co., New Orleans, 1979; owner, operator PK Grant & Co., Lakewood, Colo., 1979—; atty.; criminal def., comml., and civil litigator Denver, 1995—. Instr. Jr. Achievement Project Bus., Lakewood, Colo., 1984; state chmn. Libertarian Party, La., 1979, Libertarian Party candidate for gov. Colo., 1982, nat. chmn. Libertarian Party, 1983-85. Served with U.S. Army, 1971-74 Basketball scholar Pensacola Jr. Coll., Fla., 1967-69; named Nat. Merit scholar Auburn U., 1969-71; recipient Outstanding Translator award U.S. Army Def. Intelligence Agy., 1974 Office: 6053 S Quebec St #101 Centennial CO 80111 Office Phone: 303-771-1908.

GRANT, PETER RAYMOND, biologist, researcher, educator; b. London, Oct. 26, 1936; came to U.S., 1978; m. B. Rosemary Matchett, Jan. 4, 1962; children: Nicola, Thalia. BA with honors, Cambridge U., Eng., 1960; PhD, U. B.C., Vancouver, Can., 1964; PhD (hon.), U. Uppsala, 1986; DSc (hon.), McGill U., 2000, U. San Francisco, Quito, 2005. Prof. McGill U., Montreal, 1965-78, U. Mich., Ann Arbor, 1978-85, Princeton (N.J.) U., 1985—. Author: Ecology and Evolution of Darwin's Finches, 1986, 99; co-author: Evolutionary Dynamics of a National Population, 1989; editor: Evolution on Islands, 1998; co-editor: Molecules, Molds and Metazoa, 1992. Fellow AAAS, Am. Acad. Arts and Scis., Royal Soc. London, Royal Soc. Can.; mem. Am. Philos.l Soc. Office: Princeton U Dept Ecol Evol Biology Princeton NJ 08544-1003

GRANT, RICHARD EARL, retired medical and legal consultant; b. Spokane, Wash., Aug. 27, 1935; s. Conrad Morrison and Sylva Celeste (Sims) G.; m. Susan Kimberly Hawkins, Mar. 17, 1979; children: Paaqua A., Camber Do'otsie O. BSc cum laude, U. Wash., 1961; MEd, Whitworth Coll., 1974; PhD, Wash. State U., 1980. Cert. disability mgmt. specialist; cert. case mgr. Supr. nursing Providence Hosp., Seattle, 1970-72; asst. prof. nursing Wash. State U., Spokane, 1972-78; dir. nursing Winslow (Ariz.) Meml. Hosp., 1978-79; adminstr. psychiat. nursing Ariz. State Hosp., Phoenix, 1979-80; asst. prof. Ariz. State U., Tempe, 1980-83; assoc. prof. Linfield Coll., Portland, Oreg., 1983-86, Intercollegiate Ctr. for Nursing Edn., Spokane, 1986-88; sr. med. care coord. Fortis Corp., Spokane, 1988-92; med. svcs. cons. CorVel Corp., Spokane, 1992-94; owner Richard Grant & Assoc., Spokane, 1995-99; med./vocat. case mgr. Genex Svcs., Seattle, 1999—2003; ret., 2003; cons. Assurance Case Mgmt., 2004—. Cons. Ariz. State Hosp., 1980-82, Pres.'s Commn., Washington, 1981-83, U. No. Colo., Greely, 1985-86, Assurance Case Mgmt., 2004-; area med. svcs. cons., 1992—. Author: The God-Man-God Book, 1976, Publications of the Membership (Conaa), 1983, 4th rev. edit., 1988, Predetermined Careplan Handbook-Nursing, 1988, Duhikya: The Hopi Healer, 1996; contbr. articles to profl. jours. Judge Student Space Shuttle Project, Portland, 1983, N.W. Sci. Expo, Portland, 1983. With U.S. Army, 1953-56. Grantee NIMH, U. Wash., 1961; named one of top Hopi Scholars, Hopi Tribe, Second Mesa, Ariz., 1981. Mem. AAAS, Nat. League for Nursing, Wash. League for Nursing (v.p. 1988-90), Coun. on Nursing and Anthropology (editor 1982-90), N.Y. Acad. Scis., Case Mgmt. Soc. Am., Sigma Theta Tau. Avocations: painting, scuba diving. E-mail: dr.regrant@comcast.net.

GRANT, RICHARD W., lawyer; b. Oct. 25, 1945; AB, Brown U., 1968; JD, Boston U., 1971. Bar: D.C. 1972, Pa. 1984. Assoc. dir. divsn. investment mgmt. SEC, Washington, 1981-83; ptnr., chmn. investment mgmt. practice group Morgan, Lewis & Bockius, LLP, Phila. Office: Morgan Lewis & Bockius LLP 1701 Market St Philadelphia PA 19103-2903 also: Morgan Lewis & Bockius LLP One Oxford Ctr 32nd Fl Pittsburgh PA 15219-6401 Office Phone: 215-963-5000, 412-560-3340. Office Fax: 412-560-7001. Business E-Mail: rgrant@morganlewis.com.

GRANT, ROBERT JEFFREY, writer, actor; b. Norwood, Mass., Dec. 28, 1967; s. Robert Leo and Elaine Marie Grant. BA, Stonehill Coll., 1990; cert. paralegal, Mass. CC, 1993. Youth counselor Pilgrim Ctr., Braintree, Mass., 1990—93; corr. Putnam Investments, Franklin, Mass., 1994—97; cash contr. State St. Bank and Trust co., Quincy, Mass., 1997—2000. Actor Lipstick Model and Talent, Miami, Fla., 2001—, Extras Group, North Miami, Fla., 2003—. Author: (novels) Two Bottled Dolphins, 2004, short stories. Campaign worker Joseph Moakley, Boston. Mem.: Internat. Game and Fish Assn. Roman Catholic. Avocations: fishing, reading, swimming, snorkeling, surfing.

GRANT, ROBERT MCQUEEN, humanities educator; b. Evanston, Ill., Nov. 25, 1917; s. Frederick Clifton and Helen McQueen (Hardie) G.; m. Margaret Huntington Horton, Dec. 21, 1940; children: Douglas McQueen, Peter Williams, Susan Hardie, James Frederick. AB, Northwestern U., 1938; postgrad., Episcopal Theol. Sch., 1938-39, Columbia U., 1939-40; BD, Union Theol. Sem., 1941; STM, Harvard U., 1942, ThD, 1944; DD, Seabury-Western Theol. Sem., 1969, U. Glasgow, 1979; LHD, Kalamazoo Coll., 1979; DD, Ch. Div. Sch. Pacific, 1992. Ordained to ministry Episcopal Ch., 1942. Minister St. James Ch., South Groveland, Mass., 1942-44; instr. to prof. N.T. U. of South, 1944-53, acting dean, 1947; vis. lectr. U. Chgo., 1945, research assoc., 1952-53, assoc. prof., 1953-58, prof., 1958-87, emeritus, 1988—, Carl Darling Buck prof. humanities, 1973-87, Carl Darling Buck prof. emeritus, 1988—. Vis. lectr. Vanderbilt U., 1945-47, Seabury-Western Theol. Sem., 1954-55, 89, Augustinianum (Rome), 1990; lectr. Am. Council Learned Socs., 1957-58; vis. prof. Yale U., 1964-65, Fla. State U., 1989. Author: Second-Century Christianity, 1946, 2d edit., 2003, The Bible in the Church, 1948, rev. edit. (with David Tracy), 1984, Miracle and Natural Law, 1952, The Sword and the Cross, 1955, The Letter and the Spirit, 1957, Gnosticism and Early Christianity, 1959, 63, Gnosticism: An Anthology, 1961, The Earliest Lives of Jesus, 1961, Historical Introduction to the New Testament, 1963, The Apostolic Fathers, vol. I, 1964, vol. II (with H. H. Graham), 1965, vol. IV, 1966, U-Boats Destroyed 1914-1918, 1964, 2002, The Formation of the New Testament, 1965, History of Early Christian Literature (revision from E. J. Goodspeed), 1966, The Early Christian Doctrine of God, 1966, After the New Testament, 1967, U-Boat Intelligence 1914-1918, 1969, 2002, Augustus to Constantine, 1970, new edit., 2004, Theophilus of Antioch Ad Autolycum, 1970, Early Christianity and Society, 1977, Eusebius as Church Historian, 1980, Christian Beginnings: Apocalypse to History, 1983, Gods and the One God, 1986, Greek Apologists of the Second Century, 1988, Jesus after the Gospels, 1989, Heresy and Criticism, 1993, Irenaeus of Lyons, 1997; author: (with D. N. Freedman) The Secret Sayings of Jesus, 1960, (with G. Menzies) Joseph's Bible Notes, Hypomnestikon, 1996, Early Christians and Rome, 1999, Paul in the Roman World, 2001, U-Boat Hunters, 2003; assoc. editor Vigiliae Christianae. Fulbright research prof. U. Leiden, 1950-51; Guggenheim fellow, 1950, 54, 59. Fellow Am. Acad. Arts and Scis.; mem. Soc. Bibl. Lit. (pres. 1959), Am. Soc. Ch. History (pres. 1970, co-editor 1962-87), Chgo. Soc. Bibl. Research (pres. 1963-64, editor 1956-61), Phi Beta Kappa. Home: 5807 Dorchester Ave 11E Chicago IL 60637

GRANT, ROBERT NATHAN, lawyer; b. Newburgh, NY, Mar. 7, 1930; m. Barbara Weil, Feb. 10, 1952; children— Susan, Elizabeth Grant Ellerton, Nancy Grant Gray. BA, Yale U., 1951; LLB, Harvard U., 1956. Bar: Ill. 1956, N.Y. 1990. Assoc. Sonnenschein Nath & Rosenthal, Chgo., 1956-65; ptnr. Sonnenschein, Nath & Rosenthal, Chgo., 1965—. Contbr. articles to profl. jours. Pres. Legal Aid Soc. Ill., 1988—94; founding chmn. Winnetka (Ill.) Pub. Schs. Found., 1995—98, Winnetka Cmty. House, 2000—01; pres. Winnetka Bd. Edn., 1980—81, mem., 1974—81, Winnetka Planning Commn., 1975—77, New Trier Twp. Caucus, 1974; bd. dirs. United Charities, 1984—94, mem. legal aid com., 1982—, vice chmn., 1986—87, chmn., 1987—94; founding chmn. New Trier HS Ednl. Found., 2000—03, chmn., 2001—05. 1st lt. USAF, 1951—53. Recipient William H. Avery award for 10 yrs. svc. as chmn. Legal Aid Soc., 1994. Mem. ABA (vice-chmn. commercial leasing com.), Scholarship and Guidance Assn. (bd. dirs. 1968-92, pres. 1979-83), Harvard Law Sch. Spl. Gifts, Yale Alumni Recruiting Com., Standard Club, Yale Club (N.Y.C.), Phi Beta Kappa. Avocations: tennis, jogging, travel, reading. Home: 1165 Hamptondale Ave Winnetka IL 60093-1811 Office: Sonnenschein Nath & Rosenthal 233 S Wacker Dr Ste 8000 Chicago IL 60606-6491 Office Phone: 312-876-8072. E-mail: rgrant@sonnenschein.com.

GRANT, ROBERT ULYSSES, retired manufacturing company executive; b. Laramie, Wyo., Sept. 19, 1929; s. Guy Reid and Martha Clotilda (Krehmke) G.; m. Patricia Anne Towle, Feb. 12, 1955; children— Elizabeth, Sheila, Guy, Wilson, Mary BS in Civil Engring., U. Wyo., 1951; MBA, Harvard U., 1957. Fin. analyst, dir. acquisition analysis, v.p. mgmt. services, sr. v.p. corp. devel. Lear Siegler, Inc., Santa Monica, Calif., 1964-87. Served to lt. USNR, 1952-55 Mem.: Jonathan (Los Angeles), Masons. Democrat. Lutheran. Avocations: sailing, jogging. Home: 6549 Via Lorenzo Palos Verdes Peninsula CA 90275-6571

GRANT, RONALD ALFRED, psychiatrist, pastoral counselor, psychoanalyst; b. Providence, May 28, 1938; s. Alfred Edward and Althea G.; children: Andrew Edward, Kathryn Caroline. AB, Tufts U., 1959; MDiv, Andover Newton Theol. Sem., 1963, STM, 1964, D in Ministry, 1972; MD, Boston U., 1969. Cert. psychoanalysis, med. psychotherapy, group therapy. Intern Mary Imogene Bassett Hosp. (affiliate Columbia U. Med. Ctr.), Cooperstown, NY, 1969—70, resident, 1970—71, N.Y. State Psychiat. Inst. and Columbia Med. Ctr., NYC, 1971—73; pvt. practice pastoral counselor, 1972—; pvt. practice psychiatry, Westport, Greenwich, Conn., 1973—; pvt. practice psychoanalysis, 1981—. Mem. faculty, tng. and supervisory analyst C.G. Jung Inst. N.Y., 1981—, med. dir., 1983—87; psychiat. cons. Montessori Sch., Wilton, Conn., 1987—97; staff psychiatrist, supr. Temenos Inst., Westport, Conn., 1987—, med. dir., 1998—2000; mem. adj. faculty Andover Newton Theol. Sem., 1991—98. Mem. editorial bd. Human Devel. Jour., 1986-94. Named one of Outstanding Young Men in Am., 1970. Mem. AMA, Am. Psychiat. Assn., Am. Inst. Homeopathy, N.Y. Assn. Analytical Psychology, Internat. Assn. Analytical Psychology. Avocations: stamp collecting/philately, sports, reading, skiing, golf. Office: 45 E Putnam Ave Greenwich CT 06830-5438 also: 1465 Post Rd E Westport CT 06880 Office Phone: 203-629-3880, 203-254-3557.

GRANT, SONIA VIVIENNE, secondary school educator; b. Spanish Town, Jamaica, Jan. 27, 1947; arrived in US, 1967; d. Alfred Constantine and Mavis Adassah Jones; m. Gaffel Fritz Grant, June 23, 1968 (div. Dec. 15, 1989); children: Gaffel Sean, Nadique Tamika, Cynette Sonja. BA in Econs., Queens

Coll., Flushing, N.Y., 1975; MS, Long Is. U., Bklyn., 2000—. Cert. tchr. N.Y. Author: A Client's Point of View, 2001. Achievements include invention of grapha-phonic-bar. Home: 531 W 152nd St Apt 1 D New York NY 10031

GRANT, STEPHEN ALLEN, lawyer; b. N.Y.C., Nov. 4, 1938; s. Benton H. and Irene A. Grant; m. Anne. K. Bagley, Feb. 11, 1961 (div. Nov. 1975); children: Stephen, Katharine, Michael; m. Anne-Marie Laignel, Dec. 8, 1975; children: Natalie, Elizabeth, Alexandra. AB, Yale U., 1960; LLB, Columbia U., 1965. Bar: N.Y. 1965, U.S. Supreme Ct. 1969. Law clk. to judge U.S. Ct. Appeals (2d cir.), N.Y.C., 1965-66; assoc. Sullivan & Cromwell, N.Y.C., 1966-73, ptnr., 1973—2002. Mem. Japan-U.S. Friendship Commn., U.S.-Japan Conf. on Cultural and Ednl. Interchange, 1989-92. Lt. (j.g.) USNR, 1960-62. Mem. ABA, N.Y. State Bar Assn., Assn. of Bar of City of N.Y., Coun. Fgn. Rels. Clubs: Down Town, Links. Office: 118 Friendship Farm RD Millbrook NY 12545

GRANT, SUSAN J., federal agency administrator; Grad., Professional Military Comptroller Sch., Maxwell Air Force Base, 1982, Sr. Exec. Fellows Program, John F. Kennedy Sch. of Govt., Harvard U., Cambridge, 1992, Fed. Exec. Inst., Charlottesville, Va., 1994. Various positions including budget officer, manpower mgr., program analyst, logistics mgmt. specialist US Dept. Def., Washington, 1972—99, former dep. dir. for budget, resource mgmt. directorate, defense fin. acctng. svc., 1999—2001, CFO, dir. corp. resources, defense fin. acctng. svc., 2001—04; CFO, dir. office of mgmt., budget and evaluation US Dept. Energy, Washington, 2004—. Office: US Dept Energy Rm 4A-253 Washington DC 20585-0701*

GRANT, SYDNEY R., education educator, consultant; b. N.Y.C., Feb. 3, 1926; s. Herman S. and Ethel H. G.; m. Margarita Henderson, Sept. 4, 1951. BS in Edn. cum laude, CCNY, 1950; MA in Spanish Letters, Nat. U. Mex., Mexico City, 1951; EdD, Columbia U. Tchrs. Coll., 1961. Program asst. Sch. Gen. Studies CCNY, 1951-52, instr. Spanish Sch. Gen. Studies evening program, 1952-64; tchr. Spanish and common brs., cons. The P.R. study N.Y.C. Bd. Edn., 1952-60; dir. of instrn. K-12 Verona (N.J.) Pub. Schs., 1961-64; assoc. chief of party, assoc. prof. Columbia U. Tchrs. Coll., US./AID contract team, Lima, Peru, 1964-68; assoc. supt. for curriculum Bellevue (Wash.) Pub. Schs., 1968-69; dir. office internat. edn. Coll. Edn. Fla. State U., Tallahassee, 1969-72, assoc. prof., dir. Ctr. for Ednl. Tech., 1972-75, assoc. dean for grad. studies Coll. Edn., 1975-78, prof. Coll. Edn., 1972—, prof., head dept. ednl. founds. and policy studies, 1986-89, prof. internat.-intercultural devel. edn., 1979-85, prof. emeritus, 1994—. Cons. U.S./AID, UN Devel. Program, UNESCO, Fundacion Natura, Fla. State U., Latin Am., S.E. Asia, Africa, 1969-90; sr. resident tech. adv. Min. Edn. and Culture for Fla. State U. in Windhoek, Namibia, 1991-93. With U.S. Army, 1944-46, ETO. Recipient Esso award Esso Standard Oil Co., 1960, Palmas Magisteriales Peruvian Ministry of Edn., 1967, Pres.'s Teaching award Fla. State U., 1978; Downer scholar CCNY, 1950. Mem. Nat. Soc. for Study Edn., Comparative and Internat. Edn. Soc., Common Cause, Amnesty Internat. Avocations: short wave radio, reading. Office: 1503 Belleau Wood Dr Tallahassee FL 32308-0911

GRANT, THERESA EVLA, dental hygienist; b. Mobile, Ala., June 11, 1935; d. McCena N. and Evla (Goode) Hannon; m. Warren H. Grant, Oct. 16, 1933; children: Carliss D., Warren H. III, Kevin A. Cert. in hygiene, Howard U., 1964. Cert. RDH Washington, DC. Tchg. handicapped DC Children's Ctr., Wash., DC, 1978—85; dental hygienist Children's Dental Health, Adams Morgan Health Ctr., Wash., DC, 1986—2000, Watergate Dental Assoc., Wash., DC, 2000—. Author: A Faithful Choice, 2000, Hope and Desire, 2005, FrankenChild, 2005. Mem.: Children's Books Insider, Romance Writer's of Am. Avocations: writing, sewing, reading, cooking, boating. Home: 4917 Morning Glory Ct Rockville MD 20853 E-mail: grant.theresa@msn.com.

GRANT, VERNE EDWIN, biology professor; b. San Francisco, Oct. 17, 1917; s. Edwin and Bessie (Swallow) G.; m. Alva Day, June 12, 1946 (div. Aug. 1959); children: Joyce Grant Mixon, Brian, Brenda; m. Karen Alt, Nov. 3, 1960. AB, U. Calif., Berkeley, 1940, PhD, 1949. Teaching asst. botany U. Calif., Berkeley, 1946-49; NRC fellow Carnegie Inst., Stanford, Calif., 1949-50; geneticist Rancho Santa Ana Bot. Garden, Claremont, Calif., 1950-67; asst. prof. Claremont Grad. Sch., 1951-53, assoc. prof., 1953-57, prof., 1957-67; prof. biology Inst. Life Sci., Tex. A&M U., College Station, 1967-68; prof., dir. Boyce Thompson Southwestern Arboretum U. Ariz., Superior, 1968-70; prof. botany U. Tex., Austin, 1970-87, prof. emeritus, 1987—. Author: Natural History of the Phlox Family, 1959, The Origin of Adaptations, 1963, The Architecture of the Germplasm, 1964, (with Karen Grant) Flower Pollination in the Phlox Family, 1965, (with Karen Grant) Hummingbirds and Their Flowers, 1968, Plant Speciation, 1971, 2d edit., 1981, Genetics of Flowering Plants, 1975, Organismic Evolution, 1977, The Evolutionary Process, 1985, 2d edit., 1991, The Edward Grant Family and Related Families in Massachusetts, Rhode Island, Pennsylvania, and California, 1997; mem. editl. bd. Ency. Americana, 1955-64, Brittonia, 1957-62, Evolution, 1960-62, Am. Naturalist, 1964-67, Biologisches Zentralblatt, 1974-97; contbr. articles to profl. jours. Recipient Sci. award Phi Beta Kappa, 1964 Fellow Am. Acad. Arts and Scis.; mem. NAS, Soc. for Study of Evolution (pres. 1968), Bot. Soc. Am. (cert. of merit 1971), Internat. Soc. Plant Taxonomists, Am. Soc. Plant Taxonomists, Acad. Medicine, Engring. and Sci. of Tex. Home: 2811 W Fresco Dr Austin TX 78731-5028 Office: U Tex Sect Integrative Biology Austin TX 78712

GRANT, WALTER MATTHEWS, retired lawyer; b. Winchester, Ky., Mar. 30, 1945; s. Raymond Russell and Mary Mitchell (Rees) G.; m. Ann Carol Straus, Aug. 5, 1967; children— Walter Matthews II, Jean Ann, Raymond Russell II. ABJ, U. Ky., Lexington, 1967; JD, Vanderbilt U., 1971. Bar: Ga. 1971, Tenn. 1992. Assoc. Alston & Bird, Atlanta, 1971-76, ptnr., 1976-83; v.p., gen. counsel, sec. Contel Corp., Atlanta, 1983-91; sr. v.p., gen. counsel Smith & Nephew N.Am., Memphis, 1991-93; sr. v.p., gen. counsel, sec. The Actava Group Inc., Atlanta, 1993-96, Bruno's Supermarkets, Inc., Birmingham, Ala., 1996—2002. Bd. dirs. SCB Computer Tech., Inc., Memphis, 2002—04, Hat Shack, Inc., Atlanta. Editor in chief Vanderbilt Law Rev., 1970-71, Ga. State Bar Jour., 1979-82. Baptist.

GRANT, WILLIAM DAVIS, family medicine educator, dean; BS, U. Rio Grande, 1967; MEd, The Am. U., 1972; EdD, U. So. Calif., 1977. Asst. prof. family medicine U. Okla., Oklahoma City, 1982-87; adj. prof. marriage and family therapy Syracuse (N.Y.) U., 1995—; asst. prof. New Sch. for Social Rsch., N.Y.C., 1996—; prof. family medicine SUNY Health Sci. Ctr., Syracuse, 1987—, assoc. dean grad. med. edn., 1997—. Founding dir. Ctr. for Evidence Based Practice, SUNY Health Sci. Ctr., Syracuse, 1997-98. Pres. bd. dirs. McKenzie Inst., Syracuse, 1992-95; mem. internat. bd. dirs. McKenzie Internat., Waikanae, New Zealand, 1992-95. Recipient Excellence in Rsch. Edn. award South-Ctr. Rsch. Consortium, San Antonio; named Outstanding Alumnus U. Rio Grande. Fellow Royal Statis. Soc.; mem. Am. Coll. Legal Medicine (assoc.), World Orgn. Family Drs. Office: SUNY Health Sci Ctr at Syracuse 750 E Adams St Syracuse NY 13210-2306

GRANT, WILLIAM FREDERICK, geneticist, educator; b. Hamilton, Ont., Can., Oct. 20, 1924; s. William Aitken and Myrtle Irene (Taylor) Grant; m. Phyllis Kemp Harshaw, July 23, 1949; 1 child, William Taylor. BA, McMaster U., Hamilton, 1947, MA, 1949; PhD, U. Va., Charlottesville, 1953; DSc (hon.), McMaster U., 2000. Botanist, geneticist under Colombo Plan to Dept. Agr., Malaysia, 1953-55; asst. prof. McGill U., Montreal, Que., 1955-61, assoc. prof., 1961-66, prof. depts. plant sci. and biology, 1967-90, prof. emeritus, 1990—. Mem joint WHO and Int Program Chemical Safety Collaborative Study on Short Term Tests for Genotoxicity and Carcinogenicity, 1984—94; environ contaminants adv comt Ministers Environ and Nat health and Welfare, Ottawa, Ont, Canada, 1978—86; co-dir workshop higher plant mutagen bioassays UN Environ Program Quingao Ocean Univ, China, 1995. Editor: Lotus Newsletter, 1970—85, Can Jour Genetics and Cytology, 1974—82; mem ed bd: Mutation Research, 1978—85, Plant Species Biol, 1985—92, Revista Internacional de Contaminacion Ambiental, 1991—; editor (hon ed): Plant Species Biol, 1993—. Named award of Excellence, Grant- Moens, 2004; named to Alumni Gallery, McMaster Univ, 1996; recipient Andrew Fleming Award, 1953, Gov Gen Silver Medal commemorating 25th Ann Accession of H M Queen Elizabeth to Throne, 1977, Distinguished Alumni/Alumnae Scholar Award, McMaster Univ, 1990; fellow Blandy Research, 1950—53. Fellow: AAAS, Royal Soc Can, Linnean Soc London; mem.: Biol Coun Can (treas 1974—78), Soc Study Evolution (vpres 1972), Am Soc Plant Taxonomists, Int Orgn Plant Biosystematists (life; pres 1981—86), Can Botany Asn (George Lawson Medal 1989), Environ Mutagen Soc, Genetics Soc Can (pres 1975, archivist 1984—, Presdl Citation 1991), Sigma Xi (chpt pres 1975). Home: 43 St Andrews Rd Baie d'Urfe PQ Canada H9X 2T9 Office: McGill U Macdonald campus Box 4000 Dept Plant Sci Sainte Anne de Bellevue PQ Canada H9X 3V9 Office Phone: 514-398-7851. Business E-Mail: william.grant@mcgill.ca.

GRANT, WILLIAM WEST, III, banker; b. NYC, May 9, 1932; s. William West and Katherine O'Connor (Neelands) G.; m. Rhondda Lowery, Dec. 3, 1955. BA, Yale U., 1954; postgrad., NYU Grad. Sch. Bus., 1958, Columbia U. Grad. Sch. Bus., 1968, Harvard U. Grad. Sch. Bus., 1971. With Bankers Trust Co., N.Y.C., 1954-58, br. credit adminstr., 1957-58; with Colo. Nat. Bank, Denver, 1958-93, pres., 1975-86, chmn. bd., 1986-93. Chmn. bd. Colo. Capital Advisors, 1989-94; bd. dirs. Barrett Resources Corp. With Episc. Ch. Found., Nat. Trust Hist. Preservation; trustee Rocky Mountain Nat. Park Assocs., Denver, Midwest Rsch. Inst., Kansas City; mem. adv. bd. Rocky Mtn. Pub. Broadcasting Sys.; dir. Colo. Energy Sci. Ctr.; bd. dirs. Mountain State Employers Coun. Mem.: Denver Country Club. Episcopalian. Home: 545 Race St Denver CO 80206-4122 Office Phone: 303-321-1566. Business E-Mail: petergrant1155@comcast.net.

GRANTE, JULLIAN IRVING, criminologist, consultant; b. Washington, Oct. 18, 1950; s. Mamie Elmara Landis; m. Jo Draper; children: Jamil Patricia, Dusan Arthur. BBA, U. Md., 1972; M in Spl. Edn., So. Ill. U., Carbondale, 1976. Sr. ptnr. J. Irving & Draper, Spotsylvania, Va. Testified before U.S. Congress subcom. hearing on youth empowerment; apptd. advisor release rev. com. Dept. Juvenile Justice, State of Va., 1995—, past mem. Criminal Justices Svcs. Bd.; developer program The Broken Classroom: A Dialogue on Youth and Community Violence-Problems and Solutions, 1999; spkr. in field. Named Vol. of Yr. D.C. Pub. Schs., 1988; recipient award Nat. Capitol Area Region, 1990, Recognition for Volunteerism in Edn., White House Points of Light, 1992, Finalist Kellogg Nat. Fellowship Program Group XIII, 1993, finalist Entrepreneur of Yr., Washington Post Inc. Mag., 1995, 96. Mem. Phi Delta Kappa. Office: 535 Mount Pleasant Dr Locust Grove VA 22508-5208 E-mail: jgrante2@aol.com.

GRANTER, SHARON SAVOY, restaurateur, caterer; b. Hammond, Ind., Oct. 21, 1940; d. Theodore Grummer and Marie Theresa (Vincent) Kocur; m. John Albert Savoy, Aug. 14, 1959 (div. Nov. 1974); children: Renee Savoy Heuss, Jennifer Lynn Savoy, Elizabeth Anne Savoy, Ericca Marie Savoy, Caroline Savoy Sanders; m. Donald Ralph Granter, Feb. 10, 1979. Student, Ohio State U., 1958-59; grad., Lancaster Bus. Coll., 1959. Sec., bookeeper Manpower, Inc., Albany, N.Y., 1960-64; owner, operator, caterer Granter's Deli Catering Svc., Mansfield, Ohio, 1979-94; restaurateur, operator Perkins of Mansfield, 1989-94; co-owner, operator Paisley Park Gourmet Deli and Granter's Catering, Mansfield, 1996—; co-owner EZ Meals, Inc., Mansfield, 1998—. Editor newsletter NCO Rehab. Ctr., 1971-74. Vocalist Ohio State U. Jazz Forum Big Band, 1955-59; founder, dir. New Start Seminar, Mansfield, 1973-79; sec. Miss Ohio Scholarship Pageant, Mansfield, 1974-80, traveling companion, 1974-80, judge, 1974-86; mem. procurement com. Mansfield Gen. Hosp., 1973-74; pres. aux. AMA Riverside Hosp., Columbus, 1972; bd. dirs. Am. Cancer Soc. Mem. Nat. Restaurant Assn., Ohio Restaurant Assn. Republican. Home: 660 Brae Burn Rd Mansfield OH 44907-1916 Office: 1400 Park Ave E Mansfield OH 44905-2989

GRANTHAM, DONALD, composer, educator; b. Duncan, Okla., Nov. 9, 1947; s. Donald Jewel and Patricia Lewis Grantham; m. Suzanne Pearson Pearson, July 11, 1975; children: Ellen Suzanne, Mark Andrew, Paul Benjamin. MusD, U. So. Calif., 1975. Prof. composition U. Tex., Austin, Tex., 1975—. Composer (librettist): The Boor (First prize Nat. Opera Assn. Composition Competition, 1992); composer: Fantasy on Mr. Hyde's Song (First prize Nissim ASCAP Orchestral Composition Contest, 1992), Southern Harmony (First prize ABA, 1998, Ostwald award, 1998, First prize NBA/William D. Revelli, 1998), Hymn to the Earth, 2001; author: The Technique of Orchestration, 6th edition (Prentice Hall); composer: Fantasy Variations (First prize ABA Ostwald Competition, 1999, First prize NBA William D. Revelli Competition, 1999). Trustee KMFA Classical Radio Sta., Austin, 1994—2005. Recipient Music citation, Am. Acad. and Inst. of Arts and Letters, 1980; fellow, Guggenheim Found., 1991; grantee, NEA, 1980, 1983, 1995. Mem.: Town and Gown Club. Home: 8831 Mountain Path Circle Austin TX 78759 Office: University of Texas at Austin School of Music 1 University Station Austin TX 78712-0435 Office Phone: 512-471-0522. Home Fax: 512-343-7460; Office Fax: 512-471-7836. Personal E-mail: piquant@piquantpress.com. E-mail: dgrantham@mail.utexas.edu.

GRANTHAM, JARED JAMES, nephrologist, educator; b. Dodge City, Kans., May 19, 1936; married, 1958; 4 children. AB, Baker U., 1958; MD, U. Kans., 1962. Assoc. prof. med. U. Kans., Kansas City, 1969-76, head nephrology sect., 1970-96, prof., 1976-96, disting. prof., 1996—. Founder and chmn. Polycystic Kidney Rsch. Found.; dir. Kidney Inst., 2000. Fellow NIH, 1964-66; grantee Nat. Inst. Diabetes Digestive and Kidney Diseases, 1969-03; recipient Homer Smith award Am. Soc. Nephrology and Am. Heart Assn., 1992, David Hume award Nat. Kidney Found., 1998. Mem. Am. Soc. Nephrology, Am. Soc. Clin. Investigation, Am. Physiol. Soc., Am. Fedn. Clin. Rsch., Assn. Am. Phys. Achievements include research in fluid and electrolyte metabolism, electrolyte transport, mechanism of action of antidiuretic hormone and polycystic kidney disease. Office: U Kans Dept Medicine/ Nephrology 3901 Rainbow Blvd Kansas City KS 66160-0001 E-mail: jgrantha@kumc.edu.

GRANTHAM, KIRK PINKERTON, lawyer, insurance company executive; b. Tupelo, Miss., Oct. 12, 1941; s. Homer Kirk and Lucile (Pinkerton) G.; m. Damaris Dodson, Aug. 25, 1964 (div. 1980); 1 child, Dodson Kirk; m. Cheryl Norman, Apr. 25, 1983; 1 child, Tyler Kirk. B in Pub. Adminstrn., U. Miss., 1963, JD, 1966. Bar: Miss. 1966, Fla. 1971; cert. real property law and wills, trusts and estate planning. Estate tax atty. IRS, W. Palm Beach, Fla., 1966-72; ptnr. Day, Grantham & Hess, Lake Worth, Fla., 1972-81; assoc. Shutts & Bowen, Lake Worth, 1981-86; pvt. practice, West Palm Beach, 1986—; pres. Std. Title Ins. Agy., Inc., West Palm Beach. Pres. Palm Beach County Heart Assn., 1991. Sgt. USAR, 1966-72. Recipient Leadership award YMCA, 1987. Mem. ABA, Fla. Bar Assn., Miss. Bar Assn., Tuskawillow Club. Republican. Episcopalian. Office: 1860 Forest Hill Blvd West Palm Beach FL 33406-6086

GRANTHAM, RICHARD ROBERT, financial consultant; b. Ogden, Utah, July 25, 1927; s. Arthur and Dorothy (Taylor) G.; m. Charlotte Blackwood, Aug. 10, 1951; children: Robert Arthur, Scott Ford, Ann Margaret, Susan Marie. BS magna cum laude, Claremont Men's Coll., 1950. C.P.A., Calif. Acct., Price Waterhouse & Co., Los Angeles, 1950-57; asst. controller Cyprus Mines Corp., Los Angeles, 1957-64, div. controller, 1964-65, budget dir., 1965-72, v.p., treas., 1972-74, sr. v.p., treas., 1975-79, sr. v.p., controller, 1979-81; controller Amoco Minerals Co., Denver, 1980-81; sr. v.p., treas. Trust Co. of the West, L.A., 1982-88; sec., treas. TCW Convertible Securities Fund, Inc., 1986-89; mng. dir. Trust Co. of the West, L.A., 1989, cons. on oil and gas matters, 1989-92; sr. ptnr., chief adminstrv. officer TCW Realty Advisors, 1989-95; cons. earthquake repair and ins. matters Westmark Realty Advisors, 1995-99; fin. cons. San Marino, Calif., 1999—. Lectr. in field. Trustee Claremont McKenna Coll., 1953-54, 65-68, 74—, vice chmn., 1976-96; dir. Pasadena (Calif.) Symphony Assn., 1995-2005, v.p. finance 1996-99, exec. v.p., 1999-2000, pres., 2000-2002, mem. adv. bd., 2004—. Mem. AICPA, San Marino Men's Republic Club (pres. 1967), Calif. Soc. CPAs, Claremont Men's Coll. Alumni Assn. (pres. 1953-54), Republican Assocs. Clubs: California, Valley Hunt. Home: 1660 Oak Grove Ave San Marino CA 91108-1109 Fax: (626) 585-1682. E-mail: rgrantham1@socal.rr.com.

GRANTON, ELIZABETH MARLENE, artist, school director; b. Chgo., May 4, 1959; d. Marvin Hyman and Jarie Rose (Vavra) G.; m. Craig William Hunter, Apr. 22, 1989. BFA, U. Ill., Chgo., 1982; postgrad., Sch. Art Inst. Chgo., 1992-93; MLS, Dominican U., 2003. Muralist USAF, Chanute, Ill., 1979; sch. dir. Oak Park (Ill.) Art League, 1993-94. Exhibited in group shows at Old Town Triangle Art Ctr., Chgo., 1991, 1992, Countryside Arts Ctr., Arlington Heights, Ill., 1991, North Ctrl. Coll., Naperville, Ill., 1992, Contemporary Art Ctr., Arlington Heights, 1992, Nineteenth Century Women's Club, Oak Park, Ill., 1992, 2191 Cafe, Chgo., 1992-93, Oak Park (Ill.) Village Hall, 1993, Chgo. (Ill.) Cultural Ctr., 1993, Oak Park River Forest H.S., 1993. Recipient Gold Keys, Hallmark, 1975, 76, 77, Nat. Scholastic Art award Hallmark, Midwest Region, 1977. Mem. NOW (surveyor), Ill. Arts Coun., Chgo. Soc. Artists, Chgo. Women's Caucus of Art. Jewish. Avocations: writing, swimming, travel. Home: 142 N Humphrey Ave Oak Park IL 60302-2542

GRANVILLE, LAURA, professional tennis player; b. Chgo., May 12, 1981; d. Charles and Elizabeth. Student, Stanford U., 1999—2001. Profl. tennis player, 2001—. Named Coll. Player of the Yr., Tennis Mag./ITA, 2000, 2001, NCAA Singles Champion, 2000, 2001; recipient 2 Women's Circuit Singles Title, ITF. Office: WTA Tour Corporate Headquarters One Progress Plz Ste 1500 Saint Petersburg FL 33701

GRAPHIA, GARY P., lawyer; b. Baton Rouge, La., Sept. 4, 1962; m. Rene Graphia. Degree in fin., La. State U., JD, 1991. Various positions to asst. v.p. Tex. Commerce Bank, Houston; assoc. Phelps Dunbar LLP, Kean, Miller, Hawthorne, D'Armond, McCowan & Jarman LLP, Baton Rouge, 1995—99, ptnr., 1999; sec., gen. counsel The Shaw Group Inc., Baton Rouge, 1999—. Bd. trustees La. Arts & Sci. Mus., 2002—, La. State U. Paul M. Hebert Law Ctr., 2003—. Named one of "40 under 40", Baton Rouge Bus. Report, 2001. Office: The Shaw Group Inc 4171 Essen Ln Baton Rouge LA 70809

GRAPIN, JACQUELINE G., economist; b. Paris, Dec. 15, 1942; came to U.S., 1985; d. Jean and Raymonde (Ledru) G.; m. Michel Le Goc, June 4, 1971; children: Claire, Julien. Degree, Institut d'Etudes Politiques, Paris, 1966; Degree in Law, U. Paris, 1967; Auditeur, Inst. des Hautes Etudes de Def. Nat., Paris, 1980. Staff writer LeMonde, Paris, 1967-81; dir.-gen. Interavia Pub. Group, Geneva, 1982-86; pres. The European Inst., Washington, 1989—; assoc. prof. Am. U. Econ. corr. Le Figaro, Washington, 1987—; prof. Inst. d'Etudes Politiques, Paris, 1974-77. Author: Guerre Civile Mondiale, 1977, Radioscopie des Etats-Unis, 1980, Fortress America, 1984, Pacific America, 1987, Transatlantic Interoperability in Defense Industries, 2002; pub. European Affairs; contbr. articles to profl. jours. Trustee Aspen Inst. for Humanistic Studies, N.Y.C., 1981—96; bd. dirs. French Am. C. of C., Washington, Internat. Action Against Hunger. Recipient Prix Vauban Inst. des Hautes-Etudes, Paris, 1977, Officer in Order of Legion of Honor, 2001. Mem.: Internat. Inst. Strategic Studies, Cosmos Club, Nat. Press Club, Pen Club. Office: The European Inst 5225 Wisconsin Ave NW Ste 200 Washington DC 20015-2014 Home: 4201 Cathedral Ave NW Washington DC 20016

GRASER, ALFRED J., airport terminal executive, director; Dep. dir. Port Authority NY, Jamaica, 2000—01; gen. mgr. John F. Kennedy Internat. Airport, Jamaica, 2001—. Mem.: Am. Assn. Airport Exec. (pres. NE chpt. 2002—03).

GRASES, CRISTIAN, conductor; b. Caracas, Venezuela, Dec. 22, 1973; arrived in U.S., 2002; s. José Pablo Grases and Mariella Amalia Feo; m. Mirtha Fatima Martinez, July 29, 1998; children: Camila, Juan Miguel, Santiago. B in Biology (CDCH scholar), Universidad Ctrl. de Venezuela, Caracas, 1996; M in Choral Conducting, Simón Bolivar U., Caracas, 2001. Founder, condr. CINCOPAM, Caracas, 1995—2001; condr. Schola Contorum de Caracas, 1996—2002; asst. condr. Orfeón Universitario Simón Bolivar, Caracas, 1996—98; musical dir. Pequeños Cantores de Chacao, Caracas, 1997—2002; chief choral divsn. FESNOJIV, Caracas, 2001—02; artistic dir. Iowa Youth Chorus, Des Moines, 2003—. Asst. prof. I Ctrl. U. Venezuela, Caracas, 1994—95, asst. prof., 1995—96; piano tchr., 1997—2000; substitute tchr. Jefferson Sch., Caracas, 1999—2000; asst. prof. Simon Bolivar U., Caracas, 2001—02, prof. history and evolution vocal music, 2001—02. Composer: A donde Iran?, Bourrée, Calipso Carqueño, Chuao, Coral Variado, Crux Fidelis, El Estero, Hoy, others. Recipient Jose Felix Ribas, Venezuelan Govt., 1998, 2 silver medals, Choral Olympics, Bermen, Germany, 2004. Mem.: Am. Choral Dirs. Assn., Internat. Fedn. Choral Music. Home: 608 SE Chaparal Ct Clarkston GA 30021 Office: Iowa Youth Chorus 206 6th Ave Ste 1015 Des Moines IA 50309

GRASMICK, NANCY S., school system administrator; b. Balt. m. Louis J. Grasmick. BS in Elem. Edn., Towson State U., 1961; MS in Deaf Edn., Gallaudet U., 1965; PhD in Communicative Scis. with distinction, Johns Hopkins U., 1979; LHD (hon.), Towson State U., 1992, Goucher Coll., 1992, U. Balt., 1996, Villa Julie Coll., 1998. Tchr. deaf William S. Baer Sch., Balt., 1961-64; tchr. hearing and lang. impaired children Woodvale Sch., Balt., 1964-68; supr. Office Spl. Edn. Balt. County Pub. Schs., 1968-74; prin. Chatsworth Sch., Balt., 1974-78; asst. supt. Balt. County Pub. Schs., 1978-85, assoc. supt., 1985-89; sec. juvenile svcs. Dept. Juvenile Svc., Balt., 1991; spl. sec. children, youth and families Gov.'s Exec. Office, Balt., 1989-94; supt. schs. Md. Dept. Edn., Balt., 1991—. Mem., chmn. interagy. com. on sch. constrn. Gov.'s Subcabinet for Children, Youth and Families; mem. Gov.'s Workforce Investment Bd.; mem. profl. stds. and tchr. edn. bd. Md. Assocs. for Dyslexic Adults and Youth; mem. State Bd. Edn. profl. adv. bd. Met. Balt. Assn. Learning Disabled Children. Trustee Md. Retirement and Pension Sys.; active Women Execs. in State Govt.; mem. adv. coun. Scholastic, Inc. Recipient Medallion award Jimmy Swartz Found., 1989, Louise B. Makofsky Meml. award Md. Conf. Social Concern, 1990, Child Advocacy award Am. Acad. Pediat., 1990, Humanitarian award March of Dimes, 1990, Disting. Citizen's award Md. Assn. Non-pub. Spl. Edn. Facilities, 1991, Women of Excellence award Nat. Assn. Women Bus. Owners, 1991, Andrew White medal Loyola Coll., 1992, Nat. Edn. Adminstr. of Yr. award Nat. Assn. Ednl. Office Profls., 1992, Nat. award computing to asst. persons with disabilities Johns Hopkins U., 1992, Vernon E. Anderson Disting. Lecture award for outstanding leadership in edn. Coll. Edn., U. Md., 1992, DuBois Circle Award of Honor, 1992, Disting. Alumna of Yr. award Johns Hopkins U., 1992, Pub. Affairs award Md. C. of C., 1994, Educator of the Yr. award Am. Coun. on Rural Spl. Edn., Profl. Legal Excellence-Advancement of Pub. Understanding of Law award Md. Bar Found., Inc., Pressley Ridge award, Victorine Q. Adams Humanitarian award; named Communicator of Yr. by Speech and Hearing Agy., 1990, Marylander of Yr. by Advt. and Profl. Club of Balt., 1990, Marylander of Yr. by The Balt. Sun, 1997, Most Disting. Woman Girl Scouts Ctrl. Md., 1994, Cmty. Honoree 9th Ann. Heartfest Johns Hopkins Hosp., 1999; selected as one of Md.'s Top 100 Women, Warfields Bus. Record, 1996, 98. Fellow Nat. Assn. Pub. Adminstrs.; mem. Phi Delta Kappa (Excellence in Edn. award), Pi Lambda Theta. Office: Md Dept Edn 200 W Baltimore St Baltimore MD 21201-2595*

GRASS, ALEXANDER, retail company executive; b. Scranton, Pa., Aug. 3, 1927; s. Louis and Rose (Breman) G.; m. Lois Lehrman, July 30, 1950; children: Linda Jane, Martin L., Roger L., Elizabeth Ann; m. Louise B. Gurkoff, Apr. 26, 1974. LLB, U. Fla., 1949; D (hon.), Hebrew U., 2000, Doctorate (hon.) of Philosphy, 2000. Bar: Fla. 1949, Pa. 1953. Pvt. practice, Miami Beach, Fla., 1949-51; v.p. Rite Aid Corp., Shiremanstown, Pa., 1952—62, pres., 1966-69, 77-89, chmn., chief exec. officer, 1969-95, chmn. exec. com., 1995-99; chmn., CEO Super Rite Foods, Inc., 1983-95. Chmn. bd. govs. Hebrew U. of Jerusalem, 1996-99, exec. com. mem., 1999-. Mem. nat. exec. com. United Jewish Appeal, 1968-79, nat. vice chmn., 1970-79, gen. chmn., 1984-86, chmn. bd. trustees, 1986-88, mem. bd. trustees,

1988-99; pres. Harrisburg (Pa.) Jewish Fedn., 1970-72; chmn. Israel Edn. Fund, 1975-78; bd. dirs. Pa. Right to Work Found., 1972-74, Harrisburg Hosp., 1977-81; vice chmn. Harrisburg Hosp., 1988-95; bd. dirs. Pinnacle Health Sys., 1995-2001; mem. Pa. Coun. Arts, 1982; bd. dirs. Keystone State Games, 1982-92, Israel Ctr. Social and Econ. Studies, 1983; trustee Jerusalem Inst. Mgmt., 1983; mem. exec. com. Jewish Agy. for Israel, 1984-88, bd. govs. 1984-90, chmn. bd. govs., 1999-2003, exec. com. mem., 2003-; treas. United Israel Appeal, 1986-90. With USNR, 1945-46. Recipient Disting. Alumnus award U. Fla., 1992, Nat. Scopus award Hebrew U., 1993, Americanism award Anti Defamation League, 1995. Mem. Nat. Am. Wholesale Grocers Assn. (bd. dirs. 1971-73), Nat. Assn. Chain Drug Stores (bd. dirs. 1972-95, chmn. 1985-86, Nat. Achievement award 1995). Jewish (dir. temple). Office: Grass Cos 1000 N Front St Ste 503 Wormleysburg PA 17043-1043 Personal E-mail: agrass2140@aol.com.

GRASSANO, THOMAS DAVID, minister; b. Greenwood, S.C., June 19, 1961; s. Thomas and Atha Elizabeth (Watts) G.; m. Lidia Angélica Minay, Aug. 20, 1983; children: Gabrielle Angélica, Thomas David Jr. MusB, Furman U., 1983; MusM, U. S.C., 1984; MusD, Fla. State U., 1988. Ordained to ministry Ch. of God, 1981, bishop, 1990. Evangelist Ch. of God, 1980-85; assoc. pastor Pkwy. Ch. of God, Tallahassee, Fla., 1985-86; instr. music Fla. State U., Tallahassee, 1986-88, campus min., 1986-88; min. youth and music Br. St. Ch. of God, Tallahassee, 1987-88; dir. worship, campus pastor Univ. Ch. of God, Tampa, Fla., 1988-89; coord. short-term missions and collegiate ministry internat. dept. youth and Christian edn. Ch. of God, 1989-94; founder, dir. Urban Harvest Ministries, N.Y.C., 1994—; pastor Harvest Ch., Bronx, N.Y., 1995—. Lectr. Internat. Bible Schs., Mex., Guatemala, Chile, Argentina, Cuba, 1981—; founder Alpha Omega Campus Outreach Ministry, Ch. of God. Cmty. svc. chaplain, 1996—; dir. Exodus Drama Ministry, 1996—; mem. Nat. Youth Leaders Assn., Ctr. Cmty. Devel. Mem. Southeastern Composers League, Nat. Assn. Composers, Promise Keepers, March for Jesus. Republican. Office: Urban Harvest Ministries PO Box 143 East Meadow NY 11554-0143 E-mail: tdgrassano@urbanharvestministries.org. *Success is not found through position, money or power. True success is found when selfish ambitions are pushed aside to accomplish the will of Christ.*

GRASSELLI, MARGARET MORGAN, curator; b. Worcester, Mass., Mar. 1, 1951; d. Paul Shepard and Anne Piersol (Murray) Morgan; m. Nicholas Eugene Grasselli, May 24, 1981; children: James, Juliana, Anne Regina. AB magna cum laude, Radcliffe Coll., 1973; AM in Fine Arts, Harvard U., 1977, PhD, 1987. Curatorial asst. drawing dept. Fogg Art Mus., Cambridge, Mass., 1974-75, curatorial asst. print dept., 1977-78; asst. curator prints and drawings Nat. Gallery of Art, Washington, 1984-89, curator of Old Master Drawings, 1989—. Tutor fine arts dept. Harvard U., Cambridge, Mass., 1977; guest curator exhbn. Nat. Gallery of Art, Washington, 1980-84; professorial lectr. Georgetown U., Washington, 1988. Author: (exhbn. catalogs) Eighteenth-Century Drawings from the Collection of Mrs. Gertrude Laughlin Chanler, 1982, Colorful Impressions: The Printmaking Revolution in Eighteenth-Century France, 2003; co-author: (exhbn. catalogs) Renaissance and Baroque Drawings from the Collection of John and Alice Steiner, 1977, Old Master Drawings and Bronzes from the Cottonian Collection, 1979, Watteau 1684-1721, 1984-85, Master Drawings from the Armand Hammer Collection, An Inaugural Celebration, 1989, Art for the Nation, Gifts in Honor of the 50th Anniversary of the National Gallery of Art, 1991, Dürer to Diebenkorn: Recent Acquisitions of Art on Paper, 1992, Drawings from the O'Neal Collection, 1993, The Touch of the Artist: Master Drawings from the Woodner Collections, 1995, Mastery and Elegance: Two Centuries of French Drawings from the Collection of Jeffrey E. Horvitz, 1998, The Drawings of Annibale Carracci, 1999; mem. editl. bd. Master Drawings, 1994—; contbr. articles to profl. jours. Agnes Mongan Travelling fellow Harvard U., 1978-79, Samuel H. Kress Pre-doctoral fellow Samuel H. Kress Found., 1979-80, Ailsa Mellon Bruce Curatorial fellow Ctr. for Advanced Study in Visual Arts, 1989-90. Mem. Print Coun. Am. (bd. dirs. 1993-96). Office: Nat Gallery of Art 2000B S Club Dr Landover MD 20785-0001

GRASSER, GEORGE ROBERT, lawyer, real estate developer, consultant; b. Staten Island, NY, Oct. 21, 1939; s. George J. and Anita F. (Spinetta) G.; m. Cecelia Frizziola, July 13, 1968; children: Mark, Eric. BBA, Iona Coll., 1960; JD, Fordham U., 1964. Asst. office mgr. Chgo. Title Ins. Co., N.Y.C., 1966-67; assoc., then ptnr. Moot & Sprague, Buffalo, 1967-75; ptnr. Willig, Grasser & Sheffer, Williamsville, N.Y., 1975-77; prin. Albrecht, Maguire, Heffern & Gregg, Buffalo, 1977-85, Law Offices of George R. Grasser, Buffalo, 1985-87; ptnr. Phillips, Lytle, Hitchcock, Blaine & Huber, LLP, Buffalo, 1987—2002; prin. Grasser & Assocs., LLC, Buffalo, 2002—. Mem. adv. bd. Ticor Title Ins. Co., Buffalo, 1981— Author: Property Taxes and Homeowners Associations, 1980, 94, 95, 2002; contbg. author: Condominium Development, 1990; bd. editors N.Y. Land Report, Albany, 1980-83; contbr. articles to profl. jours. Pres. Ptnrs. for Livable Western N.Y., 2001—; mem. bd. advisors Friends of Sch. of Architecture and Urban Planning SUNY at Buffalo, 1999—2003; mem. bd. advisors Daemen Coll. Ctr. for Sustainable Communities. and Civic Engagement, 2002—; bd. dirs. Baker Victory Svcs., 2004—. Recipient Cmty. Svc. award, AIA, 2001, Citizen of Achievement award, NY State LWV, 2004, Exemplary Civic Action award, Buffalo Niagara Region All Am. City Com., 2004, Burchfield-Penney Art Ctr. Espirit de Corps award, 2004. Mem. NY State Bar Assn. (condominium and coop. com. 1978—, co-chmn. 1990-96, unlicensed practice of real estate law com. 1999-2002, co-chmn. 1999-2002), NY State Builders Assn. (trustee legal def. fund 1987-2000, dir. 1989-2000), Erie County Environ. Mgmt. Coun. (Friend of Environment award 2002), Erie County Bar Assn. (chmn. real estate com. 1978-82), Niagara Frontier Builders Assn. (bd. dirs. 1978-80, 89-99, sec. 1980-81, v.p. 1981, Svc. award 1977-98), Cmty. Assns. Inst. (trustee 1988-90, Svc. award 1986), Coll. Cmty. Assn. Lawyers (bd. govs. 1996-99), Buffalo Niagara Partnership (Pres.'s award 2000). Roman Catholic. Office: Grasser & Assocs LLC 11 Summer Street Buffalo NY 14209 Office Phone: 716-883-5070. Business E-Mail: ggrasser@irdprojectmanagers.com.

GRASSERBAUER, DORIS, computer scientist, mathematician, educator; Diplom-Ingenieurin, Vienna U. Tech., 2003. Hardware and software engr. Andronic Gmbh, Vienna, 1991—95; dir. of the multimedia ctr. CCNY, 2001—. Exhibitions include photographs, videos Www.dograba.com. Office Phone: 212-650-5795. Personal E-mail: doris@dograba.com. Business E-Mail: dgrasserbauer@ccny.cuny.edu.

GRASSHOFF, ALEX, scriptwriter, television producer; b. Boston; Student, Tufts Coll., U. So. Calif. Writer, producer, dir.: TV series Rockford Files, CHiPs, Nightstalker. Recipient Acad. award nomination for Really Big Family, 1966; recipient Acad. award nomination for Journey to the Outer Limits, 1974, Acad. award for documentary Young Americans, 1968, Emmy award for Journey to the Outer Limits, 1974, Emmy award for The Wave, 1982 Office: 7845 Torreyson Dr West Hollywood CA 90046-1228

GRASSI, JOSEPH F., lawyer, mediator, arbitrator; b. NYC, Dec. 6, 1949; BA, Queens Coll., 1970; JD, NYU, 1974. Bar: NY 1974, U.S. Dist. Ct. (so. and ea. dists.) NY 1977, U.S. Ct. Appeals (2d cir.) 1975, U.S. Claims Ct. 1996. Law asst. appellate divsn., 2d judicial dept. Supreme Ct. State of N.Y., 1975-76; assoc. Milbank, Tweed, Hadley & McCloy, N.Y.C., 1976-79; asst. corp. counsel Corp. Counsel of N.Y.C., 1979-83; pvt. practice N.Y.C., 1983—. Mem.: ABA, N.Y. County Lawyers' Assn., N.Y. Bldg. Congress. Office: 100 Park Ave 20th Fl New York NY 10017 Office Phone: 212-983-3274. Personal E-mail: jfgrassi@aol.com.

GRASSIA, THOMAS CHARLES, lawyer, writer; b. Westfield, Mass., Aug. 26, 1946; s. Thomas C. and Assunta (Abatiell) Grassia; m. Judith Chace Cranshaw, Aug. 15, 1970; children: Susan C., Joseph C. BA, Boston U., 1968; JD, Suffolk U., 1974. Bar: Mass. 1974, U.S. Dist. Ct. Mass. 1976, U.S. Supreme Ct. 1980. Asst. v.p. Plymouth Rubber Co., Canton, Mass., 1969-71; ptnr. P.T.S. Computer Svcs., Waltham, Mass., 1971-81, D'Angio & Grassia, Waltham, 1974-85, Grassia & Assocs., P.A., Natick, Mass., 1985—98, Grassia, Murphy & Whitney, P.A., Natick, 1998—2002, Grassia, Murphy & Lupan, P.A., Natick, 2002—. Agt. Lawyers Title Ins. Co., First Am. Title Ins. Co., Fiedilty Nat. Title Ins. Co., Stewart Title Ins. Co.; bd. dirs. regional corps.; pres., treas., bd. dirs. Lender's Title & Abstract Co. Ltd., Natick; lectr. law. Author: Campfires, 2000; contbr. articles to profl. publs. Mem., team leader Sherborn Fire and Rescue Dept., 1974—; bd. health City of Sherborn, Mass., 1976—81, bd. selectmen, 1981—85, mem. police chief selection com.; mem. Met. Boston Hosp. Coun., Burlington, Mass., 1983—84; former mem. long planning com. Sherborn Sch. Bd.; mem. Sherborn Emergency Med. Com.; trustee Leonard Morse Hosp., Natick, 1981—84. Mem.: ABA, Am. Arbitration Assn. (comml. arbitration bd.), Mass. Conveyances Assn., Mass. Bar Assn., Helicopter Assn. Internat. (Augusta Cmty. Svc. award 2003), New Eng. Helicopter Pilots Assn. (past pres., chmn. bd. dirs.). Office: Grassia Murphy and Lupan PA 5 Commonwealth Rd Natick MA 01760-1526 Office Phone: 508-650-9252. Business E-Mail: tgrassia@gmllaw.com.

GRASSIAN, ESTHER STAMPFER, librarian, educator; d. Elijah David and Ann Stampfer; life ptnr. Howard Cowan; children: David Victor, Daniel Steven. BA in Hebrew, U. Calif., 1967, MLS, 1969. From reference libr. Coll. Libr. to info. literacy outreach coord. U. Calif., L.A., 1969—2002, info. literacy outreach coord., 2002—. Vice-chmn., chmn. Calif. Clearinghouse Libr. Instrn., South, L.A., 1985—87, curator, depository collection, 1980—96; chmn. Internet Tng. Group U. Calif., L.A., 1993—96, leader Libr. Info. Literacy Initiative, Instrnl. Devel. Group, 2001—03, chmn. Libr. Info. Literacy Program, Blended Instrn. Course Task Force, 2005—, mem. Libr. Info. Literacy Program, Steering Com., 2005—, mem. Libr. Info. Literacy Initiative, Steering Com., 2001—05; adv. bd. ALA, ACRL Info. Literacy Inst., 1997—99. Co-author: Information Literacy Instruction: Theory and Practice, 2001, Learning to Lead and Manage Information Literacy Instruction, 2005; co-editor: Directory of Library Instruction Programs in California Academic Libraries, 1986; author: (web page) Thinking Critically About World Wide Web Resources; mem. editl. bd.: Rsch. Strategies, 1995—97; contbr. articles to profl. jours. Recipient Farband award, U. Calif. Dept. Near. Ea. Langs., 1967; grantee, U. Calif. Office Instrnl. Devel., 2000—01. Mem.: ALA (co-chmn. conf. com. 1987—88, chmn. nominating com. 1990—92, chmn. task force 1992—94, chmn. 1994—97, chmn. Miriam Dudley Instrn. Libr. of Yr. award 1996—97, editl. cons. 2001, mem. various coms. 2003—, ACRL instrn. sect., Pub. award 2004), Librs. Assn. U. Calif. (chmn. 1990—93, pres. 2001—04, grantee 1999, named libr. of Yr. 1995), Calif. Assn. Rsch. Librs. Jewish. Avocations: reading science fiction, cooking. Office: UCLA College Library Box 951450 Los Angeles CA 90095-1450 Office Phone: 310-206-4410.

GRASSLEY, CHARLES ERNEST, senator; b. New Hartford, Iowa, Sept. 17, 1933; s. Louis Arthur and Ruth (Corwin) G.; m. Barbara Ann Speicher; children: Lee, Wendy, Robin, Michele, Jay. BA, U. No. Iowa, 1955, MA, 1956; postgrad., U. Iowa, 1957-58. Farmer; instr. polit. sci. Drake U., 1962, Charles City Community Coll., 1967-68; mem. Iowa Ho. of Reps., 1959-75, U.S. Ho. Rep. 94th-96th Congresses from 3d Iowa Dist.; senator from Iowa U.S. Senate, Washington, 1980—; chmn. Senate Fin. Com., Washington, 2001—; mem. Senate Judiciary Com. Mem. Am. Farm Bur., Iowa Hist. Soc., Masons, Pi Gamma Mu, Kappa Delta Pi. Republican. Baptist. Office: US Senate 135 Hart Senate Bldg Washington DC 20510-0001*

GRASSO, JAMES ANTHONY, public relations executive, educator; b. Providence, Jan. 12, 1954; s. Forte T. and Eleanor Marie (D'Angelo) Grasso; m. Kimberly I. Maher, Sept. 14, 1986; children: Lauren Patricia, James A. Jr., Michael Robert. BS in Pub. Communication cum laude, Boston U., 1976, MS in Pub. Relations, 1983. Land and pub. relations rep. Algonquin Gas Transmission Co., Boston, 1978-83, asst. mgr., 1983-85, mgr. land, pub. relations, govt. relations, 1985-94, dir. pub. & govt. rels., 1994-97; v.p. pub. & govt. affairs, investor rels. Providence Energy Corp./Providence Gas Co., 1998—99; v.p. pub. and govt. affairs New England divsn. So. Union Co., 1999—2000; pres., CEO Grasso Assocs., LLC, Needham, Mass., 2001—. Mem. adj. faculty Coll. Comm. Boston U., 1997—98. Bd. dirs. Ctrl. R.I. Devel. Corp., mem. exec. com.; mem. exec. com. Narragansett Coun. Boy Scouts Am.; bd. dirs. Beth Israel Deaconess Med. Ctr., Needham, New Eng. Coun., New Eng. Can. Bus. Coun., Nat. Conf. Cmty. and Justice; mem. exec. com. Narragansett coun. Boy Scouts Am. Mem.: New Eng. Gov.'s conf., Northeast Gas Assn., Pub. Rels. Soc. Am., Greater Boston C. of C., Greater Providence C. of C., Univ. Club R.I., Capitol Hill Club. Roman Catholic. Office: Grasso Assocs LLC 17 Avery Sq Needham MA 02494 Office Phone: 781-455-0226. Business E-Mail: jgrasso@grassoassociates.net.

GRATALO, JOHN, JR., banker, small business owner; b. Sommerville, N.J., May 2, 1963; s. John and Anna Mae (Tylka) Gratalo. BS in Fin., DePaul U. Banker Sears Mortgage Corp., Libertyville, Ill., 1987—94; sr. loan officer Lincoln Home, Bloomingdale, Ill., 1994—99, United Banc, Northbrook, Ill., 1999—. Owner The Cichild Hideout, Northbrook, Ill.; loan officer First Chgo. Mortgage, 1994—. Mem.: Philipino-Am. C. of C. (officer 1996—). Roman Catholic. Avocation: rare exotic tropical fish. Office: Cichlid Inc 1108 Whitfield Rd Northbrook IL 60062-3947

GRATCH, SERGE, retired mechanical engineering educator; b. Monte San Pietro, Italy, May 2, 1921; s. Isaak F. and Tatiana (Dermaner) G.; m. Rosemary Delay, June 30, 1951; children: Susan, Mary, Lucia, Karen, Elizabeth, Ann, Barbara, Amy, Ellen, Thomas Charles. BSChemE, U. Pa., 1943, MS, ME, 1945, PhD, ME, 1950. Instr., U. Pa., 1943-45, asst. prof., 1945-50, assoc. prof., 1950-51; rsch. scientist Rohm & Haas Co., Phila., 1951-59; assoc. prof. mech. engring. Northwestern U., Evanston, Ill., 1959-61; supr. processes and devices Ford Motor Co., Dearborn, Mich., 1961-62, mgr. chem. processes and devices, 1963-69, asst. dir. engring. sci., 1969-72, dir. chem. sci. lab., 1972-85, dir. vehicles and component rsch. lab., 1985-86; prof. mech. engring. GMI Inst., Flint, Mich., 1986-96; prof. emeritus Kettering U. (formerly GMI Inst.), Flint, 1999—; ret. Mem. adv. bd. Coll. Engring. U. Iowa, 1969-73, Coll. Engring. U. Detroit, 1971-88; adv. bd. dept. mech. engring. U. Pa., 1973-88; chmn. air pollution rsch. adv. com. Coord. Rsch. Coun., 1983-85; mem. Nat. Alcohol Fuels Commn., 1979-81. Regional editor Internat. Jour. Fracture, 1965-91; contbr. articles to profl. jours. Mem. ASME (hon., past v.p. rsch., past pres., John Fritz medal 1992, Internal Combustion Engine award 1999), NAE, AAAS, Am. Soc. Engring. Edn., Am. Chem. Soc., Engring. Soc. Detroit (past pres.), Soc. Automotive Engrs. (chmn. lubricant rev. bd. 1982-83), Sigma Xi, Tau Beta Pi, Sigma Tau. Roman Catholic. Home: 32475 Bingham Rd Bingham Farms MI 48025-2427 Office Phone: 248-646-0010. Personal E-mail: sgratch112358MI@comcast.net.

GRATHWOL, JAMES NORBERT, lawyer; b. St. Paul, Dec. 19, 1930; s. John E. and Bozena R. (McKeon) G.; m. Lael Dudley, Aug. 2, 1954; children: Robert, John, Joan, James, Katharine, Margaret. BA, Coll. of St. Thomas, 1952; LLB, William Mitchell Coll. of Law, 1958. Bar: Minn. 1958, U.S. Supreme Ct., 1966. Pvt. practice, Minn., 1958-99; ret., 1999. Bd. dirs. Friends of Southshore Sr. Ctr., Shorewood, Minn., 1996-99; Lake Minnetonka Conservation Dist., Wayzata, Minn., 1967-76, 88-95; mem. city coun. City of Excelsior, Minn. 1st lt. USAF, 1954-56. Mem. ABA, Minn. State Bar Assn., Hennepin County Bar Assn., Rotary (pres. Excelsior chpt. 1978-79). Office: 216 Water St Excelsior MN 55331-1895

GRATTAN, PATRICIA ELIZABETH, retired art gallery director; b. Sault Ste. Marie, Ont., Can., Sept. 19, 1944; d. David Andrew and Virginia (Graham) G.; m. Ian Bowmer, June 29, 1968. BA with honours, U. Western Ont., London, 1966; BFA, Concordia U., Montreal, 1974; grad., Mus. Mgmt. Inst., Berkeley, Calif., 1995. Exhbns. coord. Art Gallery, Meml. U. Nfld., St. John's, 1978-80, acting curator, head visual and performing arts, 1980-81; acting chief curator Nfld. Mus., Govt. Nfld. and Labrador, St. John's, 1981-82; curator Art Gallery, Meml. U. Nfld., St. John's, 1982-88, dir., 1988-94; exec. dir. Art Gallery Nfld. and Labrador, St. John's, 1994—2003. Chmn. adv. com. Art Purchase Program, Govt. Nfld. and Labrador, 1984-89; mem. The Can. Coun., 1995-98. Author: (exhbn. catalogues) 25 Years of Art in Newfoundland, 1986, Flights of Fancy: Yard Art in Newfoundland, 1983, David Blackwood: Prints' 1960-1985, 1986, Pam Hall: The Coil, 1994. Bd. dirs. Resource Ctr. for Arts, St. John's, 1981-82, Arts Atlantic Mag., 1982-95, Anna Templeton Ctr., St. John's, 1997-99; treas. St. Michael's Printshop, 1985-87; mem. Provincial Govt. Spl. Anniversaries and Celebrations Com., 1987-89, Lakecrest Ind. Sch., 1998-2000. Mem. Can. Mus. Assn. (nat. councillor 1987-89), Can. Art Mus. dirs. Orgn. (pres. 1993-95). E-mail: pgrattan@mun.ca.

GRATTON, ROBERT, diversified financial services company executive; b. Montreal, Que., Can., Oct. 23, 1943; s. Bernard and Judith (Dufour) G.; m. Nicole Marcil, Aug. 1966; 3 children. LLL, U. Montreal; LLM, London Sch. Econs. & Polit. Sci.; MBA, Harvard U. Asst. to Hon. Paul Gérin-Lajoie, Quebec City, 1966—68; COO Credit Foncier, 1971—79, pres., CEO, 1979—82; chmn., pres., CEO Montreal Trust, 1982—89; pres., CEO Power Fin. Corp., Montreal, 1989—2005, chmn., 2005—. Chmn., bd. dirs. Great-West Life & Annuity, U.S., Investors Group, Inc., Great-West Life, London Ins. Group, London Life Assurance Co., The Can. Life Assurance co., Can. Life Fin. Corp.; bd. dirs. Power Corp. Can., Power Fin. Corp., Pargesa Holding S.A. Mem. Mt. Royal Club, St.-James's Club, St.-Denis Club. Office: Power Fin Corp 751 Victoria Sq Montreal PQ Canada H2Y 2J3

GRATWICK, JOHN, management consulting executive, writer, consultant; b. Langley, Eng., Mar. 2, 1923; emigrated to Can., 1956, naturalized, 1970; s. Ernest Frank and Doris Hilda (Shepherd) G.; m. Dorothy Shirley Vincent, Aug., 1945 (div. 1957); children: Jane Mary, Paul Vincent; m. Gwendoline Johnston, Mar. 23, 1957; 1 son, Adrian. Cert. in Physics, London U., 1942, B.Sc., 1948. Chmn. Transp. Devel. Agy., Montreal, 1970-72; v.p. research and devel. Canadian Nat., Montreal, 1972-76, corp. v.p., 1980-82; pres. CN Marine, Montreal, 1976-80; prof. Sch. Bus. Adminstrn. Dalhousie U., Halifax, NS, 1983-87, dir. Can. Marine Transp. Ctr., 1983-86, exec. dir. Internat. Inst. Transp. & Ocean Policy Studies, 1986-88; chmn. Halifax Industries Ltd., 1978-84; pres. Gratwick Hickling Inc., 1985-98; dir. Oceans Inst. Can., 1989-91. Bd. dirs. Hickling Corp., Ottawa; bd. dirs. CPCS Transcom Ltd.; chmn. Ctr. for Marine Vessel Design and Rsch., Tech. U. N.S., 1989-91; chmn. Halifax-Dartmouth Port Devel. Commn., 1991-96. Gov. Mt. St. Vincent U., 1989-98; mem. Nat. Transp. Act Rev. Commn., 1992-93. Recipient Achievement award Nat. Transp. Week, 1990. Fellow Royal Statis. Soc., Chartered Inst. of Transport; mem. Can. Operational Rsch. Soc. (pres. 1969-70), Can. Transp. Rsch. Forum (hon. life mem., pres. 1971-72), Internat. Fedn. Operational Rsch. Socs. (v.p. 1977-79). Home: 984 Bellevue Ave Halifax NS Canada B3H 3L7 Business E-Mail: johngrat@eastlink.ca.

GRATZ, JAY M., steel company executive; b. N.Y.C. m. Pam Gratz; 1 child, Kimberly. B in Econ. and Chemistry, SUNY, Buffalo, 1973; M of Mgmt. in Fin. and Acctg., Northwestern U., 1975. CPA, Ill. Various positions Inland Steel Industries, Inc., Chgo., 1975-81, asst. mgr., 1981-84, asst. mgr. cash and investments, 1984-86, mgr. fin. planning and analysis, 1986, v.p. fin., v.p. fin. Ryerson Tull, Inc., 1994-96, v.p., CFO, 1996—. Office: 30 W Monroe St Ste 100 Chicago IL 60603-2402

GRAU, JEAN ELIZABETH, retired insurance agent; b. New Orleans, June 8, 1932; d. Adolph Eugene and Katherine Caroline (O'Nion) Grau; divorced; children: Steven, Marilyn, Laurence, Lorraine. EdB, Loyola U., New Orleans, 1953, MS, 1972. Cert. tchr. La., 1953. Tchr. French Orleans Parish Pub. Sch. Dist., New Orleans, 1953—54; tchr. French, English Notre Dame Acad., Washington, 1954—55; tchr. French Orleans Parish Pub. Sch. Dist., New Orleans, 1972—86; pvt. ins. agt. New Orleans, 1980—95; tchr. gifted students Plaquemines Parish Pub. Sch., 1987—89; tchr. French East Baton Rouge, La., 1989—90, St. Charles Parish, La., 1990—91; registered rep. Jackson Nat. Fin. Svc., New Orleans, 1993—95, ret., 1995. Invited reader Internat. Soc. Poets. Author numerous poems; editor: Lyric Louisiana, 2003—. Pres. Aurora, Hyman, Kabel Civic Orgn., New Orleans, 1982—, del. Pres. Coun. of Civic Orgn., 1984—; adv. bd. Algiers Community Network, 1985-86; active Algiers Priorities Conv., 1986, Non-Pack Police Support Group, West Bank Action Com., Right to Life Orgn. Mem. Codofil, France Amerique, Am. Assn. Teachers French, La. Edn. Assn., L'Athenee Louisinais, Internat. Platform Assn., New Orleans Poetry Forum, La. State Poetry Soc. (editor jour. 2003-), Kappa Kappa Iota (hon.), Delta Epsilon Sigma (hon.), Kappa Delta Pi (hon.). Republican. Roman Catholic. Avocations: amateur radio, violin, sewing, bicycling, gardening. Home and Office: 1601 Kabel Dr New Orleans LA 70131-3633

GRAU, JOHN MICHAEL, trade association executive; b. St. Joseph, Mich., May 22, 1952; s. Otto R. and Esther P. (Spitzer) G.; m. Gayle Luedeman, May 7, 1983 (div. Nov. 1996); m. Kristine Sweeney, Aug. 30, 1997; 1 child, Brendan Sweeney. BBA, U. Mich., 1974. Realty specialist HUD, Washington, 1974-75; field rep. Nat. Elec. Contractors Assn., San Mateo, Calif., 1975-76, chpt. mgr., Milw. chpt., 1976-85, asst. exec. v.p., Bethesda, Md., 1985-86, exec. v.p., CEO, 1986—2003, CEO, 2004—. Chmn., trustee Nat. Elec. Benefit Fund, Washington, 1986-2002; co-chmn. Coun. Indsl. Rels., Washington, 1986—; bd. mem. Plan for Settlement Jurisdictional Disputes in Constrn. Industry, Washington, 1986—; co-chmn. Nat. Joint Apprenticeship and Tng. Com. for Elec. Industry, Washington, 1986—; trustee Associated Specialty Contractors, Washington, 1987—. V.p. Elec. Contracting Found., Bethesda, 1989—, vice chmn., 1999—; bd. dir. Underwriters Lab., Northbrook, Il., 2000-05, Elec. Safety Found. Internat., Rosslyn, Va., 1996—, treas., 1996-98, 2001-04; trustee Nat. Labor-Mgmt. Coop. Com., Washington, 1997—. Fellow Acad. Elec. Contracting (bd. dirs. 1986—); mem. Am. Soc. Assn. Execs. (key industries assn. com. 1987—, chmn. 2003-04), Am. Soc. Assn. Execs. Found. (bd. dirs. 2001-04), Internat. Assn. Elec. Contractors (assoc. bd. dirs. 1993—), US C. of C. (Com. of 100 1990—), Ctr. for Assn. Leadership (bd. dirs. 2004—) Lutheran. Home: 4805 Jamestown Rd Bethesda MD 20816-2710 Office: Nat Elec Contractors Assn 3 Bethesda Metro Ctr Ste 1100 Bethesda MD 20814-6302

GRAU, MARCY BEINISH, real estate broker, former investment banker; b. Bklyn., Aug. 7, 1950; d. Joseph Beinish and Gloria (Rosenbaum) Bennett; m. Bennett Grau, Nov. 19, 1978; 3 children. AB with high honors, U. Mich., 1971; postgrad., Columbia U., 1972, N.Y. Inst. Fin., 1973. Asst. to chmn. Bancroft Convertible Fund, N.Y.C., 1973-75; precious metals trader J. Aron & Co., N.Y.C., 1975-81, mgr. metals mktg., 1981-83; v.p. Goldman, Sachs & Co/J. Aron, N.Y.C., 1983-88; investment banking cons. N.Y.C., 1988-90; real estate broker Fox Residential Group, 1998-99, Stribling & Assoc., N.Y.C., 1999—2004, v.p., 2004—. Editor Precious Metals Rev. and Outlook, 1980—; contbr. article to profl. jours. Vol. worker pediatrics dept. Lenox Hill Hosp., N.Y.C., 1978-79; asst. The Holiday Project, The Hunger Project, N.Y.C., 1978-83; vol. Yorkville Common Pantry, N.Y.C., 1984; tutor Yorkville Neighborhood Assn., N.Y.C., 1984; assoc. Child Devel. Ctr., N.Y.C.; trustee Congregation B'nai Jeshurun, 1989—, pres., 1991-94, chair, 1994-97; trustee Ethical Fieldston Fund, 1994-2000. Mem. Phi Beta Kappa. Avocations: interior design, fashion, cooking, piano. Home: 300 West End Ave New York NY 10023-8156 Office: 924 Madison Ave New York NY 10021-3577 Office Phone: 212-452-4361. Personal E-mail: marcyg300@aol.com.

GRAU, SHIRLEY ANN (MRS. JAMES KERN FEIBLEMAN), writer; b. New Orleans, July 8, 1929; d. Adolph and Katherine (Onion) G.; m. James Kern Feibleman, Aug. 4, 1955; children: Ian, James, Nora Miranda, William, Katherine. BA, Tulane U., 1950. Author: (short stories) The Black Prince and Other Stories, 1955, The Hard Blue Sky, 1958, The House on Coliseum Street, 1961, The Keepers of the House, 1964 (Pulitzer prize for fiction 1965), The Condor Passes, 1971, The Wind Shifting West and Other Stories, 1973, Evidence of Love, 1977, Nine Women, 1986, Roadwalkers, 1994; writer publs. including Holiday, New Yorker, New World Writing, Mademoiselle, Saturday Evening Post, Atlantic, The Reporter, 1954—. Mem. Phi Beta Kappa. Office: PO Box 9058 Metairie LA 70055-9058 Personal E-mail: shirleygrau@bellsouth.net.

GRAUBARD, STEPHEN RICHARDS, historian, educator, editor; b. N.Y.C., Dec. 5, 1924; s. Harry and Rose (Polk) G.; m. Margaret Cavendish-Bentinck Georgiades, Aug. 5, 1978; stepsons: William J. Georgiades, David C. Georgiades. AB, George Washington U., 1945; AM, Harvard U., 1946, PhD, 1951; DHL, Providence Coll., 1971, Suffolk U., 1984, Union Coll.,

1987; DLitt, U. Vt., 1990. Instr. history and gen. edn. Harvard U., 1952-55, asst. prof., 1955-60, lectr., 1960-63, exec. sec. com. on gen. edn., 1952-59, research assoc. in internat. affairs, 1963-65; vis. prof. history Brown U., 1965-66, prof. history, 1966-94, prof. history emeritus, 1994—; mng. editor Daedalus, 1960-61, editor, 1961-2000; asst. editor Confluence, 1952-55; dir. studies Assembly on Univ. Goals and Governance, 1969-75. Author: British Labour and the Russian Revolution, 1956, Burke, Disraeli and Churchill: The Politics of Perseverance, 1961, Kissinger, Portrait of a Mind, 1973, Mr. Bush's War: Adventures in the Politics of Illusion, 1992, Command of Office: How War, Secrecy, and Deception Transformed the Presidency from Theodore Roosevelt to George W. Bush, 2004, The Presidents: The Transformation of the Presidency from Theodore Roosevelt to George W. Bush, 2005; editor: (with G. Holton) Excellence and Leadership in a Democracy, 1962, A New Europe?, 1964, (with G. Ballotti) The Embattled University, 1970 (with F. Gilbert) Historical Studies Today, 1972, (with S.N. Eisenstadt) Intellectuals and Tradition, 1973, (with F. Cavazza) Il Caso Italiano, 1974, A New America?, 1979, Generations, 1979, The State, 1980, Reading in the 1980s, 1983, Australia: The Daedalus Symposium, 1985, Art and Science, 1987, The Artificial Intelligence Debate, 1989, In Search of Canada, 1990, Living with Aids, 1990, Showa: The Japan of Hirohito (with Carol Gluck), 1992, The Research University in a Time of Discontent (with Jonathan R. Cole and Elinor G. Barber), 1994, (with Daniel Bell) Toward the Year 2000, 1997, A New Europe for Old, 1998. Served with AUS, 1943. Social Sci. Rsch. Coun. fellow, 1948-50, Acad. fellow Carnegie Corp., 1999—. Fellow Am. Acad. Arts and Scis. (editor 1963—2000), Council on Fgn. Relations, Mass. Hist. Soc. Clubs: Century, Signet. Home: 22 Elm Park Gardens London SW10 9NY England Office Phone: 44-1832 720 636. Personal E-mail: stephengraubard@aol.com.

GRAUER, DAVID W., lawyer; b. Marysville, Kans., 1954; BS in Pharmacy, U. Kans., 1977; MS, Ohio State U., 1982; JD, Capital U., 1984. Bar: Ohio 1984. Pharmacist; ptnr. Squire, Sanders & Dempsey LLP, Columbus, Ohio, co-chmn., Health Care Strategic Bus. Unit & Health Care Practice Group. Mem.: Nat. Health Lawyers Assn., Ohio State Bar Assn. (health care law com.). Office: Squire Sanders & Dempsey LLP 1300 Huntington Ctr 41 South High St Columbus OH 43215-6197 Office Phone: 614-365-2786. Office Fax: 614-365-2499. Business E-Mail: sgrauer@ssd.com.

GRAULE, RAYMOND (SIEGFRIED), metallurgical engineer; b. Phila., Feb. 7, 1932; s. Oscar P. and Elizabeth Keim (Merkle) G.; m. Beatrice D. Miller, Sept. 4, 1954 (div. Nov. 1982); children: Melissa, Jon; m. Marlys Ann Sunkle, Sept. 21, 1985 (div. Jan. 1995); children: Troy, Tara, Tiffany. BSChemE, N.J. Inst. Tech., Newark, 1955; MS in Metallurgy, Stevens Inst. of Tech., Hoboken, N.J., 1961. Process engr. Wilbur B. Driver Co., Newark, 1954-62; supr. of prod. engring. G.T.E. Corp., Newark, 1962-77; engring. mgr. Amax Corp., Parsippany, N.J., 1977-84; specialist Carpenter Tech. Corp., Orangeburg, SC, 1984—2003; cons. metallurgist RSG Electronic Alloys Practice, LLC, 2003—. Adj. instr. Essex County Coll., Newark, 1979-81, Orangeburg Calhoun Tech. Coll., 1984-87. County committeeman Rep. Party, Parsippany, 1965-81; advisor Bd. of Edn., 1969-73. With U.S. Army, 1956-58. Mem. Rep. Club (Parsippany), Goodyear Blimp Club, Exptl. Aviation Assn., Orangeburg Pilots Assn. Avocations: woodworking, flying, boating. Home: 433 Gue Rd NW Orangeburg SC 29115-4128 E-mail: raygraule@bellsouth.net.

GRAULTY, ROBERT THOMAS, engineer, consultant; b. Troy, N.Y., July 22, 1928; s. Thomas Joseph and Elsie (Connor) Graulty; m. Jacqueline Anne Shields, Feb. 18, 1950; children: Kevin, James, Mark, Karen, Dianne, Daniel, John. BS, U.S. Merchant Marine Acad., Kings Point, N.Y., 1949; diploma, Westinghouse Mgmt. Program, U. Pitts., 1959. Registered profl. engr., Pa., 68, S.C., 86. Diesel engr. Am. Locomotive Co., Schenectady, NY, 1949—55; nuc. engr. Westinghouse Bettis Lab., Pitts., 1955—69, mgr., reactor engring., 1969—73, mgr., core mfg., 1977—82; spl. assignment to Adm. H.G. Rickover U.S. Navy, Naval Reactors Br., 1973—77; mgr., fuel mfg. Westinghouse Elec. Corp., Columbia, SC, 1982—86; cons. Columbia, SC, 1986—. Instr. Midlands Tech. Coll., Columbia, SC, 2002—. Author: (design manual) Shock and Vibration Design, 1966. Midshipman USNR, 1945—49, Atlantic. Mem.: Soc. Mfg. Engrs. (sr.). Achievements include patents in field. Home: 109 Miles Rd Columbia SC 29223

GRAUSAM, JEFFREY LEONARD, lawyer; b. Newark, Sept. 21, 1943; s. John G. and Angela G.; m. Anne Jenks Boynton, Dec. 20, 1969; children: Daniel Carpenter, Elizabeth Wiley. BA, Wesleyan U., 1965; JD, U. Chgo., 1968; LLM in Taxation, NYU, 1975. Bar: Calif. 1969, N.Y. 1970, U.S. Supreme Ct. 1981. Law clk. to chief justice Roger J. Traynor Supreme Ct., State of Calif., San Francisco, 1968-69; assoc. Debevoise, Plimpton, Lyons & Gates, N.Y.C., 1969-75; officer, mem. firm Tuttle & Taylor, Inc., L.A., 1975-89; ptnr. Morgan, Lewis & Bockius, LLP, L.A., 1989—. Editor-in-chief law rev. U. Chgo., 1967-68. Dir. Libr. Found. L.A., 1993-98, 99—. Mem. L.A. County Bar Assn. (exec. com. taxation sect. 1994-95), Order of Coif. Avocation: bicycling. Office: Morgan Lewis & Bockius LLP 300 S Grand Ave Fl 22 Los Angeles CA 90071-3109

GRAUSMAN, PHILIP, sculptor; b. N.Y.C., July 16, 1935; 1 child, David. Student, Sch. Painting and Sculpture, Skowhegan, Maine, 1956-57; BA cum laude, Syracuse U., 1957; student, Art Students' League, 1959; MFA, Cranbrook Acad. Art, 1959. Critic of archtl. drawing Grad. Sch. Architecture, Yale U., New Haven, 1974—. Instr. design Cooper Union, 1965-67; instr. design and drawing Pratt Inst., 1965-69; artist-in-residence Dartmouth Coll., 1972; instr. sculpture and drawing Skowhegan Sch. Painting and Sculpture, 1973; vis. asst. prof. art Yale U., 1974-76. Solo exhbns. include Frederik Meijer Gardens and Sculpture Park, Grand Rapids, Mich., 2001, Ice Gallery, N.Y.C., 1998, Borgenicht Gallery, N.Y.C., 1966, 74, 79, Alpha Gallery, Boston, 1968, 75, Dartmouth Coll., Hanover, N.H., 1972, U. Conn., 1976, Pa. State U., 1977, Washington Art Assn., Washington Depot, Conn., 1978, 82, Robert Schoelkopf Gallery, N.Y.C., 1983, 87, Babcock Galleries, N.Y.C., 1993, 2000, Tremaine Gallery, Conn., 1997, Ice Gallery, NY, 1998, Nat. Acad. Art & Design, 173rd Ann. Exhbn., NY, 1998, (Alex Ettl Award), 174 Ann. Exhbn., 1999, Ctrl. Conn. State U., 1999, Aldrich Mus., Figure Show, Conn., 1999, Sculpture Exbhn, Pier Walk, Navy Pier, Chgo., 2000, Meijers Gardens and Sculpture Park Mich., 2001, Chesterwood Nat. Trust, Mass., 2001, Art Omi, The Fields Sculpture Park, Ghent NY, 2003; exhibited in group shows at The Aldrich Mus., Whitney Mus. Am. Art, Am. Acad. in Rome, Nat. Acad. Design, Art OMI Internat. Arts Ctr., Ohio State U., Boston Coliseum, Wadsworth Atheneum, Chgo. Arts Club, Fine Arts Mus. San Diego, U. N.C., Paris/N.Y./Kent Gallery, Kent, Conn., numerous others; represented in collections at Vassar Coll., U. Mich., U. Mass., U. Conn., Newark Mus., Met. Mus. Art, Jewish Mus., N.Y.C., De Cordova Mus. Art, Lincoln, Mass., Cornell U., Bklyn. Mus., Rose Art Mus./Brandeis U., Balt. Mus. Art, Akron Art Mus., others. Recipient Gold medal of honor in sculpture Audubon Artists, 1956, Alfred G.B. Steel Meml. prize Pa. Acad. Fine Aarts, 1962, Solon H. Borglum award Silvermine Guild, Conn., 1980, Albert Jacobson Meml. award Silvermine Guild, 1984, Alex Ettel award, Nat. Acad. of Design, 1998, others; Huntington Hartford fellow, 1957, Louis Comfort Tiffany Found. grantee, 1959, Nat. Inst. Arts and Letters grantee, 1961, Prix de Rome fellow, 1962-65. Fellow Am. Acad. in Rome; mem. NAD (Dessie Greer prize 1981, Gold medal in sculpture 1988, cert. of merit in sculpture 1993). Office: Yale U Sch of Architecture New Haven CT 06520*

GRAVEL, CAMILLE FRANCIS, lawyer; b. Alexandria, La., Aug. 10, 1915; s. Camille F. and Aline Delvaille G.; m. Katherine Yvonne David, Nov. 26, 1939 (dec. 1979); children: Katherine Ann Gravel Vanderslice, Mary Eileen Gravel Cappel, Martha Louise Antoon, Camille Francis III (dec.), Grady David, Eunice Holloman Gravel, Virginia Maureen Gravel Carbo, Margaret Lynn, Mark Alan, Charles Gregory, Richard Alvin (dec.); m. Evelyn Gianfala, 1980. BA, U. Notre Dame, 1935, La. State U., 1935-37, Cath. U. Am., 1937-39; LLD (hon.), Loyola U., New Orleans, 1976. Bar: La. 1940, U.S. dist. ct. La. 1940, U.S. Ct. Appeals (5th cir.) 1953, U.S. Supreme Ct. 1954. Asst. dist. atty. 9th Jud. Dist., Rapides Parish, La., 1942; atty. State Inheritance Tax Collector, Rapides Parish, 1943-45; asst. city atty. Alexandria (La.), 1946-48; atty. La. Tax Commn., 1948-52. Mem. Gov.'s Commn. on Higher Edn. Svcs., 1978-82; mem. Gov.'s Adv. and Rev. Commn. on Asst. Dist. Attys., 1979-88, exec. counsel, 1976-80, exec. asst., 1984-88 to gov. La.; mem. bd. suprs. La. State U. and A&M Coll., 1975-90, chmn. bd., 1981-82. Mem. U.S. Capitol Police Force, 1937-39. Invested Knight of St. Gregory by Pope Pius XII, 1954; hon. fellow Harry S Truman Library Inst., 1975. Fellow Internat. Acad. Trial Lawyers, Internat. Soc. Barristers; mem. AAUP, ABA, Nat. Assn. Criminal Def. Lawyers, La. Bar Assn., Alexandria Bar Assn. (pres. 1949-50), Notre Dame Law Assn., La. Trial Lawyers Assn., Lamar Soc., Am. Assn. Ret. Persons, Am. Heart Assn., Cath. U. Am. Alumni Assn. (nat. bd. govs. 1977—), Alexandria-Pineville C. of C., Am. Legion, Elks (past exalted ruler), KC, Order of Coif, Phi Delta Phi, Kappa Sigma. Roman Catholic. Office: PO Box 1792 711 Washington St Alexandria LA 71301-8030

GRAVELINE, JOHN LAWRENCE, lay worker, minister; b. Bay City, Mich., Sept. 1, 1971; s. Paul Dennis and Regina Margaret Graveline. BA, Magdalen Coll., Warner, NH, 1994; ThM, John Paul II Pontifical Inst. Studies on Marriage and Family, Washington, 1999. Diploma religious instrn. Sacred Congregation for the Clergy, 1997. Coord. religious edn. Prince of Peace Cath. Ch., Muskegon, Mich., 1999—2001; coord. young adult ministry Archdiocese of Washington, 2001—. Confirmation catechist St. Martin of Tours Cath. Ch., Gaithersburg, Md., 2004—. Co-founder Cath. Adults Living Leadership (CALL), Washington, 2003—; chmn. Magdalen Coll. Alumni Assn., Warner, NH, 2004—. Mem.: Nat. Cath. Young Adult Ministry Assn., Fellowship of Cath. Scholars (assoc.), KC. Office: Archdiocese of Washington PO Box 29260 Washington DC 20017 Office Phone: 301-853-4559.

GRAVER, JACK EDWARD, mathematics professor; b. Cin., Apr. 13, 1935; s. Harold John and Rose Lucille (Miller) G.; m. Yana Regina Hanus, June 3, 1961; children: Juliet Rose, Yana-Maria, Paul Christopher. BA in Math., Miami U., Oxford, Ohio, 1958; MA in Math., Ind. U., 1961, PhD in Math., 1964. Instr. Ind. U., Bloomington, 1964; John Wesley Young Rsch. instr. Dartmouth Coll., Hanover, N.H., 1964-66; asst. prof. math. Syracuse (N.Y.) U., 1966-69, assoc. prof., 1969-76; vis. prof. U. Nottingham (Eng.), 1971-72; prof. math. Syracuse U., 1976—, chmn. dept. math., 1979-82. Co-author: (books) (with M. Watkins) Combinatorics with Emphasis on Graph Theory, 1977, Locally Finite, Planar, Edge-Transitive Graphs, 1997, (with J. Baglivo) Incidence and Symmetry in Design and Architecture, 1982, (with B. and H. Servatius) Combinatorial Rigidity, 1993, Counting on Frameworks, 2001; contbr. articles to profl. jours. With USN, 1953—55. Fellow Inst. Combinatories and its Applications; mem. Soc. Indsl. and Applied Math., Nat. Coun. Tchrs. of Math., Assn. Math. Tchrs. N.Y. State, Math. Assn. Am. (bd. govs. 1985-88, Seaway sect. chair 1995-97), Am. Math. Soc. Home: 871 Livingston Ave Syracuse NY 13210-2935 Office: Syracuse Univ Dept Math Syracuse NY 13244-1150 Office Phone: 315-443-1576. Business E-Mail: jegraver@syr.edu.

GRAVER, LAWRENCE STANLEY, language educator; b. N.Y.C., Dec. 6, 1931; s. Louis and Rose (Pearlstein) G.; m. Suzanne Levy, Jan. 28, 1960; children: Ruth, Elizabeth. BA, CCNY, 1954; MA, U. Calif., Berkeley, 1959, PhD, 1961. Asst. prof. English UCLA, 1961-64, Williams Coll., Williamstown, Mass., 1964-67, assoc. prof. English, 1967-72, prof. English, 1972—, William R. Kenan, Jr. prof. English, 1977-81, John H. Roberts prof. English, 1981-97, Roberts prof. emeritus English, 1997—. Author: Conrad's Short Fiction, 1969, Carson McCullers, 1969; editor: Mastering the Film, 1977, Samuel Beckett, 1979, (Landmarks of World Lit. series) Waiting for Godot, 1989, 2d edit., 2004, An Obsession With Anne Frank: Meyer Levin and the Diary, 1995; asst. editor: Columbia Companion to the Twentieth Century American Short Story, 2001. Served with U.S. Army, 1954-56. NEH fellow, 1980-81. Mem. MLA, AAUP. Democrat. Home: 117 Forest Rd Williamstown MA 01267-2028 Office: Williams Coll Dept English Williamstown MA 01267 E-mail: lgraver@williams.edu.

GRAVER, SUZANNE LEVY, English literature educator; b. NYC, Aug. 17, 1936; BA summa cum laude, CUNY, 1958; MA, U. Calif., Berkeley, 1960; PhD, U. Mass., 1976. Tchr. English Berkeley High Sch., 1960-61, Culver City High Sch., 1961-62; asst. prof. Berkshire Community Coll., 1966-72; vis. asst. prof. Tufts U., 1976-78; assoc. ind. study Empire State Coll., SUNY, 1978; lectr. Williams Coll., Williamstown, Mass., 1976, 78-82, coord. writing workshop, 1981-85, asst. prof., 1983-87, chair dept. women's studies, 1988-89, assoc. prof. English, 1988-91, assoc. dean faculty, 1990-91, prof., 1991—2002, John Hawley Roberts prof. English prof. emerita, 2002—, vis. prof. English, 2003—05, dean of faculty, 1991-94. Manuscript reader Ind. U. Press, Victorian Studiesm, A Victorian Periodicals Review, PMLA; fellowship and grants application reader NEH, Nat. Humanities Ctr., The Grad. Ctr., CUNY; Andrew W. Mellon emeritus fellow, 2005—. Author: George Eliot and Community: A Study in Social Theory and Fictional Form, 1984, and numerous essays and revs. in Victorian lit. and culture. U. fellow U. Mass., Amherst, 1974-76, Am. Coun. Learned Socs. fellow, 1985-86, 89-90, Nat. Humanities Ctr. fellow, 1989-90, NEH fellow, 1995-96, Andrew W. Mellon Emeritus fellow, 2005-. Mem. AAUP, ACLU, NOW, MLA (rep. to del. assembly 1988-91), Amnesty Internat., Wilderness Soc., N.E. MLA (chair English novel sect. 1980). Office: Williams Coll Stetson Hall Williamstown MA 01267-0141 Business E-Mail: sgraver@williams.edu.

GRAVES, ANNA MARIE, lawyer; b. Arlington, Va., Sept. 26, 1959; d. George W. and Anna (Czikora) G. AB cum laude, Cornell U., 1981; JD, U. Va., 1985. Bar: Calif. 1985, U.S. Dist. Ct. (cen. dist.) Calif. 1986. Corp. assoc. Memel, Jacobs, Pierno, Gersh & Ellsworth, L.A., 1985-87, Stroock & Stroock & Lavan, L.A.; ptnr., co-chmn. Restaurant Food & Beverage industry group Pillsbury Winthrop Shaw Pittman, LA. Chmn. UCLA Extension Calif. Restaurant Industry Conf. Named a So. Calif. Super Lawyer, LA Mag., 2004. Mem. ABA, Beverly Hills Bar Assn., Calif. Women Lawyers. Democrat. Office: Pillsbury Winthrop Shaw Pittman 725 S Figueroa St Los Angeles CA 90017 Office Phone: 213-488-7164. Office Fax: 213-226-4017. Business E-Mail: anna.graves@pillsburylaw.com.

GRAVES, BENJAMIN BARNES, business administration educator; b. Jones County, Miss., Nov. 5, 1920; s. Thomas Cannon and Velma (Barnes) G.; m. Hazeline Wood, May 25, 1946; children— Benjamin Barnes, Janis Elizabeth, Cynthia Wood. BA, U. Miss., 1942; MBA, Harvard, 1947; PhD, La. State U., 1961; LL.D., U. Ala., 1970. Staff and supervisory positions Exxon Co., 1947-60; spl. lectr. Coll. Bus. Adminstrn., La. State U., 1959-60, asst. prof., 1960-62; assoc. prof. U. Va., 1962-64; Milner prof. indsl. econs. U. Miss., 1964-65; pres. Millsaps Coll., Jackson, Miss., 1965-70; prof. bus. adminstrn. U. Ala. in Huntsville, 1970-90, pres., 1970-79, prof. emeritus, 1990—. Guest lectr. Mid-South Exec. Devel. Program, La. State U., 1962-68, also asso. dir. program, 1961-62; guest lectr. mgmt. program Natural Resources Mgrs., Pa. State U., 1962-72, Va.-Md. Sch. Banking, U. Va., 1962-73; vis. prof. bus. adminstrn. U. N.C. at Charlotte, 1976-77 Author articles in field. Pres. Miss. Found. Ind. Colls., 1967-68; mem. com. human investigation U. Miss. Sch. Medicine, 1964-70; v.p. Miss. Jr.-Sr. Coll. Conf., 1968-69; pres. Miss. Assn. Colls., 1969-70; mem. exec. com. Ind. Coll. Funds Am.; mem. adv. com. Am. Council on Edn.'s Inst. for Coll. and U. Adminstrs.; mem. Am. Assn. Schs. and Colls. univ. pres.'s del. to People's Republic of China, 1975, Republic of China, 1976; Pres. Huntsville Research Park Adv. Bd., 1973; Mem. exec. bd. Andrew Jackson council Boy Scouts Am., 1966—; bd. dirs. Jackson Symphony Assn., 1965-70; mem. pres.'s coun. U. Ala., Huntsville. Served to lt. (s.g.) USNR, 1942-46. Recipient Humanitarian of Yr. award The Arthritis Found. of Ala., 1999. Mem. Acad. Mgmt., Am. Mktg. Assn., Southwestern Social Sci. Assn., So. Econ. Assn., A.I.M. (pres.'s council), Jackson C. of C., Pi Kappa Alpha (mem. centennial com. 100), Phi Kappa Phi, Omicron Delta Kappa, Rotary (Paul Harris fellow; Vocat. Excellence award 2001). Clubs: Rotarian (dir. Huntsville 1973). Methodist. Home: 1317 Carlton Cove Blvd Huntsville AL 35802

GRAVES, C. DOUGLAS, music educator; s. Henry Abrams and Olive Taylor Graves. BS in music edn., West Chester U., 1960; MEd, Ind. U., 1965; PhD, Mich. State, 1971. Music instr. Cherry Hill Pub. Sch., Cherry Hill, NJ, 1960—66; string tchr. Phila. Pub. Sch., Phila., 1966—67; prof. music No. Mich. U., Marquette, Mich., 1967—87, Ga. So. U., Statesburg, Ga., 1987—2004. Cellist Augusta Symphony, Augusta, Ga., 1987—, Savannah Symphony, Savannah, Ga., 1990—2002. Arranger: numerous orch. arrangements. Conductor Strings Program, Statesboro, Ga., 1987—2004; reader Regional Libr., Bulloch County, Ga., 2000—; bd. mem. San Island Bank, Stateboro, Ga., 2003—; adv. bd. Ga. So. U., Coll. of Liberal Arts and Social Scis., Ga. Home: 119 Greenbriar Tr Statesboro GA 30458-6034

GRAVES, EARL GILBERT, publishing executive; b. Bklyn., 1935; s. Earl Godwin and Winifred (Sealy) G.; m. Barbara Kydd, July 2, 1960; children: Earl Gilbert, John, Michael. BA in Econs., Morgan State U., Balt., 1958, LLD (hon.), 1973, Rust Coll., 1974, Wesleyan U., 1982; LHD (hon.), Dowling Coll., 1980; LLD (hon.), Va. Union U., 1976, Fla. Meml. Coll., 1978, J.C. Smith U., 1979; LittD (hon.), Hampton Inst., 1979; PhDBA (hon.), Bryant Coll., 1983; LLD (hon.), Talladega Coll., 1983, Baruch Coll., 1984; LittD (hon.), St. Josephs, N.Y., 1985; LLD (hon.), Ala. State U., 1985; HHD (hon.), Morehouse Coll., 1986; LLD (hon.), Mercy Coll., 1986, Iona Coll., 1987, Elizabeth City State U., 1987; DCS (hon.), Suffolk U., 1987; LLD (hon.), Brown U., 1987, Lincoln U., 1988, Cen. State U., 1988; LittD (hon.), Meharry Med. Coll., 1989; LLD (hon.), Howard U., 1989, Livingstone Coll., 1989, Northwood Inst., 1991, U. D.C., 1991, Tougaloo U., 1992; DCL (hon.), Univ. South, 1993, U. Vt., 1994; degree (hon.), N.C. Ctrl. U., 1997, Manhattanville Coll., 1998. Adminstrv. asst. to Senator Robert F. Kennedy, 1965-68; owner mgmt. cons. firm, 1968-70; editor, pub. Black Enterprise Mag., N.Y.C., 1970—. Chmn., CEO Pepsi-Cola of Washington, L.P., chmn. customer adv. and ethnic mktg. com.; pres. Earl G. Graves Pub. Co., Inc.; bd. dirs. Rohm & Haas Corp., DaimlerChrysler Corp., Mag. Pub. Assn., N.Y. State Urban Devel. Corp., Nat. Supplier Devel. Coun., New Am. Schs. Devel. Corp., Glass Ceiling Commn., TransAfrica Forum, Aetna Life & Casualty Co., Federated Dept. Stores, Inc., AMR Corp. (Am. Airlines); keynote spkr. for small and large corps., pub. and non-profit sectors of bus. in Am. Author: How to Succeed in Business Without Being White, 1997 (finalist Fin. Times/Booz-Allen & Hamilton Global Bus. Book award 1997). Mem. adv. coun. Character Edn. Partnership; bd. dirs. New Am. Schs. Devel. Corp., TransAfrica Forum, Steadman-Hawkins Sports Medicine Found., Am. Mus. Natural History and Planetarium, trustee; nat. commr. scouting Boy Scouts Am.; bd. trustees Howard U., Washington; mem. vis. com. Harvard U. John F. Kennedy Sch. Govt.; mem. Pres.'s Com. Small and Minority Bus.; mem. nat. adv. bd. Nat. Underground R.R. Freedom Ctr.; trustee Howard U., Com. for Econ. Devel.; mem. pres.'s coun. for bus. adminstrn. U. Vt. Capt. U.S. Army, 1958-60. Recipient Silver Beaver award Boy Scouts Am., 1969, Scroll of Honor, Nat. Med. Assn., 1971, Nat. award of excellence U.S. Dept. Commerce, 1972, Pub. for Freedom award Operation PUSH, Black Achiever award Talk mag., 1972, Key award Nat. Assn. Black Mrs., 1972, Chgo. Econ. Devel. Corp. award, 1974, Nat. Alliance Black Sch. Educators award, 1974, Silver Antelope award Boy Scouts Am., 1988, Silver Buffalo award Boy Scouts Am., 1988, Free Enterprise award Internat. Franchise Assn., 1991, Entrepreneurial Excellence award Dow Jones & Co., 1992, Ernst & Young N.Y.C. Entrepreneur of Yr. award, 1995, Sci. and Industry Divsn. award Bklyn. Pub. Libr.'s Centennial Celebration, 1997, award DRUM Orgn./Bell Atlantic Corp., 1998, Marietta Tree award for pub. svc., Citizens Com. for N.Y.C., Inc., 1998, Charlse Evans Hughes gold medal NCCJ, 1998, Ronal H. Brown Leadership award Dept. Commerce Minority Bus. Devel. Agy., 1998, N.Y. Black 100 award Schomburg Ctr. for Rsch. in Black Culture/Black New Yorkers/Black N.Y. Consortium, 1998, Merrick-Moore Spaulding Nat. Achievement award N.C. Mut. Life Ins. Co.-100th Anniversary, 1998, Legacy award Rush Philanthropic Arts Found./Rush Comm., 1998; named One of Ten Most Outstanding Minority Businessman in Country by Pres. U.S., 1973, Outstanding Citizen of Yr., Omega Psi Phi, 1974, also one of 200 Future Leaders of Country, Time mag., Outstanding Black Businessman, Nat. Bus. League, one of 100 influential Blacks, Am. Ebony mag.; Poynter fellow Yale U., 1978; inducted Nat. Sales Hall of Fame, 1995, Morgan State U. Hall of Fame, 1998. Mem. NAACP (bd. dirs. spl. contbns. fund, Spingarn medal 1999), SCLC, Interracial Coun. Bus. Opportunity (award), Young Pres. Orgn., Mag. Pubs. Assn. (dir.), Advt. Coun., Bus. Mktg. Corp. N.Y.C., N.Y. Econs. Club (trustee), Sigma Pi Phi, Omega Psi Phi. Clubs: N.Y. Econ. (trustee). Democrat. Episcopalian. Office: Black Enterprise Mag and Earl G Graves Pub Co Inc 130 5th Ave Fl 10 New York NY 10011-4399*

GRAVES, EARL WILLIAM, JR., journalist; b. Kodiak, Alaska, June 30, 1950; s. Earl William Graves, Sr. and Lola (Olson) Raab; m. Karin Ann Steichen, July 30, 1972; children: Emma, Mark, Max. BA in English with honors, U. Puget Sound, 1972; MA in English, Western Wash. State U., 1976. Tchr. English Naselle (Wash.) High Sch., 1972-74, Clatskanie (Oreg.) High Sch., 1975-77; police reporter Coeur d'Alene (Idaho) Press, 1978-79, city editor, 1980-82, mng. editor, 1983-84; sr. reporter Bulletin, Bend, Oreg., 1984-86; edn. reporter News and Observer, Raleigh, N.C., 1986-87; state edn. reporter News and Observer/Raleigh Times, 1987-89; edn. reporter The Oregonian, Portland, 1990—. Author: Poisoned Apple, 1995. Recipient Outstanding Svc. award N.C. chpt. Phi Delta Kappa, 1988, Third Prize So. Journalism Feature Reporting award Inst. for So. Studies, 1989, N.C. Sch. Bell award N.C. Assn. Educators, 1989, Benjamin Fine award Nat. Assn. Secondary Sch. Prins., 1989, First Pl. Gen. News Reporting award N.C. Press Assn., 1990, First Pl. Edn. Reporting award Pacific Northwest Excellence in Journalism, Soc. Profl. Journalists, 1991, 92, 2001, Media award Assn. Retarded Children Oreg., 1992, Seconad Pl. Spot News Reporting award Best of West, 1992, Second Pl. Best Writing award Oreg. Newspaper Pubs. Assn., 1993, Excellence in Edn. award Oreg. Assn. Supervision and Cirriculum Devel., 1993; Nieman fellow Harvard U., 1998-99. Mem. Edn. Writers Assn. (pres., sec., bd. dirs. 1990—, Spl. Citation Nat. Awards for Edn. Reporting 1987, 91, Second Pl. Newspaper Series award 1989, Second Pl. Nat. Awards Edn. Reporting 1989). Democrat. Avocations: gardening, photography, outdoors, running, travel. Office: Oregonian 1320 SW Broadway Portland OR 97201-3499

GRAVES, ERNEST, JR., retired army officer, consultant, engineer; b. N.Y.C., July 6, 1924; s. Ernest and Lucy (Birnie) G.; m. Nancy Herbert Barclay, May 12, 1951; children: Ralph Henry, Robert Barclay, William Hooper, Emily Birnie. BS, U.S. Mil. Acad., 1944; PhD, M.I.T., 1951; postgrad., Engr. Sch., Ft. Belvoir, Va., 1954-55, Command and Gen. Staff Coll., Ft. Leavenworth, Kans., 1957-58, Army War Coll., Carlisle Barracks, Pa., 1964-65, Harvard Bus. Sch., 1968. Commd. 2d lt. U.S. Army, 1944, advanced through grades to lt. gen., 1978, ret., 1981; with (SHAPE), Paris, 1951-54, (Army Package Power Reactor), Ft. Belvoir, 1955-57; comdr. (44th Engr. Constrn. Bn.), Korea, 1958-59; dir. (Army Nuclear Cratering Group, Lawrence Radiation Lab.), Livermore, Cal., 1962-64; exec. to sec. army Washington, 1967-68; comdr. (34th Engr. Group), Vietnam, 1968-69; div. engr. (U.S. Army Engr. Div., N. Central), Chgo., 1970-73; asst. gen. mgr. for mil. application U.S. AEC, Washington, 1973-75; dir. civil works Office Chief Engrs., Washington, 1975-77, dep. chief engr., 1977-78; dir. Def. Security Assistance Agy., Washington, 1978-81; sr. advisor Ctr. for Strategic and Internat. Studies, Washington, 1982-99. Contbr. articles to profl. jours. Decorated D.S.M., Legion of Merit, Bronze Star, Air medal. Mem. Soc. Am. Mil. Engrs. Home: 2328 S Nash St Arlington VA 22202-1548

GRAVES, H. BRICE, retired lawyer; b. Charlottesville, Va., Sept. 1, 1912; BS, U. Va., 1932, MS, 1933, PhD, LL.B., 1938. Bar: N.Y. 1940, Va. 1949. Assoc. Cravath, Swaine & Moore, N.Y.C., 1938-42, 45-48; ptnr. Hunton & Williams, Richmond, Va., 1949—2005, ret., 2005. Planning com. U. Va. Ann. Tax Conf., 1971-82, trustee emeritus, 1989—; lectr. in field Contbr. articles to profl. jours. With USNR, 1942—45. Mem. Richmond Bar Assn., Va. Bar Assn. (chmn. taxation com. 1971-73), ABA (chmn. com. exempt orgns. tax sect. 1963-65, com. mem. 1975-77), Am. Law Inst., Richmond Estate Planning Council, Am. Coll. Tax Counsel Home: 10,000 Cedarfield Ct Cottage 20 Richmond VA 23233 Office: Hunton & Williams PO Box 1535 Richmond VA 23218-1535 Office Phone: 804-788-8404.

GRAVES, JAMES E., state supreme court justice, educator; BA in Sociology, Millsaps Coll.; JD, Syracuse U.; MPA, Syracuse U. Maxwell Sch. Citizenship & Public Affairs; LLD (hon.), Millsaps Coll. Clerk Dept. of Community Devel., Syracuse, NY, 1978—79; staff atty. Central Miss. Legal Services, Jackson, Miss., 1980—83; ptnr. Murrain and Graves, 1983—84; assoc. atty. Walker and Walker, 1984—86; legal counsel Health Law Div., Miss. Atty. Gen. Office, 1986—89, Human Services Div., Miss. Atty. Gen. Office, 1989—90; special asst. atty. Miss. Atty. Gen. Office, 1986—90; dir. child support enforcement div. Miss. Dept. Human Services, 1990—91; cir. ct. judge 7th Cir. Dist., 1991—2001; justice Miss. Supreme Ct., 2001—. Adj. prof. media and civil rights law Jackson State U., 1980—97; instr. trial advocacy Harvard Law Sch., 1998, 99, 2000. Active pub. sch. activities; coach student mock trial teams. Named Parent of Yr., 2000—01; recipient Judge of Yr. award, Nat. Conf. Black Lawyers, 1992, Thurgood Marshall award, Jackson's Martin Luther King Celebration, 1994, 2002, Commissioner's award, US Dept. Health & Human Services, 2001, Special Achievement award, Jackson Federal Exec. Assn., 2002, Humanized Ed. award, Miss. Assn. of Educators, 2002. Mem.: Miss. Bar Found. (Law-Related Public Ed. award 2002), Magnolia Bar Assn. (Govt. Service award 1993, R. Jess Brown award 1994, Govt. Service award 1998), Hinds County Bar Assn. (Innovation award 2000), Nat. Bar Assn. (Disting. Jurist award 1996). Office: PO Box 249 Jackson MS 39205

GRAVES, JERRELL LOREN, demographic studies researcher; b. Humansville, Mo., Feb. 10; s. Loren Silas and Edith Lucille (Childress) G. AA, San Jose City Coll., 1986. Lic. gen. contractor, Calif. Farm laborer Guy McDaniel, Bolivar, Mo., 1952-54; laborer Standard Milk Co., Bolivar, 1952-55; constrn. worker Local Union # 676, Springfield, Mo., 1957-59; wood worker Bolivar Wood Products, 1959-61; rschr. life cycles and coop. living, coord. S.W. Dem. Studies, Half Way, Mo., 1961—. Instr. hatha yoga San Jose City Coll., 1973. Coord. Caring and Sharing, San Jose, 1977-81, San Jose Coop., Inc., 1985-87; vol. Getting out the Vote Friends of John Vasconselles, San Jose, 1980. Mem. ACLU, UN Assn. U.S.A., World Federalists Assn., Common Cause, Greenpeace, World Watch, World Future Soc., Self-Realization Fellowship, Internat. Platform Assn., Rosicrucian. Avocations: studying mysticism and metaphysics, swimming, yoga. Home and Office: SW Demographic Studies 4282 Hwy P Half Way MO 65663-9133

GRAVES, JOHN WILLIAM, historian; b. Little Rock, June 25, 1942; s. William A. and Mabel (Morehart) G. BA in History, U. Ark., 1964, MA, 1967; PhD in History, U. Va., 1978. Grad. tchg. asst. U. Ark., 1965-66; instr. history U. S.W. La., LaFayette, 1966-68; rsch. asst. U. Va., Charlottesville, 1971-72; instr. history S.W. Tex. State U., San Marcos, 1972-77; coll. assistance migrant program, freshman studies coord., basic skills specialist, lectr. St. Edward's U., Austin, Tex., 1979—85; assoc. prof. then prof. history Henderson State U., Arkadelphia, Ark., 1985—, chmn. dept. social scis., 2002—. Rep. Sch. Liberal Arts Faculty Senate, 1987-88; Rep., Dept. Social Sci. Faculty Senate, 2002-03. Author: Town and Country: Race Relations in an Urban-Rural Context, Arkansas, 1865-1905, 1990 (Arkansiana award Ark. Libr. Assn. 1991, Commendation award Am. Assn. for Study of State and Local History 1993); contbr. articles to profl. jours. Bd. dirs. Soc. for Preservation of Mosaic Templars of Am. Bldg., Hillcrest Residents Assn., Little Rock, Black History Adv. Com. State of Ark.; adv. bd. dept. Ark. heritage Mosaic Templars Am. Ctr.; rep. Coalition of LIttle Rock Neighborhoods. Recipient Disting. Svc. award Henderson State U., 1999-2000, Disting. Rsch. award Henderson State U., 2001-2002; Stonewall Jackson Meml. fellow Ark. History Commn., 1965, Philip Francis DuPont fellow U. Va., 1969-71. Mem. AAUP (pres. chpt. 1999-2001), So. Hist. Assn., Ark. Hist. Assn. (v.p. 1987-92, pres. 1992-96), Ark. History Coun. (Ark. sec. of state), Audubon Soc. (pres. Bastrop County Tex. 1985), Defenders of Wildlife, Environ. Def. Fund, Ark. Nature Conservancy, Nat. Trust for Hist. Preservation, Hist. Preservation Alliance Ark., Quapaw Qtr. Assn., Student Sen. U. Ark. (grad. sch. rep. 1965-66), Tau Kappa Epsilon (pres. 1964), Phi Alpha Theta. Home: 5218 G St Little Rock AR 72205-3517 Office: Henderson State U Dept History Arkadelphia AR 71999-0001 Fax: (870) 230-5144. E-mail: johnwgrav@aol.com, gravesj@hsu.edu.

GRAVES, JOHN WILLIAM, state supreme court justice; b. Paducah, Ky., Oct. 17, 1935; m. Mary Ann Breivo; children: James Anthony, Kevin Andrew. BS, U. Notre Dame, 1957; postgrad., U. Louisville Sch. of Medicine, 1957—58; JD, U. Ky., 1963; attended, Command & Gen. Staff Coll., Airwar Coll., Nat. Defense U. Bar: Ky. 1963. Jud. law clerk to Judge James B. Milliken Ky. Ct. of Appeals, 1963—64; atty. priv. practice, Ky., 1964—84; judge Ky. Dist. Ct., 1984—88; circuit ct. judge McCracken Cir., 1989-95; justice Ky. Supreme Ct., 1995—. Colonel USAR. Decorated Army Commendation medal, Army Meritorious Service medal, Defense Meritorious Service medal. Office: Kentucky Supreme Ct 222 Kentucky Ave PO Box 993 Paducah KY 42003-0993 Office Phone: 270-575-7039.*

GRAVES, JOSEPH SCOTT, economics and management consultant; b. St. Louis, Apr. 20, 1948; s. Joseph Whitaker Jr. and Mary Frances (Scott) G.; m. Elizabeth Mather, Oct. 16, 1983; 1 child, Lindsay Mather. BA in Math., Chem. Engring., M in Chem. Engring., Rice U., 1971; MS in Indsl. Adminstrn., Carnegie Mellon, 1973, PhD in Ops. Rsch., 1978. Process design engr. Hudson Engring. Corp. (now part of McDermott Internat.), Houston, 1969-71; asst. prof. Washington U., St. Louis, 1974-78; prin. Resource Planning Assoc., Washington, 1978-84; mng. dir. Putnam, Hayes & Bartlett, Inc., Washington, 1984-98; sr. v.p. PHB Hagler Bailly, Inc., Washington, 1998-2000; mem. mgmt. group PA Cons. Group, Washington, 2000—. Spkr. in field. Author: Transmission Services Costing Framework, 1995; contbr. articles to profl. jours. Treas. Potomac Overlook Owners Assn., Washington, 1983-84. Mem. IEEE, Inst. for Ops. Rsch. and Mgmt. Scis. (chmn. computer sci. tech. 1977-78), Strategic Mgmt. Soc. (charter), Engr.'s Club St. Louis, Beta Gamma Sigma, Tau Beta Pi. Episcopalian. Avocations: sports, music, biking, camping. Office: PA Cons Grp Ste 1000 1750 Pennsylvania Ave NW Washington DC 20006-4506 Office Phone: 202-442-2348.

GRAVES, JUDSON, lawyer; b. Jacksonville, Fla., Dec. 13, 1947; s. A. Judson and Martha A. (Lively) G.; children: Ashley, Judson, Mallory. AB in Psychology, Dartmouth Coll., 1969; JD with distinction, Emory U., 1975. Bar: Ga. 1975, Fla. 1975. Assoc. Jones Bird & Howell, Atlanta, 1975-80, ptnr., 1980-83; ptnr., prod. liability group Alston & Bird LLP, Atlanta, 1983—. Lt. USN, 1969-72. Mem. Lawyers Club Atlanta, Am. Coll. Trial Lawyers, Order of Coif. Office: Alston & Bird LLP 1 Atlantic Ctr 1201 W Peachtree St NW Atlanta GA 30309-3424 Office Phone: 404-881-7279. Office Fax: 404-881-7777. Business E-Mail: jgraves@alston.com.

GRAVES, LORRAINE ELIZABETH, dancer, educator, coach; b. Norfolk, Va., Oct. 5, 1957; d. Thomas Edward and Mildred Fayette (Odom) G. BS, Ind. U., 1978. Dancer, Regisseuse Dance Theatre of Harlem, N.Y.C., 1978—, ballet mistress, 1980—, prin. dancer, 1980, artistic asst., 1998—. Artistic advisor Va. Ballet Theatre, 1997—; tchr./coach Dance Theatre of Harlem, 1998-99, 2001, guest ballet mistress, 2001—; guest tchr. N.C. Sch. of Arts, Winston-Salem, 1987, 93, Gov.'s Sch. for Arts, U. Richmond, 1990—, Carlton Johnson Acad. of Dance, 1991-95, Okla. Summer Arts Inst., 1993-94, The Flint Sch. Performing Arts, Flint Youth Ballet, 2001—, Dance Theatre of Harlem, Kennedy Ctr. Residency Program, 1993-95, 98—, Worcester Sch. Performing Arts, 1997, Greenville Ballet, 2001; resident guest tchr. Gov.'s Sch. for Arts, Norfolk, Va., 1988-91, mem. faculty, 1996—; guest tchr. Worcester Sch. Performing Arts, 1997; resident guest tchr. S.C. Gov.'s Sch. for Arts, 1995-97; guest tchr. Va. Ballet Theatre, 1996—, artistic advisor, 1998—; guest tchr. Va. Sch. for the Arts, 1997—, resident guest tchr., 2003—; educator, judge Dance Olympus, 1997—; judge Internat. Dance Challenge, 1998—; guest faculty Mid-States Regional Dance Festival, 1999; mem. faculty SERBA Festival, Roanoke, Va., 2003. Dancer Dance Theatre of Harlem as Princess of Unreal Beauty in live TV prodn. of Firebird, 1982, as Myrta, Queen of the Willis in NBC prodn. of Creole Giselle, 1987, performed at White House, 1981, also at the closing ceremonies of the 1984 Olympics, toured with Dance Theatre of Harlem, USSR, 1988, South Africa, 1992, guest artist Young People's Concert series, N.Y. Philharm., 1988, Detroit Symphony, 1989, River City Ballet, Memphis, 1991, 1992, N.W. Fla. Ballet, 1994, prin. dancer Va. Ballet Theatre, Norfolk, 1996—, Dance Theatre of Harlem, 1999, guest ballet mistress, 1999—, regisseuse Dance Theatre of Harlem, 1989—96. Mem. artistic com. Young Audiences of Va.; sec. Norfolk Commn. on the Arts and Humanities, 2002—; mem. program com. Young Audiences Va. Fellow Am. Guild Mus. Artists. Episcopalian. Avocations: modeling, teaching younger dancers.

GRAVES, MICHAEL, architect, educator; b. Indpls., July 9, 1934; s. Thomas Browning and Erma Sanderson (Lowe) Graves; children from previous marriage: Sarah Browning, Adam Daimhin stepchildren: Anne Gilbert, Liza Gilbert. BS in Architecture, U. Cin., 1958, DFA (hon.), 1982; MArch, Harvard U., 1959; postgrad. (Acad. fellow), Am. Acad. in Rome, 1960—62; PhD (hon.), U. Cin., 1982; LHD (hon.), Boston U., 1984; HHD (hon.), Savannah Coll. Art and Design, 1986; DFA (hon.), RISD, 1990, N.J. Inst. Tech., 1991; LHD (hon.), Rutgers U., 1994, U. Colo., 1995; PhD (hon.), Internat. Fine Arts Coll., 1996, Pratt Inst., 1996, Drexel U., 2000. Lectr. architecture Princeton (N.J.) U., 1962—67, assoc. prof., 1967—72, Schirmer prof. architecture, 1972—2001, emeritus, 2001—; pres. Michael Graves & Assocs., Princeton, 1964—. Arch. in residence Am. Acad. in Rome, 1979. Exhibited in group shows including Mus. Modern Art, N.Y.C., 1967, 68, 75, 78, 79, 80, 81, 84, Cooper-Hewitt Mus., 1976, 78, 79, 80, 82, 85, 87, Triennale, Milan, Italy, 1973, 85, Roma Interrotta, Rome, 1978, Venice Biennale, Italy, 1980, Met. Mus. Art, 1985, 86, 87, Emory U. Mus. Art and Archaeology, Atlanta, 1985, Denver (Colo.) Art Mus., 2002; one-man shows include U. So. Calif., 1981, No. Ill. U., 1982, Inst. for Architecture and Urban Studies, N.Y.C., 1982, Colby Coll., Maine, 1982, Moore Coll. Art, Phila., 1983, Fla. Internat. U., Miami, 1983, Pa. State U., University Park, 1984, Royal Inst. Brit. Archs., Heinz Gallery, London, 1984, Wadsworth Atheneaum, Hartford, Conn., 1984, Carleton Coll., Northfield, Minn., 1986, W.Va. U., 1986, Hamilton Coll., Clinton, NY, 1987, Archivolto Gallery, Milan, Italy, 1987, U. Va., Charlottesville, 1987, U. Md., College Park, 1988, Duke U. Mus. Art, Durham, NC, 1988, Butler Inst. Art, Youngstown, Ohio, 1989, 1989, Deutsches Architekturmuseum, Frankfurt, German Dem. Republic, 1989, Washington Design Ctr., 1989, Syracuse U. Sch. Architecture, 1990, Kunstemes Hus, Oslo, 1990, Mikimoto Hall, Tokyo, 1992, Pitts. Cultural Trust, 1993, Richard Stockton Coll., 1993, Clark County Libr., 1994, Thessaloniki Design Mus., Greece, 1996, The Min. Bldg., Seoul, Korea, 1996, Princeton Arts Coun., 1996, 99, U. Conn. Aronoff Ctr. Design and Art, 1996, NJ Sch. Arch., NJ Inst. Tech., 2000; prin. works include Hanselmann House, 1967 (AIA Nat. Honor award, 1975), Newark (NJ) Mus., 1968, Rockefeller House, 1969 (Progressive Architecture Design award, 1970), Gunwyn Ventures Office, 1971 (AIA Nat. Honor award, 1979), Snyderman House, 1972, Crooks House, 1976 (Progressive Architecture Design award, 1977), Schulman House, 1976, (AIA Nat. Honor award, 1982), Fargo-Moorhead Cultural Ctr., 1977-79 (Progressive Architecture Design award, 1978), Plocek House, 1978 (Progressive Architecture Design award, 1979), pvt. residence in Green Brook, NJ, 1978 (Progressive Architecture Design award, 1980), Sunar showrooms N.Y.C., 1979, 81 (Interiors award, 1981), Chgo., 1979, Houston, 1980, LA, 1980, London, 1985, Loveladies Beach House, 1979 (Progressive Architecture Design award, 1979) Environ. Edn. Ctr., 1980 (Progressive Architecture award, 1983), Portland (Oreg.) Bldg., 1980 (AIA Nat. Honor award, 1983), San Juan Capistrano Pub. Libr., Calif., 1980 (AIA Nat. Honor award, 1985), Newark Mus. Master Plan and Renovation, 1982 (AIA Nat. Honor award, 1992), Human Bldg., Louisville, 1982 (Interiors award, 1985, AIA Nat. Honor award, 1987), Emory U. Mus. Art and Archaeology, 1982 (Interiors award 1985, AIA Nat. Honor award, 1987), Riverbend Music Ctr., 1983, Whitney Mus. Am. Art, N.Y.C., 1984, Diane Von Furstenburg Boutique, 1984, Clos Pegase Winery, Calif., 1984 (AIA Nat. Honor award, 1990), Sotheby's Tower, N.Y.C., 1985, Warehouse Renovation (Graves House), 1985 (Progressive Architecture Design award, 1978), Aventine Devel., La Jolla, Calif., 1985, Shiseido Health Club, Tokyo, 1985, Disney Co. Corp. Office Bldg., Burbank, Calif., 1985, Crown Am. Hdqs., Johnston, Pa., 1985, Walt Disney World Dolphin and Walt Disney World Swan hotels, Fla., 1986 (Progressive Architecture award, 1989), Youngston (Ohio) Hist. Ctr. Industry and Labor, 1986 (Progressive Architecture Design award, 1987), 10 Peachtree Pl., Atlanta, 1987, Henry House, Rhinebeck, NY, 1987 (Progressive Architecture award, 1989), U. Va. Arts. and Scis. Bldg., Charlottesville, 1987, Portside Dist. Condominium Tower, Yokohama, Japan, 1987, Momochi Dist. Apt. Bldg., Fukuoka, Japan, 1987, Metropolis Master Plan LA, 1988, stores and galleries for Lenox, Tysons Corner, Va., 1988, Palm Beach, 1988, N.Y.C., 1988, Mpls., 1988, Costa Mesa, 1989, Frankfurt, 1989, Phila., 1989, Nashville, 1989, Midousuji Minami Office Bldg., Osaka, 1988, Tajima Office Bldg., Tokyo, 1988, Hotel NY, 1988, Euro Disneyland, France, 1988, Inst. for Theoretical Physics, U. Calif., Santa Barbara, 1989, Detroit Inst. of Arts Master Plan, 1989, Indpls. Art Ctr., 1989, Emory U. Mus. Art and Archaeology Addition, 1989, Fukuoka Internat. Office Project, 1990, Kasumi Group Rsch. and Tng. Ctr., Tsukaba City, Japan, 1990, Clark County Libr., Las Vegas, 1990, U. Cin. Sci. and Engring. Rsch. Ctr., 1990, Richard Stockton Coll. Arts and Scis. Bldg., Pomona, NJ, 1991, Denver Ctrl. Libr., 1991 (AIA-NJ Design award, 1992, 95, AIA Nat. Honor award for Interior Architecture, 1998, AIA and Am. Libr. Assn. Excellence award, 2001), Astrid Park Plz. Hotel and Bus. Ctr., Antwerp, Belgium, 1992, Thomson Consumer Electronics Hdqs., Indpls., 1992 (AIA-NJ Design award, 1994), Rome Reborn Vatican Exhibit, Libr. Congress, 1992 (Casebook award Print Mag., 1993), Pitts. Cultural Trust Theater and Office Bldg., 1992, Taiwan Mus. Pre-History, Taipei, 1993 (AIA-NJ Design award, 1994), Archdiocesan Ctr., Newark, 1993, Internat. Fin. Corp. Hdqs., Washington, 1993 (AIA-NJ Design award, 1997), 1500 Ocean Dr. Condominiums, Miami, 1994, Del. River Port Authority Hdqs., Camden, NJ, 1994 (AIA-NJ Design award, 1998), St. Martin's Coll. Libr., Lacey, Wash., 1994, Topeka (Kans.) and Shawnee County Pub. Libr., 1995, Miramar Hotel, Egypt, 1995 (AIA-NJ Design award, 1996), NJ Inst. Tech. Residence Hall, 1995, Jiang-to Blvd. Master Plan, Xiamen, China, 1995, Alexandria (Va.) Ctrl. Libr., 1996, U.S. Courthouse Annex, Washington, 1996, Life Mag. Dream House, 1996, Lake Hills country Club, Seoul, Korea, 1996, World Trade Exch., Manila, 1996, new residence Hall, Drexel U., Phila., 1997, Miele Appliances Americas Hdqs. Bldg., Princeton, 1997 (AIA-NJ Design award, 2002), NovaCare Sports Training Facility, 1997 (AIA-NJ Design award, 2002), El Gourna Golf Villas, Egypt, 1997 (AIA-NJ Design award, 2002), French Inst. Libr, N.Y.C., 1997, Hyatt Regency Taba Heights Hotel, Egypt, 1997, St. Mary's Ch., Rockledge, Fla., 1998, Rice U. Master Plan, Houston, 1998, The Impala Bldg., N.Y.C., 1998, Wash. Monument Restoration Scaffolding, 1998 (AIA-NJ Design award, 1998), Rolex Watch Technicum Tng. and Svc. Ctr., Lancaster County, Pa., 1999, Theater Square: Pitts. Cultural Trust Svc. Ctr., 1999, Mus. Shenandoah Valley, Winchester, Va., 1999, 425 Fifth Ave. Tower, N.Y.C., 2000, Mahler IV Mixed-Use Bldg., Amsterdam, 2000, Fed. Res. Bank Dallas: Houston Br., 2000, Famille-Tsukishima Bldg., Tokyo, 2000, U.S. Embassy, Seoul, 2000, Dept. Transp. Hdqs., Washington, 2001, Detroit Inst. Arts, 2001, St. Coletta's Sch., Washington, 2002, NJ City U. Arts and Scis. Bldg., 2002, Nat. Automobile Mus., The Netherlands, 2003, U.S. Courthouse, Nashville, 2003; designer furniture, artifacts, textiles, and consumer products, V'Soske, 1979-80, Sunar, 1980-83, Alessi, 1981—Baldinger Archtl. Lighting, 1983—, Swid Powell, 1985—, Steuben, 1986—, Munari, 1986—Tajima, 1987-88, WMF, 1987—, Atelier Internat., 1987—Vorwerk, 1987—, Lenox Inc., 1988—, Markuse Corp., 1989—, Dunbar Furniture, 1989—, Arkitektura, 1989—, Moeller Internat. Design, 1992—, Target Stores, 1997—, Glen Eden Wool Carpet, 2002—, Delta Faucets, 2003—; monographs include: Five Architects, 1972, Michael Graves, Academy Editions, 1979, Michael Graves: Buildings and Projects 1966-1981, 1981, Michael Graves: Buildings and Projects 1982-1989, 1990, Michael Graves: Buildings and Projects 1990-1994, 1995, The Master Architect Series III: Michael Graves: Selected and Current Works, 1999, Michael Graves: Buildings and Projects 1995-2002, 2003. Named Designer of Yr., Interiors, 1981; recipient Arnold W. Brunner Meml. prize in Architect., 1981, 61 awards, N.J. Soc. Architects, Euster award, 1984, Ind. Arts award, 1984, Henry Hering Meml. medal, Am. Sculpture Soc., 1986, profile Best Architects and Designers Working Today, Architectural Digest, 1990, 1995, 2000, Nat. Medal Arts, Nat. Endowment Arts, 1999, Frank Annunzio award, 2001, AIA Gold medal, Sigma Tau Delta, 2003. Fellow: AIA (Gold medal, 2001); mem.: N.Y. Sch. Interior Design (bd. trustees), Mus. Arts and Design (bd. trustees), Am. Acad. in Rome (bd. trustees, Rome prize 1960—62), Am. Acad. Arts and Letters. Office: Michael Graves & Assoc 341 Nassau St Princeton NJ 08540 also: Michael Graves Architect 560 Broadway Ste 401 New York NY 10012 E-mail: info@michaelgraves.com.

GRAVES, PAMELA KAY, music educator; b. Cleve., Ohio, Oct. 29, 1953; d. Frank Michael and Harriet Gertude Duncan; m. Garry Thomas Graves, Aug. 17, 1979; 1 child, Tyler Logan. MusB, BE, Capital U., 1976. Bookkeeper McDonald Restaurants, Mayfield, Ohio, 1970—80; music tchr., instrumental dir. St. Joseph & John Sch., Stongsville, Ohio, 1985—2000; adj. music Ohio Music Educator Assn., Ohio, 1993—. Instrumental dir., tchr. Wickliffe Mid. Sch., Ohio, 1993—; freelance musician, Ohio, 1985—; guest conductor Ohio State Fair Band, Ohio, 1980—; piano tchr. Piano Turner Sch., Ohio, 1986. Contbr. articles to profl. jour., 2002. Mem.: Nat. Assn. of Music Edn., Levy Com., Wickliffe Parent and Tchr. Together (sec. 2001—03). Avocations: photography, crafts, gardening, family. Home: 1717 Robindale St Wickliffe OH 44092 Office: Wickliffe Mid Sch 29240 Eudid Ave Wickliffe OH 44092

GRAVES, RAY REYNOLDS, retired judge; b. Tuscumbia, Ala., Jan. 10, 1946; s. Isaac and Olga Ernestine (Wilder) Graves; children: Claire Elise, Reynolds Douglass. BA, Trinity Coll., Hartford, Conn., 1967; JD, Wayne State U., 1970. Bar: Mich. 1971, U.S. Dist. Ct. (ea. dist.) Mich. 1971, U.S. Ct. Appeals (6th cir.) 1972, U.S. Supreme Ct. 1976, D.C. 1977. Defender Legal Aid and Defender Assn., Detroit, 1970-71; assoc. Liberson, Fink, Feiler, Crystal & Burdick, 1971-72, Patmon, Young & Kirk, 1972-73; ptnr. Lewis, White, Clay & Graves, 1974-81; mem. legal dept. Detroit Edison Co., 1981; judge U.S. Bankruptcy Ct., Ea. Dist. Mich., Detroit, 1982-2002; chief judge U.S. Bankruptcy Ct., 1991-95; prin. BBK, Ltd., Southfield, Mich., 2002—. Mem. U.S. ct. com. State Bar Mich. Trustee Mich. Opera Theatre, 1986—88; vestry Christ Ch. Episcopal, Grosse Pointe, Mich., 1994—97; del Diocesan Conv. Episcopal Ch., Mich., 1997; bd. dirs. Mich. Cancer Found. Fellow: Am. Coll. Bankruptcy; mem.: D.C. Bar Assn., Detroit Bar Assn., Wolverine Bar Assn., Assn. Black Judges Mich., World Peace Through Law Conf., World Assn. Judges, Nat. Conf. Bankruptcy Judges (bd. govs. 1984—88), Iota Boulè (Sire Archon 1999—2001), Sigma Pi Phi, Delta Kappa Epsilon. Episcopalian. Office: BBK Ltd 300 Galleria Officentre # 103 Southfield MI 48034 Office Phone: 248-603-8373. Business E-Mail: rgraves@e-bbk.com.

GRAVES, ROBERT J., lawyer; b. Hinsdale, Ill., 1958; BA cum laude, Ill. Wesleyan Univ., 1980; JD magna cum laude, Univ. Ill., 1984. Bar: Ill. 1984. Law clerk Judge Thomas Gibbs Gee, US Ct. of Appeals, Fifth Cir., 1984—85; ptnr., chair, lending/structured fin. practice Jones Day. Author: numerous articles in profl. publications. Fulbright Scholar, Univ. Erlangen, Germany, 1980—81. Mem.: ABA, Chgo. Bar Assn. (past chair, comml. fin. com.), Order of Coif. Fluent in German. Office: Jones Day 77 W Wacker Chicago IL 60601-1692 Office Fax: 312-782-8585.

GRAVES, SAMUEL B., congressman, retired state legislator; b. Fairfax, MO, Nov. 7, 1963; BS, Univ. Missouri-Columbia. State rep. Dist. 4 Mo. Gen. State Assembly, 1993-94, state senator Dist. 12, 1995-2001; mem. U.S. Congress from 6th Mo. dist., 2001—. Mem.: Transp. & Infrastructure Com., Small Bus. Com., Agriculture Com., U.S. Congress from 6th Mo. dist. Republican. Office: US Ho Reps 1513 Longworth Ho Office Bldg Washington DC 20515-2506 also: Dist Office 113 Blue Jay Dr Ste 200 Liberty MO 64068

GRAVES, TODD PETERSON, prosecutor; b. 1965; m. Tracy Graves; 4 children. BA summe cum laude, U. Mo., 1988; MS, JD, U. Va., 1991. Bar: Mo. 1991, cert.: U.S. Dist. Ct. Mo. 1991, U.S. Ct. Appeals 8th Cir. 1993. Assoc. Skadden Arps, N.Y.C.; asst. atty. gen. State of Mo., 1991; assoc. Bryan Cave law Firm, 1992—94; prosecutor Platte County Ct., Mo., 1994—2001; U.S. atty. (we. dist.) Mo U.S. Dept. Justice, 2001—. Republican. Office: 400 E 9th St 5th Fl Kansas City MO 64106

GRAVES, VICKI LLOYD, retired mechanical engineer; b. Phoenix, Ariz., Aug. 5, 1935; d. Margarite Marie Hogue and Lonnie Hershal Lloyd, Ivan Burton and Dorothy Carol Lloyd; m. William S. Graves, June 24, 1966; stepchildren: Kay Levy, Lynn Neilson, Diane Graves-Dolk children: Darlene Ann Clow, Diane Jeanette Clow, Anthony Thomas Clow. Mech. Engring. Design, Marietta Cobb Tech., 1969. Cons. Engring. Cons. Designer, St. Petersburg, Fla., 1968—82; art designer Vicki Quail Run Art Studio, Mesa, Ariz., 1992—. Membership chmn. Scottsdale Artist League, Ariz., 1998—2000. Mem.: Scottsdale Artist League, Mesa Artist League. Address: 234 E Bakerview Rd Apt # 106 Bellingham WA 98226

GRAVES, VIRGINIA BETH, elementary school educator; b. Oceanside, Calif., Sept. 19, 1950; d. Joe Howard and Bertha Elizabeth (Denney) Long; children: Betsy Lynn, John Howard. BS in Edn. with distinction, U. Okla., 1972; M in Reading, U. Ctrl. Okla., 1996. Cert. elem. edn. early childhood, reading specialist, elem. prin. Okla. Tchr. 5th grade Oklahoma City Pub. Schs., 1972-75; tchr. 1st grade Westminster Day Sch., Oklahoma City, 1989-94, tchr. 2d grade, co-chair lang. arts curriculum, 1994—98, reading recovery tchr., 1998—99, reading recovery tchr. leader, 1999—, program coord. reading recovery pre-k and kindergarten, 2004—. Mem. Jr. League Oklahome City, 1985-89, 92-95. Mem.: ASCD, Internat. Reading Assn. Home: 1605 Brighton Ave Oklahoma City OK 73120 Office: Putnam City Schs 5401 NW 40th St Oklahoma City OK 73122 E-mail: vgraves1@cox.net.

GRAVES, WALLACE BILLINGSLEY, retired university executive; b. Ft.Worth, Feb. 10, 1922; s. Ellery George and Edith (Billingsley) G.; m. Barbara Jeanne Abey, Nov. 20, 1943; children: David W., Emily Graves Mc Donald, John R., Julie Graves Williams. BA, U. Okla., 1943; MA, Tex. Christian U., 1947; PhD, U. Tex., 1953; LLD (hon.), Ind. State U., 1970, Valparaiso U., 1972; LHD (hon.), Morningside Coll., 1971, U. Evansville, 1989. Teaching fellow Tex. Christian U., Ft. Worth, 1946-47, U. Tex., Austin, 1947-50; prof. polit. sci. DePauw U., Greencastle, Ind., 1950-58; Armstrong prof. govt., dean of men Tex. Wesleyan Coll., Ft. Worth, 1958-63, asst. to pres., 1963-65; acad. v.p. U. Pacific, Stockton, Calif., 1965-67; pres. U. Evansville, Ind., 1967-87, chancellor, 1986-89, pres. emeritus, 1989—. Vis. prof. Butler U., summer 1956; bd. dirs. Citizens Nat. Bank, Evansville, Herrburger Brooks P.L.C., Nottingham, Eng. Author: The United Nations, Great Britain and the British Non-Self Governing Territories, 1954, The One Semester Course in International Relations, 1956, Harlaxton College: The Camelot of Academe, 1990; contbr. articles to profl. jours. Mem. exec. bd. Tarrant County chpt. ARC, 1960-65, chmn. home svc. com.; chmn. ARC of Southwestern Ind., 1994—; midwest region com. ARC, 2000-02; bd. dirs. Ft. Worth Assn. Retarded Children, 1963-65; mem. Met. Ft. Worth Devel. Coordinating Com., World Affairs Coun., Chgo. and Stockton, adv. bd. Supplementary Edn. Ctr., Stockton; v.p. Buffalo Trace coun. Boy Scouts Am., Evansville, 1968, exec. bd., 1968-74, adv. coun, 1974—; bd. dirs. Jr. Achievement Inc., Evansville, 1968-73; mem. comm. ecumenical affairs United Meth. Ch., Evansville, 1968-72, univ. senate, 1972-76, Ind. area study commn., 1972-74; bd. dirs. Evansville Day Sch., 1967-76; mem. Ind. State Scholarship Commn., 1969-77, adv. bd. St. Mary's Med. Ctr., Evansville, 1970—, Evansville's Future Inc., 1967—, pres., 1974-77; bd. dirs. Ind. Health Careers Inc., 1974-75; mem. Govs. Adv. Com. Pub. Health, 1971-72; bd. dirs. Leadership Evansville, 1975-71, Evansville Mus., 1978—, Lincolnland Hist. Trust, 1978—; pres. Beethoven Found., Indpls., 1980-88; mem. organizing com. Pan Am. Games, 1987; bd. dirs. Sta. WNIN Pub. TV, Evansville, 1973—, chmn. bd., 1982-84. With U.S. Army, 1943. Recipient Best Tchr. award DePauw U., 1954, medal of honor U. Evansville, 1977, medal of merit Govt. Thailand, 1984, medal of honofr DAR, 1999; Wallace B. Graves Day named in his honor Office Mayor City Evansville, 1977; rsch. scholar U. Tex., 1947; Ford Found. fellow, summer 1951, 55; Paul Harris (Rotary) fellow, 1995. Mem. AAUP, Am. Assn. Acad. Deans, Am. Coll. Pub. Relations Assn., Am. Polit. Sci. Assn., Ind. Colls. and Univs. Ind. Inc. (pres. 1970-71, 76-77), North Cen. Assn. Colls. and Secondary Schs. (cons., investigator), Am. Assn. Pres. Ind. Colls. and Univs. (exec. com. 1969-70), Am. Assn. Colls. (various coms.), Associated Colls. Ind. (pres. 1972-74), Carl

Duisberg Soc. (pres. Am. assn. 1973-74), Internat. Assn. Univ. Pres. (bd. dirs. N.Am. council 1975-87), Ind. Consortium Computer and High Tech. Edn., Ft. Worth C. of C. (chmn. econ. edn. com. 1963-64), Gold Key, Blue Key, Phi Kappa Phi, Phi Mu Alpha, Alpha Sigma Lambda, Pi Sigma Alpha, Sigma Nu. Clubs: Knife and Fork (pres. 1964-65) (Ft. Worth); Commonwealth (San Francisco); Columbia (Indpls.); Petroleum; Evansville Country, Kennel (Evansville). Lodges: Rotary (pres. Ft. club 1964-65). Personal E-mail: wexprex@aol.com.

GRAVES, WILLIAM PRESTON, governor; b. Salina, Kans., Jan. 9, 1953; s. William Henry and Helen (Mayo) G.; m. Linda Richey, Apr. 1990; 1 child, Katie. BBA, Kans. Wesleyan U., Salina, 1975; postgrad., U. Kans., 1978-79. Dep. asst. sec. of state State of Kans., Topeka, 1980-85, asst. sec. of state, 1985-87, sec. of state, 1987-95, gov., 1995—2003. Former mem. Competitiveness Policy Coun. Mem. Kans. Cavalry; trustee Kans. Wesleyan U., 1987—; bd. trustes Sunflower State Games, Harry S. Truman Scholarship Found., 2003—. Named Outstanding Young Alumnus, Kans. Wesleyan U., Salina, 1975, Outstanding Young Kansan, Salina Jaycees, 1986, Kans. Jaycees, 1986, Outstanding Kans. Citizen, Jayhawk area BSA, 2002; named to Athletic Hall of Fame, Kans. Wesleyan U., Salina, 1986. Mem. Kans. C. of C. and Industry. Republican. Methodist. Avocations: running, reading, travel.

GRAVES-ROMAN, PATRICIA ANN, language educator, writer; b. Jan. 8, 1959; d. Frank X. Graves and Grace Elizabeth Flowers; m. Roman, Aug. 24, 2000; children: Chassie, Willow, O'Her, Karen, Britten; children: Denise Genname, Sarhrona, Baby Shamon. AAS in Humanity of Arts, Passaic County C.C., 1987; MA in Eng. & Lit., Fairleigh Dickinson U., 1994; degree (hon.), U. London, 1989. Asst. dir. William Jefferson Clinton Sch., N.Y.C., 1997—2001; prof. Fairleigh Dickinson U., Teaneck, NJ, 2001—. Rschr. Sen. Frank R. Lautenberg, Washington. Author: Blood on The Dagger, 1998, Secrets, 1998. Mem.: Sheriff Soc. U.S.A. Home: 56 Park Ave Paterson NJ 07501 Office: Oval Office of George Bush Jr Pennsylvania Ave Washington DC 20002

GRAVETT, MICHAEL GLEN, obstetrician, gynecologist, researcher; b. Clarinda, Iowa, Aug. 11, 1951; s. Glen Cecil and Wanda Mae (Williams) G.; m. Yvonne Marie Olson, Dec. 29, 1973 (div. Apr. 1989); children: Erin Elizabeth, Courtney Ann, Geoffrey Glen; m. Claudia Jean Payne, May 5, 1990; 1 child, Diana Payne. BS, Oreg. State U., 1973; MD, UCLA, 1977. Diplomate Am. Bd. Ob-Gyn. Resident in ob-gyn. U. Wash., Seattle, 1977-81, fellow in infectious diseases, 1981-82, fellow in maternal-fetal medicine, 1981-83, asst. prof. ob-gyn., 1983-84; dir. maternal-fetal medicine St. Luke's Regional Med. Ctr., Boise, 1986-90; asst. prof. ob-gyn. Oreg. Health Scis. U., Portland, 1990-96; dir. maternal-fetal medicine Legacy Emanuel Hosp., Portland, 1994—; assoc. prof. ob-gyn. Oreg. Health Scis. U., Portland, 1996—. Collaborative scientist Oreg. Regional Primate Rsch. Ctr., Beaverton, Oreg., 1990-97, assoc. scientist, 1997—; dir. ob-gyn. grad. med. edn. Legacy Emanuel Hosp., Portland, 1994-97. Contbr. numerous chpts. to textbooks and articles to profl. jours. Fellow ACOG; mem. Soc. Perinatal Obstetricians (perinatal resource award 1982, Perinatal Soc. award 1984), Infectious Disease Soc. for Ob-Gyn. (best paper award 1993, 98), Pacific Coast Ob-Gyn. Soc., Phi Kappa Phi. Lutheran. Achievements include development of first nonhuman primate research model to study infectious causes of preterm labor and delivery. Office: 501 N Graham St Ste 280 Portland OR 97227-2000

GRAVITZ, MELVIN A., psychologist, consultant; b. Balt., Dec. 8, 1927; s. Philip B and Sophie Gravitz; m. Harriet D Gravitz, June 1950; children: Ronald, Karen, Nancy, Susan. BA in psychology, George Wash. U., 1950; MA in psychology, George Wash.U., 1951; PhD in clin. psychology, Adelphi U., 1955. Diplomate Am. Bd. Profl. Psychology (pres. 1980-81), Am. Bd. Psychol. Hypnosis (pres. 1975-78), Am Bd. Forensic Psychology. Clin. psychology intern Springfield State Hosp., Sykesville, Md., 1953—54; staff psychologist County Mental Health Clin., 1955—57; chief psychologist, adult clinic D.C. Health Dept., 1957—64; pvt. practice Washington, 1964—; clin. prof. of psychiatry George Wash. U., 1980—. Contbr. chpts. to books, articles to profl. jours. With USN, 1945—47. Named Disting. Practitioner Nat. Acad. Practice, 1982. Fellow Am. Soc. Clin. Hypnosis (pres. 1978-79), APA (coun. rep. 1988-91, 98—, pres. divsn. hypnosis, Heiser award). Avocation: collecting antique books. Office Phone: 202-331-9722.

GRAVLEE, GLENN P(AGE), anesthesiologist, educator; b. Birmingham, Ala., Aug. 15, 1950; BS in Medicine, Northwestern U., 1972, MD, 1974. Diplomate Am. Bd. Anesthesiology. Intern Hartford (Conn.) Hosp., 1974—75; resident anesthesiology Mass. Gen. Hosp., Harvard Med. Sch., Boston, 1975—77, chief resident, cardiac anesthesia fellow, 1977—78, instr., 1978—79; from asst. prof. to prof. Wake Forest U., 1978—94; prof. Allegheny U. Health Scis., Pitts., 1994—99, chair, 1994—99; prof. Dept. Anesthesiology Coll. Med. and Pub. Health Ohio State U., Columbus, 1999—, chmn. Dept. Anesthesiology Coll. Med. and Pub. Health, 1999—2001. Editor: Cardiopulmonary Bypass: Principles and Practice, 1994, 2000; co-editor: A Practical Approach to Cardiac Anesthesia, 2003; contbr. articles to profl. jours. Mem.: Am. Soc. Anesthesiologists, Internat. Rsch. Soc., Soc. Cardiovasc. Anesthesiologists (pres. 2003—05), Am. Bd. Anesthesiologists (dir. 1999—). Office: Ohio State U Dept Anesthesiology Coll Medicine and Pub Health 410 W 10th Ave Columbus OH 43210 Office Phone: 614-293-9081. Business E-Mail: gravlee.1@osu.edu.

GRAW, LEROY HARRY, diversified financial services company executive; b. Dupree, S.Dak., Jan. 10, 1942; s. Harry Fred and Luella (Eichmann) G.; m. Kyong Hee Yuk, Sept. 25, 1969 (div. Feb. 1979); 1 child, Natasha; m. Anat Harari, July 3, 1981; children: Byron, Karen. BS, U.S. Mil. Acad., 1964; M Commerce, U. Richmond, 1974; EdD, U. So. Calif., 1980. Govt. contracting officer worldwide, 1971-88; mgr. govt. contracts Fluor Corp., Dallas, 1988-89; mgr. contracts Superconducting Super Collider, Dallas, 1989-95; dir. contract adminstnr. Los Angeles County MTA, L.A., 1995-96; pres. Internat. Resource Mgmt. Assocs., Upland, Calif., 1996—. Ccons., Dallas, 1991-95; adj. prof. U. Dallas, 1990-95, U. Calif., Riverside, 1996—, UCLA, Westwood, 1996—, Keller Grad. Sch., 1997—. Author: Service Purchasing, 1994, Cost/Price Analysis, 1994; editor: Global Purchasing, 1990; contbr. articles to profl. jours. Dist. commr. Boy Scouts Am., Portland, Oreg., 1987, mem. troop com. troop 608, La Crescenta, 1997. Capt. U.S. Army, 1964-70, Vietnam. Recipient dist. award of merit Boy Scouts Am., Honolulu, 1985. Fellow Nat. Contract Mgmt. Assn. (cert., chpt. pres. 1997—); mem. Nat. Assn. Purchasing Mgmt. (cert., nat. officer 1992—). Avocations: skiing, hiking, camping, chess. Home and Office: Paperless PMB 101325 PO Box 7334 San Francisco CA 94120-7334

GRAWITCH, MATTHEW J., researcher, educator; b. Belleville, Ill., Dec. 16, 1975; s. Joseph Grawitch and Eileen M Cason; m. Kristie M. Ailshire, July 26, 2003; children: Lyric N. Ailshire, Hope J. BA, St. Louis U., 1999, MS, 2001. Rschr. St. Louis U., 2000—04, orgnl. cons., 2000—, adj. faculty, 2001—, asst. prof. rsch., 2004—. Recipient Olson award, Dept. of Psychology, St. Louis U., 2001, 2004, Nick J. Colarelli award, 2004. Mem.: Acad. Mgmt., Gateway Indsl. and Orgnl. Psychologists, APA, Soc. for Indsl. and Orgnl. Psychology. Office: Saint Louis U 3511 Laclede Ave Saint Louis MO 63103-2010 Personal E-mail: grawitch@netwitz.net. Business E-Mail: grawitch@slu.edu.

GRAY, ALFRED ORREN, retired journalism educator; b. Sun Prairie, Wis., Sept. 8, 1914; s. Charles Orren and Amelia Katherine (Schadel) G.; m. Nicolin Jane Plank, Sept. 5, 1947; children— Robin, Richard BA, U. Wis.-Madison, 1939, MA, 1941. Reporter-correspondent-intern U. Wis.-Madison and Medford newspapers, 1937-39; free-lance writer, 1938-41, 51-57; intelligence investigator U.S. Ordnance Dept., Ravenna, Ohio, 1941-42; hist. editor, chief writer U.S. Ordnance Service, ETO, Paris and Frankfurt, Germany, 1944-46; asst. prof. journalism Whitworth Coll., Spokane, Wash., 1946-48, assoc. prof., 1948-56, head dept. journalism, adviser student publs., 1946-80, prof., 1956-80, prof. emeritus, 1980—, chmn. div. bus. and communications arts, 1958-66, chmn. div. applied arts, 1978-79; rschr. writer Spokane, 1980—; dir. Whitworth News Bur., 1952-58. Prin. researcher, writer 12 hist. and ednl. projects. Author: The History of U.S. Ordnance Service in the European Theater of Operations, 1942-46, Not by Might, 1965, Eight Generations From Gondelsheim: A Genealogical Study, 1980; co-author: Many Lamps, One Light: A Centennial History, 1984; editor: The Synod Story, 1953-55; mem. editl. adv. bd. Whitworth Today mag., 1989-90; contbr. articles to newspapers, mags., jours.; reader Am. Presbyns.: The Jour. of Presbyn. History, 1992-94. Scoutmaster Troop 9, Four Lakes Coun., Boy Scouts Am., Madison, Wis., 1937-41; chmn. Pinewood Addition Archtl. Com., Spokane, 1956—; dir. Inland Empire Publs. Clinic, Spokane, 1959-74; mem. ho. of dels. Greater Spokane Council of Chs., 1968-71; judge Goodwill Worker of Yr. awards Goodwill Industries Spokane County, 1972; vice-moderator Synod Wash.-Alaska, Presbyn. Ch. (U.S.A.), 1966-67; bd. dirs. Presbyn. Hist. Soc., 1984-90, 91-94, exec. com., 1986-90, chmn. hist. sites com., 1986-90; mem. Am. Bd. Mission Heritage Commn. for Sesquicentennial of Whitman Mission, 1986; elder Spokane 1st Presbyn. Ch., 1962—, clk. of session, 1984-86, mem. Inland Empire Presbytery Com. for Bicentennial of Gen. Assembly, 1988-89; mem. com. justice and peacemaking Presbytery of the Inland Northwest, 1988-95; mem. Care and Equipping of Congregations Com., 1995-2000; Dem. precinct official, Spokane, 1988-92. Served with AUS, 1942-46. Decorated Bronze Star and Army Commendation medals; recipient citation Nat. Coun. Coll. Publ. Advisers, 1967, Outstanding Teaching of Journalism award Whitworth Coll. Alumni Assn., 1972; named Disting. Newspaper Adviser in U.S. among colleges and univs., Nat. Coun. Coll. Publ. Advisers, 1979. Mem. Assn. for Edn. in Journalism and Mass Comms., Ea. Wash. Hist. Soc., Coll. Media Advisors (hon.), N.Am. Mycol. Assn., U. Wis. Alumni Assn. Half Century Club, Phi Beta Kappa (pres. profl. chpt. 1949-50, 67-68, 70-71), Sigma Delta Chi, Phi Eta Sigma. Democrat. Avocations: genealogy, travel. Home: 101 E Hawthorne Rd B-8 Spokane WA 99218

GRAY, ALLEN (ERNEST BUNGAARD), communications executive; b. Council Bluffs, Iowa, Nov. 13, 1920; s. Jeppe and Martha (Petersen) Bundgaard; m. Mary Lee Burden; children; Bruce Burden, Kurt Jepson, Robert Lee. BA in Speech and Radio Broadcasting, U. Iowa, 1943. Announcer Sta. KFAB, Omaha, 1947-50; dir. Housewives Protective League Sta. WCCO (CBS), Mpls., 1951-58, Sta. WCBS, N.Y.C., 1959-63; owner Food Brockerage Co., Mpls., 1963-71; freelance broadcaster, creator Coffee Breaks various stas., Mpls., 1971-77; owner Advt. Agy., Mpls., 1978-84; owner, founder, chmn. bd. Lakes Broadcasting Group, Sta. KLKS-FM, Breezy Point, Minn., 1984—. Author: The Lore of Uncle Fogy, 1971; creator, dir.: (cassette) Uncle Fogy's Bird Calls, 1974, (album) Nature's Choir, 1979. Founder Uncle Fogy Conservation Found., Mpls., 1973, hon. chmn. for life, 1983—. 1st lt. inf. U.S. Army, 1943—46, ETO. Recipient Minn. Pioneer Broadcaster of Yr. award Minn. Broadcasters Assn., 1997; inducted into Pavek Mus. Broadcasters Hall of Fame, 2001. Mem.: Pres. Club U. Iowa, he 1847 Soc. U. Iowa. Avocation: outdoor activities. Home: PO Box 300 Pequot Lakes MN 56472-0300 Office: Sta KLKS-FM PO Box 300 Pequot Lakes MN 56472-0300

GRAY, ANTHONY ROLLIN, retired finance company executive; b. Des Moines, Nov. 26, 1939; s. James W. and Pauline (Frink) G.; m. Janet Eicher, June 26, 1971 (div. Mar. 1987); m. Barbara Lacey Whittaker, June 14, 1991. BA, Grinnell Coll., 1961; MS, U. Iowa, 1963. Securities analyst Lincoln Nat. Life Ins. Co., Ft. Wayne, Ind., 1966—69; dir. rsch. 1st Wis. Trust, Milw., 1969—71; chief investment officer Oak Park (Ill.) Trust, 1971—74; asst. v.p. Union Ctrl. Life Ins. Co., Cin., 1974—79; dir. rsch. Sun Banks, Orlando, Fla., 1979—85; past pres. Sun Bank Capital Mgmt. Co., Orlando, past chmn. bd., CEO, 1985—2000; ret., 2002. Founder, ptnr. Graybeard Capital LLC, 2002—. Capt. USPHS, 1963-66. Avocations: biking, golf. Office: Graybeard Capital LLC 1211 Orange Ave #101 Winter Park FL 32789 Office Phone: 407-622-5925.

GRAY, ARCHIBALD DUNCAN, JR., lawyer; b. Houston, July 12, 1938; s. Archibald Duncan and Lucie (Hill) G.; m. Suzanne Curtis, July 27, 1963 (div. Nov. 1978); 1 child, Archibald Duncan III; m. Nina Carol Wheeley, June 9, 1984; children: Matthew Hill, Joseph Sharp, Michael Branch. AB with distinction, Dartmouth Coll., 1960; JD, U. Mich., 1963; LLM in Taxation, NYU, 1964. Bar: Tex. 1963, U.S. Dist. Ct. (so. dist.) Tex. 1968, U.S. Ct. Appeals (5th cir.) 1976, Colo. 1982. Assoc. Baker & Botts, Houston, 1964-72; gen. atty. Pennzoil Co., Houston, 1972-74, v.p., 1977-79, Pennzoil Producing Co., Houston, 1974-79; of counsel Ireland, Stapleton, Pryor & Pascoe, Denver, 1981; ptnr. Mayer, Brown & Platt, Denver, 1981-82, ptnr. in charge Houston, 1982-96, ptnr., 1982-97; also sr. mgmt. com., 1992-96; co-founder, ptnr. Baker & McKenzie, Houston, 1997-2000; ptnr. King & Spalding, Houston, 2000—. Mem. ABA, Colo. Bar Assn., Tex. Bar Assn., Houston Bar Assn. Clubs: Houston Country, Houston, Cherry Hills Country (Denver), Hills Country Club (Austin). Republican. Methodist. Avocations: golf, hunting, skiing. Home: 6046 Riverview Way Houston TX 77057-1450 Office: King & Spalding 1100 Louisiana St Ste 4000 Houston TX 77002-5219 E-mail: duncangray@kslaw.com.

GRAY, ARLENE, music educator, musician; b. The Dalles, Oreg., Dec. 15, 1948; d. Irving Bernard and Sarah Grace (Adamson) Elle; m. David Leroy Gray, Oct. 20, 1972; children: Mark, Stephanie, Brian, Timothy. BS in Elem. Edn., Oreg. State U., 1970; BA in Music Performance, U. Mary, 1994. Tchr. kindergarten, Fairview, Mont., 1972; pvt. piano tchr. Mandan, ND, 1973—, Bismarck, ND. Coll. choir accompanist Bismarck State Coll., ND, 1994—2003, tchr. piano and organ, 1998—. Chair Piano Guild, Bismarck, 1987—; organist Presby. Ch., Mandan, 1982—98. P.E.O. grantee, 1992, Profl. Devel. grante, N.D. Coun. on Arts, 2004—05. Mem.: Jr. Fed. Music Club (chmn. The Playing Keys 1980—), ND Fed. of Music Clubs, Nat. Fed. of Music Clubs, N.D. Music Tchrs. Assn. (sec. 1996—98, chmn. state conv. 1997, co-chmn. 2003, chmn. state conv. 2003), Am. Coll. Musicians (chmn. 1987—, judge 1997—), Am. Guild Organists, Nat. Music Tchrs. Assn. (state bd. dirs.). Avocations: reading, gardening, swimming. Home: 4525 Camden Loop Bismarck ND 58503 Office: Bismarck State Coll 1500 Edwards Ave Bismarck ND 58501 Office Phone: 701-224-5510. Business E-Mail: Arlene.Gray@bsc.nodak.edu.

GRAY, BARBARA BRONSON, nurse, foundation administrator, writer, public relations executive; b. Van Nuys, Calif., June 3, 1955; d. Gerald M. and Jane Marie (Strauss) Bronson; m. Thomas Stephen Gray, Aug. 27, 1977; children: Jonathan Thomas, Katherine Marie. BS, UCLA, 1977, M in Nursing, 1981. RN, Calif. Staff nurse Valley Presbyn. Hosp., Van Nuys, Calif., 1977—80; asst. adminstr. Calif. Med. Ctr., L.A., 1981—84; freelance writer Oak Park, 1984—96; exec. dir. Nurseweek, 1995—96, editor-in-chief, 1996—99; mng. editor WebMD Corp., Atlanta, 1999—2000; sr. mgr. found. and cmty. affairs Amgen, 2000—02, assoc. dir. corp. comm., 2002—03; prin. Barbara Bronson Gray Comms., 2003—. Cons. St. John's Hosp. and Health Ctr., Santa Monica, Calif., 1986-90, Los Robles Regional Med. Ctr., Thousand Oaks, Calif., 1993-95; lectr. UCLA Sch. Nursing, 1991-98, asst. clin. prof., 1998—. Author: 120 Years of Medicine in Los Angeles County, 1991; contbr. articles to jours., mags. and newspapers; syndicated by L.A. Times Syndicate. Mem. City of Thousand Oaks Mayor's Bus. Roundtable, 2001—02; Bishop's com. Ch. of the Epiphany, Oak Park, Calif., 2002—03; bd. dirs. New West Symphony, 2001—, Ventura County Econ. Devel. Assn., Conejo/Las Virgenes Futures Found., 2001—02, Sr. Concerns, 2001—02, Boys and Girls Clubs Conejo's Las Virgenes, 2002—. Named Writer of Yr., Nurseweek, 1991; recipient Outstanding Achievement award, Perinatal Network, Santa Clara County, Calif., 1994, Prism award, Pub. Rels. Soc. Am., L.A. chpt., 2004, Mktg. and Comms. award, Boys & Girls Clubs Am., 2005; Kellogg fellow, 1979—81. Mem. Nat. Assn. Sci. Writers, Am. Orgn. Nurse Execs., Assn. Calif. Nurse Leaders (bd. dirs. 1999-2001, Leadership award 1999), Valley Industry Commerce Assn. (bd. dirs. 2000-2002), Westlake/Thousand Oaks C. of C. (bd. dirs. 2001-2002), Sigma Theta Tau (Cert. of Appreciation 1994, Internat. Media award 1995). Republican. Avocations: swimming, hiking, kayaking. Office Phone: 818-889-5415. Personal E-mail: bbgray@sbcglobal.net.

GRAY, BRADFORD HITCH, public health service officer, researcher; b. Greenwich, Conn., Dec. 31, 1942; s. John Bradford and Joyce (Hitch) G.; m. Anne Morgan, Aug. 6, 1966 (div. 1980); children: Carrie Elizabeth, Joshua Bradford; m. Helen Darling, Jan. 15, 1983. BS, Okla. State U., 1964; PhD, Yale U., 1973. Asst. prof. U. N.C., Chapel Hill, 1971-74; staff sociologist Nat. Commn. for the Protection of Human Subjects of Rsch., Washington, 1975-77; study dir. Inst. of Medicine NAS, Washington, 1977-88; prof. pub. health Yale Sch. Medicine, New Haven, 1989-96; exec. dir. Program on Non-Profit Orgns. Yale U., New Haven, 1989-96, dir. Inst. for Social and Policy Studies, 1992-96; dir. divsn. health and sci. policy N.Y. Acad. Medicine, N.Y.C., 1996—2004; prin. rsch. assoc. Urban Inst., Washington, 2004—. Author: Human Subjects in Medical Experimentation, 1975, The Profit Motive and Patient Care, 1991; editor: New Health Care for Profit, 1983, For-Profit Enterprise in Health Care, 1986. Grantee Lilly Endowment, Indpls., 1990, Ford Found., N.Y., 1989, Rockefeller Bros. Fund, N.Y., 1989, Robert Wood Johnson Found., 1989, 93, 96, Commonwealth Fund, 1997. Mem.: Inst. of Medicine, Grolier Club, Yale Club of N.Y. Office: Urban Inst 2100 M St NW Washington DC 20037 Home: 1648 32nd St NW Washington DC 20007

GRAY, C. BOYDEN (CLAYLAND BOYDEN GRAY), lawyer; b. Winston-Salem, N.C., Feb. 6, 1943; s. Gordon and Jane (Craige) G. BA in History magna cum laude, Harvard U., 1964; JD with high honors, U. N.C., 1968. Bar: D.C. 1970, N.C. Law clk. to Chief Justice Earl Warren US Supreme Ct., Washington, 1968; assoc. Wilmer Cutler Pickering LLP, Washington, 1969, ptnr., 1976-81, 1993—; legal counsel & dep. chief of staff to v.p. The White House, Washington, 1981-85, counselor to v.p., 1985-89, counsel to the Pres., 1989-93. Chmn. Citizens for a Sound Economy, 1993—, Summit Comms., Inc., Atlanta, 1982-89. Mem. com. to visit coll. and com. on univ. devel., Harvard U. With USMC, 1964-70. Mem. ABA (chmn. adminstrv. law and regulatory practice sect. 2001-02), D.C. Bar Assn., N.C. Bar Assn., Fed. Bar Assn., Met. Club, Chevy Chase Club, Alibi Club. Republican. Episcopalian. Home: 1534 28th St NW Washington DC 20007-3058 Office: Wilmer Cutler Pickering LLP 2445 M St NW Ste 9NW Washington DC 20037-1487

GRAY, CAMPBELL, museum director; Art degree, City Art Inst., Sydney Coll. Advanced Edn., Alexander Mackie Coll. Advanced Edn.; PhD in art hist., U. Sussex, Eng. Faculty mem., coord. postgraduate studies visual arts & art hist. U. Western Sydney; dir. Brigham Young U. Mus. Art, Provo, Utah, 1996—. Office: Mus Art Brigham Young U Provo UT 84602*

GRAY, CARLOS GIBSON, restaurant manager, agricultural products supplier, entertainer, television producer; b. Shelbyville, Ind., Sept. 5, 1937; s. Gibson Tull and Edna Frances (Wicker) G.; m. Elizabeth Vivian Stickrod, Aug. 30, 1959 (div. 1971); children: Carla Elizabeth Christine Gray Stokes, Zarrell Thomas Gibson Gray; m. Carolyn June Breeden, 1971. BSEE, Purdue U., 1960. Cert. secondary tchr. Ind. Tchr. math. Reynolds H.S., Ind., 1960—61, Jefferson H.S., Lafayette, Ind., 1961—63, Warren Ctrl. H.S., Indpls., 1963—64; sys. engr. IBM, Indpls., 1964—67, mktg. rep., 1967—69; asst. v.p., mgr. data processing Aero Mayflower Transit Co., Indpls., 1969—74; asst. v.p. application devel. Ind. Nat. Bank, Indpls., 1974—76; co-owner Gray's Seed, Inc., Fairland, Ind., 1976—; owner Boggstown Inn and Cabaret-TDCC, Corp., Ind., 1984—99; co-owner Jacray Corp., 1994—98, Branson Stage Theatre Corp., 1996—97; owner, dir. Ind. Receptive Co., 1998—2002. Data processing cons. Meth. Hosp., Indpls., 1968, Ford Motor Corp., Dearborn, Mich., 1967, Army, Naval Class of Indsl. Coll. Nat. Security, Indpls., 1967; pilot Angel Flights. Ragtime music video and audio cassettes This is Boggstown, 1986; prodr., dir. Ragtime Lil & Banjo-Banjo, Branson, Mo., 1994-97. Active Hoosier Internat. Ragtime Soc. (developed home for preservation and promotion of Am.'s ragtime music), Boggstown, 1986, U.S. C.G. Aux., 2003. Mem. Fretted Instrument Guild Am., Exptl. Aircraft Assn., Purdue Pilots, Inc. (pres. 1959-60), Angel Flight Avocations: multi-engine, instrument rated pilot, scuba diving, entertaining. Home: 2410 Palo Duro Blvd Herons Glen North Fort Myers FL 33917 E-mail: carlos@swfla.rr.com.

GRAY, CHARLES AUGUSTUS, banker; b. Syracuse, N.Y., Sept. 16, 1928; s. Charles William and Elizabeth Marie (Koch) G. Cert., Am. Inst. Banking, 1958, Sch. Bank Adminstrn., 1961. Cert. internal auditor. With Mchts. Nat. Bank & Trust Co. of Syracuse, 1946-77, auditor, 1959-77, v.p., 1970-77; N.Y. State dir. Bank Adminstrn. Inst., 1970-72; regional auditor cen. N.Y. region Irving Bank Corp., 1977-82, v.p. cen. N.Y. region, 1982-89. Author: A History of Brantingham, 2000. Treas. Upper N.Y. Synod, Luth. Ch. in Am., 1966-87, Upstate N.Y. Synod, Evang. Luth. Ch. in Am., 1988-2002, Meml. Masonic Temple Corp., 1996—, Luth. Found. Upstate N.Y., 1977-78, bd. dirs., 1980—; pres. Interfrat. Alumni Coun., Syracuse U., 1980-83; treas. N.Y. State Coun. Deliberation, 1997—. Mem. Bank Adminstrn. Inst. (pres. central N.Y. chpt. 1970-72), Inst. Internal Auditors (treas. cen. N.Y. chpt. 1974-76, pres. 1985-86), Lions (pres. local club 1973-75), Masons, Shriners. Republican. Home and Office: 1321 Westmoreland Ave Syracuse NY 13210-3436

GRAY, CHARLES ELMER, lawyer, rancher, investor; b. Elvins, Mo., July 23, 1919; s. Grover P. and Martha Elizabeth (Sullivan) G.; m. Beulah Henrich Gray, July 4, 1942; children— Karen Lee, Cecilia Jean, Bette Sue, Marsha Dawn. Student, Flat River Jr. Coll., 1937-38, U. Hawaii, 1940-41; LL.B., Washington U., St. Louis, 1947. Bar: Mo. 1947. Pvt. practice, St. Louis, 1947—; ptnr. Gray and Ritter. Gen. counsel, dir. United Mo. Bank, St Louis; mem. Mo. Appellate Jud. Commn.; mem. rules com. Supreme Ct. Mo., 1970-81 Served to capt. USAF, 1939-45. Fellow Internat. Acad. Trial Lawyers (dir.), Am. Coll. Trial Lawyers, Internat. Soc. Barristers (state chmn., dir.); mem. ABA, Mo. Bar Assn., St. Louis Bar Assn., Lawyers Assn. St. Louis (v.p. 1954, bd. govs., Honor award 1977), Harbour Ridge Yacht Club (commodore 1991-92), Phi Delta Phi. Home: PO Box 709 Farmington MO 63640-0709 Office: Gateway One on the Mall 701 Market St Fl 8 Saint Louis MO 63101-1850 also: Apt 312 4800 Highway A1A Vero Beach FL 32963 Personal E-mail: cgray34957@aol.com.

GRAY, CHARLES ROBERT, lawyer; b. Kirksville, Mo., Aug. 22, 1952; s. George Devon and Bettie Louise (McCormick) G.; m. Dana Elizabeth Kehr, June 1, 1974; children: Jennifer, Jessica, Marcus, Gregory, Victoria. BS, N.E. Mo. State U., 1974; JD, U. Mo., Kansas City, 1978. Bar: Mo. 1978, Va. 1993, U.S. Dist. Ct. (we. dist.) Mo. 1978, U.S. Ct. Appeals (fed. cir.) 1992, U.S. Ct. Appeals (4th cir.) 1995, U.S. Supreme Ct. 1981; cert. mediator; cert. hearing officer Va. Supereme Ct., 1997. Pvt. practice, Parkville, Mo., 1978-81; asst. pub. defender 5th Jud. Cir. Ct. Mo., St. Joseph, 1978-79; pub. defender 6th Jud. Cir. Ct. Mo., Platte City, 1981; asst. dist. counsel Army Corps of Engrs., Kansas City, 1981-82, Vicksburg, Miss., 1982-83; chief counsel space shuttle, MX missile U.S. Army, Vandenberg AFB, Calif., 1983-85, chief counsel troop support agy. Ft. Lee, Va., 1985-87; fraud counsel Def. Gen. Supply Ctr. Dept. of Def., Richmond, Va., 1987-93; pvt. practice, Chester, Va., 1993-99; asst. atty. gen. Atty. Gen.'s Office State of Va., 1999—; owner Pvt. Jud. Svcs., Inc., Chester, 1993—. Adj. prof. St. Leo Coll., Ft. Lee, 1986-91, John Tyler Coll., Chester, Va., 1994—; mem. dispute resolution coun. VA, 2002, mem. adv. oversite panel. Mem. Selective Svc. Draft Bd., Brookfield, Mo., 1972-74; pres. Old Towne Parkville Assn., 1979-81, Chester (Va.) Youth Sports Boosters, 1989-91; den leader Boy Scouts Am., Chester, 1991—. Victor Wilson honor scholar, 1977; recipient Am. Jurisprudence award Coop-Bancroft-Whitney, 1989. Mem. ATLA, Am. Arbitration Assn. (mem. nat. panel arbitrators 1994—, mem. govt. disputes panel 1995—, mem. constrn. panel 1995—, mem. comml. panel 1995—), Def. Rsch. Inst. (approved mem. panel on mediation and arbitration), Mo. Bar Assn., Va. Bar Assn., Va. Trial Lawyers Assn. Methodist. Avocations: coaching youth sports, cub scouts, softball, tennis, basketball. Home: 3813 Terjo Ln Chester VA 23831-1839 Office: Pres Presiding Ofcl PO Box 34386 Chester VA 23834 Office Phone: 804-786-7372. E-mail: cgray@oag.state.va.us.

GRAY, DAVID LAWRENCE, retired air force officer; b. Portland, Oreg., Aug. 19, 1930; s. Thomas Graham and Helen Lee (Brown) G.; m. Nelda Joyce Ryan, Nov. 17, 1951 (dec. June 1987); children: David Scott, Vicki

Lynn, Steven Mark; m. Patricia F. Umstead, Mar. 22, 1991. BS, U. Colo., 1958; MBA, George Washington U., 1962. Registered rep. United Services Planning Assn. & Ind. Research Agy., Montgomery, Ala., 1982-83, dist. agt. Charleston, S.C., 1983-86; exec. dir. Air Force Assn., Arlington, Va., 1986-87. Host: TV talk show Def. Issues, 1982-83 Exec. dir. Air War Coll. Found., 1982-94. Maj. gen. USAF, 1951-82; Korea, Vietnam. Mem. Air Force Assn. (pres. Charleston chpt. 1985-86, nat. exec. dir. 1986-87), Daedallians. Republican. Avocations: golf, boating. E-mail: dgray3@cfl.rr.com.

GRAY, DEBBIE L., music educator; b. Independence, Mo., Mar. 7, 1956; d. Thurman L. and Alice F. Smithee; m. Mike Gray, Nov. 17, 1979; children: Micah, Jessica. BME, U. Mo., Kansas City, 1979; M in Tchg., Webster U., 1988. Lifetime cert. music edn. K-12 band and vocal Kans., Mo. Tchr. music Blue Springs (Mo.) Sch. Dist., 1980—. Workshop presenter; performer, entertainer USO, 1977, 79. Author: These Tricks Are for Kids, 2004; vocal dir. (children's album) Sniggles, Squirrels and Chicken Pox, vocal talent (commls.) Toastmaster, Mo. Tourism, Country Club Plz., Blockbuster Video. Mem. tchr. edn. adv. com. U. Mo., Kansas City, 2002—; team mem. Critical Incident Stress Mgmt., Blue Springs, 2001—. Named a Disney Tchr. of Yr., 1999, 2000, 2002. Mem.: mO. mUSIC eDUCATORS, Mo. State Tchrs. Assn., Music Educators Nat. Conf. (del. 1980—), Sports Car Club Am., Delta Kappa Gamma. Republican. Avocations: writing, reading. Home: 2112 SW 22d Terr Blue Springs MO 64015 Office Phone: 816-224-1335.

GRAY, DOLORES, author; b. Chgo., Apr. 11, 1941; d. Mitchell and Leah (Weiner) Ruda; m. Joseph LaRue Gray, Jan. 14, 1963; children: Jason David, Jonathan Spencer Stedman. BA with hons., Mich. State U., 1963; MA, Ohio State U., 1968; MRC, Bowling Green State U., 1981. Author: The Sitter's Survival Manual, 1971; contbr. numerous articles to profl. jours.; author rev. Jour. of Neurology, 1988. Mem. Nat. League Am. Pen Women, AAUW. Avocations: art, music.

GRAY, DONALD MELVIN, molecular and cell biology educator; b. Milton, Pa., Apr. 4, 1938; s. Harry Seal and Edith Sophia (Larrison) G.; m. Carla Christine Winlund, Sept. 10, 1970. BA, Susquehanna U., 1960; MS, Yale U., 1963, PhD, 1967. Postdoctoral fellow U. Calif., Berkeley, 1967—70; asst. prof. molecular and cell biology U. Tex. at Dallas, Richardson, 1970—76, assoc. prof., 1976—83, prof., 1983—, program head, 1989—95, 2004—. Contbr. articles to profl. jours. Fogarty Sr. Internat. fellow European Molecular Biology Lab., Heidelberg, Fed. Republic of Germany, 1977-78; NIH grantee U. Tex. at Dallas, 1972-93, NSF grantee, 1994-98, Welch Found. grantee, 1972—. Fellow AAAS; mem. Am. Chem. Soc., Biophys. Soc. Office: Univ Tex at Dallas Molecular and Cell Biology PO Box 830688 Richardson TX 75083-0688

GRAY, DOROTHY LOUISE ALLMAN POLLET, librarian; b. Billings, Mont., Dec. 17, 1945; d. Lee F. and Ruth H. (Behner) Allman; m. Michael Haslam Gray, Aug. 11, 1980; children: M. Alexander, Timothy Haslam. BA, U. Colo., 1969; MSLS, Syracuse U., 1972. Reference libr., bibliographer Libr. of Congress Div. Blind and Physically Handicapped, Washington, 1972-75; reference specialist Libr. of Congress Gen. Reference and Bibliography Div., Washington, 1975-77; ednl. liaison officer nat. programs Libr. of Congress, Washington, 1977-82; rsch. assoc. Nat. Commn. on Librs. and Info. Sci., Washington, 1982-88; info. ctr. mgr. Nat. Assn. Inveterate and Obdurate Politicos, Arlington, Va., 1988-92; libr. dir. Nat. Sch. Bds. Assn., Alexandria, Va., 1992—. Editor: Sign Systems for Libraries, 1979; editor Leads, the newsletter of Internat. Rels. Roundtable, ALA, 1979-82; cons. editor: The Bowker Annual of Library and Book Trade Information, 1986-88. Recipient Superior Svc. award Libr. of Congress, Washington, 1981. Mem. ALA, CEC, Spl. Librs. Assn. Avocations: music, calligraphy. Office: Nat Sch Bds Assn 1680 Duke St Ste 100 Alexandria VA 22314-3455

GRAY, DOUGLAS D., child and adolescent psychiatrist; b. Dickinson, N.D., Mar. 18, 1955; s. Darrold and Darlene Gray; m. Anne S. Stouffer, Nov. 26, 1983; children: Stacy, Matthew, Melissa. BS in Bioengring., U. Colo., 1978, MD, 1985. Diplomate Am. Bd. Psychiatry with subspecialty in child and adolescent psychiatry. Intern in pediat. U. Utah, Salt Lake City, 1985—86, resident in child psychiatry, 1986—88; resident in gen. psychiatry U. Colo., 1988—90; med. dir. Primary Children's Ctr. Counseling, Salt Lake City, 1990—98; med. dir. child and adolescent psychiatry Nelson, New Zealand, 1998—99; dir. Splty. Clinic, U. Utah, Salt Lake City, 1999—, residency tng. dir. child psychiatry programs and triple bd. program, 1999—. Assoc. clin. prof. medicine U. Utah, 1990—; prin. investigator Utah Youth Suicide Stidy, Salt Lake City, 1994—; chmn. Utah Youth Suicide Prevention Task Force, Salt Lake City, 1997—; cons. in field. Contbr. articles to profl. jours. Mem. adv. coun. Allies for Families, Salt Lake City, 1993—94. Named one of Best Pediat. Drs. in Salt Lake City, Salt Lake Mag., 2000, Best Doctors, Best Drs. Inc., 2001; recipient Ebaugh award, U. Colo. Med. Sch., 1985. Mem.: Am. Acad. Child and Adolescent Psychiatry, Nat. Alliance for the Mentally Ill, Am. Assn. of Suicidology. Avocations: skiing, hiking, basketball, music, art. Office: 650 S Komas Dr Ste 208 Salt Lake City UT 84108 Office Phone: 801-585-1212.

GRAY, D'WAYNE, retired marine corps officer; b. Navarro County, Tex., Apr. 9, 1931; s. Henry Oliver and Myrtle Daisy (Lee) G.; m. Mary Joan Sobieck, Oct. 11, 1955; children: Stephen D'Wayne, Elizabeth Joan Gray Hendrickson, Theresa Mary Gray Croghan. Student, N. Tex. Agrl. Coll., 1948-49; BA, U. Tex., 1952; MS in Internat. Affairs, George Washington U., 1971; postgrad., Naval War Coll., 1970-71, Harvard U., 1980. Commd. 2d lt. USMC, 1952, advanced through grades to lt. gen., 1983; combat svc. in Korea, 1953, in Vietnam, 1965, 71-72; asst. div. comdr. 1st Marine Div. Camp Pendleton, Calif., 1977-79; dir. plans Hdqrs. Washington, 1979-80; dir. ops. Hdqrs., 1980-81; dir. personnel mgmt. Hdqrs., 1981-83; chief of staff Hdqrs., 1983-85; comdg. gen. Fleet Marine Force, Pacific; comdr. Marine Corps Bases, Pacific, Camp H.M. Smith, Hawaii, 1985-87; ret., 1987; ind. cons., 1987-89; exec. dir. Montgomery County Revenue Authority, Rockville, Md., 1989-90; undersec. veterans affairs for benefits Dept. Vet. Affairs, Washington, 1990-93. Chmn. bd. dirs. TROA EdPlus, Inc., Alexandria, Va., 2000—; del. Inter-Am. Def. Bd., 1980; bd. dirs. U.S. Naval Inst., 1980-85; mem. bd. govs. Uniformed Svcs. Benefit Assn. Kansas City, 1982-83, 85-88; mem. sec. of state's Adv. Panel on Overseas Security, 1984-85. Chmn. editorial bd., U.S. Naval Inst., 1980-83. Mem. maritime policy study group Ctr. for Strategic and Internat. Studies, Georgetown U., 1981-85. Decorated D.S.M., Legion of Merit with gold star and V, Bronze Star medal with V, Meritorious Svc. medal with gold star, Air medal with bronze numeral 5, Joint Svc. Commendation medal with V, Navy Commendation medal with V. Mem. Marine Corps Assn., U.S. Naval Inst., Marine Corps Heritage Found., Marine Corps Scholarship Found., Mil. Officers Assn. Am. (bd. dirs. 1994-2000, 1st vice chmn. 1998-2000), Cath. War Vets. Roman Catholic. Home: 3423 Barger Dr Falls Church VA 22044-1202 *The military way of life is not for everyone. But, to those for whom it is right, it offers an unequalled opportunity for both personal adventure and service to one's fellow Americans. I wish I could do it all again!.*

GRAY, ELIZABETH VAN DOREN, lawyer; b. Columbia, S.C., Jan. 3, 1949; d. Robert Lawson and Elizabeth Dacus (Gaines) Van Doren; m. James Cranston Gray, Jr., Apr. 30, 1982; children: James Cranston III, Elizabeth Gaines. BA in Internat. Studies, U. S.C., 1970, JD cum laude, 1976; student, St. Mary's Coll., Raleigh, N.C., 1966-67. Bar: S.C. 1977, U.S. Dist. Ct. S.C. 1977, U.S. Ct. Appeals (4th cir.) 1980, U.S. Ct. Appeals (6th cir.) 1989, U.S. Supreme Ct. 1998. Assoc. McNair Law Firm, PA, Columbia, 1977-82, shareholder, 1982-87; ptnr. Glenn Irvin Murphy Gray & Stepp, Columbia, 1987—2000; now ptnr. Sowell Gray Stepp & Lafitte, LLC, Columbia. Contbr. articles to profl. jours. Mem. ABA, Am. Coll. Trial Lawyers, John Belton O'Neal Inn of Ct., S.C. Bar (pres. 2001-02), S.C. Women Lawyers Assn. (bd. dirs. 1995-99, sec. 1997-98), Richland County Bar Assn. Episcopalian. Office: Sowell Gray Stepp & Lafitte LLC PO Box 11449 Columbia SC 29211 Home: 8 Mahalo Ln Columbia SC 29204-3380

GRAY, FARRAH, entrepreneur, writer; Co-host Backstage Live radio show, Las Vegas; founder Farr-Out Foods, NYC, New Early Entrepreneur Wonders; owner INNERCITY mag. Founder Urban Neighborhood Econ. Enterprise Club; cons. Minority Bus. Devel. Agency U.S. Dept. Commerce; bd. dirs. Nat. Assn. Real Estate Brokers, Inc.; spkr. in field. Author: (book) Reallionaire: Nine Steps to Becoming Rich from the Inside Out, 2005; contbg. author: book Chicken Soup for the African-American Soul; guest appearances Good Morning America, Tom Joyner Radio Show, Tavis Smiley Radio Show. Bd. dirs. United Way So. Nev.; bd. advisors Las Vegas C. of C. Achievements include acquiring millionaire status at the age of 14 through 1.5 million in sales of Farr-Out Food product. Office: Farrah Gray Found 67 Wall St Ste 2212 New York NY 10005 also: Farrah Gray Found PO Box 11351 Las Vegas NV 89111-1351 Office Phone: 212-859-5028. Office Fax: 702-926-9662. E-mail: fg@farrajgrayfoundation.org, farrahgray@aol.com.*

GRAY, FESTUS GAIL, electrical engineer, educator, researcher; b. Moundsville, W.Va., Aug. 16, 1943; s. Festus P. and Elsie V. (Rine) G.; m. Caryl Evelyn Anderson, Aug. 24, 1968; children: David, Andrew, Daniel. BSEE, W.Va. U., 1965, MSEE, 1967; PhD, U. Mich., 1971. Instr. W.Va. U., Morgantown, 1966-67; asst. prof. Va. Poly. Inst. and State U., Blacksburg, 1971-77, assoc. prof., 1977-82, prof., 1983—2003, prof. emeritus, 2003—. Vis. scientist Rsch. Triangle Inst., N.C., 1984-85; faculty fellow NASA, 1975; cons. Inland Motors, Radford, Va., 1980, Rsch. Triangle Inst., 1987—; researcher Rome Air Devel. Ctr., N.Y., 1980-81, Naval Surface Weapons Ctr., Dahlgren, Va., 1982-83, Army Rsch. Office, 1983-86, NSF, 1991-93, 98-2001, ARPA, 1993-96, Wright-Patterson AFB, 1995-99; publs. chmn. Internat. Symposium on Fault Tolerant Computing, Ann Arbor, Mich., 1985. Co-author: Structured Logic Design with VHDL, 1993, VHDL Representation and Synthesis, 2d edit., 2000; contbr. articles to sci. jours. Assoc. treas. Northside Presbyn. Ch., Blacksburg, 1986—, bd. deacons, 1980-83; coach S.W. Va. Soccer Assn., Blacksburg, 1980-86; asst. scoutmaster Boy Scouts Am., 1990—. Grantee NSF, Office Naval Rsch., NASA, Adv. Rsch. Projects Agy; Teaching fellow U. Mich., 1967-70. Mem. IEEE (chpt. chmn. 1979-80), Computer Soc. IEEE, Sigma Xi. Democrat. Achievements include research on fault tolerance, diagnosis, testing and reliability issues for VLSI, distributed and multiprocessor computer architectures, modeling and synthesis with VHDL, modeling and design with hardware description languages. Home: 304 Fincastle Dr Blacksburg VA 24060-5036 Office: Va Poly Inst and State U Blacksburg VA 24061-0111

GRAY, FRANCINE DU PLESSIX, author; b. Warsaw; came to U.S., 1941, naturalized, 1952; d. Bertrand Jochaud and Tatiana (Iacovleff) du Plessix; m. Cleve Gray, Apr. 23, 1957; children: Thaddeus Ives, Luke Alexander. BA, Barnard Coll., 1952; Litt.D. (hon.), CUNY, Oberlin Coll., U. Santa Clara, St. Mary's Coll., U. Hartford. Annenberg fellow Brown U., 1997. Disting. vis. prof. CCNY, 1975; vis. lectr. Yale U., New Haven, 1981-82; Ferris prof. Princeton U., 1986; Disting. vis. prof. Vassar Coll., 1999. Author: Divine Disobedience: Profiles in Catholic Radicalism, 1970 (Nat. Cath. Book award), Hawaii: The Sugar-Coated Fortress, 1972, Lovers and Tyrants, 1976, World Without End, 1981, October Blood, 1985, Adam & Eve and the City, 1987, Soviet Women: Walking the Tightrope, 1989, Rage and Fire: A Life of Louise Colet, 1994, At Home with the Marquis de Sade: A Life, 1998, Simone Weil, 2001, Them: A Memoir of Parents, 2005. Guggenheim Found. fellow, 1991-92. Fellow, Am. Acad. Arts & Sci.;mem. Am. P.E.N., Am. Acad. Arts and Letters. Democrat. Roman Catholic.

GRAY, FRANK TRUAN, lawyer; b. Prince Frederick, Md., Oct. 22, 1920; s. John B. and Aimée Atlee (Truan) Gray; m. Sally A. Jackson, Dec. 31, 1976; children: John W., Edward A., Philip L., Theodora R. AB, Princeton U., 1942; student, Cambridge (Eng.) U., 1945; LL.B., Harvard U., 1948. Bar: Md. 1949. Assoc. firm Piper & Marbury, Balt., 1948-56, ptnr., 1957-90. Asst. atty. gen. State Md., 1955—56; pres. Balt. Estate Planning Coun., 1975—76. Editor: Harvard Law Rev., 1947—48. Pres. Citizen's Planning Housing Assn., Balt., 1960—62; bd. dirs. Balt. Neighborhoods, Inc., 1959—85, Balt. Bar Found., 1985—93; trustee Provident Hosp., Inc., 1961—74, Leonard and Helen R. Stulman Charitable Found., 1991—. Fellow: Md. Bar Found., Am. Bar Found. (chmn. Md. 1993—98); mem.: ABA, Balt. Bar Assn., Md. Bar Assn., Am. Law Inst. Office: DLA Piper Rudnick Gray Cary LLP 111 S Calvert St Ste 1950 Baltimore MD 21202-6193

GRAY, FRED DAVID, lawyer; b. Montgomery, Ala., Dec. 14, 1930; s. Abraham and Nancy G.; m. Bernice Hill, June 17, 1956; children: Deborah R., Vanessa, Fred D., Stanley F. BS, Ala. State U., 1951; JD, Case Western Res. U., 1954. Bar: Ala. 1954, Ohio 1954, U.S. Dist. Ct. (mid. dist.) Ala. 1955, U.S. Supreme Ct. 1956, U.S. Ct. Appeals (5th cir.) 1958, U.S. Dist. Ct. (no. dist.) Ala. 1963, U.S. Tax Ct. 1968, U.S. Ct. Appeals (11th cir.) 1982. Sr. ptnr. Gray, Langford, Sapp, McGowan, Gray & Nathanson, Montgomery and Tuskegee, Ala., 1983—. Vis. prof., Charles Hamilton Houston Chair N.C. Central Univ. Sch. of Law, Durham, NC. Author: (book) Bus Ride to Justice, 1995, The Tuskegee Syphilis Study, 1998. City atty. City of Tuskegee, 1965—; cooperating atty. NAACP Legal Def. Fund, Inc.; local gen. counsel Tuskegee U.; spl. asst. to atty. gen. State of Ala., 1975; past mem. Ala. Adv. Com. U.S. Commn. on Civil Rights; mem. Tuskegee Civic Assn. (life, award 1981); elder Tuskegee Ch. of Christ; chmn., trustee Southwestern Christian Coll., Terrell, Tex. Recipient Constl. Law award Ala. Civil Liberties Union, 1968, Disting. Alumni award Ala. State U., 1974, Social Engr.'s citation, 1975, Martin Luther King, Jr. Meml. Drum Major award So. Christian Leadership Conf., 1980, Black Achievers award, Ala. chpt. SCLC 1981, Fletcher Reed Andrews Grad. Yr. award Case Western Res. U., 1985, Man Yr. award Southwestern Christian Coll., 1986, Charles Hamilton Medallion of Merit Washington Bar Assn., 1986; honored by Miller Brewing Co. Gallery of Greats: Black Attys. Counsels for the Cause, 1989. Mem. ABA, Assn. Trial Lawyers Am., Ala. Trial Lawyers Assn., Ala. State Bar Assn. (pres.-elect 2001-02, pres. 2002-03), Nat. Bar Assn. (pres. 1985-86, 1st Ann. Equal Justice award 1977), Macon County Bar Assn. (past pres.), Nat. Bar Inst., NAACP (life), Soc. Benchers, Omega Psi Phi, Sigma Pi Phi. Represented Rosa Parks when she was arrested for not giving up her seat on a Montgomery bus, 1955. Office: Gray Langford et al PO Box 830239 Tuskegee AL 36083-0239 also: 400 S Union St Ste 205 Montgomery AL 36104-4316*

GRAY, FREDERICK THOMAS, JR., (RICK GRAY), journalist, actor, educator; b. Hopewell, Va., Mar. 22, 1951; s. Frederick Thomas and Evelyn (Helms) Johnson Gray. BA with distinction, U. Va., 1972, JD, 1975, MEd, 1990, postgrad., 1991-94, U. Richmond, 1981-82. Bar: Va. 1976. Law clk. Williams, Mullen & Christian, Richmond, Va., 1975-76, assoc., 1976-78; sec. Commonwealth of Va., Richmond, 1978-81; high sch. tchr., 1982—89, 1999—2000, 2002—04; asst. prin., 1991—92; op-ed columnist, 2004—. Appeared in TV series In the Heat of the Night, profl. stage prodns. My Fair Lady, Macbeth, To Kill a Mockingbird, also others. Mem. Va. Dem. state ctrl. com., 2001—; 3d vice-chair Chesterfield County Dem. Com. Mem. SAG, Raven Soc. (U. Va.), Actor's Equity Assn. Address: 4701 Bermuda Hundred Rd Chester VA 23836-3257 Office Phone: 804-530-2231. E-mail: deinikes@yahoo.com.

GRAY, GEORGE TRUMON, test development professional; b. Indpls., June 1, 1946; s. Trumon Lloyd and Helen Louise (McClain) G.; m. Beverly Diane Liebenow, Aug. 24, 1974; children: Elizabeth Diane, Steven Trumon. B in Music Edn., Ind. U., 1968, MS in Edn., 1969, EdD, 1973. Asst. prof. Tenn. Tech. U., Cookeville, 1973-75; coord. Office of Curriculum, Devel. and Evaluation Rush U., Chgo., 1976-80, dir. Office of Curriculum, Devel. and Evaluation, 1980-92; program assoc. health programs dept. Profl. Devel. Svcs. ACT, Iowa City, 1993-94; asst. dir. Health Programs Dept., PDS, ACT, Iowa City, 1994-99, dir., 1999—. R & D com. bd. registry Am. Soc. Clin. Pathologists, Chgo., 1985-91, computer adaptive testing com., 1988-93. Contbr. articles to profl. jours. Mem. Nat. Coun. Measurement in Edn., Am. Ednl. Rsch. Assn. Presbyterian. Office: ACT Inc 2201 N Dodge St Iowa City IA 52243-0001 Office Phone: 319-337-1168. Business E-Mail: george.gray@act.org.

GRAY, GORDON L., communications educator; b. Hampton, Iowa, May 18, 1924; s. Leroy Ernest and Arianna (Oldham) G.; m. Barbara Ann Smith, Feb. 5, 1949; children: David Gordon, Jonathan William. BA, Cornell Coll., 1948; MA, Northwestern U., 1951, PhD, 1957. Radio announcer and newsman, 1948-50; broadcast coordinator NBC-TV, Chgo, 1951; instr. to asso. prof. television and radio Mich. State U., 1953-67; prof. communications Temple U., Phila., 1967-96, prof. emeritus, 1996—, chmn. dept. radio, TV, and Film, 1967-74, 78-82, 1994-95. Program assoc. Ednl. TV and Radio Ctr., Ann Arbor, Mich., 1956-57. Served to staff sgt. AUS, 1943-46. Fulbright scholar Inst. Edn. U. Leeds, U.K., 1965-66

GRAY, HANNA HOLBORN, historian, educator; b. Heidelberg, Germany, Oct. 25, 1930; d. Hajo and Annemarie (Bettmann) Holborn; m. Charles Montgomery Gray, June 19, 1954. AB, Bryn Mawr Coll., 1950; PhD, Harvard U., 1957; MA, Yale U., 1971, LLD, 1978; LittD (hon.), St. Lawrence U., 1974, Oxford (Eng.) U., 1979; LLD (hon.), Dickinson Coll., 1979, U. Notre Dame, 1980, Marquette U., 1984; LittD (hon.), Washington U., 1974; HHD (hon.), St. Mary's Coll., 1974; LHD (hon.), Grinnell (Iowa) Coll., 1974, Lawrence U., 1974, Denison U., 1974, Wheaton Coll., 1976, Marlboro Coll., 1979, Rikkyo (Japan) U., 1979, Roosevelt U., 1980, Knox Coll., 1980, Coe Coll., 1981, Thomas Jefferson U., 1981, Duke U., 1982, New Sch. for Social Research, 1982, Clark U., 1982, Brandeis U., 1983, Colgate U., 1983, Wayne State U., 1984, Miami U., Oxford, Ohio, 1984, So. Meth. U., 1984, CUNY, 1985, U. Denver, 1985, Am. Coll. Greece, 1986, Muskingum Coll., 1987, Rush Presbyn. St. Lukes Med. Ctr., 1987, NYU, 1988, Rosemont Coll., 1988, Claremont U. Ctr. Grad Sch., 1989, Moravian Coll., 1991, Rensselaer Poly. Inst., 1991, Coll. William and Mary, 1991, Centre Coll., 1991, Macalester Coll., 1993, McGill U., 1993, Ind. U., 1994, Med. U. of S.C., 1994; LLD (hon.), Union Coll., 1975, Regis Coll., 1976, Dartmouth Coll., 1978, Trinity Coll., 1978, U. Bridgeport, 1978, Dickinson Coll., 1979, Brown U., 1979, Wittenburg U., 1979, Dickinson Coll., 1979, U. Rochester, 1980, U. Notre Dame, 1980, U. So. Calif., 1980, U. Mich., 1981, Princeton U., 1982, Georgetown U., 1983, Marquette U., 1984, W.Va. Wesleyan U., 1985, Hamilton Coll., 1985, Smith Coll., 1986, U. Miami, 1986, Columbia U., 1987, NYU, 1988, Rosemont Coll., 1988, U. Toronto, Can., 1991; LDH, LHD, Haverford Coll., 1995; LDH (hon.), Tulane U., 1995; LLD, LLD, Harvard U., 1995; LHD (hon.), McGill U., 1993, Macalester Coll., 1993, Ind. U., 1994, Med. U. S.C., 1994, Haverford Coll., 1995, Tulane U., 1995; LLD (hon.), Harvard U., 1995, U. Chgo., 1996. Instr. Bryn Mawr Coll., 1953—54; tchg. fellow Harvard, 1955—57, instr., 1957—59, asst. prof., 1959—60, vis. lectr., 1963—64; asst. prof. U. Chgo., 1961—64, assoc. prof., 1964—72; dean, prof. Northwestern U., Evanston, Ill., 1972—74; provost, prof. history Yale U., 1974—78, acting pres., 1977—78; pres. U. Chgo., 1978—93, prof. dept. history, 1978—, Harry Pratt Judson disting. svc. prof. history, 1994—. Fellow Ctr. for Advanced Study in Behavioral Scis., 1966—67, vis. scholar, 1970—71; vis. prof. U. Calif., Berkeley, Calif., 1970—71. Co-editor (with Charles Gray): Jour. Modern History, 1965—70; contbr. articles to profl. jours. Mem. Nat. Coun.on Humanities, 1972—78; trustee Yale Corp., 1971—74; former mem. bd. regents The Smithsonian Instn.; former chmn. bd. Andrew W. Mellon Found.; mem. Harvard Univ. Corp., 1986—; chmn. bd. Howard Hughes Med. Inst., Marlboro Sch. Music. Named Grosse Verdienstkreuz, Germany; recipient Grad. medal, Radcliffe Coll., 1976, Yale medal, 1978, Medal of Liberty award, 1986, Medal of Freedom, 1991, Frontrunner award, Sara Lee, 1991, Laureate Lincoln Acad. Ill., 1988, Charles Frankel prize, 1993, Centennial medal, Harvard U., 1994, Disting. Svc. award in edn., Inst. Internat. Edn., 1994, Medal of Distinction, Barnard Coll., 2000; fellow Newberry Libr., 1960—61, St. Anne's Coll., Oxford U., 1978—; scholar Fulbright scholar, 1950—51. Fellow: Am. Acad. Arts and Scis.; mem.: Coun. Fgn. Rels. N.Y., Coun. Fgn. Rels. Chgo., Nat. Acad. Edn., Am. Philos. Soc. (Jefferson medal 1993), Renaissance Soc. Am., Phi Beta Kappa (vis. scholar 1971—72). Office: U Chgo Dept History 1126 E 59th St Chicago IL 60637-1580 Business E-Mail: h-gray@uchicago.edu.

GRAY, HARRY BARKUS, chemistry professor; b. Woodburn, Ky., Nov. 14, 1935; s. Barkus and Ruby (Hopper) Gray; m. Shirley Barnes, June 2, 1957; children: Victoria Lynn, Andrew Thomas, Noah Harry Barkus. BS, Western Ky. U., 1957; PhD, Northwestern U., 1960, DSc (hon.), 1984, U. Chgo., 1987, U. Rochester, 1987, U. Paul Sabatier, 1991, U. Göteborg, 1991, U. Firenze, 1993, Columbia U., 1994, Bowling Green State U., 1994, Ill. Wesleyan, 1995, Oberlin Coll., 1996, U. Ariz., 1997, Carleton U., 2001, U. SC, 2003, U. Copenhagen, 2003. Postdoctoral fellow U. Copenhagen, 1960—61; faculty Columbia U., 1961—66, prof., 1965—66; prof. chemistry Calif. Inst. Tech., Pasadena, 1966—, now Arnold O. Beckman prof. chemistry and founding dir. Beckman Inst. Vis. prof. Rockefeller U., Harvard U., U. Iowa, Pa. State U., Yeshiva U., U. Copenhagen, U. Witwatersrand, Johannesburg, South Africa, U. Canterbury, Christchurch, New Zealand, U. Hong Kong; George Eastman prof. Oxford (Eng.) U., 1997—98; cons. govt., industry; Kistiakowsky lectr. Harvard U., 1999. Author: Electrons and Chemical Bonding, 1965, Molecular Orbital Theory, 1965, Ligand Substitution Processes, 1966, Basic Principles of Chemistry, 1967, Chemical Dynamics, 1968, Chemical Principles, 1970, Models in Chemical Science, 1971, Chemical Bonds, 1973, Chemical Structure and Bonding, 1980, Molecular Electronic Structures, 1980, Braving the Elements, 1995. Named Calif. Scientist of Yr., 1988, Achievement Rewards for Coll. Scis. Man of Sci., 1990; recipient Franklin Meml. award, Stanford U., 1967, Fresenius award, Phi Lambda Upsilon, 1970, Shoemaker award, U. Louisville, 1970, award for excellence in tchg., Mfg. Chemists Assn., 1972, Centenary medal, Royal Soc. Chemistry, 1985, Nat. medal of Sci., 1986, Alfred Bader Bioinorganic Chemistry award, 1990, Gold medal, Am. Inst. Chemists, 1990, Linderstrom-Lang prize, 1992, Priestly award, Dickinson Coll., 1991, Chandler medal, Columbia U., 1999, Harvey prize, Technion Israel Inst. Tech., 2000; fellow Guggenheim, 1972—73; scholar Phi Beta Kappa, 1973—74. Fellow: AAAS; mem.: NAS (Nichols medal 2003, award in chem. scis. 2003), Royal Danish Acad. Scis. and Letters, Am. Philos. Soc., Royal Soc. (London), Royal Swedish Acad., Am. Chem. Soc. (award pure chemistry 1970, Harrison Howe award 1972, award inorganic chemistry 1978, Remsen Meml. award 1979, Tolman medal 1979, award for disting. svc. in advancement of inorganic chemistry 1984, Pauling medal 1986, Priestley medal 1991, Willard Gibbs medal 1992, Wolf prize for chemistry 2004, Benjamin Franklin medal in chemistry 2004), Phi Lambda Upsilon, Alpha Chi Sigma. Office: Calif Inst Tech 408 Beckman MC 127-72 1200 E California Blvd Pasadena CA 91125-0001

GRAY, HARRY JOSHUA, retired engineering educator; b. St. Louis, June 24, 1924; s. Harry Joshua and Mary Margaret (Davis) Gray; m. Cecilia M. McNulty, Apr. 23, 1949; children: Margaret, Cecilia, Kathleen(dec.), Mary Ellen. Student, Lehigh U., 1941—43; BSEE, U. Pa., 1944, PhD, 1953. Registered profl. engr., Pa. Instr. Moore Sch. Elec. Engring., U. Pa., Phila., 1947-51, assoc., 1951-53, asst. prof., 1953-54, assoc. prof., 1957-64, prof. elec. engring. and computer and info. sci., 1964-89, prof. emeritus, 1989—. Mem. staff ENIAC, 1947; with Remington Rand Univac, Phila., 1954—57; cons. in field. Author: Digital Computer Engineering, 1963, High Speed Digital Circuits and Memories, 1976; contbr. articles to profl. jours. With USN, 1943—46. Recipient 50th Anniversary medal, ENIAC, 1997; grantee, U.S. Army Electronics Command, 1966—69, NSF, 1966—68, NIMH, 1971—73, Burroughs Corp., 1973—75. Mem.: IEEE (life; mem. profl. groups, mem. EMC group), Phi Eta Sigma, Pi Mu Epsilon, Eta Kappa Nu, Tau Beta Pi, Sigma Xi. Achievements include patents in field.

GRAY, HAZEL IRENE, retired special education educator, counselor, consultant; b. Van Nuys, Calif., July 2, 1921; d. Charles Clayton Cramer and Ida Mae (Leffler); m. Reed A. Gray; children: Mildred Lorene(dec.), Paul Charles; m. Neil Chapin Smith (dec.). BA, San Jose (Calif.) State Coll., 1964, MA, 1968; EdD, U. So. Calif., LA, 1977. Itinerant tchr. hearing impaired Santa Cruz County Office of Edn., 1964—66; resource specialist Santa Cruz Pub. Schools, 1966—68; psychologist Santa Cruz County Office of Edn., 1968—71; psychologist, cons. and parent counselor Project Idea, San Jose, 1971—72; dir. spl. edn. Live Oaks schs. Santa Cruz County Office of Edn., 1972—74; cons. Calif. State Dept. of Edn., Sacramento, 1975—76; adminstr. San Jose City Coll., 1976—78; dir. pupil pers. Campbell Union Sch. Dist., Calif., 1978; pvt. practice marriage counseling, 1971—. Cons. Catholic

Pre-Sch., LA; lectr. Calif. State U, San Jose, U. Calif., Santa Clara, Santa Cruz; with Med. Info. Svcs. Co-author: (book) Behavior Modification, 1971. Mem. rescue Calif. Coast Guard, 1971—76; team mem. marriage family and child counseling license rev. Calif. State Dept. of Licensing, Sacramento. Mem.: San Jose Movie TC Club, Camera Club. Republican. Mem. Lds Ch. Achievements include vis. numerous countries Japan, So. Africa, Israel, Greece, Egypt, England, Can., Ireland, France and Portugal. Avocations: travel, photography, grandchildren.

GRAY, HELEN THERESA GOTT, editor; b. Jersey City, July 2, 1942; d. William E. and Cynthia B. Gott; m. David L. Gray, Aug. 15, 1976; 1 child, David Lee Jr. BA, Syracuse U., 1963; M in Internat. Affairs, Columbia U., 1965. Editor religion sect. The Kansas City (Mo.) Star, 1971—. Tchr. Bible sch. Pleasant Green Bapt. Ch., Kansas City, Kans., 1975—, counselor, 1978—; former owner of a Christian book store. Co-author, editor several books; contbr. articles to profl. jours. Recipient writing award Valley Forge Freedom Found., 1967-97; John Hay Whitney Found. grantee, 1963-64; named 100 Most Influential African Ams. in Greater Kansas City. Mem. Religion Newswriters Assn., Kansas City Assn. Black Journalists (Life Achievement award 1998). Baptist. Office: The Kansas City Star 1729 Grand Blvd Kansas City MO 64108-1458 Office Phone: 816-234-4446. E-mail: hgray@kcstar.com.

GRAY, HOWARD RICHARD, science educator; b. Downey, Idaho, Oct. 5, 1944; s. Elmo Austin and Nadine Dunn Gray; m. Sharon Pearl Reed; children: Austin, Sheridan, Jordan, Mardi. BS, Brigham Young U., 1969, MA, 1970; PhD, Pa. State U., 1977. Asst. exec. dir. Casper (Wyo.) Cmty. Recreation, 1970—72; fellow Pa. State U., State Coll., 1973—75; chmn., asst. prof. Radford (Va.) Coll., 1975—79; asst. prof. Brigham Young U., Provo, Utah, 1979—86, prof. therapeutic recreation and gerontology, 1986—, chmn. recreation dept., 1987—93, dir. gerontology, 1994—98. Co-author: Master Plan Process, 1985 (AAHPERD award, 1985), Leisure Resources, 1999, Feasibility Study Process, 2005 (Phi ta Sigma award, 2005). Pres. Utah Spl. Olympics, 1984, Am. Assn. Leisure and Recreation, Reston, Va., 1992—93, Lions Club, Pleasant Grove, Utah, 2001; amb. Huntsman World Senior Games, St. George, Utah, 1987—2005; internat. client svcs. Salt Lake Winter Olympic Games, Salt Lake City, 2002. With USNG, 1960—68. Recipient Lifelong Learning award, Nat. Art Edn. Assn., 1998; Sr. fellow, Am. Leisure Acad., 1997. Mem.: AAHPERD (v.p.), Brigham Young Gerontology Assn. (exec. com., dir.), Am. Gerontology in Higher Edn. (institutional rep. 1999). Mem. Lds Ch. Avocations: writing, gardening, sports, travel. Home: 288 West 130 South Lindon UT 84042 Office: Brigham Young Univ Ste 273 L RB Provo UT 84602-2024 Office Phone: 801-422-3506. Office Fax: 801-422-0609. Business E-Mail: howard-gray@byu.edu.

GRAY, INA TURNER, fraternal organization administrator; b. Eagleville, Mo., July 25, 1926; d. Farris T. and Teloir (Anderson) Turner; m. Wallace G. Gray Jr., Dec. 18, 1948; children: Toni Jo, Tara Joy. BS with high honors, Cen. Meth. Coll., 1948; MA, Scarritt Coll., 1952; postgrad., U. Hawaii, 1969. Tchr. Rutherford-Met. Sch. Bus., Dallas, 1948-49; dir. Christian edn. 1st Meth. Ch., Lawton, Okla., 1953-54, Winfield, Kans., 1957-58; dir. religious life Southwestern Coll., Winfield, 1958-59; dir. commn. on archives and history Kans. West Conf., Winfield, 1960-78; exec. dir. Pi Gamma Mu, Winfield, 1976-96. English tchr. JoGakuin Jr. High, Hiroshima, Japan, 1971-72, Kitakyushu U., Japan, 1997-98. Mem. editorial bd. Fire on the Prairie, 1961-69; mem. editorial and pub. coms. The Lure of Kansas, 1990. Mem. Cowley County Bd. Dirs., 2004—. Mem. Assn. Coll. Honor Socs. (del. 1986-96), Commn. Archives and History (local Ch. History award 1982—), Kans. State Assn. Parliamentarians (v.p. Walnut Valley unit 1991-92, 99-2000), Faculty Dames (pres. 1981-82). Republican. Avocations: travel, historical research, Japanese flower arranging. Home: 1701 Winfield Ave Winfield KS 67156-1919 Personal E-mail: gray@sckans.edu.

GRAY, JAMES, English literature educator; b. Montrose, Scotland, May 11, 1923; s. James and Matilda (Smythe) G.; m. Pamela Doris Knight, July 26, 1947; 1 child, Caroline Gordon. MA, U. Aberdeen, 1946; BA with honours, U. Oxford, Eng., 1948, MA, 1951; PhD, U. Montreal, 1970. Prof. English Bishops U., Lennoxville, Que., Can., 1948-72, chmn. humanities div., 1971-72; prof., chmn. dept. English Dalhousie U., Halifax, N.S., 1972-75, dean Faculty Arts and Sci., 1975-80, Thomas McCulloch prof. English, 1980-88, prof. emeritus, 1988—. Mem. Humanities Rsch. Coun. Can.; vis. prof. Queen's U., Kingston, Ont., 1955, 70, U. B.C., 1958, Acadia U., 1991. Author: The Sermons of Samuel Johnson: A Study, 1972, Dr. Johnson's French, 1986, Miracles in the 18th Century, 2002, Dr. Johnson's Oxford, 2003; co-editor: The Religious Writings of Samuel Johnson, 1978; mem. editl. bd. Yale U. Press edit. Works of Samuel Johnson, The Age of Johnson; contbr. articles to profl. jours. Served with Brit. and Indian Armies, 1942—46. Recipient Queen Elizabeth II Coronation medal, Jubilee medal. Fellow Royal Soc. Arts, Royal Soc. Can.; mem. Can. Inst. Internat. Affairs (br. pres.), MLA, English Inst., Am. Assn. for Eighteenth Century Studies, Can. Assn. for Eighteenth Century Studies, Internat. Assn. for Eighteenth Century Studies, Assn. Can. Univ. Tchrs. English (pres. 1982-84), Humanities Assn. Can. (past pres.) Mem. Liberal Party. Presbyterian. Club: University Faculty. Home: Ward MTN RR 2 3856 Prospect Rd Kentville NS Canada B4N 3V8 Office: Dalhousie U Dept English Halifax NS Canada B3H 3J5 Office Phone: 902-494-3384. Personal E-mail: jgray000@ns.sympatico.ca.

GRAY, JAMES N., computer scientist; BS in Math. and Engring., U. Calif., Berkeley, 1966, PhD in Computer sci., 1969; D of Natural Sci. (hon.), U. Stuttgart, Germany, 1990. Sys. rschr. Bell Labs, Whippany, NJ, 1966—67; rsch. asst., computer sci. U. Calif., Berkeley, Calif., 1967—69; ops. sys. rschr. T.J. Watson Rsch. Lab IBM, Yorktown Heights, NY, 1971—72; UNESCO expert Polytech. Inst., Bucharest, Romania, 1972; database rschr. IBM, San Jose, Calif., 1972—80; rschr. Tandem Computers, Cupertino, Calif., 1980—90; corp. cons. engr. Digital Equipment Corp., 1990—94; sr. rschr. Microsoft Corp., 1995—; and disting. engr. Scaleable Servers Rsch. Group Microsoft Bay Area Rsch. Ctr., San Francisco, 2000—. Vis. scholar U. Calif., Berkeley; pres. Adv. Com. on Info. Tech.; mem. adv. bd. Sch. Engring., Stanford U. Editor: Morgan Kaufmann Data Management Series, Data Mining and Knowledge Discovery; moderator database sect. Computer Sci. Online Rsch. Repository; past editor in chief and endowment bd. VLDB Jour. Recipient A.M. Turing award Assn. Computer Machinery, 1998, Phi Beta Kappa, Sigma Chi. Fellow Assn. Computing Machinery; mem. NAE, NRC (mem. computer sci. and telecomm. bd.). Office: Microsoft Bay Area Rsch Ctr 16th Fl 455 Market St San Francisco CA 94105 E-mail: gray@microsoft.com.

GRAY, JAN CHARLES, lawyer, business owner; b. Des Moines, June 15, 1947; s. Charles Donald and Mary C. Gray; 1 child, Charles Jan. BA in Econs., U. Calif., Berkeley, 1969; MBA, Pepperdine U., 1986; JD, Harvard U., 1972. Bar: Calif. 1972, D.C. 1974, Wyo. 1992. Law clk. Kindel & Anderson, L.A., 1971-72; assoc. Halstead, Baker & Sterling, L.A., 1972-75; sr. v.p., gen. counsel and sec. Ralphs Grocery Co., L.A., 1975-97; pres. Am. Presidents Resorts, Custer, S.D., Casper/Glenrock, Wyo., 1983—; owner Big Bear (Calif.) Cabins-Lakeside, 1988—; pres. Mt. Rushmore Broadcasting, Inc., 1991—; owner Sta. KGOS/KERM, Torrington, Wyo., 1993—, Sta. KRAL/KIQZ, Rawlins, Wyo., 1993—, Sta. KZMX, Hot Springs, S.D., 1993—, Sta. KFCR, Custer, S.D., 1992—, Sta. KQLT-FM, Casper, Wyo., 1994—, Sta. KASS-FM, Casper, 1995—, Sta. KVOC-AM, Casper, 1997—, KAWK-FM, Rapid City, S.D., 1997—, KHOC, Casper, Wyo., 1998—, KMLD, Casper, Mt. Rushmore Farms Horse Racing, 1999—. Judge pro tem L.A. Mcpl. Ct., 1977-85; instr. bus. UCLA, 1976-85, Pepperdine MBA Program, 1983-85; arbitrator Am. Arbitration Assn., 1977-97; media spokesman So. Calif. Grocers Assn., 1979-90, Calif. Grocers Assn., 1979-97, Calif. Retailers Assn., 1979-97; real estate broker, Calif., 1973—. Contbg. author: Life or Death, Who Controls?, 1976; contbr. articles to profl. jours. Trustee South Bay U. Coll. Law, 1978-79; mem. bd. visitors Southwestern U. Sch. Law, 1983—; mem. L.A. County Pvt. Industry Coun., 1982-96, exec. com. 1984-88, chmn. econ. devel. task force, 1986-89, chmn. mktg. com. 1991-93; mem. L.A. County Martin Luther King, Jr. Gen. Hosp. Authority, 1984—94; mem. L.A. County Aviation Commn, 1986-92, chmn., 1990-91; L.A. Police Crime Prevention Adv. Coun., 1986—97; Angelus Plaza Adv. Bd., 1983-85; bd. dirs. RecyCAL of So. Calif., 1983-89; trustee Santa Monica Hosp. Found., 1986-91, adv. bd., 1991—94; mem. L.A. County Dem. Cen. Com., 1980-90, L.A. City Employees' Retirement System Commn., 1993—; del. Dem. Nat. Conv., 1980. Recipient So. Calif. Grocers Assn. award for outstanding contbns. to food industry, 1982, appreciation award for No on 11 Campaign, Calif./Nev. Soft Drink Assn., 1983; Tyler Price Meml. award Mex.-Am. Grocers Assn., 1995, Radio Affiliate of Yr.-Classic Rock ABC, 1998. Mem.: ABA, Harvard Club of So. Calif., U. Calif. Alumni Assn., Town Hall L.A., Food Mktg. Inst. (govt. rels. com. 1977—97, chmn.lawyers, economists 1993—95, benefits coun. 1993—97), Calif. Retailers Assn. (supermarket com.), L.A. World Affairs Coun., L.A. Pub. Affairs Officers Assn., San Fernando Valley Bar Assn. (chmn. real property sect. 1975—77), L.A. County Bar Assn. (exec. com. corp. law depts. sect. 1979—2000, exec. com. barristers sect. 1974—75, exec. com. corp. law depts. sect. 1974—76, exec. com. barristers sect. 1979—81, chmn. 1989—90, trustee 1991—93, jud. evaluation com. 1993—96, nominating com. 1994), Calif. Bar Assn., Ephebian Soc. L.A., So. Calif. Bus. Assn. (bd. dirs. 1981—99, mem. exec. com. 1982—99, sec. 1986—91, chair 1991—98), Casper Country Club, L.A. Athletic Club, Phi Beta Kappa. Office: PO Box 826 Los Angeles CA 90078 Personal E-mail: jcg4321@aol.com.

GRAY, JANET ETHEL, elementary school educator; b. Snyder, Tex., Dec. 15, 1942; d. James Lavern and Irene McClain (Brown) Cotton; m. Richard Lee Gray, June 24, 1960; children: Melinda, Eric, Heidi, Keith. BS in Edn., Abilene Christian U., 1964; degree in kindergarten-early childhood, Tex. Christian U., 1972. Tchr. Abilene (Tex.) Pub. Schs., 1964-67, Castleberry Ind. Sch., Fort Worth, 1967-84, Conroe (Tex.) Ind. Sch., 1984—2002. Tech Elem. Coord. Conroe ISD, 2002—03. Recipient Presdl. award for excellence in sci. and math. teaching NSF, 1994, Presdl. award for excellence in sci., Tex., 1994. Mem. Sci. Tchrs. Assn. Tex., Nat. Sci. Tchrs. Assn., Soc. Elem. Presdl. Awardees, Coun. for Elem. Sci. Internat., Tex. State Tchrs. Assn. (bldg. rep. 1992-95), ASCD. Office: Anderson Elem Sch 1414 E Dallas St Conroe TX 77301-2100 Business E-Mail: jgray@conroeisd.net.

GRAY, JEFFREY T., automotive executive; BS in bus., Va. Polytechnic U. CPA. CPA KPMG LLP, 1987—93; contr. Hollins U., 1993—94; v.p., inventory mgmt. Advance Auto Parts, Roanoke, Va., 1994—2000, sr. v.p., CFOcontr., asst. sec., 2000—. Office: Advance Auto Parts 5673 Airport Rd Roanoke VA 24012

GRAY, JEREMY J.F., lawyer; b. Oxford, Eng., July 17, 1961; BA, Concordia Coll., 1984; JD magna cum laude, Loyola University, LA, 1990. Bar: Calif. 1990. Assoc. Irell & Manella, England, Whitfield, Schroeder & Tredway; ptnr. Katten Muchin Zavis Rosenman, LA. Mem.: ABA, LA County Bar Assn. Office: Katten Muchin Zavis Rosenman Ste 2600 2029 Century Park E Los Angeles CA 90067 Office Phone: 310-788-4592. Office Fax: 310-712-8452. E-mail: jeremy.gray@kmzr.com.

GRAY, JIM C., artist, art gallery owner; b. Middleton, Tenn., June 4, 1932; s. Jerry Franklin and Mamie Pearl Gray; life ptnr. Painting workshop Greenbriar Inc., Gatlinburg, Tenn., 1970—80. Author: (book) Roads I've Traveled, 2000. Scout master Boy Scouts USA, 1971—74; rotarian Rotary Club, 1968—76. Sgt. USAF, 1951—55. Recipient Gov. disting. artist award, Tenn. Arts Commn., 2003. Achievements include patents for for medical splints. Avocations: music, reading, boating. Home and Studio: 2405 Alcoa Hwy Knoxville TN 37920

GRAY, JOHN WALKER, mathematician, educator; b. St. Paul, Oct. 3, 1931; s. Clarence Walker and Helen (Ewald) G.; m. Eva Maria Wirth, Dec. 30, 1957; children— Stephen, Theodore, Elisabeth. BA, Swarthmore Coll., 1953; PhD, Stanford U., 1957. Temp. mem. Inst. for Advanced Study, Princeton, N.J., 1957-59; Ritt instr. Columbia U., 1959-62; asst. prof. math. U. Ill., Urbana, 1962-64, asso. prof., 1964-66, prof., 1966—, dir. grad. studies, 1995—2000, prof. emeritus, 2000—. Organizer Category Theory Session, Oberwolfach, Germany, 1971, 72, 73, 75, 77, 79 Contbr. to: Springer Lecture Notes in Mathematics, 1974. NSF sr. fellow, 1966-67; Fulbright-Hays sr. lectr., 1975-76 Mem. Am. Math. Soc., AAAS. Home: 303 W Michigan Ave Urbana IL 61801-4945 Office: U Ill Dept Math Urbana IL 61801

GRAY, JONI NADINE, state agency administrator; b. St. Joseph, Mo., Mar. 24, 1959; d. Albert Benjamin and M. Nadine (Harris) G.; children: John Charles, Haley Brooke, Jordan Roselle Gray-DeKraai. BA in Psychology, U. Nebr., 1982, JD, MA in Psychology, 1990. Rsch. policy analyst Gov.'s Policy Rsch. Office, Lincoln, 1985-86; dir. trainee Lancaster Cmty. Mental Health Ctr., Lincoln, 1987-88; policy analyst Ea. Nebr. Cmty. Office of Mental Health, Omaha, 1989; sys. developer Ctr. for Children, Families and the Law, Lincoln, 1989-90; law and psychology instr. U. Nebr., Lincoln, 1987, 90-91; rschr., analyst Nebr. Advocacy Svcs., Lincoln, 1993-94; policy analyst Ctr. for Children, Families and the Law, Lincoln, 1993-94; mental health program specialist Dept. Pub. Instns., Lincoln, 1995-96. Mem. adv. bd. Child Care and Early Childhood Edn. Coord. Com., Lincoln, 1996—, Nebr. Ctr. for Women, York, 1996—, Nebr. chpt. Nat. Mgr.'s Assn., Lincoln, 1996—. 1st author: Ethical and Legal Issues in AIDS Research, 1995; contbr. chpt. to book. Recipient Nat. Rsch. Svc. award NIMH, 1984-87, 92-93, Am. Jurisprudence award, 1989. Mem. Am. Psychology-Law Soc. (newsletter columnist 1984-85), Alpha Lambda Delta, Phi Eta Sigma.

GRAY, JUDITH A., retired school librarian, educator; b. Pitts., Nov. 30, 1942; d. John and Helen Ondich; m. N. Gordon Gray, June 13, 1964; 1 child, Ameena. BS in Edn., Indiana U. Pa., 1963; MLS, U. Pitts., 1964. Cert. sch. libr., pub. libr., secondary tchr. English, N.Y. Peace Corps vol., libr. Tanzanian Nat. Libr., 1964-67; reference libr. Syracuse U., 1967; sch. libr. H.W. Smith Jr. H.S., Syracuse, N.Y., 1967-69; substitute tchr. Syracuse City Sch. Dist., 1971-72; sch. libr. Nottingham H.S., Syracuse, 1972—2001. Pres. coun. Good Shepherd Luth. Ch., Fayetteville, N.Y., 1988-89. Mem. Peoples Choice award for photography N.Y. State Fair, 1987. Mem. ALA, N.Y. Libr. Assn. (bd. dirs. sch. libr. media sect. 1988-92, pres. 1992-93), Am. Assn. Sch. Librs. (nat. guidelines revision com. 1995-98), Librs. Unltd. (sec. 1998-2000, pres. 2000-01), Syracuse Tchrs. Assn. (chair elections com. 1974-2001), Monday Evening Club (historian 1996—). Avocations: gardening, hiking and camping, knitting, photography, travel. Home: 302 Pleasant St Manlius NY 13104-1816

GRAY, JUSTIN Y., lawyer; BS magna cum laude, Fla. A&M U., 1996; JD, U. Va., 1999. Bar: Pa. 1999, DC 1999, Va. 1999. Assoc. Shaw Pittman LLP, Sonnenschein Nath & Rosenthal LLP, Washington, 2003—. Corp. adv. coun. Congl. Black Caucus Found. Office: Sonnenschein Nath & Rosenthal LLP Ste 600, E Tower 1301 K St NW Washington DC 20005 Office Phone: 202-408-9111. Office Fax: 202-408-6399. Business E-Mail: jgray@sonnenschein.com.

GRAY, KAREN KAY, counselor; b. Tulsa, Okla., Aug. 5, 1957; d. Bobby Ray Phillipe and Ruth Marie Kay. BS in Mktg. & Econ., Okla. State U., 1979, MS in Recreation Adminstrn., 1980. Cert. drug and alcohol profl. counselor Okla.; therapeutic recreation specialist Nat. Coun. for Therapeutic Recreation Cert., internat. cert. alcohol and drug counselor. Recreation therapist Rader Children's Ctr., Sand Springs, Okla., 1981—89, St. John Med. Ctr., Tulsa, Okla., 1989—. Mem. adv. bd. Tulsa C. C., Tulsa, 1999—; bd. mem. Therapeutic Recreation Symposium of S.W., chmn., 1997—99. Mem. Gov.'s Adv. Coun. on Homeless, Okla. City, Okla., 2000—; precinct chmn. Rep. Party, Tulsa, 2000—. Mem.: LWV (mem. mental health com. 2000—, spkrs. bureau 2000—, bd. dirs. 2002—, edn. com. 2002—), Mental Health Assn. (edn. com. 1998—). Republican. Mem. United Ch. Of Christ. Avocations: reading, tennis, soccer, yardwork. Home: 1452 N Evanston Ave Tulsa OK 74110-4814 Office: St John Med Ctr 1923 S Utica Ave Tulsa OK 74104

GRAY, KARLA MARIE, state supreme court justice; b. Escanaba, Mich., May 10, 1947; BA, MA in African History, Western Mich. U.; JD, Hastings Coll. of Law, San Francisco, 1976. Bar: Mont. 1976, Calif. 1977. Law clk. to Hon. W. D. Murray U.S. Dist. Ct., 1976-77; staff atty. Atlantic Richfield Co., 1977-81; pvt. practice law Butte, Mont., 1981-84; staff atty., legis. lobbyist Mont. Power Co., Butte, 1984-91; justice Mont. Supreme Ct., Helena, 1991-2000, chief justice, 2000—. Mem. Mont. Supreme Ct. Gender Fairness Task Force. Fellow Am. Bar Found., Am. Judicature Soc., Internat. Women's Forum; mem. State Bar Mont., Silver Bow County Bar Assn. (past pres.), Nat. Assn. Women Judges. Avocations: travel, reading, piano, family genealogy, cross-country sking. Office: Supreme Ct Mont PO Box 203001 Helena MT 59620-3001

GRAY, KATHERINE MARIE GANZAUGE, artist; b. Seneca Falls, N.Y. d. Max Theodor and Benigna Schmid Ganzauge; m. Edward Wyllys Taylor Gray III (div. Nov. 1987); children: Taylor, Peter, Carolyn. BA, Wells Coll., 1958. Judge Passaic County (N.J.) Teen Arts Festival, 1990, Art in the Park Exhibit, Montclair, N.J., 1988, PSE&G Employee Art Exhibit, Newark, 1990. One-woman shows include Maine Statehouse, Augusta, 1985, Bowdoin Coll., Brunswick, Maine, 1987, Somerset Art Assn., Far Hills, N.J., 1988, Crum & Forster Corp. Hqrs., Morristown, N.J., 1988, Montclair Cmty. Hosp., N.J., 1984, 89, Ortho Diagnostics Sys., Inc., Raritan, N.J., 1989, Claremont Gallery, Bedminster, N.J., 1990, Georgetown (Maine) Town Office, 1990, Burgdorff Realtors, Montclair, N.J., 1991, Ten Park Gallery & Restaurant, Montclair, 1989, 90, 91, Children's Specialized Hosp., Mountainside, N.J., 1993, West Caldwell Libr. Gallery, N.J., 1992, 94, Mt. Kemble Gallery at Rehab. Inst. of Morristown Hosp., 1995, Not Just Framing Gallery, Maine, 1995, Audobon Naturalist Soc., Chevy Chase, Md., 1996, Riverdell Winery Gallery, New Paltz, N.Y., 1997, Burgess Bus. Solutions Inc., Maine, 1997, Robinhood Free Meeting House, Georgetown, Maine, 1998, Barnes & Noble, Poughkeepsie, N.Y., 1998, Woodstock Artists Assn., Woodstock, 1999, The Grenwich Art Ctr., Greenwich, Conn., 2000, Lyric Gallery, Highland, N.Y., 2000; exhibited in group shows at Ctr. for Arts, Bath, Maine, Art Gallery at 6 Deering St., Portland, Maine, Phila. Watercolor Club, Pa., Mountain Art Show, Bernardsville, N.J., Art Centre of N.J., Ridgewood Art Inst., N.J., Summit Art Ctr., N.J., Nabisco Brands Gallery, East Hanover, N.J., Arts Coun. Annual Juried Art Show for N.J. Artists, Trenton City Mus., N.J., Bergen Mus., Paramus, N.J., Garden State Watercolor Soc., N.J. Watercolor Soc., Am. Artists Profl. League's Open Juried Shows, N.Y. and N.J., Catharine Lorillard Wolfe Club, N.Y.C., Salmagundi Club, N.Y.C., Nat. Arts Club, N.Y.C., Nat. Assn. Women Artists, N.J.; exhibited in galleries at Huston-Tuttle & Gallery One, Rockland, Maine, The Gallery, Five Islands, Maine, Maine Art Gallery, Wiscasset, Boothbay Region Art Found., Boothbay Harbor, Maine, Riverside Gallery, Pottersville, N.J., Heritage Art Gallery, Rhinebeck and Poughkeepsie, N.Y., Mark Gruber Gallery, New Paltz, N.Y., Peel Gallery, Danby, Vt., Albert Shahinian Fine Art, Poughkeepsie, N.Y., West Island Gallery, Peel Gallery, Louisa Melrose Gallery, Frenchtown, N.J. Recipient Merit award Millburn Outdoor Show, 1993, N.J. Portrait award Tewksbury Hist. Soc., 1993, Best in Show, Somerset Art Assn., 1993, Merit award Livingston Art Assn., 1994, 95, 96, 1st Place Watercolor award 1994; Merit awards Millburn-Short Hills Art Assn., 1993, 94, award of Excellence, 1997; Merit award Mountain Art Show, 1994, Merit awards Essex Watercolor Club N.J., 1990, 93, 94, Hon. Mention, N.J. Watercolor Soc., 1995, Ida Wells and Clara Stroud award for Best Watercolor Am. Artists Profl. League, 1989, Merit award, 1990; 3d prize in Watercolor and Tempera Northeast Art Festival, 1993, 95, Merit award Highland Cultural Ctr., 1994, Edgar A. Whitney Meml. award Catharine Lorillard Wolfe Art Club, Inc., 1994, Winifred E. Morse award Salmagundi Club, 1992, Amelia Peabody Meml. award Nat. Assn. Women Artists, 1992, C.L. Mason and A.V. Mason Meml. award Nat. Assn. Women Artists, 1993; recipient Elizabeth Morse Genius award The Pen and Brush Club, 1990, Cecilia Cardman Meml. award, 1990, Grumbacher, Inc. award, 1991, Catherine Ballantyne Meml. award, 1991, Gene Alden Walker award, 1992, Margaret Sussman award, 1992, Hors Concours Hon. Mention award, 1993, Margery Soroka award, 1995, Cheap Joe's Art Supplies award, 1995, Millburn Merit award Short Hills Arts Assn., 1997, 2nd prize in watercolor N.E. Art Festival, 1997, award West Essex Art Assn., 1998, 99, Merit award Kent Art Assn., 2000. Mem. Nat. Assn. Women Artists, Am. Artists Profl. League, The Woodstock Artists Assn., Catharine Lorillard Wolfe Art Club, The Pen & Brush Club, N.J. Water Color Soc., Phila. Watercolor Club, Maine Art Gallery. Avocations: hiking, gardening, contra dancing, maine travels. Home: 3 Wood Lot Rd New Paltz NY 12561-3730 E-mail: okaykayg@aol.com.

GRAY, KIMBERLY S., lawyer; b. Waynesboro, Pa., May 25, 1959; d. Harold Richard and Lillian May Null. BA in Psychology, Shippensburg (Pa.) U., 1989; JD, Dickinson Sch. Law, Carlisle, Pa., 1994. Bar: Pa. 1994, U.S. Dist. Ct. (mid. dist.) Pa. 1995. Shareholder/mng. atty. Martin & Gray, P.C., Chambersburg & Waynesboro, Pa., 1995-98; assoc. counsel Highmark Inc., Camp Hill, Pa., 1998-2001, chief privacy officer, 2001—. Adj. prof. law The Dickinson Sch. of Law, Carlisle, 1997-99. Bd. dirs. Cumberland Valley Mental Health, Chambersburg, 1996-98, Family Health Svcs., Chambersburg, 1995-98, Coyle Free Libr., Chambersburg, 1997-98; mem. Health Cmtys. Partnership Preventive Health Task Force, Chambersburg, 1997-98; mem. adv. bd. Big Bros. Big Sisters Franklin County, 1997-98. Recipient Monroe E. Trout Law and Medicine award Dickinson Sch. Law, 1994, Disting. Alumni award Hagerstown Bus. Coll., 1999. Mem. Nat. Health Lawyers Assn., Pa. Bar Assn. (health law com., co-vice chair 2000—, legis. subcom. 1995—, chair 1998—, interdisciplinary com. on med. and health related issues 1996-97, zone 3 del. to Ho. of Dels. 1997—), Franklin County Bar Assn. (chmn. law and you com. 1996-98, co-chmn. bench/bar conf. com. 1995). Republican. Methodist. Avocations: foreign language, culture and travel, horseback riding, music, art. Office: Highmark Inc 1800 Center St Camp Hill PA 17089-0001 E-mail: kimberly.gray@highmark.com.

GRAY, KIRK LAMOND, social investment firm executive, anthropologist; b. Keene, N.H., Mar. 9, 1948; s. Norman Hamblin and Ann Elaine (Lamond) G. BA in Anthropology, Prescott Coll., 1969; MA in Anthropology, We. Mich. U., 1974. Site monitor The Rand Corp., Green Bay, Wis. and Santa Monica, Calif., 1973-78; regional dir. Common Cause, Washington, 1978-79; sr. adv. Quadel Consulting Corp., Bethesda, Md., 1980-81; dep. dir. housing and cmty. devel. divsn. Advanced Tech., Inc., Reston, Va., 1982-83; dir., founder Howland & Assocs., Ltd., McLean, Va., 1983-84; regional dir. US Dept. Housing and Urban Devel., Phila., 1984-89, program adv. office of asst. sec. Washington, 1988-89; founder, pres., CEO The Gray Group, Inc., Columbia, Md., 1990; chmn., CEO Cornerstone Housing, LLC, Columbia, Md., 1996—. Contbr. chpt. to book, articles to profl. jours. Mem. Chesapeake Bay Found., Annapolis, Md., 1992—; sustaining mem. Rep. Nat. Com., Washington, 1995. Recipient White House Commendation Office of Pres., Washington, 1989, Disting. Svc. award HUD, 1988, Disting. Alumnae award We. Mich. U., 1986. Fellow Soc. Applied Anthropology (mem. exec. com. 1984-87, 86—); mem. Washington Assn. Profl. Anthropologists (pres. 1982-84), Nat. Assn. Housing and Redevelopment Officials, Pa. Assn. Housing and Redevelopment Officials (Partnership award). Office: The Gray Group 7188 Cradlerock Way Ste 106 Columbia MD 21045-5066 also: Cornerstone Housing LLC Ste 301 5950 Symphony Woods Rd Columbia MD 21044-3590

GRAY, KRIS DIANE, nursing consultant, forensic specialist; ASN, Fresno C.C., 1993; BA in Biology, Calif. State U., 1985. Diplomate Am. Bd. Medicolegal Death Investigators (registered), lic. paramedic Calif., cert. emergency nurse Bd. Cert. Emergency Nursing, flight nurse Bd. Cert. Emergency Nursing; RN Calif. Cardiac rsch. assoc. U. Calif. San Francisco, Fresno, 1984—85; paramedic Fort Bend County Emergency Svcs., Rosenberg, Tex., 1987—90, Am. Med. Svcs., Fresno, 1990—94; RN Sierra View Dist. Hosp., Porterville, Calif., 1994—2004; instr. Porterville C.C., 1994—95; RN Holland Am.-West Tours Inc., Seattle, 1996—2000; owner Gray Forensics and Consulting, Visalia, Calif., 2003—. Peer counselor Ctrl. Valley Emergency Svcs. Support Team, Fresno, 1990—95; forensic autopsy asst. Tulare County Sheriff's Office, Visalia, 1998—; safety officer Disaster Mortuary Ops./Recovery Team, Washington, 2002—; founding mem. Dept. Homeland Security U.S. Govt. Rschr. (book) Visalia's Fabulous Fox, 2000, unit prodn. mgr. (feature film) Legend of Jake Kincaid, 2001, interviewer (oral history project) Tulare County and WWII, 2004. Crisis counselor Help in Emotional Trouble, Fresno, 1983—85; bd. dirs. Citizens Adv. Bd., Visalia, 1987. Mem.: Am. Bd. Forensic Nurses, Air and Surface Transport Nurses Assn., Am. Bd. Forensic Examiners (cert. med. investigator), Am. Assn. Legal Nurse Consultants, Calif. State Coroners Assn. (assoc.). Avocations: golf, snorkeling, guitar. Office: Gray Forensics and Consulting 2115 S Ashton Ct Visalia CA 93277 Office Phone: 559-734-3980.

GRAY, MARVIN LEE, JR., lawyer; b. Pitts., May 9, 1945; s. Marvin L. and Frances (Stringfellow) G.; m. Jill Miller, Aug. 14, 1971; children: Elizabeth Ann, Carolyn Jill. AB, Princeton U., 1966; JD magna cum laude, Harvard U., 1969. Bar: Wash. 1973, U.S. Supreme Ct. 1977, Alaska 1984. Law clk. to judge U.S. Ct. Appeals, N.Y.C., 1969-70; law clk. to justice U.S. Supreme Ct., Washington, 1970-71; asst. U.S. atty. U.S. Dept. Justice, Seattle, 1973-76; ptnr. Davis Wright Tremaine, Seattle, 1976—, mng. ptnr., 1985-88. Staff counsel Rockefeller Commn. on CIA Activities in U.S., Washington, 1974; lectr. trial practice U. Wash. Law Sch., Seattle, 1979-80. Lay reader Episcopal Ch. of Ascension, Seattle, 1982-94. Capt. USAF, 1971-73. Fellow Am. Coll. Trial Lawyers; mem. ABA, Am. Law Inst. Office: Davis Wright Tremaine 1501 4th Ave Ste 2600 Seattle WA 98101-1688 Business E-Mail: montygray@dwt.com.

GRAY, MARY WHEAT, statistician, lawyer; b. Hastings, Nebr., 1939; d. Neil C. and Lillie W. (Alves) Wheat; m. Alfred Gray, Aug. 20, 1964. AB summa cum laude, Hastings Coll., 1959; postgrad., J.W. Goethe U., Frankfurt, Fed. Republic Germany, 1959-60; MA, U. Kans., 1962, PhD, 1964; JD summa cum laude, Am. U., 1979; LLD (hon.), U. Nebr., 1993; LHD (hon.), Hastings Coll., 1996. Bar: D.C. 1979, U.S. Supreme Ct. 1983, U.S. Dist. Ct., D.C. 1980. Physicist Nat. Bur. Standards, Washington, summers 1959-63; asst. instr. U. Kans., Lawrence, 1963-64; instr. dept. math. U. Calif., Berkeley, 1965; asst. prof. Calif. State U., Hayward, 1965-67, assoc. prof., 1967-68; assoc. prof. dept. math., stats. and computer sci. Am. U., 1968-71, prof., 1971—, chmn. dept., 1977-79, 80-81, 83—; statis. cons. for govt. agys., univs. and pvt. firms, 1976—. Vis. prof. King's Coll., London, 2004. Author: A Radical Approach to Algebra, 1970; Calculus with Finite Mathematics for Social Sciences, 1972; contbr. numerous articles to profl. jours. Nat. treas., dir. Women's Equity Action League, from 1981, pres., from 1982; bd. dirs. treas. ACLU, Montgomery County, Md.; mem. adv. com. D.C. Dept. Employment Services, 1983—; dir. Amnesty Internat. USA, 1985—, treas., 1988-93, chair, 1993—; mem. Commn. on Coll. Retirement, 1984-86; bd. dirs. Am.-Middle East Edn. Found., 1983—, chair, 1998--. Recipient U.S. Presdl. award for excellence in sci., engring. and math. mentoring, 2001; Fulbright grantee, 1959-60; NSF fellow, 1963-64, NDEA fellow, 1960-63 Fellow AAAS (chmn. com. on women, com. on investments, com. on sci. freedom and responsibility, Lifetime Mentoring award 1995); mem. AAUP (regional counsel 1984—, com. on acad. freedom 1978—, dir. Legal Def. Fund 1974-78, bd. dirs. Exxon Project on Salary Discrimination 1974-76, com. on status of women 1972-78, Georgina Smith award), Am. Math. Soc. (v.p. 1976-78, coun. 1973-78), Amnesty Internat. (internat. treas. 1995-2001, chair USA 1993-95), Conf. Bd. Math. Scis. (chmn. com. on affirmative action 1977-78), Math. Assn. Am. (chmn. com. on sch. lectrs. 1973-75, vis. lectr. 1974—), Assn. for Women in Math (founding pres. 1971-74, exec. com. 1974-80, gen. counsel 1980—), D.C. Bar Assn., ABA, Am. Soc. Internat. Law, London Math. Soc., Societe de Mathematique de France, Brit. Soc. History of Math., Can. Soc. History of Math., Assn. Computing Machinery, N.Y. Acad. Scis., Am. Statis. Assn., Phi Beta Kappa, Sigma Xi, Phi Kappa Phi, Alpha Chi, Pi Mu Epsilon. Home: 6807 Connecticut Ave Chevy Chase MD 20815-4937 Office: Am U Math & Stats Dept Washington DC 20016 Office Phone: 202-885-3171. Business E-Mail: mgray@american.edu.

GRAY, MYLES MCCLURE, retired insurance company executive; b. Lansing, Mich., Aug. 28, 1932; s. Carlyle Avery and Lucile (Meitz) G.; m. Marilyn Ida Osberg, Feb. 14, 1953; children: Kathleen (Mrs. Mark Abraham), David, Patricia. BBA with distinction, U. Mich., 1954. Div. mgr. Nat. Life & Accident Ins. Co., Nashville, 1954-58; from asst. actuary to exec. v.p., actuary United Benefit Life Ins. Co., Omaha, 1958-67; v.p., actuary Gen. Reins. Life Corp., N.Y.C., 1967-69, Cal. Western States Life Ins. Co., Sacramento, 1969-74; v.p. Alexander & Alexander, N.Y.C., 1974-75, Nat. Life & Accident Ins. Co., Nashville, 1975-81, NLT Corp., Nashville, 1981-83; sr. v.p., chief actuary Life Investors, Inc., Cedar Rapids, Iowa, 1983-86; v.p. Cal Farm Life Ins. Co., Sacramento, 1986-96; ret., 1996. Cons. in field. Docent Calif. State Railroad Mus., 1996—. Fellow Soc. Actuaries (sec., mem. exec. com. 1977-80, bd. govs. 1977-83); mem. Am. Acad. Actuaries (bd. dirs. 1986-87), Alpha Kappa Psi, Phi Kappa Phi, Beta Gamma Sigma. Republican. Home: 11454 Mother Lode Cir Gold River CA 95670-3042

GRAY, NICOLE P. H., mathematics educator; b. Chgo., Ill., May 6, 1971; d. Sandra Henley; m. Jamison R. Gray, Aug. 19, 2000; 1 child, Stephanie Lane. BA, Dartmouth Coll., Hanover, N.H.; MS, U. Ill., Urbana-Champaign, Ill. Faculty mem. Foothill Coll., Los Altos Hills, Calif., 1996. Recipient President's Faculty Excellence Award, Pres. of Foothill Coll., 2000. Mem.: Calif. Math. Coun. for Cmty. Colls. Office: Foothill Coll 12345 El Monte Rd Los Altos Hills CA 94022 Office Phone: 650-949-7175.

GRAY, OSCAR SHALOM, lawyer; b. N.Y.C., Oct. 18, 1926; BA, Yale U., 1948, JD, 1951. Bar: Md. 1951, D.C. 1952, U.S. Supreme Ct. 1952. Atty.-adviser legal adviser's office U.S. Dept. State, Washington, 1951-57; sec. Nuclear Materials and Equipment Corp., Apollo, Pa., 1957-64, treas., 1957-67, v.p., 1964-71, dir., 1964-67; spl. counsel Presdl. Task Force on Communications Policy, Washington, 1967-68; cons. U.S. Dept. Transp., Washington, 1967-68, acting dir. office environ. impact, 1968-70; sole practice Washington, 1970—, Balt., 1971—. Adj. prof., professorial lectr. Law Ctr. Georgetown U., Washington, 1970-71; lectr. Cath. U. Am., Washington, 1970-71; assoc. prof. U. Md., Balt., 1971-74, prof., 1974-93, Jacob A. France prof. of torts, 1993-96, prof. emeritus, 1996—; vis. prof. U. Tenn., 1977. Author: Cases and Materials on Environmental Law, 1970, 2d edit., 1973, supplements, 1974, 1975, 1977; author: (with F. Harper and F. James Jr.) The Law of Torts, 2d edit., 1986; author: 3d edit., vol. 1, 1996; author: (with H. Shulman and F. James Jr.) Cases and Materials on the Law of Torts (with D. Gifford) 4th edit., 2003; contbr. articles to profl. legal jours. Mem.: ABA, D.C. Fedn. of Civic Assns. (parliamentarian 1991—99, 2000—04), D.C. Bar, Am. Law Inst. (adviser Restatement of the Law, Third, Torts: Products Liability), Selden Soc. (state correspondent Md.), Phi Beta Kappa, Order of Coif. Office: 500 W Baltimore St Baltimore MD 21201-1602 Office Phone: 410-706-7174. Business E-Mail: ogray@law.umaryland.edu.

GRAY, PAUL EDWARD, academic administrator; b. Newark, Feb. 7, 1932; s. Kenneth Frank and Florence (Gilleo) G.; m. Priscilla Wilson King, June 18, 1955; children: Virginia Wilson, Amy Brewer, Andrew King, Louise Meyer. SB, MIT, 1954, SM, 1955, DSc, 1960. Mem. faculty MIT, 1960-71, 90—, Class of 1922 prof. elec. engring., 1968-71, dean Sch. Engring., 1970-71, chancellor, 1971-80, pres., 1980-90; mem. MIT Corp., 1971—, chmn., 1990-97. Trustee Wheaton Coll., Norton, Mass., 1971-97, trustee emeritus 1997—, chmn. bd. trustees, 1976-87. 1st lt. AUS, 1955-57. Fellow IEEE (life, publs. bd. 1969-70), Am. Acad. Arts and Scis.; mem. NAE (treas. 1994-01), AAAS, Mex. Nat. Acad. Engring. (corr.), Sigma Xi, Eta Kappa Nu, Tau Beta Pi, Phi Sigma Kappa. Mem. United Ch. Christ Office: MIT Dept Elec Engring Rm 38-344 77 Massachusetts Ave Cambridge MA 02139-4307 Office Phone: 617-253-4665. Business E-Mail: pogo@mit.edu.

GRAY, PAUL RUSSELL, academic administrator, electrical engineering educator; b. Jonesboro, Ark., Dec. 8, 1942; married; 2 children. BS, U. Ariz., 1963, MS, 1965, PhD, 1969. Vis. lectr. dept. elec. engring. and computer sci. U. Calif., Berkeley, 1971—72, asst. prof., 1972—74, assoc. prof., 1974—78, prof., 1978—, acting dir. Electronics Rsch. Lab., 1985—86, vice chmn. EECS Dept. for Computer Resources, 1988—90, chmn. Dept. Electrical Engring. and Computer Scis., 1990—93, dean Coll. Engring., 1996-2000, Roy W. Carson chair in engring., 1996, exec. vice chancellor, provost, 2000—, Andrew S. Grove chair in electrical engring., 2000—. Mem. tech. staff Semiconductor Div. Fairchild Camera and Instrument Corp., 1969—71; project mgr. Telecommunications Filter Prog., Intel Corp., 1977—78; dir. CMOS Product Develop. Microlinear Corp., 1984—85. Co-author: Analysis and Design of Analog Integrated Circuits; contbr. articles to profl. jours. Recipient Solid-State Circuits award IEEE, 1994. Fellow IEEE (Baker prize 1980, Morris N. Liebmann Meml. award 1983); mem. NAE. Office: U Calif Office Chancellor 200 California Hall Berkeley CA 94720-1502 Office Phone: 510-642-1961, 510-642-5179. Office Fax: 510-643-5499. E-mail: pgray@berkeley.edu.*

GRAY, PAULETTE STYLES, biologist; b. Chattanooga, Feb. 21, 1944; d. Paul Styles and Louise (Hill) Dennis; m. Walter Leonard, May 10, 1964; children: Walter Leonard Jr., Daniel Allen. BS, Tuskegee Inst., 1966; MS, Atlanta U., 1976, PhD, 1978. Asst. prof., dir., electron microscopy lab. Atlanta U., 1978-79; research assoc. U. Kaiserslautern, Fed. Rep. Germany, 1979-81; instr. U. Maryland, Kaiserslautern, 1980-82; supr. clin. microbiology sect. Landstuhl Army Regional Med. Ctr., Fed. Rep. Germany, 1981-82; exec. sec. Nat. Cancer Inst. div. of Extramural Activities, Bethesda, Md., 1983-84, spl. review officer, 1984—, chief, rev. logistics br., 1988—, dep. dir., acting dir. Mem. Nat. Cancer Inst. Div. Extramural Activities awards com., Bethesda, 1983—, exec. sec. working group of subcom. on agenda adv. bd., 1989—, adv. com. Comprehensive Minority Program, Bethesda, 1983—; chmn. orgn. subcom. NIH Women's Adv. com., Bethesda, 1986-88; assignee profl. devel. health sci. adminstr. program NIH, Bethesda, 1986-88; co-coord. Nat. Cancer Adv. Bd. Activities, NCI, 1989—; mentor presenter Am. Inst. Biol. Scis., 1990; keynote speaker Fed. Exec. Inst., 1990. Contbr. articles to profl. jours. Tchr. Sun. Sch. Alfred St. Bapt. Ch., Alexandria, Va., 1982-89, supt., 1988-89; judge sci. and engring. fair Fairfax County pub. schs., 1984-89; speaker Med. Coll. Ga., Augusta, 1985. Recipient Lederle Labs. award, 1977, H.E. Finley Meml. award Atlanta U., 1978, Outstanding Performance award Nat. Cancer Inst., 1983—; Josiah Macy Jr. fellow, 1979, Hon. Fulbright Hays fellow, 1979-81, Spl. Act. of Achievement award 1992, 93, EEO Spl. Recognition award, 1991, NIH Dir.'s award, 1990, Cert. Recognition and Spl. Achievement award, HHS, 1988-93. Mem. Am. Soc. Zoology, Nat. Inst. Sci., Atlanta U. Ctr. Honor Soc. (biology), Am. Assn. Cancer Rsch., Inc., Am. Assn. Cell Biology, Internat. Platform Assn., Women in Cancer Rsch., Assn. Women in Govt., Nat. Assn. Exec. Women. Avocations: cooking, reading, jogging, writing. Office: Nat Cancer Inst 6116 Exec Blvd MSC 8327 Bethesda MD 20892

GRAY, PHILIP HOWARD, former psychologist, writer, educator; b. Cape Rosier, Maine, July 4, 1926; s. Asa and Bernice (Lawrence) G.; m. Iris McKinney, Dec. 31, 1954; children: Cindelyn Gray Eberts, Howard. MA, U. Chgo., 1958; PhD, U. Wash., 1960. Asst. prof. dept. psychology Mont. State U., Bozeman, 1960—65, assoc. prof., 1965—75, prof., 1975—92; ret., 1992. Vis. prof. U. Man., Winnipeg, Can., 1968-70, U. N.H., 1965, U. Mont., 1967, 74, Tufts U., 1968, U. Conn., 1971; pres. Mont. Psychol. Assn., 1968-70 (helped write Mont. licensing law for psychologists); chmn. Mont. Bd. Psychologist Examiners, 1972-74; spkr. sci. and geneal. meetings on ancestry of U.S. presidents; presenter, instr. grad. course on serial killers and the psychopathology of murder; founder Badger Press of Mont., 1998. Organizer folk art exhbns. Mont. and Maine, 1972-79; author: The Comparative Analysis of Behavior, 1966, (with F.L. Ruch and N. Warren) Working with Psychology, 1963, A Directory of Eskimo Artists in Sculpture and Prints, 1974, The Science That Lost Its Mind, 1985, Penobscot Pioneers vol. 1, 1992, vol. 2, 1992, vol. 3, 1993, vol. 4, 1994, vol. 5, 1995, vol. 6, 1996, Mean Streets and Dark Deeds: The He-Man's Guide to Mysteries, 1998, Ghoulies and Ghosties and Long-leggety Beasties: Imprinting Theory Linking Serial Killers, Child Assassins, Molesters, Homosexuality, Feminism and Day Care, 1998, Egoteria of a Psychologist: Poetry, Letters, Memos from Nether Montana, 2001; contbr. numerous articles on behavior to psychol. jours.; contbr. poetry to lit. jours. With U.S. Army, 1944—46. Decorated EAME medal Ctrl. Europe and Rhineland Campaigns, Victory medal WWII; recipient numerous rsch. grants. Fellow: APA, AAAS, Internat. Soc. Rsch. on Aggression, Am. Psychol. Soc.; mem.: SAR (trustee 1989, v.p. Sourdough chpt. 1990, pres. 1991—2004, v.p. gen. intermountain dist. 1997—98, pres. state soc. 1998—99, trustee 2001—03, v.p. gen. intermountain dist. 2003—04), NRA (life), Order of the Crown of Charlemagne, Gallatin County Geneal. Soc. (charter, pres. 1991—93), Nat. Geneal. Soc., New Eng. Hist. Geneal. Soc., Deer Isle-Stonington Hist. Soc., Flagon and Trencher, Order Descs. Colonial Physicians and Chirugiens, Internat. Soc. Human Ethology, Descs. Illegitimate Sons and Daus. of Kings of Britain, Bozeman Rifle and Pistol Club. Republican. Avocations: collecting folk art, first and signed editions of novels, pistol shooting. Home: 1207 S Black Ave Bozeman MT 59715-5633 E-mail: phgray@mcn.net. *We are human to the extent that we have bondings and the more bondings we have the more human we are. These attachments include familial bonding (imprinting), friendship bonding, marital bonding, ethnic-religious bonding, possession and goal bondings, and bonding to the land and ocean. My life's work is the study of these bondings and I am thereby more firmly connected to the human race.*

GRAY, RICHARD, art dealer, consultant, holding company executive; b. Chgo., Dec. 30, 1928; s. Edward and Pearl B. Gray; m. Mary Kay Lackritz, Mar. 28, 1953; children: Paul, Jennifer, Harry. Pres. The Grayline Co., 1952-63; sec.-treas. The Edward Gray Corp., 1952-63; prin., dir. GrayCor, 1963—; founder, ptnr. The Richard Gray Gallery, Chgo. and N.Y.C., 1963—. Lectr., juror, panelist Guggenheim Mus., N.Y.C., Art. Inst. Chgo., Harvard U., U. Ill., Mich. State U., Milw. Art Mus., New Sch. for Social Research, N.Y., Met. Mus., N.Y.C., Colloquium-The Getty Mus., U. Chgo., Seattle Art Mus.; mem. art adv. panel U.S. Internal Revenue Svc., 1988-98. Contbr. articles to Chgo. Tribune, Chgo. Daily News, Crain's Chgo. Bus., Chgo. Mag., Collector Investor Mag. Bd. dirs. Sta. WFMT-FM, 1992-, Ill. Humanities Coun.; trustee, vice chmn. WTTW Channel 11—Chgo. Pub. TV; bd. dirs. Goodman Theatre, Chgo.; life trustee Chgo. Symphony Orch., Art Inst. Chgo.; former chair bd. Chgo. Internat. Theater Festival; adv. com. Smithsonian Inst.; bd. dirs. Art Inst. Chgo., Old Masters Soc.; mem. steering com. Friends of the Libraries; mem. capital devel. bd. State of Ill., pub. arts adv. com., former mem. selection com. Gov.'s Awards for Arts; former mem. nat. adv. bd. Ohio State U. Wexner Ctr. for Visual Arts; pres. Art Dealers Assn. Am., 1997-2003; former pres. Chgo. Art Dealers Assn., 1968-80; former chmn. Navy Pier Task Force, City of Chgo., 1986-88; mem. vis. com. U. Chgo. Humanities Div., chmn., bd. govs. Alfred Smart Mus. U. Chgo., 1992-; former vice-chmn., bd. dirs. Chgo. Humanities Festival. Mem. Chgo. Pub. Schs. Alumni Assn. (former chmn. bd. dirs.), Chgo. Coun. Fgn. Rels. (Chgo. com.), Chgo. Club, Quadrangle Club, Arts Club of Chgo. Achievements include specializing in contemporary, modern and impressionist masters. Office: Richard Gray Gallery 875 N Michigan Ave Ste 2503 Chicago IL 60611-1876 also: 1018 Madison Ave New York NY E-mail: rgray@richardgraygallery.com.

GRAY, RICHARD ALEXANDER, JR., retired chemical company executive; b. Pitts., Apr. 28, 1927; s. Richard Alexander and Margaret Katheryn Gray; m. Lucia I. Long, Sept. 8, 1956; children: Richard Alexander III, James W. Midshipman, U.S. Mcht. Marine Acad., 1945-47; BA, Princeton U., 1950; LL.B., Harvard U., 1954; postgrad., Univ. Coll., Southampton, Eng., 1949. Bar: Pa. bar 1955, U.S. Supreme Ct. bar 1975. Asso. firm Reed Smith Shaw & McClay, Pitts., 1954-62; with Air Products and Chems., Inc., Allentown, Pa., 1962-90, asst. gen. counsel, 1976-78, corp. sec., 1978-90, assoc. gen. counsel, 1980-84, v.p., 1984-90. Trustee Kutztown (Pa.) U., 1988-96, chmn., 1995-96; mem. bd. regents Mercersburg (Pa.) Acad., 1971-80. Trustee First Presbyn. Ch. of Allentown. Served to lt. (j.g.) USNR, 1950-51. Mem. ABA, Am. Soc. Corp. Secs. (bd. dirs. 1985-89), Lehigh Country Club (bd. govs. 1993-96). E-mail: ragjr28hh@aol.com.

GRAY, RICHARD MOSS, retired college president; b. Washington, Jan. 25, 1924; s. Wilbur Leslie and Betty Marie (Grey) G.; m. Catherine Claire Hammond, Oct. 17, 1943; children: Janice Lynn Gray Armstrong, Nancy Hammond Gray Schultz. BA, Bucknell U., 1942; MDiv summa cum laude, San Francisco Theol. Sem., 1961; PhD, U. Calif., Berkeley, 1972; doctorate degree (hon.), World Coll. West, 1988. Writer, creative dir. N.W. Ayer & Son, Phila., 1942-58; univ. pastor Portland State U., Oreg., 1961-68; founder, pres. World Coll. West, Petaluma, Calif., 1973-88, pres. emeritus, 1988—. Bd. dirs. World Centre, San Francisco, Life Plan Ctr.; founder Presidio World Coll., 1992—. Author poetry Advent, 1989. Bd. dirs. Citizens Found. Marin, San Rafael, Calif., 1988—, Marin Ednl. Found.; ruling elder Presbyn. Ch. U.S.A. Named Disting. Alumnus of Yr. San Francisco Theol. Sem., 1988, Marin Citizen of Yr. Citizens Found., 1988; recipient Svc. to Humanity award Bucknell U., 1992. Mem. Phi Beta Kappa. Avocations: song-writing, poetry.

GRAY, ROBERT DONALD, retired mayor; b. Quincy, Ill., May 6, 1924; s. James Arthur and Katherine Elnora (Moore) G.; m. Marie Dolores Albert, July 15, 1951; children: Michael S., Sheilah C. Student, Washington & Jefferson Coll., 1945-47; BSEE, Okla. State U., 1949; postgrad., Northwestern U. Electrolysis engr. Sinclair Refining Co., 1949-50; North Atlantic field mgr. navigation/communication systems USAF, 1950-51; cons. Lockheed Aircraft Ga. Co., 1951-52; sr. devel. engr. Harris Corp., 1952-54; dir. Gen. Telephone Electronics, Mountain View, Calif., 1954-66; dir. reliability and quality control Gen. Dynamics/Electronics, Rochester, N.Y., 1961-62; v.p. rsch./devel. Lockheed Missiles/Space Co., Sunnyvale, Calif., 1966-79; pres. Gray Assocs., Internat. Air Traffic Control System, Los Altos, Calif., 1980-87; mem. Los Altos City Coun., 1993-97; mayor City of Los Altos, Calif., 1994-95. With USN, 1941-45; ETO. Mem. IEEE (sr.), Phi Kappa Psi. Republican. Avocations: golf, amateur radio, electronics, aircraft. Home: 2880 Carey Way Hollister CA 95023-2300

GRAY, ROBERT F., JR., lawyer; BBA, Univ. Mich., 1972, MA, 1974; JD, Univ. San Diego, 1977; LLM, NYU, 1978. Bar: Calif. 1977, Tex. 1978, DC 1979. With Fulbright & Jaworski LLP, Houston, 1978—, now ptnr. and co-head tech. and emerging companies dept. Bd. dir. Jr. Achievement of Houston/Gulf Coast, 1996—2001; adv. bd. dir. Houston Tech. Ctr., 2000—; bd. dir. Houston Entrepreneur's Found., 2000—; bd. mgrs. Cougar Investment Fund, 2001—; dean's adv. bd. Univ. Houston C.T. Bauer Coll. Bus., 2002—. Named a Tex. Super Lawyer, Tex. Monthly Mag., 2003. Fellow: Tex. Bus. Law Found.; mem.: ABA (Tex. State Liaison, com. on corp. laws 1990—98), State Bar Tex. (chmn. bus. law sect. 1995—96), State Bar of Calif., Houston Bar Assn., DC Bar. Office: Fulbright & Jaworski LLP Ste 5100 1301 McKinney Houston TX 77010-3095 Office Phone: 713-651-5151. Office Fax: 713-651-5246. Business E-Mail: rgray@fulbright.com.

GRAY, ROBERT STEELE, publishing executive, editor, writer; b. Beaumont, Tex., Oct. 6, 1923; s. Fred and Ruth Louise (Lewelling) G.; m. Nellie Frances McGuinness, July 3, 1945; children: Robert Steele, Laura, Ruth Ellen (Mrs. Sommy L. Ham). BS, U. Houston, 1954. Newscaster Sta. KPRC-AM, Houston, 1947; news dir. Sta. KNUZ, Houston, 1948-49; reporter Citizens Papers, Houston, 1950; newsfilm dir. Sta. KPRC-TV, 1951-56; writer Houston Post, 1956-60; founder, pub. editor Cordovan Corp., Houston, 1960—, chmn. bd., 1982—; pub. Cordovan Bus. Jours., Houston, 1971; co-founder Golfer Mags., Inc., 1984—. Author: Survivor, 1998. 2nd lt. USMCR, 1942-46, to 1st lt. 1951-52, Korea. Mem.: Soc. Profl. Journalists. Office: 13662 Mansfield Point Ln Houston TX 77070

GRAY, ROBERT WARD, art association administrator; b. Tallahassee, Fla., June 26, 1916; s. Joseph Henry and Welia (Ward) Gray; m. Lenorma Verdelle Connell, Dec. 15, 1943. Degree in civil engring., U. Fla.; degree, Tri-State Coll., Sch. for Am. Craftsmen, 1949. Project engr. Fla. State Highway Dept., Fla., 1946—47; mgr. Pottery Shop, Old Sturbridge Village, 1949—51; coord. of craft program Old Sturbridge Village, 1951; dir. Worcster Craft Ctr., 1951—61; exec. dir. Southern Highland Craft Guild, Asheville, NC, 1961—80, dir. emeritus, 1980, dir. devel., 1980—83. Charter mem. bus. cabinet Ga. State Coll., Milledgeville, Ga., 1974—77; fellow Am. Craft Coun., N.Y.C., NY, 1980. Pres. Asheville Tourism Assn., Asheville, NC, 1975—76; adv. coun. Haywood C.C., Clyde, NC, 1975; honoarary lifetime mem. Asheville Tourism Assn., Asheville, NC, 1985. Tech. sgt. USMC, 1942—46. Recipient Dist. Svc. award, Asheville Tourism Assn., 1985, Lifetime Achieve. award, Southern Highland Craft Guild, 1980, Fine Art's award, Gov. of NC, 1998. Home: 17 Botany Ct Asheville NC 28805-1605

GRAY, ROLAND WILLIAM, pediatrician; b. Nashville, Feb. 10, 1947; s. William Thurman and Margaret Helen (Miller) G.; m. Gloria Diane Gray, Mar. 14, 1969; children: Roland, Jr., Camilla, Andrew. BA, Vanderbilt U., 1969; MD, U. Tenn., 1972. Diplomate Am. Bd. Pediat. Asst. prof. U. Fla., Gainesville, 1976-78; pediatrician Children's Clinic Donelson, Nashville, 1978—. Med. dir., addictionist Koala Ctr., Nashville; clin. instr. pediat. Vanderbilt U., Nashville; med. dir. Physicians Health Program, Tenn. Med. Found., 2002. Bd. dirs. Recovery Residence, Nashville. Named Tenn. Vol. Hero, 2001. Mem. AMA, Am. Acad. Pediatrics, Am. Bd. Pediatrics, Am. Soc. Addiction Medicine, Tenn. Med. Assn., Fla. Med. Assn. Episcopalian. Avocations: gardening, fishing. Office: 216 Centerview Dr Ste 304 Brentwood TN 37027 Office Phone: 615-467-6411.

GRAY, SARAH VIRGINIA, retired librarian; b. Durham, N.C., Oct. 1, 1934; d. Irving Emory and Virginia Rose (Gearhart) G. AB in History, Duke U., 1956; MLS, U. N.C., 1964. Asst. to curator of manuscript Duke U. Library, Durham, N.C., 1956-58; asst. supr. res. reading rm. U. N.C., Chapel Hill, 1959-61, supr. reserve reading room, 1961-64; exchange librarian U. Exeter, England, 1968; periodicals librarian Coll. of William & Mary, Williamsburg, Va., 1964-81; circulation librarian Williamsburg Regional Library, 1981-85; systems adminstr. Colonial Williamsburg Found., Williamsburg, 1988—2001; ret., 2001. Author: Index to Commonwealth Little Magazines, 2 vols., 1976-79, 1 vol. 1980-82, 1 vol., 1983-84, 85. Mem. Lord Chamberlain Soc. Va. Shakespeare Festival, Williamsburg, 1987—. Democrat. Presbyterian. Avocations: historical cooking, antiques, travel, indexing. Home: 405 Tyler St Williamsburg VA 23185-4214

GRAY, SHEILA HAFTER, psychiatrist, researcher; b. N.Y.C., Oct. 19, 1930; MD, Harvard U., 1958. cert. Washington Psychoanalytic Inst., 1969. Intern St. Elizabeths Hosp., Washington, 1958-59; resident McLean Hosp., Belmont, Mass., 1959-61; clin. and rsch. fellow Mass. Gen. Hosp., Boston, 1961-62; staff psychiatrist Chestnut Lodge, Inc., Rockville, Md., 1962-64; practice medicine, specializing in psychiatry and psychoanalysis Washington, 1964—; clin. asst. prof. psychiatry U. Md. Sch. Medicine, Balt., 1968-75, clin. assoc. prof., 1975-83, clin. prof., 1983-96; instr. Washington Psychoanalytic Inst., 1971-75, tchg. analyst, 1975-96, Balt.-Washington Inst. for Psychoanalysis, 1996—; clin. prof. psychiatry Uniformed Svcs. U. Health Scis., 1997-99, adj. prof. psychiatry, 1999—. Staff U. Md. Hosp., Balt., 1970-96; physician mem. Commn. on Mental Health, Superior Ct. of D.C., 1972-98; bd. govs. Nat. Capital Reciprocal Ins. Co., 1981-98; treas. NCRIC Physicians Orgn., 1994-97; cons. Walter Reed Army Med. Ctr., Washington, 1983—. Active Mayor's Adv. Com. on Mental Health Svcs. Reorgn., Washington, 1984; adv. panel Mayor's Environ. Design Awards Program, 1988-89; exec. com. D.C. Fedn. Civic Assns., 1984—, asst. rec. sec., 1985, rec. sec., 1986-88, 2d v.p., 1989-90, pres., 1991-92, del.-at-large, 1993—; v.p. programs Women's Equity Action League Met. D.C., 1986; commr. D.C. Adv. Neighborhood Commn., 1986-88; mem. Met. Washington Coun. of Govt.'s Partnership for Regional Excellence, 1992; trustee Accreditation Coun. for Psychoanalytic Edn., Inc., 2002—, sec., 2004—. Fellow: Am. Psychiat. Assn. (chair com. quality assurance and improvement, Coun. on Econ. Affairs, 1996—97); mem.: Washington Psychoanalytic Soc. (chmn. bd. dirs. psychoanalytic clinic and councillor ex officio 1987—90), Med. Soc. D.C. (exec. bd. 1982, ho. dels. 1992—97), Washington Psychiatric Soc. (councillor 1981—83), Am. Acad. Psychoanalysis (trustee 1996—99, pres.-elect 1999—2000, pres. 2000—01, editl. bd. jour. 2002—), Am. Psychoanalytic Assn. (diplomate Bd. Profl. Stds.), Palisades Citizens Assn. (bd. dirs. 1980—, treas. 1983—84, pres. 1984—86). Office: PO Box 40612 Palisades Sta Washington DC 20016 Office Phone: 202-338-1955.

GRAY, SIMON JAMES HOLLIDAY, writer, educator; b. Oct. 21, 1936; s. James Davidson Gray and Barbara Cecelia Mary (Holliday) Davidson; m. Beryl Mary Kevern, 1965 (div. 1997); 2 children; m. Victoria Rothschild, 1997. Student, Westminister Sch., Dalhousie U., Halifax, N.S.; MA, U.

Cambridge. Supr. English U. B.C., 1960-63. Sr. instr., 1963-64; lectr. Queen Mary Coll., U. London, 1965-84. Author: (novels) Colmain, 1963, Simple People, 1965, Little Portia, 1967, A Comeback for Stark, 1968, Breaking Hearts, 1997, (non-fiction) An Unnatural Pursuit and Other Pieces, 1985, How's That For Telling 'Em Fat Lady, 1988, Fat Chance, 1995, Enter a Fox, 2001, The Smoking Diaries, 2005, (plays) Wise Child, 1968, Sleeping Dog, 1968, Dutch Uncle, 1969, The Idiot, 1971, Spoiled, 1971, Butley, 1971 (Evening Std. award), Otherwise Engaged, 1975 (Best Play, N.Y. Drama Critics Cir., Evening Std. award), Plaintiffs and Defendants, 1975, Two Sundays, 1975, Dog Days, 1976, Molly, 1977, The Rear Column, 1978, Close of Play, 1979, Quartermaine's Terms, 1981, Tartuffe, 1982, Chapter 17, 1982, The Common Pursuit, 1984, Plays One, 1986, Melon, 1987, Hidden Laughter, 1991, The Holy Terror, 1992, Cell Mates, 1995, Simply Disconnected, 1996, Life Support, 1997, Just the Three of Us, 1997, The Late Middle Classes, 1999, Japes, 2000, (TV movies) After Pilkington, 1987, Quartermaine's Terms, 1987, Old Flames, 1990, They Never Slept, 1991, The Common Pursuit, 1992, Running Late, 1992, Unnatural Pursuits, 1993, Femme Fatale, 1993, (film) A Month in the Country, (radio plays) The Holy Terror (rev.), 1989, The Rector's Daughter, 1992, With a Nod and a Bow, 1993, Suffer the Little Children, 1993. Mem. Dramatists Guild. Mailing: c/o Angela Rose/Granta Agy 2/3 Hanover Yard Noel Rd London N1 8BE England*

GRAY, SUE, elementary school educator; d. Wilbur and Naomi Jacobsen; 1 child, Jedidiah. BA in History, U. Calif., Davis, 1968. Tchg. credential U. Calif. Davis, 1969. Tchr. Gibson Elem. Sch. Woodland Unified Sch. Dist., Woodland, Calif., 1968—70, Whitehead Elem. Sch., 1970—83, Willow Spring Elem. Sch., 1983—89, Prairie Elem. Sch., 1989—. Workshop presenter Nat. Coun. Tchrs. Math. Hawaii/Calif., 1990—91, N. Calif. Math Project U. Calif. Davis, 1988—91; math mentor Woodland Unified Sch. Dist., 1987—90, curriculum coach, GATE advisor, mem. leadership team. Named Outstanding Tchr., Woodland Unified Sch. Dist., 1997. Mem.: AAUW (pres. Woodland chpt. 1998, 1999), Nat. Math. Coun., Delta Kappa Gamma (pres. Woodland chpt. 1986, 1987). Avocations: reading, painting, travel. Office: Woodland Prairie Elem Sch 1444 Stetson St Woodland CA 95776-6722

GRAY, SUZY, recreation director, educator; b. Little Rock, July 28, 1960; d. James Haughton Gray, Sr., Susan East and Ronald A. May (Stepfather). BA, Trinity U., San Antonio, 1982; MEd, Tex. Tech U., 1983; PhD, U. Tex., 2004. Cert. Recreational Sports Specialist Nat. Intramural Recreational Sports Assn., 1983. Recreational sports dir. USAA, San Antonio, 1985—94; asst. dir. wellness and leadership programs Our Lady of the Lake U., 1995—98; exec. dir. campus recreation U. Tex. at San Antonio, 1998—. Key vol. San Antonio Sports Found., 1985—; mem. Stonewall Democrats, 2000—; mem., vol. Human Rights Campaign, 1987—; elder Madison Sq. Presbyn. Ch., 2000—. Mem.: Nat. Intramural-Recreational Sports Assn. (nat. conf. co-chair 2002—03). Liberal. Avocations: sports, reading, travel. Home: 151 Thorain Blvd San Antonio TX 78212-1227 Office: Univ Texas at San Antonio 6900 N Loop 1604 W San Antonio TX 78249-0693 Office Phone: 210-458-6262. Office Fax: 210-458-7272. E-mail: suzy.gray@utsa.edu.

GRAY, THOMAS ALVA, JR., writer, minister, retired protective services official; b. Ridgeway, Mo., Mar. 2, 1935; s. Thomas Alva and Claudia Ladine (Brown) Gray; m. Barbara Elisabeth Locke (Haug), Jan. 18, 1974; children: Paul David, Daniel Lawrence, Douglas Eric 1 stepchild, Derek Brundage Locke. BA in Sociology, Northwestern U., Evanston, Ill., 1961; MDiv magn cum laude, Nazarene Theol. Sem., Kansas City, 2003. Lic. min. Ch. of Nazarene, 2002. Pres. Gray Furniture, Inc., Smithville, Mo., 1961—65; spl. agt. FBI, 1966—86; pvt. investigator Clarence M. Kelley & Assocs., Kansas City, 1987—89; tchg. asst. Nazarene Theol. Sem., Kansas City, 2000—01; pastor Freeman Christian Ch., Mo., 2002; writer Leawood, Kans. Columnist (Little Known Facts About Authors): Potpourri Lit. Mag., 1991—96; editor: Red Herring Mystery Mag., 1996, The Seedling, 1996—99; author: (short stories) Handprint in the Woods, 1997, Mobius, The Journal of Social Change, 1996; author, editor: A Journey of Faith, 2005. Vol. assoc. chaplain Kingswood Manor Retirement Ctr., Kansas City; vol. tutor Vanderberg Youth Ctr., City Union Mission, Kansas City; exec. v.p. adminstn. bd. Nazarene Theol. Sem. Student Assn., Kansas City, 2000—01; sec. World Mission Fellowship coun. Nazarene Theol. Sem., Kansas City, 2001—02, treas. Women in Ministry coun., 2002—03; mem. 1st Bapt. Ch. Kansas City; founding mem., bd. dirs. Arts and Humanities Assn. Johnson County, Overland Park, Kans.; bd. dirs. Friends of Powell Gardens, Inc., Kingswood, Mo. With U.S. Army, 1958—61. Mem.: Phi Eta Sigma. Baptist. Avocations: reading, travel, volunteer work, golf. Home: 2007 Condolea Dr Leawood KS 66209

GRAY, THOMAS STEPHEN, writer; b. Burbank, Calif., Aug. 22, 1950; s. Thomas Edgar and Lily Irene (Ax) G.; m. Barbara Ellen Bronson, Aug. 27, 1977; children: Jonathan Thomas, Katherine Marie. BA, Stanford U., 1972; MA in English, UCLA, 1976. Tchg. assoc. UCLA, 1976-77; reporter LA Daily News, 1977-79, editl. writer, 1979-84, editl. page editor, 1984-95; sr. editor Investor's Bus. Daily, LA, 1995-98; v.p. and account group mgr. Investor Rels. Internat., 2003—. Author: Teach Yourself Investing Online, 1999, Investing Online for Dummies-Quick Reference, 2000, Online Investing Bible, 2001; contbg. writer: Convergence: Mag. of Sci. and Enging., UC Santa Barbara. Recipient 1st Place award Editl. Writing Greater LA Press Club, 1988, Inland Daily Press Assn., 1993. Office Phone: 818-889-4999. E-mail: tsgray@sbcglobal.net.

GRAY, VIRGINIA HICKMAN, political science professor; b. Camden, Ark., June 10, 1945; d. George Leonard and Ethel Massengale (Bell) Hickman; 1 child, Brian Charles. BA with honors, Hendrix Coll., 1967; MA, Washington U., St. Louis, 1969, PhD, 1972. Asst. prof. polit. sci. U. Ky., Lexington, 1971-73; from asst. prof. to assoc. prof. U. Minn., Mpls., 1973-83, prof., 1983-2000, chairperson dept. polit. sci., 1985-88; Winston Disting. prof. polit. sci. U. N.C., Chapel Hill, 2001—. Guest scholar Brookings Inst., Washington, 1977-78; vis. prof. U. Oslo, 1985, Nankai U., 1988, U. B.C., 1992, U. N.C., 1993-94; NSF vis. prof. for women, 1993-94. Co-author: The Organizational Politics of Criminal Justice, 1980, Feminism and the New Right, 1983, Politics in the American States, 1983, 8th edit., 2004, American States and Cities, 1991, 2d edit., 1997, The Population Ecology of Interest Representation, 1996, Minnesota Politics and Government, 1999. Bd. dirs. Health Ptnrs. Inc., 1992-2001, chair, 1999-2001. Fellow Woodrow Wilson Found., 1970, NDEA, 1969-70; grantee Swedish Bicentennial Found., 1985; recipient rsch. assistantship NSF, 1968-69, rsch. grant NSF, 1997-2001; scholar in residence Rockefeller Ctr., Bellagio, Italy; Investigator award Robert Wood Johnson Found., 2003-05; named Disting. Alumnus Hendrix Coll., 2005 Mem. Am. Polit. Sci. Assn. (coun. 1990-92), Midwest Polit. Sci. Assn. (coun. 1984-86, v.p. 1997-99, pres. 2003-2004), Policy Studies Orgn. (coun. 1977-79), So. Polit. Sci. Assn., Western Polit. Sci. Assn. Democrat. Unitarian Universalist. Home: 2 Heather Ct Chapel Hill NC 27517 Office: U NC Dept Polit Sci CB 3265 Hamilton Hall Chapel Hill NC 27599-3265 E-mail: vagray@email.unc.edu.

GRAY, WALTER P., III, historian, archivist, consultant; b. San Francisco, Aug. 8, 1952; s. Walter Patton II and Elsie Josephine (Stroop) G.; m. Mary Amanda Helmich, May 23, 1980. BA in History, Calif. State U., Sacramento, 1976. Rschr. Calif. State R.R. Mus., Sacramento, 1977-80, curator, 1980-81, 85-90, archivist, 1981-85, mus. dir., 1990-98; Calif. state archivist, 1998—2004; state hist. records coord., 1999—2004; chief cultural resources divsn. Calif. State Parks, 2004—. Trustee Golden State Mus., 2003-04; cons. in field, 1976—. Contbr. articles to profl. jours. Buddhist. Avocations: woodworking, antique automobiles, photography. Office: California State Parks 1416 9th St Ste 905 Sacramento CA 95814 Office Phone: 916-653-9946. E-mail: wgray@parks.ca.gov.

GRAY, WHITMORE, lawyer, educator; b. 1932; AB, Principia Coll., 1954; JD, U. Mich., 1957; postgrad., U. Paris, 1957—58, U. Munich, 1962; LLD, Adrian Coll., 1982. Bar: Mich. 1958. Assoc. Casey, Lane & Mittendorf, N.Y.C., 1958—60; asst. prof. U. Mich., 1960—63, assoc. prof., 1963—66, prof., 1966—93; assoc. Cleary, Gottlieb, N.Y.C., 1981; of counsel LeBoeuf, Lanb, Greene & MacRae, N.Y.C., 1994—2001. Mem. adv. bd. Bull. on Rsch. in Soviet Law and Govt. and Soviet Status and Decisions; lectr. contract law Chinese Acad. Social Scis., 1982; summer faculty Jilin U., China, 1985; vis. prof. Fordham Law Sch., NY, 1989—; advisor on contract and arbitration law, Thailand, 1993, Cambodia, 94, Indonesia, 1995—96. Contbr. articles on comml. arbitration and alternative dispute resolution to profl. jours.; translator: Russian Republic Civil Code, General Principles of Civil Law of People's Republic of China; past editor-in-chief: Mich. Law Rev., bd. editors: Am. Jour. Comparative Law. Japan Found. fellow, U. Tokyo, 1977—78. Mem.: Assn. Asian Studies, Japanese-Am. Soc. Legal Studies (bd. dirs.), Internat. Acad. Comparative Law, Am. Fgn. Law Assn. (dir.), Am. Assn. Law Schs. (past chmn. comparative law sect.). Home: 150 S 5th Ave Ann Arbor MI 48104 Office: U Mich Law Sch 625 S State St Ann Arbor MI 48109-1215 also: 271 W 47th St 30G New York NY 10036 Office Phone: 212-757-9264. Personal E-mail: whitgray@aol.com.

GRAY, WILLIAM GUERIN, engineering educator; b. San Francisco, Jan. 9, 1948; BS, U. Calif., 1969; MA, Princeton U., 1971, PhD, 1974. Asst. prof. dept. civil engring. Princeton U., N.J., 1975-80, dir. grad. studies dept. civil engring., 1977-84, assoc. prof. dept. civil engring., 1980-84; prof. dept. civil engring. U. Notre Dame, Ind., 1984-88, chmn. civil engring., geol. scis., 1984-95, Massman prof. civil engring. and geol. scis., 1988—. Office: U Notre Dame Dept Civil Engring Sc Notre Dame IN 46556 Home: 759 Pyrula Ave Sanibel FL 33957-6604

GRAY, WILLIAM H., III, lawyer, former non profit association administrator; b. Baton Rouge, Aug. 20, 1941; m. Andrea Dash, Apr. 17, 1971; children— William H. IV, Justin Yates, Andrew Dash. BA, Franklin and Marshall Coll., 1963; M.Div., Drew Theol. Sem., Madison, N.J., 1966; Th.M., Princeton Theol. Sem., 1970; postgrad., U. Pa., 1965, Temple U., 1966, Oxford U., 1967. Ordained to ministry Baptist Ch.; asst. minister Bright Hope Baptist Ch., Phila., 1963-64; dir. 1st Baptist Ch., Montclair, N.J., 1964-65; co-pastor, sr. minister Union Baptist Ch., Montclair, 1966-72; asst. prof., dir. St. Peter's Coll., Jersey City, 1970-74; sr. minister Bright Hope Baptist Ch., 1972—; lectr. Jersey City State Coll., 1968, Rutgers U., 1971, Montclair State Coll., 1970-72; mem. 96th-101st Congresses from 2d Dist. Pa., 1979—91; Ho. majority whip, 1989—91; pres., CEO United Negro Coll. Fund, N.Y.C., 1991—2004; sr. advisor Loeffler Jonas & Tuggey LLP, Washington, 2004—. Chmn. house budget com., 1985; mem. house appropriations com. Congl. Black Caucus, Nat. Economic Commn.; vice chmn. Dem. Leadership Coun.; envoy to Haiti, 1994; bd. dirs., Dell Inc., 2000-, J. P. Morgan Chase & Co., Prudential Financial, Inc., Rockwell Automation Inc., Visteon Corp., 2000-, Pfizer Inc., 2000-. Trexler Found. scholar, 1962; Rockefeller Protestant fellow, 1965 Mem. Phila. Pastor's Conf., Phila. Baptist Assn., Progressive Nat. Baptist Assn., Am. Baptist Conv., Alpha Phi Alpha. Clubs: Frontier Internat. Lodges: Masons, Elks. Democrat. Office: Loeffler Jonas & Tuggey LLP 1801 K St NW Ste 340 Washington DC 20006

GRAY, WILLIAM R., lawyer; b. Peoria, Ill., Aug. 25, 1941; s. John J. and Alverna K. (Kennedy) G.; m. Tiana M. Yeager, June 12, 1982; children: Ann Katherine, Thomas William. BA, U. Colo., 1963, JD, 1966. Bar: Colo. 1966; U.S. Dist. Ct. Colo. 1966; U.S. Ct. Appeals (10th cir.) 1976. Dep. dist. atty. Dist. Atty.'s Office/10th Jud. Dist., Pueblo, Colo., 1967-69, Dist. Atty.'s Office/20th Jud. Dist., Boulder, Colo., 1969-70; dep. state pub. defender Colo. State Pub. Defender, Boulder, 1970-72; ptnr. Miller & Gray, Boulder, 1973-85, Purvis, Gray, Murphy, LLP, Boulder, 1985—. Mem./vice chair, chmn., Colo. Supreme Ct. grievance com., 1983-88, mem. criminal rules com., 1982-84; adj. prof. law U. Colo. Sch. of Law, Boulder, 1984. Bd. dirs. Mental Health Ctr. of Boulder County, 1972—78. Fellow Am. Coll. Trial Lawyers (Courageous Advocacy award 1985), Internat. Soc. Barristers (bd. govs. 2004—), Internat. Acad. Trial Lawyers, Am. Bar Found., Colo. Bar Foun., Colo. Bar Assn. (Professionalism award 1995), Am. Bd. Trial Advs. (Colo. chpt. pres. 2003-04). Democrat. Office: Purvis Gray Murphy LLP Ste 501 1050 Walnut St Boulder CO 80302-5144 Office Phone: 303-442-3366. Business E-Mail: bgray@purvisgray.net.

GRAYBEAL, BARBARA, editor, writer; b. Mountain City, Tenn., Sept. 21, 1935; d. Claude Harold and Ruby Lucille (Hodge) G.; m. Lewis N. Kremer, June 7, 1958 (div.); m. Charles L. Ring, May 8, 1982(div.). BA magna cum laude, Marietta Coll., 1957; grad. Pub. Procedures Course, Radcliffe Coll., 1957. With New Yorker mag., N.Y.C., 1957-58; assoc. editor Saturday Evening Post, Phila., 1958-62, Voter Registration in Mississippi, 1964, Episc. mag., Phila., 1962-69; editl. asst. Luth. mag., Phila., 1971-72; instr. journalism Temple U., Phila., 1972-81; founding editor CGA World mag., 1980-82, sr. editor, 1982-83. Editor, writer: Fast and Fresh (by Julie Dannanbaum), 1981, The CGA Cookbook, 1984; editl. cons. Good Ideas for Decorating; contbr. articles, photographs and poetry to various publs. Mem. com. interpretation and promotion, dept. overseas missions Nat. Coun. Chs., 1966-68; mem. Phila. Dem. Com., 1968; bd. dirs., sec. Friends of Free Libr. Phila.; bd. dirs. N.C. Sch. Arts, The Assocs. of N.C. Sch. Arts, 1983-86; lay reader Episc. Ch.; vol. 1964 Miss. Freedom summer, Registration Project, Hattiesburg, Miss. Mem. AAUW (pres. br.), Women in Comms. (v.p. chpt.), Marietta Coll. Alumni Assn., Internat. Platform Assn., Phi Beta Kappa, Sigma Delta Chi, Alpha Xi Delta. Address: 1525 Woods Rd Apt 106 Winston Salem NC 27106-3135 Office Phone: 336-924-6913. Fax: 336-922-0261.

GRAYBEAL, JACK DANIEL, chemist, educator; b. Detroit, May 16, 1930; s. Paul Herman and Polly Dale (McClintic) G.; m. Evelyn Alice Nicolai, June 13, 1954; children: Daniel Lee, David Eugene, Dale Kevin. BS in Chemistry, W.Va. U., 1951; MS in Chemistry, U. Wis., 1953, PhD in Chemistry, 1955. Mem. tech. staff Bell Tel. Labs., Holmdel, NJ, 1955-57; asst. prof. chemistry W.Va. U., Morgantown, 1957-63, assoc. prof., 1963-68; assoc. prof. chemistry Va. Poly. Inst. and State U., Blacksburg, 1968-69, prof., 1969-97, assoc. head dept., 1975-95, prof. emeritus, 1997—. Author: Molecular Spectroscopy, 1988; contbr. articles to profl. jours. Mem. Am. Chem. Soc., Phi Lambda Upsilon (nat. editor 1981-87, nat. sec. 1987-96, nat. pres. 1996-2002, nat. historian 2002—), Sigma Xi. Avocations: stamp collecting/philately, photography. Home: 312 Apperson Dr Blacksburg VA 24060-3641 Office Phone: 540-552-4073. E-mail: graybealea@aol.com.

GRAYBURN, PAUL ARTHUR, cardiologist, educator; b. Cin., July 24, 1954; m. Rose L. Heicken, Jan. 16, 1983; children: Lynn, Michelle, John Paul, Juliet. BA in Chemistry, Tex. A&M U., 1976; MD, U. Tex. Med. Br., 1981. Resident St. Paul Hosp., Dallas, 1981-84, chief resident, 1983-84; fellow in cardiology U. Ky. Med. Ctr., Lexington, 1984-87, instr. in medicine, 1987-88; asst. prof. U. Tex. Southwestern Med. Ctr., Dallas, 1988-92, assoc. prof., 1992—, assoc. dir. cardiology fellowship tng. program, 1992—. Dir. echocardiography lab. VA Med. Ctr., Dallas, 1988—, acting chief of cardiology, 1990-92, chief sect. cardiovascular diseases, 1992—; mem. nat. adv. panel consequences of geographic variation in care of acute MI patients VA; grant reviewer VA Merit Rev. Program. Manuscript reviewer numerous profl. jours.; contbr. chpts. to books and articles to profl. jours. Fellow Am. Heart Assn., 1985-86, 86-87; NIH grantee, 1988-89, 88-90, 89-94. Fellow Am. Coll. Cardiology, Am. Heart Assn. Coun. on Clin. Cardiology; mem. Am. Heart Assn., AMA, Am. Soc. Echocardiography (mem. task force on digital formatting standards, spl. procedures com.), Acad. Med. Arts and Scis., Tex. Med. Assn. Home: 1405 Sagewood Dr De Soto TX 75115-7711 Office: U Tex Southwestern Med Ctr 5323 Harry Hines Blvd Dallas TX 75390-7208

GRAYDOSH, ANNE RENAE, literature and language professor; b. Richmond, Ind., July 30, 1976; d. Jack Carl and Carol Ann Graydosh; 1 child, Isabella. BS, Miami U., 1998; Med, Brock U., 2002. Realtor Re/Max, Richmond, Ind., 1997—99; tchr. Spanish Troy City Schs., Ohio, 1999; tchr. French Brantford Schs., 2000—01; tchr. English Hamilton-Wentworth Schs., 2001—02, Eaton Cmty. Schs., Ohio, 2002—; rep. Silpada, Inc., Richmond, 2003—; instr. English Sinclair C.C., Dayton, Ohio, 2005—. Mem.: Ohio Edn. Assn., Kappa Alpha Theta. Office: Eaton High Sch 600 Hillcrest Dr Eaton OH 45320

GRAYER, ELIZABETH L., lawyer; b. Boston, June 19, 1964; BA magna cum laude, Amherst Coll., 1986; JD cum laude, Harvard Univ., 1989. Bar: NY 1990. Law clk., Hon. Miriam Goldman Cedarbaum US Dist. Ct., So. Dist. NY; assoc. Cravath Swaine & Moore LLPq, NYC, 1990—97, ptnr., litig., 1997—. Mem.: ABA, Assn. of Bar of City of NY, NY State Bar Assn., Phi Beta Kappa. Office: Cravath Swaine & Moore LLP Worldwide Plz 825 Eighth Ave New York NY 10019-7475 Office Phone: 212-474-1604. Office Fax: 212-474-3700. Business E-Mail: egrayer@cravath.com.

GRAYER, JONATHAN, education company executive; AB, Harvard Coll.; MBA, Harvard U., 1990. Mktg. dir. Newsweek, Inc., 1990; regional ops. dir. Kaplan, Inc., N.Y.C., 1991—94, pres., CEO, 1994—2002, chmn., CEO, 2002—. Bd. mem. BrassRing Inc., N.Y.C. Partnership, New Sch. U. Mem.: Harvard Bus. Sch. Club N.Y. Office: Kaplan Inc 888 7th Ave New York NY 10106

GRAY-FUSON, JOAN LORRAINE, lawyer; b. Glendale, Calif., Mar. 25, 1938; d. Stanley Wayne Brune and Maxine Lorraine (Falconer) Talkin; m. Darrell Herbert Gray, June 26, 1959 (div. 1972); children: Michael Herbert Gray, Thomas Edward Gray; m. Arnold Max Fuson, Dec. 18, 1977; stepchildren: Marie Fuson Hudson, Karen Fuson, Gregory J. Fuson. BA in Edn., Calif. State U., 1960; JD, U. of the Pacific, 1978. Bar: Calif. 1978, U.S. Dist. Ct. (ea. dist.) Calif. 1978. Tchr. Rio Linda Union Sch. Dist., Sacramento, Calif., 1960-65; pvt. practice Sacramento, 1978-81; staff counsel State of Calif. Water Resources Control Bd., Sacramento, 1982-91; sr. staff counsel State of Calif. Dept. of Conservation, Sacramento, 1991—. Elder on session Fremont Presbyn. Ch., Sacramento, 1995-97. Avocations: gardening, folk dancing, exercise. Office: Dept of Conservation 801 K St # Ms24-3 Sacramento CA 95814-3500

GRAYHACK, JOHN THOMAS, urologist, educator; b. Kankakee, Ill., Aug. 21, 1923; s. John and Marie (Keckich) G.; m. Elizabeth Houlehin, June 3, 1950; children: Elizabeth, Anne Marie, Linda Jean, John, William. BS, U. Chgo., 1945, MD, 1947. Diplomate Am. Bd. Urology. Intern medicine Billings Hosp., Chgo., 1947; intern gen. surgery Johns Hopkins Hosp., 1947-48, asst. resident, 1948-49, fellow urology, 1949-50, asst. resident, 1950-52; resident urology, 1952-53; dir. Kretschmer Lab., Northwestern U. Med. Sch., 1956-75, prof. urology, 1963—, chmn. dept., 1961-90. Cons. VA Rsch. Hosp. Editor Year Book of Urology, 1963-78; editor Jour. Urology, 1985-94. Served to capt. USAF, 1954-56. Recipient Outstanding Achievement award USAF, Ferdinand C. Valentine award N.Y. Acad. Medicine, Disting. Svc. award U. Chgo., 1978, Pioneer award Internat. Symposium Biology Prostate Growth, 1998; fellow Am. Cancer Soc., 1949-50, Damon Runyon Fund, 1953-54, Johns Hopkins Soc. Scholars. Mem. AMA, ACS (dedication honoree, surg. forum, 2003), Ill., Chgo. Med. Socs., Am. Assn. Genitourinary Surgeons (Barringer medal, Keyes medal), Am. Urology Assn. (Hugh H. Young award, Fuller award, Mary Hugh and Russell Scott award, Ramon Guiteras award 1994), Soc. Urol. Oncology (Huggins medal 2002), Chgo. Urology Soc. (John T. Grayhack lectr.), Endocrine Soc., Clin. Soc. Genitourinary Surgeons, Am. Surg. Assn., Soc. Univ. Urologists, Phi Beta Kappa, Alpha Omega Alpha. Home: 95 N Park Rd La Grange IL 60525-5938 Office: Northwestern Meml Hosp Superior St Fairbanks Ct Chicago IL 60611

GRAYSMITH, ROBERT, political cartoonist, author; b. Pensacola, Fla., Sept. 17, 1942; s. Robert Gray and Frances Jane (Scott) Smith; m. Melanie Krakower, Oct. 15, 1975 (div. Sept. 1980); children: David Martin, Aaron Vincent, Margot Alexandra. BA, Calif. Coll. Arts and Crafts, 1965. Polit. cartoonist: Oakland (Calif.) Tribune, 1964-65, Stockton (Calif.) Record, 1965-68, San Francisco Chronicle, 1968-83; author: Zodiac, 1986, Trailside, 1986, The Sleeping Lady, 1990, The Murder of Bob Crane, 1993, Unabomber: A Desire to Kill, 1997, The Bell-Tower, A True Detective Story of Gas-lit San Francisco, 1999, Ghost Fleet, 1999, Zodiac Unmasked, 2002, Amerithrax: The Hunt for the Anthrax Killer, 2003, (films) Auto-Focus, 2002, Zodiac, 2005; cons Zodiac, Phoenix Pictures, 2004; illustrator: I Didn't Know What to Get You, 1993. Recipient 2d place Fgn. Press Awards 1973, World Population Contest 1976. Democrat. Presbyterian. Office: San Francisco Chronicle 901 Mission St San Francisco CA 94103-2905 Office Phone: 415-731-4069.

GRAYSON, ALBERT KIRK, social studies educator; b. Windsor, Ont., Can., Apr. 1, 1935; s. Albert Kirk and Helen (Smith) Grayson'; m. Eunice Marie Service, Aug. 3, 1956; children: Vera Lorraine, Sally Frances. BA, U. Toronto, Ont., 1955; MA, U. Toronto, 1958; postgrad., U. Vienna, Austria, 1959-60; PhD, Johns Hopkins U., 1962. Research asst. Chgo. Assyrian Dictionary Oriental Inst., Chgo., 1962-63; asst. prof. history Temple U., Phila., 1963-64; asst. prof. Near Eastern studies U. Toronto, 1964-67, assoc. prof., 1967-72, prof., 1972-2000, prof. emeritus, 2000—. Dir. Royal Inscriptions of Mesopotamia project, 1981—; vis. lectr. U. Pa., Phila., 1963-64; spl. asst. dept. Western Asiatic Antiquities Brit. Mus., London, intermittently, 1967-76; invited lectr. various univs., mus., U.S., Germany, Iraq, Eng., Austria, Italy Author: Assyrian Royal Inscriptions vol. I, 1972, Assyrian Royal Inscriptions vol. II, 1976, Assyrian and Babylonian Chronicles, 1975, Babylonian Historical-Literary Texts, 1975, Assyrian Rulers of the Third and Second Millennia, B.C. 1987, Assyrian Rulers of the Early First Millennium BC I-II, 1991-96; contbr. chpts. to books. Can. Council fellow, 1959-61; Samuel S. Fels Fund fellow, 1961-62; Social Scis. and Humanities Research Council Can. editorial grantee, 1981— Fellow Royal Soc. Can. (hon. sec. 1989-92); mem. Soc. Mesopotamian Studies (pres. 1980-92), Fondation Assyriologique Georges Dossin (Belgium), Oriental Club Toronto (sec. 1969-70, pres. 1979-80), Rencontre Assyriologique Internationale (sessional chmn. Berlin 1978, Vienna 1980, Leiden, Netherlands 1983), Am. Oriental Soc. (sec. Midwest br. 1965-68). Mem. Anglican Ch. of Canada. Office: 56 Rathnelly Ave Toronto ON Canada M4V 2M3

GRAYSON, DAVID S., paper company executive; b. Binghamton, N.Y., Oct. 16, 1943; s. Milton M. and Helen A. (Oretskin) G.; m. Wendy W. Grayson (div. June 1986); children: Natalie, Marc, Dana. BS, Coll. Forestry, Syracuse, N.Y., 1965; MS, Rensselaer Poly., 1967. Various positions Riegel Paper div. James River Co., Milford, N.J., 1967-80; sales mgr. Kerwin Paper, Appleton, Wis., 1980-81; pres., founder Am. Fine Paper, Appleton, 1981—. Jewish. Office: Am Fine Paper PO Box 2638 Appleton WI 54912-2638

GRAYSON, EDWARD DAVIS, lawyer, manufacturing executive; b. Davenport, Iowa, June 20, 1938; s. Charles E. and Isabelle (Davis) G.; m. Alice Ann McLaughlin; children: Alice Anne, Maureen Isabelle, Edward Davis Jr. BA, U. Iowa, 1960, LLB, 1964. Bar: Iowa 1964, Mass. 1967. Atty. Goodwin, Procter & Hoar, Boston, 1967-74; sr. v.p., gen. counsel Wang Labs., Inc., Lowell, Mass., 1974-92; v.p., gen. counsel Honeywell, Inc., Mpls., 1992—99. Trustee U. Lowell, Mass., 1981-87, chmn. bd. trustees, 1982-85, 87; dir. Bus. Econs. Edn. Found., 1992—. Capt. USAF, 1964-67. Mem. ABA (com. corp. law depts.), Mass. Bar Assn. (bd. dels. 1977-80), Greater Mpls. C. of C. (dir. 1992—).

GRAYSON, GERALD HERBERT, economist, educator, arbitrator, writer; b. Bklyn., June 23, 1940; s. Frank and Sylvia (Cohen) G.; m. Florence M. Herbstman, Dec. 27, 1964; children— Todd Zachary, Douglas Philip. BA, Bklyn. Coll., 1961; MA, U. Ill., 1963; PhD, N.Y. U., 1973. With Dept. Labor, Washington, 1963; labor economist N.Y.C. Bd. Edn., 1963-66; prof., chmn. Dep. Social Sci. N.Y.C. Coll. Tech., 1966—98; pub., editor Labor Edn. Pub. Co., N.Y.C., 1995—. Adj. prof. Adelphi U., Garden City, NY, 1974-81, Farmingdale State, 2002—; exec. dir. NY State Conf. AAUP, 1992-2002; labor arbitrator Fed. Mediation and Conciliation Svc., NY State Employees Rels. Bd., Suffolk Pub. Employees Rels. Bd., 2002-; securities arbitrator NASD. Served with USAR, 1962-68. Mem. Labor and Employment Rels. Assn. Jewish. Home: 43 Northcote Dr Melville NY 11747-3924 Office Phone: 931-920-7201. Personal E-mail: jerryarb@optonline.net.

GRAYSON, MARK, educational association administrator, director; b. Akron, Ohio, June 15, 1957; s. Thomas David G. and Suzanne Marie (Miller) Rowins; m. Sarah Richardson Houghton, Dec. 3, 1988; children: William Parker, Philip Houghton. BA cum laude, Harvard U., 1979; MBA, Columbia U., 1987. Asst. acct. exec. AC&R Advtsg., Inc., N.Y.C., 1981-83; acct. exec. North Castle Pntrs., Greenwich, Conn., 1983-85; tv packaging agent, v.p. internat. t.v. Triad Artists, Inc., L.A., 1987-92; pres., dir. Rabbit Ears Prodns., Inc., Rowayton, Conn., 1992-96; prin. Graybark Enterprises, Norwalk, Conn., 1996-98; CEO, exec. dir. All Kinds of Minds, Chapel Hill, NC, 1998—. Contbr. articles to profl. jours. Mem. The Fly Club, Beta Gamma Sigma. Office: All Kinds of Minds PO Box 3580- Chapel Hill NC 27515

GRAYSON, RICHARD STEPHEN (LORD OF MURSLEY), news correspondent, management consultant, finance educator; came to the U.S., 1995; s. Bernard Lewis and Lucille Ruth (Kliston) G.; m. Katherine Lilian Hunston, June 4, 1971; children: Karyn Elizabeth, Lindsey Anne. BA, BS, Cambridge U., 1967; MA, Sch. Internat. Svc., 1968; PhD, Oxford (Eng.) U., 1974. Research and lectr. in internat. law and politics Oxford (Eng.) U., 1970-74; adviser, negotiator 2d Diplomatic Conf., Geneva; mem. secretariat and sec. Round Table Diplomatic Conf., Italy; also research fellow, writer and editor Inst. Henry Dunant, Geneva, 1974; internat. legal and polit. adviser Geneva, 1974; asso. dir. Inst. World Affairs, 1975, exec. dir., 1976-77; internat. legal and polit. mgmt. cons. N.Y.C., and Washington, 1975; internat. legal and polit. cons., univ. lectr., speaker in field and adviser various internat. and nat. orgns., TV and radio programs on fgn. policy, 1976—; pres. Grayson Assos. Internat., Inc., 1978—. Adj. assoc. prof. NYU; bur. chief and sr. corr. British TV News; bd. dirs. Cambridge U., Oxford U. Alumni, Internat. Emmys Judge, British Acad. Film & Television Arts. Author: Basic Background Study of Southeast Asia, 3 vols, 1968, Political and International Legal Implications of the Problems of Civil War. Bd. dirs. Royal Buckingham Theatre, Fgn. Press Assn., pres., UNESCO Assn. USA, Center for Farm and Food Research, Am. Ibsen Theatre, Ibsen Soc. Am.; bd. dirs., corp. mem. Assn. for World Univ.; trustee InterFuture; del. Fed. Trust Edn. and Research Conf., Eng., 1969; mem. legis. adv. com. N.Y. State Legislature. Avalon fellow, 1966-68; grantee Inst. Henry Dunant, 1971-73 Mem. Internat. Inst. Strategic Studies, Inst. Hist. Research, Inst. Advanced Legal Studies, Inst. U.S. Studies, Mensa, Am. Soc. Internat. Law, Am. Polit. Sci. Assn., Internat. Law Assn., Internat. Polit. Sci. Assn., Am. Acad. Polit. and Social Sci., Oxford Soc., Brit. and Commonwealth Inst. (charter), Brit. Inst. Internat. and Comparative Law, Brit. Acad. of Film and TV Arts, Internat. Inst. Humanitarian Law, Cambridge U. Grad. Soc. (pres. 1969-70), U.S. Polo Assn., Oxford and Cambridge Soc., Fgn. Press Assn. (pres.), Fgn. Press Ctr., UN Corrs. Assn., St. George's Soc., English-Speaking Union, Westchester Council for the Arts, Am. Film Inst., Nat. Trust (U.K.), Nat. Press Club, Nat. Acad. Television Arts and Scis., Radio and Television News Directors Assn., Pi Sigma Alpha, Pi Gamma Mu. Clubs: University (N.Y.C.); United Oxford and Cambridge Univ. (London, internat. Emmy's judge), Savage (London); Pilgrims (N.Y.C. and London). Office: Oxford U Pembroke Coll Oxford OX1 1DW England

GRAYSON, TREY, state official; b. Ky. m. Nancy Humphrey; children: Alex, Kate. AB in Govt., Harvard Coll., 1994; MBA, JD, U. Ky., 1998. Atty. Greenbaum Doll & McDonald, Keating, Muething & Klekamp; sec. of state State of Ky., Frankfort, 2004—. Adv. bd. Just Democracy, Inc.; adv. mem. HelpingAmericansVote.org. Named one of 44 Ky. Leaders for New Century, Ky. Press Assn. & Shakertown Roundtable, 1999; Toll Fellowship, Coun. State Govt., 2004. Mem.: Nat. Assn. of Secretaries of State (vice chmn., com. voter participation, election com., bus. svcs. com., subcom. presidential primaries). Republican. Office: Office of Sec of State State Capitol Rm 150 Frankfort KY 40601-3493 Office Phone: 502-564-3490. Office Fax: 502-564-5687. Business E-Mail: tgrayson@mail.sos.state.ky.us.

GRAZER, BRIAN, film company executive; m. Gigi Levangie. Grad., U. So. Calif., 1974. Co-chair Imagine Films Entertainment. Prodr. films including: Night Shift, 1982, Splash, 1984, Real Genius, 1985, Spies Like Us (with George Folsey Jr.), 1985, Armed & Dangerous (with James Keach), 1986, Like Father, Like Son (with David Valdes, 1987, Parenthood, 1989, Cry Baby (with Jim Abrahams, 1990, Kindergarten Cop (with Ivan Reitman), 1990, Closet Land (with Ron Howard), 1991, The Doors (with Nicholas Clainos & Mario Kassar), 1991, Backdraft (with Raffaella DeLaurentiis), 1991, My Girl, 1991, Far and Away (with Ron Howard), 1992, Boomerang (with Warrington Hudlin), 1992, Housesitter, 1992, CB4 (with Sean Daniel), 1993, For Love or Money, 1993, The Paper (with Frederick Zollo), 1994, My Girl 2, 1994, Greedy, 1994, The Cowboy Way, 1994, Apollo 13 (with Ron Howard), 1995 (Acad. Award Nom. Best Picture, 1996), Sgt. Bilko, 1996, Ransom, 1996, Bowfinger, 1999, Beyond the Mat, 1999, Curious George, 2000, Nutty Professor II: The Klumps, 2000, How the Grinch Stole Christmas, 2000, A Beautiful Mind, (with Ron Howard), 2001, (Acad. Award Best Picture, 2002), Undercover Brother, 2002, Blue Crusch, 2002, 8 Mile, 2002, Intolerable Cruelty, 2003, The Cat in the Hat, 2003, The Missing, 2003, Friday Night Lights, 2004, Inside Deep Throat, 2005, Cinderella Man, 2005; prodr. TV miniseries: From the Earth to the Moon, 1998 (Emmy Outstanding Miniseries) exec. prodr. TV series: The PJs, 1999, Wonderland, 2000, "24", 2001-, The Beast, 2001, Miss Match, 2003, Arrested Development, 2003, The Big House, 2004, The Inside, 2005-. Named one of 50 Most Powerful People in Hollywood, Premiere mag., 2004, 2005. Office: Imagine Films Entertainment 9465 Wilshire Blvd Fl 7 Beverly Hills CA 90212-2606*

GRAZIANI, LEONARD JOSEPH, pediatric neurologist, researcher; b. Phila., Nov. 17, 1929; m. Amelia Honeyford, June 29, 1956; children: Paul, Amy, Virginia, David. BA, LaSalle Coll., Phila., 1951; MD, Jefferson Med. Coll., Phila., 1955. Diplomate Am. Bd. Pediat., Am. Bd. Psychiatry and Neurology. Intern Valley Forge (Pa.) Army Hosp., 1956; resident Brooke Army Hosp., San Antonio, 1959; chief pediatric svc. Ireland Army Hosp., Ft. Knox, Ky., 1960-61; neurology fellow Bronx Mcpl. Hosp. Ctr., 1961-64; interdisciplinary fellow Albert Einstein Coll. Medicine, Bronx, 1964-66, asst. prof. pediat. and neurology, 1964-68; career scientist Health Rsch. Coun., N.Y.C., 1967-68; attending pediatrician, neurologist Thomas Jefferson U. Hosp., Phila., 1968—; chief div. pediatric neurology dept. pediat. Jefferson Med. Coll., Thomas Jefferson U., Phila., 1974-99, vice chair dept. pediat., 1988-96, prof. pediat., neurology, 1968—. Cons. neurologist Woods Svcs., Langhorne, Pa., 1968—; staff E.I. duPont Inst., Wilmington, 1984—. Contbr. articles to profl. jours. Capt. U.S. Army, 1955-61. Fellow Am. Acad. Neurology, Am. Acad. Pediat.; mem. Am. Pediatric Soc., Soc. Pediatric Rsch., Child Neurology Soc., Alpha Omega Alpha, Sigma Xi.

GRAZIANI, LINDA ANN, secondary school educator; b. Erie, Pa., Aug. 16, 1951; d. Edward and Christine (Karsznia) Grzelak; m. Richard Martin Graziani, Aug. 4, 1973; 1 child, Kristen Lynn. BS, Pa. State U., 1973; MBA, Gannon U., 1978. Asst. twsp. sec. Lawrence Park Twsp., Erie, Pa., 1968-73; bus. edn. tchr. Millcreek Sch. Dist., Erie, 1973-74, Fairview (Pa.) Sch. Dist., 1983—, Girard (Pa.) Sch. Dist., 1976; adult edn. instr. Erie (Pa.) County Tech. Sch., 1978-85. Active Bus. Adv. Coun., Millcreek, Pa., 1994-2002. Bd. dirs. Lake Erie Jr. Women's Club, Erie, 1977-83, St. Stephen's Preschool, Fairview, 1982-83; mem. adv. com. Erie Bus. Adventure, 2002—; eucharistic min. Holy Cross Ch., Fairview, 1982—, steering com., 2002-03. Mem.: Inst. Mgmt. Accts., Erie County Bus. Edn. Assn., Nat. Bus. Edn. Assn., Pa. State Alumni Assn., Beginners Luck Investment Club, Phi Chi Theta. Democrat. Roman Catholic. Avocations: aerobics, tennis, golf, cross country skiing, reading, cooking. Home: 680 Hawthorne Trce Fairview PA 16415-1723 Office: Fairview HS 7460 Mccray Rd Fairview PA 16415-2401 Office Phone: 814-474-2600.

GRAZIANO, CRAIG FRANK, lawyer; b. Des Moines, Dec. 7, 1950; s. Charles Dominic and Corrine Rose (Comito) G. BA summa cum laude, Macalester Coll., 1973; JD with honors, Drake U., 1975. Bar: Iowa 1976, U.S. Dist. Ct. (no. and so. dists.) Iowa 1978, U.S. Ct. Appeals (8th cir.) 1977, U.S. Supreme Ct. 1988. Law clk. to Hon. M. D. Van Oosterhout U.S. Ct. Appeals (8th cir.), Sioux City, Iowa, 1976-78; pvt. practice Dickinson, Mackaman, Tyler & Hagen, PC, Des Moines, 1978-98; with Office of Consumer Advocate, Iowa Dept. Justice, Des Moines, 1999—. Mem. Gov.'s Task Force on Quality and Efficiency in Govt., 1999—2000. Mem. Iowa Bar Assn. (chair specialization com. 1993-96, chair adminstrv. law sect. 1996-99), Order of Coif, Phi Beta Kappa. Home: 500 44th St Des Moines IA 50312-2408 Office: 310 Maple St Des Moines IA 50319-0063 E-mail: craig.graziano@mchsi.com, cgraziano@mail.oca.state.ia.us.

GRAZIANO, FRANK MICHAEL, medical educator, researcher; b. Easton, Pa., June 5, 1942; s. Michael and Grace (Farace) G.; m. Mary Helen Ashton, Feb. 4, 1967; children: Teresa Ann, Frank Jr., Alicia Grace. BS, St. Joseph's Coll., 1964; MS, Villanova Univ., 1967; PhD, Univ. Va., 1970, MD, 1973. Diplomate Am. Bd. of Internal Medicine, Am. Bd. of Allergy and Clinical Immunology. Internship Univ. Wis. Hosp., Madison, 1973-74; residency in medicine Univ. Wis., Madison, 1974-76, asst. prof., 1978-84, assoc. prof., 1984-89, prof. medicine, 1989—, chief section of Rheumatology, 1989—. Author numerous books, articles, papers in field. Admissions com. Univ. Wis. Medical Sch., 1983-86, Minority subcom. chmn., 1985-86; medical and scientific com. Wis. Arthritis Found., 1979-80, Univ. Wis. Madison AIDS Task Force Com., 1986-89; Bd. dirs. Wis. Arthritis Found., 1990—, Wis. Com. Based Rsch. Consortium, 1990—. Recipient Am. Acad. Travel grant, 1978, NIH Young Investigator award, 1980, NIH Allergic Disease Acad. award, 1985. Fellow Am. Acad. Allergy/Immunology, Am. Coll. Physicians; mem. Am. Assn. Immunologists, Am. Assn. Advancement of Sci., Am. Thoracic Soc., Am. Coll. Pheumatology, Clinical Immunology Soc., Wis. Allergy Soc., Wis. Rheumatism Assn., Sigma Xi. Home: 853 Tipperary Rd Oregon WI 53575-2641 Office: Univ Wis Hosp & Clinics 600 Highland Ave # H6 363 Madison WI 53792-0001

GRAZIER, DIANA LYNN, community health nurse, medical/surgical nurse, writer; b. Washington, Oct. 17, 1958; d. Leroy Bone and Carol Lee Griswold; m. James Edward Grazier, Aug. 5, 1989; m. Merrill Kendrick Williams, Sept. 11, 1976 (div. June 1989); 1 child, Carmen Jennetta Williams. Diploma, Rockford Area Vocat. Ctr., 1976; AS in Nursing, Waubonsee C.C., Sugar Grove, Ill., 1985; BS in Health Arts, U. St. Francis, 1999. Rn, Ill., 1985. Nurse Sycamore Mcpl. Hosp., Ill., 1977—85, Valley Hosp., Las Vegas, 1985—86; charge nurse El-Jen Convalescent Ctr., Las Vegas, 1987—91; head nurse, asst. dir. nursing Vegas Valley Convalescent Hosp., 1991—95; case mgr. Sierra Health Svcs., Las Vegas, 1996—99; charge nurse La Paz Regional Hosp., Parker, Ariz., 1999—2000; pub. health nurse La Paz County Health Dept., 2001—, dir. nursing, 2003—. Author: The Price of Fame, 2001, One Last Dance, 2002, The Heart of Hidden Secrets, 2003. Recipient Best Poets of 2002, Internat. Libr. of Poets, 2002. Avocations: writing, reading, crocheting, piano. Office: La Paz County Health Dept 1112 Joshua Ave Ste 206 Parker AZ 85344 Office Phone: 928-669-1100. Personal E-mail: jeg91dlg@citlink.net.

GRAZIN, IGOR NIKOLAI, law educator, state official; b. Tartu, Estonia, June 27, 1952; came to U.S., 1990; s. Nikolai V. and Dagmar R. (Kibe) G.; children: Anton, Kaspar. Jurist degree, U. Tartu, Estonia, 1975; candidate of sci. in law, Moscow Inst. Law, 1979; DSc in Law, Inst. State and Law, Moscow, 1986. Cert. jurist, USSR. Lectr., prof. U. Tartu, Estonia, 1977-86, prof., 1986-89, assoc. dean Law Sch., 1986-89; mem. of the coun. Popular Front of Estonia, Tallinn, 1988-90; atty. Bachman and Ptrns., Tallinn, Estonia; pub. policy scholar Kennan Inst., Woodrow Wilson Ctr., Wash., 2004—05. Prof. U. Notre Dame, Ind., 1990-2000; faculty fellow Kellogg Inst. for Internat. Studies, Notre Dame, 1994-2000; adj. fellow Hudson Inst., 1994-2000; dir. Estonian Privatization Trust Fund; v.p. U. Nord. Author: Law as Text, 1983, Jeremy Bentham, 1990, Anglo-American Philosophy of Law, 1983, Right Course, 1994; editor: Studia Juridica, 1988-90; contbr. articles to profl. jours. Dep., Congress of Peoples Deps. of USSR, 1989-91; mem. Supreme Soviet, Moscow, 1989-91; counsellor to Pres., Republic of Estonia, 1993-97, V.P., pres. nat. assembly, 1999—; mem. Nat. Parliament of Estonia, 1995-99. Mem. AAUP, AALS (bd. dirs.), Estonian Bar Assn., Federalist Soc. U.S.A., Acad. Soc. of Estonian Lawyers (co-founder, vice chmn. 1989-90), Acad. Arts (Estonia, bd. dirs.), Rotary, Roman Club (founding). Republican. Lutheran. E-mail: igorveel@hotmail.com.

GREALY, MARY R., medical association administrator; Sr. Washington counsel Am. Hosp. Assn., 1996—99; pres. Healthcare Leadership Coun., Washington, 1999—. Office: Healthcare Leadership Coun 1001 Pennsylvania Ave NW Ste 550 S Washington DC 20004 Business E-Mail: mgrealy@hlc.org.

GREANEY, JOHN M., state supreme court justice; b. Westfield, Mass., Apr. 8, 1939; s. Patrick Joseph and Margaret Irene (Fitzgerald) G.; m. Susan H. Greaney, Nov. 23, 1967. 1 child, Jessica S. BA summa cum laude, Holly Cross Coll., 1960; JD, NYU, 1963; LLD (hon.), Westfield State Coll., 1967, Western New England Coll., 1969; LLD, New England Law Sch., 1991. Bar: Mass., Supreme Judicial Ct., U.S. Dist. Ct., U.S. Supreme Ct. Ptnr. Ely & King, Springfield, Mass., 1963-73; presiding judge Hampden County Housing Ct., Springfield, Mass., 1973-75; assoc. judge Mass. Superior Ct., Boston, 1975-76; assoc. justice Mass. Appeals Ct., Boston, 1976-84, 1976-84, chief justice, 1984-89; assoc. justice Mass. Supreme Jud. Ct., Boston, 1989—. Former faculty mem. Western New England Law Sch., Westfield State Coll.; co-chair. Supreme Judicial Ct's Gender Bias Study Commn; mem. bd. Tribunes WGBY-Channel #57. Former assoc. editor Mass. Law Review. Trustee, dir. Westfield Atheneum, participant Child and Family Svcs. Program. Fellow Am. Bar Found.; mem. ABA (litigation, judicial adminstrn. section), Hampden County Bar Assn.(former mem. exec. com., grievance com., treas.), Mass. Bar Assn. (former chmn. Young Lawyers section, bd. delegates, exec. com., grievance com., legal svc. to the poor com., civil litigation, criminal law sections), Am. Law Inst. Avocations: competitive running, reading. Office: Mass Supreme Jud Ct 1 Beacon St 3rd Fl Boston MA 02108-1701*

GREANEY, MICHAEL E., lawyer; b. June 15, 1952; BA, Loyola Univ., 1974; JD, Univ. So. Calif., 1977. Bar: Calif. 1977, NY 1999. Former co-ptnr.-in-charge NYC office Gibson Dunn & Crutcher LLP, NYC, now ptnr. corp. transactions and securities. Mem. exec. com. Gibson Dunn & Crutcher. Mem. Univ. So. Calif. Law Rev., 1975—76. Mem.: ABA (fed. regulation of securities com.). Office: Gibson Dun & Crutcher LLP 47th fl 200 Park Ave New York NY 10166-0193 Office Phone: 212-351-4065. Office Fax: 212-351-5260. Business E-Mail: mgreaney@gibsondunn.com.

GREANEY, THOMAS L., law educator, lawyer; BA magna cum laude, Wesleyan Univ., 1970; JD, Harvard Univ., 1973. Legis. asst. U.S. Rep. Elizabeth Holtzman, Washington, 1973—74; law clk. FCC, Washington, 1974—76; sr. trial atty. U.S. Dept. Justice, Antitrust div., Washington, 1976—81, asst. chief, 1982—85; Victor Kramer vis. fellow Yale Univ., 1985—86, NIMH fellow, 1986—87, lectr., Law Sch., 1986—87; prof., Sch. Law Saint Louis Univ., 1987—, assoc. prof., Sch. Pub. Health, 1987—; dir. Ctr. for Health Law Studies, Saint Louis Univ., 1987—. Vis. prof. Universite d'Orleans, France, 2001—02; Merck vis. scholar Seton Hall Univ., 2002, vis. prof., 04. Author: Bioethics, Liability; co-author: Health Law: Cases, Materials and Problems, Internat. Ency. Laws, Medical Law, U.S. Nat. ed., Health Law Statutes & Regulations. Fulbright Fellow, European Cmty. Rsch. Program, Brussels, Belgium, 1993—94. Mem.: Phi Beta Kappa. Office: Saint Louis University School of Law 3700 Lindell Blvd Saint Louis MO 63108

GREASER, CONSTANCE UDEAN, retired automotive executive; b. Jan. 18, 1938; d. Lloyd Edward and Udean Greaser. BA, San Diego State Coll., 1959; postgrad., U. Copenhagen Grad. Sch. Fgn., 1963, Georgetown U. Sch. Fgn. Svc., 1967; MA, U. So. Calif., 1968; exec. MBA, UCLA, 1981. Advt., publicity mgr. Crofton Co., San Diego, 1959-62; supr. Mercury Publs., Fullerton, Calif., 1962-64; supr. engring. support svcs. divsn. Arcata Data Mgmt., Hawthorne, Calif., 1964-67; mgr. computerized typesetting dept. Continental Graphics, LA, 1967-70; v.p., editl. dir. Sage Publs., Inc., Beverly Hills, Calif., 1970-74; head publs. RAND Corp., Santa Monica, Calif., 1974-90; mgr. svc. comms. Am. Honda Motors Co., Torrance, Calif., 1990—2002; ret., 2002. Co-author: Quick Writer-Build Your Own Word Procesing Users Guide, 1983, Quick Writer-Word Processing Center Operations Manual, 1984; editor: Urban Research News, 1971-74; mng. editor: Comparative Polit. Studies, 1971-74; contbr. articles to profl. jours. Nat. com. Million Minutes of Peace Appeal, 1986, Nat. Info. Stds. Orgn., 1987-93, Global Cooperation for Better World, 1988. Recipient Berber award Graphic Arts Tech. Found., 1989. Mem. Women in Bus. (pres. 1977-78), Graphic Comm. Assn. (bd. dirs. 1994-99), Soc. for Scholarly Pubs. (nat. bd. dirs.), Women in Comm., Soc. Tech. Comm., So. Calif. Women for Understanding (chair Westside chpt., 2004—)

GREASER, MARION LEWIS, science educator; b. Vinton, Iowa, Feb. 10, 1942; s. Lewis Levi and Elisabeth (Sage) G.; m. Marilyn Sue Pfister, June 12, 1965; children— Suzanne, Scott BS, Iowa State U., 1964; MS, U. Wis., 1967, PhD, 1969. Postdoctoral fellow Boston Biomed. Research Inst., 1968-71; asst. prof. sci. U. Wis., Madison, 1971-73, assoc. prof., 1973-77, prof., 1977—, Cambell-Bascom prof., 2004—. Contbr. articles to profl. jours. Recipient Outstanding Researcher award Am. Heart Assn.-Wis., 1985 Mem. AAAS, Am. Soc. Biochem. Molecular Biology, Biophys. Soc., Am. Meat Sci. Assn. (Disting. Rsch. award 1981), Am. Soc. Animal Sci. (Meat Rsch. award 2000). Home: 2374 Branch St Middleton WI 53562-2809 Office: U Wis Muscle Biology Lab 1805 Linden Dr W Madison WI 53706-1110 Business E-Mail: mgreaser@ansci.wisc.edu.

GREASON, ARTHUR LEROY, JR., retired university administrator; b. Newport, R.I., Sept. 13, 1922; s. Arthur LeRoy and Pauline (Brown) G.; m. Pauline Schaaf, Dec. 29, 1945; children— Randall Mark, Katherine, Douglas Bradford. BA, Wesleyan U., Middletown, Conn., 1945; MA, Harvard U., 1947, PhD, 1954; LittD (hon.), Wesleyan U., 1987; LHD (hon.), Colby Coll., 1989, Bowdoin Coll., 1990, Bates Coll., 1990, U. Maine, 1992. Asst. to dean Wesleyan U., 1945-46; teaching fellow English Harvard, 1948-52; mem. faculty Bowdoin Coll., 1952-90, assoc. prof. English, 1961-66, prof., 1966-90, dean students, 1962-66, dean of coll., 1966-75, acting pres., 1981, pres., 1981-90. Trustee Portland Stage Co., 1991-97, Westbrook Coll., 1992-96, Maine Hist. Soc., 1994-97, U. New England, 1996—2004, Maine Bd. Bar Examiners, 1997—2003, DLF Charitable Found., 1997—. Kent fellow Soc. Religion Higher Edn., 1946 Mem. Maine Bar Assn. (fee arbitration commn. 1997-2002), Phi Beta Kappa. Congregationalist. Home: 20 Birch Meadow Brunswick ME 04011-2955 E-mail: algreason@gwi.net.

GREASON, MURRAY CROSSLEY, JR., lawyer; b. Wake Forest, N.C., Dec. 12, 1936; s. Murray Crossley and Evelyn Elizabeth (Hackney) G.; m. Joan Millicent Wilder. BS magna cum laude, Wake Forest U., 1959, JD magna cum laude, 1962. Bar: N.C. 1962. Assoc. firm Womble Carlyle Sandridge & Rice, PLLC, Winston-Salem, N.C., 1965-70; mem. firm Womble Carlyle Sandridge & Rice, Winston-Salem, N.C., 1970—; mng. ptnr. firm Womble Carlyle Sandridge & Rice, PLLC, Winston-Salem, 1988-96. Vis. lectr. Wake Forest U., 1972-74. Pres. Winston-Salem Estate Planning Coun., 1973; trustee Denmark Loan Fund, scholarships to Wake Forest U.; bd. visitors Wake Forest Law Sch., 1983—, chmn. 1994-2000; trustee Wake Forest U., 1990, vice chmn., 1997-2002, chmn., 2003-05; chmn. N.W. N.C. chpt. ARC, 1996; chmn. bd. United Way Forsyth County, 1995; mem. Commn. on Ministry Episcopalian Diocese N.C., 1983-93; bd. dirs. Winston-Salem Alliance, 2000-05, Idealliance, 1998—, Wake Forest U. Health Scis., 2000—, DoctorsCare, 2004—. Capt. JAG, AUS, 1962-65. Fellow Am. Coll. Tax Coun.; mem. ABA, N.C. Bar Assn. (I. Beverly Lake Pub. Svc. award 2005), Forsyth County Bar Assn. (pres. 1986-87), Winston-Salem C. of C. (bd. dirs., vice chmn. 2001, chmn. 2002), Wake Forest U. Alumni Assn. (pres. 1973), Forsyth Country Club, Phi Beta Kappa, Omicron Delta Kappa. Episcopalian. Home: 745 Arbor Rd Winston Salem NC 27104-2209 Office: Womble Carlyle Sandridge PLLC One W 4th St Winston Salem NC 27101 Office Phone: 336-721-3616. Business E-Mail: mgreason@wcsr.com.

GREATBATCH, WILSON, biomedical engineer; b. Buffalo, Sept. 6, 1919; married; 5 children. BEE, Cornell U., 1950; MSEE, U. Buffalo, 1957; ScD (hon.), Houghton Coll., 1971, SUNY, Buffalo, 1984, Clarkson U., 1987, Roberts Wesleyan Coll., 1988, D'Youville Coll., 2002. Project engr. Cornell Aeronaut Lab. Inc., 1950—52; asst. prof. elec. engring. U. Buffalo, 1952—57; mgr. electronics div. Taber Instrument Corp., 1957—60; v.p. Mennen Greatbatch Electronics Inc., 1962—78. Adj. prof. elec. engring. SUNY, Buffalo, 1981—; adj. prof. engring. Cornell U., Ithaca, NY, 1989—; adj. prof. physical scis. Houghton (N.Y.) Coll., 1978—; adj. prof. phys. scis. Kingston U., Niagara Falls, Ont., Canada, 2001—. Contbr. over 100 articles to sci. jours.; holder over 320 U.S. and fgn. patents. Named Paul Harris fellow, Rotary Internat., 1993; named to, Nat. Inventors Hall of Fame, 1986, U.S. Space Tech. Hall of Fame, 1993, Sci. and Engring. Hall of Fame, 1997; recipient Holley medal, ASME, 1986, Chancellor Morton medal, U. Buffalo, 1990, disting. svc. award, NSPE, 1984, Pacemaker award, Prince Rainier of Monaco, 1988, Nat. Medal of Tech., Pres. Bush, 1990, Vladimir Karapetoff award, Eta Kappa Nu, 1992, Washington award, Western Engring. Soc., Chgo., 1995, Lemelson/MIT Career Achievement award, 1996, Russ Prize, Nat. Acad. Engring., 2001. Fellow: ASME, IEEE, AAAS, N.Y. Acad. Scis., Am. Inst. Med. and Biol. Engring. (founder), Am. Soc. Angiology, Am. Coll. Cardiology, Royal Soc. Health; mem.: NAE (Russ prize 2001), Assn. Advancement Med. Instrumentation (Laufman award 1982), Eta Kappa Nu., Tau Beta Pi, Sigma Xi. Achievements include invention of implantable cardiac pacemaker; research in implantable power supplies for medical uses, biomass energy, genetic engineering. Office: Greatbatch Technologies Inc 9645 Wehrle Dr Clarence NY 14031*

GREAUX, CHERYL PREJEAN, federal agency administrator; b. Houston, July 30, 1949; m. Robert Bruce Greaux. BA, Tex. So. U., 1967; MA, U. Tex., 1973. Mgr. compliance programs Dept. Labor, N.Y.C., 1973-80; corp. human resources mgr. Allied Signal Inc., Morristown, NJ, 1980-85; account exec., sourcing specialist Dean Witter Reynolds, N.Y.C., 1986-88; dir. civil rights staff USDA Rural Devel., Washington, 1994—. Cons. Seagrams, N.Y.C., 1984, Gen. Foods, White Plains, NY, 1985. Author: Struggling Within or Success from Within?, 1973. Lectr. Nat. Urban League, 1980—; cons. Nat. Urban Affairs Coun., NY, 1981—86; bd. dirs. Ednl. Opportunity Fund, NJ, 1985—87. Mem.: Edges Group, Delta Sigma Theta. Office: Dept Agr 14th And Independence SW Washington DC 20250-0001 Office Phone: 202-692-0204. Business E-Mail: cheryl.greaux@usda.gov.

GREAVER, HARRY, artist; b. LA, Oct. 30, 1929; s. Harry Jones and Lucy Catherine (Coons) G.; m. Hanne Synnestvedt Nielsen, Nov. 30, 1955; children: Peter, Paul, Lotte. BFA, U. Kans., 1951, MFA, 1952. Assoc. prof. art U. Maine, Orono, 1955-66; exec. dir. Kalamazoo Inst. Arts, 1966-78; dir. Greaver Gallery, Cannon Beach, Oreg., 1978—. Mem. visual com. Mich. Coun. Arts, 1976-78. One-man exhbns. include Baker U., Baldwin, Kans., 1955, U. Maine, Orono, 1958, 59, Pacific U., 1985; group exhbns. include U. Utah Mus. Fine Arts, 1972-73, Purdue U., 1977, Drawings, USA, St. Paul, 1963, San Diego Mus., 1971, Rathbun Gallery, Portland, Oreg., 1988; 10-yr. print retrospective Cannon Beach Arts Assn., 1989, 20-yr. retrospective, 1998, 25th Anniversary exhibit. Mem. adv. bd. Haystack Ctr. for the Arts, Cannon Beach, 1988-91. Recipient Purchase award Nat. Endowment Arts, 1971; grantee U. Maine, 1962-64. Address: PO Box 120 Cannon Beach OR 97110-0120 Office Phone: 503-436-1185.

GREAVER, JOANNE HUTCHINS, mathematics educator, writer; b. Louisville, Aug. 9, 1939; d. Alphonso Victor and Mary Louise (Sage) Hutchins; 1 child, Mary Elizabeth. BS in Chemistry, U. Louisville, 1961, MEd, 1971; MAT in Math., Purdue U., 1973. Cert. tchr. Pres. Math Mentors Inc., 1962—. Part-time faculty Bellarmine Coll., Louisville, 1982-2002, U. Louisville, 1985—; project reviewer NSF, 1983—; advisor Council on Higher Edn., Frankfort, Ky., 1983-86; active regional and nat. summit on assessment in math., 1991, state task force on math., assessment adv. com., Nat. Assessment Ednl. Progress standards com.; charter mem. Commonwealth Tchrs. Inst., 1984—; mem. Nat. Forum for Excellence in Edn., Indpls., 1983; metric edn. leader Fed. Metric Project, Louisville, 1979-82; mem. Ky. Ednl. Reform Task Force, Assessment Com., Nat. Framework, Nat. Assessment Ednl. Progress

Rev. Com.; lectr. in field. Author: (workbook) Down Algebra Alley, 1984; co-author curriculum guides. Named Outstanding Citizen, SAR, 1984; named to Hon. Order Ky. Cols.; recipient Presdl. award for excellence in math. tchg., 1983; grantee, NSF, 1983, Louisville Cmty. Found., 1984—86. Mem. Greater Louisville Coun. Tchrs. of Math. (pres. 1977-78, 94-95, Outstanding Educator award 1987), Nat. Coun. Tchrs. of Math. (reviewer 1981—), Ky. Coun. Tchrs. of Math. (pres. 1990-91, Jefferson County Tchr. of Yr. award 1985), Math. Assn. Am., Phi Delta Kappa Internat., Kappa Delta Pi, Delta Kappa Gamma, Zeta Tau Alpha. Republican. Presbyterian. Avocations: tropical fish, gardening, handicrafts, travel. Home: 11513 Tazwell Dr Louisville KY 40241 E-mail: jogreaver@aol.com.

GREAVES, ALISON ASH, retired physician; b. Evanston, Ill., Dec. 15, 1928; d. William Henry and Edythe E. Tower Ash; m. Robert George Greaves, June 9, 1962; children: Edmund, Cordelia Ann. B in Philosophy, Northwestern U., 1953; MD, U. Ill., 1962, MPH, 1974. Diplomate Am. Bd. Pediats. Med. technologist Northwestern U. Med. Sch., Chgo., 1949-51, G.D. Searle, Skokie, Ill., 1951-53, Evanston Hosp., 1953-56, Aramco, Saudi Arabia, 1956-58; pediatrician Chgo. Bd. Health, 1966-67; med. dir. Infant Welfare Soc. Chgo., 1967-73; physician Northwestern U. Student Svc., Evanston, 1974-85, Cook County Hosp. Employee Health Svc., Chgo., 1986-92. Organizer cropwalk Christ the King Episcopal Ch., Sturgeon Bay, Wis., 1995, 96; reading buddy Sturgeon Bay Pub. Sch. 1997—; singer Door County Peninsula Chamber Singers, 1993-2005, So. Germany, Austria, 1998; alto Hope Ch. Choir, 2000-, Hope UCC Ch. Choir, 1997-; active Cornell Lab. Ornithology Project Feeder Watch, 1998—; co-leader book discussion group Sturgeon Bay Pub. Libr. Fellow Am. Acad. Pediats.; mem. AMA, LWV, AAUW, Chgo. Med. Soc., Wis. State Med. Soc., Med. Soc. Door Kewaunee County, Alpha Omega Alpha. Home: 806 Memorial Dr Sturgeon Bay WI 54235-2661 E-mail: agreaves@charter.net.

GREAVES, ROGER F., health maintenance organization executive; b. 1937; BA, Calif. State U., Long Beach, 1962. With Allstate Ins. Co., Chgo. and Pasadena, Calif., 1962-68; various positions, then v.p. human resources Blue Cross So. Calif., 1968-82; pres., CEO Health Net, Inc., Woodland Hills, Calif., 1982—91, chmn. bd., 1989-95; co-chmn bd., co-pres., co-CEO Health Systems Internat., Woodland Hills, 1991-95, non-exec. bd. dir., 1996—2004, non-exec. chmn., 2004—. Mem. Calif. Wellness Found. (bd. dirs.). Office: Health Net 21650 Oxnard St Woodland Hills CA 91367*

GREAVES, WILLIAM WEBSTER, chemist; b. Queenstown, Md., Jan. 10, 1951; s. William Emory and Mary Elizabeth (Wood) G. BS in Chemistry, Bucknell U., 1973; PhD in Inorganic Chemistry, Iowa State U., 1978. Tech. publ. editor Standard Oil of Ind., Naperville, Ill., 1978-81, rsch. info. scientist, 1981-84; assoc. editor Science mag., Washington, 1984-86; supr. chem. data systems SK&F Labs., Upper Merion, Pa., 1986-88; sr. patent searcher Abbott Labs., Abbott Park, Ill., 1988-90; patent analyst Amoco Corp., Chgo., 1990-99; sr. staff chemist ExxonMobil Rsch. and Engring. Co., 1999—2002. Dir., cmty. liaison Chgo. Adv. Coun. on Lesbian, Gay, Bisexual and Transgender Issues, 2000—. Contbr. articles to profl. publs.; contbr. revs. to Lambda Book Report. Active Frontrunners Chgo., 1988—, sec., 1991, v.p., 1992, pres., 1993, past pres., 1994, Proud to Run com., 1996-99; active D.C. Front Runners, 1984—; mem. Chgo. Adv. Coun. on Gay and Lesbian Issues, 1994-99; Chgo. coord. track and field and marathon events Gay Games, N.Y.C., 1994; mem. Honorary bd. for Chgo. 2006, 2000-02; trustee Adler Sch. Profl. Psychology, Chgo., 2005—. Mem. AAAS, Am. Chem. Soc. (sec. chem. info. divsn. 1994-96, edn. com. Chgo. chpt. 1981-84, mgr. Chgo. chpt. student symposium 1982), Soc. Tech. Comm. (sr., sec. Chgo. chpt. 1983), USA Track and Field, Chgo. Area Runners Assn., Stockton (N.J.) Runners Club, Sigma Xi. Office: Chgo Commn on Human Rels 740 N Sedgwick St Ste 300 Chicago IL 60610

GREBNER, BERNICE PRILL, author, astrological counselor; b. Peoria, Ill. d. John Elmer and Emma (Duhs) Prill; m. Arthur Conrad Grebner (div. 1974); children: David Arthur, Marjorie Welsch. Astrological counsellor. Pres. Grebner Books Pub. Author: Lunar Nodes, 1980, The Decannates, 1980, Everything Has a Phase, 1982, Mercury, The Open Door I, 1988, Mercury, The Open Door II, 1990, Day of Your Birth, 1990, Bee's Flight, 1991., ABCs of Astrology and Astronomy, 1993. Chmn. Woodford County (Ill.) Citizens for John Kennedy. Mem. Am. Fedn. Astrologers (accreditd profl.). Avocation: music: composing and performing for audiences. Home and Office: 5137 N Montclair Ave Peoria IL 61616-5221

GREBOW, EDWARD, finance company executive; b. Lakewood, NJ, July 17, 1949; s. Benjamin and Ruth (Blume) G.; m. Cynthia Miller, Feb. 23, 1985. BBA, George Washington U., 1971; postgrad., George Washington, 1972. V.p. Morgan Guaranty Trust Co., N.Y.C., 1972-80, J.P. Morgan & Co., Inc., N.Y.C., 1980-85; exec. v.p. Bowery Savs. Bank, N.Y.C., 1985-88; sr. v.p. CBS, Inc., N.Y.C., 1988-94, exec. v.p., 1994-95; pres. Tele-TV Sys., Reston, Va., 1995-97; pres., CEO, Chyron Corp., Melville, N.Y., 1997-99; pres. Sony Electronics Broadcast and Profl. Co., 1999—2002; dep. pres. Sony Electronics, Inc., 2000—02; pres. Met. TV Alliance, NYC, 2002—04, Ullico, Inc., Washington, 2003—, Union Labor Life Ins. Co., 2003—. Chmn. Morgan Data Svcs. Inc., Wilmington, Del., 1981-84; pres. J.P. Morgan Lease Funding Corp., NYC, 1982-84; bd. dirs. CBS Studio Ctr. Inc., Panavision, Inc. Bd. dirs., treas. Theater Devel. Fund, George Washington U., Ave of Americas Assn., Delaware Valley Opera, Am. Film Inst.; mem. N.Y. Hosp. Rev. and Planning Coun. Mem. Nat. Assn. Bank Cost and Mgmt. Acctg. Avocation: deep sea fishing. Home: 1136 Fifth Ave New York NY 10128-0122 Office: Ullico Inc 1625 Eye St NW Washington DC 20006 Office Phone: 202-962-8409. Business E-Mail: egrebow@ullico.com.

GREBOWSKY, JOSEPH MARK, physicist; b. Hazelton, Pa., Aug. 20, 1941; s. Joseph Anthony and Mary (Dagilus) G.; m. Margaret Louise Alpert, June 21, 1963; children: Bret, Amorette. BS in Physics, Manhattan Coll., 1963; MS in Physics, Pa. State U., 1965, PhD in Physics, 1968. Physicist Naval Ordinance Lab., White Oak, Md., 1963; rsch. asst. Pa. State U., University Park, 1963-65; astrophysicist Goddard Space Flight Ctr., NASA, Greenbelt, Md., 1968—. Contbr. articles to profl. jours. Mem. AIAA, Am. Geophys. Union. Buddhist. Home: 10902 Devin Pl Kensington MD 20895-2302

GREBSTEIN, SHELDON NORMAN, university administrator; b. Providence, Feb. 1, 1928; s. Sigmund and Sylvia (Skotkin) G.; m. Phyllis Strumar, Sept. 6, 1953; children: Jason Lyle, Gary Wade. BA cum laude, U. So. Calif., 1949; MA, Columbia U., 1950; PhD, Mich. State U., 1954. Instr. then asst. prof. English U. Ky., 1953-62; asst. prof. U. South Fla., 1962-63; mem. faculty SUNY, Binghamton, 1963-81, prof. English, 1968-81, asst. to pres., 1974-75; dean arts and scis. Harpur Coll., 1975-81; pres. SUNY, Purchase, 1981-93, univ. prof. of lit., 1993-95; dir. edn. Westchester Holocaust Edn. Ctr., 1995—. Fulbright-Hays lectr. U. Rouen, France, 1968-69; vis. lectr. Caen U., Hull U., and Edinburgh U., 1969. Author: Sinclair Lewis, 1962, John O'Hara, 1966, Hemingway's Craft, 1973; Editor: Monkey Trial, 1960, Perspectives in Contemporary Criticism, 1968, Studies in For Whom The Bell Tolls, 1971; editorial cons. univ. presses, publishers.; Contbr. articles to profl. jours. Office Phone: 914-696-0738. E-mail: shelwhc@bestweb.net.

GRECH, DAVID JOHN, lawyer, writer; s. Tristan and Kathleen Grech. BA summa cum laude, Hofstra U., 1998; JD with hons., St. John's U., Jamaica, NY, 2004. Internet/intranet mgr. Sid Paterson Advt., Inc., New York, 1998—2000; paralegal Queens County Dist. Atty.'s Office, Kew Gardens, NY, 2000—02; dean's fellow St. John's U. Sch. Law, Jamaica, 2004—05; assoc. Scher Law Firm, LLP, Carle Place, NY, 2005—. Cons. RA Entertainment, New York. Co-author (book of humor) It Was a Dark and Stormy Night and Other Attention Grabbing Opening Lines; author: (case comment) People v. DePallo: The Ethical and Procedural Implications of Narrative Testimony; articles and notes editor St. John's Law Review. Scholar, Hofstra U., 1994—98, St. John's U. Sch. Law, 2002—04. Mem.: N.Y. State Bar Assn. (Law Student Legal Ethics award 2004), St. John's U. Sch. of Law Entertainment and Sports Law Soc., St. John's U. Sch. of Law Corp. and Securities Law Soc., Pi Sigma Alpha, Phi Beta Kappa. Avocations: fitness and nutrition, tennis, basketball, golf. Office Phone: 516-746-5040. Personal E-mail: davidgrech@msn.com.

GRECHANIK, JEFFREY, operations research specialist; s. Walter and Cynthia Grechanik; m. Connie Lana Remaley. BS in Engring. Scis., USAF Acad., 1978; MS Strategic and Tactical Scis., Air Force Inst. of Tech., 1987. Commd. 2d lt. USAF, 1978, advanced through grades to lt. col.; instr. weapon systems officer 20th Tactical Fighter Wing, 79th Tactical Fighter Squadron, Royal Air Force Upper Heyford, England, 1979—82, 27th Tactical Fighter Wing, 524th Tactical Fighter Tng. Squadron, Cannon Air Force Base, N.Mex., 1982—85; ops. analyst Air Force Wargaming Ctr., Maxwell Air Force Base, Ala., 1987—90; chief, current ops. 20th Fighter Wing, 20th Ops. Support Squadron, Royal Air Force Upper Heyford, England, 1990—93; dep. chief, treaty plans and policy Hdqs. Air Force, Plans Directorate, Washington, 1993—94; student, internat. tng. course in security policy and arms control Geneva Ctr. for Security Policy, Geneva, 1994—95; nuc. policy planner Joint Chiefs of Staff, Plans and Policy Directorate, Washington, 1995—98; prof. George C. Marshall European Ctr. for Security Policy, Garmisch-Partenkirchen, Germany, 1998—99; chief, airborne systems basing Air Combat Command, Plans and Programs Directorate, Langley Air Force Base, Va., 1999—2003; ops. rsch. analyst Air Combat Command, Requirements Directorate, Langley AFB, Va., 2003—. Decorated DFC, Air medal. Mem.: Mil. Ops. Rsch. Soc., Inst. for Ops. Rsch. and Mgmt. Scis. Republican. Avocations: modeling and simulation, bicycling, skiing, swimming.

GRECICH, DARYL GEORGE, marketing communications executive; b. Beaver Falls, Pa., Mar. 26, 1966; s. George William and Patricia Joan (Scassa) G. BA, U. Pitts., 1988, MA Public and Internat. Affairs, 1991. Dir. publs. and mktg. Inst. for the Study of Diplomacy, Georgetown U., Washington, 1992—95; dir. comm. Inst. for a Drug-Free Workplace, Washington, 1995—98; mktg. comm. mgr. Data Warehousing Inst., Washington, 1998—2000; v.p. mktg. and comms. Idealliance, Washington, 2000—01; dir. mktg. and comms. Internat. Trademark Assn., N.Y.C., 2002—. Recipient Wolves Club scholar, 1984. Mem. Delta Tau Delta Fraternity. Avocations: skiing, literature, raquetball, running, history. Office: Internat Trademark Assn 1133 Ave of Ams Fl 33 New York NY 10036 Home: Apt 3E 308 Mott St New York NY 10012-2814 E-mail: dgrecich@inta.org.

GRECO, ANTHONY JOSEPH, artist, educator, dean; b. Cleve., Apr. 24, 1937; s. Joseph Anthony and Catherine C. (Corrao) G.; m. Astrida Paeglis, 1962 (div. July 1984); children: Joseph, Vivan, Regina; m. Elizabeth Vernon Shackelford, June 23, 1990. BFA, Cleve. Inst. Art, 1960, Kent State U., 1964, MFA, 1966. Head dept. drawing Atlanta Coll. Art, 1966-75, chmn. divsn. advanced studio, 1974-76, asst. to pres., 1975-76, acad. dean, 1976-82, acting acad. dean, 1985-86, prof. painting and drawing, 1988—2001, prof. emeritus, 2001—. Solo exhbns. include Armstrong State Coll., Savannah, Ga., 1976, Javo Gallery, Atlanta, 1978, Atlanta Coll. Art Libr., 1986, Chattahoochee Valley Art Mus., LaGrange, Ga., 1992; exhibited in group shows at Auburn U., 1987, Dekalb Coun. for Arts, 1989, U. Montevallo, Ala., 1989, Fay Gold Gallery, Atlanta, 1990, McIntosh Gallery, Atlanta, 1991, 92, 93, Spruill Ctr. Arts, Atlanta, 1999, Lazzaro Signature Gallery Fine Art, Stoughton, Wis., 1999; represented in collections at Jimmy Carter Presdl. Libr., Coca-Cola U.S.A., Atlanta, Chase Manhattan Bank, Summit Bank Corp., Atlanta, Kilpatrick and Cody Law Offices, Atlanta, Kent State U., Ga. State Art Commn., Atlanta, Butler Inst. Am. Art., King & Spalding Attys., Atlanta. Bd. dirs. Auditory Ednl. Clinic for Hearing Impaired, Atlanta, 1979-82; mem. adult programs adv. bd. High Mus. Art, Atlanta, 1985; mem. MARTA Coun. for the Arts, Atlanta, 1976-82, 85-86; mem. panel So. Arts Fedn., Visual Arts Dirs. Job-Alike Meeting, Atlanta, 1990. So. Arts Fedn./NEA regional fellow, 1988; recipient purchase awards and other awards for art. Office: Atlanta Coll Art 1280 Peachtree St NE Atlanta GA 30309-3502 Personal E-mail: ajgrec@mindspring.com.

GRECO, CHRISTOPHER JON, musician, composer, educator; b. Inglewood, Calif., July 19, 1959; s. Donald Rudolph and Sharon Marie Greco; m. Yvette Marcia Ybarra, Dec. 26, 1995. MusB, Calif. State U., LA, 1990—93, MA in Composition, 1993—95; at, UCLA, 2004—. Free-lance performer/rec. artist- woodwinds, LA, 1982—; leader of ensembles (duo, trio, quartet, quintet, sextet), 1985—; composer Am. Soc. of Composers, Authors and Publishers, 1988—, pub. (pleiadian music), 1995—; rec. artist (composer/woodwinds) GWSFourwinds Records, Pasadena, 1995—; contr. writer (new music column) Saxophone Jour., Medfield, Mass., 2002—; featured artist, Sept. Euro Club de Jazz, England, 2003. Composer: (compact disc) Trane of Thought, Pleiadian Call/Music for Trio; musician: Well You Needn't/Standards. Named dedication, A Stroll Down the Free Jazz/Avant-Garde Ave., All About Jazz, 2003; recipient Highly Recommended Performances, LA Weekly, 1990, 1991, 1992, 1993, 1994, 1996, Julius Hemphill Composition Award, Jazz Composers Alliance, 2001, Critics' Choice Performance, LA Reader, 1994, 1995, 1996, Recommended Performance, LA Times, 1997, Highly Recommended CD Rev., Jazz Jour. Internat., London U.K., 1996. Mem.: ASCAP (Plus award 2002, 2003, 2004), The Coll. Music Soc., Music Teachers Nat. Assn., Am. Music Ctr. Avocations: walking, gardening. Office Phone: 626-440-9861. E-mail: c.j.greco@worldnet.att.net.

GRECO, ERIC JOSEPH, music educator; b. New Brighton, Pa., Sept. 14, 1978; s. Joseph L. and Rebecca A. Greco. BS in Edn., Ind. U. Pa., 2002. Cert. std. tchr. Del., 2002. Band dir. Polytech H.S., Woodside, Del., 2002—. Mem.: NEA, Nat. Assn. Music Educators. Democrat. Methodist. Office Phone: 302-697-3255. Personal E-mail: ejgreco@hotmail.com.

GRECO, JOSEPH DOMINIC, JR., lawyer; b. Jersey City, Aug. 22, 1955; s. Joseph Dominic Sr. and Bernice Amelia (Tamburello) G.; m. Sharon K. Hayes, Apr. 17, 1982; children: Meghan Kathleen, Joseph Dominic III, Christine Anne. BS in Bus. Mgmt. cum laude, St. Peters Coll., Jersey City, 1977; JD, Fordham U., 1980. Bar: N.J. 1980, U.S. Dist. Ct. N.J. 1980. Law clk. to Hon. Frederick W. Kuechenmeister Bergen County Dist. Ct., Hackensack, NJ, 1980—81; assoc. Carluccio & Carluccio, Hoboken, NJ, 1981—83, ptnr., 1983—2001; mng. ptnr. Carluccio, Greco & Machese, Hoboken, NJ, 2002—. Benjamin Darling scholar. Mem. ABA, N.J. Bar Assn., Hudson County Bar Assn. (pro bono legal svcs. program). Democrat. Roman Catholic. Office: Carluccio Greco & Machese PO Box 230 51 Newark St Ste 404 Hoboken NJ 07030-5617

GRECO, MICHAEL S., lawyer; b. Rende, Cosenza, Italy, Nov. 22, 1942; came to U.S., 1950; s. Raphael and Rose (Felicetti) G.; children: Christian Raphael, Jordan Phillip, Elizabeth Elena. AB in English, Princeton U., N.J., 1965; JD, Boston Coll., 1972. Bar: Mass. 1972, U.S. Supreme Ct. 1979, U.S. Ct. Appeals (1st Cir. & Armed Forces), U.S. Tax Ct., U.S. Dist. Ct. (Mass. Dist.). Clk. U.S. Ct. Appeals for 2d Circuit, N.Y.C., 1972-73; assoc. Hill & Barlow, Boston, 1973-79, ptnr., 1979—2003, Kirkpatrick & Lockhart LLP, 2003—. Mem. Mass. Bd. Bar Overseers, 1978-81, vice chmn., 1980-81; mem. Kennedy Commn. on Fed. Appointments, 1993; pres. Mass. Continuing Legal Edn., Inc., 1994—; mem. acad. com. Flaschner Jud. Inst., 1990—; mem. adv. com. Mass. Supreme Jud. Ct., 1990-93; spl. asst. atty. gen. Dorchester Ct. Case, 1988-90; mem. exec. com. Jud. Nominating Coun. Commonwealth of Mass., 1990—; charter mem. overseers Mass. Supreme Jud. Ct. Hist. Soc., 1989—. Editor-in-Chief Boston Coll. Law Rev., 1971-72 Mem. permanent sch. accommodations com. Wellesley, Mass., 1980-83; bd. overseers Newton (Mass.)-Wellesley Hosp., 1990—; founder Mass. Gov.'s Commn. on Unmet Legal Needs of Children, 1986-89; chmn. Mass. Legal Svcs. Plan for Action, 1986-89; co-founder, co-chmn. Nat. Bar Leaders for Preservation Legal Svcs. for Poor, 1986. Fellow Inst. Comparative Law, U. Florence, Italy, 1974. Fellow Am. Bar Found. (life), Mass. Bar Found. (treas., trustee 1982-90); mem. ABA (del. 1985—, chmn. pvt. bar involvement project 1988-90, mem. standing com. on fed. judiciary 1993—, mem. consortium 1988-91, chmn. IRR sect. com. on nuclear disarmament 1990—, mem. standing com. on law and nat. security 1991-93, Mass. state del. 1993— pres.-elect 2002-05, pres. 2005-), Am. Law Inst., Am. Judicature Soc. (bd. dirs. 1988-92), New Eng. Bar Found. (pres. 1987-92), New Eng. Bar Assn. (pres. 1986-87), Mass. Bar Assn. (pres. 1985-86), Mass. Lawyers Alliance for Nuclear Arms Control (pres. 1988-91), Boston Coll Law Sch. Class of 1972 (pres.), Princeton U. Class of 1965 (v.p. 1985—), Princeton Club (N.Y.C.), Wellesley Club. Democrat. Office: Kirkpatrick & Lockhart LLP 75 State St Boston MA 02109 E-mail: mgreco@kl.com.

GREDEN, JOHN FRANCIS, psychiatrist, educator; b. Winona, Minn., July 24, 1942; m. Renee Mary Kalmes; children: Daniel John, Sarah Renee, Leigh Raymond. BS, U. Minn., 1965, MD, 1967. Diplomate Am. Bd. Psychiatry and Neurology. Assoc. dir. psychiat. rsch. Walter Reed Army Med. Ctr., Washington, 1972-74; asst. prof. dept. psychiatry U. Mich., Ann Arbor, 1974-77, assoc. prof., 1977-81, dir. clin. studies unit for affective disorders, 1980-85, prof., 1981—, chmn., prof., 1985—, chmn. faculty group practice, 1996—98, exec. dir. Depression Ctr., 2001—. Editor 3 books; contbr. more than 200 articles to profl. jours., more than 30 chpts. to books. Served to maj. U.S. Army, 1969-74. Recipient A.E. Bennett research award Cen. Neuropsychiat. Found., 1974, Nolan D.C. Lewis Vis. Scholar award Carrier Found., 1982. Fellow Am. Psychiat. Assn. (chair coun. on rsch. 2000—); mem. AAAS, Soc. Biol. Psychiatry (past pres., co-editor-in-chief Jour. Psychiatry Rsch. 1984-2000), Am. Coll. Neuropsychopharmacology (coun. 2001—, Psychiat. Rsch. Soc. (past pres.). Office: U Mich Med Ctr Dept Psychiatry 1500 E Medical Center Dr Ann Arbor MI 48109-0295

GREDER, GREGORY ARTHUR, lawyer; b. Valentine, Nebr., Mar. 6, 1963; s. Gary Arthur and Doris Marie (Best) G. BS in Agr., U. Nebr., 1986, JD, 1990. Bar: Nebr. Terminal mgr./salesman Consol. Freightways, Laramie, Wyo., 1991-92; pvt. practice, Lincoln, Nebr., 1992—. Bd. dirs. Nebr. Human Resources Inst., Lincoln, 1993—; counselor Big Bros. Nebr. Human Resources Rsch. Found., Lincoln, 1992—. Mem. Nebr. Bar Assn. (young lawyers sect.), Lincoln Bar Assn. (barrister). Republican. Methodist. Avocations: skiing, travel, Karate, playing guitar. Home: 518 Pier 1 Lincoln NE 68528 Office: 6040 S 58th St Ste D Lincoln NE 68516-3695 Office Phone: 402-423-9020.

GREEAR, DEBORAH LYNN, secondary school educator; b. Ft. Chaffee, Ark., Mar. 3, 1955; d. Howard K. and Mattye Gwendolyn Hinds. BS in Chemistry Edn., Ctrl. State U., Edmond, Okla., 1977. Nat. bd. cert. tchr., Okla., 2004. Tchr. chemistry and physics Edmond Pub. Schs., 1977-78; field chemist Halliburton Svcs., Oklahoma City, 1978-83; tchr. Crooked Oak Pub. Schs., Oklahoma City, 1983-87; tchr. chemistry Edmond Pub. Schs., 1987—. Republican. Mem. Ch. of Christ. Home: 707 Rockridge Cir Edmond OK 73034-7251 Office: Edmond North HS 215 W Danforth Rd Edmond OK 73003-5206

GREEF, CHARLES E. (STORMY GREEF), lawyer; b. Amarillo, Tex., Jan. 16, 1949; AB, Yale U., 1971; JD, U. Tex., 1974. Bar: Va. 1975, Tex. 1976. Shareholder Jenkens & Gilchrist, P.C., Dallas, firm leader fin. institutions practice group. Mem.: Va. State Bar Assn., Tex. State Bar Assn. Office: Jenkens & Gilchrist PC Ste 3200 1445 Ross Ave Dallas TX 75202-2799 Office Phone: 214-855-4337. Office Fax: 214-855-4300. Business E-Mail: cgreef@jenkens.com.

GREEFF, DOUGLAS HAVEN, cosmetics executive; b. N.Y.C., Jan. 18, 1956; BA in Econs., Williams Coll., 1978; MS in Acctg., NYU, 1979. CPA, 1978. V.p. leverage capital dept. and global loans Citibank N.A., 1986-98; mng. dir. fixed income global loans Salomon Smith Barney, 1998-2000; CFO, exec. v.p. Revlon Inc., N.Y.C., 2000—03; exec. v.p. Strategic Fin., 2004—. Office: Revlon Inc 237 Park Ave New York NY 10017 Office Phone: 212-527-6455. Business E-Mail: douglas@greeff.us.

GREEHEY, WILLIAM EUGENE, energy company executive; b. Ft. Dodge, Iowa, 1936; married. BBA, St. Mary's U., San Antonio, 1960. Auditor Price Waterhouse & Co., 1960-61; sr. auditor Humble Oil and Refining Co., 1961-63; sr. v.p. fin. Coastal Corp. (and predecessor), 1963-74; with Valero Energy Corp. (formerly Coastal States Gas Producing Co.), San Antonio, 1974—, pres., chief exec. officer, 1979-83, chmn. bd., 1983—, also chmn., chief exec. officer numerous subsidiaries. Office: Valero Energy Corp PO Box 500 San Antonio TX 78292-0500*

GREEK, DAROLD I., lawyer; b. Kunkle, Ohio, Mar. 30, 1909; s. Albert F. and Iva (Shaffer) G.; m. Catherine Johnson, Oct. 12, 1935 (dec. 1962); 1 child, Darold I (dec.); m. Elizabeth Tracy Ridgley, Sept. 18, 1970 (dec. May 1972); stepchildren— Thomas B., David Ridgley; m. Nadine Berry Weisheimer Bivens, Dec. 23, 1976; stepchildren— Richard A. Weisheimer, Jon B. Weisheimer. Student, Bowling Green State U., 1926-28; LL.B., Ohio State U., 1932. Bar: Ohio 1932. Treas., Williams County, Ohio, 1932-33; atty. Ohio Dept. Taxation, 1934-36; practiced in Columbus, 1937-89; ptnr. George, Greek, King, McMahon & McConnaughey (and predecessors), 1937-79; of counsel Baker & Hostetler, 1979-89. Mem. Ohio Bar Assn., Columbus Bar Assn. (pres. 1966-67), The Golf Club, Naples Yacht Club, Hole in the Wall Golf Club. Presbyterian. Home (Summer): 6638 Lake of Woods Pt Galena OH 43021 Office: 65 E State St Columbus OH 43215-4213 Home (Winter): 2901 Gulf Shore Blvd Naples FL 34103

GREELEY, ANDREW MORAN, sociologist, writer; b. Oak Park, Ill., Feb. 5, 1928; s. Andrew T. and Grace G. AB, St. Mary of Lake Sem., 1950, STL, 1954; MA, U. Chgo., 1961, PhD, 1962; LHD (hon.), Bowling Green State U., 1986, No. Mich., 1993; HHD (hon.), St. Louis U., 1991; LHD, LLD, Ariz. State U., 1998; LHD (hon.), U. San Francisco, 2002, Bard Coll., 2002; LLD (hon.), Nat. U. Ireland, Galway, 2003. Ordained priest Roman Cath. Ch., 1954. Asst. pastor Ch. of Christ the King, Chgo., 1954-64; sr. study dir. Nat. Opinion Rsch. Ctr., Chgo., 1962-68; dir. Ctr. for Study Am. Pluralism, from 1973; lectr. sociology U. Chgo., 1963-72; prof. sociology U. Ariz., Tucson, from 1978, now adj. prof.; prof. social sci. U. Chgo., 1991—. Cons. Hazen Found. Commn. Columnist Daily Southtown; guest columnist Chgo. Sun Times, 1985—; Author: The Church and the Suburbs, 1959, Strangers in the House, 1961, Religion and Career, 1963, (with Peter H. Rossi) Education of Catholic Americans, 1966, Changing Catholic College, 1967, Come Blow Your Mind With Me, 1971, Life for a Wanderer: A New Look at Christian Spirituality, 1971, The Denominational Society: A Sociological Approach to Religion in America, 1972, Priests in the United States: Reflections on A Survey, 1972, That Most Distressful Nation, 1972, New Agenda, 1973, Jesus Myth, 1971, Unsecular Man, 1974, Ethnicity in the United States: A Preliminary Reconnaissance, 1974, Ecstasy: A Way of Knowing, 1974, Building Coalitions: American Politics in the 1970's, 1974, Sexual Intimacy, 1975, Denomination Society, 1975, The Great Mysteries: An Essential Catechism, 1976, The Communal Catholic: A Personal Manifesto, 1976, Death and Beyond, 1976, The American Catholic: A Social Portrait, 1977, The Making of the Popes, 1978, 79, The Magic Cup: An Irish Legend, 1979, Women I've Met, 1979, Why Can't They Be Like Us?, 1980, Death In April, 1980, The Cardinal Sins, 1981, Religion: A Secular Theory, 1982, Thy Brother's Wife, 1982, Ascent Into Hell, 1983, Lord of the Dance, 1984, Virgin & Martyr, 1985, Piece of My Mind on Just About Everything, 1985, Happy are the Meek, 1985, The Magic Cup, 1985, God Game, 1986, Happy Are the Clean of Heart, 1986, Confessions of a Parish Priest, 1986, Patience of a Saint, 1987, Rite of Spring, 1987, Angels of September, 1986, Happy Are Those Who Thirst For Justice, 1987, The Final Planet, 1987, Angel Fire, 1988, (photography) Andrew Greeley's Chicago, 1989, Love Song, 1989, St. Valentine's Night, 1989, The Bible and Us, 1990, The short stories All About Women, 1990, (photography) The Irish, 1990, The Catholic Myth: The Behavior and Beliefs of American Catholics, 1990, The Cardinal Virtues, 1990, Faithful Attraction: Discovering Intimacy, Love, and Fidelity in American Marriage, 1991, The Search for Maggie Ward, 1991, An Occasion of Sin, 1991, Happy Are the Merciful, 1992, Wages of Sin, 1992, Fall from Grace, 1993, Sacraments of Love: A Prayer Journal, 1994, Irish Gold, 1994, Happy are the Poor Spirit, 1994, Happy are Those Who Mourn, 1995, Angel Light: An Old-Fashioned Love Story, 1995, Windows: A Prayer Journal, 1995, Religion as Poetry, 1995, Sociology and Religion, 1995, White Smoke,

1996, Irish Lace, 1996, Happy Are The Oppressed, 1996, (with J. Neusner) Common Ground: A Priest and a Rabbi Read Scripture Together, 1996, Summer at the Lake, 1997, Star Bright!, 1997, The Bishop at Sea, 1997, I Hope You're Listening, God: A Prayer Journal, 1997, Irish Whiskey, 1998, Contract with an Angel, 1998, The Bishop and the Three Kings, 1998, A Mid-Winter's Tale, 1998, Furthermore! Memories of a Parish Priest, 1999, 2000, The Bishop and the Missing L Train, 2000, Christmas Wedding, 2000, Irish Love, 2001, The Bishop and the Begger Girl of St. Germain, 2001, September Song, 2001, Irish Stew, 2002, The Bishop in the West Wing, 2002, Irish Cream, 2005, (with Mary Durkin) The Book of Love, 2002, The Bishop Goes to The University, 2003; (with Chilton, Green, and Neusner) Forging a Common Future, 1996, The Catholic Imagination, 2000, (with Albert Bergesen) God in the Movies, 2000, My Love: A Prayer Journal, 2001, Letters to a Loving God, 2002, Second Spring, 2003, Religion in Europe at the End of the Second Millennium, 2003; The Catholic Revolution: New Wine, Old Wineskins, and the Second Vatican Council, 2004; Priests: A Calling in Crisis, 2004; The Priestly Sins, 2004; editor: Emerald Magic, 2004, Golden Years, 2004, Irish Cream, 2005; contbr. articles to profl. jours. Recipient Cath. Press Assn. award for best book for young people, 1965, Thomas Alva Edison award for radio broadcast, 1962, C. Albert Kobb award Nat. Cath. Edn. Assn., 1977, Mark Twain award Soc. Study Midwestern Lit., 1987, Popular Culture award Ctr. Study of Popular Culture, 1988, Freedom to Read award Friends Chgo. Pub. Libr., 1989, U.S. Cath. award, 1993, Ill. Outstanding Citizen award Coll. Lake County, 1993, Quigley Disting. Alumni award, 1997; named to Top 100 Irish Ams. Irish Am. Mag, 1992, named Irish Am. of Century Irish Am. Mag., 1999. Mem. Am. Sociol. Assn., Soc. for Sci. Study Religion, Religious Research Assn.

GREELEY, BURNHAM H., lawyer; b. Mapleton, Minn., Feb. 13, 1934; BA, Grinnell Coll., 1956; LLB, Harvard U., 1959. Bar: Hawaii 1960. Ptnr. Greeley Walker & Kowen, Honolulu. Bd. dir. Kuakini Medical Ctr.; mem. Hawaii Federal Jud. Selection comm. Fellow Am. Bar Found.; mem. ABA (ho. of dels. 1989-91, bd. gov. 2003-, chmn. Coalition for Justice comm.), Hawaii State Bar Assn. (pres. 1987), Am. Inn of Ct. IV Hawaii chptr., Am. Judicature Soc. Hawaii chptr. (dir., chmn. Civil Justice comm.). Office: Ste 900 745 Fort Street Mall Honolulu HI 96813-3815

GREELEY, JENNIFER ANN, military officer, educator; d. Horace; children: Travis, Tyler. AA, Chaminate U., Honolulu, 1992; BA in sociology, U. Okla., Norman, 1995; EdM, U. R.I., Kingston, 1999; M Human Rels., U. Okla., 2004. Lt. USN, 1985—; yearbook editor U. Okla. NROTC, Norman, 1993—95; adminstrn. officer dept. head sch. surface warfare USN, Newport, RI, 1996—99, officer recruit trng. command Great Lakes, Ill., 1999—2002; adj. prof. Coll. of Lake County, Grayslake, 2001; transp. dir. military sealift command USN, Yokohama, Japan, 2002, officer in charge naval support facility Kamiseya, 2002—03, navy recruiting dist. Chgo. Ft. Sheridan, Ill., 2003—; adj. prof. Coll. Lake County, 2003—. Chmn. civilian adv. bd. Salvation Army, Waukegan, Ill., 2002—, mem., 2003—; mem. spl. events com. Highland Pk. C. of C., Ill., 2000—; bd. mem. civilian adv. bd. Salvation Army, Newport, RI, 1997—99, Sunday soup kitchen organizer, 1997—99. Ex-officio mem. human rels. Commn. Highland Park, Ill., 2003—. Named a Cited Vol., USO, Honolulu, 1991; recipient Community Spirit award, Combined Fed. Campaign United Way, 2001. Mem.: Women Officer Prof. Assn., Am. Assn. Pub. Adminstrn., Am. Assn. of U. Profs., Rotary Internat., City Club of Chgo., Kappa Delta Pi. Achievements include founding local branch of Drug Edn. for Youth in Atsugi, Japan, community outreach programs. Avocations: travel, writing. E-mail: ltjenn45@hotmail.com.

GREELY, HENRY T. (HANK GREELY), law educator; b. 1952; AB in Polit. Sci., Stanford U., 1974; JD, Yale U., 1977. Law clk. to Hon. John Minor Wisdom US Ct. Appeals 5th Cir., 1977—78; law clk. to Hon. Potter Stewart US Supreme Ct., 1978—79; spl. asst. to gen. counsel Deanne C. Siemer US Dept. Def., 1979; staff asst. to Sec. Energy Charles W. Duncan, Jr., 1979—81; assoc. Tuttle & Taylor, LA, 1981—84, ptnr., 1984—85; assoc. prof. Stanford Law Sch., 1985—92, prof., 1992—, C. Wendell and Edith M. Carlsmith prof. law, 2002—04, Deane F. and Kate Edelman Johnson prof. law, 2004—; dir. Stanford Program in Law, Sci. & Tech., 2000—01, co-dir., 2001—, Stanford Program on Genomics, Ethics, and Soc., 1995—; dir. Stanford Ctr. for Law and Biosciences. Mem. Calif. Adv. Com. on Human Cloning, 1999—, Calif. Adv. Com. on Ethical Issues in Biotechnology, 2003—. Office: Stanford Law Sch Crown Quadrangle 559 Nathan Abbott Way Stanford CA 94305-8610 Office Phone: 650-723-2517. Business E-Mail: hgreely@stanford.edu.*

GREEN, AHMAN, professional football player; b. Omaha, Nebr., Feb. 16, 1977; m. Heather Green; 2 children. BS in Geology, U. Neb. Running back Seattle Seahawks, 1998—2000, Green Bay Packers, 2000—. Founder Ahman Green Foundation for Youth Development, 2001. Named to NFC Pro-Bowl Team, 2001—04. Office: Green Bay Packers PO Box 10628 Green Bay WI 54307-0628*

GREEN, AL, congressman; b. New Orleans, La., Sept. 1, 1947; Attended, Fla. A&M Univ., Tuskegee Inst. Tech.; JD, Tex. So. Univ., 1974. Founder, mng. ptnr. Green Wilson Dewberry & Fitch, Houston, 1974; justice of the peace Houston, 1977—2004; mem. U.S. Ho. Reps., 109th Congress, 9th Dist. Tex., 2005—. Past pres. NAACP, Houston. Recipient Disting. Svc. award, Houston Citizens C. of C., 1978, Outstanding Leadership award, Black Heritage Soc., 1981, Citation for Svc., Am. Fedn. Teachers, 1983. Democrat. Baptist. Office: 1529 Longworth House Office Bldg Washington DC 20515-4309 Office Phone: 202-225-7508.*

GREEN, ALVIN, lawyer, consultant; b. Elgin, Ill., Mar. 13, 1931; s. Samuel and Rose (Brustein) G.; m. Miriam E. Blau, June 13, 1954 (dec.); children: Andrew, Marie, Jennifer. BA, U. Mich., 1953, MA, 1954; LLB, Harvard U., 1957. Bar: NY. Atty. Eastern Air Lines, Inc., N.Y.C., 1957-65; asst. to gen. counsel C.I.T. Corp., N.Y.C., 1965-70, gen. counsel, 1970-72; v.p. Condren, Walker & Co., N.Y.C., 1972-75; v.p., gen. counsel, sec. Seatrain Lines, Inc., N.Y.C., 1975-81, exec. v.p., co-CEO, sr. counsel, 1981-90; exec. v.p. Seatrain Tankers Inc., 1987-90, Bay Tankers Inc., 1981-90, Bay Ocean Mgmt. Inc., Englewood Cliffs, NJ, 1990—95. NASD arbitrator; ptnr. Seham, Seham Meltz & Petersen; cons. in field. Bd. dirs. Inst. for Child, Adolescent and Family Studies, N.Y.C., Learning Leaders, Gray Matters. Woodrow Wilson fellow, 1953—54. Mem.: ABA, Am. Bur. Shipping, Assn. of Bar of City of N.Y. (mem. com. on aeronautics), Harvard Club (N.Y.C.), Phi Beta Kappa, Phi Kappa Phi. Home: 145 E 48th St New York NY 10017 Office: 145 E 48th St 5F New York NY 10017 Office Phone: 212-644-3707. Personal E-mail: green_alvin@hotmail.com.

GREEN, AMY, psychiatrist; b. N.Y.C., May 5, 1939; d. Alex and Fannie Green; m. Jack M. Clemente (dec.); children: Laura, David. BA in Psychology, Bard Coll., 1960; MD, McGill U., 1964. Diplomate Am. Bd. Psychiatry. Intern U. Ill. Rsch. & Ednl. Hosps., Chgo., 1964—65; resident N.Y. Med Ctr., Met. Hosp. Ctr., N.Y.C., 1965—68; acting chief psychiat. walk-in svc. Cmty. Mental Health Svcs., San Diego, 1968—70; liaison psychiatrist Beth Israel Med. Ctr., N.Y.C., 1970—74; staff psychiatrist Mental Health Resource Ctr., Montclair, NJ, 1974—76; pvt. practice psychiatry N.Y.C., 1970—78, Montclair, 1974—. Psychiat. cons. Montclair State Coll., 1982—88; staff psychiatrist Mountainside Hosp., Montclair, 1988—. Fellow: Am Acad. Psychoanalysis (cert.); mem.: Soc. Med. Psychoanalysts (pres. 1989—90), NJ Psychiat. Assn. (life), Am. Psychiat. Assn. (life). Avocations: nature walks, snorkeling, gardening, reading. Office: 326 Park St Montclair NJ 07043

GREEN, ANGEL YVONNE, literature educator; b. N.Y.C., Oct. 24, 1955; d. Henry Arthur Moss and Lillie Vera Harris; m. Joseph Cecil Green, Nov. 18, 1975 (div. Feb. 1979); 1 child, Gabriel Veran. Baccalaureate English, U. R.I., 1986, Masters English, 1997, PhD English, 2001; Baccalaureate Psychology, Coll. Continuing Edn./U. R.I., Providence, 1995. On-call police matron Newport and Jamestown Police Depts., RI, 1986—95; tchg. asst. U. R.I., Kingston, 1995—2000, fellow Grad. Sch., 2000—01, adj. faculty, 2001—. Vol. Literacy Vol. Am., Newport, RI, 1995—2002; enrichment instr. Talent Devel., U. R.I., Kingston, 1996—2002. Author short stories. Bd. mem. Wahid, Newport, 1986—90, First Step Newport County, Newport, 1990—95. With USN, 1973, with USNR, 1976—98. Recipient MLK Scholarship award, Providence Pub. Schs., 1995—98. Mem.: MLA, NAACP, Mensa. Home: 21-E Rolling Green Rd Newport RI 02840 Office: Univ RI Feinstein Coll Continuing Edn 80 Washington St Providence RI 02903 Personal E-mail: blublocker21@aol.com.

GREEN, ASA NORMAN, university president; b. Mars Hill, Maine, July 22, 1929; s. Clayton John and Annie Glenna (Shaw) G.; m. Elizabeth Jean Zirkelbach Ross, May 27, 1965; 1 son, Stephen Richard Ross. AB cum laude, Bates Coll., Lewiston, Maine, 1951; MA, U. Ala., 1955; LL.D., Jacksonville (Ala.) U., 1975. Rsch. dir. Ala. League Municipalities, Montgomery, 1955-57; city mgr. Mountain Brook, Ala., 1957-65; exec. sec. Ala. Assn. Ins. Agts., 1965-66; dir. devel. Birmingham-So. Coll., 1966-71; dir. devel. and communications Dickinson Coll., Carlisle, Pa., 1971-73; pres. Livingston (Ala.) U., 1973-93; pres. emeritus Livingston U., 1993—; pres. U. So. Ala. Found., 2004—. Cons. NCAA Pres.'s Commn., 1993—99; instr. polit. sci. U. Ala. Ext. Ctr., Montgomery and Birmingham, 1955—57, 1958—60. Author: Revenue for Alabama Cities, 1956. Mem. adminstrv. bd. Livingston United Methodist Ch., 2005—; bd. dirs. U. South Ala. Found., 1997—, pres., 2004—. Served with CIC U.S. Army, 1952—54. Grad. fellow So. Regional Tng. Program in Pub. Adminstrn., 1951 Mem.: Phi Beta Kappa. Independent. Methodist. Office: PO Box 1466 Livingston AL 35470-1620

GREEN, BARBARA MARIE, publisher, journalist, poet, writer; b. N.Y.C., Mar. 21, 1928; d. James Matthew and Mae (McCarter) G. BA, CCNY, 1951, MA, 1955; ABD, NYU, 1978. Adminstr., tchr. English, 1952-82; tchr. English Newtown High Sch., Elmhurst, Queens, N.Y., 1961; asst. prin. Jr. High Sch. 142, Queens, N.Y., 1963; founder, pub. The "Creative" Record, Virginia Beach, Va., 1988-92. Keynote speaker; pres. Bar 'JaMae Comm. Inc. Founder, publisher The Good News, East Elmhurst, N.Y., 1985-88; author: (book of poetry) Love Pain Hope, 1990, More Poetic Thoughts, 1993, Dreams and Memories, 1996, Spirit, 1997; contbr. poetry to publs. Ch. and cmty. reporter N.Y. Voice; mem. libr. action com. Corona (N.Y.)-East Elmhurst, Inc.; mem. Langston Hughes Cmty. Libr. and Cultural Ctr., Corona, Harpers Ferry Hist. Assn., Va. Symphony League; mem. Crispus Attucks Theater Restoration Com., Norfolk. Recipient Profl. award Nat. Assn. Negro Bus. and Profl. Women's Club Inc., 1964, Trophy "Career Woman of Yr.", County Line Guild of Career Women, 1967, Cert. of Appreciation Women's Equality Action League, 1978, First Lynnhaven Bapt. Ch., Virginia Beach, Va., 1982, Cert. of merit City of N.Y., 1982, Community Svc. award Arlene of N.Y., 1990, N.Y. State Resolution commemorating the "Good" News, 1985, participation award Coalition of 100 Black Women, Valuable Service citation Phi Delta Kappa, cert. of appreciation Houston C.C., 1998, plaque U.S. Army and USAF N.G. Bur., Ageless Hero for Creativity award Blue Cross/Blue Shield, 1998; named Star Among Stars, 1991, Keeper of the Flame, 1997, Hampton Roads Poet Laureate, 2002; named to African-Am. Biographies Hall of Fame, Atlanta, 1994; elected to Hunter Coll. Alumni Hall of Fame, 1997; named poet laureate-in-residence First Lynnhaven Bapt. Ch., Virginia Beach, Va., 1996—, Hampton Roads Poet Laureate, New Jour.-Guide Newspaper, 2002. Mem. Am. Bus. Women's Assn. (Elizabeth River Charter chpt.), Nat. Assn. Negro Musicians (life; bd. dirs. Chgo. 1984-91, ea. region dir. 1990-91), Harpers Ferry Hist. Assn., Poetry Soc. Va., Nat. Assn. Black Journalists, Zonta Internat., Va. Fedn. Bus. and Profl. Women's Clubs (corr. sec. 1992, 1st v.p. 1993, pres. 1993, chair coastal region pub. rels. com. state level 1994-95), N.Y.C. Ret. Suprs. Assn., Phi Delta Kappa, Alpha Kappa Alpha. Baptist. Office: PO Box 15442 Chesapeake VA 23328-5442 Office Phone: 757-547-7440.

GREEN, BARBARA R., artist; b. N.Y.C., Nov. 7, 1942; d. Morris and Irene Edith Korr; m. Francis Eugene Green, Feb. 14, 1980. BS, NYU, 1964; MFA, Inst. Allende, San Miguel de Allende, Mex., 1974. Tchr. N.Y.C. Sch. Sys., 1964—73, 1975—76, 1982—84; chromiste Eleanor Ettinger Publisher, N.Y.C., 1976—82; tchr. Greene Correctional Facility, Russel Sage Coll., 1986—88. Recipient Silver Crown, Columbia U., 1985; grantee, Meml. Found. for Jewish Culture, 2000. Mem.: Greene County Coun. of the Arts, Woodstock Artists Assn. Home: 10 Rte 23A Catskill NY 12414

GREEN, BARBARA STRAWN, psychotherapist; b. Cleve., May 31, 1938; d. Charles Everard and Dorothy Haring (Strawn) G. BA, Pa. State U., 1960; MS, Columbia U., 1962; postgrad. in psychotherapy and psychoanalysis, Postgrad. Ctr. for Mental Health, N.Y.C., 1975. Ordained Dharma tchr., 2003; cert. social worker, N.Y.; cert. Rutgers Summer Sch. Alcoholism Studies, 1982. Social worker VA, N.Y.C., 1962-66; sr. psychiat. social worker in child psychiat. Downstate Med. Ctr., Bklyn., 1966-71; staff therapist Inst. for Contemporary Psychotherapy, N.Y.C., 1971-73; social worker Lower East Side Service Ctr., N.Y.C., 1975-77; intake coordinator alcoholism program Postgrad. Ctr. for Mental Health, N.Y.C., 1981-82; program coordinator Bowery Residents Com., N.Y.C., 1984—; pvt. practice psychotherapy N.Y.C., 1973—, Dingmans Ferry, Pa., 1994-2000; interpreter VAn Cortlandt Manor, Croton-on-Hudson, 2003—. Sec. alcoholism com. N.Y.C. chpt. NASW, 1987-89. Author: Jogging the Mind, 1995. Sec. Middle-Way Mediation Ctr., Danbury, Conn.; leader Buddhist meditation group Fed. Correctional Inst., Danbury, 2000—; participant N.Y.C. Marathon, 1991, 1992. Avocations: pottery, travel. Office: 108 1/2 E 37th St New York NY 10016

GREEN, BERT FRANKLIN, JR., psychologist; b. Honesdale, Pa., Nov. 5, 1927; s. Bert Franklin and Emily May (Brown) G.; m. Hasseltine Beck Robinson, Apr. 29, 1961 (div. 1974); children: Malcolm, Edward. AB, Yale, 1949; MA, Princeton, 1950, PhD, 1951. Mem. psychology group Lincoln Lab., Mass. Inst. Tech., 1951-62, leader, 1958-62; cons. RAND Corp., 1961; prof. psychology Carnegie Inst. Tech., Pitts., 1962-69, head psychology dept., 1962-67; prof. psychology Johns Hopkins, Balt., 1969-98, prof. emeritus, 1998—. Author: Digital Computers in Research, 1963. Mem. Am. Psychol. Assn., Am. Statis. Assn., Psychometric Soc., Am. Edn. Rsch. Assn. (Lindquist award for Excellence Rsch. Measurement, 2001). Home: 311 Eastway Ct Baltimore MD 21212-4710 Personal E-mail: bfgreen@verizon.net. Business E-Mail: bfgreen@jhu.edu.

GREEN, CAROL H., lawyer, educator; b. Seattle, Feb. 18, 1944; BA in History/Journalism summa cum laude, La. Tech. U., 1965; MSL, Yale U., 1977; JD, U. Denver, 1979. Reporter Shreveport (La.) Times, 1965-66, Guam Daily News, 1966-67; city editor Pacific Jour., Agana, Guam, 1967-68, reporter, editl. writer, 1968-76, legal affairs reporter, 1977-79; asst. editor editl. page Denver Post, 1979-81, house counsel, 1980-83, labor rels. mgr., 1981-83; assoc. Holme Roberts & Owen, 1983-85; v.p. human resources and legal affairs Denver Post, 1985-87, mgr. circulation, 1988-90; gen. mgr. Distbn. Systems Am., Inc., 1990-92; dir. labor rels. Newsday, 1992-95, dir. comm. and labor rels., 1995—96; v.p. Weber Mgmt. Cons., 1996—98; v.p. human resources and labor rels. Denver Post, 1998—2000; v.p. human resources, labor rels. Denver Newspaper Agy., 2001—. 1985 speaker for USIA, India, Egypt; mem. Mailers Tech. Adv. Com. to Postmaster Gen., 1991-92. Recipient McWilliams award for juvenile justice, Denver, 1971, award for interpretive reporting Denver Newspaper Guild, 1979. Mem.: ABA, Soc. Human Resources Mgmt., Colo. and Internat. Women's Forum, Denver Bar Assn. (co-chair jud. selection and benefits com. 1982—85, 2nd v.p. 1986), Newspaper Assn. Am. (mem. human resources and labor rels. com.), Colo. Bar Assn. (bd. govs. 1985—87, chair BAR-press com. 1980), Leadership Denver. Episcopalian.

GREEN, CAROLE L., lawyer; b. Queens, NY, Mar. 17, 1959; d. Gerald Harry and Mary (Clark) Green. AB cum laude with distinction, Dartmouth Coll., 1980; JD, Harvard Law Sch., 1983. Bar: NY. Congl. aide to rep. John Conyers U.S. House of Reps., Washington, 1980; assoc. real estate Kaye Scholer LLP, NY, 1983—85, Richards & O'Neil, N.Y.C., 1985—87; gen. counsel Petrie Stores Corp., Secaucus, N.J., 1987-88; assoc. counsel Mfrs. Hanover Trust Co. (now JP Morgan Chase Bank), N.Y.C., 1988-91; v.p., asst. gen. counsel Chem. Bank (now JP Morgan Chase Bank), N.Y., 1991-96; contract atty. N.Y.C., 1996—; pub. arbitrator NASD Dispute Resolution, 1996—. Mem.: ABA, Practicing Attys. for Law Students, Inc. (founding mem. 1986—95, bd. dirs. 2004—), Assn. Bar City N.Y., N.Y. State Bar Assn., Black Alumni of Dartmouth Assn. Avocations: travel, jazz, cinema. Office Phone: 212-613-0099.

GREEN, CATHERINE COOPER, artist; b. Bozeman, Mont., Oct. 2, 1948; d. David Lawrence and Mary Francis Cooper; m. Timothy Haskell Green, June 14, 1970. BFA, Temple U., 1970. Art tchr. Rumford (Maine) Sch. Sys., 1970-72, Newburyport (Mass.) Sch. Sys., 1972-86; instr. divsn. continuing edn. U. N.H., Durham, 1979-89; artist Stratham, NH, 1989—. Yankee Mag., 1985, exhibited in group shows at Westfield Art Festival, 1993, Stamford Art Festival, 1993, On the Green Art Show, 1994, 1995, Nat. Print Biennial, 1996, Nat. Print Competition Artlink, Ft. Wayne, 1997, 1998, 2000—05, Calif. State U., 1997, 2002, Works on Paper, U. W. Fla., 2000, Prescott Park Arts Festival, 2005 (Hon. mention, 2005). Recipient Yankee Print award, Yankee Mag., 1983, Most Creative Print award, League of N.H. Craftsmen, 2005. Mem.: N.H. Art Assn., League N.H. Craftsmen (mem. stds. com. 1988—, print jury mem. 1989—, v.p. bd. trustees), Exeter League N.H. Craftsmen Jury (chair 1989—95). Avocations: sailing, racquetball, organic gardening, tai chi, cooking. Home: 128 Bunker Hill Ave Stratham NH 03885-2411 E-mail: info@catherinegreenart.net.

GREEN, CATHERINE GERTRUDE, retired secondary school educator; b. Indpls., Nov. 23, 1945; d. Gentry L. and Helen G. (Peters) Kirby; m. Alan E. Matz, June 3, 1967 (div. May 1972); m. James G. Green, Mar. 8, 1975 (div. 1996); 1 child, Heather Vanessa. BA, Purdue U., 1967; MA, Northwestern U., 1970; cert. in adminstrn., No. Ill. U., 1985, EdD. Cert. in curriculum and instrn. No. Ill. U., 2000. English and speech tchr. Wellington (Mo.)-Napoleon High Sch., 1967-68; communication and English tchr. Crystal Lake (Ill.) Cen. High Sch., 1968-85, chair English dept., 1985-86, dean of students, 1986-87; asst. prin. Cary Grove H.S., Cary, Ill., 1987-88, prin., 1988-94, curriculum dir. H.S. Dist. 155, 1994—2000, ret., 2000—; asst. prof. dept. edn. St. Mary's Coll., Notre Dame, Ind., 2000—. Speech instr. Purdue U., West Lafayette, Ind., 1974-75; speech tchr. McHenry County Coll., Crystal Lake, 1968-70; analyst, mentor, bd. trustees Ednl. Svc. Ctr. #1 Ill. State Bd. of Edn., 1991—, presenter, 1991—. Named Dinsting. Tchr., Crrystal Lake Jaycees, 1986; fellow 75th Anniversary Paul Harris. Mem. ASCD, Assn. Tchr. Educators, Rotary, Delta Kappa Gamma (state corr. sec. 1989-91, chpt. pres., mem. various coms.scholar 1983), Zeta Phi Eta, Alpha Omicron Pi. Avocation: rosarian. Office: 95 Madeleva Hall Saint Mary's Coll Notre Dame IN 46556

GREEN, CHARLES ADAM, retired education educator, psychologist; b. Detroit, Mich., Oct. 17, 1927; s. Fred Green and Charlena Cragwall; m. Marilyn Anderson Anderson, Aug. 22, 1987; m. Mildred Saphronia Wilson, Jan. 4, 1957 (div. May 23, 1975); children: Iris Denise Diop, Robin Charles. BA, U. of Mich., 1952; MEd, Wayne State U., 1957, PhD, 1974. Diplomate Am. Coll. Forensic Examiners; lic. psychologist Mich. Tchr. Detroit Bd. of Edn., 1954—58; dir. of spl. edn. Northville (Mich.) State Hosp., 1958—62; sch. psychologist Detroit Bd. of Edn., 1962—68, rsch. assoc., 1968—2001. Pres. Met. Cmty. Housing Devel. Orgn., Detroit, 1995—. Contbr. articles to profl. jours. Chmn., Thunder Bird dist. Boys Scouts of Am., Detroit, 1973—75; chairperson The Westsider Orgn., Detroit, 2000—03; bd. chmn. Highland Park (Mich.) YMCA, 1981—85. Pvt. USAF, 1945—46. Recipient Ability is Ageless award, Operation Able of Mich. Fellow: Am. Assn. on Mental Deficiency; mem.: APA, Phi Delta Kappa. Liberal. Avocations: boating, photography, travel, writing. Home: 398 Lodge Dr Detroit MI 48214 Personal E-mail: marilyn.green6@gte.net.

GREEN, CHERYL KAYE, dean, writer; b. Houston, Tex., Feb. 24, 1970; d. Frank D. and Velma R. Green. BA, Yale U., 1993; Master's, Ohio State U., 1995; PhD, So. Meth. U., 2004. Program assoc. Meadows Found., Dallas, 1996—98; CEO Child of Promise Found., Dallas, 1998—2001; program coord. Sen. Robert J. Dole Found., Wash., 1992—98; dean Resource & Cmty. Devel. Eastfield Coll., Mesquite, Tex., 2001—. Nonprofit cons., Cedar Hill, Tex., 1996—; dir. nonprofit bd. Ctrl. Dallas Ministries, 1996—2003, Women & Philanthropy, Wash., 1998—2001, Disability Funders Network, Wash., 2000—03. Author: (nonfiction book) World Wide Search: The Savvy Christian Singles Guide to Online Dating, (biography) Child of Promise: One Woman's Journey Through Tragedy to Triumph. ADA trainer Americans with Disabilities Act Tng. and Implementation Network, Wash., 1993—2000; bd. mem. representing interests of women with disabilities Women & Philanthropy, Wash., 1996—2000. Recipient Mellon Undergrad. Fellowships, Mellon Found., 1990—93, Everret Chandler Prize for Character, Courage and High Moral Purpose, Yale U., 1993, grad. fellowship, NSF, 1993—95, Nat. Rsch. Svc. award, Nat. Inst. Health/Nat. Inst. Mental Health, 1996—2000. Independent. Christian. Office: Eastfield Coll 3737 Motley Dr Mesquite TX 75150 Home Fax: 214-853-5668; Office Fax: 972-860-7294. Personal E-mail: txsunshine_2@yahoo.com. Business E-Mail: ckgreen@dcccd.edu.

GREEN, DAN, publishing company executive; b. Passaic, N.J., Sept. 28, 1935; s. Harold and Bessie (Roslow) G.; m. Jane Oliphant, Sept. 20, 1959; children— Matthew Kenan, Simon Pom. BA, Syracuse (N.Y.) U., 1956. Publicity dir. Dover Press, 1957-58, Sta. WNAC-TV, 1958-59, Bobbs-Merrill Co., 1959-62; with Simon & Schuster Inc., 1962-85, assoc. publisher, 1976-80, v.p., pub., 1980-84, pres. trade pub. group, 1984-85; founder, pub. Kenan Press, 1979-80; chief exec. officer Wheatland Pub., N.Y.C., 1985-89; pub. Weidenfeld & Nicolson N.Y., 1985-89; chief exec. officer Grove Press, Inc., N.Y.C., 1985-89; pres. Kenan Books, N.Y.C., 1989—. Pres. Pom Literary Agy., 1989. Office: Pom Inc 611 Broadway Rm 907B New York NY 10012-2608 Office Phone: 212-673-3835. Personal E-mail: pominc@verizon.net.

GREEN, DANA I., lawyer, human resources specialist; b. 1949; BA, Ind. Univ., 1971, JD, 1974; LLM in taxation, DePaul Univ., 1990. Bar: Ill. 1974. Atty. through dept. dir., employee rels. Walgreen Co., 1974—98, div. v.p., employee rels., 1998—2000, corp. v.p., human resources, 2000—04, sr. v.p., 2004—05, sr. v.p., gen. counsel, corp. sec., 2005—. Office: Walgreen Co 200 Wilmot Rd Deerfield IL 60015 Office Phone: 847-914-2500. Office Fax: 847-914-2804.*

GREEN, DAVID, manufacturing executive; b. Chgo., Mar. 22, 1922; s. Harry B. and Carrie (Scheinbaum) G.; m. Mary I. Winton, June 15, 1951; children: Sara Edmond, Howard Benjamin, Jonathan Winton. BA in Econs., U. Chgo., 1942, MA in Social Scis., 1949. Mgr. Toy Co., Chgo., 1950—54; founder, chmn., pres. Quartet Mfg. Co., Skokie, Ill., 1954—90, chmn., prin. officer, 1990—97. Pres. Colleague, Inc., Booneville, Miss., 1967-87; chmn. bd., cons. DG Group, Chgo., 1977-2005. Pres.'s circle Chgo. Botanic Garden; playwright's circle Stratford Festival; founder dir. circle Steppenwolf Theatre Co.; trustee Chgo. Symphony Orch.; chmn. Winnetka (Ill.) Caucus, 1971; chmn. Ill. state Dan Walker for Gov., 1972, 1976; governing mem. Chgo. Symphony Orch., Art Inst. Chgo.; spl. cons. to White House-Trade Expansion Act Washington, 1962; spl. asst. to Gov. for intergovtl. relations Ill., 1973—77; mem. pres.'s coun., vis. com. social scis. U. Chgo., mem. vis. com. on the coll. and student activities. Served with U.S. Army, 1942—45, PTO. Recipient 1st Non-Smoking Office Bldg. award Skokie Clean Air Coalition, 1987; named Office Products Divsn. Man of Yr., Richard Karasik Humanitarian award, UJA, 1997, Alumni Svc. citation U. Chgo., 2002, 1st Green Gargoyle award for Outstanding Achievement, U. Chgo., 2002, Writers' Theatre Founder's award, 2003; named Alumni Emeritus chair U. Chgo., 2002. Mem. Bus. Products Industry Assn., Office Products Wholesale Assn. (named Office Product Mfr. of Yr. 1989, 93, 94), Chgo. Soc. of Clubs, Met. Club Chgo., Bay Colony Club Naples, Fla. Home: 311 Woodley Rd Winnetka IL 60093-3740 Office: 650 Dundee Rd Ste 456 Northbrook IL 60062-2758 also: 8171 Bay Colony Dr Naples FL 34108-7561 Business E-Mail: davidgreen456@ameritech.net.

GREEN, DAVID, hematologist; b. Phila., 1934; AB, U. Pa., 1956; MD, Jefferson Med. Coll., 1960; PhD, Northwestern U., 1974. Cert. Am. Bd. Internal Medicine, 1967, in Hematology 1972. Intern Cook County Hosp.,

Chgo., 1960—61; resident, internal medicine Jefferson Hosp., Phila., 1961—63, fellow, hematology, 1963—64; attending physician Northwestern Meml. Hosp., Chgo., 1975—; prof. Northwestern U., 1975—; attending physician Rehab. Inst. Chgo., 1993—. Office Phone: 312-695-0990.

GREEN, DAVID, nonprofit organization administrator; BA, U. Mich., 1978, MPH, 1982. With Seva Found. Aravind Eye Hosp., Madurai, India, 1983—2000, founder Aurolab, 1992; founder Project Impact, Inc., 2000—. Named MacArthur Fellow, John D. and Catherine T. MacArthur Found., 2004, Ashoka Fellow. Achievements include first to establish a non-profit manufacturing facility in a developing country which produces, manufactures and distributes affordable medical technologies. Office: Project Impact 1782 Fifth St Berkeley CA 94710 Office Phone: 510-981-1103. Office Fax: 313-668-6861.*

GREEN, DAVID CHARLES, surgeon; b. Honeoye, N.Y., Apr. 25, 1929; s. Pierpont Lewis and Anna Mary (Motycka) G.; m. Susan Ash, June 28, 1958; children: Lane Hollins, Rebecca Green Edland, Suzan Green Dallam, Pierpont Lewis II, Caroline Ash. BS, St. Lawrence U., 1954; MD, SUNY, Syracuse, 1954. Intern U. Md. Hosp., Balt., 1954-55; commd. 1st lt. U.S. Army, 1955, advanced through grades to col., 1969; resident in gen. surgery Walter Reed Army Med. Ctr., Washington, 1955-60, chief cardiothoracic surgery, 1970-77; resident in thoracic surgery Brooke Army Med. Ctr., Ft. Sam Houston, Tex., 1965-67; ret. U.S. Army, 1977; pvt. practice Silver Spring, Md., 1977-79, Annapolis, Md., 1986—; prof. surgery U. Md. Coll. Medicine, Balt., 1979-86. Prof. surgery Uniformed Services Univ., Bethesda, Md., 1976—; cons. to surgeon gen. in thoracic surgery, Washington, 1970-77. Contbr. numerous articles to profl. jours. Fellow Am. Coll. Surgeons, Am. Coll. Chest Physicians; mem. Soc. Thoracic Surgeons, Ea. Vascular Soc., Chesapeake Vascular Soc., Soc. Med. Cons. to Armed Forces, Annapolis Yacht Club, Annapolitan Club. Republican. Episcopalian. Avocations: sailing, gardening. Home: 1489 Brookside Common Annapolis MD 21401-6469 Office: 1489 Brookside Common Annapolis MD 21401-1001 Office Phone: 410-841-5217. E-mail: dsgreen9@comcast.net.

GREEN, DAVID EDWARD, librarian, priest, translator; b. Adrian, Mich., June 22, 1937; s. Edward Robert Alexander and Fannie Amelia (Nadler) G.; m. Sharon Weiner, June 1, 1961; children: Alexis Ann, Philip DeWitt. BA, Harvard U., 1960; BD, Ch. Div. Sch. of Pacific, Berkeley, Calif., 1963; MLS, U. Calif., Berkeley, 1970. Ordained priest Episc. Ch., 1964. Assoc. librarian Grad. Theol. Union, Berkeley, 1970-82; libr. dir. Gen. Theol. Sem., N.Y.C., 1982—. Translator many German theol. works. Mem. Am. Theol. Libr. Assn., N.Y. Area Theol. Libr. Assn., Beta Phi Mu. Avocation: english country dancing. Home and Office: Gen Theol Sem St Mark's Libr 175 9th Ave New York NY 10011-4924 E-mail: green@gts.edu.

GREEN, DAVID F., biochemist, researcher; b. London, Ont., Canada, Dec. 23, 1975; s. Margaret A. and Francis J. A. Green; life ptnr. Faye Yu. BS in Chemistry with honors, Simon Fraser U., 1997; PhD in Biol. Chemistry, MIT, 2002. Postdoctoral assoc. MIT, Biol. Engring. Divsn., Cambridge, Mass., 2002—. V.p., bd. mem. MolySym, Inc., Cambridge, 2002—. Contbr. articles to profl. jours. Recipient BC Provincial Exam Gold medal, BC Dept. Edn., 1993; scholar, Simon Fraser U., 1993—97. Mem.: Protein Soc. (assoc.), Am. Chem. Soc. (assoc.). Achievements include patents pending for Method and system for interactive molecular docking and feedback; Method and system for integrating a physical molecular model with a computer-based visualization and simulation model; research in Methods for analysis and design of electrostatic interactions in protein-ligand binding systems. Office: MIT 77 Massachusetts Ave Room 32-211 Cambridge MA 02139 Office Phone: 617-253-5438. E-mail: dfgreen@alum.mit.edu.

GREEN, DAVID WILLIAM, chemist, educator; b. Hudson, Mich., Nov. 19, 1942; s. Francis Harger and Dorotha Louise (Onweller) G.; m. Mary Sarah McCullough, July 8, 1967; children: Laura, Brenda, Mark, Brian, William. BA, Albion Coll., 1964; PhD, U. Calif., Berkeley, 1968; MBA, U. Chgo., 1985. Instr. U. Calif., Berkeley, 1968; rsch. assoc. U. Chgo., 1968-71; asst. prof. Albion (Mich.) Coll., 1971-75; chemist Argonne (Ill.) Nat. Lab., 1975-82, mgr. analytical chemistry, 1982—2001; prof. chemistry Coll. DuPage, Glen Ellyn, Ill., 1991-93. Vis. prof. chemistry Albion Coll., 2001—. Editor Mng. the Modern Lab. 1995-2003, mem. editl. bd., 1994—. Pres. Dist. 58 Bd. Edn., Downers Grove, Ill., 1976-79. Mem. Analytical Lab. Mgrs. Assn. (pres. 1986-87, treas. 1989). Home: 602 Bidwell Albion MI 49224-Office: Putnam Hall Albion College Albion MI 49224- Office Phone: 517-629-0656. Business E-Mail: dwgreen@albion.edu.

GREEN, DENNIS, professional football coach; b. Harrisburg, Pa., Feb. 17, 1949; BS, U. Iowa, 1971. Asst. coach U. Iowa, 1972, 74-76, U. Dayton, 1973, Stanford U., 1977-78, 80, San Francisco 49ers, 1979; head coach Northwestern U., 1981-85; asst. coach San Francisco 49ers, 1986-88; head coach Stanford U., 1989-91, Minn. Vikings, 1992—2002, Arizona Cardinals, 2004—. Office: c/o Ariz Cardinals PO Box 888 Phoenix AZ 85001-0888

GREEN, DENNIS JOSEPH, lawyer; b. Milw., Sept. 28, 1941; m. Janet McQueen; children: Karla Pope, Cheryl Ashley, Deborah. BS in Mgmt., U. Ill., 1963, JD, 1968. Bar: Ill. 1968, Mo. 1968. Atty. Monsanto Co., St. Louis, 1968-75, asst. co. counsel, 1975-76, counsel, 1976-79; gen. counsel, sec. Fisher Controls Internat. Inc., Clayton, Mo., 1979-85, v.p., gen. counsel, sec., 1985-93; v.p. Emerson Electric Co., St. Louis, 1999—, assoc. gen. counsel, 1999—2004, dep. gen. counsel, 2004—. 1st lt. U.S. Army, 1963-65. Office: Emerson Electric Co PO Box 4100 8000 W Florissant Ave Saint Louis MO 63136-1494 E-mail: dennis.green@emrsn.com.

GREEN, DON WESLEY, chemical and petroleum engineering educator; b. Tulsa, July 8, 1932; s. Earl Leslie and Erma Pansy (Brackins) G.; m. Patricia Louise Polston, Nov. 26, 1954; children: Guy Leslie, Don Michael, Charles Patrick. BS in Petroleum Engring., U. Tulsa, 1955; MSChemE, U. Okla., 1959, PhD in Chem. Engring., 1963. Rsch. scientist Continental Oil Co., Ponca City, Okla., 1962-64; asst. to assoc. prof. U. Kans., Lawrence, 1964-71, prof. chem. and petroleum engring., 1971-82, chmn. dept. chem. and petroleum engring., 1970-74, 96-200, co-dir. Tertiary Oil Recovery project, 1974—, Conger-Gabel Disting. prof., 1982-95, Deane E. Ackers Disting. prof., 1995—. Faculty rep. to NCAA. Editor: Perry's Chemical Engineers' Handbook, 1984, 1997; co-author: Enhanced Oil Recovery, 1998; contbr. articles to profl. jours. 1st lt. USAF, 1955-57. Fellow Am. Inst. Chem. Engrs.; mem. Soc. Petroleum Engrs. (Disting. Achievement award 1983, chmn. edn. and accreditation com. 1980-81, Disting. mem. 1986, Disting. lectr. 1986). Democrat. Avocations: handball, baseball, mountain hiking. Home: 1020 Sunset Dr Lawrence KS 66044-4546 Office: U Kans Dept Chem & Petroleum Engring 4008 Learned Hall Lawrence KS 66045-7526 E-mail: dgreen@ku.edu.

GREEN, DONALD HUGH, lawyer; b. Elizabeth, N.J., May 26, 1929; s. Mortimer Jordan and Edna (Reinherz) G.;m. Carol Margaret Medsger, Sept. 20, 1960; children: Michael, Margaret, Matthew, Mark. AB, Syracuse U., 1951; LLB, Harvard U., 1954. Bar: Fla. 1956, N.Y. 1957, D.C. 1960. Atty. Office of Legal Counsel, U.S. Dept. Justice, Washington, 1958-60, atty. civil div., 1960-61; assoc. Bergson & Borkland, Washington, 1961-65; ptnr. Wald, Harkrader & Ross, Washington, 1966-87; vice chmn. exec. com. mng. ptnr., of counsel Pepper, Hamilton LLP, Washington, 1987—, mem. exec. com., mng. ptnr. DC office, 1995—2000. Mem. faculty curriculum com. Legal Edn. Inst., U.S. Dept. Justice, Washington, 1985-92; lectr. Georgetown Law Ctr., Washington, 1981—, various symposia D.C. Bar; adj. prof. Georgetown Law Ctr., 1992-03; apptd. def. adv. com. on women in the svcs. Sec. of Def., 1999, exec. com. 1999-01. Contbr. articles to profl. jours. Mem., chmn. trustees Cedar Lane Unitarian Ch., Bethesda, 1972-75; coxswain USCG Aux., 2001—. Col. USMCR, 1954-85. Decorated Legion of Merit. Mem. ABA, Internat. Assn. Women Judges (mem. bd. mng. trustees 2002—), Fed. Bar Assn., Am. Arbitration Assn., Joint Svcs. Com. on Profl. Ethics, Nat. Panel Arbitrators, Fed. Am. Inn of Ct. (pres. 1994-95). Democrat. Avocations: painting, boating, tennis. Home: 5610 Wisconsin Ave Apt 18A Chevy Chase MD 20815-4415 Office: Pepper Hamilton LLP Hamilton Sq 600 14th St NW Washington DC 20005-2008 Office Phone: 202-220-1213. Business E-Mail: greendh@pepperlaw.com.

GREEN, DONALD PHILIP, political scientist, educator; b. Chgo., June 23, 1961; s. Burton and Isabel (Engelhardt) G.; m. Ann Gerken, June 18, 1989; children: Aaron, Rachel. BA in Polit. Sci., UCLA, 1983; MA in Polit. Sci., U. Calif., Berkeley, 1984, PhD, 1988. From asst. to assoc. prof. dept. polit. sci. Yale U., New Haven, 1989-94, prof., 1994—, dir. Instn. for Social and Policy Studies, 1996—, A. Whitney Griswold chair, 2001. Author: Pathologies of Rational Choice Theory, 1994, Partisan Hearts and Minds, 2002, Get Out the Vote, 2004; contbr. articles to profl. jours.; inventor abstract strategy games. Recipient Nat. Young Investigator award NSF, 1993—. Fellow: AAAS. Office: Yale Univ 77 Prospect St New Haven CT 06520-8209 Office Phone: 203-432-3237. Business E-Mail: donald.green@yale.edu.

GREEN, DOUGLAS ALVIN, retired library director; b. Gilmer, Tex., Feb. 17, 1925; s. Arthur Elmer and Evalena (Loyless) G.; m. Clovis Wayne Elwell, Dec. 15, 1945; 1 child, Danis (dec.). BA, U. N. Tex., 1950; MA, E. Tex. State U., 1951, EdD, 1980; MS, La. State U., 1968. Chief bibliographer U. Ark. Gen. Libr., Fayetteville, 1963-67; libr. dir. Bee County Coll., Beeville, Tex., 1968-73; chmn. learning resources Richland C.C., Decatur, Ill., 1973-75; libr. dir. Laredo (Tex.) State U., 1975-76, Amb. Coll., Big Sandy, Tex., 1976-77, Pasadena, 1977-78, U. Ctrl. Ark., Conway, 1981-84; ret. Ark. State U., Beebe, 1990. Author: An Index to Collected Essays on Educational Media and Technology, 1982; contbg. author: The Smaller Academic Library - A Management Handbook, 1988. With USNR, 1943-46. HEA Title II scholar, 1967-68. Avocations: piano, organ, keyboards, fishing. Home: 3414 Lee St Tyler TX 75702-1628

GREEN, DOUGLAS G., lawyer; MA with honors, Bowdoin Coll., 1968; MA in English, U. Va., 1969; JD, Georgetown U., 1973. Bar: DC 1973. Ptnr. & vice chmn., Electric Power, Antitrust, Toxic Torts & Comml. Litig. Steptoe & Johnson LLP, Washington, mem. exec. com. Spkr. in field; editor: Georgetown Law Jour.; contbr. articles to jour. Office: Steptoe& Johnson LLP 1330 Connecticut Ave NW Washington DC 20036 Office Phone: 202-429-6212. Office Fax: 202-429-3902. Business E-Mail: dgreen@steptoe.com.

GREEN, EDWARD LEWIS, mathematics professor; b. N.Y.C., Apr. 4, 1946; s. Benjamin and Ruth (Simpson) G.; m. Diane Pearl Weinstein, Aug. 14, 1966; children: Jessica, Benjamin. BA, Cornell U., 1967; MS, Brandeis U., 1968, PhD, 1973. Lectr. U. Pa., Phila., 1973-75; vis. prof. U. Ill., Urbana, 1975-77; asst. prof. Va. Tech., Blacksburg, 1977-79, assoc. prof., 1979-81, prof. math., 1981—. Co-author: Module With Cores; editor Communications in Algebra, 1990—; contbr. articles to profl. jours. Rsch. grantee NSF, 1974—.

GREEN, EDWARD THOMAS, JR., education educator; b. Oxford, N.J., Apr. 19, 1921; s. Edward Thomas and Euphemia (Lanterman) G.; m. Margaret Evelyn Tuttle, Jan. 30, 1944; children: Marsha, Margaret, Barbara. BS cum laude, Ithaca Coll., 1942; MS, Syracuse U., 1947, EdD, 1965. Music instr. high sch., Palmyra, N.Y., 1942-50; dir. guidance, vice-prin., 1946-50; prin. Palmyra-Macedon Ctrl. Sch., 1950-54; supervising prin. New Berlin (N.Y.) Ctrl. Sch., 1954-58, Rondout Valley Ctrl. Sch., Accord, N.Y., also supt. schs., 1958-66; supt. schs. Oneida (NY) City Schs., 1966-77; prof. edn. Ga. So. U., Statesboro, 1977-87, prof. emeritus, 1987—. Pres. Ithaca (N.Y.) Alumni Coun., Palmyra Betterment Club 1952, Mid-Hudson Sch. Study Coun., New Paltz, N.Y., 1960, Ind. Residents Coun., Longview, Ithaca, N.Y., 2004—, co-founder and moderator men's group; vice chmn. CHE-MAD-HER-ON, Inc.; area sec. Ctrl. Sch. Study; mem. exec. com. Catskill Study on Small Sch. Design; v.p. N.Y. State Tchrs. Retirement Bd.; v.p. Rip Van Winkle coun. Boy Scouts Am., 1964-66, v.p., then pres. Madison County coun., chmn. Madison Dist., pres. Iroquois coun.; mem. Ulster County Cmty. Action Program; bd. dirs. Ithacare Sr. Citizens Ctr., Ithaca, N.Y., 2003—. Served with AUS, 1942—46, ETO. Mem. N.Y. State Sch. Dist. Adminstrs. (pres.), Am. Assn. Sch. Adminstrs., Assn. for Supervision and Curriculum Devel., Nat. Sch. Pub. Rels. Assn., Nat. Assn. Secondary Sch. Prins., Nat. Assn. Elem. Sch. Prins., Ga. Assn. Ednl. Leaders, So. Assn. Colls. and Schs. (Ga. sec. com. 1991-95), Ga. Accrediting Commn., Nat. Orgn. for Legal Problems in Edn., Masons, Shriners, Rotary Internat., Lions Club, Phi Delta Kappa (chpt. pres., area coord.), Phi Mu Alpha. Republican. Presbyterian. Home: 301 Bella Vista Dr Ithaca NY 14850-5774 Personal E-mail: edgreen21@yahoo.com.

GREEN, ELBERT P., retired academic administrator; b. Laneview, Va., June 9, 1935; s. James H. and Levallia C. (DeLeaver) G.; m. Mary M. Green, July 6, 1961; children: Mark B., Marsha B. BS, Va. State Coll., 1957; BD, Felix Adler Meml. U., Chapel Hill, N.C., 1969; MS in Edn., Troy State U., Montgomery, Ala., 1988; MBph, Am. Bible Sch., Kansas City, Kans., 1968; PhD, S.W. U., New Orleans, 1991. Cert. tchr., Ala., cert. hypnotherapist; ordained minister. 2d lt. U.S. Army, 1958, advanced through grades to maj.; ret., 1979; dir. jr. ROTC, Indianola (Miss.) City Schs., Macon County (Ala.) Schs.; dir. residence hall Tuskegee (Ala.) U. Author: Poetry Is Soul, 1988, Poetry Is Gold, 1982, The Light of the World Is Poetry, 1995, Daily Bread for Living, 2004; contbr. articles to newspapers. Inductee Internat. Poetry Hall of Fame, 1997, Who Is Who of Contemporary Achievers Hall of Fame, 1997, Phi Beta Sigma Hall of Fame, 1999, Am. Biographical Inst. Hall of Fame, 2002. Mem. Internat. Soc. of Poets, Profl. Educators Orgn., Am. Legion, Lions Internat., Scabbard and Blade, Phi Beta Sigma, Phi Delta Kappa, Gamma Beta Phi. Home: 2910 W Martin L King Hwy Tuskegee AL 36083

GREEN, ELEANOR MYERS, veterinarian, educator; b. Phila., Feb. 10, 1948; d. Wade Cooper and Eleanor Ruth (McWherter) Myers; children: George Ashby Jr., Stacy Elizabeth, William Wade. Student, U. South Fla., 1965-67, U. Fla., 1967-69; DVM, Auburn U., 1973. Diplomate Am. Coll. Vet. Internal Medicine, Am. Bd. Vet. Practitioners (pres. 1993-95, past pres. 1995-96). Ptnrship, owner Guntown (Miss.) Vet. Clinic, 1973-76; asst. prof. Miss. State U., Starkville, 1976-84; assoc. prof. U. Mo., Columbia, 1984-91; prof. U. Tenn., Knoxville, 1991-96; prof., chair dept. U. Fla., Gainesville, 1996—. Named Disting. Practitioner Nat. Acads. of Practice, CALS award of distinction, 2004. Mem. Am. Assn. Equine Practitioners (bd. dirs. 1997-99), Fla. Vet. Med. Assn., Am. Vet. Med. Assn., Internat. Soc. Vet. Perinatology, Am. Assn. Vet. Clinicians (Faculty Achievement award 1999, pres. 1995-96, past pres. 1996-97), Nat. Acad.'s Practice (Disting. Practitioner 1998—), Fla. Thoroughbred Owners and Breeders Assn., Fla. Quarter Horse Assn. (bd. dirs.), Rotary Internat. Presbyterian. Avocations: horseback riding, tennis, painting. Office: U Fla Coll Vet Medicine Dept Large Animal Clin Scis Gainesville FL 32610-0136 E-mail: greene@mail.vetmed.ufl.edu.

GREEN, ERIC HOWARD, lawyer; b. N.Y.C., Jan. 5, 1950; s. Bernard and Edith Green; m. Mona M. Green, July 10, 1982; children: Zachary Samuel, Shawn Alexander. BA, SUNY, Buffalo, 1972, JD, 1976. Bar: N.Y. 1977, U.S. Dist. Ct. (so. and ea. dist.) N.Y. 1979, U.S. Supreme Ct. 1985. Assoc. Pops & Estrin, N.Y.C., 1976-77, Karp & Silver, Queens, N.Y., 1977-81, Edward Leshaw, Esq., N.Y.C., 1981-82; mng. ptnr. Eric H. Green, Esq., N.Y.C., 1982—. Instr. Nat. Inst. of Trial Advocacy, Cardoza Law Sch., N.Y.C., 1987—, U. Buffalo, coll. of Urban Studies, 1974-76; lectr. NYU, Sch. Continuing Edn., N.Y.C., 1986-90; arbitrator Am. Arbitration Assn., 1987—. Mem. N.Y. Dem. Judicial Screening Panel, N.Y.C., 1989; advisor, vol. N.Y.C. Open Doors Edn. Program, 1985-89. Mem. ATLA, N.Y. County Lawyers Assn., N.Y. State Bar Assn., N.Y. State Trial Lawyers Assn. (bd. dirs., speaker cmty. speakers bur. 1988—), N.Y. County Lawyers Assn. (fee dispute com., Supreme Ct. com.), Assn. Bar City N.Y. (tort litigation com., chmn. mediation subcom.). Avocations: sports, theater, antiques. Office: 295 Madison Ave New York NY 10017-6304 E-mail: greenlegal@msn.com.

GREEN, ERIC ROGER, librarian; b. Scobey, Mont., July 29, 1963; s. Roger Iarve and Joyce Rogers Green. BA in sociology, Western State Coll., 1986; MA in sociology, Am. U., 1996; M in libr. sci., Emporia State, 2003. Support staff Denver Pub. Libr., Denver, 1990—93, 2000—04; libr. C.C. of Colo., Lowry Campus, Denver, 2000—02; libr. dir. Lamar C.C., Lamar, Colo., 2004—. Libr. internship Regis U. Libr., Denver, 2003. Vol. Peace Corps, Sienna Leave, South Africa, 1989—90. Libr. Sch. scholarship, Denver Pub. Libr., 2000. Mem.: Am. Sociological Assn., Colo. Assn. of Libr., Am. Libr. Assn. Home: 1601 S Ninth St 2 Lamar CO 81052 Office: Lamar CC 2401 S Main La Junta CO 81050 Office Phone: 719-336-1541.

GREEN, FRANCIS EUGENE, artist, educator; b. San Diego, Apr. 3, 1946; s. Charles Green, Jr. and Lois Lavonne (Simmerman) Adelman; m. Bonnie Weigle, Oct. 8, 1966 (div. Apr. 1979); m. Barbara Korr, Feb. 14, 1980. AA in Painting, San Diego Mesa Jr. Coll., 1968; BA in Painting, San Diego State U., 1971; MFA, Temple U., 1973. Dept. head printmaking Instituto Allende, San Miguel de Allende, 1972-75; master printer Atelier Ettinger, N.Y.C., 1975-79; cons. fine art editions N.Y.C., 1979-84; vocat. comml. arts instr. Greene Correctional Facility, Coxsackie, 1984—; represented by Pierce Galleries, Inc., Nantucket, Mass., Deborah Davis Fine Art, Hudson, NY. Instr. Olana State Hist. Site, Hudson, N.Y., 1990-2000, Columbia/Greene C.C., Hudson, 1996-97. Exhibits in N.Y., N.J. and Conn. Democrat. Jewish. Home: #10 Rte 23A Catskill NY 12414

GREEN, FRANK EARL, civil engineer; b. Joplin, Mo., Nov. 24, 1931; s. Lloyd Cuthbertson and Gladys Alberta (Kennedy) G.; m. Joan Imogene (Wheeler),July 25, 1953; children: Kevin Joe, Keely Sue Green LaNoue. BS in Math., S.W. Mo. State U., 1953; BSCE, Kans. State U., 1958. Registered profl. engr., Mo., land surveyor, Mo. Hwy. designer Mo. Hwy. and Transp. Dept., Kansas City, 1958-61, sr. hwy. designer, 1962-65, dist. hwy. design engr., 1966-96; ret., 1996. Usher, mem. Grandview (Mo.) United Meth. Ch., 1970—. With Army Corps. of Engrs., 1953-55. Mem. ASCE (life, bd. dirs. Kansas City sect. 1987-91, sec.-treas. and pres.-elect 1992, pres. 1993), Nat. Soc. Profl. Engrs. (life), Mo. Soc. Profl. Engrs. (bd. dirs. Western chpt. 1985-91). Republican. Home: 5608 E 100th Ter Kansas City MO 64137-1312

GREEN, GEORGE EDWARD, retired surgeon; b. N.Y.C., Jan. 18, 1932; s. Robert and Hannah Augusta (Berkowitz) G.; m. Sheila Ellen Greenwald, Feb. 18, 1960; children: Samuel, Benjamin. Student, Yale Coll., 1952, MD, 1956. Diplomate Am. Bd. Thoracic Cardiovascular Surgery, Am. Bd. Surgery. Asst. attending surgeon NYU Hosp., N.Y.C., 1968-70; attending surgeon St. Lukes Roosevelt Hosp., 1970-94, Columbia Presbyn. Hosp., N.Y.C., 1992-94; attending surgeon, chief cardiothoracic surgery L.I. Jewish Hosp., N.Y.C., 1982-83; prof. clin. surgery Columbia U., N.Y.C., 1992-94; ret., 1994. Author, editor: Surgical Revascularization of the Heart, 1991; contbr. articles to profl. jours. Lt. comdr. USN, 1962-63. Rsch. grantee Nat. Heart and Lung Inst. NIH, 1966-68. Mem. Am. Assn. Thoracic Surgery, Soc. Thoracic Surgeons, Soc. Vascular Surgery, Internat. Cardiovascular Soc. Democrat. Jewish. Home: PO Box 364 Millerton NY 12546-0364

GREEN, GEORGE JOSEPH, publishing executive; b. NYC, May 6, 1938; s. Monroe and Ruth (Gast) G.; m. Wilma H. Jordan. BA, Yale U., 1960. Trainee advt. dept. Burlington Industries, N.Y.C., 1961-62; with The New Yorker Mag., 1962-84, salesman retail advt. N.Y.C. div., 1962-64, salesman advt. Atlanta div., 1964-66, salesman advt. N.Y.C. div., 1966-67, asst. treas., 1967-71, dir. circulation, v.p., 1971-75, pres., 1975-84; exec. v.p. Hearst Mags., N.Y.C., 1984—; pres. Hearst Mags. Internat., N.Y.C., 1989—. Bd. dirs. Nat. Magazine Co. Served with USAR, 1960-65. Mem. Mag. Publs. Assn. (bd. dirs.). Office: Hearst Mags 959 8th Ave New York NY 10019-3795 E-mail: ggreen@hearst.com.

GREEN, GERALD B., state legislator; Freeholder Union County; assemblyman dist. 22 N.J. State Assembly. Chmn. fin. Union County Freehold, 1991, chair bd. dirs., 1990. Pvt. industry coun. Union County Coll. Bd. Sch. Estimate. Mem. Union County Police Chiefs Assn. Office: 17 Watchung Ave Plainfield NJ 07060-1228 Office Phone: 908-561-5757. Business E-Mail: asmgreen@njleg.org.

GREEN, GERARD LEO, priest, educator; b. Batavia, NY, July 27, 1928; s. George Leo and Marian (Powers) G. BS, Mt. St. Mary's Coll., 1952; MA, St. Bonaventure U., 1958; postgrad., U. Notre Dame, summers 1961-62, U. Buffalo, 1965-66; EdM, SUNY, 1968. Ordained priest Roman Catholic Ch., 1956. Lab technician Eastman Kodak Co., 1947-48; chemist Xerox Co., 1952; parish asst. Diocese Buffalo, 1956-59; instr. chemistry Bishop Turner H.S., Buffalo, 1959-74, dir. sci., 1959-70, 72-74; adminstr. Our Lady of the Rosary Parish, Wilson, N.Y., 1968, St. Barnabas Parish and Sch. Depew, N.Y., 1973-75, pastor, 1976-90; prelate of honor, 1984; mem., supr., leader tng. team, 1979-90; pastor Sts. Peter and Paul Parish, Hamburg, N.Y., 1990-99; rector pro tem St. Joseph's Cathedral, Buffalo, 2001. Mem. sci. curriculum com. Dept. Edn. Diocese Buffalo, 1960-70, chmn. diocesan chemistry textbook evaluation com., 1961-70, mem. diocesan pastoral coun. for handicapped, 1976-82, sec. 1978-79, diocesan regional coord., 1979-80, mem. diocesan fin. com., 1984-94, diocesan priests coun., 1990-99, 2003—, mem. diocesan coll. of consultors, 1994-99; active Diocesan Cons. Parish Computers, 1983-98, Diocesan Bd. Priests Retirement, 1985-91, 99—, Diocesan Cemetary Bd., 1994—, Sch. Bd. St. Francis H.S., 1992-98; diocesan bd. dirs. for TV prodn. 1986-94; chaplain Hyview Fire Co., 1976-81, Cheektowaga Police PBA, 1976-90, West End Fire Co., 1977-90, Depew Village Fire Co., 1980-88. Contbr. articles to profl. publs. Mem. Western N.Y. Sci. Congress Com., 1960-74, sec., 1968, co-chmn. 1969, chmn. 1972-73, state chmn. 1970; mem. gen. chemistry exam. com. N.Y. State Edn. Dept., 1970-73; mem. Maryvale Schs. Planning Bd., 1977-79; cons. sci. facilities in secondary schs.; mem. local IUE-AFL-CIO Scholarship Fund Com., 1968-71; mem. dist. com. Boy Scouts Am., Buffalo, 1957-74; bd. dirs. Tifft (Conservation) Farm, 1978-82, Hamburg Meals on Wheels, 1999-00; active Nat. Cath. Cemetary Conf., N.Y. State Fire Chaplains. With AUS, 1946-47, VFW. Recipient Disting. Svc. award in sci. edn., 1975, Justice and Charity award First Cath. Charities, 1999, Cure of ARS award Outstanding Priest, 1999, Eagle Scout. Mem. Sci. Tchrs. Assn., N.Y. (dir. 1971-73), Nat. Cath. Edn. Assn., Order of Arrow, KC 4th degree past grand knight), VFW. Address: 9686 Oak Grove Dr Angola NY 14006-8904 E-mail: msgrgreen@hotmail.com.

GREEN, GINGER E., retired nurse; b. Chicago, Ill., Apr. 8, 1949; d. William H. and Elizabeth L. (Falk) Power; m. Ronald K. Green, June 6, 2002; children: Charles W. Power, Tomas R. Power. A, Triton Coll., 1979; A in Liberal Sci., Elgin (Ill.) C.C., 1991; degree, Army War Coll., 1991; BSN, U. N.Y., 1991. Registered profl. nurse, Ill., 1979. Registered profl. nurse Elmhurst (Ill.) Meml. Hosp., 1979—2003. Preceptor Elmhurst Meml. Hosp., 1979—2004; head nurse combat support hosp. U.S. Army Res., 1979—2000. Writer: newsletter Surgical Synopsis. Maj. USAR, 1979—2000. Decorated Presdl. Citation Pres. of the U.S. Mem.: Am. Legion. Independent. Roman Catholic. Avocations: hunting, fishing, boating.

GREEN, GRANT S., JR., former federal agency administrator; b. Seattle, June 16, 1938; s. Grant S. and Eveleth (Solberg) G.; m. Virginia Dondy; children: Kelley, Shelley, Tana. BA, U. Ark., 1960; MS, George Washington U., 1978. Commd. 2d lt. U.S. Army, 1961, advanced through grades to col., ret., 1983; various mgmt. positions Sears World Trade, Washington, 1983-86; spl. asst. to pres. for nat. security affairs NSC, Washington, 1986-87; asst. sec. def. Office Sec. Def., Washington, 1987-88; v.p. IPAC, Washington; chmn. & pres. GMD Solutions; under sec. for mgmt. U.S. Dept. State, Washington, 2001—05. Cons. Carlyle Group, Washington, 1988—; mem. bd. USO, Nat. Def. Univ., 1987—. Decorated Bronze Star, DFC, DDSM, DSSM, others; recipient Disting. Pub. Svc. award Dept. of Def., several fgn. awards. Mem. World Affairs Coun., Ctr. for Excellence in Govt., Assn. U.S. Army, Army Aviation Assn., Ret. Officers Assn., Am. Legion. Republican. Avocations: antique cars, boating, golf, skiing.

GREEN, HARRY WESTERN, II, geology-geophysics educator; s. Harry Buetel and Mabel (Hendrickson) G.; children from previous marriage: Mark, Stephen, Carolyn, Jennifer; m. Maria Manuela Marques Martins, May 15,

1975; children: Alice, Miguel, Maria. AB in Geology with honors, UCLA, 1963, MS in Geology and Geophysics, 1967, PhD in Geology and Geophysics with distinction, 1968. Postdoctoral rsch. assoc. materials sci. Case Western Res. U., Cleve., 1968-70; asst. prof. geology U. Calif., Davis, 1970-74, assoc. prof., 1974-80, prof., 1980-92, chmn. dept., 1984-88, prof. geology and geophysics Riverside, 1993-99, disting. prof. geology and geophysics, 1999—, dir. Inst. Geophysics and Planetary Physics, 1993-95, 2001, dir. analytical electron microscopy facility, 1994—2000, vice chancellor for rsch., 1995-2000, dir. ctrl. facility advanced microscopy and microanalysis, 2000—. Exch. scientist U. Nantes, France, 1973, vis. prof., 1978-79; vis. prof. Monash U., Melbourne, Australia, 1984; specialist advisor World Bank Program, China U. of Geoscis., Wuhan, 1988; adj. sr. rsch. scientist Lamont-Doherty Earth Obs., Columbia U., 1989-95, Vetlesen vis. prof., 1991-92; expert advisor geophysics rev. panel NSF, 1991-94; co-founder Gordon Conf. on Rock Deformation, 1995, chmn. 2d conf., 1997; hon. faculty China U. Geoscis., Wuhan, 1998—; vis. scientist Carnegie Inst. Washington, 2000—, Abelson lectr., 2000, vis. rev. com., 2004; faculty rsch. lectr. U. Calif., Riverside, 2002-03; mem. facilities com. Consortium for Materials Properties Rsch. in Earth Scis., 2002-04, chmn. exec. com., 2004-. Contbr. articles to books and profl. jours. Grantee NSF, 1969—, Dept. Energy, 1988-94. Fellow AAAS, Mineral Soc. Am., Am. Geophys. Union (N.L. Bowen award 1994, Francis Birch lectr. 1995); Cosmos Club (Washington), Sigma Xi. Achievements include discovery and characterization of new mechanisms of deep earthquakes; discovery of exhumation of rocks from hundreds of km depth in subduction zones. Office: U Calif IGPP Earth Scis 900 University Ave Riverside CA 92521 Office Phone: 951-827-4505. Business E-Mail: harry.green@ucr.edu.

GREEN, HARVEY, history educator; b. Buffalo, Sept. 15, 1946; s. Herman and Bessie Green; m. Susan Reynolds Williams, June 21, 1980. BA, U. Rochester, 1968; MA, Rutgers U., 1970, PhD, 1976. Historian Strong Mus., Rochester, N.Y., 1976-83, v.p. interpretation, 1983-89; assoc. prof. history Northeastern U., Boston, 1989-93, prof. history, 1993—. Fulbright bicentennial prof. Am. studies Helsinki, Finland, 1999-2000. Author: Light of the Home, 1983, Fit for America, 1986, The Uncertainty of Everyday Life 1915-1945, 1992; mem. editorial bd. Northeastern U. Press, 1990-96; contbr. articles to profl. jours. Trustee Landmark Soc. Western N.Y., Rochester, 1985-89; bd. overseers Strawbery Banke Mus., 1991-96; bd. corporators Canterbury Shaker Mus., 1994-2000. Univ. fellow Rutgers U., 1973; NEH grantee, Washington, 1982, 83, 85; Fulbright award to Turku, Finland, 1995. Fellow Am. Antiquarian Soc., Winterthur Mus.; mem. Orgn. Am. Historians, Am. Studies Assn., Am. Hist. Assn., Am. Assn. State and Local History (coun. mem., cons. various museums 1987—). Avocations: woodworking, golf, gardening, conservation. Office: Northeastern U 249 Meserve Hall Boston MA 02115 E-mail: h.green@neu.edu.

GREEN, HOLCOMBE TUCKER, JR., investment company executive; b. Atlanta, Sept. 29, 1939; s. Holcombe Tucker and Mary Katherine (Woltz) Green; m. Nancy Reade Hall, June 18, 1966. AB, Yale U., 1961; LLB, U. Va., 1967; DBA (hon.), Piedmont Coll., 1995. Bar: Ga. 1967. Assoc. firm Hansell & Post, Atlanta, 1967-70, mem. firm, 1970-87, mgmt. com., 1980-87; CEO Green Capital Investors L.P., Atlanta, 1987—; chmn., CEO WestPoint Stevens, Inc., 1992—2003. Bd. dirs. Vytech Industries, Inc., Access Integrated Networks, Inc., Cumulus Media, Inc.; bd. dirs., chmn. Rhodes, Inc., 1988—96; chmn. HBO & Co., 1990—98. Bd. dirs. Child Svc. and Family Counseling Ctr., 1972—85, pres., 1982—84; active Leadership Atlanta, 1974—75; trustee Atlanta Bot. Garden, 1976—92, pres., 1982—84; bd. dirs. High Mus. Art, 1982—96, Yale U. Art Gallery, 1992—, Atlanta Ballet, 1987—89, Atlanta Hist. Soc., 1993—96; trustee, vice chmn. investments Taft Sch., 1987—2000; trustee Woodruff Arts Ctr., 1990—98; chmn. Yale Devel. Bd., 1998—; fellow Yale Corp., 1999—; hon. Swedish consul State of Ga., 1988—96. Served to lt. (j.g.) USN, 1961—64. Mem.: Raven Soc. Va., Ocean Forest Golf Club, Doubles Club, Chatooga Club, Wade Hampton Club, Capital City Club, Piedmont Driving Club, Nine O'Clocks Club, Homosassa Fishing Club, Royal Order Polar Star, Order Coif. Democrat. Presbyterian. Home: 4295 Club Dr Atlanta GA 30319

GREEN, JACK PETER, pharmacologist, educator; b. N.Y.C., Oct. 4, 1925; s. Maurice and Tillie (Herman) G.; m. Arlyne Genevieve Frank, Oct. 25, 1958. BS, Pa. State U., 1947, MS, 1949; PhD, Yale, 1951, MD, 1957; postgrad., Poly. Inst., Copenhagen, 1953-55, Inst. de Biologie Physico-Chimique, Paris, 1964-65. Vis. scientist Poly. Inst., Copenhagen, 1953-55, Inst. de Biologie Physico-Chimique, Paris, 1964-65; asst. prof. Yale, 1957-61, asso. prof., 1961-66, Cornell U. Med. Coll., 1966-68; prof., chmn. dept. pharmacology Mt. Sinai Sch. Medicine, 1968—98. Mem. research grant rev. com. USPHS; mem. N.Y.C. Health Research Council, Dysautonomia Found., Irma T. Hirsch Trust. Contbr. articles profl. jours.; Mem. editorial bds. profl. jours. Recipient Claude Bernard Vis. Professorship U. Montreal, 1966 Mem. N.Y. Acad. Sci., Am. Chem. Soc., Am. Soc. Biol. Chemists, Soc. Drug Research, N.Y. Acad. Medicine, Harvey Soc., A.A.A.S., Am. Soc. Pharmacology and Exptl. Therapeutics, Internat. Soc. Quantum Biology, Am. Coll. Neuropsychopharmacology, Am. Soc. Neurochemistry, Soc. for Neurosci., Sigma Xi, Alpha Omega Alpha, Phi Lambda Upsilon, Gamma Sigma Delta. Home: 1212 5th Ave New York NY 10029-5218 Office: Mt Sinai Sch Medicine Dept Pharmacology Fifth Ave at 100th St New York NY 10029

GREEN, JAMES SAMUEL, lawyer; b. Berwick, Pa., May 24, 1947; m. Carla Eyer; children: Jennifer, Emily, James Samuel Jr., Jared. AB, Princeton U., 1969; JD, Villanova U., 1972. Bar: Del. 1972, Pa. 1973, U.S. Dist. Ct. Del. 1973, U.S. Ct. Appeals (3d cir.) 1981, U.S. Supreme Ct. 1990. Assoc. Connolly, Bove, Lodge & Hutz, Wilmington, Del., 1972-74, ptnr., 1977-90; dep. atty. gen. State of Del., Wilmington, 1975-76; ptnr. Duane Morris & Heckscher, Wilmington, 1990-99, Seitz, Van Ogtrop & Green, P.A., Wilmington, 1999—. Bd. dirs. David Wellborn Found.; del. Bd. Unauthorized Practice of Law, chmn., 1994—99. Fellow Am. Coll. of Trial Lawyers; mem. ABA, Am. Bd. Trial Advocates (nat. bd. dirs. 1991-2000), Del. Bar Assn. (treas. 1980-81, chmn. litigation sect. 1988-91), Ivy Club (Princeton), Wilmington Country Club, Princeton Club NY. Home: 2603 W 17th St Wilmington DE 19806-1108 Office: Seitz Van Ogtrop & Green PA PO Box 68 Wilmington DE 19899-0068 Office Phone: 302-888-7603. E-mail: jgreen@svglaw.com.

GREEN, JAMES WYCHE, sociologist, anthropologist, consultant, psychotherapist; b. Alton, Va., Aug. 5, 1915; s. William Ivey and Mary (Crowder) G.; m. Pearl O'Neal Cornett, Mar. 2, 1940 (dec. 1982); 1 child, Margaret Lydia.; m. Arlene Borkenhagen, Mar. 26, 1983. BS with honors, Va. Poly. Inst., 1938, MS, 1939; postgrad., Duke U., 1947—48; PhD, U. N.C., 1953; postgrad., Sch. Advanced Internat. Studies, Johns Hopkins U., 1959. Rsch. fellow Va. Poly. Inst., 1938—39; rsch. field supr. Va. Expt. Sta., 1939; asst. specialist program planning N.C. State Coll. Extension Svc., 1939—42; v.p. Greever's, Inc., 1946; tchr. h.s., farm operator, 1946—47; asst. prof. rural sociology N.C. State Coll., 1949—54; from assoc. chief to chief cmty. devel. adv. Govt. of Pakistan, Karachi, 1954—59; prof. rural sociology dept. Cornell U., Ithaca, NY, 1960; cmty. devel. adviser Govt. of So. Rhodesia, AID, 1960—64; chief cmty. devel., local govt. adviser Govt. of Peru, 1964—67; chief urban cmty. devel. adviser Govt. of Panama, 1967—69; prof., chmn. dept. sociology and anthropology U. N.C., Charlotte, 1969—70; chief methodology divsn. Bur. Tech. Assistance, AID, Washington, 1970—74; sociologist/anthropologist cons. AID, Washington, 1974—75, contractor Yemen, 1975; pvt. practice cons., 1975—. Author: Integrative Meditation: Towards Unity of Mind/Body/Spirit, 1994, And It Was Never Dull: A Memoir, 2003, Publications and Writings of James Wyche Green, 30 vols., 2003 (Libr. of Congress permanent collection, 2004); author monographs; contbr. chpts. to books and articles to profl. jours. Served from 1st lt. to capt. AUS, 1942-46; lt. col. Res. ret. 1975. Decorated Croix de Guerre with Silver Star France; Croix de Guerre with Palm Belgium; Bronze Star with cluster; named Outstanding Alumnus Hargrave Mil. Acad., 1979 Fellow Am. Anthrop. Assn., AAAS, Soc. Applied Anthropology; mem. Res. Officers Assn., Public Citizen, ACLU, Common Cause, Amnesty Internat., Omicron Delta Kappa, Alpha Zeta, Phi Kappa Phi. Democrat. Lutheran. Home and Office: 6430 Lily Dhu Ln Falls Church VA 22044-1409 *I have found few joys in life which are as deep and lasting as "cracking a culture," i.e. understanding how it really works, and then using that understanding for its people's good as they see the good.*

GREEN, JERRY HOWARD, investment banker; b. Kansas City, Mo., June 10, 1930; s. Howard Jay and Selma (Stein) G.; m. Betsy Bozarth, July 18, 1981. BA, Yale U., 1952. Pres. Union Chevrolet, 1955-69, Union Securities, Inc., Kansas City, 1969—, Union Bancshares, Inc., Kansas City, 1969-76; chmn. Union Bank, Kansas City, 1976—, Budget Rent-A-Car Mo., Inc., 1961—, Budget Rent-A-Car Memphis, Inc., Budget Rent-A-Car, Wichita, Kans.; pres. Pembroke Bancshares, Kansas City, 1983—. Chmn. Union Broadcasting, Inc., Union Sports Broadcasting, (KCTE-AM) and (WHB-AM), Inc.; bd. dirs. Century City Artists Corp., L.A. Bd. dirs. Jackson County Pension Plan Com.; bd. dirs., chmn. bd. Mo. Higher Edn. Loan Authority, 1987—; chmn. bd. Mo. Valley Bancshares, Mountain Grove, Mo.; chmn. Yale Class of 1952 Reunion Gift. 1st lt. USAF, 1952-55. Mem. Am. Bankers Assn., Yale Alumni Assn. (bd. dirs.), Kansas City Club, Oakwood Country Club, Saddle and Sirloin Club, University Club. Republican. Office: Union Bank 9300 Blue Ridge Blvd Kansas City MO 64138-3844

GREEN, JOANNE MARIE, special education coordinator; b. Stoneham, Mass., June 20, 1951; d. Frederick and Beatrice Marie Munroe; m. Mark Emerson Russell, June 28, 1975 (dec. Jan. 26, 1991); children: Mark Emerson Russell, Jennifer Marie Russell, Matthew Munroe Russell; m. Laurence Dutton Green, May 28, 1993. BS, U. Mass., 1973; EdM, Lesley Coll., 1991; PBIS Cert., Rivier Coll., 2004. Cert. elem. edn. tchr. N.H., gen. spl. edn. tchr. N.H., learning disabilities tchr. N.H. Tchr. grade 2 Franklin Elem. Sch., Wakefield, Mass., 1974—77; spl. edn. tchr. Timberlane Regional Mid. Sch., Plaistow, NH, 1987—2001; spl. edn. coord. James Mastricola Elem. Sch., Merrimack, NH, 2001—; diagnostic summer sch. dir. Merrimack Sch. Dist., 2003—. Positive Behavioral Interventions and Supports project mgr. Mastricola Elem. Sch., 2002—, Write Traits group co-facilitator, 2004—; spl. edn. onsite evaluation team mem. Southeastern Regional Edn. Svc. Ctr., Bedford, NH, 2003—04; mentor Merrimack Sch. Dist., NH, 2003—; mem. NH Spl. Edn. Administrators Acad., 2004—. Sch. rep. Merrimack Edn. Week Com., 2004—05. Mem.: N.H. Coun. for Exceptional Children (exec. bd. sec. 2005), Coun. for Children with Behavior Disorders, Coun. for Exceptional Children. Avocations: travel, walking, reading, sewing, crafts. Home: 62 Mammoth Rd Windham NH 03087 Office: James Mastricola Elem Sch 7 School St Merrimack NH 03054 Office Phone: 603-424-6218. Business E-Mail: joanne.green@merrimack.k12.nh.us.

GREEN, JODY, real estate company executive, real estate broker; b. Iowa City, Nov. 13, 1942; d. George A. and Clare Walton (Wiggs) Olson; m. Samuel C. Wolgemuth, 1964 (div. 1976); children: Amy Clare Wolgemuth-Bordoni, George Robert Wolgemuth; m. John I. Green, 1977. Student, Greenville Coll., 1961—63, Taylor U., Upland, Ind., 1963—64. Lic. real estate broker Ill., Mich. Real estate sales Dixon Gallery Homes, Glen Ellyn, Ill., 1974—75, real estate mgr., 1975—77; real estate sales Coldwell Banker, Wheaton, Ill., 1977—82; real estate recruiter Westdale Better Homes & Gardens, Grand Rapids, Mich., 1985—96, real estate sales trainer, 1992—96; real estate recruiter, trainer Coldwell Banker Schweitzer, Sterling Heights, Mich., 1996—99; real estate sales Keller Williams Realty, Northville, Mich., 1999—. Spkr. in field. Vol. Wheaton (Ill.) Ctrl. Hosp., 1974—79, Butterworth Hosp., Grand Rapids, 1985—95. Scholar, Wheaton Coll., 2002. Mem.: Hosp. Guild (sec. 1982—84), Homeowners Assn. (v.p. 1992—2000, 2004—). Independent. Avocations: reading, boating, travel. Office: Kellwer Williams Realty 22260 Haggerty Ste 250 Northville MI 48167

GREEN, JOHN F., headmaster; BA, Wesleyan U.; MEd, Harvard U. Various positions including prof. history, admissions dir., interim head of history dept. and dean of faculty St. Paul's Sch., 1986—2001; head of sch. Peddie Sch., Hightstown, NJ, 2001—. Office: Peddie Sch PO Box A S Main St Hightstown NJ 08520-1010*

GREEN, JOHN I., engineering executive; b. Akron, Ohio; s. Walter Lewis and Carmen Ruth Green; m. Jody O. Green, 1977; 3 children. BSChemE, Purdue U.; MBA, U. Chgo. Asst. treas. UOP subs. Signal Oil, Des Plaine, Ill.; exec. v.p. Sackner Products, Grand Rapids, Mich.; pres. Crown Assocs., Inc., Novi, Mich., 1986—. Cons. Mich. Modernization Svc., Grand Rapids, 1987; writer in field. Apptd. Auto Mich. Project, Grand Rapids, 1986. Mem.: AIChE, Soc. Automotive Engrs., Project Mgmt. Inst. (pres. 2003). Avocations: golf, boating, gardening. Office: Crown Assocs Inc Novi MI 48375 Office Phone: 248-761-9544. Business E-Mail: jgreen@crownassociates.com.

GREEN, JOHN LAFAYETTE, JR., educational association administrator; b. Trenton, N.J., Apr. 3, 1929; m. Harriet Hardin Hill, Nov. 8, 1962; 1 child, John Lafayette III BA, Miss. State U., 1955; MEd, Wayne State U., 1971; PhD, Rensselaer Poly. Inst., 1974. Asst. to treas. Internat. Paper Co., 1955-57; mem. faculty U. Calif., Berkeley, 1957-65; v.p. U. Ga., Athens, 1965-71, Rensselaer Poly. Inst., Troy, N.Y., 1971-76; exec. v.p. U. Miami, 1976-80; sr. v.p. U. Houston, 1980-81; pres. Washburn U., Topeka, Kans., 1981-88; exec. dir. Assn. Collegiate Bus. Schs. and Programs, Overland Park, 1988-95. Pres., chmn. bd. dirs. Strategic Planning/Mgmt. Assocs., Inc., Overland Park, Kans., 1981—; CEO Internat. Assembly for Collegiate Bus. Edn., Overland Park, 1997—; past. pres. Kansas City and Topeka chpts. Planning Forum; chmn. bd., CEO ARP-US, 2005—. Author: Budgeting, 1967, (with others) Cost Accounting, 1969, Administrative Data Processing, 1970, Strategic Planning, 1980, Strategic Planning: A System for Businesses, 1986, A Strategic Planning System for Higher Education, 1987, Strategy Development and Implementation for Banks, 1988, co-author: Outcomes Assessment in Higher Education Linked to Strategic Planning and Budgeting, 1997, Outcomes Assessment in Higher Education, 2002. Bd. dirs. Boy Scouts Am., Topeka, 1983-85. With U.S. Army 1951-53 Recipient Disting. Kansan of Yr. in Pub. Adminstrn. award Topeka Capital Jour., 1984, Kans. Pub. Adminstr. of Yr. award Am. Soc. Pub. Adminstrn., 1984, Disting. Exec. award Mktg. Exec. Kans., 1984, Edn. Leader's Hall of Fame award, 1995. Mem. AAUP, Conf. Bd., Am. Mgmt. Assn., Fin. Execs. Inst., Demographics Inst., Masons, Shriners, Royal Order of Jesters, Phi Delta Kappa, Beta Alpha Psi, Phi Kappa Phi, Pi Kappa Alpha, Delta Sigma Pi. Republican. Presbyterian. (elder, deacon). Avocations: golf, tennis. Home: 12568 Farley Overland Park KS 66213-2526 Office: PO Box 25217 Shawnee Mission KS 66225-5217

GREEN, JOHNNIE D., government agency administrator, finance educator; b. Malvern, Ark., Feb. 5, 1961; s. Edward and Edessia Green. AAS, Vincennes U., 1998; BBA, Ark. Bapt. Coll., 1999; MBA, Webster U., 1999, MA in Internat. Bus. and Fin., 2000. Admin., fin. and personnel specialist U.S. Army, 1981—84; asst. br. mgr. Twin City Bank, North Little Rock, Ark., 1984—94; asst. v.p., loan officer Bank of Malvern, Ark., 1994—95; comml. loan officer U.S. SBA, Little Rock, 1995—. Adj. prof. Vincennes U., North Little Rock, Ark., 2000—; CEO, chmn. Ark. Cmty. Recreational Svcs.; adj. prof. Webster U., Memphis, 2000—, Embry Riddle Aeronautical Univ. Little Rock AFB, Jacksonville, Ark., 2001—, Ctrl. Bapt. Coll., Conway, Ark., 2001—, Philander Smith Coll., Little Rock, 2002—, Nova Southeastern U., Ft. Lauderdale, Fla., 2003—. Past pres. Malvern Stella Smith Boys and Girls Club; bd. dirs. Teen Promise, Inc.; CEO, chmn. Ark. Cmty. Recreation Svcs. E-5 N.G. U.S. Army, 1987—2002. Decorated Meritorious Svc. Medal; recipient Cert. of Appreciation, Ark. N.G., 2002, Cert. of Svc. award, Ark. Guard Bur., 2002, Commendation medal, State of Ark., 2002. Mem.: ACLU, NAACP, Assn. for Fin. Profls., Fin. Mgmt. Assn. Internat., Nat. Assn. Urban Bankers, Acad. of Mgmt., Non-Commn. Officers Assn., Little Rock Club. Home: 507 Maurice Dr Malvern AR 72104 Office: US SBA 2120 Riverfront Dr Ste 100 Little Rock AR 72202 Office Phone: 501-324-5871 233. Business E-Mail: johnnie.green@sba.gov.

GREEN, JOSEPH LIBORY, lawyer; b. St. Louis, Mar. 20, 1960; s. Joseph Richard and Kathleen Ann Green; m. Sherry Michelle Fedder, Oct. 7, 1989; children: Bryan Smith, Samantha Joe Green, Jacob Fedder Green, Jacqueline Michelle Green. BSBA, Truman State U., 1982; JD, St. Louis U., 1987. Bar: Mo. 1988, U.S. Dist. Ct. (ea. dist.) Mo. 1993, U.S. Dist. Ct. (we. dist.) Mo. 1996, U.S. Ct. Appeals (8th cir.) 1998, U.S. Supreme Ct. 1998. Asst. pub. def. St. Joseph (Mo.) Pub. Def.'s Office, 1988; chief trial atty. St. Louis County Pub. Def.'s Office, Clayton, Mo., 1989-90; capital litigation atty. Mo. State Pub. Def.'s Office, St. Louis, 1990-93; assoc. Wittner, Poger, Rosenblum & Spewak, P.C., Clayton, 1993-96; sole practitioner St. Charles, Mo., 1996; ptnr. Baerveldt, Bagsby, Lee & Green, L.L.C., St. Charles, 1996—. Dem. candidate for county prosecutor, St. Charles, 1994, 98. Mem. Nat. Assn. Criminal Def. Lawyers, Mo. Assn. Criminal Def. Lawyers. Office: Baerveldt Bagsby Lee & Green LLP 566 1st Capitol Dr Saint Charles MO 63301-2726

GREEN, JOSHUA, III, retired bank executive; b. Seattle, June 30, 1936; s. Joshua, Jr. and Elaine (Brygger) G.; m. Pamela K. Pemberton, Nov. 1, 1974; children: Joshua IV, Jennifer Elaine, Paige Courtney. BA in English, Harvard U., 1958. With Peoples Nat. Bank Wash., Seattle, 1960-88, exec. v.p., 1972-75, pres., 1975—, chief exec. officer, 1977-78, chmn. bd., 1979-88, U.S. Bank Washington (merger PeoplesBank and Old Nat. Bank), 1988-96; chmn., CEO Joshua Green Corp., Seattle, 1996—. Bd. dirs., chmn., CEO, Joshua Green Corp., Safeco, Port Blakely Tree Farms, Va. Mason Hosp. Found., Virginia Mason Hosp. Rsch; dir. Va. Mason Health Sys. Pres. Joshua Green Found.; trustee Downtown Seattle Assn., Arts Fund. Mem. Pacific Sci. Ctr., Univ. Club, Rainier Club, Seattle Tennis Club, Wash. Athletic Club. Home: 414 McGilvra Blvd E Seattle WA 98112-2308 Office: Joshua Green Corp 1425 4th Ave Ste 420 Seattle WA 98101-2218

GREEN, JOYCE, book publishing company executive; b. Taylorville, Ill., Oct. 22, 1928; d. Lynn and Vivian Coke (Richardson) Reinerd; m. Warren H. Green, Oct. 8, 1960. AA, Christian Coll., 1946; BS, MacMurray Coll., 1948. Pres. Warren H. Green, Inc., St. Louis, 1992—, Affirmative Action Register, 1977—, InterContinental Industries, Inc., 1980—; chief exec. officer Pubs. Svc. Ctr.; pres. Epoch Press, 2004—. Mem. St. Louis C. of C., Jr. League Club, Media Club, Mo. Athletic Club. Home (Winter): 10000 Ocean Blvd Apt 905 Jensen Beach FL 34957 Office: 8356 Olive Blvd Saint Louis MO 63132-2814 Home (Summer): 12120 Hibler Dr Saint Louis MO 63141 E-mail: JRG1036@aol.com.

GREEN, JOYCE HENS, federal judge; b. N.Y.C., Nov. 13, 1928; d. James S. and Hedy (Bucher) Hens; m. Samuel Green, Sept. 25, 1965 (dec.); children: Michael Timothy, June Heather, James Harry. BA, U. Md., 1949; JD, George Washington U., 1951, LLD, 1994. Practice law, Washington, 1951-68, Arlington, Va., 1956-68; ptnr. Green & Green, 1966-68; assoc. judge Superior Ct., D.C., 1968-79; judge U.S. Dist. Ct. for D.C., 1979—; judge presiding U.S. Fgn. Intelligence Surveillance Ct., 1988-95. Bd. advisors George Washington U. Law Sch., 1991-2001; jud. br. com. Jud. Conf. U.S., 1995-2001. Co-author: Dissolution of Marriage, 1986, supplements, 1987-89, Marriage and Family Law Agreements, 1985, supplements, 1986-89. Chair Task Force on Gender, Race and Ethnic Bias for the D.C. Cir. Recipient Alumni Achievement award George Washington U., 1975, Profl. Achievement award, 1978, Outstanding Contbn. to Equal Rights award Women's Legal Def. Fund, 1976, hon. doctor of Laws George Washington U., 1994, U.S. Dept. Justice Edmund J. Randolph award, 1995, Professionalism award D.C. Cir., Am. Inns Ct., 2004. Fellow Am. Bar Found.; ABA (jud. adminstrn. divsn., chair nat. conf. fed. trial judges 1997-98), Fed. Judges Assn., Nat. Assn. Women Judges, Va. Bar, Bar Assn. D.C. (jud. honoree of Yr. 1994), D.C. Bar, D.C. Women's Bar Assn. (pres. 1960-62, woman lawyer of yr. 1979), Exec. Women in Govt. (chmn. 1977), Woman's Forum of Washington D.C. Office: US Dist Ct E Barrett Prettyman US Courthouse 333 Constitution Ave NW Washington DC 20001-2802

GREEN, KAREN F., lawyer; b. 1956; AB magna cum laude, Radcliffe Coll., 1978; JD cum laude, Harvard Univ., 1981. Bar: Mass. 1981. Law clk. Judge W. Arthur Garrity, US Dist. Ct. (Mass. dist.), 1981—82; assoc. Hale & Dorr, Boston, 1982—84; asst. U.S. atty. civil div., U.S. Dept. of Justice, Boston, 1984—86; assoc. Hale & Dorr, Boston, 1987—88, jr. ptnr., 1988—90, sr. ptnr., 1990—93; chief of staff Mass. Gov. William F. Weld, 1993; dep. U.S. atty. U.S. Dept. of Justice, Boston, 1994—96; sr. ptnr. Hale & Dorr, Boston, 1996—2004; ptnr., co-chmn. Litigation dept., mem. exec. com. Wilmer Cutler Pickering Hale & Dorr, Boston, 2004—. Co-chmn., transition team for exec. office of health & human svc. Mass. Gov.-elect William F. Weld, 1990—91; bd. dir. Fiduciary Trust Co.; mem. spl. commn. on Suffolk County Sheriff's Dept. for Mass. acting Gov. Jane Swift; vice chmn. com. on pro bono legal svc. Mass. Supreme Judicial Ct.; mem. gender bias com. US Ct. Appeals (1st cir.); mem. com. to revise local criminal rules & com. on alternative dispute resolution US Dist Ct. (Mass. dist.); instr. Harvard Law Sch. Trial Advocacy Workshop, U.S. Atty. Gen. Advocacy Inst. Mem. exec. com. Mass. Judicial Nominating Council; dir. Children's Trust Fund. Named one of Boston's Top Women Lawyers, Boston Globe, 1996, Top 100 Mass. Super Lawyers & Top 50 Female Mass. Super Lawyers, Boston Mag., 2004; recipient award for Outstanding Svc. to City of Boston, Park St. Forum, 1997, Leading Women award, Patriot's Trail Girl Scout Council, 2000, Women's Bus. Hall of Fame award, 2001, honoree for pro bono legal work, Granada House, 2002. Mem.: Boston Bar Found. (trustee), Boston Bar Assn. (council mem. & chmn. Fed. Practice & Procedure com.), Boston Club (dir.), Phi Beta Kappa. Office: Wilmer Cutler Pickering Hale & Dorr 60 State St Boston MA 02109 Office Phone: 617-526-6207. Office Fax: 617-526-5000. Business E-Mail: karen.green@wilmerhale.com.

GREEN, KEVIN PATRICK, career officer; b. Aug. 28, 1949; m. Kate Donohue; 3 children. Grad., U.S. Naval Acad., 1971; MS, Naval Postgrad. Sch., 1977; Grad., Nat. War Coll., 1992. Ensign USN, 1971, advanced through grades to rear adm., 1996; assigned to frigate USS Voge (DE 1047), 1971-74; weapons officer USS Richard L. Page (FFG 5), 1978-80; ops. officer USS Preble (DDG 46), 1980-82; exec. officer USS Dahlgren (DDG 43), 1984-85; comdr. USS Taylor (FFG 50), 1989-91; comdr. destroyer squadron twenty-three, 1994-95; duty in spl. ops. br. Atlantic fleet hqrs., 1982-84; instr. combat sys., tactics prospective comdg. officer course, 1985-88; mil. asst. office of Sec. of Def., 1992-94; dir. surface officer disbn. divsn. bur. naval personnel, 1995-97; comdr. Naval Tng. Ctr., Great Lakes, Ill., 1996-98, Cruiser-Destroyer Group Three, 1998-99, U.S. Naval Forces So. Command, 1999—2002; Deputy Chief Naval Operations for Plans, Policy, Operations, 2002—. Decorated Legion of Merit.

GREEN, KIM RENE, trade association administrator, researcher; m. James Paul Pastorick, Oct. 26, 1985. BSc in chemistry, So. Oreg. U., 1976—80; MSc in geochemistry, Colo. Sch. of Mines, 1980—84. Cert. Ground Water Profl., Nat. Ground Water Assn./Ohio, 1993. Rsch. scientist U.S. Geol. Survey, Denver, 1982—86; sr. assoc. ICF, Inc., Fairfax, Va., 1986—93; mgr. ENVIRON, Arlington, 1990—93; br. mgr. Ogden Environ. Svcs., Fairfax, 1993—96; sr. assoc. The Weinberg Group, Washington, 1996—2003; v.p. rsch. sci. & tech. affairs Internat. Bottled Water Assn., Alexandria, Va., 2003—; rsch. dir. Drinking Water Rsch. Found., Alexandria, Va., 2003—. Dir. Internat. Chinese Snuff Bottle Soc., Balt., 2000—. Mem.: Assn. of Ground Water Scientists and Engineers (dir. 1995—2000). Avocations: bicycling, animal rescue, art collecting. Office: Internat Bottled Water Assn 1700 Diagonal Rd Ste 650 Alexandria VA 22314 Office Phone: 703-863-5213 114. E-mail: kgreen@bottledwater.org.

GREEN, LAUREN, news anchor and correspondent, concert pianist; Degree in piano performance, U. Minn.; grad., Northwestern U. Medill Sch. Journalism. Gen. assignment reporter KSTP-TV (ABC), St. Paul, 1988—93; weekend news anchor & correspondent WBBM-TV (CBS), Chgo., 1993—96; news update anchor "FOX & Friends," FOX News Channel, 1996—. Pianist: debut CD, Classic Beauty, 2004, interviewed some of most prominent people in classical music: Placide Domingo, Pierre Boulez & Joshua Bell, covered events such as: Van Cliburn Internat. Piano Competition, opening night of The Metropolitan Opera. Mailing: c/o Fox News Channel 1211 Avenue Of The Americas New York NY 10036 E-mail: lauren.green@foxnews.com.

GREEN, LINDA C., education specialist administrator, researcher; b. Memphis, Nov. 21, 1947; d. Frank Allen and Mary Elizabeth (Hankins) Green; m. John Newton Osborne, Feb. 7, 1975 (div. June 1979); 1 child, Suzanne; m. Phillip Harold James, Oct. 17, 1980 (div. Aug. 2003); 1 child, Sarah Elizabeth. BA, U. Tenn., 1970; MA, Calif. State U., Long Beach, 1975; EdD in Higher Edn., U. Memphis, 1995. Instr. Memphis State U., 1979—85, dir. Wordsmith, 1984—85; asst. prof. Jackson State C.C., Tenn., 1985—90; adminstrv. intern State Tech. Inst. Memphis, 1990—91; asst. dir. Mid South Quality Productivity Ctr., Memphis, 1991—92; dir. acad. devel. State Tech. Inst. Memphis, 1992—93; edn. specialist Nat. Inst. Stds. and Tech., Gaithersburg, Md., 1993—94; specialist sys. mgmt. U. Tenn., Martin, 1994—95; dir. assessment State Tech. Inst. Memphis, 1995—2000; v.p. acad. affairs Nat. Grad. Sch., 2000—01. Bd. dirs., v.p. Greater Memphis Area Award for Quality; mem. adv. com. Nat. Govs. Conf. Edn., 1994; cons. City of Memphis Dept. Planning, 1993; mem. editl. bd. CQI Newsletter, 1994—; mem. adv. coun. Total Quality Learning Sys. Am. Soc. Quality, 1995—; trainer Koalaty Kids, 1996; bd. dirs. ASQ; Koalaty Kid Alliance, 1997—; mem. adj. faculty Nat. Grad. Sch., 1997—; bd. examiners Malcolm Baldrige Nat. Quality award, 1995-98, 99. Facilitator Leadership Memphis Diversity Program, 1993; vol. Girl Scouts, N.W. Tenn., 1986-89. Recipient grant Bell-South, 1991-93, fellow Tenn. Collaborative Acad., 1990-91. Mem. Am. Assn. Higher Edn., Am. Soc. Quality Control (assoc., Memphis sect. co-chair quality forum 1992-93), Tenn Assn. Devel. Educators, Phi Delta Kappa. Home: 30 Benjamin Nyes Ln North Falmouth MA 02556

GREEN, LISA CANNON, online editor; b. Marshall, Ky., May 7, 1962; d. Walter L. and Phyllis (Jones) Cannon; m. Bob Dale Green, May 31, 1980; children: Emily, Ethan. BA in Journalism and English, Murray State U., 1983. With The Post-Intelligencer, Paris, Tenn., 1983-84, The Jackson (Tenn.) Sun, 1984-90, The Tennessean, Nashville, 1990—. Office: The Tennessean 1100 Broadway Nashville TN 37203-3134 Office Phone: 615-259-8275. Business E-Mail: lgreen@tennessean.com.

GREEN, LOUIS HARRY, retired surgeon; b. Houston, Jan. 21, 1923; MD, U. Tex. Med. Br., 1947. Diplomate Am. Bd. Surgery. Intern D.C. Gen. Hosp., Washington, 1947—48; resident surgery Meml. Hosp., Houston, 1948—49, Houston VA Hosp., 1951—54, Baylor Affiliated Hosps., Houston; emeritus clin. assoc. prof. Baylor Coll. Medicine, Houston; emeritus staff Meth., St. Luke's Episcopal, Tex. Children's, Hermann Hosps. Commencement spkr. U. Houston, 2005. Named Disting. Alumnus U. Houston, 1989, Great Texan Chron's and Colitis Found. Am., 1975. Fellow: ACS; mem.: AMA, Houston Surg. Soc. (pres. 1991—92). Personal E-mail: louis@300kbps.com.

GREEN, MADELEINE F., educational association administrator; BA magna cum laude, Harvard U.; PhD Columbia U. V.p., dir. ctr. instl. and internat. initiatives Am. Coun. Edn. Interim pres. Mt. Vernon Coll., Washington, 1990—91; mem. bd. trustees Wilson Coll., Pa., 1988—93, Sweet Briar Coll., Va., 1994—2002; bd. dirs. Juniata Coll., Pa.; mem. adminstrv. bd. Internat. Assn. Univs. (IAU). Co-author: Internationalizing the Campus: A User's Guide, On Change series, The American College President: 2000 Edition; editor: Leaders for a New Era: Strategies for Higher Education, 1988, Minorities on Campus: A Handbook for Enhancing Diversity, 1989, Investing in Higher Education: A Handbook of Leadership Development, 1991, Transforming Higher Education: Views from Leaders Around the World, 1997. Office: Am Coun Edn One Dupont Cir NW Washington DC 20036 Office Phone: 202-939-9418.

GREEN, MARK ANDREW, congressman, lawyer; b. Boston, June 1, 1960; s. Jeremy Raleigh and Elizabeth Pamela (Roome) G.; m. Susan Keske, Aug. 5, 1985; children: Rachel Eve Libinu, Anna Faith Kitali, Alexander Mark Amutavi. BA, U. Wis., Eau Claire, 1983; JD, U. Wis., Madison, 1987. Bar: Wis. 1987. Tchr., intern World Teach Project, Kakamega, Kenya, 1987-88; of counsel Godfrey & Kahn, S.C., Green Bay, Wis., 1989-98; mem. Wis. Assembly, Madison, 1992-98, chmn. assembly majority caucus, chmn. assembly jud. com., 1994-98; state chmn. Am. Legis. Exch. Coun.; mem. U.S. Congress from 8th Wis. dist., 1999—; mem. fin. svcs. com., judiciary com. Legal counsel Rep. Assembly Campaign Com., Madison, 1993—. Chmn. mcpl. affairs Brown County Taxpayers Assn., Green Bay, 1990-92; chmn. Brown County Rep. Party, 1991-92; bd. dirs. Nat. R.R. Mus., Green Bay, 1992—; chmn. resolutions com. Wis. Rep. Conv., Milw., 1993. Recipient Wis. award Ind. Bus. Assn., 1996; named Wis. Outstanding Legislator of 1995, Wis. Builders Assn., Healthcare Leader of Wis., State Med. Soc., 1996; scholar U. Wis., Eau Claire, 1982. Mem. ABA, Wis. Bar Assn., Am. Legis. Exch. Coun., Nat. Conf. State Legislators, Brown County Home Builders Assn., Kiwanis. Republican. Office: Ho of Reps 1314 Longworth Ho Office Bldg Washington DC 20515-4908

GREEN, MARSHALL MUNRO, lawyer; b. Staten Island, N.Y., Feb. 23, 1938; s. Thomas Marshall and Mary (Tibbitts) G.; m. Lucy Featherstone Abbott, June 15, 1959; children: Eleanor Thurston, John Marshall, Lucy Gatewood. AB, Harvard U., 1959, LLB cum laude, 1965. Bar: N.Y. 1965, Conn. 1976, Fla. 1976, U.S. Dist. Ct. Conn. 1984. Assoc. Breed, Abbott & Morgan, N.Y.C., 1965-72; ptnr. Williamson & Green, N.Y.C., 1972-76, Bisset, Atkins & Green, N.Y.C., 1976-82, LeBoeuf, Lamb, Leiby & MacRae, N.Y.C., 1982-90; v.p. Carter-Wallace, Inc., N.Y.C., 1990—. Adj. prof. N.Y. Law Sch., N.Y.C., 1993—. Trustee Childrens Aid Soc., N.Y.C., 1972—, Fedn. Protestant Welfare Agys., N.Y.C., 1980—, United Charities Inc., N.Y.C., 1983—; mem. bd. mgrs. Episcopal Social Svcs., N.Y.C., 1995—; mem. Nat. Choral Council, 1976—. Fellow Am. Coll. Trusts and Estates Counsel; mem. The Century Assn. (N.Y.C.), Univ. Club (N.Y.C.), Harvard Club (N.Y.C.), City Island Yacht Club. Democrat. Episcopalian. E-mail: greenm@earthlink.net.

GREEN, MARTIN LINCOLN, investor, retired health institute executive; b. Des Plaines, Ill., Feb. 22, 1940; s. Martin Lincoln and Madelyne Mae (Larson) G.; m. Carolyn Elizabeth Johnson, Jan. 19, 1968; children: Peter Cranston, Edward Reavy. BA in Econs., Lawrence U., 1963; MBA, U. Chgo., 1977. News asst. N.Y. Times, N.Y.C., 1963—64; reporter Sheffield Telegraph, England, 1964—66, Balt. Sun, 1966—67; sales rep. 3M Co., Chgo., 1967—70; stockbroker Bache & Co., Chgo., 1970—71; sales mgr. Xerox Corp., Chgo., 1971—77, mgr. strategic planning Rochester, NY, 1977—81; dir. sales, mktg. Bausch & Lomb, Inc., Rochester, 1981—84, v.p. sales, mktg., 1984—87; v.p. strategic planning Cambridge Instruments, Buffalo, 1987—88, pres. ophthalmic inst. divsn., 1988—90, Leica, Inc., Buffalo, 1988—97; pres. The Thornell Inst., Pittsford, NY, 1998—2002; ret., 2002. Republican. Avocations: investing, walking, reading, weightlifting, writing. Home: 16 Forest Knoll Pittsford NY 14534-3602

GREEN, MAURICE, molecular biologist, educator, virologist; b. N.Y.C., May 5, 1926; s. David and Bessie (Lipschitz) G.; m. Marilyn Glick, Aug. 20, 1950; children: Michael Richard, Wendy Allison Green Lee, Eric Douglas. BS in Chemistry, U. Mich., 1949; MS in Biochemistry and Chemistry, U. Wis.-Madison, 1952, PhD in Biochemistry and Chemistry, 1954. Instr. biochemistry U. Pa. Med. Sch., Phila., 1955-56; asst. prof. St. Louis U. Health Scis. Ctr., 1956-60, assoc. prof., 1960-63, prof. microbiology, 1963-77; prof., chmn. Inst. for Molecular Virology, 1964—. Office: St Louis U Health Sci Ctr Inst for Molecular Virology 3681 Park Ave Saint Louis MO 63110-2511 Business E-Mail: green@slu.edu.

GREEN, MAURICE RICHARD, neuropsychiatrist; b. Chgo., Oct. 28, 1922; divorced; children: Melissa, Suzanne, Constance. BS, Northwestern U., 1942; BM, Northwestern U. Med. Sch., 1945, MD, 1946; cert. in Psychoanalytic Tng., William Alanson White Inst., N.Y.C., 1954. Diplomate Am. Bd. Psychiatry and Neurology. Intern Passavant Hosp., Chgo., 1945-46; resident in psychiatry Bronx (N.Y.) VA Hosp., 1948-51; cons. psychiatrist Brookwood Hall, East Islip, L.I., N.Y., 1955-58; staff psychiatrist Psychiatric Clinic Ct. Spl. Sessions, 1956-60; cons. psychiatrist Bleuler Psychotherapy Ctr., Queens, N.Y., 1956-68; rsch. psychiatrist, mem. psychiat. epidemiology sect. William Alanson White Inst., N.Y.C., 1968-72; attending geriat. psychiatrist Albert Einstein Med. Sch., 1974-76; attending child and adolescent psychiatry Harlem Hosp. of Columbia Presbyn. Med. Ctr., N.Y.C., 1974-75; med. dir. geriat. and family psychiatry Lincoln Hosp., 1974-76; chief psychiatrist Family Ct. Svcs. divsn. South Beach Psychiat. Ctr., S.I., N.Y., 1976-80; sr. attending pyschiatrist Columbia-Presbyn. at St. Luke's-Roosevelt Hosp., N.Y.C., 1978—; cons. psychiatrist Liaison-Consultation Svc. NYU Med. Ctr., N.Y.C., 1985-86; psychiatrist spl. evaluation and treatment unit Rockland Psychiat. Ctr., 1985-87. Mem. faculty William Alanson White Inst., N.Y.C., 1957—; cons. Goddard Coll., 1961-68; assoc. attending psychiatrist Bellevue Hosp., 1962-85, presently attending physician; supervisory and tng. analyst William Alanson White Inst., 1962—2003; clin. prof. psychiatry NYU Med. Sch., 1964—2003; mem. med. bd. Roosevelt Hosp., 1965-76; prin. investigator Diamox-Thiamine Research Unit Nathan S. Kline Research Inst., 1987; project dir. Brain Chemistry of Schizophrenia at Nathan Kline Inst., 1988-93; med. dir. Neurologic Sys., Inc., 1987; presidium Inst. for Brain Function Rsch., Inc., 1987; mem. Treatment Innovations Task Force-Soc. for Traumatic Stress Studies, 1987. Author: Interpersonal Psychoanalysis: Selected Papers of Clara Thompson, 1971, Psicoanalisi interpersonale, 1972, L'Esperiencze Prelogica, 1972, Violence and the Family, 1980; (with Edward S. Tauber) Prelogical Experience, 1959; assoc. editor Contemporary Psychoanalysis jour., 1968-80; contbr. articles to profl. jours. Project dir. Nathan Kline Rsch. Inst., 1988—. Fellow: N.Y. Acad. Medicine, Am. Acad. Child and Adolescent Psychiatry (com. on hospitalization of children, nat. legis. network 1982—86), Am. Psychiat. Assn. (com. on aging N.Y. Dist. br.), Am. Orthopsychiat. Assn. (publs. com. Anniversary Vol. 1968—71); mem.: Am. Assn. Geriat. Psychiatry, Internat. Soc. Psychoneuroendocrinology, Am. Assn. Psychosocial Rehab., Soc. Biol. Psychiatry, Nat. Assn. Patients Rights and Advocacy, Physicians for Social Responsibility, William Alanson White Psychoanalytic Soc., N.Y. Soc. Clin. Psychiatry, N.Y. Coun. Child Psychiatry. Home and Office: 275 Central Park W Apt 15 D New York NY 10024-3058 Office Phone: 212-595-9774. *We are all much more simply human than otherwise; what enhances our individual humanity will also enhance the common humanity of those around us.*

GREEN, MONICA H., history professor; BA, Barnard Coll., 1978; MA, Princeton U., 1981; PhD in History of Sci., Princeton (N.J.) U. Fellow U. N.C., Chapel Hill; assoc. prof. history Duke U.; prof. history Ariz. State U., Tempe, 2001—. Author: (essays) Women's Helathcare and the Medieval West: Texts and Contexts, 2000; contbr. articles; editor, translator: The Trotula: A Medieval Compendium of Women's Medicine, 2001. Fellow, NEH, Inst. Advanced Study, Princeton U., Nat. Humanities Ctr., John Simon Guggenheim Meml. Found., 2003. Office: Ariz State U Dept History PO Box 872501 Tempe AZ 85287-2501

GREEN, MORRIS, pediatrician, educator; b. Indpls., May 27, 1922; s. Coleman and Rebecca (Oleinick) Green; m. Janice Barber Gorton, Mar. 11, 1955; children: David Schuster, Alan Coleman, Carolyn Ann, Susan Elaine, Marcia Ruth, Sylvia Rebecca. AB, Ind. U., 1942, MD, 1944. Intern Ind. U. Med. Ctr., 1945; resident pediat. U. Ill. Rsch. and Ednl. Hosps., 1947—49; instr. pediat. U. Ill. Coll. Medicine, 1949—52; asst. prof. Yale Sch. Medicine, 1952—57; faculty Ind. U. Sch. Medicine, Indpls., 1957—, Perry W. Lesh prof. pediat., 1963—; chmn. dept. pediat., physician-in-chief James Whitcomb Riley Hosp. for Children, Indpls., 1967—88. Commr. health State of Ind., 1990—91. Author: Pediatric Diagnosis, 6th edit., 1998; co-editor: Ambulatory Pediatrics, 1968, 5th edit., 1999, Bright Futures, 2d edit., 2000; mem. editl. bd.: Pediat. Rev., Contemporary Pediat., Current Problems Pediat., Jour. Devel. Behavioral Pediat., Jour. Ambulatory Pediat. Assn., Social Work in Health Care, nat. adviser: Children Today. Served to capt. M.C. U.S. Army, 1945—47. Recipient George Armstrong award in ambulatory pediat., 1971, C. Anderson Aldrich award in child devel., 1982, Irving S. Cutter award, Phi Rho Sigma, 1984, Ross award for pediat. edn., 1985, Simon Wile award, Am. Acad. Child and Adolescent Psychiatry, 1990, Joseph W. St. Geme award, Fedn. Pediat. Orgns., 1992, Disting. Career award, Ambulatory Pediat. Assn., 1996, Lifetime award for disting. svc. in years of health advancement, Ind. Pub. Health Found., 2003. Mem.: AMA (Abraham Jacobi award 1990), Soc. Rsch. Child Devel., Inst. Medicine, Am. Orthopsychiat. Assn., Am. Acad. Pediat. (Abraham Jacobi award 1990), Am. Fedn. Clin. Rsch., Soc. Pediatric Rsch., Am. Pediatric Soc., Alpha Omega Alpha, Sigma Xi, Phi Beta Kappa. Home: 1840 Brewster Rd Indianapolis IN 46260-1561 Office: 702 Barnhill Dr Indianapolis IN 46202-5128

GREEN, NANCY JOYCE, librarian; b. LaFollette, Tenn. d. Everett H. and Evelyn L. (Kidwell) Huddleston; children: Elizabeth Maria, Autumn Rebecca. Libr. LaFollette (Tenn.) Pub. Libr. Mem. Tenn. Libr. Assn., Campbell County Hist. Soc. (1st v.p.), Goodwill PAC, LaFollette Book Club. Baptist. Office: LaFollette Pub Libr 201 S Tennessee Ave La Follette TN 37766-3606 Office Phone: 423-562-5154. E-mail: laflib@comcast.net.

GREEN, NANCY LOUGHRIDGE, publishing executive; b. Lexington, Ky., Jan. 19, 1942; d. William S. and Nancy O. (Green) Loughridge. BA in Journalism, U. Ky., 1964, postgrad., 1968; MA in Journalism, Ball State U., 1971; postgrad., U. Minn., 1968; EdD, Nova Southeastern U., 2003. Tchr. English, publs. adv. Clark County H.S., Winchester, Ky., 1965-66, Pleasure Ridge Park H.S., Louisville, 1966-67, Clarksville (Ind.) H.S., 1967-68, Charleston (W.Va.) H.S., 1968-69; asst. publs., pub. info. specialist W.Va. Dept. Edn., Charleston, 1969-70; tchr. journalism, publs. dir. Elmhurst H.S., Ft. Wayne, Ind., 1970-71; adviser student publs. U. Ky., Lexington, 1971-82; gen. mgr. student publs. U. Tex., Austin, 1982-85; pres., pub. Palladium-Item, Richmond, Ind., 1985-89, News-Leader, Springfield, Mo., 1989-92; asst. to pres. newspaper divsn. Gannett Co., Inc., Washington, 1992-94; exec. dir. advancement Clayton State Coll., Morrow, Ga., 1994-96; v.p. advancement Clayton Coll. & State U., Morrow, Ga., 1996-99; v.p. comm. Ga. GLOBE U. Sys., 1999-2000; dir. circulation/distbn., sales & mktg. Lee Enterprises, Davenport, Iowa, 2000—02; v.p. circulation LEE Enterprises, Davenport, 2002—; pub. Waterloo-Cedar Falls Courier, 2004—. Dir. urban journalism program Harte-Hanks, 1984, various Louisville and Lexington newspaper pubs., 1976-82; pres. Media Cons., Inc., Lexington, 1980; sec. Kernel Press, Inc., 1971-82. Contbr. articles to profl. jours. Bd. dirs. Studen Press Law Ctr., 1975-2005, Richmond Cmty. Devel. Corp., 1987-89, United Way of the Ozarks, 1990-92, ARC, 1990-92, Springfield Arts Coun., 1990-91, Bus. Devel. Corp., 1991-92, Bus. Edn. Alliance, 1991-92, Caring Found., 1991-92, Cox Hosp. Bd., 1990-92, Springfield Schs. Found., 1991-92, Jr. League, Lexington, 1971-82, Manchester Ctr., 1978-82, pres., 1979-82; chmn. Greater Richmond Progress Com., 1986-87, bd. dirs., 1986-89; pres. Leadership Wayne County, 1986-87, bd. dirs. 1985-89; adv. bd. Ind. U. East, 1985-89, Richmond C. of C., 1987-89, Ind. Humanities Coun., 1988-89, Youth Comm. Bd., 1988-92, Opera Theatre No. Va., 1992-94, Atlanta chpt. AIWF, 1995-2000. Recipient Coll. Media Advisers First Amendment award, 1987, Disting. Svc. award Assn. Edn. Journalism and Mass Comm., 1989; named to Ball State Journalism Hall of Fame, 1988, Coll. Media Advisers Hall of Fame, 1994. Mem. Student Press Law Ctr. (bd. dirs. 1975—, pres. 1985-87, 94-96, v.p. 1992-94), Assoc. Collegiate Press, Journalism Edn. Assn. (Carl Towley award 1988), Nat. Coun. Coll. Publs. Advs./Coll. Media Advisers (pres. 1979-83, Disting. Newspaper Adv. 1976, Disting. Bus. Adviser 1984), Columbia Scholastic Press Assn. (Gold Key 1980), So. Interscholastic Press Assn. (Disting. Svc. award 1983), Nat. Scholastic Press Assn. (Pioneer award 1982), Soc. Profl. Journalists, Internat. Newspaper Mktg. Assn. N.Am. (bd. dirs. 2002—), Newspaper Assn. Am. (postal com. 2001—, readership adv. group 2002—, diversity subcom. 1991—, circulation fed. bd. 2002-), Clayton County C. of C. (adv. bd. 1995-99, chmn. internat. com. 1996-98), Cedex Falls C. of C. (bd. dirs. 2005—) Office Phone: 563-383-2126, 319-291-1500. Business E-Mail: nancy.green@lee.net. *An opportunity each day to make the best of every situation to help others, your community, your profession and employees to be successful.*

GREEN, NORMAN KENNETH, retired oil industry executive, former naval officer; b. Columbus, Ind., July 1, 1924; s. Otto and Bernice Escalene (Snyder) G.; m. Mary Ann McCarthy, Mar. 12, 1949; children: David Bruce, Norman K., Penny Ann, Michael Anthony, Patricia Elizabeth. BS, U.S. Naval Acad., 1947; MS, Naval Postgrad. Sch., 1959. Joined U.S. Navy, 1943, advanced through grades to rear adm., 1974; comdg. officer USS St. Louis, 1970-72; comdg. officer USS Ticonderoga, 1972-73; capt. aviation assignment officer Bur. Naval Personnel Washington, 1973-74; comdr. Sea Based ASW Wings Atlantic Fleet, 1974-77; comdr. Carrier Group 6 and Carrier Strike Force Mayport, Fla., 1977-79; dep. dir. command and control Office Chief Naval Ops., Navy Dept. Washington, 1979-80; ret., 1980; sr. v.p. Charter Co., Jacksonville, Fla., 1980-87. Mem. Com. of 100, Jacksonville, Fla., 1974-77; mem. exec. bd. United Way, 1974-77. Decorated Def. Superior Service medal, Legion of Merit.; recipient Brotherhood award NCCJ, 1979 Mem. Jacksonville C. of C. (bd. govs. 1974-77, 83-86) Clubs: Army-Navy, Ponte Vedra, Marsh Landing Country. Roman Catholic. Home: 550 Granada Ter Ponte Vedra Beach FL 32082-2304

GREEN, NORMAN MARSTON, JR., retired minister; b. Oakland, Calif., June 27, 1932; s. Norman Marston and Gladys Marian (Meads) Green; m. Dolores Antoinette Taylor, June 27, 1953; children: Russell Norman, Cynthia Louise, Sharon Marie, Deona Lynn. BA, U. Calif., Berkeley, 1954; BD, Berkeley Bapt. Div. Sch., 1957; postgrad., U. Chgo., 1957-59; DMin, Ea. Bapt. Theol. Sem., Phila., 1982. Ordained to ministry Am. Baptist Ch., 1957. Pastor Grace Bapt. Ch., Downers Grove, Ill., 1959-62; field rep. Am. Bapt. Home Mission Soc., Valley Forge, Pa., 1962-66, field dir., 1966-76; dir. office planning resources Am. Bapt. Nat. Ministries, Valley Forge, Pa., 1977-95; ret. Rec. clk. Ctrl. Bapt. Ch., Wayne, Pa., 1986—90, treas., 1990—96, 2002—, bookkeeper, 1997—; championship statistician masters long distance running com. U.S.A. Track and Field, 1988—, sec., 1997—2001, chair, 2002—, bd. dirs. Co-author: Local Church Planning Manual, 1977, Key Steps in Local Church Planning, 1980, Churches and Church Membership in the United States, 1990, 1992. Mgr. U.S.A. Track and Field Masters Hall of Fame, 1997—; insp. elections Tredyffrin Twp., Berwyn, Pa., 1976—81; U.S. del. World Assn. Vet. Athletes, 1988—2001; bd. dirs., sec. Springdell Village Homeowners Assn., 1994—98. Named Mid-Atlantic Assn. Long Distance Runner of the Yr., 1982—90, U.S.A. Track and Field Male Athlete of the Yr., age 50-54, 1982—87, Male Athlete of the Yr., age 55-59, 1987—91, age 60-64, 1993—95, Mid-Atlantic Assn. Long Distance Runner of the Yr., 1994—95, Male Athlete of the Yr., age 65-69, 1997, Mid-Atlantic Assn. Long Distance Runner of the Yr., 1998; named to Masters Hall of Fame, U.S.A. Track and Field, 1996; recipient Otto T. Essig award, 1990, Lifetime Achievement award, 1999, Pres.'s award, U.S.A. Track and Field, 2003. Mem.: Am. Running and Fitness Assn. (pres. 1991—94), Mid-Atlantic Assn. U.S.A. Track and Field (v.p. 1988—96, coord. grand prix 1991—, treas., membership chair 1997—98, sec. 1999—, membership processor 2000—, sanctions adminstr. 2005), Am. Bapt. Mins. Coun., Phila. Masters Track and Field Assn. (life), Rd. Runners Club Am. (named to Hall of Fame 1992). Democrat. Avocations: long-distance running, reading. Home: 407 Freedom Blvd Coatesville PA 19320-1559 Personal E-mail: runrnorm@comcast.net.

GREEN, PATRICIA PATAKY, school system administrator, consultant; b. NYC, June 18, 1949; d. William J. and Theresa M. (DiGianni) P.; m. Stephen I. Green, Dec. 7, 1975. BS, U. Md., 1971, MEd, 1977, PhD, 1994. Tchr. Prince George's County Pub. Sch., Md., 1971-83; elem. instrnl. adminstrv. specialist Thomas Stone Sch., Mt. Ranier, Md., 1984-85, Glenridge Sch., Lanham, Md., 1984, Greenbelt Ctr. Sch., Md., 1983-84, Prince George's County Pub. Schs., 1985-91; prin. Columbia Pk. Sch., Landover, Md., 1985-91; asst. supt. Prince George's County Pub. Sch., 1991-95, assoc. supt., chief divsn. adminstr., 1995-99, assoc. supt. for pupil svc., 1999—2001, acting dep. supt. for instrn., 2000—02, fellow Broad Ctr. Supt., Bd. Found., 2002; supt. sch. North Allegheny Sch. Dist., Pitts., 2002—. Exec. dir. North Allegheny Found.; cons. nationwide sch. systems; presenter in field. Featured in numerous mag. and on TV shows; contbr. articles to profl. jour. Apptd. commr. Prince George's Commn. for Children, Youth and Families; mem. Prince George's County Cmty. in Sch., 1998—2002; trustee North Allegheny Found., 2002, exec. dir., 2002—. Recipient Nat. Sch. Recognition award US Dept. Edn., 1988, Outstanding Adminstr. award Prince George's County C. of C., 1990, Outstanding Rsch. award Md. Assn. Supervision and Curriculum Devel., 1995, Outstanding Educator award Prince George's County, 1983, Spotlight on Prevention award Md. State Atty. Gen., 1998, Disting. Achievement award North Allegheny Sch. Dist., 2002, Outstanding Profl. award U. Md. Coll. Edn., 2003. Mem. NAESP (Excellence of Achievement award 1988), ASCD, Phi Kappa Phi. Kappa Delta Pi. Avocations: landscape gardening, photography, reading, writing, bicycling. Business E-Mail: pgreen@northallegheny.org.

GREEN, PAUL ELIOT, JR., retired optical engineer; b. Durham, NC, Jan. 14, 1924; s. Paul Eliot and Elizabeth Atkinson (Lay) G.; m. Dorrit L. Gegan, Oct. 30, 1948; children: Dorrit Green Rodemeyer, Nancy E., Judith Green Godin, Paul M., Gordon M. AB, U. N.C., 1943; MS, N.C. State U., 1948; ScD, MIT, 1953. Group leader MIT Lincoln Lab., Lexington, 1951-69; sr. mgr. rsch. divsn. IBM, Yorktown Heights, N.Y., 1969-97; dir. optical networking tech. Tellabs, Hawthorne, N.Y., 1997-2000. Radio engring. adv. com. USIA, 1984—93; panel on survivable comm. NRC, 1982—89. Author: Fiber Optic Networks, 1992; co-editor: Computer Communications, 1974; editor: Computer Network Architectures and Protocols, 1982, Network Interconnection and Protocol Conversion, 1988. Served to lt. comdr. USNR, 1943—60, ret. Named Disting. Engring. Alumnus N.C. State U., 1983; recipient Data Comm. award Assn. Computing Machinery, SIGCOM, 1994. Fellow: IEEE (chmn. info. theory group 1960, pres. Comm. Soc. 1992—93, Aerospace Pioneer award 1981, E.H. Armstrong award 1989, Simon Ramo medal 1991); mem.: NAE, Russian Popov Soc. (hon.). Home: 35 Roseholm Pl Mount Kisco NY 10549-4619 Office Phone: 914-666-3473. E-mail: pegreen@earthlink.net.

GREEN, PAUL WARREN, state supreme court justice; b. San Antonio, Mar. 6, 1952; s. Hubert William and Leah (Tritt) G.; m. Judith Ellen Keppler, Aug. 4, 1973; children: W. Paul, John K. BBA, U. Tex., 1974; JD, St. Mary's U., San Antonio, 1977. Bar: Tex. 1977, U.S. Dist. Ct. (we. dist.) Tex. 1982, U.S. Ct. Appeals (5th cir.) 1985, U.S. Dist. Ct. (so. dist.) Tex. 1990. Ptnr. Green, McReynolds & Reed, San Antonio, 1977—95; judge San Antonio Ct. of Appeals, 1995—2004; justice Tex. Supreme Ct., 2005—. Bd. dirs., Halfway House of San Antonio, 1978-90, pres., 1985. Fellow Tex. Bar Found., San Antonio Bar Found.; mem. ABA (mem. house of delegates 1991-93), State Bar Tex. (dir. 1993-94), San Antonio Bar Assn. (pres. 1991-92). Avocations: golf, sailing, hunting. Office: Tex State Supreme Court PO Box 12248 Austin TX 78711

GREEN, PETER MORRIS, classics educator, writer, translator; b. London, Dec. 22, 1924; came to U.S., 1971; s. Arthur and Olive Emily (Slaughter) G.; m. Lalage Isobel Pulvertaft, July 28, 1951 (div.); children: Timothy Michael Bourke, Nicholas Paul, Sarah Francesca; m. Carin Margreta Christensen, July 18, 1975. BA, Cambridge U., 1950, MA, PhD, Cambridge U., 1954. Dir. studies in classics Selwyn Coll., Cambridge, Eng., 1952-53; freelance writer, journalist, translator, London, 1954-63; lectr. Greek history and lit. Coll. Yr. in Athens, 1966-71; prof. classics U. Tex., Austin, 1971-97, James R. Dougherty Centennial prof., 1982-97, prof. emeritus, 1997—. Vis. prof. classics UCLA, 1976; vis. prof. history U. Iowa, 1997-98, adj. prof. classics, 1998—; vis. prof. history, Athens, 1999; Mellon chair in humanities Tulane U., 1986; vis. fellow, writer-in-residence Hellenic studies program Princeton U., 2001; King Charles II Disting. vis. prof. in classics and ancient history, East Carolina U., 2004. Fiction critic: Daily Telegraph, London, 1954-63; sr. cons. editor: Hodder & Stoughton Ltd., London, 1959-63; cons.: (Odyssey project) Nat. Radio Theatre, Chgo., 1980-81; author: The Sword of Pleasure, 1957 (Heinemann award for Lit. 1957), The Laughter of Aphrodite, 1965, Armada from Athens, 1970, The Shadow of the Parthenon, 1972, Alexander of Macedon 356-323 BC: A Historical Biography, 1974, 2d edit., 1991, Classical Bearings, 1989, ed edit., 1998, Alexander to Actium: The Historical Evolution of the Hellenistic Age, 1990, rev. edit., 1993, The Greco-Persian Wars, 1996, From Ikaria to the Stars, 2004; translator, editor: Juvenal, The Sixteen Satires, 1967, 3d edit., 1998, Ovid: The Erotic Poems, 1982, Yannis Ritsos: The Fourth Dimension, 1993, Hellenistic History and Culture, 1993, Ovid: The Poems of Exile, 1994, rev. edit., 2005, Apollonios Rhodios, The Argonautika, 1997, The Poems of Catallus, a bilingual edit., 2005; editor-in-chief Syllecta Classica, 1999—. Served to sgt. RAF, 1943-47. NEH fellow, 1983-84; Craven scholar Cambridge U., 1950; Obermann Ctr. for Advanced Rsch. fellow U. Iowa, 1997; recipient 1st prize Nat. Poetry Libr., 1997. Fellow Royal Soc. Lit. (council 1959-63); mem. Soc. for Promotion of Hellenic Studies (U.K.), Classical Assn. (U.K.), Am. Philol. Assn., Archaeol. Inst. Am., Mem. Liberal Party. Club: Savile (London). Office: Dept Classics U Iowa Iowa City IA 52242 Office Phone: 319-341-6573. Business E-Mail: peter-green-1@uiowa.edu. *Prime aims, then, now always; to have maximum possible time for writing, travel, sport, relationships; to avoid any job that threatens my solitude or independence; to shun mature opinions; to go on, forever if possible, finding every day exciting, new, a fresh challenge, mentally and physically; to love and be loved always, to write all the books I have in me, and be healthy in mind and body until I die, preferably at well over the century, in Greece.*

GREEN, PHYLLIS HARTMAN, writer, playwright; b. Pitts., June 24, 1932; d.Victor Geyer and Phyllis (Sailer) Hartman; m. Robert Bailey Green, Aug. 15, 1959; children: Sharon Buell, Bruce. BS in Edn, Westminster Coll., 1953; MEd, U. Pitts., 1955. Writer, playwright, 1972—. Author: The Fastest Quitter in Town, 1972, Nantucket Summer, 1974, Ice River, 1975, Wild Violets, 1977, Grandmother Orphan, 1977, Mildred Murphy, How Does Your Garden Grow?, 1977, Walkie-Talkie, 1978, Nicky's Lopsided, Lumpy, But Delicious Orange, 1978, A New Mother for Martha, 1978, Gloomy Louie, 1980, Bagdad Ate It, 1980 (Calif. Young Reader Medal 1984), The Empty Seat, 1980, Uncle Roland, The Perfect Guest, 1983, Eating Ice Cream with a Werewolf, 1983 (Maud Hart Lovelace award 1989), Bummer Summer, 1988, Chucky Bellman Was So Bad, 1991; playwright: Deer Season, 1980, Physically Handicapped Singles Dance, 1983, Acapulco Holiday, 1988. Named Best Actress in Del., Del. Play Festival, 1956.

GREEN, RAYMOND EUGENE (GENE GREEN), congressman; b. Houston, Oct. 17, 1947; s. Garland B. and Evelyn (Clark) G.; m. Helen Lois Albers; children: Angela, Christopher. BS in Bus. Adminstrn., U. Houston, 1971; student, Bates Coll., Sch. of Law. Bar: Tex. 1977. Mgr. printing co.; atty.; mem. Tex. Ho. of Reps., 1973-85, Tex. Senate, 1985-92, U.S. Congress from 29th Tex. dist., 1993—; mem. energy and commerce com., standards of official conduct com., ethics com. Recipient Outstanding Legis. award Houston Park Police Assn., Appreciation award Dem. Nat. Com., Appreciation award Harris County Sheriff's Deputy Assn., Legis. Support award AFL-CIO, Support award Tex. Dem. Party. Mem. Baytown C. of C., Tex. Hist. Soc., Coastal Conservation Assn. Democrat. Methodist. Office: US House of Reps 2335 Rayburn Ho Office Bldg Washington DC 20515-4329 also: 11811 I-10 East Ste 430 Houston TX 77029*

GREEN, RAYMOND FERGUSON ST. JOHN, marketing and advertising executive; b. Phila., Aug. 15, 1950; Raymond Silvernail and Rose Dorathea (Basile) G.; BA in Psychology, Lafayette Coll., 1972; postgrad. Temple U., 1972-75; m. Lisa Rose Wardzinski, June 24, 1972; children: Katharine Amanda, Ian Ferguson Paul. Prodn. asst. Franklin Broadcasting Co., Phila., 1972-73, asst. sec., 1973-75, v.p. corp. affairs, 1975-78, exec. v.p., 1978-84; pres., gen. mgr., COO Franklin Broadcasting Co., 1983-88, pres. Magnetik Prodns., Inc., 1982-88; pres. Greenrose Corp., 1988—, also bd. dirs.; pres. Greenrose Broadcasting Svcs., WWPR Bradenton, Fla., 1996—; sec./treas. Liebert & Co.; bd. dirs. Young Audiences Eastern Pa., co-chmn., 1989-90. Associated Bio-Med. Svcs.; dir. Northwestern Corp., 1988-93; v.p. Amica Co., 1985-93; treas. NW Ctr. MH/MR, 1986-93. Mem. adv. bd. Phila. Boys Choir & Chorale, 1986—, Musical Fund Soc. of Phila. Mem. Northwest Center; mem. Musical Fund Soc. Phila., Phila. Art Alliance; dir. choral Arts Soc. of Phila., 1991-98, v.p., 1995-97, pres., 1997-98. Mem. Internat. Soc. Bacchus (trustee, chmn. Phila. chpt. 1988-91), Center Internat. Gastronomic Studies (trustee), Union League Club, Commonwealth Club, Rotary. Roman Catholic. Office: 308 Manor Rd Lafayette Hill PA 19444-1741 Home: 6320 Arlingham Rd Flourtown PA 19031-1637

GREEN, RICHARD ALAN, retired lawyer; b. Springfield, Mass., Apr. 25, 1926; s. Herman and Emma (Rudnick) G.; m. Lorna H. Paul, Sept. 6, 1957; children: Charles C., Thomas F. AB cum laude, Harvard U., 1947, LL.B., 1952. Bar: N.Y. 1954, D.C. 1975, Md. 1987. Assoc. Steinberg & Patterson, N.Y.C., 1954-57; asst. U.S. atty. So. Dist. N.Y., 1957-59; 1st asst. counsel N.Y. State Commn. Investigation, 1960; individual practice law N.Y.C., 1961-64; dir. ABA Project on Standards for Criminal Justice, 1964-73; dep. dir. Nat. Commn. on Reform of Fed. Criminal Laws, 1967-71; lectr. U. Va. Sch. Law, 1971; dep. dir. Fed. Jud. Center, Washington, 1971-74; partner Rowley and Green, Washington, 1974-80, Stohlman, Beuchert, Egan & Smith, Washington, 1981-2000; ret., 2000. Served with USN, 1944-46. Mem. ABA, Am. Law Inst., DC Bar Assn., Assn. of Bar of City of NY, Harvard (NYC) Club. Home: 1050 N Stuart St Apt 714 Arlington VA 22201-5749 E-mail: richagreen@hotmail.com.

GREEN, RICHARD C., lawyer; b. Phoenix, Ariz., 1944; BA, Yale U., 1966; JD, Georgetown U., 1976. Bar: Md. 1976, DC 1980. Of counsel, Energy Transactions Andrews Kurth LLP, Washington, mng. ptnr. DC office. Mem. Georgetown Law Jour., 1975—76. Mem.: Fed. Energy Bar Assn., Bar State Md., DC Bar. Office: Andrews Kurth LLP 1701 Pennsylvania Ave NW Ste 300 Washington DC 20006 Office Phone: 202-662-2742. Office Fax: 202-662-2739. Business E-Mail: rgreen@andrewskurth.com.

GREEN, RICHARD CALVIN, JR., electric power and gas industry executive; b. Kansas City, Mo., May 6, 1954; s. Richard C. and Ann (Gableman) G.; m. Nancy Jean Risk, Aug. 6, 1977; children: Allison Thompt, Ashley Jean, Richard Calvin III. BSBA, So. Methodist U., 1976. With Mo. Pub. Service, Kansas City, 1976-85, exec. v.p., 1982-85; pres., CEO UtiliCorp United Inc., Kansas City, 1985—89, pres., chmn. bd., 1989—, CEO, 1985—2002, chmn., 1989—; pres., CEO Aquila, Inc. (formerly UtiliCorp United Inc.), Kansas City, 2002—. Bd. dirs. Midwest Rsch. Inst., The BHA Group, Inc., Urban Inst. Washington.*

GREEN, RICHARD FREDERICK, astronomer; b. Omaha, Feb. 13, 1949; m. Joan Auerbach; children: Alexander Simon, Nathaniel Martin. AB in Astronomy magna cum laude, Harvard U., 1971; PhD in Astronomy, Calif. Inst. Tech., 1977. Physics lab instr. Harvard U., Cambridge, 1970-71; NSF trainee Calif. Inst. Tech., Pasadena, 1971-72, grad. teaching asst. in astronomy, 1972-74, grad. rsch. asst. in astronomy, 1974-77, rsch. fellow in astronomy, 1977-79; asst. astronomer Steward Observatory, U. Ariz., Tucson, 1979-83, Kitt Peak Nat. Observatory, Tucson, 1983-85, assoc. astronomer, 1986-90, astronomer, 1990—, dir., 1997—; acting dir. Nat. Optical Astronomy Observatories, Tucson, 1992-93, acting dep. dir., 1993-94, dep. dir., 1994-99. Rsch. asst. Smithsonian Astrophys. Observatory, 1970-71; adj. asst. prof. Steward Observatory, U. Ariz., 1983-85, adj. assoc. astronomer and prof., 1986-90, adj. astronomer, 1990—; mem. users' com. Internat. Ultraviolet Explorer Satellite, NASA, 1979-81, chair proposal rev. panel, 1986-88, 93, final sci. program com., 1993, mem. sci. team Far Ultraviolet Spectroscopic Explorer Satellite, 1981—, Space Telescope Imaging Spectrograph, 1982—, guest observer working group Extreme Ultraviolet Explorer Satellite, 1988-92, chair proposal rev. panel ROSAT Guest Observer Program, 1989, 92, ROSAT Users' Coms., 1990-93, chair HST Cycle 2 Porposal Rev. Panel, mem. time allocation com., 1991, STSDAS users' com., 1991-92, Hubble Space Telescope Program Rev., 1997; mem. panel ultraviolet and optical astronomy from space, astronomy survey com. Nat. Acad. Scis., 1989-90; mem. panel HST and Beyond AURA, 1994-95; mem. proposal rev. panels NSF, 1996-97; instrument scientist Gemini 8-m Telescopes Project, 1991-92; mem. U.S. Gemini sci. adv. com., Gemini (Internat.) sci. com. U.S. Gemini Project Office, 1991-93, acting U.S. Gemini Project scientist, 1992-93, mem. instrument forum, optical instrumentation sci. working group, chair multi-object spectrograph critical design rev., 1997. Nat. Merit scholar; Hon. scholar Harvard U. Mem. AAAS (astronomy divsn. nominating com. 1992, coun. astronomy rep. com. coun. affairs 1995-97), Am. Astronomical Soc., Internat. Astronomical Union, Astronomical Soc. of the Pacific, Phi Beta Kappa. Office: Kitt Peak Nat Observatory 950 N Cherry Ave MS KPS PO Box 26732 Tucson AZ 85726-6732

GREEN, RICHARD JOHN, architect; b. Painesville, Ohio, Mar. 14, 1944; s. Robert Franklin and Hazel (Ruble) G.; m. Judith Marie Ellen Niemi, Aug. 25, 1965 (div. 1985); children: Kevin Ward, Tyler Andrew. BArch with honors, N.C. STate U., 1968. Registered architect, Mass., Calif., Pa., Ill., Ind., N.H., N.C., Nev., Conn., Minn., N.Y., Mich. Project designer The Stubbins Assocs., Inc., Cambridge, Mass., 1968-74, assoc., 1974-77, v.p. deisgn, 1977-83, pres., COO, 1983-92, chmn., pres., 1992—2003, consulting prin., 2004—05; dir. scis. group CBT Archs., Boston, 2004—. Vis. instr. Calif. State Poly. U., Pomona, 1980—84; vis. lectr. Nat. U. Mex., Mexico City, 1981; instr. Boston Archtl. Ctr., 1971—72, 1975—76; thesis advisor Harvard U., Cambridge, 1981—82; part-time adj. faculty dept. arch. N.C. State U., 1998; adj. prof. arch. U. Hawaii, 1998—. Drawings, projects and photographs pub. in books. Bd. dirs. Sch. Design Found., N.C. State U. Fellow AIA (internat. com., corr. mem., com. design and urban design and planning, Cert. Merit 1968, Rotch Travelling scholar 1972); mem. Boston Soc. Architects, AIA Mass., Nat. Coun. Archtl. Registration Bds., Archtl. League N.Y., Corinthian Yacht Club. Avocations: athletics, travel, sailing, Tae Kwon Do. Home: 22 Oak St Marblehead MA 01945-1947 Office Phone: 781-631-6438.

GREEN, RICHARD M., academic administrator, internist; b. Chgo., Jan. 28, 1960; s. Henry and Reva Green; m. Marianne M. Green. MD, Duke U., 1986. Diplomate ABIM, 1993. Chief, divsn. gastroenterology Chgo. VAMC-Lakeside Divsn.; chief, divsn. hepatology Northwestern U. Feinberg Sch. Medicine, 2002—. Grantee, NIH, 2000—02. Office: Northwestern U Divsn Hepatology Searle 10-544 303 E Chicago Ave Chicago IL 60611

GREEN, RIVA LEE, social worker, minister; b. Denmark, S.C., May 18, 1953; d. Rious and Elizzillia (Banks) G.; m. George E. Collins, June 19, 1974 (div. June 1985); children: Corey E., Kevin L., Monique N. AAS, Cumberland County Coll., Vineland, N.J., 1992. Ordained to ministry Jamison Sch. Ministry, Phila., 1995. Caseworker Salem County Women's Svcs., Salem, N.J., 1992-97; family non-violence training U.S. Army, Ft. Dix, N.J., 1995—; family svc. specialist III State of N.J. Divsn. Youth and Family Svcs., Camden, 1997—. Pastor Strings of Faith ministry, Seabrook, N.J. Active NAACP (area coord. Bridgeton, N.J., 1995, 1st v.p. Cumberland County, 1995—); adv. bd. Maple Garden Tenant Assn., 1991-93; natural leader Martin Luther King Academy, 1995—; mem. C.O.R.E. Mem. C.O.R.E. Home: 32 Tower Ln Willingboro NJ 08046-4114

GREEN, ROBERT EDWARD, JR., physicist, researcher; b. Clifton Forge, Va., Jan. 17, 1932; s. Robert Edward and Hazle Hall (Smith) G.; m. Sydney Sue Truitt, Feb. 1, 1962; children: Kirsten Adair, Heather Scott. BS, Coll. William and Mary, 1953; PhD, Brown U., 1959; postgrad., Aachen (Germany) Technische Hochschule, 1959-60. Physicist underwater explosions rsch. divsn. Norfolk Naval Shipyard, Va., 1959; asst. prof. mechanics Johns Hopkins U., Balt., 1960-65, assoc. prof., 1965-70, prof., 1970—, chmn. mechanics dept., 1970-72, chmn. mechanics and materials sci. dept., 1972-73, chmn. civil engring./materials sci. and engring. dept., 1979-82, chmn. materials sci. and engring. dept., 1982-85, 91-93, dir. ctr. for nondestructive evaluation, 1985—2002. Ford Found. resident sr. engr. RCA, Lancaster, Pa., 1966-67; cons. U.S. Army Ballistic Rsch. Labs., Aberdeen Proving Ground, Md., 1973-74; physicist Ctr. for Materials Sci., U.S. Nat. Bur. Standards, Washington, 1974-81; program mgr. Def. Advanced Rsch. Projects Agy., 1981-82; cons. to various indsl. firms, govt. labs., legal offices; spkr., presenter internationally. Author: Ultrasonic Investigation of Mechanical Properties (Treatise on Materials Science and Technology, vol. 3), 1973; co-editor 11 books; also articles. Fulbright grantee. Mem. ASM Internat., Am. Phys. Soc., Acoustical Soc. Am., Met. Soc. AIME, Am. Soc. Nondestructive Testing, Soc. for the Advancement of Material and Process Engring., Materials Rsch. Soc., Sigma Xi, Tau Beta Pi, Alpha Sigma Mu, Sigma Nu. Methodist. Achievements include research in recovery, recrystallization, elasticity, plasticity, crystal growth and orientation, X-ray diffraction, electro-optical systems, linear and non-linear elastic wave propagation, light-sound interactions, high-power ultrasonics, ultrasonic attenuation, dislocation damping, fatigue, acoustic emission, non-destructive testing, polymers, biomaterials, synchrotron radiation, composites, sensors and process control. Office: Johns Hopkins U Materials Sci and Engring Dept 102 Maryland Hall 3400 N Charles St Baltimore MD 21218-2689 Office Phone: 410-516-8924. Business E-Mail: robert.green@jhu.edu.

GREEN, RONALD MICHAEL, bioethics educator; b. N.Y.C., Dec. 16, 1942; s. Daniel David and Beatrice (Friedlander) G.; m. Mary Jean Matthews, June 25, 1965; children— Julie Elisabeth, Matthew Daniel AB, Brown U., 1964; PhD, Harvard U., 1973. Instr. Dartmouth Coll., Hanover, NH, 1969-73, asst. prof., 1973-79, assoc. prof., 1979-85, John Phillips prof. of religion, 1985-98, chmn. dept. religion, 1980—83, 1985, 2000—, adj. prof. Amos Tuck Sch. Bus. Adminstrn., 1985-92, Cohen prof., 1998—. Vis. assoc. prof. Stanford U., Calif., 1984-85; adj. prof. dept. cmty. medicine Dartmouth Med. Sch., 1980—; dir. Dartmouth Ethics Inst., 1993—, Office of Genome Ethics Nat. Human Genome Rsch. Inst. NIH, 1996-97; human embryo rsch. panel NIH, 1994; chmn. ethics adv. bd. Advanced Cell Tech. Author: Population Growth and Justice, 1975, Religious Reason, 1978, Religion and Moral Reason, 1988, Kierkegaard and Kant, 1992, The Ethical Manager, 1994, The Human Embryo Research Debates, 2001; assoc. editor Jour. Religious Ethics, 1973-91, mem. editorial bd., 1991—; mem. editorial bd. Jour. Am. Acad. Religion, 1985-91. Kent fellow, 1965-69, Guggenheim fellow, 2005-; recipient Fulbright award, 1964-65, Dartmouth Disting. Teaching award, 1978 Mem. Am. Acad. Religion (sec. 1995—), Soc. Christian Ethics (bd. dirs., v.p. 1997-98, pres. 1998-99), Soc. Bus. Ethics, Am. Soc. for Study Religion. Jewish. Office: Dartmouth Coll Dept Religion Hanover NH 03755 E-mail: ronald.m.green@dartmouth.edu. *I continue to believe in the ideals of the enlightenment: that human beings can use their reason to expand opportunity, freedom and community.*

GREEN, RONALD MICHAEL, lawyer; b. N.Y.C., Nov. 17, 1943; s. Morris Joseph and Sally (Sutel) G.; children: Rachel, Micah, Joshua. BS, NYU, 1965; JD, Bklyn. Law Sch., 1968; LLM, George Washington U., 1973. Bar: N.Y. 1969, U.S. Ct. Mil. Appeals 1970, U.S. Dist. Ct. D.C. 1971, U.S. Tax Ct. 1971, U.S. Ct. Appeals D.C. 1972, U.S. Ct. Appeals (1st cir.) 1973, U.S. Supreme Ct. 1973, U.S. Dist. Ct. (so. dist.) N.Y. 1976, U.S. Ct. Appeals (2nd cir.) 1976, U.S. Dist. Ct. (ea. dist.) Wis. 1978, U.S. Dist. Ct. (ea. dist.) N.Y. 1978, U.S. Dist. Ct. (we. dist.) N.Y. 1985, U.S. Ct. Appeals (3rd cir.) 1986, U.S. Dist. Ct. (no. dist.) Calif. 1988, U.S. Ct. Appeals (11th cir.) 1991, U.S. Ct. Appeals (9th cir.) 1993, U.S. Dist. Ct. (no. dist.) N.Y. 1988. Head of civil rights divsn. U.S. Dept. Labor, Washington, 1970-73; gen. counsel, head N.Y. State Racing & Wagering, N.Y. State Consumer Protection, 1974; ptnr. Vedder Price, N.Y.C., 1975-78, Epstein Becker & Green, PC, N.Y.C., 1978—. Author: (books) Negligent Hiring, Fraud, Defamation and Other Emerging Areas of Employment Liability, An Executive's Guide to Equal Employment Opportunity Compliance, The Equal Employment Compliance Manual - A Systematic Approach to Effective Management Practice, Laws and Regulations Impacting on the Banking Industry, Age Discrimination in the Workforce and Its Implications, Personal Liability of Corporate Officials Under title VII of the Civil Rights Act of 1964: A Doctrine Still in the Formative Stages; co-author: Employer's Guide to Workplace Torts. Capt. U.S. Army, 1968-72. Mem. ABA, N.Y. State Bar Assn., Masons. Avocations: driving race cars, collecting cars, flying, squash, basketball. Office: Epstein Becker & Green PC 250 Park Ave Ste 1200 New York NY 10177-1211

GREEN, RONALD SIMONDS, retired history educator; b. Seattle, Wash., Nov. 24, 1942; s. Ronald Simonds and Eleanor Catherine (Bird) Green; children: Erika Tana, Elizabeth Deming. AB, Harvard Coll., 1965; MA, U. Wash., Seattle, 1970; PhD, U. Okla., 1998. Cert. Tchr. Wash., 1967. Tchr. history and film art Redmond H.S., Wash., 1967—88; bluegrass disc jockey WFNR Radio, Christiansburg, Va., 1988—89; ops. mgr., disc jockey WPUV Radio, Pulaski, Va., 1989—90; tchg. asst. U. Okla., Norman, 1990—98; history tchr. Casady Sch., Oklahoma City, 1998—2004, chair history dept., 2001—04; ret. Bd. mem. Seattle Film Soc., 1973—78. Aviation officer candidate USN, 1966. A.K. and Ethel T. Christian fellow, 1997. Mem.: Orgn. Am. Historians, Am. Hist. Assn. Avocations: movies, bluegrass music, travel, gardening, reading.

GREEN, RUTHANN, marketing and management consultant; b. Streator, Ill., July 14, 1935; d. John Joseph and Edna Marie (Peters) G. BS in Edn., U. Ill., 1957. Elem. tchr. Jefferson Sch., Davenport, Iowa, 1957-59; tchr. Hinsdale (Ill.) Jr. High Sch., 1959-62; ednl. cons. Harcourt Brace & World, Chgo., 1962-63; exec. sec. Everpure, Inc., Oakbrook, Ill., 1963-68; ednl. cons. Houghton Mifflin Co., Europe, 1968-69, Palo Alto, Calif., 1969-77, sr. mktg. mgr. Boston, 1977-87; v.p., nat. sales mgr. Riverside Pub. Co., Chgo., 1987-89; v.p., dir. mktg. McDougal, Littell & Co., Evanston, Ill., 1990-92; v.p., gen. mgr. Open Court Pub. Co., Chgo., 1992-94; pres. Peters & Green, Inc. Seminars & Bus. Devel., Chgo., 1994—. Author: WSIL: Why Should I Listen, 1987, 1993, 2004, A Garfield Memoir, 1995. Bd. dirs. Ritchie Tower Condo Assn. Recipient Svc. award Am. Arbitration Assn., 1987, Golden Reel of Excellence Internat. TV Assn., 1983. Mem. Am. Mktg. Assn., Nat. Assn. Women Bus. Owners, Internat. Reading Assn., People for Am. Way, Common Cause, Am. Arbitration Assn., Urban Gateways (bd. dirs.). Avocations: reading, fitness activities, travel, art. Home and Office: 1310 N Ritchie Ct Apt 21A Chicago IL 60610-8405 Office Phone: 312-787-2767. E-mail: petersgreen@att.net.

GREEN, SHAWN, professional baseball player; b. Des Plaines, Ill., Nov. 10, 1972; Player Toronto Blue Jays, 1993—99, L.A. Dodgers, 2000—04, Arizona Diamondbacks, 2005—. Named to Am. League All-Star team, 1999, Nat. League All-Star team, 2002; recipient Am. League Gold Glove Award, 1999. Office: c/o Arizona Diamondbacks 401 E Jefferson St Phoenix AZ 85004

GREEN, SHIRLEY MOORE, retired communications executive, public information officer; b. Graham, Tex., Dec. 21, 1933; d. N. Edgar and Cora Day (Morrow) Moore; m. Paul M. Green, Aug. 26, 1967 (div. 1981); children: Ruth Lynn, Tracy Moore Anderson. Student, Midwestern U., Wichita Falls, Tex., 1952; BBA, U. Tex., 1956. Staff asst. Rep. Party, Austin, Tex., 1965-67; press asst. Bob Price U.S. Rep., Washington, 1967; coordinator Tex. and Ark. Bush for Pres. Campaign, Houston, 1979-80; dep. press sec. V.p. Bush, Washington, 1980-85, acting press sec., 1983; dir. pub. affairs NASA, Washington, 1985-86, dep. assoc. adminstr. communications, 1987-89; spl. asst. to the Pres. White House, Washington, 1989-92, dep. asst. to Pres., 1992; dir. Pres. Bush Transition Office, Washington, 1993; dir. program support Internat. Rep. Inst., Washington, 1993-96; dir. corr. and constituent svcs. Gov. George W. Bush, Austin, 1996-2001; dir. comm. svcs. Atty Gen. John Cornyn, 2001—03. Local chmn. Jim Baker for Atty. Gen., 1978, Pres. Ford Com., San Antonio, 1976; trustee S.W. Found. Forum, San Antonio, 1974-78; bd. dirs. Child Welfare Bd. Bexar County, 1975-79; presdl. apptd. mem. J. William Fulbright Scholarship Bd. Recipient Exceptional Svc. medal NASA, 1989. Mem.: Tex. Fedn. Rep. Women (editor Partyline mag. 1969—72, one of 10 Outstanding Rep. Women Tex. 1979). Presbyterian. Avocations: reading, travel. Home: 1513 W 30th St Austin TX 78703-1403

GREEN, STANLEY E., military officer; BS in Polit. Sci., U. Tex.; MA in Bus., Webster U. Enlisted U.S. Army, 1969, commd. 2d lt., 1971, advanced through grades to brig. ben.; early assignments include svc. with 7th bn., 61st air def. mil., U.S. Army, Spangdahlem AFB, Germany; then battery comdr. 1st bn., 7th air def. arty., Ft. Bliss, Tex.; battery comdr., then bn. S-3 Illesheim, Germany; comdr. 1st bn., 52s air def. arty., Ft. Lewis, Wash., 1989-91; with office of Asst. Dep. Chief of Staff for Force Devel. Hdqrs., Dept. of Army, 1991-94; comdr. 31st air def. arty. brigade Ft. Hood, Tex., 1994-96; asst. dep. chief of staff USFK and Chief of Staff, 8th U.S. Army, 1996-98; asst. dep. chief of staff for combat devels. U.S. Army Tng. and Doctrine Command, 1998, dep. chief of staff for doctrine, 1999—. Decorated Def. Superior Svc. medal, Legion of Merit with oak leaf cluster, Meritorious Svc. medal with 4 oak leaf clusters, Army Commendation medal with 1 oak leaf cluster, others.

GREEN, STEPHEN J., surgeon; b. Apr. 5, 1954; AB, Dartmouth Coll., 1976; MD, Tufts U., 1980. Intern then resident North Shore U. Hosp./Cornell, 1980-83; fellow in cardiology North Shore U. Hosp., 1983-85, assoc. dir. Cardiac Cath Labs Manhasset, NY, 2000—, chmn. cardiovascular svcs., performance improvement, 1994—; assoc. prof. medicine NYU. Office: North Shore Univ Hosp Divsn of Cardiology 300 Community Dr Manhasset NY 11030-3801 Office Phone: 516-562-4100. E-mail: sgreen@nshs.edu, stevegreen@optonline.net.

GREEN, SUZY AMBER, education educator; b. Pomeroy, Ohio, Oct. 6, 1959; d. Hollie Edison Green and MaryAlice (Williams) Samuels. BA in internat. studies, Ohio U., 1982, MBA, 1983, PhD in edn., 1992. Instr. Ohio U., 1985—87; program evaluation specialist/asst. prof. Meharry Med. Coll., 1991—93; asst. prof. Ohio U., 1994—99; assoc. prof. U. of the Virgin Is., St. Thomas, 1999—. Cons. Creative Assoc. Internat., Washington, 1998. Grant, 1994. Mem.: Am. Ednl. Rsch. Assn. Office: Univ Virgin Islands Divsn Edn 2 John Brewers Bay St Thomas VI 00802 Office Phone: 340-693-1308. Business E-Mail: sgreen@uvi.edu.

GREEN, THOMAS ANDREW, law and history educator, lawyer; b. 1940; AB, Columbia U., 1961, MA, 1962, PhD, 1970; JD, Harvard U., 1972. Asst. prof. Bard Coll., Annandale, NY, 1967—69; prof. law and hist. U. Mich. Law Sch., Ann Arbor, John P. Dawson Collegiate Prof. Law. Vis. prof., Harvey and Susan Perlman Disting. Vis. Prof. Law U. Nebr., 2003. Co-editor: Studies in Legal History, 2003; mem. editl. bd. Am. Jour. of Legal History, Jour. of British Studies, and Law and Soc. Review; contbr. articles to law jours. Mem.: Am. Soc. Legal History (pres. 2000—01), Am. Hist. Assn., Selden Soc. Office: U Mich Law Sch 342 Hutchins Hall 625 S State St Ann Arbor MI 48109-1215 Office Phone: 734-764-1457. Office Fax: 734-763-9395. E-mail: tagreen@umich.edu.*

GREEN, THOMAS CHARLES, lawyer; b. Mpls., Feb. 7, 1941; s. Myron Bernard and Donna (Lavine) G.; m. Rochelle K. Green (div. 1974); children: Joshua L., Marisa A.; m. Pamela Kellogg, Aug. 31, 1979; children: David Swiler, Michael Curtis. AB, Dartmouth Coll., 1962; LLB, Yale U., 1965. Bar: Minn. 1965, D.C. 1967, U.S. Supreme Ct. 1968, U.S. Ct. Military Appeals. Asst. U.S. atty., Washington, 1967-70; pvt. practice, 1967—90; sr. litigation ptnr. Sidley & Austin (now Sidley, Austin, Brown & Wood LLP), Washington, 1990—, head, white collar criminal def. practice. Instr. civil and criminal trial practice various law schs., bar assnsn., Nat. Inst. Trial Advocacy; lectr., panelist various profl. programs. Capt. and arty. battery commdr. U.S. Army, 1965-67; attached 1st Air Cavalry Divsn., Vietnam. Named one of Top 10 Litigators, Nat. Law Jour., 2003, 75 Best Lawyers in Washington, Washingtonian survey mag. Fellow: Am. Coll. Trial Lawyers; mem.: Nat. Assn. Criminal Def. Lawyers (past. chmn. com. on environ. crime), Asst. U.S. Attys. Assn. (past pres.). Democrat. Jewish. Avocations: sailing, tennis, bicycling. Office: Sidley Austin Brown & Wood LLP 1501 K St NW Washington DC 20005 Office Phone: 202-736-8069. Office Fax: 202-736-8711. Business E-Mail: tcgreen@sidley.com.

GREEN, THOMAS GEORGE, retired architect; b. Ackley, Iowa, July 12, 1931; s. Thomas Chalmers and Marie Angeline (Dentel) G. BA, U. Chgo., 1951, B.D., 1955; M.Arch., Yale U., 1959. Ordained to ministry United Ch. of Christ, 1955. With Architects Collaborative, 1959-65, assoc., 1964-65; ptnr. Benjamin Thompson & Assocs., architects, Cambridge, Mass., 1966-80; assoc. Wallace, Floyd, Assocs., Architects, Boston, 1981-88; commd. minister United Ch. Bd. of Homeland Ministries, 1962-69, mem. archtl. adv. panel, 1979—; prin. Benjamin Thompson & Assocs., Cambridge, Mass., 1988—2001. Vis. critic Harvard Grad. Sch. Deisgn, 1981, Yale Sch. Architecture, 1983-84 Prin. works include Greylock Residential Houses, Williams Coll., high sch., Bennington, Vt., Design Rsch. Bldg., Harvard Sch. Edn. Libr., Cambridge, music bldg. Amherst Coll., Berkshire Community Coll., Pittsfield Mass., Soldiers Field Park, Harvard U., Faneuil Hall Markets, Boston, Inter-Continental Hotels, Abu Dhabi, Al Ain, Cairo, Trinitarian Ch.,

Scituate, Mass., United Ch., Norwell, Mass., Custom House Docks, Dublin, Ireland, Harumi Waterfront, Tokyo, Spitalfields Market Redevel., London, Navy Pier Expn. Ctr., Chgo., J.F. Kennedy Performing Arts Ctr. Masterplan, Washington, Abasto Marketplace, Buenos Aires. Mem. Boston Zoning Commn., 1975-85, Boston Landmarks Commn., 1996—. Eliel Saarinen Traveling fellow Yale U., 1959 Fellow AIA; mem. Boston Soc. Archs. Office Phone: 617-227-7707.

GREEN, TRENT JASON, professional football player; b. Cedar Rapids, Iowa, July 9, 1970; m. Julie Green; children: T.J., Derek Green. Degree in Bus., Ind. U. Football player San Diego Chargers, 1993, Washington Redskins, 1995—99, St. Louis Rams, 1999—2001, Kans. City Chiefs, 2001—. Established Trent Green Family Found., 1999; supporter Star Bright Rm. at Kans. Children's Mercy Hosp. Named to AFC Pro-Bowl Team, 2003. Avocations: basketball, golf, hunting, fishing. Office: 1 Arrowhead Dr Kansas City MO 64129

GREEN, VINCENT MICHAEL, music educator; b. Suffern, NY, July 17, 1965; s. Edward Vincent and Frances Alice Green; m. Michele P. Phelan, June 20, 1990; children: Justin, Shannon. MusB Edn., Crane Sch. of Music, 1991; MS, Western Conn. State U., 1996; Cert. of Advanced Study, SUNY, New Paltz, 2001—01. Cert. tchr. NY, sch. dist. administr. NY. Vocal music tchr. Mahopac (NY) Mid. Sch., 1992—94, South Orangetown Mid. Sch., Blauvelt, NY, 1994—98; dir. of bands Nyack H.S., Upper Nyack, NY, 1998—; music dept. chairperson Nyack (NY) Schs., 2001—. Permanent guest condr. Rockland County Cath. Choir, Nyack, 1991—; cantor St. Anns Ch., Nyack, 1990—. Mem.: NY State Sch. Music Assn. (pres. 1990—91), NY State Coun. Adminstrs. Music Edn. (area rep. 2002—), Music Educators Nat. Conf. Home: 74 Lake Rd Valley Cottage NY 10989 Office: Nyack HS 360 Christian Herald Rd Nyack NY 10960 Personal E-mail: nyackjazz@yahoo.com.

GREEN, WILLIAM, archaeologist; b. Chgo., May 30, 1953; s. David and Lillian (Kerdeman) G. AB, Grinnell Coll., 1974; MA, U. Wis., 1977, PhD, 1987. Staff archaeologist State Hist. Soc. of Wis., Madison, 1978-86; asst. prof. archaeology Western Ill. U., Macomb, 1980, 81; state archaeologist U. Iowa, Iowa City, 1988-2001, adj. asst. prof. anthropology, 1988-94, adj. assoc. prof. anthropology, 1994-2001; dir. Logan Mus. Anthropology, Beloit (Wis.) Coll., 2001—, adj. prof. anthropology, 2001—. Editor jour. The Wis. Archaeologist, 1983-88; editor: Midcontinental Jour. Archaeology, 1998-02; contbr. articles and revs. to profl. jours. Chair Johnson County Hist. Preservation Commn., Iowa, 1991-93. Grantee NSF, 1990-91, State Hist. Soc. Iowa, Leopold Ctr. for Sustainable Agr., Iowa Acad. Sci., 1988-91, 95, Inst. Mus. and Libr. Svcs., 2003—. Fellow Am. Anthropol. Assn., Midwest Arch. Conf., Inc. (pres. 2002-04). Jewish. Office: Logan Mus Anthropology Beloit Coll Beloit WI 53511

GREEN, WILLIAM L., lawyer; b. Syracuse, NY, Oct. 13, 1954; BA in Polit. Sci. cum laude, Middlebury Coll., 1976; JD magna cum laude, Boston Coll., 1980. Bar: Mass. 1980, NY 1981, Wash. 1986. Assoc. Quint, Marx, Chill & Greene, NY, 1980—82, Skadden, Arps, Slate, Meagher & Flom, NY, 1982—86; ptnr., Comml. Transaction Practice Area Perkins Coie LLP, Seattle. Limited Practice Bd. Wash. State Supreme Ct., 1993—2000; trustee Intiman Theatre Co., 1996—2002. Mem.: Wash. State Bar Assn. (Real Property, Probate & Trust Sect 1995—97), Mt. Baker Cmty. Club (pres. 1993—95). Office: Perkins Coie LLP 1201 Third Ave Ste 4800 Seattle WA 98101-9000 Office Phone: 206-359-8513. Office Fax: 206-359-9000. Business E-Mail: wgreen@perkinscoie.com.

GREEN, WILLIAM PORTER, lawyer; b. Jacksonville, Ill., Mar. 19, 1920; s. Hugh Parker and Clara Belle (Hopper) G.; m. Rose Marie Hall, Oct. 1, 1944; children: Hugh Michael, Robert Alan, Richard William. BA, Ill. Coll., 1941; JD, Northwestern U., Evanston, Ill., 1947. Bar: Ill. 1947, Calif. 1948, U.S. Dist. Ct. (so. dist.) Tex. 1986, U.S. Ct. Customs and Patent Appeals, U.S. Patent and Trademark Office 1948, U.S. Ct. Appeals (fed. cir.) 1982, U.S. Ct. Appeals (5th and 9th cir.), U.S. Supreme Ct. 1948, U.S. Dist. Ct. (cen. dist.) Calif. 1949, (so. dist.) Tex.1986. Pvt. practice, L.A., 1947—; mem. Wills, Green & Mueth, L.A., 1974-83; of counsel Nilsson, Robbins, Dalgarn, Berliner, Carson & Wurst, L.A., 1984-91; of counsel Nilsson, Wurst & Green L.A., 1992—. Del. Calif. State Bar Conv., 1982—, chmn., 1986. Bd. editors Ill. Law Rev., 1946; patentee in field. Mem. L.A. world Affairs Coun., 1975—; deacon local Presbyn. Ch., 1961-63. Mem. ABA, Calif. State Bar, Am. Intellectual Property Law Assn., L.A. Patent Law Assn. (past. sec.-treas., mem. bd. govs.), Lawyers Club L.A. (past treas., past sec., mem. bd. govs., pres. 1985-86), Los Angeles County Bar Assn. (trustee 1986-87), Am. Legion (past post comdr.), Northwestern U. Alumni Club So. Calif., Big Ten Club So. Calif., Town Hall Calif. Club, PGA West Golf Club (La Quinta, Calif.), Phi Beta Kappa, Phi Delta Phi, Phi Alpha. Republican. Home: 3570 Lombardy Rd Pasadena CA 91107-5627 Office: 707 Wilshire Blvd Ste 3200 Los Angeles CA 90017-3514 Office Phone: 213-362-9501. Personal E-mail: wpgreen@aol.com.

GREENAWALT, KENT, law educator; BA, Swarthmore U., 1958; B. Phil., Oxford U., 1960; LLM, Columbia U., 1963. Law clk. to Justice John M. Harlan US Supreme Ct. Atty. Lawyers Com. for Civil Rights, Jackson, Miss.; faculty mem. Columbia U. Law Sch., NYC, 1965—, Univ. prof.; dep. US solicitor gen., 1971—72. Contbr. articles to profl. jours. Vis. fellow, Clare Hall, Cambridge, 1972—73, All Souls Coll., Oxford, 1979. Fellow: Am. Acad. Arts and Scis., Am. Coun. Learned Societies; mem.: Assn. Bar of City of NY (mem. Civil Rights Com.), Am. Soc. for Polit. and Legal Philosophy (pres. 1991—93), Am. Philos. Soc. Office: Columbia Law Sch 435 W 116th St New York NY 10027 Office Phone: 212-854-2637. Office Fax: 212-854-7946. E-mail: kgreen@law.columbia.edu.

GREENAWALT, ROBERT KENT, lawyer, educator; b. Bklyn., June 25, 1936; s. Kenneth William and Martha (Sloan) G.; m. Sanja Milic, July 14, 1968 (dec. Nov. 1988); children: Robert Milic, Alexander Kent Anton, Andrei Milenko Kenneth; m. Elaine Pagels, June 1995; children: Sarah Pagels, David. AB with honors, Swarthmore Coll., 1958; Ph.B.; Keasbey fellow, Oxford (Eng.) U., 1960; LL.B.; Kent scholar, Columbia U., 1963. Bar: N.Y. 1963. Law clk. to Justice Harlan, U.S. Supreme Ct., 1963-64; spl. asst. AID, Washington, 1964-65; mem. faculty Columbia U. Law Sch., 1965—, prof. law, 1969—, Cardozo prof., 1979—, Univ. prof., 1990—. Dep. solicitor gen. U.S., 1971-72; assoc. dir. N.Y. Inst. Legal Edn., 1969; vis. prof. Stanford U. Law Sch., 1970, Northwestern U. Law Sch., 1983, Marshall-Wythe Sch. Law, 1985, N.Y.U. Law Sch., 1989-90; atty. Lawyers Com. Civil Rights, 1965, trustee, 1992; mem. staff Task Force Law Enforcement N.Y.C., 1965; vis. fellow All Souls Coll. Oxford (Eng.) U., 1979 Co-author: The Sectarian College and The Public Purse, 1970; author: Legal Protections of Privacy, 1976, Discrimination and Reverse Discrimination, 1983, Conflicts of Law and Morality, 1987, Religious Convictions and Political Choice, 1988, Speech, Crime and the Uses of Language, 1989, Law and Objectivity, 1992, Private Consciences and Public Reasons, 1995, Fighting Words, 1995, Statutory Interpretation: Twenty Questions, 1999, Does God Belong in Public Schools, 2005; editor-in-chief Columbia U. Law Rev., 1962-63; contbr. articles to legal jours. Recipient Ivy award Swarthmore Coll., 1958; fellow Am. Council Learned Soc., 1972-73. Fellow Am. Acad. Arts and Scis.; mem. Am. Philos. Soc., Am. Law Inst., Am. Soc. Polit. and Legal Philosophy (pres. 1992-93). Office: Columbia U Law Sch 435 W 116th St New York NY 10027-7201 Office Phone: 212-854-2637.

GREENAWALT, WILLIAM SLOAN, lawyer; b. Bklyn., Mar. 4, 1934; s. Kenneth William and Martha Frances (Sloan) G.; m. Jane DeLano Plunkett, Aug. 17, 1957 (div. May 1986); m. Peggy Ellen Freed Tomarkin, Oct. 31, 1987; children: John DeLano, David Sloan, Katherine Downs. AB, Cornell U., 1956; LLB, Yale U., 1961. Bar: N.Y. 1962, U.S. Dist. Ct. (so. and ea. dists.) N.Y. 1962, U.S. Ct. Appeals (2d cir.) 1962, U.S. Supreme Ct. 1966. Assoc. Sullivan & Cromwell, N.Y.C., 1961—65; dir. N.E. regional legal svcs. U.S. Office Econ. Opportunity, N.Y.C., 1965—68; assoc. Rogers & Wells, N.Y.C., 1968—69, ptnr., 1969—77, sr. ptnr., 1977—81, Halperin, Shivitz, Eisenberg, Schneider & Greenawalt, N.Y.C., 1981—86, Eisenberg Honig Fogler Greenawalt & Davis, N.Y.C., 1986—91, Bangser Klein Rocca & Blum, N.Y.C., 1991—93, Loselle Greenawalt Kaplan Blair & Adler, N.Y.C., 1993—97, Loselle Greenawalt Kaplan & Blair, N.Y.C., 1997—99, Meyer Greenawalt Taub & Wild, LLP, N.Y.C., 1999—2001; pvt. practice N.Y.C., 2001—. Lectr. in field. Bd. editors: Yale Law Jour., 1959-61; contbr. articles in field to profl. jours. Chmn. bd. dirs. Applied Resources, Inc., N.Y.C., 1968-70; chmn. Cmty. Aid Employment Ex-Offenders, Westchester, N.Y., 1971; pres. Westchester Legal Svcs., 1971-74, bd. dirs., 1975-91; mem. N.Y. State Gov.'s Task Force on Elem. and Secondary Edn., 1974-75; mem. Pres. Carter's Task Force on Criminal Justice, 1976; adv. coun. N.Y. State Senate Dems., 1978—; asst., acting treas. N.Y. State Dem., 1990-96, vice chair, 1996-2000, 9th jud. dist. rep. 2002—, state com., 1974—, exec. com. 1990-2000, 2002—; chair Greenburgh Dem., 1997-2002; mem. Greenburgh Recreation Commn., 1976-83, Dem. Statewide Spl. Commn. on Polit. Ethics, 1986-87, Statewide Spl. Commn. on Election Law and Campaign Spending Reform, 1989-95; pres. Westchester Crime Victims Assistance Agy., 1981-82; commr. Taconic State Pk., Recreation and Hist. Preservation Commn., 1984-96, 2004—, Nat. Recreation and Pk. Assn., 1998—, N.Y. State Recreation and Pk. Soc., 1998—; chmn., 1989-96; vice chmn. N.Y. State Coun. on Pk., Recreation and Hist. Preservation, 1989-94, 2004—; moderator Scarsdale Congl. Ch., 1988-90; mem. Westchester County Parks, Recreation and Conservation Bd., 1998—, vice chmn., 1999-2004, chmn. 2004—; mem. Westchester County Execs. Transition Team on Planning, 1997. Lt. comdr. USN, 1956-58, with Res., 1961-68. Fellow N.Y. Bar Found.; mem. ABA, Am. Arbitration Assn. (panel comml. arbitrators 1977—), N.Y. State Bar Assn. (chmn. com. on availability of legal svcs. 1968-70, chmn. action unit 3 1979-81, chmn. spl. commn. on alternatives to jud. resolution of disputes 1981-85), Assn. of Bar of City of N.Y., Nat. Legal Aid and Defenders Assn., Sphinx Head, Aleph Samach, County Tennis Club Westchester (Scarsdale, N.Y., pres. 1979-80), Yale Club, Phi Alpha Delta, Chi Psi. Democrat. Congregationalist. Home: 24 Lewis Ave Hartsdale NY 10530 Office: Law Offices William S Greenawalt 230 Park Ave Ste 2525 New York NY 10169-0199 Office Phone: 212-972-2604. Personal E-mail: wsgreenawalt@aol.com.

GREENAWAY, JOSEPH ANTHONY, JR., judge; b. London, Nov. 16, 1957; came to U.S., 1959; s. Joseph Anthony Sr. and Brucel May (Lynch) G BA in History, Columbia U., 1978; JD, Harvard U., 1981. Law clk. to Hon. Vincent L. Broderick U.S. Dist. Ct. (so. dist.) N.Y., N.Y.C., 1982-83; lawyer Kramer, Levin, Nessen, Kamin & Frankel, N.Y.C., 1981-82, 83-85; chief narcotics divsn., asst. U.S. atty. Dept. Justice, Newark, 1985-90; in-house counsel Johnson & Johnson, New Brunswick, N.J., 1990-96; dist. judge U.S. Dist. Ct., Newark, 1996—; adj. prof. Rutgers Law Sch., 2002—. Weintraub lectr. Rutgers U. Law Sch., 1998. Presenter in field. Past sec. Columbia U. Alumni Assn., bd. dirs., N.Y.C.; bd. dirs. Columbia U. Nat. Coun.; chair Columbia Coll. Black Alumni Coun. Named Minority Achiever of Yr. East Orange YMCA, 1997; recipient proclamation Newark City Coun., 1990, medal of excellence Columbia U., 1997. John Jay award Columbia U., 2003; Earl Warren Legal scholar. Mem. ABA, Nat. Bar Assn., Garden State Bar Assn., Fed. Judges Assn., Am. Corp. Counsel Assn. (Disting. Svc. award 1997), Columbia Coll. Alumni Assn. Avocation: golf. Office: Martin Luther King Jr Fed Bldg PO Box 999 Newark NJ 07101-0999

GREENBAUM, LEWIS, lawyer; b. NYC, July 29, 1948; BA with honors, NYU, 1970; JD, Georgetown U., 1973. Bar: NY 1974, Ill. 1978. Ptnr. pub. fin. Katten Muchin Zavis Rosenman, Chgo. Office: Katten Muchin Zavis Rosenman 525 W Monroe St, Ste 1600 Chicago IL 60661 Office Phone: 312-902-5418. Office Fax: 312-577-8960. E-mail: lewis.greenbaum@kmzr.com.

GREENBAUM, MAURICE COLEMAN, lawyer; b. Detroit, Apr. 3, 1918; s. Henry and Eva (Klayman) G.; m. Beatrice Wiener, June 28, 1942. BA, Wayne State U., 1938; JD, U. Mich., 1941; LLM, NYU, 1947. Bar: Mich. 1941, N.Y. 1947, Conn. 1948. Assoc. Herman H. Copelon, New Haven, 1948—50, Greenbaum, Wolff & Ernst, N.Y.C., 1950—54, ptnr., 1955—82, Katten, Muchin, Rosenman LLP (formerly Rosenman & Colin, LLP), N.Y.C., 1982—91, counsel, 1991—. Mem. vis. com. Rosenstiel Sch. Marine and Atmospheric Sci.; mem. adv. com. Great Neck Sr. Citizen Ctr.; mem. adv. com. Helen Merrill Fund; bd. dirs. Humanity in Action, Rosenstiel Found., World Rehab. Fund. Co-author: Estate Tax Techniques; grad. editor Tax Law Rev., 1946-47. Village Justice, Kings Point, N.Y., 1985—; assoc. trustee North Shore U. Hosp., Manhasset, N.Y.; bd. trustees N.Y. Found., 1967-83. Served to maj. U.S. Army, 1941-45. Democrat. Jewish. Home: 24 Cow Ln Kings Point NY 11024-1517 Office: Katten Muchin Rosenman LLP 575 Madison Ave New York NY 10022-2585 Office Phone: 212-940-8837.

GREENBAUM, STUART I., dean, economist, educator; b. N.Y.C., Oct. 7, 1936; s. Sam and Bertha (Freimark) G.; m. Margaret E. Wache, July 29, 1964; children: Regina Gail, Nathan Carl. BS, NYU, 1959; PhD, Johns Hopkins U., 1964. Fin. economist Fed. Res. Bank of Kansas City, Mo., 1962-66; sr. economist Office of the Comptroller of the Currency, Washington, 1966-67; assoc. prof. econs. U. Ky., Lexington, 1968-74, prof., 1974-76, chmn. dept. econs., 1975-76; vis. prof. fin. Kellogg Grad. Sch. Mgmt., Northwestern U., Evanston, Ill., 1974-75, prof. fin., 1976-78, Harold L. Stuart prof. banking and fin., 1978-83, Norman Strunk disting. prof. fin. instns., 1983-95, dir. Banking Research Ctr., 1976-95, assoc. dean for acad. affairs, 1988-92; dean John M. Olin Sch. of Bus. Washington U., St. Louis, 1995—, Bank of Am. prof. mgrl. leadership, John M. Olin Sch. bus., 2000—. Cons. Fed. Res. Bank Chgo., 1994-95; mem. Fed. Savs. and Loan Adv. Coun., 1986-89; vis. prof. banking and fin. Leon Recanati Grad. Sch. Bus. Adminstrn., Tel Aviv (Israel) U., 1980-81. Assoc. editor Nat. Banking Rev., 1966-67, So. Econ. Jour., 1977-79, Jour. Fin., 1977-83, Jour. Banking and Fin., 1980-92, Jour. Fin. Rsch., 1981-87, Fin. Rev., 1985-89, Managerial and Decision Econs., 1989-94, Jour. Econs., Mgmt. and Strategy, 1991-95; founding and mng. editor Jour. Fin. Intermediation, 1989-96. With U.S. Army, 1958—64. Mem.: Am. Econ. Assn. Office: Washington U Campus Box 1133 One Brookings Dr Saint Louis MO 63130-4899 Business E-Mail: greenbaum@wustl.edu.

GREENBAUM, VICKY, music and English educator; b. Denver, May 17, 1957; d. Joseph and Ruth Marianne Claire (Schonfeld) G. BA, Calif. State U., Northridge, 1980; MA, Calif. State U., 1984. Cert. secondary educator, English and music. Staff summer program Meadowmount Sch. for Music, Elizabethtown, N.Y., 1980-84; grad. asst. English Calif. State U., Northridge, 1980-82; violinist Houston Grand Opera Orch., 1982-84; conducting asst. Berkeley (Calif.) Opera, 1985-88; tchr. English Newark (Calif.) and Alameda Pub. Schs., 1985-88; music dir. Morristown (N.J.) Beard Sch., 1988-89; master tchr. English Phillips Acad., Andover, Mass., 1988-90; tchr. English, music dir. Frisch Sch., Paramus, N.J., 1989-90; tchr., orch. dir. Northfield (Mass.) Mt. Hermon Sch., 1990-95; orch. dir. Menlo Sch., Atherton, Calif., 1995—. Conductor Northampton (Mass.) Cmty. Music Ctr., 1993-94; guest conductor Springfield (Mass.) Young Peoples Symphony, 1993—. Contbr. articles to profl. English jours. Vol. counselor Pacific Ctr. for Human Growth, Berkeley, 1985-87; mem. acad. com. Northfield Mt. Herman Sch., 1991-94, sec. to faculty exec. com., 1994-95. Recipient fellowship NEH, 1992, Pflug fellowship Northfield Mt. Herman Sch., 1994, named Tchr. of Yr. Rotary, 2002; grantee Northfield Mt. Herman Sch., 1993. Mem. Mensa, Hemingway Soc. Office: Menlo Sch 50 Valparaiso Ave Atherton CA 94027-4401 E-mail: vgreenbaum@menloschool.org.

GREENBERG, ABBY J., physician; b. N.Y.C., July 8, 1935; d. Irving and Ruth (Gellert) Schlein; m. Gerald Martin Greenberg, June 23, 1955; children: Leonard Marc, Scott Kenneth, Carolyn Beth. Student, Barnard Coll., 1952-53; BA, U. Rochester, 1955; MD, SUNY, Bklyn., 1959. Clinician pediats. Nassau County Dept. Health, Mineola, N.Y., 1967-83; dir. spl. children's svcs., 1984-86; dir. Cmty. Health Ctr., 1987-89; dir. divsn. epidemiology, 1990-93; acting commr. health, 1993-94; dir. divsn. disease control, 1994—; asst. prof. dept. preventive medicine and pediats. Med. Sch. SUNY, Stony Brook, 1973—; attending physician Nassau U. Med. Ctr., East Meadow, NY, 1973—. Contbr. articles to profl. jours. Fellow Am Acad. Pediats.; mem. Am. Pub. Health Assn., Am. Thoracic Soc., Assn. Tchrs. Preventive Medicine, Internat. Union Against TB and Lung Disease. Avocations: travel, theater, concerts. Office: Nassau County Dept Health 240 Old Country Rd Mineola NY 11501-4250

GREENBERG, ALAN COURTNEY (ACE GREENBERG), securities trader; b. Wichita, Kans., Sept. 3, 1927; s. Theodore H. and Esther (Zeligson) G.; m. Kathryn Olson, June 27, 1987; children: Lynn, Theodore. Student, U. Mo., 1949. With Bear Stearns & Co., N.Y.C., 1949—, gen. ptnr., 1958—, chmn. bd., CEO, 1978-93, chmn. bd., 1993—2001, chmn. exec. com., sr. mng. dir., 2001—. Bd. dirs. Viacom, 2003—. Winner Nat. Bridge Championship, 1977; recipient Horatio Alger award, 1997. Mem. Soc. Am. Magicians, Harmonie Club, Bond Club, Deep Dale Club.*

GREENBERG, ALBERT, art director; b. N.Y.C., Mar. 15, 1924; s. Samuel David and Mary (Miller) G.; m. Marilyn Hoffner, May 29, 1949; children: Doren Roe, Peter Cooper. BFA, Cooper Union, 1948. Art editor Gentry, Am. Fabric Mags., N.Y.C., 1951-56; art dir. Gentlemen's Quar. Mag., Esquire, Inc., N.Y.C., 1956-70; sales promotion art dir. Lampert Agy., N.Y.C., 1970-71; v.p., sales promotion art dir. Wells Rich Greene Inc., N.Y.C., 1971-83; chmn. dept. comms. design Parsons Sch. Design, N.Y.C., 1983-94. Tchr. Pratt Inst., 1964-65, 73-74, Cooper Union, 1967-68, Finch Coll., 1973-75, Manhattanville Coll., 1974-75, Parsons Sch. Design, 1975-82. Contbg. editor: Typographic Directions, 1964, Advertising Directions, Photography, 1962, Advertising Directions, Visual Advertising, 1961. Trustee Cooper Union, 1979-82. Served with USAAF, 1943-45, ETO. Decorated air medal with silver oak leaf cluster; recipient more than 100 profl. awards, including Gold Medal, Art Dirs. Club, 1979, Pres.'s citation for profl. achievement Cooper Union, 1982; named Alumnus of Yr., Cooper Union, 1968. Mem. Art Dirs. Club N.Y. (designer 43d ann.), Cooper Union Alumni Coun. (1st v.p. 1970-71, pres. 1971-73). Office Phone: 845-229-8469. Personal E-mail: cu1948@aol.com.

GREENBERG, ALLAN, advertising and marketing research consultant; b. NYC, Dec. 8, 1917; s. Solomon and Rose (Honik) G.; m. Rosalie Katz, Nov. 7, 1943; children— Barbara L. Gutman, Roy J. BS, CCNY, 1942; postgrad., U. Wis., 1944, New Sch. for Social Research, 1946-54. Assoc. Psychol. Corp., N.Y.C., 1937-38; research analyst Serutan, Inc., Jersey City, 1939-41; research mgr./asst. dir. research Grey Advt., Inc., N.Y.C., 1948-55; sr. v.p., dir. research and planning Doyle Dane Bernbach, Inc., N.Y.C., 1955-74; research cons. to advt. agys. and mfrs., 1974—. Former chmn. tech. rsch. com. Advt. Rsch. Found.; former pres. joint coun. Empire Blue Cross/Blue Shield-HMO. Author: (with Mary Joan Glynn) A Study of Young People; booklet, 1966; contbr. articles to profl. jours. Former pres. mems. coun. Cmty. Health Program Queens-Nassau; mem. Profls. and Execs. in Retirement Group at Hofstra U. With AUS, 1942-45. Mem.: B'nai Zion (past mem. nat. exec. bd.; past pres. L.I. region). Home and Office: 5333 Zelzah Ave Apt 140 Encino CA 91316-2207

GREENBERG, AMY SCHILDHOUSE, artist; b. Cleve., Mar. 2, 1957; d. Burton and Ruth (Schaffer) Schildhouse; m. Moises Zabludorsky, Oct. 17, 1987 (div. July 1992); 1 child, Daniel; m. Joshua Greenberg, Jan. 15, 1995; children: Bess, Jake. BA, Vassar Coll., Poughkeepsie, N.Y., 1979. Production mgr. Crown Publishers, N.Y.C., 1980—85; artist in schools Greater Columbus (Ohio) Arts Coun., 1991—; artist in edn. Ohio Arts Coun., Columbus, 1997—. Mem. editl. bd. Story Quarterly, Chgo., 2001—. Author: (short stories) Best Ohio Fiction (Anthology), 1989, Into the Silence (anthology), 1990, A Loving Voice (anthology), 1990; contbr.; translator (short stories). Bd. trustees Congregation Torat Emet, Columbus, Ohio, 2001—. Nominee Pushcart Prize in Essay, 1988; recipient Hon. Mention award, Greater Cleve. Poets and Writers' Orgn., 2001; fellow Director's fellowship, Ind. U. Writers' Conf., Bloomington, 1986. Democrat. Jewish.

GREENBERG, BARBARA LEVENSON, literature educator, poet; b. Boston, Aug. 27, 1932; d. Louis B Levenson, Esther Harrison Levenson; m. Harold L Greenberg; children: David A, Russell S. BA, Wellesley Coll., 1953; MA, Simmons Coll., 1973. Faculty MFA writing program Goddard Coll., Plainfield, Vt., 1976—80; faculty, mem. adv. bd. Warren Wilson MFA Program for Writers, Swannanoah, NC, 1981—83; faculty writing program MIT, Cambridge, Mass., 1988—90; sr. lectr. Suffolk U., Boston, 1998—2000; affiliated scholar Brandeis U. Women's Studies Rsch. Ctr., Waltham, 2000—. Author: (poems) The Spoils of August, 1974, The Never Not Sonnets, 1989, What Nell Knows, 1997, (short stories) Fire Drills, 1982.

GREENBERG, BARRY MICHAEL, talent executive; b. Bklyn., Nov. 9, 1951; s. Aaron Herbert and Alice Rhoda (Strauss) Greenberg; m. Susan Kay Greenberg, Feb. 19, 1990; 1 child, Samuel Jacob; 1 child from previous marriage, Seth Grahame-Smith. BA, Antioch U. Dir. B'nai B'rith, Phila., 1976-80; acting dir. Jewish Nat. Fund, L.A., 1980-81; chmn. Celebrity Connection, L.A., 1981—. Co-founder Beverly Hills Air Force Co.; adj. faculty U. So. Calif. Annenberg Sch. Journalism; bd. dirs. Entertainment Industry Devel. Corp. Emeritus mem. Air Force adv. bd. USAF; Wilshire cmty. police adv. bd. L.A. Police Dept.; fin. co-chair, past chair Cmty.-Police Adv. Bd. Summit; 50th Anniversary of WWII com. U.S. Dept. Def.; pub. safety steering com. L.A. 4th Councilmanic Dist.; exec. bd. CDC Bus. Responds to AIDS program; co-founder Windsor Watch; adv. bd. Windsor Sq. Assn.; charter past pres. entertainment industry unit B'nai B'rith; past pres. Temple Israel of Hollywood Men's Club; bd. mgrs. Hollywood-Wilshire YMCA; treas. Fuller Ave. Sr. Housing. Recipient Chief of Chaplains Meritorious Svc. award, USAF. Mem. Def. Orientation Conf. Assn., Air Force Pub. Affairs Alumni Assn. Jewish. Avocations: pilot, music. Office: Celebrity Connection 4311 Wilshire Blvd # 300 Los Angeles CA 90010-3713 Office Phone: 323-650-0001. Business E-Mail: info@celebconn.com.

GREENBERG, BENJAMIN, physician; b. N.Y.C., Sept. 10, 1914; s. Moses and Beatrice (Kasten) G.; children: William Michael, Harvey Herman, Barry Edward. BA, Ind. U., 1936; MD, U. Edinburgh, Scotland, 1941. Intern Maimonides Hosp., N.Y.C., 1942-43; resident in surgery Maimonide Hosp., N.Y.C., 1943-44; pvt. practice N.Y.C., from 1946. Contbr. articles to profl. jours. Bd. dirs. Rockwood Park Security Assn.; chmn. adv. bd. Rep. Party; mem. Inner Circle Nat. Rep. Party, mem. Round Table; mem. Citizens Ambassador Program. Recipient Medal of Freedom award Sen. Rep. Party, 1994; named Comdr. of Honor, Eng. Mem. AMA, Am. Acad. Family Practice, Am. Acad. Sports Medicine and Rsch., Rockwood Park Civic Assn. (bd. dirs. 1960-70), Poan Am. Med. Assn., N.Y. State Med. Assn., Queens County Acad. Medicine. Republican. Jewish. Avocations: tennis, golf, photography. Address: 132 W 31st St Fl 15 New York NY 10001-3406

GREENBERG, BERNARD, retired entomologist; b. N.Y.C., Apr. 24, 1922; s. Isidore and Rose (Gordon) Greenberg; m. Barbara Muriel Dickler, Sept. 1, 1949; children: Gary, Linda, Deborah, Daniel. BA, Bklyn. Coll., 1944; MA, U. Kans., 1951, PhD, 1954. Asst. prof. biology U. Ill. Med. Ctr., Chgo., 1954-61, assoc. prof., 1961-66, prof. geophys. scis., 1966-90, prof. emeritus, 1990—. Vis. scientist Istituto Superiore di Sanita, Rome, 1960—61, Fulbright-Hays sr. rsch. scholar, 1967—68; vis. scientist Instituto de Salubridad y Enfermedades Tropicales, Mexico City, 1962, Mexico City, 63; pres. Bioconcern; nat. lectr. Sigma Xi, 1996—; cons. in field; expert witness forensic entomology. Author: Flies and Disease, vol. 1, 1971, Flies and Disease, vol. 2, 1973, Entomology and the Law: Flies as Forensic Indicators, 2002; contbr. articles to profl. jours. With USAF, 1944—46. NSF grantee, 1959—60, 1979—81, NIH grantee, 1960—67, U.S. Army Med. R & D Command grantee, 1966—72, Electric Power Rsch. Inst. grantee, 1976—85, Office Naval Rsch. grantee, 1977—78. Fellow: AAAS; mem.: Chgo. Acad. Sci. (sci. gov. 1981—), Entomol. Soc. Am. Home: 1463 E 55th Pl Chicago IL 60637-1875 Office: Dept Biol Scis M/C 066 U Ill Chgo Chicago IL 60607 Business E-Mail: bugaboo@uic.edu.

GREENBERG, BRADLEY SANDER, communications educator; b. Toledo, Aug. 3, 1934; s. Abraham and Florence (Cohen) G.; m. Delight Thompson, June 7, 1959; children: Beth, Shawn, Debra. BA in Journalism; Univ. scholar, Bowling Green State U., 1956; MS in Journalism; Univ. fellow, U. Wis., 1957, PhD in Mass Communication, 1961. Postdoctoral fellow Mass. Comms. Rsch. Ctr., 1960-61; research asso. Inst. Communication Research, Stanford U., 1961-64; asst. prof. Mich. State U., East Lansing, 1964-66, assoc. prof., 1966-71, prof. dept. communication, 1971—2004, Univ. Disting. prof., 1990, chmn. dept., 1977-84, prof. telecommunication, 1975—2004, chmn. dept., 1984-90. Vis. prof. U. Mich., 2004, U. Ga., Athens, 1999, U. Calif., Berkeley, 1992; fellow Ctrs. Disease Control and Prevention, Atlanta, 1999; sr. fellow East-West Ctr., Comms. Inst., Honolulu, 1978-79, 81; rsch. fellow Ind. Broadcasting Authority, London, 1985-86; cons. Pres.'s Commn. on Causes and Prevention Violence, 1968-69, Surgeon Gen.'s Sci. Adv. Com. on TV and Social Behavior, 1970-72, 82. Author: The Kennedy Assassination and the American Public: Social Communication in Crisis, 1965, Use of Mass Media by the Urban Poor, 1970, Life on Television, 1980, Mexican Americans and the Mass Media, 1983, Cableviewing, 1988, Teletext in the U.K., 1988, Mass Media, Sex and the Adolescent, 1993, Desert Storm and the Mass Media, 1993, The Alphabet Soup of TV Ratings, 2001, Communication and Terrorism, 2003. Served to maj. U.S. Army Res., 1973. Recipient Chancellors award for disting. svc. in journalism U. Wis., 1978, disting. faculty award Mich. State U., 1979; named to Journalism Hall of Fame Bowling Green State U., 1980; rsch. grantee NIH, NSF, USPHS, Carnegie Corp., Hoso Bunka Found., Nat. Assn. Broadcasters. Fellow Internat. Comm. Assn. (pres. 1994-95); mem. Assn. for Edn. in Journalism, Phi Kappa Phi (pres. 1993-94). Home: 350 Winterberry Ln Okemos MI 48864-4166 Office: Mich State U Dept Telecommunication 569 Communication Arts Sci East Lansing MI 48824-1212 Office Phone: 517-353-6629. E-mail: bradg@msu.edu.

GREENBERG, BYRON STANLEY, newspaper and business executive, consultant; b. Bklyn., June 17, 1919; s. Albert and Bertha (Getleson) G.; m. Helena Marks, Feb. 10, 1946; children: David, Eric, Randy. Student, Bklyn. Coll., 1936-41. Circulation mgr. N.Y. Post, 1956-62, circulation dir., 1962-63, bus. mgr., 1963-72, gen. mgr., COO, 1973-79; sec., dir. N.Y. Post Corp., 1966-75, treas., dir., 1975-76, v.p., 1976-81. V.p., dir. Leisure Systems, Inc., 1978-80; pres., chief exec. officer, dir. Games Mgmt. Services, Inc., 1979-80 Bd. dirs. 92d St YMHA, 1970-71, Friars Nat. Found., 1981-82. Served with AUS, 1942-45. Mem. Friars Club. Home and Office: 2560 S Grade Rd Alpine CA 91901-3612 E-mail: slugger19@cox.net.

GREENBERG, CAROLYN PHYLLIS, anesthesiologist, educator; b. San Francisco, July 7, 1941; AB, Stanford U., 1962; MD, U. Calif., San Francisco, 1966. Diplomate Am. Bd. Anesthesiology. Rotating intern L.A. County Hosp., 1966-67; resident in anesthesiology Presbyn. Hosp., N.Y.C., 1967-69, vis. fellow in anesthesiology, 1969-70, asst. attending anesthesiologist, 1971-90, assoc. attending anesthesiologist, 1990-99, med. dir. ambulatory surgery, 1986-96, attending anesthesiologist, 1999; asst. attending anesthesiologist N.Y. Hosp., 1970-71; attending anesthesiologist N.Y. Presbyn. Hosp., 1999—. Instr. anesthesiology Cornell Med. Sch., 1970—71; assoc. anesthesiology Columbia U., N.Y.C., 1971—74, asst. prof. clin. anesthesiology, 1974—90, assoc. prof. clin. anesthesiology, 1990—99, prof. clin. anesthesiology, 1999, prof. emerita anesthesiology, 1999—; clin. prof. anesthesiology Cornell Med. Sch., 1999—. Contbr. book chpts., articles to profl. jours. Mem. Am. Soc. Anesthesiologists, N.Y. State Soc. Anesthesiologists (Media award 1992), Med. Soc. N.Y., Soc. Ambulatory Anesthesia (treas. 1994-98, 2nd v.p. 1998-99, 1st v.p. 1999, Ambulatory Anesthesia Rsch. Found. award 1992), Malignant Hyperthermia Assn. of U.S. (hotline cons. 1983-99, partnership award 1996). Jewish. Avocations: swimming, reading, piano, travel. Office Phone: 212-746-2959. Personal E-mail: agfbogie@yahoo.com.

GREENBERG, DANIEL, electronics rental company executive; b. Mpls., May 14, 1941; s. Mayer and Ruth G.; m. Susan L. Steinhauser, Oct. 19, 1985. BA, Reed Coll., 1962; JD, U. Chgo., 1965. Staff atty. State of Calif. Dept. Water Resources, 1965-67; various positions, then pres., ceo Telecor, Inc., 1967-79; with Electro Rent Corp., Van Nuys, Calif., 1973—, chmn., chief exec. officer, 1979—. Former mem. U.S./Mex. Counsultive Group. Trustee Reed Coll., chmn., 2002--; trustee Nat. Pub. Radio Found.; former mem. visiting com. U. Chgo. Law Sch.; former mem. adv. com. Dept. Commerce, Fgn. Comml. Svc. Mem. Am. Bus. Conf. (charter, past bd. dirs.), Earthjustice(chmn. 1991-94), Bus. Execs. for Nat. Security. Office: Electro Rent Corp 6060 Sepulveda Blvd Van Nuys CA 91411-2512

GREENBERG, DANIEL LAWRENCE, lawyer; b. Bklyn., Oct. 14, 1945; s. Irving and Beatrice (Rabinowitz) G.; m. Karen R. Nelson, Apr. 4, 1987; children: Ilana Nelson-Greenberg, Mara Nelson-Greenberg. BA, Bklyn. Coll., 1966; JD, Columbia U., 1969; Hon. Fellow, U. Pa. Law Sch., 1996. Elem. tchr. N.Y.C. Pub. Sch. 208, 1969-71; atty. MFY Legal Svcs., N.Y.C., 1971-73, mng. atty., 1973-87; dir. clin. edn. Harvard U. Law Sch., Cambridge, Mass., 1987-94; pres./atty.-in-chief The Legal Aid Soc., N.Y.C., 1994—2004; spl. counsel pro bono initiatives Schulte Roth & Zabel LLP, NYC, 2005—. Bd. visitors CUNY Law Sch., Queens, 1989—, Columbia Law Sch., 1995—, Boston Coll. Law Sch., 1996—; Sibley lectr. U. Ga. Sch. Law, 1999. Contbr. guest editls. N.Y. Times, Daily News, 1989-97. Mem bd. advisors The Workplace Project, Hempstead, N.Y., 1995—, Programs on the Legal Profession of the Open Soc. Inst., 1997-2000, Stein ethics program, Fordham Law Sch., 1996—; mem. selection panel Root-Tilden Project NYU Law Sch., 1997. Recipient First Ann. Pub. Interest Honoree award Columbia U. Law Sch., 1991, Disting. Pub. Interest Lawyer in Residence award Touro Coll. Sch. of Law, 1998, Emory Buckner award for pub. svc. Fed. Bar Coun. 2002. Mem. Nat. Lawyers Guild (pres. NYC chpt. 1985-87, Ann. award 2001), Assn. of the Bar of the City of N.Y., N.Y. County Lawyers, N.Y. State Bar Assn. Dem. Jewish. Office: Schulte Roth & Zabel LLP 919 Third Avenue New York NY 10022 Office Fax: 212-756-2069. E-mail: danny.greenberg@srz.com.

GREENBERG, DAVID BERNARD, chemical engineering educator; b. Norfolk, Va., Nov. 2, 1928; s. Abraham David and Ida (Frenkil) G.; m. Helen Muriel Levine, Aug. 15, 1959 (div. Aug. 1980); children: Lisa, Jan, Jill BS in Chem. Engring., Carnegie Inst. Tech., 1952; MS in Chem. Engring., Johns Hopkins U., 1959; PhD, La. State U., 1964. Registered profl. engr., La. Process engr. U.S. Indsl. Chem. Co., Balt., 1952-55; project engr. FMC Corp., Balt., 1955-56; asst. prof. U.S. Naval Acad., Annapolis, Md., 1958-61; from instr. to prof. La. State U., Baton Rouge, 1961-74; prof. chem. engring. U. Cin., 1974—, head dept., 1974-81. Program dir. engring. divsn. NSF, Washington, 1972-73, chem. and thermal scis. divsn., 1989-90; sr. scientist Chem. Sys. Lab., Dept. Army, Edgewood, Md., 1981-83; cons. Burk & Assocs., New Orleans, 1970-78. Contbr. numerous articles on chem. engring. to profl. jours. Mem. Cin. Mayor's Energy Task Force, 1981—. Served to lt. USNR, 1947-52 Esso research fellow, 1964-65, NSF fellow, 1961 Fellow Am. Soc. for Laser Medicine and Surgery; mem. Am. Inst. Chem. Engrs., Am. Chem. Soc., Am. Soc. for Engring. Edn., Sigma Xi, Tau Beta Pi, Phi Lambda Upsilon. Jewish. Home: 8547 Wyoming Club Dr Cincinnati OH 45215-4243 Office: Univ Cin Dept Chem and Materials Engring PO Box 210012 Cincinnati OH 45221-0012 Business E-Mail: david.greenberg@uc.edu.

GREENBERG, E. PETER, microbiologist; BA in biology, Western Wash. U.; MS in microbiology, U. Iowa; PhD in microbiology, U. Mass., 1977. With Cornell U., U. Iowa, 1988—2004, Sheppard prof. molecular pathogenesis; chair dept. microbiology U. Wash. Sch. Med., 2005—. Sci. advisor Integrated Genomics Inc. Editor: Jour. Bacteriology; assoc. editor Annual Reviews Microbiology. Mem.: Am. Acad. Microbiology, Am. Acad. Advancement Sci., Nat. Acad. Scis. Office: U Wash Sch Medicine Dept Microbiology 1959 NE Pacific St Box 357242 HSB G-328 Seattle WA 98195-7242 Office Phone: 206-616-2881. E-mail: epgreen@u.washington.edu.

GREENBERG, EDWARD SEYMOUR, political science professor; b. Phila., July 1, 1942; s. Samuel and Yetta (Kaplan) G.; m. Martha Ann Baker, Dec. 24, 1964; children: Joshua, Nathaniel. BA, Miami (Ohio) U., 1964, MA, 1965; PhD, U. Wis., 1969. Asst. prof. polit. sci. Stanford (Calif.) U., 1968-72; assoc. prof. Ind. U., Bloomington, 1972-73; prof. U. Colo., Boulder, 1973—, dir. research program polit. and econ. change Inst. Behavioral Sci., 1980—, chair dept. polit. sci., 1985-88. Author: Serving the Few, 1974, Understanding Modern Government, 1979, Capitalism and the American Political Ideal, 1985, The American Political System, 1989, Workplace Democracy, 1986 (Dean's Writing award Social Scis. 1987), The Struggle for Democracy, 1993, 7th edit., 2005, 4th brief edit., 2002, The American Democratic Republic, 2005; contbr. articles to profl. jours. Recipient fellowship In Recognition of Disting. Tchg., 1968, Jeffrey Pressman award Policy Studies Assn.; grantee Russell Sage Found., 1968, U. Wis., 1968, NSF, 1976, 82, 85, NIH, 1991-94, 96-2001. Mem.: Internat. Polit. Sci. Assn., Am. Polit. Sci. Assn., Western Polit. Sci. Assn. (mem. exec. bd. 1986—89). Avocations: reading, bicycling, travel. Home: 755 11th St Boulder CO 80302-7512 Office: U Colo Inst Behavioral Sci PO Box 487 Boulder CO 80309-0487 Office Phone: 303-492-2141. Business E-Mail: edward.greenberg@colorado.edu.

GREENBERG, ELINOR MILLER, director, consultant; b. Bklyn., Nov. 13, 1932; d. Ray and Susan (Weiss) Miller; m. Manuel Greenberg, Dec. 26, 1955; children: Andrea, Julie, Michael. BA, Mt. Holyoke Coll., 1953; MA, U. Wis.-Madison, 1954; cert. in Mgmt. Lifelong Edn., Harvard U., 1980; EdD, U. No. Colo., 1981; LittD (hon.), St. Mary-of-the-Woods, Ind., 1983; LHD (hon.), Profl. Sch. Psychology, Calif., 1987. Cert. lifelong edn. Harvard U., 1980. Speech pathologist U. Colo., Denver, 1954—69, mem. faculty, 1967—69, exec. dir., Arapahoe Inst. for Cmty. Devel., 1969—71; founding dir. Univ. without Walls, Loretto Heights Coll., Denver, 1971—79, asst. acad. dean, 1982—84, asst. to pres., 1984—85; regional exec. officer Coun. for Adult and Experiential Learning, Chgo., 1979—91; founding exec. dir. US West Comm.-CWA, Pathways to the Future, 1986—91; rsch. assoc. Inst. Rsch. on Adults in Higher Edn., U. Md., U. Coll., 1991; exec. dir. project leadership, 1986—. Project dir. Healthcare Seminars, Colo. Rural New Economy Initiative, 2000-02; pres., CEO EMG and Assocs.; cons. US West Found., No. Telecom, Rose Found., U. Colo. at Denver, Cogeoinfo., 1992-96, NEON Project, Western Interstate Commn. Higher Edn., 2003—, NEAT Project, U. Wis., 2003—, Colo. Dept. Labor and Employment, 04-, Colo. AHEC Sys., U. Colo. Health Scis. Ctr.; founding regional coord. Mountain and Plains Partnership, 1996-02; adminstr. Visible Human Project-Undergrad., U. Colo. Health Scis. Ctr., 2002-04. Co-editor, contbr.: Educating Learners of All Ages, 1980; co-author: Designing Undergraduate Education, 1981, Widening Ripples, 1986, Leading Effectively, 1987, In Our Fifties: Voices of Men and Women Reinventing Their Lives, 1993, MAPP Online Voices, 2000; editor, contbr.: New Partnerships: Higher Education and the Nonprofit Sector, 1982, Enhancing Leadership, 1989, Liberal Education Journal, 1992; author: Weaving: The Fabric of a Woman's Life, 1991, Journey for Justice, 1994; guest editor Liberal Edn., 1992; gen. editor Seven MAPP Studies, 2002; feature writer Colo. Woman News, 1993-96, Women's Bus. News, 1995-96; contbr. Sculpting The Learning Organization, 1993; contbr. articles to profl. jours. Bd. dirs., exec. com. Anti Defamation League of B'nai B'rith, Denver, 1981-99, chair women's leadership com., 1991-93, bd. dirs., 1985-95; mem. Colo. State Bd. C.C. and Occupl. Edn., 1981-86, vice-chair, 1984-85; bd. dirs. Internat. Women's Forum, 1986-88, Internat. Women's Forum Leadership Found., 1991-95, Griffith Ctr., Golden, Colo., 1982-86, Colo. Bd. CLE and Jud. Edn., 1984-96; bd. dirs. Colo. Jud. Inst., 2004—, v.p., 2005-; mem. Women's Forum Colo., 1981-, pres. 1986; v.p. Women's Forum Colo. Found., 1987; adv. bd. Anchor Ctr. Blind Child, Colo. Coalition Prevention Nuclear War, Mile Hi Girl Scouts, Nat. Conf. on Edn. Women's Devel.; cmty. adv. bd. Colo. Woman News; adv. com. Colo. Pvt. Occupl. Sch., 1990-98, Colo. Cmty. Incentive Fund; co-chair Gov.'s Women's Econ. Devel. Taskforce, Women's Econ. Devel. Coun., 1988-96; bd. visitors U. Hosp., U. Colo., 1990-91, gov. apptd. Colo. Math., Sci. and Tech. Commn., chair, 1991-93, co-telecom. adv. commn. TAC 14, chair, 1993-95; founding steering com. Colo. Women's Leadership Coalition, 1988-96; mem. interdisciplinary telecomm. program, exec. bd. U. Colo., 1992-03; U.S. Dept. Edn., mem. Tech. Panels, 1991—, mem. Expert Panel on Lifelong Learning, 1999-02, Western AHEC Reg. Learning System, chair, coursework com., 1998; bd. dirs. Colo. Rural Tech. Program, 1996-00, Housing for All/Metro Denver Fair Housing Ctr., 1999-03, chair, 2002-03; chair Colo. Coalition for the Advancement of Telehealth, 2002-03; co-chair Colo. Coun. on Telehealth, 2003; mem. U. Physicians Inc. Task Force on Telehealth, 2003; mem. industry adv bd. MESA, 2002-05, bd. dirs., 2005-; mem. planning com. Colo. Women's Health Rsch. Symposium, 2004-05. Named Citizen of Yr., Omega Psi Phi, Denver, 1966, Woman of Decade Littleton Ind. Newspapers, 1970; grantee W. K. Kellogg Found., 1982, Weyerhaeuser Found., 1986, Fund for Improvement of Post Secondary Edn., 1977, 80, Robert Wood Johnson Found., 1997-2002; recipient Sesquicentennial award Mt. Holyoke Coll. Alumni Assn., 1987, Minoru Yasui Cmty. Vol. award, 1991, Women of Excellence award Colo. Women's Leadership Coalition, 1996, Founding Mothers award, 1997, Woman of Dist., Mile High Girl Scouts, 1997, Martin Luther King Disting. Svc. award to Little Coun. for Human Rels., Arapahoe C.C., 2003, Arthur and Bea Branscombe Meml. award Housing for All: The Metro Denver Fair Housing Ctr., 2003. Mem. Kappa Delta Pi. Democrat. Jewish. Home: 6725 S Adams Way Littleton CO 80122-1801 Personal E-mail: ellie.greenberg@uchsc.edu.

GREENBERG, GARY HOWARD, lawyer; b. N.Y.C., Mar. 2, 1948; s. Leo and Elizabeth P. (Weissman) G.; m. Sherri Snyder, June 21, 1987; children: Benjamin, Laura, Nicholas. BA, Johns Hopkins U., 1970; JD, N.Y.U., 1974. Bar: N.Y. 1975, U.S. Dist. Ct. (so. dist.) N.Y. 1975, U.S. Dist. Ct. (ea. dist.) N.Y. 1975, U.S. Ct. Appeals (2nd cir.) 1984. Assoc. Orans, Elsen & Lupert, N.Y.C., 1975—83, ptnr., 1983—2002; of counsel Vinson & Elkins LLP, N.Y.C., 2002—. Instr. trial acad. direct and cross exam. skills N.Y. County Lawyers' Assn.-Nat. Inst. of Trial Advocacy, 1995. Mem. ABA, Assn. of Bar of City of N.Y. (mem. com. on fed. legis. 1983-86), N.Y. State Bar Assn., N.Y. County Lawyers' Assn. (chair appellate cts. com. 1996-99). Office: Vinson & Elkins LLP 666 Fifth Ave New York NY 10103-0040

GREENBERG, GERALD STEPHEN, lawyer; b. Phila., July 27, 1951; s. Bernard and Elaine Alice (Shapiro) G.; m. Pamela Sue Meyers, Aug. 24, 1975; children: David Stuart, Allison Brooke. BA, Dickinson Coll., 1973; JD, Harvard U., 1976. Bar: N.Y. 1977, U.S. Dist. Ct. (so. dist.) N.Y. 1977, Ohio 1988. Assoc. Kaye, Scholer, Fierman, Hays & Handler, N.Y.C., 1976-86; atty. Exxon Corp., N.Y.C., 1986-87; assoc. Taft, Stettinius & Hollister LLP, Cin., 1987-89; ptnr. Taft, Stettinius & Hollister, Cin., 1990—. Mem. ABA, Assn. of Bar of City of N.Y., Cin. Bar Assn. Office: 1800 Firstar Tower 425 Walnut St Cincinnati OH 45202-3923 E-mail: greenberg@taftlaw.com.

GREENBERG, GORDON ALAN, lawyer; b. Chgo., July 2, 1954; s. Henry and Ruth (Bluestien) G.; m. Patricia L. Collins; children: Haley, Danielle. BA, U. Ill., 1976; JD with honors, Ill. Inst. Tech./Chgo.-Kent, 1980. Bar: Ill. 1980, U.S. Dist. Ct. (no. dist.) Ill. 1980, U.S. Ct. Appeals (7th cir.if. 1980, Calif. 1984, U.S. Ct. Appeals (9th cir.) 1984. Asst. state atty. Cook County, Chgo., 1980-83; spl. asst. U.S. atty. No. Dist. Ill., Chgo., 1982-83; asst. U.S. atty., chief Fin. Investigations Unit L.A. U.S. Atty. Office, 1983-89; ptnr. Sheppard, Mullin, Richter & Hampton, L.A., 1989—; ptnr.-in-charge L.A. Office McDermott Will & Emery LLP, L.A. Instr. U.S. Dept. Justice, 1985-89, lawyer rep. 9th cir., L.A., 1993-96. Contbr. articles profl. jours. Named one of top 50 trial lawyers in L.A., L.A. Bus. Jour. Mem. ABA, State Bar Assn. Calif., L.A. County Bar Assn. (chmn. White Collar Def. Com.). Office: McDermott Will & Emery 2049 Century Park E Fl 34 Los Angeles CA 90067-3101 Office Phone: 310-551-9398. Office Fax: 310-277-4730. Business E-Mail: ggreenberg@mwe.com.

GREENBERG, HINDA FEIGE, library director; b. Bayreuth, Germany, Feb. 26, 1947; arrived in U.S., 1951; d. Samuel Leon and Sima (Schampagnere) F.; m. Joseph Lawrence, July 6, 1968; children: David Micah, Jacob Alexander. BA, Temple U., 1969; MLS, Rutgers U., 1981; PhD, Drexel U., 1999. Assoc. librarian Ednl. Testing Svc., Princeton, NJ, 1981-86; dir. info. ctr. Carnegie Found., Princeton, 1986-97, Robert Wood Johnson Found., Princeton, 1997—. Pres. Consortium of Found. Librs. Avocation: travel.

GREENBERG, IRA ARTHUR, psychologist; b. Bklyn., June 26, 1924; s. Philip and Minnie (S.) G.; m. Martha Estelle Cantrell, 1949 (div. 1950); m. Judith Linda Burgard-Rials, 1952 (div. 1954); m. Monita Ruth Nibord, 1961 (div. 1965). Grad. Scouts and Raiders Sch., US Naval Amphibious Tng. Base, Ft. Pierce, Fla., 1944; BA in Journalism, U. Okla., 1949; MA in English, U. So. Calif., 1962; MS in Counseling, Calif. State U., L.A., 1963; PhD in Psychology, Claremont (Calif.) Grad. Sch., 1967; Grad., Marine Corps Inst.'s Command and Staff Coll., 1992. Editor Ft. Riley (Kans.) Guidon, 1950-51; copy editor, reporter Columbus (Ga.) Enquirer, 1951-55; reporter Louisville Courier-Jour., 1955-56, L.A. Times, 1956-62; free-lance writer L.A., Montclair, Camarillo, Calif., 1960-69, 76—. Counselor Claremont Coll. Psychol. Clinic and Counseling Ctr., 1964-65; lectr. psychology Chapman Coll., Orange, Calif., 1965-66; psychologist Camarillo State Hosp., 1967-69, supervising psychologist, 1969-73, part-time clin. psychologist, 1973-93; part-time asst. prof. edn. San Fernando Valley State Coll., Northridge, Calif., 1967-69, lectr. psychodrama, social welfare U. Calif. Extension Divsn., Santa Barbara, 1968-69; vis. prof. edn. U. Nev., Reno, 1977—; vol. psychologist Free Clinic, L.A., 1968-70; staff dir. Calif. Inst. Psychodrama, 1969-71; tng. cons. Topanga Ctr. for Human Devel., 1970-75, bd. dirs., 1971-74, faculty Calif. Sch. Profl. Psychology, 1970-80; founder, exec. dir. Behavioral Studies Inst., mgmt. cons., L.A., 1970—; pvt. practice cons. in psychology, psychodrama, hypnosis, 1970—; founder, exec. dir. Psychodrama Ctr. for L.A., Inc., 1971—, Group Hypnosis Ctr., L.A., 1976—; prodr., host TV talk show Crime and Pub. Safety, Adelpial, Channel 98, 1983—. Author: Psychodrama and Audience Attitude Change, 1968; editor (author): Psychodrama: Theory and Therapy, 1974, Group Hypnotherapy and Hypnodrama, 1977, The Hebrew National Orphan Home: Memories of Orphanage Life, 2001. Vol. humane officer State of Calif., 1979-89; res. officer L.A. Police Dept., 1980-86; bd. dirs. Humane Educators Coun., 1982-86; mem. Nat. Coun. Employer Support of Guard and Res., 1998—. With AUS 78th inf. divsn., 1943, army specialized tng. program, 1944, 11th engr. combat battalion XXI corps 7th Army, ETO, 1944-46; USAR, 1950-51, sgt. 1st class; capt. Calif. State Mil. Res., 1986-93, maj., 1993-2000; lt. col. U.S. Svc. Command, 2000-02; col. Emergency Disaster Assistance Corps, 2002—. Fellow Am. Soc. Clin. Hypnosis, Am. Soc. Group Psychotherapy and Psychodrama; mem. Am. Psychol. Assn., Calif. Psychol. Assn., L.A. County Psychol. Assn., So. Calif. Soc. Clin. Hypnosis (pres. 1977-78), Group Psychotherapy Assn. So. Calif. (pres. 1987-88), So. Calif. Psychotherapy Affiliation (dir. 1976-85), Am. Soc. Psychical Rsch., Assn. Rsch. and Enlightenment, Peace Officers Assn., L.A. County, Acad. TV Arts and Scis., Nat. Acad. Cable Programming, UDT/SEAL Assn., Navy Amphibious Scouts and Raiders Assn., 11th Engr. Combat Battalion Assn., 78th Infantry Divsn. Assn., VFW, Am. Legion, Jewish War Vets., State Def. Forces Assn. Am., State Def. Forces Assn. Calif., Mensa, Am. Zionist Fedn., NRA, Calif. Rifle and Pistol Assn., SW Pistol League, Animal Protection Inst. Am., L.A. SPCA, Hebrew Nat. Orphan Home Alumni Assn., Sigma Delta Chi. Clubs: Sierra, Greater L.A. Press; B'nai B'rith; Beverly Hills Gun. Office Phone: 310-472-2662.

GREENBERG, IRA GEORGE, lawyer; b. NYC, May 8, 1946; s. Julius M. and Florence Greenberg; children: Amanda, Glenn. AB, Harvard U., 1968, JD, 1971. Bar: NY 1972. Asst. to gen. counsel Office of Sec. of Army, Washington, 1971-74; assoc. Dewey Ballantine, N.Y.C., 1974-81, Summit Solomon & Feldesman and predecessor firms, N.Y.C., 1981-83, ptnr., 1983-92, Edwards & Angell LLP, N.Y.C., 1992—. Capt. U.S. Army, 1971-74. Mem. ABA, Assn. Bar City N.Y. Democrat. Office: Edwards & Angell LLP 750 Lexington Ave New York NY 10022-1200 Office Phone: 212-912-2756. E-mail: igreenberg@edwardsangell.com.

GREENBERG, JACK, lawyer, educator; b. N.Y.C., Dec. 22, 1924; s. Max and Bertha (Rosenberg) G.; m. Sema Ann Tanzer, 1950 (div. 1970); children: Josiah, David, Sarah, Ezra; m. Deborah M. Cole, 1970; children: Suzanne, William Cole. AB, Columbia U., 1945, LLB, 1948, LLD, 1984, Morgan State Coll., Central State Coll., 1965, Lincoln U., 1977, John Jay Coll. Criminal Justice, 1983, De Paul U., 1994, Howard U., 2004, Notre Dame, 2005. Bar: NY 1949. Rsch. asst. N.Y. State Law Revision Commn., 1949; asst. counsel NAACP Legal Def. and Ednl. Fund, 1949-61, dir.-counsel, 1961-84; argued in sch. segregation, sit-in, employment discrimination, poverty, capital punishment, other cases before U.S. Supreme Ct.; adj. prof. Columbia U. Law Sch., 1970-84, prof., vice-dean, 1984-89; dean Columbia Coll., 1989-93; prof. Columbia U. Law Sch., 1993—. Cons. Ctr. Applied Legal Studies, U. Witwatersrand, 1978; vis. lectr. Yale U. Law Sch., 1971; vis. prof. CCNY, 1977, Tokyo U., 1993-94, 99, St. Louis U. Law Sch., 1994, Lewis and Clark Law Sch., 1994-98, Princeton U., 1995, U. Munich, 1998; lectr. Harvard U. Law Sch., 1983, Hebrew U., 2005; disting. lectr. humanities Columbia Coll. Physicians and Surgeons, 1998, U. Nurenberg-Erlangen, 1999, Hebrew U., 2005. Author: (with H. Hill) Citizens Guide to Desegregation, 1955, Race Relations and American Law, 1959, Judicial Process and Social Change, 1976, (with James Vorenberg) Dean Cuisine or the Liberated Man's Guide to Fine Cooking, 1990, Crusaders in the Courts, 1994, Crusaders in the Courts: Legal Battles of the Civil Rights Movement, 2004, Brown v. Board of Education: Witness to a Landmark Decision, 2004; contbg. author: Race, Sex and Religious Discrimination in International Law, 1981; contbr. articles to profl. jours. Bd. dirs. NYC Legal Aid Soc., Internat. League for Human Rights, Mex.-Am. Legal Def. Fund, 1968-75, Asian Am. Legal Def. Fund, 1980—, Human Rights Watch, 1978-98, NAACP Legal Def. and Ednl. Fund. Co-recipient Grenville Clark prize, 1978; hon. fellow, U. Pa. Law Sch., 1975. Fellow AAAS, Am. Coll. Trial Lawyers; mem. ABA (commn. to study FTC, adv. com. to spl. com. on crime prevention, sect. on individual rights and responsibilities, Silver Gavel award, Thurgood Marshall prize, Presdl. Citizens medal 2001), NY State Bar Assn. (exec. dir. spl. com. study state antitrust laws 1956), Am. Law Inst., Bar Assn. City NY (Cardozo lectr. 1973) Adminstrv. Conf. U.S. Home: 118 Riverside Dr New York NY 10024-3708 Office: Columbia Law Sch 435 W 116th St New York NY 10027-7297 Office Phone: 212-854-8030. Business E-Mail: jg25@columbia.edu.

GREENBERG, JACK M., former food products executive; b. Sept. 28, 1942; s. Edith S. Scher; m. Donna Greenberg; children: David, Ilyse, Allison. BSc in Acctg., DePaul U., Chgo., 1964, JD, 1968. CPA Ill.; bar:. With Arthur Young & Co., 1964-82; vice chmn., CFO McDonald's Corp., Oak Brook, Ill., CFO, exec. v.p., 1982, vice chmn., CFO, 1992, vice chmn., 1991—98, pres., 1998—99, pres. US Bus., 1997, CEO, 1998—2002, chmn., 1999—2002. Bd. dirs. Abbott Labs, Abbot Park, Ill., Allstate Corp., Northbrook, Ill., Hasbro, Inc., Pawtucket, RI, First Data Corp., Greenwood Village, Colo., Manpower Inc., Milw. Bd. dirs. DePaul U. Field Mus., Inst. Internat. Edn., Chgo. (Ill.) Symphony, Chgo. (Ill.) Cmty. Trust. Mem.: AICPA, Ill. Inst. Cert. Pub. Accts.

GREENBERG, JACOB, biochemist, educator, consultant; b. Haifa, Israel, Mar. 10, 1929; came to U.S., 1961; s. Shlomo and Temima Greenberg; m. Esther Kahana, May 19, 1957; children: Abraham, Daphne. PhD, Hebrew U., Jerusalem, 1958. Assoc. rsch. biochemist biochem. dept. NYU, 1962-67, assoc. rsch. scientist Sch. Medicine, 1969-71; assoc. rsch. scientist Mt. Sinai Med. Sch., N.Y.C., 1967-68; asst. prof. N.Y. Med. Coll., 1972-76; dir. R&D quality assurance Advanced Biofactures, N.Y.C., 1971-83; dir. R&D Protos, N.Y.C., 1983—. Cons. Columbia U., N.Y.C., 1965-67. Editor Autism Now; contbr. articles to profl. jours. Mem. White House Inner Cir., Washington, 1984-93, Autistic Soc. NIH fellow, 1961-62, grantee, 1972-76. Mem. AAUP, Internat. Congress Biochemistry, Am. Chem. Soc. (grantee 1967), N.Y. Acad. Scis. Avocations: swimming, chess, writing. Office: Protos A Co 130-16 Francis Lewis Blvd Jamaica NY 11413-1841 Personal E-mail: jacobautie@aol.com.

GREENBERG, JERROLD, education educator; b. NYC, Feb. 20, 1947; s. Max and Ida (Myman) G.; m. Toby F. Block, Dec. 25, 1977; children: Mark E., Ann B., Simon M. BS in Chemistry, Bklyn. Coll., 1967; PhD in Biochemistry, Columbia U., 1975. Rsch. assoc. lab. molecular biology U. Wis., Madison, 1976-79, fellow in molecular genetics, 1977-78; vis. asst. prof. chemistry and biochemistry So. Ill. U., Carbondale, 1979-80; chmn. sci. div. Yeshiva HS, Atlanta, 1980—99, mem. organizing com. 11th biennial conf. chem. edn., 1990; vis. prof. chemistry Ga. Coll. and State U., Milledgeville, 2003—05; asst. prof. sci. dept. Ga. Perimeter Coll. Dunwoody

Campus, Atlanta, 2005—. Vis. asst. prof. Sch. Chemistry and Biochemistry, Ga. Inst. of Tech., Atlanta, 1992. Contbr. articles to profl. jours. Mem. Am. Soc. Microbiology, N.Y. Acad. Scis., Phi Lambda Upsilon. Achievements include research in theoretical and medical problems of antibiotic resistance.

GREENBERG, JERROLD SELIG, health education educator; b. NYC, Jan. 19, 1942; s. David and Bess G.; m. Karen Lider, Aug. 29, 1970; children: Todd, Keri. BS, CCNY, 1964, MS, 1965; EdD, Syracuse U., 1969. Tchr. N.Y.C. and Syracuse Pub. Sch. Dists., 1964-67; instr. Syracuse U., 1968-69; asst. prof. Boston U., 1969-71; prof. health edn. SUNY, Buffalo, 1971-79; prof. pub. and cmty. health U. Md., 1979—. Presenter in field. Author: Student Centered Health Instruction: A Humanistic Approach, 1978, Health Through Discovery, 1980, 1989, Sexuality Education: Theory and Practice, 1981, 2004, Comprehensive Stress Management, 1983, 2006, Sexuality: Insights and Issues, 1986, 1993, Physical Fitness: A Wellness Approach, 1986, 1989, Stress and Sexuality, 1987, Health Education: Learner-Centered Instructional Strategies, 1989, 1998, Coping With Stress: A Personal Guide, 1990, The College Student's Health Self-Care Diary, 1991, Exploring Health, 1992, Your Personal Stress Profile and Activity Workbook, 1992, 2006, The Health Education Ethics Book, 1992, The Caregiver's Guide, 1992, Holt Health, 1994, 1999, Physical Fitness and Wellness, 1995, 2004, Wellness: Creating a Life of Health and Fitness, 1997, The Code of Ethics for the Health Education Profession, 2001, Service Learning in Health Education, 2000, Dimensions of Human Sexuality, 2002, 2004, Health Education and Health Promotion: Learner-Centered Instructional Strategies, 2004. With U.S. Army, 1967. Grantee We. N.Y. chpt. Am. Heart Assn., 1977-78; Rsch. Found. of SUNY, 1979-80, Met. Life Found., 1985-86, Consumer Health Found., 2003. Fellow AAHPERD (Alliance scholar), Am. Sch. Health Assn. (Disting. Svc. award), mem. APHA, Am. Assn. for Health Edn. (Presdl. citation, Profl. Svc. to Health Edn. award, Scholar award), Soc. Pub. Health Edn., Eta Sigma Gamma (finalist Thomas Ehrlich Faculty award). Jewish. Home: 9412 Reach Rd Rockville MD 20854-2852 Business E-Mail: jerry@umd.edu.

GREENBERG, JERRY A., information technology executive; b. NJ; Degree in Econs., Harvard U. With Cambridge Technology Inc.; co-founder, co-chmn., co-CEO Sapient Corp., Cambridge, Mass., 1991—. Spkr. in field. Named one of Top 25 Most Influential Consultants, Consulting mag., 2005. Office: Sapient Corp 25 First St Cambridge MA 02141

GREENBERG, JOEL I., lawyer; BS, NYU, 1967; JD, Yale U., 1974. Bar: NY 1974. Ptnr., co-chair Corp. & Fin. Dept. Kaye Scholer LLP, NYC. Mem.: ABA, Assn. Bar of City NY. Office: Kaye Scholer LLP 425 Park Ave New York NY 10022 Office Phone: 212-836-8201. E-mail: jigreenberg@kayescholer.com.

GREENBERG, JOSHUA F., lawyer, educator; b. Bklyn., Feb. 27, 1933; s. Emil and Betty (Fierer) G.; m. Reva Frances Messeloff, June 28, 1959; children: Elizabeth, James, Anne. BA, Columbia U., 1954, LLB, 1956. Bar: N.Y. 1956. Assoc. firm Kaye, Scholer, Fierman, Hays & Handler, N.Y.C., 1956-65, ptnr., 1966-96; chmn. advanced antitrust workshop Practising Law Inst., N.Y.C., 1969-98; adj. prof. in residence Sch. Law Pace U., White Plains, N.Y., 1997-2000; dir. N.Y. Eye & Ear Infirmary, N.Y.C., 2000—. Adj. prof. NYU Law Sch., N.Y.C., 1970-87. Pres. Camp Ella Fohs, N.Y.C., 1965-85; trustee Beth Israel Med. Ctr., N.Y.C., 1986—; chmn. Mapplethorpe Residential Treatment Facility, 1995—. Recipient Disting. Trustee award United Hosp. Fund, 1998. Mem. ABA (council antitrust law sect. 1981-85), N.Y. State Bar Assn. (chmn. antitrust law sect. 1971) Jewish.

GREENBERG, JUDITH HOROVITZ, geneticist; b. Phila., Apr. 2, 1947; d. Monty B. and Evelyn (Cohen) Horovitz; m. Warren Greenberg, June 8, 1969; 1 child, Elyssa H. BS in Biology, U. Pitts., 1967; MA in Biology, Boston U., 1970; PhD in Biology, Bryn Mawr Coll., 1972. Rsch. assoc. ARC, Bethesda, Md., 1971—74; postdoctoral fellow NIH, Bethesda, 1974—75, sr. staff fellow, 1975—81, health scientist adminstr., 1981—88; dir. divsn. genetics and devel. biology NIH, Nat. Inst. Gen. Med. Scis., Bethesda, 1988—; acting dir. Nat. Inst. Gen. Med. Scis. NIH, Bethesda, 2002—03. Recipient Pub. Health Svc. Spl. Recognition award, 1991, Presdl. Meritorious Exec. award, 1999, NIH Dirs. award, 2004. Mem. Soc. Devel. Biology, Am. Soc. Cell Biology, Am. Soc. Human Genetics, AAAS, Sigma Xi. Office: NIGMS NIH 45 Center Dr Bldg 45 Bethesda MD 20892-6200 E-mail: greenbej@nigms.nih.gov.

GREENBERG, KAREN ALAINE, lawyer; b. St. Louis, Nov. 20, 1960; d. Burton Marvin and Phyllis Ann (Trugman) Greenberg; m. Andrew Feist Wasserman, Oct. 12, 1991. BA, Washington U., St. Louis, 1983; JD, St. Louis U., 1986. Bar: Mo. 1986, Ill. 1987, U.S. Dist. Ct. (ea. dist.) Mo. 1986, U.S. Dist. Ct. (so. dist.) Ill. 1987. Assoc. Portman, Edwards, Cooper and Singer, Clayton, Mo., 1986-88, Greenberg and Pleban, St. Louis, 1988-2000; atty. Law Offices of Karen A. Greenberg, 2000—. Trustee United Hebrew Congregation, St. Louis, 1994-97, 2003-; bd. dirs. Delcrest, St. Louis, 1994-98, Women's Self Help Ctr., St. Louis, 1994-98. Mem. ABA, Assn. Trial Lawyers Am., Ill. Bar Assn., Mo. Bar Assn., Met. St. Louis. Office Phone: 314-241-4141. E-mail: kgreenberg@sbcglobal.net.

GREENBERG, KAREN K., lawyer; b. Boston, Apr. 28, 1950; d. Arthur and Dorothy (Sheinfeld) Konowitz; m. Benjamin Greenberg, July 23, 1972; children: Jed, Jenna Rose. BS in Edn., Boston U., 1972; MS in Edn., Wheelock Coll., Boston, 1979; JD, Suffolk U., 1983. Bar: Mass. 1983, U.S. Ct. Appeals 1984, U.S. Dist. Ct. 1984. Tchr. Quincy (Mass.) Pub. Schs., 1973-80; assoc. Law Firm of Steven Konowitz, Needham, Mass., 1983-88; ptnr. Konowitz & Greenberg, Needham, 1988—. Mem. hearing com. Mass. Bd. Bar Overseers, Boston, 1990-97. Mem. town meeting Town of Natick, Mass.; trustee, chmn. pers. Temple Israel, Natick, 1993—; mem. ethics com. Faulkner Ctr. for Reproductive Medicine, Boston, 1995—. Mem. Am. Acad. Adoption Attys., Jewish Women Internat. (connect card listing mem. 1989—), Women's Bar Assn. Avocations: personal fitness, reading. Office: Konowitz & Greenberg 210 Cedar St Wellesley Hills MA 02481-5435

GREENBERG, LENORE, public relations professional; b. Flushing, N.Y. d. Jack and Frances Orenstein. BA, Hofstra U.; MS, SUNY. Dir. pub. rels. Bloomingdale's, Short Hills, N.J., 1977-78; dir. comms. N.J. Sch. Bds. Assn., Trenton, 1978-82; dir pub. info. N.J. State Dept. Edn., Trenton, 1982-90; assoc. exec. dir. Nat. Sch. Pub. Rels. Assn., Arlington, Va., 1990-91; pres. Lenore Greenberg & Assocs., Inc., 1991—. Adj. prof. pub. rels. Rutgers U. Freelance feature writer N.Y. Times. Mem. bd. assocs. McCarter Theatre, Princeton, N.J.; mem. Franklin Twp. Zoning Bd. Adjustment; mem. Franklin Twp. Human Rels. Commn.; chair Somerset County LWV; instr. Bus. Vols. for the Arts. Recipient award Am. Soc. Assn. Execs., award Women in Comms., award Internat. Assn. Bus. Communicators; Gold Medallion awrd Nat. Sch. Pub. Rels. Assn. Mem. Pub. Rels. Soc. Am. (accredited; pres. N.J. State chpt., nat. nominating and accreditation coms., Silver Anvil award), Nat. Health/Edn. Consortium. Home and Office: 30971 Carrara Rd Laguna Niguel CA 92677-2757

GREENBERG, LON RICHARD, energy executive, lawyer; b. N.Y.C., Sept. 4, 1950; s. Ralph Austin and Miriam (Kenner) G.; m. Bonnie Small, June 25, 1972; children: Jody B. Scott B., Daniel A. BS, U. Pa., 1972; JD, Villanova U., 1975; postgrad., Harvard U., Boston, 1994. Bar: Pa. 1975. Law clk. to Hon. J. Sydney Hoffman, Superior Ct. Pa., Phila., 1975-76; assoc. Morgan, Lewis & Bockius, Phila., 1976-80; corp. devel. counsel UGI Corp., Valley Forge, Pa., 1980-82, corp. sec., 1982-87, v.p., gen. counsel, 1983-87, v.p. legal and corp. devel., 1987-89, sr. v.p. legal and corp. devel., 1989-94, pres., 1994-95, pres., CEO, 1995-96, chmn., pres., CEO, 1996—2005, chmn., CEO, 2005—, also bd. dirs. Bd. dirs. AmeriGas Propane, Inc., chmn., CEO, 1996—; bd. dirs. World LP Gas Assn.; former mem. bd. dirs. Mellon PSFS, Phila. Bd. dirs., mem. fin. com., chmn. investment com., mem. nominating com. Reading Is Fundamental, Washington, 1995—; mem. policy com., treas. Pa. Bus. Roundtable, Harrisburg, 1995—2005, chmn., 2005—; former mem. bd. trustees Chestnut Hill Healthcare; former mem. nat. indsl. adv. coun. Industrialization Ctrs. Am.; former mem. task force com. United Way Leadership Giving Southeastern Pa., Phila.; mem. bd. dirs. United Way Southeastern Pa., Phila.; mem., coach Chestnut Hill Fathers Club, Phila.; adv. bd. Ea. Pa. chpt. Arthritis Found.; bd. dir. Greater Phila. (Pa.) C. of C., CEO Coun. on Growth. Recipient Good Samaritan award N.W. Victim Svcs., 1994, Disting. Svc. award Chestnut Hill Cmty. Assn., 1994. Mem.: ABA, Pa. Bar Assn. Avocations: swimming, tennis, golf, family activities. Office: UGI Corp 460 N Gulph Rd King Of Prussia PA 19406*

GREENBERG, MAURICE RAYMOND (HANK GREENBERG), retired insurance company executive; b. NYC, May 4, 1925; s. Jacob and Ada (Rheingold) G.; m. Corinne Phyllis Zuckerman, Nov. 12, 1950; children: Jeffrey W., Evan G., L. Scott, Cathleen J. Pre-law cert., U. Miami, Fla., 1948; LLB, N.Y. Law Sch., 1950, also JD (hon.); JD (hon.), New Eng. Sch. Law, 1970, Bryant Coll., Middlebury Coll., Brown U., Pace U. Bar: NY 1953. With Continental Casualty Co., 1952-60, Am. Internat. Group Inc., NYC, 1960—2005, pres. subs. Am. Home Assurance Co., 1962-67, pres., CEO, 1967—89, chmn. bd., CEO, 1989—2005, non-exec. chmn., 2005; v.p. C.V. Starr & Co., NYC, 1960—65, dir., 1965—68, pres., CEO, 1968—2005, chmn., CEO, 2005—. Mem. Bus. Roundtable, pres.'s adv. com. Trade Policy and Negotiations; vice-chmn. Ctr. for Strategic and Internat. Studies; chmn. US-China Bus. Coun., US-Korea Bus. Coun., US-ASEAN Bus. Coun.; hon. vice-chmn. Coun. on Fgn. Rels.; founding chmn. US-Philippine Bus. Com.; former chmn., dep. chmn., dir. Fed. Res. Bank NY. Bd. govs. NY Hosp.; mem. Pres.'s adv. com. on trade negotiations Ctr. for Strategic and Internat. Studies, mem. bus. roundtable; chmn. emeritus NY Presbyn. Hosp., 1995, NY Presbyn. Hosp. Found. Inc.; mem. bd. overseers Weill Med. Sch. Cornell U.; trustee Am. Mus. Nat. History; trustee emeritus Rockefeller U.; life trustee NYU; trustee Sch. Risk Mgmt., Ins., Actuarial Sci.; hon. trustee Mus. Modern Art; chmn. Acad. Medicine Devel. Co.; bd. dirs. Internat. Rescue Com. Capt. US Army, ETO, Korea. Decorated Bronze Star. Mem. NY Bar Assn., The Asia Soc. (chmn.), Police Athletic League, Lotos Club, Harmonie Club. Office Phone: 212-759-5999. Business E-Mail: maurice.greenberg@cvstarrco.com.

GREENBERG, MICHAEL HOWARD, lawyer; b. Bklyn., Aug. 3, 1933; s. Joseph and Lillian (Newman) G.; m. Eulalia Virgili Elias, June 11, 1960; children: Peter E., Edward L. BS magna cum laude, Cornell U., 1955; JD magna cum laude, Harvard U., 1958; student, Institut de Droit Comparé, Luxembourg, 1959. Clk. to Hon. Charles M. Metzner U.S. Dist. Ct. (So. Dist.) N.Y., 1959-60; from assoc. to ptnr. Graubard Moskovitz et al, N.Y.C., 1960-88; of counsel Sharretts Paley Carter & Blauvelt, P.C., N.Y.C., 1989-92. Chair Bi-national Art 19 Panel, U.S.-Can. Free Trade Agreement, 1992; corp. sec. Spain-U.S. C. of C. Editor Harvard Law Rev., 1956-58; contbr. articles to profl. jours. Committeeman, Democratic Party, Nassau County, N.Y., 1973-92. Mem. ABA, N.Y. County Lawyers Assn. Avocations: gardening, tennis. Home: 239 E 79th St Apt 13P New York NY 10021-0816 Office: 37 Madison Ave Ste 2310 New York NY 10017-5202

GREENBERG, MICHAEL JAY, accountant; b. Buffalo, Apr. 17, 1958; s. Melvin J. and Anna C. (Pavlakis) G.; m. Christa M. Rao, May 14, 1983; 1 child, Mary J. BS in Acctg., Canisius Coll., 1980. Staff acct. Seligman Sunshine & Co., CPA's, Amherst, N.Y., 1979-81; acctg. supr. City Mattress, Inc., Amherst, 1981-83; pres., owner, mng. ptnr. M. Greenberg and Assocs., Inc. Acctg., Bookkeeping, Tax Svc., North Tonawanda, NY, 1988—; controller Savage Litho Co., Buffalo, 1983-86; CFO Avinda Video Inc., Amherst, 1986-88. Mem. Internat. Assn. Approved Basketball Officials, 1978—, audit com. Hellenic Greek Orthodox Ch., 1984-88, 96-99. Mem. Region 3 Jr. Coll. Ofcls. Assn. Republican. Avocations: sports activities, reading, travel. Home: 113 Maplegrove Ave Tonawanda NY 14150-9148 Office: Ste 111 1089 Kinkead Ave North Tonawanda NY 14120-2840 Personal E-mail: mgreen13@yahoo.com.

GREENBERG, MICHAEL RICHARD, urban studies and community health educator; b. N.Y.C., Aug. 22, 1943; s. Sidney Saul and Mildred (Saletra) Greenberg; m. Gwendolyn Barker, Jan. 19, 1978; children: Seana Pappas, Heather Wilkerson, Joshua Suggs, Alexandra Greenberg. BA, CUNY, 1965; MA, Columbia U., 1966, PhD, 1969. Asst. prof. Columbia U., N.Y.C., 1969-71; assoc. prof. Rutgers U., New Brunswick, NJ, 1971-73, prof., 1973-78, disting. prof., 1978-82, prof. urban studies and cmty. health, 1982—, assoc. dean faculty, 2000—. Co-dir. pub. health N.J. Grad. Progam in Pub. Health, New Brunswick, 1983—. Author: Urbanization and Cancer Mortality, 1983, Public Health and the Environment, 1988, Environmental Risk and the Press, 1989 (award 1988), Environmental Reporter's Handbook (award 1989), Environmentally Devastated Neighborhoods, 1996, Restoring America's Neighborhoods, 1999. Recipient Spl. Merit award, EPA, 1977, Dennis Sullivan award, Pub. Health Assn., 2001. Mem. APHA, Assn. of Am. Geographers (Disting. Scholars award 1997 Disting. Achievement award 2003), Soc. for Risk Analysis. Avocation: walking. Office: Rutgers U Dept Urban Studies Civic Sq Bldg 33 Livingston Ave Ste 100 New Brunswick NJ 08901-1900 E-mail: mrg@rci.rutgers.edu.

GREENBERG, MILTON, political science professor; b. Bklyn., Feb. 20, 1927; s. Samuel and Fannie (Schnell) G.; m. Sonia B. Brown, June 20, 1948; children: Anne Greenberg Bookin, Nancy R. BA, Bklyn. Coll., 1949; MA, U. Wis., 1950, PhD (univ. scholar), 1955; LLD (hon.), Am. U., 1993. Instr. polit. sci. U. Tenn., Knoxville, 1952-55; from asst. prof. to prof. Western Mich. U., Kalamazoo, 1955-64, chmn. polit. sci. dept., 1965-69; dean Coll. Arts and Scis., Ill. State U., Normal, 1969-72; v.p. acad. affairs, dean faculties Roosevelt U., Chgo., 1972-80; provost, v.p. acad. affairs Am. U., Washington, 1980-93, prof. govt., 1980-97, interim pres., provost, 1990-91, prof. emeritus, 1997—; freelance writer, 1993—. Rsch. assoc. Cleve. Met. Svcs. Commn., 1957; cons. Citizens for Mich. (constl. reform movement), 1960; cons. Supreme Ct. Hist. Soc., 1997—, Coun. for Higher Edn. Accreditation, 1997—. Author: (companion book to PBS show) The GI Bill: The Law That Changed America, 1997, (with J.C. Plano) The American Political Dictionary, 1962, 11th edit., 2002; (with others) The Poltical Science Dictionary, 1973; contbr. to Collier's Yearbook, 1959-93, Chronicle of Higher Education Career Network, 1999-; mem. editl. bd. Ednl. Record, 1985-97, guest editor, 1994; cons. editor ASHE-ERIC Higher Edn. Reports, 1986-90; contbr. articles to profl. jours., mags. and newspapers. Mem. Mich. Gov.'s Commn. on Legis. Apportionment, 1962, Kalamazoo Community Rels. Bd., 1964-65; mem. bd. dirs. Combined Health Appeal of Nat. Capital Area, 1982-93, v.p., 1983-85, pres., 1986-88. Social Sci. Rsch. Coun. grantee, 1959, 61. Mem. AAUP, Am. Polit. Sci. Assn., Midwest Polit. Sci. Assn. (exec. coun. 1972-75), Mid. States Assn. Colls. and Schs. (cons.-evaluator 1983-97), Law and Soc. Assn., Am. Assn. Higher Edn. (vis. scholar 1994, 2004), North Ctrl. Assn. Colls. and Schs. (commn. on instns. higher edn. 1975-80, exec. bd. 1979-80, cons.-evaluator 1975-80), Nat. Coun. Chief Acad. Officers, Am. Coun. on Edn. (exec.com. 1983-85, chmn. 1985). Office: Am U 4400 Massachusetts Ave NW Washington DC 20016-8022 E-mail: mgreenb@american.edu.

GREENBERG, MORTON IRA, federal judge; b. Phila., Pa., Mar. 20, 1933; s. Harry Arnold and Pauline (Hofkin) Greenberg; m. Barbara-Ann Kissel, May 29, 1987; children from previous marriage: Elizabeth, Suzanne, Lawrence. AB, U. Pa., 1954; LLB, Yale U., 1957. Bar: N.J. 1958, U.S. Dist. Ct. N.J. 1958, U.S. Ct. Appeals (3d cir.) 1972, U.S. Supreme Ct. 1973. Law clk.office of atty. gen. State of NJ, Trenton, NJ, 1957—58, dep. atty. gen., 1958—60, asst. atty. gen., 1971—73; pvt. practice Cape May, 1960—71; judge law div. Superior Ct. NJ, New Brunswick, 1973—76, judge chancery and gen. equity divs. Trenton, 1976—80, judge appellate div., 1980—87; judge US Ct. Appeals (3d cir.), Trenton and Phila., 1987—2000, sr. judge, 2000—. Office: US Ct Appeals US Courthouse Rm 219 402 E State St Trenton NJ 08608-1507*

GREENBERG, MORTON PAUL, lawyer, consultant, life settlement broker; b. Fall River, Mass., June 2, 1946; s. Harry and Sylvia Shirley (Davis) Greenberg; m. Louise Beryl Schindler, Jan. 24, 1970; 1 child, Alexis Lynn. BSBA, NYU, 1968; JD, Bklyn. Law Sch., 1971. Bar: N.Y. 1972; CLU Am. Coll., 1975. Atty. Hanner, Fitzmaurice & Onorato, N.Y.C., 1971—72; dir., counsel, cons. on advanced underwriting The Mfrs. Life Ins. Co., Toronto, 1972—98; mng. gen. agt. for life settlements Viaticus, Inc., Chgo., 1999—2001; prin. life settlement broker Parker, Co., 1998—. Mem. sales ideas com. Million Dollar Roundtable, Chgo., 1982—83, 4th ann. George M. Graves meml. lectr., 1991; mem. adv. bd. Keeping Current, 1999—; spkr. on law, tax, life settlements, and advanced underwriting various profl. groups. Contbr. articles to profl. jours.; author: (tech. jour.) ManuBriefs. Mem.: ABA, Soc. Fin. Svcs. Profls., Nat. Assn. Ins. and Fin. Advisors, Internat. Platform Assn., Assn. for Advanced Life Underwriting (mem. bus. ins. and estate planning steering com. 1989—93), N.Y. State Bar Assn., Stern Sch. Bus. Alumni Assn., NYU Alumni Assn. Office: PO Box 183 7617 E Sunrise Trail Parker CO 80134-6915 Office Phone: 303-841-0891. Personal E-mail: mpgjd@aol.com.

GREENBERG, MYRON SILVER, lawyer; b. L.A., Oct. 17, 1945; s. Earl W. and Geri (Silver) G.; m. Shlomit Gross; children: David, Amy, Sophie, Benjamin. BSBA, UCLA, 1967; JD, 1970. Bar: Calif., 1971, U.S. Dist. Ct. (middle dist.) Calif. 1971, U.S. Tax Ct. 1977; cert. splst. in taxation law bd. legal specialization State Bar Calif.; CPA, Calif. Staff acct. Touche Ross & Co., L.A., 1970-71; assoc. Kaplan, Livingston, Goodwin, Berkowitz, & Selvin, Beverly Hills, Calif., 1971-74; ptnr. Steefel, Levitt, & Weiss, 1975—82, Myron S. Greenberg, a Profl. Corp., Larkspur, Calif., 1982—. Professorial lectr. tax. Golden Gate U.; instr. U. Calif., Berkeley, 1989-2003. Author: California Attorney's Guide to Professional Corporations, 1977, 79; bd. editors UCLA Law Rev., 1969-70. Mem. San Anselmo Planning Commn., 1976-77; mem. adv. bd. cert. program personal fin. planning U. Calif., Berkeley, 1991-2003; bd. dirs. Marin County Estate Planning Coun., 2001—, pres., 2004. Mem.: ABA, AHA (bd. dirs. Marin county chpt. 1984—90, pres. 1988—89), Calif. Bd. Legal Specialization (mem. tax commn. 1998—2001, chmn. 2001, bd. dirs. 2003—, vice chair bd. 2005—), Real Estate Tax Inst. Calif. Cont. Edn. Bar (planning com.), Marin County (Calif.) Bar Assn. (bd. dirs. 1994—2001, pres. 1999), L.A. County Bar Assn., Larkspur C. of C. (bd. dirs. 1985—87). Democrat. Jewish. Office: # 205 700 Larkspur Landing Cir Larkspur CA 94939-1711 Office Phone: 415-461-5844. Business E-Mail: msg@eplaw.com.

GREENBERG, NATHAN, accountant; b. Worcester, Mass., May 17, 1919; s. Samuel and Ida (Katz) G.; m. Mimi Aaron, Mar. 12, 1950 (dec.); children: Henry Aaron, Ruthanne; m. Barbara Rudnick, Feb. 9, 1979. BS in Bus. Adminstrn, Boston U., 1942. CPA, Mass. With IRS, 1945-47; v.p. finance, dir. Gt. Am. Plastics Co., Fitchburg, Mass., 1948-68, Gt. Am. Chem. Corp., Fitchburg, 1968-80; founder Greenberg, Rosenblatt, Kull & Bitsoli, P.C., Worcester, 1958—. Bd. dirs. Xsirius, Inc., Kleinert's, Inc. Trustee Nathan and Barbara Greenberg Charitable Trust, Jewish Home for Aged, Jewish Community Center, Jewish Fedn. Served with AUS, 1942-45, ETO. Decorated Bronze Star. Fellow AICPA, Mass. Soc. CPA's, Fla. Soc. CPA's, Controllers Inst. Am.; mem. Mu Sigma. Home: 19 Sloans Curve Dr Palm Beach FL 33480 Office: The Day Bldg 306 Main St Worcester MA 01608-1550 Office Phone: 508-791-0901.

GREENBERG, OSCAR WALLACE, physicist, researcher; b. N.Y.C., Feb. 18, 1932; s. Joseph Jacob and Betty Greenberg; m. Yael Shapiro, May 27, 1969 (div. Apr. 1997); children: Joshua Daniel, Jeremy Hillel, Benjamin Gideon; m. Pearl Katz, June 27, 1999. BS, Rutgers U., 1952; A.M., Princeton U., 1954, PhD, 1957. Instr. Brandeis U., 1956-57; NSF postdoctoral fellow MIT, 1959-61; mem. faculty U. Md., College Park, 1961—, prof. physics, 1967—. Mem. Inst. Advanced Study, 1964-65; vis. assoc. prof. Rockefeller U., 1965-66; vis. prof. Tel-Aviv U., 1968-69, Johns Hopkins U., fall, 1977, NASA/Goddard Space Flight Center, spring 1978; vis. scientist Fermilab, 1984-85; vis. scholar U. Chgo., 1984-85 Divisional assoc. editor: Phys. Rev. Letters, 1976-78. Served to 1st lt. USAF, 1957-59. Recipient award in phys. scis. Washington Acad. Scis., 1971; Sloan research fellow, 1964-66; Guggenheim fellow, 1968-69 Fellow Am. Phys. Soc. Home: 9404 Saint Andrews Way Silver Spring MD 20901-4859 Office: Univ Md Dept Physics College Park MD 20742-4111 Office Phone: 301-405-6014. Business E-Mail: owgreen@physics.umd.edu.

GREENBERG, PAUL, editor; b. Shreveport, La., Jan. 21, 1937; s. Ben and Sarah (Ackerman) G.; m. Carolyn Levy, Dec. 6, 1964; children: Daniel, Ruth Elizabeth. B. Journalism, U. Mo., 1958, MA in History, 1959; student, Columbia Grad. Sch., 1960-62; LittD, Rhodes Coll., 1995. Lectr. Am. history Hunter Coll., 1962; editorial page editor Pine Bluff (Ark.) Comml., 1962-66, 67-92; syndicated columnist, 1970—; editorial page editor Ark. Dem. Gazette, Little Rock, 1992—. Editl. writer Chgo. Daily News, 1966-67; adj. faculty history U. Ark., Pine Bluff, 1978-82, vis. Fulbright fellow, 1985, mem. faculty in journalism, 1991; commentator BBC, 2004; media fellow Hoover Inst., 2005. Author: Resonant Lives, 1991, Entirely Personal, 1992, No Surprises, 1996, To Life, 1999. Served to capt. U.S. Army, 1969. Recipient Grenville Clark award for best editl., 1964, Pulitzer prize editl. writing, 1969, award Nat. Newspaper Assn., 1968, U. Mo. Sch. Journalism award, 1983, Walker Stone award for editl. writing, 1985, 86, Pulitzer Prize finalist for editl. writing, 1986, H.L. Mencken Writing award, 1987, William Allen White Journalism award U. Kans., 1988, Green Eyeshade award, 1997, 2005, Katie award Dallas Press Club, 1999, 2000, Carmage Walls award, 2003. Jewish. Office: Arkansas Democrat Gazette Capitol at Scott Little Rock AR 72202

GREENBERG, RAYMOND SETH, academic administrator, educator, health facility administrator; b. Chapel Hill, N.C., Aug. 10, 1955; s. Bernard George and Ruth Esther (Marck) G.; m. Leah Daniella Dacus, Oct. 23, 1988. BA in Chemistry, U. N.C., 1976, PhD in Epidemiology, 1983; MD, Duke U., 1979; MPH, Harvard U., 1980; DMS (hon.), The Citadel, 2001; DS (hon.), Simpson Coll., 2002. Asst. prof. sch. medicine Emory U., Atlanta, 1983-86, assoc. prof., 1986-90, dep. dir. Winship Cancer Ctr., 1985-90, chair epidemiology/ biostat., 1988-90, prof., dean sch. pub. health, 1990-95; v.p. for acad. affairs, provost Med. U. SC, Charleston, 1995-99, pres., 2000—. Chair preventive medicine Nat. Bd. Med. Examiners, Phila., 1991-93; chair epidemiology study sect. NIH, Bethesda, Md., 1992-94; bd. sci. counselors Nat. Inst. for Dental and Craniofacial Rsch., Bethesda, 1994-99, mem. blue ribbon panel on rsch. tng. and career devel., 1999; chair adv. coun. Prudential Ctr. for Health Care Rsch., Atlanta, 1994-96; chair Harvard Adv. Com. on Electromagnetic Fields and Human Health, Boston, 1994-98; adv. com. on rsch. and med. grants, Am. Cancer Soc., Atlanta, 1994-96; breast and cervical cancer early detection and control adv. com., Ctrs. for Disease Control and Prevention, Atlanta, 1996-2000; adv. com. on agrl. health risks, Harvard Ctr. for Risk Analysis, Boston, 1996-99; clin. adv. bd. Deloitte and Touche Healthcare Consulting Group, 1997-99; chair sci. adv. panel 3M Corp., 1998-2002; chair bd. trustees S.C. Gov.'s Sch. Sci. and Math., 2004—. Author: Medical Epidemiology, 1993, 4th edit., 2005, Epidemiologia Medica, 1995, 3d edit., 2004; contbr. articles to profl. jours. Bd. dirs. Ga. divsn. Am. Cancer Soc., 1987-93, Carolina Art Assn., 1996-98, Trident United Way, 1999-2002; bd. sci. counselors Nat. Ctr. Health Stat., 2004—. Recipient SC Order of Palmetto, 2005. Fellow Am. Coll. Epidemiology (pres. 1990-91); mem. APHA, Am. Epidemiology Soc., SC Order of Palmetto. Democrat. Jewish. Office: Med Univ SC Rm 101 135 Cannon St PO Box 250001 Charleston SC 29425 Office Phone: 843-792-9005. Business E-Mail: greenber@musc.edu.

GREENBERG, RICHARD T., lawyer; b. Bklyn., June 10, 1952; s. Melvin David and Dolores Ruth (Siegartd) Greenberg; m. Penny W. Cutler; children: Brett, Matthew, Jodi. BA with distinction, Northwestern U., 1974; JD, NYU, 1977. Bar: Ill. 1977, US Dist. Ct. No. Dist. Ill. 1977, US Ct. Appeals 7th Cir. 1982. From assoc. to ptnr. Peters & Ross, Chgo., 1977-87; ptnr. McCullough, Campbell & Lane, Chgo., 1987-96, Ross & Hardies, Chgo., 1996—2003, McGuireWoods LLP, Chgo., 2003—, mng. ptnr. Chgo. office, 2005—. Bd. dirs. Temple B'nai Torah, Highland Park, Ill., 1995—. Mem. ABA, Ill. Bar Assn., Chgo. Bar Assn. Avocations: reading, politics, running. Office: McGuireWoods LLP Ste 4100 77 W Wacker Dr Chicago IL 60601-1815 Office Phone: 312-750-5755. Office Fax: 312-558-4377. Business E-Mail: rgreenberg@mcguirewoods.com.

GREENBERG, ROBERT Y., semiconductor company executive; BSEE, BSCE, U. Mich. Elec. engring. positions Floating Point Sys., Inc., Sperry Corp.; sys. developer Integrated Measurement Sys., Inc., 1987—88; sys. designer InFocus Sys., 1988—96; co-founder, v.p., product devel. and customer support Pixelworks, Inc., Tualatin, Oreg., 1997, sr. v.p., CTO. Office: Pixelworks Inc Ste 300 8100 SW Nyberg Rd Tualatin OR 97062

GREENBERG, RONALD DAVID, lawyer, educator; b. San Antonio, Sept. 9, 1939; s. Benjamin and Sylvia (Ghetlzer) G. BS, U. Tex., 1957; MBA, Harvard U., 1961, JD, 1964. Bar: N.Y., 1966, U.S. Dist. Ct. (ea. and so. dists.) N.Y. 1970, U.S. Ct. Appeals (2d cir.) 1975, U.S. Supreme Ct. 1975. Engring. lab. instr. U. Tex., 1957; engr. Redstone Arsenal, Army Ballistic Missile Agy., 1957; engr., bus. analyst Exxon Corp., N.Y.C., 1957-64; rsch. asst. Harvard Bus. Sch.; with Smithsonian Astrophys. Observatory and Ednl. Testing Svc., N.J., 1961-62; atty., engr. Allied Corp., N.Y.C., 1964-67; assoc. Arthur, Dry, Kalish, Taylor & Wood, N.Y.C., 1967-69, Valicenti, Leighton, Reid & Pine, N.Y.C., 1969-70; instr. faculty Columbia U., N.Y.C., 1972-81, adj. prof. bus. law and taxation, 1970-71, 82-98; of counsel Delson & Gordon, N.Y.C., 1973-87; sole practitioner Harrison, N.Y., 1988—. Lectr., cons. AICPA, Inst. Internal Auditors, New Haven C. of C., Citibank, Mfrs. Hanover Trust Co., Harcourt, Brace, Jovanovich, Inc., Prudential-Bache, Drexel, Burnham & Lambert, E.F. Hutton; vol. instr. vol. income tax program, Columbia U., N.Y.C., 1991-92; vis. prof. Stanford U., Palo Alto, Calif., 1978, Harvard U., Boston, 1981; adv. bd. Am. Law Rev, 2004— Author: Business Income Tax Materials, 1994; (with others) Business Organizations: Corporations, General Practice in New York, 1998, Business/Corporate Law and Practice, 5th edit., 2004; editor: The Compleat Lawyer, 1985-88, Tax Lawyer, 1982-95; editor in chief NY Internat. Law Rev., 1988-91, chair adv. bd., 1992—; editor in chief Internat. Law Practicum, 1987-91; contbr. chpts. to books, articles to profl. jours. Cons. coun. City of N.Y., 1971-72, Manhattan C.C., 1974-76. Lt. USNR, 1957-59. Recipient Outstanding Prof. award Columbia U. Grad. Sch. Bus., 1973, MIT fellow Mech. Engring. Dept., 1959, Harvard U., Teagle Found., 1959-61; grantee Ford Found., 1977, Columbia U. Ctr. Internat. Studies, Sch. Internat. Pub. Affairs, 1992, Columbia Bus. Sch., 1976, 92-94. Mem. AAAS, ABA (chmn. com. on taxation gen. practice sect. 1978-83, chmn. com. on corp. banking and bus. law. gen. practice sect. 1985-87, moderator, chair profl. edn. programs 1986, 87), ASME, NSPE, N.Y. State Bar Assn. (gen. practice sect., chmn. tax law com. 1983-92, chmn. bus. law com. 1985-88, internat. law & practice sect., chmn. pubs. com. 1988-91, coord. study com. on med. malpractice legislation, 1980-82), Assn. Bar City N.Y., N.Y. Acad. Scis., Mensa, Tau Beta Pi, Pi Tau Sigma, Phi Eta Sigma, Am. Assn. for the Advancement of Sci. Achievements include adv. bd., American Law Rev.(Law Press China), 2004-. E-mail: rdgreenberg@hotmail.com.

GREENBERG, ROSALIE, child psychiatrist; b. Bklyn., Dec. 21, 1950; d. Sam and Molly G.; BA, NYU, 1972; student Upstate Med. Ctr., Syracuse, 1972-73; MD, Columbia U., 1976. Intern Overlook Hosp., Summit, N.J., 1976-77; resident in gen. psychiatry Columbia Presbyn. Med. Ctr., N.Y. State Psychiatric Inst., N.Y.C., 1977-80, fellow in child and adolescent psychiatry, 1979-81, dep. dir. pediatric psychiatry outpatient clinic, 1981-82; dir. child and adolescent outpatient services Fair Oaks Hosp., Summit, N.J., 1982—; instr. Columbia U., 1981—. Mem. Am. Psychiat. Assn., Am. Acad. Child and Adolescent Psychiatry, AMA. Office: Fair Oaks Hosp 19 Prospect St Summit NJ 07901-2531

GREENBERG, SHOSHANA (SHIRLEY E. GREENBERG), artist; b. N.Y.C., Feb. 28, 1926; d. Alexander and Bessie (Fleischman) Singer; m. Arnold E. Greenberg, Aug. 2, 1952; children: Noah J., Seth M. BFA with Distinction, Calif. Coll. of Arts/Crafts, Oakland, 1972, MFA with highest distinction, 1979. Exhbns. include: A Mosaic of Jewish Experience, 1991, Jewish Community Mus., San Francisco, 1989, 1991, Jewish Comm. Libr., San Francisco, 1990, Judah L. Magnes Mus., Berkeley, 1986-87, Skirball Mus., L.A., 1985, Judah Magnes Mus., Berkeley, Calif., 1983, 1993 (Max and Sophie Adler award), Nat. Jewish Mus., Washington, 1996, numerous others; contbr. to art catalogs, including Forms for Faith, 1986-87, Location/Dislocation, 1980; contbr. profl. jours. and publs. Mem. Jewish Arts Community of the Bay (founding mem., pres. 1989-93). Home: 1816 Virginia St Berkeley CA 94703-1325

GREENBERG, STEVEN M., physician; b. N.Y.C., N.Y., June 26, 1956; s. Nathan and Jean Greenberg; m. Elizabeth Anne Altanasio, June 6, 1999; children: Aaron, Adam, Lauren. BS, SUNY, 1977; MD, Albany Med. Coll., 1983. Lic. N.Y., 1984, cert. diplomate Nat. Bd. Med. Examiners, 1983, Am. Bd. Internal Medicine, 1986, Am. Bd. Internal Medicine Subspecialty in Cardiovasc. Disease, 1989. Intern, resident internal medicine Bronx Med. Hosp. and Hosp. of Albert Einstein Coll. of Medicine, 1983—86; dir. clin. evaluation unit Weiler Hosp. of Albert Einstein Coll. of Medicine, Bronx, 1986, asst. attending physician, 1986; rsch. fellow cardiology Albert Einstein Coll. of Medicine, Bronx, 1986—87; asst. attending physician Queens Hosp. Ctr., 1986—89, Bronx Mcpl. Hosp. Ctr., 1986—90; fellow cardiology Mt. Sinai Hosp., N.Y.C., 1987—90, attending physician NY, 1989—90, St. Francis Hosp., Roslyn, NY, 1990—, coord., pacemaker ctr., 1991, dir. CCU, 1994—. Co-author articles in numerous profl. jours. Fellow: Am. Coll. Physicians, Am. Coll. Cardiology. Avocations: kayaking, coin collecting/numismatics. Office: St Francis Hosp 100 Pt Washington Blvd Roslyn NY 11576

GREENBERG, STEVEN MOREY, lawyer; b. Jersey City, Apr. 9, 1949; s. Joseph and Rhoda (Weisenfeld) Greenberg. AB cum laude, Syracuse U., 1971; JD, U. Pa., 1974. Bar: N.J. 1974, U.S. Dist. Ct. N.J. 1974, N.Y. 1980, U.S. Dist. Ct. (so. and ea. dists.) N.Y. 1986, U.S. Ct. Appeals (3d cir.) 1987, U.S. Ct. Fed. Claims 1989. Assoc. Carpenter, Bennett & Morrissey, Newark, 1974—77, Cole, Berman & Belsky, Rochelle Park, NJ, 1977-79; pvt. practice Hackensack, NJ, 1979—94; atty. Bergenfield (N.J.) Rent Leveling Bd., 1985-89, 92-93, 99, Bergenfield Planning Bd., 1993-96; ptnr. Greenberg & Marmorstein, Hackensack, 1994-97, Greenberg & Lanz, Hackensack, 1997—. Numerous offices Jewish Ctr. Teaneck, NJ, 1978—, Jewish Home and Rehab. Ctr., Jersey City, River Vale, NJ, 1982—; active United Jewish Appeal Fedn., Bergen County, N. Hudson, 1997—2004, com. mem. Jewish Family Svc. Inc., Rockleigh, NJ, 1986—96; v.p. Jewish Home, 2003—; treas. UJA Fedn. No. N.J., 2004—05, bd. trustees, 2004—, campaign chair, 2004—05; pres. Jewish Inst. Bioethics, NYC, 1998—2004, bd. dirs., 1998—; trustee Jewish Assn. Devel. Disabilities, 1999—, Bergen County HS Jewish Studies, 2000—; active Jewish Cmty. Rels. Coun. No. N.J., 1986—93, 1999—; trustee Assn. Jewish Fedns., NJ, 2002—03, exec., ops. com., 2002—03; governing body Jewish Home Found. North Jersey, Inc., NJ, 2003—, sec., 2005—; dir. Union Traditional Judaism, 1993—97; active Jewish Family Svc., Inc., 1986—96, 2005—; NJ regional adv. bd. Anti-Defamation League, 1989—, exec. com., 1989—; v.p. UJA Fedn. No. N.J., 2005—; active N.J. Leadership Think Tank The Allen and Joan Bildner Ctr. Study of Jewish Life Rutgers U., 2001—. Recipient Second Century award, Jewish Theol. Sem. Am., 1988, Cmty. Svc. award, Friends Lubavitch, 1997, Jewish Ctr. Teaneck award, 1997, Ma'Ayanot Yeshiva HS Girls award, 2001, Americanism award, Anti-Defamation League, 2003, Gates of Jerusalem award, Boys Town Jerusalem, 2004. Mem.: ABA, N.Y. State Bar Assn., Bergen County Bar Assn., N.J. Bar Assn., Pi Sigma Alpha, Phi Kappa Phi. Home: 96 Westminster Ave Bergenfield NJ 07621-3916 Office: 2 University Plz Hackensack NJ 07601-6202 Office Phone: 201-487-7755. Business E-Mail: smg@greenberglanz.com.

GREENBERG, WILLIAM MICHAEL, psychiatrist; b. Bklyn., Oct. 19, 1946; s. Benjamin Greenberg and Marilyn (Berger) Hamberg; m. Wendy Faith Megerman, June 14, 1992. BA, Queens Coll., 1968; postgrad., U. Medicine & Dentistry N.J., 1974—76; MD, Albert Einstein Coll. Medicine, 1978. Diplomate Am. Bd. Psychiatry Neurology, Am. Bd. Geriatric Psychiatry, Am. Bd. Forensic Psychiatry, Am. Bd. Addiction Psychiatry, cert. clin. psychopharmacology. Computer programmer We. Electric Co., N.Y.C., 1970—73; rsch. asst. Bklyn. Jewish Hosp., 1973—74; resident psychiatry Bronx Mcpl. Hosp. Ctr., NY, 1978—83, pres. house staff, 1981—82; acting med. dir. Met. Ctr. Mental Health, N.Y.C., 1983; staff psychiatrist Bronx Psychiat. Ctr., 1983—84; dir. psychiatry clinic North Ctrl. Bronx Hosp., 1984—88; psychiatrist, cons. Montefiore Mental Health Svcs. Rikers Island, East Elmhurst, NY, 1985—86; pvt. practice Bronx, NY, 1985—88, NJ, 1997—; mem. spkr.'s bur. Bergen Pines County Hosp. (now Bergen Regional Med. Ctr.), Paramus, NJ, 1988—2000; chief psychiatrist, attending staff mem. Bergen Regional Med. Ctr., Paramus, 1988—96, dir. psychiat. rsch., 1993—2000, interim med. dir. psychiatry, 1996—98, dir. psychiatry residency tng. program, 1997—2000, chmn. instrnl. rev. bd., 1996—2000; dir. outpatient rsch. ctr. Nat. Kline Inst., Orangeburg, NJ, 2001—. Asst. clin. prof. Albert Einstein Coll. Med., Bronx, NY, 1988—90; vis. asst. prof. Med. Coll. Pa., 1990—94, adj. asst. prof., 1994—2000; adj. assoc. prof. Drexel U. Coll. Medicine, 2000—04; adj. assoc. prof. environ. medicine NYU Sch. Medicine, 2001—02; prin. investigator clin. drug trials; clin. assoc. prof. psychiatry NYU Sch. Medicine, 2002—. Editor: N.J. Psychiatrist, 2001—; asst. editor: Cmty. Psychiatrist, 1985—89, mem. editl. bd.: Einstein Quar. Jour. Biology and Medicine, 1987—2000; contbr. articles to profl. jours. Union rep. Cmty. Interns Residents, N.Y.C., 1979—81; spkr.'s bur. Physicians Social Responsibility, N.Y.C., 1982—84; mem. NJ Physicians Assn., 2004—05. Recipient Psychiatrist Recognition award, NJ Alliance Mentally Ill, 1996; scholar Rock Sleyster Mem., AMA, 1977. Mem.: AAAS, N.J. Psychiat. Assn. (pres. 2004—05), Assn. Advancement Philosophy Psychiatry, Am. Psychiat. Assn. (pres. 2004—). Avocations: analytic philosophy, meditation, computers, photography. Office: Nathan S Kline Inst Psychiatry Outpatient Rsch Orangeburg NY 10962

GREENBERGER, BETTE JO, retired art teacher; b. Irwin, Penn., Apr. 28, 1937; d. William and Rose (Reisberg) Bergad; m. Howard Leroy Greenberger. BS, Chatham Coll., 1959; postgrad., Carnegie Mellon U., 1959-61; MS, Queens Coll., 1964. Cert. art tchr., N.Y. Elem. tchr. Pitts. Pub. Sch., 1959-61, Lawrence Pub. Sch., Woodmere, N.Y., 1961-62. Instr. N.Y. State Tchrs. Assn., 1983-89; critic for tchr. tng. program C.W. Post Coll., Molloy Coll., Adelphi U., Dowling Coll., N.Y. Inst. Tech., 1977-89; ednl. art cons. Recipient Gt. Tchr. award Lawrence Pub. Schs. PTA, 1974, Jenkins Meml. award N.Y. State PTA, 1976; Henry Clay Frick scholar, 1960. Mem. N.Y. State Art Tchrs., Assn., L.I. Art Tchrs. Assn., Early Am. Ind. Assn. Jewish. Avocations: travel, photography, cooking, arts and crafts. Home: 4 Washington Square Vlg New York NY 10012-1936

GREENBERGER, ELLEN, psychologist, educator; b. N.Y.C., Nov. 19, 1935; d. Edward Michael and Vera (Brisk) Silver; m. Michael Burton, Aug. 26, 1979; children by previous marriage: Kari Edwards, David Silver. BA, Vassar Coll., 1956; MA, Harvard U., 1959, PhD, 1961. Instr. Wellesley (Mass.) Coll., 1961—67; sr. rsch. scientist Johns Hopkins U., Balt., 1967-76; prof. psychology and social behavior U. Calif., Irvine, 1976—. Author: (with others) When Teenagers Work, 1986; contbr. articles to profl. jours. USPHS fellow, 1956-59; Margaret Floy Washburn fellow, 1956-58; Ford Found. grantee, 1979-81; Spencer Found. grantee, 1979-81, 87, 88-91. Fellow Am. Psychol. Assn., Am. Psychol. Soc.; mem. Soc. Rsch. in Child Devel., Soc. Rsch. on Adolescent Devel. Office: U Calif 3340 Social Ecology II Irvine CA 92697-7085 Business E-Mail: egreenbe@uci.edu.

GREENBERGER, HOWARD LEROY, lawyer, educator; b. Pitts., July 16, 1929; s. Abraham Harry and Alice (Levine) G.; m. Bette Jo Bergad, June 15, 1959. BS magna cum laude, U. Pitts., 1951; JD cum laude, NYU, 1954; diploma in law (Fulbright scholar), Oxford (Eng.) U., 1955. Bar: Pa. 1955, D.C. 1954, N.Y. 1969, U.S. Supreme Ct. 1964. Law clk. U.S. Ct. Appeals (3d cir.), 1958-60; assoc. Kaufman & Kaufman, Pitts., 1960-61; assoc. prof. law NYU, 1961-65, prof., 1965—2001, prof. emeritus, 2001—; assoc. dean NYU Sch. Law, 1968-72; dean and dir. Practising Law Inst., 1972-75; senator NYU, 1994—. Cons. in field.; v.p. Nat. Ctr. Para-Legal Tng.; pres. Early Am. Industries Assn., 1979-82; chmn. Commn. on Fgn. Grad. Study, AALS. Author: (with G. Cole) The Meriden Experiment, 1973; Study of the Quality of Continuing Legal Education in the U.S, 1980; contbr. articles to legal publs.; chmn. editorial bd. Jour. Legal Edn, 1974-77. Pres. N.Y.C. chpt. Am. Jewish Com., 1977-79, nat. bd. govs., 1979-85; vice chmn., gen. counsel Coalition to Free Soviet Jews, 1977—; trustee Law Ctr. Found., 1973-91, Am. Friends of Hebrew U. Jerusalem, 1986—; chair New Amsterdam dist. Boy Scouts Am., 1990—, Ctr. on Social Welfare Policy and Law, 1991—, Blaustein Inst. on Human Rights, 1992—. Capt. JAGC, U.S. Army, 1955-58. Recipient Alumni Meritorious Svc. award NYU, 1977, Stanley Isaacs award Am. Jewish Com., 1982, Gt. Tchr. award NYU, 1993, Friendship award Govt. of Germany, 1988, Robert B. McKay Disting. Svc. award N.Y.U. Sch. of Law, 1997, Great Tchr. award 1999; Root-Tilden grantee NYU, 1954. Fellow Am. Bar Found.; mem. ABA, Assn. of Bar of City of N.Y., N.Y. County Lawyers Assn. (bd. dirs. 1990—), Am. Law Inst., Assn. Am. Law Schs., NYU Club (pres. 1981-83, Masons, Sojourners, Vigil Hon. Order Arrow Bay, Scouts Am., Order of Coif, Phi Epsilon Pi. Democrat. Jewish. Home: 4 Washington Square Vlg Apt 16 New York NY 10012-1936 Office: NYU Sch Law Vand Hall 40 Washington Sq S New York NY 10012-1005 Office Phone: 212-998-6221.

GREENBERGER, I. MICHAEL, lawyer; b. Scranton, Pa., Oct. 30, 1945; s. David and Betty (Kabatchnick) G.; m. Marcia Devins, July 19, 1969; children: Sarah Devins, Anne Devins AB, Lafayette Coll., 1967; JD, U. Pa., 1970. Bar: D.C. 1971, U.S. Dist. Ct. D.C. 1971, U.S. Ct. Appeals (D.C. cir.) 1971, U.S. Supreme Ct. 1975. Law clk. to Judge Carl McGowan U.S. Ct. Appeals for D.C. Circuit, Washington, 1970-71; legis. asst. to U.S. Congresswoman Elizabeth Holtzman, 1972-73; atty., advisor Office of Criminal Justice, Office U.S. Atty. Gen., 1973; assoc. Shea & Gardner, Washington, 1973-77, ptnr., 1977-97; dir. divsn. of trading and markets U.S. Commodity Futures Trading Commn., 1997-99; counselor to U.S. Atty. Gen., 1999, prin. dep. assoc., atty. gen., 1999-2001; vis. prof. U. Md. Law Sch., 2001—02, prof., 2002—; dir. U. Md. Ctr. for Health and Homeland Security, Md., 2002—. Bd. govs. D.C. Bar, 1995—98, com. on legal ethics, 1993—95; mem. D.C. Cir. Adv. Com. on Procedures, 1983—89; mem. steering com. D.C. Pro Bono Partnership, 1994—97, Lafayette Coll. Leadership Coun., 1994—99; mediator office of cir. exec. U.S. Cts. for D.C., 1989—97; mem. D.C. Cir. Jud. Conf., 1983—; legal cons. Software Engring. Inst. Carnegie-Mellon U., Pitts., 1986—87; mem. steering com. Pres.'s Working Group on Fin. Markets, 1997—99; mem. hedge fund task force Internat. Orgn. Secs. Commrs., 1999. Editor-in-chief U. Pa. Law Rev., 1969-70; contbr. articles to profl. jours. Bd. dirs. Washington Legal Clinic for the Homeless, 1993-98, Am. Rivers, 1993-98, sec., 1995-98; bd. dirs. MIT Enterprise Forum Washington, 1984-87, Advanced Tech. Assn. Md., 1985-87, D.C. Prisoners' Legal Svc. Project, 1997-98. Fellow: Am. Bar Found.; mem.: ABA (chair criminal justice com. 2003—, mem.individual rights and responsibilities section 2003—), Am. Law Inst., Phi Beta Kappa. Address: 2757 Brandywine St NW Washington DC 20008-1041 E-mail: mgreenberger@law.umaryland.edu.

GREENBERGER, MARTIN, biotechnologist, information scientist, educator; b. Elizabeth, N.J., Nov. 30, 1931; s. David and Sidelle (Jonas) G.; m. Ellen Danica Silver, Feb. 2, 1959 (div. June 1974); children: Kari Edwards, David Silver; m. Liz Attardo, Dec. 11, 1982; children: Beth Jonit, Jonah Ben, Jilly Sal. Grad. with hons., USAF Officer Candidate Sch., 1953; AB, Harvard U., 1955, AM, 1956, PhD, 1958. Teaching fellow, resident adviser, staff mem. Computation Lab., Harvard U., Cambridge, 1954-58; mgr. applied sci. Cambridge IBM, 1956-58; asst. prof. mgmt. Mass. Inst. Tech., Cambridge, 1958-61, assoc. prof., 1961-67; prof., chmn. computer sci., dir. info. processing Johns Hopkins U., Balt., 1967-72; prof. math. scis., sr. research assoc. Center for Met. Planning and Research, 1972-75, prof. math. scis., 1978-82; IBM chair in tech. and info. systems UCLA Anderson Grad. Sch. Mgmt., 1982—; dir. UCLA Ctr. Digital Media, 1995-2000; pres. Council for Tech. and the Individual, 1985—; sr. fellow Milken Inst., 1999—. Mgr. systems program Electric Power Research Inst., Palo Alto, Calif., 1976-77; Isaac Taylor vis. prof. Technion-Israel Inst. Tech., Haifa, 1978-79; vis. prof. Internat. Energy Program, Grad. Sch. Bus., Stanford U., 1980, MIT Media Lab., 1988-89, Harvard U., 2001; computer sci. and engring. bd. NAS, 1970-72; chmn. COSATI rev. group NSF, 1971-72; evaluation com. Internat. Inst. for Applied Systems Analysis, Laxenburg, Austria, 1980; adv. panels, Office Tech. Assessment, GAO, U.S. Congress; adv. com. Getty Info. Inst.; cons. IBM, AT&T, CBS, Rand Corp., Morgan Guaranty, Arthur D. Little, TRW, Munger Tolles, Bolt, Beranek & Newman, Brookings Inst., Resources for Future, Electric Power Rsch. Inst., Atlantic Richfield, Rockwell Internat., Security Pacific Corp., John F. Kennedy Sch. of Govt. Harvard U., Bell Atlantic Corp., Sony Corp., Applied Minds, Mitchell Silberberg and Knupp, Am. Online, Kirkland and Ellis, Vertex Pharmaceuticals, Nat. Cancer Inst. Author: (with Orcutt, Korbel and Rivlin) Microanalysis of Socioeconomic Systems: A Simulation Study, 1961; (with Jones, Morris and Ness) On-Line Computation and Simulation: The OPS-3 System, 1965; (with Crenson and Crissey) Models in the Policy Process: Public Decision Making in the Computer Era, 1976; (with Brewer, Hogan and Russell) Caught Unawares: The Energy Decade in Retrospect, 1983; editor: Management and The Computer of the Future, 1962, republished as Computers and the World of the Future, 1964; Computers, Communications, and the Public Interest, 1971; (with Aronofsky, McKenney and Massy) Networks for Research and Education, 1973; Electronic Publishing Plus: Media for a Technological Future, 1985, Technologies for the 21st Century, Vol. 1, On Multimedia, 1990, Vol. 3, Multimedia in Review, 1992, Vol. 5, Content and Communication, 1994, Vol. 7, Scaling Up, 1996. Mem. overseers' vis. com. Harvard U., 1975-81; founder and mem. working groups Energy Modeling Forum, Stanford U., 1978-81; mem. adv. com. Nat. Center Analysis of Energy Systems Brookhaven Nat. Lab., 1976-80, chmn., 1977; mem. rev. com. Energy and Environment div. Lawrence Berkeley Lab., 1983, applied sci. div., 1986-88; chmn. forum on electronic pub. Washington program Annenberg, 1983-84; co-founder ICC Forum, 1985; chmn. CTI Roundtable, 1990-99; trustee Educom, Princeton, N.J., 1969-73, chmn. council, 1969-70. With USAF, 1952-54, USAFR, 1954-60. Named a Disting. Grad. Officer Candidate Sch., USAF, 1953; NSF fellow, 1955-56; Guggenheim fellow U. Calif., Berkeley, 1965-66. Fellow: AAAS (v.p., chmn. sect. T 1973—75); mem.: Sigma Xi, Phi Beta Kappa. Office: UCLA Anderson Grad Sch Mgmt Los Angeles CA 90095-1481

GREENBERGER, PAUL ALLEN, allergist, immunologist, educator, medical researcher; b. Pitts., May 28, 1947; s. Lawrence Fred and Jean (Half) G.; m. Rosalie Simon, Dec. 29, 1974; children: Rachel, Daniel. BS, Purdue U., 1969; MD, Ind. U., 1973. Intern Meth. Hosp., Indpls., 1973; resident in medicine Washington U., St. Louis, 1974-76; allergy, immunology fellow Northwestern U., Chgo., 1976-78, asst. prof. medicine, 1979-83, assoc. prof., 1983-88, prof., 1988—. Contbr. articles to profl. jours. Fellow ACP, Am. Thoracic Soc., Am. Coll. Chest Physicians, Am. Acad. Allergy and Immunology, Am. Coll. Allergy Asthma and Immunology, Cen. Soc. for Clin. Rsch. Office: Northwestern U Dept Medicine 676 N St Clair St #14018 Chicago IL 60611 Office Phone: 312-695-4000. Business E-Mail: p-greenberger@northwestern.edu.

GREENBLATT, DAVID J., pharmacologist; b. Boston, Apr. 8, 1945; s. Milton and Gertrude A. (Rogers) G.; m. Lisa L. von Moltke, Nov. 29, 1991. BA, Amherst Coll., 1966; MD, Harvard Med. Sch., 1970. Diplomate Am. Bd. Clin. Pharmacology. Intern in medicine Montefiore Hosp., Bronx, N.Y., 1970-71; resident in medicine Harvard Med. Svc. Boston City Hosp., 1971-72; fellow clin. pharmacology Mass. Gen. Hosp., Boston, 1972-74, mem. staff clin. pharmacology unit, 1974-76, chief clin. pharmacology unit, 1976-79; dir. clin. pharmacology program Tufts-New England Med. Ctr., Boston, 1979—; prof. pharmacology/exptl. therapeutics, psychiatry, medicine, anesthesia Sch. Medicine, Tufts U., Boston, 1979—; chmn. dept. pharmacology and exptl. therapeutics Sch. Medicine, Tufts U., Boston, 1994—, Louis Lasagna chair in pharmacology and exptl. therapeutics, 1997—. Author, co-author 11 books; contbr. over 800 articles to profl. jours. Recipient T. George Bidder award UCLA, 1988. Fellow Am. Coll. Clin. Pharmacology (bd. regents 1987-91, McKeen-Cattell award 1985, Disting. Svc. award 2001, pres.-elect 1994-96, pres. 1996-98, Dist. Investigator award 2002); mem. Am. Soc. Clin. Pharmacology and Therapeutics (bd. dirs. 1983-85, Rawls-Palmer award 1980), Am. Soc. Clin. Investigation, Am. Coll. Neuropsychopharmacology. Avocation: baseball. Office: Tufts U Sch Medicine 136 Harrison Ave Boston MA 02111-1817 E-mail: dj.greenblatt@tufts.edu.

GREENBLATT, DEANA CHARLENE, elementary school educator; b. Chgo., Mar. 13, 1948; d. Walter and Betty (Lamasky) Beisel; m. Mark Greenblatt, June 22, 1975. BEd, Chgo. State U., 1969; MA in Guidance and Counseling, Roosevelt U., 1973. Cert. tchr. K-9 Ill., Ohio, personnel guidance Ill., Ohio. Tchr., counselor Chgo. Pub. Schs., 1969—75, tchr., 1993—; tchr., counselor City Colls. Chgo. GED-TV, Chgo., 1976; tchr. Columbus (Ohio) Pub. Schs., 1976—86. Participant learning exchange, Chgo. Vol. Right-to-Readmem, Columbus; active Cmty. Learning Exchange, Acad. Yr. in USA Com. Counselor, 1989—, B'nai B'rith. Mem.: Internat. Platform Assn., Am. Pers. and Guidance Assn., B'nai B'rith Women Club (chpt. v.p.). Democrat. Home: 3820 W Touhy Ave Lincolnwood IL 60712-1026

GREENBLATT, EDWARD LANDE, lawyer; b. Augusta, Ga., Mar. 16, 1939; s. Robert B. and Gwendolyn (Lande) G.; m. Sherry Agoos, June 1, 1967; 1 dau., Susan. Student Duke U.; B.A., Birmingham So. Coll., 1961; LL.B., Emory U., 1964; LL.M., NYU, 1965. Bar: Ga. 1963, D.C. 1966, U.S. Supreme Ct. 1971. Atty., U.S. Dept. Treasury, Washington, 1965-66; assoc. Lipshutz, Greenblatt, & King, and predecessors, Atlanta, 1967-71, ptnr., 1971—. Bd. dirs. Atlanta Legal Aid Soc., Atlanta Community Ctr., Paces Battle Assn.; bd. dirs., chmn. Atlanta B'nai B'rith Youth Orgn., 1973-75; pres. The Temple, 1985-87; chmn. Southeastern Med. Rsch. Found., 1987—; pres. coun. Case Western Res. U., 1990-91. Fellow Royal Soc. Arts; mem. ABA, State Bar Ga., Atlanta Bar Assn., Lawyers Club Atlanta, Am. Judicature Soc. Jewish. Home: 3257 Teton Dr NW Atlanta GA 30339-4341 Office: Lipshutz Greenblatt & King Attys at Law 2400 Harris Tower Peachtree Ctr 233 Peachtree St NE Atlanta GA 30303-1504

GREENBLATT, HELLEN CHAYA, immunologist, microbiologist; b. Frankfurt au Main, Germany; came to U.S., 1948; d. Gedaljie and Sara (Glass) Greenblatt. BA, CCNY, 1968; MS, U. Okla., 1971; PhD, SUNY Downstate Med. Ctr., Bklyn., 1977. Microbiologist Walter Reed Army Inst., Washington, 1978-80; sr. rsch. immunoparasitologist Merck Sharp & Dohme, Rahway, N.J., 1980-81; assoc. Albert Einstein Coll. Medicine, Bronx, N.Y., 1981-84; dir. rsch. and devel. Clin. Scis. Inc., Whippany, N.J., 1984-86, dir. new bus. and sci. devel., 1986-88; sr. devel. virology E.I. DuPont, Wilmington, Del., 1988-90; mng. dir. M-CAP Techs. Internat./DCV, Wilmington, 1990-93; tech. rep. BTR Separations, Wilmington, 1993-94; v.p. R & D, DCV Biol. Scis., Wilmington, 1994-97; v.p. devel. Life Scis. divsn. DCV BioNutrition, Wilmington, 1997-2000; v.p. Legacy USA, Melbourne, Fla., 1999—2002; exec. v.p. Legacy for Life, 2002—04, chief sci. officer, 2004—. Numerous internat. and domestic tech. presentations in field. Contbr. chpt. to book, numerous articles to peer-review profl. jours. Tutor Lit. Vols. Am., 1992—97; bd. dirs. Interfaith Housing of Del., 1993—97. Recipient Outstanding Young Woman award Competitive Resident Rsch. Coun., Washington, 1978; grantee NRC, 1978-80; fellow NRC. Mem.: NY Acad. Scis., Am. Acad. Anti-Aging Medicine, Del. Acad. Medicine. Achievements include patents for gastroprotective, anti-inflammatory and anti-diarrheal properties of immune egg; among the foremost authorities on polyvalent hyperimmune egg (PHIE) for human and pet applications. Office: Legacy for Life 2725 Ctr Pl Melbourne FL 32940 Office Phone: 800-746-0300. Business E-Mail: hgreenblatt@legacyforlife.net.

GREENBLATT, MARTIN ELLIOTT, lawyer; b. Boston, Apr. 26, 1939; s. Harry J. and Mollie (Brown) G.; m. Linda Rosenbleet, Mar. 5, 1965; children: Robin A., Richard B. BA, Brandeis U., 1960; LLB, Cornell U., 1963. Bar: Mass. 1963, U.S. Dist. Ct. Mass., U.S. Ct. Appeals (1st cir.), U.S. Supreme Ct. Staff atty. Fed. Communications Commn., Washington, 1964-65; asst. city solicitor City of Newton (Mass.), 1965-70; ptnr. Greenblatt & Greenblatt, Boston, 1970-73, Kaplan, Soshnick, Greenblatt & Goodman, Boston, 1973-78, Tyler & Reynolds, Boston, 1978-81, Casner & Edwards, Boston, 1981—. Bd. dirs. N.E. Regional Bd. Anti-Defamation League, Boston, 1975—.

Served as 1st lt. M.I. Corps, U.S. Army, 1968-69. Mem. ABA, Mass. Bar Assn., Phi Alpha Delta. Republican. Jewish. Avocation: amateur radio. Office: Casner & Edwards LLP 303 Congress St Boston MA 02210

GREENBLATT, MIRIAM, writer, editor, educator; b. Berlin; d. Gregory and Shifra (Zemach) Baraks; m. Howard Greenblatt (div.). BA magna cum laude, Hunter Coll.; postgrad., U. Chgo. Editor Am. People's Ency., Chgo., 1957-58, Scott Foresman & Co., Chgo., 1958-62; pres. Creative Textbooks, Chgo., 1972—. Tchr. New Trier (Ill.) HS, 1978—81. Author (with Chu): The Story of China, 1968; author: (with Cuban) Japan, 1971; author: The History of Itasca, 1976; author: (with others) The American People, 1986; author: James Knox Polk, 1988, Franklin Delano Roosevelt, 1989, John Quincy Adams, 1990; author: (with Welty) The Human Expression, 1992; author: Cambodia, 1995; author: (with Jordan and Bowes) The Americans, 1996; author: Hatshepsut and Ancient Egypt, 2000, Alexander the Great and Ancient Greece, 2000, Augustus and Imperial Rome, 2000, Peter the Great and Tsarist Russia, 2000; author: (with Lemmo) Human Heritage, 2001; author: Genghis Khan and the Mongol Empire, 2002, Elizabeth I and Tudor England, 2002, The War of 1812, 2003, Iran, 2003, Charlemagne and the Early Middle Ages, 2003, Suleyman the Magnificent and the Ottoman Empire, 2003, Lorenzo de Medici and Renaissance Italy, 2003, Afghanistan, 2003, Julius Caesar and the Roman Republic, 2005, Han Wu Di and Ancient China, 2005; editl. cons. Peoples and Cultures Series, 1976—78, subject area cons. World Geography and Cultures, 1994; contbg. editor: A World History, 1979. Mem. nat. exec. coun. Am. Jewish Com., 1980—84, v.p. Chgo chpt., 1977—79; treas. Glencoe Youth Svcs., 1981—83. Mem.: Cliff Dwellers, Nat. Assn. Scholars. Jewish. Address: 2754 Roslyn Ln Highland Park IL 60035-1408

GREENBLATT, RAY HARRIS, lawyer; b. Milw., June 29, 1931; s. Charles and Ethel (Harris) G.; m. Betty Goldsmith, July 11, 1955 (dec. Mar. 1967); children: Walter, Robert, Edward; m. Helen Judith Pick, Mar. 29, 1969 (div. Dec. 1969). BS in Econs., U. Pa., 1953; JD magna cum laude, Harvard U., 1956. Bar: Ill. 1956. Assoc. Mayer, Brown, Rowe & Maw, 1956-64, ptnr., 1965-94. Arbitrator, mediator Am. Arbitration Assn., 1970-96; hearing officer Ill. State Banking Bd., 1989; lectr. Sch. for Bankers U. Wis., Madison, 1964, 73, Ill. Inst. Continuing Legal Edn., 1973. Contbr. articles to profl. jours. Pres. Winnetka (Ill.) Bd. Edn., 1973-74, mem. 1969-75; vol. tchr. economics, poetry and debate, Providence-St. Mel Sch., Chgo., 1994-98. Mem. Chgo. Literary Club (pres. 2000-01), Cliff Dwellers Club, Lake Shore Country Club. Jewish. Home: 1003 Westmoor Rd Winnetka IL 60093-1855 E-mail: rayofsunsh@aol.com.

GREENBLATT, STEPHEN JAY, literature and language professor, writer; b. Cambridge, Mass., Nov. 7, 1943; s. Harry J. and Mollie (Brown) G.; m. Ramie Targoff; children: Joshua, Aaron, Harry. BA, Yale U., 1964, MPhil, 1968, PhD, 1969; BA, Cambridge U., England, 1966, MA, 1969. Asst. prof. Dept. English U. Calif., Berkeley, 1969—74, assoc. prof., 1974—79, prof., 1979—97, The Class of 1932 Prof., 1984—97; Harry Levin Prof. Lit. Harvard U., Cambridge, Mass., 1997—2000, John Cogan U. Prof. of the Humanities, 2000—. Non-resident permanent fellow, Wissenschaftskolleg zu Berlin, vis. prof. 1996-97, 2003-04, U. Calif. Santa Cruz, 1981, Peking U., Beijing, 1982, Northwestern U., 1984, U. Bologna, Italy, 1988, U. Chgo., 1989, Ecole des Hautes Etudes en Sciences Sociales, Paris, 1989, Harvard U., 1990, 91, 93, 94, U. Trieste, 1991, Dartmouth U., 1992, U. Florence, 1992, 96, U. Torino, 1998, Kyoto U., 1998, Queen Mary and Westfield Coll., U. London, 1999; sr. fellow, Soc. for the Humanities, Cornell U., 1983. Author: Three Modern Satirists: Waugh, Orwell, and Huxley, 1965 (Lloyd Mifflin Prize), Sir Walter Raleigh: The Renaissance Man and His Roles, 1973, Renaissance Self-Fashioning: From More to Shakespeare, 1980 (Brit. Coun. Prize in the Humanities), Shakespearean Negotiations: The Circulation of Social Energy in Renaissance England, 1988 (James Russell Lowell Prize, MLA, 1989), Learning to Curse: Essays in Early Modern Culture, 1990, Marvelous Possessions: The Wonder of the New World, 1991, Hamlet in Purgatory, 2001 (Erasmus Inst. Book Prize, 2002), Will in the World: How Shakespeare Became Shakespeare, 2004; co-author (with Catherine Gallagher): Practicing New Historicism, 2000; editor: Allegory and Representation: Selected Papers from the English Institute, 1979-80, 1981, The Power of Forms in the English Renaissance, 1982, Representing the English Renaissance, 1988, New World Encounters, 1993; co-editor (with Giles Gunn): Redrawing the Boundaries: The Transformation of English and American Literary Studies, 1992; co-editor: The Norton Shakespeare, 1997; co-editor: (with M.H. Abrams) Norton Anthology of English Literature, 7th edit., 1999. Recipient Mellon Disting. Humanist Award, 2002; fellow, Rockefeller Found. Study and Conf. Ctr., Bellagio, 1999; NDEA Title IV Fellowship, 1966—69, Robert C. Bates Fellowship, 1967—68, Sterling Fellowship, 1968—69, Fulbright Scholarship, 1964—66, NEH Fellowship for Younger Humanists, 1971—72, Howard Found. Fellowship, 1978, Humanities Rsch. Fellowship, 1978, 1983, Guggenheim Fellowship, 1975, 1983, Am. Coun. Learned Societies Travel Grant, 1986. Fellow: Am. Acad. Arts and Sciences. Office: Harvard U Dept English and Am Lit and Lang Barker Ctr 12 Quincy St Cambridge MA 02138 E-mail: greenbl@fas.harvard.edu.

GREENBURG, DAN, author; b. Chgo., June 20, 1936; s. Samuel and Leah (Rozalsky) G.; m. Nora Ephron, Apr. 9, 1967 (div.); m. Suzanne O'Malley, June 28, 1980 (div.); m. Judith Wilson, Oct. 17, 1998. BFA, U. Ill., 1958; MFA, UCLA, 1960. Copywriter Lansdale Co., Los Angeles, 1960-61, Carson Roberts Advt., Los Angeles, 1961-62; mng. editor Eros mag., N.Y.C., 1962-63; copywriter Papert, Koenig, Lois (advt.), N.Y.C., 1963-65; freelance writer N.Y.C., 1965—. Author: How to Be a Jewish Mother, 1964, Kiss My Firm but Pliant Lips, 1965, How to Make Yourself Miserable, 1966, Chewsday: A Sex Novel, 1968, Jumbo the Boy and Arnold the Elephant, 1969, 89, Philly, 1969, Porno-Graphics, 1969, Scoring: A Sexual Memoir, 1972, Something's There: My Adventures in the Occult, 1976, Love Kills, 1978, What Do Women Want?, 1982; (with Suzanne O'Malley) How to Avoid Love and Marriage, 1983, True Adventures, 1985, Confessions of a Pregnant Father, 1986, How to Make Yourself Miserable for the Rest of the Century, 1987, The Nanny, 1987, Exes, 1990, The Guardian, 1990, The Bed Who Ran Away From Home, 1991, Young Santa, 1991, Great Grandpa's in the Litter Box, 1996, A Ghost Named Wanda, 1996, Through the Medicine Cabinet, 1996, Zap! I'm a Mind-Reader, 1996, Moses Supposes, 1997, Dr. Jekyll, Orthodontist, 1997, I'm Out of My Body, Please Leave a Message, 1997, My Son, the Time Traveler, 1997, Never Trust a Cat Who Wears Earrings, 1997, The Volcano Goddess Will See You Now, 1997, Bozo the Clone, 1997, How to Speak Dolphin in Three Easy Lessons, 1997, Now You See Me, Now You Don't, 1998, The Misfortune Cookie, 1998, Elvis the Turnip and Me, 1998, Hang a Left at Venus, 1999, Evil Queen Tut and the Great Ant Pyramids, 1999, Yikes! Grandma's a Teenager, 1999, How I Fixed the Year 1000 Problem, 1999, The Boy Who Cried Bigfoot, 2000, The Day I Went from Bad to Verse, 2000, Don't Count on Dracula, 2000, This Body Isn't Big Enough for Both of Us, 2000, Greenish Eggs and Dinosaurs, 2001, My Grandma, Major League Slugger, 2001, How I Became a Superhero, 2001, The Day Everything Tasted Like Broccoli, 2001, Invasion from the Planet of the Cows, 2001, Maximum Girl Unmasked, 2002, Attack of the Soggy Underwater People, 2002, Trapped in the Museum of Unnatural History, 2002, Me and My Mummy, 2002, Meet Super Sid, Crime-Fighting Kid, 2002, My Teacher Ate My Homework, 2002, If You Tell a Lie, Your Butt Will Grow, 2002, The Worst Bully in the Entire Universe, 2003, Just Add Water and Scream, 2003, It's Itchcraft, 2003, The Onts, 2005, Treachery and Betrayal at the Jolly Days Orphanage, 2005; (films) I Could Never Have Sex with Any Man Who Has So Little Regard for My Husband, 1973, Private Lessons, 1981; (with Suzanne O'Malley) Private School, 1983, The Guardian, 1990; (plays) Arf, 1969, The Great Airplane Snatch, 1969; contbr. to Broadway revue Oh, Calcutta, 1969. Recipient Silver Key award Advt. Writers Assn., N.Y.C., 1964, Playboy Humor award, 1964, 72, 76. Mem. Dramatists Guild, Authors Guild Am., AFTRA, Screen Actors Guild, Writers Guild Am., Mystery Writers Am. Personal E-mail: dan.greenburg@verizon.net.

GREENE, ALBERT LAWRENCE, healthcare executive; b. N.Y.C., Dec. 10, 1949; s. Leonard and Anne (Birnbaum) G.; m. Jo Linda Anderson, Sept. 3, 1972; children: Stacy, Jeremy. BA, Ithaca Coll., 1971; MHA, U. Mich., 1973. Adminstrv. asst. Harper Hosp., Detroit, 1973-74, asst. adminstr., 1974-77, assoc. adminstr., 1977-80; adminstr. Grace Hosp., Detroit, 1980-84, Harper Hosp., Detroit, 1984-87; pres., CEO Sinai Samaritan Med. Ctr., Milw., 1988-90, Alta Bates Med. Ctr., Berkeley, Calif., 1990-98; CEO Sutter Health East Bay Svc. Area, Berkeley, Calif., 1998-99, HealthCtrl., Emeryville, Calif., 1999—2001, Hollywood Presbyn. Med. Ctr., L.A., 2002—. Bd. dirs. Sierra Health Svcs.; chmn. Calif. Assn. Hosps. and Health Sys., 1998. Trustee Huron Valley Hosp., Milford, Mich., 1984-87. Mem.: Am. Coll. Healthcare Execs., World Pres. Orgn., City Ctr. Club, Braemar Country Club. Avocations: tennis, golf. Home: 25948 Wellington Ct Calabasas CA 91302 Office: Hollywood Presbyn Med Ctr 1300 N Vermont Ave Los Angeles CA 90027

GREENE, ALVIN, management consultant; b. Aug. 26, 1932; s. Samuel David and Yetta Kroff Greene; m. Louise Sokol, Nov. 11, 1977; children: Sharon, Aaron, Ami, Ann, Daniel. BA, Stanford U., 1954, MBA, 1959. Asst. to pres. Narmco Industries, Inc., San Diego, 1959—62; adminstrv. mgr., mgr. mktg. Whittaker Corp., L.A., 1962—67; sr. v.p. Cordura Corp., L.A., 1966—75; chmn. bd. Sharon-Sage, Inc., L.A., 1975—79; exec. v.p., COO Republic Distbrs., Inc., Carson, Calif., 1979—81, also dir.; COO Memel, Jacobs & Ellsworth, 1981—87, 1987—; pres. SCI Cons., Inc. Bd. dirs. Sharon-Sage, Inc., True Data Corp.; vis. prof. Am. Grad. Sch. Bus., Phoenix, 1977—81. Chmn. bd. commrs. Housing Authority City of L.A., 1983—88; tchr., mentor Anderson Grad. Sch. Bus., UCLA, 2002—; bd. dirs. Spl. Olympics, 2003. 1st lt. U.S. Army, 1955—57. Mem.: Bradley Group, Safety Helmet Mfrs. Assn., Direct Mail Assn. Business E-Mail: sciconsultants@aol.com.

GREENE, BERNARD HAROLD, lawyer; b. Bklyn., Sept. 21, 1925; s. Max and Clara (Pasweg) G.; m. Magda C. Schwartz, Sept. 19, 1948; children: Michael, Edith, Susan, Jonathan, David. BBA magna cum laude, CCNY, 1948; LLB cum laude, Yale U., 1951. Bar: NY 1952. Assoc. Paul, Weiss, Rifkind, Wharton & Garrison, N.Y.C., 1951-60, ptnr., 1960-94, of counsel, 1995—. Vis. lectr. Yale Law Sch., New Haven, 1972-78, 81-83; adj. prof. N.Y. Law Sch., N.Y.C., 1985-88. Chmn. deferred giving and estate planning com. Cmty. Svc. Soc., N.Y.C., 1975-82. 1st lt. U.S. Army, 1943-47. Mem.: Assn. Bar City N.Y. (mem. surrogate's ct. com. 1958—61). Home: 153 Union St Montclair NJ 07042-2102 Office: Paul Weiss Rifkind Wharton & Garrison Rm 200 1285 Avenue of the Americas New York NY 10019-6065

GREENE, CHARLES HILTON, biological oceanographer; b. N.Y.C., Oct. 19, 1956; s. Neil Richard and Paula Marylin (Pecker) G.; m. Catherine Drew Harvell, Sept. 1, 1984; children: Nathaniel Harvell, Morgan Harvell. BA, U. Colo., 1978; PhD, U. Washington, 1985. Postdoctoral fellow Woods Hole (Mass.) Oceanographic Instn., 1985-86, vis. scientist, 1986—; vis. asst. prof. Cornell Univ., Ithaca, N.Y., 1986-90, dir., biol. resources program, 1989-92; dir. ocean resources and ecosystems program Cornell U., Ithaca, 1992—, adj. asst. prof., 1991-93, adj. assoc. prof., 1994-95, assoc. prof., 1995—. Contbr. articles to Sci., Limnology Oceanography, Nature. Recipient Chancellor's medal Univ. Colo., 1978, Havana Bradner scholar Univ. Washington, 1982, Seaspace scholar Univ. Washington, 1983. Mem. Am. Soc. Limnol. Oceanography, Ecol. Soc. Am., Oceanography Soc., Am. Geophysical Union, Phi Beta Kappa. Democrat. Jewish. Home: 3 Sunny Knoll Rd Ithaca NY 14850-9616 Office: Cornell U Suee Hall Ithaca NY 14853

GREENE, CHRISTINE ELIZABETH, artist; b. Chelm, Poland, Mar. 29, 1945; came to the U.S., 1949; d. Stanley and Irene (Gering) Lipert; m. Stephen M. Greene, Aug. 25, 1974; 1 child, Valerie I. Diploma, Newark Sch. Fine Indsl. Arts, 1965; BFA, Moore Coll. Art, 1968. Textile designer Lowenstein & Sons, N.Y.C., 1968-71, Schwartz & Leibman Textiles, N.Y.C., 1971-77; caricaturist Syosset, N.Y., 1981—. Recipient Art award Grumbacker Art Supplies, 1981, Award of Excellence Channel 21 Art Show, 1982, Huntington Twp. Art League, 1983. Mem. Pastel Soc. Am., Nat. Caricaturist Network. Avocations: tropical fish breeding, gardening. Home and Office: 17 Edward Ln Syosset NY 11791-3502 Office Phone: 516-921-6892. E-mail: chris@artistchrisgreene.com.

GREENE, CLAYTON, JR., state appeals court judge; b. Glen Burnie, Md., Jan. 22, 1951; s. Clayton Sr. and Evelyn Greene; m. Janice Elizabeth Butler, Dec. 21, 1974; children: Clayton III, Jonathan. BA in History, U. Md., 1973, JD, 1976. Bar: Md. 1977, Ct. Appeals, Md., 1977, U.S. Bankruptcy Ct., 1978, U.S. Dist. Ct., Md., 1978, Supreme Bench Balt. City, 1978, Anne Arundel County Bar Assn., Md., 1978, D.C. 1980, Ct. Appeals D.C., 1980. Law clerk Anne Arundel County Pub. Defender T. Joseph Touhey Jr., Md., 1974-76, various firms, Md., 1976-77; asst. county solicitor Anne Arundel County, Md., 1977-78; sole practioner Md., 1977-88; asst. pub. defender Anne Arundel County, 1978-85, dep. pub. defender, 1985-88, assoc. judge dist. ct., 1988-90, adminstrv. judge dist. ct., 1990-95, assoc. judge circuit ct., 1995-96, adminstrv. judge 5th Jud. Cirduit, 1996—2002; judge Ct. Special Appeals, 5th Appellate Circuit, 2002—04, Md. Ct. of Appeals, 2004—. Bd. dirs. Anne Arundel County Offender Aid and Restoration, Md., 1978-79; title ins. agent, 1980-88; mock trial judge citizenship law related edn. program, 1988-93; tchr. MICPEL trial adv. course, trial procedures for law enforcement officers, 1990-95; lectr. Anne Arundel C.C., Md., 1990-98, Jud. Inst. Md.; mem. standing com. practice and procedures Ct. Appeals, 1991-95; ex-oficio mem. Anne Arundel County Criminal Justice Coordinating Coun., 1993-95; co-chmn. Ad Hoc com. for implementation of family law divsn., 1997-2002; mem. Public Awareness Com., Md. Jud. Conference, 2000-02; spkr. in field. Asst. coach St. Jane Frances Clinic Soccer League, 1986, Arthur Slade basketball, 1988, Severna Park Green Hornets basketball, 1988, coach Arthur Slade basketball, 1994; mem. Gender Equality Com., 1990-92. Recipient Pub. Svc. award U. Md., 1987, Govs. Citation, 1988, Civic Betterment award Frontiersmen's Internat., 1989, cert. appreciation Kiwanis Club of Odenton, Morris H. Blum Humanitarian award, 1995, Morris H. Blum Humanitarian award Dr. Martin Luther King, Jr. Awards Dinner Foundation, 1995, Donald C. Roane award for Public Service NAACP, 1998. Mem. Hall United Meth. Ch. (bd. dirs. 1978-86, mem. bldg. com. 1984-87, trustee 1978-86), Anne Arundel County Bar Found., Md. (dir. 1993). Avocations: tennis, basketball, alto-saxaphone, clarinet. Office: Md Ct Appeals Robert C Murphy Bldg 361 Rowe Blvd Annapolis MD 21401*

GREENE, DANIEL E., pastel artist; b. Cin., Feb. 26, 1934; Attended, Art Acad. Cin., Art Students League. Prof. Nat. Acad. Design, NY, 1969—74, Art Students League, NY, 1974—82; guest lectr. - Animation Dept. Disney Studios, 1993. Author: Pastel, 1974; Exhibited in group shows at Works on Paper, Janet Nessler Gallery, NY, 1960, Current Am. Painting, Invitational Butler Inst. Am. Art, Ohio, 1976, Recent Acquisitions, Cin. Mus. Fine Art, 1984, The Detailed Image, Realism Here and Abroad Invitational, Harcourts Contemporary Gallery, San Francisco, 1986, Art at the Armory, NY, 1988, Objects Observed: Contemporary Still Life, Gallery Henoch, NY, 1990, Subway Series, 1993, Am. Figurative Painters, 1999, Artists of Am. Invitational, Denver, 1991, Homage To, John Pence Gallery, San Francisco, 2001, Still Life and Interiors, 2003, US Artists, 33rd St. Armory, Phila., 2004, one-man shows include Driscol Gallery, Denver, 1978, Miller Gallery, Cin., 1981, Gallery Henoch, NY, 1985, John Pence Gallery, San Francisco, 2002. Named to Pastel Soc. of Am. Hall of Fame, 1983; recipient Grumbacher Prize, Allied Artists of Am., 1969, Gold Medal, Pastel Soc. of Am., 1988, 2001, Len Everett Meml. award, Allied Artists of Am., 1988, Best of Show, Kans. Pastel Soc., 1989, Pastel Laureate award, Pastel Soc. West Coast, 2003, Medal of Honor, Salmajundi Club, NYC, 2003. Mem.: Portrait Soc. Am. (adv. bd.). Mailing: Portrait Soc America PO Box 11272 Tallahassee FL 32302*

GREENE, DAVID, surgeon, researcher; b. N.Y.C., Nov. 15, 1966; s. Martin and Carole Greene; m. Denise Altman; 1 child, Jonathan. BA magna cum laude, Harvard U., 1989; MD, Yale U., 1993. Diplomate Am. Bd. Med. Examiners, Am. Bd. Otolaryngology, Am. Bd. Facial Plastic Surgery. Rsch. fellow NIH, Bethesda, Md., 1990—90; resident otolaryngology head and neck surgery U. Calif., San Francisco, 1993—98, chief resident head and neck surgery, 1997—98; fellow facial plastic surgery Stanford (Calif.) U., 1998—99; clin. instr. facial plastic surgery Stanford U. Med. Ctr., 1998—99; staff surgeon Palo Alto (Calif.) Vets. Health Sys., 1998—99; staff otolaryngologist, head and neck surgeon Cleveland Clinic, Naples, Fla., 1999—, dept. head, 2001—. Contbr. articles to profl. jours. Recipient Spl. Thanks and Recognition award, VA, 1999, Physician Recognition award, AMA, 2001; scholar John Harvard scholar, Harvard U., 1986, Harvard Coll. scholar, 1986. Fellow: Am. Rhinologic Soc., Am. Acad. Otolaryngology (Achievement award 2001); mem.: Am. Acad. Facial Plastic Surgery (Best Clin. Rsch. Paper award 1999), Phi Beta Kappa. Office: Cleveland Clinic Florida 6101 Pine Ridge Rd Naples FL 34119 Office Phone: 239-348-4000.

GREENE, DAVID LOUIS, language professional educator, genealogist; b. Middletown, Conn., Sept. 24, 1944; s. George Louis and Margaret Elsie (Chindahl) G.; m. Elizabeth Larrabee Johnson, Nov. 1974 (div. Feb. 1986); children: Jennifer Helen, Christopher Douglas; m. Amelia Jane McFerrin, July 30, 1988; stepchildren: Elizabeth Johnson, Laura Johnson. BA, U. So. Fla., 1966; MA, U. Pa., 1967, PhD, 1974. Prof. English Piedmont Coll., Demorest, Ga., 1970—. Author: The Oz Scrapbook, 1976; editor The Am. Genealogist, 1983—. Fellow Am. Soc. Genealogists; mem. Am. Antiquarian Soc., Nat. Geneal. Soc., New Eng. Hist. Geneal. Soc., N.Y. Geneal. and Biog. Soc. Democrat. Episcopalian. Home: 299 Ostrich Dr Cleveland GA 30528-4151 Office: English Dept Piedmont Coll Demorest GA 30535

GREENE, DIANE, information technology executive; m. Mendel Rosenblum. BS in mech. engring., U. Calif., Berkeley; M in computer sci. and naval architecture, MIT. Joined Sybase, 1986; various tech. leadership positions Tandem, Silicon Graphics Inc.; co-founder, CEO Vxtreme (sold to Microsoft Corp.), Palo Alto, Calif., 1995—98; founder, pres. VMware (sub. of EMC), 1998—. Named one of 50 Most Powerful People in Networking, Network World mag., 2003. Office: VMware Inc 3145 Porter Dr Palo Alto CA 94304 Office Phone: 650-475-5000, 877-486-9273. Office Fax: 650-475-5005.

GREENE, DONALD RICHARD, dermatologist, educator; b. Buffalo, Aug. 20, 1947; s. Norman Sanborn and Helen Jean (Secord) Powers; m. JoAnne D'Amico, Mar. 5, 1982; children: Patrick Ryan, Claire Elizabeth. BA, SUNY, Buffalo, 1970, MD, 1974. Diplomate Am. Bd. Dermatology. Intern Buffalo Gen. Hosp., 1974-75; resident Hosp. of U. Pa., Phila., 1975-76, Yale-New Haven Hosp., 1976-79, chief resident, 1978-79; clin. instr. Yale U. Sch. Medicine, New Haven, 1979-82, clin. asst. prof., 1982—. Attending physician Yale-New Haven Hosp., Hosp. St. Raphael, 1979—; med. bd. Branford (Conn.) Health Care Ctr., 1983—. Grantee, Am. Cancer Soc., 1972. Fellow Am. Acad. Dermatology; mem. AMA, Conn. State Med. Soc. (pres. dermatology sect. 1984-85), New Haven County Med. Assn., New Haven City Med. Assn., New England Dermatologic Soc., N.Y. Acad. Sci., Assn. of Attendings at Yale U. Sch. Medicine, Mensa, Yale Club New Haven, Penn Club N.Y., Madison Winter Club, Mory's Assn. Episcopalian.

GREENE, DOUGLAS A., internist, educator; AB in Biol. Scis., Princeton U., 1966; MD, Johns Hopkins U., 1970. Intern Johns Hopkins U. Hosp., Balt., 1970-71, asst. resident, 1971-72; postdoctoral rsch. fellow George S. Cox Med. Rsch. Inst. U. Pa. Hosp., Phila., 1972-75; asst. prof. medicine U. Pa., Phila., 1975-80; assoc. prof. medicine, dir. clin. rsch. unit and diabetes rsch. labs. U. Pitts., 1980-86; prof. internal medicine, dir. Mich. Diabetes Rsch. and Tng. Ctr. U. Mich., Ann Arbor, 1986—, mem. faculty neuroscience, 1988—, chief divsn. endocrinology and metabolism, 1991—, prof. internal medicine, dir. clin. investigation and therapeutics; dir. Mich. Diabetes Rsch. Tng. Ctr.; dir. JDF Ctr. Diabetes U. Mich., N.Y.C., 2000—. Chmn. endocrinologic and metabolic adv. com. U.S. FDA, 1991-94. Contbr. over 116 articles to Jour. Clin. Investigation, Frontiers in Diabetes, Diabetic Neuropathy, Diabetes, Diabetes Care, Am. Jour. Physiology, others. Office: JDF Ctr Complications Diabetes 120 Wall St New York NY 10005-3904

GREENE, EDWARD FORBES, chemistry educator; b. N.Y.C., Dec. 29, 1922; s. Roger Sherman and Kate (Brown) G.; m. Hildegarde Forbes, June 11, 1949; children: Susan Curtis, Judith Elizabeth, David Forbes, Roger Cobb. AB, Harvard U., 1943, A.M., 1947, PhD, 1949. Jr. research chemist Shell Oil Co., Wood River, Ill., 1943-44; mem. staff Los Alamos Sci. Lab., 1949; research assoc. Brown U., Providence, 1949-51, instr., 1952-53, asst. prof. chemistry, 1953-57, assoc. prof., 1957-63, prof., 1963-92, dept. chmn., 1980-83, Jesse H. and Louisa D. Sharpe Metcalf prof. chemistry, 1985-92; prof. emeritus, 1993—. Vis. prof. Tougaloo (Miss.) Coll., 1965; resident visitor Bell Labs., Murray Hill, N.J., 1976-77 Co-author: (with J.P. Toennies) Chemical Reactions in Shock Waves, 1964. Served with USN, 1944-46. NSF fellow, 1959-60, 66-67 Fellow Am. Phys. Soc.; mem. Am. Chem. Soc. Office: 1395 Massa Ave #213 Arlington MA 02476-4101 E-mail: Edward_Greene@Brown.edu.

GREENE, ELLIN, library service educator; b. Elizabeth, NJ, Sept. 18, 1927; d. Charles M. and Dorothea (Hooton) Peterson. A.B., Rutgers U., 1953, M.L.S., 1957, Ed.D., 1979. Children's librarian Free Pub. Library, Elizabeth, 1953-57, specialist in group work with children, 1957-59; asst. group work specialist NY Pub. Libr., NYC, 1959-64, supervising children's librarian, Bronx, 1964, asst. coord. children's services, 1965-67, dir. Early Childhood Project, NY Pub. Libr., 1986-89; adj. faculty Rutgers U. Grad. Sch. Libr. and Info. Studies, New Brunswick, NJ, 1968-97; vis. prof. Nat. Coll. Edn.-McGaw Grad. Sch., Chgo., 1976-77; dean students U. Chgo. Grad. Libr. Sch., 1980-82, assoc. prof., 1980-85; cons. libr. svcs. to children, 1985—; vis. prof. U. Ill. Grad. Sch. Libr. and Info. Sci., 1979; adv. com. NY Pub. Libr. Early Childhood Resource & Info. Ctr., 1982—89; adv. bd. Nat. Clearing House for Info. on Storytelling, 1986-88. Author: Recordings for Children, 1964; A List of Stories to Tell and to Read Aloud, 1965; Films for Children, 1966; (with Augusta Baker) Storytelling: Art and Technique, 1977, 3d edit., 1996; (with Madalynne Schoenfeld) A Multimedia Approach to Children's Literature, 1972, 2d edit., 1977; (with George Shannon) Storytelling: A Selected Annotated Bibliography, 1986, Books, Babies, and Libraries: Serving Infants, Toddlers, Their Parents and Caregivers, 1991; Roger Duvoisin: The Art of Children's Books, 1989, Read Me a Story: Books & Techniques for Reading Aloud and Storytelling, 1992; (with others) Best-Loved Stories Told at the National Storytelling Festival, 1992; co-author, contbr. to numerous edn. books and profl. jours.; mem. nat. editorial bd. Arrow Book Club, 1975-85; adv. com. Bull. of Ctr. for Children's Books, 1980-85; mem. editl. bd. Library Quar., 1980-85; editl. coun. Nat. Storytelling Jour., 1983—85. Books for children include: The Pumpkin Giant, 1970; Princess Rosetta and the Popcorn Man, 1971; The Rat-Catcher's Daughter: A Collection of Stories by Laurence Housman, 1974; Clever Cooks, 1973, 1977; Midsummer Magic, 1977, The Legend of the Christmas Rose, 1990, The Legend of the Cranberry, 1993, Billy Beg and His Bull, 1994, Li-Ling and the Phoenix Fairy, 1996, The Little Golden Lamb, 2000. Acad. specialist grantee U.S. Info. Agy. Bur. Ednl. and Cultural Affairs, 1989. Recipient Lifetime Achievement award Nat. Storytelling Network Oracle, 2002. Mem. ALA, Assn. Libr. Svc. to Children, Authors Guild Inc., Nat. Storytelling Network, Soc. Children's Book Writers and Illustrators, Douglass Soc., Psi Chi Office: 113 Chatham Ln Point Pleasant NJ 08742-2005

GREENE, ENID, retired congresswoman; b. San Rafael, Calif., Oct. 5, 1958; BS in Pol. Sci., U. Utah, 1980; JD, Brigham Young U., 1983. Caseworker, rsch. asst. U.S. Rep. Dan Marriott, R., 1980; atty. Ray, Quinney & Nebeker, 1983-90; dep. chief of staff Gov. Norman H. Bangerter, 1990-92; corp. counsel Novell, Inc., 1993-94; mem. 104th Congress from 2nd Utah dist., Washington, 1995-97; atty. Smith & Glauser, Salt Lake City, 1998—.

GREENE, ERNEST RINALDO, JR., anesthesiologist, chemical engineer; b. Mobile, Ala., Jan. 26, 1941; s. Ernest Rinaldo and Dorris Rolinha (Lassiter) G.; m. Lois Ellen Laura Zullig, Sept. 23, 1967; children: Laura Rolinha, Ernest Rinaldo III, Ellen Victoria, Max McKeen. BA, Rice U., 1962, BS, 1963; MA, Princeton U., 1966, PhD, 1968; MD, Washington U., St. Louis, 1981. Diplomate Am. Bd. Anesthesiology; diplomate, Nat. Bd. Med. Examiners; registered profl. engr., Ala. Tenured asst. prof. engring. U. Ala., Birmingham, 1970-84, asst. prof. anesthesiology, 1986-88; chief anesthesiology Cooper Green Hosp., Birmingham, 1986-90, VA Med. Ctr., Birmingham, 1987-90; assoc. prof. anesthesiology U. Ala., Birmingham, 1988-90; chief anesthesiology Vaughan Regional Med. Ctr., Selma, Ala., 1990-92; adjunct assoc. prof. biomed. engring. U. Ala., Birmingham, 1990—; founder, CEO Hivex, Inc.; with AnesCare, Phenix City, Ala., 1994-98; anesthesiologist clin. svcs. E. A. Mangieri, PC, Northport, Ala., 1998-2000; anesthesiologist Michael Pesce and Assocs., Birmingham, 2000—; co-founder Aesthetic Laser Clinic, Tuscaloosa, Ala., 2000—, Southside Anesthesia Assoc., P.C., Birmingham, 2001—, Decatur Anesthesiology Assocs., LLC, 2003—. Reviewer (bioengring.) NSF, Washington, 1981-90; guest reviewer Anesthesiology (jour.), Phila., 1988-90; co-founder Aesthetic Laser Clin., Tuscaloosa, Ala., 2000—. Author: Homogenous Enzyme Kinetics, 1984, Immobilized Enzyme Kinetics, 1984; (with others) New Anesthetic Agents, Devices and Monitoring Techniques, 1984, Pain Management of AIDS Patients, 1991. Mem.: SAR, Sigma Tau, The Huguenot Soc. S.C. (founding chartered mem.), Gen. Soc. of War of 1812, Soc. Colonial Wars, S.R., Huguenot Soc. S.C., Internat. Anesthesia Rsch. Soc., Am. Soc. Anesthesiologists, AIChE, The Summit Club, Phi Lambda Upsilon, Tau Beta Pi, Sigma Xi (assoc.). Republican. Methodist. Office: PO Box 43858 Birmingham AL 35243-0858

GREENE, FRANK EDWARD WADE, foundation administrator, writer; b. Syracuse, N.Y., Jan. 17, 1933; s. Melville Hart Greene and Nan Wade Pearson; m. Susanne Cavanagh, Apr. 1, 1966; children: Nathanael Wade, Jennifer Robin. AB, Princeton U., 1956; MS, Columbia U., 1962. Reporter Hartford Courant, Conn., 1956-57; writer Look Mag., N.Y.C., 1958-59; editor Am. Heritage, N.Y.C., 1962-64, Newsweek, N.Y.C., 1964-69, Saturday Rev., San Francisco, 1972-73; writer, editor Commn. Pvt. Philanthropy and Pub. Needs, Washington, 1975-76; editor N.Y. Times Mag., N.Y.C., 1976-77; philanthropy adviser Rockefeller Family and Assocs., N.Y.C., 1979—. Bd. dirs. Environ. Media Svcs., Washington. Author: Disarmament, Challenge of Civilization, 1966, Giving in America, 1976. Liaison Pres.'s Coun. Sustainable Devel., Washington, 1993—95; mem. Coun. Fgn. Rels., 1994—, League Conservation Voters, Washington, 1995—; trustee Whitehead Found., N.Y.C., 1999—, Beldon Fund, N.Y.C., 2000—, Nantucket Sustainable Devel. Corp., 2000—, Nantucket Land Coun., 2001—. With U.S. Army, 1953—55, Korea. Recipient Eleanor Roosevelt Peace award Peace Action, 1997; Profl. Journalism fellow Stanford U., 1967-68, Alicia Patterson fellow Alicia Patterson Found., 1977-78. Mem. Century Assn. Office: Rockefeller Family and Assocs 30 Rockefeller Plz New York NY 10112

GREENE, FRANK SULLIVAN, JR., investment company executive; b. Washington, Oct. 19, 1938; s. Frank S. Sr. and Irma O. Greene; m. Phyllis Davison, Jan. 1958 (dec. 1984); children: Angela, Frank. BS, Washington U., St. Louis, 1961; MS, Purdue U., 1962; PhD, U. Santa Clara, Calif., 1970. Part-time lectr. Washington U., Howard U., Am. U., 1959-65; pres., dir. Tech. Devel. Corp., Arlington, Tex., 1985-92; pres. Zero One Systems Inc. (formerly Tech. Devel. of Calif.), Santa Clara, Calif., 1971-87, Zero One Systems Group subs. Sterling Software Inc., 1987-89. Asst. chmn., lectr. Stanford U., 1972—74; mng. mem. New Vista Capital, LLC, Palo Alto, Calif., 1993—; pres. Networked Picture Sys. Inc., 1989—91, chmn., 1991—94; bd. dirs. Reach Comms., Compliance Coach; observer ZNYX. Author two indsl. textbooks; also articles; patentee in field. Bd. dirs. NCCJ, Santa Clara, 1980—2005, NAACP, San Jose chpt., 1986-89, Am. Musical Theatre of San Jose, 1995—2005; bd. regents Santa Clara U., 1983-90, trustee, 1990-2000; mem. adv. bd. Urban League, Santa Clara County, 1986-89, East Side Union High Sch., 1985-88. Capt. USAF, 1961-65. Mem IEEE, IEEE Computer Soc. (governing bd. 1973-75), Assn. Black Mfrs. (bd. dirs. 1974-80), Am. Electric Assn. (indsl. adv. bd. 1975-76), Fairchild Rsch. and Devel. (tech. staff 1965-71), Bay Area Purchasing Coun. (bd. dirs. 1978-84), Security Affairs Support Assn. (bd. dirs. 1980-83), Sigma Xi, Eta Kappa Nu, Sigma Pi Phi. Business E-Mail: fgreene@nvcap.com.

GREENE, FREDERICK DAVIS, II, chemistry professor; b. Glen Ridge, N.J., July 9, 1927; s. Phillips Foster and Ruth (Altman) G.; m. Theodora Elizabeth Whatmough, June 5, 1953; children— Alan, Carol, Elizabeth, Phillips. Grad., Phillips Andover Acad., 1944; BA, Amherst Coll., 1949, D.Sc. (hon.), 1969; PhD, Harvard, 1952. Research assoc. U. Calif., Los Angeles, 1952-53; instr. dept. chemistry Mass. Inst. Tech., Cambridge, 1953-55, asst. prof., 1955-58; assoc. prof. MIT, 1958-62, prof., 1962-95; prof. emeritus, 1995—. Editor-in-chief: Jour. Organic Chemistry, 1962-88; contbr. articles to sci. jours. Served with USNR, 1945-46. Alfred P. Sloan fellow, 1958-62; NSF Sr. Postdoctoral fellow, 1965-66 Fellow AAAS; mem. Am. Chem. Soc., Royal Soc. Chem. (U.K.), Am. Acad. Arts and Scis., Phi Beta Kappa. Office: Mass Inst Tech Dept Chemistry Bldg 18-297 77 Massachusetts Ave Cambridge MA 02139-4301

GREENE, GLADSTONE FITZPATRICK, education educator, consultant; b. Liverpool, Corentyne, Guyana, Dec. 17, 1944; s. Gosnel Greene and Victoria Gibbs; m. Fleur Bonita Ainsworth; children: Karon, Kevin. BA, U. Guyana, Turkeyen, 1973; MSc in Econs., Cardiff Bus. Sch., Wales, 1987; PhD, Columbia Pacific U., 2000. Cert. respiratory asst., med. billing; trained class 1 grade 1 tchr.'s cert. Graduate Teacher Ministry of Education, Georgetown, Guyana, 1967—76; Education Officer Guyana Defence Force, Georgetown, Guyana, 1976—79; Principal Kuru Kuru College, Georgetown, Guyana, 1980—87; Lecturer University of Guyana, Turkeyen, Guyana, 1987—90; Resource Project Teacher New York City Board Of Education, Brooklyn, 1990—2002. Mgmt. cons. Guyana Mgmt. Inst., Georgetown, 1988—90. Contbr. poetry to anthologies, 2002. Faculty rep. Faculty of Edn., Guyana, Georgetown, 1974—75; pres. student coun. Tchrs.' Tng. Coll., Georgetown, 1965—66. Capt. Tng. Corps, 1976—79, Timehri, Guyana. Recipient Cert. Merit, 2001, 2002. Mem.: Am. Mgmt. Assn., Caribbean Mgmt. Devel. Assn. Office: Erasmus Hall Campus Bus and Tech 911 Flatbush Ave Brooklyn NY 11206 Personal E-mail: saggaboy2000@yahoo.com.

GREENE, HANS, warehouse manager; BFA in Ceramics, Ohio State U., 1979; M in Energy Resources, U. Pitts., 1996. Dir. facilities Pitts. Ctr. Arts, 1996—98; energy mgr., utility budget adminstr. Drexel U., Phila., 1998—. Mem.: Assn. Energy Engrs. (cert.). Achievements include music copyrights. Office: Drexel Univ 3330 Market 16-103 Philadelphia PA 19104 E-mail: h.greene@drexel.edu.

GREENE, HERBERT BRUCE, lawyer, investor, entrepreneur; b. NYC, Apr. 13, 1934; s. Joseph Lester and Shirley (Kasen) G.; m. Judith Jean Metricks, Dec. 31, 1958; children: Pamela S., Scott L. AB, Harvard U., 1955; JD, Columbia U., 1958. Bar: N.Y. 1959, Conn. 1975. Asst. U.S. atty So. Dist. N.Y., Dept. Justice, N.Y.C., 1958-61; assoc. Kaye, Scholer, Fierman, Hays & Handler, N.Y.C., 1961-66; asst. to gen. counsel CIT Fin. Corp., N.Y.C., 1966-67; group gen. counsel Xerox Corp., Rochester, N.Y., 1967-68, v.p. adminstrn., 1968-71; sr. v.p. Xerox Edn. Group, Stamford, Conn., 1971-75; v.p., gen. counsel, sec. Lone Star Industries, Inc., Greenwich, Conn., 1976-79, sr. v.p., asst. to chmn., 1979-82; chmn., CEO Earle and Greene & Co., Westport, 1982-96, Portland, Oreg., 1997—. Mem. Phi Delta Phi. Republican. Home and Office: Herbert B Greene & Co 4233 W Redondo Ave Portland OR 97239

GREENE, HOWARD E., JR., pharmaceutical executive; b. 1943; Diploma, Harvard U., 1967. With McKinsey & Co., Chgo., 1967-74, Baxter Travenol, San Diego, 1974-78; CEO Hybritech, Inc., San Diego, 1979-86; gen. ptnr. Biovest Ptnrs., San Diego, 1986-91; with Cytel Corp., 1991—, now chmn. bd.

GREENE, JAMES S., III, school administrator; b. Harlan, Ky., Nov. 10, 1943; s. James S. Jr. and Elizabeth (Howard) G.; m. Glenda Hollors, Feb. 2, 1968; children: Laurel Elizabeth, Amy Janine, James McKeehan. Postgrad., U. N.C., 1961-62; BS in Edn. French and History, U. Wis., 1965; MA in Edn., Union Coll., Barbourville, Ky., 1973; PhD in Edn., Ohio State U., 1982. Cert. tchr. secondary edn., sch. adminstrn. and supervision, Ky. Tchr. French and History Harlan H.S., 1965-83; supr. instrn. Harlan Ind. Sch. Dist., 1983—. Adj. instr. history S.E. Cmty. Coll., Cumberland, Ky., 1977-83; humanities scholar multimedia project The Lynch Legacy Project, 1987. Reviewer The History Tchr., 1973-83; contbr. (book): The Kentucky Ency., 1992. Bd. dirs. Southeastern Ky. Spl. Edn. Coop., Harlan, 1983-88; mem. adv. coun. Stokely Inst. for Liberal Arts Edn., U. Tenn., Knoxville, 1982-89; trustee Pine Mountain (Ky.) Settlement Sch., 1989—; coord. Harlan Christian Arts Festival, 1973, 76; mem. Ky. Bicentennial Commn., Frankfort, 1988-93; pres. bd. dirs. Romance of the Hills Corp., Harlan, 1992-93; elder First Presbyn. Ch., Harlan, 1968-73, 80-83, 90-95, 97-2003, organist, 1982—; mem. Ky. State Hist. Records Adv. Bd., 1996—; curriculum advisor Am. Legacies Project, 2002—. Recipient Award for Outstanding Contbns. to Math. Edn., Ky. Coun. Tchrs. Math., 1992; Humanities scholar So. Mountains Settlement Symposium, 1999-2000. Avocation: composing and choral arranging. Office: Harlan Ind Sch Dist 420 E Central St Harlan KY 40831-2372 E-mail: jgreene@harlan-ind.k12.ky.us.

GREENE, JERRY GEORGE, physician; b. Regina, Sask., Can., May 13, 1937; came to U.S., 1962, naturalized, 1981; s. David Robert and Fae (Woodman) G.; m. Waltra Laguniak, Feb. 27, 1960; children: Deidre, Cheryl, Michael. MD, U. Man., 1960. Diplomate: Am. Bd. Internal Medicine. Rotating intern St. Boniface Hosp., Winnipeg, Man., Can., 1960-61, jr. asst. resident medicine, 1961-62; teaching fellow U. Man., 1961-62; fellow in medicine Mayo Clinic, 1962-66, asst. in pulmonary diseases, 1966; chief pulmonary lab. St. Joseph's Hosp., St. Paul, 1966-69; asst. prof. medicine U. Minn. St. Paul, 1968-71; practice medicine specializing in internal medicine, 1966-68, Med. Assos. Saranac Lake, N.Y., 1972-78; asso. cardiac catheterization lab. St. Mary's Hosp., Mpls., 1967, dir. inhalation therapy program, 1967; chief pulmonary disease St. Paul Ramsey Hosp., 1968-71; med. dir. Will Rogers Hosp., Saranac Lake, N.Y., 1971-72; chief dept. medicine Saramac Lake Gen. Hosp., 1977-78; chief pulmonary disease sect. VA Hosp., Fargo, N.D., 1978-90; clin. assoc. prof. Mt. Sinai Sch. Medicine, 1991—. Asst. prof. medicine in internal medicine U. Minn., 1968-71; prof. medicine U. N.D. Sch. Medicine; chief pulmonary svc. VA Hosp., Fargo, 1978-91; chief of staff VAMC, Castle Point, N.Y.; med. dir. VA Upstate N.Y. Healthcare, N.Y.; cons. N.D. Lung Assn., PSRO, Blue Cross/Blue Shield N.D.; mem. adv. com. med. edn. NIH 1980—, mem. pulmonary acad. award com. on pulmonary testing 1979-84; comdr. 105th USAF Clinic, Stewart Field, Newburgh, N.Y. Assoc. editor RT mag.; contbr. articles to profl. jours. Bd. dirs. N.D. Lung Assn., 1979. Served with RCAF, 1960-62; to lt. col. M.C., USAF, Air N.G., 1982, comdr. Air Nat. Guard, 2000-2004, ret. col. USAF, 2004. Recipient Recognition award Mayo Clin. Fellow's Assn., 1966, Pulmonary Acad. award NIH, 1978 Fellow A.C.P., Am. Coll. Chest Physicians (com. on respirator pathophysiology); mem. VA Pulmonary Physicians, Mayo Clinic Alumni Assn. Office: 113 Holland Ave Albany NY 12208-0980

GREENE, JESSE J., JR., former computer company executive; b. N.Y.C., Mar. 7, 1945; s. Jesse Johnson and Ann (Cox) G.; m. Christine Sofijczuk, Aug. 6, 1972; children: Bryan Michael, Colin Jesse. BSME, NYU, 1969, MSME, 1971; JD and MBA in Bus., Columbia U., 1975. Engr. Grumman Aerospace, Bethpage, N.Y., 1969, IBM Corp., Yorktown Heights, N.Y., 1971-72, tax atty. Armonk, N.Y., 1975-83, IBM Credit Corp., Stamford, Conn., 1983-86, dir. taxes, 1989-91; asst. treas. IBM Corp., Armonk, N.Y., 1991—; CFO, sen. v.p. Compaq Computer Corp., Houston, 2000—01, senior v.p. strategic planning, 2001. NDEA fellow NYU, 1970; N.Y. State Regents scholar, 1963. Mem. ABA, ASME, N.Y. State Bar Assn. Avocations: aviation, boating, fishing, autos, woodworking. Home: 11 Overlook Dr Bedford Corners NY 10549-4908

GREENE, JOHN CLIFFORD, dentist, retired dean; b. Ashland, Ky., July 19, 1926; s. G. Norman and Ella R. Greene; m. Gwen Rustin, Nov. 17, 1957; children: Alan, Lisa, Laura. AA, Ashland Jr. Coll., 1947; student, Marshall Coll., 1948; D.MD, U. Louisville, 1952, Sc.D. (hon.), 1980; M.P.H., U. Calif., Berkeley, 1961; Sc.D. (hon.), U. Ky., 1972, Boston U., 1975. Diplomate Am. Bd. Dental Pub. Health. Intern USPHS Hosp., Chgo., 1952-53, staff San Francisco, 1953-54; asst. regional dental cons. Region IX, San Francisco, 1954-56; asst. to chief dental officer USPHS, Washington, 1958-60; chief epidemiology program Dental Health Center, 1961-66; dep. dir. Div. Dental Health, 1966-70, acting dir., 1970, dir., 1970-73; acting dir. Bur. Health Resources Devel., 1973-74, dir., 1974-75; chief dental officer USPHS, 1974-81, dep. surgeon gen., 1978-81; with Epidemic Intelligence Service, Communicable Disease Center, Altanta and Kansas City, Mo., 1956-57; epidemiology and biometry br. Nat. Inst. Dental Research, NIH, Bethesda, Md., 1957-58; prof. and dean sch. dentistry U. Calif., San Francisco, 1981-94; prof. and dean emeritus, 1994—. Spl. cons. WHO, India, 1957; mem. adv. com. rsch. women's health NIH, Bethesda, Md., 1995—97. Contbr. articles to profl. jours. With USN, 1945—46. Recipient citation, Sch. Grad. Dentistry Boston U., 1971, U. of the Pacific, 1977, Meritorious and Disting. Svc. awards, HEW, 1972, 1975, Outstanding Alumnus award, U. Louisville, 1980, award of merit, FDI, 1978, Alumnus of Yr. award, U. Calif. Sch. Pub. Health, Berkeley, 1984, John W. Knutson award, APHA, 1997, U. Calif. San Francisco medal, 1999, Disting. Svc. award, Am. Dental Edn. Assn., 2001, Bill Tuttle award, 2002. Fellow: Am. Coll. Dentists, Internat. Coll. Dentists; mem.: ADA, Inst. of Medicine of NAS, Am. Assn. Pub. Health Dentistry (Disting. Svc. award 1996), Am. Assn. Dental Schs. (former v.p., chair coun. of deans), Am. Assn. Pub. Health Dentistry, Am. Assn. Dental Rsch. (past pres.), Internat. Assn. Dental Rsch. (past pres.), San Francisco Dental Soc., Calif. Dental Assn., Delta Omega, Omicron Kappa Upsilon. Home: 103 Peacock Dr San Rafael CA 94901-1551

GREENE, JOHN COLTON, retired historian; b. Indpls., Mar. 5, 1917; s. Edward Martin and Helen (Carter) G.; m. Ellen Wiemann Greene, Nov. 3, 1945; children: Ruth, Ned, John David. BA, U. S.D., 1938, DHL (hon.), 1986; MA, Harvard U., 1939, PhD, 1952. Instr. U. Chgo., 1948-52; asst. prof. U. Wis., Madison, 1952-56; from assoc. prof. to prof. Iowa State U., Ames, 1956-62; vis. prof. U. Calif., Berkeley, 1962-63; prof. U. Kans., Lawrence, 1963-67, U. Conn., Storrs, 1967-87, prof. emeritus, 1987—. Author: The Death of Adam, 1959, Darwin and the Modern World View, 1961, Science, Ideology and World View, 1981, American Science in Age of Jefferson, 1984, paperback edit., 2004, Debating Darwin: Adventures of a Scholar, 1999, A Scholar Goes to War, 2005. Capt. U.S. Army, 1942-46. Jr. fellow Harvard U., 1941-42, 46-48, Guggenheim fellow, 1966-67, Am. Antiquarian Soc. fellow, 1983—; vis. scholar Cambridge U., 1974. Mem. AAUP, History of Sci. Soc. (sec. 1960-70, pres. 1975-77, George Sarton medal 2002), Midwest Junto History of Sci. (pres. 1961-62), Internat. Acad. History of Sci. (corr.). Democrat. Episcopalian. Avocation: singing.

GREENE, JOHN EDWARD, JR., music educator; b. Burlington, NC, June 13, 1966; s. John E. Sr. Greene; children: Demario Rayshon, Jade Ericka. BS in Instrumental Music, A&T State U., Greensboro, NC, 1991. Cert. tchr. SC. Band dir. McCormick (SC) H.S., 1991—. Named Tchr. of Yr., McCormick H.S., 1992. Mem.: NEA, SC Edn. Assn., Music Educators Nat. Conf. (licentiate), Phi Mu Alpha Sinfonia (life). Home: 1410 Dans Rd Greensboro NC 27401 Office: McCormick Mid/HS 516 Mims Dr Mc Cormick SC 29835

GREENE, JOHN JOSEPH, lawyer; b. Marshall, Tex., Jan. 19, 1946; s. William Henry and Camille Anne Greene. BA, U. Houston, 1969, MA, 1974; JD, South Tex. Coll., 1978. Bar: Tex. 1978, U.S. Supreme Ct. 1982. Asst. atty. City of Amarillo, Tex., 1978-79, Harris County, Tex., 1979-83; pvt. practice, 1983—; city atty. City of Conroe (Tex.), 1983-89; sr. asst. city atty. City of Austin (Tex.), 1990—. Served to capt. USAR, 1969—76. Decorated Bronze Star, Air medal. Roman Catholic. Office: 723 E 6th St Austin TX 78701-3008

GREENE, JOHN THOMAS, judge; b. Salt Lake City, Nov. 28, 1929; s. John Thomas and Mary Agnes (Hindley) G.; m. Dorothy Kay Buchanan, Mar. 31, 1955; children: Thomas Buchanan Greene, John Buchanan Greene, Mary Kay Greene Platt. BA in Polit. Sci., U. Utah, 1952, JD, 1955. Bar: Utah 1955, U.S. Dist. Ct. (10th cir.) 1955, U.S. Supreme Ct. 1966. Pvt. practice, Salt Lake City, 1955-57; asst. U.S. atty., 1957-59; ptnr. Marr, Wilkins & Cannon (and successor firms), Salt Lake City, 1959-75; ptnr., pres., chmn. bd. dirs. Greene, Callister & Nebeker, Salt Lake City, 1975-85; judge U.S. Dist. Ct., Salt Lake City, 1985—. Author: (manual) American Mining Law, 1960; contbr. articles to profl. jours. Chmn. Salt Lake City Cmty. Coun., 1970-75, Utah State Bldg. Authority, Salt Lake City, 1980-85; Regent Utah State Bd. Higher Edn., Salt Lake City, 1982-86. Recipient Order of Coif U. Utah, 1955, Merit of Honor award, 1994, Utah Fed. Bar Disting. Svc. award, 1997. Fellow ABA Found. (life); ABA ho. of dels. 1972-92, bd. govs. 1987-91; mem. Dist. Judges Assn. (pres. 10th cir. 1998-2000), Utah Bar Assn. (pres. 1971-72, Judge of Yr. award 1995), Am. Law Inst. (life, panelist and lectr. 1980-85, advisor 1986-98); Phi Beta Kappa. Mem. Lds Ch. Avocations: travel, reading, tennis. Office: US Dist Ct 350 S Main St Ste 447 Salt Lake City UT 84101-2180 Office Phone: 801-524-6180. Personal E-mail: JTGJR@hotmail.com. Business E-Mail: Thomas_Greene@utd.uscourts.gov.

GREENE, JOSEPH E., material science researcher; PhD in Materials Sci., U.S.C., 1971. Prof. U. Ill., 1971—; Erlander prof. Physics Linkping U., Sweden. Editor: CRC Critical Revs. in Solid State and Materials Sci., Thin Solid Films. Recipient Tage Erlander Physics prize 1992-95, Tech. Excellence award Semiconductor Rsch. Corp. 1994, Dept. Energy Sustained Outstanding Rsch. award 1996, David Adler Lectrship. award 1998. Mem. Am. Vacuum Soc. (bd. dirs., pres.), Am. Inst. Physics (gov. bd. mem.), Am. Physical Soc., AVS, TMS, MRS. Office: Dept Materials Sci and Engring U Ill 1101 W Springfield Ave Urbana IL 61801-3005

GREENE, JULE BLOUNTE, lawyer; b. Dublin, Ga., Aug. 15, 1922; s. Jule B. and Bette (O'Neal) G.; m. George Williams, Aug. 22, 1952; children: James Herschel, Bradley O'Neal. AB, Mercer U., 1949, LL.B., 1950. Bar: Ga. 1950, U.S. Supreme Ct. 1960. Atty. SEC, Atlanta, 1950-53, Washington, 1956-58, atty.-in-charge Miami, Fla., 1958-69, regional adminstr. Atlanta, 1969-82; regional counsel Nat. Assn. Securities Dealers, Atlanta, 1982-90; pvt. practice law Macon and Waycross, Ga., 1953-56, Dublin, Ga., 1990—. Former mem. Atlanta Fed. Exec. Bd., Interagy. Bd. U.S. Civil Service Examiners; former v.p., dir. Peachtree Fed. Credit Union.; former treas., dir. Mental Health Assn. Met. Atlanta. Served with A.C. AUS, 1942-46. Recipient award for exemplary achievement in pub. adminstrn. William A. Jump Meml. Found., 1958 Methodist. Home: 507 Woods Ave Dublin GA 31021-3542 Personal E-mail: juleg@aol.com.

GREENE, KEVIN C., lawyer; b. Cheverly, Md., Oct. 4, 1952; BA with highest honors, U. Md., 1974; JD, Cath. U. Am., 1977. Bar: Ga. 1977, D.C. 1979, U.S. Dist. Ct. (no. dist.) Ga., 1979. Law clk. to Hon. Charles A. Moye, Jr. U.S. Dist. Ct. (no. dist.) Ga., 1977-79; assoc. Troutman Sanders LLP, Atlanta, 1977—85, ptnr., 1986—, group co-leader, energy dept. Named a Super Lawyer, Atlanta Mag., 2004. Mem. ABA, D.C. Bar, State Bar Ga. Office: Troutman Sanders LLP 600 Peachtree St NE Ste 5200 Atlanta GA 30308-2216 Office Phone: 404-885-3146. Office Fax: 404-962-6575. Business E-Mail: kevin.greene@troutmansanders.com.

GREENE, LEONARD MICHAEL, manufacturing executive, aerospace transportation executive; b. N.Y.C., June 8, 1918; s. Max and Lyn (Furman) G.; m. Beverly Kaufman, June 27, 1943 (div. 1957); children: Randall Ashley, Bonnie LeVar, Laurie Baldwin; m. Phyllis Saks, June 8, 1958 (dec. Oct. 1965); children: Douglas, Charles, Donald (dec.), Stephen, Terry; m. Joyce Teck, Jan. 2, 1967; stepchildren: Jeffrey Meller, William Meller, Gary Meller, Amy Meller Gerbe. BS in Engring., CCNY, 1937, MS in Engring., 1939; postgrad., Guggenheim Sch. Aeronautics, NYU; D in Civil Law (hon.), Pace U., 1977. Rsch. chemist Rubber & Asbestos Corp., NJ, 1938-41; aerodynamicist, engring. test pilot Grumman Aircraft Corp., L.I., NY, 1941-45; hon. chmn. Safe Flight Instrument Corp., White Plains, NY, 1946—. Pres., founder SoundTitles, Inc., 1989; bd. dirs. Nationwide Ins. Author: Free Enterprise Without Poverty, 1981, The National Tax Rebate: A New America With Less Government, 1998, Inventorship: The Art of Innovation, 2001, (monographs) A Plan for a Nat. Demogrant Fianced by a Value-Added Tax, The Medical Costs Recovery Program. Mem. adv. bd. Martha's Vineyard Hosp.; pres., founder Inst. for SocioEcon. Studies, 1970; v.p., co-founder Corp. Angel Network, White Plains, 1981—; mem. spl. com. on income maintenance and council on trends and perspectives U.S. C. of C., 1975-76; bd. dirs. Blythedale Children's Hosp., Urban League Westchester Inc., Nationwide Ins.; chmn. Income Assistance/Community Devel. Program of Westchester Council of Social Agys.; pres., founder Fair Share Found., Inc.; mem. income maintenance com. Community Svc. Soc.; mem. work group on welfare reform Task Force on N.Y.C. Fiscal Crisis; mem. Westchester Coordinating Coun. on Handicapped; mem. Conf. Bd.'s Econ. Forum, 1979. Recipient Air Safety award Flight Safety Found., 1949, 81, Pilot Safety award Nat. Bus. Aircraft Assn., 1961, Employer Merit award Pres.'s Com. on Employment of Handicapped, Albert Gallatin award for Civic Leadership, Flight Safety Found award for Meritorious Svc., Disting. Svc. award Human Rights Commn. of White Plains, 1976, Medallion award Found. for Westchester C.C., 1988, U.S. EPA, Region I Spl. Act award, 1989, Meritorious Svc. to Aviation award Nat. Bus. Aircraft Assn., 1996, AlliedSignal Bendix trophy for aviation safety Flight Safety Found., 1999, Carrels award Outstanding Achievement Elecs. Aviation Week & Space Tech., 1999, Laureate award for lifetime achievement as a pioneer in flight safety, performance and innovation Aviation Week & Space Tech., 2001, Contbn. to Am. Innovation award U.S. Patent and Trademark Office, 2002; nominated N.Y. State Employer of Yr; cited by N.Y. Gov.'s Com. to Employ Handicapped, 1966; commendation from sec. dept. HEW, private sector initiative commendation Pres. of U.S.; inducted into Nat. Inventors Hall of Fame, 1991. Fellow AIAA (assoc.); mem. Soc. Exptl. Test Pilots (life), Nat. Aviation Assn., Internat. 12 Meter Assn. (voting), Edgartown Yacht Club, N.Y. Yacht Club, Sheldrake Yacht Club (Mamaroneck, N.Y.), Royal Hamilton Amateur Dinghy Club (Bermuda), Quaker Ridge Golf Club (Scarsdale, N.Y.), Alpha Beta Gamma. Achievements include co-founding Courageous Sailing Ctr., Inc., Boston, to which donated 12-meter yacht Courageous IV, winner America's Cup, 1974, 77. Office: Safe Flight Instrument Corp 20 New King St White Plains NY 10604-1204 Home: 1010 Greacen Point Rd Mamaroneck NY 10543

GREENE, LILIANE, literature and language educator, editor; b. Salonica, Greece, Oct. 10, 1928; came to U.S., 1941; d. Maurice and Daisy (Kohn) Massarano; m. Thomas McLernon Greene, May 20, 1950; children: Philip James, Christopher George, Francis Richard BA, Hunter Coll., 1948; MA, Columbia U., 1949; PhD, Yale U., 1969. Asst. in instrn. French Yale U., New Haven, 1964-65, instr., 1967-68, lectr., mng. editor Yale French Studies, 1980-94 (ret.); instr. Conn. Coll., New London, 1968-69, asst. prof., 1970-75. Contbr. articles to profl. jours. Fullbright fellow, 1949-50. Mem. MLA, Am. Assn. Tchrs. French, Ctr. Ind. Study (founding mem., pres. 1978-79, bd. dirs. 1977-89), Conn. Acad. of Arts and Scis. Democrat. Avocations: travel, theater. Home: 125 Livingston St New Haven CT 06511-2428

GREENE, LINDA KAY, retired secondary school educator; b. Elk City, Okla., Nov. 8, 1943; d. Granville E. and Edna (Nicholson) G. BA, U. N.Mex., 1966, MA in Teaching of English, 1970. Cert. tchr. Calif., lic. N.Mex. English tchr. Albuquerque Pub. Schs., 1971—96, English dept. chair, 1989-91; English tchr. Orange (Calif.) Unified Sch. Dist., 1970-71, Muroc Unified Sch. Dist., Edwards Air Force Base, Calif., 1966-69; ret., 1996. Mem. Sch. Restructuring Team, 1990-92; mem. Tchr. Adv. Coun., 1991-93, Supt. Tchr. Adv. Coun., 1992-93, exec. com., 1992-93, South Region adv. com., 1993-94. Author: numerous poems. Named Tchr. of Yr. (twice) Harrison Jr. High Sch., 1970's, Most Improved Bowler WIBC, 1970's; recipient 3rd and 6th place N.Mex. Poet Soc. Contests, 1970's. Mem. NEA (chair, co-chair), Albuquerque Press Club. Avocations: writing, drawing, painting, bowling, swimming, reading. Home: 6107 Del Campo Pl NE Chimney Ridge Albuquerque NM 87109-2529

GREENE, LYDIA ABBI JWUAN, elementary school educator; b. La Fayette, Tenn, Sept. 20, 1963; d. Thomas and Icy (Daniel) G. BBA, Tenn. State U., 1985, M in Elem. Edn., 1993; MLIS, Trevecca NAzarene U., 2001. Rep. customer svc. JC Penney Telemarketing Ctr., Nashville, 1986—93; tchr. Paragon Mills Elem. Sch., Nashville, 1993—2004; media specialist Wright Mid. Sch., Nashville, 2004—. Tchr. Youth Hobby Shop Camp, Nashville, 1981-83, Met. Nashville Edn. Assn., 1994—; mem. Faculty Adv. Com.; sci. facilitator Paragon Mills Elem. Mem. NEA, NSTA, Tenn. Edn. Assn., Fed. Aviation Assn. (educator 1995—), Tenn. Reading Assn., Nashville Inst. Arts,

Libr. Congress, Title I (com. 1999—), MNEA (sch. rep 1999-2000). Mem. Ch. Christ. Avocations: personal computing, reading, travel. Office: Paragon Mills Elem Sch 260 Paragon Mills Rd Nashville TN 37211-4075

GREENE, MARC ELLIOT, educational association administrator; b. Englewood, N.J., July 3, 1958; s. Leonard I. and Myrna J. Greene; 1 child, Cassandra Renee. BS, Ithaca Coll., 1980; MS, Coll. St. Rose, 1985; grad., LI U., 1998. Cert. music tchr. N.Y., 1985, sch. dist. adminstrn N.Y., 1998. Music tchr. Bethlehem Ctrl. Schools, Delmar, NY, 1981—88, Scotia-Glenville Ctrl. Schools, 1988—90, Solvay Pub. Schools, 1990—92; choral/theatre dir. Mid. Country Ctrl. Schools, Centereach, 1993—97, dir. music & fine arts, 1997—. Pres. NY State Coun. Adminstrs. Music Eduation, Seaford, 2003—; curriculum com. mem. NY State Sch. Music Assn., 1999—, cert. vocal and choral adjudicator, 1996—; ho. mgr. Saratoga Performing Arts Ctr., 1982—90. Contbr. new york state music curriculum; singer: Charis Vocal Ensemble, Saint Cecilia Choral Society. Bd. dirs. St. Cecilia Choral Soc., N.Y.C., 2003—. Mem.: Sch. Administrators Assn., Am. Choral Directors Assn., NY State Art Teachers Assn., NY State Sch. Music Assn., Phi Delta Kappa, Tri-M Music Honor Soc. (life), Phi Mu Alpha Sinfonia. Home: 21 Harrison Ave Coram NY 11727 Office: Middle Country Central School District 14 Forty-Third Street Centereach NY 11720 Office Phone: 631-285-8185. Personal E-mail: meg@marcgreene.com.

GREENE, MARGARET H., telecommunications industry executive; b. Nebr. JD, U. Nebr., 1972; LLD (hon.), Georgetown Coll., 1975. Assoc. solicitor Dept. Energy, Washington; atty. pvt. practice; with legal dept. South Ctrl. Bell, 1983; pres. Bellsouth Corp., Ky., 1991—95; cabinet sec. Gov. Commonwealth Ky., 1996; v.p., gen. counsel Bellsouth Telecomm., 1996—98; pres. regulatory and external affairs Bellsouth Corp., Atlanta, 1998—. Mem. adv. com. rsch., devel. and tech. So. Govs. Assn.; bd. dors. High Mus. Art, Atlanta; mem. nat. bd. vis. U. Louisville Bus. Sch. Mem.: ABA, Nebr. Bar Assn., Ky. Bar Assn., D.C. Bar Assn., Ala. Bar Assn., U.S. Telecom Assn. (chair). Office: Bellsouth Corp 1155 Peachtree St NE Atlanta GA 30309-3610

GREENE, MARK A., music educator; b. Monroe, N.C., Aug. 27, 1970; s. James Wilson and Nancy Helms Greene; m. Hoy Lee, Nov. 3, 2001. MusB, Appalachian State U., 1993; M in Music Edn., Winthrop U., 1995. Cert. grades K-12 music tchr. N.C., 2004. Band dir. Anson Jr. H.S., Wadesboro, NY, 1995; kindergarten asst. East Elem. Sch., Monroe, 1995—96; music tchr. Shiloh Elem. Sch., Monroe, 1996—. Musician and musical dir. Reflection Big Band, Monroe, 1995—2005. Mem.: Music Educators Nat. Conf. Republican. Baptist. Avocations: fishing, music, computers. Office Phone: 704-296-3035. Personal E-mail: mgreene@vnet.net.

GREENE, MARK I., lawyer; b. Neponsit, NY, July 18, 1967; BA, Cornell Univ., 1989; JD, Univ. Pa., 1993. Bar: NY 1995. Law clk., Hon. Charles A. Legge US Dist. Ct., No. Dist. Calif.; assoc. Cravath Swaine & Moore LLP, NYC, 1994—2001, ptnr., corp, 2001—. Mem.: ABA, Assn. of Bar of City of NY (European Affairs Com.), NY State Bar Assn. Office: Cravath Swaine & Moore LLP Worldwide Plz 825 Eighth Ave New York NY 10019-7475 Office Phone: 212-474-1150. Office Fax: 212-474-3700. Business E-Mail: mgreene@cravath.com.

GREENE, MAURICE, Olympic athlete, track and field athlete; b. Kansas City, Kans., July 23, 1974; Gold medalist 100m and 4x100m, 2000; U.S. indoor 60m champ, 2001; world indoor 60m champion, 1999; placed 1st at Home Depot invitational outdoors, 2003; placed 1st in Athens, 2002; placed 1st in Monaco, 2002; won3rd US 100m title, 2002; ranked #3 in the world (#2 in US) T&FN, 2002. Recipient USATF's Visa Humanitarian of the Yr. award, 2001, Jesse Owens award, 1999. Holder record time Grand Prix meet, Athens, 1999, world's fastest man, Sydney, 2000; became first man to win both 100 and 200 meter races at World Championship, 1999. Office: USA Track and Field Team One RCA Dome Ste 140 Indianapolis IN 46225

GREENE, MELINDA JEAN, retail maintenance analyst; b. Warren, Pa., Jan. 15, 1963; d. Nancy Louise Stanko, Gerald Paul Stanko (Stepfather). BA, Malone Coll., 1999. Customer svc. Blair Corp., Warren, Pa., 1980—92; retail clerk BP Products N.Am. Inc., Wexford, Pa., 1992—95, asst. maintenance and constrn., 1995—96, maintenance asst. Warrensville, Ohio, 1996—98, account svc. rep. Cuyahoga Heights, Ohio, 1998—2000, retail maintenance analyst Alpharetta, Ga., 2000—. Protestant. Office: BP Products NAm Inc 2475 Northwinds Pkwy Ste 400 Alpharetta GA 30004 Home: 566 Declaration Ln Aurora IL 60504-7341 Personal E-mail: greenemj@bp.com.

GREENE, MICHAEL F., obstetrician; m. Greene. BA, Rutgers Coll., 1970; MD, SUNY, 1976. Maternal Fetal Medicine Mass., 1982. Dir. maternal fetal medicine Mass. Gen. Hosp., Boston, 1994—; prof. obstetrics, gynecology and reproductive biology Harvard Med. Sch. Office: Mass Gen Hosp 55 Fruit St Founders 445 Boston MA 02114 Office Phone: 617-724-2229.

GREENE, MONICA LYNN BANKS, recreational therapist, director; b. Washington, Sept. 24, 1963; d. John Thomas and Pricilla (Sneed) Banks; m. Edward Ray Greene, Sept. 12, 1991. BS in Microbiology and Therapeutic Recreation, Howard U., 1986; MBA, U. Md. Cert. therapeutic recreation specialist, activity cons. Therapeutic recreation specialist Dept. Human Svcs., Washington, 1986-91; dir. activities, vols., transp. Independence Ct. Hyattsville, Md., 1991-93; dir. therapeutic activity svcs. Asbury Meth. Village, Gaithersburg, Md., 1993—; dir. therapeutic activities and vol. svcs. Presdl. Woods Health Care Ctr., Adelphi, Md.; owner, pres. Excell Eldercare Mgmt., Inc.; asst. adminstr. St. Thomas More Nursing & Rehab. Ctr., Hyattsville, Md.; exec. dir. Morningside HOuse of St. Charles, Waldorf, Ind., 2003—. Democrat. Baptist. Avocations: swimming, reading, needlecrafts, quilting. E-mail: edmonicaathome@msn.com.

GREENE, NORMAN L., lawyer; b. Mt. Vernon, NY, Aug. 31, 1948; s. Martin M. and Vera R. Greene. BA, Columbia U., 1970; JD, NYU, 1974. Bar: N.Y. 1975, U.S. Supreme Ct., U.S. Ct. Appeals (2d, 3d and 5th cirs.), U.S. Dist. Cts. (so., ea. and no.) N.Y. Assoc. Paskus Gordon & Hyman, NYC, 1974-76, Guggenheimer and Untermyer, NYC, 1976-83, ptnr., 1983-85, Rosenman & Colin, NYC, 1985—92; now ptnr. Schoeman, Updike & Kaufman, LLP, NYC. Mem. NY State Uniform Law Commn., drafting com. model punitive damages act Nat. Conf. Commrs. Uniform State Laws. Contbr. articles to profl. jours. Mem. Assn. Bar City NY (exec. com., chmn. com. capital punishment, chmn. com. on lectures and continuing edn., chmn. com. uniform state laws, mem. product liability com.), Nat. Conf. Commrs. on Uniform State Laws, NY State Bar Assn. (spl. com. court structure and jud. selection). Office: Schoeman Updike & Kaufman LLP 60 E 42nd St Fl 39 New York NY 10165-0006 Office Phone: 212-661-5030. E-mail: ngreene@schoeman.com.

GREENE, RICHARD H., journalist, writer, policy analyst; b. Milford, Conn., Aug. 12, 1955; s. Eugene Harold and Bebe (Bender) G.; m. Katherine Barrett, Feb. 21, 1982; children: Benjamin, Sandra. BS in Journalism, Northwestern U., 1977. Rschr. Forbes mag., N.Y.C., 1977-79, reporter, 1979-81, staff writer, 1981-82, assoc. editor, 1982-84, contbg. editor, 1984-89; freelance writer N.Y.C., 1984—; pres. Barrett & Greene, N.Y.C., 1996—. Adv. bd. Govtl. Acctg. Stds. Bd.; spkr. in field; sr. project coord. Pen Ctr. on the States, 2005—. Author (with Katherine Barrett): The Man Behind the Magic, 1991, Frankly My Dear..., 1996, Powering Up, 2000, Inside the Dream, 2001; corr. Governing mag.; co-prodr. Walt Disney biographical CD-ROM; co-prodr., writer TV documentary Walt: The Man Behind the Myth; contbr. articles to mags., including Newsweek, Glamour, Ladies' Home Jour., Reader's Digest, Redbook, Working Woman, others. Curator Walt Disney Family On-line Mus. Named one of ten best articles of yr., Forbes' Media Guide, 1993; recipient Amos Tuck award, Dartmouth Coll., 1978, award for excellence in fin. journalism, N.Y. Soc. CPAs, 1984, 1991, cert. of merit, 1987, Children's Choice award, Internat. Reading Assn., 1992, Wash. Monthly Journalism award, 1999, Folio Editl. Excellence award, 2002, Excellence in Health Case Reporting award, Nat. Inst. Health Care Mgmt., 2004. Home and Office: 25 Waterside Plz Apt GG New York NY 10010-2621 E-mail: greenebarrett@cs.com.

GREENE, RICHARD LAWRENCE, lawyer; b. L.A., Oct. 16, 1938; s. Robert and Mildred (Dorfman) G.; m. Lorrie Lee Levin, Jan. 27, 1963; children: Dana Michele, Julie Alyson, Elisa Suzanne. AA, U. Calif., Berkeley, 1958, BS, 1960, LLB, 1963. Bar: Calif. 1964. Ptnr. Bronson, Bronson & McKinnon, San Francisco, 1971-84, Greene, Radovsky, Maloney & Share, San Francisco, 1984—. Adj. prof. law U. Calif., Berkeley, 1984; lectr. tax insts. Contbr. articles to profl. jours. Bd. dirs. Koret Found., San Francisco, 1981—, San Francisco Hearing and Speech Cen., 1982-86. Served with USAR, 1963-69. Mem. Calif. Bar Assn. (V. Judson Kelin award taxation sect. 1981), Order of Coif, Concordia Club, Phi Beta Kappa. Jewish. Avocations: tennis, sports, kachina dolls, contemporary art. Office: Greene Radovsky Maloney & Share LLP 4 Embarcadero Ctr Ste 400 San Francisco CA 94111

GREENE, ROBERT ALLAN, former university administrator; b. Boston, Nov. 6, 1931; s. Merrill Francis and Alice Josephine (Anderson) G.; m. Mary E. Mahoney, July 20, 1957; children— Robert, Merrill, Helen, Priscilla. BA, Boston Coll., 1953, MA, 1954; PhD, Harvard U., 1961. Lectr. dept. English Univ. Coll., U. Toronto, Ont., Can., 1958-61, asst. prof., 1962-65, assoc. prof., 1966-69, prof., 1969-80; dean U. Toronto Faculty of Arts and Sci., 1972-77; Leverhulme vis. lectr. Durham (Eng.) U., 1962-63; vice-chancellor for acad. affairs, provost U. Mass., Boston, 1980-87. Editor: (With H.R. MacCallum) Nathaniel Culverwell's Discourse of the Light of Nature, 1652, 1971, 2002. Office: U Mass Harbor Campus Boston MA 02125 E-mail: robert.greene@umb.edu.

GREENE, ROBERT MICHAEL, lawyer; b. Buffalo, Jan. 14, 1945; s. Gerald Henry and Dorothy Louise (Doll) G.; m. Catherine Ellen Ostanski, Sept. 28, 1974; children: Amy, Megan, Timothy, Daniel. BA, Canisius Coll., 1966; JD, U. Notre Dame, 1969; LLM, NYU, 1971; DHL (hon.), Canisius Coll., 2005. Bar: NY 1970, U.S. Dist. Ct. (we. dist.) NY 1970, U.S. Ct. Appeals (2d cir.) 1970. Atty. VISTA, N.Y.C., 1969-71; assoc. Phillips Lytle LLP, Buffalo, 1971-75, ptnr., 1976-81, mng. ptnr., 1982—95, CEO, 1982—2003, ptnr., 2003—. Del. White House Conf. on Small Bus., 1986; bd. dirs. Cello Pack Corp., Gioia Mgmt., Inc. Author: Managing Partner 101: A Primer on Law Firm Leadership, 1990, Making Partner, A Guide for Law Firm Associates, 1992; co-author: Summary of Land Use Regulation in the State of New York and State Land Use Programs, 1974; editor: The Quality Pursuit: Assuring Standards in the Practice of Law, 1989; bd. editors Law Practice Mgmt. mag., 1989-93, articles editor, 1992-93. Trustee Canisius Coll., 1971-77, 92-2000, chmn. 1993-97; chmn. Shea's Ctr. for Performing Arts, Buffalo, 1981-85; pres. Zool. Soc. of Buffalo, 1987-92; chmn. Buffalo Philharm. Orch., 1997-99; pres. bd. Cath. Edn. Diocese of Buffalo, 1987-97; trustee Western NY Pub. Broadcasting Assn., 1984—, chmn. 1993-96; Greater Buffalo Devel. Found., 1992-93; bd. dirs. Greater Buffalo Partnership, 1993-2000, sec. 1996-2000; trustee Buffalo Philharm. Orch. Found., 2001-04, chmn., 2003-04; trustee Found. of Diocese of Buffalo, 2000—, Zool. Soc. Buffalo Found., 1999—, WNED Found., 2001—; bd. dirs. Albright-Knox Art Gallery, 2000—. Recipient LaSalle award Canisius Coll., 1980, Bd. Regents Dist. Citizens Achievement award, 1987, Disting. Alumni award 1991, Signum Fidei award St. Joseph's Collegiate Inst., 1990, Golden Marquee award Shea's Buffalo Theatre, 1984, Theodore Roosevelt Exemplary Citizen award, 1993, Person of Yr. award Notre Dame Club of Buffalo, 1994, Brotherhood award Nat. Conf., 1997, Chmn.'s award Buffalo Niagara Partnership, 1999, Humanitarian award Niagara Luth. Health Found., 2000, Caritas award St. Joseph Hosp. Found., 2002, Reflections award Trocaire Coll., 2003, Bishop's medal, Diocese Buffalo, 2005. Mem. NY State Bar Assn., Erie County Bar Assn., U. Notre Dame Law Assn. (bd. dirs. 1988—, pres. 2003-04), Buffalo Club (bd. dirs. 1997-2000, 2005-), Cherry Hill Club. Democrat. Roman Catholic. Office: Phillips Lytle LLP 3400 HSBC Ctr Buffalo NY 14203-2887 Fax: 716-852-6100. Office Phone: 716-847-7038. Business E-Mail: rgreene@phillipslytle.com.

GREENE, ROBERT OLIVER, consumer products company executive; s. Albert Herman and Florence Greene; m. Stacy Easton Greene, Aug. 27, 1988. BA, U. Md., 1969. CEO, designer Amazing Grain Woodworking, Inc., Rockville, Md., 1976—. Recipient A.W.I. Design Solutions & Washington Building Congress Award for Craftsmanship. Office: Amazing Grain Woodworking Inc 4930 Boiling Brook Parkway Rockville MD 20852 Office Phone: 301-230-2500.

GREENE, ROBERT WILLIAM, communications educator, media consultant; b. Jamaica, N.Y., July 12, 1929; s. Francis McLaughlin and Mary Virginia (Clancy) G.; m. Kathleen A. Greene, Jan. 28, 1951; children: Robert William, Lea Marie (dec.). Student, Fordham U., 1947-50. Reporter Jersey Jour., 1949-50; sr. investigator N.Y.C. Anti-Crime Com., 1950-55; reporter Newsday, Garden City, N.Y., 1955, leader investigative team, 1967-73, sr. editor, 1970-92, Long Island editor, 1972-78, asst. mng. editor, 1978-93; ret., 1993; Disting. Stessin prof., chair dept. journalism and mass media studies Hofstra U., 2001—03; ret. Staff investigator U.S. Senate Select Com. on Unfair Practices in Labor/Mgmt. Field, 1957; dir. Ariz. Project, 1976-77; pres., CEO Greene Assocs.; lectr. in field; journalism program coord. SUNY, Stony Brook, 1986-95. Author: Naked Came the Stranger, 1969, The Heroin Trail, 1973, The Sting Man, 1981. Chmn. publicity Smithtown Tercentenary, 1967; founding mem., bd. dirs. Suffolk County Happy Landings Fund; bd. visitors Inst. on Polit. Journalism Georgetown U.; bd. dirs. Smithtown Hist. Soc., Mus. at Stony Brook, Cleary Sch. for Deaf; founder, former pres. L.I. Press Club; founder St. Anthony's Gridiron Club; mem. Pres.' Coun. Xavier H.S.; chmn. Mollenhoff Journalism Award Comn. Named Hon. mem. Class of 1996, U. Md. Coll. Journalism, Hon. Alumnus, Hofstra U., 1999, Tchr. of Yr., 2000, hon. pres., Norwegian Investigative Reporters, Oslo, 1991; named to, L.I. Hall of Fame, 1991; recipient George Polk award, L.I. U, Peter Zenger award, U. Ariz., James Wright Brown award, Gold Medal Pulitzer prize, 1970, 1974, Mo. medal for disting. svc. to Am. journalism, 1979, Front Page award, 1982, Edgar award, Mystery Writers Am., 1982, Disting. Achievement award, Fordham U. Grad. Sch. Edn., 1994, Pres.'s medal, Hofstra U., 2001. Fellow Soc. Profl. Journalists; mem. Investigative Reporters and Editors Group (pres. 1976-77, chmn. exec. bd.), Assn. Edn. Journalism & Mass Comms., Radio & TV News Dirs.'s Assn. Clubs: Hofstra Univ. Club, L.I. Press (pres. 1976). Republican. Roman Catholic. Office: 4 Ardmore Pl Kings Park NY 11754-4002 E-mail: RGreene455@aol.com.

GREENE, SHEREE' JEANE, elementary school educator, consultant; d. Floyde Eugene and Betty Etheridge Greene. B in Early Childhood Edn., Wesleyan Coll., 1984; M in Early Childhood Edn., Piedmont Coll., 1996. In-Tech Certification Ga. State Bd. Edn., 2005; PBT-5 tchg. cert. in early childhood edn. Ga. State Bd. Edn., 2005, cert. tchr. support specialist Ga. State Bd. Edn., 1997. Elem. educator Northside Elem. Sch., Griffin, Ga., 1984—86; receptionist/sec. Athens (Ga.) Regional Youth Devel. Ctr., 1986—87; elem. educator Ila (Ga.) Elem. Sch., 1987—. Motivational spkr./cons. Nat. and State Inclusion Confs., Athens, 1992—; ednl. rsch. cons. U. Ga. Sch. Edn., Athens, 1993—94, vol. mentor (open door classroom observations), 1994—96; ednl. rsch. cons. U. Ga., Athens, 1994—95; portfolio evaluator Madison County Tchr. of the Yr. Evaluation Com., Danielsville, Ga., 1996—97; so. accreditation of colleges and schools steering com. co-chairperson Ila Elem. Sch., 1999—2004; motivational spkr. Emmanuel Coll., Franklin Springs, Ga., 2003—. Composer: (written lyrics and melody) Single Married Man (Ga. Songwriters Association's Top Ten Songwriters, 1992). Exec. com. co-chairperson/social events coord. Friends of the Madison County Libr., Danielsville, Ga., 1994—96; motivational spkr./singer various chs., Ga., 2004—. Recipient Leadership/Future Tchr. award, Alpha Delta Kappa, 1980, Tchr. of Yr. Cmty. award, Madison County Optimist Club, 1996, Tchr. of the Yr., Ila Elem., 1995, Madison County Sch. Sys., 1996; Future Tchr. scholar, Kappa Delta Epsilon, 1980. Avocations: songwriting, singing, gardening, creative writing, event planning. Office: Ila Elementary School 150 Sewell Mill Rd Ila GA 30647 Office Phone: 706-789-3445. Business E-Mail: sgreene@madison.k12.ga.us.

GREENE, STEPHEN CRAIG, lawyer; b. Watertown, NY, Apr. 27, 1946; s. Harold Adelbert and Mildred Esther (Baker) G.; m. Nancy Jean Adams, Mar. 28, 1965; children: Kathryn, Stephen, Hilary. AB, Syracuse U., 1967, JD, 1970. Bar: NY 1971, US Tax Ct., 1977. Asst. to pres. SUNY, Oswego, NY, 1970-73; assoc. firm Leyden E. Brown, Oswego, NY, 1973-75; ptnr. Brown and Greene, 1976-81; pvt. practice law, 1981—. Bd. dirs. Found. Corp. Legal Studies, Inc., 1968-70, United Way of Oswego County, Inc., 1985-88, Campbell's Point Assn., 1994-96; bd. dir. Oswego Hosp., 1981-2000, mem. exec. com., 1985-2000, pres., 1996-98; bd. dirs. Oswego Health, Inc., 1997—, pre, 1997-02; town atty. Oswego, 1972—; counsel Oswego County Bd. Realtors, 1978—; mem. Oswego County Rep. Com., 1974-85, counsel, 1980-83; gen. counsel Express Abstract Co., 1992-95. Recipient Inst. Counsel, 1970. Mem. ABA, NY Bar Assn., Oswego County Bar Assn., Greater Oswego C. of C. (bd. dir. 1980-87), Oswego Country Club (counsel 1977-81), Masons, Shriners, Phi Delta Phi. Home: 611 W 1st St Oswego NY 13126-4137 Office: 85 W Bridge St Oswego NY 13126-2011

GREENE, TENA LORRAINE, singer, educator, actor; d. Roy and Kathryn Correen (Case) Greene. MusM in Voice Performance, Converse Coll., Spartanburg, S.C., 2001. Voice tchr. Limestone Coll. Acad., Gaffrey, SC, 1995—97, Converse Pre-Coll., Spartanburg, 1999—2002, U. S.C., Spartanburg, 1999—2003, Mars Hill (N.C.) Coll., 2003—. Singer: various local cmty. theater and opera cos. Sec. bd. dirs. Tryon Little Theater, 1993—, fund raising performer, ARC, Tryon, Columbus, NC, 2000—05. Named Dist. winner, Nat. Assn. Tchrs. Singing, 2001; A. J. Fletcher Found. scholar, Gardner-Webb U., 1987. Mem.: Foothills Music Club. Home: 49 Locust St Columbus NC 28722 Office: Mars Hill Coll Music Dept PO Box 370 Mars Hill NC 28754-0370

GREENE, THOMAS HARDY, architect; b. Washington, Apr. 19, 1948; s. Thomas Elbert and Marie Dabney (Sitton) G.; m. Linda Louise Weaver, June 16, 1978. Student, Montgomery Coll., 1966-68, 72-73; BArch cum laude, U. Md., 1979. Registered arch., D.C., Md., Tex., Wis., Va., Mass., N.Y., Fla., Conn., Calif., Okla., Pa., N.C., S.C.; cert. NCARB, LEED Accredited Professional. Archtl. designer, technologist Clifton B. White, Silver Spring, Md., 1965, Cohen, Haft & Assocs., Silver Spring, Md., 1966-69, 70-72, Sullivan, Clark, Almy & Savage, Bethesda, Md., 1973; archtl. model builder Roger Lewis & Assocs., Washington, 1974-75; archtl. designer Thomas H. Greene Design, Chevy Chase, Md., 1976; designer, technologist David M. Schwarz Archtl. Svcs., Washington, 1976-78; architect, chmn. bd. dirs. David M. Schwarz Archtl. Svcs., Inc., Washington, 1978—; ptnr. David M. Schwarz & Ptnrs., Washington, 1990—. Bd. dirs. Glen Briar Condominium Owners' Assn., Silver Spring, 1982, pres., 1983. Recipient U. Md. Divsn. Arts and Humanities cert. scholarship, 1977. Mem. AIA, Nat. Fire Protection Assn., Nat. Trust Hist. Preservation, Internat. Code Coun., Amnesty Internat., U. Md. Alumni Assn., Phi Kappa Phi. Avocations: travel, photography, t'ai chi chuan, reading. Home: 2304 Ashboro Dr Chevy Chase MD 20815-3048 Office: David M Schwarz Archtl Svcs Inc 1707 L St NW Ste 400 Washington DC 20036 Office Phone: 202-862-0777. Business E-Mail: thg@dmsas.com.

GREENE, TIMOTHY GEDDES, lawyer; b. Lewiston, Idaho, May 12, 1939; s. George and Norma (Geddes) G.; m. Patricia Apcar, Sept. 13, 1969; children: Andrew Apcar, Jonathan Apcar. BA cum laude, U. Idaho, 1961; LLB, George Washington U., 1965. Bar: D.C., 1966, Tex., 1990, 97. Exec v.p., gen. counsel Sallie Mae, Washington, 1965—69; exec. asst. to the chmn. SEC, Washington, 1969—71; spl. asst. to gen. counsel U.S. Treasury Dept., Washington, 1971—73; sec. U.S. Emergency Loan Guarantee Bd., Washington, 1971—73; exec. v.p., gen. counsel Student Loan Mktg. Assn. Sallie Mae, Washington, 1973—79; prin. Eggers & Greene, Dallas, 1979—90, Stuart Mill Capital, Inc., Arlington, Va., 1997—. Bd. dirs. Wolf Trap Found. for the Performing Arts, Vienna, Va., 1991-97, NCCJ, 1993-98. Ford Found. fellow Brown U. Grad. Sch. Econs., 1961-62. Republican. Mem. Lds Ch. Avocations: sports, golf, tennis. Home: 1026 Wallen Rd Moscow ID 83843

GREENE, TIMOTHY JAMES, industrial engineering educator; b. Lafayette, Ind., Oct. 18, 1952; s. James H. and Barbara H. (Holt) G.; m. Nancy E. Van Kuren, Nov. 16, 1996. BS in Aero. and Astron. Engring., Purdue U., 1975, MS in Indsl. Engring., 1977, PhD, 1980. Instr., rsch. asst. sch. indsl. engring. Purdue U., West Lafayette, Ind., 1975-80; asst. prof. indsl. engring. Va. Tech., Blacksburg, 1980-85, assoc. prof. indsl. engring., 1985-91, asst. head dept. indsl. engring., 1986-91; prof., head dept. indsl. engring. and mgmt. Okla. State U., Stillwater, 1991-96, assoc. dean for rsch. Coll. Engring., Arch. and Tech., 1995-99; dean coll. engring. U. Ala., Tuscaloosa, 2000—04, asst. v.p. rsch. and acad. affairs, 2004—. Contbr. 5 chpts. to books, over 30 articles to profl. jours. Fellow Inst. Indsl. Engrs. (trustee 1991-99, sr. v.p. tech. ops. 1994-96, sr. profl. devel. 1992-94, Outstanding Young Indsl. Engr. 1987, pres. elect 1996-97, pres., 1997-98, past pres. 1998-99), Soc. Mfg. Engrs. (Outstanding Young Mfg. Engr. 1986); mem. Am. Soc. Engring. Educators. Home: 1626 Teal Cir Tuscaloosa AL 35405

GREENE, TRISTAN DORIAN, state agency administrator; b. New Orleans, Feb. 22, 1969; s. Richard Carl Greene and Cheryl Jean Arceneaux. BA, U. New Orleans, 1990, MA, 1992, MS in Urban Studies, 1993. Spl. asst. for rsch. Ark. Dept. Edn., Little Rock, 1993—; spl. advisor to atty. gen. Ark. Atty. Gen.'s Office, Little Rock, 1993—. Chmn. bd. dirs. NestEGG Prodns., New Orleans, 1996—2001. Author: (Book) How Does Arkansas Fund Its Schools?, 2000, (Monograph) Performance-Based Program Budgeting: A Government Worker's Guide to the Process, 1999, (invited paper) Overview of Education Finance Litigation, 2002, Performance Pay in Arkansas: Results from a School Finance Adequacy Study, 2003. Mem. Nat. Edn. Stats. Adv. Com., Washington, 1996—99; bd. dirs. Storer Boone Theater Awards, New Orleans, 1992—98. Mem.: Winthrop Rockefeller found. Edn. Funding Adv. Com., Am. Edn. Rsch. Assn., Am. Soc. Internat. Law, Am. Edn. Fin. Assn., Am. Polit. Sci. Assn., Am. Acad. Polit. Sci., Peace Sci. Soc., Internat. Studies Assn. Roman Catholic. Avocations: chess, golf, classical guitar, theater, travel. Office: Ark Dept Edn 323 Center St Ste 200 Little Rock AR 72201 Business E-Mail: Tristan.Greene@ag.state.ar.us.

GREENE, VICTOR ROBERT, history educator; b. Newark, Nov. 15, 1933; s. Jerome Harold and Sally (Colt) G.; m. Laura Judith Offenhartz; children: Jessica, Geoffrey. BA cum laude, Harvard U., 1955; MA, U. Rochester, 1960; PhD, U. Pa., 1963. Asst., assoc. prof. Kans. State U., Manhattan, 1963-71; assoc. prof. to prof. U. Wis., Milw., 1971—2003, prof. emeritus, 2003—. Mem. history com. Statue of Liberty-Ellis Island Com., 1989—; mem. planning com. Harvard Encyclopedia of Am. Ethnic Groups, 1971-79. Author: Slavic Community on Strike, 1968, For God and Country, 1975, Immigrant Leaders, 1987, A Passion for Polka, 1992, A Singing Ambivalence, 2004. Recipient summer rsch. grant NEH, 1967, Nat. Humanities Inst. fellowship Yale U., 1975-76, sr. Fulbright award Fed. Rep. of Germany, 1980-81, Fulbright grant U.K., 1990, NEH sr. fellowship, 1987-88; USIA lectr. grantee, Poland, 1999; Fulbright Sr. Specialist award 2003. Mem.: Mem. Immigration History Soc. (editor 1968—71, pres. 1985—88, exec. bd. 2004—). Office: U Wis-Milw History Dept Milwaukee WI 53201 Office Phone: 414-229-3965. E-mail: vicgre@uwm.edu.

GREENE, WILLIAM CASWELL, investment company executive; b. Dover, Mass., June 5, 1933; s. Whitney Eastman Greene and Maude Victoria Larsson; m. Davis Crane, Nov. 27, 1954 (div. 1983); children: William, Bruce, Josephine, Winnie, Leo, Amy; m. Catherine Radzewicz, Jan. 16, 1988; children: Whitney, Jill, Jeffrey. AB, Princeton (N.J.) U., 1954; MBA, Babson Coll., 1956; postgrad., Harvard Bus. Sch., 1956-57; cert., Hague Acad. of Internat. Law, The Netherlands, 1953. CPA, Mass. Rsch. assoc. Harvard Bus. Sch., Boston, 1957-59; auditor, cons. Coopers & Lybrand, Boston, 1959-65; ptnr. Greene & Vecchi, Wellesley, Mass., 1965-80, Greene and Co., Natick, Mass., 1980-87; prin. Lost Nation Mgmt., Lancaster, N.H., 1987—; ptnr.

Natick Investments, 1965—. Trustee VAR Estates and Trusts; bd. dirs. VAR Corps., Mass., N.H.; lectr. Mgmt. Growth Inst., Wellesley, 1965-88. Author: Cases in Cost Administration, 1963, Stories for Kids, 2000; co-author: Small Business Workbook, 1975. Chmn. Dover Sch. Com., 1964-70; state committeeman 2nd Norfolk Dist., Mass., 1966-68; trustee town funds Northumberland, 1994—; bd. dirs. Mass. Gen. Hosp., 1985-91. Recipient Svc. award Small Bus. Assn. of N.E., 1981, Hist. Preservation award Town of Natick, 1980. Mem. New Bedford Yacht Club, Harvard Faculty Club Republican. Avocations: cattle and timber, sailing, carpentry, tennis, gardening. Home: Lost Nation Rd Lancaster NH 03584 Office: Greene & Co 70 Star of the Sea Dr South Dartmouth MA 02748 Personal E-mail: whitneygre@aol.com.

GREENE, WILLIAM HENRY L'VEL, academic administrator; b. Richburg, S.C., July 28, 1943; s. Malachi and Mattie Greene; m. Ruth Lipscomb; children— Omari, Jamila BA, Johnson C. Smith U., 1966; MA, Mich. State U., 1970, PhD, 1972. Asst. prof. U. Mass., Amherst, 1972-76; dir. in-service tchr. edn. Ctr. for Urban Edn., 1974-76; asst. to chancellor, dir. devel. and univ. relations Fayetteville State U., N.C., 1976-79; dir. career counseling and placement Johnson C. Smith U., Charlotte, N.C., 1979-83; pres. Livingstone Coll., Salisbury, N.C., 1983-88; assoc. dean of curriculum and faculty devel. Gaston Coll., Dallas, N.C., 1989-91, dean, instr., 1991-92; assoc. v.p. curriculum & instrn., dean liberal arts & scis., 1992-2000; dir. devel. The Ohio State U., 2000—. Mem. Gov.'s N.C. Internship Council, Gov.'s Task Force on Racial, Religious and Ethnic Violence and Intimidation; dir. First Union Nat Bank, Salisbury Bd. dirs. Salisbury Rowan Symphony, Salisbury Rowan YMCA, Salisbury Rowan United Way Found., Gov.'s Task Force on Racial, Religious, and Ethnic Violence and Intimidation, Gaston County YMCA, Gastonia, N.C., Mint Mus., Charlotte; chmn. Gaston County Art and History Mus.; mem. Gaston County United Arts Coun.; mem. planning com. U. N.C. State Bd. Cmty. Colls. Recipient Community Service award Delta Zeta chpt. Zeta Phi Beta, 1984, Advisor of Yr. award Fayetteville State U., 1978-79, Achievement Recognition award Am. Heart Assn., 1984; named Outstanding Black Educator, Black Caucus, 1976, one of Outstanding Young Men Am. Mem. ASCD (bd. dirs., exec. bd. Mass. chpt., chmn. of Black Caucus), Fayetteville Bus. League (exec. bd.), Salisbury C. of C. (bd. dirs.), N.C. Am. Heart Assn., Salisbury-Rowan C. of C., Rotary Club of Gastonia, William Upton Lodge, Edward Evans Consistory, Phi Delta Kappa, Omega Psi Phi, Sigma Pi Phi. Home: 1000 Clifton St Charlotte NC 28216-5404

GREENE, WILLIAM L., marketing professional, consultant; b. Tallahassee, Fla., July 31, 1964; s. Larry R. Greene and Patricia C. Wilkins; m. Nancy L. Jorgensen; children: Jordan, Jessica. AA, Brevard (N.C.) Coll., 1984; BA, U. N.C., Asheville, 1986; MA, U. N.C., Greensboro, 1991; postgrad., Fla. Internat. U., Miami, 1992—95; PhD, Miami Christian U., 1997. Adj. prof. Fla. Internat. U., Miami, 1991—94; internet mgr. Jesus Fellowship, Inc., Miami, 1994—97; dir. internet mktg. Grizzard Advt., Atlanta, 1997—99; v.p. internet mktg. and devel. Am. Target Advt., Inc., Manassas, Va., 1999—2001; pres. Strategic Internet Campaign Mgmt., Inc., Buford, Ga., 2002—. GOP nominee Fla. Ho. of Reps., Miami, 1996. Mem.: Direct Mktg. Assn. of Atlanta. Avocations: walking, bicycling, church and family activities. Office: Strategic Internet Campaign Mgmt 3285 Windgate Dr Buford GA 30519 Business E-Mail: William.Greene@SICM.com.

GREENE, WILLIAM P., JR., federal judge; b. Bluefield, W.Va. m. Madeline Sinkford; children: William Robert, Jeffrey. BA, W. Va. State Coll., 1965; JD, Howard Univ., 1968; attended, Judge Adv. Gen. Sch., Charlottesville, Va., U.S. Army Command & Gen. Staff Coll., Fort Leavenworth, Kans., U.S. Army War Coll., Carlisle, Pa. Bar: W. Va. 1968. Immigration judge U.S. Dept. Justice, Washington, 1993—97; judge U.S. Ct. Appeals Vets. Claims, 1997—. Colonel Judge Adv. Gen. Corps U.S. Army, 1968—93. Decorated Legion of Merit (3 awards); named Hon. Col. Judge Adv. Gen. Corps, 1997, disting. mem. Judge Adv. Gen. Corps, 2000. Mem.: Nat. Bar Assn. (co-founder Mil. Law sect., NBA Mil. Law Hall of Fame 2002). Office: US Ct Appeals Vets Claims Ste 900 625 Indiana Ave NW Washington DC 20004-2950

GREENEBAUM, LEONARD CHARLES, retired lawyer; b. Langgoens, Germany, Feb. 6, 1934; arrived in U.S., 1937, naturalized, 1952; s. Norbert and Henny Lisa (Greenbaum) Greenebaum; m. Barbara Rosendorf, Feb. 10, 1957; children: Beth Lynn, Cathy Sue, Steven I. BS in Commerce cum laude, Washington and Lee U., 1956, JD cum laude, 1959. Bar: DC 1959, Va. 1959, Md. 1965. Atty. Sachs, Greenebaum & Tayler and predecessor firms, Washington, 1959-64, ptnr., 1964-75, mng. ptnr., 1975-90; ptnr., D.C. coord. litig. Baker & Hostetler, Washington, 1990-95, firmwide litig. group chair, 1996-2000; ret., 2001. Arbitrator Am. Arbitration Assn., Washington, 1975—2000; mem. law coun. Washington and Lee U.; mentor Citadel student mentoring program U. SC, SC, 2004—. Chmn. bd. dirs. Davis Meml. Goodwill Industries, Washington, 1979—82; bd. dirs. Coun. Ct. Excellence, Cold War Submariner Meml. Found., Charleston, 1999—; mem. citizen's advisory bd. Med. U. SC, SC, 2003—; mentor Citadel U. SC, 2003—; dir. Cold War Sub. Meml. in Charlston Habor and Found.; mem. citizens adv. bd. Hollins Cancer Ctr., Med. U. SC, 2003—. Capt. U.S. Army, 1957. Recipient Svc. to Handicapped award, Davis Meml. Goodwill Industries, 1982. Fellow: Am. Bar. Found. (life); mem.: Md. Bar Assn., D.C. Bar Assn., County Club Estates Cmty. Assn. (bd. dirs. 2004—), Country Club Charleston. Jewish. Personal E-mail: curlyccc@comcast.net.

GREENER, SIR ANTHONY, telecommunications industry executive; b. 1940; Dir. Reed Internat., 1990-98, Reed Elsevier, 1993-98; chmn. Guinness plc, 1993—97, Diageo plc, 1997-2000, Uf Industry Ltd., London, 2000—04, Robert Mondavi, 2000—; dep. chmn. Brit. Telecom, 2001—; chmn. Qualifications & Curriculum Authority, 2002—. Office: QCA 83 Piccadilly London W1J 8QA England Office Phone: 020 7509 5893.

GREENER, RALPH BERTRAM, lawyer; b. Rahway, N.J., Sept. 23, 1940; s. Ralph Bertram and Mary Ellen (Esch) G.; m. Jean Elizabeth Wilson, Mar. 21, 1964; children: Eric Wilson, Erin Hope, Nicholas Christian. BA, Wheaton Coll., 1962; JD, Duke U., 1968. Bar: Minn. 1969. With Fredrikson & Byron P.A., Mpls., 1969—. Chmn. bd. Minn. Lawyers Mutual Ins. Co., Mpls. 1981—; pres. Nat. Assn. of Bar-Related Ins. Cos., 1989-90. 1st Lt. USMCR, 1962-65. Recipient award of profl. excellence Minn. State Bar Assn., 1993. Mem. Rotary Club (pres. Mpls. 2002-03). Home: 1018 W Minnehaha Pky Minneapolis MN 55419-1161 Office: Fredrikson & Byron PA 200 S 6th St Ste 4000 Minneapolis MN 55402-1425 E-mail: rgreener@fredlaw.com.

GREENES, ROBERT A., medical educator; MD, Harvard U., 1966, PhD, 1977. Prof. radiology Med. Sch. Harvard U., Boston, prof. health scis. and tech., prof. health policy and mgmt. Sch. Pub. Health. Contbr. articles to profl. jours. Mem.: NIH. Office: Brigham and Women's Hosp Dept Radiology 75 Francis St Boston MA 02115-6106 Fax: 617-732-6317. E-mail: greenes@harvard.edu.

GREENFIELD, DAVID W., lawyer; b. Greenville, Pa., May 6, 1950; m. Carla Greenfield; 2 children. BA magna cum laude, U. Pitts., 1972; JD, Wake Forest U., 1975. Bar: Pa. 1975, U.S. Dist. Ct. Pa. (We. dist.) 1975, U.S. Supreme Ct. 1984. Atty. G.C. Murphy Co., 1975—79; counsel, asst. sec. Westinghouse Electric Corp., 1979—82; asst. gen. counsel Rockwell Internat. Corp., 1982—95, assoc. gen. counsel, 1995—97; sr. v.p., gen. counsel, sec. Meritor Automotive, Inc. (now ArvinMeritor, Inc.), 1997—99, spl. counsel, 1999—2000; with Buchanan Ingersoll P.C., Pitts., 2000—01; v.p., sec., gen. counsel Kennametal, Inc., Latrobe, Pa., 2001—. Mem.: Am. Corp. Counsel Assn., Am. Soc. Corp. Secretaries. Office: Kennametal Inc 1600 Technology Way PO Box 231 Latrobe PA 15650-0231 Office Phone: 724-539-5000. Office Fax: 724-539-4710.

GREENFIELD, GEORGE B., radiologist; b. N.Y.C., May 4, 1928; s. Jacob and Rose (Wolf) G.; m. Barbara Anne O'Driscoll, Mar. 3, 1956; children: Edward James, Sheelagh Anne. BA, NYU, 1949; MD, State U. Utrecht, Netherlands, 1956. Diplomate: Am. Bd. Radiology, Am. Bd. Nuclear Medicine. Intern Bridgeport (Conn.) Hosp., 1956-57; resident radiology Presbyn.-St. Lukes Hosp., Chgo., 1957-60; practice medicine, specializing in radiology Chgo., 1960—; radiologist Cook County Hosp., 1961-66, asst. dir. diagnostic radiology, 1966-69; assoc. prof. radiology U. Ill., 1966-69; prof., chmn. dept. radiology Chgo. Med. Sch., 1969-74, Mt. Sinai Hosp. Med. Center, 1969-89; prof. diagnostic radiology Rush Med. Coll., 1975-87; pres. med. staff Mt. Sinai Hosp. Med. Center, 1983-85; prof. radiology Cook County Grad. Sch. Medicine., Chgo. Med. Sch., 1987-89, vice chmn. dept. radiology, 1988-89; prof. radiology U. South Fla., Tampa, 1989—2003, prof. emeritus, 2004—. Attending radiologist H. Lee Moffitt Cancer Ctr. and Rsch. Inst., Tampa. Author: Radiology of Bone Diseases, 5th edit., 1990; sr. author: A Manual of Radiographic Positioning, 1973, Computers in Radiology, 1985, Imaging of Bone Tumors, 1995 Imaging of Arthritis, 2001; contbr. articles to profl. jours. Trustee Mt. Sinai Hosp., 1986-89. Served with U.S. Army, 1951. Fellow Am. Coll. Radiology; mem. AMA, AAAS, Chgo. Med. Soc., Chgo. Roentgen Soc., Am. Roentgen Ray Soc., Radiol. Soc. N.Am., Inst. Medicine Chgo., Internat. Skeletal Soc., Soc. Skeletal Radiology, Sigma Xi. Office: Moffitt Cancer Ctr & Rsch Inst PO Box 17 Tampa FL 33601-0017 Personal E-mail: gbgreenfield@worldnet.att.net. Business E-Mail: greenfield@moffitt.usf.edu.

GREENFIELD, GREGG SCOTT, lawyer; b. Sioux Falls, S.D., Sept. 1, 1963; s. Russell R. and Caroline B. (Reuter) G.; m. Julie D. Greenfield, July 21, 1990; children: Paul T., Michael J. BA, George Wash. U., 1985; JD, U. S.D., 1989. Bar: S.D. 1989, U.S. Dist. Ct., S.D. 1989, U.S. Ct. Appeals (8th cir.) 1989. Assoc. to U.S. Sen. Jim Abdnor U.S. Senate, Wash., 1989—94; ptnr. Boyce, Greenfield, Pashby & Welk, LLP, Sioux Falls, 1994—. Mem. S.D. Bd. Natural Resources, Pierre, 1997—99; chmn. S.D. Bd. Water & Natural Resources, Pierre, 1999—; mem. Vols. of Am., Sioux Falls, 1989—92, chmn., 1992—95. Mem.: Order of Barristers. Republican. Lutheran. Office: Boyce Greenfield Pasbhy & Welk LLP PO Box 5015 Sioux Falls SD 57117 Business E-Mail: gsgreenfield@bgpw.com.

GREENFIELD, JAMES ROBERT, lawyer; b. Phila., Mar. 31, 1926; s. Milton and Katherine E. (Rosenberg) G.; m. Phyllis Chaplowe, Aug. 17, 1947 (dec. May 1978); m. Joyce MacDonald Koehler, Mar. 22, 1980. BS, Bates Coll., 1947; JD, Yale U., 1950. Bar: Conn. 1950, U.S. Dist. Ct. Conn. 1951, U.S. Ct. Appeals (2d cir.) 1966, U.S. Supreme Ct. 1959. Atty. Chaplowe & Greenfield, 1950-54, Markle & Greenfield, New Haven, 1954-58; sr. ptnr. Lander, Greenfield & Krick, New Haven, 1958-80, Greenfield, Krick & Jacobs, New Haven, 1980-90, Greenfield & Murphy, New Haven, 1990-98; of counsel Tyler Cooper & Alcorn, New Haven, 1998—. Lectr. U. Conn. Law Sch., 1966-67, 71-72, 75-76. Mem. editl. bd. Conn. Bar Jour., 1963-77. Pres. New Haven Symphony, 1976-78, Conn. Bar Found., 1976-77; bd. dirs. Nat. Jud. Coll., 1978-84. With USNR, 1944-46. Fellow Am. Bar Found. (state chmn. 1985-90); mem. ABA (state del. 1975-78, bd. govs. 1978-81, ho. of dels. 1972-83, spl. com. on goverance 1983-84, chmn. various coms.), Conn. Bar Assn. (pres. 1973-74, Disting. Profl. Svc. award 1989), Am. Judicature Soc. (bd. dirs. 1983-87, 2002-03), Am. Law Inst., Am. Acad. Matrimonial Lawyers (pres. Conn. chpt. 1993-94), Internat. Acad. Matrimonial Lawyers, New Haven County Bar Assn. (pres. 1969-70, Lifetime Achievment award 1993, Conn. Law Tribune Svc. to the Profession award 2002), Yale Law Sch. Assn. (sec. 1977-80), Quinnipiack Club, Mory's. Office: Tyler Cooper & Alcorn 205 Church St New Haven CT 06510-1805 Office Phone: 203-784-8200. Business E-Mail: greenfield@tylercooper.com.

GREENFIELD, JEFF (HENRY JEFF GREENFIELD), news analyst; b. NYC, June 10, 1943; s. Benjamin and Helen Evelyn (Greenwald) Greenfield; m. Carrie Carmichael, May 11, 1968 (div. 1993); children: Casey Carmichael, David Carmichael; m. Karen Gannett, 1993 (div. 1997); m. Dena Sklar, June 21, 2002. BA with honors, U. Wis., 1964; LLB cum laude, Yale U., 1967. Legis. aide to Senator Robert F. Kennedy, Washington, 1967-68; speechwriter to Mayor John V. Lindsay, NYC, 1968-70; media critic CBS News, NYC, 1979-83; polit. media analyst ABC News, NYC, 1983-97; sr. analyst CNN, NYC, 1998—. Contbr. Inside Politics with Judy Woodruff, American Morning and NewsNight with Aaron Brown; host Greenfield at Large, CNN, CEO Exchange, PBS; guest host Larry King Live; moderator CNN town hall meeting Investigating the President: Media Madness?, 1998, Listening after Littleton, 1999. Columnist Universal Press Syndicate, 1981—96, Time mag., 1996—; contbr. articles to NY Times, Esquire and Nat. Lampoon; co-author: The Advance Man, 1971, A Populist Manifesto, 1972; author: No Peace, No Place, 1973, The World's Greatest Team, 1975, Television: The First 50 Years, 1977, Playing to Win, 1980, The Real Campaign, 1982, The People's Choice, 1995, Oh Waiter! One Order of Crow!, 2001. Recipient Emmy Award, NATAS, 1986, 1991, 1993, 1999, Quill Award for Profl. Achievement, 2002. Office: CNN 10 Columbus Cir New York NY 10019*

GREENFIELD, JOHN CHARLES, bio-organic chemist; b. Dayton, OH, 1945; s. Ivan Ralph and Mildred Louise (House) G.; m. Liga Miervaldis, aug. 2, 1980; children: John Hollen, Mark Richard. BS cum laude, Ohio U., 1967; PhD, U. Ill., 1974. Instr. sci. area h.s., Dayton, 1968-71; grad. rsch. asst. U. Ill., 1971-74; postdoctoral rsch. fellow Swiss Fed. Inst. Tech., Zurich, 1975-76; rsch. chemist infectious diseases rsch. Upjohn Co., Kalamazoo, 1976-82, sr. rsch. scientist drug metabolism rsch., 1982-93; sr. project mgr. Upjohn Labs., Kalamazoo, 1993-95, Pharmacia & Upjohn Inc., Kalamazoo, 1995-96; acquisitions review specialist, bus. devel. Pharmacia and Upjohn, Inc., Kalamazoo, 1996-98, clin. monitor, U.S. market co. med. affairs, 1998-2000; dir. global med. svcs. Pharmacia Inc., Kalamazoo, 2000—03, Pfizer, Inc., Kalamazoo, 2003—04; v.p. bus. devel. Biomedical and Pharmaceutical Info. Solutions, Kalamazoo, 2004—. Contbr. articles to sci. jours.; patentee in field. Adult leader Boy Scouts Am. Am.-Swiss Found. for Sci. Exchange fellow, 1975; NSF-NATO postdoctoral fellow, 1975-76 Mem. AAAS, Am. Chem. Soc. (chmn. Kalamazoo sect. 1994, Disting. Svc. award 1996), Am. Assn. Pharm. Scientists, Am. Assn. Microbiology, Drug Info. Assn., Sigma Xi, Phi Eta Sigma, Blue Key, Phi Lambda Upsilon, Delta Tau Delta. Achievements include identification, evaluation, and management of worldwide research and development projects for new pharmaceutical agents. Home: 6695 E E Ave Richland MI 49083-9471 Office: Biomedical and Pharmaceutical Info Solutions Ltd 7107 Elm Valley Dr Kalamazoo MI 49009 Office Phone: 269-488-3302. Business E-Mail: jcgreenfield@biomedpharmis.com.

GREENFIELD, JOSEPH CHOLMONDELEY, JR., physician, educator; b. Atlanta, July 20, 1931; s. Joseph Cholmondeley and Agnes (Game) Greenfield; m. Mary Ruth Fordham, Aug. 13, 1955; children: Mary Agnes, Ruth Ann, Susan Lee. AB in History, Emory U., 1954, MD, 1956. Intern, resident in medicine Duke Med. Ctr., Durham, NC, 1956—59; mem. staff Vets. Affairs Med. Ctr., 1962—, Duke Med. Ctr., 1962—2001; dir. heart sta. Vets. Affairs Med. Ctr., Durham, 1962—; asst. prof. medicine Duke Med. Ctr., Durham, NC, 1962—65, assoc. prof. medicine, 1965—70, prof. medicine, 1970—, dir. heart sta., 1972—2001, James B. Duke disting. prof., 1981—, chief cardiovasc. divsn., 1981—89, chmn. dept. medicine, 1983—95, chief med., 2005; clin. assoc. NIH, USPHS, 1959—62, mem. cardiovasc. and pulmonary study sect., 1974—78, chmn., 1975—78, 1983—84, mem. cardiovasc. rev. com., 1980—84. Author: A Quail Hunter's Odyssey, 2004, Duke Cardiology Fellows Training Program, Origin to the Present, 2004, Bawna Babu, 2005, Duke Chief Medical Residents, 2005; contbr. 200 articles to profl. jours. Fellow: ACP, Am. Coll. Cardiology (disting. sci. award 1985); mem.: NRA (life), Inst. Medicine, Assn. Am. Physicians, Am. Physiol. Soc., Am. Soc. Clin. Investigation, Sons Confederate Vets., Safari Club Internat., Kappa Alpha, Alpha Omega Alpha, Phi Beta Kappa. Methodist. Home: 1212 Virginia Ave Durham NC 27705-3264 Office: Duke U Med Ctr PO Box 3246 Durham NC 27715-3246

GREENFIELD, LAZAR JOHN, surgeon, educator; b. Houston, Dec. 14, 1934; s. Robert G. and Betty B. (Greenfield) Heath; m. Sharon Dee Bishkin, Aug. 29, 1956; children: John, Julie, Jeff. Student, Rice U., 1951-54; MD, Baylor U., 1958. Diplomate: Am. Bd. Surgery (dir. 1976-82), Am. Bd. Thoracic Surgery, cert. gen. vascular surgery, 1991. Intern Johns Hopkins Hosp., Balt., 1958-59, resident, 1961-66; chief surgery VA Hosp., Oklahoma City, 1966-74; prof. dept. surgery U. Okla. Med. Center, 1971-74; Stuart McGuire prof., chmn. dept. surgery Med. Coll. Va., Richmond, 1974-87; F.A. Coller prof., chmn. dept of surgery U. Mich., 1987—2002; CEO U. Mich. Health System, 2002—03; interim exec. v.p. med. affairs U. Mich. Med. Sch., 2002—03; sabbatical FDA, 2003—04. Mem. surgery A study sect. NIH. Author: Surgery in the Aged, 1975; editor-in-chief Surgery, Scientific Principles and Practice, 1993, 96, 3d edit., 2001, Surgery News, 2004-; editor Complications in Surgery and Trauma, 1983, 2d edit., 1990; contbr. to profl. publs. Served with USPHS, 1959-61. Recipient Disting. Alumni award Rice U., 1999; Thomas R. Franklin scholar, 1952, John and Mary Markle scholar in med. sci., 1968-73. Mem. Inst. of Medicine of NAS, Am. Surg. Assn., Am. Assn. Thoracic Surgery, Assn. Acad. Surgery, Soc. Univ. Surgeons, Johns Hopkins Soc. Scholars, Phi Delta Epsilon. Home: 505 E Huron St Ann Arbor MI 48104-1573 Office: UMMC Surgery 1327 Jones Dr # 201 Ann Arbor MI 48105 Office Phone: 734-936-6398. E-mail: lazarg@umich.edu.

GREENFIELD, LEE, state legislator; b. Bklyn., July 29, 1941; s. Solomen and Edith (Herschman) G.; m. Marcia Greenfield, Nov. 25, 1965. BS in Physics, Purdue U., West Lafayette, Ind., 1963; postgrad., U. Minn., 1963-73. Instr. applied math. U. Minn., Mpls., 1964-73; prin. asst. Hennepin County Bd. Commrs., Mpls., 1975-77; mgmt. analyst Office of Planning & Devel., Hennepin County, Mpls., 1977; rep. Minn. Ho. of Reps., St. Paul, 1979-2000; prin. adminstrv. asst. Hennepin County Dept. Human Svcs. and Pub. Health, 2001—. Mem. steering com. Reforming State Group, N.Y.C., 1993—, chmn., 1994-96. Bd. dirs. Twin City Cmty. Program for Affordable Health Care, Mpls., 1982-84, Arthritis Found., Mpls., 1988-90, Minn. Aids Project Mpls., 2002-, Minn. Vis. Nurse Agy., Mpls., 2003-, Ams. for Dem. Action, Mpls., 1979—, v.p., 1976-78. Recipient Dwight V. Dixon award Mental Health Assn. Minn., 1994. Mem. Mental Health Assn. Minn. (Disting. Svc. award 1987), Planned Parenthood of Minn. (Pub. Svc. award 1993). Dfl. Jewish. Office: Hennepin County Health Policy Ctr A-1702 Government Center Minneapolis MN 55487-0172 Office Phone: 612-348-3553. Business E-Mail: lee.greenfield@co.hennepin.mn.us.

GREENFIELD, LINDA SUE, nursing educator; b. Dover, Del., Aug. 5, 1950; d. Norman Raymond and Eleanor Henrietta (Harmon) Connell; m. Douglas Herman Greenfield, Dec. 27, 1976; children: Leah, Paige. BSN, Cath. U., 1972; MSN cum laude, Boston U., 1977; postgrad., Coll. New Rochelle, 1986-88; PhD, Adelphi U., 1998. RN, N.Y. Staff nurse emergency rm. and ICU Washington Hosp. Ctr., 1974-75; operating rm. nurse Mass. Eye & Ear, Boston, 1975; ICU nurse Peter Bent Brigham Hosp., Boston, 1975-76; surg. nurse practitioner Kingsbrook Jewish Hosp., Bklyn., 1976-79; nurse anesthetist student Metropolitan Hosp., 1979—81; cert. registered nurse anesthetist Brookdale Hosp., Bklyn., 1981-92, Winthrop U. Hosp., Mineola, N.Y., 1992-94; adj. prof. Adelphi U., Garden City, N.Y., 1995-99; adj. prof. nursing N.Y. Inst. Tech., Old Westbury, 1998-99; clin. supr. Midtown Ctr. Complementary Care, N.Y.C., 1999-2000; clin specialist St. Francis Hosp., Roslyn, N.Y., 2000-01; asst. prof. nursing Adelphi U., 2001—. Bd. officer Manhasset Newcomers, N.Y., 1988-90; bd. dirs. Friends of Manhasset Libr., N.Y., 1990-94; mem. Make a Wish Found., Port Washington, N.Y., 1990—. Lt. U.S. Army, 1970-74. Mem.: ANA, Nat. Assn. U. Women, Nat. Assn. for Holistic Nurses, Nat. Assn. Homeopathy, Noetic Soc., Sch. Cmty. Assn., Am. Assn. Nurse Anesthetists, Sigma Theta Tau. Avocations: skiing, sailing, dance. Office Phone: 516-877-4515. E-mail: greenfi2@adelphi.edu.

GREENFIELD, MICHAEL DENNIS, biology educator, researcher; b. N.Y.C., Mar. 2, 1952; s. Raymond Arthur and Sylvia (Geller) G.; m. Valery Jane Terwilliger, June 27, 1982. BA in Biology, NYU, 1973; PhD in Entomology, U. Wis., 1978. Rsch. asst. dept. entomology U. Wis., Madison, 1973-78; postdoctoral fellow Smithsonian Tropical Rsch. Inst., Republic of Panama, 1978-79; postdoctoral researcher USDA, Gainesville, Fla., 1979-81; asst. prof. dept. biology UCLA, 1981-87, assoc. prof., 1987-91; assoc. prof. dept. entomology U. Kans., Lawrence, 1991-94, prof., 1994—, chair dept. entomology, 1995—. Vis. lectr. dept. zoology Hebrew U., Jerusalem, 1989; mem. panel animal behavior and learning NSF. Contbr. articles to profl. jours. and chpts. in books. Smithsonian Instn. fellow, 1978; NSF grantee, 1983—, Nat. Geographic Soc. grantee, 1983. Mem. Animal Behavior Soc., Ecol. Soc. Am., Orthopterist's Soc., Sigma Xi. Achievements include research in sexual selection in insects, acoustic and olfactory communication, territorial behavior, animal behavior, animal ecology, behavioral ecology and sociobiology, physiol. entomology. Office: U Kans Dept Entomology Lawrence KS 66045-0001

GREENFIELD, NORMAN SAMUEL, psychologist, educator; b. N.Y.C., June 2, 1923; s. Max and Dorothy (Hertz) G.; m. Marjorie Hanson Klein, May 17, 1969; children— Ellen Beth, Jennifer Ann, Susan Emery. BA, NYU, 1948; MA, U. Calif., Berkeley, 1951, PhD, 1953. Fellow med. psychology Langley Porter Clinic, U. Calif. Med. Center, 1949-50; VA Mental Health Clinic trainee San Francisco, 1950-53; instr. clin. psychology U. Oreg. Med. Sch., 1953-54; from asst. prof. to prof. psychiatry U. Wis. Med. Sch. at, Madison, 1954—; assoc. dir. Wis. Psychiat. Inst., U. Wis. Center for Health Scis., 1961-74. Emeritus prof. psychiatry, 1991—. Co-editor: The New Hospital Psychiatry, Handbook of Psychophysiology, Psychoanalysis and Current Biological Thought; contbr. articles to profl. jours. Served with USAAF, 1943-46. Mem. AAUP, Am. Psychol. Assn., Soc. Psychophysiol. Rsch., Am. Psychosomatic Soc. Office: U Wis Psychiat Inst 6001 Research Park Blvd Madison WI 53719-1176 E-mail: ngreen5921@aol.com.

GREENFIELD, ROBERT KAUFFMAN, retired lawyer; b. Phila., Mar. 30, 1915; s. William I. and Bertha (Kauffman) G.; m. Louise Rose Stern, June 20, 1937; children: Linda Greenfield Baldwin, Mary Greenfield Davenport, William Stern, James Robert. AB, Swarthmore Coll., 1936; JD, Harvard U., 1939; LHD (hon.), Pa. Coll. Podiatric Medicine, 1990. Bar: Pa. 1939. Pvt. practice, Phila., 1939-87; with firm Goodis, Greenfield, Henry & Edelstein (and predecessors), 1939-77; of counsel Montgomery, McCracken, Walker & Rhoads, 1977-87; ret. Chmn. bd. Phila. Theatre Co., 1983-85. Bd. dirs. Conv. and Tourist Bur., Phila., 1942-84; commr., v.p. Phila. Fellowship Commn., 1965-74; pres. Jewish Cmty. Rels. Coun., 1962-65; chmn. bd. Moss Rehab. Hosp., 1974-77; pres. Alexis Rosenberg Found., 1983-91; fin. chmn. Inst. Contemporary Art, 1974-83; exec. com. Coun. Performing Arts, 1964-70; v.p. Nat. Comty. Rels. Adv. Coun., 1965-68; pres. Phila. chpt. Am. Jewish Com., 1966-68; trustee Pa. Coll. Podiatric Medicine, 1967-91, chmn., 1989-90; pres. Greenfield Found., 1991—2005; dir. Asolo Theatre Co., 1997-2002, v.p. 1999-2001; trustee Asolo Endowment Fund, 2003—, Hermitage Artist Retreat, 2004—. Mem. Landings Racquet Club (pres. 1994-96), Phi Beta Kappa. Home: 1650 Landings Blvd Sarasota FL 34231-3223 E-mail: rkg1650@comcast.net.

GREENFIELD, SANFORD RAYMOND, architect; b. N.Y.C., Feb. 3, 1926; s. Harry Leon and Dorothy (Shaefer) G.; m. Stella Berger, Oct. 12, 1952; children— Lise, Daniel, Stefanie. Student, Mich. State Coll. Liberal Arts, 1946-48; B.Arch., M.I.T., 1952, M.Arch., 1954; postgrad., New Sch. Social Research, N.Y.C., 1953, L'Inst. d'Urbanisme, Paris, 1954-55; Ed.M., Harvard U., 1975. Faculty Sch. Architecture and Planning, M.I.T., 1955-57; with Samuel Glaser, Boston, 1958-60; ptnr. Carroll & Greenfield (architects), Boston, 1960-73; dir. edn. Boston Archtl. Ctr. Sch. Architecture, 1967-75; research mgr. AIA Research Corp., 1975-76; cons. Sanford R. Greenfield & Asso., Boston; chmn. dept. architecture Iowa State U., Ames, 1976-81; dean Sch. Architecture, N.J. Inst. Tech., 1981-91, prof. architecture emeritus, 2001—. Lectr. Inst. Urban Design, Krakow (Poland) Politechnika, 1978; dir. edn. Boston Archtl. Ctr.; cons. ednl. planning; lectr. Mass. Coll. Art; mem. task force on edn. and tng. for internat. constrn. Bldg. Rsch. Bd. NRC, 1987; examiner archtl. registration exam. in design, 1984, 85, 86, 87, 90. Editor: Architecture and the Computer, 1964, Forces Shaping the Role of The Architect, 1966, Systems, 1968; contbr. articles to profl. jours.; Important works include Library St. John's Sem. Mem. 5-Presidents' Task Force on Edn., 1972-73; chmn. Nat. Adv. Coun. Continuing Edn., 1972-73; mem. adv. bd. Ctr. for Study of Profl. Edn., U. Cin., 1992—. Served with USNR, 1944-46. Recipient Centennial Educator award Boston Archtl. Ctr., 1989; Fulbright scholar, 1954-55; Nat. Endowment for Arts grantee, 1978; Sch. of Architecture Libr. Coll. named in his honor, N.J. Inst. Tech., 1996. Fellow

AIA (bd. dirs. AIA/ACSA rsch. coun. 1989-91); mem. Iowa Assn. Architects, Assn. Collegiate Schs. Architecture (v.p. 1972-73, pres. 1973-74, also dir.), N.J. Soc. Architects (bd. dirs. 1982-91), Boston Archtl. Ctr. Task Force Limits of Growth, 2002.

GREENFIELD, SUSAN L., lawyer; m. Lawrence Abramson; children: Rebecca, Kate. BA, Wayne State U., 1970, JD, 1975. In house atty. Fruehoff Trailer Corp., Valeron Corp., 1977—87; staff atty. Guardian Industries Corp., 1987—94; with Palace Sports and Entertainment Inc., 1994—, v.p. & gen. counsel; v.p. - legal Detroit Pistons. Office: Palace Sports & Entertainment Inc 4 Championship Dr Auburn Hills MI 48326

GREENFIELD, VAL SHEA, ophthalmologist; b. N.Y.C., Apr. 20, 1932; s. Frank Lynne and Helen (Meyers) G. Student, Brown U., 1948-49, 50-51, St. John's U., 1949; BA cum laude, Bklyn. Coll., 1952; MD, Yale U., 1956. Diplomate Am. Bd. Ophthalmology. Intern Walter Reed Army Hosp., Washington, 1956-57; asst. chief U.S. Army Dispensary, Phila., 1957-59, chief, 1959-60; postgrad. preceptorship in ophthal. under co-chief ophthal. Presby.-U. Pa. Med. Ctr., Phila., 1963-66; practice medicine specializing in obstetrics Phila., Riveride, N.J., 1960-63; practice medicine specializing in ophthalmology Phila., 1966—. Assoc. dir., lectr. in neuro-ophthalmology Hahnemann U., Phila., 1978—, from asst. prof. to assoc. prof. ophthalmology Sch. Medicine, 1977-88; assoc. clin. prof. Robert Wood Johnson Med. Sch.-N.J. U. Medicine and Dentistry, 1988—; attending surgeon in ophthalmology Frankford and Rolling Hills Hosps., Phila., 1970—; lectr. Bibl. topics U.S., Israel, Europe, New Zealand, USSR; guest speaker TV stas. and clubs; speaker, Gideons Internat. Gospel Soc. Internat., 2001. Contbr. articles to profl. jours., chpts. to textbooks. Mem. bd. deacons Cmty. Ch., Mt. Laurel Chapel and Fellowship, 1970—; bd. dirs. Hebrew Christian Outreach of Ch. of Our Lord Jesus Christ, 1958—; v.p. NJ MOorestown Camp of Gideons Internat. Bible Distbn. and Lectr. Soc., 2004—; spkr. ann. meeting G.I. Gospel Soc. Internat., 2001; trustee The Delaware Valley Pa. Vision Rsch. Charitable Trust, Comell Inst. for Med. Rsch., Red Cross, Fedn. Allied Jewish Appeal, 2003—. Served to capt. M.C., U.S. Army, 1955-60. Inducted into Chapel of 4 Chaplains, Temple U., 1981; inducted Hon. Brave Cherokee Indians by Chief Rising Sun, Chief and High Priest of N.Am. and S.Am. Indian Tribes and Couns., 1947; recipient AMA Physicians Recognition award in med. edn., tri-annually, 1974—. Fellow ACS, ACP, Am. Geriatrics Soc., Phila. Coll. Physicians; mem. AMA, Pa. Med. Soc., Phila. County Med. Soc., Am. Acad. Ophthalmology, N.Y. State Ophthal. Soc., Pa. Acad. Ophthalmology, Pan-Am. Soc. Ophthalmology, Soc. Contemporary Ophthalmology, Christian Med. Soc., Am. Soc. Cataract and Refracture Surgery, Internat. Platform Soc., Am. Judeo-Christian Fellowship, Alpha Kappa Kappa. Avocations: book collecting, bible lectures and writings. Office Phone: 856-234-7268. E-mail: greenfieldv@aol.com. *In over forty years of studying and applying the principles of medicine to my patients, I have seen the devastating toll that anger, hatred, fear, doubt, anguish, inordinate lust and jealousy have taken on men's and women's bodies and souls. I continually advise my patients that conventional medicines and therapies alone cannot heal or cure these "spiritual diseases". I add to my therapeutic armamentarium the concepts of the Ten Commandments and the Sermon on the Mount, which I suggest that my patients apply to their daily lives. The happiest moments in my professional life have been when I observe the salubrious effects that faith, hope and love have upon my patients' afflictions. Jesus, the Annointed One of God, prophetically called "The Mighty God, the Everlasting Father, the Prince of Peace", summed up His whole religion, which I heartily recommend to my patients, colleagues, friends, as well as to myself, as follows: "Thou shalt love The Lord thy God with all thy heart and with all thy soul and with all thy mind. Thou shalt love thy neighbor as thyself. On these two commandments hang all the law and Prophets." Unless mankind in general, and each and every man and woman in particular, appropriate and follow these commandments, then we will face the dire consequences that are already evolving worldwide: the scourges of war, pestilence and famine.*

GREENGARD, PAUL, neuroscientist, educator; b. N.Y.C., Dec. 11, 1925; married; 3 children. AB, Hamilton Coll., 1948; PhD, Johns Hopkins U., 1953. NSF fellow in neurochemistry U. London (Eng.)Inst. Psychiatry, 1953—54; Nat. Found. Infantile Paralysis fellow U. Cambridge (Eng.) Molteno Inst., 1954—55; Paraplegia Found. fellow Nat. Inst. Med. Rsch., England, 1955—56; fellow Nat. Inst. Neurological Diseases and Blindness, 1956—58; dir. biochemistry dept. Ciba-Geigy Rsch. Labs., 1958—67; prof. pharmacology and psychiatry Yale U. Sch. Medicine, New Haven, 1968—83; Andrew D. White prof.-at-large Cornell U., Ithaca, NY, 1981—87; Vincent Astor prof. Rockefeller U., N.Y.C., 1983—. Vis. scientist Nat. Heart Inst., 1958—59; vis. assoc. prof. Albert Einstein Coll. Medicine, 1961—68, vis. prof., 1968—83, Vanderbilt U., 1967—68; Harvey Soc. lectr., 1980; lectr. in field. Recipient Dickson prize and medal in medicine, U. Pitts., 1977, Ciba-Geigy Drew award, 1979, Biol. and Med. Scis. award, N.Y. Acad. Scis., 1980, 3M Life Scis. award, Fedn. Am. Socs. Exptl. Biology, 1987, Bristol-Myers award for disting. achievement in neurosci. rsch., 1989, Goodman and Gilman award in receptor pharmacology, 1992, Karl Spencer Lashley prize, Am. Philos. Soc., 1993, Biochem. Soc. Thudichum medal, 1996, Charles A. Dana Found. award for pioneering achievements in health, 1997, Met. Life Found. award for excellence in sci. and tech., 1999, Nobel prize in physiology or medicine, 2000. Mem.: NAS (award in neuroscis. 1991), Nat. Alliance for Rsch. on Schizophrenia and Depression (Lieber prize Outstanding Achievement Schizophrenia Rsch. 1996), Soc. for Neurosci. (Grass lectr. 1986, Gerard prize 1994), Am. Acad. Arts and Scis., Am. Neurol. Assn. (hon.). Office: Rockefeller U 1230 York Ave New York NY 10021-6399*

GREENGRASS, PAUL, film director; b. Cheam Surrey, Eng., Aug. 13, 1955; Attended, Cambridge U. Dir., writer: (TV films) Open Fire, 1994; The One That Got Away, 1996; The Fix, 1997; The Murder of Stephen Lawrence, 1999; (films) Bloody Sunday, 2002; writer, prodr.: (TV films) Omagh, 2004; dir.: (films) Resuurected, 1989, The Theory of Flight, 1998, The Bourne Supremacy, 2004; (TV films) When the Lies Run Out, 1993; (TV series) Kavanagh QC, 1995—2001; co-author: (book) Spycatcher, 1988. Address: c/o Universal Pictures 100 Universal City Plz Universal City CA 91608*

GREENGUS, SAMUEL, academic administrator, theology studies educator; b. Chgo., Mar. 11, 1936; s. Eugene and Thelma (Romirowsky) G.; m. Lesha Bellows, Apr. 30, 1957; children: Deana, Rachel, Judith. Student, Hebrew Theol. Coll., Chgo., 1950-58; MA, U. Chgo., 1959, PhD, 1963. Prof. semitic langs. Hebrew Union Coll.-Jewish Inst. Religion, Cin., 1963-89, Julian Morgenstern prof. bible and near eastern lit., 1989—, dean rabbinic sch., 1979-84, dean Cin. campus, 1985-87, dean sch. grad. studies, 1985-90, dean faculty, 1987-98, v.p. for Acad. affairs, 1990-96. Vis. lectr. U. of Dayton, Ohio, 1964-69, Leo Baeck Coll., London, 1976-77; area supr. Tel Gezer Excavation, Israel, 1966-67; mem. bd. editors Hebrew Union Coll. Ann. Author: Old Babylonian Tablets from Ishchali and Vicinity, 1979, Studies in Ishchali Documents, 1986; mem. bd. editors Zeitschrift fur Altorientalische und Biblische Rechtsgeschichte; contbr. articles to profl. jours. Mem. Cin. Community Hebrew Schs. Bd., 1970-75; mem. vis. com. Sch. for Creative and Performing Arts, Cin., 1980-82; chmn. acad. officers, Greater Cin. Consortium Colls. and Univs., 1984-85, mem. exec. com., 1989-96. Am. Council Learned Socs. fellow, 1970-71, Am. Assn. Theol. Schs. fellow, 1976-77. Mem. Am. Oriental Soc., Assn. Jewish Studies, Soc. Bibl. Lit., Phi Beta Kappa. Jewish. Office: Hebrew Union Coll Jewish Inst Religion 3101 Clifton Ave Cincinnati OH 45220-2404 Office Phone: 513-221-1875. E-mail: sgreengus@huc.edu.

GREENHALGH, DOUGLAS BRUCE, secondary school educator; b. Niagara Falls, N.Y., Mar. 1, 1957; s. Frederick Edward and Doris May (Campbell) G.; m. Therese Gerard Nellesen, Sept. 30, 1978; children: Amber, Natel, Amanda. Student, U. Wis., Stevens Point, 1975-78; BS in Music and History Edn., U. Wis., Superior, 1983; M in Edn. Profl. Devel., U. Wis., Eau Claire, 1998. Cert. tchr. music edn. K-12, secondary history, Wis. Instrumental music tchr. Chippewa Falls (Wis.) H.S., 1983—, music dept. chmn., 1986—. Visual adjudicator Drum Corps Midwest, 1988-99, music clinician and arranger, 1981—; concert mgr. Chippewa Vly. Cmty. Concerts, 1989-93. Recipient Excellence in Edn. award Chippewa Falls Adv. Bd., 1988, 89, 91, 92, 93, 94, 96, 97, 98, 99, 2000, 02, 03, 05. Mem. Nat. Band Assn., Gold Wing Road Riders Assn. (asst. dist. dir. 2003-05). Avocations: dogs, walking, motorcycle touring. Home: 10172 65th Ave Chippewa Falls WI 54729-5710 Personal E-mail: whitewng@discover-net.net. Business E-Mail: greenhdb@chipfalls.k12.wi.us.

GREENHILL, H. GAYLON, retired academic administrator; Chancellor U. Wis., Whitewater, 1991-99, chancellor emeritus, 1999—. Address: PO Box 507 Whitewater WI 53190-0507 E-mail: greenhig@mail.uww.edu.

GREENHILL, JOE ROBERT, retired judge, lawyer; b. Houston, July 14, 1914; s. Joe R. Jr. and Violet (Stanuell) G.; m. Martha Shuford, June 15, 1940; children: Joe IV, William D. BBA, BA, U. Tex., 1936, LLB, 1939; LLD (hon.), So. Meth. U., 1977. Briefing atty. for chief justice Alexander Tex. Supreme Ct., Austin, 1941, 46; 1st asst. atty. gen. Tex. Austin, 1947-50; co-founder Graves, Dougherty & Greenhill, Austin, 1950-57; justice Supreme Ct. of Tex., Austin, 1957-72, chief justice, 1972-82; of counsel Baker & Botts, Austin, 1982—. Co-incorporator Tex. Ctr. for Professionalism and Ethics, Austin, 1991—; pres. elect Conf. Chief Justices and Nat. Ctr. for State Courts, Williamsburg, Va., 1982. Editor Tex. Law Rev., 1937-39 (Outstanding Ex-Editor 1975). Lt. USNR, 1942-46, PTO. Named Disting. Alumnus U. Tex., 1974, Disting. Alumnus U. Tex. Law Sch., 1977, Disting. Alumnus U. Tex. Coll. Bus. Adminstrn., 1974. Fellow Tex. Bar Found. (life, Outstanding 50 yr. lawyer 1989, exec. dir. 1984—), Am. Bar Found. (life); mem. Masons (33 degree). Office: Baker & Botts 98 San Jacinto Blvd Ste 1600 Austin TX 78701-4078

GREENHILL, ROBERT FOSTER, investment banker; b. Mpls., June 20, 1936; s. J. Raymond and Mary (Foster) G.; m. Mary Gayle Gussett, Sept. 13, 1958; children: Sarah B., Robert Foster, Mary B. AB, Yale U., 1958; MBA, Harvard U., 1962. Assoc. Morgan Stanley & Co., Inc., N.Y.C., 1962-70, mng. dir., 1970-93, pres., 1991-93; chmn., chief exec. officer Smith Barney Shearson, Inc., N.Y.C., 1993-96, Greenhill & Co., LLC, N.Y.C., 1996—. Trustee Am. Enterprise Inst. Served to lt. (j.g.) USNR, 1960-62. Mem. Ausable Club (Keene Valley, N.Y.), Field Club, Links Club, River Club. Clubs: Ausable (Keene Valley, N.Y.); Field (Greenwich); Links; River (N.Y.C.). Office: Greenhill & Co LLC 300 Park Ave New York NY 10022 Office Phone: 212-389-1510.

GREENHOUSE, LINDA JOYCE, journalist; b. NYC, Jan. 9, 1947; d. Herman Robert and Dorothy Eleanor (Greenlick) Greenhouse; m. Eugene R. Fidell, Jan. 1, 1981; 1 child, Hannah Margalit Fidell. BA, Radcliffe Coll., 1968; M of Studies in Law, Yale U., 1978; D.H.L. (hon.) (hon.), Brown U., 1991; LLD (hon.) (hon.), Colgate U., 1993, Northeastern U., 1997, CUNY, 1997; LLD (hon.), U. Miami, 2004, Georgetown U., 2004. Asst. to James Reston The N.Y. Times, N.Y.C., 1968—69, met. reporter, 1970—74, state polit. reporter, 1974—77, supreme ct. corr. Washington, 1978—85, 1988—, congl. corr., 1986—88. Author: Becoming Justice Blackmun: Harry Blackmun's Supreme Court Journey, 2005. Adv. com. Schlesinger Libr. on the History of Women in Am., Radcliffe Coll., 1995—2002; mem. Schlesinger Libr. Coun., 2003—; bd. dirs. Yale Law Sch. Fund, New Haven, 1984—91. Recipient Pulitzer prize in journalism for beat reporting, 1998, Carey McWilliams award, Am. Polit. Sci. Assn., 2002, Henry J. Friendly medal, Am. Law Inst., 2002, Golden Pen award, Legal Writing Inst., 2002, Goldsmith Career award, John F. Kennedy Sch. Govt., Harvard U., 2004, Pres.'s Spl. award, N.Y. Women's Bar Assn., 2004, Anvil of Freedom award, Estlow Internat. Ctr. for Journalism and New Media, U. Denver, 2005, John Chancellor award for excellence in journalism, 2004, William Green award Profl. Excellence, U. Richmond Law Sch., 2005. Fellow: Am. Acad. Arts and Scis. (mem. coun. 2004—); mem.: Women's Forum of Washington (v.p. 2003—05), Yale Law Assn. (exec. com. 1993—97), Am. Law Inst. (hon.), Am. Philos. Soc., Harvard Club of Washington (bd. dirs. 1989—92). Office: The NY Times 1627 I St NW Washington DC 20006-4007 Office Phone: 202-862-0371. Business E-Mail: ligree@nytimes.com.

GREENHUT, MELVIN LEONARD, economist, educator; b. NYC, Mar. 10, 1921; s. Ab and Lillian (Frudman) G.; m. Elmara Margaret Griffith, Mar. 24, 1944; children: Margaret Lee, Pamela Jo, John Griffith, Patricia Lynn. PhD, Washington U., 1951. Prof. econ. various univ., 1948-62; prof., head dept. econ. Tex. A&M U., Coll. Sta., 1966-69, disting. prof. econ., 1969—, alumni disting. prof. econ., 1980-85, Abell Prof. Liberal Arts, disting. prof. econ., 1986—, Abell Prof. Liberal Arts, disting. prof. econ. emeritus, 1992—, chmn. disting. prof., 1988-89. Vis. prof., lectr. in field. Co-author (with John Greenhut): (book) Sci. and God, 2002, Our Teleological Econ. World, 2002; author: 19 books; contbr. articles to profl. jour. Mem. nat. econ. policy com. and econ. adv. coun. US C. of C., 1960-63. Maj. US Army. Mem. Am. Econ. Assn., So. Econ. Assn. (past v.p.), Regional Sci. Assn. (councillor), Royal Econ. Soc., Econometric Soc., Delta Chi, Omicron Delta Gamma. Lutheran. Home: 5814 Constellation Cir Rockwall TX 75032-5770 Office: Tex A&M U Dept Econs College Station TX 77843-0001

GREENLAND, LEO, advertising executive; b. N.Y.C., Mar. 4, 1920; s. Jack and Ida (Abrams) G.; m. Rita Levine, June 29, 1955 (dec. Sept. 7, 1991); m. Eileen Ludwig, Feb. 2, 2004 children: Seth, Andrew. Student, New Sch. for Social Rsch., 1945—47. Pres. Sherwood Prodns., 1949-52; exec. various advt. agys., 1952-59; pres. Smith/Greenland Co., Inc., N.Y.C., 1959—, chmn., CEO, 1974—. Guest lectr. Fordham U. Sch. Communication Arts, 1967-, Cornell Sch. Hotel Mgmt., NYU. Nat. commr. Anti-Defamation League, chmn. radio-TV dept.; bd. dirs., pres. Friars Found.; trustee ADL Found., hon. vice-chmn.; hon. chief N.Y.C. Fire Dept.; mem. adv. bd. bus. coun. UN; mem. Am. Forces Info. Svc. Task Force; bd. dirs. Nat. Libr. Mus., Phila., Am. Interfaith Inst. Served with AUS, 1943-46. Mem. Am. Advt. Agys. (bd. govs. N.Y.), Nat. Advt. Rev. Bd., Am. Mgmt. Assn. (lectr. 1969—), Am. Arbitration Assn., Nat. Businessmen's Coun., Fgn. Policy Assn. Interracial Businessmen's Coun., Ea. Frosted Foods Assn. (pres. 1965-67, bd. dirs.), Chief Execs. Orgn., Met. Pres. Orgn., Sales Execs. Club N.Y., Newcomer Soc. N.Am., Def. Orientation Conf. Assn., Am. Forces Info. Svc. Task Force, Young Presidents Orgn., World Bus. Coun., Sierra Club, Econs. Club, Gilda's Club (founding mem.), Rockrimmon Country Club, Friars Club (pres. found.), Palm Beach Round Table. Home: PO Box 806 Bedford NY 10506-0806 Office: Smith/Greenland Inc 1056 5th Ave # 10A New York NY 10028-0112 Office Phone: 646-672-9233. Personal E-mail: leobald@aol.com.

GREENLAW, MARILYN JEAN, retired adult education educator; b. St. Petersburg, Fla., Apr. 1, 1941; d. Hinckley and Dorothy Rebecca (Ball) G. BA, Stetson U., 1962, MA, 1965; PhD, Mich. State U., 1970. Elem. tchr. Broward County schs., Ft. Lauderdale, Fla., 1962-64; ele. cons. Harper and Row Publs., Evanston, Ill., 1965-69; from asst. to assoc. prof. U. Ga., Athens, 1970-78; from assoc. to full prof. U. North Tex., Denton, 1978-87, regents prof., 1987—2005, ret., 2005. Cons. Scholastic Publs., N.Y.C., 1978-87, Houghton Mifflin Co., Boston, 1984-94, Tex. Instruments, Dallas, 1981-85, Coordinating Bd., Austin, Tex., 1987-91. Author: Ranch Dressing: The Story of Western Wear, 1993, Welcome to the Stock Show, 1997; co-author: Storybook Classrooms, 1985, Educating the Gifted, 1988; editor book rev. column Jour. Reading, 1981-84, The New Adv., 1987-94. Mem. Friends of the Denton Pub.Libr., 1984—, pres., 1995-97, 2001-, Keep Denton Beautiful, pres., 2003; bd. dirs. Denton Libr., 1992-97, chair, 1995-96. Recipient Arbuthnot award, 1992, Disting. Svc. award Tex. State Reading Assn., 1996, Pres.'s Coun. Disting. Svc. award U. North Tex., 1996. Mem.: ALA (com. chairperson 1984—85), Internat. Reading Assn. (com. chairperson 1980—90, Arbuthnot award 1992), Nat. Coun. Tchrs. of English (com. chairperson 1980—, Outstanding Leadership in Edn. award 1976), Kiwanis (pres. 2002—), Phi Kappa Phi (v.p. 1986—87), Phi Delta Kappa (pres. 1982—83, Outstanding Young Educator award 1981). Republican. Avocations: reading, gardening, photography. Home: 2600 Sheraton Rd Denton TX 76209-8620

GREENLAW, ROGER LEE, interior designer; b. New London, Conn., Oct. 12, 1936; s. Kenneth Nelson and Lyndell Lee (Stinson) Greenlaw; children: Carol Jennifer, Roger Lee. BFA, Syracuse U., 1958. Interior designer Cannell & Chaffin, 1958-59, William C. Wagner, Arch., L.A., 1959-60, Gen. Fireproofing Co., L.A., 1960-62, K-S Wilshire, Inc., L.A., 1963-64; dir. interior design Calif. Desk Co., L.A., 1967-67; sr. interior designer Bechtel Corp., L.A., 1967-70; sr. interior designer, project mgr. Daniel, Mann, Johnson & Mendehall, L.A., 1970-72, Morganelli-Heumann & Assocs., L.A., 1972-73; owner, prin. Greenlaw Design Assocs., Glendale, Calif., 1973—96, Greenlaw Interior Planning & Design, 1996—. Lectr. UCLA; mem. adv. curriculum com. Mt. San Antonio Coll., Walnut, Calif., Fashion Inst. Design, LA; bd. dirs. Calif. Legis. Conf. Interior Design, treas., 1992—94, v.p., 1990—92, pres., 1994—98. Past scoutmaster Verdugo coun. Boy Scouts Am.; pres. bd. dirs. Unity Ch., La Crescenta, Calif., 1989—91. Mem.: ASID (treas. Pasadena chpt. 1983—84, 1st v.p. 1985, chmn. So. Calif. Regional Conf. 1985, pres. 1986—87, nat. dir. 1987—89, v.p., treas. 1992, pres. 1994—98, mem. nat. com. legis., chmn. stds. task force, mem. nat. com. jury catalog award, spkr. ho. dels., nat. bd. dirs., regional v.p., nat. chair ethics com., nat. exec. com., medallist award), Adm. Farragut Acad. Alumni Assn., Glendale C. of C. (bd. dirs. 1998), Kiwanis (bd. dirs.), Delta Upsilon. Republican. Office: 1145-4 Willowbend Cir Colorado Springs CO 80918-7035 Office Phone: 719-547-0885. Business E-Mail: greenlawdesign@msn.com.

GREENLEAF, JOHN L., JR., lawyer; b. Ft. Campbell, Ky., July 27, 1953; s. John L. Sr. and Betty R. G.; m. Carol K. Hood, Dec. 18, 1971; children: Sara E., J. Luke, Danielle H. BS, U. Ill., 1975; JD, John Marshall Law Sch., 1978. Bar: Ill. 1978, U.S. Dist. Ct. (so. and cen. dists.) Ill. 1978, U.S. Supreme Ct. 1982. Assoc. Byers & Byers, Inc., Decatur, Ill., 1978-80; ptnr. Byers, Byers & Greenleaf, Inc., Decatur, 1980-89; pvt. practice Decatur, 1989-98; assoc. Frank H. Byers, Decatur, 1998-2001; assoc. pastor Decatur Foursquare Ch., 1998—. Dir. Decatur Foursquare Broadcasting--WFHL TV 23, 1980-98; adv. dir. New Life Pregnancy Ctr., Decatur, 1994—; treas. Decatur Jaycees, 1982, Com. to Elect Frank H. Byers, II as State's Atty., 1988. Named Leading Ill. Attys., Am. Rsch. Corp., 1996. Mem. Ill. Bar Assn. Avocations: teaching and preaching the Bible, skiing, swimming, golf. Office: 4670 Needle Rd Decatur IL 62526 E-mail: attylaw7@msn.com.

GREENLEE, HERBERT BRECKENRIDGE, surgeon, educator; b. Rockford, Ill., Sept. 6, 1927; s. Harvey James and Abbie (McCathran) G.; m. Shirley Claire Rurik, June 12, 1955; children: Herbert, William, Kenneth, Anne. AB, Beloit Coll., 1951; MD, U. Chgo., 1955. Diplomate: Am. Bd. Surgery. Intern U. Chgo. Clinics, 1956, resident in surgery, 1956-62; practice medicine specializing in surgery Chgo., 1964-66; staff surgeon VA Hosp., Madison, Wis., 1966-67, asst. chief surg. service Hines, Ill., 1967-72, chief surg. service, 1972—; asso. prof. surgery Stritch Sch. Medicine, Loyola U., Maywood, Ill., 1967-72, prof. surgery, 1972—; prof. emeritus dept. surgery, 1995—. Author: Surgery of the Small and Large Intestine, 1973, Spanish edit, 1976; contbr. articles to sci. jours. Served with M.C. AUS, 1962-64. Recipient Raymond W. McNealy award Chgo. Surg. Soc., 1956 Fellow Am. Cancer Soc., A.C.S. (coordinator gen. surgery film sessions 1976—, chmn. motion picture com. 1978—, mem. program com. 1978—), Inst. Medicine Chgo.; mem. Am. Gastroenterology Assn., AMA, Soc. Surgery Alimentary Tract, Midwest Gut Club, Chgo. Soc. Gastroenterology (pres. 1973-74, counselor 1974-75), Am. Surg. Assn., Ill. Surg. Soc. (pres. 1975-76, trustee 1976—), Chgo. Surg. Soc. (sec. 1974-77, pres. 1980-81), Charles B. Puestow Surg. Soc., N.Y. Acad. Sci., Assn. VA Surgeons (pres. 1981-82), Assn. Acad. Surgery, Collegium Internat. Chirurgiae Digestivae, Western, Midwest, Central surg. assns., Internat. Soc. Surgery, Pancreas Club, Phi Beta Kappa, Sigma Xi, Alpha Omega Alpha. Home: 1917 Wyman School Rd Caledonia IL 61011-9528 Office: Loyola U Sch Medicine Dept Surgery 2160 S 1st Ave Dept Surgery Maywood IL 60153-3304 E-mail: hbgreenlee@earthlink.net.

GREENLEE, JIM MING, prosecutor; B in Engring., JD, U. Miss. Atty. Taylor and Whitwell, 1981—85; ptnr. Taylor, Jones, Alexander, Greenlee, Seale and Ryan, 1985—87; asst. U.S. atty. (no. dist.) Miss. U.S. Dept. Justice, 1987—2001, U.S. atty. (no. dist.) Miss., 2001—. Office: 900 Jefferson Ave Oxford MS 38655 Office Phone: 662-234-3351.

GREENLER, ROBERT GEORGE, physics professor, researcher; b. Kenton, Ohio, Oct. 24, 1929; s. Dallas George and Ruth Edna (Mallett) G.; m. Barbara Stacy, May 30, 1954; children: Leland S., Karen R., Robin A. BS in Physics, U. Rochester, 1951; PhD in Physics, Johns Hopkins U., 1957. Rsch. scientist Allis-Chalmers Mfg. Co., Milw., 1957-62; assoc. prof. physics U. Wis., Milw., 1962-67, prof., 1967-91, adj. prof., 1991-98, prof. emeritus, 1998—. Sr. vis. fellow U. East Anglia, Norwich, Eng., 1971-72; traveling lectr. Optical Soc. Am., 1973-74; lectr. Coop. Edn. Program, Malaysia, 1990-91; organizer pub. outreach program Sci. Bag; prodr. 25 ednl. videos; did field rsch. on optical atmospheric effects at U.S. Antarctic Rsch. Station, South Pole, 1976-77, 97-98, 98-99. Author: Rainbows, Halos and Glories, 1980, Chasing the Rainbow: Recurrences in the Life of a Scientist, 2000; contbr. 90 articles to profl. jours. Grantee, NSF, Petroleum Rsch. Fund, Am. Chem. Soc.; Sr. Fulbright scholar, Fritz Haber Inst. of Max Planck Soc., West Berlin, 1983. Fellow AAAS, Optical Soc. Am. (v.p. 1985, pres.-elect 1986, pres. 1987, 1st Esther Hoffman Beller award 1993); mem. Am. Assn. Physics Tchrs. (Milikan Lectr. award 1988). Achievements include research in surface science, infrared spectroscopy of absorbed molecules, meteorological optics, irridescent colors in biological systems. Home: 6225 Mineral Point Rd Apt 17 Madison WI 53705 Business E-Mail: greenler@uwm.edu.

GREENLEY, BEVERLY JANE, lawyer, educator; b. Cleve., Sept. 24, 1947; d. Gaylord H. and Joan C. (Gurklis) G. BA, Principia Coll., 1969; JD, U. Mo., 1976; LLM, Washington U., 1981. Bar: Mo. 1976, Ill. 1977, U.S. Tax Ct. 1979. Ptnr. McCarter & Greenley, St. Louis, 1976-81, McCarter, Snyder & Greenley, St. Louis, 1981-85; assoc. prof. law Stetson U. Coll. Law, St. Petersburg, Fla., 1981-85; ptnr. Gage & Tucker, St. Louis, 1985-87, Husch, Eppenberger, Donohue, Cornfeld & Jenkins, St. Louis, 1987-90, McCarter & Greenley, LLC, St. Louis, 1990—. Estate planning lectr. for CLE programs, 1997—; estate planning expert witness, 2000—. Co-author: Missouri Lawyer's Guide, 1984. Mem.: Ill. Bar Assn., Mo. Bar Assn. Office: 1 Metropolitan Sq Ste 2100 Saint Louis MO 63102-2797 E-mail: bgreenley@mccartergreenley.com.

GREENLY, COLIN, artist; b. London, Jan. 21, 1928; came to U.S., 1939, naturalized, 1948; s. Arthur John and Caroline Matilda (Fantini) G.; m. Laurie Ann Zadek, May 8, 1976; 1 child, Katharine Lydia Caro Herman. AB, Harvard Coll., 1948; student, Columbia U. Sch. Painting and Sculpture, 1951-53; attended Grad. Sch. Fine Arts, Am. U., 1956. Dir. art Madeira Sch., Greenway, Va., 1955-68; Dana prof. fine arts Colgate U., 1972-73; vis. artist numerous colls., univs. One-man shows Corcoran Gallery of Art, Washington, 1968, Royal Marks Gallery, N.Y.C., 1968, 70, Everson Mus., Syracuse, N.Y., 1971, Andrew Dickson White Mus. (now Herbert F. Johnson Mus.), Cornell U., 1972, Picker Gallery, Colgate U., 1973, Finch Coll. Mus., N.Y.C., 1974; group shows include Mus. Modern Art, N.Y.C., 1953, 73, De Cordova Mus., Lincoln, Mass., 1965, Des Moines Art Ctr., 1967, Nat. Collection Fine Arts, Washington, 1968, Krannert Art Mus., Champaign, Ill., 1969, 74, Emmerich Gallery Downtown, N.Y.C., 1972, John Weber Gallery, N.Y.C., 1975, Whitney Mus. Am. Art, N.Y.C., 1978, N.Y. State Mus., Albany, 1981; represented in permanent collections Albright Knox Art Gallery, Buffalo, Corcoran Gallery Art, Des Moines Art Ctr., Everson Mus., High Mus. Art, Atlanta, Mus. Modern Art, N.Y.C., Phila. Mus. Art, Nat. Gallery Art, Washington, Nat. Collection Fine Arts (now Smithsonian Am. Art Mus.), Washington, Herbert F. Johnson Mus., Ithaca, N.Y.; restoration and contemporary adaptation of Hulse Barn, Campbell Hall, N.Y.; contbr. to World Trade Ctr. Site Meml. Competition, 2003; contbr. works of art, videos, photographs to CDROM Images of the Whole, 1998; contbr. articles to profl. jours. Ptnr. Leaning Post Prodns. Grantee Nat. Endowment for Arts, 1967, Com. for Visual Arts, 1974, Creative Artists Pub. Svc. Program, 1972, 78, N.Y. State Coun. on Arts, 1993; named winner nat. competition playground sculpture Art in Am. and Corcoran Gallery Sch. Art, 1967. Mem. Nat. Audobon Soc., Nature Conservancy, Wilderness Soc., Nat. Trust for Hist. Preservation, Sierra

Club. Achievements include incorporating the characteristics of a circle and a square into a single image, thereby discovering an effective visual symbol for the concepts of transition and change, 1964; Intangible Sculpture. Address: 487 Hulsetown Rd Campbell Hall NY 10916-3201 Personal E-mail: greenly@leaningpost.com. *Developing one's abilities may require a measure of commitment and excellence, but committing excellence to indiscriminate ends is artless. The synthesis of life and art is art.*

GREENMAN, FREDERICK F., JR., lawyer; b. NYC, Feb. 22, 1933; s. Frederick F. and Mildred G.; m. Angela Lancieri; children: Paul Rudolph, Jodi La Bourene. BA, Harvard U., 1954, LLB, 1961, LLM, 1963. Bar: NY 1962. Assoc. Hays, Sklar & Herzberg, NYC, 1962-66; asst. U.S. atty. So. Dist. NY, NYC, 1966-69; assoc. Linden and Deutsch, NYC, 1969-70; ptnr. Deutsch Klagsbrun & Blasband (and predecessor firm), NYC, 1971-2001; lawyer pvt. practice, 2001—. Legal advisor Am. Adoption Congress. Mem. Assn. Bar City of NY, NY State Bar Assn. Jewish. Office: 641 Lexington Ave New York NY 10022-4503 Office Phone: 212-758-1158. E-mail: FFGreenman@aol.com.

GREENMAN, JANE FRIEDLIEB, lawyer, human resources executive; b. N.Y.C., Sept. 9, 1950; d. Morton Jerome and Isabelle Irene (Bisgyer) F.; m. Charles P. Greenman, Nov. 23, 1975; children: Margot, Jaclyn, Danielle. BS, Cornell U., 1972; JD, NYU, 1975, LLM in Labor Law, 1981. Bar: NY 1976, NY 1986. Assoc. Wolf Haldenstein, N.Y.C., 1975-79; faculty NYU Law Sch., 1979-81, Bklyn. Law Sch., 1981—82; assoc., counsel Hughes Hubbard & Reed, N.Y.C., 1982-91, ptnr., chair employee benefits dept., 1991-96; v.p., dep. gen. coun. human resources Honeywell Internat., Inc., Morristown, NJ, 1996—2003; v.p. compensation, benefits and labor rels. Tyco Internat., N.Y.C., 2003—. Adj. prof. Bklyn. Law Sch., 1982-92, 95, Hofstra U.; bd. dirs. Women's Fund of N.J., NYC Bound Outward. Mem. Temple Sinai of Summit, Religious Action Ctr. Commn. for Social Action. Mem. ABA, N.Y.C. Bar Assn., N.Y. State Bar Assn. Jewish. Office: Tyco Internat Inc 9 Roszel Rd Princeton NJ 08540

GREENMAN, PAULA S., lawyer; b. Putnam, N.Y., 1951; BA cum laude, Yale U., 1972; JD, Boston (Mass.) Coll., 1976. Bar: Conn. 1976, N.Y. 1995. Atty. Skadden, Arps, Slate, Meagher & Flom LLP, N.Y., ptnr., 2001—. Office: Skadden Arps Slate Meagher & Flom LLP Four Times Sq New York NY 10036

GREENMAN, RICHARD LEONARD, retired physician, educator; b. Chgo., Aug. 29, 1943; s. Albert and Gladys (Krause) G.; m. Bernadine Heller, Jul. 31, 1966; children: Benjamin, Aaron, Joshua. BA, Cornell Univ., 1964; MS, Univ. Iowa, 1965; MD, Chgo. Medical Sch., 1969. Diplomate Am. Bd. Nat Bd. Medical Examiners, Diplomate Am. Bd. Internal Medicine. Asst. prof. medicine Univ. Miami Sch. of Medicine, 1974-80, assoc. prof. medicine, 1980-92, prof. of medicine, 1992-98; ret., 1998. With USAF Res., 1973-80. Fellow ACP, Infectious Diseases Soc. of Am.; mem. Fla. Infectious Diseases Soc. (pres. 1995-96), Alpha Omega Alpha (pres. 1968). Democrat. Jewish. Avocations: sailing, skiing, scuba diving. Office: Univ Miami Medical Sch PO Box 16960 Miami FL 33101-6960

GREENO, JOHN LADD, chemicals executive; b. Syracuse, New York, June 6, 1949; s. John Stuart and Mary Jane (Pfohl) G.; m. Grace Marie (Misiano), Feb. 7, 1981; children: Meredith, Jane. BBA, U. Okla., 1971; postgrad., U. Hawaii, 1975; MBA, Harvard U., 1978. cert. profl. environ. auditor. Ensign USN, 1971, advance through grades to lt., 1971—75, surface warfare officer, 1971—76; human resource mgmt. specialist Human Resource Mgmt. Sch., USN, Memphis, 1975, Human Resource Mgmt. Ctr. USN, Honolulu, 1976, resigned, 1976; cons. Arthur D. Little, Inc., Cambridge, Mass., 1977—2002, dir., 1985—89, v.p., 1986—92, sr. v.p., 1993—2002, mng. dir., 1989—2000, COO, 2000—02; pres. Arthur D. Little of Can., Ltd., 1993—96, chmn., CEO, 1997—2002; pres., CEO, bd. dirs. AgION Tech., Inc., Wakefield, Mass., 2003—, chmn., 2004—. Mem. bd. environ. auditors cert., chmn. bd. dir., Arthur D. Little of Can., Ltd., 1998-2002, pres., 1999-2002; bd. dir. Pyxsys Corp.; chmn. Cambridge Cons. Ltd.; mem. Registrar Accreditation Bd. Author: Environmental Auditing: Fundamentals and Techniques, 1985, Environmental, Health and Safety Auditors Handbook, 1988, Guide to Effective Environmental Auditing, 1991; contbg. author Environmental Auditing Handbook, 1984, Environmental Strategies Handbook, 1993, Risk Assessment and Management Handbook, 1995. Served in USN, 1971-76. Mem. Environ. Auditing Roundtable (founding mem., chmn. steering com. 1984-85, Extra Ordinary Svc. Award 1991), Conf. Bd. Environ. Coun. (charter mem., bd. environ. auditor cert. 1998—, cert. profl. environ. auditor 1997, bd. dir. registrar accreditation bd. 1998-2002) Home: 363 Mattison Dr Concord MA 01742-4142 Office: AgION Tech Inc 60 Audubon Rd Wakefield MA 01880

GREENOUGH, WILLIAM BATES, III, medical educator; b. Providence, Jan. 3, 1932; s. William Bates Jr. and Dorothy Garrison (Rand) G.; m. Jane Cheney Woodruff, Aug. 14, 1954 (dec. 1964); children: William Beckley, Kate, Thomas Clark, Elisabeth Bates; m. Quaneta Ahmed, 1965; 1 child, Zarin Farah Naz. BA magna cum laude, Amherst Coll., 1953; MD cum laude, Harvard U., 1957. Intern, asst. resident Columbia U. Coll. Physicians and Surgeons, N.Y.C., 1957-59; sr. rsch. fellow Mary Imogene Bassett Hosp., Cooperstown, N.Y., 1959-61; sr. resident Peter Bent Brigham Hosp., Boston, 1961-62; staff assoc. Nat. Heart Inst. Cholera Rsch. Lab., Dhaka, Bangladesh, 1962-65; chief infectious diseases div. Johns Hopkins U. Sch. Medicine, Balt., 1970-76, dir. Robert Wood Johnson Clin. Scholars Program, 1974-77, prof. medicine, 1983—, prof. internat. health sch. pub. health, 1985—; dir. Internat. Ctr. for Diarrhoeal Disease Rsch., Dhaka, Bangladesh, 1979-85; mem. geriatric medicine div. Johns Hopkins U., 1985—. Cons. infectious diseases Perry Point VA Hosp., 1972-77, Internat. Rescue Com., NYC, 1971-72; bacteriology and mycology study sect. NIH, 1972-76, chmn., 1974-76; ad hoc study group on enteric disease Walter Reed Army Inst. Rsch., 1975-77; pres. Bangladesh Info. Ctr., Washington, 1971-84; adv. coun. Bangladesh Found., Chgo., 1972; active Md. Gov.'s Commn. on Phys. Fitness and Marathon Commn., 1971-77; pres., chmn. bd., trustee Internat. Child Health Found., Columbia, Md., 1985-95, pres., 1998—; chmn. Internat. Ctr. for Diarrhoeal Disease Rsch., Bangladesh Endowment Fund, 1997—; cons. Cera Products Inc., 1993-. Editor Infection and Immunity, 1975-78, Topics in Infectious Disease, 1976—, Jour. Diarrhoeal Disease Rsch., 1983-85, 93-2000; internat. adv. Kuwait Med. Jour., Jour. Health Population and Nutrition, 2000—; contbr. articles to profl. jours., chpts. to books Sr. surgeon USPHS, 1962-67. Recipient Internat. prize in medicine, King Faisal Found., 1984, Maurice Pate prize UNICEF, 1984, recognized for svc. to children, 1983; Howard Florey Meml. lectr. U. Adelaide, 2001. Fellow: ACP, AAAS, Infectious Diseases Soc. Am. (mem. internat. affairs com. 2000—03); mem.: Bangladesh Med. Soc., Am. Soc. Microbiology, Bangladesh Assn. for Advancement Scis., Am. Geriatric Soc., Am. Soc. for Clin. Investigation, Assn. Am. Physicians. Muslim. Achievements include patents in field. Home: 1300 Hollins Ln Baltimore MD 21209-2237 Office: Johns Hopkins Geriatrics Ctr 5505 Hopkins Bayview Cir Baltimore MD 21224-6822 Office Phone: 410-550-0782. Personal E-mail: wgreenou@hotmail.com. Business E-Mail: wgreenou@jhmi.edu. *"Assuredly The Creation of The Heavens And The earth Is a greater matter Than The creation of man: Yet most men understand not.".*

GREENSLADE, CINDY LOUISE, psychologist; b. Balt., Nov. 9, 1959; d. John Robert and Doris Ann Weeks; m. Ivor David Greenslade, Sept. 11, 1982. AA in Nursing, Catonsville (Md.) C.C., 1980; BS in Psychology cum laude, Liberty U., 1993; MA in Clin. Psychology, Biola U., 1997, PhD in Clin. Psychology, 2001. Lic. psychologist Calif.; RN Calif. Psychotherapist Deaf Journey Counseling Program, Orange, Calif., 1997—99; instr. West Coast Deaf Bible Coll., Long Beach, Calif., 1998—99; intern and staff psychotherapist St. John's Child and Family Devel. Ctr. and Deaf Program, Santa Monica, Calif., 1999—2001; staff psychologist deaf program Patton (Calif.) State Hosp., 2001—02; ednl. psychologist Calif. Sch. for the Deaf, Riverside, 2000; psychotherapist Meier Clinics, Long Beach, 2002—. Cons. forensic deaf mental health Patton State Hosp., 2001—; cons. deaf and hearing mental health Meier Clinics, 2002—. Mem.: APA, Adv. Coun. Abused Deaf Children, Nat. Assn. of the Deaf, Am. Deafness and Rehab. Assn. Achievements include co-establishment of the first deaf community counseling center in California. Avocations: backpacking, music, bicycling, stain glass. Office: Meier Clinics 4401 Atlantic Ave Ste 430 Long Beach CA 90807 Office Phone: 562-428-3266.

GREENSPAN, ALAN, Chairman of Federal Reserve Board, economist; b. N.Y.C., Mar. 6, 1926; s. Herman Herbert Greenspan and Rose Goldsmith; m. Andrea Mitchell, Apr. 6, 1997. BS summa cum laude, NYU, 1948, MA, 1950, PhD, 1977; degree (hon.), Harvard, Yale, Notre Dame, Wake Forest, Colgate U., U. Pa., U. Leuven, Belgium. Rsch. assoc. Nat. Indsl. Conf. Bd., N.Y.C., 1948—53; Pres., CEO Townsend-Greenspan & Co., Inc., N.Y.C., 1954-74, 77-87; cons. Council Econ. Advisers, 1970-74, chmn., 1974-77; cons. Congressional Budget Office, 1977-87; mem. Pres.'s Econ. Policy Adv. Bd., 1981-87; chmn. Nat. Commn. on Social Security Reform, 1981-83; mem. Task Force on Econ. Growth, 1969, Pres.'s Fgn. Intelligence Adv. Bd., 1983-85; commn. on an All-Vol. Armed Force, 1969-70; commn. on Fin. Structure and Regulation, 1970-71; sr. adviser panel on econ. activity Brookings Instn., 1970-74, 77-87; corp. dir. Aluminum Co. of Am., Automatic Data Processing, Inc., Capital Cities/ABC, Inc., General Foods, Inc., J.P. Morgan & Co., Inc., Morgan Guarantee Trust Co. of N.Y., Mobil Corp., The Pittston Co.; chmn. bd. govs. Fed. Res. System, 1987—. Mem. bd. economists Time mag., 1971-74, 77-87, bd. trustees, Rand Corp., chmn., Fed. Open Market Com., US alt. gov., IMF, 1987- Bd. overseers Hoover Instn. on War, Revolution and Peace, 1973—74, 1977—87. Decorated comdr. Legion of Honor France, hon. knight comdr. Brit. Empire; recipient John P. Madden medal, 1975, Pub. Svc. Achievement award, 1976, William Butler Meml. award, 1977, Gerald R. Ford medal for disting. pub. svc., 2003. Fellow: Am. Statis. Assn., Nat. Assn. Bus. Economists (past pres.); mem.: Harmonie Club. Office: Federal Reserve System Office of Chmn 20th & C St NW Washington DC 20551-0001

GREENSPAN, DANIEL S., molecular biologist, educator; b. Jersey City, Aug. 31, 1951; s. Aaron and Doris Greenspan; m. Leslie Herman, June 27, 1999; children: Ilana Rina, Jonathan Meir. BA, NYU, 1974, MS, 1978, PhD, 1981. Postdoctoral fellow dept. human genetics Yale U., New Haven, 1981-84, rsch. scientist, mem. faculty, 1984-86; asst. prof. pathology and lab. medicine U. Wis., Madison, 1986-92, assoc. prof., 1992-97, prof., 1997—, vice chair for rsch., 2003—, mem. Comprehensive Cancer Ctr., 1996—, mem. Cardiovascular Ctr., 1999—, vice chair rsch., 2003—. Affiliate Waisman Ctr. for Human Devel. and Devel. Disabilities, 2003—, prof., 2004—. Contbr. articles pub. to profl. jours.; editl. bd. Jour. of Biological Chemistry, 2005—. Arthritis Found. fellow, 1984-87; prin. investigator NIH. Mem. Am. Soc. Biochemistry and Molecular Biology, Am. Soc. Microbiology, Am. Soc. Human Genetics, N.Y. Acad. Scis., Sigma Xi. Office: U Wis Dept Pathology 1300 University Ave Madison WI 53706-1509

GREENSPAN, DEBORAH, dental educator; 2nd BDS, U. London, 1960, BDS, 1964, DSc, 1991; fellow in Dental Surgery (hon.), Royal Coll. Surgeons, Edinburgh, 1994; LDS, Royal Coll. Surgeons, Eng., 1964; ScD (hon.), Georgetown U., 1990. Registered dental practioner, U.K.; diplomate Am. Bd. Oral Medicine. Vis. lectr. oral medicine U. Calif., San Francisco, 1976-83, asst. clin. prof., 1983-85, assoc. clin. prof., 1985-89, clin. prof., 1989-96, prof. clin. oral medicine, 1996—. Lectr. in oral biology, U. Calif., San Francisco, 1972, clin. dir. Oral AIDS Ctr., 1987—, active Sch. Dentistry coms. including admissions com., 1985—, chair task force on infection control, 1987—; cons. Joint FDI/WHO Working Group on AIDS, 1989—, EEC, 1990, WHO, 1990, 91, Dept. Health State Calif., 1991, others; ad hoc reviews Epidemiology and Disease Control Sect. Div. Rsch. Grants NIH, 1987—; mem. programs adv. com. Nat. Inst. Dental Rsch., 1989—, mem. spl. ad hoc tech. rev. panel, 1991, mem. panel Fed. Drug Adminstrn., 1991-94; other svc. to govtl. agys.; participant numerous sci. and profl. workshops, meetings, and continuing edn. courses, numerous radio, TV, and press interviews concerning AIDS and infection control in dentistry. Author: (with J.S. Greenspan, Pindborg, and Schiødt), AIDS and the Dental Team, 1986 (transl. German, French, Italian, Spanish, Japanese), AIDS and the Mouth, 1990, (with others) San Francisco General Hospital AIDS Knowledge Base, 1986, Dermatologic Clinics, 5th edit., 1987, Infectious Disease Clinics of North America, 2nd. edit., 1988, Oral Manifestations of AIDS, 1988, Contemporary Periodontics, 1989, Opportunistic Infections in AIDS Patients, 1990, AIDS Clinical Review, 1990, Oral Manifestations of Systemic Disease, 1990, others; mem. editl. bd. rev. Jour. Am. Coll. Dentists, 1991; mem. editl. bd. Oral Diseases, 1999; ad hoc referee Jour. Oral Pathology, 1983—, Cancer, 1985—, Jour. Acad. Gen. Dentistry, 1986—, European Jour. Cancer & Clin. Oncology, 1986, Archives of Dermatology, 1988—, Jour. AMA, 1988—, AIDS, 1991; contbr. numerous articles to profl. jours. Mem. dental subcom. of profl. edn. com. Calif. div. Am. Cancer Soc., 1982-90, profl. health care providers task force, 1991. Nat. Cancer Inst. fellow, 1978-79, Am. Coll. Dentists fellow, 1988; recipient Woman of Distinction award, London, 1986, Commendation cert. Asst. Sec. for Health, 1989; named Seymour J. Kreshover lectr. Nat. Inst. Dental Rsch., 1989, Hon. Lectr. United Med. and Dental Schs. of Guys and St. Thomas Hosps., U. London, 1991. Fellow AAAS, Royal Soc. Medicine, Royal Coll. Surgeons; mem. ADA (vis. lectr. speaker's bur. 1988—, cons. coun. on dental therapeutics 1988—, mem. coun. sci. affairs 1999—), Am. Assn. Dental Rsch. (session chair 1986-87, constitution com. 1988-91, chair 1990-91, pres. San Francisco sect. 1990—, treas. 1992—), Am. Acad. Oral Pathology, Am. Soc. Microbiology, Am. Assn. Women Dentists, Am. Acad. Oral Medicine, Am. Assn. Dental Schs., Internat. Assn. Dental Rsch. (pres. exptl. pathology group 1989-90, v.p. 2005-, other coms. and offices), Internat. Assn. Oral Pathologists, Calif. Dental Assn., San Francisco Dental Soc., Internat. AIDS Soc., Inst. of Medicine. Achievements include rsch. on oral candidiasis in HIV infection, on HIV-associated salivary gland disease, on oral hairy leukoplakia, and on the prevalence of HIV-associated gingivitis and periodontitis in HIV-infected patients. Office: U Calif Sch Dentistry Dept Stomatology S 612 513 Parnassus Ave Box 0422 San Francisco CA 94143-0422

GREENSPAN, DONALD, mathematician, educator; b. N.Y.C., Jan. 24, 1928; BS, NYU, 1948; MS, U. Wis., 1949; PhD, U. Md., 1956. Instr. U. Md., 1948-56; research engr. Hughes Aircraft Co., 1956-57; asst. prof. Purdue U., 1957-61, asso. prof., 1961-62; permanent mem. U. Wis. Math. Research Center, Madison, 1962-68; prof. computer scis., cons. to U. Wis. Computing Center, 1965-78; prof. math. U. Tex., 1978—. Lectr. Am. Math. Assn., 1963-64, U. Mich. Summer Conf., 1964; referee NRC, NSF. Author: Theory and Solution of Ordinary Differential Equations, 1960, Introduction to Partial Differential Equations, 1961, 2d edit., 2000, Introductory Numerical Analysis of Elliptic Boundary Value Problems, 1965, Introduction to Calculus, 1968, Lectures on the Numerical Solutions of Linear, Singular, and Nonlinear Differential Equations, 1968, Introduction to Numerical Analysis and Application, 1970, Discrete Models, 1973, Discrete Numerical Methods in Physics and Engineering, 1974, Arithmetic Applied Mathematics, 1980, Computer-Oriented Mathematical Physics, 1981, (with U. Bulgarelli and V. Casulli) Pressure Methods for the Numerical Solution of Free Surface Fluid Flow, 1984, (with V. Casulli) Numerical Analysis for Applied Mathematics, Science and Engineering, 1988, Quasimolecular Modelling, 1991, Particle Modeling, 1997, A Science Handbook for Musicians, Entrepreneurs and Candidates for Public Office, 2002, N-Body Problems and Models, 2004; editor: Numerical Solutions of Nonlinear Differential Equations, 1966, (with Pal Rosza) Numerical Methods, 1988, 2d rev. edit., 1991; editl. bd. Jour. Computers and Math. with Applications, Systems Analysis-Modelling-Simulation, CDC Handbook of Fluid Dynamics; contbr. articles to profl. jours. Active Common Cause, NAACP. Mem. ACLU, Am. Math. Soc., Am. Phys. Soc., Assn. Computing Machinery, Ams. for Dem. Action. Office: U Tex Math Dept Arlington TX 76019-0001 Business E-Mail: dgx@uta.edu.

GREENSPAN, FRANCIS S., physician; b. Perth Amboy, N.J., Mar. 16, 1920; s. Philip and Francis (Davidson) G.; m. Bonnie Jean Fisher, Oct. 25, 1945; children: Richard L., Robert H., Susan L. BA, Cornell U., 1940, MD, 1943. Diplomate Am. Bd. Internal Medicine. Mem. endocrinology staff U. Calif.-San Francisco; chief endocrinology Stanford (Calif.) Hosp., 1949-59; chief thyroid clinic U. Calif. Med. Ctr., San Francisco, 1959—, now clin. prof. medicine and radiology; practice medicine specializing in endocrinology San Francisco; chief of staff U. Calif. Hosps. and Clinics, San Francisco, 1976-78. Editor: Textbook of Endocrinology; contbr. articles to med. jours. Served with USNR, 1944-45. Mem. San Francisco Med. Soc., Calif. Med. Assn., AMA, Endocrine Soc., Am. Thyroid Assn., Western Soc. Clin. Rsch., Western Assn. Physicians, Calif. Acad. Medicine. Office: U Calif Med Ctr Ste 553 400 Parnassus Ave San Francisco CA 94143-1222 Office Phone: 415-353-2350. Business E-Mail: N520@itsa.ucsf.edu.

GREENSPAN, HARVEY PHILIP, applied mathematician, educator; b. N.Y.C., Feb. 22, 1933; s. Louis and Jessie (Scholnick) G.; m. Mirian Gordon, Sept. 6, 1953; children— Elizabeth, Judith. BS, CCNY, 1953; MS, Harvard U., 1954, PhD, 1956; D Tech. (hon.), Royal Inst. Tech., Stockholm, 1991. Asst. prof. applied math. Harvard, 1957-60; faculty MIT, Cambridge, 1960—, prof. applied math., 1964—2002, prof. emeritus, 2002—. Author: Theory of Rotating Fluids, 1968, Calculus: An Introduction to Applied Mathematics, 1973; editor: Studies in Applied Mathematics, 1969; patentee centrifugal spectrometer. Home: 15 Chatham Cir Brookline MA 02446-5410 Office: Mass Inst Tech 77 Massachusetts Ave Cambridge MA 02139-4301 Office Phone: 617-253-4982. Business E-Mail: hpg@math.mit.edu.

GREENSPAN, JAY SCOTT See ALEXANDER, JASON

GREENSPAN, JOHN S., dental and medical educator, scientist, administrator; b. London, Jan. 7, 1938; came to U.S., 1976; s. Nathan and Jessie (Dion) G.; m. Deborah, Dec. 1962; children: Nicholas J., Louise C. BSC in Anatomy with 1st class honors, U. London, 1959, B in Dental Surgery, 1962, PhD in Exptl. Pathology, 1967; ScD (hon.), Georgetown U., 1990. Licentiate in dental surgery Royal Coll. of Surgeons of Eng. Asst. house surgeon in conservation and periodontology Royal Dental Hosp. London, 1962; asst. lectr. oral pathology Sch. of Dental Surgery Royal Dental Hosp. of London, U. London, 1963-65, lectr. oral pathology Sch. of Dental Surgery, 1965-68, sr. lectr. oral pathology Sch. of Dental Surgery, 1968-75; prof. oral biology and oral pathology Sch. of Dentisty, U. Calif., San Francisco, 1976—, vice chmn. dept. oral medicine and hosp. dentistry, 1977-82, chmn. div. oral biology, 1981-89, coord. basic scis., 1982-96; chmn. dept. stomatology Sch. of Dentistry, U. Calif., San Francisco, 1989—2000, dean rsch., 2001—; dir. AIDS Rsch. Inst. U. Calif., 2004—. Cons. oral pathology St. John's Hosp. and Inst. of Dermatology, London, 1973-76; cons. dental surgeon St. George's Hosp., 1972-76; prof. dept. pathology Sch. Medicine U. Calif., San Francisco, 1976—; dir. U. Calif. AIDS Specimen Bank, San Francisco, 1982—, U. Calif. Oral AIDS Ctr., San Francisco, 1987—; assoc. dir. dental clin. epidemiology program U. Calif., San Francisco, 1987—; dir. U. Calif. AIDS Clin. Rsch. Ctr., San Francisco, 1992—; Burroughs Wellcome vis. prof. Royal Soc. Medicine, U.K., 1996-97; dir. UCSF Aids Rsch. Inst., 2004—; fellow Kings Coll., London, Eng., 2003; presenter, lectr. in field. Author: (with others) Opportunistic Infections in Patients with the Acquired Immunodeficiency Syndrome, 1989, Contemporary Periodontics, 1989, Gastroenterology Clinics of North America, 1988, Perspectives on Oral Manifestations of AIDS, 1988, AIDS: Pathogenesis and Treatment, 1988, others; contbr. articles to profl. jours.; editorial cons. Achives of Oral Biology, 1968—, Jour. of Calif. Dental Assn., 1980—; editoral adv. bd. Jour. of Dental Rsch., 1977—; editorial bd. AIDS Alert, 1987-89, Brit. Dental Jour., 1998—; sr. editor Oral Diseases, 1994-98. Rsch. grantee NIH-Nat. Inst. Dental Rsch., 1978-82, 86—, U. Calif. Task Force on AIDS, 1983—, rsch. com. Royal Dental Hosp., London, 1964-76, Med. Rsch. Coun. of U.K., 1974-77, chmn. U. Calif. San Francisco Acad. Senate, 1983-85; Nuffield dental scholar, 1958-59; fellow Am. Coll. Dentists, 1982—, AAAS, 1985—; recipient Seymour J. Kreshover Lecture award Nat. Inst. Dental Rsch., NIH, 1989, Rsch. in Oral Biology award Internat. Assn. Dental Rsch., 1992. Fellow: Royal Coll. Surgeons Faculty of Dental Surgery, Royal Coll. Pathologists; mem.: AAAS, ADA, King's Coll. London, Am. Assn. Pathologists, Calif. Soc. Oral Pathologists Histochem. Soc., Calif. Dental Assn., San Francisco Dental Soc., Internat. Assn. Oral Pathologists, Bay Area Tchrs. Oral Pathology, Am. Acad. Oral Pathology, Oral Pathology Soc. (U.K.), Pathological Soc. (U.K.), Royal Soc. Medicine (U.K.), Internat. Assn. Dental Rsch. (pres. 1996—97), Am. Assn. Dental Rsch. (pres. 1988—89), Inst. Medicine of Nat. Acad. Scis. Avocations: skiing, gardening, travel, wine. Office: U Calif PO Box 422 San Francisco CA 94143-0001 Office Phone: 415-476-2220. Business E-Mail: greenspanj@dentistry.ucsf.edu.

GREENSPAN, LEON JOSEPH, lawyer; b. Phila., Feb. 10, 1932; s. Joseph and Minerva (Podolsky) G.; m. Irene Gordon, Nov. 2, 1958; children: Marjorie, David, Michael, Lisa. AB, Temple U., 1955, JD, 1958. Bar: N.Y. 1959, N.J. 1985, Fla. 1985, Pa. 1986, Conn. 1991, U.S. Tax Ct. 1973, U.S. Supreme Ct. 1969. Pvt. practice law, White Plains, N.Y., 1959-64; ptnr. Greenspan and Aurnou, White Plains, 1964-77, Greenspan, Jaffe & Rosenblatt, White Plains, 1987-91, Greenspan & Greenspan, White Plains, 1992—. Counsel Brown, Boston; lectr. Fla. Bar CLER Program, 1991, 92, 99; atty. Tarrytown (N.Y.) Housing Authority. Pres. Hebrew Inst., White Plains; vice chmn. ann. dinner NCCJ. Recipient Pres.'s award Union Orthodox Synagogues, 1982, Owl Club award Temple Univ., 2001; honoree Hebrew Inst., White Plains, 1983. Mem. ABA, N.J. Bar Assn., Fla. Bar Assn., Westchester County Bar Assn., White Plains Bar Assn., N.Y. State Trial Lawyers Assn., Criminal Cts. Bar Assn. Westchester County, N.J. Bar Assn. Home: 14 Pinebrook Dr White Plains NY 10605-4713 Office: Greenspan & Greenspan 150 Grand St 6th Fl White Plains NY 10601-4400 Office Phone: 914-946-2500. Business E-Mail: leon@greenspans-law.com.

GREENSPAN, MICHAEL ALAN, lawyer; b. Bklyn., Dec. 16, 1940; s. Abe and Leona (Peckerar) G.; m. Heather Gold, Aug. 2, 1964; children: Lisa, David. BA, Cornell U., 1962; LLB, Columbia U., 1965. Bar: N.Y. 1965, D.C. 1968. Assoc. Melrod Redman & Gartlan, Washington, 1969; asst. sec., sr. atty. Bd. Govs. Fed. Res. System, Washington, 1969-73; ptnr. Metzger, Noble, Schwarz & Kempler, Washington, 1973-78, Noble, Greenspan & Austin, Washington, 1978-82, Thompson Mitchell, Washington, 1982-96, Thompson Coburn, Washington, 1996—. Adj. prof. U. Balt. Law Sch., 1998—. Author: (with others) Direct Investment and Development in the U.S., 1978; contbr. articles to profl. jours. Trustee Temple Emanuel, Kensington, Md., 1986-88; prin. Coun. for Excellence in Govt., Washington, 1990—. With U.S. Army, 1966-68. Mem. ABA (chmn. com. on fin. markets & instns. sect. antitrust law), Fed. Bar Assn. (coun. banking law com.). Republican. Jewish. Avocations: chess, sign lang., photography, performing. Office: Thompson Coburn 1909 K St NW Ste 600 Washington DC 20006-1167 E-mail: mgreenspan@thompsoncoburn.com, mikegreenspan2@aol.com.

GREENSPAN, SUSAN LYNN, medical researcher; d. Francis Sorrell Greenspan and Bonnie Jean Fisher; m. Neil Martin Resnick, May 15, 1977; children: Jennifer, David. BA, Stanford U., 1975; MD, Harvard U., 1979. Diplomate Am. Bd. Internal Medicine, Am. Bd. Endocrinology, Am. Bd. Geriatric Medicine. Intern Beth Israel Hosp., Boston, 1979—80, resident in internal medicine, 1980—82; from instr. medicine to assoc. prof. Harvard Med. Sch., Boston, 1985—99; asst. in medicine Beth Israel Deaconess Med. Ctr., Boston, 1985—86, assoc. in medicine, 1986—2001, dir. Osteoporosis Prevention and Treatment Ctr., 1990—99, assoc. program dir. Gen. Clin. Rsch. Ctr., 1995—98, program dir., 1998—99; assoc. physician Brigham & Women's Hosp., 1986—99; dir. bone health program Magee-Women's Hosp., Pitts., 1999—2002; dir. Osteoporosis Prevention and Treatment Ctr. U. Pitts., 1999—, assoc. program dir. Gen. Clin. Rsch. Ctr., 1999—, prof. Mem. panel on osteoporosis U.S. Surgeon Gen., 2002—04. Contbr. articles to profl. jours. Named one of Best Drs. in Pitts., Pitts. Mag., 2002, 2005; recipient Albert P. Rowe, MD Meml. award, Found. Osteoporosis Rsch. and Edn., 2001. Mem.: Internat. Soc. Clin. Densitometry (bd. trustees 2001—04), Am. Gerontol. Soc., Am. Soc. Bone and Mineral Rsch. (councilor 2002—), Endocrine Soc. Office: U Pitts Kaufmann Med Bldg Ste 1110 3471 5th Ave Pittsburgh PA 15213

GREENSPAN-MARGOLIS, JUNE E., psychiatrist; b. NYC, June 28, 1934; d. Benjamin Robert and Theresa (Cooperstein) Edelman; divorced; 1 child, Alisa Greenspan; m. Gerald J. Margolis. AB, Bryn Mawr Coll., 1955;

MD, Med. Coll. Pa., 1959; grad., Inst Phila Assn Psychoanalysis, Bala Cynwyd, 1975. Intern Albert Einstein Med. Ctr., Phila., 1959-60; pvt. practice medicine specializing in pediatrics Cinnaminson, N.J., 1961-67; psychiat. resident Hahnemann Med. Coll., Phila., 1967-71; practice medicine specializing in adult and child psychiatry, psychoanalysis Jenkintown, Pa., 1971—. Instr. U. Pa. Sch. Medicine, Phila., 1975—77, clin. assoc., 1977—81, clin. asst. prof., 1981—86, clin. assoc. prof., 1986—; tng. and supervisory analyst Psychiat. Ctr. Phila., Bala Cynwyd, Pa., 1986—. Fellow Am. Coll. Psychoanalysts, Am. Psychiat. Assn.; mem. AMA, Am. Psychoanalytic Assn. (cert. adult and child psychoanalysis), Am. Acad. Child Psychiatry, Ctr. for Advanced Psychoanalytic Studies (Princeton). Office: The Pavilion Ste 434 261 Old York Rd Jenkintown PA 19046 Office Phone: 215-887-5355.

GREENSPON, ROBERT ALAN, lawyer; b. Hartford, Conn., Apr. 17, 1947; s. George Arthur and Shirley Jean (Shelton) G.; m. Claire Alice Stone, Aug. 21, 1971; children: Colin Haynes, Alison Shelton. AB, Franklin and Marshall, 1969; JD, Columbia U., 1972. Bar: Conn. 1973, N.Y. 1998, U.S. Dist. Conn. 1973, U.S. Ct. Appeals (2d cir.) 1983. Assoc. Robinson & Cole, Hartford, Conn., 1972-78, ptnr., 1978-81, Stamford, Conn., 1981-86; sr. v.p., gen. counsel Guinness Peat Aviation Corp., Stamford, N.Y.C., 1985-92, Shannon, Ireland, 1985—92; ptnr. Latham & Watkins, N.Y.C., 1992—. Contbr. articles to profl. jours. Mem. ABA (comml. fin. services, aircraft fin.), Conn. Bar Assn., N.Y. State Bar Assn., Internat. Bar Assn., Southwestern Legal Found. (bd. advisors internat. and comparative law ctr.). Home: 49 Old Farm Rd Darien CT 06820-6119 Office: Latham & Watkins 885 3rd Ave Fl 10 New York NY 10022-4834 Office Phone: 212-906-1375. Business E-Mail: robert.greenspon@lw.com.

GREENSPUN, DAVID TODD, plastic and reconstructive surgeon; s. Simon Asher and Madelaine Greenspun. BS with distinction, McGill U., 1994, MS, 1997; MD with hons., NY Med. Sch., 1999. Physician License NY, 2001. Resident Montefiore Med. Ctr., Bronx, 2000—03; attending surgeon St. Luke's, Roosevelt Hosp. Ctr., NYC, 2004—, Albert Einstein Coll. Medicine, Weiler Hosp., Bronx, 2004—, Montefiore Med. Ctr., 2004—; pvt. practice NYC, 2004—. Resident in surgery Cornell U., NY Hosp., NYC, 1999—2002; chief resident in plastic and reconstructive surgery Montefiore Med. Ctr., Bronx, 2003—04. Contbr. articles to profl. jours. Recipient Alpha Omega Alpha Nat. Med. Honor Soc., Beta Chpt., NJ. Med. Sch., 1998—99; grantee Merit Award for Rsch. in Biol. Sciences, Fonds De La Recherché En Santé Du Que., 1994—95. Mem.: NY County Med. Soc., Med. Soc. State of NY, AMA. Avocations: travel, photography, running. Office: David T Greenspun MD MSc 50 E 79th St New York NY 10021 Office Phone: 212-744-1200. E-mail: davidgreenspun@yahoo.com, davidgreenspun@mac.com.

GREENSTEIN, ABRAHAM JACOB, mortgage company executive, accountant; b. Munich, Fed. Republic of Germany, May 5, 1949; came to U.S., 1950; s. Morris and Bella (Yeger) G.; m. Ruth Sanik, June 5, 1974; children: Pinchus, Yisroel, Shlomo. BS in Acctg., Bklyn. Coll., 1972. Sr. auditor State Comptrollers Office, N.Y.C., 1972-75; asst. dir. Office of Spl. Dep. Comptroller, N.Y.C., 1978-82; sr. v.p. fin. N.Y.C. Housing Devel. Corp., 1983-88, exec. v.p., 1988-98. Treas. Housing Assistance Corp., N.Y.C., 1985-98, Residential Mortgage Ins. Co., N.Y.C., 1993-98; exec. v.p., chief oper. officer Housing for N.Y. Corp., N.Y.C., 1986-93, pres., 1993-98; v.p. Greystone & Co., N.Y.C., 1998—. Trustee Congregation Chasdi Gur, Bklyn., 1982-87 Mem. Am. Mgmt. Assn., Govt. Fin. Officers Assn., Council of State Housing Agys., Mortgage Bankers Assn. Jewish. Avocations: swimming, tennis. Office: Greystone & Co 60th Fl 152 W 57th St Fl 60 New York NY 10019-3310 Office Phone: 212-649-9700. Business E-Mail: agreenspein@greyco.com.

GREENSTEIN, FRED IRWIN, political science professor; b. N.Y.C., Sept. 1, 1930; s. Arthur Aaron and Rose (Goldstein) G.; m. Barbara Elferink, July 14, 1957; children: Michael, Amy, Jessica. BA, Antioch Coll., 1953; MA, Yale U., 1956, PhD, 1960. Instr. Yale U., New Haven, 1959-62, vis. prof., 1965-68; mem. faculty Wesleyan U., Middletown, Conn., 1963-73, prof. polit. sci., 1966-73; Henry Luce prof. politics, law and society Princeton U., 1973-81, prof. politics, 1973—2000, prof. emeritus, 2000—. Vis. prof. U. Essex, Eng., 1968-69, 91. Author: Children and Politics, 2d edit., 1969, The American Party System and the American People, 1970, Personality and Politics, 2d edit., 1975, The Hidden-Hand Presidency: Eisenhower as Leader, 1982, The Reagan Presidency: An Early Appraisal, 1983, Leadership in the Modern Presidency, 1988, How Presidents Test Reality: Decisions on Vietnam, 1954 and 1965, 1989, The Presidential Difference: Leadership Style from FDR to Clinton, 2000, 2d edit., 2004, The George Bush Presidency: An Early Assessment, 2003; co-author (with R.E. Lane and J.D. Barber): Introduction to Political analysis, 2d edit., 1965; co-author: (with M. Lerner) A Source Book for the Study of Personality and Politics, 1971; co-author: (with N.W. Polsby) The Handbook of Political Science, 8 vols.; co-author: (with R. Wolfinger and M. Shapiro) Dynamics and American Politics, 1976; co-author: (with L. Berman and A. Felzenberg) The Evolution of the Modern Presidency: A Bibliographical Review, 1977. Served with AUS, 1953-55. Fellow Ctr. Advanced Study Behavioral Scis., 1964-65; NSF sr. postdoctoral fellow, 1968-69 Fellow Am. Acad. Arts And Scis.; mem. Am. Polit. Sci. Assn. (editorial bd. 1968-72, sec. 1976-77), Internat. Soc. Polit. Psychology (pres. 1996-97). Home: 340 Jefferson Rd Princeton NJ 08540-3475 Office: Princeton Univ Dept Politics Princeton NJ 08544-0001 Business E-Mail: fig@princeton.edu.

GREENSTEIN, GARY, periodontist, dental educator; b. Nyc, Ny, Feb. 2, 1947; s. Sidney and Anne Greenstein; m. Helene Cohen, Nov. 13, 1951; children: Benjamin, Jaclyn, Michele. BA, Queens Coll., New York City, 1964—68; DDS, NYU Coll. of Dentistry, New York City, 1968—72; Periodontal Certification, Eastman Dental Ctr., Rochester, New York, 1978—80; MS, U. of Rochester, Rochester, New York, 1980—81. Periodontal Certification Eastman Dental Ctr., 1980, Board Diplomate Am. Acad. of Periodontology, 1993. Clin. prof., periodontology UMDNJ, Dept. of Periodontology, Newark, 1993—; pvt. practice Dr. Gary Greenstein, Freehold, NJ, 1983—; chief of periodontics Monmouth Med. Ctr., Long Branch, NJ, 1990—97. Cons. US Army Dental Corp, Ft. Gordon, Ga., 1988—; trustee Am. Acad. of Periodontology, Chgo., 1993—99, sci., rsch. and therapy com., 1992—2002. Author: (contributions to periodontal literature) 95 Publications, Jour. of Periodontology, Jour. of Am. Dental Assoc., Compendium of Continuing Ed. in Dentistry, Internat. Jour. of Restorative Dentistry and Periodontics. Maj. US Army, 1972—78, Kans., South Korea, New Jersey. Decorated Cert. of Achievement for Meritorious Svc. US Army, Army Commendation Medal; recipient Gies Award, Am. Acad. of Periodontology, 1997, Fellowship Award, 2000, Hirschfeld Meml. Award, NE Soc. of Periodontists, 2000. Mem.: NJ. Soc. of Periodontists (licentiate), NE Soc. of Periodontists (licentiate), ADA (licentiate), Am. Acad. of Periodontology (licentiate; trustee 1993—99). R-Consevative. Jewish. Achievements include research in Periodontal Therapy; Over 100 Guest Lectures. Avocations: tennis, rafting, mountain biking. Office: Dr Gary Greenstein 900 West Main Street Freehold NJ 07728 Office Phone: 732-780-1450. Personal E-mail: ggperio@aol.com.

GREENSTEIN, JEFFREY IAN, neurologist; b. Durban, South Africa, July 27, 1947; s. Joseph and Miriam (Shamos) G. MD, U. Cape Town, S. Africa, 1971. Diplomate Am. Bd. Neurology and Psychiatry. Asst. to assoc. prof. neurology Temple U. Sch. Med., Phila., 1983-89, prof., 1989—2002, chmn. neurology, 1989—2000; pres. Multiple Sclerosis Inst., 2002—. Chair Dept. of Neurology Grad. Hosp., 1999—; clin. prof. of neurology Drexel U. Sch. Medicine. Pres. Multiple Sclerosis Rsch. Inst., 2004—. Mem. AAAS, Am. Acad. Neurology, N.Y. Acad. Sci., Nat. Multiple Sclerosis Soc. (chmn. profl. adv. com. Phila. 1992-95, bd. of trustees, Del. Valley Chpt. 1996-). Office: Multiple Sclerosis Inst 1740 South St Ste 401 Philadelphia PA 19146-2246 Office Phone: 215-985-2245.

GREENSTEIN, JOEL SANDOR, industrial engineering educator; b. Chgo, May 7, 1952; s. Benjamin and Muriel Greenstein; m. Katherine Marie Lodenkamp, Sept. 1, 1982; children: Claire Elizabeth, Seth Michael, Paul David BS, U. Ill., 1973, PhD, 1979; MS, Stanford U., 1974. Asst. prof. indsl. engring. and ops. rsch. Va. Poly. Inst. & State U., Blacksburg, 1979-85; assoc. prof. indsl. engring. Clemson U., SC, 1985—. Contbr. articles in field to profl. jours. Mem. Am. Soc. Engring. Edn., Assn. for Computing Machinery, Human Factors and Ergonomics Soc., Inst. Indsl. Engr., Usability Profl. Assn. Office: Clemson U Dept Indsl Engring Clemson SC 29634-0920 Office Phone: 864-656-5649. Business E-Mail: iejsg@clemson.edu.

GREENSTEIN, RUTH LOUISE, think-tank executive, lawyer; b. N.Y.C., Mar. 28, 1946; d. Milton and Beatrice (Zutty) G.; m. David Seidman, May 19, 1972. BA, Harvard U., 1966; MA, Yale U., 1968; JD, George Washington U., 1980. Bar: D.C. 1980. Fgn. service info. officer USIA, Washington and Tehran, Iran, 1968-70; adminstrv. asst. Export-Import Bank U.S., Washington, 1971-72; asst. dean Woodrow Wilson Sch. Pub. and Internat. Affairs, Princeton U., 1972-75; budget examiner U.S. Office Mgmt. and Budget, Washington, 1975-79; budget coordinator U.S. Internat. Devel. Coop. Agy., 1979-81; dep. gen. counsel NSF, 1981-84; treas., then v.p. and gen. counsel Genex Corp., Gaithersburg, Md., 1984-90; v.p. fin. and adminstrn., gen. counsel Inst. for Def. Analyses, Alexandria, Va., 1990—. Mem. acad. adv. panel to tech. transfer intelligence com. CIA, 1983-90; mem. def. trade adv. group U.S. Dept. State, 1994-96; mem. com. for protection of human subjects ARC, 1996—; dir. VSA arts, 1998—, PLATO Learning Inc., 2002-. Mem. NAS (panel on future design and implementation of nat. security export controls 1989-91), AAAS (com. on sci. freedom and responsibility 1987-93), D.C. Bar Assn. Home: 2737 Devonshire Pl NW Apt 511 Washington DC 20008-3458 Office: Inst for Def Analyses 4850 Mark Center Dr Alexandria VA 22311-1882 Business E-Mail: rgreenst@ida.org.

GREENSTEIN, SCOTT, broadcast executive; b. 1959; BA, Tulane U.; JD, George Washington U. Atty. Cahill Gordon & Reindel, NYC, 1984—87, Loeb & Loeb, Los Angeles, 1987—89, Viacom Entertainment, NYC, 1989—92; v.p. law dept. Viacom Internat., NYC, 1992—93; senior v.p. motion pictures, music, new media and publishing Miramax Films, NYC, 1993—97; co-pres. October Films, NYC, 1997—99; chmn. USA Films, NYC, 1999—2004; pres. entertainment & sports Sirius Satellite Radio, NYC, 2004—. Office: SIRIUS Satellite Radio 1221 Ave of the Americas New York NY 10020 Office Phone: 212-584-5100.

GREENSTEIN, SHANE MITCHELL, education educator; s. Morey and Eleanor Greenstein; m. Ranna Adina Rozenfeld, Aug. 20, 1995; children: Noah, Rebecca, Ilana, Eli. BA, U. Calif., Berkeley, Calif., 1983; PhD, Stanford U., Stanford, Calif., 1989. Asst. prof. U. Ill., Urbana, Ill., 1990—97; elinor and wendell hobbs prof. Northwestern U., Evanston, Ill., 1997—. Chair, mgmt. and strategy dept., kellogg sch. of mgmt. Northwestern U., Evanston, Ill., 2002—. Author: Diamonds are Forever, Computers are Not. Rsch. assoc. Nat. Bur. of Econ. Rsch., Cambridge, Mass., 1992—2005. Achievements include research in economic geography of the Internet in the US. Office Phone: 847-467-5672.

GREENSTEIN, STUART MARK, surgical educator; b. Bklyn., Feb. 16, 1955; s. Saul and Anne (Stillman) G.; m. Gayle Suzette Shulman (div. Jan. 1987); 1 child, Samuel; m. Sylvia Redner, July 2, 1989; children: Brian Liedman, Leah Chaya Ruth, Talia Miriam Rachel. BS, CUNY, 1976; MD, Harvard U., 1979. Diplomate Am. Bd. Surgeryy. Intern, instr. surgery NYU Med. Ctr., N.Y.C., 1979-80; resident in surgery, clin. instr. U. Med. and Dentistry N.J., Newark, 1980-84; instr. vascular surgery Hosp. of U. Pa., Phila., 1984-85; clin. asst. instr. SUNY Downstate Med. Ctr., Bklyn., 1985-86; asst. prof. surgery Hahnemann U., Phila., 1986-88, Albert Einstein Coll. Medicine, Yeshiva U., Bronx, N.Y., 1988-93, assoc. prof. surgery, 1993—2002, prof. surgery, 2002—. Mem. staff Montefiore Med. Ctr., Bronx, 1988—. Contbr. articles to med. jours. Salk scholar CUNY, 1975. Fellow ACS (1st prize N.J. chpt. 1982, 2d prize 1983); mem. AAAS, Am. Soc. Transplant Surgeons, Transplantation Soc., N.Y. Acad. Scis. Democrat. Achievements include construction of a competent phonatory neoepiglottis using cervical skin flaps. Office: Montefiore Med Ctr 111 E 210th St Bronx NY 10467-2401 Office Phone: 718-920-8146. Business E-Mail: sgreenst@montefiore.org.

GREENSTONE, MICHAEL, economics professor, researcher; b. Chgo., Dec. 6, 1968; s. J. David and Joan Greenstone; m. Katherine Ozment, July 21, 2000; 1 child, William Pryor. BA, Swarthmore Coll., 1991; PhD, Princeton U., 1998. Robert Wood Johnson scholar U. Calif., Berkeley, 1998—2000; rsch. assoc. Nat. Bur. Econ. Rsch., Cambridge, 2000—; asst. prof. econ. U. Chgo., 2000—03; 3M assoc. prof. econ. MIT, Cambridge, Mass., 2003—. Mem. EPA Environ. Econ. Sci. Adv. Bd., Washington, 2003—. Avocations: basketball, hiking. Office: MIT Dept Econ E52-359 50 Meml Dr Cambridge MA 02142 Office Phone: 617-452-4127. Office Fax: 617-253-1330. E-mail: mgreenst@mit.edu.

GREENSTREET, JENNIFER KENNIS, librarian; b. Stockton, Calif., Nov. 12, 1945; d. Kenneth and Betty Jean (Lewis) Roberts; m. Robert Wayne Greenstreet, Sept. 1, 1973; 1 child, Dacia Erin. BA, Calif. State U., Sacramento, 1969; MLS, U. Okla., 1989. Substitute tchr. Lamoni (Iowa) Community Schs., 1983-84; ref. clk. Graceland Coll., Lamoni, 1980-84; children's libr. Ada (Okla.) Pub. Libr., 1986-87, libr. dir., 1987—. Adj. instr. Fresno (Calif.) City Coll., 1975-76, Graceland Coll., 1979-80, East Cen. U., Ada, 1985, 91; community mem. Humanity Diversity Com., East Cen. U., Ada, 1992; founding mem. Ada Libr. Friends Inc., 1991—; del. Govs. Conf. Libr. and Info. Svcs., Okla., 1990. Bd. mem. Pontotoc County Adult Day Care; bd. dirs. Pontotoc County Literacy Coalition, Ada, 1990—, treas. Mem.: ALA, Mountain Plains Libr. Assn., Okla. Libr. Assn., Rotary. Avocations: golf, walking, photography. Home: PO Box 837 Ada OK 74821-0837 Office: Ada Pub Libr 124 S Rennie St Ada OK 74820-5189 Office Phone: 580-436-8121. Business E-Mail: jgreenstreet@ada.lib.ok.us.

GREENSTREET, ROBERT CHARLES, architect, educator; b. London, June 8, 1952; s. Joseph Philip Henry and Joan (Dean) G.; m. Karen Eloise Holland, Sept. 6, 1975. Diploma in architecture, Oxford Brookes U., 1976, PhD in Architecture, 1983. Registered architect, Eng. Vis. asst. prof. Kans. State U., 1978-79; asst. prof. U. Kans., 1979-80; vis. prof. Ball State U., Muncie, 1980-81; prof. U. Wis., 1981—, asst. vice chancellor, 1985-86, chmn. dept. architecture, 1986-90, dean Sch. Architecture and Urban Planning Milw., 1990-2000, dep. chancellor for campus and urban design, 2000—, interim chancellor, 2003—04; dir. planning and design City of Milw., 2004—. Author, co-author 7 books; contbr. more than 150 articles to profl. jours. Fellow Royal Soc. Arts; mem. AIA (assoc.), Royal Inst. Brit. Architects, Wis. Soc. Architects, Chartered Inst. Arbitrators; mem. Am. Arbitration Assn., Assn. Collegiate Schs. of Architecture (pres. 1995-96). Anglican. Office: U Wis Dept Architecture PO Box 413 Milwaukee WI 53201-0413

GREENWALD, ALFRED EMANUEL, retired cosmetic surgeon; b. New Brunswick, N.J., Feb. 25, 1920; s. Louis and Ethel (Weiss) G.; m. Leatrice Joy Fleishman, June 15, 1947 (div. June 1995); children: Melvin Alan, Bryna Jane Pomp. Student, George Washington U., 1938-40; BA, NYU, 1942, MS in Chemistry, 1943; MD, N.Y. Med. Coll., 1947, postgrad., 1950-51. Diplomate Am. Bd. Surgery, Am. Bd. Cosmetic Surgery, Nat. Bd. Med. Examiners. Rotating intern Newark Beth Israel Hosp., NJ, 1947-48; surg. intern Flower and Fifth Avenue Hosps., N.Y.C., 1948-49; resident in surgery Hackensack (N.J.) Hosp., 1949-50, Martland Med. Ctr.-Univ. Hosp., Newark, 1951-54; gen. practice medicine Hackensack, 1950-51; pvt. practice surgery, Paramus, N.J., 1954, New Brunswick, N.J., 1957-92; ret., 1992. Examining physician 1 N.Y. State Workers' Compensation Bd., Bklyn., 1994-95; former staff mem. Middlesex Gen. Hosp., Robert Wood Johnson Univ. Hosp., St. Peter's Univ. Hosp., Meml. Med. Ctr. South Amboy, N.J., Surgicare Ctrl. Jersey. Author: The Aging Face, 1985; contbr. articles to med. jours. Capt. M.C., U.S. Army, 1955-57. Mem. AMA, Am. Assn. Cosmetic Surgeons, Am. Soc. Cosmetic Surgeons, Am. Acad. Cosmetic Surgery, Pan Am. Med. Assn., Internat. Coll. Surgeons, Internat. Soc. Cosmetic, Plastic and Reconstructive Surgery, Internat. Acad. Cosmetic Surgery, French Soc. Esthetic Surgery, Med. Soc. N.J., N.J. Soc. Cosmetic Surgery, Phila. Soc. Facial Plastic Surgeons, Middlesex County Med. Soc., Am. Physicians Fellowship for Israel Med. Assn., Med. Amateur Radio Coun. (founder 1965, treas. 1986-00, conf. chmn. 1984), Princeton Personal Computer Users Group. Jewish. Achievements include pioneer work on high cheek bones, malar augmentation and the lip lift cheilopexy for cheiloptosis. Home: Ten Llewellyn Pl New Brunswick NJ 08901-3027 Office Phone: 732-247-5578. E-mail: ALFREDGR@aol.com.

GREENWALD, ANDREW ERIC, lawyer; b. NYC, May 31, 1942; s. Harold and Lillian G.; m. Paula S., Aug. 20, 1967; children: Brooke Ellen, Karen Michelle. BS, U. Wis., 1964; JD, Georgetown U., 1967. Bar: D.C. 1968, Md. 1969, U.S. Ct. Appeals Md. 1969. Lawyer Nat. Labor Rels. Bd., Washington, 1967-68; asst. corp. counsel D.C. Govt., 1968-69; shareholder Joseph, Greenwald & Laake PA, Greenbelt, Md., 1969—. Past mem. dept. family and cmty. devel. U. Md. Contbr. articles to profl. jours. Active adv. com. Georgetown U. Continuing Legal Edn., 1991, Georgetown U. Law Ctr. Alumni Bd., 1995. Named Top Lawyer, Washingtonian Mag., 2004. Mem. ATLA (chmn. tort sect. 1985, co-chair birth trauma litigation group 2005), ABA, Nat. Inst. Trial Advocacy, Am. Bd. Profl. Liability Attys., Am. Bd. Trial Advocates, William B. Bryant Inn, Am. Inns of Ct. Office: Joseph Greenwald & Laake PA 6404 Ivy Ln Ste 400 Greenbelt MD 20770-1407 Office Phone: 301-220-2200. Personal E-mail: aegatty@yahoo.com. Business E-Mail: agreenwald@jgllaco.com.

GREENWALD, BRIAN H., history professor; MA, George Wash. U., 1999. Asst. prof. dept. history Gallaudet U., Washington, 2001—. Fellow, Gallaudet U. Rsch. Inst., 2002. Mem.: Disability History Assn. (treas. 2004), Am. Hist. Assn. Office: Gallaudet U Dept History 800 Florida Ave NE Washington DC 20002-3695 Office Fax: 202-651-5652. Business E-Mail: brian.greenwald@gallaudet.edu.

GREENWALD, CAROL SCHIRO, professional services marketing research executive; b. Phila., Mar. 2, 1939; d. Sidney L. and Adele R. (Rosenheim) Schiro; children: David Bruce, William Michael. BA cum laude, Smith Coll., 1961; MA, Hunter Coll., 1965; PhD in Polit. Sci., CUNY, 1972. Instr. polit. sci. Queen's Coll., CUNY, 1970-73; asst. dir. Evaluation N.Y.C. Adminstrv. Decentralization Project, 1971-73; asst. prof. Richmond Coll., CUNY, 1973-76, Bklyn. Coll., CUNY, 1976-77; research assoc. Bunting Inst., Radcliffe Coll., 1977-79; project dir. Jobs in the 1980s Pub. Agenda Found., N.Y.C., 1979-81; assoc. dir. Grant Thornton acctg. firm, 1984-86; sr. mgr. Seidman and Seidman, 1986-87; market research mgr. KPMG Peat Marwick, 1988-90; cons., 1990-91, 2002—; mktg. dir. Haight, Gardner, Poor & Havens, 1991-92; dir. comm. Richard A. Eisner & Co., LLP, 1993-97; dir. mktg. Hamilton, HMC divsn. Kurt Salmon Assoc., 1997—, Whitman Breed Abbott & Morgan LLP, 1998-2000; cons. MarketForce, a divsn. of Hildebrandt, Internat., 2002; pvt. practice, 2002—. Author: Group Power: Lobbying and Public Policy, 1977; mem. editl. bd. Mktg. Rev., 1997—; contbr. articles on polit. sci. to profl. jours. Lilly Found. fellow Mem. Am. Mktg. Assn. (chair profl. devel. leadership coun. 1995—, mem. edtl. bd. 1996—), Common Cause (chmn. N.Y. 1981-83, nat. dir. 1978-84), Westchester Women in Comm. (treas. 1993-95). Home: 688 Forest Ave Larchmont NY 10538-1535 E-mail: greenwaldcarol@hotmail.com.

GREENWALD, DAVID, lawyer; b. NYC, July 31, 1968; BA summa cum laude, Harvard Univ., 1990; JD with high honors, Univ. Chgo., 1993. Bar: NY 1995, US Dist. Ct., So. and Ea. Dists., NY 1995, US Ct. of Appeals, 2nd Cir. 1998, US Ct. of Appeals, 4th Cir. 2002. Law clk., Hon. Richard A. Posner US Ct. of Appeals, 7th Cir.; summer assoc. Cravath Swaine & Moore, NYC, 1992, assoc., 1994—97, 2000—05, ptnr., litig., 2005—; asst. US atty., So. Dist. NY, criminal divsn. US Attorney's Off., 1997—2000. Editor: Univ. Chgo. Law Rev. Mem.: Order of Coif, Phi Beta Kappa. Office: Cravath Swaine & Moore LLP Worldwide Plz 825 Eighth Ave New York NY 10019-7475 Office Phone: 212-474-1922. Office Fax: 212-474-3700. Business E-Mail: dgreenwald@cravath.com.

GREENWALD, JOHN DOYLE, lawyer; b. N.Y.C., July 27, 1945; s. Joseph Adolph and Virginia (Doyle) G.; m. Maria Teresa Tarujo de Almeida, Dec. 23, 1972; children— Nicholas, Fransisco, Katherine. A.B., U. N.C., 1967; J.D., Columbia U., 1972. Bar: N.Y. 1973. Assoc. Sullivan & Cromwell, N.Y.C., 1972-74; dep. gen. counsel Office of U.S. Trade Rep., 1974-80; dep. asst. sec. commerce for import adminstrn., 1980-81; counsel Verner, Liipfert, Bernhard & McPherson, 1981-83; ptnr. Wilmer, Cutler & Pickering, Washington, 1983—; adj. prof. law Georgetown U. Sch. Law, 1981— . Office: Wilmer Cutler Pickering Hale and Dorr LLP 1899 Pennsylvania Ave, NW Washington DC 20006 Office Phone: 202-663-6743. Office Fax: 202-663-6363. E-mail: john.greenwald@wilmerhale.com.*

GREENWALD, JOHN EDWARD, publishing executive, journalist; b. N.Y.C., Oct. 28, 1942; s. Herbert and Carrie (Weisberg) G.; m. Rita Lynn Lipman, May 16, 1987. BA, Syracuse U., 1963. Copy boy N.Y. Post, N.Y.C., 1963-64; assoc. editor Air Force Times, Washington, 1967-70; editor The Times Mag., Washington, 1970-80; editorial dir. Jour. Newspapers, Inc. (Fairfax Jour., Arlington Jour., Alexandria Jour., Prince George's Jour., Prince William Jour., Montgomery Jour.), Springfield, Va., 1980-90; editor Am. Legion Mag., Indpls., 1991-94; asst. mng. editor/Sunday & Spl. Projects The Sun, Lowell, Mass., 1994-98; entertainment columnist Waterbury (Conn.) Republican-Am., 2000—; free-lance writer, 1999—; art critic Lowell (Mass.) Sun, 2002—. Film reviewer Times Jour. Co., Springfield, Va., 1967-85. Exhibitions include Nude 2002, Lexington (Ky.) Art League, La Boniche, Whistler House Mus. of Art, 2002, 2003, Higher Ground, 2003. Coord. Lowell Cultural Roundtable, 1998-; mem. Arts League of Lowell, 2003-; served with U.S. Army, 1964-67. E-mail: johnedit@bigfoot.com.

GREENWALD, MARTIN, publishing company executive; b. Bronx, N.Y., Apr. 25, 1942; s. David and Jean (Kaufman) G.; m. Irma Heldman; children: Karen Sue, Craig Mitchell. AB, Lafayette Coll., 1963; MBA, Columbia U., 1965. Mgr. acquisition planning, fin. analyst Macmillan Inc., N.Y.C., 1965-69, bus. mgr., trade div., 1970-72; new bus. devel. analyst Holt div. CBS, N.Y.C., 1969-70; v.p., gen. mgr. Hagstrom Co. Inc., N.Y.C., 1972-76; pres. Paddington Press, N.Y.C., 1976-80; dir. mktg. Facts On File, Inc., 1980-82, v.p. mktg., 1982-88, sr. v.p., 1988-90, pub., exec. v.p., 1990-95; pres. Martin Greenwald Assocs., Inc., N.Y.C., 1995-96; exec. dir. The Pub. Strategists, Bronxville, N.Y., 1996—, Krugosvet Encyclopedia, Moscow, 1996—; pub. mgr. Open Soc. Inst., 1998—. Author: Maps on File, 1981, Historical Maps on File, 1984 V.p. Green Acres Libr. Bd., Hempstead, NY, 1976—80, Green Acres Civic Assn., 1976—89; mem. Nassau County (N.Y.) Rep. Com., 1973—80; bd. dirs. Non-Profit Found. for the Support of Cultural, Ednl. and New Info. Techs.-Russia, 1999—, Internat. Debate Edn. Assn., 2002—, Krugosvet 000, Russia, 2005—. Mem. Assn. Am. Pubs., Canadian Booksellers Assn., Internat. Debate Edn. Assn., N.Y. Road Runners Club. Jewish. Home: 275 Central Park W New York NY 10024-3015 Office: The Publishing Strategists 29 Palmer Pl Leonia NJ 07605 also: Open Soc Inst 400 W 59th St New York NY 10019 Office Phone: 212-547-6932. Personal E-mail: mgaig@aol.com.

GREENWALD, PETER, epidemiologist, researcher; b. Newburgh, N.Y., Nov. 7, 1936; s. Louis and Pearl (Reingold) G.; m. Harriet Reif, Sept. 6, 1968; children— Rebecca, Laura, Daniel BA, Colgate U., 1957; MD, SUNY Coll. Medicine, 1961; MPH, Harvard U., 1967, DrPH, 1974. Intern Los Angeles County Hosp., 1961-62; resident in internal medicine Boston City Hosp., 1964-66; asst. in medicine Peter Bent Brigham Hosp., 1967-68; mem. epidemiology and disease control study sect. NIH, 1974-78; mem. N.Y. State Gov.'s Breast Task Force, 1976-78; with N.Y. State Dept. Health, Albany, 1968-81, dir., 1968-76, dir. epidemiology, 1976-81; prof. medicine Albany Med. Coll., 1976-81; attending physician Albany Med. Ctr. Hosp., 1968-81; adj. prof. biomed. engring. Rensselaer Poly. Inst., Troy, N.Y., 1976-81; assoc. scientist Sloan-Kettering Inst. for Cancer Research, N.Y.C., 1977-81; dir. div. cancer prevention Nat. Cancer Inst., NIH, Bethesda, Md., 1981-97, 98—. Mem. VA Merit Rev. Bd. Med. Oncology, Washington, 1972-74 Editor-in-chief Jour. Nat. Cancer Inst., NIH, 1981-87; contbr. articles to profl. jours. Rear adm. USPHS, 1962-64, 81—. Recipient Disting. Svc. award N.Y. State Dept. Health, 1975; Redway medal and award for med. writing N.Y. State Jour. Medicine, 1977, N.Y. State Gov.'s Citationfor pub. health achievement, 1981, PHS commendation 1983, 88, Disting. Svc. medal, 1993, Disting. Svc. award, Am. Cancer Soc., 1997, Outstanding Rsch. award Am. Inst. Cancer Rsch., 1997, Pub. Svc. award Cancer Treatment and Rsch. Found., 1997; named to SUNY Honor Roll of Disting. Grads., 1997. Fellow ACP, APHA (epidemiology sect. chmn. 1981), Am. Coll. Preventive Medicine, Am. Soc. Nutritional Scis.; mem. Am. Assn. Cancer Rsch. (DeWitt Goodman lectr. 1998), Am. Soc. Clin. Oncology, Am. Coll. Epidemiology (bd. dirs. 1981-82), Am. Soc. Preventive Oncology (Disting. Achievement award 1998), Internat. Epidemiology Soc., Nat. Acad. Scis. (food and nutrition bd. 1982-88), Am. Cancer Soc. (Cancer Prevention award 2002). Office: NIH/NCI Divsn Cancer Prevention EPN/2040 6130 Exec Blvd Bethesda MD 20892-7309 Office Phone: 301-496-6616. Business E-Mail: pg37g@nih.gov.

GREENWALD, RICKY, psychologist, human services administrator; b. Boston, Dec. 10, 1958; s. Alan Robert and Sondra Esther (Cohen) Greenwald; m. Hannah de Vries, Nov. 18, 2004. BS in Psychology, Lesley Coll., Cambridge, Mass., 1988; MA in Psychology, Forest Inst. Prof. Psychology, 1989; D in Psychology, Forest Inst. Psychology, 1994; cert. in couple/family therapy, Kantor Family Inst., 1991. Lic. psychologist N.Y. Postdoctoral fellow Cmty. Svcs. Inst., Springfield, Mass., 1995—96; sr. psychologist Mokihama Project Dept. Edn., Kauai, Hawaii, 1997—99; asst. clin. prof., dir. tng., cons. dept. psychiatry & pediat. Mt. Sinai Sch. Medicine, N.Y.C., 2000—03; founder, exec. dir., sr. trainer Child Trauma Inst., Greenfield, Mass., 2002—. Faculty mem. Art Inst., Mexico City, 2003—; moderator, co-founder EMDR Rsch. Inst., 1999—. Author: EMDR in Child/Adolescent Psychotherapy, 1999, Child Trauma Handbook, 2005; editor: Trauma & Juvenile Delinquency, 2002; mem. editl. bd. Traumatology, 2001—, Jour. EMDR Rsch. and Practice, 2005—. Mem.: Network EMDR Tng. (co-founder), Internat. Soc. Traumatic Stress Studies (past founder), EMDR Internat. Assn. (mem. rsch. com., past bd. dirs.). Green Party. Jewish. Office: Child Trauma Inst PO Box 544 Greenfield MA 01302

GREENWALD, ROBERT, public relations executive; b. NYC, Jan. 14, 1927; s. Louis and Rebecca (Shapiro) G.; m. Genevieve Kushnir, Apr. 15, 1957 (div. 1960); m. Dorothy Pearl Brand, Apr. 19, 1963; children: Liza, Mark. BA, NYU, 1949, postgrad., 1951-54; postgrad, Columbia U., 1950, New Sch., 1950-51. Account exec. Ruder & Finn, Inc., N.Y.C., 1954—, sr. assoc., 1955-56, v.p., 1957-65; sr. v.p. Ruder, Finn & Rotman, Inc., N.Y.C., 1965-79; exec. v.p. Ruder, Finn & Rotman Inc., N.Y.C., 1980-83, sr. counsel, 1983-85; vice-chmn. Makovsky & Co. Inc., N.Y.C., 1987—; pvt. quality control cons. N.Y.C., 1994—. Author: (with Dorothy Brand) Learning To Live with The Love of Your Life, 1979. Chmn. pub. relations com. UNICEF, N.Y.C., 1976-82, dir., 1976-82, mem. nat. adv. com., 1983-97, mem. nominating com., 1983-87; bd. dirs. Jewish Family Services, N.Y.C., 1972-75. Served with U.S. Army, 1945-46, ETO. Recipient Silver Anvil award Pub. Relations Soc. Am., 1955, 73, 81; recipient Paul B. Zucker award Ruder & Finn Inc., 1976, 82 Democrat. Jewish. Home: 73 Alexander Ave Montclair NJ 07043 Office Phone: 973-509-3934. Personal E-mail: bobdott1@aol.com.

GREENWALD, SHEILA ELLEN, writer, illustrator; b. N.Y.C., May 26, 1934; d. Julius and Florence (Friedman) Greenwald; m. George E. Green, Feb. 18, 1960; children: Samuel Green, Benjamin Green. BA, Sarah Lawrence Coll., 1956. Author over 24 children's books, including Give Us a Great Big Smile Rosy Cole, 1980, Valentine Rosy, 1984, Rosy Cole's Great American Guilt Club, 1987, Write on Rosy, 1988, Rosy's Romance, 1989, Here's Hermione, 1991, The Mariah Delany Author of the Month Club, 1990, Rosy Cole Discovers America, 1992, My Fabulous NewLife, 1993, Rosy Cole, She Walks in Beauty, 1994, Rosy Cole: She Grows and Graduates, 1997, Stucksville, 2000, Mariah Delany Lending Library Disaster (The Mariah Delany Author of The Month Club 1999), Stucksville, 2001, The Hot Day reissued by Silver Mountain, 2002, Rosy Cole's Worst Ever, Best Yet Tour of New York City, 2003. Mem. PEN, Authors League. Jewish. Office: Melanie Kroupa Books Ferrar Straus & Geroux 19 Union Sq W New York NY 10003 E-mail: sheilagreenwald@usa.net.

GREENWALD, THERESA MCGOWAN, rehabilitation nurse; b. Scranton, Pa., Feb. 8, 1950; d. Robert Bell and Agnes (Butler) McGowan; m. David Jeffrey Greenwald, Oct. 26, 1996; 1 child, Jennifer Emilie Nicole Drescher. Diploma nursing, Hosp. U. Pa., 1970. RN, Ohio; cert. rehab. nurse, case mgr. Staff nurse, asst. head nurse Riddle Meml. Hosp., Media, Pa., 1971-80; rehab. nurse, mgr. Upjohn Rehab. Scvs., Phila. and Cin., 1980-85; cons., life care planner Occupl. Health Resources, Cin., 1985-87, Springfield, Va., 1987-88; dir. life care planning Rehab. Experts, Vienna, Va., 1988-89; program mgr., account exec. Comprehensive Rehab. Assocs., Cin., 1989-93; dir. managed care case mgmt. Sheakley Med. Mgmt. Sys., Cin., 1993-95; clin. program coord. Mayfield Clinic and Spine Inst., Cin., 1996—; dir. Nat. Bd. Certification Continuity of Care, 1998-99. Mem. cmty. adv. bd. Drake Ctr., Inc., 1998-2000. Mem. Nurse Case Mgrs. of S.W. Ohio (membership chair 1994-99), Case Mgmt. Resource Network (v.p., pres. elect, 2005). Office: Mayfield Spine Inst 506 Oak St Cincinnati OH 45219-2507 Office Phone: 513-755-1950. E-mail: TGreenwald@Mayfieldclinic.com.

GREENWALD, THOMAS ALBERT, lawyer; b. Brookfield, Wis., Aug. 12, 1962; s. Albert Donald and Sharon Lee Greenwald; m. Deborah Lynn Hannon, June 25, 1963; children: Thomas Albert, Asher Hill. BBA in Fin., U. of Wis., Milw., 1987; JD, Tex. Tech Sch. of Law, Lubbock, Texas, 1989—92. Bar: Tex. 1992, cert.: Tex. Bd. of Legal Specialization (family law) 1997, bar: US. Dist. Ct. (no. dist.) Tex. 2000. Ptnr. McKnight, McKnight & Greenwald, L.L.P., Dallas, 1992—94, Goranson, Bain Larsen & Greenewald, L.C., Dallas, 1994—. Mem. ct. rules com. State Bar Tex., Austin, 2001—. Contbr. articles to profl. jours. Bd. of edn. Calvary Sch., Dallas. Named Tex. Super Lawyer, Tex. Monthly; named one of Best Lawyers in Dallas Under 40, D Mag. Fellow: Am. Acad. Matrimonial Lawyers, Collin County Bench Bar Found. (life; bd. dirs. family law sect.), Dallas Bar Found. (life; bd. dirs. family law sect., officer family law sect.); mem.: Collin County Bar Assn., Dallas Bar Assn. Office: Goranson Bain Larsen & Greenwald LC 8150 N Central Expy Ste 1850 Dallas TX 75206 E-mail: tgreenwald@gblg-law.com.

GREENWAY, HUGH DAVIDS SCOTT, journalist; b. Boston, May 8, 1935; s. James Cowen and Helen Livingston (Scott) G.; m. Joy Beverly Brooks, June 11, 1960; children: Julia Livingston, Alice Lauder, Sarah Davids. BA, Yale U., 1958; postgrad., Oxford U., Eng., 1960-62. Corr. Time mag., London, 1962-63, Washington, 1963-64, Boston, 1964-66, Saigon, 1967-68, Bangkok, 1968-70, UN, N.Y.C., 1970-72; corr. Washington Post, Hong Kong, 1973-76, Jerusalem, 1976-78; assoc. editor for nat. and fgn. news Boston Globe, 1978-91, sr. assoc. editor, 1991-93, editl. page editor, 1994-2000, fgn. affairs columnist, 2000—. Trustee, Woods Hole (Mass.) Oceanographic Inst. Served with USNR, 1958-60. Nieman fellow Harvard U., 1971-72 Mem.: Internat. Press Inst., Coun. on Fgn. Rels., Am. Soc. Newspaper Editors. Home: 634 Charles River St Needham MA 02492-1031 Office Phone: 781-235-0353. Personal E-mail: greenway@globe.com.

GREENWAY, JOAN M., dean; b. Adelaide, South Australia, Australia; d. John Francis Matthew and Ida Gladys Wilding; m. Elliott D. Full, Feb. 9, 1997; m. Ian MacKinnon Disher, Aug. 30, 1944 (dec. Mar. 16, 1957); children: Carolyn Wilding Whitting, Susan MacIntosh Miller, Jamie Sutherland MacDonald. BA, U. Colo., Boulder, CO, 1968, MA, 1969, PhD, 1970. TV journalist NEWS Ltd., South Australia, Australia, 1957—62, Australian Broadcasting Commn., Australia, 1962—66; asst. prof. Regis Coll., Denver, 1969—71; prof. and chmn. Calif. State U., Pomona, Calif., 1971—76; dean Continuing Edn. Calif. State U., Pomona, Calif., 1976—88. Spl. adv. children Superior Ct. LA County, Los Angeles, Calif., 1993—97. Recipient Disting. Prof. Am., Wash., D.C., 1975. Mem.: Phi Beta Kappa Colo. Chpt.

GREENWELL, ARNOLD, editor, photographer; b. Tokyo, Mar. 3, 1956; came to U.S., 1958; s. Charles Warren Greenwell and Miyoko (Takahashi) Wallace. AS cum laude, Lees-McRae Coll., 1976; BA, U. N.C., 1979. Research technician dept. zoology U. N.C., Chapel Hill, 1977-79; research technician Howard Hughes Med. Inst., Durham, N.C., 1979-80; biol. lab. technician Nat. Inst. Environ. Health Scis., Research Triangle Park, N.C., 1980-84, research biologist, 1984-2000; tech. info. specialist, 2000—; assoc. editor, photographer Eviron. Health Perspectives, 2000—. Pvt. pilot, 1982—; free-lance photographer, 1977—. Mem. editl. adv. bd. The Southern Aviator, 1993-95; contbr. articles to profl. jours.; pub. numerous photographs in aviation pubs., calendars, mus. exhbns. Mem.: Nat. Inst. Environ. Health Scis. Camera Club (v.p. 1981—83, sec. 1987—94), Nat. Press Photographers Assn., Exptl. Aircraft Assn., Aircraft Owners and Pilots Assn., Wings of Carolina Flying Club, Phi Theta Kappa. Republican. Avocations: flying, hunting, fishing, photography. Home: 6211 Dawn Dr Hurdle Mills NC 27541 Office: Nat Inst Environ Health Scis PO Box 12233 Research Triangle Park NC 27709 Office Phone: 919-541-3393. Business E-Mail: greenwe1@niehs.nih.gov.

GREENWELL, RAYMOND N., mathematician, educator, writer; b. Alhambra, Calif., Apr. 14, 1953; s. Robert N. and Katherine M. Greenwell; m. Karla Harby, June 10, 1978. BA, Univ. San Diego, 1974; PhD, Mich. State U., 1979. Asst. prof. math. Albion (Mich.) Coll., 1979—83; prof. math. Hofstra U., Hempstead, NY, 1983—. Author: (mathematics textbooks) Finite Mathematics, 2005, Calculus with Applications, 2005; contbr. articles to profl. jours. Trip leader Sierra Club Inner City Outings, N.Y.C., 1986—. Mem.: Math. Assn. Am. (gov. met. N.Y. sect. 2002—05). Home: 264 National Blvd Long Beach NY 11561 Office: Dept of Mathematics 103 Hofstra University Hempstead NY 11549 Office Phone: 516-463-5573. E-mail: matrng@hofstra.edu.

GREENWELL, RONALD EVERETT, communications executive; b. Louisville, Oct. 28, 1938; s. Woodrow M. and Christine (Comer) Gossett G.; m. Diane J. Greenwell, Mar. 18, 1967; children: Wendy, Robin. With Motorola Inc., Schaumburg, Ill., 1962-94, sr. v.p., gen. mgr. communications internat. group, 1986-94; pres. Motorola Communications Internat. Inc., Schaumburg, Ill., 1986-94, ret., 1994. Bd. dirs. ALTELA, Inc., Albuquerque. Home: 30 Canyon Ridge Dr Sandia Park NM 87047-8506

GREENWOOD, DANN EDWARD, lawyer; b. Dickinson, N.D., Sept. 21, 1952; s. Lawrence E. and Joyce E. (Henley) G.; m. Debra K. Ableidinger, June 15, 1975; children: Jay, Lindsey, Paige. BSBA magna cum laude, U. N.D., 1974, JD, 1977. Bar: N.D. 1977, U.S. Dist. Ct. N.D. 1980. Ptnr. Greenwood, Greenwood & Greenwood and predecessor firms, Dickinson, 1977-98, Greenwood & Ramsey PLLP, 1998—. Mem. N.D. Supreme Ct. Disciplinary Bd., 1983-89, Northern Lights Boy Scouts Council, Dickinson, 1985—; bd. dirs. Legal Assistance N.D., Bismarck, 1980-86. Mem. N.D. Bar Assn. (pres. 1998-99), Stark-Dunn County Bar Assn., N.D. Trial Lawyers Assn. (sec. 1983-84, treas. 1984-85, v.p. 1985-86, pres. 1987-88), Kiwanis, Masons, Shriners, Elks. Lutheran. Home: PO Box 688 Dickinson ND 58602-0688 E-mail: shadyln@ndsupernet.com, grlawdg@ndsupernet.com.

GREENWOOD, DAVID A., lawyer; b. Salt Lake City, Aug. 9, 1946; BA magna cum laude, U. Utah, 1970; JD, U. Chgo., 1973. Bar: Utah 1973. Shareholder Van Cott, Bagley, Cornwall & McCarthy, Salt Lake City; shareholder, comml. litig. Bendinger Crockett Peterson Greenwood & Casey, Salt Lake City. Fellow Am. Bar Found., Am. Coll. Trial Lawyers (vice chmn. Utah state com.); mem. ABA, Am. Bd. Trial Advocates (assoc., past pres. Utah chapt.), Utah State Bar, Phi Beta Kappa, Phi Kappa Phi. Office: Bendinger Crockett Peterson Greenwood & Casey Ste 400 170 S Main St Salt Lake City UT 84101 Office Phone: 801-533-8383. Office Fax: 801-531-1486.

GREENWOOD, FRANK, information scientist, educator; b. Rio de Janeiro, Mar. 6, 1924; came to U.S., 1935; s. Heman Charles and Evelyn (Heyns) G.; m. Mary Mallas, Oct. 24, 1972; children: Margaret, Ernest, Nicholas. BA, Bucknell U., 1950; MBA, U. So. Calif., 1959; PhD, UCLA, 1963; hon. doctorate, Commonwealth Open U. Brit. VI, 1999. Cert. systems profl., project mgmt. profl. Various positions The Tex. Co., U.S., Africa and Can., 1950-60; assoc. prof. U. Ga., Athens, 1961-65; chmn. dept. computer sys. Ohio U., Athens, 1966-76; dir. computer ctr. U. Mont., Missoula, 1977-84; prof. mgmt. info. sys. Southea. Mass. U. (now U. Mass.), North Dartmouth, 1985-89, Ctrl. Mich. U., Mt. Pleasant, 1990-93; pres. Greenwood & Assocs., Ltd., Bloomfield Hills, Mich., 1993. Instr. on-line clases Jones Internat. U., Englewood, Colo., Gatlin Ednl. Svcs., Ft. Worth, Tex., Touro U. Internat., Cypress, Calif. Author: Casebook for Management and Business Policy: A Systems Approach, 1968, Managing the Systems Analysis Function, 1968; (with Nicolai Siemens and C.H. Marting Jr.) Operations Research: Planning, Operating and Information Systems, 1973; (with Mary Greenwood) Information Resources in the Office Tomorrow, 1980, Profitable Small Business Computing, 1982, Office Technology: Principles of Automation, 1984, Business Telecommuncations: Data Communications in the Information Age, 1988, Introduction to Computer-Integrated Manufacturing, 1990, How to Raise Office Productivity, 1991, Meeting the Challenges of Project Management: A Primer, 1998; columnist: Computerworld mag., 1972-73, The Daily Record, 1982-83, (with Mary Greenwood) Herald News, 1986, The Beacon, 1986, Morning Sun, 1990-93; contbr. monographs, articles to profl. jours. and chpts. to books. Sgt. AUS, 1943-45. UCLA Alumni scholar, 1961; Ford Found. fellow, 1962-63. Mem. Wamsutta Club (New Bedford, Mass.). Greek Orthodox. Avocation: exercise. Home and Office: 7426 Deep Run Apt 1322 Bloomfield Hills MI 48301-3844 Personal E-mail: fgreenw617@aol.com. *Do what you believe you should (and not what others do). Put your trust in your own capacity to provide products/services others need (and don't seek security as a "corporate slave"). Mental and physical health are the key to all else.*

GREENWOOD, JANE, costume designer, educator; b. Liverpool, England, Apr. 30, 1934; d. Harold Ralph Pate and Florence Sarah Mary (Humphrey) G.; m. Ben Edwards, children: Sarah, Kate. Attended, Central Sch. of Arts & Crafts, London, England. Teacher Lester Polakov Design Studio, New York, NY, Julliard Sch., New York, NY; assoc. prof. of design Yale U., New Haven, 1977—. Stage work includes: The Ballad of the Sad Cafe, 1963, Hamlet, 1964, Incident at Vichy, 1964-65, Tartuffe, 1965, Half a Sixpence, 1965-66, A Race of Hairy Men!, 1965, Nathan Weinstein, 1966, Where's Daddy?, 1966, How's the World Treating You?, 1966, More Stately Mansions, 1967-68, The Prime of Miss Jean Brodie, 1968, Seven Descents of Myrtle, 1968, I'm Solomon, 1968, The Wrong Way Light Bulb, 1969, The Penny Wars, 1969, Angela, 1969, Sheep on the Runway, 1970, Othello, 1970, Gandhi, 1970, Hay Fever, 1970, Les Blancs, 1970, Antigone, 1971, Wise Child, 1972, Look Away, 1973, Finishing Touches, 1973, A Moon for the Misbegotten, 1973-74, Cat on a Hot Tin Roof, 1974, 2003-04, Same Time Next Year, 1975-78, A Matter of Gravity, 1976, California Suite, 1976, A Texas Trilogy, 1976, Otherwise Engaged, 1977, Anna Christie, 1977, Vieux Carre, 1977, The Night of the Tribades, 1977, An Almost Perfect Person, 1977, A Touch of the Poet, 1977, Cheaters, 1978, The Kingfisher, 1978, Faith Healer, 1979, Knockout, 1979, Romantic Comedy, 1979, To Grandmother's House We Go, 1981, The Supporting Cast, 1981, The West Side Waltz, 1981-82, Duet for One, 1981, Medea, 1982, The Queen and the Rebels, 1982, Plenty, 1983, Heartbreak House, 1983-84, The Golden Age, 1984, Alone Together, 1984, The Iceman Cometh, 1985, Lillian, 1986, So Long on Lonely Street, 1986, Ah, Wilderness, 1988, Long Day's Journey into Night, 1988, Our Town, 1988, The Secret Rapture, 1989, Lisbon Traviatta, The Circle, 1989, The Tenth Man, 1990, The Big Love, 1991, I Hate Hamlet, 1991, Park Your Car in Harvard Yard, 1991, A Streetcar Named Desire, 1992, The Price, 1992, Lips Together, Teeth Apart, The Sisters Rosensweig, 1993-94, Abe Lincoln in Illinois, 1993, She Loves Me, 1993, Passion, 1994, The Heiress, 1995, A Month in the Country, 1995, Sylvia, Death Defying Acts, Master Class, 1995, A Delicate Balance, 1996, Once Upon a Mattress, 1996, The Last Night of Ballyhoo, 1997, An American Daughter, 1997, The Little Foxes, 1997, Proposals, 1997, The Scarlet Pimpernel, 1997, The Deep Blue Sea, 1998, Honour, 1998, High Society, 1998, James Joyce's The Dead, 2000, A Moon for the Misbegotten, 2000, The Dinner Party, 2000-01, Major Barbara, 2001, Bea Arthur on Broadway, 2002, Fortune's Fool, 2002, The Retreat from Moscow, 2003-04, The Violet Hour, 2003, The Caretaker, 2003-04, Oldest Living Confederate Widow Tells All, 2003, Who's Afraid of Virginia Woolf?, 2005, On Golden Pond, 2005, Lennon, 2005; TV work includes: The House Without a Christmas Tree, 1972, The Easter Promise, 1975, Beyond the Horizon, 1976, Addie and the King of Hearts, 1976, The Royal Romance of Charles and Diana, 1982, The Shady Hill Kidnapping, 1982, The File on Jill Hatch, 1983, Kennedy, 1983, Johnny Bull, 1986, Ike, 1986, Heartbreak House, 1986, Lyndon Johnson, 1987, Dialogue of the Carmelites, 1987, Liberace: Behind the Music, 1988, Our Town, 1989, The Ivory Hunters, 1990, Sensibility and Sense, 1990, Three Hotels, 1991, The End of a Sentence, 1991, A Life in the Theatre, 1993, The Mother, 1994; film work includes: Last Embrace, 1979, Can't Stop the Music, 1980, The Four Seasons, 1981, Arthur, 1981, Wetherby, 1985, Sweet Liberty, 1986, The Squeeze, 1987, Jacknife, Mr. Destiny, 1990, Glengarry Glen Ross, 1992, Oleanna, 1994, Other Voices, Other Rooms, 1995. 14 Tony nominations. Office: 54 W 22nd St New York NY 10010-5811*

GREENWOOD, JANET KAE DALY, psychologist, academic administrator, marketing professional; b. Goldsboro, N.C., Dec. 9, 1943; d. Fulton Benton and Kelminy Ethel Esther (Ball) Daly; 1 child, Gerald Thompson. AA, Peace Coll., 1963; BS in English and Psychology, East Carolina U., 1965, MEd in Counseling, 1967; postgrad., N.C. State U., 1967-69, U. London, 1969; PhD in Counseling and Higher Ednl. Adminstrn., Fla. State U., 1972. Tchr. English Kinston (N.C.) City Schs., 1965-66, Goldsboro City Schs., 1966-67; counselor and psychometrist primary and secondary schs. County of Wake, N.C., 1967-69; coord. Am. Inst. for Fgn. Study, 1969; supr. student tours in Eng., France, Switzerland, Italy, and Capri, 1969; counselor Fla. State U., Tallahassee, 1969-72; asst. dir. counseling Rutgers U., New Brunswick, N.J., 1972-73, cons. to v.p. for student svcs., 1973-74, lectr. in counseling psychology, 1972-74; coord. and assoc. prof. counselor edn. U. Cin., 1974-77, adviser to grad. students, 1974-77, vice provost student affairs, 1977-81; pres. Longwood Coll., Farmville, Va., 1981-87, U. Bridgeport, Conn., 1987-92; cons., ptnr., dir. Heidrick & Struggles, Washington, 1992-2000; v.p. A.T. Kearney, Inc., 2000—04; owner, ptnr. Greenwood & Assocs., Inc., 2004—. Guidance cons. South Plainfield Pub. Schs., 1973-76; adviser Parents without Ptnrs., 1976; bd. dirs. Hydraulic Co.; mem. Gov.'s Partnership To Prevent Substance Abuse in the Workforce, mem. audit com. and cmty. and govt. rels. com. Contbr. articles to profl. jours. Mem. Gov.'s Ad Hoc Edn. Com. on Tchr. Edn. and Counselor Edn., State of Ohio, 1975; mem. state planning commn. Nat. Identification of Women Project; chair Twin Rivers Tenants Rights Assn., 1972-74; bd. dirs. Bridgeport Hosp., Bridgeport Bus. Coun.; mem. adv. com. Bridgeport Pub. Edn. Fund; bd. dirs. Conn. Ballet Theatre, chair South End streeting com; mem. mgmt. adv. com. City of Bridgeport; mem. adv. com. United Way Tri-State; chair South End Partnership Com; mem. The Schiavone Steering Com./Downtown Bridgeport Project, YWCA Bd., Champion/United Way, United Way Community Human Svcs. Planning Coun., Bridgeport Symphony Bd., Bridgeport Opera Bd., Bridgeport Area Coll./Univ. Consortium, Conn. Conf. Ind. Colls., The Newcomen Soc. of U.S., The United Way Ea. Fairfield County; mem. adv. bd. Sacred Heart/St. Anthony Sch., Roosevelt Sch; mem. ct. com. Regional Plan Assn. Fairfield 2000; bd. dirs. Conn. Ballet Theatre; chair The Bridgeport Regional Bus. Coun. Brass Ring Task Force on Leadership; bd. govs. Fairfield County Study; mem. hon. bd. dirs. Conn. Earth Day 20, Inc.; chair L.I. Sound Western Regional Coun.; founding mem. L.I. Sound Assembly; mem. membership com., campus partnership subcom. Drugs Don't Work program, 1989-91. Recipient Spl. award Black Arts Festival, Meritorious Svc. award Am. Assn. State Colls. and Univs. Mem. AAUP, Am. Coll. Pers. Assn. (editor and chair media bd. 1975—), Am. Pers. and Guidance Assn., Cin. Pers. and Guidance Assn., Ohio Psychol. Assn., Cin. Psychol. Assn., Organizational Behavior Assn., Am. Sch. Counselors Assn., Ohio Sch. Counselors Assn., Assn. for Women Faculty, Ohio Counselor Edn. and Supervision Assn., Kappa Delta Pi.

GREENWOOD, JOEN ELIZABETH, economist, consultant; b. Mineral Point, Wis., Aug. 29, 1934; d. John Edward and Lillian Laile (Rohr) G. BS, MA, U. Wis., 1956, 57; postgrad., U. Calif., Berkeley, 1957—61, Newnham Coll. Cambridge U., Eng., 1961-62; diploma in Advanced Mgmt. Program, Harvard Bus. Sch., 1983. Instr. econs. Wellesley (Mass.) Coll., 1962-68; sr. assoc. Charles River Assocs., Boston, 1968-79, v.p., 1979—2003, sr. cons., 2003—. Mem. bd. editors Energy Jour., 1979-83; mem. Nat. Coal Coun., 1993-2000. Co-author: Folded, Spindled and Mutilated: Economic Analysis and U.S. v. IBM, 1983; contbr. to profl. publs. Mem. Commonwealth of Mass. Pub. Health Coun., Boston, 1973—79; chairwoman Women's Philantropy Coun. U. Wis. Found., 2001—04, bd. dirs., 2001—04. Earhart fellow U. Calif.-Berkeley, 1960-61; Fulbright scholar U.K., 1961-62 Mem. Internat. Assn. Energy Economists (v.p. 1978-84, exec. v.p. 1981-84), U. Wis. Alumni Assn. (bd. dirs. 1987-93), Wis. Alumni Assn. Greater Boston (pres. 1987-89), Boston Club, Harvard Club, Phi Beta Kappa. Home: 130 Mt Auburn St Unit 304 Cambridge MA 02138 Office: Charles River Assocs 200 Clarendon St Fl 33 Boston MA 02116-5092 Business E-Mail: jeg@crai.com.

GREENWOOD, JOHN E., investment advisor; b. Gas City, Ind., May 15, 1922; s. Elmer Middleton and Lenora Cassinda (Reynolds) G.; m. Valerie Louise Komanich, Dec. 26, 1947. Student, W.Va. U., 1940—42, Cornell U., 1942—43; BSBA, U. Mo., 1949. Registered rep. N.Y. Stock Exchange. Stockbroker Newhard, Cook & Co., Inc., St. Louis, 1949-50, Alton, Ill., 1950-89, resident mgr., 1977-88, v.p. St. Louis and Alton, 1984-89; v.p. investments Newhard, Cook/Advest, Inc., 1989-92, Longrow Securities, Inc., St. Louis, also Alton, Ill., 1992-96; v.p. Alton Securities Group, Inc., 1996—. Founder Midcoast Aviation Svcs., Inc., St. Louis, 1957, bd. dirs., 1970-78. Editor: Alton Rotary Historical Building Survey, 1972; contbr. articles and book revs. to hist. publs. Campaign chmn. March of Dimes, Alton, 1957; chmn., bd. dirs. Hayner Pub. Libr., Alton, 1964-77; chmn. Alton Hist. Commn., 1972-74; founder, bd. dirs. 8th Air Force Meml. Mus. Found., Inc., pres., 1985-86, 86-97, chmn., CEO, 1998—; governing trustee Air Force Hist. Found., 1986—; life mem. Commemorative Air Force, Midland, Tex.; mem. The Mighty Eighth Air Force Heritage Mus., Savannah, Ga.; trustee Am. Airpower Heritage Found., 1987-89, Alton Jr. C. of C., 1951-56, v.p. bd.; bd. dirs. Am. Air Mus. in Britain, 1992—, Imperial War Mus.; gov. trustee Air Force Hist. Found., 1986-2002, emeritus, 2003—. 1st lt. USAAF, 1942-45, England. B-17G navigator USAF, European, African and Middle EAst campaing, Am. Campaign. Decorated Air medal with four oak leaf clusters, Two Presdl. Unit citations, Marksman-Pistol medal Mem. 8th Air Force Hist. Soc. (founder, bd. dirs., pres. 1975—), Army and Navy Club (Washington), Lockhaven Country Club, Rotary (bd. dirs., treas. Alton 1960—, President's award for outstanding svc. 1965), Air Force Assn., VFW, Friends of U.S. Air Force Mus., Retired Officers Assn., Air Crew Assn. (Gt. Britain), U. Mo. Alumni Assn., Culver Mil. Acad. Alumni Assn., Sigma Chi Frat. Republican. Methodist. Avocations: aviation research, photography, golf, travel. Home: 607 State St Alton IL 62002-6141 Office: Alton Securities Group 2410 State St PO Box 160 Alton IL 62002-0160 Office Phone: 618-466-9700.

GREENWOOD, JONATHAN RICHARD GUY (JONNY GREENWOOD), musician; b. Oxford, England, Nov. 5, 1972; married. Student in Psychology, Oxford (Eng.) Poly. Lead guitarist Radiohead, 1992—; composer in residence BBC, 2004—. Musician: (albums) Pablo Honey, 1993, The Bends, 1995, OK Computer, 1997 (Grammy award, 1997), Kid A, 2000 (Grammy award, 2000), Amnesiac, 2001, I Might Be Wrong: Live Recordings, 2001, Hail to the Thief, 2003. Office: Capital Records 1750 North Vine St 10th Fl Hollywood CA 90028

GREENWOOD, LAWRENCE GEORGE, banker; b. Briercrest, Sask., Can., June 16, 1921; s. Goerge Tuckfield and Mildred Jane (Clifford) G.; m. Margaret Purser, June 28, 1947 (dec.). Grad., Regina Central Collegiate, 1938; LLD (hon.), Queens U., Ont., 1980. With Cn. Bank Commerce, Regina, Sask., 1938—, merged to form Can. Imperial Bank Commerce, 1961; pres. Can. Imperial Bank Commerce, Toronto, 1968-71, vice chmn., Toronto and Montreal, 1971-76; dir. emeritus Can. Imperial Bank of Commerce, Toronto.

Mem. Nat. Trust for Scotland; hon. trustee Hosp. for Sick Children, Toronto. Served with RCAF, 1941-45. Mem.: York. Home: 7 Tudor Gate Willowdale ON Canada M2L 1N3 Office: PO Box 63 Commerce Ct N Ste 2601 Toronto ON Canada M5L 1B9

GREENWOOD, LOREN, toy manufacturing executive; BS in bus., Calif. State U., Fullerton. Various positions with Ace Novelty, Walt Disney Co.; v.p.-sales Hasbro, Inc., 1996—99, sr. v.p.- global sales and internat. offices, 1999—2001, exec. v.p.- global sales, mktg. and organized play, 2001—02; exec. v.p. and COO Wizards of the Coast, Inc., subs. Hasbro, Inc., 2002—. Avocations: reading, bicycling. Mailing: 1801 Lind Ave SW Renton WA 98055

GREENWOOD, M. R. C., college dean, biologist, nutrition educator; b. Gainesville, Fla., Apr. 11, 1943; d. Stanley James and Mary Rita (Schmeltz) Cooke; m. (div. 1968); 1 child, James Robert. AB summa cum laude, Vassar Coll., 1968; PhD, Rockefeller U., 1973; LHD (hon.), Mt. St. Mary Coll., 1989. Rsch. assoc. Inst. of Human Nutrition, Columbia U., N.Y.C., 1974-75, adj. asst. prof., 1975-76, asst. prof., 1976-78; assoc. prof. dept. biology Vassar Coll., Poughkeepsie, N.Y., 1978-81, prof. biology, 1981-86, dir. animal model, CORE Lab. of Obesity Rsch. Ctr., 1985-89, dir. undergrad. rsch. summer inst., 1986-88, dir. Howard Hughes biol. scis. network program, 1988, chmn. of biology dept., John Guy Vassar prof. natural scis., 1986-89; prof. nutrition and internal medicine, dean grad. studies U. Calif., Davis, 1989-96, chancellor Santa Cruz, 1996—2004; sr. v.p. academic affairs U. Calif. sys., 2004—. Mem. nutrition study sect. NIH, 1983-87; mem. NRC; assoc. dir. for sci. White House Office Sci. and Tech., 1993-95. Editor: Obesity, Vol. 4, 1983; contbr. over 250 articles and abstracts to profl. jours., 1974-89. Recipient Rsch. Career Devel. award NIH, 1978-83; Mellon scholar-in-residence St. Olaf Coll., Northfield, Minn., 1978; N.Y. State Regents fellow, 1968. Mem. Inst. Medicine of Nat. Acad. Scis. (chair food and nutrition bd., diet and health subcom. 1986—), N.Am. Soc. for Study of Obesity (pres. 1987-88), Am. Inst. Nutrition (BioServ 1982), Am. Physiol. Soc., The Harvey Soc., Am. Diabetes Assn., Internat. Assn. for Study of Obesity (treas. 1991—). Home: 5033 El Cemonte Ave Davis CA 95616 Office: U Calif Office of the Pres 1111 Franklin St Oakland CA 94607

GREENWOOD, MONIQUE, innkeeper, writer, restaurant owner; b. Wash., DC; m. Glenn Pogue. Grad. magna cum laude, Howard U. Lifestyle dir., style editor Essence mag., 1996—98, exec. editor, 1998—2000, editor-in-chief, 2000—01; owner, innkeeper Akwaaba Mansion Bed & Breakfast, Bklyn., 1995—, Akwaaba by the Sea, Cape May, NJ, 2001—; owner Akwaaba Cafe, Bklyn. Co-founder, pres. Go On Girl! Book Club. Author: Having What Matters: The Black Woman's Guide to Creating the Life You Really Want, 2001. Bd. mem. Bklyn. Urban League, Central Bklyn. Partnership, Bridge St. Devel. Corp. Recipient Points of Light award, Pres. Bush. Avocations: reading, antiques, travel, interior decorating. Mailing: Akwaaba Mansion Bed & Breakfast 347 MacDonough St Brooklyn NY 11233 Office Phone: 718-455-5958. Office Fax: 718-774-1744.

GREENWOOD, NAOMI, social worker; b. Phila., Feb. 12, 1941; d. David Nisan and Emma (Morgenstern) Greenwood; m. Burton S. Kolko, June 17, 1962 (div. 1993); children: David Joseph, Joshua Howard; m. Thomas E. Dahl, Jan. 2, 1999. BA in Sociology with honors, U. Pa., 1962; MSW, Smith Coll., 1964. Cert. Am. Bd. Examiners of Clin. Social Work; lic. clin. social worker. Clin. social worker St. Elizabeths Hosp., Washington, 1964-69; social worker children's unit Psychiat. Inst., Washington, 1972-76, assoc. dir. social work, 1976-79; acting dir., summer, 1979; pvt. practice clin. social work Bethesda, Md., 1979-84; co-founder, ptnr. North Bethesda Assocs., 1984-86; founder The Bethesda Group, 1993. Cons. Community Psychiat. Clinic, Wheaton, Md., 1980-83, Gaithersburg, Md., 1983-85; provisional vice chmn. Precinct 7-14, Montgomery County, Md., 1982-84. Fellow Am. Orthopsychiat. Assn.; mem. Nat. Assn. Social Workers, Greater Wash. Soc. Clin. Social Workers, Hadassah Club. Democrat. Jewish. Home: 8313 Beech Tree Rd Bethesda MD 20817-2934 Office: Wyngate Med Park 5654 Shields Dr Bethesda MD 20817-3574 Office Phone: 301-530-9563. E-mail: rngreenwood@comcast.net.

GREENWOOD, RICHARD HOPSON, lawyer, minister; b. Ann Arbor, Mich., Apr. 12, 1949; m. Deborah Anne Rundlett, Oct. 17, 1987; 1 child, Elizabeth Donaldson. BA, U. Va., Charlottesville, Va., 1970; JD, U. Tex., Austin, Tex., 1979; MDiv, Yale U., New Haven, Conn., 1987, MST, 1989. Bar: Tex. 1976, N.Y. 1997, Conn. 1997, Calif. 2003; Ordination Min. United Ch. of Christ, 1989, Min. of Word and Sacrament Presbyteries of Hudson River, 1992, Pitts. 2000, San Diego 2002. Atty., counselor at law Pvt. Practice, San Diego, 2003—; min. of word and sacrament Presbytery of San Diego, San Diego, 2002—. Mem., permanent jud. commn. Presbytery of San Diego, San Diego, 2003—. Recipient Norenberg Prize for Excellence in Preaching and Leadership of Pub. Worship, Yale U., 1986. Office: San Diego CA Personal E-mail: rgreenwood3@cox.net.

GREENWOOD, W. R., III, investment banker; b. Albany, N.Y., Apr. 21, 1941; s. Wilbur R. Jr. and Jean (McOrmond) G.; m. Pamela Sheridan Sutton, Nov. 8, 1974; children: Jennifer, Trevor. BA, Yale U., 1963; MBA, Cornell U., 1968. Investment banker Smith Barney, N.Y.C., 1968-75, Foster & Marshall, Seattle, 1976-82, Dain Bosworth, Seattle, 1982-86; pres., CEO Spider Staging Corp., Seattle, 1986-93, chmn. bd. dirs.; pres., CEO, Windswept Capital, Seattle, 1996—. Bd. dirs. Foster & Marshall, Seattle, Advanced Imput Devices, Flow Internat., Foster & Marshall, Advanced Input Devices, Output Tech., Skyland Sci. Svcs., Port Townsend Paper. Lt. USNR, 1963-65. Mem. Wash. Athletic Club, Overlake Golf Club, Rainier Club. Office: Windswept Capital LLC 1001 4th Ave Ste 3000 Seattle WA 98154-1101

GREENWOOD, WILLIAM WARREN, journalist; b. Richmond, Va., Mar. 28, 1942; s. William Rogers and Gloria Vivian (Brown) Warren; m. Marsha Ann Sheppard, Dec. 21, 1968; 1 child, Kelly. Student, Fla. State U., 1960-63; BA, Am. U., 1970. Announcer Sta. WZRO, Jacksonville Beach, Fla., 1956-60; newscaster Sta. WMBR, Jacksonville, Fla., 1960-64, Sta. WPDQ, Jacksonville, 1964-66, Sta. WWDC, Washington, 1966-67; dir. pub. affairs Nat. Edni. Radio, Washington, 1967-68; news corr. U.P.I., Washington, 1968-70; corr. MBS, Washington, 1970-74, v.p. news, 1974-76; news corr. Sta. WCBS-TV, N.Y.C., 1976-79, ABC News, N.Y.C., 1979, White House corr. Washington, 1980-81, Washington corr., 1981—. Guest lectr. NYU, 1975, 76; chmn. Congl. Radio-TV Galleries, Washington, 1975; guest lectr. Am. U., 1967; v.p. Nat. Press Bldg. Corp., 1974, Nat. Press Club, 1974; ABC coverage participant Peabody award, 2002, ABC coverage participant Alfred i. DuPont award, 2002. Recipient award of merit ARC, 1960, 61; Emmy award, 1978, N.Y.C. Firefighters award, 1979, Am. Bankers Assn. award ABC coverage participant, 1981, Edward R. Morrow award 1999, 03, 05; Emmy nomination, 1979. Mem. Radio and TV Corrs. Assn. (pres. 1975), White House Corrs. Assn., Fla. State U. Alumni Assn. (founding v.p. Washington chpt. 1974-75), ARC Lifeguard Alumni Assn. Episcopalian. Office: ABC Washington Bur 1717 Desales St NW Washington DC 20036-4407 Office Phone: 202-222-7261. Business E-Mail: bill.greenwood@abc.com.

GREENZANG, KATHERINE, lawyer, insurance company executive; b. 1964; BA, Johns Hopkins Univ.; JD, NYU. Bar: NY 1990. Assoc. Dewey Ballantine, NYC, 1990—94; corp. counsel Assurant Inc., NYC, 1994—95, asst. v.p., corp. counsel, 1995—96, v.p., corp. counsel, 1996—2001, sr. v.p., gen. counsel, sec., 2001—. Mem.: ABA, Assn. Corp. Counsel, NY State Bar Assn. Office: Assurant Inc 41st Fl 1 Chase Manhattan Plz New York NY 10005

GREER, ALAN GRAHAM, lawyer; b. El Dorado, Ark., May 31, 1939; s. Arthur W. and Marie (Ross) G.; m. Patricia A. Seitz, Aug. 14, 1981. BS, U.S. Naval Acad., 1961; JD, U. Fla., 1969. Ptnr. Richmnan, Greer Weil Brumbaugh, Miami, Fla., 1969—. Chmn. emeritus WLRN Pub. Radio and TV Sta.; bd. dirs. probono.net Past chmn. Dade County Coun. Arts and Scis.; past mem. Fla. State Task Force on Water Issues, Gov.'s Bus. Adv. Coun. on Edn.; co-chmn. site selection com. Dem. Nat. Com., 1992, also trustee; past bd. dirs. Camillus Ho. With USN, 1961-67. Fellow Internat. Soc. Barristers, Am. Coll. Trial Lawyers (chmn. professionalism com.); mem. ABA, Fla. Bar Assn. (cert., past chmn. internat. law com.). Home: 224 Ridgewood Rd Miami FL 33133-6614 Office: Richman Greer Weil Brumbaugh Miami Ctr 10th Fl 201 S Biscayne Blvd Miami FL 33131-4332 Office Phone: 305-373-4000. E-mail: agreer@richmangreer.com.

GREER, ALLEN CURTIS, II, lawyer, investment company executive; b. New Rochelle, N.Y., Dec. 6, 1951; s. Allen Wilkinson and Nancy (Carroll) G.; children: Katharine Burrage, Constance Carroll, Genevieve Forbes. AB, Harvard U., 1972, JD, 1975. Assoc. Cadwalader, Wickersham & Taft, N.Y.C., 1975-79, Palmer & Dodge, Boston, 1979-82; ptnr. Gaston & Snow, Boston and N.Y.C., 1982-91, Rogers & Wells, 1991-97, Cadwalader, Wickersham & Taft, N.Y.C., 1997-99, of counsel, 1999—; with Westbrook Ptnrs., 1999—2004, SCG Capital Ptnrs., Boston, 2004—. Bd. dirs. various pvt. cos. Mem.: Urban Land Inst., Nat. Assn. Real Estate Investment Trusts. Office: SCG Capital Ptnrs 222 Berkeley St 22d Fl Boston MA 02116 Address: RECAP Investments Ptnrs 390 Orchard Rd #09-03/04 Palais Rennissanu 238871 Singapore Office Phone: 617-646-6114. E-mail: curt.greer@cnet.com.

GREER, BERNARD LEWIS (BEN), JR., lawyer; b. Knoxville, Tenn., Sept. 11, 1940; s. Bernard Lewis and Margaret Strickland (Vinsinger) G.; m. Lynda Lea Kidd, June 11, 1966; children: Andrew Scott, William Vinsinger. BA magna cum laude, U. Tenn., 1962, postgrad., 1964-65; JD, Emory U., 1968. Bar: N.Y. 1969, Ga. 1975; conseil juridique France, 1971. Assoc. Willkie Farr & Gallagher, N.Y.C., 1968-71, 73-74, Willke, Farr & Gallagher, Paris, 1971-73, Shoob, McLain, Merritt & Lyle, Atlanta, 1974-77, O'Callaghan, Saunders & Stumm, 1977-85; ptnr. to sr. ptnr., internat. practice group Alston & Bird LLP, Atlanta, 1985—. Participant various seminars; lectr. on European bus. instns. and practice internat. legal Emory U. Law Sch., Atlanta, 1975—, Ga. State U. Law Sch., 1975—. Mem. Emory U. Law Rev., 1967-68; mem. edit. bd. The European Lawyer; contbr. to legal publs. Lifetime trustee Atlanta Bot. Garden, Inc.; mem. exec. com., bd. dirs. Ga. Coun. for Internat. Visitors, 1986-93, pres., 1989-90; bd. visitors U. Tenn. Coll. Liberal Arts, Knoxville, 1988-91. 1st lt. U.S. Army, 1962-64. Internat. bus. fellow S.E. region, 1988. Mem. ABA, Internat. Bar Assn. (coun. bus. law sect. 1990-94, sec. gen. 2000-02, chmn. WTO working group), State Bar Ga. (chmn. internat. law sect. 1982-83, chmn. com. on internationalization of practice of law 1989—), State Bar N.Y., Atlanta Bar Assn., Assn. Bar City N.Y., Soc. Internat. Bus. Fellows, Am. Arbitration Assn. (panel of arbitrators 1987—), Lex Mundi (chair-elect, treas., mem. exec. com.), Scabbard and Blade, Omicron Delta Kappa, Pi Sigma Alpha, Pi Delta Phi, Phi Eta Sigma. Office: Alston & Bird 1 Atlantic Ctr 1201 W Peachtree St NW Atlanta GA 30309-3400 Office Phone: 404-881-7458. Business E-Mail: bgreer@alston.com.

GREER, CARL CRAWFORD, petroleum company executive; b. Pitts., June 12, 1940; s. Joseph Moss and Gene (Crawford) G.; m. Jerrine Ehlers, June 16, 1962 (div.); children: Caryn, Michael, Janet; m. Patricia Taylor, Feb. 4, 1989. BS, Lehigh U., 1962; PhD, Columbia U., 1966; PsyD, Ill. Sch. Profl. Psychology, Chgo., 1993. Lic. clin. psychologist and Jungian analyst. Assoc. in bus. Columbia U., 1964-66, asst. prof. banking and finance, 1966-67; retail mktg. mgr. Martin Oil Service Inc., Alsip, Ill., 1967-68, exec. v.p., 1968, pres., dir., 1968-76, chmn. bd., pres., 1976-85; pres., dir. Gen. Ptnrs. Martin Oil Mktg. Ltd., 1982—, Martin Exploration Mgmt. Co., 1985—. Bd. dirs. Fin. Assocs., Inc. Mem. Beta Theta Pi, Tau Beta Pi, Beta Gamma Sigma, Omicron Delta Kappa. Presbyterian.

GREER, DAVID S., dean, educator, physician; b. Bklyn., Oct. 12, 1925; s. Jacob and Mary (Zaslawsky) Greer; m. Marion Clarich, June 25, 1950; children: Jeffrey, Linda. BS, U. Notre Dame, 1948; MD, U. Chgo., 1953; MA (hon.), Brown U., 1975; LHD (hon.), Southeastern Mass. U., 1981. Diplomate Am. Bd. Internal Medicine. Intern Yale-New Haven Med. Center, 1953—54; resident in medicine U. Chgo. Clinics, 1954—57; instr. endocrinology and medicine U. Chgo., 1957; practice medicine specializing in internal medicine Fall River, Mass., 1957—74; chief staff dept. medicine Fall River Gen. Hosp., 1959—62; med. dir. Earle E. Hussey Hosp., Fall River, 1962—75; chief staff dept. medicine Truesdale Clinic and Truesdale Hosp., Fall River, 1971—74, pres. med. staff, 1968—70; sr. clin. instr. medicine Tufts U. Coll. Medicine, 1969—71, asst. clin. prof., 1971—78; clin. asso. prof. community health Brown U., 1973—75, dir. family practice residency program, 1975—78, prof. community health, 1975—93, prof. emeritus, 1993—, assoc. dean medicine, 1974—81, dean medicine, 1981—92, dean emeritus, 1992—, chmn. sect. community health, 1978—81. Mem. Gov.'s Task Force on Quality of Care, Medicaid Program, Commonwealth of Mass., 1969—70; del. White House Conf. Aging, 1971, 81; pres. Ind. Living Authority, State of R.I., 1975—81; mem. exec. com. Cancer Control Bd. R.I., 1975—80; mem. R.I. Gov.'s Task Force for Inst. of Mental Health, 1976—81; bd. dirs. Health Planning Coun., Inc., Providence, 1976—78; chmn. com. on aging Jewish Fedn. R.I., 1978—80; chmn. Gov.'s Commn. on Provision of Comprehensive Mental Health Svcs. in R.I., 1980—81; trustee Southeastern Mass. U., 1970—81, chmn., 1973—74, Providence Mayor's Sr. Citizens Task Force, 1975; bd. dirs. Assn. Home Health Agys. R.I., 1975—80; founding dir. Internat. Physicians for Prevention of Nuc. War, Inc., 1980—85; vis. prof. dept. medicine Georgetown U., 1992—93; scholar-in-residence Assn. Am. Med. Colls., 1992—93. Contbr. articles to profl. jours. Named Prof. of the Yr., Brown U., 1992; recipient Outstanding Svc. award, Mass. Easter Seal Soc., 1970, Outstanding Citizens award, Jewish War Vets. Aux., 1973, Disting. Svc. award, U. Chgo. Med. Alumni Assn., Cutting Found. medal, Andover Newton Theol. Sem., 1976; fellow in health, Kellogg Found. Internat., 1986—89, vis. fellow, Green Coll. Oxford U., 1985. Master: ACP; mem.: R.I. Med. Soc., Internat. Soc. Rehab. Medicine, Am. Congree Rehab. Medicine, Gerontol. Soc., Inst. Medicine. Jewish. Office: Brown U Box G Providence RI 02912 Office Phone: 401-729-3644. Business E-Mail: David_Greer@brown.edu.

GREER, FRANK ROLAND, pediatrician, neonatologist; b. Gainesville, Fla., Mar. 3, 1946; s. Charles Francis and Elizabeth French Greer; m. Catherine West West, June 15, 1946; children: Natalie Greer Nicholson, Jonathan West. BS, Washington & Lee U., 1968; MD, U. Pa., 1972. Pediatircs Am. Bd. of Pediat., Chapel Hill, NC, 1977, Neonatal-Perinatal Medicine Am. Bd. of Pediat., NC, 1981. Prof. of pediat. U. of Wis., Madison, Wis., 1980—. Maj. U.S. Army, 1975—78, West Berlin Germany. Office: Dept Pediats Univ Wisconsin 600 Highland Ave Madison WI 53792 Office Phone: 608-262-6561. Office Fax: 608-267-6377. E-mail: frgreer@wisc.edu.

GREER, GEORGE W., judge; b. Bklyn., 1942; BS, Fla. State U., 1964; JD, U. Fla., 1966. Bar: 1966. Pvt. practice zoning and land use real estate law, 1969—92; commr. Pinellas County, Fla., 1985—93; chief judge sixth jud. cir. Fla., 1993—. Office: 315 Court St Rm 484 Clearwater FL 33756 Office Phone: 727-464-3933.*

GREER, GERMAINE, author; b. Melbourne, Australia, Jan. 29, 1939; d. Eric Reginald and Margaret May Mary (Lafrank) G. BA with honors in English, French Lit., U. Melbourne, 1959; MA with honors in English, U. Sydney, Australia, 1961; PhD (Commonwealth scholar), Newnham Coll. of Cambridge U., Eng., 1967; Doctorate (hon.), U. Griffith, 1996, U. York, Toronto, 1999, Manchester Inst. Tech., 2000. Sr. tutor U. Sydney, 1963-64; lectr. English U. Warwick, Eng., 1967-72; prof. modern letters U. Tulsa, 1980-83; dir. Tulsa Ctr. for Study of Woman's Lit.; prof. English and comparative studies U. Warwick, 1998—. Vis. prof. grad. faculty modern letters U. Tulsa, fall 1979; founder-dir. Tulsa Centre for the Study of Women's Lit.; founder, editor Tulsa Studies in Women's Lit., 1981; dir. Stump Cross Books, 1988—; spl. lectr. and unofcl. fellow Newnham Coll., Cambridge, 1989-98; lectr. in N.Am. Am. Program Bur., 1973-78. Author: The Female Eunuch, 1969, The Obstacle Race: The Fortunes of Women Painters and their Work, 1979, Sex and Destiny: The Politics of Human Fertility, 1984, Shakespeare, 1986, The Madwoman's Underclothes, 1986, Daddy, We Hardly Knew You, 1989 (J.R. Ackerly Prize, Premio Internazionale Mondello), The Change: Women, Aging and the Menopause, 1991, Slip-Shod Sibyls: Recognition, Rejection and the Woman Poet, 1995, The Surviving Works of Anne Wharton, 1997; editor: (with Susan Hastings, Jeslyn Medoff, Melinda Sansone) Kissing the Rod: An Anthology of Seventeenth Century Women's Verse, 1988, The Uncollected Verse of Aphra Behn, 1989, The Change: Women, Aging and the Menopause, 1991, Slip-Shod Sibyls: Recognition, Rejection and the Woman Poet, 1995, The Whole Woman, 1999, The Whole Woman, 1999, John Wilmot, Earl of Rochester, 1999 The Boy, 2003; editor 101 Poems by 101 Women, 2001, Poems for Gardeners, 2003; selected journalism published as The Madwoman's Underclothes, 1986, columnist Sunday Times, London, 1971-73, broadcaster/journalist/reviewer various publs. 1972-79. Jr. Govt. scholar, 1952, Diocesan scholar, 1956, Sr. Govt. scholar, 1956, Commonwealth scholar, 1964, Teacher's Coll. Studentship, 1956, Hon. Doctorate Univ. of Griffith, 1996.

GREER, GORDON BRUCE, retired lawyer, writer; b. Butler, Pa, Feb. 17, 1932; s. Samuel Walker and Winifred (Fletcher) G.; m. Nancy Linda Hannaford, June 14, 1959; children: Gordon Bruce, Alison Clark. BA, Harvard U., 1953, JD cum laude, 1959. Bar: Wis. 1959, Mass. 1961. Assoc. Foley, Sammond & Lardner, Milw., 1959-61; assoc. Bingham Dana LLP, Boston, 1961-67, ptnr., 1967-97, of counsel, 1997—2002; ret., 2002. Lectr. Boston U. Sch. Law, 1998-2002. Author: World in Conflict, 2003, The First Decade, 2004, What Price Security?, 2005; editor: Harvard Law Rev. Vols. 71, 72. Maj. USAFR (ret.) Mem.: Harvard Club (Boston), Brae Burn Country Club. Republican. Home: 45 Fieldmont Rd Belmont MA 02478-2606

GREER, K. GORDON, banker; b. Tulsa, Oct. 28, 1936; s. H.K. and Afton (Goodman) G.; m. Nancy Lang, Nov. 22, 1958; children— Keith G., Scott A. BS in Banking and Fin., Okla. State U., 1958. Pres. Liberty Nat. Bank, Oklahoma City, 1958-84; CEO The First Nat. Bank and Trust Co., Tulsa, 1984—89; pres. Bank IV, Wichita, Kans., 1989—96; vice chmn. BancFirst Corp., Tulsa, 1996—. With Air Force N.G., 1958-64 Named to Hall of Fame, Bus. Adminstrn. Sch. Okla. State U., 1984 Mem. Am. Bankers Assn., Okla. Bankers Assn. (pres. 1983-84), So. Hills Country. Republican. Methodist. Avocation: golf.

GREER, KENNETH E., dermatologist; b. Marion, Va., 1941; MD, U. Va., 1967. Intern Strong Meml. Hosp., Rochester, N.Y., 1967-68, resident, 1968-69, U. Va., Charlottesville, 1971-74, mem. med. staff; prof. dermatology, dept. chmn. U. Va. Sch. Medicine, Charlottesville. Mem. AMA, Am. Dermatology Assn., NWDS, Va. Dermatology Soc., Am. Bd. of Dermatology (exec. dir. 1994-2002).

GREER, MELVIN, medical educator; b. N.Y.C., Oct. 14, 1929; s. Aaron and Ceil (Cohen) Jefkel; m. Arline Ebert, Dec. 16, 1951; children: Jonathan, Richard, Alison, David. BA magna cum laude, NYU, 1950, MD, 1954. Intern, resident Bellevue Hosp., N.Y.C., 1954-56; fellow N.Y. Neurol. Inst., Columbia, 1958-61; prof., chmn. dept. neurology U. Fla. Coll. Medicine, Gainesville, 1963-2000. Cons. NIH, 1971—, Fla. Div. Corrections, 1971—; lectr., cons. Navy Dept.; prof. dept. neurol. dept. psychiatry, dept. pediatrics, U. Fla. Coll. Medicine; endowed professorship neurology U. Fla. Coll. Medicine, Gainesville, 1991—. Author: Mass Spectrometry of Biologically Important Aromatic Acids, 1969, Differential Diagnosis of Neurological Diseases, 1977; also articles.; Editorial bd.: Neurology, Geriatics, 1968— . Served to lt. comdr. USNR, 1956-58. Recipient Medallion award Columbia U., 1968, Hippocratic award U. Fla., 1970, Outstanding Clin. Tchr. award, 1975, 79; NIH grantee, 1962-71 Fellow Am. Acad. Neurology (councillor, sec.-treas. 1977-81, pres.-elect 1983-85, pres. 1985-87), Am. Acad. Pediatrics; mem. Am. Neurol. Assn. (councillor), Soc. Pediatric Research, Am. Pediatric Soc., Phi Beta Kappa, Alpha Omega Alpha. Home: 2058 NW 14th Ave Gainesville FL 32605-5245

GREER, MONTE ARNOLD, endocrinologist, educator; b. Portland, Oreg., Oct. 26, 1922; s. William Wallace and Rose (Rasmussen) G.; m. Peggy Johnson, Dec. 31, 1943; children: Susan Elizabeth, Richard Arnold. Student, Oreg. State U., 1940-43; AB, Stanford U., 1944, MD, 1947. Intern San Francisco Gen. Hosp., 1946—47; rsch. fellow endocrinology New England Med. Ctr., Boston, 1947—49; resident internal medicine Mass. Meml. Hosp., Boston, 1949—50; rsch. assoc. in endocrinology New England Med. Ctr. Hosp., 1950—51; sr. investigator, sr. asst. surgeon USPHS, Nat. Cancer Inst., NIH, Bethesda, Md., 1951—55; chief radioisotope unit D.C. Gen. Hosp., Washington, 1951—55; clin. asst. prof. medicine UCLA, 1955—56; chief radioisotope svc. VA Hosp., Long Beach, Calif., 1955—56; head div. endocrinology Oreg. Health & Sci. U. (formerly U. Oreg. Med. Sch.), Portland, 1956—80, assoc. prof., 1956—62, prof. medicine, 1962—, prof. physiology, 1992—, head divsn. endocrinology, metabolism and clin. nutrition, 1980—84, head sect. endocrinology, 1984—90. Author: (with H. Studer) The Regulation of Thyroid Function in Iodine Deficiency, 1968, (with P. Langer) Antithyroid Drugs and Naturally Occurring Goitrogens, 1977; editor: The Thyroid Gland, 1990, (with D.H. Solomon) The Thyroid, 1974; mem. editorial bd. Endocrinology, 1960-72, Neuroendocrinology, 1965-76, Endocrine Regulations, 1971—; contbr. articles to profl. jours. Mem. Thyroid Task Force NIH Com. for Evaluation of Endocrinology and Metabolic Diseases, 1977-80, Endocrinology Study Sect., NIH, 1977-80. Pharmacol. and Endocrinology fellowship study sect. NIH, 1968-72; recipient Oppenheimer award Endocrine Soc., 1958, Rsch. Career award NIH, 1962-81, Discovery award Med. Rsch. Found. Oreg., 1985, DeMolay Legion of Honor award, 1988. Mem. AAAS, Am. Fedn. for Clin. Rsch. (chmn. Western sect. 1958-59), Western Soc. for Clin. Rsch. (v.p. 1963-64, pres. 1967-68), Endocrine Soc. (mem. council 1965-68, v.p. 1976-77), Am. Thyroid Assn. (v.p., dir. 1974-77, pres. 1980, Disting. Service award 1985), Am. Soc. Clin. Investigation, Soc. Exptl. Biology and Medicine, Western Assn. Physicians (sec.-treas. 1974-77), Assn. Am. Physicians, Internat. Brain Rsch. Orgn., Internat. Soc. Neuroendocrinology, European Thyroid Assn., Japan Endocrine Soc. (hon.), Czechoslovak Endocrine Soc. (hon.), Rotary, Sigma Chi. Office: Oreg Health and Sci Univ Portland OR 97201

GREER, ROBERT BRUCE, III, orthopedist, educator; b. Butler, Pa., 1934; BA, Haverford Coll., 1956; MD, Harvard U., 1960. Diplomate Am. Bd. Orthopaedic Surgery (bd. dirs. 1985-94, pres. 1990-91). Intern Mich. Med. Ctr., 1960-61, resident in surgery, 1961-62; resident in orthopaedic surgery Pitts. Med. Ctr., 1964-67, asst. prof. orthopedic surgery, 1967-71; orthopaedist MS Hershey Med. Ctr., Pa.; prof., chief orthopaedic surgery Pa. State U., 1971-91; ret. Med. dir. Howmedica, Inc., 1997-99. Capt. USAR, 1962-64. Mem. ACS, Am. Acad. Orthopaedic Surgeons, Am. Orthopaedic Assn., Ea. Orthopaedic Assn., Alpha Omega Alpha.

GREER, SUZANNE MICHELLE, music educator; b. Duluth, Minn., May 14, 1968; d. Robert Leonard Moore and Beatrice Mae Sandum; m. David Lee Greer, May 20, 2000. MusB in Piano Performance, St. Olaf Coll., Northfield, Minn., 1990; MusM in Piano Performance, U. Minn., 1994. Cert. music tchr. Music Teachers Nat. Assn., 2001, motorcycle safety instr. Motorcycle Safety Found., 1999. Music dir. Trinity Episc. Ch., Anoka, Minn., 1997—98; piano instr. SG Studio, Minnetonka, Minn., 2002—; depot outreach artist-in-residence Depot Cmty. Outreach Program, Duluth, Minn., 1990—91; motorcycle safety instr. Mpls., 1999—; rider's edge new rider course instr. St. Paul Harley Davidson, 2001—; music instr. North Hennepin C.C., Brooklyn Park, Minn., 1994—2002, Anoka-Ramsey C.C., Coon Rapids, Minn., 2001—02; piano instr. Son-Sheim Music Sch., Anoka, Minn., 1994—2002; piano accompanist Robbinsdale All-District Choir, Robbinsdale, Minn., 2000—02. Liaison for bd. of dirs. Magnum Chorum (St. Olaf Alumni Choir), St. Paul, 1998—2001; honors concert vol. coord. Minn. Music Tchrs. Assn., Mpls., 2002—. Scholar Music scholar, St. Olaf Coll., 1986, U. of Minn., 1993, Shar Products scholar, Suzuki Assn. of the Ams., 2002. Mem.: Suzuki Assn. for the Ams. (Shar Products Co. Scholarship for Tchr. Tng. 2004, Tchr. Tng. Scholarship 2004), Mpls. Music Tchrs. Forum (recital com. chair 2004—),

Suzuki Piano Tchrs. Guild (pres.-elect 2004—), Music Tchrs. Nat. Assn., West Suburban Music Tchrs. Assn., Minn. Music Tchrs. Assn. (honors concert vol. coord. 2002). Democrat. Presbyterian. Avocations: motorcycling, travel. E-mail: sgstudio@mn.rr.com.

GREER, WILLIS ROSWELL, JR., finance educator; b. Memphis, Nov. 16, 1938; s. Willis Roswell and Myra Bell (Bridges) G.; m. Melinda S. Scott, June 28, 1963; children: Howard Willis, Catherine Irene Grubbs, Charles Walker. BS, Cornell U., 1961, MBA with distinction, 1966; PhD in Acctg., U. Mich., 1971. Cert. Mgmt. Acct., Cert. Bus. Appraiser. Lectr. acctg. and stats. U. West Indies, Trinidad, 1966-67; teaching asst., Paton fellow U. Mich., 1967-71; asst. prof. acctg. U. Oreg., 1971-75, assoc. prof., 1975-76; vis. prof. acctg. Dartmouth Coll., Amos Tuck Sch., 1976-77, assoc. prof., 1976-82; vis. scholar Manchester (Eng.) Bus. Sch., 1981; prof. acctg. Naval Postgrad. Sch., 1982-88, acad. assoc. fin. mgmt., 1983-84, chmn. dept. adminstrv. scis., 1984-87; prof. acctg. U. Iowa, Iowa City, 1988-96, assoc. dean grad. programs, 1989-92, head dept. acctg., 1992-95; lectr. acctg. and fin. analysis Tohoku U., Japan, 1993-94; dean Coll. Bus. Adminstrn. U. No. Iowa, Cedar Falls, 1996—2001. Cons. U.S. Small Bus. Adminstrn. Minority Bus. Devel. Program, several large firms in various mfg. and svc. industries; presenter numerous seminars and workshops. Co-author: (with Paul Wasserman) Consultants and Consulting Organizations, 1966, (with J. Peter Williamson) Interim Inventory Estimation Error, 1979, (with Shu Liao) Cost Analysis for Dual Source Weapon Procurement, 1983, Cost Analysis for Competitive Major Weapon Systems Procurement: Further Refinement and Extension, 1984; author: A Method for Estimating and Controlling the Cost of Extending Technology, 1988; editor: (with Dan Nussbaum) Cost Analysis and Estimating: Tools and Techniques, 1990; contbr. articles to profl. jours. Treas. Oaknoll Retirement Cmty., 1993—. Mem. Inst. Mgmt. Accts. (dir. Cedar Rapids chpt. 1990—), Am. Acctg. Assn., Decision Scis. Inst., Inst. Bus. Appraisers, Inc. Republican. Achievements include research on conditions under which dual source procurement of major weapon systems is beneficial to goverment; building an accurate model for forecasting research and development costs for specified technology advancement. Home: PO Box 224 Rollins MT 59931-0224

GREEVER, JOHN, retired mathematics professor; b. Pulaski, Va., Jan. 30, 1934; s. John Jay Greever and Hulah Lily (Loyd) Bentley; m. Margaret LeSueur Quarles, Aug. 29, 1953; children: Catherine Patricia, Richard George, Cynthia Diane. BS in Math., U. Richmond, 1953; MA in Math., U. Va., 1956, PhD in Math., 1958. Asst. prof. math. Fla. State U., Tallahassee, 1958-61; mem. faculty Harvey Mudd Coll., Claremont, Calif., 1961-95, prof. math., 1970-95, chmn. math. dept., 1972-75, founding dir. math. clinic, 1973-75. Faculty Claremont Grad. Sch., 1962-95; vis. prof. Kyoto (Japan) U. Rsch. Inst. for Math. Sci., 1967-68, U. B.C. Inst. Animal Resource Ecology, Vancouver, 1984-85; rsch. assoc. dept. biology U. Calif., Riverside, 1975-78; vis. rsch. mathematician dept. entomology U. Calif., 1978. Author Theory and Examples of Point Set Topology, 1967; contbr. articles to profl. jours. Mem.: Soc. of the Cin., Math. Assn. Am. (sec.-treas. So. Calif. sect. 1973—76, pres. 1981—82), Coun. on Undergrad. Rsch. (councilor 1989—95, vice-chmn. math. and computer scis. sect. 1991—92, chmn. 1992—94), Am. Math. Soc., Wash. State U. (master gardener 2005), San Juan County Park Bd., Pole Pass Power Squadron (comdr. 2001), Orcas Island Garden Club (pres. 2005), Orcas Island Yacht Club (commodore 2002), Sigma Xi, Phi Kappa Sigma, Kappa Mu Epsilon, Pi Mu Epsilon. Avocations: boating, gardening. Home: 260 Grey Havens Loop PO Box 413 Orcas WA 98280-0413 E-mail: greever@hmc.edu.

GREEVER, MARGARET QUARLES, retired mathematics educator; b. Wilkensburg, Pa., Feb. 7, 1931; d. Lawrence Reginald and Ella Mae (LeSueur) Quarles; m. John Greever, Aug. 29, 1953; children: Catherine Patricia, Richard George, Cynthia Diane. Cert. costume design, Richmond Profl. Inst., 1952; student, U. Va., 1953—56; BA in Math., Calif. State U., L.A., 1963; MA in Math., Claremont Grad. Sch., 1968. Cert. tchr. specializing in Jr. Coll. math., Calif. Tchr. math. Chaffey Unified H.S. Dist., Alta Loma, Calif., 1963—64, L.A. Unified Sch. Dist., 1964—65, Chino Unified Sch. Dist., Calif., 1965—81; from asst. prof. to prof. Chaffey Coll., Rancho Cucamonga, 1981—96, chmn. phys. sci. divsn. Alta Loma, 1985—92, dean, phys., life, health sci., 1992—96. Mem. AAUW (pres. local chpt. 1998-2000), Orcas Island Garden Club (treas. 1997-2000, pres.-elect 2000, pres. 2001), Orcas Island Yacht Club, Pi Lambda Theta. Avocations: quilting, cooking, sewing, gardening. E-mail: greever@rockisland.com.

GREGAN, EDMUND ROBERT, landscape architect; b. New Haven, Feb. 4, 1936; s. Edmund Arthur and Elizabeth (Kochiss) G.; m. Janet Lamson Shaw, Aug. 22, 1959; children: Edmund Robert, Darianne Lee, Christyn Elizabeth. BS in Landscape Architecture, R.I. Sch. Design, 1960. Lic. landscape architect, Conn. Landscape architect and site planner Morton S. Fine & Assocs., Hartford, Conn., 1960-62; landscape architect New Haven Redevel. Agy., 1962—66, chief landscape architect, 1966-78; landscape architect, cons., lectr. E. Robert Gregan Landscape Architect, Northford, Conn., 1965—; chief landscape architect New Haven City Plan Dept., 1978-91. Instr. landscape architecture Guilford/Madison (Conn.) Adult Edn. Programs, 1979-88; tchr., critic Yale, R.I. Sch. Design, U. Conn. Conway Sch. Landscape Design, So. Conn. State U.; tchr. environ. design Yale Sch. of Forestry and Environtl. Studies Elem. Schs. New Haven, 1992; tchr. Federated Garden Clubs Conn. Sch. Landscape Design, 1979—; lectr. various orgns. and clubs. Contbr. numerous profl. jours. Bd. dirs. North Branford Land Conservation Trust, 1968-72, v.p., 1973—; mem. North Branford Conservation Commn., 1969-73, chmn., 1971-72, assoc. mem., 1973-92; cons. North Branford Ctr. Improvement Com., 1991-95; mem. North Branford-Northford Town Design Dists. Adv. Com., 1995—; bd. dirs. New Haven Urban Resources Initiative, 1991-96; mem. steering com. Long Wharf Nature Preserve, 1995-2000; landscape arch., vice chair spl. events 1995 Spl. Olympics World Games. Recipient Cert. of Achievement award Federated Garden Clubs. Conn., 1981, Bronze medal Federated Garden Clubs Conn., 1991, Cert. of Merit for Excellence in Study of Landscape Architecture, RISD, 1960, Outstanding Urban Forestry Profl. award Urban Forest Coun., 2001, numerous profl. design awards. Fellow Am. Soc. Landscape Architects; mem. Conn. Soc. Landscape Architects (bd. dir. 1981-86, hist. and landscape preservation com. 1987—, George A. Yarwood Cert. Svc. award 1987), Totoket Hist. Soc. (mem. design cons. 1972—), Garden Club New Haven (hon. mem.), Federated Garden Clubs of Conn., Inc. (hon. mem. landscape design critics coun. 1993). Episcopalian. Avocations: design, gardening, photography, travel. Home and Office: 7 Stair Brook Way Northford CT 06472-1495 Office Phone: 203-484-2724.

GREGANTI, MAC ANDREW, physician, medical educator; b. Cleveland, Miss., Apr. 13, 1947; s. Mack Americo and Grace Margaret (Barbati) G.; m. Susan Taylor, Aug. 8, 1971; children: Paul Andrew, Mack Taylor, Mary Catherine. BS summa cum laude, Millsaps Coll., 1969; MD summa cum laude, U. Miss., 1972. Diplomate Am. Bd. Internal Medicine, Am. Bd. Geriat. medicine. Intern U. Rochester, N.Y., 1972-73, resident, 1973-75; instr. dept. medicine U. Miss. Sch. Medicine, Jackson, 1975-76, asst. prof., 1976-77, U. N.C. Sch. Medicine, Chapel Hill, 1977-83, assoc. prof., 1983-90, prof., 1990—, chief div. gen. medicine, 1986-91, assoc. chair for clin. affairs, 1991-99, acting chmn., 1999-2000, vice-chmn., 2000—. Dir. med./pediatric residency U. N.C. Dept. Medicine, Chapel Hill, 1980-86, dir. medicine residency, 1981-86. Contbr. articles on med. edn. and patient care to profl. jours. Fellow ACP; mem. Am. Geriatrics Soc., Alpha Omega Alpha. Roman Catholic. Avocations: computers, tennis, golf, photography. Office: Univ NC Chapel Hill Dept of Medicine 3029 Old Clinic Bldg Cb 7005 Chapel Hill NC 27599-7005 Office Phone: 919-966-3063.

GREGERSEN, R(OALD) GEORGE, newspaper publishing executive; b. Copenhagen, Mar. 14, 1935; came to U.S., 1948; s. Richard Vilhelm and Eva (Giertsen) G.; m. Gayle Froerer Richards, May 1, 1964 (div. 1978); m. Penney Losse, Dec. 21, 1982; children: Mary Anne Georgia, John Christian. Student, U. Utah, 1953-55. Pres., CEO Mortgage Investment Corp., Salt Lake City, 1955-68; pres., CEO Gregersen & Co., Salt Lake City, 1968-74; pub., CEO The Enterprise (weekly), Salt Lake City, 1974—. Editl. writer The Enterprise, 1974—. Bd. dirs. Utal Mil. & Vets. Affairs com., Salt Lake City, 1982-92. Named Utah Mil. Citizen of Yr., 1986; recipient Assn. U.S. Army Exceptional Svc. award, 1990. Mem. Alta Club (bd. dirs. 1993-96), Rotary. Republican. Episcopalian. Avocation: flyfishing. Home: 1427 Circle Way Salt Lake City UT 84103-4433 Office: Enterprise Newspaper Group Inc 136 S Main St Ste 721 Salt Lake City UT 84101-1676 Office Phone: 801-533-0556.

GREGERSON, DANIEL P., retired computer company executive; s. Donald Carl and Sue Gregerson; m. Virginia M. Moore, Apr. 3, 1990; children: Lily Anne, John Luke. BA with honors, U. Calif., Santa Cruz, 1981. Founder, COO Intelligent Technologies, Inc., Palo Alto, Calif., 1982—84; founder, CEO PeerLogic, Inc., San Francisco, 1986—2000. Chmn. Mindfabric, Inc., Saratoga, Calif., 2001—04. Author: Playground of the Fleas. Vol. cons. Hertz Found., Livermore, Calif., 2004—05. Mem.: Commonwealth Club Calif. (assoc.). Achievements include patents in field.

GREGERSON, LINDA KAREN, poet, language educator, critic; b. Elgin, Ill., Aug. 5, 1950; d. Olaf Thorbjorn and Karen Mildred Gregerson; m. Steven Mullaney, 1980; children: Emma Mullaney, Megan Mullaney. BA, Oberlin Coll., 1971; MA, Northwestern U., 1972; MFA, U. Iowa, 1977; PhD, Stanford U., 1987. Actress Kraken Theater Co., 1972—75; asst. poetry editor The Atlantic Monthly Press, 1982—86; staff editor Atlantic Monthly, Boston, 1982—87; asst. prof. Dept. English U. Mich., 1987—91, William Wilhartz asst. prof. English, 1991—94, assoc. prof. Dept. English, 1994—2001, prof. Dept. English, 2001—03, Frederick G. L. Huetwell prof., prof. English, 2003—, dir. MFA program in creative writing, 1997—2000. Mem. usage panel Am. Heritage Dictionary, 1987—; vis. asst. prof. creative writing program Dept. English Boston U., 1985—86; instr. lit. MIT, 1985—87; asst. editor Mich. Quarterly Rev., 1987—; editl. cons. Cambridge Univ. Press, 1989—, Harvard Univ. Press, 1989—, Oxford Univ. Press, 1989—, Wesleyan Univ. Press, 1989—, Ind. Univ. Press, 1989—, Bedford Books, 1989—, Univ. Mich. Press, 1989—, Wayne State Univ. Press, 1989—. Author: Fire in the Conservatory, 1982, The Reformation of the Subject: Spenser, Milton, and the English Protestant Epic, 1995, The Woman Who Died in Her Sleep, 1996, Negative Capability: Contemporary American Poetry, 2001, Waterborne, 2002, (poems) Illinois Again, 1975, Alone, 1977, Man Sitting in the Sun, 1979, To Albert Speer, 1980, (poetry) Ex Machina, 1982, Halfe a Yard of Rede Sea, 1983, Mother Ruin, 1984, Blazon, 1984, An Arbor, 1990, For the Taking, 1993, Fish Dying on the Third Floor at Barney's, 1996, Eyes Like Leeks, 2000, Pass Over, 2001, A History Play, 2002, Maculate, 2002. Recipient Levinson Prize award Poetry, 1991, Consuelo Ford award, Poetry Soc. Am., 1992, Isabel MacCaffrey award, Spenser Soc. Am., 1992, Pushcart prize, 1994, 2004, Acad. award in Lit., Am. Acad. Arts and Letters, 2002; fellow, Nat. Endowment Arts, 1985, 1992, Mellon, Nat. Humanities Ctr., 1991—92, Guggenheim, 2000; grantee Arts Found., Mich., 1994; Ingram Merrill grant, 1982—84. Mem.: MLA, Inst. Advanced Study (vis. mem. 1993—94), Milton Soc., Internat. Spenser Soc. (Isabel MacCaffrey award 1992), Renaissance Soc.Am., Shakespeare Assn. Am. Office: U Mich Dept English Lang and Lit 3147 Angell Hall Ann Arbor MI 48109-1045

GREGG, BILLY RAY, seed industry executive, consultant; b. Taylorsville, Miss., Aug. 31, 1930; s. Hinds and Lillie Mae (Moore) G.; m. Mary Frances Barber, Aug. 12, 1950 (div. Jan. 1987); children: Kathryn, Patricia, Lisa; m. Orawan Chonlavorn, Dec. 20, 1988; 1 child, Nathan Paul. AA, Perkinston (Miss.) Jr. Coll., 1950; BS, Miss. State U., 1954, MS, 1956, PhD, 1968; postgrad., Wash. State U., 1957-63. Asst. prof. Wash. State U., Pullman, 1956-63; mgr. Ala. Crop Improvement Assn., Auburn, Ala., 1964-66; seed technologist Miss. State U., 1966-68; chief party/processing specialist seed improvement project U.S. AID, New Delhi, India, 1968-72, chief party and seed specialist seed project Brasilia, Brazil, 1972-74, chief, seed industry devel. specialist Bangkok, 1977-87, seed industry devel. specialist Cairo, 1987-93; chief party and seed industry specialist IDB and GOB Agiplan Project, Brasilia, 1974-76; seed industry specialist Internat. Plant Breeders, Maringa, Parana, Brazil, 1976, Interam. Agrl. Sci. Inst., Brasilia, 1976-77; seed industry devel. specialist internat. programs Miss. State U., 1993—. Cons./advisor on seed tech. matters, mgmt., quality control and industry devel. nat. govts., pvt. cos., World Bank, Interam. Devel. Bank, FAO, GTZ, U.S. AID in more than 80 countries, 1960-95. Contbr. over 500 articles to profl. jours.; author 2 books. With U.S. Army, 1950-52; ETO. Indian Soc. Seed Technologists fellow, 1987. Mem. Kiwanis Internat. (dir., Kiwanian of the Yr. 1968), Agrl. Sci. Soc. Thailand (hon.), Wash. State Crop Improvement Assn. (hon. life), Phi Kappa Phi, Sigma Xi, Phi Theta Kappa. Buddhist. Avocations: vegetable and flower gardening, writing, travel. Home: PO Box 1756 Starkville MS 39760-1756 Office Phone: 662-323-0035. Personal E-mail: billgregg1@bellsouth.net. E-mail: topgregg@bully.net.

GREGG, CHARLES THORNTON, research and development company executive, researcher, molecular biologist; b. Billings, Mont., July 27, 1927; s. Charles Thornton and Gertrude (Hurst) G.; m. Elizabeth Whitaker, Dec. 20, 1947; children: Paul, Diane, Brian, Elaine. BS in Physics, Oreg. State U., 1952, MS in Organic Chemistry, 1955, PhD in Biochemistry, 1959. Postdoctoral fellow Nat. Cancer Inst., Johns Hopkins Sch. Med., Balt., 1959-63; mem. staff Los Alamos (N.Mex.) Nat. Lab., 1963-85; sr. scientist Mesa Diagnostics, Los Alamos, 1985-86; v.p. rsch. Los Alamos Diagnostics, 1986-90; pres. Innovative Surg. Tech. Inc., 1991—. Pres. Bethco, Inc., 1972—; vis. prof. The Free U., Berlin, 1973-74; cons. internat. tech. div. Los Alamos Nat. Lab., 1985-90. Author: Plague, 1978, The Virus of Love, 1983, Tarawa, 1985; patentee bacterial identification apparatus, safe surg. knife. Bd. dirs. Friends of Mesa Pub. Libr., Los Alamos, 1981-83, County Libr. Los Alamos, 1983-85, Los Alamos Arts Coun., 1985-87, bd. dir., Lukens Med. Corp., 1996-97. Served in U.S. Navy, 1944-46. Fellow AAAS; mem. Am. Soc. Biochemistry and Molecular Biology, Am. Soc. Microbiology, Sigma Xi, Sigma Pi Sigma, Phi Lambda Upsilon. Democrat. Unitarian Universalist. Avocation: hiking. Office: 190 Central Park Sq Los Alamos NM 87544-4001 Office Phone: 505-662-3240. Personal E-mail: cgregg3@yahoo.com. Business E-Mail: president@1stmedmart.com.

GREGG, DAVID, III, investment banker; b. N.Y.C., Jan. 29, 1933; s. David Gregg and Virginia (Wyckoff) Macgregor; m. May Foster Bowers, Dec. 21, 1963 (div. Apr. 1984); children: Justine Simms Barkstrom, David; m. Sarah Choate Massengale, Dec. 8, 1984. Assoc. Eastman Dillon Union Securities & Co., N.Y.C., 1959-67, ptnr., 1967-69; v.p. Blyth & Co., Inc., N.Y.C., 1969-72; 1st v.p. Blyth, Eastman, Dillon & Co., N.Y.C., 1972-73; exec. v.p. Overseas Pvt. Investment Corp., Washington, 1973-77; mng. dir. Pierce Internat., Ltd., Washington, 1978-85, Pierce Investment Banking Corp., 1985-97, Pierce Fin. Corp., Arlington, Va., 1986-2000, sr. advisor, 2000—03. Chmn. bd. dirs. Gator Broadcasting Corp., Del., 1986—; trustee Calvert Tax Free Res. Fund, 1978-83; dir. No. Ireland and Border Counties Trade and Investment Coun., 1994-98; dir. Monument Funds, 2000-02. Served with U.S. Army, 1955-57. Mem. Onteora Club (Tannersville, N.Y.) (dir. 1969-72), Chesapeake Bay Yacht Club (Easton, Md.), Amateur Ski Club N.Y. Republican. Episcopalian.

GREGG, ELLEN M., lawyer; b. Elkton, Md., July 9, 1961; BA summa cum laude, Campbell U., 1983; JD cum laude, Campbell U. Sch. Law, 1986. Bar: NC 1986, admitted to practice: All NC Fed. Dist. Cts., Ct. Appeals (4th Cir.). Intern Md. State Atty. Office, Cecil County, 1982; clerk to Hon. Gerald Arnold NC Ct. Appeals, 1984, jud. clerk to Hon. John C. Martin, 1986—87; mem. Womble Carlyle Sandridge & Rice, PLLC, Winston-Salem, NC. Membership editor Campbell Law Review; contbr. articles to profl. jours. Mem. jail manual adv. bd. Inst. Govt., Univ. NC. Named Region Champion, Nat. Trial Competition, 1986; recipient Lewis F. Powell Medallion for Excellence in Advocacy, Book Awards in Civil Procedure, Trial Advocacy, Criminal Procedure & Jurisprudence. Mem.: ABA (mem. litig. sect.), Forsyth County Young Lawyers Assn. (mem. litig. sect., mem. career develop. com., mem. trial practice general curriculum com.), NC Bar Assn. (mem. young lawyers divsn., mem. litig. sect.), Forsyth County Bar Assn. (mem. young lawyers sect.), Omicron Delta Kappa, Phi Kappa Phi. Office: Womble Carlyle Sandridge & Rice PLLC One W 4th St Winston Salem NC 27101 Mailing: Womble Carlyle Sandridge & Rice PLLC PO Box 84 Winston Salem NC 27102 Office Phone: 336-721-3729. Office Fax: 336-733-8384. Business E-Mail: egregg@wcsr.com.

GREGG, HUGH, retired manufacturing executive, retired governor; b. Nashua, N.H., Nov. 22, 1917; s. Harry A. and Margaret R. (Richardson) G.; m. Catherine M. Warner, July 24, 1940; children: Cyrus Warner, Judd Alan. Grad., Phillips Exeter Acad., 1935; AB, Yale U., 1939; LLB, Harvard U., 1942; LLD, U. N.H., 1953; MA, Dartmouth Coll., 1953; DCL, New England Coll., 1954. Bar: N.H. 1942, Mass 1948. Mem. Sullivan & Gregg, Nashua; former pres., treas. Gregg & Son, Inc., Nashua; gov. of N.H., 1953-55. Chmn. bd. dirs., treas. Gregg Cabinets Ltd., Chambly, Que., Can.; former owner Greggs Greenhouse Restaurant, Sarasota, Fla.; clk., former co-pub. N.H. Profiles; pres. Resources of N.H., Inc., Nashua. Author: The Candidates: See How They Run, 1990, A Tall State Revisited, 1993, Birth of the Republican Party, 1995, Why NH?, 2003. Mem. Nat. Exec. Res.; alderman-at-large, City of Nashua, 1948-50, mayor, 1950; bd. dirs. New England Coun., 1952-55, pres., 1955-57; Rep. nat. committeeman from N.H., 1988; law commr. N.H. Ballot, 1992—; founder N.H. Polit. Libr., 1997—. Spl. agt. CIC, U.S. Army, 1942-46, 50-52. Mem.: VFW. Home: 17 Gregg Rd Nashua NH 03062-1002 E-mail: hgresources@charter.net.

GREGG, JAMES R., optometrist, educator; b. Napoleon, Ohio, Oct. 26, 1914; s. Edgar Macmillan Gregg, Minnie Lauerman Gregg; m. Bernice Rose Klopf; children: Janell Rose Gregg Bassett, Ronald Edgar. BSBA, Ohio State U., 1937, BS Optometry, 1942; D Optometry, L.A. Coll. Optometry, 1948, D (hon.) Ocular Science, 1955, DHL (hon.), 1965. Lic. optometrist 1944. Assoc. prof. L.A. Coll. Optometry, 1947—58; optometrist pvt. practice, Inglewood, 1947—73; prof. L.A. Coll. Optometry, 1958—73, So. Calif. Coll. Optometry, Fullerton, 1973—84, interim dean, 1975—76, grants adminstr., 1976—84, prof. emeritus, 1984—2002; freelance writer Anaheim, Calif., 1947—. Cons. U.S. Dept. of Health, Edn. and Welfare, Washington, 1967—69; bd. trustees AOA Members Retirement Plan, St. Louis, 1971—90. Author: The Story of Optometry, 1965 (AOA Distinguished Journalism award, 1970), The Sportman's Eye, 1971; editor: The Business of Optometric Practice, 1981; contbr. articles to profl. jours. Scoutmaster Boy Scouts Am. Troop 292, Inglewood, Calif., 1962—65; pres. Am. Field Svcs., 1968—69. Staff sgt. U.S. Army, 1943—46. Named Disting. Grad., Ohio State U., 1961. Mem.: Calif. Optometric Assn. (pres. 1958—59, Optometrist of Yr. 1956), Friends of Canyon Hills Libr. (pres. 1989—90), Rotary (bd. trustees 1984—86, Rotarian of Yr. 1985). Avocations: photography, writing, travel, hiking, camping. Home: 412 S Rolling Hills Pl Anaheim CA 92807

GREGG, JAY MASON, geology educator; b. Pitts., Jan. 24, 1951; s. Jay Buell and Patricia Louise (Mason) G.; m. Elizabeth Michelle Prudot, Sept. 3, 1977; children: Patricia Michelle, Nicholas Mason, Jay William. BS in Geology and Biology, Bowling Green State U., 1974; MS in Geology, Okla. State U., 1976; PhD in Geology, Mich. State U., 1982. Assoc. geologist Sun Exploration and Prodn. Co., Midland, Tex., 1976-78; sr. rsch. geologist St. Joe Minerals Corp., Viburnum, Mo., Tucson, 1982-87; prin. scientist Westinghouse Hanford Co., Richland, Wash., 1987-88; asst. prof. geology U. Mo., Rolla, 1988—91, assoc. prof. geology, 1991—95, prof., 1995—2000, Gulf Oil Found. Prof., 2000—. Co-editor SEPM Spl. Publ. on Basin-Wide Diagenetic Patterns; mem. editl. bd. Soc. of Econ. Geologists 75th Anniversary Volume. Fulbright scholar U. Coll., Dublin, 1995-96. Mem. AAAS, Geol. Soc. Am., Soc. for Sedimentary Geology. Democrat. United Methodist. Achievements include investigating, with others, the sources and flow-paths of hydrothermal mineralizing fluids in southern Missouri and the Irish Midlands using distribution of trace and minor elements, cathodoluminescence petrography, and fluid inclusions; co-development of classification system for dolomite rock textures. Home: 1321 Woodlawn Dr Rolla MO 65401-2591 Office: U Mo 125 Mcnutt Hall Rolla MO 65401

GREGG, JOHN BAILEY, surgery educator, researcher; b. Sioux Falls, S.D., June 5, 1922; s. John B. and Anna Elida (Bailey) G.; m. Pauline Benfer Snyder, June 29, 1946; children: Michele Lee, John Benfer, Stewart David, Rebecca Jo Anderson. BA, Iowa U., 1943, MD, 1946; DSc (hon.), U. S.D., 1989. Diplomate Am. Bd. Otolaryngology. Asst. prof. otolaryngology U. Iowa Hosps., Iowa City, 1959-60; prof. anthropology U. Tenn., Knoxville, 1972—; chmn. div. otolaryngology Sch. of Medicine U. S.D., Sioux Falls, 1968-72, vis. prof. Sch. of Medicine, 1972-75, dir. specialties of surgery Sch. Medicine, 1972-88. Cons. VA Hosps, Iowa City and Sioux Falls, 1946-79, USPHS Indian Hosps., Rosebud, Pine Ridge and Wagner, S.D., 1956-75, U. S.D. Speech & Hearing Clinic, Vermillion, 1960—; dir. med. svcs. S.D. Dept. Health, 1982-84, dir. Div. Pub. Health, 1983-84. Author: Dry Bones, 1987, 2d rev. edit., 1989; author: (with others) Benigh Diseases of the Esophagus, 1982; contbr. over 200 articles to profl. jours. Speaker Ho. of Dels., S.D. State Med. Assn., Sioux Falls, 1973-75. Lt. (j.g.) USNR, 1942-49. Mem. Sioux Falls Elks, Sioux Falls Rotary. Republican. Episcopalian. Achievements include research on medicine, anthropology, archeology, history and epidemiology. Home: 4510 S Prince of Peace Pl Sioux Falls SD 57103-5873

GREGG, JON MANN, lawyer; b. Louisville, Oct. 22, 1943; s. James Willard and Margaret Josephine (Mann) G.; m. Jeanette Ruth Brandner, June 18, 1966 (div. Oct. 1980); children: Heather Suzanne, Douglas Robert; m. Carol Ruth Slonneger, July 9, 1983; children: Catherine Marie, Emma Celeste. BS in Acctg., U. Ill., 1965; LLB, Harvard U., 1968. Bar: Ill. 1968. Assoc. Sidley & Austin, Chgo., 1968-74, ptnr., 1974—. Mem. ABA, Chgo. Bar Assn. Avocations: flying, aerobatics, tennis, sailing. Home: 344 W Wisconsin St Unit D Chicago IL 60614-5452 Office: Sidley Austin Brown & Wood 10 S Dearborn Bank One Plz Chicago IL 60603-2000 Business E-Mail: jgregg@sidley.com.

GREGG, JUDD ALAN, senator, former governor; b. Nashua, NH, Feb. 14, 1947; m. Kathleen MacLellan, 1973; children— Molly, Sarah, Joshua AB, Columbia U., 1969; JD, Boston U., 1972, LL.M., 1975. Bar: N.H. 1972. Ptnr. Sullivan, Gregg and Horton, Nashua, N.H.; mem. 97th-100th Congresses from 2d N.H. dist., Washington, 1981-89; gov. State of N.H., Concord, 1989-93; U.S. senator from N.H., 1993—. Mem. Budget/Appropriations Com.; chmn. Appropriations Subcom. on Commerce, Justice, State, Judiciary; chmn. Labor and Human Resources Subcom. on Children & Families; mem. N.H. Gov.'s Exec. Coun., 1978-80. Pres. Crotched Mountain Rehab. Found. Mem. ABA, N.H. BAr Assn., Nashua Bar Assn. Republican. Office: US Senate 393 Senate Russell Bldg Washington DC 20510-0001*

GREGG, LUCIUS PERRY, JR., aerospace transportation executive; b. Henderson, N.C., Jan. 16, 1933; s. Lucius Perry and Rachel (Jackson) G.; m. Doris Marie Jefferson, May 30, 1959 (dec. Nov. 1980); 1 child, Lucius Perry III; m. Beverly E.E. Ward, Jan. 3, 1994. BSEE with distinction, U.S. Naval Acad., 1955; MS in Aero and Astronautics, MIT, 1961; AMP Program, Harvard Bus. Sch., 1975; D of Sci. (hon.), Grinnell Coll., 1973. Pilot, aircraft commdr. mil. air command USAF, 1956-59; project scientist Air Force Office Scientific Rsch., Washington, 1961-65; dir., rsch. coord., assoc. dean sci. Northwestern U., Evanston, Ill., 1965-69; program officer Alfred P. Sloan Found., N.Y.C., 1969-72; pres. First Chgo. U. Finance Corp., Chgo., 1972-79; v.p. First Nat. Bank Chgo., 1972-79; v.p. corp. planning Bristol-Myers Co., N.Y.C., 1979-83; dir. nat. pub. affairs, v.p. gov. rels. Citibank/Citicorp, N.Y.C., 1983-87; v.p. pub. affairs N.Y. Daily News, N.Y.C., 1987-89; v.p. corp. communications Hughes Electronics Corp., L.A., 1989—99. Vis. com. on aero and astronautics MIT, Cambridge, 1971-79; vis. com. on physics Harvard U., Cambridge, 1973-79; mem. commn. on human resources Nat. Acad. Sci., Washington, 1973-78; founding trustee Fermi Nat. Accelerator Lab., Batavia, Ill., 1968-72; chmn. White House Fellows selection com. (Midwest), 1977-79; chmn. bd. dirs. Negro Ensemble Co., NYC, 1984-89; bd. dirs. U.S.-South Africa Leadership Exchange Program, Wash., 1975-1982; vice chmn., bd. dirs. Corp. for Pub. Broadcasting, Washington, 1975-81; bd. trustees WNET Pub. TV, N.Y.C., 1981-89; bd. dirs. Chgo. Coun. on Fgn. Rels., Chgo., 1975-79; mem. academic adv. bd. U.S. Naval Acad., Annapolis, Md., 1971-81; mem. civilian adv. bd., Chief of Naval Personnel, 1975-80;

mem. NASA U. Rels., Washington, 1968-72; chmn. bd. visitors Tulane U., New Orleans, 1972-77; mem. intelligence rev. com. Chgo. Police Depart., 1977-79. Maj. USAF, 1965-85. Named Engr. of Yr. Washington Acad. Sci., 1964, One of 10 Outstanding Young Men Chgo. Jr. Assn. Commerce and Industry, 1966. Office: 4143 Via Marina (PH16) Marina Del Rey CA 90292 E-mail: lu@lugregg.com.

GREGG, MARIE BYRD, retired farmer; b. Mount Olive, NC, Jan. 12, 1930; d. Arnold Wesley and Martha (Reaves) Byrd; m. Robert Allen Gregg, (deceased) July 11, 1953; children: Martha Susan, Kathryn Elizabeth, Kenneth Allen. BA in Elem. Edn., Furman U., 1951. Tchr. 3rd grade Greenville City Sch., SC, 1951-53; med. social worker Ctrl. Carolina Rehab. Hosp., Greensboro, NC, 1959-61; window display designer Kerr Rexall Drugs, Durham, NC, 1960's; shop owner Something Else Antiques, Lima, Ohio, 1979-81; farm owner Mt. Olive, 1978-92. Democrat. Methodist. Avocations: collecting antiques, travel, reading, interior decorating. Home and Office: 212 Baucom Park Dr Greer SC 29650-2972

GREGG, PHILLIP MARTIN, political scientist, educator; b. Portland, Oreg., Oct. 22, 1940; s. Robert Wesley and Ellen Pitkanen Gregg; m. Nancy Gale Jensen, June 12, 1966 (div. June 1982); children: Thomas Robert, Mary Catherine Gregg Zilliot. BS in Math., Oreg. State U., 1963; MA in Govt., Ind. U., 1965, PhD in Polit. Sci., 1972. Exec. trainee Office of Sec. Def., Washington, 1963; exec. sec. Internat. Devel. Rsch. Ctr., Bloomington, Ind., 1964—66; from instr. to prof. polit. sci. U. Mich., Ann Arbor, 1968—74; from assoc. prof. to prof. emeritus U. Ill., Springfield, 1976—2001, prof. emeritus, 2001—. Mem. bd. editors Policy Studies Orgn., Campaign, Ill., 1973—82; dir. Local Govt. Internship Program, Springfield, 1977—82; mem. coord. com. Work-Study Program, 1978—81. Editor: Problems of Theory in Policy Analysis, 1976. Project dir. rsch. Springfield Arts Assn., 1978—80; mem., pres. bd. Abraham Lincoln Inst., 1984—95; mem., chair Kwen Inst., 1983—88. Recipient Aaron Wildausky Book award, Policy Studies Orgn., 1997, Disting Svc. award, U. Ill., 1991; fellow, NSF, Bloomington, Ind., 1967—68. Mem.: Phi Kappa Phi. Avocations: dance, hiking, writing, fly fishing. Home: 22 Knollcrest Ln Chatham IL 62629 Office: U Ill Pub Adminstrn Dept Springfield IL Office Phone: 217-206-6310. E-mail: gregg_phil1@msn.com.

GREGG, RODMAN WALTER, motion picture and television producer, publisher; b. Wilmington, Del., Sept. 1, 1953; s. Rodman I. and Elizabeth W. Gregg. BS in Plant Sci., U. Del., 1975. Asst. mgr. So. States Coop., Richmond, Va., 1977-79; tchr. New Castle County Sch. Dist., Wilmington, 1979-80; ind. prodr. L.A., 1981-90; prodr., ptnr. O'Hara/Gregg Films, Beverly Hills, Calif., 1990-94; pres. Mount/Kramer T.V., L.A., 1997-98, The Mount Co., Hollywood, Calif., 1998-2001; exec. RKO Pictures, 2001—02; cons., prodr. Idiom Films, 2002—03; prodr. RGO Pictures, 2003—. Pub. Packard House Books, Beverly Hills, 1984—; cons. Hollywood Broadcasting.com, L.A., 1999—2000; exec. sr. v.p. TV RKO Pictures, 2001; ind. prodr. and cons., 2002—03; exec. Lightmotive TV, 2005. Editor: (book series) Who's Who in the Motion Picture Industry, 1981—; writer (T.V. movie) The Prisoner of Zenda, 1996, (feature film) Manhattan Cowboys; prodr. (feature film) Jesus the Driver, 2004; co-exec. prodr. (TV documentary) Tarawa, 2005. With USMC, 1970-73, Vietnam. Producing fellow Am. Film Inst., Hollywood, 1984-86. Mem. Prodrs. Guild Am. Democrat. Avocations: writing, automobile restoration. Office: PO Box 2187 Beverly Hills CA 90213-2187 E-mail: filmbiz200@aol.com.

GREGG, STEPHEN THOMPSON, political scientist, consultant; s. David Almus Gregg II and Virginia Thompson Gregg; m. Karen Hein Gregg; 1 child, John Jefferson. BS in Bus. and Orgnl. Behavior magna cum laude, SUNY, Albany, 1973; MPA, Ind. U., 1996. Relapse Prevention Specialist #438 CENAPS, Inc. - Homewood, IL, 1994, Cognitive-Behavioral Therapist # 10881 NACBT - Weirton, WV, 1996, Extra Class Amateur Radio Operator - N9RKS Fed. Comm. Commn., 2001. Elected selectman, bd. chmn. Town of Holderness, NH, 1985—89; candidate for U.S. Rep., Rep. Primary, Congressional District 2, NH, 1988; counselor S.T. Gregg & Assocs., Indpls., 1992—, pub. affairs, policy, & mgmt. facilitator, 1995—. Disaster radio group ARC, Indpls., 1998—. With U.S. Army, 1965—68, Vietnam. Named to Hon. Order of Ky. Cols., 1981. Mem.: ASPA (assoc.), Am. Radio Relay League (assoc.), Pemigewasset Valley Fish & Game Club (assoc.; v.p., dir. 1986—88), VFW (life). Moderate. Congregationalist. Avocations: scuba diving, radio communications, red cross volunteer. Office: ST Gregg & Assocs PO Box 36366 Indianapolis IN 46236-0366

GREGGS, ELANORA, social worker; b. Barnwell County, SC, Nov. 10, 1933; d. Daniel and Georgia (Cobb) Young; children: John, Christopher, Paulette, Doris. BA, Coll. New Rochelle, 1985; MSW, Yeshiva U., 1987. Para-profl. Bd. Edn., Bklyn., 1965—67; salesperson Tira Exclusive, Laurelton, NY, 1982—85, Mary Kay Cosmetics, Stanley Home Products; human svcs. supr. Cath. Charities, Bklyn., 1986—87, social work supr. Jamaica, NY, 1987—95, Jamaica Support Sys., 1995. Tchr. Maranatha Bible Inst., 2001—; cons., spkr. in field. Author: Broken Pieces, 1998. Alumni Coll. New Rochelle, NY, 1985—, Yeshiva U., N.Y.C., 1987—; pub. rels. Lake Arbor Found., Mitchellville, Md., 2000—; vol. in nursing homes, 1996—; active Christian Women of Faith, Mitchellville, Md., 2001—; acting min. Evangel Cathedral, 1995—. Avocations: reading, writing, walking, swimming, gardening.

GREGOIRE, CHRISTINE O., governor, former state attorney general; b. Auburn, Wash., Mar. 24, 1947; m. Michael Gregoire; children: Courtney, Michelle. BA in Speech & Sociology, U. Wash., 1969; JD cum laude, Gonzaga U., 1977, LLD (hon.), 1995. Clerk, typist Wash. State Adult Probation/ Parole Office, Seattle, 1969; caseworker Wash. Dept. Social and Health Scis., Everett, 1974; asst. atty. gen. State of Wash., Spokane, 1977—81, sr. asst. atty. gen., 1981—82, dep. atty. gen., 1982—88, atty. gen., 1992—2005, gov. Olympia, 2005—; dir. Wash. State Dept. Ecology, 1988—92. Chair States/B.C. Oil Spill Task Force, 1989—92, Puget Sound Water Quality Authority, 1990—92, Nat. Com. State Environ. Dirs., 1991—92. Bd. dirs. Wash. State Dept. Ecology, 1988—92. Named Woman of Yr., Am. Legion Aux., 1999; named one of 25 Most Influential Working Mothers, Working Mother mag., 2000; recipient Conservationist of Yr. award, Trout Unlimited/N.W. Steelhead & Salmon Coun., 1994, Gov.'s Child Abuse Prevention award, 1996, Myra Bradwell award, 1997, Wyman award, 1997—98, Bd. of Gov.'s award for professionalism, WSBA, 1997, Kick Butt award, The Tobacco Free Coalition of Pierce County, 1997, Wash. State Hosp. Assn. award, 1997, Citizen Activist award, Gleitsman Found., 1998, Woman of Achievement award, Assn. for Women in Comm. Matrix Table, 1999, Pub. Justice award, WSTLA, 1999, Excellence in Pub. Health award, Wash. State Assn. Local Pub. Health Ofcls., 1999, Women in Govt. award, Good Housekeeping, 1999, Spl. Recognition award, Wash. State Nurses Assn., 2000. Mem.: Nat. Assn. Attys. Gen. (consumer protection and environment com., energy com., children and the law subcom., pres. 1999—2000). Democrat. Office: Office of Gov PO Box 40002 Olympia WA 98504*

GREGOIRE, MICHAEL P., software company executive; BS in Physics and Computing, Wilfred Laurier U., Ont., Can.; MBA, Calif. Coast U.; diploma in Internat. Exec. Program, Thunderbird Am. Sch. Internat. Bus. From mgmt. to mng. dir. svcs. Global Fin. Mkts. Group Electronic Data Sys. Corp., 1988—2000, mng. dir. svcs. Global Fin. Mkts. Group; sr. v.p. PeopleSoft Consulting N.Am. PeopleSoft Inc., Pleasonton, Calif., 2000—03, exec. v.p. Global Svcs., 2003—. Mem.: Assn. Mgmt. Consulting Firms (bd. dirs.). Office: PeopleSoft Inc 4460 Hacienda Dr Pleasanton CA 94588

GREGOIRE, TIMOTHY GORDON, forestry researcher; b. Dover, N.H., Oct. 10, 1949; s. Albert Rene and Fernande Geneva (Hayes) G.; m. Judith Ann Wright, Sept. 12, 1981; children: Taylor Albert Gregoire-Wright, Logan Carl Gregoire-Wright. BS, Princeton U., 1971; MS, U. N.H., 1980; MPhil, Yale U., 1982, PhD, 1985. Assoc. prof. Va. Poly. Inst. and State U., Blacksburg, 1985-90, 1990—. Co-author: Sampling Techniques for Multiresource Forest Inventories, 1993; assoc. editor Forest Sci., 1989—; contbr. over 80 articles to profl. jours. Mem. Soc. Am. Foresters (working group officer), Am. Stats. Assn., Internat. Biometric Soc. Avocations: woodworking, stamp collecting/philately. Office: Va Poly Inst and State Univ Dept Forestry Blacksburg VA 24061

GREGOR, DOROTHY DEBORAH, retired librarian; b. Dobbs Ferry, N.Y., Aug. 15, 1939; d. Richard Garrett Heckman and Marion Allen (Richmond) Stewart; m. A. James Gregor, June 22, 1963 (div. 1974). BA, Occidental Coll., 1961; MA, U. Hawaii, 1963; MLS, U. Tex., 1968; cert. in Library Mgmt., U. Calif., Berkeley, 1976. Reference libr. U. Calif., San Francisco, 1968-69; dept. libr. Pub. Health Libr. U. Calif., Berkeley, 1969-71, tech. services libr., 1973-76; reference libr. Hamilton Libr., Honolulu, 1971-72; head serials dept. U. Calif., Berkeley, 1976-80, assoc. univ. libr. tech. svcs. dept., 1980-84, univ. libr., 1992-94; chief Shared Cataloging div. Libr. of Congress, Washington, 1984-85; univ. libr. U. Calif.-San Diego, La Jolla, 1985-92, OCLC asst. to pres. for acad. and rsch. libr. rels., 1995—98; docent Asian Art Mus., San Francisco, 1997—, ret. Instr. sch. libr. and info. studies U. Calif., Berkeley, 1975, 76, 83; cons. Nat. Libr. of Medicine, Bethesda, Md., 1985, Ohio Bd. Regents, Columbus, 1987; trustee Online Computer Libr. Ctr., 1988-96; dir. Nat. Coordinating Com. on Japanese Libr. Resources, 1995-98; docent Asian Art Mus., San Francisco, 1997-. Mem.: ALA, Libr. Info. Tech. Assn., Program Com. Ctr. for Rsch. Librs. (bd. chair 1992—93, Hugh Atkinson award 1994). E-mail: dgregor@mcn.org.

GREGOR, MELINDA L., literature and language educator; b. Lima, Ohio, Feb. 18, 1952; d. Walter Scott and Evelyn E. Sousley; m. Warren T. Gregor, Apr. 7, 1973; children: Kerin, Andrew, James, Joseph. BS in Music Edn., Findlay Coll., 1974; postgrad., Dominican U., 2005—. Tchr. English Lincolnview Schs., Van Wert, Ohio, 1974—75, Ft. Myers Christian Sch., Fla., 1989—95, St. Henry Local Schs., St. Henry, Ohio, 2000—05. Advisor Nat. Honor Soc., St. Henry, 2004—05. Composer Christian music songs. Mem.: NEA, Ohio Edn. Assn., Delta Kappa Gamma (2d v.p. 2003—05). Home: 315 N Buckeye St Celina OH 45822

GREGOR, TIBOR PHILIP, retired management consultant; b. Levoca, Czechoslovakia, Apr. 25, 1919; arrived in Can., 1951; s. Philip and Emma (Aufricht) Gregor; m. Helen Frances Lorenz, Sept. 15, 1942 (dec. 1989); children: Jan Michael, Charlotte Anne; m. Valma Costa, Dec. 17, 1994 (dec. 2003). Student, U. London, 1938—40. Gen. sales mgr. Eastern Steel Products Ltd., Toronto, Canada, 1952-57; pres., gen. mgr. Roneo Co. Ltd., Toronto, 1957-63, Roneo, Inc., Phila.; pres. Mcpl. Sand & Gravel Co., Kingston, Canada, 1964-71; exec. dir. Can. Soft Drink Assn., Toronto, 1972-86; pres. T.P. Gregor Assocs., Toronto, 1986—98, ret., 1998. Mem. Ont. Comml. Registration Appeals Tribunal, 1987—93. Vice chmn. Toronto Centennial Com., 1964—67; pres. Met. Toronto Assn. Mentally Retarded, 1961—64; past pres. Can. Assn. Mentally Retarded, 1969—71; founder, chmn. Friends Royal Can. Acad. Arts, 1985—89; past chmn. Can. Fund Czech and Slovak Univs. Served as col. Czechoslovak Armoured Brigade, ret., 1945. Decorated Medal of Merit 1st class France; recipient Freedom award, City of Winnipeg, 1970, Centennial medal, Royal Can. Acad., 2000, commendation, City of Toronto. Mem.: Am. Soc. Assn. Execs., Can. Soc. Assn. Execs., Royal Can. Legion, Royal Can. Mil. Inst., Rotary (past gov. Rotary Dist. 7070, Toronto-Eglinton), Rotary Internat. (bd. dirs., treas. Rotary Found. R.I., past trustee, v.p. Rotary Found. Can.), Toronto Lawn Tennis Club. Mem. United Ch. Home and Office: 218 Glen Rd Toronto ON Canada M4W 2X3

GREGORATOS, GABRIEL, medical educator; b. Athens, Greece, Aug. 20, 1929; came to U.S., 1948. s. Panos and Catherine (Monopoli) G.; m. Eva Gallay, Jan. 2, 1953; children: Katherine M., Barbara A., Nicholas S. AB, Hamilton Coll., 1950; MD, N.Y. Med. Coll., 1954. Intern St. Vincent's Hosp., N.Y.C., 1954-55; resident in internal medicine Tripler Army Med. Ctr., Honolulu, 1959-62; resident in cardiology Walter Reed Army Med. Ctr., Washington, 1962-64; commd. 1st lt. U.S. Army, 1956, advanced through grades to col., 1970; chief cardiology Letterman Army Med. Ctr., San Francisco, 1971-76; ret. U.S. Army, 1976; assoc. prof. to prof. of medicine U. Calif., San Diego, 1976-84; chief cardiology Pacific Presbyn. Med. Ctr., San Francisco, 1984-89; prof. medicine, dir. clin. cardiology U. Calif. Davis, Sacramento, 1989-97; prof. medicine, dir. cardiology cons. svcs. U. Calif., San Francisco, 1997—2001. Cons. FDA, Washington, 1973-2000, VA, San Francisco, 1986-89, Letterman Army Med. Ctr., 1985-92, NAval Hosp., San Diego, 1979-84; chair FDA adv. panel (circulatory system), 1992-93. Co-editor: Coronary Care, 1981; contbr. articles to profl. jours. Pres. San Francisco Heart Assn., 1988-89. Decorated Legion of Merit. Fellow ACP, Am. Coll. Cardiology (councillor Calif. chpt. 1989-92, pres. Calif. chpt. 1994-95, gov. No. Calif. 1994-97), Coun. of Clin. Cardiology, Am. Heart Assn. Democrat. Greek Orthodox. Office: U Calif Box 0214 505 Parnassus Ave San Francisco CA 94143-0214 Office Phone: 415-353-9156. Business E-Mail: gpggrego@medicine.ucsf.edu.

GREGORIAN, DAREH ARDASHES, reporter; b. Austin, Tex., Mar. 24, 1970; s. Vartan and Clare Russell Gregorian; m. Maggie Lindsy Haberman, Nov. 9, 2003. BA, Boston U., 1988—92. Reporter/rshcr. NY Observer, 1992—93; typist/part time reporter NY Post, 1993—95, police reporter, 1996—97, gen. assignment exchange reporter, 1997—98, supreme ct. reporter, 1998—. Recipient NYPD Crimestoppers award, NYC Police Found., 1997. Mem.: NY Press Club. Office: NY Post 1211 6th Ave 10th Fl New York NY 10036 Office Phone: 212-930-8500. E-mail: dgregorian@nypost.com.

GREGORIAN, RAFFI, diplomat; b. Redwood City, CA, Jan. 15, 1964; s. Vartan Gregorian, Clare Russell Gregorian; m. Bernadette Mary Dawson. PhD, Johns Hopkins School of Advanced International Studies, Washington, D.C., 1991—98; MA, King's College, University of London, London, 1988—89; BA (Hons), University of Pennsylvania, Philadelphia, PA, 1982—86. Historian U.S. Army Ctr. for Mil. History, Washington, 1986—88; policy analyst Ctr. for Arms Control and Tech. Assessment, EOS Technologies, McLean, Va., 1990—92; sr. analyst Sci. Applications Internat. Corp., McLean, Va., 1992—98; sr. adviser Dept. of Def. Interagency Task Force for Mil. Stblzn. in the Balkans, Washington, 1998—98; sr. advisor and chief of staff Office of the Spec. Adviser to the Pres. and Sec. of State for Kosovo and Dayton Implementation, Dept. of State, Washington, 1999—2001; acting office dir. Office of Kosovo Implementation Dep. of State, Washington, 2001—01; dir. for Bosnia policy Office of South Ctrl. Europe Dept. of State, Washington, 2001—. Author: (Book) The British Army, the Gurkhas, and Cold War Strategy in the Far East, 1947-54, 2002. Commd. officer USNR, 1993—. Mem.: Army-Navy Club, Society for Military History, Royal United Services Institute, International Institute for Strategic Studies. Home: 507 Queen Street Alexandria VA 22314 Office: Department of State 2201 C Street NW Washington DC 20520 Office Phone: 202-647-1880. Business E-Mail: gregorianr@state.gov.

GREGORIAN, VARTAN, foundation administrator; b. Tabriz, Iran, Apr. 8, 1934; came to U.S., 1956; s. Samuel B. and Shushanik G. (Mirzaian) G.; m. Clare Russell, Mar. 25, 1960; children: Vahe, Raffi, Dareh. Grad., Coll. Armenian, 1955; BA, Stanford U., 1958, PhD, 1964; degree (hon.), Boston U., 1983, Brown U., 1984, Jewish Theol. Sem., 1984, SUNY, 1985, Johns Hopkins U., 1987, NYU, 1987, U. Pa., 1988, Dartmouth Coll., 1989, Rutgers U., 1989, CUNY, 1990, Tufts U., 1994, Johnson and Wales U., 1999, Julliard Sch., 2000, U. Ill., 2001, Fordham U., 2003, Pa. State U., 2003, San Francisco State U., 2004, Am. U. Beirut, 2004, U. Notre Dame, 2005. From instr. to assoc. prof. history San Francisco State Coll., 1962—68; assoc. prof. UCLA, 1968; from assoc. prof. to prof. U. Tex., 1968—72, dir. spl. programs, 1970—72; Tarzian prof. Armenian and Caucasian history U. Pa., Phila., 1972—80; dean U. Pa. (Faculty Arts and Scis.), Phila., 1974—78, provost, 1978—80; pres. N.Y. Pub. Libr., 1981—89; prof. New Sch. Social Rsch., N.Y.C., 1984—89; prof. History and Near Eastern studies NYU, 1984—89; pres., prof. History Brown U., Providence, 1989—97; pres. Carnegie Corp., N.Y.C., 1997—. Author: The Emergence of Modern Afghanistan, 1880-1946, 1969, The Road to Home: My Life and Times, 2003, Islam: A Mosaic, Not a Monolith, 2003. Bd. dirs. Aaron Diamond Found., 1990-97, Brookings Instns., 1994-97, Inst. for Internat. Edn., 1989-95, Internat. League of Human Rights, 1984-97, Inst. for Advanced Study, 1987—, J. Paul Getty Trust, 1988-2000, Aga Khan U., 1995-2000, Human Rights Watch, 1996—; chmn. bd. visitors Grad. Sch. and Univ. Ctr., CUNY, 1984-90; bd. trustees Mus. Modern Art, 1994—, Providence Jour., 1998-, Cell Therapeutics, Inc., 2001-, Nat. Constn. Ctr., 2002-, Qatar Found., 2003-; bd. mem. Am. Acad. Berlin, 2003-, World Trade Ctr. Meml. Found., 2004-. Decorated Officier de l'Ordre des Arts et Lettres (France), Grand Oficial Ordem Infante D. Henrique Portuguese Govt., 1995; recipient Danforth E.H. Harbison Tchg. award 1969, Cactus Tchg. award 1971, award of distinction Phi Lambda Theta and Phi Delta Kappa, 1980, Silver Cultural medal Italian Ministry Fgn. Affairs, 1977, Gold medal of honor City and Province of Vienna, Austria, 1976, 1st Disting. Humanist award Pa. Humanities Coun., 1983, Nat. Fellowship award Fellowship Commn., Phila., 1984, Gold medal Nat. Inst. Social Scis., 1985, Disting. Svc. to the Arts award Third St. Music Sch. Settlement, 1997, Disting. Svc. to Pub. Edn. award N.Y. Acad. Pub. Edn., 1998, Friends of the Arts award Town Hall, 1998, Nat. Humanities medal, Pres. William J. Clinton, 1998, Eleanor Roosevelt Val-Kill award Eleanor Roosevelt Ctr., 1999; fellow Social Sci. Rsch. Coun., 1960, Ford Found. Fgn. Area Tng., 1960-62, Am. Coun. Learned Socs.-Social Sci. Rsch. Coun., 1965, John Simon Guggenheim Found., 1971-72, Social Sci. Rsch. Coun., 1971-72, Am. Coun. Edn., 1973. Fellow Acad. Arts Scis., Am. Philos. Soc.; mem. Am. Antiquarian Soc., Am. Hist. Assn. (program chmn. 1972), Am. Philos. Soc. (grantee 1965, 66), Internat. Fedn. Libr. Assns. (co-chmn. program com. 1985), Assn. Advancement Slavic Studies (program chmn. Western Slavic Conf. 1967), Mid-East Studies Assn., Coun. Fgn. Rels., Grolier Club, Round Table, Century Club, Econ. Club, Phi Beta Kappa. Office: Carnegie Corp Office of the Pres 437 Madison Ave Fl 27 New York NY 10022-7001 Office Phone: 212-371-3200.

GREGORIE, CORAZON ARZALEM, operations research specialist; b. Bethesda, Md., Aug. 6, 1947; d. Faustino and Rosalina Arzalem. AA in Bus. Adminstrn., Palm Beach Coll., 1967; postgrad., Fla. Atlantic U., 1967; BA in Bus. Adminstrn., U. Fla., 1969. Mgmt. trainee Burdines Dept. Store, West Palm Beach, Fla., 1969; adminstrv. asst. divsn. econs. Nat. Food Processors Assn., Washington, 1970-71, statis. analyst divsn. econs. and stats., 1972-77, acting dir. divsn. econs. and stats., 1978; asst. editor Airfare Pub. Co., Washington, 1979-81; product specialist Arbitron Co., Beltsville, Md., 1982-83, tng. supr. Laurel, Md., 1984-87, night shift ops. supr. Columbia, Md., 1988—95, survey supr., 1996—. Collective mem., bd. dirs. Glut Food, Mt. Rainier, Md., 1973-78. Force vol. Nat. Park Svc., Washington, 1973-76; coord. College Park Food Coop., Md., 1970-72. Mem. Lotus Ltd. (bd. dirs. 1974—, treas., parts and tech. chmn., membership dir., corr. sec.). Avocations: photography, sports cars. Office: Arbitron Co 9705 Patuxent Woods Dr Columbia MD 21046-1572

GREGORY, ANN YOUNG, editor, publisher; b. Apr. 28, 1935; d. David Marion and Pauline (Adams) Young; m. Allen Gregory, Jan. 29, 1957; children: David Young, Mary Peyton. BA with high distinction with departmental honors, U. Ky., 1956. Sec. Ky. Edit. TV Guide, Louisville, summer 1956; traffic mgr. Sta. WVLK, Lexington, 1956-61; part-time tchr. adult basic edn. Wise County (Va.) Sch. Bd., St. Paul, 1966-72; adminstrv. asst. Appalachian Field Svcs., Children's TV Workshop, St. Paul, 1971-74; editor, co-pub. Clinch Valley Times, 1974—. Pres. Clinch Valley Pub. Co., Inc., St. Paul, 1974—; mem. mktg. com. Mountain Empire TechPrep Consortium, 1993—. Editor, text writer: The Flood of '77 in the St. Paul Area, 1977; weekly newspaper columnist: Of Shoes...and Ships...and Sealing Wax, 1974—. V.p. St. Paul PTA, 1970-73; trustee Lonesome Pine Regional Libr. Bd., 1972-80, chmn., 1978-80; chmn. com. to establish br. libr. in St. Paul, opened 1975; mem. adv. bd. Pro-Art, Wise County chpt. Va. Mus. Fine Arts, 1979-86; co-leader Brownie troop Girl Scouts U.S.A., 1971-76, bd. dirs. Appalachian coun., 1983-95, 1st v.p., 1985-91; mem. adv. bd. Wise County YMCA, 1977-80; mem. Wise County Bd. Edn., 1975—, vice-chmn., 1981-95, 99, chmn., 2000-01; pres. So. Region Sch. Bds. Assn., 1987-88; mem. Va. Edn. Block Grants Adv. Com., 1981-86, Region I State Literacy Coun., 1989-91; mem. Local Vocat. Adv. Coun., 1980—, chmn., 1981—; mem. statewide planning coun. Va. Dept. Edn.; mem. Va. Coun. on Vocat. Edn., 1987-95, chmn., 1989-91; mem. exec. com. Va. H.S. League, 1984-88 (Lifetime Achievement award, 2001); past pres. Wise County Humane Soc., Inc.; bd. dirs. Va. Sch. Bds. Assn., 1979-89, pres., 1985-86; bd. dirs. Va. Literacy Found., 1987-89, Appalachian Edn. Lab., 1995-2001, bd. chmn., 2000, amb., 2005—, Quarter Century Club, Va. Sch. Bd. Assn., 2002; sec., treas. S.W. Va. Pub. Edn. Found. Bd., 1993—; mem. Mountain Empire C.C. Found. Bd., 1994—; mem. adv. com. Va. State Supt. Pub. Instrn., 1993-96; mem. devel. and comty. rels. com., mem. music adv. com. Clinch Valley Coll.; mem. adv. bd. Wise Appalachian Regional Hosp., 1995-98; mem. Wise County Info. Tech. Task Force, 1998—; bd. dirs., sec. St. Paul Tomorrow Steering Com., 1998-2000; mem. adv. com. WISE-FM, U. Va. Coll., Wise; sec., bd. dirs. St. Paul Tomorrow, Inc., 2001— Named Outstanding Clubwoman of Yr., St. Paul Jr. Women's Club, 1964, 66, Outstanding Citizen, S.W. Va. dist. Va. Fedn. Women's Clubs, 1968, Woman of Yr. Wise County/Norton Dem. Women's Club, 1986, Citizen of Yr., Wise County C. of C., 1990; recipient Rufus Beamer award Va. Poly. Inst., 1989, William P Kanto Meml. award for contbns. to edn. Clinch Valley Coll., Mountain Empire C.C. and Wise County and Norton Pub. Schs., 1990, Literacy award S.W. Reading Coun., 1994, Lifetime Achievement award Va. H.S. League, 2001; Ky. Broadcasters Assn. scholar, 1956 Mem. Va. Press Assn. (1st pl. award for editl. writing 1976), Nat. Press Women, Va. Press Women, Nat. Newspaper Assn., Women in Comms., Nat. Sch. Bds. Assn. (pub. rels. com., nominating com. 1987, Quarter Century Club award Va. chpt., 2002), Mortar Bd., Delta Kappa Gamma (hon. mem. Alpha Psi chpt.), Phi Beta Kappa, Alpha Delta Pi, Chi Delta Phi, Alpha Epsilon Rho, Alpha Lambda Delta, Theta Sigma Phi. Democrat. Methodist. Home: PO Box 303 Saint Paul VA 24283-0303 Office: PO Box 817 Saint Paul VA 24283-0817 Office Phone: 276-762-7671. Business E-Mail: agregory@naxs.com.

GREGORY, ARTEMIS CHRISTINA, elementary school educator; b. Santa Monica, Calif., Sept. 3, 1963; d. Richard Palmer and Mary Thiras Benjamin; children: Kosta, Michael, George. B of Liberal Arts, Hellenic Coll., 1986; MEd in Reading & Lang., U. Mass., 2005. Cert. literary specialist. Tchr. 4th grade St. Andrew Sch., Jamaica Plain, Mass., 1987—89; tchr. 5th grade Delay Mid. Sch., Lowell, 1996—2001; tchr. 4th grade Lincoln Elem. Sch., 2001—. Lead tchr. Lowell Sch. Dept., 2004—; teach first facilitator Lincoln Elem. Sch., 2005; coach girls mid. sch. basketball, 1998—2001; coach boys mid. sch. volleyball, 2001. Creator, dir. vacation bible sch. Boston Diocese Greek Orthodox Ch., 1995—2000. Mem.: Internat. Reading Assn. Democrat. Eastern Orthodox.

GREGORY, BETTINA LOUISE, journalist; b. N.Y.C., June 4, 1946; d. George Alexander and V. Elizabeth Friedman; m. John P. Flannery, II, 1981 (div. 2001); 1 child, Diana Elizabeth. Student, Smith Coll., 1964-65; diploma in acting, Webber-Douglas Sch. Dramatic Art, London, 1968; BA in Psychology, Pierce Coll., Athens, Greece, 1972; PsyD, George Washington U., 2002; LittD (hon.), Susquehanna U., 1988, St. Thomas Aquinas U., 1992; LLD (hon.), Wilmington Coll., 1989; D in Journalism (hon.), U. Findlay, 1990; LittD (hon.), Bethany Coll., 2000. Reporter Sta. WVBR-FM, Ithaca, 1972-73, Sta. WCIC-TV, Ithaca, 1972; reporter, anchorwoman Sta. WGBB, Freeport, N.Y., 1973, Sta. WCBS, N.Y.; freelance reporter, writer AP, N.Y.C., 1973-74; freelance reporter N.Y. Times, 1973-74; with ABC News, 1974—2001, corr. Washington, 1977-79, White House corr., 1979, sr. gen. assignment corr., 1980, host The American Family, Goodlife TV Network, 2002—; pres. Sunshine State Telephone Co., Miami, Fla., 2004—. Elected rep. for corrs. ABC News Women's Adv. Bd.; adj. prof. Robert H. Smith Sch. Bus.; adj. prof. exec. masters in bus. adminstrn. U. Md. Reporter TV spl. Flaws in the Shield, 1989 (1st pl. Headliner award), A&E's Biography of Hillary Rodham Clinton, 1994 (Best Documentary ACE award 1994), Murder Trial O.J. Simpson (Edward R. Murrow award Best News Series 1996), Hannibal Lecter: the Honey in the Lion's Mouth, Am.Journal Psychotherapy, 2002. Recipient 1st Place award Nat. Feature News, Odyssey Inst., N.Y., 1978, Clarion award Women in Communications, Inc., 1979, hon. mention Nat.

Commn. on Working Women, 1979, Media award for Am. Agenda segment on homeless World Hunger Found., 1990, Cable Ace Best Documentary award, 1995, Edward R. Murrow award for coverage of O.J. Simpson Murder trial, 1996, Telly award for Bipolar Teens, 2004; named one of top 10 investigative reporters, TV Guide, 1983. Mem. Radio TV Corrs. Assn., White House Corrs. Assn. Clubs: Newswomen's N.Y. (recipient Front Page award 1976); Nat. Press; Washington Press. Office: ABC News Washington Bur 1717 Desales St NW Washington DC 20036-4407 Personal E-mail: bettinagre@aol.com.

GREGORY, CALVIN, real estate investor; b. Bronx, N.Y., Jan. 11, 1942; s. Jacob and Ruth Gregory; m. Rachel Anna Carver, Feb. 14, 1970 (div. Apr. 1977); children: Debby Lynn, Trixy Sue; m. Carla Deane Deaver, June 30, 1979. AA, L.A. City Coll., 1962; BA, Calif. State U., L.A., 1964; MDiv, Fuller Theol. Sem., 1968; M in Religious Edn., Southwestern Sem., Ft. Worth, 1969; PhD in Religion, Universal Life. Ch., Modesto, Calif., 1982; DDiv (hon.), Otay Mesa Coll., 1982. Ordained to ministry Am. Bapt. Conv., 1970; cert. notary pub., real estate lic., casualty lic. Calif. Youth minister First Bapt. Ch., Delano, Calif., 1964—65, 1969—70; youth dir. St. Luke's United Meth. Ch., Highland Park, Calif., 1969—70; tchr. polit. sci. Maranatha High Sch., Rosemead, Calif., 1969—70; aux. chaplain U.S. Air Force 750th Radar Squadron, Edwards AFB, Calif., 1970—72; pastor First Bapt. Ch., Boron, Calif., 1971—72; ins. agt. Prudential Ins. Co., Ventura, Calif., 1972—73, sales mgr., 1973—74; casualty ins. agt. Allstate Ins. Co., Thousand Oaks, Calif., 1974—75; pres. Ins. Agy. Placement Svcs., Thousand Oaks, Calif., 1975—; head youth minister Emanuel Presbyn. Ch., L.A., 1973—74; owner, investor real estate. Counselor YMCA, Hollywood, Calif., 1964, Soul Clinic-Universal Life Ch. Inc., Modesto, Calif., 1982. Mem.: Life Underwriter Tng. Coun., Apt. Assn. L.A., Kiwanis (club spkr. 1971), X32 Club (Ventura, Calif.), Forensic Club (L.A.). Republican. Office: PO Box 4407 Thousand Oaks CA 91359-1407

GREGORY, CLAIRE DISTELHORST, television producer; b. Chgo., Mar. 6, 1926; d. Robert Henry and Genevieve (McCall) Distelhorst; children: Charles, Martha. Student, Cornell Coll., 1943-46; AB, Ind. U., 1947, MS, 1954. Tchr. pub. schs., Bismarck and Rossville, Ill., 1947-50, Helmsburg, Ind., 1950-51; grad. asst. Audio Visual Ctr. of Ind. U., 1953-55; dir. women's, children's/social svc. programs radio/TV, 1956-59; lectr., 1956-59; exec. dir. Cmty. Svc. Coun., Inc., Bloomington, Ind., 1971-75; asst. supr. instructional TV program devel. Ind. U. Radio and TV Svc., 1975-81, dir. spl. projects, 1982-92; chmn. Bloomington Telecomms. Coun., 1975-80. Writer, prodr: Russian Revolution and Arts, Parts I and II, 1976, Intro. to Immediate Access, 1977-80, Teleconference on Mass Transp., 1976, Transp. Briefing, 1977, videotapes on profl. devel. Internat. Devel. Inst., 1975-80, 16 videotapes on computer instrn., 1978-80, Getting There, 1980, Living Africa, 1979-82, Programming for Microcomputers, 1982, Negotiation, 1984, Ind. Collection, 1987, Joshua's Battle: The Story of Lyles Station, 1988, Charting New Courses teleconferences, 1988; prodr., videodisc instructional Clarity; prodr., dir., editor videotape SOUTH SHORE LINE: A Good Investment, 1990; prodr., editor Autism: Learning to Live, 1990 (Excellence award Autism Soc. Am. 1991), Autism: Stubborn Love, 1991 (Excellence award Autism Soc. Am. 1992), Autism: Being Friends, 1991; TV advisor Mostly Moliere Troupe, 1981-89; lay reader A Moment of Silence prodn., 1996. Recipient Communication Industry Silver award Assn. Visual Communicators, 1989. Mem. Blue Ridge Assn. (treas. 1978-81), Theta Sigma Phi, Psi Iota Xi.

GREGORY, DEIRDRE DIANNE, secondary school educator; b. Fairview Park, Ohio, Feb. 12, 1958; d. Richard Whiting and Ruth Elizabeth (Moody) Mason; m. Thomas Bradford Gregory, July 15, 1995. BS, Ashland U., 1981; MS, Ohio State U., 1986; MEd, Ashland U., 1989, U. Dayton, 1993. Cert. tchr., Ohio; cert. vocat. family and consumer sci. sch. guidance counselor and supr.; Praxis III assessor. Tchr. home econs. Mansfield (Ohio) City Schs., 1981-93, GRADS coord., 1993-99, guidance counselor, 1999—. Mem. adv. bd. Mansfield (Ohio) City Schs. Parents as Tchrs., 1993—, Pioneer Career and Tech. Ctr. GRADS Adv. Bd., Shelby, Ohio, 1993—; chair Children Family Health Svcs. Consortium, Mansfield, 1996-98; adj. prof. Ashland U., 2003-. Mem. AAUW (pres. 1997-99), NEA, Mansfield Sch. Employee Assn. (pres. 1994-95), Am. Assn. Family and Consumer Sci., Order of Eastern Star, Ashland U. Alumni Assn. (pres.), Local Profl. Devel. Com. (co-chair), Local Profl. Devel. Trainer, Ohio Assn. Coll. Admission Counseling, Ohio Sch. Counseler Assn, Ohio Edn. Assn., Kappa Omicron Phi, Phi Delta Kappa (pres. 1994-96, historian 1996-98), Am. Sch. Counselor Assn. Democrat. Presbyterian. Avocations: reading, singing, music, cross stitch, walking. Home: 411 Overlook Rd Mansfield OH 44907-1533 Office: Mansfield Sr H S 124 N Linden Rd Mansfield OH 44906-2621 Office Phone: 419-525-6369 20303. Business E-Mail: DGregory@mansfield.k12.oh.us.

GREGORY, DICK, comedian, volunteer; b. St. Louis, Oct. 12, 1932; m. Lillian Smith, 1959; children: Michele, Lynne, Paula, Pamela, Stephanie, Gregory, Christian, Ayanna, Miss, Yohance. Student, So. Ill. U., 0951—1953, student, 1955—56. Lectr. univs. throughout U.S.; nutritionist world-heavyweight boxing champion Riddick Bowe, 1992. Entertainer, Esquire Club, Chgo., opened night club, Apex, Robbins, Ill., master ceremonies, Roberts Show Club, Chgo., 1959-60, night club appearances, Akron, Milw., Chgo., 1960, San Francisco, Hollywood, numerous other cities, 1961-, comedy act, Playboy Club, Chgo., 1961; TV guest appearances Jack Paar show, others; record albums Dick Gregory: The Light Side-Dark Side; others; Author: The Back of the Bus, 1962, Nigger, 1964, What's Happening, 1965, The Shadow That Scares Me, Write Me In, No More Lies, 1971, Dick Gregory's Political Primer, 1971, Dick Gregory's Natural Diet for Folks Who Eat, Cookin' With Mother Nature, 1973, Dick Gregory's Bible Tales, with Commentary, 1974, Up From Nigger, 1976, (with Mark Lane) Code Name Zorro: The Murder of Martin Luther King, Jr, 1977, Murder in Memphis, 1993, Callus on My Soul, 2002. Peace and Freedom Party presdl. candidate, 1968. Served with AUS, 1953-55. Winner Mo. mile championship, 1951, 52; named Outstanding Athlete So. Ill. U., 1953; recipient Ebony-Topaz Heritage and Freedom award, 1978. Achievements include invention of Dick Gregory's Bahamian Diet Drink. Office: Dick Gregory Hlth Enterprises PO Box 3270 Plymouth MA 02361-3270 Office Phone: 508-746-7427.

GREGORY, FREDERICK DREW, federal agency administrator; b. Washington, Jan. 7, 1941; s. Francis Anderson and Nora Drew Gregory; m. Barbara Ann Archer, June 3, 1964; children: Frederick D. Jr., Heather Lynn Gregory Skeens. BS in Aerospace Engring., USAF Acad., 1964; MS in Info. Systems, George Washington U., 1977; DSc, U. D.C., 1986. Cert. astronaut shuttle comdr., FAA comml. and instrument cert. for singlr- and multi-engine airplanes and helicopters. Commd. 2nd lt. USAF, 1964, advanced through grades to col., 1983, helicopter pilot, 1964-69, fighter pilot, 1969-70; exptl. test pilot NASA and USAF, 1971-78; retired as colonel USAF, 1993; astronaut NASA, Houston, 1978-93, assoc. adminstr., Office of Safety and Mission Assurance Washington, 1992—2001, assoc. adminstr. for space flight, 2001—02, deputy adminstr., COO, 2002—, acting adminstr., 2005. Astronaut pilot, Orbiter Challenger (STS-51B), 1985, spacecraft comdr. aboard Discovery (STS-33), 1989, spacecraft comdr. aboard Atlantis (STS-44), 1991. Bd. dirs. Young Astronaut Coun., Washington, Kaiser Permanente Mid-Atlantic States, Nat. Capital Area coun. Boy Scouts Am., Challenger Ctr. for Space Sci. Edn., Va. Air and Space Ctr.-Hampton Roads History Ctr.; bd. visitors Air Force Inst. Tech., Maxwell AFB, Ala. Decorated Legion of Merit, Air medal (16), Disting. Flying Cross (2), NASA Space Flight medals (3); recipient Def. Meritorious Svc. medal, Meritorious Svc. medal, Air Force Meritorious Svc. medal USAF, Air Force Commendation medal, Def. Superior Svc. medal Dept. Defense, Nat. Intelligence Achievement medal CIA, Black Sci. award, Nat. Tech. Assn., Pres. award Black Enterprise Mag., Disting. Nat. Scientist award, Nat. Soc. Black Engrs., George Washington U. Outstanding Alumni award. Mem. AMVET, Am. Helicopter Soc., Order of Daedalians, The Naval Order, Soc. Experimental Test Pilots, Assn. Space Explorers, Air Force Acad. Assn. of Graduates, Air Force Assn.(Ira Eaker Fellow), Sigma Pi Phi, Nat. Tech. Assn., Tuskegee Airmen. Avocations: audio/video equipment, reading, world travel, specialty cars, hunting, water-skiing.*

GREGORY, GWEN MEYER, librarian; b. Albuquerque, N.Mex., Aug. 24, 1965; d. Bobby Lee Gregory and Margaret Elizabeth Brown; m. Donald Francis Meyer. BA in Anthropology, U. N.Mex, Albuquerque, 1986; MPA, N.Mex State U., Las Cruces, 1998; MLS, U. Ariz., Tucson, 1988. Head of bibliographic svcs. Colo. Coll., Colo. Springs, Colo., 2001—. Editor: The Successful Academic Librarian. Office: Tutt Library Colo Coll 1021 N Cascade Ave Colorado Springs CO 80903 Office Phone: 719-389-6662.

GREGORY, HENRY D., JR., real estate company executive; Exec. v.p. fgn. indsl. devel. LJ Hooker, 1984—89; pres., CEO Indsl. Devel. Internat. (IDI) Svcs. Group, Inc., Atlanta, 1989—. Office: IDI Corp Monarch Tower Ste 1500 3424 Peachtree Rd NE Atlanta GA 30326

GREGORY, JACKIE SUE, critical care nurse; b. Amarillo Potter County, Tex., Nov. 26, 1946; d. Albert Ray and Rosa Inez (Bryson) Horner; children: Larry, Paula, Justin. BSN, West Tex. State U., 1989; MSN, West Tex. A&M U., 1997. RN, Tex., Okla.; cert. FNP. Staff nurse vascular ICU Baylor U. Med. Ctr., Dallas, 1991-93; adminstr. Assocs. Home Health Inc., Jacksonville, Tex., 1994-95, Angel Home Health Inc., Malakoff, Tex., 1995-96; charge nurse, case mgr. South Plains Health Provider, Amarillo, Tex., 1996-97, Coalition of Health Svcs, Inc., 1997-99, Cmty. Neighborhood Clinic, 1999-2001; HIV coord. Dallas County Inmate Health Svcs., 2001—. Clin. instr. Cameron U., Lawton, Okla., 1990-93; part-time PCP Spl. Health Resources of Est Tex., 2002--. Contbr. articles to profl. jours. Vol. hospice program Vis. Nurse Assn., 1989-90. USPHS scholar, 1989. Mem. AACN, ANA, Am. Acad. Nurse Practitioners, Tex. Nurse Practitioners, Panhandle Nurse Practitioners, Okla. Nurses Assn., Sigma Theta Tau.

GREGORY, JAMES ALEXANDER, editor, writer, film producer; b. Marshall, Mich., Apr. 11, 1930; s. Alexander and Chrissoula (Shoupilla) Gregory; life ptnr. Mayer Olortegui; children: Ben Tea, Robert Nuñez, Jim Davidson, Daniel G. B of English with honors, U. Mich., 1951, MA in English, 1952. Publicist Columbia Pictures, N.Y.C., 1956; press book editor-in-chief RKO Radio Pictures, N.Y.C., 1956—57; editor-in-chief Movieland and TV Time, N.Y.C., 1958—61; West Coast editor, writer Silver Screen, Screenland, Movieland and TV Time, L.A., 1960—69; staff reporter Nat. Enquirer, 1974—76, freelance writer, 1976—80; editor, writer Larry Flynt Publ., L.A., 1980—83; editor Landscape and Irrigation, Van Nuys, Calif.; sr. editor Arbor Age, 1984—91, ret., 1992. Author: David David David, 1972, The Soul of the Jackson 5, 1973, Donny!, 1973, Donny and the Osmond Family, 1974, The Lucille Ball Story, 1974; co-author: The Wallaces of Alabama with George Wallace, Jr., 1975; author, editor: The Elvis Presley Story, 1960; prodr.: (films) Flaco and the Wizard of Hugs, Lucy Luvs Flaco. Lt. (j.g.) USNR, 1953-55. Democrat.

GREGORY, JEANNETTE T., publisher, writer; b. Newport News, Va., Sept. 25, 1954; d. Charlie James and Maggie Harris Tyson; m. Eric Gregory, Jan. 17, 1973; children: Derrick, Deitre, Alicia. AA, Rutledge Coll., Charlotte, NC, 1980. Mem. Bell South Advt. and Pub., Charlotte, NC, 1980—95; freelance motivational spkr. Charlotte, 1998—; life skill trainer and facilitator Transformation Ctr., Charlotte, 2000—; pres. Chosen Word Pub., Charlotte, 2000—. Author: (books) The Corridor of My Heart, 2000, Who Am I, 2002; contbr. columns in newspapers. Mentor Youth Network, Charlotte, NC, 2003. Recipient Editors Choice award, 1997. Avocations: writing, music, grandchildren. Office: Chosen Word Publishing Ste 307 1101 Tyvola Charlotte NC 28217

GREGORY, JOSEPH F., art gallery director, art educator; PhD, SUNY, Binghamton. Asst. prof. art history, dept. visual studies Drexel Univ., Phila., and dir., Design Arts Gallery. Office: Drexel Univ Design Arts Gallery 209 Nesbitt Hall 33rd & Market Sts Philadelphia PA 19104 Office Phone: 215-895-2548. Office Fax: 215-895-4917. Business E-Mail: jfg22@drexel.edu, joseph.f.gregory@drexel.edu.*

GREGORY, JOSEPH M., investment company executive; m. Niki Gregory; 5 children. BA, Hofstra U., 1974. Joined as comml. paper trader Lehman Brothers Holdings Inc., 1974, various mgmt. positions, fixed income div., 1980—91, co-head, fixed income divsn., 1991—96, head, global equities divsn., 1996—2000, chief adminstrv. officer, 2000—02, co-COO, 2002—04, pres., COO, 2004—. Bd. trustees The Millbrook Sch.; bd. dirs. The Posse Found., Inc., Dorothy Rodbell Cohen Found. Office: Lehman Brothers Holdings Inc 745 Seventh Ave New York NY 10019

GREGORY, KARL DWIGHT, economics professor, consultant; b. Detroit, Mar. 26, 1931; s. Bertram and Sybil Gregory; m. Tenicia Ann Banks, June 7, 1959; children: Karin Diane, Sheila Therese, Kurt David. BA, Wayne State U., 1952, MA, 1957; PhD, U. Mich., 1962. Fiscal economist Office of Mgmt. and Budget, Washington, 1961-64; prof. Wayne State U., Detroit, 1960-61, 64-68, Oakland U., Rochester, Mich., 1968-96, disting. prof. emeritus, 1996—, ret. Chmn. bd. dirs., CEO Greater Detroit Bidco, Inc., 1990—96, Accord, Inc., Detroit, 1969—71; mem. coun. econ. advisors Gov. Engler of Mich., 1992—96, Gov. Granholmd of Mich., 2003—; cons. UN Devel. Program, Beijing, 1991; chief organizer, dir. First Ind. Nat. Bank Detroit, 1968—81, interim pres., 1980—81; vis. prof. SUNY, Buffalo, 1975; vis. scholar, mem. exec. staff U.S. Congl. Budget Office, Washington, 1975—76. Author (with others): State of Black Michigan, 1984—87, 1991; contbr. articles to publs. Mem. Gov.'s Entrepreneurial Commn., Lansing, Mich., 1984—88, Regional Devel. Initiative S.E. Mich. Coun. Govts., 1990—91, Gov.'s Task Force Tourism, Lansing, 1986—89; bd. dirs. United Way S.E. Mich., Mich. Ctr. High Tech., 1991—95, Detroit Alliance Fair Banking, 1992—2004, Adult Well-Being Svcs., 1999—; mem. Detroit Workforce Devel. Bd., 2002—; trustee Episcopal Diocese of Mich., Detroit, 1981—83, 1984—87, 1990—92. 1st lt. U.S. Army, 1953—56. Recipient Rsch. award, Detroit chpt. NAACP, 1987, Entrepreneurial award, SBA, 1989, Mich. Dept. Commerce, 1992. Mem.: Booker T. Washington Bus. Assn., Nat. Econ. Assn. Avocations: reading, music, photography, computers, travel. Home: 18495 Adrian St Southfield MI 48075-1803 Personal E-mail: gregory_karl@hotmail.com.

GREGORY, MEL HYATT, JR., retired insurance company executive; b. Frankfort, Ky., Mar. 28, 1936; s. Mel Hyatt and Audrey (Fraley) G.; m. Joyce Klein, Sept. 9, 1955; children: Susan Gregory Lawson, Scott, Lisbeth Gregory Olesky. BS, Stetson U., 1958. Mgr., agt. Equitable Life Ins. Co., Louisville, 1959-66, agy. mgr. Dayton, Ohio, 1966-70, Atlanta, 1970-73, v.p. Cin., 1974-77, sr. v.p. N.Y.C., 1978-85, pres. so. ops. Atlanta, 1985-90, exec. v.p. N.Y.C., 1990-93; ret., 1993. Bd. dirs. Stetson U. Sch. Bus. Capt. U.S Army, 1958-62. Mem. Gen. Agts. and Mgrs. (pres. 1966-74), Cherokee Country Club. Republican. Home: 4570 Jett Rd NW Atlanta GA 30327-4562 Personal E-mail: mel_gregory@hotmail.com.

GREGORY, NELSON BRUCE, retired motel owner, retired naval officer; b. Syracuse, N.Y., Aug. 4, 1933; s. Nelson Bruce and Josephine (Sully) G.; m. Bonnie K. Bannowsky, May 2, 1961 (div. 1970); children: Elizabeth Jo, Jennifer Kay; m. Patricia Ann Greenhalgh, Oct. 15, 1977 (div. 1994); children: Peter Ward, Annette Frances, Michael John, Geoffrey Charles. BS, N.Y. Maritime Coll., 1955; postgrad., USN Pilot Tng., Pensacola, Fla., 1955-57; grad., NATO Weapons Sch., Oberammergau, Fed. Republic of Germany, 1966; diploma, Joint Warfare Sch., Salisbury, Eng., 1967, USN Counter Insurgency, Little Creek, Va., 1968, USAF Space Ops., Montgomery, Ala., 1969. Commd. ens. USN, 1955, advanced through grades to lt. comdr., 1964, operational pilot airborne Early Warning Squadron 2 Patuxent River, Md., 1957-60, flight instr. Airborne Early Warning Tng. Unit, 1960-63, command pilot Air Devel. Squadron 6 McMurdo Sound, Antarctica, 1963-64; airspace control officer NATO, Naples, Italy, 1964-68; chief pilot Naval Support Activity, Danang, Vietnam, 1968-69; space intelligence analyst NORAD, Colorado Springs, Colo., 1969-71; operational pilot Electronic Warfare Squadron 33 USN, Norfolk, Va., 1971-74, ops. officer Nat. Parachute Test Range El Centro, Calif., 1974-75, ret., 1975; owner, gen. mgr. Bonneville Motel, Idaho Falls, Idaho, 1975-99; ret., 1999. Bd. dirs. Am. Travel Inns, 1976-78. Newspaper contbr. Decorated Combat Air medals (3) USN; recipient Vietnamese Gallantry Cross Republic of Vietnam, 1969; Gregory Ridge in Antarctica named for him, 1964. Mem. VFW, Ret. Officers Assn. (life), Am. Legion, Heritage Found., Cato Inst., Elks. Republican. Presbyterian. Avocations: yachting, camping, travel. Home: 474 Whittier St # 18 Idaho Falls ID 83401-2632

GREGORY, RALPH J., historian, curator; b. Washington, Mo., Sept. 27, 1909; s. Roy R. Gregory and Rose Virginia Engelhardt; widowed; 1 child, Nancy Rose Gregory Kimball. Curator Washington Hist. Soc., 1959—66, 1998—, Mark Twain Shrine and Mark Twain Boyhood Home, Mo., 1960—75; active Mark Twain Home Bd., Hanibal, 1975—78; pres. Monroe County Hist. Soc., Paris, 1964—75, Phoebe A. Hearst Soc., St. Clair, 1963—88; dir. Boone-Duden Soc., New Melle, 1985—, Warren County Hist. Soc., Warrenton, 1999—2001; pres. Franklin County Hist. Soc., Union, 2003—. Mem. Lewis & Clark Commn. of Missions, Jefferson City, Mo., 1966—70. Author: Mark Twain's First America, 1965, A History of Washington Mo., 1971, Price's Road in Franklin County, 1990, over 200 articles published in science, philosophy, state, and local history. Mem. Preservation Commn. Washington, Mo., 1991—; dir. Park Bd., Marthasville, 1991—. Democrat. Avocations: gardening, walking. Home: 308 E South Marthasville MO 63357 Office: Washington Hist Soc 401 Market St Washington MO 63090

GREGORY, ROBIN N., lawyer; b. Syracuse, NY, Feb. 16, 1956; BS magna cum laude, Syracuse U., 1978; JD, Villanova U., 1981. Bar: NY 1982, US Dist. Ct. So. Dist. NY, US Dist. Ct. Ea. Dist. NY. Asst. dist. atty., Kings County, NY, 1981—85; ptnr. Wilson, Elser, Moskowitz, Edelman & Dicker LLP, NYC. Mem.: Am. Bd. Trial Advocates, Assn. of the Bar of the City of NY. Office: Wilson Elser Moskowitz Edleman & Dicker LLP 23rd Fl 150 E 42nd St New York NY 10017-5639 Office Phone: 212-490-3000 ext. 2650. Office Fax: 212-490-3038. Business E-Mail: gregoryr@wemed.com.

GREGORY, ROGER LEE, federal judge; b. Phila., July 17, 1953; s. George Lee and Fannie Mae (Washington) G.; m. Carla Eugenia Lewis, Sept. 6, 1980; children: Adriene Leigh, Rachel Leigh. BA, Va. State U., 1975; JD, U. Mich., 1978. Bar: Mich. 1978, Va. 1980, US Ct. Appeals (6th cir.) 1978, US Ct. Appeals (4th cir.) 1980. Assoc. atty. Butzel, Long, Gust, Klein & Van Zile, Detroit, 1978-80, Hunton & Williams, Richmond, Va., 1980-82; mng. ptnr., chmn. litigation sec. Wilder & Gregory, Richmond, 1982—2001; judge US Ct. Appeals (4th cir.), Richmond, 2001—. Bd. visitors Va. Commonwealth U., Richmond, 1985-;adj. prof. Va. State U., 1981-1985. Bd. dirs. Indsl. Devel. Authority, Richmond, 1984—, Richmond chpt. YMCA, 1989—. Me. Cen. Va. Legal Aid Soc. (exec. com.), Old Dominion Bar Assn. (pres.), Richmond Bar Assn. (bd. dirs.), Metro C. of C. (bd. dirs. 1989—), Alpha Kappa Mu, Alpha Mu Gamma. Baptist. Office: US Ct Appeals 4th Cir 1000 E Main St Rm 212 Richmond VA 23219*

GREGORY, ROGER THORPE, surgeon, consultant; b. Rocky Mount, N.C., July 17, 1939; s. Richard Henry and Virginia Thorpe Gregory; m. Elizabeth Kjeldsen Kjeldsen, Mar. 25, 1967; 1 child, Roger Thorpe Gregory, Jr. AB in Zoology, Duke U., Durham, N.C., 1961; MD, Med. Coll. Va., 1965. Chief of vascular surgery Ea. Va. Med. Sch., Norfolk, 1995—2000, prof. of surgery, 1995—. Contbr. articles to profl. jours. Maj. U.S. Army, 1970—73, Fort Wainwright, Alaska. Decorated Army Commendation Medal. Mem.: Soc. of Vascular Surgery (mem. 1990—2004), Michael E. DeBakey Internat. Surg. Soc. (pres. 2002—04). Conservative. Christian. Achievements include design of Vascular instrumentation. Avocations: tennis, chip carver, acting, singing, writing. Home: 5008 Lauderdale Ave Virginia Beach VA 23455 Office Phone: 757-363-0267. Home Fax: 757-363-0384. Personal E-mail: okdin@cox.net.

GREGORY, ROSS, retired history educator, author; b. Washington, Ind., Feb. 11, 1933; s. Norrell and Bertha Beatrice (Jones) G.; m. Shirley Ann Heines, Dec. 15, 1961; children: Theresa M., Graham T., Darren M. AB, Ind. U., 1959, MA, 1961, PhD (U. fellow), 1964. Asst. prof. history W.Va. Inst. Tech., Montgomery, 1963-66; asst. prof. history Western Mich. U., Kalamazoo, 1966-69, assoc. prof., 1969-73, prof., 1973—2005; ret., 2005. Author: Walter Hines Page: Ambassador to St. James's, 1970 (Frederick Jackson Turner award), The Origins of American Intervention in the First World War, 1971, America 1941: A Nation at the Crossroads, 1989, Almanacs of American Life: Modern America, 1914-1945, 1995, Almanacs of American Life: Cold War America, 1946-1990, 2003; contbg. author: To Do Good in the World: Woodrow Wilson and America's Mission in Makers of American Diplomacy, 1974, The Domino Theory of Ency. Am. Fgn. Policy, 1978, Wendell Willkie: Hoosier Internationalist, 1992; contbr. articles to profl. jours. Served with AUS, 1954-56. Am. Philos. Soc. grantee, 1967; Western Mich. U. fellow, 1969, 83 Mem. Soc. for Historians of Am. Fgn. Rels. Home: 2812 Romence Rd Portage MI 49024-7851 E-mail: ross.gregory@umich.edu.

GREGORY, SARA SUSAN (SUDIE), musician, singer, lyricist, poet, recording industry executive, sound recording engineer, archivist; b. De-Queen, Ark., June 24, 1952; d. Eugene Cluran Gregory and Maxine Louise Fulton; m. Steven Eugene Thomas, Nov. 18, 1977 (div. Dec. 1, 1995). Student, East Tex. State U., 1964—66, So. Meth. U., 1967—69, U. Okla., 1971, Southeastern Okla. State U., 1972—75, U. Denver, 1974, Oklahoma City U., 1981, San Francisco State U., 1996, U. North Tex.; Master classes in trumpet, Nat. Trumpet Symposium, North Tex. State U. Auditor, payroll, ins. agt. Okla. Employment Svc., Oklahoma City, 1975—80; acct. Steven E. Thomas, CPA, Oklahoma City, 1980—82; musician, audio engr., record prodr. World Evangelism Svcs., Oklahoma City, 1983—94; owner Times Two Records and Pub., Oklahoma City and San Francisco, 1986—94, North Beach Rec., San Francisco, 1990—94; receptionist San Francisco Planning and Urban Rsch., 1996—; audio/video engr. Bill Graham Presents, San Francisco, 1996, archivist, 1996; event staff San Francisco Performing Arts Found., 1996—98, Bay Area Music Awards, 1996—98, Black and White Ball, 1996; publicist Daniel Castro Blues Band, 1996—98; prodr. Kimpton Prodns. Live from the Starlight Room TV show, 1998; hostess Little City & Tavolino Restaurants, 1998; enumerator U.S. Dept. Commerce-Census 2000, 2000; archivist George Tsongas, 2001. Judge No. Calif. Songwriters Assn., San Francisco, 1997; prodr./engr. performance and program com. Upper Grant Ave Fall Art Fair, 2003—. Prodr.: (rec.) Sheer Joy, 1983; prodr., engr., writer, musician: rec. Steve & Sara, 1986, prodr., engr., writer, performer, distbr.: Frontlines, 1988; prodr., engr., writer, performer, distbr.: Songs of the Street, 1992; prodr., engr., writer, performer, distbr.: Streetsinger, 1992, Christmas by the Sea, 1992; author: Collected Lyrics and Poetry, 1999; mem. prodn. crew 150th Anniversary Statehood Celebration, Sacramento, Calif., 1999, audio engr. Trieste Music, North Beach, San Francisco, 2003—, City Lights 50th Anniversary and Landmarking Celebration, 2002, 2003, Tele-Hi Neighborhood Ctr., 2002—, Indonesian Consultate and Telegraph Hill Dwellers Tsunami Relief Benefit, 2005; co-editor: Trieste Music News. Mem. Common Cause, Telegraph Hill Dwellers Assn., San Francisco, 1994—; mem. comm. com. Pioneer Park Project at Coit Tower, San Francisco, 1996—2001, 400 Trees Project Telegraph Hill Dwellers and Friends of the Urban Forest, San Francisco, 1996—98; mem. jazz band S.E. Okla. State U., 1972—75; concert band trumpet soloist Madrigal Singers and Opera Workshop; founder Nat. Campaign for Tolerance, 2005; poll worker presdl. election, 1996, 2000, 2004. Named to, Okla. All Dist. Band, 1965—70, Okla. All-State Band, 1969, 1970; recipient John Philip Sousa award, Broken Bow H.S., 1970, pvt. endowment, Elizabeth Styll Smith, 1983—94. Mem.: LWV, NARAS (staff 1997), Audio Engring. Soc., Music Educators Nat. Conf., Brass Quintet (outstanding brass ensemble 1969—70), Dixieland Combo-SE Okla. Dist. Tchrs., Okla. Music Educator's Conv., Four States Band Masters Conv., 4H Club, Dist. 3 Dem. Club. Democrat. Roman Catholic. Avocations: cooking, sewing, ceramics. Home: PO Box 330522 San Francisco CA 94133 E-mail: sarasgregory@yahoo.com.

GREGORY, SHARON E., neonatal clinical nurse specialist, nurse practitioner; b. San Francisco, Aug. 26, 1955; d. Donald J. and Nadalie S. Goldstein; m. John Karl Gregory, Aug. 31, 1986; 1 child, Leah Nicole. BSN,

U. Fla., 1977; MSN, Emory U., 1985. Cert. CNNP. Staff RN Children's Med. Ctr., Dallas, St. Paul's Hosp., Dallas, Meth. Hosp., Dallas; clin. nurse specialist DeKalb Med. Ctr. Neo-Natal Svcs., Decatur, Ga. Contbr. chapters to books, articles to profl. jours. Mem.: Ga. Assn. Neonatal Nurses, Acad. Neonatal Nursing. Home: 603 Collingwood Dr Decatur GA 30032-1721

GREGORY, SHAWN ALEN, physician, researcher; b. Gallatin, Tenn., Nov. 4, 1971; s. Gerald Alen and Donna Marjorie Gregory; m. Mary Lucia Partin, Aug. 18, 2001. BS, U. Ala., Tuscaloosa, 1994; MD, U. Va., 1998. Diplomate Am. Bd. Internal Medicine, in nuc. cardiology Am. Bd. Nuc. Cardiology. Instr. of medicine U. Ala. Sch. of Medicine, Birmingham, Ala., 2001—02; rsch. fellow in medicine Harvard Med. Sch., Boston, 2002—; fellow in cardiology Mass. Gen. Hosp., Boston, 2002—; scholar in clin. sci. Harvard Med. Sch., Boston, 2004—. Physician Mass. Gen. Hosp., Boston, 2002—, U. Ala. Hosp., Birmingham, 1998—2002. Contbr. articles pub. to profl. jour., chapters to books. Grantee Scholars in Clin. Sci. Program, Harvard Med. Sch., 2004-2006; scholar Presdl. scholar, U. Ala., 1990-1994; Nat. Rsch. Svc. awardee, NIH, 2004-2006, Teresa Thomas scholar, U. Va. Sch. of Medicine, 1998, Lawson scholar, 1997. Mem.: Paul Dudley White Soc. of Mass. Gen. Hosp., ACP/Am. Soc. Internal Medicine (assoc.), Am. Coll. Cardiology (assoc.), Phi Beta Kappa, Alpha Omega Alpha, Lambda Chi Alpha. Achievements include research in non-invasive imaging And clin. cardiovascular disease. Avocations: travel, history. Office: Mass Gen Hosp-Yawkey 5800 55 Fruit St Boston MA 02114 Office Phone: 617-726-2677.

GREGORY, STEPHANIE ANN, hematologist, educator; b. Vineland, N.J., June 23, 1940; d. Andonetta Gregory; m. Sheldon Chertow; children: Elizabeth Chertow, Jennifer Chertow, Daniel Chertow, Erica Chertow. BS cum laude, Boston Coll., 1961; MD cum laude, Med. Coll. Pa., 1965. Diplomate Am. Bd. Internal Medicine, subspecialty hematology, Am. Bd. Hematology. Intern in internal medicine Presbyn.-St. Luke's Hosp., Chgo., 1965-66, resident in internal medicine, 1966-68, fellow in hematology, 1969—72; chief resident Presbyn.-St. Lukes Hosp., Chgo., 1968-69; chief spl. morphology lab. sect. hematology Rush-Presbyn.-St. Luke's Med. Ctr., Chgo., 1972-76, dir. sect. hematology and stem cell divsn. hematology/oncology, 1994—, Elodia Kehm prof. medicine, dir. hematology and stem cell transplantation, 1995—; from asst. prof. medicine to assoc. prof. medicine Rush Med. Coll., Chgo., 1972-86, prof. medicine, 1986—; adminstr., dir., cons. Rush U. Medical Ctr., Chgo., 1985—, sr. attending physician, 1982—, dir. sect. hematology & stem cell transplant divsn. hematology, 2004—. Coord. continuing edn. sect. hematology Rush-Presbyn.-St. Luke's Med. Ctr., Chgo., 1970-76, dir. transfusion therapy svc. sect. hematology, 1972-76, asst. chmn. dept. medicine, 1972-76, clin. dir. Sheridan Rd. Pavilion, 1976-77, acting dir. sect. clin. hematology, 1980-81, assoc. dir. sect. hematology, 1993-94, asst. chairperson dept. medicine, 1993-94; co-dir. Lymphoma Ctr., Rush Univ Medical Ctr., Chgo., 1992—; mem. UN Security Coun. Commn. Experts, 1994; mem. med. adv. bd. Leukemia Rsch. Found., 1996—, Leukemia/Lymphoma Soc. Am., Lymphoma Rsch. Found. Mentor Lean on Me support group for young adults with cancer Rush Univ. Medical Ctr., Chgo., 1992—. Recipient award Am. Women's Med. Assn., 1965, William B. Peck Sci. award for rsch. in hematopoietic stem cell studies Sci. Assembly of Interstate Postgrad. Med. Assn., 1973, Outstanding Alumni award MCP-Hahneman Med. Sch., 1998; grantee Schweppe Found. Rsch., 1969-72, NIH tng. grantee Nat. Heart, Lung and Blood Inst., 1974-79; Schweppe fellow, 1969-72. Fellow ACP (mem. Ill. coun. 1994—, mentor physician mems. for advancement to fellowship designation ann. meeting 1996, Ill. Laureate award 1996); mem. AMA, Internat. Soc. Hematology (Inter-Am. divsn.), Internat. Soc. Exptl. Hematology (charter), Leukemia Soc. Am. (bd. trustees Ill. chpt. 1987—, chmn. patient aid com. Ill. chpt. 1988-90, treas. Ill. chpt. 1992-93, chairperson patient fin. aid com. Ill. chpt. 1992—, v.p. Ill. chpt. 1991-94, mem. med. adv. bd. Ill. chpt. 1996—), Am. Soc. Clin. Oncology, Am. Soc. Hematology, Cell Proliferation Soc., Ea. Coop. Oncology Group, Inst. Medicine Chgo., Chgo. Soc. Internal Medicine (exec. com. 1992—, sec.-treas. 1992-93, v.p. 1993-94, pres. 1994-95), Aplastic Anemia Found. Am. (hon. bd. trustees 1988—), Mark H. Lepper M.D. Soc. Tchrs. (elected), Alpha Omega Alpha, Sigma Xi. Office: Rush Univ Medical Ctr 1725 W Harrison St Ste 834 Chicago IL 60612-3861 Office Phone: 312-942-5982. Business E-Mail: stephanie-gregory@rush.edu.

GREGORY, TERENCE VAN BUREN, clergyman; b. Atlanta, Nov. 29, 1950; s. Vic Odell and Evelyn Ora (Gardner) G.; m. Leslie Christine Lytle, July 29, 1972; children: Joshua Adam, Rachel Leigh, Matthew Jordan. BA in Bible, Antioch Bapt. Coll., 1973; MRE, Mid-Am. Bapt. Theol. Sem., 1975. Ordained to ministry So. Bapt. Conv., 1972; lic. min. Youth min. 1st Bapt. Ch., Minden, La., 1976-77, Spencer Meml. Bapt. Ch., Tampa, Fla., 1977-80; pastor Crestview Bapt. Ch., Lakeland, Fla., 1980-83; min. pastoral care 1st Bapt. Ch., Lakeland, 1983-87; pastor Seminole Bapt. Ch., Tallahassee, 1987—. Del., messenger So. Bapt. Conv., Atlanta, 1990-91, 95, 99. Mem. Fla. Bapt. Assn. (mem. exec. com., evangelism com. 1992-94, nominating com. 1990-91, keynote speaker ann. mtg. 1994, 99). Republican. Office: Seminole Bapt Ch 2280 W Mission Rd Tallahassee FL 32304-2627 Office Phone: 850-562-8069. E-mail: tgregory55@comcast.net.

GREGORY, THOMAS BRADFORD, mathematics professor; b. Traverse City, Mich., Dec. 13, 1944; s. Philip Henry and Rhoda Winslow (Hathaway) G.; m. Deirdre Dianne Mason, July 15, 1995. *Father, Philip Henry Gregory, received a BS from Bowdoin College in 1926, a Bachelor of Sacred Theology from Yale Divinity School in 1935, and an MA from Oberlin College in 1937. A registered pharmacist, he became a minister, serving Baptist, Congregational and Presbyterian churches in Vermont, Massachusetts, Michigan and Ohio. Mother, Rhoda Winslow Hathaway, a member of the Massachusetts Society of Mayflower Descendants, studied at Massachusetts School of Art. Wife Deirdre Dianne Mason received a BSEd from Ashland College in 1981 and an MEd in 1989. She received an MS from Ohio State University in 1986 and an MEd from the University of Dayton in 1993. She is the former president, Mansfield School Employees Association and is currently guidance counselor, Mansfield City Schools.* BA, Oberlin (Ohio) Coll., 1967; MA, Yale U., 1969, M of Philosophy, 1975, PhD, 1977. Lectr. Ohio State U., Mansfield, 1977-78, asst. prof. math., 1978-84, assoc. prof. math., 1984—, pres. faculty, 2001—02. Reviewer: Math. Revs., 1984—; contbr. articles to profl. jours. Active Mansfield (Ohio) Symphony Chorus, 1977—, Presbytery Youth Ministries Com., New Philadelphia, Ohio, 1980-87, Ohio State U. Cmty. Singers, Mansfield, 1985—; mem. Presbytery Bibl. Authority task force, 1994-95; bd. dirs. Lay Acad. Religion, Wooster (Ohio) Coll., 1997—; commd. lay min. Presbytery of Muskingum Valley, New Philadelphia, Ohio, 1998—; mem. Presbytery Com. on Ministry, 2004-. Comdr. USNR, 1969-96. Fellow NSF, Washington, 1967; hon. fellow U. Wis., Madison, 1987-88, 92. Fellow Phi Beta Kappa; mem. Am. Math. Soc. (translator 1974-82), Ohio Coun. Tchrs. Math., Am. Soc. Naval Engrs., Res. Officers Assn., Naval Res. Assn., Navy League, Sigma Xi. Avocations: classical piano, singing. Home: 411 Overlook Rd Mansfield OH 44907-1533 Office: Ohio State U 1680 University Dr # O-15 Mansfield OH 44906-1547 Office Phone: 419-755-4247. Business E-Mail: tgregory@math.ohio-state.edu.

GREGORY, VALISKA, writer; b. Chgo., Nov. 3, 1940; d. Andrej and Stephania (Lascik) Valiska; m. Marshall W. Gregory, Aug. 18, 1962; children: Melissa, Holly. BA cum laude, Ind. Ctrl. Coll., 1962; MA, Univ. Chgo., 1966; postgrad., Vassar Inst. Pub. Writing, 1984, Simmons Coll., 1986. Music and drama tchr. White Oak Elem. Sch., Whiting, Ind., 1962-64; tchr. Oak Lawn (Ill.) Meml. H.S., 1965-68; lectr. English U. Wis., Milw., 1968-74; adj. prof. English U. Indpls., 1974-83, Butler U., Indpls., 1983-85, writer-in-residence, 1993—; fellow Butler Writer's Studio, 1989-92. Founding dir. Butler U. Midwinter Children's Litf. Conf., 1989—; spkr., workshop leader schs., libr., confs., 1993—. Author: Sunny Side Up, 1986 (Chickadee Mag. Book of Month award 1986), Terribly Wonderful, 1986 (Grandparent's Mag. Best Book award 1986), The Oatmeal Cookie, 1987 (Best of Best Book list Chgo. Sun-Times), Riddle Soup, 1987 (Best of Best Book list Chgo. Sun-Times), Through the Mickle Woods (named Pick of List Am. Booksellers Assn. 1992, Parent's Choice award, 1992; State Ind. Read Aioud-List 1993), Happy Burpday, Maggie McDougal!, 1992 (State Ind. Read-aloud List 1993), Babysitting for Benjamin (Parent's Choice Honor award 1993), Kate's Giants, 1995, Loooking for Angels, 1996, (named Picked of the List Am. Book Sellers Assn., 1996), When Stories Fell Like Shooting Stars, 1996, (Family Circle Mag. Critics Choice, 1996), A Valentine for Norman Noggs, 1999, Shirley's Wonderful Baby, 2002. Recipient Ill. Wesleyan U. Poetry award, 1982, hon. mention Billee Murray Denny Nat. Poetry Award Bilee Murray Denny Poetry Found., 1982, Hudelson award Children's Fiction Work-In-Progress, 1982, Artistic Excellence and Achievement award State Art Treasure Arts Ind., 1989; Individual Artist Master fellow Ind. Arts Commn. and Nat. Endowment for Arts, 1986. Mem. AAUW (Creative Writer's pres. 1984-86), Author's Guild, Authors League Am., Soc. Children's Book Writers and Illustrators, Nat. Book Critic's Circle, Children's Reading Round Table, Soc. Midland Authors. Democrat. Office: Butler U 4600 Sunset Ave Indianapolis IN 46208-3487

GREGORY, WILLIAM ROGER, real estate company executive; BS in Bus. Adminstrn., La. Coll. CPA Tex., La. Sr. mgr. comml. svcs. group Arthur Andersen LLP, 1994—2002; sr. v.p., CFO PM Realty Group, Houston, 2002—. Trustee devel. coun. La. Coll. Mem.: R-Club (pres.). Office: PM Realty Group Ste 1000 910 Travis St Houston TX 77002

GREGORY, WILTON D., archbishop; b. Chgo., Dec. 7, 1947; s. Wilton and Ethel Duncan Gregory. Student, Niles Coll., Loyola U., Chgo., St. Mary of Lake Sem., Mundelein, Ill.; PhD in Sacred Liturgy, Pontifical Liturgical Inst., Sant'Anselmo, Rome, 1980. Ordained priest Roman Cath. Ch., 1973; assoc. pastor Our Lady of Perpetual Help Parish, Glenview, Ill.; mem. faculty St. Mary of the Lake Sem.; master of ceremonies to Cardinals Cody and Bernardin; elevated to bishop Roman Cath. Ch., 1983; aux. bishop Archdiocese of Chgo., 1983—94; bishop Diocese of Belleville, 1994—2005; archbishop Archdiocese of Atlanta, 2005—. Avocations: travel, music, racquetball, golf. Office: Archdiocese of Atlanta 680 W Peachtree St NW Atlanta GA 30308 Office Phone: 404-888-7802.*

GREGORY, YVONNE ELIZABETH HEYNING, interior designer; b. The Hague, The Netherlands, Apr. 2, 1952; arrived in U.S., 1953, naturalized, 1966; d. Joan Marinus Heyning and Johanna Alving; m. Hugh Martin Smith, Apr. 24, 1976 (div. Jan. 1990); 1 child, Erica Renee Smith; m. Walker Shelton Gregory, Aug. 8, 1992. AA, El Camino Coll., 1974; student, Harbor Coll., San Pedro, Calif., 1974-76, Torrance (Calif.) Art Ctr., 1976-79. Owner, designer HM Smith Constrn., San Pedro, Calif., 1974—90, San Pedro Renaissance Gallery, 1983—88, Nuhome Designs, Mt. Pleasant, SC, 1989—, Comml. Designs, Mt. Pleasant, 1997—2003. Bd. dirs. Wild Dunes (S.C.) Cmty. Archtl. Rev. Bd., 1998-2001; v.p. Leads for Women, San Pedro, 1985-88. Recipient Best Model Home Merchandising award Charleston (S.C.) Homebuilders, Best Lobby Remodel award Clear Channel Comm., Charleston, 1999. Mem. Charleston Trident Homebuilders Assn., Am. Soc. Interior Designers, Internat. Furnishings and Design Assn., BBB, S.C. Real Estate Commn., The Gibbes Art Mus. Democrat. Avocations: painting, reading, craft work, art work, jewelry making. Office: 3036 Intracoastal View Dr Mount Pleasant SC 29466-9022 Office Phone: 843-881-1597.

GREGORYANZ, EUGENE, physicist, researcher; s. Andronik and Rimma Gregoryanz; life ptnr. Chrystele Sanloup; 1 child, Philipp. Diploma in Physics, Moscow State U., Russia, 1989; PhD, Meml. U. Nfld., St. John's, 1998. Rsch. scientist Carnegie Instn., Washington, 1998—2001, sr. rsch. scientist, 2002—. Vis. scientist U. de Marie et Pierre Curie, Paris, 2001—02. Contbr. scientific papers. Fellow, U. de Marrie et Pierre Curie, 2002. Achievements include pioneering research in high pressure physics. Office: Carnegie Inst Washington 5251 Broad Branch Rd NW Washington DC 20015 Office Phone: +1(202)-478-8953. Office Fax: +1(202)-478-8901.

GREGORY-GOODRUM, ELLNA KAY, educator, artist; b. Houston, Oct. 3, 1943; d. A. N. and Harriet (Christensen) Gregory; m. Craig R. Goodrum, Aug. 11, 1983; 1 child, Emily K. BFA, U. Okla., 1965; MFA, North Tex. State U., 1979. Tchr., Dallas Ind. Schs., 1965-85; instr. art Richland Coll., Dallas, 1981—; lectr. in field; group exhibits include: Watercolor Soc. of Ala., 1979, Clifford Gallery, Dallas, 1982-83; Nat. Watercolor Soc., 1985, 87, 88, San Diego Watercolor Soc., 1985, Edith Baker Gallery, 1986, 87, Women and Watercolor, Transco. Energy Ctr., Houston, 1988, Watercolor U.S.A., 1988, Rocky Mountain Nat. Watermedia, 1988, Springfield Art Mus.; works represented in permament collections: Rockwell Internat., Brown Found. and Cons., Atlantic Richfield, Renaissance Ctr., Detroit, Southwestern Watercolor Soc. (mem.). Recipient Cash awards Tex. Watercolor Soc., 1978, Dallas Art Mus., 1978, So. Watercolor Soc., 1979. Mem. Pastel Soc. Am. (best abstract 1979, Mixed Media award 1987), Pastel Soc. S.W. (2d award 1987), Coll. Art Assn., Nat. Watercolor Soc., Tex. Watercolor Soc., Pastel Soc., Women's Caucus on Art. Methodist. Home: 7214 Lane Park Dr Dallas TX 75225-2454

GREGOV, MARIA IRMA POTT, elementary school educator; b. Ruma, Srem, Yugoslavia, Dec. 5, 1932; arrived in U.S., 1950; d. Adam and Theresia (Kuppek) Pott; m. Slavko, July 7, 1964; children: Slavko Stephan Joseph, Elizabeth Rose, Maria Louise, Antonio Rudolf. BS in Edn., Loyola U., Chgo., 1969, MEd, 1977. Lic. elem. and high sch. tchr. Tchr. 4th grade St. Joseph's Elem. Sch., Conway, Ark., 1953-55, tchr. 1st and 2d grades, 1955-57, tchr. 1st grade Nokomis, Ill., 1957-58; tchr. 4th grade St. Mary's Grade Sch., Herrin, Ill., 1958-59; tchr. 5th and 6th grades St. Joseph's Sch., Cobden, Ill., 1959-60; tchr. 4th grade St. Jerome Elem. Sch., Chgo., 1960-64; tchr. 3d and 4th grades St. Cecilia's Sch. # 57, Bartelso, Ill., 1964-65; tchr. 4th grade Wesclin Sch. Dist. # 3, Trenton, Ill., 1965-93; prin. St. Anthony Sch., Beckemeyer, Ill., 1993-94; substitute tchr. Ill., 1994—. Pres Mater Dei Mothers & Friends, Breese, Ill., 1990-91; treas. St. Judes Sch., Aviston, Ill., 1987-88. Active Mater Dei PTA. Recipient Cert. of Achievement, Office of Edn., Diocese of Belleville, Ill., 1980-81, Catechist cert., 1985, Catechist Cert. for Faithful Svc. Pastoral Assoc., New Baden, Ill., 1987-88. Mem. NEA, ASCD, ILTAWL Reading Assn., Ill. Edn. Assn., Altar Sodality St. George, Ret. Tchrs. Assn. Roman Catholic. Home: 412 E Oak St New Baden IL 62265-1012 Personal E-mail: kuppek@hotmail.com.

GREHAN, KEVIN J., lawyer; b. Mt. Kisco, NY, Jan. 5, 1956; BA summa cum laude, Fordham Coll., 1978; JD, Columbia Univ., 1981. Bar: NY 1984. Assoc. Cravath Swaine & Moore LLP, NYC, 1981—88, ptnr., corp., 1988—. Trustee Convent of the Sacred Heart. Mem.: ABA, Assn. of Bar of City of NY, NY State Bar Assn. Office: Cravath Swaine & Moore LLP Worldwide Plz 825 Eighth Ave New York NY 10019-7475 Office Phone: 212-474-1490. Office Fax: 212-474-3700. Business E-Mail: krehan@cravath.com.

GREIDER, CAROL WIDNEY, molecular biology educator; b. San Diego, Apr. 15, 1961; BA in Biology, U. Calif., Santa Barbara, 1983; PhD in Molecular Biology, U. Calif., Berkeley, 1987. Fellow Cold Spring Harbor (N.Y.) Lab., 1988-90, asst. investigator, 1990-92, assoc. staff investigator, 1992-94, investigator, 1994-97; assoc. prof. dept. molecular biology and genetics, Johns Hopkins U. Sch. Medicine, Balt., 1997—99, prof., 1999—2002, acting dir., 2002—03, Daniel Nathans prof. and dir., 2003—; prof., dept. oncology Johns Hopkins U. Sch. Medicine, Balt., 1999—. Contbr. numerous articles, revs., book chpts. Regents scholar U. Calif., 1981, Pew Biomed. Scis. scholar; recipient Allied Signal Outstanding Project award, 1992, Gertrude Elion Cancer Rsch. award Am. Assn. Cancer Rsch., 1994, Cornelius Rhoads award, 1996, Glenn Found. award Am. Assn. Cell Biology, 1995, Schering-Plough Sci. Achievement award, 1997, Ellison Medical Found. Sr. Scholar award, 1998, Gairdner Found. award 1998, Passano Found. award 1999, Rosenstiel award 1999, Harvey Soc. Lecture, 2000, Richard Lounsbery award, 2003. Mem. Phi Beta Kappa. Elected mem., Nat. Acad. Sciences, 2003, fellow, Am. Acad. Arts and Sciences, 2003. Office: Johns Hopkins U Sch Med 617 Hunterian Bldg 725 N Wolfe St Baltimore MD 21205-2105

GREIF, AVNER, economics professor; b. 1955; m. Estee; 3 children. BA, Tel Aviv U., 1981, MA, 1985, Northwestern U., 1988, PhD, 1989. Asst. prof., dept. of econ. Stanford U., Calif., 1989—94, assoc. prof., dept. of econ., 1994—98, assoc. prof., dept. of hist., 1995, prof., dept. of econ., 1999—, Bowman Family Endowed Prof., Humanities & Sci., 2001—. Visiting prof. Tel Aviv U., 1993, 95, 97, 2000, 02, U. of Tokyo, 1993. Author: Genoa and the Mghribi Traders; Historical and Comparative Institutional Analysis, 1998; contbr. articles to profl. jours. MacArthur fellow John D. and Catherine T. MacArthur Found., 1998 Fellow, Am. Acad. Arts & Sci.; Mem. Am. Econs. Assn., ASSHA, EHA, Cliometrics Soc. Achievements include research in economic history; use of game theory and other modelling techniques to demonstrate the connection of random beliefs, institutions and social ties to cultural norms of trust and reciprocity in order to understand the conditions leading to social conflict and cooperation. Office: Stanford U Econs Dept Ralph Candan Econs Bldg Stanford CA 94305-6072 E-mail: avner@leland.stanford.edu.*

GREIF, ROBERT, mechanical engineering educator; b. N.Y.C., Jan. 17, 1938; s. Harry and Anne (Reiter) G.; m. Joyce Ambrose; children: Jessica, Andrew. BSME, NYU, 1958; SM, Harvard U., 1959, PhD, 1963. Registered profl. engr., Mass. Staff scientist Missile Systems div., Avco Corp., Wilmington, Mass., 1963-65, sr. staff scientist, 1965-67; asst. prof. mech. engring. Tufts U., Medford, Mass., 1967-70, assoc. prof., 1970-78, prof., 1978—, chmn. dept. mech. engring., 1981-89. Cons. Stone & Webster, Boston, 1971-78, U.S. Dept. Transp., Cambridge, Mass., 1977—; vis. scholar Harvard U., Cambridge, 1981; vis. research fellow U. Sussex, Eng., 1974; sr. rsch. assoc. NASA Langley Rsch. Ctr., 1988. Fellow AIAA (assoc.), ASME; mem. AAUP. Office: Tufts U Dept Mech Engring 200 College Ave Anderson Hall Medford MA 02155 Office Phone: 617-627-3238. Business E-Mail: robert.greif@tufts.edu.

GREIF, TONI ANNE, mortgage banker; b. N.Y.C., June 2, 1954; d. Murray W. and Adele (Buchsbaum) G. BA in Psychology, Fairfield U., 1976; MBA, U. Conn., 1981; MA in Human and Orgnl. Devel., The Fielding Inst., 1996. Various positions to asst. auditor Conn. Bank and Trust Co., N.A., Norwalk, 1972-76; various positions including br. mgr. Old Greenwich br. People's Bank, Bridgeport, Conn., 1976, asst. v.p., 1983-85; exec. v.p. Williamsburg Mortgage Corp., Greenwich; sr. v.p. Bank of Darien, Conn., 1985-87; founder, owner, pres., chief operating officer Sound Beach Fin. Corp., Riverside, Conn.; co-founder, prin. Parallel Comml. Capital-Con./Westchester LLC, Riverside. Ad hoc prof. real estate fin. Norwalk (Conn.) C.C.; ad hoc prof. New Eng. Sch. Banking, Williams Coll. Former bd. dirs. United Way Greenwich; mem. adv. bd. Youth Shelter; past pres. Norwalk Cmty.-Tech. Coll. Found. Bd.; former mem. bd. dirs. S.W. Fairfield County chpt. Am. Cancr Soc.; former mem. adv. coun. Fairfield County Coop. Found. Recipient Disting. Svc. award Greenwich Jaycees, 1981, Outstanding Personal Achievement Alumni merit award Fairfield U., 1985, Bravo award YMCA/Town of Greenwich, 1988. Mem. Am. Mgmt. Assn., Greenwich Bd. Realtors, Stamford Bd. Realtors, Women in Mgmt. (bd. dirs., past pres., Outstanding Recognition award 1992), Kiwanis (bd. dirs., chmn. cmty. devel. com.). Avocation: baseball memorabilia. Office: Sound Beach Fin Corp 1171 E Putnam Ave Ste 4 Riverside CT 06878-1433

GREIFELD, ROBERT A., stock exchange executive; BA Eng., Iona Coll., 1979; MBA, NYU, Stern Sch. of Bus., 1986. Pres. and chief op. officer Automated Securities Clearance, Inc., 1991—99; serves Bd. of Knight Securities, 1993; ECN Automated Securities Clearance, Inc., 1998; v.p. Sunguard Data Sys. Inc. and group CEO, Sunguard Brokerage Sys., 1999—2000; sr. v.p. Sunguard Data Sys., Inc., 2000—02; pres., CEO The Nasdaq Stock Market, Inc., NYC, 2003—. Chmn. USA Track & Field Found., 2004—. Office: The Nasdaq Stock Market Inc 1 Liberty Plz #49 New York NY 10006-1404*

GREIFINGER, DAVID ROSS, lawyer; b. L.A., June 25, 1957; s. Carl and Phyllis (Stoliar) G. BS in Physics, UCLA, 1979; JD, Loyola U., 1982. Bar: Calif. 1982, U.S. Dist. Ct. (cen. dist.) Calif. 1983, U.S. Ct. Appeals (9th cir.) 1985. V.p., gen. counsel Athletics Internat. Inc., L.A., 1985—. Mem. Santa Monica Track Club (v.p. 1975—), USA Track & Field (bd. dirs. 1980-96, counsel to bd. 1999—). Avocation: long distance running. Office: 1801 Ocean Park Blvd Apt 201 Santa Monica CA 90405-4924 Office Phone: 310-452-7923.

GREIG, BRIAN STROTHER, lawyer; b. Austin, Tex., Apr. 10, 1950; s. Ben Wayne Greig and Virginia Ann (Strother) Higgins; m. Jane Ann Sentilles, June 17, 1972; children: Travis Darden, Grace Hanna. BA, Washington and Lee U., 1972; JD, U. Tex., 1975. Bar: Tex. 1975, U.S. Dist. Ct. (ea. dist.) Tex. 1976, U.S. Ct. Appeals (5th cir.) 1976, U.S. Dist. Ct. (so. dist.) Tex. 1977, U.S. Dist. Ct. (we. dist.) Tex. 1980, U.S. Supreme Ct. 1980, U.S. DIst. Ct. (no. dist.) Tex. 1984, U.S. Ct. Appeals (11th cir.) 1984. Law clk. to chief judge U.S. Dist. Ct., Beaumont, Tex., 1975-76; sr. ptnr. Fulbright & Jaworski L.L.P., Austin, 1976—, mem. policy com., 2004—. Mem. Austin Tomorrow On-Going Goals Assembly Com., 1981; pres. Austin Mgmt. Lawyers Forum, 1987, 93. Editor-in-chief Tex. Assn. Bus. Employment Law Handbook; mem. editl. bd. Tex. Labor Letter, 1994-2001. Pres. Austin Lawyers and Accts. for Arts, 1981; trustee Laguna Gloria Art Mus., Austin, 1983-91, pres., 1989-90, chmn., 1990-91; bd. dirs. Zachary Scott Theater Ctr., Austin, 1981; mem. devel. bd. Inst. Texan Cultures, 1991-98; trustee Westminster Manor Health Facilities Corp. of Travis County, Tex., 1991-96, sec., 1995-96; trustee St. Stephen's Episcopal Sch., 1995-2001; pres. Austin Mus. Art, 1991-92, trustee, 1991-93; bd. dirs. The Capital of Tex. Pub. Telecomms. Coun., Inc. (KLRU-TV), 2001—. Fellow Tex. Bar Found. (life), Am. Coll. Labor and Employment Lawyers; mem. ABA, FBA, Am. Arbitration Assn. (employment adv. coun. 1995—), Tex. Bar Assn., Travis County Bar Assn., Tex. Commn. on Human Rights (chmn.'s task force), Tex. Assn. Bus. (bd. dirs. 2000—), Tarry House Club, Headliners Club (trustee 1998—, pres.-elect 2005), Austin Assembly, Pan Tex. Assembly. Methodist. Avocations: hunting, fishing. Office: Fulbright & Jaworski LLP 600 Congress Ave Ste 2400 Austin TX 78701-3271 Office Phone: 512-536-4510. Business E-Mail: bgreig@fulbright.com.

GREIG, WILLIAM TABER, II, publishing company executive; b. Mpls., Apr. 16, 1924; s. William Taber and Margaret Naomi (Buckbee) G.; m. Doris Jane Walters, June 23, 1951; children: Kathryn Ann Greig Rowland, William Taber, III, Gary Stanley, Doris Jane. B.Arch., U. Minn., 1945. Jr. exec. Bur. Engraving, Mpls., 1946-48; partner, mgr. Praise Book Publns., Mound, Minn., 1948-50; v.p., exec. v.p., gen. mgr. Gospel Light Publs., 1950-76, pres., owner Ventura, Calif., 1976—, chmn., 1983—. Bd. dirs. Lighthouse Ptnrs. Bookstores; founder, chmn., Gospel Light Worldwide, 2000-; founder, chmn. bd. Credo Pub., St. Petersburg, Russia. Ruling elder Presbyn. Ch. (U.S.A.); co-founder Minn. Sunday Sch. Assn., 1953; bd. dirs., chmn. Joy of Living Bible Studies, 1978—; trustee Concerts of Prayer Internat., 1988—; chmn. bd. dirs. John M. Perkins Found. for Christian Cmty. Devel., Jackson, Miss. Lt. (j.g.) USNR, 1943-46. Mem. Evang. Christian Pubs. Assn. (co-founder 1974, bd. dirs., pres. 1981-83) Clubs: Tower. Republican. Home: 347 Lupine Way Ventura CA 93001-2201 Office: Gospel Light Publs 1957 Eastman Ave Ventura CA 93003 Office Phone: 805-644-9721 x1212.

GREIGG, CATHRYN O., music educator, musician; b. Sioux City, Iowa, Oct. 15, 1941; d. Gerald Niles Thomson and Honsen Louise Phillips; m. Stanley Lloyd Greigg, June 26, 1965; children: Valerie Dugan, Heather, Cathryn Greigg-Murphy. Student, Oberlin Coll., 1960—61; MusB cum laude in Music Edn., Morningside Coll., 1964; MusM, Cath. U. Am., 1989. Music tchr. Maurice-Orange City (Iowa) Schs., 1960—61, 1964—65; piano instr. Bethesda, Md., 1965—; music dir. Grace Luth. Ch., Washington, 1974—, organist, 1974—. Mem.: Am. Guild Organists, Montgomery County Music Tchrs., Md. State Music Tchrs., Congl. Club. Democrat.

GREILSHEIMER, JAMES GANS, lawyer; b. N.Y.C., Oct. 14, 1937; s. Jerome J. and Lillian (Gans) G.; m. Louise B. Steiner, Aug. 11, 1974; children: Lauren, Julie, Michael, Jeremy. AB cum laude, Princeton U., 1959; LLB, Harvard U., 1962. Bar: N.Y. 1963, D.C. 1969. Asst. U.S. atty. So. Dist. N.Y., 1963-68; litigating asst. corp. counsel City of N.Y., 1974-77, 1st asst. corp. counsel, 1978-80; ptnr. Blank Rome LLP and predecessor firms, N.Y.C., 1993—. Mediator mediation program U.S. Dist. Ct. (so. dist.) N.Y., 1993—. Mem., sec. N.Y.C. Charter Rev. Commn., 1982-83; pres. N.Y. chpt. Am. Jewish Com., 1981-84; v.p. Jewish Cmty. Rels. Coun. N.Y., 1981-85, bd. dirs., 1995-2001; bd. dirs. Com. on Decent Unbiased Campaign Tactics, 1983-93, Non-profit Coordinating Com., N.Y., 1985—, Vol. Cons. Group, Inc., 1986—; v.p., bd. dirs. Fund for Pub. Schs., Inc., 1986-91, pres., 1992-2002; mem. Citizens Budget Commn., Inc., 1991-93. Mem.: Assn. Bar of City of N.Y. (mcpl. affairs com. 1979—81, govt. ethics com. 1990—98, com. on condemnation and tax certiorari 1993—95, 2001—), N.Y. County Lawyers Assn. (bd. dirs. 1981—87, chmn. fed. cts. com. 1977—80, spl. com. on condemnation 1990—), N.Y. State Bar Assn. (spl. com. on cts. and cmty. 1975—81). Office: Blank Rome LLP 405 Lexington Ave New York NY 10174-0002 Office Phone: 212-885-5381. Business E-Mail: jgreilsheimer@blankrome.com.

GREINER, CHARLES H., paper company executive; Attended, Old Dominion U. Exec. v.p., fine paper, dist., chemical products Union Camp Corp., 1997—99; sr. v.p., printing and comm. papers Internat. Paper Comp., 1999—. Office: Internat Paper Co 6400 Poplar Ave Memphis TN 38197

GREINER, HELEN, mechanical engineer, robotic company executive; b. London, Dec. 6, 1967; BS in Mech. Engring., MIT, 1989, MS in Computer Sci., 1990. Worked with NASA Jet Propulsion Lab., MIT, Artificial Intelligence Lab.; co-founder IS Robotics (now iRobot Corp.), Burlington, Mass., 1990—, pres., head of rsch.; also chmn. bd. iRobot Corp., Burlington, Mass. Lectr. in field; invited to the World Econ. Forums as a Global Leader of Tomorrow. Named Innovator for the Next Century, Technology Review Mag., (with Colin Angle) Ernst and Young New England Entrepreneurs of Yr., 2003; named one of Top 10 Innovators in the US, Fortune Mag.; recipient DEMO God award, DEMO conf. Achievements include inventor of the ROOMBA robotic vacuum. Avocations: reading, gardening, kayaking, mountain climbing, snowboarding. Office: iRobot Corp 63 South Ave Burlington MA 01803 Office Phone: 781-345-0200. Office Fax: 781-345-0201.*

GREINER, KENNETH DONALD, JR., management consultant; b. Cushing, Okla., Aug. 19, 1938; s. Kenneth Donald Greiner and Billie Alene (Williams) Greiner; m. Leitner Louise Jarrell, Sept. 2, 1961; children: Katherine Louise Pierce, Kenneth Donald III, Jennifer Lee, Cheryl Sue. BS in Econs., Okla. State U., 1960; MBA, Harvard U., 1962; BS in Health Care Adminstrn., Okla. Bapt. U., 1977. Adminstrv. asst. Doric Corp., Oklahoma City, 1962-64; asst. to treas. Skelly Oil Co., Tulsa, 1964-66; loan officer AID, Lahore, Karachi, Pakistan, 1966-69; ptnr. Resource Analysis and Mgmt. Group, Oklahoma City, 1969-74; v.p., dir. Texas Internat. Co., Oklahoma City, 1974-76; chmn. Grace Living Ctrs. (formerly Amity Care Corp.), Oklahoma City, 1976—2002; pres. Nursing Home Properties, 2002—; ptnr. Ams. Mgmt. Svcs. LLC, 2003—. Asst. trustee in bankruptcy Four Seasons Nursing Ctrs. Am., 1972—73; bd. dirs., mem. exec. com. Will Rogers Bank, 1983—94; br. adv. dir. Oklahoma City Nations Bank, 1994—97; trustee in bankruptcy Gulf South Corp., 1974, Cleanerator Corp., 1974, Preferred Commodity Options Corp., 1974—75; pres. Nursing Home Properties Inc., 2002—; partner Am. Mgmt. Svcs., 2003—; bd. dir. Secret Harbour Beach Resort; bd. dirs. Comty. Bank, Bettany, Okla. Treas., bd. dirs. Neighborhood Svcs. Orgn., Oklahoma City Met. Area, 1978—83; chmn. bd. New World Sch., Oklahoma City, 1973—74; mem. Putnam City Sch. Bd., 1988—93, pres., 1992—93; dir. Cowboy Golf, Inc., 1992—2003; trustee Hillcrest Hosp., Oklahoma City, 1989—93; dir. Emergency Med. Svcs. Authority, Oklahoma City, Tulsa, 1998—2001; mem. bd. govs. Okla. State U. Found., 1994—, trustee, 1998—, vice chmn., 2004—; chmn. Cath. Social Ministries, Archdiocese of Oklahoma City, 1977—86. Mem.: Nat. Assn. Bds. Examiners Nursing Home Adminstrs. (pres. 1994—96), Okla. State Bd. Nursing Homes (bd. dirs. 1988—92), Nursing Home Assn. Okla. (exec. bd. 1988—2003, v.p. 1990—92), Okla. State U. CBA Assocs. (pres. 1993—94), Equestrian Order Holy Seplechre, Ski Island Lake Inc. (pres. 1984—87), Quail Creek Golf and Country Club (v.p., dir. 1998—2001), Bus. Boosters Club (pres. 1985), Harvard Bus. Sch. Alumni Club (pres. Oklahoma City 1970—71), Phi Delta Theta Alumni (pres. Oklahoma City 1969—71). Republican. Roman Catholic. Office: Ams Mgmt Svcs 4700 Estate Charlotte Amalie 201 First Bank Plz St Thomas VI 00802 Home: 6280 Estate Nazareth St Thomas VI 00802

GREINER, STEPHEN W., lawyer; b. N.Y.C., Dec. 14, 1944; BA, Syracuse U., 1965; JD, NYU, 1968. Bar: N.Y. 1969. Mem. Willkie Farr & Gallagher LLP, N.Y.C. Mem. Assn. Bar City N.Y., Order of Coif. Office: Willkie Farr & Gallagher LLP 787 7th Ave New York NY 10019-6018 E-mail: sgreiner@willkie.com.

GREINKE, EVERETT DONALD, management consultant; b. Elmhurst, Ill., Oct. 31, 1929; s. Herman and Marie Barbara (Kline) G.; m. Clara Joan Plasil, Sept. 29, 1951; children: Donald James, David Carl, Mark Andrew. BS with honors, No. Ill. U., 1951, MS with honors, 1956; postgrad., U. Wis., 1956, George Washington U., 1957. Project officer Bur. Aeronautics USN, Washington, 1956-60, asst. br. head Bur. Aeronautics, 1960-61, tech. advisor Automatic Data Processing Office Chief Naval Ops., 1961-65, asst. dir. command/control Office Chief Naval Ops., 1965-67; sr. staff specialist reconnaissance Office Dir. Def. Research and Engring., Washington, 1967-73, sr. staff specialist tactical command, control and intelligence, 1973-76, asst. dir. combat support, 1976-77, dir. combat support, 1977-80, dir. NATO/Europe affairs, 1980-82; acting dep. undersec. internat. programs and tech. Office UnderSec. Def. Research & Engring., Washington, 1982; scientific advisor to Supreme Comdr. NATO/Supreme Hdqrs. Allied Powers Europe, Casteau, Belgium, 1982-86; dep. undersec. internat. programs and tech. Office Undersec. Def. (Acquisition), Washington, 1986-88; internat. programs cons., 1988-90; v.p. corp. devel. Internat. Partnerships Group (Interpar), 1990-93; v.p. Internat. Planning and Analysis Ctr., 1993-96, Global Mktg. Devel. Solutions, 1996—. Lectr. on armaments cooperation various orgns., 1977—; mem. Army Sci. Bd., 2002—; cons. Def. Sci. Bd., 1988—, U.S. Industry on Internat. Coop. and High Tech. Programs, 1988—. Contbr. articles to profl. jours. Pres. Chapel Sq. Sch. PTA, Annandale, Va., 1966-67, v.p. 1965; pres. W.T. Woodson High Sch. PTA, 1972-73; pres. Hope Luth. Ch. Coun., Annandale, 1970-71, mem. ch. coun., 1987-89, mem. bd. elders, 1974-82, mem. planning com., 1986-87, chmn. bldg. com., 1987-92, trustee, 1993—; com. chmn. Boy Scouts Am., Annandale, 1966-68, chmn. Explorer Post, Annandale, 1972-73, scoutmaster, 1968-78; Santa Claus for local civic orgns., Annandale, 1961-94. Comdr. USNR, 1951-55. Decorated Def. D.S.M. (3), Def. Meritorious Service Medal; Comdr.'s Cross (Austria); recipient Def. Outstanding Pub. Service award, Service plaque W.T. Woodson High Sch. PTA, 1973, Service award Boy Scouts Am., 1975, Disting. Alumni award No. Ill. U., 1987. Mem. Nat. Def. Indsl. Assn. Lutheran. Avocations: gardening, fishing. Home: 8315 Toll House Rd Annandale VA 22003-4630 Office Phone: 703-299-6649. Business E-Mail: greinkee@gmdsinc.com.

GREISEN, KENNETH INGVARD, physicist, emeritus educator; b. Perth Amboy, N.J., Jan. 24, 1918; s. Ingvard C. and Signa (Nielsen) G.; m. Elizabeth C. Chase, Apr. 12, 1941 (dec.); children: Eric Winslow, Kathryn Elise; m. Helen A. Leeds, Mar. 27, 1976 (dec. 1996). Student, Wagner Coll., 1934-35; BS, Franklin and Marshall Coll., 1938; PhD, Cornell U., 1942. Instr. Cornell U., 1942-43, asst. prof., 1946-48, assoc. prof., 1948-50, prof. physics, 1950-84, prof. emeritus, 1984—, chmn. dept. astronomy, 1976-79, univ. ombudsman, 1975-77, dean faculty, 1978-83; scientist Manhattan Project, Los Alamos, 1943-46. Fellow Am Phys. Soc.; mem. Am. Astron. Soc., Internat. Astron. Union, Nat. Acad. Sci., AAUP. Rsch. cosmic rays. Home: 379 Savage Farm Dr Ithaca NY 14850-6505

GREIST, MARY COFFEY, dermatologist; b. Ft. Wayne, Ind., Jan. 31, 1947; d. George Alma and Irene Katherine (Zollinger) Coffey; m. Timothy William Greist, June 10, 1972; children: Heather Maria, Thomas Coffey, Timothy Michael. BA, Valparaiso U., 1969; MD, Ind. U., 1973. Intern in family medicine Duke U., Durham, NC, 1973—74, resident in dermatology, 1974—77; asst. prof. dermatology sch. medicine Ind. U., Indpls., 1977—82, clin. asst. prof. dermatology sch. medicine, 1982—; pvt. practice Indpls., 1982—. Dermatology cons. Eli Lilly and Co., Indpls., 1977-86, Elizabeth Arden and Co., Indpls., 1978-88, Medicare-Blue Cross/Blue Shield, Indpls., 1989—. Mem. Ind. State Dermatological Soc. (sec. 1985, v.p. 1986, pres. 1987-88). Democrat. Avocation: gardening. Office: Greist Ozols & Wilson Dermatology 6820 Parkdale Pl Ste 211 Indianapolis IN 46254-6600 Office Phone: 317-329-7050. Personal E-mail: greist@sbcglobal.net.

GREJDA, GAIL FULTON, dean; b. Clarion, Pa., Aug. 31, 1937; d. Ralph Jay and Virginia Agnew Fulton; m. Edward Stanley Grejda, Aug. 31, 1958; children: Richard Edward, Steven Douglas. BS, Clarion U., 1966, MEd, 1968; PhD in Instrnl. Sys. Design, Pa. State U., 1988. Cert. level 2 in elem. edn. and spl. edn., Pa. Tchr. Brookville (Pa.) Area Sch. Dist., 1966-69, Clarion (Pa.) Area Sch. Dist., 1969-87, dir. gifted programs, 1977-82; tchr. Beijing Internat. Embassy Sch., 1980-81; computer instr. Sch. of Am. Embassy, Bridgetown, Barbados, 1987-88; asst. prof. Clarion U., 1988-93, assoc. prof., 1993-97, prof., 1997-98, dean Coll. Edn. and Human Svcs., 1998—. Author: (book chpt.) Guidelines for Interpreting Educational Research, 1994; contbr. articles to profl. jours. Grantee U.S. Dept. Edn., 1999, Bell Atlantic Found., 1998, NSF, 1999-2003, 2003—. Mem. Am. Assn. Colls. for Tchr. Edn., Assn. Tchr. Educators (commn. on utilizing tech. for ednl. reform 1988—), Tchr. Edn. Coun. State Colls. and Univs., Assn. for Ednl. Comms. and Tech., Pa. Assn. Coll. Tchr. Educators (bd. dirs. 1988—), Phi Delta Kappa (v.p. 1982—), Pi Lambda Theta. Avocations: travel, reading, golf. Office: Clarion U 101 Stevens Hall Clarion PA 16214 E-mail: grejda@mail.clarion.edu.

GRELLA, MELISSA A., nurse; b. Glen Cove, N.Y., Nov. 23, 1978; d. Anthony Joseph Grella and Janice Ann Burns. B, Hartwick Coll., 2000; postgrad., U. Phoenix, 2002—. RN N.Y., 2000. Nurse Winthrop U. Hosp., Mineola, NY, 2000—. Mem.: N.Y. Nurses Assn. Roman Catholic. Home: 128 Cambridge Ave Holbrook NY 11741

GREMSE, DAVID ALBERT, pediatrician, educator; b. Montgomery, Ala., Oct. 14, 1956; s. Albert Rudolph and Jean (Faust) Gremse; m. Diane Blackwell, June 13, 1981; children: Jennifer, Albert, Christopher. BChE summa cum laude, Ga. Inst. Tech., 1970; MD, U. S. Ala., 1983. Lic. Ala., Ohio, diplomate Am. Bd. Pediat. and Pediat. Gastroenterology, Nat. Bd. Med. Examiners. Prof., chair pediats. U. Nev. Sch. Medicine, 2004—; dir. pediats. U. South Ala. Gastroenterology and Nutrition Divsn., 1990—2003. Asst. prof., assoc. prof. Pediat. U. South Ala., Mobile, 1990—99, asst. prof. Pharmacology, 1997—99, prof. pediat., 1999—2003, assoc. prof. Pharmacology, 1999—2003. Contbr. chpts. in books, articles to profl. jours. Recipient Eagle Scout award, Boy Scouts Am., 1970; fellow, NIH, 1988—90; grantee, Cystic Fibrosis Found., 1994—95, 1996—97, TAP Holdings, Inc., 1998—99, 1998, Cell Pathways, Inc., 1999—2000, AstraZeneca, Inc., 1999—2000, Glaxo Wellcome, 1999—2000, 2000—01, Omnicare Clin. Rsch., Inc., 2001, 2002, Glaxo Wellcome, 2001—03, TAP Holdings, Inc., 2002, Wyeth Ayerst, 2002, GlaxoSmithKline, 2002—04. Fellow: Am. Coll. Gastroenterology (credentials com. 2001—, Pediat. Gastroenterology com. 2001); mem.: AMA (Physician's Recognition award 1997—2000), Soc. Pediat. Rsch. (reviewer Gastroenterology Abstract 2003), So. Soc. Pediat. Rsch. (moderator Gastroenterology session ann. meeting 1994, moderator Clin. Pharmacology ann. meeting 1997), Crohn's and Colitis Found. Am., Med. Soc. Mobile (Bd. Censors 1995—97), Mobile Pediat. Soc. (pres. 1994—95), Am. Bd. Pediat. (assoc.), So. Med. Assn., Med. Assn. State of Ala., N.Am. Soc. Pediat. Gastroenterology and Nutrition, Am. Gastroent. Assn., Am. Acad. Pediat. (chmn. Acad. Issues com. Ala. chpt. 1997—, Com. mem. Gastroenterology and Nutrition Edn. sect. 2001—, Nutrition com. 2001—, exec. bd. dist. VII rep. Ala. chpt. 2001—), Alpha Omega Alpha, Tau Beta Pi, Phi Kappa Phi, Phi Eta Sigma. Home: 4885 Staranger Ln Las Vegas NV 89147 Office: U Nev Med Sch 2040 W Charleston Blvd Ste 402 Las Vegas NV 89102

GRENDELL, JAMES HENRY, medical educator; b. Cleve., Dec. 7, 1949; married; 3 children. BS in Biology magna cum laude, John Carroll U., 1971; MD cum laude, Ohio State U., 1975. Diplomate Nat. Bd. Med. Examiners, Am. Bd. Internal Medicine with subspecialty in gastroenterology; lic. physician, N.Y. Intern in medicine Beth Israel Hosp., Boston, 1975-76, resident in medicine, 1976-78; fellow in gastroenterology U. Calif., San Francisco, 1978-81, asst. prof. medicine and physiology, 1981-88, assoc. prof., 1989-94; chief gastroenterology sect. San Francisco VA Med. Ctr., 1990-94; prof. medicine Cornell U., N.Y.C., 1994—99; chief divsn. digestive diseases New York Hosp.-Cornell U. Med. Ctr., N.Y.C., 1994-98; chief divsn. gastroenterology, hepatology and nutrition Winthrop U. Hosp., Mineola, NY, 1999—; prof. medicine SUNY, Stony Brook, 2003—. Mem. gastroenterology subsplty. bd. Am. Bd. Internal Medicine, 1995-99; lectr. in field. Editor: Current Diagnosis and Treatment in Gastroenterology, 1996, 2003; assoc. editor Internat. Jour. Pancreatology, 1989—, Pancreas, 1993—; cons. editor Gastroenterology, 1982; ad hoc referee Sci. Jour. of Clin. Investigation, Annals of Internal Medicine, Gastroenterology, Am. Jour. Physiology, Digestive Diseases and Scis., Neuroendocrinology, Western Jour. Medicine, Fedn. Proc., Can. Jour. Physiology and Pharmacology, Endocrinology, Am. Jour. Gastroenterology, Jour. Lab. and Clin. Medicine; contbr. numerous articles and abstracts to profl. jours., chpts. to books. Mem.: ACP (gastroenterology subcom. med. knowledge self-assessment program IX 1989—91), Internat. Assn. of Pancreatology, Western Assn. Physicians, Western Soc. for Clin. Investigation, Am. Pancreatic Assn. (governing coun. 1989—95, pres. 1993—94), Gastroenterology Rsch. Group, Am. Gastroenterol. Assn. (com. on tng. and edn. 1990—94, chmn. tng. subcom. 1991—94, Fall postgrad. course assoc. dir. 1992, co-chair pancreatic disorders sect. 1993—95, chair 1995—97, coun. 1997—2000, governing bd. 1997—2000, course dir. 1998, pub. affairs and advocacy com. 2003—), Am. Fedn. Clin. Rsch., Landacre Soc., Alpha Omega Alpha. Office Phone: 516-663-4624. Business E-Mail: jgrendel@winthrop.org.

GRENDLER, PAUL FREDERICK, historian, educator; b. Armstrong, Iowa, May 24, 1936; s. August Paul and Josephine Lucy (Girres) G.; m. Marcella T. McCann, June 16, 1962; children: Peter, Jean. BA, Oberlin Coll., 1959; MA, U. Wis., 1961, PhD, 1964. Lectr. history U. Pitts., 1963-64, U. Toronto, Ont., Can., 1964-65, asst. prof., 1965-69, assoc. prof., 1969-73, prof., 1973-98; prof. emeritus, 1998; postdoctoral fellow Inst. for Research in Humanities, U. Wis., 1967-68. Author: Critics of the Italian World, 1530-1560, 1969, The Roman Inquisition and the Venetian Press, 1540-1605, 1977 (Marraro prize 1978), rev. Italian transl., 1983, Culture and Censorship in Late Renaissance Italy and France, 1981, Schooling in Renaissance Italy, 1989 (Marraro prize 1989), paperback, 1991, 1995, Italian transl., 1991, Books and Schools in the Italian Renaissance, 1995, The Universities of the Italian Renaissance, 2002 (Marraro prize 2002), 2nd edit., 2004; editor: An Italian Renaissance Reader, 1987, 2d edit., 1992, Roman and German Humanism 1450-1550, 1993, Renaissance Quarterly, 2000-03; editor-in-chief: Ency. of Renaissance, 6 vols., 1999, 2d printing, 2000 (Dartmouth medal 2000, Roland H. Bainton prize 2000), Renaissance. An Encyclopedia for Students, 4 vols., 2004; assoc. editor Europe 1450-1789, 6 vols., 2004; mem. editl. bd., exec. com.: Collected Works of Erasmus, from 1976; contbr. articles to profl. jours. Fulbright fellow Italy, 1962-63; Can. Council fellow, 1970-71; Am. Council Learned Socs. fellow, 1971-72; I Tatti fellow Harvard U. Ctr. for Italian Renaissance Studies, Florence, Italy, 1970-72; sr. fellow Soc. for Humanities Cornell U., 1973-74; Guggenheim Meml. fellow, 1978-79; Social Scis. and Humanities Research Council Can. fellow, 1979-80, 85-86; Woodrow Wilson Internat. Ctr. for Scholars fellow, 1982-83; Nat. Humanities Ctr. fellow, 1988-90; grantee NEH, 1989-92; Connaught fellowship, 1998. Mem. Renaissance Soc. Am. (v.p. 1991-92, pres. 1992-94), Am. Hist. Assn., Am. Cath. Hist. Assn. (pres. 1984), Am. Philos. Soc., Soc. Italian Hist. Studies (sr. scholar citation 1998; v.p. 2001-03, pres. 2003-05). Address: 110 Fern Ln Chapel Hill NC 27514-4206 E-mail: pgrendler@cs.com.

GRENELL, JAMES HENRY, retired manufacturing company executive; b. Mpls., Feb. 19, 1924; s. Harrison Morton and Harriet Elizabeth (Kuch) G.; m. Naomi Betty Callerstrom, Sept. 15, 1945; children: Bonita (Mrs. Michael Wolfe), Suzanne Naomi, Andrea Bergine. BBA, U. Minn., 1947; postgrad. Advanced Mgmt. Program, Harvard U., 1974. With Honeywell Inc., Mpls., 1951-86, accountant, 1951-56, div. controller, 1956-68, group controller, 1968-71, asst. corp. controller, 1971-74, v.p., controller, 1974-82, v.p., staff exec., 1982-86. Instr. Mgmt. Inst. U. Wis.-Madison, 1960-69, Inst. Tech. U. Minn., Mpls., 1963-65; asso. dir. Mgmt. Center U. St. Thomas, 1959-69 Contbr. articles to profl. jours. Bd. dirs. Mpls. Soc. for Blind, 1963-71, pres., 1970-71; bd. dirs. U. Minn. Coll. Bus. Alumni Bd., 1975-82; mem. Acctg. Adv. Coun. U. Minn., 1977-83. Served to 1st lt. 1943-46, European Theatre Operations. Decorated 4 Battle Star US Army. Mem. Fin. Execs. Inst., Alpha Kappa Psi, Harvard Club of Ariz., Ariz. Club. Republican. Home: 10056 E Calle De Cielo Scottsdale AZ 85258-5652 Home (Summer): 1201 Skyview Flagstaff AZ 86004-8718

GRENEVICKI, LANCE FRANCIS, surgeon; b. Plainfield, N.J., May 21, 1967; s. Lawrence Francis and Joann Frances (Bengivenga) Grenevicki; m. Amy Lavonne Bridgers, Apr. 13, 1996; 1 child, Anna Lavonne. BS, Va. Poly. Inst. and State U., 1989; DDS cum laude, Med. Coll. Va., 1993; MD, U. Mo., Kansas City, 1997. Diplomate Am. Bd. Oral and Maxillofacial Surgery. Intern Truman Med. Ctr., Kansas City, Mo., resident, 1993-99; attending med. staff, chmn. med. records com. Holmes Regional Med. Ctr., Melbourne, Fla.; mem. med. staff, chmn. med. records com. Palm Bay (Fla.) Cmty. Hosp.; courtesy clin. asst. prof. surgery U. Fla.; active med. staff mem. Wuesthoff Hosp., Melbourne, Fla. Mem. adv. coun. Fla. Cancer Control and Rsch.; bd. dirs. Isaac Walton League of Am., Christiansburg, Va., 1988—89. Named Surg. Resident of Yr., Isaac Walton League Am., 1997; recipient Victim's Advocate award, State Atty.'s Office, 2002. Fellow: ACS, Am. Acad. Cosmetic Surgery, Am. Coll. Oral and Maxillofacial Surgeons, Am. Assn. Oral and Maxillofacial Surgeons (alt. del. Fla.); mem.: ADA, AMA (Brevard County del.), Fla. Soc. Dental Anesthesiology (v.p. 2004), Brevard County Med. Soc. (bd. govs.), Brevard County Dental Soc. (co-editor, newsletter, mem.-at-large), So. Med. Assn., Ctrl. Dist. Dental Soc., Fla. Dental Assn., Fla. Med. Assn. (Brevard county del.), Fla. Soc. Oral and Maxillofacial Surgeons (trustee 2001—, Young Eagle award 2001), Southeastern Soc. Oral and Maxillofacial Surgeons, Psi Omega, Alpha Omega Alpha, Pi Kappa Alpha. Roman Catholic. Avocations: trap and skeet shooting, hunting, fishing. Office: Inst Facial Surgery 1093 S Wickham Rd Melbourne FL 32904-1652 Home: 2306 N Riverside Dr Indialantic FL 32903-3619 Office Phone: 321-674-3900.

GRENIER, EDWARD JOSEPH, JR., lawyer; b. N.Y.C., Nov. 26, 1933; s. Edward Joseph and Jane Veronica (Farrell) G.; m. Patricia J. Cederle, June 22, 1957; children; Victoria-Anne, Edward Joseph III, Peter C. BA summa cum laude, Manhattan Coll., N.Y.C., 1954; LLB magna cum laude, Harvard U., 1959. Bar: D.C. 1959, N.Y. 1983, U.S. Ct. Appeals (D.C. cir.) 1959, U.S. Ct. Mil. Appeals 1960, U.S. Ct. Appeals (3d cir.) 1966, U.S. Supreme Ct. 1966, U.S. Ct. Appeals (9th cir.) 1973, U.S. Ct. Appeals (10th cir.) 1977, U.S. Ct. Appeals (5th cir., 11th cir.) 1982. Law clk. U.S. Ct. Appeals (D.C. cir.), 1959-60; assoc. Covington & Burling, Wahsington, 1960-68; ptnr. Sutherland, Asbill & Brennan, Wahsington, 1968—. Speaker in field of energy related issues to profl. orgns. Contbr. articles in field to legal jours. Chmn. bd. trustees, mem. exec. com. Connelly Sch. Holy Child, Potomac, Md., 1976-85, trustee, 1976-88; bd. dirs. D.C. Recording for the Blind, Washington, 1977-89. 1st lt. USAF, 1954-56. Fellow: Am. Bar Found.; mem.: ABA (chmn. sec. adminstrv. law 1986—87, sec., del. Ho. of Dels. 1991—97), Am. Inns of Ct. (master of bench Prettyman-Leventhal Inn of Ct. 1988—2000, pres. 1991—92, counselor 1997—98), Energy Bar Assn. (bd. dirs. 1986—89, 1995—2001, v.p. 1995—96, pres.-elect 1996—97, pres. 1997—98, del. Ho. of Dels. 1999—2001), D.C. Bar Assn., Fed. Bar Assn., Congl. Country Club, Met. Club. Office: Sutherland Asbill & Brennan LLP 1275 Pennsylvania Ave NW Washington DC 20004-2415 Office Phone: 202-383-0138. Business E-Mail: edward.grenier@sablaw.com.

GRENIER, JOSEPH JEFFREY, medical physicist, neurology researcher; b. Detroit, Dec. 19, 1961; s. Alfred Joseph and Evangeline M. (Murray) G.; m. Bonnie Cass, Nov. 17, 1994. BA, Swarthmore Coll., 1980-83; MD, CM, McGill U., Montreal, Can., 1984-89; postgrad., U. B.C., 1991-92, Oakland U., Rochester, Mich. Rschr. Sloan-Kettering Cancer Ctr., N.Y.C.; brain rschr. Mass. Gen. Hosp., Boston, 1983-84; vision rschr. U. Mich., Ann Arbor, 1987; intern in surgery Providence Hosp., Southfield, Mich., 1989-90; intern in medicine Med. Coll. Va., Richmond, 1991; neural devel. rschr. U. Mich., Ann Arbor, 1994-95; cerebrovascular rschr. Wayne State U., Detroit, 1992; rschr. Stanford U., Palo Alto, Calif., 1994-95; neurology rschr. Henry Ford, Detroit, 1996—; resident nuc. medicine U. Ala., Birmingham, 1999—; vision sci. rschr. psychology Brain Rsch. Inst. U. Chgo., 2000. CEO Rohl & Assocs., Novi, Mich., 1992-94, Neurosurg. & Brain Rsch. Cons., Ann Arbor, 1994; neurosurg. cons., Auburn Hills, Mich., 1994-95, Troy, Mich., 1995-98. Author: Textbook of Cerebral Blood Flow, 1998. Friends of McGill scholar McGill Med. Sch., Montreal, 1985-87; vision grantee NIH, 1987; Nat. Sci. and Engring. Rsch. Coun. grantee Govt. of Can., 1990-91. Mem. AAAS, Soc. Nuclear Medicine. Republican. Roman Catholic. Avocations: golf, squash, baseball, theater, quarto. Home and Office: Apt 103 2145 Walcott Rd Aurora IL 60504-7714

GRENIER, LAURA MARGIOTTA, medical/surgical nurse; b. L'Aquila, Italy, Jan. 18, 1963; arrived in U.S., 1964; d. Guido and Linda (Tedeschi) Margiotta; m. Arthur Jacob Grenier, III, May 3, 1986; children: Danielle Monique, Anthony James, Zachary Jon. Nursing degree, U. Conn., 1986; ADN, Greater Hartford C.C., 1998. Lic. arrhythmia interpretation, cert. health unit coord. Cardiology nurse Hartford (Conn.) Hosp., 1986—. Contbr. poetry to anthologies; author: (poetry) Beyond the Garden Gate, 2003, Convoluted Dream, 2003 (Pres.'s award, Hon. Mention, 2003). Mem. Hilstead Mus., Farmington, Conn., 2001—. Recipient Editor's Choice awards for poetry, 1997, 1998, 2001, Pres.'s award Literacy Excellence for poem "Convoluted" Dream, Illiad Press, 2003, hon. mention for poem "Convoluted" Dream, Summer Competition Illiad Press, 2002. Mem.: Brain Injury Assn. Conn., Am. Brain Tumor Soc., Copper Canyon Press (assoc.), Copper Canyon Press (assoc.), Poetry Soc. Am., Acad. Am. Poets, Quarter Century Club, Hartford Hosp. Qtr. Century Club (assoc.). Roman Catholic. Avocations: poetry, playing piano, going to the beach, travel, tennis. E-mail: bmw6263@aol.com.

GRENIG, JAY EDWARD, law educator; b. Salt Lake City, Apr. 18, 1943; s. Robert Edward and Betty (Gifford) G.; m. Sharon Flanigan, Dec. 22, 1967; children: Robert Jay, Alejandro Edward, Christian Michael. Student, U. Ariz., 1961-63; BA, Willamette U., Salem, Oreg., 1966; postgrad., Ariz. State U., 1968-69; JD, U. Calif.-Hastings Coll. Law, 1971. Bar: Calif. 1972, U.S. Dist. Ct. (no. dist.) Calif. 1973, U.S. Ct. Appeals (9th cir.) 1974, U.S. Ct. Claims 1974, Wis. 1980. Asst. dean Coll. of Law Willamette U., Salem, 1971-72; assoc. firm Johnson & Stanton, San Francisco, 1972-73; sole practice San Mateo, Calif., 1973-77; assoc. prof., dir. Employment Law Inst., Pepperdine U. Sch. Law, Malibu, Calif., 1977-79; prof. law Marquette U. Sch. Law, Milw., 1980—. Lectr. U. So. Calif. Grad. Sch. Pub. Adminstrn., L.A., 1978; reporter civil justice reform act adv. group U.S. Dist. Ct. (ea. dist.) Wis., 1991-97; pres., bd. dirs. Ctr. Pub. Representation, 1993-97; mem. Wis. Judicial Council, 2002—; reporter U.S. Dist. Ct. (ea. dist) Wis., 1991—. Author: (with others) Private Sector Labor Law, 1980, West's Federal Jury Practice and Instructions, 5th edit., 2001, West's California Education Code Forms, 1992, California Government Codes Forms with Practice Commentaries, 1998, Labor Arbitration Advocacy, 1989, West's Federal Forms, 1992, Wisconsin Civil Procedure, 1994, Wisconsin Civil Discovery, 1996, Alternative Dispute, 1997; editor Calif. Sch. Law Digest, 1973-84, Wisconsin Civil Discovery, 1996, West's Alternative Dispute Resolution, 1997, Illinois Civil Discover, 2000, West's Federal Jury Practice and Instructions (5th edit.), 2000; contbr. articles to legal publs. Bd. trustees Univ. Lake Sch., 1992-95. With U.S. Army, 1966-68. Mem.: Nat. Acad. Arbitrators (bd. govs.), State Bar Assn. Wis., Assn. Am. Law Schs. (chmn. labor and employment law sect. 1991—92), Am. Law Inst., Thurston Soc., Order of Coif. Home: 122 Birch

Rd Delafield WI 53018-1305 Office: Marquette U Law Sch 1103 W Wisconsin Ave Milwaukee WI 53233-2313 Office Phone: 414-288-5377. Personal E-mail: jgrenig@earthlink.net.

GRENLEY, HENRY WALKER, lawyer; b. Memphis, Sept. 24, 1944; s. Henry Woodrow and Julia (Hawn) G.; m. Connie Lynn Grenley, Jan. 27, 1979; children: David, Marc, Kim. BA, So. Meth. U., 1967, JD, 1969. Bar: Tex. 1969, Hawaii 1971, Wash. 1974. Ptnr. Mullavey, Prout, Grenley & Foe, 1977—; apptd. Com. Wash. State Bar Examiners, 1986; part time instr. Edmonds C.C. Arbitrator, mediator King County; mem. numerous coms. Active North Seattle Alliance; bd. dirs. Sr. Svcs. Bd. Served to lt. JAGC USN, 1969-74. Mem. Wash. Bar Assn., Seattle King County Bar Assn., Wash. Trial Lawyers Assn., Bar Com. Lawyers Guild Client Protection, Lodges: Exchange (pres. 1983). Home: 20505 86th Pl W Edmonds WA 98026-6615 Office: PO Box 70567 2401 NW 65th St Seattle WA 98117-5831 Business E-Mail: henryg@nwlink.com.

GRENQUIST, PETER CARL, publishing executive, consultant; b. East Orange, N.J., Feb. 15, 1931; s. Ernst Alexander and Carmela (Anastasia) G.; m. Barbara Ross Krone, Dec. 20, 1967; children: Carl Robert (dec.), Louisa Beatrice. BA, Dartmouth Coll., 1953; MA, Columbia U., 1957, PhD, 1963. V.p. Am. Assembly Columbia U., 1957-62; dir. Spectrum Books, Prentice-Hall, Inc., 1962-70; v.p. coll. divsn. Prentice-Hall, Inc., 1970-72, pres. Trade Book divsn., 1972-80; CEO Arco Pub., Inc. (subs.), 1981-85; gen. mgr. gen. books divsn. McGraw-Hill Book Co., 1986-89; exec. dir. Assn. Am. Univ. Presses, Inc., N.Y.C., 1990-97; sr. assoc. Moseley Assocs. Inc., 1997—. Served to lt. (j.g.) USNR, 1953-56. Woodrow Wilson fellow, 1956-57. Mem. Devon Yacht Club, Phi Beta Kappa. Office: Moseley Assocs Inc 1202 Lexington Ave # 356 New York NY 10028 Office Phone: 212-988-2834. E-mail: grenquist@aol.com.

GRENROCK-WOODS, STACEY, comedian, actress; b. L.A., Nov. 22, 1971; m. Kenny Woods, 1999. Editor: (column) Esquire mag.; co-founder, co-editor: L.A. Innuendo mag., 2003—; actor: (TV series) The Daily Show with Jon Stewart, 1998—, Arrested Development, 2003—. Office: The Daily Show 513 W 54th St New York NY 10019

GRENZ, M. KAY, manufacturing executive; b. Minn., Dec. 1946; m. Rod Grenz; 1 child, Jenni. BA in Sociology, U. SD. Cord. 3M Co., 1969—71, salary adminstr., 1971—76, mgr., 1976—84, dir. human resources, 1984—96, v.p. human resources, 1996—98, sr. v.p. human resources, 1998—. Bd. dirs. Gillette Children's Specialty Healthcare. Mem.: Human Resource Planning Soc.*

GRENZIG, GAIL A., school system administrator, consultant; d. Daniel Tkatch and Virginia Mary Cosgrave; m. Edward W. Grenzig, June 23, 1990; children: Christopher Edward, Brittany Marie. Post Grad. Profl. Diploma, L.I. U., 1989; MS, Adelphi U., 1985, BS, 1983. Cert. SDA Ednl. Adminstrn. NY State Bd. of Regents, 1994. Tchr. spl. edn. Glen Cove City Sch. Dist., NY, 1985—94; ednl. cons. Grenzig Consulting, Nesconset, NY, 1993—; adj. prof. Dowling Coll., Oakdale, NY, 1994; coord. of pupil pers. svcs. Mid. Country Ctrl. Sch. Dist., Centereach, NY, 1999—2002; asst. prin. Harry B. Thompson Mid. Sch. Syosset (NY) Ctrl. Sch. Dist., 2002—04; asst. to asst. supt. for pers. Sachem Cen. Sch. Dist., Holbrook, NY, 2004—. Varsity coach Glen Cove City Sch. Dist., 1985—94. Vol. soccer coach Smithtown Kickers, NY, 1997—2003; editor - newsletter Nesconset Elem. PTA, 1996—2003; religion tchr. Parish of Holy Cross, Nesconset, 1999—2004. Mem.: ASCD, NASSP, L.I. Assn. Sch. Pers. Adminstrs., Nat. Mid. Sch. Assn., Coun. of Exceptional Children (spkr., presenter N.Y. State Conf. 2002), L.I. Assn. of Spl. Edn. Adminstrs. Avocations: reading, travel, gardening, sports. Office: Sachem Cen Sch Dist Office Pers 245 Union Ave Holbrook NY 11741 Personal E-mail: gail@grenzig.com.

GREPPIN, JOHN AIRD COUTTS, philologist, editor, educator; b. Rochester, N.Y., Apr. 2, 1937; s. Ernest Haquette and Edna Barbara (Kill) G.; m. Mary Elizabeth Cleland Hannan, Sept. 30, 1961; children: Sarah Cleland Coutts, Carl Hannan Haquette. AB in Greek, U. Rochester, N.Y., 1961; MA in Classics, U. Wash., 1966; PhD in Indo-European Studies, UCLA, 1972; postdoctoral student, Yerevan State U., USSR, 1974-75. Tchr. Greek, Latin Stowe (Vt.) Prep. Sch., 1961-62; tchr. Woodstock (Vt.) Country Sch., 1962-65, admissions dir., 1968-69; interim asst. prof. U. Fla., Gainesville, 1971-72; tchr. Isidore Newman Sch., New Orleans, 1972-74; from asst. to assoc. to prof. linguistics Cleve. State U., 1975—, dir. program in linguistics, 1979-83, 99—. Vis. prof. linguistics Philipps U., Marburg, Germany, 1993. Author: Initial Vowel and Aspiration in Classical Armenian, 1973, Classical Armenian Nominal Suffixes, 1975, Classical and Middle Armenian Bird Names: A Taxonomic and Mythological Study, 1978, An Etymological Dictionary of the Indo-European Components of Classical Armenian, 1984, Bark Galianosi: The Greek Armenian Dictionary to Galen, 1985, A Handbook of Armenian Dialectology, 1986, An Arabic-Armenian Pharmaceutical Dictionary, 1997, The Diffusion of Greco-Roman Medicine into the Middle East and the Caucasus, 1999; editor: Proc. of 1st Internat. Conf. on Armenian Linguistics, Phila., 1979, (with others) Interrogativity: A Colloquium of the Grammar, Typology and Pragmatics of Questions in Seven Diverse Languages, 1984, When Worlds Collide: The Indo-Europeans and the Pre-Indo-Europeans: The Bellagio Papers, 1990, Studies in Classical Armenian Literature, 1994, Studies in Honor of Jaan Puhvel, Part One: Ancient Languages and Philology, 1997, Part Two: Mythology and Religion, 1997; founding editor Ann. Armenian Linguistics, 1980-2002, Armenian and Anatolian Studies, 1979—, Proc. 4th Internat. Conf. on Armenian Linguistics, 1992, Classical Armenian Literature: Studies in Early Armenian Authors; mng. editor Raft, A Jour. of Armenian Poetry and Criticism, 1987-2000; editor Jour. Soc. Armenian Studies, 2002—; contbr. over 200 articles to Am., European and Soviet jours., over 260 revs. to London Times Lit. Supplement, N.Y. Times Book Rev., Boston Book Rev., others. Recipient Silver medal Congregazione Mekhitarista, Venice, Italy, 1979, Medal of David the Invincible award Armenian Philos. Acad., 2003; fellow Am. Coun. Learned Socs., 1965, NEH, 1978-79, NIH, 1984, Internat. Rsch. and Exchs. Bd., 1974-75, grantee, 1979-81, 84-87, 89, 92, 94, 98; grantee AGBU Manoogian Fund, 1977, 79-2003, Gulbenkian Found., 1982, 85, 96, Rockefeller Found., 1987, Am. Coun. Learned Socs., 1987. Mem. Assn. Internat. des Études Arméniennes, Soc. for Study of the Caucasus, Am. Philol. Soc., Linguistic Soc. Am., Soc. for Armenian Studies (mem. exec. bd. 1982-86, 2002—, sec. 1983-85), Am. Oriental Soc., Soc. Caucasologia Europaea. Avocations: piano, chamber music, birdwatching. Home: 3349 Fairmount Blvd Cleveland OH 44118-4262 Office: Cleve State U Dept Linguistics Cleveland OH 44115 Office Phone: 216-687-3967. Business E-Mail: j.greppin@csuohio.edu.

GRESHAM, GLEN EDWARD, physician; b. Ft. Worth, Dec. 1, 1931; s. Perry Epler and Elsie Inez (Stanbrough) G.; m. Phyllis Elaine Kilmer, Nov. 9, 1957; children: Stephen Deane, David Epler, Elizabeth Anne Kilmer, Jennifer Gordon. BA, Harvard Coll., 1953; MD, Columbia U., 1958. Intern, then resident in internal medicine Univ. Hosps., Cleve., 1958-60, 62-64; asst. prof. preventive medicine Ohio State U., Columbus, 1964-69; asst. prof. medicine Yale U., New Haven, 1969-70; assoc. prof. rehab. medicine, medicine and cmty. medicine Tufts U., Boston, 1970-78; prof., chmn. dept. rehab. medicine SUNY, Buffalo, 1978-98, deans adv. coun., 1998—, Gresham vis. prof., 1989, med. dir. Erie County Med. Ctr., 1990-92. Bd. dirs. Presbyn. Sr. Care Found. NY. With USPHS, 1960—62. Nat. Found. fellow rehab., 1962-64; recipient Disting. Service award Mass. Council Orgns. Handicapped, 1972 Fellow ACP, Am. Coll. Rheumatology (emeritus); mem. Am. Acad. Phys. Medicine and Rehab. (hon.), Renaissance Acad., Columbia U. Club (NYC), Harvard Club (Boston), Gross Med. Club. Achievements include research in epidemiology chronic disease, functional assessment, stroke disability. Office: SUNY Buffalo Dept Rehab Medicine 462 Grider St Buffalo NY 14215 Office Phone: 716-898-3218. Personal E-mail: greshdoc@aol.com.

GRESHAM, ZANE OLIVER, lawyer; b. Mobile, Ala., Dec. 16, 1948; S. Charles Brandon and Lillian Ann (Oliver) G. BA cum laude, Johns Hopkins U., 1970; JD magna cum laude, Northwestern U., 1973. Bar: Calif. 1973. Assoc. Morrison & Foerster, San Francisco, 1973-79, ptnr., 1980—, co-chair land use and environ. law group, 1987-97, co-chair airports and aviation law group, 1996—; chair Latin Am. Group, 1998—. Dir., v.p. (Latin Am.) Internat. Private Water Assn., 1999—; dir. Fromm Inst., 2000—. Cons. editor: Environ. Compliance and Litigation Strategy. Pres. San Francisco Forward, 1980-85; bd. dirs. Regional Inst. Bay Area, Richmond, Calif., 1989-95, Regional Parks Found., Oakland, Calif., 1992—, pres., 1995; spl. counsel Grace Cathedral, San Francisco, 1991—; dir., exec. v.p. Pan Am. Soc. Calif., 1995-97, pres. 1998—; vice chmn. Nat. Youth Sci. Found., 1997—; bd. dir. Found. San Francisco (Calif.) Archl. Heritage, 2004—. Mem. State Bar Calif., Urban Land Inst., Lambda Alpha. Avocations: opera, sketching. Office: Morrison & Foerster 425 Market St Ste 3100 San Francisco CA 94105-2482 Office Phone: 415-268-7000. Business E-Mail: zgresham@mofo.com.

GRESSAK, ANTHONY RAYMOND, JR., sales executive; b. Honolulu, Jan. 22, 1947; s. Anthony Raymond and Anne Tavares (Ferreira) G.; m. Catherine Streb, Apr. 11, 1981; children: Danielle Kirsten, Anthony Raymond III, Christina Michelle. AA, Utah State U., 1967; postgrad., U.S. Army Inf. Officers Candidate Sch., 1968. Restaurant mgr. Ala Moana Hotel, Honolulu, 1970-72; gen. mgr. Fred Harvey, Inc., Ontario, Calif., 1972-73; regional mgr. So. Calif., 1972-73, regional mgr. tollway ops., 1973; divisional mgr. Normandy Lane, 1973; resident mgr. Royal Inns of Am., San Diego, 1974; food and beverage dir. Asso. Inns & Restaurant Co. of Am. (Aircoa), Big Sky, Mont., 1974-75; condominium mgr. Big Sky, 1975; asst. gen. mgr. Naples (Fla.) Bath and Tennis Club, 1975-76; food and beverage dir. Nat. Parks, Grand Canyon, Ariz., 1976-77; gen. mgr. Grand Canyon Nat. Park Lodges, 1977-79; divisional v.p. food services The Broadway, Carter Hawley Hale, Inc., Los Angeles, 1979-82; exec. v.p. Silco Corp., Los Angeles, 1982-84; mktg. mgr. Interstate Restaurant Supply, 1984-85; dir. mktg. and merchandising S.E. Rykoff & Co., Los Angeles, 1986-91; nat. accounts sales mgr. healthcare and hospitality Rykoff-Sexton, Inc., L.A., 1991-93; v.p. distbr. sales The Cheesecake Factory Bakery Inc., Calabasas Hills, Calif., 1993—. Mem. edn. culinary steering com. LA Trade Tech. Coll. With U.S. Army, 1967-70. Decorated Silver Star, Bronze Star, Purple Heart; South Vietnamese Cross of Gallantry. Mem.: Internat. Foodservice Mfrs. Assn., Smithsonian Assocs., Nat. Restaurant Assn. (assoc.), Am. Culinary Fedn. (assoc. Presdl. Medallion award 1991), Calif. Restaurant Assn. (assoc.), Internat. Order DeMolay (life; chevalier). Roman Catholic. Home: 20301 Minnehaha St Chatsworth CA 91311-2540 Office: The Cheesecake Factory 26950 Agoura Rd Agoura Hills CA 91301-5335 Office Phone: 818-871-3000. E-mail: tgressak@thecheesecakefactory.com. *Common sense isn't so common. Self discipline and respect for yourself will achieve success. Strive for perfection and you will attain it. Never give up. You never get a second chance to make a first impression.*

GRESSMAN, EUGENE, lawyer; b. Lansing, Mich., Apr. 18, 1917; s. William Albert and Bess Beulah (Nagle) G.; m. Nan Alice Kirby, Aug. 6, 1944 (dec. May 2004); children: William, Margot and Nancy (twins), Eric. AB, U. Mich., 1938, JD with distinction, 1940; LLD, Seton Hall U., 1994. Bar: Mich. 1940, U.S. Supreme Ct. 1945, D.C. 1948, Md. 1959. Atty. SEC, Washington, 1940-43; law clk. to Justice Frank Murphy, U.S. Supreme Ct., 1943-48; ptnr. firm Van Arkel, Kaiser, Gressman, Rosenberg & Driesen, Washington, 1948-77, of counsel, 1977-81, Bredhoff & Kaiser, Washington, 1981-84, Brand & Frulla, Washington, 1984—. Spl. counsel U.S. Ho. of Reps., 1976-84; William Rand Kenan Jr. prof. law U. N.C., Chapel Hill, 1977-87, prof. emeritus, 1987—; disting. vis. prof. Fordham U. Law Sch., 1982-83, 1987-88; Disting. vis. prof. Seton Hall U. Law Sch., 1987-94; vis. prof. law Ohio State U., 1967, Mich. Law Sch., 1969, George Washington U., 1971-77, Ind. U., 1976, Cath. U. Am., 1977; judge Appeals Tax Ct. Montgomery County, Md., 1959-62; chmn. rules com. U.S. Ct. Appeals for 4th Cir., 1984-89. Author: (with Robert L. Stern and others) Supreme Court Practice, 1950, 8th edit., 2002; (with Charles A. Wright and others) Federal Practice and Procedure: Jurisdiction, vol. 16, 1977; (with David Crump and David Day) Cases and Materials on Constitutional Law, 1989, 4th edit., 2002; contbr. articles to profl. jours. Fellow Am. Acad. Appellate Lawyers (hon.); mem. ABA, Fed. Bar Assn., D.C. Bar, Am. Law Inst. (life), Am. Judicature Soc., Order of the Coif, Order of Barristers, Phi Beta Kappa, Delta Theta Pi (Lifetime Achievement award). Home: 325 Glendale Dr Chapel Hill NC 27514-5915 Office: U NC Sch Law Chapel Hill NC 27599-3380 Office Phone: 919-962-3688. Business E-Mail: egressma@email.unc.edu.

GRETES, FRANCES CONSTANCE, information specialist; d. Ernest Peter Gretes. BFA, Coll. William and Mary, 1970; M in Librarianship, Emory U., 1973. Archtl. libr. John Portman & Assoc., Atlanta, 1973—76; adminstrv. libr. U.S. Army Libr., Grafenwoehr, 1976—79; army libr. Pentagon, Washington, 1980; mktg. coord., info. dir. Skidmore, Owings & Merrill, N.Y.C., 1980—93; pres. Gretes Rsch. Svcs. Info. Broker, 1993—. Dir. new bus. Rafael Viñoly Architects, 2002—. Author: Directory of International Periodicals and Newsletters on the Built Environment; contbr. articles to profl. jours. Recipient Cert. of Achievement, U.S. Dept. Army, 1979. Mem.: Assn. Ind. Info. Profls., Art Libr. Soc. N.Am., Spl. Libr. Assn. Greek Orthodox.

GRETZ, RONALD JOHN, music educator, conductor; b. Balt., Oct. 17, 1944; s. Charles William and Ida May Gretz. MusB, Peabody Conservatory, 1966, MusM, 1968. Tchr. Brunswick Sch., Greenwich, Conn., 1968—69; instr. Harford C.C., Bel Air, Md., 1969—71; dir. admissions Peabody Conservatory, Balt., 1971—72; prof. music C.C. Balt., 1972—. Conductor, artistic dir. Annapolis Opera, 1985—; opera coach Peabody Conservatory, 1992—96; conductor Gettysburg Symphony, Balt., 1993—2003; conductor, founder Md. Philharmonic Orch., Balt., 2004—. Organist, choir dir. U. Bapt. Ch., 1989—. Home: 1904 Eutaw Pl Baltimore MD 21217 Office: Cmty Coll Balt Essex Campus 7201 Rossville Blvd Rosedale MD 21237

GRETZINGER, RALPH EDWIN, III, retired management consultant; b. Louisville, Sept. 7, 1948; s. Ralph Edwin Jr. and Martha Irene (Jennings) G.; m. Jewel Jean Rocker, Mar. 21, 1970; children: Ralph Edwin IV, Sarah Elizabeth. BS in Applied Math., Ga. Inst. Tech., 1970; MBA, U. Utah, 1974. Group mgr. Prudential Ins. Co., Cin., 1974-76; owner, regional office mgr. Hewitt Assocs., Lincolnshire, Ill., 1976-78, Dayton, Ohio, 1978-81, Dallas, 1981—2005, ret., 2005. Trustee Child Care Partnership of Dallas, 1985-90; mem. adv. bd. Ga. Tech. Coll. Scis., 2004—. Served with U.S. Army, 1971-74. Mem. S.W. Pension Conf., Ga. Tech. Club of North Tex. (pres. 1986-88), Beta Gamma Sigma. Roman Catholic. Avocations: wine collecting, golf. Office: Hewitt Assocs 2201 W Royal Ln Ste 100 Irving TX 75063-3205 Office Phone: 972-402-8700. Personal E-mail: regretzi@aol.com.

GRETZKY, WAYNE DOUGLAS, retired professional hockey player, businessman; b. Brantford, Ont., Can., Jan. 26, 1961; s. Walter and Phyllis Gretzky; m. Janet Jones, July 16, 1988; children: Paulina, Ty Robert, Trevor Douglas. Center Peterborough Petes, Jr. Ont. Hockey Assn., 1977—78, Sault Ste. Marie Greyhounds, 1977—78, Indpls. Racers, World Hockey Assn., 1978, Edmonton Oilers NHL, Edmonton, Canada, 1988, L.A. Kings, NHL, 1988—96, St. Louis Blues, NHL, 1996, N.Y. Rangers, NHL, 1996—99, ret., 1999; investor Los Arcos Sports LLC/Phoenix Coyotes, 1999—; head coach Phoenix Coyotes, 2005—; dir. Can. Nat Team, Olympic Games, Salt Lake City, 2002, Can. Nat Team, World Cup of Hockey, 2004. Named Rookie of Yr., World Hockey Assn., 1978—79, Sportsman of Yr., Sports Illustrated, 1982, Sporting News NHL Player of Yr., 1980—81, 1986—87, Sporting News Man of Yr., 1981, Can. Athlete of Yr., 1985, Dodge Performer of Yr., 1984—85, 1986—87, All-Star Game MVP, 1983, 1989, 1999; named to NHL All-Star Team, 1980—94, 1997—99; recipient Art Ross Meml. Trophy, NHL, 1981—87, 1989—90, 1990—91, 1993—94, Conn Smythe Trophy, 1985, 1988, William Hanley Trophy, 1977—78, Lemms Family award, 1977—78, Hart Meml. Trophy, 1974—80, Lady Byng Meml. Trophy, 1979—80, 1990—91, 1991—92, 1993—94, Lester B. Pearson award, 1982, 1984—85, 1986—87, Emery Edge award, 1983—84, 1984—85, 1986—87, Lester Patrick Trophy, 1993—94. Achievements include the record holder for points, goals, assists, overtime assists and others; mem. Stanely Cup Champion Edmonton Oilers, 1984, 1985, 1987, 1988; inducted into Hockey Hall of Fame, 1999. Office: c/o Phoenix Coyotes Cellular One Ice Den 9375 E Bell Rd Scottsdale AZ 85260-0101*

GREVE, GUY ROBERT, lawyer; b. Bay City, Mich., Oct. 25, 1947; m. Nancy Lisbeth Mueller, Sept. 21, 1991; 1 child, Tyler James. BA, U. Mich., 1970; postgrad., U. Kent, Canterbury, Eng., 1974; JD, Detroit Coll., 1975. Bar: Mich. 1975, U.S. Dist. Ct. (ea. dist.) Mich. 1975. Ptnr. Patterson & Greve, Bay City, 1975-78; asst. atty. City of Bay City, 1975-76, atty., 1976-78; pvt. practice Bay City, 1978—. One-man shows include; co-chair Day in Life of Bay Country Photo Project, 2000. Bd. dirs. Am. Cancer Soc., 1975—2001, pres., 1982—83, Muse-Hopper Mobile Mus., Mich., 1980—82; co-chair Delta Coll. Scholarship Fundraiser, 2001; mem. steering com., capital campaign com. Friends State Theater, 2001—, vice chair, 2005; bd. dirs. Bay Arts Coun., 1999—, Women's Crisis Ctr., Bay City, 1977—79. Named Disting. Alumnus, Handy HS, 1985; recipient Disting. Svc. award, Bay City Jaycees, 1981. Mem.: ATLA, ABA, Mich. Trial Lawyers Assn., Bay County Bar Assn. (Liberty Bell chmn. 1994—98, bd. dirs. 1994—2000, pres. 1998—99), Mich. Bar Assn. (rep. assembly 1999—2001), Bay Area C. of C., Studio 23 (hon.), U.S. Power Squadron, Saginaw Bay Yacht Club, U. Mich. Alumni Club (Bay City chpt. pres. 1994—97), Elks Club (lodge # 88), Optimists (pres. Bay City 1979—80, lt. gov. Mich. 1985—86, chmn. new club bldg. 1986—87, chmn. club svcs. 1989—90, founder, chair travel series 1993—, asst. gov. Mich. 1996—97, internat. conv. com. 1997). Home: 2300 Nurmi Dr Bay City MI 48708-6872 Office: PO Box 851 817 Washington Ave Bay City MI 48707 Office Phone: 989-893-9578. Personal E-mail: ggreve@sbcglobal.net.

GREVE, JOHN HENRY, veterinary parasitologist, educator; b. Pitts., Aug. 11, 1934; s. John Welch and Edna Viola (Thuenen) G.; m. Sally Jeanette Doane, June 21, 1956; children— John Haven, Suzanne Carol, Pamela Jean BS, Mich. State U., East Lansing, 1956, D.V.M., 1958, MS, 1959; PhD, Purdue U., West Lafayette, Ind., 1963. Assoc. instr. Mich. State U., East Lansing, 1958-59; instr. Purdue U., West Lafayette, 1959-63; asst. prof. Iowa State U., Ames, 1963-64, assoc. prof., 1964-68, prof. dept. vet. pathology, 1968-99, interim chair dept. vet. pathology, 1992-95, counselor acad. and student affairs, 1991-92. Cons. to dean on alumni affairs Coll. Vet. Medicine; cons. parasitologist various zoos. Mem. editl. bd. Lab. Animal Sci., 1971-83, Vet. Rsch. Comm., 1977-84, Vet. Parasitology, 1984-98; contbr. articles to sci. jours., chpts. to books. Dist. chmn. Broken Arrow Dist., Boy Scouts Am., Ames, Iowa, 1975-77; mem. devel. bd. Octagon Ctr. for the Arts, Ames, 2004—. Named Disting. Tchr. Norden Labs., 1965, 99, Outstanding Tchr. Amoco Oil, Iowa State U., 1972, Faculty Mem. of Yr., Coll. Vet. Medicine, 1999; recipient Faculty Citation Iowa State U. Alumni Assn., 1978. Mem. AVMA (mem. editl. bd. jour. 1975-98, Excellence in Teaching award student chpt. 1990), Iowa Vet. Med. Assn., Am. Soc. Parasitologists, Midwestern Conf. Parasitologists (sec.-treas. 1967-75, presiding officer 1975-76), Am. Assn. Vet. Parasitologists (pres. 1968-70), Helminthological Soc. Washington, World Assn. for Advancement Vet. Parasitology, Am. Assn. Vet. Med. Colls., Izaak Walton League (bd. dirs. Iowa 1968-70), Honor Soc. Cardinal Key, Gamma Sigma Delta, Phi Eta Sigma, Phi Kappa Phi, Phi Zeta. Lodges: Kiwanis (Town and Country-Ames pres. 1967, 2006, Nebr.-Iowa lt. gov. 1972-73). Republican. Avocations: stamp collecting/philately, camping, gardening. Office: Iowa State U Coll Vet Med Found Ames IA 50011-1250 Office Phone: 515-294-0867. Business E-Mail: sdgreve@isunet.net.

GREVEN, KATHRYN MCCONNELL, radiologist, oncologist; b. Richmond, Va., Dec. 28, 1956; d. Robert William and Kathryn Paine McConnell; m. Craig Greven, Sept. 12, 1981; children: Margaret, William, Alexander. MD, Wake Forest U., 1983; AB in Chemistry, Duke U., 1979. Diplomate Am. Bd. Radiology, 1983. Resident Wake Forest U. Med. Ctr., 1983—87; asst. prof. radiology U. Pa., 1987—89; prof. Wake Forest U., WinstonSalem, NC, 2001—. Office: Department of Radiation Oncology Medical Center Boulevard Winston Salem NC 27157 Business E-Mail: kgreven@wfubmc.edu.

GREVESEN, CHRIS WILLIAM, management consultant, educator; b. South Amboy, NJ, Apr. 28, 1955; s. Chris Eugene and Alice Louise Grevesen; m. Bella Marie Ryan, Aug. 18, 1979; children: Kara, Jessica, Kristen. BA, Rutgers Coll., 1978; MBA, Rutgers U., 1987, PhD, 2001. Cert. tchr. NJ. Tchr. Woodbridge (NJ) Twp. Schs., 1978—82; dean gen. den. DeVry Tech. Inst., Woodbridge, 1982—93; prof. dept. bus. DeVry Coll. Tech., North Brunswick, NJ, 1993—. Mem.: Acad. Internat. Bus., Strategic Mgmt. Soc., Acad. Mgmt., Phi Delta Kappa, Phi Beta Kappa. Roman Catholic. Office: DeVry Coll Tech 630 US Hwy 1 North Brunswick NJ 08902 E-mail: cgrevese@nj.devry.edu.

GREVING, ROBERT C., insurance company executive; BS in Math., Quincy U., 1975. Exec. v.p., chief actuary Southwestern Fin. Svcs. Corp., 1990—97; sr. v.p., chief actuary Provident, 1997—2001, sr. v.p. fin., 2001—02; sr. v.p., CFO UnumProvident Corp., Chattanooga, 2002—03, exec. v.p., CFO, 2003—. Office: Unum Provident Corp 1 Fountain Sq Chattanooga TN 37402

GREW, PRISCILLA CROSWELL, academic administrator, geologist, educator; b. Glens Falls, NY, Oct. 26, 1940; d. James Croswell and Evangeline Pearl (Beougher) Perkins; m. Edward Sturgis Grew, June 14, 1975. BA magna cum laude, Bryn Mawr Coll., 1962; PhD, U. Calif., Berkeley, 1967. Instr. dept. geology Boston Coll., 1967-68, asst. prof., 1968-72; asst. rsch. geologist UCLA, 1972-77, adj. asst. prof. environ. sci. and engring., 1975-76; dir. Calif. Dept. Conservation, 1977-81; commr. Calif. Pub. Utilities Commn., San Francisco, 1981-86; dir. Minn. Geol. Survey, St. Paul, 1986-93; prof. dept. geology U. Minn., Mpls., 1986-93; vice chancellor for rsch. U. Nebr., Lincoln, 1993-99, prof. dept. geoscis., 1993—, prof. conservation/survey divsn. Inst. Agr., 1993—, dir. U. Nebr. State Mus., 2003—, fellow Ctr. for Great Plains Studies, 2003—; coord. Native Am. Graves Protection and Repatriation Act, 1998—. Vis. asst. prof. geology U. Calif., Davis, 1973-74; chmn. Calif. State Mining and Geology Bd., Sacramento, 1976-77; exec. sec., editor Lake Powell Rsch. Project, 1971-77; cons., vis. staff Los Alamos (N.Mex.) Nat. Lab., 1972-77; com. on minority participation in earth sci. and mineral engring. Dept. Interior, 1972-75; chmn. Calif. Geothermal Resource Task Force, 1977, Calif. Geothermal Resources Bd., 1977-81; earthquake studies adv. panel US Geol. Survey, 1979-83, adv. com., 1982-86; adv. coun. Gas Rsch. Inst., 1982-86, rsch. coord. coun., 1987-98, vice-chmn., 1994-96, chmn., 1996-98, sci. and tech. coun., 1998-2001; bd. on global change rsch. NAS, 1995-99, subcom. on earthquake rsch., 1985-88, bd. on earth scis. and resources, 1986-91, bd. on mineral and energy resources, 1982-88, Minn. Minerals Coord. Com., 1986-93, US nat. com. for internat. union of geological scis. (IUGS), 1985-93, US nat. com. for the internat. union of geodesy and geophysics 2001—, chmn., 2003—; mem. US Nat. Com. on Diversitas, 2000—, vice chmn., 2004—; adv. bd. Stanford U. Sch. Earth Scis., 1989—, Sec. of Energy Adv. Bd., 1995-97; com. on equal opportunities in sci. and tech. NSF, 1985-86, adv. com. on earth scis., 1987-91, adv. com. on sci. and tech. ctrs. devel., 1987-91, adv. com. on sci. and tech. ctrs., 1996, adv. com. on geoscis., 1994-97; mem. State-Fed. Tech. Partnership Task Force, 1995-99, Fed. Coun. for Continental Sci. Drilling, 1992-98, Gt. Plains Partnership Coun., 1995-99; trustee Am. Geol. Inst. Found., 1988— (Ian Campbell medlist 1999). Contbr. articles to profl. jours. Trustee 1st Plymouth Congl. Ch., Lincoln, 1997—2000; mem. edn. and outreach steering com. Earth Scope, 2005—; bd. dirs. Abendmusik:Lincoln, 1995—97. Fellow, NSF, 1962—66. Fellow AAAS (chmn. electorate nominating com. sect. E 1980-84, mem.-at-large 1987-91, chmn.-elect 1994, chmn. 1995, coun. del. 1997-98), Geol. Soc. Am. (nominations com. 1974, chmn. com. on geology and pub. policy 1981-84, audit com. 1988-90, chair 1990, com. on coms. 1986-87, 91-92, chmn. com. on coms. 1995, chair Day medal com. 1990, councilor 1987-91), Mineral. Soc. Am. (mem. Roebling medal com. 1999-2003), Geol. Assn. Can., Ctr. Great Plains Studies; mem. Am. Geophys. Union (chmn. com. pub. affairs 1984-89), Soc. Mayflower Descs., Nat. Parks and Conservation Assn. (trustee 1982-86), Nat. Assn. Regulatory Utility Commrs. (com. on gas 1982-86, exec. com. 1984-86, com. on energy conservation 1983-84), Interstate Oil and Gas Compact Commn.

(mem. Petroleum Profls. Task Force, 2001-03), Cosmos Club, Rotary, Country Club of Lincoln, Sigma Xi (pres. U. Minn. chpt. 1990-91). Congregationalist. Office: U Nebr State Mus 307 Morrill Hall Lincoln NE 68588-0338 Office Phone: 402-472-3779. Business E-Mail: pgrew1@unl.edu.

GREW, RAYMOND EDWARD, mechanical engineer; b. Metamora, Ohio, Jan. 11, 1923; s. Edward F. and Coletta (Minck) G.; children: Elizabeth, Mary, Janet, John. BSME, U. Mich., 1948. Registered profl. engr., Calif. Prin. engr. Hoffmann La Roche, Nutley, NJ, 1957—83. Navigator USAF. Mem. English Speaking Union, Pilgrims of U.S., Caterpiller Club. Achievements include patent for chromatographic device. Home: 28124 Hamden Ln Escondido CA 92026-6648

GREWAL, RAJDEEP, marketing professional, educator; b. Ludhiana, Punjab, India, July 18, 1968; arrived in U.S., 1994; s. Ranjit and Rana Grewal; m. Rima Baidwan, Jan. 5, 1997; children: Kabir children: Angad. B.Tech, Indian Inst. of Tech., New Delhi, 1990; PGDM in Bus. Adminstrn., Indian Inst. Mgmt., Lucknow, 1994; MS in Bus. Stats., U. Cin., 1997, PhD in Bus. Adminstrn., 1998. Asst. prof. mktg. Wash. State U., Pullman, 1998—2001, Pa. State U., State Coll., 2001—. Mem. editl. bd.: Jour. of Mktg., Decision Scis.; contbr. articles to profl. jours. (Young Contr. award, Jour. of Consumer Psychology, 2003). Mem.: Acad. of Mgmt., Mktg. Sci. Inst. (Young Scholar 2003), Am. Mktg. Assn. Achievements include research in modeling issues in strategic mktg; interfirm relationships. Home: 1465 N Foxpointe Dr State College PA 16803 Office: 701 BAB 1 Smeal Coll of Bus Pa State Univ University Park PA 16802-3007 Office Phone: 814-863-0728. Personal E-mail: rug2@psu.edu.

GREWCOCK, BRUCE E., mining executive; BS, Colo. Sch. Mines, 1976. With Utah Internat., 1976—82; chief engr. Peter Kiewit Sons', Inc., 1982—85; v.p., ops. mgr. Kiewit Mining Group, 1986—91, pres., 1992—95; pres., COO Peter Kiewit Sons', Omaha, 2000—; exec. v.p. Peter Kiewit Sons', Inc., Omaha, 1996—2002; also bd. dirs. Bd. dirs. Kiewit Materials Co., Kinross Gold Corp. Coun. mem. Knights of Ak-Sar-Ben Found., 2002—; bd. dirs. Omaha Cmty. Found., Coll. World Series. Office: Peter Kiewit Sons 1000 Kiewit Plz Omaha NE 68131-3374

GREWELL, JOHANNE H. FAIRS, retired librarian; b. Pittsfield, Mass., June 30, 1938; d. John H. and Eleanor (Brooks) Fairs; m. Donald Robert Grewell, Aug. 5, 1961 (div. Feb. 1970); 1 child, Dawn Rebecca. BS in Edn., Ea. Ill. U., Charleston, 1960; MS in LS, U. Ill., 1965. Cert. in h.s. teaching, instructional materials, Ill. Tchr. English, 10th grade Mattoon (Ill.) H.S., 1960-64; tchr. lang. arts, 8th grade Ctrl. Jr. H.S., Mattoon, 1964-66; 1st asst. cataloger Ea. Ill. U., 1966-71; media specialist Armstrong Jr. H.S., Jacksonville, Ill., 1971-77; libr. media specialist Peoria (Ill.) HS, 1977—2000; sch. libr. devel. cons. Alliance Libr. Sys., East Peoria, Ill., 2000—05; ret., 2005. Instr. media/libr. svcs. Ill. Ctrl. Coll., East Peoria, 1978-95; subcom. on sys. Ill. State Libr. Adv. Coun., Springfield, 1994-97; cons. Libr. Book Selection Svc., Bloomington, Ill., 1992-2000, Alliance Libr. Sys. Adv. Coun., 1995-2000. Costume chmn. for numerous plays in cmty. theaters. Mem. ALA, Am. Assn. Sch. Librs., Ill. Sch. Libr. Media Assn. (bd. dirs., past pres.), PEO, Delta Kappa Gamma.

GREY, BRAD, motion picture studio executive; b. Bronx, NY, Dec. 29, 1957; m. Jill Grey; children: Sam, Max, Emily. Student, SUNY; BS in Comm. & Bus., U. Buffalo, 1979; LHD (hon.), SUNY, 2003. With Harvey & Corky Productions, Brillstein-Grey Entertainment, Beverly Hills, Calif., 1985—92, ptnr., 1992—96, chmn. CEO, 1996—2005; co-founder (with Jennifer Anniston and Brad Pitt) Plan B Entertainment, 2002; chmn., CEO Paramount Motion Pictures Group, Hollywood, Calif., 2005—. Bd. dirs UCLA Sch. Medicine, Project ALS, KCET LA Pub. TV, Dean's Coun., NYU Tisch Sch. Arts; bd. dirs. Environ. Media Assn., Comic Relief; bd. councilors U. So. Calif. Sch. Cinema. Exec. prodr.: (films) Opportunity Knocks, 1990; exec. prodr.: (films) The Celluloid Closet, 1995, Happy Gilmore, 1996, The Cable Guy, 1996, Bulletproof, 1996, The Replacement Killers, 1998, The Wedding Singer, 1998, Dirty Work, 1998, What Planet Are You From?, 2000, Screwed, 2000, Scary Movie, 2000; prodr. (films) City by the Sea, 2002, View From the Top, 2003, Charlie and the Chocoloate Factory, 2005, prodr., writer The Burning, 1981; exec. prodr.: (TV films) Don't Try This at Home!, 1990, Three Sisters Searching for a Cure, 2004; (TV series) The Boys, 1989, Good Sports, 1991, The Larry Sanders Show, 1992, NewsRadio, 1995, Mr. Show, 1995, The Naked Truth, 1995, The Steve Harvey Show, 1996, The Dana Carvey Show, 1996, Just Shoot Me!, 1997, Alright Already, 1997, C-16: FBI, 1997, Politically Incorrect, 1997—98, 2000—01, Applewood 911, 1998, The Sopranos, 1999— (Golden Globe award for best dramatic series, Emmy award for best dramatic series, 2004), Sammy, 2000, Pasadena, 2001, Real Time with Bill Maher, 2003, My Big Fat Greek Life, 2003, The Lyon's Den, 2003, Cracking Up, 2004, Married to the Kellys, 2003, Jake in Progress, 2005—. Named one of 50 Most Powerful People in Hollywood, Premiere mag., 2005; recipient George Foster Peabody award (4 times). Office: Paramount Studios 5555 Melrose Ave West Hollywood CA 90038

GREY, DEBORAH CLELAND, former Canadian government official; b. Vancouver, B.C., Can., July 1, 1952; d. Mansell Caverhill Grey and Lilian Joyce (Russell) Levy; m. Lewis Larson, Aug. 7, 1993. Student, Burrard Inlet Bible Inst., 1973; student in Sociology and English, Trinity Western Coll., Langley, British Columbia, 1978; BA, U. Alta., Edmonton, Can., 1978, B of Edn. after degree, 1979. Tchr. Frog Lake (Alta.) Indian Res., 1979-80; tchr. jr. and sr. H.S. Dewberry (Alta.) Sch., 1980-89; M.P. Ho. of Commons, Ottawa, 1989—2004. Author: (autobiography) Never Retreat, Never Explain, Never Apologize: My Life, 2004. First mem. Reform Party Ho. Commons; Caucus chmn. Reform Party, 1993-2000, apptd. dep. parliamentary leader, 1995-2000, apptd. leader ofcl. opposition, 2000; dep. critic Human Resources Devel., 1998; caucus chair PC-DR Coalition Caucus, 2001; critic Aboriginal Affairs, 2001. Recipient Can. 125 medal, 1993, Alumni award of distinction Trinity Western U., 1996. Reform. Avocations: kayaking, gospel singing, motorcycles, drama, hiking.

GREY, FRANCIS JOSEPH, accountant, educator; b. Yeadon, Pa., Nov. 30, 1931; s. William and Delia (Mullin) G.; m. Marlene M. Ward, June 24, 1961; children: Francis Joseph Jr., Melissa Ann. BS in Econs., Villanova U., 1958. CPA. Tax profl. Coopers & Lybrand, Phila., 1958-64, tax ptnr. in charge, 1964-72, mng. ptnr. tax, 1972—. Mem. devel. com. Villanova (Pa.) U., 1972—; bd. dirs. Del. County Hosp., Upper Darby, Pa.; adj. prof. Villanova Law Sch. Author: Tax Planning for Real Estate, 1978, 88, Pa. Taxation of Corporations, 1980; contbr. articles to profl. jours. Adv. com. Wharton Sch. Tax Conf., Phila., 1970-88, Internat. Bus. Forum, Phila., 1980-88. Sgt. U.S. Army, 1952-53, Korea. Mem. AICPAs, Pa. Inst. CPAs (v.p. 1988), Internat. Fiscal Assn. (treas. 1975), Phila. C. of C. (bd. dirs. 1975—), Phila. Country Club (bd. dirs. 1980-84), Union League of Phila., Locust Club, Beta Gamma Sigma. Republican. Roman Catholic. Avocations: golf, tennis, sports.

GREY, JOEL, actor; b. Cleve., Apr. 11, 1932; s. Mickey and Grace Katz; m. Jo Wilder, June 29, 1958; children: Jennifer, Jimmy. Litt.D. (hon.), Cleve. State U., 1974. Began stage career in childhood, traveling with father as song and dance man, played Chez Paris, Chgo., at age 18; N.Y. stage debut in The Littlest Revue, 1956; appeared with nat. touring co. of Stop the World on Broadway, 1963, Come Blow Your Horn, 1961, Half a Sixpence, 1965, George M, 1969, Harry, Noon and Night, 1965, Marco Polo Sings a Solo, 1977; appeared on stage in Goodtime Charley, 1975, The Grand Tour, 1979, Silverlake, 1981, Pal Joey, 1983, 1988-89, (off-Broadway), The Normal Heart, 1986, When We Dead Awaken, 1991; starring role (Broadway prodn.) Cabaret, 1966-67, (Tony award 1967) (revival 1987-88, nat. tour 1988—), also motion picture, 1972 (Acad. award 1972); TV appearances include Evening at Pops, 1979, Dallas, 1991, Alias, 2005, others; (TV spls.) George M, 1970, Twas the Night Before Christmas, 1974, Jubilee!, 1976, Night of 100 Stars, 1982, The Yeoman of the Guard, 1984; (TV movie) The Wizard of Oz in Concert, 1995; (TV miniseries) Queenie, 1987, Marilyn and Me, 1991, The Dangerous, 1995; (films) About Face, 1952, Calypso Heat Wave, 1957, Come September, 1961, Man on a Swing, 1974, Buffalo Bill and the Indians, 1975, The Seven Percent Solution, 1976, Remo Williams: The Adventure Begins, 1985, Kafka, 1992, The Music of Chance, 1993, Venus Rising, 1995, The Fantasticks, 1995, The Empty Mirror, 1996, My Friend Joe, 1996, Reaching Normal, 1999, Just Desserts, 1999, Dancer in the Dark, 2000. Address: Innovative Artists Talent and Literary Agy 1999 Ave Of Stars Ste 2850 Los Angeles CA 90067-4612*

GREY, JOSEPH EDWARD, II, artist; b. Lancaster, Ohio, May 20, 1927; s. Joseph E. and Lyla Belle (Goodwin) G.; m. Mary Gargiulo, Aug. 15, 1957; children: Catherine Alexandra, Anthony Joseph. CFA, Columbus Coll. of Art & Design, 1950, M Visual Arts, 1986. Graphic designer N.Y.C. Housing Authority, 1953-56; illustrator Chas Bracket Studio, N.Y.C., 1956-57; designer M&M Studio, N.Y.C., 1958-60, Paul Klemptner, N.Y.C., 1960-61; art dir. Hockaday Assocs., N.Y.C., 1961-65, Sullivan, Stoffer, Cowell & Bayles, N.Y.C., 1965-69; creative dir. McCann Erickson, Jamaica, W.I., 1969-72, art dir. N.Y.C., 1972-76, Troy, Mich., 1976-80; sr. art dir. Campbell Ewald, Warren, Mich., 1980-90; art dir. McCann SAS, Troy, 1990-92; fine art painter Beverly Hills, Mich., 1992—. Pub. in: The Best of Watercolor 1996, Best of Watercolor Painting Composition, 1997, New Art Internat., 1997, Portrait Inspirations, 1997. Recipient Chevrolet-One Car Co. award Am. Film Festival, N.Y., 1986, Caddy/Gold award, Detroit, 1978, N.Y. Ad Club/Gold, N.Y., 1975, Am. Film Festival/Gold, N.Y., 1968, awards Ariz. WS Assn., 1995, Art Birmingham, 1996, Watercolor Soc., Houston, 1997, Fort North, 1997, Nat. Watercolor Soc., 1999, N.E. Watercolor Soc., 1999, Fine Arts Inst. 34th Ann. Int., 1999. Mem. Nat. Watercolor Soc., Watercolor West, Tex. Watercolor Soc., Ariz. Watercolor Soc., Pa. Watercolor Soc., Ft. Worth Watercolor Soc., Art Birmingham, Houston Watercolor Art Soc., Emily Lowe Nat. Watercolor Competition. Roman Catholic. Avocations: tennis, classical and jazz music. Home: 19100 Beverly Rd Beverly Hills MI 48025-3901

GREY, ROBERT DEAN, academic administrator, biology educator; b. Liberal, Kans., Sept. 5, 1939; s. McHenry Wesley and Kathryn (Brown) G.; m. Alice Kathleen Archer, June 11, 1961; children: Erin Kathleen, Joel Michael. BA, Phillips U., 1961; PhD, Washington U., 1966. Asst. prof. Washington U., St. Louis, 1966-67; from asst. prof. to full prof. zoology U. Calif., Davis, 1967—, chmn. dept., 1979-83, dean biol. scis., 1985—, interim exec. vice chancellor, 1993-95, provost, exec. vice chancellor, 1995—2001, sr. advisor to chancellor, 2001—02, provost, exec. vice chancellor emeritus, 2002—, exec. asst. to chancellor health affairs Riverside, 2005—. Author: (with others) A Laboratory Text for Developmental Biology, 1980; contbr. articles to profl. jours. Recipient Disting. Tchg. awrd Acad. Senate U. Calif., Davis, 1977, Magnar Ronning award for tchg. Associated Students U. Calif., Davis, 1978, Disting. Alumnus award Phillips U., 1991. Mem. Am. Soc. Cell Biology, Soc. Developmental Biology, Phi Sigma. Avocations: music, hiking, gardening.

GREY, ROBERT J., energy executive, lawyer; b. N.Y.C., Sept. 6, 1950; m. Susan Grey; children: Lisa, Laura. BA, Columbia U., 1972; JD, Emory U., 1975; LLM taxation, George Washington U., 1979. Bar: Ga. 1975, U.S. Dist. Ct. (no. dist.) Ga. 1975, D.C. 1976, Md. 1976, N.Y. 1978, Oreg. 1982, U.S. Dist. Ct. Oreg. 1984, Wash. 1988, Pa. 1995. Atty., advisor, legal asst. U.S. EPA, 1975-77; staff counsel N.Y. State Pub. Svc. Commn., 1977-82; assoc. Preston Gates & Ellis, Seattle, 1982—83, ptnr., 1983-92; gen. counsel L.I. Lighting Co., 1992—95; v.p., gen. counsel, sec. PPL Corp., Allentown, Pa., 1995—96, sr. v.p., gen. counsel, sec., 1996—. Mem. exec. com. Energy Assn. Pa.; mem. Conference Bd. Council of Chief Legal Officers. Pres. & dir. Jewish Fedn. Lehigh Valley. Mem. ABA. Office: PPL Co 2 N 9th St Allentown PA 18101-1170

GREY, ROBERT J., JR., lawyer; b. Richmond, Va., Aug. 5, 1950; BS, Va. Commonwealth U., 1973; JD, Washington & Lee U., 1976. Bar: Va. 1978. Ptnr. Grey & Wesley, 1978—82; asst. prof. Va Commonwealth U., Sch. of Bus., 1979—82; ptnr. Mays & Valentine, 1985—95, LeClair Ryan, Richmond, Va., 1996—2002, Hunton & Williams LLP, 2002—. Chmn., Va. State Alcoholic Beverage Control Bd., 1982-85; pres., Richmond Crusade for Votes, 1988-90; chmn., Youth Matters, 1995-98; co-chmn., MAPS steering com., 1997-2000; chmn., Greater Richmond Partnership, 1999-2000; bd. dir. Margaretten Corp., 1994; bd. dir & mem. ea. reg. adv. bd., Jefferson Nat. Bank, 1995-97; mem. Va. State bd. adv., Wachovia Bank, 1999-2000; bd. dir., Va Biotechnology Rsch. Park Corp., 2000-. Alumni Star award, Va. Commonwealth U. Sch. of Bus.; 1995, Disting. Leader award, Nat. Assn. for Community Leadership, 1997; Flame Bearer award, UNCF, The College Fund, 1998; Hon. mem., Washington and Lee U. Sch. of Law, 1993. Mem. ABA (chair ho. dels., 1998-2000, bd. govs., exec. com., 1998-2000, president, 2003-04, pres., 2004-05), Grtr. Richmond C. of C. (chair, 1996-97); mem. Va. State Bar (pres., Young Lawyers Conf., 1982-83, chair., Commn. on Women & Minorities in the Profession, 1985-86, chair, Legal Ethics Com., 1986-87); Am. Law Inst.; Nat. Bar Assn. (Wiley A. Branton award 1998, Gertrude E. Rush award 2003); Old Dominion Bar; Richmond Bar Assn.; D.C. Bar; Va. Bar Assn. Office: Hunton & Williams LLP Riverfront Plz E Tower 951 E Byrd St Richmond VA 23219-4074 E-mail: rgrey@hunton.com.

GREY, RUTHANN E., communications specialist, management consultant; b. Buffalo, May 13, 1945; d. Wilson Campbell and Rosalie (Briggs) Evege; m. Daine A. Grey, Aug. 25, 1990; children: Daine, Jr., Keenan, Nichole. BS, SUNY, Buffalo, 1966, MS, 1970, PhD, 1980; postgrad., Harvard U., 1988. Tchr. Bennett H.S., Buffalo, 1966-69; prof. Erie C.C., Buffalo, 1970-73; adminstr. No. Va. C.C., Annandale, 1975-76, Wayne State U., Detroit, 1978-80; dir. pub. affairs Burroughs Corp., Detroit, 1981-86; exec. asst. to chmn. bd. dirs. The Equitable, N.Y.C., 1986-89; mgr. pub. affairs N.Y. Times, N.Y.C., 1989-90; mgr. divsn. corp. rels. Pub. Svc. Corp. Colo., Denver, 1990-93; v.p. comm. and pub. affairs Hoechst Celanese, Bridgewater, NJ, 1993—; v.p. global media and external rels. Hoechst Marion Roussel, Bridgewater, NJ, 1996—; comm. chief Ednl. Testing Svc., Princeton, NJ; with The Caunos Group, Watchung, NJ, 1998—. Cons. A+ For Kids, Newark, 1989-90, Rockefeller Found., N.Y.C., 1989-90. Bd. dirs. Citizens Scholarship Found., Minn., 1990-94. Mem. Pub. Rels. Seminar, Arthur Page Soc., The Wisemen, Pub. Rels. Rsch. Found. Avocations: gardening, walking. Home and Office: The Caunos Group 107 Rockafellow Mill Rd Flemington NJ 08822 Office Phone: 908-377-0180. Personal E-mail: regrey1@earthlink.net.

GREY, SAMUEL T., lawyer; b. Christiansted, St. Croix, V.I., Aug. 1968; BS, U. V.I., 1991; JD, Creighton U., Omaha, 1994. Bar: V.I. 1994. Atty. Legal Services, V.I., 1994—97; assoc. Nichols Newman Logan & D'Eramo, P.C., Christiansted. Mem.: Virgin Islands Bar Assn. (pres. 2003). Office: Nichols Newman Logan & D'Eramo 1131 King St Ste 204 Christiansted VI 00820

GREY, THOMAS C., law educator; b. Sept. 1, 1941. BA, Stanford U., 1963; BA, Oxford U., Eng., 1965; LLB, Yale U., 1968; LLD (hon.), Chgo.-Kent Law Sch., 1998. Bar: DC 1969. Law clk. to Hon. J. Skelly Wright US Ct. Appeals DC Cir., 1968-69; law clk. to Hon. Thurgood Marshall US Supreme Ct., 1969-70; staff atty. Washington Rsch. Project, 1970-71; asst. prof. Stanford Law Sch., 1971-74, assoc. prof., 1974-78, prof., 1978—, Nelson Bowman Sweitzer and Marie B. Sweitzer prof. law, 1990-. Office: Stanford Law Sch Crown Quadrangle 559 Nathan Abbott Way Stanford CA 94305-8610 Office Phone: 650-723-3579. Business E-Mail: tgrey@law.stanford.edu.*

GREYBECK, BARBARA JEAN, education educator; d. Edward Harry and Helen Regina Greybeck. BA, Ohio U., 1970, MS, 1974; PhD, U. of Calif., Berkeley, 1995. Sch. psychologist Sunnyside Sch. Dist., Tucson, 1974—77, Marana Sch. Dist., Ariz., 1977—81; dir. Ctr. for Human Devel., Guadalajara, Mexico, 1981—85, The Reading Game Ctr., Los Angeles, Calif., 1985—86; program specialist/sch. psychologist Oxnard Sch. Dist., Calif., 1986—90; coord. of grad. programs in edn. ITESM Guadalajara, Mexico, 1996—2000; tenured prof. U. of Guadalajara, Mexico, 1996—2000; assoc. prof. Tex. A & M Internat. U., Laredo, Tex., 2000—. Rsch. asst. U. of Calif. at Berkeley, 1992—93; field supr. for student teachers Devel. Tchr. Edn., U. of Calif. at Berkeley, 1993—95; lectr. in virtual u. ITESM, Monterrey, Mexico, 1997—2000, cons. for the ctr. for instl. effectiveness, Mex. City, Mexico, 1998; coord. of doctoral program in edn. U. of Guadalajara, 1998—2000; dir. of the hinojosa reading rsch. ctr. Tex. A & M Internat. U., 2002—. Contbr. articles to profl. jours., chapters to books. Bd. mem. Literacy Volunteers of Am., Laredo, Tex., 2005. Recipient Rsch. Scholar of the Yr., Coll. of Edn., Tex. A & M Internat. U., 2004, Tchr. Effectiveness award, U. of Calif. at Berkeley, Grad. Divsn., 1993, Outstanding Grad. Student Instr. in Edn., 1992, Distinction on Oral Qualifying Exam., Sch. of Edn., U. of Calif. at Berkeley, 1993; Regents' Initiative Collaborative grant, Tex. A & M Internat. U., 2001—04, Fellowship Grant for the Regents' Initiative, 2000, 2004. Mem.: Tex. Assn. of Reading Professors, Tex. State Reading Assn. (jour. editor 2005), Nat. Coun. of Teachers of English, Internat. Reading Assn., Phi Delta Kappa, Delta Kappa Gamma, Kappa Delta Pi (found. rep. 2004—05). Avocations: reading, travel, walking, hiking. Office: Texas A & M Internat Univ 5201 University Blvd Laredo TX 78041 Office Phone: 956-326-2923.

GREYSER, LINDA LORRAINE, education educator; b. Lynn, Mass., Oct. 8, 1942; d. Paul and Minnie E. (Sogoloff) Segel; m. Stephen A. Greyser, June 30, 1968; 1 child, Naomi Judith. BA, Lake Erie Coll., 1964; MA, Middlebury Coll., 1965; EdM, Harvard U., 1990, EdD, 1994. Tchr. Beverly (Mass.) Pub. Schs., 1965-67, Wayland (Mass.) Pub. Schs., 1967-73; cons. Edn. Coop., Wellesley, Mass., 1991-94; assoc. dir. programs in profl. edn. Grad. Sch. Edn. Harvard U., Cambridge, Mass., 1994—. Mem. Comm. for Common Core of Learning, Mass. Dept. Edn., 1993-94. Mem. sch. bd. Wayland Pub. Schs., 1981-90; mem. learning svcs. com. Pub. Broadcasting Svc., 1994-97. Democrat. Office: Harvard U Grad Sch Edn PPE 14 Story St Cambridge MA 02138 Home: Apt A121 330 Beacon St Boston MA 02116-1179

GREYSON, CHARLES BRUCE, psychiatrist; b. Bklyn., Oct. 25, 1946; s. William Lawrence and Augusta Celia (DeBare) G.; m. Jane Alice Chapman, Mar. 23, 1968; children: Devon Lara, Eric Chapman. AB, Cornell U., 1968; MD, SUNY, Syracuse, 1973. Diplomate Nat. Bd. Med. Examiners, Am. Bd. Psychiatry and Neurology. Psychiat. resident U. Va., Charlottesville, 1973-76, asst. prof. psychiatry, 1976-78, U. Mich., Ann Arbor, 1978-84; assoc. prof. psychiatry U. Conn., Farmington, 1984-93, prof. psychiatry, 1993-95, U. Va., Charlottesville, 1995—, Bonner-Lowry prof. personality studies, 1998—2002, Carlson prof. psychiatry, 2002—. Editor: The Near-Death Experience, 1984; editor Jour. Near-Death Studies, 1982—; contbr. sci. articles to profl. jours. Recipient William C. Menninger award Central Neuropsychiat. Assn., 1976. Fellow Am. Assn. Social Psychiatry, Am. Psychiat. Assn.; mem. Am. Assn. Suicidology, Parapsychol. Assn., Internat. Assn. for Near-Death Studies (pres. 1982-83, dir. rsch. 1981—). Home: 2700 Gray Fox Spur Charlottesville VA 22901-8867 Office: U Va Health Sys Divsn Personality Studies PO Box 800152 Charlottesville VA 22908-0152 E-mail: cbg4d@virginia.edu.

GREYSON, CLIFFORD RUSSELL, internist; b. N.Y.C., 1958; AB, Harvard Coll., 1980; MSEE, Stanford U., 1985, MD, 1987. Cert. internal medicine and cardiovascular diseases, critical care medicine. Resident in internal medicine Stanford U. Hosp., 1987-90, fellow in critical care, 1990-91; fellow in cardiovasc. disease U. Calif., San Francisco, 1991-95, faculty cardiology divsn., 1995-99, U. Colo. Health Scis. Ctr., Denver, 1999—. Co-dir. med. intensive care unit San Francisco VA Med. Ctr., 1998-99. Elected to city coun. Town of Woodside, Calif., 1995. Recipient Clinician Scientist award Am. Heart Assn., 1995-96, Clin. Investigator Devel. award NIH, 1996-01, R01 rsch. award NIH, 2003. Fellow Am. Coll. Cardiology; mem. ACP, Western Soc. Clin. Investigation. Office: Denver VA Med Ctr Cardiology 111B 1055 Clermont St Denver CO 80220-3808

GREYSON, TREY (C.M. GRAYSON), state official; b. Apr. 18, 1972; m. Nancy Greyson; children: Alexandra, Kate. BA in Govt., Harvard U., 1994; MBA, JD, U. Ky., 1998. Chmn. Young Profls. for Bush/Cheney in Ky., 2000; atty. Keating, Muething and Klekamp, 2001—03; sec. of state Commonwealth of Ky., 2004—. Office: State Capitol Ste 152 700 Capitol Ave Frankfort KY 40601 Office Phone: 502-564-3490. E-mail: tgrayson@kysos.com.

GREYSON D'OTAZZO, MEAGHAN REGINA, literary critic; b. Havana, Cuba, Sept. 7, 1942; arrived in US, 1962; d. Miguel Blanco and Virginia Mary de Barzaga-De Herrera; m. Neil Alfred D'Otazzo, Sept. 8, 1958; children: Jesse, Vivian, Patrick, Ann Shirley. B in psychology, U. Ga., 1972, M in hist. and lit., 1973, M in edn., 1976, PhD in hist. and lit., 1984. Tchr. Clark County Dist., Athens, Ga., 1971—75; rschr. Emory U., Psychology Dept., Atlanta, 1975—85; journalist freelance, N.Y.C., 1986—94, Orlando, Fla., 1995; literary critic various newspapers and mags., Los Angeles, Calif., 1995—97, London, 1997—; rschr. US Capitol Hist. Soc., Wash., DC, 2000—02, Smithsonian Inst., Wash., DC, 2003—04, Libr. of Congress, Wash., DC, 2004—. Author: La Musica de Haiti & Others, 1960, Literary Criticism: Conceptual Approach to Theatrical Reviews, 2004; contbr. articles various profl. jours. Poll judge Rep. Party, N.Y.C., NY, 1980—2004; tchr., autistic and deaf children. Mem.: Assn. Am. Writers, Assn. Reviewers and Editors. Republican. Catholic. Avocation: piano. Home: 6150 Forland Garth 204 Columbia MD 21045 E-mail: meaghan7@aol.com.

GRIBBLE, CHARLES EDWARD, editor, language educator; b. Lansing, Mich., Nov. 10, 1936; s. Charles P. and Elizabeth K. Gribble. BA, U. Mich., 1957; AM, Harvard U., 1958, PhD, 1967; postgrad., Moscow State U., 1960-61. Instr., asst. prof. Russian Brandeis U., Waltham, Mass., 1961-68; asst. prof. Slavic langs. Ind. U., Bloomington, 1968-75; assoc. prof. Slavic langs. Ohio State U., Columbus, 1975-89, prof. Slavic lang., 1989—, chairperson of dept., 1990-96. Pres., editor Slavica Pub., Inc., Columbus, 1966-97; vis. assoc. prof. Slavic lang. U. Va., 1977. Author: Russian Root List, 1973, A Short Dictionary of 18th Century Russian, 1976; editor-in-chief Folia Slavica, 1977-88; editor: Studies Presented to Professor Roman Jakobson by His Students, 1968, Medieval Slavic Texts, vol. 1, 1973; contbr. articles to profl. jours. Woodrow Wilson fellow, 1957-58, Am. Coun. Learned Soc. fellow, 1972; Internat. Rsch. and Exch. Bd. grantee, 1960-61, 72, 80, Fulbright grantee, 1987. Mem. MLA, Am. Assn. Advancement Slavic Studies, Am. Assn. Tchr. Slavic and Ea. European Lang. (Disting. Contbn. to the Profession award 1992), Linguistic Soc. Am., Linguistic Soc. Europe, Bulgarian Studies Assn. (pres. 2002-03), Phi Beta Kappa. Office: Ohio State Univ Slavic Lang Dept 1775 College Rd #400 Columbus OH 43210-1340 E-mail: gribble.3@osu.edu.

GRIBBON, DANIEL MCNAMARA, lawyer; b. Youngstown, Ohio, Jan. 27, 1917; s. James Edward and Loretta (Hogan) G.; m. Jane Retzler, Sept. 13, 1941; children: Diana Jane Gribbon Motz, Deborah Ann Gribbon Alt. AB, Case Western Res. U., 1938; JD, Harvard U., 1941. Bar: N.Y. 1942, D.C. 1946, U.S. Supreme Ct. 1950. Clk. Judge Learned Hand, N.Y.C., 1941-42; assoc. Covington & Burling, Washington, 1946-50, ptnr., 1950—. Chmn. adv. com. on procedures U.S. Ct. Appeals (D.C. cir.), 1983-88 Served with USNR, 1942-46. Fellow Am. Bar Found.; mem. Am. Coll. Trial Lawyers, D.C. Bar Assn. (chmn. bd. profl. responsibility 1976-79). Clubs: Met. (Washington) (pres. 1981-82); Chevy Chase (Md.). Roman Catholic. Office: Covington & Burling 1201 Pennsylvania Ave NW Washington DC 20004-2401 Office Phone: 202-662-5310. Office Fax: 202-778-5310. Business E-Mail: dgribbon@cov.com.

GRIBBON, DEBORAH, museum director; b. Washington, June 11, 1948; d. Daniel M. Gribbon and Mary Jane Retzler Gribbon; m. Winston Alt; children: Sarah Alt, Jane Alt. PhD, Harvard U., 1982, MA, 1971; BA, Wellesley Coll., 1970. Tchg. fellow Dept. Fine Arts Harvard U., Cambridge, Mass., 1972—74; curator Isabella Steward Gardner Mus., Boston, 1976—84; asst. dir. curatorial affairs The. J. Paul Getty Mus., L.A., 1984—87; assoc. dir. curatorial affairs The J. Paul Getty Mus., L.A., 1987—91, assoc. dir., chief curator, 1991—98, dep. dir., chief curator, 1998—2000, dir., 2000—04. Instr. Ext. Sch. Harvard U., Cambridge, 1982—84; v.p. J.Paul Getty Trust, L.A., 2000—04; bd. dirs.

Courtauld Inst. Art, London. Co-author: The J. Paul Getty Museum and Its Collections: A Museum for a New Century, 1997; author (book): Sculpture in the Isabella Stewart Gardner Museum, 1978; contbr. articles to profl. jours. Recipient Plogsterth Prize for Art History, Wellesley Coll., 1970; fellow Theodore Rousseau Fellowship for Mus. Studies, Harvard U., 1982. Mem.: Assn. Art Mus. Dirs., Internat. Women's Forum.

GRIBOU, JULIUS M., architecture educator; B in Design, U. Fla., 1971; MArch, U. Ill., 1977. Sr. designer Rathert and Roth Archs., St. Louis, 1971—74; rsch. assoc., archtl. specialist Nat. Clearinghouse for Criminal Justice Planning and Arch., 1974—78; assoc., cons. Perkins Guidry, Young Archs., Lafayette, La., 1978—83; asst. prof. arch. U. St. Louis, 1978—81, 1983—85; assoc. prof. Tex. A&M U., 1985—99, arch. prof., 1999—2000, assoc. dept. head, 1991—92, dept. head, 1992—2000; dean, prof. Sch. Arch. U. Tex., San Antonio, 2000—. Prin. Julius M. Gribou, AIA, La., Tex.; cons. Cmty. Rsch. Assocs., Champaign, Ill., 1992. Contbr. articles to profl. jours. Named Outstanding Adminstr., Women's Week, Tex. A&M U., 1996; Fulbright scholar, Poland, 1991. Mem.: AIA (treas. Brazos chpt. 1992, sec. Brazos chpt. 1993, pres.-elect Brazos chpt. 1994, pres. Brazos chpt. 1995, Design award Brazos chpt. 1998, Photography Merit award 1990), Preservation Tex., San Antonio Conservation Soc., Nat. Trust for Hist. Preservation, Tex. Soc. Archs. Office: U Tex Sch Arch Divsn Arch and Interior Design 501 W Durango Blvd San Antonio TX 78207

GRICE, RICHARD W., lawyer; b. Green Bay, Wis., Feb. 12, 1959; BS, Univ. Wis., Madison, 1981; JD, Cornell Univ., 1984. Bar: NY 1984, Ga. 1987. Assoc. Milbank, Tweed, Hadley & McCloy, NYC, 1984—87; ptnr., chmn., leveraged capital group Alston & Bird LLP, Atlanta. Sr. editor Cornell Internat. Law Jour. Named one of Atlanta's Super Lawyers. Mem.: Phi Beta Kappa. Office: Alston & Bird LLP One Atlantic Ctr 1201 W Peachtree St NW Atlanta GA 30309-3424 Office Phone: 404-881-7576. Office Fax: 404-881-7777. Business E-Mail: rgrice@alston.com.

GRICE, ROBERT E., JR., music educator, composer; b. Dothan, Ala., Sept. 27, 1964; s. Robert E. and Linda Hughes Grice. B in Music Edn., Troy State U., 1987, MS, 1996. Dir. Troy (Ala.) State Wesley Singers, 1983—87; band dir. Geneva (Ala.) City Schs., 1987—97, Enterprise (Ala.) City Schs., 1997—; mem. adj. faculty Enterprise State Jr. Coll., 1999—. Co-dir. Enterprise Indoor Percussion, 1997—2002; dir. Chamber Ensemble, Enterprise, 2002—. Composer: (symphonic music) Red Eclipse, 2000, Pinnacle, 2002, Myths and Legends, 2002. Recipient Golden Apple Tchr. award, WDHN-TV, Dothan, 2002. Mem.: Music Educators Nat. Conf., Phi Mu Alpha (pres. 1985—2002), Kappa Delta Pi. Methodist. Home: 464 Sandy Oak Enterprise AL 36330 Office: Daughin Jr HS 425 Dauphin St Enterprise AL 36330 E-mail: rgrice2607@aol.com.

GRIDLEY, MARK CHARLES, psychologist; b. Detroit, Jan. 5, 1947; s. Frederick William and Helen Lucille (Jones) Gridley. BS, Mich. State U., 1969; MS, Case Western Res. U., 1970, PhD, 1977. Psychometrist, research asst. Case Western Res. U. Hosp., 1971-73; saxophonist/flutist free-lance Cleve., 1969—; cons., psychologist Cleve. Bd. Edn., 1977-81; vis. asst. prof. John Carroll U., University Heights, Ohio, 1981-84; prof. psychology Heidelberg Coll., Tiffin, Ohio, 1987—. Author: Jazz Styles: History and Analysis, 1978, 1985, 1988, 1991, 1994, 1997, 2000, 2003, 2005, Concise Guide to Jazz, 1992, 2003; contbr. articles to profl. jours., chapters to books. Recipient Best Flutist award, Notre Dame Collegiate Jazz Festival, 1968, Disting. Achievement award, Ednl. Press Assn. Am., 1987. Mem.: N.E. Ohio Jazz Soc., Soc. Am. Music, Col. Music Soc., Internat. Assn. Jazz Educators. Home: 47 Maple St Tiffin OH 44883-2719

GRIEB, ELIZABETH, lawyer; b. Chestertown, Md., Nov. 14, 1950; d. Henry Norman and Lillian (Ballard) Grieb; m. George Stewart Webb, Aug. 18, 1979 (div. 1990); children: Timothy Stewart, Margaret Elizabeth; m. Walter George Lohr, Jr., Feb. 15, 2003. BA English, Wells Coll., 1972; JD cum laude, U. Balt., 1977. Bar: Md. 1977. Assoc. Piper & Marbury, Balt., 1977-84; ptnr. Piper & Marbury (now Piper Marbery Rudnigh & Wolfe LLP), Balt., 1984—2002; pres., CEO The Md. Zoo (formerly Balt. Zoo), 2002—. Adv. bd. U. Md. Sys. Downtown Ctr., Balt., 1990-92; bd. dirs., sec. Choice Jobs, Inc., Balt., 1991-93; pres. U. Balt. Alumni Assn., 1994-95; bd. dirs. Balt. Zoo, 1995-2002, pres. bd. dirs., 1999-2002. Mem. Md. State Bar Assn. (chair securities laws com. 1990-92), Ho. of Ruth (bd. dirs. 1994-97), Ctr. Club. Episcopal. Office Phone: 410-396-7102. E-mail: bgrieb@marylandzoo.org.

GRIECO, MICHAEL HENRY, allergy and infectious diseases physician; b. N.Y.C., Aug. 10, 1932; s. Henry and Angelina G. m. Dorothy; children: Michael, Angela, Susan. BA, NYU, 1954; MD, SUNY, Bklyn., 1957; JD, Fordham U., 1979. Diplomate Am. Bd. Legal Medicine, Am. Bd. Diagnostic Lab. Immunology, Am. Bd. internal Medicine; bd. cert. in allergy and clin. immunology, infectious diseases, pulmonary diseases, rheumatology, geriatric medicine, clin. tropical medicine and travelers' health. Intern in medicine St. Luke's Med. Ctr., N.Y.C., 1957-58, resident in medicine, 1960-61, resident in cardiology, 1961-62; resident in allergy The Roosevelt Hosp., N.Y.C., 1962-63; resident chest svc. Bellevue Hosp., N.Y.C., 1963-64; asst. attending physician The Roosevelt Hosp., 1964—, St. Luke's Hosp. Ctr., 1965-69, assoc. attending physician, 1969, assoc. dir. medicine, 1970, attending physician, 1973; prof. emeritus of clin. medicine Columbia U. Coll. of Physicians and Surgeons. Resident infectious disease svc. Cornell Med. Divsn., Bellevue Hosp., 1963-64; asst. outpatient dept. St. Luke's Hosp. Ctr., 1964-65, dir. allergy lab., 1965, dir. allergy and infectious disease sect., 1968; asst. in medicine Vanderbilt Clinic Presbyn. Hosp., N.Y.C., 1964; dir. Robert A. Cooke Inst. Allergy and Divsn. Allergy, The Roosevelt Hosp., 1973; attending, chief divsn. allergy, clin. immunology and infectious diseases, St. Luke's/Roosevelt Hosp. Ctr., 1980, dir. AIDS Ctr., 1987-97, dir. dept. medicine, 1993-97; v.p. med. affairs Christ Hosp., Jersey City, 1998—2003. Fellow ACP, Am. Coll. Legal Medicine, Infectious Diseases Soc. Am.; mem. Am. Soc. Microbiology (com. chmn. 1984-87), N.Y. Allergy Soc. (pres. 1971-72, sec. 1968-70), N.Y. County Med. Soc. (v.p. 1989, sec. 1985-88, mem. health com. 1968-73, mem. CME com. 1978-79), N.Y. State Bar Assn. (mem. spl. com. on AIDS and the law 1988-89), Phi Beta Kappa, Alpha Omega Alpha. Home: 9 Mayflower Dr Tenafly NJ 07670-3129 E-mail: michael.grieco@verizon.net.

GRIECO, PAUL ANTHONY, chemistry professor; b. Framingham, Mass., Oct. 27, 1944; married; 4 children. BA, Boston U., 1966; MA, Columbia U., 1967, PhD in Organic Chemistry, 1970. NSF fellow Harvard U., 1970-71; from asst. prof. to prof. chemistry U. Pitts., 1971-80; prof. chemistry Ind. U., Bloomington, 1980-85, Earl Blough prof. chemistry, 1985—, chmn. dept., 1988-97; head of chemistry and biochemistry dept. Mont. State U., 1999—. William P. Timmie lectr. Emory U., 1977; Abbott lectr. Yale U., 1984; H.C. Brown lectr. Purdue U., 1984; Disting. lectr. U. Wyo., 1986; Conv. Intercantonale Romande pour L'Enseignement du Troisième Cycle en Chimie, Switzerland, 1987; Centennial lectr. Abbott Labs., Chgo., 1988; H. Martin Friedman lectr. Rutgers U., 1988; Centennial Anniversary lectr. 1st Internat. Conf. on Organic Chem. Nomenclature, Geneva, 1992. Fellow Alfred P. Sloan Found., 1974-76, Japan Soc. Promising Scientists, 1978-79; recipient Ernest Guenther award, 1982, NIH-Nat. Cancer Inst. Merit award, 1988. Mem. Am. Chem. Soc. (Akron sect. award 1982, Arthur C. Cope Scholar award 1990, award for creative work in synthetic organic chemistry 1991, lectr. French.-Am. socs. meeting in France 1992), Royal Soc. Chemistry, Chem. Soc. Japan, Swiss Chem. Soc. Achievements include rsch. in the devel. of new synthetic methods for constrn. of complex natural products. Office: Mont State U Dept Biochem & Chem 108 Gains Hl Bozeman MT 59717-0001

GRIECO, STEPHEN, music educator, department chairman; b. N.Y., Feb. 19, 1974; BA in Music Composition, SUNY, Fredonia NY; MusM in Music Composition, Bowling Green (Ohio) State U.; DMA in Music Composition, Ariz. State U. Prof., chmn. Dept. Music Phoenix (Ariz.) Coll., 1999—2003; chmn. Dept. Music C.C. Phila., 2003—. Composer: (songs) Christopher's Lament for Full Orchestra (North Am. Artists Found. award), Musical Area Recognition System, The Monkey's Paw (Victoria Bohlen award). Mem.: Broadcast Music Inc. Office: Community College of Philadelphia: Music 1700 Spring Garden Street Philadelphia PA 19130

GRIEFEN, JOHN ADAMS, artist, educator; b. Worcester, Mass., Nov. 24, 1942; s. Robert John and Faith (Adams) G.; 1 child, Katherine Abigail Jacqueline. Student, Chgo. Art Inst., 1964-65, Bennington Coll., 1965-66; BA, Williams Coll., 1966; postgrad., Hunter Coll., 1966-68. Instr. Bennington Coll., 1968-69, Great Neck Adult Edn., N.Y., 1971-76. One-man shows Kornblee Gallery, 1969, 70, 73, Deitcher O'Reilly Gallery, N.Y.C., shows, William Edward O'Reilly Inc., N.Y.C., Martha Jackson Gallery, N.Y.C., Frank Watters Gallery, Sydney, Australia, 1979, Salander O'Reilly Galleries, N.Y.C., 1981, 82, 84, 85, 91, 93, 99, Harcus-Hrakow Gallery, Boston, Phyllis Kind Galley, Chgo., B.R. Kornblatt Gallery, Balt., Diane Brown Gallery, Washington, 1978, Sunne Savage Gallery, Boston, 1979, Williams Coll. Mus. Art, Williamstown, Mass., 1980, Martin Gerard Gallery, Edmonton, Alta., Can., 1981, Gallery Moos Ltd., Toronto and Calgary, 1981, Edmonton Art Gallery, 1984, Hirondelle Gallery, N.Y.C., 1986, Salander O'Reilly Galleries, L.A., 1991, Edmonton Art Gallery, Alberta, Can., 1993, Swift Current Art Gallery, Sask., 1993, S.C. Schultz Gallery, N.J., 1994; exhibited group shows Indpls. Mus. Art, Phoenix Mus., Sydney Mus., Whitney Mus. Purdue U., N.Y. Mus. Modern Art, Santa Barbara Mus., Boston Mus. Fine Arts; represented in pub. collections Larry Aldrich Mus. Contemporary Art, Allen Art Mus., Arthur A. Anderson Co., Bank of Ill., Calgary (Can.), Boston Mus. Fine Arts, Bklyn. Mus., Carnegie Inst. Mus. Art, Chase Manhattan Bank, Continental Resources Inc., Hines Indsl., Boston, N.Y.C., Washington, Dallas, Hirshhorn Mus. and Sculpture Garden, Washington, Met. Mus. Art, Michner Collections-U. Tex., Musnson-William-Proctor Art Inst., Mus. Modern Art, Newark Mus. Fine Arts, Reader's Digest Assn. Inc., Rose Art Mus., Brandeis U., Rothmans Art Gallery, St. Lawrence U., Sydney Mus., Australia, Whitney Mus., Williams Coll. Art Mus., Worcester Mus. Art, Mass., Met. Mus. Art, N.Y.C., Vassar Coll. Mus. Art, Poughkeepsie, N.Y., Lowcart Gallery, Miami. Recipient Esther Forbes award Bancroft Sch., Worcester, Mass., 1996. Home: 275 Park Ave Apt 6R Brooklyn NY 11205 Office: care Salander O'Reilly Galleries 20 E 79th St New York NY 10021-0106 Personal E-mail: jgriefen@aol.com.

GRIEGO, DAYNA JUNE, art educator, writer, artist; b. Denver, June 10, 1947; d. Winston Horton Jowers and Maria Cruz Chavez; m. Rudolfo Ricardo Griego, Feb. 10, 1944; children: Jon Shannon, Quinn Christopher, Sarah Maria Rodriquez, Juan Jose. BFA, Corcoran Coll. of Art and Design, 1997; MA in Edn., Western N.Mex U., 2001. Cert. K-12 tchr. N.Mex. Tchr. elem. art Deming Pub. Schs., N.Mex., 2000—. Writer Silver City Daily Press, N.Mex., 2000—, The Ink, Las Cruces, N.Mex., 2002—04; adj. prof. Western N.Mex. U., Silver City, 2001—. Newspaper articles, Artist Profiles (First Pl., N.Mex Press Women's Communication Contest, 2004), one-woman shows include Ctr. Cultural Francaise, Kinshasa, Zaire, 1984. Vista vol., Silver City, N.Mex., 1998—2000. Recipient Cert. for Svc. on Sch. Bd., Am. Sch. of Kinshasa Zaire, 1985, Cert. of Appreciation, Embassy of USA, Lima, Peru, 1991, Cash Performance award, U.S. Dept. of State, 1992, Cert. of Excellent Performance, 1992, Fine Arts award, Corcoran Coll. of Art and Design, 1996; grantee, Barbara Bush Literacy Found., 1998, PNM Found., 2003. Mem.: Nat. Assn. of Art Educators, N.Mex Press Women (newsletter editor 2001—03, Communication award 1st place 2001, 2003). Avocations: art, reading. Home: PO Box 682/1900 Cottonwood Santa Clara NM 88026 Office: Deming Pub Schs 501 Florida Deming NM 88030 Personal E-mail: daynajgriego@hotmail.com.

GRIEM, HANS RUDOLF, physicist, researcher; b. Kiel, Schleswig-Holstein, Germany, Oct. 7, 1928; came to U.S., 1954; s. Rudolf H. and Paula D. (Schwarz) Griem; m. Irmgard H. Hoehling, May 11, 1957; children: Jens, Torsten, Rowena, Bridget. Abitur, Max-Planck Sch. Kiel, 1949; PhD, U. Kiel, 1954; PhD (hon.), Ruhr U., Bochum, Fed. Republic Germany, 1990. Rsch. asst. U. Md., College Park, 1954-55, asst. prof., 1957-61, assoc. prof., 1961-63, prof., 1963-94; prof. emeritus, sr. rsch. scientist, 1994—; Wissenschaftlicher asst. U. Kiel, 1955-57; dir. Lab. for Plasma Rsch. U. Md., 1980-87. Cons. Naval Rsch. Lab., Washington, 1957-96, Lawrence Livermore (Calif.) Nat. Lab., 1979—. Author: Plasma Spectroscopy, 1964, Spectral Line Broadening by Plasmas, 1974, Principles of Plasma Spectroscopy, 1997; editor: Methods of Experimental Physics, Vol. 9A, 1970; contbr. articles to sci. jours., chpts. to books. NSF sr. postdoctoral fellow, 1963; Guggenheim Found. fellow, 1968; European Space Rsch. Orgn. fellow, 1971; recipient Humboldt prize, 1978, William F. Meggers award Optical Soc. Am., 1987. Fellow Am. Phys. Soc. (councilor 1983-87, J.C. Maxwell prize 1991). Achievements include development of quantitative spectroscopic methods for high temperature plasma diagnostics. Office: Univ of Md Inst Rsch in Electronics and Applied Physics College Park MD 20742-3511 Office Phone: 301-405-4981. Business E-Mail: griem@umd.edu.

GRIEM, JOHN MICHAEL, management consultant; b. San Francisco, Apr. 29, 1945; s. John Drysen and Gwendolyn (Pyeatt) G.; m. Peggy Clarke, Sept. 16, 1967; children: John Michael Jr., Marjorie Lynne. ScBE magna cum laude with high honors, Brown U., 1965, ScME, 1966; MBA, U. Chgo., 1968. Sr. economist USPHS, 1968-70; assoc. to v.p., dir. Cresap, McCormick and Paget, Chgo., 1970-81; mng. ptnr. subs. Cresap, McCormick and Paget do Brasil Servicos Ltda., 1978-81; v.p. A.T. Kearney, Chgo., 1981-95; pres. Kearney, Health Svcs. Cons., Chgo., 1981-87; pres., CEO, Griem & Co., Lake Bluff, Ill., 1995—. Bd. govs. Am. Soc. Sao Paulo, Brazil, 1979-81, John G. Shedd Aquarium, Chgo., 1992-98. Fellow NDEA, 1965-66, Ford Found., 1965, 67-68. Mem. Inst. Mgmt. Cons. (cert.; bd. dirs. 1998-2003, pres. 2000-01), Mid Am.-Arab C. of C. (bd. dirs. 1989-91) Chgo. Coun. Fgn. Rels., Ill. Curling Assn. (bd. dirs. 2000—, pres. 2002—), Exmoor Country Club, Brown U. Club, Sigma Xi, Tau Beta Pi, Beta Gamma Sigma. Home and Office: 120 Indian Rd Lake Bluff IL 60044-2714 Office Phone: 847-234-6923. Business E-Mail: m.griem@comcast.net.

GRIER, DAVID ALAN, actor; b. Detroit, June 30, 1955; m. Maritza Grier, 1987 (div.). Grad., U. Mich.; MFA, Yale U., 1981. Actor (Broadway plays) The First (Tony award nomination, Theatre World award), Dreamgirls, A Funny Thing Happened on the Way to the Forum, The Mambo Kings, 2005 (off-Broadway plays) A Soldier's Play, various other stage credits; (TV series) All is Forgiven, 1986, In Living Color, 1990-94, The Preston Episodes, 1995, "DAG," 2000, Life with Bonnie, 2002-04 Tough Crowd with Colin Quinn, 2002; (TV films) Kingpins, 1987, A Saintly Switch, 1999, The 60s, 1999, Angels in the Infield, 2000, King of Texas, 2002, Rock Stars Do the Dumbest Things, 2003, The Muppets' Wonderful Wizard of Oz, 2005; (films) Streamers, 1983, A Soldier's Story, 1984, Beer, 1985, Ich und Er, 1987, From the Hip, 1987, Amazon Women on the Moon, 1987, I'm Gonna Git You Sucka, 1988, Off Limits, 1988, Almost an Angel, 1990, Loose Cannons, 1990, The Player, 1992, Boomerang, 1992, In the Army Now, 1994, Blankman, 1994, Tales from the Hood, 1995, Jumanji, 1995, Top of the World, 1997, McHale's Navy, 1997, East of A, 1999, Damned If You Do, 1999, (voice) Stuart Little, 1999, The Adventures of Rocky and Bullwinkle, 2000, Tiptoes, 2003, The Woodsman, 2004, Bewitched, 2005. Mailing: c/o Golden Gate Theatre 1 Taylor St San Francisco CA 94102*

GRIER, JAMES EDWARD, hotel executive, lawyer; b. Ottumwa, Iowa, Sept. 7, 1935; s. Edward J. and Corinne (Bailey) G.; m. Virginia Clinker, July 4, 1959; children: Michael, Susan, James, John, Thomas. BSc, U. Iowa, 1956, JD, 1959. Bar: Iowa 1959, Mo. 1959. Mng. ptnr. Hillix, Brewer, Hoffhaus & Grier, Kansas City, Mo., 1964-77, Grier & Swartzman, Kansas City, 1977-89; pres. Doubletree Hotels Corp., Phoenix, 1989-94; chmn. Sonoran Hotel Capital, Inc., Phoenix, 1994-96; mng. ptnr. Copa Investments, 1996—, Gainey Hotel Co., 1996—. Bd. dirs. Iowa Law Sch. Found., Iowa City, St. Joseph Healthcare Ariz., Phoenix, Homeward Bound, Phoenix. Home: 3500 E Lincoln Dr Phoenix AZ 85018-1010 Office: Gainey Hotel Co 7300 E Gainey Suites Dr Ste 169 Scottsdale AZ 85258-2061 Office Phone: 480-367-4664. Business E-Mail: jegrier@gaineysuiteshotel.com.

GRIER, MELINDA W., lawyer; Dir., legal svcs. and compliance Ore. U. Sys.; gen. counsel U. Ore. Sch. Law, 1998—. Adj. prof. U. Ore. Sch. Law, 1992—. Mem.: Nat. Assn. of Coll. and Univ. Atty. (past second v.p., pres.-elect). Office: U Ore Sch Law 1515 Agate St Eugene OR 97403 Office Phone: 541-346-3852.

GRIER, TERRY B., school system administrator; s. O. F. and Alfreda Grier; m. Nancy Kay Miller, Jan. 24, 1998; children: Danielle Peckham, Anna Peckham, Jason Brooks children: Cynthia Leigh. D of Edn., Vanderbilt U., Nashville, 1983. Cert. sch. adminstrn. N.C. Dept. Pub. Instrn. Supt. McDowell County Schs., Marion, NC, 1984—87, Amarillo (Tex.) Ind. Sch. Dist., 1987—88, Darlington (S.C.) County Schs., 1988—91, Akron (Ohio) Pub. Schs., 1991—94, Sacramento City Schs., 1994—95, Williamson County Schs., Franklin, 1996—2000, Guilford County Schs., Greensboro, NC, 2000—. Cons. New Brunswick (Can.) Sch. Supts. Contbr. articles to profl. jours. Bd. dirs. Nat. Sch. Pub. Rels. Assn., Rockville, Md., 2002—04; bd. dirs., past pres. Horace Mann League of USA, Wash., 1985—2005; mem. membership com. Coll. Bd., N.Y.C., 2004—05; bd. dirs. Forward Greensboro III, 2004—05; bd. govs. 2 Those Who Care, NC, 2000—05. Named Lion of Yr., St. Pauls Lions Club, 1982, Regional Supt. of Yr., Piedmont Triad Edn. Consortium; named to Exec. Educator 100, Exec. Educator Mag.; recipient Silver Ladle award, Leukemia Found., State Svc. award, N.C. United Way, Outstanding Alumni award, East Carolina U., Gold Award of Excellence, S.C. Sch. Pub. Rels. Assn. Mem.: N.C. Assn. Supervision and Curriculum Devel. (pres. 2004—05, Disting. Educator award). Avocation: travel. Office: Guilford County Schs 712 N Eugene St Greensboro NC 27402 Office Phone: 336-370-8992. Office Fax: 336-370-8992. E-mail: griert@guilford.k12.nc.us.

GRIERSON, WILLIAM, retired agriculturist; b. Boscombe, Eng., Dec. 15, 1917; came to U.S., 1952; s. Edward James and Winifred (Burridge) Grierson-Jackson; m. Agnes Cray; children: Peter Robert, John Patrick (dec.). BSc in Agr., Ont. Agrl. Coll., Guelph, Can., 1938; PhD, Cornell U., 1951. Asst. prof. U. B.C., Vancouver, Can., 1945-51, U. Fla., Lake Alfred, 1952-60, prof., 1964-82; assoc. dir. Food Industries Rsch. and Engring., Yakima, Wash., 1960-64; prof. emeritus, cons. Winter Haven, Fla., 1983—. Author, editor: (textbook) Fresh Citrus Fruits, 1986; author: (World War II memoir) We Band of Brothers, 1997, also 4 manuals; contbr. over 200 articles to sci. jours. Maj. RCAF, 1940-45. Fla. Citrus Packers grad. fellow, 1992; named Rschr. of Yr. Fla. Fruit and Vegetable Assn., 1972; named to Fla. Citrus Hall of Fame, 1995. Fellow Am. Soc. Hort. Sci. (assoc. editor 1970-74); mem. Fla. State Hort. Soc. (hon. mem., pres. 1981-82, editor 1972-79, Gold medal 1969). Achievements include devel. of designs for citrus degreening rooms now used world wide, of methods for the marketing of Florida lemons; first identification of two physiological diseases of citrus ("zebraskin" and "sloughing"). Home and Office: 18 Golf View Cir NE Winter Haven FL 33881-4302

GRIES, JAMES R., psychologist; b. Bklyn., N.Y., Feb. 23, 1973; s. Leonaid T. and Susanne L. Gries. BA in Psychology, Brandeis U., 1995; MA in Clin. Psychology, Ga. Sch. Profl. Psychology, 1997; PsyD in Clin. Psychology, Ill. Sch. Profl. Psychology, 2001. Lic. clin. psychologist N.Y. Assoc. psychologist Sagamore Children's Psychiat. Ctr., Dix Hills, NY, 2001—04; clin. psychologist R. G. Psychol. Svcs., N.Y.C., 2004—; program dir. Inst. for Emotional Health, East Hills, NY, 2004—. Cons. on adoption Wide Horizons, Waltham, Mass., 2003—. Mem.: APA. Office: Inst for Emotional Health 29-11 Jordan St Flushing NY 11358

GRIES, ROBBIE RICE, geologist, gas and petroleum company executive; Student, Del Mar Junior Coll., Corpus Christi, Tex.; BS in Geology, Colo. State U.; MS in Geology, U. Tex., Austin, 1970. Cert. petroleum geologist 1985. Geology tchr. Wichita State U.; with Texaco, Inc., Denver, 1973—76; staff geologist Reserve Oil Inc., 1976—80; ind. geologist, cons., 1980—92; founder Priority Oil & Gas, LLC, Denver, 1992—, pres., CEO, 1995—. Dir. Colo. Oil and Gas Assn. Mem. adv. coun. Geology Found., U. Tex., Austin. Named Leadership Honoree, Key Women in Energy awards, RaderEnergy, 2004; recipient Disting. Svc. award, Rocky Mountain Assn. Geologists. Mem.: Soc. Sedimentary Geology, Geol. Soc. Am., Am. Assn. Petroleum Geologists (hon.; sec. 1995—97, pres. 2001—02, A.I. Leverson award 1985, Disting. Svc. award 1991, named hon. mem. 1998). Achievements include First woman to serve as president of the Amernican Association of Petroleum Geologists. Office: Priority Oil & Gas PO Box 27798 Denver CO 80227-0798

GRIESA, THOMAS POOLE, federal judge; b. Kansas City, Mo., Oct. 11, 1930; s. Charles Henry and Stella Lusk (Bedell) G.; m. Christine Pollard Meyer, Jan. 5, 1963. AB cum laude, Harvard U., 1952; LL.B., Stanford U., 1958. Bar: Wash. 1958, N.Y. 1961. Atty. Justice Dept., 1958-60; with firm Symmers, Fish & Warner, N.Y.C., 1960-61, Davis Polk & Wardwell, N.Y.C., 1961-72, partner, 1970-72; judge U.S. Dist. Ct. So. Dist. N.Y., 1972—, chief judge, 1993-2000. Mem.: Stanford Law Rev., 1956-58. Bd. visitors Stanford Law Sch., 1982-84; bd. dirs. Greater N.Y. Coun. Boy Scouts Am. Served to lt. (j.g.) USCG, 1952-54. Mem. Bar Assn. City N.Y., Union Club N.Y.C. Christian Scientist. Office: US Dist Ct US Courthouse 500 Pearl St New York NY 10007-1316

GRIESCHE, ROBERT PRICE, hospital purchasing executive; b. Berkeley, Calif., July 21, 1953; s. Robert Bowen and Lillian (Price) G.; m. Susan Dawn Albers, June 8, 1985 (div. Apr. 1989); 1 child, Sara Christine. AA, Coll. of the Canyons, Valencia, Calif., 1984; BS in Health Care Mgmt., Century U., 2005. Warehouse supr. John Muir Hosp., Walnut Creek, Calif., 1973-82; purchasing mgr. Henry Mayo Newhall Hosp., Valencia, 1982-85; materials mgr. Foothill Presbyn. Hosp., Glendora, Calif., 1985-87; materials mgmt. dir. Huntington Meml. Hosp., Pasadena, Calif., 1987-96; sys. dir. purchasing So. Calif. Healthcare Sys., Pasadena, 1996—2002; materials mgmt. dir. Univ. Med. Ctr. of So. Nev., Las Vegas, 2002—05; equipment program planner HDR Architecture, Las Vegas, 2005—. Chmn. Huntington Employee Campaign, 1990-92. V.p. Coll. of Canyons Found., Valencia, 1985-90. Named to Outstanding Young Men of Am., 1988. Mem. Am. Soc. Healthcare Materials Mgmt Republican. Presbyterian. Avocations: swimming, gardening, photography. Home: 9621 Kinlock Ct Las Vegas NV 89117 Office: 770 E Warm Springs Rd Las Vegas NV 89119 Office Phone: 702-938-6000.

GRIESEMER, ALLAN DAVID, retired museum director; b. Mayville, Wis., Aug. 13, 1935; s. Raymond John and Leone Emma (Fischer) G.; m. Nancy Jean Sternberg, June 6, 1959; children: David, Paul, Steven. AB, Augustana Coll., 1959; MS, U. Wis., 1963; PhD, U. Nebr., 1970. With intern program Newark Mus., 1961—62; curator earth sci. & planetarium Dayton Mus. Natural History, 1962—65; curator; coordinator ednl. services U. Nebr., Lincoln State Museum, 1965-77, assoc. prof., assoc. dir., 1977-79, acting dir., 1980-81, assoc. dir. and coordinator, 1981-82, interim dir., 1982-84; dir. San Bernardino County Mus., Calif., 1984-97, dir. emeritus, 1997—; mem. faculty dept. geology U. Nebr., Lincoln, 1968-80; lectr. geology U. Nebr., Lincoln State Mus., 1968-80; CEO, dir., curator Mousley Mus. Natural History, San Bernardino County Mus., Yucaipa, Calif., 1984-97, ret., 1997. Adj. prof. Calif. State U., San Bernardino, 1986. Contbr. articles to sci. jours., mus. publs., 1965— . Bd. dirs. San Bernardino County Mus. Assn., Redlands Hist. Mus., Redlands Cmty. Hosp. Found., Friends of Calico, 1999—2005, Redlands Theatre Festival; mem. adv. bd. Redlands Cmty. Hosp.; mem. Fortnightly Club, Inland Harvest, Redlands Symphony Bd., 2005—. Recipient Hon. award Sigma Gamma Epsilon, 1958 Mem. Paleontol. Soc., Nebr. Mus. Conf. (pres. 1976-79), Nebr. Geol. Soc., Nebr. Acad. Scis., Mountain Plains Conf., Mountain Plains Mus. Assn. (pres. 1979), Am. Assn. Museums (v.p. 1983), Rotary. Lutheran. Home: 306 La Colina Dr Redlands CA 92374-8247

GRIEVES, FOREST LESLIE, political science professor, department chairman; b. Beatty, Nev., Sept. 19, 1938; s. William Arthur and Alice Louise (Parman) G.; m. Irmgard Katharina Spengler, Mar. 31, 1963; children: Kevin Michael, Emily Katharina. BA in Polit. Sci., Stanford U., 1960; MA in Polit. Sci., U. Nev., 1964; PhD in Govt., U. Ariz., 1967. Tchg. assoc. U. Ariz.,

Tucson, 1964-67; asst. prof. Western Ill. U., Macomb, 1967-69; asst. prof. polit. sci. U. Mont., Missoula, 1969-72, assoc. prof., 1972-76, prof., 1976—2004, dept. chmn., 1990—91, 1997—2001, prof. emeritus, 2004—. Guest prof. U. Saarlandes, Saarbrücken, Germany, 1978-79, 81; scholar-diplomat U.S. Dept. State, Washington, 1980; participant Friedrich Ebert Found. Seminar, Saarbrücken, 1982, Konrad Adenauer Found.-U.S. Dept. State Seminar, Bosen, Germany, 1982; Fulbright sr. lectr., Germany, 1978-79. Author: Supranationalism and International Adjudication, 1969, Conflict and Order, 1977; editor: Transnationalism in World Politics and Business, 1979; contbr. over 100 articles to profl. jours. and encys. 1st lt. U.S. Army, 1960-62. Rsch. grantee NEH, 1973, German Acad. Exch. Svc., 1978, 87; rsch. fellow Alexander von Humboldt Found., Germany, 1979, 81; Fulbright-Hays sr. scholar, Germany, 1984, 98. Mem. German Studies Assn. Office: U Mont Dept Polit Sci Missoula MT 59812-5832 E-mail: forest.grieves@umontana.edu.

GRIEVES, LETA M., librarian, director; b. Portland, Oreg., Feb. 9, 1960; d. William Aitchison Grieves and Lilly Viola Henderson; life ptnr. Deb Ramirez; children: Zachary David, Lisa Michelle. Degree in mktg., West Ga. Tech. Coll., 2002. Br. mgr. Chattahoochee Regional Libr. Svc., Lumpkin, Ga., 2005—. Math. tutor West Ga. Tech. Coll., LaGrange, Ga., 2002—03. Achievements include development of mathematics tutoring center at West Georgia Technical College. Office: Lumpkin Pub Libr PO Box 727 117 Main St Lumpkin GA 31815 Office Phone: 229-838-6472. E-mail: lgrieves@cvrls.net.

GRIFF, HARRY, lawyer; b. Worcester, Mass., May 27, 1952; s. Joseph J. and Dorothy J. (Goldsmith) Griff; m. Joan G. Garovoy, May 27, 1973; children: Joshua, Jordana. BA with high distinction, U. Mich., 1973, JD with distinction, 1977. Bar: Mich. 1977, Colo. 1982. Legal counsel Social Security Adminstrn., HHS, Balt., 1978—79; trial atty. U.S. Dept. Justice, Washington, 1979—81; assoc. Dufford, Waldeck, Ruland, Wise & Milburn, Grand Junction, Colo., 1981—83; atty. Harmon & Griff, P.C., Grand Junction, 1983—86; ptnr. Foster, Larson, Laiche & Griff, Grand Junction, 1986—99, Griff, Larson, Laiche & Volkmann, Grand Junction, 1999—2001, Griff, Larson & Laiche, Grand Junction, 2001—03, Griff, Larson, Laiche & Brennan, Grand Junction, 2004—. Legal counsel Grand Junction br., NAACP, Colo., 1983—84, Walker Field, Colo. Pub. Airport Authority, Grand Junction, 1984—97; bd. dirs. Paradise Hills Homeowners Assn., Grand Junction, Colo., 1984—87, Ptnrs., Inc., 1988—94, KPRN Pub. Radio Sta., 1989—91. Bd. dirs. Grand Junction Jewish Cmty. Ctr., 1984—89, Colo. Lawyers Trust Acct. Found., 1986—92, Mus. We. Colo., 1997—2001, Vol. Ctrl., 1996—99, Downtown Devel. Authority, 2002—, Avalon Theatre, 2002—, Friends of Kulture and Entertainment for the Grand Valley, 2003—; vol. KAFM Cmty. Radio, 1996—. Mem.: ABA, ATLA, Mesa County Bar Assn. (pro bono program 1984—89, bd. dirs. 1999—2001), Colo. Bar Assn. Democrat. Home: 2636 Chestnut Dr Grand Junction CO 81506-8390 Office: Griff Larson Laiche & Brennan 422 White Ave Fl 3 Grand Junction CO 81501-2555 Office Phone: 970-245-8021. Business E-Mail: harry@gllblaw.com.

GRIFFEL, L. MICHAEL, music educator, researcher; b. NYC, Nov. 12, 1942; s. Joseph and Klara Griffel; m. Margaret Ross, Sept. 15, 1968; 1 child, David S. BA, Yale U., 1963; MS, Juilliard Sch. Music, NYC, 1966; MA, Columbia U., 1968, PhD, 1975. Adj. lectr. music Hunter Coll., CUNY, N.Y.C., 1970—71, instr. music, 1971—75, asst. prof. music, 1975—77, assoc. prof. music, 1978—84, prof. music, 1985—; asst. prof. music Grad. Sch., CUNY, N.Y.C., 1977, assoc. prof. music, 1978—84, prof. music, 1985—; asst. dean arts and scis. Hunter Coll., N.Y.C., 1999—2000, assoc. dean arts and scis., 2000—02, acting assoc. provost, 2002—05. Grad. faculty Mannes Coll. Music, N.Y.C., 1980—99, Juilliard Sch., N.Y.C., 1997—; artist-tchr. Merrywood Music Sch., Lenox, Mass., 1965—67; editor-in-chief Current Musicology, N.Y.C., 1970—71, co-editor-in-chief, 1971—72. Contbr. chapters to books, articles to profl. jours. Mem.: Shubert Soc. USA (mem. adv. bd. 2003—), Am. Musicol. Soc. (coun. 1969—71), Am. Schubert Inst. (bd. advisors 1995—), Am. Beethoven Soc. (v.p. N.Y. chpt. 1995—). Achievements include research in Schubert's symphonies. Home: 3135 Johnson Ave Apt 9E Bronx NY 10463 Office: Hunter Coll 695 Park Ave New York NY 10021 Business E-Mail: lgriffel@hunter.cuny.edu.

GRIFFEN, CLYDE CHESTERMAN, retired historian; b. Sioux City, Iowa, July 29, 1929; s. Clyde Rumbaugh and Rosanna Susan (Chesterman) G.; m. Sarah Goldsborough Donoho, Feb. 14, 1959; children: John Winslow, Sarah Bolling, Robert Henry. BA, State U. Iowa, 1952; MA, Columbia U., 1953, PhD, 1960. Lectr. Columbia U., N.Y.C., 1954-57; instr. history Vassar Coll, Poughkeepsie, N.Y., 1957-61, asst. prof., 1961-67, assoc. prof., 1967-75, Lucy Maynard Salmon prof. Am. history, 1975-92, chmn. dept. history, 1982-85, dir. Am. culture program, 1977-79. Author: (with Sally Griffen) Natives and Newcomers: The Ordering of Opportunity in Mid-Nineteenth-Century Poughkeepsie, 1978; editor: New Perspectives on Poughkeepsie's Past, 1988; co-editor: Meanings for Manhood: Constructions of Masculinity in Victorian America, 1990; co-author: Full Steam Ahead in Poughkeepsie: The Story of Coeducation at Vassar, 1966-1974, 2000; mem. editl. bd. Social Sci. History Assn., 1976-89. NSF grantee, 1973-74; Nat. Humanities Inst. fellow, 1976-77; Fulbright rsch. scholar N.Z., 1984; N.Z. Forst Rsch. fellow, 1996, 98. Home: 9 MacCracken Ln Poughkeepsie NY 12604-0001

GRIFFEN, WARD O., JR., surgeon, educator, medical association administrator, director; b. New Orleans, July 21, 1928; s. Ward O. and Dorothea (Rosenberg) G.; m. Margaret Mary Taylor, Dec. 27, 1952; children— Peter, Mary Ellen, Steven, Colleen, Timothy, Margaret Mary, Leah. AB, Princeton U., 1948; MD, Cornell U., 1953; PhD, U. Minn., 1963. Diplomate Am. Bd. Surgery, Am. Bd. Thoracic Surgery. Asst. prof. dept. surgery U. Minn, Mpls., 1962-65; assoc. prof. U. Ky. Coll. Medicine, Lexington, 1965-67, prof., chmn. dept. surgery, 1967-84; exec. dir., sec.-treas. Am. Bd. Surgery, Phila., 1984-94; prof. surgery U. Ky. Coll. Medicine, Lexington, 1994—. Contbr. articles to profl. jours. Served to comdr. USNR, 1955-67 John R. Markle Found. scholar, 1962-67 Fellow ACS (bd. govs. 1972-78, 2d v.p. 1995-96); mem. Am. Surg. Assn. (2d v.p. 1989), So. Surg. Assn. (1st v.p. 1995-96, pres. 1997-98), Assn. Acad. Surgery (pres. 1971), Ctrl. Surg. Assn. (sec. 1980-82, pres. 1984), Soc. Surgery Alimentary Tract (v.p. 1984-85), Halsted Soc. (sec. 1983-85, pres. 1986). Republican. Roman Catholic. Avocations: cooking, gardening, fishing. Personal E-mail: popswog@coslink.net.

GRIFFENHAGEN, GEORGE BERNARD, trade association executive; b. Portland, Oreg., June 9, 1924; s. Richard Bernard and Clara (Schoenian) G.; m. Joan Helen Houston, June 21, 1946; children: Gary Bernard, Gordon Wesley, Barbara Clare. BS in Pharmacy, U. So. Calif., 1949, MS, 1950; student, Fresno State Coll., 1946, U. London, 1948. Dir. research Nion Corp., Hollywood, Calif., 1950-52; curator div. med. scis. Smithsonian Instn., Washington, 1952-59; sec. sect. history of pharmacy Am. Pharm. Assn., Washington, 1952-59, pres. local chpt., 1958-59, assoc. exec. dir., 1959-89, hon. pres., 1990-91; trustee Am. Pharm. Assn. Found., Washington, 1989-94; editor Jour. Am. Pharm. Assn., Washington, 1960-76; sec.-gen. 4th Pan Am. Congress Pharmacy and Biochemistry, Washington, 1957; sec. organizing com. 31st Internat. Congress Pharm. Scis., Washington, 1971; sec.-gen. Internat. Congress History of Pharmacy, Washington, 1983, Japan-U.S. Congress of Pharm. Scis., Honolulu, 1987; v.p. Pan Am. Pharm. and Biochem. Fedn., 1963-82, 85-91, Pharmacy World Congress, Washington, 1991. U.S. del. Internat. Pharm. Fedn. Gen. Assemblies, London, 1955, Brussels, 1958, Copenhagen, 1960, Vienna, 1962, Amsterdam, 1964, Hamburg, 1968, Geneva, 1970, Lisbon, 1972, Rome, 1974, Warsaw, 1976, Cannes, 1978; U.S. del. FIP Coun., Bucharest, 1969, Dublin, 1975, Montreal, 1985, Helsinki, 1986, Amsterdam, 1987, Sydney, 1988, Munich, 1989, Istanbul, 1990, Lyon, 1992, Tokyo, 1993, Lisbon, 1994, Jerusalem, 1996, Vancouver, 1997, The Hague, 1998, Barcelona, 1999, Vienna, 2000; congress coord., The Hague, 1977; U.S. del. Pan Am. Fedn. Pharmacy Congress, Mexico City, 1963, Buenos Aires, 1966, Caracas, 1969, Panama, 1972, Guatemala City, 1985, Santo Domingo, 1988, Buenos Aires, 1994, San Jose, Costa Rica, 1997, Rio de Janeiro, 2000; U.S. del. Internat. Congress History of Pharmacy, Budapest, Hungary, 1981, Fedn. Asian Pharm. Assns. Congress, Seoul, Korea, 1982; mem. Nat. Action Com. on Drug Edn., Office of Edn., 1970-71, Va. Gov.'s Coun. on Narcotic and Drug Abuse Control, 1970-72. Editor: Scalpel and Tongs, 1972-73; Contbr. articles to profl. jours. Mem. Fairfax County (Va.) Rep. Com., 1962-97; adminstrv. asst. to chmn. Va. State Rep. Com., 1969-71; life mem. Rep. Nat. Com., 1979—; founding pres. Nat. Coordinating Coun. on Drug Edn., 1968-69. Served with C.E. AUS, World War II, ETO. Recipient Pfizer Merit award U.S. CD Coun., 1964, U. So. Calif. Alumnus award, 1969; Hugo H. Schaefer award Am. Pharm. Assn., 1984; Disting. Svc. award Pharmacy Guild of Australia, 1988, Internat. Pharmacy Jour. Editor's prize, 1989, 95, Remington Honor medal Am. Pharm. Assn., 1991; named to Nat. Philatelic Writers Hall of Fame, 1990. Mem. Am. Inst. History of Pharmacy (pres. 1960-61, Edward Kremers award 1969, sec. 1991-2005), Friends of Hist. Pharmacy (pres. 1957-58), Pharm. Wholesalers Assn. (Distinguished Service award 1971), Am. Topical Assn. (1st v.p. 1972-75, pres. 1976-79, pres. med. subjects unit 1969-72, Distinguished Topical Philatelist award 1970, Myrtle Watt Med. Philately Topicalist award 1980, editor Topical Time 1992—), Am. Philatelic Congress (Jere Hess Barr award 1969), Am. Philatelic Soc. (sec.-treas. Writers Unit 1982—; U.S. commr. to Internat. Exhbn. Thematic Philately, Basel, Switzerland 1983, Luff award 2003), Am. Revenue Assn. (named to Sterling Meml. Roll of Disting. Fiscalists 1979), Council Philatelic Orgns. (treas. 1983-91), Internat. Pharm. Fedn. (hon.), Philatelic Lit. Assn., Académie Internationale d'Histoire de la Pharmacie (treas. 1971-81, 1989-97), Pharm. Soc. Gt. Britain (hon.), Sigma Xi, Rho Chi, Phi Kappa Psi. Home: 2501 Drexel St Vienna VA 22180-6906 Office: Am Pharm Assn 2215 Constitution Ave NW Washington DC 20037-2907 Business E-Mail: ggriffenhagen@aphanet.org.

GRIFFETH, LANDIS KING, nuclear medicine physician; b. Greenville, SC, Aug. 3, 1956; s. Jesse Ellis and Mary Alice (King) G.; m. Terri Blount, Aug. 6, 1978. BA in Chemistry and Zoology summa cum laude, Duke U., 1977, PhD in Pharmacology, 1983, MD, 1984. Diplomate Am. Bd. Nuc. Medicine. Postdoctoral rsch. fellow Duke U. Sch. Pharmacology, Durham, NC, 1983-84; resident in diagnostic radiology Mallinckrodt Inst. of Radiology, Washington U., St. Louis, 1984-86, resident in nuclear medicine, 1986-87, chief resident in nuc. medicine, 1987-88, asst. prof. radiology, 1988-93; dir. nuc. medicine Baylor U. Med. Ctr., Dallas, 1993—; med. dir. North Tex. Clin. P.E.T. Inst., Dallas, 1998—. Dir. nuc. medicine and P.E.T., Am. Radiology Assn., Dallas, 1993—, nat. med. dir., P.E.T., U.S. Oncology, 2000—. Assoc. editor Radiology Jour., 1993-2000; cons. to editor Radiology, 2000-02; contbr. numerous articles to profl. jours; reviewer med. jours; edit. bd. Molecular Imagingand Biology, 2004-. Mem. Univ. Park United Meth. Ch.; bd. dirs. Cavalier Health Found.; mem. devel. coun. Tex. A&M Coll. Vet. Medicine. Mem. Am. Coll. Radiology, Am. Coll. Nuc. Physicians, Soc. Nuc. Medicine, Acad. Molecular Imaging (nat. patient adv. com.), Inst. for Clin. P.E.T., Radiol. Soc. N.Am., Am. Soc. for Law Enforcement Tng., Tex. Med. Assn., Tex. Radiol. Soc., Dallas County Med. Soc., Phi Lambda Upsilon, Alpha Omega Alpha. United Methodist. Methodist. Avocations: target shooting, reading, dogs, travel. Office: Baylor U Med Ctr 3500 Gaston Ave Dallas TX 75246-2096 Office Phone: 214-826-8822. Business E-Mail: lk.griffeth@baylorhealth.edu.

GRIFFEY, JACQUELINE JETT, journalist, writer; d. Otis Nathaniel Jett and Mary Lodema Kinnaird (maiden); m. James Howard Griffey, Sr., Dec. 3, 1947; children: James Howard Jr., Marita Ann. Columnist North Shelby Times, Memphis. Mem. Sisters in Crime, Kans., 2000—. Author: (novel) Welcome To Lazarus, 2000 (Darrell Award Hon. Mention, 2003), Recycling Humanity, 2000, 2004, Memphis In Our Heart, 2003, Once Burned, 2005, The Devil in Maryvale. Mem.: The Penpoint Group (vice pres./treas. 2002—03). Protestant. Avocations: baking, freelance writing, travel, reading.

GRIFFEY, KEN, JR., (GEORGE KENNETH GRIFFEY JR.), professional baseball player; b. Donora, Pa., Nov. 21, 1969; s. Ken Griffey Sr. Grad., H.S., Cin. Outfielder Seattle Mariners, 1987—99, Cin. Reds, 2000—. Named Most Valuable Player, All-Star Game, 1992, Am. League MVP, 1997; named to All-Star Team, 1990—2000, MLB All-Century Team, 1999; recipient Gold Glove award, 1990—99. Achievements include led the Am. League in Home Runs, 1994, 1997-1999; Hit his 500th career Home Run on June 22, 2004. Office: Cincinnati Reds 100 Cinergy Fld Cincinnati OH 45202-3543

GRIFFEY, LINDA BOYD, lawyer; b. Keokuk, Iowa, Aug. 6, 1949; d. Marshall Coulter and Geraldine Vivian (White) Boyd; m. John Jay Griffey, June 24, 1972. BS in Pharmacy, U. Iowa, 1972; JD, Duke U., 1980. Bar: Calif. 1980; lic. pharmacist, Iowa, N.C. Pharmacist Davenport (Iowa) Osteo. Hosp., 1972-75, Wagner Pharmacy, Clinton, Iowa, 1975-77, Durham (N.C.) County Gen. Hosp., 1977-80; assoc. O'Melveny & Myers, L.A., 1980-88, ptnr., 1988—. Spkr., writer in field of employee benefits and exec. compensation; former pres. L.A. chpt. Western Pension and Benefits Conf., 1998-99. Active L.A. Philharm. Bus. & Profl. Assn.; bd. dirs. Hillsides Home for Children, Pasadena Playhouse. Mem. ABA (employee benefits com. tax sect.), Am. Law Inst., L.A. County Bar Assn. (former chair employee benefits com. 1994-95), L.A. Duke Bar Assn. (pres. 1987-90, 91-92), Rotary (L.A. chpt. bd. dirs. 1995-97). Avocations: golf, reading, swimming. Office: O'Melveny & Myers 400 S Hope St Los Angeles CA 90071-2899 E-mail: lgriffey@omm.com.

GRIFFEY, MARIAN LOVENE, counselor; b. Hickory, NC, Dec. 26, 1954; d. Joseph Wesley Friffey and Treva Ayers Griffey; m. Clifford Kenneth Dodd, Jr., Jan. 1, 1999; children: Jonathan Scott, Orion Jahosa. B in psycho. devel., Canyon Coll., 2004. Cert. domestic violence emergency first responder Am. Assn. Experts in Traumatic Stress, 2005. Counselor Peaceful Paths Domestic Abuse Network, Gainesville, Fla., 2002—04, Reaven Found., Gainesville, 2004—; reverand, spiritual counselor Universal Ministries, 2004—. Vol. K5 Geological Survey, Gainsville, Fla., 1995—; facilitator Am. Chronic Pain Assn., Gainesville, Fla., 2002. Author: (poetry) numerous publications, (short stories) Not So Long Ago, 1995, The Girl From Sandpit Road, 1998 (1st Place, The Modern Mag. of the Mts., 1998); contbr. articles various profl.jours.; author: A Layman's Look at Edible and Medicinal Plants of Florida, 1998, In Search of the Grapevine, 1995, Backhills Summer Sundays, 1996, Take a Look At Alice, 1997, Dark Side of a Big-Bole Tree, 1999, He Gave Me His Heart: Honoring the Fathers, 1999, The Butterfly Girl, The Problem Box. Vol. Rockin' Readers, Alachu County Sch. Sys., Gainesville, 1995—99. Recipient Principal's award, Pattillo Elem. Sch., 1992. Mem.: Am. Chronic Pain Assn., Am. Mental Health Counselors Assn., Am. Acad. of Experts in Traumatic Stress, NC Poetry Soc., Am. Poetry Soc. Avocations: poetry, creative artwork. Home: 5222 NW 56th Ct Gainesville FL 32653 Office: Reaven Found 5222 NW 56th Ct Gainesville FL 32653 E-mail: mariangriffey@yahoo.com, kdodd@nervm.nerdc.ufl.edu.

GRIFFIN, ADELE, writer; b. Phila., Pa., July 29, 1970; d. Robert Earnest Watson and Priscillsa Goodwyn Sands; m. Erich Paul Mauff, Aug. 16, 1997. BS, U Pa., 1993. Writer Hyperion Books, 1996—, Putnam/G.P. Putnam's Sons, N.Y.C., 2000—. Author: Split Just Right, 1997 (Parents Choice Award), Sons of Liberty, 1997 (Nat. Book Award Finalist, Am. Lib. Assn. Best Book), The Other Shepards, 1998 (Pub. Weekly Bes Book of the Yr., Am. Lib. Assn. Best Book, Sch. Lib. Jour. Best Book of the Yr.), Dive, 1999, Amandine, 2001 (Pub. Weekly Bes Book of the Yr.), Hannah Divided, 2002 (Am. Lib. Assn. Best Book), Overnight, 2003, Witch Twins, Witch Twins at Camp Bliss, Witch Twins and Melody Malady, Witch Twins and the Ghost of Glenn Bly, books have been translated into Spanish, German, and Italian. Mem.: Soc. of Children's Book Writers adn Illustrators, N.Y. Pub. Lib., Southern Poverty Law Ctr. Democrat. Avocations: yoga, painting. Home: 163 East 71st St New York NY 10021

GRIFFIN, ALAN NASH, psychologist; b. Dallas, Oct. 23, 1943; s. Jack Forrest and Mary Helen (Nash) G. BA, U. North Tex., 1965, MA, 1966; PhD, U. Fla., 1971. Lic. psychologist, Tex.; cert. group psychotherapist; cert. cons. in clin. hypnosis. Psychologist Hillsborough County MHMR Ctr., Tampa, Fla., 1972-73; asst. prof. U. North Tex., Denton, 1973-74; pvt. practice Dallas, 1973-88, Austin, Tex., 1988—. Cons. Tex. Rehab. Commn., 1974-93, U.S. Dept. Labor, 1987-88, Plano, Tex. Sch. System, 1974-81, Mesquite Tex. Sch. System, 1974-75, Dallas Soc. for Crippled Children, 1974-75; asst. prof. psychology U. North Tex., 1973-74; adj. prof. So. Meth. U., 1975-77, U. South Fla., 1972-73; staff psychologist Dallas Child Guidance Clinic, 1969, Beverly Hills Hosp., 1967-69, Rusk, Tex. State Hosp., 1966-67. Editor (video series) Psychology Century Series, 1992; contbr. articles to profl. jours. Pres. Frontier Toastmasters, 1990; state del. Dem. Party, 1982-86, precinct chair 1968-69; pres., bd. dirs. Suicide Prevention Ctr., Dallas, 1978. Mem. Assn. of Psychol. Type (life), Am. Psychol. Assn., Am. Group Psychotherapy Assn. (clin. mem.), Am. Soc. of Clin. Hypnosis (clin. mem.), Am. Assn. of Marriage and Family Therapists (clin. mem.), Am. Assn. of Sex Educators, Conselors and Therapists (life). Avocations: travel, sailing, concerts, reading, writing. Home: 2704 Oakhaven Dr Austin TX 78704-3832 Office: 1600 W 38th St Ste 428 Austin TX 78731-6409 E-mail: dralangriffin@austin.rr.com.

GRIFFIN, ANNE, political scientist, educator; d. John Bastin and Elizabeth McCue Griffin; m. Jay Lefer, July 26, 1968; children: David G. Lefer, Theodore B. Lefer. BA, Wellesley Coll.; MA, NYU, 1973, PhD, 1975. Asst. to dean NYU, N.Y.C, NY, 1965—68, asst. prof., politics N.Y.C., NY, 1977—78; asst. prof. to prof., polit. sci. Cooper Union for Advancement of Sci. & Art, N.Y.C., NY, 1978—; adj. assoc. prof., politics NYU, N.Y.C., NY, 1987—89; vis. scholar Ctr. for European Studies, NYU, N.Y.C., NY, 2000—. Assoc. Columbia U. Seminar, Am. Civilization, N.Y.C, NY, 1978—, Columbia U. Seminar, Hist. and Memory, N.Y.C., NY, 2002—; cons. Rsch. & Forecasts, N.Y.C., NY, 1979—81; mem., adv. bd. Women in Sci. Sect., NY Acad. of Sciences, N.Y.C., NY, 1981—2003; mem. Ad Hoc Com. on Animal Rsch., NY Acad. of Sciences, N.Y.C., NY, 1982—87; cons. Cornell U, NY Hosp., N.Y.C., NY, 1983—87, St. Martin's Press, N.Y.C., NY, 1992—92. Author: Quebec: The Challenge of Independence, Les Nationalismes au Quebec du XIXe au XXIe siecle; contbr. articles various profl. jours.;, co-editor various profl. pamphlets, author various book reviews. Mem., com. chair Cmty. Planning Bd. 8, Manhattan, N.Y.C., NY, 1972—77; v.p. NYU Alumni Assn., N.Y.C., NY, 1999—2001; pres. NYU, Grad. Sch. of Arts & Sci. Alumni Assn., N.Y.C., NY, 1985—87. Summer Seminar fellow, NEH, 1981, Summer Stipend grant, 1995, 2000, Que. Studies grant, Govt. of Que., 1993-94, 1996-97, Sr. Rsch. fellowship, Fulbright Found., 2001-2002, Fellow, NEH, 2002. Mem.: NY State Polit. Sci. Assn. (Can. polit. chair, dir. 1995—2001), Am. Coun. for Que. Studies, Am. Polit. Sci. Assn., Assn. for Can. Studies in the US (life). Democrat. Office: Cooper Union for the Advancement of Science & Art 51 Astor Pl Rm 113 New York NY 10003 Office Phone: 212-353-4276. Personal E-mail: griffinphd@hotmail.com. E-mail: griffin@cooper.edu.

GRIFFIN, BETTY LOU, not-for-profit developer, educator; d. Julius Craven and Rachel Idell Best; m. Jack Wayne Griffin, May 28, 1960; children: Cheryle Louann, Melanie Lynn Young, Penelope. BS in Elem. Edn. magma cum laude, Campbell U., 1967; ME in Adult and Cmty. Coll. Edn., N.C. State U., 1974; ME in Adminstrn. and Supervision, Fayetteville State U., 1995. Tchr. Sampson County Schs., Clinton, NC, 1965-67, Clinton City Schs., 1967-87; founder, exec. dir. U Care Inc., Sampson County Domestic Violence and Sexual Assault Program, Clinton, 1996—; CEO, bd. dirs., exec. dir. On Track Youth Svcs., Clinton, 2000—02. Evening bus. math. instr. Sampson CC, 1973—75, instr., 1975—77; notary pub. State of N.C., 1995—. Author: (poems) Poetry Collection, 1997, Rhyme in Time, 1999. Founder, dir. Sampson County Women's Assembly, 1994, 1996, 1998; legis. chmn., monitor chmn. Youth Adv. Coun., Sampson, 1994—98; founder, pres., exec. dir. Sampson County Coun. Women, 1995—. Named N.C. Dem. Women Poet Laureate, 1997, Sampson County Disting. Woman of the Yr., Sampson County Coun. Women, 1998; recipient Carpathian award, N.C. Equity, 1996. Mem.: DAR U. D.C., N.C. Dem. Women (mem. exec. bd. 1995—99, 1st poet laureate 1997—), Sampson County Dem. Women (v.p. 1993, 2d v.p. 1996—97, 2000—03, pres. 1994—95, 1998—99), Order of Eastern Star, Delta Kappa Gamma. Democrat. Methodist. Avocations: reading, creative writing, arts and crafts, hunting, fishing. Home and Office: 2535 Rosebory Hwy Clinton NC 28328

GRIFFIN, CAMPBELL ARTHUR, JR., retired lawyer; b. Joplin, Mo., July 17, 1929; s. Campbell Arthur and Clara M. (Smith) G.; m. Margaret Ann Adams, Oct. 19, 1958; children: Campbell A., Laura Ann. BA, U. Mo., 1951, MA in Acctg., 1952; JD, U. Tex., 1957. Bar: Tex. 1957. Assoc. Vinson & Elkins, LLP, Houston, 1957-67, ptnr., 1968-92, mgmt. com., 1981-90, mng. ptnr. Dallas, 1986-89. Adj. prof. adminstrv. sci. Jones Grad. Sch. Adminstrn., Rice U., 1992-94. Mem. ofcl. bd. Bethany Christian Ch., Houston, 1962-69, chmn. bd. elders, 1968; bd. dirs. Houston Pops Orch., 1982-87; councilman City of Hunters Creek Village, Tex., 1993-95; pres. Windcliff Property Owners Assn., Estes Park, Colo., 1995-96; bd. dirs. Cornell Cos., Inc. (NYSE), 1996-2000; active St. Martin's Episcopal Ch., Houston. Mem. Houston Bar Assn., State Bar Tex. (bus. law sect. chmn. 1974-75), Tex. Bus Law Found. (chmn. 1988-89, dir. 1988-2000), Houston Racquet Club (dir. 1992-94), St. Charles Bay Hunting Club (sr.).

GRIFFIN, CARLETON HADLOCK, accountant, educator; b. Richmond Heights, Mo., Oct. 30, 1928; s. Merle Leroy and Bernice Hilder Edwards (Nelson) G.; m. Mary Lou Goodrich, Dec. 26, 1953; children: Julia, Anne. BBA, U. Mich., 1950, JD, MBA, U. Mich., 1953. Mem. audit and tax staff Touche Ross & Co., Detroit, 1955-59, adminstrv. partner Denver, 1959-71, nat. tax dir. N.Y.C., 1971-72, nat. dir. ops. and adminstrn., 1972-74, chmn. bd., 1974-82, sr. ptnr., 1982-85, regional ptnr., 1983-85; prof. acctg. U. Mich., 1985-95. Dir. Paton Acctg. Ctr., U. Mich., 1997-2001. Contbr. articles to profl. jours. Sr. warden St. Paul's Episcopal Ch., Darien, Conn., 1979-81; trustee Siena Heights Coll., Adrian, Mich., 1988-2000. Served with Fin. Corps AUS, 1953-55. Mem. AICPA, Colo. Soc. CPAs (pres. 1970-71), N.Y. Soc. CPAs, Mich. Soc. CPAs. Republican.

GRIFFIN, CATHY MCWHORTER, elementary school educator; b. Monroe, N.C., Apr. 3, 1956; d. Samuel Edward and Grace (Couick) McWhorter; m. Eric Steven Griffin, Apr. 21, 1979. BS in Early Childhood, Appalachian State U., 1978; M in Human Devel. and Learning, U. N.C., Charlotte, N.C., 1985. Cert. tchr. grades K-4. Tchr. elem. Prospect Elem. Sch., Monroe, N.C., 1979—. Mem. softball com. Bethlehem Meth. Ch., Monroe, 1993—. Named Tchr. of Yr., Prospect Sch., 1982, Outstanding Young Educator, Prospect Sch., 1983; recipient UNW membership pin, 2004. Mem. Prospect PTA, Bethlehem United Meth. Women (sec. 1981-92). Democrat. Methodist. Avocations: music, art, running, gardening, collecting antiques. Home: 4108 S Rocky River Rd Monroe NC 28112-7595 Office: Prospect Elem Sch 3005 Ruben Rd Monroe NC 28112-8039 Office Phone: 704-764-2920.

GRIFFIN, CLAYTON HOUSTOUN, retired electric power industry executive; b. Atlanta, June 14, 1925; s. George Clayton and Eugenia (Johnston) G.; m. Gloria Giegel Handley; 1 child, Clayton Houstoun; m. Lela Lounsbery Griffin, June 6, 1953; children: Lela Griffin Lofgren, George Duncan Bryan, Phillips Lounsbery B.E.E., Ga. Inst. Tech., 1945, MS in E.E., 1950. Registered profl. engr., Ga. Tester Ga. Power Co., Atlanta, 1949-51, test engr., 1953-58, protection engr., 1958-63, chief protection engr., 1963-79, mgr. system protection and control, 1979-89. Contbr. tech. papers to profl. publs. Trustee Ga. Tech Nat. Alumni Assn., Atlanta, 1977-80. Served to lt. comdr. USNR, 1943-47, 51-53 Named Engr. of Yr., Ga. Power Engring. Soc., Atlanta, 1966, Ga. Soc. Profl. Engrs., Atlanta, 1984; named to Sch. of Engring. Hall of Fame, Ga. Inst. Tech., 2002. Fellow IEEE (chmn. Atlanta chpt. 1974, chmn. stds. com. on dispersed generation 1982-89, chmn. power sys. relaying com. 1987-89, Disting. Svc. award power sys. relaying com. 1990, Charles Proteus Steinmetz Major Contbns. to Devel. Elec. Engring. Stds. award 1994). Clubs: Cherokee Town and Country (Atlanta). Republican. Episcopalian. Avocations: stamp collecting/philately, golf. Home: 221 The South Chace NE Atlanta GA 30328-4262

GRIFFIN, CLEMENT M., information technology executive; b. Vicksburg, Miss., June 22, 1950; s. Howard Clement and Lena Lucille Griffin; m. Hannah Kay Morris, July 26, 1998; m. Sharon G Walker, Sept. 7, 1987 (div. Jan. 7, 1995); m. Cynthia Ann Kruithof, Mar. 12, 1978 (div. July 12, 1984); children: Leanna Morris, Jessi Lynn, Damien Brent. BS in computer sci., Kennesaw

State U., 1989—95; PhD in computer sci., Kennedy Western U., 2000—02; tech. degree computer programming, Midwest Automation Tng., 1967—68. Installer/repairman South Ctrl. Bell Tel. & Telegraph, Vicksburg, Miss., 1968—72; dir., mis United Am. of Tenn., Memphis, 2000—01, v.p., mis, 2001—02; systems analyst/programmer lead Sedgwick Claims Mgmt. Svcs., Memphis, 2002—05; cable splicing technician South Ctrl. Bell Tel. & Telegraph, Vicksburg, Miss., 1972—73, cable repair technician, 1973—74, sr. systems technician, 1974—85; integrated systems specialist AT&T Comm., Huntsville, Ala., 1986—88; tech. trainer/developer AT&T Computer Systems Tng., Atlanta, 1988—92; tech. support mgr. AT&T Bell Labs, Alpharetta, Ga., 1992—96; data networking tech. cons. AT&T Bus. Comm. Services, Memphis, 1996—99; bus. systems analyst United Am. of Tenn., Memphis, 1999—2000; sr. program analyst Hilton Hotels Corp., Memphis, 2005—. Recipient Most Outstanding Computer Sci. Student, Kennesaw State U., 1995, Presdl. Scholar, Kennesaw State U. (SALT program), 1994—95, Nat. Dean's List, Kennesaw State U., 1996, Outstanding Scholastic Achievement, 1996. Mem.: Golden Key Nat. Honor Soc. (life), Phi Kappa Phi (life). Avocations: music composition, singing, fishing. Office: Hilton Hotels Corp 765 Crossover Ln Memphis TN 38117 Office Phone: 901-374-5462. E-mail: clement.griffin@earthlink.net.

GRIFFIN, DANIEL BERNARD, JR., writer, scriptwriter, lyricist; b. New Milford, Conn., Jan. 20, 1971; s. Daniel Bernard Griffin, Sr. and Patricia Ann Griffin; m. Alice Rose Arnts, Oct. 26, 2002. Student, U.S. Mil. Acad., 1989—90, Western Conn. State U., 1993—96. Mgr., co-founder Anna's Collectibles, Brewster, NY, 1991—97; bouncer Down the Hatch, Brookfield, Conn., 1993—97; head gymnastics coach Brookfield YMCA, 1993—97; electrician Drew Stephensen, Brookfield, 1995—97; barista Coffee Bean, West Hollywood, Calif., 1997—98; mgr. Brewster Amusements, Red Rooster, 1999—2003; tax clk. Greenburgh Town Hall, Elmsford, NY, 2000—02; pub. mgr. Blue Hawk Pub., Monmouth U., West Long Branch, NJ, 2002—03; CEO Lazarus Prodns., Inc., Queens, NY, 2003—. Prodr.: (music video) Right Now, 2003; writer, prodr.: Beauty in a Jar, 2003; dir.: (animation CD) The Adventures of Merlin the Mouse, 2003; stage mgr.: (TV films) Life As We Know It, 2003; bass player, songwriter, background vocals: Celtic Rock band The Ruffians, 1998—2003; actor: Jingle All the Way, Keeping the Faith, Gattaca, The Long Gray Line, Central Park West. Assoc. mem. West Long Branch Fire Dept. #1, 2003. Cpl. U.S. Army, 1989—90. Mem.: Ancient Order Hibernians. Roman Catholic. Avocations: comic book collecting, wing chun kuen, bushido ryu, making movies, walking. Home: Apt 8 1 West End Ct West End NJ 07740 Office: Lazarus Prodns Inc 31-30 35th St Astoria NY 11006

GRIFFIN, DENNIS JOSEPH, middle school principal; b. Chgo., Feb. 4, 1943; s. Dennis Joseph and Ruth G.; m. Janet A. Maender; children: Nathan, Jonathan. BA, Western Mich. U., 1969; MA, Portland State U., 1980; postgrad., U. South Fla. Counselor U.S. Job Corps, Ft. Custer, Mich.; tchr. Kalamazoo (Mich.) Ctrl. H.S., Charlotte Amalie H.S., St. Thomas, U.S. Virgin Islands; tchr., head basketball coach Eudora Kean H.S., St. Thomas; program coord. CATCH Program Portland (Oreg.) Pub. Schs.; counselor Blanton Elem./St. Petersburg H.S., Fla.; asst. prin. Southside Fundamental Mid. Sch., St. Petersburg; prin. Bay Point Mid. Sch., St. Petersburg. Bd. dirs. Ctr. Against Spouse Abuse, St. Petersburg; vol. Boy Scouts Am., 1988; pres. Pinellas City Adminstrn. Assn., 2003; mem. edn. practices commn. State of Fla., 2002—; mem. Leadership St. Petersburg, 1987—, mem. planning com., 1989-91; commr. Southside Youth Soccer, 1988. Recipient Mayoral Proclamation, City of St. Petersburg, 2005. Mem. Nat. Assn. Secondary Sch. Prins., Mid. Sch. Prin. Assn. (pres. Largo, Fla. chpt.), Pinellas Adminstrs. Assn. (pres. 2003-2004), Rotary (leadership com. St. Petersburg, 1987, planning com., 1989-91).

GRIFFIN, DONALD WAYNE, retired diversified chemical company executive; b. Evansville, Ind., Mar. 1, 1937; s. Pauline Marie (Rahm) G.; m. Kristanya Johnson; children: Kristanya Anne, Kirstin Alyson. Student, Ind. U., 1954-57; BSBA, Evansville Coll., 1961. Sales rep. organics and explosives Olin Corp., Knoxville, Tenn., 1961-62; sales rep., dist. sales mgr. brass sales dept. Olin Corp., Indpls., 1964-69; dist. sales mgr. Milw., 1969-73; asst. to dir. field sales, s.w. region sales mgr. East Alton, Ill., 1973-77; dir. field sales, 1977-80; dir. internat. bus. devel., 1980-81; v.p. mktg. brass group Olin Corp., East Alton, 1981-83, pres. brass group, 1983-85, pres. Winchester group, 1985-86, pres. def. systems group, 1986-87, exec. v.p., pres. def. systems, 1987-93, vice chmn. bd. ops., 1993-94, pres., CEO, chmn. Norwalk, Conn., 1996—. Bd. dirs. Riverbend Bancshares, Inc., Ill. State Bank, East Alton, Olin Corp., Rayonier, Inc., Rayonier Forst Resources Co. Bd. dirs. Leadership Coun. S.W. Ill., Edwardsville, 1984—, Alton Meml. Hosp., Ill., 1983-89, St. Louis Regional Growth Assn., 1986-89. Mem. Assn. U.S. Army, Am. Def. Preparedness Assn., Navy League U.S. (life), Am. Soc. Metals, Small Arms Ammunition Mfrs. (bd. dirs. 1985—), S.W. Ill. Indsl. Assn. (bd. dirs. 1985—), Ill. C. of C. (bd. dirs. 1985-89), Wildlife Mgmt. Inst. (bd. dirs. 1986—), Nat. Shooting Sports Found. (bd. dirs. 1985—, trustee Buffalo Bill Hist. Ctr. 1991—), Chem. Mfrs. Assn. (bd. dirs. 1994—). Office: Olin Corp 501 Merritt 7 Ste 1 Norwalk CT 06851-6261

GRIFFIN, ELEANOR, publishing executive, editor; BA in Journalism and Political Sci., U. Ind. Merchandising mgr., So. Living So. Progress Corp., 1977—87, promotions mgr. So. Living and So. Accents mags., 1987—91, creative services dir., So. Living, So. Accents and Travel South, 1991—92, editorial coord. So. Living, 1992—93, exec. editor So. Living Birmingham, 1993—2001, custom Publishing editorial dir., 2001—02, corp. mag. develop., editorial dir., v.p. and editor Cottage Living, 2003—. Office: Southern Progress Corp 2100 Lakeshore Dr Birmingham AL 35209-6721

GRIFFIN, HENRY CLAUDE, chemistry professor; b. Greenville, S.C., Feb. 14, 1937; s. Arthur Gwynn and Christa Lou (Wilson) G.; m. Barbara Jean Pierson, Sept. 3, 1960; children: Gwen Meredith Van Ark, Lyle Deborah Warshauer. BS, Davidson Coll., 1958; PhD, MIT, 1962. Instr. math. New Prep. Sch., Cambridge, Mass., 1960-61; rsch. assoc. Argonne Nat. Lab., Lemont, Ill., 1962-64, guest scientist, 1964-70; asst. prof. chemistry U. Mich., Ann Arbor, 1964-70, assoc. prof., 1970-89, prof., 1989—. Vis. scientist Swiss Fed. Reactor Inst., Wurenlingen, 1971-72; vis. rsch. engr. U. Calif., Berkeley, 1978-79; chairperson senate assembly U. Mich., 1993-94; dir. nuc. studies Environ. Rsch. Group, Ann Arbor, 1980-81. Inventor process for separation of Na-22. Mem. AAAS, Am. Chem. Soc. (chairperson steering com. Ctrl. region 1994-95), Am. Phys. Soc. Home: 1410 Harbrooke Ave Ann Arbor MI 48103-3618 Office: Univ Mich Dept Chemistry 930 N University Ave Ann Arbor MI 48109-1055 Office Phone: 734-764-1438.

GRIFFIN, JAMES ANTHONY, bishop; b. Fairview Park, Ohio, June 13, 1934; s. Thomas Anthony and Margaret Mary (Hanousek) Griffin. BA, Borromeo Coll., 1956; JCL magna cum laude, Pontifical Lateran U., Rome, 1963; JD summa cum laude, Cleve. State U., 1972; DHL (hon.), Ohio Dominican Coll., 1994. Priest Roman Cath. Ch., 1960. Bishop Roman Cath. Ch., 1979; assoc. pastor St. Jerome Ch., Cleve., 1960—61; sec.-notary Cleve. Diocesan Tribunal, 1963—65; asst. chancellor Diocese of Cleve., 1965—68, vice chancellor, 1968—73, chancellor, 1973—78, vicar gen., 1978—79; pastor St. William Ch., Euclid, Ohio, 1978—79; aux. bishop Diocese of Cleve., vicar of western region Lorain, Ohio, 1979—83; bishop Diocese of Columbus, Ohio, 1983—2004. Mem clergy rels. bd. Diocese Cleve., 1972—75, mem clergy retirement bd., 1973—78, mem clergy pers. bd., 1979—83; disting. prof. theology Ohio Dominican U., 2005—. Author (with A. J. Quinn): (book) Thoughts for Our Times, 1969, Thoughts for Sowing, 1970; author: (with others) Ashes from the Cathedral, 1974, Sackcloth and Ashes, 1976, The Priestly Heart, 1983, Reflections on the Law of Love, 1991, Summary of the New Catholic Catechism, 1994, A Lenten Walk, 1998; author: They Were There, 2004. Chmn. bd. govs. N. Am. Coll., Rome, 1984—88; co-chair Columbus Comty. Rels. Comn., 1992—95; mem Am's Promise, Columbus, 1997—2001, Columbus Coalition Domestic Violence, 2001—04; mem. adv. coun. Cmty. Shelter Bd., 2001—04; mem. adv. team Cmtys. in Sch., 2002—04; chmn. Mayor's Coun Youth, 1986—90; trustee St Mary Sem, 1976—78; bd. dirs., mem pension comt Cath Cemeteries Assn., 1978—83; vice-chancellor Pontifical Col. Josephinum, 1983—2004; treas. Cath. Relief Svc. Bd., 1988—91, pres., 1991—96; bd. dirs. Holy Family Cancer Home, 1973—78, Meals on Wheels, Euclid, 1978—79, Franklin County United Way, 1984—90. Decorated Knight of the Holy Sepulchre; recipient Human Rights award, Anti-Defamation League B'nai B'rith, 1987, Gov's award, State of Ohio, 1994, Jessing award, Pontifical Coll., 1993, Don Bosco medal, 1997, NG Minuteman award, 1999, Cmty. Svc. award, Columbus Urban League, 1999, Bronze Pelican award, Cath. Boy Scouts, 2002, Charity Newsies award, 2002, St. Thomas More award, 2004. Mem.: Columbus Bar Assn. (chmn. jud. advt. com. 1987—91, Liberty Bell award 1989), Am. Canon Law. Soc. Roman Catholic.

GRIFFIN, JEAN LATZ, political scientist, writer; b. Joliet, Ill., Mar. 6, 1943; d. Carl Joseph and Helene Monica (Bradshaw) Latz; m. Dennis Joseph Griffin, Sept. 16, 1967; children: Joseph, Timothy, Peter. BS in Chemistry, Coll. St. Francis, Joliet, 1965; MS in Journalism, U. Wis., 1967. Clin. investigation coord. Baxter Labs., 1967-68; reporter Joliet Herald News, 1968-70, Raleigh (N.C.) Times, 1974-75, Suburban Trib, Hinsdale, Ill., 1976-78, regional edn. reporter, 1978-82; gen. assignment reporter Chgo. Tribune, 1982-84, edn. writer, 1984-88, pub. health writer, 1988-94, govt., politics, and pub. policy reporter, 1994-97, econ. devel. reporter, 1997; strategist The Strategy Group, Chgo., 1998—; owner CyberINK, 1998—. Adj. journalism instr. Roosevelt U., Chgo., 2001—; facilitator U. Phoenix, 2004—. Bd. dirs. Residents for Emergency Shelter, Chgo., 1978-82, Genesis House, Chgo., 1995-98, vol. cook, 1994-98; devel. com. mem. Hope Now, Inc., 1998-2000; membership chair Arlington Hts. C. of C., 2001-2002; vol. Taoist Tai Chi instr., 2001—, pres. Taoist Chi Soc., Ill., 2003—. Recipient Writing award Am. Dental Assn., 1969, Alumna Profl. Achievement award Coll. St. Francis, Joliet, 1985, First Prize in ednl. writing Edn. Writers Am., 1986, Grand prize, 1988, Benjamin Fine award Nat. Assn. Secondary Sch. Prins., 1988, Edward Scott Beck award for reporting Chgo. Tribune, 1988, Peter Lisagor award for pub. svc. Soc. Profl. Journalists, Chgo. chpt., 1988, Mark of Excellence Chgo. Assn. Black Journalists, 1992, Cushing award for Journalistic Excellence, Chgo. Dental Soc., 1992, Human First award Horizon Cmty. Svcs., Chgo., 1993, Robert F. Kennedy Grand Prize in Journalism, 1994, Editl. Excellence award Ill. Merchandising Coun., 1994; finalist Pulitzer Prize, 1994. Mem. Taoist Tai Chi Soc. USA-Ill. Office: CyberINK 621 N Belmont Ave Arlington Heights IL 60004 E-mail: jlgrif@earthlink.net. *Keep climbing mountains. Invent challenges if you have to. Love all life--amoeba to stars. Dive into the flow of the universe. And wash your dishes when you're done.*

GRIFFIN, JEFFREY FARROW, surgeon; b. Dallas, 1946; MD, Tulane U., 1974. Diplomate Am. Bd. Surgery, Am. Bd. Colon and Rectal Surgery. Intern Ochsner Found. Hosp., New Orleans, 1974-75, resident in gen. surgery, 1975-79; fellow in colon and rectal surgery U. Minn., Mpls., 1979-80; now pvt. practice New Orleans. Mem. staff East Jefferson Gen. Hosp., Metairie, La., So. Bapt. Hosp., La.; clin. asst. prof. medicine Tulane U. Mem. ACS, Am. Soc. Colon and Rectal Surgery. Office: 4429 Clara St Ste 600 New Orleans LA 70115-6951

GRIFFIN, JO ANN THOMAS, retired financial planner, tax specialist; b. Dallas, July 20, 1933; d. John Baxton and Joan Marion (Ament) Thomas; m. John Barrett Brown, June 29, 1963 (div. 1972); children: John Barrett Jr., Daniel Thomas; m. Thomas Reese Griffin, Jan. 25, 1976; stepchildren: Gregory Crawford, Kevin Bradley. BA, U. Miss., 1955; BS magna cum laude, Lamar U., 1964; MEd, U. Del., 1972. CFP; enrolled agt. U.S. Treasury Dept. Site mgr. Motivational Ctr., Inc., Wilmington, Del., 1976-78; asst. dir. Indochinese social svcs. Assoc. Cath. Charities, New Orleans, 1978-79; dir. continuing edn. St. Mary's Dominican Coll., New Orleans, 1979-80; with fin. mgmt. USDA, New Orleans, 1981; tax auditor IRS, New Orleans, Phila., Del., 1981-86, revenue agt. Wilmington, 1987-92; tax specialist Horty & Horty, CPA's, Wilmington, 1986-87; quality control H&R Block, Wilmington, 1992-94; counselor Svc. Corps Ret. Execs., Wilmington, 1992—96; dir. Wilmington River-City Com., 1997-2000. Docent Winterthur, New Orleans Mus. Art, Wilmington and New Orleans, 1966—85; sustaining mem., advisor Jr. League, Wilmington, 1989—92, 1998—2000, mem. cmty. adv. bd., 1998—2000; regent Vieux Carre chpt. DAR, New Orleans, 1984; bd. dirs. Neighborhood Watch, New Orleans, 1983—85, Waterfront Coalition, Inc., 1998—2000; sec., mem. exec. bd. Henrietta Johnson Med. Ctr., 1998—2001; treas., exec. bd. Civil War Round Table Wilmington, Inc., 1999—2002; bd. dirs. Common Cause Del., 2000—, Del. Medicare and Medicaid Fraud Project, 2000—; CASA vol. Family Ct., State of Del., 2000—01; pres. Wilmington chpt. Nat. Assn. Ret. Fed. Employees, 2001—03; lay reader, mem. outreach com. Episc. Ch. Diocese of Del., Wilmington, 1971—2000. Recipient Grad. Scholarship award AAUW, 1971, Sustained Superior Performance award IRS, New Orleans, 1984, Spl. Achievement awards IRS, Wilmington, 1988, 89, Customer Svc. awards, 1989, 90. Mem. Am. Soc. Women Accts. (sec. 1986-89), Del. Valley Soc. CFPs, Wilmington Tax Group, Estate Planning Coun. Del., Wilmington Women in Bus., Rotary, Blue and Gold Club, Mortar Bd., Phi Kappa Phi, Delta Delta Delta. Democrat. Episcopalian. Home: 900 N Broom St Unit 16 Wilmington DE 19806-4546

GRIFFIN, JOHN JOSEPH, JR., chemist, video producer; b. Chgo., Sept. 11, 1946; s. John Joseph, Sr. and Louise (Griswold) G.; m. Ramona Rodriguez, Apr. 19, 1969; 1 child, Marcus. BS, Tex. A&M U., 1972, MS, 1974. With Johns-Manville, Chgo., 1964—66; chemist, rsch. chemist Dow Chemical USA, Tex. Divsn., Freeport, 1974—78; sr. chemist Soltex Polymers, Deer Pk., Tex., 1978—80; plant chemist Air Products & Chemicals, Pasadena, Tex., 1980—84; quality assurance supr. Core Lab., Chromaspec Divsn., Houston, 1984—88; plant chemist and quality assurance supr. Ga. Gulf Corp., Pasadena, Tex., 1988—95; synthesis chemist, quality coord. KMCO, L.P., Crosby, Tex., 1995—2004; propr. Petro-Star, Houston, 1995-96, owner, 1996—97; cons. R&D chemist Technisource, Houston, 2004—. Propr. owner JJ's Quality Custom Video, Houston, 1986—88, 20-Minute Video, 2001—; propr. Pro-Star Video Prodns., Houston, 1988—, prodr., 1988—; video prodr. J. Frank Dobie H.S. Graduation, U. Houston Graduation, also weddings and seminars; v.p., 1996—. Pres. Kirkwood Civic Club, Houston, 1991-96, v.p. 1996-2002; bd. dirs. Southbelt Security Alliance, Houston, 1988-2003, Houston Better Bus. Bur., 1996. With USAF, 1966-70. Mem. ASTM (D-16 com. aromatic compounds and D-2 petro products and lubricants, D-2 petroleum products and lubricants), Am. Chem. Soc. Office: Pro-Star PO Box 750102 Houston TX 77275-0102 Office Phone: 713-907-7807. E-mail: griffinrjj@earthlink.net.

GRIFFIN, JOHN W., neurologist, medical educator; b. Nebr. BA, Grinnell Coll., 1963; MD, Stanford U., 1968. Cert. Am. Bd. Psychiatry and Neurology. Internship Internal Medicine Stanford U. Hosp., 1968—69, resident, 1969—70; resident Neurology Johns Hopkins Hosp., 1970—73; clin. assoc. Med. Neurology Branch NINDS, NIH, 1973—75; asst. prof. Dept. Neurology Johns Hopkins U., Sch. Medicine, Baltimore, 1975—79, assoc. prof., 1979—86, dir. Peripheral Nerve Labs., 1986—, prof. Dept. Neurology and Neuroscience, 1986—, chair, Neurologist-in-Chief, 1998—, prof. Dept. Pathology, 1999—. Hon. prof. Neurology Hebei Med. Coll., Second Tchg. Hosp., Shijiazhuang, China, 1993; hon. attending physician Hebei Province Min. Health, 1995. Editl. bd. Neurotoxicology, 1982—93, Muscle and Nerve, 1987—91, 1998—2001, Neuromuscular Disorders, 1990—94. Recipient Frank R. Ford Tchg. Award, Dept. Neurology, Johns Hopkins U. Sch. Medicine, 1986, Jacob K. Javits Award, Nat. Insts. Neurological Diseases and Stroke, NIH, 1987. Mem.: Soc. Experimental Neuropathlogy, Soc. Neuroscience, Nat. Adv. Neurological Disorders and Stroke (coun. 1999—), Soc. Experimental Neuropathology (pres. 1993—95), Am. Neurological Assn. (pres. elect 2001—03), Am. Acad. Neurology, Alpha Omega Alpha, Phi Beta Kappa. Office: Dept Neurology Johns Hopkins Hosp Meyer Bldg Rm 6-113 600 N Wolfe St Baltimore MD 21287

GRIFFIN, JUDITH ANN, elementary school educator; d. James Robert Thompson and Leona Geraldine Thompson-Ours; m. Stephen Blaine Griffin, July 20, 1968; children: Nathan Blaine, Katrina Ann. BS, Eureka Coll., 1971; MEd, Olivet Nazarene U., 2003. Cert. First Aid and AIDS Instr. ARC, 1995; Tchr. Ill. State Bd. Edn., 1971. Biology, phys. edn. instr. Morton HS, Morton Jr. HS, Ill., 1971—73; phys. edn., health educator Morton Jr. HS, 1973—97, health, computer tech. educator, 1997—, volleyball coach, 1974—79, student coun., scholastical bowl, chess club advisor, 1982—92, dept. chairperson, 1985—, computer club, potter pantagraph advisor, 1996—. Biology lab. instr. Bradley U., Peoria, Ill., 1971—72. Jump rope for heart coord. Am. Heart Assn., Peoria, Ill., 1981—2004, bd. mem. midwest affiliate, 1994—98. Named a Disney Am. Tchr. award honoree, 2002—03; recipient Healthy Me award for Exemplary Health Edn. Program, Met. Life Found., 1985, Devel. Vol. of Yr., Ill. Affiliate Am. Heart Assn., 1998, Health Tchr. of Yr., Ill. Sch. Health Assn., 2002; First grant, Am. Bank, 1994, grant, Office of Edn., 1999, Nat. City Bank, 2000, Recycling grant, Ill. Dept. Commerce and Cmty. Affairs, 2001. Mem.: ASCD, Morton Edn. Assn. (increment rep. 1985—95, Named an Outstanding Tchr. 1985), Ill. Assn. Health, Phys. Edn., Recreation, and Dance, Ctrl. Ill. Rock Club. Roman Catholic. Achievements include research in the effects of hormones in plants. Avocations: rock/geode hunting, reading, hiking, scrapbooks. Office: Morton Unit Sch Dist 709 225 E Jackson Morton IL 61550 Personal E-mail: grif2@dpc.net. Business E-Mail: judy.griffin@morton709.org.

GRIFFIN, KATHY, actress; b. Oak Park, Ill., Nov. 4, 1966; d. John and Maggie Griffin; m. Matthew Moline, Feb. 18, 2001. Studied acting, Lee Strasberg Inst. Actress playing Vicki Groener on Suddenly Susan NBC-TV, 1996—. Appearances include (TV series) Saturday Night Special, 1996, Suddenly Susan, 1996-2000, (voice) Dilbert, 1999-2000, My Life on the D-List, 2005-, (TV episodes) ER, 1994, Caroline in the City, 1995, Comedy Central, 1995, Mad About You, 1995, Seinfeld, 1996, Partners, 1996, (TV spls.) HBO Comedy Half-Hour: Kathy Griffin, 1996, The VH1 Fashion Awards, 1996, (TV movie) The Barefoot Executive, 1995, A Diva's Christmas Carol, 2000, (films) The Unborn, 1991, Shakes the Clown, 1992, It's Pat, 1994, Pulp Fiction, 1994, Courting Courtney, 1995, Four Rooms, 1995, The Cable Guy, 1996, Trojan War, 1997, Can't Stop Dancing, 1999, Dill Scallion, 1999, Muppets From Space, 1999, (voice) Lion of Oz, 2000, The Intern, 2000, On Edge, 2001, (voice) Dinotopia: Quest for the Ruby Sunstone, 2005, Her Minor Thing, 2005; also various stage and stand-up comedy performances. Office: care Warner Bros TV 300 Television Plz Burbank CA 91505*

GRIFFIN, KEITH BROADWELL, retired economics professor; b. Colon, Republic of Panama, Nov. 6, 1938; came to U.S., 1988; s. Marcus Samuel Griffin and Elaine Ann (Broadwell) Fabick; m. Dixie Beth, Apr. 2, 1956; children: Janice, Kimberley. BA, Williams Coll., 1960, DLitt (hon.), 1980; PhB, Oxford (Eng.) U., 1962, PhD, 1965. Fellow and tutor in econs. Magdalen Coll. Oxford (Eng.) U., 1965-76, fellow Magdalen Coll., 1977-79, pres., 1979-88, hon. fellow, 1988; acting warden, dir. Queen Elizabeth House, Inst. Commonwealth Studies, 1973, 77-78, warden, dir., 1978-79; prof. U. Calif., Riverside, 1988—2004, chmn. dept. econs., 1988-93, Presdl. prof., 1988-90, Disting. prof., 1997—2004. Vis. prof. Inst. Econs. and Planning U. Chile, 1962-63, 64-65; chmn. bd. UN Rsch. Inst. for Social Devel., 1988-95, sr. cons., 1971-72; mem. UN com. for devel. planning, 1987-94; mem. coun. UN Univ., 1986-92, chmn. fin. and budget com., 1988-90; mem. Marshall Aid Commemoration Commn., 1984-88; mem. World Commn. on Culture and Devel., 1994-95; chief ILO Employment Adv. Mission to Ethiopia, 1982; econ. advisor Govt. of Bolivia, 1989-91; pres. Devel. Studies Assn., U.K., 1978-80; chief rural and urban employment policies br. ILO, 1975-76; cons. ILO on rural devel. in Ecuador, 1974; sr. adviser OECD Devel. Centre, Paris, 1986-91; adviser to Inter-Am. Com. for Alliance for Progress on copper expansion programme in Chile, 1968, to FAO/ICO/IBRD World Coffee Study in Guatemala, El Salvador and Colombia, 1967; rsch. advisor Pakistan Inst. Devel. Econs., Karachi, 1965, 70; expert on agrl. planning to Govt. of Algeria, acting chief FAO Mission, Algiers, 1963-64; cons. IBRD on land reform in Morocco, 1973; head UN Devel. Program Poverty Alleviation Mission to Mongolia, 1994; head ILO Social Policy Rev. Mission to Uzbekis, 1995; cons. on econ. reform in Vietnam, UNDP, 1997; head ILO Employment and Social Protection Mission to Kazakstan, 1997; head UNDP mission to Mongolia, 2001, Armenia, 2002; leader UNDP program evaluation team in China, 2004-05. Author: Underdevelopment in Spanish America, 1969, 2d edit., 1971, Spanish edit., 1972, The Green Revolution: An Economic Analysis, 1972, The Political Economy of Agrarian Change, 1974, 2d edit., 1979, Spanish edit., 1982, Hindi edit., 1983, Land Concentration and Rural Poverty, 1976, 2d edit., 1981, Spanish edit., 1983, International Inequality and National Poverty, 1978, Spanish edit., 1984, World Hunger and the World Economy, 1987, Alternative Strategies for Economic Development, 1989, 2d edit., 1999, Chinese edit., 1992, Studies in Globalization and Economic Transitions, 1996, Studies in Development Strategy and Systemic Transformation, 2000; co-author: Comercio Internacional y Politicas de Desarrollo Economico, 1967, Planning Development, 1970, Spanish edit., 1975, The Transition to Egalitarian Development, 1981, Globalization and the Developing World, 1992, Implementing a Human Development Strategy, 1994; editor: Financing Development in Latin America, 1971, Institutional Reform and Economic Development in the Chinese Countryside, 1984, The Economy of Ethiopia, 1992, Poverty and the Transition to a Market Economy in Mongolia, 1995, Social Policy and Economic Transformation in Uzbekistan, 1996, Economic Reform in Vietnam, 1998, Poverty Reduction in Mongolia, 2003; co-editor: Ensayos Sobre Planificacion, 1967, Growth and Inequality in Pakistan, 1972, The Economic Development of Bangladesh, 1974, Human Development and the International Development Strategy for the 1990s, 1990, The Distribution of Income in China, 1993, also numerous articles. Vis. fellow Oxford Ctr. Islamic Studies, 1998. Fellow: AAAS. Avocation: travel. Office: Univ Calif Dept Econs Riverside CA 92521-0001 Personal E-mail: keithdixiegriffin@sbcglobal.net.

GRIFFIN, KELLY ANN, public relations executive, consultant; b. Buffalo, May 20, 1964; d. Michael Gerald and Patricia Frances (Lippert) G.; m. Thomas Richard Kleinberger, Oct. 11, 1992. B in Polit. Sci., SUNY, Geneseo, 1986; postgrad., CUNY, Bklyn., 1994—96. Legis. asst. to N.Y. State Assembly Spkrs. Stanley Fink and Mel Miller, Buffalo, 1986-87; acct. exec. Griffin Media Group, N.Y.C., 1987-88, acct. supr., v.p., 1988-90, pres., CEO, 1990-94; pub. rels. cons. N.Y.C., 1994—. Assoc. dir. N.Y. State Funeral Dirs. Assn., N.Y.C., 1992-94, Met. Funeral Dirs. Assn., N.Y.C., 1992-94, County Execs. of Am., N.Y.C. and Washington, 1993-2000; dep. exec. dir. County Execs. Am., 2000—; instr. remedial reading Cornell U. Sch. Industry/Lab. Rels., Buffalo, 1987; v.p. Fairfield Owners Cooperative, Riverdale, 1996-2000. Editor N.Y. State AFL-CIO Unity, 1988-90, County Execs. News, 1993—, N.Y. State Funeral Dirs. Assn./Met. Funeral Dirs. Assn. News, 1992-94, Amalgamated Transit Union News, 1988-90. Cons. Interfaith Assembly on Homelessness, N.Y.C., 1994-97, Voter Assistance Commn., N.Y.C., 1990-92; participant, cons. Erie County Dem. Party, Buffalo, 1985-87; mem. assocs. steering com. Children's Health Fund, N.Y.C., 1991-97; bd. dirs. Kingsbridge Hts. Cmty. Ctr., Bronx, 1999—, sec., 2000-01, chair, 2001-04; mem. Parents' Assn., Frances Schervier Home and Hosp. Childcare Ctr., Bronx, 1997-2000, Support Our Schs. Com., Bronx, 1999-2000; class parent Prospect Hill Sch. PTA, Pelham Manor, 2001—, rec. sec., 2003-04, pres.-elect, 2004—; mem. fundraising com. Transition Learning Ctr., New Rochelle, NY. Recipient Acad. award DAR, 1978. Mem. Pub. Rels. Soc. N.Y.C., The Manor Club (Pelham Manor, N.Y.). Roman Catholic. Avocations: reading, running, yoga, ice skating. Home: 1061 Hunter Ave Pelham NY 10803-3409 Office: Griffin Media Group 3rd fl 1010 Massachusetts Ave NW Washington DC 20001-5402 Office Phone: 800-296-8438. E-mail: kgrif@optonline.net.

GRIFFIN, KENNETH C., investment company executive; b. Boca Raton, Fl. m. Anne Dias. BA in Economics, Harvard U., 1989. With Glenwood Investment Corp.; founder, pres, CEO Citadel Investment Group, 1990—. Bd. trustees Chgo. Museum Contemporary Art; bd. dirs. Chgo. Public Education Fund, 2003—, Chgo. Public Library Found. Named to Top 200 Collectors, ARTnews mag., 2004. Avocation: Collector of Imprssionism and Post-Impressionism Art. Office: Citadel Investment Group LLC 131 S Dearborn St Chicago IL 60603 Office Phone: 312-395-2100. Office Fax: 312-368-1348.

GRIFFIN, MARVIN ANTHONY, industrial engineer, educator; b. Pine Apple, Ala., Mar. 28, 1923; s. Randolph Simpson and Linnie (Barrett) G.; m. Jane Pearle A. L'Herisson, Sept. 4, 1949 (dec. Dec. 1992); children: Margaret Lynn, John Marvin, Barbara Lee, Elizabeth Ann. BS, Auburn U., 1949; MS Engring, U. Ala., 1952; D.Eng., Johns Hopkins, 1960. Registered profl. engr., Ala. Chief ops. analysis Anniston Ordnance Depot, Ala., 1949-51; sr. mfg. engr. Western Electric Co., Winston-Salem, N.C., 1952-55; chief engring. Cumberland Mfg. Co., Chattanooga, 1955-57; instr. Johns Hopkins, 1957-60; chief indsl. engr. Matson Navigation Co., San Francisco, 1960-61, v.p. corporate devel., 1977-78, group v.p., 1978-79; prof. indsl. engring. U. Ala., 1961-76, chmn. dept., 1965-71, chmn. dept. computer sci. and ops. research, 1971-76, dir. computer sci., 1969-76, prof. indsl. engring. and computer sci., 1980—, prof. emeritus indsl. engring., 1987—, chmn. dept., 1983—. Mem. maritime transp. research bd., maritime info. com. Nat. Acad. Sci., 1976—; mgmt. cons. to industry, govt.; labor arbitrator Fed. Mediation and Conciliation Service, Am. Arbitration Assn.; cons. indsl. engring., ops. rsch., arbitration, mediation svcs., 1987-92. Contbr. articles to profl. jours. Served to comdr. USNR, 1943-47, PTO. Sr. postdoctoral fellow Johns Hopkins U., 1969 Mem. Operations Research Soc. Am., Am. Inst. Indsl. Engrs. (dir. 1954-55, chpt. pres. 1959-60), Am. Soc. Engring. Edn., Inst. Mgmt. Sci., Assn. Computing Machinery, Johns Hopkins Soc. Scholars. Home: 2013 Fox Ridge Rd Tuscaloosa AL 35406-3056

GRIFFIN, MARY FRANCES, retired media consultant; b. Cross Hill, S.C., Aug. 24, 1925; d. James and Rosa Lee (Carter) G. BA, Benedict Coll., 1947; postgrad., S.C. State Coll., 1948-51, Atlanta U., 1953, Va. State Coll., 1961; MLS, Ind. U., 1957. Tchr., libr. Johnston (S.C.) Tng. Sch., Edgefield County Sch. Dist., 1947-51; libr. Lee County Sch. Dist., Dennis High, Bishopville, S.C., 1951-52, Greenville County (S.C.) Sch. Dist., 1952-66; libr. cons. S.C. Dept. Edn., Columbia, 1966-87; ret. Vis. tchr. U. S.C., 1977. Bd. dirs. Greater Columbia Lit. Coun.; mem. Richland County unit Assault on Illiteracy. Recipient Cert. of Living the Legacy award Nat. Coun. Negro Women, 1980. Mem. ALA, Assn. Ednl. Comms. and Tech., S.C. Assn. Curriculum Devel., AAUW (pres. Columbia br. 1978-80), Southeastern Libr. Assn. (sec. 1979-80), S.C. Libr. Assn. (sec. 1979), S.C. Assn. Sch. Librarians, Nat. Assn. State Ednl. and Media Pers. Baptist. Home: PO Box 1652 Columbia SC 29202-1652 also: 1100 Skyland Dr Columbia SC 29210-8127

GRIFFIN, MICHAEL D., federal agency administrator, aerospace scientist; b. Aberdeen, Md., 1949; BS, MS in applied physics, Johns Hopkins U.; MS in aerospace sci., Cath. U.; MS in elec. engring., U. So. Calif.; MS in civil engring., George Washington U.; MBA, Loyola Coll.; PhD in aerospace engring., U. Md. Registered engr., Md., Calif. With Computer Scis, Corp., Jet Propulsion Lab.; dep. for tech. Strategic Defense Initiative Orgn., 1986—91; chief engr., assoc adminstr. for exploration NASA, Washington, DC, 1991—94; sr. v.p. program devel. Space Industries Internat., gen. mgr. Houston; exec. v.p., chief tech. officer Orbital Scis. Corp., Dulles, Va., 1995—2002; pres., COO In-Q-Tel, Arlington, Va., 2002—04; head Space Dept. Applied Physics Lab., Johns Hopkins U., Laurel, Md., 2004—05; adminstr. NASA, 2005—. Adj. prof. U. Md., Johns Hopkins U., George Washington U. Author: (textbook) Space Vehicle Design. Recipient Exceptional Achievement Medal, NASA, Disting. Pub. Svc. Medal, Dept. Defense. Fellow: AIAA (Space Sys. Medal); mem.: Internat. Acad. Astronautics. Avocations: golf, flying, skiing, scuba diving, amateur radio. Office: NASA Two Independence Sq 300 E St NW Rm 9F44 Washington DC 20546*

GRIFFIN, MICHAEL F., lawyer; b. 1954; AB magna cum laude, Dartmouth Coll., 1976; JD cum laude, NYU, 1980. Bar: NY 1981. Assoc. Townley & Updike, 1980—88, ptnr., 1989—95; ptnr., corp group Dorsey & Whitney LLP, NYC, 1995—2005, and chmn, hedge fund practice group; ptnr., corp., securities group Arnold & Porter LLP, NYC, 2005—. Bd. dir. Boys Choir of Harlem. Mem.: ABA, Managed Funds Assn., Futures Industry Assn., Assn. Bar City NY, Order of Coif. Office: Arnold & Porter LLP 399 Park Ave New York NY 10022-4690 Office Phone: 212-715-1136. Office Fax: 212-715-1399. Business E-Mail: Michael.Griffin@aporter.com.

GRIFFIN, OSCAR O'NEAL, JR., writer, former oil company executive; b. Daisetta, Tex., Apr. 28, 1933; s. Oscar O'Neal and Myrtle Ellen (Edgar) G.; m. Patricia Lamb, July 28, 1955; children: Gwendolyn Ann, Amanda Karen, Gregory O'Neal, Marguerite Ellen. B. Journalism, U. Tex., 1958; grad., Harvard U. Sch. Bus., 1982. Editor Canyon (Tex.) News, 1959-60, Pecos (Tex.) Ind., 1960-62; reporter Houston Chronicle, 1962-66, White House corr., 1966-69; asst. dir. pub. affairs U.S. Dept. Transp., Washington, 1969-74; pres. Griffin Well Service, Inc., El Campo, Tex., 1974-88; sr. v.p. 395 Enterprises, Inc., 1986-88; free-lance writer Houston, Tex., 1988—. Served with AUS, 1953-55. Recipient award for investigative reporting Southwest Journalism Forum, 1963; Pulitzer prize for local reporting not under pressure of edit. time, 1963 Mem. Houston Livestock Show and Rodeo (life), U. Tex. Alumni Assn. (life), Harvard Bus Sch. Club of Houston, Soc. Profl. Journalists (Disting. Svc. in Journalism award Ft. Worth chpt. 1962, Courage in Journalism award Des Moines chapt. 1963, award for gen. reporting nat. orgn. 1963). Clubs: National Press. Home and Office: PO Box 156 New Waverly TX 77358-0156 E-mail: oscargriffin@msn.com.

GRIFFIN, PATTI ELAINE, medical educator, consultant; d. Edgar Heerwald and Eva Irene Smith; m. Dennis W. Griffin; children: Lisa, Pat, Tim. BA, Stephens U., 1979; MA, U. Minn., 1984; MBA, S.W. Mo. State U., 1986; PhD in Healthservices and Social Change, Walden U., 1987. V.p. St. John's Regional Med. Ctr., Joplin, Mo., 1973—84, Franciscan Health Sys., Dayton, Ohio, 1987—93; cons. edn. specialist Johnson & Johnson, Cin., 1994—98; prof. Coll. Bus. Harding U., Searcy AR, 1998—99; prof. Coll. Bus. Lipscomb U., Nashville, 1999—2000, asst. provost, 2002—. Missionary Latin Am. Missions, Valdosta, Ga., 1987—99, Health Talents, Internat., Birmingham, Ala., 2000—02. Contbr. articles to profl. jours. Fellow: Am. Coll. Healthcare Exec. Mem. Ch. Of Christ. Avocations: singing, running, golf. Home: Apt 17306 101 Gillespie Dr Franklin TN 37067-7573 Office: Lipscomb Univ 3901 Granny White Pk Nashville TN 37204

GRIFFIN, PAUL, not-for-profit executive; s. James and Eileen Griffin; m. Sevanne Martin, Sept. 19, 1998; 1 child, Cyrus James. BA, Ind. U., 1988. Dir. No-Neck Monsters Theater of Youth, Washington, 1991—93; founding dir. City at Peace - D.C., Washington, 1994—2000; founder, pres. City at Peace, N.Y.C., 2000—. Dir.: (original theatrical mus.) City in Flames, ReVisions, 24 Hours/Divided by Life, Who's to Blame, I of the Storm, Picture This, Lockdown, Beyond Me, Difference is Beautiful, Cracks in the Concrete Canvas. Ally, cmty. organizer Pub. Allies, Washington, 1993—94. Named Visionary Founder, City at Peace - D.C., 2005; recipient Tomorrow's Leaders Today award, Pub. Allies, 1993. Achievements include development of innovative creative process using the performing arts for youth development, social change and the creation of new theatrical works written and performed by youth; Leading creation of national network of programs using the performing arts with diverse groups of teenagers for their positive development and social change. Avocations: travel, skiing, reading, exploring cities, writing. Office: City at Peace 12th Fl 104 W 27th St New York NY 10001 Office Phone: 212-924-2300. Office Fax: 212-924-2167. E-mail: info@cpnational.org.

GRIFFIN, PAUL, JR., navy officer, engineer, educator; b. Aiken, S.C., Mar. 13, 1961; s. Paul and Mamie Lou (Curry) G. AS, Fla. Keys C.C., 1985; BS, Fla. A&M U., 1986, MEd, M in Applied Social Sci., 1993. Asst. produce mgr. Winn-Dixie Store, Goose Creek, S.C., 1977-79; enlisted USN, 1979, commd. ensign, 1986, advanced through grades to lt. comdr., 1990, data systems technician, 1979-86; electrical officer, asst. safety officer USS Leyte Gulf, Mayport, Fla., 1986-88; anti-submarine officer USN, Mayport, Fla., 1988-90; asst. prof. Fla. A&M U./USN, Tallahassee, 1990-93; quality assurance officer, 1993-97; chief engr. USS Stump, 1993-97; master tng. specialist USN, 1992—, dept. head, engr. officer, 1993-97, chmn. cash verification bd., 1993-97; 1st lt. USS Enterprise (CVN 65), 1997-99, 99-2000; comdr., gen. staff coll. Staff Coll., 2000—02; dir. quota mgmt. Navy Enlisted Quota Mgmt. Office, 2000—02; asst. dir. Navy Selection and Classification Mgmt. Office, 2001—02; registrar Tng. Quality Performance Transp. Adminstrn., 2002—03; dep. dir. distributed learning and tng. support Transp. Security Adminstrn., 2002—03; program analyst workforce, performance and tng. Transp. Security Adminstrn., Dept. Homeland Security, 2003—. Project handclasp and cmty. rels. coord. La Guardia, Salvador, Rio de Janeiro, Puerto Ingeniero White, Valparaiso, S. Am., 1994; propulsion and control sys. analyst Comdr. Naval Surface Forces Atlantic, 1997; chmn. Integrated Tng. Requirements and Planning Databases Configuration Control Bd., 2000-2002. Mentor Griffin Mid. Sch., Tallahassee, 1990-92; asst. coord. Family Support Group for Desert Storm, Tallahassee, 1991; spkr., vol. Hugh O'Brien Youth Leadership Program, Tallahassee, 1991; judge Capital Regional Sci. and Engring. Fair, Tallahassee, 1992; advisor City of Tallahassee Examination of Drug and Crime Activity Project, 1992; vol., spkr. Gadsden County GED and Dropout Prevention Program, 1992-93; vol. Riley Elem. Sch. Say No To Drug's Program; founder, coord. Men of Faith Support Group 1st Missionary Bapt. Ch., 1999-2000; chmn. tech. rsch. com. Command and Gen. Staff Coll. 2000 LLC, 1999-2002; others. Delores Auzenne fellow, 1992. Mem. 100 Black Men of Am., Fla. A&M U. Nat. Alumni Assn. (life), Nat. Naval Officers Assn. (life). Democrat. Baptist. Avocations: photography, chess, tennis. Home: 7401 Georgian Dr Upper Marlboro MD 20772 Office: US Dept Homeland Security Transp Security Adminstrn Hdqrs 601 S 12th St East Tower TSA-12 Arlington VA 22202 Business E-Mail: pgjrlg@bellatlantic.net.

GRIFFIN, PENNI ONCKEN, dean, social worker; b. Cedar Rapids, Iowa, Nov. 11, 1945; d. Edward Charles and Rita Margaret Oncken; m. Walt Griffin, Dec. 6, 1980; children: Rebecca, Kathleen, Shawn, Megan. BA, Coe Coll., 1970; MSW, U. Cinn., 1992. LMSW S.C. Lead social worker Iowa Dept. Social Svcs., 1975—79; dir. homemaker svcs. Family Svc. Agy., Cedar Rapids, 1979—80; investigator protective svcs. Iowa Dept. Social Svcs., Waterloo, Iowa, 1982—89; med. social worker S.C. Dept. Health and Environl. Control, SC, 1992—95; asst. prof. and dir. Social Work Program Limestone Coll., Gaffney, SC, 1995—2002, asst. dean and dir. Social Work Program, 2002—. Founding bd. dir. LinnHaven Home Retarded Adults, Cedar Rapids, 1976—78; mem. adv. bd. Make Today Count, Cedar Rapids, 1976—79, Cherokee County Alcohol and Drug Abuse Commn., Gaffney, SC, 2001—. Chmn. fin. Linn County Dems., Cedar Rapids, 1979—80, Steve Sovern U.S. Congress, Cedar Rapids, 1980; bd. dirs. Gaffney (S.C.) Little Theatre, 1994—2001. Mem.: NASW, Internat. Assn. Social Workers, Social Work Baccalaureate Program Dirs., Coun. Social Work Edn. Democrat. Avocations: reading, travel. Home: 1008 College Drive Gaffney SC 29340 Office: Limestone College 1115 College Drive Gaffney SC 29340 Office Phone: 864-488-4526. Business E-Mail: pgriffin@limestone.edu.

GRIFFIN, RICHARD ALLEN, federal judge; b. Traverse City, Mich., Apr. 15, 1952; m. Christine Griffin; 3 children. BA magna cum laude, We. Mich. U., 1973; JD, U. Mich., 1977. Bar: Mich. 1977, Fla. 1978. Law clk. to Hon. Ross W. Campbell Mich. Ct. Appeals (23rd cir.), 1975—77; assoc. Williams, Coulter, Cunningham, Davison & Read, 1977—81; ptnr. Coulter, Cunningham, Davison & Read, 1981—85; founder, ptnr. Read & Griffin, Traverse City, Mich., 1985—88; judge Mich. Ct. Appeals (3rd dist.), 1989—2005, US Ct. Appeals (6th cir.), 2005—. Office: US Ct Appeals 540 Potter Stewart Courthouse 100 E Fifth St Cincinnati OH 45202

GRIFFIN, RICHARD J., federal agency administrator; b. Chgo., Oct. 9, 1949; m. Mary Jean Lang; three children. B in Econs., Xavier U., 1971; grad., Nat. War Coll., 1983; MBA, Marymount U., 1984, LHD (hon.), 2004. Agt. U.S. Secret Svc., Chgo., 1971, agt. in charge L.A., dep. asst. dir. Office of Investigations, asst. dir. protective ops., dep. dir.; insp. gen. US Dept. Vets. Affairs, Washington, 1997—2005; asst. sec. (diplomatic security) US Dept. State, Washington, 2005—, dir. Office Fgn. Missions, 2005—. Office: US Dept State 2201 C St NW Washington DC 20520

GRIFFIN, ROBERT ARTHUR, communications educator; b. Cleve., Feb. 6, 1926; s. Elbert Nolan and Martha May (Stephens) G.; m. Helen Frances McClure, Jan. 25, 1952 (div. Aug. 1980); children: Karen, Linda; m. Geraldine Mazzei, Aug. 26, 1980; stepchildren: Ernest, Paul, Steven. ThB, Cleve. Bible Coll., 1948; BA, Geneva Coll., Beaver Falls, Pa., 1951; MDiv, Pitts. Theol. Sem., 1954; PhD, Ohio State U., 1967. Cert. tchr., Ohio. Instr. Berlitz Schs., Brunswick, Fed. Republic Germany, 1954-55, German C. of C. Inst., Goettingen, Fed. Republic Germany, 1956-57; tchr. pub. schs., Kenton and Springfield, Ohio, 1959-64; grad. teaching asst. Ohio State U., Columbus, 1964-67; prof. corp. communication and econ. history So. Conn. State U., New Haven, 1967—, mem. senate, 1981-86. Mem. adj. faculty Urbana (Ohio) Coll., 1962-63; rsch. fellow Yale U., New Haven, 1978-79; vis. prof. U. Florence, Italy, 1987-88, Martin-Luther U., Halle-Wittenberg, German Dem. Republic, 1988-89, Sapienza U., Rome, 1989; vis. scholar NYU, N.Y.C., 1987-88. Author: Thorstein Veblen, 1982, High Baroque Culture, 1982; contbr. articles to profl. jours. Pres. UN Assn.-USA, New Haven, 1980-82; mem. Yale Bach Chorus, 1985-86. Mem. AAUP, Am. Econ. Assn., History Econs. Soc., Assn. for Social Economists, Assn. for Instnl. Economists, Internat. Soc. for Intercommunication New Ideas, Conn. Fedn. Tchrs. (v.p. 1970-75), New Haven Colony Hist. Assn. Democrat. Avocations: architecture, horticulture, music, travel, essay writing. Office: So Conn State U 501 Crescent St New Haven CT 06515-1330

GRIFFIN, ROBERT H., career military officer; b. Atlanta, Oct. 4, 1947; BS in Mech. Engring., MS in Geotech. Engring., Auburn U.; MBA, Long Island U.; grad., U.S. Army War Coll., Army Command/Gen. Staff Coll. Registered profl. engr., Va. Commd. 2d lt. U.S. Army, advanced through grades to major gen.; served in Dharan, Saudi Arabia; chief of staff US Army CE, Washington, comdr. & divsn. engr. Northwestern divsn. Portland, Oreg., 1997—99, comdr. & divsn. engr. Great Lakes/Ohio River Divsn. Cincinnati, Ohio, 1999—2001, dir. civil works program, 2001—03, dep. chief of engineers, dep. commdg. gen. Washington, 2003—. Chair U.S. section Internat. St. Lawrence River Bd. of Control, 1999—. Decorated Legion of Merit with oak lead cluster, Bronze Star medal, Meritorious Svc. medal with three oak leaf clusters, Army Commendation medal, Army Achievement medal. Office: US Army Corps Engrs 441 G St NW Washington DC 20314 E-mail: robert.h.griffin.bg@usace.army.mil.

GRIFFIN, ROBERT JAMES, radiobiologist; b. Madison, Wis., June 7, 1969; s. James Otto and Karen Delta Griffin; m. Amy Kristine Johnson, Sept. 30, 1995; children: Sylvia Kate children: Grace Karen, Anna Viola. BA, St. Olaf Coll., Minn., 1991; PhD, U. Minn., 1998. Asst. prof. U. Minn., Mpls., 1998—. Study grant, NIH, 2005—. Office: Univ Minn 420 Delaware St SE MMC 494 Minneapolis MN 55455 Office Phone: 612-626-6064. Office Fax: 612-626-6245. E-mail: griff007@umn.edu.

GRIFFIN, ROBERT THOMAS, automotive company executive; b. Somerville, Mass., July 3, 1917; s. Michael and Cecelia (Rourke) G.; m. Mary Ellen Mulcahy, Sept. 10, 1960; children: Mary Catherine, Christiane Marie, Justine Dufresne, Joseph Michael. BS, Boston Coll., 1939; MA in Pub. Adminstrn, Boston U., 1954; postgrad., Harvard U. Grad. Sch. Pub. Adminstrn., 1954-55. Regional mgr. War Assets Adminstrn., 1946-49; with GSA, Washington, 1950-56, 58-80, spl. asst. to adminstr., 1961-62, asst. adminstr., 1962-70, asst. commr. property mgmt., 1970-73; spl. asst. to adminstr. for coordination John F. Kennedy Library, 1973-77, acting adminstr., 1977—; dep. adminstr. GSA, 1977-78; sr. advisor Pres.'s Spl. Trade Rep., White House, 1977-78; sr. advisor to Personal Rep. of Pres. to Middle East Negotiations, White House, 1978-80. Staff exec. to pres. Chrysler Corp., 1980—; dir. Van Pool Services, Inc.; mem. Pres.'s Inflation Task Force, 1978-79; conferee White House Conf. Natural Beauty, 1964, Pres.'s Fed. Agy. Task Force on Cost Reduction, 1965; adminstrv. cons. Govt. of Iran, 1956-58; mem. Pres.'s Com. Minority Enterprise. Bd. dirs. Hamlet Citizens Assn., Chevy Chase, Md., 1981—, John F. Kennedy Libr., 1991— (dir. emeritus). Served with USCGR, 1943-46. Mem. Am. Soc. Pub. Adminstrn., DAV Clubs: Washington Athletic, Columbia Country. Office: 1100 Connecticut Ave NW Washington DC 20036-4101

GRIFFIN, RONALD CHARLES, law educator; b. Washington, Aug. 17, 1943; s. Roy John and Gwendolyn (Points) G.; m. Vicky Tredway, Nov. 26, 1967; children: David Ronald, Jason Roy, Meg Carrington. BS, Hampton Inst., 1965; JD, Howard U., 1968; LLM, U. Va., 1974. Bar: D.C. 1970, Kans., 1986, U.S. Supreme Ct. 1973. Asst. corp. counsel Govt. of D.C., 1970; asst. prof. law U. Oreg., 1974-78; assoc. prof. law Washburn U., Topeka, 1978-81, prof. law, 1981—. Vis. prof. U. Notre Dame, 1981-82; vis. scholar Faculty of Law Queen's U., Kingston, Ont., Can., 1988; dir. Council on Legal Ednl. Opportunity, Summer Inst., Great Plains Region, 1983; grievance examiner Midwest region EEOC, 1984-85; arbitrator consumer protection complaints Northeast Kans. Better Bus. Bur., 1989—; commr. Continuing Legal Edn. Commn. for Kans., 1989-95; external examiner Sch. Law U. Limerick, Ireland, 2004-2005. Contbr. articles to legal jours. Chmn., bd. dirs. Brown Found, 1996-1999; chmn., bd. dirs. Midwest People of Color Legal Scholarship Conf., 2003-2005. JAGC, U.S. Army, 1970-74. Named William O. Douglas Outstanding Prof. of Yr., 1985-86, 94-95; Rockefeller Found. grantee Howard U., 1965-68; fellow Parker Sch. Fgn. and Comparative Law, Columbia U., summer 1981; Kline sabbatical rsch. and study, Japan, 1985. Mem. ABA, Kans. Bar, Ctrl. States Law Sch. Assn. (pres.-elect 1987, pres. 1987-1988), Phi Kappa Phi, Phi Beta Delta. Home: 3448 SW Birchwood Dr Topeka KS 66614-3214 Office: Washburn U Sch Law Topeka KS 66621 Business E-Mail: ronald.griffin@washburn.edu.

GRIFFIN, SHARON L., lawyer; b. Toledo, June 14, 1939; d. Werner Gustave and Martha Lou (Doyle) Knauf; m. John Anthony Griffin, May 21, 1963 (div. 1975); children: Simone Louise, Matthew Compton. BA, U. Mich., 1961; JD, U. Toledo, 1982. Bar: Ohio 1983, U.S. Dist. Ct. (no. dist.) Ohio 1985, U.S. Ct. Appeals (6th cir.) 1987, U.S. Supreme Ct. 1988. Editorial asst. Am. Jour. Comparative Law, U. Mich. Law Sch., Ann Arbor, 1962-64; adminstrv. asst. dept. edn. U. Melbourne (Australia), 1965; legal sec. Papua New Guinea, 1969-71; office mgr. engring. firm, Papua New Guinea, 1969-71; employment placement counselor Snelling and Snelling Pers., Toledo, 1972-74; adminstrv. asst. to dean U. Toledo Coll. Law, 1974-77; adminstrv. asst. Met. Toledo Consortium, 1977-83, acting program coord., 1983; litter control grant coord. dept. community devel. City of Toledo, 1984-85; pvt. practice Toledo, 1983—. Mediator citizens settlement dispute program Toledo Mcpl. Ct. Vol. numerous local polit. campaigns; mem. legal svcs. com. Battered Women's Shelter, YWCA, Toledo; trustee YWCA, Toledo; mem. allocations com. United Way Greater Toledo, also team leader children svcs. panel; v.p. for fund raising, mem. adv. bd., past membership chmn. Democratic Women's Campaign Assn.; precinct chmn. Toledo Dem. Com., 1986—. Mem. ABA (family law com.), Ohio Bar Assn., Lucas County Bar Assn., Toledo Bar Assn. (pro bono program, citizens dispute settlement program com., family law com., cert. of commendation 1986), Toledo Law Assn., Women's Bar Assn. (pub. rels. com., newsletter com.), Ohio Acad. Trial Lawyers, ACLU (bd. dirs., legal com.), NOW (adv. counsel Toledo chpt.). Office: Spitzer Bldg 520 Madison Ave Ste 837 Toledo OH 43604-1355

GRIFFIN, SYLVIA GAIL, reading specialist; b. Portland, Oreg., Dec. 13, 1935; d. Archie and Marguerite (Johnson) G. AA, Boise Jr. Coll., 1955; BS, Brigham Young U., 1957, MEd, 1967. Cert. advanced teaching, Idaho. Classroom tchr. Boise Pub. Sch., Idaho, 1957-59, 61-66, 67-69, reading specialist, 1969-90, 91-95, 98-2001, inclusion specialist, 1995-98, early childhood specialist, 1990-91. Tchr. evening Spanish classes for adults, 1987-88; lectr. in field; mem. cons. pool US Office Juvenile Justice and Delinquency Prevention, 1991—. Author: Procedures Used by First Grade Teachers for Teaching Experience Readiness for Reading Comprehension, The Short Story of Vowels, A Note Worthy Way to Teach Reading, The Little Black Schoolhouse, Hellside Elementary School, Reading, Righting, and Revenge, Memorandum: Murder, Once Upon a Trial. Advisor in developing a program for dyslexics Scottish Rite Masons of Idaho, Boise. Mem.: NEA, Actor's Guild, Idaho Edn. Assn. (pub. rels. dir. 1970—72), Boise Edn. Assn. (pub. rels. dir. 1969—72, bd. dirs. ednl. polit. involvement com. 1983—89), Alpha Delta Kappa. Avocations: music, creative writing. Home: 9948 W Sleepy Hollow Ln Boise ID 83714-3665 Personal E-mail: readwell2@yahoo.com.

GRIFFIN-BROWN, DIANNA LYNN, entrepreneur, educator; b. Moline, Ill., Oct. 9, 1957; d. Robert Edward and Bonita Pearl (Myers) Kirklin; m. Scott Martin Griffin, Dec. 1, 1982 (div. May 1995); 1 child, Robert Edward Griffin; m. William Brown Jr., 1978 (div. 1982); 1 child, Heidi Lynn Brown. Student, Black Hawk Coll., 1977, student, 1996. Shipper, truck driver, mail expediter Desaulniers Printing Co., Moline, Ill., 1975—89; propr. Angelic Fashions, Moline, Ill., 1989—94; dir., propr. Angelic Pageants, Mystical Starr Pageants, Moline, Ill., 1988—; propr. Golden Birthday Co., 1995—. Inventor numerous bridal and party goods. Author: The Complete Guide to Children in Pageants, 1995, 2002; creator: (party goods line) Golden Birthday, 1995, Star Birthday, 1995. Tchr. Literacy is for Everyone, Moline, Ill., 2001, 2002; tchr. poise and charm Y and Cmty. Pk. Bd., Moline, Ill., 2002; electoral judge Voter Registration, Moline, Ill., 1998. Democrat. Avocations: dance, sewing, crafts, writing, reading. Office: Angelic Enterprises 2800 81/2 Ave Rock Island IL 61201

GRIFFIN-BURRILL, KATHLEEN R. F. See BURRILL, KATHLEEN R. F.

GRIFFIS, KIRBY T., lawyer; b. Bo, Sierra Leone, Dec. 19, 1967; BA summa cum laude, MA summa cum laude, Emory U., 1990; JD, U. Va., 1995. Bar: Va. 1995, DC 1997, US Dist. Ct. (Central Dist.), Ill., US Dist. Ct. (We. & Ea. Dist.), Va., US Ct. of Appeals, Fourth Circuit, Seventh Circuit & Tenth Circuit. Clerk to Judge Glenn Williams US Dist. Ct., Va.; assoc. then ptnr., pharm. products Spriggs & Hollingsworth, Washington, 1997—. Mem.: ABA (mem. litigation section 1995—98). Office: Spriggs & Hollingsworth 1350 I St NW Ste 900 Washington DC 20005 Office Phone: 202-898-5800. Office Fax: 202-682-1639. Business E-Mail: kgriffis@spriggs.com.

GRIFFITH, ALAN RICHARD, retired banker; b. Mineola, N.Y., Dec. 17, 1941; s. Charles Ernest and Amalia (Guenther) G.; m. Elizabeth Ferguson, Nov. 28, 1964; children: Timothy, Elizabeth. BA, Lafayette Coll., Easton, Pa., 1964; MBA, CUNY, 1971. Asst. credit officer The Bank of N.Y., N.Y.C., 1968-72, asst. v.p., 1972-74, v.p., 1974-82, sr. v.p., 1982-85, exec. v.p., 1985-88, sr. exec. v.p., 1988-90, pres., 1990-94, vice chmn., 1994—. Trustee Amyothrophic Lateral Sclerosis Assn., Sherman Oaks, Calif., Chesapeake Bay Found., Annapolis, Md., Chesapeake Bay Maritime Mus., St. Michaels, Md.; chmn. bd. trustees Lafayette Coll. Mem. Univ. Club, (N.Y.C.). Address: 300 Piney Point Farm Ln Centreville MD 21617

GRIFFITH, ARNOLD KOONS, computer consultant; b. Providence, July 1, 1942; s. John Ramsbottom and Barbara Koons G.; m. Patricia Martino, July 10, 1971. BA, Swarthmore (Pa.) Coll., 1964; PhD, MIT, 1970. Divsn. mgr. Info. Internat., Inc., Culver City, Calif., 1971-82; owner A/P Systems, Santa Monica, Calif., 1982—. Contbr. articles to profl. jours. Mem. IEEE, Assn. for Computing Machinery, Jonathan Club, Phi Beta Kappa. Avocations: tennis, music, photography. Home: 802 Washington Ave Santa Monica CA 90403 E-mail: griffitha@acm.org.

GRIFFITH, B. HEROLD (BEZALEEL HEROLD GRIFFITH), retired plastic surgeon, retired educator; b. N.Y.C., Aug. 24, 1925; s. Bezaleel Davies and Henrietta (Herold) G.; m. Jeanne B. Lethbridge, 1948; children: Susan, Tristan. BA, Johns Hopkins U., 1992; MD, Yale U., 1948. Cert. Am. Bd. Plastic Surgery. Asst. in anatomy Yale U., New Haven, 1947—48, asst. in surgery, 1948—49; intern Grace New Haven Cmty. Hosp.-Yale U., 1948-49; resident in surgery VA Hosp., Newington, Conn., 1949-50; asst. resident in surgery 2d (Cornell) Surg. Divsn., Bellevue Hosp., N.Y.C., 1952-53; instr. surgery Cornell U., 1956; resident in plastic surgery VA Hosp., Bronx, 1953-55; resident (sr. registrar) in plastic surgery U. Glasgow, Scotland, 1955; chief resident in plastic surgery N.Y. Hosp. Cornell Med. Ctr., N.Y.C., 1956; rsch. fellow in plastic surgery Cornell U. Med. Coll., 1956-57; pvt. practice specializing in plastic surgery Chgo., 1957-96; attending plastic surgeon

Northwestern Meml., Children's Meml., VA Lakeside hosps., Rehab. Inst. Chgo.; instr. surgery Northwestern U., 1957-59, assoc. in surgery, 1959-62, asst. prof. surgery, 1962-67, assoc. prof., 1967-71, prof., 1971-96, prof. emeritus, 1996, chief divsn. plastic surgery, 1970-91; chief plastic surgery Shriners Hosp. for Crippled Children, Chgo., 1994-96; ret., 1996. Chmn. Am. Bd. Plastic Surgery, 1981—82. Mem. editl. bd.: Plastic and Reconstructive Surgery, 1972—78; contbr. articles to profl. jours. Lt. M.C. USNR, 1950—52. Fellow ACS, Am. Assn. Plastic Surgeons, Chgo. Surg. Soc., Royal Soc. Medicine; mem. AAAS, AMA, Am. Bd. Plastic Surgery (dir. 1976-82), Am. Soc. Plastic and Reconstructive Surgeons (sec. 1972-74), Brit. Assn. Plastic Surgeons, Plastic Surgery Rsch. Coun. (chmn. 1969), Am. Cleft Palate Assn., N.Y. Acad. Scis., Ill., Chgo. Med. Socs., Midwestern Assn. Plastic Surgeons, Soc. Head and Neck Surgeons, Ill., Chgo. Hist. Socs., Civil War Round Table, Evanston Hist. Soc. (trustee 1974-78), Sigma Xi (pres. Northwestern U. 1986-87, 94-95). Clubs: Yale (Chgo.). Lodges: Masons. Achievements include research in transplantation, skin tumors, cleft palate, paraplegia.

GRIFFITH, BRYANT EDWARD, education educator; s. Glen Owen and June Mavis Griffith; m. Karin Frances Yolton, Aug. 7, 1969; children: Emily Alice, Jane Rosalind. PhD, U. Toronto, 1984; BA in History with honors, York U., Toronto, 1968, BA in Philosophy with honors, 1970; BEd, U. Toronto, 1972, MA in Edn. Theory, 1976. Permanent specialist tchg. cert. Ont. Dept. head and tchr. Peel Bd. of Edn., Brampton, Canada, 1982—89; assoc. dean and prof. grad. divsn. ednl. rsch. U. Calgary, Canada, 1989—98; dir. and prof. sch. edn. Acadia U., Wolfville, Canada, 1998—2002; prof. coll. of edn. Tex. A&M U., Corpus Christi, 2003—. Vis. scholar Cambridge U., Wolfson Coll., 1995; vis. faculty Antioch U., 1996; vis. scholar dept. edn. Oxford U., 1996. Author: Where do we start?. Chair bd. dirs. York Montessori Schs., Toronto, 1979—82. Mem.: ASCD (assoc.), Can. Soc. Studies in Higher Edn. (hon.; pres. 1997—98), Coll. Reading Assn. (assoc.), Am. Ednl. Rsch. Assn. (assoc.), Am. Assn. for Advancement of Curriculum Studies (assoc.). Office: Texas A&M U - Corpus Christi 6300 Ocean Dr Corpus Christi TX 78412 Office Phone: 361-825-2446. Personal E-mail: bryant.griffith@mail.tamucc.edu.

GRIFFITH, CHARLES DEE, JR., state official; BA in Philosophy, Elon Coll., 1978; JD, Washington and Lee U., 1982. Bar: Va., 1982. Asst. commonwealth atty. Commonwealth of Va., Norfolk, 1983-87, commonwealth atty., 1992-2000; asst. U.S. atty. Ea. Dist. Va., 1987-92; cir. ct. judge Norfolk, 2000—. Former bd. dirs. Southampton Rds. YMCA. Mem. Va. Bar Assn., Va. Assn. Commonwealth Attys. Office: Norfolk Cir Ct Commonwealth of Va 100 Saint Pauls Blvd Norfolk VA 23510-2721

GRIFFITH, DANIEL ALVA, geography educator; b. Pitts., Nov. 15, 1948; s. Donald Sanford and Mary Jane (McClain) G.; m. Diane Elaine Swartz, Jan. 3, 1970; children: Darren Lee, Michele Renee. BS, Indiana U. of Pa., 1970, MA, 1972; MS, Pa. State U., 1985; PhD, U. Toronto, Ont., Can., 1978. Instr. Ryerson Polytech. U., Toronto, 1975-78; from asst. prof. to full prof. SUNY, Buffalo, 1978-88; prof. geography Syracuse (NY) U., 1988—2003, dir. stats. program, 1991—95, chair, 1995—97; prof. geography U. Miami, Fla., 2003—05; prof. geospatial info. scis. U. Tex., Dallas, 2005—. Adj. prof. Coll. Environ. Sci. and Forestry, 1992-2003; vis. EPA/EMAP rsch. affiliate stats. dept. Oreg. State U., Corvallis, 1990-93; vis. rsch. prof. Erasmus U., Rotterdam, 1992, U. Rome, 1995; dep. dir. NY State program in geographic info. and analysis Syracuse U., 1989-90; ASI dir. NATO Sci. Affairs, Brussels, 1979-82, 85, cons. Peru Minister Edn., 2000-01; Leverhulme vis. prof. Cambridge U., 2004; vis. rschr. Max Planck Inst. Demographic Rsch., Rostock, Germany, 2005 Author: Spatial Autocorrelation, 1987, Advanced Spatial Statistics, 1988, Statistical Analysis for Geographers, 1991, Spatial Regression Analysis on the PC, 1993, Multivariate Statistical Analysis for Geographers, 1997, A Casebook for Spatial Statistical Data Analysis, 1999, Spatial Autocorrelation and Spatial Filtering, 2003; contbr. articles to profl. jours. Recipient Award Pa. Geog. Soc., 1999; NSF grantee, 1981, 83-85, 88-90, 92-93, 95-97, 99, 2002, 2004—; Fulbright fellow, 1992-93, 2005—, rsch. fellow ASA/USDA-NASS, 1999, Guggenheim fellow, 2001-02; named to Ashbel Smith Endowed chair U. Miami, 2005 Fellow N.Y. Acad. Scis.; mem. Am. Statis. Assn., Regional Sci. Assn. (pres. 1996-97), Assn. Am. Geographers (chair 1987-88, Nystrom Dissertation award 1980, Pub. Domain Computer Software award 1994, 97), Sigma Xi (Syracuse chpt. pres. 1999-2000). Democrat. Methodist. Avocation: travel. Office: U Miami Geography & Regional Studies Dept Miami FL 33157-2221 Address: 15824 SW 82nd Court Palmetto Bay FL 33157 Business E-Mail: dagriffith@miami.edu.

GRIFFITH, DENNISON W., academic administrator, art educator, artist; BFA, Ohio Wesleyan U.; MFA, Ohio State U. Individual artists program coord. Ohio Arts Coun., 1978—83; exec. dir. Ohio Found. Arts; dep. dir. Columbus Mus. Arts, 1988—98; pres. Columbus Coll. Art & Design, 1998—, prof. painting, 1998—. Trustee Ross Art Mus., Delaware, Ohio, 2004—. Mem.: Nat. Assn. Schs. Art and Design (chair ethics com.), Higher Edn. Coun. Columbus (chmn.), Assn. Ind. Coll. Art & Design (exec. com.), Greater Columbus C. of C. (co-chmn. creative svcs. com., bd. mem.). Office: Office of President Columbus College Art & Design 107 N Ninth St Columbus OH 43215 Office Phone: 614-222-3220. Business E-Mail: dgriffith@ccad.edu.

GRIFFITH, DEWEY MAURICE, mechanical engineer, investor; b. Conway, S.C., Feb. 13, 1938; s. Edwin Dewey and Addie Lee (Pittman) G.; m. Margaret Louise Taylor, Aug. 18, 1963 (div.); 1 child, Jeffrey Scott. BSME, N.C. State Coll. Agr. & Engr., 1959. Mfg. engr. Westinghouse Electric Corp., Richmond, Ky., 1960-63, design adminstrv. engr. Bloomfield, N.J., 1963-70; project mech. engr. PPG Industries, Shelby, N.C., 1970-71, GE, Lexington, Ky., 1971-72, E.D. Griffith Renaissance, Greenville, N.C., 1972-74, Catalytic Inc., Charlotte, N.C., 1974-75; profl. engr. D.M. Griffith Design and Rsch., Charlotte, N.C., 1975-79; The Delta Error-Sq. investor The Master E. with Accent Entity, Charlotte, N.C., 1979—. Inventor flashing miniature lamp. Mem. Math. Assn. Am. Republican. Methodist. Avocations: art, design, finance, geometry, mathematics. Home: Stonehaven Subdivision 5959 Kirkpatrick Rd Charlotte NC 28211-4200 E-mail: desadept@earthlink.net.

GRIFFITH, DONALD KENDALL, lawyer; b. Aurora, Ill., Feb. 4, 1933; s. Walter George and Mary Elizabeth G.; m. Susan Smykal, Aug. 4, 1962; children: Kay, Kendall. Grad. in history with honors, Culver Mil. Acad., 1951; BA, U. Ill., 1955, JD, 1958. Bar: Ill. 1958, U.S. Supreme Ct. 1973. Assoc. Hinshaw & Culbertson, Chgo., 1959-65, ptnr., 1965-98, of counsel, 1999—. Spl. asst. atty. gen. Ill., 1970-72; lectr. Ill. Inst. Continuing Legal Edn., 1970-90. Mem. editl. bd. Ill. Civil Practice After Trial, 1970; co-editor The Brief, 1975-83; contbg. author Civil Practice After Trial, 1984, 89; contbr. articles to profl. jours. Trustee Lawrence Hall Youth Svcs., 1967-2000, v.p. for program, 1969-74; bd. dirs. Child Care Assn. Ill., 1970-73; bd. edn. Lake Forest HS, 1983-84; 2d lt. USAF, 1956. Fellow Am. Acad. Appellate Lawyers; mem. ABA (chmn. appellate advocacy com., tort and ins. practice sect. 1983-84), Ill. Bar Assn., Appellate Lawyers Assn. Ill. (pres. 1973-74), Univ. Club Chgo., Knollwood Club, Alpha Chi Rho (chpt. pres.), Phi Delta Phi. Office: Hinshaw & Culbertson 222 N LaSalle St Ste 300 Chicago IL 60601-1081 Office Phone: 312-704-3460. E-mail: dkg5558@earthlink.net.

GRIFFITH, EDWARD, judge; b. Wilkes-Barre, Pa., Feb. 9, 1948; s. Edward Meredith Griffith and Jane (Randall) Griffith Jones; m. Linda Christine Scribner, Aug. 9, 1969 (div. July 1982); children: Trevor Scribner, Stewart Randall; m. Katherine Greybill, Oct. 24, 1987 (div. Dec. 2004). BA, Lehigh U., 1970; JD, Dickinson Sch. Law, 1973. Bar: Pa. 1973, U.S. Dist. Ct. (ea. dist.) Pa. 1973, U.S. Ct. Appeal (3rd cir.) 1973, U.S. Supreme Ct. 1978. Ptnr. Duane, Morris LLP, Phila., 1973—2003; judge Ct. of Common Pleas of Chester County, Pa., 2004—. Cons. Pa. State Bd. Law Examiners, Phila, 1974-77. Master John E. Stively Inn of Ct.; mem. Pa. Bar Assn., Chester County Bar Assn. Republican. Presbyterian. Avocations: hunting, fishing, gardening. Office: Chester County Courthouse 2 N High St West Chester PA 19380 E-mail: egriffith@chesco.org.

GRIFFITH, ERIC MICHAEL, choral director; b. Lancaster, Pa., Oct. 6, 1978; s. Robert Michael and Robin Ann Griffith. BS in Music Edn., Slippery Rock (Pa.) U., 2001. Cert. tchr. Pa. Dept. Edn. Mem. Bach Choir of Pitts., 2001; choral dir. Reid Ross Classical Sch., Fayetteville, NC, 2001—02, Waynesboro (Pa.) Area Sr. H.S., 2002—. Choral dir. Am. Music Abroad, NJ, 2004—. Mem. Cmty. Concert Assn., Waynesboro, 2002—05. Mem.: NEA, Am. Choral Dirs. Assn., Pa. Music Educators Assn., Music Educators Nat. Conf. Democrat. Lutheran. Avocation: travel. Home: 13121 Welty Rd # 12 Waynesboro PA 17268 Office: Waynesboro Area Sr HS 550 E 2nd St Waynesboro PA 17268 Office Phone: 717-762-1191 x 12131. Office Fax: 717-762-3787. Personal E-mail: egriffith@wasd.k12.pa.us.

GRIFFITH, F. LEE, III, lawyer; b. Buffalo, Sept. 3, 1947; s. Forrest Lee Jr. and Helen Elizabeth (Lines) G.; children: Amanda, Abigail. BA, Williams Coll., 1969; JD cum laude, Boston U., 1972. Bar: Conn. 1972. Assoc. Day, Berry & Howard, Hartford, Conn., 1972-78, ptnr. Stamford, Conn., 1979—, exec. com., 1989—. Mem. numerous bar and profl. assns. Office: Day Berry & Howard 1 Canterbury Grn Ste 7 Stamford CT 06901-2047

GRIFFITH, G. LARRY, lawyer; b. Keokuk, Iowa, Mar. 6, 1937; s. Charles Floyd and Lillian Mae (McClinton) G.; children: Randall Dale, Kristin Lin, Barry Wynn. BA, DePauw U., 1959; JD, U. Iowa, 1962. Bar: Iowa 1962, Minn. 1963. Ptnr. Dorsey & Whitney, Mpls., 1962-2000, chair real estate dept., 1991-95, of counsel, 2001—04. Instr. modern real estate transactions U. Minn., Mpls., 1970-71; bd. dirs. Brock-White Co. Comment editor U. Iowa Law Rev., 1961-62. Scout master Boy Scouts Am., Mpls., 1965-69; bd. dirs. Jr. Achievement, 1991-2005. Rector scholar De Pauw U., 1955-59 Mem. ABA, Minn. Bar Assn., Hennepin County Bar Assn., U.S. Ski Assn. (alpine competition com. cen. div. 1981-87, chmn. region I 1984-86), Mpls. Athletic Club, Burnsville Athletic Club (bd. dirs., legal advisor 1980-92), Phi Alpha Delta. Avocations: skiing, tennis, hunting, scuba diving, golf. Home: 8308 40th Ave N New Hope MN 55427 Office: H Enterprises Internat Inc 120 S 6t St Minneapolis MN 55402-1553 Office Phone: 612-340-2747. Business E-Mail: lgriffith@heii.us.

GRIFFITH, GAIL, performing arts educator, actress; b. Fort Benning, Ga., Feb. 21, 1959; d. James Lee and Sherry Sue Griffith. BFA, Ohio U., 1977—82, M in edn., 1996—97. Actress/dir. Shadowbox Cabaret, Columbus, Ohio, 1989—96; tchr./drama dir. Hilliard Darby H.S., Hilliard, Ohio, 1997—. Actress Shadowbox/2 Co's Cabaret, Columbus, Ohio, 1997—2003. Mem.: Ednl. Theatre Assn. (assoc.), Theatre Comm. Guild (assoc.), Internat. Thespian Assn. (hon.). Office: Hilliard Darby High School 4200 Leppert Rd Hilliard OH 43026 Office Phone: 614-527-4200.

GRIFFITH, HENRY RANDALL, psychologist; b. Ft. Meade, Md., June 1, 1971; s. Larry Randall and Cheryl Diane Griffith; m. Nichole Jean Lariscy, Sept. 4, 1994; children: Eamon Randall, Seona Nichole. BA, Mercer U., Macon, Ga., 1993; MS, Ga. Coll., Milledgeville, Ga., 1995, Chgo. Med. Sch., North Chicago, Ill., 1998; PhD, Chgo. Med. Sch., North Chgo., Ill., 2001. Lic. Psychology Ala. Bd. of Examiners in Psychology, 2002. Behavior specialist Ctrl. State Hosp., Milledgeville, Ga., 1995—96; asst. prof. Dept. of Neurology, U. of Ala. at Birmingham, Birmingham, Ala., 2003—. Contbr. articles pub. to profl. jour. Recipient W.G. Lee Scholar in Comm., Mercer U., 1993, Best Grad. Presentation, Ga. Coll., 1995, Postdoctoral Career Enhancement Award, U. Ala. at Birmingham, 2002; fellow Pre-Doctoral Rsch. Fellowship, Epilepsy Found., 2000-2001; grantee Epilepsy Found. Rsch. Grant, Epilepsy Found. of Am., 2004-2005, Epilepsy Found. Targeted Rsch. Initiative, 2004-2005, Clin. Rsch. Feasibility Funds, UAB Gen. Clin. Rsch. Ctr., 2004-2005, Rsch. Grant, Alzheimer's of Ctrl. Ala., 2002-2005. Mem.: Am. Epilepsy Soc., Internat. Neuropsychological Soc., Nat. Acad. of Neuropsychology (assoc.), Phi Eta Sigma. Christian. Achievements include research in Cermak Award - Outstanding Contrn. in memory rsch. Avocations: music, boating, skiing. Office: Univ Ala at Birmingham 1216 JT 625 19th St So Birmingham AL 35233-7340 Office Phone: 205-934-2334. Office Fax: 205-975-3094. Personal E-mail: rlgriffith@uabmc.edu.

GRIFFITH, H(OWARD) MORGAN, lawyer; b. Phila., Mar. 15, 1958; s. A. Hundley and Charlotte Virginia (Burford) G. BA with honors, Emory and Henry Coll., 1980; JD, Washington and Lee U., 1983. Bar: Va. 1983, U.S. Dist. Ct. Va. 1985. Assoc. Lutins & Shapiro, Roanoke, Va., 1983—84; pvt. practice Salem, Va., 1984—87, 1989—; ptnr. Griffith & Varney, Salem, 1987—89; del. 8th legis. dist. Va. Gen. Assembly, 1994—; house majority leader, 2000—; mem. commerce and labor com.; mem. cts. of justice com.; mem. militia, police and pub. safety com.; mem. rules and joint rules com. Dir. FNB Salem Bank & Trust. Bd. visitors Emory and Henry Coll.; mem. Freedom of Info. Adv. Coun., Joint Legis. Audit and Rev. Commn.; mem. joint subcommittee SW Va. Econ. Devel.; vice-chmn. Joint Commn. Adminstrv. Rules; mem. Blue Ridge Mountains Coun. Boy Scouts Am., advisor, sponsor Legal Explorers Post Salem, 1988—89, chmn. Catawba dist. Blue Ridge Mountains coun., 1984—86, vice chmn., 1987—88, dist. chmn., 1988—91, v.p. rels. and membership, 1991—93; mem. Shawsville Ruritan; mem. state ctrl. com. Rep. Party of Va.; chmn. Rep. Party Salem, 1986—88, 1991—94; mem. St. Paul's Episc. Ch., Salem; mem. state bd. dirs. Easter Seals Va.; mem., bd. trustees Jamestown-Yorktown Found.; bd. dirs. Legal Aid Soc. of Roanoke Valley, 1991—92; com. mem. Stonegate Swim Club, Salem, 1984—88, bd. dirs., 1991—. Recipient Dist. Award of Merit, Boy Scouts Am., 1990—91, Silver Beaver award, 1994. Mem. Va. State Bar Assn., Salem/Roanoke County Bar Assn. (pres. 1995-96), Joint Legislative Audit and Review Comm., Freedom of Info. Adv. Coun., State Ctrl. Com. Rep. Party of Va., Lions (bd. dirs. 1988-90). Episcopalian. Episcopalian. Avocations: swimming, ornithology, ichthyology. Office: 113 E Main St Salem VA 24153-3804 Office Phone: 540-389-4498. E-mail: hmg1993@aol.com.

GRIFFITH, HURDIS M., dean; BSN, Jamestown Coll., N.D.; MSN, U. Washington; cert. adult, primary care nurse, PhD, U. Md. Fellow Robert Wood Johnson Health Policy, 1986-87; dean Coll. Nursing, prof. Rutgers U., Newark. Mem. Nat. Acads. Practice (pres.-elect). Office: Rutgers U Coll Nursing Ackerson Hall 180 University Ave Newark NJ 07102-1897 Fax: 973-353-1277. E-mail: griffith@nightingale.rutgers.edu.

GRIFFITH, JAMES LEIGH, lawyer; b. Knoxville, Tenn., May 25, 1951; s. James M. and Marguerite B. Griffith; m. Catherine West; children: Catherine Leigh, James Leigh. BA, U. Va., 1973; JD, Vanderbilt U., 1976; LLM, NYU, 1977. Bar: Tenn. 1977, N.Y. 1977, D.C. 1978; CPA, Tenn., Miss. Sr. tax acct. Ernst & Whinney, Nashville, 1977-81; mem. Waller, Lansden, Dortch & Davis PLLC, Nashville. Contbr. articles to profl. jours. Past bd. dirs. Grace Eaton Day Home, Nashville, Sneed Forest Homeowners Assn., Franklin, Tenn.; past pres., chmn. bd. Versailes Homeowners Assn., Nashville. Fellow Am. Coll. Tax Counsel, Nashville Bar Assn.; mem. ABA (tax sect., various coms.), Tenn. Bar Assn., D.C. Bar Assn., Tenn. Soc. CPA's (coun. mem.), Am. Tax Policy Inst. (life), Phi Beta Kappa. Achievements include development of new standards and Poor's and Moody's asset class and first rated security of misurance arbitrage. Office: Waller Lansden Dortch & Davis PLLC 511 Union St Ste 2700 Nashville TN 37219-1760 Office Phone: 615-850-8534. Business E-Mail: lgriffith@wallerlaw.com.

GRIFFITH, JAMES W., manufacturing executive; B in Indsl. Engring, MBA, Stanford U. Formerly with Homestake Mining Co., Bunker Hill Co., Martin Marietta; with The Timken Co., Canton, Ohio, 1984—, head rail bus., 1996—98, pres., COO, bd. dirs., 1999—2002, pres., CEO, 2002—. Bd. dirs. Goodrich Corp. Trustee United Way of Ctrl. Stark County. Mem.: Mfrs. Alliance/MAPI (exec. com., trustee). Office: The Timken Co 1835 Dueber Ave SW Canton OH 44706-2798

GRIFFITH, JAMES WILLIAM, systems engineer, consultant; b. Waco, Tex., Apr. 11, 1922; s. Paul Isaac and Willie Elizabeth (Rawlin) G.; m. Dorothy Louise Cannon., Oct. 17, 1949; children: Pamela D. (Mrs. John Fletcher Freeman), James William. Student, Tex. Tech U., 1940-41, U. Utah, 1943-44; BS, So. Meth. U., 1949, MS, 1956. Dir. engring. grad. div. So. Meth. U., 1960-67, chmn. dept. indsl. engring., 1965-67, prof., chmn. dept. systems engring., 1967-69; prin. K-G Assocs., 1970-80; prin. James W. Griffith Inc., Dallas, 1980—. U.S. expert in daylighting Commn. Internat. Eclairage, 1957—; cons. to govt. agys. including HUD, HEW, NAS; tech. cons. Nat. Fenestration Coun., 1984-87, LBL Windows and Daylighting, 1980-85; tech. cons. profl. devel. program AIA, 1982-86, instr., 1982-86, now cons.; mem. AIA Found. Contbr. articles to profl. jours. Served with USAAF, 1942-46. Named to Engrs. of Distinction Engrs. Joint Council, 1970 Fellow Illuminating Engrs. Soc. (nat. pres.); mem. ASHRAE, NSPE, Illuminating Engring. Rsch. Inst., Bldg. Environment and Thermal Envelope Coun., Nat. Fenestration Rating Coun., Bldg. Rsch. Inst. (bd. dirs. 1965-67, 73-75), Tex. Soc. Profl. Engrs., Soc. Mayflower Descs., Sigma Tau, Eta Kappa Nu. Achievements include a patent on the method of and assembly for measuring equiv alent sphere illumniation. Home and Office: 31 Brookline Ct The Woodlands TX 77381 E-mail: billgsr@juno.com.

GRIFFITH, JASON SCOTT, education educator; b. Sioux City, Iowa, May 26, 1971; s. James Joseph and Linda Faye Griffith; m. Heather Dawn Griffith, June 22, 1996; children: Noah Bryce, Emma Paige. BA, West Liberty State Coll., W.Va., 1989—93; MM, Ohio U., Athens, 1999—2001. Cert. profl. tchng. Ohio Dept. of Edn., 2002. Adj. prof. Kenyon Coll., Gambier, Ohio, 2004—; twp. trustee Howard Twp., Ohio, 2004—; tchr. East Knox Local Schools, Howard, 2001—; grad. tchg. asst. Ohio U., Athens, 1999—2001; tchr. Morgan Local Schools, McConnelsville, Ohio, 1994—99. Arts edn. cons. Gov. Taft's Tchr. Adv. Bd., Columbus, 2002—; mem.-township cons. Knox County Citizen Corps, Mt. Vernon, Ohio, 2004—04; mem. Knox County Regional Planning Commn., Mt. Vernon, Ohio, 2003—. Mem. Knox County Democrats, 2002—04. Master: Mt. Zion #9 Masonic Lodge; mem.: Ohio Music Edn. Assn., Music Educators Nat. Conf., Ohio Edn. Assn., NEA, Apple Valley Lions Club. Methodist. Avocations: music, baseball, history. Home: 552 Baldwin Drive Howard OH 43028 Office Phone: 740-599-7000.

GRIFFITH, JERRY DICE, energy executive, management consultant; b. Sturgis, Mich., Sept. 8, 1933; s. Levi Robert and Vivian Marie (LeVeck) G.; m. Gloria Louise Hessie, June 25, 1965; children: Jennifer Lynn, Bradley Jerome. BS summa cum laude, Mich. State U., 1955, MS, 1957; ME, Calif. Inst. Tech., 1959; PFPA, Princeton U., 1967. Dir. nuclear safety C.E., U.S. Army, Washington, 1967-72; chief research and devel. br. AEC and ERDA, Washington, 1972-76; asst. dir. for reactor safety Dept. Energy, Washington, 1976-79, dir. div. nuclear power devel., 1979-80, dir. office light water reactors, 1980-84, assoc. dept. asst. sec. reactor systems devel. and tech., 1985-94, acting asst. sec. for nuclear energy, 1989, acting prin. dept. asst. sec. for nuclear energy, 1990-92; energy and mgmt. cons. Rockville, Md., 1994—. U.S. rep. to OECD Nuclear Energy Agy., Paris, 1976-86, 89-94. Contbr. articles to profl. jours., 1967—; patentee inherent reactor control concept, small reaction turbine. Served to capt. U.S. Army, 1959-62. Recipient Meritorious Civilian Service award U.S. Army, 1970; Congl. fellow, 1969. Mem. Am. Nuclear Soc. Home: 14711 Bauer Dr Rockville MD 20853-3621 Office Phone: 301-460-1059. E-mail: jerrygriffith@comcast.net.

GRIFFITH, JOHN RANDALL, health facility administrator, educator; b. Balt., Mar. 22, 1934; s. Richard Robinson and Eleanor (Bond) G.; m. Helen Klenner, Sept. 17, 1955; children: Julia, Alison, Richard. BS Indsl. Engring., The Johns Hopkins U., 1955; MBA Hospital Adminstrn., U. Chgo., 1957. From asst. prof. to prof. U. Mich. Sch. Pub. Health Dept. Health Mgmt. Policy, Ann Arbor, 1960—, interim dept. chair, 1987-88, dept. chair, 1988-91, Andrew Pattullo Collegiate prof. Hosp. Adminstrn., 1982—; dir. program, chmn. dept. Bur. Hosp. Adminstrn., Ann Arbor, Mich., 1970-82. Examiner Baldridge Nat. Quality Award, 1997—98. Author: Quantitative Techniques for Hospital Planning and Control, 1972, Measuring Hospital Performance, 1978, The Well Managed Community Hospital, 1987 (award, 1988), Moral Challenges of Health Care Management, The Well-Managed Health Care Organization, 1995 (award, 1999, 2000), The Well-Managed Health Care Organization, 5th edit., 2002, Designing 21st Century Healthcare: Leadership in Hospitals and Health Systems, 1998; author: (with others) Thinking Forward: Six Strategies for Highly Successful Organizations, 2003. Bd. dirs., pres., Assn. Univ. Programs Health Adminstrn., 1974-75, Pattullo lectr., 1999; bd. dirs. Accredation Commn., 1977-83, Nat. Ctr. Healthcare Leadership, 2002-. Recipient Filerman Prize for Ednl. Leadership, Assn. Univ. Programs in Health Adminstrn., 2002. Fellow Am. Coll. Health Care Execs. (gold medal 1992, James A. Hamilton award), Tau Beta Pi, Omicron Delta Kappa. Home: 333 Rock Creek Ct Ann Arbor MI 48104-1857 Office: U Mich SPH II 109 Observatory St Ann Arbor MI 48109-2029 Office Phone: 734-936-1304. Business E-Mail: jrg@umich.edu.

GRIFFITH, JOHN VINCENT, academic official; b. Oneida, NY, Dec. 24, 1947; s. William F. and Dorothy (Roberts) G.; m. Nancy E. Snell, Jan. 25, 1969; children: Matthew, Christopher. BA cum laude, Dickinson Coll., 1969; MDiv magna cum laude, Harvard U., 1972; PhD, Syracuse U., 1980. Dean admissions Davidson Coll., NC, 1979-85, v.p. inst. advancement, 1985-89; pres. Lyon Coll., Batesville, Ark., 1989-97, Presbyn. Coll., Clinton, SC, 1998—. Mem. Omicron Delta Kappa, Sigma Alpha Epsilon, Phi Mu Alpha Sinfonia. Office: Presbyn Coll Office of Pres PO Box 975 Clinton SC 29325-0975 Office Phone: 864-833-8700. Business E-Mail: griffith@presby.edu.

GRIFFITH, KATHERINE SCOTT, retired communications executive, retired librarian; b. Atlanta, Jan. 16, 1942; d. Robert Sherrill and Emily Howell (Reynolds) G.; m. Henry Armand Terjen, Sept. 4, 1970 (div. Nov. 1979); 1 child, Henry Foster Terjen (dec.); m. Michael Christopher Healy, May 20, 1995. AB, Sweet Briar Coll., 1964; Masters, Emory U., 1968. Editor South Today, So. Regional Coun., Atlanta, 1969-72; editor Phoenix, Bklyn., 1972-73; dir. comm. N.Y. C. of C. and Industry, N.Y.C., 1978-79; dir. pub. liaison N.Y.C. Dept. Ports and Terminals, 1979-80; sr. pub. affairs officer Citicorp/Citibank, N.Y.C., 1981-83; asst. v.p., pub. rels. mgr. Citicorp Diners Club Media Svcs., N.Y.C., 1983-84; asst. v.p., pub. rels. dir. Citicorp Pub., N.Y.C., 1985-86, asst. v.p. corp. comms., 1986-87; v.p. First Atlanta Corp., Atlanta, 1984; sr. mgr. Can. Imperial Bank of Commerce, N.Y.C., 1987-88, v.p. USA corp. comm., 1989-95; dir. mktg. and comm. Can. Imperial Bank Commerce Wood Gundy, N.Y.C., 1995-97; v.p., dir. corp. comm. Signet Banking Corp., Richmond, Va., 1997; comm. cons. Greenwich, Conn., 1998-99; pub. rels. supr. Ferguson Libr., Stamford, Conn., 1999—2000; dir. comms. and external rels. NY Regional Assn. Grantmakers, 2000—03; libr. Bedford Free Libr., 2003—04; ret., 2004. Pres. 150 Joralemon Street Corp., Bklyn., 1987-89. Pres. 78th Precinct Cmty. Coun., Bklyn., 1977-78; mem. com. Cmty. Bd. 6, Bklyn., 1978-80; mem. coun. So. Regional Coun., Atlanta, 1984-98; bd. dirs. Atlanta Chamber Players, 1984; active Friends of Ferguson Libr., 2000—, Friend of Pittsboro Meml. Libr., 2005—. Mem. LWV, Fin. Women's Assn. NY (bd. dirs. 1995-96), Jr. League, Success by Six (mem. com. 1999-2002), UN Assn., Dem. Club (Fearrington Village), Beta Phi Mu. Democrat. Episcopalian. Home: 342 Fearrington Post Pittsboro NC 27312-2941 Personal E-mail: kittygriffith4@msn.com.

GRIFFITH, LAWRENCE STACEY CAMERON, cardiologist, educator; b. Washington, Sept. 16, 1937; s. Ernest Stacey and Margaret Dyckman (Davenport) G.; m. Anne Gorman Young, June 20, 1959; children: Lawrence, John, Melinda, Gordon. BA, Haverford Coll., 1959; MD with honors, U. Rochester, 1963. Diplomate Am. Bd. Internal Medicine, Am. Bd. Cardiovascular Disease. Intern in medicine and surgery Strong Meml. Hosp., Rochester, N.Y., 1963-64, asst. resident in surgery, 1964-65, asst. and assoc. resident in medicine, 1967-69; rsch. fellow in cardiology Johns Hopkins U., Balt., 1969-71, asst. prof. medicine Sch. Medicine, 1971-76, asst. prof. radiology, 1974-80, assoc. prof. medicine, 1976-88, prof. medicine, 1988—; med. dir. Johns Hopkins Medicine Internat., 1999—. Cons. VA Coop. Study Surgery for Coronary Artery Disease, Program on Surg. Control of Hyperlipidemias, U. Minn. Contbr. articles to profl. jours. Bd. dirs. Julia Dychman Andrus Meml., Inc., Yonkers, N.Y., 1971—, chmn., 1976—; bd. dirs. John E. Andrus Meml. Home for Aged, Hastings-on-Hudson, N.Y., 1974-97; bd. dirs. Surdna Found., N.Y.C., 1976—, v.p., 1988-94; chmn. adv. bd. Balt. Pastoral Counseling Svc., 1971-80. With USPHS, 1965-67. Fellow ACP, Coun. Clin.

Cardiology of Am. Heart Assn., Am. Coll. Cardiology; mem. Alpha Omega Alpha. Democrat. Methodist. Home: 802 W Saint Georges Rd Baltimore MD 21210-1409 Office: Johns Hopkins Hosp Halstad 500D 600 N Wolfe St Baltimore MD 21287-0005 Office Phone: 410-955-6173.

GRIFFITH, LEAH MARIE, librarian; b. Astoria, Oreg., Mar. 4, 1956; d. Frank Howard and Patricia (Kemmerer) G. BS in Social Scis., So. Oreg. State Coll., Ashland, 1978; MLS, Clarion (Pa.) U., 1987. Clk. libr. Multnomah County Libr., Portland, Oreg., 1979-83; libr. asst. Hillsboro (Oreg.) Pub. Libr., 1983; libr. dir. Cornelius (Oreg.) Pub. Libr., 1983-89; extension libr. Ohio Valley Area Librs., Wellston, Ohio, 1989-92; libr. dir. Newberg (Oreg.) Pub. Libr., 1992—. Mem. ALA, Ohio Libr. Assn., Oreg. Libr. Assn. (chair pub. rels. com. 1985-86, founder small librs. round table, chair pub. libr. divsn., 1994-95, chair Conf. 2000, pres. 2005-2006). Democrat. Avocations: travel, reading, gardening. Office: Newberg Pub Libr 503 E Hancock St Newberg OR 97132-2899 Home: 1201 Foothills Dr Newberg OR 97132-6011

GRIFFITH, LINDA G. (LINDA GRIFFITH-CIMA), biomedical engineer, chemical engineer, educator; BS in Chemical Engring., Georgia Tech., 1982; PhD in Chemical Engring., U. Calif., Berkeley, 1988. Postdoctoral assoc. chemical engring. MIT, 1988—96, prof. mechanical engring. & biological engring., 1996—, principal investigator Biotechnology Process Engring. Ctr., 1998—2001, dep. dir. Biotechnology Process Engring. Ctr., 2001—03, dir. Biotechnology Process Engring. Ctr., 2003—. Editorial bd. mem. Jour. of Biomaterials Sci. Named one of Brilliant 10, Popular Sci. mag., 2002; recipient Presidential Young Investigator award, Nat. Sci. Found., 1991; fellow Am. Inst. of Med. & Biological Engineers, 1998, Biomaterials Sci. & Engring., Internat. Union of Soc. for Biomaterials Sci. & Engring., 2000. Renowned for human tissue engineering research and development. Office: MIT Mechanical Engring Dept Room 16-429 Cambridge MA 02139

GRIFFITH, MELANIE, actress; b. N.Y.C., Aug. 9, 1957; d. Tippi Hedren; m. Don Johnson, Jan. 1972 (div. July 1976); m. Steven Bauer May 1982 (div. 1987); 1 child, Alexander; m. Don Johnson, June 26, 1989 (div. Feb. 1996); 1 child, Dakota; m. Antonio Banderas, 1996; 1 child, Stella. Student, Hollywood Profl. Sch., 1981; studied acting with, Stella Adler. Acting debut in Night Moves, 1975, other films include The Drowning Pool, 1975, Smile, 1975, One on One, 1977, Roar, Joyride, 1977, Underground Aces, Body Double, 1984, Fear City, Something Wild, 1986, Cherry 2000, 1988, The Milagro Beanfield War, 1988, Stormy Monday, 1987, Working Girl, 1988 (Acad. Award nominee), In the Spirit, The Grifters, Pacific Heights, 1990, Bonfire of the Vanities, Shining Through, Paradise, 1991, A Stranger Among Us, 1992, Born Yesterday, 1993, Milk Money, 1994, Nobody's Fool, 1994, Two Much, 1996, Mulholland Falls, 1996, Now and Then, 1996, Shadow of Doubt, Another Day in Paradise, Lolita, 1996, Celebrity, 1998, Crazy in Alabama, 1999, Cecil B. DeMented, 2000, Forever Lulu, 2000, Tart, 2001, Stuart Little 2 (voice), 2002, The Night We Called It a Day, 2003, Tempo, 2003, Shade, 2003; TV appearances include (series) Carter Country, (mini-series) Once an Eagle, Buffalo Girls, 1995, (TV movies) She's in the Army Now, 1981, Golden Gate, 1981, Alfred Hitchcock Presents, 1985, Women and Men: Stories of Seduction, 1990, Buffalo Girls, 1995, RKO 281, 1999, Heartless, 2005, (pilots) Golden Gate; (TV series) Twins, 2005; (Broadway plays) Chicago, 2003. Recipient Golden Globe award, 1989.

GRIFFITH, MELVIN EUGENE, entomologist, public health service officer; b. Lawrence, Kans., Mar. 24, 1912; s. George Thomas and Estella (Shaw) G.; m. Pauline Sophia Bogart, June 23, 1941. AB, U. Kans., 1934, AM, 1935, PhD, 1938; postgrad., U. Mich., summers 1937-40. Instr. zoology N.D. Agrl. Coll., Fargo, 1938—39, asst. prof., 1939—41, assoc. prof., 1941—42; commd. officer USPHS, 1943—71; malaria control state entomologist State Dept. Health, Oklahoma City, 1943—46; assoc. prof. zool. scis. U. Okla., Norman, 1945—52, prof., 1952—; extended malaria control program, 1946—51; chief malaria adviser ICA, Bangkok, 1951—60, Vientiane, 1956—58; assoc. dir. Malaria Eradication Tng. Ctr., Kingston, Jamaica, 1960; regional malaria advisor SE Asia, AID, New Delhi, 1960—62, Near East and South Asia, AID, 1962—64; dep. chief malaria eradication br. AID, Washington, 1964—67, chief, 1967—71; ret. as capt. USPHS, 1971. Rapporteur founding conf. SE Asia antimalari coord. bd., Saigon, 1956; cons. Office of Health, AID, Washington, 1971—75; mem. rev. team ind. status assessment of advanced nat. malaria eradication programs WHO, Iran, 1962, Philippines. Contbr. articles and monographs on entomology, malaria control and pub. health. Recipient citation for disting. svc. U. Kans., 1962. Mem. APHA, Am. Soc. Tropical Medicine and Hygiene, Am. Soc. Limnology and Oceanography, Entomol. Soc. Am., Explorers Club, N.Y. Acad. Scis., Siam Soc., Phi Beta Kappa, Sigma Xi. Achievements include chairman of first all-Asia malaria eradication conference in Bangkok in 1953; initial development of national malaria eradication program in Thailand and Laos. Address: PO Box 3550 Williamsburg VA 23187-3550 E-mail: melvinegriffith@cs.com.

GRIFFITH, NANCI, singer, songwriter; b. Austin, Tex., 1954; d. Griff and Ruelene G. BA Edn., U. of Tex., Austin. Former kindergarten & 1st grade teacher Austin SD; recording artist, 1978—. Albums include: There's a Light Beyond These Woods, 1978, Poet in My Window, 1982, Once in a Very Blue Moon, 1985, Last of the True Believers, 1986, Lone Star State of Mind, 1987, Little Love Affairs, 1988, One Fair Summer Evening, 1988, Storms, 1989, Late Night Grande Hotel, 1991, The MCA Years - A Retrospective, 1993, Other Voices, Other Rooms, 1993 (Grammy award Best Folk album), The Best of Nanci Griffith, 1993, Flyer, 1994, Country Gold, 1997, Blue Roses From the Moons, 1997, Other Voices, Too, 1998, The Dust Bowl Symphony, 1999, Wings to Fly and a Place to Be, 2000, The Millennium Collection, 2001, Clock Without Hands, 2001, From A Distance: The Very Best Of Nanci Griffith, 2002, Winter Marquee, 2002, Complete MCA Studio Recordings, 2003; appeared in Nanci Griffith on Broadway, 1994. Office: care Gold Mountain Entertainment 2 Music Cir S Ste 212 Nashville TN 37203-5708

GRIFFITH, OSBIE HAYES, chemistry professor; b. Torrance, Calif., Sept. 14, 1938; s. Osbie and Mary Belle (Neathery) G.; m. Karen Hedberg; 2 sons BA, U. Calif.-Riverside, Riverside, 1960; PhD, Calif. Inst. Tech., 1964; postgrad., Stanford U., 1965. NAS-NRC postdoctoral Stanford (Calif.) U., 1965; asst. prof. chemistry U. Oreg., Eugene, 1966-69, assoc. prof., 1969-72; prof. chem. Inst. Molecular Biology, 1972—2003, prof. emeritus of chemistry, 2003—. Co-editor: Lipid-Protein Interactions, 1982; mem. edtl. bd. Biophysical Jour., 1974-78, Chemistry & Physics of Lipids, 1974-95, Microscopy and Microanalysis, 1995-2002; contbr. articles to profl. jours. Camille and Henry Dreyfus Found. scholar, 1970; Career Devel. award Nat. Cancer Inst., 1972-76; fellow Sloan Found., 1967-69, Guggenheim Found., 1972-76; Faculty Achievement award for Tchg. Excellence, Burlington No. Found., 1987, Dean's Devel. award, 1991, Creativity Ext. NSF, 1992, Outstanding Faculty award U. Oreg. Office of Multicultural Affairs, 2004. Mem. Am. Chem. Soc., Biophys. Soc., Microscopy Soc. Am. Home: 2550 Charnelton St Eugene OR 97405-3216 Office: Univ Oreg Dept Chemistry Eugene OR 97403 Business E-Mail: griffith@uoregon.edu.

GRIFFITH, OWEN WENDELL, biochemistry professor; b. Oakland, Calif., June 19, 1946; s. Charles H. and Gladys C. (Farrar) G. BA, U. Calif., Berkeley, 1968; PhD, Rockefeller U., 1975. Asst. prof. Cornell U. Med. Coll., N.Y.C., 1978-81, assoc. prof., 1981-87, prof., 1987-92; prof., chmn. biochemistry Med. Coll. of Wis., Milw., 1992-2001, prof. biochemistry, 2001—; sci. founder, bd. dirs. ArgiNOx, Inc., Milw., 2000—. Mem., chmn. med. biochemistry study sect. NIH, Bethesda, Md., 1988-92. Contbr. more than 160 articles to profl. jours. Grantee NIH. Mem. Am. Chem. Soc., Am. Soc. Biochemistry and Molecular Biology, Am. Soc. Pharmacology and Exptl. Therapeutics. Achievements include more than 40 patents and patent applications in biomedical research. Office: Med Coll Wis Dept Biochemistry 8701 W Watertown Plank Rd Milwaukee WI 53226-3548 Business E-Mail: griffith@mcw.edu.

GRIFFITH, PATRICIA KING, journalist; b. San Francisco, Jan. 20, 1934; d. Earl Beardsley and Frankie Mae (Kelly) King; m. Winthrop Gold Griffith, Oct. 4, 1958 (div. Jan. 1986); children: Kevin Winthrop, Christina Suzanne. BA, Stanford U., 1955. Copy asst., reporter Washington Post, 1956-57, 60-64; reporter San Francisco Examiner, 1957-59; Washington bureau chief Monterey Herald and Toledo Blade, Washington, 1979-81; investigative reporter Monterey (Calif.) Peninsula Herald, 1973-79, city editor, 1981-83, mng. editor, 1983-88; Washington bureau chief, White House corr. Toledo Blade and Pitts. Post-Gazette, Washington, 1988-99. Bd. dirs. Lyceum of Monterey Peninsula, 1977-79, All Sts. Episcopal Day Sch., Carmel, Calif., 1977-79, Monterey Coll. Law, 1978-79; sr. warden St. Dunstan's Episcopal Ch., Carmel Valley, Calif., 1983-84; warden St. Margaret's Episcopal Ch., Belfast, Maine, 2004—. Recipient Silver Gavel award ABA, 1978. Mem.: Stanford Alumni Assn., Nat. Press Club, Gridiron Club, Stanford Cap and Gown Soc. Home: 103 Dockside Ln Belfast ME 04915

GRIFFITH, RICHARD LATTIMORE, lawyer; b. Abilene, Tex., Feb. 8, 1939; s. Richard Allan and Lorayne (Lattimore) G.; m. Sarah Brewster, Feb. 16, 1963 (dec. 1979); 1 child, Grey; m. Betsy Brooks, Apr. 19, 1980. BA, U. Okla., 1961; LLB, U. Tex., 1963. Bar: Tex. 1965, U.S. Dist. Ct. (no. dist.) Tex. 1966, U.S. Ct. Appeals (5th cir.) 1981, U.S. Dist. Ct. (ea. dist.) Okla. 1976, U.S. Dist. Ct. (we. dist.) Okla. 1967. Ptnr., chmn. health law sect. Cantey & Hanger, Ft. Worth, Tex., 1965—. Chmn. Health Law Sect. State Bar of Tex., 1988. Co-author: Texas Hospital Law, 1988, 3d edit., 1998; contbr. articles to profl. jours. 1st lt. U.S. Army, 1963-65. Fellow Am. Coll. Trial Lawyers, Tex. Bar Found. (life); mem. Am. Bd. Trial Advocates (chpt. pres. 1985, state chmn. 1995), Def. Counsel Trial Acad. (faculty 1988), Tex. Assn. Def. Counsel (v.p. 1984-85, regional v.p. 1986-88, 92-93), Tarrant County Bar Assn., Tex. Bar Assn. Eldon Mahon Inn of Ct. (emeritus), Def. Rsch. Inst. (dir. 1993-2000). Avocations: gardening, fishing, hunting, cooking. Home: 6332 Curzon Ave Fort Worth TX 76116-4604 Office: Cantey & Hanger 2100 Burnett Plaza 801 Cherry St Ste 2100 Fort Worth TX 76102-6821 Office Phone: 817-877-2845.

GRIFFITH, ROBERT CHARLES, allergist, educator, planter; b. Shreveport, La., Jan. 9, 1939; s. Charles Parsons and Madelon (Jenkins) G.; m. Loretta Dean Secrist, July 15, 1969; children: Charles Randall, Cameron Stuart, Ann Marie. BS, Centenary Coll., 1961; MD, La. State U., 1965. Intern, Confederate Meml. Med. Ctr., Shreveport, 1965-66, resident in internal medicine, 1966-68; fellow in allergy and chest disease, instr. U. Va. Med. Sch. Hosp., Charlottesville, 1968-70; practice medicine specializing in allergies, Alexandria, La., 1970-72, The Allergy Clinic, Shreveport, 1972; pres. Griffith Allergy Clinic, Shreveport, 1973—; faculty internal medicine La. State U., 1972—; owner, planter Riverpoint Plantation, Caddo Parish, La. and Miller and Lafayette Counties, Ark. Bd. dirs. Caddo-Bossier Assn. Retarded Citizens, 1977-84, Access (fomerly Child Devel. Ctr.), Shreveport, 1979-85; mem. (life) NRA, med. adv. com., spl. edn. adv. com. Caddo Parish Sch. Bd., 1977-89; mem. commission on missions and social concerns First Methodist Ch., 1981-84, mem. adminstrv. bd., 1981-84; mem. med. panel for transfer Caddo Parish Sch. Bd., 1974-94; mem. adopt a flag program Confederate Meml. Mus. New Orleans; co-chair Loyola Fund Drive, 1994-95. Served to maj. M.C., U.S. Army, 1965-71. Recipient Physician of the Yr. award Shreveport-Bossier Med. Assts., 1984. Fellow Am. Coll. Asthma, Allergy and Immunology, Am. Coll. Chest Physicians (assoc.), Am. Thoracic Soc.; mem. AMA, SAR (chpt. surgeon 1994—), Am. Acad. Allergy, Asthma and Immunology, Am. Legion, Jamestowne Soc., So. Med. Assn., La. Med. Soc., Shreveport Med. Soc. (allergy spokesman 1984—), La. Allergy Soc. (charter; past pres.), U. Va. Med. Alumni Assn. (life), Pace Soc. Am., La. State U. Med. Alumni Assn., Confederate Soc. Am., Heritage Preservation Assn., League of the South (charter, sustainer), League of the South La. (bd. dirs.), Legion South, Am. Legion (Viet Nam), Mil. Order Stars and Bars, Order of So. Cross, Shreveport C. of C., Kappa Alpha, Methodist. Lodges: Masons (32 degree). Clubs: Shreveport Country, Petroleum of Shreveport, Shreveport, Ambs., Cotillion, Royal, Plantation, Shriners (El Kahruba Temple), Jesters, Les Bon Temps., Demoiselle Club. Home: 7112 E Ridge Dr Shreveport LA 71106-4749 also: Riverpoint Plantation Ida LA 71044

GRIFFITH, ROBERT DEAN, non-commissioned officer, nurse; b. McAllen, Tex., Jan. 6, 1962; s. Roger Leroy and Susan Lynn (Disney) G.; m. Dianne Mary Clark, July 6, 1995; children: Lee Austin, Jayna Lynn. BSN magna cum laude, Old Dominion U., 1996, Degree in Biology and Chemistry. Enlisted E-1 USN, 1980; commd. ensign USN Naval Nurse Corps, 1996; student US Naval Schs., Gt. Lakes, Ill., 1980-81; profl. USS Monongahela, Norfolk, Va., 1981-82, Naval Spl. Warfare, Norfolk, 1982-93; RN Nat. Naval Med. Ctr., Bethesda, Md., 1996—, mem. staff edn. com. surg. ward, 1996-98, mem. staff ICU, 1998-99, unit mgr. cardiac rehab., 1999—. Mem. AACN, Emergency Nurses Assn., Old Dominion U. Alumni Assn., Sigma Theta Tau, Phi Kappa Phi. Avocations: family time, reading, running, bicycling, camping. Office: Nat Naval Med Ctr 8901 Wisconsin Ave Bethesda MD 20889-0001

GRIFFITH, ROY LLOYD, design engineer; b. Shrewsbury, Salop, U.K., Feb. 17, 1972; R&D mgr. Barclay Leisure, Macclesfield, England, 1991—97; tech. mgr. Ultrabronz Am., Richmond, Va., 1997—99; tech. dir. HOTRS, Inc., Kansas City, 1999—2000; design engr. Spectrum Products, Indpls., 2000—. Achievements include patents pending for shoulder tanner evice; flat panel tanning lamp device; variable wattage ballast. Home: 1211 N Ogden St Indianapolis IN 46202 Office: ETS Inc 6270 Corp Dr Indianapolis IN 46278 Office Phone: 317-290-8982 2088. Personal E-mail: roygrif@hotmail.com.

GRIFFITH, SIMA LYNN, investment banker, consultant; b. N.Y.C., Sept. 7, 1960; d. Morris Benjamin and Mary (Buberoglü) Nahum; m. Clark Calvin Griffith, Sept. 13, 1987. BA in English, Amherst Coll., 1982. Account exec. D.F. King & Co., Inc., N.Y.C., 1982-84, asst. v.p., 1984-86, v.p., 1986-88, Wells & Miller, Mpls., 1988; with Griffith, Levi Capital, Inc, Mpls., 1988-96; prin. Aethlon, Capital LLC, Mpls., 1996—. Co-chmn. PRSA, IR seminars, 1987; bd. adv. Pacer, Inc. Bd. dirs. Children's Hosps. and Clinics, 2004—; bd. govs. Children's Theater Co. Mem.: Pub. Rels. Soc. Am. (bod. govs., investor rels. sec. 1987—89), Assn. Bus. Communicators (bd. govs. 1987—88). Office: Aethlon Capital LLC 4920 IDS Ctr 80 S 8th St Minneapolis MN 55402-2100

GRIFFITH, STEVEN FRANKLIN, SR., lawyer, insurance agent; b. New Orleans, July 14, 1948; s. Hugh Franklin and Rose Marie (Teutone) G.; m. Mary Elizabeth McMillan Frank, Dec. 9, 1972; children: Steven Franklin Jr., Jason Franklin. BBA, Loyola U., New Orleans, 1970, JD, 1972. Bar: La. 1972, U.S. Dist. Ct. (ea. dist.) La. 1975, U.S. Ct. Appeals (5th cir.) 1975, U.S. Supreme Ct. 1976. With Law Offices of Senator George T. Oubre, Norco, La., 1971-75; sole practice Destrehan, La., 1975—. Pres. 29th Jud. Dist. Bar Assn., 1999—2002. Fellow: La. State Bar Found.; mem.: ATLA, ABA, St. Charles Parish Bar Assn. (pres. 1999—2002), Fed. Bar Assn., New Orleans Trial Lawyers Assn., La. Trial Lawyers Assn., La. State Bar Assn. (ho. of dels. 1987—). Democrat. Home: 34 Shadow Ln Destrehan LA 70047-3623 Office: PO Box 999 13358 River Rd Destrehan LA 70047-5000 Office Phone: 985-764-6862. Business E-Mail: griffithlawfirm@aol.com.

GRIFFITH, THEA R. L., psychologist, researcher; d. Terrill A. and Richard S. Billstein (Stepfather); life ptnr.; 1 child, Joshua J. AA in Psychology, Mineral Area Coll., Park Hills, Mo., 2002; BA in Psychology, Washington U., St. Louis, 2005. Rsch. asst. Washington U., St. Louis, 2003—; recruiter Washington U. Med. Sch., St. Louis, 2004—. Applied behavior analysis therapist Spl. Sch. Dist. & First Steps, St. Louis, 2002—04; rsch. asst. cognitive devel. lab. Washington U., 2003—, rsch. intern neuropsychology lab., 2003. Contbr. articles to profl. jours. Chair com. - vol. St. Francois County Cmty. Outreach Ctr., Park Hills, Mo., 2001—02; tutor Upward Bound, Park Hills, Mo., 2001—02; mem. TRIO, Park Hills & St. Louis, 2000—05, Internat. Student Assn., Park Hills, Mo., 2000—02; bd. advisors Career Ctr. Student Adv. Bd., St. Louis, 2003—04; mem. student adv. bd. Career Ctr. Washington U., 2003—04. Mem.: APA, Psi Chi, Psi Beta (life), Phi Theta Kappa (life; chpt. pres. 2001—02, named leader of promise 2001, scholar 2002—05). Office: Washington U 1 Brookings Dr Box 1125 Saint Louis MO 63130 Office Phone: 314-935-4357. Personal E-mail: thea.griffith@wustl.edu.

GRIFFITH, THOMAS BEALL, federal judge; b. Yokohama, Japan, July 5, 1954; s. Robert Elmon and Jane (Beall) Griffith; m. Susan Ann Stell; children: Chelsea, Megan, Robert, Erin, Victoria, Tanne. BA, Brigham Young U., 1978; JD, U. Va., 1985. Bar: NC 1985, DC 1991. Assoc. Robinson, Bradshaw & Hinson P.A., Charlotte, NC, 1985—89, Wiley, Rein & Fielding LLP, Washington, 1989—93, ptnr., 1993—95, 1999—2000; legal counsel US Senate, Washington, 1995—99; asst. to the pres., gen. counsel Brigham Young U., Provo, Utah, 2000—05; judge US Ct. Appeals (DC cir.), Washington, 2005—. Mem. advisory bd., Ctrl. European & Eurasian Law Initiative ABA, 1995—, ex officio council mem., Adminstrv. Law & Regulatory Practice, 1996—99; gen. counsel Advisory Commn. on Electronic Commerce, 1999—2000; mem. Sec. Edn.'s Commn. on Opportunity in Athletics (Title IX Commn.), 2002—03. Office: US Ct Appeals 333 Constitution Ave NW Washington DC 20001

GRIFFITH, W.E.B. See BUTTERWORTH, WILLIAM III

GRIFFITH, WILLIAM HENRY (BILL GRIFFITH), cartoonist; b. Bklyn., Jan. 20, 1944; s. James Louis and Barbara Marion (Jackson) G.; m. Diane Noomin, Nov. 18, 1980. Student, Pratt Inst., 1962-64. Cartoonist East Village Other, N.Y.C., 1969-70; comic book cartoonist (comic books) Print Mint, Last Gasp, Rip-off Press, San Francisco, 1970—; founder, editor, cartoonist Cartoonists Co-op Press, San Francisco, 1973-74; cartoonist, co-editor Arcade, the Comics Revue, San Francisco, 1974-75; owner, cartoonist Zipsynd, San Francisco, 1976—; cartoonist Nat. Lampoon, N.Y.C., 1982-84, San Francisco Examiner, 1985, E.P. Dutton, Inc., N.Y.C., 1985-89, King Features Syndicate, N.Y.C., 1985—; screenwriter Pacific Arts Corp., Beverly Hills, Calif., 1986-87; Penguin Books, 1991—. Author: Zippy Stories, 1981, Nation of Pinheads, 1982, Pointed Behavior, 1984, Are We Having Fun Yet?, 1985, Pindemonium, 1986, King Pin, 1987, Pinhead's Progress, 1989, Get Me a Table Without Flies Harry, 1990, From A to Zippy, 1991, Zippy: From Here to Absurdity, 2004, (screenplays) ZippyVision, 1987; exhibited in group shows at Whitney Mus. of Am. Art, 1983, Smithsonian Instn., 1990, Masters of Cartoon Art Show, 1991. Recipient Pulcinella award 6th Internat. Exhibition of Comics and Animation, 1984. Mem. Nat. Cartoonists Soc., Writers Guild of Am., Cartoon Art Mus., 1987—. Office: King Features Syndicate Ph 2 888 7th Ave New York NY 10106-0003*

GRIFFITH, WILLIAM R., lawyer; AB in polit. sci., Brown U., 1970; JD, George Washington U., 1974. Bar: NY 1975. With Certilman Haft Balin Buckley Kremer & Hyman; ptnr. Rivkin Radler Dunne & Bayh, 1988—89, Parker Duryee Rosoff & Haft (combined with Reed Smith in 2002), 1989—2002, Reed Smith LLP, NYC, 2002—, also practice group leader life sciences transactions group. Dir. Nat. Hospice and Palliative Care Orgn.; chmn. bd. Nat. Hospice Found. Office: Reed Smith LLP 599 Lexington Ave 29th Fl New York NY 10022 Office Phone: 212-549-0238, 212-521-5450. Business E-Mail: wgriffith@reedsmith.com.

GRIFFITH, YOLANDA EVETTE, professional basketball player; b. Chgo., Mar. 1, 1970; d. Harvey G.; 1 child, Candace Michelle. Student, Palm Beach Jr. Coll., Fla. Atlantic U. Basketball player Palm Beach Jr. Coll., Fla. Atlantic U., 1992—93; profl. basketball player Germany, 1993—97, Long Beach StingRays, ABL, 1997—98, Sacramento Monarchs, WNBA, 1999—. Mem. USA Basketball Women's Sr. Nat. Team, 1998, 99, 2000, 04. Named ABL Defensive Player of Yr., 1997-98; recipient MVP award, 1999. Achievements include mem. US Women's Basketball Gold Medal Team, Sydney Olympics, 2000; mem. US Women's Basketball Team, Athens Olympics, 2004. Avocations: softball, music. Office: Sacramento Monarchs One Sports Pkwy Sacramento CA 95834

GRIFFITH-BARBARA, MARTHA JAYNE, music educator; b. Ft. Smith, Ark., Aug. 12, 1968; d. Bob D. and Mary Jane Griffith; m. Donovan Scott Barbara, Dec. 20, 2002. MusB in Edn., U. Ctrl. Ark., 1990, MusM, 1993; PhD in Music Edn., U. Okla., 2003. Music dir. Norfork (Ark.) Pub. Sch., 1990—91; grad. asst. U. Ctrl. Ark., Conway, 1991—92; band dir. Lonoke (Ark.) Pub. Schs., 1993—94; beginning band coord. Pleasant Grove Ind. Sch. Dist., Texarkana, Tex., 1995—97; grad. tchg. asst. U. Okla., Norman, 1997—2000, vis. asst. prof., 2000—01. Dir. New Horizons Band, Norman, 2000—01. Pres. Columns Homeowner Assn., Norman, 2002—03. Mem.: Music Educators Nat. Conf. (life), Grad. Music Student Assn. (life; sec./treas. 1997—99), Pi Kappa Lambda (life), Sigma Alpha Iota (life; v.p., historian 1988—90). Home: 1303 Rebecca Ln Norman OK 73072 Personal E-mail: wheester@yahoo.com.

GRIFFITHS, JEFFREY W., electronics executive; Merchandising mgr. Electronics Boutique Inc., 1984—84, v.p., merchandising, 1987—96, sr. v.p., merchandising & distribution, 1996—98, Electronics Boutique Holding Corp., 1998—2001, pres., CEO, dir., 2001—. Office: c/o Electronics Boutique 931 South Matlack St West Chester PA 19382*

GRIFFITHS, JEM, singer; b. Cardiff, Wales, 1975; JD, Sussex U. Singer: (albums) Finally Woken, 2004; composer (films) The Prince & Me, 2004, guest appearance (TV series) The O.C., 2004, Kelly, 2005, T4, 2005, composer (TV series) Desperate Housewives, The O.C., 24. Office: ATO Records Sam Shah 157 Chambers St 12th Fl New York NY 10007*

GRIFFITHS, PHILLIP A., mathematician, former academic administrator; b. Raleigh, N.C., Oct. 18, 1938; s. Phillip and Jeanette (Field) G.; m. Ann Lane Crittenden, 1958-67; children: Jan Kirsten, David; m. Marian Folsom Jones, 1968; children: Sarah, Rebecca. BS, Wake Forest U., 1959; PhD, Princeton U., 1962; D (hon.), Angers U., France, 1979; DSc (hon.), Wake Forest U., 1973, U. Peking, China, 1983; DSc (hon.), U. Oslo, 2002. Mem. staff U. Calif., Berkeley, 1964-67; prof. math. Princeton (N.J.) U., 1968-72; prof. Harvard U., Cambridge, Mass., 1972-83, Dwight Parker Robinson prof. math., 1983; provost, James B. Duke prof. math. Duke U., Durham, N.C., 1983-91; dir. Inst. for Advanced Study, Princeton, NJ, 1991—2003, prof. math., 2004—; sr. advisor Mellon Fedn., 2001—; Disting. Presdl. fellow for acad. affairs NAS, 2002—. Bd. dirs. Oppenheimer Funds, GSI Lumonics; vis. prof. Princeton U., 1967-68, mem. Inst. Advanced Study, 1968-70; chmn. bd. on math. scis. NRC, 1986-91, chmn. commn. on phys. scis., math. and applications, 1992, chmn. com. on sci., engring. and pub. policy, 1992-99; mem. Nat. Sci. Bd., 1991-96; sec. Internat. Math. Union, 1999—; chair Sci. Initiative Group, 1999—. Editor Jour. Differential Geometry, 1980-90, Compositio Mathematica, 1980-92, Duke Math. Jour., 1983—, Selecta Mathematica, 1994—, Annals of Math., 1997—, Advances in Function Theory, 2002, Annals of Math. Studies, 2001. Bd. dirs. Rsch. Triangle Inst., 1983-91; trustee Woodward Acad., N.C. Sch. Sci. and Math. Decorated Nat. Order of Sci. Merit (Brazil); recipient LeRoy P. Steel prize Am. Math. Soc., 1971, Dannie Heineman Preis, Acad. Scis. Gottingen, 1979, Ordem Nat. Mérito Cientifico, Ministry of Sci. and Tech., Brazil, 2002; Miller fellow U. Calif. Berkeley, 1962-64, 1975-76, Guggenheim fellow, 1980-82. Fellow: Accademia Lincei (assoc.; fgn.), Third World Acad. Scis. (assoc.; fgn.); mem.: NAS (disting. sr. pres. fellow internat. rels. 2002—), Coun. on Fgn. Rels., Am. Acad. Arts and Scis., Am. Philos. Soc., N.Y. Yacht Club.

GRIFFITHS, RACHEL, actress; b. Melbourne, Australia, June 4, 1968; m. Andrew Taylor, 2002; 1 child, Banjo Patrick. BEd in Drama and Dance, Victoria Coll. Actor: (films) Muriel's Wedding, 1994 (Best Supporting Actress Australian Film Critics award, Best Supporting Actress Australian Film Inst. award, 1995), Jude, 1996, To Have and To Hold, 1997, My Best Friend's Wedding, 1997, Hilary and Jackie, 1998 (nominee Best Supporting Actress Oscar, 1999), My Son, the Fanatic, 1998, Among Giants, 1998, Amy,

1998, Me Myself I, 1999, Blow, 2001, The Rookie, 2002, The Hard Word, 2002, Ned Kelly, 2003; (TV series) Secrets, 1993, Jimeoin, 1994, Six Feet Under, 2001—05 (Best Suppporting Actress Golden Globe award, 2001).

GRIFFITHS, ROBERT BUDINGTON, physics professor; b. Etah, India, Feb. 25, 1937; s. Walter Denison and Margaret (Hamilton) H. AB, Princeton U., 1957; MS, Stanford U., 1958, PhD, 1962. Postdoctoral fellow U. Calif. at San Diego, 1962-64; asst. prof. Carnegie-Mellon U., Pitts., 1964-67, assoc. prof., 1967-69, prof. physics, 1969—, Otto Stern prof., 1979—, univ. prof., 1998—. NSF fellow, 1962-64, Alfred P. Sloan Rsch. fellow, 1966-68, J.S. Guggenheim fellow, 1973; recipient Sr. Scientist award Humboldt Found., 1973, A. Cressy Morrison award Acad. Scis., N.Y., 1981, Dannie Heineman prize for math. physics, 1984. Mem. Am. Phys. Soc., Am. Sci. Affiliation, U.S. Nat. Acad. Scis., Phi Beta Kappa, Sigma Xi. Presbyterian. Achievements include research in statistical and quantum mechanics.

GRIFFITHS, SYLVIA PRESTON, physician, educator; b. London, Dec. 25, 1924; d. Wheeler Bate and Dorothy (Hartley) Preston; m. Raymond B. Griffiths; 1 dau., Wendy Elizabeth. BA, Hunter Coll., 1944; MD, Yale U., 1948. Intern Grace-New Haven Community Hosp., 1948-49, resident, 1949-52; fellow in pediatric cardiology Yale U., 1952-54; asst. to prof. clin. pediatrics Columbia U., N.Y.C., 1955, prof. clin. pediatrics, 1977-90, prof. emerita, 1990—. Recipient career scientist award Health Research Council, City of N.Y., 1963-69 Mem. N.Y. Heart Assn. (dir. 1977-83), Am. Acad. Pediatrics, Am. Pediatric Soc., Am. Heart Assn., Am. Coll. Cardiology, Babies Hosp. Alumni Assn. (pres. 1991-92). Office: Columbia Presbyterian Med Ctr 622 W 168th St New York NY 10032-3720

GRIFFY, THOMAS ALAN, physics professor; b. Oklahoma City, Dec. 16, 1936; s. Judson H. and Dicie (Johnston) G.; m. Peggy Lynn Walker, June 6, 1958; children— David, Alan, Marjorie BA, Rice U., 1959, MA, 1960, PhD, 1961. Asst. prof. physics Duke U., Durham, NC, 1961—62; research assoc. High Energy Physics Lab., Stanford U., Calif., 1962-65; assoc. prof. physics U. Tex., Austin, 1965—68, prof., 1968—2004, chmn. dept., 1974—84, assoc. dean grad. sch., 1970—73, 1996—2000, prof. emeritus, 2004—. Contbr. articles to profl. jours. Fellow: Am. Phys. Soc. Methodist. Office: U Tex Dept Physics Austin TX 78712 E-mail: tgriffy@sbcglobal.net.

GRIFFY, TIMOTHY T., human resources specialist, finance company executive; BA, M in Acctg., Rice U. With Ernst & Young, NYC, 1980—, ptnr., 1992—95, dir. human resources (S.W. area), 1995—98, area mng. ptnr., 1998—2002, global mng. ptnr. people, 2002—. Office: Ernst & Young Internat 5 Times Square New York NY 10036 Office Phone: 212-773-3000. Office Fax: 212-773-6350.*

GRIGG, EDDIE GARMAN, minister, educator; b. Shelby, NC, Feb. 20, 1957; s. Gaston Theodore and Sylvia Evlyn (Davis) G.; m. Susan Wanda Ray, May 28, 1977; children: Mark Zolton, Jamie Ray, Steven Russell. BA, Gardner-Webb Coll., 1980; MDiv, Southeastern Bapt. Theol. Sem., 1985; D Ministry, Emmanuel Bapt. U., 1994, DRE, 1995; DD (hon.), New Life U., 1998. Ordained to ministry So. Bapt. Conv., 1976. Pastor Victory Bapt. Ch., Kings Mountain, N.C., 1975-79, Christian Freedom Bapt. Ch., Kings Mountain, 1979-81, Sanford Meml. Bapt. Ch., Brodnax, Va., 1981-85, Pleasant Hill Bapt. Ch., Shelby, N.C., 1985-89; sr. min. Wilson Grove Bapt. Ch., Charlotte, N.C., 1989-93; founder, pastor New Life Bapt. Ch., Charlotte, 1993—2003; co-founder, pres. New Life Theological Seminary, Charlotte, 1996—; ch. adminstr. Ebenezer Bapt. Ch., 2004—. Mem. Bapt. Metrolina Ministers Pastor's Conf. (pres. 1995-97), Bapt. Metrolina Ministries Assn. (evangelism com. 1990-93, urban ch. com. 1990-94). Republican. Office: New Life Theol Sem PO Box 790106 Charlotte NC 28206 Office Phone: 704-334-6882. Personal E-mail: eddieggrigg@aol.com.

GRIGGER, JANE ELIZABETH, earth science educator, photographer; b. Phila., June 7, 1947; d. John Casimer and Rozanne Marie (Peters) G. BS in Geology, Bucknell U., 1969; EdM in Earth Sci. Edn., Temple U., 1971. Tchr. secondary sci. Bensalem Twp. Sch. Dist., Cornwells Heights, Pa., 1970-72, Princeton Regional Schs. (N.J.), 1972-75; tchr. middle sch. earth sci. and phys. sci. Princeton Day Sch., 1975—. Tchr. ptnrs. in edn. geology program Princeton U., 1985, photographer jours. Troop advisor S.E. Pa. coun. Girls Scouts U.S.A., 1969—; photographer Girl Scout Internat. Event, 1975, 76. Mem. Phila. Geol. Soc., Field Conf. Pa. Geologists, N.J. Sci. Tchrs. Assn., Roster Women Geoscis., N.J. Earth Scis. Tchrs. Assn., Nat. Assn. Geology Tchrs., Nat. Sci. Tchrs. Assn., Bucknell Alumni Club. Episcopalian. Home: 6413 Ravens Crest Dr Plainsboro NJ 08536-2430 Office: Princeton Day Sch PO Box 75 Princeton NJ 08542-0075 Office Phone: 609-924-6700. Business E-Mail: jane_grigger@pds.org.

GRIGGS, CAROLYN MITCHELL, accountant, communications specialist; b. Columbus, Ohio, Mar. 3, 1949; d. Carold and Ivy D. (Harper) Mitchell; m. Andrew R. Griggs I, Feb. 28, 1987; children: Mark, Deana, Katina, Lonnie, Andrew II. AB in EDP Auditing, Columbus State U., 1984; BA in Computer Mgmt., Acctg., Franklin U., 1987, MBA in Mgmt. Info. Sys., 2004. Acct. Dial-A-Ride, Columbus, 1972—75, Ctrl. Cmty. House, Columbus, 1976—80; supr. comm. tech. Columbus Police Radio, 1980—. Cons. Columbus Police Dept., 1982—, CAD sys. group, 1992—; treas. St. Philip Episcopal, Columbus, 1990—; v.p. Block Watch/Columbus Police, 1990—; tchr.'s aide Pilgrim Sch., Columbus, 1994—, v.p., 1996—, hiring com., 1997; chmn. Quality Work Life, Columbus, 1994-97, vice chmn., 1998—. Recipient award John Galbreath Co., 1979. Mem. AICPA, Ohio Bd. Accts., Ea. Star (treas. 1994—). Episcopalian. Avocations: gardening, horseback riding, tutoring. Office: CM Griggs Acctg Svc Inc PO Box 83401 Columbus OH 43203-0401 Office Phone: 614-258-3906.

GRIGGS, ERLAYNE ANN, music educator; b. Burlington, Iowa, June 5, 1956; d. Warren Earl and Frances Elaine (Kelley) Gillaspie; m. LaVerne F. Griggs, June 13, 1992; 1 child, Angela M. B, Ctrl. Coll., 1978; postgrad., U. Iowa, 1985, Drake U., 1999, postgrad., 2000, postgrad., 2002. Cert. tchg. Iowa, 1978. Music tchr. Hedrick Schs., Hedrick, Iowa, 1978—80; vocal music tchr. Norway Schs., Norway, Iowa, 1980—84, Valley Cmty. Schs., Elgin, Iowa, 1985—89, Grinnell (Iowa)-Newburg Schs., 1989—. Chair, mid. sch. planning Grinnell Mid. Sch., Iowa, 2001—; chair Grinnell Mid. Sch., NCA Local Cmty., Grinnell, 1997—2000; bldg. rep. Grinnell Schs., Sch. Improvement Team, Grinnell, 2000—. Music and Tech. in the Classroom grant, Iowa Valley Continuing Edn., 2000. Mem.: NEA, Am. Choral Dirs. Assn. Democrat. Meth. Avocations: gardening, reading, singing, travel. Office: Grinnell Mid Sch 132 E St S Grinnell IA 50112 Office Phone: 641-236-2750. E-mail: egriggs@grinnell.k12.ia.us.

GRIGGS, FARRAR O'NEAL, JR., lawyer; b. Kannapolis, N.C., Jan. 17, 1948; s. Farrar O'Neal Sr. and Katherine Long (Turbyfill) G.; m. Peggy Jane Link, Apr. 27, 1974 (div. Aug. 1991); children: Rebekah Lauren, Emily Farrar, Ethan Link, Eleanor Jane; m. Cynthia Lynn Scott, Dec. 2, 1995. Student, Duke U., 1966-68; BA in English, U. N.C., 1970; JD, John Marshall Law Sch., Chgo., 1977; postgrad., Northwestern U., 1976. Bar: N.C., U.S. Dist. Ct. (we. dist.) N.C., U.S. Tax Ct. Account rep. Cannon Mills, Inc., N.Y.C., 1972-75; owner law practice Farrar Griggs Jr., Atty., Kannapolis, N.C., 1977—; owner Griggs Properties, Kannapolis, 1983—. Mem. Kannapolis Bd. Edn., 1988-92; past. treas., mem. coun. Boy Scouts Am.; coach Youth Soccer, 1991, 92, 96, baseball, 1990. Lt. U.S. Navy, 1970-72; owner Griggs Properties. Mem.: Kannapolis C. of C. (past pres. elect, bd. dirs.), N.C. Bar Assn., Am. Legion, Kannapolis Rotary Club (past treas., bd. dirs., young life steering com.). Republican. Presbyn. Avocations: whitewater rafting, fishing, hiking. Office: 601 Coach St Kannapolis NC 28083-6023 E-mail: fog@carolina.rr.com.

GRIGGS, GARY BRUCE, science administrator, oceanographer, geologist, educator; b. Pasadena, Calif., Sept. 25, 1943; s. Dean Brayton and Barbara Jayne (Farmer) G.; m. Venetia Gina Bradfield, Jan. 11, 1980; children: Joel, Amy, Shannon, Callie, Cody. BA in Geology, U. Calif., Santa Barbara, 1965; PhD in Oceanography, Oreg. State U., 1968. Registered geologist, Calif.; cert. engr. geologist, Calif. Rsch. asst., NSF grad. fellow in oceanography Oreg. State U., 1965-68; from asst. prof. to prof. earth scis. U. Calif., Santa Cruz, 1969—; Fulbright fellow Inst. for Ocean & Fishing Rsch., Athens, Greece, 1974-75; oceanographer Joint U.S.A.-N.Z. Rsch. Program, 1980-81; chair earth scis. U. Calif., Santa Cruz, 1981-84, assoc. dean natural scis., 1992-95; dir. Inst. of Marine Scis., 1991—. Vis. prof. Semester at Sea program U. Pitts., 1984-96; guest lectr. World Explorer Cruises, 1987; chair marine coun. U. Calif., 1999—; bd. govs. Consortium for Oceanographic Rsch. and Edn., 1995—. Author: (with others) Geologic Hazards, Resources and Environmental Planning, 1983, Living with the California Coast, 1985, Coastal Protection Structures, 1986, California's Coastal Hazards, 1992; mem. editl. bd. Jour. of Coastal Rsch., Geology; contbr. numerous articles to profl. jours. Mem. Am. Geophys. Union, Am. Geol. Inst., Coastal Found. Achievements include research in coastal processes; coastal erosion and protection; coastal engineering and hazards; sediment yield, transport and dispersal; geologic hazards and land use. Office: U Calif Inst Marine Scis Santa Cruz CA 95064 E-mail: griggs@emerald.ucsc.edu.

GRIGGS, JOYCE L., secondary school educator; d. Milo Roger and Mary Louise Hulsebus; m. Thomas J. Griggs, May 26, 1973; children: Brian, Jeffrey. BA, Simpson Coll., 1973; MA, Ariz. State U., 1991. Tchr. Southeast Warren Schs., Liberty Center, Iowa, 1973—75, Marshall U. High Sch., Mpls., 1975—76; sec. Watermation Engring., St. Paul, 1976—79; adminstrv. asst. Neiser, Campara & Horne Law Firm, Phoenix, 1980—84; tchr. Lamson Coll., Glendale, 1984—86; tchr., instructional specialist Ironwood High Sch., 1987—. Author of poems. Grantee, Peoria Ednl. Enrichment. Mem.: ASCD, Phi Kappa Phi. Methodist. Avocations: graphic arts, computers, writing.

GRIGGS, KAREN, university educator, technical writer; b. Ft. Wayne, Ind., Nov. 4, 1946; BA, Purdue U., 1972, PhD, 1994; MSEd, Ind. U., Ft. Wayne, 1986. Instr. Purdue U., West Lafayette, Ind., 1987-93; asst. prof. James Madison U., Harrisonburg, Va., 1995-96. Vis. asst. prof. No. Ill. U., DeKalb, 1994-95. Mem. Girl Scout coun., Ft. Wayne, 1972-78; editor Ind. divsn. Izaak Walton League Am., Gaithersburg, Md., 1983-92, regional gov. 1985-78, environ. health and air com. 1986—, tech. adv. com. 1996—. Grantee M.W. Pollution Prevention Conf. Environ. Def. Fund, 1991, 92. Mem. Soc. Tech. Comm., Assn. Bus. Comm., Rhetoric Soc. Am., Nat. Coun. Tchrs. Eng., Coll. Composition and Comm. Conf., Speech Comm. Assn. Home: 635 County Road 35 Ashley IN 46705-9744

GRIGGS, LEONARD LEROY, JR., air transportation executive, consultant; b. Norfolk, Va., Oct. 13, 1931; s. Leonard LeRoy and Mary (Blair) G.; m. Denise Ziegler, Mar. 18, 1977; children: Margaret Rosalyn, Virginia Lorraine Williams, Julia Blair Havey, Deborah Branham Taylor. BS, U.S. Mil. Acad., 1954; MS in Aero. Engring., Air Force Inst. Tech., 1960; MS in Internat. Affairs, George Washington U., 1967; disting. grad., Naval War Coll., 1967, Army War Coll., 1971. Registered profl. engr., Mo. Commd. 2d lt. U.S. Army, 1954; advanced through grades to col. USAF, 1970; served in Vietnam; ret., 1977; dir. Lambert St. Louis Internat. Airport, 1977-87; v.p. Ross & Baruzzini, Inc., 1987-89, Bangert Bros. Constrn. Co., St. Louis and Denver, 1989—; asst. adminstr. for airports FAA, Washington, 1990-93; airport dir. St. Louis Internat. Airport, 1993—2004; aviation cons., 2005—. Adj. prof. St. Louis U.; apptd. to Nat. Civil Aviation Rev. Commn., 1997. Bd. dirs. USO, St. Louis/Lambert, Airports Coun. Internat., 1997-98. Decorated Silver Star, D.F.C. with 4 oak leaf clusters, Bronze Star, Meritorious Svc. medal, Air medal with 22 oak leaf clusters, Purple Heart, Air Force Commendation medal with 2 oak leaf clusters, Army Commendation medal; Medal of Honor; Medal of Gallantry (Vietnam); recipient Aviation Engring. Safety award FAA, 1979. Mem. Airport Operators Coun. Internat., Am. Assn. Airport Execs., Profl. Engring. Soc. St. Louis, Order of Dadelians, St. Louis Air Force Assn., Engr. Club, Mo. Athletic Club, Army Navy Club, Univ. Club, Order DeMolay. Home: 1609 Tradd Ct Chesterfield MO 63017-5627 Office: LL Griggs Assocs 232 N Kingshighway Blvd Ste 202 Saint Louis MO 63108 Office Phone: 314-361-4449. Business E-Mail: colgriggs@sbcglobal.net.

GRIGGS, LEWIS BROWN, executive producer, speaker, trainer; b. Mpls./St.Paul, Minn., Aug. 16, 1948; s. Charles Edward Bayliss Griggs and Mary Barbara Brown; children: Ashley Copeland, Ian Copeland. BA, Amherst Coll., Amherst, Mass., 1970; MBA, Stanford U. Grad. Sch. of Bus., Stanford, Calif., 1980. Asst. adminstr. office GSA, Washington, 1970—72; sales & mktg. dir. Spellbinder Inc, Concord, Mass., 1972—74; devel. office WGBH / Channel 2 / PBS, Boston, 1974—76, KQED / Channel 9 / PBS, San Francisco, 1976—78; pres. & CEO Griggs Prodn., San Rafael, Calif., 1982—. Bd. dirs. Geog. Expeditions, San Francisco, 1996—. Author: Going International, Valuing Diversity; prodr.: (6-part series of training videos/guides) Human Energy at Work, (3-part series of interactive cd-roms) No Potential Lost, (7-part series of training videos/guides) Going International, Valuing Diversity (Nat. Edn. Film Festival, 1988), (3-part series of training videos/guides) Valuing Relationship (Internat. TV Assn., 1993); cross-cultural diversity speaker/trainer (Valuing Diversity workshops) (Internat. HRD Practitioner Award, 1989, Achieving Performance Excellence Award, 2003). Mem.: Soc. Intercultural Edn. Tng. Rsch., Acad. Mgmt., Am. Soc. for Tng. & Devel., Soc. for Human Resource Mgmt., Diversity Leadership Forum, Assn. for Spirit at Work, Spirit in Bus., World Bus. Acad. Office: Griggs Production 905F Irwin St San Rafael CA 94901 Office Phone: 415-455-1500. Office Fax: 415-455-5585. E-mail: lewis@griggs.com.

GRIGGS, NINA M., realtor; b. NYC, Sept. 21, 1932; d. John Malcolm Miller and Kathryn Ruth Wilenzick; m. Charles Guy Moseley, Aug. 28, 1954 (dec. Feb. 1970); children: Charles Edward Keeble Moseley, Kathryn Drew Moseley Kristofik; m. Bancroft Gerardi Davis, Dec. 31, 1971 (dec. Dec. 1980); m. Richard Curtis Miles, Feb. 5, 1983 (dec. Sept. 1987); m. Northam Lee Griggs, Feb. 13, 1993 (dec. Mar. 2002). BA, Vassar Coll., 1954; MA, U. Va., 1956; postgrad., Columbia U. Exec. assoc., part-time rsch. assoc., 1961-63; founder, pres. Adventures Abroad, Ltd., 1964-71; also asst. to dir. profl. exams. divn. Psychol. Corp., N.Y.C., 1968-71; program officer Internat. Inst. Ednl. Planning/UNESCO, Paris, 1971-72; program adminstr. French and German lang. tchg. asst. prog. Inst. Internat. Edn., N.Y.C., 1973-85; dir. women's program Internat. Exec. Svc. Corps, 1988-91; real estate associate New England Land Co, Greenwich. Founder, dir. Women's Talent Corps, 1965-67; mem. N.Y. Jr. League; dir. Masters Nursery and Children's Ctr., 1962-81. Author: U.S. Citizenship Today, 1963; editor: (with Kertis, O'Driscoll) English Language and Orientation Programs in the United States, 1978, 80; contbr. articles to profl. jours. Trustee, chmn. nominating com. Dobbs Sch., 1968-71. Mem. Hyannisport Club, N.Y. Jr. League, Harvard Club of N.Y., Regency Club, Delta Delta Delta. Episcopalian. Home: 9 Country Rd Westport CT 06880-2524 Office: New England Land Co 783 North St Greenwich CT 06831-3105 Personal E-mail: ninagriggs@aol.com.

GRIGGS, ROBERT CHARLES, physician; b. Wilmington, Del., Jan. 8, 1939; s. Albert Bertin and Virginia (Robertson) G.; m. Rosalyne Hoggard, June 16, 1964; children Jennifer, Heather. AB, U. Del., 1960; MD, U. Pa., 1964. Intern Case Western Reserve U., Cleve., 1964-65, resident, 1965-66, Nat. Inst. Neurol. Disease and Blindness, Bethesda, Md., 1966-68; resident in medicine at Strong Memorial Hosp. Rochester Sch. Medicine, 1969—70, attending physician, neurology, Strong Memorial Hosp., 1971—; hon. cons. Univ. Coll. Hosp., London, 1981-82; Edward A. & Alma Vollersten prof. neurophysiology U. Rochester Sch. Med. & Dentistry. Author: Evaluation and Treatment of Myopathies; editor in chief Neurology, 1997—. Served to lt. comdr. USPHS, 1966-68. ACP Rsch. and Teaching grantee, 1971-74. Office: Strong Meml Hosp Dept Neurology 601 Elmwood Ave Dept Box 681 Rochester NY 14642-0002

GRIGGS, ROBERT F., military officer; s. Philip D. and Carmen A. Griggs; m. Jerah G. Gregory, Mar. 5, 1994; children: Jake, Anna. BBA, Campbell U., 1994; MEd, Pa. State U., 2005. Co. comdr./staff officer 504th PIR, 82nd Airborne Divsn., Fort Bragg, NC, 1999—2003; asst. prof. mil. sci. US Army ROTC, University Park, Pa., 2003—. Maj. U.S. Army, 1988—2005, Penn State University. Decorated Combat and Expert Infantryman's Badge 82nd Airborne Divsn., Bronze Star Medal, Coalition Task Force 82 - Afghanistan, Master Parachutist Badge with Combat Star 82nd Airborne Divsn. Mem.: 82nd Airborne Divsn. Assn. (life), Assn. of the US Army (life), Pi Lambda Theta (assoc.). Catholic. Avocations: golf, basketball, volleyball, running, weightlifting. Home: 332 W Fairmount Ave State College PA 16801 Office Phone: 814-863-0368. Personal E-mail: griggsrf@msn.com.

GRIGGS, STEPHEN L., management consultant; b. Morristown, NJ, 1947; s. Paul and Frances G.; m. Margaret Anne Hastings, 1970; children: Jocelyn Hastings, Diana Hastings. BSME, Villanova (Pa.) U., 1969; MS, MIT, 1971; MBA, Harvard U., 1974. Mem. tech. staff Bell Telephone Labs., Holmdel, N.J., 1969-72; div. mgr. Norlin Industries, Carlisle, Pa., 1974-77, contr., chief fin. officer, 1977-79; sr. assoc. Booz Allen & Hamilton, N.Y.C., 1979-82; v.p. ops., chief fin. officer Phys. Acoustics Corp., Princeton, N.J., 1982-83; sr. ptrn. KSM Group Inc., Short Hills, N.J., 1983-88; pres. The Tewksbury Group Inc., Oldwick, N.J., 1988—. Mem. IEEE, Am. Inst. Ultrasound Medicine, Am. Assn. Clin. Chemists, Soc. Competitive Intelligence Profls., Parenteral Drug Assn., Med. Mktg. Assn., Am. Soc. Materials, Soc. for Advancement of Materials and Process Engring., Am. Soc. for Microbiology, Am. Soc. Echocardiography, Hunterdon County Hist. Soc., Geneal. Soc. N.J., Nat. Geneal. Soc., New Eng. Hist. Geneal. Soc., Controlled Release Soc., Sigma Xi, Tau Beta Pi, Pi Tau Sigma. Republican. Episcopalian. Avocations: trout fishing, architecture. Office: Tewksbury Group Inc PO Box 48 Oldwick NJ 08858-0048

GRIGONIS, RICHARD WILLIAM, technical editor; b. Passaic, N.J., Sept. 24, 1956; s. William Vincent and Louise Medla (DiServio) G. BA in Journalism, Rowan U., 1978. Prodn. asst. Sesame Street prodn. dept. Children's TV Workshop, N.Y.C., 1980-85; Wang office info. sys. technician Peat, Marwick, N.Y.C., 1985-86; MIS dir. Squadron, Ellenoff, Plesent & Sheinfeld, N.Y.C., 1987-94; tech. editor Computer Tel. Mag., N.Y.C., 1994-98, chief tech., editor, 1998—. Pres. Grigonis Rsch., Harrison, N.J., 1992—; cons., multimedia programmer AT&T Bell Labs., Holmdel, N.J., 1992—. Author: Fault Resilient PCs, 1996, Encyclopedia of Computer Telephony, 1999. Avocations: writing, photography. Office: Miller Freeman 12 W 21st St Fl 2 New York NY 10010-6999

GRIGORIAN, VREJ, surgeon; b. Tehran, Iran, Apr. 15, 1938; came to U.S., 1957; s. Hairapet and Varsening (Sayranian) G.; m. Setta Daghestanian, June 29, 1963; children: Vera, Sonia, Vivian, Armen. AA, El Camino Coll., 1959; BA, U. Calif., L.A., 1961; D in Medicine, Wayne State U., 1965. Diplomate Am. Bd. Surgery. Intern Hosp. Good Samaritans, L.A., 1965-66; resident in gen. surgery Zion Hosp., San Francisco, 1966-70; pvt. practice Lombard Med. Group, Thousand Oaks, Calif., 1970—, chmn. bd., 1980-85; attending surgeon Los Robles Hosp. and Regional Med. Ctr., Thousand Oaks, 1970—. Chmn. bd. dirs. Lombard Med. Group, Inc., 1980-85. Fellow ACS; mem. Soc. Clin. Vascular Surgery. Republican. Avocations: tennis, travel. Business E-Mail: vrej.grigorian@verizon.net.

GRIGORIEV, SERGEI ALEKSANDROVICH, political scientist, researcher; b. Moscow, Feb. 16, 1957; came to U.S., 1991; s. Aleksandr Mironovich Grigoriev and Antonina Nikolayevna Barinova-Sitnikova; m. Valentina M. Maliukovskaya, Nov. 14, 1975 (div. June 1986); 1 child, Helen S. Grigoriev-Pogosyan; m. Elena Borisovna Kostritsyna, June 3, 1989. MA in History, Regional Studies, Langs., Moscow State U., 1979; MPA, Harvard U., 1993; PhD in Interdisciplinary Studies, Tufts U., 1996. Exec. sec. Soviet Chinese Friendship Assn., 1979-84; sr. exec. N.Am. sect. Communish Party of the Soviet Union, Moscow, 1984-90; asst. press spokesman Office Pres. USSR, Moscow, 1990-91; fellow in residence Princeton (N.J.) U., 1991-92; fellow Harvard U., Cambridge, Mass., 1992, sr. rsch. assoc., 1992—, exec. dir. Russian fellows program, 1996-99; vis. prof., lectr. Northeastern U., Boston, 1992-96; chief of staff, sr. adviser to Hon. Vladimir Kozhin Head of Office for Gen. Mgmt. and Bus. Adminstrn., 2000—. Cons. ABC News, N.Y.C., 1991-92; cons., lectr. Leigh Bur., Sommerville, N.J., 1991-94; adviser, cons. to chmn. All-Russian TV and Radio Broadcasting Co., Moscow, 1999-2000; adviser CNN, 2000, Eruasia Group Moscow Trip, 2000. Contbr. articles to newspapers and profl. jours. Cons. Yeltsin for Pres. Campaign, Boston, Moscow, 1996, City Legislature Election, 1998, TV-Ctr., Moscow, 1998; advisor to Hon. Sergei V. Yastrzhembsky, Dep. Premier Moscow City Govt., 1998-99, Hon. Sergei V. Kiriyenko, leader New Force Movement, 1999. Mem. Am. Acad. Polit. Sci. Home: 110A Inman St Cambridge MA 02139-1206 also: # 108 Prospect Mira Apt 342 124626 Moscow Russia Office: Ria Vest News Agy # 2 Nikithikov 121099 Moscow Russia

GRIGSBY, L. LANE, manufacturing executive; Pres., CEO Cajun Constructors, Inc., Baton Rouge, 1973—94, chmn., bd. dirs.; bd. dirs. The Shaw Group, Inc., Baton Rouge, 1995—. Officer or dir. various charitable orgns. Mem.: La. Assn. Bus. and Industry, Associated Builders and Contractors. Office: Cajun Constructors Inc PO Box 104 Baton Rouge LA 70817

GRIJALVA, RAUL, congressman; b. Tucson, Feb. 19, 1948; m. Ramona F. Grijalva; children: Adelita, Raquel, Marisa. BA in Sociology, U. Ariz., 1988. Dir. El Pueblo Neighborhood Ctr.; asst. dean Hispanic student affairs U. Ariz.; mem. Pima County Bd. Suprs., 1989—2003, U.S. Congress from 7th Ariz. dist., 2003—; mem. Edn. and Workforce com., Resources com. and Small Bus. com. U.S. Ho. Reps. Democrat. Roman Catholic. Office: 1440 Longworth House Office Bldg Washington DC 20515-0307

GRIJALVA, SANTIAGO, energy executive, consultant; PhD, U. Ill., 2002. Cert. CIEEPI, 2004. Head software dept. Nat. Ctr. of Energy Control, Quito, Ecuador, 1994—97; sr. cons. PowerWorld Corp., Champaign, Ill., 2001—. Pres. ElectriMarts, Quito, Ecuador, 2004—. Author: (technical paper) Conplex-Flow Based Nonlinear ATC Screening (IEEE Transactions in Power Engring.). Adv. to exec. dir. Nat. Ctr. of Energy Control, Quito, Ecuador, 2003—04. Recipient Best Power Engring. Grad., Escuela Politecnica Nacional, 1994; fellow Outstanding Internat. Student award, La. State U., 1997; fellowship, Fulbright, 1997-1999. Mem.: IEEE (assoc.), Counseil Internat. des Grandes Reseaux Electriques (corr.). Achievements include invention of consideration of reactive power in Ppwer transfer capability algorithm; optimal location of renewal generation to enhance grid security algorithm; design of methodology for reduction of losses in electric distribution systems; research in physical issues of power system static voltage collapse. E-mail: santiago@electrimarts.com.

GRILES, J. STEVEN (JAMES STEVEN GRILES), lobbyist, former federal agency administrator; b. Clover, Va., Dec. 13, 1947; s. Frazier Lee and Elsie (Neal) G.; m. Mary L. Disque, Mar. 26, 1978; children— Matthew Disque, Maegan Elizabeth; children by previous marriage— Kimberly Neal, Timothy Neal BA, Univ. Richmond, 1970. Exec. asst. Va. Dept. Conservation, Richmond, Va., 1968-81; dep. dir. Office Surface Mining U.S. Dept. Interior, Washington, 1981-83, dep. asst. sec. land and minerals, 1983-85, asst. sec. for land & minerals mgmt., 1985-89; sr. v.p. environ. and pub. affairs The United Co., Bristol, Va., 1989—95; dep. sec. U.S. Dept. Interior, Washington, 2001—05; ptnr. Lundquist, Nethercutt & Griles LLC, Washington, 2005—. Served with Va. USNG, 1970-78 Republican. Office: Lundquist Nethercutt & Griles LLC 101 Constitution Ave NW Ste 525 E Washington DC 20001

GRILL, LAWRENCE J., lawyer, accountant, bank executive; b. Chgo., Nov. 5, 1936; s. Samuel S. and Evelyn (Wollack) G.; m. Joan V. Krimston, Dec. 16, 1961; children: Steven Eric, Elizabeth Anne. BS with honors, U. Ill., 1958; postgrad., U. Chgo., 1959—60; LLB, Northwestern U., 1963. CPA Ill.; bar: Ill. 1963, Calif. 1965. Audit and tax mgr. Arthur Anderson & Co., Chgo., 1958-60; with firm Aaron, Aaron, Schimberg & Hess, Chgo., 1963-64, Gendel, Raskoff, Shapiro & Quittner, LA, 1964-66; sec., gen. counsel Traid Corp., LA, 1966-69; v.p., sec., gen. counsel Kaufman & Broad, Inc., LA, 1969-78; pres. Kaufman & Broad Asset Mgmt., dir. subs.; v.p., sec., gen. counsel AM Internat., Inc., Century City, Calif., 1979-82, dir. subs.; sr. v.p., group ops. officer, dir. subs. Wickes Cos., Inc., Santa Monica, Calif., 1982-85; acting CEO, COO, mem. exec. com. Barco of Calif., Gardena, 1985-86; pres. Lawrence J. Grill & Assocs., LA, 1985-94; pres., CEO Pan Am. Bank and United Pan Am. Fin. Corp., San Mateo, Calif., 1994-2000; also bd. dirs. Chmn., pres., CEO Universal Savs. Bank, Orange, Calif., 1988-90; cons. bd. dirs. World Trade Bank, N.A., 1992, Marathon Nat. Bank, 1992-93; spl. advisor to Fed. Home Loan Bank Bd. San Francisco, FDIC for Distressed Savs. Instns., 1986-88; arbitrator Am. Arbitration Assn. Served with AUS, 1958-59. Home: 48437 Vista Palomino La Quinta CA 92253 Office: 1300 S El Camino Real San Mateo CA 94402-2963 Personal E-mail: lar36@yahoo.com.

GRILLER, DAVID, management consultant; b. London, Eng., May 29, 1948; came to Can., 1977; s. Lewis and Renee (Kellinger) G.; m. Alexis Myers, Aug. 22, 1971; children: Hannah, Mark, Nadia. BS, U. Coll. London, 1969, PhD, 1972. Salters Co. fellow, London, 1973; postdoctoral fellow NRC of Can., Ottawa, 1973-75, head organic chemistry, 1977-91; mgmt. cons. Deloitte, Haskins and Sells, London, 1975-77; sr. ptnr. Secor Inc., Ottawa, Ont., Can.; 1991—. Author over 180 sci. papers and books. Recipient CNC-Iupac award Internat. Union Pure and Applied Chemists, 1984, Rutherford medal Royal Soc. Can., 1986, Organic Reaction Mechanisms award Royal Soc. of Chemistry, 1986. Fellow Royal Soc. Can., Can. Inst. Chemistry (Merck Sharp and Dohme award 1985). Avocations: squash, skiing. Office: Groupe Secor 38 McArthur Ave Ste 200 Ottawa ON Canada K1L 6R2 E-mail: dgriller@secor.ca.

GRILLER, GORDON MOORE, legal association administrator, consultant; b. Sioux City, Iowa, Feb. 3, 1944; s. Joseph Edward and Arlene (Searles) G. m. Helen Mary Friederichs, aug. 20, 1966; children: Heather, Chad. BA in Political Sci., U. Minn., 1966, MA in Pub. Affairs, 1969. Mgnt. analyst Hennepin County Adminstr., Mpls., 1968-72; asst. court adminstr. Hennepin County Municipal Ct., Mpls., 1972-77, ct. adminstr., 1977-78; judicial dist. adminstr. 2nd Dist. Ct. Minn., St. Paul, 1978-87; ct. adminstr. Superior Ct. Ariz., Phoenix, 1987—2002, Trial Cts. in Maricopa County Ariz., Phoenix, 2002—03; v.p. Justice Practice Group, ACS, Inc. Bd. dirs. Nat. Conf. Metro Cts., 1999—. Vice-chmn. Bloomington Sch. Bd., Minn., 1981-87. Sgt. USAAF, 1968-74 Res. Recipient Warren E. Burger award Inst. Ct. Mgnt.,1988, Leadership Fellows award Bush Leadership Program, 1974. Mem. Nat. Assn. Trial Ct. Adminstrs.(pres. 1983-84), Ariz. Ct. Assn., Nat. Assn Ct. Mgmt. (award of merit), Am. Judicature Soc., (bd. dirs. 1997-2003). Lutheran. Avocations: running, scuba diving, kayaking, hiking. Home: 8507 E San Jacinto Dr Scottsdale AZ 85258-2576 Office: Ste 1750 101 N 1st Ave Phoenix AZ 85003

GRILLO, HERMES CONRAD, surgeon; b. Boston, Oct. 2, 1923; s. Giacomo and Rose G.; children: Andrea York, Hermes Conrad, Paula, Amy Whittier. AB, Brown U., 1943; MD, Harvard U., 1947. Diplomate Am. Bd. Surgery, Am. Bd. Thoracic Surgery (dir. 1979-84). Intern Mass. Gen. Hosp., Boston, 1947-48, resident, 1948-51, 53-55, mem. surg. staff, 1955—, chief gen. thoracic surgery, 1969-94; pvt. practice medicine specializing in thoracic surgery Boston, 1955—. Prof. surgery Harvard U. Med. Sch., 1973—2000, emeritus, 2000—. Author: Surgery of Trachea and Bronchi, 2004; editor 3 books; mem. editl. bd. Jour. Thoracic and Cardiovasc. Surgery, 1975-82; contbr. over 350 sci. articles to profl. jours. Served with USMC, 1951-52; with USN, 1952-53. Decorated Commendation medal with Combat V, Cavaliere dell'Ordine al Merito della Repubblica Italiana, Order Civil Merit (Korea), Korean campaign ribbon with 3 battle stars; recipient Hermes C. Grillo Professorship of Thoracic Surgery Harvard Med. Sch., 2002. Mem. ACS, Am. Assn. Thoracic Surgery, Soc. Thoracic Surgeons (pres. 1987-88, Bakken Sci. Achievement award 2002), Am. Surg. Assn., Am. Coll. Chest Physicians (Medallist 1994), Am. Thoracic Soc., Thoracic Surgery Dirs. Assn. (pres. 1983-85), Am. Broncho-Esophagological Assn. (hon.), Belgian Surg. Soc. (hon.), Can. Soc. Cardiovasc. and Thoracic Surgeons (hon.), European Soc. Thoracic Surgeons (hon.), French Surg. Assn. (hon.), Italian Thoracic Surg. Soc. (hon.), Italian Surg. Soc. (hon.), Japanese Assn. for Chest Surgery (hon.), Korean Med. Assn. (hon.), Soc. Thoracic and Cardiovasc. Surgeons Gt. Britain and Ireland (hon.), Assn. Thoracic Surgeons Asia (hon.), Boston Surg. Soc. (pres. 1997, Bigelow medal 2003), Mass. Thoracic Soc. (Chadwick medal 1996), N.E. Surg. Soc. (Nathan Smith award 2000), Italian Surg. Soc. (hon.), World Soc. Thoracic Surg. (hon.), World Soc. Cardiothoracic Surgery (hon.). Office: Mass Gen Hosp 55 Fruit St/Blake 1570 Boston MA 02114-2620 Office Phone: 617-726-2811. Business E-Mail: pguerriero@partners.org.

GRILLO-LOPEZ, ANTONIO J., physician; b. Hato Rey, P.R., Nov. 20, 1939; s. Antonio Grillo-Ramírez and Lolita López-Grillo; m. Maria S. Marxuach-Grillo, Nov. 7, 1964; children: Antonio G. Grillo, Miguel A. Grillo, Javier J. Grillo. BS, U. P.R., Rio Piedras, 1960; MD, U. P.R., San Juan, 1964. V.p. clin. rsch. Parke Davis, Ann Arbor, Mich., 1980—92; exec. med. dir. DuPont Merck Pharm., Wilmington, Del., 1987—92; chief med. officer IDEC Pharms., San Diego, 1992—2001; chmn. Neoplastic and Autoimmune Diseases Rsch. Inst., Rancho Santa Fe, Calif., 2001—. Contbr. articles to profl. jours. Lt. comdr. USNR, 1974, 1965. Recipient Discovery Health Channel Med. Honors, 2004. Roman Catholic. Avocations: music, theater, opera, travel, cars. Office: Box 3797 Rancho Santa Fe CA 92067

GRILLONE, GREGORY ANGELO, otolaryngologist; b. N.Y., Feb. 17, 1953; s. Gregory and Rose Marie Grillone; m. Diane Marie Raymond, May 29, 1988; children: Gregory James, Deanna Rose. MD, Mt. Sinai U., 1983. Diplomate Am. Bd. of Otolaryngology, 1988. Vice chmn. Dept. Otolaryngology Boston (Mass.) U., 1999—, assoc. prof. Dept. Otolaryngology, 2004—. Residency program dir. Dept. Otolaryngology Boston (Mass.) U. Med. Ctr., 1997—. Fellow: ACS; mem.: AMA, Am. Acad. Otolaryngology (Honor award 2000), Soc. U. Otolaryngologists, Am. Head and Neck Soc., The Voice Found., Mass. Soc. Otolaryngology (bd. of directors 1992), New Eng. Otolaryn. Soc. (sec., treas. 1994—99, v.p. 1999—2000, pres. 2000—01). Office: Boston University Medical Center 88 E Newton Street Boston MA 02118 Office Phone: 617-638-7934. Home Fax: 617-638-7965; Office Fax: 617-638-7965. Personal E-mail: gregory.grillone@bmc.org.

GRILLY, EDWARD ROGERS, physicist; b. Cleve., Dec. 30, 1917; s. Charles B. and Julia (Varady) G.; m. Mary Witholter, Dec. 14, 1942 (dec. 1971); children: David, Janice; m. Juliamarie Andreen Langham, Feb. 1, 1973. BA, Ohio State U., 1940, PhD, 1944. Rsch. scientist Carbide & Carbon Chemicals Corp., Oak Ridge, Tenn., 1944-45; asst. prof. Chemistry U. N.H., Durham, 1946-47; mem. staff U. Calif. Nat. Lab., Los Alamos, N.Mex., 1947-80, cons., 1980—. Contbr. articles to books and profl. jours. Mem. N.Mex. House of Reps., Santa Fe, 1967-70, Los Alamos County Coun., Los Alamos, 1976-78. Mem. Am. Physical Soc., Kiwanis Club, Los Alamos Golf Club (pres. 1974-75). Republican. Avocation: golf. Home: 705 43rd St Los Alamos NM 87544-1807 *The key to my life is discovery. It always amazes me how learning can be so fascinating. Of course, the ultimate is discovery in my own vocation-physics-whether it is of my own doing or learning of a colleague's work. But, I also found that intense involvement in community work can lead to surprising results.*

GRIM, CHARLES W., federal agency administrator; Grad., U. Okla., 1983; M in Health Svcs. Adminstrn., U. Mich. Clin. assignment Claremore Svc. unit Indian Health Svc., U.S. Dept. Health and Human Svcs., Okmulgee, Okla., asst. area dental officer Oklahoma City, area dental officer, 1989—92, dir. divsn. oral health Albuquerque, 1992, acting dir. Oklahoma City, 1999—2000, area dir., 2000—02, acting svc. unit dir. Albuquerque, dir. divsn. clin. svcs. and behavioral health, assoc. dir. office health programs Phoenix, 1998—99, interim dir., 2002—03, dir. Rockville, Md., 2003—. Rear adm. Commd. Corps USPHS. Mem.: ADA, Soc. Am. Indian Dentists, Am. Assn. Pub. Health Dentistry, Am. Bd. Dental Pub. Health, Commd. Officers Assn. Office: Indian Health Svcs US Dept HHS 801 Thompson Ave Rockville MD 20852-1627

GRIM, PATRICK NEAL, philosophy logician educator; b. Pasadena, Calif., Oct. 29, 1950; s. Elgas Shull Grim and Dorothy Mae O'Neal; m. L. Theresa Watkins. AB in Philosophy and Anthropology, U. Calif., Santa Cruz, 1971; BPhil, U. St. Andrews, 1975; PhD, Boston U., 1976. Mellon faculty fellow Wash. U., St. Louis, Md., 1977-78; from asst. prof. to prof. SUNY, Stony Brook, 1978-94, prof., 1994—2001, disting. tchg. prof., 2001—. Author: The Incomplete Universe, 1991, The Philosophical Computer, 1998, Questions of Value, 2005; editor: The Philosopher's Annual, Vols. 1-25, 1979-2003, Philosophy of Science and the Occult, 1982, 91; contbr. articles to profl. jours. Fulbright fellow, St. Andrews, Scotland, 1971-72, Mellon Faculty fellow Washington U., St. Louis, 1977-78. Fellow Acad. of Tchr./Scholars; mem. Internat. Assn. Philosophy of Law, Am. Philosophical Assn., Cognitive Sci. Soc., Internat. Soc. Artificial Live. Avocations: art, music. Home: Toad Hall 99 Swezey St Patchogue NY 11772 Office: Dept of Philosophy Suny At Stony Brk Stony Brook NY 11794-3750 Office Phone: 631-632-7578. Business E-Mail: pgrim@notes.cc.sunysb.edu.

GRIM, SAMUEL ORAM, chemistry professor; b. Landisburg, Pa., Mar. 11, 1935; s. Oram Michael and Esther Blanche (Gable) G.; m. Faith H. Rojahn, June 8, 1957 (div. 1982); children: Stephen W., Amy R., Lucy G.; m. Caren L. Klarman, Mar. 11, 1983 (div. 1993); 1 child, Christina K.; m. Rebecca A. Allen, Aug. 11, 2001. BS, Franklin and Marshall Coll., 1956; PhD, MIT, 1960. Faculty U. Md., College Park, 1960—, prof. chemistry, 1968—2003, prof. emeritus, 2003—, chmn. inorganic chemistry divsn., 1970-77, 80-86, 1995—96, assoc. chmn., chemistry dept., 1996-98. Program officer in inorganic chemistry NSF, 1988-90. Contbr. articles to profl. jours. Union Carbide Co. scholar, 1954-56; NSF fellow, 1958-60; summer teaching fellow, 1960; research fellow Imperial Coll., London, 1961-62; Sir John Cass's Found. sr. research fellow City of London Poly., 1979-80 Fellow AAAS, Am. Inst. Chemists, Royal Soc. Chemistry (London); mem. Am. Chem. Soc., N.Y. Acad. Scis., Internat. Union Pure and Applied Chemistry, Internat. Coun. Main Group Chemistry, Chem. Soc. Washington, Phi Beta Kappa, Sigma Xi (Sci. Achievement award 1983), Phi Lambda Upsilon, Alpha Chi Sigma. Clubs: Terrapin (College Park). Republican. Home: 1280 Highland Greens Dr Venice FL 34285-5665 E-mail: sogrim@umd.edu.

GRIMALDI, JAMES THOMAS, investment fund executive; b. Elizabeth, N.J., Dec. 8, 1928; s. Anthony and Helen (Bernatt) G.; m. Norma Miriello, June 17, 1951; children: Patricia Ann, Pamela Gay, Donna Lynne. BS in Econs., U. Pa., 1951; MBA, Columbia U., 1955. CLU, 1964. Br. acct. Watson-Flagg Engring. Co., Paterson, N.J., 1953-56; from agt. to sr. asst. dist. mgr. Met. Life Ins. Co., Paterson, Ridgewood, N.J., 1956-61; reg. agy. dir., asst. v.p. Am. Amicable Life Ins. Co., Ft. Lauderdale, Fla., 1961-66; v.p. mktg. Inland Life Ins. Co., Chgo., 1966-69; exec. v.p. Peoples Home Life Ins. Co. Ind., 1969-71, Fed. Life & Casualty Co., Battle Creek, 1970-71; pres., chief exec. officer, also dir. Peoples Home Life Ins. Co. of Ind., 1971-74; pres., CEO, bd. dirs. Fed. Life & Casualty Co., 1971-74, Keystone Co., Boston, 1974-76, Cornerstone Fin. Svcs., Inc., Boston, 1974-76; exec. v.p. sales Keystone Custodian Funds, Inc., Boston, 1974-76; engaged in pvt. investments, 1976—. Mem. faculty De Paul U., Chgo., 1969. 1st lt. USAF, 1951-53; bd. dirs., Mich. C. of C., 1972-74; trustee, Cmty. Hosp. Assn., Battlecreek, Mich. 1971-74. Recipient Spl. Tribute as Outstanding Citizen, State of Mich., 1974 Mem. Sales Mktg. Execs. Internat., Am. Soc. CLU, Nat. Assn. Life Underwriters, Am. Mktg. Assn., Assn. Individual Investors, Life Assn. Mich. (pres. 1973, exec. com.), Nat. Assn. Security Dealers, Acad. Polit. Sci., U. Pa. Alumni Assn., Columbia U. Alumni Assn. Home: 4904 Sentinel Post Rd Charlotte NC 28226-7445

GRIMALDI, NEIL VINCENT, lawyer; b. N.Y.C., Jan. 27, 1947; s. Vincent and Frances Grimaldi. B in Fgn. Svc., Georgetown U., 1968; JD, St. John's U., 1973. Bar: N.Y.; ordained min. Interfaith Sem., 1999. Prosecutor Bronx Dist. Atty. Office, N.Y.C., 1974—77; pvt. practice N.Y.C., 1979—. Pres. Grimaldi Corp., N.Y.C., 1999—. Author: The Grand Jury, 1999. Mem.: Masonic Order Free Masons. Democrat. Home: 2860 Buhree Ave New York NY 10461

GRIMALDI, NICHOLAS LAWRENCE, fundraising executive; s. Dominick Lawrence and Marian Theresa G. Student, Manhattan Coll.; BA summa cum laude, Fordham U. Exec. assoc. Nat. Assn. Regional Ballet, N.Y.C., 1979-87; exec. dir. Nikolais/Louis Found. for Dance, Inc., N.Y.C., 1987-89; dir. devel. Hartley House, N.Y.C., 1989-93, Fountain House, Inc., N.Y.C., 1993—. Cons. mgmt. and fund raising; mem. steering com./pastoral coun. Ch. of St. Francis Xavier, N.Y.C., 1993-97. Mem.: Assn. Fundraising Profls., Phi Sigma Tau, Phi Kappa Phi, Alpha Sigma Nu. Office: Fountain House Inc 425 W 47th St New York NY 10036-2397

GRIMES, DALE MILLS, physics and electrical engineering educator; b. Marshall County, Iowa, Sept. 7, 1926; s. LeRoy and Helen (Mills) G.; m. Janet LaVonne Moore, Mar. 22, 1947; children: Prudence Rae, Craig Alan. BS in Physics, Math. and Chemistry, Iowa State U., 1950, MS in Physics and Math, 1951; PhD in Elec. Engring, U. Mich., Ann Arbor, 1956. From rsch. assoc. to assoc. prof. elec. engring. U. Mich., 1951-61, prof. elec. engring., 1961-76; chief scientist Conductron Corp., Ann Arbor, 1960-63; prof. elec. engring., chmn. dept. U. Tex., El Paso, 1976-79; prof. elec. and computer engring. Pa. State U., 1979-91, prof. emeritus, 1992—, chmn. dept., 1979-86. Adj. prof. physics U. Ky., 1996—2000; cons. Environ. Rsch. Inst. Mich., U.S. Dept. Transp., GM Corp., 1968—91; vis. prof. elec. and computer engring. U. Tex.-Austin, 1985—86; chief scientist Crale, Inc., 1985—95. Author: Electromagnetism and Quantum Theory, 1969, Automotive Electronics, 1974, Advanced Electromagnetics: Foundations, Theory, Applications, 1995, Electromagnetic Origin of Quantum Theory and Light, 2002, 2005, also articles on automotive radar, biconical antennas, quantum theory, electromagnetic radiation; patentee in field. Served with USNR, 1943-46. Fellow AAAS; mem. IEEE, Am. Phys. Soc., Lexington Acad. Sr. Profls. Home: 1325 Megan Dr State College PA 16803 Personal E-mail: dmg6@psu.edu.

GRIMES, DAVID LYNN, communications company executive; b. Oklahoma City, June 9, 1947; s. Glenn Ross and Kathleen Sue G.; m. Sandra Kay Belt, Mar. 6, 1970; children: David Edwin, Emily Kathleen. BBA in Mktg., Ctrl. State U., Edmond, Okla., 1978; grad. internat. sr. mgrs. program, Harvard U., 1988. With Southwestern Bell Tel., 1970-83, rates and tariff Oklahoma City, 1975-77, industry mgr., 1977-79, dist. mgr. sales ops. St. Louis, 1979-80, mktg. mgr. Kansas City, Mo., 1980-82, Houston, 1982-83; divsn. mgr. Am. Bell, Houston, 1983-84; br. mgr. nat. accts. AT&T, Houston, 1984-85, v.p. sales Dallas, 1986-98; COO Sharetech, Parsippny, NJ, 1985-86; pres., COO Sykes Enterprises, 1998-2000, pres., CEO, 2000; sr. v.p. Tropic Networks, 2001—04, pres., 2004—. Mem. Nat. Bd. of Visitors Tex. Christian U., 1990-96; mem. adv. coun. Sch. Nat. Sci., U. Tex., Austin, 1988-93; bd. dirs. Tex. Bus. Hall of Fame Found., Dallas, 1988-93. Mem. Dallas C. of C. (mem. exec. com. econ. devel. 1991-93), Harvard Bus. Club Dallas, Univ. Club (Dallas), Avila Country Club, Pinnacle Country Club, Tampa C. of C. (bd. dirs. 2000-01). Republican. Methodist. Avocations: golf, tennis, fishing, hunting. Home: 5510 Merrimac Ave Dallas TX 75206 Office Phone: 214-824-9961. Personal E-mail: dgrimes647@aol.com. Business E-Mail: dgrimes@tropicnetworks.com.

GRIMES, GARY JOE, communications executive; b. Aug. 19, 1947; s. Joseph E. Jr. and Norma M. (Good) G.; m. Sharon J. Hanson; children: David, Jennifer. BS in Physics, Colo. Coll., 1969; MS in Physics, U. Wis., 1970; PhD in Elec. Engring., U. Colo., 1973. Project mgr., sr. engr. Kappa Systems Inc., Colorado Springs, Colo., 1974-78; disting. mem. tech. staff Bell Labs. Lucent Technologies, Denver, 1978—; W.R. Bunn prof., exec. dir. Ctr. Telecom. Edn. and Rsch., 1994—. Contbr. articles to profl. jours. and chpts. to books. Mem. IEEE, Soc. Photo-optical Instrumentation Engrs., Phi Beta Kappa. Achievements include 72 issued US patents. Office: U Ala 1150 10th Ave S Birmingham AL 35294-0001 E-mail: telesnoozer@yahoo.com.

GRIMES, HEILAN YVETTE, publishing executive; b. Hamilton, Ohio, Sept. 16, 1949; d. J and Claudette (Hinkle) G. Grad., New Eng. Sch. Photography, 1987. Founder, pres. Dot & Line Graphics, 1975—, Color Computer Weekly, 1982—, Hollow Earth Pub., 1983—. Adj. prof. U. Mass., Lowell. Author: Norse Mythology, 1984, Legend of Niebelungenlied, 1984, Using QuarkXPress 3.3, 1994, Beginning Internet, 1994, Filemaker Pro Developer's Guide, 1997, Netiquette and E-Commerce Marketing, 2004, Runes, 2005; founder Byte Mag., 1974, Macpower Mag., 1993 Democrat. Avocations: magic, juggling, hiking, travel. Office: PO Box 51480 Boston MA 02205-1480 Office Phone: 617-249-0161. Personal E-mail: yvettegr@hotmail.com.

GRIMES, HOWARD RAY, management consultant; b. Manilla, Iowa, July 24, 1918; s. Ray Herb and Sarah Alice (Saunders) G.; m. Nancy Palmer, Nov. 17, 1993; children from previous marriage: Patricia, Susan, Nancy, Sarah, Laura. Student, U. Wis., 1939; BA, Grinnell Coll., 1940. With Aetna Life & Casualty Co., 1940-82, field supr., regional mgr. Boston, 1950-74, regional dir., v.p. field, 1974-82; mgmt. cons., 1983-95; chmn. Benefit Svcs. Inc., 1968-93. Bd. dirs. Waterville Co. Inc. Served with USAAF, 1942-45. Sports-Illustrated Silver Anniversary All-Am. Mem. Weston Golf Club (Mass.), Bald Peak Colony Club (N.H.), The Moorings Club (Fla.), Harvard Club (Boston). Home: PO Box 513 Waterville Valley NH 03215-0513 also: 1180 Reef Rd Vero Beach FL 32963-2971 E-mail: hrgrimes8@aol.com.

GRIMES, JAMES GORDON, geologist; b. Kenosha, Wis., Mar. 18, 1951; s. James Gordon Bennett Jr. and Alyce Louise (Gannaway) G. BS in Earth Sci., U. Wis., Parkside, 1974; MS in Geology, Mich. Tech. U., 1977. Registered profl. geologist, Tenn. Geologist nat. uranium resource evaluation project Union Carbide Corp. Nuclear Div., Oak Ridge, 1977-84; geol. cons. UCC-ND Mercury Task Force, Oak Ridge, 1983; geologist Lockheed Martin Energy Systems Inc., Oak Ridge, 1984-99. Tech. mgr. Y-12 plant Meterol. Info. Support System, 1987-96, ind. cons., Kenosha, 1999—. Mem. Geol. Soc., Air and Waste Mgmt. Assn. E-mail: xjg@worldnet.att.net.

GRIMES, MARGARET WHITEHURST, artist, educator; b. New Bern, N.C., June 5, 1943; d. Alan Pendleton and Margaret (Whitehurst) G. BA, Gov. State U., 1975, MA, 1976; postgrad., Notre Dame U., 1977; MFA, U. Pa., 1980. Instr. drawing and design Thornton C.C., Chgo., 1974-79; prof. painting and drawing Western Conn. State U., Danbury, 1980—, asst. chair, 1991-92, coord., master fine arts program, 2000—. Guest lectr./critic Vt. Coll. of Norwich U., Montepelier, 1995-96, Vt. Studio Ctr., Johnson, 1995, Tanglewood Inst., Lenox, Mass., 1997, S.V.A. Conf. on Liberal Arts and the Edn. of Artists, 1997, Ctrl. Conn. State U., New Britain, 1997, Weir Farm Nat. Hist. Site, Wilton, Conn., 1998, Gunn Mus., Washington, 2000; vis. artist Am. U., Corciano, Italy, 2001-05, Hendrix Coll., Conway, Ark., 2002, Chautauqua (N.Y.) Inst., 2003, 05, Am. U., Washington, 2004; artist-in-residence Writz Farm Trust, 2003; Univ. prof. Conn. State U., 1992. Co-editor New Art Assn. Newsletter, 1971; one woman shows include Green Mountain Gallery, N.Y., 1979, (biaunally) Blue Mountain Gallery, N.Y., 1980-2003, Fischbach Gallery, N.Y., 1986, Moravian Coll., Bethlehem, Pa., 1990, Western Conn. State U., 1990, 98, Ctrl. Conn. State U., 1997, Washington Art Assn., 1990, 2000, Weir Farm Nat. Trust, Wilton, Conn., 2003, 100 Pearl Gallery, Conn., 2003, Hartford; three-person show Provincetown Group Gallery, Mass., 1987; exhibited in group shows at Internat. Women's Art Festival, Walker Art Inst., 1976, Woodmere Mus., Phila., 1977, Provincetown Art Mus., Mass., 1978, Reading Mus., Pa., 1983, Queens Mus., N.Y., 1983, Rahr-West Mus., Manitowoc, Wis., 1983, Columbus (Ohio) Mus. of Art, 1987, Katherina Rich Perlow Gallery, 1987, 88, 89, 76th Am. ann. show Newport (R.I.) Mus., 1988, Erector Sq. Gallery, New Haven, 1994, Kline Gallery, Santa Fe, N.Mex., 1994, Creiger-Dane Gallery, Boston, 1995, Park Ave. Atrium, N.Y.C., 1995, Wilmington (Del.) Ctr. for Contemporary Art, 1996, Conn. State U. biennial, 1987-99, Blue Mountain Gallery, 1980-2001, Bachelier-Cardonsky Gallery, Kent, Conn., 1996, 97, 98, Philbrook Museum, Tulsa, Ringling Museum of Art, Sarasota, Fla., Davenport Mus., Iowa, 1999-2000, NAS, 2001-02,Nat.Acad. Design, 2004; represented in permanent collections at Pitts. Plate Glass Co., Conn. Ins. Group, N.Am. Christian Sci. Ch. Ctr., Boston, U.S. Tobacco Co., Bellevue Hosp., N.Y., NAS, Washington, Nat. Acad. Sci. Recipient Disting. Lectureship award Henry Barnard Found., 1990; rsch. grantee in painting Conn. State U., 1985, Benjamin Altman prize in painting NAD, 2003 Mem. AAUP (grantee 1986, 90, 91, 93, 95, 99, 2003), Coll. Art Assn. Home: 27 Wykeham Rd Washington CT 06793-1308

GRIMES, MARTHA, author; b. Pittsburgh, Pa. d. D.W. and June (Dunnington) G.; div.; 1 s.: Kent Van Holland BA, MA, U. Md. Formerly instr. English U. Iowa, Iowa City; asst. prof. Frostburg State Coll., Frostburg, Md.; prof. Montgomery Coll., Takoma Park, Md., 1970—; instr., writing seminars program Johns Hopkins Univ. Author: mystery novels The Man With a Load of Mischief, 1981, The Old Fox Deceiv'd, 1982, The Anodyne Necklace, 1983 (Nero Wolfe Award for best mystery of yr.1983), The Dirty Duck, 1984, The Jerusalem Inn, 1984, Help the Poor Struggler, 1985, The Deer Leap, 1985, I Am the Only Running Footman, 1986, The Five Bells and Bladebone, 1987 (NY Times Bestseller), The Old Silent, 1989 (NY Times Bestseller), Send Bygraves, 1989, The Old Contemptibles, 1991 (NY Times Bestseller), End of the Pier, 1992, The Horse You Came In On, 1993, Rainbow's End, 1994, Hotel Paradise, 1996, The Case Has Altered, 1997, The Stargazey, 1998, Biting the Moon, 1999, Lamorna Wink, 2000, Hotel Paradise, 1994, Cold Flat Junction, 2001, The Blue Last, 2001 (NY Times Bestseller), The Grave Maurice, 2002, Foul Matter, 2003, The Winds of Change, 2004 (Publishers Weekly Bestseller). Mailing: c/o Viking Pub Author Mail Penguin Putnam 375 Hudson New York NY 10014*

GRIMES, MELANIE JOY, homeopath, writer; d. Leo L. and Laura O. Kornfeld; m. Charles H. Grimes, Dec. 3, 1975; children: Julian Asher, Benjamin William. BA, We. Wash. U., 1975; grad. in Advanced Screenwriting, UCLA Sch. of Theatre, Film and TV, 2001; grad. in Advanced Homeo., Dynamis Coll. of Homeopathy, England, 1996; grad. in Classical Homeopathy, New Eng. Sch. of Homeopathy, Seattle, Mass., 1994. Registered Homeopath North Am. Soc. of Homeopaths, 1992, Classical Homeopath Coun. for Homeo. Cert., 2001; Fiction Writing U. Wash., 1997. Pres. Alethea Homeopathics, Seattle, 1994—; owner M.J.Feet, Birkenstock Store, Inc., Seattle, 1972—. Pub. Alethea Book Co., Seattle, 1992—. Author: (book) Dr. John Bastyr: Philosophy and Practice, (screenplay) Dead Right (U.C. Riverside Screenwriting Contest finalist, 2003), (Quarterfinalist: v Internat. Screenwriting Competition, 2004); author: (librettist) (opera) Seijo; contbr. book; author: (book) v Tiger Shark Liver: An Exploration and Homeopathic Proving of Galeocerdo Cuvier Hepar; editor (publisher): v Dynamic Provings, volume 1, Dynamis Books; editor: v Dynamics and Methodology of Homeopathic Provings, Second edition, Dynamis Books; author: (teleplay) From Sea to Shining Sea- West Wing teleplay (Semifinalist: Austin Film Festival, 2002); contbr. articles to profl. jours. Membership chair PTA, Seattle, 1989—90; sec. Internat. Found. for Homeopathy, 1995—97; mem. Homeo. Cmty. Coun., 1997—99; sec. N.Am. Soc. of Homeopaths, 1999—2000, Pacific NW Writer's Assn., 2003—04. Mem.: N.Am. Soc. of Homeopaths (assoc.; sec. 1999—2000). Achievements include research in Homeopathic Proving of Tiger Shark LIver: Galeocerdo cuvier hepar; Homeopathic Proving of Meteorite: Fax caelestis allende; Homeopathic Proving of Blue Green Algae-Microcystic aeruginosa; Homeopathic Proving of Tule Bluet Dragonfly: Enallagma carunculatum. Office Phone: 206-284-5340. Personal E-mail: melaniegrimes@aol.com. E-mail: melaniegrimes.com.

GRIMES, MICHAEL D., investment banker; b. 1966; m. Janelle Grimes. With Bear, Stearns & Co., 1992—95; v.p. Morgan Stanley, Menlo Park, Calif., 1995—96, principal, co-head of West Coast Technol. Group, 1997—98, mng. dir., co-head of West Coast Techol. Group, 1998—. Named to Forbes Midas List, 2001, 2002, 2003, 2004. Office: Morgan Stanley 3000 Sand Hill Rd Bldg 4 Ste 250 Menlo Park CA 94025

GRIMES, MICHAEL DAVID, podiatrist; b. Berkeley, Calif., Jan. 29, 1973; s. Charlie Alfred and Ruth Elaine Grimes; stepfather, Roger Lloyd Sharpe. BS, U. Calif., Berkeley, 1994; D of Podiatric Medicine, Calif. Coll. Podiatric

Medicine, San Francisco, 1998. Resident in podiatry Houston Podiatry Found., 1998-99, surg. resident in podiatry, 2000—04. Pvt. practice, 1999—. Named one of Outstanding Young Men in Am., 1998. Mem. AAAS, Am. Podiatric Med. Assn., Am. Chem. Soc., Tex. Podiatric Med. Assn., Calif. Podiatric Med. Assn., Assn. Am. Coll. Foot and Ankle Surgeons Avocations: running, biking, swimming, hiking, fishing. Office: 1320 Tara Hills Dr Ste H Pinole CA 94564 Home: 635 Creston Rd Berkeley CA 94708-1239 Office Phone: 510-724-1530.

GRIMES, PAMELA EMELIA, writer, illustrator; b. Monroe, La., Mar. 3, 1945; d. Barney Albert and Wanda Neel Grimes; m. James C. Williams, June 3, 1967 (div. July 1990); children: Amelia, Adam, Adrienne, Amanda, Alexander. Student, Creighton U.; BA, Tex. A&M U., 1970; MA, Hood Coll., 1987. Cert. tchr., Tex. Instr. secondary polit. sci. and German Frederrick (Md.) C.C., 1987—90; tchr. French and German Palestine (Tex.) H.S., 1990-92; writer, illustrator, Palestine, 1992—. Author, illustrator: Foxes of the Field, 1998, Pilar, 2000, The Adventures of Yukiko and Her Dog ITO, 2004, The Flying Koffer, 2004, The Family Williams, 2005. Den mother Boy Scouts Am., Mont., 1978-81, Md., 1987-89; bd. dirs. Hamilton (Mont.) Pub. Libr., 1981-83; pres. Monocacy Mid. Sch. PTA, Frederick, 1985-86; v.p. Ft. Detrock (Md.) Officers Wives Club, 1986-89; tchr. citizenship class Palestine Pub. Libr., 1998. Republican. Episcopalian. Avocation: linguist. Home and Office: PO Box 27 Tennessee Colony TX 75861-0027 Office Phone: 903-928-2395. E-mail: godolphin@dctexas.net.

GRIMES, R. DALE, lawyer; b. Nashville, Mar. 30, 1953; BA cum laude, U. of the South, 1975; JD, U. Tenn., 1978. Bar: Tenn. 1978. Law clk. to Hon. L. Clure Morton chief judge U.S. Dist. Ct. (mid. dist.) Tenn., 1978-80; mem., litig. practice Bass, Berry & Sims, Nashville, 1980—. Chair fed. civil justice reform act adv. group (mid. dist.) Tenn., 1991-95. Articles editor Tenn. Law Rev., 1977-78. Bd. regents U. of the South, 1989-95, chmn., 1993-95, lectr. exec. seminars, Owen Grad. Sch. Mgmt., Vanderbilt U., pres. bd. trustees, St. Mary's Retreat Conf. Ctr., chair constn. canons com. Episcopal Diocese Tenn. Fellow Nashville Bar Found.; mem. ABA (antitrust law sect., litig. sect., health law sect.), Am. Health Lawyers Assn., Nat. Health Lawyers Assn., Tenn. Bar Assn., Nashville Bar Assn. (co-chair fed. ct. com. 1990, vice chair 1989), Omicron Delta Kappa. Office: Bass Berry & Sims Ste 2700 315 Deaderick St Nashville TN 37238-3001 Office Phone: 615-742-6244. Office Fax: 615-742-2744. Business E-Mail: dgrimes@bassberry.com.

GRIMES, RICHARD ALLEN, economics professor; b. Toledo, Apr. 24, 1929; s. Robert Howell and Mary Mildred Grimes; m. Helen Ann Schaeffer, Aug. 25, 1951; children: Gregory Allen, Julianne, Frank Edwin, Mary Ann. BS major in Chemistry, U. Ga., 1951; MS in Mgmt., Ga. Inst. Tech., 1959; postgrad., Ga. State U., 1979. Commd. lt. U.S. Army, 1951, advanced through grades to lt. col., ret. 1971; asst. prof. econs. Clayton State Univ., Morrow, Ga., 1971-74; assoc. prof. econs. Ga. Perimeter Coll., Decatur, 1974-97. Adj. prof. Jacksonville State U., 1959—63, Va. Commonwealth U., 1964—67, Ga. Mil. Coll., 1979—91, Ctrl. Tex. Coll., 1997—2001, Gordon Coll., 1998—; ednl. cons.; real estate broker, instr. Author: (book) Economics and Finance Study Guide, 2000; reviewer: Economics, 1979—99. Organizing dir. Cmty. Bank, 2001—; umpire Atlanta Area Football Ofcsl. Assn., treas., 1971—95; evaluator Ga. H.S. Football Ofcls., 1996—; active Spl. Olympics, Atlanta, 1971—; founding pres. Rex Civic Assn., 1973; sec.-treas. Villages Homeowners Assn., 1994—95; tax cons., instr. AARP, 2001—; mem. Stockbridge Urban Redevel. Agy., 2005. Decorated Soldier's medal for valor Vietnam; named Rotarian of the Yr., 1976, Football Ofcl. of the Yr., Atlanta area, 1980; recipient Eagle Scout award, 1944. Mem.: AAUP (pres. Ga. Perimeter Coll.chpt. 1987—97), VFW (life), Cmty. Banking Assn., Mil. Officers Assn. Am., Nat. Soc. Pub. Acctgs., Ga. Assn. Acctg. Profls. (past pres.), Ga. Assn. Econs. and Fin. (past pres.), Am. Acctg. Assn., So. Econ. Assn., U. Ga. Varsity Letterman, South Atlanta U. Ga. Alumni Club, So. Metro. Ga. Tech. Alumni Club (sec., scholarship chmn.), Am. Legion, Delta Pi Epsilon. Presbyterian. Avocations: football, golf, camping, swimming. Home: Eagles Landing 118 Carron Ln Stockbridge GA 30281-6302 Personal E-mail: r_grimes@bellsouth.net.

GRIMES, RUSSELL NEWELL, inorganic chemist, educator; b. Meridian, Miss., Dec. 10, 1935; s. Newell Cleveland and Marion Esther (Zehner) G.; m. Nancy Farrow Hall, Sept. 21, 1962; children— Susan, David BS in Chemistry, Lafayette Coll., 1957; PhD in Chemistry, U. Minn., 1962; postdoctoral, Harvard U., 1962, U. Calif., Riverside, 1962-63. Asst. prof. chemistry U. Va., Charlottesville, 1963-68, assoc. prof. chemistry, 1968-73, prof. chemistry, 1973—2003, chmn. dept. chemistry, 1981-84, prof. emeritus, 2003—. Guest prof. U. Canterbury, N.Z., 1974-75, U. Heidelberg, Fed. Republic of Germany, 1986, 1997-98. Author: Carboranes, 1970; editor: Metal Interactions with Boron Clusters, 1982, Inorganic Syntheses Vol. 29, 1992; contbr. over 240 articles to profl. jours. Grantee Office Naval Rsch., 1965-83, Army Rsch. Office, 1983—, NSF, 1976—; Fulbright sr. rsch. scholar, New Zealand, 1974-75; recipient Alexander von Humboldt Sr. Rsch. prize, 1996. Fellow AAAS; mem. Am. Chem. Soc. (sec.-treas. inorganic divsn. 1981-84, grantee 1965—), Corp. Inorganic Syntheses, Sigma Xi (President's and Visitors' rsch. prize 1981, 85, 96). Office: U Va Dept Chemistry Mccormick Rd Charlottesville VA 22904-0001 E-mail: rng@virginia.edu.

GRIMES, STEPHEN HENRY, retired state supreme court justice; b. Peoria, Ill., Nov. 17, 1927; s. Henry Holbrook and June (Kellar) G.; m. Mary Fay Fulghum, Dec. 29, 1951; children: Gay Diane, Mary June, Sue Anne, Sheri Lynn. Student, Fla. So. Coll., 1946—47; BS in Bus. Adminstrn. with honors, U. Fla., 1951, LLB with honors, 1954; LLD (hon.), Stetson U., 1980. Bar: Fla. 1954, U.S. Dist. Ct. (no. and so. dists.) 1954, U.S. Ct. Appeals (5th cir.) 1965, U.S. Supreme Ct. 1972. Since practiced in, Bartow, Fla.; ptnr. Holland and Knight and predecessor firm, Tallahassee, 1954-73, 98—; judge Ct. Appeals 2d Dist. Fla., Lakeland, 1973-87, chief judge, 1978-80; chmn. Conf. Fla. Dist. Cts. Appeals, 1978-80; justice Fla. Supreme Ct., Tallahassee, 1987-97, chief justice, 1994-96; chair Article V Task Force, 1994-96, Supreme Ct. Workload Study Commn., 2000—01. Mem. Fla. Jud. Qualification Commn., 1982-86, vice chmn., 1985-86; chmn. Fla. Jud. Coun., 1989-94. Contbr. articles U. Fla. Law Rev., 1951, 54. Bd. dirs. Bartow Meml. Hosp., 1958-61, Bartow Libr., 1968-78; trustee Polk C.C., Winter Haven, Fla., 1967-70, chmn., 1969-70; bd. govs. Polk Pub. Mus., 1976-97; bd. dirs., chmn. Elder Care. Lt. (j.g.) USN, 1951-53. Fellow Am. Coll. Trial Lawyers; mem. ABA, Fla. Bar Assn. (bd. govs. jr. bar 1956-58, bd. dirs. trial lawyers sect. 1967-69, sec. 1969, vice chmn. appellate rules com. 1976-77, vice chmn. tort litig. rev. commn. 1985-86), 10th Cir. Bar Assn. (pres. 1966), Am. Judicature Soc., Bartow C. of C. (pres. 1964), Rotary (dist. gov. 1960-61). Episcopalian (sr. warden 1964-65, 77). Office: Holland & Knight LLP 315 S Calhoun St Tallahassee FL 32301-1856 Office Phone: 850-224-7000. E-mail: sgrimes@hklaw.com.

GRIMES, SUZANNE, publishing executive; married; 2 children. BA in Internat. Mgmt., Georgetown U. With NY Times; advt. dir. Success; with TV Guide, 1990—94, nat. advt. dir., 1994—95, sr. v.p., pub., 1995—97; pub. Women's Sports & Fitness, 1997—2000, Allure, 2000—01; pub., v.p. Glamour Mag., 2001—04; v.p. media group Conde Nast, 2004—. Office: Conde Nast 4 Times Sq New York NY 10036-6522*

GRIMLEY, JANET ELIZABETH, newspaper editor; b. Oelwein, Iowa, Dec. 3, 1946; d. Harold E. and Ida Mae (Anderson) Teague; m. Terry L. Grimley, June 15, 1968; 1 child, Brynn Sara Mae Grimley. BA, U. Iowa, Iowa City, 1969; attended, U. Wash., Seattle, 1979-82. Asst. mng. editor Seattle Post-Intelligencer; publs. dir. Marycrest Coll., Davenport, Iowa, 1969-70; reporter Quad-Cities Times, Davenport, Iowa, 1970-74, Seattle Post-Intelligence, Seattle, 1974-76, feature editor, 1976-95, asst. mng. editor, 1995—. Past pres. Am. Assn. Sunday and Feature Editors; mem. Newspaper Features Coun. Mem. Shoreline Strategic Planning Com., Seattle, 1993, Shorewood Site Coun., 1997-99, Shorewood Boosters; co-chair Shoreline Capitol/Bond Com., Seattle, 1994, Einstein Site Coun., Seattle, 1994-96; bd. dirs. Ctr. for Human Svcs. Mem. Junior League of Seattle (bd. dirs. 1989-90, exec. bd. 1991-92), City Club Seattle. Avocations: sailing, skiing, gardening. Office: Seattle Post Intelligencer 101 Elliott Ave W Ste 200 Seattle WA 98119-4295

GRIMLEY, JEFFREY MICHAEL, dentist; b. Alton, Ill., Feb. 3, 1957; s. John Richard and Joyce Imogene (Mallin) G.; m. Julie Ellen Gardner, Aug. 2, 1980; children: Joel Michael, Christopher Mark, Benjamin Jeffrey. BS, U. Iowa, 1979, DDS, 1983; cert., Miami Valley Hosp., Dayton, Ohio, 1984. Gen. practice dentistry, Naperville, Ill., 1984—. Mem. ADA, Acad. Gen. Dentistry, Ill. Dental Soc., Chgo. Dental Soc. Methodist. Avocations: sports, photography. Office: Ste 112 1980 Three Farms Ave Naperville IL 60540-5365 Personal E-mail: grimleydds1@aol.com.

GRIMLEY, ROBERT THOMAS, chemistry professor; b. North Attleboro, Mass., Jan. 3, 1930; s. John Thomas and Ivy (Frost) G.; m. Margaret Rockwood, June 21, 1952 (dec. Feb. 8, 2005); children: Mark, Maureen, Kevin, Terrence, Peter. BS, U. Mass., 1951; PhD, U. Wis., 1958. Rsch. chemist Corning (N.Y.) Glass, Inc., 1957-59; fellow U. Chgo., 1959-61; prof. chemistry Purdue U., West Lafayette, Ind., 1961-94, prof. emeritus, 1995—. Vis. prof. Calif. Inst. Tech., Pasadena, 1992—96; vis. scholar Dartmouth Coll., 2001—. 1st lt. USAF, 1951—53. Mem. Am. Chem. Soc. (chmn. Purdue U. sect.), Am. Phys. Soc., Sigma Xi, Alpha Chi Sigma. Home: PO Box 550 Grantham NH 03753-0550

GRIMM, BEN EMMET, library director, consultant; b. Jersey City, Sept. 27, 1924; s. Benjamin Harrison and Eunice Blanche (Whitenack) G.; m. Jean Kay Bohrer, Aug. 19, 1950 (div. 1982); children: Jeffrey, Kevin, Mark, Wendy; m. Lucy Ann Taylor, Jan. 21, 1989. BA, Washington and Lee U., 1949; MS, Columbia U., 1950. Librarian youth services Detroit Pub. Libr., 1950-52; sr. librarian Fair Lawn (N.J.) Pub. Libr., 1952-54; reference and reading librarian Montclair (N.J.) Pub. Libr., 1955-56; asst. dir. Montclair (N.J.) Pub. Libr., 1956-61; dir. Belleville (N.J.) Pub. Libr., 1961-72, Jersey City Pub. Libr., 1973-85; prin. Grimm/McPherson Assocs., Montclair, N.J., 1988-92; ind. libr. cons., 1992-93. Chmn. Hudson County Audio-Visual Aids Commn., 1975-85; cons. libr. bldgs., svcs. and adminstrn., 1966-93; cons., mem. state aid constrn. adv. bd. N.J. State Libr., 1985-88, chmn. adv. coun. Libr. Svcs. and Constrn. Act, 1979-83. Mng. editor Libr. Trustee Newsletter, 1978-80. Bd. dirs. Orange County (Va.) Hist. Soc., 1994-96, pres., 1995; bd. dirs. Orange County Libr. Found., 1995-98, v.p., 1997-98; bd. dirs. Rapidan Found., 1999—, treas., 2003—; bd. dirs. The Arts Ctr. in Orange, 2002-03. With USAAF, 1942-45. Decorated D.F.C., Air medal with oak leaf clusters. Mem. N.J. Libr. Assn. (pres. 1968-69). Home and Office: PO Box 145 Rapidan VA 22733-0145 Personal E-mail: bgrimm92@yahoo.com. Business E-Mail: bengrimm@ns.gemlink.com.

GRIMM, JAMES R. (RONALD GRIMM), b. Monroe, Mich., Nov. 5, 1935; s. Carl S. and Annie B. (Platt) G.; m. Carol Ann Forman, Aug. 24, 1957; children: James R., Phillip H. BS in Bus. Adminstrn, Ariz. State U., 1958. Dir. internal audit Motorola, Inc., Phoenix, 1961-68; bus. and fin. mgr. Europe Motorola Semicondr. Co., Geneva, 1968-70; dir. internat. fin. Fairchild Camera & Instrument Co., Mountain View, Calif., 1970-71; v.p. internat. fin. Computer Scis. Corp., Los Angeles, 1971-74; sr. v.p., chief fin. exec. Pertec Computer Corp., Los Angeles, 1974-80; exec. v.p. fin. and adminstrn. MAPCO, Inc., Tulsa, 1980-84; v.p., chief fin. officer Greyhound Corp., Phoenix, 1984-88; pres. Internat. Bus. Cons., Phoenix, 1988—; sr. v.p., CFO Gulf States Steel Ala., Gadsden, 1998-2000. Bd. dirs. Petro Star Inc., Fairbanks, Alaska, Infinite Tech. Corp., Dallas. Contbr. articles to Inst. Internal Auditors publs., 1964-68. Inducted into Ariz. State U. Hall of Fame, 1982 Mem. Inst. Internal Auditors (founder and 1st pres. Phoenix chpt. 1963), Fin. Exec. Inst., Gadsden Country Club. Home: 527 Mistletoe Holw Gadsden AL 35901-5739 Personal E-mail: gjim4al@aol.com.

GRIMM, JANE BOLLES, artist; b. San Francisco, Feb. 21, 1942; d. John Savage and Mary Vande Water (Piper) Bolles; m. Rupert Edwin Grimm, Aug. 1968; children: Jacqueline, John Piper. AB, Sarah Lawrence Coll., 1965; MFA, Calif. Coll. Arts & Crafts, 1992. Pres. Jane Bolles, Inc., N.Y., 1965-70; pres., designer Bolles Jewelry, San Francisco, 1975-89; artist San Francisco, 1989—. Trustee Cambridge Sch. Weston, Weston, Mass., 1992-99, Calif. Coll. Arts & Crafts, 1996—. Recipient Murphy fellowship San Francisco Found., 1991, Merit award Calif. State Fair, 1994, 99, award Assn. Clay and Glass Artists of Calif., 1999. Avocation: tennis. Office: 743 Harrison St San Francisco CA 94109 Home: 1895 Pacific Ave #305 San Francisco CA 94117

GRIMM, JEFFERY WILLIAM, psychologist, educator; b. Bremerton, Wash., Sept. 22, 1970; s. Fred Milo and Wilene Marie Grimm; m. Stephanie Dawn Davis, May 1, 1993; children: Anya Manzanita, Ella Marie. BA, Whitman Coll., 1992; MS, Wash. State U., 1995, PhD, 1999. Postdoctoral rsch. assoc. Nat. Inst. on Drug Abuse, Balt., 1999—2001; assoc. prof. psychology Western Wash. U., Bellingham, Wash., 2001—.

GRIMM, JOHN LLOYD, marketing professional; b. N.Y.C., Oct. 21, 1945; s. Judson and Nanette Grimm; m. Stephanie L. Cassagne, Dec. 23, 1969; children: Samantha, Jonathan. BBA, Tulane U., 1967, MBA, 1969. Asst. prof. Dillard U., New Orleans, 1969-82; pres. Multi-Quest Internat. Inc., New Orleans, 1966—, Analytical Studies Inc., New Orleans, 1966—, Sybersurveys Inc., New Orleans, 1966—. Author: Interviewer's Handbook & Training Manual, 1970. Chmn. rsch. com. United Way, New Orleans, 1988-89, 94—, mem. mktg. com., 1986-88; mem. mktg. com. YMCA, New Orleans, 1985-98; mem. pub. rels. com. Goodwill Industries, New Orleans, 1986-89. Named Prof. of the Yr., Dillard U., 1981. Mem. Am. Mktg. Assn. (pres. New Orleans chpt. 1985-87, 94-95, treas. 1984-85, sec. 1983-84), Market Rsch. Assn., New Orleans Camellia Club. Avocation: growing and showing camellias. Office: Multi-Quest Internat Inc 708 Rosa Ave Metairie LA 70005-2145 Office Phone: 504-835-3507. Business E-Mail: research@eatel.net.

GRIMM, LOUIS JOHN, mathematician, educator; b. St. Louis, Nov. 30, 1933; s. Louis and Florence Agnes (Hammond) G.; m. Barbara Ann Mitko, May 6, 1967; children: Thomas, Mary. BS, St. Louis U., 1954; MS, Ga. Inst. Tech., 1960; PhD, U. Minn., 1965. Chemist USPHS, Savannah, Ga., 1958-61; asst. prof. U. Utah, Salt Lake City, 1965-69; assoc. prof. U. Mo., Rolla, 1969-74, prof., 1974—, chmn. dept. math. and stats., 1981-87, dir. Inst. Applied Math., 1983-87. Vis. asst. prof. U. Minn., Mpls., 1966; vis. prof. U. Nebr., Lincoln, 1978-79, U. So. Calif., L.A., 1987-88; exch. scientist Polish Acad. Scis., Warsaw, 1981. Contbr. articles to profl. jours. With Med. Svc. Corps, AUS, 1956-58. Jefferson Smurfit fellow Univ. Coll. Dublin (Ireland), 1984; NSF rsch. grantee. Mem. AAUP, Soc. for Indsl. and Applied Math., Polish Math. Soc., Gesellschaft für angewandte Mathematik und Mechanik, Math. Assn. Am. (Disting. Tchg. award 2001), Sigma Xi. Office: U Mo Dept Math & Stats Rolla MO 65409-0001

GRIMM, TERRY M., lawyer; b. Bloomington, Ill., Apr. 3, 1942; BA, Ind. U., 1964, JD cum laude, 1967. Bar: Ill. 1967, U.S. Dist. Ct. No., Ctrl. & So. Calif., No. & Ctrl. Ill., No. Ind., So. N.Y., Wyoming. Spl. prosecutor DuPage County (Ill.) Prosecutors Office, 1975-76; assoc. to ptnr. Winston & Strawn LLP, Chgo., 1968—, mem. exec. com. Fellow Am. Coll. Trial Lawyers; mem. Ill. State Bar Assn., Order of the Coif. Office: Winston & Strawn 35 W Wacker Dr Ste 4200 Chicago IL 60601-9703 Office Phone: 312-558-5782. Office Fax: 312-558-5700.

GRIMMER, STEPHEN ANDREW, lawyer; b. St. Louis, June 9, 1953; s. Ralph J. and Rosemary Patricia G.; m. Ruth Ann Gerhart, June 14, 1975 (div. 1997); children: Nick, Alex, Samuel, Anna. BSCE, Tex. Tech. U., 1975; JD, U. Tex., 1981. Bar: Tex. 1981, U.S. Dist. Ct. (no. dist.) Tex. 1982, U.S. Dist. Ct. (we. dist.) Tex. 1987, U.S. Ct. Appeals (5th cir.) 1987, U.S. Supreme Ct. 1989, U.S. Patent Office 1983. Assoc. Underwood, Wilson, Berry, Stein & Johnson, Amarillo, Tex., 1981-85; assoc. Haynes & Boone, Dallas, 1985-89; ptnr. Cantey & Hanger, Dallas, 1990-93; shareholder Turner, Dealey, Zimmermann & Grimmer, Dallas, 1993-97; pvt. practice Dallas, 1997—; of counsel Jones, Allen & Fuquay, Dallas, 1997—. Contbr. articles to profl. jours. Troop com. chmn., asst. scoutmaster Boy Scouts Am., Dallas, 1992-97; Little League mgr., Dallas, 1994—. Mem. Dallas Bar Assn. (chmn. judicial evaluation com. 1997—, judicial preference poll com. 1997—), State Bar Tex. (vice chmn. com. 1988), Tex. Pro Bono Coll. Avocations: coaching baseball and soccer, golf, running, church activities, baseball. Office: Jones Allen & Fuquay 8828 Greenville Ave Dallas TX 75243-7160 Office Phone: 214-343-7400. Business E-Mail: sgrimmer@jonesallen.com.

GRIMMETTE, MARK, Olympic athlete; b. Ann Arbor, Mich., Jan. 23, 1971; Mem. U.S. Olympic Luge Men's Doubles Team, 1989. Named U.S. Nat. Champion in Doubles, 1996, winner 6 World Cup medals, World Cup champion, 1998, Bell Atlantic Nat. champion Silver medal, 1998; recipient Bronze medal Luge Men's Doubles, Nagano Olympics, Japan, 1998, Bronze medal, Lillehammer Olympics, 1996, All-Japan Championships, Nagano, Silver medal, Luge Challenge Cup, 2000, Bronze medal, World Championship, 2000, 2005. Office: US Luge Assn 35 Church St Lake Placid NY 12946-1805*

GRIMSHAW, JAMES ALBERT, JR., retired language educator; b. Kingsville, Tex., Dec. 10, 1940; s. James A. and John Maurine (Haley) G.; m. Glenda Darlene Hargett, June 10, 1961; children: Courtney Anne, James A. IV. BA in English, Tex. Tech. U., 1962, MA in English, 1968; PhD in English, La. State U., 1972. Commd. 2d lt. USAF, 1962, advanced through grades to lt. col., ret., 1983; instr. in English USAF Acad., Colorado Springs, 1968-70, asst. prof., 1970-74, assoc. prof., 1974-80, prof., 1980-83; prof. and dept. head Tex. A&M U. (formerly East Tex. State U.), Commerce, 1983-90, prof., 1990—2003, regent's prof., 1995—2003, 2005, ret., 2005. Pres. Northeast Tex. Orgn. of Lang. Educators, Commerce, 1984-85, S. Cen. Assn. Depts. English, 1984-85, Tex. Assn. Depts. English, Commerce, 1988-89; chmn. Robert Penn Warren Adv. Group, Bowling Green, Ky., 1990-98; pres. Robert Penn Warren Circle, Durham, N.C., 1991-93. Author: The Flannery O'Connor Companion, 1981, Understanding Robert Penn Warren, 2001; compiler: Robert Penn Warren: A Descriptive Bibliography, 1981; editor: Cleanth Brooks at the United States Air Force Academy, 1980, Robert Penn Warren's A Brother to Dragons, 1983, Time's Glory: Original Essays on Robert Penn Warren, 1986, The Paul Wells Barrus Lectures, 1983-89, 1990, Friends of Their Youth: Cleanth Brooks and Robert Penn Warren, 1993, Cleanth Brooks and Robert Penn Warren: A Literary Correspondence, 1998, (with James A. Perkins) Robert Penn Warren's All the King's Men: Three Stage Rersions, 2000. Mem. vestry Epiphany Episcopal Ch., Commerce, Tex., 1989-91, sr. warden, 95-96. Decorated Bronze Star medal USAF, Vietnam, 1965-66; recipient Disting. Faculty award, Faculty Senate East Tex. State U., Commerce, 1988, 95, East Tex. State U. Honors Prof. of Yr. award, 1993, Tex. Assn. of Coll. Tchrs. Disting. Faculty Tchg. award, 1992-93; named to the Flannery O'Connor Vis. Professorship, Ga. Coll., Milledgeville, 1977, vis. fellow in bibliography, Beinecke Rare Book & Manuscript Libr., Yale U., New Haven, Conn., 1979-80. Mem. Soc. for Study of So. Lit. Avocations: swimming, gardening, cross country skiing, chess, 5-string banjo, raising bison and peafowl. Home: 248 County Rd 4101 Greenville TX 75401-4799 Office: Tex A&M U-Commerce Dept of Lit & Langs Commerce TX 75429 E-mail: james_grimshaw@tamu-commerce.edu.

GRIMSLEY, MEREDITH RE', art educator; d. Peter and Gail Re'; m. James Grimsley, July 20, 2002. BFA, U. Ga., 1999, MFA, 2002. Archive photographer/design intern Glen Raven (NC), Inc., 2002—03; adj. instr. art U. Ga., Athens, 2002—03; instr. mixed media and crafts Bloomsburg (Pa.) U., 2003—04, asst. prof. mixed media, 2004—. Workshop leader Arrowmont Sch. Arts and Crafts, Gatlinburg, Tenn., 2004—05. Solo exhibition, Subtext, juried exhibition, Decay/Growth: Forgiveness (Best in show purchace Award, Rocky Mt. Arts Ctr., Rocky Mt., NC, 2003), juried entry, Identity (Selection for publ. in Fiber Arts Design Book 7, Lark Books, 2004), solo exhibition performance, What Do You Say?, juried exhibtion, Living Out My Fantasy Panties (Selection for 2004 Nat. Juried Exhbn. of Contemporary Crafts, Wayne Art Ctr., Wayne, PA). Bd. dirs. Lyndon House Arts Found., Inc., Athens, 2002. Grantee, Commn. on the Status of Women, Bloomsburg U., 2005. Mem.: Assn. Pa. State Coll. Faculties, Surface Design Orgn., Coll. Art Assn., P.E.O. Sisterhood (life; chmn. internat. peace scholarship fund 2005—). Avocations: travel, reading, exercise. Office: Bloomsburg U 400 East 2d St Bloomsburg PA 17815 Personal E-mail: mgrimsle@bloomu.edu.

GRIMSLEY, SEAN C., lawyer; BA with highest honors, Univ. Tex., 1994; JD summa cum laude, Univ. Mich., 2000. Law clk. U.S. Ct. Appeals (D.C. cir.), Washington, 2000—01; law clk. to Hon. Sandra Day O'Connor U.S. Supreme Ct., Washington, 2003—04; assoc. Bartlit Beck Herman Palenchar & Scott, Denver, 2004—. Editor (article): Mich. Law Rev. Office: Bartlit Beck Herman Palenchar & Scott 8th Fl 1899 Wynkoop St Denver CO 80202

GRIMSTE, CHRISTY H., music educator, management consultant, real estate agent; b. New Orleans, July 11, 1978; d. Charles and Carolyn Chestnutt; m. Robert Grimste, Jr., Mar. 29, 2003. BSBA, U. Md. Assn. mgr. U.S. Embassy, Vienna; mgmt. specialist U.S. Dept. State, Wash.; piano tchr.; real estate agt. ESL tchr. Immanuel Bible Ch. Mem.: Fgn. Affairs Recreation Assn. Conservative. Christian. Avocations: travel, languages, skiing, writing. Personal E-mail: christygrimste@yahoo.com.

GRIMSTED, PATRICIA KENNEDY, historian, archivist, writer, consultant; b. Elkins, W.Va., Oct. 31, 1935; BA in History with honors, U. Calif., 1957, MA in Modern European History, 1959, PhD in Russian History, 1964. Sr. rsch. assoc. Ukrainian Rsch. Inst., Harvard U., Cambridge, Mass., 1974—; lectr. Bucknell U., 1965—67, U. Md., 1968—70; rsch. assoc. Russian Inst., Columbia U., N.Y.C., 1969—74; project dir. Fed. Archival Svc. Russia, State Pub. Hist. Libr., Internat. Inst. Social History, Moscow, 1991—. Vis. assoc. prof. dept. history Am. U., Washington, 1971—72, adj. prof. dept. history, 1971—72; lectr., mem. archival bd. Ctrl. European U., Open Soc. Archives, Budapest, 1996, 2001. Author: Trophies of War and Empire: The Archival Heritage of Ukraine, World War II and the International Politics of Restitution, 2001, The Odyssey of the Turgenev Library from Paris 1940-2002, 2003; contbr. articles to profl. jours.; editor: Archives of Russia: A Directory and Bibliographic Guide to Holdings in Moscow and St. Petersburg, 2000. Active Ukrainian Commn. Cultural Restitution Ukraine, 1993—98. Recipient Waldo Gifford Leland prize, Soc. Am. Archivists, 1973, Disting. Alumna award, Katherine Branson Sch., 1980; fellow, Russian Rsch. Ctr., Harvard U., Cambridge, 1964, 1967—68, 1974—97, Internat. Inst. Social History, Amsterdam, 1997—; grantee, Internat. Rsch. and Exchs. Bd., 1991, 1992—93, 1993—94, 1994—95, 1995—96, 1996—97, 1996—97, 1998—99, 2004; Rsch. grantee, NEH, 1971—91, 2004, Nat. Coun. East Europeans and Eurasian Rsch., 2000—02. Fellow: Internat. Inst. Social History (hon.); mem.: Am. Assn. Baltic Studies, Am. Assn. Ukrainian Studies, Internat. Coun. Archives, Soc. Am. Archivists, Am. Hist. Assn., Am. Assn. Advancement Slavic Studies (Lifetime Achievement award 2002). Avocation: photography. Office: Ukrainian Rsch Inst Harvard U 1583 Mass Ave Cambridge MA 02138

GRIMWADE, RICHARD LLEWELLYN, lawyer; b. Chgo., Apr. 26, 1945; s. Eric Illingworth and Pauline J. (Crandall) G.; m. Alexandra M. Galbraith, Feb. 22, 1981; children: Eric Montgomery, Sara Elizabeth. BA, Lawrence U., 1967; JD cum laude, U. Wis., 1971. Bar: Wis. 1971, N.Y. 1971, Ill. 1978, Calif. 1981, U.S. Dist. Ct. (so. and ea. dists.) N.Y., 1971, U.S. Dist. Ct. (no. dist.) Wis., 1971, U.S. Dist. Ct. (no. dist.) Ill., 1978, U.S. Dist. Ct. (ctrl. dist.) Calif., 1981, U.S. Ct. Appeals (2d cir.) 1971, U.S. Ct. Appeals (7th cir.) 1978, U.S. Ct. Appeals (9th cir.) 1981. Atty. Davis Polk, N.Y.C., 1971—76; ptnr. Barton Klugman, L.A., 1983—93; pvt. practice L.A., 1993—. Mem. U. Wis. Law Rev., 1969-71. Bd. mgrs. Ketchum Downtown YMCA, L.A., 1991-97; trustee Reform L.A. Pub. Schs. (LEARN), 1993-97. Recipient 3 Am. Jurisprudence awards for evidence, legis., and acctg. and law Bancroft-Whitney, 1970. Mem.: State Bar Calif., Toastmasters (Best Performer award 1996, Best Table Topics award 1997, Best Spkr. award 1997), Order of Coif.

Avocations: gardening, poetry, running, public speaking, history. Home: 22372 Dardenne St Calabasas CA 91302 Office Phone: 818-591-3151. Personal E-mail: rlgrimwade@yahoo.com.

GRIMWOOD, HELEN PERRY, lawyer; b. Phoenix, Aug. 9, 1953; BSBA magna cum laude, Univ. Ariz., 1973; JD magna cum laude, Ariz. State Univ., 1980. CPA Ariz., 1979. Law clerk Judge L. Ray Haire, Ariz. Ct. of Appeals, 1980—81, Judge William C. Canby Jr., U.S. Ct. of Appeals, Ninth Cir., 1981—82; judge pro tempore Ariz. Superior, Maricopa County, 1993—, Ariz Ct. of Appeals, 1998; ptnr. Grimwald Law Firm plc, Phoenix. Named a Fellow, Am. Bar Found., 2000; named one of the Valley's Most Influential in Law, Bus. Journal, 2000; recipient Friedman award for excellence in legal edn., Maricopa County Bar Assn., 1995, Justice Gordon award for pro bono svc., 1996, Solin award for outstanding leadership, Ariz. Women Lawyer's Assn. Mem.: Ariz. Women Lawyer's Assn. (pres. 1996—97), Nat. Conf. of Women's Bar Assn. (dir. 1977—), Maricopa County Bar Assn. (dir. 1992—96, chair, comml. litig. CLE Com. 1993—96), Ariz. State Bar Assn. (mem., bd. gov. 1997—, pres.-elect 2004). Office: Grimwood Law Firm plc Ste 940 3101 N Central Ave Phoenix AZ 85012-2666

GRINALDS, JOHN SOUTHY, military officer, retired academic administrator; b. Balt., Jan. 5, 1938; Grad., West Point Mil. Acad., 1959; B in Geography, M in Geography, Oxford (Eng.) U.; MBA with distinction, Harvard U. Commd. 2d lt. USMC, 1959, advanced through grades to maj. gen.; commdg. gen. Marine Corps Recruit Depot, San Diego, 1989—91; headmaster Woodberry Forest Sch., Woodberry Forest, Va., 1991—97; pres. The Citadel, Charleston, SC, 1997—2005. Decorated Silver Star; recipient Legion d'Honneur, French Pres., Francois Mitterand. Office: The Citadel 171 Moultrie St Charleston SC 29409

GRINDE, DONALD ANDREW, JR., historian, educator; b. Savannah, Ga., Aug. 23, 1946; s. Donald Andrew Sr. and Bernice (Woodrum) G.; m.Ann Upchurch, Oct. 31, 1966 (div. Jan. 1971); 1 child, Donald Andrew III; m. Sarah Nez, July 19, 1978; 1 child, Kee Nez. BA, Ga. So. Coll., 1966; MA, U. Del., 1968, PhD, 1971. Instr. Am. history Mercyhurst Coll., Erie, Pa., 1971-73; asst. prof. Am. history SUNY, Buffalo, 1973-77; assoc. prof. Am. history Calif. Poly. State U., San Luis Obispo, 1977-78, 79-81, prof. Am. history, 1984—; visiting assoc. prof. Am. history U. Calif., Los Angeles, 1978-79; assoc. prof. Am. history and dir. native Am. studies U. Utah, Salt Lake City, 1981-84. Author: Readings in American History, 1976, Iroquois and the Founding of the American Nation, 1977. Sec. N.Am. Indian Ctr., Buffalo, 1974-77; mem. resolutions com. Nat. Indian Edn. Assn., 1981-83; chmn. Salt Lake Indian Ctr., Salt Lake City, 1983-84. Mem. Am. Indian Hist. Assn. (bd. dirs. 1975—), Am. Indian Historians Assn. (charter), Am. Indian Hist. Soc. Democrat. Yamasian. Avocations: golf, stamp collecting/philately, bridge.

GRINDEL, PATRICIA DIANE, writer, educator, consultant; b. Pitts., May 29, 1957; s. Richard Edward Grindel and Dorothy June (Peffer) Preuhs. BA in Journalism/Communications, Point Park Coll., 1980, MA in Journalism/Communications, 1987; postgrad., Ga. State U. Editor/writer Three Rivers Mag., Sewickley, Pa., 1983-84; asst. to dir. Point Park Coll., Pitts., 1985; publs. specialist Ga. Inst. Tech., Atlanta, 1986, sr. writer, 1986-87, asst. dir. publs., 1987-88, acting dir. publs., 1988-89, dir. publs., 1989-90; dir. edn. AID Atlanta, 1990-93; freelance writer Atlanta, 1983—; pres. Wellness Resource Group, 1993-95; mgr. hosp. devel. Life Link of Ga., Atlanta 26275496, 1995—2000; comm. and pub. rels. cons., 2000—; instr. Kennesaw State U.,dept. of comm., 2002—. Instr. Ga. Inst. Tech., 1988-90. Contbr. articles to publs.; editor of newsletter Human Relations com. Ga. Inst. Tech., 1989-90, editor 1995— Mem. AIDS Task Force, Ga. Inst. Tech. Recipient Writing award Women's Press Club, 1979. Democrat. Avocations: tennis, running, swimming, bicycling.

GRINDLAY, JONATHAN ELLIS, astrophysics educator; b. Richmond, Va., Nov. 9, 1944; s. John Happer and Elizabeth (Ellis) G.; m. Sandra Kay Smyrski, Oct. 10, 1970; children: Graham Charles, Kathryn Jane. AB, Dartmouth Coll., 1966; MA, Harvard U., 1969, PhD, 1971. Jr. fellow Harvard U., Cambridge, Mass., 1971-74, asst. prof., 1976-81, prof. astronomy, 1981—2001, Robert Treat Paine prof. astronomy, 2001—, chmn. dept. astronomy, 1985—90, 2001—03; astrophysicist Smithsonian Obs., 1974—76. Cons. MIT Lincoln Lab., Bedford, Mass., 1982—; mem. vis. com. astronomy U. Chgo., 1983, Astrophys. Lab. Saclay, France, 1988—, NASA/Goddard Space Flight Ctr., 1995—96, chmn., 1997; mem. vis. com. dept. physics Columbia U., 1998; mem. vis. com. Naval Rsch. Lab., 1998; mem. vis. com. dept. astronomy and space physics Rice U., 1999; mem. users com. Cerro Tololo Interam. Obs., La Serena, Chile, 1981—84; mem. Aspen Ctr. for Physics, Colo., 1991—2001, trustee, 1989—90; chmn. high energy astrophysics mgmt. ops. group NASA, 1986—88; mem. users com. Compton Gamma Ray Obs., 1992—94; chair users com. NASA High Energy Astrophysics Sci. Archive Ctr., 2000—02; mem. space sci. bd. NAS, 1986—89; mem. com. astronomy and astrophysics NRC, 1992—98, mem. com. on internat. programs, 1996—98, mem. high energy astronomy forum space panel, 1998—99; mem. Space Telescope Inst. Coun., 1993—96, 1989—90, Space Telescope Ind. Sci. Rev. Com., 1996—97; chmn. binary panel Space Telescope Cycle 7 Time Allocation Commn.; chmn. space sci. working group AAU, 1990—92; mem. sci. orgn. com. for numerous internat. mtgs.; mem. NASA Space Sci. Adv. Commn., 2003—; chmn. Gamma-Ray Large Area Space Telescope Users Com., 2004—. Contbr. articles to profl. jours. and books. Recipient Bart J. Bok prize dept. astronomy Harvard U., 1976; NSF and NASA rsch. grantee, 1978—; Guggenheim fellow, 1991-93, Sloan fellow, 1981-84. Fellow: AAAS, Am. Astron. Soc. (high energy divsn. nat. sec.-treas. 1982—84, councilor 1989—90, nat. v.p. 1994—97, nat. vice chair 2000—02, nat. chair 2002—04), Am. Phys. Soc. (nat. chair divsn. astrophysics 1998—99); mem.: Internat. Astron. Union (pres. commn. 6 1991—94, organizing com. 1997—). Home: 195 Lincoln Rd Lincoln MA 01773-4102 Office: Harvard-Smithsonian Ctr Astrophysics 60 Garden St Cambridge MA 02138-1516 Office Phone: 617-495-7204. Business E-Mail: jgrindlay@cfa.harvard.edu.

GRINDLEY, BRUCE ALAN, real estate agency executive; b. Woking, England, Mar. 1, 1948; s. Ernest and Ivy (Mummery) G.; children: Andrée, Paul. Brokerage clk. Leslie & Godwin, Lloyds Brokers, London, 1965-67; from enquiry clk. to br. mgr. Abbey Life, London, Croydon, Crawley, England, 1967-86; dir. Sunway Properties, Tenerife, Spain, 1986-94, Tenerife Property Shop, 1994—. Recipient Winner Best Internat. Estate Agt. Gold award 1996-, Best Internat. Residential Estate Agent, 1997-, Best Spanish Estate Agent Gold award, 1998-99, 99-2000, 2001-, 2002-, Best Property Website award, 2000, 2002-03, Safe Home award, 2000, Best Property Advt., 2001-02, Best Internat. Estate Agt., 2002-, Five Star award Best Property Adv., 2003, Five Star award Best Spl. Estate Agt, 2004 Fellow Life Ins. Assn.; mem. Internat. Real Estate Inst., Nat. Assn. Estate Agts., Liga Internat. de Representacion y Agencia Comml., Coll. Ofcl. Agts. Comml., The Personal Fin. Soc. (life). Office: Tenerife Property Shop SL 117 Puerto Colon Playa de las Americas Adeje Tenerife Spain Office Phone: 34-922-714700. E-mail: info@tenerifepropertyshop.com.

GRINDSTAFF, GENE ARTHUR, engineer, information scientist; b. Banner Elk, NC, Dec. 27, 1947; s. Charles Thomas and Nancy Louise Grindstaff; m. Linda Sue Usrey, June 18, 1971; children: Jennifer Marie Ellis, Heather Lynn Murphy. BS, Tenn Tech U., 1969, MS, 1973. Cert. metrologist, USAF, 1972. Assoc. engr. Tex. Instruments, Dallas, 1975—77; CAD/CAM mgr. Arnold AFB, Tullahoma, Tenn., 1977—84; chief scientist Intergraph Corp., Huntsville, Ala., 1984—. Contbr. articles to profl. jours. Poll watcher trainer Rep. Party, Morgan County, Ala., 1992—2005. Staff sgt. USAF, 1971—75, SJ AFB, Goldsboro, NC. Named to Space Tech. Hall of Fame, Nat. Space Symposium, 2001. Mem.: IEEE (assoc.). Republican. Ch. Of Christ. Avocations: radio, plasma physics. Home: 2202 Essex Dr SW Decatur AL 35603 Office: Intergraph Corp 170 Graphics Dr Madison AL 35758 Office Fax: 256-730-2424. Personal E-mail: gagrinds@yahoo.com. Business E-Mail: gene.grindstaff@intergraph.com.

GRINELL, SHEILA, museum director; b. N.Y.C., July 15, 1945; d. Richard N. and Martha (Mimiless) G.; m. Thomas E. Johnson, July 15, 1980; 1 child, Michael; stepchildren: Kathleen, Thomas. BA, Radcliffe Coll., 1966; MA, U. Calif., Berkeley, 1968. Co-dir. exhibits and programs The Exploratorium, San Francisco, 1969-74; promotion dir. Kodansha Internat., Tokyo, 1974-77; traveling exhbn. coord. Assn. Sci. Tech. Ctrs., Washington, 1978-80, exec. dir., 1980-82, project dir. traveling exhbn. Chips and Changes, 1982-84; assoc. dir. N.Y. Hall of Sci., 1984-87; pres., CEO Ariz. Sci. Ctr., Phoenix, 1993—. Cons. Optical Soc. Am., 1987, Nat. Sci. Ctr. Found., 1988, Interactive Video Sci. Consortium, 1988, Assn. Sci. Tech. Ctrs., 1988-89, Found. for Creative Am., 1989-90, Am. Assn. for World Health, 1990, Children's TV Workshop, 1991, Sciencenter, 1991, SciencePort, 1991, The Invention Factory, 1992, N.Y. Bot. Garden, 1992-93. Author: Light, Sight, Sound, Hearing: Exploratorium '74, 1974; editor A Stage for Science, 1979, A New Place for Learning Science: Starting and Running A Science Center, 1992, 2d edit., 2003, (with Mark St. John) Vision to Reality: Critical Dimensions in Science Center Development, Vol. I, 1993, II, 1994. Fulbright teaching asst., 1966; hon. Woodrow Wilson fellow, 1967 Fellow AAAS; mem. Am. Assn. Mus., Phi Beta Kappa. Office: Ariz Sci Ctr 600 E Washington St Phoenix AZ 85004-2303 Office Phone: 602-716-2010. E-mail: grinells@azscience.org.

GRINER, G. CHRISTOPHER, lawyer; BA, Lehigh U., 1971; JD, Rutgers U., 1973. Bar: Pa. 1973, DC 1976. Atty. advisor Office of Gen. Counsel, Dept. of Defense, 1973—77; mng. ptnr. Kaye Scholer LLP, Washington, DC. Mem.: Pa. Bar Assn., DC Bar. Office: Kaye Scholer LLP McPherson Bldg 901 Fifteenth St, NW, Ste 1100 Washington DC 20005 Office Phone: 202-682-3619. E-mail: cgriner@kayescholer.com.

GRINER, PAUL FRANCIS, physician; b. Phila., Jan. 1, 1933; s. John and Josepha (Snyder) G.; m. Miriam Millard; children: Laura, Paul Jr. BA, Harvard U., 1954; MD with honors, U. Rochester, 1959. Diplomate Am. Bd. Internal Medicine, Nat. Bd. Med. Examiners. Intern in medicine Mass. Gen. Hosp., Boston, 1959-60, asst. resident, 1960-61, sr. resident, 1963-64; chief resident in medicine Strong Meml. Hosp., Rochester, N.Y., 1964-65; fellow in pathology U. Rochester Sch. Medicine & Dentistry, 1956-57, instr. medicine, fellow in hematology, 1964-65, clin. instr., 1965-66, clin. sr. instr., 1966-67, asst. prof. medicine, 1967-69, assoc. prof., 1969-73, Samuel E. Durand prof. medicine, 1973-95, head. gen. medicine unit, 1976-84, acting chmn. dept. medicine, 1977-79, chmn. dept. health svcs., 1985-94; gen. dir. Strong Meml. Hosp., 1984-95; v.p. Assn. Am. Med. Colls., Washington, 1995-2000. Dir. med. edn. Rochester Gen. Hosp., 1965—67, cons., 1969—95, Genesee Hosp., 1969—95, Highland Hosp., 1969—95; chmn. bd. dirs. Acad. Med. Ctr. Consortium, 1991—92; emeritus prof. medicine U. Rochester Sch. Medicine and Dentistry; sr. fellow Inst. for Healthcare Improvement, 2002—. Contbr. numerous articles to profl. jours., chpts. to books. Mem. N.Y. Gov.'s Health Care Adv. Bd., 1990-94, Mayoral Commn. on Health and Hosps. Corp. of City of N.Y., 1991-92. Capt. USAF, 1961-63. Decorated Air Force Commendation medal; recipient Doran Stephens prize, U. Rochester, 1959. Master: ACP (mem. health and pub. policy com. 1981—84, 1987—88, chmn. 1988—90, chmn. bd. regents 1991—92, chmn. clin. efficacy assessment subcom. 1986—88, pres. 1993—94); mem.: Inst. Medicine Nat. Acad. Scis. (com. quality rev. and assurance in Medicare 1987—90, mem. bd. healthcare svcs. 1987—2000, mem. com. on future primary care 1994—95), Soc. Med. Adminstrs., So. Gen. Internal Medicine Soc., Assn. Am. Physicians, Am. Clin. and Climatol. Assn., Alpha Omega Alpha. Avocations: skiing, golf, surf fishing, travel.

GRINNAN, KATIE, artist; b. Richmond, Va., 1970; Attended, Studio Arts Ctr. Internat., Florence, Italy, 1991; BFA in Painting, Carnegie Mellon U., 1992; attended, Skowhega Sch. Painting & Sculpture, Skowhegan Maine, 1992; MFA in Sculpture, UCLA, 1999. One-woman shows include Rock Bottom, ACME, L.A., 2001, 2003, Whitney Mus. Am. Art at Altria, 2003, exhibited in group shows at UCLA MFA Thesis Exhbn., New Wight Gallery, LA, 1998, As I love you you become more pretty, 937 Hudson Ave., LA, 2000, Legal Paper Work, Beyond Baroque, LA, 2000, katie grinnan alice konitz christie frields, Guggenheim Gallery, Chapman U., Calif., 2000, Snapshot, UCLA Hammer Mus., 2001, Sharing Sunsets, Mus. Contemporary Art, Tucson, 2001, Bommerang: Collector's Choice, Exit Art, NYC, 2001, Anti-Form, Soc. Contemporary Photog., Kans. City, Mo., 2002, Officina Am., Galeria D'Arte Monderna, Bologna, Italy, 2002, Drive-By, Reynolds Gallery, Richmond, Va., 2002, Strolling Through an Ancient Shrine & Garden, ACME, LA, 2002, Out of the Ground Into the Sky Out of the Sky Into the Ground, Pond, San Francisco, 2002, Wit Form Rainbow (Part I), The Project, LA, 2003, Whitney Biennial, Whitney Mus. Am. Art, NYC, 2004, Material Faith, Kontainer Gallery, LA, 2004, Real World: Dissolving Space of Experience, Modern Art Oxford, England, 2004, Art on Paper, Weatherspoon Art Mus., U. NC, 2004. Mailing: c/o ACME 6150 Wilshire Blvd #1 Los Angeles CA 90048*

GRINNELL, ALAN DALE, neuroscientist, educator; b. Mpls., Nov. 11, 1936; s. John Erle and Swanhild Constance (Friswold) G.; m. Verity Rich, Sept. 30, 1962 (div. 1975); m. Feelie Lee, Dec. 23, 1996. BA, Harvard U., 1958, PhD, 1962. Jr. fellow Harvard U., 1959-62; research assoc. biophysics dept. Univ. Coll. London, 1962-64; asst. research zoologist UCLA, 1964-65, from asst. prof. to prof. dept. biology, 1965-78, prof. physiology, 1972—; dir. Jerry Lewis Neuromuscular Research Ctr. UCLA Sch. Medicine, 1978—2003; head Ahmanson Lab. Cellular Neurobiology UCLA Brain Research Inst, 1977—; dir. tng. grant in cellular neurobiology UCLA, 1968—, rsch. assoc. Fowler Mus. Cultural History, 1990—, chmn. dept. physiol. sci., 1997—2001. Author: Calcium and Ion Channel Modulation, 1988, Physiology of Excitable Cells, 1983, Regulation of Muscle Contraction, 1981, Introduction to Nervous Systems, 1977, others; contbr. editorial revs. to profl. jours., pub. houses, fed. granting agys. Guggenheim fellow, 1986; recipient Sr. Scientist award Alexander von Humboldt Stiftung, 1975, 79, Jacob Javits award NIH, 1986. Mem. AAAS (mem.-at-large neurosci. steering group 1998-2002), Muscular Dystrophy Assn. (mem. med. adv. com. L.A. chpt. 1980-92), Soc. for Neurosci. (councilor 1982-86), Am. Physiol. Soc. (mem. neurophysiol. steering com. 1981-84), Soc. Fellow, Phi Beta Kappa, Sigma Xi, others. Avocations: music, anthropology, archaeology, travel. Home: 510 E Rustic Rd Santa Monica CA 90402-1116 Office: UCLA Sch Medicine Dept Physiology Los Angeles CA 90095-0001 Office Phone: 310-825-4468.

GRINNELL, HELEN DUNN, musicologist, arts administrator; b. N.Y.C., Nov. 22, 1936; d. Kempton and Susan Barret (Gill) Dunn; m. Alexander Grinnell; children: Taylor, James Bodman. Ed., New Eng. Conservatory, 1957-60; BMus in Music Theory, San Francisco Conservatory, 1968; MA in Musicology, Am. U., 1982. Dir. Opera and Symphony Previews, San Francisco, 1966-67; arts coord. Del. State Arts Coun., 1977-78; mgr. Performing Arts Libr. Am. U., 1981-84; pres. Music Info. Specialists, 1984—. Cons. Met. Mus. Art, 1996—, China Inst. in Am., 1999, Carnegie Hall, 2000—; vis. com. Mus. Fine Arts, Boston, 2002—. Author: Chinese Musical Inconography: A History of Musical Instruments Depicted in Chinese Art, 1987; program annotator Dumbarton Concert Series, Smithsonian Instn., Kennedy Ctr., Stagebill; editor: Am. Women Composers' Forum, 1986—88; contbr. Orientations, Music in Art, 1995—. Steering com. Friends of Music Smithsonian Instn., 1978—88; pres. Cambridge Music Assn., 2004—; mem. adv. bd. East-West Music Exch. Assn., 2000—; bd. dirs. Nat. Sympony Orch., Washington, 1979—82, Nat. Orchestral Assn., 1993—95, Spring Opera San Francisco, 1967—71, Jr. League of San Francisco, 1967—71, Wilmington Music Sch., 1973—78, Washington Performing Arts Soc., 1980—90, Bargemusic Ltd., N.Y.C., 1992—94, Shelter Island Hist. Soc., 1993—95, New Eng. Conservatory Alumni Coun., 1994—; bd. overseers New Eng. Conservatory, 1985—90; bd. dirs. Cape Cod Chamber Music Festival, 2000—; chair acad. policy com., trustee San Francisco Conservatory of Music, 1967—71; chair archtl. rev. bd. Village of Dering Harbor, NY, 1991—95; mem. adv. bd. East-West Music Exch. Assn., 2000—. Mem. Am. Musical Instruments Soc., Am. Musicol. Soc., Soc. Ethnomusicology, Cambridge Mus. Assn. (pres. 2003—), Cosmopolitan Club.

GRINNELL, JOSEPH FOX, lawyer; b. July 4, 1923; s. Robert L. and Mary King G.; m. Marjorie Volwiler, Aug. 24, 1946; children: Stephen F., Christine K. Burcham, James W. BA, Yale U., 1945; JD, Northwestern U., 1949. Bar: Ill. 1949, U.S. Dist. Ct. (no. dist.) Ill. 1949, Minn. 1954. Assoc. Winston-Strawn, Chgo., 1949-54; sr. v.p. law Investors Diversified Svcs., Mpls., 1954-83; of counsel Pepin Dayton Herman Graham & Getts, Mpls., 1983-87. Bd. dirs. Guthrie Theater, Mpls., 1970-71, Minn. Orch. Assn., Mpls., 1976-78; bd. dirs., chmn. Minn. Pollution Control Agy., Mpls., 1973-81. Served to lt. (j.g.) USN, 1942-46, PTO. Democrat. Presbyterian. Home: 8155 Parkview Ln Bloomington MN 55438 Personal E-mail: jo-margie@msn.com.

GRINNEY, JAY, health facility company executive; b. Racine, Wis., Mar. 20, 1951; s. Leo Richard and June Louise (Christensen) G.; children: Naomi Hope, Rachel June, Matthew Jay; m. Ellen Heath, May 4, 1988. BA in Psychology, St. Olaf Coll., 1973; Master's in Hosp. Adminstrn., Washington U., St. Louis, 1981; MBA, Washington U., 1981. Adminstrv. resident The Methodist Hosp. System, Houston, 1982-83, asst. v.p., 1982-84, sr. v.p., 1985; CEO, Rosewood Med. Ctr. HCA Healthcare Co., Houston, 1990—92, COO, Houston region, 1992—93, pres., Houston region, 1993—96, pres. Ea. group Nashville, 1996—2004; pres., CEO HealthSouth Corp., Birmingham, 2004—. Treas., bd. dirs. The People's Community Clinic, St. Louis, 1979-81; adj. instr. Washington U., Houston, 1988—. Mem. allocations com. Houston United Way, 1988. Mem. Am. Coll. Healthcare Execs. (mem. regent's adv. coun. 1986—), Am. Hosp. Assn., Tex. Hosp. Assn., Greater Houston Hosp. Coun. (fin. com. 1985). Avocations: weightlifting, running, skiing, horseback riding. Office: HealthSouth Corp One HealthSouth Pkwy Birmingham AL 35243

GRINSHPAN, ARCADII ZAKAROVICH, mathematician; b. St. Petersburg, Russia, Nov. 28, 1945; s. Zahar Lazarevich and Lidiya Aronovna (Rabinovich) G.; m. Asya Markovna Margolina, June 5, 1970; 1 child, Anatolii. MS in Math. summa cum laude, St. Petersburg U., Leningrad, 1969, PhD in Math., 1973. Rschr., mathematician Sci. and Prodn. Union for Fuel Sys. of Engines (CNITA), St. Petersburg, 1969-76, sr. rschr., mathematician, 1976-91; leading rschr. Russian Acad. Scis., Internat. Environ. Coop. (INENCO), St. Petersburg, 1991—. Vis. prof. U. South Fla., Tampa, 1992—. Reviewer Math. Rev. of Am. Math. Soc., 1983—; contbr. articles to profl. jours. With Russian Navy, 1964-65. Mem. Am. Math. Soc., St. Petersburg (Russia) Math. Soc., SAE Internat. (The Engring. Soc. for Advancing Mobility Land, Sea, Air and Space). Home: Slava prospect h 16 f66 Saint Petersburg Russia 192071 Office: Russian Acad Scis INENCO 4 Chernomorskii Ln Saint Petersburg 190000 Russia Address: Univ So Fla Math Dept 4202 E Fowler Ave Tampa FL 33620-8000

GRINSTEIN, GERALD, air transportation executive; b. 1932; m. Lyn Grinstein; 4 children. BA, Yale U., 1954; LL.B., Harvard U., 1957. Bar: (D.C.), (Wash.). Counsel to merchant marine and transp. subcoms., chief counsel U.S. Senate Commerce Com., Washington, D.C., 1958-67; adminstrv. asst. U.S. Senator Warren G. Magnuson, Washington, D.C., 1967-69; ptnr. Preston Thorgrimson Ellis & Holman, 1969-83; chmn. bd. Western Air Lines Inc., Los Angeles, 1983-84, pres., COO, 1984-85, CEO, 1985-86, chmn., CEO, 1986-87; vice chmn. Burlington Northern Inc., Ft. Worth, 1987-88; pres., CEO Burlington Northern, Inc., Ft. Worth, 1989-90, chmn., CEO, 1990-95; pres., CEO, Burlington No. R.R. Co., 1989-90; chmn., CEO Burlington Northern R.R. Co., 1990-95; chmn. Delta Air Lines, Inc., 1997-99, also bd. dirs.; chmn. Agilent Techs., 1999—2002; CEO Delta Air Lines, Inc., 2004—. Bd. dirs. Paccar, Inc., Vans Inc., Delta Air Lines, 1987—, Brinks Co. Office: Delta Airlines 1030 Delta Blvd Dept 940 Atlanta GA 30354-1989*

GRINTER, DONALD W., metal processing executive; b. 1936; married BA, Mich. State U., 1961, MBA, 1962. With Borg-Warner Corp., 1962-81; v.p. Abex Corp., Stamford, Conn., from 1981, exec. v.p., 1984—87, also bd. dirs.; pres. supermarket group Hussmann Corp., 1987—89; chmn., CEO ABC Rail Products Corp., 1991—2000; chmn. ABC-NACO Inc., 1999—2000, bd. dirs., 1991—; sr. advisor Whitestone Assocs. LLC. Office: 100 Centershore Rd Northport NY 11768*

GRIPE, ALAN GORDON, minister; b. Indpls., Sept. 8, 1920; s. Otto Herman and Bertha (Anderson) G.; m. Elizabeth Howell, Sept. 29, 1951 (div. 1972); children: Stephen, David. BA, Lake Forest (Ill.) Coll., 1942; BD, Princeton Theol. Sem., 1946; STM, Union Theol. Sem., N.Y.C., 1953. Ordained to ministry, Presbyn. Ch. (U.S.A.), 1946. Asst. prof. Silliman U., Dumaguete City, Philippines, 1946-50; chaplain Davidson Coll., NC, 1951-52; asst. chaplain U.S. Mil. Acad., West Point, 1952-55; pastor First Presbyn. Ch., Westfield, NY, 1955-65; exec. coord. Personnel Svcs., United Presbyn. Ch. USA, 1965-88; interim pastor Genesee Valley Presbytery, Rochester, NY, 1991-99, acting exec. presbyter, 2001—02, ret., 2002; clergy visitor Strong Meml. Hosp., Rochester, NY, 1999—2002. Author: The Interim Pastor's Manual, rev. edit., 1997. Treas. John Milton Soc. for Blind, N.Y.C., 1988-90. Mem. Assn. of Presbyn. Interim Ministry Specialists (coun. mem. 1987-90). Home: 95 Penarrow Rd Rochester NY 14618-1721

GRIPPI, SALVATORE WILLIAM, artist; b. Buffalo, Sept. 30, 1921; s. Leonardo and Josephine (Orlando) G.; m. Rosalind Ratzenberg, Apr. 14, 1945. Student, Mus. Modern Art, N.Y.C., 1944—45, Art Students' League, 1945—48, Atelier 17, 1951—53, Instituto Statale d'Arte, Florence, Italy, 1953—55. Instr. Atelier 17, summer 1953, Cooper Union Art Sch., 1956-59, Sch. Visual Arts, N.Y.C., 1961-62; assoc. prof. art Claremont Grad. Sch., 1962-68, Pomona Coll., 1962-68; prof., founder art dept. Ithaca (NY) Coll., 1968—. Invited participant Ford Found. Conf. Visual Artists, 1961. One-man shows include, NYU, N.Y.C., 1958, Zabriskie Gallery, N.Y.C., 1956, 59, Krasner Gallery, N.Y.C., 1962, 64, 79, 81, Feingarten Galleries, 1967, 70, Everson, Mus., Syracuse, N.Y., 1978, Handwerker Gallery, Ithaca Coll., 1978, group shows include, Met. Mus. Art, N.Y.C., 1952, Schneider Gallery, Rome, 1954, Galleria La Fontanella, Rome, 1955, Whitney Mus. and Smithsonian Inst. Traveling show, 1958-59, Corcoran Gallery Art, Washington, 1959, 63, Whitney Mus., N.Y.C., 1960, Mus. Modern Art, N.Y.C., 1962, 1994-95, Hunter Coll. Leubsdorf Gallery, N.Y.C., 1995; represented in permanent collections, Whitney Mus., Met. Mus. Art, N.Y. Pub. Libr., N.Y.C., Joseph Hirshorn Collection, Washington, Milw.-Downer Coll., Ithaca Coll., St. Lawrence U., Everson Mus., Annex Gallery, Santa Rosa, Calif. Served with USNR, 1942-45. Fulbright grantee, Instituto Statale d'Arte, 1953—55. Mem. Art Students' League (life, treas. 1961-62, bd. control 1961-64), Coll. Art Assn. Home: 9 Orchard Hill Rd Ithaca NY 14850 Office: Ithaca Coll Art Dept Ithaca NY 14850

GRISCHKOWSKY, DANIEL RICHARD, research scientist, educator; b. St. Helens, Oreg., Apr. 17, 1940; s. Oscar Edward and Christine Hazel (Olsen) G.; m. Frieda Rosa Bachmann; children: Timothy and Stephanie (twins), Daniela BS, Oreg. State U., 1962; AM in Physics, Columbia U., 1965, PhD in Physics, 1968. Postdoctoral studies Columbia U., N.Y.C., 1968-69; mem. rsch. staff IBM Watson Rsch. Ctr., Yorktown Heights, N.Y., 1969-77; sci. advisor to dir. rsch. div. IBM, Yorktown Heights, 1978; mgr. atomic physics with lasers group IBM Watson Rsch. Ctr., Yorktown Heights, 1979-83, mgr. ultra-fast sci. with lasers group, 1983-93; Regents prof., Bellmon chair optoelectronics Sch. Elec. and Computer Engring. Okla. State U., Stillwater, 1993—. Chmn. Internat. Coun. on Quantum Electronics, 1989-93, Am. Phys. Soc./Optical Soc. Am./IEEE Joint Coun. on Quantum Electronics, 1989-93. Contbr. articles to profl. jours.; patentee in field. Recipient Boris Pregel award N.Y. Acad. of Sci., 1985. Fellow IEEE, Am. Phys. Soc. (chmn. laser sci. topical group 1993-94), Optical Soc. Am. (R.W. Wood prize 1989, William F. Meggers award 2003). Office: Okla State U Sch Elec Computer Engring Stillwater OK 74078-0001 Business E-Mail: grischd@ceat.okstate.edu.

GRISEZ, JAMES LOUIS, physician, plastic surgeon; b. Modesto, Calif., Feb. 25, 1935; s. John Francis and Josephine Marie (Tournahu) G.; m. Diane Madeline Skidmore, Mar. 7, 1989; children: James, Stephen, Suzanne, Kathleen. MD, St. Louis Sch. Medicine, 1960. Diplomate Am. Bd. Plastic and Reconstructive Surgery. Intern D.C. Gen. Hosp., Washington, 1960-61;

resident med. ctr. Georgetown U., Washington, 1961-64; resident plastic and reconstructive surgery ctr. St. Francis Meml. Hosp., San Francisco, 1964-66; military surgeon Brook Army Med Ctr., San Antonio, 1966, Second Gen. Hosp., Landstuhl, Germany, 1966-69; pvt. practice Napa, Calif., 1969-82, Salinas, Calif., 1982-90, Kailua-Kona, Hawaii, 1990-93, South Valley Plastic Surgery, Gilroy, Calif., 1993—. Active staff mem. St. Louise Regional Hosp.; chief of staff South Valley Hosp., Hazel Hawkins; chief staff St. Helena Hosp., 1977-78, exec. com. 1973-80; radio talk show host All About Plastic Surgery, sta. KRNY, 1986-88. Contbr. articles to med. jours. Mem. Am. Cancer Soc. (pres. 1988-90), Am. Soc. Plastic Surgeons, Calif. Soc. Plastic and Reconstructive Surgeons, Hawaii Plastic Surgery Soc. Home: 1595 Chesapeake Pl Arroyo Grande CA 93420 Office: 354 South Halcyon Rd Ste C Arroyo Grande CA 93420 Personal E-mail: jgrisez5@cs.com.

GRISHAM, JOE WHEELER, cell biologist, educator; b. Smith County, Tenn., Dec. 5, 1931; s. William Wince and Grace (Allen) G.; m. Jean Evelyn Malone, July 2, 1955. BA, Vanderbilt U., 1953, MD, 1957. Intern Washington U.-Barnes Hosp., St. Louis, 1957-58, resident in pathology, 1958-60; mem. faculty Washington U., Med. Sch., 1960-73; prof. pathology and anatomy Washington U. Med. Sch., 1969-73; assoc. pathologist Barnes Hosp., 1969-73; vis. instr. Makerere Med. Coll., Kampala, Uganda, 1961; prof. pathology, chmn. dept. U. N.C. Med. Sch., Chapel Hill, 1973-99; also pathologist-in-chief U. N.C. Hosp., Chapel Hill, 1973-99; Kenan prof. U. N.C. Med. Sch., Chapel Hill, 1992—2003; sr. scientist Nat. Cancer Inst., Bethesda, 2003—. Bd. sci. counsellors Nat. Inst. Environ. Health Scis., 1974-78; mem. sci. advisory panel Chem. Industry Inst. Toxicology, 1977-88, chmn., 1980-88; adv. bd. Given Inst. Pathobiology, 1983-87; mem. pathology study sect. A NIH, 1969-73, chmn. 1970-73, chmn. pathology study sect. B, 1979-83; lectr. in field. Contbr. articles to med. jours. Served to lt. comdr. USNR, 1961-63. Fogarty scholar NCI/NIH, 2000—02; John and Mary R. Markle scholar Acad. Medicine, 1964-69; fellow Life Ins. Med. Rsch. Fund, 1959-61, Nat. Cancer Inst., 1958-59; Brindley prof. U. Tex. Med. Br., 1993; named Disting. Med. Alumnus Vanderbilt U., 1994; named to Order of Long Leaf Pine, State of N.C., 1996. Mem. Am. Assn. Pathologists (pres. 1984-85), Am. Assn. Cancer Research, Fedn. Am. Soc. Exptl. Biology (pres., chmn. bd. 1984-85), Am. Assn. Study Liver Diseases, Am. Soc. Cell Biology, Univ. Assn. Rsch. and Edn. in Pathology (v.p. 1985-86), Tissue Culture Assn., Internat. Acad. Pathology, Cell Kinetics Soc., AMA, AAAS. Home: 1703 Curtis Rd Chapel Hill NC 27514-7614 Office: Lab Expl Carcinogensis CRC NCI NIH Bldg 37 Rm 4146A 37 Convent Dr MSC 4262 Bethesda MD 20892-4262

GRISHAM, JOHN, writer; b. Jonesboro, Ark., Feb. 8, 1955; m. Renee Jones; children: Ty, Shea. BS, Miss. State U., 1977; JD, U. Miss., 1981. Bar: Miss. 1981. Practiced law, Southaven, Miss., 1981-91; mem. Miss. Ho. Reps., 1984-90. Author: A Time to Kill, 1989, The Firm, 1991, The Pelican Brief, 1992, The Client, 1993, The Chamber, 1994, The Rainmaker, 1995, The Runaway Jury, 1996, The Partner, 1997, The Street Lawyer, 1998, The Testament, 1999, The Brethren, 2000, A Painted House, 2001, The Summons, 2002, Skipping Christmas, 2002, The King of Torts, 2003, Bleachers, 2003, The Last Juror, 2004, The Broker, 2005; (screenplay) The Gingerbread Man, 1998. Office: Doubleday Pub 1540 Broadway New York NY 10036-4039 Address: c/o Agent David Gernert 18th Fl 136 E 57th St New York NY 10022

GRISHAM, LARRY RICHARD, physicist; b. Henderson, Tex., Feb. 2, 1949; s. James Marion and Eva Fay Grisham; m. Jacqueline Lea Criswell, June 24, 1972; children: Austin Nathanial, Rachel Nicole, Hilary Jane. BS in Physics, U. Tex., 1971; PhD in Physics, Oxford (Eng.) U., 1974. Postdoctoral fellow Plasma Physics Lab. Princeton (NJ) U., 1974—75, staff rsch. physicist, 1975—82, rsch. physicist, 1982—89, prin. rsch. physicist, 1989—, head beam physics, 1988—. Cons. Northrop Corp., L.A., 1985, Phys. Dynamics, La Jolla, Calif., 1986-88, Teledyne Brown Engring., Huntsville, Ala., 1989—; mem. and chmn. various rev. panels U.S. Army Strategic Def. Command, 1986—. Contbr. numerous articles to profl. jours. Mem. NJ Rhodes Scholar Selection Com., Morristown, 1986—. Recipient Tex. Exes Centennial Honored Alumnus award U. Tex., Austin, 1985, Wolfson Grad. award, 1972, Kaul Found. prize for excellence in plasma physics and tech. devel., 2001; winner Westinghouse Sci. Talent Search, Washington, 1967; Rhodes scholar, 1971; Woodrow Wilson fellow, 1971, invited rsch. fellow Japan Atomic Energy Rsch. Inst., 1996. Methodist. Achievements include research in energy confinement properties of tokamak plasmas as a fuction of major and minor radius; physics and technology of high power neutral beam systems physics of excited nuclear states. Home: 2 Dennick Ct Princeton NJ 08540-2202 Office: Princeton Univ Plasma Physics Lab PO Box 451 Princeton NJ 08543-0451

GRISKEY, RICHARD GEORGE, chemical engineering professor; b. Pitts., Jan. 9, 1931; s. George and Emma (Maskell) G.; m. Pauline Anne Becker, June 11, 1955; children: Paula Louise, David Richard. BChemE, Carnegie-Mellon U., 1951, MChemE, 1955, PhD, 1958. Registered profl. engr., Wis. Sr. engr. E. I. duPont Co., Seaford, Del., 1958-60; asst. prof. U. Cin., 1960-62; assoc. prof. Va. Poly. Inst., 1962-64, prof., 1964-66; prof., head chem. engring. dept. U. Denver, 1966-68; dir. rsch. and found. rsch. prof. Newark Coll. Engring., 1968-71; prof. chem. engring., dean U. Wis., Milw., 1971-82; prof. chem. engring., dean engring. U. Ala., Huntsville, 1982-85; v.p., provost Stevens Inst. Tech., 1985-86, exec. v.p., provost, 1986-88, The Institute prof. chemistry and chem. engring., 1988—. Vis. scientist Polish Acad. Sci.-NAS, 1971; OAS vis. prof. Multi Nat. Food Project, Brazil, 1973; vis. prof. Monash U., Australia, 1974, Algerian Inst. Petroleum, 1975-76; cons. in field. Editor, Marcel Dekker Inc., 1974—; referee, reviewer: Canadian Jour. Chem. Engring., Am. Inst. Chem. Engrs. Jour., Jour. Polymer Sci., Jour. Fluid Mechanics, Jour. Heat Transfer; author: Chemical Engineering for Chemists, 1997; author: Polymer Process Engineering, 1995, Chemical Engineers Portable Handbook, 2000, Transport Phenomena and Unit Operations, 2001; contbr. articles to profl. jours. With AUS, 1951-53. Fellow ASME, Am. Inst. Chemists, Am. Inst. Chem. Engrs.; mem. Soc. Rheology, Am. Soc. Engring. Edn., Am. Assn. Higher Edn., Plastics Inst. Am. (bd. dirs. 1986—), Soc. Plastics Engrs., Am. Chem. Soc. (congl. counselor, Exceptional Achievement award 1991), Tau Beta Pi, Sigma Xi, Triangle, Scabbard and Blade. Office: Stevens Inst Tech Dept Chem & Chem Engring Hoboken NJ 07030

GRISMORE, ROGER, physics professor, researcher; b. Ann Arbor, Mich., July 12, 1924; s. Grover Cleveland and May Aileen (White) G.; m. Marilynn Ann McNinch, Sept. 15, 1950; 1 child, Carol Ann. BS, U. Mich., 1947, MS, 1948, PhD, 1957; BS in Computer Sci., Coleman Coll., 1979. From asst. to assoc. physicist Argonne (Ill.) Nat. Lab., 1956-62; assoc. prof. physics Lehigh U., Bethlehem, Pa., 1962-67; specialist in physics Scripps Inst. Oceanography, La Jolla, Calif., 1967-71, 75-78; prof. physics Ind. State U., Terre Haute, 1971-74; from mem. staff to sr. scientist JAYCOR, San Diego, 1979-84; lectr. Calif. Poly. State U., San Luis Obispo, 1984-92, rsch. prof., 1992—, lunar sample investigator, 1994—. Contbr. numerous articles to profl. jours. Served as ensign USNR, 1945-46, PTO. Mem. Am. Phys. Soc., Am. Geophys. Union, N.Y. Acad. Scis., Sigma Xi. Achievements include co-discovery of the radioisotope silver-108m in the general marine environment, and development of the technique of radiosilver dating. Home: 535 Cameo Way Arroyo Grande CA 93420-5574 Office: Calif Poly State U Dept Physics San Luis Obispo CA 93407 Office Phone: 805-756-2424. Personal E-mail: r_grismore@charter.net.

GRISSOM, GARTH CLYDE, lawyer, director; b. Syracuse, Kans., Jan. 24, 1930; s. Clyde and Bernice Minnie (Eddy) Grissom; m. Elena Joyce Kerst, Aug. 17, 1958; children: Colin, Grady, Cole, Kent. BS, Kans. State U., 1951; LLB, Harvard U., 1957. Bar: Colo. 1957, U.S. Dist. Ct. (fed. dist.) Colo., 1957, U.S. Ct. Appeals (10th cir.) 1957, U.S. Supreme Ct. 1989. Ptnr., mem., counsel Sherman & Howard, L.L.C., Denver, 1963—. Sec., counsel, trustee Mile High United Way, Denver, 1985-88; trustee Kans. State U. Found., Manhattan, 1962-89; mem. Colo. Gov.'s Commn. on Life and the Law, 1990-99, chmn., 1996-99. Mem. ABA, Colo. Bar Assn., Denver Bar Assn. (pres. 1985-86, award of merit 1994), Rotary (sec. Denver 1983-84, bd. dirs. 1983-86, pres. 1989-90), Pi Kappa Alpha (pres. 1968-70). Home: 1777 Larimer St Apt 1610 Denver CO 80202-1548 Office: Sherman & Howard LLC 633 17th St Ste 3000 Denver CO 80202-3665 Office Phone: 303-299-8156. Business E-Mail: ggrissom@sah.com.

GRISSOM, J. DAVID, private investor, bank executive; b. Portsmouth, Ohio, 1939; 3 children. BA, Centre Coll., 1960; LL.B., U. Louisville, 1962. Ptnr. Greenebaum, Grissom, Doll, Matthews & Boone, Louisville, to 1969; exec. v.p., sec. Humana, Inc., until 1969, now dir.; with Citizens Fidelity Corp. (acquired by PNC Fin. Corp.), Louisville, 1973-89, former chmn., former vice chmn., chief exec. officer, also bd. dirs.; chmn., chief exec. officer Citizens Fidelity Bank & Trust Co. (subs. Citizens Fidelity Corp.), Louisville, until 1989, also bd. dirs.; chmn. Mayfair Capital, Louisville, 1989—, The Glenview Trust Co., 2001—. Bd. dirs. Capital Holding Co., Churchill Downs, Louisville Gas & Electric Co., Transco Energy, Yum! Brands, Inc. Chmn., dir. bd. trustees Centre Coll., Ky.; mem. exec. com. Ky. Econ. Devel. Com.; mem. Ky. Coun. Econ. Edn.

GRISSOM, MARQUIS DEON, professional baseball player; b. Atlanta, Apr. 17, 1967; Student, Fla. A & M. Outfielder Montreal Expos, 1988—94; with Atlanta Braves, 1994—97, Milw. Brewers, 1997—2000, L.A. Dodgers, 2001—02, San Francisco Giants, 2002—. Named to All-Star Team, Nat. League, 1993, 1994; recipient Golden Glove award, 1993—96. Achievements include leading the Nat. League in stolen bases, 1991-92. Office: Milwaukee Brewers 1 Briwers Way Milwaukee WI 53214-3651

GRISSOM, MARY ANNE, speech educator; d. Joe Bryan Grissom and Mary Elizabeth Askins. BA, Baylor U., 1968, MA, 1969; PhD, U. North Tex., Denton, 1985. Asst. dir. forensics Calif. State U., Fullerton, 1969—70, San Fernando Valley State Coll., Northridge, Calif., 1970—71; instr. speech comm. El Centro Coll., Dallas, 1971—78; prof. speech comm. Mountain View Coll., Dallas, 1978—. Coord. svc. learning Mountain View Coll., Dallas, 1998—. Mem.: AAUW, Tex. Speech Comm. Assn., Tex. C.C. Tchrs. Assn., Phi Theta Kappa, Phi Delta Kappa. Office: Mountain View Coll 4849 W Illinois Ave Dallas TX 75211 Office Phone: 214-860-8748. E-mail: agrissom@dcccd.edu.

GRISSOM, ROBERT JESSE, SR., retired criminal justice educator; b. Little Rock, June 4, 1927; s. Robert Clarence and Eva Snowden (Downs) G.; m. Mildred Louise Cossey, Aug. 29, 1966; children: Robert Jesse, Eva Dawn, Syble Louise. BS, U. Ctrl. Ark., 1951; MA, Harding U., 1958; EdS, Pittsburg State U., 1972; EdD, U. Fla., 1977, PhD, 1997. Tchr. pub. schs., Ark., 1951-52, 56-60, 1962-68; vocat. rehab. counselor Mo. Dept. Edn., Farmington, 1968-71; tng. officer Fla. Divsn. Youth Svcs., Ocala, 1972-73; state supr. rsch. and planning Ark. Dept. Corrections, Pine Bluff, 1978-79; state dir. corrections data Ala. Dept. Corrections, Montgomery, 1979-80; prof. criminal justice Ctrl. Fla. C.C., Ocala, 1980-87. Cons., rsch. in field. Served with USN, 1952-56. Recipient J. Edgar Hoover commendation, 1954, Nat. Jaycee award, 1980, Ark. Traveler award Gov. Bill Clinton, 1985. Mem. Internat. Platform Assn., Kiwanis Internat., Lions Internat., Alpha Kappa Delta, Alpha Psi Omega, Kappa Delta Pi, Phi Kappa Phi. Home and Office: 720 NE 45th St Ocala FL 34479-1918

GRIST, JOHN, retired government official, engineering executive; b. Nov. 17, 1928; (parents Am. citizens); s. John Rivers and Raphaela Matilda (Santiesteban) Grist; m. Ana Dolores D'Almonte, Nov. 22, 1961; children: Anna Cecilia, John Alexander, Paul Steven. Lic. realtor Fla. Aircraft indsl. engrng. cons. Parr Engring., Atlanta, 1958; food mfg. indsl. engring. cons. USDA, Washington, 1958—60; postal mechanization indsl. engr. U.S. Post Office Dept., Washington, 1962—64; hosp. indsl. engr. cons. VA, Washington, 1962—64; bldgs. mgmt. indsl. engr. cons. GSA, Washington, 1964—65; parks mgmt. sr. mgmt. analysis cons. Nat. Park Svc., Washington, 1965—71; White House presdl. fellow Md. U., 1970—71; sr. indsl. engring. cons. U.S. Postal Svc., N.Y.C., 1971—74, sr. indsl. cons. Western Mass. Springfield, 1974—89; internat. bilingual export-import tech. cons., 1958. Pres. Parents' Coun., Lexington Sch. for Deaf, Queens, NY, 1972—74; mem. fund raising com. Clarke Sch. for Deaf, Northampton, Mass., 1975—76. With USAF, 1951—55. Mem.: Ga. Tech. Nat. Alumni Assn. Home: 15102 SW 104 St #809 Miami FL 33196 Personal E-mail: gristmiami@bellsouth.net.

GRISWELL, J. BARRY, insurance company executive; b. Ga. Bachelor's, Berry Coll., 1971; master's, Stetson U., 1972. Pres., CEO MetLife Mktg. Corp. (subs. MetLife Ins. Co.); agy. v.p. The Prin. Fin. Group, Des Moines, 1986-91, sr. v.p. individual ins. dept., 1991-96, exec. v.p., 1996-98, pres., CEO, 2001—, chmn., 2002—; dir. Prin. Life Ins. Co., Des Moines, 1998—, pres., 1998—2000, pres. and CEO, 2000—, chmn., 2002—. Past chair LIMRA Internat.; past chair bd. trustees Life Underwriting Tng. Coun.; chair elect Am. Counsel Life Insurers; bd. mem. Bus. Roundtable, Am. Coun. Capital Formation; dir. Herman Miller Inc. Dir. Bus. Com. for Arts; trustee Central Coll., Berry Coll., Ga. Fellow: LIMRA Leadership Inst. Office: The Prin Fin Group 711 High St Des Moines IA 50392-0002*

GRISWOLD, FRANK TRACY, III, bishop; b. Bryn Mawr, Pa., Sept. 18, 1937; s. Frank Tracy Jr. and Louisa Johnson (Whitney) G.; m. Phoebe Wetzel, Nov. 27, 1965; 2 children. AB, Harvard Coll., 1959; student, Gen. Theol. Sem., 1959—60; BA, Oxford U., 1962, MA, 1966. Ordained deacon Episc. Ch., 1962, ordained priest Episc. Ch., 1963. Bishop coadjutor Diocese of Chgo., 1985—87, bishop, 1987—97; presiding bishop Episcopal Ch. in USA, N.Y.C., 1998—. Former dep. to Gen. Conv.; former chmn. Pa. Liturgical Commn. Former chair Standing Liturgical Commn., Episcopal Ch. U.S.; former co-chair Anglican-Roman Cath. Dialogue U.S., Anglican-Roman Cath. Internat. Episcopalian. Office: Episcopal Ch Ctr 815 2d Ave New York NY 10017 E-mail: pboffice@episcopalchurch.org.

GRISWOLD, GEORGE, marketing, advertising and public relations executive; b. N.Y.C., Mar. 5, 1919; s. George and Isabel (Bridgman) G.; m. Tracy Haight, May 15, 1942 (div. 1985); children: Tracy Griswold Glass, Mariana Van Rensselaer Griswold Geer, Alice Bradford Griswold Stetson; m. Joan Loosley McNamara, Mar. 11, 1986 (div. 1992); m. Nancy Cox Holbrook, Apr. 3, 1993. Student, Ecole des Beaux Arts, Fontainebleau, France, 1939; BA, Yale U., 1941; postgrad., NYU, 1947. Editor Fairchild Publs., N.Y.C., 1945-46; pub. rels., operating positions long lines dept. AT&T, 1946-49, pub. rels. exec. N.Y.C., 1962-79; exec. Newsweek mag., N.Y.C., 1950-55; exec. dir. pub. rels. and publs. divsn. Bell Labs., Inc., N.Y., N.J., 1955-62; pres. Litchfield Distbrs., Inc., Conn., 1949-52; tchr. Fairleigh Dickinson U. Grad. Sch., 1961; sr. v.p. Sheldon Satin Assocs., Inc., N.Y., 1979-83; pres. Griswold Comm., Hilton Head, S.C., 1983-89; v.p. mktg. and pub. rels. Environ. Am. Inc., Hilton Head, 1989-92. Pres. Norfolk (Conn.) Libr., 1965-75. Comdr. USNR, 1941-45, WWII, ret. Mem. AAAS, SAR, Pub. Rels. Soc. Am. (accredited), Nat. Assn. Sci. Writers, Soc. Mayflower Descs., Soc. Colonial Wars, Huguenot Soc. Am., Huguenot Soc. S.C., Soc. First Families S.C., Yale Club (N.Y.C.), S.C. Yacht Club, Piedmont Club. Home: 509 Claridge Cir Winston Salem NC 27106-6301

GRISWOLD, KATHY ANN KING, academic administrator; b. Danville, Pa., Apr. 25, 1957; d. Kenneth Albert and Mattle Jane (Boone) King; m. Keith E. Griswold, July 1, 1978; children: Kelsey A., Kyle K.E. AA in Gen. Studies, Eastern Nazarene Coll., Quincy, Mass., 1978; BS in Acctg., SUNY, Rochester, 1982; MA in Bus. and Policy Studies, SUNY, Empire State Coll., Rochester, 1998. Cert. treasury profl., bus. mgr. Acct., bookkeeper Brophy Daily & Bonn CPAs, Rochester, 1978-81; asst. to contr. Bathtique Internat. Ltd., Rochester, 1981-84; treas., contr. Sugar Creek Stores, Inc., Rochester, 1984-93; treasury mgr. Wegmans Food Markets, Inc., Rochester, 1993-2000; asst. treas. U. Rochester, 2000—. Treas. Campaign to Elect Keith Griswold, Brighton, N.Y., 1985, 93. Mem. Assn. Fin. Profls. (retail task force), Assn. for Fin. Profls. Western NY (pres. 1992), Inst. Mgmt. Accts. (past dir.). Republican. Methodist. Home: 1442 Crittenden Rd Rochester NY 14623-2310 Office Phone: 585-275-6968. Business E-Mail: kathy.king-griswold@rochester.edu.

GRISWOLD, SARA Y., language educator; arrived in U.S., 1988; m. George Griswold; children: Carlos, George. BA in Edn., Nat. U. Trujillo, 1977; Cert. D'aptitude Dans L'enseignement Du Français langue etrangere, U. Grenoble, France, 1981; MA in Edn., U. Kans., 1986; doctoral student language edn., U. Georgia. ESL tchr. Santa Rosa H.S., Trujillo, 1977—79; ESL instr. Cath. U., Trujillo, 1979; French tchr. Alliance Française, Trujillo, 1979—84; ESL tchr. Inst. Cultural Peruano-Americano, Trujillo, 1979—88, acad. coord., 1988; part-time ESL instr. Prince George's C.C., Largo, Md., 1989; part-time Spanish instr. Augusta (Ga.) State U., 1989—90, temporary full time Spanish instr., 1992—93, full time Spanish instr., 1993—99, full time Spanish asst. prof., 1999—. Recipient Study award, French Govt., 1980—81, Delta Kappa Gamma, 1984—86; scholar, Fulbright, 1984—86, U. Kans., 1984—86. Mem.: Peru-TESOL, Fgn. Lang. Assn. for Internat. Rapport, Am. Assn. Tchrs. Spanish and Portuguese, Cultural Hispanic Assn. of the Ctrl. Savannah River Area, Augusta, Ga. 1992, Alpha Mu Gamma (advisor/sponsor Iota Phi chpt. 1992—). Avocations: travel, collecting post cards, reading. Office: Augusta State Univ 2500 Walton Way Augusta GA 30904

GRISWOLD, THOMAS L., lawyer; b. Kansas City, Mo., Sept. 23, 1949; s. Thomas L. and Betty L. Griswold; m. Noreen M. Puhala, Apr. 23, 1988; children: Alisha Beth, Shannon Blake. BA cum laude, Washburn U., Topeka, Kans., 1973; MPA, U. Kans., 1976, JD, 1981. Bar: Kans. 1981, Mo. 1990, U.S. Dist. Ct. (we. dist.) Mo. 1990. Staff planner Topeka-Shawnee County Met. Planning Agencies, Topeka, 1968—74; chief planner City of Topeka Dept. of Labor Svcs., Topeka, 1974—75; audit supr. State of Kans. Legis. Divsn. of Post Audit, Topeka, 1975—78; mem. firm Payne & Jones, Chartered, Overland Park, Kans., 1981—. Editor in chief Kans. Law Rev., 1980. Contbr. articles to profl. jours. Bd. mem. City of Topeka Legal Aid Soc., Topeka, Kans., 1973—74. With USMCR, 1969. Recipient Burdick Prize, U. of Kans. Sch. of Law, 1979, various awards, Am. Jurisprudence, 1978—80, Am. Judicature Soc. award, 1980. Mem.: ABA, The Mo. Bar, Kans. Bar Assn., Order of the Coif. Office: Payne & Jones Chartered 11000 King St Overland Park KS 66210

GRISWOLD, TONY JAMES, music educator, director; b. Kans. City, Kans., Feb. 3, 1956; s. James Park and Janet Louise Griswold; m. Kathleen Patricia Wilson, June 30, 1979; children: Jeffrey Scott, Allison René. MusB in Edn., Ctrl. Mo. State U., 1978. Dir. band Cass R-V Sch. Dist., Archie, Mo., 1978—80, Maries R-I Sch. Dist., Vienna, Mo., 1980—94, Steelville (Mo.) R-3 Sch. Dist., 1994—2004. Mem. choir Cuba (Mo.) United Meth. Ch., Cuba, Mo., 1994. Recipient Educator of Yr. award, Steelville (Mo.) C. of C., 2000. Mem.: NEA (life), Ctrl. Mo. Choral Dirs. Assn. (Tchr. of Yr. award 2002), South Ctrl. Mo. Music Educators Assn. (pres. 1998—99, Tchr. of Yr. award 2002), Music Educators Nat. Conf., Phi Beta Mu. Avocations: collecting sports memorabilia, collecting christmas ornaments. Personal E-mail: tjgris@misn.com.

GRISWOLD, WILLIAM M., museum director, curator; BA in Art History, with honors, Trinity Coll., Conn.; PhD, The Courtauld Inst. Art, London. Assoc. curator dept. drawings and prints Met. Mus. Art, NYC; Charles W. Engelhard curator, head dept. drawings and prints Pierpont Morgan Libr., NYC, 1995—2001; assoc. dir. collections J. Paul Getty Mus., LA, 2001—04, acting dir., chief curator, 2004—05; dir. & pres. Mpls. Inst. of Arts, 2005—. Bd. dir. The Courtauld Inst. Art, London. Office: Mpls Inst of Arts Office of the Pres 2400 Third Ave South Minneapolis MN 55404*

GRITSCH, RUTH CHRISTINE LISA, editor; b. Duisburg, Germany, July 18, 1931; came to the U.S., 1941; d. Carl and Maria Augusta (von Schuman-Janssen) Sandman; m. Eric Walter Gritsch, June 4, 1955 (div. 1993); children: Deborah, Erika. BA, NYU, 1953. Assoc. Inst. for Internat. Edn., N.Y.C., 1953-55; sec. Zeigler Bros., Inc., Gardners, Pa., 1993—2003. Translator: (books) Liberty, Equality, Sisterhood, 1978, Office of the Ministry, 1981, Huldrich Zwingli, 1983, Unity of the Churches, 1984, I Am a Palestinian Christian, 1995, Violence, 1996; co-translator: Luther's Works, Vols. 39, 41, 1966, 67; editor: Roly, 1988; translator, editor: Justification of the Ungodly, 1968; editor, co-translator: Thomas Müntzer, A Tragedy of Errors, 1989. Active So. Poverty Law Ctr., Adams Co. Arts Coun. Mem.: LWV (bd. dirs., v.p. 1969—90, 1999—2001), Internat. Platform Assn. Democrat. Lutheran. Avocations: reading, collecting art. Home: 1 West St Gettysburg PA 17325-2130 E-mail: ruth@superpa.net.

GRITTON, EUGENE CHARLES, nuclear engineer, director; b. Santa Monica, Calif., Jan. 13, 1941; s. Everett Mason and Matilda (Benne) Gritton; m. Gwendolyn O. Gritton; children: Dennis Mason, Kathleen Wanda. BS, UCLA, 1963, MS, 1965, PhD, 1966. Research engr., def. systems analyst RAND, Santa Monica, Calif., 1966-73, project leader advanced undersea tech. program, 1973-76, program dir. marine tech., 1974-76, program dir. applied sci. and tech., 1976-94, head dept. phys. scis., 1975-77, head engring. and applied scis. dept., 1977-86, RAND resident scholar for tech., 1990-93, dep. v.p. Nat. Security Rsch. Divsn., 1986-93, dep. v.p. Rsch. Ops. Group, 1986-90, dir. Acquisition and Tech. Policy Ctr., 1994—2004, acting dir. Nat Security Rsch. divsn., 1997—98, v.p. Nat Security Rsch. divsn., 2004—. Bd. dirs. Nat. Def. Rsch. Inst.; vis. lectr. dept. mech. engring. U. So. Calif., LA, 1967-72; vis. lectr. dept. energy and kinetics UCLA, 1971, 73; mem. Def. Sci. Bd. Study, 1996, 98. Recipient Engring. Alumnus of Yr. award UCLA Sch. Engring. and Applied Sci., 1985-86; AEC fellow, 1963, NSF Coop. Grad. fellow, 1964-66. Mem. Am. Nuclear Soc. (mem. exec. com. aerospace and hydrospace div. 1974-75), AIAA Home: 819 Dickson St Marina Del Rey CA 90292 Office: Rand PO Box 2138 1776 Main St Santa Monica CA 90407-2138 Office Phone: 310-393-0411 ext. 6933. Business E-Mail: gene@rand.org.

GRIVER, JEANETTE A., human services administrator, consultant; b. NY, NY, July 2, 1932; d. Lawrence Maurice Rosenthal and Selma Demby-Rosenthal; m. David M Griver, Mar. 15, 1951 (div. Apr. 1991). BA in psychology, U. of Calif. at Los Angeles, 1961; MA in psychology human factor, U. Southern Calif., 1964. V.p. Jan Engring. Electronic Components, Santa Monica, 1955—62; pres. Jan Engring. Human Factors Divsn., Santa Monica, 1962—89; CEO Compsych Systems, Inc., Los Angeles, 1969—. Cons. to several org., 1962—. Author: Applied Problem Analysis Plus, 1988, Oh No! Not Another Problem, 2000, Curio a Shetland Sheepdog Meets the Crow, 2004, Curio a Shetland Sheepdog and Friends, 2005; contbr. articles to jours. Mem. Pacific Palisades C. of C., 1990—2003. Mem.: Human Factors Soc. (sec. 2003), Lions Club Pacific Palisades (pres. 1990). Avocations: travel, tennis. Office: Compsych Systems Inc PO Box 1568 Pacific Palisades CA 90272 Office Phone: 310-454-6426. E-mail: res04wq4@gte.net.

GRIZZAFFI, KIMBERLY ANNE, music educator, secondary school educator; b. Bronx, Feb. 20, 1978; d. Peter and Loretta Grizzaffi. B, Ithaca Coll., 2000; M, SUNY, 2005. Educator 7th - 8th grade band Sayville Pub. Schs., NY, 2000—. Tchr. summer music program Island Trees, Levittown, NY, 1996—2002; dir. marching band Sayville Mid. Sch., 2000—05, dir. jazz band, 2000—05; mem. Stony Brook Wind Ensemble, 2000—05, L.I. South Shore Jazz Band, 2002—05. Dir. Flute Choir, Sayville, 2000—05, Clarinet Choir, 2000—05, Saxophone Quartet, 2000—05, Trumpet Trio, 2003—04, Summer Jazz Band, 2004. Mem.: Sayville Tchrs. Assn., NY State Sch. Music Assn., NY State United Tchrs., Suffolk County Music Educators Assn., Music Educators Nat. Conf., Tri-M Music Honor Soc. (hon.). Avocation: bowling. Home: 31 Shepherd Ln Levittown NY 11756 Office: Sayville Mid Sch 291 Johnson Ave Sayville NY 11782 Office Phone: 631-244-6650.

GRIZZARD, GEORGE, actor; b. Roanoke Rapids, N.C., Apr. 1, 1928; s. George Cooper and Mary Winifred (Albritton) G. BA, U. N.C., 1949. Appeared at Arena Stage, Washington, 1950, 52-54; Broadway appearances include The Desperate Hours, 1955, The Happiest Millionaire, 1956-57, The Disenchanted, 1958-59 (nominee Tony award), Face of a Hero, 1960, Big Fish, Little Fish, 1961 (nominee Tony award), Mary, Mary, 1962, Who's Afraid of Virginia Woolf?, 1962, The Glass Menagerie, 1965, You Know I Can't Hear You When the Water's Running, 1967, Sweet Potato, 1968, The

Gingham Dog, 1969, Inquest, 1970, The Country Girl, 1972, The Creation of the World and Other Business, 1972, Crown Matrimonial, 1973, The Royal Family, 1975, California Suite, 1976, Man and Superman, 1978, A Delicate Balance, 1996 (Best Leading Actor Tony award 1996), Judgement At Nuremberg, 2001; also appeared with Assn. of Producing Artists, N.Y.C., 1961-62, Tyrone Guthrie Theatre, Mpls., 1963-65, Show Boat, Toronto, 1995, London, 1998; film appearances include From the Terrace, 1960, Advise and Consent, 1961, Warning Shot, 1967, Happy Birthday, Wanda June, 1971, Comes a Horseman, 1978, Firepower, 1979, Seems Like Old Times, 1980, Wrong is Right, 1981, Bachelor Party, 1983, The Wonder Boys, 2000, Small Time Crooks, 2000; TV appearances include Twilight Zone, The Adams Chronicles (nominated Emmy award), 1976, The Oldest Living Graduate (recipient Emmy award 1980), Caroline?, 1988, Simple Justice, 1993, Breaking the Silence, 1993, Queen, 1993, Scarlett, 1994, Suspicion of Innocence, 1997. Mem. Kappa Alpha. Office: PO Box 2275 New Preston Marble Dale CT 06777-0275

GRIZZARD-BARHAM, BARBARA LEE, artist; b. Roanoke, Va., Apr. 4, 1935; d. Alton Lee and Mable (Jewell) Grizzard; m. Charles Thomas Barham, Sr., June 25, 1955; children: Charles Thomas, Christopher. BS, Va. Commonwealth U., 1971, postgrad. Educator Colonial Heights (Va.) Sch. Sys., 1971—88; represented by Agora Gallery, NYC, 1999—2001, 2002, Amsterdam Whitney Gallery, NYC, 2003—05. One-woman shows include Wakefield (Va.) Ctr. for Arts, 1992, 1993, 1994, Petersburg (Va.) Area Art League, 1993, 1995, 2000, Rappahannock Westminster-Canterberry Gallery, Va., 1995, Assn. for Visual Artists Gallery, Chattanooga, Tenn., 1999, Rappahannock Westminster Canterberry Gallery, Va., 1999, Williamsburg Regional Libr./Gallery/Theater Complex, 1999, exhibited in group shows at Richmond (Va.) Jewish Cmty. Ctr., 1991, 1993, Rappahannoc Art League Show, Va., 1995, Assoc. Artists Winston-Salem, N.C., 1991, 1992, 1996, Hoyt Inst. Fine Arts, Pa., 1998, Fredericksburg (Va.) Creative Ctr. Art, 1999, Richmond Shockoe Creative Ctr. Art, 1999, Richmond Women's Caucus for Art, 1999—2000, Shockoe Bottom (Va.) Art Ctr., 1999—2000, Agora Gallery, 1999, 2000, N.Y.C., 2001, 2002, Amsterdam Whitney Gallery, 2003, 2004, 2005, Limner Gallery, 2001. Recipient awards for art. Mem. Petersburg Area Art League, Va. Mus. Art, Whitney Mus. Art, Mus. Modern Art. Republican. Episcopal. Avocations: judging and breeding American Cocker Spaniels, piano. Home: 701 Forestview Dr Colonial Heights VA 23834-1116

GROAT, CHARLES GEORGE, geologist; b. Westfield, N.Y., Mar. 25, 1940; married, 1963; 2 children. AB, U. Rochester, 1962; MS, U. Mass., 1967; PhD in Geology, U. Tex., 1970. Rsch. geologist Bur. Econ. Geology, U. Tex., Austin, 1968-71, assoc. dir., 1971-75, assoc. prof. dept. geol. sci., 1971-76, acting dir. Bur. Econ. Geology, 1975-76; assoc. prof. geol. sci., chmn. U. Tex., El Paso, 1976-78; dir. La. Geol. Survey, 1978-90; exec. dir. Am. Geol. Inst., 1990-92; dir. La. State U. Ctr. Coastal Energy & Environ. Rsch. Lab., Baton Rouge, 1992-95, U. Tex. Ctr. for Environ. Resource Mgmt., El Paso, 1995-98; assoc. v.p. rsch. U. Tex., El Paso, 1998; dir. U.S. Geol. Survey US Dept. Interior, Reston, Va., 1998—2005; dir. Ctr. for Internat. Energy & Environ. Policy U. Tex., Austin, 2005—, chair energy & mineral resources, Dept. Geological Sciences, 2005—. Mem. Geol. Soc. Am., Am. Assn. Petrol Geologists, Am. Geophys. Union, Am. Assn. for Higher Edn. Achievements include research in geology of energy resources, environmental aspects of resource extraction, geomorphology of coastal and arid areas, water resources, science education. Office: U Tex Austin Charles Groat Dept Geological Sciences 1 University Station C1100 Austin TX 78712

GROB, GEORGE FREDERICK, health science association administrator; M in Math., Georgetown U., 1969. Comptr. Office of Asst. Sec. Def.; ops. rsch. analyst Office of Asst. Sec. Navy for Fin. Mgmt.; dir. planning and policy coordination Office of Asst. Sec. Planning and Evaluation, USHHS, 1976-88; chair evaluation and inspection round table PCIE, Washington, 1994—2002; dep. insp. gen. for evaluation and inspections USHHS, Washington, 1988—2002, asst. insp. gen. for evaluation and inspections, 2004—05, dep. insp. gen. mgmt. and policy, 2002—05; exec. dir. Citizens Health Care Working Group, 2005—. Mem. Am. Evaluation Assn. (co-chair Evaluation Mgrs. and Suprs. Group). Home: 38386 Millstone Dr Purcellville VA 20132-3739 Office: USHHS 330 Independence Ave SW Washington DC 20301-0001 Office Phone: 301-443-1530. Personal E-mail: georgegrob@cs.com.

GROB, GERALD N., historian, educator; b. N.Y.C., Apr. 25, 1931; s. Sidney and Sylvia G. Grob; m. Lila Kronick, Dec. 25, 1954; children: Bradford S., Evan D., Seth A. BS, CCNY, 1951; MA, Columbia U., 1952; PhD, Northwestern U., 1958; D.Litt. (hon.), Clark University, 2002. From instr. history to prof. Clark U., Worcester, Mass., 1957—69; Henry E. Sigerist prof. of the history of medicine Rutgers U., New Brunswick, NJ, 1969—, chmn. dept., 1969—71, 1973—74, 1981—84. Mem. fellowship adv. com. NEH, 1975—76; chmn. study sect. history of medicine NIH, 1975—77, 1987—89, 1993—98. Author: books including Ed Jarvis and the Medical World of 19th Century America, 1978, Workers and Utopia, 1961, The State and the Mentally Ill, 1966, Mental Institutions in America, 1973, Mental Ilness and American Society, 1875-1940, 1983, The Inner World of American Psychiatry, 1890-1940, 1985, From Asylum to Community, 1991, The Mad Among Us, 1994, The Deadly Truth: A History of Disease in America, 2002; contbr. articles to profl. jours. Elected to inst. medicine NAS. With U.S. Army, 1955—57. Fellow, NEH, 1972—73, 1989—90, Am. Coun. Learned Socs., 1976—77, Guggenheim fellow, 1980—81, Davis Ctr., Princeton U., 1985—86; grantee, NIH, 1960—65, 1967—81, 1984—92. Mem.: Orgn. Am. Historians, Am. Antiquarian Soc., Am. Assn. History of Medicine (coun. mem. 1978—81, v.p. 1994—96, pres. 1996—98, William H. Welch medal 1986). Jewish. Home: 821 Starview Way Bridgewater NJ 08807-1824 Office: Rutgers U Inst Health Care Policy 30 College Ave New Brunswick NJ 08901-1293 Office Phone: 732-932-8377. Business E-Mail: ggrob@rci.rutgers.edu. *My philosophy of history is essentially a tragic one; a study of the past, if undertaken in as honest and objective a manner as is humanly possible, should render us less certain about our omniscience and ability to control the future.*

GROBAN, JOSH, vocalist; b. L.A., 1981; Student, Interlochen Arts Acad. Performer Inauguration ceremonies of Gov. Joseph Graham 'Gray' Davis Jr., 1999; performer with Sarah Brightman in concert, Rotterdam, Netherlands, 2000; performer Closing ceremony of the 2002 Winter Olympics, Salt Lake City, 2002. Singer: (albums) Josh Gordon, 2001, Josh Groban in Concert (live), 2002, Closer, 2003; singer: (duet with Lara Fabian) (songs) For Always, 2001; singer: (duet with Charlotte Church) The Prayer, 2001; singer: (TV series) Ally McBeal, 2001, (TV spls.) A Home for the Holidays with Mariah Carey, 2001, Great Performances, 2003. Office: Warner Bros Records 75 Rockefeller Plaza New York NY 10019

GROBAN, MARK D., health care company executive; b. Cin., Ohio, Nov. 10, 1941; MD, Albany Med. Coll., 1967. Cert. Psychiatry 1976. Joined Mid Atlantic Med. Svcs., Inc., 1990, pres. Alliance Preferred Provide Orgn. Rockville, Md., pres. MAPSI, med. dir. behavioral health and quality improvement, chmn., 1999—. Office: Mid Atlantic Med Svcs Inc 4 Taft Ct Rockville MD 20850*

GROBE, CHARLES STEPHEN, lawyer, accountant; b. Columbus, Ohio, May 5, 1935; s. Harry A. and Bertha S. (Swartz) G.; m. Ila Silverman, Aug. 30, 1964; children— Eileen, Kenneth. BS, UCLA, 1957; JD, Stanford U., 1961. Bar: Calif. 1962; CPA, Calif. Tax acct., Beverly Hills, Calif., 1961—63; tax atty. L.A., 1963—. Author: Guide to Investing Pension and Profit-Sharing Trust Funds, 1973, Guardianship, Conservatorship and Trusts on Behalf of Persons Who Are Mentally Retarded— An Assessment of Current Applicable Laws in the State of California, 1974, Using an Individual Retirement Savings Plan and the Related Rollover Provisions of the Pension Reform Act of 1974, 1975, Guide to Setting Up a Group Term Life Insurance Program Under IRC Section 79, 1976, Practical Estate Planning, 1988, Planning for Incapacity, 1989, Planning to Reduce the Generation Skipping Tax, 1989, Estate Planning Considerations for Community Property Interests, 1990, Legal and Tax Problems of Joint Tennancy as a Form of Ownership, 1990, The Tax Economics of Using the Generating Skipping Tax Exemptions, 1992, The Tax Economics of Gifting Property, 1992, Saving Estate Taxes with Life Insurance and a Life Insurance Trust, 1992, Family Wealth Transfer Planning, The Tax Economics of a Qualified Personal Residence Trust, also articles. Capt. AUS, 1957-64. Mem. ABA, State Bar Calif., L.A. County Bar Assn., Beverly Hills Bar Assn., Calif. Soc. CPAs. Office: 12110 Wilshire Blvd Los Angeles CA 90025-1104 Home: 172 S Woodburn Dr Los Angeles CA 90049-3041

GROBERG, JAMES JAY, information technology executive; b. Bklyn., May 29, 1928; s. David and Anna (Gross) G.; m. Marcia J. Black, June 25, 1950 (div. June 1986); children: Neil H., Richard L., Eric L.; m. Carol Ann De Barros, Sept. 4, 1986. BS in Econs., U. Pa., 1951. Asst. v.p. Economy Fin. Corp., Indpls., 1959-62; v.p. Rosenthal & Rosenthal, Inc., N.Y.C., 1962-68, Brandon Applied Systems, Inc., N.Y.C., 1970-71; fin. v.p. Telco Mktg. Svcs., Inc., Chgo., 1971-73; exec. v.p. Volt Info. Scis., Inc., N.Y.C., 1973-81, sr. v.p., CFO, 1985—, bd. dirs.; chmn., CEO Multivest, Inc., Ft. Lauderdale, Fla., 1981-82, Mego Corp., N.Y.C., 1982-85, also bd. dirs. Chmn. bd. dirs. Am. Community Pubs. Inc., 1989-91; bd. dirs. Autologic Info. Internat., Inc. Capt. USAFR, 1950-66. Mem. Fin. Execs. Inst. Office: Volt Info Scis Inc 560 Lexington Ave New York NY 10022-6828 Office Phone: 212-704-2480. Personal E-mail: jgroberg@volt.com.

GROBMAN, ARNOLD BRAMS, retired biology educator, retired academic administrator; b. Newark, Apr. 28, 1918; s. Samuel H. and Sophia (Brams) G.; m. Hulda Gross, Feb. 20, 1944; children: Marc Ross, Beth Burruss. BS, U. Mich., 1939; MS, U. Rochester, 1941, PhD, 1943. Instr. zoology U. Rochester, 1943-44; research asso. Manhattan project, 1944-46; from asst. prof. to asso. prof. biology U. Fla., 1946-59; research participant Oak Ridge Inst. Nuclear Studies, summer 1950, research specialist, med. center study, 1951-52; dir. Fla. State Mus., 1952-59; dir. biol. scis. curriculum study U. Colo., 1959-65, dean Coll. Arts and Scis.; prof. zoology Rutgers U., New Brunswick, N.J., 1965-72, dean Rutgers Coll., 1966-72; vice chancellor for acad. affairs, prof. biol. scis. U. Ill., Chgo., 1973-74, spl. asst. to pres., 1974-75; chancellor U. Mo.-St. Louis, 1975-85, chancellor emeritus, 1985—, prof. biology, 1975—, research prof., 1986—; adj. curator Fla. Mus. Natural History, 1982—. Vis. lectr. Utah State U., U. Ind./Purdue U., U. So. Ill., Nat. Taiwan Normal U., U. Campinas, Brazil, U. New Delhi, India, U. No. Sumatra, Indonesia, U. Sind, Pakistan, Chulalongkorn U., Bangkok, Thailand, U. Singapore, Sophia U., Japan, Internat. Christian U., Japan, Chiang Mia U., Thailand; cons. to govt., industry, founds. and ednl. instns., 1954—; Mem. div. biology and agr. NRC-Nat. Acad. Scis., 1954-58, com. adult edn., 1956-58; sec. U.S. nat. com. Internat. Union Biol. Scis., 1966-69; Chmn. Ednl. Opportunity Center of Met. St. Louis, 1976-78; mem. advisory team sci. soc., Thailand, 1971; fgn. observer Treaty Plebiscite, Gov. Panama, 1977-78; mem. Commn. on Adult Learner Author: (with others) Island Life: A Study of the Land Vertebrates of Eastern Lake Michigan, 1948, Our Atomic Heritage, 1951, Genetics Effects of Chronic X-irradiation Exposure in Mice, 1960, BSCS Biology Implementation in the Schools, 1964, The Changing Classroom, 1969, Urban State Universities, 1988; editor: Social Implications of Biological Education, 1970; also articles to profl. jours., encys. and newspapers. Bd. dirs. in St. Louis United Way, Laumeier Sculpture Park, Narcotics Service Council, Regional Commerce and Growth Assn., St. Louis Higher Edn. Ctr., St. Louis Pub. Libr.; v.p. St. Louis Conf. on Edn., 1980-82; adv. bd. Indian River County Pub. Libr., 1997-2003. Recipient Fred H. Stoye prize Am. Soc. Ichthyologists and Herpetologists, 1941; A Cressy Morrison prize N.Y. Acad. Scis., 1943; Macalaster award Nat. Assn. Biology Tchrs., 1966; award of merit Urban League, 1984; Commanders Cross, Order of Merit, Fed. Republic Ger., 1985. Mem. Acad. Zoology in India (exec. com. 1967-69), Am. Assn. Higher Edn., AAAS (council 1961-65), Am. Assn. Museums (mus. tng. com. 1960-63), Am. Assn. State Colls. and Univs. (urban affairs com. 1977-85), Am. Ednl. Research Assn., Am. Inst. Biol. Scis. (exec. com. 1958-61, Disting. Service award 1984), Am. Soc. Ichthyologists and Herpetologists (bd. govs. 1952—, pres. 1964), Am. Soc. Naturalists, Am. Soc. Zoologists, Assn. Am. Med. Colls., Assn. Southeastern Biologists, Assn. Supervision and Curriculum Devel., Assn. Tropical Biology, Asian Assn. Biol. Edn., Biol. Scis. Curriculum Study (chmn. steering com. 1965-69), Biol. Soc. China, Biol. Soc. Washington, Council on Fgn. Relations, NEA, Edn. Programs Improvement Corp. (trustee 1970-74), Colo.-Wyo. Acad. Sci., AAUP, Explorers Club, Fla. Acad. Sci., Fla. Found. Future Scientists (chmn. 1957-59), Herpetologists League, Mo. Council Pub. Higher Edn. (exec. com. 1977-82, v.p. 1978, pres. 1979), Mo. Bot. Garden, Nat. Council Accreditation Tchr. Edn. (chmn. 1970-71), Genetics Soc., Herpetologists League, Philippine Assn. Sci. Tchrs., Nat. Assn. Biology Tchrs. (pres. 1966, editorial bd. 1974-77, dir. 1978-80), Nat. Assn. Research Sci. Teaching, Nat. Assn. State Univs. and Land Grant Colls. (exec. com. 1979-80, council on acad. affairs 1974-76, chmn. div. urban affairs 1978-79), Nat. Sci. Tchrs. Assn., Nature Conservancy, Newcomen Soc., N.J. Acad. Scis., Orgn. Tropical Studies, Sci. Soc. Thailand, Soc. Study Amphibians and Reptiles, Soc. Study Evolution, Soc. Systematic Zoology, Soc. Vertebrate Paleontology, Southeastern Museums Conf. (pres. 1955-57), Phi Beta Kappa, Sigma Xi, Phi Kappa Phi, Phi Sigma, Alpha Sigma Lambda, Alpha Epsilon Delta. Home: 5000 SW 25th Blvd Apt 1115 Gainesville FL 32608 E-mail: agrobman@aol.com.

GROBMAN, HULDA GROSS (MRS. ARNOLD B. GROBMAN), health science educator; b. Phila., Aug. 2, 1920; d. Joseph and Dora (Abrahams) Gross; m. Arnold B. Grobman, Feb. 20, 1944; children— Marc Ross, Beth Alison Burruss. AB, U. Pa., 1940; MPA, U. Mich., 1941; EdD, U. Fla., 1958. Rsch. asso. Western Interstate Commn. on Higher Edn., Boulder, Colo., 1959-60; staff cons. Biol. Scis. Curriculum Study, Boulder, 1960-65, Joint Council on Econ. Edn., N.Y., 1965-66; prof. edn. N.Y. U., 1966-72, Bklyn. Coll., City U. N.Y., 1972-73; sr. rsch. assoc. ADA, Chgo., 1973-74; dir. edn./career mobility, area health edn. system, prof. med. edn. U. Ill. Med. Center, 1973-75; prof. health scis. edn. St. Louis U. Med. Ctr., 1975-88; prof. emeritus St. Louis U. Med. Center, 1988—. Cons. Sci. Edn. Center, U. Sao Paulo, Brazil; vis. prof. Asian Assn. Biol. Edn., Hebrew U. Jerusalem Inst. on Test Writing, 1972; cons. Fundacao Carlos Chagos, Sao Paulo, Brazil. Author: Developmental Curriculum Projects, 1970, Evaluation Activities of curriculum Projects, 1968, also articles; cons. editor Jour. Ednl. Rsch., 1973-80, Am. Ednl. Rsch. Jour.; mng. editor Serin Press. Bd. dirs. LWV Fla., 1950-55; candidate for City Commn., Gainesville, Fla., 1955; mem. Bd. State Dept. Children and Families, Dist. 15, 1997-2000. Recipient A-Individual Achievement award 3d Army Res. Command, 1956. Fellow AAAS (council 1967-73); mem. Asian Assn. Biology Edn. (charter hon. mem.), Am. Ednl. Research Assn. (sec. div. I 1979-81). Home: 5000 SW 25th Blvd Unit 1115 Gainesville FL 32608 E-mail: agrobman@aol.com.

GROCE, WILLIAM HENRY, III, environmental engineer, consultant; b. Greer, S.C., Feb. 9, 1940; s. William Henry Jr. and Mary Alvis (Williams) G.; 1 child, William H. IV. BS in Chemistry, Newberry Coll., 1964. Registered profl. engr., S.C.; diplomate environ. engring.; master hazardous material mgmt. Chemist FDA, Atlanta, 1966-68; chemist, engr. Celanese Corp., Greer, 1968-74; prin. engr. Groce Labs., Greer, 1974-86; dir. rsch. Aqua-Tech Corp., Port Washington, Wis., 1986-89; cons. Chemotech Corp., Greer, 1989-90; sr. scientist Savannah River Site U.S. Dept. of Energy, Aiken, S.C., 1990—. Cons. Environ. Resource Tech., Greer, 1990. Recipient Silver Beaver award Boy Scouts Am., 1990. Fellow Am. Inst. Chemists; mem. NSPE, Am. Inst. Chem. Engrs. Achievements include research in process and treatment methods for hazardous waste including reclaimation, detoxification, in situ treatment, and deactivation of highly reactive materials.

GROCHOWSKI, JELSIA, music educator; b. Bklyn., Oct. 4, 1936; d. Frank and Maria (Pollifrone) Artuso; m. Anthony Joseph Grochowski, Oct. 6, 1956; children: Robert, Thomas, Maria. Student, NYU, Manhattan Sch. Music; cert. program ch. music, Lebanon Valley Coll. Choir dir. P.S. 127, Bklyn., 1975-80; tchr. music Our Lady of Angels Sch. (formerly St. Peter Sch.), Columbia, Pa., 1990—. Dir. sr. citizens choir YMCA, Lancaster, Pa., 1982-84; accompaniest St. John Neumann Folk Group, Lancaster, 1982-87; dir. St. John Neumann Youth Choir, 1988—; organ tchr. Dominican Nuns, Lancaster, 1996—. Mem. Nat. Guild Piano Tchrs., Pa. Music Tchrs. Assn., Am. Organist Guild, Music Edn. Nat. Conf., Choristers Guild, Pastoral Musicians-Music Edn. Republican. Roman Catholic. Avocations: reading, walking, stitchery. Home: 2627 Pinewood Rd Lancaster PA 17601-4865

GROCHOWSKI, JUDITH ANNE, art educator; d. Gerald J. and Mary P. Nevins; m. Francis S. Grochowski, June 21, 1980; children: John J, Mary C. BS in Art Edn., U. Wis., 1976; MA in Curriculum, Nat. Loius U., 1989. Cert. tchr. Wis., 1976. Art tchr. Sch. Dist. Greenfield, Wis., 1976—. Bd. dirs. Libr. Bd., Greenfield, Wis., 2002—04. Mem.: Wis. Art Edn. Assn. (secondary rep to the bd. 2001—04, President's Recognition award 2003). Office: Greenfield High School 4800 South 60th Street Greenfield WI 53220 Office Phone: 414-281-6200. E-mail: jgrochowski@greenfield.k12.wi.us.

GRODD, LESLIE ERIC, lawyer; b. N.Y.C., Feb. 18, 1946; s. Abe and Celia G.; m. Judith Cota, June 18, 1967; children: Elissa, Katharine, Matthew. BA, U. Vt., 1966; JD, St. John's U., 1969; MBA, NYU, 1971. Bar: N.Y. 1969, Conn. 1974, D.C. 1982, U.S. Dist. Ct. Conn. 1975, U.S. Tax Ct. 1980, U.S. Supreme Ct. 1975. With tax dept. Coopers & Lybrand, N.Y.C., 1969-74; prin. Blazzard, Grodd & Hasenauer, PC, Westport, Conn., 1974—. Mem. ABA (chair closely held bus. com., tax sect. 1998-99, vice chair 2000-2001, chair 2001-03), AICPA, Conn. Soc. CPAs (chmn. fed. tax com. 1988-89), Conn. Bar Assn. (chmn. tax sect. 1991-94), N.Y. Bar Assn., D.C. Bar Assn., fellow, Am. Coll. of Tax Counsel, 2003-. Jewish. Office: Blazzard Grodd & Hasenauer PC 943 Post Rd E PO Box 5108 Westport CT 06880-5399 Office Phone: 203-226-7866. Personal E-mail: lgrodd@aol.com. Business E-Mail: leslie.grodd@bghpc.com.

GRODE, SUSAN A., lawyer; BFA, Cornell U., 1964; JD, U. So. Calif., 1977. Bar: Calif. 1977. V.p. Harry N. Abrams, Inc.; ptnr. Kaye, Scholer, Fierman, Hays & Handler, LLP; ptnr., co-chair Entertainment and Media Dept. Katten Muchin Zavis Rosenman, LA. Author: Visual Artist Manual, 1985. Mem.: ABA, Calif. Women's Law Ctr., State Bar Calif., LA County Bar Assn., Beverly Hills Bar Assn., Alpha Alpha Gamma, Phi Kappa Phi. Office: Katten Muchin Zavis Rosenman Ste 2600 2029 Century Park E Los Angeles CA 90067 Office Phone: 310-788-4410. Office Fax: 310-712-8422. E-mail: susan.grode@kmzr.com.

GRODMAN, MARC D., lab administrator, physician, medical educator; BA, U. Pa., 1973; MD, Columbia U., Coll. Physicians and Surgeons, 1977; studied, Kennedy Sch. Govt., Harvard U., 1980—83. Primary care clin. fellow Mass. Gen. Hosp., 1980—83; founder, pres., CEO, chmn., bd. dirs. Bio-Reference Labs., Inc., Elmwood Park, NJ, 1981—; med. cons., med. trades dept. AFL-CIO, 1982—84; med. cons. Uniformed FireFighters Assn. of N.Y.C., 1984—; asst. prof., clin. medicine Columbia U., Coll. of Physicians and Surgeons, N.Y.C.; asst. attending physician Presbyn. Hosp., N.Y.C. Office: Bio-Reference Labs Inc 481 Edward H Ross Dr Elmwood Park NJ 07407-3118

GRODSKY, GEROLD MORTON, biochemistry professor; b. St. Louis, Jan. 18, 1927; s. Louis and Goldie B.; m. Kayla Deane Wolfe, Dec. 6, 1952; children: Andrea, Jamie. BS, U. Ill., 1946, MS, 1947; PhD, U. Calif., Berkeley, 1954; postgrad., Cambridge (Eng.) U., 1954-55. Prof. biochemistry U. Calif. Med. Sch., 1961-92, prof. emeritus (active status), 1992—. Vis. prof. U. Geneva, 1968—69, U. Paris VII, 1989; Somogyi Meml. lectr., 72; Helen Martin lectr., 76; Herman Rosenthal lectr., 86; cons. various pharm. houses; cons. to UCSF Diabetes Ctr., 1993—. Mem. editl. bd. Diabetes, 1965-73, 86-90, Am. Jour. Physiology, 1977-94, Diabetologia, 1990-92, Endocrinology, 1992-96; founding adv. editor: Diabetes Tech. and Therapy, 1998—, Diabetes New World (China); contbr. chpts. to books; contbr. over 200 articles on diabetes and storage, secretion of insulin to profl. jours. Mem. med. adv. bd. Juvenile Diabetes Found., 1974-77, 80-85; program dir. NIH Diabetic Animal Program, 1978-82, chmn. diabetes rsch. adv. bd. to Sec. Health, 1982-87. Lt. (s.g.) USNR, 1944-54. Recipient David Rumbough Internat. award Juvenile Diabetes Found., 1984, Williams-Levine award, 1990, NIH Merit award, 1987, Juvenile Diabetes Found. annual endowed Grodsky award for basic rsch. in diabetes, 1994—, Western Region Islet Study Group annual Gerold M. Grodsky Disting. Scientist award, 2004—; named as one of 1000 most cited world scientists. Mem.: Am. Diabetes Assn. (rsch. bd. 1974—77, chmn. rsch. policy com. 1977, bd. dirs. Calif. chpt. 1989—91, nat. grant rev. com. 1992—96), Endocrine Soc., European Diabetes Assn., Am. Fedn. Clin. Rsch., Soc. Exptl. Biology, Am. Soc. Biol. Chemists, Internat. Diabetes Found., Meadowood Club, Harborpoint Club, Calif. Tennis Club. Home: 3969 Washington St San Francisco CA 94118-1613 Office: U Calif Sch Medicine Diabetes Ctr PO Box 0540 San Francisco CA 94143-0001

GRODSKY, JAMIE ANNE, law educator; b. San Francisco; d. Gerold Morton and Kayla Deane (Wolfe) G. BA in Human Biology/Natural Scis. and History with distinction, Stanford U., 1977; MA in Econ. Geography, U. Calif., Berkeley, 1986; JD, Stanford Law Sch., 1992. Ednl. dir. Oceanic Soc., San Francisco, 1979-81; rsch. asst. Woods Hole (Mass.) Oceanographic Inst., 1983; analyst Office Tech. Assessment U.S. Congress, Washington, 1984-89; counsel Com. Natural Resources, U.S. Ho. of Reps., Washington, 1993—95; counsel to Com. on Judiciary U.S. Senate, Washington, 1995-97; jud. clk. with chief judge U.S. Ct. Appeals (9th cir.), 1997-98; sr. advisor to the gen. counsel U.S. EPA, Washington, 1999—2001; assoc. prof. law U. Minn. Law Sch., Mpls., 2001—. Articles editor Stanford Law Rev.; contbr. articles to profl. jours. Trustee Desert Rsch. Inst. Found. Mem.: D.C. Bar Assn., Calif. Bar Assn., Supreme Ct. Bar Assn. Home: 2900 Thomas Ave S Apt 2112 Minneapolis MN 55416-4106

GRODY, DONALD, actor, judge, lawyer; b. N.Y.C., Dec. 18, 1927; s. Charles E. and Jeannette (Kessler) G.; m. Judith Anderson Weston, Oct. 21, 1989; children by previous marriage: Dion, Gordon, James, Jeremy. Student, Royal Acad. Dramatic Art, 1949-50; BA cum laude, Hunter Coll., 1951; LLB, N.Y. Law Sch., 1959. Bar: N.Y. State bar 1959. Profl. actor, singer, 1950-58; atty. U.S. Dept. Labor, Washington, 1959-60; labor union atty. N.Y.C., 1960-65; atty.-advisor NLRB, Washington, 1965-67; asst. gen. counsel Retail Clks. Internat. Assn., Washington, 1967-69; gen. counsel dist. 65 Distributive Workers, UAW, N.Y.C., 1970-73; exec. sec. Actors Equity Assn., N.Y.C., 1973-80; asst. exec. dir. NFL Players Assn., Washington, 1980-81, arbitrator, mediator, 1984-93; sole practice law N.Y.C., 1981-89; supervising adminstrv. law judge N.Y.C. Parking Violations Bur., 1989-93. Mem. theatre adv. panel Nat. Endowment for the Arts; mem. exec. bd., dept. profl. employees AFL-CIO; chmn. Equity-League Pension and Welfare Trust Funds, 1973-80 Appeared: (pre-Broadway tour) Yiddle with a Fiddle, 1994-95, Little Shop of Horrors, Tenn. Repertory Theatre, 1995, Sweeney Todd, Pitts. Pub. Playhouse, 1995-96, Let's Do It, Long Wharf Theatre, 1996, Jekyll & Hyde, Broadway, N.Y.C., 1997-98, Gypsy, Paper Mill Playhouse, 1998, Golf With Alan Shepard, Buffalo Studio Arena Theatre, 1998, Guys and Dolls, Dallas Theater Ctr., 2000, Parade (nat. tour), 2000, (returned to theatre) Nat. Co. Guys & Dolls, 1993-94 (nat. tour 2000), (TV show) Law & Order, 1999, 2002, Law & Order: Criminal Intent, 2003, (world premiere) Tooth and Claw, Arden Theatre, Phila., 2004, Caroline or Change, Broadway, NYC, 2004, She Stoups to Conquer, Irish Repertory Theatre, NYC. Served with AUS, 1945-47. Mem. AFTRA, SAG, Actors Equity Assn., Dramatists Guild.

GRODY, MARK STEPHEN, public relations executive; b. Milw., Jan. 1, 1938; s. Ray and Betty (Rothstein) G.; m. Karen Goldstein, Mar. 6, 1965 (div. 1972); 1 child, Laura; m. Susan Tellem, Mar. 25, 1979 (div. 1989); 1 child, Daniel; m. Jackie Black, June, 2, 2002. BS, U. Wis., 1960. Pub. rels. exec. GM, Detroit, 1961-74; v.p. pub. affairs Nat. Alliance of Businessmen, Washington, 1973-74; v.p. Carl Terzian & Assocs., L.A., 1974-75; chmn. Mark Grody Assocs. and Grody Tellem Comm., Inc. (now The Rowland Co.), L.A., 1975-90; pres. Mark Grody Assocs., L.A., 1990-93; exec. v.p., gen. mgr. Ogilvy Pub. Rels., L.A., 1993-96; pres. Mark Grody Assocs., L.A., 1996—. Ptnr. Mktg. Golf Resources, L.A., 1996-99, thegolfspot.com, 1998; founder corporategolf.com, L.A., 1999—. Co-author: Corporate Golf: How to Play the Game for Business Success, 1996. Capt. U.S. Army, 1960. Mem. Internat. Network Golf (bd. dirs.), Pub. Rels. Soc. Am., The Lakes Country Club. Avocations: golf, bridge. E-mail: mgrody@aol.com.

GRODY, WAYNE WILLIAM, physician; b. Syracuse, NY, Feb. 25, 1952; s. Robert Jerome and Florence Beatrice (Kashdan) G.; m. Gaylen Ducker, July 8, 1990. BA, Johns Hopkins U., 1974; MD, Baylor Coll. Medicine, 1977, PhD, 1981. Diplomate Am. Bd. Pathology, Am. Bd. Med. Genetics; lic. physician, Calif. Intern, resident UCLA Sch. Medicine, 1982-85, postdoctoral fellow, 1985-86, asst. prof., 1987-93, dir. DNA Diagnostic Lab., 1987—, assoc. prof., 1993-97, prof. depts. pathology and lab. medicine, pediat., human genetics, 1997—. Panelist Calif. Children's Svcs., 1987—, U.S. FDA, Washington, 1989—; DNA tech. com. Pacific Southwest Regional Genetics Network, Berkeley, Calif., NIH Task Force on Genetic Testing, others, 1987—; med., tech. cons., writer Warner Bros., NBC, Tri-Star, CBS, Twentieth Century Fox, Universal, others, 1987—; chair, molecular genetics com. Coll. Am. Pathologists, Am. Coll. Med. Genetics, Assn. Molecular Pathology, others. Contbg. editor, film critic: MD Mag., 1981-91; assoc. editor Diagnostic Molecular Pathology, 1993—; contbr. articles to profl. jours., chpts. to books. Recipient best paper award L.A. Soc. Pathology, 1984, Joseph Kleiner Meml. award Am. Soc. Med. Technologists, 1990; Basil O'Connor scholar March of Dimes Birth Defects Found., 1989, Nakamura Lectureship Scripps Clinic, 1996, Moss Lectureship LSU, 1998, Stop Cancer Fdn. Rsch. award, 1998, Hill Lectureship Baylor Coll. Medicine, 2003; named One of Am.'s Top Doctors, 2001—. Mem. AAAS, AMA, Am. Soc. Clin. Pathology, Am. Soc. Human Genetics, Am. Coll. Med. Geneticist (bd. dirs. 2001-), Soc. Inherited Metabolic Disorders, Soc. Pediat. Rsch. Democrat. Jewish. Achievements include application of molecular biology to clinical diagnosis and genetic screening, molecular genetics research and AIDS and cancer research. Office: UCLA Sch Medicine Divsns Med Genetics and Molecular Pathology Los Angeles CA 90095-1732 Office Phone: 310-825-5648. Business E-Mail: wgrody@mednet.ucla.edu.

GROENING, MATTHEW (MATTHEW ABRAM GROENING), writer, cartoonist; b. Portland, Oreg., Feb. 15, 1954; s. Homer Philip and Margaret Ruth (Wiggum) Groening; m. Deborah Lee Caplan (div.); children: Homer, Abe. BA, Evergreen State Coll., 1977. Cartoonist Life in Hell weekly comic strip (syndicated by Acme Features Syndicate), Sheridan, Oreg., 1977—; creator, writer, cartoonist Simpson Shorts, The Tracey Ullman Show, 1987—; creator Akbar and Jeff; pres. Matt Groening Prodns., Inc., L.A., 1988—; writer, story, prodr., exec. prodr., creator, developer The Simpsons, 1989—; writer, creator, exec. prodr., developer Futurama, 1999—; founder, pub. Bongo Comic Group, 1993—, Bongo Comics, 1995; exec. prodr. Olive, The Other Reindeer, 1999; writer, exec. prodr. Boo Boo Runs Wild. Author: Work is Hell, Love is Hell, School is Hell, The Big Book of Hell, The Huge Book of Hell, Love is Hell, Akbar & Jeff's Guide to Life, Binky's Guide to Love, The Simpsons: A Complete Guide to Our Favorite Family, The Simpsons Xmas Book, The Simpsons Rainy Day Fun Book, Making Faces With The Simpsons, Bart Simpson's Guide To Life, The Simpsons' Uncensored Family Album, Cartooning With The Simpsons, Simpsons Illustrated mag., Simpsons Comics Simps-O-Rama, Simpson Comics & Stories comic book, Simpsons Comics Extravaganza, Simpsons Comics Spectacular, Bartman: The Best of The Best; creater, developer, exec. prodr. The Simpsons Christmas Special, 1989, writer The Simpsons: Family Therapy, 1989, creater Bart vs the Space Mutants, 1991, original character designer The Simpsons Wrestling, 2001, creative consultant The Simpsons: Hit & Run, 2003, exec. prodr. The Simpsons: Bart's Nightmare, 1993, Bart Wars, the Simpsons Strike Back, 1999, voice of Arturo Olive, the Other Reindeer, 1999, voice of Dill Hair High, 2004, guest appearances The Tracey Ullman Show, 1988, Space Ghost Coast to Coast, 1996, The Big Breakfast, 2000, Great Performances, 2000, (voice) The Simpsons, 2004. Named New Pub. Yr., Diamond Distbn. Gem awards, 1993; recipient The Simpsons, Emmy award for Outstanding Animated Program, 1990, 1991, 1995, 1997, 1998, 2000, 2001, 2003, Futurama, Emmy Award for Outstanding Animated Program, 2002. Achievements include The expression "d'oh!" from The Simpsons was added to the Oxford English Dictionary in 2001. Office: The Simpsons c/o Twentieth Television Matt Groening's Office PO Box 900 Beverly Hills CA 90213 Address: Bongo Comics Group 1999 Avenue of Stars 15th Fl Los Angeles CA 90067 Office Phone: 310-788-1367. Office Fax: 310-788-1200.*

GROESBECK, ROLF ALFRED, music history and ethnomusicology educator; b. Detroit, Aug. 26, 1957; s. Byron Lou and Lois Johnson Groesbeck. BA, BM, Oberlin Coll., 1979; MA, NYU, 1985, PhD, 1995. Tchg. asst. Oberlin Coll., NYU, 1979, 1984—88, 1990—91; asst. prof. Vanderbilt U., Nashville, 1993—98; assoc. prof. U. Ark., Little Rock, 1998—. Adj. prof. Bklyn. Coll., 1987—88; adj. instr. Marymount Coll., 1991, NYU, N.Y.C., 1993; vis. prof. U. Va., Charlottesville, 1992; spkr. in field. Contbr. articles to profl. jours. Mem. Amnesty Internat., 1978—; mem. cultural com. Ark. Kerala Assn., Fgn. Lang. and AreaStudies grantee, 1988, 1991, Am. Inst. for Indian Studies fellow, 1988—89. Mem.: Soc. for Ethnomusicology, Internat. Coun. Traditional Music, Coll. Music Soc., Phi Beta Kappa, Pi Kappa Lambda. Democrat. Avocations: music, reading. Office: U Ark Music Dept 2801 S Univ Little Rock AR 72204 Office Phone: 501-569-3101. E-mail: ragroesbeck@ualr.edu.

GROETZINGER, JON, JR., lawyer, pharmaceutical executive; b. NYC, Feb. 12, 1949; s. Jon M. and Elinor Groetzinger; m. Carol Marie O'Connor, Jan. 24, 1981; 3 children. AB magna cum laude, Middlebury Coll., 1971; JD in Internat. Legal Affairs, Cornell U., 1974. Bar: N.H. 1974, N.Y. 1980, Mass. 1980, Fla. 1982, Md. 1985, Ohio 1991, U.S. Supreme Ct. 1980. Assoc. McLane, Graf, Greene, Raulerson and Middleton, P.A., Manchester, N.H., 1974-76; atty. John A. Gray Law Offices, Boston, 1978-81; pvt. practice N.H., Boston, 1977-81; chief internat. counsel Martin Marietta Corp., Bethesda, Md., 1981-88; pres., exec. v.p. Martin Marietta Overseas Corp., Bethesda, 1984-88; sr. v.p., gen. counsel, corp. sec. Am. Greetings Corp., Cleve., 1988—2003; CEO, pres. LifePill, Cleve., 2004—. Chmn. internat. adv. bd. Case Western Res. U. Law Sch., 1995—, disting. adj. prof., 1992—. Trustee Middlebury (Vt.) Coll., 1974—76, bd. overseers, 1977—; bd. dirs. Cleve. Coun. on World Affairs, 1992—98, 2000—, vice chmn., 2002—, chmn. strategic planning com., 2000—02, exec. com., 2000—05, trustee, 1992—96, 1998—2005; bd. dirs. Can.-U.S. Law Inst., 1990—, The Conf. Bds. Coun. Chief Legal Officers, 1996—2003, membership chmn., 1997—98, program chair, 1999—2000, coun. chmn., 2000—02; chmn., pres. Greater Cleve. Gen. Counsel Assn., 2001—04; bd. dirs. Lake Erie Coll., 2002—. Mem. ABA, N.H. Bar Assn., Fla. Bar Assn., Ohio Bar Assn., Cleve. Bar Assn., Md. Bar Assn., Am. Soc. Corp. Secs. (sec. Ohio chpt. 1995—, v.p. 1996-97, pres. 1997-98, adv. com. 1998—), Soc. of Benchers, Phi Beta Kappa. Office: LifePill 37455 Miles Rd Moreland Hills OH 44022 Office Phone: 440-247-8287. Personal E-mail: jgroetzi@yahoo.com.

GROFF, ARTHUR M., controller; b. Easton, Pa., June 24, 1964; s. Arthur M. and Margaret A. (King) Groff; m. Cynthia L. Hutton, Oct. 25, 1997; children: Jacob, Joseph. BA in Bus. Adminstrn., Vt. Coll., 2000; MBA, Norwich U., 2003. Nat. sales mgr. Filtration Engring., Portland, Pa., 1995—2000; contr. Omega Tools Inc., Mt. Bethel, Pa., 2000—04, gen. mgr. fin. and adminstrn., 2004—. Mem. com. Northampton County Rep. Party, Easton, 1988—92. Mem.: Soc. Human Resource Mgmt., Inst. Mgmt. Accts. Roman Catholic. Avocations: fly fishing, travel. Office: Omega Tools Inc 4136 Church St PO Box 217 Portland PA 18351 Home: 512 Stonybrook Rd Nazareth PA 18064 Office Phone: 570-897-8338. Office Fax: 570-897-7484. Personal E-mail: art@groff-family.com. Business E-Mail: groffmba@rcn.com.

GROFF, STANLEY ALLEN, social services administrator, educator; b. Madison, Minn., Oct. 24, 1942; s. Sherwood Allen and Rosella Belinda (Hanson) G.; m. Margaret Louise Parsons, May 5, 1990; children: Beth Ann, Steve; stepchild, Marco Parsons. BA in Sociology, U. Minn., Morris, 1965; MSW, Fla. State U., 1971. Dir. McLeod County Welfare Dept., Glencoe, Minn., 1967-69; supr. Stearns County Social Svcs., St. Cloud, Minn., 1971-72; dir. Faribault County Social Svcs., Blue Earth, Minn., 1972-75; mgmt. analyst Gov.'s Office Human Svcs., St. Paul, 1975-77; supr. Dakota County Social Svc., South St. Paul, Minn., 1977-80; dir. Steele County Human Svcs., Owatonna, Minn., 1980—, Steele County Transit Authority, Owatonna, 1997—. Founder, leader Steele County Coun. of Dirs., 1982—; grad. adj. asst. prof. St. Mary's U. Minn., Mpls., 1989—; vice chair Region 6 Health Coordinating Bd., S.E. Minn., 1994—. Author: Minnesota Public Social Welfare Administrators in Times of Change, 1994. Founder, bd. dirs. Exch. Club Ctr. for Family Unity, Owatonna, 1982-94; mem. Healthy Owatonna 2000, 1993-98; trustee Owatonna Hosp. Bd., 1995—; founder, bd. dirs. Steele County Clothesline, Inc., 1997, Crossroads Youth Shelter of Owatonna, 1990. Mem. NASW, Minn. Social Svcs. Assn. (pres. 1996), Minn. Assn. County Social Svcs. Adminstrs. (pres. 1983), Owatonna Rotary Club, Owatonna C. of C. Avocations: flying, motorcycling, classic cars, boating, reading. Office: Box 890 630 Florence Ave Owatonna MN 55060-4704

GROGAN, DAVID R., work saver company executive; m. Susie Grogan; 2 children. Founder Toter, Inc., 1983—, pres., chmn., CEO Statesville, NC. Office: Toter Inc 841 Meacham Rd Statesville NC 28677-2983

GROGAN, KATE ANN, music educator, choreographer; b. New Haven, Conn., Mar. 14, 1980; d. Ann Lousie Grogan and Lawrence Stephen Gaechter. BA in Music, BS in Edn., U. Conn., 2003. Cert. Conn., 2003. Voice, piano, dance tchr. Cmty. Sch. of Arts, Pvt. Studios, U. Conn., Storrs, Glastonbury, Middletown, North Branford, Conn., 1994—; early childhood music and movement tchr. Cmty. Sch. Arts, Storrs, Conn., 2000—03; choreographer Middletown Pub. Sch, IDS, Conn. Sch. of Performing Arts, 2003; gen. choral music tchr. Middletown BOE, 2003—. Dance team coach, dir. musical performances, dance club leader Middletown BOE, 2003—. Singer solo recitals, choral works; actor: (musicals). Student ednl. embassador Sister City Program, New Haven/Leon, Conn., 1998. Mem.: Music Educators Nat. Conf., Conn. Music Educator' Assn., Am. Choral Dirs. Assn. Avocations: travel, baking, tennis, theater, dance. Office: Moody Elem Sch 300 Country Club Rd Middletown CT 06457 Office Phone: 860-347-2561. Personal E-mail: misskgrogan@yahoo.com. E-mail: grogank@mps1.org.

GROGAN, LYNN LANGLEY, lawyer; b. Rockingham, N.C., Jan. 16, 1957; d. John Wesley and Hilda Maske Langley; m. Lee Roy Grogan Jr., Oct. 29, 1983; children: Erin Margaret, Hannah Elizabeth, Mary-Stamper. AB, Davidson Coll., 1979; JD, Mercer U., 1983. Counselor Jack Eckerd Found., Tampa, Fla., 1979-80; assoc. Hirsch, Beil & Partin, P.C., Columbus, Ga., 1983-86, ptnr., 1986-89, Hirsch, Partin, Grogan & Grogan, P.C., Columbus, 1989—. Chmn. Child Fatality/Abuse Protocol, Columbus, 1990-93; lectr. CLE, Atlanta. Bd. dirs. Muscogee Edn. Excellence Found., Columbus, 1994-97; founding bd. dirs. Easter Seal Soc. West Ga., Columbus, 1986; bd. dirs. March of Dimes, Columbus, 1984-86; chmn. State Public Affairs Com., Atlanta, 1991-92. Recipient Leadership award Leadership Columbus, 1995, Woman of Achievement award Concharty Order of Girl Scouts U.S., 1998. Fellow Am. Acad. Matrimonial Lawyers; mem. Ga. State Bar Assn., Columbus Bar Assn., Jr. League of Columbus (pres. 1996-97). Avocations: biking, reading, stitchery. Home: 2715 Lynda Ln Columbus GA 31906-1248 Office: Hirsch Partin Grogan & Grogan PC 1021 3d Ave Columbus GA 31901

GROGAN, MICHAEL WAYNE, columnist, editor-in-chief, poet; b. Mabelvale, Ark., Feb. 15, 1940; s. Horace Milton and Charmel Elaine Grogan. BA in Art, Henderson Coll., Arkadelphia, Ark., 1963. Freelance work Ark. Gazette, 1961—91; newspaper columnist Southern Standard, Arkadelphia, Ark., 1979—87, Daily Siftings Herald, 1987—94; editor and publisher Heroes from Hackland mag., 1995—. Contbg. editor: The Best of Grogan Essay Collection, 1987. Democrat. Methodist. Avocations: comic book collecting, juvenile book series collecting. Office: Heroes from Hackland 1225 Evans Arkadelphia AR 71923 Office Phone: 870-246-6223.

GROGAN, PAUL J., retired engineering educator; b. Adrian, Minn., Nov. 20, 1918; s. William Edward and Amelia (Steinbach) Grogan; m. Dorothy Wells, Sept. 7, 1946; children: William, Jane, Katherine, Mary, JoAnne, Tom. BSME, Purdue U., 1943; student in diesel engring., Pa. State U., 1943; student in naval architecture, U. Mich., 1944—45; MSME, U. Wis., 1949. Cert. profl. engr., Wis. Asst. prof. U. Notre Dame, Ind., 1950—51; dir. OSTS, Dept. Commerce, Washington, 1966—68; from instr. to asst. prof. U. Wis., Madison, 1947—50, from asst. prof. to prof., 1951—66, prof., 1968—85, prof. emeritus, 1985—. Power cons. City of Marshfield, Wis., 1952—56; loss analysis Madison Gas and Electric, 1972—85. Editor: (two volume set) History of Tech.: Tech. in Western Civilization 1961-1965; contbr. articles to profl. jours.; illustrator:. Mem. various state and county coms. Lt. USN, 1943—46, PTO. Recipient various awards. Mem.: Am. Soc. Engring. Edn. (life), Nat. Soc. Power Engrs. (life), Am. Legion, Triangle Fraternity. Avocations: crossword puzzles, mathematics, science, word games, puzzles. Home: 18 Southwick Cir Madison WI 53717 E-mail: pjgrogan@facstaff.wisc.edu.

GROGAN, VIRGINIA S., lawyer; b. Pasadena, Calif., Nov. 19, 1951; d. Bruce Mason and Helen Maude Gorsuch; m. Aug. 17, 1973 (div. June 1975); m. Allen R. Grogan, Jan. 10, 1982; children: Travis, Tess. BS, Occidental Coll., Eagle Rock, Calif., 1973; JD, U. So. Calif. Bar: Calif. 1979. Assoc. Latham & Watkins, LA, 1979-86, ptnr., 1987-97, chmn. assocs. com., 1995-97, mng. ptnr. Orange County Office Costa Mesa, Calif., 1997—. Mem. exec. roundtable U. Calif., Irvine, 1998—; mem. adv. com. Orange County Performing Arts, Costa Mesa, 1998—. Mem. ABA, Los Angeles County Bar Assn., Orange County Bar Assn. (judiciary com. 1998—), Legion Lex. Avocations: travel, classic music. Office: Latham & Watkins 650 Town Center Dr Costa Mesa CA 92626-1989

GROH, JENNIFER CALFA, law librarian; b. Patchogue, NY, Mar. 28, 1970; d. Anthony Bernard and Mary (Fogerty) C.; m. William Matthew Groh, May 10, 1997. BA in Social Sci., St. Joseph's Coll., 1992; MA in Internat. Edn., NYU, 1993; MSLS, Pratt Inst., Bklyn., 1996. Reference page Patchogue (N.Y.)-Medford Libr., 1986-93; from libr. asst. to libr. mgr. Morgan & Finnegan, N.Y.C., 1994—. NYU grad. scholar, 1992, Law Libr. Assn. scholar, N.Y. 1995, Am. Assn. Law Librs. scholar, 1996. Mem. ALA, Spl. Librs. Assn., Law Libr. Assn. Greater N.Y. Home: 21 Mohawk Dr North Babylon NY 11703-3303 Office: Morgan & Finnegan 3 World Fin Ctr New York NY 10281-2101 Office Phone: 212-303-2672. Business E-Mail: jgroh@morganfinnegan.com.

GROHS, ROBERT LOUIS, computer scientist; b. Washington, Jan. 19, 1943; s. Louis Henry and Bessie Jones Grohs; m. Grace Patti Musumeci, Sept. 12, 1963; children: Patti Ann, Robert Louis. AA, Montgomery Coll., 1964. Computer specialist Dept. of Army, Arlington, Va., 1970—95. Author: Merchandise Manual, 1978; inventor elec. grill with adjustable cooking surfaces, 2002, elec. grill with food divider, 2004. Office: Emerson St Ptnrs PO Box 5775 Bethesda MD 20824 Office Phone: 301-774-5643. E-mail: esp@olg.com.

GROISS, FRED GEORGE, lawyer; b. Glen Cove, NY, Mar. 12, 1936; s. Frederick F.W. and Dorothy C. (Roberts) G.; m. Jacqueline C. Grosse; children— Frederick C., Katherine E., Jennifer L. AB, Cornell U., 1958, LL.B., 1961. Bar: N.Y. 1961, Wis. 1963, U.S. Dist. Ct. (ea. dist.) Wis., 1963, U.S. Ct. Appeals (7th cir.) 1965. Assoc. Sage, Gray, Todd & Sims, N.Y.C., 1961-63; assoc. Porter, Quale, Porter & Zirbel, Milw., 1963-65, Brady, Tyrrell, Cotter & Cutler, Milw., 1965-70; ptnr. Quarles & Brady, Milw., 1970-2000; ret. Mem. Gov.'s Commn. on Civil Service Reform, Madison, Wis., 1977—78. Mem.: Wis. Bar Assn. (bd. dirs. labor law sect. 1975—77), Greencroft ACAC Club. Republican. Avocation: sports. Home: 2460 Dunmore Rd Charlottesville VA 22901-9447 E-mail: fgg@cstone.net.

GROL, REGINA, literature educator, translator; b. Dubno, Poland, Jan. 19, 1945; d. Teofil Meir Grol and Maria (Masza) Pinczuk; m. Czeslaw Zygmunt Prokopczyk, Feb. 21, 1970 (div. Apr. 1992); children: Hanna, Benjamin. MA in English, Warsaw U., 1967; MA in Comparative Lit., SUNY, 1970, PhD in Comparative Lit., 1973. Asst. prof. SUNY, Binghamton, 1973—74, Empire State Coll., Buffalo, 1974—, prof. comparative lit., 1991—. Vis. asst. prof. Rutgers U., New Brunswick, NJ, 1976—77; vis. assoc. prof. U. Buffalo, 1988, Hunter Coll., CUNY, N.Y.C., 1990—91; mem. adv. artistic coun. Irish Classical Theatre, Buffalo, 2000—. Translator: (book) Poems by URzula Koziot, 1989, Between Dawn and the Wind, 1991, Ambers Aglow, 1996, And Yet I Still Have Dreams, 2004. Mem.: Polish Inst. Arts & Scis., Polish-Jewish Studies Assn., Am. Assn. Slavic Studies, Polish Arts Club (bd. dirs. 1994, 2001—03, chair programs com. 1999—2003). Office: Empire State Coll SUNY 617 Main St Buffalo NY 14203-1498

GROLLI, FRANK THOMAS, retired pharmacist; b. Bklyn., July 25, 1933; s. Frank and Theresa D. G.; m. Maria T. Cerbone, Mar. 30, 1974. BS in Pharmacy, Bklyn. Coll. Pharmacy, 1956. Registered pharmacist Ferro's Pharmacy, Bklyn., 1959-61; mgr., owner Associated Drugs, NYC, 1961-66; mgr., pharmacist Frank's Pharmacy, Staten Island, 1966-76; asst. mgr., pharmacist Savon SuperX, Staten Island, 1976-84, asst. mgr., pharmacy supr., 1984-88, pharmacy coord., 1988-94; n.e. region pharmacy coord. H.S.I., Rutherford, NJ, 1994; pharmacy supr. Revco D.S., Carteret, NJ, 1994-95, ret., 1995. Col. Med. Svc. Corps, 1961-86. Decorated Nat. Def. Svc. medal. Army Reserve Comp. Achievement medal, Meritorous Svc. medal. Mem. APHA, Pharm. Soc. NY, N.Y.C. Pharm. Soc., Italian Pharm. Soc., Res. Officers Assn., Assn. Mil. Surgeons. Avocations: gardening, stamp collecting/philately, fishing, home repairs.

GROMACKI, SUSAN JEAN, optometrist; b. Greenfield, Mass., Oct. 03; d. George Peter and Jean Klocko Gromacki; m. Scott David Lathrop, June 2, 2001; 1 child, Sarah Jean Lathrop. BS, U. Notre Dame, 1989; OD, MS in Physiol. Optics, Ohio State U., 1993. Lic. optometrist. Resident in hosp.-based optometry U. S. Dept. of Veterans Affairs Med. Ctr., Chillicothe, Ohio, 1993—94; asst. prof. optometry New Eng. Coll. Optometry, Boston, 1994—98; faculty dept. ophthalmology and visual scis. U. Mich., Ann Arbor, 1998—2001; optometrist Hudson Valley Eye Surgeons, Fishkill, NY, 2002—03, Kaiser Permanente, Fairfax, Va., 2004—. Speakers' bur. Vistakon (Johnson & Johnson), Jacksonville, Fla., 1995—2003; cons. Westcon Contact Lens Co., Grand Junction, Colo., 1999; examiner Nat. Bd. of Examiners in Optometry, 1998—; speakers' bur. Sunsoft Contact Lens Co., Albuquerque, 1996—99; adv. bd. Cooper Vision, Rochester, NY, 1996—; cons. Danker Contact Lens Co., Miami, Fla., 2001—. Contbr. articles to profl. jours. V.p. Mil. Coun. of Cath. Women, West Point, NY, 2002—03; mem. parish coun. . Most Holy Trinity Parish, West Point, NY, 2002—03; provider Vision USA, Various, 1994—. Recipient Contact Lens Achievement award, CIBA Vision, 1993, Harold F. Kohn award, Am. Optometric Found., 1993, Allergan Optometry award, Allergan, 1993, Wesley-Jessen award for Excellence, Wesley-Jessen, 1993, Alcon NOVA award, Alcon, 1993, America's Top Optometrists, Consumers' Rsch. Coun. of Am., 2002, 2003, 2004, 2005; Ednl. grant, Vistakon/ Johnson & Johnson, 1992, Optometry Class of 1953 Endowed scholarship, Ohio State U., 1992, U. of Notre Dame scholar, U. of Notre Dame, 1985—89, Bausch & Lomb Contact with the Future Ednl. Travel grant, Bausch & Lomb, 1992. Fellow: Am. Acad. Optometry (nat. comm. com. 2001—); mem.: Va. Optometric Assn., Ohio Optometric Assn., Mass. Soc. Optometrists, Mich. Optometric Assn., NY State Optometric Assn., Am. Optometric Assn., Assn. Contact Lens Educators, Ohio State U. Alumni Assn., U. Notre Dame Alumni Assn. (Boston bd. dirs. 1996—98), Epsilon Psi Epsilon. Roman Catholic. Avocations: physical fitness, golf, tennis, cooking, travel.

GROMADA, THADDEUS V., historian, academic administrator; b. Passaic, NJ, July 30, 1929; s. John W. and Aniela (Pudzisz) Gromada; m. Theresa M. Michalski, Aug. 25, 1951; children: Joseph, John, Ann. BS magna cum laude, Seton Hall U., 1951; MA, Fordham U., 1953, PhD, 1966. From asst. prof. history to prof. European history N.J. City U., 1959-92; v.p., exec. dir. Polish Inst. Arts and Scis., N.Y.C., 1991—. Chmn. Gov.'s Commn. Ea. European History, Trenton, NJ, 1985—89; cons. ethnic heritage Dept. Edn., Washington; cons. NEA, 1975—. Author, editor: book Essays on Poland's Foreign Policy 1918-1939, 1969; co-editor: Polonia Amerykanska, 1988; editor: Jadwiga of Anjou & Rise of East Central Europe, 1991; founder, co-editor: Tatra Eagle, 1947—. Mem. awards com. Korczak Lit. prize, 1980—85; co-organizer Conf. Germany, Poland & Europe, 1992; organizer Conf. Jagiellonian U.and Polish Acad. Arts and Scis., Cracow, Poland, 2000; vice chmn., trustee Kosciusko Found., N.Y.C., 1981—; mem. dialog com. Nat. Polish Am.-Jewish Am. Coun., Washington, 2001—. Sgt. U.S. Army, 1953—55. Decorated Officer's Cross of Merit Pres. Poland, Comdrs. Cross, L'Ordre du Merite Culturel Poland's Min. of Culture and Arts; recipient Haiman medal, Polish Am. Hist. Assn., 1985. Mem.: Polish Am. Hist. Assn. (pres. 1995—96), Am. Hist. Assn., Am. Assn. Advancement Slavic Studies. Roman Catholic. Avocations: classical music, violin, polish highlander folklore, hiking. Home: 2722 Old Oak Walk Johns Island SC 29455-6213 Office: Polish Inst Arts & Scis 208 E 30th St New York NY 10016-8202 E-mail: tgromada@mindspring.com.

GRONER, BEVERLY ANNE, retired lawyer; b. Des Moines; d. Benjamin L. and Annabelle (Miller) Zavat; m. Jack Davis; children: Morrilou Davis Morell, Lewis A. Davis, Andrew G. Davis; m. Samuel Brian Groner, Dec. 17, 1962. Student, Drake U., 1939-40, Cath. U., 1954-56; JD, Am. U., 1959. Bar: Md. 1959, U.S. Supreme Ct. 1963, D.C. 1965. Pvt. practice, Bethesda Md., Washington, 1959-99; ret., 1999. Chmn. Md. Gov.'s Commn. on Domestic Relations Laws 1977-87; exec. com. trustee Montgomery-Prince George's Continuing Legal Edn. Inst., 1983-99, pres., 1992-98; lectr. to lay, profl. groups; speaker to Bar Assns. and numerous seminars; participant continuing legal edn. programs, local and nat.; participant, faculty mem. trial demonstration films Am. Law Inst.-ABA Legal Consortium; participant numerous TV, radio programs; seminar leader, expert-in-residence Harvard Law Sch., 1987, Family Law, Georgetown U. Law Ctr., 1988, 89; mem. gov.'s com. ERA, 1978-80; faculty mem. Montgomery County Bar Assn. Law Sch. for the Pub., 1991, Inst. on Professionalism, 1992. Cons. editor Family Law Reporter, 1986-90, MD Family Law Monthly, 1993-99; mem. bd. editors Fairshare 1992-97; contbr. numerous articles to profl. jours. Pres. Am. Acad. Matrimonial Lawyers Found., 1994-98. Named One of Leading Matrimonial Practitioners in U.S., Nat. Law Jour., 1979, 87, Best Divorce Lawyer in Md., Washingtonian Mag., 1981, One of Best Matrimonial Lawyers in U.S., Town and Country mag., 1985, Best Lawyers in Am., 1987—; recipient Disting. Svc. award Va. State Bar Assn., 1982, Okla. Bar Assn., 1987, Md. Gubernatorial citation, 1987. Fellow Am. Acad. Matrimonial Lawyers (pres. Md. chpt. 1992-98, pres.-elect found. 1993-94); mem. Bar Assn. Montgomery County (exec. com. chmn. family law sect. 1976, chmn. fee arbitration panel 1974-77, legal ethics com.), Md. State Bar Assn. bd. of govs., (gov., chmn. family law sect. 1975-77, vice chmn. com. continuing legal edn., ethics com. 1991-99, mem. inquiry panel and grievance com., 1991-99, faculty mem. on Professionalism 1992), ABA (chmn. family law sect. 1986-87, rep. to White House conf. on Yr. of Child 1984, sec. family law sect. 1983-84, vice chmn. 1984-85, chmn. sect. marital property com., assn. adv. to nat. conf. commrs. on uniform marital property act, mem. faculty family law advocacy inst. 1988, 90), Am. Acad. of Matrimonial Lawyers, Md. State Bar Assn. (mem. inquiry panel and grievance com. 1991—), Phi Alpha Delta. Home: 5600 Wisconsin Ave Apt 1602 Chevy Chase MD 20815-4413

GRONLUND, ROBERT B., art collector, fund raising consultant; b. Duluth, Minn., May 2, 1926; s. Bernard S. and Lena J. (Manske) G.; m. Dorothy M. Dahlstrom, June 2, 1951; children: Gaye, Robin, Gregg, Jamie. BA, Wartburg Coll., Waverly, Iowa, 1949; MDiv, Wartburg Sem., Dubuque, 1953; LittD, Thiel Coll., Greenville, Pa., 1973. Ordained Luth. Ch., 1953. Pastor Newport Harbor Luth. Ch., Newport Beach, Calif., 1953-56; exec. dir. Inter Ch. Fellowship, L.A., 1956-59; asst. to pres. Calif. Luth. U., Thousand Oaks, Calif., 1959-62; exec. dir. Am. Luth. Ch. Found., Mpls., 1962-63; v.p. devel. Capital U., Columbus, Ohio, 1963-69, U. Tampa, Fla., 1969-76; founding ptnr. Gronlund Sayther Brunkow, West Palm Beach, Fla., 1976—; pres. Fla. campus Northwood U., West Palm Beach, 1981-83. Mem. works of art com. Norton Mus., West Palm Beach, 1993-96; chair PBCC Art Gallery, Palm Beach Gardens, Fla., 1995-96; chair Tampa Bay Art Ctr., Tampa, 1973-74;

chair Vision for Mission Com., Evang. Luth. Ch. Am., Chgo., 1995-99. Exhibited collection at Norton Mus., Pensacola Mus., Tampa Mus., Wartburg Coll., Lighthouse Gallery, Tequesta, Fla., Ctr. for Arts, Vero Beach, Fla., others. Chair Fla. Repertory Theater, West Palm Beach, 1990—92; founding pres. Planned Giving Coun., West Palm Beach, 1982—84; sr. warden Bethesda By Sea Episcopal Ch., 1995; founding chair S.E. Diocese Episcopal Found., 1999—2002. Cpl. U.S. Army, 1943—46, ETO. Mem.: Men of Bethesda (chair 2002—). Republican. Episcopalian. Avocations: golf, travel, grandchildren. Home: 2320 Saratoga Bay Dr West Palm Beach FL 33409-7222 E-mail: bobgronlund@gsbfr.com.

GRONSTAL, TOM, commissioner, bank executive; Chmn. Carroll County State Bank; commr. Iowa Divsn. Banking, 2001—. Mem. Iowa Workforce Devel. Regional Adv. Bd., Carroll Area Devel. Corp. Former pres. Carroll C. of C., Iowa Bankers Assn. Named to Iowa Vol. Hall of Fame, 1994. Office: 200 E Grand Ste 300 Des Moines IA 50309*

GROOM, WINSTON FRANCIS, JR., writer; b. Washington, Mar. 23, 1943; s. Winston Francis and Ruth (Knudsen) G.; m. Ruth Noble, Dec. 10, 1969 (div. Mar. 1985); m. Anne-Clinton Bridges, June 6, 1987. AB, U. Ala., 1965. Reporter The Washington Star, 1968-77; author Simon & Schuster, N.Y.C., 1977-81, G.P. Putnams, N.Y.C., Doubleday & Co., N.Y.C., 1984—. Author: Better Times Than These, 1978, As Summer's Die, 1981, Only, 1984, Forest Gump, 1986 (#1 NY Times Bestseller), Gone the Sun, 1988, Gumpisms: The Wit and Wisdom of Forrest Gump, 1994, The Bubba Gump Shrimp Co. Cookbook: Recipes & Reflections from Forrest Gump, 1994, Shrouds of Glory, 1995, Such a Pretty Girl, 1999, The Crimson Tide, 2000, A Storm in Flanders, 2002, 1942: The Year That Tried Men's Souls, 2005; (co-author) Conversations with the Enemy, 1983 (Pulitzer Prize nomination, 1984). Served to cpt. U.S. Army, 1965-68, Vietnam. Recipient Best Novel award So. Library Assn., 1982, Pulitzer Prize nomination, 1984. Mem. Writers Guild Am. Presbyterian. Office: c/o Theron Raines Raines & Raines Agy 103 Kenyon Rd Medusa NY 12120*

GROOMS, BRUCE ESTES, career military officer; b. Cleveland, Ohio; m. Emily Penn; children: Geoff, Jared. BS, U.S. Naval Acad., Annapolis, 1980; M in nat. security & strategic studies, Naval War Coll.; Nat. Security Affairs Fellow, Stanford Univ. Commd. ensign USN, advanced through grades to capt.; exec. officer USS Pasadena (SSN 752); commdg. officer USS Asheville (SSN 758); co. officer U.S. Naval Acad., Annapolis; sr. inspector Atlantic Fleet nuclear propulsion examining bd.; sr. mil. aide to under sec. for policy U.S. Dept. Def., Washington; comdt. of midshipmen U.S. Naval Acad., Annapolis, 2005—. Decorated Def. Superior Svc. medal, Legion of Merit (2 awards), Meritorious Svc. medal; recipient Vice Adm. Stockdale Inspirational Leadership award, 1999. Office: US Naval Academy Commandant of Midshipmen 121 Blake Rd Annapolis MD 21402-5000

GROOMS, HENRY RANDALL, civil engineer; b. Cleve., Feb. 10, 1944; s. Leonard Day and Lois (Pickell) G.; m. Tonie Marie Joseph; children: Catherine, Zayne, Nina, Ivan, Ian, Athesis, Shaneya, Yaphet, Rahsan, Dax, Jevay, Xava. BSCE, Howard U., 1965; MSCE, Carnegie-Mellon U., 1967, PhD, 1969. Hwy. engr. D.C. Hwy. Dept., Washington, 1965; structural engr. Peter F. Loftus Corp., Pitts., 1966; structural engr., engring. mgr. Rockwell Internat. (now Boeing), Downey, Calif., 1969—. Contbr. articles to profl. jours. Scoutmaster Boy Scouts Am., Granada Hills, Calif., 1982-87; basketball coach Valley Conf., Granada Hills, 1984—; coach Am. Youth Soccer Orgn., Granada Hills, 1985-90, 94—; tutor Watts Friendship Sports League, 1989—; co-founder Project Reach Scholarship Found., 1993. Recipient Alumni Merit award Carnegie-Mellon U., 1985, Lifetime Achievement award Black Engr. of Yr. Awards Conf., 2004, Lifetime Achievement in Industry award Nat. Soc. Black Engrs., 2004; honoree Black History Project Western Res. Hist. Soc., 1989. Fellow Inst. Advancement Engring. (Outstanding Engring. Vol. award, 1999), African Sci. Inst.; mem. ASCE, Tau Beta Pi, Sigma Xi. Office: Boeing Mail Code H013-C326 5301 Bolsa Ave Huntington Beach CA 92647-2099 E-mail: henry.r.grooms@boeing.com.

GROOMS, RED (CHARLES ROGERS GROOMS), artist; b. Nashville, June 2, 1937; Student, Peabody Coll., Chgo. Art Inst., New Sch. Social Research, Hans Hofmann Sch., Provincetown, Mass. One-man exhbns. include, Sun Gallery, Provincetown, 1958, Reuben Gallery, N.Y.C., 1960, Tibor de Nagy Gallery, 1963, 65-67, 69-70, Artists Guild, Nashville, 1962, Allan Frumkin Gallery, Chgo., 1967, John Bernard Myers Gallery Discount Store, 1971, Happenings: A Play Called Fire, Sun Gallery, 1958, Burning Bldgs, N.Y.C., 1958, Rutgers Gallery Art, New Brunswick, N.J., 1973, N.Y. Cultural Center, 1973, Mus. de Arte Contemporaneo, Caracas, Venezuela, 1973, Brooke Alexander Gallery, N.Y.C., 1975, Ft. Worth Art Mus., 1976, Stanford Mus., 1976, SUNY-Purchase, 1978, Hudson River Mus., Yonkers, N.Y., 1979, Lowe Art Mus., U. Miami, 1980, Aspen Ctr. Visual Arts, 1981, Seibu Mus., Tokyo, 1982, Marlborough Gallery N.Y.C., 1984, 86, 87, 89, 90, 92, 95, 96, Marlborough Fine Art, London, 1985, Hokin/Kaufman Gallery, Chgo., 1985, Benjamin Mangel Gallery, Phila., 1985, Circulo de Bellas Artes, Madrid, 1985, Sette Pub. Co., Tempe, Ariz., 1985, Pa. Acad. Fine Arts, 1985-86, Stanton Gallery Denver Art Mus., 1986, Mus. Contemporary Art, Los Angeles, 1986, Tenn. State Mus., Nashville, 1986, Cumberland Gallery, Nashville, 1985-86, 1986, Marlborough Fine Art, Tokyo, 1986, Fine Arts Ctr., Cheekwood, Nashville, 1986—, Muscarelle Mus. Art Coll. William and Mary, Williamsburg, Va., 1986—, Ruth Eckerd Hall, Clearwater, Fla., 1986—, Erie (Pa.) Art Mus., 1986—, William Benton Mus. Art U. Conn., Storrs, 1986—, S.D. Meml. Art Ctr., Brookings, 1986—, The Nelson-Atkins Mus. Art, Kansas City, Mo., 1986—, Arvada (Colo.) Ctr. Arts and Humanities, 1986—, Carpenter Ctr. Visual Arts Harvard U., Cambridge, Mass., 1986, Whitney Mus., N.Y.C., 1973, 87, Marlborough Gallery, Paris, 1990, Arvada Ctr. for Arts and Humanities, Colo., 1992, Cabaret Voltaire, Turin, Italy, 1992, Grand Ctrl. Terminal, N.Y.C., 1993, Nagoya City Mus., Japan, 1993, others; group exhbns. include, Chgo. Art Inst., 1964, Delancey St. Mus., N.Y.C., 1959, 60, also, Provincetown/Chrysler Mus., Tibor de Nagy Gallery, N.Y.C., 1969, Walker Art Center, Mpls., 1970, 88-89, Guggenheim Mus., N.Y.C., 1972, Ruckus Manhattan, N.Y.C., 1975-76, 81, SUNY, Purchase, 1978, Lowe Art Mus. U., Miami (Fla.), 1980, The New Gallery, Cleve., 1982, ICA, Phila., 1982, Allen Frumkin Gallery, N.Y.C., 1985, Open Air Mus. Sculpture, Middelheim, Antwerp, Belgium, 1985, Sewell Art Gallery Rice U., Houston, 1985, Artists' Choice Mus., N.Y.C., 1986, Mus. Art, Ft. Lauderdale, Fla., 1986, Wilson Art Ctr., Rochester, N.Y., 1986, Allentown (Pa.) Art Mus., 1986, N.Y. Acad. Art, 1986, Whitney Mus. Am. Art at Philip Morris, N.Y.C., 1986-87, Nat. Mus. Am. History Smithsonian Instn., Washington, 1986—, Saxon Lee Gallery, L.A., 1988, Baruch Coll., N.Y.C., 1988, Lockport Gallery, Ill., 1988-89, Bucknell U., Lewisburg, Pa., 1989, others; (with Rudy Burckhardt) movie Shoot the Moon, 1962, Big Sneeze, 1965, Before'n After, 1966, Washington's Wig Whammed!, 1966, Fat Feet, 1966, (with Rudi Burckhardt) Meow, Meow!, 1967, Small Fry Gangster, 1985; represented in permanent collections, Mint Mus. Art, Charlotte, N.C., Chgo. Art Inst., Mus. Modern Art, N.Y.C., Chrysler Mus. Art, Provincetown, Mass., Cheekwood Fine Arts Mus., Nashville, Met. Mus. Art, N.Y.C., Moderna Mus., Stockholm, Agrl. Bldg. Des Moines Art Ctr.; (theatre) set design The Mysteries and What's So Funny, 1991; commd. (with Lysiane Luong) for Am. Mus. of Moving Image, N.Y., for movie theater titled Tuts Fever. Recipient Pres.'s award R.I. Sch. Design, 1985, Ten Best Illustrated Childrens' Books award N.Y. Times, 1986, Gov.'s award in Art, State of Tenn., 1986, Nat. Arts Club award, 1986, N.Y.C. Mayor's award of Honor, 1988, Founders medal Pa. Acad. Arts, 1990. Mailing: c/o Tibor de Nagy Gallery 724 Fifth Ave New York NY 10019*

GROOS, ARTHUR BERNHARD, JR., German studies educator, music educator; b. Fullerton, Calif., Feb. 5, 1943; s. Arthur Bernhard and Nancy Elizabeth (Stowe) G.; m. Bonnie Cleo Buettner, May 16, 1979; children: Peter, Jan. AB magna cum laude, Princeton U., 1964; MA, Cornell U., Ithaca, N.Y., 1966; PhD, Cornell U., 1970; postgrad., Freie Universitat Berlin, 1966-67. Asst. prof. UCLA, 1969-73; asst. prof. German lit. Cornell U., 1973-76, assoc. prof., 1976-82, prof., 1982—, dir. medieval studies, 1974-86, chmn. dept. German studies, 1986-91, 96-99, prof. German studies and music, 2003—. Chmn. German dept. adv. coun. Princeton U., N.J., 1981-85; vis. prof. U. Paderborn, W.Ger., 1982, Freie U. Berlin, 2001-02, U. Amiens, 2004; bd. dirs. Centro Studi Giacomo Puccini (Lucca). Author: Puccini: La Boheme, 1986, Romancing the Grail, 1995; co-author: Medieval Christian Literary Imagery, 1988; editor: Dichtkunst und Lebenkunst, 1981, Magister Regis, 1986, Reading Opera, 1988, Cambridge Opera Jour., 1988-98, Studi pucciniani, 1998—, Perceval/Parzival, 2002, Madama Butterfly: Fonti e documenti, 2005; gen. editor: Cambridge Opera Monographs; co-editor: Kulturen des Manuskriptzeitalters, 2004, Transatlantische Studien. Fulbright fellow Berlin, 1966, Fulbright sr. fellow Munich, 1979, Guggenheim fellow Munich, 1979; recipient ASCAP-Deems Taylor prize, 1993, Humboldt Rsch. prize 1999. Mem. MLA, Internat. Arthurian Soc., Medieval Acad. Am., Wolfram v. Eschenbach Gesellschaft, Internat. Courtly Lit. Soc., Am. Musicol. Soc., Phi Beta Kappa. Home: 492 Valley Rd Brooktondale NY 14817-9701 Office: Cornell U Dept German Studies 185 Goldwin Smith Hall Ithaca NY 14853-3201 Office Phone: 607-255-5265. Business E-Mail: abg3@cornell.edu.

GROOTHUIS, DOUGLAS RICHARD, minister, educator; b. Anchorage, Jan. 3, 1957; s. Harold Fred and Lillian (Cominetto) G.; m. Rebecca Merrill, Aug. 4, 1984. BS in Philosophy, U. Oreg., 1979; MA in Philosophy, U. Wis., 1986; PhD in Philosophy, U. Oreg., 1993. Instr., writer McKenzie Study Ctr., Eugene, Oreg., 1979-84; rschr. Probe Ministries, Seattle, 1986-89; adj. in religion dept. Seattle Pacific U., 1987—; campus min. Restoration Campus Ministry, Eugene, Oreg., 1989—93; assoc. prof. philosophy Denver Sem., 1993—2003, prof., 2003—. Vis. instr. U. Oreg., 1992. Author: Unmasking the New Age, 1986, The New Age Movement, 1986, Confronting the New Age, 1988, Revealing the New Age Jesus, 1990, New Age, New Life, 1990, The New Age Jesus, 1992, Christianity That Counts, 1994, Deceived By The Light, 1995, Jesus in an Age of Controversy, 1996, The Soul in Cyberspace, 1997, Are All Religions One?, 1996, Truth Decay, 2000, On Jesus, 2003, On Pascal, 2003, In Defense of Natural Theology, 2005; contbr. Christian Rsch. Jour., 1988—; contbr. articles to profl. jours. Mem. Evangel. Philos. Soc., Evang. Theol. Soc. Mem. Evang. Ch. Avocation: book collecting. Office: Denver Sem PO Box 100000 Denver CO 80201-1000 Office Phone: 303-762-6895.

GROPP, LOUIS OLIVER, editor-in-chief; b. LaPorte, Ind., June 6, 1935; s. Hosea Howard and Carol Gladys (Pagel) G.; m. Jane Margaret Goodwin, Aug. 15, 1965; children: Amy Alison Forbes, Lauren Elizabeth Lowry. BA in Communication Arts, Mich. State U., 1957. Design editor Home Furnishings Daily, Chgo. and N.Y.C., 1960-67; v.p. Milo Baughman Design, Wellesley, Mass., 1967; exec. editor House & Garden Guides, Conde Nast Co., N.Y.C., 1968—72, editor-in-chief, 1973—80, House and Garden mag., N.Y.C., 1981—88; v.p. design and creative svcs., consumer products div. Westpoint-Pepperell, N.Y.C., 1988-89; editor in chief Elle Decor, Hachette Pub. co., N.Y.C., 1990-91; editor-in-chief House Beautiful, Hearst Mags. Div., N.Y.C., 1991-2000. Author: Solar Houses, 1978. Chmn. bd. deacons Riverside Ch., N.Y.C., 1973-75; pres. bd. Christianity and Crisis, 1988-90; bd. dirs. Am. Soc. Mag. Editors, 1990-94, N.Y. Theol. Sem., 1999—, N.Y. Sch. Interior Design, N.Y.C., 2001—, Long House Res., Easthampton, N.Y., 2001—. Home: 140 Riverside Dr Apt 6G New York NY 10024-2605 also: 44 Old Depot Rd Quogue NY 11959 E-mail: lougropp@earthlink.com.

GROPPER, ALLAN LOUIS, bankruptcy judge; BA, Yale U., 1965; JD, Harvard U., 1969. Bar: N.Y. 1969, U.S. Dist. Ct. (so. and ea. dists.) N.Y. 1971, U.S. Ct. Appeals (2d cir.) 1971, U.S. Supreme Ct. 1974. Atty. Civil Appeals Bur., Legal Aid Soc., N.Y.C., 1969-71; assoc. White & Case, N.Y.C., 1972-77, ptnr., 1978-2000; bankruptcy judge U.S. Bankruptcy Ct., N.Y.C., 2000—. Adj. prof. Fordham Law Sch., 2003—. Bd. dirs. Browning Sch., 1990—. pres., 1997-2000; bd. dirs. Legal Aid Soc., 1990-2000, v.p., 1996-2000; bd. dirs. N.Y. Lawyers for Pub. Interest, 1990-2000. Mem. ABA, Assn. of Bar of City of N.Y. (v.p. 1995-96, mem. exec. com. 1991-96, chmn. 1994-95). Office: US Bankruptcy Ct Alexander Hamilton Custom House 1 Bowling Green New York NY 10004 Office Phone: 212-668-5629.

GROPPER, SAREEN ANNORA STEPNICK, dietician, educator; b. Washington, July 9, 1959; d. Edward William and Barbara Claryce Stepnick; m. Daniel Michael Gropper, July 31, 1982; children: Michelle Lauren, Michael James. BS, U. Md., 1981; MS, Fla. State U., 1984, PhD, 1987. Prof. Auburn U., Ala., 1988—. Adj. prof. Fla. State U., Tallahassee, 1987-88; mem. Study Inborn Errors metabolism, 1991—; cons. in field. Author: Advanced Nutrition/Human Metabolism, 4th edit., 2005, Biochemistry of Human Nutrition, 2d edit., 2000; contbr. articles to profl. jours. Asst. leader Girl Scout Troop 361, Auburn, 1984-2001. Recipient Faculty of Yr. award Student Dietetic Assn., 2001-2003, Camp War Eagle Faculty Honoree, 1998, Alumni Undergraduate Tchg. award Alumni Assn., 1998-99, Favorite Educator award Mortar Bd., 1999-2000. Mem. Am. Dietetic Assn., Am. Soc. Nutritional Scis., Am. Soc. Parenteral & Enteral Nutrition, Ala. Dietetic Assn. (scholarship chair 2001-2002), Auburn Dietetic Assn. (pres. 1999-2000), Alpha Chi Omega (former scholarship advisor). Avocations: aerobic and anaerobic exercise, reading. Office: Dept Nutrition Food Sci Auburn U 101 Poultry Sci Bldg Auburn AL 36849 Office Phone: 334-844-3271. E-mail: groppss@auburn.edu.

GROSBARD, ULU, film director; b. Antwerp, Belgium, Jan. 9, 1929; came to U.S., 1948; s. Morris and Rose (Tennenbaum) G.; m. Rose Gregorio, Feb. 25, 1965 BA, U. Chgo., 1950, MA, 1952; postgrad., Yale U. Sch. Drama, 1952-53. Dir. plays The Days and Nights of Beebeem, 1962, The Subject Was Roses, 1964 (Tony nomination 1965), A View from the Bridge, 1965 (Obie award 1965), The Investigation, 1966, The Price, 1968, American Buffalo, 1977 (Tony nominations), The Woods, 1980, The Floating Light Bulb, 1981, Weekends Like Other People, 1982, The Wake of Jamie Foster, 1982, The Tenth Man, 1989, Family Week, 2000; (films) The Subject Was Roses, 1968, Who is Harvey Kellerman, 1971, Straight Time, 1978, True Confessions, 1981, Falling in Love, 1984, Georgia, 1994, The Deep End of the Ocean, 1999. Served with U.S. Army, 1953-55 Mem. Dirs. Guild Am., Soc. Dirs. and Choreographers Jewish. Office Phone: 212-586-1616.

GROSCH, LAURA DUDLEY, artist, educator; b. Worcester, Mass., Apr. 1, 1945; d. Daniel Swartwood and Edith Dudley (Taft) G. BA in Art History, Wellesley Coll., 1967; BFA in Painting, U. Pa., 1968. Solo exhbns. include Mint Mus. Art, Charlotte, N.C., 1974, Jerald Melberg Gallery, Charlotte, 1984, 87, Greenville (N.C.) Mus. Art, 1987, Greenville County Mus. Art, 1987, Christa Faut Gallery, Davidson, N.C., 1990, 93, 96, Rock Sch. Arts Found., Valdese, N.C., 2000, Millennium exhbn., Valdese, 2000, others; group exhbns. include Impressions Gallery, Boston, 1973, Rose Mus. Glenbow-Alberta Gallery, Can., 1974, New Orleans Mus. Art, 1975, Bklyn. Mus., 1976, Visual Arts Ctr. Alaska, 1978, Print Club, Phila., 1980, Palazzo Venezia, Rome, 1984, Syracuse U., N.Y., 1987, Wellesley (Mass.) Coll., 1997, Mint Mus. Art, Charlotte, N.C., 2002, Christa Faut Gallery, Cornelius, N.C., 2003, 04, Charlotte Wine and Food, 2004; represented in pub. collections Boston Pub. Libr., Brit. Mus., London, Bklyn. Mus., Fla. State U., Manhattan Coll., Mus. Fine Arts, Boston, N.Y. Pub. Libr., Ringling Mus., Sarasota, Fla., Smithsonian Inst., Washington, UCLA, Newark Pub. Libr., Minn. Inst. Arts, Honolulu Acad. Arts, Dayton (Ohio) Art Inst., Carnegie Mellon U., Pitts., Free Libr. Phila., Victoria and Albert Mus., London, many others. Office: PO Box 10 Davidson NC 28036-8006

GROSE, CHARLES FREDERICK, pediatrician, epidemiologist; b. Faribault, Minn., Apr. 15, 1942; s. Frederick G. and Marie A. (Swelland) G. BA, Beloit Coll., 1963; MD, U. Chgo., 1967. Bd. cert. in pediatric infectious disease. Resident Albert Einstein Coll. Medicine, Bronx, N.Y., 1967-68, fellow, 1970—75, U. Calif., San Francisco, 1975-76; asst. prof. Health Sci. Ctr. U. Tex., San Antonio, 1976-84; prof. pediatrics U. Iowa Hosp., Iowa City, 1985—. Cons. NIH, Bethesda, Md., 1988—. Editor Pediat. Infectious Disease Jour., 2003—; mem. editl. bd. Virology Jour.; contbr. articles to profl. and sci. jours. Capt. U.S. Army Med. Corps, Vietnam, 1968-70. Grantee NIH, 1978—. Fellow Infectious Disease Soc. Am., Pediatric Infectious Disease Soc., Am. Acad. Pediatrics, Am. Soc. Virology. Achievements include research on diagnosis and treatment of chickenpox and shingles, and on the etiologic agent which is varicella virus. Office: U Iowa Hosp Pediatrics 200 Hawkins Dr Iowa City IA 52242-1009 Office Phone: 319-356-2270. Business E-Mail: charles-grose@uiowa.edu.

GROSE, WILLIAM RUSH, publishing executive; b. Charleston, W.Va., Jan. 29, 1939; s. William Ellis and Mary W. (Morrison) G. Grad., Haverford Coll., 1961. With Prentice-Hall, Inc., Englewood Cliffs, N.J., 1962-70, Warner Communications, Inc., N.Y.C., 1970-72; editor-in-chief Dell Pub. Co., Inc., N.Y.C., 1972-79; v.p., pub. Jove Publs., Inc., N.Y.C., 1979-81; v.p., editorial dir. Berkeley/Jove Pub. Group, 1981-82; v.p., editor-in-chief New Am. Library Inc., 1982-83; exec. v.p., editorial dir. Pocket Books, 1983—. Mem.: Knickerbocker; Groucho (London). Democrat. Episcopalian. Home: 929 Park Ave New York NY 10028-0211 also: 128 Blackville Rd Washington CT 06794-1209 Office: Simon and Schuster Ste 383 1230 Avenue Of The Americas Fl Conc1 New York NY 10020-1586

GROSECLOSE, CLARA RITA, retired secondary school educator; b. Kingsport, Tenn. d. Murry Clyde and Gladys Elizabeth (Roller) Groseclose. BS East Tenn. State U., 1944; MA, Columbia U., 1951, George Peabody Coll., 1962. Instr. Tusculum Coll., Greeneville, Tenn., 1947—50; tchr., libr. Dobyns-Bennett H.S., Kingsport, 1950—82. Commr. Govt. Sullivan County, 1986—94; mem. Tenn. Hist. Commn., 1987—97; state pres. Nat. League Am. Pen Women, 2002—04. Mem.: DAR, Sullivan County Farm Bur. (dir.), Delta Kappa Gamma. Home: 774 Bloomingdale Pike Kingsport TN 37660

GROSECLOSE, EVERETT HARRISON, retired editor; b. Childress, Tex., June 25, 1938; s. Everett Jackson and Eula Margaret (Snider) G.; m. Edna Kathryn Hunter, Dec. 24, 1962 (div. 1986); children: Kirsten Lee, Megan Margaret; m. Susan Kahne Greer, Dec. 22, 1990. BA in Journalism, Tex. Tech. U., Lubbock, 1961. Reporter Wall St. Jour., Dallas and N.Y.C., 1965-70; asst. mng. editor Cleve., 1970-76; dir. pub. affairs Dow Jones & Co., N.Y.C., 1976-80; mng. editor Dow Jones News Services, N.Y.C., 1980-88; exec. editor Dow Jones Profl. Investor Report, N.Y.C., 1988-92; dir. product devel. Dow Jones Info. Services, N.Y.C., 1988-92; dir. internat. mktg., news and database svcs. Telerate, Inc. subs. Dow Jones, N.Y.C., 1992-94; mng. editor Dow Jones Emerging Markets Report, N.Y.C., 1994-97, Servicio Dow Jones Americas, N.Y.C., 1996-97; founder Internet Pub. Group, Inc. (formerly VertiNews.com, Inc.), 1999—2003, Back-Country Angler, 2003—. Served with AUS, 1961-64. Decorated Army Commendation medal. Unitarian Universalist. Home: 57 Goodnight Trl E Santa Fe NM 87506-7925 Office Phone: 505-989-8999. E-mail: egroseclose@starband.net.

GROSECLOSE, JOANNE STOWERS, special education educator; b. Bland, Va., Dec. 15, 1956; d. Claude Swanson and Josephine (Mustard) Stowers; m. John Vincent Groseclose, June 24, 1979; children: Jouette Nicole, Nicholas Vincent. BS, Radford Coll., 1979; MS, Radford U., 1983. Cert. tchr., Va, exceptional needs specialist, Nat. Bd. Profl. Tchg., 2001. Tchr. kindergarten Bland (Va.) Combined Sch., Bland County Sch. Bd., 1979; tchr. 4th grade Marion (Va.) Intermediate Sch., Smyth County Sch. Bd., 1979-80, tchr. learning disabled 4th, 5th, 6th grades, 1980—. Instr. adult basic edn. Smyth County Schs., Marion, 1989-90. Technician Bland County Rescue Squad, 1975-78; bd. dirs. Am. Cancer Soc., 1985-88, Marion United Way, 1989-91, Smyth County Assn. for Retarded Citizens, 1982-85, Smyth County Cmty. Hosp., 1993-98; sec., vice chair Smith County Cmty. Found., 1998—; vol. Mt. Rogers Smyth House Group Home for Retarded Adults, 1983-85; mem. Hospice of Smyth County; mem. S.W. Va. Reading Coun., 1989-91, 94—, Smyth County Humane Soc.; mem. area Luth. ch. coun., 1996-99. Named Outstanding Young Careerist Marion Bus. and Profl. Women, 1983, Outstand Young Woman of Am., Marion Bus. and Profl. Women, 1981, Radford U. Outstanding Alumi, 1990, Va. Tchr. of Yr. Ency. Britannica/Good Housekeeping/Coun. of Chief State Sch. Officers, 1991. Mem. NEA (del. conv.), Smyth County Edn. Assn. (rep. 1979, 82, 93—, treas. 1981-83, pres. 1985), Smyth County C. of C., Va. Edn. Assn. (del. conv.), Marion Book and Study Club, Phi Kappa Phi, Kappa Delta Pi. Avocations: reading, travel, camping, playing bridge, tennis. Home: 241 Magnolia St Marion VA 24354-4413 Office: Marion Intermediate Sch 820 Stage St Marion VA 24354-4000 Office Phone: 276-783-2609.

GROSECLOSE, WANDA WESTMAN, retired elementary school educator; b. Clarks, Nebr., Oct. 5, 1933; m. B. Clark Groseclose; children: D. Kim, Byron C. Jr., Eric P., A. Glenn. B degree, Brigham Young U., 1976; M in Tchg., St. Mary's Coll., Moraga, Calif., 1981. Cert. tchr., Calif. 5th grade tchr. Brentwood (Calif.) Union Sch. Dist., 1977-97; ret. Art tchr., mentor tchr. Contra Costa County Program of Excellence. Author: American Music in Time, 1992, In the Shadow of Our Ancestors, vol. I, vol. II, 2004, The Lees of Southwest Virginia, 2004. Human rels. bd. dirs. City of Livermore, 1968—70. Republican. Mem. Lds Ch. Avocations: painting, sewing, gardening, genealogy. Home: 603 Campania Ct Brentwood CA 94513-4701 Personal E-mail: grosclose@ecis.com.

GROSFELD, JAMES, real estate development company executive; b. N.Y.C., 1938; LLB, Columbia U., 1962. Atty. Kelly, Drye, Newhall, Maginnes and Warren, 1962—65; former house counsel Goodbody & Co.; v.p. Pulte Home Corp., West Bloomfield, Mich., 1972, vice chmn., 1972, pres., 1973—74, chmn., CEO, 1974—90; former owner MultiVest, Inc.; ret. Bd. mem. Black Rock, Inc., Championship Auto Racing Team, Copart, Inc., Ramco-Gershenson Properties Trust, Lexington Corp. Properties.

GROSFELD, JAY LAZAR, surgeon, educator; b. N.Y.C., May 30, 1935; m. Margie Faulkner; children: Lisa, Denise, Janice, Jeffrey, Mark. AB cum laude, NYU, 1957, MD, 1961. Diplomate Am. Bd. Surgery (spl. qualification Pediatric Surgery). Gen. surgery intern Bellevue and Univ Hosps. NYU, N.Y.C., 1961—62; resident in gen. surgery Bellevue and Univ. Hosps. NYU, N.Y.C., 1962—66; resident in pediatric surgery Ohio State U. Coll. Medicine, Children's Hosp., 1968—70; instr. surgery Ohio State U. Coll. Medicine, 1968—70; clin. instr. surgery NYU Sch. Medicine, N.Y.C., 1965—66, asst. prof. surgery and pediatrics, 1970—72; prof., dir. pediatric surgery Ind. U. Sch. Medicine, Indpls., 1972—, Lafayette F. Page prof., 1981—, chmn. dept. surgery, 1985—2003; surgeon-in-chief James Whitcomb Riley Hosp. Children, 1972—. Author: Common Problems in Pediatric Surgery, 1991, Central Surgical Association: The First 50 Years, 1991, Progress in Pediatric Trauma, 1992, Essentials of Pediatric Surgery, 1995, Pediatric Surgery, 5th edit., 1998, The Surgery of Childhood Tumors, 1999, Principles of Pediatric Surgery, 2003; editor-in-chief: Jour. Pediat. Surgery; editor: Seminars in Pediat. Surgery; contbr. over 560 papers, reports, book chpts., articles for med. jours. Capt. M.C. U.S. Army, 1966—68. Decorated Commendation medal; named Sagamore of the Wabash, 2002; recipient numerous fellowships, grants, teaching awards. Fellow: ACS (bd. govs. 1985—91), Am. Acad. Pediat. (exec. com. surg. sect. 1989—95, chmn. surg. sect. 1994—95, sec. surg. sect., Ladd medal 2002—), Royal Coll. Physicians and Surgeons Glasgow (hon.), Royal Coll. Surgeons of Eng. (hon.); mem.: AMA, Halsted Soc. (v.p. 1995—96, pres. 1996—97), Accreditation Coun. Grad. Med. Edn. (surg. residency rev. com. 1996—2001, vice chair 2000—01), Am. Bd. Med. Specialities, World Fedn. Assns. Pediat. Surgeons (pres. 1998—2001, v.p.), Am. Bd. Surgery (bd. dirs. 1989—97, vice chair 1995, chmn. 1996—97, chmn.-elect), Am. Pediatric Surg. Assn. Found. (chmn. bd. dirs.), Internat. Soc. Surgery (sec., treas. Internat. Soc. Surgery Found. 2001—), Western Surg. Assn. (pres. 1997—98), Soc. Surg. Oncology, Brit. Assn. Pediat. Surgeons (exec. coun. 1990—93, Denis Browne Gold medal 1998), Ctrl. Surg. Assn. (sec. 1987—, pres.-elect 1988, pres. 1990), Soc. Surgery Alimentary Tract, Am. Trauma Soc., Ind. State Med. Assn., Marion County Med. Soc., Soc. Univ. Surgeons, Am. Surg. Assn. (first v.p. 2005—), Am. Pediat. Surg. Assn. (pres. 1994—95, bd. govs., pres.-elect), N.Y.C. Cancer Soc., Assn. Acad. Surgery, Pediat. Surgery Biology Club, Alpha Omega Alpha, Phi Beta Kappa. Office: J W Riley Childrens Hosp 702 Barnhill Dr Rm 2500 Indianapolis IN 46202-5128 Business E-Mail: jgrosfel@iupui.edu.

GROSH, RONALD CHAMBERLAIN, meteorologist, researcher; s. Lawrence Chamberlain and Dorothy Cecelia (Hammersley) Grosh; children: Jason, Ryan. BA, U. Wis., 1967, MS, 1971. Rsch., tchg. asst. U. Wis., Madison, 1969—72; rschr. U. Ill., Champaign-Urbana, 1972—79, U. Wis., 1980—81; expert UN/WMO, Jakarta, Indonesia, 1983, Seoul, 1987; dir. CSIR, Pretoria, South Africa, 1986—91. Vis. prof. U. Sao Paulo, 1985—86. Contbr. articles to profl. jours. Active Sr. Olympics. Mem.: Nat. Weather Assn. (charter), Weather Modificatin Assn., Royal Meteorol. Soc. Avocation: bridge.

GROSHNER, MARIA STAR, nuclear engineer; b. Las Vegas, Nev., Aug. 31, 1961; d. Robert Leroy and Stepheny (Higby) Groshner; m. Robert Clay Singleterry, Jr., May 18, 1984. BS in Nuc. Engring., U. Ariz., 1984; MBA, Averett U., 2003. Engr. in tng., Idaho; cert. pvt. pilot 2003. Reactor operator EG&G Idaho, Inc., Idaho Falls, 1985-89, engr., 1989-90, sr. engr., 1990-91; export control reviewer EG&G Idaho Inc., Idaho Falls, 1990-91; engr. III Westinghouse Idaho Nuc. Co., Idaho Falls, 1991-92, sr. engr. I, 1992-94; prin. engr., safety analyst Lockheed Martin Idaho Techs. Co., Idaho Falls, 1994-96, staff engr., 1996-97; prin. mem. Quantum Solutions LLC, 1995-96; sr. engr. BWX Techs., Inc., Lynchburg, Va., 1999—. Sci-by-mail mentor, 1998—2000. Mem. Citizen Energy Alert Network Nuc. Energy Inst., Washington, 1987—96; mem. Planned Parenthood, 1992—96; troop leader Girl Scouts; vol. Big Brothers Big Sisters, 2004. Mem.: Soc. Women Engrs. (chpt. sect. rep. 1990—91, treas. 1993—96, v.p. southeastern Idaho chpt. 1989, coord. young women's conf. 1990), Am. Nuc. Soc. (media rels. chmn. Idaho chpt. 1990, comm. 2001), Toastmasters Internat. (chpt. pres. 1990, chpt. pres. Lynchburg unit 2000, adminstrv. v.p. Jack C. High unit 1989, v.p. pub. rels. 1995, Competent Toastmaster, Able Toastmaster), U.S. Golf Assn. Avocations: aviation, golf, camping, crafts, amateur radio. Home: 407 Chadwick Drive Lynchburg VA 24502- Office: BWX Techs Inc PO Box 785 Lynchburg VA 24505-0785 Personal E-mail: kittyzulu@yahoo.com.

GROSJEAN, SEBASTIEN RENE, professional tennis player; b. Marseille, France, May 29, 1978; m. Marie-Pierre Grosjean, Nov. 16, 1998; children: Lola, Tom. Profl. tennis player ATP Tour, 1996—. Achievements include Finished as the number one ranked jr. in the world in both singles and doubles in 1996; Winner of 3 singles titles: Nottingham, 2000, Paris TMS, 2001, St. Petersburg, 2002; Winner of 4 doubles titles: Casablanca, 2000, Los Angeles, 2002, Marseille, 2003, Indian Wells TMS, 2004. Office: c/o ATP Tour Internat Hdqs 201 ATP Tour Blvd Ponte Vedra Beach FL 32082

GROSKOPF, AUBREY BUD, broadcast executive, lawyer; b. Milw. s. George Norman and Rose (Becker) G.; 1 child, James E.; m. Mary Jo Gregory. BS, U. Wis., 1952, LLB, 1956. Bar: Wis. 1957. Dir. bus. affairs CBS-TV Network, N.Y.C., 1958-73; exec. v.p. Four Star Internat., L.A., 1973-76; pres. Republic Pictures Corp., L.A., 1976-87; ind. motion picture and TV prodr., 1987—. Prodr. motion picture Boys of Paul Street, 1969 (Best Fgn. Film award 1969); writer, prodr., dir. TV spl. and video A Norman Rockwell Christmas, 1994; creator Tales of Edgar Allan Poe, 1998. 1st lt. U.S. Army, 1952-54, Korea; selectman Town of Yarmouth, Cape Cod, 2005—. Decorated Bronze Star. Mem. NATAS, Acad. Motion Picture Arts and Scis.

GROSLAND, EMERY LAYTON, retired banker; b. Holden, Alta., Can., July 19, 1929; s. Arne and Lillie Olivetta (Jacobson) G.; m. Margaret Grace Woodward, Sept. 3, 1952; 1 child, Roberta Jayne Student pub. schs., Holden; student Amos Tuck Sch. Exec Program, Dartmouth Coll., 1980. With The Royal Bank of Can., 1949—, sr. v.p. Toronto, Canada, 1983—87; ret., 1987. Cons. in field. Mem.: N. Halton Golf and Country. Avocation: golf.

GROS LOUIS, KENNETH RICHARD RUSSELL, humanities educator; b. Nashua, N.H., Dec. 18, 1936; s. Albert W. and Jeannette Evelyn (Richards) Gros L.; m. Dolores K. Winandy, Aug. 28, 1965; children: Amy Katherine, Julie Jeannette. BA, Columbia U., 1959, MA, 1960; PhD (Knapp fellow), U. Wis., 1964. Asst. prof. Ind. U., Bloomington, 1964—67, assoc. prof. English and comparative lit., 1967—73, prof., 1973—, assoc. chmn. comparative lit. dept., 1967—69, assoc. dean arts and scis., 1970—73, chmn. dept. English, 1973—78, dean arts and scis., 1978—80, v.p., 1980—88, chancellor, 1988—2001, v.p. acad. affairs, 1994—2001, trustee prof., 2001—. Bd. dirs. Anthem, Inc.; exec. coun. acad. affairs Nat. Assn. Univ. and Land Grant Colls., 1986-97, bd. dirs. Bd. dirs. Editor Yearbook of Comparative and Gen. Lit., 1968—, Vol. I: Literary Interpretations of Biblical Narratives, 1974, Vol. II, 1982; contbr. articles to profl. jours. Bd. dirs. Assoc. Group, 1983-95, Anthem Blue Cross and Blue Shield, 1995—; mem. Ind. Com. Humanities, chmn., 1980-81; chmn. Com. on Instnl. Coop., 1986-2000; mem. Nat. Commn. on Libr. Preservation and Access, 1986-93; vice chmn., bd. dirs. Ctr. for Rsch. Librs., 1986—, chmn. bd. dirs., 1987-88. Recipient Disting. Teaching award Ind. U., 1970 Mem. MLA, Nat. Coun. Tchrs. English, AAUP, Phi Beta Kappa. Home: 4965 E Heritage Woods Rd Bloomington IN 47401-9313 Office: Ind U Wylie Hall Bloomington IN 47405 E-mail: grosloui@indiana.edu.

GROSMAN, ALAN M., lawyer; b. Mar. 13, 1935; s. Charles M. and Grace (Fishman) G.; m. Bette Bloomenthal, Dec. 27, 1967; children, Ellen, Carol. BA, Wesleyan U., 1956; MA, Yale U., 1957; JD, N.Y. Law Sch., 1965. Bar: N.J. 1965, U.S. Dist. Ct. N.J. 1965, U.S. Supreme Ct. 1969. Ptnr. Grosman & Grosman and predecessors, Millburn, NJ, 1965—; asst. prosecutor Essex County, NJ, 1968—69; prosecutor Millburn, 1981—. Mem. family practice com. NJ Supreme Ct., 1984—88, mem. dispute resolution task force, 1987—88, mem. com. on women in the cts., 1991—93; chmn. NJ Trade Coun., 1975—77, dir., 1978—; adj. prof. family law Rutgers U. Sch. Law, 2002—; lectr. in field. Author: New Jersey Family Law, 1999, with annual supplement; reporter: New Haven Jour., 1959—60, Newark Evening News, 1961—62; contbr. articles to profl. jours. Mem. ABA (chmn. alimony, maintenance and support com. family law sect. 1983-87, editor ABA Family Law Quar. 1993—), N.J. State Bar Assn. (exec. editor N.J. Family Lawyer 1980-91, mem. exec. com. family law sect. 1980—, chmn. sect. 1987-88, appellate practice com. 1995—), Am. Acad. Matrimonial Lawyers (pres. N.J. chpt. 1983-85, nat. bd. govs. 1984-88, editor Jour. AAML 1980-90), Essex County Bar Assn. (chmn. family law com. 1970-72), N.Y. Law Sch. Alumni Assn. (bd. dirs. 1988-98), Millburn-Short Hills Rep. Club, Inc. (counsel 1988—), Phi Beta Kappa. Address: PO Box 597 75 Main St Ste 205 Millburn NJ 07041-1322 E-mail: alan.grosman@verizon.net.

GROS-PIETRO, GIAN MARIA, economics professor; b. Turin, Italy, Feb. 4, 1942; Degree in econs., U. Turin. Tchr. prodn. econs. Sch. Indsl. Adminstrn. U. Turin, 1965-72, prof. indsl. econs., 1974—, full prof. indsl. policy and econs., 1994—2004; head Dept. Econs. and Bus. Luiss U., Rome, 2004—. Rschr. CERIS-Istituto di Ricerca sull'Impresa e lo Sviluppo, Nat. Rsch. Coun., 1965-72, dir., 1977-95; coord. plan for instrumental mechs. Ministry of Industry, Italy, 1977-80; econ. cons. Italian Union Machine Tool Constructors, 1983—; mng. dir. Fincimu, 1983-85; rep. Ministry Public Investment; mem. various sci. couns., sci. com. Nomisma; chmn., CEO IRI, 1997-99; chmn. ENI, 1999-2002, Autostrade, 2002—. Author numerous texts in field. Bd. dirs. U. Turin, 1985—96. Mem. Soc. Italiana degli Economisti, Federtrasporto (pres. 2003—). Office: Autostrade Via Bergamini 50 00159 Rome Italy

GROSS, ALAN MARC, lawyer; b. Trenton, N.J., June 9, 1960; s. William and Lois G. BBA, Emory U., 1982; JD with honors, U. Fla., 1985. Bar: Fla. 1985, U.S. Dist. Ct. (mid. dist.) Fla. 1986, U.S. Tax Ct. 1988, 11th Cir. Ct. Appeals, 2000; CPA, Fla. Accountant, tax sr. Arthur Andersen & Co., Tampa, Fla., 1985-87; ptnr. Battaglia, Ross, Dicus & Wein, P.A., St. Petersburg, Fla., 1987-95, Powell, Carney, Hayes & Silverstein, P.A., St. Petersburg, 1995-00, Powell, Carney, Gross, Maller & Ramsay, P.A., 2001—. Participant Leadership St. Petersburg, 1991, Leadership Tampa Bay, 1994; treas. Congregation Bnai Israel, St. Petersburg. Mem. Fla. Bar Assn., Fla. Inst. CPAs, Am. Assn. Attys. and CPAs, St. Petersburg Bar Assn. (chmn. tax sect. 1990, Pro Bono award), Suncoast Estate Planning Coun. (charter), Fla. Region Fedn. Jewish Men's Clubs (pres. 2000-01). Home: 11346 Heritage Way Largo FL 33778-2901 Office: Powell Carney Gross Maller Ramsay PA 1 Progress Plz Ste 1210 Saint Petersburg FL 33701-4335 Office Phone: 727-898-9011. E-mail: agross@tampabay.rr.com.

GROSS, ALLEN JEFFREY, lawyer; b. Wheeling, W.Va., May 2, 1948; s. Arthur and Bertyl (Kahn) G.; m. Carolyn McGuire, May 2, 1982; children: Alexander, Lindsay, Matthew. BS, Ohio State U., 1970; JD, Georgetown U., 1974. Bar: Pa. 1974, U.S. Dist. Ct. (ctrl. and we. dists.) Pa., Calif. 1989, U.S. Dist. Ct. (no., so. and ctrl. dists.) Calif. 1989, U.S. Ct. Appeals (3d and 6th cirs.). Ptnr. Morgan, Lewis & Bockius, Phila., 1974-89, Orrick, Herrington & Sutcliffe, L.A., 1989-93; now with Mitchell, Silberberg & Knupp, L.A. Mem. Corp. Counsel Inst. adv. bd. Georgetown U. Law Ctr; vice chair Georgetown Corp. Coun. Inst; co-chair Georgetown ELLI, 1993-. Author: Survey of Wrongful Discharge Cases in the United States, 1979, Employee Dismissal Laws, Forms, Procedures, 1986, 2d edit. 1992. Fellow Coll. Labor and Employment Lawyers Inc.; mem. ABA (chair trial advocacy supcom. 1989-93, employee rights and responsibilities com. 1991—, co-chair Nat. Advocacy Inst. 1992, com., Sect. Insts. Spl. Programs sub-com, gov. coun., 1998), L.A. County Bar Assn. Office: Mitchell Silberberg & Knupp 11377 W Olympic Blvd Los Angeles CA 90064-1625

GROSS, AMY, editor-in-chief; Features editor and spl. projects editor Vogue, 1978—88; founding editor Mirabella, 1988—93, editor-in-chief, 1995—97; editl. dir. Elle, NYC, 1993—96; editor-in-chief O, The Oprah Mag., 2000—. Co-author: (books) Women Talk About Breast Surgery: Diagnosis to Recovery, 1991, Women Talk About Gynecological Surgery: From Diagnosis to Recovery, 1992. Office: O The Oprah Mag 224 W 57th St New York NY 10019-6708*

GROSS, BENEDICT H., mathematician; b. South Orange, NJ, June 22, 1950; BA, Harvard U., 1971, PhD, 1978; MSc, Oxford U., 1974. Asst. prof. Princeton U., 1978—82; assoc. prof. Brown U., 1982—85; prof. Harvard U., 1985—98, George Vasmer Leverett prof. math., 1998—, dean undergraduate edn., 2002—03, dean, 2003—. Selection com. Sloan Postdoctoral Fellowships, 2003—. Author: Arithmetic on Elliptical Curves with Complex Multiplication, 2000; co-author: The Magic of Numbers, 2004. Recipient Cole prize in number theory, AMS, 1987; fellow, Sloan, 1980—83, MacArthur, 1986—91. Mem.: Am. Acad. Arts and Scis., Nat. Acad. Scis. Office: Harvard U Math Dept 1 Oxford St Cambridge MA 02138-2901 Business E-Mail: gross@math.harvard.edu.

GROSS, CHARLES GORDON, psychology professor; b. NYC, Feb. 29, 1936; s. Frank and Sara (Gordon) G.; m. Gaby Ellen Peierls, Sept. 23, 1961 (div. Mar. 1985); children: Melanie, Monica (dec.), Derek, Rowena; m. Greta Berman, May 1, 1988. BA, Harvard U., 1957; PhD, Cambridge U., Eng., 1961. From postdoctoral fellow to asst. prof. psychology MIT, 1961-65; vis. lectr., asst. prof., then lectr. Harvard U., 1963-70; prof. psychology Princeton U., 1970—. Vis. prof. U. Calif., Berkeley, 1970-71, MIT, 1975-76, Beijing U., 1986; vis. scientist Tokyo Met. Inst. Neurosci., 1988-89, Nencki Inst. Exptl. Biology, Warsaw, Poland, 1961; Fulbright lectr. Inst. Biophysics, Fed. U. Rio de Janeiro, 1986; U.S. Nat. Program vis. scientist Shanghai Inst. Physiology, 1987; vis. fellow Magdalen Coll., Oxford U., 1990, vis. scholar Wolfson Coll., 1995, McDonnell-Pew vis. fellow Med. Rsch. Coun. Ctr. in Brain and Behaviour, 1995, chair, Psychology Section (J), Am. Assoc. for the Advancement of Science. Author books and papers on brain, visual function and history of science. Grantee NIH, NSF, Spencer Found., Sloan Found., McDonald-Pew Found., Office Naval Rsch. Fellow APA (Disting. Contbn. to Psychology award 2005), AAAS, Soc. Exptl. Psychologists, Brazilian Acad. Sci.(fgn.), Nat. Acad. Sci., am. Acad. Arts and Sci. Home: 45 Woodside Ln Princeton NJ 08540-5417 Office: Princeton Univ Green Hall Princeton NJ 08544 Office Phone: 609-258-4430.

GROSS, CHARLES ROBERT, bank executive, state senator; b. St. Charles, Mo., Aug. 20, 1958; s. Jack Robert and Margaret Ellen (Stumberg) G.; m. Leslie Ann Goralczyk, May 27, 1984; children: Megan Marie, Madelynn Ann. BS in Pub. Adminstrn., U. Mo., 1981, MPA, 1982. Pers. mgr. Army and Air Force Exch. Svc., various cities, 1983-89; pers., safety dir. Ever-Green Lawns Corp., St. Charles, 1989-92; state rep. Mo. Legislature, Jefferson City, 1993—; real estate appraiser, 1994—2001; v.p. UMB Bank, 2001—. Pres. St. Charles County Young Reps., 1990-92; active Youth in Need, Bridgeway Counseling. Mem. St. Charles DARE, Kiwanis, Pacaderms, Alpha Kappa Psi (life). Lutheran. Avocations: golf, scuba diving, ice hockey. Home: 3019 Westborough Ct Saint Charles MO 63301-4550 Office Phone: 573-751-8635. E-mail: chuckgross58@hotmail.com.

GROSS, CYNTHIA SUE, petrochemicals manufacturing executive; b. Palmyra, Mo., Aug. 14, 1959; d. Floyd Raymond and Carolyn Elizabeth (Howell) Mette; m. Edward Lee Gross, June 8, 1985; 1 child, Ray E.; stepchildren: Troy A., Christina M. BS in Metall. Engring., U. Mo., Rolla, 1980. Metallurgist Bryon Jackson Pump, Tulsa, Okla., 1981-82; metall. engr. Conoco, Inc., Ponca City, Okla., 1982-84, Vista Chem., Houston, 1984-89; staff maintenance engr. Hoechst Celanese, Clear Lake, Tex., 1989-92; instr. of welding metallurgy San Jacinto Coll., 1992; sect. leader maintenance engring. Hoechst Celanese, Bishop, Tex., 1992-93, sect. leader maintenance, 1993-95; prodn. supt. for polyester Hoechst Celanese, Trevira, Spartanburg, S.C., 1995-97; process hazards prevention leader Celanese, Clear Lake, 1997-98, methanol and maintenance mgr., 1999-2000, tech. and maintenance mgr., 2000—01, corp. reliability, maintenance and engring. dir., 2001—. Spkr. symposium Nat. Petroleum Refiners Assn., San Antonio, 1993, San Antonio, 2000, San Antonio, 02; instr. welding metallurgy San Jacinto Coll., Houston, 1992. Quality mgmt. com. Houston Bus. Roundtable, 1990-92, chmn. Quality Day '91. Mem. NPRA (maintenance com. 2001-05, vice-chair 2005), Alpha Chi Sigma. Avocations: antiques, piano. Office: Celanese Clear Lake Plant 9502 Bayport Blvd Pasadena TX 77507-1402 Business E-Mail: cindy.gross@celanese.com.

GROSS, DAVID ARLEN, psychiatrist; b. N.Y.C., June 6, 1947; s. Samuel Charles and Debra Gross; m. Myrna Sheila Margolis, June 28, 1970; children: Samuel Mark., Shaari Beth. BA in Psychology magna cum laude, U. Rochester, N.Y., 1968; MD, U. Fla., Gainesville, 1973; postgrad., Yale U., 1976. Resident Yale U.-Yale New Haven Hosp., Conn. Mental Health Ctr.; dir. spl. svcs. Waterbury (Conn.) Hosp. Health Ctr., 1976-84; pvt. practice psychiatry Bethany, Conn., 1972-84; clin. dir. Fair Oaks Hosp., Delray Beach, Fla., 1984-90, med. dir., 1990-92; pvt. practice psychiatry Delray Beach, 1992—. Bd. dirs. IMX Corp., Delray Beach, 1995—. Author: Common and Uncommon School Problems, 1978; mem. editl. bd. Jour. Neuropsychiatry and Clin. Neurosci., 1994—, Jour. Clin. Psychiatry, 1994—; contbr. articles to profl. jours., chpts. to books. Bd. dirs. Mental Health Assn. Palm Beach County, Fla., 1992—; chair internat. Med. and Sci. Adv. Coun. on Drug Abuse. Recipient Golden Bell award Mental Health Assn., Palm Beach, 1997, Mental Health Advocate award Mental Health Assn., Palm Beach, 1998. Fellow Am. Psychiat. Assn., Fla. Psychiat. Assn. (pres. 1996). Avocations: photography, music, tennis. Office: 4800 Linton Blvd Ste D503 Delray Beach FL 33445-6593 Office Phone: 561-496-1281.

GROSS, DAVID JONATHAN, physicist; b. Washington, Feb. 19, 1941; s. Bertram M. and Nora (Faine) G.; m. Shulamith Toaff, Mar. 30, 1962; children: Ariela, Elisheva; m. Jacquelyn Savani, Aug. 12, 2001. BSc, Hebrew U., Jerusalem, 1962; PhD, U. Calif., Berkeley, 1966; Doctorate (Docteur Honoris Causa) (hon.), U. Montpellier, 2000, Hebrew U., 2001. Harvard Soc. of Fellows jr. fellow Harvard U., 1966-69; asst. prof. physics Princeton U., 1969-71, assoc. prof., 1971-73, prof., 1973-86, Eugene Higgens prof. physics, 1986—95, Jones prof. physics, 1995—97, Jones prof. physics emeritus, 1997—; dir. U. Calif., Santa Barbara, Inst. for Theoretical Physics, Santa Barbara, Calif., 1997—; prof. U. Calif., Santa Barbara, Calif., 1997—, Frederick W. Gluck prof. theoretical physics, 2001—. Vis. prof. CERN, Geneva, 1968—69, Geneva, 1993, Ecole Normale Superioure, Paris, 1983, Paris, 1988—89, Hebrew U., Jerusalem, 1984, Lawrence Radiation Lab., Berkeley, Calif., 1992; invited lecturer for several universities; chair, evaluation com. Scuola Internazionale Superiore di Studi Avanzati, Italy, 1994—. Assoc. editor Nuclear Physics, 1972—. Dir. Jerusalem Winter Sch., 1999—. Recipient Alfred P. Sloan fellow, 1970-74, MacArthur Prize fellow, 1987, Dirac medal, 1988, Harvey prize, Technion-Israel Inst. Tech., 2000, Oscar Klein medal, Stockholm U., 2000, grande médaille, French Academy Sciences, 2004; co-recipient High Energy and Particle Physics prize, European Physical Soc., 2003, Nobel Prize in Physics, 2004. Fellow AAAS, Am. Phys. Soc. (J. J. Sakurai prize 1986), Am. Acad. Arts and Scis.; mem. Nat. Acad. Scis. Research, numerous publs. in field; discovered asymptotic freedom, 1973; proposal of non-Abelian gauge theories of the strong interactions, 1973, heterotic string theory, 1984; discovery of (with H. David Politzer and Frank Wilczek) the asymptotic freedom in the theory of the strong interaction. Office: Kavli Inst for Theoretical Physics Univ Calif Santa Barbara Kohn Hall 1219 Santa Barbara CA 93106 Office Phone: 805-893-7337. Office Fax: 805-893-2431. Business E-Mail: gross@kitp.ucsb.edu.

GROSS, DAVID LEE, geologist; b. Springfield, Ill., Nov. 20, 1943; s. Carl David and Shirley Marie (Northcutt) G.; m. Claudia Cole, June 11, 1966; children: Oliver David, Alexander Lee AB, Knox Coll., 1965; MS, U. Ill., 1967, PhD, 1969. Registered profl. geologist, Ill., Calif. Asst. geologist Ill. State Geol. Survey, Champaign, 1969-73, assoc. geologist, 1973-80, geologist, 1980—, coord. environ. geology, 1979-84, head environ. studies, 1984-89, asst. chief, 1991-99, sr. geologist emeritus, 1999—. Exec. dir. Gov.'s Sci. Adv. Com., Chgo., 1989-91; bd. dirs. First State Bank, Beardstown, Ill., chmn. 2001—. Contbr. numerous articles to profl. jours. Bd. govs. Channing-Murray Found., 1973-76, pres., 1976; trustee Unitarian Universalist Ch., Urbana, 1977-80, 99—, chmn., 1977-79, 99-2001; bd. dirs. Vol. Action Ctr., 1981-85, chmn., 1984-85; bd. dirs. United Way Champaign County, 1984-89, exec. com., 1984-85, chmn. United Way Campaign, U. Ill., 1986, chair Youth Vision Coun., 2003-05; bd. dirs. Vol. Ctr., 1994-97; mem. Gov.'s Sci. Adv. Com., 1989-97; vol. summer camp counselor for teenage youth, 1984-2005; bd. dirs. Ill. Prairie chpt. ARC, 1997—2003. NDEA fellow, 1969 Fellow Geol. Soc. Am., AAAS; mem. Internat. Union Quaternary Rsch., Am. Quaternary Assn., Am. Inst. Profl. Geologists (pres. Ill.-Ind. sect. 1980), Ill. State Acad. Sci., Rotary (pres. Urbana, Ill. chpt. 1986-87), Columbia (Chgo.) Yacht Club, Sigma Xi. Home: 3 Flora Ct Champaign IL 61821-3216 Office: Ill State Geol Survey 615 E Peabody Dr Champaign IL 61820-6918 *Strive for reasonable balance among family, volunteer and professional responsibilities. All are essential for a healthy life.*

GROSS, DORINE MILES, artist; b. Detroit, Oct. 29, 1945; d. Theodore and Janet Catherine (Szymanek) Miles; m. Charles William Gross, June 17, 1966; children: Darcy, Alecia Kay. A in Fine Arts, W.R. Harper Coll., 1983; BA, Govs. State U., 1984; MFA, Northwestern U., 1986. Grad. tchr. Northwestern U., Evanston, Ill., 1984-86, instr., 1985-86; freelance artist Rye, N.H., 1986—. Guest lectr. W.R. Harper Coll., Palatine, Ill., 1984-85, Acad. Fine Art & Design, Bratislava, Slovakia, 1993, J. Koniarek Gallery, Tranava, Slovakia, 1993; adj. prof. U. N.H., Durham, 1987-89, Notre Dame Coll., Manchester, N.H., 1991; panel discussionist Karl Drerup Gallery, Plymouth (N.H.) State Coll., 1990; key note spkr. Internat. Symposium on Art, Moravani, Slovakia, 1993. One woman shows include Women's Bd. Rm., Art Inst. Chgo., 1980, Paul Waggoner Gallery, Chgo., 1982, Kemper Group, Long grove, Ill., 1983, Dittmar Gallery, Evanston, Ill., 1986, Capricorn Galleries, Bethesda, Md., 1990, Notre Dame Coll., Manchester, N.H., 1993, Pierce Gallery, Portsmouth, N.H., David Gary Ltd. Fine Art, Milburn, N.J., 1996, Tom James Gallery, Westwood, N.J., 1996, Biennial, 1997, N.H. Inst. of Art, Manchester, N.H., 1997, N.H. Soc. Preservn. Forests, 1999; represented in permanent collections Brenau U., Gainesville, Ga., Butler Inst. Am. Art, Youngstown, Ohio; creator image-coordinated project Patty's Gift, 1996-97; artist-in-residence 1st N.H. All State Art Festival, Currier Gallery Art, 1999. Commr., sec. Lake Barrington (Ill.) Park Dist., 1982-86. Recipient Muriel T. Lagasse Meml. award Springfield Art League, 1988, Pub. Art commn. State of N.H., 1995. Mem. Nat. Soc. Painters, Coll. Art Assn., N.H. Art Assn. (award 1988-89, 90-91), Seacoast Cultural Art Alliance, Rye Art Study. Avocations: botany, geology, skiing, walking. Home: PO Box 761 Rye NH 03870-0761

GROSS, EDWARD, retired sociologist; b. Nagy Genez, Romania; s. Samuel and Dora (Levi) G.; m. Florence Rebecca Goldman, Feb. 18, 1943; children— David P., Deborah L., Teagardin. *Ancestor Frigyes Grósz (1798-1858) founded the first Jewish ophthalmology clinic in 1829 in Nagyvarad, Hungary and was chief of medicine at the Jewish Hospital. He was politically active, leading a delegation to the Hungarian Diet which demanded a declaration of emancipation. Abraham Goldman, father of Florence, studied clothing design in Paris, France, later emigrating to Edmonton, Alberta, Canada, where he accompanied bush pilots to northern Alberta to trade for fur with Inuit. In 1906, along with his wife Rose Zand, he founded a leading fur retailer establishment in Edmonton.* BA, U. B.C., Can., 1942; MA, U. Toronto, Ont., Can., 1945; PhD, U. Chgo., 1949; JD, U. Wash., 1991. Prof. Wash. State U., Pullman, Wash., 1947-51, 53-60; prof. U. Wash., Seattle, 1951-53, 65-89, prof. emeritus, 1990—; prof. sociology U. Minn., Mpls., 1960-65. Vis. prof. Australian Nat. U., Canberra, 1971, U. Queensland, U. New South Wales, Griffith U., Australia, 1977; invited lectr. Cen. China Poly. Inst., 1987; lectr. arts and sci. honor program U. Wash., 1998—; pres. resident coun. Ida Culver Broadview Vet. Facility, 2005—. Author: Work and Society, 1958, Univ. Goals and Academic Power, 1968, Changes in Univ. Orgn., 1964-71, The End of a Golden Age: Higher Ed. in a Steady State, 1981, Embarrassment in Everyday Life, 1994; co-author (with A. Etzioni) Orgn. in Soc., 1985; contbg. author: Handbook of Sociology and Encyclopedia of Sociology, 2d edit.; former assoc. editor Social Problems, Symbolic Interaction, Can. Jour. Sociology; contbr. numerous articles to profl. jour. Trustee Temple Beth Am, Seattle, 1993-97. Fulbright scholar Australia, 1977, 87. Mem.: Am. Sociol. Assn. (emeritus), Pacific Sociol. Assn. (pres. 1971, coun. 1983—85). Office: U Wash Dept Sociology Seattle WA 98195-0001

GROSS, FELIKS, sociologist, educator, writer; b. Cracow, Poland, June 17, 1906; came to U.S., 1941; s. Adolf and Augusta (Alexander) G.; m. Priva Baidaff, July 25, 1937; 1 child, Eva Helena Gross Friedman. LLM, Jagiellonian U., 1930; LLD, Jagiellanian U., 1931. Bar: Poland 1937. Sec., gen. Cen. Ea. European Planning Bd., 1941-45; editor New Europe and World Reconstrn. jour., N.Y.C., 1942-45; prof. sociology and anthropology grad. ctr. Bklyn. Coll., N.Y.C., 1946-77, prof. emeritus, 1977—, resident prof. CUNY grad. ctr., 1988—. Vis. prof. NYU, 1945-68; vis. prof., dir. Inst. Internat. Affairs, U. Wyo., Laramie, summers 1945-52; vis. prof. Woodrow Wilson Sch. Fgn. Affairs, U. Va., Charlottesville, 1951, 54-56, U. Vt., Burlington, 1957; sr. Fulbright sr. lectr. U. Rome, 1957-58, 64-65, 74; lectr. other European, Am. univs.; mem. rsch. coun. Fgn. Policy Rsch. Inst., Phila., 1966—; vis. prof. Columbia U., N.Y.C., 1973; lectr. U. Florence, 1977, Italian Fgn. Office, Rome; cons. Nat. Com. on Causes and Prevention of Violence, 1968. Pres., Taraknath Das Found., N.Y., 1965; hon. pres. CUNY Acad. Humanities and Scis., 1985; co-founder, bd. dirs. Non-Profit Coordinating Com. N.Y., 1984-86. Author: Nomadism, 1936; Polish Worker, 1945; Foreign Policy Analysis, 1954; Seizure of Political Power, 1957; Valori Sociali e Struttura, 1967; World Politics and Tension Areas, 1967; Violence in Politics, 1973; Il Paese, Values and Social Change in an Italian Village, 1974; The Revolutionary Party, 1974; Ethnics in the Borderland, 1979; Ideologies, Goals and Values, 1986; Working Class and Culture (in Polish), 1986, Toleration and Pluralism (in Polish), 1992, European Federation & Confederations, Origin and Visions (in Polish), 1994, The Civic and the Tribal State, 1998, Citizenship and Ethnicity, 1999, The Civic and Tribal State, (translated, pub. Chinese Acad. Scis.), 2002, others; contbr. numerous articles to profl. jours. Decorated Golden Cross of Phoenix (Greece); Order Polonia Restituta (Poland); Carnegie scholar, Paris, 1931, Pub. Affairs Found. NYU, 1962-63; recipient Ethnic New Yorker award N.Y.C., 1987, Alfred Jurzykowski Price award for scholarship contbn., Polish Nat. Archives award, 1995, award Polish Ministry Culture and Art, 1995, N.Y.C. commendation for serving the Polish-Am. Cmty., 1998; ILO/League of Nations scholar, Geneva, 1930, Carnegie Scholarship, 1931; grantee Sloan Found., 1963, City U. Rsch. Found., 1971-74, NSF, 1972, Rockefeller Found., 1974; Fulbright grantee, 1956-57, 64-65, 74. Fellow Polish Inst Arts and Scis. (pres. E-7 1988-99);

mem. Internat. League Rights of Man (dir. 1960-88), Am. Sociol. Assn., Acad. Polit. Sci., N.Y. Acad. Scis., Polish Acad. Scis. (fgn.), Polish Sociology Soc. (hon.), Sigma Xi. Home: 310 W 85th St New York NY 10024-3819 Office: CUNY Acad for Human and Science 365 Fifth Ave New York NY 10016-4309

GROSS, GARY NEIL, allergist, physician; b. Fort Lewis, Wash., July 25, 1944; s. Norman Harold and Dorothy Naomi (Bercie) G.; m. Elaina Wee, Mar. 23, 1974; children: Risa, Lara. BA, U. Tex., 1967; MD, Southwestern Med. Sch., Dallas, 1969; MBA, Southern Methodist U., Dallas, 1987. Diplomate Am. Bd. Internal Medicine, Am. Bd. Allergy and Clin. Immunology. Intern U. Utah Med. Ctr. Hosp., Salt Lake City, 1969-70, resident, 1970-71; fellow Nat. Jewish Hosp., Denver, 1971-74; founding physician Dallas Allergy and Asthma Ctr., Tex., 1979—; med. dir. Pharm. Rsch. and Cons., Dallas, 1992—; clin. prof. internal medicine Southwestern Med. Sch., Dallas, 1994—. Contbr. articles to profl. jours. Bd. dirs. Am. Jewish Com., Dallas, 1990-94, Am. Lung Assn., 1978-88, Temple Emanuel Brotherhood, 1978-80. Fellow Am. Coll. Physicians (Disting. Svc. award 2003), Am. Acad. Allergy Asthma and Immunology (chmn. seminars com., 1987-88, chmn. pub. edn. com., 1989-90, Outstanding Vol. Clin. Faculty award 2004); mem. Fedn. Regional State Local Allergy Socs. (gov. reg. 5, 1992-, chmn. 1993-94), Joint Coun. Allergy Clin. Immunology (sec. bd. dirs. 1992-96, exec. v.p. 1998-). Jewish. Avocations: bicycling, skiing, photography. Office: 5499 Glen Lakes Dr Ste 100 Dallas TX 75231-4383 Office Phone: 214-691-1330. Personal E-mail: ggross144@yahoo.com.

GROSS, GEOFFREY FRIES, systems architect; b. Cin., Apr. 26, 1950; s. Merrill Jay and Ann Fries Gross; m. Diantha Louise Perry, May 9, 1970 (dec. July 1998); 1 child, Abraham Hart; m. Wendy Robin Levine, Aug. 12, 2000. BA in Math. cum laude, SUNY, Buffalo, 1973, MEd in Math. Instrn., 1976. Acting chmn. math. dept., instr. U. New Eng., Biddeford, Maine, 1979-80; tchr. math. Laconia (N.H.) H.S., 1980-81; programmer Franklin, N.H., 1982; project leader Mellen Co., Webster, N.H., 1983-87; sys. engr. Analysis and Computer Sys. Inc., Burlington, Mass., 1987-90; sys. arch., project mgr. Sys. Resources Corp., Burlington, 1990-95; sr. prin. sys. arch. Raytheon, St. Petersburg, Fla., 1996—2004. Mem. Sch. Budget Com., Milford, N.H., 1990-91; pres. Congregation Betenu, Amherst, N.H., 1991-97; trustee Congregation B'nai Israel, St. Petersburg, 2002—; bd. dirs. Sun Island Assn., South Pasadena, Fla., 2002-03; cons. Mus. Fine Arts, Boston, 1995. Mem. N.Y. Acad. Scis., Phi Beta Kappa (Omicron chpt.). Jewish. Avocations: american art, presidential campaign materials, chess, photography. E-mail: grossg@tampabay.rr.com.

GROSS, HANNS, history professor; b. Stockerau, Austria, June 20, 1928; came to U.S., 1961; s. Arthur and Gabriele (Schneider) G.; m. Bonnie Jean Rotter, July 20, 1991. *Had to leave Austria in July 1939 at the age of eleven because of racial persecution. Spent teenage years at a boarding school and in my twenties at the Attached Bible College. Arrived in Chicago on December 23, 1961 to visit dying father who had fled to Shanghai after being released from Dachau Concentration Camp in December 1938.* BA with honors, U. London, 1950; AM, U. Chgo., 1963, PhD, 1966. Tchr. Emmanuel Grammar Sch., Swansea, Wales, 1950-61; tutor Bible Coll. Wales, Swansea, 1950-61; asst. prof. So. Ill. U., Carbondale, 1966-67; asst. prof., assoc. prof. history Loyola U., Chgo., 1967-78, prof., 1978-99, emeritus, 1999—. Author: Empire and Sovereignty, 1973, Rome in the Age of Enlightenment, 1990. Elder Moody Ch., 1998-2005. Mem.: Deutsche Gesellschaft fuer Erforschung des 18. Jahrhundert, Soc. Italian Hist. Studies, Conf. on Faith and History, Am. Soc. for 18th Century Studies, Am. Soc. for Legal History, Am. Hist. Assn. Avocations: travel, walking, conversation. Office: Loyola U Dept History 6525 N Sheridan Rd Chicago IL 60626-5344 Personal E-mail: stockerau11@msn.com.

GROSS, HARRIET P. MARCUS, religious studies and writing educator; b. Pitts., July 15, 1934; d. Joseph William and Rose (Roth) Pincus; children: Sol Benjamin, Devra Lynn. AB magna cum laude, U. Pitts., 1954; cert. in religious tchg., Spertus Coll. of Judaica, Chgo., 1962; MA, U. Tex., Dallas, 1990, postgrad., 1998—. Assoc. editor Jewish Criterion of Pitts., 1955-56; publs. writer B'nai B'rith Vocat. Svc., 1956-57; group leader Jewish Cmty. Ctrs. Met. Chgo., 1958-63; columnist Star Publs., Chicago Heights, Ill., 1964-80; pub. info. specialist Operation ABLE, Chgo., 1980-81; dir. religious sch. Temple Emanu-El, Dallas, 1983-86; freelance writer, 1986—; columnist Dallas Jewish Life Monthly, 1992-96, Dallas (Tex.) Jewish Week, 2000—04, Tex. Jewish Post, Dallas, 2004—. Lectr. U. Tex., Dallas, 1994-98; tchr. writing Homewood-Flossmoor (Ill.) Park Dist., Brookhaven Jr. Coll., Dallas; advisor journalism program Prairie State Coll., Chicago Heights, 1978-80; mem. adv. bd. The Creative Woman Quar. Publ., Gov.'s State U., Governors Park, Ill., The Mercury U. Tex., Dallas. Bd. dirs., sec. Family Svc. and Mental Health Ctr. of South Cook County, Ill., 1965-71; active Park Forest (Ill.) Commn. on Human Rels., 1969-80, chmn., 1974-76; bd. dirs. Ill. Theatre Ctr., 1977-80, Jewish Family Svc. of Dallas, 1982-95, Dallas Jewish Hist. Soc., 1995—; mem. Dallas Jewish Edn. Com., 1992-95. Recipient Humanitarian Achievements award Fellowship for Action, 1974, Honor award Anti-Defamation League of B'nai B'rith, 1978, Cmty. Svc. award Dr. Charles E. Gavin Found., 1978, 1st Ann. Leadership award Jewish Family Svc., 1990, Katie award Dallas Press Club, 1995; inducted into Park Forest (Ill.) Hall of Fame, 2000, Tex. Press Women State Writing award, 2003. Mem. Nat. Fedn. Press Women, Press Women of Tex., Ill. Woman's Press Assn. (named Woman of Yr. 1978), Intertel (pres. Gateway Forum of Dallas 1984-85), Nat. Assn. Temple Educators, Mensa, Soc. Profl. Journalists, Dallas Press Club, Nat. Soc. of Newspaper Columnists, Am. Jewish Press Assn., Phi Sigma Sigma. Jewish. Achievements include development of 1st community newspaper action line column. Office: 8560 Park Ln Apt 23 Dallas TX 75231-6312 Office Phone: 214-691-8840. Business E-Mail: hgross@utdallas.edu.

GROSS, IAN, academic pediatrician, neonatologist; b. Pretoria, Oct. 15, 1943; came to U.S., 1971; s. Kenneth and Gladys Bakst (Cooper) G.; m. Melanie Belman, Dec. 3, 1967; children: David Anthony, Adam Charles. BS, U. Witwatersrand, Johannesburg, Republic of South Africa, 1963, MBBCh, 1967. Diplomate Am. Bd. Pediat., Am. Bd. Neonatal-Perinatal Medicine. Rotating intern Johannesburg Gen. Hosp., 1968; pediatric resident U. Witwatersrand Hosps., Johannesburg, 1970-71, Children's Hosp. Harvard Med. Sch., Boston, 1971-72; postdoctoral fellow in pediat. Harvard Med. Sch., Boston, 1972-73; postdoctoral fellow in pediatrics Yale U., New Haven, 1973-74; asst. prof. Yale U. Sch. Medicine, New Haven, 1974-78, assoc. prof., 1978-85, prof., 1985—. Dir. newborn spl. care unit Yale-New Haven Hosp., 1982—; mem. study sect. NIH, Bethesda, Md., 1981-85; mem. adv. bd. Hood Found., Boston, 1988-94. Editor Pediat. Rsch., 1992-98, Seminars in Perinatology, 1997—; contbr. chpts. to books, numerous articles to profl. jours. Named Most Disting. Med. Grad. U. Witwatersrand, Johannesburg, 1967, Mentor of Yr., Ea. Soc. Pediatric Rsch., 2005; James Hudson Brown fellow, Yale U., 1973; rsch. grantee NIH and Am. Heart Assn. Fellow Am. Acad. Pediat.; mem. Soc. Pediatric Rsch., Am. Physiol. Soc. Avocations: bicycling, photography. Office: Yale Sch Medicine 333 Cedar St New Haven CT 06520-8064 E-mail: ian.gross@yale.edu.

GROSS, JAMES DEHNERT, pathologist; b. Harvey, Ill., Nov. 15, 1929; s. Max A. and Marion (Dehnert) G.; m. Marilyn Agnes Robertson, Jan. 9, 1960; children: Kathleen Ann, Terrence Michael, Brian Andrew, Kevin Matthew. BS in Biology, U. Chattanooga, 1951; MD, Vanderbilt U., 1955. Diplomate Am. Bd. Pathology, Am. Bd. Med. Mgmt. Rotating intern U.S. Naval Hosp., St. Albans, N.Y., 1955-56; resident in anatomic and clin. pathology Nat. Naval Med. Ctr., Bethesda, Md., 1956-59; dir. labs. U.S. Naval Hosp., Memphis, 1959-62, St. Mary's Hosp., Streator, Ill., 1962-93, pres. med. staff, 1972-73. Instr. pathology and microbiology U. Tenn. Med. Sch., 1960-62; bd. dirs. La Salle County bd. Am. Cancer Soc., 1966-68 Mem. parish council St. Anthony's Roman Catholic Ch., Streator, 1969-72. Served to lt. comdr. M.C., USNR, 1955-68 Fellow Am. Soc. Clin. Pathologists, Coll. Am. Pathologists, Assn. Clin. Scientists (founder); mem. AMA, Ill. Med. Soc., Sigma Chi, Alpha Kappa Kappa Lodges: K.C., Rotary (past bd. dirs.). Republican. Home and Office: 374 MacEwen Dr Osprey FL 34229-9233 Office Phone: 941-966-3763. Personal E-mail: marigro@comcast.net.

GROSS, JAMES GEORGE, lawyer; b. Chgo., Apr. 14, 1949; s. George Dean and Geraldine Veronica (Wilson) G.; m. Michele P. Armstrong, July 12, 1975; children: Colin, Corinne. BA in Sociology, Mich. State U., 1973; JD, Wayne State U., 1977. Bar: Mich. 1977, U.S. Dist. Ct. (ea. dist.) Mich., 1977, U.S. Ct. Appeals (6th cir.) 1982, U.S. Supreme Ct., 1981. Pre-hearing atty. Mich. Ct. Appeals, Detroit, 1977, clk. to Daniel Walsh, 1977-78; assoc., ptnr. Gromek Bendure & Thomas, Detroit, 1978-80, 80-84; assoc., prin. MacArthur Cheatham Acker & Smith, Detroit, 1984-87, 87-90; assoc. Garan & Lucow, Detroit, 1990-91; ptnr. Gross Nemeth & Silverman (formerly Gross & Nemeth), Detroit, 1991—. Guest lectr. Inst. Cont. Edn., Ann Arbor, Mich., 1986—, U. Detroit, 1991-94; founding mem. Appellate Bench Bar Conf. Found., Detroit, 1994—; lectr. Mich. Def. Trial Counsel, Detroit, 1995—; moderator settlement conf. pilot program Ct. Appeals, Detroit, 1995—. Contbr. articles to profl. jours. Recipient Robert E. Dice Def. Lawyer of Yr. award Mich. Physicians Mut. Liability Co., 1988. Fellow Am. Acad. Appellate Lawyers; mem. ABA, Detroit Met. Bar Assn., Assn. Trial Lawyers Am., Mich. Trial Lawyers Assn., Mich. Def. Trial Counsel (bd. dirs. 1995-2001, treas. 2001-02, sec. 2002-03, v.p. 2003-04, pres. 2004-05), Assn. Def. Trial Counsel, Def. Rsch. Inst. Office: Ste 1305 615 Griswold St Detroit MI 48226-3994 E-mail: jgross@grsappeals.com.

GROSS, JAMES HOWARD, lawyer; b. Springfield, Ohio, Sept. 21, 1941; s. Cyril James and Virginia (Stieg) G.; m. Gail Sue Helmick, July 13, 1968; children: Karin G. Cramer, David James. BA, Ohio State U., 1963; LLB, Harvard U., 1966. Bar: Ohio 1966, D.C. 1975. Assoc. Vorys, Sater, Seymour and Pease, Columbus, Ohio, 1966-75, resident ptnr. Washington, 1975-77; ptnr. Vorys, Sater, Seymour and Pease LLP, Columbus, 1975—. White House fellow, spl. asst. to sec. HUD, Washington, 1972-73; city atty. City of Bexley, Ohio, 1985—. Mem. Franklin County Rep. Cen. Com., 1973-75, Bexley City Coun., 1981-85. Lt. comdr. USNR, 1968-74. Mem. ABA, Ohio Bar Assn. (corp. law com.), Columbus Bar Assn. (securities law com.), D.C. Bar Assn. Lutheran. Home: 5 Sessions Dr Bexley OH 43209-1440 Office: Vorys Sater Seymour and Pease LLP 52 E Gay St PO Box 1008 Columbus OH 43216-1008 Office Phone: 614-464-6231. Business E-Mail: jhgross@vssp.com.

GROSS, JEREMY V. (JERRY GROSS), finance company executive; B in Acctg. and Fin., Monash U., Melbourne, Australia. Formerly with tech. mgmt. dept. KMPG, Andersen Consulting (now Accenture); former mng. dir., chief tech. officer Countrywide Credit Industries, Calabasas, Calif.; former group exec. of tech., ops. and eCommerce Westpac Banking Corp., 1999—2001; exec. v.p., chief info. officer Washington Mut., Inc., Seattle, 2001—. Office: Washington Mut Inc 1201 3d Ave Seattle WA 98101

GROSS, JOHN H., lawyer; b. Cleve., Apr. 2, 1942; BS, U. Pa., 1964; JD, George Washington U., 1967. Bar: N.Y. Asst. U.S. atty. (so. dist.) N.Y., 1969-75, asst. chief criminal divsn., 1974-75; assoc. spl. counsel U.S. Dept. Justice, 1979; ptnr. Anderson, Kill, Olick & Oshinsky, N.Y. Adj. prof. law N.Y.U., 1983-89. Mem. Assn. of the Bar of the City of N.Y. Office: Proskauer Rose LLP 1585 Broadway Fl 27 New York NY 10036-8299 E-mail: jgross@proskauer.com.

GROSS, JONATHAN LIGHT, computer scientist, mathematician, educator; b. Phila., June 11, 1941; s. Nathan K. and Henrietta E. (Light) G.; m. Susan Fay Kodner, Aug. 29, 1976; children: Aaron, Jessica, Joshua, Rena Lea, Alisa Sharon BS, M.I.T., 1964; MA, Dartmouth Coll., 1966, PhD, 1968. Instr. math. Princeton (N.J.) U., 1968-69; asst. prof. math. stats. Columbia U., N.Y.C., 1969-72, assoc. prof., 1973-78, prof. computer sci., math. and stats., 1978—, vice-chmn. dept. computer sci., 1982-89; dir. edn. Ctr. for Advanced Tech., 1989-93. Cons. Russell Sage Found., Inst. Def. Analyses., AT&T Bell Labs., Alfred P. Sloan Found., IBM, Oak Ridge Nat. Lab.; vis. scientist Carnegie-Mellon U., Pitts., 1984-85. Co-author: Fundamental Programming Concepts, 1972, FORTRAN 77 Programming, 1978, Introduction to Computer Programming, 1979, Pascal Programming, 1982, Measuring Culture, 1985, PASCAL, 1984 FORTRAN 77 Fundamentals and Style, 1985, Topological Graph Theory, 1987, WATFIV-S Fundamental Style, 1986, Graph Theory and Its Applications, 1999; editor: Handbook of Discrete and Combinatorial Mathematics, 2000, Handbook of Graph Theory, 2004; adv. editor: Columbia U. Press, Jour. Graph Theory, Computers and Electronics, CRC Press; contbr. articles to profl. jours. Mem. exec. bd. United Jewish Fedn. of Princeton Mercer-Bucks, 2004—. IBM postdoctoral fellow, 1972-73; Sloan fellow in math., 1973-75; rsch. grantee NSF, Office of Naval Rsch., Exxon Found., ARCO Found., Mellon Found., Russell Sage Found., N.Y. State Sci. and Tech. Found., Citicorp. Mem. Am. Math. Soc., Assn. Computing Machinery, Soc. Indsl. and Applied Math. (sec. discrete math. 1994-96), Jewish Ctr. of Princeton (v.p. 1997-99, pres. 2000-02). Jewish. Home: 3 Stuart Ln W Princeton Junction NJ 08550-1844 Office: Columbia U Dept Computer Sci New York NY 10027 *If I ever fail to overstate the case, please call an ambulance.*

GROSS, JOSEPH H., lawyer, educator; b. Tel Aviv, Feb. 28, 1934; s. Woolf and Mali (Timberg) G.; m. Zvia Armon, July 21, 1959; children: Raz, Aeyal, Vardit. LLB, Tel Aviv U., 1955, LLM, 1958; PhD, U. London, 1962. Bar: Israel 1959, N.Y. 1989. Legal advisor Discount Bank Investment Co., Tel Aviv, 1963-76; prof. law Tel Aviv U., 1968—, assoc. dean Law Sch., 1973-78; chmn. law firm Gross, Kleinhandler, Hodak, Halevy, Greenberg & Co., Tel Aviv, 1979—. Vis. scholar Harvard U. Law Sch., Boston, 1977; chmn. com. on mergers Govt. of Israel, 1975—77, com. to reform co. law, 1985—94, chmn. adv. bd. govt. cos., 1986—91, com. to reform tax law, 2002; chmn. Israel Bar Pub. House; bd. dirs. Ta'agidim Ltd., Sano Ltd., Carmel Holdings Co. Ltd.; chmn. transparency internat. Israel br. Bloostein-Genosar Ltd.; ct. appeals on mergers and monopolies, 1995—2000; pub. com. on taxing nonprofit orgns. Israel Income Tax Authority, 1989—90. Author: Israel's Company Law, 1970, Company Promoters, 1972, Securities Law, 1973, Directors in Government Companies, 1977, Tax Planning of Investments, 1984, Corporation Tax, 3 edits., 1987, V.A.T., 1987, Directors and Officers of Corporations, 1989, Director's Manual, 9th edit., 1999; editor: The Director in Practice, 2d edit., 1997, The New Companies Law, 1999, 3d edit., 2003, The New Tax Law, 3th edit., 2003, The Meaning of Control and Its Applications, 2003. Maj. Israeli Army, 1954-57. Mem.: N.Y. Bar Assn., Israel Bar Assn. Home: 10 Berkovitz St 64238 Tel Aviv Israel Office: 1 Azrieli Ctr 67021 Tel Aviv Israel Office Phone: 972 3 6074444. E-mail: joseph@gkh-law.com.

GROSS, JUDY E., publishing executive; B in Math. cum laude, Vassar Coll., 1984; MBA, U. Chgo., 1988. Asst. mgr. Chem. Banking Corp.; planning analyst prodn. dept. N.Y. Times, N.Y.C., 1990—92, planning mgr. in prodn. dept., 1992—95, mgr. in strategic planning dept., 1995—97, mng. dir. gen. classified advt., 1997—99, mng. dir. customer order fulfillment, 1999—2001, group dir. customer order fulfillment, 2001—04, v.p. pub. ops., 2004—. Office: NY Times 229 W 43rd St New York NY 10036-3959

GROSS, KAREN CHARAL, lawyer; b. NYC, Nov. 25, 1940; d. Harry B. and Adele (Hook) Charal; m. Meyer A. Gross, Aug. 16, 1964; children: Dana Leslie, Jennifer P., Pamela A. AB, Barnard Coll., 1962; JD, NYU, 1965. Bar: N.Y. 1965. Atty. Wolder & Gross, NYC, 1965-78, Wolder, Gross & Yavner, NYC, 1978-86; sr. v.p. legal and bus. affairs GoodTimes Entertainment LLC, NYC, 1986—2004; of counsel Schweitzer Cornman Gross & Bondell LLP, NYC, 2005—. Editor NYU Law Rev., 1963-65. Parent liaison Ramaz Sch., N.Y.C., 1980-86; del. Dem. County Com., N.Y.C., 1988—; legal mentor to students Barnard Coll., N.Y.C. John Norton Pomeroy scholar NYU, 1963-65. Mem. Internat. Trademark Assn., Copyright Soc. USA. Avocation: travel. Office: Schweitzer Cornman Gross & Bondell LLP 292 Madison Ave New York NY 10017 Office Phone: 646-424-0770.

GROSS, KENNETH ANDREW, lawyer; b. NYC, Jan. 22, 1951; s. Robert Emanual and Gloria (Polansky) F.; m. Karin Goldsmith, June 29, 1986; 1 child, Jennifer Gail. BS cum laude, U. Bridgeport, 1972; JD, Emory U. Sch. Law, 1975. Bar: Ga. 1975, DC 1976, US Ct. Appeals (5th cir.) 1975, US Ct. Appeals (DC cir.) 1977, US Ct. Appeals (11th cir.) 1979, US Supreme Ct. 1978, N.Y. 2003. Assoc. Lipshutz, Zusmann & Sikes, Atlanta, 1975-77; atty. Fed. Election Commn., Washington, D.C., 1977-78, asst. gen counsel, 1978-79, assoc. gen. counsel, 1980—86; ptnr. political law Skadden, Arps, Slate, Meagher & Flom, Washington, 1986—. Adj. prof. NYU, 2003; co-chmn. Practicing Law Inst. annual seminar on "Corporate Political Activities"; served as appointee of former Senator Daniel P. Moynihan on the Fed. Jud. Screening Com. Author Corporate Political Activities--Bureau of National Affairs, 2003, Federal Regulations of Campaign Finance, 1980, co-author: Ethics Handbook for Entertaining and Lobbying Pub. Officials, BNA's Corporate Political Activities; guest appearances on CNN, Fox News, NPR Radio and other media outlets. Bd. trustee Campaign Fin. Inst.; mem. exec. com., counsel Am. Coun. Young Polit. Leaders. Mem. ABA (std. com. election law). Home: 10 Eagle Ridge Ct Bethesda MD 20817-3922 Office: Skadden Arps Slate Meagher & Flom LLP 1440 New York Ave NW Ste 600 Washington DC 20005 Office Phone: 202-371-7000. Office Fax: 202-661-7956. Business E-Mail: kgross@skadden.com.

GROSS, LARRY PAUL, communications educator; b. Washington, Nov. 22, 1942; s. Bertram Myron and Nora (Faine) G. BA, Brandeis U., 1964; PhD, Columbia U., 1968; MA (hon.), U. Pa., 1973. Asst. prof. U. Pa., Phila., 1968-73, assoc. prof., 1973-82, prof., 1982—, Sol Worth prof., 1998—, assoc. dean for grad. studies, 1989-93, chair faculty senate, 2000-01, dep. dean, 2001—03; prof., dir. Sch. Comm., U. So. Calif., 2003—. Author: Contested Closets: The Politics and Ethics of Outing, 1993; editor: Communications Technology and Social Policy, 1973, Between Men-Between Women book series, 1991—, Studying Visual Communication, 1981, Image Ethics, 1988, Studies in Visual Communications, 1977-85, On the Margins of Art Worlds, 1995, The Columbia Reader on Lesbians and Gay Men in Media, Society and Politics, 1999, Up From Invisibility: Lesbians, Gay Men and the Media in America, 2001; author, editor: Image Ethics in the Digital Age, 2003; assoc. editor Internat. Ency. Comm., 1989; contbr. articles to profl. jours. Chair Phila. Lesbian and Gay Task Force, 1981-2000; mem. Pa. Humanities Coun., 1985-90. Guggenheim fellow, 1998-99. Fellow Am. Anthrop. Assn. (co-chmn. rsch. group on homosexuality 1981-84); mem. Internat. Comm. Assn. (chair task force on diversity 1992—, lesbian and gay studies interest group 1993-96), Nat. Comm. Assn., Phi Beta Kappa, Sigma Xi. Home: 329 S Sycamore Los Angeles CA 90036 Office: U So Calif Annenberg Sch Los Angeles CA 90089 Office Phone: 213-740-3770. Business E-Mail: lpgross@usc.edu.

GROSS, LAURA ANN, marketing and communications professional, acupuncturist, herbalist; b. Kew Gardens, N.Y., July 11, 1948; d. Melvin Fredericks and Harriette (Levy) G. BA, Boston U., 1970; MA, Columbia U., 1974; MS, Pacific Coll. Oriental Medicine, 1996. Staff writer Am. Banker, N.Y.C., 1974-82, assoc. editor, 1982-88; dir. fin. svcs., instns., communications Am. Express Travel/Related Svcs. Co., N.Y.C., 1988-89; dir. sales promotion and pub. rels. Am. Express Travelers Cheque Group/Am. Express Travel Svcs., N.Y.C., 1989-92; dir. strategic bus. comm. Am. Express Travel Related Svcs., N.Y.C., 1992-93; pres. Strategic Comm. Cons., N.Y.C., 1993-2000; founder Alternative Ctr. for Natural Healing, 1997—; exec. v.p. mktg. Letsgotrade, Inc., 2000-01; sr. v.p. mktg./ebusiness Muriel Siebert & Co., Inc., 2001—. Spkr. fin. svcs. and Chinese medicine. Author, editor consumer surveys and articles. Recipient editorial awards Pannell Kerr Forster, 1984, N.E. Bus. Press Editors, 1986, N.Y. Bus. Press. Editors, 1987, first Boston U. Coll. of Liberal Arts Young Alumni award, 1985. Avocations: fiction writing, travel, snorkeling.

GROSS, LAWRENCE ALAN, lawyer; b. Phila., Oct. 1, 1952; s. Herbert and Rita Lila (Garelik) G.; m. Lynda Kinsfather, May 27, 1979; 1 child, Alyssa Rachel. AB with highest honor, U. Mich., 1973, AM in Philosophy, 1978, JD magna cum laude, 1979. Bar: Pa. 1979. Assoc. Blank, Rome, Comisky & McCauley, Phila., 1979-86; v.p., gen. counsel Sungard Data Sytems Inc., Wayne, Pa., 1986—. Bd. dirs. Sungard Data Sytems Inc. and subs. Mem. ABA, Corp. Counsel Assn., Am. Soc. Corp. Secs., Pa. Bar Assn., Phila. Bar Assn., U. Mich. Alumni Assn. Home: 1433 Evans Rd Ambler PA 19002-1203 Office: Sungard Data Systems 680 E Swedesford Rd Wayne PA 19087

GROSS, LEE STEVEN, physician, researcher; s. Sanford Gross and JoAnn Israel; m. Janice K Konya, July 27, 1997; 1 child, Steven A. MD, Case Western Res. U., Cleve., 2000. Diplomate Am. Bd. of Family Practice, 2003. Rsch. coord. Cleve. Clinic Found., 1993—96; chief resident U. Hosps. of Cleve., 2001—02; staff physician U. Hosps. Suburban Urgent Care Ctr., South Euclid, Ohio, 2001—02; physician, assoc. Inter-Medic Med. Group, PA, Port Charlotte, Fla., 2002—04; physician, owner Prime Health of North Port, LLC, North Port, Fla., 2004—. Adj. prof. of pharmacy Ohio No. U. Coll. of Pharmacy, Cleve., 2001—03. Researcher (original research) Increased consumption of refined carbohydrates and the US diabetes epidemic: An ecological assessment (Am. Acad. of Family Physicians, Resident Scholar Award; .Am J Clin Nutr 2004;79:774-779, 2003); contbr. articles to profl. jours.; peer reviewer European Jour. Clin. Nutrition, 2004. Dir. of diabetes and nutrition edn. Fawcett Meml. Hosp., Port Charlotte, Fla., 2003—04; mem. Cmty. Health Improvement Project, North Port, Fla., 2003—04; adv. bd. mem. Cert. Diabetic Edn. Svcs., Naples, Fla., 2003—04; v.p. North Port Area C. of C., 2002—04; bus. adv. bd. Sarasota County Bd. of Edn., Sarasota, Fla., 2004—04; adv. bd. mem. Mederi Home Health Care, Port Charlotte, Fla., 2003—04; bd. dirs. Charlotte County YMCA, Port Charlotte, Fla., 2003—04; exec. bd. Fawcett Meml. Hosp., Port Charlotte, Fla., 2003—04, chmn., utilization rev. com., 2003—04, physician advisor, case mgmt. / utilization rev. dept., 2003—04. Recipient Alfred S. Maschke award for excellence in the art and practice of Medicine, Case Western Res. U., 2000, Resident Tchg. award, Case Western Res. U., Sch. of Medicine, 2002, Resident Scholar's award, Am. Acad. of Family Physicians, 2002, Resident Tchr. award, Soc. of Tchrs. of Family Medicine; fellow Rsch. fellow, Cleve. Clinic Found., 1997. Mem.: Fla. Med. Assn. (assoc.), Charlotte County Med. Soc. (assoc.), Am. Acad. of Family Physicians (assoc.), AMA (assoc.). Achievements include research in Conducted first U.S. study of coronary artery stenting without anticoagulation, pioneering cardiac stent placements; Conducted first national study linking diabetes epidemic to refined carbohydrate consumption with Harvard Medical School and Centers for Disease Control and Prevention; development of Assisted with the concept and development of City of North Port Community Health Services Center and Social Service Center. Office: Prime Health of North Port LLC 2630 Bobcat Village Center Rd North Port FL 34288 Office Phone: 941-423-9936.

GROSS, LEONARD, mathematics professor; PhD, U. Chicago, 1958. Prof. Yale U., 1959; rsch. fellow NSF, 1959—60; asst. prof. mathematics Cornell U., 1960—68, prof. mathematics, 1968—. Bd. mem. NSF Inst. for Mathematics & Applications, U. Minnesota; editorial bd. mem. Jour. Functional Analysis, Reviews of Mathematical Physics, Potential Analysis, Soochow Jour. of Mathematics. Recipient Senior Scientist award, Humboldt Found., 1993; grantee Guggenheim Found. fellowship, 1974—75. Fellow: Am. Acad. Arts & Sciences; mem.: Inst. of Mathematics (bd. govs. 1989—91), Am. Mathematical Soc. (co-organizer special session meeting 1998). Office: Cornell U Mathematics Dept 310 Malot Hall Ithaca NY 14853*

GROSS, LEROY, retired sugar company executive; b. N.Y.C., Aug. 11, 1926; s. Morris and Sarah (Leichter) G.; m. Betty Koch, Aug. 28, 1949; children: Michael Stephen, Kenneth Richard, Emily Jayne Gross Eider. BS in Acctg., NYU, 1948; postgrad., Fordham U., 1951-53; MBA in Acctg., NYU, 1955. With SuCrest Corp., N.Y.C., 1948-77, internal audit mgr., 1962-65, corp. acctg. mgr., 1965-69, contr., 1969-75, asst. sec., 1971-77; v.p. N.Y.C., 1975-77; v.p., contr. Revere Sugar Corp., 1977-86. Lectr. NYU, 1968-71; cons. in field. With USAAF, 1946-47. Mem. Inst. Internal Auditors, Nat. Assn. Accountants, Fin. Execs. Inst. Home and Office: 118 Winder Rd Yorktown VA 23693-3222

GROSS, LESLIE JAY, lawyer; b. Coral Gables, Fla., July 24, 1944; s. Bernard Charles and Lillian (Adler) G.; m. Frances L. Londow, June 16, 1968; children: Jonathan Eric, Jason Marc. BA magna cum laude, Harvard U., 1965, JD, 1968. Bar: Fla. 1971, U.S. Dist. Ct. (so. dist.) Fla. 1971, U.S. Ct. Appeals (5th cir.) 1971, U.S. Tax Ct. 1971, U.S. Supreme Ct. 1971; registered real estate broker, registered mortgage broker. Rsch. aide Fla. 3d Dist. Ct. Appeal, Miami, Fla., 1968-69; prof. social sci. Miami-Dade Community Coll., 1969-70; assoc. Greenberg, Traurig, et al., Miami, 1969-70, Patton, Kanner, et al., Miami, 1970-71, Fromberg, Fromberg, Roth, Miami, 1971-72; ptnr. Fromberg, Fromberg, Gross, et al., Miami, 1973-88; assoc. Thornton, David, Murray, et al., Miami, 1988-94. Atty. agt. Atty.'s Title Ins. Fund, First Am. Title, Miami, 1971-94; adj. prof. U. Miami Sch. Law, 1984; lectr. seminar Nat. Aircraft Fin. Assn., 1990. Contbr. articles to profl. jours. Mem. transp. com. Greater Miami C. of C., 1984-85; v.p., pres., bd. dirs. Kendale Homeowners Assn., Miami, 1970-81; vol. Dem. candidates in state and nat. elections, Miami, 1968, 70, 72, 87, 88; mem. Vision Coun. Land Use Task Force, Miami, 1988-89; judge Silver Knight awards Miami Herald, 1987, 92, 93, 94, 95, judge spelling bee, 1987; bd. dirs. Internat. Assn. Fin. Planning, 1983-84; founding mem., bd. dirs. The Actors Playhouse, 1987—, sec., 1990—. Mem. Harvard Law Sch. Assn., Harvard Club of Miami (v.p. 1985-90, pres. 1990-94, dir. 1985-99). Democrat. Jewish. Avocations: gardening, humorous creative writing, photography, aerobics, travel. Home: 10471 SW 126th St Miami FL 33176-4749

GROSS, LOIS, elementary school educator; b. Ames, Iowa, June 23, 1951; d. Elmer Herman Gross and Beth Maxine Jensen. BS, Iowa State U., Ames, 1973, MS, 1987, PhD, 1989. Cert. tchr. k-9 Iowa State U., supt./prin. k-12 Iowa State U. Tchr. grade 2 and grade 5 social studies Collins Cmty. Sch., Iowa, 1979—83; tchr. grade 2 Collins-Maxwell Cmty. Sch., Maxwell, 1983—91, tchr. grade 5 Collins, 1991—.

GROSS, MARK, lawyer, food products executive; b. 1963; BA, Dartmouth Coll.; JD, U. Pa. Law Sch. Mergers and acquisitions ptnr. Skadden, Arps, Slater, Meagher & Flom, N.Y.C.; sr. v.p. C & S Wholesale Grocers, Inc., Keene, NH, 1997—2002, gen. counsel, 1997—, CFO, 2001—, corp. exec. v.p., 2002—, bd. dir., 1997—; exec. v.p. GU Markets, 2001—03, pres., 2003—. Mem. board of dir. Monadnock Waldorf School; bd. dir. Food Industry Alliance, NY. Office: C & S Wholesale Grocers 7 Corporate Dr Keene NH 03431

GROSS, MARY ANNE, author, educator; b. Cornwall, N.Y., Aug. 10, 1943; d. Anthony Louis and Anne Malvina (Buckneberg) Gross; m. Angelo Carl Ferraro, Jan. 31, 1974; children: Antonia Anne, Daniel James. BA, BS, SUNY, New Paltz, 1965. Cert. tchr., N.Y. Tchr. pub. and pvt. schs., N.Y., 1965-75. Author: Baking Bread the Way Mom Taught Me, 1979; editor: Mother, These Are My Friends, 1969, Ah, Man, You Found Me Again, 1972. Founder Save Our Streams, Woodbury Falls, N.Y., 1986. Recipient Ray Bergman Trout Unlimited Conservation award, 1989. Mem. Kappa Delta Pi. Avocations: watercolor painting, photography. Home: PO Box 597 Highland Mills NY 10930-0597

GROSS, MELISSA RASMUSSEN, library and information scientist, educator; b. Marshall, NC, Oct. 1, 1955; d. Robert Cody and Jo Ann Ethridge; m. Joshua Miller Gross, Sept. 29, 1978; children: Rachel Elspeth, Max. BA in English Lit., UCLA, 1977, MLS, 1994, PhD, 1998. Cert.: Fla. (county mediator) 2004. Asst. libr. San Marino Pub. Libr., 1991—92; substitute libr. Glendale Pub. Libr., 1994—97, LA Pub. Libr., 1994—97; children's libr. Beverly Hills Pub. Libr., 1994—99; lectr. UCLA, 1998—99; Sara K. and Ted Srygley lectr. Fla. State U., Tallahassee, 1999, asst. prof., 1999—2004, assoc. prof., 2004—. Cons. LA Pub. Libr., 1998—99, Santa Monica Pub. Libr., 1998; field reviewer, spkr. in field. Co-author: HIV/AIDS Information for Children: A Guide to Issues and Resources, 1996, Statistics and Measures, and Quality Standards for Assessing Digital Reference Library Services, Guidelines and Procedures, 2002, Implementing Digital Reference Services: Setting Standards and Making it Real, 2003; manuscript referee: Libr. Quar., 1996—2003; mem. editl. adv. bd. Libr. Quar., 2003—; manuscript referee: Children's Lit. Edn., 1999—, Jour. Am. Soc. Info. Sci., 1999, Jour. Youth Svcs., 2000, Annual Rev. Info. Sci. and Tech., 2003, Can. Jour. Info. and Libr. Sci., 2004; mem. editl. adv. bd. Reference and User Svcs. Quar., 2000—, Libr. and Info. Sci. Rsch., 2002—; contbr. articles to profl. jours. Recipient Outstanding Faculty Mem. award, Fla. State U., 2002—03, Recogntion award for Emerging Scholars, AAUW, 2001; fellow, UCLA, 1994—95, 1995—96, 1997—98; Dept. Edn. grantee, 1995—96, 1996—97, Faculty Travel grantee, Fla. State U., 2000. Mem.: Beta Phi Mu. Office: Fla State U Coll Info 246 Louis Shores Bldg Tallahassee FL 32306-2100

GROSS, MICHAEL LAWRENCE, chemistry professor; b. St. Cloud, Minn., Nov. 6, 1940; s. Ralph J. and Margaret T. (Iten) G.; m. Kathleen M. Trammer, June 13, 1966 (div. 1981); children: Matthew R. and Michele R. (twins); m. Judith L. Stewart, 1994. BA, St. John's U., St. Cloud, 1962; PhD, U. Minn., 1966. Postdoctoral fellow U. Pa., Phila., 1966-67, Purdue U., Lafayette, Ind., 1967-68; asst. prof. chemistry U. Nebr., Lincoln, 1968-72, assoc. prof., 1972-78, prof., 1978-83, 3M alumni prof., 1983-88, C. Petrus Peterson prof., 1988-94; dir. Midwest Ctr. for Mass Spectrometry, Lincoln, 1978-94; prof. chemistry, pathology, and medicine Washington U., St. Louis, 1994—. Mem. metallobiochemistry study sect. NIH, Washington, 1985-88; mem. bd. on chem. scis. and tech. NRC, 1986-91; vis. prof. Internat. Grad. Sch., U. Amsterdam, The Netherlands, 1990, U. Warwick, Eng., 1988. Editor: High Performance Mass Spectrometry, 1978, Biological Mass Spectrometry: A Tutorial, 1991, Biological Mass Spectrometry: Present and Future, 1994, Practical Electrospray Ionization Mass Spectrometry, 2001; editor Mass Spectrometry Revs., 1982-90, Jour. Am. Soc. Mass Spectrometry, 1990—; contbr. 430 chpts. to books and numerous articles to profl. jours. Mem. instnl. rev. bd. St. Elizabeth, Lincoln Gen. and Bryan Meml. hosps., 1982-90. Recipient award for disting. tchg. U. Nebr., 1978, Pioneer award Commonwealth of Mass., 1987, Outstanding Mentor award Washington U., 2001, Sommer award U. Nebr., 2004; identified as one of Top 50 Cited Chemists in World, 1984-91. Mem. Am. Chem. Soc. (Field and Franklin award 1999, Midwest award 2002), Am. Soc. for Mass. Spectrometry, Union Concerned Scientists, Sigma Xi, Phi Lambda Upsilon. Democrat. Roman Catholic. Home: 6958 Waterman Ave Saint Louis MO 63130-4332 Office: Washington U Dept Chemistry Saint Louis MO 63130 Office Phone: 314-863-2221. E-mail: mgross@wustl.edu.

GROSS, MICHAEL ROBERT, writer, editor; b. NYC, July 16, 1952; s. Milton and Estelle (Murov) G.; m. Barbara Hodes, June 21, 1986. BA, Vassar Coll., Poughkeepsie, N.Y., 1974. Music columnist Andy Warhol's Interview, N.Y.C., 1973—74; editor-in-chief Rock Mag., N.Y.C., 1976—78, Fire Island News, N.Y.C., 1978; contbg. editor, columnist Manhattan, Inc., N.Y.C., 1984—85; reporter, columnist N.Y. Times, N.Y.C., 1985—88; contbg. editor N.Y. Mag., N.Y.C., 1988—94; commentator CBS This Morning, N.Y.C., 1992—93; sr. writer Esquire Mag., N.Y.C., 1994—95; contbg. editor Tatler mag., London, 1994—99; writer at large GQ Mag., N.Y.C., 1996—2000; contbg. editor N.Y. Mag., N.Y.C., 1997—2000, Travel and Leisure mag., N.Y.C., 1997—; sr. editor George Mag., N.Y.C., 2000; contbg. writer Talk mag., N.Y.C., 2001—02; columnist Daily News, N.Y.C., 2002—03; contbg. writer Radar mag., 2003. Author: Robert Plant, 1975, Bob Dylan, 1978, Model: The Ugly Business of Beautiful Women, 1995, My Generation: Fifty Years of Sex, Drugs, Rock, Revolution, Glamour, Greed, Valor, Faith and Silicon Chips, 2000, The More Things Change: Why the Baby Boom Won't Fade Away, 2001, Genuine Authentic: The Real Life of Ralph Lauren, 2003, 740 Park, 2005; co-author: The Rock Yearbook, 1980, Temple Kent, 1982, Shattered Mask, 1983, Precious Objects, 1984; contbr. articles to profl. jours. Mem. Am. Soc. Journalists and Authors, Authors Guild, Century Assn. Office: Trident Media Group 41 Madison Ave New York NY 10010

GROSS, PATRICK WALTER, information technology executive; b. Ithaca, N.Y., May 15, 1944; s. Eric T. B. and Catharine B. (Rohrer) G.; m. Sheila Eve Proby, Apr. 12, 1969; children: Geoffrey Philipp, Stephanie Lovell. Student, Cornell U., 1962-63; B in Engring. Sci., Rensselaer Poly. Inst., 1965; MSE in Applied Math., U. Mich., 1966; MBA, Stanford U., 1968. Cons. info. mgmt. operation Gen. Electric Co., Schnectady, 1965-67; sr. staff mem. Office Sec. Def., Washington, 1968-69, spl. asst., 1969-70; founder, prin. exec. officer, chmn. exec. com. Am. Mgmt. Systems, Inc., Arlington, Va., 1970—2002, also bd. dirs.; chmn. The Lovell Group, 2002—. Also bd. dirs.; chmn. bd. dirs. Medlantic Enterprises, Inc., 1988-94, Baker and Taylor Holdings, Inc., 1994-2003, dir., 1992-2003, Capital One Fin. Corp., 1995-, Mobius Mgmt. & Sys., Inc. Sarnott Corp., several pvt. cos., Computer Network Tech. Corp.; adv. coun. Stanford Grad. Sch. of Bus., 1999-2004, Ctr. for Strategic and Internat. Statis., 1998-2003. Trustee Washington Hosp. Ctr., 1977-87, Georgetown Med. Ctr., 2000—, Sidwell Friends Sch., 1980-88, 92-2000, Wolf Trap Found. Performing Arts, 1997-2002, Com. for Econ. Devel., Georgetown U. Hosp., 2000—, Aspen Inst., 2001—; mem. exec. com., treas. Youth for Understanding, 1984-90, 93—, vice chmn., 1996-2001, Youth for Understanding Found., Germany, 1989-2002; mem. Coun. on Competitiveness, Fed. City Coun., Washington, 1992-; mem. adv. bd. Ctr. Strategic Internat. Studies; adv. coun. Stanford Grad. Sch. Bus.; adv. bd. Stanford Inst. for Econ. Policy Rsch. Mem. Fgn. Policy Assn. (bd. govs., bd. dirs., mem. exec. com. 1977-86, 87—), World Affairs Coun. Washington (bd. dirs., founding vice chmn. 1980-91, chmn. 1991-2002), Coun. Excellence in Govt. (bd. dirs. 1996—, vice chmn. 1999—), Jamestown Found. (bd. dirs. 1997—), Aspen Inst. (bd. dirs. 2001—), Coun. Fgn. Rels., Washington Inst. Fgn. Affairs, Internat. Inst. Strategic Studies (London), World Econ. Forum (Geneva), Econ. Club Washington, Nat. Economists Club, Aspen Inst. Soc. Fellows, Pilgrims of U.S., Smithsonian Luncheon Group, Met. Club Washington, Chevy Chase Club, Univ. Club N.Y.C., Useless Bay Country Club (Wash.), Sigma Xi, Tau Beta Pi. Home: 7401 Glenbrook Rd Bethesda MD 20814-1327 Office: Lovell Group 1725 I St NW Ste 300 Washington DC 20006 Office Phone: 703-407-6700. E-mail: pat.gross@thelovellgroup.com.

GROSS, PAUL ALLAN, health products executive; b. Va., VA, Oct. 1, 1937; s. Albert and Cynthia (Saxe) G.; m. Gail Byrd, Nov. 19, 1966; children: Lorri, Garry, Randy. Degree, U. Richmond, 1959; BA, U. Ga., 1961; MHA, Va. Commonwealth U., 1964; cert. in hosp. adminstrn., U. Miami, Jackson Meml. Hosp. Adminstrv. resident in hosp. adminstrn. Tampa Gen. Hosp., Fla., 1964; adminstrv. asst. Dallas County Hosp. Dist., 1964-66, asst. adminstr., 1966-69, sr. asst. adminstr., 1969-70, assoc. adminstr., 1971-72; clin. assoc. prof. hosp. med. care U. Tex. Southwestern Med. Sch., 1964-72, Sch. Allied Health Scis., Dallas, 1964-72; exec. dir. Humana Inc. Suburban Hosp., Louisville, 1972-76; v.p. Fla. region Humana Inc., Miami, 1976-81; sr. v.p. Pacific Region Humana Inc., Newport Beach, Calif., 1981-84, exec. v.p., pres. hosp. div., 1984-92; ret. Humana Inc., 1992; prof., health adminstr. Va. Commonwealth U./Med. Coll. Va., 1992-95, prof. emeritus, 1996—. Nat. cons. emeritus Surgeon Gen. USAF, 1987—; vice chmn. bd. trustees MedEcon, Inc., Louisville, 1993-96, also bd. dirs.; bd. dirs. St. Anthony Pub. Co., Washington, 1993-96; advisor KBL Healthcare Inc., Comprehensive Med. Mgmt., Inc., N.Y.C. 1993-96. Contbr. articles to profl. jours. Mem., chmn. U.S. Selective Svc. System Local Bd. 154, Newport Beach, 1983, Bd. 13, Louisville, 1982-2002; bd. assocs. U. Richmond, Va., 1990-96; bd. dirs. St. Francis High Sch., Louisville, 1989-92; bd. dirs. Louisville Zool. Found., 1989-96, chmn. investment com., 1992; mem. adv. bd. Sch. Nursing, 1992-96, Spalding U., 1997; chmn. devel. bd. Jefferson County C.C., Kentuckiana Edn. and Work Force Com.; bd. dirs U.S. Selective Svc. Bd., 1981-2002, emeritus 2002—; preceptor Fellowship Program-Edn. with Industry, USAF, 1986-92; bd. dirs. Spaulding U., 1996-97, Lake/Sumter County United Way, 2004—, LifeStream Behavioral Ctr., 2004—; bd. mem. chair, Comprehensive Med. Mgmt Inc, 1993-96; bd. dirs. Med. Coll. Va. Found., chmn. audit and applications com., 1993-2000; pres. bd. dirs. Pelican Cove Two Condo Assn.; bd. dirs. Hospice of Lake and Sumter County, Fla, 2005—, United Way of Lake and Sumter Counties, 2004-05, Lifestream Behavioral Ctr., Leesburg, Fla., 2004-05; CRA adv. bd., mem, chmn. City of Tauares Fla., 2005-. With USNR, 1955—63. Named Outstanding Adminstr., Ctrl Region Humana, 1975, 1976; recipient Humana Club award, Ctrl. Region, Louisville, 1974—76, Presdl. medallion, Va. Commonwealth U., 1995. Fellow Am. Coll. Health Care Execs. (ethics com., chmn. inv. droped sect. 1993—); mem. Tex. Hosp. Assn., Hosp. Coun. So. Calif. (chmn. multi-instnl. corp. liaison com. 1983—), United Hosp. Assn. Calif., Fedn. Am. Healthcare Sys. & Am. Hosp. Assn. (hon. life). Mailing: 1730 Peninsula Dr Tavares FL 32778 E-mail: pagross144@comcast.net.

GROSS, PAUL HANS, emeritus chemistry educator; b. Berlin, Apr. 17, 1931; came to U.S., 1962; s. Paul Karl Friedrich and Olga Frieda (Saacks) G.; m. Uta Maria Freudiger, June 8, 1957; children: Thomas, Klaus, Michael, Eva. Diploma, F.U., Berlin, 1958, Dr.rer.nat., 1961. Rsch. chemist Schering A.G., Berlin, 1961-62; postdoctoral fellow U. Pacific, Stockton, Calif., 1962-64; rsch. fellow, instr. Harvard Med. Sch., Boston, 1965-66, Mass. Gen. Hosp., Boston, 1965-66; assoc. prof. U. Pacific, Stockton, Calif., 1966-70, prof., 1970-99, prof. chemistry emeritus, 1999—. Vis. prof., vis. scientist Tech. Hochschule, Munich, 1973, Freie U., Berlin, 1978, U. Autonoma, Baja Calif., Mex., 1978, Med. Hochschule Hannover, Germany, 1983, U. de Sevilla, Spain, 1988; cons. United Pharms., 1984—, Cell Pathways, Inc., Phila., 1990—, Dupont Merck, 1992—, Kimberly Clark, 1993—. Contbr. articles to profl. jours. Rsch. grantee NSF, 1968, 69-71, Rsch. Corp., 1972-74, Med. Sch. Hann., 1983, NIH, 1987-89. Mem. Gesellschaft Deutscher Chemiker, Am. Chem. Soc., Alpha Chi Sigma, Sigma Xi, Phi Kappa Phi. Achievements include patents in field. Office: U of the Pacific Dept Chemistry Stockton CA 95211-0001 Fax: (209) 946-2607.

GROSS, PETER ALAN, epidemiologist, researcher; b. Newark, Nov. 18, 1938; s. Meyer P. and Nathalie (Bass) Denburg) G.; m. Regina Teri Gittlin, May 30, 1964; children: Deborah Karen, Michael Philip, Daniel Brian. BA cum laude, Amherst Coll., 1960; MD, Yale U., 1964. Diplomate Am. Bd. Internal Medicine. Intern Yale-New Haven Hosp., 1964-65, jr. resident, 1965-66; sr. resident Peter Bent Brigham Hosp., Boston, 1968-69; research and edn. assoc. Va Hosp., West Haven, Conn., 1971-73, acting chief infectious disease sect., 1972-73; chief infectious disease sect. VA Hosp., West Haven, Conn., 1973-74, Hackensack (N.J.) U. Med. Ctr., 1974—, chmn. dept. medicine, 1980—, chmn. med. bd., 1986; prof. medicine N.J. Med. Sch., Newark, 1981—, vice chmn. dept. medicine, 1994—. Assoc. clin. prof. medicine Columbia U. Coll. Physicians and Surgeons, N.Y.C., 1971—81, asst. clin. prof., 1974—77; asst. prof. medicine Yale U. Sch. Medicine, New Haven, 1971—74; ad hoc reviewer rsch. grants NIH, Nat. Inst. Allergy and Infectious Diseases; investigator Ctr. for Biologic Evaluation and Rsch. FDA, 1974—95; chmn. drug safety and risk mgmt. adv. com. Ctr. for Drug Evaluation and Rsch. FDA, 2002—; mem. clin. indicators task force Joint Commn. on Accreditation of Healthcare Orgns., 1987—89, chmn. pneumonia clin. adv. panel, 1999—2001; chmn. Sentinel Event Adv. Group; project dir. Phase I-111 Robert Wood Johnson Found. and Inst. for Healthcare Improvement; mem. expert panels on cmty.-acquired pneumonia, HCQIP and surg. dir. prevention HCQIP Ctrs. for Medicare and Medicaid Svc., 1998—2002; co-chmn. N.J. Quality Improvement Adv. Com. Author: Gram Strain Recognition, 1975, 2d edit., 1980, Managing Your Health, 1991; past assoc. editor: Clinical Performance and Quality Health Care; mem. editorial bd. Jour. Clin. Microbiology, 1980—, Infection Control, 1980-90; mem. editl. bd. Managed Care, 1998—; past editl. adv. bd. Joint Commn. Jour. Quality Improvement. Served to lt. comdr. USPHS, CDC, 1966-68. NIH fellow Yale U., 1969-71. Fellow Infectious Diseases Soc. Am. (clin. affairs com., past chair practice guidelines com., councillor 2000-02); mem. ACP (task force on adult immunization), Am. Acad. Microbiology, Am. Soc. Virology, Am. Soc. Microbiology, Soc. Healthcare Epidemiologists Am. (councillor 1986-88, v.p. 1992, pres.-elect 1993, pres. 1994, past pres. 1995), Assn. Profs. Medicine. Office: Hackensack U Med Ctr Dept Internal Medicine Hackensack NJ 07601

GROSS, RICHARD BENJAMIN, lawyer, film producer; b. Santa Monica, Calif., Sept. 26, 1947; s. Edward L. and Adele P. Gross; m. Pamela McGovern, June 1, 1985; 1 child, Hannah McGovern. Student, UCLA, 1965-68; BA, U. Calif., Berkeley, 1970; JD, Harvard U., 1973; postgrad., Cambridge (Eng.) U., 1973-74. Bar: N.Y. 1975, U.S. Dist. Ct. (so. dist.) N.Y. 1975, U.S. Ct. Appeals (2d cir.) 1975, Ill. 1987. Assoc. White & Case, N.Y.C., 1974—77; assoc. counsel Am. Express Co., N.Y.C., 1977—82; sr. v.p., gen. counsel and sec. Citicorp Diners Club, Inc., Chgo., 1982—90; sr. v.p., gen. counsel Citicorp Ins. Group, Inc., N.Y.C., 1990—91; sr. v.p., gen. counsel, sec. Ambac Fin. Group, Inc., N.Y.C., 1991—98; mng. dir., gen. counsel U.S. Trust Corp., N.Y.C., 1998—2001; co-pres., chief legal officer GoldenRich Films, LLC, N.Y.C., 2003—. Mem. bd. mgrs. Robeco-Sage Triton Fund, LLC, 2004—. Bd. dirs. Randall's Island Sports Found., 1999—, sec., treas., 2000—. Mem. ABA, N.Y. State Bar Assn., Assn. Bar of the City of N.Y., Assn. Corp. Counsel, Am. Film Inst., Ind. Film Project, Assn. Ind. Video and Film Makers. Office Phone: 917-974-6717. E-mail: rich@goldenrichfilms.com.

GROSS, RICHARD M., chemicals executive; Mem. staff hydrocarbons and energy rsch. divsn. Dow Chem. Co., Midland, Mich., 1974—79, mem. staff coal gasification rsch. La. divsn., 1979, tech. dir. consumer products rsch. applied sci. and tech. labs., dir. R&D and tech. svc. and devel. for chems. and metals, R&D dir. N.Am. chems. and metals/hydrocarbons R&D, 1992—95, global v.p. core techs. R&D, 1995—98, v.p., dir. Mich. ops., 1997—98, corp. v.p. R&D, 1998—. 1st vice chmn. chem. engring. bd. Worcester Poly. Inst.; mem. adv. bd. Nat. Sci. Resources Ctr., Coll. Chemistry, U. Calif., Berkeley; mem. adv. bd. on chem. scis. and tech. NRC; bd. dirs. Mich. Molecular Inst. Mem.: AIChE, Coun. Chem. Rsch. (mem. governing bd. exec. com.), Indsl. Rsch. Inst., Am. Chem. Soc. Office: Dow Chem Co 47 Building Midland MI 48067

GROSS, ROBERT ALAN, history professor; b. New Haven, Feb. 17, 1945; s. Samuel and Roslyn (Chadys) G.; m. Ann Leslie Goldman, May 22, 1966; children: Matthew Benjamin, Stephen Alexander, Eleanor Elizabeth. BA, U. Pa., 1966; MA (Woodrow Wilson nat. fellow), Columbia U., 1968, PhD, 1976; MA (hon.), Amherst Coll., 1986. Gen. sec. U.S. Student Press Assn., Washington, 1966-67; asst. editor Newsweek, N.Y.C., 1968-70; NIMH trainee in social history Columbia U., 1970-72; adj. asst. prof. Worcester Poly. Inst., 1973-76; asst. prof. history and Am. studies Amherst Coll., 1976-80, assoc. prof., 1980-86, prof., 1986-88; prof. Am. studies and history, dir. Am. studies Coll. of William and Mary, 1988-98, Forrest D. Murden prof. Am. studies, 1992—2003; James L. and Shirley A. Draper chair of early Am. hist. U. Conn., 2003—. Prof. Am. studies U. Sussex, Brighton, England, 1981-83; vis. prof., dir. studies Ecoles des Hautes Etudes en Sciences Sociales, Paris, 1985; vis. assoc. prof. Brandeis U., 1985; core scholar New England and the Constitution, 1986-88; Am. Studies specialist U.S. Info. Agy., 1991-92; dir. NEH Summer Inst., 1993; Fulbright chair of Am. studies Odense (Denmark) U., 1998-99, Fulbright sr. specialist (Brazil), 2003; book rev. editor William and Mary quar., 1999—2002. Author: The Minutemen and Their World, 1976, 25th Anniversary edit., 2001 (Nat. Hist. Soc. Book award, Bancroft prize), Books and Libraries in Thoreau's Concord, 1988, In Debt to Shays: The Bicentennial of an Agrarian Rebellion, 1993; mem. editl. bd. Jour. Am. History, 1995-98. Bd. dirs. Rare Brook Sch., 2003—. Guggenheim fellow, 1979-80, Charles Warren fellow Harvard U., 1979-80, Amherst Coll. Trustees faculty fellow, 1979-80, Bibliog. Soc. Am. fellow, 1984, Kate and Hall Peterson fellow Am. Antiquarian Soc., 1984, Howard Found. fellow, 1988-89, Old Sturbridge Village Rsch. fellow, 1991, NEH fellow, 1994; residency Rockefeller Found.'s Study and Conf. Ctr., Bellagio, Italy, 1994. Fellow: Soc. Am. Historians; mem.: New Eng. History Tchrs. Assn. (Kidger award 1987), Mass. Hist. Soc., Am. Antiquarian Soc. (chair program in the history of the book in Am. culture 1993—98, coun. 1999—2002, Mellon Disting. scholar in residence 2002—03), Am. Studies Assn. (Mary C. Turple award 2001), Orgn. Am. Historians, Am. Hist. Assn., Colonial Soc. Mass., Grolier Club, Phi Beta Kappa. Democrat. Jewish. Home: 92 Krivarec Rd Willington CT 06279 Office: U Conn 241 Glenbrook Rd Unit 2103 Storrs Mansfield CT 06269-2103 Office Phone: 860-486-6088. Business E-Mail: robert.gross@uconn.edu.

GROSS, RONALD MARTIN, forest products executive; BA, Ohio State U., 1955; MBA, Harvard U., 1960. With Battelle Meml. Inst., Columbus, Ohio, 1957-58, Champion Internat., 1960-68, Can. Cellulose Co. Ltd., Vancouver, B.C., 1968-78, pres., CEO, dir., 1973-78; pres., COO ITT Rayonier, Inc., Stamford, Conn., 1978-81, pres., CEO, 1981-84, chmn., pres., CEO, 1984-96; chmn., CEO, 1996-98; chmn. emeritus, 1999—. Bd. dirs. Rayonier Inc., Brink's Co., Corn Products Internat. Office: 6 Landmark Sq Ste 400 Stamford CT 06901-2704

GROSS, SALLY LUCILLE, retired librarian; b. Cleve., Feb. 17, 1943; d. John Albert and Harriette Frances (Galbraith) Sekerak; m. Douglas Hale Gross, June 17, 1967. BA, Baldwin Wallace Coll., 1965; MSLS, Western Res. U., 1967. Cert. libr., N.Y. Libr. I Denver Pub. Libr., 1967-68, libr. II, 1968-69; libr. grad. sch. internat. studies U. Denver, 1969-70; asst. libr. dept. rare books U. Rochester, N.Y., 1970-75; assoc. libr. DeGolyer Libr. So. Meth. U., Dallas, 1982-86; head spl. collections U. Tex., Arlington, 1988—2003; ret., 2003. Vol. libr. Mayfield State Hosp., Upper St. Clair, Pa., 1977, Blount County Pub. Libr., Maryville, Tenn., 2003—. Mem. ALA, Tex. Libr. Assn. (sec. local history roundtable 1986-87), Tex. State Hist. Assn., Am. Assn. State and Local History, Soc. S.W. Archivists, Phi Alpha Theta, Beta Phi Mu. Avocations: gardening, reading. Home: 128 N Panoscenic Dr Maryville TN 37803-4108

GROSS, SAMUEL R., law educator; Grad., Columbia Coll., 1968; JD, U. Calif., Berkeley, 1973. Atty., San Francisco, United Farm Workers Union, Calif., Wounded Knee Legal Defense Com., Nebr.; cooperating atty. NAACP Legal Defense and Ednl. Fund Inc., NY, Nat. Jury Project, Oakland, Calif.; faculty mem. Stanford Law Sch., U. Mich. Law Sch., Ann Arbor, Thomas and Mabel Long Prof. Law. Vis. lectr. Yale Law Sch.; vis. prof. Columbia Law Sch., NYC, 2001. Office: U Mich Law Sch 965 Legal Research 625 S State St Ann Arbor MI 48109-1215 Office Phone: 734-764-1519. Office Fax: 734-764-8309. E-mail: srgross@umich.edu.

GROSS, STEPHEN MARK, pharmacist, dean; b. Bklyn., July 31, 1938; s. Arthur S. and Hazel F. (Marks) Gross; m. Susan S. Farber, Nov. 5, 1961; 1 child, Julie S. BS, Columbia U., 1960, MA, 1969, EdD, 1975. Registered pharmacist N.Y., 1961. Pharmacist/mgr. C.O. Bigelow Chemists Inc., N.Y.C., 1960-65, Bigelow-Americana Chemists Inc., N.Y.C., 1963-65; asst. to dean Coll. Pharm. Scis., Columbia U., 1965-68, asst. dean, 1968-71, assoc. dean, 1971-72, acting dean, 1972-74, dean, 1974-76; dean grad. studies Arnold & Marie Schwartz Coll. Pharmacy and Health Scis. L.I. U., 1976-79; dean Sch. Bus. and Pub. Adminstrn., Bklyn. Ctr. L.I. U., 1983-84; dean grad. studies and research Conolly Coll. L.I. U., 1979-83, dean Faculties Pharmacy and Health Professions, 1984-88, dean Schwartz Coll. Pharmacy, 1985—, dean Sch. of Health Professions, 1990—. Mem. health care quality improvement steering com. Island Profl. Rev. Orgn., 1995—2000; mem. NY State Bd. Pharmacy, 1991—2002, chmn., 1997—98, extended mem., 1991—. Contbr. articles to profl. publs. Recipient numerous grants instnl. improvement. Mem.: Am. Soc. Health-Sys. Pharmacists, Nat. Cmty. Pharmacists Assn., Pharm. Soc. State N.Y., Am. Assn. Colls. Pharmacy (chmn. sect. continuing edn. 1979—80), Am. Pharm. Assn., Soc. Am. Magicians (v.p. N.Y. Assembly 1981—83, pres. 1983—84). Home: 43 Knott Dr Glen Cove NY 11542-4116 Office: LI U 1 University Plz Brooklyn NY 11201-5301 Office Phone: 718-488-1004. Business E-Mail: sgross@liu.edu.

GROSS, STEPHEN RANDOLPH, accountant; b. Newark, Oct. 8, 1947; s. Edward Thomas and Frances (Randolph) G.; m. Barbara Louise Schutz, June 14, 1969 (div. Jan. 1981); children: David Randolph, Matthew Jeffrey; m. Tami Marie Haddad, Dec. 30, 1999. AB, Duke U., 1970. CPA Ga.; cert. CFE, fraud examiner, CVA, valuation analyst Ga. From staff acct. to ptnr. Lester Witte & Co., Atlanta, 1970—74, ptnr. Chgo., 1974—79, nat. dir. tng., 1978—79, exec. com.; founder HLB Gross Collins, Atlanta, 1979—. Trustee nds; bd. dirs. ebank.atlanta, Anderson Calhoun, Ltd., Healthfield, Inc.; treas. Henry Aaron Ent., Inc., Milw.; v.p. Coventry Holding Group, Inc., Decatur, Ga.; sec. Carint of NA, Milan; mng. dir. Next Tech. Golf, LLC. Bd. dirs. Henry Grady Found.; active Atlanta Symphony Orch., 1975—, High Mus. Art, Atlanta, 1985—, Ga. Pub. Policy Found., 1991—. Mem. AICPA, Ga. Soc. CPAs, Nat. Assn. Cert. Valuation Analysis, Assn. Cert. Fraud Examiners, Inst. Bus. Appraisers, Cherokee Town and Country Club, Chaine des

Rotisseurs (Paris), Reynolds Plantation Club. Home: 175 River North Dr NW Atlanta GA 30328-1111 Office: HLB Gross Collins PC 2625 Cumberland Pkwy SE Ste 400 Atlanta GA 30339-3993 E-mail: sgross@grosscollins.com.

GROSS, STEVEN ROSS, lawyer; b. NYC, June 15, 1946; s. Alexander and Lola (Mandelbaum) Gross; m. Georgette Francine Kleinhaus, Dec. 14, 1968; children: Amy, Jillian. BA, Columbia U., 1968, MA, 1969; LLB, Cambridge U., 1971; JD, Yale U., 1973. Bar: US dist. Ct. (ea. and so. dists.) NY 1974. Assoc. Debevoise & Plimpton LLP, NYC, 1973-80, ptnr., 1981—, head Bankruptcy and Restructuring Practice Group. Co-author: Collier Business Workout Guide; contbr. Mem.: ABA, Assn. of Bar of City of N.Y. Jewish. Home: 145 E 74th St New York NY 10021-3225 Office: Debevoise & Plimpton 919 3rd Ave 42nd Fl New York NY 10022-3094 Office Phone: 212-909-6586. E-mail: srgross@debevoise.com.

GROSS, THEODORE LAWRENCE, university administrator, author; b. Bklyn., Dec. 4, 1930; s. David and Anna (Weisbrod) G.; m. Selma Bell, Aug. 27, 1955 (dec. 1991); children: Donna, Jonathan; m. Joellen Gross, 2001. BA, U. Maine, 1952; MA, Columbia U., 1957, PhD, 1960. Prof. English CCNY, 1958-78, chmn. dept., 1970-72, assoc. dean and dean humanities, 1972-78, v.p. instl. advancement, 1976-77; provost Capitol Campus, Pa. State U., Middletown, 1979-83; dean Sch. Letters and Sci. SUNY Coll., Purchase, 1983-88; chmn. SUNY-Purchase Westchester Sch. Partnership, 1984-88; pres. Roosevelt U., Chgo., 1988—2002, chancellor, 2002—03. Vis. prof., Fulbright scholar, Nancy, France, 1964-65, 68-69, Dept. State lectr., Nigeria, Israel, Japan, Austria. Author: Albion W. Tourgée, 1964, Thomas Nelson Page, 1967, Hawthorne, Melville, Crane: A Critical Biography, 1971, The Heroic Ideal in American Literature, 1971, Academic Turmoil: The Reality and Promise of Open Education, 1980, Partners in Education: How Colleges Can Work with Schools to Improve Teaching and Learning, 1988, Roosevelt University: From Vision to Reality, 2002, The Rise of Roosevelt University: Presidential Reflections, 2005; editor: Fiction, 1967, Dark Symphony: Negro Literature in America, 1968, Representative Men, 1969, A Nation of Nations, 1971, The Literature of American Jews, 1973; gen. editor: Studies in Language and Literature, 1974, America in Literature, 1978; contbr. also essays, revs. With AUS, 1952-54. Grantee, Rockefeller Found., 1976-77, Am. Coun. Learned Socs. Mem. MLA, PEN, Nat. Coun. Tchrs. of English (chmn. lit. com.), Century Assn., Univ. Club, Chgo. Club. Home: 1100 N Lake Shore Dr Chicago IL 60611-1070 Business E-Mail: tgross@roosevelt.edu.

GROSS, WILLIAM H. (BILL GROSS), financial analyst, investment company executive; b. Middletown, Ohio, Apr. 13, 1944; m. Sue Gross; children: Jeff, Jennifer, Nick. BA in Psychology, Duke U., 1966; MBA in Fin., UCLA, 1971. Chartered Fin. Analyst. Investment analyst Pacific Mut. Life Ins. Co., Newport Beach, Calif., 1971-73, sr. analyst, 1973-76, asst. v.p., Fixed Income Securities, 1976-78, 2d v.p., Fixed Income Securities, 1978-80, v.p. Fixed Income Securities, 1980-82; from mng. dir. to chief investment officer Pacific Investment Mgmt. Co. subs. Pacific Mut. Life Ins. Co., Newport Beach, Calif., 1982—. Regular panelist Wall Street Week with Louis Rukeyser TV program. Author: Everything You've Heard About Investing Is Wrong!, 1997, Bill Gross on Investing, 1998. Served tour of duty USN, Vietnam. Recipient Fixed Income Mgr. of the Year, Morningstar, 1998, 2000, Disting. Svc. award, Bond Market Assn., 2000. Mem. L.A. Soc. Fin. Analysts. Office: 840 Newport Center Dr Newport Beach CA 92660-6310

GROSSBERG, BERNARD M., lawyer; b. Fayetteville, N.C., May 10, 1945; s. David and Evelyn (Goodman) G.; m. Jill Braut, Aug. 27, 1967; children: Blythe, Joshua. BA, SUNY, 1967; JD, Univ. Wis., 1971. Bar: Mass. 1974, U.S. Dist. Ct. (ea. dist.) Wis. 1971, U.S. Dist. Ct. Mass. 1972, U.S. Dist. Ct. R.I. 1971, U.S. Ct. Appeals (1st cir.) 1979, U.S. Supreme Ct. 1987. Lawyer Reginald Herber Smith Fellowship, Providence, R.I., 1971-72, Cmty. Law Fellowship, Boston, 1973-77; pvt. practice Boston, 1977—. Active Prisoners Rights Project. Mem. Mass. Assn. Criminal Def. Lawyers, Nat. Assn. Criminal Def. Lawyers. Avocation: bicycle touring. Office: 99 Summer St Boston MA 02110-1213

GROSSBERG, GEORGE THOMAS, psychiatrist, educator; b. Hungary, Aug. 20, 1948; came to the U.S., 1957; s. Henry and Barbara (Rothman) G.; m. Darla Jean Brown, June 13, 1976; children: Jonathan, Anna-Leah, Aviva, Aliza Rebecca, Jeremy. BA, Yeshiva U., 1971; MD, St. Louis U., 1975. Diplomate Am. Bd. Psychiatry and Neurology. Chief resident in psychiatry St. Louis U., 1977-78, instr., 1979-81, asst. prof., 1982-86, assoc. prof., 1986-90, prof., 1990-98, Samuel W. Fordyce prof. and chmn. dept. psychiatry, 1995-98, Samuel w. Fordyce prof., dir. divsn. geriat. psychiatry, 1998—. Cons. on aging U.S. VA Hosps. Assn., Washington, 1990—. Contbr. articles to profl. jours. Adv. bd. St. Louis Alzheimers Assn., 1983—. Recipient Pub. Svc. award, St. Louis Alzheimers Assn., 1989, Donovan-Sheer award, St. Louis Mental Health Assn., 1999, Fleischman-Hilliard award, Jewish Ctr. for Aged, 2000, Physician of Year award, Mo. Adult Daycare Assn., 2001. Mem. Am. Assn. Geriat. Psychiatry (pres. 1989-90), Am. Psychiat. Assn. (cons. on aging 1990—, Falk fellow 1977-79), Am. Geriat. Soc., Gerontol. Soc. Am., Internat. Psychogeriat. Assn. (treas. 1997—, pres. 2003-05). Avocations: collectibles, art, skiing. Office: Saint Louis U Med Ctr 1221 S Grand Blvd Saint Louis MO 63104-1016 Office Phone: 314-577-8721. Business E-Mail: grossbgt@slu.edu.

GROSSBERG, MARC ELIAS, lawyer; b. Houston, Dec. 26, 1940; s. Sylvester and Leah (Hochman) G.; m. Eva M. Wolski, Jan. 3, 1981; 1 child, Nicole; children from previous marriage: Lee Ann Krishnan, Toni Oreck. BS in Polit. Sci., U. Houston, 1961; JD with honors, U. Tex., 1965. Bar: Tex. 1965, Calif. 1966, Fla. 1980, U.S. Supreme Ct. 1980; bd. cert. fed. income taxation, Tex. Acct. Brochstein Toomim & Co CPAs (now Deloitte Touche), Houston, 1961-62; law clk. hon. Walter Ely U.S. Ct. Appeals (9th cir.), L.A., 1965-66; assoc. Fulbright & Jaworski, Houston, 1966-71; ptnr. Schlanger Mills Mayer & Grossberg, LLP, Houston, 1974-99, Thompson & Knight LLP, Houston, 1999—. Pres. Imprint, Inc., 2000—02, chmn. bd. dirs., 2002—04. Articles editor: Tex. Law Rev. Advanceman, speech writer 1968 Hubert Humphry Presdl. Campaign; pres. Tex. Bill of Rights Found., Houston, 1971-72, Jewish Family Svc., Houston, 1986-87, U. Tex. Law Rev. Assn.; commr. Housing Authority City of Houston, 1974-78. Mem. ABA (tax sect. and litig. sects.), Order of Coif. Democrat. Jewish. Avocations: family, writing, reading, exercise. Office: Thompson & Knight LLP Ste 3300 333 Clay St Houston TX 77002 Office Phone: 713-951-5824. Business E-Mail: marc.grossberg@tklaw.com.

GROSSBERG, MICHAEL LEE, film critic, writer; b. Houston, Sept. 7, 1952; s. Fred Samuel and Esther R. (Rosenstein) G. BA, U. Tex., 1979, BS in Journalism, 1983. Film, theater critic, reporter Victor Valley Daily News, Victorville, Calif., 1983-85; film, theater critic Columbus (Ohio) Dispatch, 1985-87, theater critic, 1987—. Co-founder Free Press Assn., Mencken awards for outstanding journalism, dir., 1981-94. Contbr. Otis Guernsey/Burns Mantle Theater Yearbook: Best Plays, 1993-02; regional report columnist Backstage, 1997—. Mem. Outer Critics Cir., Am. Theatre Critics Assn. (chmn. awards new plays com. 1993-99, exec. com. 1996-2002, vice chmn. 2001-02), Libertarian Futurist Soc. (chmn. Prometheus award judges com. 1997-, pres. bd. 1999-2002, bd. sec. 2003-). Avocations: reading, travel, meditation, public speaking. Home: 3164 Plymouth Pl Columbus OH 43213-4236 Office: Columbus Dispatch 34 S 3rd St Columbus OH 43215-4241 Office Phone: 614-461-5266. Personal E-mail: mikegrossb@aol.com. Business E-Mail: mgrossberg@dispatch.com.

GROSSER, BERNARD IRVING, psychology professor; b. Boston, Apr. 19, 1929; s. John and Katherine (Russman) G.; children: Steven, Mark, Minda; m. Karen Grosser. BA, U. Mass., 1950; MS, U. Mich., 1953; MD, Case-Western Res. U., 1959. Diplomate Am. Bd. Psychiatry and Neurology. Intern U. Utah, 1959-60, resident in psychiatry, 1960-65; asst. prof. psychiatry U. Utah Sch. Medicine, Salt Lake City, 1967-71, assoc. prof., 1971-75, prof., 1975—, chmn. dept., 1978—. Mem. pre-clin. and clin. psychopharm. rev. com. NIMH, Washington, 1974-79, 80-84, mem. sci. adv. bd., 1984-88; mem. merit rev. bd. VA, Washington, 1988-91; sr. sci. advisor Alcohol, Drug Abuse and Mental Health Adminstrn., Washington, 1987-88; ad hoc mem. Mental Health Clin. Rsch. Ctr. rev. com. NIMH, 1997, ad hoc mem. mental health clin. contracts rev. com., 1998, ad hoc mem. spl. emphasis panel, 2000-05 Contbr. chpts. to books, articles to profl. jours. Capt. USAF, 1965-67. Grantee NIMH, 1959-84, FDA, 1985-88; recipient Exemplary psychiatrist award Nat. Alliance for Mentally Ill, 1997. Fellow Am. Psychiat. Assn. (disting. life); mem. Internat. Soc. Psychoneuroendocrinology (treas. 1974-88), Utah Psychiat. Assn. (pres. 1995-96), Psychiat. Rsch. Soc. (pres. 1986-87), Am. Coll. Neuropsychopharmacology, Soc. Neurosci., N.Y. Acad. Scis., Collegium Internat. Neuro-psychopharmacologicum, Am. Assn. Psychiatry Dept. Chairmen (coun. 1997—2005, sec.-treas. 2005-). Republican. Jewish. Home: 511 Perrys Hollow Rd Salt Lake City UT 84103-4245 Office: U Utah Sch Medicine Dept Psychiatry 50 N Medical Dr Salt Lake City UT 84132-0001 Office Phone: 801-581-4888. Business E-Mail: bernard.grosser@hsc.utah.edu.

GROSSER, T.J., not-for-profit fundraiser; b. Milw., Oct. 17, 1938; s. Owen Henry and Ethel Clare (Hathazy) G.; m. Mary Janet McClanahan, Apr. 3, 1976; children: Paul Howard, Julie Anne, Philip Owen, Peter John, Elizabeth Michelle. BA, U. Wis., 1958, MA, 1962, EdD, 1971; DD (hon.), Union Theol. Sem., Richmond, Va., 1972. Min. edn. Cross Luth. Ch., Milw., 1957-62; assoc. Christ Luth. Ch., Oshkosh, Wis., 1962-65; preacher/tchr. Trinity Luth. Ch., Santa Barbara, Calif., 1966-71; pres. Amigos de las Ams., Houston, 1972-79, Vols. in Internat. Svc. & Awareness, L.A., 1980-84; v.p. Pacific Clinics, Pasadena, Calif., 1985-87; pres., CEO Children's Aid Internat., San Diego, 1987-97, Angelcare, 1998—. Bd. dirs. Am. Devel. Found., Washington, 1981-95; bd. dirs., pres. End Hunger Network, L.A., 1983-87; bd. dirs., v.p. Ind. Charities of Am., San Francisco, pres., 1988—; bd. dirs. Children's Charities Am.; advisor numerous internat. and religious agys. Contbr. 200 artices to profl. jours. Advisor African Refugee Ctr., L.A., 1989—; worker priest Hope Luth. Ch., Hollywood, Calif., 1983—. Named Educator of Yr. Am. Luth. Ch., Mpls., 1966, exec. of Yr. Coun. Internat. Vol. Orgn., Geneva, 1975, 76; recipient Papal medal Pope John Paul II, Rome, 1979. Mem. Fund Raising Execs., Rotary (Paul Harris fellow 1987). Democrat. Avocations: reading, speaking, travel, promoting internat. adoptions. Home: 6457 Elmhurst Dr San Diego CA 92120-3959 Office: Anglecare PO Box 600370 San Diego CA 92160-0370 Office Phone: 619-795-6234. E-mail: tjgrosser@angelcare.com.

GROSSETT, DEBORAH LOU, psychologist, consultant; b. Alma, Mich., Feb. 16, 1957; d. Charles M. and Margaret A. (Roethlisberger) G. BS, Alma Coll., 1979; MA, Western Mich. U., Kalamazoo, 1981, PhD, 1984. Lic. psychologist, Tex.; cert. in diagnostic evaluation, Tex.; bd. cert. behavior analyst, Tex. Grad. rsch. and tchg. asst. Western Mich. U., 1979-84; asst. group home supr., cmty. outreach Residential Opportunities, Kalamazoo, 1982-84; psychologist Richmond (Tex.) State Sch., 1984-87, Shapiro Devel. Ctr., Kankakee, Ill., 1987-88; clin. coord. Monroe Devel. Ctr., Rochester, NY, 1988; chief psychologist Denton (Tex.) State Sch., 1989-90; dir. psychol./behavioral svcs. Ctr. for the Retarded, Houston, 1990—2002; psychologist Mental Health and Mental Retardation Authority of Harris County, Houston, 2002—; pvt. practice, 2004—. Behavioral cons. Ctr. for Developmentally Disabled Adults, Kalamazoo, 1984, Goodman-Wade Enterprises, Houston, 1987; instr. psychology Houston C.C., 1985-86, U. Houston-Clear Lake, 1987, 92, 95—. Contbr. chpt. to book, articles to profl. jours. Western Mich. U. fellow, 1984. Mem. Am. Psychol. Assn., Am. Assn. on Mental Retardation, Assn. for Behavior Analysis (chair Outreach Bd. 1989-91), Tex. Assn. for Behavior Analysis (bd. dirs. 1989-91, program chair 1996, pres. 1997). Democrat. Presbyterian. Avocations: golf, camping, gardening. Home: 9750 Ravensworth Dr Houston TX 77031-3130 Office: MHMRA Harris County 7011 SW Freeway Houston TX 77074 Office Phone: 713-970-8217. Personal E-mail: degrosset@msn.com. Business E-Mail: deborah.grossett@mhmraharris.org.

GROSSMAN, BARBARA, artist, educator; b. NYC, Nov. 10, 1943; d. Emil Carl and Rose (Lehrberger) G.; m. Charles F. Cajori, June 23, 1967; 1 child, Nicole Antonia. Student in Sign Lang. Interpretation, Yale U. Sch. of Music & Art, 1964; BFA, Cooper Union, 1965; postgrad., Academie der Kunst, Munich, 1967-68. Instr. Westover Sch., Middlebury, Conn., 1975, 81, Mattatuck Mus., Waterbury, Conn., 1978-80, Tunxis Community Coll., Farmington, Conn., 1981, Washington (Conn.) Art Assn., 1974-77, 1992, 1996, 2002; resident faculty Chautauqua (N.Y.) Instn., 1987—90, N.Y. Studio Sch., 1989—90, 1993—94, 1996, 1996, 1998, 2001; resident critic Vt. Studio Ctr., Johnson, 1991-94, 95; tchr. MFA program Vt. Coll. Norwich U., Montpelier, Vt., 1991—. Vis. critic summer program Caumsett-Queens Coll., Huntington, N.Y., 1988, Yale Sch. Art and Architecture, New Haven, 1986-98, 2003, 04, Hampshire Coll., Amherst, Mass., 1992, Dartmouth Coll., Hanover, N.H., 1992, 2002; adj. prof. art U. Hartford, 1992—; assoc. adj. prof., 1993-, Yale Sch. of Architecture, 1986-2005, Brooklyn Coll., 2002; adj. assoc. prof. U. Pa. Grad. Sch. Fine Arts, 1994-2000; vis. critic Am. U., Washington, 1997, 2003; vis. prof. Knox Coll., Galesburg, Ill., 1999, Brandeis U., 1999, 2004; adj. prof. We. Conn. State U., 1983-94, Lafayette Coll., 2001, We. Conn. State U., 2002, U. Wash., 2002, U. Utah-Salt Lake, 2002, Brooklyn Coll., 2002, Union Coll., 2003, Hollins U. Roanoke, 2003; MFA faculty, Western Carolina U., 2004-05; artist in res./faculty, Hollins U., 2003; lectr. Yale Sch. of Art, 2003-05; master class Nat. Acad. Sch. Fine Arts, 2005. One woman shows include Lyman Allyn Mus., New London, 1977, Mattatuck Mus., Waterbury, 1979, Washington Art Assn., Washington Depot, Conn., 1985, Bowery Gallery, N.Y.C., 1973, 77, 81, 85, 88, 92, 95, 98, 2001, Paessagio Gallery, Hartford, Conn., 1991, Hurlbutt Gallery, Greenwich, Conn., 1994, Pa. Sch. of Art and Design, Lancaster, 1996, Hollins Coll., Roanoke, Va., 1997, Wayne Arts Ctr., Wayne, Pa., 2000, Jaffe Fried & Strays Galleries, 2002, Dartmouth Coll., 2002, Hollins U., Roanoke, Va. 2003, Union Coll., Schenecktady, NY, 2003, New Arts Gallery, Litchfield, Conn., 2004, Washington & Lee U. Dupont Gallery, 2005; exhibited in group shows at Wadsworth Atheneum, 1983, Coll. of William and Mary, 1987, Nat. Acad. Design, 1986, 90, 92, 94, 97, 98, 99, Guamann Cicchino Gallery, 1990, Bachelier Cardonsky, Kent, Conn. 1990, 92, 96, N.Y. Studio Sch., 1974, 76, 89, 93, 95, Ind. U., 1987, Margaret Lipworth Fine Art, 1991, Bryn Mawr (Pa.) Coll., 1993, Muscarelle Mus. of Art, Williamsburg, Va., 1994, Munson Gallery, New Haven, Conn., 1995, U. Pa., Phila., 1995, 96, Nat. Acad., N.Y., 1986, 90, 92, 94, 97, 98, 2001, 02, 03, U. Hawaii, Hilo, 1997, Western Carolina U., Cullowhee, 1998, Mangel Gallery, Phila., 1998, Marymount Coll., Tarrytown, N.Y., 1999, 55 Mercer St. Gallery, 2000, Ct. Commn. Arts, 2002, Andrews Gallery, William & Mary Coll., 2002, Wayne Art Ctr., 2002, Wash. Art. Assn., 2003, Westport Arts Ctr., Conn., 2005; solo exhbns. include Hollins U., 2003, Atrium Gallery, Union Coll., Schenectady, 2003, New Arts Gallery, Litchfield, Conn., 2004, A Survey, 2004-05: Wright State U., Dayton, Ohio, Lafayette Coll., Easton, Pa., Wash. & Lee Coll., Lexington, Va., N.Y. Studio Sch.; group exhbns. include Wash. Art Assn. Painting on Paper, 2003, Paessagio Gallery, W. Hartford, Conn., Spring Print Exhbn., 2004, Marymount Coll., Tarrytown, N.Y. Women By Women, 2004, Lohin-Geduld, N.Y., Languor, 2004, New Arts Gallery, Litchfield, Conn., 2005. Participant applied arts adv. com. Tunxis Community Coll., 1979-84, participant art program State of Conn. Evaluation Team, 1984; co-chair exhibition com. Washington Art Assn., 1988—; chair book selection com. Oliver Wolcott Libr., Litchfield, 1984-89; sec., founding mem. Bowery Gallery, 1969—. Fulbright/Hayes grantee, 1967-68, Conn. Commn. on the Arts grantee, 1978-79, Ingram Merrill Found. grantee, 1982-83, Grumbacher Art award and Gold medal, 1995, Adolp & Clara Obrie Prize, Nat. Acad., 2000, Henry Ward Ranger Purchase Award, Nat. Acad., 2001; Fellowship grant, Conn. Commn. Arts, 2002. Mem. Washington Art Assn. (trustee 1985—), Coll. Art Assn., Nat. Acad. (award for painting 1995). Mailing: c/o Bowery Gallery 530 West 25th St New York NY 10001 Personal E-mail: barbaragrossman@earthlink.net.

GROSSMAN, BONNIE, art gallery director; m. Sy Grossman. Former kindergarten teacher; founder The Ames Gallery, Berkeley, Calif., 1970—. Lectr. on Am. folk art and outsider art. Exec. prod., co-dir., prod. nine TV programs on Calif. artists; contbr. articles to profl. publs. Avocations: cake sculpture, knitting. Office: The Ames Gallery 2661 Cedar St Berkeley CA 94708 Office Phone: 510-845-4949. Office Fax: 510-845-6219. E-mail: amesgal@comcast.net.

GROSSMAN, CAROLYN SYLVIA CORT, retired elementary school educator; b. Cleve., Apr. 26, 1928; d. Louis J. and Esther (Matyas) Cort; m. Melvin J. Grossman, Aug. 7, 1949; children: Richard, Susan, Elaine. BS in Edn., Flora Stone Mather Coll., 1949; MS in Edn., Kent State U., 1974. Tchr. Columbus City Schs., Ohio, 1949—52; tchr. presch. Jewish Cmty. Ctr., Cleve., 1965—68, Carol Nursery, University Heights, Ohio, 1968—70; tchr. Cleveland Heights Schs., Ohio, 1970—93; ret., 1993. Bd. dirs., officer, pres. S. Euclid Lyndhurst (Ohio) LWV, 1957-74; coord. John W. Raper Open Sch., Cleve., 1965-73; bd. dirs. Greater Cleve. Tchr. Ctr., 1974-80; founder, pres., bd. dirs. Heights Parent Ctr., Cleveland Heights, 1975-80, hon. life trustee, 1985; co-chair Hello Israel program Nat. Coun. Jewish Women, Cleve., 1995-00, chair, 2000—. Martha Holden Jennings Found. scholar, 1975; recipient Achievement award City of University Heights, 1992, Arline B. Pritcher award Nat. Coun. Jewish Women-Cleve. Sect., 1998; named Carolyn Grossman award in her honor Heights Parent Ctr., 2003. Mem. Cleve. Heights Tchrs. Union (v.p. 1985-90, Ellen Krebs award 1983), Heights Ret. Tchrs. (founder, officer, bd. dirs. 1993-96). Jewish.

GROSSMAN, CISSY, curator, art historian; b. N.Y.C., 1932; BA, Lehman Coll., N.Y., 1972; MA in Art History, Hunter Coll., N.Y., 1979; PhD in Art History, CUNY, 1998. Asst. curator judaica The Jewish Mus., N.Y., 1972-79; lectr. art history Rutgers U., New Brunswick, N.J., 1978-86; lectr. George Washington U., Washington, D.C., 1979; curator Cen. Synagogue, N.Y., 1986-98; appraiser of Judaica N.Y., 1992—. Sr. rschr. Mus. of Jewish Heritage, N.Y., 1992—; curator Michael and Judy Steinhardt Collection; cons. curator Cong. Emanu-El, N.Y., 1980-89. Author: A Temple Treasury, 1989, A Jewish Family's Book of Days, 1989; curator, author catalog The Collector's Room: Selections From the Michael and Judy Steinhardt Collection, 1993; curator Fragments of Greatness, Walters Art Gallery, Balt., Americana from The Jewish Mus., N.Y.C. Bd. dirs. Grad. Ctr. for Jewish Art, Jerusalem, Textile Conservation Workshop, South Salem, N.Y. Mem. Am. Assn. Mus. (curator's com.), Appraiser's Assn. of Am. E-mail: cissyg@nyc.rr.com.

GROSSMAN, CLAUDIO M., dean, law educator; b. Valparaiso, Chile, Nov. 26, 1947; came to U.S., 1982; s. David and Berta (Guiloff) G.; m. Irene Klinger, Aug. 14, 1971; children: Sandra, Nienke. DSc in Law, U. Amsterdam, The Netherlands, 1980; JD, U. Chile, 1971. Dir., Internat. Legal Studies Prog. Washington Coll. Law, Am. U., 1983—93, acting dean, 1993, dean grad. studies, 1994, dean, 1995—, Raymond Geraldson Scholar of Internat. and Humanitarian Law. Coun. mem. Inter-Am. Inst. Human Rights; Leo Goodwin Disting. Vis. Prof. NOVA Southeastern Sch. Law, 2000; pres. Coll. of Am., 2003. Mem., vice chmn. UN Com., 2004; adv. bd. Latino and Latin Am. Inst. of the Am. Jewish Commn., 2005. Recipient Immigrant Achievement Award, D.C. Chap. Am. Immigration Lawyers Assn. and Internat. Law Soc. of Georgetown U. Law Ctr., 1996, René Cassin award, 1997, Henry LeRoy Jones Award, Washington Foreign Law Soc., 1999, Outstanding Dean of Yr. Award, Nat. Assn. for Pub. Interest Law, 2000, Chapultepec Grand Prize, Inter-Am. Press Assn (IAPA), 2002. Fellow: Am. Bar Found.; mem.: ABA (mem. Task Force on UN 2003—, chair nominating com. 2003—), Assn. Am. Law Schs., Orgn. Am. States (IACHR) (mem. Inter-Am. Commn. on Human Rights 1993—2001, pres. 1996—97, 2001), Inter-Am. Bar Assn. (coun. 1989—, gen. rapporteur 1992). Office: Washington Coll Law 4801 Massachusetts Ave NW Washington DC 20016-8001

GROSSMAN, DAN STEVEN, lawyer; b. N.Y.C., Apr. 6, 1953; s. George M. and Jeanne L. (Stickle) G.; m. Patrice Irene Michaelson, June 27, 1976; children: Deborah, Andrea. BA, SUNY, Albany, 1975; JD, Albany Law Sch., 1978; LLM, Georgetown Law Ctr., 1980. Bar: D.C. 1978, N.Y. 1979. Law clk. to judge U.S. Tax Ct., Washington, 1978-80; assoc. Webster and Sheffield, N.Y.C., 1980-84, Finley Kumble Wagner, N.Y.C., 1984-87, Willkie Farr and Gallagher, N.Y.C., 1987-90, ptnr., 1991—. Mem. ABA (tax sect.), N.Y. State Bar Assn. (tax sect.), Assn. of Bar of City of N.Y., D.C. Bar Assn. Office: Willkie Farr and Gallagher 787 7th Ave New York NY 10019-6018 Office Phone: 212-728-8226. Business E-Mail: dgrossman@willkie.com.

GROSSMAN, DANIEL V, investor; b. NY, NY, May 21, 1941; s. Nathan F and Rose G Grossman; m. Martha F Fine, Dec. 10, 1967; children: James B(dec.), Kate H. BA magna cum laude, Harvard Coll., 1958—62; JD cum laude, Harvard Law Sch., 1962—65. Bar: State of NY 1966. Ptnr. Holtzmann, Wise & Shepard, NYC, 1970—80, Werbel, Grossman & McMillin, NYC, 1981—88; chmn. Canfield Technologies, Inc., Sayreville, NJ, 1986—2000; co-founder and exec. v.p. Cytopharm, Inc., Menlo Park, Calif., 1988—; chmn. Tridan Internat., Inc., Danville, Ill., 1989—2000, KW Parts Inc., Pompano Beach, Fla., 1993—, Tech Comm, Inc., Sunrise, Fla., 1997—; founder & chmn. Ind. Precision, Inc., Crawfordsville, Ind., 1998—2000; chmn. Friends Mktg. Inc., Glastonbury, Conn., 2003—. Office: KW Parts Inc 2504 NW 19th St Pompano Beach FL 33069 Office Phone: 954-973-8400.

GROSSMAN, DAVID MICHAEL, academic administrator, educator; b. NYC, Feb. 1, 1944; s. Joseph Grossman and Ida Bogdonoff; m. Phyllis Wilson Grossman, Jan. 27, 1967; 1 child, Serge Philip Bogdonoff. BA with honors, CCNY, 1964; MA, Johns Hopkins U., 1965; PhD, Washington U., St. Louis, 1973. Dir. continuing edn. No. Ill. U., Dekalb, 1976—80; dir. U. Minn., Mpls., 1980—88, exec. assoc. dean, 1988—2000; dean Fla. Internat. U., Miami, 2000—04; vice provost Thomas Edison Coll., Trenton, NJ, 2004—. Mem.: Univ. Continuing Edn. Assn. (bd. dirs. 1978—2005). Home: 3729 Solora Rd Coconut Grove FL 33133 Office: Thomas Edison Coll Trenton NJ 08608

GROSSMAN, DOROTHEA G., poet, freelance writer; b. Phila., Aug. 27, 1937; d. Nathan Theodore and Shirley (Gerson) Dwartzin; m. Richard Grossman, June 29, 1958 (dec. Oct. 1992). BA in English Lit., Temple U., 1959. Registrar So. Calif. Inst. Architecture, Santa Monica, 1987-91. Author: (books of poetry) Cuttings, 1988, Poems from Cave 17, 1996, Museum of Rain, 2002; recording: (CD) Dorothea Grossman& Michael Vlatkovich, Call & Response, pfMentum Records, 2004. Performance grantee Meet the Composer, Calif., 1996, 2003. Avocation: music. Home: 2414 S Barrington Ave Apt 302 Los Angeles CA 90064-2934 E-mail: dottieg@pon.net.

GROSSMAN, EDITH MARIAN, translator; b. Phila., Mar. 22, 1936; d. Alexander and Sally (Stern) Dorph; children: Matthew, Kory. BA, U. Pa., 1957, MA, 1959; postgrad., U. Calif., Berkeley, 1960-62; PhD, NYU, 1972. Translator: Love in Time of Cholera (Garcia Márquez), 1988, General in his Labyrinth (Márquez), Maqroll (Alvaro Mutis), 1992, Strange Pilgrims (Márquez), 1993, Of Love and Other Demons (Márquez), 1995, The Adventures of Maqroll (Mutis), 1995, Death in the Andes (Vargas Llosa), 1996, In The Palm of Darkess (Mayra Montero), 1997, The Feast of the Goat (Vargas Llosa), 2001, The Red of His Shadow (Mayra Montero), 2001, Monstruary (Julian Rios), 2001, Don Quixote (Miguel de Cervantes), 2003; also others. Avocations: reading, music.

GROSSMAN, ELMER ROY, pediatrician; b. LA, Jan. 30, 1929; s. Harry and Reta (Frankel) G.; m. Rosalind Nagin, June 24, 1951 (div. 1976); children: Deena, Marianna; m. Pamela Canfield Antoncich, July 29, 1976; stepchildren: Camilla Sutter, Michael A. Antoncich. AB, U. Calif.-Berkeley, 1949; MD, U. Calif. Sch. Medicine, San Francisco, 1953. Intern Orange County Gen. Hosp., Orange, Calif., 1953-54; resident U. Calif. Hosps., San Francisco, 1957-59; practice medicine specializing in pediatrics Berkeley Pediatric Med. Group, Calif, 1959-92. Assoc. clin. prof. health and med. scis. U. Calif., Berkeley, 1978-80; clin. prof. pediat. emeritus U. Calif. Sch. Medicine, San Francisco; chmn. dept. pediat. Alta Bates Hosp., Berkeley, 1972-74, chmn. infant care ethics com., 1984-90. Author: Everyday Pediatrics, 1993, Everyday Pediatrics for Parents, 1996; columnist The Everyday

Pediatrician; contbr. articles to nat. mags. Mem. Berkeley Schs. Master Plan Com., 1966—68, Berkeley Schs. Child Care Com., 1968—70, Berkeley Cmty. Environ. Adv. Commn., 2000—02, Berkeley Cmty. Health Commn., 2002; pres. Temple Beth El, Berkeley, 1970—72. Served to capt USAF, 1954—56. Fellow Am. Acad. Pediatrics; mem. Alameda-Contra Costa Med. Assn., Physicians for Social Responsibility, Physicians for a Nat. Health Program. Democrat. Jewish. Avocations: wine making, gardening. Home and Office: 899 Euclid Ave Berkeley CA 94708-1305 Office Phone: 510-526-9614. Personal E-mail: elmer@grossmanfamily.com.

GROSSMAN, FRANCES KAPLAN, psychologist; b. Newport News, Va., May 28, 1939; d. Rubin H. and Beatrice (Fischlowitz) Kaplan; m. Henry Grossman, July 26, 1970; children: Jennifer, Benjamin. BA, Oberlin (Ohio) Coll., 1961; MS, PhD, Yale U., 1965. Diplomate Am. Bd. Profl. Psychology. Asst. prof. Yale U., New Haven, 1965-69, Boston U., 1969-71, assoc. prof. psychology, 1971-82, prof. psychology, 1982—2002, prof. emeritus, 2002—. Author: Brothers and Sisters of Retarded Children, 1971, Pregnancy, Birth and Parenthood, 1980, With the Phoenix Rising, 1999. Trustee Oberlin Coll., 1990-92, pres. Alumni Assn., 1979-80. Recipient Cert. of Appreciation Oberlin Coll. Alumni Assn., 1983. Fellow APA (mem. ethics com. 1994-97); mem. New Eng. Soc. Study Treatment Trauma and Dissociation (bd. dirs. 1995-99), Mass. Psychol. Assn. (chair ethics com. 1989-91, Career Contbn. award 1991), Sigma Xi, Phi Beta Kappa. Jewish. Office: Boston Univ Dept Psychology 64 Cummington St Boston MA 02215-2407 Office Phone: 617-332-6505. E-mail: frang@bu.edu.

GROSSMAN, HERBERT BARTON, urologist, researcher; b. Tampa, Fla., June 25, 1945; s. Benjamin and Pauline (Mattis) G.; m. Amy C. Becker, Aug. 24, 1969; children: Beth, Sara, Rebecca. BA, La Salle Coll., Phila., 1966; MD, Temple U., 1970. Diplomate Am. Bd. Urology. Surg. intern U. Mich. Med. Ctr., Ann Arbor, 1970-71; surg. resident St. Joseph Mercy Hosp., Ann Arbor, 1973-74; urology resident U. Mich. Med. Ctr., Ann Arbor, 1974-77; instr. U. Mich. Med. Sch., Ann Arbor, 1977-78; rsch. and clin. fellow Meml. Sloan-Kettering Cancer Ctr., N.Y.C., 1978-80; asst. prof. U. Mich. Med. Sch., Ann Arbor, 1980-85, assoc. prof., 1985-90, prof., 1990-94; dir., urologic oncology U. Mich. Cancer Ctr., Ann Arbor, 1986-94; prof. U. Tex. M.D. Anderson Cancer Ctr., Houston, 1994—, dep. chair Dept. Urology, 1998—. Cons. Taubman Med. Libr., 1985-94, The Med. Letter, 1991, Jour. Vascular Surgery, 1991; reviewer VA Merit Rev. Bd. for Surgery, 1986, NIH Pathology B Ad Hoc (SI) Study Sect., 1988, NIDDK Ad Hoc Rev. Groups 12 and 13, 1992; spl. reviewer NIH Exptl. Therapeutics Study Sect., 1986, reviewer spl. study sect., 1995, reviewer cancer ctr. support grant, 1996; reviewer NCI Rev. Group/subcom. 4, 1997; external reviewer Alberta Cancer Bd., 1998; mem. surg. quality control and edn. com. S.W. Oncology Group, 1980-90, GU com., 1980—, organ site chmn. for local bladder cancer, 1991-2000; surg. oncology adv. com. dept. surgery U. Mich. Med. Ctr., Ann Arbor, 1981-82, dept. surgery computer sys. adv. com., 1983-88, cancer ctr. clin. rsch. com., 1987-94, laser safety com., 1987-94, med. sch. admissions com., 1988-94, patient care com., 1989-90, hosps. quality mgmt. com., 1990-94, rsch. coord. sect. urology, 1991, fin. adv. com., adv. promotion com. for primary rsch. staff dept. surgery, 1993-94; med. practice subcom. U. Tex. M.D. Anderson Cancer Ctr., Houston, 1994—, grad. med. edn. com., 1994—2004, surveillance com., 1994-95, dir. clin. rsch., 1994—2004, dep. chmn. dept. urology 1998—; prostate cancer adv. com. Mich. Dept. Pub. Health, 1993-94, clin. rsch. com. mem. 1994-2000, chmn. 1997-2000, dir. bladder cancer multidisciplinary rsch. program, 1999-2004; mem. scientific adv. bd. Anthra Pharms., Inc., 1994-2004, Fujirebio Diagnostics Inc., 2003-; reviewer Med. Rsch. Coun., U.K., 1999, Dutch Cancer Soc., 1999, NCI Spl. Emphasis Panel, 1999, 2000, 03, cons. NCI early detection rsch. network, 2002, ad hoc reviewer NCI sub com. E, 2003-04, mem. NCI PACCT strategy group, 2004-; molecular biology review panel, FAMRI, 2001, 02, 03, 04; ad hoc reviewer U.S. Army Med. Rsch. and Materiel Command, 1999; clin. study sect. revue grants program M.D. Anderson Cancer Ctr., 2002-, vice chmn. 2002-03, chmn. 2003-04; mem. NCI program for assessment of clin. cancer tests strategy group, 2003-. Mem. editl. bd. Oncology Reports, 1998-, Jour. Urology, 1999-; sect. editor Urologic Oncology, 2000-; contbr. 209 articles to profl. jours.; authored 25 book chpts. Capt. USAF, 1971—73. Recipient 2d prize Ferdinand C. Valentine Urology Essay Contest, 1980, also numerous rsch. grants; named to W.A. "Tex" and Deborah Moncrief, Jr. Disting. Chair in Urology, 1994, Vis. Professorship award in urology, Pfizer/AUA, 2004; Ferdinand C. Valentine fellow N.Y. Acad. Medicine, 1979-80, clin. fellow Am. Cancer Soc., 1979-80. Office: U T MD Anderson Cancer Ctr 1515 Holcombe Blvd # 1373 Houston TX 77030-4009

GROSSMAN, JACK, advertising agency executive; b. N.Y.C., Mar. 22, 1925; s. Benjamin Robert and Sarah Dora (Bender) G.; m. Esther Arline Goldman, Nov. 23, 1949; children— Barbara Ruth, Neil David. B.Sc., NYU, 1950, MBA, 1952. With Biow Co., Inc., N.Y.C., 1952-56, mgr. sales research, 1954-56; with William Esty Co., Inc., N.Y.C., 1956-87, mgr. research dept., then v.p. research, 1964-73, sr. v.p., dir. research, 1973-87; pres. MBN Research Assocs., N.Y.C., 1987—. Adj. asso. prof. mktg. Pace U., 1962-74, adj. prof., 1988; adj. prof. mktg. Parsons Sch. Design, 1988; lectr. Baruch Coll., CUNY, 1990. Bd. dirs. L.I. Cons. Center, 1979— . Served with AUS, 1943-47. Decorated Bronze Star with oak leaf cluster, Purple Heart. Jewish. Office: MBN Rsch Assocs 1365 York Ave New York NY 10021-4035

GROSSMAN, JAMES A., public relations executive; b. Altoona, Penn., Feb. 24, 1942; s. Irwin Isaac and Ruthe (Hytowitz) Grossman; m. Sarah A. Reyes, July 29, 1968; children: Liliana Michelle, Luis Manuel. BA magna cum laude, U. Pitts., 1964; MS cum laude, Columbia U., Grad.Sch. Journalism, 1968. Reporter Pitts. Press, 1967, Charlotte Observer, NC, 1968, San Juan Star, PR, 1969; copy editor Wall St. Jour., N.Y., 1969—70; asst. editor Consumer Reports, Mt. Vernon, NY, 1970—76; asst. dir. pub. rels. Muscular Dystrophy Assn., N.Y., 1976—77; exec. asst. N.Y. State Assembly, Albany, 1977—82; exec. v.p. Rubenstein Assoc., Inc., N.Y., 1982—. 1st lt. U.S. Army, 1964—66, Korea. Mem.: Phi Beta Kappa. Democrat. Jewish. Achievements include pub. rels. clients including David Merrick, Marv Albert, Michael Bolton, Pamela Harriman, Madame Dewi Sukarno, F. Lee Bailey, John Jay Coll. Criminal Justice, CUNY, Becket Fund for Religious Liberty; Cardiovascular Rsch. Found., The U. of Medicine and Dentistry of N.J., SUNY Downstate Med. Ctr. Avocation: photography. Home: 525 W 238th St Bronx NY 10463 Office: Rubenstein Assoc 1345 Ave of Americas New York NY 10105 Office Phone: 212-843-8000.

GROSSMAN, JEFFREY A., language educator; b. Mt. Vernon, N.Y., Jan. 19, 1961; s. David W. and Marilyn Klein Grossman. BA, Tufts U., 1982, MA, 1986; PhD, U. Tex., 1992. Postdoctoral fellow Hebrew U., Jerusalem, 1992-95, Ctr. for Judaic Studies, U. Pa., Phila., 1995-96; asst. prof. U. Va., Charlottesville, 1996—, mem. exec. com. Jewish studies, 2000—01. Author: (book) The Discourse on Yiddish in Germany from the Enlightenment to the Second Empire, 2000; contbr. numerous articles to profl. jours. DAAD Rsch. grantee, 1989-90; Fulbright postdoctoral fellow, 1992-94. Mem. MLA, German Studies Assn., Yivo Inst. for Jewish Rsch. Office: U Va Dept Germanic Lang & Lit 108 Cocke Hall Charlottesville VA 22903

GROSSMAN, JEFFREY W., utilities company professional; BSBA, Drexel U. CPA. Various positions including auditor, mgr. gen. audit Columbia Gas, Svc. Corp., Columbia Gulf's Treasury Dept., Houston, Wilmington, Del., 1979-92; asst. controller Columbia Energy Group, Herndon, Va., 1992-96, v.p., controller, 1996—. Office: Columbia Energy Group 200 Civic Center Dr Columbus OH 43215-4157

GROSSMAN, JEROME HARVEY, medical educator, medical association administrator; b. Maplewood, N.J., Sept. 23, 1939; s. Abraham and Sally Grossman; m. Barbara Nan Grossman, June 9, 1968; children: Elizabeth, Katherine, Amelia. BS, MIT, 1961; MD, U. Pa., 1965; DHL (hon.), Lesley Coll., 1996. Fellow Mass. Gen. Hosp., Boston, 1966—69; physician, 1969—79; physician (hon.), 1979—; assoc. dir. computer sci. Mass. Gen. Hosp., Boston, 1969—72, dir. ambulatory care, 1974—79; asst. prof. Harvard Med. Sch., Boston, 1971-72, 74-79; pres. New Eng. Med. Ctr., Boston, 1979—84, chmn., CEO, 1984—95, Health Quality Inc., Boston, 1996—99; chmn. Lion gate Mgmt. Corp., 1999—; prof. Tufts U. Sch. Medicine, Boston, 1979—96; program dir. Commonwealth Fund Acad. Health Ctr. Program, 1982—87; chmn. The Health Inst., 1988—95; scholar in residence Inst. of Medicine, 1996—97. Bd. dirs. Stryker Corp., Kalamazoo, Fed. Res. Bank, Boston, chmn., 1992—96; bd. dirs., mem. nat. adv. com. Boston Pub. Libr. Found. Bd. dirs. Boston Pvt. Industry Coun., 1982—96, chmn., 1990—93; trustee Wellesley Coll., 1983—; mem. Bd. Edn., Commonwealth Mass., 1991—96, Jobs Coun., Commonwealth Mass., 1991—96; chair Bd. Transition Sys., Inc., 1985—96. Lt. col. USAF, 1972—74. Recipient Karl Taylor Compton prize, MIT, 1961. Fellow: ACP; mem.: Acad. Med. Ctr. Consortium (chmn. 1992—95), Assn. Am. Med. Colls. (adminstrv. bd. 1986—92, chmn. 1990—91, Disting. Svc. membership), Am. Fedn. Clin. Rsch., Inst. Medicine of NAS, Mill Reef Club, Cosmos Club, Tavern Club, Somerset Club, Country Club.

GROSSMAN, JOAN DELANEY, literature and language professor; b. Dubuque, Iowa, Dec. 12, 1928; d. Francis Joseph and Opal (Desmond) Delaney; m. Gregory Grossman, June 16, 1972. BA, Clarke Coll., Dubuque, 1952; MA, Columbia U., 1962; PhD, Harvard U., 1967. Asst. prof. Russian Mundelein Coll., Chgo., 1967-68; asst. prof., assoc. prof. then prof. Slavic langs. and lit. U. Calif.-Berkeley, 1968-93, prof. emeritus, 1993—, prof. grad. sch., 1995—. Author: Edgar Allen Poe in Russia: A Study of Legend and Literary Influence, 1973, Valery Bryusov and the Riddle of Russian Decadence, 1985; co-editor: Creating Life: The Aesthetic Utopia of Russian Modernism, 1994. Guggenheim fellow, 1978; Soviet Acad. Scis. fellow, Am. Acad. Learned Socs., 1978, 86, NEH fellow, 1992. Mem. Am. Assn. Advancement of Slavic Studies (v.p. 1988, pres. 1989), Am. Assn. Tchrs. Slavic and Eastern European Langs., Western Slavic Assn. (pres. 1984-86). Office: Univ Calif Dept Slavic Langs And Lits Berkeley CA 94720-2979

GROSSMAN, JOEL B(ARRY), political science educator; b. N.Y.C., June 19, 1936; s. Joseph and Selma G.; m. Mary Hengstenberg, Aug. 23, 1964; children: Alison, Joanna, Daniel. BA, Queens Coll., 1957; MA, U. Iowa, 1960, PhD, 1963. Faculty dept. polit. sci. U. Wis., Madison, 1963-96, prof., 1971-96, chmn. dept., 1975-78; prof. Johns Hopkins U., 1996—. Fellow in law and polit. sci. Harvard Law Sch., Cambridge, Mass., 1965-66; Fulbright lectr. U. Strathclyde, Glasgow, 1968-69; vis. prof. law U. Stockholm, 1973, John Hopkins U., 1995-96. Editor: Law and Soc. Review, 1978-82; author: Lawyers and Judges, 1965, Frontiers of Judicial Research, 1969, Law and Change in Modern America, 1971, Constitutional Law and Judicial Policy Making, 1972, 80, 88; contbr. articles to profl. jours. Chmn. Wis. Jud. Commn. 1985-87. Served with USAR, 1960-66. Mem. Wis. Civil Liberties Union (vice chmn. 1970-72), Am. Polit. Sci. Assn., Midwest Polit. Sci. Assn. (v.p. 1988-90), So. Polit. Sci. Assn., Law and Soc. Assn. Democrat. Home: 6606 Walnutwood Cir Baltimore MD 21212-1213 E-mail: jbgrossm@jhu.edu.

GROSSMAN, JOYCE RENEE, pediatrician, internist; b. Bklyn., Nov. 15, 1951; d. Norman and Sydell (Rashbaum) Katz; m. Arthur Robert Grossman (div.); 1 child, Justin. BS, Bklyn. Coll., 1973; MS, Cornell Med. Coll., 1980; MD, Downstate Med. Coll., 1986. Adj. prof. Downstate Med. Ctr., Bklyn., 1994—; attending physician NY Hosp. Network, Bklyn., 1996—97, Beth Israel Med. Ctr., Bklyn., 1997; assoc. med. dir. Cigna of NY, NYC, 1998—. Author: (with others) Pediatric Aspects of Tuberculosis & Clinical Handbook, 1995. Fellow: Am. Acad. Physicians, Am. Acad. Pediat. Achievements include patents in field of gene therapy, antibiotics and chemotherapeutic agents.

GROSSMAN, LAWRENCE, geochemist; b. Toronto, Canada, Feb. 2, 1946; arrived in US, 1968; s. David Saul and Marian Lillian (Jacobs) Grossman; m. Karen Lee Fruitman, Aug. 11, 1968; children: Sheryl Gloria, Daniel Martin. BSc with honors, McMaster U., 1968; MPhil in geochemistry, Yale U., 1970, PhD in geochemistry, 1972. Geological field asst. McMaster U., Geology Dept., Hamilton, Canada, 1965; mineralogist, chemist Ctr. for Forensic Sci., Ontario Dept Atty. Gen., Toronto, Canada, 1966—68; curatorial asst. Peabody Mus, Yale U., New Haven, 1968—72; asst. prof. geochemistry U. Chgo., Dept Geophysical Sci., 1972—76; rsch. assoc. Field Mus. Nat. Hist., Chgo., 1976—; assoc. prof. geochemistry U. Chgo., Enrico Fermi Inst., 1976—81; prof. geochemistry U. Chgo., 1981—. Cons. editor, geochemistry McGraw-Hill Encyclopedia of Sci. and Tech., 1988—97. Contbr. articles various profl. jours. Mem. NASA Planetary Geosciences Strategy Com., Wash., DC, 1986—87, Coun. of Meteoritical Soc., 1983—86. Recipient F.W. Clarke medal, The Geochemical Soc., 1974, James B. Macelwane award, Am. Geophysical Union, 1980; fellow, Royal Soc. of Can., 1998. Fellow: Am. Geophysical Union, Meteoritical Soc., Mineralogical Soc. of Am. Office: U Chgo Geophysical Sci Dept 5734 S Ellis Ave Chicago IL 60637 Office Phone: 773-702-8153. Office Fax: 773-702-9505. E-mail: yosi@midway.uchicago.edu.

GROSSMAN, LAWRENCE KUGELMASS, former communications executive, advertising executive; b. N.Y.C., June 21, 1931; s. Nathan F. and Rose (Goldstein) G.; m. Alberta S. Nevler, Mar. 1, 1954; children: Susan Lee, Jennifer Nancy, Caroline Ann. BA, Columbia, 1952; student, Harvard Law Sch., 1953. Editor, promotion exec. Look mag., 1953-56; advt. exec. CBS-TV, 1956-62; v.p. advt. NBC, 1962-66; pres. Lawrence K. Grossman, Inc., N.Y.C., 1966-76, Forum Communications, Inc., 1969-76, PBS, Washington, 1976-84, NBC News, N.Y.C., 1984-88, Brookside Prodns. Ltd., Westport, Conn., 1989—; co-chmn., prin. Digital Promise Project. Vis. lectr. Frank Stanton Chair on 1st Amendement, Kennedy Sch. Govt., Harvard U., 1989—, chair; sr. fellow, vis. scholar Columbia U. Gannett Media Ctr.; trustee Conn. Pub. Broadcasting and various nonprofit health orgns.; bd. dir. Fedn. Am. Scientists. Assoc. editor: A Candid Portrait of the 1964 Presidential Election, 1965; author: The Electronic Republic: Reshaping Democracy in the Information Age, 1996; TV columnist, Columbia Journalism Review; juror, Dupont-Columbia Journalism award. Address: Digital Promise Project 1717 K St NW Ste 209 Washington DC 20036*

GROSSMAN, MARC ISSAIAH, former federal agency administrator; b. L.A., Sept. 23, 1951; s. Melvin and Estelle Grossman; m. Mildred Patterson, May 29, 1982; 1 child, Anne. BA, U. Calif., Santa Barbara, 1973; MSc in Internat. Rels., London Sch. Econs./Polit. Sci., 1974. Polit. officer U.S. Embassy, Islamabad, Pakistan, 1977-79; staff asst. Bur. Near Eastern and South Asian Affairs US Dept. State, 1979-80; dep. spl. adviser to Pres. Carter The White House, Washington, 1980; chief profl. staff State Dept. Transition Team, 1980; country officer for Jordan US Dept. State, 1981-83; polit. officer U.S. Mission to NATO, 1983; dep. dir. pvt. office of sec. gen. NATO, 1984-86; exec. asst. to dep. sec. US Dept. State, 1986-89; dep. chief U.S. Mission in Turkey, 1989-92; exec. sec., spl. asst. to sec. US Dept. State, Washington, 1993-94, U.S. amb. to Turkey Ankara, 1995-97, asst. sec. for Europe and Can. affairs Washington, 1997-98, asst. sec. European affairs, 1998-2000, dir. gen. Fgn. Svc., 2000-01, under sec. polit. affairs, 2001—05; vice chmn. The Cohen Group, Washington, 2005—. Mem. Am. Friends of the London Sch. of Econs., Army and Navy Club (Washington). Avocations: reading, travel, sports. Office: The Cohen Group 1200 19th St NW Washington DC 20036

GROSSMAN, MARSHALL BRUCE, lawyer; b. Omaha, Mar. 24, 1939; s. Lee and Elsie (Stalmaster) G.; m. Marlene Belle Delson, Aug. 19, 1962; children: Rodger Seth, Leslie Erin. Student, U. Calif. at Los Angeles, 1957-59; BSL., LL.B., U. So. Calif., 1964. Bar: Calif. 1965. With Alschuler, Grossman Stein & Kahan, LA, 1965-67, ptnr., 1967—. Lectr. law U. So. Calif., Los Angeles, 1966-69; lectr., author on comml. litigation, 1968—; mem. Calif. Commn. Jud. Performance, 2001—, chmn., 2005—. Mem. Calif. Coastal Commn., 1981-86; bd. dirs. Bet Tzedek Legal Services, 1986—, United Way, 1992-95, Jewish Big Brothers, 1995-, Amer. Jewish Com., 2000-. Mem. ABA, LA Bar Assn., Beverly Hills Bar Assn. (bd. govs. 1971-76), Barristers Bar Assn. (pres. 1972-73), Assn. Bus. Trial Attys. (bd. govs. 1974-75), LA Jewish Fedn. (chmn. commn. on law and legislation 1973-74, chmn. commn. on Soviet Jewry 1981, chmn. cmty. rels. com. 1984-86), Calif. Commn. Jud. Performance (chair 2005-), Order of Coif, Tau Delta Phi, Phi Alpha Delta. Clubs: Mason. Office: Alschuler Grossman Stein & Kahan LLP The Water Garden 1620 26th St Fourth Fl N Tower Santa Monica CA 90404-4060 Office Fax: 310-907-2000.

GROSSMAN, MARY MARGARET, elementary school educator; b. East Cleveland, Ohio, Sept. 26, 1946; d. Frank Anthony and Margaret Mary (Buda) G. Student, Kent State Univ., 1965-67; BS in Elem. Edn. cum laude, Cleveland State Univ., 1971; postgrad, Lake Erie Coll., 1974-77, John Carroll Univ., 1978, 81, 82, 83, 85, Cleveland State Univ., 1985. Cert. elem. sch. tchr. grades 1 to 8 Ohio, cert. data processing Ohio. Tchr. Cleve. Catholic Diocese, Cleve., Ohio, 1971-72, Willoughby-Eastlake Sch. Dist., Willoughby, Ohio, 1972—. Participant Nat. Econ. Edn. Conf., Richmond, Va., 1995. Eucharistic min. St. Christine's Ch., Euclid, 1988—, mem. parish pastoral coun., 1995-00. Recipient Samuel H. Elliott Econ. Leadership award, 1986-87, Consumer Educator award N.E. Ohio Region, 1986, 1st pl. award for excellence in tchg. Tchrs. in Am. Enterprise, 1984-85, 89-90; Martha Holden Jennings scholar, 1984-85. Mem. NEA, Ohio Edn. Assn. (human rels. award 1986-87, cert. merit 1987-88), N.E. Ohio Edn. Assn. (Positive Tchr. Image award 1988). Roman Catholic. Avocations: racquetball, softball, walking, tennis, bicycling. Home: 944 E 225th St Cleveland OH 44123-3308 Office: McKinley Elem Sch 1200 Lost Nation Rd Willoughby OH 44094-7324

GROSSMAN, MELANIE, dermatologist; AB in Biology, Princeton U., N.J., 1984; MD, NYU, 1988. Diplomate Am. Bd. Dermatology. Intern Yale U. Med. Ctr., New Haven, 1988—89; resident in dermatology Presbyn. Hosp./Columbia U., N.Y.C., 1989—92; fellow in laser dermatology and photodynamic therapy Mass. Gen. Hosp. and Wellman Labs., Boston, 1993—95; pvt. practice dermatology N.Y.C., 1992—. Asst. attending dermatology Presbyn. Hosp., N.Y.C., 1992—, Cornell U., N.Y.C., 1998—, N.Y. Hosp., N.Y.C., 1998—, St. Luke's Roosevelt Hosp. Ctr., N.Y.C., 1995—; attending physician dept. plastic surgery N.Y. Eye and Ear Infirmary, N.Y.C., 1996—; assoc. clin. in dermatology Columbia U., N.Y.C., 1992—; dir. clin. and laser rsch. studies Laser and Skin Surgery Ctr. of N.Y., N.Y.C., 1995; clin. affiliate dermatology N.Y. Hosp., N.Y.C., 1996—97; clin. instr. dermatology Cornell U. Med. Ctr., N.Y.C., 1996—97; clin. fellow dermatology Mass. Gen. Hosp.-Harvard Med. Sch., Boston, 1993—95. Contbr. articles to profl. jours. Fellow: Am. Soc. for Dermatologic Surgery, Am. Soc. for Laser Medicine and Surgery (socioecon. affairs com. 1997—2000, nominating com. 2000); mem.: Women's Dermatologic Soc., Women's Med. Soc. N.Y., Dermatologic Soc. Greater N.Y. (comm. com., exec. com.), Med. Soc. State of N.Y., Am. Acad. Dermatology (chair photobiology task force 1998—99, melanoma task force, comm. com. 1998—2000, comm. study group for 21st century, sports ad hoc com., chair socioecon. affairs com. 1999—2000). Office: 161 Madison Ave Ste 4 NW New York NY 10016 Office Phone: 212-725-8600.

GROSSMAN, MICHAEL, economics professor; b. Bklyn., July 12, 1942; s. Mortimer and Doris (Orent) G.; m. Ilene Joy Gordon, Sept. 11, 1966; children: Sandra Diane, Barri Lynn. BA, Trinity Coll., Hartford, Conn., 1964; PhD, Columbia U., 1970. Asst. prof. Ctr. Health Adminstrn. Studies, Grad. Sch. Bus., U. Chgo., 1969-71; rsch. assoc., co-program dir. health econs. rsch. Nat. Bur. Econ. Rsch., N.Y.C., 1972—; prof. econs. CUNY Grad. Sch., 1974, disting. prof. econs, 1988. Cons. in field. Author: (Book) The Demand for Health: A Theoretical and Empirical Investigation, 1972 (Nomination for Kulp Award of the American Risk and Insurance Association, 1976); editor: The Economic Analysis of Substance Abuse: An Integration of Econometric and Behavioral Economic Research, 1999, Economic Analysis of Substance Use and Abuse: The Experience of Developed Countries and Lessons for Developing Countries, 2001; assoc. editor Jour. Health Econs., Amsterdam, Netherlands, 2000—01; contbr. articles to profl. jours. Mem. Social Scis., Nursing, Epidemiology and Methods Study sect. Ctr. for Sci. Rev., NIH, Washington, 2000—01. Ford Found. fellow Columbia U. Mem.: APHA, Health Econs. Rsch. Orgn., Population Assn. Am., Internat. Health Econs. Assn., Am. Econ. Assn., Pi Gamma Mu, Phi Beta Kappa. Independent. Jewish. Avocations: tennis, skiing, boating. Home: 115 E 9th St Apt 14C New York NY 10003 Office: Nat Bur Econ Rsch 365 5th Ave 5th Flr New York NY 10016-4309 Office Phone: 212-817-7959. Business E-Mail: mgrossman@gc.cuny.edu.

GROSSMAN, NANCY, artist; b. NYC, 1940; d. Murray and Josephine G. BFA, Pratt Inst., 1962. Mem. jury sculpture N.Y. State Council on Arts, 1973, Prix de Rome fellowships Am. Acad. in Rome, 1974 Exhibited in one-woman shows, Krasner Gallery, N.Y.C., 1964, 65, 67, Cordier & Ekstrom, N.Y.C., 1968, 69, 71, 73, 75, 76, Church Fine Arts Gallery, U. Nev., Reno, 1978, Barbara Gladstone Gallery, N.Y.C., 1980, 82, Heath Gallery, Atlanta, 1981, 86, Terry Dintenfass Gallery, 1984, Exit Art, N.Y.C., 1991, Sculpture Ctr., N.Y.C., 1991, Hillwood Art Mus., Brookville, N.Y., 1991, Exit Art, N.Y.C., 1991, Hillwood Art Mus., Brookville, N.Y., 1991, Sculpture Ctr., N.Y.C., 1991, Artemisia, Chgo., 1992, Beacon St. Gallery, Chgo., 1992, Ark. Art Ctr., Little Rock, 1992, Contemporary Mus., Honolulu, 1992, Binghamton U. Art Gallery, 1992, Hooks-Epstein Galleries, Houston, 1993, 95, LedisFlam, N.Y.C., 1994, Weatherspoon Art Gallery, Greensboro, N.C., 1994, Greenville Cty Museum of Art, 2004; exhibited in numerous group shows, including, Whitney Mus. Am. Art, N.Y.C., 1968, 69, 69, 73, 80, 81, 93, 95, Fogg Art Mus., Cambridge, Mass., 1972, Am. Acad. Arts and Letters/Nat. Inst. Arts and Letters invitational, N.Y.C., 1974, 1987, New Mus. New American Painting exhbn., Hungary, Czechoslovakia, Poland, 1978, Betté Stoler, 1983, Whitney Mus. at Phillip Morris, 1984, Exit Art, N.Y.C., 1991, Michael Rosenfeld Gallery, N.Y.C., 1996, Nat. Acad., N.Y.C., 1996, The Geffen Contemporary, L.A., 1999, Beacon Street Gallery, Chicago, 2001, George Adams Gallery, N.Y.C, 2003, Chelsea Art Museum, N.Y.C., 2004; represented in permanent collections, Whitney Mus. Am. Art, Hirshhorn Mus., Washington, Smithsonian Inst., Dallas Mus. Fine Arts, Balt. Mus., Mus. Boymans Van Beuningen, Rotterdam, Netherlands, U. Calif., Berkeley, Princeton U. Art Mus., N.J., Contemporary Arts Mus., Houston, Met. Mus. Art, N.Y.C., Va. Mus. Fine Arts, Richmond, Weatherspoon Art Gallery, Greensboro, N.C., Contemporary Mus., Honolulu. Recipient Inaugural Contemporary Achievement award Pratt Inst., 1966, award AAAL and Nat. Inst. Arts and Letters, 1974, Hassam, Speicher, Betts and Symons purchase award Am. Acad. and Inst. Arts and Letters, 1989, Alumni Achievement award Pratt Inst., 1995, Joan Mitchell Found. fellowship, 1996; Ida C. Haskell scholar, 1962; Guggenheim fellow, 1965, fellow for sculpture Nat. Endowment for Arts, 1991; grantee Nat. Endowment for Arts, 1984. Mem. Nat. Acad. Address: 105 Eldridge St New York NY 10002-4405 Office: Michael Rosenfeld Gallery 24 W 57th St New York NY 10019-3918*

GROSSMAN, ROBERT ALLEN, transportation executive; b. Port Jervis, N.Y., July 24, 1941; s. George and Helen (Garson) G.; m. Joan Ward, June 15, 1962 (div.); children: Jeffrey, Wendy; m. Gloria Schwartz, Nov. 22, 1987. Student, Cornell U., 1959-60, U. Pa., 1960-62. Fin. divsn. North Shore Packing Co., Inc., North Bellmore, N.Y., 1962-64; mgr. refin. and legal dept. Coburn Corp. Am., Rockville Centre, N.Y., 1964-67; stockbroker Weis, Volson & Cannon, Inc., N.Y.C., 1967-69, Nadel & Co., N.Y.C., 1969-70; v.p. Emons Industries, Inc., York, Pa., 1971—79, chmn. bd., CEO, 1979—2002; chmn., CEO Emons Transp. Group, 1986—2002; exec. v.p. Genesee & Wyoming Inc., Greenwich, Conn., 2002—. Mem. legis. policy com. Am. Assn. Shortline and Regional R.R. Assn., 1998—. Bd. dirs. Better York, Inc., 1996-2003. Mem. Am. Assn. Short Line and Regional R.R.s (dir. 1998—), York Area C. of C. (dir. 1978-83), Pa. Rail Freight (adv. com. 1993-2002), Maine Rail Task Force, Keystone State Ra.R. Assn. (pres. 1996-99, exec. com. 1996-2002), Nat. Indsl. Transp. League, R.R.s of N.Y. (pres. 2004—), Oreg. Rail Users League (bd. dirs. 2005—). Office: Genesee & Wyoming Inc 204 North George St Ste 230 York PA 17401

GROSSMAN, ROBERT GEORGE, neurosurgeon, department chairman; b. N.Y.C., Jan. 24, 1933; s. Ferenc and Vivian (Isenberg) Grossman; m. Ellin Friedman, June 26, 1955; children: Amy, Kate, Ruth. BA, Swarthmore Coll., 1953; MD, Columbia U., 1957. Diplomate Am. Bd. Neurosurgery. Intern Strong Meml. Hosp., Rochester, NY, 1957-58; resident Presbyn. Hosp., Columbia U., N.Y.C., 1960-63; acad. practice medicine, specializing in neurol. surgery Houston, 1973—; from instr. to assoc. prof. neurol. surgery U. Tex. S.W. Med. Sch., 1963-68; from assoc. prof. to prof. neurol. surgery Albert Einstein Coll. Medicine, 1969-73; prof., chmn. div. neurol. surgery U. Tex. Med. Br., Galveston, 1973-80; prof., chmn. dept. neurol. surgery Baylor Coll. Medicine, 1980—2005; assoc. dean clin. affairs Baylor Coll. Medicne, 2002—05; dir. Neurol. Inst., chmn. dept. neurosurgery Meth. Hosp., Houston, 2005—. Chmn. neurology B study sect. USPHS, NIH, 1972—74; mem. bd. sci. counsellors Nat. Inst. Neurol. Diseases and Strok, NIH, 1993—96. Author (with W. D. Willis): Medical Neurobiology, 3d edit., 1981; chmn. editl. bd.: Jour. Neurosurgery, 1987. With U.S. Army, 1958—60. Mem.: ACS, Soc. Neurol. Surgeons (pres. 1995), Am. Acad. Neurol. Surgery (v.p.), Am. Bd. Neurol. Surgery (chmn. bd. dirs. 1989—90), Soc. Univ. Surgeons, Am. Assn. Neurol. Surgeons. Home: 2002 Sunset Blvd Houston TX 77005-1651 Office: Tex Med Ctr Scurlock Tower 6560 Fannin St Ste 944 Houston TX 77030-2706 Office Phone: 713-441-3800. Business E-Mail: rgrossman@tmh.tmc.edu.

GROSSMAN, ROBERT JAMES, retired architect; b. Spokane, Wash., Feb. 3, 1936; s. George Christian and Corinne (Shelton) G.; m. Charleigh Rozelle, Aug. 7, 1956; children: Kevin James, Heidi Rozelle. B Archtl. Engring. with highest honors, Wash. State U., 1959. Lic. architect, Wash. Architect Heylman-Trogdon, Spokane, 1962-64, Trogdon-Smith, Architects, Spokane, 1964-72; prin. architect Trogdon-Smith-Grossman, TSG Architects, Spokane, 1973-83; mng. prin. N.W. Archtl. Co. (A Joint Venture), Spokane, 1979-83; pres., prin. N.W. Archtl. Co., P.S., Seattle, 1983-85, 98-99, mng. prin., 1986-99; ret., 1999. Coord. architect for site planning and devel. Expo'74 World's Fair, Spokane, 1971-74; mem. adv. coun. Sch. Architecture Wash. State U., Pullman, 1986-93, mem. adv. bd. Coll. Engring. and Architecture, 1991-99, 2001—; bd. dirs. Evergreen Bancorp. Inc. Prin. works include 40 sch. projects throughout Wash.; Wash. State U. Alumni Ctr., Pullman; instnl. and comml. projects. Bd. dirs., pres. Salvation Army-Booth Care Ctr., Spokane, 1972-85; bd. dirs. Med. Svc. Corp., Spokane, 1984-86; mem. state adv. bd. Lien Law Reform, 1990; founding pres. Downtown Exch. Club of Seattle Found., 1990—; mem. adv. bd. for master planning Children's Hosp., Seattle, 1991-94; chair Wash. State Archs. and Engrs. Legis. Coun., 1994-97. 1st lt. C.E., U.S. Army, 1960-62. Recipient Disting. Svc. award Govt. State of Wash. and State Commn. for Expo '74, 1974. Mem. AIA (pres. Spokane chpt. 1976), Wash. State Coun. Architects (bd. dirs. 1975-78), Wash. State U. Alumni Assn. (Alumni Achievement award 1990), Exch. Club (bd. dirs. 1988-91). Avocations: travel, music.

GROSSMAN, ROBERT LOUIS, lawyer; b. Cleve., Dec. 20, 1954; s. Sidney and Lillian Belle (Davis) G.; m. Rochelle Carol Shear, Nov. 7, 1987; children: Zachary, Jonathan, David, Andrew. BA with honors, Ohio State U., 1975, JD with Honors, 1978, MA with honors, 1979. Bar: Ohio 1978, Fla. 1982, U.S. Ct. Appeals (5th cir.) 1979. Law clk. U.S. Dist. Ct. (so. dist.) Ohio, Columbus, 1977-78; sr. atty. U.S. Govt. EEOC, Houston, 1979-82; shareholder Greenberg, Traurig, P.A., Miami, 1982—. Editor: Florida Corporate Practice, 2d edit., 1991. Chmn. South Dade Jewish Leadership Coun., 1997-99; bd. dirs. Greater Miami Jewish Fedn. South Dade, 1987—, campaign chmn., 1995-97, chmn., 1997-99; bd. dirs. Greater Miami Jewish Fedn., 1995—, mem. exec. com., 1997-99; bd. dirs. Alper Jewish Cmty. Ctr., 1997-00, exec. com., 1998-00; bd. dirs. Children's Bereavement Ctr., 2000—, Orgn. Leadership Advancement Miami, 2001-; chmn. Exec. Inst. OLAM, 2001-; bd. dirs. Beacon Coun., 2000—; chmn. Exec. Inst. for Orgn. for Leadership Advancement in Miami, 2001-03; chmn. Fedn. Agy., Day Sch. and Synagogue Campaign, 2003-; bd. dirs. Temple Beth Am., 2003-05, Project Interchange, 2005-, Jewish Nat. Fund, 2005-, United Jewish Cmtys. Israel Advocacy Com., 2005-. Donald Becker Meml. scholar Ohio State U., 1975, 76, fellow, 1978; Robert Russell fellow Greater Miami Jewish Fedn., 1998; recipient Stanley C. Myers Young Leadership award Greater Miami Jewish Fedn., 1999, Put Something Back Cmty. award, 2003. Mem. ABA (corp. securities sect.), The Fla. Bar, Dade County Bar Assn., Order of Coif. Avocations: sports, reading, travel. Office: Greenberg Traurig 1221 Brickell Ave Miami FL 33131-3224 Office Phone: 305-579-0756. Business E-Mail: grossmanb@gtlaw.com.

GROSSMAN, SANFORD JAY, economics professor; b. Bklyn., July 21, 1953; s. Sloane and Florence G.; m. Naava. BA in Econs. with honors, U. Chgo., 1973, MA in Econs., 1974, PhD in Econs., 1975. Asst. prof. econs. Stanford U., Calif., 1975-77; economist Bd. Govs. Fed. Res., 1977-78; assoc. prof. econs. U. Pa., Phila., 1978-79, prof. econs., 1979-81, U. Chgo., 1981-85; John L. Weinberg prof. econs. Princeton U., N.J., 1985-89; Steinberg trustee prof. fin. U. Pa., Phila., 1989—2000; dir. Wharton Ctr. Quantitative Fin., 1994—2001, Quantitative Fin. Strategies, Inc., Stamford, Conn., 2001—. Pub. dir., bd. dirs. Chgo. Bd. Trade, 1992-96. Mem. editl. bd. Finance India, 1994—; mem. adv. bd. Math. Finance, 1994—; contbr. articles to profl. jours. Trustee U. Chgo., 2003—. Recipient Irving Fisher grad. monograph award, award for best article, Graham and Dodd Scroll, Fin. Analyst Jour., 1988, Roger F. Murray 1st Prize award, Q Group, 1988, Math. Fin. Best Paper award, 1993, Profl. Achievement citation, U. Chgo., 2002, 2002, Mathematical Fin. Best Paper award, 1993; fellow, Lilly Found., Guggenheim Meml., Sloan Found., Am. Econometric Soc., 1980, Lilly Found. Fellow AAAS, Econometric Soc., Am. Fin. Assn. (v.p. 1992, pres.-elect 1993, pres. 1994, bd. dirs., fellow 2000); mem. Am. Econ. Assn. (John Bates Clark medal 1987). Office: Quantitative Fin Strategies 10 Glenville St Greenwich CT 06831 Business E-Mail: qfs@qfsfunds.com.

GROSSMAN, STEVEN L., lawyer; b. Chgo., 1957; BA, Stanford U., 1979; JD, U. So. Calif., 1982. Bar: Calif. 1982, US Dist. Ct. (Ctrl. Dist. Calif.) 1982, US Ct. Appeals (9th Cir.) 1982, DC 1992. Corp. and securities ptnr. O'Melveny & Myers LLP, Los Angeles, Calif., co-chair. mergers and acquisitions/private equity practice group. Staff mem. So. Calif. Law Review, 1980—81, mng. editor, 1981—82. Mem.: State Bar Calif. (mem. bus. law sections), ABA. Office: O'Melveny & Myers LLP 1999 Avenue of the Stars 7th Fl Los Angeles CA 90067-6035 Office Phone: 310-246-6727. Office Fax: 310-246-6779. Business E-Mail: slgrossman@omm.com.

GROSSMAN, THEODORE MARTIN, lawyer; b. N.Y.C., Dec. 31, 1949; s. Albert and Sylvia Pia (Greenstein) G.; m. Linda Gail Steinbook, Dec. 5, 1976; children: Andrew Scott, Michael Steven. AB, Cornell U., 1971, JD, 1974. Bar: N.Y. 1975, U.S. Ct. Appeals (D.C. cir.) 1981, U.S. Ct. Appeals (2nd cir.) 1982, U.S. Ct. Appeals (5th cir.) 1984, U.S. Dist. Ct. (no. dist.) Ohio 1986, Ohio 1987, U.S. Dist. Ct. (so. dist.) N.Y. 1988, U.S. Dist. Ct. (ea. dist.) N.Y. 1988, U.S. Ct. Appeals (6th cir.) 1988, U.S. Supreme Ct., 2004. Assoc. Debevoise, Plimpton, Lyons & Gates, N.Y.C., 1974-77, Rosenman Colin Freund Lewis & Cohen, N.Y.C., 1977-80; trial and appellate counsel fed. programs br. of civil div. U.S. Dept. Justice, Washington, 1980-84; assoc. Jones Day, Cleve., 1984-86, ptnr., 1987—. Lectr. on cross-examination, deposition techniques, oral advocacy, trial tactics, and product liability law in ABA presentations and other seminars.; guest lectr. on internat. trade litigation Georgetown U. Law Ctr.; counsel on behalf of the Lawyers' Com. for Civil Rights. Editor Cornell U. Law Rev., 1974. Trustee Cleve. Ctr. for Contemporary Art, 1992-96, treas., 1992-94. Named one of Top 10 Litigators, Nat. Law Jour., 2003. Fellow: Am. Coll. Trial Lawyers; mem.: ABA. Home: 2979 Broxton Rd Shaker Heights OH 44120 Office: Jones Day 901 Lakeside Ave E Cleveland OH 44114-1190 Office Phone: 216-586-3939, 216-586-7268. E-mail: tgrossman@jonesday.com.

GROSSMAN, WILLIAM, medical researcher, educator; b. N.Y.C., 1940; MD, Yale U., 1965. Intern Peter Bent Brigham Hosp., Boston, 1965-66, resident in medicine, 1968-69, rsch. fellow in cardiology, 1969-71; dir. cardiac catheterization labs. N.C. Meml. Hosp., Chapel Hill, 1971-75, Peter Bent Brigham Hosp., Boston, 1975-81; chief cardiovasc. divsn. Beth Israel Hosp., Boston, 1981-94; tchg. fellow in medicine Harvard U., Boston, 1968-71, assoc. prof., 1975-81, prof., 1981-84, Herman Dana prof. medicine, 1984-94; exec. dir. cardiovasc. rsch. Merck & Co., West Point, Pa., 1994-95, v.p., 1996-97; prof. medicine U. Calif., San Francisco, 1997—, chief cardiology, 1997—. Served as sr. asst. surgeon USPHS, 1966-68. Fellow Am. Coll. Cardiology, Am. Heart Assn., Assn. Am. Physicians, Am. Physiol. Soc., Am. Soc. Clin. Investigation. Office: UCSF Med Ctr Dept Cardiology Box 0124 San Francisco CA 94143-0124

GROSSMANN, EDWARD A., lawyer; b. NYC, Apr. 8, 1948; BA cum laude, Univ. Wis., 1970; JD, Univ. Mich., 1973. Bar: NY 1974, US Dist. Ct. (so. & ea. dist. NY 1974), US Ct. Appeals (2d cir. 1975, 3d cir. 1990, 9th cir. 1991, 5th cir. 1993, 11th cir. 1996). Founding ptnr., litigation, class action Bernstein Litowitz Berger & Grossmann LLP, NYC, 1983—. Mem. com. vis. Univ. Mich. Law Sch.; treas. UJA Fedn. Bergen County NJ. Mem.: Assn. Trial Lawyers Am. (past chmn. Comml. Litigation sect.), ABA (past chmn. Class & Derivitative Action Trials subcom.), NY State Bar Assn. Office: Bernstein Litowitz Berger & Grossmann 1285 Ave of the Americas New York NY 10019 Office Phone: 212-554-1404. Office Fax: 212-554-1444. Business E-Mail: edward@blbglaw.com.

GROSSMANN, ERIK MICHAEL, surgeon; b. St. Louis, Mar. 8, 1970; s. Ralph Leonard and Mary Francis Grossmann; m. Karen Marie Camille, June 5, 1999; children: Mary Kathryn, Christopher Aaron. MD, U. Mo., 1996. Bd. cert. gen. surgery Am. Bd. Surgery, 2003, bd. cert. colorectal surgery Am. Bd. Colon and Rectal Surgery, 2004. Asst. prof. surgery St. Louis U. Hosp., 2003—05. Mem.: AMA, ACS, Am. Soc. Colon and Rectal Surgeons, Assn. Acad. Surgery. Office: St Louis Univ Hosp 3635 Vista Ave PO Box 15250 Saint Louis MO 63110-0250 Office Phone: 314-577-8619. Office Fax: 314-577-8635.

GROSSMANN, RONALD STANYER, lawyer; b. Chgo., Nov. 9, 1944; s. Andrew Eugene and Gladys M. Grossmann; m. Jo Ellen Hanson, May 11, 1968; children: Kenneth Frederick, Emilie Beth. BA, Northwestern U., 1966; JD, U. Mich., 1969. Bar: Oreg., 1969. Law clk. Oreg. Supreme Ct., Salem, 1969-70; assoc. Stoel Rives LLP, Portland, Oreg., 1970-76, ptnr., 1976—. Mem.: Am. Coll. Employee Benefits Counsel, Oreg. Bar Assn., ABA. Office: Stoel Rives LLP 900 SW 5th Ave Ste 2600 Portland OR 97204-1268

GROSSO, DOREEN ELLIOTT, management consultant; d. John and Hilda Elliott; m. Joseph Anthony Grosso, May 30, 1971; children: John Cesar, Michael Steven, Joseph Armando. BS, Fordham U., 1971; MBA, Pace U., 1979. V.p. Chem. Bank, NYC, 1981—91; pres. Change Creates Opportunity, Inc., Fresh Meadows, NY, 1991—. Dir. ARIL/CrossCurrents, NYC, 1995—2003. Participant, alum Coro-Leadership NY, NYC, 1990—90. Named Woman of Future, NY Women's Agenda, 2001. Mem.: Orgn. and Devel. Network Greater NY, World Future Soc. Roman Catholic. E-mail: ccoi@nyc.rr.com.

GROSTICK, RANDY, musician, director, music educator; b. Wichita Falls; AA, AS, Pierce Coll., Tacoma, Wash., 1996; MusB Music Edn., Ctrl. Wash. U., Ellensburg, Wash., 2000, MusM Percussion Performance, 2002. Cert. profl. edn. Supt. of Pub. Instrn. / Wash., 2000. Owner Floral Expressions & Gifts, Olympia, Wash., 1994—96; stage crew / prodn. asst. Wash. Ctr. for the Performing Arts, Olympia, 1994—96; band dir. Olympia H.S., Wash., 2000—01; grad. tchg. asst. Ctrl. Wash. U., Ellensburg, Wash., 2000—02; music dir. Cle Elum - Roslyn Sch. Dist., Wash., 2002—03, North Mason H.S., Belfair, Wash., 2003—05; band dir. Shelton (Wash.) H.S., 2005—; tech. dir. Valley Musical Theatre, Ellensburg, Wash., 2001—04; freelance musician Olympia, Seattle, Yakima, Ellensburg, Wash., 1994—. Percussionist Yakima Symphony Orch., Wash., 2000—02, Olympia Symphony Orch., Wash., 1995—, NW Wind Symphony, Centralia, Wash., 1995—2005, Tacoma Concert Band, Tacoma, 1995—2005, Bremerton Symphony Orch., Wash., 2003—04. Musician undergraduate percussion recital, graduate percussion recital. Recipient Nat. Dean's List, Ednl. Comm., 1995-1996. Mem.: Percussive Arts Soc., Wash. Music Educators Assn. - Music Educators Nat. Conf. (assoc.). Achievements include Premiered music by composers: Timothy Brock, David Maslanka, Gloria Swisher, & Dave Hollinden. Personal E-mail: grostick@hotmail.com.

GROSVENOR, GILBERT MELVILLE, journalist, educator, business executive; b. Washington, May 5, 1931; s. Melville Bell and Helen (Rowland) Grosvenor; m. Donna C. Kerkam, June 16, 1961 (div.); children: Gilbert Hovey II, Alexandra Rowland; m. Wiley Jarman, June 1, 1979; 1 child, Graham Dabney. BA, Yale U., 1954; D in Pub. Svc. (hon.), George Washington U., 1983; LHD (hon.) (hon.), U. Colo., 1983, Curry Coll., 1984; LLD (hon.) (hon.), Coll. of Wooster, Ohio, 1983; LHD (hon.) (hon.), Coll. William and Mary, 1987, Miami U., Oxford, Ohio, 1988, Syracuse U., 1989, R.I. Coll., 1991, Old Dominion U., 1993, Longwood Coll., Worcester, Mass., 1997, Ind. Univ., 1998, Univ. S.C., 1998, Pa. State Univ., 1999, S.W. Tex. State U., 2002, Appalachian State U., 2004. With Nat. Geog. Soc., 1954—, trustee, 1966—, v.p., 1966—80, assoc. editor, 1967—70, editor, 1970—80, pres., 1980—96, chmn. bd. dirs., 1987—. Bd. dirs. Chevy Chase Bank, FSB, Saul Ctrs., Inc.; former fellow Yale Corp. Bd. visitors Duke U. Nicholas Sch. Environment and Earth Scis.; former bd. visitors Coll. William and Mary; former mem. Pres.'s Commn. on Environ. Quality; mem. Washington Cathedral Bldg. Com.; trustee Nat. Wildflower Rsch. Ctr., B.F. Saul Real Estate Trust, Saul Ctrs., Inc.; past vice chmn. Pres.'s Commn. Ams. Outdoors; chmn. emeritus, found. bd. Alexander Graham Bell Assn. for Deaf; bd. dirs. Conservation Fund, Dian Fossey Gorilla Fund Internat. Recipient Editor of Yr. award, Nat. Press Photographers Assn., 1975, Disting. Achievement award, U. So. Calif. Sch. Journalism and Alumni Assn., 1977, Pres. medal, George Washington U., 1993, Golden Plate award, Am. Acad. Achievement, 1996, Presdl. medal of freedom, 2004. Mem.: Assn. Am. Geographers, Chevy Chase (Md.) Club, Cosmos Club, Alibi Club, Alfalfa Club, Newcomen Soc., Explorers Club (citation of merit 1997). Office: Nat Geog Soc 1145 17th St NW Washington DC 20036-4701

GROSZ, BARBARA JEAN, computer science educator; b. Phila., July 21, 1948; d. Joseph Eugene and Judith Phyllis (Zander) Gross. AB in Math., Cornell U., 1969; MA in Computer Sci., U. Calif., Berkeley, 1971, PhD in Computer Sci., 1977. Rsch. mathematician Artificial Intelligence Ctr., SRI Internat., Stanford, Calif., 1973-77, computer scientist, 1981-82, sr. computer scientist, 1981-82, program dir. nat. lang. and representation, 1982-83, sr. staff scientist, 1983-86; co-founder, mem. exec. com., prin. researcher Ctr. for Study of Lang. and Info. Stanford U. and SRI Internat., 1983-86; with divsn. engring. and applied scis. Harvard U., Cambridge, Mass., 1986—, interim assoc. dean for affirmative action, 1993-94, Higgins prof. natural scis., 2001—, dean of sci. Radcliffe Inst. Advanced Study, 2001—. Vis. faculty dept. computer sci. Stanford U., fall 1982, cons. assoc. prof. computer sci. and linguistics, 1984-85, computer sci., 1985-87; vis. scholar dept. computer and info. sci. U. Pa., Jan.-June 1982; conf. chair Internat. Joint Conf. on Artificial Intelligence (IJCAI-91), chair bd. trustees IJCAI Inc., 1989-91, mem. bd. trustees, 1987-97, program com. 1982; Harold Perlman vis. prof. faculty sci. Hebrew U., Jerusalem, 1992; invited spkr. numerous nat. and internat. profl. assns., confs., symposia; reviewer program proposals NSF; participant adv. meetings for rsch. and funding various govtl. agys. Author: (with others) Elements of Discourse Understanding, 1982, Understanding Spoken Language, 1982, Foundations of Cognitive Science, 1988, Intentions in Communications, 1988; editor: (with Sparck Jones, Webber) Readings in Natural Language Processing, 1986; assoc. editor: Ann. Rev. Computer Sci., 1982-1985; editl. bd.: Artificial Intelligence Jour., 1982—, Am. Jour. Computational Linguistics, 1981-83; contbr. articles and papers to profl. jours., workshops and conf. procs. Recipient Disting. Alumna award in computer sci. and engring., U. Calif., Berkeley, 1997, Donald E. Walker Disting. Svc. award, IJCAI, 2001. Fellow Am. Acad. Arts & Sci., Am. Assn. Artificial Intelligence (exec. coun. 1981-84, 86-89, pres.-elect 1991-93, pres. 1993-95, past pres. 1995-97, disting. svc. award, 1999), Assn. Computing Machinery (vice chair 1979-81, chair 1981-83, mem. SIGART), Am. Acad. Arts & Sci.; mem. NRC (computer sci. & telecom. bd. 1994-98), Assn. Computational Linguistics (exec. com. 1986-88), Am. Philos. Soc. Avocations: hiking, wildflower photography, snorkeling. Address: 33 Oxford St Rm 249 Cambridge MA 02138-2901*

GROTA, BARBARA LYNN, academic administrator, educator; d. Jerome A. and Laura B. Grota; m. James William Murphy, Apr. 30, 1988 (dec. Sept. 30, 1991). BA, Southeastern Mass. U., North Dartmouth, MA, 1976—79; MS, Syracuse U., Syracuse, NY, 1980—82; PhD, Walden U., 2005. Orgnl. devel. cons. Carrier Corp., Syracuse, NY, 1980—81; social sci. - adj. faculty New Eng. Inst. of Tech., Warwick, RI, 1982—85, coop. edn. founder/coord., 1983—85; coop. edn. asst. dir. Roger Williams U., Bristol, RI, 1985—2000, social sci. adj. faculty, 1988—2000, asst. prof. of mgmt., 2000—, asst. dean, asst. prof., 2000—. Pres. New Eng. Assn. for Coop. Edn. and Field Experience, Boston, 1990—90; supervising editor NEACEFE newsletter, New Eng. Assn. for Coop. Edn. and Field Experience, Boston, 1991—92; mem. bd. of directors Riverwood Rehab. Services Inc., Bristol, RI, 1995—2000, co-president bd. of directors, 1997—99; strategic planning cons./facilitator Bristol Econ. Devel. Commn., Warren, RI, 2000—00; facilitator/trainer RI Probate Ct., West Greenwich, RI, 2002—02. Author (co-author): (rsch. article) Procs. of the 2002 Symposium for the Mktg. of Higher Edn. of the Am. Mktg. Assn., (pub. rsrch.) Procs. of the 1987 Nat. Coop. Edn. Assn. Conf. Canvas com. mem. Fairhaven Unitarian Universalist Ch., Fairhaven, Mass., 1999—99; exec. dir. evaluation com. mem. Riverwood Rehab. Services, Inc., Bristol, RI, 1995—2000; mem. Child and Family Services of Newport County, Newport, RI, 1999—99. Recipient The Excellence in Tchg. Award, Alpha Chi - Nat. Honor Soc., 1997, Psi Chi - Psychology Nat. Honor Soc., 2000, Honor Soc. Induction, Sigma Beta Delta - Internat. Honor Soc. in Bus., Mgmt., and Adminstrn., 2000, Outstanding Women On Campus award, Roger Williams U. Women's Ctr., 1998, 2002. Mem.: Am. Mktg. Assn., Am. Psychol. Assn. (APA), Roger Williams U. Dean's Diversity Coun., Nat. Academic Advising Assn. Avocations: hiking, gourmet cooking, reading. Office: Roger Williams University One Old Ferry Rd Bristol RI 02809 Office Phone: 401-254-3092.

GROTE, DICK (RICHARD CHARLES GROTE), management consultant, educator, writer, radio commentator; b. NYC, Dec. 14, 1941; s. Charles Henry and Muriel (Steele) G.; m. Jacqueline Center, May 11, 1991. BA, Colgate U., 1959; M Liberal Arts, So. Meth. U., 1992. Pers. mgr. GE, Schenectady, 1964—67; mgr. mgmt. devel. United Air Lines, Chgo., 1967-72; mgr. tng. and devel. Frito-Lay, Inc., Dallas, 1972-77; pres. Performance Systems Corp., Dallas, 1977-87; prin. Grote Cons. Corp., Dallas, 1987—. Adj. prof. U. Dallas Grad. Sch. Mgmt., 1977—; commentator NPR, 1993—; reviewer Inst. Mus. Svcs., 1974-77. Author: Positive Discipline, 1985, Discipline Without Punishment, 1995, The Complete Guide to Performance Appraisal, 1996, The Performance Appraisal Q&A Book, 2002, Forced Ranking, 2005; host (film series) Respect and Responsibility; contbr. articles to profl. jours. Trustee, pres. Schaumburg (Ill.) Pub. Libr., 1969-72; bd. dirs. Shakespeare Festival Dallas, 1981-84, Dallas Opera, 1981-88; chmn. So. Meth. U. Conservatory Soc., 1988—; bd. councillors U. Dallas, 1989—. Recipient Torch award ASTD, 1979, Disting. Svc. award Malaysian Soc. for Tng. and Devel., 1984, Bapindo award Govt. of Indonesia, 1984. Republican. Office: Grote Consulting Corp 15303 Dallas Pkwy Ste 645 Addison TX 75001-6725 Office Phone: 972-702-7555. Business E-Mail: dickgrote@groteconsulting.com.

GROTEN, BARNET, energy executive; b. Bklyn., Oct. 25, 1933; s. Irving and Pearl G.; m. Iris Diane Brand, Aug. 1955; children: Eric Allen, Kurt David, Jessica Amy. BS, Bklyn. Coll., 1954; PhD, Purdue U., 1961. Joined Exxon Co., various locations, 1961; dir. rsch. and bus. devel. Tex. Eastern Corp., Houston, 1977-87; exec. v.p. Tex. Eastern Devel., Inc., 1980-87; sec. Gulf Univs. Research Consortium, 1980-81; chmn. bd. Gulf Univs. Rsch. Consortium, 1982-83; exec. dir. Energy Ctr. U. Okla., Norman, 1987-91; v.p. Energy Internat., Inc., Bellevue, Wash., 1991-99; pres., CEO Grait Techs., LLC, Bellevue, 1999—, Power Genix Systems, Inc., Bellevue, 2001—03. Contbr. articles to profl. jours. Mem. Gov.'s Energy Adv. Coun.; chmn. Natural Gas Vehicle Task Force. Office: Grait Techs LLC 13706 NE 36th Pl Bellevue WA 98005-1413 Office Phone: 425-883-8040. Personal E-mail: bargro@comcast.net.

GROTH, ALEXANDER JACOB, political science professor; b. Warsaw, Mar. 7, 1932; came to U.S., 1947; s. Jacob and Maria (Hazenfuss) Goldwasser; m. Marilyn Ann Wineburg, Dec. 15, 1961; children: Stevin James, Warren Adrian. BA magna cum laude, CCNY, 1954; MA, Columbia U., 1955, PhD, 1960. Instr. polit. sci. Trinity Coll., Hartford, Conn., 1957-58, CUNY, 1960-61; asst. prof. Harpur Coll., Binghamton, N.Y., 1961-62, U. Calif., Davis, 1962-71, prof., 1971—. Author: Revolution and Elite Access, 1966, Comparative Politics, 1971, Major Ideologies, 1971, 2d rev. edit., 1983, People's Poland, 1972, Progress and Chaos, 1984, Lincoln: Authoritarian Savior, 1995, Democracies Against Hitler, 1999, Holocaust Voices, 2003; co-author: Contemporary Politics: Europe, 1976, Comparative Resource Allocation, 1984, Public Policy Across Nations, 1985; editor: Revolution and Political Change, 1996; mem. editl. bd. Political Crossroads, 1996-; contbr. Encyclopedia Americana Annuals, Poland, 1965-2001, The Encyclopedia of Political Revolutions, 1998; contbr. numerous articles to encys., scholarly jours. Recipient Ward medal dept. govt. CCNY, 1954, T. R. Dye award, 2000; grantee Am. Co. Learned Socs. and Social Sci. Research Council, 1965-66; nominee Panunzio award, U. Calif., Davis, 2004, 05. Mem. Western Polit. Sci. Assn., Policy Studies Assn., Far West Slavic Assn., Phi Beta Kappa. Republican. Avocations: baseball, basketball, writing, painting. Home: 1848 Rushmore Ln Davis CA 95616-6654 Office: U Calif Dept Polit Sci Davis CA 95616 Personal E-mail: marilynag@aol.com.

GROTHE, DONALD SINCLAIR, counselor, educator; b. Charles City, Iowa, Sept. 5, 1926; s. Jens and Helen Marie Grothe; m. Martha Alice Katzer, June 14, 1952; children: Pamela Sue, Holly Jo, Gretchen Annette, Todd Alan. BA, Iowa U., 1950, MA, 1952. Tchr., counselor Washington Jr. High Sch., Dubuque, Iowa, 1951—53; counselor, tchr. Seaholm High Sch., Birmingham, Mich., 1953—89; substance abuse counselor Schoolcraft County Health Dept., Mainstigue, 1990—96; clin. therapist Cmty. Mental Health, 1996—98; counselor Friend of the Ct., 1998—. Owner Grothe Career Testing and Counseling Svc., Birmingham, 1965—89. Author 35 children's books. Vol. organist Med. Care Facility, Mainstigue, 1991—. With USN, 1944—46. Mem.: NEA, Mich. Edn. Assn. Democrat. Avocations: motorcycling, horseback riding, sports, organ. Home: 15511 Portage Bay Rd Garden MI 49835 Office Phone: 906-341-3650.

GROTHENDIECK, ALEXANDRE, retired mathematician; b. Berlin, Mar. 28, 1928; s. Alexander Shapiro and Hanka Grothendieck. Student, Monpellier U., Ecole Normale Supérieur, Paris, 1948-49; PhD, U. Nancy; postgrad., U. San Paulo, 1953-55, U Kans., 1956. With Centre Nat. de la Recherche Scientifique, 1950-53, 56-59; chair Institut des Hautes Etudes Scientifique, 1959-70; vis. prof. Coll. France, 1970-72, Orsay, 1972-73; prof. U. Montpellier, 1973-84; dir. rsch. Centre Nat. de la Recherche Scientifique, 1984-88. Recipient Fields medal, 1966. Achievements include unifying themes in geometry, number theory, topology and complex analysis. Address: c/o Roy Lisker 8 Liberty St Apt 306 Middletown CT 06457-2751*

GROTKOWSKI, EDWARD MICHAEL, music educator, director; b. Erie, Pa., June 20, 1954; s. Edward John Grotkowski and Dorothy Patricia Nickerson. BA, Mercyhurst Coll., 1976; MA, Middlebury Coll., 1979; MusM, U. Miami, 1991; postgrad., U. So. Calif., L.A., 1992—95. Various tchg. positions, Pa., 1978—90; asst. conductor Greater Miami Youth Symphony, Fla., 1990—91; dir. music West Jefferson H.S., L.A., 2000—01, East Jefferson H.S., L.A., 2001—. Dir. music St. Philip the Apostle Ch., Pasadena, Calif., 1991—95; music dir. Our Lady of Gulf Ch., Bay St. Louis, Mo., 1996—; adj. prof. Nunez C.C., La., 1998—. Bd. dirs. Erie Dhicharoronie Youth Orchestra. Mem.: Am. Fedn. Tchrs., Am. Guild Organists, Music Educators Nat. Avocations: boating, reading, travel. Home: 6640 Alii Pl Diamondhead MS 39525 Office: East Jefferson HS 400 Palox Ave Metairie LA 70001

GROTON, JAMES PURNELL, lawyer, arbitrator; b. Newport News, Va., Oct. 29, 1927; s. Lafayette Watson and Mary (Skidmore) Groton; m. Lora Frances Webster, June 13, 1953 (dec. Mar. 1999); children: James Purnell,

Hunter W., Molly Groton Urban, Lora Groton Rust. AB cum laude, Princeton U., 1949; LLB, U. Va., 1954. Bar: D.C. 1954, Ga. 1955, U.S. Supreme Ct. 1964. Assoc. Sutherland, Asbill & Brennan, Atlanta, 1954—61, ptnr., 1961—2001. Lectr. to profl. socs. on alternative dispute resolution and constrn. Editor: (articles) Va. Law Rev., 1953—54; contbr. articles to profl. jours. Chmn. Constrn. Industry Dispute Avoidance and Resolution Task Force, 1991—94; bd. dirs. Atlanta Coun. for Internat. Visitors, 1968—75; bd. dirs., treas. N.W. Ga. coun., Girl Scouts U.S., 1973—79; trustee South Kent Sch., Conn., 1973—77, Nat. Assn. Women in Constrn. Edn. Found., 1993—98. Sgt. USMC, 1946—48, capt. USMC, 1950—52. Recipient medal excellence, Engring. News-Record, 1993. Fellow: Chartered Inst. Arbitrators, Coll. of Comml. Arbitrators, Am. Coll. Constrn. Lawyers (pres. 2000—01); mem.: AIA (hon. Bronze medal 1984), Princeton Alumni Assn. Ga. (v.p. 1964—77), Ctr. for Pub. Resources (Alternative Dispute Resolution award 1988, 1994), Ga. Coun. Sch. Bd. Attys. (exec. com. 1971—78), Nat. Assn. Coll. and Univ. Attys., Nat. Sch. Bds. Assn. Coun. of Sch. Attys., Am. Arbitration Assn. (nat. panel constrn. arbitrators 1970—, bd. dirs. 1990—2002, nat. constrn. dispute resolution com. 1992—, Whitney North Seymour medal 1983), Atlanta Bar Assn. (chmn. constrn. sect. 1992—93), State Bar Ga., Nat. Acad. of Constrn., Old War Horse Lawyers Club, Piedmont Driving Club, Peachtree Club, Phi Delta Phi. Democrat. Episcopalian. Home: 7 Park Ln NE Atlanta GA 30309 Office: Suite 2300 999 Peachtree St NE Atlanta GA 30309-3996 Office Phone: 404-853-8071. Business E-Mail: jim.groton@sablaw.com.

GROTTA, DANIEL, writer, editor; b. Phila., Oct. 23, 1944; s. Victor and Cecile Louise Grotta; m. Sally Wiener, June 24, 1978. Student, Temple U., 1962—64, Phila. Coll. Art, 1965—66, Radcliffe Coll., 1967, Cambridge (Eng.) U., 1969. Freelance writer, author, reviewer, columnist, Newfoundland, Pa., 1968—; contbg. editor Phila. Mag., 1974—79; consulting editor Running Press, 1974—76; contbg. editor Computer Shopper, N.Y.C., 1989—93; digital products update editor Photo Dist. News, N.Y.C., 1989—94; contbg. editor PhotoPro Mag., Titusville, Fla., 1990—92, PC Mag., N.Y.C., 1995—2000; pres. Digital Benchmarks, 2000—. Author: J.R.R. Tolkien: Architect of Middle-earth. Historian The Mann Music Ctr., Phila., 1979—80; mem. Phila. Journalism Rev., 1975—77, Scranton (Pa.) Cmty. Concerts, 2000—. Writer-in-Residence fellow, Edna St. Vincent Millay Colony for the Arts, 1978. Mem.: Computer Press Assn. (treas. 1994—95, Best Product Rev. of Yr. award 1998), Sci. Fiction Writers Am., Authors Guild, Nat. Book Critics Cir., Overseas Press Club, Cambridge Arts Lab. Democrat. Secular Humanist. Home: Pixel Hall Newfoundland PA 18445-9601 Office Phone: 570-676-5500. Personal E-mail: daniel@grotta.net.

GROTTEROD, KNUT, retired paper company executive; b. Sarpsborg, Norway, Feb. 12, 1922; emigrated to Can., 1945, naturalized, 1954; s. Klaus and Maria Magdalena (Thoresen) G.; m. Isabel Edwina MacMaster, Feb. 25, 1950; children: Ingrid, Christopher, Karen. Grad., Tech. Coll., Horten, Norway, 1945; BME, McGill U., Can., 1949, postgrad, 1951; DSc (hon.), U. Maine, 1987; Exec. in Residence (hon.), U. N.B., 1989. With Consol. Bathurst Ltd., Canada, 1951-70; v.p. prodn., gen. mgr. N.S. Forest Industries, Port Hawkesbury, Canada, 1970-73; from v.p. mfg. to chmn. rsch. productivity coun. Fraser Cos. Ltd., Edmundston, Canada, 1973—86; chmn. rsch. productivity coun. Fraser Inc., Edmundston, 1986—. Chmn. bd. Atlantic Waferboard, Chatam, N.B., 1985-87, Island Paper Mills, Vancouver, B.C., 1985-87, Alta. Newsprint Co. Ltd., Whitecourt, 1988-90, Rsch. and Productivity Coun., Fredericton, N.B., 1986—, Incutech Brunswick, 1988-94, Potato Devel. and Mktg. Coun., Fredericton, 1989-90. Bd. dirs. Can.-Scandinavian Found., Montreal, 1974-75, v.p., 1975-77, pres., 1978-94; mem. bd. govs. U. N.B. With Norwegian Underground Army, 1941-45. Mem. N.B. Forest Products Assn. (dir. 1983-88, pres. 1985-88), Pulp & Paper Assn. Can., Corp. Profl. Engrs. N.B., Rotary Internat. (dist. gov. 1996-97). Home: 67 Castleton Ct Fredericton NB Canada E3B 6H3 Office: Rsch & Productivity Coun 921 College Hill Rd Fredericton NB Canada E3B 6Z9

GROTZINGER, LAUREL ANN, librarian, educator; b. Truman, Minn., Apr. 15, 1935; d. Edward F. and Marian Gertrude (Greeley) G. BA, Carleton Coll., 1957; MS, U. Ill., 1958, PhD, 1964. Instr., asst. libr. Ill. State U., 1958-62; asst. prof. Western Mich. U., Kalamazoo, 1964-66, assoc. prof., 1966-68, prof., 1968—, asst. dir. Sch. Librarianship, 1965-72, chief rsch. officer, 1979-86, interim dir. Sch. Libr. and Info. Sci., 1982-86, dean grad. coll., 1979-92, prof. univ. libr., 1993—. Author: The Power and the Dignity, 1966; mem. editl. bd. Jour. Edn. for Librarianship, 1973-77, Dictionary Am. Libr. Biography, 1975-77, Mich. Academician, 1990—; contbr. articles to profl. jours., books. Trustee Kalamazoo Pub. Libr., 1991-93, v.p., 1991-92, pres., 1992-93; pres. Kalamazoo Bach Festival, 1996-97, bd. dirs. 1992-98, exec. com. 1996-98. Mem. ALA (sec.-treas. Libr. History Round Table 1973-74, vice chmn., chmn-elect 1983-84, chmn. 1984-85, mem.-at-large 1991-93), Spl. Librs. Assn., Assn. Libr. Info. Sci. Edn., Mich. acad. Sci., Arts and Letters (mem.-at-large, exec. com. 1980-86, pres. 1983-85, exec. com. 1990-94, pres. 1991-93, vice chmn. libr./info. scis. 1996-97, chair 1997-98), Internat. Assn. Torch Clubs (v.p. Kalamazoo chpt. 1992-93, pres. 1993-94, exec. com. 1989-95), Soc. Collegiate Journalists, Phi Beta Kappa (pres. S.W. Mich. chpt. 1977-78, sec. 1994-97, pres. 1997-99), Beta Phi Mu, Alpha Beta Alpha, Delta Kappa Gamma (pres. Alpha Psi chpt. 1988-92), Phi Kappa Phi. Home: 2729 Mockingbird Dr Kalamazoo MI 49008-1626 Office Phone: 269-387-5418. Business E-Mail: laurel.grotzinger@wmich.edu.

GROUDINE, MARK T., oncologist; married. BS in Zoology, U. Wis., 1970; MD, U. Pa., 1975, PhD, 1976. Lic. physician Wash., 1990, diplomate Am. Bd. Radiation Oncology. Vis. scientist dept. molecular biology Swiss Inst. Exptl. Cancer Rsch., Lausanne, Switzerland, 1972—73; vis. fellow dept. biochem. scis. Princeton U., Princeton, NJ, 1975—76; intern and resident in radiation oncology U. Wash., Seattle, 1976—80, asst. prof. radiation oncology, adj. asst. prof. dept. pathology, 1979—83, assoc. prof. radiation oncology, adj. assoc. prof. pathology, 1983—86, full prof. radiation oncology, adj. full prof. pathology, 1986—; asst. mem. basic scis. divsn. Fred Hutchinson Cancer Rsch. Ctr., 1979—83, assoc. mem. basic scis. divsn., 1983—86, program head molecular medicine program, 1986—95, full mem. basic scis. divsn., 1995—, dep. dir., 1998—. Mem. bd. sci. counselors divsn. cancer treatment Nat. Cancer Inst., 1986—91. Recipient, Allison Eberlein Fund award, 1989; fellow Clin. fellow, Am. Cancer Soc., 1979—80, Leukemia Soc. fellow, 1977—79, Med. Scientist Tng. Program fellow, NIH, 1970—72. Fellow: AAAS; mem.: Inst. Medicine, 2004 (life). Avocations: reading, exercise, collecting and studying tribal art. Office: Univ Washington Sch Medicine Radiation Oncology UW Box 356043 Seattle WA 98195

GROULX, AIMÉ RENÉ, artist, photographer; b. Goffstown, N.H., Oct. 12, 1942; s. René Robert and Cecile Jeanie Groulx; m. Adele Elizabeth Freedman (div.); m. Ly Thi Le, Oct. 9, 1999. Diploma in photography, Manchester Inst. Arts & Scis., 1992. Exhbn. technician Wadsworth Antheneum, Hartford, Conn., 1968-69; artist-in-residence Elliot U. Ctr. U. N.C., Greensboro, 1972. Exhbns. include Morehead Planetarium, U. N.C., Chapel Hill, 1973, Washington and Lee U., Lexington, Va., 1974, Lisbon Pub. Libr., Wadworth Athneum, Huntington Gallery, 1968-69, Greensboro Pub. Libr., 1975, Robert Frost House, Franconia, N.H., 1977, others. Mem. U.S. Naval Inst. Avocations: conceptual biology, medical science, natural science. Home: PO Box 1385 Manchester NH 03105 Office: Inter Net Work Gallery PO Box 1385 Manchester NH 03105

GROUNDS, VERNON CARL, seminary administrator; b. Jersey City, July 19, 1914; s. John and Bertha Barbara (Heimburg) G.; m. Ann Barton, June 17, 1939; 1 child, Barbara Ann Grounds Owen. BA, Rutgers U., 1937; BD, Faith Theol. Sem., 1940; DD (hon.), Wheaton Coll., 1954; PhD, Drew U., 1960; LHD (hon.), Gordon Coll., 1977. Pastor Paterson (NJ) Gospel Tabernacle, 1935-45; dean, prof. theology Bapt. Bible Sem., Johnson City, 1945-51; dean Denver Conservative Bapt. Sem., 1951-55, pres., 1955-79, chancellor, 1979—. Author: Yes, But How?, Emotional Problems and the Gospel, Evangelicalism and Social Responsibility, The Reason for Our Hope, Revolution and the Christian Faith; contbg. editor Christianity Today, 1980—. Sec. Evang. Theol. Soc., Lynchburg, Va., 1963-76; bd. dirs. Radio Bible Class Ministries. Home: 3455 S Corona St Apt 513 Englewood CO 80110-2878 Office: PO Box 100000 Denver CO 80113-3139

GROUSBECK, WYC, professional sports team executive; s. H. Irving Grousbeck. BA in History, Princeton U.; JD, U. Mich.; MBA, Stanford U. Atty. Brobeck, Phleger & Harrison, 1986—90; founder, pres. MedWise, 1990—95; gen. ptnr. Highland Capital Ptrs., 1995—2002; mng. ptnr. Boston (Mass.) Celtics, 2002—, CEO, 2002—. Office: 151 Merrimac St Boston MA 02114

GROUT, ROBERT W., lawyer; b. Memphis, Nov. 2, 1944; s. M. Wayne and Evelyn (McClure) G.; m. Marsha Karkula, Aug. 12, 1967; children: Brad, Taylor. BA in Econs., Vanderbilt U., 1966; LLB, U. Va., 1969. Bar: Ga. 1969, Ga. Supreme Ct. 1970, Ga. Ct. of Appeals 1970, U.S. Dist. Ct. (no. dist.) Ga. 1975, U.S. Supreme Ct. 1975. Assoc. Troutman, Sanders, Lockerman & Ashmore, Atlanta, 1969-73; ptnr. Troutman Sanders LLP, Atlanta, 1974-85, sr. ptnr., sect. chief, corp. dept., 1986—, mem., exec. com, ptnr. compensation com., opinion com., tech. com. Seminar speaker Atlanta Bar Assn., 1986-99. Bd. dirs. Ashford-Dunwoody YMCA, 1984-93, Met. Atlanta YMCA, 1998-2004, Boy Scouts of Am. Troop, 1986-92; pres. Neighborhood Civic Assn., 1984—2004; mem. fin. com. Cherokee Town & Country Club, 1991—2003, pres. 2003-04. Named a Super Lawyer, Atlanta Mag., 2005; named one of America's Leading Bus. Lawyers, Chambers USA, 2003—04, Legal Elite, Ga. Trend Mag., 2004. Mem. ABA, State Bar Ga., Atlanta Bar Assn., Dunwoody Rotary Club (dir. 1984-91), Ravinia Club, Cherokee Town and Country Club (mem. fin. com. 1991—). Avocations: hunting, fishing, computers, photography. Office: Troutman Sanders LLP 600 Peachtree St NE Ste 5200 Atlanta GA 30308-2216 Office Phone: 404-885-3152. Office Fax: 404-962-6789. Business E-Mail: bob.grout@troutmansanders.com.

GROVE, ANDREW STEVEN, electronics company executive; b. Budapest, Hungary, Sept. 2, 1936; m. Eva Kaston, 1958; 2 children. BS in Chemical Engring., CCNY, 1960, DSc (hon.), 1985; PhD, U. Calif., Berkeley, 1963; DEng (hon.), Worcester Poly. Inst., 1989; LLD (hon.), Harvard U., 2000. With Fairchild Camera and Instrument Co., 1963—67, asst. dir. rsch. & devel., 1967—68; co-founder Intel Corp., Santa Clara, Calif., 1968, v.p., dir. ops., 1968—74, exec. v.p., 1975—76, COO, 1976—87, pres., 1979—97, CEO, 1987—98, chmn. bd., 1997—. Mem. bd. dirs. Intel Corp., 1974—; lectr. Stanford Grad. Sch. of Bus. Author: Physics and Technology of Semiconductor Devices, 1967, High Output Management, 1983, One on One with Andy Grove, 1987, Only the Paranoid Survive: How To Exploit the Crisis Points That Challenge Every Company and Career, 1996, Swimming Across, 2001, of articles in Fortune, The Wall Street Journal, and The NY Times. Named Exec. of Yr., U. Ariz., 1993, Citizen of Yr., World Forum Silicon Valley, 1993, Statesman of Yr., Harvard Bus. Sch., 1996, Tech. Leader of Yr., Industry Week, 1997, Man of Yr., Time mag., 1997, CEO of Yr., CEO mag., 1997, Distinguished Exec. of Yr., Acad. Mgmt., 1998; recipient Am. Inst. Chemists medal, 1960, Merit cert., Franklin Inst., 1975, Townsend Harris medal, CCNY, 1980, Hall of Fame award, Information Industries Assn., 1984, Enterprise award, Profl. Advt. Assn., 1987, George Washington award, Am. Hungarian Found., 1990, Achievement medal, Am. Electronics Assn., 1993, Heinz Family Found. award, 1995, John von Neumann medal, Am. Hungarian Assn., 1995, Steinman medal, CCNY, 1995, Internat. Achievement award, World Trade Club, 1997, Cinema Digital Technols. award, Internat. Film Festival, 1997, Cinema Digital Tech. award, Cannes Film Festival, 1997, Disting. Exec. of the Yr., Acad. of Mgmt., 1998, Lifetime Achievement award, Strategic Mgmt. Soc., 2001. Fellow: IEEE (Achievement award 1969, J.J. Ebers award 1974, Engring. Leadership Recognition award 1987, Computer Entrepreneur award 1997, Medal of Honor award 2000), Am. Acad. Arts and Scis.; mem.: Nat. Acad. Engring. (award 1979). Achievements include patents in field. Office: Intel Corp 2200 Mission College Blvd Santa Clara CA 95052 Office Phone: 408-765-8080. Office Fax: 408-765-9904.

GROVE, BRANDON HAMBRIGHT, JR., diplomat; b. Chgo., Apr. 8, 1929; s. Brandon Hambright and Helen Julia (Gasparska) G.; m. Marie Cheremeteff, 1959 (div. 1983); children: John C., Catherine C.G. Jones, Paul C., Mark C.; m. Mariana Alfaro Moran, 1988; 1 step child, Michele Parsons Shotts. AB, Bard Coll., 1950; M.P.A., Princeton U., 1952. Joined U.S. Fgn. Svc., 1959; vice consul Abidjan, Ivory Coast, also Upper Volta, Niger, and Dahomey, 1959-61; staff asst. to undersec. state, 1961-62; spl. asst. to dep. undersec. state for adminstrn., 1962-63; spl. asst. to Am. amb. to India, New Delhi, 1963—65; U.S. liaison officer to city govt. West Berlin Germany, 1965—69; dir. Office Panamanian Affairs, State Dept., 1969-71; mem. Sr. Seminar in Fgn. Policy, 1971-72; dep. dir. State Dept. policy planning staff, Washington; also staff dir. Under Secretaries Com. of NSC, 1972-74; chargé d' affaires, then dep. chief of mission Am. Embassy to German Dem. Republic, Berlin, 1974-76; fgn. svc. sr. insp. Dept. State, 1976-78; dep. asst. sec. state for Inter-Am. affairs, 1978-80; consul gen. Jerusalem, 1980—83; Capstone fellow Nat. Def. U., Fort McNair, Washington, 1984; ambassador to Zaire, Kinshasa, 1984-87; coord. State Dept. Budget Rev., Washington, 1987-88; dir. Fgn. Service Inst., Washington, 1988-92; diplomat-in-residence Georgetown U., Washington, 1992-93; sr. advisor State Dept. Policy Planning Staff, Washington, 1993-94; retired U.S. Fgn. Svc., 1994. Asst. instr. Princeton U., 1953; sr. cons. APCO Assocs., Inc., Washington, 1996-2000, Sol M. Linowitz prof. internat. affairs, Hamilton Coll. Author: Behind Embassy Walls: the Life and Times of an American Diplomat, 2005; chmn. editl. bd. Fgn. Svc. Jour., 1992-94. Served to lt. USNR, 1954-57. Recipient Pres.'s Meritorious Service award, 1985, 90, 92, John Dewey medal for disting. pub. svc. Bard Coll., 1990. Mem. Am. Acad. Diplomacy (bd. dirs.), Am. Fgn. Svc. Assn. (achievement award 2000), Washington Inst. Fgn. Affairs, Coun. on Fgn. Rels., Georgetown U. Inst. for Study of Diplomacy (bd. dirs.), Assn. for Diplomatic Studies and Tng. (bd. dirs.), Diplomatic and Consular Officers Ret., Met. Club Washington, Cosmos Club. Home: 2029 Connecticut Ave NW Washington DC 20008-6141 E-mail: brandongrove@earthlink.net.

GROVE, DAVID D., anthropology professor; PhD Anthropology, UCLA, 1968. Faculty SUNY, Binghamton, Calif. State U., Northridge; prof. U. of IL, Urbana-Champaign, 1970—2001, prof. emeritus, 2001—; prof. U. of FL. Pres., Anthropology div. Am. Anthropology Assoc., 1992—93. Recipient Distinguished Teaching Award, College of Liberal Arts & Sci. Fellow: Am. Acad. Arts & Sci.; mem.: Am. Anthropology Assoc. Office: Dept of Anthropology University of Florida 1112 Turlington Hall PO Box 117305 Gainesville FL 32611*

GROVE, DAVID LAVAN, lawyer; b. Johnstown, Pa., Nov. 4, 1937; s. William Morgan and Edith Elizabeth (Boyd) G.; m. Barbara Pearson Fogg, Aug. 26, 1961; children: Jonathan Morgan, Amy Pearson. BA in Polit. Sci. with honors, Dickinson Coll., 1959; LLB, Yale U., 1962. Bar: Pa. 1965, U.S. Dist. Ct. (ea. dist.) Pa. 1966, U.S. Ct. Appeals (3d cir.) 1972, U.S. Supreme Ct. 1976, U.S. Ct. Internat. Trade 1977, U.S. Dist. Ct. (mid. dist.) Pa. 1990. Vol. U.S. Peace Corps, Nigeria, West Africa, 1962-64, atty-advisor Washington, 1967-69; assoc. Montgomery, McCracken, Walker & Rhoads, LLP, Phila., 1964-67, 69-72; ptnr. Montgomery, McCracken, Walker & Rhoads, Phila., 1972—. Asst. lectr. law faculty U. Lagos, Nigeria, 1962-64, Office of Peace Corps Gen. Counsel, Washington, 1967-69; advisor on fed. law and regulations Peace Corps ofcls.; U.S. del. to Coun. Internat. Secretariat for Vol. Svc., Washington, 1968, Geneva, 1969. Bd. sch. dirs. Wallingford (Pa.)-Swarthmore Sch. Dist., 1975-87, bd. pres., 1977-79, 82-84; mem. Wallingford-Swarthmore Sch. Authority, 1988-99, pres., 1995-99; bd. dirs. Recs. for Blind and Dyslexic, Phila., 1994-2003; mem. Corp. Am. Friends Svc. Com., Phila., 2002—; mem. Swarthmore Borough Planning Commn., 2004—; Swarthmore Borough rep. Ctrl. Delaware County Authority, 2004—. Fellow: Am. Coll. Trial Lawyers; mem.: ABA, Phila. Bar Assn., Rolling Green Golf Club (Springfield, Pa.), Theta Chi, Omicron Delta Kappa, Pi Gamma Mu, Delta Phi Alpha. Democrat. Mem. Soc. Of Friends. Avocations: tennis, golf, snorkeling, scuba diving. Home: 80 Yale Ave Swarthmore PA 19081-1607 Office: Montgomery McCracken Et Al 123 S Broad St 24th Fl Philadelphia PA 19109 Office Phone: 215-772-7234. Personal E-mail: dlgrove@gmail.com. Business E-Mail: dgrove@mmwr.com.

GROVE, ERIC JOHN, military analyst; b. Dec. 3, 1948; m. Elizabeth Jane Grove. MA with honors in hist., U. Aberdeen, 1970; MA in war studies, Kings Coll., U. London, 1971; PhD in security studies, U. of Hull, 1996. Lectr. to sr. lectr., deputy head of dept. Britannia Royal Naval Coll., Dept. of Strategic Studies and Internat. Affairs, Dartmouth, 1971—85; sr. rsch. officer Coun. for Arms Control, London, 1985—86; assoc. dir. Found. for Internat. Security, Common Security Program, 1986—88; naval rsch. dir. Found. for Internat. Security, Adderbury, 1988—93; vis. lectr. Ctr. for Internat. Sutidies, U. Cambridge, 1986—94; visit. lectr. Royal Naval Coll., Greenwich, 1986—93; rsch. fellow Mountbatten Ctr., U. Southampton, 1991—93. Dir. Ctr. for Security Studies and Reader, Dept of Polit. and Internat. Studies, U. of Hull. Co-author: Fundamentals of British Maritime Doctrine, 1995; author: Vanguard to Trident: British Naval Policy Since 1945, 1987, Crucible of Peace, 1988, Some Principles of Maritime Strategy, 1988, The Future of Sea Power, 1990, Maritime Strategy and European Security, 1990, Sea Battles in Close-up, World War Two, 1990, The Riddle of the Sands, 1991, Fleet to Fleet Encounters: Tsuskima, Jutland, Philippine Sea, 1993, Great Battles of the Royal Navy, 1994, Narvik, 1996, The Battle and The Breeze, The Naval Reminiscenses of Admiral of the Fleet Sir Edward Ashmore, 1997, The Defeat of the Enemy Attack Upon Shipping, 1997, Jane's War at Sea 1897-1997, 1997, The Dynamics of Sea Power: Global Strategic Change In The Modern World, 1998, The Price of Disobedience, The Battle of the River Plate Reconsidered, 2001, The Royal Navy Since 1815, A New Short History, 2005; contbr. chapters to books various profl. books, articles various profl. jours. Recipient Hutton and Fullerton Bursary, U. Aberdeen, 1966, mem., Russian Acad. of Natural Scis., 1991. Fellow: Royal Hist. Soc.; mem.: Navy Records Soc., Internat. Studies Assn. Avocations: music, motor racing. Office: Ctr for Security Studies Dept Polit and Internat Sudies U of Hull HU6 7RX England E-mail: e.j.grove@hull.ac.uk.

GROVE, JEFFREY SCOTT, family practice physician; b. Paxton, Ill., Sept. 21, 1964; s. Ronald Edwin and Delores Ann (Martensen) G.; m. Karen Beth Hanlon, June 17, 1989; children: Garrett Jeffrey, Victoria May. BS in Biology, Fla. So. Coll., 1986; DO, Southeastern Coll. Osteo Med., North Miami Beach, Fla., 1990. Diplomate Am. Bd. Quality Assurance and Utilization Rev. Physicians; bd. cert. family practice and in geriatrics. Intern Suncoast Hosp., Largo, Fla., 1990-91, resident in family practice, 1991-93; pvt. practice SunCoast Family Med. Assocs., Largo, 1993—. Med. dir. Barrington Properties, Largo, 1994-97, Oak Manor Nursing Ctr., Largo, 1993-2000, Drew Village Nursing Ctr., Clearwater, Fla., 1996-99, Highland Pines Nursing Ctr., 1999-2000; rep.-at-large exec. com. Suncoast Hosp., 1995-2000, chief adminstrv. resident, 1992-93, family practice tchg. staff, geriatrics program dir., 1993-96, faculty devel. com., 1994—, legal compliance comm., 1998—; mem. quality assurance/utilization rev. com., 1993—, med. dir. of quality assurance/utilization rev. dept., 1995—; bd. dirs. Suncoast Cmty. Care PHO, Largo, 1994-98, med. dir., 1998; clin. asst. prof. family medicine Nova Southeastern U. Coll. Osteo. Medicine, North Miami Beach, 1994-2000, clin. assoc. prof., 2000—; clin. instr. Kirksville Coll. Osteo. Medicine, 1993—; trustee SunCoast Hosp. Found., 1996-2002, SunCoast Hosp., 1998—; regional med. dir. Tampa Bay for Elder Health. *Dr. Jeffrey S. Grove practices primarily through SunCoast and Morton Plant Hospital in Pinellas County. SunCoast Hospital is the West Coast Academic Center for Nova Southeastern University, College of Osteopathic Medicine. He also has staff privileges at Largo Medical Center.* Vice-chmn. bd. trustees SCH Found., 1997-98, chmn., 1998-99; trustee St. Paul's Sch., 2003—, chmn. devel. com., 2005—. Named to Outstanding Young Men of Am.; recipient Disting. Trustee award SCH Found., 2000. Mem.: Am. Coll. Family Practitioners (nat. bd. govs. 2004—), Pinellas County Osteo. Med. Soc. (bd. govs. 1995—, treas. 1996—99, pres. 2000—03, Physician of Yr. 2002—03), Fla. Soc. Am. Coll. Osteo. Family Physicians (chmn. membership com. Fla. chpt. 1997—99, trustee 1997—, treas. 1999—2000, v.p. 2000—01, pres. 2001—02, Physician of Yr. 2003—04), Fla. Osteo. Med. Assn. (trustee 2001—, exec. com. 2005—), Am. Osteo. Assn. (bur. state govt. affairs, mem. Bur. of State Govt. Affairs), Nova Southeastern U. Coll. Osteo. Medicine Alumni Assn. (v.p. 2000—01, pres. 2002—03, Disting. Alumni award 2001, Disting. Alumni Achievement award 2003), Scouting Res., Nat. Eagle Scout Assn. (life). Republican. Methodist. Avocations: golf, stamp collecting/philately, travel, skiing. Home: 301 Osceola Rd Clearwater FL 33756-1453 Office: SunCoast Family Med Assocs 12020 Seminole Blvd Largo FL 33778 Office Phone: 727-588-9572. Personal E-mail: scfma2@earthlink.net.

GROVE, RICHARD CHARLES, retired power tool company executive; b. Bethlehem, Pa., Aug. 13, 1940; s. Dale Addison and Mary Elizabeth (Ripple) G.; m. Cynthia Ann Dimmick, Dec. 7, 1963; 1 child, Jeffrey. BEE, Cornell U., 1962; MBA, U. Pitts., 1967. Mgmt. cons. Touche Ross & Co., Detroit, 1967-72; mgr. bus. planning Amstar Corp., N.Y.C., 1972-75, treas. Spreckels Sugar div. San Francisco, 1975-82, treas. N.Y.C., 1983-84, v.p., controller Stamford, Conn., 1985-88, v.p., chief fin. officer, 1988-89; sr. v.p. Esstar Inc., New Haven, 1989, exec. v.p., dir., 1995; exec. v.p. Milw. Electric Tool Corp., 1990-91, pres., CEO, 1991—2000. Bd. dirs. Carolinas Concert Assn., bd. pres., 2004—. Served to 1st lt. U.S. Army, 1964—66. Mem.: The Point Lake and Golf Club. Republican. Avocations: golf, reading, travel. Personal E-mail: richardgrove@adelphia.net.

GROVE, TIMOTHY LYNN, geology educator; b. York, Pa., July 15, 1949; s. Arthur Leib and Ruby Janette (Finger) G.; m. Madeline Scadden, June 15, 1971; m. Ann Marie Reilly, June 19, 1979; children: Matthew Brian, Michael Thomas. BA, U. Colo., 1971; AM, Harvard U., 1975, PhD, 1976. Rsch. asst. SUNY, Stony Brook, 1975-79; from asst. prof. to assoc. prof. dept. earth, atmospheric and planet sci. MIT, Cambridge, 1979-91, prof. dept. earth, atmospheric and planet sci., 1991—. Vis. prof. CalTech divsn. geology and tech., Pasadena, 1979; vis. prof. divsn. isotope geology and ore deposits Swiss Eidgenossische Tech. Hochschule, Zurich, Switzerland, 2001. Editor Contbns. to Mineralogy and Petrology, 1985—. Fellow: Am. Geophys. Union (Bowen award 1993), Mineral Soc. Am.; mem.: Geochem. Soc., Geol. Soc. Am. Home: 87 Menotomy Rd Arlington MA 02476-6111 Office: MIT Earth Atmospheric & Planet Sci 77 Massachusetts Ave # 541220 Cambridge MA 02139-4307 Office Phone: 617-253-2878. Business E-Mail: tlgrove@mit.edu.

GROVER, CAROL NOELLE, controller, accountant; b. Canandaigua, N.Y., 1970; d. Robert Charles and June Nona Ellis; m. Trevor Thomas Grover, Sept. 12, 1992; children: Felicia, Caitlyn. Diploma, Marcus Whitman Coll., 1989; AA, Fingerlakes C.C., 1991, AA, 1997; BA, Keuka (N.Y.) Coll., 2000. CPA N.Y., 2002. Auditor Bonadio & Co., LLP, Pittsford, NY, 1999—2003; controller Keuka (N.Y.) Coll., Keuka Pk., 2003—. Mem.: N.Y. State Soc. CPAs (Outstanding Achievement in Acctg. award 1999). Home: 4546 Ridge Rd Canandaigua NY 14424 Office: Keuka College 141 Central Ave Keuka Park NY 14478 Office Phone: 315-279-5252. Business E-Mail: cgrover@mail.keuka.edu.

GROVER, CHARLES D., mathematics educator; b. Greenville, Pa., June 4, 1971; s. Charles F. and Margaret R. Grover; m. Janet B. Blades, June 28, 2003; 1 child, Kaitlyn Elizabeth. BS, Pa. State U., 1993; MEd, Salisbury U., Md., 1997. Advanced Professional Teaching Certificate Md., 2003. H.s. math. tchr. Col. Richardson H.S., Federalsburg, Md., 1993—2002, Brunswick H.S., Md., 2002—. Ch. choir mem. St. John the Evangelist Cath. Ch., Frederick, Md., 2002—. Mem.: Internat. Soc. for Tech. in Edn., Md. Instrnl. Computer Coords.Assn., Nat. Coun. of Tcgrs. Math. Home: 4918 Sutherland Dr Frederick MD 21703 Office: Brunswick High Sch 101 Cummings Dr Brunswick MD 21716 Office Phone: 240-236-8600.

GROVER, JAMES ROBB, chemist, editor; b. Klamath Falls, Oreg., Sept. 16, 1928; s. James Richard and Marjorie Alida (van Groos) G.; m. Barbara Jean Ton, Apr. 14, 1957; children: Jonathan Robb, Patricia Jean. BS summa cum laude, valedictorian, U. Wash., Seattle, 1952; PhD, U. Calif., Berkeley, 1958. Rsch. assoc. Brookhaven Nat. Lab., Upton, N.Y., 1957-59, assoc.

chemist, 1959-63, chemist, 1963-67, chemist with tenure, 1967-77, sr. chemist, 1978-93, rsch. collaborator, 1993—. Cons. Lawrence Livermore (Calif.) Nat. Lab., 1962; assoc. editor Ann. Rev. of Nuclear Sci., Ann. Revs., Inc., Palo Alto, Calif., 1967-77; vis. prof. Inst. for Molecular Sci., Okazaki, Japan, 1986-87; vis. scientist Max-Planck Inst. für Strömungsforschung, Göttingen, Fed. Republic Germany, 1975-76. Contbr. numerous articles to profl. jours. With USN, 1946-48. Mem. Am. Chem. Soc. (chmn. nuclear chemistry and tech. 1989), Am. Phys. Soc., Triple Nine Soc., Sigma Xi, Phi Beta Kappa, Phi Lambda Upsilon, Zeta Mu Tau, Pi Mu Epsilon. Libertarian. Presbyterian. Achievements include naming of the nuclear yrast levels and discovery of their importance in nuclear reactions; invention of use of short-lived radioactivity in molecular beams; first to successfully use radioactivity for detection in chemically reactive scattering experiments; invention of threshold photoionization method for measuring the dissociation energies of neutral weak complexes in molecular beams. Home and Office: 1536 Pinecrest Ter Ashland OR 97520-3427 E-mail: jrobbgrover@cs.com.

GROVER, KATHY JO, school system administrator, mathematics educator; b. Miami, Okla., Oct. 30, 1956; d. Wilber Ray and Joanne Edna Kaylor; m. Dennis Lee Grover, Aug. 16, 1974; children: Lee Michael, Anthony Daniel. BSEdn in Math. and German, S.W. Mo. State U., 1992, MSEd in Math., 2001. Math. tchr. Billings (Mo.) Pub. Schs., 1992—94, Springfield (Mo.) Pub. Schs., 1994—99; math tchr., curriculum dir. Clever (Mo.) Pub. Schs., 1999—. Mem. exec. com. S.W. Regional Profl. Devel. Ctr., Springfield, 2004—. Team capt. ACS Relay for Life, Springfield, 2003—05. Mo. Incentive grantee, Mo. Dept. Edn., 1994. Mem.: ASCD, Nat. Coun. Tchrs. Math. Avocations: reading, gardening. Office: Clever Pub Schs 103 S Public Ave Clever MO 65631 Business E-Mail: groverk@clever.k12.mo.us.

GROVER, MARK DONALD, computer scientist; b. Augusta, Maine, July 12, 1955; s. Donald William and Aletha D. (Wells) G. BA, U. Fla., 1976; MS, Northwestern U., Evanston, Ill., 1978, PhD, 1982. Cert. EMT and CPR instr. Instr. Northwestern U., Evanston, Ill., 1978—81; mem. tech. staff TRW Def. Sys., Redondo Beach, Calif., Fairfax, Va., 1981—85; sr. computer scientist Advanced Decision Sys., Arlington, Va., 1985—89; prin. software engr. Oberon Software Inc., Cambridge, Mass., 1990—94; sr. software engr. DeLorme Mapping, Yarmouth, Maine, 1995. Program chmn. Nat. Symbolics User Group Conf., Washington, 1986; mem. computer sci. dept. adv. bd. U. So. Maine; presenter to conferences in field. Contbg. articles to sci. journals. Mem. mcpl. comprehensive plan com. Town of Gray, Maine; exec. dir. Gray Region Citizen Corps, Maine; vol. EMT Gray Fire Rescue, Gray, Maine; trustee First Congl. Ch., Gray, Maine. Mem. NRA (life endowment), Phi Beta Kappa, Tau Beta Pi. Avocations: travel, rare books, drama, marksmanship, history. Office: DeLorme Mapping PO Box 298 Yarmouth ME 04096-0298 Office Phone: 207-846-7000. Business E-Mail: mark.grover@delorme.com.

GROVER, NORMAN LAMOTTE, theologian, philosopher; b. Topeka, Feb. 9, 1928; s. LaMotte and Virginia Grace (Alspach) G.; m. Anne Stottler, June 24, 1950; children: Jennifer Jean, Peter Neal, Rebecca Louise Grover Verna, Sandra Christine Grover Mason. B. Mech. Engring., Rensselaer Poly. Inst., 1948; B.D., Yale, 1951, S.T.M., 1952, PhD, 1957. Mem. faculty, chaplain Hollins (Va.) Coll., 1954-57, asst. prof. religion, 1956-57; ordained to ministry Presbyn. Ch., 1952; head dept. philosophy and religion Va. Poly. Inst. and State U., 1957-75, prof. philosophy and religion, 1961-83, prof. religion, 1983-91, prof. emeritus, 1991—. Adj. prof. Ctr. for Study Sci. in Soc., 1983-86, guest lectr. computer sci., 2005; mem. supervising com. So. leadership tng. project Fund for Republic, 1955-56; assoc. Danforth Found., 1958—, sr. assoc., 1962—, chmn. Va., N.C. and S.C. conf., 1962; psychotherapeutic counsellor Blacksburg Community Counselling Center, 1962-65 Bd. dirs. YMCA at Va. Tech. (Gold Triangle award 1962); bd. dirs. United Campus Ministries of Blacksburg, 1986-95; mem. Blacksburg Master Chorale and Va. Tech. Concert Choir Concert Tour in Berlin, Poland, Czech Republic, Salzburg, 1992, Germany, Austria, Czech Republic, 1995, England, Scotland, 2003; concert under Robert Shaw, 1998; study trip to Costa Rica, Nicaragua, El Salvador and Guatemala Presbyn. Ch. U.S.A. Presbytery of Peaks Partnership with CEDEPCA, 1989, 91; mem. Habitat for Humanity, New River Valley chpt., Montgomery County Race Rels. Work Group, Ecumenical Alliance of New River Valley; mem. local convening com. Interfaith Social Concerns Network, 1999—; mem. Montgomery County Dem. Com., 2004—. Mem. AAUP (pres. Va. Poly. Inst. and State U. chpt. 1961-62, 81-82, sec.-treas. chpt. 1959-60, 77-80, v.p. chpt. 1960-61, 80-81, 92-94), NAACP (life, exec. bd. Montgomery, Floyd, Radford br. 1999—, Mountain Climber award 2000), ACLU, Amnesty Internat., Va. Philos. Assn. (pres. 1969), So. Soc. Philosophy and Psychology, Am. Acad. Religion (chmn. S.E. region theology/philosophy religion sect. 1983-85, mem. citizen amb. team to Ukraine and Russia 1993, China 1994), Coalition for Justice in Ctrl. Am. (bd. dirs., v.p. 1990-94), Bread for the World, Sierra Club, Smithsonian Assocs., Wilderness Soc., Am. Assn. Ret. Persons, People to People Internat. (Am. People amb. del. to India, Nepal and Tibet 1996, China 2000). Home: Warm Hearth Village 1622 Hawthorne Ridge Blacksburg VA 24060-6143 Office Phone: 540-552-3833. Business E-Mail: ngrover@warmhearthva.org.

GROVER, ROSALIND REDFERN, oil and gas company executive; b. Midland, Tex., Sept. 5, 1941; d. John Joseph and Rosalind (Kapps) Redfern;m. Arden Roy Grover, Apr. 10, 1982; 1 child, Rosson. BA in Edn. magna cum laude, U. Ariz., 1966, MA in History, 1982; postgrad. in law, So. Meth. U. Libr. Gahr H.S., Cerritos, Calif., 1969; pres. The Redfern Found., Midland, 1982—; ptnr. Redfern & Grover, Midland, 1986—; pres. Redfern Enterprises Inc., Midland, 1989—. Chmn. bd. dirs. Flag-Redfern Oil Co., Midland. Sec. park and recreation commn. City of Midland, 1969-71, del. Objectives for Convocation, 1980; mem., past pres. women's aux. Midland Cmty. Theatre, 1970; chmn. challenge grant bldg. fund, 1980, chmn. Tex. Yucca Hist. Landmark Renovation Project, 1983, trustee, 1983-88; chmn. publicity com. Midland Jr. League, Midland, Inc., 1972, chmn. edn. com., 1976, corr. sec., 1978; 1st v.p. Midland Symphony Assn., 1975; chmn. Midland Charity Horse Show, 1975-76; mem. Midland Am. Revolution Bicentennial Commn., 1976; trustee Mus. S.W., 1977-80, pres. bd. dirs., 1979-80; co-chmn. Gov. Clements Fin. Com., Midland, 1978; mem. dist. com. State Bd. Law Examiners; mem. bd. visitors Hockaday, 2001-03; trustee Midland Meml. Hosp., 1978-80, Permian Basin Petroleum Mus., Libr. and Hall of Fame, 1989-98, Midland Cmty. Theatre, 2005—. Recipient HamHock award Midland Cmty. Theatre, 1978. Mem. Ind. Petroleum Assn. Am., Tex. Ind. Producers and Royalty Owners Assn., Petroleum Club, Racquet Club (Midland), Horseshoe Bay (Tex.) Country Club, Phi Kappa Phi, Pi Lambda Theta. Republican. Office: PO Box 2127 Midland TX 79702-2127 Office Phone: 432-683-9137. E-mail: rozgrover@aol.com.

GROVER, WILLIAM HERBERT, architect; b. Phila., Feb. 10, 1938; s. William Oliver Grover and Lucy Gertrude (Whetzel) Grover Lott; m. Dora Bradford Apted, Feb. 24, 1962; children: Virginia Lucy, Amy Ellen. Student in mech. engring., Cornell U., 1955-58; B in Profl. Art, Art Ctr. Coll., Pasadena, Calif., 1962; MArch, Yale U., 1969. Registered architect, N.Y., N.H., Conn., Mass., Md. Designer Gen. Motors Corp., Warren, Mich., 1962-65; draftsman MLTW/Moore Turnbull, New Haven, 1969-70; architect, mgr. Charles W. Moore Assocs., Essex, Conn., 1970-75; architect, pres. Moore Grover Harper P.C., Essex, Conn., 1975-84; architect, ptnr. Centerbrook Architects, Essex, Conn., 1984—. Pres. Centerbrook, Architects LLC, Essex, 1984—, bd. dirs.; pres. Mainstream, Inc., 1984—. Prin. works include Jones Lab., 1973 (AIA Honor award 1981), Grace Auditorium, 1986, Neurosci. Ctr., Cold Spring Harbor Lab., 1991, DeKalb Discovery Rsch. Ctr., 1992, Phelps Sci. Bldg., Phillips Exeter Acad., 2003; designer (light fixtures) Slice of Light, 1981 (Progressive Architecture award 1982, 85, Eidolon 1984). Member Essex Zoning Commn., 1972-77, Essex Rep. Town Com., 1973-74; bd. dirs. Essex Art Assn., 1989-2000, Community Music Sch., 1991-2003, Essex Land Conservation Trust, 2004—. Recipient Builders' Choice award Nat. Home Builders, 1987, Sportmanship award U.S. Sailing Assn., 1990; named to Domino's Top 30 Architects, 1991, Architectural Digest's Top 100 Architects, 1991. Fellow AIA (Honor award 1981, N.Eng. honor award 1994, 95, Firm award 1998); mem. Conn. Soc. Architects (Honor awards 1980, 85, 92, 93, 94, 95, 2002), Internat. Etchells Class Assn., Pettipaug Yacht Club (Commodore Essex chpt. 1984-86), Essex Yacht Club, Duck Island Yacht Club. Avocations: yacht racing, jazz musician, watercolor artist. Home: 123 Main St Centerbrook CT 06409 Office: Centerbrook Architects PO Box 955 Centerbrook CT 06409-0955

GROVES, AMANDA SIMS-, music educator, singer; b. Murray, Ky., Dec. 30, 1969; d. Arvy Glen and Moyna Arnett Sims; m. James William Groves, Nov. 16, 1991. MusB in Vocal Performance, Murray (Ky.) State U., 1992; MusM in Vocal Performance, So. Ill. U., 1995. Cert. tchr. Ill., 1997. Choral dir. Du Quoin (Ill.) H.S. and Mid. Sch., 1996—2003, Herrin (Ill.) H.S. & Mid. Sch., 2003—04, So. Ill. Children's Choir, Carbondale, Ill., 2004—. Co-founder Sing On!; guest choral dir., clinician in field. Singer: Metropolitan Opera Council St. Louis District Competition (Dist. winner, 2000), Metropolitan Opera St. Louis District Competition (Dist. winner, 1999), with Paducah Symphony Chorus. Bd. dirs. Thompsonville (Ill.) Grade Sch., 1998—2004. Mem.: Nat. Educators Assn., Ill. Music Educators Assn. (co-chmn. dist. 6 jr. high festival 2002—03), Am. Choral Dirs. Assn. Democrat. Protestant. Avocations: singing, antiques. Home: 4457 Olive Hamlett Rd Benton KY 42025 Personal E-mail: agroves1@yahoo.com.

GROVES, B. C., educational consultant, writer; d. James Alvis Cowan and Jean Maxine Wilkinson; m. Winford E. Groves, Dec. 16, 1955; 1 child, Cheryl J. BA, North Tex. State U., 1962; MS, Okla. State U., 1976. Cert. tchr. Tex., Okla., 1966. Tchr. Carrollton (Tex.) ISD, 1966—74; supr. Right to Read, Stillwater, Okla., 1974—75; writing tchr. Dallas County Cmty., 1976—78, Dallas C.C., El Centro Coll.; tchg. asst. Tex. A&M, Coll. Sta., 1979—82; real estate broker self-employed, Dallas and Denton, 1982—90; mayor City of Lewisville (Tex.), 1991—93; author, cons. self-employed, Oreg., 1994—. Bd. dirs. Crimestoppers, Denton, Tex., 1989—91. Contbg. author: Reflections on the Umpqua, 1999; co-author: Keeping Christmas, 2002; author: Heros of Lively County, 2003; contbr. articles to profl. jours., local newspapers. Mem. Dallas Crime Commn., 1989—90; precinct chair Denton County Rep. Lewisville, Tex., 1990—93; precinct person Douglas County Rep. Party, Oreg., 2004—. Recipient Outstanding Woman, Dallas Times Herald, 1972. Mem.: AAUW, DAR (com. chair 2003—05, 2nd vice regent Umpqua chpt. 2003—05), Tex. State Tchrs. (life). Republican. Episcopalian. Avocations: hiking, gardening, travel. Business E-Mail: greayfeather@rosenet.net.

GROVES, BERNICE ANN, retired elementary and secondary school coordinator, educator; b. Bklyn., Feb. 5, 1928; d. Charles and Mary (Silverman) Lichtenstein; m. Stuart Weiss, June 5, 1949 (div. June 1978); children: Joel Weiss, Patricia Weiss Levy; m. Sidney Groves, July 30, 1978 (dec. May 2000). MA, Adelphi U., 1971; MS in Edn., Coll. of New Rochelle, 1975. Cert. adminstr., supr., N.Y. K-6th grade tchr., reading tchr. Ossining (N.Y.) Schs., Byram Hills Schs., Armonk, NY, Bedford (NY) Schs., 1964—84; reading specialist The Hallen Sch., Mamaroneck, NY, 1984-88, coord. testing and curriculum New Rochelle, NY, 1988—2001; ret., 2002. Mgr. nutrition ctr. GNC, Scarsdale, NY, 1981—82; mem. curriculum adv. coun. Lower Westchester BOCES, 1988—2001. Pres. Mineola (N.Y.) Elem. Sch. PTA, 1962-63. Mem. ASCD, Lower Hudson Coun. Adminstrv. Women in Edn., Westchester Reading Coun., Orton Dyslexia Soc., Am. Mensa Ltd. Avocations: tennis, gourmet cooking, nutrition.

GROVES, EDGAR STEPHENS, music educator, conductor; b. Leechburg, Pa., May 16, 1935; s. William Edgar and Alice Stephens Groves; m. Merry Ann Dille, Apr. 5, 1980; children: Edgar John, Heather Jean. BS in Music Edn., Ind.(Pa.) U., 1957; MS in Edn., Westminster Coll., Pa., 1963. Cert. Tchr. Pa., 1957. Music tchr. Hermitage (Pa.) Sch. Dist., 1959—93; part time asst. prof. Edinboro U. of Pa., Farrell, 1970—76; adj. instr. Westminster Coll., New Wilmington, Pa., 1971—78; choral condr. Youngstown (Ohio) State U., 1979—80; vis. lecture Grove City (Pa.) Coll., 1993—; adj. instr. Pa. State U., 1984—97; music dir. Shenango Valley Chorale, Sharon, Pa., 1995—. Mem. Greenville (Pa.) Symphony, 1995—2000. Recipient Citation, Pa. Ho. of Reps., 1985, Congratulation, Pa. Senate, 1989, Pa. Tchr. of Yr. Finalist, Pa. Dept. of Edn., 1991. Mem.: Hermitage Edn. Assn. (pres. 1971—73), NEA, Am. Choral Dirs. Assn., Music Educators Nat. Conf. Liberal-Conservative. Presbyterian. Avocations: exercise, bicycling, backpacking, reading. Home: 570 Carley Ave Sharon PA 16146 Office: Grove City Coll 100 Campus Dr Grove City PA 16158 Office Phone: 724-458-2086. Personal E-mail: jiged@infonline.net. E-mail: esgroves@gcc.edu.

GROVES, JOHN TAYLOR, III, chemist, educator; b. New Rochelle, NY, Mar. 27, 1943; s. John Taylor and Frances (Gaylor) G.; m. Karen Joan Morrison, Apr. 15, 1967; children: Jay, Kevin. BS, M.I.T., 1965; PhD, Columbia U., 1969. Asst. prof. U. Mich., Ann Arbor, 1969-76, assoc. prof., 1976-79, prof. organic chemistry, 1979-85; prof. organic and inorganic chemistry Princeton (N.J.) U., 1985—, chmn. dept. chemistry, 1988-93, Hugh Stott Taylor prof. chemistry, 1991—. Morris S. Kharasch Vis. Prof. U. Chgo., 1993; cons. in field; dir. Mich. Center for Catalytic and Surface Scis., Ann Arbor, 1981-85; disting. vis. prof., U. Hong Kong, 2003. Bd. editors: Bioorganic Chemistry, 1984—, Bioorganic and Medicinal Chemistry, 1994—, Bioorganic and Medicinal Chemistry Letters, 1994—; mem. editl. bd.: Reaction Kinetics and Catalysis Letters, 1989—, Jour. of Biol. Inorganic Chemistry, 1995—; contbr. articles to profl. jours.; mem. adv. bd. Inorganic Chemistry, 1995-97. Recipient Phi Lambda Upsilon award for outstanding teaching and leadership, 1978, NSF Extension award, 1990—92. Fellow AAAS, Am. Acad. Arts and Scis.; mem. Am. Chem. Soc. (Arthur C. Cope Scholar award 1991, Alfred Bader award in bio-organic and bioinorganic chemistry 1996), N.Y. Acad. Sci., Sigma Xi. Office: Princeton U Dept Chemistry 203 Hoyt Lab Princeton NJ 08544-0001 Business E-Mail: jtgroves@princeton.edu.

GROVES, RAY JOHN, accountant; b. Cleve., Sept. 7, 1935; m. Anne Keating, Aug. 18, 1962; children: David, Philip, Matthew. BS summa cum laude, Ohio State U., 1957. CPA, Conn., NY, Ohio. With Ernst & Whinney, Cleve. and N.Y.C., 1957-94, ptnr., 1966-71, nat. ptnr., 1971-77, chmn., chief exec. officer NYC, 1977-89; co-CEO, Ernst & Young, NYC, 1989-91, chmn., CEO, 1991-94; chmn. Legg Mason Merchant Banking, Inc., 1995—2001; sr. officer Marsh, Inc., 2001—. Bd. govs. Am. Stock Exch., 1987-93; bd. dirs. Boston Sci. Corp., Gillette, EDS. Bd. overseers Wharton Sch. U. Pa., 1986-95; vice chmn. bd. trustees Ursuline Coll., Cleve., 1970-86; mng. dir. Met. Opera Assn., 1988—; trustee Pub. Policy Inst. NY State, 1988—, Bus. Coun UN, 1993-99; dir. Ohio State U. Found., 1994—, chmn., 1999-2001. Mem. AICPA (chmn. bd. dirs. 1984-85), Nat. Assn. Securities Dealers (bd. govs. 1981-84), Union Club, Pepper Pike Club, Links Club, Met. Club, Blind Brook Club. Republican. also: 1120 Park Ave Apt 11B New York NY 10128-1242 Office: Marsh Inc 1166 Ave of Americas 44th Flr New York NY 10036-2774 Office Phone: 212-345-1823.

GROWCOCK, TERRY D., agricultural products executive; BS Business Management, U. of St. Francis. Exec. King-Seeley Corp., United Technologies, Universal Nolin, Paragon Electric; v.p., gen. mgr Robertshaw Automotive; exec. v.p., gen. mgr. Manitowoc Ice, 1994—95; pres. Manitowoc Foodservice Group, 1995—98; pres., CEO, bd. dir Manitowoc Co. Inc., 1998—, chmn., 2002—. Bd. dir. Harris Corp., 2005—. Office: c/o Manitowoc 2400 S 44th St Manitowoc WI 54221*

GROWNEY, ROBERT L., former communications company professional, venture capitalist; BSME, Ill. Inst. Tech., Chgo., 1974, MBA, 1982. Various mgr. positions to gen. mgr. Fixed Products Divsn. Motorola, Inc., Schaumburg, Ill., 1966-89, sr. v.p., gen. mgr. Radio Technologies Group, 1989-91, sr. v.p., gen. mgr. Paging and Telepoint Systems Group, 1991-92, exec. v.p., gen. mgr. Paging and Wireless Data Group, 1992-94, pres., gen. mgr. Messaging, Info. and Media Sector, 1994-97, pres., COO, 1997—2001, bd. dirs., 1997—2002, vice chmn., 2001—02; ptnr. Edgewater Funds, Chgo., 2002—. Exec. com. mem. bd. trustees Ill. Inst. Tech., chmn. oversight bd. Stuart Grad. Sch. Bus. Office: Edgewater Funds 900 N Mich Ave Ste 1800 Chicago IL 60611

GROZBEAN, STUART HARVEY, lawyer; b. Washington, Nov. 3, 1948; s. Albert and Ann Grozbean; m. Laurie Smiler, Jan. 24, 1950; children: Michelle, Stephanie. JD, U. Balt., 1974; BA, Jacksonville U., 1971. Bar: Md. 1975, D.C. 1976, U.S. Supreme Ct., Md. Ct. Appeals, U.S. Ct. Mil. Appeals. Founder, CFO Belli, Weil & Grozbean, P.C., Rockville, Md., 1989—. Former instr., lectr. law U. Md. Mem.: ABA, Md. State Bar Assn. Achievements include development of Developed child support software used by the Courts in Maryland to determine child support; In 2003, Tom DeLay, Majority Leader of the House of Representatives appointed Mr. Grozbean as Honorary Co-Chairman of the Business Advisory Council. Office: Belli Weil & Grozbean PC 111 Rockville Pike Ste 980 Rockville MD 20850 Office Phone: 301-738-5700. Personal E-mail: shgroz@grozbean.us. Business E-Mail: shgroz@bwglaw.com. E-mail: shgroz@bwg-law.com.

GRUB, PHILLIP DONALD, business educator; b. Medical Lake, Wash., Aug. 8, 1931; s. Carl Dryer and Barbara Rosalie (Johnson) G. BA in Econs. and Bus. Edn. with honors, Eastern Wash. State U., 1953; MBA (Scottish Rite Found. fellow), George Washington U., 1960, DBA (Am. Security and Trust scholar), 1964; DBus (hon.), U. Internat. Bus. and Econs., Beijing, 1986. Pres. Phillip D. Grub, Inc., Spokane, Wash., 1953-54; pvt. practice, 1956-62; co-owner, co-mgr. 7G Ranch, Medical Lake, 1962-70; assoc. prof., dir. programs in internat. bus. George Washington U., Washington, 1964-70, chmn. dept. bus. adminstrn., 1968-70, prof. bus. adminstrn., 1971-73, Aryamehr prof. multinat. mgmt., 1974-94, Aryamehr prof. emeritus, 1994—, spl. asst. to pres., 1974-80; chmn. Phillip Grub and Assocs., 1994—; disting. internat. exec. in residence Ea. Washington U., Cheney, 1997—. Cons. Summa Group, Jakarta, Indonesia, 1991-92; mgmt. cons. to industry and govts.; sr. ptnr. C & P Properties, Medical Lake, Wash., 1988—, Pacific Costal Investments, Medical Lake, Wash., 2001—; mem. Md.-D.C. Export Expansion Coun., 1968-89; vis. prof. internat. bus. adminstrn., acting dir. Ohio World Trade Edn. Ctr., Cleve. State U., 1972-73; dir., chmn. exec. com. Diplomat Nat. Bank, 1978-80; mem. bd. adv. Donaldson, Luftkin & Jenrette, 1980-83; bd. dirs. U.S.-Japan Culture Ctr.; dir. Washington World Trade Inst., 1983-91, pres., 1983-86; dir. U.S. Vietnam Ednl. Found., 1990—; sr. advisor Shanghi Ctr. Internat. Studies, 1987—. Author: A Guide to Personnel Development, 1966, A Handbook for Term Papers, Theses and Dissertations, 1967, American-East European Trade: Controversy, Progress, Prospects, 1968; (with Norma M. Loeser) Executive Leadership: The Art of Successfully Managing Resources, 1969, Management U.S.A., 1968; (with Mika S. Kakimies) International Marketing in Perspective, 1971; (with Ashok Kapoor) The Multinational Enterprise in Transition, 1972, 3d edit., 1986; (with Ghadar and Khambata) Asia Dimensions of International Business, 1982, Foreign Investment Analysis: Cases and Country Studies, 1986, Global Business Management in the 1990's, 1990, Foreign Direct Investment in China, 1991, The Re-Emerging Securities Market in China, 1992, Vietnam, The New Investment Frontier in Southeast Asia, 1992, (with Dara Khambata) The Multinational Enterprise: Strategies for Global Competitiveness, 1993, Global Business Strategies for the Year 2000, 1995; contbr. articles to profl. jours. Bd. dirs. U.S. Forestry, 1987-90; sr. advisor Shanghai Ctr. Internat. Studies, 1987—. With U.S. Army, 1954-56. Named a Univ. Prof. in Peoples Republic of China, 1986. Mem. Acad. Internat. Bus. (pres. 1975-77), Acad. Mgmt., Am. Mgmt. Assn., U.S.-Japan Culture Soc. (bd. dirs., exec. sec.), Fellows Acad. Internat. Bus., Masons, Alpha Kappa Psi, Beta Gamma Sigma. Home: 4810 S Saint Andrews Ln Spokane WA 99223-4304 Office: C & P Properties PO Box 220 Medical Lake WA 99022-0220 Office Phone: 509-299-5133. E-mail: phillip54@aol.com.

GRUBB, DANIEL STUDD, literature and language professor, priest; b. London, Eng., Apr. 1, 1928; arrived in U.S., 1947; s. Norman Percy Grubb and Pauline Evangeline Priscilla Studd; m. Rosemary Callan, June 4, 1960; 1 child, Daniel Studd Jr. BA, Wheaton Coll., Wheaton, Ill., 1953; MA in Tchg., Duke Univ., Durham, N.C., 1957; MA in Eng. Lit., Univ. Mich., Ann Harbor, Mich., 1964, PhD, 1967. Ordained priest and deacon Episcopal Ch., 1984. 6th grade tchr. Episc. Acad., Phila., 1953; 7th grade tchr. Woodlawn Elem. Sch., Augusta, Ga., 1955; 10th grade tchr. Greenbrier Mil. Sch., Lewisburg, W.Va., 1956—57; tchr. jr. coll. Caney (Ky.) Coll., 1957; H.S. tchr. Evart (Mich.) H.S., 1957—58, Zeeland (Mich.) H.S., 1955—62; prof. Eng. Ind. Univ. of Pa., Ind., Pa., 1967—93. With U.S. Army, 1953—55. Republican. Episc. Avocations: reading, painting, walking. Home: 4770 W Pk Rd New Era MI 49446 Business E-Mail: ghh4000@voyger.net.

GRUBB, DAVID H., construction company executive; b. Jan. 22, 1936; married BSCE, Princeton U.; MSCE, Stanford U. With Swinerton and Walberg Co., San Francisco, 1964—, then exec. v.p. Structural divsn., exec. v.p. ops., pres., also bd. dirs.; pres. Swinerton Inc., 1993-96, CEO and chmn. bd. Chmn. bd. Swinerton Builders. Office: Swinerton Incorp 260 Townsend St San Francisco CA 94107-1790

GRUBB, DONALD HARTMAN, paper industry company executive; b. West Chester, Pa., Oct. 22, 1924; s. Donald C. and Bessie (Hanthorne) G.; m. Jean Louise Flounders, Sept. 7, 1946; children: Donna Jean (Mrs. Robert Kanich), Deborah Anne (Mrs. James R. Jackson), Donald Philip. BA, U. Pa., 1949; MA, Am. U., 1954; postgrad., NYU, 1963-64. With U.S. Treasury Dept., Washington, 1949-57, recruitment officer, 1951-53, dir. personnel, 1953-57; mgr. personnel Westvaco Corp., N.Y.C., 1957-59, regional adminstrv. mgr. Hoboken, N.J., 1959-61, mgr. sales, 1961-64; asst. to v.p. Huyck Corp., Stamford, Conn., 1964, v.p. adminstrn. and mktg., 1969-70, exec. v.p., 1970-73, pres., dir., chief exec. officer, 1973-81; chmn. BTR Paper Group, 1981-82; pres. Gedon Enterprises, 1982—; v.p., gen. mgr. Formex Co. of Can., Kentville, N.S., 1965-67; also dir.; v.p., gen. mgr. Huyck Formex Co. of U.S., Greeneville, Tenn., 1967-69. Mgr. Grubb Assocs., LLC dba Fasteners Supply of Goldsboro; retired dir. various cos. in U.S. and U.K. Bd. dirs. Blanchard-Fraser Meml. Hosp., Kentville, N.S., Can., 1966-67, Wake County Hosp. System, Raleigh, 1983-87, N.C. State U. Pulp and Paper Found.; mem. N.C. State U. Sch. Engring. Foun., N.C. State U. Sch. Humanities Found. Served with AUS, 1943-46. Mem. Raleigh C. of C. (dir. 1976-78), Phi Beta Kappa. Presbyterian. Personal E-mail: dongrubb@earthlink.net.

GRUBB, GEOFFREY JOSEPH, academic administrator, religious studies educator; s. Francis Charles and Mary L. Grubb; m. Jenna Marie Giudici, Nov. 18, 1978; children: Gretchen Giudici Grubb Sabin, Geoffrey Francis, Marcus Emmanuel. AB, St. Louis U., 1974, PhD, 1986; MA, Cath. U. Am., 1977. Chairperson dept. religion Nerinx Hall, Webster Groves, Mo., 1977—79; prof. religious studies Lourdes Coll., Sylvania, Ohio, 1985—, dean Sch. Arts and Scis., 2001—, interim v.p. for academic affairs, 2003—05. Mem.: Coll. Theology Soc., Cath. Theol. Soc. Am., Alpha Sigma Nu, Phi Beta Kappa. Roman Catholic. Avocation: genealogy. Office: Lourdes College 6832 Convent Blvd Sylvania OH 43560 Office Phone: 419-824-3818.

GRUBB, ROBERT L., JR., neurosurgeon; b. Charlotte, N.C., May 9, 1940; MD, U. N.C., 1965. Intern Barnes Hosp., St. Louis, 1965-66, resident in gen. surgery, 1966-67, resident in neurosurgery, 1969-73; fellow NIH, Bethesda, Md., 1968-69; mem. staff Barnes-Jewish Hosp., St. Louis, St. Louis Children's Hosp.; prof. neurosurgery Washington U., St. Louis. Fellow ACS; mem. Am. Acad. Neurol. Surgery, AANS, CNS, SNS. Office: Washington U Sch Medicine 660 S Euclid Ave Box 8057 Saint Louis MO 63110-1010 Office Phone: 314-362-3567. Business E-Mail: grubbr@nsurg.wustl.edu.

GRUBB, STEVEN CARL, music educator; b. Stockton, Calif., May 25, 1949; s. Jack Gordon and Edna Mae Grubb; m. Shelly Sneed (div.); 1 child, Kevin Robert; m. Helen Vivian Grubb. AA, Medesto Jr. Coll., 1970; BA, Calif. State U., Hayward, 1972, MA, 1976. Dir. ch. music Grace Luth. Ch., Modesto, Calif., 1971—; chmn. organ dept. Modesto Jr. Coll., Calif., 1991—. Founding bd. dir. Townsend Opera Players, Modesto, Calif., 1981—89. Mem.: Music Tchr.'s Assn. (v.p. 1985), Am. Guild Organists (dean 1995), Alpha Gamma Sigma (Superior Instr. award 1983, Outstanding Tchr. award 1992). Office: 3709 Rexford Dr Modesto CA 95356-1833

GRUBB, WILLIAM FRANCIS XAVIER, consumer products company executive, marketing professional; b. N.Y.C., Aug. 11, 1944; s. William Martin and Eileen F. (Donnelly) G.; m. Eileen B. O'Leary, Apr. 4, 1964; children: Catherine E., William M., Kerri A., Christopher M. BA in Econs., Fordham U., 1966; MBA in Mktg. and Fin., Seton Hall U., 1972. bd. dirs. several privately-held cos. Mktg. and sales exec. Black & Decker, Towson, Md., 1968-79; v.p. mktg. Atari, Sunnyvale, Calif., 1979-81; chmn., pres. New West Mktg., Mountain View, Calif., 1981; pres., chief exec. officer, chmn. Imagic, Los Gatos, Calif., 1981-84; exec. v.p. Dataspeed, 1984-85; pres. Axlon Inc., 1985-86; exec. v.p., gen. mgr. Worlds of Wonder, Inc., Freemont, Calif., 1986-87; pres., chief exec. The Complete PC, San Jose, Calif., 1987-93; CEO, ICTV Inc., Los Gatos, Calif., 1994-96; CEO Millenia Software Inc., Saratoga, Calif., 1996—; pres. Toolz Ltd., Palo Alto, Calif., 1998-99; CEO Grubb Enterprises LLC, Pawleys Island, S.C., 1999—. Bd. regents Holy Names Coll. Office: Grubb Enterprises LLC 93 Rookery Trl Pawleys Island SC 29585-5266 Home: 109 Black Duck Rd Pawleys Island SC 29585-5266 Personal E-mail: wfxgrubb@aol.com.

GRUBBS, MISTY D., music educator; b. Auburn, Ind., July 14, 1974; d. Robert W. and Jerilyn A. Farver; m. James C. Grubbs, May 17, 1996; 1 child, Clay Cecil. B, Ind. State U., 1996; M, U. Ky., 2003. Band dir. Thomas Edison Mid. Sch., Indpls., 1996—97, Westfield H.S., 1997—98; band and choir dir. Speedway Jr. High, 1999—2001; band dir. Beaumont Mid. Sch., Lexington, Ky., 2001—02; orch. dir. Clark County Schools, 2002—04; choir dir. Bourbon County Sch., 2004—. Mem.: Music Educators Nat. Conf. Home: 3840 Plantation Dr Lexington KY 40514 Personal E-mail: misteryd@msn.com.

GRUBBS, R(OBERT) HOWARD, lawyer; b. Wilkinsburg, Pa., Mar. 28, 1946; s. Jack H. and Margaret Charlotte (Weaver) G.; m. Mary Jo Grubbs; 1 child, Margaret Elizabeth. BA, Denison U., 1968; JD, U. SC, 1977. Bar: SC 1977, NC 1985, US Dist. Courts SC, US Ct. Appeals 4th Cir. Assoc. McKay, Sherill, Walker & Townsend, Columbia, SC, 1977-81; ptnr. McKay, McKay, Grubbs & Nunn, Columbia, 1981-85; assoc. Womble Carlyle Sandridge & Rice PLLC, Winston-Salem, NC, 1985-91, mem., 1991—, chair environ. law & toxic tort litig. practice group. Sgt. U.S. Army, 1968-71. Mem.: ABA (litig. sect., torts and ins. sect.), Am. Arbitration Assn. (panel arbitrators), Def. Rsch. Inst. (environ. concerns com.), Richland County Bar Assn., SC Bar Assn., NC Bar Assn. (environ. & natural resources sect.). Office: Womble Carlyle Sandridge & Rice PLLC PO Box 10208 Greenville SC 29603-0208 Office Phone: 864-255-5413. Office Fax: 864-255-5493. Business E-Mail: hgrubbs@wcsr.com.

GRUBBS, ROBERT W., computer services company executive; Grad., U. Mo. Joined Anixter Internat. Inc., 1978; pres. Anixter U.S.A.; pres., CEO, Anixter Inc. subs. Anixter Internat. Inc., 1994—98, Anixter Internat. Inc., 1998—, bd. dirs., 1997—. Former dir. A. M. Castle & Co., 2000. Office: Anixter Internat Inc 2301 Patriot Blvd Glenview IL 60025-8020

GRUBBS, SUSAN KYLE, language educator; b. Roanoke, Va., Sept. 30, 1964; d. Leonard Helm and Elizabeth Anne (Brinkman) Grubbs. BA in Spanish, East Carolina U., 1986. Tchr. Spanish Burnt Hills (NY) Continuing Edn.; tchr. Spanish and French Northwood Elem., Jacksonville, NC; tchr. Spanish Halifax (Va.) HS. Author: numerous poems. Fundraising vol. Diabetic Assn., Lowell, Mass.; pres. resident coun. Lowell Health Care Nursing Home. Avocations: reading, travel, languages, music, singing. Home: 19 Varnum St Lowell MA 01850

GRUBE, ELIZABETH, investment company executive; b. Indpls., 1917; d. Emery Warner and Jessie (Foster) Hanes; m. William F. Grube, Mar. 15, 1937; children: Carol Buck, F. William. Student, Consol. Bus. Coll., 1936, Ind. U.-Purdue U., Indpls., 1984. Pres. Prospect Investment Co. Bd. dirs. Indpls. Water Co., IWC Resources Corp., Indpls. Bd. dirs. Jameson Camp for Children, Indpls., 1981—, Greenwood Village South, Indpls., 1982—; mem. Rep. Senatorial Inner Circle, Washington, 1984. Methodist. Avocation: travel. Home: 285 Celtic Cir Greenwood IN 46143-2458

GRUBE, KARL BERTRAM, judge; b. Elmhurst, Ill., Jan. 13, 1946; s. Karl Ludwig and Gerturde (Bertram) G.; m. Mary B. Harr, May 4, 1974 (div. Aug. 1991); m. Julia Ross, Dec. 28, 1998. BSBA, Elmhurst Coll., 1967; JD, Stetson U., 1970; M in Judicial Studies, U. Nev., 1992. Asst. pub. defender State of Fla., Clearwater, 1970-73, county ct. judge St. Petersburg, 1977—; pvt. practice Seminole, Fla., 1973-76; city atty. City of Redington Beach, Fla., 1975-76. Asst. dean Fla. Jud. Coll., Tallahassee, 1984-85; faculty mem., course coord., mem. faculty coun. Nat. Jud. Coll., chair faculty coun., 2000—; mem. Nat. Hwy. Traffic Safety Jud. Tng. Implementation Bd. Contbr. articles to profl. jours. Dir. Pinellas Comprehensive Addiction Svcs., Clearwater, 1982-88. Jud. fellow U.S. Dept. Transp., 1998, Nat. Hwy. Traffic Safety Adminstn., 1999. Mem. ABA (conf. chmn. divsn. jud. adminstrn. 1992, del. to jud. divsn. coun. 1997—, Dedicated Svc. award 1991, Gov.'s Commendation, N.C. 2000, Nev. 2001), Nat. Jud. Coll. (mem. faculty coun. 1998-2003, chmn. 2001), Nat. Highway Traffic Safety (adminstrn. jud. outreach liaison 2003-), Fla. Bar Assn. (civil rule com.), Colo. Bar Assn., Fla. Conf. County Ct. Judges (pers. com. 1984-85), Rolls Royce Owner's Club (editor 1982-84). Lutheran. Avocations: collecting fountain pens, collecting antique watches, auto restoration. Office: Pinellas County Ct 501 1st Ave N Ste A212 Saint Petersburg FL 33701-3732 Office Phone: 727-582-7880.

GRUBE, REBECCA SUE, elementary school administrator, educator, consultant; b. Lancaster, Pa., June 27, 1945; d. Warren Landis and Ruth Rebecca (Hackman) Newcomer; m. Terry Wayne Grube, Aug. 27, 1966; children: T. David, Joy Lynn, Matthew Warren. Student, Juniata Coll., 1963-65; BA, Franklin and Marshall Coll., 1976; MEd, Millersville U., 1979; postgrad., Temple U. Cert. spl. edn., neurolinguistic programmer. Grad. asst. Millersville U., Pa., 1978-79; tchr. gifted and learning disabled Sch. Dist. of Lancaster, 1979-80; tchr. pvt. sch. Lancaster, 1980-81; elem. tchr. Lancaster Country Day Sch., 1981-85, tchr. resource room, 1985-90, chmn. elem. lang. arts curriculum, 1985-88, mem. curriculum com., 1986-87, tchr. psychology, 1989—, dir. spl. projects, 1990-91, head lower sch., 1991—. Instr. Franklin and Marshall Coll., 1991; pvt. practice ednl. cons., tutor, Lancaster, 1981—; dir. program Tchg. Talented and Outstanding Pupils for Success, 1987, 88—; instr. Performance Learning Systems, 1987—, Wilkes Coll., 1987—. Contbr. articles to profl. quars.; author rsch. report. Pres. bd. dirs. Contact Lancaster, 1986, chairperson support workers, 1987-88; mem. Listening Ear, Parents of Adoptive Children Orgn., 1981-85, Martin Luther King Scholarship Fund, Janus L.D. Sch.; mem. Leadership Pa., 1990. Fellow Christa McAulife U.S. Dept. Edn., 1988-89, Leadership Lancaster, 1989; recipient award Lancaster Assn. Retarded Citizens, 1978-79, cert. of appreciation AFL-CIO Cmty. Svcs., 1983, CONTACT award City of Lancaster, 1988, Literacy award for Tchg. Talented and Outstanding Pupils for Success, Lancaster-Lebanon Reading Coun., 1988. Mem. Assn. Supervision and Curriculum, Orton Dyslexia Soc., Assn. for Children with Learning Disabilities (past bd. dirs. Lancaster Lebanon chpt.), Pa. Assn. for Gifted Children, Coun. Exceptional Children, Nat. Assn. for Gifted Children, Ctrl. Pa. Friends of Jazz, Pi Lambda Theta (chmn. Lehman Home Project 1984-86), Delta Kappa Gamma. Republican. Lutheran. Avocations: tennis, walking, piano, drums, reading. Home: PO Box 4036 Lancaster PA 17604-4036 Business E-Mail: grubeb@e-lcds.org.

GRUBEN, WILLIAM CHARLES, economist, writer; b. Sacramento, Calif., Sept. 29, 1943; s. Virginia Dorothy Gruben; m. Maria de Lourdes Flores; children: Adrienne Sigrid, Anna Patricia. PhD, U. Tex., Austin, 1977. Staff economist InterFirst Corp., Dallas, 1975—82; v.p., sr. economist Fed. Res. Bank Dallas, 1982—; dir. Ctr. Latin Am. Economics, Fed. Res. Bank Dallas, 1992—; adj. prof. So. Meth. U., Dallas, 1985—98. Contbr. articles to fin. publs. Achievements include research in Financial Crises, Banking Panics, International Capital Flows, Capital Account Liberalization, Trade And Trade Liberalization. Office: Fed Reserve Bank Dallas 2200 North Pearl St Dallas TX 75201

GRUBER, IRA DEMPSEY, historian, educator; b. Phila., Jan. 6, 1934; married; 3 children. AB, Duke U., 1955, AM, 1959, PhD, 1961. Instr. history Duke U., 1961-62; fellow Inst. Early Am. History and Culture, 1962-65; asst. prof. Occidental Coll., 1965-66; from asst. prof. to assoc. prof., 1966-74; prof. Rice U., Houston, from 1974, now Harris Masterson prof. history, chmn. dept. history, 1983-87. Master Hanszen Coll., Rice U., 1968-73; John F. Morrison prof. U.S. Army Command and Gen. Staff Coll., 1979-80; vis. prof. mil. history U.S. Mil. Acad., 1984-85, 92-93; mem. hist. adv. com. USAF, 1987-91, Dept. Army, 1992-95; trustee Soc. for Mil. History, 1987-95. Author: Lord Howe and Lord George Germain, 1965, The American Revolution as a Conspiracy: The British View, 1969, The Howe Brothers and the American Revolution, 1972, The Education of Sir Henry Clinton, 1990; co-author: Classical Traditions in Early America, 1976, Reconsiderations on the Revolutionary War, 1978, Limits of Loyalty, 1980, Arms and Independence, 1984, Against All Enemies, 1986, America's First Battles, 1986, Warfare in the Western World, 1996; editor: John Peebles American War, 1998; mem. editl. bd. Jour. of Mil. History, 1995—, chair editl. bd., 1999—. Office Phone: 713-348-4947. E-mail: gruber@rice.edu.

GRUBER, JACK, virologist, medical researcher; b. Bklyn., Apr. 18, 1931; s. Harry and Rose (Kramer) Gruber; m. Patricia Ann Mason, June 28, 1964; 1 child, Harry Mason. BS, CUNY, Bklyn., 1954; PhD, U. Ky., 1963. Rsch. asst., lab. instr. dept. microbiology U. Ky., Lexington, 1955-61; rsch. bacteriologist U.S. Army Biol. Labs., Ft. Detrick, Frederick, Md., 1962-63; bacterial immunology microbiologist Med. Scis. Lab., Ft. Detrick, 1963-67, viral immunology microbiologist, 1967-70; microbiologist, rsch. program adminstr. viral biology br. Nat. Cancer Inst., NIH, Bethesda, Md., 1970-72, chief office of program resources and logistics, viral oncology program, 1972-78, asst. chief biol. carcinogenesis br., divsn. cancer etiology, 1978-80, dep. chief biol. carcinogenesis br., divsn. cancer biology, 1980—84, chief, 1984—2003, chief cancer etiology br., divsn. cancer biology, 2003—. Editor (with others): Primates and Human Cancer, 1979; contbr. articles to profl. jours. Achievements include research in and publications on rheumatic fever and group A streptococci; on highly pathogenic bacteria; on development of various arbovirus vaccines; on the role of biological and chemical agents, especially viruses and carcinogenic polycyclic aromatic hydrocarbons in the etiology of human cancer. Office: National Cancer Institute NIH Exec Plz N # 5012 Bethesda MD 20892-0001 Office Phone: 301-496-9740. Business E-Mail: jg65y@nih.gov.

GRUBER, JOHN BALSBAUGH, physics professor; b. Hershey, Pa., Feb. 10, 1935; s. Irvin John and Erla R. (Balsbaugh) G.; m. Judith Anne Higer, June 20, 1961; children: David Powell, Karen Leigh, Mark Balsbaugh. BS, Haverford (Pa.) Coll., 1957; PhD, U. Calif. at Berkeley, 1961. NATO postdoctoral fellow Inst. Tech. Physics, Tech. U. Darmstadt, Germany, 1961-62, gastdozent, 1961-62; asst. prof. physics UCLA, 1962-66; asso. prof. physics Wash. State U., Pullman, 1966-71, prof. chem. physics, 1971-75; asst. dean Wash. State U. (Grad. Sch.), 1968-70, assoc. dean, 1970-72; prof. physics, dean Coll. Sci. and Math., N.D. State U., Fargo, 1975-80; prof. physics and chemistry, v.p. for acad. affairs Portland (Oreg.) State U., 1980-84; prof. physics San Jose State U., 1984—2005, acad. v.p., 1984-86, v.p. devel., 1986, dir. Inst. for Modern Optics, 1992—2005, chmn. dept. physics, 2001—05; prof. rsch. in laser physics Univ. Tex., San Antonio, 2005—. Vis. prof. Joint Ctr. Grad. Study, Richland, Wash., 1964, 65, 66, Ames Lab., Dept. of Energy, Iowa State U., 1976-80; Disting. vis. prof. U.S. Navy Naval Weapons Ctr., China Lake, Calif., 1984-93, Stanford U., 1993-2005; invited lectr., U.S., Can., Europe, 1966—; cons. in laser physics and spectroscopy Aerospace Corp., El Segundo, Calif., 1962-65, Douglas Aircraft and McDonnell Douglas Astronautics Co., Santa Monica, Calif., 1963-69, N.Am. Aviation, Space and Info. Systems, Downey, Calif., 1964-66, Battelle-Northwest, Richland, Wash., 1964-69, Los Alamos (N.Mex.) Sci. Lab., 1969-71, 73-74; mem. task force lunar exploration sci. Apollo, NASA, 1964-69, 71-73; cons. Army Rsch. Lab., Adelphi Ctr., U.S. Army, 1991—, IBM, 1985-90, GTE, 1986-89, Lasergenics, 1986—, Night Vision Lab. U.S. Army, Ft. Belvoir, 1993—, Deltron, 1990-91, Rey Tech Corp., 1998-2002, Laser Sci. and Tech., 1999—, Bicron Corp., 2000—03, Spectragen Corp., 2000, SAIC, 2002-, Battelle, 1994-2003, Aculight Corp., 2003—, Newteck Corp., 2003-05, CACI Techs., 2004; mem. Rare Earth Rsch. Conf. Com., 1976-83, exec. com., 1977-83, sec. bd. dirs., 1979-84; gen. conf. chmn. XIV Internat. Rare Earth Rsch. Conf., 1979, Novel Laser Sources and Materials, 1992; exec. sec. Internat. Frank H. Spedding Award, 1979, 83, Willig award, 1986, Internat. Spencer prize for outstanding contbrn. to sci., 1987, Pres.'s Scholar, 1994-95, Outstanding Achievement awards U.S. Dept. Def., 1995, 96, 98, 01, 02, 03, 04, Nom. U.S. Asst. Sec. Def. (Spl. Ops.), 1986-87; chmn. U.S. Navy/ASEE Postdoctoral Selection Bd., 1988-2002, U.S. Nat. Inst. Sci. and Tech. Postdoctoral Selection Bd., 1989-91; mem. rev. panel U.S. Navy/ASEE Grad. Fellowship Program, 1990-2002; chmn., mem. NASA/ASEE program rev. bd., 1994-98; chmn. Internat. Conf. on Novel Laser Sources and Applications, San Jose, Calif., 1993, chmn. Battelle U.S. Dept. Def. Scholarship Program, 1994-2001; mem. Battelle Sci. Bd. for selection of grad. scholarship fellows, 1998-99; vis. scholar Stanford U., 1993-2005, Darpha, 2005—. Contbr. articles to profl. jours., chpts. to books; holder numerous patents in laser sci. and tech. Trustee Symphony Bd. Fargo-Moorhead Symphony Orch., 1978-80; mem. N.D. State Bd. PTA; chmn. Univ., Coll. and Pub. Sch. Rels. Bd., 1979-80; active Boy Scouts Am.; trustee Pullman Pub. Libr., 1973-75, N.D. Symphony Orchs. Assn., 1978-80; mem. planning commn. City of Pullman, 1972-75; bd. dirs. Westminster Found., 1982-84. Recipient Outstanding Merit and Performance award San Jose State U., 1990, San Jose State Pres.'s Scholar, 1994-95, Dist. Tchr./scholar award, 1996, 97, 99, award in the field of lasers and electro-optics U. Chgo., 1995, Citation for Svc. and Achievement Dept. of Def., 1996, Award for Rsch. into night vision devices U.S. Army, 1997, Outstanding World Leadership in Sci. award Acad. Scis., Poland, 1998, Outstanding Rsch. award San Jose State Univ., 2005; grantee AEC-ERDA, 1963-75, NSF, 1966-72, 76-78, 92—, U.S. Army Rsch. Office, Durham, 1979-80, Am. Chem. Soc. Petroleum Rsch. Funds, 1979-80, Dept. Energy, 1979-84, Dept. Def., 1984—, Office Naval Rsch., 1987—, Office Naval Tech., 1988-93, Dept. Def., DARPA, 1998—; fellow NASA Ames Lab., 1993-95; vis. scholar Stanford U., 1993—. Fellow Am. Soc. Engring. Edn. (disting.), Am. Phys. Soc. (chmn. nat. mtg. sessions), Am. Acad. Spectral Scis.; mem. AAAS, IEEE (sec. lasers and electro-optics 1995-96), NSF (reviewer and panel mem. divsn. material sci. 1994—), N.Y. Acad. Scis., N.D. Acad. Sci., Oreg. Acad. Sci., Acad. Scis. of Ukraine, Nat. Acad. Scis. (com. on lasers and electro-optics), Coun. Colls. Arts and Scis., Optical Soc. No. Calif. (v.p. 1992, pres. 1993), Lasers and Electro-optics Soc. (mem. program com. nat. meeting 1995), Internat. Soc. Optical Engring. (bd. dirs. 1993), Phi Beta Kappa, Sigma Xi, Phi Kappa Phi, Sigma Pi Sigma, Phi Sigma Iota. Office: Univ Tex at San Antonio Dept Physics and Astronomy San Antonio TX 78249-0601 Business E-Mail: jbgruber@utsa.edu.

GRUBER, JOHN EDWARD, editor, historian, photographer; b. Chgo., May 18, 1936; s. Edward David and Leah Elizabeth (Diehl) G.; m. Bonnie Jean Barstow, May 12, 1962; children: Richard J., Timothy J. BA in Journalism, U. Wis., 1959, postgrad., 1981-84. Editor, writer U. Wis., Madison, 1960-95; editor Vintage Rails, Waukesha, Wis., 1995-99. Author: Focus on Rails, 1989, (pamphlet) Madison's Pioneer Buildings, 1987; co-author: Caboose, 2001, (posters) Travel by Train, 2002, Railway Photography, 2003; acting editor Rail News, 1999; also articles; contbr. photographs to Trains mag., 1960—; contbg. editor: Classic Trains, 2000—; coord. Representatives of Railroad Work 2003—. Dir. Historic Madison, Inc., 1981-89. Recipient Nat. Award in R.R. History for photography Rwy. and Locomotive Hist. Soc., 1994; James J. Hill Rsch. grant Hill Reference Libr., 1986. Mem. Mid-Continent Railway Hist. Soc. (bd. dirs. 1984-97, pres. 1988-89, sec. 1990-95, v.p. 1995-97, editor Mid-Continent Railway Gazette 1982-99), Ctr. for R.R. Photography and Art (pres. 1997—). Home: 1430 Drake St Madison WI 53711-2211 Office Phone: 608-251-5785. E-mail: jgruber@execpc.com.

GRUBERG, MARTIN, political science professor; b. N.Y.C., Jan. 28, 1935; s. Benjamin and Mollie (Stolnitz) G.; m. Rosaline Kurfirst, Mar. 25, 1967 (dec. 1980); m. Humaira Sayeed, Aug. 15, 1983. BA, CCNY, 1955; PhD, Columbia U., 1963. Agt.-adjudicator Passport Agy., Dept. State, N.Y.C, 1960-61; tchr. social studies Pelham (N.Y.) High Sch., 1961-62; instr. polit. sci. CUNY-Hunter Coll., 1961-62; tchr. social studies James Monroe and Seward Park High Schs., N.Y.C., 1962-63; asst. prof. polit. sci. U. Wis., Oshkosh, 1963-66, assoc. prof., 1966-69, prof., chmn. dept., 1969-72, dir. pre-law program, 1966-69, 83—, coord. criminal justice program, 1983-87. Author: Women in American Politics, 1968, A Case Study in U.S. Urban Leadership: The Incumbency of Milwaukee Mayor Henry Maier, 1996, A History of Winnebago County Government, 1998, Introduction to Law, 2003; newspaper column: Women: Our Largest Minority, The Paper for Ctrl. Wisc., 1970-71, Spotlight on Women for Oshkosh Northwestern, 1971-73; Broadcast 16 weeks Civil Rights Revolution, Wis. State FM Network, 1974; editor: Wis. Polit. Scientist, 1986-91; contbr. articles to encys., profl. jours. Pres. Oshkosh Human Rights Coun., 1966-68; v.p. Winnebago chpt. NOW, 1970-71, sec. Oshkosh chpt., 1980-81, pres., 1981-83; pres. Women's Caucus of Midwest Polit. Scientists, 1980-81; pres. Fox Valley ACLU, 1985—. Recipient Am. Legion Aux. Americanism award, 1949, Buckvar award, 1955, Steigman award, 1955; N.Y. State scholar, 1952; Columbia grantee, 1961, 62, Wis. Regents' rsch. grantee, 1964-70, 73-75. Mem. AAUP (state sec. 1975-81, pres.-elect 1981-82, 91-92, pres. 1982-83, 92-93), Am. Polit. Sci. Assn., Midwest Polit. Sci. Assn., Wis. Polit. Sci. Assn. (pres. 1974-75), Law and Soc. Assn., Acad. Criminal Justice Scis., Candlelight Club, Optimists. Home: 2121 Oregon St Oshkosh WI 54902-7058 Office: U Wis Clow Hall Oshkosh WI 54901 Office Phone: 920-424-0146. Business E-Mail: gruberg@uwosh.edu.

GRUBICH, DOUGLAS LEO, cartoonist, writer; s. Leo Francis Grubich and Audrey Carol Hedman. AA, Otero Jr. Coll., La Junta, Colo., 1982. Staff cartoonist High Plains Trader, La Junta, 1980—82; cartoonist Ordway (Colo.) New Era, 1984; owner Grubich Cartoons Prodns., Ordway, Colo., 1984—92; T-shirt designer Crowley County Days Fair Bd., Ordway, Colo., 1993—99. Asst. art instr. Otero Jr. Coll., 1982; window muralist Crowley County Dem. Party, Ordway, 1990; artist cons. Crowley County C. of C., Ordway, 1992. Comic strip series, That Kid Show, 1984—92, Fuzzies, 1999—2000; author: Beyond the Haunted Sky, 2002. Donor muralist La Junta Theater Entertainment, 1981; donor sign painter Crowley County Fair Bd., 1989—90; census enumerator U.S. Dept. Commerce, Ordway, 1990. With USAF, 1978. Democrat. Avocations: antiques, videotaping, comic book collecting, model starships, digital video disk recording.

GRUBIN, SHARON ELLEN, lawyer, former federal judge; b. Newark, Feb. 9, 1949; d. Harold and Blanche (Dultz) G. AB with honors, Smith Coll., 1970; JD with honors in Legal Writing and Analysis, Boston U., 1973. Bar: N.Y. 1974, U.S. Dist. Ct. (so. and ea. dists.) N.Y. 1974, U.S. Ct. Appeals (2nd cir.) 1974. Litigator White & Case, N.Y.C., 1973-84; judge U.S. Dist. Ct. (so. dist.) N.Y., N.Y.C., 1984-2000; gen. counsel Metroplitan Opera, N.Y.C., 2000—. Chair 2d Cir. Task Force on Gender, Racial and Ethnic Fairness in the Cts.; lectr. NYU Sch. Law, Yale Law Sch., Bklyn. Law Sch., N.Y. Law Sch.; dir., sec., exec. com. Lawyers' Com. on Violence, Inc. Author: (with others) Advocacy-The Art of Pleading a Cause, 1985, Removal, Federal Civil Practice, 1989, and supplement, 1993; spkr. seminars in field. Mem. ABA (chair spl. projects com. 1996-97, nat. conf. fed. trial judges, jud. adminstrn. divsn.), Nat. Assn. Women Judges (chair fed. gender bias com., publicity and pub. affairs com., newsletter com.), Fed. Bar Coun. (trustee, exec. com., chair nominating com. 1994, v.p. 1990-94, award com. 1988-94, com. on 2d cir. cts. 1982-96, long-range planning com. 1992-96), N.Y. State Bar Assn. (exec. com., nominations com., fed. cts. task force, comml. and fed. litig. sect.), N.Y. State Assn. Women Judges (bd. dirs.), Assn. of Bar of City of N.Y. (long-range planning com., chair nominating com. 1995—, chair spl. com. on legal history 1994-96, chair spl. com. on Orison S. Marden Meml. lectrs., chair 1994-96, exec. com. 1990-94, spl. com. on gender bias in fed. cts. 1991-94, coun. on jud. adminstrn. 1986-90, prof. and jud. ethics com. 1986-89, nominating com. 1984-85, 95-96, com. on jud. 1982-83, chair young lawyers com. 1979-81, com. on entertainment law, 2001-), Am. Judicature Soc. (editl. com. 1994-97). Office: Metropolitan Opera Lincoln Ctr New York NY 10023

GRUBISICH, TOM, screenwriter, editor, writer; b. Peoria, Ill., Dec. 31, 1936; s. Michael Bernard and Mary (Pintar) G.; m. Marilyn J. Burson, Oct. 30, 1965 (div. 1982); children: Emily, Miranda. Student, Spalding Inst., Peoria, 1950-54; BS, Marquette Univ., Milw., 1958. Copy boy New Yorker Mag., 1959; reporter Worcester (Mass.) Telegram, 1959-61; copy editor New York Post, 1961-64; reporter New York Herald Tribune, 1964-66; editor, reporter Washington Post, 1966-81; founding editor The Connection Newspapers, Reston, Va., 1981-94; exec. editor Times Community Newspapers, Reston, Va., 1995-96; resident adviser Press of Slovak Republic, Bratislava, 1996—97; mng. editor Digital City/America Online, 1997—2001. Author: Reston: First 20 Years, 1985, contbr. Variety, 2003—, On-Line Journalism Rev., 2005; op-ed articles in Washington Post and mags. Co-founder Planned Cmty. Archives, George Mason U., 1986, Robert E. Simon Jr. Children's Ctr., 1988, Reston Hist. Trust, 1997; pres. Wash.-Balt. Newspaper Guild, 1976. Recipient In My Backyard award Fairfax United Way, 1993, Best of Reston award Reston Interfaith and Greater Reston C. of C., 1992, Citation of Merit Fairfax Fedn. Citizens Assn., 1994; Wash. Post fellow Duke U., 1979; 10-yr. honoree The No. Va. Women's Ctr., 1995. Mem. D.C. chpt. Soc. Profl. Journalists (Dateline award/editing, writing 1987, 91, 93, Disting. Svc. in Local Journalism award 1987), Va. Press Assn. (editl., writing 1st prize 1987), Suburban Newspapers Am. (Cmty. Svc. award 1987, editl. writing 1995), Ctr. for Fgn. Journalists (vol. faculty, 10th anniversary honoree 1995). Roman Catholic. Office: PMB 123 1247 Lincoln Blvd Santa Monica CA 90401-1711 Office Phone: 310-917-1197.

GRUBMAN, ALLEN J., lawyer; b. Bklyn., Dec. 30, 1942; BBA, CCNY, 1965; JD, Bklyn. Law Sch., 1967. Bar: N.Y. 1968. Ptnr. Grubman Indursky P.C., N.Y.C., 1974—. Office: Grubman Indursky 152 W 57th St New York NY 10019-3310

GRUCA, PAWEL PIOTR, neuroradiologist; b. Warsaw, Oct. 13, 1959; came to U.S., 1977, naturalized, 1996; s. Jerzy and Stefania Maria (Swigon) G.; m. Renata Maria Olejnik, June 15, 1989 (div. May 1993). BS in Radiologic Tech. cum laude, St. Mary's Coll., Orchard Lake, Mich., 1981; DO, Coll. Osteo. Medicine, 1987. Diplomate Am. Osteo. Bd. Radiology. Intern Muskegon (Mich.) Gen. Hosp., 1987-88; instr., resident Mich. State U., East Lansing, 1988-92; fellow in neuroradiology Henry Ford Hosp., Detroit, 1992-94; pvt. practice radiology and neuroradiology, Pottsville, Pa., 1994-95, Aberdeen, S.D., 1995—; asst. med. dir. dept. radiology Avera St. Luke's, 1995—; med. dir. health sci. program in radiologic tech. Presentation Coll., Aberdeen, 1998—. Vis. lectr. neuroradiology Temple U., Phila., 1994; lectr. diagnostic radiology S.D. State U., 1996; lectr. ultrasound S.D. Soc. Radiologic Technologists Conv., 1997. Mem. AMA, Am. Coll. Radiology, Am. Osteo. Coll. Radiology, Radiol. Soc. N.Am., Am. Soc. Neuroradiology, Am. Soc. Spine Radiology, Am. Soc. Pediat. Neuroradiology, S.D. State Med. Assn. Republican. Roman Catholic. Home: 1006 N 2d St Apt 5 Aberdeen SD 57401-2316 Office: St Luke's Midland Radiology 305 S State St Aberdeen SD 57401-4527

GRUCCI BUTLER, DONNA, fireworks company executive; d. Felix and Concetta Grucci; m. Philip Butler; children: Jeffrey, Danielle. Pres. Fireworks by Grucci, Brookhaven, NY, 2001—. Prodr.: (firework prodn.) Bi-Centennial Celebration on Charles River for Arthur Fielder's Boston Pops, 1976, Six consecutive Presdl. Inaugurations, 1981, 1985, 1989, 1993, 1997, 2001, Bklyn. Bridge, 1983, Centennial Celebration of Statue of Liberty, 1986, Wedding of Prince Abu Dhabi, Olympics, 1981, 1985, 2002, World's Fair, 1982, 1984, 1993; spokesperson for firework tours Wisk Bright Nights, Lever Brothers', Merit Harbor Lights, Philip Morris. Tchr. Cath. religious edn. classes to 1st graders; mem. local C. of C. events, local Head Start Programs; vol. fundraiser Am. Heart Assn.; established two scholarships Bellport H.S., 1992. Recipient Gold medal, Monte Carlo Internat. Fireworks Competition,

1979, Ellis Island medal of Honor for Outstanding Achievements in Arts and Entertainment Field, Nat. Ethnic Coalition Orgns., 1995. Avocations: gardening, reading. Office: Fireworks By Grucci 1 Grucci Ln Brookhaven NY 11719 E-mail: info@grucci.com.

GRUCHACZ, ROBERT S., real estate executive; b. Bloomfield, N.J., May 15, 1929; s. Stanley A. and Mae (Zalenski) G.; m. LaVerne T. Stein, Mar. 2, 1957; children— Robert S., Thomas A., Christopher J. BS, Seton Hall U., 1950; MBA, NYU, 1971; student, Advanced Mgmt. Program, Harvard U., 1973. C.P.A., N.J. With Arthur Young & Co., C.P.A.'s, 1955-58, Sterling Drug Inc., N.Y.C., 1958-65; controller Nabisco Inc., 1965-72, asst. to pres., 1973-74, 76—, v.p., 1979-84; broker Dunes Mktg. Group and Sea Pines Realty, 1985-2001; exec. v.p. Aurora Products, 1974-76. Served as 1st lt. USAF, 1952-54. Mem. AICPA. Home: 11 Timber Marsh Ln Hilton Head Island SC 29926-2790 Office: 6 Queens Folly Rd Hilton Head Island SC 29928-5110 E-mail: bobgruchacz@aol.com.

GRUDEN, JON, professional football coach; b. Sandusky, Ohio, Aug. 17, 1963; Student, U. Dayton. Asst. coach U. Tenn., 1986-87, U. Southeast Mo., 1988-89, San Francisco 49ers, 1990, U. Pitts., 1991, Green Bay Packers, 1992-94; offensive coord. Phila. Eagles, 1994-97; head coach Oakland Raiders, 1998—2002, Tampa Bay Buccaneers, 2002—. Office: Tampa Bay Buccaneers One Buccaneer Pl Tampa FL 33607*

GRUE, SETH MICHAEL, educational association administrator; b. Mass., July 23, 1975; s. Beverly Ann and Robert Francis Grue. BS, Roger Williams U., 1994—98; M in edn., U. of Tex. - Austin, 1998—2000. Asst. hall coord. U. of Tex. - Austin, 1998—2000, hall coord., 2000—01; residence life coord. Ga. Inst. of Tech., Atlanta, 2001—04; assitant dir. of residence life Emerson Coll., Boston, 2004—. Recipient Seth M. Grue Resident Appreciation award, Ga. Tech, Residence Hall Assn., Outstanding New Profl., Ga. Coll. Pers. Assn., 2004.

GRUEBELE, MARTIN, chemistry professor, biophysics profefssor; b. Stuttgart, Federal Republic of Germany, Jan. 10, 1964; came to U.S., 1980; s. Helmut and Edith Victoria (Berner) G.; m. Nancy Makri, July 10, 1992; 2 children. BS in Chemistry, U. Calif., Berkeley, 1984, PhD in Chemistry, 1988. Rsch. fellow Calif. Inst. Tech., Pasadena, 1989-92; asst. prof. dept. chemistry U. Ill., Urbana, 1992-98, assoc. prof., 1998-99, prof. chemistry and biophysics, 1999—2000, prof. chemistry, physics, and biophysics, 2000—01, Alumni Scholar prof. chemistry, prof. physics, biophysics and computational biology, 2002—. Sr. editor Jour. Phys. Chemistry; mem. editl. bd. Jour. Chem. Physics., Chem. Phys. Lett., Ann. Rev. Phys. Chem., Chem. Physics. Recipient New Faculty award Dreyfus Found., 1992, Nat. Young Investigator award NSF, 1994, Coblentz award, 2000, Wilhelm Friedrich Bessel Prize, Von Humbaldt Soc., 2005; fellow IBM, 1986-87, Dow Chem. Co., 1987-88, David and Lucile Packard Found., 1994, Sloan fellow, 1997; Cottrell scholar, 1995, Camille and Henry Dreyfus scholar, 1998, Alfred P. Sloan fellow, 1998; Univ. scholar U. Ill., 1998; Baker symposium lectr. Cornell U., 2004. Fellow: Am. Phys. Soc.; mem.: Biophys. Soc., Am. Chem. Soc., Sigma Xi. Achievements include research of theoretical and experimental studies of novel transient molecular species, studies in laser-control of chemical reactions and molecular vibrational relaxation, as well as fast time-resolved protein folding dynamics. Office: U Ill Dept Chemistry Box 5-6 600 S Mathews Ave Urbana IL 61801-3602

GRUEN, DAVID HENRY, financial analyst; b. Buffalo, Aug. 12, 1929; s. Edward Charles and Florence (Knoche) G.; m. Joan Willard, Jan. 3, 1976; children by previous marriage: David E., Stephen P., Cathryn E., Edward Charles II, William A. BA, Cornell U., 1951, MBA, 1954. C.P.A., N.Y. Sr. accountant Arthur Andersen & Co., N.Y.C., 1954-59; asst. treas. Marine Midland Banks, Inc., 1959-60, asst. v.p., 1960-63, v.p., treas., 1963-69; sr. v.p. Marine Midland Bank-Western, 1969-74; sr. v.p., treas. Marine Midland Banks, Inc., Buffalo, 1974-80; sr. v.p., gen. auditor, 1980-85; cons. Gruen Assocs., Buffalo, 1986—; v.p., chief fin. officer Niagara Envelope Group Inc., Buffalo, N.Y., 1986-89. Served from 2d lt. to 1st lt. USAF, 1951-53. Mem. Am. Inst. C.P.A.s, Tax Execs. Inst., N.Y. Soc. C.P.A.s, Fin. Execs. Inst. Home: 34 Middlesex Rd Buffalo NY 14216-3616

GRUEN, GERALD ELMER, psychologist, educator; b. Granite City, Ill., July 19, 1937; s. Elmer George and Velma Pearl G.; m. Karol Jane Selvidge, Mar. 20, 1960; children— Tami Jane, Christy Lynn. BA, So. Ill. U., 1959; MA, U. Ill., 1963, PhD, 1964. Postdoctoral fellow Heinz Werner Inst. of Developmental Psychology, Clark U. and Worcester (Mass.) State Hosp., 1964-66; asst. prof. dept. psychol. scis. Purdue U., West Lafayette, Ind., 1966-69, assoc. prof., 1969-74, prof., 1974—, head dept. psychol. scis., 1987-97. Author: (with T. Wachs) Early Experience and Human Development; contbr. chpt. to The Structuring of Experience, 1977; contbr. articles to profl. jours. Deacon Calvary Baptist Ch., West Lafayette. Recipient USPHS rsch. awards, 1968-71, Nat. Rsch. Svc. award NIMH, 1976-80, Research award Nat. Insts. Child Health and Human Devel., 1981—; recipient Ind. Psychol. Assn. Gordon Barrows award for disting. career contbns., 2000. Fellow APA, Am. Psychol. Soc. (charter mem.); mem. Midwestern Psychol. Assn., Soc. for Rsch. in Child Devel., Sigma Xi. Home: 3738 Westlake Ct West Lafayette IN 47906 Office: Purdue U Psychology Dept West Lafayette IN 47907 Personal E-mail: jjgruen@insightbb.com. Business E-Mail: gruen@psych.purdue.edu.

GRUEN, MARGARET, actress; b. N.Y.C., July 24, 1949; d. Arno G. and Judith (Goldstein) Milenbach. Student, Yale Sch. Drama. Actress. Writer, performer (theatre) Tanya Talks: The Last Jew, 1997, The Young Sophisticate, 1994, What A Wonderful World, 1990, Dracula, 1970; one-woman show: Grenfell's Eccentric Characters; appeared in theatre, TV, and radio prodns., including Uncle Vanya, Garcia Lorca's New York; mem. comedy team The Chamansky Sisters. Mem. Am. Fedn. Television & Radio Artists, Actors Equity Assn., Screen Actors Guild. Office Phone: 917-968-3662. Personal E-mail: gruen_margaret@yahoo.com.

GRUENBERG, ELLIOT LEWIS, electronics engineer and company executive; b. N.Y.C., Mar. 16, 1918; s. Lewis and Sadie (Schoenbrun) G.; m. Ruth Frankel, Apr. 19, 1947. BEE, CCNY, 1938. Engr., inspector U.S. Signal Corps Line Inspection, Newark, N.J., 1939-43; quality control mgr. Tech. Devices, Roseland, N.J., 1943-48; sr. engr. J.H. Bunnell, Bklyn., 1948-51, Freed Radio, N.Y.C., 1951; sr. engr., mgr. W.L. Maxson, N.Y.C., 1951-58; sr. engrng. mgr. Fed. Systems div. IBM, Bethesda, Md., 1958-73; cons. West New York, N.J., 1974-79; chmn. BroadCom, Inc., Secaucus, N.J., 1979-88, also bd. dirs.; chmn., pres. CompFax Corp., West N.Y., N.J., 1988-92; pres. Digital Compression Tech., L.P., N.Y.C., 1993—. Editor: Handbook of Telemetry and Remote Control, 1967; inventor SYNAPZ Microwave Comm., radar, electronic telecomm., telemetry, BGET Secure Comm., DTIC Digital Transmission Bandwidth Compression, Superresonant Digital Modulation and Filtering; patentee in field; contbr. articles to profl. jours. Fellow Am. Inst. Aeronautics and Astronautics (assoc.); mem. IEEE (sr. life mem. 1940—). Democrat. Mem. Ethical Culture. Avocations: puzzles, astronomy, art collecting, artificial intelligence. Home: 6040 Boulevard E Apt 30G West New York NJ 07093-3866

GRUENBERG, MARTIN J., federal agency administrator, lawyer; BA, Princeton U., 1975; JD, Case Western Res. Law Sch., Cleve. Past pro. staff mem. Subcommittee Econ. Stabilization House Com. on Banking, Fin. & Urban Affairs, Washington; past staff dir. Subcommittee on Intern. Fin. & Monetary Policy Senate Banking Com., Washington; staff mem. to sr. counsel Senate Com. on Banking, Housing & Urban Affairs, Washington, 1987—2005; mem., vice chmn. bd. dir. FDIC, Washington, 2005—. Office: FDIC 550 17th St NW Rm 6000 Washington DC 20429-9990

GRUENBERGER, PETER, lawyer; b. Czechoslovakia, May 19, 1937; came to U.S., 1941; s. Leslie and Olga (Zollman) G.; m. Carin Lamm; children: Karen, Richard, Lauren. AB, Columbia U., 1958, LLB, 1961. Bar: N.Y. 1962, U.S. Dist. Ct. (so., ea. and no. dists.) N.Y. 1962, U.S. Ct. Appeals (1st and 2d cirs.) 1963, U.S. Supreme Ct. 1964. Assoc. Hughes, Hubbard & Reed, N.Y.C., 1962-69; ptnr. Weil, Gotshal & Manges, N.Y.C., 1970—, mng. ptnr. Tex. office Houston, 1988-90. Contbr. articles on litigation to profl. jours. Served as 1st lt. U.S. Army, 1961-62. Harlan Fiske Stone scholar, 1959-61. Mem. ABA (chmn. various coms. 1973-75, 79-86, spl. com. on class actions and discovery 1977-86, governing council 1975-78, litigation sect.), Assn. of Bar of City of N.Y. (grievance com. 1975-77). Office: Weil Gotshal & Manges 767 5th Ave Fl Concl New York NY 10153-0119

GRUENDER, RAYMOND W., federal judge, former prosecutor; b. St. Louis, July 5, 1963; BA, Washington U., 1984, MBA, JD, Washington U., 1987. Assoc. Lewis, Rice and Fingersh, 1987—90; ptnr. Thompson Coburn LLP, 1994—2000; asst. U.S. atty., (ea. dist.) Mo. U.S. Dept. State, St. Louis, 1990—94, 2000—01, U.S. atty. (ea. dist) Mo, 2001—04; judge U.S. Ct. Appeals, (8th cir.), 2004—. Office: US Courthouse 111 S Tenth St Saint Louis MO 63102*

GRUENWALD, JAMES HOWARD, association executive, consultant; b. Cin., Aug. 30, 1949; s. Howard Francis and Geraldine Emma (Mueller) G. BS, Xavier U., 1971. Cert. profl. in recreation and leisure svc., Ill. Rep. pub. rels. Cath. Youth Orgn., Cin., 1969—72; sales rep. Spade Trucking Co., Cin., 1972—73; field rep. Ohio Dept. Transport, Columbus, 1973—75; editl., sales rep. Cin. Suburban Newspaper, 1977—79; nat. exec. dir. Say Soccer USA, Cin., 1979—93; co-founder, exec. dir. U.S. Indoor Soccer Orgn., 1985—93; bd. dirs. Buckeye Men's Baseball, Cin., 1982—90, chmn., 1982—86, 1989—90; dir. Amateur Athletic Union, Indpls., 1983—85; nat. membership coord. Am. Youth Soccer Orgn., L.A., 1993—2001; assoc. customer svc. Sam's Club, Loveland, Ohio, 2001—. Cert. trainer Am. Coaches Effectiveness Program, Champaign, Ill., 1983-92. Editor Touchline jour., 1980-92, Parents Guide to Soccer, 1985-92. Bd. dirs. Mid West Soccer Ofcls. Assn., bd. mem., 2003—05; adv. bd. Ch. Parish, Cin., 1974—76. Recipient cmty. svc. award State of Mich., 1986. Mem. Nat. Coun. Youth Sports Dirs., Nat. Recreation and Parks Assn., Mich. Recreation and Parks Assn. (cmty. svc. award 1986), Soc. for Non Profits. Avocations: hiking, reading, writing, teaching, conducting workshops. Home: 1143 Dennis Ln #2 Hamilton OH 45013-3983 Office Phone: 513-677-8341. E-mail: jimmygee94@aol.com.

GRUFT, JAMES HARRIS, physiatrist, educator; b. N.Y.C., Mar. 22, 1954; s. Miriam and Mortimer Gruft; m. Ewa Zofia Osysko, Mar. 12, 1978. BA in Psychology, SUNY Suffern, 1976; MD, George Wash. U. Sch. of Medicine, 1986. Cert. Am. Acad. of Phys. Medicine & Rehab., 1992, Pain Medicine Am. Acad. of Phys. Medicine & Rehab., 2002. Med. dir. pain mgmt. program Marianjoy Rehab. Hosp. and Clinics, Oakbrook Terrace, Ill., 1990—2004; pres. and med. dir. Complete Pain & Rehab. Mgmt., LLC, Hinsdale, Ill., 2003—. Asst. prof. Rush Med. Coll., Chgo., 1990—. Author: (book) Understanding Pain and Healing (Schmerz verstehen und heilen). Named, Best Doctors, 2002, 2003, 2004. Fellow: Am. Acad. Phys. Medicine & Rehab.; mem.: Am. Acad. Pain Medicine, Internat. Assn. for Study of Pain, Dramatist Guild. Avocation: back-packing. Office: Complete Pain & Rehab Mgmt LLC Ste 126E 40 S Clay St Hinsdale IL 60521 Office Phone: 630-920-0015.

GRUHL, ANDREA MORRIS, librarian; b. Ponca City, Okla., Dec. 9, 1939; d. Luther Oscar and Hazel Evangeline (Anderson) Morris; m. Werner Mann Gruhl, July 10, 1965; children: Sonja Krista, Diana Krista. BA, Wesleyan Coll., 1961; MLS, postgrad., U. Md., 1968, postgrad., 1971—73, Johns Hopkins U., 1970—71, Oxford U., 1996. Tchr. Broward County, Fla., U.S. Dept. Def. Montgomery County, Md., 1061—66; libr. Prince Georges County (Md.) Pub. Libr., 1966—68, 1981—83, U. Md., College Park, 1970—72; art. history rschr. Joseph Alsop, Washington, 1972—74; libr. Howard County Pub. Libr., Columbia, Md., 1969—70, 1974—79; European exch. staff Libr. of Congress, Washington, 1982—86; cataloger fed. documents GPO, Washington, 1986—93, supervisory libr., 1993—2001. Women's program adv. com., processing dept. rep. Libr. of Congress, 1983-86, mem. ofcl. Libr. of Congress delegation to Internat. Fedn. Libr. Assn. ann. conf., Munich, 1983, Chgo., 1985; state del. White House Conf. on Librs., 1978, 90. Indexer, editor: Learning Vacations, 3d edit., 1980; editor: Federal Librarian, 1994-99, NCA News & Notes, 2003-04; LCPA Index to Libr. of Congress Info. Bull., 1984. Trustee Howard County (Md.) C.C., 1989-95, Howard County Pub. Libr., Columbia, Md., 1979-87; publ. chmn. LWV Howard County, 1974, bd. dirs., 1996-97, 2005-, sec., 2002-2004, co-pres., 2004-05; bd. dirs. LWV Nat. Capital Area, 2002—; chair Homeland Security Com., 2003—, LWV U.S. Task Force on Civil Liberties, 2004-05; citizens rep. Howard County, exec. bd. Balt. Regional Planning Coun. Libr. com., 1976-79; Friends of Libr., Howard County, pres., 1976; vol. Nat. Gallery Art Libr., Washington, 1978-80. Mem.: ALA (govt. documents roundtable 1986—, fed. libr. round table 1988—, editor 1994—99, IFLA rep. 1996—, v.p. 1997—98, councilor 1997—2001, pres. 1998—99, co-chair coun. caucus 2000—01), Fed. and Armed Forces Librs. Round Table (chmn. constn. and bylaws com. 2001—, Disting. Svc. award 2001), Md. Libr. Assn. (pres. trustee divsn. 1982—83), Libr. Congress Am. Fedn. State, County and Mcpl. Employees Union (program chair 1984—86), Libr. Congress Profl. Assn. (coord. ann. staff art shows 1982—83, chair libr. sci. interest group 1985—87), Art Librs. Soc. N.Am. (coord. mems.' publ. exhbn. 1980—82), Internat. Fedn. Libr. Assns. and Instns. (sect. on cataloging, internat. std. bibliog. description/cartographic materials working gro), Assn. Coll. and Rsch. Librs., DC Libr. Assn. (co-chair mgmt. interest group 1996—97, v.p. 2001—02, pres. 2002—03), Libr. Adminstrn. and Mgmt. Assn. (planning and evaluation libr. svcs. 1996—97), Oxford U. Soc., Md. Assn. C.C. (bd. dirs. 1993—95), UN Assn. Nat. Capital Area Chpt. (Md. tel. chair 1992—94, membership com. 1992—, co-chair endowment com. 2004—), Md. Assn. C.C. Trustees (sec. 1991—92, bd. dirs. 1992—93), Women's Nat. Dem. Club, Beta Phi Mu (pres. Washington Area chpt. 2005—). Democrat. Lutheran. Home: 5990 Jacobs Ladder Columbia MD 21045-3817

GRUHL, JAMES, energy scientist, artist; b. Milw., Apr. 9, 1945; s. Alfred and Helen (Vanderveer) G.; m. Nancy Lee Huston, July 4, 1974; children: Amanda Natalie, Steven Christopher. BS, MS, MIT, 1968, PhD, 1973. Lectr. MIT, 1969-83; rsch. scientist MIT Energy Lab., Cambridge, 1973-83, program mgr., 1978-83, rsch. affiliate, 1984; sci. adv. bd. U.S. EPA, 1986-93; energy cons. U.S. Congress, rsch. insts., internat. energy industries, 1973—. Ednl. counselor MIT, 1978—. Recipient Silver Beaver award Boy Scouts Am., 1986, numerous art awards, 1990—; NSF grantee. Mem. IEEE, AAAS, Math. Programming Soc., MIT Alumni Assn. (officer 1978—), Tau Beta Pi, Eta Kappa Nu. Achievements include research on uncertainties and validity of analytic models, validity of government and industry energy policy models, and climate change models. Office: Gruhl Assocs PO Box 36524 Tucson AZ 85740-6524 E-mail: gruhl1@mindspring.com.

GRULING, KAY ANN, family physician; b. Merrill, Wis., Sept. 28, 1961; d. Robert Herman and Esther Martha (Schulz) G.; m. Timothy Charles Buttke, June 11, 1988; children: Calla Kay, Isaac Friedrich. Student, U. Wis., Wausau, 1982, U. Wis., 1984, Rheinische Frederick-Wilhelms U., Bonn, West Germany, 1984, U. Wis., 1988. Diplomate Am. Bd. Family Practice. Intern and resident in family medicine U. Wis. Wausau Program, 1988-91; family physician Marshfield Clinic,Wausau Med. Ctr., Wis., 1991—. Mem. edn. com., exec. com. Wausau Family Practice Ctr., 1988-91, bioethics com., 1989-91; mem. pediat. sedation task force Wausau Hosp., 1991-93, edn. com., 1992— (chairperson 1993-95, 98—); mem. physician extender task force Wausau Med. Ctr., 1991—, mktg. com., 1992-99, physician charging practices subcom., 1993-95, walk-in dept. task force, 1994, sect. head Family Practice dept., 2002—; mem. Shadowing Program U. Wis. Stevens Point, 1992-95; vol. faculty Residency Program Wausau Family Practice, 1991—; mem. domestic abuse task force, med. dir. Marathon County Med. Soc., 1993; v.p. U. Wis. Marathon Ctr. Found., 1994-95; bd. dirs. U. Wis. Marathon Ctr. Bd. dirs., mem. public edn. com. Marathon Unit Am. Cancer Soc., 1992-95; active Trinity Lutheran Ch., 1988—; active local and regional polit. campaigns, 1988—; mem., vol. Farm Bureau, 1993-96. Mem. Wis. Acad. Family Physicians, 1983— (publs. and pub. rels. com. 1991—, chairperson, 1992-95), legis. affairs com., 1991, women's task force, 1991-92, access to health care task force, 1992—, newsletter editor, 1992-95, Wis. Valley Dist., 1988—, pres. 1991—). Democrat. Lutheran. Avocations: walking, cooking, travel, decorating, sports. Home: 620 County O Rd Wausau WI 54401 Office: Marshfield Clinic Wasau Med Ctr 2727 Plaza Dr Wausau WI 54401-4129 Office Phone: 715-847-3450.

GRUMAN, JESSIE CHRISTINE, not-for-profit developer; b. Berea, Ky., Dec. 7, 1953; d. Lawrence Lowell and Eleanor Angell (Weekes) Gruman; m. Richard Peter Sloan, June 21, 1984. BA, Vassar Coll., 1975; PhD in Social Psychology, Columbia U., 1984. Counselor, cmty. organizer Greenwich House Counseling Ctr., N.Y.C., Greenwich Settlement House, N.Y.C., 1979—84; mgr. employee health promotion AT&T Comm., Basking Ridge, NJ, 1984—86; nat. dir. pub. edn. Am. Cancer Soc., N.Y.C., 1986—88; project officer Nat. Cancer Inst. NIH, Bethesda, Md., 1988—92; pres., founding exec. dir. Ctr. Advancement Health, Washington, 1992—. Mem. editl. bd. Annals Family Medicine, 2003—; contbr. articles to profl. jours. Chair adv. panel Health Care Financing Adminstrn. Evidence Report and Evidence-Based Recommendations: Health Risk Appraisals and Medicare, 2001; trustee Mind Brain Body and Health Initiative, Galveston, Tex., 2001—; mem. adv. bd. U.S. Cochrane Ctr., 2003—; trustee Sallen Found., 2004—. Fellow: Soc. Behavioral Medicine; mem.: APA, Nat. Orgn. Tobacco Use Rsch. Funders, Pub. Health Inst., Am. Psychosocial Oncology Soc., Nat. Adv. Coun., Nat. Health Coun. Office: Ctr Advancement Health 2000 Florida Ave NW Ste 210 Washington DC 20009-1231

GRUMBACH, MELVIN MALCOLM, pediatrician, educator; b. N.Y.C., Dec. 21, 1925; s. Emanuel and Adele (Weil) G.; m. Madeleine F. Butt, Dec. 1, 1951; children: Ethan Malcolm, Kevin Lawrence, Anthony Havemeyer. Student, Columbia Coll., 1945; MD, Columbia U., 1948; DM honoris causa (hon.), U. Geneva, 1991; D honoris causa (hon.), U. René Descartes Paris V, 2000. Diplomate Am. Bd. Pediatrics, Am. Bd. Pediatric Endocrinology (com. mem. 1975-79). Resident in pediatrics Babies Hosp., Presbyn. Hosp., Columbia U. Med. Ctr., N.Y.C., 1949-51; vis. fellow Oak Ridge Inst. Nuclear Studies, 1952; postdoctoral fellow, asst. pediatrics Johns Hopkins Sch. Medicine, 1953-55; mem. faculty Columbia U. Coll. Physicians and Surgeons, N.Y.C., 1955-65, from instr. to assoc. prof. pediatrics, 1961-65; from asst. to assoc. attending pediatrician Babies Hosp. and Vanderbilt Clin., Columbia-Presbyn. Med. Ctr., 1955-65, founding head postdoctoral tng. program pediat. endocrinology Pediat. Endocrine Divsn., 1955—65; dir. pediatric svc. U. Calif. Hosps., 1966-86; prof. pediatrics, chmn. dept. U. Calif. Sch. Medicine, San Francisco, 1966-86, first Edward B. Shaw prof. pediatrics, 1983-94, acting dir. Lab. Molecular Endocrinology, 1987-89, Edward B. Shaw prof. emeritus pediatrics (active), 1994—. Vis. prof. Vanderbilt U., 1961, Emory U., 1962, U. Western Ont., 1962, U. N.C., 1963, U. Rochester, 1972, UCLA, 1981, U. N.C., 1982, U. Tex.-Dallas, 1983, Peking Union Med. Coll. and Hosp., 1986, U. Hong Kong, 1986; cons. Letterman Gen. Hosp., 1966-94, Children's Hosp., San Francisco, U.S. Naval Hosp., Oakland, Calif., 1966-94, HEW, NIH, 1961-; Nat. Bd. Med. Examiners, 1964-68; mem. human embryology and devel. study sect. NIH, 1962-66, endocrinology study sect., 1967-71; bd. sci. counselors Nat. Inst. Child Health and Human Devel., 1971-75; mem. gen. clin. rsch. ctrs. com., divsn. rsch. resources NIH, 1976-80; mem. com. for rev. NIH Clin. Ctr., 1984-85, nat. adv. coun. Nat. Inst. Child Health and Human Devel., NIH, 1991-96; mem. sci. adv. com., clin. rsch. adv. com. Nat. Found.-March of Dimes, 1969-94, chmn. clin. rsch. adv. com., 1974-82, Basil O'Connor starter scholar rsch. award comm., 1995-99, grant screening com., 2000-; mem. awards com. Lita Annenberg Hazen Award for Excellence in Clin. Rsch., 1981-86; mem. sci. adv. bd. Scripps Clinic and Rsch. Found., 1977-78, Princesse Marie Christine Found., Brussels, 1981-91, U. Mich. Ctr. for Human Growth and Devel., 1982-89, U. Colo. Health Scis. Barbara Davis Ctr., 1986-93, Hosp. for Sick Children, Toronto, 1984-88, Children's Hosp. of Los Angeles, 1987-92; sci. and med. adv. bd. Whittier Inst. Diabetes and Endocrinology, 1987-92; mem. adv. bd. Nat. Pituitary Agy., 1965-69; mem. NIH Evaluation of Endocrinology and Metabolic Diseases, 1977-79; Dean's bd. vis. Mt. Sinai Sch. Medicine, N.Y.C., 1986-87; mem. sci. adv. coun. Cin. Children's Hosp. Rsch. Found., 1997-98; pres. bd. trustees Internat. Pediatric Rsch. Found., Inc., 1984-89; mem. sci. coun. Aid Pour la Recherche Medicale a l'enfance, Paris, 1981-89; del. to Chinese Acad. of Med. Scis., 1986; numerous lectrs. in field; chmn. various confs. Assoc. editor, mem. editorial bd. Jour. Clin. Endocrinology, 1957-70; adv. editor Jour. Pediatrics, 1966-73; editorial bd., 1973-79; assoc. editor Pediatric Rsch., 1970-84, Barnett Pediatrics, 14th-15th edits., Rudolph Pediatrics, 16th-21st edits., Current Topics in Experimental Endocrinology; mem. internat. editorial bd. pediatrics and pediatric surgery: Excerpta Medica, 1974—; editorial bd. Biology of Reproduction, 1968-70; editorial com. Endocrinologic Clinica Metabolismo, 1981—; editorial bd. Pediatrics in Rev., 1982-84, Jour. Endocrinol. Investigation, 1982-90, Endocrine Revs., 1984-88, Jour. Pediatric Endocrinology Metabolism, 1984—, Trends in Endocrinology, 1989—, Monographs on Endocrinology, Springer-Verlag, 1975-90, Clinical Pediatric Endocrinology (Jour. of the Japanese Soc. for Pediatric Endocrinology), 1992—, Jour. Endocrine Genetics, 1999—; contbr. articles to med. and sci. books and jours. Mem. Com. Report Future of Public Health, 1986—87, Com. Study AIDS Rsch. Program of the Nat. Inst. of Health, 1989—91. Capt. USAF, 1951—53. Postdoctoral fellow Nat. Found. Infantile Paralysis, 1953-55; recipient Joseph M. Smith prize Columbia U., 1962; Career Scientist award Health Research Coun. City N.Y., 1961-66; Silver medal Bicentennial Columbia Coll. Physicians and Surgeons, 1967, Gold medal, 1988, Borden award, Am. Acad. Pediatrics, 1971; Clin. Endocrinology Trust medal (U.K.), 1985, Centennial Medallist award Babies Hosp., Columbia-Presbyn. Med. Ctr., 1987, Collège de France medal, 1979, Robert H. Williams Disting. Leadership award, Endocrine Soc., 1980, Winthrop award, Am. Fertility Soc., 1981, Fred Conrad Koch award Endocrine Soc., 1992, Lifetime Achievement award Am. Acad. Pediatrics, 1996, John Howland award Am. Pediatric Soc., 1997, Sci. Patron, The Liggins Inst. Faculty Med. Health Sci., U. Auckland, New Zealand, 2001—. Fellow: AAAS, NY Acad. Scis., Am. Acad. Pediats., Am. Acad. Arts & Scis.; mem.: NAS, Inst. Medicine Nat. Acad. Sci., Am. Pediat. Soc., Am. Pediat. Soc. (pres.-elect 1988—89, pres. 1989—90), Calif. Acad. Medicine, Western Assn. Physicians, Internat. Neuroendocrinology Soc., Internat. Endocrine Soc. (del. to ctrl. com. 1976—92, exec. com. 1984—92, hon. pres. 2000—04), Endocrine Soc. (coun. 1968—71, pres. elect 1980—81, coun. 1980—83, pres. 1981—82), Teratology Soc., Soc. Pediat. Rsch., Western Soc. Pediat. Rsch. (pres. 1978—79), Lawson Wilkins Pediat. Endocrine Soc. (pres. 1975—76), Harvey Soc., Am. Soc. Human Genetics, Assn. Am. Physicians, Am. Soc. Clin. Investigation, Assn. Med. Sch. Pediat. Dept. Chmn. (exec. coun. 1967—72, pres. 1973—75, task force on Pediat. Scientist Tng. Program 1984—91, chmn. selection com. 1986—91), Argentine Soc. Endocrinology and Metabolism (hon.), Can. Soc. Endocrinology and Metabolism (hon.), Japanese Soc. Pediat. Endocrinology (hon.), Pacific Coast Fertility Soc. (hon.), Israel Endocrine Soc. (hon.), European Soc. Pediat. Endocrinology (corr.), Société Française de Pediatrie (corr.), Inst. Medicine Nat. Acad. Scis. (mem. com. 1985—87, 1989—91, chmn. adolescent devel. and biology of puberty 1998—99, mem. com. 2000—01), Johns Hopkins U. Soc. Scholars, U. Club NYC, Alpha Omega Alpha, Sigma Xi. Office: U Calif Sch Medicine Dept Pediatrics S672 San Francisco CA 94143-0434 Business E-Mail: grumbac@itsa.ucsf.edu.

GRUMBACHER, TIM, retail executive; m. Nancy Grumbacher. Grad., Dartmouth. Joined Bon-Ton Stores, Inc., York, Pa., 1964, dir., 1967—, CEO, 1985—95, 2000—04, chmn., 1991—. Served U.S. Army. Office: Bon-Ton Stores 2801 E Market St York PA 17402 Office Phone: 717-757-7660.*

GRUMBLES, BENJAMIN H., federal agency administrator; BA, Wake Forest U.; JD, Emory U.; LLM, George Washington U. Sr. counsel water resources and environ. subcom. U.S. Ho. of Reps., Washington, dep. chief of staff and environ. counsel ho. sci. com., 2001—02; dep. asst. adminstr. office of water EPA, Washington, 2002—04, acting asst. adminstr. for water programs, 2004, asst. adminstr. for water programs, 2005—. Adj. prof. George Washington U. Office: EPA 1201 Pennsylvania Ave NY Rm 3219 Washington DC 20460 Office Phone: 202-564-5700. Office Fax: 202-564-0488.*

GRUMMER, EUGENE MERRILL, commodity futures market development executive; b. Luzerne, Iowa, Aug. 12, 1924; s. William Henry and Louise Wilhamena (Schroeder) G.; m. Priscilla Ann Storrs, Sept. 17, 1955; children: James Hollister, Nancy Louise, Sarah Storrs. BA, Brown U., 1947. Sr. v.p. Merrill Lynch, N.Y.C., 1950-80, ptnr., 1974—; chmn. N.Y. Cotton Exch., N.Y. Citrus Exch., N.Y.C., 1970-74; dir. N.Y. Commodity Exch., N.Y.C., 1969-72, N.Y. Wool Futures Exch., N.Y.C., 1954-60. Originated N.Y. market for frozen concentrated orange juice futures market; helped develop futures market in crude oil, live cattle and lumber; tchr. Merrill Lynch Commodity Tng. Sch.; lectr. to U.S. and internat. industry groups on hedging use of future markets, 1951-74; chmn. Internat. Futures Exch., Bermuda, 1981-85. Mem. Anglers Yacht Club. Republican. Avocations: hunting, fishing, snowmobiling, cross country skiing, golf. Home: Ste 1108 5275 S Atlantic Ave Apt 1108 New Smyrna Beach FL 32169-4564

GRUNBERG, NANCY R., lawyer; b. Mankato, Minn., Sept. 26, 1953; BA with distinction, Stanford U., 1975; JD, Columbia U., 1979. Bar: Pa. 1979, DC 1983, Md. 1996. Litigation assoc. Davis Polk & Wardwell, Washington, 1981—88; atty. securities, banking and commercial litigation priv. practice, Washington, 1992—96; lead trial atty., enforcement div. US Securities and Exchange Commn., 1996—99, litigation counsel, office of internat. affairs, 1999—2000, asst. dir., div. of enforcement, 2000—02; ptnr. Venable LLP, Washington, 2002—. Mem.: ABA, Md. Bar Assn., DC Bar Assn. Office: Venable LLP 575 7th St NW Washington DC 20004 Office Phone: 202-344-4730. Office Fax: 202-344-8300. Business E-Mail: nrgrunberg@venable.com.

GRUNBERG, ROBERT LEON WILLY, nephrologist, educator; b. Bucharest, Romania, July 23, 1940; arrived in U.S., 1972, naturalized, 1977; s. William A. and Isabelle L. (Rosen) Grunberg; m. Donna M. Fishman, Oct. 19, 1975; children: Wendie I., Andrea B. MD, U. Orleans-Tours, France, 1969. Diplomate Am. Bd. Internal Medicine, Am. Bd. Nephrology, cert. hypertension specialist in clin. hypertension. Intern, then resident in cardiology Vichy (France) Hosp., 1968-72; resident in internal medicine Albert Einstein Med. Ctr., Phila., 1972-74; fellow in nephrology-hypertension Hahnemann Univ. Hosp., Phila., 1974-76, sr. clin. instr. then asst. clin. prof. div. nephrology, 1976; pvt. practice medicine specializing in nephrology Allentown, Pa., 1976—. Attending physician St. Luke's Hosp., Bethlehem, Pa., Lehigh Valley Ctr. (name now Lehigh Valley Hosp.), Allentown; attending charge divsn. nephrology Easton (Pa.) Hosp., dir. Renal Dialysis Ctr., 1989; courtesy staff Hahnemann U. Hosp.; chief dialysis Warren Hosp., Phillipsburg, NJ, 1999. Fellow: ACP; mem.: AMA (Physician's Recognition award 1975, 1979, 1982, 1985, 1988—98, 2001), N.Y. Acad. Scis., Nat. Kidney Found., Internat. Soc. Peritoneal Dialysis, Assn. Advancement Med. Instrumentation, Internat. Soc. Nephrology, Internat. Soc. Artificial Organs, Am. Soc. Parenteral and Enteral Nutrition, Internat. Soc. Hypertension, Am. Soc. Artificial Internal Organs, Am. Soc. Nephrology, Pa. Med. Soc. Office: 50 S 18th St Easton PA 18042-3912 also: 401 N 17th St Allentown PA 18104-5034 Office Phone: 610-258-3608.

GRUNBERG, STEVEN MARC, medical educator; b. Paterson, N.J., June 5, 1950; s. Emanuel and Eleanor (Hoffman) G.; m. Kelly Jean McLeod, July 1, 1984; children: Elizabeth, Katherine, Alexandra. BA, Cornell U., 1971, MD, 1975. Diplomate Am. Bd. Internal Medicine. Asst. prof. U. So. Calif., L.A., 1981-87, assoc. prof., 1987-93; prof. U. Vt., Burlington, 1993—. Contbr. articles to profl. jours. Fellow ACP; mem. Am. Soc. Clin. Oncology (proceedings editor, 2000—), Am. Assn. Cancer Rsch., No. New England Clin. Oncology Soc. (bd. dirs. 1995—, pres. 2003-04), Nat. Cancer Inst. Initial Review Group Subcommittee G- Edn. (chair 2002-04). Office: Fletcher Allen Health Care UHC Campus St Joseph 3400 1 S Prospect St Burlington VT 05401

GRUNDER, FRED IRWIN, industrial hygienist, consultant; b. Detroit, Aug. 17, 1940; s. Fritz and Mary Kathrine (Irwin) G.; m. Barbara Ann Ward, May 7, 1966; children: John Frederick, Robert William. BS in Engr. Physics, U. Mich., 1963, MS in Physics, 1967. Diplomte Am. Bd. Indsl. Hygiene; cert. indsl. hygienist. Rsch. assoc. U. Mich., Ann Arbor, 1960-69; chemist G.D. Clayton & Assocs., Southfield, Mich., 1969-72; lab. dir. Bethlehem (Pa.) Steel Corp., 1972-85; dir. indsl. hygiene Am. Med. Labs., Fairfax, Va., 1985-92; mgr. lab. accreditation programs Am. Indsl. Hygiene Assn., Fairfax, 1992—2002; indsl. hygiene cons. Fishersville, Va., 2002—. Evaluation coord. Nat. Coop. Lab. Accreditation, Fishersville, Va., 2005—. Sect. editor: Methods for Biological Monitoring, 1988. Scoutmaster Boy Scouts Am., Bethlehem, 1972-84; pres. U. Mich. Club, Lehigh Valley, 1980-84; mem. toxic planning and oversight panel Chesapeake Rsch. Consortium, Solomons Island, Md., 1990-91, site assessor AIHA Lab., 1992, 2004—; bd. dirs., vice-chair Nat. Coop. Lab. Accreditation, 1997-98, pres., 1998-2000, past pres., 2000-01, evaluation coord., 2004—; bd. dirs. SAW Habitat for Humanity. Fellow Am. Indsl. Hygiene Assn.; mem. ASTM, Am. Chem. Soc., Am. Acad. Indsl. Hygiene. Democrat. Methodist. Avocations: reading, stamp and coin collecting, gardening. Personal E-mail: fgrunder@mindspring.com.

GRUNDER, HERMANN A., science administrator; b. Basel, Switzerland; MS in Mech. Engring., Karlsruhe Inst. Tech., Germany; PhD in Exptl. Nuc. Physics, U. Basel, Switzerland; doctorate, laudatio (hon.), U. Frankfurt, 2000. Dep. dir. gen. sci. Lawrence Berkeley Nat. Lab., Calif.; dir. Thomas Jefferson Nat. Accelerator Facility, 1985—2000, Argonne Nat. Lab., 2000—. Lab. rep. to lab. ops. bd. Sec. Engery Adv. Bd. (SEAB); chair Nat. Ignition Facility Program Rev.; bd. dirs. vis. com. U. Chgo. Divsn. Physical Scis.; bd. dirs. Ill. Coalition; mem. steering com. U.S. Particle Accelerator Sch.; mem. adv. com. physics Los Alamos AOT Divsn. Named Scientist of Yr., Commonwealth Va., 1998; recipient U.S. Sr. Scientist award, Alexander von Humboldt Found., Germany, 1979, Disting. Assoc. award, U.S. Dept. Energy, 1996, Sec. of Energy Gold award, 2004. Fellow: AAAS, Am. Physical Soc.; mem.: Swiss Physical Soc., European Physical Soc. Office: Argonne Nat Lab 9700 S Cass Ave Argonne IL 60439 Office Phone: 630-252-2481. Business E-Mail: grunder@anl.gov.

GRUNDFAST, KENNETH MARTIN, otolaryngologist; b. Bklyn., Mar. 12, 1944; s. Theodore Harvey and Anne Gertrude (Goldberg) G.; m. Ruthanne Blatt Grundfast, May 26, 1974; children: Rena Brett, Dara Beth. BA, Johns Hopkins U., 1965; MD, SUNY, Syracuse, 1969. Clin. instr. dept. of community medicine Georgetown U. Sch. of Medicine, Washington, 1972-74, prof. depts. otolaryngology and pediat., 1996-99, interim chmn. dept. otolryngology; resident otolaryngology Boston U. Hosp., 1974-77; fellow in pediatric otolaryngology Childrens Hosp. of Pitts., 1977-78, staff otolaryngologist, 1978-79, asst. prof. of otolaryngology, 1978-79; prof. dept. otolaryngology, 1980-96; chmn. dept. otolaryngology Children's Nat. Med. Ctr., Washington, 1980-94, vice-chmn., 1994-96; prof., chmn. dept. otolaryngology Sch. Medicine Boston U., 1999—. Lectr. in field. Author: (with others) Ear Infections in Your Child, 1987, Pediatric Otology/Neurotology, 1997; contbr. articles to profl. jours. Lt. comdr. USPHS, 1971-73. Recipient Sylvan Stool Achievement award Sentac, 2000. Fellow ACS, Am. Acad. Pediat.; mem. AMA (Humanitarian award 1973), Soc. for Ear, Nose and Throat Advancement in Children (bd. dirs. 1985, v.p. 1988, pres. 1989), Am. Bronchoesophagologic Soc.,Soc. of U. Otolaryngologists, Am. Neurotology Soc., Trilogical Soc. (hon. mention clin. rsch. thesis), Am. Soc. Pediatric Otolaryngology (pres. 1993-94), Am. Acad. Otolaryngology (v.p. 1994-96, Presdl. Citation award 1996). Avocations: swimming, bicycling. Office: Dept Otolaryngology One Boston Med Ctr Pl Boston MA 02118-2393

GRUNDFEST, JOSEPH ALEXANDER, law and business educator; b. NYC, Sept. 8, 1951; s. Michael A. and Esther Grundfest: m. Carol Chia-Ming Hsu, Aug. 6, 1978. Student MSc program in math. economics and econometrics, London Sch. Econometrics, 1971—72; BA, Yale U., 1973; JD, Stanford U., 1978, doctoral studies in Economics, 1975—78. Bar: Calif. 1978, DC 1979, US Supreme Ct. 1987. Economist, cons. Rand Corp., Santa Monica, Calif., 1973-78; rsch. assoc. The Brookings Instn., 1978—79; assoc. Wilmer, Cutler & Pickering, Washington, 1979-84; counsel, sr. economist legal and regulatory matters Pres.'s Coun. Econ. Advisers, Washington, 1984-85; commr. SEC, Washington, 1985-90; assoc. prof. law Stanford Law Sch., 1990—94, prof., 1994—97, William A. Franke prof. law and bus., 1997—, John M. Olin faculty fellow, 1991—92, Helen L. Crocker faculty scholar, 1996—97, dir. George R. Roberts Program in Law, Bus. and Corporate Governance, 1993—2002, co-dir. Program in Law, Economics and Bus., 2002—. Mem. legal adv. com. NY Stock Exch., 1993—96; nat. fellow Hoover Instn. Stanford U., 1992—93. Recipient John Bingham Hurlbut Award for Excellence in Tchg., Stanford Law Sch., 1992, 2001. Fellow Coun. Fgn. Rels.; mem. ABA, Am. Law Inst., Am. Fin. Assn., Am. Economics Assn., Am. Law and Economics Assn. Avocations: swimming, jogging. Office: Stanford Law Sch Crown Quadrangle 559 Nathan Abbott Way Stanford CA 94305-8610 Office Phone: 650-723-0458. Business E-Mail: grundfest@stanford.edu.*

GRUNDHOFER, JERRY A., bank executive; BA, Loyola Marymount U., 1967. With Union Bank, 1967-81; pres. Alliance Bank, 1981-83; sr. v.p. So. Calif. corp. banking, sr. v.p. So. Calif. retail banking ops. Wells Fargo Bank, 1983-85, exec. v.p. 440 br. statewidef retail banking sys., 1985-87; vice chmn. Security Pacific Nat. Bank, 1987-90, pres., CEO, 1990-93, Star Banc Corp., Cin., 1993—, also chmn. bd. dirs.; pres., CEO Star Bank, N.A., 1993—, also bd. dirs.; CEO Firstar Corp., Milw.; pres. US Bancorp (formerly Firstar Corp.), Minneapolis, 2001—04; CEO US Bancorp, 2001—, chmn., 2002—. Bd. dirs. Arete Assocs., Cin. Equity Fund, L.L.C., Hennegan Co., Visa Internat., Visa U.S.A., Inc., mem. exec. com. Trustee Children's Hosp. Med. Ctr., Health Found. Greater Cin., Cin. Symphony Orch., United Appeal/Cmty. Chest, United Way, U. Cin. Found., Xavier U.; co-chair Fine Arts Fund Campaign, 1995, chmn., 1996; co-chmn. Urban Capital Campaign, 1995, 96; chmn. corp. exec. com. 13th ann. tribute dinner Jewish Inst. Rel. Hebrew Union Coll., 1995; chmn. ann. dinner Nat. Conf. Christians and Jews, 1997; bd. dirs. Nat. Underground Railroad Freedom Ctr. Honoree 15th ann. tribute dinner Jewish Inst. Rel. Hebrew Union Coll., 1997. Mem. Am. Bankers Assn. (bd. dirs.), Internat. Fin. Conf. (bd. dirs.), Bankers Roundtable (bd. dirs.), Greater Cin. C. of C. (bd. dirs.), Over-the-Rhine C. of C. (bd. dirs.), Birnan Woods, Cin. Country Club, Comml. Club (mem. exec. com.), Double Eagle Golf Club, Queen City Club. Office: US Bancorp US Bank Pl 601 2nd Ave S Minneapolis MN 55402*

GRUNDHOFER, JOHN F., bank executive; b. L.A., 1939; Student, Loyola U., 1960, U. So. Calif., 1964. Formerly with Wells Fargo & Co., San Francisco, also vice chmn.; now chmn., pres., CEO U.S. Bancorp (formerly First Bank System, Inc.), Mpls., 1990—2001, chmn., 2001—, also dir. Office: US Bancorp 601 2nd Ave S Minneapolis MN 55402-4303

GRUNDISH, LEE ANNE, small business owner; b. Kalamazoo, Mich., Apr. 13, 1959; d. Allen Grundish and Jeane Gratop. BA in Psychology, U. Toledo, 1984. Bus. owner, pres. Grafix Services, Etc., Toledo, 1989—. Lyricist (song) Love Is What We Need (No. 1 song in Negril, Jamaica, 1999). Parent counselor Family and Child Abuse Prevention Ctr., Toledo, 1984, fundraising vol., 1998; youth mentor Big Bros. & Big Sisters, Toledo, 1990—91, fundraising vol., 1995—98, Arts Commn. of Greater Toledo, 1998; voters' rights vol. Nat. Voice, Toledo, 2004. Mem.: ASCAP, ACA, Nat. Resume Writers Assn., Nat. Employment Counselors Assn. Democrat. Avocations: poetry, politics. Home and Office: Grafix Svcs Etc 2242 Portsmouth Ave Toledo OH 43613 Business E-Mail: grafixservices@aol.com.

GRUNDLER, MARY JANE LANG, business education educator; b. Wentworth, Mo., Oct. 26, 1919; d. Charles Fremont and Angeline Rose (Baker) Lang; m. Francis Edward Grundler, Dec. 26, 1963. BS in Edn., U. Mo., 1944, MEd, 1947, EdD, 1960. Tchr. Shiloh Sch., Carthage, Mo., 1940-41, Duenweg (Mo.) Elem. Sch., 1941-42; bus. tchr. Duenweg High Sch., 1942-43, Seneca (Mo.) High Sch., 1943-45, Lindenwood Coll., St. Charles, Mo., 1945-47; instr. bus. tchr. edn. U. Mo., Columbia, 1947-60, asst. prof., 1960-67, assoc. prof., 1967-76, prof., 1976-85, prof. emeritus, 1985—. Coord. bus. edn. Coll. Edn. U. Mo., Columbia, 1968-80. Contbr. articles to profl. bus. edn. jours. and yearbooks. Bd. dirs. Koinonia House, Columbia, 1988—. Recipient Disting. Svc. award U. Mo. Alumni Assn., 1986, Outstanding Alumnus award Mo. So. State Coll., Joplin, 1988. Mem. AAUW (state treas. 1988-90), Am. Vocat. Assn. (Outstanding Svc. cert. Divsn. Bus. Edn. 1980), Nat. Assn. Tchr. Educators Bus. Edn. (Recognition award 1984), Nat. Bus. Edn. Assn., Ret. Tchrs. Assn. Mo. (newsletter editor 1988-90), Mo. State Tchrs. Assn., Mo. Vocat. Assn., Mo. Bus. Edn. Assn. (Outstanding Bus. Educator 1979, Disting. Svc. award 1985, past pres., v.p., sec., charter inductee Who's Who in Mo., Bus. Edn. 1992), U. Mo. Alumni Assn. (life, sec. bd. dirs. 1972-86, historian 1994—), Pi Lambda Theta (sponsor Alpha chpt. 1989—, mem. nat. nominating com. 1992-93), Delta Kappa Gamma. Roman Catholic. Avocations: reading, music. Home: 1406 Business Loop 70 W #13 Columbia MO 65202-1324

GRUNDY, KENNETH WILLIAM, political science professor; b. Phila., Aug. 6, 1936; s. William and Alma (Hahn) G.; m. Martha Jonet Paxson, June 25, 1960; children: William MacIntyre, Thomas Paxson, Anne Edmunds. BA with honors, Ursinus Coll., 1958; MA, Pa. State U., 1961, PhD, 1963. Asst. prof. polit. sci. San Fernando Valley State Coll., Northridge, Calif., 1963-66; assoc. prof. Case Western Res. U., Cleve., 1966-74, prof., 1974-88, Marcus A. Hanna prof., 1988—2005, prof. emeritus, 2005—, chmn. dept. polit. sci., 1974-76, dir. Ctr. for Policy Studies, 1998-2000. Vis. sr. lectr. Makerere U. Coll., Kampala, Uganda, 1967-68; vis. scholar Inst. Social Studies, The Hague, The Netherlands, 1972-73, U. Pretoria, 1998; vis. Fulbright prof. U. Zambia, Lusaka, 1977, Nat. U. Ireland, Galway, 1979-80; vis. adj. prof. Cleve. State U., 1992—; editl. adv. bd. Ctr. Internat. Race Rels., 1968—. Author: Conflicting Images of the Military in Africa, 1968, Guerrilla Struggle in Africa, 1971, Confrontation and Accommodation in Southern Africa, 1973, (with Weinstein) The Ideologies of Violence, 1974, We're Against Apartheid, But, 1974, Defense Legislation and Communal Politics, 1978, (with V. McHale and B. Hughes) Evaluating Transnational Programs in Government and Business, 1980, Soldiers Without Politics, 1983, The Militarization of South African Politics, 1986, rev. edit., 1988, South Africa: Domestic Crisis and Global Challenge, 1991, The Politics of the National Arts Festival, 1993; also articles; book rev. editor Internat. Jour. Comparative Sociology, 1973-83; assoc. editor Jour. African Policy Studies, 1991—; contbg. editor Current History, 1982-2003; mem. editl. adv. bd. African Affairs, 1983-93; mem. editl. bd. Jour. Third World Studies, 1988—, South African Jour. Internat. Affairs, 1993-98. Fellow NDEA, 1959-62, Rhodes U., Grahamstown, South Africa, 1989-90, Ctr. Internat. Race Rels., 1969-70; 1st Bradlow fellow South African Inst. Internat. Rels., 1982; grantee Rockefeller Found., 1967-68, Social Sci. Rsch. Coun., 1972, 79-80, Earhart Found, 1979. Mem. African Studies Assn. (mem. exec. coun.), Inter-Univ. Seminar on Armed Forces and Soc., Internat. Studies Assn. Home: 2602 Exeter Rd Cleveland OH 44118-4246 Office: Case Western Res U Dept Polit Sci Cleveland OH 44106 Business E-Mail: kwg@case.edu.

GRUNE, STEVEN, publishing executive; Acct./bus. mgr. McCalls; sales positions Parents Mag., adv. dir., 1994—97, Redbook, 1997, assoc. pub., 1998; pub. Midwest Living, 1999—2000, Country Living, 2000—, Country Living Gardener, 2000; v.p. Country Living, 2002—, Country Living Gardener, 2002—. Office: Country Living 224 West 57th St New York NY 10019*

GRUNEICH, JEFFREY ALAN, biotechnologist, director; b. Berkeley, Calif., July 27, 1973; s. John A Gruneich and Angie A Holdaway. BS in Chemistry and Math., U. Calif., Berkeley, 1996, MA in Chemistry, 1997; PhD, U. Pa., 2002. Chief bus. officer Infoceutics, Inc., Phila., 2001—; subject matter expert IBM, Phila., 2003—. Chief strategy officer eTechtransfer.com, Phila., 1999—2000. Musician: (performance) Dear Mandy (Conan O'Brien, Best Coll. Band, 1995). Co-pres. U. Pa Biotech Club, Phila., 1999—2000. Recipient Magna cum laude, So. Meth. U., 1996; fellow Grad. Student fellowship, Chemistry, NSF, 1996-2001. Mem.: Am. Soc. of Gene Therapy, Am. Assn. of Pharm. Scientists (assoc.), World Future Soc. (assoc.), Am. Assn. for the Advancement of Sci. (assoc.), Am. Chem. Soc. (assoc.), Phi Beta Kappa. Achievements include patents pending for synthesis and use of reagents for improved DNA lipofection and/or slow release prodrug and drug therapies. Avocations: skiing, weightlifting, travel, guitar, trumpet. Home: Apt GR 250 Marlborough St Boston MA 02116 Office Phone: 215-738-3852.

GRUNES, ROBERT LEWIS, engineering executive, consultant; b. Bklyn., Aug. 15, 1941; s. Abe and Doris (Dicker) G.; m. Eleonora Grasselli, Oct. 14, 1972; children: Natalie, Daniel, Ian. BS in Engring., Poly. Inst. Bklyn., 1963, MS in Engring., 1965, PhD in Phys. Metallurgy, 1970. Registered profl. engr., N.Y., N.J., Pa. Engr. Pratt & Whitney div. United Aircraft Corp., East Hartford, Conn., 1963; rsch. fellow Poly. Inst. Bklyn., 1963-64, rsch. assoc., 1966-70; rsch. engr. Lewis Rsch. Ctr. NASA, Cleve., 1965; pres. R. L. Grunes & Assocs., Inc., N.Y.C., 1970—. Mem. adj. faculty N.J. Inst. Tech., Newark, 1974-78. Author: Pollution Control Market and Industries, 1971; contbr. articles to profl. jours. 1st lt. CE U.S. Army, 1964-66. Mem. ASME, ASCE, ASTM, Metall. Soc., Soc. Automotive Engrs., Nat. Fire Protection Assn., Am. Boat & Yacht Coun. Office: R L Grunes & Assocs Inc 521 5th Ave New York NY 10175-0003

GRUNEWALD, DONALD, former college president, educator; b. N.Y.C., Feb. 9, 1934; s. Harry A. and Tina (Gegner) G.; m. Barbara Susan Frees, Feb. 7, 1981; children: Donald Frees, Susan Christina Irene. AB, Union Coll., 1954; MA, Harvard U., 1955, MBA, 1959, DBA, 1962; LLD, Emerson Coll., 1973; LittD, Suffolk U., 1974; DSc, Far East U., 1979, Medaille Coll., 1983; D of Polit. Sci., Kyung Hee U., 1983; LHD, Mercy Coll., 1984; PhD honoris causa, U. Mindanao, 1981. Cert. profl. mgr. Instr. U. Kans. Sch. Bus., 1959-60; lectr. Boston U. Coll. Bus. Adminstrn., 1961-62; research agt. Harvard U. Grad. Sch. Bus., 1962; asst. prof. Rutgers U. Grad. Sch. Bus., 1962-65, assoc. prof., 1965-67; dean, prof. Coll. Bus. Adminstrn., Grad. Sch. Adminstrn. Suffolk U., 1967-69, v.p., dean Coll. Liberal Arts and Scis., Coll. Journalism, 1969-72; pres. Mercy Coll., Dobbs Ferry, N.Y., 1972-84, disting. prof., 1984-86; prof. Iona Coll., 1986—. Ednl. cons., propr. Boston Athenaeum; life gov. Manchester Coll., Oxford, Eng.; former trustee Trinity Coll., Washington, chmn. bd., 1984-87. Author: Cases in Business Policy, 1962, (with Moranian and Reidenbach) Business Policy and Its Environment, 1964, (with H. Bass) Public Policy and the Modern Corporation, 1966, Small Business Management, 1966, (with Fenn and Katz) Business Decision Making and Government Policy, 1966, (with Flink) Managerial Finance, 1969, I Am Honored to Be Here Today, 1985, (with Shaviro and Baron) Cases in Strategic Management, 1989, 2d. edit., 1993, (with Andersson, Baron & Shaviro) Readings in Business Policy and its Environment, 1991, Cases in Strategic Management and Policy, 1997, 2d edit., 2000, (with Shaviro) The Complete Book of Management, 1998. Trustee Dobbs Ferry Hosp., Lab. Inst. Merchandising. Lt. USAF, 1955-57. Decorated knight Sovereign Order St. John of Jerusalem, Comdr., Order of St. Lazarus, Knight Grand Cross with Collar, Order of St. Gregory the Illuminator, 5 other knighthoods. Fellow Royal Soc. Arts, Inst. Commerce, Coll. Preceptors; mem. Internat. Assn. Univ. Pres.'s (exec. com.), Harvard Club, Cosmos Club. Home: PMB # 307 5 River Rd Wilton CT 06897-4069 E-mail: dgrune34@aol.com. *I have always relied on the old motto: "Never rest until you have made the good better and the better best.".*

GRUNIG, JAMES ELMER, communications educator, researcher, public relations consultant; b. Storm Lake, Iowa, Apr. 18, 1942; s. Roy Albert and Gladys Erma (Harjes) G.; m. Juretta Ann Weisgerber, Sept. 11, 1965 (dec. May, 1984); children: Andrew, John, Neil; m. Larissa Ann Johnson, May 11, 1985; 1 stepchild, Lara Schneider. BS, Iowa State U., 1964; MS, U. Wis., 1966, PhD, 1968. Asst. prof. Land Tenure Ctr. U. Wis., Madison, 1968-69; asst. prof. communications Coll. Journalism, U. Md., College Park, 1969-72, assoc. prof., 1972-78, prof., 1978-99, prof. dept. comm., 1999—2005, emeritus prof., 2005—. Pub. rels. cons. numerous orgns. Author: Decline of the Global Village, 1976, Managing Public Relations, 1984, Excellence in Public Relations and Communication Management, 1992, Public Relations Techniques, 1993, Manager's Guide to Excellence in Public Relations and Communication Management, 1995, Excellent Public Relations and Effective Organizations, 2002; co-editor Pub. Rels. Rsch. Ann., 1989-91, Jour. Pub. Rels. Rsch., 1992-94; contbr. articles to profl. jours. Scoutmaster Boy Scouts Am., Hyattsville, Md., 1985-90; tchr. Rockville (Md.) United Ch., 1980-92. Recipient Pathfinder award for rsch., Inst. for Pub. Rels. Rsch. and Edn., N.Y., 1984, James W. Schwartz award, Greenlee Sch. Journalism and Comm., Iowa State U., 2002; grantee, Internat. Assn. Bus. Communicators Found., 1986—95. Mem. Assn. for Edn. in Journalism and Mass Comm. (Paul J. Deutschmann award 2000), Internat. Comm. Assn., Pub. Rels. Soc. Am. (Outstanding Educator award 1989, Jackson, Jackson and Wagner award for behavioral sci. rsch. 1992), Internat. Assn. Bus. Communicators, Nat. Comm. Assn., Internat. Pub. Rels. Assn., Cosmos Club (Washington). Democrat. Avocation: sport. Office: U Md Dept Comm 2130 Skinner Bldg College Park MD 20742-7635 E-mail: jgrunig@umd.edu.

GRUNSFELD, ERNEST ALTON, III, architect; b. Chgo., June 5, 1929; s. Ernest Alton Jr. and Mary Jane (Loeb) G.; m. Sally Riblett, July 10, 1954 (dec. 1999); children: Marcia Grunsfeld, John Mace. Student, Inst. Design, Chgo., 1945, Art Inst. Chgo., 1946; BArch, MIT, 1952. Registered architect, Ill., Conn., Ind., Mich., N.C., Ohio, Mo., Wis. Ptnr. Yerkes & Grunsfeld, Chgo., 1956-65; owner Grunsfeld & Assocs., Architects, Chgo., 1965-75, sr. ptnr., 1975-84, owner, 1984—2001; prin. Grunsfeld Shafer Architects, LLC, 2001—. Corp. mem. Woodlawn Hosp., Chgo., 1968-70; mem. Highland Park (Ill.) Planning Commn., 1969-75; pres. Grunsfeld Meml. Fund, Chgo., 1970—. Contbr. articles to profl. jours. Bd. dirs. Urban Gateways, Chgo., 1968-89, mem. adv. bd., 1989—; life mem. Field Mus. Natural History, Chgo., 1970—, Chgo. Symphony Orch. Assn., 1975—, governing mem., 1995—; mem. exec. com. Coun. for Arts MIT, Cambridge, 1977-89, bd. dirs., 1977—; hon. life mem. Chgo. Hort. Soc., 1995—, governing mem., 2001—; benefactor, hon. governing mem. Art Inst. Chgo., 1980—. Recipient 1st Honor award Burlington Mills, 1968. Fellow AIA (corp. mem. Chgo. chpt., Honor award 1962, citation of merit 1969); mem. Tavern Club, Lake Shore Country Club, Arts Club of Chgo. Office: Grunsfeld Schafer Architects LLC 211 E Ontario St Chicago IL 60611-3219 Office Phone: 312-202-1800.

GRUPE, ROBERT CHARLES, corporate communications specialist; b. Alice, Tex., Sept. 3, 1948; m. Dorothy E. Cleveland, Nov. 22, 1975; children: Amber, Robert, Elisabeth, Jonathan. BA, MBA, Calif. Coast U., 1977, PhD, 1992. Announcer Stein Broadcasting Co., Sweetwater, Tex., 1966-68; news announcer Ea. Okla. TV Co., Ada, 1969-72; announcer Anadarko (Okla.) Broadcasting Co., 1972-74; news dir. Cleveland County Broadcasting Co., Norman, Okla., 1974-75; instr. Elkins Inst., Oklahoma City, 1975-77; mng. editor Okla. World Media, Oklahoma City, 1977-78; pres., owner Quality Prodns. Inc., Oklahoma City, 1978—. Job skills cons. Okla. Pvt. Industry Coun., Oklahoma City, 1989; vol. trainer U.S. Olympic Festival, Oklahoma City, 1989; mem. Total Quality Mgmt. Faculty Okla. State U., 1990-95; TV prodr./host Cox Cable Pub. Programming, Oklahoma City, 1990-96; syndicated radio commentator, 1993-99; talk show host WKY Radio, Oklahoma City, 1999-2000, ind. networking specialist, 2000—; TV host Pathways to Success, produced for Oklahoma City Ednl. TV Consortium, 2001—. Author: The Miracle of Speech, 1981, The Change, 1993, Creating The Future, 1994, Creating Your Future in Network Marketing, 2002; contbr. articles to profl. jours. Vol. media devel. Vol. Action Com. Oklahoma City, 1991. Mem. ASTD (v.p. 1992), Internat. Assn. Bus. Communicators (v.p. 1996-97), Neuro Linguistic Programming Assocs. (v.p. 1991-92), World Assn. of Persons with Disabilities (bd. dirs. 2005-) Avocation: historical research. Office: Quality Prodns Inc 4230 NW 36th St Oklahoma City OK 73112-2910 Office Phone: 800-781-2722. E-mail: dgrupe@drgrupe.com.

GRUSH, ERIC SCOTT, music educator; b. Pitts., Pa., Nov. 29, 1969; s. Larry Lee and Nancy Eklund Grush; m. Marianne Williamson Sikes, Apr. 5, 1997. MusB in Edn., U. N.C., 1991. Cert. tchr. N.J. Band dir. Daniels Mid.

Sch., Raleigh, NC, 1991—93, Athens Dr. H.S., Raleigh, 1993—94; dir. of instrumental music Cary (N.C.) Acad., 1997—2001, band dir., 2001—. Lead tchr. Summer Tech. Camp, Cary, 2000—; assoc. dir. Triangle Wind Ensemble, Cary, 1999—2002. Dir.: (performance) Cary Acad. Wind Ensemble Performance at Meymandi Concert Hall, 2001. Mem. Raleigh Jaycees, 1993—94; min. music Fairmont United Meth. Ch., Raleigh, NC, 1995—97. Named Outstanding 1st Yr. Tchr., Sallie Mae, 1992. Mem.: N.C. Bandmaster's Assn. (bd. dirs. 1992—93), N.C. Music Educators Assn. Avocations: singing, scrapbooking, collecting Disney memorabilia. Office: Cary Acad 1500 N Harrison Ave Cary NC 27513 E-mail: eric_grush@caryacademy.org.

GRUSHEVSKY, ALLA, microbiologist; b. Kiev, Ukraine, Oct. 24, 1948; d. Arnold and Ludmila Rozenfeld; m. Val Goldfine, July 8, 1972; children: Zhanna Goldfine, Leo Goldfine. BS in Biology, Donetsk State U., Ukraine, 1971. Cert. microbiologist Am. Acad. Microbiology, 1993. Scientist Inst. Pesticides Rsch., Kiev, Ukraine, 1969—74; med. technologist Children Hosp. #3, Kiev, Ukraine, 1974—89; sr. microbiologist Wesley-Jessen Corp., Chgo., 1990—; staff microbiologist Aksys Ltd., Lincolnshire, Ill., 1995—. Mem.: Am. Soc. Microbiology, Am. Assn. Med. Instrumentation. Avocations: painting, reading, gardening, travel, crafts. Home: 1307 Crabtree Dr Arlington Heights IL 60004 Business E-Mail: allag@aksys.com.

GRUSHKIN, JAY D., lawyer; b. N.Y.C., 1957; BA magna cum laude, Univ. Pa., 1979; JD, Vanderbilt Univ., 1982. Bar: D.C. 1982, N.Y. 1991. Atty. Milbank Tweed Hadley & McCloy, Washington, Hong Kong, ptnr. in charge Tokyo, ptnr. Global Fin. Group & mem. recruiting com. N.Y.C., 1997—. Adj. prof. Temple Univ. Law Program, Japan; mem. bd. adv. Vanderbilt Jour. Transnational Law. Contbr. articles to profl. jours.; editor (exec.): Vanderbilt Jour. Transnational Law. Mem.: Structured Fin. Inst., ABA, N.Y. State Bar Assn., D.C. Bar, Tokyo Bar Assn. (gaikokuho jimu bengoshi), Order of the Coif. Office: Milbank Tweed Hadley & McCloy 1 Chase Manhattan Plz New York NY 10005-1413 Office Phone: 212-530-5346. Office Fax: 212-530-5219. Business E-Mail: jgrushkin@milbank.com.

GRUSHOW, SANDY, broadcast executive; BA in Communication, UCLA, 1983. Former v.p. creative advtg. 20th Century Fox Film Corp.; sr. v.p. advtg. and promotion Fox Broadcasting Co., 1988—90, exec. v.p. programming and scheduling, 1990—91; exec. v.p. Fox Entertainment Group, 1991—92, pres., 1992—95, Tele-TV Media, 1995—97, Twentieth Century Fox TV, LA, 1997—99; chmn. Fox Entertainment Group, 1999—2004.

GRUSKY, ROBERT R., investor; b. NYC, Aug. 19, 1957; s. Burton and Barbara (Rudoy) G.; m. Hope Holmes Eiseman, Feb. 25, 1989; children: Robert R. Jr., Katherine Elizabeth, Alexandra Rose. BA in History cum laude, Union Coll., 1979; MBA with distinction, Harvard U., 1985. Banking assoc. to banking officer to 2nd v.p. U.S. Banking Dept. Continental Ill. Nat. Bank and Trust Co., Chgo., 1979-83; assoc. to v.p. investment banking divsn. Goldman Sachs & Co., N.Y.C., 1985-93, v.p., prin. investment, 1993-97; asst. to the sec. of def. for spl. projects The Pentagon, Washington, 1990-91; sr. advisor Hon. Ronald S. Lauder, N.Y.C., 1997-2000; pres. RSL Investments Corp., N.Y.C., 1998-2000; co-founder, prin. New Mountain Capital, N.Y.C., 2000—05; sr. advisor New Mountain Capital L.C.C., 2005—. Mng. mem., gen. ptnr. Hope Capital Ptnrs., 2000—. Trustee Hackley Sch., Tarrytown, N.Y., 1992—. White House fellow, 1990-91. Mem. Harvard Club N.Y.C., Manursing Island Club. Presbyterian. Office: 787 South Ave 49th Fl New York NY 10019 Office Phone: 212-720-0300. Business E-Mail: rgrusky@newmountaincapital.com.

GRUSON, MICHAEL, lawyer; b. Berlin, Sept. 17, 1936; came to U.S., 1962; s. Rudolf and Barbara Gruson; m. Hiroko Tsubota, July 11, 1964; children: Rudolf, Andreas, Sebastian, Matthias, Florian, Konrad. LLB, U. Mainz, Fed. Republic of Germany, 1962; M in Comparative Law, Columbia U., 1963, LLB, 1965; Dr. iur, Freie Univ., Berlin, 1966. Bar: N.Y. 1969, U.S. Ct. Appeals (2d cir.) 1969, U.S. Dist. Ct. (so. dist.) N.Y. 1971, U.S. Supreme Ct. 1977. Assoc. Shearman & Sterling, N.Y.C., 1966-73, ptnr., 1973—2000, of counsel, 2000—. Bd. dirs. Mizuho Corp. Bank. Author: Die Bedurfniskompetenz, 1967; co-author: Sovereing Lending: Managing Legal Risk, 1984, Legal Opinions in International Transactions, 4th edit., 2003, Regulation of Foreign Banks, 2 vols., 4th edit., 2003, Acquisition of Shares in a Foreign Country, 1993; contbr. articles to profl. jours. Mem. Am. Law Inst., Internat. Bar Assn. (past vice chmn. com. banking law, past chmn. subcom. on legal opinions), N.Y. State Bar Assn. (com. internat. banking, securities and fin. transaction, internat. law and practice sect.), Internat. Law Assn. (com. on internat. monetary law, hon. treas. Am. br.). Home: 108 E Hook Cross Rd Hopewell Junction NY 12533 Office: Shearman & Sterling Rm 1060 599 Lexington Ave New York NY 10022-6069 Office Phone: 212-848-8060.

GRUSS, MARTIN DAVID, investor; b. N.Y.C., Mar. 1, 1943; s. Joseph Saul and Caroline (Zelaznik) G.; m. Agneta Peterson; m. Audrey Butvay, June 28, 1988; children: Joshua, Amanda. BSE, U. Pa., 1964; LLB, N.Y. U., 1967. Sr. ptnr. Gruss Ptnrs., N.Y.C. Bd. trustee Solomon R Guggenheim Mus., NYC. Mem. N.Y. Bar Assn. Office: Gruss & Co 667 Madison Ave New York NY 10021 Office Phone: 212-688-1500. Office Fax: 212-688-2138.

GRUSSENDORF, STEVEN CARL, music educator, director; b. Mpls., Nov. 7, 1961; s. Wesley Edward Grussendorf and Elaine Della Peikert; m. Robin Kathleen LaFollette, Feb. 6, 1982; children: Joshua, Amy, Adam. BMusEd, U. Wyo., Laramie, 1985; post grad., Casper Coll., Wyo., 1980—82, Colo. State U., 1982. Cert. tchr. music k-12 Wyo., music adjudicator Wyo. Tchr. elem. music grade 5-6 Natrona County Sch. Dist. #1, Casper, Wyo., 1985—89; dir. choir Green River H.S., 1989—96; choral dir. Western Wyo. Coll., Rock Springs, 1991—95, Natrona County H.S., Casper, 1996—. Choral v.p. Wyo. Music Educators, 1998—99; dir. musicals Casper Coll., 1998—2001; music minister First Assembly of God, 2002—. Composer: (songs) Take My Hand, Today, 1993, Songs of Worship and Praise, 2004. Choral dir. civic orgns., nursing homes, cmty. events Natrona County H.S. Choirs, 1996—. Recipient medallion of Excellence, Natrona County Sch. Dist. #1, 2001. Mem.: Internat. Assn. Jazz Educators, Music Educators Nat. Conf. Republican. Avocations: fishing, hunting, camping. Office: Natrona County HS 930 S Elm St Casper WY 82601-3697 Home: 4911 E 15th St Casper WY 82609

GRUSSING, BRUCE DOUGLASS, lawyer; b. Mpls., June 25, 1939; s. Bon Dirck and Evelyn Florence (Pearson) G.; m. Jean Louise Christianson, Aug. 17, 1963; children: Andrea J., Katherine M. BA, Carleton Coll., Northfield, Minn., 1961; JD, U. Minn., 1965. Bar: Minn. 1965. Prin., chair employee stock options group Gray, Plant, Mooty, Mooty & Bennett PA, Mpls., 1965—. Former chmn. bd. dirs. Gray, Plant, Mooty, Mooty & Bennett. Contbr. articles to profl. jours. Past pres. Ensemble Capriccio, Mpls., 1992. Mem. Minn. Bar Assn. (past chair employee benefits sect.), Employee Stock Ownership Plan Assn. (chair legis. and regulation com. 1995-97), Midwest Pension Conf. (past bd. dirs.), Mpls. Pension Conf. (past pres.). Unitarian/Universalist. Avocations: golf, fly fishing, skiing. Office: 80 S 8th St #500 Minneapolis MN 55402-5383 Office Phone: 612-632-3030. E-mail: bruce.grussing@gpmlaw.com.

GRUTMAN, JEWEL HUMPHREY, lawyer, writer; b. N.Y.C., Mar. 13, 1931; d. Robert and Gladys Humphrey; m. Robert W. Bjork, June 26, 1954 (div. Apr. 22, 1975); 1 child, Bruce Bjork; m. Roy Grutman, Oct. 30, 1975 (wid. 1994); m. Fredrick Yonkman, July 4, 1998. BA magna cum laude, Mt. Holyoke Coll., 1952; LLB, Columbia U., 1955. Bar: N.Y., U.S. Dist. Ct. (So. Dist.) N.Y. 1971, U.S. Dist. Ct. (ea. dist.) N.Y. 1974, U.S. Dist. Ct. Conn. 1984, U.S. Supreme Ct. 1983. Atty. Debevoise & Plimpton, N.Y.C., 1954-60; ptnr. Eaton Van Winkle, N.Y.C., 1976-79, Grutman Greene & Humphrey, N.Y.C., 1979—. Co-author: (with CD-ROM) The Ledgerbook of Thomas Blue Eagle, 1994 (Christopher award 1995, Internat. Reading Assn. award), The Sketchbook of Thomas Blue Eagle, 2001, (CD-ROM) The Journey of Thomas Blue Eagle, 1995 (Best Project award Intermedia, Asia, 1995, Creative NGee ANN Disting. award 1995, EMMA award best visual content 1996); asst. prodr., editor (ednl. film on art) Where Time is a River (1st prize Women's Film Festival); contbr. photograph illustrations: The Reforming Power of the Scriptures, 1996; developer series of designs based on Native Am. art; contbr. articles to mags. and newspapers. Dir. Inwood Ho., N.Y.C., 1970-80; past mem. various coms. Mt. Holyoke Coll.; mem. com. sr. advisors N.Y. Commn. for Internat. Bus. and UN, 1997; past chmn. com. to establish Barbara Black Fellowship at Columbia U. Law Sch.; past pres. 85th St. Playground Assn., N.Y.C.; active supporter The Children's Storefront, Harlem, N.Y.C., N.Y. Jr. League. Mem.: Assn. Bar City N.Y., Coral Ridge Country Club (Ft. Lauderdale, Fla.)., The Stanwich Club (Greenwich, Conn.). Avocations: opera, golf, tennis, poetry. E-mail: bijou203@optonline.net, bijou203@bellsouth.net.

GRUVER, NANCY, publishing executive; Founder, pub. New Moon Pub., Duluth, Minn., 1992—. Author: How To Say It To Girls, 2004; prodr. (mag.) New Moon: The Magazine for Girls and Their Dreams, 1992—. Office: New Moon Publishing 34 E Superior St #200 Duluth MN 55802-3003 Office Phone: 218-728-5507. Business E-Mail: nancyg@newmom.org.

GRUVER, WILLIAM ROLFE, investment banker; b. Denver, May 31, 1944; s. John and Marion Jean (Plummer) G. AB with distinction, Dartmouth Coll., 1966; MBA, Columbia U., 1968. Ptnr. Goldman, Sachs & Co., N.Y.C., 1972-99; ret., 1999. Disting. exec. in residence, prof. Bucknell U., 1993—; dir. The Street.com., 2004-; dir. Geisinger Found., Danville, Pa., 2005—; mem. adv. bd. Hirtle, Callaghan & Co., West Conshocken, Pa., 1996—, Cornell U. Park Leadership Fellows, Ithaca, N.Y., 2002—. Vol. Big Bros., Morristown, NJ, 1981—84; mayor Eagles Mere Borough, 1994—2005; dir. Eagles Mere Hist. Village, Inc., 2004—; trustee Eagles Mere (Pa.) Cmty. Ch., 1993—; chmn. bd. trustees Woodbridge (N.J.) Devel. Ctr., 1982—87; trustee Berea Coll., 1995—, Eagles Mere Found., 1998—; mem. advisor bd. The Lymphoma Found., N.Y.C., 1985—; arbitrator NASD, 1993—. Lt. USN, 1968—72. Mem. Am. Legion. Home: PO Box 359 Eagles Mere PA 17731-0359 Business E-Mail: gruver@bucknell.edu.

GRYKA, GEORGE EDWIN, chemical company executive; b. Belmont, Mich., Nov. 22, 1932; s. George John and Helen Elizabeth (Powlowski) G.; m. Madeline E. Barko, Sept. 28, 1957 (dec.); 1 child, Cynthia Mary (dec.) BSChemE, U. Mich., 1954, MS, 1955. With Monsanto Co., St. Louis, 1955-68, planning mgr., 1966-68; corp. planning analyst GAF Corp., N.Y.C., 1969; with Stauffer Chem. Co., Westport, Conn., 1970-84; pres. Mt. Pleasant Chem. Co., Westport, 1978-81, divsn. gen. mgr., 1981-84; prin. Phoenix Internat. Enterprises, Southport, Conn., 1984—. Bd. dirs. TODD Credfeld Inc., Roanwell Corp., PIPco, Inc. Mem. Planning Forum (past pres. N.Y. chpt., past nat. v.p.), Soc. Chem. Industry, Am. Coun. Sci. and Health Comml. Devel. Assn., Southport Racquet Club. Home: 893 Sasco Rd Southport CT 06490 Office: PO Box 656 Southport CT 06890-0656 E-mail: g.gryka@att.net.

GRYSON, JOSEPH ANTHONY, orthodontist; b. Rahway, N.J., Feb. 11, 1932; s. Elmer Joseph Anthony and Joyce Asher (Toms) G.; m. Patricia Ann Huddleston, Nov. 22, 1961; children— Karen Ann, David Joseph. M.Chem. Engring., Cornell U., 1954; D.D.S., U. Calif., San Francisco, 1964. Diplomate: Am. Bd. Orthodontics. Engr. div. refinery tech. service Standard Oil of Calif., Richmond, 1954, 58-60; individual practice dentistry specializing in orthodontics San Rafael, Calif., 1964-96; clin. instr. orthodontics U. Calif., San Francisco, 1965-87, assoc. clin. prof. orthodontics, 1987-99, clin. prof. orthodontics, 1999—. Referee Am. Jour. Orthodontics and Dentofacial Orthopedics. Contbr. articles to profl. jours. Treas., pres., dir. Homeowners Assn., San Rafael, 1970-74. Served as carrier pilot USN, 1954-58. Mem. ADA, Pacific Coast Soc. Orthodontists (dir. 1980-85, pres. 1985-86, award of merit 1992), Am. Assn. Orthodontists (ho. of dels. 1982-87, 94-95, spkr. ho. of dels. 1988-91, James E. Brophy Disting. Svc. award 1996), Calif. Dental Assn. (Disting. Svc. award 1994), E.H. Angle Soc. (sec. No. Calif. component 1992-96). Home: 1060 Lea Dr San Rafael CA 94903-3726 E-mail: jagryson@comcast.net.

GRZANKA, LEONARD GERALD, writer, consultant; b. Ludlow, Mass., Dec. 11, 1947; s. Stanley Simon and Claire Genevive Grzanka; m. Christine Duncan Pearson, May 15, 1997 (div. Dec. 2000). BA, U. Mass., 1972; MA, Harvard U., 1974. Asst. prof. Gakushiun U., Tokyo, 1975-78; pub. rels. specialist Pacific Gas and Electric Co., San Francisco, 1978-80; sales promotion writer Tymshare Transaction Svcs., Fremont, Calif., 1980-81; account exec. The Strayton Co., Santa Clara, Calif., 1981-82; mng. editor Portable Computer Mag., San Francisco, 1982-84; prin. Grzanka Assocs., San Francisco, 1984-86; San Francisco bur. chief Digital News, 1986-91; battery program cons. Bevilacqua Knight Inc., Oakland, Calif., 1991-97; freelance writer, cons., 1997—. Staff asst. Electric Power Rsch. Inst./U.S. Advanced Battery Consortium, Palo Alto, Calif., 1991-96; lectr. Golden Gate U., San Francisco, 1985-87; instr. Diablo Valley Coll., Pleasant Hill, Calif., 2002--. Author: Neither Heaven Nor Hell, 1978; translator, editor: (art catalog) Masterworks of Japanese Crafts, 1977; translator: (book chpt.) Manajo: The Chinese Preface to the Kokinwakashu, 1984 (Literary Transl. award 1984), Spanish translation, 1994. Sgt. USAF, 1965—69. Fellow, Danforth Found., 1974. Mem. Harvard Club of San Francisco (bd. dirs. 1984-88, Cert. Appreciation 1986, 88), Phi Beta Kappa, Phi Kappa Phi. Avocations: writing, fishing. Home: 2909 Madison St Alameda CA 94501-5426

GRZANNA, DONALD EDWARD, music educator, musician, composer, publishing executive; b. Milw., Aug. 22, 1931; s. Rudolph and Edna Martha (Lutsen) Grzanna; m. Maureen Ann Schroeder; children: Christine, Donald M. Jr., Suzanne, Mark, Michelle. MusB, Rizzo Sch. Music, 1954; B in Music Composition, Roosevelt U., 1967, M in Music Edn., 1974. Music tchr. Cascio Music Co., Milw., 1953—68, Rizzo Sch. Music, Chgo., 1952—55, Alverno Coll., Milw., 1961—64; choir, band dir. Wells Jr. H.S., Milw., 1967—68, Fritsche Mid. Sch., Milw., 1968—97, Sarah Scott Mid. Sch., Milw., 1997—. Owner, pub. Don Grzanna Music, Caledonia, Wis., 1950—; musician John Ernst Restaurant, Bavarian Inn Restaurant, Lake Park Bistro Restaurant. Composer: 70 accordian solos, 30 other songs, classical arrangements for band, piano and accordian. Recipient awards, ASCAP, 1999, 2000, 2001. Republican. Lutheran. Home and Office: 1013 Sherwood Ln Caledonia WI 53108 E-mail: grzannde@mail.milwaukee.k12.wi.us.

GRZESIAK, KATHERINE ANN, primary school educator; BS, Ctrl. Mich. U., 1968; MA in Tchg., Saginaw Valley State U., 1975; postgrad., various univs., 1975—. 6th grade tchr. Buena Vista Sch. Dist., Saginaw, Mich., 1968-69, 70-71; tchr. Carrollton Pub. Schs., Saginaw, 1972-80, St. Peter and Paul Elem. Sch., Saginaw, 1981-84, Sch. Dist. of City of Saginaw, 1984-90; instr. Ctr. for Innovation in Edn., Saratoga, Calif., 1989—; tchr. Midland (Mich.) Pub. Schs., 1991—; 5th grade tchr. Eastlawn Elem., Midland. Adj. faculty Saginaw Valley State U., University Center, Mich., 1976-80, 88-90; presenter in field. Contbr. articles to profl. jours. Recipient Presdl. award for Excellence in Sci. and Math. Tchg., 1994, Top Tchr. in Mich. Met. Woman mag., 1997, Nat. Educator award Milken Family Found., 1998; named Mich. Tchr. of Yr., 1998. Home: 3115 McGill St Midland MI 48642-3928 Office: Eastlawn Elem Sch 115 Eastlawn Dr Midland MI 48640-5561 Office Phone: 989-923-7112. E-mail: grzesiakka@mps.k12.mi.us.

GRZESIK, JAN ALEXANDER, electronics engineer, mathematician; b. Rybnik, Upper Silesia, Poland, Aug. 7, 1939; arrived in U.S., 1952; s. Aleksander Franciszek Grzesik and Anna Makowska; m. Ewa Wiktoria Michalak, July 24, 1965 (div. Dec. 1970); m. Renata Ewa Wisniewska, Jan. 4, 1971; children: Renata Katarzyna, John Michael. BA in Physics summa cum laude, UCLA, 1960, PhD in Nuc. Engring., 1977; MA in Physics, Harvard U., 1961. Physicist U. Calif. Lawrence Livermore Lab., 1963; tchg. fellow dept. physics Harvard U., Cambridge, Mass., 1963—64; sr. staff antennas TRW Space and Electronics, Redondo Beach, Calif., 1968—; physicist RAND Corp., Santa Monica, Calif., 1973—75; rsch. engr. Sch. Engring. Applied Sci. UCLA, 1975—76. Contbr. articles to profl. jours. Fellow, Woodrow Wilson Found., 1960—61, NSF, 1961—62. Mem.: Math. Assn. Am., IEEE Antennas and Propogation Soc. Avocation: music. Home: 5517 Babcock Ave Valley Village CA 91607-1530 Office: Northrop Grumman Space Tech One Space Pk R11/2856AA Redondo Beach CA 90278 Business E-Mail: jan.grzesik@ngc.com.

GSCHWIND, DONALD, management and engineering consultant; b. Youngstown, Ohio, July 3, 1933; s. Mark Leon and Esther Lillian (Wauschek) G.; s. Eleanor Ann Tyken, May 27, 1961; children: Sandra J., Kurt L. BSME, Case Western Res. U., 1955; MS in Auto Engring., Chrysler Inst. Engring., 1957; MBA, Mich. State U., 1975. With Chrysler Corp., Detroit, 1955-58, mgr. steering and suspension engring., 1968-72, mgr. product engring., 1972-74, mgr. quality control, 1974-76, dir. chassis engring., 1976-80, v.p. product planning, 1980-84, v.p. program mgmt., 1984-88; dir., master automotive engring. Lawrence Tech. U., 1994-96. Served to capt. USAF, 1957—59. Mem. Soc. Auto Engrs., Tau Beta Pi

GSCHWIND, MICHAEL KARL, engineering educator; b. Vienna, Nov. 21, 1968; arrived in U.S., 1997; s. Karl Friedrich and Elfriede Lieselotte (Hager) G.; m. Valentine Salepura, Feb. 1998; 1 child, Katharina Valentina Lieselotte. BS in Computer Sci., Tech. U. Wien, 1990, MS in Computer Sci. summa cum laude, 1991, PhD in Computer Sci. summa cum laude, 1996. Teaching asst. Technische Univ. Wien, Vienna, 1988-89, studien asst., 1989-91, asst. prof., 1993—; rsch. scientist IBM Thomas J. Watson Rsch. Ctr., Yorktown Heights, N.Y., 1997—. Cons. in field, Vienna, 1988-91; rschr. European Union ESPRIT program, Brussels, Vienna, 1990-91; mem. acad. computer ctr. bd. Tech. Univ. Wien, 1990, mem. various coms. and bds., 1994. Contbr. articles to profl. jours. Fulbright scholar, 1991; Suksdorf fellow Washington State U., 1991. Mem. IEEE, IEEE Computer Soc., USENIX, Anglo-Austrian Soc., Austro-Am. Soc., Alt-Piaristner Austrian Fulbright Alumni Assn. (founding), Phi Kappa Phi. Avocations: languages/linguistics, travel, scuba diving, ethnic food, charitable work. Office: IBM TS Watson Rsch Ctr PO Box 218 Yorktown Heights NY 10598-0218

GU, BIN, research scientist; b. Nanjing, Jiangsu, China, June 24, 1974; s. Huaisu Gu and Meidi Su; m. Linglan Wang, July 13, 2000. PhD, Penn. State U., 2003. Rschr. Fudan U., Shanghai, 1996—99, Penn. State U., U. Pk, Pa., 1999—. Organizer Chinese Friendship Assn., State Coll. Pa., 2001—02. Mem.: Am. Chem. Soc., Sigma Xi. Office: Penn State U Dept Material Sci 187 MRL Bldg University Park PA 16802 E-mail: bingu@chem.psu.edu.

GU, BINHE, environmental scientist; b. Qingyuan, Guangdong, China, Mar. 28, 1957; s. Zaizhong Gu and Lianzhen Luo; m. Le Xu; children: Steven B., Diana S. PhD in Oceanography, U. Alaska, 1993. Post doctoral rsch. assoc. U. Fla., Gainesville, 1993—97; environ. specialist III St. Johns River Water Mgmt. Dist., Palatka, Fla., 1993—97; sr. environ. scientist South Fla. Water Mgmt. Dist., West Palm Beach, 1997—. Guest prof. Zhanjiang Ocean U., Guangdong, 2004—. Contbr. articles to profl. jours. Mem.: Chinese Assn. Sci., Edn. and Culture South Fla. (bd. dirs. 2002—06), World Aquaculture Soc., Soc. for Wetland Scientists (registered profl. wetland scientist 2001), Ecol. Soc. Am., Am. Soc. Limnology and Oceanography, Sino-Ecologists Club Overseas. Home: 3911 Hamilton Key West Palm Beach FL 33411 Office: S Fla Water Mgmt 3301 Gun Club Rd West Palm Beach FL 33406 Office Phone: 561-682-2556. Personal E-mail: bengu@netzero.com. E-mail: bgu@sfwmd.gov.

GU, HENRY HONGSHENG, pharmacist, researcher; s. Yuanqing Gu and Xiuwen Cao; m. Linda Yihong Yihong Ding, Mar. 20, 1993; children: Rachel Shinran, Sophie Yiran. MS, Ohio U., 1996; BS, Shanghai Jiao Tong U., 1987; postgrad., Rutgers U. Rsch. scientist Bristol-Myers Squibb Co., Princeton, NJ, 1997—2002; rsch. chemist Sanle GE, Nanjing, China, 1987—93. Patent advisor, agt. Bristol-Myers Squibb Co., Princeton, NJ, 2002—. Mem. 80-20. Scholar Nanyang Scholarship, Shanghai Jiao Tong U., 1987, Scholarship, Ohio U., 1993—96, U. of Pa, 1996. Mem.: Am. Intellectual Property Law Assn., Am. Chem. Soc. Achievements include patents for Us 6, 624, 184, Us 6, 596, 747, Us 6, 399, 773; Us 5, 990, 109; patents pending for Wo 0026197, Wo 0181340, Wo 2003059269, Wo 2003055447, Wo 2002143176; research in Jour. of Bioorganic & Medicinal Chemistry; Jour. of Medicinal Chemistry; Organic Letters; Tetrhedron Letters; Synlett; discovery of new drugs discovery. Office: Bristol-Myers Squibb Co Po Box 4000 Princeton NJ 08543-4000

GU, JIANHUI, process engineer, educator; b. Wuhan, China; married. BS in Engring., Huazhong U. Sci. and Tech., China, 1986; MSc, Huazhong U. Sci. and Tech., 1989; PhD, Nat. Tech. U., Singapore, 2002. Lectr. Huazhong U. Sci. and Tech., Wuhan, 1989—95, assoc. prof., 1995—98; rsch. assoc. Nanyang Technol. U., Singapore, 1998—2000; elec. engr. Hewlett-Packard Co., Singapore, 2000—. Contbr. over 80 articles to profl. jours. Mem.: Hubei Provincial Assn. Lasers, Internat. Soc. Optical Engring. Achievements include patents pending for laser cleaning of debris from laser ablated polyimide surface; invention of discloure on fs laser micromachining; research in areas of high-power lasers, laser interaction with material, laser micromachining. Office: Hewlett-Packard Co 1000 NE Circle Blvd Corvallis OR 97330 Office Phone: 541-715-2846. Business E-Mail: jianhui.gu@hp.com.

GU, JIANMIN, mechanical engineer, researcher; arrived in U.S., 1995; s. Shunfa Gu and Lingjiu. BS in Ocean Engring. Tech. Engring. Econ. with honors, Shanghai Jiao Tong U., 1988—92, MS in Structural Mechanics, 1992—95; PhDME, U. Mich., 1996—2000, postgrad., 2005—. Lab. and rsch. asst. Nat. Lab. Ocean Engring. Shanghai Jiao Tong U., 1991—92, rsch. investigator, asst. Structural Mech. Lab., 1992—95; rsch. asst. thermotractive thin film rsch. group Mich. State U., East Lansing, 1995—96; rsch. asst. Computational Mech. Lab. U. Mich., Ann Arbor, 1995—2000, instr. dept. mech. engring. and applied mech., 1999; devel. and test engr. core analysis tools Mech. Dynamics, Inc., Ann Arbor, 1997—99; rsch. engr. rsch. and vehicle tech. Ford Motor Co., Dearborn, Mich., 2000—05, tech. expert N.Am. engring., 2005—. Summer rsch. engr. Tech. and Equipment Rsch. Inst. Shengil Oil Field Complex, Shandong, China, 1992; cons., reviewer jours. in field. Contbr. articles to profl. jours. Recipient Fellowship award, Chinese Soc. Naval Arch. and Marine Engrs., 1991, 3d prize, Shanghai Sci. and Tech. Assn., 1993, Best Paper award, Nat. Conf. Offshore Engring., 1994, Coll. Engring. Disting. Achievement award, U. Mich., 1998, VEV Achievement award, Ford Motor Co., 2004; Computational Dynamics fellow, Mech. Dynamics, Inc., 1999, Horace H. Rackham Travel grant, 1999, Nat. Congress Computational Mech. scholar, 1999. Mem.: ASME, Internat. Assn. Computational Mechanics (Finalist award Robert J. Melosh medal 1999), Soc. Automotive Engrs. (Henry Ford II Disting. award for Excellence in Automotive Engring. 2004), U.S. Assn. Computational Mechanics (Computational Mechanics scholar 1999), Am. Acad. Mechanics, Sigma Xi. Baptist. Avocations: travel, reading, music, tunning. Office: Ford Motor Co Product Devel Ctr 1D-M32 MD297 20901 Oakwood Blvd Dearborn MI 48124 Business E-Mail: jgu2@ford.com.

GUADAGNINO, FRANK T., lawyer; b. Pitts., Aug. 24, 1956; BS in mktg., Pa. State U., 1978; JD cum laude, U. Pitts., 1983. Bar: Pa. 1983. Assoc. Reed Smith LLP, Pitts., 1983—92, ptnr., 1992—, practice group leader fin. services group, 2002—. Bd. dirs. Downtown Pitts. YMCA, 2002—. Mem.: ABA, Am. Arbitration Assn., Allegheny County Bar Assn. Office: Reed Smith LLP 435 Sixth Ave Pittsburgh PA 15219 Office Phone: 412-288-3236. Office Fax: 412-288-3063. Business E-Mail: fguadagnino@reedsmith.com.

GUAJARDO, ELISA, counselor, educator; b. Roswell, N. Mex., Nov. 13, 1932; d. Alejo Najar and Hortensia (Jiminez) Garcia; m. David Roberto Guajardo, Oct. 15, 1950; 1 child, Elsie Edith. BS, Our Lady of the Lake U., 1962, MEd, 1971; MA, Chapman U., 1977. Cert. tchr., adminstr., counselor, Calif. Elem. tchr. San Antonio (Tex.) Sch. Dist., 1962-63; tchr. social sci. Newport Mesa Sch. Dist., Costa Mesa, Calif., 1963-67, Orange (Calif.) Unified Sch. Dist., 1967-70, project dir., 1970-71, tchr. English, 1972-73, counselor, 1973—. Pres. Bilingual, Bicultural Parent Adv. Bd., Orange, Calif., 1971-72; reader bilingual projects Calif. State Dept. Edn., Orange, 1971-72;

vis. lectr. We. Wash. Univ., Bellingham, 1972-73; mem. curriuculum and placement couns., Orange Unified Sch. Dist., 1973-78, 95-96. Author: (Able)Adaptations of Bilingual/Bicultural Edn, Fed. Project Proposal. Mem. NEA, AAUW, Calif. Tchrs. Assn., Orange Unified Edn. Assn, Hon., Alpha Chi, Our Lady of Lake U., Tex. chpt. Democrat. Mem. Assemblies of God Church. Avocations: choir and solo singing, piano, marimba, organ. Home: 335 E Jackson Ave Orange CA 92867-5743 Office: Canyon HS 220 S Imperial Hwy Anaheim CA 92807-3945 E-mail: davielisa2@juno.com.

GUAJARDO, SALOMON A., finance director; s. Victor Caballero and Maria Dolores Guajardo. BA in Polit. Sci., UCLA, 1988; MPA in Pub. Mgmt., U. Pitts., 1990, MEd in Rsch. Methodology, 1994, PhD in Pub. Policy Rsch. and Analysis, 1996. Dir. of fin. Nassau County Legislature, Mineola, NY, 2004—; sr. mgr. pub. analysis and rsch. Govt. Fin. Officers Assn., Chicago, 1989—2000; asst. prof. pub. mgmt. CUNY, N.Y.C., 1997—98; sr. profl. assoc. NEA, Washington, 2000—01; dir. rsch. for fin. and budget Office of County Exec., Nassau County, Mineola, NY, 2002—04. Author: Revenue Analysis and Forecasting, Elected Official's Guide to Revenue Forecasting, Elected Official's Guide to Performance Management, Elected Official's Guide to Multi-year Budgeting. Office: Nassau County Legislature One West St Rm 503 Mineola NY 11501 Office Phone: 516-571-6100.

GUAN, E., research scientist; b. Liaoning Province, China; PhD, U. Sci. and Tech. China, 1997, SUNY Stony Brook, 2004. Post doctoral fellow SUNY, Stony Brook, rsch. scientist, 2001—. Mem.: Material Rsch. Soc., Am. Phys. Soc. Achievements include invention of Dynamic facial recognition technique; patents pending for An Early Diagnosis Method of Skin Diseases and facial nerve disorders with DISC; Use of Digital Speckle Image Correlation to Quantify Skin Aging; Use of DISC Technique to Measure the Deformation of the Skin Induced by a Polymer; Prosthetic Spinal Disc Nucleus. Office: Dept Materials Science State Univ New York Stony Brook NY 11794 Office Phone: 631-632-8467. Office Fax: 631-632-5764. E-mail: eguan@ic.sunysb.edu.

GUARASCIO, PHILIP, advertising executive; b. N.Y.C., June 28, 1941; s. Frank and Charlotte (Cohen) G.; m. Ruth Agness Hornick, Sept. 7, 1963, children: Lisa Marie, David Evan BA, Marietta Coll. Sr. v.p., dir. media mgmt. Benton & Bowles, Inc., N.Y.C., bd. dirs.; exec. dir. advt. svcs. Gen. Motors, Detroit, 1985—90, exec. dir. mktg. programs and advt., 1990—91, exec.-in-charge corp. mktg. and advt., 1991—92, gen. mgr. mktg. and advt. N. Am. Ops., 1992—94, v.p./gen. mgr. mktg. and advt. No. Am. Ops., 1994—2000; ind. advisor NFL, 2000—04, lead exec. mktg. and sales, 2004—. Trustee Marietta Coll., Ohio, 1981-83. Served USAR, 1963—70. Mem. Nat. Cable TV Assn., Internat. Radio & TV Found., Am. Assn. Advt. Agys., Radio Advt. Bur., Nissequogue Country Club, St. James, N.Y. Avocations: golfing, tennis. Home: 3075 Chestnut Run Dr Bloomfield Hills MI 48302-1110 Office: GM 3044 W Grand Blvd Detroit MI 48202-3037

GUARD, PATRICIA J., federal agency administrator; b. Lafayette, Ind., June 9, 1948; BS, MS, Purdue U. Therapist speech, lang. and hearing Logansport Area Joint Spl. Svcs. Coop., 1974-76, supr. speech dept., 1976-78; dir. spl. edn. Boone-Clinton-NW Hendricks Count Joint Svcs. Spl. Edn. Coop., 1978-81; rsch. asst. U.S. Ho. of Reps., 1981-82; legis. specialist Office Legis. and Pub. Affairs, 1983-84; acting dir. Office Spl. Edn. Programs Dept. Edn., 1985-86, deputy dir. Office Spl. Edn. Programs, 1984-85, 86-87, sr. legis. analyst Office Legis. and Pub. Affairs, 1987-90, dir. policy and planning staff Office Spl. Edn. and Rehabilitative Svcs., 1990-92, dep. dir. Office Spl. Edn., 1992-93, acting dir. Office Spl. Edn. Programs, 1993-94; mem. sr. exec. svc. Office Edn. Programs, Washington, 1994—. Vice chmn., trustee Arlington Cmty. Residence, Inc., 1993, bd. dirs., 1989—. Fellow Inst. Ednl. Leadership, 1981; recipient Disting. Alumni award Purdue U., 1989, Mentor award Dept. Edn., 1994. Office: Spl Edn Programs 330 C St SW Washington DC 20201-0001

GUARDO, CAROL J., association executive; b. Hartford, Conn., Apr. 12, 1939; d. C. Fred and Marion (Biase) G. BA, St. Joseph Coll., 1961; MA, U. Detroit, 1963; PhD, U. Denver, 1966. Asst. prof. psychology Eastern Mich. U., Ypsilanti, 1966-68; assoc. prof., staff psychologist U. Denver, 1968-73; assoc. prof., dean coll. Utica Coll. of Syracuse U., Utica, N.Y., 1973-76; prof., dean Coll. Liberal Arts, Drake U., Des Moines, 1976-80; provost, prof. U. Hartford, 1980-85; pres. R.I. Coll., Providence, 1986-90, Great Lakes Colls. Assn., Ann Arbor, Mich., 1990—. Mem. Iowa Humanities Bd., 1976-80, pres., 1978-80; bd. dirs. Am. Coun. Edn., People's Bank. Author: The Adolescent As Individual: Issues and Insights, 1975; contbr. articles to profl. jours. Trustee St. Joseph Coll., Monmouth Coll., Colby-Sawyer Coll., Cabrini Coll. NSF fellow, 1964, NIMH fellow, 1964-66. Mem. Am. Assn. Higher Edn., Assn. Am. Colls. (vice chair 1987, chair 1988), Am. Psychol. Assn., Assn. Gen. and Liberal Studies (pres. 1979-81), Soc. Rsch. in Child Devel., Greater Providence C. of C., Phi Beta Kappa. Office: Great Lakes Colls Assn 2929 Plymouth Rd Ste 207 Ann Arbor MI 48105-3206

GUARE, JOHN, playwright, educator; b. N.Y.C., Feb. 5, 1938; s. John Edward and Helen Clare (Grady) Guare; m. Adele Chatfield-Taylor, 1981. AB, Georgetown U., 1961; MFA, Yale U., 1963; PhD (Hon.), Georgetown U., 1991. Seminar in writing fellow Saybrook Coll., Yale U., New Haven, 1977—78; adj. prof., 1978—81; fellow Juilliard Sch., 1993—94; lectr. NYU, CCNY; vis. artist Harvard U., 1990—91. Author: (plays) Universe, 1949, Thirties' Girl, 1959, The Toadstool Boy, 1960, The Golden Cherub, 1962, Did You Write My Name in the Snow, 1962, To Wally Pantoni, We Leave a Credenza, 1964, The Loveliest Afternoon of the Year, Something I'll Tell You Tuesday, 1966, Muzeek, 1967 (Obie award, 1968), Cop-out, 1968 (N.Y. Drama Critics' award, 1969), A Play by Brecht, Home Fires, Kissing Sweet, 1969, The House of Blue Leaves, 1971 (N.Y. Drama Critics' Circle award, 1971, Outer Critics' Circle award, 1971, Obie award, 1971, Tony award, 1986), (musical) Two Gentlemen of Verona, 1971 (N.Y. Drama Critics' Circle award, 1972, 2 Tony awards, 1972, 2 Drama Desk awards, 1972), A Day for Surprises, 1971, Un Pape a New York, 1972, Marco Polo Sings a Solo, Optimism, or the Adventures of Candide, 1973, Rich and Famous, 1974, Landscape of the Body, 1977 (Joseph Jefferson award, 1977), Take a Dream, 1978, Bosoms and Neglect, 1979, In Fireworks Lie Secret Codes, 1981, Lydie Breeze, Gardenia, 1982, Hey, Stay a While, Women and Water, 1984, Gluttony, The Talking Dog, 1985, Moon Over Miami, 1989, Six Degrees of Separation, 1990 (N.Y. Drama Critics' Circle award, 1991), London, 1993 (Olivier Best Play award, 1993), Four Baboons Adoring the Sun, 1992 (Tony award nomination Best Play, 1992), Moon Under Miami, 1995, The General of Hot Desire, 1997; co-adapter, lyricist: plays Two Gentlemen of Verona, 1971; author: (screenplays) Taking Off, 1970, Atlantic City, 1981 (Academy award nomination Best Original Screenplay, 1981, N.Y. Film Critics' award, 1981, L.A. Film Critics' award, 1981, Nat. Soc. Film Critics' award, 1981, Venice Film Festival Grand prize, 1981), Six Degrees of Separation, 1993, Chuck Close: Life and Work 1988-1995, War Against the Kitchen Sink, 1996; playwright-in-residence N.Y. Shakespeare Festival, 1976—77; co-editor: Lincoln Ctr. Rev. Named Lit. Lion, N.Y. Pub. Libr., 1986; recipient Award of Merit, Am. Acad. Arts and Letters, 1981, Obie Sustained Achievement award, Village Voice, 2005; Rockefeller grantee. Mem.: Am. Acad. Arts and Letters, Dramatist Guild Council.*

GUARENTE, LEONARD P., medical geneticist, educator; b. Chelsea, Mass., June 6, 1952; s. Leonard and Norma Guarente; m. Barbara Weiffenbach, Sept. 6, 1981 (div. 1985); 1 child, Jeffrey. BS in Biology, MIT, 1974; PhD in Molecular Genetics, Harvard U., 1978. Asst. prof. biology MIT, Cambridge, 1981—85, assoc. prof. biology, 1985—, now Novartis prof. biology. Founder, dir. Elixir Pharm., Cambridge, 2000—. Author: Ageless Quest, 2003; contbr. articles to profl. jours. Recipient Presidential Young Investigator award, NSF, 1984—89. Fellow: Am. Acad. Arts & Sci.; mem.: Am. Acad. Microbiology. Achievements include patents in field; discovery of gene that regulates aging.*

GUARIGILA, DALE A., lawyer; BED, U. Kan., 1985; JD, U. Mo.-Kansas City, 1985. Bar: Mo. 1985, US Dist. Ct., Ea. and We. Dist. Mo. Ptnr., group dep. Environ. Bryan Cave LLP, St. Louis. Office: Bryan Cave LLP One Metropolitan Sq 211 N Broadway, Ste 3600 Saint Louis MO 63102 Office Phone: 314-259-2606. E-mail: daguarigila@bryancave.com.

GUARNIERI, ALBINA, Canadian legislator; b. Faeto, Italy, June 23, 1953; BA, MA, McGill U. Solicitor Gen., Can., 1980; liberal leader1981 election; press sec. Mayor of Toronto, Ont., Can.; M.P. Ho. Commons, 1988—; parliamentary sec. to min. Canadian heritage Govt. of Can., Ottawa, 1993—96, assoc. min. nat. defense, 2003—, min. state (civil preparedness), 2003—, min. VA, 2005—. Office: House of Commons Rm 450 Confederation Bldg Ottawa ON Canada K1A OA6

GUASP, SUSAN GUIHAN, painter, educator; b. Bklyn., Apr. 28, 1959; d. Robert A. and Veronica Guihan; children: Sarah Veronica, Jules Robert. BA, Queens Coll., Flushing, N.Y., 1987, M in Art Edn., 1989. Art tchr. Kings Park (N.Y.) HS, 1987—. Exhibitions include Heckscher Mus., Huntington, N.Y., 1987, 1997, Mills Pond House Gallery, St. James, N.Y., 2004, Art League's 50th Exhbn. of LI Artists, Jeannie Tongelgea Gallery, Dix Hills, NY, 2005, New England Exhbn., Bennington, Vt., 2004, HTAL's Fall Invitational Hutchins Gallery, Greenvale, NY, 1993, 35th HTAL Heckscher Mus., Huntington, NY, 1990. Avocations: painting, printmaking. Home: 106 Gull Dip Rd Ridge NY 11961 Office: Kings Park HS 200 Rt 25 A Kings Park NY 11754-3898

GUASTAFERRO, ANGELO, space science administrator, consultant; b. Hoboken, NJ, June 4, 1932; s. Carlo and Rafaela Nancy (Gioffi) G.; m. Eleanor Lago, Sept. 12, 1954; children: Carl, Mark, John Brian. BS in Mech. Engring, N.J. Inst. Tech., 1954; MBA, Fla. State U., 1963; A.M.P., Harvard U., 1984. With NASA, 1963-85, dep. mgr. Viking project, 1974-76; dir. planetary programs NASA Hdqs., Washington, 1979-81; dep. dir. Ames Research Center, Moffett Field, Calif., 1981-85; v.p., program dir. Lockheed Missiles & Space Co., 1985-96, exec. dir., 1994-96; CEO, chmn. bd. n View Corp., Newport News, Va., 1996; pres., CEO View Corp., Newport News, Va., 1996—98; exec. cons. AG Cons., Williamsburg, Va., 1998—. Bd. trustees Internat. Space U., 1993-96; chmn. bd. dirs. View Corp., 1995-2002; sci. adv. com. NJIT. Chair bd. dirs. Hampton Rds. Tech. Coun. Served with USAF, 1955-58. Recipient Langley Spl. Achievement award NASA, 1974, 77, 78, Outstanding Leadership medal, 1977, Superior Performance award, 1980, Exceptional Service medal, 1981, Presdl. Meritorious rank, 1982; Disting. Alumnus NJIT, 1997. Fellow AIAA (Space Systems medal 1982), Am. Astronautics Soc.; mem. Mars First Landing Soc. (pres. 1978-79), Internat. Astronautics Fedn. (bd. dirs.), Tau Beta Pi (eminent engr. 1989). Roman Catholic. Office: AG Cons 124 Peter Lyall Williamsburg VA 23185-8902 Office Phone: 757-258-3039. E-mail: gusg@cox.net.

GUBBINS, KEITH EDMUND, chemical engineering educator; b. Southampton, Eng., Jan. 27, 1937; came to U.S., 1962; m. Pauline Margaret Payne, June 28, 1960; children: Nick, Vanessa. B.Sc. in Chemistry, Queen Mary Coll., U. London, 1958; Diploma in Chem. Engring., King's Coll., U. London, 1959, PhD in Chem. Engring., 1962. Vis. lectr. U. London, Eng., 1960-62; postdoctoral fellow U. Fla., Gainesville, 1962-64, asst. prof., 1964-68, assoc. prof., 1968-72, prof., 1972-76; T.R. Briggs prof. engring. Cornell U., Ithaca, NY, 1976-98, T.R. Briggs prof. engring. emeritus, 1998—, dir. Sch. Engring., 1983-90; W.H. Clark Disting. Univ. prof. N.C. State U., Raleigh, 1998—, co-dir. Ctr. for High Performance Simulation, 2004—. Vis. cons. theoretical physics divsn., U.K. Atomic Energy Authority, Harwell, U.K., 1971; vis. prof. Dept. Physics U. Guelph, 1971-73, 76, U. Kent, Canterbury, Eng., 1975, Dept. Chemistry U. Oxford, 1979-80, 86-87, Chiba U., Japan, 1999, Dept. Chem. Engring., U. Calif., Berkeley, 1982, Australian Nat. U., Canberra, 1993, Imperial Coll., London, 1970-71, 94, 2002, U. Paris-Sud, 2001-02, Dept. Chem. Engring., U. Wis., 1993, Chiba U., Japan, 1999, U. Paris-Sud, 2001-2002; vis. fellow Fulbright Sr. scholar Australian Nat. U., 1993-94; mem. NAS com. to study formation of Nat. Resource Ctr. for Computing in Chemistry, 1976-77, NRC Assessment Bd. to rev. NIST programs, 1988-91; cons. in field; lectr. in field Mem. editl. bd. Molecular Physics, 1978-87, 95—, Jour. of Chem. Physics, 1995-98, Molecular Simulation, 1986—, assoc. editor, 1990—; assoc. editor Am. Inst. Chem. Engrs. Jour., 1988-91; editor: Topics in Chem. Engring., Oxford U. Press, 1991—; del. Oxford U. Press, 1991—. Recipient best paper ann. award Can. Soc. Chem. Engring., 1973; named Eppley Found. fellow Imperial Coll. London, 1970-71, Guggenheim fellow, 1986-87, sr. vis. fellow (SERC award) U. Oxford, 1986-87, vis. fellow (SERC award) Imperial Coll., London, 1994. Mem. NAE, AAAS, Am. Chem. Soc., Am. Inst. Chem. Engrs. (program com. 1974-81, Alpha Chi Sigma award 1986, William H. Walker award 2000, fellow 2003), Am. Inst. Physics, Chem. Soc. (London). E-mail: keg@ncsu.edu, kgubbins@aol.com.

GUBEN, JAN K., lawyer; b. Balt., Md., Nov. 11, 1942; BA, Tusculum Coll., 1964; LLB, U. Balt., 1967. Bar: Md. 1967, DC, 2001. Ptnr., real estate law Venable LLP (formerly Venable, Baetjer and Howard), Balt., chair. bus. div., 1995—2001. Lectr. real estate Johns Hopkins U., 1986-95, deleg. US Agy. Internat. Devel., 1997. Mem. ABA, Md. State Bar Assn., Bar Assn. Balt. City. Office: Venable LLP 1800 Mercantile Bank & Trust Bldg 2 Hopkins Plz Baltimore MD 21201 Office Phone: 410-244-7624. Office Fax: 410-244-7742. Business E-Mail: jkguben@venable.com.

GUBER, PETER, executive producer; b. Boston, Mass., Mar. 1, 1942; m. Lynda Gellis. BA, Syracuse U.; SSP, JD, LLM, U. Florence, Italy; postgrad., NYU. Bar: N.Y., Calif., D.C. Exec. asst. Columbia Pictures, studio chief, co-chmn., 1989-94; prin. Peter Guber's Filmworks; co-prin., chmn. bd. Casablanca Record and Filmworks (merger Peter Guber's Filmworks and Casablanca Records), 1976-80; prin. Polygram Pictures, 1980-83, Guber-Peters, 1983-88; co-chmn., mng. dir. Guber-Peters-Barris Entertainment Co, 1988-89, chmn., 1989; chmn., chief exec. officer Sony Pictures Entertainment, 1989-94; chmn., CEO Mandalay, incl. Mandalay Pictures, Mandalay Television, Mandalay Sports Entertainment, Mandalay Media Arts, Mandalay E-Media. Vis. prof., chmn. producer's dept. UCLA Sch. Theatre Arts. Author: Inside the Deep, Above the Title, (with Peter Bart) Shoot Out: Surviving Game and (Mis)Fortune in Hollywood, 2002; prodr.: (films) The Deep, 1977; (with Jon Peters) Vision Quest, 1985, Batman, 1989, Tango & Cash, 1989; (with Peters and Neil Canton) The Witches of Eastwick, 1987, Caddyshack II, 1988; (television) Stand By Your Man, 1981, Brotherhood of Justice, 1986, Bay Coven, 1987, Nightmare at Bitter Creek, 1988, Finish Line, 1989, Autobahn, 2005, The Jacket, 2005; exec. prodr.: Midnight Express, 1978; (with Peters) An American Werewolf in London, 1981, Six Weeks, 1982, Missing, 1982 (Academy award nomination for best picture 1982), Flashdance, 1983, D.C. Cab, 1983, Head Office, 1985, The Legend of Billie Jean, 1985, The Color Purple, 1985 (Academy award nomination for best picture 1985), Youngblood, 1986, Gorillas in the Mist, 1988, Rain Man, 1988 (Academy award for best picture 1988), Missing Link, 1989, The Bonfire of the Vanities, 1990, This Boy's Life, 1993, With Honors, 1994; (with Peters, George Folsey, Jr., and John Landis) Clue, 1985; (with Peters, Mark Damon, John Hyde, and Sydney Kimmel) The Clan of the Cave Bear, 1986; (with Peters, Kathleen Kennedy, Frank Marshall, and Steven Speilberg) Innerspace, 1987; (with Peters and Roger Birnbaum) Who's That Girl?, 1987, (with Peters, Benjamin Melniker, and Michael E. Uslan) Batman Returns, 1992, Galapagos: The Enchanted Voyage, 1999, Alex and Emma, 2003, A Thousand Roads, 2005, Into the Blue, 2005; (television) The Toughest Man in the World, 1984; (with Peters) Television and the Presidency, 1983 (Emmy award nomination 1984), Rude Awakening, 1998; asst. prodr.: High Spirits, 1988. Named Producer of Yr., NATO, 1979; Albert Gallatin fellow NYU. Office: Mandalay Entertainment Astaire Bldg 10202 W Washington Blvd Culver City CA 90232-3119*

GUBERMAN, SIDNEY, painter, writer; b. Greenville, S.C., Aug. 24, 1936; s. Morris and Louise (Cook) G.; m. Jennifer Glidden, June 5, 1965 (div. 1977); children: Maxwell, Angus; m. Rebecca Wilson, July 31, 1977; children: Elizabeth Tindall, Dore Hopkins Brooks. BA, Princeton U., 1958; MArch, U. Pa., 1967. Asst. prof. Ecole Polytechnique, Lausanne, Switzerland, 1973-75. Vis. artist U. S.C., Columbia, 1991-92, Atlanta Coll. Art, 1989, 91; vis. lectr. Princeton (N.J.) U., 1981; artist invité Federale de Lausanne Ecole des Beaux-Arts, Switzerland, 1971-73; chmn. bd. dirs. New Visions Gallery, Atlanta, 1987-93; bd. dirs. Atlanta Arts Festival, 1986-88. Solo exhbns. include Henri Gallery, Washington, 1970, 73, 75, Galerie R-B, Fribourg, Switzerland, 1975, 79, Image South Gallery, Atlanta, 1976, Harcus/Krakow/Rosen/Sonnabend, Boston, 1976, Fraser's Stable Gallery, Washington, 1978, Heath Gallery, Atlanta, 1979, Leah Levy Gallery, San Francisco, 1979, Diane Brown Gallery, Washington, 1980, Galerie Jonas, Cortaillod, Switzerland, 1980, Barbara Fiedler Gallery, Washington, 1981, Fay Gold Gallery, Atlanta, 1981, 82, 83, 85, Gertrude Herbert Gallery, Augusta, Ga., 1985, Gibbes Art Mus., Charleston, S.C., 1988, Galerie von der Milwe, Aachen, Germany, 1990, Hodges-Taylor, Charlotte, N.C., 1990, Louisa McIntosh Gallery, Atlanta, 1991, Susan Conway Carroll Gallery, Washington, 1991, "New Paintings" Weslyn Coll Gallery, Macon, Ga., 1999; group exhbns. include Prix de peinture, Vevey, Switzerland, 1974, City Gallery Contemporary Art, Raleigh, N.C., 1987, SECCA, Winston-Salem, N.C., 1988, Birmingham (Ala.) Mus. Art, 1988-89; permanent collections include The High Mus., Atlanta, The Hunter Mus., Chattanooga, Tenn., The Nat. Mus. Am. Art, Washington, Princeton (N.J.) U. Mus., Colo. Springs Fine Arts Ctr.; author: Frank Stella: An Illustrated Biography, 1995; curator Frank Stella-Imaginary Landscapes exhbn. The Gibbes Mus., 2001, Charleston, S.C., William Christenberry: Hale County on My Mind, various museums. Individual Artist's grantee NEA, 1980; Guggenheim fellow, 1988-89. Mem. The Ivy Club. Democrat. Avocations: films, tennis, opera. Home: 131 Montgomery Ferry Dr NE Atlanta GA 30309-2712 Office: 1174 Zonolite Pl NE # C Atlanta GA 30306-2002 Office Phone: 404-881-0222. Business E-Mail: st.gubie@mindspring.com.

GUBERT, WALTER ALEXANDER, investment company executive; b. Merano, Italy, June 15, 1947; LLD, U. Florence, Italy, 1970; grad., INSEAD, Fountainbleu, France, 1973. Analyst European chems. J.P. Morgan & Co., Inc., Paris, 1973-77, v.p. treasury mgmt. adv. group London, 1977-81, sr. v.p. capital markets activities U.S. N.Y.C., 1981—87; CEO J.P. Morgan Securities, London, 1987—90; chmn. London Mgmt. Com. J.P. Morgan & Co., Inc., London, 1989—92, co-head Investment Banking Europe, ME & Africa, 1992—95, sr. exec. Europe, ME & Africa, 1995—97, v. chmn., 1998—2000, global head Investment Banking N.Y.C., 1998—2000; vice chmn. J.P. Morgan Chase & Co., N.Y.C., 2001—; chmn. J.P. Morgan Investment Bank, N.Y.C., 2001—04; chmn. Europe, Middle East and Africa J.P. Morgan Chase & Co., 2004—. Office: JP Morgan Chase & Co 270 Park Ave New York NY 10017-2014 also: JP Morgan Chase & Co Investment Bank 10 Aldermanbury London EC2V7RF England Office Phone: 212-270-6000.

GUBLER, DUANE J., research scientist, educator, virologist; b. Santa Clara, Utah, June 4, 1939; s. June and Thelma (Whipple) G.; m. Bobbie J. Carroll, Mar. 1, 1958; children: Justin Chase, Stuart Jefferson. BS, Utah State U., 1963; MS, U. Hawaii, 1965; ScD, Johns Hopkins U., 1969; AS, So. Utah State U., 1962, DSc (hon.), 1988. Asst. prof. pathobiology Sch. Hygiene Johns Hopkins U., Balt. and Calcutta, 1969-71; assoc. prof. tropical medicine Sch. Medicine U. Hawaii, Honolulu, 1971-75; head virology dept. Naval Med. Rsch. Unit Number 2, Jakarta, Indonesia, 1975-78; assoc. prof. entomology and microbiology U. Ill., Urbana, 1978-79; rsch. microbiologist divsn. vector-borne viral diseases Ctrs. for Disease Control and Prevention, Fort Collins, Colo., 1980-81, dir. San Juan (P.R.) Labs., 1981-89, dir. divsn. vector-borne infectious diseases Ft. Collins, Colo., 1989—2003; dir. Asia Pacific Inst. Tropical Medicine and Infectious Diseases, U. Hawaii, Honolulu, 2004—. Cons. NRC, 1972, South Pacific Commn., 1972-76, WHO, Geneva, 1974—, AID, Washington, 1977—, Pan Am. Health Orgn., 1981—, Internat. Devel. Rsch. Ctr., Ottawa, Can., 1977—, Rockefeller Found., N.Y.C., 1987—, numerous nat. ministries of health, 1972—; Bailey K. Ashford meml. lectr. U. P.R. Sch. Medicine, 1999; chmn. bd. coun. Pediat. Dengue Vaccine Initiative, 2002; mem. scientific adv. bd. Novartis Inst. Tropical Diseases, 2003—. Contbr. numerous articles to profl. jours. Lt. USN, 1975-77; capt. USPHS. Recipient Commendation medal, 1984, Outstanding Svc. medal, 1988, Meritorious Svc. medal, 1991, Outstanding Unit citation, 1995, 98, 2000, Outstanding Alumni award for sci. and rsch. Johns Hopkins U. Sch. Pub. Health, 1997, Chuck Alexander Operational award La. Mosquito Control Assn., 1998, Disting. Svc. award Dept. HHS, 1996, 2000, 01, 03, Charles Shepard award in Sci., Ctr. for Disease Control, 2001; selected as one of 90 Illustrious Alumni in celebration of U. Hawaii's 90th year, 1997, Woodward Lectr. award USN Preventive Medicine Unit, 2000. Mem. AAAS, Am. Soc. Tropical Medicine (Charles Franklin Craig lectr. 1988, pres.-elect 1998, pres. 2000), Am. Soc. Parasitologists, Am. Mosquito Control Assn., Entomol. Soc. Am. (highlights in med. entomology lecture 1979, 95), Soc. Vector Ecologists, Infectious Disease Soc. Am., Rotary (Rotarian of Yr. San Juan chpt. 1986, Meritorious Svc. award Rotary Found., Evanston, Ill. 1990, Svc. Above Self award Fort Collins Club 1999, Internat. Svc. Above Self award 2000). Office: U Hawaii Sch Medicine Leahi Hosp 3675 Kilauea Ave Honolulu HI 96816 Office Phone: 808-732-1477. Business E-Mail: dgubler@hawaii.edu.

GUBSER, PETER ANTON, political scientist, writer, educator; b. Tulsa, May 9, 1941; s. Eugene Herbert and Mary (Douglass) G.; m. Annie Yeni-Komshian, Aug. 15, 1969; children: Sasha Mary-Helen, Christi Valerie. BA, Yale U., 1964; MA, Am. U. Beirut, 1966; PhD, Oxford (Eng.) U., 1970. Rsch. fellow U. Manchester, Eng., 1970-72; assoc. rsch. scientist Am. Insts. for Rsch., Washington, 1972-74; asst. rep. Ford Found., Beirut, 1974-77; pres. Am. Near East Refugee Aid, Washington, 1977—. Bd. dirs. Internat. Svc. Agys., Washington, Am. Coun. Vol. Internat. Action, Internat. Coll., Beirut, Nat. Coun. on U.S.-Arab Rels., Washington, Found. for Mid. East Peace, Washington, Global Devel. Forum, Amman, Jordan; adj. prof. Georgetown U., Washington, 1990—; lectr. various govt. and non-govt. instns., 1977—. Author: Politics and Change at Karak, Jordan, 1973, Jordan: Crossroads of Middle East Events, 1983, Historical Dictionary of Hashemite Kingdom of Jordan, 1991. Mem. Somerset (Md.) Town Coun., 1994-2004; mem. Montgomery County Adv. Bd., 2004—. Mem.: Washington Inst. Fgn. Affairs, Middle East Studies Assn., Middle East Inst., Am. Polit. Sci. Assn., Cosmos Club, Order of the Hosp. of St. John of Jerusalem. Democrat. Mem. Christian Ch. Avocations: hiking, reading, travel. Office: Am Near East Refugee Aid 1522 K St NW Ste 202 Washington DC 20005-1202 Office Phone: 202-347-2558. E-mail: peter@anera.org, gubser@mindspring.com.

GUCCIONE, SAMIRA, radiologist, educator; b. Tehran, Iran, Jan. 21, 1966; arrived in U.S., 1980; d. Javad and Susan Salehi-Had; children from previous marriage: Carle, Sophia. BS, U. Va., 1988; MS, Johns Hopkins U., 1995, PhD, 1999. Aquacultural rschr. Maricultura, Wilmington, NC, 1985—86; rsch. assoc. U. Va., Charlottesville, 1988—89; clin. engr. Johns Hopkins U., Balt., 1990—93, rsch. asst., 1994—97; rsch. assoc. Stanford (Calif.) U., 2003—04, asst. prof. radiology, 2004—. Cons. NIH, Bethesda, Md., 2002—, Medlumi-nal Inc., Palo Alto, Calif., 2004; lectr. in field. Contbr. chapters to books, articles to profl. jours. Resource specialist Calif. State Blue Ribbon Task Force Nanotechnology, Sacramento, 2004—. Scholar, AFLAC, 2001; NIH fellow, Stanford U., 2000—02. Mem.: Internat. Soc. Magnetic Resonance Medicine (award 2002), Am. Soc. Clin. Oncologists, Am. Assn. Cancer Rsch. Achievements include patents for drug delivery system for nucleic acid; system for protesmic analysis. Avocations: tennis, hiking, bicycling, skiing. Office: Stanford U Lucas MRS Ctr 1201 Welch Rd Stanford CA 94305

GUCKENHEIMER, DANIEL PAUL, financial advisor; b. Tel Aviv, Oct. 10, 1943; came to U.S., 1947, naturalized, 1957. s. Ernest and Eva Guckenheimer; m. Helen Sandra Fox, Dec. 21, 1969; children: Debra Ellen, Julie Susan. BBA in Fin., U. Houston, 1970; cert. hosp. adminstrn., Trinity U., San Antonio, 1973. Asst. adminstr. Harris County Hosp. Dist., Houston, 1970-76; pres. Mid Am. Investments, Kansas City, Kans., 1976; exec. dir. Allen County Hosp., Iola, Kans., 1977-78; comml. loan officer Traders Bank, Kansas City, Mo., 1979; v.p., mgr. Traders Ward Pkwy. Bank, 1980; v.p., mgr. installment loans Traders Bank, 1981, v.p., comml. loan officer, 1982; sr. v.p., mgr. comml. loans United Mo. Bank South, 1982-91; sr. v.p., mgr. lending United Mo. Bank, N.A., 1991-93; pres. Guckenheimer Fin. Svcs., 1993—.

Bd. dirs. Robert Morris Assocs., 1988-92, Food Distbn., Inc., 1983-88, Crime Stoppers Greater Kansas City, 1989—; clinic adminstr. 190th USAF Clinic, 1977-84. With USAF, 1962-66, maj. Res. ret. Mem. N.G. Assn. Tex., Olympic Soc., Internat. Platform Assn., Assn. Mil. Surgeons U.S., Mil. Officers Assn. Am., Mil. Order World Wars, B'nai Brith (v.p. 1982-83, pres. 1984-85, treas. 1986-95), Amer-Israeli Pub. Affairs Com. Office: 8439 W 113th St Overland Park KS 66210-2437 Office Phone: 913-451-0051.

GUCLU, CEYLAN CELIL, research scientist; b. Istanbul, Turkey, June 13, 1966; s. Yildirim and Sultan Guclu. PhD, U. Calif. at Irvine, Irvine, Calif., 1995. Postdoctoral rschr. U. Calif.-Irvine, Irvine, Calif., 1995—97; mr image quality scientist GE Healthcare-Technologies, Waukesha, Wis., 1997—. Tchg. (mr physics, stats.) GEHC- Diagnostic Imaging, Waukesha, Wis., 1998—. Recipient ISMRM Sci. Poster Award (Cum Laude), Internat. Soc. of Magnetic Resonance in Medicine, 1993; grantee UC-Markey Fellow, UC-Markey Found., 1996-1997; UC-Regents Fellowship, U. Calif., 1990-1991. Mem.: Internat. Soc. for Magnetic Resonance in Medicine (ISMRM). Achievements include patents for 2; patents pending for 5; research in 8 Jour. papers, 25 conf. presentations. Home: 1600 Lindsay Way Waukesha WI 53186 Office: Gen Elec Healthcare-Tech 3200 N Grandview Blvd W-832 Waukesha WI 53188 Office Phone: 262-521-6838. Home Fax: 262-521-6600; Office Fax: 262-521-6600. Personal E-mail: ceylan.guclu@med.ge.com.

GUDDATI, MURTHY N., civil engineer, researcher; b. Relangi, A.P., India, Aug. 16, 1971; s. Janaki Rama Rao and Manga Tayaru (Yerramsetti) G. BTech, Indian Inst. Tech., Madras, India, 1992; MS, U. Cin., 1994; PhD, U. Tex., 1998. Devel. engr. Schlumberger-Dowell, Sugarland, Tex., 1998—. Contbr. articles to profl. jours. Recipient Promising Young Investigator award Internat. Union Theoret. and Applied Mechanics, 1997. Mem. ASCE (assoc. mem.), Soc. Petroleum Engrs., Soc. Indsl. and Applied Math. Achievements include development of three efficient methods for analysis of wave propagation in unbounded domains.

GUDE, GILBERT, former federal official, former state official, nurseryman, writer; b. Washington, Mar. 9, 1923; s. Adolph Elbert and Inez Elinor (Gilbert) G.; m. Jane Wheeler Callaghan, June 19, 1948; children: Sharon, Gilbert Jr., Gregory, Daniel, Adrienne. BS, Cornell U., 1948; MA, George Washington U., 1958; DSc (hon.), Georgetown U., 1977. Del. Md. Gen. Assembly, Annapolis, 1953-58, senator, 1962-66; mem. U.S. Congress from Md. dist., 1967-76; dir. Congl. rsch. svc. Library of Congress, Washington, 1977-86; ind. cons. Bethesda, Md., 1987—. Mem., past chmn. consultative com. Ctr. Parliamentary Documentation Inter-Parliamentary Union, Geneva, 1984-89; mem. exec. com. Environ. and Energy Study Inst., Washington, 1986-89, 1999—; exec. dir. Potomac River Basin Consortium, Bethesda. Author: Where the Potomac Begins, 1984, Small Town Destiny, 1989; contbr. articles on rsch. and info. systems in support of legis. bodies to various publs. Trustee Montgomery County Hist. Soc., Rockville, Md., Md. Hist. Trust, 1992—; bd. dirs. Pks. and History Assn., 1999—. With U.S. Army, 1943-46, PTO. Mem. Nat. Acad. Pub. Adminstrn., Chevy Chase Club, Capitol Hill Club. Republican. Roman Catholic. Home and Office: 5411 Duvall Dr Bethesda MD 20816-1871 E-mail: gjgude@aol.com.

GUDE, NANCY CARLSON, lawyer; b. Kane, Pa., Aug. 5, 1948; d. Edward Walter and Theo Alberta (Herzog) Carlson. BA in History, Pa. State U., 1969; MS in Computer Sci., U. Central Fla., 1981; JD, Thomas M. Cooley Law Sch., 2001. Bar: Fla. 2001, U.S. Dist. Ct. (no. and so. dists.) Fla. 2003. Programmer Group Hospitalization, Inc., Washington, 1969-70; programmer analyst Space Age Computer Sys., Washington, 1970-73, Ky. Fried Chicken, Louisville, 1973-75; sys. analyst Sentinel Comm. Co., Orlando, Fla., 1975-77, programming supr., 1977-78, sys. and programming mgr., 1978-80, asst. dir. data processing, 1980, mgr. staff devel., 1981-82; mgmt. info. svcs. mgr. Sun-Sentinel Co., Ft. Lauderdale, Fla., 1982-83, v.p., dir. info. sys., 1983-94, sys. cons., 1994-98; assoc. atty. Walton Lantaff Schroeder & Carson, Ft. Lauderdale, 2002—04. Adj. instr. U. Ctrl. Fla., Orlando, 1981—82. Participant Leadership Broward X; chair LBX Artserve Intervention Group. Recipient Thomas M. Cooley Leadership Achievement award, 2001. Mem.: Broward County Bar Assn., Fed. Bar Assn., The Fla. Bar, Pa. State U. Alumni Assn. (Ft. Lauderdale chpt., treas. 1990—92, v.p. 1992—93, pres. 1993—95). Presbyterian. Home: 9 NE 20 Ave Pompano Beach FL 33060

GUDELL, VALERIE M., academic administrator, musician; d. Gary P. and Diane D. Gudell. MusB with honors in Composition, Syracuse U., N.Y., 1991; MusM, New Eng. Conservatory Music, Boston, 1993; DMA, U. Houston, 2001. Pvt. oboe instr., 1988—; faculty artist and chamber music coach Southampton Chamber Music Festival, 1997; substitute oboe and English horn Houston Ballet Orch., 1998—, Houston Grand Opera Orch., 1999—, Opera in the Heights Orch., 1999—; adj. music faculty mem. San Jacinto Coll. North, 1998—2000; John and Rebecca Moores tchg. fellow U. Houston, 1998—2001; oboe and English horn Woodlands Symphony Orch., 1998—, asst. to music dir., 2001—, libr., 2003—; oboe, English horn and oboe d'amore JS Bach Soc. Orch., 1999—; academic advisor Coll. Architecture U. Houston, 2002—04; academic coord. Coll. Natural Sciences and Math. U. Houston, 2004—. Soloist Internat. Festival Inst. at Round Top, Round Top, Tex., 1993—93, Tex. Music Festival, Houston, 1994—2001, orch. mgr. and head libr., 2001; soloist C.W. Post Chamber Music Festival, Greenvale, NY, 1997; advanced orchestral studies master classes Centre d'Arts Orford, Canada, 1997. Exhibitions include Having a Bad Reed Day., Yunya: Prickly Pear Cactus Kachina; performer (with U. N.C. Greensboro Orch.): Vaughan Williams-Oboe Concerto; performer: (with C.W. Post Festival Orch.) Haydn-Oboe Concerto; performer: (with Syracuse U. Orch.) Marcello-Oboe Concerto, Salieri-Concerto for Flute and Oboe; performer: (with Woodlands Symphony Orch.) Copland-Quiet City; performer: (with Moores Sch. Chamber Orch.) Haydn-Sinfonie Concertante, Francaix-The Flower Clock; composer: Quintet for Percussion, Duo for Oboe and Trombone, Instrumentalise for Soprano and Double Bass, Nielsen Variations (for flute and bass trombone), Chances are. (for oboe and marimba), Piano Variations, Soliloquy for Oboe and Piano, Chromatic Interlude for Solo Clarinet, Refracted Interludes for Electronic Tape. Finalist Concerto Competition, Tex. Music Festival, 1995, 1996; named Sr. Class Marshal, Syracuse U. Coll. VPA, 1991, Moores Sch. of Music Outstanding Doctoral Student, 2001; recipient Harwood Simmons award, Syracuse U. Sch. Music, 1991, spl. resentation Winners Series, Artists Internat., Inc., 1994; fellow Tex. Music Festival, 1994—2001, C.W. Post Chamber Music Festival, 1997; grantee, Tex. State Pub. Edn., 1998—2001; scholar Charles Foster scholarship, 1989—90, Marie Arnold Chapin scholarship, 1990—91, New Eng. Conservatory Music, 1991—93, Internat. Festival Inst. at Round Top, 1993, Centre d'Arts Orford, 1997; Hirsch Meml. scholarship, 1998—2000, Levin Meml. scholarship, 2000—01. Mem.: Syracuse Profl. Musician's Assn., Internat. Double Reed Soc., Am. Music Ctr., Chamber Music Am., Houston Profl. Musician's Assn., Coll. Music Soc., N.Y. Women Composers, Inc., Nat. Assn. Composers USA, Golden Key, Phi Kappa Phi, Eta Pi Upsilon, Pi Kappa Lambda, Phi Beta Delta, Sigma Alpha Iota. Office: Univ Houston Coll NSM Dean's Office Houston TX 77204-5008

GUDENBERG, HARRY RICHARD, arbitrator, mediator; b. Frankfurt, Germany, May 20, 1933; m. Sharon Rickey; children— Lori, Bruce. BS, N.Y. U., 1960, MBA, 1964; JD, Seton Hall U., 1970. Bar: N.J. bar 1970, U.S. Supreme Ct 1973. With ITT, N.Y.C., 1970-88, v.p., dir. indsl. and employee relations, employment and labor law, 1978-88; cons. on benefits, compensation and employment law William M. Mercer Inc., N.Y.C., 1988-93. Arbitrator, mediator fact finder, dispute resolution, employment and labor law, panel mem. Am. Arbitration Assn., Fed. Mediation and Conciliation Svc., N.J. State Bd. Mediation, N.J. Pub. Employment Rels. Commn., 1994—, also various pvt. panels. Served with U.S. Army, 1953-55. Mem. ABA, Nat. Acad. Arbitrators, N.J. Bar Assn., Indsl. Res. Rsch. Assn.

GUDLAVALLETI, SAURI, mechanical engineer; b. Kalpakkam, Tamil Nadu, India, Mar. 15, 1978; s. Muralikrishna and Vyjayanti Gudlavalleti. B of Tech. in Mech. Engring., Indian Inst. Tech. Madras, Chennai, 1999; MS in Mech. Engring., MIT, 2002. Mech. rsch. engr. GE Global Rsch., Niskayuna, NY, 2002—. Recipient 3rd prize, Indian Nat. Math Olympiad, 1993, 1st prize, Madras Region Math Olympiad, 1993, 10th prize, Physics Soc. India, 1993; fellow Rosenblith fellowship, MIT Dept of Mech. Engring., 1999 - 2000. Achievements include 10 patents pending on mechanical testing, fuel cells and sensors. Office: GE Global Rsch 1 Research Cir K1-3A17 Niskayuna NY 12309 Office Phone: 518-387-4403. Personal E-mail: sauri@alum.mit.edu.

GUDMUNDSDOTTIR, BERGLIND, psychologist; b. Reykjavik, Iceland, May 1, 1972; d. Gudmundur Thorkelsson and Kristjana Stefansdottir; m. Benedikt Halldorsson, July 15, 1970. BA, U. Iceland, 1998; Master, SUNY, Buffalo, 2004; postgrad., SUNY, 2004—. Asst. head of dept. Solbrekka Presch., Seltjarnarnes, Iceland, 1998—98, behavioral therapist for multi-site young autism project, 1998—99; diagnostic interviewer and therapist Car Accident Clinic, SUNY, Buffalo, 1999—; project coord./grad. rsch. asst. Ctr. for Anxiety Rsch., SUNY, Buffalo, 1999—. Mem. student editl. bd.: Behavioral Therapy; contbr. articles to profl. jours. Recipient Naman Study award, Landsbanki Islands, Reykjavik, Iceland, 2004; Dissertation fellowship, Coll. of Arts and Scis., SUNY, 2004-2005, NORDPLUS Student Exch. scholarship, U. Iceland, 1995. Mem.: APA, Assn. for the Advancement of Behavior Therapy, Psychology Grad. Student Assn., SUNY (sec. 2001—02, pres. 2002—03). Office Phone: 716-645-3650 337. Office Fax: 716-645-3801.

GUDMUNDSSON, FINNBOGI, library administrator; b. Reykjavik, Iceland, Jan. 8, 1924; s. Gudmundur Finnbogason and Laufey Vilhjalmsdottir; m. Kristjana P. Helgadottir, Oct. 1, 1955 (dec.); 1 child, Helga Laufey. Cand. mag., U. Iceland, 1949, Dr. phil., 1961. Assoc. prof. U. Man., Winnipeg, Can., 1951-56; lectr. Icelandic Univs., Oslo and Bergen, 1957-58; tchr. Icelandic Reykjavik Gymnasium, 1958-64; docent U. Iceland, Reykjavik, 1962-64; dir. Nat. Library of Iceland, Reykjavik, 1964-94. Author: Sveinbjörn Egilsson's Translations of Homer, 1960, Stephan G. Stephansson in Retrospect: Seven Essays, 1982, Poets' Letters to Gudmundur Finnbogason, 1987, The Humour of Snorri Sturluson, 1991, Talt og Skrevet, 2002, Nineteen Articles and Speeches, 2003; editor: Arbok Landsbokasafns, 1964-93, Orkneyinga saga, 1965, Andvari, 1968-82, Selected Letters Written to Stephan G. Stephansson I-III, 1971-75; contbr. articles to profl. jours. Mem. Icelandic Studies Soc. (chmn. 1962-64), Icelandic Research Librarians (chmn. 1966-73), Icelandic Patriotic Soc. (pres. 1967-82), Nordinfo (bd. dirs. 1976-79), Icelandic Nat. League (hon.), Icelandic Libr. Assn. (hon.), Rotary (sec. 1983-84). Lutheran.

GUEDRY, JAMES WALTER, lawyer, retired manufacturing executive; b. Morgan City, La., Jan. 7, 1941; s. J. Walter and P. Marie (McNulty) G. AB magna cum laude, Georgetown U., 1962; postgrad., U. Brussels, 1962-63; LL.B., U. Va., 1966. Bar: NY 1967. Assoc. Lord, Day & Lord, NYC, 1966-76; v.p., corp. sec./assoc. gen. counsel Internat. Paper Co., NYC, 1976-2000; retired, 2000. Mem. Assn. Bar City NY Home and Office: 79 Charles St New York NY 10014-2638

GUEDRY, LEO J., agricultural economics educator; b. Baton Rouge, Nov. 2, 1940; s. Leo J. and Beulah LaCour (Monger) G.; m. Nealea Ann Vosbury, Jan. 25, 1964; children: Leigh Ann, Grechen. BS, La. State U., 1962; MS, U. Ill.-Urbana, 1965; PhD, Oreg. State U.-Corvallis, 1970. Asst. prof. agrl. econs. La. State U., 1969-74, assoc. prof., 1974-81, prof. agrl. econs. Baton Rouge, 1981—, head dept. agrl. econs., 1981—; interim assoc. dean Coll. Agr., 1995-96. Mem. editorial council: So. Jour. Agrl. Econs., 1977-79, editor, 1981. Mem. Am. Agrl. Econs. Assn., Am. Econs. Assn., So. Agrl. Econs. Assn., Western Agrl. Econs. Assn., Internat. Agbus Mgmt. Assn. Office: La State U Dept Agrl Econs & Agribus 101 Agrl Adminstrn Bldg Baton Rouge LA 70803-0001

GUEHENNO, JEAN MARIE, international organization official; b. Paris, Oct. 30, 1949; s. Jean and Annie (Rospabe) G.; m. Mademoiselle de la Bardonnie, Mar. 26, 1974 (div.); m. Michele Fahy Moss, Apr. 21, 1981; 1 child, Claire Maia. Student, Ecole Normale Superieure, Paris, 1968-72, Ecole Nationale D'Administration, 1974-76, Inst. D'Etudes Politiques, 1972-73. Auditor Cour des Comptes, Paris, 1976-79, referendary counselor, 1978, 1986-87; deputy dir. Policy Planning Staff, Paris, 1979-82; cultural counselor French Embassy, N.Y.C., 1982-86; special advisor to chmn. Banque de l'Union European, Paris, 1987-89; dir. policy planning staff Ministry Fgn. Affairs, 1989—93, amb., Western European Union, 1993—95; mem., Sec. Gen. Advisory Bd. on disarmament UN, N.Y.C., 1999—2000, under sec. gen for peacekeeping ops., 2000—. Chmn. Institut des hautes études de défense nationale, 1998—2000. Contbr. articles to profl. jours. Office: UN Rm 3727B New York NY 10017 Office Phone: 212-963-8079. E-mail: guehenno@un.org.

GUELICH, ROBERT VERNON, retired management consultant; b. Dayton, Ohio, Oct. 30, 1917; m. Jane E. Schory, Dec. 6, 1941; children: Susan MacKenzie, Robert V. Jr., Helen Jane. BA, Ohio Wesleyan U., 1938; MBA, Harvard U., 1940. Reporter Dayton Jour., 1935-37; overseas corr., staff editor Air Force mag., 1942-46; asst. dir. public relations Firestone Co., Akron, Ohio, 1946-57; sr. v.p. pub. relations Montgomery Ward & Co., Chgo., 1957-81; sr. mgmt. cons. Hill & Knowlton, Chgo., 1981-83; asst. to chmn. Nat. Fitness Found., 1981-90; pres. Robert V. Guelich & Assocs., Inc., 1981—; pub. rels. cons. Exec. Svc. Corp. of Chgo., 1983-89. Chmn. Nat. Pub. Rels. Seminar, 1981. Bd. dirs. Nat. 4-H Coun., 1972-81; pres. bd. edn. New Trier Twp. High Sch., 1965-70. Maj. USAF, 1941-46. Recipient George Washington Honor medal Freedoms Found., 1977 Mem. Pub. Rels. Soc. Am. (bd. dirs. 1976-79, 3 Silver Anvil awards, 4 Presdl. Citations 1976, Outstanding Film award 1977), Chgo. Yacht Club, Mich. Shores Club, Phi Beta Kappa, Phi Gamma Delta, Sigma Delta Chi. Presbyterian. Home and Office: 380 Sterling Rd Kenilworth IL 60043-1048

GUENTER, HELEN MARIE GIESSEN, librarian, reading specialist; b. El Dorado, Ark., Dec. 21, 1944; d. Charles Henry and Thelma (Fish) G.; m. James Claude Burson, June 3, 1967 (div. 1982); children: Laura Marie, Alicia Zillana; m. Joseph Martin Guenter, June 20, 1992. BA in English, Centenary Coll., 1966; MA in Reading, La. Tech. U., 1980; MLS, U. So. Miss., 1986. Cert. tchr., Ark., La.; cert. libr. and reading specialist, cert English grades 7-12. Libr. researcher, editor, tutor for pvt. clients, Houston, also Minden, La., 1967-79; libr. asst. Shreveport (La.) Meml. Pub. Libr., 1966-67; libr. Dubberly and Heflin (La.) Elem. Schs., 1979-80, Glenbrook Sch., Minden, La., 1980-82; full-time cons. S.E. Ark. Ednl. Coop. Media Ctr., Monticello, Ark., 1982; serials and reference libr. U. Ark., Monticello, 1982—. Tchr. Caddo-Bossier Parishes Headstart, Shreveport, 1966-67; part-time tchr. Webster Parish Schs., Minden, 1977-80; asst. libr. Phillips Lab. Sch., Rustin, La., 1980; reading diagnostician, clinician Reading Ctr. La. Tech. U., Ruston, 1980; coll. reading instr. U. Ark., Monticello, 1986, 89, mem. coun. assessment of student acad. achievement, 1994-98, sec. faculty assembly, 1995-96, honors coun., 1995-2004, faculty assembly nominating com., 2004-05, gen. edn. com., 2003—. Column editor Ark. Librs., 1991-96; contr. articles to profl. publs. Mem. founders' grant com. Webster Parish Hist. Mus., Minden, 1976-79; mem. organizational com. Drew County Lit. Coun., Monticello, 1986-87; mem. grants com. Drew Hist. Soc., Monticello, 1986—; press. rep. S.E. Ark. Dist., Monticello chpt. Nat. Fedn. Music Clubs, 1986—, S.E. dist. sec., 1991-94; mem. commn. archives and history Little Rock Conf. United Meth. Ch., 2002-04, commn. archives and history Ark. conf., 2004—. Anderson Acad. scholar Centenary Coll., La., 1962-66; Wilson scholar Sch. Libr. Svc., U. So. Miss., 1986; U. Ark. Monticello faculty devel. grantee, 1986—. Mem. ALA, AAUW, Assn. Coll. and Rsch. Librs. (nat. adv. com. 1991-95, sec. Ark. chpt. 1988-90), Ark. Libr. Assn. (intellectual freedom com. 1989-93, ALA scholar 1985, publs. com. 1994-97, awards com. 1997-2000), Ark. Assn. for Instrnl. Media, Monticello Book Club, Internat. Reading Assn., Ark. Tchr. Educators of Reading (honor status com. 1989), N.Am. Serials Interest Group, Beta Phi Mu. Meth. Avocations: cats, choir handbells and piano, needlecrafts, reading, travel. Home: 315 Glenwood Dr Monticello AR 71655-5525 Office: Univ Ark Monticello Assoc Libr PO Box 3599 Monticello AR 71656-3599 Office Phone: 870-460-1680, 870-460-1080. Business E-Mail: guenter@uamont.edu.

GUENTHER, ARTHUR HENRY, research scientist, government agency administrator; b. Hoboken, N.J., Apr. 20, 1931; s. George Gregory and Florence B. (Roberts) G.; m. Joan Roth, Nov. 21, 1954; children: Tracie Katherine, Wendy Katherine. BS in Chemistry, Rutgers U., 1953; PhD in Chemistry-Physics, Pa. State U., 1957; DSc (hon.), U. Albuquerque, 1973. Dir. pulse power lab. Kirtland AFB, Albuquerque, 1959-62, dir. material dynamics lab., 1962-65, sci. advisor, chief simulation and pulsed power group, 1965-66, chief sci. support group, sci. advisor, 1966-69, chief tech. div. Air Force weapons lab., 1969-70, sci. dir. tech. div., 1970-74, chief scientist Air Force Weapons Lab., 1974-88; chief scientist for advanced def. tech. Los Alamos (N.Mex.) Nat. Lab., 1988-91; sci. advisor lab. devel. Sandia Nat. Labs., 1991-97; sci. advisor to Gov. of N.Mex., 1988-94; chmn. sci. and tech. commercialization com.; prof. Ctr. for High Tech. Materials U. N.Mex., 1997—. Vice chmn., chmn. Gordon Rsch. Conf., 1970-71; chmn. permanent sci. com. Internat Symposium on Discharges and Elec. Insulation in Vacuum; chmn. internat. steering com. Internat. Conf. on Phenomena in Ionized Gases, 1991—; fourder, co-chmn. bd. dirs., pres. ann. Symposium on Optical Materials for High Power Lasers, 1969—; char SPIE OE Laser, 1992; mem. adv. com. several NATO advanced study insts., sci. dir NATO Advanced Study Inst. on High Brightness Accelorators, Pitlochery, Scotland, 1986; mem. European Study Group on Laser-Produced Plasmas; co-chair 1st conf. on coupling tech. to national need, 1993; NAS-NRC Rev. Bd., 1974, Def. Nuclear Agy. TREE Working Group on Simulation and Instrumentation, NRC/Air FOrce Studies Bd. Rev. on High Power Optics, Air Force Systems Command 1990s; sponsor Advanced Beam Weapons Concepts Definition Project, 1983; mem. chair U.S. nat. com. for Internat. Commn. for Optics of Bd., NRC; with USAF 2000 study; Air Force mem. to microwave rev. group, 1983; chmn. PILOT Adv. Com.; mem. steering com. Tamarron MEetings on SPark Gaps and Diffuse Dishcharges; vice chmn. Fgn. Applied Ci. Assessment Ctr. Study on Macroelectronics, 1985; apptd. by Gov. of N.Mex. to Energy R&D Rev. Com., 1975-78; mem. nat. steering com. on nuclear tech. Coun. Math. and Sci. Edn., 1975; mem. search com. for AFOSR Tech. Dir., endowed chair dept. elec. and computer engring. U. N.Mex.; mem. DAPKL Rev. Group, Basillisk Rev. Group, Def. Advanced Rsch. Projects Agy., Washington; adj. prof. U. N.Mex., Tex. Tech. U., Air Force Inst. Tech.; external reader U. Salford, Eng., Indian Inst. Sci., Bangalore; chmn. Optics Tech. Transger Strategic Def. Initiative office, 1989—, mem. Blue Ribbon tech. oversight bd. on lethality, 1990; chair confs. in field. Editor Advances in Pulse Power Tech., Symposium on Optical Materials for High Power Lasers, High Brightness Accelerators, NATO Brightness Accelerators; assoc. editor Jour. Lasers and Particles Beams, Laser Interaction and Related Plasma Phenomena; mem. editorial adv. bd. Lasers and Optronics, Photonics Tech Briefs, O.E. mag.; patentee in field; contbr. more than 350 articles to tech. jours. Mem. Gov.'s Com. on Tech. Excellence, Task Force on Higher Edn. Reform, 1987, U. N.Mex. Joint Ctr. Materials Sci.; bd. dirs., past chmn., mem. Ctr. for Occupational R & D (CORD) Edn. Coun., 1989-98, trustee CORD Found.; vice chmn. sci. and tech. adv. com. State of N.Mex., 1984-86; bd. dirs. N.Mex. Math. Engring. Scientist. 1st lt. USAF, 1957-59. Recipient Disting. Pub. Svc. award State of N.Mex., 1982, 2001; Meritorious Presdl. award Pres. of U.S., 1983, Disting. Exec. Rank award, 1985. Fellow IEEE (pres. U.S., editor numerous spl. edits., chmn. standards activities, mem. Photonics del. to A. Popov Soc., USSR 1989, IEEE Harry Diamond award 1971, IEEE Peter Haas award 1989, IEEE Ben Dasher award), Laser Inst. Am. (bd. dirs. pres., Arthur L. Schawlow medal 1983), Optical Soc. Am. (bd. dirs., chmn. adv. com., chmn. fellows com. 1980, fin. com. 1982, edn. coun. 1989—, Eastman Lectr.); mem. IEEE Laser Electro-Optic Soc. (adv. com., chmn. fellows com. 1986, ad com. 1983, chmn. govt. rels. com.), Am. Chem. Soc., N.Mex. Acad. Sci. (Disting. Scientist of Yr. 1977), Russian Acad. Sci. (fgn. mem.), Forum for Mil. Applications of Directed Energy (dir.), Directed Energy Profl. Soc. (organizer 1999), AMBA (pres.), Sigma Xi, Phi Lambda Upsilon. Avocations: woodworking, the outdoors, music, bowling. Home: 989 Lynx Loop NE Albuquerque NM 87122-1313 Office: Ctr for High Tech Materials U NMex 1313 Goddard St SE Albuquerque NM 87106-4343 E-mail: agun@chtm.unm.edu, aguenther3@home.com.

GUENTHER, CHARLES JOHN, librarian, writer; b. St. Louis, Apr. 29, 1920; s. Charles Richard and Hulda Clara G.; m. Esther G. Klund, Apr. 11, 1942; children: Charles John, Cecile Anne, Christine Marie. AA, Harris Tchrs. Coll., 1940; postgrad., St. Louis U., 1952-54; BA, Webster Coll., 1973, MA, 1974; LHD (hon.), So. Ill. U., Edwardsville, 1979. Editl. asst. St. Louis Star-Times, 1938; with Social Security Commn. Mo., Dept. Labor, U.S. Employment Service, War Dept., C.E., St. Louis, 1941-43; head archives unit USAAF Aero Chart Svc., St. Louis, 1943-45, head rsch. unit, 1945-47; asst. chief, chief of library, translator, historian, geographer, supervisory cartographer, librarian USAF Aero Chart and Info. Center (name changed to DMA Aerospace Center), St. Louis, 1947-57, chief tech. libr., 1957-75. Civilian library specialist Project Crossroads, USAF, 1946; instr. creative writing Peoples Art Center, St. Louis, 1953-56; lectr., poetry workshop leader various U.S. writers confs. Author: Modern Italian Poets, 1961, Paul Valery in English, 1970, (poems) Phrase.Paraphrase, 1970, Voices in the Dark, 1974, Moving the Seasons, 1994; translator: (with others) Selected Poems in Alain Bosquet, 1963, Selected Translations, 1986; contbr. articles to profl. jours.; book reviewer: St. Louis Post-Dispatch, 1953-2003, Globe-Democrat, 1972-82; author numerous poems. Decorated commendatore Ordine al Merito della Repubblica Italiana; recipient Shell Co. Found. grant for book Phrase/Paraphrase, 1970, Witter Bynner grant, 1979; recipient Lit. award Mo. Libr. Assn., 1974, Mo. Writers Guild award, 1987, 94, 96, Mo. and St. Louis Arts awards, 2001. Mem. Poetry Soc. Am. (Midwest regional v.p., James Joyce award 1974), St. Louis Writers Guild (v.p. 1958, pres. 1959, 76-77), St. Louis Poetry Center (chmn. bd. chancellors 1965-72, pres. 1974-76), Mo. Writers Guild (v.p. 1971-73, pres. 1973-74), Spl. Libraries Assn. (pres. Greater St. Louis chpt. 1969-70), Rose Soc. Greater St. Louis; corr. mem. Academie d'Alsace (diplome d'honneur 1957); hon. mem. Les Violetti Picards et Normands, Paris, Academia de Ciencias Humanisticas y Relaciones, Mexico, Academie Chablaisienne, Thonon-les-Bains, France, Biblioteca Partenopea, Naples; asso. mem. Internat. Am. Inst. Home: 9877 Allendale Dr Saint Louis MO 63123-6450 *A poet's relation to his time is complex and mutable. A poet's temperament, attitudes, and sense of the function of poetry are all changeable and conflict with each other throughout his life. In a world which tends to be imitative, regimented, and standardized, each poet is his own definition of poet, his own conscience, his own value.*

GUENTHER, IRENE V., historian, educator; d. Peter W. and Andrea D. Guenther; 1 child, Bryn Austin Bellomy. PhD of History, U. Tex., 2000. Post-doctoral fellow in humanities U. Houston, 1996—99; prof. history Houston C.C. - NW, 1999—2005; vis. prof. history Rice U., Houston, 2005—. Founder, dir. Women's Resource Ctr. Houston C.C., 2001—. Author: (book) Nazi Chic? Fashioning Women in the Third Reich (Best History Book of 2004 written by a female historian, Sierra prize Western Assn. Women Historians, Millia Davenport award for Best Book on Fashion, Costume Soc. Am., 2004), (ency. chpt. Fascist Fashion) Ency. Clothing and Fashion, (exhibition catalogue essay) Aryanization: The Destruction of the German Fashion Industry in Broken Threads. Destruction of the High Fashion Industry — From Aryanization to Cultural Loss, exhibition catalogue. Vancouver: Holocaust Education Centre. Mem. acad. bd. Holocaust Mus. Houston, 2002—05. Recipient NISOD Nat. Tchg. Award; HCC Tchg. Excellence Award, U. of Houston Tchg. Excellence Award, 1995—2005; fellow U. of Houston Post-Doctoral Fellowship; DAAD Rsch. Fellowship; U. of Tex. Rsch. Fellowship, 1995—2000. Mem.: AAUW, Western Assn. Women Historians, German Studies Assn., Am. Hist. Assn., Coun. Women Historians (coordinating coun.). Office: Rice U Dept History 6100 Main St Houston TX 77005-1892 Office Phone: 281-701-5933. E-mail: iguenther@sbcglobal.net.

GUENTHER, JACK DONALD, banker; b. Little Rock, Jan. 21, 1929; s. Gottlob and Josephine Margaret (Presley) G.; m. Margaret Adah Beltz, June 11, 1956; children— Elizabeth, Katherine, John BA, Yale U., 1950; postgrad., King's Coll., Cambridge U., Eng., 1952-53; MA, Harvard U., 1957, PhD,

1959. Various staff positions IMF, Washington, 1960-79; sr. v.p., sr. advisor internat. ops. Citibank, N.Y.C., 1979-95; cons. MBIA, N.Y.C., 1995-98. Served as sgt. U.S. Army, 1953-55 Home: 4231 42d St Washington DC 20016

GUENTHER, JACK EGON, lawyer; b. San Antonio, Dec. 14, 1934; m. Valerie Urschel, Feb. 1, 1964; children: Abigail Guenther Kampmann, Jack Egon. BBA, U. Tex.-Austin, 1956; LLB magna cum laude, St. Mary's U., 1959; LLM in Taxation, NYU, 1960. Bar: Tex. 1959; C.P.A., Tex. Practice pub. acctg., San Antonio, 1957-59; pvt. practice, 1960—; assoc. Cox & Smith (and predecessor firm), 1961-65, ptnr., 1965-2001. Chmn. bd. BMW Ctr., Ltd., 1965—, Rivergate Toyota, Inc., 1983—, Performance Toyota, Inc., 1984—, Performance Honda, Isuzu, Chrysler and Jeep, 1987, Lexus of Nasville, 1989—, Volvo and Porsche Ctr., 1990—, Toyota of Plano, 1990—, Enercorp LLC, 1994—. Bd. dirs. Nat. Western Art Found., Nat. Fish and Wildlife, Tex. Pub. Radio Adv. Coun.; trustee V.H. McNutt Meml. Found., Amy Shelton McNutt Charitable Trust, Jack Valerie Guenther Found., Amy McNutt Endowment Fund for Gardens of S.W. Craft Ctr.; adv. dir. Tex. Highway Patrol Mus. Assn. Mem. ABA, Tex. Bar Assn., Tex. Soc. CPA's, Sigma Chi, Phi Delta Phi. Episcopalian. Office: 153 Treeline Park Ste 300 San Antonio TX 78209-1880

GUENTNER, JAMES FRANCIS, JR., art educator, artist; b. Glenshaw, Pa., Feb. 23, 1949; s. James Francis Guentner and Elizabeth McCloskey; m. Linda Louise Kauffman Guentner; 1 stepchild, Ronald Kauffman; m. Cheryl Guentner (div. Apr. 28, 1973); 1 child, Rachel. A, Allegheny C.C., Pa., 1969; BA, Carlow Coll., Pa. Art tchr. Shaler Sch. Dist., Glenshaw, Pa., 1999—; painting instr. North Hills Art Ctr., Pa., 1986—94; truck driver GAGE Co., Pa., 1979—99, Local 249 Union Hall, Pa., 1976—79; med. equipment installer Robert A. Fulton Co., Pa., 1973—76; substitute art tchr. Shaler Sch. Dist., Glenshaw, Pa., 1972—73. Exhibitions include Borelli-Edwards Gallery, Carnegie Mus. Art. Avocations: guitar, magic, bodybuilding. Home: 220 Lucille St Glenshaw PA 15116

GUEORGUIEVA, RALITZA V., biostatistician; b. Sofia, Bulgaria, Apr. 25, 1971; arrived in U.S., 1994; d. Vladislav Gueorguiev and Vesela Gueorguieva; m. Velizar T. Tchernev, Sept. 19, 1998; children: Alexander Tchernev, Liliana Tchernev. PhD, U. Fla., 1999; MS in Computer Sci., Sofia U., Bulgaria, 1994. Vis. asst. prof. U. Fla., Gainesville, 1999—2000; assoc. rsch. scientist Yale U., New Haven, 2000—04, asst. prof., 2004—. Mem.: Bulgarian Statis. Soc., Am. Statis. Assn., Internat. Biometrics Soc. Office: Yale Univ 60 College St New Haven CT 06520-8034 Office Phone: 203-974-7529.

GUEQUIERRE, JOHN PHILLIP, manufacturing executive; b. Milw., Sept. 10, 1946; s. Gerald Herbert and Louise Ann (Fenske) G.; m. Mary Rowlands Speer, Aug. 17, 1968; children: William Edward, Robert John, Elizabeth Louise. BA, U. Wis., 1968; MBA, U. Chgo., 1972. Systems analyst Inland Steel Co., East Chgo., Ind., 1968-72; analyst inventory INRYCO, Milw., 1972-73, supr. material planning, 1973-74, mgr. contract administrn., 1974-76; mgr. fin. Inland Steel Devel. Corp., Washington, 1976-78; mgr. fin. analysis Inland Steel Urban Devel. Corp., Chgo., 1978-80; v.p. administrn. Scholz Homes Inc., Tol., 1980-83; sr. v.p. administrn., dir. Schult Homes Corp., Middlebury, Ind., 1983-92, sr. v.p. ops., dir., 1992-95, pres. manufactured housing group, 1995-99; sr. v.p. mfg. Oakwood Homes, Middlebury, 1999-2000; chmn., CEO Pleasant St. Homes, LLC, 2000—. Chmn. budget subcom. United Way, Elkhart, Ind., 1983-89, bd. dirs. 1989-2000, treas., 1990-92, chmn. 1992; adult leader 4H, Elkhart County, 1983—; bd. dirs. Elkhart Chamber Found., 1993-98; bd. dirs. Ind. Assn. United Ways, 1993-2000, vice chmn., 1995-97, chmn., 1997. Mem.: Beta Gamma Sigma, Phi Kappa Phi, Phi Beta Kappa. Republican. Presbyterian. Office: Pleasant St Homes LLC 51700 Lovejoy Dr Middlebury IN 46540 Business E-Mail: johng@homesbyjps.com.

GUERIN, BILL, professional hockey player; b. Wilbraham, Mass., Nov. 9, 1970; With New Jersey Devils, 1991—98, Edmonton Oilers, 1998—2001, Boston Bruins, 2001—02, Dallas Stars, 2002—. Mem. Team U.S.A., Olympic Games, Nagano, Japan, 1998, Salt Lake City, 2002, Team U.S.A., World Cup of Hockey, 1996, 2004. Named to NHL All-Star Team, 2001, 2003, 2004. Achievements include mem. Stanley Cup Champion New Jersey Devils, 1995; mem. World Cup Champion Team U.S.A., 1996. Office: Southwest Sports Group 1000 Ballpark Way Ste 400 Arlington TX 76011

GUERIN, CHARLES ALLAN, museum director, artist; b. San Francisco, Feb. 27, 1949; s. John Warren and Charlene (Roovaart) G.; m. Katherine Riccio. BFA, No. Ill. U., 1971, MA, 1973, MFA, 1974. Co-dir. Guerin Design Group, Colorado Springs, Colo., 1972-77; dir. exhbns. Colorado Springs Fine Arts Ctr., 1977-80, curator fine arts, 1980-86; dir. U. Wyo. Art Mus., Laramie, 1986—2000. Author catalogues including various Colorado Springs Fine Arts Ctr. catalogues; contbg. author The Encyclopedia of Crafts, 1974; exhbns. include Purdue U. West Lafayette, Ind., 1974, 76, DePauw U., Greencastle, Ind., 1976, Colorado Springs Fine Arts Ctr., 1977, Mus. of Fine Arts, Santa Fe, N.Mex., 1978, Wis. State U., Platteville, 1972, Suburban Fine Arts Ctr., Highland Park, Ill., 1974, Colo. Woodworking Invitational, Silver Plume, 1977, Colo. Craft Invitational, Arvada, 1981, Leslie Levy Gallery, Scottsdale, Ariz., 1983, Robischon Gallery, Denver, 1983, Adams State Coll., Alamosa, Colo., 1984, U. Wyo. Art Mus., 1986—, Elaine Horwitch Gallery, Scottsdale, 1990; represented in permanent collections Lloyds of London, Dallas, Art Inst. Chgo., Marriott Hotel, Albany, N.Y., Ill. State Mus., Springfield, U.S. West Corp., Denver, Thresholds, Chgo., others. Grantee Nat. Endowment for the Arts, Ill. Arts Council, 1973. Mem. Coll. Art Assn. Am., Am. Assn. Mus., Western Mus. Conf. Office: U Wyo Art Mus PO Box 3807 U Laramie WY 82071-3807

GUERIN, D. MICHAEL, lawyer; b. La Crosse, Wis., Dec. 15, 1940; BS, Marquette U., 1970, JD, 1974. Bar: Wis. 1974, U.S. Dist. Ct. Wis.(Ea. and We. dist.) 1974, U.S. Ct. Appeals (7th cir.) 1974, U.S. Supreme Ct. 1995. Spl. agent Dept. Justice, 1969—71; ptnr. Gimbel, Reilly, Guerin & Brown, Milw. Lectr. at law, trial practice Marquette U., 1979—81, adj. prof. evidence, 1975—; bd. dirs., past pres. Marquette U. Law Alumni Assn., 1995—96. Mem. bd. ethics City of Milw., former police officer. Mem.: ABA, Wis. Acad. Trial Lawyers, Assn. Trial Lawyers Am., State Bar Wis. (pres.-elect 2004—, mem. bd. govs., pres.), Milw. Bar. Assn. (pres. 2000—01), Tau Epsilon Rho, Alpha Sigma Nu. Office: Gimbel Reilly Guerin & Brown Two Plaza East Ste 1170 330 E Kilbourn Ave Milwaukee WI 53202 Office Phone: 414-271-1440. Office Fax: 414-271-7680. E-mail: dmguerin@grgblaw.com.

GUERIN, DEAN PATRICK, metal products executive; b. St. Paul, Feb. 21, 1922; s. Joseph Henry and Della (Booth) G.; m. Jo Alice Maryman, Sept. 3, 1959; children: Dean William, Stephen Patrick, Mark Joseph. BSBA, Boston U., 1949. With Sperry Gyroscope Co., N.Y.C., 1940-42; registered rep. Chas. A. Day & Son, Boston, 1946-49, Dallas Rupe & Son, 1949-51; from exec. v.p. to chmn. bd. dirs. Eppler, Guerin & Turner, Inc., Dallas, 1951-89; CEO, chmn. bd. dirs. Gen. Aluminum Corp., 1990—94; ind. dir. cos., 1994—. Bd. dirs. Components Corp.; chmn. Archaea Solutions, Inc. Past trustee Marine Mil. Acad. With USMCR, 1942-46, PTO. Mem. Dallas Country Club, Dallas Petroleum Club. Republican. Episcopalian. Home: 9016 Broken Arrow Ln Dallas TX 75209-2406

GUERIN, DIDIER, magazine executive; b. Neuilly/Seine, France, Aug. 2, 1950; came to US 1973; s. Jacques Guerin and Jeanine (Vaesken) Florange; m. Margaret Moray, Dec. 31, 1982; 1 son, Didier Guy Jr. BA in Pub. Law, BA in Comm., U. Paris, 1973; MA in Journalism, Mich. State U., 1975. Editor Soc. Gen. de Presse, Paris, 1976-79; asst. pub. Look mag., NYC, 1979-81; mng. dir. Hachette Comm. Ltd., London, 1982-93; exec. v.p., dir. Hachette Publs., Inc., NYC, 1983-86, Publs. Filipacchi, NYC, 1983-86; pub. ELLE Mag., 1984-85; pres., CEO, dir. Hachette Publs., Inc., NYC, 1987-91; pres., CEO Publs. Filipacchi, NYC, 1987-91, Interdeco Inc., NYC, 1989-91, Hachette-Filipacchi Asia-Pacific, Sydney, 1991-95, Conde Nast Asia-Pacific, Sydney, 1995-2000, Media Convergence Asia-Pacific, Sydney, 2000—. Chmn. The Conde Nast Publs. Pty. Ltd. (VOGUE Australia), Sydney, 1995-2000, The Conde Nast Publs. Pte. Ltd. (VOGUE Singapore), Singapore, 1995-97, The Conde Nast China (VOGUE, GQ Taiwan), Taipei, 1996-2000, Nikkei-Conde Nast (VOGUE Nippon), Tokyo, 1997-2000, Interculture Comm. Ltd., Taipei, 1996-2000; chmn. bd. Toyo Fashion Kaihatsu, Tokyo, 1984-92, Hachette-Consol. Press. (ELLE Australia), Sydney, 1990-95, Hachette Filipacchi Australia, Sydney, 1990-95, Hachette-Interculture, (ELLE Taiwan), Taipei, 1992-95, Hachette Mags. Ltd., Hong Kong, 1993-95, ELLE Mag. Ltd. (ELLE Hong Kong), 1993-95, Hachette Filipacchi-Post, Bangkok (ELLE Thailand), 1994-95, Hachette Filipacchi Japan Ltd., Tokyo (Elle Japan); fgn. trade advisor French Govt., 1988—. Office: Media Convergence Asia-Pacific Knox Manor 17 Knox St Double Bay NSW 2028 Australia Office Phone: 612-9327-8966. E-mail: didier@mediaconv.com.

GUERIN, JOHN WILLIAM, artist; b. Houghton, Mich., Aug. 29, 1920; s. Omer Francis and Mildred Montague (Miller) G.; m. Anne Walden Dewey, Dec. 28, 1948 (dec. 1979); m. Martha McAshan, Apr. 10, 1982. Student, Am. Acad. Art, Chgo., Art Students League, N.Y.C., Escuela de Bellas Artes, San Miguel, Mexico. Prof. art U. Tex., 1953-80, prof. emeritus, 1980—. Artist in residence, Skowhegan (Maine) Sch. Painting and Sculpture, 1960; one-man shows, Kraushaar Galleries, N.Y.C., 1960, 63, 68, Ft. Worth Art Center, 1956, 64, 65, Marion Kooglar McNay Art Inst., San Antonio, 1961, 65, Centennial Mus., Corpus Christi, Tex., 1963, Carlin Galleries, Ft. Worth, 1962, 64, 67, 70, 77, 81, 87, Nat. Acad. Design, N.Y.C., 1987; one-man retrospective show, Nave Mus., Victoria, Tex., 1982, group exhbns. include, Met. Mus. Art, Whitney Mus. Art, Art Inst. Chgo., Corcoran Mus. Art, Carnegie Inst.; represented in permanent collections, Chrysler Mus., Provincetown, Mass., Joslyn Mus., Omaha, New Britain (Conn.) Mus., Houston Mus., Dallas Mus., U. Notre Dame Art Gallery, Colorado Springs (Colo.) Fine Art Center., Archives Am. Art, Smithsonian Instn., Washington. Served with USAAF, 1942-45. Grantee Am. Acad Arts, Nat. Inst. Arts & Letters, 1960, Ford Found., 1978; recipient Henry Ward Ranger Fund Purchase prize NAD, 1958; Research Inst. grant U. Tex., 1960, 66 Mem. Art Students League N.Y.C. (life), Nat. Acad. Design (academician). Episcopalian. Home and Office: 3400 Stoneridge Rd Austin TX 78746-7716

GUERIN-GONZALES, CAMILLE, history professor; b. Las Vegas, N.Mex., July 20, 1945; d. Benedict Frederick Guerin and Estella Maria Gonzales; life ptnr. Susan Lee Johnson; children from previous marriage: Kerrie Lester, Ron Lester, Mike Lester. BA, U. Calif., Riverside, 1978, MA, 1980, PhD, 1985. Asst. prof. history U. Colo., Boulder, 1987—90; asst. prof., assoc. prof. history Oberlin Coll., Ohio, 1990—95; assoc. prof. history UCLA, L.A., 1995—96, U. Colo., 1996—2001; prof. history, dir. Chicano-Am. and Latino studies U. Wis., Madison, 2001—. Author: Mexican Workers and American Dreams: Immigration, Repatriation and California Farm Labor, 1900-1939, 1994; co-editor: The Politics of Immigrant Workers: Essays on Labor Activism & Migration in the World Economy Since 1830, 1993, The Politics of Immigrant Workers: Essays on Labor Acrivism & Migration in the World Economy Since 1830, rev. edit., 1998. Fellow, U. Calif., 1986—88, Ford Found., 1991—92, NEH, 2001—02. Mem.: Orgn. Am. Historians, Am. Hist. Assn., Am. Studies Assn. Democrat. Office: U Wis Chicano & Latino Studies 1155 Observator Dr Madison WI 53706

GUERRA, ALDO BENJAMIN, plastic surgeon, cosmetic surgeon; b. Managua, Nicaragua, Dec. 10, 1969; s. Aldo Antonio and Nelly Beatriz Guerra. MD, U. Calif.-San Diego, La Jolla, 1996. Diplomate Am. Bd. of Plastic Surgery. Chief cosmetic surgeon (face and boby) Aesthetic Surg. Assocs., Metairie, La., 2004—; chief cosmetic surgeon (face and body) McCollough Inst. Appearance and Health, Gulf Shores, Ala., 2004—. Asst. prof. La. State U., New Orleans, 2002—04. Contbr. articles to profl. jours. Hipanic role model, cmty. outreach Hispanic Med. Assn. of La., Metairie, La., 2003—05. Named one of Top 100 Hispanic, New Orleans Metro Area, Vocero News Mag., 2004. Mem.: Hispanic Med. Assn. of La. (assoc.). Achievements include first to use new reconstructive techniques in children. Avocations: traveling, sailing. Office: Aesthetic Surgical Assocs 3601 Houma Blvd Ste 300 Metairie LA 70006 Office Phone: 504-459-3517. Home Fax: 504-885-1360; Office Fax: 504-885-1360. Personal E-mail: aldissimo1@hotmail.com. E-mail: drguerra@gmail.com.

GUERRA, BERTA ALICIA, elementary school educator, music educator, director; b. McAllen, Tex., July 12, 1976; d. Rogerio Arcadio Guerra and Maria del Carmen Garza Guerra. BA, U. Tex., Brownsville, TX, 2000; MA in Interdisciplinary Studies, U. Tex., Edinburg, TX, 2005. Cert. music tchr. State Bd. Educator Certification, 2000. Tchr. music St. Luke Cath. Sch., Brownsville, 1996—97, Kenmont Montessori Sch., Brownsville, 1997—99; dir. choir Faulk Mid. Sch., Brownsville, 2000—01, Besteiro Mid. Sch., Brownsville, 2001—. Mem.: Tex. Choral Dirs. Assn., Am. Choral Dirs. Assn., Tex. Music Educators Assn. (sec. 2003), Kappa Kappa Iota, Sigma Psi Delta (pres. 1999—2000). Roman Catholic. Avocations: travel, clarinet, singing, collecting postcards. Office: Besteiro Middle School 6280 Southmost Rd Brownsville TX 78521 Office Phone: 956-698-0597. Personal E-mail: baguerra@gmail.com. E-mail: baguerra@bisd.us.

GUERRA, FERNANDO A., pediatrician, health facility administrator; b. San Antonio, 1939; BS, U. Tex.; MPH Harvard U.; MD, U. Tex. Med. Br., Galveston, 1964. Diplomate Am. Bd. Pediatrics. Intern San Francisco Gen. Hosp., 1964—65; resident U. Tex. Hosps., Galveston, 1967—69, U. Tex. Bexar County Tchg. Hosps., San Antonio, 1969—71; staff pediatrician Santa Rosa Children's Hosp., San Antonio, 1970—; fellow in pub. health Harvard U., Boston, 1982—83; dir. health MetroHealth, San Antonio. Clin. prof. pediats. U. Tex. Health Sci. Ctr., San Antonio; part-time pvt. practice pediats., San Antonio; bd. trustees Urban Inst., Inst. Medicine Bd. on Children and Families, CDC Adv. Com. on Immunization Practices; founding scholar Pub. Health Leadership Inst. Contbr. numerous articles to profl. jours. Fellow: Am. Acad. Pediats. (spokesman for Internat. Yr. of the Child 1979); mem.: APHA, Tex. Med. Assn., Inst. of Medicine of NAS. Office: MetroHealth 332 W Commerce San Antonio TX 78205-2489 Office Phone: 210-207-8731.

GUERRA, JOHN MICHAEL, optical engineer; Registered profl. engr., Mass., N.H. Program mgr. near-field optics tech. Polaroid Corp., Cambridge, Mass. George Eastman lectr. Rocky Mountain Optical Soc. Am., 1991. Recipient Engring. Excellence award for invention and devel. of photon tunneling microscope Optical Soc. Am., 1994, Photonics Cir. of Excellence award, 1993, R & D 100 award, 1992. Mem. Internat. Soc. Optical Engring., Optical Soc. Am. Achievements include 18 patents in applications of near-field optics in microscopy, optical data storage and metrology. Office: Polaroid Corp 1265 Main St Waltham MA 02451-1743

GUERRA, MARY LOUISE, human resources executive; b. El Paso, Tex., Mar. 28, 1946; d. Luis and Mary Ruth Alvidrez; m. Victor Guerra, Apr. 15, 1965; children: Paul, Cristina. BSN, U. Tex., 1971. RN, 1968. Adminstrv. dir. Dallas County Mental Health, 1979-85; dir. human resources Prudential, Newark, 1985-97; sr. v.p. human resources CIT, Livingston, N.J., 1997—. Mem. Alto Lakes Country Club, Kokopelli Country Club. Office: CIT 650 CIT Dr Livingston NJ 07039

GUERRANT, DAVID EDWARD, retired food company executive; b. Elizaville, Ky., Sept. 27, 1919; s. William Upton and Claire (Jordan) G.; m. Charlotte L. Lander, Feb. 6, 1942; children: Stephen, Jeffrey. BS, Kans. State U., 1941. With Potts-Turnbull Agy., Kansas City, Mo., 1941-48; creative dir. Campbell-Ewald Co., Chgo., 1948-51; with John W. Shaw Advt., Inc., Chgo., 1951-61, pres., 1959-61, MacFarland, Aveyard & Co., Chgo., 1961-64; pres., v.p. mktg. Libby, McNeill & Libby, Chgo., 1964-68, pres., CEO, 1968-73, chmn. bd., 1971-77; chmn., pres., CEO Nestlé Co., Inc., White Plains, N.Y., 1973-81, Nestlé Enterprises Inc. (holding co. for Nestlé Co. Inc., Libby, McNeill & Libby and Stouffers Inc.), 1977-83; ret., 1983. Mem.: Island Country (Marco Island, Fla.). Presbyterian. Home: 591 Hammock Ct Marco Island FL 34145-5848

GUERRANT, RICHARD LITTLETON, medical educator; b. Roanoke, Va., July 21, 1943; s. Richard Francis and Sara Young (Davis) G.; m. Nancy Brearley, June 5, 1965; children: Jeffrey L., Amy Lee Guerrant Perkins, David I. BS, Davidson (N.C.) Coll., 1964; MD, U. Va., 1968. Intern Harvard Med. Sch./Boston City Hosp., 1968-69, asst. resident, 1969-70; clin. assoc. NIH, Dacca, Bangladesh, 1970-71, NIH/Johns Hopkins U., Balt., 1971-72; chief resident U. Va., Charlottesville, 1972-73, fellow in infectious diseases, 1973-74, from asst. to assoc. prof., 1974-81, prof. internat. medicine, 1981—. Hon. prof. Fed. U. Ceará, Fortaleza, Brazil, 1994; Hunter prof U. Va., 1991—, dir. office internat. health, 1995—; mem. study sect. NIH, Bethesda, Md., 1993-97, VA Merit Rev., Washington, 1984-87; active WHO-Sci. Working Group, Geneva, Switzerland, 1987-89. Contbr. over 400 articles to profl. jours.; editor: At the Edge of Development, 1996, Infections of the GI Tract, 1997, Tropical Infectious Diseases: Principles, Pathogens and Practice, 1999. Chmn. Va. Ptnrs. of the Ams., 1985-87; chmn. U.S.-Japan Cholera Panel, Bethesda, Md., 1991—. Recipient Horsley Meml. Rsch. prize, 1974, Emilio Ribas medal Brazilian Infectious Disease Soc., Bahia, 1997. Fellow ACP, Infectious Diseases Soc. Am. (Smadel medal 1993, Abbott award 1997), Royal Soc. Tropical Medicine and Hygiene; mem. Am. Soc. Tropical Medicine and Hygiene (pres. 1997-98), Am. Soc. Microbiology (chmn. divsn. B 1985), Inst. Medicine, 2004. Avocation: sailing. Home: 2507 Northfield Rd Charlottesville VA 22901-1230 Office: U Va Sch Medicine HSC 485 Charlottesville VA 22908 E-mail: guerrant@virginia.edu.

GUERRERO, DONNA MARIE, sales executive; b. L.A., Apr. 27, 1964; d. Henry Joseph Guerrero and Dolores Catherine Veiga. BA, Whittier Coll., 1985; MPA, Harvard U., 1988. Presdl. intern, pub. rels. mgr. U.S. EEOC, Washington, Houston, 1988—98; profl. sales & leasing cons. Toyota of Whittier, Calif., 2002—. Bd. mem. Nat. Hispanic Media Coalition, L.A., 1994—98. Adv. bd. League of United Latin Am. Citizens, Houston, 1995—97. Recipient Heroes of Reinvention Award, V.P. Al Gore's Nat. Performance Rev., 1994. Roman Catholic. Avocations: christian devotional/spirituality, holistic health, sports memorabilia/collectibles. Home: 11037 Le Grand Ln Moreno Valley CA 92557 Personal E-mail: dguerrero@adelphia.net.

GUERRERO, LISA (LISA GUERRERO-COLES), sports reporter; b. Chgo., Apr. 8, 1964; m. Scott Erickson. Cheerleader Los Angeles Rams; dir, choreographer Atlanta Falcons Cheerleaders, New England Patriots; reporter Extra, 1994; co-host Sports Geniuses, 2000; reporter The Best Damn Sports Show Period!, FoxSportsNet, 2000—03; sideline reporter Monday Night Football, ABC, 2003—04. Actress: (films) Batman Returns, 1992; Love Potion No. 9, 1992; Fire Down Below, 1997; (TV series) Wild West Showdown, 1994; Sunset Beach, 1998—99. Vol. Salvation Army, Cedar Sinai Med. Ctr. Achievements include appearing in over 200 commercials and the covers of Maxim and FHM. Office: 77 W 66th St New York NY 10023

GUERRERO, VLADIMIR, professional baseball player; b. Nizao Bani, Dominican Rep., Feb. 9, 1976; Outfielder Montreal Expos, 1996—2004, Anaheim Angels, 2004—. Named Am. League MVP, 2004; named to Nat. League All-Star Team, 1999—2002, Am. League All-Star Team, 2004, 2005. Achievements include led the Nat. League in hits (206), 2002. Office: c/o Anaheim Angels 2000 Gene Autry Way Anaheim CA 92806*

GUERRI, WILLIAM GRANT, lawyer; b. Higbee, Mo., Mar. 30, 1921; s. Grant and Pearl (Zambelli) G.; m. Millicent K. Branding; children: Paula Ann Guerri Baker, Glenda Kay, William Grant. AB, Central Meth. U., 1943; LLB, Columbia, 1946. Bar: NY 1946, Mo. 1947. Ptnr. Thompson Coburn LLP, St. Louis, 1956—. Mem. bd. editors: Columbia Law Rev, 1945-46. Hon. mem. bd. dirs. St. Louis Heart Assn., chmn., 1972-73; bd. dirs. United Way Greater St. Louis, 1976-94; curator Ctrl. Meth. U., 1981-97. Fellow The Fellows of Am. Bar; mem. ABA, Mo. Bar Assn. (trustee 1984-92), Bar Assn. Met. St. Louis, Assn. of Bar of City of N.Y., Am. Law Inst., Am. Judicature Soc., Noonday Club, Round Table Club, Phi Delta Phi. Home: Apt 308 14300 Conway Meadows Ct E Chesterfield MO 63017-9612 Office: Thompson Coburn LLP Ste 3500 1 US Bank Plz Saint Louis MO 63101-1643 Office Phone: 314-552-6000. Business E-Mail: wguerri@thompsoncoburn.com.

GUERRIERO, CAROL MARIE, librarian; b. Sept. 10, 1963; BA in Radio/TV/Film, Wayne State U., 1985, MLS, 1988. Libr. Livonia (Mich.) Pub. Librs., 1991—. Office: Livonia Pub Libr 32777 Five Mile Rd Livonia MI 48154-3045

GUERRY, WILLIAM, lawyer; b. Norfolk, Va., Apr. 3, 1961; s. William M. and Russell Adelia (Bradford) G.; m. Samantha Semerad, Sept. 8, 1990; 1 child, William. BA, U. Va., 1983, JD, 1986. Bar: Va. 1987, DC 1988, U.S. Ct. Appeals (fed. cir.) Law clk. Justice Russell Supreme Ct. Va., Richmond, 1986-87; from assoc. to ptnr. Collier Shannon, Washington, 1987—. Office: Collier Shannon 3050 K St NW Washington DC 20007-5108

GUERTAL, ELIZABETH ANDERSON, agronomist, educator; BS, Ohio State U., 1984, MS, 1988; PhD, Okla. State U., 1993. Asst. prof. dept. agronomy & soils Auburn (Ala.) U., 1993—. Recipient Novartis Agronomy award Am. Soc. Agronomy, 1997. Office: Auburn U Dept Agronomy 202 Funchess Hall Auburn AL 36849-5412

GUERTIN, ROBERT POWELL, physics professor, dean; b. Trenton, N.J., July 5, 1939; s. Alfred N. and Rhoda (Thomas) G.; m. Margaret Eipper, Aug. 13, 1966 (div. 1999); children: Lynn Frances, Laura Thomas. BS, Trinity Coll., 1961; MA, Wesleyan U., 1963; PhD, U. Rochester, 1969. Asst. prof. physics Tufts U., Medford, Mass., 1968-75, assoc. prof., 1975-83, prof., 1983—, dean Grad. Sch. Arts and Scis., 1985-96, dean Grad. Sch. Rsch. and Profl. Edn., 1994-96. Bd. govs. Univ. Press New England, Hanover, N.H., 1985-96, chmn., 1986-87, 93-94; vis. scientist Nat. High Magnetic Field Lab., Fla., 1996—. Editor books on crystalline electric fields and anomalous rare earth magnetic effects, 1980, 83, 90, 94; contbr. articles to profl. jours. Mem. Lucretia Crocker adv. council Commonwealth Mass., 1986—; bd. dirs. N.E. Assn. Grad. Schs. NSF and NIH rsch. award, 1972-90. Mem. Am. Phys. Soc. (mem. various coms. 1968—). Unitarian Universalist. Avocations: piano, swimming. Home: Apt 1 345 Commonwealth Ave Boston MA 02115-1928

GUESON, EMERITA TORRES, obstetrician, gynecologist; b. Angeles City, The Philippines, Jan. 4, 1942; came to U.S., 1964; d. Lina (Torres) Gueson. AA, U. Sto. Tomas, Manila, Philippines, 1958, MD, 1963. Resident in ob-gyn. Phila. Gen. Hosp., 1966-71; attending physician Nazareth Hosp., Phila., 1973—, Holy Redeemer Hosp., Meadowbrook, Pa., 1983—. Bd. dirs. Physicians Who Care; lectr. healthcare issues to consumer groups, Phila. Author: Doctors Under Fire, 1989, Scales of Justice: Exploring the Wilderness of Health Care and Society's Moral Conscience, 1992, Do HMO's Cut Costs...and Lives, 1997, Survival Guide for HMO Patients, 1997; pub. ThereseVision Publs.; also med. writer, screenplay writer, line dir., prodr. Hon. co-chair physicians adv. bd. Republican Nat. Com. Fellow ACOG, ACP; mem. AMA, Pa. Med. Soc., Philadelphia County Med. Soc., Pro-Life Ob.-Gynecologists (charter). Avocations: writing, painting, refinishing furniture. Office: 3336 Aldine St Philadelphia PA 19136-3802 E-mail: therese44@aol.com.

GUESS, EVELYN LOUISE, elementary school educator; d. Booker T. and Evelyn M. Murry; m. Gerald W. Guess; children: Corey, Timothy, Erin Renee. AA, Contra Costa Coll., 1968; BA, San Jose State U., 1971, MA, 1974. Educator, tchr. Oak Grove Sch. Dist., San Jose, Calif., 1971—; educator dir. Boys & Girls Club, San Jose, 1990—. ESL tchr., Senegal, Brazil. Congl. rep. Dem. Nat. Conv., NY, 1992; bd. dirs. Emmanuel Sch./Family Life Ctr., San Jose, 2002—03. Recipient Good Neighborhood award for Santa Clara County, Tchr. of Achievement award, Entertainment Club, 2004. Mem.: Calif. Tchrs. Assn. (local rep., state coun. rep.), Alpha Kappa Alpha (budget chairperson 2003—05). Avocations: travel, reading. Home: PO Box 53344 San Jose CA 95153 Office: Boys and Girls Club Silicon Valley 518 Valley Way Milpitas CA 95035

GUEST, BARBARA, author, poet; b. Wilmington, NC, Sept. 6, 1920; d. James Harvey and Anna (Hetzel) Pinson; m. Lord Stephen Haden-Guest, 1948 (div. 1954); 1 child, Hon. Hadley; m. Trumbull Higgins, 1954 (dec.); 1 child, Jonathan van Lennep. AB, U. Calif., Berkeley, 1943. Editorial assoc. Art News, 1951-59. Author: (plays) The Ladies Choice, 1953, The Office, 1961, Port, 1965; author: (with Kevin Killian) Often, 2000; author: (poems) The Location of Things, 1960, Poems, 1963, The Blue Stairs, 1968, Moscow Mansions, 1973; author: (with Sheila Isham) I Ching: Poems and Lithographs, 1969; author: The Countess from Minneapolis, 1976, The Türler Losses, 1980, Biography, 1981, Quilts, 1981, Fair Realism, 1989; author: (with June Felter) Musicality, 1989; author: (with Richard Tuttle) The Altos, 1991; author: Defensive Rapture, 1993, Selected Poems, 1995, Stripped Tales, 1995, Quill Solitary Apparition, 1996, Rocks on a Platter: Notes on Literature, 1999, If So, Tell me, 1999, The Confetti Trees: Motion Picture Stories, 1999; author: (with Laurie Reid) Symbiosis, 2000; author: Miniatures and Other Poems, 2002, (novels) Seeking Air, 1978, reprint, 1997, The Red Gaze, 2005, (biographies) The Poet H.D. and Her World, 1984, Herself Defined, 2002, (essays) Forces of Imagination: Writing on Writing, 2003, Dürer in the Window, 2003; editor: (poetry) Partisan Rev. Recipient Longview award, Longview Found., 1960, Laurence Lipton prize in lit., 1990, San Francisco State U. award for poetry, 1994, Fund for Poetry award, 1995, 2005, The America award, 1996, Pen West Josephine Miles award, 1996, Robert Frost medal, Poetry Soc. Am., 1999, Lifetime Achievement award, Small Press Traffic, San Francisco, 2003; grantee, Nat. Endowment for the Arts, 1978; Yaddo fellow, 1958. Address: 1301 Milvia St Berkeley CA 94709-1934 E-mail: barbgues@aol.com.

GUEST, FLOYD EMORY, JR., lawyer; b. Oglethorpe, Ga., May 5, 1929; s. Floyd Emory and Eula Belle (Jones) G.; m. Mary E. Vick, Oct. 12, 1955 (div. 1959); 1 child, Victoria Elizabeth; m. Martha J. Roy, Oct. 12, 1963; children: Alyson Jane, Emory Roy. AB in Bus. Adminstrn., Duke U., 1952; JD, U. Tex., 1962; MS in Fin. Svcs., Am. Coll., 1980. Bar: Tex. 1962. V.p., controller Cosmopolitan Life, Houston, 1952-59; trust officer Bank of Southwest, 1962-67, Capital Nat. Bank, 1967-69; chmn. Profl. Businessmen Assn. Retirement Plans Co., Houston, 1969—. Pres. Southgate Civic Assn., Houston, 1967, 68. Served to capt. USAFR, 1952-67. Mem. SAR, Tex. Bar Assn., Houston Bar Assn., Houston Estate Planning Coun. Delta Theta Phi Law Frat. (pres. Houston alumni 1964). Lodges: Downtown Optimist (pres. 1982-83), Masons, K.T. Republican. Home: 5826 Doliver Dr Houston TX 77057-2470 Office: Action Advisors Inc 5005 Mitchelldale St Ste 174 Houston TX 77092-7242 Office Phone: 713-680-0530. Business E-Mail: fguest@actionadvisors.net.

GUEST, GREG STEPHEN, anthropologist, researcher; arrived in U.S., 1995; s. Glen and Joyce Guest; m. Gretel Abramowsky, Sept. 9, 1999; 1 child, Hunter. BA, McGill U., 1988; cert. in Tchg. English as Fgn. Lang., St. Giles Coll., 1990; MA, U. Calgary, 1995; PhD in Anthropology, U. Ga., 2000. Sr. rschr. Sapient Corp., San Francisco, 2000—02; health analyst Ctrs, Disease Control and Prevention, Atlanta, 2002—03; assoc. scientist Family Health Internat., Durham, NC, 2003—. Author: Globalization, Health and the Environment: An Integrated Perspective, 2005; contbr. articles to profl. jours. Recipient Fgn. Goverenment award, Govt. Mex. External Affairs, Can., 1995, Harold K. Schneider Award, Soc. Econ. Anthropology, 1997; fellow, Social Sci. and Humanities Rsch. Coun. of Can., 1998—2000; grantee, NSF, 1996; scholar, U. Calgary, 1994. Fellow: Soc. Applied Anthropology; mem.: Soc. Med. Anthropology, Am. Anthrop. Assn., Delta Upsilon. Office: Family Health International 2224 E NC Highway 54 Durham NC 27713 Business E-Mail: gguest@fhi.org.

GUEST, JACQUALINE VERDELMA, psychologist; b. Indpls., June 30, 1953; d. Ben Jack and Verdelma Mae (Smith) Guest; m. Paul Richard Mueller, Oct. 21, 1958; children: Patrick Reynolds, Morgan Mueller. BA, Calif. State U., 1977—79; MA, Pacific Oaks Coll., 1984—88, Governors State U., 1997—2000. Nationally Certified School Psychologist NASP, 2004, Liscensed Specialist in School Psychology Tex., 2005, Type 73 School Psychologist Ill., 2000. Sch. psychologist Homewood Flossmoor H.S., Flossmoor, Ill., 2000—; dir. of learning enhancement ctr. David and Margaret Home, La Verne, Calif., 1990—96. Group leader Soka Gaki Internat., Chgo.; team parent AYSO, Chgo. Recipient Meritorious Achievement award, Governors State U., 2000. Mem.: NASP (licentiate), Nat. Honor Soc. of Psychology (life). Office: San Antonio Ind Sch Dist San Antonio TX 78210 Office Phone: 210-225-2406. E-mail: jguest@hfhighschool.org.

GUEST, JODIE LYNN, epidemiologist, educator; d. Vern and Barbara Otte; m. Thomas M. Guest, July 12, 1997; children: Gavin, Anna. BA, Baylor U., 1990; MPH, Emory U., 1992, PhD, 1999. Epidemiologist Am. Cancer Soc., Atlanta, 1997—98; dir., HIV rsch. Atlanta VA Med. Ctr., Decatur, Ga., 1998—. Recipient Golden Apple Tchg. Award, Emory U. Sch. of Medicine, 2002. Office: Atlanta VA Medical Center 1670 Clairmont Rd MS 111-RIM Decatur GA 30033 Office Phone: 404-321-6111.

GUEST, LINDA SAND, education educator; b. Ft. Morgan, Colo., Sept. 9, 1945; d. Robert E. and Leona Mae (Prettyman) Sand; m. Richard E. Guest, June 5, 1966; children: Elise M., Gregory D. BA, Colo. State U., 1967, MEd, 1983; EdD, Harvard U., 1990. Ednl. cons. Nat. Office for Rural Edn., Ft. Collins, Colo.; tchr. Denver Pub. Schs., East Maine Sch. Dist. 63, Niles, Ill., Poudre R-1 Sch. Dist., Ft. Collins, 1979-91; asst. prof. curriculum and instrn. U. Denver Sch. Edn., 1991-94; project coord. Rocky Mountain Tchr. Edn. Collaborative, Greeley, Colo., 1994-98; dir. curriculum Am. Honda Eagle Rock Sch. and Profl. Devel. Ctr., Estes Park, Colo., 1998—2004. Adj. faculty mem. Sch. Edn. Colo. State U., 1997—. Mem. ASCD, Am. Ednl. Rsch. Assn., Phi Delta Kappa. Personal E-mail: lsg01@msn.com.

GUEST, RITA CARSON, interior designer; b. Atlanta, Aug. 17, 1950; d. Walter Harold and Doris Rebecca Carson; m. John Franklin Guest Jr., Jan. 20, 1979. B of Visual Arts, Ga. State U., 1973. Registered interior designer Ga., Fla., D.C., Ala. Pres., dir. design Carson Guest, Inc., Atlanta, 1984—. Lectr. in field. Bd. dirs. Mus. of Design, Atlanta, 2002—. Recipient 5 1st place awards Gwinnett Home Show and Interior Design Expo, 1991. Fellow: ASID (Ga. chpt. dir. 1984, treas. 1985—86, nominating com. 1987, chmn. interprofl. devel. com. 1988—90, pres.-elect 1991—92, pres. 1992—93, nat. office coun. of pres.'s steering com. 1993—94, nat. dir. for region 14 1995—96, legis. adv. coun. 1997—98, mem. fellows coun. 1997—99, nat. bd. dirs. 2000—02, awards com. 2003, nat. nominating com. 2003, Comml. Design Project award 1983, Ga. chpt. Presdl. citation 1984, Residential Design award 1987, Ga. chpt. 1st place Office Design award 1987, Comml. Offices 1st place Project award 1989, Profl. Office Design award 1989, 1st place Libr. Design/1st place Comml. Offices award 1991, Pres. citation 1991, Designer of Yr. 1992, 2 Comml. Project awards 1992, 1st place Nat. Project award 1993, 1st place Instnl. Design award 1994, 1st place Healthcare Project award 1995, Ga. chpt. Silver Contract Design award 2000, Bronze Contract Design award 2001, Gold Instl. award 2002, Gold Comml. award 2003); mem.: Ga. Alliance Interior Design Profls. (pres. 1991—92, bd. advisors 1993—98), Atlanta C. of C. Presbyterian. Avocation: painting. Office: Carson Guest Inc 1720 Peachtree St NW Ste 1001 Atlanta GA 30309-2459 E-mail: ritaguest@carsonguest.com.

GUEST, ROBERT HENRY, state legislator, management consultant, educator; b. East Orange, N.J., May 3, 1916; s. James Henry and Charlotte (Newbould) G.; m. Kate Hay, Dec. 18, 1942; children: David Hartley, Gregory Alan, John Hay, Peter Staples. AB cum laude, Amherst Coll., 1939, LHD, 1974; MA, Columbia U., 1941, PhD, 1960; MA (hon.), Dartmouth Coll., 1963. Dir. indsl. relations Limerick Yarn Mills, Me., 1941-42; sr. field examiner NLRB, 1946-47; mem. field research staff Labor and Mgmt. Center Yale, 1948-52; assoc. dir. research tech. project, 1952-60; ptnr. Charles R. Walker Assocs. (mgmt. cons.), New Haven, 1952-61; prof. organizational behavior Amos Tuck Sch. Dartmouth, 1960-81; mng. dir. Health Mgmt. Assocs. (mgmt. cons.), 1975. Mediator Conn. Labor-Mgmt. Com. Econ. Devel., 1960; mem. N.H. Gov's. Mental Health Com., 1964, N.H. Aeros. Commn., 1968; mem. mgmt. adv. panel NASA, 1969; disting. lectr. U. Leeds, U.K. 1959, U. Strathclyde, U.K. 1969, U. Canterbury, New Zealand, 1981, U. Sapporo, Japan, 1982. Author: (with C. R. Walker) The Man on the Assembly Line, 1952, (with C. R. Walker and A. N. Turner) The Foreman on the Assembly Line, 1957, Organizational Change: The Effect of Successful Leadership, 1962, Hospital Policy: Process and Action; contbg. editor: Changing Forces In American Society, 1964, Organizational Research in Health Institutions, 1973, IL Mutamento Della Organizzazione Aziendale, 1976, (with Paul Hersey and Kenneth H. Blanchard) Organizational Change Through Effective Leadership, 1977, rev. edit., 1986, Innovative Work Practices, 1981, Robotics: The Human Dimension, 1984, Work Teams and Team Building, 1986, As Good Luck Would Have it: An Autobiography on the Light Side, 1987. Exec. com. N.H. Dem. Party; ofcl. U.S. Winter Olympics, Lake Placid, N.Y., 1980; rep. N.H. State Legislature, 1988-2000; prime sponsor First Physician-Assisted Suicide Legis. in USA, 1991. With USNR, 1942-45. Reicpient Book of Yr. award Nat. Orgn. Devel. Coun., 1963, Article of Yr. awards Can. Assn. Mgmt., 1967, Am. Coll. Hosp. Adminstrs., 1974, Disting. Svc. medal Amherst Coll., 1986; marshal Brit. Open Golf Championship, 1990. Mem. Alpha Delta Phi. Clubs: Royal and Ancient Golf (St Andrews, Scotland). Home: Harvest Hill Apt 17 121 Mascoma St Lebanon NH 03766-2634 Personal E-mail: robert.guest@valley.net.

GUETTEL, ADAM, lyricist, composer; b. NYC, 1965; s. Mary Rodgers. Lyricist/composer (plays) Lydie Breeze, Saturn Returns (released as Myths & Hymns, 1999), Love's Fire, Floyd Collins, 1996, (score films) Arguing the World, Jack, 1994, (Broadway plays) Song & Dance, 1985, Light in the Piazza, 2005 (Tony award, best original score (music and/or lyrics) written for theatre, 2005, Tony award, best orchestrations, 2005, Drama Desk award, outstanding orchestrations, 2005, Drama Desk award, outstanding music, 2005). Recipient Stephen Sondheim award, 1990, Obie award, The Village Voice, 1996, Lucille Lortel award, 1996, ASCAP New Horizons award, 1997.*

GUEVARA, AMADO, professional soccer player; b. Tegucigalpa, Honduras, May 2, 1976; married; 1 child. Midfielder CD Motagua, Honduras League, 2003, Major League Soccer, All-Star Team, 2003, 2004, MetroStars, Major League Soccer, East Rutherford, NJ, 2003—. Named Tournament Most Valuable Player, Copa América, 2001, Most Valuable Player, Major League Soccer, All-Star Game, 2004. Led MetroStars in game-winning assists in 2003. Office: MetroStars Meadowlands Sports Complex 50 State Rt 120 East Rutherford NJ 07073

GUEVARA, RAUL, physician, neurologist, neuroophthalmologist; s. Primo and Eva Guevara. BS in Psychology, U. of Philippines, 1984; MD, U. Philippines, Manila, Philippines, 1990. Neurology residency SUNY Health Scis. Ctr., Syracuse, NY, 1992—95; neuro-ophthalmology fellowship Ill. Eye and Ear Infirmary/U. of Ill. Coll. of Medicine, Chgo., 1995—96, Emory Eye Ctr./Emory U. Sch. of Medicine, Atlanta, 1996—97; pvt. practitioner/neurologist Neurol. Care Ctr., Cin., 1998—2002; pvt. practitioner/neuro-ophthalmologist North Tex. Neurology Assoc., Wichita Falls, Tex., 2003—; pvt. practice neuro-ophthalmology S.W. Neurosci. Inst., Dallas, 2005—. Chief resident Dept. of Neurology/SUNY Syracuse, NY, 1994—95. Scholar Resident Ann. Meeting Edn. Scholarship, Am. Acad. of Neurology, 1995, Outstanding Resident, Am. Neurol. Assn., 1994. Mem.: AMA (assoc.). Achievements include research in Pub. case study of longest positive temporal artery biopsy in a patient with temporal arteritis on steroid therapy. Office Phone: 214-496-0500.

GUEVARA, ROGELIO E., federal agency administrator; BS in Police Sci. and Adminstrn., Calif. State U., 1972. With Bur. Narcotics and Dangerous Drugs (now Drug Enforcement Adminstrn.), L.A., 1972, Drug Enforcement Adminstrn., Monterrey, Mexico, 1978—82, Riverside, Calif., 1982—85, with pub. affairs office L.A., 1985—87, supr. in charge S.E. Asian Heroin Enforcement Group, 1987—92, with Office Congl. and Pub. Affairs Arlington, Va., 1992—94, insp. Office Profl. Responsibility, 1994—97, asst. spl. agt. in charge L.A., 1997—2000, spl. agt. in charge Caribbean field divsn. San Juan, PR, 2002—03, chief ops. Alexandria, Va., 2002—03, chief inspector office hdqs. Arlington, 2003—. Office: Drug Enforcement Adminstrn Chief Inspector Office DEA Hdqs Arlington VA 22202 Personal E-mail: rogelio.guevara@gmail.com.

GUFFEY, TRISHA RAE, secondary school educator; b. Kans. City, Mo., May 17, 1979; d. Michael Ray and Sheila G Carver; m. Robert Dale Guffey, Apr. 13, 2002. B in sec. edn., Ctrl. Mo. State U., 1998—2001, M in sec. edn., 2002—03. Bus. and tech. educator Raytown H.S., Raytown, Mo., 2001—02, Raytown Mid. Sch., Raytown, Mo., 2002—. Exploring carer through tech. edn. adv. com. Career and Tech. Edn. (Mo.), Mo., 2004—; curriculum leader - career exploration Raytown C2 Sch. Dist., Mo., 2003—, curriculum writer, 2002—03; yearbook sponsor Raytown Mid. Sch., 2004—, blue creations creator and sponsor, 2002—, students coun. creator and sponsor, 2005—; asst. coach Nat. Forensics League, Raytown H.S., 2001—02; prof./tchg. asst. Ctrl. Mo. State U., 2000—01; mo. bus. educators assn. legislator (greater kans. city rep.) Mo. Bus. Educators Assn., 2002—; raytown c2 sch. dist. curriculum coun. Raytown C2 Sch. Dist., 2003—, raytown mid. sch. practical arts chairperson, 2003—; raytown mid. sch. student recognition com. Raytown Mid. Sch., 2003—, raytown mid. sch. dept. chair, 2002—; presenter Mo. Bus. Educators Assn., 2004—05; united way chair Raytown Mid. Sch., 2004—; curriculum leader - computer i Raytown C2 Sch. Dist., 2004—. Chmn. United Way - Raytown Mid. Sch., 2004. Recipient Best of the Best for Creativity, Donation Amount, Sch. Involvement, United Way, 2004; Gen. Motors UAW scholarship, Gen. Motors, 1999, 2000, Superintendent's Leadership grant, Blue Springs R4 Sch. Dist. Supt., 1997, 1998. Mem.: Alpha Omicron Pi (life; activities chair 1999—2001, philanthropy chair 2000—01). Office: Raytown C2 School Dist 4900 Pittman Rd Kansas City MO 64133 Office Phone: 816-268-7360. E-mail: trisha.guffey@raytownschools.org.

GUGEL, CRAIG THOMAS, advertising and strategic research executive; b. Detroit, Jan. 18, 1954; s. Paul Walter and Patricia Angela (Sullivan) G. BA, U. Windsor, Ont., Can., 1976. Asst. br. mgr. Mich. Nat. Bank, Livonia, 1975—77; analyst media rsch. Kenyon & Eckhardt, Inc., Birmingham, Mich. and N.Y.C., 1977—81, supr. media rsch. N.Y.C., 1981—82; v.p., asst. dir. media rsch. McCann-Erickson, Inc., N.Y.C., 1982—84; v.p., dir. media rsch. Foote, Cone & Belding, Inc., N.Y.C., 1984—86; sr. v.p., corp. dir. media resources Bozell, Jacobs, Kenyon & Eckhardt, Inc., N.Y.C., 1986—88; sr. v.p., dir. media research Bates Worldwide, Inc., N.Y.C., 1988—91, sr. v.p., exec. dir. media rsch. and tech., 1991—94, sr. v.p., exec. dir. interactive media and rsch., 1994—95, exec. v.p. new media and interactive rsch., 1995—97, exec. v.p., dir. media resources and rsch., 1997; pres., CEO Manhattan-Pacific Multimedia Inc., N.Y.C., 1997—; chief rsch. svcs. officer Organic, Inc., N.Y.C., 1997—98; exec. v.p., dir. strategic insights Optimedia Internat., N.Y.C., 2001—03; exec. v.p. worldwide analytics and strategy Interactive Market Sys., Inc., N.Y.C., 2003—. Mem.: Advt. Rsch. Found. (bd. dirs. 1995—2001, chmn. interactive media com., co-chmn. digital media measurement coun.). Avocations: reading, theater, computers.

GUGELOT, PIET CORNELIS, physics educator; b. Bussum, The Netherlands, Feb. 24, 1918; came to U.S., 1947, naturalized, 1954; s. Pieter Cornelis and Anna (Arnold) G.; m. Ursula Federspiel, June 27, 1944; 1 son, Oliver C. Physics degree, Fed. Sch. Tech., Zurich, Switzerland, 1940, PhD, 1945. Research asso. Phys. Inst., Fed. Sch. Tech., Zurich, 1940-47; research asso. Princeton, 1947-49, asst. prof., 1949-56; dir. Inst. for Nuclear Research, Amsterdam, The Netherlands; prof. nuclear physics U. Amsterdam, 1956-66; prof. physics U. Va., Charlottesville, 1966-92, prof. emeritus, 1992—. Vis. prof. U. Wash., 1954; vis. scientist Oak Ridge Nat. Lab., 1959, U. Calif., Livermore, 1960; vis. prof. Stanford, 1963-64, Fermi Inst., U. Chgo., 1970; dir. NASA Space-Radiation Lab., 1966; cons. NASA Langley Research Center, Los Alamos Sci. Lab.; vis. scientist dept. nuclear physics Saclay CERN, 1975-76; vis. prof. U. Lyon, France, 1977; invited lectr. Japan Soc. Promotion Sci., U. Tokyo, 1984 Contbr. articles to profl. jours. Recipient Alexander von Humboldt award Fellow Am. Phys. Soc.; mem. Swiss, European phys. socs., Gesellschaft Ehemaliger Polytechn., Sigma Xi, Sigma Pi Sigma (hon.) Office: U Va Dept Physics Mccormick Rd Charlottesville VA 22904-0001

GUGGENHEIM, FREDERICK GIBSON, psychiatrist, educator; b. Chgo., July 8, 1935; s. Melvin Elias and Marjorie Stone (Gibson) G.; m. Bethany Reed (div. Apr. 1976); m. Olivia Bishop Rogers, Nov. 23, 1984; children: Jennifer, Hannah, Russell Alderson, Rhoades Alderson. BA, Yale U., 1957; MD, Columbia U., 1961. Resident in medicine Bellevue Hosp., N.Y.C., 1961-63, Columbia Presbyn. Med. Ctr., N.Y.C., 1963-64; clin. assoc. NIMH, Bethesda, Md., 1964-66; resident in psychiatry Strong Meml. Hosp., Rochester, N.Y., 1966-69; asst. prof. Harvard Med. Sch., Boston, 1970-79; from asst. in psychiatry to assoc. psychiatrist Mass. Gen. Hosp., Boston, 1969-79; assoc. prof. Southwestern Med. Sch. in Tex., Dallas, 1979-85; Marie Wilson Howells prof. and chair dept. psychiatry U. Ark. for Med. Scis., Little Rock, 1985-2000, prof., 2001—02, prof. and chair emeritus, 2004—; chief psychiat. cons. svc. Univ. Hosp., Little Rock, 2001—02; staff psychiatrist East Bay Mental Health Ctr., Providence, 2002—05; psychiatrist Butler Hosp., 2005—. Mem. nat. adv. com. clin. scholars program Robert Wood Johnson Found., Princeton, N.J., 1988-94; mem. com. on career devel. awards VA, Washington, 1990-95; mem. nat. adv. coun. Substance Abuse and Mental Health Svcs. Adminstrn., 1993-96; chief of staff U. Hosp., 1992-94, sec. med. bd., 1998-2000. Recipient Allison travel fellowship Yale U., 1956, 57, Saybrook Fellows prize, 1957, Nancy CA Roeske cert. of recognition for excellence in med. student edn., 2002, Irma Blend MD award for excellence in tchg. residents, 2005, Lifetime Achievement award Assn. Acad. Psych., 2005. Fellow Am. Psychiat. Assn. (Irma Bland MD award for excellence in tchg. resident 2005), Am. Coll. Psychiatrists, Acad. Psychosomatic Medicine; mem. So. Assn. Rsch. in Psychiatry (pres. 1991-92), Am. Assn. Chairmen of Depts. Psychiatry (pres. 1995-96), Ark. Psychiat. Soc. (pres. 1988-89), Assn. Acad. Psychiatry (pres. 1992-93, Life Achievement award 2005), Cosmos Club of Wash., Alpha Omega Alpha (faculty). Home: 690 Angell St Providence RI 02906-5552 Office: Butler Hosp Partial Hospitalization Program 345 Blackstone Blvd Providence RI 02906 Office Phone: 401-455-6408.

GUGGENHEIM, MARTIN FRANKLIN, lawyer, educator; b. N.Y.C., May 29, 1946; s. Werner and Fanny (Monatt) G.; m. Denise Silverman, May 29, 1969; children: Jamie, Courtney, Lesley. BA, SUNY, Buffalo, 1968; JD, NYU, 1971. Bar: N.Y. 1972, U.S. Dist. Ct. (so. dist. and ea. dist.) N.Y. 1973, U.S. Ct. Appeals (2d cir.) 1974, U.S. Ct. Appeals (3d cir.) 1979, U.S. Ct. Appeals (6th cir.) 1977, U.S. Supreme Ct. 1976. Staff atty. Legal Aid Soc., N.Y.C., 1971-72, dir. spl. litig. unit, juvenile rights divsn., 1972-73; clin. instr. NYU Sch. Law, N.Y.C., 1973-75; staff atty. juvnile rights project ACLU, N.Y.C., 1975-79, acting dir., 1976-77; asst. prof. clin. law NYU, N.Y.C., 1975-77, assoc. prof. clin. law, 1977-79, prof. clin. law, 1980—; of counsel Mayerson & Stutman LLP, N.Y.C., 2001—. Exec. dir. Washington Sq. Legal Svcs., Inc., N.Y.C., 1986-2000; pres. Nat. Coalition for Child Protection Reform, 2000—; pres., founding dir. Family Def. Law Project, Inc., N.Y.C., 1992-2000; advisor program for children Edna McConnell Clark Found., 1993-2001; dir. clin. and advocacy programs NYU, 1989-2002; founding dir. Ctr. for Family Representation, N.Y.C., 2002--; cons. juvenile justice stds. project ABA/Inst. Jud. Adminstrn., 1979-81; acting dir. Clin. Advocacy Programs, Sch. of Law NYU, 1988-89. Author: (with Alan Sussman) The Rights of Parents, 1980, Abuse and Neglect Volume, 1982, The Rights of Young People, 2d edit., 1985, (with Anthony G. Amsterdam and Randy Hertz) Trial Manual for Defense Attorneys in Juvenile Court, 1991, (with Alexandra Lowe and Diane Curtis) The Rights of Families, 1996, What's Wrong With Children's Rights, 2005. Dir. William J. Brennan Ctr., NYU, 1995-2000; mem. adv. bd. N.Y.C. Adminstrn. Children, 1997—; pres. Nat. Coalition for Child Protection Reform, 2000—. Arthur Garfield Hays Civil Liberties fellow, 1970-71, Criminal Law Edn. and Rsch. fellow, 1969-70; Kathryn A. McDonald award Assn. of the Bar of the City of N.Y., 2000. Mem. ABA, Am. Assn. Law Schs., Assn. of Bar of City of N.Y. Office: NYU Sch Law 5th Fl 245 Sullivan St New York NY 10012 Business E-Mail: martin.guggenheim@nyu.edu.

GUGGENHEIM, STEPHEN, geology educator; b. N.Y.C., June 4, 1948; s. S. Frederic and Dorothy Guggenheim; m. Linda R. Brand; children: Lauren, David. BS, Marietta Coll., 1970; MS, SUNY, Stony Brook, 1972; PhD, U. Wis., 1976. Asst. prof. U. Ill., Chgo., 1976-82, assoc. prof., 1982-88, prof., 1988—. Contbr. over 90 articles and book chpts. to profl. jours. Recipient Hawley medal Mineral. Assn. Can., 1987, Jackson Mid-Career award Clay Minerals Soc., 1994, NSF, Petroleum Rsch. Fund grants, 1981—, AMEA medal, Internat. Assn. for Study of Clays, 2005. Fellow Mineral. Soc. Am., Clay Minerals Soc. (pres. 1996-97. editor-in-chief Clays and Clay Minerals, 1999—2001), Assn. Internat. pour l'etude des argiles Coun., Am. Crystallographic Soc. Office: Dept Earth and Environ Sci M/C 186 U Ill Chgo 845 W Taylor St Chicago IL 60607-7056

GUGGENHEIMER, HEINRICH WALTER, mathematician, educator; b. Nurnberg, Germany, July 21, 1924; arrived in U.S., 1959; s. Siegfried and Marguerite Erna (Bloch) G.; m. Eva Auguste Horovicz, June 6, 1947; children: S. Michael, Esther H., Tobias I.S., Hanna Y. Diploma in math., Swiss Fed. Inst. Tech., Zurich, 1947, DSc in Math., 1950. Lectr. Hebrew U., Jerusalem, 1954-56; prof. Bar Ilan (Israel) U., 1956-59; assoc. prof. Wash. State U., Pullman, 1959-60, U. Minn., Mpls., 1960-62, prof., 1962-67, Poly U. (formerly Poly. Inst. Bklyn.), 1967—; prof. emeritus Poly. U. N.Y. (formerly Poly. Inst. Bklyn.), 1989—. Author: Differential Geometry, 2d edit., 1977, Plane Geometry and Its Groups, 1967, Mathematics for Engineering and Science, 1976, Applicable Geometry, 1977, BASIC mathematical Programs for Engineers and Scientists, 1987, (with Eva H. Guggenheimer) Jewish Family Names and Their Origins: An Etymological Dictionary, 1992, German edit., 1996, The Scholar's Haggadah, 1995, Seder Olam: A Translation and Commentary, 1998, The Jerusalem Talmud, bilingual edit., vol. 1, vol. 2, 2000, vol. 3, 2001, vol. 4, 2002, vol. 5, 2003, part III vol. 6, 2004, vol. 7, 2005; contbr. articles to profl. jours. With Swiss Army, 1944-54. Mem. Swiss Math. Soc. (life), Math. Assn. Am., Soc. Indsl. Applied Math. Home: PO Box 401 West Hempstead NY 11552-0401

GUGGENHEIMER, JOAN, law administrator; BA, Binghamton Univ.; JD, Columbia Univ. Gen. coun. Citigroup's Global Corp. and Invest. Bank, Chgo.; head of diversity Smith Barney (now Citigroup), 1985—2003; Co-head of Anti-Money Laundering Citigroup, co-Gen. Coussel; assoc. Smith Barney, 1985; dep. gen. coun. for litig. Citigroup's Global Corp. and Investment Bank, Chgo., gen. counsel of the Inst. Bus., gen. coun.; clk. US Court of Appeals for the Second Circuit; litig. Davis Polk and Wardwell, 1980; Fmr. Gen. Coun. of Globil Corp. and Invest. Bank Citigroup Inc.; chief legal officer Bank One Corp., Chgo., 2003—. Editor: (tabloid) Law Rev./Columbia Univ. Office: Office of Gen Coun Bank One Corp 1 Bank One Plz Chicago IL 60670

GUGGENHEIMER, TOBIAS IMMANUEL SIMON, architect; b. Basel, Switzerland, Jan. 30, 1953; s. Heinrich Walter and Eva Augusta (Horowicz) G.; m. Lisa Ann Shapiro, June 27, 1976 (div. 1999); children: Anna Bella, Leanora Margaret. BA in Lit., SUNY, Binghamton, 1975; MArch, U. Colo., 1985. Registered architect, N.Y., N.J. Pres. Tobias Guggenheimer Arch., P.C., Dobbs Ferry, N.Y., 1991—. Educator Pratt Inst. Sch. of Architecture, Bklyn., 1987—99; asst. prof. and dir. interior design program Fordham U., Tarrytown, 1999—2003; prof. Parsons Sch. of Design, N.Y.C., 2004—; lectr. in field. Author: A Taliesin Legacy: The Architecture of Frank Lloyd Wright's Apprentices, 1995; contbg. editor: Jour. of Taliesin Fellows, 1996-97; architect: (restorations) Frank Lloyd Wright's Serlin Residence, 1996-97; (projects) Mittman Residence, Spearfish, S.D., 2000; (renovations) Yannuzzi Residence, Tuxedo Park, N.Y., 1997-99, Malek Residence, 1999, Denberg Residence, 2003, Howe Bldg., 2000-02, Holtz-Lamb Residence, 2000, Frank-Mermelstein Residence, 2002, Hunter Residence, 2002, Hanlon Residence, 2002, Shore Residence, 2003, Hellman Residence, 2003, Denberg Residence, 2003, Schmidtberger Residence, 2003, Wells Residence, 2004,

Mengel Residence, 2004, Kolleck Residence, 2004, Boukouzis Residence, 2005, Slipp Residence, 2005, Cypers Residence, 2005, others; curator: A Taliesin Legacy: The Independent Work of Frank Lloyd Wright's Apprentices, Pratt Inst. Gallery, 1993, Architectural Competitions in America, 2000. Cons. Village Tuxedo Park, 1999, Frank Lloyd Wright's Reisley Residence, 1999. Mem. AIA, Nat. Coun. Archtl. Registration Bds. Office: Tobias Guggenheimer Arch PC 145 Palisade St Dobbs Ferry NY 10522-1617 Home: 250 W 88th St #409 New York NY 10024-1745 Personal E-mail: tobiasarch@aol.com.

GUGGENHIME, RICHARD JOHNSON, lawyer; b. San Francisco, Mar. 6, 1940; s. Richard E. and Charlotte G.; m. Emlen Hall, June 5, 1965 (div.); children: Andrew, Lisa, Molly; m. Judith Perry Swift, Oct. 3, 1992. AB in Polit. Sci. with distinction, Stanford U., 1961; JD, Harvard U., 1964. Bar: Calif. 1965, U.S. Dist. Ct. (no. dist.) Calif. 1965, U.S. Ct. Appeals (9th cir.) 1965. Assoc. Heller, Ehrman, White & McAuliffe, San Francisco, 1965—71, ptnr., 1972—. Spl. asst. to U.S. Senator Hugh Scott, 1964. Mem. San Francisco Bd. Permit Appeals, 1978—86; bd. dirs. Marine World Africa USA, 1980—86; mem. San Francisco Fire Commn., 1986—88, Recreation and Parks Commn., 1989—92, 2003—04; chmn. bd. trustees San Francisco Univ. H.S., 1987—90; trustee St. Ignatius Prep. Sch., 1987—96. Mem.: Am. Coll. Probate Counsel, Mayacama Golf Club, Olympic Club (bd. dirs. 1999—2002, pres. 2002), Chevaliers du Tastevin (San Francisco), Wine and Food Soc., Bohemian Club. Home: Apt 403 1000 Mason St San Francisco CA 94108 Office: Heller Ehrman LLP 333 Bush St San Francisco CA 94104-2806 Office Phone: 415-772-6374. Personal E-mail: rguggenhime@hewm.com. Business E-Mail: rich.guggenhime@hellerenrman.com.

GUGINO, CARLA, actress; b. Sarasota, Fla., Aug. 29; Studied acting, with Gene Bua. Appearances include (TV series) Falcon Crest, 1989-90, Spin City, 1996—, (TV movies) Murder Without Motive, 1992, A Private Matter, 1992, Rebel Highway, 1994, (TV spls.) The Buccaneers, 1995, (films) Troop Beverly Hills, 1989, Welcome Home, 1990, Son-in-Law, 1993, Miami Rhapsody, 1995, Homeward Bound II: Lost in San Francisco, 1996, Michael, 1996, Red Hot, 1996, The War at Home, 1996, Wedding Bell Blues, 1996; (broadway) After the Fall, 2004, (Theatre World award, 2005). Avocations: yoga, travel. Office: William Morris Agy 151 S El Camino Dr Beverly Hills CA 90212-2704

GUGLIELMINO, JUDE PATCH, writer, humanitarian aid worker; b. San Francisco, Calif., Dec. 30, 1939; d. Richard George and Marvis Linn Patch; m. Louis Elvira Guglielmino, May 5, 1959; children: Brad Richard, Sophie Olga Collins, Louis Elvira Guglielmino II. AA, Santa Rosa Jr. Coll., Calif., 1994—96; BS in Orgnl. Behavior, U. San Francisco, 1997—99. Disaster relief level iii officer ARC, Santa Rosa - Nat. ARC, Calif., 1998—, family services coord. dshr coord. Santa Rosa, Calif., 1998—. Family services coord. ARC, Santa Rosa, Calif., 1998—, dshr coord., 1998—. Writer: Reflections on 9/11/manhattan/ pen/ink drawings Flag at Half Mast. Coord./officer ARC, Santa Rosa, 1998—2004. Recipient Chris Beck Award, ARC, 2001 and 2003, Svc., The Govt. of Guam, 2002, Cmty. Svc. Award, Calif. State Assembly, 2003, Declared a hero for work at Ground Zero, Sonoma County Bd. of Supervisors, 2003, Outstanding Svc., US Senate, 2003. Mem.: Italian/Am. Cultural Club. Roman Catholic. Avocations: travel, reading, art collector, exercise. Office: Am Red Cross 5297 Aero Dr Santa Rosa CA 95403 E-mail: judepatch@hotmail.com.

GUGLIELMINO, LUCY MARGARET MADSEN, education educator, researcher, consultant; b. Charleston, S.C., Feb. 20, 1944; d. Robert Allen and Margaret Webb (Rodgers) Madsen; m. Paul Joseph Guglielmino, July 31, 1965; children: Joseph Allen, Margaret Rose. BA in English magna cum laude, Furman U., 1965; MEd in English and Edn., Savannah Grad. Ctr., 1973; EdD in Adult Edn., U. Ga., 1977. Tchr. English various pub. schs., Mass., 1965-72; vis. asst. prof. adult and cmty. edn. Fla. Atlantic U., Boca Raton, 1978-87, asst. prof., 1987-88, assoc. prof., 1988-90, prof., 1991—, chmn. dept. ednl. leadership, 1991-94, dir. Melby Cmty. Edn. Ctr., 1994—2000. Cons. AT&T, Motorola, Westvaco, S.E. banks, 1979—; bd. dirs. South Fla. Ctr. for Ednl. Leaders. Author: Adult ESL Instruction: A Sourcebook, 1991, Community Education and Florida's Future: Proceedings of the Commissioner's Summit, 1997; co-author: Administering Programs for Adults, 1997; author: (adult form) Self-Directed Leaning Readiness Scale, 1978, 3 other forms and translations into 17 other langs., 1979—94, Learning Preference Assessment (self-scoring format for business), 1991; editor: Florida GED Teachers' Handbook, 1999, 2001, Florida GED Teachers' Lesson Bank, 2001; co-editor: Internat. Jour. Self-Directed Learning, 2003—; contbr. over 100 articles to profl. jours., chapters to books. Mem. Fla. Literacy Coalition, 1990—. Recipient Tchr. of Yr. award Coll. Edn., Fla. Atlantic U., 1990, Outstanding Achievement award 1991, Presdl. Merit award, 1993, Profl. Excellence award, 1998, Malcolm Knowles Meml. award for outstanding lifelong contbn. to rsch. in self directed learning, 2002; named to Fla. Adult and Cmty. Edn. Hall of Fame, Fla. Adminstrs. Adult and Cmty. Edn., 1992; numerous grants, 1979—. Mem. AAUW, Nat. Cmty. Edn. Assn., Am. Assn. for Adult and Continuing Edn., Commn. Profs. Adult Edn. (chmn. self-directed learning task force 1987-88, 90-91), Fla. Adult Edn. Assn. (bd. dirs. 1989-90), Phi Kappa Phi, Phi Delta Kappa. Episcopalian. Avocations: reading, swimming, bicycling, flower arranging, gardening, boating. Home: 7339 Reserve Creek Dr Port Saint Lucie FL 34986 Office: Fla Atlantic U CO 113 500 NW California Blvd Port Saint Lucie FL 34986 Office Phone: 772-873-3348. E-mail: lguglie@fau.edu.

GUGLIELMO, GRACE M., retired artist; b. Bronx, N.Y., Feb. 11, 1920; d. Francesco Paolo Porcelli and Antonia Zullo; m. Porcelli, Oct. 1, 1939; children: Thomas, Diane Dirocco, Mary Jingeleski, Joseph, Gerard, John(dec.), Peter, Michael, Stephen, Christopher, Angelo J. Guglielmo, Jr. AA, Queensborough C.C., Bayside, N.Y., 1987. Eucharistic minister, alpha coord. St. Andrew Avellino Ch., 1994—2002. Mem.: Internat. Womens Writing Guild (Artist of Life 1988, award 1987). Roman Catholic. Avocations: gardening, flower pressing, reading, cooking, antiques. Personal E-mail: agug@prodigy.net.

GUHA, SUJATA, education educator; b. Calcutta, West Bengal, India, Dec. 13, 1969; d. Ashoke Kumar and Minu Guha. *Father, Ashoke Kumar Guha, graduated from Jadavpur University in Calcutta with a degree in chemical engineering. He worked for Union Carbide India Limited as a chemical engineer, and was a manager of its Calcutta branch. Mother, Minu Guha, has a Master of Arts in classical Indian music and is also a specialist in child psychology. She is currently teaching Indian classical music and Rabindrasangeet in Calcutta. Grandparents from father's side of the family were grandfather, Anil Mohan Guha, a lawyer, and grandmother, Sapanbala Guha. Grandmother, Nanibala Ghosh, was from mother's side of the family.* BS, U. of Dubuque, Iowa, 1994; MS, Purdue U., Ind., 1997, PhD, 2000. Grad. instr. chemistry Purdue U., West Lafayette, Ind., 1994—2000; asst. prof. chemistry Rocky Mountain Coll., Billings, Mont., 2000—03, Tenn. State U., Nashville, 2003—. Author: (book chapter) Stratospheric Bromine Chemistry: Insights from Computational Studies. Presdl. Scholarship, U. of Dubuque, 1991—94. Mem.: Am. Chem. Soc., Am. Assn. for the Advancement of Sci., N.Y. Acad. of Scis., The Math. Assn. Am., Mont. Sci. and Tech. Consortium, NASA-Montana Space Grant Consortium, Phi Lambda Upsilon, Alpha Chi (bd. dirs. 1992—94). Achievements include research in Atmospheric chemistry of novel transient species in the gas phase. Office: Tenn State U 3500 John Merritt Blvd Nashville TN 37209 Home: 5160 Rice Rd Apt 137 Antioch TN 37013 Office Phone: 615-963-5334. Office Fax: 615-963-5326. Personal E-mail: sujata_guha@yahoo.com. Business E-Mail: sguha@tnstate.edu.

GUHAROY, ROY SUDIP, pharmacist; s. B M and Gita Guharoy; m. Sue Guharoy, May 3, 1983; 1 child, Victor. MBA, Claremont Grad. Sch., 1992; D of Pharmacy, U. Minn., 1982. Licensed Pharmacist NY, 1998. Clin. pharmacist Porterville (Calif.) State Hosp., 1982-83, John F. Kennedy Meml. Hosp., Indio, Calif., 1983-86, dir. phamancy svcs., clin. coord., 1986-98; dir. pharmacy svcs. Canyon Springs Hosp., Cathedral City, Calif., 1988-90, U. Hosp., Syracuse, N.Y., 1998—; assoc. prof. Union U., Albany Coll. of Pharmacy, 1998—, Wilkes-Barre U., 1999—; assoc. prof. Sch. of Nursing SUNY Health Sci. Ctr., Syracuse, 1998—, assoc. prof. Sch. Medicine, vice chmn. clin. pharmacology, 1998—. Asst. prof. U. So. Calif. Sch. Pharmacy, 1991-98; profl. rels. com. Am. Coll. of Clin. Pharmacy. Contbr. numerous articles to profl. publs. Named, NY State Pharmacist of Yr., 2003. Fellow Am. Soc. of Hosp. Pharmacists, Am. Coll. Clin. Pharm., Am. Coll. Clin. Pharmacy; mem. N.Y. Soc. of Health System Pharmacists (editl. bd.). Achievements include research in pharmacoeconomics, infectious disease, adverse drug events and patient safety. Avocations: travel, hiking, jogging. Office: Univ Hosp 750 E Adams St Syracuse NY 13210-1834

GUHR, DANIEL JOHANNES, management consultant; b. Kirch-Brombach, Germany, Oct. 22, 1967; s. Ekkehard E.F. and Sigrid G. Guhr; m. Erin Nicole Dunlop, 2001. BA Equivalent, U. Bonn, Germany, 1991; MA, Brandeis U., 1995; MSc, Oxford U., England, 1995, PhD, 1999. Intern The Libr. of the German Parliament, Bonn, Germany, 1990, Embassy of the U.S., Bonn, Germany, 1990—91; mgmt. cons. The Boston Cons. Group, Munich, 1997—99, San Francisco, 1999—2000; dir. bus. devel. SAP Markets, Inc., Palo Alto, Calif., 2000—01; mng. ptnr. Illuminate Consulting Group, 2002—. Author: (novels) Access to Higher Education in Germany and California, 2002; editor DAAD North American Studies Yearbook 1991/92, 1992. Scholar, Friedrich-Naumann-Found., 1990, Brandeis U., 1992; fellowship for doctoral studies at Oxford U., Econ. and Social Rsch. Coun., Eng., 1994, scholarship and stipend for studies at Harvard U., German Acad. Exch. Svc., 1991, Travel grantee, Heinz-Schwarzkopf-Found., 1990. Mem.: Comparative and Internat. Edn. Soc., The Acad. Polit. Sci., Turnerschaft Germania (Bonn, Germany) (life), Oxford U. Alumni Assn. (pres. San Diego br.), U. Bonn Alumni Assn., U. Calif. Berkeley Alumni Assn., Brandeis U. Alumni Assn., German Acad. Exch. Svc. Alumni Assn., U. Harvard Alumni Assn., The Commonwealth Club of Calif. Business E-Mail: guhr@illuminategroup.com.

GUI, JAMES EDMUND, architect; b. Wooster, Ohio, Aug. 13, 1928; s. Harry Ludwig and Mabel Josephine (Olson) Gui; m. Anne Louise Outram, Oct. 15, 1955; children: Linda Anne, Jeffrey Allen. BArch, Ohio State U., 1954. Assoc. firm Charles F. McKirahan & Assocs., Archs., Ft. Lauderdale, Fla., 1958—63; chief specifications Archs. Collaborative, Cambridge, Mass., 1963—67; propr. James E. Gui, Archtl. and Specifications Cons., Belmont, Mass., 1967—2005, ret., 2005. Prin. works include Archs. Collaborative, Benjamin Thompson & Assocs., Cambridge Seven Assocs., Archtl. Resources Cambridge, Inc., Harvard, MIT, Juilliard Sch. Music, Lincoln Ctr., NYC, U.S. Pavillion Expo 67, Montreal, New Eng. Aquarium, Children's Hosp. Med. Ctr., Harvard U. Law Sch. Complex, Harvard Gutman Libr., Harvard Obs., Kirkland Coll., Berkshire CC, Tufts U. Dental Health Ctr., Independence Nat. Hist. Pk. Visitors Ctr., Navy Pier, Chgo., Wilmington Jewish Cmty. Ctr., Faneuil Hall Marketplace, Boston, Harborplace, Balt., Seaport Market, NYC, Pier 17, Bayside Marketplace, Miami, Century City Market, LA, Harvard Kennedy Sch. Govt., Cambridge, Ordway Music Theater, Mpls., Union Sta. Restoration, Washington, Va. Performing Arts Ctr., Richmond, Va. Recipient Disting Alumnus award, Ohio State U., 2003. Mem.: Constrn. Specifications Inst. Office Phone: 843-785-7645.

GUICE, NANCY MARTIN, artist, fashion designer; b. Isola, Miss., Dec. 21, 1939; m. John David Wynne Guice; 1 child, Nancy Elizabeth Martin; stepchildren: Soni, Johnny. Student, U. Miss. Staff sec. Miss. Bapt. Hosp., Jackson, 1961-65; dir. Ctrl. Med. Soc., Jackson, 1965-75; designer, buyer Martin Merchandising, Laurel, Miss., 1975-88; designer, artist Designs Unlimited, Laurel, 1988—. Pres. Laurel Arts League, 1975—, Laurel Ballet Guild, 1978, Laurel/Jones County Hist. Soc., 1995; docent Lauren Rogers Mus. Art, 1976, 2d v.p., 1976-78, 98-99, 1st v.p., 1999-2000, pres., 2000-01; bd. dirs. Ptnrs. Arts, Hattiesburg, Miss., 1998—. Mem. Laurel Garden Club, Kappa Alpha Theta. Republican. Episcopalian. Avocations: gourmet cooking, collecting butterflies, collecting antique silver, collecting shells. Home: 2340 N 7th Ave Laurel MS 39440-2274

GUIDA, PAT, information broker, literature chemist; b. Highland Park, Mich. d. W.B. Graham; m. Edward Silvio Guida, Aug. 29, 1965; children: Niels Bohr, Eric Bohr. Student, Regis Coll., 1946-48, Rutgers U., 1952-55; BS cum laude, Fairleigh Dickinson U., 1961. Asst. librarian Warner-Lambert Research Inst., Morris Plains, N.J., 1961-64; librarian Reaction Motors Div. Thiokol, Denville, N.J., 1964-69; mgr., info. ctr. Foster D. Snell Div., Booz Allen & Hamilton Inc., Florham Park, N.J., 1969-80; pres. Pat Guida Assocs., Fairfield, N.J. Mem. sci. adv. bd. EPA, Washington, 1978-82, Library Com. Chemists Club, N.Y.C., 1983-89. Editor: Chemical Digest, 1971—74. Pres. PTA, Sparta, N.J., 1959-60. Avocations: theater, West Highland white terriers, music, travel. Home and Office: 101 Madison Green Pompton Plains NJ 07444

GUIDA, ROBERT ANTHONY, otolaryngologist, plastic surgeon; b. New Kensington, Pa., May 19, 1957; Attended, Franciscan U., 1979; MD, Hahnemann U., 1983. Intern Lankenau Hosp., Phila., 1983—84; resident in gen. surgery Grad. Hosp., U. Pa., Phila., 1984—85; resident NY Eye & Ear Infirmary, NYC, 1985—89; fellow Oregon Health Sci. U., Portland, 1989—90; dir. divsn. facial plastic and reconstructive surgery Cornell Med. Ctr., NY, 1992—; assoc. prof. otolaryngology Cornell Med. Coll. Named one of Top Doctors in NY, NY Mag., 2004. Office: NY Hosp Cornell Med Ctr 525 E 68th St New York NY 10028-4873 Office Phone: 212-746-2212. Office Fax: 212-746-2253.

GUIDASH, JUDITH CAROLYN, neonatal/perinatal nurse practitioner, paralegal, consultant; d. William and Loretta Romanow; m. David Eric Guidash, Jan. 11, 1992. BS in Nursing, U. Del., Newark, 1989. Cert.: Widener U. Legal Edn. Inst. (paralegal) 2001; legal nursing cons. Widener U. Legal Edn. Inst., 2001; RN Del. Staff nurse St. Christopher's Hosp. Children, Phila., 1989—96, Christiana Care Health Sys., Newark, Del., 1996—2001, Dupont Hosp. Children, Wilmington, 2002—. Legal nurse cons. First State Legal Nurse Consultants, Newark, 2001—. Mem.: Am. Assn. of Legal Nurse Consultants (assoc.; mem. nat. conf. com. 2003—04, pres. elect Diamond State chpt. 2002—03), Nat. Assn. of Neonatal Nurses (assoc.), Sigma Theta Tau (assoc.).

GUIDO, MICHAEL ANTHONY, evangelist; b. Lorain, Ohio, Jan. 30, 1915; s. Mike and Julia (DePalma) G.; m. Audrey Forehand, Nov. 25, 1943. Student, Moody Bible Inst., Chgo., 1933-35. Ordained to ministry So. Bapt. Conv., 1939. Min. youth and music lst Presbyn. Ch., Sebring, Fla., 1936-38, lst Bapt. Ch., Lake Charles, La., 1939; evangelist Moody Bible Inst., 1940-50; founder, pres., speaker Guido Evangelistic Assn., Metter, Ga., 1950—. Writer, speaker daily telecast A Seed from the Sower, 1972—, daily broadcaster The Sower, A Seed from the Sower, Seeds from the Sower, Your Favorite Ten, 1957—. Author: (autobiography) Seeds from the Sower, 1990, rev. edit., 1998, Treasury of Illustrations, 1999; editor Sowing and Reaping mag., 1957—; daily newspaper columnist Seeds from the Sower, 1957—. Named Alumnus of Yr., Moody Bible Inst., 1982, Citizen of Yr., Kiwanis Club, Metter, 1982. Baptist. Interstate bridge named in honor of Michael A. Guido, 1998. Home: PO Box 508 Metter GA 30439-0508 Office Phone: 912-685-2222. E-mail: thesower@the-sower.org. *Life to me is loving God and serving Him by finding a need and supplying it, and searching for a lost soul and bringing that one home to God.*

GUIHER, JAMES MORFORD, JR., publisher, writer; b. Clarksburg, W.Va., Feb. 21, 1927; s. James Morford and Ruth Holt (Souders) G.; m. Elizabeth Ewing Hart, Aug. 20, 1954; children: Catharine Brownfield, Deborah Hart. BA, Princeton U., 1951; postgrad., Harvard U., 1951-52, Boston Mus. Sch. Fine Arts, 1953-54. Editor coll. textbooks Prentice-Hall, Inc., Englewood Cliffs, N.J., 1954-66, exec. editor Ednl. Book div., 1966-68, editor-in-chief, 1968-74, v.p., gen. mgr., 1974-76; publishing cons. Author: (play) Aphrodite, 1999. Served with AUS, 1945-47. Home: 4 E 88th St New York NY 10128-0509

GUILAMO-RAMOS, VINCENT M., social sciences educator; MSW, N.Y. U., N.Y.C., 1995, MS in Non-Profit Mgmt., 1999; PhD, SUNY, Albany, 2000. Asst. prof. social work, population and family health Columbia U., N.Y.C., 2001—. Bd. mem. Latino Coun. on Alcohol and Tobacco, Washington, 2005—. Achievements include development of parenting program to assist urban Latino and African American families in preventing problem behavior in their adolescent children. Office: Columbia U 1255 Amsterdam Ave New York NY 10027 Office Phone: 212-851-1659. Office Fax: 212-851-2206. Personal E-mail: rg650@columbia.edu.

GUILD, ALDEN, retired lawyer; b. Boston, July 3, 1929; s. Howard Redwood and Frances Allen (Warren) G.; m. Ruth Ineta Creighton, Sept. 14, 1957; 1 child, Heather Louise. BA, Dartmouth Coll., 1952; JD, U. Chgo., 1957; LLD (hon.), Norwich/Vt. Coll., 1977. Bar: Vt. 1958, U.S. Dist. Ct. Vt. 1958. With law dept. Nat. Life Ins. Co., Montpelier, Vt., 1957-90, asst. v.p., counsel, corp. sec., 1974-83, v.p., gen. counsel, 1983-89, sr. v.p., gen. counsel, 1989-90; ret. McKee, Giuliani & Cleveland, Montpelier, of counsel, 1990-97. Author: Stock-Purchase Agreements, 1960, Professional-Partnership Purchase Agreements, 1961, Business-Partnership Purchase Agreements, 1962; contbr. articles to legal jours. Trustee Norwich U., 1972-96, Vt. Coll., 1967-72, Kimball U. Acad., 1972-74, Wood Art Gallery, 1961-72; mem. Dartmouth Coll. Alumni Council, 1975-78. Served with USAF, 1950-53, Korea. Recipient Disting. Service award Montpelier Jr. C. of C., 1962 Mem. Vt. Bar Assn., Assn. Life Ins. Counsel, Am. Coun. Life Ins., VFW, Am. Legion, Order of Coif, Lake Mansfield Trout Club (Stowe, Vt.), Masons, Elks, Phi Beta Kappa, Theta Chi. Republican. Home: 63 Murray Rd Montpelier VT 05602-8514

GUILD, RICHARD SAMUEL, trade association management company executive; b. Boston, Nov. 5, 1925; s. Walter Rayford and Anna (Hollander) G.; m. Susan Jane Coughlin, July 3, 1965; children: Laura Ann, Linda Jean. BS, Boston U., 1949. Cert. assn. exec. With Guild Assocs., Inc., Boston, 1949—, mng. dir., 1960-65, pres., 1965—. Owner Copypro, 1975-92; treas. Resource Matching System, Inc., 1982-83; exec. sec. New Eng. Marine Trade Assn., 1963, Liquified Petroleum Gas Assn. New Eng., 1972-1985; mng. dir. Shoe Pattern Mfrs. Assn., 1951-94, Mass. Automatic Merchandising Coun., 1964-99, Tel. Answering Assn. New Eng., 1983-99; exec. v.p. Am. Boat Builders and Repairers Assn., 1979-90; treas. Wet Ground MICA Assn., 1983-87. With USNR, 1944-45. Mem. Multiple Assn. Mgmt. Inst. (past pres.), Am. Soc. Assn. Execs. (past bd. dirs.), N.Am. Paddlesports Assn. (exec. v.p 1987-90), Boston Soc. Assn. Execs. (past pres.), Def. Orientation Conf. Assn., Soc. Mgmt. of Profl. Computing (exec. sec. 1985-94), New Eng. Honda Automobile Dealers Assn. (exec. sec. 1985-95), Acura Dealers of N.E. (exec. sec. 1989-93, 96—). Home: 5 Glengarry Rd Winchester MA 01890-2511 Office: 389 Main St Malden MA 02148-5017

GUILFORD, ANDREW JOHN, lawyer; b. Santa Monica, Calif., Nov. 28, 1950; s. Howard Owens and Elsie Jennette (Hargreaves) G.; m. Loreen Mary Gogain, Dec. 22, 1973; children: Colleen Catherine, Amanda Joy. AB summa cum laude, UCLA, 1972, JD, 1975. Bar: Calif. 1975, U.S. Dist. Ct. (ctrl. dist.) Calif. 1976, U.S. Ct. Appeals (9th cir.) 1976, U.S. Supreme Ct. 1979, U.S. Dist. Ct. (so. dist.) Calif. 1981, U.S. Dist. Ct. (no. and ea. dists.) Calif. 1990. Assoc. Sheppard, Mullin, Richter & Hampton, L.A. and Orange County, Calif., 1975-82, ptnr. Orange County, 1983—. Lectr. The Rutter Group, Encino, Calif., 1983—, Continuing Edn. of the Bar, Berkeley, 1978—, Hastings Ctr. for Advocacy, San Francisco, 1988; judge pro tem, arbitrator Calif. Superior Ct., 1983—; mem. commn. future legal profession and state bar; mem. adv. task force on multi-juristictional practice; task force on self-represented litigants. Author UCLA Law Review, 1975. Mem. Amicus Publico, Santa Ana, Calif., 1986; bd. dirs. Pub. Law Ctr. Orange County, 1990—, pres., 2003—; bd. dirs. Constl. Rights Found., 1990, pres., 2003—, Baroque Music Festival, 1992-96, NCCJ, 1995-99, UCLA Law Alumni Assn., 1992-95; subdeacon, warden, del. Episcopal Ch. Recipient resolution of commendation Calif. State Senate and Assembly, Outstanding Svc. award Poverty Law Ctr., 1991, Bernard E. Witkin Amicus Curiae award Calif. Jud. Coun., Jurisprudence award Anti-Defamation League, J. Reuben Clark award, cert. of recognition U.S. Congress, others; co-recipient President's Pro Bono award State Bar; Regents scholar U. Calif., Berkeley, 1968-72; named one of Calif.'s 100 Most Influential Attys., The Daily Jour., Bus. Litig. Trial Lawyer of Yr., Orange County Trial Lawyers Assn. Fellow Am. Coll. Trial Lawyers; mem. ABA, FBA (bd. dirs. 2001—), Assn. Bus. Trial Lawyers (founding officer Orange County chpt., pres. 2000-2001), Am. Arbitration Assn. (arbitrator large complex case program 1993-95), Calif. Bar Assn. (pres. 1999-2000, bd. govs. 1996-2000), Orange County Bar Assn. (bd. dirs. 1985-87, officer 1988-90, pres. 1991, chmn. bus. litigation sect. 1983, state bar conv. 1986, 87, law-motion com. 1982, standing com. trial ct. delay reduction 1987-93, Franklin G. West award 2003), 9th Cir. Jud. Conf. (rep. 1990-92, 99—2001), Phi Beta Kappa (sec.-treas. 1978-80, v.p. 1980-84), Pi Gamma Mu, Sigma Pi. Republican. Avocations: theater, photography, sports, gardening, poetry. Office: Sheppard Mullin Richter & Hampton 650 Town Center Dr Fl 4 Costa Mesa CA 92626-1993 Home: 31852 Camino del Cielo Trabuco Canyon CA 92679-3400 Office Phone: 714-424-2827. E-mail: aguilford@sheppardmullin.com.

GUILFORD, MATTHEW TODD, musician, music educator; b. Middleboro, Mass. s. Byron Fredrick Guilford and Beverly Anne Salvato; m. Rayne Belle Pdlack, Oct. 10, 1998; children: Russell, Vivianne Sarah. BMus, New Eng. Conservatory, Boston, Mass., 1986, MMus, 1988. Musician bass trombonist San Francisco Opera Orch., San Francisco, 1989—91; faculty mem. Cath. Univ. of Am., Washington, 1992—, Univ. Md., Coll. Pk., Md., 1992—; musician bass trombonist Nat. Symphony Orch., Washington, 1991—, Nat. Orch. Inst., Coll. Pk., Md., 1997—. Adj. faculty mem. Peabody Conservation at John Hopkins, 1996—97. Office: Univ Md Music Dept Tawes Bldg College Park MD 20742

GUILFORD, ROBERT E., lawyer; b. Cleve., Apr. 14, 1933; s. Isadore H. and Malvene G.; m. Edel Singer, 1960 (div. 1963); 1 child, Steven; m. Judith Cagen, May 5, 1990. BA in Philosophy with honors, U. Va., 1955; JD, Harvard U., 1958. Bar: Calif. 1959, U.S. Dist. Ct. (cen. dist.) Calif. 1959, U.S. Dist. Ct. (no. dist.) Calif. 1964, U.S. Dist. Ct. (no. dist.) N.Y. 1996, U.S. Ct. Appeals (9th cir.) 1959. Asst. U.S. atty. Dept. Justice, L.A., 1958-59; legal staff MCA Universal, Universal City, Calif., 1959-65; gen. counsel World Horizons Inst., Newport Beach, Calif., 1965-70; ptnr. Bryant, Maxwell, Guilford & Sheahan, 1970-75; outside counsel Home Savings & Loan Assn., Beverly Hills, Calif., 1975-80; pvt. practice Santa Monica, Calif., 1980-85; gen. counsel Mus. of Flying, Santa Monica, Calif., 1985-90; assoc. counsel Am. Golf Corp., Santa Monica, Calif., 1987-90; pvt. practice, 1990—93; shareholder Baum, Hedlund, Profl. Corp., L.A., 1993—. V.p., chief pilot, trustee Mus. Flying, Santa Monica; v.p. Supermarine Aviation Ltd., Liberty Aero Corp., NATO Aviation. Mem. State Bar Calif., Lawyer-Pilot's Bar Assn., Aircraft Owners and Pilots Assn., Exptl. Aircraft Assn., Classic Jet Aircraft Assn. (chmn. bd. dirs.), Warbirds Am. (co-founder), Hunter Flight Test Ltd. (v.p.), Nat. Air Disaster Found. (Safety award 2002), Mustang Pilots Club (founder, pres.), Phi Eta Sigma. Avocation: pilot. Office: Baum Hedlund PC Ste 950 12100 Wilshire Blvd Los Angeles CA 90025-7107 E-mail: rguilford@baumhedlundlaw.com.

GUILFOYLE, MARVIN C., librarian; b. Greenville, Mich., Apr. 30, 1945; s. Claude C. and Beatrice R. Guilfoyle; m. Kristi A. Miller, Dec. 27, 1988; 1 child, Ryan M. Miller. BS in Edn., Ctrl. Mich. U., Mt. Pleasant, 1963—67, MA in History, 1968—74; MS, Western Mich. U., Kalamazoo, 1972—73. Govt. docs. libr. U. Okla., Norman, 1973—78; asst. dir. for pub. svcs. N.E. Okla. State U. Libr., Tahlequah, 1978—79; dir., pub. svcs. U. Evansville Librs., Ind., 1979—87, periodicals libr., 1988—93, acquisitions and collection devel. libr., 1992—. Democrat. Avocations: skiing, hiking, white-water rafting. Office: Univ Evansville Librs 1800 Lincoln Ave Evansville IN 47722 Office Phone: 812-488-2247. E-mail: mg29@evansville.edu.

GUILIANO, FRANCIS JAMES, office products manufacturing company executive; b. Feb. 1, 1932; s. James V. and Mary C. Guiliano; m. Mary Beth Eberly, Jan. 9, 1957; children: Barbara Jean, James Francis, Janet Marie, John Alden. BBA in Fin., U. Mass., 1959; MBA, U. Pa., 1978. Salesman Continental Can Co., 1959-63; sales mgr. State of Mich., 1964-65; plant gen. mgr. Internat. Paper Co., Greensburg, Pa., 1966-67, gen. mktg. mgr. container divsn., 1967-69, world-wide gen. mktg. mgr., 1969-72, v.p., gen. mgr. Folding Carton divsn. N.Y.C., 1972-76; exec. v.p. Simkins Industries, New Haven, 1977; chmn., CEO, pres. Ampad Corp., Holyoke, Mass., 1979-90; owner, CEO Rite-Now Container Corp., East Longmeadow, Mass., 1990—. CEO 4M Corp., 1987—; dir. Shawmut First Bank & Trust; CEO and pres. PCL Industries, 1990-93. Bd. dirs. United Way, 1981-82; chmn. bus. adv. coun., mem. exec. com. U. Mass. Sch. Bus., 1980-82; bd. govs. Holyoke Libr. Served with USN, 1951-55. Mem. Am. Mgmt. Assn., Ind. Box Makers Assn., Paper Converters Assn., Nat. Office Products Assn., Wholesale Stationers Assn., Colony Club (Springfield, Mass.), Longmeadow Country Club. Office Phone: 508-240-6728. Personal E-mail: ritenow@capecod.net.

GUILIANO, MIREILLE, consumer products company executive; b. Moyeuvre, France, Apr. 14, 1946; m. Edward Guiliano. Student, Sorbonne, Paris, Institut Supérieur d'Interprétariat et de Traduction; M in English and German; cert., interpreter/translator. Pres., CEO Clicquot, Inc., NYC, 1984—; and dir. Champagne Clicquot, Reims, France. Author: French Women Don't Get Fat, 2004 (Publishers Weekly bestseller list, NY Times bestseller list); contbr. articles to food, wine, lifestyle pubs. Mem.: Com. of 200. Office: Clicquot Inc 4th Fl 717 Fifth Ave New York NY 10022*

GUILLAMA-ALVAREZ, NOEL JESUS, merchant banker, healthcare executive; b. Havana, Cuba, Nov. 30, 1959; arrived in US, 1966, naturalized, 1981; s. Jesus Mario Guillama and Rosa Maria Alvarez Guillama; 1 child, Jahziel Mikhail Guillama; m. Susan E. Darby, Dec. 13, 2002; 1 stepson, Patrick James Jacobs. Student, Palm Beach C.C., Lake Worth, Fla., 1978—80; BS in Constrn. Mgmt., Allstate Coll., Tampa, Fla., 1983; postgrad., MIT, 1997—99. Cert. bldg. contractor, Fla.; lic. real estate broker, mortgage broker, gen. ins. agt. Dir. programing Teleprompter Corp., West Palm Beach, Fla., 1976-79; pres., CEO JMG Holdings Inc, Palm Beach, Fla., 1980-90; chmn., CEO Tektonica, Inc., Tequesta, Fla., 1984—; v.p. ops. Quality Care Networks, Boca Raton, Fla., 1990-95; v.p. devel. Medpartners, Inc., Birmingham, Ala., 1995; pres., CEO Met. Health Networks, Boca Raton, 1995-2000; chmn., mng. ptnr. Millenium Capital Ptnrs., Boca Raton, 1997—; chmn. The Quantum Group, Wellington, Fla., 2000—, TargitInteractive, Portsmouth, NH, 2000—02; dir. Da Vinci Ventures Group, Inc., 2003. Vice-chair Palm Beach County Adv. Bd., West Palm Beach, 1990—92; co-founder, vice-chair Lake Worth Cmty. Devel. Corp., 1990—92; co-founder Project Lake Worth, 1989—92; dir. Palm Beach C.C.; trustee Palms West Hosp., Loyahatenee, Fla. Writer weekly column Palm Beach Latino Newspaper, 1991-92. Mem. Wellington Fla. Edn. Com., 2004—; dir. Palm Beach Cmty. Coll. Found., Lake Worth, Fla., 2005—; trustee Palms West Hosp., Loxahatchee, Fla.; bd. dir. Fla. Internat. U. Found., Miami, 2002—. Recipient award Leukemia Soc. Am., 1979, Chin de Plata award Todo Mag., Miami, Fla., 1978. Mem.: Health Info. Mgmt. Soc., Med. Group Practice Assn., Am. Fin. Assn., Am. Coll. Healthcare Execs. (assoc.). Republican. Avocations: scuba diving, tennis, golf, fishing. Office: 3460 Fairlane Farms Rd Ste 4 Wellington FL 33414 Office Phone: 561-798-9800. Business E-Mail: nguillama@qtum.com.

GUILLAUME, JUANITA CONNOR, financial analyst, minister; b. NYC, Feb. 3, 1957; d. Zinnie Pickett and Queen Esther Lipscomb; m. Odner Guillaume, June 12, 1976; children: Gary Andre, Natasha Nichelle. AA, Bethel Bible Inst., Jamaica, N.Y., 1977; DD (hon.), World Christianship, Fresno, Calif., 1994; B of Theology in Religious Edn., Open Bible Faith Ministries, Bklyn., 1998, Internat. Sem. Calif.; MTh in Counseling, Open Bible Faith Sem., Bklyn., 2005. Ordained min. Fireside Ch.; ETA cert. tchr.'s pastoral counselor. Claims devel. clerk Human Resource Adm., 1970-82; account clerk U. Hosp., Bklyn., 1983—. Author: Express of the Heart, 1997. Assoc. min. Fireside Pentacostal Ch., 1970—, supt. Sunday sch., 1995—; pres. Promises Faith Ministry, 1996—. Recipient Editor's award, 1995. Mem. Am. Assn. Christian Counselors Calif. Democrat. Home: 661 E 80th St Fl 2 Brooklyn NY 11236-3311 Office: Fireside Pentecostal Assembly 69-71 Thayer St New York NY 10040 Personal E-mail: juanita-guillaume@hotmail.com.

GUILLAUME, RAYMOND KENDRICK, banker; b. June 19, 1943; s. William Raymond and Marguerite (Lyons) G.; m. Ann Greenwell, June 26, 1965; children— Lee Kendrick, Jill Lyons Kissel. BS, Western Ky. U., 1965. Asst. cashier Liberty Nat. Bank, Louisville, 1968, asst. v.p., 1969-70, v.p., 1970-72, sr. v.p., 1973-78, exec. v.p., 1978-92, pres., 1993-95, also bd. dirs.; vice chmn., CEO Bank of Louisville, 1995—2002; pres. Ky. and Louisville metro region Br. Banking & Trust, 2002—04, chmn. Ky. Ops., 2004—, pres. Ky. Ops., 2004, CEO Ky. Ops., 2004—. Chmn., bd. dirs. ARC, Louisville, 1985; treas., bd. dirs. Met. United Way, Louisville, 1984-92, 93—, St. Anthony's Hosp., Louisville, 1985; trustee Christ Ch. United Meth., Louisville, 1984; chmn. Leadership Louisville, 1992-95; chmn. bd. dirs. Metro United Way, Western Ky. Univ. Found., Ky. Ctr. for the Arts Endowment Fund; bd. dirs. Norton Healthcare, The Healing Pl., The Housing Partnership. Mem. Western Ky. U. Nat. Alumni Assn. (pres. 1985), Ky. Bar Assn. (bd. dirs.), Pendennis Club, Louisville Boat Club, Louisville Country Club, Jefferson Club, Kentuckians of N.Y. Home: 415 Rolling Ln Louisville KY 40207-1807 Office: Br Banking & Trust PO Box 1101 Louisville KY 40201-1101 Office Phone: 502-562-5802. Business E-Mail: rguillaume@bbandt.com.

GUILLEMIN, ROGER C. L., physiologist; b. Dijon, France, Jan. 11, 1924; arrived in U.S., 1953, naturalized, 1963; BA, U. Dijon, 1941, B.Sc., 1942; MD, Faculty of Medicine, Lyons, France, 1949; PhD, U. Montreal, 1953; PhD (hon.), U. Rochester, 1976, U. Chgo., 1977, Baylor Coll. Medicine, 1978, U. Ulm, Germany, 1978, U. Dijon, France, 1978, Free U. Brussels, 1979, U. Montreal, 1979, U. Man., Can, 1984, U. Turin, Italy, 1985, Kyung Hee U., Korea, 1986, U. Paris, Paris, 1986, U. Barcelona, Spain, 1988, U. Madrid, 1988, McGill U., Montreal, Can., 1988, U. Claude Bernard, Lyon, France, 1989, Laval U., Quebec, Can., 1990, Sherbrooke U., Quebec, 1997, U. Franche-Comté, France, 1999. Intern, resident univs. hosps., Dijon, 1949-51; assoc. dir., asst. prof. Inst. Exptl. Medicine and Surgery, U. Montreal, 1951-53; asst. prof. physiology Baylor Coll. Medicine, 1953-57, assoc. prof., 1957-63, prof., dir. labs. neuroendocrinology, 1963-70; assoc. dir. dept. exptl. endocrinology Coll. de France, Paris, 1960-63; resident fellow, chmn. labs. neuroendocrinology Salk Inst., La Jolla, Calif., 1970-89, adj. rsch. prof., 1989-94; Disting. Scientist Whittier Inst., 1989-97, med. and sci. dir., 1993-94; adj. prof. medicine U. Calif., San Diego, 1995-97; disting. prof. Salk Inst., La Jolla, Calif., 1997—. Bd. dir. ICN Pharms.; cons. physiology VA Hosp., Houston, 1954—60; lectr. exptl. endocrinology dept. biology Rice U., Houston, 1958—60; dir. rsch. CNRS, Paris, 1963—68. Decorated chevalier Legion d'Honneur France, officer de la Légion d'Honneur French Republic; recipient Gold medal, 1st Internat. Congress Pharmacology, Stockholm, 1961, Saintour award for exptl. endocrinology, Coll. de France, Paris, 1961, Disting. Scientist award, Nat. Diabetes Rsch. Coalition, 1966, U.S. NIH lectureship, Bethesda, Md., 1973, La Madonnina award for medicine, The Carlo Erba Found., 1974, Gairdner Internat. award, 1974, Lasker award, Lasker Found., 1975, Dickson prize in medicine, 1976, Passano award sci., 1976, Schmitt medal neurosci., 1977, Nobel Prize in Medicine, The Nobel Found., 1977, Nat. Medal of Sci., Pres. of the U.S.A., 1977, Barren Gold medal, 1979, Dale medal, Soc. for Endocrinology, UK, 1980, Ellen Browning Scripps Soc. medal, Scripps Meml. Hosps. Found., 1988; scholar, John and Mary R. Markle Found., N.Y., 1952—56. Fellow: AAAS; mem.: NAS, Tex. Med. Ctr. Rsch. Soc. (pres. elect 1959, pres. 1960, hon. 1970), Assn. des Physiologistes, Am. Inst. Biol. Sci., Western Soc. Clin. Rsch., Internat. Soc. Neurosci. (charter), Acad. Royale de Medecine de Belgique, Acad. Sci., Academie Nat. de Medicine, French Acad. Scis., Am. Acad. Arts & Scis., Soc. Neuro-scis., Internat. Soc. Rsch. Biology Reprodn., Internat. Brain Rsch. Orgn., Soc. Exptl. Biology and Medicine, Endocrine Soc. (coun. 1969—73, nominating com. 1974—75, pres. 1986), Assn. Am. Physicians, Am. Physiol. Soc., Soc. Francaise d'Endocrinologie (hon.; pres. 1982—83), Soc. de Biology Paris (hon.), Soc. Can. Biology (hon.), Internat. Soc. for Immunology of Reproduction (hon.), Howard Florey Inst. Exptl. Physiology and Medicine (hon.), Houston Philos. Soc. (hon.), Can. Soc. Endocrinology and Metabolism (hon.), Swedish Soc. Med. Sci. (hon.), Am. Peptide Soc. (hon.), Club of Rome. Office: The Salk Inst 10010 N Torrey Pines Rd La Jolla CA 92037-1099 Address: The Salk Inst PO Box 85800 San Diego CA 92186-5800*

GUILLEN, ALITA (ALITA HAYTAYAN), newscaster; BA in English, U. N.H., 1992; MA in Broadcast Journalism, U. Miami, 1995. Anchor, prodr., reporter and host Dynamic Cable, Miami, Fla.; reporter and anchor WABU-TV, Boston, 1995—96; reporter and substitute anchor WTSP-TV, Tampa, Fla., 1997—99; morning news anchor and reporter WFOR-TV, Miami, 1999—2002; co-anchor weekend news and reporter WBBM-TV, Chgo., 2002—. Office: WBBM-TV 630 N McClurg Ct Chicago IL 60601

GUILLEN, JEROME, trucking executive; b. Cavaillon, Vaucluse, France, Aug. 27, 1972; s. Gerard Guillen and Nicole Barriere; life ptnr. Brian Ramsay. BSME, Ecole Nationale Superieure De Techniques Avancees, Paris, 1993; MSc in Nuc. Engring., Escuela Tecnica Superior De Ingenieros Industriales, Madrid, 1994; PhD in Mech. Engring., U. Mich., 1999. Engagement mgr. McKinsey & Co., Inc., Detroit, 1999—2002; gen. mgr. new product devel. Freightliner LLC, Portland, Oreg., 2002—. Contbr. articles to profl. jours. Named one of Top 40 under 40, Portland Bus. Jour., 2003. Mem.: SAE, ASME. Office: Freightliner LLC 4747 N Channel Ave C1C-P3 Portland OR 97217 Office Phone: 503-745-3354. Personal E-mail: jeromeguillen@freightliner.com.

GUILLEN, MAURO FEDERICO, sociology and management educator; b. Leon, Spain, Sept. 30, 1964; came to U.S., 1987; s. Julian and Maria Flor (Rodriguez) G. BA in Polit. Economy, U. Oviedo (Spain), 1987, D Polit. Economy cum laude, 1991; MA, Yale U., 1989, M in Philosophy, 1990; PhD in Sociology, 1992. Instr. Yale U., New Haven, 1989-91, grad. affiliate Calhoun Coll., 1990-92; asst. prof. internat. mgmt. and sociology MIT Sloan Sch. Mgmt., Cambridge, 1992-96; from asst. prof. to prof. mgmt. Wharton Sch. U. Pa., Phila., 1996—. Rsch. affiliate Ctr. for European Studies, Harvard U., 1992-96; vis. mem. Inst. for Advanced Study, Princeton U., 1998-99. Author: The AIDS Disaster, 1990 (Gustavus Myers award Outstanding Book on Human Rights 1991), La Profesion de Economista, 1989, Models of Management, 1994 (Pres.'s Book award Social Sci. History Assn. 1993), The Lines of Convergence, 2001, The Rise of Spanish Multinationals, 2005. Organizer Grad. Employees and Studen Orgn. at Yale, New Haven, 1991-92. Fulbright fellow Inst. of Internat. Edn., 1989-92, John D. Rockefeller 3d fellow Program on Nonprofit Orgns., Yale U., 1989, Guggenheim fellow, 1998-99. Mem. Am. Sociol. Assn., Internat. Sociol. Assn., Acad. Mgmt., Acad. Internat. Bus. Roman Catholic. Avocations: modernist art, opera, basketball, squash. Home: 2410 Spruce St Philadelphia PA 19103-6423 Office: U Pa Wharton Sch 2016 Steinberg Hall Philadelphia PA 19104-6370

GUILLERMO, LINDA, clinical social worker; b. Chgo., July 4, 1951; d. Triponio Pascua and Helen Elizabeth (Moskal) Guillermo. BA, U. Ill., Chgo., 1973, MSW, 1975, postgrad., 1980, Jane Addams Coll. Social Work, 1980—82. Diplomate in clin. social work, lic. real estate broker Ill. Mktg. rsch. interviewer Rabin Rsch. Co., Chgo., 1970—73; mktg. rsch. interviewer, coder Marcor Mktg. Rsch., Inc., Chgo., 1973—75; social work intern Child and Family Svcs., Chgo., 1973—74, Chgo. Bd. Edn., 1974—75; social worker, therapist child abuse and neglect, case investigator, case planning cons., social svc. program planner Ill. Dept. Children and Family Svcs., Chgo., 1975—78; social svc. program planner, contract negotiator, monitoring agt. Ctrl. Resources Contracts and Grants, 1978—79; real estate sales person Sentry Realty, Chgo., 1976—; social worker, therapist, program coord., casework supr. of child abuse assessment and intervention program, proposal writer Casa Ctrl., Chgo., 1979—82, casework cons. of child abuse assessment and intervention program, proposal writer, program dir. and casework supr. of early intervention program, 1979—85; social worker, clin. supr. Chgo. Bd. Edn., 1985—. Tng. specialist City Coll. of Chgo., 1980; adj. assoc. rschr. Asher Feren Law Office, Chgo., 1980—81. Treas. Greenleaf Condominium Assn., Chgo., 1980—81, sec., 1987—88, interim pres., 1988; regional rep. North Ill. Assn. of Sch. Social Workers, 1986—87; active various polit. campaigns, Chgo. Mem.: Ill. Cert. Lic. Social Workers, Nat. Assn. Cert. Social Workers (register clin. social workers), North Side Real Estate Bd. Home: 7405 N Kenneth Ave Skokie IL 60076 Office Phone: 847-763-0865.

GUILLERMOPRIETO, ALMA, journalist, non-fiction writer; b. Mex., May 27, 1949; Journalist, 1978—. Dancer Ballet Co. of Mex. Author: Samba, 1990, The Heart That Bleeds: Latin America Now, 1994, Looking for History, 2002, Dancing With Cuba, 2005. MacArthur fellow, 1995.

GUILLERY, RAINER WALTER, anatomy educator; b. Greifswald, Germany, Aug. 28, 1929; came to U.S., 1964; s. Hermann and Eva (Hackel) G.; m. Margot Cunningham Pepper, Dec. 21, 1954, (div. 2000); children: Peter, Edward, Philip, Jane. BSc in Anatomy, U. Coll., London, 1951, PhD, 1954. Asst. lectr. Univ. Coll., London, 1953-57, lectr., 1957-63, reader, 1963-64; assoc. prof. U. Wis., 1964-68, prof. anatomy, 1968-77; prof. dept. pharm. and physiol. Scis. U. Chgo., 1977-84; Dr. Lee's prof. anatomy Oxford U., England, 1984-96; vis. prof. anatomy U. Wis., 1996—2002, emeritus prof. anatomy, 2002—; hon. prof. Chinese U., Hong Kong, 2005. Author: (with M.S. Sherman) Exploring the Thalamus, 2001; mem. editl. bd. Jour. Comparative Neurology, 1971-2002, Jour. Neurocytology, 1972-76, Jour. Neurophysiology, 1975-81, Neurosci., 1979-2005, Jour. Neurosci, 1980-90; editor-in-chief European Jour. Neurosci., 1987-92, mem. editl. bd., 1987-. Fellow U. Coll. London, 1987. Fellow Royal Soc.; mem. Soc. Neurosci., Anatomical Soc. G.B., Ireland (pres. 1994-96). Achievements include research on central nervous system, synapses, degeneration, developmental visual pathways. Office: U Wis Dept Anatomy Sch Medicine 1300 University Ave Madison WI 53706-1510 Office Phone: 608-263-4763. Business E-Mail: rguiller@wisc.edu.

GUILLILAND, MARTHA W., academic administrator; b. Pa. BS in Geology and Math., Catawba Coll., 1966; MS in Geophysics, Rice U., 1968; PhD in environ. engring./sys. ecology, U. Fla., 1973. Rsch. fellow sci. and pub. policy U. Mo., Kan. City, Mo., 1974—77; asst. prof. civil engring. and environment sci. U. Okla., 1975—77; exec. dir. Energy Policy Studies, Inc., El Paso, Tex., 1977—82; assoc. prof. civil engring. U. Nebr., Lincoln, 1988—90, dir. Ctr. Infrastructure Rsch., 1988—99; dean grad. sch. and asst. v.p. rsch. U. Ariz., 1990—93, vice provost academic affairs, 1993—95, academic v.p. info. and human resources, 1995—97, prof. hydrology and water resources, 1995—97; provost Tulane U., New Orleans, 1997—2000; pres. U. Mo., Kans. City, 2000—. Appointee Rsch. and Adv. Panel of Gen. Acctg. Office, Energy Engring. Bd. of Nat. Rsch. Coun., NAS Com. on Strategic Assessment of Dept. of Energy Coal Program, Nat. Inst. Global Change, Pres.'s Coun. of Advisors on Sci. and Tech., 2001. Author: (book) Energy Analysis: A New Public Policy Tool, co-author books; contbr. articles to profl. jours. Recipient Hubert H. Humphrey award, Policy Studies Orgn., 2002, Gov.'s award Excellence Total Quality Efforts, Ariz.; fellow, W.K. Kellogg Found., 1985—88. Office: U Mo 5100 Rockhill Rd Kansas City MO 64110

GUILLORY, ANN VERRETT, psychologist, educator; b. New Orleans, Dec. 10, 1948; d. Wilbert A. and Augusta Bell Verrett; m. Samuel Guillory (div.); children: Elizabeth, Christine. BS, Loyola U. of the South, New Orleans, 1970; MEd in Guidance and counseling, Loyola U. of the South, 1972; MEd in Gerontology, Columbia U., N.Y.C., 1981; EdD in Applied Human Devel., Columbia U., 1983. Cert. student svcs. and sci. tchr. La., N.J. Dir. Ednl. Opportunity Fund Felician Coll., Lodi, NJ, prof. psychology. Trustee Care Plus N.J., Paramus, 1994—, Care Plus Found., Paramus, 2001—, Westside Daycare Ctr., Englewood, NJ, 2001—. Mem.: Am. Coll. Pers. Assn., Assoc. Gerontology in Higher Edn. Roman Catholic. Avocations: gardening, needlepoint. Office: Felician College 262 S Main St Lodi NJ 07644

GUIN, DON LESTER, insurance company executive; b. Shreveport, La., Nov. 5, 1940; s. Lester and Ethelyn (Dumas) G.; m. Mary Ann Guin, Feb. 3, 1979. BBA in Ins., U. Ga., 1962; BS in Law, Kensington U., Glendale, Calif., 1987, JD, 1989. Bar: Calif. 1990, U.S. Ct. Appeals (5th and 9th cirs.) 1990, U.S. Dist. Ct. (no. dist.) Calif. 1990, U.S. Ct. Appeals (fed. cir.) 1991, U.S. Dist. Ct. (ea. dist.) Tex. 1991, U.S. Ct. Internat. Trade 1991, U.S. Ct. Fed. Claims 1992, U.S. Supreme Ct. 1994. Adjuster, supr. Lindsey & Newsom, Beaumont, Tex., 1963-71, mgr. Port Arthur, Tex., 1968-71, asst. to pres. Tyler, Tex., 1971-74, v.p. ops., 1977-84, sr. v.p., 1984—; sr. v.p. adminstrn. and legal Lindsey Morden, 1990—; sr. v.p., corp. sec. Lindsey Morden Claims Svc. Inc., Lindsey Morden Claims Mgmt., 1992-93, sr. v.p., treas. U.S. Ops., 1993—, sr. v.p., corp. treas., chief legal officer, 1995—; sr. v.p., corp. treas. and sec. Vale Nat. Training Ctrs, Inc., 1993—; exec. v.p., corp. treas, corp. sec., chief legal officer, 1995—; exec. v.p. Cunningham Lindsey U.S., Inc., 2000—, Vale Nat. Tng. Ctr., 2001—. Bd. dirs. Lindsey Morden Claims Svc., Inc., Lindsey Morden Claims Mgmt., Inc., exec. com., mgmt. com., compensation com., incentive com., Vale Nat. Tng. Ctrs., Lindsey & Newsom Inc.; trustee Lindsey and Newsom Benefit Trusts, 1990-91, plan adminstr. Lindsey Morden Profit Sharing Retirement Trust, 1994, Lindsey & Newsom Retirement Funds, 1990—; sr. v.p., corp. sec., CLO Lindsey Morden Group, Inc., 1996—; mem. adv. bd. Kemper Ins. Group; sr. v.p., corp. sec. Lindsey & Newsom, Vale Nat; bd. dirs. Tyler Mus. Art, chmn. pers. policy com., chair fin. com., 1999; exec. v.p. Cunningham Lindsey, U.S., Inc., 2000. Author: Analysis of Garage Liability, 1972, Dishonesty Claims Handling, 1973, Casualty Reporting Manual, 1975, Sexual Harassment in the Workplace, 1986, (audio cassette) Beating the Bears of Bad Faith, 1991, (video cassette) Bad Faith and Preventing Errors and Omissions Claims, 1987. Trustee Lindsey Morden Benefit Trusts, Lindsey Morden Retirement Trusts, 1992—; dir. assoc. U. Tex Health Ctr., 1995; budget allocation panelist United Way Tyler/Smith County, Tex., 1995; bd. dirs. Tyler Mus. of Art, 1996. Mem. ABA (internat. law sect., corp. law sect.), Can. Bar Assn., Nat. Assn. Def. Counsel, Nat. Assn. Ind. Ins. Adjusters (data processing com. 1976, legis. com. 1990), Bar Assn. D.C., Bar Assn. U.S. Fed. Cir., Defense Inst. Trial Lawyers Assn. (ins. law com.), State Bar Calif. (internat. law sect., tort sect., litigation sect., labor and employment law sect.), Nat. Employee Benefit Found., Def. Rsch. Inst., Alameda County Bar Assn., Inter-Pacific Bar Assn., Italian-Am. Bar Assn., Bar Assn. 5th Fed. Cir., Optimist Club, Kiwanis Club, Sabre Club, Lawyers Club San Francisco, Ins. Soc. U. Ga. (charter mem.), Circle K-Kiwanis. Home: 17389 Hidden Valley Ln Flint TX 75762-9611 Office: Lindsey Morden Claims Svcs Inc 211 Brookside Dr Tyler TX 75711

GUINIER, LANI, law educator; BA cum laude, Radcliffe Coll., 1971; JD, Yale U., 1974; MA (hon.), U. Pa., 1992; LLD (hon.), Northeastern U., 1994, Swarthmore Coll., 1996, Smith Coll., 1999, U. DC, 2001; D in Civil Law (hon.), Hunter Coll., 1994, Spelman Coll., 1998; LHD (hon.), U. RI, 1999. Bar: Mich. 1975, U.S. Supreme Ct. 1979, D.C. 1980, U.S. Ct. Appeals (5th, 6th, 8th and 11th cirs.). Law clk. to Hon. Damon J. Keith US Ct. Appeals 6th Cir., 1974—76; juvenile ct. referee Wayne County Juvenile Ct., Detroit, 1976—77; spl. asst. to asst. atty. gen. civil rights divsn. US Dept. Justice, 1977—81; asst. counsel NAACP Legal Def. and Ednl. Fund, Inc., NYC, 1981—88; assoc. prof. U. Pa. Law Sch., Phila., 1988—92, prof. law, 1992—98, Harvard Law Sch., Cambridge, Mass., 1998—2001, Bennett Boskey prof., 2001—. Adj. prof. NYU Sch. Law, 1985—89; of counsel NAACP Legal Def. Fund, Inc., 1988—91; trustee Phila. Cmty. Legal Svcs., 1989—90, Open Soc. Inst., 1996—; mem. adv. bd. com. on acad. freedom and tenure Assn. Am. Law Schs., 1992—93; mem. small grants adv. com. So. Regional Coun., 1992—95; founder, pres. Commonplace, Inc., 1994—99; vis. prof. Harvard Law Sch., 1996; mem. Penn Nat. Commn. on Soc., Cmty. and Culture, 1996—98; mem. vis. com. for diversity Brown U., 2000; presenter in field. Author: Lift Every Voice: Turning a Civil Rights Setback into a New Vision of Social Justice, 1987, The Tyranny of the Majority: Fundamental Fairness in Representative Democracy, 1994; co-author (with Michelle Fine and Jane Balin): Becoming Gentlemen: Women, Law Schools and Institutional Change, 1997; co-author: (with Susan Sturm) Who's Qualified: A New Democracy Forum on Creating Equal Opportunity in School and Jobs, 2001; co-author: (with Gerald Torres) The Miner's Canary: Enlisting Race, Resisting Power, Transforming Democracy, 2002; contbr. articles to profl. jours. Mem.: Am. Law Inst. Office: Harvard Law Sch 1563 Massachusetts Ave Cambridge MA 02138-2903 Office Phone: 617-496-1913. Office Fax: 617-495-4299. E-mail: lguinier@law.harvard.edu.*

GUINN, KENNY C., governor; b. Garland, Ark., Aug. 24, 1936; m. Dema Guinn; 2 children. BA, MA, Calif. State U., Fresno; EdD, Utah State U. Supt. Clark County Sch. Dist.; v.p. adminstrn. Nev. Savs. and Loan Assn. (PriMerit Bank), 1978-80, pres., chief operating officer, 1980-85, chief exec. officer, 1985-92, now chmn. bd.; pres. Southwest Gas Corp., 1987-88, chmn., chief exec. officer, 1988-93; chmn. bd. S.W. Gas Corp.; gov. State of Nev., Carson City, 1999—; interim pres. U. Nev., Las Vegas, 1994. Republican. Episcopalian. Office: Governors Office 101 N Carson St Carson City NV 89701

GUINN, STANLEY WILLIS, lawyer; b. Detroit, June 9, 1953; s. Willis Hampton and Virginia Mae (Pierson) Guinn; m. Patricia Shirley Newgord, June 13, 1981; children: Terri Lanae, Scott Stanley. BBA with high distinction, U. Mich., 1979, MBA with distinction, 1981; MS in Taxation with distinction, Walsh Coll., 1987; JD cum laude, U. Mich., 1992. CPA Mich., cert. mgmt. acct.; bar: Calif., U.S. Dist. Ct. (so. dist.) Calif., U.S. Tax Ct. Tax mgr. Coopers & Lybrand, Detroit, 1981-87; tax cons. Upjohn Co., Kalamazoo, 1987-89; litig. atty. Brobeck, Phleger & Harrison, 1992-94, Coughlan, Semmer & Lipman, San Diego, 1994-95; consumer fin. atty. Bank Am. NT & SA, San Francisco, 1995-98, GreenPoint Credit, LLC, San Diego, 1998—. With USN, 1974—77. Mem.: Atty.-CPA, Inc., San Diego County Bar, Calif. State Bar Assn., Delta Mu Delta, Beta Alpha Psi, Beta Gamma Sigma, Phi Kappa Phi. Avocations: tennis, racquetball, hiking. Home: 3125 Crystal Ct Escondido CA 92025-7763 Office: GreenPoint Credit 10089 Willow Creek Rd San Diego CA 92131-1603 Office Phone: 858-530-9491. Personal E-mail: sguinn1234@cox.net.

GUINSBURG, PHILIP FRIED, alcohol and substance abuse counselor; b. NYC, Sept. 13, 1946; s. Theodore and Elena (Fried) G.; m. Debrah Josias Guinsburg, June 15, 1968; children: Mark, Michael. BA, Columbia Coll., 1968; MA, U. N.D., 1970, PhD, 1973. Diplomate Am. Bd. Med. Psychotherapy; lic. alcohol and drug abuse counselor. Clin. dir. Nashville Drug Treatment Ctr., Dede Wallace Ctr., 1973-78; pvt. practice Nashville, 1974—. Asst. clin. prof. psychiatry Vanderbilt U., Nashville, 1987-93; cons. Crisis Intervention Ctr., 1974-99; pres. Dreammakers, Inc., Nashville, 1989-91; cons. Campus For Human Devel. Co-author: Making Love Safe, 2003. Baseball coach Brentwood (Tenn.) Civitan Little League, 1982-92. Named U.S. Profl. Yr., Nat. Assn. Alcohol and Drug Abuse Counselors. Mem. ACA, Am. Group Psychotherapy Assn., Am. Acad. Psychoterhapists (pres.), Assn. for Spiritual, Ethical and Religious Values in Counseling, Nat. Assn. Addiction Counselors (profl. of the yr.), Tenn. Assn. Alcohol and Drug Abuse Counselors (pres., Tenn. Profl. of Yr. 2002, Lifetime Achievement award 2003). Jewish. Avocations: gardening, sports, gourmet foods. Home: 8121 Maryland Ln Brentwood TN 37027-7341 Office: 2313 21st Ave S Nashville TN 37212-4908 Office Phone: 615-386-3333. E-mail: PFG1946@aol.com.

GUION, ROBERT MORGAN, psychologist, educator; b. Indpls., Sept. 14, 1924; s. Leroy Herbert and Carolyn (Morgan) Guion; m. Mary Emily Firestone, June 8, 1947; children: David Michael, Diana Lynn, Keith Douglas, Pamela Sue, Judith Elaine. BA, State U. Iowa, 1948; MS, Purdue U., 1950, PhD, 1952. Vocat. counselor Purdue U., 1948-51, research fellow, 1951-52; mem. faculty Bowling Green (Ohio) State U., 1952—, prof. psychology, 1964—, univ. prof., 1983-85, univ. prof. emeritus, 1985—, chmn. dept., 1966-71. Vis. prof. U. Calif., Berkeley, 1963—64, U. N.Mex., 1965; tech. adviser Dept. Pers. Svcs., State of Hawaii, 1970; vis. rsch. psychologist

Ednl. Testing Svc., 1971—72; cons. in field. Author: (book) Personnel Testing, 1965, Assessment, Measurement and Prediction for Personnel Decisions, 1998; editor: Jour. Applied Psychology, 1983—88. With AUS, 1943—46. Recipient Stephen E. Bemis award, Internat. Pers. Mgmt. Assn., 2000. Mem.: APA (pres. divsn. 14 1972—73, pres. divsn. 5 1982—83, James McKeen Cattell award divsn. 14 1965, 1981, Disting. Sci. Contbn. award divsn. 14 1987, Disting. Svc. award divsn. 14 1993, Lifetime Contbn. award divsn. 5 1997), Am. Psychol. Soc. (James McKeen Cattell award 2000). Methodist. Home: 632 Haskins Rd Bowling Green OH 43402-1615 Personal E-mail: rmguion@wcnet.org.

GUIRGUIS, RAOUF ALBERT, health science association administrator; b. Cairo, Aug. 25, 1953; came to U.S., 1983; s. Albert Amin Guirguis and Georgette Dahabi; m. Dana Lynn Lebo, Aug. 26, 1982 (div. June 1988); 1 child, Sandra Gene; m. Loretta Elisabeth Moschetti, July 14, 1989; 2 children. MD, U. Alexandria, Arab Republic of Egypt, 1980, MS, 1983, Georgetown U., 1987, PhD, 1988. Intern Alexandria U. Sch. Medicine, 1979-80, navy capt., 1980—83; rsch. assoc. Lombardi Cancer Ctr., Washington, 1983-84; pathology fellow Nat. Cancer Inst., NIH, Bethesda, Md., 1984—89; chmn. bd. Antibody Resources Inc., Gaithersburg, Md., 1989-93; pres., CEO Cancer Diagnostics Inc., Rockville, Md., 1989-94; chmn. bd. Fingerprint Diagnostics, Inc., Rockville, Md., 1989—94; owner, operator Biotech Pharma, LLC, 1992—; chmn. Comprehensive Cancer Care Ctrs. LLP, 1994—, Cancer Diagnostics Holding Co., Fairfax, Va., 1995—; founder, pres. Point of Care Techs., Inc., 1999—; founder, pres., CEO MonoGen, Inc., 1996—99; owner, operator Diplomatic Lang. Svcs. LLC, 2001—; founder, pres., CEO Lamina Equities Corp., 2001—; owner, operator Fingerprint Biotech, LLC, 2002—. Cons. Nephrology Cancer Ctr., Mansura, Arab Rep. of Egypt, 1988-94; adj. prof. dept. physiology and biophysics Georgetown U. Med. Sch., Washington, 1988-93. Contbr. articles to profl. jours. Assoc. Smithsonian, Washington, 1990; mem. Kennedy Ctr., Washington, 1990, Georgetown Club, Washington, 1989; mem. Balt. Coun. on Fgn. Affairs; bd. dirs. U.S. Israel Biotech. Coun. Georgetown U. scholar, 1985-88, Saudi Minister of Health scholar, 1986-88; Nat. Coun. of Churches Rsch. grantee, 1986, Hoffmann-LaRoche Innovation Rsch. grantee, 1986. Mem. AMA (chief exec. divsn.), AAAS, IEEE, Am. Math. Assn., Am. Assn. for Clin. Chemistry, Am. Soc. for Microbiology, Am. Chem. Soc., Am. Mgmt. Assn., NY Acad. Sci., Soc. for Computer Simulation, Sigma Xi (presdl. roundtable). Republican. Coptic Orthodox. Achievements include patents for CDI Shuttle System, a cancer screening and laboratory testing device, a method for CytoShuttle a monolayer cytology device, a method for LC-Shuttle a chromatography device for multiple marker panels, for Assay-Shuttle a bead based immuno-assay, a Cell Chamber for chemotaxis assay, a Modular Multiple Fluid Sample Preparation Assembly, a Blood Withdrawing Apparatus and a Antigen Testing Method, a Enviromental Sample Collection and Testing Device, a Blood Testing and Fingerprint Identification Method; patents pending for Preparation and Isolation of Intact Pseudopodia Fragments, a Urine Testing Apparatus with Urinary Sediment Device, a Intact and Isolated Pseudopodia Fragments/A Model SYstem for Cell Migration, a Possible Role for Membrane Fusion in Tumor Cell Invasion and Metastasis, and a New Method and Device for the Early Detection of Cancer Using Body Fluids (mainly urine). Office: Lamina Equities Corp Ste 800 1901 N Fort Myer Dr Arlington VA 22209

GUISE, DAVID EARL, architect, educator; b. N.Y.C., Dec. 29, 1931; s. Jack I. and Frances (Haberman) G.; m. Gretchen Grunenfelder, Nov. 21, 1962; children: Gabrielle Ann, John George, Jacqueline Alexis, Ursula Claire. BArch with honors, U. Pa., 1957. Job capt. Kahn & Jacobs, Architects, N.Y.C., 1957-60; designer draftsman E.J. Robin, Architect, N.Y.C., 1961; architect David Guise, Architect, N.Y.C., 1962—; asst. prof. Sch. Architecture, CCNY, 1966-70, assoc. prof., 1970-76, prof., 1976-91; prof. emeritus CCNY, 1991—. Adj. prof. Columbia U., 1983-85, CCNY, 1993—; vis. prof. U. Pa., 1990. Author: Design and Technology in Architecture, 1985, rev. edit., 1991; contbr. articles to profl. jours., Ency. Britannica yearbook; architect numerous comml. and residential bldgs. Mem. nat. panel Am. Arbitration Assn., 1967—; sec. Irvington Planning Bd., N.Y., 1974-88. Mem. Bldg. Rsch. Inst. Home: PO Box 295 Ardsley On Hudson NY 10503 Office: PO Box 295 Ardsley On Hudson NY 10503

GUITRY, LORAINE DUNN, community health nurse; b. Bryan, Tex., Apr. 12, 1930; BS Elem. Edn., Paul Quinn Coll., 1954. Registered nurse U. Tex. Med. Br., Galveston, 1958—67, U.S. Pub. Health Svc., Galveston, 1967—. Home: 701 Chadley Ct Bryan TX 77803

GUKENBERGER, VICKIE LYNN, dean, nursing administrator; b. Stevens Point, Wis., Feb. 18, 1955; d. Robert Dale and Nancy Jean (Eberhardt) O'Keefe; m. Jeffrey A. Gukenberger, Apr. 9, 1991. BSN, U. Wis., Eau Claire, 1977; PhD, U. Wis., Madison, 2000; MSN, Marquette U., 1981. Staff nurse Mt. Sinaie Med. Ctr., Milw., 1977—81; tchr. St. Joseph's Hosp., Marshfield, Wis., 1981—83; DON Adams County Meml., Friendship, Wis., 1983—85, Riverside Med. Ctr., Waupaca, Wis., 1985—88; dean health programs Mid-State Tech. Coll., Wisconsin Rapids, Wis., 1989—2001; dean acad. affairs Allen Coll., Waterloo, Iowa, 2001—02; dean life scis. and human svcs. Harper Coll., Palatine, Ill., 2002—. Bd. dirs. Wis. Orgn. Nurse Execs., 1983—88. Mem.: Wis. Nurses Assn. (bd. dirs., pres. 1986—2001, Nurse Educator award 1998). Avocations: reading, scrapbooks. Home: 1552 W Ethans Glen Palatine IL 60067 Office Phone: 847-925-6682, 847-925-6047. Business E-Mail: vgukenbe@harpercollege.edu.

GULAN, BONNIE MARION, writer, researcher; b. Kenosha, Wis., Feb. 27, 1922; d. Matthew and Elizabeth Ummy Thomas; m. Edward J. Gulan, Nov. 26, 1949; children: John, Michael, Kathryn. Beauty cons. Globe Dept., Kenosha, Wis., 1950—54; inventor & pitch artist Beauty Blush Cosmetic Line, Waukegan, Ill., 1954—56; creator & founder Felture's Inc., Brookfield, Ill., 1956—59; gen. mgr. & designer Eichling's Flowers Inc., Skokie, Ill., 1960—64; founder, dir. An-Oix-Is In-home Youth Ministry, Winnetka, Ill., 1965—75; founder & ceo The Christmas Tree Story Ho. Mus., Multiple Locations, Ill., 1970—90; author & rschr. Milwaukee, Wis., 1990—98; author Saukville, Wis., 1998—. Founder, pres. World-Wide Women's Inventor's Orgn., Libertyville, Ill., 1961—65; creator, lectr. Miracle Thinking Lecture Series, Mundelein, Ill., 1965—69; spkr. in field. Author: (book) Family Miracles, 1981, Stories From The Christmas Tree Story House, 1981, The Great Bible Dig, 2001, The House of the Seven Cats - An Adventure, 2001, Lost Adventures-House of the 7 Cats, 2001, 7 Cats Promised Land Adventure, 2001, Over the Fence Non-Sense Tales, 2001, Lamp Of Hope, 2001, Back Yard Critter Tales, 2001, A Collection Of Mrs. Claus' Christmas Stories, 2001, The Master Toy Maker, 2001, Adventures Down Nursery Rhyme Lane, 2001, A Collection Of Nodding Off Stories, 2001, Christmas In Our Town, 2002, The Great Journey in Pursuit of Jesus' Way, Truth & Life, 2002; composer: (albums) Sounds of The Christmas Tree Story House, 1975. Founder, pres. & lectr. T.H.E Anti-Drug Youth Program, Winnetka, 1971—75. Home: 1053 South Main Street Saukville WI 53080 Office Phone: 262-268-1224. Personal E-mail: bmgulan@aol.com.

GULATI, SUNIL, sports administrator; b. Allahabad, India, 1959; m. Marcela Gulati; 1 child, Emilio. BA magna cum laude, Bucknell U.; MA, MPhil in Econs., Columbia U. Asst. prof. econs. Columbia U., 1986-90; with World Bank, 1991; former dep. commr. Major League Soccer, 1995—99; mng. dir. Kraft Soccer Properties, 1999—. Mng. dir. nat. teams, chmn. internat. games com., nat. teams com., US Cup 1992 and 1993 US Soccer Fedn., 1987-94; exec. v.p., chief internat. officer, mem. mgmt. com. World Cup U.S.A., 1994; bd. dirs. 1999 Women's World Cup, US Soccer, US Soccer Found., Nat. Soccer Hall of Fame (bd. trustee), bd. dir. Women222s World Cup 226 mem.; bd. dir., exec. v.p. US Soccer; bd. govs (alternate) Major League Soccer, Soccer United Mktg.; mem. Fedn. Internat. Football Assn. World Cup Championship Com. and Youth Competitions Com.; mng. dir. US Soccer Fedn. Project 2010. Mem. Phi Beta Kappa. Office: 725 5th Ave Ste 1700 New York NY 10022-2519

GULBRANDSEN, NATALIE WEBBER, religious association administrator; b. Beverly, Mass., July 7, 1919; d. Arthur Hammond and Kathryn Mary (Doherty) Webber; m. Melvin H. Gulbrandsen, June 19, 1943 (dec. Feb. 23, 1991); children: Karen Ann Bean, Linda Jean Goldsmith, Eric Christian, Ellen Dale Williams, Kristin Jane Morgan. BA, Bates Coll., 1942, LLD (hon.), 1996; LHD (hon.), Meadville/Lombard Theol. Sch., Chgo., 1991. Social worker Bur. Child Welfare, Bangor, Maine. Leader Girl Scouts USA, Auburn, Maine, 1940—44, exec. dir. Belmont, Mass., 1943—45, leader Wellesley, Mass., 1952—65, leadership trainer, 1946—63, bd. dirs., 1950—63, pres., 1960—63; mem. Wellesle Town Meeting, 1967—91; trustee Unitarian Universalist Women's Fedn., 1971—81, pres., 1977—81, mem. commn. on appraisal, 1981—85; moderator Unitarian Universalist Assn., U.S. and Can., Boston, 1985—93; bd. dirs. Unitarian Universalist Ch. of the Larger Fellowship, 1992—98, chairperson bd. dirs., 1996—98, ch. search com., 1998—99, chair ministerial rels. com., 1999—2001; bd. dirs. Unitarian Universalist Women's Heritage Soc., 1994—2002, ch. bd., 2001—02; chair denominational affairs Unitarian Universalist Soc. Wellesley Hills, 2002—; bd. dirs. Wellesley program Am. Field Svc., 1964—70; mem. permanent sch. accomodations com. Wellesley, 1970—76; mem. Wellesley Youth Commn., 1968—70; trustee Wellesley Human Rels. Svc., 1964—76, pres., 1973—76; bd. dirs. Newton Wellesley Weston Needham Area Mental Health Assn., 1975—78; co-chairperson METCO Program of Wellesley, 1965—69. Co-recipient Wellesley Ctr. Cmty. award, 1981; recipient Unitarian Universalist Disting. Svc. award, 2002. Mem. AAUW, Boston Bates Alumnae Assn. (pres. 1966-69), Internat. Assn. Religious Freedom (mem. coun. 1981-90, v.p. 1990-93, pres. 1993-96, co-pres. U.S. chpt. 1997-2003, Clara Barton birthplace com. 1997-01). Unitarian Universalist. Home: 2251 Commonwealth Ave Auburndale MA 02466-1817

GULBRANDSEN, NORMAN RALPH, retired music educator; b. Salt Lake City, Oct. 3, 1918; s. Ole and Halvorine Gulbrandsen; m. Joy Katharine Scott, Mar. 21, 1969; children: Glenn, Kevin McClure; m. Lois Stirling, Sept. 7, 1943 (div. 1968); children: Stephen, Douglas, James, Robert, Richard, Gina. BS, U. Utah, 1943; MM, Northwestern U., 1945; postgrad., U. So. Calif., 1950. Dir. of choral act Montana State U., 1945—51; asst. dir. choral act Northwestern U., 1944; dir. glee clubs U. So. Calif., 1949; instr. voice and choral Brigham Young U., 1952—61; dir. choral Lake Forest Coll., 1962—63; prof. voice and opera Northwestern U., 1963—89; adj. prof. voice DePaul U., 1989—2003; ret., 2003. Dir. choir Glenview C.C.; org., found., condr. Cmty. Male Chorus, Missoula, Mont., 1945—51; condr. Glenview C.C. Fellow: Lions Club; mem.: Pi Kappa Lambda, Phi Mu Alpha, Phi Delta Kappa. Republican. Avocations: tennis, golf. Home: 1911 Oak Knoll Dr Lake Forest IL 60045 Office: DePaul U 804 W Belden Chicago IL 60614

GULBRANDSEN, PATRICIA HUGHES, physician; b. May 9, 1940; d. Patrick Boland and Anne Hughes; m. Jon Alf Gulbrandsen, Mar. 6, 1972 (dec. Oct. 1984). BA, Cornell U., 1962; MD, U. Pa., 1967; MPH, Johns Hopkins U., 1980. Cert. Am. Bd. Disability Analysts; diplomate Am. Bd. Phys. Medicine and Rehab., Am. Bd. Occupl. Medicine. Rotating intern Chgo. Wesley Meml. Hosp., 1967-68; resident in neurology Pa. Hosp., Phila., 1968-69, Georgetown U. Hosp., Washington, 1972-74; fellow in gynecologic endocrinology Chelsea Hosp. for Women, London, 1969-71; resident in phys. medicine and rehab. Good Samaritan Hosp., Phoenix, 1974-76; commd. maj. U.S. Army, 1979, advanced through grades to lt. col., 1982; with Walter Reed Army Med. Ctr., Washington, 1979-81; occup. medicine officer U.S. Army/Army Environ. Hygiene Agy., Aberdeen Proving Ground, Md., 1981-83; resigned U.S. Army, 1983; med. dir. USN/Naval Surface Warfare Ctr., White Oak, Md., 1984-89, NASA Hdqs., Washington, 1990-93; acting chief med. officer Hdqs. FBI, Washington, 1995; med. officer Orgn. Am. States, Washington, 1999—2001; occupl. health phys., cons. Def. Intelligence Agy., Bolling AFB, Washington, 2001—03; NIOSH occupl. medicine physician Dept. Energy Worker Advocacy Program, 2004. Occupl. medicine Profl. Occupl. Health Svcs., 1997-98; staff physiatrist, head consultation svc. New Eng. Med. Ctr. Hosps., Boston, 1977-78; instr. neurology and phys. medicine and rehab. Tufts U. Sch. Medicine, Boston, 1977-78; cons. in field Mem. Am. Coll. Preventive Medicine, Am. Coll. Occupl and Environ. Medicine, Montgomery County Med. Soc., Med. and Chirurg. Faculty Md. Office Phone: 301-585-6519. Office Fax: 301-585-6519. Personal E-mail: mddocg@yahoo.com.

GULCHER, ROBERT HARRY, air transportation executive; b. Columbus, Ohio, Aug. 26, 1925; s. Alban H. and Beatrice (Plohr) G.; m. Barbara Witherspoon, June, 1949 (div.); 1 child, Robert; m. Anne Cummings, Dec. 14, 1959 (dec.); children: Jeffrey, Donald; m. Suzanne K. Kane, Apr. 12,1969; children: Andrew, Kristin. BS, U.S. Marine Acad., 1945; B.E.E., Ohio State U., 1950. Third asst. engr. Am. Petroleum Transp. Co., N.Y.C., 1945-46; engr. Capital Elevator & Mfg. Co., Columbus, Ohio, 1949-51, Columbus div. N. Am. Aviation, 1951-53, various mgmt. engring. positions, 1953-66; chief engr. Columbus div. Rockwell Internat., 1966-79, v.p. rsch. and engring. N.Am. aircraft ops. El Segundo, Calif., 1979-85, v.p. advanced programs N.Am. aircraft ops., 1985-87, v.p., program mgr. nat. aerospace plane, 1987-90, v.p. hypersonic programs Downey, Calif., 1990-91; retired, 1991; aerospace cons., 1992—. Trustee Little Company of Mary Hosp. Found., 1992—2005, chmn. bd. trustees, 1996-97; trustee coun. LCMH Hosp., 1997—2002; pres. St. Paul Lutheran Ch., 2004-. Fellow AIAA, IEEE (sr. mem.); mem. Rotary Internat. Republican. Lutheran. E-mail: rgulcher@aol.com.

GULDA, EDWARD JAMES, diversified financial services company executive; b. Detroit, Oct. 28, 1945; s. Alfred and Lucy Irene (Ball) G.; m. Nancy Mary Greenlee, Nov. 28, 1964; children: Kimberly Sue Marsh, Nicholas Edward. BS in Aerospace Engring., U. Mich., 1968, MBA, 1979. Systems engr. LTV Aerospace Corp., Sterling Heights, Mich., 1966-72; mgr. systems engring. Ford Motor Co., Dearborn, Mich., 1972-78; mgr., prodn. plan. Rockwell Internat. Corp., Dearborn, Mich., 1978-79, dir. prod. plan. Troy, Mich., 1979-80, dir. mkt. electronics, 1980-81, gen. mgr. auto electronics, 1981-84, v.p. rsch. and engring., 1984-85; pres. ITT Teves Am., Troy, 1985-87; group v.p. engring. ITT Auto, Inc., Troy, 1987-88; pres., chief exec. officer Dayton Walther (Varity) Corp., Dayton, Ohio, 1988-89; pres. Varity Brake Group Kelsey-Hayes Brake Group N.Am., Romulus, Mich., 1989-94; pres. Kelsey-Hayes Co., Romulus, Mich., 1994-95, chief exec. Livonia, Mich., 1995; chmn. and CEO Peregrine Inc., Southfield, Mich., 1996-98; pres. Kinnick Group LLC, 1998—. Mem.: Mensa. Avocations: hunting, golf. Home: 4395 Forest Ave Waterford MI 48328-1110 Office Phone: 248-618-9809. Business E-Mail: ejgulda@gulda-associates.com.

GULDEN, SIMON, lawyer, management consultant, consultant; b. Montreal, Que., Can., Jan. 7, 1938; s. David and Zelda (Long) G.; m. Ellen Lee Barbour, June 12, 1977. BA, McGill U., Montreal, 1959; cert., U. Rennes, 1961; LL.L., U. Montreal, 1962; cert., Wharton Sch., 1979; alt. dispute resolution cert., York U., Toronto, 1999. Bar: Que. Ptnr. Genser, Philips, Friedman & Gulden, Montreal, 1963-68; sec., legal counsel Pl. Bonaventure, Inc., 1969-72; legal counsel real estate Steinberg Inc., Montreal, 1972-74; solicitor, prime atty. Bell Can., Montreal, 1975-76; v.p., gen. counsel, sec., dir. Nabisco Ltd, Toronto, 1975-98; pres., dir. Interlude Capital Corp., Markham (Unionville), 1997—; dir. legal affairs Stream Intelligent Networks Corp., 2000-2001; v.p. corp. and legal affairs Canderel Stoneridge Equity Group, 2001—02. Mem.: ABA, Bar of Que., Inst. Chartered Secs. and Adminstrs. (cert.), Osgoode Law Soc., Lord Reading Law Soc. Que., Can. Bar Assn. Home and Office: 23 Danbury Ct Markham ON Canada L3R 7S1 Office Phone: 905-477-9130. E-mail: simongulden@rogers.com.

GULEK, JAMES CENGIZ, school system administrator, educator; b. Edirne, Turkey, Feb. 1, 1968; s. Halit and Zehra Gulek. BA, Bogazici U., Turkey, 1992, MA, 1994; PhD, Boston Coll., 1999. Preliminary Adminstrv.Svcs. Credential Calif., 2003, Pupil Pers. Svcs. Credential Calif., 2003, Sch. Counselor Ministry of Turkish Edn., 1992. Adj. prof. St. Mary's Collge of Calif., Moraga, 2003—; sch. counselor Koc Sch., Istanbul, Turkey, 1992—94; rsch. asst. Boston Coll., Chestnut Hill, Mass., 1994—99; rsch. scientist Harvard Med. Sch., Boston, 1998—99; supr. of assessment, rsch. & accountability Sun Prairie Area Sch. Dist., 1999—2001; dir. of assessment, evaluation Pleasanton (Calif.) Unified Sch. Dist., 2001—. Cons. Edn. Devel. Ctr., Inc., Newton, Mass., 1996—97. Contbr. articles to profl. jours. Choreographer Yore Folk Dance Ensemble, Stanford,Berkeley, Calif., artistic dance dir., 2003—. Mem.: ASCD, Internat. Sch. Psychology Assn., Assn. of Calif. Sch. Administrs., Am. Ednl. Rsch. Assn. (assoc.), Anatolian Folklore Found. Achievements include Choreographed a Turkish Folk Dance Piece That was Invited for Performance at the 26th Annual San Francisco Ethnic Dance Festival. Avocation: traditional folk dance. Home: 3306 Santa Rita Rd Pleasanton CA 94566 Office: Pleasanton Unified Sch Dist 4665 Bernal Ave Pleasanton CA 94566 Office Fax: 925-462-8216. Personal E-mail: gulek_c@yahoo.com. E-mail: cgulek@pleasanton.k12.ca.us.

GULGOWSKI, PAUL WILLIAM, German language, social science, and history educator; b. Oberhausen, Germany, July 4, 1940; s. Paul and Katharina (van Look) G.; m. Heide Anna Maria Hegenscheidt, July 6, 1989; children: Audrey-Annette, Paul William. BSc, U. Tex., El Paso, 1970; MA, Marquette U., 1992; PhD, U. Bremen, Germany, 1981. Cert. tchr., social sci., German and history. Commd. 2d lt. U.S. Army, 1970, advanced through grades to maj., 1981; gen. staff officer, comdr. combat and support forces U.S. Army, worldwide, 1970-80; polit. advisor, forces comdr. U.S. Army, Germany, 1980-82; prof. German U.S. Mil. Acad., West Point, N.Y., 1982-85; personal rep. of NATO Land Forces comdr., Heidelberg, Germany, 1985-87; ret. U.S. Army, 1987; lectr. German and fgn. lang. study methodology U. Wis., Whitewater, 1993—. Author: U.S. Military Government in Germany, 1983, Flucht aus Ostpreussen, 1986, Die unglaubliche Story des Peter V., 2001; author articles. Chief historian USCG Aux., Washington, 1992-94; comdr. northwestern USCG 9th, 1994—; v.p. Wis. Profl. Edn. & Info. Coun., 1997-99, pres., 2000—. Decorated D.S.M. with four oak leaf clusters; comdr.'s cross German Order of Merit. Mem. Phi Kappa Phi. Roman Catholic. Avocations: classical music, literature, skiing, boating, travel. Home: PO Box 180347 Delafield WI 53018-0347 Personal E-mail: phgulgow@milwpc.com.

GULICK, ROBERT T, technology trainer, educator; s. Thomas and Rosemary Gulick; m. Carmella Veneziano, Aug. 5, 1968; children: Rebecca, Sarah. B of Edn., U. Akron, 1989; MEd, Baldwin-Wallace Coll., 1992; EdD, Nova Southeastern U., 2002. Cert. tchr. 1-8 Ohio, 1989, computer sci. tchr. Ohio, 1995, sch. tech. leadership U. Minn., 2004. Tchr. elem. sch. Parma City Sch. Dist., Ohio, 1997—2000, tech. trainer, 2000—. Computer cons. Convergent, Parma, 2001—04. Office: Parma City Sch Dist 6726 Ridge Rd Parma OH 44129 Office Phone: 440-885-7099. Personal E-mail: robert@thegulicks.com.

GULICK, ROY MOYER, physician; b. Quantico, Va., Mar. 14, 1960; s. Roy Moyer Gulick and Anne McAfee Wheeler. BA, Johns Hopkins U., 1982; MD, Columbia U., 1986; MPH, Harvard U., 1993. Diplomate Am. Bd. Internal Medicine, Am. Bd. Infectious Disease. Instr. medicine Harvard Med. Sch., Boston, 1991-93, NYU Sch. of Medicine, 1993-97, asst. prof. of clin. medicine, 1997—. Mem. IRB Comm. Rsch. Initiative in AIDS, N.Y.C., 1995—; co-investigator AIDS Clin. Trial Group, N.Y.C., 1989—. Mem. Am. Coll. Physicians, Infectious Disease Soc. of Am., N.Y. State Infectious Disease Soc., Alpha Omega Alpha. Office: NYU Med Ctr Dept Medicine 550 1st Ave Dept Medicine New York NY 10016-6402

GULICK, WALTER LAWRENCE, psychologist, educator, retired academic administrator; b. Summit, NJ, July 4, 1927; s. Walter Lawrence and Carol (Dewey) G.; m. Winifred Bourn Frazee, Oct. 18, 1952; children: Hans, Tod, Kristina. AB, Hamilton Coll., Clinton, N.Y., 1952; MA, U. Del., 1955; PhD, Princeton U., 1957; MA (hon.), Dartmouth Coll., 1968; LHD (hon.), St. Lawrence U., 1989. Mem. faculty U. Del., 1957-65, prof. psychology, 1963-65, chmn. dept., 1964-65; prof. psychology Dartmouth Coll., Hanover, NH, 1965-74, chmn. dept., 1970-73, 74-75, Disting. Class of 1925 prof., 1973-75; dean of coll. Hamilton Coll., 1975-79, prof. psychology, 1975-81, William R. Kenan prof., 1979-81; pres. St. Lawrence U., 1981-87, Gulick Assocs., 1987—. Vis. prof. U. Vt., 1977; resident scholar U. Del., 1988-02; cons. Presbyn. Hosp., Phila., 1961-63; editl. cons. Oxford U. Press, 1963—, McGraw-Hill Pub. Co., 1966-67, Harper & Row, 1971-73, Cambridge U. Press, 1979—. Author: Hearing: Physiology and Psychophysics, 1971, Human Stereopsis: Psychophysical Analysis, 1976, Hearing: Physiological Acoustics, Neural Coding and Psychoacoustics, 1989; contbr.: Ency. of Human Behavior, 1994; contbr. articles to profl. jours. Mem. Hanover Sch. Bd., 1972-75, Dresden Bd. Sch. Dirs., 1972-75; mem. grad. coun. Princeton U., 1972-75; mem. adv. coun. Nat. Inst. for Humanities, 1975-; mem. tchg. evaluation project HEW. Served with AUS, 1946-48. Recipient nat. svc. award 1955, 81; Dale prize music Hamilton Coll., 1952, alumnni achievement medal Hamilton Coll., 1995; Theta Delta Chi fellow U. Del., 1953-55, Psychology scholar Princeton U., 1955-57. Mem. N.Y. Acad. Scis., Ea. Psychol. Assn., Psychonomic Soc., Phi Beta Kappa, Omicron Delta Kappa, Sigma Xi (pres. Dartmouth chpt. 1967-68, Gold Medal Lifetime Achievement award 1995), Psi Chi (pres. U. Del. chpt. 1954-55). Achievements include research in vision and hearing. Home: 347 Greenbriar Ln West Grove PA 19390 Office: Gulick Assocs Inc PO Box 154 Kelton PA 19346 Personal E-mail: wglg@msn.com.

GULKIN, HARRY, arts administrator, film producer; b. Montreal, Que., Can., Nov. 14, 1927; s. Peter Oliver and Raya (Shinderman) G. Portrait photographer, 1942-44; mcht. seaman, trade union organizer, 1944-49; labour journalist, critic, trade union organizer, 1950-56; market researcher, cons., 1956-71; ind. film producer, 1971—; exec. and artistic dir. Saidye Bronfman Ctr., 1983-87; dir. projects Soc. Developpement Entreprises Culturelles, 1987—; producer BAYO, 1985. Challenger Nat. Film Bd., Can., 1979; adv. coun. film dept. Concordia U. Producer: Penny and Ann (2d prize Film Festival Internat. Congress Rehab. Centres 1976, award Amtec Media Festival 1977), 1974 (Red Ribbon Am. Film Festival 1977), Lies My Father Told Me (Hollywood Fgn. Critics award as best fgn. film 1975, Grand prize V.I. Internat. Festival 1975, Christopher awards 1975, Assn. Can. TV and Radio Artists award 1976, Canadian Film award 1976, Can. Motion Picture Distbrs. Assn. award 1976, nominated Best Original Screenplay Oscar, 1976), Jacob Two Meets The Hooded Fang, 1976 (Gold medallion spl. jury award Miami Internat. Film Festival 1978, Spl. Jury award 8th Internat. Children's Film Festival, Los Angeles 1979), Two Solitudes, 1977; editor: The Marketer Jour., 1966. Mem. Motion Picture Inst. Can. (pres. 1977), Can. Film Inst. (past pres., chmn.), Assn. Que. Film Producers, Cinematheque Québecoise (v.p. 1995-2000), Am. Mktg. Assn. (past chpt. pres.), Acad. Can. Cinema, Quebec Soc. for Promotion of English Lang. Lit. (mem. adv. coun.). Home: 111 St Joseph Blvd W Montreal PQ Canada H2T 2P7 Office: Bur 800 215 Rue St JAcques Montreal PQ Canada H2Y 1M6

GULKO, RALPH, lawyer; b. Paterson, N.J., June 13, 1953; s. Benjamin and Anita (Yankelevsky) G.; m. Joan Lyttle, Feb. 6, 1983; children: Aaron, Jacob. BA, Rutgers U., 1975, JD, 1978. Bar: N.J. l978, U.S. Dist. Ct. N.J. 1978, Pa. l980, U.S. Ct. Appeals (3d cir.) 1980, U.S. Supreme Ct. 1982, N.Y. 1996. Law clk. to judge N.J. Superior Ct., Paterson, 1978-79; assoc. Celentano & Stadtmauer, Clifton, N.J., 1979-80; ptnr. Eichenbaum, Kantrowitz, Leff & Gulko, Jersey City, 1980—. Mem. ABA, N.J. Bar Assn., Comml. Law League Am.

GULLACE, MARLENE FRANCES, systems engineer, systems analyst, consultant; b. Ft. Belvoir, Va., Jan. 12, 1952; d. Amerigo Francis and Martha Arlene Guy; m. Gerald Lynn Tolley, June 26, 1970 (div. Nov. 1974); 1 child, Gerald Lynn Tolley Jr.; m. Salvatore Gullace, Nov. 19, 1976 (div. Apr. 1991). AA in Pre-Law, Cochise Coll., 1979; BA in Polit. Sci., U. Ariz., 1982; AA in Computer Sci., Bus., Chaparral Coll., 1985. Realtor, entrepreneur, inventor, Sierra Vista, Ariz., 1977-84; ADP instr. Chaparral Coll., Tucson, 1985; model Barbizon, Tucson, 1986-87; clk. HUD/FHA, Tucson, 1987-88; computer programmer DOD Inspector Gen., Arlington, 1988-89; programmer analyst US Army Corps of Engrs., USAF, Washington, 1989-91, Calibre Sys. Inc., Falls Church, Va., 1991; cons., sys. analyst/programmer EDP, Vienna, Va., 1991-93; info. engr. Ogden/Anteon Corp., Vienna, 1993-96, Orkand Corp., 1996, SRA Internat., Inc., 1997-00, SRA Internat., 2000—01, SAIC,

2002—04, Lockheed Martin, 2004—. Patented toy, registered trademark. Realtor assoc. Cochise County Bd. Realtors, 1977-84. Mem. IEEE, Fed. Women's Program at SBA (sec. 1976). Methodist. Avocations: art, design, crafts, sewing. Home: 7829 Piccadilly Dr Warrenton VA 20186-8623

GULLAHORN, JEANNE ERARD, retired psychologist, retired academic administrator; b. Springfield, Mass., Mar. 11, 1932; d. Hector Langevin and Malvina Elmire Erard; m. John T. Gullahorn, May 7, 1955 (dec. Apr. 1987); children: Gregory, Lorraine, Leslie. BA, Radcliffe Coll., 1954; MA, U. Kans., 1958; PhD, Mich. State U., 1964. Asst. prof. to assoc. prof. psychology Mich. State U., East Lansing, 1965—74, prof., 1974-86, assoc. dean grad. sch., 1982-86; health scientist adminstr. NIMH, Rockville, Md., 1979-81; v.p. rsch., dean grad. studies SUNY, Albany, 1986-98, interim exec. v.p., 1990-91; ret., 1998. Vis. scientist Sys. Devel. Corp., Santa Monica, Calif., 1965—66; vis. prof. U. Coll., Cardiff, Wales, 1972—73; bd. govs. Gt. Lakes Rsch. Consortium, Syracuse, 1988. Co-author: Women: A Psychological Perspective, 1977; editor: Psychology and Women: In Transition, 1979. Bd. dirs. Symphony Orch., 1987—92; mem. commrs. doctoral coun. N.Y. State Edn. Dept., Albany, 1990—98. Mem.: African Am. Inst. (mem. exec. com. grad. deans), Phi Beta Kappa. Avocations: tennis, travel, chamber music. Home: 4445 Novato Ct Naples FL 34109-1355 Personal E-mail: JeanneGullahorn@aol.com.

GULLAND, EUGENE D., lawyer; b. Endicott, N.Y., Aug. 27, 1947; s. George Raymond and Virginia (Fisher) G.; m. Kristin Spearing, Aug. 29, 1970; children: Michael Spearing, Molly Spearing, Samuel Spearing. AB, Princeton U., 1969; JD, Yale U., 1972. Bar: D.C., Va., U.S. Supreme Ct., U.S. Ct. Appeals (1st, 2d, 3d, 4th, 6th, 7th, 9th, D.C., Fed. cirs.), U.S. Dist. Ct. D.C., (ea. dist.) Va., Md., Ariz., Ind. Assoc. Covington & Burling, Washington, 1973-80, ptnr., 1980—. Practitioner before London Ct. Internat. Arbitration, Internat. C. of C., ICSID, Am. Arbitration Assn., also other arbitral tribunals; mem. faculty Nat. Inst. for Trial Advocacy, Am. Judicature Soc. Trustee Loudoun Day Sch., Leesburg, Va., 1986-98; vestryman, treas. Our Redeemer Ch., 1987-97; mem. alumni schs. com. Princeton U. Capt. U.S. Army, 1972-73, Woodrow Wilson scholar Princeton U., Princeton U. scholar. Mem. Nat. Assn. Coll. and Univ. Attys., Phi Beta Kappa. Am. Judicature Soc., Henlopen Acres Beach Club Home: Little River Farm Aldie VA 20105 Office: Covington & Burling 1201 Pennsylvania Ave NW Washington DC 20004-2401 Office Phone: 202-662-5504. Business E-Mail: egulland@cov.com.

GULLEDGE, SANDRA SMITH, publishing executive, film producer; b. Great Lakes, Ill., July 6, 1949; d. Dennis Murrey and Olga (Grosheff) Smith. BS, Northwestern U., 1971; MA, Annenberg Sch Comm., U. So. Calif., 1986. Columnist Camarillo Daily News, Calif., 1971-76; editor Fillmore Herald, Calif., 1976-78; pub. info. officer Oxnard Union High Sch. Dist., Calif., 1980-82, Ventura County Cmty. Coll. Dist., 1982-83; pub. rels. dir. Murphy Orgn., Oxnard, Calif., 1983-84; editor Forum and Solutions GTE, Irving, Tex., 1988-89; mktg. spec. USAA Alliance Svc., San Antonio, 1995-99; pres. Crimson Horse Entertainment & Publ.Co., LLC, 2000—. E-mail: guidepublishing@usa.net.

GULLEN, CHRISTOPHER ROY, lawyer; b. Detroit, Feb. 17, 1950; s. George Edgar and Mary Ruth Gullen; m. Sheila Rae Collins, Aug. 25, 1973; children: Brian Christopher, Katelyn Elizabeth. BA, U. Mich., 1972; JD, Ohio Northern U., 1975. Bar: Mich. 1975, U.S. Dist. Ct. (ea. dist.) Mich. 1975, U.S. Ct. Appeals (6th cir.) 1978. Law clk. Mich. Ct. Appeals, Lansing, 1975-77; ptnr. Gullen & Fitzsimmons, Rochester, Mich., 1977-82, Sarvis, Gullen & Herrmann, Birmingham, Mich., 1982-86; pub. liability atty. Kmart Corp., Troy, Mich., 1986-90, pub. liability counsel, 1990-99, dir. risk mgmt. and pub. liability, 2000—02. Mediator Oakland County Cir. Ct., 1986—. Author: Rules and Regulations of the Science Court, 1980. Mem. ABA, Mich. Bar Assn. Office: James E Logan & Assocs Ltd 7011 Orchard Lake Rd West Bloomfield MI 48322 Office Phone: 248-865-3900. E-mail: cgullen@jeloganltd.com.

GULLER, IRVING BERNARD, forensic, clinical psychologist, consultant, writer; b. NYC, July 27, 1932; s. Hyman and Mildred (Rothman) G.; m. Adele Horowitz, Apr. 5, 1955; children: Robert, Matthew. BA, CCNY, 1954, MS, 1956; PhD, NYU, 1962. Diplomate clin. psychology Am. Bd. Profl. Psychology (fellow), Am. Coll. Forensic Examiners. Dir. psychol. tng. and rsch. Maine Dept. Mental Health and Corrections, Augusta, 1962-63; asst. prof. psychology, coll. psychologist Franklin and Marshall Coll., 1963-67; assoc. prof. psychology John Jay Coll., NYC, 1967-71, prof. psychology, 1971-92, prof. emeritus, 1992—; doctoral faculty criminal justice CUNY, 1981—92, prof. emeritus, 1992—. Founder, dir. Inst. Forensic Psychology, 1971—. attending psychologist, cons. St. Joseph's Hosp., Paterson, NJ, 1970-99; cons. to police depts. and criminal justice agys. in forensic psychology; family therapist in pvt. practice, Oakland, NJ, 1962—; founding assoc. N. Jersey Mental Health Assocs., Oakland. Author: Clinical Psychology Training Guide and Handbook, 1963, The Clinical Psychologist in Institutional Settings, 1976, A Brief Introduction to Protective Techniques, 1982, Stop Panic, 2001; contbr. articles to profl. jours. Served with AUS, 1954-56. Recipient Founder's Day award NYU, 1963. Mem. Am. Psychol. Assn., Ea. Psychol. Assn., NJ Psychol. Assn., Am. Coll. Forensic Examiners. Office: 5 Fir Ct Oakland NJ 07436-1821 Office Phone: 201-337-4996. Personal E-mail: copdoc@aol.com.

GULLEY, JOAN LONG, banker; b. Balt., Sept. 10, 1947; d. Thomas F. and Florence (Waldron) Long; m. Philip Gordon Gulley, aug. 2, 1969; 1 child, Colin Jason. BA, U. Rochester, 1969; postgrad., Harvard U., 1985. Analyst U.S. Dept. Commerce, Washington, 1969-70, Fed. Res. Bd., Washington, 1970-74; sr. analyst 5, Washington, 1979-81; asst. v.p. Fed. Res. Bank Boston, 1975-79, v.p., 1981-83; sr. v.p. 5, 1983-86; exec. v.p. The Mass. Co., Boston, 1986-94, pres., CEO, 1994, also bd. dirs.; chmn., CEO PNC Bank New Eng., 1995-97; sr. v.p., mgr. strategic planning PNC Bank Corp., 1997-98, exec. v.p., dep. mgr. consumer bank, 1998—, dep. mgr. regional cmty. bank, 1999—2000; CEO PNC Bus. Banking, 2000—02, PNC Advisors, 2002—. Chmn. PNC Bank, New Eng., 1997-99. Mem. Allegheny Country Club, Nantucket Golf Club, Duquesne Club, Phi Beta Kappa. Office: PNC Bank Corp 1 PNC Plz 249 5th Ave Pittsburgh PA 15222-2709

GULLEY, WILBUR PAUL, JR., retired savings and loan association executive; b. Little Rock, Aug. 8, 1923; s. Wilbur Paul and JaJa Douglas (Ashburn) Gulley; m. Mary Elizabeth Bragg Hunt, Mar. 13, 1971; children from previous marriage: Wilbur Paul III, William H., James Ransom, Michael Pierce. AB in Bus. Adminstrn., Duke U., 1947. With Gulley Ins. Agy., Little Rock, 1947, ptnr., mng. officer, 1947-58; with Savers Fed. Savs. & Loan Assn., Little Rock, 1947-89, sec., 1948-52, v.p., 1952-58, pres., 1959-83, chmn. bd. dirs., 1983—89, also bd. dirs.; ret., 1989. Bd. dirs. Little Rock br. Fed. Res. Bank St. Louis, 1983—87. Gen. campaign chmn. United Fund, Pulaski County, Ark., 1963—64; v.p. Little Rock Boys Club, 1970—71, pres., 1971—72; commr. Metrocenter Improvement Dist., 1977—81, chmn., 1981; bd. stewards 1st United Meth. Ch. Little Rock, 1960—90, fin. chmn., 1989; trustee Savs. & Loan Found., 1977—81, Hendrix Coll., Conway, 1980—92, Roselawn Meml. Pk., 1975—, v.p. bd. trustees, 1994—; pres. BBB, Ark., 1962; trustee George W. Donaghey Found., 1958—2001, pres., 1969—72, 1981—83, 1995—96; trustee Ark. State U., 1968—73, sec.-treas., 1971—72, chmn., 1972—73. With USNR, 1943—46. Mem.: Ark. Savs. and Loan League, Pulaski County Savs. and Loan League, U.S. League Savs. Instns., Fin. Instns. Retirement Fund, Southwestern Savs. and Loans Conf., Little Rock C. of C., Little Rock Country Club, Phi Beta Kappa, Beta Omega Sigma, Sigma Alpha Epsilon. Home: 3500 Cedar Hill Rd Unit 3 Little Rock AR 72202-1914 Office: PO Box 3573 Little Rock AR 72203-3573 Personal E-mail: bgulley@bblittlerock.com.

GULLICKSON, ARLEN R., education educator, researcher, academic administrator; s. Joe A. and Marcella Gullickson; m. Janet Wuerffel; children: Amy, Jean, Karen. BA, U. of No. Iowa, 1963, MA, 1967; PhD, U. of Colo., 1971. Tchr. St. Ansgar H.S., St. Ansgar, Iowa, 1963—65, Dept. of Def., Bitburg, Germany, 1965—66; physics tchr. St. Paul Pk. H.S., St. Paul Park, Minn., 1967—69; rsch. assoc. U. of Minn., Mpls., 1971—73; prof. U. of S.D., Vermillion, SD, 1973—91; chief of staff, the evaluation ctr. Western Mich. U., Kalamazoo, 1991—2002, dir., the evaluation ctr., 2002—. Chair Joint Com. on Standards for Ednl. Evaluation, Kalamazoo, 1998—; editl. bd. mem. PARE (online jour.), U. Md., 1999—. Author: (book) Teacher Self-Evaluation Tool Kit; contbr. articles to profl. jours. Recipient Disting. Svc. award, Western Mich. U., 2002, Project Innovations Spl. Merit Award for Excellence, U. of S.D., 1988, Purple Key award, U. of No. Iowa, 1963. Mem.: Nat. Coun. on Measurement in Edn., Am. Evaluation Assn., Am. Ednl. Rsch. Assn. Avocation: woodworking. Office: Western Michigan University 1903 West Michigan Ave Kalamazoo MI 49008-5237 Home: 6642 West H Ave Kalamazoo MI 49009 Office Phone: 269-387-5895. Office Fax: 269-387-5923. E-mail: arlen.gullickson@wmich.edu.

GULLICKSON, JOANNE LOIS, writer; b. Mpls., May 18, 1931; d. Leslie Robert and Alice Maratanna (Schnabel) Johnson; m. R. Burton (div.); children: Bonnie Mae, Debra Ann, Katheryn Alice; m. Leslie Marshall Gullickson, Dec. 6, 1969. Student, Augsburg Luth. Coll., Mpls., 1949—50. Cert. lic. real estate Minn., 1975, Ariz., 1978, reservations cert., airline tng. 1962. Mgr. Radelle Products, Mpls., 1954—57; reservationist United Airlines, Mpls., 1962—69; realtor News Realty, Mpls., 1975—78, Osselear Realty, Phoenix, 1979—85; metaphysical counselor, 1986—99; writer, guest numerous radio & TV shows, 1989—. Mem. Ariz. Assocs. Astrologers, Scottsdale, 1985—2000. Author: (book) On Angels' Wings, 1998 (Cert. of Merit, 1998), A 5 Step Guide: For the Woman Just Diagnosed With Breast Cancer, 2002, (newsletter) With Light and Love, JoAnne, 1992—94. Mem. Luther League, sec./treas., 1946, pres., 1947; mem. Scottsdale Soroptamists, 1990—93; founder, chairperson Cancer Support Group, Scottsdale, Ariz., 2001—03; choir mem. Mpls. & St. Louis Pk., 1945—70. Recipient St. Louis Park award, City of St. Louis Park, Minn., 1949. Mem.: The Authors Guild, Inc. Independent. Lutheran. Avocations: writing, oil painting, travel, music. Personal E-mail: phxgolf5813@sbcglobal.com.

GULLIVER, CARL T., lawyer; b. Indpls., Mar. 6, 1951; s. Alfred and Mary (Johnston) G.; m. Polly C. Russell, Oct. 6, 1973; children: Bess, Sam. BA, Ohio Wesleyan U., 1973; JD, George Washington U., 1980. Bar: Conn. 1982, N.Y. 1985, Md. 1982, D.C. 1980, U.S. Dist. Ct. Conn. 1986, U.S. Ct. Appeals (D.C. cir.) 1981; cert. in bus. bankruptcy law Am. Bankruptcy Bd. Cert. Assoc. atty. Docter, Docter & Salus, Washington, 1980-86; from assoc. to prin. DiPietro Katrovitz & Brownstein, P.C., New Haven, 1986-94; ptnr. Coan, Lewendon, Gulliver, & Millenberger LLC, New Haven, 1994—. Mem. Am. Bankruptcy Inst., Conn. Bar Assn., New Haven County Bar Assn. Office: Coan Lewendon Gulliver & Millenberger LLC 495 Orange St New Haven CT 06511-3809 Office Phone: 203-624-4756.

GULLIVER, JOHN STEPHEN, civil engineering educator; b. Torrence, Calif., Sept. 9, 1950; s. Robert David and Jane Elizabeth (Loeffler) G.; m. Karen Lyum, Nov. 27, 1972; children: Djuna, Teigan, Hallon. BSChemE, U. Calif., Santa Barbara, 1974; MSCE, U. Minn., 1977, PhD in Civil Engring., 1980. Registered profl. engr., Minn. Rsch. assoc. U. Minn., Mpls., 1980-81, asst. prof. civil engring., 1981-87, assoc. prof., 1987-96, prof., 1996—, acting head civil engring., 1997-98, head, 1998—. Editor: Handbook of Hydropower Engineering, 1990, Air-Water Mass Transfer: Selected Papers From the Second Symposium on Gas Transfer at Water Surfaces, 1991; tech. editor Hydro Rev., 1987-2001, Hydro Rev. Worldwide, 1993-2001; contbr. 87 publs. to sci. and engring. jours. Mem ASCE (Rickey medal 1990, 2003), Internat. Assn. for Hydraulic Rsch. (editor Proc. 27th Congress, Vol. D), Internat. Assn. Water, Am. Soc. Engring. Edn., Assn. Environ. Engring. and Sci. Profs., Am. Pub. Works Assn., Minn. Surveyors and Engrs. Soc., N.Am. Lake Mgmt. Soc. Home: 942 Forest Dale Rd Saint Paul MN 55112-2517 Office: U Minn Civil Engring Dept Minneapolis MN 55455 Office Phone: 612-625-4080. Business E-Mail: gulli003@umn.edu.

GULLIVER, STUART, bank executive; MA with honors, Worcester Coll., Oxford U. With HSBC Holdings, 1980—, CEO, investment banking & markets, Asia Pacific region, 2000—03, head, global markets, 2002—03, co-chief exec., corp. investment banking and markets, 2003—. Office: HSBC Holdings plc 8 Canada Sq London E14 5HQ England

GULLO, STEPHEN PERNICE, psychologist, corporate executive; b. NYC; s. Anthony V. and Rose (Pernice) G. PhD Columbia U. Pres., chmn. bd. Inst. Health and Weight Scis., NYC, 1980—; co-dir. Family Bereavement Project Columbia U. Med. Sch., NYC. Asst. clin. prof. Columbia-Presbyn. Med. Ctr., 1980-96; chair Nat. Obesity and Weight Control Edn. Inst., Am. Inst. for Life-Threatening Illness, Columbia U., 1996-98; chair profl. adv. bd. Am. Inst. for Life Threatening Illness, Columbia-Presbyn. Med. Ctr., 1996-2000; mem. com. grants and profl. edn. NYC region Am. Cancer Soc., 1980-99; mem. sci. adv. com. Inst. Cancer Rsch.; co-chmn. Internat. Conf. Child and Health, Columbia-Presbyn. Med. Ctr., NYC, 1979; co-chair Nat. Obesity Symposium, Am. Inst. for Life Threatening Illness, Columbia U. Med. Ctr., 1994; expert witness City Coun. NY. Author: (with J. Schowalter et al) When People Die, 1978, The Child and Death, 1983, Education in Thanatology, 1984, Loveshock: How to Survive a Broken Heart and Love Again, 1988, Thin Tastes Better, 1995, (with T. Van Italie, A. Simopoulos and W. Futterweit) Obesity, 1995; cons. editor Jour. Thanatology, 1974-80, Archives Found. Thanatology, 1974—; chmn. editl. bd. Thanatology Abstract Series, 1974-76; cons. editor Advances in Thanatology, 1980-97; assoc. editor Loss, Grief & Care, 1990, Illness, Crises and Loss; contbg. editor: SELF, 1994-2002; contbr. articles and chpts. to med. textbooks. Vice chair ann. dinner Boys' Town of Jerusalem, 1981, assoc. chmn. ann. dinner Girls' Town Jerusalem, 1984; co-chmn. fundraising com. Found. Thanatology, 1982—; life hon. mem. Foss Found. Recipient gran croce al merito Accademia Italiana per lo Sviluppo Economico e Souale, Rome, 1985, Schoenberg award Am. Inst. for Life Threatening Illness, 1990; Knight Order St. John of Jerusalem, 1986; Patterson Found. fellow, 1972-73; NIH Rsch. grantee, 1973-75. Mem. NY Acad. Scis., Found. Thanatology (exec. bd., profl. adv. bd.), Columbia U. Coll. Physicians and Surgeons, Rolls Royce Owners Found. Home: 420 E 80th St Penthouse New York NY 10021-1052 Office: 16 E 65th St New York NY 10021-7030

GULOTTA, STEPHEN J., cardiologist; b. Bklyn., Mar. 5, 1933; s. Vito and Dora Gulotta; m. Lee Scaringella Gulotta, June 27, 1954; 1 child, Stephen Gulotta Jr.; children: Ronald, Eric. BS in Chemistry, Bklyn. Coll., 1954; MD, SUNY, Bklyn., 1958. Diplomate Am. Bd. Internal Medicine with subspeciality in cardiovascular diseases. Med. intern Montefiore Hosp., Bronx, NY, 1958—59, resident in medicine, 1959—61; fellow in cardiology N.Y. Hosp. Cornell Med. Ctr., N.Y.C., 1961—62; chief cardiology North Shore Univ. Hosp., Manhasset, NY, 1967—79; dir. catheterization labs. St. Francis Hosp., Roslyn, NY, 1979—2000. Mem. editl. bd. Circulation, Jour. Am. Coll. Cardiology, 1962—, Am. Jour. Cardiology, —; contbr. over 50 articles to profl. jours. Pres. Nassau Heart Assn., 1978—80, Am. Heart Assn., N.Y. Affiliate, 1981—83; bd. dirs. Commn. on Human Rights, Mt. Vernon, NY, 1964—70. Recipient Disting. Svc. award, Am. Heart Assn., 2000. Fellow: Am. heart Assn. Coun. of Clin. Cardiology, Am. Coll. Chest Physicians, Soc. Coronary Angiography and Interventions, Am. Coll. Cardiology, Am. Coll. Physicians. Avocations: skiing, collecting 20th Century American painters. Office: St Francis Hosp 100 Port Washington Blvd Roslyn NY 11576 Office Phone: 516-365-5599.

GULSEN, GULTEKIN, education educator; b. Malatya, Turkey, Jan. 10, 1971; s. Tahsin and Mujgan Gulsen; m. Mine Demir, Sept. 12, 1999; 1 child, Berk. PhD, Bogazici U., 1987—99. Postdoctral rschr. UC-Irvine, Irvine, 2000—01, asst. rschr., 2001—05, asst. prof., 2005—. Biomedical physicist Am. Hosp., Istanbul, Turkey, 1998—99; mgr. UC-Irvine, 2002—. Contbr. articles to profl. jours.; reviewer Jour. of Biomedical Optics200, 2004—05, NIH, 2003—05. Grant, DOD Army Med. Rsch., 2004—, multiple grants, NIH, 2004—. Mem.: IEEE, Internat. Soc. of Optical Engring., Optical Soc. of Am., Network for Translational Rsch. for Optical Imaging, UCI-Cancer Ctr. (assoc.). Achievements include design of multi-frequency diffuse optical tomography compatible with MRI. Home: 921 Somerville Irvine CA 92620 Office: UC-Irvine Irvine Hall Rm#164 Irvine CA 92697 Office Phone: 949-824-6557. Office Fax: 949-824-3481. Personal E-mail: ggulsen@uci.edu.

GULYA, AINA JULIANNA, neurologist, educator, surgeon; b. Syracuse, N.Y., Feb. 3, 1953; d. Aladar and Sylvia E. Gulya; m. William R. Wilson, May 21, 1983. AB cum laude, Yale Coll., 1974; MD with distinction in rsch., U. Rochester, 1978. Diplomate Am. Bd. Otolaryngology. Intern, jr. resident in gen. surgery Beth Israel Hosp., Boston, 1978-80; resident in otolaryngology Mass. Eye and Ear Infirmary, Boston, 1980-83; fellow in otology/neurotology Bapt. Hosp. Ear Found., Nashville, 1983-84; asst. prof. surgery George Washington U., Washington, 1984-87, assoc. prof. surgery, 1987-90; assoc. prof. otolaryngology and head and neck surgery Georgetown U., Washington, 1990-94, prof., 1994-96; chief clin. trials br. Nat. Inst. on Deafness and other Comm. Disorders, Bethesda, Md., 1996-2000, chief clin. trials epidemiology biostatistics sect., 2000—; clin. prof. surgery, otolaryngology, head and neck surgery George Washington U., 1998—2005; ret., 2005. Assoc. examiner Am. Bd. Otolaryngology, 1993-97, bd. dirs., 1997-2002, oral exam. leader for otology, 2000-02, chair neurotology sub-specialty cert. com., 2000-02, cons. NIDCD. Co-author: Anatomy of the Temporal Bone With Surgical Implications, 1986, 95; assoc. editor Am. Jour. Otology, 1989-99; co-editor Surgery of the Ear, 5th edit., 2002. Bd. dirs. Deafness Rsch. Found., 1994—2001. Recipient Libr. award, Rochester Acad. Medicine, 1975, presdl. citation, Am. Otol., Rhinol. and Laryngol. Soc., 1999. Mem.: Am. Acad. Otolaryngology, Head and Neck Surgery (bd. dirs. 1995—97, Honor award 1991, Disting. Svc. award 2001), Am. Neurotology Soc. (coord. for continuing med. edn. 1990—95), Am. Otological Soc. (coun. 1993—, editor-libr. 1995—2000, trustee rsch. fund 1993—2001, pres.-elect 1999—2000, pres. 2000—01). Avocation: water-skiing. Home: 111 Pleasant Grove Rd Locust Grove VA 22508

GUMBINNER, PAUL S., advertising and executive recruitment agency executive; b. NYC, Aug. 30, 1942; s. Paul G. Gumbinner and Ruth (Gumpert) Coben; m. Nancy Levin (div. 1978); children: Elizabeth Susan, Jeffrey Michael; m. Amye Hope Price, Sept. 12, 1982. BS, Temple U., 1964. Asst. account exec. Richard K. Manoff, N.Y.C., 1964-66; account exec. DKG, Inc., N.Y.C., 1966-68; v.p. Kenyon & Eckhardt, N.Y.C., 1969-73; sr. v.p. McCaffrey & McCall, N.Y.C., 1974-77; pres. Anesh, Viseltear, Gumbinner, N.Y.C., 1977-82, The Gumbinner Co., Inc., N.Y.C., 1982—. Contbr. articles to Ad Week, Advt. Age. Pres. Friends Emelin Theatre, Mamaroneck, N.Y., 1976-78; v.p. Larchmont (N.Y.) Pub. Libr., 1975-77; bd. dirs. Urban Glass, Bklyn., 1997—, chmn., 2000-05; bd. dirs. Art Alliance for Contemporary Glass; pres. Southgate Owners Assn., 2000—. Recipient Effie award Am. Mktg. Assn., 1985. Mem. Ad Club N.Y. (guest lectr.). pres. Southgate Owens Assn., 2000-. Democrat. Avocations: photography, glass collecting. Office: The Gumbinner Co Inc 509 Madison Ave Ste 708 New York NY 10022-5501

GUMERSON, JEAN GILDERHUS, health foundation executive; b. Hayfield, Minn., Mar. 19, 1923; d. Nordeen Palmer and Mable Jeannette (Scharberg) Gilderhus; m. William Dow Gumerson Sr., Mar. 5, 1943 (dec. Jan. 1978); children: William Dow Jr., Ted Lee, Jon David. Student, U. Minn., 1941-42, U. Okla., 1961-62. Adminstrv. asst. to Rep. state party chmn., Oklahoma City, 1976-77; campaign coord. 1st dist. Paula Unruh for Congress, Tulsa, 1978; dir. pub. rels. C.R. Anthony Co., Oklahoma City, 1979-87; dir. human rels. Wilson Agy., Mass. Mut. Ins. Co., Oklahoma City, 1987; adminstrv. dir. Okla. Art Ctr., Oklahoma City, 1988-89; exec. dir. Children's Med. Rsch., Inc., Oklahoma City, 1989—. Presbyn. Healh Found., Oklahoma City, 1989—. Active exec. com. Pres.'s Com. on Mental Retardation, Washington, 1986-91; So. Govs. Conf. on Infant Mortality, Washington, 1987-92; chmn. City-County Health Dept. Bd., Oklahoma City, 1980-93; gov. appointee steering com. Healthy Futures, Oklahoma City, 1988-92; bd. dirs. Children's Med. Rsch. Inc., Okla. City 1982—; nat. bd. Contact U.S.A., Okla. City, 1992—. Recipient Gov.'s Arts award for community svc. Okla. Arts Coun., Woman of Yr. award Okla. Mental Health Assn., Humanitarian award Opportunities Indsl. Ctr., Outstanding Vol. Fund Raiser award Okla. chpt. Nat. Soc. Fund Raising Execs., 1988, Humanitarian award Nat. Conf. for Comty. and Justice, 1999; inducted to Okla. Hall of Fame, 1999; Jean Gumerson Endowed Chair in Pediat. Psychology established in his honor, 1999. Mem. AIA (hon.), Exec. Women in Govt., Charter 35, Econ. Club. Okla., Oklahoma City C. of C., Theta Sigma Phi. Presbyterian. Home: 6206 Waterford Blvd Apt 50 Oklahoma City OK 73118-1109

GUMINA, GREGORY LAWRENCE, music educator, composer; b. McKeesport, Pa., June 27, 1967; s. Felix Joseph and Glenda Jean Gumina; m. Michelle Renee Nastiuk, July 8, 2000. MusB, W.Va. U., 1991; MA in Music Edn., U. Ala., 1995. Asst. band dir. Gadsden H.S., Ala., 1995—96; percussion caption head, arranger Southwind Drum and Bugle Corps, Montgomery, 1995—97; asst. band dir. Prattville H.S., 1996—97; assoc. band dir. Shades Valley H.S., Birmingham, 1997—. Arts adv. bd. Jefferson County Schs., Birmingham, 2002—04, mem., curriculum writing com., 2002—02, mem., auxilliary policy writing com., 2000—00; condr. U. of Ala. Summer Music Camp, Tuscaloosa, Ala., 2002—02; presenter and clinician Nat. Assn. for the Study and Performance of African Am. Music Conf., Birmingham, 2001—01. Composer: (music for percussion ensemble) Over 30 Compositions. Mem.: Percussive Arts Soc., Ala. Bandmasters Assn., Ala. Music Educators Assn., Music Educators Nat. Conf., Pi Kappa Lambda. Presbyterian. Avocation: building and riding motorcycles. Home: 675 Forest Lakes Dr Sterrett AL 35147 Office: Shades Valley High Sch 6100 Old Leeds Rd Birmingham AL 35210 Office Phone: 205-956-4638. Home Fax: 205-956-4638; Office Fax: 205-956-4638. Personal E-mail: gummusic@aol.com.

GUMM, ALAN JOSEPH, music educator, researcher, writer; b. Jefferson, Iowa, Mar. 27, 1960; s. Max Douglas Gumm and Norita LaVonne Elwood; m. Carolyn Gayle Reinoehl, Sept. 30, 1962; children: Jordan Nathaniel, Brandon Jeffrey. BA, McPherson Coll., McPherson, Kans., 1983; MMus, Ft. Hays State U., Hays, Kans., 1986; PhD, U. Utah, Salt Lake City, Utah, 1991. K-12 vocal music tchr. USD 302 Ransom Schs., Ransom, Kans., 1983—85; vocal music tchr. USD 465 Tonganoxie Schs., Tonganoxie, Kans., 1985—88; tchg. asst./asst. instr. U. Utah, Salt Lake City, 1988—91; asst. prof. music Ithaca Coll., Ithaca, NY, 1991—94, McPherson Coll., McPherson, Kans., 1994—2000; assoc. prof. music Ctrl. Mich. U., Mount Pleasant, Mich., 2000—. Editl. bd. mem. Jour. of Music Tchr. Edn., 2004—. Author: Music Teaching Style: Moving Beyond Tradition; contrbg. author The Music Director's Cookbook: Creative Recipes for a Successful Program; contbr. articles pub. to profl. jour. Lay min. Midland Ch. of the Brethren, Midland, Mich., 2004—. Mem.: Soc. for Rsch. in Music Edn., Soc. for Music Tchr. Edn., Music Educators Nat. Conf., Am. Choral Dirs. Assn. Achievements include research in Eight-dimension devel. theory of music tchg. style. Home: 1911 Churchill Blvd Mount Pleasant MI 48858 Office: Ctrl Mich Univ Sch of Music Mount Pleasant MI 48859 Office Phone: 989-774-1966. Office Fax: 989-774-3766. Business E-Mail: gumm1aj@cmich.edu.

GUMMEL, HERMANN KARL, retired physicist, lab administrator; b. Hannover, Germany, July 6, 1923; came to U.S., 1953; s. Johannes and Charlotte (Elgeti) G.; m. Erika Ilse Reich, Aug. 31, 1952; children— Monica Ruth, Margaret Grace MS, Syracuse U., 1952, PhD, 1957; diploma in Physics, Philipps U., Marburg-Lahn, 1952. Mem. tech. staff Bell Telephone Labs, Murray Hill, N.J., 1957-62, supr., 1962-67, dept. head, 1967-82, asst. dir., 1982-84; dir. AT&T Bell Labs, Murray Hill, N.J., 1984-86, ret., cons. Contbr. articles to profl. jours.; patentee in field Recipient Phil Kaufman award Electronic Design Automation Co., 1994. Fellow IEEE (David Sarnoff award 1983, Guillemin-Cauer prize paper award Circuits and Systems Soc. 1977, Tech. Achievement award Circuit and Systems Soc. 1990, Golden Jubilee medal 2000, Third Millennium medal 2000); mem. Am. Phys. Soc., Nat. Acad. Engring., Sigma Xi Presbyterian. Home: 123 Valley View Pompton Plains NJ 07444

GUMMERE, WALTER COOPER, finance educator, consultant; b. Columbus, Ohio, Apr. 24, 1917; s. Walter Cooper and Glenn (Becker) G.; m. Virginia Lee Jeffries, Jan. 10, 1942; children: Virginia Glenn Gummere

Stewart, Deborah Gummere Lilgendahl (dec.), Rebecca Jane Gummere Pivetta. AB, Brown U., 1940; MBA, U. Louisville, 1953. Chief indsl. engr. Colgate Palmolive Co., 1947-53; gen. supt., dir. Rich's Inc., Atlanta, 1953-57; personnel adminstr. Montgomery Ward & Co., Chgo., 1957-60; v.p., gen. mgr. Plasti-Line Inc., Knoxville, Tenn., 1960-62; mgmt. cons., 1962-63; with Tappan Co., 1963-73, exec. v.p., 1966-72, pres., chief exec. officer, 1972-73; also dir.; chmn., chief exec. officer The Vendo Co., 1974-78; pres. Square Pegs Assocs., Inc., 1978—. Exec.-in-residence U. Central Fla., 1982-83, Centre Coll. Ky., winter 1983, Am. Coll., London, spring and summer 1984; Goodyear exec. prof. Sch. Bus., U. Akron, 1984-85; vis. prof. Clemson U., 1986, Lander Coll., 1987, Am. Coll., London, 1988, Centre Coll. Ky., 1990, U. Louisville, 1990—. Served to capt. AUS, 1942-46. Mem. Newcomen Soc., Acad. Mgmt., Delta Upsilon, Phi Beta Kappa, Delta Sigma Pi, Sigma Iota Epsilon, Omicron Delta Kappa Republican. Presbyterian. Home and Office: 202 Meadowvista Ln Sun City Center FL 33573-5562

GUMP, BROOKS B., psychologist, educator; b. Balt., Aug. 5, 1964; s. Dieter W. A. Gump and Linnea D. Taylor; m. Linda S. McGlasson, May 28, 1988; children: Amelia, Avery. MA, Radford U., 1990; PhD, U. Calif., San Diego, 1995; MPH, U. Pitts., 1997. Assoc. prof. SUNY, Oswego, 1998—. Contbr. articles to profl. jours. Office: Dept Psychology SUNY Oswego Rte 104 Oswego NY 13126

GUMPEL, HUGH, artist; b. 1926; m. Virginia Peckham. Studied at, Columiba U., Grande Chaumière, Paris, Art Students League. Prof.-drawing & painting Nat. Acad. Sch., NYC; adj. prof.-watercolor painting SUNY Purchase. Mem.: Am. Watercolor Soc., Nat. Acad. Design. Office Phone: 207-236-0818. E-mail: HGumpel@aol.com.*

GUMPERT, GUNTHER, artist; b. Krefeld, Germany, Apr. 17, 1919; came to U.S., 1967, naturalized, 1971; s. Karl and Erna (Cordes) G.; m. Anita Von Kahler, Nov. 28, 1967. Grad., Human. Gymnasium, Krefeld, 1937, Sch. Fine Arts, Krefeld, 1938, Sch. Fine Arts, Wuppertal, 1939. Numerous one-man shows: Europe and U.S. including: Zurich, 1955, Winterthur, 1959, Paris, 1960, Vienna, 1961, Rome, 1962, N.Y.C., 1963, 96, 98, Chgo., 1963, 64, London, 1963, Pforzheim, 1964, Seattle, 1965, 68, 70, 73, 76, Denver, 1972, Washington, 1966, 68, 69, 72, 75, 79, 82, 85, 87, 88, 90, 93, Cleve., 1971, Santo Domingo, 1978, Wichtrach, Bern, 2004; group shows: Suermondt Mus., Aachen, Ger., 1948, Kaiser-Wilhelm Mus., Krefeld, 1949, 50, 51, Internat. Exhibit Abstract Art, Pistoia, Italy, 1961, Salon Realites Nouvelles, Paris, 1959, 60, 61, Salon De Mai, Paris, 1962, Gruppe Z, Wuppertal, 1960, Internat. Exhbn. Contemporary Art, London, 1964, European Acad. Fine Art, Trier, 2000, Die Grosse Abstraktion, Wichtrach/Bern, 2002; represented in permanent collections, Met. Mus. Art, N.Y.C., Victoria and Albert Mus., London, Albertina, Vienna, The Phillips Collection, Washington, Kaiser-Wilhelm Mus., Krefeld, Museo Nacional de Bellas Artes, Santiago, Chile, Sch. Design, Providence, R.I., Princeton U. Art Mus., Mus. Fine Arts, Dallas, Denver Art Mus., Finch Coll. Mus., N.Y.C., Wesleyan U., Middletown Conn., Ohio U. Mus. Am. Art, Athens, Roosevelt House, New Delhi, India, Museo de Arte Moderno, Santo Domingo, George Washington U., Washington, and others; TV film Gumpert At Work, 1963. Address: 3752 Mckinley St NW Washington DC 20015-2510

GUMPERT, GUSTAV, public relations executive; b. Phila., Nov. 28, 1922; s. Hibbard Gustav and Lillian (Heebner) G.; A.B., Lehigh U., 1944. Reporter, Allentown (Pa.) Morning Call, 1945-46; asso. editor Musical Digest, N.Y.C., 1946-49; health edn. dir. Dept. Public Health, Phila., 1950-52, health info. officer, 1952-60; writing unit head pub. rels. dept. SmithKline Beecham, Phila., 1962-63, mgr. writing, editorial svcs., 1965-66, mgr. planning, editorial svcs., 1966-73, dir. spl. projects, 1973-78, dir. creative sers., 1978-89; ret., 1989. Contbr. articles to profl. jours. Pres. bd. Planned Parenthood Assn. Phila., 1960-62; bd. dirs. Found. for Study Cycles, 1959-60. Mem. Phi Beta Kappa.

GUMPERT, LYNN, gallery director; Student, Sorbonne, Paris, 1971-72; cert. completion first year, Ecole du Louvre, Paris, 1971-72; BA in History of Art with honors, U. Calif., Berkeley, 1974; MA in History of Art, U. Mich., 1977. Curatorial asst. The Jewish Mus., N.Y.C., 1978-80; curator The New Mus. Contemporary Art, N.Y.C., 1980-84, sr. curator, 1984-88; adj. curator Mus. Contemporary Art, L.A., 1988-89, We. States Arts Fedn., Santa Fe, 1988-89; coord. Eighth Biennale of Sydney Art Gallery N.S.W., Sydney, Australia, 1989-90; guest curator, adminstrv. dir. Amway (Japan) Ltd. and Setagaya Art Mus., Tokyo, 1989-91, Nat. Mus. Art, Osaka, Japan, 1989-91; cons. curator Gallery at Takashimaya, Inc., N.Y.C., 1992-95; guest curator, U.S. coord. ARC/Musée d'Art Moderne de la Ville de Paris, 1994-95; guest curator Grey Art Gallery, NYU, N.Y.C., 1996-97, dir., 1997—; interim dirl mus. studies program NYU, 1999-2000. Lectr. in field; juror in field; panelist in field; ind. curator/cons., 1988-97; mem. adv. com. Asia Soc. Galleries. Exhbns. include Grey Art Gallery, The New Mus. Contemporary Art, 1980, 81, 82, 84, 86, 89, Pitts. Ctr. Arts, 1983, Mus. Contemporary Art, Chgo., 1988, Galerie Ghislaine Hussenot, Paris, 1992, The Gallery at Takashimaya, N.Y.C., 1994, 95, numerous others; author: Christian Boltanski, 1993, reprint, 1996; editor: The Art of the Everyday: The Quotidian in Postwar French Culture, 1997. Decorated chevalier Order Arts and Letters (France); Univ. fellow U. Mich., 1975. Mem. Internat. Assn. Art Critics, ArtTable (N.Y.). Office: Grey Art Gallery NYU 100 Washington Sq E New York NY 10003-6688 Fax: 212-995-4024. E-mail: greygallery@nyu.edu.

GUMPERTZ, WERNER HERBERT, structural engineering company executive; b. Berlin, Dec. 26, 1917; s. Richard and Olga H. Gumpertz; m. Elizabeth Mildred Lewit, Nov. 25, 1949; children: Richard H., Ruth O. Gumpertz Moses. BCE, Swiss Fed. Inst. Tech., 1939; SBCE, MIT, 1948, SM in Bldg. Engring. and Constrn., 1950, advanced profl. degree in bldg. engring. and constrn., 1954. Registered profl. engr., Mass., Pa., Calif., Colo., Okla., Md., Kans., Tex., Ga., La. Constrn. supr., expeditor, draftsman Homes & Gardens Inc., N.Y.C., 1940; engring. draftsman, surveyor Lockwood Kessler & Bartlett, Bklyn., 1940-41; office engr., estimator, constrn. supr. M. Shapiro & Sons Constrn. Co., N.Y.C. and Newport News, Va., 1941-43; engring. asst. to head Kaiser Co. Inc. Shipyard, Vancouver, Wash., 1943; structural engr. U.S. Army C.E., ETO, 1946-47; office and field engr. United Engrs. & Constructors Inc., Phila. and Devon, Conn., 1948-49; prof. civil engring. MIT, Cambridge, Mass., 1949-57; sr. prin. Simpson Gumpertz & Heger Inc., Waltham, Mass., 1956—. Part-time instr. structural engring. Bridgeport Engring. Inst., 1948-49, U. Mass. Extension, 1953-62; cons. bldg. constrn. and material tech., bldg. systems and assemblies of materials; lectr. Harvard Grad. Sch. Design, 1985, 87. Contbr. articles to profl. jours. Mem. Adv. Com. on Pub. Bldg. Constrn., City of Newton, Mass., 1956-68; guidance lectr. Cambridge Pub. Sch. System, 1955-57. Served to cpl. U.S. Army, 1943-46, ETO. Fellow ASCE (nat. com. on stds., sec.-treas., joint com. on profl. conduct Mass. sect.), ASTM Internat (chmn. com. D-8 on roofing, waterproofing and bituminous materials 1981-85, real estate com. 1988-95, Award of Merit 1986, Walter C. Voss award to Engr. for Outstanding Contbn. to Advancement of Bldg. Tech. 1987, William C. Cullen award 2005); mem. Am. Concrete Inst. (com. on residential concrete slabs, cellular concrete com.), U.S. Metric Assn. (cert. advanced metrication specialist), Am. Soc. Engring. Edn. (chmn. archtl. engring. divsn.), Am. Arbitration Assn. (nat. panel arbitrators), Nat. Fire Protection Assn., Midwest Roofing Contractors Assn. (assoc.), Nat. Roofing Contractors Assn. (assoc.), Sigma Xi. Office: Simpson Gumpertz & Heger Inc 41 Seyon St Waltham MA 02453-8335 Office Phone: 781-907-9000. Business E-Mail: whgumpertz@sgh.com.

GUMPPERT, KARELLA ANN, federal government official; b. N.Y.C., Oct. 16, 1942; d. Leonard Lewis and Florence M. Gumppert. AB in Polit. Sci., George Washington U., 1963, postgrad., 1963-65. Lic. in real estate sales, Md., 1984. Jr. editor to Bd. Govs. Fed. Res. Sys., Washington, 1966-67; editl. asst. Jour. of Maritime Law and Commerce, N.Y.C., 1969-71; adminstr. NYU Law Sch., N.Y.C., 1968-73; law asst. White & Case and other firms, N.Y.C., Boston, Hartford, 1974-80; vol. asst. U.S. Presdl. Inaugural Com., Washington, 1981; confidential asst. The White House Staff, Washington, 1981; publs. asst. Congressional Budget Office, Washington, 1982-84; credit summarizer Xerox Corp., Arlington, Va., 1985-86; asst. in govtl. affairs Mut. Omaha, Washngton, 1988; land law adjudicator U.S. Dept. Interior, Anchorage, 1991—. Author, illustrator: (children's book) An Adventure, 1949; founding editor lit. mag. Springboard, 1959; mem. editorial bd., copy editor newspaper Amicus Curiae, 1964-65. Charity asst. Girl Scouts U.S.A., N.Y.C., 1952-54, Christian Assn., N.Y.C., 1959-61, Wesley Found., Washington, 1962-63; vol. asst. N.Y. Rep. County Com., 1959-62, Conn. Reps. State Com., Hartford, 1979-80. Recipient numerous scholarships, 1957-60. Mem. NAFE, Nat. Trust for Hist. Preservation, Nat. Audubon Soc., Women's Nat. Rep. Club, Anchorage Opera Assn., Library of Cong. Assocs. (founding mem.). Avocations: music, nostalgia, travel, theater, sports.

GUMPRECHT, JANE CAROLINE DOERING, retired physician; b. Lewistown, Mont., Feb. 6, 1922; d. Gotthilf Johann Doering and Martha Elizabeth Strauss; m. Donald Max Gumprecht, Sept. 1944; children: Donald George, Ruth Ellen Carlson, Thomas Frank, Ernest Charles. BS, Mont. State U., 1942; BM, MD, U. Minn., 1946. Diplomate Am. Bd. Medicine. Pvt. practice, Three Forks, Mont., 1948—49, Coeur d' Alene, Idaho, 1951—87; ret., 1987. Sec., bd. dirs. Kootenai Meml. Hosp., Coeur d'Alene; inspirational spkr. Author: Holistic Health: A Medical and Biblical Critique of New Age Deception, 1986, New Age Health Care: Holy or Holistic? 2d edit., 1988, Abusing Memory: The Healing Theology of Agnes Sanford, 1997. Com. for the handicapped City of Coeur d' Alene, 1961—62; cand. for Idaho legislature Rep. Party, Boise, Idaho, 1960, state com. woman, 1962—64; founding mem. Coeur d' Alene Bible Ch., Coeur d' Alene; sec. Kootenai County Med. Soc., Coeur d' Alene, 1957—58, pres., 1959—60; grand marshal Coeur d'Alene 4th of July Parade, 2004. With USPHS, 1949—51. Named Idaho Mother of the Yr., Am. Mothers, Inc., 1981. Mem.: PEO, Alpha Omicron Pi, Phi Sigma, Phi Kappa Phi. Republican. Avocations: golf, travel, gardening. Home: 317 Military Dr Coeur D Alene ID 83814

GUMUDAVELLI, SRIDHAR, pharmacist, researcher; b. Warangal, Andhrapradesh, India, Feb. 26, 1967; arrived in U.S., 2002; s. Krishnamurthy and Annapoorna Gumudavelli; m. Padmasree Gunda, Feb. 11, 1996; children: Srinija children: Sricharan. M in Pharmacy, Kakatiya U., Warangal, 1992. Post Graduate In Packaging Technology Mumbai, India, 1999, Diploma In Export Management Bangalore, India, 1997. Prodn. mgr. Trident Pharmaceuticals Ltd., Hyderabad, India, 1992—95; dep. mgr. R&D Biological, Ltd., Hyderabad, 1995—99; mgr. R&D Cadilla Pharmaceuticals, Ahmedabad, India, 1999—2002; sr. mgr., head R&D Intas Pharmaceuticals Ltd., Ahmedabad, 2002—03; sr. mgr., head novel drug delivery systems Alembic Ltd., Vadodara, India, 2003—03; dir. tech. Capricorn Pharma Inc., Frederick, Md., 2003—05, Pharmaceutics Internat. Inc., Balt., 2005—. Prodn. cons. Adjuvant Pharmaceuticals, Hyderabad, 1994—. Author: (scientific journal) Sneezing Facts & Myths (Best Author award, 1986). Cmty. helper Warangal Youth, 1984—92. Mem.: Am. Assn. Pharm. Scientist. Achievements include patents for The Process For Manufacturing Of Clear Liquid Pharmaceutical Composition Of Azithromycin; patents pending for Site Specific Bioadherent Controlled Release Self Microemulsion Drug Delivery Composition; Pharmaceutical Zinc Acetate Dihydrate Rapid Mouth Disintegrating Mucoadherent Dosage Form Coposition And Process; Microosmosealed Controlled Drug Delivery Formulation & Process; A Process Of Preparaing Liquisolid Molecular Adsorption Compact Solid Dosage Forms Containing Loratidine; A process of preparing extended release osmo microsealed venelafaxine HCl; A Process Of Preparing Capsule Dosage Form Of Azithromycin Monohydrate; A process of preparing lozenges of bupropion HCl; A Process Of Preparing Sildenafil Citrate Trandermal Gel; A Process Preparing Of Azithromycin Microparticules By Evaporation Precipitation Method; A Process Preparing Of Antihistaminic Mucoadhesive Liquid; A Process Preparing Of Bupropion Chewing Gum. Home: Unit E 606 Knoll Crest Pl Cockeysville MD 21030 Office: Pharmaceutics Internat Inc Hunt Valley MD 21031 Personal E-mail: sricharan21@hotmail.com.

GUNBERG, EDWIN WOODROW, JR., counseling psychologist, consultant, researcher; b. Sioux Falls, S.D., Nov. 13, 1950; s. Edwin Woodrow and Eileen Marie Elizabeth (Youngdahl) G.; m. Elizabeth Ann Robbins, June 5, 1976; children: Edwin Christian, Emily Elizabeth. BA, Gustavus Adolphus Coll., St. Peter, Minn., 1972; MA, George Mason U., 1975; postgrad., Va. Poly. Inst. and State U., 1975-79; PhD, U. N.D., 1981. Diplomate Am. Bd. Forensic Examiners, Am. Bd. Forensic Medicine, Am. Bd. Psychol. Specialties. Asst. prof. counseling U. N.D., Grand Forks, 1981-82; prin. PSYCON, Round Hill, Va., 1982—; pres. MARS Assessment Tech., Inc., Sterling, 1990-2001; v.p. United Bus. Svcs., 1996-98. Cons. HumRRO Internat., Inc., Alexandria, Va., 1985-91. Bd. dirs. Loudon Symphony Assn., 1994—, pres., 1996—99; mem. Round Hill Econ. Devel. Com., 2003—04, Rep. Senatorial Inner Cir., 1989, Loudon County Rep. Com., 1992—97. Mem. Am. Assn. for Marriage and Family Therapy (clin.), Am. Psychol. Soc., Aircraft Owner and Pilot Assn., Exptl. Aircraft Assn., Mooney Aircrft Pilots Assn. Lutheran. Avocation: aviation. Address: PO Box 636 Round Hill VA 20142

GUND, AGNES, retired museum administrator; b. Cleve., Ohio; d. George Gund, Jr.; m. Daniel Shapiro, June 13, 1987; children: David, Catherine, Jessica, Anna. BA in art history, Conn. Coll., 1960; MA in art history, Fogg Mus., Harvard U., 1980; LHD (hon.), Case Western Reserve U., 1995, Brown U., 1996. Trustee Mus. Modern Art, N.Y.C., 1976—, v.p., 1988—91, pres., 1991—2002, pres. emerita, 2002—; chair Mayor's Cultural Affairs Adv. Commn., N.Y.C., 2003—. Bd. trustees Wexner Ctr. Found., 1997—; trustee Brown U., Aaran Diamond AIDS Rsch. Ctr., Inst. Advanced Study, Princeton, NJ, J. Paul Getty Trust, Malibu, Calif.; mem. mus. coun. Cleve. Mus. Art. Named one of Top 200 Collectors, The ARTnews Mag., 2004; recipient Women in the Arts award, Coll. Art Assn., Art Table award for Disting. Svc. to Arts, 1994, Montblanc de la Culture award, 1997, Nat. Medal Arts, 1997, Arts Edn. award, Am. for the Arts, 1999, Evan Burger Donaldson Achievement award, Miss Porter's Sch., 2003, Centennial Medal, Harvard U. Grad. Sch. Arts and Sciences, 2003. Fellow: Am. Acad. Arts and Sciences; mem.: Studio in a Sch. Assn. (founder, Gov.'s Art award, N.Y. 1988, Dorothy Freeman award, N.Y.C. 1988). Avocation: Collector of Contemporary, African, Chinese Art. Office: care Museum Modern Art 11 W 53rd St New York NY 10019-5401*

GUND, GORDON, venture capitalist, professional sports team executive; b. Cleve., Oct. 15, 1939; s. George and Jessica (Roesler) G.; m. Llura Liggett; children: Grant Ambler, Gordon Zachary. BA, Harvard U., 1961; DPubSvc (hon.), U. Maryland, 1980; DHL, Whittier Coll., 1993; LLD (hon.), U. Vt., 1994; PhD (hon.), Goteburg U., Sweden, 1997. Pres., chmn., CEO Gund Investment Corp., Princeton, N.J.; prin. owner Cleve. Cavaliers, NBA, 1983—. Mem. bd. govs. NBA; bd. dirs. Kellogg Co., Corning Inc. Mem. U.S. Olympic Com.; co-founder The Found. Fighting Blindness, 1971; mem. Nat. Adv. Eye Coun., 1980—84. Office: Gund Investment Corp PO Box 449 14 Nassau St Princeton NJ 08542-4523 also: Cleveland Cavaliers Gund Arena One Center Ct Cleveland OH 44115

GUNDECK, CAROLINE NYKLEWICZ, investment company executive; b. Paterson, NJ; BS econs., Marymount Coll. With Merrill Lynch, White Plains, NY, 1983, currently first v.p. investments, chair Adv. Com. to Mgmt. on Diversity, dir. Women's Bus. Devel., 2003—. Created No. NJ Women's Network for Financial Advisors. Mem. adv. com. Preservation and Use of Ellis Island appointed by Gov. Christine Todd Whitman; dir. Women Presidents' Orgn. Recipient Tribute to Women & Industry Award, YMCA, 1999, recognized for outstanding volunteerism, United Way of Passaic County, 2000. Office: 1300 Merrill Lynch Drive, 3rd Fl Pennington NJ 08534 E-mail: caroline_gundeck@ml.com.

GUNDERSEN, ALLISON MAUREEN, management consultant; b. Syracuse, N.Y., Oct. 14, 1959; d. Jerrold Paul and Rosemarie Noël (Harvey) G. AB, Cornell U., 1981; postgrad., NYU, 1982-83, Swedish Inst., 1991; MA in Intercultural Rels., Lesley Coll., 1996. Assoc. Morgan Stanley & Co., N.Y.C., 1981-84, sr. assoc., 1985-86; project mgr. Morgan Stanley Internat., Tokyo, 1987-88; cons. Computech Cons. Svcs., Winchester, N.J., 1989-90; pres. Woman About Globe, Ltd., N.Y.C., 1990-93; assoc. Cambridge (Mass.) Myotherapy, 1992-95; intern UN Indsl. Devel. Orgn., Vienna, 1996; prin. cons. Data Dimensions, 1997-98; cons. Culpeper Consulting Group, N.Y.C., 1998—. Mem. NOW (dir. membership processing N.Y.C. 1990), Internat. Feminists Japan (coord. 1987-88), Am. Massage Therapists Assn., City Island Yacht Club, Cornell Club N.Y. Democrat. Avocations: travel, languages, photography, sailing. Mailing: PO Box 356 Findley Lake NY 14736-0356

GUNDERSEN, WAYNE CAMPBELL, energy executive, consultant; b. Elgin, Ill., May 27, 1936; s. LeRoy Arthur and Jean Ellen (Campbell) Gundersen; m. Gail Andrews, Mar. 21, 1959; children: Thomas Dexter, Lori Ann, Kathy Lee. BS, U. Nebr., 1959, MS, 1961. Advisor fgn. ops. Std. Oil Calif., San Francisco, 1974-76; asst. to v.p. Chevron Overseas Petroleum, San Francisco, 1976-80; dir. oil and gas Kaiser Aluminum & Chem. Corp., Oakland, Calif., 1980-81; v.p., gen. mgr. Kaiser Energy, Inc., Oakland, 1983-85, pres., 1985-87; v.p. Kaiser Aluminum and Chem. Corp., Oakland, 1983-87; pres. Kaiser Aluminum Exploration Co., Oakland, Kaiser Exploration and Mining Co., Oakland, 1985-87; cons. in oil and gas., 1987—; CEO, chmn. bd. dirs. Petroleum Synergy Group, Inc., 1988—. Mem. geology adv. bd. U. Nebr., Lincoln, 1984—87; mgr. Western Geothermal Ptnrs., LLC. Contbr. articles to profl. jours. Pres. Parents Club Foothill Sch., Walnut Creek, Calif., 1978—79. Named Man-of-Yr., New Orleans Jaycees, 1973; Sinclair fellow, 1960—61. Mem.: Am. Assn. Petroleum Geologists. Republican. Methodist. Office: The Petroleum Synergy Group Inc PO Box 34300 Reno NV 89533 Office Phone: 775-787-6640. Personal E-mail: renooilman@aol.com.

GUNDERSHEIMER, WERNER LEONARD, library director; b. Frankfurt, Hesse, Germany, Apr. 7, 1937; s. Herman Samuel and Frieda (Siegel) G.; m. Karen Rosenwald, Oct. 16, 1939; children: Joshua, Benjamin. BA, Amherst Coll., 1959, DHL (hon.), 1984; MA, Harvard U., 1960, PhD, 1963; MA (hon.), U. Pa., 1971; DHL (hon.), Williams Coll., 1989, Muhlenberg Coll., 1991, Davidson Coll., 1998, Washington Coll., 2003. Asst. prof. history U. Wis., Madison, 1963-64; jr. fellow Harvard U., Cambridge, Mass., 1962-66; asst. prof. U. Pa., Phila., 1966-68, assoc. prof., 1968-72, prof., 1972-85, chmn. history dept., 1976-78; dir. Folger Shakespeare Library, Washington, 1984—2002, dir. emeritus, 2002—; vis. prof. history Williams Coll., 2003; vis. prof. George Washington U., 2004—. Trustee Rosenbach Mus. and Library, Phila., 1969-89, The Medici Found., Princeton, N.J., 1984-2000, Brit. Inst. of the U.S., Washington, 1985-90; vis. prof. Tel Aviv (Israel) U., 1982; adj. prof. history Amherst (Mass.) Coll., 1986-02; Phi Beta Kappa vis. scholar, 2004-05. Author: Life and Works of Louis LeRoy, 1966, Ferrara: The Style of a Renaissance Despotism, 1973, Art and Life of the Court of Ercole I d'Este, 1972; editor: The Italian Renaissance, 1965; contbr. articles to profl. jours. Cons. NEH, 1982—; trustee Shakespeare Theatre at the Folger, Washington, 1985-92, PEN/Faulkner Found., 1990-95; v.p. Nat. Humanities Alliance, 1992-95, pres., 1996-00; overseer Hancock Shaker Village, 2004-. Fellow Inst. for Advanced Study, 1970-71, Guggenheim fellow, 1974-75, I Tatti fellow Harvard Ctr. for Renaissance Study, 1974-75. Fellow Am. Acad. Arts & Sci.; mem. Am. Philos. Soc., Am. Hist. Assn., Ind. Rsch. Libr. Assn. (pres. 1994-97), Renaissance Soc. Am., Med. Acad. Am., Century Assn., Grolier Club, Phi Beta Kappa (senator 1994-2000, vis. scholar 2004-05). Democrat. Jewish. Business E-Mail: wgundersheimer@folger.edu.

GUNDERSON, CARL HARMON, neurologist, educator; b. South Bend, Ind., Nov. 6, 1933; s. Norris Elwood and Harriet Elizabeth (Harmon) G.; m. Anne Bruner, Sept. 7, 1957; children: Sarah, Carl, Katharine. BS, Notre Dame U., 1954; MS, MD, U. Chgo., 1958. Diplomate Am. Bd. Psychiatry and Neurology. Resident, fellow in neurology Yale U., New Haven, Conn., 1959-62; chief neurology svc. Womack Army Hosp., Ft. Bragg, N.C., 1962-64; chief psychiatry & neurology br. Med. Field Svc. Sch., Ft. Sam Houston, Tex., 1964-67; asst. chief neurology svc. Letterman Army Med. Ctr., Presidio of San Francisco, 1967-70; chief neurology svc. Brooke Army Med. Ctr., Ft. Sam Houston, 1970-80, Walter Reed Army Med. Ctr., Washington, 1980-96; chmn. dept. neurology Uniformed Svcs. U. Health Scis., Bethesda, Md., 1983-97, prof. neurology, 1997—. Cons. Surgeon Gen. Army, 1980-91. Author: Quick Reference to Clinical Neurology, 1982, Essentials of Clinical Neurology, 1990. Col. U.S. Army, 1972-96. Fellow Am. Acad. Neurology, Am. Heart Assn.; mem. AMA, Am. Neurologic Assn.

GUNDERSON, CLARK ALAN, orthopedic surgeon; b. Watertown, S.D., Aug. 27, 1948; s. Harvey Alfred and Eugenie (Tulson) G.; m. Robbie Gunderson; children: Ashley, Camille Student, U. Minn., 1966-69; BS, U. S.D., 1971; MD, Baylor Coll. of Medicine, 1973. Diplomate Am. Bd. of Orthopaedic Surgery, 1979. Intern in gen. surgery Charity Hosp., New Orleans, 1973-74, resident in orthopedic surgery, 1974-78; chief of surgery Lake Charles (La.) Meml. Hosp., 1980-83, 90-91, sec., treas. med. staff, 1983-87, pres. med. staff, 1992-93, also trustee, 90-94, chief of surgery, 1998-99; clin. assoc. prof. La. State U. Sch. of Medicine, New Orleans, 1987-90. Bd. dirs. Arthritic Found. La., 1987. Mem. AMA, ACS, Am. Acad. Orthopaedic Surgeons (bd. councilors 2002, com. on state com. 2002), La. Orthopaedic Assn. (pres. 1995-96), Calcasieu Parish Med. Soc., La. State Med. Soc., N.Am. Spine Assn., Mid Am. Orthopaedic Assn., La. Orthopaedic ASsn. (exec. com. 1993—), Lake Charles Country Club (pres. 1987-89), Clin. Orthopedic Rsch. Soc., Sigma Chi. Avocation: golf. Office: 2615 Enterprise Blvd Lake Charles LA 70601-7675

GUNDERSON, DONALD RAYMOND, fisheries educator and researcher; b. La Jolla, Calif., Jan. 3, 1942; s. David Elling Gunderson and Elizabeth Topping Duke; children: David John, Dean Stransham. BS, Mont. State U., 1963, MS, 1966; PhD, U. Wash., 1976. Biologist Wash. State Dept. Fisheries, Seattle, 1967-75; rsch. biologist Nat. Marine Fisheries Svc., Seattle, 1975-78; asst. prof. U. Wash., Seattle, 1978-81, assoc. prof., 1981-94; prof., 1995—. Cons. various govt. agys. and pvt. corps., 1978—. Author: Surveys of Fisheries Resources, 1993; mem. editorial bd. Fisheries Rsch., 1984-89; contbr. articles to Can. Jour. Fisheries and Aquatic Sci., Fisheries Rsch., Marine Fisheries Rev., Estuaries, others. Scoutmaster Boy Scouts Am., Seattle, 1980-83, cubmaster, 1977. Mem. Am. Fisheries Soc., Am. Inst. Fisheries Rsch. Biologists, Sigma Xi. Achievements include research in population dynamics and recruitment processes in marine fish and shellfish; surveys of fisheries resources; biology of rockfish and other marine fish. Home: 4811 Terrace Dr NE Seattle WA 98105-3923 Office: U Wash PO Box 357980 Seattle WA 98195-7980

GUNDERSON, GERALD AXEL, economics professor; b. Seattle, May 24, 1940; s. Marian A. and Ethel Ann (Hamon) G.; m. Margaret Jean Overway, Sept. 10, 1965; children: David Eric, Laura Lynn. BA in Econs., U. Wash., 1962, MA in Econs., 1965, PhD in Econs., 1967. Asst. prof. econs. U. Mass., Amherst, 1967-74; vis. assoc. prof. econs. Mt. Holyoke Coll., South Hadley, Mass., 1974-75; spl. lectr. econs. N.C. State U., Raleigh, 1975-78; prof. econs. Trinity Coll., Hartford, Conn., 1978-82, Shelby Cullom Davis prof. Am. bus. and econ. enterprise, 1982—, dir. S.C. Davis Endowment, 1982—. Bd. dirs. exec. com. Yankee Inst. for Pub. Policy Studies; acad. adv. com. Inst. on Research on Econs. of Taxation. Author: A New Economic History of America, 1976, The Wealth Creators: An Entrepenurial History of the United States, 1989; contbg. author: Explorations in Econs. History, 1973—, Jour. Econ. History, 1974, Social Sci. History, 1977, Wall Street Jour.; editor Jour. Pvt. Enterprise. Grantee Freedom Found. at Valley Forge, 1980 Mem. Assn. Pvt. Enterprise Edn. (pres. 1984-85), Econ. History Assn. Home: 6 Andrew Dr Weatogue CT 06089-9725 Office: Trinity Coll 300 Summit St Hartford CT 06106-3100 Office Phone: 860-297-2395. E-mail: gerald.gunderson@trincoll.edu.

GUNDERSON, ROBERT VERNON, JR., lawyer; b. Memphis, Dec. 4, 1951; s. Robert V. and Suzanne (McCarthy) G.; m. Anne Durkheimer, May 15, 1982; children: Katherine Paige, Robert Graham. BA with distinction, U. Kans., 1973; MBA, U. Pa., 1974; MA, Stanford U., 1976; JD, U. Chgo., 1979. Bar: Calif. 1979, U.S. Dist. Ct. (no. dist.) Calif. 1979. Assoc. Cooley, Godward, Castro, Huddleson & Tatum, San Francisco and Palo Alto, Calif., 1979-84, ptnr., 1984-88, Brobeck, Phleger & Harrison, Palo Alto, 1988-95, mem. exec. com., 1991-95, chmn. bus. and tech. practice, 1992-95; founder, ptnr. Gunderson Dettmer Stough Villeneuve Franklin & Hachigian, Menlo Park, Calif., 1995—. Panelist Venture Capital and Pub. Offering Negotiation, San Francisco and N.Y.C., 1981, 83, 85, 92, Practicing Law Inst., N.Y.C. and San Francisco, 1986; moderator, panelist Third Ann. Securities Law Inst., 1985; dir. Vitae Pharms., Ft. Washington, Pa., Theravance, Inc., South San Francisco, Inc.; sec. Dionex Corp., Sunnyvale, Calif., 1983-88, Southwall Techs., Inc., Palo Alto, 1985-88, Conductus, Inc., Sunnyvale, 1992-2001, Remedy Corp., Mountain View, Calif., 1995-97; vis. lectr. U. Santa Clara Law Sch., 1985, 89 Exec. editor U. Chgo. Law Rev., 1978-79; contbr. articles to profl. jours. Mem. ABA (bus. law sect., various coms.), State Bar Calif. (panelist continuing legal edn. 1984), San Francisco Bar Assn., Am. Fin. Assn., Wharton Club (San Francisco Bay area). Avocations: contemporary art, music, travel. Home: 243 Polhemus Ave Atherton CA 94027-5442 Office: Gunderson Dettmer Stough Villeneuve 155 Constitution Dr Menlo Park CA 94025-1106 Office Phone: 650-321-2400.

GUNDERSON, TED LEE, security consultant; b. Colorado Springs, Colo., Nov. 7, 1928; BBA, U. Nebr. Sales rep. George A. Hormel Co., Austin, Minn., 1950-51; spl. agt. in charge U.S. Dept. Justice FBI, Los Angeles, Dallas, Memphis, Phila., 1951-79; internat. security cons. Ted L. Gunderson & Assocs., Santa Monica, Calif., 1979—; chmn. bd. dirs. HEB Inc., pubs. of Am. Free Press, Washington. Cons. Calif. Narcotic Authority; lectr., cons. on terrorism, cults and related topics. Author: How to Locate Anyone Anywhere, 1989, Be Smart, Be Safe, 1994; appeared on numerous nat. and local TV and radio talk shows; prodr. TV documentary on Satanism. Named Outstanding Law Enforcement Am., AFL CIO Metal Trade Coun., 1977. Mem. Bel Air U.S. Navy League, Internat. Assn. Chiefs of Police, Internat. Footprinters Assn., Philanthropic Found. (Los Angeles chpt.), Royal Soc. Encouragement of Arts, Mfrs. and Commerce, Sigma Alpha Epsilon. Avocations: golf, racquetball.

GUNDY, ELIZABETH, writer; b. N.Y.C., Mar. 22, 1942; d. Morey and Eveyln (Blaustein) G.; William Kotzwinkle. BA, CUNY, 1964. Author: Naked in a Public Place, 1975, Bliss, 1977, Cat On A Leash, 1979, Love, Infidelity and Drinking To Forget, 1984, The Disappearance of Gregory Pluckrose, 1985, Rough Weather Ahead for Walter the Farting Dog, 2005

GUNEYI, UMIT AHMET, physician, consultant; b. Kirikkale, Turkey, Dec. 22, 1957; arrived in U.S., 1958; s. Selim S. and Muazzez A. Guneyi. BS in Molecular Biology, U. Hawaii, 1981; MD, U. Tech. Santiago, Santo Domingo, Dominican Republic, 1985; MS in Health Svcs. Adminstrn., U. St. Francis, 2003. Surgeon Washoe Med. Ctr., Reno, 1990—91; dep. coroner Washoe County Coroners Office, Reno, 1991; chief instr. med. terminology Truckee Meadows C.C., Reno, 1994—2000; ind. rschr. dept. biomed. engrng. U. Nev., Reno, 2000—04; lectr. Associated Counter-Threat Edn. Specialists, Reno, 2003—, con. bio-terrorism, 2003—. Adv. Helping Angels Home Healthcare Svcs., Sparks, Nev., 2002—03; founder, CEO Gulee Enterprises, Reno-Sparks, 1994—98; exec. v.p. med. svcs. Homeland Security Def. Coalition, Rochester, NY. Mem. Nev. Washoe County Citizen Homeland Security Coun., 2003—. Nev. Washoe County Cmty. Emergency Response Team, 2004—; lobbyist, co-dir. com. establish state P.A. program Carson City, Nev., 2002—; del. convs. Rep. Party, Nev., 1996, 2000, rep. presdl. task force Washington, 1996—, rep. nat. senatorial com., 1996—. Scholar, Pacific Health Rsch. Inst., 1978. Fellow: Am. Coll. Internat. Physicians; mem.: Am. Acad. Family Physicians, Am. Coll. Emergency Physicians. Republican. Avocations: astronomy, parapsychology, coin collecting/numismatics, stamp collecting/philately, antiques. Home: 3025 Socrates Dr Reno NV 89512 Office Phone: 775-813-6442.

GUNHUS, GAYLORD T., military career officer; b. Enderlin, N.D., May 22, 1940; m. Ann Broten; children: Kevin, Michael, Holly. BS, Seattle Pacific U., 1962; MDiv, Luth. Brethren Sem., 1967; ThM, Princeton Theol. Sem., 1976; grad., Armed Forces Staff Coll., 1980, Army War Coll., 1989. Ordained clergyman Luth. Ch., Ch. Luth. Brethren of Am. Synod, 1967. Army chaplain U.S. Army, 1967, advanced through grades to maj. gen., asst. brigade chaplain Arty. Officer Candidate Sch. Ft. Sill, Okla., 1967-68, bn.-chaplain 520th Transp. Bn. Phu Loi, Vietnam, 1968-69, asst. ctr. chaplain U.S. Army Pers. Ctr. Ft. Lewis, Wash., 1969-72, group chaplain 164th Aviation Group Can Tho, Vietnam, 1972-73, cmty. chaplain Stanley R. Mikkelson Safeguard Complex Nekoma, N.D., 1973-75, asst. cmty. chaplain Heidelberg, Germany, 1976-79, chief Concepts and Studies Divsn., chief Concepts Divsn. Ft. Benjamin Harrison, Ind., 1980-85, divsn. chaplain 9th Inf. Divsn. Ft. Lewis, Wash., 1985-87, I Corps and Installation chaplain, 1987-88, USAREUR chaplain, 1989-92, TRADOC chaplain Ft. Monroe, Va., 1992-94, dep. chief of chaplains Washington, 1994-99, chief of chaplains Arlington, Va., 1999—2003. Decorated Legion of Merit with oak leaf cluster, Bronze Star medal with oak leaf cluster, Meritorious Svc. medal with two oak leaf clusters, Air medal, Army Commendation medal with oak leaf cluster.

GUNN, ALAN, retired law educator; b. Syracuse, NY, Apr. 8, 1940; s. Albert Dale and Helen Sherwood (Whitnall) G.; m. Bertha Ann Buchwald, 1975; 1 child, William BS, Rensselaer Poly. Inst., 1961; JD, Cornell U., 1970. Bar: D.C. 1970. Assoc. Hogan & Hartson, Washington, 1970-72; asst. prof. law Washington U., St. Louis, 1972-75, assoc. prof., 1975-76; assoc. prof. law Cornell U., Ithaca, N.Y., 1977-79, prof., 1979-84, J. duPratt White prof., 1984-89; prof. law U. Notre Dame, Ind., 1989-96, John N. Matthews prof., 1996—2005, prof. emeritus, 2005—. Apptd. spl. advocate St. Joseph County Probate Ct., 2001—. Author: (with James R. Repetti) Partnership Income Taxation, 1991, 4th edit., 2005; (with Larry D. Ward) Cases, Text and Problems on Federal Income Taxation, 5th edit., 2002; (with Vincent R. Johnson) Studies in American Tort Law, 1994, 3rd edit., 2005. Methodist. Office: U Notre Dame Law Sch Notre Dame IN 46556

GUNN, ALBERT EDWARD, JR., internist, educator, health facility administrator, lawyer; b. Port Washington, N.Y., Oct. 31, 1933; s. Albert Edward and Esther Frances (Williams) G.; m. Joan Marie Jacoby, May 18, 1968; children: Albert Edward III, Emily Williams Gunn Hebert, Andrew Robert, Clare Margaret Gunn Berchelmann, Catherine Ann, Philip David. *Albert E. Gunn Sr. was born on September 16, 1891, in Port Washington, New York, and died there on October 14, 1952. His father, Edward Mott Gunn, was married to Sarah Olivia (Nelson) G. He was valedictorian at the Port Washington High School in 1910. He received an LL.B. from the Brooklyn Law School of St. Lawrence University in 1912, and was admitted to the New York Bar in 1914. He had a law practice in New York City until 1919, and then relocated to Port Washington with the firm Gunn and Gunn, and then Gunn, Neier and Gunn until 1952. He was the president of the Port Washington Chamber of Commerce in 1932. He was a Regimental Sergeant Major with the Judge Advocate Generals Department from 1918-19. He married Esther Frances (Williams) G., daughter of Edward Williams and Ellen (Bevan) W. on April 27, 1924. She was born on October 22, 1898 in New York, and died April 30, 1969 in Stuart Florida.* BS, Fordham Coll., 1955, LLB, 1958; MB BCh BAO, Nat. U. Ireland, Galway, 1967. Bar: NY 1958, U.S. Ct. Mil. Appeals 1959, DC 1972, U.S. Supreme Ct. 1972, U.S. Ct. Appeals (DC cir.) 1972; diplomate Am. Bd Internal Medicine, lic. physician Pa., NY, Fla., Va., Tex., Eng., Wales. Owner, agt. Albert E. Gunn Ins. Agy., Port Washington, 1953-65; intern Montefiore Hosp., N.Y.C., 1967-68; resident in medicine Roosevelt Hosp., N.Y.C., 1968-70; USPHS trainee in neurology U. Rochester, NY, 1970-72; asst. dir. govtl. rels. AMA, Washington, 1972-74; med. dir. Geriat. Svcs. Suffolk County, Hauppauge, NY, 1974-75, Rehab. Ctr., U. Tex./M.D. Anderson Cancer Ctr., 1975-88, chief rehab. sect., 1988-93, chief geriat. sect., 1993-2000, dep. chmn. dept. internal med. spltys., 1998-2000; prof. mgmt. and policy scis. U. Tex. Houston Sch. Pub. Health, 2001—. Asst. prof. medicine U. Tex. Med. Sch., Houston, 1976-80, assoc. prof., 1980-2000, prof., 2000—, also assoc. dean for admissions; med. dir. Region IV, Tex. Med. Found., 1986-93; del.-at-large White House conf. on Handicapped Individuals, 1977; pres. Mus. Med. Sci., 1990; cons. CDC, Legal Svcs. Corp., Nat. Libr. Medicine. Co-author: Rehabilitation of the Cancer Patient, 1976, AIDS in Africa, 1988; editor, contbg. author: Cancer Rehabilitation, 1984; mem. editl. bd. Cancer Bull., 1977-90, Gerontology and Geriatrics Edn., 1984-2003, Linacre Quar.; contbr. articles to profl. jours Pres. Cath. Evidence Guild, Fordham, N.Y., 1953-54; mem. nat. adv. health coun. HEW, 1974-75; mem. adv. com. Nat. Inst. Law Enforcement and Criminal Justice, Law Enforcement Assistance Adminstrn., U.S. Dept. Justice, 1974-76; mem. bd. regents Nat. Libr. Medicine, NIH, 1983-87, chmn., 1986-87, chmn. lit. selection tech. adv. com., 1988-91; bd. dirs. Right to Life Advs., 1977-78, Tex. Med. Ctr. Libr., 1990. With USAF SAC, 1958-61, capt. Res., 1961-75 Fellow ACP; mem. Tex. Med. Assn. (trustee ins. trust, chmn. bd. trustees 1997-2000), Harris County Med. Soc. (exec. bd. 1986-90, v.p. 1998), Royal Coll. Physicians London (licentiate), Royal Coll. Surgeons Eng., Houston Acad. Medicine (bd. dirs. 1986-90, pres. 1990), Houston Bar Assn., D.C. Bar, Cath. Med. Assn. (regional bd. dirs. 1992—, Thomas Linacre award 1997), NRA (life), Res. Officers Assn. (life), Sons of Union Vets. of Civil War, Am. Legion, KC, Army and Navy Club, Cosmos Club, Fellowship Cath. Scholars. Roman Catholic. Office: U Tex MD Anderson Cancer Ctr 1515 Holcombe Blvd Box 515 Houston TX 77030-4009 Home: 3514 Glen Haven Blvd Houston TX 77025-1306 Office Phone: 713-500-5118.

GUNN, CLARE ALWARD, travel consultant, writer, retired educator; b. Grandville, Mich., Oct. 28, 1916; s. Fred Melvin and Lila Barton (Alward) G.; married; children: Thomas, Bruce, Richard, William. BS, Mich. State U., 1940, MS in Land and Water Conservation, 1952; PhD in Landscape Architecture, U. Mich., 1965. Prof. dept. tourism-recreation devel. Mich. State U., East Lansing, 1945-66; vis. prof. tourism Sch. Travel Industry Mgmt. U. Hawaii, 1966-67; prof. tourism-recreation devel. Tex. A&M U., College Station, 1967-74, prof. dept. recreation, park and tourism scis., 1975-85, prof. emeritus, 1985—. Prof. resources recreation Oreg. State U., summer 1974; prof. Sch. Landscape Arthitecture, U. Guelph, Ont., Can., 1974-75; vis. prof. Clemson U., 1989; cons. state tourism plans N.Y., 1986, Okla., 1987, Wash., 1988, Del., 1990, Ill., 1993; cons. analysis tourism potential Whiteman Park, Perth, Australia, 1989; cons. South African Tourism Bd., 1988, natural resource potential for Tourism in Del., 1991; mem. task force Moorea & Tourism, French Polynesia, 1990, tourism potential Finger Lakes Region, N.Y., 1989-91, resort devel. plan Chun-Cheon Lake Area, Korea, 1991; tourism plan Newfoundland, Labrador, Can., 1994; prepared Agenda Item 13 World Tourism Conf., The Philippines, 1980, major destination zone study for Can., 1982. Author: A Concept for the Design of a Tourism-Recreation Region, 1965, An Annotated Bibliography of Resource Use of the Texas Gulf Coast, 1969, Vacationscape: Designing Tourist Regions, 3d edit., 1997, Chinese edit., 1998, Tourism Planning, 3d edit., 1994, 4th edit., 2002, Western Tourism: Can Paradise Be Reclaimed, 2004, others; contbr. articles to profl. jours. Mem. George Bush Libr. Com., College Station, 1994; chair adv. com. CVB of Bryan, College Station, 1992-93; mem. sch. bd. Okemos (Mich.) Dist., 1958-64. Recipient Tex. Gov. award, 1984, Disting. Alumni award Landscape Architecture Program, Mich. State U., 1999; named mem. emeritus Internat. Acad. for Study of Tourism, 2001. Fellow Am. Soc. Landscape Architects (Spl. award 1973); mem. Travel and Tourism Rsch. Assn. (bd. dirs., Lifetime Achievement award 2001), Rotary Internat. (chmn. dist. group study exch. com. 1992-93, chair dist. exch. com. 1992-94, Role of Fame award 1990), Gamma Sigma Delta, Epsilon Sigma Phi, Beta Gamma Sigma, Phi Kappa Phi, Sigma Lambda Alpha (Disting. Mem. award 1991). Republican. Methodist. Avocations: photography, travel, sketching. Home: 1602 Glade St College Station TX 77840-4365

GUNN, GILES BUCKINGHAM, language educator, religious studies educator, global and international studies educator; b. Evanston, Ill., Jan. 9, 1938; s. Buckingham Willcox and Janet (Fargo) G.; m. Janet Mears Varner, Dec. 29, 1969 (div. July 1983); 1 child, Adam Buckingham; m. Deborah Rose Sills, July 9, 1983; 1 child, Abigail Rose. BA, Amherst Coll., 1959; student, Episc. Theol. Sch., Cambridge, Mass., 1959-60; MA, U. Chgo., 1963, PhD, 1967. Prof. religion and lit. U. Chgo., 1966-74; prof. religion and Am. studies U. N.C., Chapel Hill, 1974-85; prof. English and Religion U. Fla., 1984-85; prof. English U. Calif., Santa Barbara, 1985—, chmn. English dept., 1993-97, prof. global and internat. studies, 1998—, chmn. global studies, 2001—. Vis. asst. prof. religion Stanford U., Palo Alto, Calif., 1973; Benedict Disting. vis. prof. religion Carleton Coll., Northfield, Minn., 1977; William R. Kenan Disting. vis. prof. humanities Coll. William and Mary, Williamsburg, Va., 1983-84; Humanities Disting. vis. prof. U. Colo., 1989; Eric Yoegelin Disting. prof. Am. Studies, U. Munich, 1994-95; dir. NEH summer sems. for coll. and univ. tchrs., 1979, 81, 85, 94, for sch. tchrs., 1987, 88, 89, 91; cons. Libr. of Am. Author: F.O. Matthiessen, The Critical Achievement, 1975, The Interpretation of Otherness: Literature, Religion and the American Imagination, 1979, The Culture of Criticism and The Criticism of Culture, 1987, Thinking Across the American Grain: Ideology, Intellect, and the New Pragmatism, 1992, Beyond Solidarity: Pragmatism and Difference in a Globalised World, 2001; editor: Literature and Religion, 1971, Henry James, Senior: A Selection of His Writings, 1974, New World Metaphysics: Readings on the Religious Meaning of the American Experience, 1981, The Bible and American Arts and Letters, 1983, Church, State, and American Culture, 1984, Early American Writing, 1994, William James, Pragmatism and Other Writings, 2000, A Historical Guide to Herman Melville, 2005; co-editor: Redrawing the Boundaries: The Transformation of English and American Literary Studies, 1992; contbr. numerous articles to profl. jours. Bd. dirs. Fund for Santa Barbara. Edward John Noble Leadership grantee, 1959-63; Amherst-Doshisha fellow, Kyoto, Japan, 1960-61, Kent fellow, Danforth Found., 1963-65, Guggenheim fellow, 1978-79, Nat. Endowment for Humanities fellow, 1990, U. Calif. Pres.'s Rsch. fellow, 1990; Phi Beta Kappa vis. scholar, 2000-01. Mem. MLA, Am. Acad. Religion (dir. research and pubs. 1974-77), Am. Studies Assn., Soc. Religion, Arts and Contemporary Culture, Soc. Am. Phil., Nat. Critics Book Circle. Democrat. Avocations: walking, motorcycling, travel. Office: U Calif Dept English Santa Barbara CA 93106 Home: 5488 Rincon Beach Park Dr Ventura CA 93001-9749

GUNN, JAMES E., language educator; b. Kansas City, Mo., July 12, 1923; s. J. Wayne and Elsie M. (Hutchison) G.; m. Jane Frances Anderson, Feb. 6, 1947; children: Christopher Wayne, Kevin Robert. BS, U. Kans., 1947, MA, 1951. Editor Western Printing and Litho, Racine, Wis., 1951-52; asst. dir. Civil Def., Kansas City, Mo., 1953; instr. U. Kans., Lawrence, 1955, mng. editor Alumni Assn., 1956-58, adminstrv. asst. to the chancellor for univ. rels., 1958-70, lectr. English, 1970-74, prof., 1974-93, emeritus prof., 1993—. Cons. Easton Press, Norwalk, Conn., 1985-98; lectr. in field. Author: over 25 books including Station in Space, 1958, The Immortals, 1962, The End of Dreams, 1975, Alternate Worlds: The Illustrated History of Science Fiction (World Sci. Fiction Conv. Spl. award, 1976, Pilgrim award Sci. Fiction Rsch. Assn., 1976), The Listeners, 1972, The Dreamers, 1980, Isaac Asimov: The Foundations of Science Fiction, 1982 (Hugo award World Sci. Fiction Conv., 1983), The Science of Science-Fiction Writing, 2000, The Millennium Blues, 2001, Human Voices, 2002, Speculations on Speculation: Theories of Science Fiction, 2004, numerous plays, screenplays, radio scripts; editor: The Road to Science Fictions, 6 vols., 1977—2002; editor: (with Matthew Candelarie) Speculations on Speculations: Theories of Science Fiction, 2004; editor: 8 other books; contbr. 100 stories to mags.; contbr. articles. Dir. Ctr. for Study Sci. Fiction, Lawrence, 1984—. Lt. (j.g.) USN, 1943-46, PTO. Recipient Eaton award Eaton Conf., 1992, Hugo award, 1983; Mellon fellow U. Kans., 1981, 84. Mem. Author's Guild, Sci. Fiction and Fantasy Writers Am. (pres. 1971-72), Sci. Fiction Rsch. Assn. (pres. 1981-82, Pilgrim award 1976)., Avocations: golf, bridge. Home: 2215 Orchard Ln Lawrence KS 66049-2707 Office: U Kans English Dept Lawrence KS 66045-0001 Office Phone: 785-864-3380. Business E-Mail: jgunn@ku.edu.

GUNN, JOAN MARIE, health facility administrator; b. Binghamton, N.Y., Jan. 29, 1943; d. Andrew and Ruth Antoinette (Butler) Jacoby; m. Albert E. Gunn, Jr., May 18, 1968; children: Albert E. III, Emily Williams Gunn Hebert, Andrew R., Clare M. Berchelmann, Catherine A.B., Philip D. Diploma, Binghamton State Hosp., 1966; BS summa cum laude, Tex. Women's U., 1983; MSN, U. Tex., Houston, 1989. RN, N.Y., Tex., Va., Gt. Britain. Staff nurse Columbia/Presbyn. Med. Ctr., N.Y.C., 1966-67; head nurse, ICU Montefiore Hosp. and Med. Ctr., N.Y.C., 1967-68; staff nurse Nat. Orthopedic and Rehab. Hosp., Arlington, Va., 1972-73, Woman's Hosp. of Tex., Houston, 1976-80; staff nurse geriatrics St. Anthony's Ctr., Houston, 1985-86; charge nurse gero psychiatry Bellaire Gen. Hosp., Houston, 1986; from head nurse gero psychiat. unit to dir. patient svcs. Harris County Psychiat. Ctr. U. Tex., Houston, 1986—2001, dir. patient svcs. Harris County Psychiat. Ctr., 2001—. Mem. NRA, Nat. Soc. Colonial Dames of the XVII Century, Daus. of Union Vets. of Civil War, Sigma Theta Tau. Roman Catholic. Avocation: reading history. Home: 3514 Glen Haven Blvd Houston TX 77025-1306 Office: U Tex Harris County Psychiat Ctr 2800 S Macgregor Way Houston TX 77021-1032

GUNN, JOSEPH RIDGEWAY, III, consulting economist; b. Ross, Calif., Nov. 28, 1928; s. Joseph Ridgeway, Jr. and Melvine Henrietta (Longley) G.; BS in Bus. Adminstrn., U. Calif., Berkeley, 1954, MA in Econs., 1958; spl. studies Oxford (Eng.) U., 1967; m. Marie Elsie Thurlow, June 16, 1951; children: Dana Carolyn Gunn Winslow, Anita Jayne Gunn Shirley, Janice Marie Gunn Smeallie. Econ. analyst Standard Oil Co., Calif., 1954-61; econ. adv. Ministry Commerce, Govt. Afghanistan, Kabul, sponsored by The Asia Found., 1961-67; cons. economist, 1967—95; econ. adv. Ministry of Commerce Govt. Thailand, 1974-76; bd. dirs. Nathan Assocs., Inc., Arlington, Va., 1986—, chmn. bd. dirs. 2001—. Mem. Am. Econ. Assn., Asia Soc., Cosmos Club (v.p., 2004-2005, pres. 2005—). Democrat. Episcopalian. Contrb. articles and reports to profl. jours. Home: 10917 Picasso Ln Potomac MD 20854-1711 Office: Nathan Assocs Inc 2101 Wilson Blvd Arlington VA 22201-3062

GUNN, KRISTEN JOY, music educator, composer; b. Canton, Ohio, Oct. 8, 1971; d. James Milton and Linda Lee (Overcasher) Smith; m. David William Gunn, Dec. 26, 1996. BM, So. Meth. U., 1994; MM, Northwestern U., 1996. Cert. tchr., Tex.; cert. Kindermusik. Piano instr. Keyboard Connection, Dallas, 1991-94; piano, class instr. Master's Touch Sch. Music and Performing Arts, Grapevine, Tex., 1994-95; music educator South Seneca Elem. Sch., Interlaken, N.Y., 1997, Palm Beach Gardens Elem., Jupiter, Fla., 1998—. Instr. Kindermusik, Evanston, Ill., 1996. Composer Winter Wind, Being Apart of You, Letting Go, You are My Strength, No One Makes it Alone. Scholar Women's League, 1990-93, full-artistic scholar So. Meth. U., 1990-94, artistic scholar Northwestern U., 1995-96. Mem. Music Tchrs. Nat. Assn., Pi Kappa Lambda. Avocations: reading, water sports, aerobics, travel, writing.

GUNN, MOREY WALKER, JR., secondary music educator, choir director, organist; b. Orangeburg, S.C., June 23, 1939; s. Morey Walker Sr. and Marjorie (Dusek) G.; m. Sheila Dianne Taylor, Nov. 26, 1994; 1 child, Andrew Walker. BA in Music, Furman U., 1961, MA, 1967. Cert. specialist music edn. tchr., S.C. Band dir. Holly Hill (S.C.) H.S., 1961-65, Orangeburg H.S., 1965-71, Greer (S.C.) H.S., 1971-73, Ft. Johnson H.S., Charleston, SC, 1973-77, Berkeley County Schs., Goose Creek, SC, 1978-92; organist St. Andrews United Meth. Ch., 1992—. Mem. Nat. Rep. Senatorial Com. 1978-97; deacon 1st Presbyn, Ch., 1965-71; elder James Island Presbyn. Ch., 1974-76, 78-80, choir dir., organist, 1965-94; ch. musician St. Andrews United Meth. Ch., Orangburg, 1994—; bd. dir. excellence in tchg. award com. Charleston County Youth Symphony, 1975; bd. dir. Charles Towne Landing Band Festival Com., 1988-89; class agt. Furman U., 2003-2004; mem. bd. visitors Meth. Oaks, 2004-. Mem. Am. Guild Organists, Sertoma Club (bd. dir. 1989-90), Kiwanis Club (bd. dir. 1997-2001, sec. 1998-99, pres. 1999-2000, Disting. sec. 1998-99, Disting. pres. 1999-2000, Disting. Kiwanian award 1998-2000), Hibernian Soc., Elks, Orangeburg Music Club, Phi Mu Alpha (hon. life). Avocations: dance, reading, dining out, travel. Home: 2 Waters Edge Ct Charleston SC 29414-7327

GUNNELS, LEE O., retired finance educator, retired management educator, manufacturing and research company director; b. Huntington Park, Calif., Sept. 11, 1933; s. LeRoy O. and Marrion W. Gunnels; m. Laura Gunnels, Nov. 7, 1958; children: Cornelia, Amelia, Sarah. BA in Math./Physics, U. Hawaii, 1960; MBA, Xavier U., Cin., 1970, PhD in Edn., 1983. Nuc. physicist Battelle Meml. Inst., Columbus, Ohio; ret. assoc. prof. fin. and mgmt. Zane State Coll., Zanesville, Ohio, past chmn. faculty senate; inventor, developer Gunnels Rsch. LLC. Contbr. articles to various publs. Home: 1849 Drugan Ct SW Reynoldsburg OH 43068-8181 also: Stoney Meadow Farms Adamsville OH 43802

GUNNER, MURRAY, religious organization administrator; b. NYC, Mar. 26, 1918; s. Abraham and Sadie (Schnee) G.; m. Pearl O. Katz, June 12, 1949; children: Marilyn Ruth, Janet Marie. BS, CCNY, 1938; MSW, Columbia U., 1946; cert., Hebrew U., 1971. Cert. social worker. Social worker, acting supr. N.Y.C. Dept. Welfare and Camp LaGuardia, 1940-45; adminstrv. asst. Coun. House, St. Louis, 1946-50; program dir. Jewish Community Ctr., Hartford, Conn., 1950-54, exec. dir. Newburgh, N.Y., 1954-62, Bklyn., 1962-66, Yonkers, N.Y., 1966-83; cons. Jewish Community Ctr., Jewish Fedn., 1983-89; exec. dir. Jewish Coun. of Yonkers, 1989—. Cons. Hudson River Mus., Elizabeth Seton Coll., 1989-89; co-chmn. commn. of synagogue rels. United Jewish Appeal Fedn., N.Y.C., 1980-81, co-chmn. Jewish Community Ctrs., 1981-82; co-chair adult edn. com. Greystone Jewish Ctr., Yonkers, 1980-82, bd. dirs., 1978-80. Contbr. author to various books. Active Charter Revision Commn., Yonkers, 1979, Mayor's Holocaust Commn. Yonkers, 1979, Mayor's Com. on Jewish Affairs, Yonkers, 1990—, Yonkers Crime Commn., 1975, Yonkers Mental Health Coun., 1978—83, Mayor's Cmty. Rels. Com., Yonkers, 1992—, task force City/County Youth Violence; exec. com. Edn. 2000, Yonkers, 1992; cmty. planning coun. Substance Abuse Prevention Com., 1997—; shared decision making commn. Gorton H.S., 1997; exec. com. Yonkers Mayor's Cmty. Rels. Commn., 1997; edn. com. Yonkers City Coun., 1998—; chair Yonkers Flag Day Commn., 1998; mem. Yonkers Family and Cmty. project Columbia U., 1998, N.Y. State Assemblyman Adv. Com., 1997; active Yonker Mayor's Health Commn., 1998—2002; older adults com. Yonkers Mayor Health Commn., 1999; active Older Adult Task Force, Substance Abuse Task Force; apptd. mem. partnership com. Yonkers Bd. Edn., 1999; apptd. bd. dirs. Yonkers Libr. Found., 2001; apptd. by Benedict Found. Elder-Friendly Com., City of Yonkers, 2001; apptd. sec. adv. com. Westchester Jewish Chronicle; apptd. Yonkers Libr. Found. Commn., 2001; adv. com. to senator N.Y. State Senate, 1997—; active Mentoring Com. for Youth at Risk, 1993, Mayor's Commn. on AIDS, 1997—; bd. dirs. Greystone Jewish Ctr., 2000—, Yonkers United Way, 1981—83, Cmty. Planning Agy., Yonkers, 1992—. Recipient Israel Cummings award Commn. on Synagogue Rels. Fedn., 1963, cert. of merit, 1992, Am. Com. on Italian Migration, 1992, cert. of recognition for outstanding svc. and contbns. Charles Gorton H.S., Yonkers, 1995, Yonkers Martin Luther King Commn. award, 1995, Cmty. Svc. award Mayor of City of Yonkers, 1995, Multi-Cultural Edn. award Yonkers Pub. Schs., 1998, honors for outstanding leadership Westchester County Exec. Dirs., 2001, Outstanding Leadership award S.W. Yonkers Planning Assn., 2001, Outstanding Profl. award Westchester County Execs. of U.S.A. Fedn., Humanitarian award, C. of C., 2002, Griffon award Untrmeyer Performing Arts Coun., 2002; honored for cmty. svc. Jewish Coun. Yonkers Bd. Dirs., City of Yonkers, County of Westchester, U.S. Congress, Rockland County YM-YWHA, 1998; Murray Gunner Day named in his honor City of Yonkers, 1983, County of Westchester, 1983; named guest of honor Westchester chpt. Am. Heart Assn., 1997., award Cmty. Svc. Rconstructionist Synagogue of scarsdale, N.Y., 2004, Cmty. Svc. award, Jewish Cmty Ctr.on the Hudson, 2004. Mem.: NASW (Gold Care mem., Disting. Svc. award Westchester chpt. 2001, Lifetime Achievement award N.Y. State chpt. 2001), Rotary (chair pub. rels. com. 1988, chair cmty. svcs., bd. dirs. 1993—94, Paul Harris fellow 1994, honored for 34 yrs. of service 2005). Home: 10 Gateway Rd Yonkers NY 10703-1200 Office: Jewish Coun of Yonkers 584 N Broadway Yonkers NY 10701-1731 Office Phone: 914-423-3399. *The struggle for survival we face each day, can be exhillerating or threatening. The manner, in which we handle each challenge, is dependent on the degree of our faith in God, coupled with the strength of belief in ourselves.*

GUNNING, CAROLYN SUE, dean, provost, nursing educator; b. Ft. Smith, Ark., Dec. 16, 1943; d. Laurence George and Flora Irene (Garner) G. BS, Tex. Woman's U., 1965; MS, U. Colo., 1973; PhD, U. Tex., Austin, 1981. RN, Tex. Clinician III Bexar County Hosp., San Antonio, 1968-71; instr. U. Tex. Sch. Nursing, San Antonio, 1973-74, asst. prof., 1974-83, asst. to dean, 1977-79, assoc. prof., asst. dean undergrad. programs, 1983-84, assoc. dean, 1984-88; dean Sch. Nursing Marshall U., Huntington, W.Va., 1988-90; dean Coll. Nursing Tex. Woman's U., Denton, 1991—2003, intern provost, v.p. academic affairs, 2003—04, assoc. v.p. spl. projects, 2004—. Accreditation site visitor Commn. on Collegiate Nursing Edn. Contbr. articles to profl. jours. Active Leadership San Antonio, 1978-79, Leadership Tex., 1992. Served to capt. Nurse Corps, U.S. Army, 1965-68; to lt. col. Army N.G., 1980-88. Decorated Army Commendation medal. Mem. ANA, Sigma Theta Tau, Kappa Delta Pi, Phi Kappa Phi. Office Phone: 940-898-2422.

GUNNING, FRANCIS PATRICK, lawyer, insurance company executive; b. Scranton, Pa., Dec. 10, 1923; s. Frank Peter and Mary Loretta (Kelly) G.; m. Nancy C. Hill, Aug. 10, 1951; 1 son, Brian F. Student, City Coll. N.Y., 1941-43; LLB, St. John's U., 1950. Bar: N.Y. 1950. Legal editor Prentice Hall Pub. Co., N.Y.C., 1950-51; legal specialist Tchrs. Ins. & Annuity Assn. Am.-Coll. Retirement Equities Fund, N.Y.C., 1951-53, asst. counsel, 1953-57, assoc. counsel, 1957-60, counsel, 1960-65, asst. gen. counsel, 1965-67, assoc. gen. counsel, 1967, v.p., assoc. gen. counsel, 1967-73, sr. v.p., gen. counsel, 1973-74, exec. v.p., gen. counsel, 1974-88, ret., 1988. Trustee, mem. exec. and audit coms. Mortgage Growth Investors (now MGI Properties). Contbr. articles on mortgage financing to profl. jours. With USAAF, 1943-46. Mem. ABA, N.Y. State Bar Assn., Am. Land Title Assn., Am. Law Inst., Assn. of Bar of City of N.Y., Assn. Life Ins. Counsel, Nat. Assn. Coll. Univ. Attys., Am. Coll. Real Estate Lawyers. Republican. Roman Catholic. Home and Office: 32 Kewanee Rd New Rochelle NY 10804-1324 Office Phone: 914-235-1846.

GUNNING, PATRICIA ANN, music educator; b. Spokane, Wash., Feb. 12, 1948; d. Harry S. Sullivan and Angela Marie Baker; m. Gary Ralph Gunning, June 6, 1970; children: Teya Dyan, Janelle Lynn. BA in Music Edn., U. Portland, Oreg., 1970. Elem. music tchr. Glendale Elem. Sch., Ariz., 1972—79, Spokane Sch. Dist., Wash., 1980—85, mid. sch. music tchr., 1985—; dir., founder Spokane Area Children's Chorus, Wash., 1985—92. Recipient Hidden Hero award, Spokane Rotary, 2002. Mem.: Music Educators Nat. Conf., Am. Choral Dirs. Assn. Republican. Avocations: camping, travel. Home: 1904 W Pinto Colbert WA 99005 Office: Garry Mid Sch 725 E Joseph Spokane WA 99208 Office Phone: 509-354-5112. Business E-Mail: patriciag@spokaneschools.org.

GUNNING, ROBERT CLIFFORD, mathematician, educator; b. Longmont, Colo., Nov. 27, 1931; s. Clifford Henry and Inez (Wilhelm) G.; m. Wanda S. Holtzinger, July 9, 1966. AB, U. Colo., 1952; MA, Princeton U., 1953, PhD, 1955. NSF fellow U. Chgo., 1955-56; mem. faculty Princeton U., 1956—, prof. math., 1966—, chmn. dept., 1976-79, dean of faculty, 1989-95. Vis. prof. U. São Paulo, Brazil, 1957, U. Munich, 1967, ULCA, 1972, Oxford (Eng.) U., spring 1968, fall, 1980, 88, 95; Sloan fellow, 1958-61; asst. dir. studies, math. St. Catharines Coll., Cambridge (Eng.) U., 1959-60; mem. editl. bd. Princeton (N.J.) U. Press, 1969-73. Author: Lectures on Modular Forms, 1962, (with H. Rossi) Analytic Functions of Several Complex Variables, 1965, Lectures on Riemann Surfaces, Vol. I, 1966, Vol. II, 1967, Vol. III, 1972, Complex Analytic Varieties, Vol. I, 1970, Vol. II, 1974, Generalized Theta Functions, 1976, Uniformization of Complex Manifolds, 1978, Introduction to Holomorphic Functions of Several Variables, 3 vols., 1990; editor: Problems in Analysis, 1970, Theta Functions, 1989, Collected Papers of Salomon Bochner, 4 vols., 1991; contbr. articles to profl. jours. Recipient Pres. Award Disting. Tchg., 2003. Fellow AAAS; mem. Am. Math. Soc., Princeton Club (N.Y.C.), Nassau Club (Princeton), Phi Beta Kappa, Sigma Xi. Episcopalian. Office: Fine Hall Washington Rd Princeton NJ 08544-1000

GUNNING, TIMOTHY MICHAEL, lawyer; b. Subic Bay, The Philippines, Aug. 2, 1964; s. Jean-Jacques and Irene Marie Gunning. BA in English, Boston Coll., 1986; JD, U. Md., Balt., 1990. Bar: Md. 1990, U.S. Dist. Ct. Md. 1990. Law clk. to Hon. James B. Dudley Cir. Ct. Howard County, Md., 1990—91; asst. state atty. Baltimore County, Towson, Md., 1991—96; assoc. Howell, Gately, Whitney & Carter LLP, Towson, 1996—97; pvt. practice Towson, 1997—. Mem.: Fed. Bar Assn., Md. State Bar Assn., Md. Criminal Def. Attys. Assn., Nat. Assn. Criminal Def. Attys. Avocations: fly fishing, hunting, skiing, exercise. Office: 305 Washington Ave Ste 301 Towson MD 21204 Business E-Mail: tgunning@radicus.net.

GUNNING, TOM, art educator; PhD in Cinema Studies, NYU. Prof. dept. art history U. Chgo. Author: D.W. Griffith and the Origins of American Narrative Film: The Early Years, 1991, The Films of Fritz Lang...Allegories of Vision and Modernity; contbr. articles to profl. jours. Guggenheim fellow, 1998. Office: Dept Art History U Chgo 5540 S Greenwood Ave Chicago IL 60637-1506 E-mail: tgunning@midway.uchicago.edu.

GUNNSTAKS, C. LUKE, lawyer; b. N.J. m. Maria Gunnstaks. JD, So. Meth. U., 1990. Bar: Tex. 1991, U.S. Dist. Ct. (ea. dist.) Tex. 1992. Musician, 1970-80, Vince Vance and the Valiants, Dallas, 1980-86, Sgt. Fury and the Valiant Allstars, Dallas, 1986-88; supr. ITI, Inc., Dallas, 1988-91; atty. Gunnstaks Law Office, Dallas, 1991—. Copyright holder. Mem. ABA, Am. Trial Lawyers Assn., Dallas Bar Assn., State Bar of Tex. Avocation: music. Office: Gunnstaks Law Office 15150 Preston Rd Ste 300 Dallas TX 75248-4871

GUNSEL, SELDA, chemical engineer, researcher; b. Istanbul, Turkey, Nov. 10, 1958; d. Nejat and Hikmet (Suntekin) G.; m. Donald Lee Pferdehirt, June 6, 1987; children: Melisa, Lara. BSc in Chem. Engring., Istanbul Tech. U., 1981; MSc in Chem. Engring., Pa. State U., 1983, PhD in Chem. Engring., 1986. Advanced rsch. engr. Pennzoil Prods. Co., The Woodlands, Tex., 1986-90, sr. rsch. engr., 1990-94, rsch. assoc., 1994-97, sr. rsch. assoc., 1997-98, dir. tech. devel., 1999-2000, v.p. tech. devel., 2000—02; bus. team mgr. automotive lubricants Shell Global Solutions (U.S.) Inc., Houston, 2002—. Editor: Current Research in Tribology in North Am., 1993; mem. editl. rev. bd. CRC Handbook Lubrication and Tribology, Vol. III; mem. editl. bd., Jour. of Lubrication Sci.; Assoc. editor, Lubrication Engrg. Jour., contbr. articles to profl. jours. Fellow Soc. Tribologists Lubncation Engr. (exec. com. 2000-); mem. Am. Chem. Soc., Am. Soc. Heating, Refrigeration, Air Conditioning Engrs., Soc. Automotive Engrs. (Excellence in Oral Presentation 1996, chmn. lubricant rsch. award bd. 1997-99), Soc. Tribologists and Lubrication Engrs. (Captain Alfred E. Hunt award 1998, bd. dirs. 1996—, instr. edn. courses 1990, 97, 99), Sigma Xi, Phi Lambda Upsilon. Achievements include patents for non-aqueous lamellar liquid crystalline lubricants, liquid crystal-surfactant technology; contributions in the field of lubrication science and tribology; leadership in the advancement of knowledge and application of science and lubrication and tribology; research in areas of thermal/oxidative stability of lubricants, friction/wear mechanisms in boundary and elastohydrodynamic lubrication, vapor-phase lubricants, liquid crystal lubricants, refrigeration lubricants. Office: Shell Global Solutions (US) Inc Westhollow Tech Ctr 3333 Hwy 6 S Houston TX 77082

GUNSELMAN, KENNETH DAVID, library director; b. Albemarle, N.C., Jan. 17, 1956; s. Charline Foreman and Wm. Douglass Gunselman; m. Cynthia Louise Spragg, June 16, 1979; children: Douglass Thomas, Amber Joy. BA, Oral Roberts U., 1976; M in Libr. Sci., U. North Tex., 1991; MEd in Instrnl. Sys Tech., Ind. U., 1978. H.s. libr. Chandler (Okla) Pub. Sch., 1980—85; reference libr. Faulkner U., Montgomery, 1985—86; media services libr. Abilene (Tex.) Christian U., 1986—92; instrnl. media dir. Northwestern Okla. State U., Alva, 1992—97, govt. docs. libr., 1997—2000; tchr., libr. Aline-Cleo Pub. Sch., Okla., 2000—01; libr. dir. York (Nebr.) Coll., 2001—. Deacon Coll. Hill. Ch. of Christ, Alva, Okla., 2001, East Hill Ch. of Christ, York, 2002—. Mem.: Assn. Christian Librarians, Christian Coll. Librarians Inc. (restoration serials index, indexer for the christian chronicle 0186), Nebr. Libr. Assn. R-Conservative. Mem. Church Of Christ. Office: York Coll Levitt Libr 1125 E 8th St York NE 68467 Office Phone: 402-363-5704. Office Fax: 402-363-5685. Personal E-mail: kgunselman@york.edu.

GUNSON, DOUGLAS R., lawyer; Former assoc. Moore & Van Allen, NC, 1989—90, Parker Poe Adams & Bernstein, NC, 1990—94; corp. counsel SGL Carbon Corp., NC, 1994—2000; gen. counsel Nucor Corp., Charlotte, NC, 2005—. Office: Nucor Corp 2100 Rexford Rd Charlotte NC 28211 Office Phone: 704-972-1832. Business E-Mail: dgunson@nucor.com.

GUNTER, BLANCHE HARRIS, librarian, archivist; b. Pensacola, Fla., Feb. 12, 1953; d. William Elmer Harris and Jessie Ruth Jarrell; m. Sanford Earl Gunter, Mar. 10, 1979; children: Nathanael Harris, Abigail Whitney. BSc in Edn., U. Ala., 1995, M in Libr. Sci., 1978. Reference libr. U. Ala., Tuscaloosa, 1982—83; libr. Antique Monthly Mag., Tuscaloosa, 1983—85, West End Christian Sch., Tuscaloosa, 1988—89, Martin Luther King, Jr. Elem. Sch., Tuscaloosa, 1989—90, Westwood Elem., Northport, 1990—91, Tuscaloosa Acad., 1991—; archivist Kettering Found., Dayton, Ohio, 2004—. Cons. Kettering Found., Dayton, Ohio, 2003. Sustainer Jr. League Tuscaloosa, 1986—; mem. Tuscaloosa Children's Theatre Guild, Tuscaloosa Symphony Guild; patron Westervelt Warner Mus. Art. Mem.: Am. Assn. Sch. Librs., Am. Libr. Assn., Ala. Libr. Assn. Avocations: yoga, reading, walking. Office: Tuscaloosa Acad Libr 420 Rice Valley Rd N Tuscaloosa AL 35406

GUNTER, BRADLEY HUNT, capital management executive; b. Norfolk, Va., Dec. 8, 1940; s. J.A. and Virginia (Whalen) G.; m. Susan Mason Hart, Dec. 27, 1962 (div. 1977); children: Bradley Hunt, Valerie Mason; m. Anne Macon, Nov. 7, 1985 (dec. 1994); 1 child, Bradford Macon Gunter; m. Meredith Laura Strohm, Dec. 16, 1994. BA, U. Richmond, 1962; MA, U. Va., 1963, PhD, 1969. Instr. Washington and Lee U., Lexington, Va., 1967-69; asst. prof. Boston Coll., 1969-71; editor Econ. Rev. Fed. Res. Bank, Richmond, Va., 1971—80, corp. sec., 1973—80; pres. Bartleby's Inc., Richmond, 1980-85; dir. found. rels. U. Va., Charlottesville, 1985-86; investment broker Scott and String fellow, Richmond, 1987-89; mng. dir. Scott & Stringfellow Capital Mgmt., Richmond, 1989-97, pres., CEO, 1997—2000; pres. Investment Mgmt. of Va., LLC, Richmond, Charolesttesville, 2000—05. Cons. NEH, Washington, 1975-80. Author: Studies in The Waste Land, 1971, Guide to T.S. Eliot, 1970, Checklist of T.S. Eliot, 1969; contbr. articles to profl. jours. Chmn. fund drive United Way, Richmond, 1980; mem. arts and scis. alumni coun. U. Va., mem. Emeritus Soc., Coll. Found.; pres., bd. dirs. New Va. Rev.; pres. Arts Coun. Richmond; chmn. Hist. Richmond Found.; bd. dirs. Poe Found., Va. Ctr. for the Book; bd. dirs., chmn. U. Va. Cancer Ctr., U. Va. Health Scis. Coun., U. Va. Libr. Bd.; mem. regional bd. Sorensen Inst. for Polit. Leadership; mem. U. Va. Ann. Giving Adv. Bd.; vestryman St. Paul's Ch., Richmond, 1975—78; bd. dirs. St. Christopher's Sch. Found., Richmond, 1981—85, Richmond Ballet, Big Bros. Richmond Inc., Va. Found. for Humanities and Pub. Policy, Scott and Stringfelow Ednl. Found., Elk Hill Farm; trustee St. Paul's Endowment Fund, Inc., United Way Greater Richmond. Mem. Richmond Assn. Bus. Economists, Assn. for Investment Mgmt. and Rsch., U. Va. Alumni Assn. (chpt. pres. Richmond 1981), Va. Soc. Mayflower Descs. (bd. dirs.), Country Club Va., Colonnade Club, Focus Club, Univ. Club NY, Farmington Country Club, Phi Beta Kappa, Omicron Delta Kappa. Episcopalian. Avocation: walking. Office: Investment Mgmt of Va 310 4th St NE Charlottesville VA 22902-5266 Office Phone: 434-220-0356. Personal E-mail: bradhg@adelphia.net. E-mail: bgunter@imva.net.

GUNTER, JAMES HOUSTON, JR., state supreme court justice; b. Atlanta, Tex., Mar. 8, 1943; s. James Houston and Helen Marie (Long) G.; m. Ruth Elma Miller, Jan. 23, 1965 (divl Jan. 1992); children: Christie Gunter Adams, Craig; m. Judee Thompson, May 30, 1992. BBA, Tex. A&M U., 1965; JD, U. Houston, 1972. Bar: Tex. 1972, Ark. 1973, U.S. Dist. Ct. (we. dist.) Ark., U.S. Dist. Ct. (ea. dist.) Tex., U.S. Supreme Ct. Assoc. John Wilson Law Firm, Hope, Ark., 1973-74; ptnr. Wilson & Gunter, Hope, 1974-75, Wilson, Gunter & Walker, Hope, 1975-82; pros. atty. 8th Jud. Dist., Hope, 1976-82, chancery judge, 1982-90, cir. judge, 1990—2004; assoc. justice Ark. State Supreme Ct., Little Rock, 2004—. Asst. scoutmaster Boy Scouts Am., Hope, chair Razorback dist., mem. exec. bd. Cando Area coun.; pres. Ark. Enterprises for the Blind, Little Rock, 1976; bd. dirs. World Svcs. for the Blind, 1976. Mem. ABA, Ark. Bar Assn., Lions (chmn. 1976, dist. gov. Ark. 1975). Avocations: golf, flying, canoeing. Office: Ark Supreme Ct 625 Marshall St 1320 Justice Bldg Little Rock AR 72201*

GUNTER, JOSEPH CLIFFORD, III, lawyer; b. Ft. Worth, Apr. 26, 1943; s. Joseph Cliford Jr. and Helen (Wright) G.; children: Joseph Clifford IV, Grant Norwood. BA, U. Tex., 1965, JD, 1967. Bar: Tex. 1967. Assoc. McDonald Sanders Ginsberg New Kirk Gibson & Webb, Ft. Worth, 1967-68; ptnr. Bracewell & Patterson, Houston, 1968—. Adv. Am. Bd. Trial Advocates. Lt. USNR, 1967-73. Fellow Am. Coll. Trial Lawyers, Tex. Bar Found., Houston Bar Found.; mem. ABA, State Bar Tex., State Bar Colo. Episcopalian. Avocations: golf, tennis, skiing, sailing. Office: Bracewell & Patterson 711 Louisiana St Ste 2900 Houston TX 77002-2781 E-mail: clifford.gunter@bracepatt.com.

GUNTER, MARGUERITE A., systems analyst; b. N.Y.C., Apr. 19, 1974; d. Hugh L. and Rose H. Foster. M Computer Info. Tech., Regis U., 2003. Sys. tng. coord. NY Presbyn. Hosp., N.Y.C., 1996—99; sys. analyst United Healthcare, N.Y.C., 1999—2002, Maimonides Med. Ctr., Bklyn., 2002—. Contbr. Citrix Metaframe Network Adminstrn. Mem.: HIMSS. Office: Maimonides Med Ctr 1045 39th St Brooklyn NY 11201 Home: 166 State St Apt 5 Brooklyn NY 11201 Office Fax: 718-283-1880. Personal E-mail: margo-1@mindspring.com. Business E-Mail: mgunter@maimonidesmed.org.

GUNTER, MICHAEL DONWELL, lawyer; b. Gastonia, N.C., Mar. 26, 1947; s. Daniel Cornelius and DeNorma Joyce (Smith) G.; m. Barbara Jo Benson, June 19, 1970; children: Kimberly Elizabeth, Daniel Cornelius III. BA in History with honors, Wake Forest U., 1969; JD with honors, U. N.C., 1972; MBA with honors, U. Pa., 1973. Bar: N.C. 1972, U.S. Dist. Ct. (mid. dist.) N.C. 1974, U.S. Tax Ct. 1975, U.S. Supreme Ct. 1979, U.S. Claims Ct. 1982, U.S. Ct. Appeals (D.C. cir.) 1985, U.S. Ct. Appeals (4th cir.) 1992. Mem. Womble Carlyle Sandridge & Rice PLLC, Winston-Salem, NC, 1974—; chmn. employee benefits practice group. Bd. dirs. G & J Enterprises Inc., Gastonia, Indsl. Belting Inc., Gastonia. Contbr. articles to profl. jours. Coach youth basketball Winston-Salem YMCA, 1981-90; advisor Winston-Salem United Way Christmas Cheer Toy Shop, 1975; fundraiser Deacon Club Wake Forest U., also mem. exec. com., strategic planning com., athletic coun., 1987—, v.p., pres., 1990-92; bd. dirs. Goodwill Industries, Winston-Salem, 1987—, forum chmn. bd., sec., chmn. fin. com., chair, CEO search com.; bd. dirs. Centenary Meth. Ch., 1980; mem. cmty. problem solving com. United Way, 1988-99; mem. Leadership Winston-Salem, former mem. Alumni Coun. Wake Forest U., Cert. Com. NCAA, long range planning com. athletic dept. William E. Newcombe scholar U. Pa., 1972-73; selected One of Best Employee Benefits and Corp. Lawyers in Am., Nat. Law Jour. Fellow Am. Coll. Employee Benefits Counsel (charter); mem. ABA, So. Pension Conf., N.C. Bar Assn. (former chmn. tax sect., mem. continuing legal edn. com., sports and entertainment law com.), Forsyth County Bar Assn., Forsyth County Employee Benefit Coun., Winston-Salem Estate Planning Coun. (past bd. dirs.), Profit Sharing Coun. Am., ESOP Assn., Profit Sharing Coun., Assn. of Pvt. Pension and Welfare, Forsyth Country Club (former pres., bd. dirs.) Order of Coif, Rotary (former bd. dirs. Reynolda club). Democrat. Avocations: golf, fishing. Home: 128 Ballyhoo Dr Lewisville NC 27023-9633 Office: Womble Carlyle Sandridge & Rice PLLC One West Fourth St Winston Salem NC 27101 Office Phone: 336-721-3607. Office Fax: 336-733-8392. Business E-Mail: mgunter@wcsr.com.

GUNTER, RUSSELL ALLEN, lawyer; b. Amarillo, Tex., Feb. 21, 1950; s. J.B. and Shirley Ann (Russell) G.; children: Kim, Sarah, Laura, Rachel. BS in Polit. Sci., So. Ark U., 1972; JD, Tex. Tech. U., 1975. Bar: Ark., 1975, Tex. 1975, U.S. Dist. Ct. (ea. and we dists.) Ark. 1975, U.S. Dist. Ct. (no. dist.) Tex. 1976, U.S. Ct. Appeals (8th cir.), 1980, U.S. Supreme Ct. 1986. Assoc. Gaines N. Houston, Little Rock, 1975-79, Wallace, Dover & Dixon, P.A., Little Rock, 1979-90, McGlinchey Stafford Lang P.L.L.C., Little Rock, 1990-97; Cross, Gunter, Witherspoon & Galchus P.C., Little Rock, 1997—. Mem. ABA (com. on practice and procedure before NLRB labor sect.), Soc. for Human Resource Mgmt. (cert. sr. profl. in human resources), Ark. Bar Assn., Tex. Bar Assn., Ark. State C. of C. (bd. dirs.). Office: 500 Clinton Ave Ste 200 Little Rock AR 72201-1747 Office Phone: 501-371-9999. Business E-Mail: rgunter@cgwg.com.

GUNTER, WILLIAM DAYLE, JR., physicist, consultant; b. Mitchell, S.D., Jan. 10, 1932; s. William Dayle and Lamerta Berniece (Hockensmith) G.; m. Shirley Marie Teshera, Oct. 24, 1955; children: Maria Jo, Robert Paul. BS in Physics with distinction, Stanford U., 1957, MS, 1959. Physicist Ames Rsch. Ctr. NASA, Moffett Field, Calif., 1960-81, asst. br. chief electronic optical engring., 1981-85; pvt. practice cons. Photon Applications, San Jose, Calif., 1985-98, Modesto, Calif., 1998-2000; ret. Patentee in field; contbr. articles to profl. jours. With U.S. Army, 1953-55. Recipient Westinghouse Sci. Talent Search award, 1950; Stanford U. scholar, 1950. Mem. IEEE (sr.), Am. Phys. Soc., Optical Soc. Am., Nat. Space Soc., NASA Alumni League. Personal E-mail: gunter@thevision.net.

GUNTHARP, ELIZABETH ANNE, librarian; b. Tulsa, Nov. 26, 1940; d. Edward Wallace and Anna Louise (Sims) Austin; m. John Gill Guntharp, Aug. 17, 1966. BA, U. Tex., 1962; MA, St. Mary's U., San Antonio, 1967; MLS, Our Lady of Lake Coll., San Antonio, 1972. Tchr. San Antonio Schs., 1962-65, Northside Schs., San Antonio, 1966-68; librarian Austin (Tex.) Pub. Library, 1969, Shenandoah Library, San Antonio, 1970-72, Sul Ross Sch., San Antonio, 1973-88, John Marshall High Sch., San Antonio, 1988—, ret.; libr. Covenant Presbyn. Ch. Contbr. articles to profl. jours. Ch. libr. Covenant Presbyn. Ch., San Antonio. Mem. ALA, NEA, Am. Assn. Sch. Libr., Bexar Libr. Assn., Tex. State Tchrs. Assn., Tex. Libr. Assn., S. Tex. Archael. Soc., Tex. Archeol. Soc., S.W. Archeol. Soc., Northside Tchrs. Assn., Alpha Delta Kappa (pres. 1986-88, treas. 1989-92, historian 1992-94), Phi Alpha Theta. Republican. Presbyterian. Avocations: archaeology, travel, cooking, reading, pottery. Office: John Marshall Libr 8000 Lobo Ln San Antonio TX 78240-2645

GUNTHER, BARBARA, artist, educator; b. Bklyn., Nov. 10, 1930; d. Benjamin and Rose (Lev) Kelsky; m. Gerald Gunther, June 22, 1949; children: Daniel Jay, Andrew James. BA, Bklyn. Coll., 1949; MA, San Jose State U., 1975. Instr. printmaking, drawing, painting Cabrillo Coll., Aptos, Calif., 1976-93. Instr. lithography Calif. State U., Hayward, 1978-79; instr. studio arts Calif. State U., San Jose, summer 1977, 78, 80; co-founder San Jose Print Workshop, 1975. One-woman shows include include Palo Alto (Calif.) Cultural Ctr., 1981, Miriam Pearlman, Inc., Chg., 1984, D.P. Fong and Spratt galleries, San Jose, 1991—93, Branner/Spangenburg Gallery, Palo Alto, 1991, U. Calif., Santa Cruz, 1991, Cabrillo Coll., 1997, Frederick Spratt Galleries, San Jose, 1996, San Francisco, 2000, Triton Mus. of Art, Santa Clara, 2001, Represented in permanent collections San Jose Art in Pub. Places Program, Triton Mus., Santa Clara, Calif., Mus. City NY, Santa Clara Law Sch., Found. Press, Chrysler Motors. Recipient Purchase award Palo Alto Cultural Ctr., 1975, Judges' Merit award Haggin Mus., 1988. Mem. Calif. Printmakers Soc., San Jose Inst. of Contemporary Art. Studio: 4000 Middlefield Rd Palo Alto CA 94303 E-mail: bgunther@sbcglobal.net.

GUNTHER, LEON, physicist, educator; b. Bklyn., Aug. 22, 1939; s. Joseph and Esther Gunther; m. Harriet S. Gamrin, Oct. 10, 1962; children: David Michael, Benjamin Gene, Rachel Leah; m. Johanna Ellen Cotter, Nov. 11, 1979; 1 stepchild, Erika Rae Brown; 1 child, Avi Yosef. BS, CCNY, 1960; PhD, MIT, 1964. Asst. prof. Tufts U., Medford, Mass., 1965-72, assoc. prof., 1972-78, prof., 1978—. Cons. in field; vis. prof. Technion, Tel-Aviv U., Louis Néel Lab. of Magnetism, Grenoble, France. Co-editor Proceedings of NATO Workshop in Quantum Tunneling of Magnetization, 1995; contbr. over 100 articles to profl. jours. Prin. 2d violinist Newton Symphony Orch., Mass., 1974-83; founder, dir. Mak'haylah chorus Temple Emunah, Lexington, Mass. NATO Postdoctoral fellow NSF, 1965-66, Research grantee. Mem. AAUP, Am. Phys. Soc. Office: Tufts Univ Dept Of Physics Medford MA 02155

GUNTHER, VANESSA ANN, historian, registered nurse; b. Bakersfield, Calif., Apr. 2, 1961; d. Ralph Isaac and Hester Ann Gunther. AS, Cypress Coll., 1990; BA, Calif. State U. Fullerton, 1995, MA, 1998; PhD, U. Calif. at Riverside, 2001. RN State of Calif., 1990. Lectr. Cerritos Coll., Norwalk, Calif., 2001—, Calif. State U., Fullerton, 2001—, Fullerton Coll., 2002—. Author: Ambiguous Justice, Native American's and the Law in Southern California, 1848-1890; contbr. articles to jours. and encys. Vol. Pacific Wildlife, Irvine, 2000—02. Mem.: Ninth Judicial Hist. Assn., Western Hist. Assn., Am. Hist. Assn.

GUNTHER, WILLIAM DAVID, academic administrator, economics professor; b. Balt., Oct. 11, 1940; s. Geneva (Gee) G.; m. Irene Leveja Reineks, Jan. 8, 1966; children: William B., Kristine A., Jennifer R. BS, Kent State U., 1962, MA, 1965; PhD, U. Ky., 1969. Asst. prof. econs. U. Ala., Tuscaloosa, 1968-72, assoc. prof. econs., 1972-76, prof. econs., 1976—98, assoc. dean for rsch., 1988-98; dean sch. bus. U. So. Miss., Hattiesburg, 1998—2004, prof. econs., 1998—. Contbr. articles to profl. jours. Fulbright scholar Fulbright Commn., 1972, Faculty fellow USAF, 1979. Mem. Assn. Coll. Honor Socs. (exec. coun. 1983—), Am. Econs. Assn. Avocations: boating, coin collecting/numismatics, paper money collecting. Office: U So Miss PO Box 5021 Hattiesburg MS 39406-1000 E-mail: william.gunther@usm.edu.

GUNTHEROTH, WARREN GADEN, pediatrician, educator; b. Hominy, Okla., July 27, 1927; s. Harry William and Callie (Cornett) G.; m. Ethel Haglund, July 3, 1954; children: Kurt, Karl, Sten. MD, Harvard U., 1952. Diplomate: Am. Bd. Pediatrics, Am. Bd. Pediatric Cardiology, Nat. Bd. Med. Examiners. Intern Peter Bent Brigham Hosp., Boston, 1952-53; fellow in cardiology Children's Hosp., Boston, 1953-55, resident in pediatrics, 1955-56; rsch. fellow physiology and biophysics U. Wash. Med. Sch., Seattle, 1957-58, mem. faculty, 1958—, prof. pediatrics, 1969—, head divsn. pediatric cardiology, 1964-91. Author: Pediatric Electrocardiography, 1965, How to Read Pediatric ECGs, 1981, 4th edit., 2005, Crib Death (Sudden Infant Death Syndrome), 1982, 3d edit., 1995, Climbing With Sasha, a Washington Husky, 1995; also numerous articles; mem. editl. bd. Am. Heart Jour., 1977-80, Circulation, 1980-83, Am. Jour. Noninvasive Cardiology, 1985-94, Jour. Am. Coll. Cardiology, 1988-94, Am. Jour. Cardiology, Jour. Noninvasive Cardiology, 1996-00; sect. editor Practice of Pediatrics, 1979-87. Served with USPHS, 1950-51. Spl. research fellow NIH, 1967. Mem. Soc. Pediatric Rsch., Biomed. Engring. Soc. (charter), Am. Heart Assn. (chmn. N.W. regional med. rsch. adv. com. 1978-80), Cardiovascular System Dynamics Soc. (charter), Am. Coll. Cardiology. Democrat. Home: 13201 42nd Ave NE Seattle WA 98125-4626 Office: U Wash Med Sch Dept Pediatrics PO Box 356320 Seattle WA 98195-6320 Office Phone: 206-543-3186. Business E-Mail: wgg@u.washington.edu. *My career includes medical practice, teaching and research; my hobby is mountain climbing. Both work and hobby benefit from courage. Encouraging students to ask difficult— and even embarrassing— questions, reaching a timely diagnosis, starting treatment in a dangerously ill patient, and raising challenging questions in research that may provoke anger or scorn; all require courage. Silent convictions are not enough.*

GÜNTHER-STIRN, DAGMAR DOROTHEA, retired social sciences educator; b. Tientsin, Hopeh, China, June 8, 1931; arrived in U.S., 1939; d. Wilhelm Otto Carl Franz Günther and Emilie Marcella Stirn. BA, Wellesley Coll., 1953; MIA, Columbia U., 1955, ABD, 1961. Instr. dept. polit. sci. U. Ct., Hartford, 1963—70, Ctrl. Conn. State U., New Britain, 1971; adj. prof. U. Hartford, West Hartford, 1970—83; ret., 1983. Corporator Dana Hall Sch., Wellesley, Mass., 2002—; bd. dirs. J. L. Anthony & Co., 1966—. Trustee Hartford Conservatory Music, 1983—96; from bd. dirs. to pres. Cromwell (Conn.) Hills Condominium Assn., 1996—2004. Scholar, Dept. of State, 1971—73. Mem.: Am. Polit. Sci. Assn., Musical Club Hartford (exec. bd., sec. 2000—04). Republican. United Ch. Of Christ. Avocations: travel, gardening, opera. Home: 23 Cherry Hill Ct Cromwell CT 06416

GUNTON, HOWARD E., insurance company executive; Numerous fin. mgmt. positions Am. Internat. Group Inc.; sr. v.p., CFO AIG Life Cos. (U.S.), Mass. Mutual Life Ins., Springfield, Mass., 1999—. Mem. AICPAs, Del. Soc. CPA's. Office: Mass Mutual Life Ins Co 1295 State St Springfield MA 01111-0002*

GUNTY, CHRISTOPHER JAMES, newspaper editor; b. Hometown, Ill., Oct. 13, 1959; s. Harold Paul and Therese Agnes Gunty; div.; children: William, Amy, Timothy. BA, Loyola U., Chgo., 1981. Circulation mgr. The Chgo. Catholic, 1981-83, assoc. mnging. editor, 1983, mng. editor, 1983-85; editor, mng. editor The Catholic Sun, Phoenix, 1985-96; assoc. pub. The Cath. Sun, Phoenix, 1996—. Author: He Came to Touch Us, 1987; co-author videotape script The Pope in Arizona, 1987; contbg. author: (anthologies) Freedom of Journalist, 1990, Mission and Future of the Catholic Press, 1998; contbr. articles to spl. Catholic news svcs. as well as papers where employed. Mem. Fiesta Bowl Com., Phoenix, 1987-92; bd. dirs. Catholic Journalism Scholarship Fund, 1990—, pres., 1995-96, 99-2001. Named Honoree Summer U. Internat. Cath. Union of the Press, Switzerland, 1988. Mem. Cath. Press Assn. (bd. dirs. 1988-99, sec. 1990-92, v.p. 1994-96, pres. 1996-98, St. Francis de Sales award 2000), Assoc. Ch. Press, Ariz. Newspapers Assn., Soc. Profl. Journalists. Roman Catholic. Avocations: bicycling, science fiction. Office: The Catholic Sun 400 E Monroe St Phoenix AZ 85004-2336

GUNZBURGER, SUZANNE NATHAN, municipal official, social worker; b. Buffalo, July 12, 1939; d. Lawrence Emil and Ruth Lucille (Wohl) Nathan; m. Gerard Josef Gunzburger, Apr. l0, l960; children: Ronald Marc, Cynthia Anne, Judith Lynn. BS in Edn., Wayne State U., 1959; MSW, Barry U., 1974. Tchr. pub. schs., Detroit, 1959-63, Trumbull, Conn., 1963-66, North Miami Beach, Fla., 1967-68, Broward County, Fla., 1968-72; pvt. practice clin. social work Hollywood, Fla., 1975—; vice mayor City of Hollywood, 1983-84, 85-87, city commr., 1982-92; commr. Broward County, 1992—, chair, 1994-95, 99-2000. Chmn. Met. Planning Orgn., Broward County, 1984—87, 1989, Statewide Human Rights Adv. Com., 1988—89; pres. Broward County Mental Health Bd., 1984; active Broward County Commn. Status Women, 1978—82, White House Conf. Families, Balt., 1980; del. Broward County League Cities, 1988—92; mem. adv. bd. Broward Homebound, 1991—; mem. Broward Children's Svc. Bd., 1988—92, Broward County Water Adv., 1992—94, 1997—98, Broward County Cmty. Redevel. Agy., 1992—, South Fla. Regional Planning Coun., 1992—94, 1998—99, treas., 1999; vice-chmn. Broward County Planning Coun., 1996—98, chair planning coun., 2000—01, Broward County Cultural Affairs Coun., 1996—; Broward chair Concert Assn. of Fla., Inc., 1996—; mem. Broward Children's Svc. Bd., 1998—; bd. dirs. Environ. Coalition Broward County, 1982—89, 1997—2000, Fla. Assn. of Counties, 1992—, Broward Alliance, 1992—2000, Broward Children's Svcs., 1997, Children's Svcs. Coun., 2001—. Named Broward County Woman of Yr., 1990, Humanitarian of Yr., David Posnack, Jewish Comty. Ctr., 1994, Environmentalist of Yr., Broward County Environ. Coalition, 1994, Polit. Leader of Yr., The Vanguard Chronicle, 1999, Woman of Valor, David Posnack JCC, 2003, First Lady Broward, Broward County Fair, 2004; recipient Woamn of Yr. in Govt. award Women in Comms., 1983, Disting. Achievement award Am. Jewish Congress, 1990, Fla. Philharm. Woman of Style and Substance, 1995, Woman of Distinction award March of Dimes, 1996, Heart award Children's Consortium, 1996, Disting. Alumni award Barry U., 1996, Jesse Portis Helms Dem. of Yr. award Dolphin Dem. Club, 1996, Gracias award Hispanic Unity, 1999, Polit. Alliance of Yr. award Dolphin Dem. Club, 1999; inductee Broward County Women's Hall of Fame, 1995, Woman of Distinction award City of Hollywood, 1997, Women's Polit. Caucus, 1997, Encore award Art Serve, 2004; Jewish Mus. Fla., Queen Esther Court Honoree, 2004. Mem. Nat. Assn. Social Workers (diplomate clin. social work), Internat. Acad. Behavioral Med., Counseling and Psychotherapy (diplomate profl. psychotherapy), Am. Acad. Behavioral Med. (clin. mem.), Nat. Coun. Jewish Women (pres. 1980-82, Hannah G. Solomon award 1989), Met. Planning Orgn., Israel Bond Coun., Hollywood C. of C. (leadership devel. 1990—), Kiwanis. Democrat. Avocations: reading, swimming, travel. Office: Office Bd County Commrs Govtl Ctr Rm 412 115 S Andrews Ave Fort Lauderdale FL 33301-1818

GUNZENHAUSER, GERARD RALPH, JR., management consultant, investor; b. Mt. Vernon, N.Y., Sept. 26, 1936; s. Gerard Ralph and Helen Elizabeth (Carey) G.; m. Alfa Marjorie Vendetti, Sept. 17, 1960; children: Cathy Susan, Michael Gerard, Christopher John, Eric David. BBA, Iona Coll., 1965; postgrad., NYU Sch. Bus. Adminstrn., 1967-68. Asst. mgr. fin. analysis Gen. Foods Corp., White Plains, N.Y., 1962-68; dir. fin. planning and analysis RJR Foods, Inc., Winston-Salem, N.C., 1968-76; area fin. dir. R.J. Reynolds Tobacco Internat., Winston-Salem, 1976-79; comptroller R.J. Reynolds Tobacco. Co., Winston-Salem, 1979-81, v.p., comptroller, 1981-83, v.p. fin., chief fin. officer, 1983-84; sr. v.p., chief fin. officer Del Monte Corp., San Francisco, 1984-85; sr. v.p. fin., controller RJR Nabisco, Inc., Winston-Salem, 1986-87; sr. v.p. fin. R.J. Reynolds Tobacco Co., Winston-Salem, 1987-88, exec. v.p., chief fin. officer, 1988-91, also exec. com., bd. dirs.; pres., chief exec. officer GRG Assocs., Inc., Winston-Salem, 1991—. Mem. local adv. bd. Branch Banking & Trust Co., 1987-99; mem. Consumer Credit Counseling Svc., 1983-84, 87-90; mem. Reynolds Carolina Credit Union Bd., 1973-83. Trustee Winston-Salem Arts Coun., 1987-94; bd. dirs. Winston-Salem Piedmont Triad Symphony, 1986—, Piedmont Opera Theatre, 1989—, Tanglewood Pk. Found., 1991-98; mem. N.C. Gov.'s Bus. Coun. on Arts and Humanities, 1987-91; chmn. fund appeal Bishop McGuinness High Sch., Winston-Salem, 1982-83, mem. bd. edn., 1987-90, chmn. bd., 1988-90; chmn. St. Leo's Parish Coun., Winston-Salem, 1974-77; exec. v.p. Winston-Salem Nat. Little League, 1981-84; chmn. sch. budget task force C. of C., 1976; mem. bd. advisors Catholic Conf. Ctr., 1990-93; exec. com., bd. trustees Forsyth County Park Authority, 1992-99; bd. dirs., vice chmn. Found. Roman Cath. Diocese of Charlotte. Named to Hon. Order Ky. Cols., 1983 Mem. Fin. Execs. Inst. Roman Catholic. Home: 2814 Galsworthy Dr Winston Salem NC 27106-5107 Office: GRG Assocs Inc 101 S Stratford Rd Ste 201 Winston Salem NC 27104-4224

GUO, RUYAN, engineering educator, researcher; b. Beijing; arrived in U.S., 1985, naturalized; BSEE, Xi'an Jiaoting U., China, 1982; MSEE, Xi'an Jiaotong U., China, 1984; PhD in Solid State sci., Pa. State U., 1990. Assoc. lectr. elec. engring. dept. Xi'an Jiaotong U., 1984—85; faculty rsch. assoc. Materials Rsch. Lab. Pa. State U., University Park, 1991—94, faculty rsch. assoc., asst. prof. materials, 1995—96, sr. rsch. assoc., assoc. prof. materials, assoc. prof. elec. engring., 1996—99, assoc. prof. elec. engring. and materials rsch., dept. elec. engring. and Materials Rsch. Inst., 1999—2004, prof. elec. engring., dept. elec. engring. and Materials Rsch. Inst., 2004—. Presenter in field. Editor on bd.: jour. Phase Transitions, 2001—, Jour. of Korean Ceramic Soc., 2002—; contbr. tech. papers to refereed jours., conf. procs., book chpts. Fellow: Am. Ceramic Soc.; mem.: AAAS, IEEE (sr.), SPIE Internat. Soc. for Optical Engring., Am. Soc. for Engring. Edn., Ultrasonic, Ferroelectric and Frequency Control Soc., Materials Rsch. Soc. Achievements include research in science and technology of electronic and optoelectronic materials and devices; ferroelectric oxides; low loss and tunable microwave materials; optical fiber communications and tunable wireless optical interactions. Office: Pa State U Dept Elec Engring 187 Materials Rsch Lab University Park PA 16802 E-mail: ryguo@psu.edu.

GUO, SHENG MING, retired history educator; b. Zhengjiang, Jiangsu, China, Dec. 25, 1915; came to U.S., 1989, naturalized, 1996; s. Dun Xue Guo and Xiao Chun Wu; m. Hong Yi Wang, Jan. 24, 1945; children: Victor Kuo, John Kuo, Meide Guo. BA in History, Nat. Ctrl. U., Chongching, China, 1938; MA, Ctrl. Inst. Polit. Sci., Chongching, 1941; postgrad., Tulane U., 1949. Vice consul Chinese Consulate, New Orleans, 1945-47, acting consul, 1948-50; prof. history Kuangsi (China) U., 1951-53, Hunan (China) U., 1953-56, East China Normal U., Shanghai, 1957-89. Advisor Chinese Assn. Medieval History, Beijing, 1976—, Shanghai Assn. Social Sci., 1983—; U.S. State Dept. vis. prof., Georgetown U., Harvard U., U. Chgo., Stanford U., also others, 1983. Author: A Survey of Western Historiography, 1983 (State prize 1985), An Outline of World Civilization, 1989 (State prize 1991); editor-in-chief: Dictionary of World History, 1986; editor History of Foreign Countries in Ency. Sinica, 1987. Presbyterian. Avocation: gardening.

GUO, XIN, music educator, editor; b. Beijing, Dec. 16, 1952; d. Chang-zhi Guo and Shui-lian Chen. MusB in Piano Performance, Tianjin Conservatory Music, China, 1978, MA in Music Theory, 1986; MusM in Piano Performance, Carnegie Mellon U., 1995; MA in Music Theory, U. Conn., 1999; PhD in Music Theory, Fla. State U., 2002. Certificate in Piano Pedagogy Carnegie Mellon U., 1995, YAMAHA Electone Grade 5 YAMAHA Music Fourdation, Japan, 1991, YAMAHA Fundamentals Grade 5 YAMAHA Music Fourdation, Japan, 1991. Piano accompanist Tianjin Conservatory Music, 1978—84; lectr. theory Ctrl. Conservatory Music, Beijing, 1986—92; piano instr. Prep. Sch. Carnegie Mellon U., Pitts., 1993—96; piano instr. Cmty. Sch. of Arts U. Conn., Storrs, 1997—99; rsch. asst. music theory Fla. State U., Tallahassee, 1999—2002; piano instr. Mason's Sch. Music, Tallahassee, 2000—02; asst. editor Jour. Music in China, LA, 2003—; piano instr. Waltrip's Music Ctr., Arcadia, Calif., 2003—04. Piano accompanist Conservatory China, Beijing, 1987—88; asst. libr. Ctrl. Conservatory Music, Beijing, 1987—92; tchg. asst. applied piano Carnegie Mellon U., Pitts., 1993—95; tchg. asst. ear-training and sight-reading U. Pitts., 1996; tchg. asst. class piano U. Conn., Storrs, 1996—97, tchg. asst. music theory, 1996—98, studio accompanist, 1997—99. Contbr. to Jour. Music China. Mem.: Am. Coll. Musicians, Music Tchrs. Assn. Calif. Achievements include research in Chinese famous contemporary composer Chen Yi's music. Home: 437 W Duarte Rd #1 Arcadia CA 91007 Personal E-mail: xig990809@excite.com.

GUO, ZENGKUI, research scientist; arrived in U.S., 1986; s. KaiQi H. Guo and AiYing K. Zhang; m. Lendia L. Zhou; children: Winston, Yugene. PhD, U. Mo., 1990. Rsch. fellow Chinese Acad. of Agrl. Scis., Beijing, 1983—86; postdoctoral rsch. fellow Cedars-Sinai/Harbor UCLA Med Ctr, 1990—91; rsch. assoc. U. Chgo., 1991—92; sr. rsch. assoc. U. Cin., 1993—95; NIH grant trainee Mayo Found., Rochester, Minn., 1995—98, rsch. assoc., 1998—2002, assoc. cons., 2002—. Co-author: (textbook) Animal Anatomy and Physiology. Recipient Pilot and Feasibility Project award, Minn. Obesity Ctr., 1999—2001; grantee, NIH RO1 grant, 2001—. Mem.: Am. Diabetes Assn., N.Am. Soc. for Study of Obesity, Nat. Inst. Nutritional Scis. Achievements include research in skeletal muscle lipid metabolism using stable and radioactive isotopes; establishment of techniques for removal of intramuscular adipocytes; establishment of a stress-free platform for studying rodent metabolism in vivo and pioneer research in these areas; development of models for measuring intramyocellular fatty acid oxidation and kinetics directly. E-mail: guo.zengkui@mayo.edu.

GUO, ZIBIN, medical anthropologist; b. Nanjing, China, Jan. 18, 1961; came to U.S., 1986; s. Wenxue Guo and Yueqing Wu. BA, Nanjing U., 1982; MA, U. Conn., 1988, PhD, 1994; postgrad., Harvard U., 1995-97. Dir. clin. studies New Eng. Sch. Accupuncture, Watertown, Mass., 1995; lectr. Harvard Med. Sch., Boston, 1997-98; asst. prof. dept. sociology and anthropology U. Tenn., Chattanooga, 1998—. Cons. N.Y. Task Force on Immigrant/Health, N.Y.C., 1993-94, U. Conn. Med. Ctr., Farmington, 1995, Women's Rsch. Ctr., Wellesley (Mass.) Coll., 1998-2000; mem. adv. com. Inst. Cmty. Rsch., Hartford, Conn., 2000—. Author: Ginseng and Aspirin, 2000; contbr. chpts. to books. Grantee Nat. Ctr. for Health Stats., 1992-93; fellow Nat. inst. Aging., 1995-97, summer, 1996, U. Tenn., summer 1999. Mem. Am. Anthropol. Assn., Soc. for Applied Anthropology, U.S. Judo Assn. (life). Avocations: tai chi, martial arts. Office: U Tenn 615 McCallie Ave Chattanooga TN 37403 Home: 1731 Rock Bluff Rd Hixson TN 37343-3125 E-mail: Zibin-Guo@utc.edu.

GUOKAS, JOAN ELLEN (MRS. MATTHEW GUOKAS SR.), retired elementary school educator; b. New Rochelle, N.Y., Aug. 24, 1919; d. Homer Vincent and Mary Ellen Ann (Ivory) Burnham; widowed; children: Mary Tyrrell, Matthew Jr. BS in Edn., St. Joseph U., 1961; MEd, Temple U., 1970. Elem. sch. tchr. St. Timothy's Sch., Phila., 1950-53, St. Bernard's Sch., Phila., 1953-59, Vare Elem. Sch., Phila., 1961-68, McCall Elem. Sch., Phila., 1969-81; ret., 1981. Mem. fellowship award com. Emergency Aid, 1981—; mem. alumnae bd. Chestnut Hill Coll., Phila., 1990—; mem. Jefferson Hosp. Women's Bd., 1991; mem. election day voting panel Phila. Election Bd., 1981—; vol. Ocean City's Hist. Mus.; choir mem. Frances Cabrini Roman Cath. Ch., Ocean City. Mem. AAUW. Roman Catholic. Avocations: tutoring foreign students, mentoring, church activities. Address: 500 Bay Ave Apt 305N Ocean City NJ 08226-4809

GUP, BENTON EUGENE, banking educator; b. Reading, Pa., Mar. 5, 1936; married; children: Lincoln, Andrew, Jeremy. BA, U. Cin., 1961, MBA, 1963, PhD, 1966. Economist Fed. Res. Bank of Cleve., 1967-70; prof. fin. U. of Tulsa, 1970-82, prof., chair banking, 1970-82; vis. prof., chair banking U. Va., Charlottesville, 1980-81; prof., chair banking U. Ala., Tuscaloosa, 1983—. Author: Guide to Strategic Planning, 1980, Financial Intermediaries, 2d editl., 1980, Principles of Financial Management, 1983, 2d editl., 1987, Management of Financial Institutions, 1984, The Basics of Investing, 5th edit., 1992; author: (with Charles Meiburg) Cases in Bank Management, 1986; author: Personal Investing: A Complete Handbook, 1987, Commercial Bank Management, 1989, Bank Mergers: Current Issues and Perspectives, 1989, Bank Fraud: Exposing the Hidden Threat to Financial Institutions, 1990; author: (with Donald Fraser and James Kolari) Commercial Banking: The Management of Risk, 1995; author: The Bank Director's Handbook, 1996, Bank Failures in the Major Trading Countries of the World, 1998, International Banking Crises, 1999, The New Financial Architecture, 2000, Megamergers in a Global Economy, 2002, The Future of Banking, 2003, Investing OnLine, 2003, Too Big to Fail: Policies and Practices in Government Bailouts, 2004, The New Basel Capital Accord, 2004, Capital Markets, Globalization and Economic Development, 2005. Served with USAF, 1954—58. Mem. Fin. Mgmt. Assn. (chmn. site selection 1975-85), Midwest Fin. Assn. (pres. 1982-83), Am. Fin. Assn., Fin. Execs. Inst., Acad. Fin. Svcs. (v.p., dir. 1988-91). Home: 1124 Forest Oaks Ln Tuscaloosa AL 35406-2673 Office: U Ala Dept Fin PO Box 870224 Tuscaloosa AL 35487-0154 Office Phone: 205-348-7842.

GUPCHUP, GIREESH VIJAY, pharmacist, educator; b. Bombay, Dec. 28, 1965; arrived in U.S., 1988; s. Vijay Narhar and Vijaya Gupchup; m. Chatura Chitale-Gupchup, Dec. 27, 1994; 1 child, Samay. BS in Pharmacy, U. Bombay, 1988; MS, U. Toledo, 1990, MS, 1993; PhD, Purdue U., 1996. Lic. pharmacist Maharashtra State Pharmacy Coun., India. Purdue-Merck fellow in pharm. economics, grad. asst. Purdue U., West Lafayette, Ind., 1993—96; chmn. pharmacy adminstrn. grad. program U. N.Mex, Albuquerque, 1996—2000, asst. prof. pharmacy, 1996—2002, assoc. prof. pharmacy, 2002—04; dir. N.Mex Medicaid Retrospective Drug Utilization Rev. Program, Albuquerque, 2000—03; prof., assoc. dean Sch. Pharmacy So. Ill. U., Edwardsville, 2004—. Pharmacoeconomics cons. N.Mex Medicaid Drug Utilization Rev. Program, Albuquerque, 1996—2000. Mem. editl. adv. bd.: Jour. Am. Pharm. Assn., Rsch. in Social and Adminstrv. Pharmacy; contbr. more than 25 article to profl. jours. Recipient Alumni Achiever's award, KMK Coll. of Pharmacy, U. Bombay, 2000; grantee, various state, fed. and industry sources, 1996—2002. Mem.: N.Mex Pharm. Assn. (2d v.p. 2002—03, 1st v.p. 2003—04), Internat. Soc. Pharmacoeconomics and Outcomes Rsch., Am. Pharm. Assn., Kappa Psi, Phi Kappa Phi, Rho Chi. Achievements include development of two instruments to measure health-related quality of life among Native American asthma and diabetes patients. Avocations: golf, swimming. Home: 6 Sharpsburg Ct Edwardsville IL 62025 Office Phone: 618-650-5150. E-mail: ggupchu@siue.edu.

GUPTA, ANJU, risk management consultant; b. Bangalore, India, Sept. 14, 1971; d. Dharam Singh and Neera Gupta; m. Parag Gupta. PhD, Stanford U., California, USA, 1997. Postdoctoral rsch. scholar Stanford U., Palo Alto, Calif., 1997—98; sr. engr. Risk Mgmt. Solutions Inc., Newark, Calif., 1998—2000, product mgr., weather risk, 2000—01, dir. product mgmt., 2001—02, 2002—. Cons. Wharton team on NSF project, Palo Alto, 1996; mem. Curee, L.A., 1998; mem. com. earthquake risk financing and transfer Earthquake Engring. Rsch. Inst., Oakland, Calif., 1999. Contbr. articles to profl. jours. Vol. for adult literacy, Mountain View, Calif., 1998; vol. for childhood literacy New Delhi, 1995—97. Mem.: Earthquake Engring. Rsch. Inst. Achievements include development of financial risk model for Central America; a standardized national earthquake loss estimation software tool, Hazards US (HAZUS); participation in project dealing with urban search and rescue requirements for responding to catastrophic disasters in the U.S; project to assess annualized losses from earthquakes in the U.S; project to validate and calibrate the HAZUS methodology. Office: Risk Mgmt Solutions Inc 7015 Gateway Blvd Newark CA 94560 Home: 1265 Tainan Pl San Jose CA 95131-2416 Personal E-mail: anjurisk@yahoo.com. E-mail: anju.gupta@rms.com.

GUPTA, ASHWANI KUMAR, mechanical engineering educator; b. Punjab, India, Oct. 23, 1948; s. Ram Nath and Vidya G. BSc, Panjab U., India, 1966; MSc, Southampton (Eng.) U., 1970; PhD, Sheffield (Eng.) U., 1973, DSc, 1986. Chartered engr., fuel technologist, U.K. Rsch. engr. Internat. Combustion Co., Derby, England, 1967-71; rsch. asst. Sheffield U., 1971-73, rsch. fellow, ind. rsch. worker, 1973-76; mem. rsch. staff MIT, Cambridge, 1977-82; prof. dept. mech. engring. U. Md., College Park, 1983—. Mem. sci. adv. bd. State of Md., 1985—. Author: Swirl Flows, 1984, Flowfield Modeling and Diagnostics, 1985, High Temperature Air Combustion: From Energy Conservation to Pollution Reduction, 2003; editor 12 books in Energy and Engineering Science series, 1980—; founding co-editor: Environmental and Energetics series, 1990—; author over 350 tech. papers. Recipient Pres. Kirwan Rsch. award, U. Md., 2003. Fellow AIAA (chmn. propellants and combustion tech. com. 1988-90, chmn. terrestrial energy systems tech. com. 1991-2000, dep. dir. energy 2000—, Energy Sys. award 1990, Propellant and Combustion award 1999), Inst. Energy U.K., ASME (chmn. Fuels and Combustion Tech. divsn. 1998-2000, mem. computers and info. in engring. divsn. 2002-03, George Westinghouse Gold medal 1998, James Harry Potter Gold medal 2003, Landis medal 2004); mem. Soc. Automotive Engrs., Combustion Inst., Am. Soc. Engring. Edn. Avocations: flying, swimming, squash, photography. Office: U Md Dept Mech Engring College Park MD 20742-0001 Office Phone: 301-405-5276. E-mail: akgupta@eng.umd.edu.

GUPTA, DEVENDRA, material scientist, engineer; b. Nagina, India, Feb. 15, 1931; s. Kanh Mal and Shiva Devi Gupta; m. Sudha Gupta; children: Chitra, Sudhir, Devratna. BSc, Delhi U., 1950; BSc in Engring., Banaras Hindu U., 1954; MS, NYU, 1957; PhD, U. Ill., 1961. Reader Banaras (India) Hindu U., 1961-63; asst. chief Planning Commn., Delhi, 1963-65; fellow metallurgy U. Ill., Urbana, 1966-68; rsch. staff mem. IBM T.J. Watson Rsch. Ctr., Yorktown Heights, N.Y., 1968-93, emeritus rsch. staff mem., 1993—. Mem. faculty adv. bd. U. Conn., 1990-94; adj. prof. U. Lehigh, Bethlehem, 1995—, Polytech. U., Bklyn., 1978-85; vis. scientist U. Stuttgart (Germany) and Max Planck Inst., 1997—98. Author 5 books including: Diffusion Phenonmena, 1988, Thin Films and Microelectronic Through Materials and Related Subjects, 1994; contbr. numerous articles to profl. jours. Fellow Am. Phys. Soc.; mem. The Metallurgical Soc. (councillor 1986-96, treas, chmn.), Sigma Xi. Achievements include patent on portfolio on metallization of Si-chips used in the microelectronic industry. Home: 3 Morningside Ct Ossining NY 10562-3003 Office: IBM Thomas J Watson Rsch Ctr Kitchwan Rd Yorktown Heights NY 10598 Office Phone: 914-945-1665. Business E-Mail: gupta1@us.ibm.com.

GUPTA, KISHAN CHAND, psychologist; b. Alawal Pur, Punjab, India, Mar. 19, 1932; came to U.S., 1972; s. Shri Mela Ram and Bhagwanti Gupta; m. Raj Kumari Aggarwal, Dec. 7, 1955; children: Shailesh, Neeraj. BA, Punjab U., India, 1952; BE, Jamia Millia Islamia U., New Delhi, 1954; MA in Psychology, Aligarh Muslim U., India, 1959; postgrad. cert. in counseling psychology, Cen. Bur. Edn. and Vocat. Guidance, 1961; course in vocat. rehab., Gov. India Ministry of Employment and Tng., New Delhi, 1962; D of Spl. Edn., U. Liverpool, England, 1970. Cert. psychologist, Coun. Nat. Register Health Svc. Providers Psychol., Ohio; lic. psychologist, Ohio. Head Tchrs. Tng. Dept., Rohtak, India, 1954-55; sr. tchr. psychology Tchrs. Tng. Inst. Panjab Civil Svc., India, 1955-61; regional sch. counselor Divisional Insp. Schs., Ambala, India, 1961; employment counselor Sub-Regional Employment Exch., Patiala, India, 1961-63; clin. psychologist child guidance clinic coll. nursing Ministry of Health, New Delhi, 1963-72, dir. child guidance clinic coll. nursing, 1966-69; staff psychologist, adminstrn. specialist V Western Res. Psychiat. Hosp., Northfield, Ohio, 1972—. Mem. faculty of arts Delhi U., India, 1965-68; sec. Delhi Soc. for the Welfare of Retarded Children, 1966-70; part-time cons. Family Life Ctr., New Delhi, 1970-72; part-time faculty Cuyahoga C.C., Cleve., 1972-73; faculty psychologist N.E. Clergy Tng. Inst., Hawthornden State Hosp., 1972-75; cons. S.E. Cmty. Mental Health Ctr., Cleve., 1974-75; part-time psychologist Shaker Heights, Ohio, 1974-78; staff psychologist North Coast Behavior Health Care Sys., South Campus, Northfield, Ohio, 1972-2004 Contbr. articles to profl. jours. Cons., clin. dir. Lorain County Ctr. for Youth Services, 1979-83. Recipient Commonwealth scholarship U. Liverpool, U.K., 1969-70. Hindu. Home: 1875 Surrey Pl Gates Mills OH 44040-9757

GUPTA, KRISHNA CHANDRA, mechanical engineering educator; b. 1948; m. Karuna Gupta; 1 child, Anupama. B of Tech. with distinction, Indian Inst. Tech., 1969; MS in Mech. Engring., Case Inst. Tech., 1971; PhD in Mech. Engring., Stanford U., 1974. Grad. asst. Case Inst. Tech., Cleve., 1969-71; rsch. asst. Stanford (Calif.) U., 1971-74; from asst. prof. mech. engring. to prof. U. Ill., Chgo., 1974—, assoc. dean, 2002—05. Mem. editl. adv. bd. Jour. Applied Mechanisms and Robotics 1993-2000; assoc. editor Mechanism and Machine Theory 1998-2004; contbr. articles to profl. jours. Recipient award of merit Procter & Gamble Co., 1978, South Pointing Chariot award, 1989, AM&R G.N. Sandor award, 1997; grantee in field. Fellow ASME (assoc. editor Jour. Mech. Design 1981-82, mem. editl. adv. bd. Applied Mechanics Rev. 1985-93, chmn. mechanisms com. 1989-90, gen chmn. 1990 design tech. conf., chmn. 1990 mechanisms conf., mem. design divsn. exec. com. 2001—, chair design divsn., 2005—, editor newsletter divsn. design engring., best paper computers in engring. conf. 1991, Henry Hess award 1979, Design Divsn. Mechanisms and Robotics award 2002). Avocations: investments, speed reading. Office: Univ Ill Dept Mech and Indsl Engring MC 251 842 W Taylor St Chicago IL 60607 E-mail: kcgupta@uic.edu.

GUPTA, MADHU SUDAN, electrical engineering educator; b. Lucknow, India, June 13, 1945; came to U.S., 1966; s. Manohar Lal and Premvati Gupta; m. Vijaya Lakshmi Tayal, July 9, 1970; children: Jay Mohan, Vineet Mohan; m. Manorama Vyas, May 29, 1985. BS, Lucknow U., India, 1963; MS, Allahabad U., India, 1966, Fla. State U., 1967; MA, U. Mich., 1968, PhD, 1972. Registered profl. engr., Ont. Asst. prof. elec. engring. Queen's U., Kingston, Ont., Can., 1972-73, MIT, Cambridge, 1973-78, assoc. prof. elec. engring., 1978-79, U. Ill., Chgo., 1979-84, prof. elec. engring., 1984-87, dir. grad. studies, 1980-83; vis. prof. elec. and computer engring. U. Calif., Santa Barbara, 1985-86; sr. staff engr. Hughes Aircraft Co., 1987-95; prof. elec. engring., chmn. dept. elec. engring. Fla. State U., Tallahassee, 1995-2000; prof. elec. engring., RF comm. sys. industry chair San Diego State U., 2000—; dir. Comm. Sys. and Signal Processing Inst., 2000—; adj. prof. elec. engring. U. Calif., San Diego, 2002—. Cons. Lincoln Lab. MIT, Lexington, 1976-79, Hughes Research Labs., Malibu, Calif., 1986-87. Editor: Electrical Noise, 1977, Teaching Engineering, 1987, Noise in Circuits and Systems, 1988; editor-in-chief IEEE Microwave & Guided Wave Letters, 1998-2000; contbr. articles to profl. jours. Lilly fellow, 1974-75. Fellow IEEE; mem. IEEE Microwave Soc. (vice chmn. 1984-85, chmn. 1986-87). Achievements include patents in field. Office: San Diego State U Dept Elec Engring 5500 Campanile Dr San Diego CA 92182-1309 Office Phone: 619-594-7015. Business E-Mail: mgupta@mail.sdsu.edu. *A person's level of maturity is measured by what he wants from other members of the society: something for nothing, equal return for everything, or nothing except the opportunity to put something back in the kitty.*

GUPTA, PAUL R., lawyer; b. Cambridge, Eng., Mar. 7, 1950; s. Suraj Gupta and Letty J.R. Paine; m. Mary Lee Gupta, Sept. 30, 1978; children: Adam, Margaret. BA, Yale U., 1971; JD, Harvard U., 1974. Bar: Mass., N.Y. Assoc. Simpson Thacher & Bartlett, N.Y.C., 1974-79, Cravath, Swaine & Moore, N.Y.C., 1980-83; ptnr. Sherin and Lodgen, Boston, 1983-91, Nutter, McClennen & Fish, Boston, 1991-94, Sullivan & Worcester, LLP, Boston, 1995—2002, LeBoeuf, Lamb, Greene & MacRae L.L.P., 2002—04, Mayer, Brown, Rowe & Maw, LLP, NYC, 2004—, practice leader, 2005—. Frequent lectr. Correspondent European Intellectual Property Review; mem. editl. adv. bd. Elec. Banking Law and Commerce Report, BNA's Computer Tech. Law Report, Electronic Commerce and Law Report, E-Commerce Law and Strategy; contbr. aticles to profl. jours. Mem. ABA (co-chair antitrust subcom., intellectual property litigation com.), Assn. Bar City of NY (computer law com. 1994-96), Phi Beta Kappa. Office: Mayer Brown Rowe & Maw LLP 1675 Broadway New York NY 10019-5820 Office Phone: 212-506-2670. Business E-Mail: pgupta@mayerbrownrowe.com.

GUPTA, PIYUSH, research scientist; b. Bhopal, Madhya Pradesh, India, Sept. 20, 1971; s. Surendra Kumar and Shobha Gupta; m. Naveen Aggarwal, May 15, 2002. B of Tech., Indian Inst. Tech., 1993; MS, Indian Inst. Sci., 1996; PhD, U. Ill., 2000. Design engr. Ctr. Devel. Telematics, Bangalore, India, 1993—94; mem. tech. staff Bell Labs, Lucent Techs., Murray Hill, NJ, 2000—. Editor: Advances in Network Information Theory. Grantee, NSF, 2003—. Mem.: IEEE, Ctr. Discrete Math. and Theoretical Computer Sci. Achievements include research in The capacity of wireless networks, ' P. Gupta and P. R. Kumar, IEEE Transactions on Information Theory, vol. IT-46, no. 2, pp. 388-404, March 2000; ″On cycle-time performance improvement under varying mixes by choices of scheduling policies, P. Gupta, P. R. Kumar, D. Andersen, T. Ivanova, E. Reitman, SMOMS-WMC'99, San Francisco, 1999; A system and traffic dependent adaptive routing algorithm for ad hoc networks, P. Gupta and P. R. Kumar, IEEE 36th Conf. on Decision and Control, pp. 2375-2380, San Diego, 1997; Depth-optimal O(n)-node neural networks for n-bit addition, P. Gupta and P. G. Poonacha, Intl. Conf. on Neural Networks Applications in Signal Processing, Singapore, 1993; ″Random-access scheduling with service differentiation in wireless networks, P.Gupta, Y.Sankarasubramaniam, and A.Stolyar, Proceedings of IEEE Infocom 2005, Miami, FL, March 13-17, 2005; patents pending for ″Methods and apparatus for distributed scheduling with service differentiation in wireless networks' (filed in June 2004); ″Methods and apparatus for channel prediction in wireless networks' (filed in April 2004); ″An adaptive wireless communication device and methods of operating the same' (filed in August 2002); research in Towards an information theory of large networks: An achievable rate region, P. Gupta and P. R. Kumar, IEEE Transactions on Information Theory, Vol. 49, no. 8, pp1877-1894, August 2003; Internets in the sky: The capacity of three dimensional wireless networks, P. Gupta and P. R. Kumar, Communications in Information and Systems, vol. 1, no. 1, pp.33-50, January 2001; Randomized neural networks for learning stochastic dependences, V. S. Borkar and P. Gupta, IEEE Transactions on Systems, Man & Cybernetics - Part B: Cybernetics, vol. 29, no. 4, August 1999; Critical power for asymptotic connectivity in wireless networks, P. Gupta and P. R. Kumar, Stochastic Analysis, Control, Optimization and Applications: A Volume in Honor of W.H. Fleming, W. M. McEn; Learning decentralized goal-based vector quantization, P. Gupta and V. S. Borkar, Complex Systems, vol. 11, no. 2, February 1997; Random-access scheduling with service differentiation in wireless networks, P. Gupta, Y. Sankarasubramaniam and A. Stolyar, Proceedings of 2005 IEEE INFOCOM Conference, Miami, FL, March 13-17, 2005; ″Capacity theorems for wireless relay channels, G. Kramer, M. Gastpar, and P. Gupta, Proceedings of 41st Allerton Conference, Allerton, IL, Oct. 2003; ″The multiple-relay channel: coding and antenna-clustering capacity, ' M. Gastpar, G. Kramer, and P. Gupta, IEEE International Symposium on Information Theory ISIT2002, Lausanne, July 2002. Avocations: photography, flying, hiking. Home: 210 Birchview Dr Piscataway NJ 08854 Office: Bell Labs Lucent Technologies 600 Mountain Ave 2c-374 Murray Hill NJ 07974 Office Phone: 908-582-4054. Office Fax: 908-582-3340. Personal E-mail: pgupta71@netscape.net. E-mail: pgupta@research.bell-labs.com.

GUPTA, RAJENDRA PRASAD, physician; b. Marhura, India, May 19, 1948; naturalized, 1981; s. Ramji Das and Somvati Devi Gupta; m. Vinod K. Gupta, Dec. 14, 1974; children: Vanita, Vikram, Vishal. BSc, Agra U., Mathura, 1964; B Medicine B Surgery, Rajisthan U., Udiapur, India, 1969, MD, 1973; MBA, U. South Fla., 1999. Diplomate Am. Bd. Internal Medicine, Am. Bd. Gastroenterology, Am. Bd. Utilization and Quality Review Physicians. Rotating intern R.N.T. Med. Coll., Udaipur, Ind., 1969-70, resident in internal medicine, 1970-71, casualty med. officer in internal medicine, 1972; med. officer Seema Nursing Home, Udaipur, 1972, cons. physician, 1972-73; resident tng. in internal medicine Nat. Health Svc. Hosps., 1973-75; resident in internal medicine category ″C″ St. Francis Med. Ctr., Trenton, N.J., 1975-77; fellow in gastroenterology U. Medicine and Dentistry of N.J., Newark, 1977-79; pvt. practice in gastroenterology and internal medicine Trenton, 1979—; practice medicine Hopewell Valley Med. Group PA, Trenton, N.J. Tchr. Ravindra Nath Tagore Med. Coll.; clin. instr. U. Medicine and Dentistry of NJ, 1977-79, Robert Wood Johnson Med. Sch., Piscataway, NJ, 1992-95; clin. sr. instr. Hahneman Med. Coll., Phila., 1981-92; asst. prof. Robert Wood Johnson Med. Sch., Piscataway, 1995—; affiliated Capital Health Sys., Trenton, Robert Wood Johnson at Hamilton Hosp., NJ; chmn. audit com. Mercer Med. Ctr., Trenton, 1982-83, chmn. utilization rev., 1983-88, mem. constitution and bylaws, 1984-88, med. records com., 1983-85, exec. com., 1985-88, chmn. risk mgmt. com., 1987—, chief gastroenterology sect., 1993-95, chmn. com. sect. chiefs, 1995-97, chmn. physician/hosp. orgn. com., 1993-94, steering com., 1994-95, computer com., 1993, co-chmn. joint conf. com., 1995—, strategic planning com., 1995-96, chmn. dept. medicine, 1995-97, search com., med. dir., 1995, pres. med. staff, 1995-96, fin. com., 1995-97; assoc. med. dir. Ctrl. NJ Mercer, Middlesex Preferred Orgn., Prucare, 1985-86; pres. Healthpath Mercer County, Aetna Health Plan Ind. Practice Assocs., Mt. Laurel, NJ, 1992-94; chmn. med. adv. bd. Morris Hall Home for Aged, Lawrenceville, NJ, 1987-90; treas. Physician's Healthcare Plan NJ, Lawrenceville, 1993-95, sec., 1995-96, v.p., 1996-97, fin. com., 1993-97; cons. gastroenterology Bd. Med. Examiners, Trenton, 1990—. Active Am. Cancer Soc. Mercer County chpt., 1990-92; bd. trustees Chapin Sch., Princeton, NJ, 1993-94; mem. Healthcare Adv. Group for Christie Whitman, 1993; chmn. Capital Health Sys. Found., Trenton, NJ, 2003—. Fellow ACP, Internat. Coll. Physicians, Am. Coll. Gastroenterology, Coll. Utilization Rev. Physicians; mem. AMA (category I award cert. 1979—, Physician Outreach award Presentation 1997, 99), Am. Soc. Gastrointestinal Endoscopy, Acad. Medicine NJ, Med. Soc. NJ (bd. trustees 1996—, legis. com. 1992-94, internat. med. grad. com. 1992-93, pres. coun. 1992-93, vice-chmn. internat medicine grad. com. 1993-94, chmn. reference com. B house of dels. 1993, chnm. house of dels. 1994, vice-chmn. coun. on legis. 1994-95, del. organized med. staff sect. 1995—, exec. com. coun. on legis. 1996—, cons. coun. legis. 1996—), NJ Gastrointestinal Soc., Mercer County Med. Soc. (v.p. 1990-91, chmn. numerous coms., pres. 1992-93), Capital Health Found. Republican. Hindu. Avocations: tennis, swimming, skiing. Office: Hopewell Valley Med Group PA 1871 Pennington Rd Trenton NJ 08618-1208 Office Phone: 609-882-5317. Personal E-mail: rguptamd@hotmail.com.

GUPTA, RAJESH, engineer, consultant; b. New Delhi, June 10, 1962; s. K.L. and Urmilla Varshney; m. Jaishree Gupta, Mar. 7, 1993; children: Sameer, Salil. BSc in Elec. Engring., Aligarh U., India, 1980—85. Asst engr. Hindustan Aeronautics Ltd., Lucknow, India; sr. systems analyst Emirates Airlines Group, Dubai, United Arab Emirates, 1989—94; cons. Compaq Can. Inc., Toronto, Canada, 1995—99; prin. cons., pres. E3i Technologies Inc., Mississauga, Canada, 2000—. Mem.: Metro. Profl. and Exec. Registry (hon.). Home: 3724 Crabtree Crescent Mississauga ON Canada L4T 1S6 Office Phone: 905-677-4606. Personal E-mail: rajeshguptaji@msn.com.

GUPTA, RAJIV LOCHAN, chemical company executive; b. Muzzafarnagar, India, Dec. 23, 1945; s. Phool Prakash and Rukmini (Sahai) G.; m. Kamla Varshney, Jan. 24, 1968; children: Amita, Vanita. B of Tech. in Engring. with honors, Indian Inst. Tech., Bombay, 1967; MS in Ops. Rsch., Cornell U., 1969; MBA in Fin., Drexel U., 1971. Mgmt. sci. analyst Scott Paper Co., Phila., 1969-71; treasury mgr. Rohm & Haas Co., Phila., 1971-74, asst. to chief exec. officer, 1974-76, fin. planning mgr., 1976-79, fin. dir. East Croydon, Eng., 1979-81, planning dir. London, 1981-83, dir. gen. adj. Paris, 1983-84; dir. gen. Duolite Internat. SA, Paris, 1984-87; bus. dir. plastics Rohm & Haas Co., London, 1987-89, global bus. dir., 1989-93, v.p. Pacific Region Phila., 1993-96; chmn. comm. electronic materials bus. group Rohn & Haas Co., Phila., 1996-98, vice-chmn., 1999, chmn., CEO, 1999—. Bd. dirs. Agere Sys., Vanguard Group, Technitool. Sec. Indian Children Orgn., Phila., 1970-71. Hindu. Avocations: bridge, tennis, golf, travel, reading. Office: Rohm and Haas Co Independence Mall W Philadelphia PA 19105*

GUPTA, RAM, software company executive; BS in Engring., Birla Inst. Tech.; MS in Computer Sci., U. Mass. Mgr. networking products devel. Ungermann Bass, Philips; mgr. operating sys. devel. IBM; dir. Multimedia Networking Group Silicon Graphics, 1994—97; sr. v.p., gen. mgr. Healtheon WebMD Corp., 1997—2000; exec. v.p. products and tech. PeopleSoft Inc., Pleasonton, Calif., 2000—. Bd. advisors Certive Corp.; bd. dir. VA Software. Achievements include patents in field. Office: PeopleSoft Inc 4460 Hacienda Dr Pleasanton CA 94588

GUPTA, RITESH, cardiologist, researcher; b. New Delhi, Delhi, India, Mar. 5, 1976; arrived in U.S., 1999; s. Dharam Paul and Sneh Gupta; m. Shikha Khullar, May 30, 1975. MBBS, All India Inst. Med. Scis., 1999; MPH, No. Ill. U., 2002; MD, Cleve. Clinic Found., 2003. Diplomate 1999, cert. Am. Bd. Internal Medicine, 2003, lic. permanent licensure 2004. Rsch. asst. No. Ill. U., DeKalb, 1999—2000; house staff internal medicine Cleve. Clinic Found., 2000—03; cardiology fellow U. Ala., Birmingham, 2003—. Grad. asst. No. Ill. U., Dekalb, Ill., 1999—2000. Contbr. scientific papers, articles to profl. jours. Recipient Nat. Talent Search Examination, Nat. Coun. Edn. Rsch. and Tng., Govt. India, 1991—99. Mem.: Am. Coll. Cardiology, Am. Coll. Physicians, Aiimsonian Alumni Assn. Avocations: travel, history. Office: Univ Alabama 306 LHRB 19th South Birmingham AL 35214 Home Fax: 205-975-8568; Office Fax: 205-975-8586. E-mail: ritg@hotmail.com.

GUPTA, SANDEEP K. S., computer science educator, engineering educator; PhD, Ohio State U., Columbus, Ohio, 1995. Assoc. prof. Ariz. State U., Tempe, Ariz., 2001—. Fellow Adaptive Middleware Svcs. for Situation-Aware Comm. in Ubiquitous Computing Environ., NSF, 2001-2004; grantee ITR/SII: Wireless Networking Solutions for Smart Sensor Biomedical Applications, 2000-2004, Location Based Access Control Arch. for Wireless Home Network, Consortium for Embedded Sys., 2004, Integrated Infrastructure for Identity Assurance, 2005, Mobility Tolerant Adaptive Multicast Protocols for Ad Hoc Networks, NSF, 2000-2003. Achievements include discovery of Compilation techiques for High-Performance Computing; Data Caching Technique for Mobile Computing; Techniques for Ensuring Thermal Safety of Biosensor Networks. Office: Dept CSE Ariz State Univ 699 South Mill Ave Tempe AZ 85281 Office Phone: 480-965-3806.

GUPTA, SANJAY, psychiatrist; b. Bombay, Sept. 24, 1959; s. Parkash Ram and Sarla Rani; m. Sadhna Kayastha, Jan. 14, 1992; children, Sheila, Shawn. MD, The U. Delhi, India, 1984. Diplomate Am. Bd. Psychiatry and Neurology, Am. Bd. Forensic Examiners, Am. Bd. Addiction Medicine, Am. Bd. Forensic Medicine, Am. Bd. Geriat. Psychiatry, Am. Bd. Adolescent Psychiatry. Resident in psychiatry SUNY, Syracuse, 1987-91; rsch. fellow U. Iowa Hosps. and Clinics, Iowa City, 1991-94; asst. prof. psychiatry U. Nebr., Omaha, 1994-95; clin. assoc. prof. psychiatry health scis. ctr. SUNY Health Scis. Ctr., 1996—; clin. prof. dept. psychiatry U. Buffalo, 1997—; pres. Global Rsch. and Cons.; CEO, East West Network. Rschr. brain imaging U. Iowa, 1991-94; examiner Am. Bd. Psychiatry & Neurology Examinations, 1993-95; bd. advisors profl. standards Am. Bd. Forensic Medicine, Springfield, Mo., 1995-96; dir. psychiatry Olean (N.Y.) Gen. Hosp., 1995—, chmn. dept. psychiatry, 1997—; pres. Global Rsch. and Consulting; spkr. in field. Contbr. articles to profl. jours. Travel fellow Am. Coll. Neuropsychopharmacology, 1992. Mem. Am. Psychiat. Assn., Am. Assn. Geriatric Psychiatrists, Am. Bd. Forensic Examiners, Internat. Soc. Neuroimaging in Psychiatry, Am. Assn. Physicians from India, U. Iowa Alumni Assn. Hindu. Achievements include involvement in trials of new drugs for psychiatric illness. Office: Psychiatric Network Olean Gen Hosp 515 Main St Olean NY 14760-1921 Office Phone: 716-373-1094.

GUPTA, SUDHIR, immunologist, educator; b. Bijnor, India, Apr. 14, 1944; came to U.S., 1971; s. Tej S. and Jagdishwari Gupta; m. Abha, Jan. 28, 1980; children: Ankmalika Abha, Saurabh Sudhir. MD, King George's Med. Coll., Lucknow, India, 1966, PhD, 1970. Diplomate Am. Bd. Allergy and Immunology, Am. Bd. Diagnostic Lab. Immunology, Clin. Immunology Bd., Royal Coll. Physicians and Surgeons Can. Intern King George's Med. Coll., Lucknow, 1966, resident in medicine, 1967-70; teaching faculty fellow dept. medicine Tufts U. Med. Sch., Boston, 1971-72; vis. fellow in medicine Columbia U., N.Y.C., 1972-74; rsch. fellow Sloan-Kettering Inst. Cancer Rsch., N.Y.C., 1974-76, asst. prof., 1976-78, assoc. prof., 1978-82; instr. Cornell U., N.Y.C., 1976-77, asst. prof., 1977-79, assoc. prof., 1979-82; prof. medicine U. Calif., Irvine, 1982—, prof. microbiology and molecular genetics, 1984—, prof. pathology, 1986—, prof. neurology, 1988—2004, vice chair dept. medicine, 1994—2002. Mem. adv. panel FDA, Washington, 1989—; sci. advisor Inst. Immunopathology, Kohn, Germany, 1990—; mem. allergy-immunology subcom. NIH, Bethesda, Md., 1985-89; vis. prof. Hematologic Rsch. Found., Roslyn, N.Y., 1992. Editor-in-chief Jour. Clin. Immunology, 1980—; editor: Immunology of Clinical and Experimental Diabetes, 1984, Mechanisms of Lymphocyte Activities and Immune Regulation I-VII, 1985-98, New Concepts in Immunbodeficiency Diseases, 1993, Multidrug Resistance in Cancer, 1996, Immunology of HIV Infections, 1996. Pres. Nargis Dutt Meml. Found., So. Calif., 1990; vice-chair AIDS Task Force, Orange County (Calif.) Med. Assn., 1987-95; mem. Indo-Am. Republican Club, Orange County, 1991—. Recipient Arthur Manzel Rsch. award R.A. Cooke Inst., N.Y.C., 1976, Outstanding Achievement award in med. scis. Nat. Fedn. Asian Indians in N.Am., 1986, Lifetime Achievement award Jeffrey Modell Found., N.Y.C., 1990, Disting. Scientists award Assn. Scientists Indian Origin in Am., 1994, Disting. Physician award Indian Med. Assn. Master ACP; fellow Royal Coll. Physicians and Surgeons Can., Am. Soc. Medicine (London); mem. Am. Assn. Immunologists. Achievements include description of the presence of K+ channels in human T cells, their role in T cell function and assn. with exptl. autoimmune diseases, reversal of multidrug resistance of cancer cells by cyclosporin A both in vitro and in vivo, described a new human intracisternal retrovirus associated with CD4+ cell deficiency without HIV infection; increased apoptosis in T cells in human aging. Office: U Calif Dept Medicine C240 Med Sci I Irvine CA 92697-0001 Fax: 949-824-4362. Office Phone: 949-824-5818. E-mail: sgupta@uci.edu.

GUPTA, SURAJ NARAYAN, physicist, researcher; b. Haryana, India, Dec. 1, 1924; came to U.S., 1953, naturalized, 1963; s. Lakshmi N. and Devi (Goyal) G.; m. (Letty) J. R. Paine, July 14, 1948; children: Paul, Ranee. MS, St. Stephen's Coll., India, 1946; PhD, U. Cambridge, Eng., 1951. Imperial Chem. Industries fellow U. Manchester, Eng., 1951-53; vis. prof. physics Purdue U., 1953-56; prof. physics Wayne State U., Detroit, 1956-61, disting. prof. physics, 1961-99, disting. prof. emeritus physics, 1999—. Author: Quantum Electrodynamics, 1977. Fellow Am. Phys. Soc., Nat. Acad. Scis. of India. Achievements include research in high energy physics, nuclear physics, relativity and gravitation, quantum theory with negative probability and quantization of the electromagnetic field; flat-space interpretation of Einstein's theory of gravitation and quantization of the gravitational field; regularization and renormalization of elementary particle interactions; development of the theory of bound states in quantum electrodynamics and quantum chromodynamics; mass matrix formulation of quark mixing and CP violation in weak interactions; investigation of phenomena at supercollider energies. Home: 30001 Hickory Ln Franklin MI 48025-1566 Office: Wayne State U Dept Physics Detroit MI 48202 Business E-Mail: doctorgupta@ameritech.net.

GUPTA, SURENDRA KUMAR, chemicals executive; b. Delhi, India, Apr. 5, 1938; arrived in US, 1963, naturalized, 1971; s. Bishan Chand and Devki Gupta; m. Karen Patricia Clarke, Oct. 12, 1968; children: Jay, Amanda. BSc with honors, Delhi U., 1959, MSc, 1961; MTech, Indian Inst. Tech., Bombay, 1963; PhD, Wayne State U., 1968. Rsch. assoc. Western Mich. U., Kalamazoo, 1968—73; indsl. fellow Starks Assocs., Buffalo, 1973—74; group leader New Eng. Nuc. Co., Boston, 1974—80, Pathfinder Labs., St. Louis, 1981—83; chmn. bd., chemist Am. Radiolabeled Chem., Inc., St. Louis, 1983—; owner Precision Biochem., Inc., Vancouver, Canada, 2003—. Contbr. articles to profl. jours. Mem.: Am. Chem. Soc. (chmn. pub. rels. com. 1970—73). Hindu. Avocations: ping pong/table tennis, stamp collecting/philately, travel. Home: 22 Muirfield Ln Saint Louis MO 63141-7380 Office: Am Radiolabeled Chems Inc 101 ARC Dr Saint Louis MO 63146-3506 Office Phone: 314-991-4545. Business E-Mail: drgupta@arc-inc.com.

GUPTA, VIJAY KUMAR, retired chemistry professor; b. Ambala Cantt, Haryana, India, Apr. 27, 1941; m. Surjit Mohini Aggarwal, Sept. 5, 1968; children: Sonia, Angela, Ashish. BS in Chemistry with honors, Panjab U., Chandigarh, India, 1961, MS in Chemistry with honors, 1962, PhD in Chemistry, 1969. Asst. prof. chemistry Punjab Engring. Coll., Chandigarh, India, 1962-64, 67-68; postdoctoral rsch. assoc. Wright State U., Dayton, Ohio, 1968-69; rsch. chemist Lawrence Livermore Nat. Lab., Livermore, Calif., summer 1980; adj. faculty mem. Lebanon Correctional Inst., Ohio, fall 1977, 78, summer 1982; fellow Wright Patterson AFB, Dayton, summer 1981, with aero-propulsion lab., 1981-83, with materials lab., 1984, fellow materials lab., 1985, summers 1987, 88, 91, vis. scientist materials lab., 1985-87; adj. faculty mem. Wright State U., 1985; adj. faculty in chemistry Wilberforce U., Ohio, spring/summer 1981, 82, 83, 84, 1983-84, fall 1986-87; prof., chmn. chemistry, researcher Cen. State U., Wilberforce, Ohio, 1969-98, prof. emeritus, 1998—. Cons. E.G.&G. Mound Labs., summer, 1989, 90, 92, 93; researcher in environ. pollution, lubricant devel. and characterization, devel. of radioluminescent light sources, thermodynamics, electrochemistry, chem. kinetics, trace metals analysis, energy conversion and storage, for IBM Corp., Pitts. Plate Glass Fiber Glass Tech. Ctr., NASA, Johnson Johnson Controls Inc., Lawrence Livermore Nat. Lab., Wright Patterson AFB, Universal Energy Systems Inc., AF Office of Sci. Research, San Jose State U., United Tech. Systems Inc., SCEEE, Systran Corp., E.G.&G. Mound Techs., Inc., U. Dayton Rsch. Inst. Contbr. numerous articles to profl. jours. Vol. aux. svcs. Greene Meml. Hosp., 2000—. Recipient Appreciation award Ctrl. State U., 1975-76, Talmadge McKinney award, 1986, Excellence in Rsch. award, 1995, Outstanding Svc. to Cmty. award India Club of Greater Dayton, 1985, Clarence E. Bowman award for Comm. Svcs., 1991, others; Nat. Urban League fellow, IBM Corp. fellow, summer 1973, Pittsburgh Plate Glass Fiberglass Tech. Ctr., summer 1976, Johnson Johnson Control Inc. fellow, 1979, NSF summer fellow, 1979; USAF grantee, 1982-83, NASA grantee, 1976-79, U.S. Army grantee, 1994-98, USN grantee, 1995-96. Mem.: Divine Love Mission, Am. Chem. Soc. (chmn. Dayton sect. 1988, Outstanding Sect. award 1988), India Club (Dayton). Democrat. Hindu. Home: 2810 Dennis Ct Beavercreek OH 45434-6522

GUPTA, VIKAS, reliability engineer, research scientist; s. Ramesh Chandra and Mithilesh Gupta; m. Sabrina Forni, Nov. 9, 2002. BS, Coll. of Tech., Pantnagar, India, 1993; MS, Indian Inst. of Sci., Bangalore, 1996; PhD, U. Mo., Rolla, 2001. Design engr. Lucent Techs./Agere Systems, Breinigsville, Pa., 2001—03; vis. rsch. scientist Lehigh U., Bethlehem, Pa., 2003—; reliability engr. Tex. Instruments, Inc., Dallas, 2004—. Scholarship, U. Mo., Rolla, 1996-2000. Mem.: Sigma Xi. Achievements include patents pending for Interferometer having improved modulation depth and free-spectral range and method of manufacturing same; MEMS Integrated Submount Alignment for Optoelectronics; development of Optoelectronics Laser Pump Development; Pb-free Microelectronics Packaging; research in Polymer Matrix Woven Composites. Office Phone: 972-995-8528.

GUPTA, VIPIN, management educator; s. Surender Nath and Manju Gupta; m. Bhakti Jain, July 29, 1998. Grad., Inst. Cost & Works Accts. India, Delhi, 1988; BS in Commerce with honors, U. Delhi, 1988; MBA, Indian Inst. Mgmt., 1990; MA, Wharton Sch., 1994, PhD, 1998. Internat. product mgr. Unilever India, Mumbai, 1990—91; rsch. fellow U. Tokyo, 1994—95; sr. fellow Wharton Sch., Phila., 1999—2003; prin. co-investigator Globe Rsch. & Ednl. Found., Phila., 1999—; dir. Globe India Devel. Ctr., Delhi, 2000—. Instr. Wharton Sch., 1991—97; asst. prof. Fordham U., NYC, 1997—2003; assoc. prof. Grand Valley State U., Grand Rapids, Mich., 2003—. Editor, author (books) Culture, Leadership, and Organizations: The Globe Study of 62 Societies, Transformative Organizations: Perspectives from Around the Globe, Creating Performing Organizations; editor: IBAT Jour. Mgmt. Mem. Dhruva Coll., Hyderabad, India, 2004—05. Recipient 3d Rank in all of India, Inst. Cost & Works Accts. India, 1988, Gold medal for outstanding scholastic performance, Indian Inst. Mgmt., 1990, 5th Rank in all of India, Govt. of India, 1985, M. Scott Myers award for applied rsch. in the workplace, APA, 2005; grantee fellow, Marsh and McLennan, 1999—2003, NSF, 2001—04, Family Owned Bus. Inst., 2004—05; Nat. Talent Search scholar, Govt. of India, 1984—88, Indsl. fellow, Indian Inst. Mgmt., 1988—90, Rsch. fellow, Japan Found., 1994—95. Mem.: Acad. Mgmt. Home: 3341 Falcon Ridge Dr Grand Rapids MI 49525 Office: Grand Valley State U 456C DeVos Ctr 401 W Fulton St Grand Rapids MI 49504 Office Fax: 616-331-7445. Personal E-mail: guptavi@gvsu.edu.

GUPTA, YASH, dean; b. New Delhi; m. Nisha Gupta; children: Ashish, Ashwin. BS in engring., Punjab U., 1973; M in prodn. mgmt., Brunel U., 1974; PhD in mgmt. sci., U. Bradford, 1976. Sr. cons. Coopers and Lybrand, London, 1978—80; asst. prof. Meml. U., Newfoundland, 1980—82; assoc. prof. U. Manitoba, Canada, 1982—88, prof., 1988; Frazier Family prof. and sr. rsch. fellow Telecom. Rsch. Ctr., U. Louisville Sch. Bus., 1988—92; dean, prof. mgmt. U. Colo., Coll. Bus. and Adminstrn., Denver, 1992—99; dean, Kirby L. Cramer endowed chair bus. U. Wash. Bus. Sch., 1999—2004; dean Marshall Sch. Bus., U. So. Calif., 2004—. Vis. prof. U. Toledo, Ohio, 1985—86; adj. prof. U. Manitoba, Canada, 1991—94; mem. publ. com. Decision Sci. Inst., 1992—95. Mem. editl. bd.: Internat. Jour. Mgmt. and Sys., 1985—88, Technovation: Internat. Jour. Tech. Innovation and Entrepreneurship, Mid-Atlantic Jour. Bus.; area editor Prodn. and Ops. Mgmt. Jour. Mem.: Soc. Orgnl. Behavior, Acad. Mgmt. Achievements include ranked number one prodn. and ops. mgmt. scholar in country in terms of contbns. made to field in Jour. Ops. Mgmt., 1996. Office: Marshall Sch Bus Univ So Calif 701 Exposition Blvd Ste 800 Los Angeles CA 90089-1425 Office Phone: 213-740-6422. Business E-Mail: yash.gupta@marshall.usc.edu.

GUPTA, YOGENDRA M., physicist, researcher; b. New Delhi, July 24, 1949; came to U.S., 1968; s. Brij M. and Prabha (Garg) G.; m. Barbara MacKay, June 21, 1975; children: Anjuli Monica, Sonia Michelle. BS in Physics, Chemistry and Math., BITS, Pilani, India, 1966, MS in Physics, 1968; PhD in Physics, Wash. State U., 1972. Postdoctoral rsch. assoc. Wash. State U. and Brown U., Providence, 1973—74; from physicist to sr. physicist SRI Internat., Menlo Park, Calif., 1975—81, cons., 1981—; from assoc. prof. to prof. Wash. State U., Pullman, 1981—; dir. Inst. for Shock Physics. Editor: Shock Waves in Condensed Matter, 1986; contbr. articles to profl. jours. Mem. AAAS, Am. Phys. Soc., Am. Acad. Mechanics, Phi Kappa Phi. Office: Wash State U Dept Physics Pullman WA 99164-2814 Business E-Mail: ymgupta@wsu.edu.

GUPTA, YOGESH, computer company executive; b. India; BEE, Indian Inst. Tech.; M in Computer Sci., U. Wis. With Burroughs Corp.; from sr. mgmt. to chief tech. officer Computer Assoc. Internat., Islandia, NY, 1989—. Office: Computer Assoc Internat One Computer Assoc Plz Islandia NY 11749

GUPTAN, RAJ, physician, researcher; s. Rajkumar and Sumalika. MD, MAMC, India, 1990. Dir. Venous Rsch. Found., Schaumburg, Ill., 2003—. Dir. of rsch. Vein Clinics Of Am., Schaumburg, Ill., 2001—03; founder and dir. Venom Rsch. Found. Contbr. articles to over 80 rsch. publs. (Internat. Assn. of Study of Liver young investigator award, 1998, INASL Gold medal,

1995, World Congress of Gastroenterology Young clinician award, 2002), chapters to books. Fellow: Royal Soc. Medicine (London); mem.: Am. Coll. of Phlebology, Indian Soc. of Gastroenterology (life). Achievements include development of original clinical research, medical device invention, and hypertext medical publishing. Home: 5500 Carriageway Dr Ste 214 Rolling Meadows IL 60008 Office: Venous Rsch Found PO Box 59444 Schaumburg IL 60008 Personal E-mail: rguptan@hotmail.com. E-mail: rguptan@venousresearchfoundation.com.

GUPTILL, JOHN RANDAL, music educator; b. Wilmington, NC, Nov. 27, 1951; s. Mary Lou Crook Guptill; m. Susan B. Bowers, Oct. 29, 1952; children: James Randal, Christopher John. MusB in Edn., East Carolina U., 1975; MusM In Edn., U. NC, 1996. NC Tchg. Cert. NC, 1975. Band dir. Pender County Sch., Burgaw, NC, 1975—79, Lowe's Grove Jr. High, Mid. Sch., Durham, NC, 1979—98, Brogden Mid. Sch., 1998—2004; condr. Duke U. Wind Symphony. Prin. euphonium Triangle Brass Band, NC, 1985—; co-founder Durham Cmty. Concert Band, NC; co-founder, condr. Triangle Youth Brass Band; founding mem. NC Wind Orch., Raleigh; charter mem. Carolina Gold Sr. Drum & Bugle Corps, Raleigh, NC. Bd. mem., treas. Mallarme Chamber Players, Durham, 2004. Recipient Tchr. Yr., Lowe's Grove Mid. Sch., 1996. Mem.: Tubists Universal Brotherhood Assn., Music Educators Nat. Conf., Coll. Band Dirs. Nat. Assn. Episcopalian. Avocations: drum collecting, camping, canoeing, kayaking. Home: 902 West Carver St Durham NC 27704 Office: Duke Univ Wind Symphony Box 90665 Durham NC 27708 Office Phone: 919-660-3306. Office Fax: 919-660-3301. Personal E-mail: rsjc@mindspring.com. E-mail: guptiljr@duke.edu.

GURA, KATHLEEN MARIE, pediatric pharmacist; b. Worcester, Mass., Aug. 17, 1960; d. Philip J. and Catherine Joyce Kozak; m. Scott Gura, May 5, 1984; children: Alessandra Jeanne, Samantha Anne. BS, Mass. Coll. Pharmacy and Allied Health Scis., 1982; PharmD, Mass. Coll. Pharmacy and Health Scis., 1999. Registered pharmacist Mass. Bd. Pharmacy, 1982, D.C. Bd. Pharmacy, 1983, bd. cert. nutrition support pharmacist Bd. Pharm. Specialties, 1993. Clin. staff pharmacist Children's Hosp. Nat. Med. Ctr., Washington, 1982—84; clin. pharmacy specialist GI/nutrition Children's Hosp. Boston, 1984—. Adj. asst. prof. Mass. Coll. Pharmacy, Boston, 1999—, Northeastern U., Boston, 2002—; preceptor for experiential edn. U. N.C. Coll. Pharmacy, Chapel Hill, 2003—, Wash. State U., 2004—, U. of Wash. Sch. Pharmacy, Seattle, 2004—. Author: (textbook) Manual of Pediatric Nutrition, 2000, 2005, Pediatric Nutrition in Your Pocket, 2002, Nutrition in Pediatrics, 3d edit., 2003, Geriatric Nutrition, The Health Professional's Handbook, 3d edit., 2004. Leader Girls Scouts Am., Norfolk, Mass., 1999. Fellow: Am. Soc. Health System Pharmacists (ho. dels. 1996—2003, chair coun. profl. affairs 2000—01); mem.: European Soc. for Clin. Nutrition and Metabolism, Am. Coll. Clin. Pharmacy, Pediatric Pharmacy Advocacy Group (bd. dirs. 2000—04, v.p., finance 2004—), Am. Soc. for Parenteral and Enteral Nutrition, Mass. Soc. of Health Sys. Pharmacists (pres. 2000—01, Practitioner Excellence award 1994), Rho Chi, Rho Pi Phi (sec. 1980—81). Avocations: travel, photography. Home: 5 Barnstable Rd Norfolk MA 02056 Office: Children's Hospital Boston 300 Longwood Ave Boston MA 02115 Office Phone: 617-355-2336. Business E-Mail: kathleen.gura@childrens.harvard.edu.

GURA, PHILIP FRANCIS, English and American literature educator; b. Ware, Mass., June 14, 1950; s. Oswald Eugene and Stephanie (Koziara) G.; m. Leslie Ann Cohig, Aug. 4, 1979; children: David Austin, Katherine Blair, Daniel Alden. BA, Harvard Coll., 1972; PhD, Harvard U., 1977. Instr. Am. Lit. Middlebury (Vt.) Coll., 1974-76; asst. prof. U. Colo., Boulder, 1976-80, assoc. prof., 1980-85, prof., 1985-87, U. N.C., Chapel Hill, 1987—98, prof., English, adj. prof. Religious Studies, 1998—2000, William S. Newman disting. prof. Am. lit. and culture, 2000—. James Russell Wiggins lectr. U. N.C., 2005. Author: The Wisdom of Words, 1981, Critical Essays on American Transcendentalism, 1982, A Glimpse of Sion's Glory, 1984, The Memoirs of Stephen Burroughs, 1988, The Crossroads of American History and Literature, 1996, C.F. Martin and His Guitars, 1796-1873, 2003, Buried from the World: Inside the Massachusetts State Prisin, 1829-1831, 2001, Jonathan Edwards: America's Evangelical, 2005, (with James Bollman) America's Instrument: The Banjo in the Ninteenth Century, 1999; editor Early Am. Lit., 1989-99. Recipient Post-Baccalaureate Disting. Tchg. award, U. N.C., 2004; Peterson fellow Am. Antiquarian Soc., 1989, 1998, 2003, sr. fellow NEH, 1985-86, Charles Warren Ctr. fellow Harvard U., 1980-81. Mem. MLA, Am. Studies Assn., Colonial Soc. Mass., Am. Antiquarian Soc., Inst. Early Am. History and Culture (nat. coun. 1991-94). Office: Wm Newman Disting Prof CB3520 U NC Dept English Chapel Hill NC 27599-3520 Office Fax: 919-962-4033. E-mail: gura@email.unc.edu.

GURAL, JEFFREY R., real estate company executive; Degree in Civil Engring., Rensselaer Poly. INst. With Morse-Diesel Constrn. Co.; joined Newmark & Co. Real Estate Inc., N.Y.C., 1972—, prin., 1978—, co-pres., 1992—2000, chmn., 2000—. Co-sponsor Chelsea-Elliott "I Have A Dream" Project; bd. dirs. Eldridge St. Synagogue, Jewish Cmty. Ctr. of the Upper West Side, Cooper Union. Mem.: IHAD-NY (chmn.), USO (bd. mem.), 14th St.-Union Sq. Dist. Mgmt. Assn. (bd. dirs.), Dist. Mgmt. Assn. for the Times Sq. Bus. Improvement Dist. (chmn. bd. dirs.), Real Estate Bd. N.Y. (bd. dirs.), UJA-Fedn. (bd. dirs.), The Starlight Found. (pres. N.Y. chpt.), Real Estate Lodge B'nai B'rith (v.p.). Avocation: owner, breeder Standardbred racehorses. Office: Newmark & Co Real Estate Inc 125 Park Ave New York NY 10017 Office Phone: 212-372-2400. Business E-Mail: jgural@newmarkre.com.

GURALNICK, SIDNEY AARON, engineering educator; b. Phila., Apr. 25, 1929; s. Philip and Kenia (Dudnik) G.; m. Eleanor Alban, Mar. 10, 1951; children: Sara Dian, Jeremy. BSc, Drexel Inst. Tech., Phila., 1952; MS, Cornell U., 1955, PhD, 1958. Registered profl. engr., Pa.; lic. structural engr., Ill. Instr., then asst. prof. Cornell U., 1952-58, mgr. structural research lab., 1956-58; mem. faculty Ill. Inst. Tech., Chgo., 1958—, prof. civil engring., 1967—, disting. prof. engring., 1982—, dir. structural engring. labs., 1968-71, dean Grad. Sch., 1971-75, exec. v.p., provost, 1975-82, trustee, 1976-82, dir. Advanced Bldg. Materials and Sys. Ctr., 1987—. Devel. engr. Portland Cement Assn., Skokie, Ill., 1959-61; participant internat. confs.; cons. to govt. and industry. Author numerous papers in field. Trustee Inst. Gas Tech., 1976-81, Rsch. Inst. of Ill. Inst. Tech., 1976-82; commr.-at-large North Ctrl. Assn. Schs. and Colls., 1985-89, cons., evaluator, 1989-93. With C.E., U.S. Army, 1950-51. McGraw fellow, 1952-53; Faculty Rsch. fellow Ill. Inst. Tech., 1960; European travel grantee, 1961 Fellow: ASCE (Collingwood prize 1961, Lifetime Achievement award Ill. sect. 1997, Civil Engr. of Yr. award Ill. sect. 1998); mem.: Ill. Univs. Transp. Rsch. Consortium (adminstrv. com. 1983—93), Transp. Rsch. Bd., Structural Engrs. Assn. Ill. (bd. dirs., pres.-elect 1989—90, pres. 1990—91, John F. Parmer award 1993), Soc. Exptl. Mechanics, Am. Concrete Inst., Chi Epsilon, Tau Beta Pi, Phi Kappa Phi, Sigma Xi. Office: Ill Inst Tech 3300 S Federal St Chicago IL 60616-3793 Office Phone: 312-567-3549. Business E-Mail: guralnick@iit.edu.

GURAM, GURPAL SINGH, mathematician, educator; b. Ludhiana, India, Aug. 12, 1946; s. Arjan Singh and Bhagwant (Kaur) G.; m. Mohinder Kaur Guram, Aug. 17, 1975; children: Gurpreet, Jaspreet. BSc, Panjab (India) U., 1965; MSc, U. Roorkee, India, 1968; MS, U. Windsor, Can., 1971; PhD, U. Windsor, 1974. Assoc. prof. math. N.Y. Inst. Tech., Old Westbury, 1982—. Home: 106 Bagatelle Rd Dix Hills NY 11746

GURDAK, MICHAEL P., lawyer; b. Springfield, Vt., 1962; BA, Univ. Notre Dame, 1984, JD, 1987. Bar: Md. 1987, DC 1991, admitted to practice: US Dist. Courts for DC and Dist. of Md. and US Ct. of Fed. Claims. Ptnr., chair, trade, regulatory law and telecom.practice Jones Day, Washington, 1998—. Mem.: Md. Bar Assn., DC Bar Assn. Office: Jones Day 51 Louisiana Ave NW Washington DC 20001-2113 Office Fax: 202-626-1700.

GUREVICH, GRIGORY, visual artist, educator, mime; b. St. Petersburg, Russia, Dec. 26, 1937; came to U.S., 1976; s. Abram Grigoryevich Gurevich and Klara Mihailovna (Olshvang) Fleitman; m. Mongita Zalmanovna Freedman, Aug. 8, 1958 (div. Feb. 1967); 1 child, Jelena Gurevich Scherbina; m. Erika Wittmann, Jan. 17, 1987; d. Sept. 6, 2001. 1 child, Alexander. Diploma, Acad. Fine & Indsl. Art, St. Petersburg, 1966. Interior designer Lenprojekt, St. Petersburg, Lenzneeap, 1961-63, 63-65; founder Grigur's Pantomime Theater, St. Petersburg, 1966-69; founder mime sch. St. Petersburg, 1969-75; founder Grigur's Pantomime Theater, N.Y.C., 1977; tchr. visual arts Bergen Sch., Jersey City, 1980-82; instr. sculpture Newark Sch. Fine and Indsl. Art, 1982-96; prof. St. Johns U., Jamaica, N.Y., 1994-97. Conductor workshops on sculpture U.S., Italy, Denmark; founder Art Workshops Festival, Arts on the Hudson, Jersey City. Exhibited in solo and group exhbns. U.S., Russia, France, Denmark, Germany; bronze sculpture tableau Commuters for Newark Penn Sta., 1985, bronze bust Kazuo Hashimoto, 1996; represented in numerous pvt. collections, Russia, U.S. and Europe, Hermitage Mus., N.Y. Pub. Libr., Libr. Newark Mus., Montclair Mus., Libr. St. Bonaventure U., Yad Vashem Mus., Israel; pub. poetry Reflections, 1992; author: Book of Numbers 1-10, 10-1, 1993 (collections Bklyn. Mus. 1994, Columbia U. Chgo. Libr.); inventor process of wood firing, 1963, manifolding book, 1995; actor: David Letterman Show, 2002, Law and Order, 2003. Founder Arts on the Hudson Sch., Jersey City, N.J., 1998. Recipient Grumbacher award, Marian Reitman award, others. Mem. N.Y. Artists Equity Assn., Am. Artists Profl. League (1st Place Nat. award 1993, 98), Hudson Artists (Artist of Yr. 1995, other awards), Screen Actors Guild. Home: 282 Barrow St Jersey City NJ 07302-3502 E-mail: grigur@netzero.net.

GUREVICH, RACHEL, writer, editor; b. Pitts., May 13, 1977; d. Richard and Iris Mendlowitz Bollinger; m. Ilya Gurevich, Aug. 16, 1998; children: Menachem, Eliezer. BS cum laude, U. Pitts., 1999. Asst. editor Coincide Media, Kingston, Ohio, 2000—04; sr. editor FabJob.com, Canada, 2003—04; writing instr. Long Ridge Writer's Group, 2004—. Author: (non-fiction) FabJob Guide to Become a Doula, 2000, The Doula Advantage: Your Complete Guide to Having an Empowered and Positive Birth with the Help of a Professional Childbirth Assistant, 2003; editor: FabJob Guide to Become an Image Consultant, 2004; contbr. articles to profl. jours. Mem.: Nat. Assn. of Women Writers, Soc. of Children's Book Writers and Illustrators (assoc.). Office Phone: 410-585-0252. Business E-Mail: rachel@doyoudoula.com.

GUREWITZ, THOMAS MARK, lawyer; b. Chgo., Nov. 5, 1949; s. Jerome and Miriam (Kass) G.; m. Sarah Ward, Aug. 12, 1972 (div. Apr. 1976). BA, Beloit Coll., 1971; JD, John Marshall Law Sch., Chgo., 1975. Bar: Ill.1975. Staff atty. Legal Svcs. Lake County, Waukegan, Ill., 1976-78; asst. prosecutor City of Waukegan (Ill.), 1977-85; pvt. practice Waukegan, 1978—. Dir. Prairie State Legal Svcs., Waukegan, 1981-85. Bd. dirs., founding mem. Lake County Crisis Ctr., Waukegan, 1978-82. Mem. ABA, Ill. Bar Assn. (family law sect. council), Lake County Bar Assn. (sec. 1981-83, 1985-88; chmn. family law com. 1988-2005, pres. 1999-2000), Ill. Trial Lawyers Assn., Am. Assn. Matrimonial Lawyers (bd. dirs.). Home: 15245 W Oak Spring Rd Libertyville IL 60048-1619 Office: 20 Martin Luther King Jr Waukegan IL 60085-4326

GURFEIN, PETER J., lawyer; b. N.Y.C., Sept. 13, 1948; m. Pamela Hedin, June 23, 1976; children: Diana, William, Eva. BA, NYU, 1969; JD, George Washington U., 1973. Bar: N.Y. 1976, U.S. Supreme Ct. 1976, US. Dist. Ct. (so. and ea. dists.) N.Y. 1976, U.S. Ct. Appeals (2d cir.) 1979, Internat. Ct. Trade 1979, U.S. Ct. Appeals (9th cir.) 1986, Calif. 1986, U.S Dist. Ct. (no., ea., so. and cen. dists.) Calif. 1987, D.C. 1993. Project dir. Commn. on Correctional Facilities and Scs. ABA, Washington, 1973-76; asst. dist. atty., spl. narcotics prosecutor Dist. Atty.'s Office N.Y. County, N.Y.C., 1976-81; assoc. Zalkin, Rodin & Goodman, N.Y.C., 1981-83, Moses & Singer, N.Y.C., 1983-86; ptnr. Morrison & Foerster, San Francisco, 1986-92, Sonnenschein, Nath & Rosenthal, L.A. and San Francisco, 1993-2000, Akin, Gump, Strauss, Hauer & Feld, LLP, L.A., 2001—. Editor-in-chief The Calif. Bankruptcy Jour., 1995-2000; contbr. articles to handbooks and profl. jours. Mem. Bar Assn. San Francisco (chmn. bankruptcy and comml. law sect. 1993), L.A. County Bar Assn.; dir. L.A. Bankruptcy Forum, 1995—. Office: Akin Gump Strauss Hauer & Feld LLP Ste 2400 2029 Century Park E Los Angeles CA 90067 Office Phone: 310-229-1000. E-mail: pgurfein@akingump.com.

GURGANUS, ALLAN, writer; b. Rocky Mount, N.C., June 11, 1947; s. M.F. and Ethel Morris Gurganus. BA, Sarah Lawrence Coll., 1972; MFA, Iowa Writers' Workshop, 1975. Prof. writing and lit. Stanford (Calif.) U., 1976-78, Duke U., Durham, N.C., 1978-79, Sarah Lawrence Coll., Bronxville, N.Y., 1979-89, Iowa Writers' Workshop, Iowa City, 1989-90. Guest Eng. lectr. Cambridge U., 1995. Author: Oldest Living Confederate Widow Tells All, 1989 (Sue Kaufman prize Am. Acad. Arts and Letters, 1989), White People, 1990 (La. Times Book prize, 1990), Plays Well With Others, 1997, The Practical Heart, 2001. With USN, 1966-70. Recipient Amb. Book award English Speaking Union, 1989, Nat. Mag. prize Nat. Mag. Assn., 1994. Mem. PEN, Soc. Values in Higher Edn., Boston Atheneum. Democrat. Avocations: painting, drawing, gardening. Office: Internat Creative Mgmt c/o Amanda Urban 40 W 57th St New York NY 10019-4001

GURGOVITS, STEPHEN J., trust company executive; b. 1944; BA in Econs., Youngstown State U. Teller First Nat. Bank Pa., 1961, pres., 1988; vice chmn. bd. dirs. FNB Corp., Hermitage, Pa., 1998—2004; pres., CEO First Nat. Bank Pa., Hermitage, Pa., 2004; chmn. Regency Fin. Co. Office: FNB Corp One FNB Blvd Hermitage PA 16148-3301

GURIAN, BENNETT SHEPPE, psychiatrist; b. New Haven, Conn., May 21, 1932; s. Harry and Pauline (Caplan) G.; m. Elaine Gurian; children: Aaron, Josef, Eve; m. Tanya T. Terry, May 22, 1983; children: Amy, Andrew. AB, Brandeis U., 1954; MS, Brown U., 1956; MD, Boston U., 1965. Diplomate Am. Bd. Psychiatry and Neurology with added qualifications in geriatric psychiatry. Ind. rschr. Mass. Gen. Hosp., Boston, 1956-61; dir. geriatrics Mass. Mental Health Ctr., Boston, 1969-92; sr. cons. geriatric psychiatry Deaconess Hosp., Boston, 1992-95; N.E. regional dir. UPBEAT Dept. Vet.'s Affairs, Brockton/West Roxbury, Mass., 1995-97; psychiatrist Beth Israel Deaconess Med. Ctr., Boston, 1997—; medical dir. Jewish Family and Children's Svcs., Newton, Mass., 2000—. Editor: Jour. Geriatric Psychiatry, 1995—; contbr. articles to profl. jours. Founder For Fathering project Med. Found., Boston, 1995—; bd. dirs. SPRY Found., Washington, 1990-2000, Boston Soc. for Gerontol. Psychiatry, 1995-2001; v.p. Physicians for Social Responsibility, 1961-70. Recipient Significant Achievement award Am. Psychiat. Assn., 1990, resolution and recognition Mass. Ho. Reps., 1989. Fellow Am. Geriatrics Soc., Gerontol. Soc. Am. Avocation: watercolorist. Home: 328 Mason Ter Brookline MA 02446-2779

GURIAN, MAL, telecommunications executive; b. NYC, Nov. 17, 1926; s. George Joseph and Rose (Graff) G.; m. Gloria Dickler; children: Randy Harlan, Nancy Ellen Newman. Ptnr. Mal Gurian Assocs., N.Y.C., 1946-77; v.p. Radio Telephone Corp., N.Y.C., 1960-83; sr. v.p. Aerotron, Inc., Raleigh, N.C., 1965-81; v.p. Oki Advanced Comm., Hackensack, N.J., 1981-84; pres. Oki Telecom, Fairlawn, N.J., 1984-88, Cartell, Inc., Romulus, Mich., 1988, Cellcom Cellular Corp., Fairfield, N.J., 1989-91; CEO Universal Cellular, Inc., Anaheim, Calif., 1992; chmn., CEO Global Link Comm., Inc., Irvine, Calif., 1993—; pres., CEO Authentix Network, Inc., Tucson, 1995-98, 99—, chmn., 1998-2001; pres., CEO SimplySay, LLC, Tucson, 2001—02, Mal Gurian Assocs., Bradenton, Fla., 2002—. Adv. I-Control, Campbell, Calif., 2002-03; bd. adv. pres. Ea. Profl. Photographers Assn., NYC, 1951-53; exec. advisor TRW Wireless Commn., Sunnyvale, Calif., 1994; advisor Sims Comms., Inc., Delray Beach, Fla., 1994-98; arbitrator Am. Arbitration Assn., 1994-2002; bd. electronic comm. Rangestar Internat., San Jose, Calif., 1996-98; bd. advisor Genesis Campus, LP, 2003—; bd. dirs. Airbee Wireless; bd. advisor Mobility Ventures, 2005-, Longboard Venture Ptnrs. LLC, 2005—. Active Old Tappan (NJ) First Aid Corp., 1966—. Cpl. USMC, 1943-46. Decorated Air medal; recipient Alexander S. Popov Hon. medal, St. Petersburg Electrotech. U., Russia, 1995. Fellow Radio Club Am. (life mem., v.p. 1976-92, exec. v.p. 1993, pres. 1994, pres. emeritus 1995—, Spl. Svcs. award 1986, Sarnoff citation 1988, Fred Link award 1989, inducted into Wireless Hall of Fame, 2003); mem. Am. Assn. Pub. Safety Comm. Officers, Nat. Assn. Bus. and Ednl. Radio (bd. dirs. 1977-84, Chmn.'s award 1986, named to Wireless Hall of Fame 2003). Office Phone: 941-752-1133. Business E-Mail: mgurian@malgurianassoc.com. *Advances in technology is rapidly moving on. Mankind must strive to utilize our developments in a positive vein and promote compatibility amongst each other.*

GURKA, JAMES JOHN, meteorologist; b. Lawrence, Mass. s. John and Mary Gurka; m. Johanna Katherina Roth; children: Matthew James, Kirsten Marie Gurka-Dell. BS in Meteorology, Lowell Technol. Inst., 1970; MS in Meteorology, Pa. State U., 1972. Rsch. meteorologist NOAA/NESDIS, Camp Springs, Md., 1972—82, phys. scientist, team leader Silver Spring, Md., 2000—; meteorologist, forecaster NOAA/Nat. Weather Svc., Boston, 1982—94, meteorologist, satellite program leader Silver Spring, 1994—2000. Contbr. articles to profl. jours. Mem. Jaycees, Crofton, Md., 1977—82; pres. Ea. New Eng. chpt. Nat. Weather Assn., Boston, 1984—86. Recipient award, Nat. Weather Assn., 1989. Mem.: Am. Meteorol. Soc. Avocations: golf, tennis, travel, bicycling. Office: NOAA/NESDIS Rm 5136 1335 East-West Hwy Silver Spring MD 20910-3226 Office Phone: 301-713-2789 148.

GURNETT, DONALD ALFRED, physics professor; b. Cedar Rapids, Iowa, Apr. 11, 1940; s. Alfred Foley and Velma (Trachta) G.; m. Marie Barbara Schmitz, Oct. 10, 1964; children: Suzanne, Christina. BS in Elec. Engring., U. Iowa, 1962, MS in Physics, 1963, PhD in Physics, 1965. Prof. physics and astronomy U. Iowa, Iowa City, 1965-75, 76-79, 80—; rsch. scientist Max-Planck Inst., Garching, Fed. Republic Germany, 1975-76; vis. prof. UCLA, 1979-80; mem. space physics com. Nat. Acad. Sci., Washington, 1975-78, mem. com. on solar terrrestrial research, 1976-79, mem. com. on planetary and lunar exploration, 1982-85. Recipient Alexander von Humboldt Found. award, 1975, Disting. Sci. Achievement award NASA, 1981, Space Act award NASA, 1986, Sci. Achievement medal Gov. of Iowa, 1987, Disting. Iowa Scientist award Iowa Acad. Sci., 1989, Marion L. Huit award U. Iowa, 1990, Iowa Bd. Regents award for faculty excellence, 1994. Fellow Am. Geophys. Union (assoc. editor Jour. Geophys. Rsch. 1974-77), Am. Acad. Arts & Sci., Fleming medal 1989, Am. Phys. Soc. (award for excellence in plasma physics 1989); mem. Internat. Union Radio Sci. (Dellinger gold medal 1978), Soaring Soc. Am. (Iowa State gov. 1983-86), Nat. Acad. of Sci. Home: 4664 Canterbury Ct Iowa City IA 52245 Office: U Iowa Dept Physics and Astronomy 715 Van Allen Hall Iowa City IA 52242-1403 Business E-Mail: donald-garnett@uiowa.edu.

GURNEY, ALBERT RAMSDELL, playwright, educator; b. Buffalo, Nov. 1, 1930; s. Albert Ramsdell and Marion (Spaulding) Gurney; m. Mary Forman Goodyear, June 8, 1957; children: George, Amy, Evelyn, Benjamin. BA, Williams Coll., 1952, DDL (hon.), 1984; MFA, Yale U., 1958; LLD (hon.), Buffalo State U., 1992. Mem. faculty MIT, 1960-96, prof. lit., 1970-96. Contbr. works to Best Short Plays, 1955—56, works to Best Short Plays, 1957—58, works to Best Short Plays, 1969, works to Best Short Plays, 1970, works to Best Short Plays, 1992; author: (plays) The Golden Fleece, 1969, Public Affairs, 1970, Scenes from American Life, 1971, Children, 1974, Richary Cory, 1976, The Middle Ages, 1977, The Wayside Motor Inn, 1977, The Golden Age, 1980, The Dining Room, 1981, What I Did Last Summer, 1982, The Perfect Party, 1985, Another Antigone, 1985, Sweet Sue, 1986, The Cocktail Hour, 1988, Love Letters, 1988, The Snow Ball, 1991, The Old Boy, 1991, The Fourth Wall, 1992, Later Life, 1993, A Cheever Evening, 1994, Sylvia, 1994, Overtime, 1995, Let's Do It!, 1996, The Guest Lecturer, 1998, Labor Day, 1998, Far East, 1999, Ancestral Voices, 1999, Human Events, 2000, Buffalo Gal, 2001, The Fourth Wall (revised), 2002, O Jerusalem, 2003, Big Bill, 2003, Strictly Academic, 2003, Mrs. Farnsworth, 2004, Screen Play, 2004, (teleplays) O Youth and Beauty, 1979, The Hit List, 1988, Love Letters, 1999, (novels) The Gospel According to Joe, 1974, Entertaining Strangers, 1977, The Snow Ball, 1984, (one-act opera) Strawberry Fields, 1999. With USNR, 1952—55. Named to Theatre Hall Fame, 2005; recipient award, N.Y. Drama Desk, 1971, Rockefeller Playwrights, 1977, Playwriting award, Nat. Endowment Arts, 1981—82, Award of Merit, Am. Acad. and Inst. Arts and Letters, 1987, Lucille Lortel award for Body of Work, 1994, William Inge award, 2000. Mem.: Dramatists Guild, Writers Guild, Authors League Am. Home: 40 Wellers Bridge Rd Roxbury CT 06783-1616 Personal E-mail: a.r.gurney@charter.net.

GURNIS, MICHAEL CHRISTOPHER, geological sciences educator; b. Boston, Oct. 22, 1959; s. George Albert and Barbara (Dempsey) G. BS, U. Ariz., 1982; PhD, Australian Nat. U., Canberra, 1987. Rsch. fellow in geophysics Calif. Inst. Tech., Pasadena, 1986-88, assoc. prof. geophysics, 1994-96; asst. prof. geol. scis. U. Mich., Ann Arbor, 1988-93, assoc. prof., 1993—2003; assoc. dir. Seismological Lab. Calif. Inst. Tech., Pasadena, 1995—, prof. geophysics, 1996—; dir. Computational Infrastructure for Geodynamics, 2004—; John and Hazel Smits prof. geophysics Caltech, 2005—. Recipient Presdl. Young Investigator award NSF, 1989, fellowship David and Lucile Packard Found., 1991. Fellow Am. Geophys. Union (Macelwance medal 1993), Geol. Soc. Am. (sr., Donath medal 1993). Achievements include research in the linkage of sedimentary rocks deposited in the interiors of continents to geodynamic processes within the earth; global dynamics, mantle convection, plate tectonics, sea level changes, evolution of mantle and crust; computational and visual fluid mechanics. Office: Calif Inst Tech Seismol Lab-252-21 Pasadena CA 91125-0001

GURR, DIANNE BUCHANAN, educational consultant; b. Columbus, Ga., Mar. 17, 1947; m. J. Douglas Gurr, July 8, 1967; children: Ashley, Stuart. BS, Fla. State U., 1969; MEd, Brenau U., 2000. Tchr. Deagherty County, Albany, Ga., 1969—70; dir. tchr. Antioch Kindergarten, Marietta, Ga., 1977—83; tchr. Bells Ferry, Marietta, Ga., 1984—87, Murdock, Marietta, 1987—99; instr. lead tchr. East Side, Marietta, 1999—. Staff devel. trainer Cobb County, Marietta, Ga., 1990—97; nat. cert. trainer Talents Unlimited, Mobile, Ala., 1990—97. Named Tchr. of Yr., 1986—87, 1996—97. Mem.: Delta Kappa Gamma. Home: 1509 Waynesbourough Ct Marietta GA 30062 Office: East Side Elem 3850 Roswell Rd Marietta GA 30062 Office Phone: 770-578-7200. Office Fax: 770-578-7202. E-mail: dgurr@bellsouth.net.

GURRIA TREVINO, JOSÉ ANGEL, former Mexican government official; b. Mexico, May 8, 1950; BA in Econs., Nat. Autonomous U., 1972; MA in Pub. Fin., Leeds U., Eng.; studentInternat. Rels., U. So. Calif.; student Fin., Harvard U. Analyst Fed. Electricity Commn., Mexico, 1968-71; pvt. sec. to Sec. Gen. Fed. Dist. dept. Govt. of Mexico, Mexico City, 1971-74, pvt. sec. to dir. gen. pub. fin. dept.; permanent rep. Internat. Coffee Orgn., London, 1976-78; adv. pub. debt. Secretariat of Treasury, Mexico, 1978, dir. pub. debt., 1979; dir. gen. pub. credit, negotiator pub. fgn. debt Govt. of Mexico, Mexico City, 1983-88, undersec. internat. fin., negotiator free trade treaty, 1989-93; dir. gen. Nat. Bank for Fgn. Trade, Mexico, 1993-94; sec. fgn. affairs Govt. of Mexico, Mexico City, 1995—98, sec. fin. and pub. credit, 1998—2000. Mem. Com. Internat. Affairs, Modernization and Ideology. Institutional Revolutionary Party. Office: Partido Revolucionario Inst Insurgentes Norte No 9 Edif 2 Col Buenavista Deleg Cuauhtemoc 06359 Mexico City Mexico

GURSKY, ANDREAS, artist; b. Leipzig, Germany, Jan. 15, 1955; Student, Folkwangschule, Essen, 1978—81, Kunstakademie, Dusseldorf, 1981—87; studied with Bernd Becher, 1985. One-man shows include Flughafen Dusseldorf, 1987, Galerie Johnen and Schottle, Cologne, 1988, 1991, 303 Gallery, N.Y.C., 1989, 1991, 1995, Mus. Haus Lange, Krefeld, 1989, P.S. 1 The Clocktower, N.Y., 1989, Ctr. Genevois de Gravure Contemporaine, Geneva, 1989, Kunstlerhaus, Stuttgart, 1991, Galerie Rudiger Schottle, Paris, 1991, Munich, 1991, Hypobank, N.Y., 1992, Galeria Lia Rumma, Naples, 1992, Victoria Miro Gallery, London, 1992, Kunsthalle, Zurich, 1992, Monika Spruth Galerie, Cologne, 1993, Deichtorhallen, Hamburg, 1994, De Appel Found., Amsterdam, 1994, Le Case D'Arte, Mailand, 1994, Portikus, Frankfurt, 1995, Tate Gallery, Liverpool, Eng., 1995, Galerie Mai 36, Zurich, 1995, Rooseum Ctr. Contemporary Art, Malmo, 1995, Galerie Ghislaine Hassenot, Paris, 1996, Matthew Marks Gallery, N.Y., 1997, Milw. Art Mus., 1998, others, exhibited in group shows at Kunstlerwerkstatt Lothringer Str.,

Munich, 1985, Galerie Rudiger Schottle, 1986, 1988, Galerie Wittenbrink, 1987, Galerie Mosel and Tschechow, 1988, Galleria Lia Rumma, Naples, 1989, Nat. Mus. Modern Art, Tokyo, 1990, Castello di Rivoli, 1991, Musee d'art Moderne de la Ville de Paris, 1992, Hayward Gallery, London, 1992, Mus. Folkwang, 1993, Galerie des Archives, Paris, 1994, Matthew Marks Gallery, N.Y.C., 1995, Berlinische Galerie, 1997, The Photographer's Gallery, London, 1998, numerous others. Office: care Matthew Marks Gallery 523 W 24th St New York NY 10011-1104

GURSPAN, MITCHELL SCOTT, technology architect, writer; b. New York, NY, Jan. 12, 1962; s. Wallace Gurspan, Liliane Gurspan; m. Susan J Weiss; 1 child, Marcy Corinne. BS in Physics and Math., CUNY, 1984. Lic. mortgage broker Fla. President Digitech Software Systems, New York, NY, 1985—87; Systems Analyst Standard and Poor's Trading Systems, New York, NY, 1987—89, ILX Systems, New York, NY, 1989—91; Senior Systems Analyst Garban Inc., New York, NY, 1991—95; Principal Technology Specialist Sybase, Rockaway, NJ, 1995—2001; pres. Tanglewood Mortgage Inc., Boynton Beach, Fla., 2003. Author: (book) Upgrading and Migrating to Sybase SQL Server11, 1996. Event committee member Crohn's and Colitis Association, New York, NY, 1994—2001. Mem.: IEEE. Avocation: Third degree black belt instructor, Tai chi chuan instructor, author, tennis. E-mail: mgurspan@optonline.net.

GURSPAN, SUSAN JUDITH, language educator; b. New York, Dec. 6, 1964; d. Samuel Abraham and Alice Weiss; m. Mitchell Scott Gurspan; 1 child, Marcy Corinne. BA in Arts/Applied Linguistics and Edn. summa cum laude, Queens Coll., Flushing, NY, 1981—86, MS in Edn. summa cum laude, 1988; Hebrew Lang. and Judaic Studies, Orot Coll., Petach Tikvah, Israel, 1982—83. Cert. tchr. ESL N.Y.C. Bd. of Edn., 1986, realtor N.J. Bd. of Realtors, 2001. Adj. lectr., intensive english lang. immersion program English Lang. Inst., Queens Coll., Flushing, NY, 1986—88; tchr. of English as a second lang. Pub. Sch. 9, New York, NY, 1988—99; model teacher/staff developer/teacher-trainer Dist. 3 Office of Multilingual/Multicultural Edn., New York, NY, 1990—99; presenter/trainer NYC Bd. of Edn., New York, NY, 1990—99, Staff Devel. Resources, Torrance, Calif., 1998—2001. Curriculum developer/editor Libros: Encouraging Cultural Literacy, Long Beach, NY, —; real estate agt. Century 21/JJ Laufer, Highland Park, NJ, 2001—. Author: The "SPEED" Approach to Effective Business-English Skills in the Corporate Environment, 2001, Accelerating the Progress of ESL Students, 2001. Recipient Elaine Goran Newman award in TESOL Achievement, Queens Coll., 1989, Jonas E. Salk scholarship, 1990. Mem.: TESOL, ASTD, NJ. Assn. of Realtors. Avocations: skiing, tennis, travel.

GURSTEL, NORMAN KEITH, lawyer; b. Mpls., Mar. 24, 1939; s. Jules and Etta (Abramowitz) G.; m. Jane Evelyn Golden, Nov. 24, 1984; children: Todd, Dana, Marc. BA, U. Minn., 1960, JD, 1962. Bar: Minn. 1962, U.S. Dist. Ct. Minn. 1963, U.S. Supreme Ct. 1980. Assoc. Robins, Davis & Lyons, Mpls., 1962-67; prin. Gurstel & Gurstel, Mpls., 1967-97; pres. Marc Shawn, Inc., 1997—2003, Q, LLC, 2003—05. Arbitrator Hennepin County Dist. Ct., 1988-91; parttime referee family ct. Hennepin County Dist.; lectr. U. Minn. Family Law Seminar. Mem. ABA (corp. banking and bus. law and family law sects.), Minn. Bar Assn. (co-chmn. family ct. com. bankruptcy law sect. 1966-67, family law and bankruptcy law), Hennepin County Bar Assn. (chmn. family law com. 1964-65, vice chmn. 1981-91, fee arbitration bd., creditors remedy com.), Fed. Bar Assn., Assn. Trial Lawyers Am., Minn. Trial Lawyers Assn., Am. Acad. Matrimonial Lawyers, Nat. Council Juvenile and Family Ct. Judges, Comml. Law League Am. (recording sec. 1980-81, bd. govs. 1983-89, pres. 1987-88), Comml. Law League Fund for Pub. Edn. (sec. 1981-83, pres. 1989-92, bd. dirs. 1989-94), Phi Delta Phi. Clubs: Oak Ridge Country (Mpls.). Lodges: Shriners, Masons. Jewish. Office Phone: 952-465-0100. E-mail: norman@qfashions.com.

GURTIN, MORTON EDWARD, mathematics professor; b. Jersey City, Mar. 7, 1934; children: Amy Lynn, William Robert. B.M.E., Rensselaer Poly. Inst., 1955; PhD, Brown U., 1961; PhD in Civil Engring. (hon.), U. Rome, 1994. Structures engr. Douglas Aircraft Co., 1955-56, Gen. Electric Co., 1956-59; research asso. Brown U., 1961-62, asst. prof., 1962-64, assoc. prof., 1964-66; prof. math. Carnegie Mellon U., 1966—; alumni prof. math., 1992—. Sr. Fulbright-Hays fellow, Guggenheim fellow U. Pisa, Italy, 1974; lectr., Europe, South Am., Japan, Can; cons. to industry. Author: (with B.D. Coleman, I Herrera, and C. Truesdell) Wave Propagation in Dissipative Media, 1965, An Introduction to Continuum Mechanics, 1981, Thermomechanics of Evolving Phase Boundaries, 1993, Configurational Forces as Basic Concepts of Continuum Physics, 2000; assoc. editor Archive for Rational Mechanics and Analysis, Jour. Elasticity; contbr. articles to profl. jours., including Handbuch der Physik. Recipient Disting. Grad. Sch. Alumnus award Brown U., 1995, Agostinelli prize Acad. dei Lincei, Rome, 2001, Timoshenko medal ASME, 2004. Mem. Soc. Natural Philosophy, Sigma Xi. Office: Dept Math Carnegie-Mellon U Pittsburgh PA 15213

GURUBHAGAVATULA, INDIRA, medical educator; MD, Johns Hopkins U. Sch. of Medicine, 1990; MPH, Harvard U., 1994. Diplomate Internal Medicine Am. Bd. of Internal Medicine, 1993, Pulmonary Diseases Am. Bd. of Internal Medicine, 1997, Critical Care Medicine Am. Bd. of Internal Medicine, 1999, Sleep Disorders Medicine Am. Bd. of Sleep Medicine, 1999. Resident, internal medicine Wash. U. Med. Ctr., St. Louis, 1990—93; fellow, pulmonary, critical care and sleep disorders medicine U. Pa. Med. Ctr., Phila., 1994—2004, asst. prof. medicine, 2001—. Dir., sleep disorders medicine clinics Phila. VA Med. Ctr., 1998—. Contbr. articles various profl. rsch. jours. Recipient Clin. Assoc. Physician award, NIH, 2000 - present; grantee Competitive Pilot Project Fund, Veterans Adminstrn., 1999 - 2004; Clin. grant, Am. Lung Assn., 1999, Beginning grant, Am. Heart Assn., 1999 - 2003. Mem.: Adv. Com., Gen. Clin. Rsch. Ctrs., Am. Thoracic Soc. Achievements include research in screening for obstructive sleep apnea in high risk populations; assessment of cardiovascular outcomes of treatment of sleep apnea; economics of sleep apnea acreening. Office Phone: 215-662-4000.

GURWITCH, ARNOLD ANDREW, communications executive; b. Hamburg, Germany, Jan. 29, 1925; came to U.S., 1946; s. Max and Bertha Ida (Schereschevsky) G.; m. Barbara Anne Guthrie, July 21, 1961; children: Laurence Andrew, Sara Anne. Student, U. Basle, Switzerland, 1943-46; LLB, Bklyn. Law Sch., 1955. Bar: N.Y. Resident atty. Leeds Music Corp., N.Y.C., 1956-60; ptnr. Rosen, Seton and Sarbin, N.Y.C., 1960-64; internat. rep. ASCAP, N.Y.C., 1964-74, head fgn. dept., 1974-78, fgn. mgr., 1978-89, dir. internat. rels., 1989-94, cons. internat. rels., 1995-96. Editor: Guide to Jazz, 1956. V.p., bd. dirs. Statesmen of Jazz, Ltd. Mem. N.Y. State Bar Assn., Copyright Soc. U.S.A. Office Phone: 914-834-4625.

GURWITZ, KELLY ANN, public relations executive, writer; b. Miami, Oct. 2, 1978; d. Barry Lawrence and Patricia Mary Gurwitz. BA minor: Women's Studies, Ethnic Studies, Fla. Atlantic U., 2000. Dir. pub. rels. Saks Fifth Ave., Boca Raton, Fla., 2001—02, East Coast Jewelry, Deerfield Beach, Fla., 2002—. Freelance writer Capture Life Mag., Boca Raton, 2002—. Author: various articles (Charlie award, 2003). Home: 5646 Wellesley Pk Dr #101 Boca Raton FL 33433 Business E-Mail: kellyg@eastcoastjewelry.com.

GUSCHEL, TIMOTHY JAMES, pharmacist; s. Girard Francis and Marion Ann Guschel; m. Bette Ann Jensen, May 26, 1989; children: Shawn, Steven. BS in Pharmacy, St John's U., NYC, 1981; D in Pharmacy, U. Fla., 2003. Lic. pharmacist Pa., 1983, NY, 1981. Intern in pharmacy Lenox Hill Hosp., NYC, 1978—81; poison control tech. LI Regional Poison Control Ctr., Nausau County, NY, 1979—81; pharmacist Mt. Sinai Hosp., NYC, 1981—86, Genovese Drugs, Lindenhurst, NY, 1986—89, Geisinger Med. Ctr., Danville, Pa., 1989—2000; clin. pharmacist Bloomsburg (Pa.) Hosp., Bloomsburg, 1998—. Cons. Inst. Safe Medication Practices, Huntington Valley, Pa., 1998—. Bd. dirs. Boy Scouts of Am., Bloomsburg, 1997—2003. Mem.: Pa. Soc. Healthcare Pharmacists (assoc.). Republican. Roman Catholic. Avocation: computers. Home: PO Box 73 Riverside PA 17868 Office: Bloomsburg Hosp 549 E Fair St Bloomsburg PA 17815 E-mail: tgusl@mail.com.

GUSEWELLE, CHARLES WESLEY, journalist, writer; b. Kansas City, Kans., July 22, 1933; s. Hugh L. and Dorothy (Middleton) G.; m. Katie Jane Ingels, Apr. 17, 1966; children— Anne Elizabeth, Jennifer Sue. BA in English, Westminster Coll., 1955; LHD (hon.), Park Coll., 1990. Reporter Kansas City (Mo.) Star, 1955-66, editorial writer of fgn. affairs, 1966-76, fgn. editor, 1976-79, asso. editor, columnist, 1979—. Author: A Paris Notebook, 1985, An Africa Notebook, 1986, Quick as Shadows Passing, 1988, Far from Any Coast, 1989, A Great Current Running, 1994, Another Autumn, 1996, The Rufus Chronicle, 1998, A Buick in the Kitchen, 2000, On the Way to Other Country, 2001; contbr. short stories to Brit., Am. lit. quars.; writer, narrator, host: A Great Current Running, This Place Called Home (Regional Emmy 1998), Water and Fire: A Story of the Ozarks, Stories Under the Stone. 1st lt. AUS, 1956-58. Recipient Aga Khan prize for fiction, 1977, Thorpe Menn Lit. award, 1989; inducted Writers Hall of Fame, 2000. Home: 1245 Stratford Rd Kansas City MO 64113-1325 Office: 1729 Grand Ave Kansas City MO 64108-1413 Office Phone: 816-333-0994.

GUSHEE, RICHARD BORDLEY, lawyer; b. Detroit, Aug. 25, 1926; s. Edward Tisdale and Norine Amelia (Bordley) G.; m. Marilyn Lucy Flynn, June 9, 1951; children: Jacqueline Lowe (dec. 1977), Peter Hale. BA, Williams Coll., 1947; JD, U. Mich., 1950. Bar: Mich. 1951, U.S. Supreme Ct. 1961. Assoc. Miller, Canfield, Paddock and Stone, Detroit, 1950-58, ptnr., 1959-93, of counsel, 1994—. Chmn. Tri-county Hearing Panel #18 of Atty. Discipline Bd. Former trustee United Community Svcs.; former chancellor Episc. Diocese Mich. With USAF, 1945. Mem. ABA. Office: Miller Canfield Paddock & Stone 150 W Jefferson Ave Ste 2500 Detroit MI 48226-4416 Office Phone: 313-496-7572. Business E-Mail: gushee@millercanfield.com.

GUSKEY, THOMAS ROBERT, education educator; b. Johnstown, Pa., Feb. 15, 1950; s. Robert C. and Evelyn M. (Yarnick) G. BA, Thiel Coll., 1972; MEd, Boston Coll., 1975; PhD, U. Chgo., 1979. Tchr. St. Andrew's Sch., Erie, Pa., 1972-74; rsch. asst. Boston Coll., Chestnut Hill, Mass., 1974-75; teaching asst. U. Chgo., 1975-78; rsch. cons. Chgo. Bd. Edn., 1975-76, dir. R&D, 1976-78; dir. rsch. Ctr. for Improvement of Teaching, Chgo., 1980-82; asst. prof. edn. U. Ky., Lexington, 1978—81, assoc. prof., 1981—85, prof., 1985—. Chmn. dept. edn. policy studies and evaluation U. Ky., Lexington, 1995-96; vis. prof. various colls. and univs.; cons. edn. systems. Author: Implementing Mastery Learning, 1985, 2d edit., 1997, Improving Student Learning, 1988, High Stakes Performance Assessment, 1994, (with J. Block and S. Everson) School Improvement Programs, 1995, (with M. Huberman) Professional Development in Education, 1995, Communicating Student learning, 1996, (with J. Block and S. Everson) Comprehensive School Reform: A Program Perspective, 1999, Evaluating Professional Development, 2000, (with J. Bailey) Implementing Standard-Led Conferences, 2001, (with Bailey) Developing Grading and Reporting Systems for Student Learning, 2001, How's My Kid Doing? A Parents' Guide to Grades, Marks, and Report Cards, 2002; editor Elem. Sch. Jour., 1990—, Focus on Learning, 1996—, Ednl. Measurement: Issues and Practice, 1997—. Named to Outstanding Young Men of Am., 1981; Ky. Col., 1994; recipient U. Ky. Wethington award, 2004, 05, Disting. Alumnus award Thiel Coll., 2005. Mem. APA, ASCD, Am. Ednl. Rsch. Assn., Nat. Soc. for Study of Edn., Nat. Staff Devel. Coun. (Article of Yr. award 1996, 99, 2002, Book of Yr. award 1996, 2002, Best Non-Disseration Rsch. Award, 2003), Nat. Coun. on Measurement in Edn., Phi Delta Kappa. Home: 2108 Shelton Rd Lexington KY 40515-1170 Office: U Ky Coll Edn 145 Taylor Edn Bldg Lexington KY 40506-0001 Office Phone: 859-257-8666. E-mail: guskey@uky.edu.

GUSKIN, ALAN E., university president; b. Bklyn., Mar. 22, 1937; s. David N. and Frances (Midler) G.; m. Lois La Shell, 1990; children from previous marriage: Sharon, Andrea. BA with honors, Bklyn. Coll., 1958; PhD, U. Mich., 1968; LHD (hon.), Saybrook Inst., 1989, Antioch U., 1997. Instr., Peace Corps. vol. Chulalongkorn U., Thailand, 1961-64; dir. of selection VISTA, 1964-65; asst. dir. Ctr. for Research on the Utilization of Scientific Knowledge, Inst. for Social Research, 1968-69; lectr. dept. of psychology and residential coll. U. Mich., 1968-71, dir. ednl. change team, Sch. of Edn., 1969-71, assoc. prof. edn., 1971; provost Clark U., Worcester, Mass., 1971-73, acting pres., 1973-74, prof. sociology and edn., 1973-75; chancellor, prof. edn. U. Wis.-Parkside, Kenosha, 1975-85; pres., prof. Antioch Coll. and Antioch U., Yellow Springs, Ohio, 1985-94; chancellor, Disting. univ. prof. Antioch U., 1994-97, disting. prof., 1997—. Author: (with Samuel Guskin) A Social Psychology of Education, 1970; editor New Directions on Teaching and Learning, The Administrator's Role in Effective Teaching, 1981; contbr. numerous articles and reports to profl. jours. Chmn. bd. Coun. on Adult and Experiential Learning, 1993-95. Mem. Am. Assn. Higher Edn. Business E-Mail: aguskin@antioch.edu.

GUSKOV, SERGEY, security firm executive; b. Moscow, Aug. 31, 1973; BS in Engring. and Econs. with honors, Moscow Aviation Inst., 1995; MBA, U. Pa., 2000. Sr. auditor KPMG, Moscow, 1995—98, Leeds, England, 1998; assoc., mgmt. consulting A.T. Kearney, New York, NY, 2000—01; mgr. bus. analysis Brink's Inc., Darien, Conn., 2001—. Investment banking summer assoc. CIBC World Markets, N.Y.C., 1999. Co-author: (study book) Securities, 1998. Co-founder, v.p. Russian Digital Alliance, Washington, 2001—03. Home: 150 E 37th St Apt 2C New York NY 10016

GUSSIN, ROBERT ZALMON, retired health products executive; b. Pitts., Jan. 5, 1938; s. Carl and Yetta G. BS in Pharmacy, Duquesne U., 1959, MS in Pharmacology, 1961; PhD in Pharmacology, U. Mich., 1965. Rsch. fellow dept. pharmacology SUNY, 1965-67; rsch. pharmacologist Lederle Labs., N.Y.C., 1967-69, group leader dept. cardiovascular renal pharmacology, 1969-73, dir. cardiovascular renal disease therapy sect., 1973-74; exec. dir. rsch. McNeil Labs., Ft. Washington, Pa., 1974-78, v.p. rsch. div., 1978, v.p. R & D, 1978-79; v.p. sci. affairs McNeil Pharm., Pa., 1979-86; corp. v.p., sci. and tech. Johnson & Johnson, New Brunswick, N.J., 1986-2000. Author: Introduction to Cardiovascular Pharmacology, 1976; mem. editorial bd. New Drug Evaluations, Drug Devel, Pharmaco Therapy; contbr. in field. Mem. Am. Soc. Clin. Pharmacology and Therapeutics, Am. Soc. Nephrology, Am. Soc. Pharmacology and Exptl. Therapeutics, Am. Fedn. Clin. Research, AAAS, N.Y. Acad. Scis., Am. Heart Assn. Office: Johnson & Johnson 410 George St New Brunswick NJ 08901-2021 Office Phone: 941-387-7321. Personal E-mail: bobgnpate@aol.com.

GUSSOW, SUE FERGUSON, artist, educator; b. Bklyn., Aug. 2, 1935; d. Samuel Nathan and May (Sheinin) Shapiro; m. Donald L. Gerard, Jan. 10, 1999. Student, Bklyn. Mus., 1956-57; Diploma in Fine and Graphic Arts, The Cooper Union, 1956; BS, Columbia U., 1960; MFA, Tulane U., 1964. Prof. The Cooper Union Sch. of Architecture, N.Y.C., 1970—2005, prof. emerita, 2005—. Asst. adj. prof. in painting and drawing NYU, 1973-81; assoc. adj. prof. dept. painting and sculpture, Columbia U., 1977—; vis. asst. prof. in printmaking Manhattanville Coll., Purchase, N.Y., summer 1971; assoc. prof. printmaking Alfred U., summer 1971, others; vis. pof. The Frick Coll., 2002-2005; Pamela Djerassi Artist-in-Residence, Stanford (Calif.) U., 1982-83; vis. juror Yale U., 1987, 88, Newspace Gallery, Wilkinson Pl., New Orleans, 1977. Work exhibited in Cooper-Hewitt Mus./Smithsonian Inst., N.Y.C., Dalls Mus. of Fine Arts, Seattle Art Mus., New Orleans Mus. Art, New Orleans Jazz Mus., Phila. Free Libr., Mus. of Modern Art, N.Y.C., others; one-woman shows include Hall of the Journalists, St. Petersburg, Russia, 1992, Marcelle Fine Arts, Southhampton, N.Y., 1989, 90, Loyola Marymount U., L.A., 1983, Window/Rm., Tokyo, others; represented in the pvt. collection of Dore Ashton, Eero Saarinen's C.B.S. Bldg., Van Deren Coke, Morley Safer, George and Mary Schmidt Campbell, others. Recipient scholarships Parsons Sch. Design, 1952, Pratt Inst., 1952-53, Bklyn. Mus., 1956-57, Columbia U., 1956-60, Tulane U., 1962-63; fellowships Columbia U., 1961, Tulane U., 1963-64; recipient purchase prizes The St. Paul (Minn.) Art Ctr., 1966, 1965 Artists of La., 1965, Isaac Delgado Mus., New Orleans, 1965, SUN Y, Potsdam, 1964, Olivet (Mich.) Coll. Festival of the Arts, 1963-64, others; recipient jurors spl. mention Ark. Art Ctr., Little Rock, 1964, 1st prize Dallas Mus. Fine Art, 1964. Office Phone: 212-219-8154, 631-267-8016.

GUST, ANNE BALDWIN, former retail apparel company executive; b. Grosse Pointe Farms, Mich., Mar. 15, 1958; d. Rockwell Thomas Jr. and Anne Elizabeth (Baldwin) G.; m. Jerry Brown, June 18, 2005 BA, Stanford U., 1980; JD, U. Mich., 1983. Bar: Calif. 1983, U.S. Dist. Ct. (no. dist.) Calif. 1983, U.S. Ct. Appeals (9th cir.) 1983. Assoc. Orrick, Herrington & Sutcliffe, San Francisco, 1983-86, Brobeck, Phleger & Harrison, San Francisco & Palo Alto, Calif., 1986—91; assoc. gen. counsel The Gap, Inc., San Francisco, 1991—94, sr. v.p., gen. counsel, 1994—98, exec. v.p., human resources, legal & corp. adminstrn., 1998—99, exec. v.p., human resources, legal, global compliance & corp. adminstrn., 1999—2000, exec. v.p., chief adminstrv. officer, 2000—05. Mem. bd. dirs., Jack in the Box Inc., 2003- Contbr. articles to labor trade jours. Mem. ABA (labor subcom.), Calif. Bar Assn.

GUST, JOHN DEVENS, lawyer; b. Phoenix, Aug. 31, 1918; s. John Lewis and Ada Lee (Rebstock) G.; m. Mary Elizabeth Montgomery, Sept. 1, 1942; children— John Devens, Morgan M. A.B., Stanford U., 1940, J.D., 1942. Bar: Ariz. 1943. Ptnr., Gust, Rosenfeld, Divelbess & Henderson, Phoenix, 1946-86, sr. ptnr., 1968-86; sr. counsel, 1986—; dir. Valley Nat. Bank Ariz. Served to lt. j.g. USNR, 1941-46. Mem. ABA, State Bar Ariz. (past pres., dir.), Maricopa County Bar Assn. (past pres., dir.). Republican. Club: Ariz.

GUSTAFSON, ALBERT KATSUAKI, lawyer, engineer; b. Tokyo, Dec. 5, 1949; arrived in U.S., 1951; s. William A. and Akiko (Osada) Gustafson; m. Helen Melissa Laird, July 31, 1971 (div. 1975); m. Karen Jane Ekblad, Dec. 31, 1978 (div. 1987). BA with distinction, Stanford U., 1972; JD, U. Wash., 1980. Bar: Wash. 1981, U.S. Dist. Ct. (we. dist.) Wash. 1981, U.S. Ct. Appeals (9th cir.) 1984, NY 1993. Acoustics analyst Boeing Co., Seattle, 1973—74, material buyer, 1974; legal editor Book Pub. Co., Seattle, 1975—76; rsch. analyst Batelle Inst., Seattle, 1975—76; legal intern Office of U.S. Atty., Seattle, 1976; engr. U.P.R.R., 1977—85; corp. counsel Dorden, Inc., Centralia, Wash., 1984—87, Ansette Fin. Corp., Inc., Seattle, 1987—89, Precision Forms, Inc., 1988, Endo and Mamba, 1989—93; of counsel Barkats and Assocs., 1991—98; prin. Albert K. Gustafson, P.S., Seattle, 1981—93; pres. Shomei Corp., 1990—95, Shomei, Kokusai, Kabushki, Kaisha, 1991—95; v.p. Sierra Capital Mgmt., Inc., 1992—93; prof. internat. bus. law Sch. Internat. Studies Nichibei Kaiwa Gakuen, Tokyo, 1989—90, Nippon Tel. & Tel., 1989—90. Bd. dirs. Daiki, Inc.; v.p. ops. BND Sea and Airlines Corp., 1997—98; dir., counsel Zinza K.K., 1998—2002, pres., rep. dir., 2002—04; rep. dir. Multipro K.K., 1998—2002. Mem. nat. bd. editors Prentice-Hall Rigos CPA Review, 1991—93. Sec. local 117-E United Transp. Union, 1984, local vice-chmn., 1984; Dem. precinct chmn., 1984. Named Kraft scholar, 1968, Calif. State scholar, 1968—72. Mem.: ABA, Japan-Am. Soc., Roppongi Bar Assn., Seattle-King County Bar Assn., Inter-Pacific Bar Assn., Asian Bar Assn., Internat. Bar Assn., Rockefeller Ctr. Club, Imperial Club, Century Ct. Club, City Club, College Club, Rotary, Order of DeMolay (master councilor 1968), Shriners, Masons. Presbyterian. also: 75 Shoe Ln London England EC4 BQ also: 3917 Interlake Ave N Seattle WA 98103 also: 5 Krasnoznamenny By-str 690000 Vladivostok Russia also: PO Box 12 600 Main St Cobleskill NY 12043 Office: 67 Wall St 22nd Fl New York NY 10005: MBE 156 1 3 6 Miramiaoyama Mintorku Tokyo 107 0062 Japan Office Phone: 518-231-5040. Business E-Mail: ananda@gol.com.

GUSTAFSON, ALICE FAIRLEIGH, lawyer; b. Houston, Dec. 1, 1946; d. William H. and Mary Davis (McCord) Bell; m. Charles R. Gustafson, May 30, 1971. BA in Econs., Wellesley (Mass.) Coll., 1968; JD, U. Puget Sound, 1976. Bar: Wash. 1976. Various positions U.S. Dept. HEW, various locations, 1968-75; assoc. Graham & Dunn, Seattle, 1977-83, ptnr., 1983—. Bd. dirs. King County Am. Cancer Soc., Seattle, 1983-85, Women & Bus., Inc., Seattle, 1984-87; mem. nominating com. YWCA Seattle-King County, 1985-88. Mem. ABA, Wash. State Bar Assn. (chair Bench-Bar-Press com. 1988-90), Seattle-King County Bar Assn. (trustee young lawyers divsn. 1980-83, treas. 1985-87), N.W. Comm. Lawyers, Met. Seattle Urban League (bd. dirs. 1991-93). Avocations: sailing, bicycling, skiing. Home: 13560 Riviera Pl NE Seattle WA 98125-3845

GUSTAFSON, CRAIG THOMAS, theater director, playwright, graphics designer; b. Oak Park, Ill., Aug. 26, 1958; s. Eric O. and Mary Louise (Howlett) G.; m. Marjorie L. Weitzenfeld, July 11, 1998. Student, Second City, Chgo., 1978; AA, Coll. DuPage, 1979. Board operator Wells Fargo Alarm, Elmhurst, Ill., 1978-81; ops. employee Coll. DuPage, Glen Ellyn, 1981—. Prodr., dir. Ad Hoc Theatre Co., Lisle, Ill., 1986-89; dir., writer The Summer Place, Naperville, Ill., 1989-96, Village Theatre Guild, Glen Ellyn; dir., composer, graphic artist Wheaton (Ill.) Drama, Inc., 1990—; artistic dir. Top Banana, Oakbrook Terrace, Ill., 1997-99; v.p., dir., composer, graphic artist First St. Playhouse, Batavia, Ill., 2002-; actor, dir., prodr., composer, choreographer, others, Village Players, Oak Park, Ill., 1995, West Suburban Players, Villa Park, Ill., 1996-98, Music On Stage, Palatine, Ill., 2001, Village Theatre of Palatine, 2002. Actor: The Foreigner, The House of Blue Leaves, Chicago, Bobby Gould in Hell, Rumors, Waiting for Godot, The Fantasticks, Twelfth Night; dir.: Assassins, Luv, Lucky Stiff, Lend Me a Tenor, The Odd Couple, Tartuffe, A Funny Thing Happened on the Way to the Forum, Nunsense, Mingle, Among the Demons; writer, performer (with Joy Kenyon) Tongues and Animal Crackers, Vic Theatre, Chgo., 1992. Named Funniest Person in Chgo., Chgo. Sun-Times, 1981, Best Cmty. Prodn. for "The Nerd," Acad. Theatre Artists and Friends, Chgo., 1996. Mem. Sons of the Desert (vice-shiek 1994-95). Democrat. Avocations: studying history of comedy, irritating conservatives.

GUSTAFSON, DAVID HAROLD, industrial engineering and preventive medicine educator; b. Kane, Pa., Sept. 11, 1940; s. Harold Edward and Olive Albertina (McKalip) G.; m. Rea Corina Anagnos, June 23, 1962; children: Laura Lynn, Michelle Elaine, David Harold BS in Indsl. Engring., U. Mich., 1962, MS in Indsl. Engring, 1963, PhD, 1966. Dir. hosp. div. Community Systems Found., Ann Arbor, Mich., 1961-64; asst. prof. indsl. engring. U. Wis.-Madison, 1966-70, assoc. prof., 1970-74, prof., 1974—, Robert A. Ratner prof. indsl. engring., 2000—, dir., founder Ctr. for Health Systems and Analysis, 1974—, chmn. dept. indsl. engring., 1984-88, adminstrv. com. Grad. Sch., 1995-98, mem. athletic bd., 2000—; sr. analyst Dec. and Designs Inc., McLean, Va., 1974. Dir. rsch. Govt. Health Policy Task Force, State of Wis., 1969-71; prin. cons. Medicaid Mgmt. Study Team, 1977-78; prin. investigator Nursing Home Quality Assurance System, 1979, Computer System for Adolscent Health Promotion, 1983, Computer System to Support Breast Cancer and People with AIDS, 1993; vis. prof. London Sch. Econs., 1983, Harvard U., 1999; developer computer-based support to measure and improve health care quality; chair Fed. Sci. Panel on Interactive Comms. in Health; dir. TECC Ctr. for Excellence in Cancer Comms., 2004, Network for Improvement of Addiction Treatment. Author: Group Techniques, 1975, Health Policy Analysis, 1992, Sustainability, 2005; contbr. articles to profl. jours. Adviser conflict resolution Luth. Ch., 1973-79; active numerous civic orgns. Recipient numerous grants, 1968—, Ragnar Onstad award for cmty. svc., 1990. Fellow Assn. for Health Svcs. Rsch., Inst. for Health Care Improvement (bd. dirs. 1990—), Am. Med. Informatics Assn.; mem. Inst. Indsl. Engring., Ops. Rsch. Soc., Med. Decision Making Avocations: jogging, guitar, water sports, cross country skiing, parenting. Office: U Wis Ctr Health Systems 610 Walnut St Madison WI 53705-2336

GUSTAFSON, ERIC WILLIAM, real estate investor, wildlife habitat conservationist; b. Monterrey, Mex., Feb. 12, 1945; s. Bertel and Elenor (Ceder) G.; m. Mina Villarreal, June 16, 1973; children: Eric Alain, Karini, Elyn Michelle. BS, Duke U., 1966; MBA cum laude, Monterrey Inst. Tech., 1970; PhD, U. Mass., 1975. Founder, dir. ITESM, 1971-73, Univ. Tchg. Excellence Ctr. and LASCA Computer Degree, Monterrey, 1973-74; from strategic planning mgr. to internat. v.p. Cuauhtemoc Brewing Co., Monterrey, 1975-80; internat. dir. Femsa/Visa Group, Monterrey, 1980-82; C.E.O. & nat. v.p. Ducks Unltd. of Mex. Wildlife Conservation Orgn., 1982-97; ptnr. Metroalianza SA, 1998—. Assoc. World Bus. Coun. Sustainable Devel., Switzerland, 1991—, pres. U.S.-Mex. C. of C., NE Mexico, 1996—; founder, ptnr. Craidero Estrella, S.A., 1999; cons. U. Nuevo Leon, 1975-76, Clemente Jacques Food Corp.; Mex. rep. Can./U.S./Mex. Trilateral Wildlife Com., 1997; rep. of Mex. at UNCED World Summit Brazil, 1992, rep. of Mex. on

N.Am. Waterfowl Mgmt. Plan, 1995—. Author: Organization and Development of Teaching Improvement Center, 1975, Eco-efficiency and Sustainable Development, 1992, The White Winged Dove in Ne Mexico, 2000, Laguna Flamingos, 2001, Soto La Marina, 2002 editor: Mexico: Monterrey and You, 1984. Pres. bd. dirs. Am. Sch. Found., Monterrey, 1988-90; nat. bd. dirs. Mex. Nat. Coun. Parks and Res., 1996; Mex. rep. N.Am. Waterfowl Mgmt. Plan, 1995—; pres. Conservation Mex., 1999-2004. Recipient Excellence in Environment Spain-Mex. award, 1995; N.Am. Wetlands Conservation Act grantee, 1999-2002; Ford Found. scholar, Nat. Coun. Sci. & Tech. Mex. scholar. Mem. Valle Alto Golf Club, Casino de Monterrey, U.S.-Mex. C. of C. (pres. 1996—), Phi Kappa Psi, Union ch., ASFM Devel. (chmn.); bd. mem. USMCOC Biational, 2002, Avocations: hiking, hunting, tennis, horseback riding, golf. Office: Arbol 182 Santa Engracia Garza Garcia Nuevo Leon 66267 Mexico Fax: (52) 818-356-5010. E-mail: karini@usa.net, drericgustafson@hotmail.com.

GUSTAFSON, JOHN ALFRED, biology professor; b. Boston, Mar. 31, 1925; s. Walter Alfred and Lilly Christine (Anderson) Gustafson; m. Nancy Gay Johnson, June 30, 1951; children: Walter A., Laura E., Paul E.(dec.), Daniel D., Martha E., J. Olaf. AB, Dartmouth, 1948; PhD, Cornell U., 1954. Asst. prof. biology State U. N.Y. Coll., Brockport, 1954-55, asst. prof. biology Cortland, 1955-57, asso. prof. biology, 1957-63, prof. biology, 1963-81, chmn. dept. biol. scis., 1965-77; project dir. NSF Grant for Outdoor Sci. Edn., 1980-82. Participant NSF Inst., 1962; pres. Alliance for Environ. Edn., 1974; mem. Temporary State Commn. on Youth Edn. in Conservation, N.Y., 1969-73; owner, pub. Slingerland-Comstock Co., 1976-91. Author: (with B.A. Hall) Laboratory Studies in Botany, 1960; Editor: Nature Study, Jour. Environ. Edn. and Interpretation, 1965-79, Alliance Exchange, 1975-76. Chmn. Town of Homer (N.Y.) Zoning Bd., 1959-69, Town of Homer Planning Bd., 1969-75; chmn. Homer Plan Rev. Com., 2001-02, vice chmn. Eastern Susquehanna Water Resources Bd., 1969-76; pres. Highvista Nature Center, Inc., 1973-92; mem. Labrador Hollow Unique Area Adv. Coun., 1978—; chmn. Cortland County Environ. Mgmt. Council, 1980-82, Cortland County Anderson-Lucey campaign, 1980; mem. bd. edn. Homer Cen. Sch. Dist., 1982-88; treas. Pocono Environ. Edn. Ctr., 1988-91, Lime Hollow Nature Ctr., 1992—; Cortland County rep. to open space com. N.Y. State, Region 7, 1996—; bd. dirs. Iroquois Assn., Am. Baptist Chs., 1986-89, 97-2004, moderator, 1987; pres. Cortland County Council of Chs., 1986-89; adminstr. 1st Bapt. Ch., Homer, N.Y., 1990-94, treas., 1995-99, bd. elders, 2001-02, bd. deacons, 2002-03, dir. visitation, 2003-04; mem. steering com. N.Y. State Grazing Lands Conservation Initiative, 1997—. Served with USMCR, 1943-46, 51-53. Recipient Taft Campus award No. Ill. U., 1989, Griffith-Balcom Leadership award Am. Bapt. Chs., 1998. Fellow AAAS (coun. 1968-73); mem. Am. Nature Study Soc. (pres. 1962-63, treas. 1964-75, 79-97, Disting. Svc. award 1969, John Gustafson award for exemplary svc., 1995), Nature Conservancy (dir., treas., chmn. ctrl. N.Y. chpt., chmn. N.Y. State bd. dirs. 1983-87, vice chmn., ctrl/western N.Y. chpt. 1994-96, Oak Leaf award 1984), Phi Delta Kappa. Republican. Baptist. Home: 5881 Cold Brook Rd Homer NY 13077-9709 *As I think back over my life, I am impressed by the evidence that God, through my commitment to him, has given guidance and direction at those times when crucial decisions were made. So often what seemed at the time to be a relatively insignificant decision turned out to have been a key turning point. It is God's Spirit within me, and his love and concern, that gives meaning to what I do.*

GUSTAFSON, JOHN PERRY, geneticist, researcher; s. Elmer and Barbara Gustafson; m. Christine S. McKinstry, Mar. 14, 1977; children: Kathryn, Nicholas. PhD, U. Calif., Davis, 1972. Rsch. geneticist USDA-ARS, Columbia, Mo., 1981—. Recipient Honoris causa, Banat U., 1997; fellow Fulbright Disting. Prof., 1986. Mem.: AAAS, Am. Genetics Assn., Am. Soc. Am., Genetics Soc. Can., Genetics Soc. Am., Crop Sci. Soc. Am. Achievements include research in cereal genetics and crop improvement. Home: 3103 Crawford Columbia MO 65203 Office: USDA-ARS 206 Curtis Hall University of Missouri Columbia MO 65211 Office Phone: 573-882-7318.

GUSTAFSON, KAREN AILEEN ELSA, music educator; b. Saskatoon, Sask., Can., Sept. 27, 1963; d. Alvin Martin and Audrey Ann Gustafson. MusB, U. Victoria, B.C., 1987; MusM, Northwestern U., 1991; D in Musical Arts, U. Minn., 2001. Asst. prof. music-trumpet Okla. City U., 2001—04, U. Alaska, Fairbanks, 2004—. Prin. trumpet Enid (Okla.) Symphony Orch.; trumpet Borealis Brass, Fairbanks; prin. trumpet Fairbanks Symphony Orch., 2004—; adjudicator Nat. Trumpet Competition, Fairfax, Va., 2005—; preliminary adjudicator Internat. Trumpet Guild Competition, 2005—. Musician Immaculate Conception Ch., Fairbanks. Recipient Faculty Recognition and Appreciation award, U. Alaska Coll. Liberal Arts. Mem.: Internat. Womens Brass Conf., Internat. Trumpet Guild. Home: 689 Steele Creek Rd Fairbanks AK 99712 Office: Univ Alaska Fairbanks PO Box 755660 Fairbanks AK 99775-5660 Home Fax: 907-474-6420; Office Fax: 907-474-6420. Personal E-mail: ffkg@uaf.edu.

GUSTAFSON, MARDEL EMMA, secondary school educator, writer; b. Waukesha, Wis., June 10, 1922; d. Otto Robert and Emma Bertha (Steffan) Hoppe; m. Wayne Carroll Gustafson, Nov. 1, 1950; children: Faith, Keith, Richard, Wayne, John, Beverly. BS in Edn., U. Wis., 1946. Sec. Waukesha Motor Co., 1944—45, Wis. Gen. Hosp., Madison, 1945—46; tchr. Hannibal HS, Wis., 1946—49, St. John Pub. Sch., ND, 1949—50. Author: What Is Happening To Our Children? How to Raise Them Right, 1993, Why A Role Mother?, 2001, All My Love, 2001. Mem.: Wis. Alumni Assn., TOPS Club (sec. 1978—83). Lutheran. Avocations: sewing, knitting, crocheting, gardening, walking. Home: W289 S2915 Hwy Dt Waukesha WI 53188-9581 Personal E-mail: waynemardel@aol.com.

GUSTAFSON, RICHARD ALRICK, university president emeritus; b. Peekskill, N.Y., May 15, 1941; s. Richard Alrick Sr. and Faye Alice (Jones) G.; m. Joanne Marie Walters, Sept. 5, 1964; children: Richard III., Peter. AB in Biology and Chemistry, Boston U., 1963, MEd in Sci. Edn., 1964; PhD in Statistics and Measurement, U. Conn., 1970; attended, Harvard Inst. Ednl. Mgmt., 1982; MEd in TESOL, Notre Dame Coll., 1997. Tchr. sci. Newtown (Conn.) Pub. Sch., 1964-65; tchr. chemistry Greenwich (Conn.) Pub. Schs., 1965-68; rsch. specialist Ctr. for Planning and Evaluation, San Jose, Calif., 1970-71; dir. mgmt. svcs. New Eng. Resource Ctr. for Occupl. Edn., Newton, 1971-73; asst. dean career studies Keene (N.H.) State Coll., 1973-78, assoc. dean acad. affairs, 1978-81, v.p. acad. affairs, 1981-87; pres. So. N.H. U. (formerly N.H. Coll.), Manchester, 1987—2003, pres. emeritus, 2003—05, interim pres., 2005—. Bd. dirs. Optima Health, 1997-98. Bd. dirs. Keene Family YMCA, 1975-80, Cheshire Med. Ctr., Keene, 1986-88, Federated Arts., 1989-92, Leadership Manchester., 1989-91, Hillcrest Terr., 1991-93, Elliot Hosp., 1999-; bd. dirs. Manchester United Way, 1990-97, chmn., 1993; vice chair N.H. Tuition Savs. Plan Commn., 1997—2003; mem. ops. com. Forum for Higher Edn. in N.H., 2000-03; bd. dirs. N.H. Symphony Orch., 2003—, AAA No. New Eng., 2000—, Friends of Valley Cemetery, 2003-. Recipient Granite State award, 2000; Augustus Howe Buck scholar Boston U., 1960-62; named Manchester Citizen of Yr., 2003; Fulbright sr. rsch. fellow, Thailand, 1999. Mem. Am. Vocat. Assn. (Svc. award 1980), Nat. Assn. Ind. Colls. and Univs. (bd. dirs. 1991-94), N.H. Coll. and U. Coun. (bd. dirs. 1987-03, chmn. 1995-97), N.H. Postsecondary Edn. Commn. (chmn. 1994-96, bd. dirs. 1987-04), Hellenic-Am. U. (bd. trustees 2004-, vice chair 2004-) Greater Manchester C. of C. (bd. dirs. 1990-97, chmn. 1996), Rotary (bd. dirs. Keene 1985-87). Episcopalian. Avocations: skiing, tennis. Office Phone: 603-645-9688. Business E-Mail: r.gustafson@snhu.edu.

GUSTAFSON, THOMAS, medical association administrator; b. Mar. 31, 1947; married; 3 children. BA magna cum laude, Williams Coll., 1969; PhD in Econs., Yale U., 1982. Rsch. asst. Boston Cons. Group, 1970-71; acting dir. divsn. policy rsch. Office of Income Security Policy, U.S. Dept. Health and Human Svcs., 1983-84, economist, 1976-85; dir. divsn. Medicaid and long term care Office Legis. and Policy, Health Care Financing Adminstrn., Washington, 1985-88, dir. office policy analysis, 1988-90, dep. dir., 1990-96; dep. dir. Office Rsch. & Demonstration Health Care Financing Adminstrn., Balt., 1996-97, dep. dir. Office Strategic Planning, 1997-98, dir. Hosp. and Ambulatory Policy Group, Ctrs. Medicare and Medicaid, 1998—2003; dep. dir. Ctr. for Medicare Mgmt., Balt., 2003—. Presenter in field. Contbr. articles to profl. jours. Office: Ctr Medicaid Mgmt 7500 Security Blvd # 40126 Baltimore MD 21244-1849

GUSTAFSON, WINTHROP ADOLPH, engineering educator; b. Moline, Ill., Oct. 14, 1928; s. Gustav A. and Katherine (Wenger) G.; m. Sarah Elizabeth Garner, Aug. 3, 1957; children: Charles Lee, Stanley Scott, John Winthrop, Richard Neil. BS, U. Ill., 1950, MS, 1954, PhD, 1956. Rsch. scientist Lockheed Missiles & Space Co., Palo Alto, Calif., 1956—60; assoc. prof. Sch. Aero. and Astronautics Purdue U., Lafayette, Ind., 1960—66, prof. Sch. Aero. and Astronautics, 1966—98, assoc. head Sch. Aero. and Astronautics, 1980—98, acting head Sch. Aero. and Astronautics, 1984—85, 1993, prof. emeritus Sch. Aero. and Astronautics, 1998—. Vis. prof. U. Calif. San Diego, 1968; rsch. engr. Allison divsn. GM., Indpls., summer 1962; mem. tech. staff Bell Telephone Labs., Whippany, N.J., summer 1966, NASA-Dryden Flight Rsch. Ctr., summer 1976; cons. Goodyear Aerospace Corp., Akron, Ohio, 1964, Los Alamos Sci. Lab., 1977, U.S. Army, 1986-87. Contbr. articles to profl. jours. Served to 1st lt. USAF, 1951-53. Mem. AIAA. Home: 209 Lindberg Ave West Lafayette IN 47906-2109 Office: Purdue U Sch Aeros & Astronautics Lafayette IN 47907

GUSTAFSSON, LARS ERIK EINAR, writer, educator; b. Västerås, Sweden, May 17, 1936; came to U.S., 1983; s. Einar H. and Lotten Margaretha (Carlson) G.; m. D. Alexandra Chasnoff, 1982 (div. 2002); children: Benjamin, Karen. PhD, Uppsala (Sweden) U., 1978. Editor-in-chief Bonners Pub. House, Stockholm, 1961-72; rsch. fellow Ctr. Advanced Studies, Bielefeld, Germany, 1980-81; Aby Warburg rsch. prof. Warburg Found. U. Hamburg, Germany, 1997-98. Bd. dirs. Svenska Dagbladet Found.; bd. regents Uppsala (Sweden) U., 1994-97; adj. prof. U. Tex., Austin, 1983—; Jamail Disting. prof., 1998—, Michener Regents chair in writing, 2004; fellow Berlin Inst. for Advanced Study, 2004-2005. Author numerous novels and poetry collections. John Simon Guggenheim Meml. fellow of poetry, 1993. Mem. Acad. of Arts (Berlin), Acad. Scis. and Lit. (Mainz, Germany), Royal Swedish Acad. Engring. (Stockholm), Bavarian Acad. Fine Arts (Munich). Avocation: painting. Office: U Tex Austin Dept Philosophy Austin TX 78712 Business E-Mail: lars.gustafsson@mail.utexas.edu.

GUSTAVSON, TODD F., curator; b. Jamestown, N.Y., Nov. 4, 1957; s. Harry R. Gustavson. BFA in Photography, La. Tech U., 1980. Curatorial asst., tech. collection George Eastman Ho., Rochester, NY, 1988—94, archivist tech. collection, 1994—97, asst. curator tech. collection, 1998—98, curator tech. collection, 1998—. Mem.: The Photographic Hist. Soc. Can. (hon.). Home: 222 Rockingham St Rochester NY 14620 Office: George Eastman House 900 East Avenue Rochester NY 14607 Office Phone: 585-271-3361 x369. Business E-Mail: todd@geh.orh.

GUSTIN, BRENDA SUE, art educator, painter; b. Kenosha, Wis., July 22, 1949; d. Ralph Burt and Alene Margaret Robinson; m. John Julius Gustin, Mar. 25, 1972; children: Amy Beth Farr, John Andrew, Daniel Adam. BA, U. Wis. Parkside, Kenosha, 1971. Cert. unltd.life cert. State of Wis. Dept. Pub. Instrn., 1977, art tchr. grades K-8, secondary sch. tchr. grades 7-12. Art tchr. Kenosha Unified Sch. Dist. 1, 1974—2005, coord. art exhibit elem. children, 1991. Art coord., advertiser Animal Rehab. Kinship, Racine, Wis., 1987—91; coord. art exhibit Anderson Art Ctr., Kenosha, 2004, Bose Elem. Sch. Artist (exhibitions) local restaurants, Kenosha, 1969—71, U. Wis., Racine, Parkside Art Gallery, Kenosha, 1987, 1991, 1997, 1999, 2000, 2005, Anderson Art Ctr. Recipient Blue Ribbon, Kenosha County Fair, Wilmot, Wis., 1976, Cert. of Appreciation, Kenosha Unified Sch. Dist., 1999. Mem.: Wis. Edn. Assn. Coun., Kenosha Edn. Assn., Kenosha Unified Twenty-Five Yr. Club. Republican. Lutheran. Avocations: collecting vintage dog figurines, travel, visiting Southwestern art galleries. Home: 1802 83rd St Kenosha WI 53143-1652 Office Phone: 262-597-4044. Business E-Mail: bgustin@kusd.edu.

GUSTIN, CARL E., JR., manufacturing executive; Sr. v.p., dir. mktg. svcs. affiliates of Young & Rubicam; pres., gen. mgr. Doyle Dane Bernbach (Midwestern ops.); sr. v.p./ptnr. Doyle Dane Bernbach (regional agency); bus. develop. exec., southeast region Apple Computer, 1988, dir., sales, southern ops., exec. aide to chmn. & CEO, v.p., worldwide comm. and mktg. support; v.p., product and market strategy Digital Equipment Corp., 1994, v.p., computer systems divsn.; v.p. and gen. mgr., digital and applied imaging divsn. Eastman Kodak Co., Rochester, NY, 1994—95, acting pres., gen. mgr., digital and applied imaging divsn., 1995—96, sr. v.p., chief mktg. officer, 1995—. Mem., sr. exec. coun. Eastman Kodak Comp., Rochester, NY, chmn., corp. brand mgmt. coun., chmn., e-business mgmt. coun. Named Corp. Mktg. Exec. of Yr., Delaney Report, 1996, Top 50 marketers, Ad Age, 1996. Office: Eastman Kodak Co 343 State St Rochester NY 14650-0001

GUSTIN, MARK DOUGLAS, healthcare executive; b. Bklyn. BS in Acctg., N.Y. Inst. Tech., 1969, MBA in Bus. Mgmt., 1973; M Profl. Studies, L.I. U., 1975; residency diploma in hosp. adminstrn., Kings County Hosp. Ctr., 1979; health care fin. mgmt. cert., Molloy Coll., 1993, elder care studies cert., 1994. Cert. Behavioral Healthcare Exec. 1983. Acct. Fass, Tuchler & Muster, N.Y.C., 1969-74; asst. adminstr. Manhattan Kidney Ctr. Nat. Nephrology Found., Inc., N.Y.C., 1974-76; adminstr. Carter Cmty. Health Ctr., Jamaica, NY, 1976-77; resident in hosp. adminstrn. Kings County Hosp. Ctr., N.Y.C. Health and Hosps. Corp., Bklyn., 1978-79, evening dir. (asst. dir.), 1979-80, assoc. dir., 1980-92, sr. assoc. dir., 1992—. Panel mem. surrogate decision making program N.Y. State Commn. on Quality of Care for the Mentally Disabled, 1993—; mem. Nat. Coun. Cmty. Behavioral Healthcare, 1999-2001, bd. dirs. 1999-2001. Vol. Disaster Psychiatry Outreach, PC, 2004—. Fellow Am. Acad. Med. Adminstrs., Am. Coll. Healthcare Execs., Assn. Behavioral Healthcare Mgmt. (pres. N.Y. chpt. 1999-, adv. coun. chair 2000-01, adv. coun. mem. 2003-, Harold Piepenbrink award 2003), Am. Coll. Addiction Treatment Adminstrs., Am. Coll. Mental Health Adminstrn., Am. Coll. Managed Care Adminstrs., Royal Soc. Health; mem. Healthcare Execs. Club, Mental Health News (adv. coun. mem. 2002-), Mental Health Assn. in N.Y. State (bd. chair 2004-, Caroline Cash award, 2004). Home: 32 Jasmine Ln Valley Stream NY 11581-2412 Office: Kings County Hosp Ctr 451 Clarkson Ave Brooklyn NY 11203-2097 Office Phone: 718-245-5674.

GUTBERG, INGRID MARIA, music educator; b. Riga, Latvia, July 6, 1934; arrived in U.S., 1952; d. Emily (Tosché) Gutberg; children: Birgit, Erica. MA Music Piano, Mozarteum, Salzburg, Austria, 1948, MA Music Organ, 1949; MA Music Conducting, Mozarteum, 1950; D in Musical Arts, Boston U., 1958. Music dir., tchr. Covenant Congl. Ch. of Eastern Mass., Chestnut Hill, 1977—2003; organist, choir dir. Church of the Redeemer, Chestnut Hills, Mass., 1958—73; tchr. assoc. on piano, organ and ensemble Boston U., 1956—63; lectr. music, organist in residence MIT, Cambridge, Mass., 1978—82. Adjudicator for auditions and competition Nat. Guild of Piano Tchrs.; audition Met. Opera, N.Y.C., 1963—65, N.Y.C., 1980. Musician (duo-piano recitale w Dr. Karin Gutberg); musician: (duo piano recordings including) Two Piano Music of Latvia and France. Mem.: Nat. Music Tchrs. Assn., Am. Guild of Organists, Nat. Guild of Piano Tchrs., Latvian Heritage Found. (pres. 2000—), Latvian Guild of Organists in Am; (pres. 1999—), Pi Kappa Lambda, Sigma Alpha Iota. Avocations: art, literature, nature. Home: 45 Drabbington Way Weston MA 02493

GUTCH, ELIZABETH RIGGS, historian; b. S.D. d. Robert Irvine and Florence Harriet (Moseley) Riggs; m. Charley Franklin Gutch, June 15, 1943; 1 child, John Marion. BS in Commerce, U. Iowa, 1942. Chairperson Hist. com. S.D. Conf. United Ch. Christ, Sioux Falls, 1983-88. Cons. Ctr. for Western Studies, Augustana Coll., Sioux Falls, 1986, bd. dirs., 1990-91. Author: Papers Dakota History Conf., 1987—. Pres. Oahe Chapel Preservation Soc., Pierre, S.D., 1989-91. Mem. S.D. Hist. Soc., Congregational Christian Hist. Soc., M.W. United Ch. Christ Historians, Ctr. for Western Studies. Republican. Avocations: gardening, camping.

GUTEKUNST, CARL GEORGE, surgeon; b. Phila., Nov. 25, 1951; s. Albert William and Edna Loraine Gutekunst; m. Kathy Zatavekas, July 25, 1992 (div. Oct. 2002); m. Joanne Johnson, May 17, 2003. BS, Pa. State U., 1979; DO, Pa. Coll. Medicine, 1984. Diplomate Am. Bd. Surgery. Intern Hosp. Coll., Phila., 1984—85; resident Flint Oseopathic Hosp., 1985—89; gen. surgeon Surg. Assocs., Flint, Mich., 1990—; chief surgery Genesys Regional Med. Ctr., Grand Blanc, Mich., 2002—, sec. dept. gen. surgery, 2001—. With USN, 1970—76. Mem.: Am. Osteo. Assn., Soc. Critical Care Medicine, Flint Acad. Surgery. Avocations: flying, golf. Office: Surgical Assocs PLC G-3169 Beecher Rd Flint MI 48532

GUTEKUNST, RICHARD RALPH, microbiology educator; b. Allentown, Pa., Jan. 20, 1926; s. George D. and Jennie L. (Alsop) G.; m. Anna Frances Fetterman, Dec. 27, 1946; children: Mary Jane Ellickson, Richard M., Jo Anne Loughery. BS, Phila. Coll. Pharmacy and Sci., 1951; MS, Cornell U., 1957, PhD, 1958. Commd. ensign USN, advanced through grades to comdr., 1968; mem. faculty Hahnemann Med. Coll. and Hosp., Phila., 1968-80, prof. microbiology and immunology, 1974-80; dir. Clin. Micro Lab., 1968-75; dean Coll. Allied Health Professions, 1975-80, Coll. Health Related Professions; prof. dept. med. tech. and microbiology U. Fla., Gainesville, 1980-95; dean emeritus, 1995—.,.p. Lower Gwynedd (Pa.) Twp. Commrs., 1972-80; mem. coun. St. Peter's Luth. Ch., North Wales, Pa., 1972-77, pres., 1974-77; No. Ctrl. Fla. Regional Planning Coun., 1987-92; bd. dirs. Citizens' Crime Commn., Alachua County, 1984-88, vice-chmn., 1986-87; bd. dirs. United Way Alachua County, 1984-90, 98—, pres., 1988; bd. dirs. ARC of Alachua County, 1989-93; pres. Fla. Alliance of 100, Healthcare Manpower, 1988-90; mem. adv. bd. AIDS Inst., UF; mem. com. on pub. health FMA, 1986-95, mem. com. on allied health, 1991-94, mem. task force on nursing shortage, 1990-95; bd. dirs. DAYTOP Fla., 1996-98, chmn. 1998; bd. dirs. Phoenix Ho. of Fla., 1999—, chmn. 1999—. Recipient Lindback award, 1975; Faculty Achievement award Coll. Allied Health Professions; Faculty Achievement award Hahnemann Med. Coll. and Hosp., Phila., 1980 Fellow Am. Acad. Microbiology, Am. Soc. for Allied Health Professions (pres.-elect 1981-82, pres. 1982-83); mem. Assn. Practitioners Infection Control, Am. Soc. Microbiology, N.Y. Acad. Scis., Masons. Republican. Lutheran. Office: U Health Sci Ctr PO Box 100014 Gainesville FL 32610-0014 Office Phone: 352-392-3621. E-mail: RGutekun@gator.net.

GUTELIUS, JOSEPHA SOPHIA DEBRA, writer, editor, illustrator; b. White Plains, N.Y., Aug. 18, 1952; d. Edward Warner and Dorothy (Payne) G.;m. Benno Schmidbaur, July 27, 1978. Student, U. Munich, 1973-74; BA, Bard Coll., 1975. Journalist Christian Sci. Monitor, Boston, 1975-78; prodn. editor W.W. Norton & Co., Inc., N.Y.C., 1978-82. Contbg. editor Berliner Blaetter, 1975-78; illustrator Greenfield (Vt.) Rev. Press, 1980—, Rat & Mole Press, Amherst, Mass., 1980—. Author: To the Perfect Love that Prepares a Table Beyond Us, 1977, Rapt Meat, 1978, (plays) Atomica World Machine, 1983, Veronica Cory, 1987, Miracle Mile, 1989, Two Hands, 1999, Desperate Alien, 2004, Is It June Where You Are?, 2004, Bad Ex, 2005, RASP, 2005. Chair Citizens Action Against Besicorp/Empire, Inc.; vol. Hudson River Partnerships, N.Y., 1980—, Amnesty Internat., 1975—; comprenensive plan com., 2000—; mem. League of Women Voters, 2000—. Recipient Dramarama award Playwrights Ctr. San Francisco, 1988, Theatre Conspiracy New Play award, 2004; Pushcart Prize nominee, 1990. Mem. Dramatists Guild, Poets and Writers, Internat. Women's Writing Guild. Address: 122 Burt St Saugerties NY 12477-1910 Office Phone: 845-399-8302.

GUTENMACHER, VICTOR, mathematician, educator; b. Yoshkar-Ola, Russia, July 8, 1943; arrived in US, 1989; s. Lev Gutenmacher and Yelena Lipskerova; m. Lena Moskovich, Aug. 30, 1962; 1 child, Olga Moska. PhD, Moscow U., 1974. Sr. rsch. fellow Moscow State U., Moscow, 1977—88; sr. software engr. Computervision Corp., Beford, Mass., 1990—94; adv. engr. Auto-Trol Tech., Denver, 1994—96; sr. software engr. SDRC, Boston, 1996—2001, Vistagy, Inc., Waltham, Mass., 2001—. Sr. cons. BBN, Cambridge, Mass., 1989—98. Author: Homotopic Topology, 1986, Lines and Curves, 2004, Math Olympiads by Correspondence, 1987. Editl. bd. Kvant, Russia, 1981—88; chmn., methodological com. Gelfand Correspondence Sch., Russia, 1969—88; mem. com for USSR Math. Olympiads, Russia, 1966—79; adv. panel Com. for Am. Math. Competitions, 1996—98. Home: 21 Westbourne Terr Apt 4 Brookline MA 02446 Office: Vistagy Inc 200 Fifth Ave 5th Fl Waltham MA 02451 Office Phone: 781-250-6854. Office Fax: 781-250-6804. E-mail: vaguten@yahoo.com.

GUTENTAG, PATRICIA RICHMAND, social worker, family counselor, occupational therapist; b. Newark, Apr. 10, 1954; d. Joseph and Joan (Miller) Leflein; m. Herbert Norman Gutentag; children: Steven, Jesse. BS in Occupational Therapy, Tufts U., 1976; MSW, Boston Coll., 1979. Lic. family and marriage counselor, lic. clin. social worker, N.J.; diplomate Am. Bd. Examiners in Clin. Social Work; registered occupational therapist, N.J. Social worker Jewish Family Svc., Salem, Mass., 1979-82; pvt. practice family and marriage counselor Westfield and Red Bank, N.J., 1982—. Cons. high stress, Westfield and Red Bank, 1982—. Fellow N.J. Soc. for Clin. Social Work; mem. NASW, Am. Occupational Therapists Assn., Registered Occupational Therapists Assn., Soc. for Advancement Family Therapy in N.J., Am. Anorexia-Bulimia Assn., Am. Assn. Marriage and Family Therapy. Avocation: reading. Office: 200 Maple Ave Red Bank NJ 07701-1732

GUTFELD, NORMAN E., lawyer; b. Pitts., Dec. 8, 1911; s. Adolph and Fannie (Haupt) G.; m. Evelyn Kirtz, Aug. 9, 1938 (dec. Jan. 1989); children: Nancy Gutfeld Brown, Howard, Charles, Joan Gutfeld Miller, Rose Gutfeld Edwards, Steven. BA, Case-Western Res. U., 1933, LL.B., 1935. Bar: Ohio 1935. Individual practice law, Cleve., 1935-43; atty. U.S. Regional War Labor Bd., Cleve., 1944; assoc. firm Benesch, Friedlander & Morris, Cleve., 1944-53; treas. Builders Structural Steel Corp., Cleve., 1953-59; partner Garber, Gutfeld & Jaffe, Cleve., 1959-73, Simon, Haiman, Gutfeld, Friedman and Jacobs, Cleve., 1973-80; of counsel Hertz Kates Friedman & Kammer, Cleve., 1981-93; pvt. practice Cleve., 1993-95; retired, 1995. Mem. Cleveland Heights-University Heights Bd. Edn., 1956-63, pres., 1958-59; treas. Bur. Jewish Edn. Cleve., 1974-79; trustee Cleve. Jewish Community Fedn., 1976-77. Mem. Bar Assn. Greater Cleve., Ohio State Bar Assn., Citizen's League Cleve. Clubs: Cleve. City. Home: Apt 6008 4625 Knightsbridge Blvd Columbus OH 43214-4350

GUTFREUND, JOHN HALLE, investment company executive, consultant; b. N.Y.C., Sept. 14, 1929; s. B. Manuel and mary Halle G.; m. Joyce L. Gutfreund, Apr. 11, 1958 (div. July 18, 1980); children: Nicholas J., Joshua L., Owen David; Susan Kaposta Gutfreund, Feb. 5, 1981; 1 child, John Peter. BA, Oberlin (Ohio) Coll., 1951. Pres. Salomon Bros. Inc., N.Y.C., 1953-91, Gutfreund & Co., Inc., N.Y.C., 1993—. Chmn. bd., CEO Saloman Bros., Inc.; co-chmn. Phibro Corp., 1981-83; co-chief exec. officer, 1983-84, CEO, 1984-86, Phibro-Salomon Inc.; dir. AccuWeather, Inc., Nutrition 21, Inc., Evercel, Inc., LCA-Vision, Inc., Masicare Health Plans, Inc., The Universal Bond Fund., Montefiore Med. Ctr.; mem. exec. com. of bd. trustees and fin. Real Estate Coms.; life mem., bd. trustees N.Y. Pub. Libr., Astor, Lenox, Tilden Found.; hon. trustee Oberlin (Ohio) Coll; trustee Aperture Found. Mem. Downtown Lower Manhattan Assn., Bond Club of N.Y. (past pres., mem. bd. govs.). Home: 834 Fifth Ave New York NY 10021 Office: Gutfreund and Co Inc 350 Madison Ave New York NY 10017 Office Phone: 212-389-8287. E-mail: jgutfreund@unterberg.com.

GUTH, CARYL JOY, retired anesthesiologist; b. Peoria, Ill., 1935; m. John Faistad, 1968 (dec. 2001). AA, Mars Hill Coll., 1955; BS, Wake Forest U., 1957, MD, 1962. Diplomate Am. Bd. Anesthesiology. Intern U. Kans. Med. Ctr., Kansas City, 1962-63; resident in anesthesiology U. Pa. Hosp., Phila., 1963-65; instr. dept. anesthesiology Wake Forest U. Bapt. Hosp., Winston-Salem, NC, 1965; fellow in anesthesiology Queen Victoria Hosp., Sussex, Eng., 1966; instr. U. Nijmegan, Netherlands, 1966; former chmn. dept anesthesiology Mills-Peninsula Hosps., San Mateo, Calif., ret.; ind. Nikken wellness cons., 1996—; spl. interest-holistic and integrative medicine physician San Mateo, and Advance, NC, 1998—. Bd. dirs. Mills-Peninsula Health Sys., Mills Hosp. San Mateo, Calif.; bd. sci. and policy advisors Am. Coun.

Sci. and Health, 1995— Bd. visitors Wake Forest U. Bapt. Med. Ctr., Winston-Salem, NC, 2004—. Recipient Dis. Svc. award, Calif. Soc. Anesthesiologist, 2005. Mem. AMA, Am. Soc. Anesthesiology (del. 1976-2000, chair com. on comms. 1987-90, chair com. profl. diversity 1995-97, ann. meeting program organizer 1983-84, 87-88, 94, 97), Calif. Med. Assn. (chair com. splty. socs. 1983-84), Calif. Soc. Anesthesiology (past pres., editor bull. 1976-79, asst. treas. 1979-81, pres.-elect 1981-82, pres. 1982-83), San Mateo County Med. Assn. (bd. dirs. 1984-86, chair med. staff affairs com. 1985-86), Coy C. Carpenter Philanthropic Soc., Wake Forest U. Soc. (pres. club Wake Forest U.), Wake Forest U. Bapt. Med. Ctr. (bd. vis.), Wake Forest U. Med. Alumni Assn. (bd. dirs. 1999-, sec. 2003-, pres. 2005, established endowed chair Holistic and integrative medicine 2002). Home: 105 Willowbrook Pl Advance NC 27006-9480 Office Phone: 336-998-6112. Personal E-mail: wellconsultant@5pillars.com.

GUTH, SHERMAN LEON (S. LEE GUTH), psychologist, educator; b. NYC; s. Arthur and Caroline (Laub) G.; children from previous marriage: Melissa, Victoria; m. Ling Zhao; 1 child, Lillian. BS, Purdue U., 1959; MA, U. Ill., 1961, PhD, 1963. Lectr. dept. psychology Ind. U., Bloomington, 1962-63, instr., 1963-64, asst. prof., 1964-67, assoc. prof., 1967-70, prof., 1970—; dir. research and grad. devel. Sch. Optometry, 1980-88, chmn. dept. visual scis., 1982-85. Vis. assoc. prof. psychology Mich. State U., 1968-69; NIH spl. research fellow in psychology U. Calif., Berkeley, 1971-72; NSF program dir. for sensory physiology and perception, 1977-78 NIH research grantee, 1964—70, NSF research grantee, 1963—86. Fellow Optical Soc. Am. Achievements include being the creator of the ATD model for visual adaption and color perception. Office: Ind U Dept Psychology Bloomington IN 47405 Business E-Mail: guth@indiana.edu.

GUTHART, LEO A., electronics executive; b. N.Y.C., Sept. 26, 1937; s. Harry and Lillian (Singer) G.; m. Laura Carrol, June 16, 1960; children: Rebecca, Margaret. AB, Harvard U., 1958, MBA, 1960, D in Bus. Adminstrn., 1966. Rsch. assoc. Bus. Sch Harvard U., Boston, 1960-62; with Pittway Corp., 1963—, vice chmn. Chgo., 1988—; exec. v.p. Ademco divsn., Syosset, N.Y., 1963-71, pres., 1971-99; chmn., CEO Pittway Security Group, Syosset, 1999—; exec. v.p. Home and Bldg. Control, Honeywell Internat.; mng. ptnr. Topspin Ptnrs., LP, Roslyn Heights, N.Y., 2000—. Chmn. bd. trustees Hofstra U., Hempstead, N.Y., 1993-96; bd. dirs. Aptargroup, 1993-, Acorn Fund, 1994-2005, Symbol Technologies, L.I., 2000-04, Venture Fund; chmn. Cylink Corp., Sunnyvale, Calif., 1996-2004; chmn. Alarm Industry Rsch. and Edn. Found., 1997—. Contbr. articles to profl. jours. Fellow Ford Found., 1961; named Baker scholar, Harvard U., 1960. Mem. Harvard Club, Racquet Club, Beta Gamma Sigma (hon.). Avocation: tennis. Office: 3 Expressway Plz Roslyn Heights NY 11577-2045

GUTHEINZ, JAMES O'LEARY, military officer, law clerk; b. Munich, Sept. 24, 1982; s. Joseph Richard Gutheinz Jr. and Lori Ann Gutheinz; m. Stephanie Hamm, Jan. 15, 2005. BA magna cum laude, U. St. Thomas, 2005. Law clk. Law Office of Joseph R. Gutheinz, Jr., Houston, 1997—; cadet capt. Army ROTC, Houston, 2001—05; second lt., adj. gen. br. Tex. N.G., Ellington Field, 2003—. ROTC scholarship, US Army, 2001 to 2003, Academic scholarship, U. of St. Thomas, 2001 to 2005, scholarship, Tex. N.G., 2003 to 2005. Mem.: ROTC Honor Soc., Aquinias Nat. Honor Soc., Theology Nat. Honor Soc., Social Sci. Nat. Honor Soc., Polit. Sci. Nat. Honor Soc. Roman Catholic. Avocations: running, weightlifting, politics. Home: 205 Woodcombe Houston TX 77062 Office: Law Office of Joseph Richard Gutheinz 205 Woodcombe Houston TX 77062 Office Phone: 281-488-1280. Personal E-mail: jgutheinz@sbcglobal.net.

GUTHEINZ, JOSEPH RICHARD, JR., lawyer, politician, fraud examiner, retired army officer, NASA official, educator, author; b. Camp Lejune, N.C., Aug. 13, 1955; s. Joseph R. Sr. and Rita C. (O'Leary) G.; m. Lori Ann Bentley, Jan. 16, 1976; children: Joseph, Christopher, Michael, Jim, Bill, Dave. AS, AA, Monterey Peninsula Coll., Calif., 1975; BA, Calif. State U., Sacramento, 1978, MA, 1979; postgrad., U. Calif., Davis, 1979-80; grad. U.S. Army Mil. Intelligence Officer Basic Course, U.S. Army Tactical Intelligence Sch., 1980; grad., U.S. Army Flight Sch., 1984; MS in Sys. Mgmt., U. So. Calif., 1985; JD, S. Tex. Coll. Law, 1996; grad. Criminal Investigators Basic Course (hon.), Fed. Law Enforcement Tng. Ctrs., 1988; grad. (disting.), Fed. Law Enforcement Tng. Ctrs. Office Inspector Gen., 1989. Bar: Tex. Supreme Ct. 1997, U.S. Dist. Ct. (so. dist.) Tex. 1997, U.S. Vets. Ct. Appeals 1998, U.S. Armed Forces Ct. Appeals 1998, U.S. Ct. Appeals (5th, 10th, 11th and fed. cirs.) 1998, U.S. Tax Ct. 1998, U.S. Supreme Ct. 2001; lic. FAA comml. pilot, cert. fraud examiner, tchr. credentials in aeronautics, mil. sci., bus. and indsl. mgmt., pub. svcs. and adminstrn., sociology and police sci. Calif. Officer U.S. Army, Kitzigen, Fed. Rep. Germany, 1980-82, capt., mil. intelligence officer Stuttgart, Fed. Rep. Germany, 1982-84, capt., aviator Ft. Polk, La., 1984-86; spl. agt. civil aviation security FAA, Oklahoma City, 1986-87; spl. agt. U.S. Dept. Transp., Denver, 1987-90; sr. spl. agt., acting sr. resident agent in charge Office Insp. Gen. NASA, Houston, 1990-2000; pvt. practice atty. Houston, 1996—; mentor, instr. organized crime U. Phoenix, 2002—; instr. criminal justice Alvin C.C., 2004—. Police sci. instr. Ctrl. Tex. Coll., Nelligan, 1983; case agt. in charge of investigating space shuttle temperature transducers which grounded Shuttle Fleet, 91; apptd. mem. adv. com. on offenders with med. or mental impairments Tex. Dept. Criminal Justice, 2004—; guest spkr. in field; criminal justice instr.; nine agy. task force leader Omniplan Investigation, 1994—97; lead NASA OIG criminal investigation MIR Space State Fire and Crash, 1997; lead investigator Jerry Whittredge, The Astronaut Impersonator, 1998; under cover agent Operation Lunar Eclipse, 1998. Author: Moon Rock Con, 2003, Is it Legal to Privately Own Space ShuttleTiles, 2002, Sterling the Dream, 2002, In Search of the Goodwill Moon Rocks, 2004, There Will Be a Day After Tomorrow, 2004, Building 265, 2005, Marketing an Asteroid Threat, 2005, The Great Astronaut Impersonator, 2005, Cover-up in Space, 2005, Cumbre Vieja: A Terrorist Time Bomb, 2005, Making Safety a Priority: NASA's Path to Mars, 2005; contbr. columns in newspapers. Pres. Calif. State U. United Students for Life, 1976—79; chairperson Calif. Rally for Life, 1980; atty./activist against San Jacinto C.C. spl. election to annex parts of Clear Lake Texas, 2003; proponent Calif. Pro-Life Initiative, 1977; rally organizer Morton Downey Dem. Presdl. Campaign rallies, 1979; del. Tex. senatorial resolutions com. Rep. Party, 2000, 2004, del. conv., 2004; bd. dirs. Sea Isle Property Owners, 2001—02; briefed Pres. Yeltsin's econ. advisors, 1995. Decorated U.S. Army Meritorious Svc. medal, 1986, Army Commendation medal, 1984; recipient letter of commendation FBI Dir. Louis Freeh, 1995, Tex. Spl. Commendation U.S. Atty. Office So. Dist., 1996, NASA Exceptional Svc. medal, 2000, Pres.'s Coun. for Integrity and Efficiency Career Achievement award, 2000, Cert. of Appreciation U.S. Atty. (so. dist.) Tex., 2003, Cert. of Commendation Univ. Phoenix, 2003, U. Phoenix writing honorarium, 2004, 05; named Hon. Lt. Gov. Okla., 1987; Merit scholar South Tex. Coll. Law Mem.: Tex. Pro Bono Coll., Haris County Lawyers assn., Nat. Rep. Lawyers Assn. (mem. spkrs. panel on Calif. recall election), Tex. Criminal Def. Lawyers Assn., Tex. Bar Assn., Cert. Fraud Examiners. Republican. Roman Catholic. Avocations: reading, teaching, public speaking, political activism, helping the poor. Office: 205 Woodcombe Houston TX 77062 Office Phone: 281-488-1280. Personal E-mail: jgutheinz@sbcglobal.net.

GUTHEINZ, MICHAEL JOHN, military officer, law clerk; b. Fort Huachuca, Ariz., Aug. 6, 1980; s. Joseph Richard Gutheinz Jr. and Lori Ann Gutheinz. BA, U. St. Thomas, 2003; attending, South Tex. Coll. Law, 2003—. US Army Commn. Sec. of Army, 2003. Law clk. Law Office of Joseph Richard Gutheinz, Jr., Houston, 1997—2005, Harris County Civil Atty.'s Office, Houston, 2005. Vol. Gabriel Project, Houston, 1995—; reading tutor Am. Reads Project, Houston, 2003—. Law student mem. Rep. Nat. Lawyers Assn., Houston, 2003—05; mem. Res. Officers Assn., DC, 2003—05; law student mem. Tex. Criminal Def. Lawyers Assn., Austin, 2003—05. Cadet capt. US Army ROTC, 2001—03, lt. U.S. Army, 2003—05, Houston. Recipient Superior Cadet award, US Army ROTC Command, 2003, Phys. Fitness award, 2003. Mem.: Pi Sigma Alpha, Delta Theta Phi. Roman Catholic. Avocations: politics, running, weightlifting. Home: 205 Woodcombe Houston TX 77062 Office: Law Office of Joseph R Gutheinz Jr 205 Woodcombe Houston TX 77062 Personal E-mail: jgutheinz@sbcglobal.net.

GUTHERY, JOHN M., lawyer; b. Broken Bow, Nebr, Nov. 22, 1946; s. John M. and Kay G.; m. Diane Messineo, May 26, 1972; 1 child, Lisa. BS, U. Nebr., 1969, JD, 1972. Bar: Nebr. 1972. Pres. Perry, Guthery, Haase & Gessford, P.C., L.L.O., Lincoln, Nebr., 1972—. Bd. govs. Nebr. Wesleyan U. Mem. ATLA, ABA (mem. litigation sect.), Nebr. Bank Attys. Assn. (past pres., 1985-86), Nebr. Assn. Trial Attys., Nebr. State Bar Assn. (pres. 1998-99, mem. Nebr.State Bar Found. mem. ho. dels. 1979-83, 87-95, exec. coun. 1988-94 pres. 1998-99, chair Nebr. bankruptcy sect.), Lincoln Bar Assn. (trustee 1985-88, pres. 1990-91). Office: Perry Guthery Haase & Gessford PC LLO 233 S 13th St Ste 1400 Lincoln NE 68508-2003 Office Phone: 402-476-9200. E-mail: jguthery@perrylawfirm.com.

GUTHKE, KARL SIEGFRIED, language educator; b. Lingen, Germany, Feb. 17, 1933; arrived in U.S., 1956, naturalized, 1973; s. Karl Hermann and Helene (Beekman) Guthke; m. Dagmar von Nostitz, Apr. 24, 1965; 1 child, Carl Ricklef. MA, U. Tex., 1953; PhD, U. Göttingen, Germany, 1956; MA (hon.), Harvard U., 1968. Faculty U. Calif., Berkeley, 1956-65, prof. German lit., 1962-65, U. Toronto, Canada, 1965-68, Harvard U., 1968-78, Kuno Francke prof. German art and culture, 1978—. Vis. prof. U. Colo., 1963, U. Mass., 1967; vis. fellow Sidney Sussex Coll., Cambridge U., Nat. Rsch. Ctr., Wolfenbüttel, Inst. Advanced Studies, U. Edinburgh, Humanities Rsch. Ctr., Australian Nat. U., Canberra. Author: Englische Vorromantik und deutscher Sturm und Drang, 1958; author: (with Hans M. Wolff) Das Leid im Werke Gerhart Hauptmanns, 1958; author: Geschichte und Poetik der deutschen Tragikomödie, 1961, Gerhart Hauptmann: Weitbild im Werk, 1961, rev. edit., 1980, Haller und die Literatur, 1962, Der Stand der Lessing-Forschung: Ein Bericht über die Literatur, 1932-1962, 1965, Modern Tragicomedy: An Investigation into the Nature of the Genre, 1966, Wege zur Literatur: Studien zur deutschen Dichtungs-und Geistesgeschichte, 1967, Hallers Literaturkritik, 1970, die Mythologie der entgötterten Welt: Ein literarisches Therna vond der Aufklärung bis zur Gegenwart, 1971, Das deutsche bürgerliche Trauerspiel, 1972, 5th rev. edit., 1994, G.E. Lessing, 3d edit., 1979, Literarisches Leben im 18. Janrhundert in Deutschland und in der Schweiz, 1975, Das Abenteuer der Literatur, 1981, Haller im Halblicht, 1981, Der Mythos der Neuzeit, 1983, Erkundungen, 1983, Das Geheimnis um B. Traven entdeckt, 1984, B. Traven: Biographie eines Rätsels, 1987, The Last Frontier: Imagining Other Worlds, 1990, Letzte Worte, 1990, B. Traven: The Life Behind the Legends, 1991, Last Words, 1992, Trails in No-Man's Land, 1993, Die Entdeckung des Ich, 1993, Schillers Dramen, 1994, Schillers Dramen, 2nd edit., 2005, Ist der Tod eine Frau, 1997, The Gender of Death, 1999, Der Blick in die Fremde, 2000, Goethes Weimar und die grosse Öffnung in die weite Welt, 2001, Epitaph Culture in the West, 2003, Lessings Horizonte, 2003, Die Erfindung der Welt, 2005, others; translator: Die moderne Tragikomödie: Theorie und Gestalt, 1968; editor: Haller, Die Alpen, 1987; editor: (with Hanser) Gotthold Ephraim Lessing, Werke, 1970—72; co-editor: Joh. H. Füssli, Sämtliche Gedichte, 1973, B. Traven: Briefe aus Mexiko, 1992, Lessing Yearbook, Colloquia Germanica, Twentieth Century Literature, German Quar., Honored in History and Literature: Essays in Honor of Karl S. Guthke, 2000. Fellow: Rsch. Ctr., Wolfenbuttel, Inst. Advanced Studies, Edinburgh, Humanities Rsch. Ctr., Canberra; mem.: Inst. Germanic Studies (London corr. fellow). Office: Harvard U Dept German Cambridge MA 02138

GUTHMAN, JACK, lawyer; b. Cologne, Germany, Apr. 19, 1938; came to U.S., 1939, naturalized, 1945; s. Albert and Selma (Cahn) G.; m. Sandra Polk, Nov. 26, 1967. BA, Northwestern U., 1960; LL.B., Yale U., 1963. Bar: Ill. bar 1963. Law clk. to dist. judge U.S. Dist. Ct. No. Ill., 1963-65; since practiced in Chgo.; ptnr. Sidley & Austin, 1970-94, Shefsky & Froelich Ltd., Chgo., 1995—. Mem. City Chgo. Zoning Bd. Appeals, 1970-75, chmn., 1975-87. Democrat. Jewish. Office: Shefsky & Froelich Ltd 111 E Wacker Dr Ste 2800 Chicago IL 60601 Office Phone: 312-836-4034.

GUTHRIDGE, BILL, university basketball coach; b. Parsons, Kans., July 27, 1937; m. Leesie Guthridge; children: Jamie, Stuart, Megan. BS in Math., Kans. State U., 1960, MEd, 1963. Coach Scott City (Kans.) H.S; asst. football coach Kans. State U.; freshman basketball coach, co-asst. varsity coach U. NC, Chapel Hill, from 1973, asst. coach, 1968-97, head coach, 1997—2000. Coach Puerto Rican AAU Summer Leagues; coach Puerto Rican Olympic Team, 1968. Named Coach of Yr., Puerto Rican AAU, Nat. Coach of Yr., Nat. Assn. Basketball Coaches, Sporting News, CBS/Chevrolet, Columbus Touchdown Club, Atlantic Coast Conf., 1998; recipient Naismith award Atlanta Tipoff Club.

GUTHRIE, DIANA FERN, nursing educator; b. N.Y.C., May 7, 1934; d. Floyd George and A. May (Moler) Worthington; m. Richard Alan Guthrie, Aug. 18, 1957; children: Laura, Joyce, Tammy. AA, Graceland Coll., 1953; RN, Independence (Mo.) Sanitarium, 1956; BS in Nursing, U. Mo., 1957, MS in Pub. Health, 1969; EdS, Wichita State U., 1982; PhD, Walden U., 1985. Cert. diabetes educator, bd. cert. advanced diabetes mgmt.; RN Mo., Kans., cert. holistic nursing, RN advanced practitioner; lic. profl. counselor Kans., cert. stress mgmt. edn., clin. hypnosis, healing touch, lic. marriage and family therapist. Instr. red cross U.S. Naval Sta., Sangley Point, Philippines, 1961-63; acting head nurse newborn nursery U. Mo., Columbia, 1963-64, birth defect nurse dept. pediat., 1964-65, nursing dir. clin. research ctr., 1965-67, research asst., 1967-73; diabetes nurse specialist Sch. Medicine U. Kans., Wichita, 1973—, asst. then assoc. prof. Sch. Medicine, 1974-85, prof. dept. pediat. and psychiatry Sch. Medicine, 1985-99, prof. emeritus, 2000; prof. dept. nursing Kans. U. Med. Ctr., Wichita, 1985-99, ret., 1999. Nurse cons. diabetes Mo. Regional Med. Program, Columbia, 1970-73; nat. advisor Human Diabetes Ctr. for Excellence, Lexington, Ky., 1982-90, Phoenix, 1983-92, Charlottesville, Ky., 1990-95; adj. prof. Sch. Nursing Wichita State U., 1985—. Author: Nursing Management of Diabetes, 1977, 5th edit., 2002, The Diabetes Source Book, 1990, 5th edit., 2003, Alternative and Complementary Diabetes Case, 2000; contbr. articles to profl. jours. Health adv. bd. Mid-Am. All Indian Ctr., Wichita, 1978-80; bd. dirs. Wichita Urban Indian Health Clinic, 1980-82; bd. trustees Graceland U., Lamoni, Iowa, 1996-2001, bd. trustees emeritus, 2002—. Fellow: Am. Acad. Nursing; mem.: APHA, ANA, Am. Assn. Med. Psychotherapists (profl. adv. bd. 1985—), Am. Assn. Diabetes Educators (Kans. area Disting. Svc. award 1999), Am. Diabetes Assn. (Kans. area prof. edn. and youth com. 1988—, affiliate bd. dirs. 1979—83, pres. Kans. affiliate 1980—81, 1990—91, Outstanding Educator award 1979, Regional Outstanding Svc. award 1984), Sigma Theta Tau (Exemplary Recognition award Epsilon Gamma chpt. 1996). Democrat. Mem. Cmty. Of Christ Ch. Avocations: harp, piano, painting, crafts, reading. Office: 200 S Hillside Wichita KS 67211-2127 Office Phone: 316-681-3100. Business E-Mail: dguthrie@kumc.edu.

GUTHRIE, EDGAR KING, artist; b. Chenoa, Ill., May 12, 1917; s. David McMurtrie and Emily Henrietta (Streid) G.; m. Eva Ross Harvey, Dec. 8, 1945 (dec. Jan. 1978); children: Melody Bliss Johnson, Mark King Guthrie. BEd, Ill. State U., 1939; MA, Am. U., 1958; graduate, Command and General Staff Coll., Ft. Leavenworth, Kan., 1967. Artist W.L. Stensgaard Co., Chgo., 1939-40, The Diamond Store, Phoenix, 1941-42; presentation artist CIA, Washington, 1955-72; instr. Columbia Tech. Inst., Arlington, Va., 1966-72; owner, later ptnr. Guthrie Art & Sign Co., Winchester, Va., 1976—; instr. U. Hawaii, Lihue, 1980-81; cartoonist The Kauai Times, Lihue, 1981-90; owner Alo-o-oha-ha-ha Caricatures, Lihue, Honolulu, 1980—. Cons., artist Shenandoah Apple Blossom Festival, Winchester, 1975-78; cartoonist Internat. Salon of Caricature, Montreal, Can., 1976-77; co-chmn. Kauai Soc. of Artists Art Show, Lihue, 1981. One man shows include 50 Yrs. of Painting-A Retrospective, Lihue, 1984; inventor Artists' Kit; Filmic Artist: (documentary film) The River Nile, 1960 (NBC Emmy Award). Bd. dirs. Civil Def., Virginia Hills, 1954; publicity com. Frederick County Taxpayers Assn., Winchester, 1973, Exch. Club, Winchester, 1977. Lt. col. U.S. Army, 1942-54. Decorated Purple Heart, Bronze Star with oak leaf cluster; recipient Spl. Merit award Boy Scouts Am. Aloha Coun., Lihue, 1982. Mem. Mus. of Cartoon Art, U.S. Naval Combat Artist, Daniel Morgan Mus. (contbr. 1976), Nat. Soc. Mural Painters (contbr. 1976), Allied Artists of Am. (contbr. 1977), Pastel Soc. Am. (contbr. 1977-78), Am. Watercolor Soc. (contbr. 1982—), Greek Expeditionary Forces (hon.). Mem. Ch. LDS. Avocations: animation, cinematography, hiking, swimming, genealogy. Home and Office: 2444 Hihiwai St Apt 703 Honolulu HI 96826-5104 Office Phone: 808-955-2644. E-mail: eg@edguthrie.com. *Have short term and long term righteous goals. Be able to take risks in those things that most interest you, and gain wisdom from those risks that are least effectual. Instead of merely abandoning a project, try to give it more quality.*

GUTHRIE, FRANK ALBERT, chemistry professor; b. Madison, Ind., Feb. 16, 1927; s. Ned and Gladys (Glick) G.; m. Marcella Glee Farrar, June 12, 1955; children: Mark Alan, Bruce Bradford, Kent Andrew, Lee Farrar. AB, Hanover Coll., 1950; MS, Purdue U., 1952; PhD, Ind. U., 1962. Mem. faculty Rose-Hulman Inst. Tech., Terre Haute, Ind., 1952—, assoc. prof., 1962-67, prof. chemistry, 1967-94, prof. emeritus, 1994—, chmn. dept., 1969-72, chief health professions adviser, 1975-94. Kettering vis. lectr. U. Ill., Urbana, 1961-62; vis. prof. chemistry U.S. Mil. Acad., West Point, N.Y., 1987-88, 93-94, admissions coord., 1989—; vis. prof. chemistry Butler U., spring 2000. Mem. exec. bd. Wabash Valley coun. Boy Scouts Am., 1971-87, scoutmaster, 1979-82, adv. bd., 1988—, v.p. for scouting, 1976; mem. selection chmn. Leadership Terre Haute, 1978-80. Served with AUS, 1945-46. Recipient Vigil Honor Order of Arrow, Boy Scouts Am., 1975, Wood badge, 1976, Dist. award of merit, 1976, Silver Beaver award, 1980. Fellow Ind. Acad. Sci. (treas. 1966-68, pres. 1970, chmn. acad. found. trustees 1986—); mem. Am. Chem. Soc. (sec. 1973-77, editor directory 1965-77, chmn. divsn. analytical chemistry 1979-80; local sect. activities com. 1982-86, nominations and elections com. 1988-94, sec. 1992-94, coun. policy com. 1995, constn. and bylaws com. 1996-2002, membership affairs com., 2003—, chmn. Wabash Valley sect. 1958, counselor 1980—, steering com. for joint ctrl.-Gt. Lakes regional meetings, Indpls., 1978, 91, vis. assoc. com. profl. tng. 1984—, chmn. analytical chemistry exam. inst. std. exam. 1994, Disting. Svc. award 2005), Coblentz Soc., Midwest Univs. Analytical Chemistry Conf., Hanover Coll. Alumni Assn. (pres. 1974, Alumni Achievement award 1977), Masons (32 deg.), Sigma Xi (treas. Wabash Valley chpt. 1994-98), Phi Lambda Upsilon, Phi Gamma Delta, Alpha Chi Sigma (E.E. Dunlap scholarship selection com. 1986—, chmn. 1990—, dir. expansion 1995-99, profl. rep. 1997-2000). Presbyterian. Home: 120 Berkley Dr Terre Haute IN 47803-1708 Office: Rose Hulman Inst Tech 5500 Wabash Ave Terre Haute IN 47803-3999 Office Phone: 812-877-8312. Personal E-mail: fguthrie@chilitech.com. Business E-Mail: frank.guthrie@rose-hulman.edu.

GUTHRIE, HELEN A., nutritionist, educator, dietician; b. Sarnia, Ont., Can., Sept. 25, 1925; d. David and Helen Andrews; m. George Guthrie, June 4, 1949; children: Barbara, Jane, James. BA, U. Western Ont., 1946, DSc (hon.), 1982; MS, Mich. State U., 1948; PhD, U. Hawaii, 1968; DSc, U. Guelph, 1996. Registered dietitian, Pa. From instr. to prof. Pa. State U., University Park, 1949-73, chair dept., 1974-89, endowed prof. nutrition, 1989-91, prof. emerita, 1991—. V.p. Heinz Inst. Nutrition Sci., 1993—; nutrition cons. to industry, govt. and academia. Chmn. Bd. of Health, State College, Pa., 1977-82. Recipient Borden award Am. Home Econs. Assn., 1976, W.O. Atwater award USDA, 1989, Pacemaker award Pa. Nutrition Coun., 1994. Fellow Am. Inst. Nutrition (councillor 1982—, pres. 1987—, Elvehjhem award for pub. svc. 1989), Soc. Nutrition Edn. (pres. 1978-79, fellow, 1992), Internat. Life Sci. Inst.-Nutrition Found. (trustee 1979-92, v.p. nutrition 1986-89, editor Nutrition Today 1987-97, Philippine Assn. Nutrition and Dietetics (hon.). Office: Pa State U S-125 S Human Devel University Park PA 16802 Home: 5260 S Landings Dr Apt 907 Fort Myers FL 33919-4677 Business E-Mail: hag@psu.edu.

GUTHRIE, HUGH DELMAR, chemical engineer; b. Murdo, S.D., May 11, 1919; s. John Arlington and Farol Venus (Smith) Guthrie; m. Elizabeth Anne Harris, Mar. 4, 1950; children: Katherine Farol, Gretchen, Mary Melissa, Elizabeth Lenore, Emily Jo. BSChemE with highest distinction, State U. Iowa, 1943. Jr. engr., engr., group leader Shell Devel. Co., San Francisco, 1943-52; technologist, sr. technologist, asst. dept. mgr. Shell Oil Co., Wood River, Ill., 1952-56, staff engr., group leader N.Y.C., 1956-60, dept. mgr. Wood River, 1960-62, asst. mgr. to mgr. mktg. N.Y.C., 1962-70, from dept. mgr. to sr. staff Houston, 1970-76; div. dir. ERDA, Dept. Energy, Washington, 1976-78; dir. Energy Ctr., Stanford Rsch. Inst., Menlo Park, Calif., 1978-80; v.p. licensing, mgr. tech. assessment Occidental Rsch. Corp., Irvine, Calif., 1980-83; v.p. licensing, mgr. rsch. planning Cities Svc., Tulsa, 1983-86; dir. extraction divsn. Morgantown (W.Va.) Energy Tech. Ctr. Dept. Energy, 1987-92, gen. engr. products tech. mgmt., mgr. gas products, 1992-97, sr. mgmt., tech. advisor, 1997-99, Dept. Energy Strategic Ctr for Natural Gas, Morgantown, WVa., 1999—. Cons. Hugh D. Guthrie & Assocs., Tulsa, 1986—87; mem. adv. bd. U. Iowa, U. Calif., Berkeley, Tulsa U., U. Tex., U. Pitts., W.Va. U. Former sr. warden Episcopal chs., Conn. Named Outstanding Older Worker, W.Va. Experience Works Orgn., 2004. Fellow: AIChE (pres. 1969, chair Assembly Fellows 1990—92, chair mgmt. divsn. 1991, chair membership campaign found. 1992—98, Founder's award 1974, F. J. Van Antwerpen award 1986, Robert L. Jacks Meml. award 1992); mem.: AAAS, N.Y. Acad. Scis., Soc. Petroleum Engrs., Am. Chem. Soc., Sigma Xi, Omicron Delta Kappa, Phi Lambda Upsilon, Tau Beta Pi. Republican. Achievements include patents for distillation equipment. Home: 901 Stewart Pl Morgantown WV 26505-3688 Office: Dept Energy Morgantown Energy Fed Ctr 3610 Collins Ferry Rd Morgantown WV 26505-2353 Office Phone: 304-285-4632. E-mail: hguthr@netl.doe.gov.

GUTHRIE, JANET, professional race car driver; b. Iowa City, Mar. 7, 1938; d. William Lain and Jean Ruth Guthrie. BS in Physics, U. Mich., 1960. Comml. pilot and flight instr., 1958-61; research and devel. engr. Republic Aviation Corp., Farmingdale, N.Y., 1960-67; publs. engr. Sperry Systems, Sperry Corp., Great Neck, N.Y., 1968-73; racing driver Sports Car Club Am. and Internat. Motor Sports Assn., 1963-86; profl. racing driver U.S. Auto Club and Nat. Assn. for Stock Car Racing, 1976-80; pres. Janet Guthrie Racing Enterprises Inc., 1978—2004; owner Guthrie Racing LLC, 2004—. Highway safety cons. Met. Ins. Co., 1980-87. Author: Janet Guthrie: A Life at Full Throttle, 2005. Named to Women's Sports Hall of Fame, 1980; recipient Curtis Turner award, Nat. Assn. for Stock Car Racing-Charlotte World 600, 1976, First in class award, Sebring 12-hour, 1967, 1970. Mem. Madison Ave. Sports Car Driving and Chowder Soc., Women's Sports Found., Les Dames d'Aspen, Internat. Wine and Food Soc., Nat. Spkrs. Assn. Achievements include being the first woman to qualify for and race in Daytona 500, 1977, Top Rookie; first woman to qualify for and race in Indpls. 500, 1977, finished 9th, 1978; North Atlantic Road Racing Champion, 1973.

GUTHRIE, JOSEPH RANDALL, music educator; b. Morehead City, N.C., Aug. 20, 1954; s. Joseph Reginald and Blonnie Mae Guthrie; m. Betty Ann Ford, Dec. 21, 1974; children: Heather Ann, Heidi Jo. AA in Music, Emmanuel Coll., Franklin Springs, Ga., 1974; BA in Music Edn., U. N.C., Pembroke, 1977; MA in Ch. Music, Oral Roberts U., Tulsa, 1989; DMA in Musical Arts, Southwestern Baptist Theol. Seminary, Ft. Worth, 1992. From assoc. prof. to prof., chair, grad. ch. music Oral Roberts U., Tulsa, 1988—98; min. of music Valley Christian Ctr., Dublin, Calif., 1998—2000; prof. music, v.chmn. music dept. Oral Roberts U., Tulsa, 2000—. Copyright com. chair Oral Roberts U., Tulsa, 2001—03, faculty chapel com., 2003—, curriculum com. chair, 2000—. Contbg. editor: The New Grove Dictionary of Music, 2000. Mem.: Music Educators' Nat. Conf., The Hymn Soc., Am. Choral Dirs. Assn. Home: 5722 E 62nd Pl Tulsa OK 74136 Office: Oral Roberts Univ 7777 S Lewis Ave Tulsa OK 74171 Office Phone: 918-495-7514. Business E-Mail: rguthrie@oru.edu.

GUTHRIE, JUDITH K., federal judge; b. Chgo., July 13, 1948; d. David Curtis and Kathleen McAfee G.; m. John H. Hannah, Jr., May 9, 1992 (dec. 2003). Student, Ariz. State U., 1966—68; BA, St. Mary's U., 1971; JD cum laude, U. Houston, 1980. Bar: Tex. 1981, U.S. Dist. Ct. (ea. dist.) Tex. 1982, U.S. Ct. Appeals (5th cir.) 1982, U.S. Dist. Ct. (no. dist.) Tex. 1983, U.S. Dist. Ct. (we. dist.) Tex. 1984. Editor Am. Coun. Edn., Washington, 1972-73; exec. asst. Tex. Ho. Reps., Austin, 1973-75; lobbyist Bracewell & Patterson, Austin,

1975-80, assoc. Houston, 1980-81; briefing atty. Tex. Ct. Appeals, Tyler, 1981-82; ptnr. Hannah & Guthrie, Tyler, 1982-86; magistrate judge U.S. Dist. Ct. (ea. dist.) Tex., Tyler, 1986—. Instr. legal asst. program, Tyler Jr. Coll., 1986-87; apptd. Tex. Jud. Coun., 1991-97, gender bias task force, 1991-92; lectr. in field. Contbr. articles to profl. jours. Adv. bd. Main St. Project; legal asst. adv. bd. Tyler Jr. Coll., 1986—, chmn. adv. bd., 1996—; mem. Citizens Commn. Tex. Jud. Sys., 1992—93; bd. dirs. Habitat for Humanity, 2003—; former Dem. chmn. Smith County; former bd. dirs. Found. Women's Resources, Leadership Am., Leadership Tex. Mem.: ABA (Fed. trial judges legis. com. 1991—93), Smith County Bar Assn. (chmn. law libr. com. 1985—2001), State Bar Tex. (dist. 2A grievance com. 1990—, chmn. 1995—96), 5th Cir. Bar Assn., Fed. Magistrate Judges Assn., Am. Judges Assn. Office: US Dist Ct 300 Fed Bldg & US Ct House 211 W Ferguson St Tyler TX 75702-7212 Office Phone: 903-590-1077.

GUTHRIE, LAWRENCE SIMPSON, II, law librarian, journalist; b. Thomas, Okla., Dec. 2, 1953; s. Lawrence Simpson and Helen Marie (Janning) G. BS, Georgetown U., 1976, Anna Freud Ctr., London, 1979; MA, U. Okla., 1980; MS in Libr. Sci., Cath. U. Am., 1988. Asst. prof. psychology Tulsa Cmty. Coll., 1982—86; grad. libr. nursing/biology Cath. U. Am., Washington, 1986-89; law libr. interlibr. loan George Washington U. Law Libr., Washington, 1989-95, Covington & Burling, Washington, 1995—. Author: Sports Libraries, 1995; co-author: Library of Congress Luminary on History of Cataloging, 2003contbr. articles to profl. jours. including History of Cataloging, 2003; start-up cons., D.C. corr. Urban Tulsa newspaper, 1990-93; founder Today's Events col. Tulsa World Newspaper, 1978-79; columnist Copyright Corner, Information Outlook, 1997—. Bd. dirs. Cath. U. Sch. Libr. and Info. Sci. Alumni Assn., Washington, 1990-92; moderator White House Conf. on Librs., Washington, 1991; donated Okla. flag to John F. Kennedy Ctr. Hall of States, Washington, 1988. Recipient commendation as educator of all levels Okla. Gov. & Legislature, 1989. Mem. Spl. Librs. Assn. (copyright com. 1992-95, govt. rels. com. 1995—, chmn. 1996—, chmn. legal divsn. 1999-2000, Liverpool del. 2002), Nat. Press Club, Petroleum Club. Democrat. Roman Catholic. Avocations: ice skating, baseball, sailing. Home: 2450 Virginia Ave NW Apt E317 Washington DC 20037-2654 Office: Covington & Burling 1201 Pennsylvania Ave NW Washington DC 20004-2401 Office Phone: 202-662-6158. Business E-Mail: lguthrie@cov.com.

GUTHRIE, M. PHILIP, corporate financial executive; b. Vicksburg, Miss., Mar. 26, 1945; s. Marion P. Jr. and Aileen (Perry) G.; m. Beverly Alice Blackmon, June 2, 1966; children: Philip Todd, Edward Tait, Stuart Trent. BS, La. Tech U., 1967; MBA, U. Mich., 1968. CPA, La., Tex. Sr. cons. Price Waterhouse & Co., Houston, 1968-72; v.p. fin. and mfg. Vicra div. Baxter Labs., Dallas, 1972-78; v.p. fin., CFO, treas. S.W. Airlines Co., Dallas, 1978-81; exec. v.p., CFO, Braniff Internat., Dallas, 1981-84; pres. Diamond Mgmt. Group, Dallas, 1984-89; mng. dir. Mason Best Co., Dallas, 1989—; chmn., CEO, Am. Eagle Group, Inc., Dallas, 1992—96; CEO Aircraft Interior Resources Group Inc., 1998—2003, Intech Aerospace Group, LLC, 2004—; mng. dir. Denham Ptnrs., LLC, 2004—. Bd. dirs. Mainstream Data, Inc., Salt Lake City, Safeguard Bus. Sys., Ft. Washington, Pa., Internat. Autotech, Dallas, Westmark Sys., Inc., Austin, Tex., Sunrise Pubs., Inc., Bloomington, Ind., Bristol Group (Buenos Aires), Alpargatas (Buenos Aires). Assoc. bd. dirs. So. Meth. U. Grad. Sch. Bus., Dallas, 1985—. Mem. AICPA, Fin. Execs. Inst., Nat. Assn. Casualty and Surety Execs., Soc. Internat. Bus. Fellows, Tex. Soc. CPA's, Coun. of Ins. Co. Execs., Phi Kappa Phi, Omicron Delta Kappa, Beta Gamma Sigma, Delta Sigma Pi, Beta Alpha Psi. Office: Three Lincoln Ctr 5430 LBJ Fwy Ste 1480 Dallas TX 75240 Office Phone: 972-770-2501. E-mail: pguthrie@denhampartners.com.

GUTHRIE, RANDOLPH HOBSON, JR., plastic surgeon, consultant; b. NYC, Dec. 8, 1934; s. Randolph Hobson and Mabel Edith (Welton) G.; m. Beatrice Mills Holden, Mar. 20, 1965; children: Randolph Hobson III, Michael Phipps, Philip Holden. AB, Princeton U., 1957; MD, Harvard U., 1961. Intern NY Hosp., NYC, 1961-62, resident, 1962-63, 69-71, chief resident, 1971; resident St. Luke's Hosp., NYC, 1963-66, chief resident, 1966—71; chief plastic & reconstructive surgery svc. Meml. Sloan-Kettering Cancer Ctr., NYC, 1971-77; chief dept. plastic and reconstructive surgery NY Downtown Hosp., NYC, 1979-2000; asst. prof. Cornell U. Med. Coll., 1971-74, assoc. prof., 1974-89, prof., 1989—. Asst. attending surgeon, NY Hosp., 1971-74, assoc. attending surgeon, 1974-89, attending surgeon, 1989—; attending surgeon Sloan-Kettering Cancer Ctr., 1977-93, cons., 1994—. Author: The Truth About Breast Implants, 1994; co-author: Reconstruction and Esthetic Mammoplasty, 1989; contbr. articles to profl. jours., books. Pres. East River Med. Found., NYC, 1970-80, Acacia Found., NYC, 1980-94; alumni dir. St. Paul's Sch., Concord, NH, 1979-83, form agt., 1983-87, term trustee, 1985-89, life trustee, 1989-94; trustee Epsicopal Sch., NYC, 1976-84; bd. dirs. Am.-Italian Found. Cancer Rsch., NYC, 1985-94; bd. dirs., treas. Save Venice, Inc., 1985-89, pres., 1989-97, chmn., 1997—; trustee NY Downtown Hosp., 1985-92, Isabella Stewart Gardner Mus., Boston, 1998-2000. Maj. M.C. AUS, 1966-69. Decorated Cavaliere nell 'Ordine Al Merito della Republica Italiana; rsch. fellow Sloan Kettering Cancer Ctr., 1971-77. Mem. ACS, Plastic Surgery Rsch. Coun., Am. Geriat. Soc., Am. Soc. Plastic and Reconstructive Surgeons, Pan Am. Med. Soc., NY Soc. Plastic and Reconstructive Surgery, NY Med. Soc., Med. Soc. County NY, Herbert Conway Soc., Doubles Club, Century Club, Knickerbocker Club (NYC). Home and Office: 15 E 74th St New York NY 10021-2604 E-mail: rhgnyc@aol.com.

GUTHRIE, RICHARD ALAN, physician; b. Pleasant Hill, Ill., Nov. 13, 1935; s. Merle Pruitt and Cleona Marie (Weaver) G.; m. Diana Fern Worthington, Aug. 18, 1957; children: Laura, Joyce, Tamara. AA, Graceland Coll., 1955; MD, U. Mo., 1960. Diplomate Am. Bd. Pediatrics, Am. Bd. Pediatric Endocrinology; cert. Nat. Bd. for Diabetes Educators. Intern U.S. Naval Hosp., Camp Pendleton, Calif., 1960-61, dir. dependent svcs. Sangley Point, The Philippines, 1961-63; asst. instr., resident in pediatrics U. Mo., 1963-65, NIH fellow in endocrinology and metabolism, 1965-68, asst. prof., dir. newborn svcs., 1968-71, assoc. prof. pediat., 1971-73; prof., chmn. dept. pediatrics U. Kans. Med. Sch., Wichita, 1973-82; exec. dir. Kans. Regional Diabetes Ctr., Wichita, 1982-84; pres. Mid-Am. Diabetes Assocs., Wichita, 1984—. Dir. Robert L. Jackson Diabetes Treatment, Edn. and Rsch. Ctr., 1985—. Author: Nursing Management in Diabetes Mellitus, 1976, 1997, 2003, The Child with Diabetes, 1970, Physiologic Management of Diabetes in Children, 1986, Diabetes Source Book, 1990, 2003; mem. editl. bd.: Practical Diabetology, 1982—92, Diabetes Self-Management, 1984—97, Diabetes Educator, 1985—89, assoc. editor: Diabetes Spectrum, 2000—05; contbr. articles to profl. jours. Mem. health ministries bd. Reorganized Ch. Jesus Christ Latter-day Saints; mem. adv. bd. Kans. Action for Children, 1978—, Kans. State Diabetes, 1988-93, 95—. With USN, 1960-63. Recipient grants NIH, 1968—, Outstanding Faculty award Wichita State U., 1976, 2000, Disting. alumnus award Graceland Coll., 1984, Humanitarian award Wesley Med. Found., 1997, award for outstanding cmty. svc. Am. Diabetes Assn., 2001; Dr. McIver Furman Disting. lectureship in health scis. Del Mar Coll., Corpus Christi, Tex., 1986. Fellow Am. Acad. Pediatrics, Am. Coll. Endocrinology; mem. AMA, Am. Diabetes Assn. (bd. dirs. 1972-77, Outstanding Contbn. to Camping award 1992, Outstanding award for Reaching People 2003, Outstanding Physician Clinical award 2003), Kans. Diabetes Assn. (pres. 1974, chmn. bd. 1974-77, 85-87), Kans. State Med. Soc., Sedgewick County Med. Soc., Am. Pediat. Soc., Soc. Pediat. Rsch., Wichita Pediat. Soc. (bd. dirs. 1988, pres. 1990-92), Lawson Wilkins Pediat. Endocrinology Soc., Midwest Soc. Pediat. Rsch., Internat. Soc. for Pediat. and Adolescent Diabetes (edn. com. 1995—), Am. Assn. Diabetes Educators (bd. dirs. 1994-97), Am. Assn. Clin. Endocrinology 1992—), Sigma Xi, Alpha Omega Alpha. Home: 14210 SW 60th St Andover KS 67002-8237 Office: Mid-Am Diabetes Assocs 200 S Hillside St Wichita KS 67211-2127 Office Phone: 316-687-3100. Personal E-mail: rag33@hotmail.com.

GUTHRIE, TARA SONALI, librarian, music educator, soprano; d. Phillip L. Lewis and Lavinia G. Guthrie. MusB in Edn., U. N.C., 1993; MLS, U. N.C., Greensboro, N.C., 1996. Music tchr. Carteret County Pub. Schs., Beaufort, NC, 1993—94; acquisitions libr. Carteret C.C., Morehead City, NC, 1996—. V.p. gen. staff team Carteret C.C., 1997—98. Author: numerous poems. Choir dir. LDS Ch., 1990—93, 1996—, counselor children's orgn., 1996—99, sec. relief soc. orgn., 1999—2000, family history cons., 2000—. Recipient Danforth award, East Carteret H.S., 1987; scholar, Nat. BETA Club, 1986—88, Beaufort (N.C.) Women's Club, 1988, Morehead City Noon Rotary Club, 1988, Parents for Advancement Gifted Edn., Beaufort, N.C., 1988. Mem.: NC CC Learning Resources Assn. Mem. Lds Ch. Avocations: singing, genealogy, cooking, computers. Office Phone: 252-222-6214. Business E-Mail: tsg@carteret.edu.

GUTHRIE, WALLACE NESSLER, JR., naval officer; b. N.Y.C., Feb. 22, 1939; s. Wallace Nessler and Rena Otis (Robertson) G.; m. Virginia Dale Sargeant, June 7, 1961; children: Wallace Edward, Gail Elizabeth, Virginia Lynn. BS, U.S. Naval Acad., Annapolis, Md., 1961; MS, Rollins Coll., 1972, EdS, 1981. Commd. ensign USN, 1961, advanced through ranks to rear adm., 1987; edn. specialist Naval Tng. Systems Ctr., Orlando, Fla., 1967-89; dep. dir. Naval Res., Washington, 1989-92; dir. tng., supt. schs. Am. Forces Info. Svc., 1993-97. Past head Naval Acad. Candidate Selection Com., 9th Congl. Dist., Fla. Sr. officer adv. panel Joint Mil. Intelligence Coll.; bd. dirs., trustee Navy Mut. Aid Assn. Mem. Naval Res. Assn. (life), Res. Officers Assn. (life), Surface Navy Assn. (life), Naval Submarine League. Republican. Avocations: camping, boating, fishing, hiking. E-mail: wallaceg5@aol.com, wgguthrie@tampabay.rr.com.

GUTHRIE, WILLIAM G., retired economics professor; b. Detroit, June 25, 1948; s. William G. and Kathryn (Snyder) Guthrie; m. Rose Bursey. AA in Liberal Arts, Oakland CC, Union Lake, Mich., 1972; BA in Econs., Western Mich. U., 1973, MA in Econs. & Stats., 1974; PhD in Econs., U. N.C., 1981; cert. in non-profit mgmt., Duke U. Traffic engr. Gen. Tel. Mich., Muskegon, 1974—75; prof. econs. Appalachian State U., Boone, NC, 1980—98, prof. emeritus, 2002—; asst. fin. mgr. Children's Coun., Watauga County, NC, 1999; prof. Lees-McRae Coll., Banner Elk, NC, 2000—04; ret., 2004. Contbr. articles to profl. jours. Advisor N.C. Gov.'s Hwy. Safety Coun., 2001—05; life mem. N.C. Zool. Assn., Asheboro, 1999—; vol. Daniel Boone Native Gardens, Boone, 1995—; mem. Sierra Club, 2004—; corp. treas. First Presbyn. Ch., Boone, 1994—95. With U.S. Army, 1967—71. Mem.: NRA, Phi Kappa Phi. Avocations: photography, target shooting, Celtic music.

GUTIERREZ, CARL T. C., former governor; b. Agana Heights, Guam, Oct. 15, 1941; s. Tomas Taitano Gutierrez and Rita Benavente Cruz; m. Geraldine Chance Torres, 1963; children: Carla Stahl, Tommy, Hannah. Mem. Senate Guam, beginning 1972, spkr., chmn. of ways and means com., chmn. HUD; vice chmn. rules com., tourism com., transp. com.; gov. Guam, Agana, 1994—2003. Democrat. Roman Catholic. Mailing: PO Box 404 Hagatna GU 96932-0404

GUTIERREZ, CARLOS M., secretary of commerce, former grocery manufacturing company executive; b. Havana, Cuba, Nov. 4, 1953; m. Edilia Gutierrez; 3 children. Student, Monterrey Inst. Tech., Queretaro, Mex. Sales rep., various sales and mktg. positions Kellogg de Mex., Mexico City, 1975-82, gen. mgr., 1984-89; pres., CEO, Kellogg Can., 1989-90; supr. L.Am. mktg. svcs. Kellogg Co., Battle Creek, Mich., 1982-83, mgr. internat. mktg. svcs., 1983-84, corp. v.p. product devel., 1990, v.p., 1990-93, exec. v.p., 1994-96, exec. v.p. bus. devel., 1996-98, COO, 1998-99, pres., 1998—2000, CEO, 1999—2004, chmn., 2000—04; sec. US Dept. Commerce, Washington, 2005—. Exec. v.p. sales and mktg. Kellogg USA, Battle Creek, 1990—93, exec. v.p., 1993—94, gen. mgr. cereal divsn., 1993—94; pres. Kellogg Asia-Pacific, 1994—96. Mem.: Grocery Mfrs. Am. (bd. dirs.). Office: US Dept Commerce 14th St & Constitution Ave NW Rm 5858 Washington DC 20230*

GUTIERREZ, CAROLYN ANN, librarian; b. Tahlequah, Okla., June 27, 1952; d. Fred Earl and Lanora Annabelle (Weaver) Coldwell; m. Santiago Samaniego, Jan. 16, 1981. BSBA, Northeastern State U., 1978; MLS, U. Okla., 1984. Med. libr. VA Med. Ctr., Oklahoma City, 1984—85, Muskogee, Okla., 1985—89; ref. libr. John Brown U., Siloam Springs, Ark., 1989—90; med. libr. Springdale Meml. Hosp., Ark., 1991—92, Jane Phillips Meml. Hosp., Bartlesville, Okla., 1993—99. Mem. ALA, Okla. Health Scis. Libr. Assn., Tulsa Area Libr. Coop., Med. Libr. Assn. Republican. Avocations: travel, reading, cats, birdwatching. Office: Jane Phillips Med Ctr 3500 E Frank Phillips Blvd Bartlesville OK 74006-2411

GUTIERREZ, EDITH G., freelance/self-employed music educator, composer, lyricist; b. Houston, Tex., Nov. 29, 1914; d. John Monroe Gribbin and Maria Paulina Viglini; m. Patricio Gutierrez, June 10, 1955 (dec.); m. John Bernardo Oliveros II (dec. Sept. 15, 1985); children: Pauline, John Bernardo. Cert. tchr. piano Am. Coll. of Musicians. Jobbing musician Houston Profl. Musicians Orgn., Houston, 1930—; pvt. piano instr. Houston, 1930—. Lyracist, composer of children's plays. Author (author-composer): (plays) Rumplestiltskin, 1991, Magic of the Woods, 1992, Pocahontas, 1993, Boogie Woogie Aesop, 1994. Mem.: Houston Music Tchrs. Assn. (bd. dir. 1950—, charter mem.). Avocations: hosting foreign students, pets. Home and Studio: 2202 Colquitt St Houston TX 77098 E-mail: egg@webtv.net.

GUTIERREZ, JAY MATTHEW, lawyer; b. June 10, 1951; BS, Georgetown U., 1973; JD, Rutgers U. Sch. Law, 1979. Bar: D.C. 1991. Hearing atty. Office Exec. Legal Dir- U.S. Nuc. Regulatory Commn., 1980—83; regional counsel U.S. Nuc. Regulatory Commn.-Region I, 1983—89; counsel Newman & Holtzinger (now Newman Bouknight & Edgar), 1989—94; ptnr., mem. energy practice group Morgan, Lewis & Bockius LLP, 1994—. Author: Fundamentals Nuc. Regulation U.S., 1995. Mem.: ABA. Office: Morgan Lewis & Bockius LLP 1111 Pennsylvania Ave NW Washington DC 20004 Office Phone: 202-739-5466. Office Fax: 202-739-3001. Business E-Mail: jgutierrez@morganlewis.com.

GUTIERREZ, JONI MARIE, landscape architect, political organization worker; BS in Horticulture, N.Mex. State U.; MLA in Landscape Arch., U. Ariz. Founder, prin. Gutierrez Borowski Assocs., Las Cruces, N.Mex.; vice chmn. Dem. Party, N.Mex., 2003, acting chmn., 2003. Office: Democratic Party Chmn 1301 San Pedro NE Albuquerque NM 87110

GUTIERREZ, LUIS V., congressman, elementary education educator; b. Chgo., Dec. 10, 1953; m. Soraida Aracho; children: Omaira, Jessica. BA magna cum laude in English, Northeastern Ill. U., 1975. Social worker Ill. Dept. Children and Family Svcs.; adminstrv. asst. Mayor's Subcom. on Infrastructure, 1984-85; alderman for 26th ward Chgo. City Coun., 1986-93, pres. pro tempore, 1992; mem. U.S. Congress from 4th Ill. Dist., 1993—; mem. banking and fin. svcs. com., vet. affair com. Chmn. Housing, Land Acquisition and Disposition com., 1989—93. Democrat. Office: US Ho of Reps 2367 Rayburn House Off Bldg Washington DC 20515-1304*

GUTKNECHT, GILBERT WILLIAM, JR., congressman, former state legislator; b. Cedar Falls, Iowa, Mar. 20, 1951; s. Gilbert William Sr. and Joan (Kerns) G.; m. Mary Catherine Keefe, June 3, 1972; children: Margaret, Paul, Emily. BA, U. No. Iowa, 1973. Sales rep. J. S. Latta, Cedar Falls, 1973-78, Valley Sch. Supplies, Appleton, Wis., 1978-81; auctioneer Rochester, Minn., 1978-95; state legis. State of Minn., Rochester, 1982-95; mem. U.S. Congress from 1st Minn. dist., 1995—, mem. sci. com., budget com., agriculture com., 1997—. Republican. Avocations: fishing, boating, baseball. Office: US House Reps 425 Cannon House Office Bldg Washington DC 20515-2301 also: Midway Office Plaza 1530 Greenview Dr SW Ste 108 Rochester MN 55902-1080*

GUTMAN, LUCY TONI, social worker, educator; b. Phila., July 13, 1936; d. Milton R. and Clarissa (Silverman) G.; divorced; children: James, Laurie. BA, Wellesley Coll., 1958; MSW, Bryn Mawr Coll., 1963; MA in History, U. Ariz., 1978; MEd, Northwestern State U., 1991, MA in English, 1992; postgrad., U. So. Miss., 1992—. Cert. sch. social work specialist, Nat. Bd. Cert. Counselor; diplomate in clin. social work; cert. secondary tchr., La.; cert. counselor, La.; cert. Acad. Cert. Social Workers, La. Bd. Cert. Social Workers. Social worker Phila. Gen. Hosp., 1963-65; sr. social worker Irving Schwartz Inst. Children and Youth, 1965-66; sr. psychiat. social worker Child Study Ctr. Phila., 1966-68; chief social worker Framingham (Mass.) Ct. Clinic Juvenile Offenders, 1968-72; dir. clinic, supr. social work Tucson East Cmty. Mental Health Ctr., 1972-74; coord. spl. adoptions program Cath. Social Svcs. So. Ariz., Tucson, 1974-75; social worker Met. Ministry, 1983; supr. social work Leesville (La.) Mental Health Clinic, 1984; sch. social worker Vernon Parish Sch. Bd., Leesville, 1984—. Cons. Nashua (NH) Cmty. Coun., 1969-72; adj. instr. English, sociology, Am. and European history Northwestern State U., Ft. Polk, La., 1984-1994; part time counselor River North Psychol. Svcs., Leesville, 1989-92; presenter in field. Contbr. articles to profl. jours. Nat. Soc. Colonial Dames scholar, 1978-79; fellow Pa. State, 1961-62, NIMH, 1962-63. Mem. NASW (diplomate), La. Hist. Assn., So. Hist. Assn., So. Assn. Women Historians, Gamma Beta Phi, Phi Alpha Theta, Phi Kappa Phi. Home: 2004 Allison St Leesville LA 71446-5104 Office: Spl Edn Svcs Vernon Parish Sch Bd 201 Belview Rd Leesville LA 71446 Office Phone: 337-239-1689.

GUTMAN, RICHARD EDWARD, lawyer; b. New Haven, Apr. 9, 1944; s. Samuel and Marjorie (Leo) G.; m. Jill Leslie Senft, June 8, 1969 (dec.); 1 child, Paul Senft; m. Rosann Seasonwein, Dec. 10, 1987. AB, Harvard U., 1965; JD, Columbia U., 1968. Bar: N.Y. 1969, U.S. Ct. Appeals (2d cir.) 1969, U.S. Dist. Ct. (so. and ea. dists.) N.Y. 1975, U.S. Supreme Ct. 1982, Tex. 1991. Counsel Exxon Corp., N.Y.C., 1978-90, Dallas, 1990-91, asst. gen. counsel, 1992-99, Exxon Mobil Corp., Dallas, 1999—. Pres. 570 Park Ave Apts., Inc., NYC, 1984—89, past bd. dirs. Fellow Am. Bar Found. (life); mem. ABA (fed. regulation securities com., vice-chmn. 1995-98), Am. Law Inst., N.Y. State Bar Assn. (exec. com. 1983-86, 1993-2005, securities regulation com. 1980—, chmn. 1993-97, chmn. bus. law sect. 2001-02), Assn. of Bar of City of N.Y. (securities regulation com. 1980-81, 83-86), Dallas Bar Assn., Coll. of the State Bar of Tex., N.A.M. (corp. fin. and mgmt. com.), Harvard Club (N.Y.C., admissions com. 1983-86, chmn. 1985-86, nominating com. 1986-87, bd. dirs. 1988-91, v.p. 1990-91), Harvard Club (Dallas bd. dirs. 1998-2001)

GUTMAN, ROBERT WILLIAM, retired art educator; b. N.Y.C., Sept. 11, 1925; s. Theodore and Elsie G. BA, NYU, 1945, MA, 1948. Instr. New Sch. for Social Research, 1955-57; founder, lectr. Bayreuth Festival Master Classes, 1959-61; lectr. design history art and design div. Fashion Inst. Tech., SUNY, N.Y.C., 1957-66, asst. prof., 1966-71, assoc. prof., 1971-76, prof., 1971-88, dean div. art and design, 1974-79, dean grad. studies, 1979-88, ret., 1988. Vis. prof. Bard Coll., 1991; lectr. PBS Telecast of Bayreuth Festival, 1983, U Melbourne, 2004. Author: Richard Wagner, The Man, His Mind, and His Music, 1968, German transl., 1970, Italian transl., 1983, Mozart, A Cultural Biograpghy, 1999; editor: Volsunga Saga (transl. by William Morris), 1961. Bd. dirs. Am. Friends of Internat. Found. Mozarteum, 1991—, The Collegiate Chorale, 1990—. Biography juror Nat. Book Awards, 1973; Guggenheim fellow, 1979 Mem.: Nat. Arts (N.Y.C.), Princeton (N.Y.C.), Lotos (N.Y.C.). Home: 37 W 12th St New York NY 10011-8559

GUTMAN, ROY WILLIAM, reporter; b. N.Y.C., Mar. 5, 1944; s. Ira H. and Linda (Snyder) Gutman; m. Elizabeth Jane Dribben, May 17, 1979; 1 child, Caroline. BA, Haverford Coll., 1966; MS, London Sch. Econs., 1968; DLitt (hon.), Haverford Coll., 1995. Reporter UPI, Frankfurt, Germany, 1968—70; corr. Reuters News Agy., Bonn, Germany, 1971—72, bur. chief Belgrade, Yugoslavia, 1973—75, Dept. State corr. Washington, 1976—80, Capitol Hill bur. chief, 1981; nat. security reporter Newsday, Washington, 1982—89, European bur. chief Bonn, 1990—94, fgn. affairs reporter Washington, 1994—2000; corr. Newsweek, Washington, 2001—. Jennings Randolph sr. fellow U.S. Inst. Peace, 2002—03; adj. prof. Medill Sch. Journalism, 2003. Author: (book) Banana Diplomacy, 1988 (named one of best 200 books of 1988, N.Y. Times, Best Am. Book of the Yr., Times Lit. Supplement, London, 1988), A Witness to Genocide, 1993; co-editor: Crimes of War, 1999; contbr. articles to profl. jours. Named one of best fgn. affairs reporters in Washington, The Washingtonian, 1989; recipient Human Rights in Media award, Internat. League for Human Rights, 1992, Pulitzer Prize for internat. reporting, 1993, George Polk Fgn. Reporting award, 1993, Selden Ring Investigative Reporting award, U. So. Calif., 1993, Nat. Headliner Outstanding News Reporting award, 1993, Heywood Brown award, Newspaper Guild, 1993, Excellence in Series/Investigation award, Deadline Club, 1993, Hal Boyle award, Overseas Press Club, 1993, Exemplary Cmty. Svc. Alumni award, Haverford Coll., 1994. Mem.: Inst. Current World Affairs. Jewish. Avocations: gardening, photography. Home: 13132 Curved Iron Rd Herndon VA 20171-2930 Office: Newsweek 1750 Pennsylvania Ave NW Washington DC 20006 E-mail: RoyGut@Newsweek.com. *Facts matter. And collecting them requires a readiness to get your fingernails dirty.**

GUTMANN, AMY, academic administrator, political science and philosophy educator; b. Bklyn., Nov. 19, 1949; m. Michael Doyle, 1976; 1 child: Abigail. BA magna cum laude, Harvard-Radcliffe Coll., 1971; MSc in polit. sci., London Sch. Economics, 1972; PhD in polit. sci., Harvard U., 1976. Asst. prof. politics Princeton U., NJ, 1976—81, assoc. prof. politics, 1981—86, prof. politics, 1987—2004, Andrew W. Mellon Professor, 1987—90, dir. grad. studies dept. politics, 1986-88, dir. polit. philosophy program, 1987-89, dir. ethics and pub. affairs program, 1990-95, 1997—2000, founding dir. U. Ctr. for Human Values, 1990—95, 1998—2001, dean faculty, 1995-97, academic advisor to pres., 1997—98, Laurance S. Rockefeller U. Prof. of Politics and the U. Ctr. for Human Values, 1990—2004, provost, 2001—04; pres. U. Pa., Phila., 2004—. Visitor Inst. for Advanced Study, Princeton U., 1981-82; vis. Rockefeller Faculty Fellow, Ctr. for Philosophy and Pub. Policy, U. Md., 1984-85; vis. prof., Kennedy Sch. Govt., Harvard U., 1988-89, adv. coun., 1996-2001; Tanner lectr., Stanford U., 1994-95; academic adv. bd. Inst. Human Sciences, Vienna, 2001-; mem. bd. dirs., exec. com., Centers for Advanced Study in Behavioral Sciences, Stanford U., 1998-, Princeton U. Press, 1996-; secondary faculty appointment Annenberg Sch. for Comm., 2004—. Author: Liberal Equality, 1980, Democratic Education, 1987, 2nd edit., 1999; co-author: (with Dennis Thompson) Democracy & Disagreement, 1996, (with Anthony Appiah) Color Conscious, 1996 (award N.Am. Soc. Social Philosophy), Identity in Democracy, 2003, (with Dennis Thompson) Why Deliberative Democracy? 2004; editor: Democracy and the Welfare State, 1988, Multiculturalism, 1992, Freedom of Association, 1998, U. Ctr. for Human Values Series, Princeton U. Press, 1992-; co-editor: (with Dennis Thompson) Ethics and Politics, 3d edit., 1997; mem. editl bd. Teachers' Coll. Record, 1990-95, Cambridge Studies in Philosophy and Pub. Policy, 1991-, Raritan, 1995-, Jour. Polit. Philosophy, 1995-, Handbook of Polit. Theory, 1999-, Annual Reviews, 2001-05; internat. adv. bd. Ethnicities, 2000-. Fellowship, NEH, 1977, Am. Coun. Learned Societies, 1978-79, U. Hong Kong, 1998-99; Grant, Spencer Found., 1995-98, Sr. Scholar Award, 1999-2003; recipient Gustavus Myers Ctr. for Study of Human Rights in N.Am. Award, 1997, N.Am. Soc. for Social Philosophy Book Award, 1996-97, Ralph J. Bunche Award, Am. Polit. Sci. Assn., 1997, Bertram Mott Award, Am. Assn. Univ. Profs., Rider Coll., 1998, President's Disting. Tchg. Award, 2000, Centennial Medal, Harvard U., 2003, others. Mem. Assn. Practical and Profl. Ethics (exec. com., 1990-), Am. Soc. Political and Legal Philosophy (pres. 2001-04); fellow Am. Academy of Arts and Sciences, Nat. Academy of Edn., Am. Academy Polit. and Social Sci. Office: Univ Pa 100 College Hall Philadelphia PA 19104-6380*

GUTMANN, DAVID LEO, psychology professor; b. N.Y.C., Sept. 17, 1925; s. Isaac and Masha (Agronsky) G.; m. Joanna Redfield, Aug. 18, 1951; children: Stephanie, Ethan. MA, U. Chgo., 1956, PhD, 1958. Lectr. psychology Harvard U., Cambridge, Mass., 1960-62; prof. U. Mich., Ann Arbor, 1962-76, Northwestern U., Chgo., 1976-97, prof. emeritus, 1998—, chief of psychology, 1976-81, dir. older adult program, 1978-95. Vis. emeritus prof. Hebrew U., Jerusalem, 1997. Author: Reclaimed Powers: Toward a New Psychology of Men and Women in Later Life, 1987, Reclaimed Powers: Men and Women in Later Life, 1994, The Human Elder in Nature, Culture, and Society, 1997; co-author: (with Bardwick, Douvan and Horner) Feminine

Personality and Conflict, 1979. With U.S. Mcht. Marine, 1943-46. Recipient Career Devel. award, NIMH, 1964—74. Fellow Gerontol. Soc. Am.; mem. Am. Vets. of Israel, Nat. Assn. Scholars. Jewish. Home: 277 W Hill Rd Wallingford VT 05773-9479 Office Phone: 312-908-8852. Personal E-mail: dgutmann2004@yahoo.com.

GUTMANN, REINHART BRUNO, priest, social worker; b. Munich, May 1, 1916; came to U.S., 1942, naturalized, 1946; s. Franz and Berta G.; m. Vivian Carol Brunke, Oct. 7, 1944 (dec. Jan. 2003); children: Robin Peter Edward, Martin Francis. Student, History Honours Sch., Manchester U., Eng., 1936-38; MA in Social Scis, St. Andrews U., Scotland, 1939; postgrad., Coll. of Resurrection, Eng., 1939-41, Coll. Preachers, Washington, 1948, 52, U. Wis., summer, 1951, St. Augustine's Coll., Eng., 1964. Ordained deacon Ch. of Eng., 1941, ordained priest, 1942; curate St. Michael's Parish, Golders Green, London, 1941-42; rector St. Mark's Parish, Green Island, N.Y., 1944-45, St. Andrew's Parish, Milw., 1952-54; chaplain and mem. faculty Hoosac (N.Y.) Sch., 1943-45; founder, exec. dir. Neighborhood House and Episcopal City Mission, Milw., 1945-60; exec. dir. Friendship House, Washington, 1960-62; cons. Indian Social welfare Exec. Council of Episcopal Ch., N.Y.C., 1962-64; exec. sec. div. community services Exec. Council of Episcopal Ch., 1964-68, exec. for social welfare and field services, 1968-71; part-time priest-in-charge St. Thomas of Alexandria, Pittstown, N.J., 1968-75; hon. asst. priest St. Martin's Ch., Pawtucket, R.I., 1980; pres. Cedar Brook Cons., Inc., 1982—86; ret., 1987. Priest-in-charge St. Peter's Mission, North Lake, Wis., 1958-60, hon. asst. priest St. Ambrose Parish, Fort Lauderdale, Fla., 1984-98, asst. priest emeritis, 1996, hon. asst. priest emeritus, 1998—; mgr. spl. projects Human Resources Adminstrn., NYC, 1971-72, spl. asst. to asst. adminstr., 1972-73, dir. mgmt. office cmty. svcs., 1973, spl. asst. to dep. adminstr. social svcs., 1973-75; nat. exec. dir. Foster Parents Plan, Inc., Warwick, R.I., 1975-82. Organizer Gordonstoun Am. Found., 1983, exec. sec., 1983-87; chmn. dept. Christian social relations Province of Midwest, Episcopal Ch., 1954-60; chmn. social edn. and action Nat. Fedn. Settlements, 1960-62; hon. canon All Saints Cathedral, Milw., 1971; founder Silver Spring Neighborhood Ctr., Milw., 1958; founder Northcott Neighborhood House, Milw., 1959. Mem. Acad. Cert. Social Workers, Nat. Assn. Social Workers. Democrat. E-mail: parsongutmann@aol.com. *Personal success is not measured by wealth or public recognition. It is the knowledge that one has done everything possible to help people achieve dignity, security, and fulfillment; and in so doing has transmitted a sense of personal caring for the needs of others.*

GUTNIK, ZHANNA, gastroenterologist, consultant; b. Novomoskovsk, Ukraine, Apr. 30, 1966; came to U.S., 1991; d. Valerey and Yelizaveta Keybol; m. Igor Gutnik, Apr. 20, 1986; children: Liliya, Annette. MD, Ivano-Frankovsk Med. Inst., Ukraine, 1989. Diplomate Am. Bd. Internal Medicine, Am. Bd. Gastroenterology. Resident in internal medicine Brooklyn Hosp. Ctr., N.Y.C., 1994-97, fellow in gastroenterology, 1997-2000. Mem. Am. Gastroenterol. Assn., Am. Soc. for Gastrointestinal Endoscopy. Home: 2873 Valerie Ct Merrick NY 11566

GUTOW, BERNARD SIDNEY, packaging manufacturing company executive; b. Chgo., Nov. 11, 1939; s. Max and Betty (Warshawsky) G.; m. Carol Lerch, June 5, 1960; children: Jeffrey, Bryon. BS in Engring., U. Ill., 1961, MS in Engring., 1962; MBA, U. Santa Clara, 1965; JD, Golden Gate U., 1997, LLM, 1998. Registered profl. engr., Ill. Sr. engr. Lockheed Missiles, Sunnyvale, Calif., 1962-65; project engr. U.S. Steel Co., Chgo., 1965-67; engr., prin. A.T. Kearney Co., Chgo., 1967-78; dir. Shaklee, San Francisco, 1978-79; v.p. H.S. Crocker, San Bruno, Calif., 1979-85; v.p., gen. mgr. First Data Resources subs. Am. Express Corp., Tustin, Calif., 1985-88; gen. ptnr. Mgmt. Resource Ptnrs., Redwood Shores, Calif., 1988-96; pres., CEO Bayline Ptnrs./Bayline Paper Supply, Union City, Calif., 1991—. Pres. CEO Bayline Ptnrs., Bayline Paper Supply, Union City, Calif., 1991—. Editor: Plant Engineering Management, 1974; contbr. articles to profl. jours. Pres. Morton Grove Park Dist., Ill. 1973-78; mem. Morton Grove Youth Commn., 1973-78. Recipient Plaque, Morton Grove Park Dist., 1978, cert. Soc. Mfg. Engrs., Chgo., 1975, Bronze award Internat. Film and TV Festival N.Y., N.Y.C., 1984, 1st place internat. law writing competition award N.Y. State Bar Assn., 1998. Mem. ASME (chpt. chmn. 1972-73). Home: 3263 La Mesa Dr San Carlos CA 94070-4244 E-mail: bgutow@gguol.ggu.edu.

GUTOWICZ, MATTHEW FRANCIS, JR., radiologist; b. Camden, N.J., Feb. 23, 1945; s. Matthew F. and A. Patricia (Walczak) G.; m. Alice Mary Bell, June 27, 1977; 1 child, Melissa. BA, Temple U., 1968; DO, Phila. Coll. Osteo. Medicine, 1972. Diplomate Am. Bd. Radiology, Am. Bd. Nuclear Medicine. Intern Mercy Hosp., Denver, 1972-73; resident in diagnostic radiology Hosp. of U. Pa., Phila., 1973-76, fellow in nuclear medicine, 1976-77; chief dept. radiology and nuclear medicine Fisher Titus Med. Ctr., Norwalk, Ohio, 1977—; pres. Firelands Radiology, Inc., Norwalk, 1977—. Ptnr. Pacifica in the Desert Restaurant, Palm Desert, Calif. Republican. Roman Catholic. Avocations: photography, tennis, scuba diving. Home: 23 Patrician Dr Norwalk OH 44857-2463 Office Phone: 419-668-8101 x 6205. Personal E-mail: matthewg@neo.rr.com.

GUTSCH, WILLIAM ANTHONY, JR., astronomer; b. Newark, Jan. 14, 1946; s. William Anthony and Mary (Ellenback) G. BS, St. Peter's Coll., 1967; MS, U. Va., 1973, PhD, 1978; LHD, St. Peter's Coll., 1995. Staff astronomer Rochester Museum and Sci. Ctr., N.Y., 1973-82; chmn. Am. Mus.-Hayden Planetarium, N.Y.C., 1982-95; ind. cons., writer, prodr. for sci. ctrs., pubs., and TV, computer & multi-media, 1995—; pres., CEO Challenger Ctr. for Space Sci. Edn., Alexandria, Va., 2004—. Cons., lectr. in field; news columnist Rochester Times-Union, 1980-82; sci. reporter Sta.-WOKR-TV, Rochester, N.Y., 1976-82; sci. corr. Sta.-WABC-TV, N.Y.C., 1982-84, sci. editor., 1984-88; on-air meteorologist, spl. sci. corr. ABC Network, 1986-93; sci. columnist Gannett, 1980-90; cons. U. Santiago, Chile, 1982, NASA 2003-; sci. corr. USA Network, 1993—; pres. Great Ideas, 1995-. Author: The Search for Extraterrestrial Life, 1991, 1001 Things Everyone Should Know About the Universe, 1998, (with Isaac Asimov) The Exploding Suns, 1996; author other books, also newspaper articles, TV news and planetarium scripts; writer, contbg. editor New Book of Knowledge, 1992—; writer Discovery Channel, 1994-95. Recipient award of svc. U. Santiago, 1982, City of Buenos Aires, 1983, City of San Juan, 1991, City of Jaharta, Indonesia, 1991; Emmy nominee, 1987. Mem. Am. Astron. Soc., Am. Meteorol. Soc., Am. Assn. Physics Tchrs., Internat. Planetarium Soc. (pres. 1992-94, past pres. 1994-96). Office: Challenger Ctr for Space Sci Edn 1250 N Pitt St Alexandria VA 22314 E-mail: BillGutsch@cs.com.

GUTSCHE, CARL DAVID, chemistry professor; b. LaGrange, Ill., Mar. 21, 1921; s. Frank Carl and Vera (Mutchler) G.; m. Alice Eugenia Carr, June 4, 1944; children: Clara Jean, Betha Lynn, Christopher Glenn. BA, Oberlin Coll., 1943. With Office Sci. Devel., USDA, 1943-44; instr. chemistry Washington U., St. Louis, 1947-48, asst. prof., 1948-51, assoc. prof., 1951-59, prof., 1959-89, prof. emeritus, 1989—, chmn. dept., 1970-76; Robert A. Welch prof. chemistry Tex. Christian U., Ft. Worth, 1989—2002; vis. scholar U. Ariz., Tucson, 2002—. Cons. in field; mem. adv. bd. Petroleum Rsch. Fund., 1971—74; chmn. medicinal chemistry study sect. NIH, 1978—81. Author: The Chemistry of Carbonyl Compounds, 1967, Carbocyclic Ring Expansion Reactions, 1968, Fundamentals of Organic Chemistry, 1975, Calixarenes, 1989, Calixarenes Revisiited, 1998; mem. adv. bd.: Jour. Organic Chemistry, 1979-83; mem. editorial bd.: Organic Preparations and Procedures Internat., 1968—, Jour. Inclusion Phenomena, 1993-2000; contbr. articles to profl. jours. Bd. dirs. St. Louis Conservatory and Schs. for Arts, 1978—82, Ft. Worth Chamber Music Soc., 1999—2002. Recipient Alumni award Washington U., 1977; Guggenheim fellow, 1981. Fellow AAAS; mem. Am. Chem. Soc. (chmn. St. Louis sect. 1959, mem. pub. com. 1974-77, com. on coms. 1977-80, com. on profl. tng. 1980-89, cons. to com. 1990-98, councilor and dir., St. Louis sect. award 1971, Midwest award 1988, Doherty award 1998, Izatt-Christensen award 2002), Chem. Soc. (London), AAUP, Phi Beta Kappa (mem. qualifications com. 1992—2003), Sigma Xi. Home: 7607 S Galileo Ln Tucson AZ 85747 Business E-Mail: d.gutsche@tcu.edu.

GUTTAU, MICHAEL K., state agency administrator, banker; b. Council Bluffs, Iowa, Nov. 8, 1946; s. Detlef Hugo and Ethel Evelyn (Schmidt) G.; m. Judith Ann Frazier, June 28, 1968; children: Heidi Ann, Joshua Michael. BS in Farm Operation, Iowa State U., 1969; postgrad., U. Nebr., Omaha, 1975. Administrv. asst. to dean students, asst. instr. sociology Iowa State U., Ames, 1969; trainee, asst. cashier, cashier Treynor (Iowa) State Bank, 1972-78, pres., chmn., CEO, 1978—. Appt. Iowa Supt. Banking, 1995; bd. dirs. Mercy Midlands Corp., Omaha; advisor N.Y. Fed. Res. Bank, Russian Am. Bankers Forum Acad. for Advanced Studies in Banking and Fin.; presenter Internat. Russian Banking Conf. 1992-93, mem. steering com., 1992-93; mem. U.S. Dept. State-U.S./Slovakian Counterpart Team Agr. Fin. and Credit. Chmn. steering com. Pottawattamie County Riverbend Indsl. Site, Western Iowa Devel. Assn., Mercy Hosp., Council Bluffs, Treynor Cmty. Devel. Com.; bd. dirs. Deaf Missions Worldwide Christian Ministry for Deaf; mem. youth com. Pottawattamie County 4-H; founder, pres., bd. dirs. Treynor Devel. Found. Corp.; deacon, moderator, adult and H.S. Sunday sch. tchr. Zion Congl. Ch., Treynor. With U.S. Army, 1969-72, Vietnam; with Nebr. Army NG, 1972-80. Decorated DFC with oak leaf cluster, Bronze Star, Air medal with V device, 28 Air medals; Recipient Outstanding Citizen award Treynor Town and Country Club, Swords to Plowshares award Bus.-Banks Exch. Newspaper, Moscow, 1992. Mem. Am. Bankers Assn. (chmn. future of cmty. banking study, cmty. bankers adv. bd. and coun., dir. edn. coun., mem. adminstrv. com. govt. rels. com.), Iowa Bankers Assn. (pres.-elect 1994-95, chmn. legis. com., bd. dirs.), S.W. Iowa Bank Adminstrn. Inst. (pres.), Treynor Bus. Assn. (founder, past pres., bd. dirs.), Scabbard and Blade, Gamma Gamma, Theta Delta Chi. Republican. Avocation: aviation. Home: RR 2 Box 82B Council Bluffs IA 51503-9802 Office: Treynor State Bank 15 E Main St Treynor IA 51575

GUTTENBERG, ALBERT ZISKIND, planning educator; b. Chelsea, Mass., Nov. 6, 1921; s. Harry and Edith (Bernstein) G.; m. Mariella Mascardi, June 29, 1964. AB in Social Rels., Harvard U., 1948; postgrad. in sociology, U. Chgo., 1949-51; postgrad. in city planning, U. Pa., 1958-59. Planning asst. Planning Bd., City of Portland, Maine, 1954-56; planning analyst Planning Commn., City of Phila., 1956-60; chief gen. plans and programming sect. Comprehensive Planning div., 1960-61; sr. planner Nat. Capital Downtown Com., Washington, 1962-63; assoc. prof. urban planning U. Ill., 1964-69, prof. urban and regional planning, 1969-89; chair in urban and regional renewal Dept. Geodesy, Delft U. Tech., The Netherlands, 1977-78. Cons. in field. Author: (with others) Explorations Into Urban Structure, 1964, New Directions in Land use Classification, 1965, (with others) Human Ecology, 1975, The Language of Planning, 1993; editor Planning and Public Policy, 1974-89; contbr. articles on land use planning to profl. pubs. Served with U.S. Army, 1942-46. Guggenheim fellow, 1970-71; Brookings Inst. guest scholar, 1970-71; Gelderman Fund grantee Delft U. Tech., 1977; German Marshall Fund Travel grantee, Holland, 1979; recipient Fulbright Travel award Italy, 1986. Mem. Am. Planning Assn., Am. Inst. Cert. Planners (coll. fellows), Soc. Am. City and Regional Planning History, Fulbright Alumni Assn. Home: 711 Hamilton Dr Champaign IL 61820-6811 Office: 111 Temple Hoyne Buell Hall 611 E Lorado Taft Dr Champaign IL 61820-6921

GUTTENPLAN, HAROLD ESAU, retired food company executive; b. Flushing, N.Y., Oct. 12, 1924; s. Adolph and Millie (Penner) G.; m. Jeanette Harris, Apr. 17, 1948 (dec. Nov. 28, 2004); children: Bruce David, Mark Stuart. BA, Queens Coll., 1948; MBA, NYU, 1951. Statistician printing ink div. Sun Chem. Corp., 1948-49; cost accountant, chief accountant, asst. treas. DCA Food Industries, Inc., N.Y.C., 1949-66, treas., 1966-96, asst. sec., 1972-73, sec., dir., 1973-96; ret., 1996. Bd. dirs. Nisshin-DCA. Co-chmn. Queens Coll. 50th Alumni Day Reception, 1998; cub Scout leader Nassau County Thunderbird coun. Boy Scouts Am., 1955-63. With USAAF, 1943-45, PTO. Recipient Anti-Defamation League citation award, 1968. Mem. Daus. of Jacob Relatives Assn. (pres. 1976-77), Alpha Phi Omega (pres. 1947-48), B'nai B'rith (pres. Sagamore lodge 1963-64), Am. Assn. Ret. Persons (asst. state coord. Driver Safety Program 1998). Home: 69 Joyce Ln Woodbury NY 11797-2124

GUTTENTAG, LUCAS, advocate, lawyer; b. San Francisco, Mar. 12, 1951; s. Otto Ernst and Erika Guttentag. AB, U. Calif., Berkeley, 1973; JD, Harvard U., 1978. Bar: Calif. 1979, N.Y. 1988, U.S. Supreme Ct. 1982, U.S. Ct. Appeals (2d, 5th, D.C. cirs.) 1989, (9th cirs.) 1980, (6th cirs.) 1988, (4th cirs.) 1990, U.S. Dist. Ct. Calif. (ctrl. dist.) 1979, (no. dist.) 1990, (ea. dist.) 1992, N.Y. (so. dist., ea. dist., we. dist.) 1988. Law clk. to judge William Wayne Justice U.S. Dist. Ct. (ea. dist.) Tex., Tyler, 1978-79; staff atty. Ctr. for Law in the Pub. Interest, L.A., 1979-83; clin. prof. Columbia U. Sch. Law, N.Y.C., 1983-88; dir. immigrants rights project ACLU Nat. Hqrs., N.Y.C. and San Francisco, 1987—. Adj. prof. Columbia U. Law Sch., 1989-98, U. Calif. at Berkeley Law Sch., 1997—. Co-author: Rights of Aliens and Refugees, 1990; contbr. books and TV shows, profl. law jours. Recipient Wasserman Excellence in Litigation award Am. Immigration Lawyers Assn., 1990, 91, 97, King Contbn. to Immigration Law award Nat. Immigration Project of NLG, 1991. Mem. ABA (co-chair labor law sect., immigration law com. 1991-94, coordinating com. immigration law 1995-98. Office: ACLU Ste 300 405 14th St Oakland CA 94612

GUTTERIDGE, THOMAS G., academic administrator, consultant, arbitrator; b. Flint, Mich., Oct. 31, 1942; s. George Ernest and Mary Ruth (Stewart) G.; m. Judith Kay Grubbs Gutteridge, Aug. 28, 1965; children: Theresa, Debbie, Cindy. BS in Industrial Engring., Gen. Motors Inst., 1965; MS in Ind. Admin., Purdue U., 1966, PhD, 1971. Teaching asst. Purdue U., Lafayette, Ind., 1967-70; asst., assoc. prof. SUNY, Buffalo, 1970—83; dean, full prof. So. Ill. U., Carbondale, 1983—92; dean, disting. prof. U. Conn., Storrs, 1992—2002, emeritus dean, disting. prof., 2002—03; dean, prof. mgmt. Coll. Bus. Adminstrn. U. Toledo, 2003—. Safety engr. Buick Motors, Flint, Mich., 1964-65; corp. recruiter Industrial Nucleonics, Columbus, Ohio, 1966-67; labor arbitrator Am. Arbitration Assn., Fed. Mediation and Conciliation Svc., 1972—; mem. Conn. State Bd. Labor Rels., 1995-98. Co-author: Organizational Career Development: Benchmarks for Building a World-Class Workforce, Organizational Career Development: State of the Practice; contbr. numerous articles to profl. jours. Recipient Career Devel. awards Am. Soc. for Tng. and Devel., 1983. Mem. Acad. of Mgmt. Human Resource Planning Soc., Golden Key Honor Soc., Beta Gamma Sigma. Democrat. Avocation: sports. Home: 523 Forest Lake Holland OH 43528 Office: U Toledo Coll Bus Adminstrn Mail Stop # 103 2801 W Bancroft St Toledo OH 43606 Office Phone: 419-530-4612. E-mail: thomas.gutteridge@utoledo.edu.

GUTTERSEN, MICHAEL, rancher, investor; b. San Francisco, Mar. 26, 1939; s. William L. and Grace Tooee (Smith) Vogler; m. Penny Leonora Quinn, Aug. 29, 1959; children: Michael William, Arthur Roy, Shawn Patrick. Student, U. Col., 1957-58. Foreman Crow Creek Ranch, Ault, Colo., 1960-61; owner/mgr. Flying G Ranch, Briggsdale, Colo., 1961-86; pres. Two E Ranches Inc., Greeley, Colo., 1969-86, PX Ranch, Elko, Nev., 1969-71, Indian Creek Ranch, Encampment, Wyo., 1970-83, Lake Farms Co., Eaton, Colo., 1969-86; gen. ptnr. Guttersen & Co./Guttersen Ranch, Kersey, Colo., 1986—. Mgr. Am. Nat. Ins. Co., Greeley, 1962—70; owner FGF Ins. Brokers, Inc., Greeley, 1962—70. Bd. dirs. United Way, Weld County, Colo., 1979—81, Greeley Philharm. Orch., 1991—94, Nat. Cowboy Hall of Fame, Oklahoma City, 1994—. With U.S. Army, 1958—60. Mem.: Weld County Livestock Assn., Tex. and S.W. Cattle Raisers Assn., Colo. Cattle Feeders Assn., Colo. Cattlemens Assn., Nat. Cattlemens Assn., Galveston Country Club, Galveston Arty. Club, Greeley Country Club. Republican. Roman Catholic. Avocations: fishing, hunting in Africa. Home: Woods Lake Farm 13696 RD 74 Eaton CO 80615 Office: Guttersen and Co PO Box 528 Kersey CO 80644-0528 Office Phone: 970-590-5505.

GUTTI, JOGESH BABU, statistician, educator; b. Uppada, Andhra Pradesh, India, Aug. 14, 1947; arrived in U.S., 1974; s. Mallayya and Nagaratnam Gutti; m. Sudha Babu Gutti, May 5, 1974; children: Vinay Babu, Vijay Babu. BSc, Andhra U., 1968; M in Stats., Indian Statis. Inst., 1970, PhD, 1974. Vis. lectr. U. Ill., Urbana, 1974—75; vis. asst. prof. U. Oreg., Eugene, 1975—76; assoc. prof. Indian Statis. Inst., Calcutta, 1976—82, prof., 1982—85, Pa. State U., University Park, 1985—, dir. Ctr. Astrostatistics. Editor in chief: Statis. Methodology, 2004—. Fellow, Inst. Math. Stats., 1987, Am. Statis. Assn., 1997, AAAS, 1997. Mem.: Internat. Statis. Inst. Office: Pa State Univ Dept Stats 319 Thomas Bldg University Park PA 16802-2111

GUTTMAN, EGON, law educator; b. Niewruppin, Netherlands, Jan. 27, 1927; came to U.S., 1958, naturalized, 1968; s. Isaac and Blima (Liss) G.; m. Inge Weinberg, June 12, 1966; children: Geoffrey David, Leonard Jay. Student, U. Cambridge, 1945-48; LLB, U. London, London, England, 1950, LLM, 1952; post grad., Northwestern U. Sch. Law, 1958-59. Barrister: Eng. 1952. Sole practice, England, 1952-53; faculty Univ. Coll. and U. Khartoum, 1953-58; legal advisor to chief justice, 1953-58; founder, editor Sudan Law Jour. & Reports, Sudan, 1956-57; researcher, lectr. Rutgers U. Sch. Law, Newark, 1959-60; asst. prof. U. Alta., Edmonton, Canada, 1960-62; prof. Howard U. Law Sch., Washington, 1962-68, vis. adj. prof., 1968-96; adj. prof. law Washington Coll. Law, Am. U., Wash., 1964-68, Levitt Meml. Trust scholar-prof., 1968—, dir. JD-MBA joint degree program, 1990-2000; lectr. Practicing Law Inst., 1964—. Adj. prof. law Georgetown U. Law Ctr., 1972-74, Johns Hopkins U., Balt., 1973-81; vis. prof. Faculty of Law, U. Cambridge, Wolfson Coll., Eng., 1984, U. Haifa, Israel, 2000; atty.-fellow SEC, 1976-79; cons. to various U.S. agys. and spl. commns.; U.S. rep. to UNCITRAL working groups; mem. various ALI-ABA working groups on the revision of the uniform comml. code; mem. Sec. of State's Adv. Com. on Pvt. Internat. Law; arbitrator NY Stock Exch. and NASD, 1997—. Author: Crime, Cause and Treatment, 1956; author: (with A. Smith) Cases and Materials on Domestic Rels., 1962; author: Modern Securities Transfers, 3d edit., 2002, 4th edit., 2005; author: (with R.G. Vaughn) Cases and Materials on Policy and the Legal Environment, 1973, rev., 1978, 3d edit., 1980; author: Problems and Materials on Sales Under the Uniform Comm. Code and the Convention on Internat. Sale of Goods, Comm. Transactions, vol. 2, 1990; author: (with F. Miller) supplement, 1996—98; author: (with L.F. Del Duca) Secured Transactions Under the Uniform Comm. Code, Comm. Transactions, vol. 1, 1992; author: supplement, 1997, Problems and Materials on Negotiable Instruments Under the Uniform Comm. Code and the UN Conv. on Internat. Bills of Exch. and Internat. Promissory Notes, Comm. Transactions, vol. 3, 1993, supplement, 1995; author: (with R.B. Lubic) Secured Transactions-A Simplified Guide, 1996; author: Securities Laws in the United States-A Primer for Fgn. Lawyers, 1996—99; author: (with L.F. Del Duca, F.H. Miller, P. Winship, W.H. Henning) Secured Transactions Under the Uniform Comm. Code and Internat. Commerce, 2002; author: (with L.F. Del Duca, F.H. Miller, P. Winship) Sales Under the Uniform Commercial Code and the UN Convention on International Sale of Goods, 2005; contbr. numerous articles, revs., briefs to profl. lit. Howard U. rep. Fund for Edn. in World Order, 1966-68; trustee Silver Spring Jewish Ctr., Md., 1976-79; mem. exec. com. Sha'are Tzedek Hosp., Washington, 1971-72, 97—. Leverhulme scholar, 1948-51; U. London studentship, 1951-52; Ford Found. grad. fellow, 1958-59, NYU summer workshop fellow, 1960, 61, 64; Levitt Meml. Trust scholar-professor 1982—; recipient Outstanding Svc. award Student Bar Assn., Am. U., 1970, Law Rev. Outstanding Svc. award, 1981, Washington Coll. of Law Outstanding Contbn. to Acad. Program Devel. award, 1981. Mem. Am. Law Inst., ABA, Fed. Bar Assn. Assn. Trial Lawyers Am., Brit. Inst. Internat. and Comparative Law, Soc. Legal Scholars (Eng.), Hon. Soc. Middle Temple, Hardwick Soc. of Inns of Ct., Sudan Philos. Soc., Assn. Can. Law Tchrs., Am. Soc. Internat. Law, Can. Assn. Comparative Law, B'nai Brith, Argo Lodge, Phi Alpha Delta (John Sherman Myers award 1972). Home: 14801 Pennfield Cir Silver Spring MD 20906-1580 Office: Am U Washington Coll Law 4801 Massachusetts Ave NW Washington DC 20016-8196 Office Phone: 202-274-4213. Office Fax: 202-274-4130. E-mail: guttman@wcl.american.edu.

GUTTMAN, HELENE NATHAN, biomedical researcher, consultant, recreational therapist; b. N.Y.C., July 21, 1930; d. Arthur and Mollie (Bergovoy) Nathan. BA, Bklyn. Coll., 1951; AM, Harvard U., 1956; MA, Columbia U., 1958; PhD, Rutgers U., 1960. Registered and cert. profl. past-life regression therapist; bd. cert. nutrition specialist; bd. cert. and registered hypnotherapist; registered and cert. transpersonal counselor; cert. and registered neurolinguistic therapist. Rsch. technician Pub. Health Rsch. Inst., N.Y.C., 1951-52; control bacteriologist Burroughs-Wellcome, Inc., Tuckahoe, NY, 1952-53; vol. rschr. Haskins Labs., N.Y.C., 1952-53, rsch. asst., 1953-56, rsch. assoc., 1956-60, staff microbiologist, 1960-64; lectr. dept. biology Queens Coll., N.Y.C., 1956-57; rsch. collaborator Brookhaven Nat. Labs., Upton, L.I., NY, 1958; guest investigator Botanisches Institut der Technisches Hochschule, Darmstadt, Germany, 1960; rsch. assoc. dept. biol. scis. Goucher Coll., Towson, Md., 1960-62; vis. asst. rsch. prof. dept. medicine Med. Coll. Va., Richmond, 1960-62; asst. prof., then assoc. prof. dept. biology NYU, 1962-67; from assoc. prof. to prof. dept. biol. scis. U. Ill.-Chgo., 1967-75, prof., 1969-75; prof. dept. microbiology U. Ill. Med. Sch., 1969-75; assoc. dir. for rsch. Urban Systems Lab. U. Ill., 1975; expert Office of Dir. Nat. Heart, Lung and Blood Inst., NIH, Bethesda, Md., 1975-77, coord. rsch. resources Office Program Planning and Evaluation, 1977-79; dep. dir. Sci. Adv. Bd., Office of Adminstr., EPA, 1979-80; program coord., post-harvest tech., food safety and human nutrition, sci. and edn. adminstrn. USDA, 1980-83, assoc. dir. Beltsville (Md.) Human Nutrition Rsch. Ctr., Agrl. Rsch. Svc., 1983-89; pres. HNG Assocs., 1983—; nat. animal care coord. Nat. Program Staff Agr. Rsch. Svc./USDA, Beltsville, 1989-95. Bd. advisors The Monroe Inst., 1993—. Sr. author: Experiments in Cellular Biodynamics, 1972; co-editor (procs.) First Joint USA-USSR Joint Symposium on Blood Transfusion, Moscow, 1976, DHEW Publ. No. (NIH) 78-1246, 1978; editl. bd. Jour. Protozoology, 1972-75, Jour. Am. Med. Women's Assn., 1978-81, Methods in Cell Sci., 1994-2004; sr. editor: Science and Animals: Addressing Contemporary Issues, 1989; editor: Guidelines for Well-being of Rodents in Research, 1990, Rodents and Rabbits: Current Research Issues, 1994; (with others) Rodents and Rabbits: Addressing Current Issues, 1994; contbr. articles to profl. jours. Mem. edn. com. Ill. Commn. on Status Women, 1974-75; cons. EPA, sci. adv. bd., 1974-79; bd. dirs. Du Page County Comprehensive Health Care Agy., 1974-75. Andelot fellow Harvard U., 1956, Rutgers scholar Rutgers U., 1960; recipient Thomas Jefferson Murray prize Theobald Smith Soc., 1959; spl. award for work in Germany Deutscher Forschungs Gemeinschaft, 1960; Fellow Dazian Found., 1956; rsch. grantee. Fellow: AAAS, N.Y. Acad. Scis., Am. Acad. Microbiology, Am. Inst. Chemists (chmn. com.); mem.: Univ. and Coll. Women Ill. (past v.p.), Fed. Orgn. Profl. Women (past chmn. task force, past pres.), Assn. Women in Sci., Soc. Protozoology (past mem. exec. com., past com. chmn.), Am. Soc. Clin. Nutrition, Am. Soc. Cell Biology (past com. chmn.), Am. Soc. Microbiologists, Neuroscis. Soc., Am. Soc. Biol. Chemistry and Molecular Biology, Tissue Culture Assn. (com. chmn. Nat. Capital Area br. 1988—90), Soc. Sci. Exploration, Soc. for In Vitro Biology (chmn. constn. and bylaws com. 1994—2002, Disting. Svc. award 1995, 1999), Assn. for Transpersonal Psychology (profl. mem.), Soc. Am. Bacteriologists (pres.'s fellow), Internat. Assn. Regression Therapies (life profl.), Am. Running and Fitness Assn. (bd. dirs., mem. editl. bd., mem. bd. advisors 1993—95), Sigma Xi, Sigma Delta Epsilon (past coord. regional ctrs.). Home and Office: 5607 Mclean Dr Bethesda MD 20814-1021 *Personal philosophy: If it's worth having, it's worth fighting for.*

GUTWIRTH, MARCEL MARC, literature educator; b. Antwerp, Belgium, Apr. 11, 1923; s. Jacob Nahum and Frieda (Willner) G.; m. Madelyn Katz, June 20, 1948; children: Eve, Sarah, Nathanael. Student, NYU, 1941—42; AB, Columbia U., 1947, MA, 1948, PhD, 1950. Mem. faculty Haverford (Pa.) Coll., 1948-87, William R. Kenan, Jr. prof. French lit., 1977-82, John Whitehead prof., 1983-87; Disting. Prof. Grad. Ctr. CUNY, 1987-94, exec. officer PhD program in French, 1987-93. Vis. prof. Johns Hopkins U., 1967, Queens Coll., 1968, Bryn Mawr Coll., 1969, 76; Andrew Mellon vis. prof. humanities Tulane U., 1980; lectr. Folger Inst., 1985. Author: Molière ou l'Invention comique, 1966, Jean Racine: Un Itinéraire poétique, 1970, Stendhal, 1971, Michel de Montaigne ou le Pari d'exemplarité, 1977, Un merveilleux sans éclat: La Fontaine ou la poésie exilée, 1987, Laughing Matter, 1993, Madame de Sévigné-Classique à son insu, 2004. Bd. dirs. Childbirth Edn. Assn. Greater Phila., 1961-64. With AUS, 1943-46, ETO. Fulbright postdoctoral fellow Paris, 1953-54, Am. Coun. Learned Socs.

fellow, 1964-65, Guggenheim fellow, 1971-72, 85, Nat. Humanities Ctr. fellow, 1985-86. Mem. ACLU, MLA (mem. editl. bd. publs. 1973-76), Am. Assn. Tchrs. of French. Jewish. Home: 640 Valley View Rd Ardmore PA 19003-1029

GUTZWILLER, MARTIN CHARLES, theoretical physicist, research scientist; b. Basel, Switzerland, Oct. 12, 1925; married; 2 children. BS, Swiss Fed. Inst. Tech., Zurich, 1947, MS, 1950; PhD in Physics, U. Kans., 1953; DSc honoris causa, U. Lausanne, Switzerland, 1995, U. Freiburg, Germany, 2000. Physicist Brown, Boveri & Co., Baden, Switzerland, 1950-51; with exploration and production divsn. Shell Devel. Co., Tex., 1953-60; with rsch. divsn. Internat. Bus. Machines, Zurich, 1960-63; IBM Corp., N.Y.C., 1963-70, rsch. sci., physicist Yorktown Heights, N.Y., 1970-93, rsch. sci. emeritus, 1993—77. Adj. prof. Columbia U., 1963-83, Yale U., 1993—. Recipient Max-Planck medal, German Phys. Soc., 2003. Fellow Am. Phys. Soc. (Dannie N. Heineman prize for math. physics 1993), Am. Acad. Arts and Sci.; mem. NAS. Achievements include research in propagation of waves, electron correlation in metals, quantum and classical mechanics, especially the chaotic phenomenon, celestial mechanics. Office: 370 Riverside Dr 14B New York NY 10025 E-mail: moongutz@aol.com.

GUY, ARTHUR WILLIAM, electrical engineering educator, researcher; b. Helena, Mont., Dec. 10, 1928; s. Arthur Jack and Evelyn (Hebb) G.; m. Vivian Ruth Walker, June 12, 1952; children: William, Sandra, Fred, Arla. BSEE, U. Wash., 1955, MSEE, 1957, PhDEE, 1966. Rsch. asst. elec. engring. dept. U. Wash., Seattle, 1956-57; rsch. engr. Boeing Airplane Co., Seattle, 1957-63; cons. engr. rehab. medicine U. Wash., Seattle, 1963-65, rsch. engr. elec. engring. dept., 1964-66, prof. elec. engring. dept., rehab. medicine, 1966-83, prof., dir. bioelectromagnetics rsch. lab. Ctr. for Bioengineering, 1983-91, prof. emeritus, 1991—. Cons. Bioelectromagnetics Cons., Seattle, 1991-2000; mem. telecomms. facilities adv. com. Seattle City Coun., 1991-92; mem. Sci. Adv. Group on Wireless Tech., 1993-95; active Wireless Tech. Rsch., L.L.C., 1993-97. Contbr. articles to profl. jours. Mem. Electromagnetic Field Task Force State Dept. Health, Olympia, Wash., 1991-92. Sgt. USAF, 1947-52. Recipient Achievement award, Westinghouse Co., 1954, spl. award for the decade internat., Power Inst. for Med. and Biol. Rsch., 1980. Fellow AAAS, IEEE (life, vice chair SCC 28 stds. bd. 1989-94, mem. COMAR 1974-89, 92-98, chair COMAR 1987-89); mem. Nat. Coun. on Radiation Protection and Measurements (hon.), Bioelectromagnetic Soc. (charter mem., pres. 1984, d'Arsenval award 1987). Methodist. Home and Office: 18122 60th Pl NE Kenmore WA 98028-8901 E-mail: gbemc@comcast.net.

GUY, ELEANOR BRYENTON, retired writer; b. Pitts., Sept. 6, 1930; d. Lloyd Charles and Verda Eleanor (Hooper) Bryenton; m. Daniel Sowers Guy, Dec. 22, 1962; children: Stanley, Sharon. BA, Ohio Wesleyan U., 1953. Program dir. Lakewood Br. Cleve. Met. YWCA, Lakewood, Ohio, 1953-56, ctr. dir., 1956-57; residence dir., mem. faculty St. Luke's Hosp. Sch. Nursing, Shaker Heights, Ohio, 1957-59; pers. asst., counselor Acacia Mutual Life Ins. Co., Washington, 1959-62; admissions counselor Ohio No. U., Ada, 1963-64; freelance writer, photographer Kenton (Ohio) Times, 1984-88, Ada Herald, 1988-96; coord. external affairs, editor the Writ, Pettit Coll. of Law, Ohio No. U., 1995-96, ret., 1996. Sec. bd. trustees, chmn. pub. rels. com. Ada Pub. Libr., 1982—86; mem. pub. rels. com., bd. dirs. Hardin County Alcohol and Drug Abuse Ctr., Kenton, 1989—92; chmn. publicity Town and Gown Planning Com., Ada, 1988; tchr., mem. co-chair edn. com., mem. missions com., mem., sec. adminstrv. coun., mem. centennial com., publicist United Meth. Ch., 1985—2003; lay dist. del. to West Ohio Ann. conf. local ch., 1998—2004; dist. spiritual growth coord. Ch. United Meth. Women, 2000—03. Mem. AAUW (pres. local br. 1978-80), Ohio No. U. Women (parliamentarian, pub. rels. chair Christmas Arts Festival 1990-96), P.E.O. (v.p. 1994-96, sec. 1998-99), Twice Ten Art Club (pres. 1984-85, 90-91, 97-98, sec. 1988-89, 99-01, mem. v.p. 2003—). Methodist. Avocations: photography, travel, music.

GUY, MARY ELLEN JOHNSTON, political science professor; b. Carlinville, Ill., Dec. 2, 1947; d. Charles Oren and Marilyn Elinor (Denby) Johnston; divorced. BA cum laude, Jacksonville U., 1969; M of Rehab. Counseling, U. Fla., 1970; MA in Psychology, U. SC, 1976, PhD in Polit. Sci., 1981. Rehab. counselor Ga. Dept. Human Resources, Augusta, 1970-73; psychologist SC State Hosp., Columbia, 1973-80, quality assurance coord., 1980-82; Collins prof. pub. adminstrn. Fla. State U., 1997—; prof. polit. sci. and pub. affairs U. Ala., Birmingham, 1982-97. Adv. bd. Cooper Green Hosp., Birmingham, 1991-97. Editor: Women and Men of the States, 1992, Public Personnel Administration, 2001-; author: Ethical Decision Making, 1990, From Organizational Decline, 1989, Professionals in Organizations, 1985. Mem. ASPA (Disting. Rsch. award 1992, Outstanding Paper award 1992, coun. mem. 1987-90, pres. 1997-98), So. Polit. Sci. Assn. (pres. 2001-02), Am. Polit. Sci. Assn., Women's Caucus in Polit. Sci./South (pres. 1990-92). Unitarian Universalist. Avocations: golf, breeding and showing purebred dogs. Office: Fla State U Askew Sch Pub Adminstrn & Policy Tallahassee FL 32306-2250

GUY, RALPH B., JR., federal judge; b. Detroit, Mich., Aug. 30, 1929; s. Ralph B. and Shirley (Skladd) G. AB, U. Mich., 1951, JD, 1953. Bar: Mich. 1953. Sole practice, Dearborn, Mich., 1954—55; asst. corp. counsel City of Dearborn, 1955—58, corp. counsel, 1958—69; chief asst. U.S. Atty.'s Office (ea. dist.), Detroit and Mich., 1968—70, U.S. Atty., 1970—76; judge U.S. Dist. Ct. (ea. dist.) Mich., Ann Arbor, 1976—85, U.S. Ct. Appeals (6th cir.), Ann Arbor, 1985—94, sr. judge, 1994—. Treas. Detroit-Wayne County Bldg. Authority, 1966—73; chmn. sch. study com. Dearborn Bd. Edn., 1973; mem. Fed. Exec. Bd., 1970—, bd. dirs., 1971—73. Recipient Civic Achievement award, Dearborn Rotary, 1971, Distinguished Alumni award, U. Mich., 1972. Mem.: FBA (pres. 1974—75), ABA (state chmn. sect. local govt. 1965—70), Cin. Bar Assn., Out-County Suprs. Assn. (pres. 1965), Mich. Municipal League, Mich. Assn. Municipal Attys. (pres. 1962—64), Nat. Inst. Municipal Law Officers (chmn. Mich. chpt. 1964—69), Am. Judicature Soc., Dearborn Bar Assn. (pres. 1959—60), Detroit Bar Assn., State Bar Mich. (commr. 1975—), U. Mich. Alumni Club (local pres. Dearborn 1961—62), Rotary (local pres. 1973—74), Lambda Chi Alpha, Phi Alpha Delta. Office: US Ct Appeals PO Box 7910 200 E Liberty St Rm 226 Ann Arbor MI 48107 also: Potter Stewart US Courthouse 100 E 5th St Cincinnati OH 45202-3988

GUY, WILLIAM LEWIS, III, lawyer; b. Mpls., Apr. 27, 1946; s. William L. and Elizabeth Jean (Mason) G.; m. Marilyn J. Walter, July 11, 1969; children: Stephanie J., Mark W. BBA, U. N.D., 1968, JD, 1976. Bar: Minn. 1976, N.D. 1976, U.S. Tax Ct. 1976. Ptnr. Gunhus, Grinnell, Klinger, Swenson & Guy, Ltd. (formerly Vogel Law Firm), Moorhead, Minn., 1976—. Vice-chmn. Bd. Pensions Am. Luth. Ch., Mpls., 1980-88. Lt. USNR, 1968-73. Fellow Am. Coll. Trust & Estate Counsel; mem. Minn. Bar Assn., N.D. Bar Assn. (chaired) chmn. subcom. corp. sect., revised N.D. Bus. Corp. Act 1984), N.D. Soc. CPAs, Minn. Soc. CPAs. Democrat. Avocations: reading, skiing, sailing. Home: 3651 Fairway Rd Fargo ND 58102-1278 Office: Vogel Law Firm 215 30th St N Moorhead MN 56560-2546 E-mail: wguy@gunhuslaw.com.

GUYER, BERNARD, maternal and child health educator; Sr. acad. adv. Urban Health Inst. John Hopkins U.; assoc. prof. MCH Harvard Sch. Public Health, 1986—89; dir. Maternal and Child Health Agy., State Mass. Dept. Public Health, 1979—86, DrPH program; chair dept. Maternal and Child Health, 1989—98; chair dept. Population and Family Health Scis. John Hopkins U., 1998—2004; officer, med. epidemiologist Ctr. for Disease Control, Atlanta, Yaounde, Cameroon. Dir. maternal and child health agy., State Mass. Dept. Pub. Health, 1979-86. Contbr. articles to profl. jours. Recipient Martha May Eliot award, Am. Public Health Assn., 2003. Mem. Inst. Medicine Nat. Acad. Sci.

GUYER, CHARLES GRAYSON, II, psychologist; b. High Point, N.C., May 22, 1949; s. Charles Grayson Sr. and Mildred Louise (Wrokman) G.; m. E.R. Ward, June 24, 1986; children: Charles Grayson III, Jarvis Griffith. BA, Appalachian State U., 1972, MA, 1974; EdD, Coll. William & Mary, 1978. Bd. cert. in counseling psychology and family psychology Am. Bd. Profl. Psychology. Resident N.C. Wyo. Mental Health, Buffalo, 1978-80; pvt. practice High Point, N.C., 1980-83, Greensboro, NC, 1988—98; chief sch. psychologist Perquimans County Schs., Hertford, NC, 1998—2002; pvt. practice Jacksonville, NC, 2002—. Pres. Am. Bd. Family Psychology, 1992-94, bd. dirs., 1991-96, 2000-03, Am. Bd. Counseling Psychology, 1991-93. Contbr. chapters to books, articles to profl. jours. Lt. USN, 1983—88. Recipient Irving I. Sector award, Am. Soc. Clin. Hypnosis, 1997. Fellow APA, Am. Soc. Clin. Hypnosis (chmn. ethics com. 1993-97), Acad. Family Psychology (pres. 1995-96), Am. Acad. Counseling Psychology (bd. dirs. 1991-93, pres. 1993-95), Soc. Clin. Exptl. Hypnosis; mem. Am. Group Psychotherapy Assn., Va. Acad. Clin. Psychologists, Va. Psychol. Assn., NC Soc. Clin. Hypnosis, NC Psychol. Assn., Guilford County Psychol. Assn. (treas. 1997-98). Methodist. Avocations: running, reading. Home: 307 Tryon Ct Jacksonville NC 28546 Office: 1703 Country Club Rd Ste 204 Jacksonville NC 28546 Office Phone: 910-347-3010.

GUYER, HEDY-ANN KLEIN, special education educator; b. Phila., Dec. 25, 1947; d. Edward Chuck Klein and Gladys Selma (Shapiro) Sussman; m. Eugene August Guyer, Aug. 24, 1980 (div. Mar. 2002). BS in Secondary Edn., St. Joseph's U., Phila., 1981; MEd in Spl. Edn., Arcadia Univ., 1996. Cert. in social studies, elem. edn., spl. edn. of mentally and/or physically handicapped, Pa. Tchr. spl. edn. Sch. Dist. Phila., 1996—. Mem. ASCD, Women in Edn., George Washington H.S. Alumni Assn., B'nai B'rith (educators unit), Coun. Exceptional Children. Home: 1033 Bloomfield Ave Philadelphia PA 19115-4829 Office: Sch Dist Phila William Penn HS Broad and Master Sts Philadelphia PA 19122-4097

GUYMON, GARY LEROY, civil engineering educator; b. Farmington, N.Mex., Nov. 5, 1935; s. Leland W. and Grace E. (Cumming) G.; m. Lucinda A. Kemmis, June 11, 1988; children by previous marriage: Gary Jr., Richard, Marisa, Michael. BS, U. Calif., Davis, 1966, MS, 1967, PhD, 1970. Asst. civil engr. Calif. Dept. Water Resources, L.A., 1955-66; asst. rsch. engr. U. Calif., Davis, 1969-71; assoc. prof. U. Alaska, Fairbanks, 1971-74; prof. U. Calif., Irvine, 1974-94, chmn. dept. civil engring., 1984-88, prof. emeritus, 1994—. Mem. coordinating bd. U. Calif. Water Resources Ctr., Berkeley, 1985-89; del. Univs. Coun. on Water Resources, Carbondale, Ill., 1980-94. Author: Unsaturated Zone Hydrology, 1994; contbr. numerous articles to profl. jours.; assoc. editor Advances in Water Resources, Southampton, U.K., 1981-89. Fellow ASCE; mem. Am. Geophys. Union, U.S. Com. on Large Dams, Phi Beta Kappa, Tau Beta Pi, Chi Epsilon. Independent. Avocations: woodworking, physical fitness. Office Phone: 760-635-0233. Business E-Mail: gguymon@att.net.

GUYNES, DEMI See MOORE, DEMI

GUYNN, JACK, bank executive; b. Staunton, Va. BS in Indsl. Engring., Va. Polytech. Inst. and State U., 1964; MS in Indsl. Mgmt., Ga. Inst. Tech., 1969. Joined Fed. Res. Bank Atlanta, 1964, first v.p., COO, 1984—96, pres., CEO, 1996—. Bd. trustees Furman U.; advisory bd. Va. Tech.; bd. councilors Carter Ctr.; bd. trustees Oglethorpe U. Mem.: Atlanta Rotary Club. Office: Fed Res Bank Atlanta 104 Marietta St NW Atlanta GA 30303-2702

GUYNN, ROBERT WILLIAM, psychiatrist, educator; b. Streator, Ill., Oct. 27, 1942; s. William Digby and Helen Louise (Dancey) G. BA, Mich. State U., 1963; MD, Johns Hopkins U., 1967. Diplomate Am. Bd. Psychiatry and Neurology. Clin. fellow Nat. Inst. of Mental Health, Washington, 1970-73; asst. prof. Dept. of Psychiatry and Behaviorial Scis. U. Tex., Houston, 1973-76, assoc. prof., 1976-83, vice-chmn., prof. psychiatry, 1983-87, interim chmn., 1987-89, chmn., 1989—. Dir. U. Tex. Mental Scis. Inst., 1987—; exec. dir. Harris County Psychiat. Ctr., 1988—; sr. oral examiner Am. Bd. Psychiatry and Neurology, 1994—2003, mem. written exam com., 1998—. Contbr. articles to profl. jours. and book chpts.; mem. editl. bd. Internat. Rev. Psychiatry, 1988-93, editor-in-chief, 1989-93. Bd. dirs. Vols. of Am., Houston, 1982—88; with Passages, 1991—94; adv. bd. The Gathering Place, 2002—, The Club House, 2004—. Surgeon USPHS, 1970—73. Recipient Psychiatric Excellence award, Tex. Soc. Psychiatric Physicians, 2000. Dist. Fellow Am. Psychiat. Assn. (disting.); fellow Am. Coll. Psychiatrists; mem. Am. Soc. Biol. Chemistry, Tex. Rsch. Soc. on Alcoholism (pres. 1985-87), Tex. Soc. of Am. Assn. Psychiat. Adminstrs. (treas. 1990-91, pres. 1992-93), Biochem. Soc., Rsch. Soc. on Alcoholism, Houston Psychiat. Soc. (v.p. 1989-90, pres. 1991-92), Harris County Med. Soc. (bd. ethics 1989-92), Tex. Dept. Mental Health and Mental Retardation (med. adv. com. 1997—), Mental Health and Mental Retardation Auth. (adv. bd., 1992—) Avocations: printmaking, painting. Office: U Tex Health Sci Ctr PO Box 20708 Houston TX 77225-0708 Office Phone: 713-500-2554. Business E-Mail: robert.w.guynn@uth.tmc.edu.

GUYON, JOHN CARL, retired university administrator; b. Washington, Pa., Oct. 16, 1931; s. Carl Alexander and Sara Myrle (Bumgarner) G.; m. Elizabeth Joyce Smith, Nov. 12, 1955; children— Cynthia Joan, John Carl, II. BA, Washington and Jefferson Coll., 1953; MS, Toledo U., 1958; PhD, Purdue U., 1961. Mem. faculty U. Mo., 1961—71, prof. chemistry, chmn. dept., 1970—71, Memphis State U., 1971—74; dean Coll. Sci., So. Ill. U., Carbondale, 1974—75, Coll. Sci., So. Ill. U. (Grad. Sch.), assoc. v.p. research, 1976—80, v.p. acad. affairs and research, 1980; pres. So. Ill. U., 1987—95, chancellor, 1996—97; ret., 1997—. Author: Aanlytical Chemistry, 1965, Qualitative Analysis, 1966, Solution Equilbria, 1969; also articles, abstracts.; Gen. editor: Instrumental Methods of Analysis. Served with AUS, 1954—56. Eli Lilly Co. fellow, 1959-61; Owens Ill. Co. fellow, 1958; Jesse W. Lazear scholar, 1953 Mem. Am. Chem. Soc., AAAS, Phi Beta Kappa, Sigma Xi, Phi, Lambda Upsilon.

GUYTON, SAMUEL PERCY, retired lawyer; b. Jackson, Miss., Mar. 20, 1937; s. Earl Ellington and Eulalia (Reynolds) G.; m. Jean Preston, Oct. 11, 1959; children: Tamara Reynolds, William Preston, David Sage. BA, Miss. State U., 1959; LLB, U. Va., 1965. Bar: Colo. 1965, U.S. Dist. Ct. Colo. 1965, U.S. Tax Ct. 1977, U.S. Ct. Appeals (10th cir.) 1965, U.S. Ct. Appeals (5th cir.) 1981. Ptnr. Holland & Hart, Denver, 1965-92, ret., 1992. Mem. faculty Am. Law Inst. ABA, 1976-88, bd. dirs. Royal St. Corp., Royal St. Utah Inc., Deer Valley Ski Resort. Co-author: Cattle Owners Tax Manual, 1984, Supplement to Federal Taxation of Agriculture, 1983, Colorado Estate Planning Desk Book, 1984, 90; author: (chpt.) Success Briefs For Lawyers, 2000; contbr. articles to profl. jours., mags.; bd. advs. Agrl. Law Jour., 1978-82; mem. editl. bd. Jour. Agrl. Tax and Law, 1983-92. Sec., trustee Colo. Hist. Found., 1971-92, pres., 1983-87; trustee Music Assn. Aspen and Aspen Music Festival, 1980-88; precinct com. chmn. Dem. Party, 1968-70; mem. Gov.'s Mansion preservation com., 1989-92; bd. advisors Coll. Arts and Scis., Miss. State U., 1996-98; mem. com. govt. and legal affairs Hampshire Coll., 1996-2000; chmn. com. on legis. Woodmen of the World, 1972-2000. Fellow Am. Coll. Tax Counsel (bd. regents 1985-92, chmn., pres. 1989-91), Am. Tax Policy Inst. (trustee 1989-92, v.p. 1989-92); mem. ABA (sect. taxation 1967-92, chmn. sect.'s com. on agr. 1980-82), Colo. Bar Assn. (tax coun. 1983-86, sec. 1983, chmn. 1985-86), Colo. Bar Found. (life), Greater Denver Tax Csls. Assn. (chmn. 1978), Law Club Denver, Little River Lectures Assn. (bd. dirs., v.p. 1985-96, pres. 1996-2000), Am. Alpine Club (life), Colo. Mountain Club (life, joint devel. com.), Eleanore Mullen Weckbaugh Found. (trustee 1983-95), William P. Guyton Found. (co-trustee), Humphreys Found. (treas., v.p., dir.), Colo. Trail Found. (trustee 1987-99), Colo. Mountain Club Found. (dir., v.p.), Colo. Hist. Soc. (bd. dirs., chmn. nominating com. 1997-2001, co-chair dirs. coun.), Holland & Hart Found. (bd. dirs., pres. 1998-2004). Mem. Unity Ch. Home and Office: 12345 W 19th Pl Lakewood CO 80215-2516 *To live fully and consciously in the present is both challenge and reward.*

GUYTON, WADE, artist; b. Tenn., 1972; BA, U. Tenn., 1990—95; MFA, Hunter Coll., 1996—98. Exhibitions include Against the new Passeism. Understanding this is only the beginning, hope for the end. Build, Destroy, Do Nothing., Andrew Kreps Gallery, NY, 1999, After the Diagram, White Box Gallery, 2000—01, Retrofit, Lombard-Freid Fine Arts, 2001—02, X, Power House, Memphis, 2003, Elements of An Incomplete Map, Artists Space, NY, 2003, Whitney Biennial, Whitney Mus. Am. Art, 2004, Objects Are Much More Familiar, Power House, Memphis, 2004. Mailing: c/o Lombard Freid Fine Arts 531 West 26th St New York NY 10001*

GUZAK, KAREN JEAN WAHLSTROM, artist; b. Cambridge, Mass., May 21, 1939; d. Ernest E. and Kathryn E. (Kemp) Wahlstrom; m. Steven V. Guzak, Aug. 29, 1959 (div. 1983); children: Gretchen, Christopher, Lauren. BS, U. Colo., 1961; BFA, Cornish Sch. Allied Arts, Seattle, 1976. Pres. Karen Guzak Inc., Seattle, 1982—. Owner Yoga Circle Studio, Snohomish, Wash. One-woman shows include Foster White Gallery, Seattle, 1981, 1984, 1987, 1989, 1991, 1994, 1996, 1998, 2000, Davidson Galleries, 1981, 1984, 1987, Tom Luttrell Gallery, San Francisco, 1981, Harris Gallery, Houston, 1982, Laura Russo Gallery, Portland, Oreg., 1987, 1989, 1991, 1996, Musee Hyacinth Rigaud, Perpignan, France, 1988, Edmonds C.C., 2004, numerous group shows including most recently, exhibited in group shows at Portland Art Mus., 1997, Ctr. on Contemporary Art, 2000, Tacoma Art Mus., 2002, Lewis & Clark Coll., 2003, Edmonds C.C., 2005, Represented in permanent collections Portland Art Mus., Jundt Mus. Gonzaga U., Bklyn. Mus., NYC Libr., Pratt Inst., City of Seattle, King County Wash., So. Oreg. State Coll., King County Coun. Chambers, Overlake Ctr. for Sound Transit, Redmond, Wash., prin. works include South Seattle C.C., Redmond Town Ctr. Bon Macys, 2003. Bd. commrs. King County Arts Commn., Seattle, 1981—86, commr., 1984—85; arts adv. com. METRO Arts Program, Seattle, 1985—91; contemporary coun. Seattle Art Mus., 1990—96; pres., developer Sunny Arms Coop., Seattle, 1988—90; co-developer, pres. Union Arts Coop., 1992—93; chair Historic Design Rev. Bd., Snohomish, 2004—05; bd. dir. Ctr. Contemporary Art, 1987—88; pres. bd. dir. Artist Trust, 1996—99. Recipient Housing Designs that Work award, Seattle Design Commn., 1991, Home Of Yr. award, Seattle Times and AIA, 1994; Boettcher scholar, U. Colo., 1957—61. Mem.: AIA (Seattle chpt.) (hon.). Democrat. Home and Office: Karen Guzak Inc 230 Avenue B Snohomish WA 98290-2841 Office: Yoga Cir Studio 707 Pine Ave A103 Snohomish WA 98290 E-mail: karen@angelarmsworks.com.

GUZDA, HENRY PETER, industrial relations specialist; b. Stamford, Conn., Jan. 9, 1950; s. Henry and Marion (Wujcik) G. BA in History, Alliance Coll., 1971; MA in History, Edinboro U., 1974; postgrad., Cath. U., 1986—. Historian U.S. Dept. Labor, Washington, 1976-84, indsl. rels. specialist, 1984—. Hist. advisor U.S. Dept. Labor Libr.; dir. internat. visitor program Office of Am. Workplace, Washington, 1989—; cons. Readers Digest, Pleasantville, NY, 1993, Gale Rsch., Detroit. Contbr. articles to profl. jours. Block capt. Neighborhood Watch, Foxwood Cmty. Assn., Burke, Va., 1986-92; chief steward Office of Am. Workplace, Am. Fedn. Govt. Employees, Washington, 1993-94. Recipient Exceptional Achievement award, Sec. of Labor, 1997, 2002, 2004. Mem. Indsl. Rels. Rsch. Assn. (exec. bd. D.C. chpt. 1989-94, pres. 1992-93, award 1993). Democrat. Achievements include research in tracing origins and development of new forms of work organization/labor-mgmt. coop., research in covering origins of equal employment opportunity programs in Dept. of Labor. Home: 5654 Sutherland Ct Burke VA 22015-1850 Office: Office Asst Sec for Policy Dept Labor 200 Constitution Ave NW Washington DC 20210-0001 Office Phone: 202-693-5099. E-mail: guzda-henry@dol.gov.

GUZICK, DAVID S., dean, educator; b. 1952; MD, NYU, 1979, PhD. Resident in ob-gyn. John Hopkins Hosp., 1979—83; fellow in reproductive endocrinology U. Tex. Southwestern Med. Sch., 1983—85; dir. divsn. reproductive endocrinology Magee Women's Hosp., U. Pitts.; assoc. prof. U. Pitts., 1986—94, prof., 1994—95; chief svc. ob-gyn. Strong Meml. Hosp., Rochester, NY; Henry A. Thiede prof. and chair ob-gyn. U. Rochester Sch. Medicine and Dentistry, 1995—2002, dean and prof. ob-gyn., 2002—. Office: Univ Rochester Sch Medicine and Dentistry 601 Elmwood Ave PO Box 706 Rochester NY 14642 Office Phone: 585-275-0017. Business E-Mail: david_guzick@urmc.rochester.edu.

GUZMAN, BELINDA F., elementary school educator; b. Guadalajara, Jalisco, Mexico, Jan. 8, 1965; arrived in U.S., 1970; d. Ralph Loran and Modesta DeBelle; m. Alfonso Guzmán; children: Alfonso, Daniela. B in Indisciplinary studies, U. Tex. Pan Am., 1995, MEd, 2001. Cert. educator Tex., 1995. Legal sec. Law Office of Vernon Hill Jr., McAllen, Tex., 1982—93; educator Pharr, San Juan, Alamo Ind. Sch. Dist., Pharr, Tex., 1993—. Mem.: Mission Jr. Svc. League, Kappa Delta Pi (historian 2001—). Roman Catholic. Avocations: reading, dance. Office: North San Juan Elem Sch 2900 N Raul Longoria San Juan TX 78589

GUZMÀN, DAVID R., information technology executive; BA with honors, Yale Univ., New Haven, Conn., 1978, PhD studies in Econ. With Federated Dept. Stores, Deloitte & Touche, Credit Suisse/First Boston and Morgan Stanley; divisional v.p. & CTO Kmart; mng. dir. global arch. Alcoa, 1997—98; sr. v.p. sys. devel. Office Depot, 1999—2000; sr. v.p. & chief info. officer Owens & Minor, Inc., 2000—. Named one of top tech. innovators, Info. Week mag., 2000, 2001, 2004. Office: SVP & CIO Owens & Minor Inc 4800 Cox Rd PO Box 27626 Richmond VA 23261-7626

GUZMAN, IRIS VILA, music educator; b. Havana, Cuba, Oct. 26, 1953; d. Alfonso Eligio and Blanca Lydia Vila; m. Rodolfo Juan Guzman, Feb. 1, 1980; 1 child, Gabriella Maria. AA in Langs., Miami Dade Jr. Coll., 1973; BA in French, Fla. Internat. U., 1975, BFA in Music, 1976; MusM, U. Miami, 1981. From music therapist to tchr. music DCPS, Miami, 1982—99, tchr. music Ernest R. Graham Elem. Sch. Hialeah, Fla., 1999—; tchr. music Fairfax County Schs., Flerndon, Va., 1990—92. Musician: Musica Antiqua Miami, 1980—87, Washington (D.C.) Camerata, 1989—92, Potomac Consort, 1990—93; composer: various piano solos and duets for children, 1977. Mem. choir St. Thomas Episc. Ch., Coral Gables, Fla., 2003. Mem.: Nat. Guild Piano Tchrs. Avocations: reading, gardening, pets. Home: 9811 SW 119th Ave Miami FL 33186

GUZMAN, KATHLEEN MCFADDEN, antiques appraiser, auctioneer; b. N.Y.C., Dec. 31, 1955; d. Walter Michael and Mary Ann (Plummer) McFadden; m. Wilfredo Guzman, Sept. 3, 1977; 1 child, Caitlin. A degree, Finch Coll., 1975; BA, Manhattanville Coll., 1977; MA in Art History, Queens Coll., 1979; exec. program (hon.), Columbia U., 1989. Auctioneer Plaza Art Galleries, N.Y.C., 1979-80; dir. Art Deco Christie's, N.Y.C., 1981-84, mgr., 1984-90; pres. Christie's East, N.Y.C., 1990—2000; ind. appraiser, 2000—. Lectr. in field; regular featured appraiser PBS' Antiques Roadshow. Bd. mem. Heaven on Earth, Dixon Pl.; auctioneer Make-a-Wish, Juvenile Diabetes, Am. Craft Mus. Avocation: restoring old homes. Office: 200 E End Ave New York NY 10128

GUZMAN, MARIE ELVIRA, school guidance counselor; b. Quito, Ecuador, July 19, 1937; Came to U.S., 1968; d. Jose Amable Rubio and Sarah Maldonado; m. Antonio Guzman, Dec. 26, 1958; children: Miriam, Renato, Freddy, Scott. BA, 1975; MEd, Montclair State U., 1982. Cert. tchr., guidance counselor, N.J.; cert. Spanish, elem., bilingual, ESL, student pers. svcs. guidance counselor. Tchr. Pub. Pilot Sch., Quito, 1958-68, Paterson (N.J.) Pub. Schs., 1975-83, Paterson Adult Sch., Paterson, 1978—; guidance counselor Paterson (N.J.) Pub. Schs., 1983—. Mem. ASCD, N.J. Counselors Assn. Roman Catholic. Avocation: reading. Home: 4212 No Dancer Way Orlando FL 32826-4293

GUZY, CAROL, photojournalist; b. Bethleham, PA, Mar. 7, 1956; ADN, Northampton County Area C.C., Pa., 1978; AAS in Photography, Art Inst. Ft. Lauderdale, 1980. Staff photographer The Miami Herald, 1980-88, The Washington Post, 1988—. Named Newspaper Photographer of Yr., Nat. Press Photographer Assn., 1989, 1992, 1996, Photographer of Yr., White House News Photographers Assn., 1991, 1993, 1994, 1995, 1996, 1997, 1997, 1998, 2000; recipient Best Portfolio Award, Atlanta Seminar Photojournalism, 1982,

1985, 1990, Robert F. Kennedy award, 1984, Excellence Citation, Overseas Press Club, 1986, Leica Excellence medal, 1994, Pulitzer Prize in spot news photography, 1986, 1995, Pulitzer Prize in feature photography, 2000. Office: The Washington Post 1150 15th St NW Washington DC 20071-0002 Office Phone: 202-334-6000.*

GUZZETTI, BARBARA JEAN, education educator; b. Chgo., Nov. 15, 1948; d. Louis Earnest and Viola Genevive (Russell) G. BS, No. Ill. U., 1971, MS, 1974; PhD, U. Colo., 1982. Title I reading tchr. Harlem Consolidated Sch. Dist., Loves Park, Ill., 1971-72; elem. classroom tchr. Rockford (Ill.) Pub. Schs., 1972-77; diagnostic tchr. Denver Pub. Schs., 1977-78; secondary reading tchr. Jefferson County Pub. Schs., Lakewood, Colo., 1979-81, secondary reading specialist, 1981—82; rsch. and program assoc. Mid-Continent Regional Ednl. Lab., Aurora, Colo., 1983-84; evaluation specialist N.W. Regional Ednl. Lab., Denver, 1984-85; assoc. prof. Calif. State U., Ponoma, 1985-88; prof. Ariz. State U., Tempe, 1988—. Chair tech. com. Nat. Reading Conf., 1994—97. Author: Literacy Instruction in Content Areas, 1996, Reading, Writing and Talking Gender in Literacy Learning; editor: Perspectives on Conceptual Change, Literacy in America: An Encyclopedia of History, Theory and Practice; mem. editl. bd. The Reading Tchr., Jour. of Reading Behavior, Nat. Reading conf. Yearbook; contbr. articles to profl. jours. Mem. Am. Ednl. Rsch. Assn., Nat. Reading Conf., Internat. Reading Assn. (chair studies and rsch. grants com. 1992-95). Democrat. Lutheran. Avocations: reading, oenology, raising a pot-bellied pig, piglet. Office: Ariz State U Coll of Edn Tempe AZ 85287-0411 Home: 1951 E Citation Lane Tempe AZ 85284 Office Phone: 480-965-1890. Business E-Mail: guzzetti@asu.edu.

GUZZO, SANDRA ELIZABETH, newspaper columnist, writer; b. Berkeley, Calif., May 14, 1941; d. Frederick Joseph and Eva Maria (Weiskopf) Schmitz; m. Anthony Victor Guzzo; children: Phillip Anthony, Anne Marie. BA, U. Ariz., 1963; postgrad., U. Montpllier, France, 1963-64, U. Chgo., 1965. Sec. classics dept. U. Ariz., Tucson, 1961-63; women's news editor Laramie (Wyo.) Newspapers, Inc., 1973-79, columnist Laramie Rendezvous, 1986—, life styles editor, 1994—. Originator co-ed Picket Pin Supplement, Laramie Newspapers, Inc., 1976-79. Author: (children's books), Fox and Heggie, 1983, Miguel and the Santero, 1986, The Days Before Christmas, 1994, (book) Chickens in the Greenhouse, 1993, (book) West Wind, 2003; contbr. Laramie Daily Boomerang, 1973-79, 1993-2000. Columnist for Pen Pals (group for preservation of Wyo. Territorial Prison), Laramie, 1985, 90 Named Fulbright fellow U. Montpellier, France, 1963-64. Mem. Wyo. Writers, Inc., Laramie Writers Group, Children's Book Writers (sec. Rocky Mt. chpt. 1994-98), Rocky Mt. Fiction Writers. Avocation: watercolor and pastel artist. Home: 810 S 12th St Laramie WY 82070-4630 Office: Laramie Daily Boomerang 320 Grand Ave Laramie WY 82070-3712

GUÐMUNDSDOTTIR, BJÖRK See BJÖRK

GWADOSKY, DAN A., former state official; b. Fairfield, Maine, Feb. 16, 1954; m. Cheryl Norton; children: Joshua, Jessica. BS in Mgmt., LHD (hon.), Thomas Coll. Mem. Maine Ho. Reps., Augusta, 1978-96, asst. majority floor leader, house majority leader, 1988-94, spkr., 1994-96; sec. of state State of Maine, Augusta, 1997—2004. Adminstr. Atrium Hotels Corp., 1985—. Mem. adv. bd. Kennebec Valley Vocat. Tech. Coll., State YMCA; bd. trustees Thomas Coll.; bd. dirs. State Leaders Found.; mem. exec. com. Coun. of State Govts.; co-chair Fairfield Cmty. Fest; co-chair bldg. com. Lawrence Pub. Libr.; active Lawrence HS Alumni Assn., Booster Club; coach boys and girls baseball, soccer, and basketball teams. Democrat.

GWALTNEY, CORBIN, editor, publishing executive; b. Balt., Apr. 16, 1922; s. Howell Corbin and Margaret (Bell) G.; m. Doris Jean Kell, July 13, 1946 (dec.); children: Margaret Kell, Jean Corbin, Thomas Stewart; m. Jean Caryl Wyckoff, June 20, 1973 (dec.); m. Pamela I. Stokes, Sept. 11, 2003. BA, Johns Hopkins U., 1943; LHD (hon.), L.I. U., 1970; DHL (hon.), Johns Hopkins U., 1998. Instr., English Johns Hopkins U., 1946; with indsl. relations dept. Western Electric Co. and Locke div. Gen. Electric Co., 1946-49; editor Johns Hopkins Mag., 1949-59; editor, exec. dir., chmn. Editorial Projects for Edn., Inc., Balt. and Washington, 1959-78; exec. editor Chronicle Higher Edn., Washington, 1966-2000, chmn., 2000—; exec. editor Chronicle of Philanthropy, 1988—2000, chmn., 2000—. Served with AUS, 1943-45. Recipient Robert Sibley award Am. Alumni Council, 1951, 56, 59, Disting. Service to Higher Edn. awards Columbia U. Alumni Fedn., 1964, Disting. Service to Higher Edn. awards Am. Coll. Public Relations Assn., 1971; George Polk award for edn. reporting, 1979 Home: 5104 Brookview Dr Bethesda MD 20816-1602 also: 4755 Bayfields Rd Harwood MD 20776-9576 Office: Chronicle Higher Edn 1255 23rd St NW Ste 700 Washington DC 20037-1146 Business E-Mail: corbin@chronicle.com.

GWATHMEY, CHARLES, architect; b. Charlotte, N.C., June 19, 1938; s. Robert and Rosalie Dean (Hook) G.; m. Bette-Ann Damson, Dec. 15, 1974. Student, U. Pa., 1956-59; M.Arch., Yale U., 1962. Partner firm Gwathmey-Siegel and Assocs. Architects, N.Y.C., 1968—. Vis. prof. archtl. design Pratt Inst., Yale U., Princeton U., Harvard U., Columbia U., Cooper Union, UCLA; William A. Bernoudy resident architecture, Am. Acad., 2005. Pres. bd. trustees Inst. Architecture and Urban Studies, N.Y.C., 1978. Recipient Arnold Brunner prize AAAL, 1970; William Wirt Winchester traveling fellow, 1962-63; Fulbright grantee France, 1962-63; recipient AIA Nat. Honor awards for Straus residence, Purchase, N.Y., 1969, Whig Hall, Princeton U., 1976, Dormitory, Dining and Student Union SUNY, Purchase 1976, Taft Residence, Cin., 1984, Westover Sch., Middlebury, Conn., 1988, AIA N.Y. awards for Sch. Agr. Cornell U., 1991, Guggenheim Mus., N.Y.C., 1995, Yale Alumni Arts award for outstanding achievement, 1985, Lifetime Achievement medal in visual arts Guild Hall Acad., 1988, Lifetime Achievement award N.Y. State Soc. Archs., 1990. Fellow AIA (firm award 1982, Medal of honor 1983); mem. Am. Acad. Arts and Letters. Office: Gwathmey Siegel & Assoc Arch 475 10th Ave 3d Fl New York NY 10018-1198 E-mail: c.gwathmey@gwathmeysiegel.com.

GWATHMEY, GAINES, lawyer; b. Glen Cove, N.Y., Dec. 26, 1946; s. Gaines and Rachel (Parker) G.; m. Rose H. Harvey, May 16, 1987. AB, Harvard Coll., 1969; JD, Georgetown U., 1973. Bar: N.Y. 1974, D.C. 1975, N.J. 1985, U.S. Dist. Ct. (so., ea. and no. dists.) N.Y., U.S. Dist. Ct. N.J., U.S. Dist. Ct. D.C., U.S. Ct. Appeals (2d and 9th cirs.). Assoc. Poletti Freidin Prashker Feldman & Gartner, N.Y.C., 1973-77; asst. U.S. atty. So. Dist. N.Y., N.Y.C., 1977-79, chief environ. protection unit, 1979-82; assoc. Beveridge & Diamond, N.Y.C., 1983-85, ptnr., 1985-89; ptnr., Environmental Dept. Paul Weiss Rifkind Wharton & Garrison, N.Y.C., 1989—. Recipient Spl. Commendation U.S. Dept. Justice, N.Y.C., 1982. Mem. Fed. Bar Coun., N.J. Bar Assn., D.C. Bar Assn., Bar Assn. City N.Y. Office: Paul Weiss Rifkind Wharton & Garrison 1785 Ave of Americas New York NY 10019 Office Phone: 212-373-3351. Fax: 212-373-2104. E-mail: ggwathmey@paulweiss.com.

GWATHMEY, JOE NEIL, JR., broadcast executive; b. Brownwood, Tex., Jan. 4, 1941; s. Joe Neil and Grace Christine (Henry) G.; m. Linda Sue Sams, Aug. 22, 1965; children: Sara Lynn, David Alan. BA, Howard Payne Coll., 1963; postgrad., U. Denver, 1963-64, George Washington U., 1964-65. Sta. mgr. Sta. KUT-FM, Austin, 1965-71; various mgmt. positions Nat. Pub. Radio, Washington, 1971-83, v.p., 1983-88; pres. Tex. Pub. Radio, San Antonio, 1988—. Review panel chair United Way Bexar County, San Antonio, 1994-97; adv. coun. mem. Coll. Fine Arts Univ. Tex., Austin, 1990-93; trustee Tex. Student Publs., Austin, 1995-98, World Affairs Coun., San Antonio, 1999—; bd. adv. N.Y. Festivals, 1986—. Recipient Edward R. Murrow award Corp. Pub. Broadcasting, 1988. Mem. Rotary. Democrat. Protestant. Avocations: singing, acting, public speaking, reading. Home: 2926 Meadow Cir San Antonio TX 78231-1720 Office: Tex Pub Radio 8401 Datapoint Dr Ste 800 San Antonio TX 78229-5903

GWIAZDA, STANLEY JOHN, retired university dean; b. Phila., Feb. 14, 1922; s. Nicholas and Pauline (Stanczak) G.; m. Regina R. Grzeskowiak, Nov. 26, 1944; 1 dau., Marianne C. BS in Mech. Engring., Drexel Inst. Tech., 1944, MS, 1952. Mem. faculty Drexel U., 1946-87, assoc. prof. mech. engring., 1952-87, dean evening coll., 1963-87, assoc. prof. emeritus mech. engring., dean emeritus evening coll., 1987—97; ret., 1997. Bd. dirs. Phila. Govt. Tng. Inst.; mem. pres.'s coun. Holy Family Coll., 1984-89, acad. affairs com., 1989-2002. Author: (with J. H. Billings) Advanced Machine Design, 1958. Lt. (j.g.) USNR, 1944-46, PTO; lt. comdr. Res. ret. Stanley Gwiazda Professorship named in his honor Drexel U.; recipient Vol. Svc. award Holy Family Coll., 1994. Mem. Assn. Univ. Evening Colls. (chmn. com. on faculty devel. 1971-72), Am. Soc. Engring. Edn., Assn. Continuing Higher Edn. (dir. 1976-79, chmn. ethics com. 1979-83, pres. 1985-86, chmn. adv. com. 1986-87, Educator of Yr. award Region IV 1991), Res. Officers Assn. (pres. N.J. dept. 1973-74), Naval Res. Assn., Ret. Officers Assn., Cross Keys, Pi Tau Sigma, Alpha Sigma Lambda (assoc. dir. adult edn. found. 1984-90, bd. dirs. 1990-2002, Alpha Sigma Lambda Leadership award in Adult Edn. 1986). Roman Catholic. Home: 2001 Wayne Ave Haddon Heights NJ 08035-1036

GWIN, DOROTHY JEAN BIRD, psychology educator, college dean, retired; b. Smith, Tex., June 26, 1934; d. Joseph William and Elva Gracie (Elledge) Bird; m. Clinton Dale Gwin, Nov. 21, 1964; 1 child, Clinton Bird. BBA, East Tex. State U., 1954, MS, 1955; EdD, U. Kans., 1958. Lic. psychologist, La. Tchr. Thomas Jefferson High Sch., Port Arthur, Tex., 1954—55; resident dir. U. Kans., Lawrence, 1955-57; sch. psychologist Caddo Parish Schs., Shreveport, La., 1958-67, con. psychologist, 1967-70; prof. psychol., edn. Centenary Coll., Shreveport, La., 1967-79, 1996—, dean, 1979-92, dean enrollment mgmt., 1993—96, prof. edn., psychol. and dir. alumni rels., 1992-93, prof., 1996—97; exec. dir. Cmty. Found. Shreveport-Bossier, Shreveport, La., 1997—2004; bd. dirs. Christus Schumpert Med. Ctr., 2001—04; ret., 2004. Bd. dirs. Vol. of Am., Shreveport, 1967-70; pres. bd. dirs. Southfield Sch., Shreveport, 1984-86, bd. dirs. 1974-87. Fulbright U.S. Ednl. Adminstrs. grantee to Germany, 1990. Mem. Am. Pers. Guidance Assn. (life). Home: 429 Prestwick Ct Nashville TN 37205-5016 Personal E-mail: dbgwin@bellsouth.net.

GWIN, JAMES ELLSWORTH, librarian; b. Chattanooga, Mar. 1, 1947; s. Madison Taylor and Juanita Elizabeth (Wallace) G.; m. Sheena Margaret Mackenzie, Oct. 5, 1985; children; Colleen Mackenzie, Elizabeth Maureen. AB, U. Tenn., 1969; M Library, Emory U., 1970; MPA, Va. Commonwealth U., 1984. Instr., cataloger U. Chattanooga, 1970; asst. prof., asst. head U. Tenn., Chattanooga, 1972-75; head bibliographic svc. U. Richmond, Va., 1975-85, acting univ. librarian, 1985-86, acting dir. LRC, 1986, dir. tech. svc., 1987-99, acting univ. libr. Va., 1990-91, 96-98, dir. libr. collections/spl. collections and rare books, 2000—. Adj. prof. Cath. U. Am., 1994—. Editor Terminal Talk, 1980-81. Dir. Cen. Va. Union List of Serials Project, 1990—. 1st lt. U.S. Army, 1971-72. Lyndhurst Found. grantee, Chattanooga, 1974-75. Mem. ALA, Am. Soc. Pub. Adminstrn., Assn. Coll./Rsch. Libraries (chmn. Va. chpt. 1986), Va. Libr. Assn. (2d v.p. 1992-93), Phi Kappa Phi, Pi Alpha Alpha. Democrat. Episcopalian. Home: 1506 Palmyra Ave Richmond VA 23227-4422 Office: U Richmond Boatwright Meml Libr Richmond VA 23173 E-mail: jgwin@richmond.edu.

GWIN, JAMIE, retired librarian; b. Pine Bluff, Ark., Dec. 12, 1942; d. James Walter and Annette (Bryant) Boast; m. Aaron Gwin, Aug. 15, 1964; children: Marc, Quanta. BSE, U. Ctrl. Ark., 1963; postgrad., Ark. State U., 1986, U. Ark. Little Rock, 1986. Libr. Holly Grove (Ark.) Schs., 1963-64, Monticello (Ark.) Schs., 1964-66, 69-71, U.S. Army, APO 09069, 1967-68, Warren (Ark.) Schs., 1973-75, Woodlawn Sch., Rison, Ark., 1976-79, Wilmar (Ark.) Sch., 1980-87, Crawfordville (Ark.) Sch., 1987-89, West Memphis (Ark.) Sch., 1989—2002; ret. Mem. Sec. Boy Scout Dist., S.E., Ark., 1980-84; chmn. Crittenden County Rep., West Memphis, 1992-94. Recipient John C. Freemont award 1st Congrl. chmn., 1994. Mem. NEA, Ark. Edn. Assn., Wilmar Edn. Assn. (pres. 1984-85). Republican. Baptist. Avocations: crafts, walking, cooking. Home: 1402 Stratford Dr West Memphis AR 72301-2816

GWINN, CASEY, municipal official, lawyer; m. Beth Gwinn; 3 children. BA in Polit. Sci. with honors, Stanford U., 1982; JD, UCLA, 1985. Bar: Calif. 1995. Dep. city atty. City of San Diego, 1985-88, head dep. city atty., 1988-95, prin. asst. to city atty., 1995-96, asst. atty., 1996, atty., 1996—. Faculty Nat. Coll. Dist. Attys., Nat Judges Conf. on Domestic Violence, Nat. Navy Family Advocacy Conf., Nat. U.S. Marine Corps Love and Violence Conf., Calif. Dist. Attys. Assn. Contbr. articles to profl. jours. Adv. bd. Home Start, San Diego Ctr. for Children, Children' Edn. with Care; founder San Diego Task Force on Domestic Violence. Recipient Gov.'s Recognition award, 1990, Diogenes award Pub. Rels. Soc. Am., 1990, Recognition award Nat. Coun. Juvenile and Family Ct. Judges, 1993, State Resolution, Calif. Assembly, 1994; named 1 of Top 45 Pub. Lawyers in Am., American Lawyer. Mem. ABA, Calif. Dist. Attys. Assn., San Diego County Bar Assn., League of Calif. Cities, City Atty. Dept. Office: City Atty Office 1200 3rd Ave Ste 1620 San Diego CA 92101-4178

GWINN, MARY ANN, newspaper reporter; b. Forrest City, Ark., Dec. 29, 1951; d. Lawrence Baird and Frances Evelyn (Jones) Gwinn; m. Richard A. King, June 3, 1973 (div. Jan. 1981); m. Stephen E. Dunnington, June 10, 1990. BA in Psychology, Hendrix Coll., 1973; MEd in Spl. Edn., Ga. State U., 1975; MA in Journalism, U. Mo., 1979. Tchrs. aide DeKalb County Schs., Decatur, Ga., 1973—74, tchr., 1975—78; reporter Columbia (Mo.) Daily Tribune, 1979—83, Seattle Times, 1983—, internat. trade and workplace reporter, 1992—96, asst. city editor, 1996—98, book editor, 1998—. Instr. ext. divsn. U. Wash., Seattle, 1990; instr. journalism Seattle U., 1994. Recipient Edn. Reporting award, Charles Stewart Mott Found., 1980, Enterprising reporting award, C.B. Blethen Family, 1989, Pulitzer Prize for Nat. Reporting, 1990. Mem.: Newspaper Guild. Avocations: writing, gardening, reading, camping. Office: Seattle Times PO Box 70 Seattle WA 98111-0070

GWINN, MARY DOLORES, philosopher, director, writer; b. Oakland, Calif., Sept. 16, 1946; d. Epifanio and Carolina (Lopez) Cruz; m. James Monroe Gwinn, Oct. 23, 1965; 1 child, Larry Allen. Student, Monterey Peninsula Jr. Coll., 1965. Retail store mgr. Consumer's Distbg. divsn. May Co., Hayward, Calif., 1973-78; mktg. rep. Dale Carnegie Courses, San Jose, Calif., 1978-79; founder, pres. Strategic Integrations, Ariz.'s Innovative Bus. Devel. Ctr., Scottsdale, 1985—, Gwinn Genius Inst., Scottsdale, 1998—. Spkr. St. John's Coll. U. Cambridge, England, 1992, INC. Mag., U.S.A., 1996, Clemson Univ., 1996, Antelope Valley Coll., Lancaster, Calif., 1998; founder, pres. Internat. Inst. for Conceptual Edn., Scottsdale, 1993—; chairperson Keble Coll., Oxford (Eng.) U., 1997; spkr. Willard Internat. Hotel, Washington, 2000. Founder new fields of study Genestics and NeuroBus.; profiled the Thought Process of Genius; conceived Whole Brain Business Theory, 1985; author: Genius Leadership Secrets from the Past for the 21st Century, 1995; writer bus. column Gwinn on Bus., IMAGE Networker, Pa., 1996; contbr. articles to profl. jours. Chairperson Keble Coll., Oxford (Eng.) U. Republican. Avocations: reading, imagination games. Home and Office: 5836 E Angela Dr Scottsdale AZ 85254-6410

GWOZDZ, KIM ELIZABETH, interior designer, furniture designer; b. Spokane, Wash., June 10, 1958; d. Myron Marcus and Marilyn Kay (Alsterlund) Westerkamp; children: Ryan Marcus, Lauren Taylor. Student, U. Florence, Italy, 1979; BFA in Graphic Design, Illustration and Art History, U. Ariz., 1980. Interior designer Pat Bacon & Assocs., 1983-88; prin, interior designer Kim E. Gwozdz/Provenance, Phoenix, 1988—. Prin., designer Marcus Taylor Furniture. Contbr. articles to profl. jours. Mem. Mt. Cavalry Luth. Ch., Phoenix, 1981-96, trustee, 1993-96; mem. Christ Luth. Ch., Phoenix, 1996-2002; Jr. League of Phoenix, 1989—, HIV/AIDS com., 1994-2000; mem. Orpheum Theater com., 1989-94, vice chmn., 1990-91, chmn., 1992-2002, Gift Mart com. Design Decorations, 1991-92, chmn., 1991, exec. com. Orpheum Theatre Found., 1989-91, bd. dirs., 1992—; active annual gala com. Am. Cancer Soc., 1993-94, 94-95, 95-96, 97-98, 98—, March of Dimes Gourmet Gala, 1991, 93, 95, 97; design affiliate Nat. Trust for Hist. Preservation, 1986—. Recipient 1st place award Ann. Wool Rug Design Competition, Edward Fields, Inc., 1989, 2d place award, 1990, 3d place award, 1991; Internat. Illumination design awards, 1998, Cutler award, 1998, Lumen award, 1998. Mem. Am. Soc. Interior Designers (assoc. Ariz. North chpt., significant interiors survery com. 1975-91, chmn. 1990-91, Phoenix Home and Garden com. 1989-90, Herberger Theatre com. 1989-91, awards com. 1989, 91, chmn. 1990, competitions com. 1991, 96, chmn. 1989-90, Rosson House Christmas chmn. 1986-91, hist. preservation chmn. 1988-91, directory chmn. Designers Market 1991, project designer, 1996, 97, mem. nominating com. 1991-92, 98, mktg. com. 1995, 3d place award Ariz. Norh 1987, 96, 2d place award 1987, 88, 92, 95, 1st place award Nat. 1989, 94, 95, 97). Republican. Lutheran. Avocations: art, gardening, cooking. Home: 4820 E Merrell St Phoenix AZ 85018 Office: 2415 E Camelback Rd Ste 700 Phoenix AZ 85016-4245

GWYNN, ANTHONY KEITH (TONY GWYNN), former professional baseball player; b. LA, May 9, 1960; m. Alicia Gwynn; children: Anthony, Anisha Nicole. Student, San Diego State U. Player minor league teams, Walla Walla and Amarillo, Hawaii, 1981—82; outfielder San Diego Padres, 1982—2001; ret.; baseball coach San Diego State, 2002; now baseball analyst ESPN. Named MVP, N.W. League, 1981; named to All-Star Team, 1984—87, 1989—96, Silver Slugger Team, Sporting News Nat. League, 1984, All-Star Team, 1984, World Sports Humanitarian Hall of Fame, 1999, MLB All Century Team, 2000; recipient Batting Title award, Nat. League, 1984, 1987, 1988, 1989, 1995, Gold Glove award, 1986—87, 1989—91, Silver Slugger Team, Sporting News Nat. League, 1986—87, 1989—91, All-Star Team, 1986—87, 1986—87, 1989, 1994, Branch Rickey award, 1995, Roberto Clemente Man of the Yr. award, 1999, Lou Gehrig Meml. award, 1999. Achievements include being drafted by both MLB San Diego Padres and NBA LA Clippers. Mailing: care ESPN Baseball 935 Middle St Bristol CT 06010*

GYAMFI, CYNTHIA, gynecologist, obstetrician, maternal-fetal medicine specialist; b. Dusseldorf, Germany, Oct. 28, 1972; arrived in U.S., 1977; d. Anthony Ransford and Mary Gyamfi. BS, U. Miami, 1994, MD, 1998. Cert. U.S. Med. Lic. exam. Intern ob-gyn. U. Miami, Jackson Meml. Hosp., 1998—99, resident ob-gyn., 1999—2002; attending ob-gyn. Elmhurst Hosp. Ctr., NY, 2002—05; asst. clin. prof. maternal-fetal medicine Columbia U., 2005—. Fellow maternal fetal medicine Mt. Sinai Med. Ctr., N.Y.C., 2002—05. Contbr. articles to profl. jours. Mem.: Nat. Med. Assn., Am. Inst. Ultrasound Medicine, Am. Coll. Ob-Gyn. (jr. fellow, sec.-treas. Dist. II 2003—04, jr. fellow, vice chmn. dist. II 2004—05, jr. fellow, chmn. dist. II 2005—), Soc. Maternal Fetal Medicine (assoc.). Office: Columbia U Divsn Maternal-Fetal Medicine Dept Ob-Gyn 622 W 168th St PH-16 New York NY 10032

GYEMANT, ROBERT ERNEST, diversified financial services company executive, merchant banker; b. Managua, Nicaragua, Jan. 17, 1944; arrived in U.S., 1949, naturalized, 1954; s. Emery Gyemanat and Magda (Von Rechnitz) Gyemant; m. Sally Bartch Libhart, Oct. 17, 1992; children: Emily Bartch, Amanda Nancy, Katherine Libhart;children from previous marriage: Robert Ernest Jr., Anne Elizabeth. AB magna cum laude, UCLA, 1965; JD, U. Calif., Berkeley, 1968. CPA Calif.; bar: Calif. 1969, NY 1981. Tax acct. Ernst & Ernst, CPAs, Oakland, Calif., 1966—68; assoc. atty. Orrick, Herrington, Rowley & Sutcliffe, San Francisco, 1968—69; ptnr. Skornia, Rosenblum & Gyemant, San Francisco, 1969—74, Robert Ernest Gyemant PC, San Francisco, 1975; exec. v.p. fin. Topps & Trowsers, San Francisco, 1977—79; cons., pvt. investor ComDial Corp., San Francisco, 1979; co-founder Com Vu Corp., N.Y.C., 1979—83, San Francisco, 1993—97; prin. Knapp, Petersen & Clarke, P.C., Glendale, Calif., 1997—99, Hill, Farrer & Burrill, LLP, LA, 1999—2000; mng. dir. Trinity River Capital Ventures, LLC; CEO Trio Industries Holdings, LLC. Instr. U. Calif., Berkeley, 1968; gen. coun., sec. Advanced Micro Devices, Inc., Sunnyvale, Calif., 1972—74. Editor: Calif. Law Rev., 1967—68; contbr. articles to profl. jours. Hon. vice consul Republic of Costa Rica, 1981—; trustee French-Am. Bilingual Sch., San Francisco, 1978—82; mem., ptnr. Calif. Council Criminal Justice Jud. Process Task Force, 1971—73; mem. Calif. State Rep. Ctrl. Com. Mem.: AICPA, ABA, Calif. Trial Lawyers Assn., Assn. Def. Counsel, Calif. CPA Soc. (mem. accounting prins. com. 1969), State Bar Calif. (cert. specialist criminal law 1988—93, com. on unauthorized practice law 1974—76, spl. com. on juvenile justice 1974, commr. San Francisco County juvenile justice comm. 1976—), San Francisco Bar Assn. (co-chmn. sect. on juvenile justice 1971), San Francisco Downtown Assn., Racquet and Tennis Club, N.Y. Athletic Club (N.Y.C.), Brook Haven Country Club. Office: 8411 Preston Rd #850 Dallas TX 75225 E-mail: rgyemant@trioindustries.net.

GYFTOPOULOS, ELIAS PANAYIOTIS, mechanical and nuclear engineering educator; b. Athens, Greece, July 4, 1927; came to U.S., 1953, naturalized, 1963; s. Panayiotis Elias and Despina (Louvaris) G.; m. Artemis S. Scalleri, Sept. 3, 1962; children: Vasso, Maro, Rena. Diploma in Mech. and Elec. Engring., Tech. U. Athens, 1953; Sc.D. in Elec. Engring., M.I.T., 1958; Dr. (hon.), Tech. U. Athens, Greece, 1992, Tech. U. Nova Scotia, Halifax, Canada, 1997, Dalhousie U. Poly., Halifax, Can., 1997, U. Patras, Greece, 2001. Registered profl. engr., Mass. Instr. MIT, Cambridge, 1955-58, asst. prof., 1958-61, assoc. prof., 1961—65, prof., 1965—70, Ford prof. engring., 1970-96; chmn. Nat. Energy Council Greece, 1975-78. Bd. dirs. Thermo Electron Corp., Waltham, Mass., Thermo Retec Corp., Waltham, ThermoLase Corp., San Diego, ThermoCardio Systems, Woburn, Mass., Thermo Spectra Corp., Waltham, Trex Med. Corp., Dunbury, Conn., others; cons. in field. Author: Thermionic Energy Conversion, vol. 1, 1973, vol. 2, 1979, Fuel Effectiveness in Industry, 1974; editor-in-chief 17 Energy Conservation Manuals, 1982, Thermodynamics: Foundations and Applications, 1991, 2d edit., 2005. Trustee Anatolia Coll., Salonika, Greece, 1971-2001; vice chmn. bd. trustees, 1988-2001. With Greek Navy, 1948-51. Fellow: AAAS, ASME (James Harry Potter Gold medal 1995, Robert Henry Thurston award 2002, Edward Obert award 2001), NAE, Acad. Athens, Am. Acad. Arts and Scis., Am. Nuc. Soc. (bd. dirs. 1966—69); mem.: Philol. Soc. Parnassos. Greek Orthodox. Office: MIT Dept Nuclear Sci and Engring Rm 24-111 77 Mass Ave Cambridge MA 02139-4307 E-mail: epgyft@aol.com.

GYLES, MARY FRANCIS, retired history professor; b. Blackville, SC, Dec. 24, 1918; d. Ronald Corbin and Valeria Gyles. BA, U.N.C., Greensboro, 1939; MA, U. N.C., Chapel Hill, 1945, PhD, 1949. Asst. prof. Memphis State U., 1949-57; asst. prof. ancient and medieval history Bklyn. Coll., CUNY, 1957-63, assoc. prof., 1963-65, prof., 1965-79, prof. emerita, 1979—, chmn. dept. history, 1963-70. Instr. U SC, Aiken, 1981—91. Author: (essays in ancient history) Laudatores Temporis Acti, 1964, (with Caldwell) The Ancient World, 1966, Public Gardens of South Carolina 1999-2000, 2001; columnist S.C. Gardener, 1995—. Chmn. Garden Club SC, Columbia, 1989—, bd. dirs., chmn. hist. trails 1998-99, chmn. hort. 1997-99, chmn. botanic gardens 1999—, columnist, writer SC Gardener, 1995—; master flower show judge Nat. Garden Clubs, St. Louis, 1985—; creator meml. garden Christ Episcopal Ch., Denmark, SC, 2004-05 Recipient Pres.'s citation Garden Club S.C., 1997, also Dir.'s award, Helen S. Hull plaque Nat. Garden Club, Inc., 2003, Literary Horticulture Interest award, Nat. Garden Club, 2003. Mem. Judges Club S.C. (2d v.p. 1999—, ednl. displayer), DIA Study Club (pres. 2002-03), Phi Beta Kappa, Phi Alpha Theta. Democrat. Episcopalian. Avocations: reading, writing, gardening, travel.

GYLES, ROBERT, mathematics professor; b. Aiken, S.C., Aug. 18, 1945; s. Nossie Gyles Dillard; 1 child, Taisha Elaine. BS, S.C. State U., 1967; MA, NYU, 1975, PhD, 1988. Dir. math. Cmty. Sch. Dist., N.Y.C. Dept. Edn., 1983—91, dir. curriculum and profl. devel., 1991—95, dep. supt., 1996—2003; prof. math. Hunter Coll., CUNY, 2003—. Cons. math. edn. Create-A-Vision, Forest City, Calif., 1995—; mem. math. stds. adv. panel N.Y. State Edn. Dept., Albany, 2004—; mem. math. adv. com. N.Y.C. Dept. Edn., 2004—. Co-author: Math Central, 1998, Breakaway Math, 2004. With U.S. Army, 1969—71. Decorated Commendation medal. Mem.: Nat. Coun.

Tchrs. Math., Alpha Phi Alpha, Phi Delta Kappa. Avocations: jogging, spinning. Home: 301 Cathedral Pky Apt 11G New York NY 10026 Office: Hunter Coll CUNY 695 Park Ave New York NY 10021

GYLL, JOHN SÖREN, marketing executive; b. Skorped, Västernorrland, Sweden, Dec. 26, 1940; s. Josef and Gertrud G.; m. Lilly Margareta Hellman, 1974; 3 children. Higher cert. exam. and univ. degrees, D (hon.) in Tech., 2004. Mktg. mgr., v.p. Rank-Xerox AB, 1963-77; pres. Uddeholm-Sweden, 1977-79, exec. v.p., 1979-81; pres., CEO, Uddelholm-AB, 1981-84; CEO, Procordia AB, Stockholm, 1984-92; pres., CEO, AB Volvo, Göteborg, Sweden, 1992-97. Bd. dirs. SCA AB, Skanska AB, SKF AB. Mem.: Royal Swedish Acad. Engring. Scis. Avocations: hunting, golf, skiing. Office: Strand Promenaden 3 SE-131 50 Saltsjö-Duvnäs Sweden

GYLLENHAAL, ANDERS, publishing executive, editor; b. Cleve. m. Beverly Mills Gyllenhaal; children: Grey, Sam. B in journalism, George Washington U. Reporter The Daily News Record, Harrisonburg, Va., The Press, Atlantic City, The Miami Herald, 1979—89, editor Ft. Lauderdale bur., 1989—91; metro editor News & Observer, Raleigh, NC, 1991—95, mng. editor, 1995—97, exec. editor, sr. v.p., 1997—2001; sr. v.p. Star Tribune, Mpls., 2002—, editor, 2002—. Mem. Pulitzer Prize Bd., 2001—. Mem.: Am. Soc. Newspaper Editors. Office: Star Tribune 425 Portland Ave Minneapolis MN 55488 Business E-Mail: agyllenhaal@startribune.com.*

GYLLENHAAL, JAKE, actor; b. Los Angeles, Calif., Dec. 19, 1980; s. Stephen Gyllenhaal and Naomi Foner. Attended, Columbia U. Actor: (films) City Slickers, 1991, A Dangerous Woman, 1993, Josh and S.A.M., 1993, Homegrown, 1998, October Sky, 1999, Donnie Darko, 2001, Bubble Boy, 2001, Lovely and Amazing, 2001, The Good Girl, 2002, Moonlight Mile, 2002, Highway, 2002, The Day After Tomorrow, 2004, Proof, 2005; (plays) This is Our Youth (London Evening Standard Theatre award Oustanding Newcomer, 2002). Office: CAA 9830 Wilshire Blvd Beverly Hills CA 90212-1825*

GYLLENHAAL, MAGGIE, actress; b. NYC, Nov. 16, 1977; d. Stephen Gyllenhaal and Naomi Foner. BA in English, Columbia U., 1999. Actor: (TV series) Shake Rattle and Roll: An American Love Story, 1999; (TV films) Shattered Mind, 1996, The Patron Saint of Liars, 1998, Resurrection, 1999, Strip Search, 2004; (films) Waterland, 1992, A Dangerous Woman, 1993, Homegrown, 1998, The Photographer, 2000, Cecil B. Demented, 2000, Pornographer: A Love Story, 2000, Donnie Darko, 2001, Riding in Cars with Boys, 2001, Secretary, 2002, 40 Days and 40 Nights, 2002, Adaptation, 2002, Confessions of a Dangerous Mind, 2002, Casa de los babys, 2003, Mona Lisa Smile, 2003, Criminal, 2004, Happy Endings, 2005, The Great New Wonderful, 2005. Office: Creative Artists Agy 9830 Wilshire Blvd Beverly Hills CA 90212*

GYOHTEN, TOYOO, economist; b. Yokohama, Japan, 1931; married; 2 children. BA in Econs., U. Tokyo, 1955; postgrad., Princeton U., U.S.A., 1956-58. With Ministry Fin., Tokyo, 1955-89, Japan Desk, Internat. Monetary Fund, Washington, 1964-66; spl. asst. to pres. Asian Devel. Bank, Manila, Philippines, 1966-69; dir. gen. Internat. Fin. Bur., Ministry of Fin., Tokyo, 1984-86; vice min. fin. for internat. affairs Ministry of Fin., Tokyo, 1986-89; with The Bank of Tokyo, Ltd. (merged with Mitsubishi Bank Ltd.), Tokyo, 1991—; chmn. bd. dirs. The Bank of Tokyo, Ltd., Tokyo, 1992-96; sr. advisor The Bank of Tokyo-Mitsubishi, Ltd., 1996—; spl. advisor to Prime Minister of Japan, 1998. Pres. Inst. for Internat. Monetary Affairs, 1995—; chmn. working party III OECD, Paris, 1988-90; vis. prof. Harvard U., 1990, Princeton U., 1990-91, U. St. Gallen, Switzerland, 1991; trustee Princeton in Asia, N.J.; mem. adv. panel East African Devel. Bank, Uganda, Asia Pacific Adv. Comm., N.Y. Stock Exch.; mem. exec. com. Trilateral Comm., N.Y., Paris, Tokyo; mem. internat. coun. The Asia Soc., N.Y., Group of Thirty, Washington. Co-author (with Paul Volcker): Changing Fortunes, 1992. Office: Inst Internat Monetary Aff 1-3-2 Nihombashi-Hongokucho Chuo-ku Tokyo 103-0021 Japan

GYSBERS, NORMAN CHARLES, counselor, educator; b. Waupun, Wis., Sept. 29, 1932; s. George S. and Mabel (Landaal) Gysbers; m. Mary Lou Ziegler, June 23, 1954 (dec. July 1997); children: David(dec.), Debra, Daniel; m. Barbara K. Townsend, May 12, 2001. *Daughter-in-law, Cheryl Gysbers, is a special education teacher in Harrisburg, Missouri. She has two children, Melissa and Justin. Daughter, Debra Landes, is a Learning and Organizational Development Specialist, J.P. Morgan, Kansas City, Missouri. She has two children, Kaitlin and Samuel. Son, Daniel Gysbers, is a board certified anesthesiologist in Columbia, Missouri. His wife, Katherine, is Assistant Clinical Professor, General Internal Medicine, Rusk Rehabilitation, Center, Columbia, Missouri. They have three children, Jackson, David, and Emma. Wife, Barbara Townsend, is a Professor in the Department of Educational Leadership and Policy Analysis, University of Missouri-Columbia.* AB, Hope Coll., 1954; MA, U. Mich., 1959, PhD, 1963. Tchr. Elem. and Jr. H.S., Muskegon Heights, Mich., 1954-56; lectr. edn. U. Mich., 1962-63; prof. counseling psychology U. Mo., Columbia, 1963—. Cons. U.S. Office Edn.; mem. nat. adv. coms. ERIC Clearinghouses in Career Edn. and Counseling and Pers. Svcs.; rsch. and devel. com. for CEEB, Am. Insts. for Rsch. Project on Career Decision Making, Comprehensive Career Edn. Model, TV Career Awareness Project KCET-TV, L.A.; dir. 10 nat. rsch. projects and state projects in career devel.-guidance; Francqui prof. Universite Libre de Bruxelles. *With Earl J. Moore and later, Patricia Henderson, developed one of the first comprehensive school guidance and counseling program models in the United States. The model has been adopted by many states and local school districts. It served as the foundation model for the American School Counselor Association's national model. Several states have included the language model in their state education laws. The model has been adapted for use in other countries including Hong Kong and Turkey. Also known for work in career development and career counseling.* Editor: Vocat. Guidance Quar. 1962-70; (with L. Sunny Hansen) spl. issue Personnel and Guidance Jour., May 1975, Jour. Career Devel., 1979-, (with E. Moore and W. Miller) Developing Careers in the Elementary School, 1973, (with E. Moore and H. Drier) Career Guidance: Practices and Perspectives, 1973; author: (with E. Moore) Improving Guidance Programs, 1981, Designing Careers, 1984, (with E. Moore) Career Counseling, 1987, (with P. Henderson) Developing and Managing Your School Guidance Program, 1988, 3d edit., 2000, (with C. McDaniels) Counseling for Career Development, 1992, (with P. Henderson) Guidance Programs that Work, 1997, (with M. Heppner and J. Johnston) Career Counseling, 1998, 2d edit., 2003, (with P. Henderson) Leading and Managing Your School Guidance Program Staff, 1998, (with P. Henderson) Implementing Comprehensive School Guidance Programs, 2002; contbr. articles to profl. jours. and chpts. to textbooks. Elder Presbyn. Ch. Served with arty. U.S. Army, 1956-58. Recipient Am. Spirit award, USAF, 1987, Pillar of Excellence Ten Yr. award, Coll. Edn. U. Mo., 2003, Excellence in Tchg. award, Gov., 2004; William T. Kemper Excellence in Tchg. fellow, U. Mo., 2002. Mem.: ACA (pres. 1977—78, disting. profl. svc. award 1983), Internat. Assn. Ednl. and Vocat. Guidance, Mo. Guidance Assn. (outstanding svc. award 1978), Am. Vocat. Assn. (v.p. 1979—82, merit award guidance divsn. 1978), Am. Sch. Counselor Assn. (post-secondary sch. counselor of yr. 2001, Mary Gehake Lifetime Achievement award 2004), Assn. for Counselor Edn. and Supervision, Nat. Career Devel. Assn. (pres. 1972—73, nat. merit award 1981, Eminent Career award 1989). Home: 4 Bingham Rd Columbia MO 65203 Office: U Mo 201 G Student Success Ctr Columbia MO 65211-6060 Office Phone: 573-882-6386. E-mail: gysbersn@missouri.edu.

GYUROV, BOYKO, mathematics professor; s. Georgi Gyurov and Maria Gyurova. PhD in Math., U. Ark., Fayettville, 2005. Advt. dir. Digital Media Group, Blagoevgrad, Bulgaria, 1995; asst. prof. South-West U., Blagoevgrad, Bulgaria, 1996—2000; grad. asst. U. Ark., Fayetteville, 2000—05; risk analysis mgr. Wal-Mart Inc., Bentonville, Ark., 2003—04. Vis. asst. prof. U. Limerick, Ireland, 1997—98. John C. Massie fellow, U. Ark. Math. Dept., 2004. Mem.: AMS. Avocations: travel, writing. Home: 707 Treadwell Apt 8 Fayetteville AR 72701 Fax: 479-575-8630. E-mail: bgyurov@uark.edu.

HA, CHANG SIK, polymer science educator; b. Pusan, Jan. 30, 1956; s. Won Do and Bong Soon (Eh) H.; m. Sun Ja Han, Jan. 13, 1983; children: Ji Won, Ji Hyun, Jae Hun. BS, Pusan Nat. U., 1978; MS, Korea Adv. Inst. Sci. & Tech., Seoul, 1980, PhD, 1987. Engr. Lucky Chem. Co. Ltd., Pusan, 1982; from instr. to asst. prof. Pusan Nat. U., 1982-89, faculty advisor univ. English newspaper, 1987, assoc. prof., 1989-94, chmn. dept., 1992-94, prof., 1994—, assoc. dean of planning, 2000-01. Vis. scholar U. Cin., 1988-89, Stanford U., 1997-98, SUNY-Buffalo, 2004; mem. editl. adv. bd. Materials Sci. Found. (Trans Tech. Publs. Switzerland). Author: Polymer Chemistry, 1990, Polymer Processing, 1991, Polymer Engineering, I, 1995, II, 1997; editor: Polymer: Structure and Properties, 1988; mem. editl. bd. Material Sci. Found., 1998—; editor Macromolecular Rsch.; contbr. numerous articles to sci. jours. on polymer blends and composites, periodic mesoporous organosilicas, or organic electroluminescent devices. Recipient Best Paper of Yr. award, Korean Fed. Sci. Tech. Soc., 2003. Mem. Korean Acad. Sci. Tech., Nat. Acad. Engring. Korea, Am. Chem. Soc., Am. Phys. Soc., N.Y. Acad. Scis., Polymer Soc. Korea (Polymer Science award 1995), Soc. Polymer Sci. Japan, Korean Inst. Rubber Industries (Best Paper of Yr. award 1989). Roman Catholic. Avocations: classical music, climbing. Office: Pusan Nat U Dept Polymer Sci & Engring Pusan 609-735 Republic of Korea Fax: 82-51-514-4331. Office Phone: 82-51-510-2407. Business E-Mail: csha@pnu.edu. E-mail: csha@pusan.ac.kr.

HA, CHONG WAN, information technology executive; b. Chin-ju, Kyung-Nam, South Korea, Oct. 25, 1938; came to U.S., 1963; s. Kyung-sik and Kyung-Nam (Park) H.; m. Karen Hye-Ja Han, Aug. 19, 1968; children: Jean Frances, Julie Ann. BA in Econs., UCLA, 1970; MA in Mgmt., Claremont (Calif.) U., 1985. Sr. systems analyst Atlantic Richfield Co., Los Angeles, 1972-78; asst. v.p. 1st Interstate Services Co., Los Angeles, 1978-85; v.p. Ticor Title Ins. Co., Los Angeles, 1985-91; assoc. dir. MCA/Universal Studios, 1991; dir. State of Calif. Stephen P. Teale Data Ctr., Sacramento, 1991-97; v.p. LCS, Inc., Sacramento, 1997-99; pres., chief tech. officer Ha Technologies, Burbank, Calif., 1999-2000; chief tech. officer enterprise tech. svcs. 21st Century Ins. Group, Woodland Hills, Calif., 2000—. Exec. com. Calif. Forum on Info. Tech.; adv. bd. Govt. Tech. Conf., 1994. Res. police officer Monterey Park (Calif.) Police Dept., 1981-82; bd. dirs. Asian Pacific Alumni Assn., UCLA, 1988, Asian Pacific Am. Legal Found., L.A., 1988, Korean Youth Ctr.; mem. alumni coun. Claremont Grad. Sch., 1993. Recipient Peter Drucker Ctr. Alumni award, 1994, Calif. State Atty. Gen. award, 1994, Carnegie Mellon U. and AMS Achievement award in mng. info. tech., 1995. Mem.: Soc. Info. Mgmt., UCLA Chancellors Cir. Avocations: golf, classical music, reading. Office Phone: 818-715-6537. Personal E-mail: chong.ha@21st.com.

HA, YONGGANG, optical engineer; b. Nanjing, Jiangxi, China, Oct. 30, 1974; s. Genzhu Ha and Fengsheng Yang; m. Shuxin Li, July 26, 2000; 1 child, Lucy. PhD, Beijing Inst. Tech., 2000. Cert. optical designer, OSA. Postdoc CREOL, Orlando, Fla., 2000—01, assoc. dir. optical design, 2001—. Contbr. articles to profl. jours. Mem.: Sci. Rsch. Soc., Internat. Soc. Optical Engring. Achievements include patents for Compact Lenses for Head Mount Displays. Office: Univ Ctrl Fla 4000 Central Florida Blvd Orlando FL 32816-2700 Office Phone: 407-823-6830. E-mail: ha@odalab.ucf.edu.

HAACK, RICHARD WILSON, retired police officer; b. Chgo., July 7, 1935; s. Arthur Frank and Mildred Ann (Meyer) Haack; m. Ruth Marie Tietz, May 27, 1972; children: Laura Marie, Karl Richard. Grad., Sheriff's Police Acad., Cook County (Ill.), 1967; AS, Triton Coll., 1973; cert., Chgo. Police Acad., 1974; BA, Lewis U., 1975; MA, Northeastern Ill. U., 1979; BS in Bus. Adminstrn., Elmhurst Coll., 1982. Shipping clk. Am. Furniture Mart, Chgo., 1955-60; quality control insp. Nat. Can Co., Chgo., 1961-67; police officer Northlake (Ill.) Police Dept., 1967-92, watch comdr. patrol divsn., 1978-85, dept. chief of police, 1986-87, in-svc. tng. coord., 1991-92; ret., 1992. Realtor Internat. Realty World-Norton & Assocs., 1984—87. Author: Ency. Am. Judiciary; contbr. articles to profl. jours. Mem. Bill Bruce fundraising com. Aid Assn. Luths., Christ Evang. Luth. Ch., Northlake, 1981—82; mem. Gala Varsity Show, 1982, chmn. evang. bd., 1981—85; dir., emcee German-Am. Police Assn., 1980—2001; emcee Oktoberfest, 1980—99, chmn. entertainment, 1984—2001, assoc. membership chmn., 2001—; coach baseball team Northlake Little League, 1985; trustee Northlake Police Pension Fund, 1997—; active March of Dimes-Mothers March, 1997—99; dir. emcee Greeter Immanuel Luth. Ch., 2003—; ch. rep. Internat. Luth. Laymen's League, 1984—, pub. rels. dir., usher, 1973—85; choir Apostles Luth. Ch., 1985—87; membership chmn. Redeemer Luth. Ch. Men's Club, 1995—99; chmn. program com. Greeter Immanuel Luth. Ch., 2003—. With USMC, 1952—55, with USMCR, 1955—60, Korea. Recipient John Edgar Hoover Meml. Gold medal, 1987, numerous letters of commendation, competitive shooting awards. Mem.: NRA, Realtors Polit. Action Com. Ill. (inner cir. 1984—87), Internat. Platform Assn., Leyden Real Estate Bd. (inner cir. 1984—87), N.W. Real Estate Bd., Am. Polit. Sci. Assn., Emerald Soc. Ill. Irish/Am. Police Assn., Ill. Juvenile Officers Assn., Internat. Juvenile Officers Assn., Combined Counties Police Assn., Nat. Police Officers Assn., St. Jude Police League, Internat. Assn. Chiefs Police, German/Am. Police Assn. (life; bd. dirs.), Internat. Assn. Police (life), Fraternal Order Police (life; sec.-treas. Perri-Nagle Meml. Lodge 18 1977—85), Ill. Police Assn. (life), Korean War Vets.-Navy League, Northeastern Ill. U. Alumni Assn. (bd. dirs. 1980—86), Ret. and Disabled Polic Am., Kaire Ind. Distbr., Sharkhunters, Die Hard Cub Fans, Moose, Am. Legion, Schwaben Verein. Republican. Home: 244 E Palmer Ave Northlake IL 60164-1735 Office: 55 E North Ave Northlake IL 60164-1735 Office Phone: 708-562-0634. Personal E-mail: haackpack@comcast.net.

HAACKE, HANS CHRISTOPH CARL, artist, educator; b. Cologne, Germany, Aug. 12, 1936; s. Carl and Antonie Haacke; m. Linda Snyder, 1965; 2 sons. MFA, State Acad., Kassel, 1960; DFA (hon.), Oberlin Coll., 1991; D (hon.), Bauhaus U., Weimar, Germany, 1998. Asst. prof. Cooper Union for Advancement of Sci. and Art, N.Y.C., 1971—75, assoc. prof., 1975-79, prof., 1979—2002, prof. emeritus, 2002—. Guest prof. Hochschule für Bildende Künste, Hamburg, 1973, 94, Gesamthochschule, Essen, 1979. One-man shows include Galerie Schmela, Düsseldorf, 1965, Howard Wise Gallery, N.Y.C., 1966, 68, 69, Galerie Paul Maenz, Cologne, 1971, 74, 81, Museum Haus Lange, Krefeld, 1972, John Weber Gallery, N.Y.C., 1973, 75, 77, 79, 81, 83, 85, 88, 90, 92, 94, Kunstverein Frankfurt, 1976, Galerie Durand-Dessert, Paris, 1977, 78, Mus. of Modern Art, Oxford, 1978, Stedelijk Van Abbemuseum, Eindhoven, 1979, Renaissance Soc., Chgo., 1979, Galerie France Morin, Montreal, Que., Can., 1983, Tate Gallery, London, 1984, Neue Gesellschaft für Bildende Kunst, Berlin, 1984, Kunsthalle, Berne, 1985, Le Consortium, Dijon, France, 1986, The New Mus. Contemporary Art, N.Y.C., 1986, Victoria Miro Gallery, London, 1987, Centre Georges Pompidou, Paris, 1989, Biennale Venice, Italy, 1993, Fundació Antoni Tàpies, Barcelona, 1995, Mus. Boijmans Van Beuningen, Rotterdam, 1996, German Parliament Bldg., commn. permanent installation, Berlin, opened 2000, Portikus, Frankfurt, 2000, Serpentine Gallery, London, 2001, Generali Found., Vienna, 2001; group exhbns. Stedelijk Mus., Amsterdam, 1962, 65, 82, Mus. Modern Art, N.Y.C., 1968, 70, 88, 99, Tokyo Biennale, 1970, Jewish Mus., N.Y.C., 1970, 94, Documenta Kassel, 1972, 82, 87, 97, Biennale Venice, 1976, 78, Mus. van Hedendaagse Kunst, Ghent, Belgium, 1980, Hirshhorn Mus., Washington, 1984, Palais des Beaux-Arts, Brussels, 1984, Sydney (Australia) Biennale, 1984, 90, Sao Paulo (Brazil) Biennale, 1985, Nationalgalerie, Berlin, 1984, Centre Georges Pompidou, 1987, 89, 90, 92, 96, 2000, Musée d'Art Moderne de la Ville de Paris, 1981, 89, L.A. Cty. Mus., 1987, 2001, 04, Whitney Mus., NY, 1989, 1999, 2000, State Russian Mus., St. Petersburg, 1990, Irish Mus. Modern Art, Dublin, 1992, Musée d'art contemporain, Montreal, 1992, 2003, Bundeskunsthalle, Bonn, Germany, 1992, Kunsthalle Basel, Basel, Switzerland, 1994, 2004, Mus. Contemporary Art, L.A., 1995, 2004, Mus. Contemporary Art, Tokyo, 1995; Stage set: Ernst Jünger, Volksbühne, Berlin, 1994, Skulptur Projekte Münster, Germany, 1997, Deutschlandbilder, Gropius-Bau, Berlin, 1997, Berlin-Moskau, Gropius-Bau, Berlin, 2003-04, Johannesburg Biennale, 1997, Mus. Hamburger Bahnhof, Berlin, 1999, Museu Serralves, Porto, Portugal, 1999, 2004, Mus. Contemporary Art, Barcelona, 2000, 04, Tate Modern London, 2000, 05, Generali Found., Vienna, 2001, 05, Nat. Portrait Gallery, London, 2000, Hayward Gallery, London, 2000, Haus der Kunst, Munich, 2000, 05, ZKM, Karlsruhe, Germany, 2002, Moscow-Berlin, Hist. Mus., Moscow, 2004, Nat. Mus. Art, 2004; author: (with Edward F. Fry) Werkmonographie, 1972, (with others) Framing and Being Framed, 1975, Nach allen Regeln der Kunst, 1984, (with others) Unfinished Business, 1987, Artfairismes, 1989, (with others) Bodenlos, 1993, Mia san mia, 2001, (with Pierre Bourdieu) Libre-Echange, 1994, Obra Social, 1995, AnsichtsSachen/ViewingMatters, 1999, Haus Haacke, 2004; contbr. articles to profl. jours Recipient Golden Lion Venice Biennale, Peter Weiss prize, Bochum, 2004. Office: The Cooper Union Cooper Square New York NY 10003

HAAG, CAROL ANN GUNDERSON, marketing professional, consultant, hotel executive; b. Mpls. d. Glenn Alvin and Genevieve Esther (Knudson) Gunderson; m. Lawrence S. Haag, Aug. 30, 1969; 1 child, Maren Anne. BJ, U. Mo., 1969; postgrad., Roosevelt U., Chgo., 1975—. Pub. rels. writer, advt. copywriter Am. Hosp. Supply Corp., Evanston, Ill., 1969-70; asst. dir. pub. rels. Rush-Presbyn. St. Luke's Med. Ctr., Chgo., 1970-71; asst. mgr. pub. and employee comm. Quaker Oats Co., Chgo., 1971-72, mgr. editl. comm., 1972-74, mgr. employee comm. programs, 1974-77; dir. pub. rels. Shaklee Corp., San Francisco, 1978-82; pres. CH & Assocs., San Francisco, 1982-84; dir corp. comm. BRAE Corp., San Francisco, 1984; dir. mktg. St. Francis Meml. Hosp., San Francisco, 1985-89, dir. mktg. and planning svcs., 1989-91; ptnr. Haag & Rohan, San Francisco, San Diego, 1991—; pres. Sci. Symposiums Internat., Moraga, 1998—. Examiner Calif. Coun. for Quality and Svc., 1997, 98, sr. examiner, 1999; cons. in field. Bd. dirs. Calif. League Handicapped; mem. adv. bd. San Francisco Spl. Olympics; mem. pub. relations com. San Francisco Recreation and Parks Dept., San Francisco Vol. Bur. Recipient 1st place cert. Printing Industry Am., 1972, 74, 1st place spl. comm. award Internat. Assn. Bus. Communicators, 1974, 1st place citation Chgo. Assn. Bus. Communicators, 1974, gold award Healthcare Mktg. Reports, 1989, 90. Mem. NATAS, Indsl. Com. Coun., Pub. Rels. Soc. Am., San Francisco C. of C. (grad. leadership program 1991, bd. dirs. leadership coun.), Lafayette C. of C., Concord C. of C., Moraga Bus. Assn. Home and Office: 133 Fernwood Dr Moraga CA 94556-2315 E-mail: haagassoc1@aol.com.

HAAG, EVERETT KEITH, architect; b. Cuyahoga Falls, Ohio, Jan. 27, 1928; s. Arnold and Lois (Martz) H.; m. Eleanor Jean Baker, Nov. 1, 1961; children— Kurt, Paula, Pamela. BS in Architecture, Kent State U., 1951; B.Arch., Western Res. U., 1953. Founder, prin. firm Keith Haag & Assos. (architects), Cuyahoga Falls, 1955-72; founder, pres. Keith Haag Assos. Inc. (architecture-engring.-planning), Cuyahoga Falls, 1972-81; archtl. and planning cons. Cuyahoga Falls, 1981—. Instr. Kent State U., 1952-54 Pres. Tri-County Planning Commn., 1960-61; chmn. Urban Renewal Review Commn., Cuyahoga Falls, 1971—, Regional Planning Group, Northampton Twp., 1970—; mem. Akron Regional Devel. Bd.; bd. dirs. Goodwill Industries, chmn. strategic planning com., 1988—, Akron, Stan Hywet Hall Found., Inc. (pres. 1991-92); chmn. Historic Bldgs. Com., 1988—; mem. alumni bd. Kent State U., 1970-72, co-developer Polymer Housing system, 1989. Recipient 46 archtl. design awards. Fellow AIA (past pres. Akron chpt., nat. com. on office practice); mem. Architects Soc. Ohio (exec. com., sec. 1975-76, v.p. 1977-78, pres. 1979, Gold medal 1986), Northampton C. of C. (pres. 1972), Summit County Hist. Soc. (dir. 1974—) Clubs: President's (Kent State U.), Hilltoppers (Akron U.). Home: 1007 W Steels Corners Rd Cuyahoga Falls OH 44223-3111 Office: PO Box 1147 Cuyahoga Falls OH 44223-0147

HAAG, PAUL M., music educator; b. Cleve., Ohio, July 3, 1979; s. George E and Jean E Haag; m. Jennifer L Kempa, Aug. 10, 2002. MusB, Baldwin-Wallace Coll., 1997—2002. New York State Provisional Teaching Certificate NY State Dept. of Edn., 2002, Ohio Provisional Teaching Certificate Ohio Dept. of Edn., 2002. Elem. band tchr. Niagara-Wheatfield Ctrl. Sch. Dist., Sanborn, NY, 2002—03, Rush-Henrietta Ctrl. Sch. Dist., Henrietta, NY, 2003—04; band dir. West Valley Ctrl. Sch., NY, 2004—. Chair, music dept. West Valley Ctrl. Sch., NY, 2004—. Musician: (orchestra) Orchard Park Symphony Orchestra, 2002—, (wind ensemble) Erie County Wind Ensemble, 2003—. Mem.: Music Educators' Nat. Conf., NY State Sch. Music Assn., Percussive Arts Soc., Omicron Delta Kappa. Christian. Avocations: travel, golf, skiing, bowling, movies. Home: 4479 Richwood Dr Hamburg NY 14075 Office Phone: 716-942-3293 331. Personal E-mail: paulhaag@hotmail.com.

HAAHEIM, PATRICIA JANE DANDO, pastor, consultant; b. Abington, Pa., May 29, 1947; d. Eion Ephraim and Jean Barbara (Wilson) Dando; m. Robert James Thompson, July 11, 1981 (div. July 26, 1994); 1 child, Zachary Eion Dando-Thompson; m. Dale Robert Haaheim, Oct. 4, 1996. BA, U. Calif., Davis, 1969; tchg. credential, San Jose State U., 1970; MDiv, Bethel Theol. Sem., 1979; specialty in social change, Twin Cities Consortium of Sems., 1980. Tchg. credential Calif., Oreg. Tchr. McKenzie Elem. Sch., Blue River, Oreg., 1971—74; pvt. tchr., governess Selsdon Park Hotel, Sanderstead, England, 1974—75; pastor People's Congl. Ch., Bayport, Minn., 1981—84; missionary Nat. Assn. Congl. Christian Chs., Taiwan, 1985; founding pastor Promise Congl. Ch., Apple Valley, Minn., 1991—99; cons. revitalization pastor Nat. Assn. Congl. Christian Chs., Milw., 2000—. Adviser comty. edn Bldg. Youth Assets Dist. # 196 Comty. Edn., Apple Valley, 1992—95; comty. leader drug abuse prevention Searsport (Maine) Schs. and Comty., 1986—89; mem. adv. bd. Family Shelter Ministry S.O.M.E., Santa Rosa, Calif., 1989—91; co-founder Family Violence Network. Author: (booklet/Bible study guide) Saying Yes to God, 1987; contbr. articles to profl. jours. Recipient Founders award for prevention of family violence, Family Violence Network, 2001, Comty. Svc. award, Comty. Edn. Dist. # 196, 1995, Project award alcohol and drug prevention, Comty. Edn., 1988. Mem.: Internat. Congregation Fellowship (vice-chair youth commn. 2002—04), Minn. Fellowship Congregationalists (vice-chair 2002—03, chair 2003—04), Nat. Assn. Congl. Christian Chs. (mem. exec. com. 1999—2003). Congregationalist. Avocations: reading, travel, community work. Home: 13302 Ellice Ct Apple Valley MN 55124-8118 E-mail: revpatti@yahoo.com.

HAALAND, GORDON ARTHUR, retired academic administrator; b. Bklyn., Apr. 19, 1940; s. Ole E. and Ellen R. (Hansen) H.; m. Carol E. Anderson, Jan. 19, 1963; children: Lynn, Paul. AB, Wheaton (Ill.) Coll., 1962; PhD, SUNY, Buffalo, 1966. Instr. SUNY, Buffalo, summer, 1965; asst. to assoc. prof. psychology U. N.H., Durham, 1965-74, prof., 1974-83, chmn. dept. psychology, 1970-74, v.p. for acad. affairs Coll. Arts and Scis., 1979-83, interim pres. of univ., 1983-84, pres., 1984-90; dean Coll. Arts and Scis., prof. psychology U. Maine, Orono, 1975-79; pres. Gettysburg (Pa.) Coll., 1990—2004. Vis. prof. U. Bergen, Norway, 1972-73; mem. New Eng. Land-Grant Univs., chmn. 1985-86; v.p. N.H. Coll. and Univ. Coun., 1985-87; bd. dirs. New Eng. Bd. Higher Edn., 1986—, chmn., 1988-90; bd. dirs. Eisenhower World Affairs Inst.; chmn. N.H. Postsecondary Edn. Commn., 1986-88; dir. Maine Coun. Econ. Edn., 1975-79; evaluator NSF CAUSE Project, U. Maine, 1980-83; bd. dirs. First N.H. Banks, Inc., 1987—, mem. First NH Investment Svcs., 1987—; corporator Bangor (Maine) Savs. Bank, 1975-79. Contbr. articles, papers to profl. publs. and confs. procs. Incorporator N.H. Charitable Fund, 1985-88, Trust for N.H. Lands, 1986—; bd. dirs. Ctr. for N.H.'s Future, 1980—, N.H. Coun. World Affairs, 1986-89; mem. Gov.'s Commn. on N.H. in 21st Century, 1989—; trustee Theater-by-the-Sea, Portsmouth, N.H., 1980-83, N.H. Higher Edn. Assistance Found., 1986—; co-dir. series pub. workshops Dickey-Lincoln and Passamaquoddy Hydroelectric Projects; chair Coun. Higher Edn. Accreditation, dir., 1997-2002. Norwegian Rsch. Coun. fellow, 1972-73; grantee NSF, NIMH, HEW, 1966-75. Mem. AAAS, AAUP, NCAA (pres. commn. 1996-2000), Council of Colls. of Arts and Scis. (bd. dirs. 1977-79), Nat. Assn. State Univs. and Land-Grant Colls. (commn. on arts and scis. 1978-81, chair exec. com. council on acad. affairs 1983; internat. affairs com. 1985-87, exec. com. 1986—, chair commn. edn. for teaching professions 1987-88), Nat. Assn. Ind. Colls. and Univs. (bd. dirs. 1993—), Am. Psychol. Assn. (div. 8 and 26, coun. of reps. N.H., Vt., Maine and R.I. 1968-71, com. on structure and function of coun. 1968-71), Eastern Psychol. Assn., N.H. Psychol. Assn. (program dir. 1971), Eisenhower World Affairs Inst. (bd. dirs. 1991—), Soc. Exptl. Social Psychology, Phi Kappa Phi, Sigma Xi.

HAAR, ANA MARIA FERNANDEZ, advertising executive, public relations executive; b. Oriente Province, Cuba, Mar. 25, 1951; came to U.S., 1960; naturalized, 1970; d. Gilberto and Esmeralda Emiliana (Diaz) Fernández. Grad., Miami Dade C.C., 1971; student, Barry Coll., 1972-78. Adminstrv. asst. through asst. v.p. nat. accounts Flagship Bank, Miami Beach, Fla., 1971-77; v.p. comml. lending Jefferson Nat. Bank, Miami Beach, Fla., 1977-78; chmn., CEO, IAC Group, Inc., Miami, Fla., 1978—. Instr. Women in Mgmt. program Miami Dade C.C., 1980-81; hostess Sta. WPBT Program Viva; exec. com. World Trade Ctr., Miami; mem. Dade County Commn. on Status of Women, 1979-82; chmn. Econ. Devel. Task Force of Commn. on Status of Women, 1979-82; bd. dirs., chmn. Human Capital Group, New Am. Alliance; bd. dirs. Cuban Am. Nat. Found.; mem. adv. com. John S. and James L. Knight Found. Bd. dirs., vice-chmn. CAMACOL-Latin C. of C.; chmn. World Trade Ctr.; Miami dir. SCORE; mem. Exec. Assn. Greater Miami; vice chair New America Alliance; bd. dirs. Cuban Am. Nat. Found. Recipient Gran Orden Martiana of Cuban Lyceum for excellence in community svc., 1976, Up and Comers award South Fla. Bus. Jour., 1988, Red Cross Spectrum award, 2000; named one of 100 Most Infulential Hispanics, Hispanic Bus. Mag., So. Fla. Leading Women Business Owners, 1990, Entrepeneur of the Yr. Inc. Mag. (natl. finalist), 1992. Mem. Advt. Fedn. Greater Miami, Greater Miami Advt. Fedn. (bd. dirs.) Asociación de Publicitarios Latino-Americanos (v.p.), Japan Soc. (bd. dirs.), Miami Beach C. of C. (hon. life, trustee), Greater Miami C. of C., Hispanic Heritage Festival Com., Cuban Women's Club (past pres.), Assn. Hispanic Advt. Agys. (pres. 1998-99), New Am. Alliance.

HAAS, CHARLIE, screenwriter; b. Bklyn., Oct. 22, 1952; s. Philip and Eunice (Dillon) H.; m. Barbara K. Moran, Dec. 21, 1981. BA, U. Calif., Santa Cruz, 1984. Editorial dir. Warner Bros. Records, Burbank, Calif., 1974-76; contbg. editor New West Mag., Beverly Hills, Calif., 1976-80; freelance writer L.A., 1976-80, Oakland, Calif., 1980—. Co-author: (movies) Over the Edge, 1979, Tex, 1982, Gremlins 2, 1990, Matinee, 1993, Runaway Daughters, 1994; contbr. articles to mags. Mem. Friends of Oakland Parks & Recreation, Friends of Oakland Pub. Libr. Avocations: fountain pens, mountain bikes.

HAAS, DANIEL LOUIS, structural engineer; b. Bloomington, Ill., Sept. 6, 1949; s. Louis Francis and Dorothy Jean Haas; m. Joyce Lowe; children: David, Virgina. BSCE, Univ. Ill., Urbana, Ill., 1971. cert. structural, Ill., profl., Ill., Ga., Mo., Okla., Tenn., Kans., SD.; registered NCEES. Structual engr. Campbell & Wieland, St. Louis, 1972—74, Lemessurier Sci., St. Louis, 1974—76, Bendy Engring., St. Louis, 1976—82, Gillum Assoc., St. Louis, 1976, EDM Corp., St. Louis, 1983—89; sr. structual engr. Penta Engring., St. Louis, 1989—. Named Engr. of Yr., EDM Corp., 1987; recipient Michael Von-Siebach award, Penta Engring., 2004. Christian. Achievements include design of St. Louis Union Sta., Dragon Cement Thomasion Maine, TWA Dome, St. Louis and hundreds of others. Home: 14 Seabiscuit Dr Saint Charles MO 63301

HAAS, EDWARD LEE, finance company executive; b. Camden, N.J., Nov. 9, 1935; s. Edward David and Mildred Haas; m. Maryann Lind, Dec. 27, 1958; children: John Eric, Gretchen Haas Theodore. BA, LaSalle U., 1958. Cryptanalyst Nat. Security Agy., Ft. Meade, Md., 1958—59; mgr. sys. devel. RCA Corp., Cherry Hill, NJ, 1966—71; mgr. computer tech. svcs. Gencorp, Akron, Ohio, 1971—74; sr. mgr. computer applications R & D Ernst & Young LLP, Cleve., 1974—75, dir. nat. software products, 1976—77, chief info. officer, nat. dir. software products, 1977—80, nat. ptnr., 1978—82, cons. ptnr. Phila., N.Y.C., L.A., 1983—95; ind. mgmt. cons. L.A., N.Y.C., 1996—. 1st lt. arty. U.S. Army, 1958—59. Mem.: Tournament Players Club, Plantation Country Club. Republican. Roman Catholic.

HAAS, EILEEN MARIE, homecare advocate; b. Pitts., Feb. 27, 1948; d. Michael Joseph and Bridget Agnes (Connolly) McNulty; m. Jerry Albert Haas, July 19, 1975; 1 child, Melissa. Student, York Coll. of Pa., 1975-78, Messiah Coll., Grantsville, Pa., 1978-80. Clk. Exch. Bur. Pitts., 1966-67; debt. collector Nat. Account Sys., Pitts., 1967-71; preadoptive advocate Hershey, Pa., 1983-84, Phila., 1984-85; homecare advocate Dillsburg, Pa., 1985-88, Deer Lodge, Mont., 1988-92, Gibsonia, Pa., 1992—. Interpreter svcs. St. Victors Ch., Bairdsford, Pa., 1992—; presenter Harrisburg (Pa.) Area C.C., 1985, Pa. Soc. Respiratory Therapy, Ctrl. Pa. chpt., 1985; co-presenter Coun. Exceptional Children, Salt Lake City, 1997; rschr. in pulmonary rehab. With USN, 1971-74. Mem. DAV, Am. Soc. Deaf Children, Coun. Exceptional Children, Assn. Severe Handicaps, Profl. Networking for Excellence in Svc. to Deaf and Hard of Hearing. Republican. Roman Catholic. Avocations: deaf education research, dysphagia research, writing, needlepoint, knitting. Home: 90 Kaufman Rd Gibsonia PA 15044-7950

HAAS, FREDERICK CARL, retired paper and chemical company executive; b. Buffalo, Feb. 16, 1936; s. Karl A. and Marie S. (Shilling) H.; m. Dorothy A. Wittlief, Aug. 31, 1957; children— Kenneth Karl, Lawrence Frederick, Sandra Dorothy. BS in Chem. Engring, Purdue U., 1957; MS in Nuclear Engring, Rensselaer Poly. Inst., Troy, N.Y., 1959, PhD in Chem. Engring, 1960; grad., Advanced Mgmt. Program, Harvard U., 1978. Registered profl. engr., N.Y. Research engr. Cornell Aero. Lab., 1960-63; with Westvaco Corp., 1963-98, corp. research dir., then v.p., 1978-81, sr. v.p. ops. N.Y.C., 1982—. Asst. prof. Potomac State Coll., 1966; mem. curriculum com., research com. U. Maine; chmn. research adv. com. Inst. Paper Chemistry; mem. president's key exec. com. Rensselaer Poly. Inst. Author papers in field. Bd. dirs. Syracuse Pulp and Paper Found. AEC fellow, 1957, Tappi fellow, 1994; recipient Disting. Engring. Alumnus award Purdue U., 1993, Outstanding Chem. Engring. award, 1993. Mem. Am. Mgmt. Assn. (research and devel. council), Am. Inst. Chem. Engrs., Am. Chem. Soc., TAPPI, Nat. Soc. Profl. Engrs., Indsl. Research Inst., Dirs. Indsl. Research Can. Pulp and Paper Assn., Tri-State Shetland Sheep Dog Club, Sigma Xi. Methodist.

HAAS, GEORGE AARON, lawyer; b. N.Y.C., July 6, 1919; s. Herman Joseph and Violet (Cowen) H.; m. Miriam Durkin, Aug. 1942; children— Thomas Leonard, Karen Ann (Mrs. Michael Davenport), James G.D. AB, Princeton U., 1940; LL.B., Yale U., 1947. Bar: Ga. 1947. Since practiced in, Atlanta; partner Haas, Bridges & Kane (and predecessor firms), 1947—. Sec., dir. Lucerne Corp., East Freeway Corp., Crescent View Corp., Mountain View Corp., Lake Placid Corp. Mem. hosp. and health div. Atlanta Community Council, 1962-68; mem. tech. assistance com., del. White House Conf. on Children and Youth, 1970; state trustee from Ga. Nat. Easter Seal Soc. for Crippled Children and Adults, 1959-65, mem. exec. com., 1961-65, v.p., 1963-65, 1st v.p., 1965-66, mem. ho. of dels., 1965-73, pres. 1971-73; bd. dirs. 1965-73, chmn. formula rev. bd., mem. relations and standards rev. com., 1967-69, pres., 1969-71; trustee Ga. Easter Seal Soc. for Crippled Children and Adults, 1955-65, 78—, sec., 1957-58, pres., 1959-61, chmn. ho. of dels., 1967-69; Bd. dirs. Fulton-DeKalb chpt. Nat. Found.; mem. med. adv. bd. Ga. chpt. Am. Phys. Therapy Assn. Served to capt. F.A. AUS, World War II. Mem. ABA, Ga. Bar Assn., Atlanta Bar Assn. Clubs: Standard (Atlanta) (past sec., dir.). Lodges: Kiwanis. Home: 2575 Peachtree Rd NE Atlanta GA 30305-3694 Office: 2964 Peachtree Rd NW Atlanta GA 30305-2153

HAAS, HARRY, IV, history educator, youth minister; b. Wilkes-Barre, Pa., July 18, 1975; s. Harry Haas III and Shirley Ann Evans. BA in History, George Washington U., 1998, MEd in Social Studies, 2000. Cert. tchr. Pa., DC, Va. Tchr. Washington Pub. Schs., 1998—2000, Fairfax County Pub. Schs., Alexandria, Va., 2000—02, Dallas (Pa.) Mid. Sch., 2004—. Adj. prof. Luzerne County C.C., Nauticoke, Pa., 2003—. Site coord. Vista-Americorps, Washington, 1996—97; precinct committeeman Luzerne County Rep. Party, Wilkes-Barre, Pa., 2004—. Mem.: St. David's Soc., Wilkes-Barre Barbershop Chorus (bd. dirs. 2002—). Avocations: genealogy, mountain biking, skydiving.

HAAS, HOWARD GREEN, retired bedding manufacturing company executive; b. Chgo., Apr. 14, 1924; s. Adolph and Marie (Green) H.; m. Carolyn Werbner, June 4, 1949; children: Jody, Jonathan. Student, U. Chgo., 1942; BBA, U. Mich., 1948. Promotion dir. Esquire, Inc., Chgo., 1949-50; advt. mgr. Mitchell Mfg. Co., Chgo., 1950-52, v.p. advt., 1952-56, v.p. sales, 1956-58; sales mgr. Sealy, Inc., Chgo., 1959-60, v.p. marketing, 1960-65, exec. v.p., 1965-67, pres., treas., 1967-86, 87. Bd. dirs. Brogden Tool & Die Co., Aurora Custom Machinery, Inc.; adj. prof. strategic mgmt. U. Chgo. Grad. Sch. Bus., 1989—. Author: The Leader Within, 1993. Past mem. nominating com. Glencoe Sch. Bd.; mem. print and drawing com. Art Inst. Chgo.; past chmn. parent's com. Washington U., St. Louis; past bd. dirs. Jewish Children's Bur.; mem. vis. com. Oriental Inst., U. Chgo.; past pres. ORch. of Ill. (Chgo. Philharm). 1st lt. USAAF, 1943-45, ETO. Decorated Air medal with 3 oak leaf clusters; recipient Brotherhood award NCCJ, 1970, Human Relations award Am. Jewish Com., 1977 Mem. Nat. Assn. Bedding Mfrs. (past vice chmn., trustee), Birchwood Tennis Club (Highland Pk., Ill.), Masons. Jewish. Personal E-mail: hghhaas@aol.com.

HAAS, JANET CLAIRE PRESSEL, epidemiology nurse; b. Plainfield, N.J., Apr. 10, 1963; d. Richard Jay and Elinor Mae Pressel; m. Joseph Anthony John, Mar. 23, 1991; children: Morrison Eli, Maccabee Elitah. BFA in Photography, Ariz. State U., 1985; BS in Nursing, Russell Sage Coll., 1995; MS in Epidemiology, SUNY, 2003; postgrad., Columbia U., 2003—. RN N.Y., Mass. Mason tender, laborer Mason Tenders & Bricklayers, N.Y.C., 1983—89; millwright Millwright & Machinery Selectors, 1989—93; nurse Highgate Manor, Troy, 1995—99, Albany Med. Ctr., 1996—97, nurse epidemiologist, 1997—2001, surveillance epidemiologist, 1998—99; surveillance officer Columbia U. Sch. Nursing, N.Y.C., 2001—03; nurse epidemiologist N.Y. Presbyn. Hosp., 2002—. Cons. Hill Ho. Enterprises LLC, Petersburgh, NY, 2003—; mem. exec. com. Ctr. Inter Disciplinary Rsch. Antibiotic Resistance, Columbia U., N.Y.C., 2004—. Contbr. articles to profl. jours. Grantee, Gojo Industries, Ohio, 2004. Mem.: N.Y. State Nurses Assn., Assn. Profls. Infection Control & Epidemiology, Sigma Theta Tau. Avocations: gardening, photography. Office: NY Presbyn Hosp Columbia U Med Ctr Ft Washington Ave New York NY 10032

HAAS, JAY, professional golfer; b. St. Louis, Dec. 2, 1953; m. Janice Haas; children: Jay, William, Winona, Emily, Georgia. Grad., Wake Forest Coll., 1971. Profl. golfer PGA Tour, 1976—. Mem. Walker Cup team, 1975, Ryder Cup team, 1983, 95, 2004, The Presidents Cup team, 1994, 2003. Recipient Fred Haskins award, 1975; won NCAA Championship, 1975, Andy Williams-San Diego Open, 1978, Greater Milw. Open, 1981, B.C. Open, 1981, Hall of Fame Classic, 1982, Tex. Open, 1982, Big "I" Houston Open, 1987, Bob Hope Chrysler Classic, 1988, Mexican Open, 1991, Fed. Express St. Jude Classic, 1992, H-E-B Tex. Open, 1993, Franklin Templeton Shootout, 1996, CVS Charity Classic. Office: PGA Am Box 109601 100 Avenue Of Champions Palm Beach Gardens FL 33410

HAAS, JOHN C., architect; b. Columbus, Ohio, Nov. 3, 1934; s. John Clyde and Margaret (Merideth) H.; m. Jean Ann Scigliano, June 12, 1958 (dec. Apr. 1986); m. Joyce Conklin, May 9, 1987; children: Jeffrey, Joel, John, Paige. BArch, Pa. State U., 1958. Registered architect Pa., Ohio, N.J., N.Y., Del., W.Va., Md., Va., Mass., Fla., N.C. Archtl. draftsman Arthur E. Tennyson, Pitts., 1959-62; archtl. designer Diehl and Stein Architects, Princeton, NJ, 1962—63; staff architect Hankin and Hyres, Trenton, NJ, 1963—67; architect Mahony and Zvosec, Princeton, NJ, 1967-71; dir. archtl. planning dept. Gen. Housing Industries, State College, Pa., 1971-72; founder, prin. Haas Architects Engrs., State College, Pa., 1972—. Sec., treas. Pa. Archs. Licensure Bd., 1998—2002, v.p., 2002—03; mem. adv. bd. dirs. PNC Bank of Ctrl. Pa., 1998—2005; pres. Pa. Architects Licensure Bd., 2004, 05. Prin. works include Nittany Apt. Housing, The Meadows Clinic, Fraser St. Parking Garage, BCH Office Bldg., Geisinger Med. Clinic, The Bryce Jordan Convocation Ctr., Pa. State U. (all State Coll.), Beaver Stadium Expansion, Pa. State U., Recreation Ctr., Lycoming Coll., Williamsport, Pa. Active Centre County United Way Campaign Cabinet, 1994, 95, 96; county chmn. United Way Campaign, 1997; mem. bd. dirs. Chamber of Bus. and Ind. of Centre County, 1996-2003, Centre County United Way, 1998-2003. Capt. U.S. Army, 1958-59. Mem. AIA (pres. mid. Pa. chpt. 1986-87), Nat. Coun. Archtl. Registration Bds., Pa. Soc. Architects (pres. 1993), State College Area C. of C. (pres. 1990-91, bd. dirs. 1984-92), Rotary (pres. 1988-89, bd. dirs.). Republican. Presbyterian. Home: 14 High Meadow Ln State College PA 16803-1853 Office: John C Haas Assocs Inc Architects Engrs Planners 1301 N Atherton St State College PA 16803-2932 E-mail: JHaas@HaasAEP.com.

HAAS, JOSEPH MARSHALL, retired petroleum consultant; b. Alexandria, La., June 21, 1927; s. Samuel and Lulu Susan (Haupt) H.; m. Mary Louise Nance, June 4, 1949 (dec. Jan. 1950); 1 child, Samuel Douglas; m. Marion Barker, Apr. 9, 1954; children: Joseph Marshall, Suzanne M., Thomas B., Katherine L. B of Mech. Engring., Ga. Inst. Tech., 1949. With Gen. Am. Oil Co., Dallas, 1949-78, asst. v.p. prodn. and engring., 1957-60, v.p. engring., 1960-78. Pres., bd. dirs. Conejo Investments Inc., 1994—. With USNR, 1945-46. Mem. Am. Inst. Mining and Metall. Engrs., Masons (32 degree, Shriner), Dallas Petroleum Club, Tau Beta Pi, Sigma Chi, Pi Tau Sigma. Methodist. Home: 1119 Challenger St Austin TX 78734-3801 Office: 1123 Challenger St Austin TX 78734-3801

HAAS, JULIAN L., researcher, educator; b. Antonino, Kans., Sept. 27, 1938; s. Alfred A. and Thecla C. Haas. BA, St. Fidelis Coll., Herman, PA, 1961; MA, Capuchin Coll., Washington, DC, 1965; STL, Gregorian U., Rome, Italy, 1985; STD, Seraphicum Franciscan U., Rome, Italy, 1994. Prof. St. Fidelis H.S., Herman, Pa., 1966—71; dir. youth ctr. Thomas More Prep, Hays, Kans., 1971—77, dir. admissions, 1971—77; pastor St. Joseph's Parish, Hays, Kans., 1977—83; assoc. and pastor Annunciation Ch., Denver, 1985—89; rsch. staff Capuchin Hist. Inst., Rome, 1989—94; rschr., writer and lectr. Capuchin Friars, Saint Louis, Mo., 1994—2002, Colorado Springs, 2002—. Assoc. dean Diocese Salina, Hays, Kans., 1980—83; v.p. Salina Diocesan Priests' Senate, Salina, Kans., 1982—83. Chaplain KC, Hays, Kans., 1978—83; active Hays, Kans., 1979—83; bd. mem. Marian H.S., Hays, Kans., 1977—83. Recipient Fourth Degree, KC, 1982. Roman Catholic. Home: 15 W View PL Colorado Springs CO 80903 Personal E-mail: haas1938@yahoo.com.

HAAS, KAREN MARIE, secondary school educator; b. Scranton, Pa., May 2, 1973; d. Gary William Haas and Vincentina Rose (Salerno). BS (hon.), Marywood U., Scranton, PA, 1995; Secondary Certification, Marywood U., Scranton. PA, 1997; postgrad., Wilkes U., 2002—. Cert. instructional level II elem. edn. tchr. Pa., 1995, cert. instructional level II math. tchr. Pa., 1998. Math. tchr. East Stroudsburg Area H.S. North, Dingmas Ferry, Pa., 1998—, math. dept. chairperson Dingmans Ferry, Pa., 2000—; ballet instr. Illusions Performing Arts Studio, Old Forge, Pa., 1999—2004. Pvt. tutor, Old Forge/Moosic/Taylor/Scranton, Pa., 1995—97; scholastic scrimmage coach East Stroudsburg Area H.S. South, East Stroudsburg, Pa., 1998—2000; mentor East Stroudsburg Area H.S. North, Dingmans Ferry, Pa., 2000—, sch. growth/action plan team, 2000—; math tutor Club Z tutoring, Olyphant, Pa., 2003—05. Author: (poetry book) Wakiza. Recipient Editor's Choice Award for Poetry, World of Poetry, 1990, 1993-1997. Mem.: Keystone State Reading Assn., Northeastern Pa. Reading Assn., Internat. Reading Assn., Pa. Coun. of Tchrs. of Math., Math. Associaton of Am., Nat. Coun. of Tchrs. of Math., Internat. Soc. of Poets (life), Kappa Delta Pi (treas. 1994—95). Avocations: ballet, poetry. Home: 231 Pine St Old Forge PA 18518 Office: East Stroudsburg Area HS North HC 12 Box 690 Dingmans Ferry PA 18328 Business E-Mail: khaas@esasd.net.

HAAS, KAY PARKS BUSHMAN, secondary school English educator; b. Kansas City, Mo., Aug. 28, 1951; d. Jerome Patterson and Florence Alene (Howard) Parks; m. William James Haas, Dec. 12, 1997; 1 child, Eric Jerome. BS, U. Kans., 1973, MA, 1978. Cert. English, social studies tchr., Kans. Tchr. English, social studies Old Mission Jr. H.S., Shawnee Mission, Kans., 1974—80; tchr. English Ottawa Jr. H.S., Kans., 1980—81, Ottawa H.S., 1981—2000; tchr. instructional resource Olathe Dist. Schs., Kans., 2000—. Adj. lectr. U. Kans., Lawrence, 1989—; cons. Scott Foresman Pub. Co., Glenview, Ill., 1993. Co-author: Using Young Adult Literature in English Classroom, 1992, Teaching English Creatively, 1993; editor columns for English Jour., 1992-94, ALAN Rev., 1990-97. V.p. Ottawa Cmty. Theatre, 1983. Recipient Nancy Landan Kassebaum award Kans. State Bd. Edn., 1993; NEH fellow, 1983; named Kans. Master Tchr., 2000. Mem. ASCD, Nat. Coun. Tchrs. English (steering com. secondary sect., pres., mem. assembly on lit. for adolescents, exec. bd. dirs. 1995-97), Kans. Assn. Tchrs. English (bd. dirs.), Olathe Edn. Assn., Ottawa Edn. Assn. (pres. 2000). Methodist. Avocations: reading, exercise. Home: 2 E Brookside Ln Ottawa KS 66067-3616 Office: Olathe Sch Dist 14090 Blackbob Rd Olathe KS 66062 Personal E-mail: kpbhaas@yahoo.com.

HAAS, MARLENE RINGOLD, special education educator; b. Pitts., June 14, 1950; d. Rita Weisbrode and Irwin Mark Ringold; children: Melissa Beth, Ilyssa Meg, Seth Ringold. B in K-8 Elem. Edn. and K-12 Spl. Edn., Case Western Res. U., 1972; M in Spl. Edn., Duquesne U., 1975. Cert. spl. edn. K-12 Pa. Spl. edn. tchr. Pitts. Pub. Schs., 1972—. Home: 4244 Saline St Pittsburgh PA 15217 Office: Reizenstein Mid Sch 129 Denniston Ave Pittsburgh PA 15206

HAAS, PAUL RAYMOND, petroleum company executive; b. Kingston, N.Y., Mar. 10, 1915; s. Frederick J. and Amanda (Lange) H.; m. Mary F. Diedrick, Aug. 30, 1936; children: Rheta Marie, Raymond Paul, Rene Marie. AB, Rider Coll., 1934, LL.D., 1976. C.P.A., Tex. Acct. Arthur Andersen & Co. (C.P.A.s), N.Y.C. and Houston, 1934-41; with La Gloria Oil & Gas Co., Corpus Christi, Tex., 1941-59, v.p., treas., dir., 1947-59; adminstrv. v.p. Tex. Eastern Transmission Corp., Houston, 1958-59; pres., chmn. bd. Prado Oil & Gas Co., 1959-66, Wiltex Corp., 1950-65, Garland Co., 1956-65, Citronelle Oil & Gas Co., 1967-69, Corpus Christi Oil and Gas Co., 1968-90, Corpus Christi Leaseholds Inc., 1990—, Corpus Christi Exploration Co., 1976-90; ltd. partner Salomon Bros., 1973-81. Ind. oil and gas operator, 1959—. Trustee Corpus Christi Ind. Sch. Dist., 1951-58, pres., 1956-58; mem. Tex. Bd. Edn., 1962-72, vice chmn., 1970-72; mem. Gov.'s Com. Edn., 1966-69; Trustee Paul and Mary Haas Found., 1954—, Robert T. Wilson Found., 1954-72, Rider Coll., 1959-67, Moody Found., 1966-73, Found. Center, 1970-75, Council on Founds., 1970-76, Commn. on Philanthropy and Pub. Needs, 1973-75, Univ. Cancer Found. M.D. Anderson Hosp. and Tumor Inst., 1975— . Presbyn. (elder). Home: 4500 Ocean Dr Apt 9A Corpus Christi TX 78412-2572 Office: Corpus Christi Holding Co PO Box 779 Corpus Christi TX 78403-0779

HAAS, PETER E., SR., apparel company executive; b. San Francisco, Dec. 20, 1918; s. Walter A. and Elise (Stern) H.; m. Josephine Baum, Feb. 1, 1945; m. Mimi Lurie, Aug., 1981; children: Peter E., Michael Stern, Margaret Elizabeth. Student, Deerfield Acad., 1935-36; AB, U. Calif., 1940; IA cum laude, Harvard, 1943. With Levi Strauss & Co., San Francisco, 1945—, exec. v.p., 1958-70, pres., 1970-81, CEO, 1976-81, chmn. bd., 1981-89, chmn. exec. com., 1989—, also bd. dirs.; chmn. exec. com., bd. dirs. Levi Strauss Assocs. Inc. Holding Corp. Dir. emeritus AT&T. Trustee San Francisco Found., 1984—; assoc. Smithsonian Nat. Bd., 1988—; bd. dirs. No. Calif. Grantmakers, 1989—; former mem. exec. com. Strive for Five; former mem. Golden Gate Nat. Recreation Area Adv. Com.; Former pres. Jewish Welfare Fedn.; former trustee Stanford U.; former dir., vice chmn. San Francisco Bay Area Council; former trustee United Way of San Francisco Bay Area; former pres. Aid to Retarded Children; former bd. govs. United Way of Am. Recipient Alexis De Tocqueville Soc. award, United Way Am., 1985; named CEO of Yr., Fin. World mag., 1981, Bus. Statesman of Yr., Harvard Bus. Sch., 1982, Alumnus of Yr., 1996; Baker scholar, 1940. Office: Levi Strauss & Co 1155 Battery St San Francisco CA 94111-1256

HAAS, RAYMOND P., lawyer; b. Corpus Christi, Tex., Dec. 9, 1942; BA cum laude, Yale U., 1964, LLB, 1967. Bar: Calif. 1967. Law clk. to Hon. Roger J. Traynor Supreme Ct. of Calif., 1967-68; atty. Howard, Rice, Nemerovski, Canady, Falk & Rabkin, San Francisco. Trustee San Francisco U. High Sch., 1973-78, 85-88, chmn., 1973-76, treas., 1986-88; trustee Pacific Presbyn. Med. Ctr., 1979-91, vice chmn. 1986-91. Mem. ABA (forum com. on franchising, antitrust law sect., bus. law sect., internat. law sect., patent, copyright and trademarks sect., sci. and tech. sect.), State Bar Calif., Bar Assn. San Francisco (computer law sect.), Licensing Execs. Soc., Computer Law Assn., Order of Coif. Office: Howard Rice Nemerovski Canady Falk & Rabkin 3 Embarcadero Ctr Ste 7 San Francisco CA 94111-4074 Office Phone: 415-399-3090.

HAAS, RICHARD, lawyer; b. Glens Falls, N.Y., Sept. 1, 1924; s. Marc and Henrietta (Vogelsanger) H.; m. Dorothy J. Walz, Aug. 2, 1946; children: Eric, Marco, Gregory. AB, UCLA, 1951; LLB, U. Calif., Berkeley, 1950. Bar: Calif. 1951, U.S. Dist. Ct. (no., cen., ea. and so. dists.) Calif. 1951, U.S. Supreme Ct. 1970. Ptnr. Brobeck, Phleger & Harrison, San Francisco, 1959-79; mem. Lasky, Haas & Cohler, San Francisco, 1979-94. Served to lt. USNR, 1941-46. Fellow Am. Bar Found., Am. Coll. Trial Lawyers; mem. Order of Coif. Clubs: Clarmont Country (Oakland, Calif.); Berkeley Tennis. Republican. Home: 2901 Forest Ave Berkeley CA 94705-1310 Office: Lasky Haas & Cohler PC 2052 Moss Valley Dr Fairfield CA 94534-7942 E-mail: mugford389@aol.com.

HAAS, RICHARD JOHN, artist; b. Spring Green, Wis., Aug. 29, 1936; s. Joseph Francis and Marie Hilda (Nachreiner) H.; m. Cynthia Dickman, Sept. 1963 (div. 1971); m. Katherine Sokolnikoff, May 12, 1981; 1 child, Gregory. BS in Art Edn., U. Wis., Milw., 1959; MFA, U. Minn., 1964. Instr. U. Minn., Mpls., 1963-64; asst. prof. art Mich. State U., East Lansing, 1964-68; instr. printmaking Bennington (Vt.) Coll., 1968-78; mem. fine arts faculty Sch. Visual Arts, 1977-81. Instr. fresco Skowhegan Sch. Painting and Sculpture, 1984. One-man shows include Rhona Hoffman Gallery, Chgo., 1983, 90, Art and Architecture Gallery, U. Tenn., 1984, St. Louis Art Mus., 1984, Aspen Art Mus., 1985, Williams Coll. Mus. of Art, Williamstown, Mass., 1987, Brooke Alexander, 1985-89, Sam Houston State U., Huntsville, Tex., 1992, Miramar Gallery, Sarasota, Fla., 1992, Condeso/Lawler Gallery, N.Y., 1982, U. Wis., Milw., 1992, Marsha Orr Contemporary Fine Arts Gallery, Tallahassee, 1996, Huntington (W.Va.) Mus. Art, 1997, Century Assn., N.Y.C., 1997, Art on Main Street, Yonkers, N.Y., 1997, 1998, Southern Alleghenies Mus., Pa., 1999, Prinkworks, Chgo., 2000, Michael Ingbar Gallery, NYC, 2002, David Findlay Jr, NYC, 2004; solo exhibitions include Kunsthandel Elisabeth Michitsch, Vienna, Austria, 2005; group exhibitions include Am. Acad. Arts & Letters, Tuscon Mus. Art; over 125 nat. and internat. mural commns., 1973—. Trustee Hudson River Mus., 1989—, N.Y. State Preservation League, 1983-88; bd. govs. Skowhegan Sch. Painting and Sculpture, 1982—; bd. dirs. Pub. Art Fund, 1981-88; v.p. Archtl. League of N.Y., 1978-81; mem. N.Y.C. Art Commn. 1st lt. U.S. Army, 1959-67. Fellow Nat. Endowment Arts, 1978, Guggenheim Found., 1983-84, MacDowell Fellowship, 2003; recipient medal of honor AIA, 1977, award Mcpl. Art Soc., 1977, Doris Freedman award N.Y.C., 1989, Disting. Alumnus award U. Wis., Milw., 1991, Individual Artist award, Westchester Arts Coun., 2003; honoree Yonkers Friends of Arts Pub. Art, 2003, Jimmy Ernst award of art, Am. Acad. Arts & Letters, 2005. Mem. Nat. Acad. Design (v.p. 2000-); Century Club. Office: 361 W 36th St New York NY 10018-6408 E-mail: hassnyc@aol.com.

HAAS, ROBERT DOUGLAS, apparel manufacturing company executive; b. San Francisco, Apr. 3, 1942; s. Walter A. Haas Jr. and Evelyn (Danzig) Haas; m. Colleen Gershon, Jan. 27, 1974; 1 child, Elise Kimberly. BA, U. Calif., Berkeley, 1964; MBA, Harvard U., 1968. With Peace Corps, Ivory Coast, 1964-66; fellow White House, Washington, 1968-69; assoc. McKinsey & Co., 1969-72; with Levi Strauss & Co., San Francisco, 1973—, sr. v.p. corp. planning and policy, 1978-80, pres. new bus. group, 1980, pres. operating groups, 1980-81, exec. v.p., COO, 1981-84, pres., CEO, 1984-89, CEO, 1989—99, chmn. bd. dir., 1989—. Pres. Levi Strauss Found.; mem. Global leadership team. Hon. dir. San Francisco AIDS Found.; trustee Ford Found.; bd. dirs. Bay Area Coun.; past bd. dirs. Am. Apparel Assn. Fellow White House fellow, 1968—69. Mem.: Meyer Friedman Inst. (bd. dirs.),

Calif. Bus. Roundtable, Trilateral Commn., Coun. Fgn. Rels., Conf. Bd., Bay Area Com., Brookings Inst. (trustee), Phi Beta Kappa. Office: Levi Strauss & Co 1155 Battery St San Francisco CA 94111-1256*

HAAS, ROBERT JOHN, aerospace engineer; b. Dayton, Ohio, Apr. 14, 1930; s. Robert J. Haas and Harriett (Longstreth) Bevan; m. Florence A. Eldred, June 6, 1952 (div. June 1984); adopted children: Jeffrey (dec.), Lisa Haas Cappuccio; m. Gayle F. Byrne, Dec. 14, 1984; stepchildren: Patrick Barton, Marissa Barton; children: Amber Haas, Robert J. Haas III. Student, U.S. Mil. Acad., 1948-51; BS in Petroleum Engring., U. Tulsa, 1954. Petroleum engr. Skelly Oil Co., Tulsa, 1953-54; propulsion engr., supr. Marquardt, Van Nuys, Calif., 1957-64, mgr. rocket programs, 1964-69, dir. test and facilities, 1969-72, gen. mgr. environ. systems, 1972-75; plant gen. mgr. Williams Internat., Ogden, Utah, 1975-79, sr. v.p. engring. Walled Lake, Mich., 1979-86, sr. v.p. product planning and mktg., 1986-90; sr. advisor, cons. Las Vegas, Nev., 1990—; CEO Haas Enterprises, Consulting Firm, Las Vegas, 1992—. Cons. Marquardt, Van Nuys, 1961-75; bd. dirs. Verile Corp. Author: Approach to Aerospace Plane Propulsion, 1960. Lectr. and advisor Weber State Coll., U. Utah and various high schs. and clubs., 1975-79; pres. Marquardt Mgmt. Club, 1971. 1st lt. USAF, 1954-56. Mem. AIAA, Navy League (lifetime). Republican. Roman Catholic. Achievements include contribution to devel. and prodn. of world's smallest turbofan for cruise missiles; discoveries in the field of integrated propulsion modules for missiles, economical methods of testing ramjets, turbines and rocket engines. Home and Office: Haas Enterprize PO Box 33126 Las Vegas NV 89133-3126

HAAS, TOMMY (THOMAS MARIO HAAS), professional tennis player; b. Hamburg, Germany, Apr. 3, 1978; s. Peter and Brigette Haas. Profl. tennis player ATP Tour, 1996—. Achievements include Winner singles titles: Memphis, 1999, Adelaide, 2001, LI, 2001, Stuttgart TMS, 2001, Vienna, 2001, Houston, 2004, LA, 2004. Office: c/o Bollettieri Tennis Acad 5500 34th St W Bradenton FL 34210

HAAS, WILLIAM PAUL, humanities educator, retired academic administrator; b. Newark, May 31, 1927; s. Joseph J. and Elizabeth (Ryan) H. AB, Providence Coll., 1948; STL, Pontifical Inst., Washington, 1954; PhD, U. Fribourg, Switzerland, 1962; DBA (hon.), Bryant Coll., Providence, 1966; LLD, U. R.I., 1967, Brown U., 1969; DD, Conn. Wesleyan U., 1969; DHL, R.I. Coll., 1970, Salve Regina Coll., 1971. Ordained priest Roman Cath. Ch., 1953, laicized, 1973; prof. theology and philosophy Emmanuel Coll., Boston, 1954-60; prof. philosophy Providence Coll., 1962-63, 71-72, pres., 1965-71; asso. prof. U. Notre Dame, 1963-65; on leave as post-doctoral research asso. Boston U., 1972-73; vice chancellor for acad. affairs Mass. State Coll. System, 1973-79; pres. North Adams State Coll., Mass., 1979-83; prof. humanities Bryant Coll., Smithfield, R.I., 1983-96. Inaugurated spl. program religious studies Purdue U., 1963-65; vis. prof. contemporary theology Wabash Coll., Crawfordsville, Ind., 1964-65; vis. distinguished prof. U. R.I., 1971-72; Mem. R.I. Council Arts, 1967-70, R.I. Adv. Council State Tech. Services Act, 1965, 1967-71; mem. commn. learning Assn. Am. Colls., 1966-69; adv. council extension and continuing edn. Dept. Health, Edn. and Welfare, 1966-70; mem. commn. humanities in schs. Nat. Found. on Arts and the Humanities, 1967-71; chmn. R.I. Higher Edn. Council, 1969-71 Author: The Conception of Law and the Unity of Peirce's Philosophy, 1964, The Contemporary Arts, 1965; Contbr. articles to profl. jours. Bd. dirs. R.I. Philharmonic Orch., 1965-68, R.I. Found. Repertory Theatre, 1966-71, R.I. Urban Coalition, 1969-71, Packard Manse (center ecumenical studies), Boston, 1965-67; trustee John F. Kennedy Meml. Fund R.I., 1966-71, New Eng. Colls. Fund, 1970-71, Rocky Hill Sch., 1971-73, Bryant Coll., 1971-79; bd. dirs. United Fund R.I., 1967-71, Howard Found., Brown U., 1969-73; chmn. R.I. com. Rhodes Scholarship Trust, 1969, mem., 1970; bd. dirs. Humanities Forum of R.I., 1989—; mem. R.I. Com. for the Humanities, 1991-98. Mem. Am. Soc. Aesthetics, Nat. Cath. Edn. Assn. (exec. com. coll. and univ. dept. 1970-73) Home: 2 Vanderbilt Ave Newport RI 02840-4342

HAASE, ASHLEY THOMSON, microbiology educator, researcher; b. Chgo., Dec. 8, 1939; s. Milton Conrad and Mary Elizabeth Minter (Thomson) H.; m. Ann DeLong, 1962; children: Elizabeth, Stephanie, Harris. BA, Lawrence Coll., 1961; MD, Columbia U., 1965. Intern Johns Hopkins Hosp., Balt., 1965-67; clin. assoc. Nat. Inst. Allergy and Infectious Disease, Bethesda, Md., 1967-70; vis. scientist Nat. Inst. Med. Rsch., London, 1970-71; chief infectious disease sect. VA Med. Ctr., San Francisco, 1971-84, med. investigator, 1978-83; prof. microbiology U. Minn., Mpls., 1984-99, head dept., 1984—, Regents' prof., 1999—. Mem. fellowship screening com. Am. Cancer Soc., San Francisco, 1978-81; mem. UNESCO Internat. Cell Rsch. Orgn., India, 1978; mem. nat. adv. coun. Nat. Inst. Allergy and Infectious Diseases, 1986-91, mem. task force on microbiology and infectious diseases, 1991, Method to Extend Rsch. in Time investigator, 1989—, chair AIDS rsch. adv. com., 1993-96, chmn. vaccine subcom.; Javits neurosci. investigator Nat. Inst. Neurol. and Communicative Disorders and Stroke, 1988-95; chmn. panel on AIDS, U.S.-Japan Coop. Med. Sci. Program, 1988-95; mem. OAR AIDS Rsch. Evaluation Working Group, 1995-96; mem. adv. com. for career awards in biomed. scis. Burroughs-Wellcome Fund, 1995-2000; trustee Lawrence U., 1997-2000; adv. coun. NIH Office AIDS Rsch., 2002—, Inst. Medicine, 2003—. Editor: Microbial Pathogenesis, 1988-94; contbr. articles on AIDS pathogenesis and other topics in neurovirology to profl. jours. Recipient Lucia R. Briggs Disting. Achievement award Lawrence Coll., 1990. Mem. Am. Soc. Microbiology, Assn. Am. Physicians, Am. Soc. Clin. Investigation, Am. Soc. Virology, Assn. Med. Schs. Microbiology Chmn., Infectious Diseases Soc. Am., Nat. Multiple Sclerosis Soc. (adv. com. 1978-84), Am. Assn. Immunologists, Phi Beta Kappa, Alpha Omega Alpha, Inst. Medicine, 2004-. Democrat. Home: 14 Buffalo Rd Saint Paul MN 55127-2136 Office: U Minn Dept Microbiology 420 Delaware St SE Minneapolis MN 55455-0374 E-mail: haase001@umn.edu.

HAASE, LEIF WELLINGTON, foundation administrator; b. Boston, Mar. 13, 1965; s. Martin Rudolph Haase and Florence Cushing Wellington; m. Leslie Anne Teicholz, Sept. 19, 2004. BA, Princeton U., 1988; MA, Yale U., 1991, MPhil, 1993. Program officer 20th Century Fund, N.Y.C., 1998—2000; program officer, health care fellow Century Found., N.Y.C., 2001—, exec. dir. project on bioterrorism preparedness and pub. health, 2002—. Co-author: Medicine Tomorrow, 2001, author reports in field. Office: Century Found 41 E 70th St New York NY 10021 Office Phone: 212-452-7725.

HAASS, RICHARD NATHAN, federal official; b. Bklyn., July 28, 1951; s. Irving B. and Marcella Haas BA, Oberlin (Ohio) Coll., 1973; MA in Philosophy, Oxford U., Eng., 1975, PhD, 1982. Legis. asst. U.S. Sen. Claiborne Pell, Washington, 1975; research assoc. Internat. Inst. for Strategic Studies, London, 1977-79; spl. asst. to undersec. def. U.S. Dept. Def., Washington, 1979-80; dir. office regional security affairs U.S. Dept. State, Washington, 1981-82, dep. for policy bur. European and Can. affairs, 1982-85, spl. Cyprus coordinator, 1983-85; lectr. pub. policy John F. Kennedy Sch. govt. Harvard U., Cambridge, Mass., 1985-89; spl. asst. to pres. Nat. Security Affairs, 1989-93; sr. dir. near east and south Asia Nat. Security Coun., 1989-93; sr. assoc. Carnegie Endowment for Internat. Peace, Washington, 1993-94; dir. nat. security programs, sr. fellow Coun. on Fgn. Rels., Washington, 1994-96; v.p., dir. fgn. policy programs Brookings Instn., 1996—2001; dir. policy planning U.S. Dept. State, 2001—03; pres. Coun. on Fgn. Rels., Washington, 2003—. Author: Congressional Power: Implications for American Security Policy, 1979, Beyond the INF Treaty: Arms, Arms Control and the Atlantic Alliance, 1988, Conflicts Unending: The United States and Regional Disputes, 1990, The Power to Persuade, 1994, Intervention: The Use of American Military Force in The Post-Cold War World, 1994, The Reluctant Sheriff: The United State after the Cold War, 1997, The Bureaucratic Entrepreneur, 1999, The Opportunity: America's Moment to Alter History's Course, 2005; editor: Superpower Arms Control: Setting the Record Straight, 1987, Economic Sanctions and American Diplomacy, 1998, Transatlantic Tensions, 1999, Honey and Vinegar: Incentives, Sanctions, and Foreign Policy, 2000. Recipient Superior Honor award Dept. State, 1982, Presdl. Citizens medal, 1991, Disting. Honor award Dept. State, 2003; Rhodes scholar Oxford U., 1973. Mem. Internat. Inst. for Strategic Studies, Coun. on Fgn. Rels., Trilateral Commn. Office: Coun Fgn Rels 58 E 68th St New York NY 10021 E-mail: president@cfr.org.

HAAYEN, RICHARD JAN, academic administrator, insurance company executive; b. Bklyn., June 30, 1924; s. Cornelius Marius and Cornelia Florence (Muskus) H.; m. Marilyn Jean Messner, Aug. 30, 1946; children—Richard Jan, Peter Wyckoff, James Carell. BS, Ohio State U., 1948; D in Pub. Svc. (hon.), Nat. Coll. Edn., Evanston, Ill. With Allstate Ins. Co., 1950—, v.p. underwriting, 1969-75, exec. v.p. Northbrook, Ill., 1975-80, pres., 1980-86, chmn., chief exec. officer, 1986-89; exec.-in-residence So. Meth. U., Dallas, 1989—. Bd. dirs. Guaranty Fed. Savs. Bank, Dallas. Bd. dirs. Communities-in-Schs., Dallas. Mem. Am. Arbitration Assn. (arbitrator), Phi Delta Theta. Republican. Home: 9 Glenshire Ct Dallas TX 75225-2040 Office: 7557 Rambler Rd Ste 1424 Dallas TX 75231-2390

HABACHY, SUZAN SALWA SABA, development economist, non profit administrator; b. Cairo, July 15, 1933; came to the U.S., 1952; d. Saba and Gameela (Gindy) H. BA, Bryn Mawr (Pa.) Coll., 1954; MA, Harvard U., Cambridge, Mass., 1956. Teaching fellow Ohio U., Athens, 1957-58; economist Mobil Oil Co., N.Y.C., 1959-64; reporter, editor Petroleum Intelligence Weekly, N.Y.C., 1964-65, McGraw Hill News Bur., London, England, 1965-68; program officer UN, N.Y.C., 1969-75, section chief, 1975-88; focal point for women UN Office of Pers., N.Y.C., 1988-93; exec. dir. The Trickle Up Program, N.Y.C., 1994-2001. Avocations: theater, travel, reading. Home: 1056 5th Ave New York NY 10028-0112

HABECKER, EUGENE BRUBAKER, religious association executive; b. Hershey, Pa., June 17, 1946; s. Walter Eugene and Frances (Miller) H.; m. Marylou Napolitano, July 27, 1968; children: David, Matthew, Marybeth. AB, Taylor U., 1968; MA, Ball State U., 1969; JD, Temple U., 1974; PhD, U. Mich., 1981. Bar: Pa. 1974. Asst. dean Ea. Univ., St. Davids, Pa., 1970-74; dean students, asst. prof. polit. sci. George Fox U., Newberg, Oreg., 1974-78; exec. v.p. Huntington (Ind.) Coll., 1979-81, pres., 1981-91; pres, CEO Am. Bible Soc., N.Y.C., 1991—. Evaluation cons. North Ctrl. Assn., Chgo., 1982-91; dir. Christian Colls. and Univs., Washington, 1982-88; bd. dirs. Christianity Today Internat., United Bible Socs. internat. exec. com., 1992-2001, LeTourneau U. Author: Affirmative Action in Independent College, 1977, The Other Side of Leadership, 1987, Leading With a Follower's Heart, 1990, Rediscovering the Soul of Leadership, 1996; contbr. articles to profl. jours. Recipient Christian Mgmt. award Christian Mgmt. Assn., 1989. Mem. Nat. Assn. Intercollegiate Athletes (coun. of pres.' 1985-90), Nat. Assn. Evangs. (bd. dirs. 1985-90), Christian Mgmt. Assn. Republican. Presbyterian. Office: Am Bible Soc 1865 Broadway New York NY 10023-7503 Office Phone: 212-408-8661.

HABEEB, HABEEBA HUSSAIN, librarian; b. Male, Republic of Maldives, Sept. 9, 1930; d. Hussain Habeeb and Shahima Shamsuddin; m. Abdulla Zubair, May 18, 1923; children: Ibrahim, Shafeea, Shahida. Grad. High Sch. Urdu Medium, Osmania, Hyderabad, India, 1948; grad. High Sch. English Medium, Holy Family Convent, Colombo, Sri Lanka, 1952. Cert. librarian. Asst. prin. Govt. Service, Male, Maldives, 1956-62; sec. Prime Minister's Office, Male, 1962-67, Foreign Affairs, Male, 1968-70, Transp. Dept. Govt. Service, Male, 1974-78, Aid Dept. Ministry of Justice Govt. Service, Male, 1974-75; librarian Nat. Library, Male, 1978-86, deputy dir., 1986-90; dir., 1990-95; dir. gen., 1995—. Author: Mohammed Thakurufaan The Great, 1990; co-author: Innovation in Primary School Construction, 1986; translator: How to Write Short Stories, 1984, other lit. works from Urdu to Dhivehi and English to Dhivehi; editor Jour., Niru Libr. newsletter, Children's Club mag. including Faithoova mag.; author short stories in Maldivian lang.; contbr. articles to cultural publs. Recipient Pres.'s award Gold Pen, Presdl. award for 25 yrs. govt. svc., Presdl. Encouragement award transl. Mem. Nat. Ctr. for Linguistic and Hist. Rsch. (adv. mem.). Home: Mandoovilla 8 Bodufulah Str Male Machchangolhi 20-03 Maldives Office: Nat Libr 59 Majeedi Magu Galolhu Male 20-24 Maldives

HABEGGER, CYNTHIA A., medical/surgical nurse; b. Van Wert County, Ohio, Dec. 14, 1953; d. Palmer Paul and Donna Jean (Hertel) Johnson; m. Alan Duane Habegger, Oct. 13, 1979; children: Duane Alan, Rebekkah Ann. ADN, Purdue U., Ft. Wayne, 1985, AD in Supervision, 1991; BSN, Luth. Coll. Health Profls., Ft. Wayne, 1994. RN, Ind.; lic. supr. Staff nurse Swiss Village, Berne, Ind., 1985-87; staff nurse med.-surg. unit Caylor Nickel Clinic, Bluffton, Ind., 1987-88; DON geriatric Decatur (Ind.) Community Care, 1988; charge nurse Cooper Community Care Corp., Bluffton, 1988; psychiat. staff nurse and charge nurse Caylor Nickel Clinic, Bluffton, 1988-92; ADON Meadowvale Nursing Home, Bluffton, 1992-93; intermittent RN Vis. Nurse Svc. and Hospice, Fort Wayne, Ind., 1993-94; instr. nursing Ivy Tech State Coll., 1994-95; DON, ExtendaCare Bluffton (Ind.), 1995-96; pvt. duty nurse, 1996-99; staff nurse Swiss Village, Berne, Ind., 1999—; dir. Project Share Food Pantry and Compassionate Ministries Network, Inc., 2002—. Dir. local food bank, 2002—. Home: 1132 W 400 S Berne IN 46711

HABENER, JOEL FRANCIS, medical educator, researcher; b. June 29, 1937; AA in Chemistry, Santa Ana Coll., 1957; BS in Chemistry, U. Redlands, 1960; MD, UCLA, 1965. Diplomate Am. Bd. Internal Medicine. Med. intern, asst. resident in medicine Johns Hopkins Hosp., Md., 1965-67; fellow in medicine Johns Hopkins U., Balt., 1965-67; rsch. assoc. lab. physiology Nat. Cancer Inst. NIH, Bethesda, Md., 1967-69; clin. and rsch. fellow endocrine unit Mass. Gen. Hosp., Boston, 1969-72, investigator Howard Hughes Med. Inst., 1976—, chief lab. molecular endocrinology, 1979—, dir. endocrine divsn., 1991—; vis. scientist dept. biology MIT, Cambridge, 1970-80; assoc. prof. medicine Harvard Med. Sch., Boston, 1975-88, prof. medicine, 1989—. Assoc. editor: Jour. Clin. Investigation, 1982-87; editor: Molecular Endocrinology, 1987-92, Jour. Neuroendocrinology, 1988-93, Jour. Biol. Chemistry, 1996—, Pathogenesis, 1996—; reviewing editor: Jour. Lab. and Clin. Medicine; contbr. artiles to profl. jours. Recipient Rsch. Career Devel. award USPH, 1972-76, Rsch. award Am. Diabetes Assn., 1995. Mem. Am. Soc. Clin. Investigation, Am. Soc. Biol. Chemists, Assn. Am. Physicians, Soc. Experimental Biology and Medicine, Endocrine Soc. (Edwin A. Astwood lectr. award 1979, Robert H. Williams Disting. Leadership award 1999), Alpha Omega Alpha. Office: Mass Gen Hosp Lab Molecular Endocrinology 55 Fruit St WEL 306 Boston MA 02114-2696 Office Phone: 617-726-3420. Business E-Mail: jhabener@partners.org.

HABER, FREDERIC, lawyer; b. N.Y.C., June 20, 1958; s. Alan Walter and Carol (Cohen) H.; m. Jill Anne Jacobs, Oct. 9, 1988. AB, AM, Harvard U., 1979, JD, 1983. Bar: N.Y. 1984, Conn. 1985, Mass. 1997, U.S. Dist. Ct. (so. and ea. dists.) N.Y. 1984. Assoc. Weil, Gotshal & Manges, N.Y.C., 1983-90; of counsel, 1991-93; sr. atty. R.H. Macy & Co., Inc., 1993-95; gen. counsel, corp. sect. Copyright Clearance Ctr., Inc., Danvers, Mass., 1995—. Mem. ABA, Am. Corp. Coun. Assn., N.Y. State Bar Assn. Office: Copyright Clearence Ctr Inc 222 Rosewood Dr Danvers MA 01923-4510 E-mail: fhaber@copyright.com.

HABER, IRA JOEL, artist, art educator; b. N.Y.C., Feb. 24, 1947; s. Oscar and Rosalind (Tilzer) H. Student public schs. Instr. art SUNY, Stony Brook, 1981—, U. Calif.-San Diego, 1982, 84, Ohio State U. (Columbus), 1984. One-man shows include Fischbach Gallery, N.Y.C., 1971, 72, 74, Kent (Ohio) State U., 1977, Pam Adler Gallery, N.Y.C., 1978, 80, 82, Rutgers U., 1980, SUNY, Stony Brook, 1981, Phila. Art Alliance, 1984, J.N. Herlin Inc., N.Y.C., 1984, 86, 55 Mercer St. Gallery, N.Y.C., 1991; group shows include Mus. Modern Art, N.Y.C., 1970, Whitney Mus., N.Y.C., 1971, 73, Public Sch. One, L.I., N.Y., 1976, Albright-Knox Gallery, Buffalo, 1979, Ohio State U., 1984; represented in permanent collections NYU, Guggenheim Mus., N.Y.C., Hirshhorn Mus., Washington, Allen Meml. Art Mus., Oberlin (Ohio) Coll., Albright-Knox Gallery, Buffalo. NEA fellow, 1974, 77, 84; grantee Creative Artists Pub. Svc., 1974, 77, Ariana Found., 1982, Pollock-Krasner Found., 1986-87, 2001, Adolph and Esther Gottlieb Found., 2004. Address: 311 85th St Brooklyn NY 11209 E-mail: irajoel@aol.com.

HABER, JONATHAN H., lawyer; b. Los Angeles, Mar. 10, 1953; s. George Martin and Leah (Levy) H.; m. Bonnie Levin, Mar. 28, 1982; 1 child, Erin Nicole Levin. BA, UCLA, 1976; JD, U. San Francisco, 1981. Bar: Calif. 1982, U.S. Dist. Ct. (no. dist.) Calif. 1983. Assoc. Lossing & Elston, San Francisco, 1983-86, McGlynn, McLorg & McDowell, San Francisco; counsel & comm. dir., Agriculture, Nutrition, & Forestry Com. US Senate, 1989—92; CEO ATLA, 2005—. Cons. local, state, nat. polit. campaigns. Cons. Congressman Ted Weiss, Washington, 1979; mem. nat. advance com. Kennedy for pres., Washington, 1980; dep. campaign mgr. Brown for U.S. Senate, Los Angeles, 1982. Democrat. Jewish. Avocations: woodwork, backpacking, photography. Office: ATLA 1050 31st St Washington DC 20007

HABER, PIERRE-CLAUDE, psychologist; b. Landau, Germany, June 8, 1931; s. Kurt S. and Hedwig (Kuhn) H.; came to U.S., 1943, naturalized, 1949; BA, Bklyn. Coll., 1952; MA, Duke U., 1953; PhD, U. Paris, 1956; Counselor, dir. adult edn. Central Sch. Dist. 2, Yorktown Heights, N.Y., 1956-59; psychologist Manpower Devel. Program, Bklyn., 1959-65; asst. prof. Queens Coll., 1965-70; exec. sec., exec. dir. Psychology Soc., N.Y.C., 1970—; cons. forensic psychologist N.Y. State, 1978—; assoc. prof. Jersey City State Coll., 1967-80; organizer of biennial overseas study and visitation trips. Bd. advisors Nat. Reference Inst. Mem. APA, Am., N.Y. State personnel and guidance assns., Psychology Soc., N.Y. Assn. Public Sch. Adult Educators (v.p. 1957-59), Pi Delta Phi. Republican. Jewish. Author: The Social and Political Attitudes of Andre Gide, 2000; contbr. to Compton's Ency., also articles to profl. jours. Home and Office: 100 Beekman St New York NY 10038-1810 Office Phone: 212-285-1872.

HABER, RALPH NORMAN, psychology consultant, researcher, educator; b. Lansing, Mich., May 15, 1932; s. William and Fannie (Gallas) H.; m. Ruth Lea Boss, 1961 (div. 1974); children— Sabrina Beth, Rebecca Ann; m. Lyn R. Roland, 1974. BA, U. Mich., 1953; MA, Wesleyan U., Middletown, Conn., 1954; PhD, Stanford U., 1957; Postdoctoral fellow, Med. Research Council, Applied Psychology Unit, Cambridge, Eng., 1970-71. Rsch. assoc. Inst. for Comm. Rsch., Stanford, 1957-58; instr. psychology San Francisco State Coll., Calif., 1957-58; asst. prof. psychology Yale, 1958-64; assoc. prof. psychology U. Rochester, N.Y., 1964-67, prof. psychology, 1967-70, prof. psychology and visual sci., 1970-79, chmn. dept. psychology, 1967-70, mem. faculty senate, 1968-70, sec., mem. steering com., 1969-70; prof. psychology U. Ill., Chgo., 1979-91, rsch. prof., 1991-94, rsch. prof. emeritus, 1994—; ptnr. Human Factors Cons., Swall Meadows, Calif., 1988—; rsch. assoc. psychology U. Calif., Santa Cruz, 1995. Adj. prof. U. Calif., Riverside, 1997-99; vis. prof. Air Force Human Resources Lab., Williams AFB, Ariz., 1981-83; ptnr. Human Factors Cons., Highland Park, Ill.; vis. scientist Med. Rsch. Coun. Applied Psychology Unit, Cambridge, Eng., 1970-71; chmn., divisional maj. III Yale, 1959-64; vis. asst. prof. New Sch. for Social Research, 1963; research cons. VA, 1967-71; adv. editor for exptl. psychology Holt, Rinehart & Winston Book Pubs., 1969-77. Author: (with Hershenson) The Psychology of Visual Perception, 1973, 2d edit., 1980, (with Fried) An Introduction to Psychology, 1975, (with others) Discovering Psychology, 1977; editor: Current Research on Motivation, 1966, Contemporary Theory and Research on Visual Perception, 1968, Information Processing Approaches to Visual Perception, 1969; Contbr. articles to profl. jours. Committeeman 18th Ward, Brighton (N.Y.) Democratic Com., 1967-70; founding mem., trustee Coll. Admission Prep. Program, Rochester, 1968-70; commr. Wheeler Crest Fire Prevention Dist., Swall Meadows, Calif., 1995-2000; founder, 1st pres., bd. dirs. Eastern Sierra Conservancy, 2000-2002. Recipient Outstanding Achievement award U. Mich., 1977; Behavioral Sci. fellow Ford Found., 1953-54; grantee NSF, NIH, Nat. Inst. Edn., Air Force Office Sci. Research, Dept. Army Fellow APA, AAAS, Am. Psychol. Soc.; mem. Psychonomics Soc., Brit. Psychol. Assn., Optical Soc. Am., Human Factors and Ergonomics Soc., Am. Contract Bridge League (dir. Bishop unit 517 1996—), Sigma Xi, Pi Lambda Phi. Office Phone: 760-387-2458.

HABER, SCOTT R., lawyer; BA, Cornell Univ., 1980, MBA, 1983, JD magna cum laude, 1984. Bar: Calif. 1984. Law clk. Hon. Richard J. Cardamone, US Ct. of Appeals, Second Cir., 1984; joined Latham & Watkins, 1985—, now ptnr. San Francisco. Editor: Cornell Law Rev., 1984. Mem.: ABA, Calif. Bar Assn., Order of Coif. Office: Latham & Watkins Ste 2000 505 Montgomery St San Francisco CA 94111-2562 Business E-Mail: scott.haber@lw.com.

HABERMAN, CHARLES MORRIS, mechanical engineer, educator; b. Bakersfield, Calif., Dec. 10, 1927; s. Carl Morris and Rose Marie (Braun) H. BS, UCLA, 1951; MS in Mech. Engring., U. So. Calif., 1954, MS in Aeronautical Engring., 1960. Lead, sr. and group engr. Northrop Aircraft, Hawthorne, Calif., 1951-59, cons., 1959-61; asst. prof. to prof. mech. engring. Calif. State U., L.A., 1959-91. Cons. Royal McBee Corp., 1960-61. Author: Engineering Systems Analysis, 1965, Use of Computers for Engineering Applications, 1966, Vibration Analysis, 1968, Basic Aerodynamics, 1971. Served with AUS, 1946-47. Mem. Am. Soc. Engring. Edn. Democrat. Roman Catholic.

HABERMAN, F. WILLIAM, lawyer; b. Princeton, N.J., Apr. 20, 1940; s. Frederick William and Louise (Power) H.; m. Carmen Marie Duffy, June 15, 1963; children: Frederick, Sarah. BA, U. Wis., 1962; LLB, Harvard Law Sch., 1965. Bar: Wis. 1965, Fla. 1993, U.S. Dist. Ct. (ea. dist.) Wis. 1966, U.S. Dist. Ct. (we. dist.) Wis. 1967. Ptnr. Michael, Best & Friedrich, Milw., 1965—. Mem. adv. bd. Johnson Bank, 1994-97; bd. dirs. U. Wis. Milw. Found., 2003—. Co-author: Marital Property Law in Wisconsin, 1986. Trustee Pub. Policy Forum, Milw., 1998—; bd. dirs. Ctrl. YMCA, Milw., 1988-93, Richard and Ethel Herzfeld Found., Milw., 1985—, Wis. affiliate Am. Heart Assn., 1993-97; mem. Greater Milw. Com., 2000—; mem. adv. bd. Milw. Fair Housing Coun., 1989-90; mem. deferred giving adv. bd. Milw. Sch. Engring., 1989-93; bd. dirs. Milw. Children's Hosp. Found., 1994-98, Milw. Repertory Theater, 1997-2002. Fellow Am. Coll. Trust & Estate Counsel; mem. ABA, Wis. Bar Assn., Phi Beta Kappa. Home: 2727 E Shorewood Blvd Milwaukee WI 53211-2459 Office: Michael Best & Friedrich 100 E Wisconsin Ave Ste 3300 Milwaukee WI 53202-4108 Office Phone: 414-271-6560.

HABERMAN, PETER JOSEPH, music educator; b. St. Paul, July 4, 1975; s. George Gilbert and Marita Watrin Haberman; m. Erika Dane Tomten, Aug. 10, 2002. B of Music Edn., Concordia Coll.; MusM, U. Mont. Dir. band Maple Lake Sch. Dist., Minn., 1997—2000; tchg. asst. U. Mont., Missoula, 2000—02; dir. band Mercer Island High Sch., Wash., 2002—. Dir. Bellevue Cmty. Band, Wash., 2002—05. Mem.: Music Educators Nat. Conf., Internat. Trumpet Guild, Coll. Band Dirs. Nat. Assn., Wash. Music Educators Assn. Avocation: outdoor recreation. Home: 15214 NE 8th St #4 Bellevue WA 98007 Office: Mercer Island High Sch 9100 SE 42d St Mercer Island WA 98040

HABERMAN, SHELBY JOEL, statistician, educator; b. Cin., May 4, 1947; s. Jack Leon and Miriam Leah (Langberg) H.; m. Elinor Penny Levine, Feb. 18, 1979 (dec. 1996); children: Shoshanah, Chasiah, Sarah, Milcah, Boaz, Devorah. AB, Princeton U., 1968; PhD, U. Chgo., 1970. Asst. prof. to prof. U. Chgo., 1970-82; prof. Hebrew U., Jerusalem, 1982-84; prof. stats. Northwestern U., Evanston, Ill., 1984—2002, chmn. dept., 1986-88; dir. Ctr. for Statis. Theory and Practice, Ednl. Testing Svc., Princeton, NJ, 2002—. Author: Analysis of Frequency Data, 1974, Analysis of Qualitative Data, Vol. I, 1978, Vol. II, 1979, Advanced Statistics, Vol. I, 1996; contbr. articles to profl. jours. Guggenheim fellow, 1977-78. Fellow AAAS, Inst. Math. Stats., Am. Statis. Assn. Home: 414 S 4th St Highland Park NJ 08904- Office: Ednl Testing Svc Rosedale Rd 08541 Princeton NJ 08541-0001 Office Phone: 609-734-5787. Business E-Mail: SHaberman@ets.org.

HABERMANN, HELEN MARGARET, botanist, educator; b. Bklyn., Sept. 13, 1927; AB, SUNY, Albany, 1949; MS, U. Conn., 1951; PhD, U. Minn., 1956. Asst. botanist U. Conn., Storrs, 1949-51; asst. U. Minn., Mpls., 1951-53, asst. plant physiologist, 1953-55, head residence counselor, 1955-56; rsch. assoc. U. Chgo., 1956-57; rsch. fellow Hopkins Marine Sta. Stanford

(Calif.) U., 1957-58; from asst. prof. to prof. biol. scis. Goucher Coll., Towson, 1958—82, chmn. dept. biology, 1963-66, 68, 78-79, Lilian Welsh prof. biol. scis., 1982-92; prof. emeritus, 1992—. Co-author Biology: A Full Spectrum, 1973, Mainstreams of Biology, 1977. NIH spl. rsch. fellow Rsch. Inst. Advanced Study, Balt., 1966-67. Fellow AAAS; mem. Phytochem. Soc. N.Am. (sec. 1987-93), Am. Soc. Plant Physiologists, Am. Soc. Hort. Sci., Soc. Devel. Biology, Am. Soc. Photobiology, Am. Inst. Biol. Scis., Scandinavian Soc. Plant Physiology, Internat. Soc. Plant Molecular Biology, Japanese Soc. Plant Physiology, Soc. Exptl. Biology and Medicine, Am. Camellia Soc., Pioneer Camellia Soc. (pres. 1994-95, sec. 2000-01), Am. Hort. Soc., Sigma Xi. Personal E-mail: hhabermann@wans.net.

HABERMANN, JAMES HERBERT, retired pathologist; b. Cassville, Wis., June 18, 1926; s. Matthew Herbert and Clara Cordelia (Reilly) H.; m. Helen Audrey Howe, June 14, 1952; children: Thomas, Patrick, Michael, Jane, Mary Ann. MD, Marquette U., Milw., 1952. Diplomate in anat. and clin. pathology Am. Bd. Pathology. Family practice physician, Mt. Calvary, Wis., 1953-60; resident in pathology Denver Gen. Hosp., 1960-64; dir. labs. Mercy Hosp. and Luth. Hosp. (merged into Trinity Hosp.), Ft. Dodge, Iowa, 1964-77; staff pathologist Freeman Hosp., Joplin, Mo., 1977-80, St. John's Med. Ctr., Joplin, 1980-91; ret. Pres. bd. dirs. Trinity Regional Hosp., Ft. Dodge, 1973-77; chief of staff St. John's Med. Ctr., Joplin, 1984-85. 1st lt. U.S. Army, 1944-47, Germany. Fellow Am. Soc. Clin. Pathologists, Coll. Am. Pathologists. Roman Catholic. Avocation: woodworking. Home: 2111 E 36th St Joplin MO 64804-4232 E-mail: JHHabermann@webtv.net.

HABERMEHL, LAWRENCE LEROY, philosophy educator; b. Joplin, Mo., June 13, 1937; s. Roland William and Ruth Esther (Kelly) H.; m. Kathryn J. Barnes, June 18, 1958 (div. 1974); children: Elizabeth Anne, R. William, Edward Hale; m. Sue Ellen Lovejoy, Sept. 16, 1989 (div. 1996). AB, Phillips U., 1959; BD, Union Theol. Sem., 1961; PhD, Boston U., 1967. House mgr. Boston Seaman's Friend Soc., 1963-65; teaching fellow Boston U., 1965-66; asst. prof. philosophy Am. Internat. Coll., Springfield, Mass., 1966-73, assoc. prof., 1973—2001, prof., 2001—. Author: The Counterfeit Wisdom of Shallow Minds: A Critique of Some Leading Offenders of the 1980s, 1994; author/editor: Morality in the Modern World, 1976. Mem. AAUP, Am. Philos. Assn., Metaphys. Soc. Am., Common Cause, Amnesty Internat., Assn. Informal Logic and Critical Thinking. Unitarian-Universalist. Home: 1235 Enfield St Enfield CT 06082 Office: Am Internat Coll Dept Philosophy 1000 State St Springfield MA 01109 Office Phone: 413-205-3327. E-mail: LawLH@aol.com.

HABGOOD, ANTHONY JOHN, management consultant; b. Woodbastwick, Eng., Nov. 8, 1946; s. John Michael and Diana Margaret (Dalby) H.; m. Nancy Ray Atkinson, June 29, 1974; children: Elizabeth Ann, John Alan, George Michael. BA in Econs., Gonville and Caius Coll., Cambridge U., 1968; MA, Cambridge U., 1972; MS in Indsl. Adminstrn., Carnegie-Mellon U., 1970. From staff to v.p., dir. Boston Cons. Group Inc., 1970-86, exec. com., 1983-86; dir. Tootal, PLC, London, 1986-91, CEO, 1991; dir. Geest, PLC, London, 1988-93; CEO Bunzl, PLC, London, 1991-96, chmn., 1996—; dir. SVG Capital, PLC, London, 1995—, Marks & Spencer, PLC, London, 2004—; chmn. Whitbread plc, 2005—. W.L. Mellon fellow, 1968-70 Mem.: Royal Norfolk and Suffolk Yacht. Mem. Ch. Of Eng. Office: 110 Park St London W1K 6NX England

HABIB, IBRAHIM WAHBY, computer engineer, educator; b. Cairo, Aug. 16, 1959; arrived in U.S., 1988; s. Wahby Mohamed Habib and Salwa Kamel Essawy. BSEE, Ain Shams U., Cairo, 1981; MSEE, Poly. U. N.Y., 1984; PhD in Elec. Engring., CUNY, 1991. Cons., NJ, 1998—, 1998—; assoc. prof. CUNY, 1998, prof., 2004—. Part-time tech. cons. AT&T, 1997—2000, Telecordia, 2000—01; spkr. at several Am. and European univs. Guest editor IEEE JSAC, IEEE Comms. Mag., John Wiley Jour. on Wireless Networks; contbr. over 100 articles to profl. publs. Mem. IEEE (sr., reviewer 1991—, editor 1993-97, mem. tech. program com. numerous internat. confs.). Achievements include patents pending Adaptive Allocation of Resources in Communication Networks. Office: CUNY Elec Engring Dept 137 St and Convent Ave New York NY 10031 Office Phone: 212-650-7184. Personal E-mail: ibrahimhabib@hotmail.com.

HABICHT, CHRISTIAN HERBERT, history professor; b. Dortmund, Germany, Feb. 23, 1926; came to U.S., 1972; s. Hermann Christian and Emile Julie (Diefenbach) H.; m. Freia Renate Wilkowski, Aug. 15, 1952; children: Susanne, Christoph, Nikolaus. Dr.Phil., U. Hamburg, 1952, Habil, 1957. Asst. to assoc. prof. U. Hamburg, 1952-61; prof. ancient history U. Marburg/Lahn, 1961-65; prof. U. Heidelberg, 1965-73, dean, 1966-67; prof. Inst. Advanced Study, Princeton, N.J., 1973-98; vis. prof. Princeton U., 1973-80. Author books; contbr. articles to profl. jours. Mem. British Acad., Am. Philos. Soc., Acad. Heidelberg, Acad. Athens, German Archeol. Inst., Austrian Archeol. Inst., Am. Inst. Archeology, Assn. Ancient Historians (Reuchlin-Price award 1991, Moe-Price award 1996, Criticos-Price award 1998). Office: Inst Advanced Study Sch Hist Studies Princeton NJ 08540 Business E-Mail: habicht@ias.edu.

HABICHT, FRANK HENRY, retired manufacturing executive; b. Chgo., Sept. 4, 1920; s. Geroge Jr. and Gertrude A. (Tronc) H.; m. Jeanne Ellen Patrick, Mar. 9, 1943; children: Pamela, Patricia, Frank Henry II. BSME, Purdue U., 1942; postgrad., Cornell U., 1942, Am. U., 1944. From sales engr. to pres. Marshall & Huschart Machinery Co., Chgo., 1946-70; vice chmn. Cone-Blanchard Machine Co., Windsor, Vt. and Aldridge, Eng., 1971-74; chmn. bd., pres. United Tech. Corp., Chgo., 1970-81; pres. Steego Tech. Corp., West Palm Beach, 1981-86; chmn., pres. Corp. Assocs., Inc., 1986-97. Tech. cons. U.S. Dept. Def., Washington, 1963-64; pres. UNISIG Corp., 1980-86, King & Gavaris Cons. Engrs. Inc., 1980-84; U.S. projects mgr. Boehringer GmbH, Germany, 1989-95; 1997; lectr. in field; bd. dirs. Am. SIP Corp., Botemp Corp., Switzerland. Author: Modern Machine Tools, 1964; contbr. articles to profl. jours. Mem. def. indsl. plant equipment com. Dept. Def. Lt. comdr.USN, 1942-45. Mem. ASME, Am. Machine Tool Distbrs. Assn. (dir., past pres.), Fabricating Mfrs. Assn. (dir., past pres.), Assn. of RAF Warbirds, Conf. Bd. (exec. coun.), Order Knights St. John of Jerusalem, Oakbrook Polo Club, Palm Beach Club, Beach Club, Palm Beach Yacht Club, Governor's Club, Soc 4 Arts (Palm Beach, Navy League (bd. dirs.), Masons. Episcopalian. Avocations: hunting, fishing, tennis. Office: Corp Assocs Inc PO Box 746 Palm Beach FL 33480-0746

HABING, BRETT WILLIAM, music educator; b. Indpls., June 2, 1972; s. John William and Nancy Jean Habing; m. Deborah Sue Mongold, July 16, 1994; 1 child, Aidan James. MusB, Bob Jones U., 1994, MEd, 1997. Mem. voice and conducting faculty, chmn. music edn. dept. Northland Bapt. Bible Coll., Dunbar, Wis., 1997—, rec. prodr., 2002—. Choral clinician. Composer: various gen. and sacred choral and vocal works. Singer Dickinson Area Cmty. Chorus, Iron Mountain, Mich., 1999—2002; deacon Grace Bapt. Ch., Iron Mountain, 2002. Mem.: Nat. Assn. for Music Edn., Am. Choral Directors Assn. Baptist. Home: 1608 River St Niagara WI 54151 Office: Northland Bapt Bible Coll W10085 Pike Plains Rd Dunbar WI 54119 E-mail: bhabing@nbbc.edu.

HABLUTZEL, NANCY ZIMMERMAN, lawyer, educator; b. Chgo., Mar. 16, 1940; d. Arnold Fred Zimmerman and Maxine Lewison (Zimmerman) Goodman; m. Philip Norman Hablutzel, July 1, 1980; children: Margo Lynn, Robert Paul. BS, Northwestern U., 1960; MA, Northeastern Ill. U., 1972; JD, Ill. Inst. Tech. chgo.-Kent Coll. Law, 1980; PhD, Loyola U., Chgo., 1983. Bar: Ill. 1980, U.S. Dist. Ct. (no. dist.) Ill. 1980, U.S. Supreme Ct. 1995. Speech therapist various pub. schs. and hosps., Chgo. and St. Louis, 1960—63, 1965—72; audiologist U. Chgo. Hosps., 1963—65; instr. spl. edn. Chgo. State U., 1972—76; asst. prof. Loyola U., Chgo., 1981—87; adj. prof. Ill. Inst. Tech. Chgo.-Kent Coll. Law, 1982—, Lewis U., 1990—92; lectr. Loyola U., Chgo., 1990—98; legal dir. Legal Clinic for Disabled, Chgo., 1984—85, exec. dir., 1985—87; of counsel Whitted & Spain P.C., 1987—89; prin. Hablutzel & Assocs., Chgo., 1989—94, 1997—. Hearing officer Cir. Ct. of Cook County, 1994—96, supervising hearing officer, 1995—97; faculty No. Ill. U., 1997—2003; advisor Ill. Dept. Children and Family Svcs., 1997—2003; hearing officer Ill. State Bd. Edn., 1999—2005; asst. prof. Coll. Edn. U. St. Francis, Joliet, Ill., 2003—05. Co-author (with B. McMahon): Americans with Disabilities Act: Access and Accomodations, 1992; contbg. editor: Nat. Disability Law Reporter, 1991—92. Mem. Ill. Gov.'s Com. on Handicapped, 1972—75; mem., faculty moderator student divsn. Coun. for Exceptional Children, 1982—87; mem. adv. com. for disabled Ill. Atty. Gen., 1985—; mem. adv. com. Scouting for People with Disabilities, Chgo. Area Boy Scouts Am., 1988—92. Grantee Loyola-Mellon Found. grantee, 1983. Fellow: Ill. Bar Found. (sec. fellows 1992, vice chair fellow 1993, chair 1994, standing com. on leg. 1995—, com. on cable tv programs 1999—, com. lon legal edn., adminstrn. to bar and competency 2002—, edn. law sec. coun. 2005—), Chgo. Bar Found. (life); mem.: ABA, Chgo. Hearing Soc. (bd. dirs. 1992—94, Marion Goldman award 1988), Chgo. Bar Assn. (corp. law com., exec. com. 1984—94, chmn. Divsn. IV 1988—91, sec. 1991—92, vice chair 1992—93, chair 1993—94), Ill. Bar Assn. (Inst. Pub. Affairs 1985—, assoc., standing com. on juvenile justice, sec. 1986—87, vice chmn. 1987—88, chmn. 1988—89, legis. com. 1991—, mem. juvenile justice sect. coun. 1994—), Nat. Coun. of Juvenile and Family Ct. Judges (permanency planning com., continuing jud. edn. com. 1994—99). Avocations: sailing, travel, cooking, swimming. Office: 19 S LaSalle St Ste 1300 Chicago IL 60603

HABOUSH, WILLIAM JOSEPH, mathematician, educator; b. N.Y.C., June 7, 1942; s. Edward Joseph and Eva Marie (Truglio) H.; m. Jahyun Kim, Jan. 28, 1966. BA, Cornell U., 1963; PhD, Columbia U., 1970. Lectr. U. Mich., Ann Arbor, 1968-70; asst. prof. Bklyn. Coll., 1970-71, SUNY, Albany, 1972-74, assoc. prof., 1974-79, prof., 1979-85, U. Ill., Urbana, 1985—. Vis. mem. Inst. for Advanced Study, Princeton, N.J., 1974-75; fellow of the Japan Soc. for the Promotion of Scis., Nagoya U., 1972-73; vis. prof. UCLA, 1975-76, Inst. des Hautes Etudes Scietifiques, Bur. sur Yuette France, 1980; prof. chiarissimo Inst. Matematico Guido Castelnuovo, U. Degli Studi di Roma, Rome, 1979; vis. prof. Osaka U., 1985, Utrecht U., The Netherlands, 1986, Tohoku U., Sendai, Japan, 1993, The Tata Inst. for Fundamental Rsch., Bombay, 1992, 99, The So. Petroleum Industries Corp. Rsch. Found., Madras, India, 1992, 99, Aarhus U., Denmark, 1995, others; organizer summer sch. on algebraic groups and their generalizations Am. Math. Soc., 1991. Contbr. articles to profl. jours. Grantee Japan Soc. for the Promotion of Sci., 1972-73, 85, 92, Cime, 1979, NSF, 1975-81, 84-85. Achievements include the solving of the Mumford Conjecture in 1974, which was the last remaining great piece of Hilbert's 14th problem, and was crucial to the construction of moduli spaces in algebraic geomtery and for a very short proof of the Kempf Vanishing Theorem, which was a great break through in representation theory. Office: U Ill at Urbana/Dept Math 1409 W Green St Urbana IL 61801-2943 E-mail: haboush@math.uicu.edu.

HABRA, KAREN, management consultant; b. Beirut, Dec. 13, 1971; arrived in U.S., 1981; d. Nabil Habra, Hedy Habra. BA in Psychology and English, U. Mich., 1993; MBA in Mktg., Thunderbird U., 1996. Cert. project mgmt. profl. 2001. Coord. mktg. Stryker Med., Kalamazoo, 1993—94; mktg. rschr. Upjohn Co., Santiago, Calif., 1995; intern account exec. Coca Cola Co., Atlanta, 1996; mgr. product Bell South Long Distance, Atlanta, 1997—99; mgr. bus. devel. Bell South Advt. and Publicity, Atlanta, 1999—2001; mgr. project Bell South Internat., Atlanta, 2001—. Democrat. Roman Catholic. Avocations: soccer, tennis, pottery. Home: 1101 Defoors Landing Atlanta GA 30318

HABUSH, ROBERT LEE, lawyer; b. Milw., Mar. 22, 1936; s. Jesse James and Beatrice (Liebenberg) Habush; m. Miriam Lee Friedman, Aug. 25, 1957; children: Sherri Ellen, William Scott, Jodi Lynn. BBA, U. Wis., 1959, JD, 1961. Bar: Wis. 1961, U.S. Dist. Ct. (ea. and we. dists.) Wis. 1961, U.S. Ct. Appeals (7th cir.) 1965, U.S. Supreme Ct. 1986. Pres. Habush, Habush & Rottier, S.C., Milw., 1961—. Advisor restatement of torts products liability 3rd and gen. principles Am. Law Inst.; lectr. U. Wis. Law Sch., Marquette U. Law Sch., Wis., State Bar Wis., others. Author: The Art of Advocacy: Cross Examination of Non Medical Experts, 1981; contbr. articles to profl. jours. Benefactor scholarships, funds chairs, and founds. Capt. U.S. Army, 1959—75. Named one of Top Ten Litigators in U.S., Nat. Law Jour., 2001, Ten Wis. Leaders in the Law, Wis. Law Jour., 2003; recipient Evan P. Helfaer Donor award, Nat. Assn. Fundraising Execs., 2000, Cmty. Svc. Human Rels. award, Milw. chpt. AJC, 2004, UW Law Sch. Distng. Svc award, 2003. Mem.: ABA, ATLA (bd. govs. 1969—70, 1983—86, pres. 1986—87, former ATLA-PAC trustee and chmn. pub. affairs com., Harry Philo award 1999, Leonard Ring Champion of Justice award 2002, Robert L. Habush ATLA Endowment re-named in his honor), Wis. Bar Found., Trial Lawyers Pub. Justice, Inner Cir. Advs., Wis. Acad. Trial Lawyers (pres. 1968—69, 1971—72, named Robert L. Habush Trial Lawyer of the Yr. award in his honor 2000), Wis. Bar Assn., Am. Soc. Writers Legal Subjects, Am. Bd. Trial Advs., Nat. Bd. Trial Advs., Nat. Coll. Advocacy, Internat. Soc. Barristers, Internat. Acad. Trial Lawyers (bd. dirs. 1983—87, 1991—92), Roscoe Pound Found. Office: Habush Habush & Rottier 777 E Wisconsin Ave Ste 2300 Milwaukee WI 53202-5381 Office Phone: 414-271-0400. Business E-Mail: rhabush@habush.com.

HACCOUN, DAVID, electrical engineering educator; b. Bizerte, Tunisia, July 4, 1937; arrived in Can. 1957; s. Charles and Emma (Melloul) H.; m. Lyson Tobaly, Dec. 26, 1971; children: Nathalie, Laurent. B.Sc. Engring. Physics, U. Montreal, 1965; SM, MIT, 1966; PhD, McGill U., 1974. Registered profl. engr., Que. Comms. City of Montreal, 1965; rsch. asst. MIT, Cambridge, 1965-66; prof. Ecole Polytech. U., Montreal, 1966—. Vis. rsch. prof. Concordia U., Montreal, 1984-85, U. Lund, Sweden, 1989-90, Ecole Technologie Superieure, Montreal, 1996-97; project leader Can. Inst. for Telecom. Rsch. under Nat. Ctrs. Excellence of Govt. Can., 1990-2003; vis. rsch. fellow Advanced Study Inst., U. BC, Vancouver, 1992; vis. rschr. INRIA, Paris, 1992, 1998-99; co-founder, pres. Can. Soc. Into. Theory, 1986-87; vis. rsch. prof. Higher Sch. Tech., Montreal, 1999, U. Victoria, B.C., Can., 1999; mem. exec. com. Telecom. Engring. Mgmt. Inst. Can., 1997—; cons. in field. Co-author: Digital Communications by Satellite, 1981, translated in Japanese, 1984, in Chinese, 1989, The Communications Handbook, 1997, 2001, The Encyclopedia of Telecommunications, 2002; contbr. articles to profl. jours. Mem. exec. com. Can. Jewish Congress, 1996—; bd. dirs. Comm. Rsch. Ctr., Ottawa, 1999—. Commonwealth fellow London, 1965; Grass fellow MIT, 1966, MIT scholar, 1965-66; Hydro-Que. fellow, Montreal, 1969-72. Fellow IEEE (life), Engring. Inst. Can.; mem. AAAS, Order of Engrs. of Que., NY Acad. Scis., Sigma Xi. Avocations: photography, swimming, skiing. Office: Ecole Polytechnique PO Box 6079 Sta Centre Ville Montreal PQ Canada H3C 3A7 Office Phone: 514-340-4711 x 4548. Business E-Mail: david.haccoun@polymtl.ca.

HACEK, DONNA, microbiologist, researcher; b. Chgo., Apr. 20, 1961; d. George and Rita Prelac. BS in Clin. Lab. Sci., Marquette U., 1983. Cert. Am. Board Certified Medical Technologists, 1983. From bench techologist to clin. microbiologist Northwestern Meml. Hosp., Chgo., 1983—99; clin. microbiologist Northwestern Meml. Hosp. Prevention Epicenter, 1999—2002; clin. microbiologist Depts. Molecular Epidemiology and Epidemiology Rsch. Evanston (Ill.) Northwestern Healthcare, 2002—. Tchr. sunday sch. Willow Creek Cmty. Ch., South Barrington, Ill., 2000—05. Mem.: Ill. Soc. Microbiology, Am. Soc. Clin. Pathologists, Am. Soc. Microbiology. Office: Evanston Northwestern Healthcare 2650 Ridge Ave Walgreen Building SB525 Evanston IL 60201 E-mail: dhacek@enh.org.

HACHEY, MARC A., geologist; b. Waterville, Maine, Dec. 16, 1975; s. Richard and Nancy Hachey. BA, Colby Coll., Waterville, Maine. Cert. profl. geologist State of Calif., State of Utah. Technician Petra Geotechnical, San Diego, 1998—2001; geologist Consolidated Engring. Labs, San Ranch, Calif., 2001—. Mem.: Assn. Engring. Geologists. Democrat. Avocations: hiking, music, mountain biking. Home: 1174 Walker Ave #4 Walnut Creek CA 94596

HACHEY, THOMAS EUGENE, British and Irish history educator; b. Lewiston, Maine, June 8, 1938; s. Leo Joseph and Margaret Mary (Johnson) H.; m. Jane Beverly Whitman, June 9, 1962. BA, St. Francis Coll., 1960; MA, Niagara U., 1961; PhD, St. John's U., 1965. Asst. prof. history Marquette U., Milw., 1964-69, assoc. prof., 1969-77, prof., 1977—, chmn. dept. history, 1979-93, dean Coll. Arts and Scis., 1993-2000; exec. dir. Irish programs, endowed chair dept. history Boston Coll., 2000—. Vis. prof. history Sch. Irish Studies, Dublin, 1977-78; cons. investments in Ireland Frost & Sullivan, N.Y.C., 1978-82; pres. Am. Conf. Irish Studies, 1983-85; dir. Bradley Inst. for Democracy and Pub. Values, 1988-99. Author: Problem of Partition: Peril to World Peace, 1972, Britain and Irish Separatism, 1977; co-author: The Irish Experience, 1988, expanded edit., 1996, Perspectives of Irish Nationalism, 1988; editor: Voices of Revolution, 1972, Confidential Despatches, 1975; contbr. over 100 articles and revs. to Brit., Irish and Am. jours. and newspapers. Danforth assoc., 1979-85. Fellow Anglo-Am. Assocs. Roman Catholic. Home: 20 Deerpath Rd Dedham MA 02026 Office: Boston Coll Connolly House 300 Hammond St Chestnut Hill MA 02467-3930 Office Phone: 617-552-4847.

HACHMEISTER, JOHN H., mediator, lawyer, educator; b. Chgo., Nov. 24, 1944; s. Howard E. and Leah (Mace) H.; m. Lydia E. McCarver, Jan. 8, 1982; children: Steven, David, Mellissa, Rachel. BA in Polit. Sci., Cent. State U., Edmond, Okla., 1978; postgrad., Oklahoma City U., 1980-82; JD, Southwestern U., L.A., 1984. Bar: Calif. Technician Am. Chain & Cable, Franklin Park, Ill., 1972-76; assoc. Somers, Hall, et al., Gardena, Calif., 1985-90, Spray, Gould & Bowers, L.A., 1990-92, Fiore, Nordberg, et al, Irvine, Calif., 1992-94; pvt. practice Beach Cities Ctr. for Appropriate Dispute Resolution, Redondo Beach, Calif., 1994—; owner Jack's Imagination Enterprises, Redondo Beach, 1988—; former asst. prof. Calif. State U., Northridge. Co-trainer peer mediation Redondo Union H.S.; judge pro tem Calif. Sup. Ct.; cons., facilitator Oklahoma City Coalition of Neighborhood Assns., 1972-82; spkr. in field. Author: (poetry) Colorado Cowboy Poetry Gathering, 1993; co-inventor solder jig for multi-wire cables, 1992; contbr. articles to profl. jours. Candidate for state sen. Dem. party, Torrance, Calif., 1990, Ho. of Reps., Oklahoma City, 1978; del. Dem. party convs. Okla. and Calif., 1974-92; mem. Mayor's Transp. Task Force, Oklahoma City, 1976-80; lt. gov. Okla. Intercollegiate Legis., 1977-78; judge Southwestern U. Moot Ct. Competition, Santa Ana, Calif., 1993. Named to Outstanding Young Men of Am. Mem. Calif. Bar Assn., Greenpeace, Torrance Area C. of C. (mem. cultural involvement task force, v.p. internat. bus. commn.), Human Rels. Found. Torrance. Avocations: hiking, camping, reading, writing, footracing. Home: 143 Via La Soledad Redondo Beach CA 90277-6625 E-mail: jhachmeister@bcc4adr.com.

HACHTEN, RICHARD ARTHUR, II, health facility administrator; b. LA, Mar. 24, 1945; s. Richard A. and Dorothy Margaret (Shipley) H.; m. Jeanine Hachten, Dec. 12, 1970; children: Kristianne, Karin. BS in Econs., U. Calif., Santa Barbara, 1967; MBA, UCLA, 1969. Mgmt. intern TRW Systems Group, Redondo Beach, Calif., 1969-72; adminstrv. asst. Meth. Hosp., Arcadia, Calif., 1972-73, asst. adminstr., 1973-74, assoc. adminstr., 1974-76, v.p. adminstrn., 1976-80; exec. v.p., adminstr., 1980-81; pres., adminstr., 1981-84; CEO Tri-City Hosp. Dist., Oceanside, 1984-91; pres. Bergan Mercy Health Sys., Omaha, 1991-95, Algent Health, Omaha, 1996—. Instr. health care mgmt. Pasadena (Calif.) City Coll. Bd. dirs., pres. Hospice of Pasadena, Inc.; bd. dirs. ARC, Arcadia, Mercy Housing Midwest, Omaha, Metropolitan Cmty. Coll. Found. Mem. Am. Coll. Healthcare Execs. (diplomate), Hosp. Coun. San Diego and Imperial Counties (chmn., bd. dirs.), Nebr. Hosp. Assn. (chmn. bd. dirs., chmn. dist. 1), Calif. Assn. Hosps. and Health Sys. (bd. dirs.), Am. Hosp. Assn. (policy bd. mem.), Rotary, Beta Gamma Sigma. Republican. Methodist. Home: 2676 S 96th Cir Omaha NE 68124-1949 Office: Alegent Health 1010 N 96th St Ste 200 Omaha NE 68114-2595 Office Phone: 402-343-4420. Business E-Mail: rhachten@alegent.org.

HACK, GARY ARTHUR, dean; b. Abernethy, Sask., Can., Apr. 8, 1942; came to U.S., 1964; s. Arthur and Marie (Banerd) H.; m. Lynda Lloy Lewis, Sept. 5, 1964 (dec.); children: Andrew Arthur, Carolyn Sarah; m. Lynne Beyer Sagalyn, Jan. 1, 2002. BArch, U. Manitoba, 1964; MArch, U. Ill., 1966, M in Urban Planning, 1967; PhD, MIT, 1976. Project mgr. Gruen Assocs., N.Y.C., 1967-69; asst. prof. MIT, Cambridge, 1970-75; gen. mgr. Can. Mortgage and Housing Corp., Ottawa, Ont., 1975-79; prof. MIT, Cambridge, 1979-96; prin. Carr Lynch Hack & Sandell, Cambridge, 1986-94; dean, Paley prof. U. Pa., Phila., 1996—. Co-author: Site Planning, 3d edit., 1984, Global City Regions, 2000; chief planner West Side Waterfront, N.Y.C., 1986-91, Prudential Ctr. Redevel., Boston, 1988-91. Bd. dirs. William Penn Found., 2004—. Recipient 1st award Progressive Architecture, 1975. Mem. Am. Inst. Cert. Planners. Avocations: travel, architectural photography, collecting yi cheng teapots. Office: U Pa 101 Meyerson Hall/6311 Philadelphia PA 19104 Business E-Mail: gahack@design.upenn.edu.

HACK, RANDOLPH C., advocate, educator, counselor; b. N.Y.C., Feb. 14, 1947; s. Sidney and Eleanor (Bermak) Hack. BA, U. Hawaii, Honolulu, 1980. Per diem tchr. Hawaii Dept. Edn., Honolulu, 1984—92; dir. consumer adv. United Self-Help, Honolulu, 1989—95; program dir. United Self Help, Honolulu, 1992—95, exec. dir., 1995—99; consumer advisor Adult Mental Health Divsn., Honolulu, 1999—, acting dir. consumer affairs, 2003. Counselor Armed Svcs. YMCA, Schofield Barracks, Hawaii, 1987—95; mem. Statewide Ind. Living Coun., 1999—2005; participant White House Conf. Mental Health, Washington, 1999, Washington, 2005; grant application reviewer. Chair pro tem, vice chair. State Coun. Mental Health, 2005—; mem. Diamond Head Svc. Area Bd. Mental Health & Substance Abuse, Honolulu, 1989—92; precinct chmn. Dem. Com. Hawaii, Honolulu, 2000; bd. dirs. Mental Health Assn. Hawaii, 1984—86, Waikiki Health Ctr., 1999—, Mental Health Kokua, 1990—. Recipient Cmty. Svc. award, Mental Health Assn., 1991, Senator Daniel K. Inouye award, Hawaii Psychol. Assn., 1998. Mem.: Nat. Alliance Mentally Ill (bd. dirs. Hawaii 1997—, bd. dirs. Oahu 1997—, state rep., nat. consumer coun. 1998—, alt. rep. 2004—). Avocation: swimming. Home: 1117 12th Ave Apt 8 Honolulu HI 96816-3747 Office: Adult Mental Health Divsn 1250 Punchbowl St Honolulu HI 96813 Office Phone: 808-586-4688. E-mail: rchack@mail.health.state.hi.us.

HACKAM, REUBEN, electrical engineering educator; b. Baghdad, Iraq, Feb. 18, 1936; arrived in Can., 1978; s. Yechiel and Rachel (Cohen) H.; m. Estelle Malkinson, June 7, 1964; children: Judy, David, Abby, Dan. BSc, Israel Inst. Tech., Haifa, 1960; PhD, U. Liverpool, Eng., 1964, DEng, 1988. Sr. engr. GE, Stafford, Eng., 1964-69; lectr. elec. engring. U. Sheffield, Eng., 1969-73, sr. lectr., 1973-74, reader, 1974-78; prof. U. Windsor, 1978—2001, prof. emeritus, 2001—, chmn. dept., 1981-82, 84-86. Vis. staff dept. math. Staffordshire Poly., Stafford, 1964-69, Sheffield Poly, 1970-78, Hong Kong Poly. U., 1990-91; cons. Brit. Rail, Derby, Eng., 1975-78, English Electric Co., Stafford, 1975-77, Windsor Star, 1981-91, Corp. City of Windsor, 1983-92, Green Shield Prepaid Svcs., Inc., 1982—, County of Essex Libr., 1986—, Can. Salt Co., 1988—, Windsor Real Estate Bd., 1996-2004; vis. prof. Kumamoto U., Japan, 1998-99. Contbr. articles to profl. jours. Cons. Windsor Bd. Edn., 1988, Essex Bd. Edn., Windsor, 1989-94. Fellow: IEEE (bd. dirs. conf. on elec. insulation and dielectric phenomena 1985—91, gaseous dielectrics tech. com. 1985—, mem. tech. program com.IEEE-CEIDP 1986—97, asst. editor Digest IEEE Transactions on Dielectrics and Elec. Insulat 1990—99, mem. editl. bd. IEEE Insulation Mag. 1990—2001, permanent sci. com. int. synomps. on discharges and elec. insulat 1991—2001, sec. 1992—93, fellows award com. 1993—96, vice chmn. conf. on elec. insulation and dielectric phenomena 1994—95, chmn. 1996—97, various working groups 1997—, assoc. editor 1999—2001, editor-in-chief 2002—, program com. publicity and pub. chmn., fellows award com. 2005—, mem. editl. bd. Transactions on Dielectrics and Electrical Insultation, Third Millennium medal 2000; Eric O. Forster Disting. award 2000, Innuishi Meml. lecture award 1998); mem.: IEEE Dielectrics and Elec. Insulation Soc. (nominating and adv. coms. 1988—91, pub. com. 1988—96, chmn. publ. com. 1990—91, edn. com. 1990—95, asst. treas. 1991, treas. 1993—94, v.p. adminstrn. 1995—96, pres., meetings and svcs. com. 1997—98, chair

1999—2000, treas., pub. com. 1999—2001). Jewish. Office: U Windsor 401 Sunset Ave Windsor ON Canada N9B 3P4 Office Phone: 512-253-3000. Business E-Mail: hackam@uwindsor.ca.

HACKBARTH, GLENN M., human services administrator; BA, Pa. State U.; MA, JD, Duke U. Atty. advisor to asst. sec. for planning and evaluation HHS, 1981—84; dep. adminstr. Health Care Financing Adminstrn., HHS, 1986—88; sr. v.p. Harvard Cmty. Health Plan, 1988—97; founder, CEO Harvard Vanguard Med. Assocs., Boston, 1997—98; chmn. Medicare Payment Adv. Commn., Washington, 2001—. Cons. The Bard Group, 2000—01.

HACKBARTH, STEVEN LYLE, writer, educator; b. St. Cloud, Minn., July 7, 1945; s. Randall Clifford Hackbarth and Viola Maxine Geisinger; m. Teresa Fatima Palacios, Nov. 15, 1996; m. Joyce Marie Brown, Sept. 11, 1965 (div.); children: Grace Maria, Valerie Lynn. BA in Psychology, Calif. State U., Sacramento, 1967; MA in Psychology, Calif. State U., 1968; PhD, UCLA, 1976; MS in Edn., U. So. Calif., L.A., 1984; MA, NYU, 1995. Cert. tchr. NY, 1995, instr. Calif., 1990. Mem. profl. staff SW Regional Lab. R & D, L.A., 1969—71; tchg. asst., rsch. assoc. U. Calif., L.A., 1971—76; dir. office student svcs., adj. asst. prof. U. So. Calif., L.A., 1977—91; cons. UN Children's Fund, N.Y.C., 1993—96; computer specialist tchr. City of NY, N.Y.C., 1994—. Author: The Educational Technology Handbook: A Comprehensive Guide: Process and Products for Learning; cons. editor: Tech Trends: For Leaders in Education and Training, 2000—, contbg. editor: Educational Technology: The Magazine for Managers of Change in Education, 1996—; contbr. chapters to books, articles to profl. jours. Tennis and softball coach; scout leader; chair fin. com. Good Shepherd United Meth. Ch., Astoria, NY, 2004—05. Recipient Disting. Svc. Most Outstanding Grad. award, Doctoral Alumni Assn., UCLA, 1976; Academic scholar, NYU, 1993—95. Mem.: Far Western Philosophy Edn. Soc. (life; pres. 1990—91), Assn. for Ednl. Comm. and Tech. (life; membership com., consulting editor 2000—05, Ann. Achievement award 2001), Phi Delta Kappa (life Most Outstanding New Member award 1991), Tau Kappa Epsilon (life; v.p., chaplain 1966—68, Top TKE Alumnus 1968). Achievements include research on changes in computer literacy as a function of race and gender; design of The Computer Literacy Assessment Tool; development of rational for discipline-based inquiry learning; documentation of current practice in math and science education. Home: 3334 Crescent St Long Island City NY 11106 Office: The Lillie Devereux Blake School 45 East 81st St New York NY 10028 Personal E-mail: hackbarths@aol.com.

HACKEL, ADAM WILLIAM, music educator; s. William Michael and Geraldine Ann Hackel. BFA, Tulane U., 1994; MA in Ednl. Leadership, Kean U., 2000; EdD, Rowan U., 2002; postgrad., Combined Arms and Services Staff Sch., 2002—. Cert. Music tchr. 1996, Chem. Def. Tng. 1995, Combat Life saver 1996, Supr. K-12 2001, Prin. 2001, Chem. Def. Tng. 2001, Army Instr. 1999, Army Course Mgr. 2000. Band dir. Montgomery Twp. Sch. Dist., Skillman, NJ, 2002—; commdg. officer 3 BN 391st Rgt. 7th Brigade, 98th Divsn., FT Dix, NJ, 2002—; jazz band dir. Montgomery Twp. Sch. Dist., Skillman, NJ, 2002—; dep. comdt., U.S. Army Chem. Sch. region a 4th Bn. Chem., 98th Divsn., FT Dix, NJ, 1999—2002; broadcase mgr. U.S. Army, 2003—. Musician: (music education work book) Master Teacher collaborative, 2000 (NJ. Symphony Orch. Master Tchr. Award, 2000). Capt. U.S. Army, 1994. Decorated Nat. Def. Svc. Medal U.S. Army Chem. Sch.; recipient Dunnaway Medal, Valley Forge Mil. Acad., 1990, Wayne Rotary Club Medal for selfless svc., 1989, Master Music Tchr. Collaborative, N.J. Symphony Orch., 2000, Aerospace Edn. Disting. Svc. Award, CAP, 2000, Disting. Svc. Award, Tulane Police Dept., 1994, David Price Trainer Award, Valley Forge Mil. Acad., 1990, Dunnaway medal, 1998. Master: Music Honor Soc. (life; faculty advisor 1995); mem.: Music Educators Nat. Conf. (assoc.), Kappa Delta Pi (assoc.). Avocations: music composition, camping, theater, singing, hiking. Office: Montgomery Township School Burnt Hill Rd Skillman NJ 08558 Personal E-mail: tiamat9408@earthlink.net.

HACKEL, EMANUEL, science educator; b. Bklyn., June 17, 1925; s. Henry N. and Esther (Herbstman) H.; m. Elisabeth Mackie, June 24, 1950 (dec. Apr. 1978); children: Lisa M., Meredith Anne, Janet M.; m. Rachel A. Fisher, Oct. 18, 1981; stepchildren: Daniel E., Tabitha A., and Jessica K. Harrison. Student, N.Y. U., 1941-42; BS, U. Mich., 1948, MS, 1949; PhD, Mich. State U., 1953. Fisheries biologist Mich. Dept. Conservation, 1949; mem. faculty Mich. State U., East Lansing, 1949—, prof. natural sci., 1962-74, chmn. dept. natural sci., 1963-74, prof. medicine, 1974-95, prof. emeritus, 1995—, prof. zoology, 1974-95, prof. emeritus, 1995—. Asst. dean coll. 1958-63; rsch. fellow Galton Lab., U. Coll., London, 1970-71, 77-78; vis. investigator blood group rsch. unit Lister Inst., London, 1956-57; cons. Mpls. War Meml. Blood Bank, 1983-95. Author: Guide to Laboratory Studies in Biological Science, 1951, Studies in Natural Science, 1953, Natural Science, 1955, Vols. 1, 2, 3, 1952-63. Editor: The Search for Explanation-Studies in Natural Science, Vols. 1, 2, 3, 1967-68, Laboratory Manual for Natural Science, Vol. 1, 2, 3, 1967-68, Human Genetics, 1974, Theoretical Aspects of HLA, 1982, Bone Marrow Transplantation, 1983, HLA Techniques for Blood Bankers, 1984, Human Genetics 1984: A Look at the Last Ten Years and the Next Ten, Transfusion Management of Some Common Heritable Blood Disorders, 1992, Advances in Transplantation, 1993, HLA Typing Section, Clinical Laboratory Medicine, 1994, Human Genetics '94: A Revolution in Full Swing, 1994; contbr. articles on genetics, human blood group immunology and chem. nature of blood group antigens, human biochem. genetics, tissue typing, human histocompatability antigens to sci. jours. Served to lt. (j.g.) USNR, 1943-47; now lt. comdr. USNR Ret. Recipient Cooley Meml. award Am. Assn. Blood Banks, 1969, Elliott Meml. award Am. Assn. Blood Banks, 1987, alumni disting. faculty award Coll. Natural Sci. Mich. State U., 1995. Mem. Assn. Gen. and Liberal Studies (sec.-treas. 1962-65), AAUP, AAAS, Genetics Soc. Am., Am. Soc. Human Genetics, Am. Assn. Blood Banks (dir. 1983-84, chmn. sci. sect. 1983-84), Mich. Assn. Blood Banks (v.p. 1970, pres. 1975-77), Am. Inst. Biol. Sci., Biometric Soc., Transplantation Soc. Mich. (dir. 1975-84), Am. Assn. for Clin. Histocompatability Testing, N.Y. Acad. Scis., Sigma Xi, Phi Kappa Phi. Home: 244 Oakland Dr East Lansing MI 48823-4747

HACKEL-SIMS, STELLA BLOOMBERG, lawyer, former government official; b. Burlington, Vt., Dec. 27, 1926; d. Hyman and Esther (Pocher) Bloomberg; m. Donald Herman Hackel, Aug. 14, 1949; children: Susan Jane, Cynthia Anne; m. Arthur Sims, Aug. 28, 1980. Student, U. Vt., 1943-45; JD cum laude, Boston U., 1948. Bar: Vt. 1948, Mass. 1948, D.C. 1979, Va. 1982. Individual practice law, Burlington, 1948-49, Rutland, Vt., 1949-59, 73—; city prosecutor City of Rutland, 1957-63; commr. Vt. Dept. Employment Security, 1963-73; treas. State of Vt., 1975-77; dir. U.S. Mint, Dept. Treasury, Washington, 1977-81. Chmn. Vt. Municipal Bond Bank, 1975-77 Mem. Vt. Adv. Com. on Mental Retardation, Interdept. Council on Aging, Commn. on Status Women, Human Resource Inter-Agency Com., Emergency Resource Priorities Bd., Info. Planning Council, Legis. Council Equal Opportunity Com., Vt. Indsl. Devel. Authority, Vt. Housing Fin. Agy., Vt. Claims Commn., Vt. Tchrs. Retirement Fund. Bd., Vt. Home Mortgage Guaranty Bd.; chmn. Vt. State Employees Retirement Fund; ex-officio mem. Nat. Manpower Adv. Com., 1971-72, Fed. Adv. Council on Unemployment Ins., 1971-72; Pres. Rutland Girl Scouts Leaders Assn., 1949-50, Rutland League Women Voters, 1951-52, Rutland Council Jewish Women, 1955-56; chmn. womens div. Rutland Community Chest Dr., 1952, Rutland County-Vt. Assn. for Blind, 1953-56; pres. Rutland County Democratic Women's Assn., 1956-63; treas. Rutland City Dem. Com., 1957-63; former rep. office women's activities Dem. Nat. Com., Regional Council I., Women's CD Councils; mem. Vt. bd. Girl Scouts U.S.A.; chmn. Arlington County Tenant-Landlord Commn., Va., 1986— . Mem.: LWV, AAUW (pres. Rutland County br. 1961—62), Interstate Conf. Employment Security Agys. (v.p. region I 1966—68, legis. com. 1969, sr. v.p. 1970—71, pres. 1971—72), Am. Soc. Pub. Adminstrn., Vt. Coun. Social Agys., Bus. and Profl. Women's Club, Rutland County Bar Assn. (pres. 1973), Vt. Bar Assn., Emblem (dir. 1960-63), Woodmont Country; Internat. (Washington), Moorings Country Club (Naples, Fla.) (bd. dirs. 2003—), Emblem Club (dir. 1960—63), Delta Phi Epsilon. Personal E-mail: stellahs@earthlink.net.

HACKENJOS-BUTLER, GENIE MARIE, minister; b. Shreveport, La., Sept. 27, 1946; d. Reginald U. and Elizabeth Marie (Davis) Hackenjos; m. Sam Lennard Butler, Jr., Aug. 9, 1969 (div. Sept. 1981). BA in German, Southwestern U., Georgetown, Tex., 1969; MDiv, Iliff Sch. Theology, Denver, 1982. Lic. to preach 1977, Deacons Orders Rocky Mountain Conf. United Meth. Ch., 1978, Elder's Orders N.D. Conf., United Meth. Ch., 1983. Feature writer Houston Chronicle, 1969—70; substitute tchr. various locations Tex., 1970—75; ch. sec. United Meth. Ch., Glenwood Springs, Colo., 1972—75; bookkeeper Petre, Zimmerman & Shelton, P.C., Glenwood Springs, 1971—74; owner, mgr. Kwik Kopy Printing, Ft. Collins, Colo., 1977—80; tchr. German Langdon H.S., ND, 1993—94; pastor United Meth. Ch., Neche-Cavalier, ND, 1980—86, First United Meth. Ch., Lisbon, ND, 1986—92, Langdon, ND, 1992—98, Pierre, SD, 1998—. Vice-chmn. Bd. of Ordained Ministry, N.D. Conf. United Meth. Ch., 1985—97; pres. Pembina County Ministerium, Cavalier, ND, 1984—86, Cavalier County Ministerium, Langdon, 1996—98. Contbr. poetry to profl. jours. Leader Girl Scouts U.S., Lisbon, ND, 1988—92; mem. Acad. for Preaching United Meth. Bd. Discipleship, Nashville and Jerusalem, 1990—92; mem. Citizens Involvement Coun., Pierre, SD, 2000—. Grantee Study-Travel grantee, Wesley Ctr. of Religion, U. N.D., 1986. Mem.: AAUW (pres. 1983—84, N.Dak. state v.p. 1988—89, program v.p. 2001—), Pierre-Ft. Pierre Ministerial Assn. (chief chaplain, SD Legislature 2004). Methodist. Avocations: gardening, reading, travel, writing. Home: 320 W Capital Ave Pierre SD 57501

HACKER, ANDREW, political science professor; b. N.Y.C., Aug. 30, 1929; s. Louis Morton and Lilian (Lewis) H.; 1 child, Ann. AB, Amherst Coll., 1951; MA, Oxford (Eng.) U., 1953; PhD, Princeton U., 1955. Instr. govt. Cornell U., Ithaca, N.Y., 1955-56, asst. prof., 1956-60, asso. prof., 1960-66, prof., 1966-71; prof. polit. sci. Queens Coll., CUNY, 1971—. Cons. Conf. Bd., Brookings Instn., Rockefeller Bros. Fund, NBC, Ency. Brit. Author: Political Theory: Philosophy, Ideology, Science, 1960, Congressional Districting, 1963, The Study of Politics, 1973, The Corporation Take-Over, 1964, The End of the American Era, 1970, The New Yorkers, 1975, Free Enterprise in America, 1977, U.S.: A Statistical Portrait of the American People, 1983, Two Nations: Black and White, Separate, Hostile, Unequal, 1992, updated edit., 2003, Money: Who Has How Much and Why, 1997, 2d edit., 1998, Mismatch: The Growing Gulf Between Women and Men, 2003. Mem. Phi Beta Kappa. Home: 20 W 64th St Apt 16K New York NY 10023-7180 Office: CUNY Queens Coll Dept Polit Sci Flushing NY 11367

HACKER, GARY LEE, lawyer; b. Denver, Nov. 28, 1939; s. Andrew Aris and Lena May (Brandt) Hacker; m. Aleta Szemcsak, Nov. 14, 1975; 1 child, Andrew John. BA, U. Colo., 1963; MA, U. Denver, 1971; JD, Baylor U., 1976. Bar: Tex. 1977, Fla. 1978. Asst. city atty., Abilene, Tex., 1977; asst. dist. atty. Taylor County, Abilene, Tex., 1978, Whitten & Young, Abilene, Tex., 1978—. Bd. dirs. Steamboat Mountain Water Corp., Tuscola, Tex. Maj. U.S. Army, 1963. Mem.: ATLA, ABA, Abilene Bar Assn., Tex. Bar Found. Democrat. Lutheran. Avocation: golf. Office: Whitten & Young PC PO Box 208 Abilene TX 79604-0208 Business E-Mail: glhyoung@whittenyoungpc.com.

HACKER, MICHELLE WENDY, auditor, researcher, finance educator; b. Chgo., Feb. 19, 1955; d. George Edward and Katharine Rosino Hacker. BS, Fla. Met. U., 1993, MBA, 1995; DBA, U. Sarasota, 2001. Mgr. SuperAm., Mpls., 1985—92; machinist Sargent-Lelich Sci., Chgo., 1975—85; tax auditor Dept. of Revenue, Tampa, Fla., 1995—; adj. prof. internat. bus Fla. Met. U., Tampa, Fla., 2001—. Composer: (symphonies) #1 The Egotistical, 1998, #2 The Esoteric, 2000, #3 The Quintessens, Complete book of Preludes Piano Opus 30, 2002, Complete Book of Nocturnes Piano Opus 41. Counselor AA, Tampa, Fla. Mem.: LWV, NOW. Home: 17941 Sailfish Dr Apt D Lutz FL 33558-7745 E-mail: michelledoc2003@yahoo.com.

HACKERMAN, NORMAN, chemist, academic administrator; b. Balt., Mar. 2, 1912; s. Jacob and Anne (Raffel) Hackerman; m. Gene Allison Coulbourn, Aug. 25, 1940 (dec.); children: Patricia Gale, Stephen Miles, Sally Griffith, Katherine Elizabeth. AB, Johns Hopkins U., 1932, PhD, 1935. Asst. prof. Loyola Coll., Balt., 1935—39; rsch. chemist Colloid Corp., 1936—40; asst. chemist USCG, S.I., 1939—41; prof. Va. Poly. Inst., Blacksburg, 1941—43; rsch. chemist Kellex Corp., 1944—45; asst. prof. chemistry U. Tex., 1945—46, assoc. prof., 1946—50, prof., 1950—70, chmn. dept. chemistry, 1952—61, dir. corrosion rsch. lab., 1948—61, dean rsch. and sponsored programs, 1960—61, v.p., provost, 1961—63, vice chancellor acad. affairs, 1963—67, pres., 1967—70, prof. emeritus chemistry, 1985—; prof. chemistry Rice U., Houston, 1970—85, Disting. prof. emeritus, 1985—, pres., 1970—85, pres. emeritus, 1985—. Chmn. Gordon Corrosion Rsch. Conf., 1950; cons. in corrosion, 1946—; chmn. Inter Soc. Corrosion Com., 1956—58, Gordon Rsch. Conf. on Surface Chemistry, 1959; mem. nat. sci. bd. NSF, 1968—80; chmn., 1974—80; mem. Def. Sci. Bd., 1978—85; chmn. sci. adv. bd. Welch Found., 1982—; chmn. bd. energy studies NAS/NRC Commn. Natural Resources, 1974—77; mem. Energy Rsch. Adv. Bd., 1980—82, Tex. Gov.'s Task Force on Higher Edn., 1981—82; trustee MITRE Corp., 1980—85. Editor Jour. Electrochem. Soc., 1969—89, editl. bd., adv. edn. bd. Corrosion Sci., 1965—70, editl. bd. Catalysis Revs., 1968—73. Recipient Whitney award, Nat. Assn. Corrosion Engrs., 1956, Joseph J. Mattiello Meml. lectr., Fedn. Socs. Paint Tech., 1964, Gold medal, Am. Inst. Chemists, Mirabeau B. Lamar award, Assn. Tex. Colls. and Univs., 1981, Disting. Alumnus award, Johns Hopkins U., 1982, Alumni Gold medal for disting. svc. to Rice U., 1984, Vannevar Bush award, NSF, 1993, Nat. medal of Sci., 1993. Fellow: AAAS (Phillip Hauge Abelson prize 1987), N.Y. Acad. Scis., Am. Acad. Arts and Scis.; mem.: NAS, Am. Philos. Soc., Argonne Univs. Assn. (chmn. bd. trustees 1969—73), Nat. Corrosion Engrs. (bd. dirs. 1952—55, chmn. com. edn. Corrosion Rsch. Coun. 1957—60), Faraday Soc., Electrochem. Soc. (pres. 1957—58, Palladium medal 1965, Edward Goodrich Acheson award 1984), Am. Chem. Soc. (bd. editors 1955—62, exec. com. colloid divsn. 1955—58, chmn. chemistry and pub. affairs com. 1982—88, S.W. Regional award 1965, Charles Lathrop Parsons award 1987), Sigma Xi, Phi Kappa Phi, Alpha Chi Sigma, Phi Lambda Upsilon. Home: 3 Woodstone Sq Austin TX 78703 Office: The Robert A Welch Found 5555 San Felipe St Ste 1900 Houston TX 77056-2732 Office Phone: 713-961-9884. E-mail: atmar@welch1.org.

HACKERT, MARVIN LEROY, chemistry educator, biophysical researcher; b. Pella, Iowa, Sept. 23, 1944; s. Henry and Johanna Mae (Vanden Berg) H.; children: Christopher Lee, Brian Mitchell. BA, Central Coll., Pella, 1966; PhD, Iowa State U., 1970. Fellow Purdue U., West Lafayette, Ind., 1970-74; asst. prof. U. Tex., Austin, 1974-80, assoc. prof., 1980-86, prof., 1986—, grad. advisor, 1991-95, dept. chair, 1995-2000. Chair U.S. Nat. Com. Crystallography, 2000-03. Author: chemistry study guide, 1982, 87, 93, 97, 2000; contbr. articles to profl. jours. State sci. contest dir. Univ. Interscholastic League, 1984-96. Mem. AAAS, Am. Chem. Soc., Am. Crystallographic Assn. (chair BIOMAC SIG, 1991-92). Avocations: photography, computer graphics, woodworking. Office: U Tex Chemistry & Biochemistry Depts Austin TX 78712

HACKETT, CAROL ANN HEDDEN, physician; b. Valdese, N.C., Dec. 18, 1939; d. Thomas Barnett and Zada Loray (Pope) Hedden; m. John Peter Hackett, July 27, 1968; children: John Hedden, Elizabeth Bentley, Susanne Rochet. BA, Duke U., 1961; MD, U. N.C., 1966. Intern Georgetown U. Hosp., Washington, 1966-67, resident, 1967-69; clinic physician DePaul Hosp., Norfolk, Va., 1969-71; chief spl. health svcs. Arlington County Dept. Human Resources, Arlington, Va., 1971-72; gen. med. officer USPHS Hosp., Balt., 1974-75; pvt. practice family medicine Seattle, 1975—. Mem. staff, chmn. dept. family practice Overlake Hosp. Med. Ctr., 1985-86; clin. asst. prof. Sch. Medicine U. Wash. Bd. dirs. Mercer Island (Wash.) Presch. Assn., 1977-78; coord. 13th and 20th Ann. Inter-profl. Women's Dinner, 1978, 86; trustee Northwest Chamber Orch., 1984-85. Fellow Am. Acad. Family Practice; mem. King County Acad. Family Practice (trustee 1993-96, pres.-elect 1997-98, pres. 1998-99), King County Med. Soc. (chmn. com. TV violence), Wash. Acad. Family Practice, Wash. State Med. Soc., DAR, Bellevue C. of C., N.W. Women Physicians (v.p. 1978), Seattle Symphony League, Eastside Women Physicians (founder, pres.), Seattle Yacht Club, Sigma Kappa. Episcopalian. Home: PO Box 3098 Bellevue WA 98009-3098 Office: 1414 116th Ave NE Bellevue WA 98004-3801 Office Phone: 425-454-8191. Office Fax: 425-462-5313.

HACKETT, EARL RANDOLPH, neurologist; b. Moulmein, Burma, Feb. 16, 1932; s. Paul Richmond and Martha Jane (Lewis) H.; m. Shirley Jane Kanehl, May 25, 1953; children: Nancy, Raymond, Susan, Lynn, Laurie, Richard, Alicia. BS, Drury Coll., Springfield, Mo., 1953; MD, Western Res. U., 1957. Diplomate Am. Bd. Psychiatry and Neurology, Am. Bd. Electrodiagnostic Medicine. Intern, then resident in neurology Charity Hosp., New Orleans, 1957-62; resident in internal medicine VA Hosp., New Orleans, 1958-59; mem. faculty La. State U. Med. Sch., New Orleans, 1962—, prof. neurology, 1973-88, head dept., 1977-88; clin. prof. neurology U. Mo., Columbia, 1988—. Mem. med. adv. bd. Myasthenia Gravis Found. Fellow Am. Acad. Neurology; mem. Am. Assn. Electrodiagnostic Medicine, Soc. Clin. Neurologists, Mo. Med. Assn., Greene County Med. Soc., AOA. Methodist. Home: 2517 S Brentwood Blvd Springfield MO 65804-3201 Office: 1965 S Fremont Ave Ste 2800 Springfield MO 65804-2258

HACKETT, EDWARD VINCENT, investment research company executive; b. N.Y.C., Jan. 17, 1946; s. Edward Vincent and Gladys Theresa (O'Connell) H. BA, Fordham U., 1967; MBA, Columbia U., 1969. CPA, N.Y.; registered gen. securities rep. Cons. Irving Trust Co., N.Y.C., 1968; mgr. cons. svcs. Arthur Young & Co., N.Y.C., 1969-78; dir. mgmt. svcs. Insilco Corp. Group, Meriden, Conn., 1978-84; v.p. ops., COO, CFO Coatings div. Insilco Corp., Tampa, Fla., 1984-86; pres. mid-Atlantic div. Insilco Corp., Tampa, 1986-90; exec. v.p., COO Coronado Paint Co., Edgewater, Fla., 1990-92, bd. dirs.; fin. advisor Dean Witter Reynolds, Tampa, 1992-96; sr. investment officer Baybridge Fin. Group, Tampa, 1996-98; mng. dir. fin. Ned Davis Rsch. Group, Sarasota, 1998—. Editor Productivity News, 1984. Capt. U.S. Army, 1969-71. Mem. AICPA, Fla. Inst. CPAs (personal fin. planning com., acctg. show com. chair), Columbia Alumni Assn. (v.p.), Ivy League Club (treas.), Tampa Rotary Club (benefactor). Avocations: tennis, skiing, jogging. Office: Ned Davis Rsch Group 600 Bird Bay Dr Venice FL 34292 Home: 6815 Honeysuckle TRL Bradenton FL 34202-2924

HACKETT, GEORGE, editor; BA in Lit., Yale U.; MA in Journalism, U. Calif. Berkeley. With Newsweek, 1980—, editorial asst., 1980—81, reporting intern, 1981, 1982, editor Cyberscope sect., 1994—, editor Focus on Technology sect., 1995—, with nat. affairs sect., tech. editor, 1995—97, editor Periscope, Perspectives, My Turn sects., sr. editor sci. and tech., dept. chief, 1997—. Office: Newsweek 251 West 57th St New York NY 10019-1894 Office Phone: 212-445-4000.

HACKETT, JAMES P., manufacturing executive; b. Columbus, Ohio, Apr. 22, 1955; BA, U. Mich., 1977. With Proctor and Gamble Co., 1977-81; joined Steelcase Inc., Grand Rapids, Mich., 1981—, sr. v.p. sales and mktg., 1990—93, pres. Turnstone, 1993, exec. v.p. Steelcase Ventures, 1994; exec. v.p., CEO Steelcase N. Am., 1994, pres., CEO, 1994, Steelcase Inc., 1994—. Bd. dir. Northwestern Mutual Life, Fifth Third Bancorp. Mem., past pres. bd. overseers Inst. Design, Ill. Inst. Tech. Office: Steelcase Inc 901 44th St SE Grand Rapids MI 49508

HACKETT, JAMES T., oil industry executive; m. Maureen Hackett; 4 children. BS, U. Ill.; MBA, Harvard U. With NGC Corp., Burlington Resources, Amoco Oil Co.; exec. v.p. Pan Energy; pres. energy svcs. divsn. Duke Energy, 1996—98; chmn., CEO, pres. Seagull Energy Corp., 1998—99; chmn., pres., CEO Ocean Energy, 1999—2003; pres., COO Devon Energy Corp., 2003; pres., CEO Anadarko Petroleum Corp., The Woodlands, Tex., 2003—. Bd. dirs. Temple-Inland Corp., Fluor Corp., Fed. Res. Bank Houston br., Dallas. Pres. Houston Grand Opera. Mem.: Soc. Petroleum Engrs., Am. Petroleum Inst. (bd. dirs.), Domestic Petroleum Coun. (chmn.). Office: Anadarko Petroleum 1201 Lake Robbins Dr The Woodlands TX 77380-1046

HACKETT, JOHN BYRON, advertising executive, lawyer; b. N.Y.C., Dec. 28, 1933; s. John Joseph and Cecelia Elizabeth (Meehan) H.; m. Patricia P. Briordy, May 23, 1964 (div. 1980); children: Kimberly, John; m. Kathryn Meyer, Mar. 28, 1982. BBA, Iona Coll., 1956; JD, St. Johns U., 1960. Bar: N.Y. 1961. Sales adminstr. NBC, N.Y.C., 1962-65; with J. Walter Thompson Co., N.Y.C., 1965-85, v.p. legal dept., 1971-76, sr. v.p. adminstrn., 1976-80, sr. v.p., gen. mgr. entertainment div., 1980-83, sr. v.p., dir. spot broadcasting U.S.A., 1983-85; pvt. legal practice, 1985—. Home and Office: 1 Toms Point Ln Apt 10B Port Washington NY 11050-2120

HACKETT, JOHN PETER, dermatologist; b. N.Y.C., Feb. 10, 1942; s. John Thomas and Helen (Donohue) H.; m. Carol A. Hedden, July 27, 1968; children: John, Elizabeth, Susanne. AB, Holy Cross Coll., 1963; MD, Georgetown U., 1967. Diplomate Am. Bd. Internal Medicine, Am. Bd. Dermatology. Intern Georgetown U. Hosp., 1967-68, resident, 1968-69; fellow Johns Hopkins Hosp., 1972-75, chief resident, 1975; practice medicine specializing in dermatology Seattle, 1975—. Chmn. bd. dirs. NW Dental Ins. Co., 1989-92; clin. asst. prof. dermatology U. Wash., 1976-88, clin. assoc. prof., 1988—; active staff Swedish Hosp., Providence Hosp.; cons. Wash. State Dept. Labor and Industries, 1992—; pres. Psoriasis Treatment Ctr., Inc., 1978-80; cons. physician Children's Orthopedic Hosp. Contbr. articles to profl. jours. Bd. dirs. Mercer Island Boys and Girls Club, 1976-81, Seattle Ctr. for Blind, 1979-80, N.W. Chamber Orch., 1983-86. Served to lt. condr. USNR, 1969-71. Mem. Am. Acad. Dermatology, Seattle Dermatol. Soc. (pres. 1981-82), Soc. Investigative Dermatology, Am. Contact Dermatitis Soc., Wash. State Med. Soc., King County Med. Soc. (chmn. media rels. com. 1977-80, grievance com. 1991—), Wash. Physicians Ins. Exch. (chmn. actuarial subcom. 1983-85, chmn. subscribers adv. com. 1986-90, audit com. 1988-92, fin. com. 1990-92), Seattle Yacht Club, Marine Corps Meml. Office: 1605 116th Ave NE Ste1 02 Bellevue WA 98004-4601 Fax: 425 462 5313. Office Phone: 425-456-0709.

HACKETT, JOHN THOMAS, retired economist; b. Ft. Wayne, Ind., Oct. 10, 1932; s. Harry H. and Ruth (Greer) H.; m. Ann E. Thompson, July 24, 1954; children: Jane, David, Sarah, Peter. BS, Ind. U., 1954, MBA, 1958; PhD, Ohio State U., 1961. Instr. Ohio State U., 1958-61; asst. v.p., economist Fed. Res. Bank, Cleve., 1961-64; dir. planning Cummins Engine Co., Columbus, Ind., 1964-66, v.p. finance, 1966-71, exec. v.p., 1971-88, also dir.; v.p. fin. and adminstrn. Ind. U., Bloomington, 1988-91; mng. gen. ptnr. CID Equity Ptnrs., L.P., Indpls., 1991—2002, ret., 2002. Chmn. bd. dirs. Wabash Nat. Corp.; bd. dirs. Intertnhen Arts Acad., Mich. Land Use Inst. 1st lt. AUS, 1954-56. Mem.: Ind. Acad., Beta Gamma Sigma. Home: PO Box 466 Keene NH 03431 Office Phone: 603-352-9154.

HACKETT, KEVIN R., real estate company executive, lawyer; b. Atlantic City, Apr. 16, 1949; BA summa cum laude, Boston Coll., 1971; JD, Harvard U., 1974. Bar: N.Y. 1975. Ptnr. Shearman & Sterling, N.Y.C.; COO The Rockefeller Group, 2004—. Fellow Am. Coll. Real Estate Lawyers; mem. ABA, N.Y. State Bar Assn., Assn. Bar City of N.Y., Phi Beta Kappa. Office: Rockefeller Grp Dev Corp 1221 Ave of the Am 29th Fl New York NY 10020 Office Phone: 212-282-2260. Business E-Mail: khackett@rockgrp.com.

HACKETT, MARY J., lawyer; b. Pitts., Sept. 8, 1962; m. Arlie R. Nogay; children: Walter, Robert. BA in economics & politics, Mt. Holyoke Coll., 1984; JD with honors, U. Pitts., 1987. Bar: Pa. 1987, US Dist. Ct. We. Dist. Pa., US Ct. Appeals 3rd Cir., US Ct. Appeals 4th Cir., US Ct. Appeals 6th Cir., US Ct. Appeals 8th Cir. Law clk. to. Judge Donald E. Ziegler US Dist. Ct. We. Dist. Pa., 1987—89; chief counsel-litig. PNC Fin. Services Group Inc., 1998—2001; assoc. Reed Smith LLP, Pitts., 1987—89, 1990—96, ptnr., 1996—98, 2001—, practice group leader fin. services litig. group, 2003—. Mem.: ABA, Allegheny County Bar Assn., Pa. Bar Assn. Office: Reed Smith LLP 435 Sixth Ave Pittsburgh PA 15219 Office Phone: 412-288-3250. Office Fax: 412-288-3063. Business E-Mail: mhackett@reedsmith.com.

HACKETT, MIMS, JR., state legislator; b. Sept. 28, 1941; BS in Biology, Paul Quinn Coll., 1963; MS in Adminstrn. and Supervision, Seton Hall U., 1976. Mayor City of Orange Twp., NJ, 1996—; assemblyman N.J. Gen. Assembly, 2002—. Vice chair, state govt. com. N.J. Gen. Assembly, mem. appropriations com. Democrat. Office: 15 Village Plz Ste 1B South Orange NJ 07079 Office Phone: 973-762-1886. Business E-Mail: asmhackett@njleg.org.

HACKETT, PATRICIA A. DEAN, management consultant; BA, Albertus Magnus Coll.; MS, U. Pitts. Exec, dir. region II Regional Mental Health Bd., Inc., New Haven, 1979—82, exec. dir. north ctrl. region Hartford, Conn., 1982—92; dir. cmty. outreach Elmcrest Psychiat. Inst., 1992—93; adminstr. Hall-Brooke Hosp., Westport, Conn., 1995—97; from contract/mktg. adminstr. behavioral health to dir. behavioral health network Eastern Conn. Health Network, 1997—2001; exec. dir. Conn. Psychiat. Sys., Inc., 1997—2002; dir. spl. projects integrated health svcs. Eastern Conn. Health Network-Acute Care Gen. Hosp. Sys., 2001—03. Lectr., cons. in field. Mem.: NAFE, Conn. Hosp. Assn. Home: 3 Sweetbriar Ln Avon CT 06001

HACKETT, ROBERT JOHN, lawyer; b. N.Y.C., Feb. 6, 1943; s. John P. and Marie S. (Starace) Hackett; m. Anita Carlile, Apr. 19, 1969; children: Robert John Hackett Jr., John Peter, Kathryn Marie. AB, Rutgers U., 1964; JD, Duke U., 1967. Bar: NY 1967, Ariz. 1972. Assoc. Milbank, Tweed, Hadley, McCloy, NYC, 1967—71; ptnr. Evans, Kitchel & Jenckes, Phoenix, 1971—89; dir. Fennemore Craig, Phoenix, 1989—2004, course dir. seminar on mergers and acquisitions, 1996, 1999; mem. Jennings, Strouss & Salmon, P.L.C., Phoenix, 2004—. Mem. editl. bd. Duke Law Jour., 1966—67. Former bd. dirs. Xavier Coll. Prep., mem. steering com. for Fine Arts Ctr. capital campaign. Mem.: ABA (com. on fed. securities regulation), Maricopa County Bar Assn., State Bar Ariz. (past chmn. securities regulation sect.), Assn. Corp. Growth (past bd. dirs., past pres. Ariz. chpt.), Phoenix Duke U. Law Alumni Club (past pres.), Pi Sigma Alpha. Republican. Roman Catholic. Office Phone: 602-262-5914. E-mail: rhackett@jsslaw.com.

HACKETT, ROGER FLEMING, historian, educator; b. Kobe, Japan, Oct. 23, 1922; s. Harold Wallace and Anna Luena (Powell) H.; m. Caroline Betty Gray, Aug. 24, 1946; children: Anne Marilyn, David Gray, Brian Vance. BA, Carleton Coll., 1947; MA, Harvard U., 1949, PhD, 1955. Prof. history Northwestern U., Evanston, Ill., 1953-61; prof. history U. Mich., Ann Arbor, 1961-93, prof. emeritus, 1993—, chmn. dept., 1975-77; dir. Ctr. for Japanese Studies, 1968-71, 78, 79. Cons. Office of Edn., HEW; mem. sub-com., joint com. Social Sci. Rsch. Coun. Author: Yamagata Aritomo in the Rise of Modern Japan 1838-1922, 1971; Editor: Jour. Asian Studies, 1959-62; contbr. articles and chpts to profl. jours. and books. Served with USMC, 1942-46. Social Sci. Rsch. Coun. fellow; Japan Found. fellow; Fulbright-Hays fellow; fellow St. Antony's Coll. Oxford U. Mem. Japan Soc., Assn. for Asian Studies (exec. com., bd. dirs. 1966-69), Internat. House of Japan, Ann Arbor Racquet Club, Phi Beta Kappa. Home: 2122 Dorset Rd Ann Arbor MI 48104-2604 Office: U Mich Dept History Ann Arbor MI 48109 E-mail: fhackett@umich.edu.

HACKETT, STANLEY HAILEY, lawyer; b. Houston, May 31, 1945; s. Harley Benjamin and Rebecca Easterling (Willis) H.; m. Ann Elaine Aiken, May 29, 1971; children: Elizabeth Ann, Rebecca Aiken. BS in Banking Fin., U. S.C., 1967, JD magna cum laude, 1970; LLM, Harvard U., 1971. Bar: S.C. 1970, D.C. 1975, Ga. 1975. Atty, Office of Chief Counsel IRS, Washington, 1971—72; atty. Office Chief Counsel IRS, Washington, 1971-72, spl. asst. to chief counsel, 1972-73; legis. asst. to Sen. Strom Thurmond U.S. Senate, Washington, 1973-74; assoc. Henkel & Lamon, P.C., Atlanta, 1974-81; ptnr. Henkel, Hackett, Edge & Fleming, Atlanta, 1981-85; ptnr., tax dept. Troutman Sanders LLP, Atlanta, 1985—. Bd. dirs. Small Bus. Coun. Am., Washington, 1978—; mem. liaison com. S.E. region IRS, 1985—. Contbr. articles on taxation to profl. jours. Mem. Lawyers for Reagan/Bush, 1984; trustee Ga. Fed. Tax Conf.; advisor Ga. State Law Sch. Tax Clinic. Named a Super Lawyer, Atlanta Mag., 2004, Legal Elite in taxes, estates, and trusts, Ga. Trend Mag., 2004. Fellow Am. Coll. Tax Counsel; mem. ABA (tax sect.), Ga. Bar Assn. (chmn. tax sect. 1985-86), Phi Delta Theta. Republican. Episcopalian. Office: Troutman Sanders LLP 600 Peachtree St NE Atlanta GA 30308-2216 Office Phone: 404-885-3154. Office Fax: 404-962-6579. Business E-Mail: stanley.hackett@troutmansanders.com.

HACKETT, WESLEY PHELPS, JR., lawyer; b. Detroit, Jan. 3, 1939; s. Wesley P. and Helen (Decker) H.; children: Kelly D. Hackett Pell, Robin C. BA, Mich. State U., 1960; JD, Wayne State U., 1968. Bar: Mich. 1968, U.S. Dist. Ct. (we. dist.) Mich. 1971, U.S. Ct. Appeals (6th cir.) 1972, U.S. Dist. Ct. (ea. dist.) Mich. 1972, U.S. Supreme Ct. 1972, U.S. Ct. Mil. Appeals 1991. Law clk. Mich. Supreme Ct., Lansing, 1968-70; ptnr. Brown & Hackett, Lansing, 1971-73; pvt. practice Lansing, 1973-84; ptnr. Starr, Bissell & Hackett, Lansing, 1984-87; pvt. practice East Lansing, Mich., 1987-98, Saranac, Mich., 1998—. Adj. prof. Thomas M. Cooley Law Sch., Lansing, 1973—; instr. Lansing C.C., 1981-99. Author: Evidence: A Trial Manual for Michigan Lawyers, 1981, Hackett's Evidence: Michigan and Federal, 2d edit., 1995, Michigan Lawyers Manual Part L, 1994, revised, 2002; co-author: Hiring Legal Staff, 1990. Mem. City of East Lansing Planning Commn., 1969-72; mem. Village of Saranac Planning Commn., 2000—; bd. dirs. St. Vincent Home for Children, Lansing, 1974-82. 1st lt. USAF, 1961-65. Fellow Coll. Law Practice Mgmt.; mem. ABA (sec. gen. practice sect. 1990-91, vice-chair 1991-92, chair 1993-94, standing com. on lawyer referral and info. svcs. 1997-2000, sole practitioner of yr. 1994, founders award 1997), State Bar Mich. (chair legal econs. sect. 1990-91). Office Phone: 616-642-6074.

HACKFORD, TAYLOR, film director; b. Santa Barbara, Calif., Dec. 31, 1944; s. Joseph and Mary (Taylor) H.; m. Helen Mirren, Dec. 31, 1997. BA, U. So. Calif., 1968. Vol. Peace Corps, Bolivia, 1968-69; dir., prodr., reporter, writer Sta.-KCET, Community TV of So. Calif., Los Angeles, 1970-77; dir., prodr., writer Hackford Littman Films, Los Angeles, 1977-79; dir. United Artists Films, Los Angeles, 1979-80, Paramount Pictures, Los Angeles, 1981-82; prodr., dir. Columbia Pictures, Los Angeles, 1983—. Exec. prodr.: (films) Rooftops, 1989, The Long Walk Home, 1990, Sweet Talker, 1991, Queens Logic, 1991, Defenseless, 1991, Mortal Thoughts, 1991; exec. prodr., dir. (films) The Devil's Advocate, 1998; prodr., dir.: (films) Against All Odds, 1984, White Nights, 1985, Everyone's All American, 1988, Bound by Honor (Blood In, Blood Out), 1993, Dolores Claiborne, 1995, When We Were Kings, 1996, Greenwich Mean Time, 1999, Proof of Life, 2000; prodr.: (films) La Bamba, 1987, G:MT Greenwich Mean Time, 1999; dir. (films) Teenage Father, 1978 (Oscar 1979), The Idolmaker, 1980, An Officer and A Gentleman, 1982, Chuck Berry Hail! Hail! Rock and Roll, 1987; prodr., dir., writer, (films) Ray, 2004. Recipient Silver Reel award San Francisco Film Festival, 1972; recipient Emmy award Acad. TV Arts and Scis., 1974, Emmy award Acad. TV Arts and Scis., 1977, Acad. award Acad. Motion Picture Arts and Scis., 1979 Mem. Dir.'s Guild Am., Writers Guild Am. Office: Creative Artists Agency 9830 Wilshire Blvd Beverly Hills CA 90212-1825*

HACKL, DONALD JOHN, architect; b. Chgo., May 11, 1934; s. John Frank and Frieda Marie Hackl; m. Bernadine Marie Becker, Sept. 29, 1962; children: Jeffrey Scott, Craig Michael, Cristina Lynn. BArch., U. Ill., 1957, MS in Architecture, 1958. With Loebl Schlossman & Hackl Architects, Chgo., 1963—, assoc., 1967-74, exec. v.p., dir., 1974, pres., dir., 1975—. Prof. architecture Internat. Acad. Architecture, Sofia, Bulgaria; mem. Nat. Coun. Archtl. Registration Bds., 1980—; bd. dirs. Chgo. Bldg. Congress, 1983-94, v.p., 1985-94; design juries include: Reynolds Metals, Western Mont. Regional Design, Am. Inst. Steel Constrn., Precast Concrete Inst., Okla. Soc. Architects, UIA Gold Medal (6), UIA Celebration of Cities, Seoul, Korea, 2004, Sewaen Dist. 4 Internat. Design Competition, 2004; chmn. Ariz. Soc. Architects, Midwest Design Conf., 1983; design critic dept. arch. U. Ill., 1975-76, 81; vis. critic sch. architecture U. Notre Dame, 1977, 78, 80, 82; adj. prof. Kent Coll. Law, Ill. Inst. Tech., 1983—; adj. faculty Shenzhen (China) U., 1998-; guest lectr. Tongi U., Shanghai, 2004—; cons. Pub. Svcs. Adminstrn., Washington, 1974-76; cons. urban planning, Changchun, China. Prin. works include Water Tower Place, Chgo., 1976, King Faisel Specialist Hosp. and Rsch. Ctr., Riyadh, Saudi Arabia, 1978, Household Internat. Hdqrs., Prospect Heights, Ill., 1978, Shriners Hosp. for Children, Chgo., 1979, Square D Co. Hdqrs., Palatine, Ill., 1979, West Suburban Hosp., Oak Park, Ill., 1981, Allstate Pla. West, Northbrook, Ill., 1990, Sears Roebuck & Co. stores of future concept, 1985-89, Ford City Shopping Ctr. Redevel., Chgo., 1989, Commerce Clearing House, Riverwoods, Ill., 1986, Physicians' Pavilion Greater Balt. Med. Ctr., 1987, Two Prudential Plaza, Chgo., 1990, City Place with Omni Hotel, Chgo., 1990, 350 N. LaSalle, Chgo., 1990, Infinitec, Assistive Tech. Application Ctr. for United Cerebral Palsy Assn., Chgo., 1992, Shenzhen AVIC Plaza Bldg., Shenzhen, China, 1993, Ill. State U. Biol. and Chemistry Scis. Lab. Bldg., Normal, 1995, Old Orchard Shopping Ctr. Redevel., Skokie, Ill., 1994, Sun Comml. City, Changchun, China, 1993, Shekou Harbor Bldg., Shenzhen, 1995, East Shanghai Film and TV Ctr., 1995, Luo-Hu Comml. Ctr., Shenzhen, 1994, Shenzhen Internat. Exch. Plz., 1996, Jin Hui Plz., Shanghai, 1996, Shenzhen Cultural Ctr., 1997, Changchun Sun Housing Estates, China, 1999, Hdqrs. for Almacenes Paris LTDA, Santiago, Chile, 1999, John H. Stroger, Jr. Hosp. of Cook Cty., 2002, Grand Pier Ctr., Chgo., 2004 Computer/Engrng. Bldg. U. Ill., 1999—, Bank of Mauritius, Port Louis, 2004, Olympic Swimming Facility-Design Study, Tianjin, China, 2004, North Ctrl. Coll. Performing Arts Ctr., 2005. Mem. Met. Am. Cancer Crusade, 1973; life trustee West Suburban Hosp., 1983—, mem. exec. com., 1986-87; vice chmn. North Ctrl. Coll., 1990—; mem. Pres.'s Coun. U. Ill. Found.; mem. curricula adv. com. Dept. Architecture, U. Ill.; bd. dirs. World Trade Ctr., Chgo., 1995—. Fellow AIA (treas. Chgo. chpt. 1977-78, exec. com. 1978-81, v.p. 1981, pres. 1981, bd. dirs. Chgo. AIA Found. 1981-83, nat. v.p. 1985, 1st v.p. 1986, nat. pres. 1987, chmn. design com. 1985, exec. com. 1985-87, bd. dirs. 1981-87, documents com. 1974-79, chmn. 1980, exec. com. AIA Svc. Corp. 1983-84, chmn. internat. com. 1987-91), Nat. Coun. Archtl. Registration Bds., Royal Archtl. Inst. Can. (hon.), Colegios Architectos Mexicanos (hon.), Internat. Acad. Architecture (hon., prof.), Korean Inst. Archs. (hon.); mem. Internat. Union Archs. (bd. dirs., del. 1987—, 1st v.p. 1990-93, coun. 1993-96, v.p. region III 1996-99, treas. 2000—), Union Bulgarian Archs. (hon.), Soc. Cuban Archs., Japan Inst. Archs. (hon.), Colegio Arquitectos Cochabamba (Bolivia), Colegios Arquitectos Espana (hon.), Instituto do Arquiteclos do Brazil (hon.), Tavern Clubs, Carlton Club, Econ. Club, Lake Zurich Club. Office: Loebl Schlossman and Hackl Inc 233 N Michigan Ave ste 3000 Chicago IL 60601-5708 Office Phone: 312-565-4500. Business E-Mail: dhackl@lshchicago.com.

HACKLEY, CAROL ANN, public relations educator, consultant; b. Sacramento, Mar. 20, 1940; d. Charles Peter and Alice Marian (Schmidt) Cusick; m. William E. Hall, Sept. 1, 1966 (dec. Aug. 1991); children: Kevin Dennis, Kimberlee Marian Hall Floyd; m. T. Cole Hackley, Apr. 10, 1993. BA, Calif. State U., Sacramento, 1961; MA, Ohio State U., 1984, PhD, 1985. Pub. rels. dir., tchr. Lincoln Unified Schs., Stockton, Calif., 1961-63; advt. promotion copy writer, columnist Honolulu Star-Bulletin, Hawaii Newspaper Agy., 1964; instr. U. Nebr., Lincoln, 1964-66, Ohio State U., Columbus, 1972-80, 82-85; exec. dir. Jour. Assn. Ohio Schs., Columbus, 1974-80, 82-85; asst. prof. U. Hawaii, Manoa, 1980—82; prof. pub. rels. comm. dept. U. of the Pacific, Stockton, 1985—, chair comm. dept., 1992-94; pub. rels. cons. Hackley Ent. Inc., 1995—; owner, pub. rels. and sr. cons. Pacific Pub. Rels., 1999—. Pub. rels. cons. Hall & Hall Prescriptive Pub. Rels., Stockton, 1987-91; prof.-in-residence Edelman Pub. Rels. Worldwide, Sydney, London and San Francisco, 1990-92; dir. mktg. and univ. rels., U. of the Pacific, Stockton, San Francisco and Sacramento, 1997-98. Chmn. bd. Mountain Valley Multiple Sclerosis, Stockton, 1989-91, nat. v.p. pub. rels., 2001-02, 04-05, Navy League of U.S., Pacific Ctrl. region v.p. PR, 2005—; pres. Stockton coun. Navy League US, 1997-98, chair nat. pub. affairs com., 1997-99, steering com. spl. adv. pub. rels., 2003-04, Puerto Vallarta Coun., pres. amb. to Mex., 2003—. Recipient Nat. Pres. award, Navy League US, 2004. Fellow Pub. Rels. Soc. Am. (educators sect., internat. sect., internat. pub. rels. exec. com. 1995, v.p. Oakland/East Bay chpt. 1994, del. nat. assembly 1995-97, 2001-03, pres.-elect 1997, pres. 1998, ethics officer 2001-03); mem. Internat. Comm. Assn., Assn. for Edn. in Journalism and Mass Comm., Stockton C. of C. (edn. task force 1996-99), Navy League U.S. Avocations: singing, cooking, travel. Home: 2618 Sheridan Way Stockton CA 95207-3246 Office: Univ of the Pacific 3601 Pacific Ave Stockton CA 95211-0197 Office Phone: 209-946-3046. Personal E-mail: tchackley@aol.com.

HACKMAN, GENE (EUGENE ALDEN HACKMAN), actor; b. San Bernardino, Calif., Jan. 30, 1930; s. Eugene Ezra H.; m. Faye Maltese, Jan. 1, 1956 (div. 1986) children: Christopher, Elizabeth, Leslie; m. Betsy Arakawa, 1991. Appeared in stage prodns. The Natural Look, Death and the Maiden, others; film roles include Mad Dog Coll, 1961, Lilith, 1964, Hawaii, 1966, First to Fight, 1967, A Covenant With Death, 1967, Bonnie and Clyde, 1967, First to Fight, 1967, The Split, 1968, Riot, 1969, The Gypsy Moths, 1969, Downhill Racer, 1969, I Never Sang for My Father, 1969, Marooned, 1970, Doctor's Wives, 1971, The Hunting Party, 1971, The French Connection 1971 (Acad.award for Best Actor, Golden Globe award, Brit. Acad. award, N.Y. Film Critics award), Cisco Pike, 1971, Prime Cut, 1972, The Poseidon Adventure (Brit. Acad. award), 1972, Scarecrow, 1973 (Cannes Film Festival award), The Conversation, 1974, Zandy's Bride, 1974, Young Frankenstein, 1974, The French Connection II, 1975, Bite the Bullet, 1975, Night Moves, 1975, Lucky Lady, 1975, A Bridge Too Far, 1977, The Domino Principle, 1977, March or Die, 1977, Superman, 1978, Superman II, 1980, All Night Long, 1981, Reds, 1981, Two of a Kind (voice only), 1983, Under Fire, 1983, Uncommon Valor, 1983, Misunderstood, 1984, Eureka, 1984, Target, 1985, Twice in a Lifetime, 1985, Power, 1986, Superman IV: The Quest for Peace, 1987, No Way Out, 1987, Another Woman, 1988, Bat*21, 1988, Split Decisions, 1988, Mississippi Burning, 1988 (Best Actor award Nat. Soc. Film Critics, Acad. Award nomination), Full Moon in Blue Water, 1988, The Package, 1989, Postcards From The Edge, 1989, Class Action, 1989, Loose Cannons, 1990, Narrow Margin, 1990, Company Business, 1991, Unforgiven, 1992 (Acad. award for Best Supporting Actor, Golden Globes, N.Y., L.A., Boston Film Critics, Nat. Soc.Film Critics awards), The Firm, 1993, Geronimo: An American Legend, 1993, Wyatt Earp, 1994, The Quick and the Dead, 1995, Crimson Tide, 1995, Get Shorty, 1995, Extreme Measures, 1996, The Chamber, 1996, The Birdcage, 1996, The Magic Hour, 1997, Absolute Power, 1997, Enemy of the State, 1998, Antz (voice only), 1998, Twilight, 1998, The Replacements, 2000, The Mexican, 2001, Heartbreakers, 2001, Heist, 2001, The Royal Tenenbaums, 2001 (Golden Globe/Best Actor in a Comedy 2001, Chgo. Film Critics award for best actor 2002, Nat. Soc. Film Critics award 2002, AFI award 2002), Behind Enemy Lines, 2001, Runaway Jury, 2003, Welcome to Mooseport, 2004; acted, exec. prodr. Under Suspicion, 1999; (TV films) Ride with Terror, 1963, Shadow on the Land, 1968, My Father and My Mother, 1968.; (TV appearances)The United States Steel Hour, 1959, 60, 62, The Defenders, 1961, 63, Look up and Live, 1963, Naked City, 1963, The DuPont Show of the Week, 1963, East Side/West Side, 1963, The Trials of O'Brien, 1966, The F.B.I., 1967, The Invaders, 1967, The Iron Horse, 1967, I Spy, 1968; Author (with Daniel F. Lenihan) Wake of the Perdido Star, 2000, Justice for None, 2004. Hon. chmn. Permanent Charities Com. of the Entertainment Industries. USMC, 1946—49. Named Star of Year, Nat. Assn. Theatre Owners, 1974 Office: care Fred Spector 9830 Wilshire Blvd Beverly Hills CA 90212-1804*

HACKMAN, NADINE BROKAW, veterinarian; b. N.Y.C., June 17, 1950; d. David and Lillian Brokaw; m. John S. Hackman, July 7, 1973 (div. Oct. 1996); children: Melissa, Emily. BA in Biology, U. Pa., 1971, MS in Edn., 1972, DVM, 1980, M in Bioethics, 2000. Lic. veterinarian Pa. Tchr. gen. sci. Abington Sch. Dist., Pa., 1972—74; tchr. biology Phila. Sch. Dist., 1975—76; assoc. veterinarian Hickory Vet. Hosp., Plymouth Meeting, Pa., 1980—82; relief veterinarian various small animal pvt. practices, southeast Pa., 1983—87; prof., program dir. vet. tech. program Harcum Coll., Bryn Mawr, Pa., 1983—. Mem. IACUC Harcum Coll., 1983—, Drexel U., Phila., 1985—91; mem. ethics com. U. Pa. Vet. Sch., 1999—2002. Columnist: Vet. Technician, 2002—. Mem.: AVMA, Soc. Vet. Med. Ethics, Assn. Vet. Tech. Educators, Am. Assn. Lab. Animal Sci. Avocations: gardening, reading, word puzzles. Office: Harcum Coll 750 Montgomery Ave Bryn Mawr PA 19010 Office Phone: 610-526-6055. Business E-Mail: nhackman@harcum.edu.

HACKMANN, FRANK H., lawyer; b. St. Louis, Jan. 22, 1945; s. Sterling W. and Mary Elizabeth (Morrow) H.; m. Susan Kurz, Dec. 28, 1968; children: Emily, Fred, Meredith, Richard. BS, U. Ill., 1967; JD, St. Louis U., 1972. Bar: Mo. 1972, Ill. 1973. Plant process engr., environ. engr. William G. Krummrich Plant, Monsanto Co., Sauget, Ill., 1967-73; dir. environ. affairs, environ. and energy counsel Ralston Purina Co., St. Louis, 1973-90; ptnr. Sonnenschein Nath & Rosenthal, St. Louis, 1990—. Contbr. chpts. to several books. Chair clean air subcom. of environment and energy com. St. Louis Regional Commerce and Growth Assn. Office: Sonnenschein Nath & Rosenthal One Metropolitan Sq Ste 3000 Saint Louis MO 63102

HACKNEY, HUGH EDWARD, lawyer; b. McGregor, Tex., July 17, 1944; BA, So. Meth. U., 1966, JD, 1970. Bar: Tex. 1970. Ptnr. Fulbright & Jaworski, LLP, Dallas, 1970-97, Locke Liddell & Sapp LLP, Dallas, 1997—2005; shareholder Greenberg Traurig, LLP, Dallas, 2005—. Fellow: Coll. of Labor and Employment Lawyers; mem. ABA, London Ct. Internat. Arbitration, Chartered Inst. Arbitrators (London), State Bar Tex., Dallas Bar Assn., Houston Bar Assn., Phi Alpha Delta, Soc. Internat. Bus. Fellows, Internat. Bar Assn. Office: Greenberg Traurig LLP 600 Three Gallaria Tower 13155 Noel Rd Dallas TX 75240 Office Phone: 972-419-1272. Home Fax: 214-361-7052. Business E-Mail: hackneyh@gtlaw.com.

HACKNEY, JAMES ACRA, III, industrial engineer, consultant, retired manufacturing executive; b. Washington, N.C., Sept. 27, 1939; s. James Acra Jr. and Margaret Dunston (Hodges) H.; m. Constance Garrenton, June 5, 1961; children: Kenneth Ross, Jane H. Kemsley. BSME, N.C. State U., 1961, BS in Indsl. Engrng, 1962. Registered profl. engr., N.C. With Hackney Industries, Inc., Washington, N.C., 1961-95, chief engr., 1961-63, asst. gen. mgr., 1963-65, exec. v.p., gen. mgr., 1965-70, pres., chief exec. officer, 1970-90; chmn. bd. dirs. Hackney & Sons, Inc., Washington, NC, 1990-95; mng. dir. The Hackney Group, Washington, NC, 1995—. Bd. dirs. Sprint Mid-Atlantic Telecom, Wake Forest, N.C., 1987-97, Bank of Am., North Coast region, N.C., chmn., 1995—; mem. adv. coun. Sch. Engrng., East Carolina U. Chmn. Blackbeard dist. Boy Scouts Am., 1970-74, pres. East Carolina coun., 1976-77, mem. nat. exec. bd., 1987—, pres. S.E. region, 1987-89; chmn. bd. trustees Beaufort County Hosp., 1975-77; trustee N.C. State U., Raleigh, 1979-87, chmn. bd. trustees, 1985-87; mem. Interam. Scout Com., World Orgn. of Scout Movement, 1984-88; lay Eucharistic min. Zion Episcopal Ch., Washington, NC, 2002—; gen. campaign chmn. Beaufort County United Way, 1998-2000. Recipient Disting. Service award Washington Jaycees, 1970; Silver Beaver award Boy Scouts Am., 1975, Silver Antelope award, 1982, Disting. Eagle Scout award, 1980, Silver Buffalo award, 1992; Youth of the Ams. award World Orgn. Scout Movement, 1990, John Southam Journalism award Sail Am., 1997; named N.C. Small Businessman of Yr., SBA, 1971, Young Engr. of Yr., NSPE, 1971. Fellow NSPE; mem. Inst. Indsl. Engrs. (chpt. pres. 1967-68), Profl. Engrs. N.C. (pres. Ea. Carolina chpt. 1971-72, state sec. 2000-01, state treas. 2001-02, pres.-elect 2002-03, pres. 2003-04, Outstanding Young Engr. 1970-71), N.C. Engring. Found. (bd. dirs. 1977-79, N.C. Citizens for Bus. and Industry (bd. dirs. 1979-86), Washington C. of C. (pres. 1972-74, Outstanding Cmty. Svc. award 2000), N.C. State U. Alumni Assn. (bd. dirs. 1976-80, Outstanding Young Alumnus 1975, Disting. Engring. Alumnus 1984, Watauga Medal 1997), Rotary (pres. 1978-79), Pamlico Plantation Yacht Club (commodore 1993). Home and Office: PO Box 1987 117 Riverview Dr Washington NC 27889-9763 Office Phone: 252-975-2310.

HACKNEY, SHELDON, former federal agency administrator, history educator; b. 1933; Pres. Univ. of Penn., Philadelphia, Penn., 1981-93; chmn. NEH, Washington, 1993-97; prof. history U. Pa., Phila., 1997—. Author: The Politics of Presidential Appointment: A Memoir of the Culture War, 2002. Named Boies Prof. U.S. History, U. Pa. Office: U Pa Dept History 208 CH/6379 3451 Walnut St Philadelphia PA 19104*

HACKNEY, VIRGINIA HOWITZ, lawyer; b. Phila., Jan. 11, 1945; d. Charles Rawlings and Edith Wrenn (Pope) Howitz; m. Barry Albert Hackney, Feb. 15, 1969; children: Ashby Rawlings, Roby Howison, Trevor Pope. BA in Econs., Hollins Coll., 1967; JD, U. Richmond, 1970. Bar: Va. 1970. Assoc. Hunton & Williams, Richmond, Va., 1970-77, ptnr., capital fin., real estate, 1977—, also dep. gen. counsel. Pres. Am. Acad. Hosp. Attys. Chgo., 1992-93. Mem. agy. evaluation com. United Way of Greater Richmond, 1981-86; sustainer Jr. League of Richmond; mem. and fellow Am. Health Lawyers Assn. (pres. 1992-93, bd. dirs. 1988-94). Named Outstanding Woman in field of law, YWCA, Richmond, 1981, Women of Achievement award, Met. Richmond Women's Bar Assn., 1998. Fellow Am. Health Lawyers Assn.; mem. ABA (bus. law sect. 1984—, forum com. on health law 1982—), Va. State Bar (long range planning com. 1985-90, chmn. standing com. lawyer discipline 1986-90, exec. com. 1988-90, Bar Coun. mem. 1984-90). Avocations: book tapes, reading, boating, jogging/walking. Office: Hunton & Williams Riverfront Plz East Tower 951 E Byrd St Richmond VA 23219-4074 Office Phone: 804-788-8263. Office Fax: 804-788-8218. Business E-Mail: vhackney@hunton.com.

HADA, JERRIANNE, librarian; b. Alva, Okla., Dec. 19, 1944; d. David Leroy and Thelma Joyce (Rader) H. BA, Northwestern Okla. State U., 1966; MLS, Emporia State U., 1971; postgrad., Okla. State U., 1976, Kans. State U., 1985. Cert. secondary sch. libr. media specialist, Kans. Libr. jr. and sr. high sch. Unified Sch. Dist. 274, Oakley, Kans., 1966-68; libr. sr. high sch. Unified Sch. Dist. 443, Dodge City, Kans., 1968-72, Stuttgart (Germany) Am. High Sch., 1972-74, Cleveland (Okla.) Ind. Sch. Dist. 6, 1974-80, Unified Sch. Dist. 254, Medicine Lodge, Kans., 1980-81; libr. jr. and sr. high sch. Unified Sch. Dist. 397, Lost Springs, Kans., 1981-84; libr. sr. high sch. Unified Sch. Dist. 331, Kingman, Kans., 1984—. Grantee NDEA, 1967. Mem. NEA, ALA, AASL, Kans. Edn. Assn., Kans. Assn. Sch. Librs., Kappa Delta Pi, Delta Kappa Gamma. Methodist. Avocations: genealogy, travel, embroidery. Home: 540 W A Ave Kingman KS 67068-1205 Office: Unified Sch Dist 331 Kingman High Sch 260 W Kansas Ave Kingman KS 67068-1028 Business E-Mail: jhada@knusd331.com.

HADALLER, DAVID LAWRENCE, academic administrator; b. Chelsea, Mass., Oct. 21, 1954; s. David Lawrence I and Ruth M.; m. Mirela Mustaca, Mar. 19, 1990; children, David Lawrence III, Nicholas Edward. BA, Gonzaga U., 1976; MA, St. Louis U., 1979, Columbia U., 1999; PhD, Washington State U., 1993. English instr. St. Louis U., 1976-79, Washington State U., Pullman, 1980-83, 85-86; asst. prof. Mayville (N.D.) State U., 1983-84, 86-87; Fulbright prof. Iasi, Romania, 1987-88; English dept. faculty Clovis (N.Mex.) Coll., 1989-92; rschr. N.Y.C., 1993-95; coord. spl. projects Hostos C.C., CUNY, N.Y.C., 1996-98, asst. dean, 1998—2001; assoc. dean of curriculum Dutchess Cmty. Coll., Pougkeepsie, 2001—04; asst. acad. v.p. Bergen C.C., Paramus, NJ, 2004—. Tech., mktg. writer Topaz, Inc., San Diego, 1984-85. Author: Gynicide: Women in the Novels of William Styron, 1996. Mem. Fulbright Assn., Kappa Delta Pi, Alpha Sigma Nu, Phi Theta Kappa (hon.). Office: Bergen Community College 400 Paramus Rd Paramus NJ 07652 Office Phone: 201-447-7173.

HADAS, ELIZABETH CHAMBERLAYNE, editor; b. Washington, May 12, 1946; d. Moses and Elizabeth (Chamberlayne) H.; m. Jeremy W. Heist, Jan. 25, 1970 (div. 1976); m. Peter Eller, Mar. 21, 1984 (div. 1987). AB, Radcliffe Coll., 1967; postgrad., Rutgers U., 1967—68; MA, Washington U., St. Louis, 1971. Editor U. N.Mex. Press, Albuquerque, 1971-85, dir., 1985-2000, spl. acquisitions editor, 2000—. Bd. dirs. N.Mex. Humanities Coun., 2001—. Mem. Assn. Am. Univ. Presses (pres. 1992-93). Democrat. Home: 2900 10th St NW Albuquerque NM 87107-1111 Office: U New Mexico MSC11 6290 1 Albuquerque NM 87131-0001 E-mail: ehadas@unm.edu.

HADAS, RACHEL, poet, educator; b. NYC, Nov. 8, 1948; d. Moses and Elizabeth (Chamberlayne) H.; m. Stavros Kondilis, Nov. 7, 1970 (div. 1978); m. George Edwards, July 22, 1978; 1 child, Jonathan. BA in Classics, Radcliffe Coll., 1969; MA, Johns Hopkins, 1977; PhD, Princeton U., 1982.

From adj. to assoc. prof. Rutgers U., Newark, N.J., 1981-92, prof., 1992—, Bd. Govs. Prof., 2002—; adj. prof. Columbia U., N.Y.C., 1992-93. Vis. prof. Hellenic studies program Princeton U., 1995. Author: (poetry) Slow Transparency, 1983, A Son From Sleep, 1987, Pass It On, 1989, Living in Time, 1990, Mirrors of Astonishment, 1992, Other Worlds Than This, 1994, The Empty Bed, 1995, The Double Legacy, 1995, Halfway Down the Hall: New and Selected Poems, 1998, Indelible, 2001, Laws, 2004, (criticism) Merrill, Cavafy. Poems and Dreams, 2001. Recipient award Am. Acad. Inst. Arts and Letters, 1990; Guggenheim fellow in poetry, 1988-89. Fellow Am. Acad. Arts and Scis.; mem. MLA, Poets, Essayists and Novelists. Democrat. Avocation: reading. Home: 838 W End Ave Apt 3A New York NY 10025-5365 Office Phone: 973-353-5279 ext. 520. Business E-Mail: rhadas@andromeda.rutgers.edu.

HADDA, JANET RUTH, language educator, lay psychoanalyst; b. Bradford, Eng., Dec. 23, 1945; came to U.S., 1948; d. George Manfred and Annemarie (Kohn) H.; m. Allan Joshua Tobin, Mar. 22, 1981; stepchildren: David, Adam. BS in Edn., U. Vt., 1966; MA, Cornell U., 1969; PhD, Columbia U., 1975. Rsch. psychoanalyst So. Calif. Psychoanalytic Inst., LA, 1988—, tng. and supervising analyst, 1995—, Inst. Contemporary Psychoanalysis, 1993—; prof. Yiddish emerita UCLA, 2004—. Author: Yankev Glatshteyn, 1980, Passionate Women, Passive Men: Suicide in Yiddish Literature, 1988, Isaac Bashevis Singer: A Life, 1997, with New Introduction, 2003; contbr. articles to profl. jours. Mem. MLA, Assn. Jewish Studies, Am. Psychoanalytic Assn., Inst. Contemporary Psychoanalysis, So. Calif. Psychoanalytic Inst., Phi Beta Kappa. Office: UCLA Dept English 1335 Rolfe Hall Los Angeles CA 90095-0001 Address: 850 Masselin Ave Los Angeles CA 90036-4722

HADDAD, DAPHNE WHARTON, education educator; b. Stoke-on-Trent, England; came to U.S., 1978; BA in Theology, Birmingham (Eng.) U., 1966, MA in Islamic Studies, 1968; MEd in Elem. Edn., Converse Coll., 1985, MEd in Gifted Edn., 1987; PhD in Founds. of Edn., U. S.C., 1995. Tchr. pub. and pvt. schs., S.C., N.H., 1992-94, Cobb County (Ga.) Schs., 1994-96; assoc. prof. edn. Covenant Coll., Lookout Mountain, Ga., 1996—. Adv. bd. Dushkin/McGraw Hill Annual Editions, 1997—. Contbr. articles to profl. jours. Internat. adv. com. Greenville (S.C.) Tech. Coll., 1990-91. Francis Corder Clayton scholar Birmingham U., 1966-67, Leverhulme Rsch. scholar Lever Bros., 1967-68; George Poda Jr. scholar U. S.C., 1992, James A. Stoddrd fellow, 1993. Mem. Nat. Assn. Multicultural Edn., Nat. Middle Sch. Assn., Phi Delta Kappa, Sigma Delta Pi (v.p. 1992-93). Presbyterian. Office: Covenant Coll 14049 Scenic Hwy Lookout Mountain GA 30750-4100

HADDAD, EDMONDE ALEX, public affairs executive; b. L.A., July 25, 1931; s. Alexander Saleeba and Madeline Angela (Zail) H.; m. Harriet Ann Lenhart; children: Mark Edmonde, Brent Michael, John Alex. AA, Los Angeles City Coll., 1956; BA, U. Southern Calif., 1958; MA, Columbia U., 1961. Staff writer Sta. WCBS, N.Y.C., 1959-61; news commentator, editor Sta. KPOL AM-FM, L.A., 1961-67, dir., pub. affairs, 1967-73; exec. dir. L.A. World Affairs Coun., 1973-84, pres., 1984-88; dep. asst. sec. of state for pub. diplomacy Dept. State, Washington, 1987-88. Mem. steering com., moderator Conf. environ., L.A., 1989-90; pres. Nat. Coun. World Affairs Orgns., 1981-83; pres. Radio and TV News Assn. So. Calif., 1965-66; sr. fellow Ctr. Internat. Rels., U. Calif.; apptd. by Gov. Gray Davis to Gov.'s Blue Ribbon Adv. Panel on Hate Groups, 1999—. Author: Look to the Rainbow, 1997; contbg. author: How Peace Came to the World, 1985; founder, pub. World Affairs Jour. Quar., 1981; chair editl. bd. The Episcopal News, 2002-. Mem. So. Calif. exec. com. Friends of Wilton Park; with Brit. Fgn. Office Conf. Ctr., Ams. for Dem. Action, 1999—; apptd. hon. canon Episcopal Cathedral of St. Paul, L.A., 2004; mem. vestry St. Bede's Episcopal Ch., 2005. Recipient Am. Polit. Sci. Assn. award for Disting. Reporting of Pub. Affairs, 1967. Democrat. Avocations: poetry, nonfiction, and op-ed articles for newspapers, public speaking, travel. Home: 4350 Via Dolce Unit 104 Marina Del Rey CA 90292 Personal E-mail: edmondeh@aol.com.

HADDAD, EDWARD RAOUF, civil engineer, consultant; b. Mosul, Iraq, July 1, 1926; came to U.S., 1990. s. Raouf Sulaiman Haddad and Fadhila (Sulaiman) Shaya; m. Balquis Yousef Rassam, July 19, 1961; children: Reem, Raid. BSc, U. Baghdad, Iraq, 1949; postgrad., Colo. State U., 1966-67; PhD (hon.), 1995. Project engr., cons. Min. Pub. Works, Baghdad, 1949-63; arbitrator Engring. Soc. & Ct., Kuwait City, Kuwait, 1963-90; tech. advisor Royal Family, Kuwait, 1987-90; cons. pvt. practice Haddad Engring., Albuquerque, 1990-95; owner, pres. Overseas Contacts-Internat. Bus. and Consulting, Albuquerque, 1995—. Organizer reps abroad, Kuwait, 1990. Pres. Parents Assn., U. N.Mex., 1995. Recipient Hon. medal Pope Paul VI of Rome, 1973, Men of Achievement award Internat. Biog. Ctr., 1994. Mem. ASCE, NSPE, ABA (assoc.), Am. Arbitration Assn. (mem. adv. bd.), Sierra Cath. Internat. (trustee), Lions (bd. dirs. 1992), Inventors Club (bd. dirs. 1992), KC (chancellor 1992). Address: 1425 Monte Largo Dr NE Albuquerque NM 87112-6378 E-mail: edward.haddad@yahoo.com.

HADDAD, ERNEST MUDARRI, lawyer; b. Boston, Oct. 30, 1938; s. Abraham and Elaine (Mudarri) H.; m. Kathleen L. Tracy; 1 child, Barton Edward; children from previous marriage: Scott Cochrane, Mark Mudarri. BA, Trinity Coll., Hartford, Conn., 1960; LLB, Boston U., 1964. Bar: Mass. 1964, U.S. Dist. Ct. Mass. 1966, U.S. Supreme Ct. 1981. Asst. dean sch. law Boston U., 1966-71; asst. sec., gen. counsel Commonwealth of Mass. Exec. Office Human Svcs., Boston, 1971-76; gen. counsel Blue Cross and Blue Shield Mass. Inc., Boston, 1976-80; sec., gen. counsel The Mass. Gen. Hosp., Boston, 1981—2002, Ptnrs. HealthCare Sys., Inc., Boston, 1995—2002; assoc. dean, prof. law Boston U. Sch. Law, 2002—. Bd. dirs. Internat. Inst. Boston, 2002—, chmn. nominee and governance com., 2003—. Program chmn., mem. exec. com. Boston Study Group, 1979—; Bd. dirs. New Eng. Legal Found., 2001—. Recipient Trinity Coll. Alumni medal for Excellence, 1990. Mem. ABA, Am. Soc. Law, Medicine and Ethics, Boston Bar Assn. (mem. coun. 1998-2002, exec. com. 1999-2002, fin. com. 1999-2002, treas. 2001-02, mem. audit com. 2003—, chmn. 2005—), Boston Bar Found. (trustee 1998—), Boston U. Law Sch. Alumni Assn. (pres. 1998-99, bd. visitors Discovering Justice 2004). Home: 144 Mount Vernon St Boston MA 02108-1128 Office: 765 Commonwealth Ave Boston MA 02215 Office Phone: 617-353-3105. E-mail: ehaddad@bu.edu.

HADDAD, GABRIEL G., pediatrician, educator; b. Beirut, Mar. 20, 1947; arrived in U.S., 1974; s. George Gabriel and Ida (Bitar) Haddad; m. Karen Chmielski, June 14, 1975; children: Christopher, Diana, Justin. BS in Biology and Chemistry, Am. Univ. Beirut, 1969, MD, 1973. Diplomate Am. Bd. Pediat. Jr. resident pediat. Am. U. Beirut Med. Ctr., 1973—74; sr. resident pediat. U. Tex. Med. Ctr., Houston, 1974—75; fellow in pediat. pulmonary divsn. Columbia U., N.Y.C., 1975—78, asst. prof. pediat., 1978—84, assoc. prof. pediat., 1984—88, dir. sleep physiology lab. dept. pediat., 1980—88; dir. sect. and chief clin. svc. respiratory medicine Yale U. Sch. Medicine, New Haven, 1988—, assoc. prof. pediat., 1988—90, prof. pediat., 1990—, prof. cellular and molecular physiology, 1993—. Mem. NIHD study sect. NIH, Md., 1982; mem. edit. bd. Jour. Applied Physiology, 1983—85, assoc. editor, 1989—93; NIHLB site visitor NIH Program Project, Cleve., 1985; conf. chmn. NIHLB, 1987, NICHD, 1988; NIH subcom. chmn.; with dept. physiology and biophysics U. Iowa, 1986—87; with dept. genetics Yale U. Sch. Medicine, Boyer Ctr. for Molecular Medicine, 1996. Editor 2 books, contbr. over 173 articles and abstracts to profl. jours. and books. Recipient Edward Livingston Trudeau award, Am. Lung Assn., 1979—82, Pediat. Faculty Tchg. award, Yale U. Sch. Medicine, 1991, Excellence in Pediat. Rsch. award, Am. Acad. Pediat., 1992; fellow Parker B. Francis, 1976—79, Milton Singer, Columbia U. Coll. Physicians, 1977—78. Mem.: AAAS, Soc. for Neurosci., Am. Thoracic Soc. (respiratory neurobiology and sleep sect.), Am. Physiol. Soc., Soc. for Pediat. Rsch., Am. Heart Assn. (established investigator 1985—90), Alpha Omega Alpha. Office: 24 Bedford Rd Greenwich CT 06831-2533 Fax: 203-785-6337. E-mail: gabriel.haddad@yale.edu.

HADDAD, HESKEL MARSHALL, ophthalmologist, educator; b. Baghdad, Iraq, Sept. 26, 1930; came to U.S., 1953, naturalized, 1962; s. Moshe M. and Masuda (Cohen) H.; m. Doris I. Fatzer, July 4, 1963; children: Ava Masuda, Andreas Moshe, Michael Albert. Student, Royal Coll. Medicine, Baghdad, 1945-50; MD, Hebrew U., Jerusalem, 1953. Diplomate Am. Bd. Pediatrics, Am. Bd. Ophthalmology; ordained rabbi, 1997. Intern Donolo Hosp., Jaffo-Tel Aviv, Israel, 1950-51; rotating intern Hadassah U. Hosp., Jerusalem, 1951-53; pediatric resident Children's Med. Center, Boston, 1953-56; fellow in pediatric endocrinology Johns Hopkins Hosp., Balt., 1956-58; fellow in clin. endocrine br. Nat. Inst. Arthritis and Metabolic Diseases, NIH, Bethesda, Md., 1958-59, pediatrician sect. clin. endocrinology, 1959-60; asst. prof. pediatrics sch. medicine Howard U., Washington, 1959-60; resident, asst. dept. ophthalmology sch. medicine Washington U., St. Louis, 1960-64; leave of absence, 1962-63; fellow pediatric ophthalmology Inst. Visual Sci., San Francisco, 1962; research fellow Hôpital des Quinze-Vingts, Laboratoire de Physiologie de Vision, Ecole des Hautes Etudes, Paris, 1962-63; ophthalmologist Hôpital Beni Messous, Algiers, Algeria, 1964; asst. attending ophthalmic surgeon, also asst. prof. ophthalmology Mt. Sinai Hosp. and Sch. Medicine, N.Y.C., 1964-67; dir. dept. ophthalmology Beth Israel Med. Center, N.Y.C.; also assoc. prof. ophthalmology Mt. Sinai Sch. Medicine, 1967-71; clin. prof. ophthalmology N.Y. Med. Coll., 1971—. Author: Endocrine Exophthalmos, 1973, Metabolic Eye Diseases, 1974, Metabolic-Peditric Eye Diseases, 1979, Metabolic Ophthalmology: Diagnostic Techniques Vols. I and II, 1985, Jews of Arab and Islamic Countries: History, Problems and Solutions, 1984, (autobiography) Flight from Babylon, 1986; editor-in-chief: Metabolic Ophthalmology, 1976-79, Metabolic and Ophthalmology, 1976-79, Metabolic and Pediatric Ophthalmology, 1979-82, Metabolic, Pediatric and Systemic Ophthalmology, 1982—; contbr. articles to profl. jours.; holder 7 U.S. patents. Pres. Am. Com. for Rescue and Resettlement of Iraqui Jews, World Orgn. Jews from Arab Countries, Parents' Assn. of Sch. of Performing Arts, 1980-83. Fellow ACS, Am. Inst. Chemists; mem. Am. Endocrine Soc., Am. Fedn. Clin. Research, Assn. Research Ophthalmology and Vision, AMA, New York County Med. Soc., AAAS, Am. Acad. Ophthalmology, N.Y. Acad. Medicine, N.Y. Acad. Scis., N.Y. Soc. Clin. Ophthalmology, Soc. Eye Surgeons, Société Française d' Ophthalmologie, German Ophthal. Soc., Internat. Soc. Metabolic Eye Disease (founder, sec.-treas. 1973—), World Soc. on Systemic Ophthalmology (founder, sec.-treas. 1982, chmn.), N.Y. County Med. Soc. (chmn. com. fgn. med. grads. 1985-90, del. N.Y. State Med. Soc. 1985-86). Achievements include patents in field. Office: 1125 Park Ave New York NY 10128-1243 Office Phone: 212-427-1246. Personal E-mail: optoedcorp@aol.com. *The Commandment of "loving one's neighbor" should read "Thou shalt love for thy neighbor as for thy self." Whereas we cannot always control the emotion of love, we are consciously able to stop doing unto others what we do not like for ourselves.*

HADDAD, JAMES HENRY, chemical engineer, consultant; b. Willimantic, Conn., Jan. 30, 1923; s. William Addy and Nellie (Birbarie) H.; m. Isabel Serrano, Feb. 3, 1962; children: Frederick William, Francis Xavier. BS in Engring., Yale U., 1944. Chem. engr. Conn. Hard Rubber Co., New Haven, 1943-44; engr. rsch. dept. Mobil Rsch. Devel. Corp., Paulsboro, N.J., 1944-52, engr. engring. dept. N.Y.C., 1952-70, sr. engring. cons. Princeton, N.J., 1971-89; ind. cons. worldwide Catalytic Processing/Solids Sys., Princeton Junction, N.J., 1989—. Contbr. articles to profl. publs.; patentee in field, petroleum refining and shale retorting sys. Mem. budget com., trustee Princeton Area Communities United Way, 1977-90. Mem. Am. Chem. Soc., Am. Inst. Chem. Engrs., Alpha Chi Sigma. Avocation: swimming. Home and Office: 120 Tunicflower Ln Princeton Junction NJ 08550-1645 Office Phone: 609-918-1535.

HADDAD, JAMIL RAOUF, retired physician; b. Mosul, Iraq, Aug. 18, 1923; came to U.S., 1952, naturalized, 1965; s. Raouf Sulaiman and Fadhila (Shaya) Haddad; m. Mary Lou Scorsone, Aug. 1, 1959 (dec. 2001); children: Ralph J.(dec.), John L., James M. M.B., Ch.B., Iraqi Royal Coll. Medicine, Baghdad, Iraq, 1946. Med. officer Khanaqin (Iraq) Hosp., 1946-52; asst. resident pathology Crawford W. Long Meml. Hosp., Atlanta, 1953-54; resident Bellevue Hosp., N.Y.C., 1954-56; practice medicine specializing in pathology N.Y.C., 1963—, Passaic, NJ, 1981—; chmn. dept. anatomic and clin. pathology St. Clare's Hosp. and Health Center, N.Y.C., 1971-81; dir. pathology and clin. lab. Gen. Hosp. Ctr. at Passaic, 1981—2003; ret. Assoc. Sloan-Kettering Inst. for Cancer Rsch., N.Y.C., 1960—66; asst. prof. pathology NYU Coll. Medicine, 1959—65, asst. clin. prof. pathology, 1965—67, assoc. clin. prof. pathology, 1967—70, clin. prof. pathology, 1970—85; asst. prof. exptl. cell biology Mt. Sinai Grad Sch. Biol. Scis., N.Y.C., 1966—70, lectr., 1971—83, adj. asst. prof., 1983—88. Mem. Coll. Am. Pathologists, Am. Soc. Clin. Pathologists, AMA, N.Y. Pathol. Soc., N.Y. State, New York County med. socs. Home: 420 E 23rd St Apt MC New York NY 10010-5043 Office Phone: 212-982-0655.

HADDAD, LOUIS NICHOLAS, paralegal; b. Beggs, Okla., Sept. 3, 1923; s. Abraham and Tammam (Lelo) H.; m. Jacqueline Marie Pratali, Sept. 22, 1945 (div. 1952); children: Carole, Shirley, Charles; m. Martha Maria Laengst, Dec. 31, 1954; children: Sheila, Stephanie. Co-owner Haddad Bros. Wholesalers, Lancaster, Calif., 1955-57; regional v.p. Nulite Corp., No. Calif., 1957-60; owner, mgr. Shamrock Motors, Seaside, Calif., 1960-68, Gateway Liquors, Seaside, 1968-70, Wagontown Auto Sales, Seaside, 1971-73, Camptown West Motor Homes, Seaside, 1973-79; co-owner, mgr. Monterey (Calif.) Bay Tribune, 1983-89. Councilman City of Seaside, 1964-66, 78-80, mayor, 1966-72; charter bd. dirs. Monterey Peninsula Boys Club; bd. dirs. Alliance on Aging, Assn. Monterey Bay Area Govts., Monterey Peninsula Water Mgmt. Dist., 1993-97; chmn. Laguna Grande Agy., Seaside County Sanitation Dist., Monterey Overall Econ. Devel. Com.; chmn. adv. com. Project Aquarius; mem. Seaside Planning Comn.; vice chmn. So. Monterey Bay Water Pollution Control Agy.; chmn. tri-county bd. Calif. Coun. on Criminal Justice; former vice chmn. Monterey County Local Agys. Formation Com. Capt. U.S. Army, 1940-46, 50-55. Mem. VFW, NCO Assn. Am. (hon.), Am. Legion, Seaside C. of C. (bd. dirs.), K.C., Lions (past pres. Seaside chpt.), Rotary (past pres. Seaside chpt.). Republican. Roman Catholic. Home: 5 Deer Stalker Path Monterey CA 93940-6311 Business E-Mail: haddad@redshift.com.

HADDAD, MARK E., lawyer; BA magna cum laude, Boston Coll., 1980, JD cum laude, 1983. Bar: Mass. 1983, Supreme Judicial Ct. Mass., US Dist. Ct. (Mass.), US Ct. Appeals (1st & 4th cir.). Adminstrv. ptnr. & mem. mgmt. com. Kirkpatrick & Lockhart Nicholson Graham LLP, Boston. Mem.: ABA (Forum on Constrn. Industry), Mass. Bar Assn., Boston Bar Assn. (Constrn. & Real Estate Com.). Office: Kirkpatrick & Lockhart Nicholson Graham LLP 75 State St Boston MA 02109-1814 Office Phone: 617-261-3116. Office Fax: 617-261-3175. Business E-Mail: mhaddad@klng.com.

HADDAWAY, JAMES DAVID, retired insurance company official; b. Louisville, July 25, 1933; s. Charles Montgomery Jr. and Viola (Sands) H.; m. Myrna Lou (Harris), June 5, 1954 (dec. Sept. 1999); children: Peggy Ann, Robert Marshall, Susan Gayle; m. Janie Louise (Young), Mar. 25, 2000. BS in Commerce, U. Louisville, 1960; MBA, Xavier U., 1973. Cert. adminstrv. mgr., purchasing mgr., sr. profl. human resources. Ins. cons. Met. Life Ins., Louisville, 1955—59; supt. Byck Bros. and Co., Louisville, 1959—61; purchasing mgr. Liberty Nat. Bank, Louisville, 1961—63; v.p., mgr. gen. svcs. adminstrn. Citizens Fidelity Bank, Louisville, 1963—79; asst. v.p., mgr. human resources Ky. Farm Bur. Ins. Co., Louisville, 1979—95; ret., 1995. Founder, chmn. emeritus Kentuckiana Expn. Bus. and Industry, 1973-85. Served in the 11th Airbourne Divsn., U.S. Army, 1953-55. Named Boss of Yr., Louisville Chpt. Nat. Sec. Assn., 1978-79. Mem.: Nat. Assn. Purchasing Mgmt. (dir. nat. affairs 1970—71), Louisville Soc. Advancement Mgmt. (pres. 1993—94, dir. 1994—95, charter), Ky. C. of C. (chmn. banking and ins. health and welfare sub-com. project 21 1988), Nat. Assn. Ind. Insurers (pers. com. 1987—95), Soc. Human Resource Mgmt. (chmn. conf. com. region nine 1984, dist. dir., western Ky. 1984, v.p. region nine 1985—86, Ky. coun. chmn. 1986), Conf. Casualty Ins. Co. (chmn. nat. pers. conf. com. 1983), Louisville Soc. Human Resource Mgmt. (pres. 1983—84, chmn. reorgn. com. 1992, Profl. Excellence award 1993), Purchasing Mgmt. Assn. Louisville (pres. 1969—70), Adminstrv. Mgmt. Soc. (pres., Louisville 1975—76, bd. dir. 1976—92, nat. dir. 1979—81, charter mem. found.), Am. Assn. Individual Investors (life), Bass Anglers Sportsman Soc. (life), Land Yacht Port O'Call Airstream Pk. (co-chmn. computer club 1998, chmn. 1999), Good Sam Recreational Vehicle Club (life), Nat. Eagle Scout Assn. (life), Wally Byam Caravan Club Internat. (life; pres., Ky. unit 1993, chmn. long range planning com. 1994, second v.p. region five 1996—97, first v.p. region five 1998—99, pres. region five 2000—01, internat. second v.p. 2002—03, internat. first v.p. 2003—04, pres. 2004—05, chair internat. nominating com. 2005—), Univ. Club Louisville (charter), Shriners, Masons, Am. Legion, Order Ky. Col. Home: 200 Walnut Hill Ave # 90 Hillsboro TX 76645

HADDEN, JOHN WINTHROP, immunopharmacology educator; b. Berkeley, Calif., Oct. 23, 1939; s. David Rodney Hadden; m. Elba Mas, July 31, 1964; children: John W. II, Paul J. BA, Yale U., 1961; MD, Columbia U., 1965. Asst. prof. pathology U. Minn., Mpls., 1972-73; assoc. prof. Cornell Grad. Sch., N.Y.C., 1973-82; assoc. mem., dir. lab. immunopharmacology Sloan-Kettering Meml. Cancer Inst., N.Y.C., 1973-82; prof. medicine, dir. div. immunopharmacology U. South Fla., Tampa, 1982-99; founder, chief sci. officer IRX Therapeutics, NYC, 1999—. Cons. in field.; vis. prof. U. South Fla. Med. Coll., Nat. Cancer Inst., Mex. Assoc. editor Internat. Jour. Immunopharmacology, 1978-86, editor, 1986-99; editor 12 textbooks; contbr. chpts. to books, more than 300 articles to profl. jours. Mem. Am. Assn. Immunologists, Am. Soc. Pharm. & Exptl. Therapy, Internat. Soc. Immunopharmacology (v.p. 1982-85, pres. 1985-88, publ. officer 1988-99, treas. 1999-2002), Tampa Yale Club (v.p. 1986-91) Achievements include patents for methods of imparting immunomodulating activity. Home: 428 Harbor Rd Cold Spring Harbor NY 11724-2108 Office: Immuno-Rx Inc 140 W 57th St Ste 9C New York NY 10019-3326 Office Phone: 212-582-1199. E-mail: jwhadden@optonline.net.

HADDER, DONALD EVERETT, SR., urban planner; b. Albuquerque, Dec. 11, 1951; s. James Everett and Rose Carol Hadder; m. Vivian Lorraine Lowman, June 12, 1971; 1 child, Donald Everett Jr. BS in Geography, Ariz. State U., 1974, MA in Geography, 1976. Rsch. planner Mountainwest, Inc., Tempe, Ariz., 1974; assoc. planner City of Scottsdale, 1975—79, planner, 1980—84, sr. planner, 1984—86, planning coord. mgr., 1986—96, cmty. planning dir., 1996—2001, prin. planner, 2001—. Guest prof. Ariz. State U., Tempe, 1982; cons. in field. Bd. dirs., chmn. Scottsdale Nazarene, 1978—; bd. dirs. Friends Geography, Tempe, 1992—95; pres. bd. Scottsdale Leadership, Scottsdale, 1978—. Mem.: Scottsdale Hist. Soc., Am. Planning Assn., Urban Land Inst. Avocations: photography, golf, history, creative writing, landscaping. Home: 8232 E San Miguel Scottsdale AZ 85250 Office: City of Scottsdale 3939 N Drinkwater Blvd Scottsdale AZ 85251 Office Phone; 480-312-2352. Personal E-mail: dhaddersr@cox.net. E-mail: dhadder@scottsdaleaz.gov.

HADDOCK, FRED(ERICK) T(HEODORE), JR., retired astronomer; b. Independence, Mo., May 31, 1919; s. Fred Theodore Sr. and Helen (Sea) H.; m. Margaret Pratt, June 24, 1941 (div. Sept. 1976); children: Thomas Frederick, Richard Marshall; m. Deborah J. Fredericks, Dec. 7, 2003. SB, MIT, 1941; MS, U. Md., 1950; DSc (hon.), Rhodes Coll., 1965, Ripon Coll., 1966. Physicist U.S. Naval Rsch. Lab., Washington, 1941-56; assoc. prof. elec. engring. and astronomy U. Mich., Ann Arbor, 1956-59, prof. elec. engring., 1959-67, prof. astronomy, 1959-88, emeritus prof., 1988—. Lectr. radio astronomy Jodrell Bank U. Manchester, Eng., 1962; vis. assoc. radio astronomy Calif. Inst. Tech., 1966; vis. lectr. Raman Inst., Bangalore, India, 1978; sr. cons. Nat. Radio Astron. Obs., W.Va., 1960-61; founder, dir. U. Mich. Radio Astron. Obs., 1961-84. Author: (chpts. in books) Space Age Astronomy, 1962, Radio Astronomy of the Solar System, 1966; contbr. articles to prof. jours. and publs. Mem. Union Radio Sci. Internat., nat. chmn. commn. on radio astronomy, 1954-57; trustee Associated Univs., Inc., 1964-68; prin. investigator, five Orbiting Geophys. Observatories, 1960-74, and Interplanetary Probe 9, 1964-77; co-investigator on Voyager planetary probes, 1970-86, NASA, Washington; mem. astronomy adv. panel NSF, Washington, 1957-60, 63-66. With USN, 1944-45. Fellow IEEE (life), Am. Astron. Soc. (v.p. 1961-63); mem. Internat. Astron. Union (commn. on radio astronomy 1948—), NAS (adv. panel astronomy facilities 1962-64), AIA (hon. mem. Huron Valley chpt. 1980—), Sigma Xi (past pres. U. Mich. chpt. 1956—). Achievements include design and development of first submarine periscope radar antenna, 1943-44; early discoveries in microwave astronomy, gaseous nebulae in 1953 and early space detection of kilometer waves from galaxy and the sun, 1962. Home: 3935 Holden Dr Ann Arbor MI 48103-9415 Office: U Mich Astronomy Dept Ann Arbor MI 48109 Office Phone: 734-662-7245. Business E-Mail: fhaddock@umich.edu.

HADDOCK, RAYMOND EARL, retired career officer; b. Oklahoma City, Sept. 26, 1936; s.Clyde William and Ida Belle (Lemmon) H.; m. Brunhilde Ernestine Becker, Oct. 21, 1960; children: Ralph William, Ronald Raymond, Karen Elizabeth Haddock Fralen. BS in Chemistry, W. Tex. State U., 1958; MS in Pub. Adminstrn., Shippensburg Coll., 1977; grad., U.S. Army War Coll., Carlisle Barracks, Pa., 1977. Commd. 2d lt. U.S. Army, advanced through grades to maj. Gen., bn. comdr. Pershing Missile Bn., 56th F.A., 1973-75, pers. staff officer (G-1) 8th Inf. Div., 1975-76, dir. internat. programs Tng. and Doctrin Command Fort Monroe, Va., 1977-80, comdr 9th Div. Arty. Fort Lewis, Wash., 1980-83, chief of staff Tng. Ctr. Fort Dix, N.J., 1983-84, comdg. gen. Pershing Missile Command 56th F.A. Fed. Republic Germany, 1984-87; U.S. comdr. U.S. Command and U.S. Army, Berlin, 1988-90; comdg. gen. Security Assistance Command U.S. Army, Alexandria, Va., 1990-92; v.p. ITT Def. Internat., McLean, Va., 1993—2003, ret., 2003. Participator fall of Berlin wall, reunification of Germany and U.S.-Soviet nuclear forces treaty, 1987. Decorated D.S.M. with two oak leaf clusters; Fed. Order of Merit, Berlin; Order of Merit (Fed. Republic Germany); Gold Nat. Def. medal (France). Avocations: sailing, fishing, jogging, hunting, genealogy.

HADDOCK, ROBERT LYNN, information services entrepreneur, writer; b. Vallejo, Calif., May 12, 1945; s. Orville Walter and Lee Ellen (Alexander) H. BA, Union Coll., 1967; postgrad., NYU, 1977-81. Editor So. Pub. Assn., Nashville, 1969-74, controller, 1974-75; mktg. analyst Bus. Publs. div. Prentice-Hall, Englewood Cliffs, N.J., 1975-78, bus. mgr., 1978-81, Ziff-Davis Pub. Co., N.Y.C., 1981-82, dir. bus. devel., 1982-83; pres. Personal Access, Inc., N.Y.C., 1983-84; v.p., dir. product devel. Citicorp Global Report, N.Y.C., 1984-86, v.p., dir. mktg., 1986-88; v.p., dir. product devel. Citibank, N.A., N.Y.C., 1989-90; v.p., dir. product devel. and mktg. Enhanced Telephone Svcs., Inc., N.Y.C., 1990-91; pres. M-Power Corp., N.Y.C., 1991-98, Global Strategy Ptnrs., N.Y.C., 1998—2004. Author: The Broken Web, 1973, How to Stop Smoking, 1974; inventor database accessing system, 1983, enhanced telephone, 1989, digital screen phone, 1993. Mem. IEEE, Am. Assn. Artificial Intelligence, Software and Info. Industry Assn., Mensa. Home: 105 W 13th St Apt 15F New York NY 10011-7848 Business E-Mail: rhaddock@globalstrategypartners.com.

HADDON, EVA W., principal; b. Danville, Ill., July 3, 1938; d. Wills and Louella Huff; m. John C. Haddon, Dec. 31, 2003; children: Tracy, Amy, Mark, Lance. BA, East Stroudsburg (Pa.) U., 1985, EdM, 1987; postgrad., Widener U. Cert. tchr. spl. edn., supr. spl. edn. prin. Instnl. aide IU 20, Easton, Pa., 1980—84; tchr. spl. edn. IU 20 and East Stroudsburg State U., 1985—93; prin. East Stroudsburg Sch. Dist., 1993—2000, Allentown (Pa.) Sch. Dist., 2000—. Instr. East Stroudsburg State U., 1998—2002; presenter in field. Mem. edn. com. Allentown C. of C., 2000—03; mem. com. Allentown Symphony, 2003—04; chair, founder Very Spl. Arts Festival Monroe County, East Stroudsburg, 1990—94; bd. dirs. Bus. and Industry for Arts in Edn., 1996—2000, Learning Disabilities Assn., East Stroudsburg, 1995—98. Recipient Outstanding Achievement award, Pocono United Way, Stroudsburg, 1998, award for outstanding svc., East Stroudsburg Edn. Found., 1999; fellow, Inst. Devel. for Edn. Activities, 1995—2002. Mem.: ASCD, Pa. Assn.

Supervision and Curriculum Devel., Pa. Assn. Supervision and Adminstrn. (bd. dirs. 1996—). Republican. Lutheran. Avocations: gardening, golf, tennis, reading, violin. Office: Allentown Sch Dist 829 Turner St Allentown PA 18102

HADDON, HAROLD ALAN, lawyer; b. Flint, Mich., Dec. 2, 1940; s. Russell Daniel and Virginia Sibyl (Johnston) H.; m. Beverly Jean Reading, July 2, 1966. AB, Albion Coll., 1962; A.M., U. Mich., 1963; JD, Duke U., 1966. Bar: Colo. 1966, U.S. Dist. Ct. Colo. 1966, U.S. Ct. Appeals (10th cir.) 1966, U.S. Supreme Ct. 1977; cert. trial counsel U.S. Cts. Martial. Asso. firm Davis, Graham & Stubbs, Denver, 1966-70; chief trial dep. Colo. Pub. Defender, 1970-73; ptnr. Haddon, Morgan & Foreman, Denver, 1975—. Adj. prof. law in criminal trial advocacy U. Denver Sch. Law, 1972-73; spl. prosecutor Colo. State Grand Jury, 1976-78 Editor-in-chief Duke Law Jour., 1965-66. Sec. Nat. Multiple Sclerosis Soc., 1970-76; mem. Colo. U.S. Jud. Selection Com., 1977, 93; campaign mgr. U.S. Sen. Gary W. Hart, 1974-80; fin. chmn. Colo. Gov. Richard D. Lamm, 1978; nat. polit. coordinator Hart for Pres. campaign, 1987. Lt. comdr. USNR, 1968—. Fellow Am. Coll. Trial Lawyers, 1988; mem. Am., Colo., Denver bar assns., Nat. Assn. Criminal Def. Lawyers, Order of Coif, Phi Beta Kappa, ABA (commn. on complex fed. criminal cases, 1981-82, criminal justice standards com., 1991-92, 2002-). Democrat. Office: Haddon Morgan Mueller Jordan Mackey & Foreman PC 150 E 10th Ave Denver CO 80203

HADDON, JAMES FRANCIS, banker; b. Columbia, S.C., Aug. 12, 1954; s. Wallace James and Ida Beatrice (Bassette) H.; m. Sezelle Antoiniette Gereau. BA, Wesleyan U., 1976; MBA, Stanford U., 1980. Bank mgmt. trainee Mellon Bank, Pitts., 1976-78; assoc. Blyth Eastman Paine Webber Inc., N.Y.C., 1980-83; v.p. Paine Webber Inc., N.Y.C., 1983-93; mng. dir. pub. fin. Smith Barney, Inc., N.Y.C., 1993—. Mem. Sponsors for Ednl. Opportunities, N.Y.C., 1982—; trustee Wesleyan U., 1994-97. Mem. Nat. Assn. State Treas., Nat. Assn. of Securities Profls. (treas. 1993-97, sec. 1997—, Skull and Serpent Soc., Wesleyan Black Alumni Assn (steering com. 1984-86). Clubs: N.Y. Athletic. Office: Smith Barney Inc 390 Greenwich St New York NY 10013-2375

HADDOW, JAMES BUCHANAN, lawyer; b. Quincy, Mass., June 25, 1959; s. James Edward and Paula Kozodoy Haddow; m. Michelle Ritchie, June 4, 1988; children: Hamish Robert Mackintosh, Max Edward Buchanan Ritchie. BA in Philosophy, Colby Coll., 1982; JD, U. Maine, 1986. Bar: Maine 1986, U.S. Dist. Ct. Maine 1986, U.S. Ct. Appeals (1st cir.) 1990, U.S. Ct. Claims, 2001, U.S. Supreme Ct. 2000. Assoc. Kelly, Remmel & Zimmerman, Portland, Maine, 1986-87; prin. Profl. Resource Assoc., Portland, 1987-91; assoc. Petruccelli & Martin, Portland, 1991-94, ptnr., 1995—. Alumni bd. dirs. U. Maine Law Sch., 2000—. Mem. Planning Bd., Limington, Maine, 1995-98, chair, 1997-98; trustee Mad Horse Theatre Co., Portland, 1989-93, chair, 1991-93. Mem. ABA, ATLA, Maine State Bar Assn., Cumberland County Bar Assn., Portland C. of C. (mem. cmty. partnership com. 1999—). Democrat. Avocations: running, hiking, fly fishing. Office: Petruccelli & Martin LLP PO Box 9733 50 Monument Sq Portland ME 04104-5033

HADDY, FRANCIS JOHN, internist, educator; b. Walters, Minn., Sept. 6, 1922; s. Thomas J. and Frances (Shaheen) H.; m. Theresa Eileen Brey, Sept. 21, 1946; children: Richard, Carol, Alice. Student, Luther Coll., Decorah, Iowa, 1940-42; BS, U. Minn., 1943, M.B., 1946, MD, 1947, MS in Physiology, 1949, PhD in Physiology (Am. Heart Assn. fellow), 1953. Diplomate: Am. Bd. Internal Medicine. Intern Mpls. Gen. Hosp., 1946—47; fellow internal medicine Mayo Found., 1949—51; asst. prof. physiology and medicine Northwestern U. Med. Sch., 1953—61; clin. investigator VA Rsch. Hosp., Chgo., 1957—59; prof. physiology, chmn. dept., assoc. prof. medicine U. Okla. Med. Center, 1961—66; prof. physiology, chmn. dept. Mich. State U., East Lansing, 1966—76; prof. physiology Uniformed Svcs. U., Bethesda, Md., 1976—99, chmn. dept. physiology, 1976—87. Mem. cardiovasc. study sect. NIH, 1963-69; tng. com. Nat. Heart and Lung Inst., NIH, 1970-73; mem. atherosclerosis and hypertension adv. com. Nat. Heart, Lung and Blood Inst., NIH, 1983-86; rsch. com. Am. Heart Assn., 1974-80; mem. life scis. adv. com. NASA, 1986-92, chmn., 1988-92, mem. aerospace med. adv. com. 1988-93, mem. NASA-NIH adv. com., 1993-95; sr. scientist NASA/Johnson Space Ctr. S.C. med. scis. divsn., Houston, 1989-90; cons., peer rev. adminstr. for cardiopulmonary, integrative physiology, and clin. areas NASA, 1995—. Mem. editl. bd. Am. Jour. Physiology, 1963-69, 80-86, Jour. Applied Physiology, 1963-69, Procs. Soc. Exptl. Biology and Medicine, 1969-72, Circulation Rsch., 1975-81, Microvascular Rsch., 1978-81, Hypertension, 1978-81, Jour. Am. Coll. Nutrition, 1993-99. Recipient Med. Sci. Achievement award Am. Heart Assn., 1987, Scientist Emeritus awrd Soc. Exptl. Biology and Medicine, 1996-97, Disting. Alumnus award Mayo Found., 2003, Disting. Svc. award Luther Coll., 2004. Fellow Am. Coll. Nutrition (coord. hypertension and cardiovasc. diseases 1992-98, bd. dirs. 1993-97, publs. com. 1994-99, ann. award 1986); mem. Am. Physiol. Soc. (steering com. circulation group 1972-75, chmnm. com. on coms. 1974-77, coun. 1976-79, pres. 1981, fin. com. 1983-89, chmn. fin. com. 1985-89, select com. on animal care 1988-91, chmn. long range planning com. 1990-93, hon. com. 1993-95, chmn. 1995, Carl J. Wiggers award 1966), Am. Soc. Clin. Investigation, Fedn. Am. Socs. Exptl. Biology (bd. dirs. 1980-83, treas. 1990-92, rep. to Am. Assn. Accreditation Lab. Animal Care trustees 1993-96, exec. com. 1995-96), Internat. Union Physiol. Scis. (U.S. nat. com. 1976-79, 81-84), Nat. Hypertension Assn. (trustee 1979—, v.p. 2003—), NAS (basic biomed. scis. panel, com. on nat. needs for biomed. and behavioral rsch. pers. Inst. Medicine 1983-86), Assn. Chairmen Depts. Physiology (chmn. animal welfare com. 1986-87), Aerospace Med. Assn. (publ. com. 1994-95), Am. Soc. for Gravitational and Space Biology (awards com. 1994-99), Montgomery County Art Assn. (pres. 1997-98), Mayo Found. (Disting. Alumnus award, 2003). Achievements include left heart catherization, small vein and artery catherization, mechanisms of pulmonary edema, fluid flux across the capillary membrane, local regulation of blood flow, ionic action on blood vessels, and low renin hypertension. Home: 211 2nd St NW Apt 1607 Rochester MN 55901-2896 Business E-Mail: fhaddy@hq.nasa.gov.

HADEE, HASAN A., digital media consultant, content designer; s. Raheem and Patricia Hadee. BA in Philosophy, Wash. State U., 1995; A in Applied Arts, Art Inst. of Seattle, 1998; M in Comm. in Digital Media, U. Wash., 2005. Assoc. dir. mktg. and promotions N.W. Internat. Entertainment, Seattle, 1997—98; broadcast ops. technician Denver, 1998—99; broadcast ops. supr. New Frontier Media, Boulder, Colo., 1999—2001; broadcast media systems cons. Encoda Systems Inc., Denver, 2001; digital media lab .support specialist U. Wash., Seattle, 2004—. Mem.: Broadcast Edn. Assn., Nat. Assn. TV Program Execs., Nat. Black MBA Assn., Omega Psi Phi (assoc. Natioal Creative Grant award 2004). Office Phone: 206-543-2660. Office Fax: 206-616-3762.

HADEN, BENJAMIN, minister, retired publishing executive, broadcast executive; b. Fincastle, Va., Oct. 18, 1925; s. Benjamin and Anne Spiller Haden; m. Charlene Gay Edwards, July 22, 1950; 1 child, Dallas Haden Gibbons. BA in polit. sci., U. Tex., Austin, 1947; JD, Washington and Lee U., Lexington, Va., 1949; MDiv magna cum laude, Columbia Theol. Sem., Atlanta, 1963; DD (hon.), King Coll., Bristol, Tenn., 1968. Bar: DC 1953; ordained minister 1962. Owner and pres. Long Oil Co., Harrisonburg, Va., 1949—50; with CIA, Washington, 1950—51; news, advt., circulation Mansfield News Jour., Ohio, 1951—53; nat. advt. Jefferson City News Tribune, Mo., 1953—54; CEO Kingsport Times News, Tenn., 1954—60; interim pastor Riviera Presbyn. Ch., Miami, Fla., 1962; youth dir. North Ave. Presbyn. Ch., Atlanta, 1962—63; sr. pastor Key Biscayne Presbyn. Ch., Miami, 1963—67; spkr. Bible Study Hour, NBC radio, Phila., 1967—68; sr. pastor First Presbyn. Ch., Chattanooga, 1967—99; founder, spkr. Changed Lives TV/Radio Internat., Chattanooga, 1968—. Mem. Am. Newspaper Pubs. Assn., 1954—60, So. Newspaper Pubs. Assn., 1954—60; dir. The Bible For You, Atlanta, 1963—70; assoc. evangelist Billy Graham Crusade, Vancouver, Canada, 1965; Bible tchr. Leadership Inst., Atlanta, 1968, Monterey, Calif., 70; trustee King Coll., Bristol, Tenn., 1968—74; mem. Nat. Religious Broadcasters, 1968—2001; mem. originating bd. Debbie Fox Found., 1969; dir. Christianity Today, Chgo., 1975—2000, Electric Sys., Chattanooga, 1985—2000; spkr. first Conv. of Evangelists, Moscow, 1990; dir. Race Found., Cedar Rapids, Iowa, 1965—2002, Electric Motor Sales, Chattanooga, 1985—, Metal Sys., Inc., Chattanooga, 1994—. Author: (books) Kingsport - Modern Am. City, 1962, I See Their Faces, 1962; co-author: Why I am at Seminary, 1961; author: Rebel to Rebel, 1971, Pray!, 1974; contbr. articles to newspapers; interviewer (in print and broadcast media). Pres. Kingsport Rotary Club, 1959; mem. race rels. com. Mayor Jim Rose, Chattanooga, 1970; chmn. Salvation Army Bd., Kingsport, 1954; deacon First Presbyn. Ch., Kingsport, 1955, mem. pulpit com., 1956; mem. exec. com. Kingsport C. of C., 1956; pres. Community Chest, Kingsport, 1957; dir. Ridgefields Country Club, Kingsport, 1957. Recipient Merit in Program Prodn. award, Nat. Religious Broadcasters, 1987, Love of Chattanooga award, 1986, Nat. Heritage award, Chattanooga Sertoma Club, 1988. Mem.: Tenn. Bar Assn., Chattanooga Golf and Country Club, Mountain City Club, Rotary Club of Chattanooga, Kappa Sigma (pres. Washington and Lee chpt. 1948). Avocations: current events, hiking, writing. Office: Changed Lives Ste 200 1200 Mountain Creek Rd Chattanooga TN 37405

HADEN, CLOVIS ROLAND, retired academic administrator, engineering educator; b. Houston, Apr. 10, 1940; s. Clovis Newton and Mary Aline (Baker) H.; m. Joyce Elaine Weathers, Aug. 8, 1956; children: Cathy, Kimberly, Clay. Student, Navarro Coll., 1958-59; BSEE, U. Tex.-Arlington, 1961; MSEE, Calif. Inst. Tech., 1962; PhD, U. Tex., 1965. Lic. profl. engr., Tex., Okla. Asst. prof. U. Okla., 1965-68; dir. Sch. Elec. Engring. and Computing Scis., 1972-78; asso. prof. Tex. A&M U., College Station, 1968-71, prof., 1971-72, dir. Inst. Solid State Electronics, 1969-72; dean Coll. Engring and Applied Scis. Ariz. State U., Tempe, 1978-87, 89-91, v.p. for acad. affairs, 1987-88, provost west campus Phoenix, 1988-89, mem., pres. Research Park bd. Tempe, 1983-91; bd. dirs. Ariz. Transp. Research Ctr., 1980-91; vice chancellor for acad. affairs La. State U., Baton Rouge, 1991-93; vice chancellor/dean engring., dir. engring. experiment sta. Tex. A&M U., 1993—2002. Mem. Ariz. Gov.'s Commn. on Sci. and Tech., 1980-82, chmn. transp. subcom., 1981-83, mem. adv. coun. for engring., 1979-91; mem. Ariz. Gov.'s High Tech. Coun., 1990-91; mem. Tex. Gov.'s Coun. Sci. & Tech., 1997-2002; chair strategic planning La. Ednl. Quality Support Fund, 1991-93; mem. Nat. Engring. Dean's Exec. Bd., 1984-87, 95-2000; mem. adv. group Coun. on Competitiveness, 1994-95; chmn. bd. Ariz. R&D Co., 1983-90; mem. adv. bd. A.T. Kearney, 1986-90; mem. Tex. Bd. Profl. Engrs., 2002—. Exec. editor: Electric Power Sys. Rsch. Jour., 1978—. Bd. mgrs. Tempe YMCA, 1982-84; mem. Ariz. Econ. Devel. Bd., 1982-85; bd. dirs. Harrington Arthritis Rsch. Ctr., 1983-87, Inter-tel, Inc., 1983—, Square D. Co., 1985-91, E-Sys., 1994-95, WAVO Corp., 1990-99, Crosstex Energy, 2002—, Res. Valley Partnership, 2004—. Recipient George Washington Honor medal Freedoms Found., 1989, Disting. Alumnus award U. Tex., Arlington, 1995, Econ. Devel. award Phoenix area, 1985; Bur. Engring. rsch. fellow, 1964. Fellow IEEE (Oklahoma City Engr. of Yr. award 1977), Am. Soc. Engring. Edn. (chair pub. policy com. 1997-99, Marlowe award 1998); mem. NSPE, Ariz. Soc. Profl. Engrs. (Engr. of Yr. award 1983), Ariz. Assn. Indsl. Devel., Coun. Tex. Engring. Deans (chmn. 1995-98), Tex. Soc. Profl. Engrs. (bd. dirs. 1995-98), Soc. Mfg. Engrs., Sons of Republic of Tex., Golden Key, Sigma Xi, Phi Kappa Phi, Eta Kappa Nu, Tau Beta Pi. Republican. Mem. Ch. of Christ. Personal E-mail: r-haden@tamu.edu.

HADFIELD, MICHAEL JAMES, electrical engineer; b. Waukesha, Wis., Jan. 25, 1934; s. Raymond James and Viola Emma (Hardke) H.; m. Arlene Rita Echaust, June 11, 1955 (dec. 1996); children: Steven Michael, Linda Frances, Mary Arlene (dec. 1998), Dayna JoAnne; m. Judy Kay Hadfield; children: Franklin Dennis, David Lawrence Miller. BSEE, Marquette U., 1955; postgrad., U. Wis., 1960, U. South Fla., 1968-69. Commd. USMC, 1955, advanced through grades to capt., 1965, resigned; project engr. GM, Milw., 1958-60; guidance sys. engr. Honeywell, Inc., Clearwater, Fla., 1960-93, prin. staff engr., 1991-93, ret., 1993; mktg. mgr., program mgr. USAF, Holloman AFB, 1994-99, ret., 1999; cons., 1999—. Pres., chmn. Sta. WQXM-FM/FM Enterprises, Largo, Fla., 1968-69; v.p. Real Property Ctr., 1975-79; v.p. Luten Properties, Inc., 1979-93; broker-salesman Prudential Fla. Realty, Clearwater, 1993-94. Contbr. chpts. to books, 32 articles to tech. jours. Pres. Ch. Coun. Recipient: Gold Medal AFCEA and SAME. Fellow: AIAA (assoc.); mem.: IEEE (program and exhibits chmn., exec. com.), Inst. of Navigation (v.p.Eastern region, chmn. Inertial div.), Air Force Assn., Fla. Bd. Realtors, Nat. Bd. Realtors, Assoc. Proposal Mgmt. Profls., Scabbard and Blade, Tau Beta Pi, Pi Mu Epsilon, Eta Kappa Nu, Alpha Sigma Nu. Republican. Home and Office: PO Box 1189 Cloudcroft NM 88317-1189

HADGES, THOMAS RICHARD, media consultant; b. Brockton, Mass., Mar. 13, 1948; s. Samuel Charles and Ethel Toli (Prifti) H.; m. Beth Evelyn Rastad, Oct. 22, 1988. BA in Biology magna cum laude, Tufts U., 1969; student, Harvard Sch. Dental Med., 1969—71. Announcer Sta. WOKW, Brockton, 1965-67, Sta. WTBS-FM, MIT, Cambridge, 1966-68; announcer, program dir. Sta. WTUR, Medford, Mass., 1967-69; announcer Concert Network, Sta. WBCN-FM, Boston, 1968-78, program dir., 1977-78, Sta. WCOZ-FM, Blair Broadcasting, Boston, 1978-80, Sta. KLOS-FM, ABC, L.A., 1980-85; sr. programming advisor Pollack Media Group, Pacific Palisades, Calif., 1985-89, pres., 1989—, Pollack/Hadges Enterprises, Pacific Palisades, 1985-89. Coordinating prodr. Live Aid Concerts, 1985; worldwide radio prodr. Live 8 Concerts, 2005. Named Program Dir. of Yr., L.A. Times, 1981. Mem. Phi Beta Kappa. Avocations: jogging, electronics. Office: Pollack Media Group 860 Via De La Paz Ste D2 Pacific Palisades CA 90272-3663

HADIDIAN, DIKRAN YENOVK, librarian, clergyman; b. Aintab, Turkey, June 9, 1920; came to U.S., 1946, naturalized, 1956; s. Yenovk Haroutune and Helen (Koundakjian) H.; m. Jean Root Wackerbarth, June 9, 1948; children: Eric Dikran, Andrew Dikran. BA, Am. U. Beirut, 1944; B.D., Hartford Theol. Sem., 1948; MA, Hartford Sch. Religious Edn., 1949; S.T.M., Hartford Sem. Found., 1950; MS in L.S, Columbia U., 1960; DD (hon.), North Park U., 1998. Instr. Oak Grove Sch., Vassalboro, Me., 1950-52, Sweet Briar Coll., 1952-55; librarian Hartford Sem. Found., 1957-66, Pitts. Theol. Sem., 1966-85, prof., librarian emeritus, 1985—; vis. lectr. U. Pitts., 1969-83; Mem. corp. bd. United Ch. World Ministries, 1971-77. Bd. dirs. Pitts. Chamber Music Soc. Chmn. editl. bd. Perspective, 1967-72; editor series: Bibliographia Tripotamopolitana, 1969-85; gen. editor: Princeton Theol. Monograph series and Pitts. Theol. Monograph Series, 1974-82, 1983-2004; dir., gen. editor: Pickwick Publs.; contbr. articles to profl. jours. Mem. Studiorum Novi Testamenti, Soc. Bibl. Lit., Am. Theol. Library Assn. Address: 215 Incline Way San Jose CA 95139-1526 E-mail: dyh1@aol.com.

HADLEY, GREGORY BROWN, lawyer; b. Dec. 5, 1946; s. LaMarr E. and Mabel (Brown) H.; m. Kay Larsen, July 26, 1990; children: Brittany, Korby, McKade, Wade, Chase, Landon; children by previous marriage: Cinamon, Gregory, Grant, Regetta. BS, Brigham Young U., 1975; JD, U. LaVern, 1979. Bar: Calif. 1981, Utah 1982, U.S. Dist. Ct. (no. dist.) Calif. 1981, U.S. Dist. Ct. (cen. dist.) Utah 1982, U.S. Supreme Ct. 1982. Pvt. practice, Provo, Utah, 1982—. Judge pro tem 4th Cir. Ct., American Fork, Utah, 1986—. Candidate Utah Ho. of Reps., 1988; active Am. Delegation to U.S./Japan Bilateral Conf. on Legal and Econ. Relations, 1988. Republican. Mem. Lds Ch. Avocations: scuba diving, tennis. Office: 2696 N University Ave Ste 200 Provo UT 84604-3884

HADLEY, JOHN LIVINGSTON, V, management executive, writer; b. Nashville, Apr. 8, 1928; s. John Livingston Hadley IV and Eugenia Margaret Johnston-Hadley; m. Mary Lou Burt, Aug. 26, 1950; children: Pamela Diane, John Livingston, Burt Alexander. Student, Peabody Coll., 1946—47; BS in Indsl. Mgmt., U. Tenn., 1951. Messenger Western Union, Pryor, Okla., 1943—45; projectionist Pryor Theater, 1944—45; supr., foreman E.I. DuPont Co., Seaford, Del., 1952—53, supr. tech. lab. Kinston, NC, 1953—60, shift supr. mfg. Old Hickory, Tenn., 1960—78, supr. power engring., 1978—88; dir. Miss Rodeo Am. Pageant, Tenn., 1985—91; pres., corp. agt. Miss Rodeo Tenn. Pageant Inc., 1991—; amb./del. Miss Rodeo Am. Pageant, Pueblo, Colo., 1985—. Author: Trail Legacy, 1998, Alien Trail, 1999, Jonas One Horse Trail, 2000, The Two Horse Trail, 2001, Vicks Gold, 2002, Black Mountain Lair, 2003, Trouble in High Town, 2004. Mem.: NRA (benefactor), Gallatin Gun Club (past pres.). Republican. Avocations: reading, genealogy, hunting, rodeo, target shooting. Home and Office: Miss Rodeo Tenn Pageant Inc PO Box 53 Madison TN 37116

HADLEY, LEILA ELIOTT-BURTON (MRS. HENRY LUCE III), writer; b. NYC, Sept. 22, 1925; d. Frank Vincent and Beatrice Boswell Eliott Burton; m. Arthur T. Hadley, II, Mar. 2, 1944 (div. Aug. 1946); 1 child, Arthur T. III; m. Yvor H. Smitter, Jan. 24, 1953 (div. Oct. 1969); children: Victoria C. Van D. Smitter Barlow, Matthew Burton Smitter Eliott, Caroline Allison F.S. Nicholson; m. William C. Musham, May 1976 (div. July 1979); m. Henry Luce III, Jan. 1990. MD, St. Timothy's Sch., 1943. Author: Give Me the World, 1958, reprinted, 1999, Give Me the World, 2003, How to Travel with Children in Europe, 1963, Manners for Children, 1967, Fielding's Guide to Traveling with Children in Europe, 1972, rev., 1974, 1984, Traveling with Children in the U.S.A., 1974, Tibet-20 Years After the Chinese Takeover, 1979; author: (with Theodore B. Van Itallie) The Best Spas: Where to Go for Weight Loss, Fitness Programs and Pure Pleasure in the U.S. and Around the World, 1988, rev., 1989; author: A Journey with Elsa Cloud, 1997, paperback edit. with afterword, 2003, Give Me the World, 1999, A Garden by the Sea, 2005; assoc. editor Diplomat mag., N.Y.C., 1964—65, Saturday Evening Post, 1965—67, contbg. editor ICON: World Monuments Mag.; contbg. editor: Tricycle, the Buddhist Rev., 1991—; editl. cons. TWYCH, N.Y.C., 1985—87, book reviewer Palm Beach Life, Fla., 1967—72, consulting editor Tricyle, The Buddhist Rev., 1991—, garden columnist Fishers Island Gazette; contbr. articles to various newspapers, mags. Bd. dirs. Wings World Quest, Inc., 1992, Tibet House, 1995, Fishers Island Conservancy, 1995, Donald & Shelley Rubin Cultural Trust, 2001, Bd. Helike Found. Recipient Norman Vincent Peale award, 2002. Mem. Acad. Am. Poets, Soc. Woman Geographers, Authors Guild, Nat. Writers Union, Nat. Press Club, PEN, Explorers Club, Central Park Conservancy, Ocean Conservancy, N.Y. Acad. Medicine (guest bd.), The Kitchen Ctr. Haleakala, Inc., Nat. Arts Club, Lansdowne Club (Eng.). Office Phone: 212-759-8640. E-mail: leilahadleyluce1@aol.com.

HADLEY, MARLIN LEROY, financial planner, consultant; b. Mankato, Kans., Jan. 5, 1931; s. Charles LeRoy and Lillian Fern (Dunn) H.; m. Clarissa Jane Payne, Sept. 17, 1949; children: Michael LeRoy, Steven Lee. BS, U. Denver, 1953; postgrad., Harvard U., 1966. Pres. Jewel Home Shopping Service div. Jewel Cos., Inc., Barrington, Ill., 1953-72; pres., chief exec. officer, dir. Beeline Fashions, Inc., Bensenville, Ill., 1972-82; chmn. bd. HAS Originals, Blairstown, NJ, 1984—; fin., bus. cons. Pres., dir. Beeline Real Estate Corp., Act II Jewelry, Inc., Home Galleries, Inc.; dir. Goulder Co., Inc., Climax Spltys., Inc. Mem.: Economics (Chgo.). Home and Office: 4298 W Lake Cir Littleton CO 80123

HADLEY, NANCY LYNNE, community foundation executive, municipal official; b. Valhalla, N.Y., Mar. 1, 1951; d. Joseph and Emelia (Scavnicky) Nassetta; m. J. Dwight Hadley, May 13, 1978 (div. Aug. 1995); children: Stephen, Elizabeth. BA in Sociology and Urban Studies with honors, Manhattanville Coll., Purchase, N.Y., 1972. Asst. dir. Urban Renewal Agy., Ossining, N.Y., 1971-74; dir. cmty. devel. program Mayor's Office, Stamford, Conn., 1974-84; asst. commr. housing N.Y. State Divsn. Housing, Albany, 1984-91; dept. transportation commr. Conn. Dept. of Transportation, Newington, 1991-93; commr. Conn. Dept. of Motor Vehicles, Wethersfield, 1993-95; sr. program dir. Conn. multi-cities program Local Initiatives Support Corp., Hartford, 1995-96; exec. dir. Cmty. Found. for Greater New Haven, Conn., 1996—2000; pres. Hadley Group LLC, Newington, 2000—. Spkr. in field. Fellow Am. Leadership Forum (sr.); mem. Nat. Assn. Housing and Redevel. Officials, Conn. Women's Coun., N.Y. State Assn. Housing and Redevel. Officials, Women Transportation Seminar (founding mem. Conn. Valley chpt.), Conn. Quality Coun.(bd. mem. 1998—). Office: Hadley Group LLC 68 Crown Ridge Newington CT 06111 Office Phone: 203-576-7221. Personal E-mail: nlhinct@aol.com.

HADLEY, PAUL ERVIN, international relations educator; b. South Ovid, Mich., July 17, 1914; s. Ervin C. and Viola M. (Barnes) H.; m. Virginia Faye Last, May 15, 1945; 1 dau., Deborah Faye. AB, Occidental Coll., Los Angeles, 1934; A.M., U. So. Calif., 1946, PhD in Comparative Lit, 1955; L.H.D., Nat. U., 1980. Tchr. El Monte (Calif.) Union High Sch., 1935-42; exec. sec. Centro Cultural Paraguayo Americano, Asunción, Paraguay, 1943-44; head Cultural Insts. unit U.S. Dept. State, Washington, 1945; instr. internat. relations U. So. Calif., Los Angeles, 1945-47, asst. prof., 1947-55, assoc. prof., 1955-64, prof., 1964-81, emeritus prof., 1981—, disting. emeritus prof., 1992. Dean summer session, 1960-73; dean Coll. of Continuing Edn., 1966-73, assoc. v.p. acad. adminstrn., 1973-77, interim acad. v.p., 1975-77, acad. v.p., 1977-81, dir. emeriti ctr., 1997-2001; exec. sec. Inst. World Affairs, 1948-73, chmn. Pacific Coast Council Latin Am. Studies, 1956-57; mem. Woodrow Wilson Fellowship selection com. Region XV, 1960-67; fgn. leader and specialist program Am. Council on Edn., 1960-62; mem. State Com. on Continuing Edn., 1966-76; mem. adv. com. Servicemembers Opportunity Colls., 1978-81; chmn. edn. sect. Town Hall of Calif., 1965-68, chmn. internat. relations sect., 1969-71; trustee Latin Am. Scholarship Program Am. Univs., 1972-74; trustee So. Calif. Presbyn. Homes(chmn. 1988-89). Pres. Assn. Retirement Orgns. in Higher Edn., 2001-03. Mem. Assn. Univ. Summer Sessions (pres. 1970-71), Inst. Internat. Edn. (adv. bd. West Coast region), Nat. U. Extension Assn. (chmn. region VI 1970-71, pres. 1976-77), Adult Educators Greater Los Angeles (chmn. 1970-71), Phi Beta Kappa, Pi Sigma Alpha, Sigma Alpha Epsilon, Phi Kappa Phi. Presbyn. (elder, stated clk. Presbytery 1983-87). Home: 1230 E Windsor Rd Apt 305 Glendale CA 91205-2642

HADLEY, RALPH VINCENT, III, lawyer; b. Jacksonville, Fla., Aug. 20, 1942; s. Ralph V. and Clare (Cason) H.; m. Carol Fox Hadley, Sept. 18, 1993; children: Graham Kimball, Christopher Bedell, Blair Vincent. BS, U. Fla., 1965, JD, 1968. Bar: Fla. 1968, Calif. 1972. Assoc. Kurz, Toole, Taylor & Moseley, Jacksonville, 1968-69; asst. atty. gen. State of Fla., Orlando, 1972-73; ptnr. Davids, Henson & Hadley, Winter Garden, Fla., 1973-80; sr. ptnr. Hadley & Asma, Winter Garden, 1980-89, Parker, Johnson, Owen, McGuire, Michaud, & Hadley, Orlando, 1989-91, Owen & Hadley, Orlando, 1991-94, Hadley, Gardner & Ornstein, P.A., Winter Park, Fla., 1994-95; Swann, Hadley & Alvarez, P.A., Winter Park, 1995-2000; with Swann & Hadley, 2000—. Vice chmn. bd. dirs. Tucker State Bank, Winter Garden, 1981-88; vice chmn. bd. dirs., sec. Tucker Holding Co., Jacksonville, 1984-88; bd. dirs. BankFIRST. Bd. dirs. Orange County Dem. Exec. Com., Orlando, 1974-81, Spouse Abuse, Inc., Orlando, 1975-81. Lt. comdr. USN, 1969-72, Vietnam. Recipient Navy Achievement medal, Award of Merit, Orange County Legal Aid Soc., 1987, Disting. Svc. award Judge J.C. Jake Stone Legal Aid Soc., 1989, Pres. Pro Bono Svc. award Fla. Bar, 1992. Mem. ABA, Fla. Bar Assn., Calif. Bar Assn., Orange County Bar Assn. (legis. chmn. 1979, 82), Am. Inn of Ct. (master), Winter Park C. of C. (bd. dirs. 1979-80), West Orange C. of C. (bd. dirs. 1979-82), Rotary. Presbyterian. Office: Ste 350 1031 W Morse Blvd Winter Park FL 32789-3715 Office Phone: 407-647-2777. Business E-Mail: ralphh@swannhadley.com.

HADLEY, ROBERT JAMES, lawyer; b. Wilmington, Ohio, Oct. 27, 1938; s. Robert Edwin and Ethel Edith (Slade) H.; m. Judith Ellen Gilbert, Aug. 11, 1962; children: Scott, Laura, Stephen. BA in History cum laude, Ohio State U., 1960; LLB, Harvard U., 1963. Bar: Ohio 1963. Assoc. Smith & Schnacke, Dayton, 1963-69, ptnr., 1970-89, Thompson Hine LLP, Dayton, 1989—2003. Pres. Man-to-Man Assocs., 1978-84, Dayton Habitat for Humanity, 1988; v.p. COPE Halfway House, Dayton, 1982-85; dir., sec. Friendship Village of Dayton, 1985—; loaned exec. United Way, 1980-82, cabinet 2001-02; mem. Kettering Civic Band, 1968—, v.p. Parish Resource Ctr., 1995-2005 pres., 1999-2000; bd. dirs. South Cmty. YMCA, 1996-98, Greater Dayton Youth for Christ, 1980-86; bd. dirs., sec. Ministry of Money, 1992—. Named Kettering Man of the Yr., 1986; Rotary Found. grantee, Israel, 1974. Mem. Dayton Bar Assn., Dayton Racquet Club, Rotary (pres. Kettering 1986-87, dist. gov., group rep. Dist. 667 1989-90, dist. gov. 1993-94), Phi Beta Kappa. Republican. Methodist. Avocations: music, travel, sports. Home: 4848 Glenmina Dr Dayton OH 45440-2002 Personal E-mail: rjh4848@earthlink.net.

HADLEY, STANTON THOMAS, manufacturing executive, director, lawyer; b. Beloit, Kans., July 3, 1936; s. Robert Campbell and Helen (Schroeder) H.; m. Charlotte June Holmes, June 9, 1962; children: Gayle Elizabeth, Robert Edward, Stanton Thomas, Steven Holmes. BS in Metall. Engring., Colo. Sch. Mines, 1958; LLB, U. Colo., 1962. Bar: Colo. 1962, U.S. Dist. Ct. 1962, U.S. Patent Office 1963. Metallurgist ASARCO, Leadville, Colo., 1957; tng. engr. Allis-Chalmers Co., West Allis, Wis., 1958-61; adminstrv. engr. Ball Corp., Boulder, Colo., 1961-62, atty., 1962-65; patent counsel Scott Paper Co., Phila., 1965-71, USG Corp., Chgo., 1971-76, gen. mgr. metals div., 1976-79, group v.p. indsl. group, 1979-84, sr. v.p. adminstrn., sec., 1984, sec., 1984-87, sr. v.p. staff services, 1987-89; pres. Ansco Photo-Optical Products Corp., Chgo., 1989-93, Visador Co., Marion, Va., 1994-98. Bd. dirs. Masonite Corp., WJE Assocs. Inc., USG Found. Bd. dirs. Ill. Safety Council, North Suburban YMCA, Northbrook Symphony Orch.; former mem. founders' council Field Mus.; mem. Chgo. United, Chgo. Assn. Commerce and Industry. Served with U.S. Army, 1959. Mem. Am. Soc. Metals, Licensing Execs. Soc., Assn. Corp. Patent Counsel. Clubs: Union League, Sunset Ridge Country, Executives. Republican. Home: 555 Valley Way Northfield IL 60093-1067 Office: STH Cons 555 Valley Way Northfield IL 60093-1067

HADLEY, STEPHEN JOHN, national security advisor; b. Toledo, Ohio, Feb. 13, 1947; m. Ann Simon; 2 children. BA, Cornell U., 1969; JD, Yale U., 1972. Analyst for the comptr. US Dept. Def., Washington, 1972—74; mem. NSC, Washington, 1974—77; assoc. Shea & Gardner, Washington, 1977—81, ptnr., 1981—89, 1993—2001; asst. sec., internat. security policy US Dept. Def., Washington, 1989—93; prin. The Scowcroft Group, Inc.; asst. to the Pres. & dep. asst. for nat. security affairs. NSC, Washington, 2001—05, asst. to the Pres. for nat. security affairs, 2005—. Counsel Presdl. Spl. Review Bd. on Arms Sales to Iran, 1986—87; former mem. Def. Policy Bd., Nat. Security Advisory Panel to the Dir. of Ctrl. Intelligence. Office: National Security Coun 1600 Pennsylvania Ave NW Washington DC 20500

HADLEY, SUSAN MARIE, librarian; b. Buffalo, Nov. 25, 1952; d. Frank Joseph and Antionette (Gerace) Coniglio; m. Steven R. Hadley, Sept. 1, 1984. BA, SUNY, Buffalo, 1975; MLS, U. Mich., 1976; cert., U. Calif., Berkeley, 1986. Reference libr. Mont. Coll. Mineral Sci. and Tech., Butte, 1977-78; rsch. libr. Sandia Nat. Labs., Livemore, Calif., 1978-85; libr. cons. Townsend & Townsend, San Francisco, 1987-97, Howe-Lewis Internat., Palo Alto, Calif., 1988-90, Beyer Weaver Thomas, 1993—, TomlinsonZisko Morosoli Maser, 1998—2001, Silicon Valley Intellectual Property Group, 2000—. Mem.: NOCALL. Avocation: travel. Home: 2385 Kilkare Rd Sunol CA 94586-9461 Office Phone: 925-862-2928.

HADLEY, WANDA MARIE, academic administrator; b. Fayetteville, Tenn., Nov. 28, 1955; d. Lawrence Claborne and Martha Jane Hadley. BS, Ohio State U., 1978, MA, 1979; postgrad., U. Dayton, 1997—. Lic. profl. counselor, Ohio. Counselor U. Dayton, Ohio, 1980-90, adminstr., 1990—.

HADLEY, WILLIAM MELVIN, retired dean; b. San Antonio, June 4, 1942; s. Arthur Roosevelt and Audrey Merle (Barrett) H.; m. Dorothy J. Hadley, Jan. 21, 1967 (div. July 1989); children: Heather Marie, William Arthur; m. Jane F. Walsh, Oct. 13, 1990. BS in Pharmacy, Purdue U., West Lafayette, Ind., 1967, MS in Pharmacology, 1971, PhD in Toxicology, 1972. Teaching and grad. asst. Purdue U., West Lafayette, 1967-72; asst. prof. U. N.Mex., Albuquerque, 1972-76, assoc. prof., 1976-82, prof., 1982—2002, asst. dean Coll. Pharmacy, 1984-86, acting dean Coll. Pharmacy, 1985, dean Coll. Pharmacy, 1986—2002; prof. and dean emeritus Coll. Pharmacy, 2002—. Bd. dirs. Ctr. Hazardous Materials Mgmt., Carlsbad; vis. scientist Lovelace Inhalation Toxicology Inst., Albuquerque, 1981, adj. scientist, 1991-2002, sr. scientist, 2002—; adv. bd. Waste Edn. Rsch. Consortium, Las Cruces, N.Mex., 1989-2003; dirs. adv. com. Nat. Ctr. for Eviron. Health, CDC, 2002-04, mem. NIH Proposal Rev. Panels, Bethesda, Md., 1983-84; mem. Gov.'s PCB Expert Adv. Panel, Santa Fe, 1985-86; sci. adv. bd. Carlsbad Environ. Monitoring Ctr., 1992-97; sci. adv. com. S.W. Regional Spaceport, Las Cruces, 1992-94; bd. dirs. Ctr. Excellence Hazardous Materials Mgmt., Carlsbad, N.Mex., 2005—; cons. in field. Steering com. United Fund, U.N.Mex., 1987, key person, 1988—97. NIH grantee, 1974-80, 83-87; Bowl of Hygeia, N.Mex. Pharm. Assn., 1998. Mem. AAAS, Am. Pharm. Assn., Am. Assn. Colls. of Pharmacy, Soc. Toxicology (pres. Rocky Mt. chpt. 1990-91), Western Pharmacology Soc., Southwestern Assn. Toxicologists. Republican. Achievements include research in biotransformation of xenobiotics with emphasis on nasal tissue; effects of heavy metals on biotransformation with emphasis on cadmium; toxic effects of xenobiotics on the immune system. Office Phone: 623-465-1813. E-mail: wmhadley@aol.com.

HADLOCK, PATRICK LANGDON, lawyer; b. Boise, Idaho, Oct. 8, 1956; s. Walter Kay Hadlock and Helen Katherine Hayes; m. Cynthia Jean Spencer, Sept. 16, 1984. BA, Reed Coll., 1978; JD, U. Oreg., 1983. Bar: Oreg., 1983, Circuit Ct. Appeals, 1989, U.S. Dist. Ct., 1986. Atty. Ringo & Stuber, Corvallis, Oreg., 1984-95, Ringo, Stuber, Ensor & Hadlock, Corvallis, 1995—. Bd. dirs. Corvallis Arts Ctr., 1989-98, Oreg. State U. Symphony, 1998-99. Mem. Oreg. State Bar. Democrat. Office: Ringo Stuber Ensor & Hadlock 605 SW Jefferson Ave Corvallis OR 97333-4509

HADYK-WEPF, SONIA MARGARET, artist, real estate manager; b. May 30, 1931; d. Albert and Margaret (Rodriguez) Wepf; m. Walter Hadyk, Feb. 14, 1957 (div.June 1976); 1 child, W. Gordon Hadyk. BS in Art Edn., Pratt Inst., 1954. Tchr. art Midland Park (N.J.) Jr. H.S., 1954-55, Lyncourt (N.Y.) Pub. Sch., 1969-70; staff artist Norcross Greeting Cards, N.Y.C., 1955-56, Spencer Advt. Art, Union City, N.J., 1956-58, L.W. Peckham Advt., Syracuse, N.Y., 1958-59; freelance artist Syracuse, 1959-74; mgr. jewelry dept. Naum's, DeWitt, N.Y., 1974-75; owner Hadyk House of Gem Design, Syracuse, 1975—; mgr. Walter Hadyk Rental Homes, Syracuse, 1993—. Guest lectr. Carrier Women's Club, Syracuse, 1972, Nat. League Pen Women, Syracuse, 1972; juror Arts and Crafts Festival, Camillus (N.Y.) Hist. Soc., 1973. Designer, craftsman (cultured pearl necklace) Golden Claws, 1971, (bracelet) Bubbles, 1971, (ring) Elipses, 1983; designer, goldsmith numerous pieces including All Done With Mirrors, 1980 (Judges prize for Most Creative); designer, platinumsmith (earrings) Snowflake, 1982 (1st Runner-up). Recipient numerous awards Diamond Info. Ctr., N.Y.C., 1973, DeBeers Mines, N.Y.C., 1977, 1st prize award Jewelers' Circular Keystone, Radnor, Pa., 1979; finalist in color catalog of winning designs "Colored Gemstone Design award 2000,"; sponsored by Signity N.Y. Ltd., Stuller, Jewelers of Am., Nat. Jeweler Mag.; numerous others. Mem. Real Estate Investors Ctrl. N.Y., Gem and Mineral Soc. Syracuse Inc. Unitarian-universalist. Avocations: gem carving, gardening. Office: 102 Dewey Ave Fayetteville NY 13066-1607

HADZI, DIMITRI, sculptor, educator; b. N.Y.C., Mar. 21, 1921; s. Theodore and Christina H.; m. Cynthia Hoyle; children: Christina, Stephen. Student, Bklyn. Poly. Inst., 1940-43, Cooper Union, 1946-50; MA (hon.), Harvard U., 1977; DFA (hon.), Lawrence U., 1987. Prof. Harvard U., Cambridge, Mass., 1975—89, prof. emeritus, 1989—. One-man shows, Galleria Schneider, Rome, 1958, 60, Galerie Van de Loo, Munich, 1961, 95, Radich Gallery, N.Y.C., 1961-62, MIT, 1963, Richard Gray Gallery, Chgo., 1972, 87-88, 96, Mekler Gallery, L.A., 1978, Gruenebaum Gallery, N.Y.C., 1978, 84, Fogg Mus. Harvard U., 1981, 84; group shows include, Venice Biennale, 1956, 58, 62, Guggenheim Mus., N.Y.C., 1979, Kouros Gallery, N.Y.C., 1995, Long Point Gallery, Provincetown, Mass., 1996, Richard Gray Gallery, Chgo., 1997; represented in permanent collections, Mus. Modern Art, N.Y.C., Guggenheim Mus., Whitney Mus., N.Y.C., Hirshhorn Mus., Washington, Yale U. Gallery, Fogg Art Mus., Phila. Mus. Art, Dallas Mus. Art, UCLA, Albright-Knox Art Gallery, Buffalo; archtl. Commns. include Bronze doors, St. Paul's Ch., Rome, 1962-76, Fed. Res. Bank, Mpls., 1971-73, Johnson Wax, Racine, Wis., 1978-79, fountain, Owens-Illinois, Toledo, 1982, fountain, Copley Pl., Boston, 1984, Harvard Square, Cambridge, Mass., 1985, Pine Manor Coll., Boston, 1987, City of Appleton, Wis., 1987, Embacadero Ctr., San Francisco, 1989, Fed. Courthouse, Birmingham, 1991. Served with USAAF, 1942-46. Recipient Louis Comfort Tiffany award, 1954, St. Gaudens award, The Cooper Union, 1987; fellow Fulbright, Athens, 1950—51; John Simon Guggenheim Found. Fellowship, 1957. Studio: III Charles St Cambridge MA 02138*

HAEBERLE, ROSAMOND PAULINE, retired music educator; b. Clearwater, Kans., Oct. 23, 1914; d. Albert Paul and Ella (Lough) H. *Rosamond Haeberle's father, Albert P. Haeberle, was a wheat grower and a member of the Kansas Crop Improvement Association. Albert realized the need for an early harvesting wheat. In 1921 he interbred a collection of various types of wheat. The Haeberle wheat was a shorter-strawed variety and had a higher protein content. It ripened approximately ten days earlier than the traditional wheat. The Haeberle or Early Blackhull Wheat was grown extensively throughout the Midwest for more than 35 years. Albert laid the foundation for the development of other new wheat varieties.* BS in Music Edn., Kans. State U., 1936; MusM, Northwestern U., 1948; postgrad., Wayne State U., 1965-66. Profl. registered parliamentarian. Tchr. sch. dist., Plevna, Kans., 1936-37, Esbon, Kans., 1937-41, Frankfort, Kans., 1941-43, Garden City, Kans., 1943-44, music supr. Waterford Twp., Mich., 1944-47, tchr. Pontiac, Mich., 1947-80, ret., 1980. Pres. Pontiac Fedn. Tchrs., 1961-63. Bd. dirs. Pontiac Oakland Town Hall; adv. coun. Waterford Sr. Citizens, chmn., 1990-93; pres. Oakland County Pioneer and Hist. Soc., 1992-94. Recipient Tchrs. Day award, Mich. State Fair, 1963. Mem. AAUW (pres. Pontiac br. 1970-72, founds. chair Pontiac br.), Mich. Fedn. Music Clubs (state pres. 1993-95, chmn. state bylaws and citations, chair parliamentarian 2001—, pres. Tuesday musicale of Pontiac 1984-86, pres. S.E. dist. 1986-90, chmn. Music for the Blind Northeastern region 2000), Mich. Fedn. Bus. and Profl. Womens Club (Woman of Achievement award dist. IX 1994), Mich. DARS (state parliamentarian 1985-2002), DAR (Gen. Richardson chpt., regent 1983-85, libr. and parliamentarian, Excellence in Cmty Svc. award 1995), Waterford-Clarkston Bus. and Profl. Womens Club (bylaws and parliamentarian), Pontiac Area Ret. Sch. Pers. (parliamentarian, pres. 1981-84), Mich. Assn. Retired Sch. Pers. (Disting. Svc. award 1994), Mich. Bus. and Profl. Women's Club (dir. dist. 10 1965-67), Mich. Fedn. Music Clubs (Honored Recognition award 2000, Citations award 2000); Pontiac Bus. and Profl. Women (pres. 1959-61, Woman of the Yr. award 1974), Pontiac Area Fedn. Women's Clubs (pres. 1976-78, 81-84), Mich. Profl. Registered Parliamentarians, Louise Saks Parliamentary Unit (pres. 1990-92), Bloomfield Rep. Women's Club (parliamentarian 1999-2003), Detroit Women's Club, Eastern Star (60 Yr. award 2004), Mu Phi Epsilon, Beta Sigma Phi (life), Zeta Tau Alpha. Republican. Methodist. Avocations: travel, playing piano, reading, bell ringing, dance.

HAEBERLE, WILLIAM LEROY, corporate director, business educator, entrepreneur; b. Marion County, Ind., May 19, 1922; s. Louis Leroy and Marjorie Ellen (Jared) H.; m. Yvonne Carlton, June 17, 1947; children: Patricia, William C., David C. BS, Ind. U., 1943, MBA, 1947, DBA, 1952. Mem. faculty Ind. U., Bloomington, 1946—, prof. mgmt., 1963-85, prof. emeritus, 1985—. Sr. fellow Johnson Ctr. for Entrpreneurship and Innovation, Kelly Sch. Bus. Ind. U., 1989—; pres., dir. Nat. Entrepreneurship Found., 1982—; chmn. Command Corp., 1996—, vice chmn. Prime Tech. Inc., 1994-2002, Syndicate Sales Inc., 1994—, Norcote Internat. Inc., 1994-2003, Impact Forge Inc., 1995—, Central Products, Inc., 2004—; bd. dirs. Wildbirds Unltd. Inc., Command Equity Group; pres. Cambridge Aircraft Leasing Co. Inc., 1969-2004; advisor to owner/ops. Statewide Aluminum, Inc. 1997—, Johnson Ventures, Inc., Ohio Valley Plastics, Inc. 2002—, Anchor industries, Inc., 2003—, Palmer Automative Group, 2004—, Productive Resources, Inc., 2004—, Wabash Valley Produce, 2004—, Crew Corp., 2004—. Capt. U.S. Army, 1943-46; lt. col. USAFR, 1982, ret. Recipient Entrepreneur of Yr. award Ernst & Young, 1989, Entrepreneur of Yr., Inst. Hall of Fame. Mem. VFW, Air Force Assn., Res. Officers Assn. Sagamore of the Wabash, Am. Legion, Met. Club N.Y., Union League Club Chgo., Columbia Club Indpls., Sigma Alpha Epsilon. Personal E-mail: whaeberle@commandequity.com.

HAECK, JAMES F., manufacturing executive; m. Carolyn Haeck; 1 child, Jessica. BA in Economics, U. Pitts. Joined The LTV Corp., 1968, v.p., gen. mgr. Tubular Prods. Co., 1991—93, v.p., gen. mgr. Cleveland Works, 1993—94, sr. v.p. flat rolled opers., 1994, sr. v.p. comml., 1995—98, exec. v.p. Cleve., 1998—2001; v.p. sales mktg. Universal Steel Co. Bd. dirs. Bayou Steel Corp., 2004—. Office: Universal Steel 6600 Grant Ave Cleveland OH 44105*

HAEFELE, EDWIN THEODORE, political scientist, consultant; b. Burnt Prairie, Ill., Oct. 5, 1925; s. Monroe Edwin and Lola Amanda (Coles) H.; m. Ruth Anne Woods, Dec. 23, 1948; children: Ann Katherine, Douglas Monroe, John Joseph. Student, Mich. State U., 1943, Ill. Wesleyan U., 1946-48, U. Chgo., 1948-50. Staff asst. Pub. Adminstrn. Clearing House, Chgo., 1951-54; asst. dir. Transp. Center, Northwestern U., 1954-62; mem. sr. staff Brookings Instn., Washington, 1962-67; mem. sr. research staff Resources for Future, Inc., Washington, 1967-73; prof. polit. sci. U. Pa., Phila., 1973-82, prof. emeritus, 1982-84, 88—, prof., chmn. dept. polit. sci., 1985-88; exec. v.p. Consortium of Govtl. Counselors Inc., 1989-96. Author: Government Controls on Transport, 1965, Representative Government and Environmental Management, 1973, What Constitutes the American Republic?, 1993; editor: Transport and National Goals, 1967, The Governance of Common Property Resources, 1974 Served with AUS, 1943-46. Decorated Purple Heart, Presdl. Unit citation. Republican. Congregationalist. Home: 1215 Box Butte Ave Alliance NE 69301-2522

HAEFNER, DON PAUL, retired psychology educator; b. Albany, N.Y., Mar. 7, 1928; s. Carl William and Mary Theresa (Diamond) H.; m. Allegra Ouida Turner, June 11, 1951 (dec. Oct. 1981); children: Carol, Ann, Thomas; m. Cynthia Jean Stewart, May 29, 1982. AB in psychology, Clark U., 1951; PhD, U. Rochester, 1956. Chief soc. psychologist Vets. Adminstrn. Ctr., Bath, NY, 1956—57; rsch. soc. psychologist VA Hosp., Brockton, Mass., 1957—60, U.S. Pub. Health Svc., Washington, 1960—62; rsch. assoc., lectr. to prof. U. Mich. Sch. Pub. Health, Ann Arbor, 1962—93, asst. dean, 1968—84, prof. emeritus, 1993—. Vis. instr. U. Rochester, N.Y., 1956-57; lectr. psychology Boston U., 1958-60; reviewer profl. jours., 1975-94; cons. to health orgns., 1975-85. Contbr. articles to profl. jours. Fellow APHA, Soc. Pub. Health Edn.; mem. APA, Sigma Xi, Delta Omega. Unitarian Universalist. Avocations: travel, photography, choral singing. Home: 2250 Pine Grove Ct Ann Arbor MI 48103-2338

HAEGELE, JOHN ERNEST, metal products executive; b. Phila., July 11, 1941; s. Ernest F. and Cecilia (Wheeler) H.; m. Victoria J. Brasten, July 31, 1965; children: John, Scott, Lisa. BS Drexel U. in Acctg. and Fin., 1964. C.P.A., N.Y. Acct. Arthur Young & Co., N.Y.C., 1964-68, mgr., 1968-71; asst. controller Indian Head Inc., N.Y.C., 1971-76, v.p., controller, 1976-82; exec. v.p. dir. Interpool, Ltd., N.Y.C., 1982-85, chmn., chief exec. officer, 1987-88; sr. v.p. fin. TBG Group, N.Y.C., 1985-87, exec. v.p., 1988-92. Pres., COO TBG Group, Inc., N.Y.C., Monte Carlo, 1992-96; chmn. bd. dirs., CEO Extruded Metals Inc., N.Y.C., 1997—, TriPoint Global Comm. Inc., 1998-2004, PartMiner, Inc., 2004. Mem. bus. sch. adv. bd. Drexel U. Served with U.S. Army, 1964-69. Mem. AICPA, N.Y. Soc. CPAs. Republican. Roman Catholic.

HAEGELE, PATRICIA, publishing executive; b. Wheeling, W.Va., Dec. 19, 1950; d. Thomas J. and Marcella (Kissell) Cook. Student, W. Liberty Coll., 1970-71, Brevard Community Bus. Coll., 1973-74, Rollins Coll., 1974-76. Retail advt. rep. Coca Today/Gannett Co., Cocoa, Fla., 1973-76, Tampa Tribune Co., Tampa, Fla., 1976-79; corp. advt. rep. Washington Post Co. Inc., Washington, 1979-82; corp. advt. mgr. USA Today/Gannett Co. Inc., NYC, 1982-84, div. sales mgr., 1984-85, v.p., eastern sales mgr., 1985, v.p., advt. dir., 1985-86; v.p., advertising dir. USA Weekend, NYC, 1986-88, pub., 1988; sr. v.p. advt. USA Today, NYC, 1988—91; pub. Travel Holiday mag. (Gannett Co.), 1991—94; pres. gen. mgr. Newspaper Nat. Network, 1994—97; sr. v.p., pub. Good Housekeeping, 1997—. Selected to YWCA's Acad. of Women Achievers, 1988; profiled On The Rise column Fortune mag., Aug., 1988. Mem. Am. Newspapers Pubs. Assn., Internat. Newspaper Advt. Mktg. Assn., Am. Mktg. Assn. Republican. Roman Catholic. Avocations: running, biking, body tng. Home: 510 E 80th St #6C New York NY 10021 Office: Good Housekeeping 250 West 55th St New York NY 10019*

HAEGER, JOHN DENIS, academic administrator; Doctoral, Loyola U., Chgo.; M, Loyola U., Chgo.; BA, Loyola U., Chgo. Prof., history dept. Ctrl. Mich. U., chair, history dept., interim dean, coll. grad. studies, assoc. dean, coll. grad. studies, dean, coll. arts & sci., dir., grad. student affairs; provost, v.p. Towson U.; provost, academic student affairs divsn. Northern Ariz. U., pres., 2001—. Contbr. articles to jours. Office: No AZ U S San Francisco St Flagstaff AZ 86011

HAEMMERICH, DIETER, biomedical engineer; PhD, U. Wis., 2002. Scientist U. Wis., Madison, 2001—04; asst. prof. dept. pediatric cardiology Med. U. SC, Charleston, 2004—. Cons. Bard Electrophysiology, Lowell, Mass., 2000—01, Richmar, Inc., Inola, Okla., 2002—03, Biosense-Webster, Diamond Bar, Calif., 2003—04; adj. prof. bioengring. Clemson U., 2004—. Contbr. chapters to books. Mem.: IEEE (assoc.). Achievements include invention of multiple probe radiofrequency ablation; radiofrequency assisted resection device. Office: MUSC 165 Ashley Ave PO Box 250915 Charleston SC 29425 Office Phone: 843-792-1396.

HAENER, JUAN A., physicist; s. Georghe Haener and Elena Frederica Roth; children: Georgina Kammel, Carmen Calica, Cristian, Juan, Mila Fadely. PhD in Physics, Tech. U., Berlin, Germany, 1947. Engineering Tech. U., Berlin-Charlottenburg, 1942. Chief scientist Whittaker Corp., San Diego, 1962—72; pres. Haener Block Co. LLC, San Diego, 1975—. Mem.: NY Acad. of Sci. (life). Achievements include patents for Interlocking Mortarless Block System. Home: 8215 Harton Pl San Diego CA 92107 Office: Haener Block Company LLC 4102 Catalina Pl San Diego CA 92107 Business E-Mail: info@haenerblock.com.

HAENICKE, DIETHER HANS, academic administrator emeritus, educator; b. Hagen, Germany, May 19, 1935; came to U.S., 1963, naturalized, 1972; s. Erwin Otto and Helene (Wildfang) H.; m. Carol Ann Colditz, Sept. 29, 1962; children: Jennifer Ruth, Kurt Robert. Student, U. Gottingen, 1955-56, U. Marburg, 1957-59; PhD magna cum laude in German Lit. and Philology, U. Munich, 1962; DHL (hon.), Cen. Mich. U., 1986; DHL, We. Mich. U., 1998. Asst. prof. Wayne State U., Detroit, 1963-68, assoc. prof., 1968-72, prof. German, 1972-78, resident dir. Jr. Year in Freiburg (Ger.), 1965-66, 69-70, dir. Jr. Year Abroad programs, 1970-75, chmn. dept. Romance and Germanic langs. and lits., 1971-72, assoc. dean Coll. Liberal Arts, 1972-75, provost, 1975-77, v.p., provost, 1977-78; dean Coll. Humanities Ohio State U., 1978-82, v.p. acad. affairs, provost, 1982-85; pres. Western Mich. U., Kalamazoo, 1985-98. Asst. prof. Colby Coll. Summer Sch. of Langs., 1964-65; lectr. Internationale Ferienkurse, U. Freiburg, summers 1961, 66, 67 Author: (with Horst S. Daemmrich) The Challenge of German Literature, 1971, Untersuchungen zum Versepos des 20. Jahrhunderts, 1962; editor: Liebesgeschichte der schonen Magelone, 1969, Der blonde Eckbert und andere Novellen, 1969, Franz Sternbalds Wanderungen, 1970, Wednesdays with Diether, 2003, University Governance and Humanistic Scholarship (Festschrift), 2002; contbr. articles to acad. and lit. jours. Mem. Mich. State Atty. Discipline Bd. Fulbright scholar, 1963-65 Mem. MLA, AAUP, Am. Assn. Tchrs. of German, Mich. Acad. Arts and Scis., Mich. Coun. for Arts and Cultural Affairs, Phi Beta Kappa. Office: Western Mich U 3019 Waldo Library Kalamazoo MI 49008-3804 Office Phone: 269-387-5510. Business E-Mail: diether.haenicke@wmich.edu.

HAERING, EDWIN RAYMOND, chemical engineering educator, consultant; b. Columbus, Ohio, Dec. 8, 1932; s. Edwin Jacob and Mary Mildred (Kunst) H.; m. Suzanne Rowe, June 9, 1956; children: Cynthia, David Arthur, Elizabeth. BChemE, MS, Ohio State U., 1956, PhD, 1966. Mem. faculty Ohio State U., Columbus, 1959-91, assoc. prof., 1973-82, prof. chem. engring., 1982-91, prof. emeritus, 1991—, vice chmn. dept., 1974-76, chmn. dept., 1977-78. Cons. in field. Author: Laboratory Manual for Unit Operations Laboratory, 1980; contbr. articles to profl. jours. Disaster svcs. vol. ARC, 1997—. Lt. (j.g.) USNR, 1956—59. NROTC scholar, 1951-56, Dow Chem. Co. scholar, 1956; Koppers tchg. fellow, 1962. Mem. AIChE (treas. Cen. Ohio sect. 1974-79), Am. Chem. Soc., Port Clinton Power Squadron (exec. com. 2003), Ohio State U. Faculty Club (pres. 1988-89), Sandusky Yacht Club, Lake Erie South Shore Hunter Sailing Assn. (treas. 1997-99), Sigma Xi, Tau Beta Pi. Avocations: golf, gardening, sailing. Home: 701 Stoutenberg Dr Lakeside Marblehead OH 43440-2049 Office: Ohio State U Dept Chem Engring 701 Stoutenberg Dr Lakeside Marblehead OH 43440-2049

HAERLE, PAUL RAYMOND, judge; b. Portland, Oreg., Jan. 10, 1932; s. George William and Grace (Soden) H.; m. Susan Ann Wagner, May 30, 1953 (div. Apr. 1973); children: Karen A. Haerle D'Or, David A.; m. Michele A. Monson, June 1, 1991. AB, Yale U., 1953; JD, U. Mich., 1956. Bar: Calif. 1956, U.S. Supreme Ct. 1962. Assoc. Thelen, Marrin, Johnson & Bridges, San Francisco, 1956-64, ptnr., 1965-67, 69-94, mng. ptnr., 1990-93; appointments sec. Office of Gov., State of Calif., Sacramento, 1967-69; assoc. justice Calif. Ct. Appeal (1st dist.), San Francisco, 1994—. Lawyer rep. 9th Cir. Jud. Conf., 1985-88. Editor-in-chief Mich. Law Rev., 1955-56 Presdl. elector, 1972; del. Rep. Nat. Conv., 1972; vice chmn. Calif. Rep. Com., 1973-75, chmn., 1975-77; mem. Rep. Nat. Com., 1975-77; trustee World Affairs Coun. No. Calif., 1997-2003; mem. adv. com. on internat. law U.S. Dept. State, 2002—; regional panelist, White House Fellowship Program, 2003-. Fellow Am. Coll. Trial Lawyers; mem. Yale Club of San Francisco, Order of Coif. Avocations: tennis, travel, hiking. Office: Calif Ct Appeal 350 McAllister St San Francisco CA 94102-3600

HAESSLE, JEAN-MARIE GEORGES, artist; b. Buhl/Haut/Rhin, France, Sept. 12, 1939; came to U.S., 1967; s. Georges and Marguerite H. Student, Ecole Nationale des Beaux Arts, Paris, France, 1965-67, Ecole de la Grande Chaumiere, Paris, 1966-67. Painter, Paris, 1965-67, N.Y.C., 1967—. One man shows include Panoras Gallery, N.Y.C., 1968, West Broadway Gallery, N.Y.C., 1973, Atlantic Gallery, Washington, 1979, Nat. Acad. Sci., Washington, 1979, RR Gallery, N.Y.C., 1980, Gabrielle Bryers Gallery, N.Y.C., 1981, Kerr Gallery, N.Y.C., 1984-85, Little John-Smith Gallery, N.Y.C., 1986, Lucien Durand Galerie, Paris, 1987-91; exhibited in groups shows U.S. and abroad including Salon de la Jeune Peinture, Musee d'Art Moderne, Paris, 1968, Palace of Fine Arts, Mexico City, 1972, Aldrich Mus. Contemporary Art, Ridgefield, Conn., 1978; represented in permanent collections U.S. and abroad including So. Ill. U., Edwardsville, Bank of N.Y., N.Y.C., Atlantic-Richfield, Los Angeles, Am. Express, Fla., IBM, Los Angeles, Exxon, Fla., Chase Manhattan Bank, Los Angeles, Citibank, Los Angeles, Oven Corning Fiberglass, Toledo; works reviewed in profl. and popular publs. Roman Catholic. Home: 106112 Spring St New York NY 10012 Personal E-mail: jmhaessle@netscape.net.

HAEUSER, MICHAEL JOHN, library administrator; b. LaCrosse, Wis., July 5, 1943; s. Loyal Eldon and Kamilla (Brenengen) H.; m. Linda Kay Johnsrud, Aug. 31, 1968 (div. 1981); 1 child, Britton; m. Irene Jeanette Morris, June 20, 1987. BS in History, U. Wis., 1970, MA in History, 1972, MLS, 1973, cert., 1986. Readers svcs. libr. Knox Coll., Galesburg, Ill., 1973-74, head readers svcs., 1974-76; head libr. Linfield Coll., McMinnville, Oreg., 1976-81; dir. learning resources, head libr. Gustavus Adolphus Coll., St. Peter, Minn., 1981-97, coll. archivist, 1997—. Co-instr. Mil. History WWII, 1979; presenter in field. Author: With Grace, Elegance and Flair: The First 25 Years of Library Associates, 2002; cons. to editor books for coll. librs., Choice mag.; contbr. articles to profl. jours. Chmn. Core Curriculum Rev. Task Force, Linfield Coll., 1977-?; mem. coll. libr. com. Nat. Comm. Preservation and Access, 1989, team Bibliographic Instrn., 1982—; bd. dirs. Minn. Humanities Commn., 1990-97. With U.S. Army, 1963-66. NEH fellow, 1978; grantee, 1980, 83; grantee: Japan Found., 1978, U.S. Office Edn., 1979, 80, Murdock Trust, 1979, Hearst Found., 1980, Collins Found., 1980, Nat.

Archives and Records Svc., 1983, Presser Found., 1983; recipient John Cotton Dana Libr. pub. rels. award 1983, 94. Mem. ALA (selected vol. pres.' program Chgo. chpt. 1985, sec. coll. libr. sect. 1990, Outstanding Pub. Rels. 1983), Assn. Coll. And Rsch. Librs., Assn. Coll. and Resource Librs. (nat. adv. coun. libr. sect. 1985), Am. Hist. Assn., Minn. Libr. Assn. (pres. 1988-90), Minn. Assn. Libr. Friends (bd. dirs. 1990), Minn. Humanities Commn. (bd. dirs. 1991-97). Lutheran. Avocations: skiing, outdoor work, reading, travel, association activities. Office: Gustavus Adolphus Coll Folke Bernadotte Meml Libr 800 W College Ave Saint Peter MN 56082-1485 Office Phone: 507-933-7572. Business E-Mail: haeuser@gac.edu.

HAFEMEISTER, DAVID WALTER, physicist; b. Chgo., July 1, 1934; s. Lester David and Alma Doris (Schmidt) H.; m. Gina Rohlander, June 10, 1961; children: Andrew, Jason, Heidi. MS in Physics, U. Ill., 1959, PhD in Physics, 1964. Asst. prof. physics Carnegie-Mellon U., Pitts., 1966-69; prof. physics Calif. Poly. State U., San Luis Obispo, 1969-2000; study dir. on arms control on beyond START NAS, Washington, 2000—02; chair external rev. com. Los Alamos Nonproliferation Divsn., 2003—05; sci. fellow Ctr. Internat. Security and Cooperation Stanford U., 2005—. Sci. advisor Sen. John Glenn U.S. Senate, Washington, 1975-77; spl. asst. to Under Sec. State Benson and Nye U.S. State Dept., Washington, 1977-79; vis. scientist U. Groningen, The Netherlands, 1971, 80, Program Sci. Tech. in Internat. Security, MIT, Cambridge, 1983-84, Ctr. for Bldg. Scis. Lawrence Berkeley (Calif.) Lab., 1985-86, Office Strategic Nuc. Policy U.S. Dept. State, 1987, Ctr. Internat. Security and Arms Control Stanford U., 1988; program on nuc. policy alternatives Princeton U., 1989; profl. staff Senate Fgn. Rels. Com., 1990-92; staff Senate Gov. Affairs Com., 1992-93, Sch. Pub. Affairs, U. Md., 1996; Foster fellow Office of Strategic Negotiations, U.S. Arms Control and Disarmament Agy., 1997-98. Author: Physics of Societal Issues, 2004; co-author: Physics of Modern Architecture, 1983; co-editor: Energy Sources: Conservation and Renewables, 1985, Arms Control Verification, 1986, Nuclear Arms Technologies in the 1990s, 1988, Physics and Nuclear Arms Today, 1990, Global Warming: Physics and Facts, 1991, Biological Effects of Low-Frequency Electromagnetic Fields, 1998. Fellow Am. Phys. Soc. (chmn. forum on physics and soc. 1985-86, chair panel on pub. affairs 1996, Leo Szilard award for Physics in the Pub. Interest 1996); mem. AAAS (congl. fellow 1975-76, arms control fellow 1987), Fedn. Am. Scientists, Arms Control Assn., Am. Inst. Physics (co-editor books). Home: 553 Serrano Dr San Luis Obispo CA 93401 Business E-Mail: dhafemei@calpoly.edu.

HAFER, BARBARA, state official; b. L.A., Aug. 1, 1943; m. Jack Pidgeon; 4 children, John, Kelly, Bethany, Regan. BS, Duquesne U., Pitts., 1969; postgrad., U. Pitts., U. London. Founder, exec. dir. Allegheny County Ctr. for Victims of Violent Crime, 1973—79; account exec. Sautel Agency, 1979—82; employee relations mgr. South Hills Health System, 1982—83; auditor gen. State of Pa., Harrisburg, 1989-96, state treas., 1997—. Commr. Allegheny County bd. commissioners, 1984—89; mem. Del. River Port Authority, 1989—, Pa Partnership for Econ. Edn., 1997—, Pa. Pub. School Employees Retirement System Bd., 1996—. Office: State of Pennsylvania Treasury Dept 129 Finance Building Harrisburg PA 17120-0018 E-mail: barbarahafer@patreasury.org.

HAFER, FREDERICK DOUGLASS, utilities executive; b. West Reading, Pa., Mar. 12, 1941; s. Charles Frederick and Irene Naugle (Renninger) H.; m. Martha Louise Gartner, Apr. 6, 1963; children: Frederick, Craig, Keith. Student, Drexel Inst. Tech., 1959-62; LHD, Alvernia Coll., 1993. With Met. Edison Co., Reading, Pa., 1962-68; with Gen. Pub. Utilities Corp., N.Y.C., 1968-78, asst. treas., 1970, treas., 1970-78; v.p. rates GPU Service Corp., 1977-86; v.p. Met. Edison Co., Pa. Electric Co., 1982-86; pres. Met. Edison Co., 1986—; pres., CEO, chmn. bd. GPU Inc, 1994—, also bd. dirs. Bd. dirs. Met. Edison Co., Pa. Electric Co., GPU Service Corp., GPU Nuclear Corp., Utilities Mut. Ins. Co., Meridian Bancorp, Inc., Meridian Bank. Bd. dirs. Reading Hosp. and Med. Ctr., Leadership Pa., Leadership, Pa.; bd. dirs. Found. For Drug-Free Pa., Berks Festivals, Inc., Berks Bus.-Edn. Coalition, Kutztown U. Found. Mem.: Pa. Electric Assn. (exec. com.), Mfrs. Assn. Berks County (bd. dirs.), Berks County C. of C. (formerly bd. dirs.), Berkshire Country. Office: GPU Inc 300 Madison Ave PO Box 1911 Morristown NJ 07962-1911

HAFETS, RICHARD JAY, lawyer; b. N.Y.C., Apr. 23, 1951; s. Meyer Hafets and Marilyn (Glanzrock) Bell; m. Claire Margolis, June 18, 1972; children: Brooke, Amy. BS in Bus. summa cum laude, Am. U., Washington, 1973, JD magna cum laude, 1976. Bar: Md. 1976, U. S. Dist. Ct. Md. 1976, U.S. Ct. Appeals (4th cir.) 1976, U.S. Supreme Ct. 1981, D.C. 1997, U.S. Dist. Ct. (D.C.) 1997. Assoc. Piper & Marbury, Balt., 1976-84, ptnr., 1984—, chmn. labor and employment practice, 1990—, chmn. hiring and assoc. coms., 1988-91. Labor atty. Balt. Symphony Orch., 1986-93; bd. dirs., gen. counsel Am. Cancer Soc., Balt., 1983-89; bd. dirs. Md. Ballet, Balt., 1978-80. Mem. ABA, Md. Bar Assn., Balt. City Bar Assn., Order of Coif. Avocations: horses, skiing. Home: 7346 Narrow Wind Way Columbia MD 21046-1262 Office: DLA Piper Rudnick Gray Cary LLP 6225 Smith Ave Baltimore MD 21209-3600 Office Phone: 410-580-4168. Business E-Mail: richard.hafets@dlapiper.com.

HAFEY, JOSEPH MICHAEL, health association executive; b. Annapolis, Md., June 25, 1943; s. Edward Earl Joseph and Verna (Hedlund) H.; m. Mary Kay Miller, Dec. 30, 1978; children: Erin Catherine, Ryan Michael. BA, Whittier Coll., 1965; MPA, UCLA, 1967. Sr. asst. health officer HHS, Washington, 1967-69; dir. govt. relations Alliance for Regional Community Health, St. Louis, 1969-71; exec. dir. Contra Costa Comprehensive Health Assn., Richmond, Calif., 1971-74, Bay Area Comprehensive Health Planning Coun., San Francisco, 1974-76, Western Ctr. for Health Planning, San Francisco, 1976-86, Western Consortium for Pub. Health, Berkeley, 1980-95; pres., CEO Pub. Health Inst. (formerly Calif. Pub. Health Found.), 1985—. Chmn. Contra Costa Pub. Health Adv. Body, Martinez, Calif., 1987-93; founder Calif. Coalition for Future of Pub. Health, Sacramento, 1988—; co-founder Calif. Healthy Cities Program, Berkeley, 1987—. Chmn. United Way Com. for the Uninsured, San Francisco, 1985-93; bd. dirs. Eugene O'Neill Found., 1980-89. With USPHS, 1967-69. Recipient fellowship WHO, Geneva, 1987. Mem. Am. Pub. Health Assn. (governing coun. 1984-87), Am. Health Planning Assn. bd. dirs., chmn. annual meeting 1982). Avocations: jogging, tennis, skiing, collecting political campaign buttons. Home: 1749 Toyon Rd Lafayette CA 94549-2111 Office: Pub Health Inst 555 12th St Oakland CA Office Phone: 510-285-5561. Business E-Mail: joehafey@phi.org.

HAFFEY, THOMAS ANTHONY, cardiologist, consultant; b. Hazleton, Pa., June 13, 1951; s. James John and Mary Agnes Haffey; m. Marilyn Ann Michelcavage, Apr. 23, 1977; children: Marie Victoria, Thomas Patrick. DO, Phila. Coll. Osteo. Medicine, 1977; BS, Kings Coll. Cert. DO Am. Osteo. Assn./IL, 1977. Clin. prof. internal medicine Western U., Pomona, Calif., 1996—; intern Pontiac Osteopathic Hosp., 1977—78, resident, 1978—80; fellowship Cardiology William Beaumont Hosp., Royal Oak. Fellow: Am. Coll. Cardiology, Am. Coll. Osteo. Internists (pres. sect. cardiology 1999—2001). Conservative. Roman Catholic. Achievements include research in Investigator LIFE Study. Avocation: photography. Home: 3535 West 110th Pl Westminster CO 80031 Office: Western Cardiology Ste 190 9141 Grant St Thornton CO 80229 E-mail: thaffey@yahoo.com.

HAFFNER, ALDEN NORMAN, academic administrator; b. Bklyn., Oct. 3, 1928; s. Irving and Irene (Gutfleisch) H. AB, Bklyn. Coll., 1948; OD, Pa. Coll. Optometry, 1952; MPA, NYU, 1960, PhD, 1964; DOS (hon.), Mass. Coll. Optometry, 1960; ScD (hon.), Pa. Coll. Optometry, 1973. Exec. dir. Optometric Center of N.Y., N.Y.C., 1957—; acting chief adminstrv. officer State Coll. Optometry, SUNY, N.Y.C., 1970-71, dean, 1971-76, pres., 1976-78; assoc. chancellor for health scis. SUNY, Albany, 1978-82, vice chancellor for research, grad. studies and profl. programs, 1982-87, pres. coll. optometry, 1987—. Pub. svc. prof. health poligy Rockefeller Coll., SUNY-Albany, 1986; chmn. N.Y. State Com. on Health Personnel and Productivity, 1990—; cons. in field. Contbr. articles in field to profl. jours. Mem. adv. com. Commn. for Blind and Visually Handicapped, State Dept. Social Services, 1966-70; mem. bd. nat. study commn. on optometry Nat. Commn. on Accrediting, 1968-70; mem. health manpower planning com. Comprehensive Health Planning Agy., N.Y.C., 1969-73; project dir. Fed. Program of Identification, Counseling, Guidance and Recruitment of Minority Students in Profession of Optometry, 1968-74; mem. Mayor's Com. for Study of Aging, N.Y.C., 1958; chmn. bd. trustees Manhattan Health Plan, Inc., 1976-81. Served to 1st lt. M.C. U.S. Army, 1953-55. Recipient Albert Fitch Meml. award, 1962; Prof. Frederick A. Woll Meml. award, 1961; Distinguished Achievement award Alumni Assn., N.Y. U. Grad. Sch. Pub. Health Adminstrn., 1974 Fellow Am. Pub. Health Assn., AAAS, Am. Sch. Health Assn., Am., N.Y. Acad. Optometry; mem. N.Y. Acad. Scis., Group Health Assn. Am., Am. Pub. Welfare Assn., Am. Soc. Pub. Adminstrn., Nat. Rehab. Assn., Illuminating Engring. Soc., Am. Optometric Assn., N.Y. State Optometric Assn., Gerontol. Soc., Am. Assn. Univ. Adminstrs., Pub. Health Assn. City of N.Y. (dir. 1967—), Nat. Assn. Land Grant Colls. and State Univs. (com. health affairs 1981), Community Family Planning Coun., Am. Coun. on Edn., Assn. Cad. Health Ctrs., Hermann Biggs Soc., Beta Sigma Kappa (Gold Medal award 1974), Home: 201 E 36th St New York NY 10016-3668 Office: SUNY Coll Optometry 33 W 42nd St New York NY 10036-8003

HAFFNER, CHARLES CHRISTIAN, III, retired printing company executive; b. Chgo., May 27, 1928; s. Charles Christian and Clarissa (Donnelley) Haffner; m. Anne P. Clark, June 19, 1970. BA, Yale U., 1950. With R.R. Donnelley & Sons Co., Chgo., 1951—62, treas., 1962-68, v.p., treas., 1968-83, vice-chmn., treas., 1983-84, vice-chmn., 1984-90; ret., 1990. Bd. dirs. DuKane Corp. Chmn. Morton Arboretum, 1975—2001, Sprague Found., 1996—2000, Newberry Libr., 1986—2000, trustee; life trustee Sprague Found.; bd. govs. Nature Conservancy, 1973—84, chmn. Ill. chpt., 1984—87, life trustee, 1987—; mem. Chgo. Plan Commn., 1986—91; trustee Art Inst., Chgo., Latin Sch., Chgo., 1974—84, Ill. Cancer Coun., 1984—92, Chgo. City Day Sch., Lincoln Pk. Zool. Soc., Brooks Sch., 1987—95. 1st lt. USAF, 1952—54. Mem.: Casino Club, Caxton Club, Racquet Club, Commonwealth Club, Comml. Club, Chgo. Club. Home: 1530 N State Pkwy Chicago IL 60610-1610 Office: 35 E Wacker Dr Ste 1078 Chicago IL 60601-2398

HAFFNER, F. KINSEY, lawyer; b. San Francisco, Feb. 20, 1948; BA with distinction, Stanford U., 1971, JD, 1974. Bar: Calif. 1974, DC. Ptnr. Pillsbury, Madison & Sutro, San Jose & Palo Alto, Calif., 1980—2000; sr. v.p. & gen. counsel Converge Inc., 2001; ptnr. Pillsbury Winthrop LLP, NYC & Palo Alto, Calif., 2002—05; ptnr., co-chmn. Global Sourcing practice Pillsbury Winthrop Shaw Pittman, NYC & Palo Alto, Calif., 2005—. Office: Pillsbury Winthrop Shaw Pittman 1540 Broadway New York NY 10036 also: Pillsbury Winthrop Shaw Pittman 2475 Hanover St Palo Alto CA 94304-1114 Office Phone: 212-858-1747. Office Fax: 212-858-1500. Business E-Mail: kinsey.haffner@pillsburylaw.com.

HAFFORD, FAYE O'LEARY, writer; b. St. John Plantation, Maine, Apr. 27, 1925; d. Lee and Clara Mills O'Leary; m. Joseph Lee Hafford, Nov. 5, 1949 (dec. 1993); children: Michael Lee, Randi Lou. Student, Colby Coll., 1942—44; BS in Edn., U. Maine, 1965. Cert. elem. sch. tchr. Maine. Tchr. towns of Allagash, Limestone, Brunswick, Ft. Kent, Maine, 1951—76; ret. Author: 16 booklets on folklore of St. John Valley, 1986—. Contbr. curriculum guide Town of Brunswick; organizer, pres., vol. librarian Allagash Pub. Libr., 1998. Recipient County All Star award, Aroostook County, Presque Isle, Maine, 2000, Calendar award, Maine Ctr. for Women, 2000, Meritorious award, Nat. Coun. Geographic Edn., 1970, commendations for work on Allagash waterway, Gov. Maine, commendation, Maine Legis., Ken York award for work on Allagash Wilderness Waterway. Mem.: NEA, Aroostook Ret. Tchrs. Assn., Maine Ret. Tchrs. Assn., AARP. Republican. Congregationalist. Avocations: knitting, crocheting, fishing, camping, reading. Home and Office: Allagash Pub Libr 894 Allagash Rd Allagash ME 04774 Office Phone: 207-398-4454.

HAFKENSCHIEL, JOSEPH HENRY, JR., cardiologist, educator; b. Youngstown, Ohio, Apr. 2, 1916; s. Joseph Henry and Anna Marie (Conroy) H.; m. Lucinda Buchanan Thomas, July 18, 1942 (dec. 1983); children: Joseph Henry III, Benjamin A. Thomas, Mark Conroy, John Proctor; m. Carol MacDonald Smith Rush, Jan. 25, 1985. AB, Swarthmore Coll., 1937; MD, Johns Hopkins U., 1941. Diplomate Am. Bd. Internal Medicine. Intern U. Pa. Hosp., Phila., 1941-42; instr. pharmacology U. Pa. Sch. Medicine, 1946-47; resident U. Pa. Hosp., 1948-49, fellow in cardiology, 1949; instr. medicine U. Pa. Sch. Medicine, 1949-51; cardiovasc. disease physician, pvt. practice, 1949-65; assoc. medicine U. Pa. Sch. Medicine, 1951-66; med. dir. West Coast Office Sandoz Pharm., San Francisco, 1965-67; clin. instr. medicine Stanford U., 1966-69, staff physician Cowell Student Health Svcs., 1967-69; cardiovasc. disease physician, pvt. practice Palo Alto, 1969-78; asst. to assoc. prof. Stanford U., 1969-84, emeritus clin. assoc. prof. medicine, 1984—. Staff physician Extended Care Svc. VA Med. Ctr., Palo Alto, 1978-84. Contbr. articles to profl. jours. Pres. Peninsula Meml. and Funeral Soc., Palo Alto, 1984. Maj. M.C., USAAF, 1942-46. Fellow ACP, Coll. Physicians Phila., Am. Heart Assn., Am. Physiol. Soc.; mem. Air Force Assn., Am. Irish Hist. Soc., San Francisco Golf Club, Gulph Mills Golf Club, Ballybunion Golf (Ireland) Club, Am. Legion (post comdr. 1960-62), Sigma Xi Republican. Roman Catholic. Avocations: world travel, golf, gardening, art history. Home: Box 191 11 Harborside Rd Northeast Harbor ME 04662-0191 also: 66 Middle Rd Bryn Mawr PA 19010-1756 Personal E-mail: joecarolrush@mailstation.com.

HAFNER, JOSEPH A., JR., food company executive; b. San Bernadino, Calif., Oct. 9, 1944; s. Joseph Albert and Mary Florence (McGowan) H.; m. Merrill Hafner; children: John Michael, Daniel Stephen, Caroline Elizabeth. AB cum laude, Dartmouth Coll., 1966; MBA with high distinction, Amos Tuck Sch. Bus. Adminstrn., 1967. C.P.A. Intern Latin Am. Cornell U.-Ford Found., Lima, Peru, 1967-69; sr. cons. Arthur Andersen & Co., Houston, 1969-71; controller C/A div. Riviana Internat., Inc., Guatemala City, Guatemala, 1972-73, treas., v.p. fin. Houston, 1973-77; v.p. Riviana Foods Inc., Houston, 1977-81, pres., chief operating officer, 1981-84, pres., chief exec. officer, 1984—2005, dir., 1985—, chmn., 2005—. Recipient C.P.A. Gold medal Ark. State Bd. Pub. Accountancy, 1969 Mem. AICPA, Coun. on Fgn. Rels. Office: Riviana Foods Inc 2777 Allen Pky Houston TX 77019-2141 Office Phone: 713-529-3251.

HAFT, GAIL KLEIN, pediatrician; b. N.Y.C., Mar. 5, 1938; d. Herbert and Pearl (Mittleman) Klein; m. Jacob I. Haft, Mar. 27, 1964; children: Bethanne, Ian. AB in Chemistry, Vassar Coll., 1959; MD, U. Rochester, 1963. Diplomate Nat. Bd. Med. Examiners, Am. Bd. Pediatrics. Intern Albert Einstein Coll. Medicine, N.Y.C., 1963-64, resident, 1964-65, Mt. Sinai Hosp., N.Y.C., 1967-68; pediatrician Dept. Health, Staten Island, N.Y., 1965-67, Head Start, Englewood, N.Y., 1969-71, Dept. Health, Hackensack, N.J., 1970-71; utilization rev. physician Hosp. Corp., N.Y.C., 1973-76; pediatrician Westchester County Health Dept., N.Y., 1974-76; sch. physician Bd. Edn., Yonkers, N.Y., 1974-76; bus. mgr. Heartronics, Newark, 1980-94; chief med. officer Bergen County Spl. Svcs., Paramus, N.J., 1984—; physician Tenafly (N.J.) Sch. Bd. Edn., 1990-94. Mem. Tenafly Bd. Edn., 1983-89, pres., 1986-88.

HAFTER, DARYL M., history professor; b. Elizabeth, N.J. d. Harry and Theresa (Rothberg) Maslow; m. Monroe Z. Hafter, June 18, 1957; children: Matthew Ian, Naomi Eve. BA, Smith Coll., 1956; MA, Yale U., 1957, PhD, 1964. Lectr. U. Mich., Ann Arbor, 1967-68; asst. prof. Ea. Mich. U., Ypsilanti, 1969-73, assoc. prof., 1973-81, history prof., 1981—2004; prof. emeritus, 2004. Bd. dirs. women's studies Ea. Mich. U., 1982—84. Mem.: Soc. for History of Tech. (pres. 2001—03). Home: 1325 Brooklyn Ave Ann Arbor MI 48104-4414 E-mail: dhafter@emich.edu.

HAFTER, JEROME CHARLES, lawyer; b. Orlando, Fla., May 16, 1945; s. Jerome Sidney and Mary Margaret (Fugler) H.; m. Jo Cille Dawkins, July 18, 1976; 1 child, Jerome Bryan. BA summa cum laude, Rice U., 1967; BA with first class honours, Oxford U., 1969, MA, 1976; JD, Yale U., 1972. Bar: Miss. 1974, U.S. Ct. Appeals (5th cir.) 1974, U.S. Dist. Ct. (no. and so. dists.) Miss. 1974. Law clk. to presiding judge U.S. Ct. Appeals (5th cir.), Jackson, Miss., 1972—73; assoc. Lake, Tindall, Hunger & Thackston (now Lake Tindall LLP), Greenville, Miss., 1973—76, ptnr., 1976—2001, Phelps Dunbar LLP, Jackson, 2001—. Chmn. Miss. Bd. Bar Admissions, Jackson, 1979-2002; sec., treas. Hafter Realty Inc., Greenville, 1969-92, pres., 1992—; mem. gov.'s constn. commn., Jackson, 1985-87; sec., gen. counsel Delta and Pine Land Co., Scott, Miss., 1993— Author: Family History of Peter Quin, 1964, 2d. rev. edit., 1970. Pres. Downtown Improvement Assn. Greenville, 1980—, Common Cause/Miss., 1976—78; mem. Greenville City Election Commn., 1978—, Greenville Mcpl. Sch. Bd., 1988—, pres., 1995—96, 1999—2000, 2002—03; chmn. com. on tax Miss. Econ. Coun., Jackson, 1985, 1987, 1996—98; pres. Greenville Area C. of C., 1992; v.p. I-69 Mid-Continent Hwy. Coalition, 1992—. Marshall scholar, 1967-69; Leadership Miss. Program fellow, 1976-77; Best Lawyers in Am., 2001-02, 2003-04, 2005-06 Fellow: Miss. Bar Found.; mem.: ABA (young lawyer divsn. 1980—82, law sch. accreditation com. 1998—2002, coun. sect. legal edn. and admissions to bar 2000—, vice chmn. com. on issues affecting legal profession), Miss. Bankruptcy Conf. (chmn. com. on bankruptcy rules 1988), Am. Law Inst., Am. Judicature Soc., Nat. Conf. Bar Examiners (MBE com. 1986—88, trustee 1989—2000, chmn. 1998—99, chmn. tech. com. 2000—), Fed. Bar Assn. (v.p. no. Miss. 1977—78, 1981—82), Miss. Bar Assn. (bd. dirs. young lawyers divsn. 1976—79, chmn. sect. corp. fin. bus. law 1989—90, pres. fellows young lawyers divsn. 2000—01), Washington County Hist. Soc. (pres. 1981), Greenville C. of C. (bd. dirs. 1976—79, pres. 1992—93), Kiwanis (Greenville pres. 1978—79, lt. gov. 1982—83), Oxford & Cambridge Golfing Soc. (Rye, Eng.), Annandale Golf Club (Madison, Miss.), Huntercombe Golf Club (Nuffield, Eng.), Greenville Golf and Country Club (v.p. 1977—79), Vincents Club (Oxford, Eng.), Phi Beta Kappa. Episcopalian. Home: 315 Wetherbee St Greenville MS 38701 Office: Phelps Dunbar LLP PO Box 23066 111 E Capitol Ste 600 Jackson MS 39201 Office Phone: 601-360-9347. Personal E-mail: hafter@tecinfo.net. Business E-Mail: hafterj@phelps.com.

HAFTER, RUTH ANNE, library director, educator; b. N.Y.C., Apr. 18, 1935; BA in History and Econs. cum laude, Brandeis U., 1956; cert. Bus. Adminstrn., Harvard-Radcliffe U., 1957; MLS, Columbia U., 1963; PhD in Libr. and Info. Studies, U. Calif., Berkeley, 1984. Supr. sch. librs. Halifax County, N.S., Can., 1965-66; asst. edn. libr. Harvard U., Cambridge, Mass., 1967-68; univ. libr. St. Mary's U., Halifax, N.S., Can., 1969-75; libr. dir. Sonoma State U., Rohnert Park, Calif., 1978-86, San Jose (Calif.) State U., 1986-91, prof. div. libr. and info. sci., 1987-99, prof. emeritus, 1999—. Instr. St. Mary's U., 1972-75, Sonoma State U., 1982-85, U. Calif., Berkeley, 1975-78, 85-86; cons. Ministry of State Urban Affairs, Can., 1975, Sonoma County Hist. Records, 1979-80; coord. Geysers Info. Project., 1980-81; project humanist Calif. Coun. for Humanities, 1981-83; dir. Indochinese Cultures project Nat. Endowment for Humanities, 1983-84, Videodisc Work Shop Calif. State U., 1987—, Online Pub. Catalog Implementation, 1989; pres. Beethoven Ctr. San Jose State U., 1987-88. Author: Academic Librarians and Cataloging Networks: Visibility, Quality and Professional Status, 1986, (with George Rawlyk) Acadian Education in Nova Scotia, 1970; contbr. articles to profl. jours. Mem. Mayor Feinstein's com. on Teaching of Holocaust, San Francisco, 1986, adv. com. Foothill Coll. Libr. Tech. Asst. Program, 1987—, San Jose Pub. Libr. Found., 1987—, bd. govs. 1987-89, exec. bd. Friends of San Jose Pub. Libr., 1989—, Calif. State Libr. Networking Task Force, 1989—, adv. bd. dirs. Frances Gullard Child Devel. Ctr., 1990—; pres. alumni bd. Sch. Libr. and Info. Sci, U. Calif., Berkeley, 1993-94. Inst. Ethnography grantee Dept. Edn., 1994-95. Mem. ALA (com. on accreditation, field site vis. bd. 1982—, libr. career resource network 1987—, program com. reference and adult svcs. div. 1989—), Coop. Libr. Agy. Systems and Svcs. (bd. govs. 1988—, acad. librs. rep.), Calif. Acad. and Rsch. Librs. (pres. 1983-84), Calif. Libr. Assn. (legis. network 1988—, chair continuing edn. com. 1997), North Bay Coop. Assn. (exec. com. 1984-85), Phi Beta Kappa, Phi Kappa Phi. Home: 177 19th St Apt 1E Oakland CA 94612-4653 E-mail: rhafter@earthlink.net.

HAGA, DAVID L., lawyer; BS, W.Va. U., 1958; LLB with high distinction, U. Ariz., 1965; LLM in Tax, NYU, 1967. Bar: Ariz. 1965, U.S. Dist. Ct. Ariz. 1965, U.S. Tax Ct. 1965, U.S. Ct. Appeals (9th cir.) 1965, U.S. Supreme Ct. 1965, cert.: Ariz. Bd. Legal Specialization (tax specialist). Law clk. to Hon. Jesse H. Udall Supreme Ct. State of Ariz., 1965—66; shareholder, atty. Gallagher & Kennedy, P.A., Phoenix, 1999—. Mem. com. exams. Ariz. Supreme Ct., 1987—94, chmn., 1993—94. Asst. editor: Ariz. Law Rev. Bd. dirs. Ariz. Found. Legal Svcs. and Edn., sec., 2002, treas., 2003; bd. visitors U. Ariz. Law Sch., 1998—2004. Mem.: ABA, Order of Coif, Ariz. Bar Assn. (mem. specialization com. 1983—87), Maricopa County Bar Assn., Ctrl. Ariz. Estate Planning Coun., State Bar Ariz. (mem. com. preparid and group legal svcs. 1974—76, mem. tax sect. 1974—, pres. 1981—82), Phoenix Country Club, Phi Delta Phi. Office: Gallagher and Kennedy PA 2575 E Camelback Rd Phoenix AZ 85016-9225 Office Phone: 602-530-8380. Business E-Mail: dlh@gknet.com.

HAGA, ENOCH JOHN, computer educator, writer; b. LA, Apr. 25, 1931; s. Enoch and Esther Bonser (Higginson) H.; m. Elna Jo Wright, Aug. 22, 1957 (dec. Aug. 22, 2004). AA, Grant Tech. Coll., 1950; AB, Sacramento State Coll., 1955, MA, 1958; PhD, Calif. Inst. Integral Studies, 1972. Tchr. bus. Calif. Med. Facility, Vacaville, 1956-60; asst. prof. bus. Stanislaus State Coll., Turlock, Calif., 1960-61; engring. writer, publs. engr. Hughes Aircraft Co., Fullerton, Calif., 1961-62, Lockheed Missiles & Space Co., Sunnyvale, Calif., 1962, Gen. Precision, Inc., Glendale, Calif., 1962-63; sr. adminstrv. analyst Holmes & Narver, Inc., LA, 1963-64; tchr., chmn. dept. bus. and math. Pleasanton (Calif.) Unified Dist., 1964-92, coord. computer svcs., adminstrn., instrn., 1984-85. Vis. asst. prof. bus. Sacramento State Coll., 1967-69; instr. bus. and computer sci. Chabot Coll., Hayward, Calif., 1970-89; instr. bus. and philosophy Ohlone Coll., Fremont, Calif., 1972; prof., v.p., mem. bd. govs. Calif. Inst. Asian Studies, 1972-75; pres., prof. Pacific Inst. East-West Studies, San Francisco, 1975-76, also mem. bd. govs.; dir. Cert. Couns., Livermore, Calif., 1975-80; mem., chmn. negotiating team Amador Vly. Secondary Educators Assn., Pleasanton, 1976-77, pres. 1984-85. Coordinating editor Total Systems, 1962; editor Automation Educator, 1965-67, Automated Educational Systems, 1967, Data Processing in Biomedicine and Medicine, 1973; contbg. editor Jour. Bus. Edn., 1961-69, Data Processing mag., 1967-70; contbr. Carlos Rivera: The Prime Puzzles & Problems Connection, N.J.A. Sloane, The On-Line Encyclopedia of Integer Sequences; author, compiler: Understanding Automation, 1965; author: Simplified Computer Arithmetic, Simplified Computer Logic, Simplified Computer Input, Simplified Computer Flowcharting, 1971-72, Before the Apple Drops, 15 Essays on Dinosaur Education, 2d edit., 1997, Exploring Prime Numbers on Your PC and the Internet, 2001, How to Prepare Your Genealogy for Publication on Your Home Computer, 2001, TAROsolution: A Complete Guide to Interpreting Tarot, 1994, The 2000-Year History of the Haga-Helgoy and Krick-Keller Families, Ancestors and Descendants, 1994; editor Data Processor, 1960-62, Automedica, 1970-76, FBE Bull., 1967-68. With USNR, 1947—49, with USNR, 1953—57, with USAF, 1949—52. Mem. Internat. Assn. Computer Info. Sys. (exec. dir. 1970-74), Sacramento Statistical Assn. Avocations: genealogy, prime numbers, mathematical sequences. Mailing: PO Box 489 Folsom CA 95763-0489 Personal E-mail: Enokh@comcast.net.

HAGAN, CLIFFORD O., retired basketball player; b. Owensboro, Ky., Dec. 9, 1931; Grad., U. Ky., 1954; MA, Washington U., St. Louis, 1958. Basketball player St. Louis Hawks, 1956-66; player-coach Dallas Chaparrals, 1967-70. Named to Basketball Hall of Fame, 1977, Nat. H.S. Hall of Fame, 1989; mem. NBA Championship Team, 1958; selected All-Am., 1952, 54, Southeastern Conf. All-Time Team, 1974, NBA All-Star Team. Office: Basketball Hall Fame 1150 W Columbus Ave Springfield MA 01101-0179

HAGAN, DENNIS M., education educator; b. Auburn, Wash., Sept. 24, 1946; s. Marcus Junior and Beatrice Mae Hagan; m. Deborah Lin Hagan, Aug. 3, 2002; children: Richard, Kaycee. BA in edn., Ctrl. Wash. U., 1975. Cert. tchr. Wash. State. Ditch digger, Enumclaw, Wash., 1963—64; choker settler Weyerhause Lumber Co., Enumclaw, Wash., 1965; scheduler Boeing

Airplane Co., Auburn, Wash., 1968—69; mail carrier U.S. Postal Office, Enumclaw, Wash., 1970—71; scheduler Boeing Airplane Co., Auburn, Wash., 1971—72; tchr. Enumclaw Sch. Dist., Enumclaw, Wash., 1975—. Pres. Wash. State Girls Basketball Coaches Assn., 1986—90; rep. Wash. Interscholastic Activities Assn., 1986—91. Named Coach of Yr., 1986, 1989, Softball Sea Mount League, 1986, 1989. Mem.: NEA, Wash. State Coaches Assn., Enumclaw Edn. Assn., Wash. Edn. Assn. Avocations: golf, travel, movies. Home: 28315 SE 451st St Enumclaw WA 98022 Office: Enumclaw Sch Dist 226 Semanski St S Enumclaw WA 98022 Office Phone: 360-802-7756. E-mail: dennis_hagan@enumclaw.wednet.edu.

HAGAN, JOHN AUBREY, retired corporate financial executive; b. Pulaski, Tenn., Sept. 30, 1936; s. Edwin Jackson and Rebecca Maria (Smith) H.; m. Nicole Emilie Thiltges, Sept. 7, 1958; children— Mark, Alex, Micheline. AB, Harvard U., 1958, MBA, 1963. With R. J. Reynolds Tobacco Co. (name later changed to R. J. Reynolds Industries, then to RJR Nabisco), Winston-Salem, NC, 1963-85, asst. contr., 1970-75, contr., chief acctg. officer internal auditing and fin. info. sys., 1975-79, v.p., contr., 1979-85; CFO Embrex Inc., Research Triangle Park, NC, 1986-95, v.p. fin. and adminstrn., 1988-95, ret., 1995. Bd. dir. United Way of Forsyth County, 1976-80, pres., 1979. Officer USN, 1958-61. Mem. Fin. Execs. Inst. (com. on corp. reporting 1979-85, pres. N.C. chpt. 1981-82), Common Cause, Greater Winston-Salem C. of C. (speakers bur. 1977-85), Am. Mgmt. Assn. (fin. coun. 1981-86). Home: 104 W Lochwood Dr Cary NC 27511-9744 Personal E-mail: njhagan@att.net.

HAGAN, JOHN CHARLES, III, ophthalmologist; b. Mexico, Mo., Oct. 7, 1943; s. John Charles Hagan II and Cleta L. (Book) Neely; m. Rebecca Jane Chapman, July 15, 1967; children: Carol Ann, Catherine Elizabeth. BA, U. Mo., 1965; MD, Loyola U., Chgo., 1969. Diplomate Am. Bd. Ophthalmology. Intern Med. Coll. Wis., Milw., 1969-70; resident in ophthalmology Emory U., Atlanta, 1972-75; practice medicine, Kansas City, Mo., 1975—. Cons. Am. Running and Phys. Fitness Assn., Washington, 1973—. Editor: Mo. Medicine: The Jour. of the Mo. State Med. Assn.; contbr. over 100 articles to med. jours. Capt. M.C., USAF, 1970-72. Fellow ACS; mem. AMA, Am. Soc. Cataract and Refractive Surgery, Mo. Soc. Eye Physicians and Surgeons (pres. 1998), Kansas City Soc. Ophthalmology. Office: Discover Vision Ctrs 9401 N Oak Trafficway Kansas City MO 64155 Office Phone: 816-478-1230.

HAGAN, JOHN P., state representative; b. Alliance, Ohio, Apr. 11, 1955; married; 4 children. Attended Sch. Arch., Kent State U. Self-employed heating and plumbing contractor; state rep. dist. 50 Ohio Ho. of Reps., Columbus, 2000—, vice chair pub. utilities com., 2000—04, chair pub. utilities and energy com., 2004—, mem. econ. devel. and tech., homeland security engrng. and archtl. design, and human svcs. and aging coms., mem. ways and means com. Trustee Marlboro Twp., 1990—2000; past commr. Stark County Regional Planning Commn.; past alt. North East Four County Regional Planning Commn., Tuscarawas County Solid Waste Dist. Bd. Mem.: Nat. Fedn. Ind. Bus., Air Conditioning Contractors Am., Stark County Twp. Assn., Stark County Farm Bur., Promise Keepers of Stark County, Marlboro Twp. Hist. Soc., NRA, Lexington Grange, Alliance Area C. of C., Massillon Rep. Club, Alliance Area Rep. Club (past pres.), Marlboro Ruritans, Lions (past pres. Marlboro chpt., Lion of Yr. 1996). Republican. Methodist. Office: 77 S High St 11th fl Columbus OH 43215-6111

HAGAN, JOSEPH HENRY, higher education consultant; b. Providence, Mar. 2, 1935; s. Joseph Henry and Claire Veronica (Gorman) H.; m. Patrice O'Malley; 1 child, Kevin O'Malley. AB, Providence Coll.; EdM, Boston U.; D. Min., EdD, Grad. Theol. Found.; DCL (hon.), Salve Regina Coll., 1968; DPA (hon.), Mt. St. Joseph Coll., 1976; MBA (hon.), Bryant Coll., 1992; LLD (hon.), Boston U., 1993; DPS (hon.), Providence Coll., 1996; EdD (hon.), Assumption Coll., 1998, Rivier Coll., 1998; LHD (hon.), John Cabor U., 2004. Tchr. Providence Public Schs., 1958-61; legis. asst. U.S. Ho. of Reps., 1961-64; staff asst. Pres.'s Com. on Juvenile Delinquency, 1964-65; spl. asst. OEO, 1965-68; dir. planning, devel. and fed. relations Bryant Coll., Smithfield, R.I., 1968-70, v.p. for public affairs, 1970-73, lectr. public adminstrn., adj. prof. social scis.; asst. to chmn. Nat. Endowment for Humanities, Washington, 1973-78; pres., lectr. politics Assumption Coll., Worcester, Mass., 1978-98, pres. emeritus, 1998—; pres. Roger Williams U., Bristol, RI, 1999—2001. Chmn. bd. trustees John Cabot U., Rome; mem. Nat. Coun. on the Humanities, 1992-2000; trustee Cardinal Tardini Charitable Trust; chmn. budget com. Little Compton, R.I., 1999-2001, chmn. zoning bd., 2001-04, town moderator, 2004—. Decorated knight of honor and devotion in Obedience of Malta, knight Grand Cross, St. Gregory the Great, comdr. Palmes Academiques (France), knight Grand Cross of Justice of the Sacred Mil. Constantinian Order St. George, knight comdr. Order of Saints Maurice and Lazarus, knight grand cross of the Holy Sepulchre, comdr. Order of Merit, Knights of Malta, Gentleman-in-Waiting to the Pope. Mem. Am. Antiquarian Soc., N.Am. Assn. Constantinian Order (pres.), Univ. Club (Providence), Sakonnet Golf Club, Circulo della Caccia (Rome), KC, Univ. Club (Washington). Roman Catholic. E-mail: jhagan67@cox.net.

HAGAN, MICHAEL PHILIP, radiation oncologist; b. May 6, 1947; PhD, U. Ill., 1978; MD, Baylor Coll. Medicine, 1989. Sr. scientist Armed Forces Radiobiology Rsch. Inst., Bethesda, Md., 1980-84; chief radiation oncology svc. Walter Reed Army Med. Ctr., Washington, 1995-96; assoc. prof. radiation oncology Med. Coll. Va., Richmond, 1998—. Contbr. numerous articles on bone marrow devel. to Exptl. Hematology, Exptl. Cell Rsch., Radiation Rsch., others. Office: Med Coll Va Hosps Dept Radiation Oncology PO Box 980058 Richmond VA 23298-0058

HAGAN, PHILIP EDWARD, JR., academic administrator; b. Roanoke, Va., Jan. 11, 1954; s. Philip Edward Hagan Sr. and Dorothy Murray. BS in Environ. Health, E. Carolina U., 1985; MPH, George Washington U., 1992; cert. in hazardous materials mgmt., Inst. Hazardous Materials, 1989. Cert. healthcare safety profl., 1990, hazard control mgr., 1990, indsl. hygienist, 1993. Engrng. lab. tech. Wright Chem. Corp., Wilmington, N.N., 1976-79, safety officer, indsl. hygienist, 1985-87; sr. indsl. hygienist AMA, Washington, 1987-88; asst. dir. med. ctr. George Washington U., Washington, 1988-92; dir. occpl. safety and environ. health programs Georgetown U., Washington, 1992—. With lab. consortium environ. excellence EPA, Boston and Washington, 1997—; exec. dir. oversight com. IAFCA, 1992—; spkr. in field. Author: Indoor Environments and Health: The Building Owner's and Manager's Guide to Resolving Indoor Environmental Problems, 1998, Occupational Health, 1995, Environmental and Workplace Safety, 1996; mng. editor Am. Biol. Safety Assn., Mundelein, Ill., 1992—, Internat. Air Filtration Certifiers Assn., Arlington, Va., 1992—, Acad. Cert. Hazardous Material Mgrs., Rockville, Md., 1990-92; tech. editor, appearance (video) Hazard Communication in Health Care Facilities, 1992-93; contbr. articles to profl. jours. Mem. APHA, Assn. Physical Plant Officers, Am. Chem. Soc., Am. Conf. Govt. Indsl. Hygienists, Am. Indsl. Hygiene Assn., Nat. Assn. Coll. and Univ. Bus. Officers, Nat. Environ. Tng. Assn. (cert.), Nat. Inst. Bldg. Scis., Nat. Fire Protection Assn., Nat. Assn. Environ. Profls., Nat. Environ. Health Assn. (registered hazardous substances profl.), Nat. Safety Coun. (mem. editl. adv. bd. tech. pub. 1997—), Internat. Air Filtration Cert. Assn., Environ. Auditing Roundtable (mng. editor newsletter 1992-94, Acad. Cert. Hazardous Material Mgrs. (mng. editor 1990-92), Campus Safety Assn. Office: Georgetown U Dept Safety & Environ Mgmt New S Bldg M-14 3700 O St NW Washington DC 20057-0002

HAGANS, FRED (WILLIAM FRED HAGANS), lawyer; b. Waco, Tex., June 24, 1947; s. Raymond Leon and Pauline Elsie (Pace) H.; m. Patricia Coyle, Jan. 2, 1971; children: William, Lindsay. BA, U. Tex., 1969, JD, 1972. Bar: Tex. 1972, U.S. Dist. Ct. (ea. dist.) Tex. 1980, U.S. Ct. Appeals (11th and 5th cirs.) 1981, U.S. Ct. Claims; bd. cert. personal injury and civil trial law Tex. Bd. of Legal Specialization. Ptnr. Bracewell & Patterson, Houston, 1972-82, O'Quinn & Hagans, Houston, 1982-86, Hagans & Sydow, Houston, 1986-90; pres. Hagans, Bobb & Burdine, P.C., Houston, 1991—. Chmn. Houston Lawyer Referral Svc. Com. 1983; plaintiffs' liaison counsel Glomar Java Sea Disaster Litigation, Houston, 1983-86; mem Fed. Ct. Adv. Com., Houston, 1986—. Contbr. articles to profl. jours. Fellow Houston Bar Found., Tex. Bar Found.; mem. State Bar Tex. (chmn. grievance com. 1986-88), Assn. Trial Lawyers Am., Tex. Trial Lawyers Assn., Houston Trial Lawyers Assn., Am. Bd. Trial Advocates, Nat. Bd. Trial Advocacy. Democrat. Roman Catholic. Office: Hagans Bobb & Burdine 3200 Travis Fourth Fl Houston TX 77006

HAGAR, RICHARD JOSEPH, music educator, musician; b. Brockton, Mass., July 15, 1954; s. Preston Irving and Marie Mahoney Hagar; m. Charlene Ann Peterson, Aug. 2, 1986. B in Music and Music Edn., Hartt Coll. of Music, 1976. Cert. tchr. music K-12 Mass., Conn., N.Y. Tchr. string instruments, orch. and chorus dir. Delaware Acad., Delhi, NY, 1976—78; tchr. string instruments, orch. dir. Bedford (Mass.) Pub. Schs., 1978—88, Westborough (Mass.) Pub. Schs., 1988—. Named Mass. Orch. Dir. of Yr., 2000; recipient Lowell Mason award for outstanding contbns. to music edn., 1999. Mem.: Mass. Music Educators' Assn. (treas. Northea. Dist. 1982—86, all-state conf. exec. bd. 1993—98, 2002—, membership coord. Northea. Dist. 1980—93, all-state orch. mgr. 1998—2000), Westborough Tchrs. Assn., Mass. Tchrs. Assn., Am. String Teachers Assn. with Nat. Sch. Orch. Assn. (pres. Mass. chpt. 1982—86, exec. bd. Mass. chpt. 1990—), Music Educators' Nat. Conf. Home: 20 Greybert Ln Worcester MA 01602 Personal E-mail: rchag@aol.com.

HAGAR, SUSAN MACK, school psychologist, school counselor; b. Phila., Apr. 5, 1948; d. Walter J. and Margaret Anne (Yurchisin) Mack; m. James Newton Hagar, Jan. 19, 1974; children: Kristin, Greg. BA in Spanish, Temple U., 1970, MEd in Elem. Edn., 1975; MS in Sch. Psychology with honors, Ea. Coll., St. Davids, Pa., 1997. Cert. sch. psychologist, sch. counselor, tchr., Pa. Tchr. St. Mary's Sch., Phila., 1971-72, Morton Elem. Sch., Phila., 1972-73, Monty St. Sch., Plattsburgh, N.Y., 1976-77; reading tchr. Gladwyne (Pa.) Montessori Sch., 1986-96; sch. psychologist Colonial Intermediate Unit, Easton, Pa., 1997-98, Bethlehem Area Sch. Dist., Bethlehem, Pa., 1998—. Recipient Congratulatory Letter, First Lady Barbara Bush, 1990. Mem. NASP, APA, NEA, Pa. Psychol. Assn., Pa. Sch. Counselors Assn. Avocations: reading, cooking, walking, travel. Home: 3414 W Union St Allentown PA 18104-5947 Office: Bethlehem Area Sch Dist 1516 Sycamore St Bethlehem PA 18017-6037

HAGART-ALEXANDER, CLAUD, software engineer; b. Edinburgh, Scotland, Nov. 5, 1963; s. Claud and Hilda Etain Hagart-Alexander; m. Elaine Susan Park, June 24, 1994; 1 child, Claud Miles Park Alexander. BS in Engring., U. of Glasgow, Scotland, U.K., 1985. Software engr. Hawker Siddeley Dynamics Engring., Welwyn Garden City, England, 1985—87, Dynamic Control Sys., Vancouver, Canada, 1987—88; control sys. software engr. Devron-Hercules, North Vancouver, Canada, 1987—92; control sys. dir. Measurex-Devron, North Vancouver, 1992—98; application controls dir. Honeywell, Cupertino, Calif., 1998—. Author: (several tech. papers) Pulp and Paper. Mem.: Pulp and Paper Tech. Assn. of Can. (assoc.). Achievements include patents for Paper stock shear and formation control; Wet end control for papermaking machine; Fast CD and MD control in a sheetmaking machine; Paper stock zeta potential measurement and control; Means of correcting a measurement of a property of a material with a sensor that is affected by a second property of that material. Home: 514 Jeter St Redwood City CA 94062 Personal E-mail: claudha@comcast.net.

HAGBERG, CARL THOMAS, financial executive; b. S.I., N.Y., Dec. 19, 1942; s. Charles W. and Dorothy (Van Hoesen) H.; m. Patricia Rasile, Sept. 21, 1972; children: Karl, Peder, Erik. BA, NYU, 1971; MS, Columbia U., 1983. V.p. Mfrs. Hanover Trust Co., N.Y.C., 1972-83, sr. v.p., 1984-92; chmn., CEO Carl T. Hagberg and Assocs., Investor Rels., Jackson, N.J., 1992—. Bd. dirs., chmn. audit com. Mfrs. Hanover Trust Co. of Calif., San Francisco, 1984-92; dir. The Minerva Fund, Inc., 1994-98, The Roundtable Ensemble, 1999-2003; pub. The Shareholder Svc. Optimizer. Mem. Am. Arbitration Assn., Am. Soc. Corp. Secs., Inc. (nat. treas. 1991-97, N.Y. chpt. pres. 1991-92), Nat. Assn. Securities Dealers (bd. arbitration), Nat. Investor Rels. Inst., Securities Transfer Assn., Inc., Tiro A. Segno of N.Y., Pamet Harbor Yacht and Tennis Club. Home and Office: 6 S Lakeview Dr Jackson NJ 08527-2703 E-mail: cthagberg@aol.com.

HAGEDORN, DONALD JAMES, plant pathologist, educator, agricultural consultant; b. Moscow, Idaho, May 18, 1919; s. Frederick William and Elizabeth Viola (Scheyer) H.; m. Eloise Tierney, July 18, 1943; 1 child, James William BS, U. Idaho, 1941, DSc (hon.), 1979; MS, U. Wis., 1943, PhD, 1948. Prof. agronomy and plant pathology U. Wis., Madison, 1948-64, prof. plant pathology, 1964—. Courtesy prof. plant pathology Oreg. State U., Covallis, 1972-73; vis. scientist DSIR Lincoln Rsch. Ctr., Christchurch, N.Z., 1980-81; cons. Asgrow Seed Co., 1987-93; affiliate prof. plant pathology U. Idaho, 1991—. Contbr. chpts. to books, articles to profl. jours. With USAAF, 1943-46. Recipient Campbell award AAAS, 1961, CIBA-Geigy award, 1974, Meritorious Svc. award Nat. Pea Improvement Assn., 1979, Bean Improvement Coop., 1979, Forty-Niners award, 1983, Citation for Outstanding Sci. Achievement, Wis. Acad. Letters, Arts and Scis., 1986; NSF sr. fellow, 1957; named Disting. Centennial Alumnus, U. Idaho, 1989; named to U. Idaho Alumni Hall of Fame, 1990. Fellow Am. Phytopath, Soc.; mem. Kiwanis, Sigma Xi, Gamma Sigma Delta, Alpha Zeta. Methodist. Home: 927 University Bay Dr Madison WI 53705-2248 Office: U Wis 583 Russell Labs 1630 Linden Dr Madison WI 53706-1520

HAGEDORN, JAMES, landscape company executive; Grad. AMP program, Harvard Bus. Sch. Sr. mgmt. roles Miracle-Gro; with The Scotts Co., 1995—, pres. N.Am. ops., pres., COO, 2000—03, chmn., pres., CEO, 2003—. Exec. v.p. Scotts' U.S. Bus. Groups. Officer USAF. Office: c/o Scotts Co. 14111 Scottslawn Road Marysville OH 43041*

HAGEE, MICHAEL W., US Marine Corps Commandant; BS in Engring. with distinction, U.S. Naval Acad., 1968; MSEE, U.S. Naval Postgrad. Sch., 1969; MA in Nat. Security/Strategic Studies, Naval War Coll., 1987; Grad., Command and Staff Coll., 1982, U.S. Naval War Coll., 1987. Commd. 2d lt. USMC, 1968, advanced through grades to brig. gen., 1996—; command positions include 1st Btn., 8th Marines, 1988-90; commanding officer 11th Marine Expeditionary Unit, 1992-93; various to exec. asst. to asst. commandant USMC, 1993-94; dir. Character Devel. Divsn. US Naval Acad., 1994-95; sr. mil. asst. to dep. sec. of def. Office of Sec. of Def., Washington, 1995-96; exec. asst. to dir. CIA, Washington, 1995-96; dep. dir. opers. Hdqtrs., U.S. European Command, Stuttgart, Germany, 1996-98; dir. strategic planning and policy US Pacific Command, 1999—2000; commd. gen. I Marine Expeditionary Force, 2000—02; commd. US Marine Corps, Washington, 2003—. Decorated Def. Disting. Svc. medal, Legion of Merit with two gold stars, Bronze Star with Combat "V", Def. Meritorious Svc. medal, Meritorious Svc. medal with one gold star, Navy Achievement medal with one gold star, Combat Action Ribbon, Nat. Intelligence Disting. Svc. medal. Office: Commd USMC Petangon Washington DC 20350

HAGEL, CHARLES, senator; b. North Platte, Nebr., Oct. 4, 1946; m. Lilibet Ziller; 2 children. Student, Brown Inst. Radio & TV, Minn., 1966; BA, U. Nebr., 1971. Dep. adminstr. VA, 1981-82; found. EVP, Vanguard Cellular Systems, 1985—87; pres./CEO World USO, 1987-90; pres. McCarthy & Co., 1991-96; U.S. senator from Nebr., 1997—. Mem. internat. fin., fgn. rels. coms. U.S. Senate, chmn. senate global climate change observer group, mem. NATO observer group; mem. coms. banking, housing and urban affairs, 1997—, spl. com. on aging, 1997—; founder/dir. Vanguard Cellular Syss. Inc. Active Bellevue U., Red Cross, No Greater Love, World USO; chair Paralyzed Veterans of Am., 10 Anniversary Vietnam Vets. Meml. With U.S. Army, 1967-68. Mem. Am. Legion VFW, Omaha C. of C. (trustee). Republican. Office: 248 Russell Senate Office Bldg Washington DC 20510-0001*

HAGEL, JOHN, III, management consultant; b. Berlin, N.H., Sept. 14, 1950; s. John Jr. and Evelyn Gertrude (Parent) H. BA, Wesleyan U., 1972; PhB, Oxford U., 1974; MBA, JD, Harvard U., 1978. Bar: Mass. 1978. Cons. Boston Cons. Group, 1978-80; pres. Sequoia Group, Larkspur, Calif., 1980-82; v.p. Atari, Inc., Sunnyvale, Calif., 1982-83, sr. v.p., 1983-84; sr. engagement mgr. McKinsey and Co., N.Y.C., 1984-87, prin. San Francisco, 1987-2000; chief strategy officer 12 Entrepreneuring, Inc., San Francisco, 2000—02; pres. Bus. Performance Network, Burlingame, 2002—. Author: Alternative Energy Strategies, 1976, Assessing The Criminal, 1977, Net Gain: Expanding Markets Through Virtual Communities, 1997, Net Worth: Shaping Markets When Customers Make the Rules, 1999, Out of the Box: Strategies for Achieving Profits Today and Growth Tomorrow through Web Services, 2002, The Only Sustainable Edge: Why Business Strategy Depends on Productive friction and Dynamic Specialization, 2005; contbr. articles to profl. jours. Keasbey Found. fellow, 1972-74; Forum fellow World Econ. Forum, 1999-. Mem. ABA, Mass. Bar Assn. Episcopalian. E-mail: jh@johnhagel.com.

HAGEL, LAWRENCE B., federal judge; b. Washington, Ind. 3 children. BS, U.S. Naval Acad., 1969; JD, Univ. Pacific, 1976; LLM with highest honors, George Washington Univ., 1983. Counsel Paralyzed Veterans Am., Washington, 1990—2003; judge U.S. Ct. Appeals Vets. Claims, Washington, 2004—. Mem. Adminstrv. Conf. U.S., 1995, rules adv. com., U.S. Ct. Appeals Vets. Claims, 1992—2003, exec. bd., Vets. Pro Bono Consortium, steering com. D.C. Bar, 1999—2003. Lt. col. (ret.) USMC, infantry, Vietnam, Judge Advocate. Decorated Combat Action Ribbon, Meritorious Svc. Medal (3 awards), Joint Svc. Commendation Medal, Army Commendation Medal. Mem.: Fed. Bar Assn. (chmn., Vets. Law com. 1994—95). Office: US Ct Appeals Vets Claims Ste 900 625 Indiana Ave NW Washington DC 20004-2950 Office Phone: 202-501-5862.

HAGEL, RAYMOND CHARLES, publishing company executive, educator; b. Jersey City, Sept. 5, 1916; s. Morris and Theresa (Feigenbaum) H.; m. Ruth Block, May 30, 1941; children: Keith W., Wendy A.; m. Alsia Triner, Dec. 24, 2002. BS cum laude, NYU, 1937. Promotion mgr. McGraw-Hill Pub. Co., 1937-38, 41-42, 45-46; with bus. dept. N.Y. World-Telegram, 1939-40; with Asso. Mag. Contbrs., Inc., 1947-48; pres. Smith, Hagel & Knudsen, Inc., N.Y.C., 1948-59, P.F. Collier & Son Corp., N.Y.C., 1959-60, chmn. bd., 1961-65; exec. v.p. Crowell-Collier Pub. Co. (name changed to Crowell Collier and Macmillan, Inc. 1965, Macmillan Inc., 1973), 1959-60, pres., 1960-76, chief exec. officer, 1963-80, chmn. bd., 1964-80, also bd. dirs. David L. Tandy exec.-in-resident, vis. prof. M.J. Neeley Sch. Bus., Tex. Christian U., 1980-81, mem. adv. bd. dept. journalism, 1981—; prof. mgmt. Barney Sch. Bus. and Public Adminstrn., U. Hartford, 1981-90, chmn. dept. mgmt., 1983-84; mem. Rockefeller Center adv. bd. Chem. Bank, N.Y.C.; mem. Council Internat. Exec. Service Corps.; disting. adj. prof. Coll. Bus. and Pub. Adminstrn., NYU, 1972-79, mem. dean's adv. council, 1973 Trustee, Coll. of New Rochelle, 1970-76, 77-80. Served with USNR, 1942-45. Recipient John T. Madden Meml. medal NYU, 1972; Disting. Service award in investment edn. Investment Edn. Inst. of Nat. Assocs. Investment Clubs, 1973; Madden asso., Gallatin asso. NYU Mem. Fgn. Policy Assn., Am. Assn. Higher Edn., Dirs. Table, Assn. Am. Pubs., Alpha Delta Sigma, Beta Gamma Sigma, Beta Alpha Psi, Econ. Club, Metro. Club, Pub.'s Lunch Club. E-mail: rhagel@sbcglobal.net.

HAGEL, WILLIAM CARL, metallurgical consultant; b. Pitts., Apr. 5, 1927; s. William and Mabel Florence (Geary) H.; m. Mary Ellen Roosa; children: Lisa Christine, Karen Andrea, Juliana Margaret. B in Metall. Engring., Cornell U., 1951; MS, PhD in Metallurgy, Carnegie-Mellon U., 1954. Metallurgist GE Co. Rsch. Lab., Schenectady, N.Y., 1954-66; prof., chmn. metallurgy dept. U. Denver, Colo., 1966-70; mgr. materials devel. GE Aircraft Engines, Evendale, Ohio, 1970-72; mgr. advanced materials Kelsey-Hayes R & D, Ann Arbor, Mich., 1972-73; mgr. R&D Climax Molybdenum Co., Ann Arbor, 1973—84; pres. Arbormet Ltd., Ann Arbor, 1984—. Disting. vis. prof. Minas Inst. Tech., Minas Gerais, Brazil, 1969. Co-editor: The Superalloys, 1972, Superalloys II, 1987; contbr. articles to profl. jours.; patentee in field. Chair adv. bd. Northside Cmty. Ch., Ann Arbor, 1993-94. With USN, 1945-46. Fellow Am. Soc. for Metals, Am. Inst. for Chemists; mem. Am. Inst. Mining and Metall. Engrs., Am. Ceramic Soc., Electrochem. Soc., N.Y. Acad. Sci., Sigma Xi, Phi Kappa Phi. Avocations: archaeology, numismatics. Home: 929 Greenhills Dr Ann Arbor MI 48105-2721 Office Phone: 734-668-8069. Business E-Mail: hagelite@umich.edu.

HAGELIN, JOHN SAMUEL, political organization administrator, theoretical physicist; b. Pitts., June 9, 1954; s. Carl William and Mary Lee (Stephenson) Hagelin; m. Margaret Hagelin (div.). AB in physics summa cum laude, Dartmouth Coll., 1975; MA in quantum physics, Harvard U., 1976, PhD in quantum physics, 1981. Sci. assoc. European Lab. for Particle Physics (CERN), Geneva, 1981-82; rsch. assoc. Stanford Linear Accelerator Ctr. (SLAC), Calif., 1982-83; assoc. prof. physics Maharishi U. Mgmt., Fairfield, Iowa, 1983-84, prof. physics, 1984—, dir. Inst. Sci., Tech. and Pub. Policy, 1992—; co-founder Enlightened Audio Designs Group, 1991—; minister of sci. & tech. Global Country of World Peace; founder, pres. US Peace Govt., 2003—. Natural Law Party candidate US Presdl. Election, 1992, 96, 2000. Author: Manual for a Perfect Government, 1998; contbr. numerous articles to sci. journals. Recipient Kilby Young Innovator Award, 1992; Tyndall Fellow, Harvard U., 1979. Mem. Iowa Acad. Sciences Office: Maharishi U Mgmt Inst Sci Tech & Pub Policy 1000 N 4th St Fairfield IA 52557 also: US Peace Govt 2000 Capital Blvd Fairfield IA 52556*

HAGELSTEIN, ROBERT PHILIP, publisher; b. NYC, Dec. 15, 1942; s. H. Robert and E. Ann (Buhrow) H.; m. Ann G. Linguvic, Apr. 26, 1970; children: Christopher R., Jonathan W. BA in English Lit., L.I. U., 1964. Prodn. mgr. Johnson Reprint Corp., N.Y.C., 1965-68, editor-in-chief, 1968-70; v.p. Greenwood Press, Inc., Westport, Conn., 1970-73; pres. Greenwood Pub. Group, 1973-99; pub. and electronic pub. cons., 1999—; pub. Reclamation Press, 2005—; exec. dir. Confrontation Press, 2004—. Bd. dirs. Aldwych Press, London. Author: New York to Boston: Travels in the 1840's, 2005; contbr. articles to profl. jours Mem.: U.S. Power Squadron, South Norwalk Boat Club, North Palm Beach Yacht Club.

HAGEMAN, RICHARD PHILIP, JR., educational administrator; b. Derby, Conn., Dec. 21, 1941; s. Richard Philip and Elizabeth (Serafinowicz) H.; m. Patricia Steele; children: Margaret Anne, Sheila Marie. BS, Cen. Conn. State U., 1964; MS, U. Bridgeport, 1968, profl. diploma, 1972. Cert. counselor Nat. Bd. Cert. Counselors; cert. tchr., Conn. Tchr. Stony Brook Sch. Stratford (Conn.) Bd. Edn., 1964—69, elem. sch. guidance counselor, 1969—81, secondary sch. guidance counselor, 1981—83; asst. prin. Stratford Acad., 1983—90; prin. Whitney Sch., 1990—95, Ctr. Sch., 1995—99; ret., 1999; univ. supr. Sacred Heart U., Fairfield, Conn. Lectr. edn. Fairfield U. Grad. Sch. Edn., 1971-93; head counselor Stratford Continuing Edn. Program, 1983-91, program facilitator, 1999—; chief examiner Gen. Ednl. Devel., 1986-91; assessor, trainer Beginning Educator Support and Tng. program Conn. State Dept. of Edn.; mem. adv. bd. counselor edn. Fairfield (Conn.) U., 1970-74; co-chmn. Stratford Juvenile Deliquency Prevention Team, 1979-81; pres. Stratford Elem. Prin. Assn., 1991-92; chief reader Conn. Adminstrs. Test, 1999—. Mem. Youth Adv. Bd. Stratford, 1981-85, chairperson, 1984-85; radio announcer Sta. WMNR, Monroe, Conn., 1982—. Mem. ACA, ASCD, NEA (life), Stratford Edn. Assn. (pres. 1978-79), New Eng. Assn. Specialists Group Work (pres. 1982-83, v.p. 1999-2003), Phi Delta Kappa. Roman Catholic. Democrat. Personal E-mail: hagemanrandp@msn.com.

HAGEMANN, ROBERT A., health facility administrator; Sr. fin. positions Ernst & Young, Crompton & Knowles, Inc., Prime Hospitality, Inc.; from mem. staff to v.p., CFO Quest Diagnostics, Teterboro, NJ, 1992—98, v.p., 1998—, CFO, 1998—. Office: Quest Diagnostics One Malcolm Ave Teterboro NJ 07608*

HAGEMOSER, TODD JON, sales executive; b. U.S. Naval Station, Argentina, Apr. 18, 1972; s. Daniel Jack and Andrea Josephine Hagemoser; m. Tracy Lea Willsie, Aug. 26, 2001; children: Chelsea Elizabeth, Tevin Jay, Colby Jordan. AA, New Eng. Tech, 1995. Assoc. Ocean State Job Lot, North

Kingstown, RI, 1990—93; programmer Response HCIA, East Greenwich, RI, 1994—97, Swarovski, Cranston, RI, 1997—99; sr. sales engr. Sane Solutions, North Kingstown, RI, 1999—. Founder RippingTheRack.

HAGEN, BARBARA C., music educator; b. Beaumont, Tex., June 3, 1952; d. Bobbie Carlyle and Doris Mae (Lindberg) Mabry; m. Keith Thomas Hagen, Dec. 21, 1973; children: Holly Hagen Buche, Heidi Noel. BS in Music Theory, Lamar U., 1974. Piano accompianist First Bapt. Ch. Youth Choir, Beaumont, Tex., 1972—73; viola player Symphony of S.E. Tex., 1972—74; viola player, music arranger various ch. activities, 1972—98, San Antonio, 1972—98; viola player profl. string quartet for weddings, Beaumont, 1990—98; tchr. piano & strings Hagen's Happy Notes, 1972—. Recipient Nat. award Gladys Robinson, Nat. Fedn. Music Clubs, 1995. Mem.: DAR, ASCAP, Tex. Music Tchrs. Assn., Music Tchrs.' Nat. Assn., Nat. Fedn. Music Clubs, Beaumont Music Tchrs. Assn. (pres. 1996—98), Kingwood/Humble Music Tchrs. Assn. (sec. 1999—2004), Delta Omicron, Delta Omega, Delta Delta Delta (music chmn. 1987—88). Avocations: composing music, piano, viola, drawing, reading. Home: 2331 Crimson Valley Ct Kingwood TX 77345-2101 E-mail: barbarachagen@yahoo.com.

HAGEN, DANIEL C., lawyer; b. Cleve., 1954; BA summa cum laude, Baldwin-Wallace Coll., 1977; JD, Univ. Va., Charlottesville, 1980. Bar: Ohio 1980. Ptnr., chair, employee benefits practice Jones Day, Cleve. Mem.: ABA, Midwest Pension and Benefits Conf., Order of Coif. Office: Jones Day North Point 901 Lakeside Ave Cleveland OH 44114-1190 Office Phone: 216-586-7159. Office Fax: 216-579-0212. Business E-Mail: dchagen@jonesday.com.

HAGEN, JOANNE R., elementary school educator; b. Sparta, Wis., Aug. 14, 1967; d. Maynard B. and Marie A. Hagen. BA, Coll. St. Scholastica, Duluth, Minn., 1989; MA, Viterbo U., LaCrosse, Wis., 2003. Tchr. presch., primary child care Wee Welcome Inn Child Ctr., Sussex, Wis., 1989—95; substitute tchr. Sparta (Wis.) Area Schs., 1995—97, tchr. title I, 1997—99, tchr. 5th grade, 1999—. Nominee Disney Tchr. of Yr.; recipient 3d pl. WebFair Competition award, U. Wis.-Stout, 2002. Mem.: Delta Kappa Gamma Alpha Upsilon (chpt. women educators). Avocations: reading, walking, crocheting, sports, computers. Home: PO Box 34 Sparta WI 54656 Office: Sparta Area Schs 506 N Black River St Sparta WI 54656 Business E-Mail: jhagen@spartan.org.

HAGEN, JOHN WILLIAM, psychology professor; b. Mpls., May 11, 1940; s. Wayne Sigvart and Elfie Marie (Erickson) H.; adopted children— Darus Gene, Lonny John, Frederick F. BA, U. Minn., 1962; PhD, Stanford U., 1965. Asst. prof. psychology U. Mich., Ann Arbor, 1965-69, assoc. prof., 1969-73, prof., 1973—, chmn. developmental program, 1971-83, dir. Ctr. Human Growth and Devel., 1982-93. Mem. Mich. Gov.'s Spl. Commn. on Age of Majority, 1970-71; dir. Reading and Learning Skills Ctr., 1985—1996; exec. officer Soc. for Rsch. in Child Devel., 1989—; adv. coun. Mich. Dept. Edn., 1972-74; chmn. Univ. Com. on Internat. Year of Child, 1979-80; rsch. rev. com. Nat. Inst. Child Health and Human Devel., 1980—. Co-author: Perspectives on the Development of Memory and Cognition, 1977; cons. editor Merrill Palmer Quar, 1968-80, Child Devel, 1972—; contbr. articles to profl. jours. Bd. dirs. Guild House Campus Ministry, Ann Arbor, 1972-83; bd. dirs. Humane Soc. Huron Valley, 1991-2000; profl. adv. bd. Nat. Assn. Learning Disabilities, 2001-. Recipient Standard Oil Found. award, 1967; USPHS trainee, 1963-65; Woodrow Wilson fellow, 1962-63; James Neubacher Award, 1997. Fellow Am. Psychol. Assn., Internat. Acad. for Rsch. in Learning Disabilities (exec. com. 2001-), Am. Psychol. Soc.; mem. Am. Edn. Rsch. Assn., Midwestern Psychol. Assn., Soc. Research in Child Devel. (chmn. program com. 1981-83), Internat. Soc. Study of Behavioral Devel., Phi Beta Kappa. Clubs: Univ. (Ann Arbor), Alumni (Ann Arbor). Unitarian Universalist. Home: 3421 Burbank Dr Ann Arbor MI 48105-1518 Office: Soc Rsch in Child Devel 3131 S State St #302 Ann Arbor MI 48108 Office Phone: 734-998-6578. E-mail: jwhagen@umich.edu.

HAGEN, LAWRENCE JACOB, agricultural engineer; b. Rugby, N.D., Mar. 6, 1940; s. Lars and Alice (Hannem) H. BS, N.D. State U., 1962, MS, 1967; PhD, Kans. State U., 1980. Agrl. engr. USDA, Manhattan, Kans., 1967—. Contbr. tech. articles to profl. publs. Capt. USAF, 1963-69. Mem. Am. Soc. Agrl. Engrs., Soil & Water Conservation Soc. Am. Office: 1515 College Ave Manhattan KS 66502 E-mail: hagen@weru.ksu.edu.

HAGEN, MICHAEL DALE, family physician educator; b. St. Louis, Nov. 11, 1949; s. Hubert Dale and Gwendel (Carden) Hagen; m. Barbara Carroll Keifer, Aug. 21, 1971; children: Laura Carrol, Sandra Ann. BS in Biology, Denison U., 1971; MD cum laude, U. Mo., Columbia, 1975. Cert. family practice bd. Pvt. practice Family Medicine Assocs., Aurora, Mo., 1978—81; asst. prof. dept. family practice U. Ky., Lexington, 1981—87, assoc. prof. dept. family practice, 1987—92, prof. dept. family practice, 1993—, interim chmn. dept. family practice, 1992—93, assoc. chmn. dept. family practice, 1993—97, project dir., computer-based assessment, 1996—; assoc. dir. assessment methods Am. Bd. Family Practice, 2003—. Fellow clin. decision making New Eng. Med. Ctr., Boston, 1987—89; at-large dir. Am. Bd. Family Practice, Lexington, 1991—96, pres., 1995—96; residency rev. com. family practice Accreditation Coun. for Grad. Med. Edn., Chgo., 1994—97. Author: Saunders Review Family Practice, 1992, 1997, 2002; contbr. articles to profl. jours. Mem.: AMA, Omicron Delta Kappa, Soc. for Med. Decision Making, Am. Acad. Family Physicians (clin. policies task force 1994—95), Phi Kappa Phi, Alpha Omega Alpha. Presbyterian. Avocations: amateur radio, gardening. Home: 2012 Blairmore Rd Lexington KY 40502-2435 Office: Assessment Techs Inc 2224 Young Dr Lexington KY 40505-4219 Office Phone: 859-268-8440. Business E-Mail: mhagen@assesstech.com. E-mail: hagenmd@prodigy.net.

HAGEN, NICHOLAS STEWARD, medical educator, consultant; b. Plentywood, Mont., Aug. 6, 1942; s. William Joseph and June Janette (Reuter) H.; m. Mary Louise Edvalson, July 26, 1969; children: Brian Geoffrey, Lisa Louise, Eric Christopher, Aaron Daniel, David Michael. BS in Chemistry, Ariz. State U., 1964; MBA in Internat. Bus., George Washington U., 1969; MD, U. Ariz., 1974. Lic. physician Ariz., Utah, Idaho.; diplomate Nat. Bd. Med. Examiners. Intern., resident Good Samaritan Hosp., Phoenix, 1974-75; pvt. practice Roy, Utah, 1975-77; dir. clin. rsch. Abbott Labs., North Chicago, Ill., 1977-84; v.p. med. affairs Rorer Group, Inc., Ft. Washington, Pa., 1984-88; clin. prof. Ariz. State U., Tempe, 1988-90. Pres. Southwestern Clin. Rsch., Tempe, 1987—, Travel Profl. Internat., Tempe, 1989-98; mem. Ariz. Bd. Med. Student Loans, 1998-2002. Author: Valproic Acid: A Review of Pharmacologic Properties and Clinical Use in Pharmacologic and Biochemical Properties of Drug Substances, 1979; contbr. articles to med. jours.; patentee in field. Bishop Ch. Jesus Christ of Latter-day Saints, Gurnee, Ill., 1981-84; various positions with local couns. Boy Scouts Am., 1988—; active Rep. campaigns, Mesa, Ariz., 1988—; 2d vice chmn. Maricopa County Rep. Assembly, 1997-99; dist. republican chmn., 1996-98; mem. governing bd. East Valley Inst. Tech., 1998-2003. Lt. comdr. USCG, 1965-69. Joan Mueller-Etter scholar Ariz. State U., 1960, Phelps-Dodge scholar Ariz. State U., 1961; NASA fellow Brigham Young U., 1964. Mem. Am. Coll. Sports Medicine, Eagle Forum, Nat. Right-to-Life Assn., Utah Hist. Soc., Nat. Geneal. Soc., Bucks County Geneal. Soc., Sons of Norway, Soc. Descendants Emigrants from Numedal, Hallingdal and Hedmark, Norway, Blue Key, Archons, Kappa Sigma (treas. Greater Phoenix alumni chpt. 1999—), Beta Beta Beta, Alpha Epsilon Delta, Phi Eta Sigma, Sophos. Republican. Mem. Lds Ch. Avocations: genealogy, swimming, stamp collecting/philately, medieval history, art collecting. Office: 9802 E Irwin Ave Mesa AZ 85209

HAGEN, PAUL BEO, pharmacologist; b. Sydney, Australia, Feb. 15, 1920; emigrated to Can., 1959, naturalized, 1965; s. Conrad and Mary (McFadzean) von H.; m. Jean Himms, Sept. 29, 1956; children— Anna, Nina. M.B., BS, U. Sydney, 1945. Intern, resident New South Wales Dept. Health, Sydney, 1945-48; lectr. physiology U. Sydney, 1948-50; sr. lectr. physiology U. Queensland, 1950-52; research fellow Oxford U., 1952-54; asst. prof. pharmacology Yale U., 1954-56, Harvard U., 1956-59; head biochemistry dept. U. Man., 1959-64, Queens U., 1964-67; dir. NRC, Ottawa, Ont., 1967-68; dean grad. studies U. Ottawa, 1968-83, chmn. pharmacology dept., 1983-86. Mem. med. bd. Muscular Dystrophy Assn. Can., 1961-87, chmn., 1976-87, nat. pres., 1980-83; vice chmn. Med. Research Council, 1967; trustee Can. Inst. Particle Physics, 1971-79 Mem. Editorial bd. Biochem. Pharmacology, 1961-66, Jour. Pharmacology and Exptl. Therapeutics, 1960-64, Can. Jour. Biochemistry, 1963-67; contbr. to books and periodicals on physiol., biochem. and pharm. subjects. Chmn. Ont. Bd. Libr. Coordination, 1971-73; trustee Ottawa Gen. Hosp., 1984-94. Recipient Lederle Faculty award Yale U., 1956, Centennial medal Govt. of Can., 1967; Jubilee medal, 1977; C.J. Martin fellow Oxford U., 1952; J.H. Brown fellow Yale U., 1954; Fulbright fellow, 1954 Fellow Chem. Inst. Can. (v.p., pres. biochem. div. 1962-64); mem. Brit. Pharm. Soc., Am. Soc. Pharmacology. Home: 507-420 MacKay St Ottawa ON K1M 2C4 Canada

HAGEN, THOMAS BAILEY, business owner, former state official, retired insurance company executive; b. Buffalo, Sept. 19, 1935; s. Walter B. and Isabella S. (Bailey) H.; m. Susan R. Hirt, May 31, 1958; children: Jonathan, Sarah. Student, Pa. State U., Erie, 1953—55; BS in Commerce, Ohio State U., 1957; DPubSvc (hon.), Edinboro U. Pa., 1996. With Erie (Pa.) Ins. Group, 1953-98, exec. v.p., 1976-82, pres., 1982-90, chmn., CEO, 1990-93, spl. asst. to chmn., 1993-95, also bd. dirs., 1979-98; sec. of commerce Commonwealth of Pa., 1995-96, sec. cmty. and econ. devel., 1996-97; chmn. bd. dirs. Custom Engrng. Co., 1997—; chmn. Team Pa. Found., 1997-2001; chmn., bd. dirs. Venango Machine Co., 1999—, Lamjen, Inc., 2000—, Custom Group Industries, Ltd., 2000—. Bd. dirs. Pa. Housing Fin. Agy., Bliley Techs., Inc., GPU, Inc., 1988-2001, Case Mgmt. Support Svcs., Inc., Erie; chmn. Pa. Indsl. Devel. Authority, 1995-97, Pa. Econ. Devel. Fin. Authority, 1995-97, Pa. Ben Franklin/IRC Partnership, 1995-97. Bd. dirs. Erie Philharmonic, 1962-75, pres., 1970-71; bd. dirs. Erie Coun. Navy League U.S., 1977-86; pres. Erie Tomorrow Corp., 1979-86; vice-chmn., bd. dirs. Bayfront East Side Taskforce, Erie, 1978-96; bd. dirs. Erie Conf. on Cmty. Devel., 1985-93, hon. dir., 1993-2003; bd. dirs. Pa. Chamber Bus. and Industry, Harrisburg, 1986-95, 99—, Pa. Econ. Devel. Partnership, 1987-94, Pa. for Effective Govt., 1987-95. Capt. USNR ret. Alumni fellow Pa. State U., 1988; recipient Ins. Mentor award U. Ala., 1976, Golden Baton award Erie Philharmonic, 1974, Disting. Pennsylvanian award Gannon U., 1987, Phila. C. of C., 1980, Outstanding Community Service award Multiple Sclerosis Soc., 1980, Alumni Citizenship award Ohio State U., 1981, Man of the Yr. award Erie and Chautauqua Mag., 1986, Preservationist of Yr. award (now Otto Haas award) Pa. Hist. and Mus. Commn., 1987, Honor award Pa. Soc. Architects, 1993. Mem. Internat. Ins. Soc. (bd. dirs. 1978-92, hon. counselor award 1982), Ins. Fedn. Pa. (bd. dirs. 1970-91, chmn. 1984-86), Ins. Inst. Am. (inst. for property and liability underwriters, trustee 1987-93), Griffith Found. (v.p. 1985-92, trustee 1985-95, trustee emeritus 1995—), The Pa. Soc. (pres. 1995-97, bd. dirs. 1990—). Office: 100 State St Ste 440 Erie PA 16507-1456 Office Phone: 814-459-7405.

HAGEN, YVONNE BORN FORREST, writer; b. Ile Aux Moines, Morbihan, France, Aug. 14, 1920; came to U.S., 1929; d. Wilbur Studley and Floss May (Springer) Forrest; m. Karl-Victor Hagen, Sept. 15, 1940 (dec. July 1948); children: Nina, Karen, Anthony; m. N.H. Stubbing, May 10, 1983 (dec. Oct. 1983). Student, Fontainbleau Sch. of Fine Arts, Columbia U., 1940-41. Interviewer Am. Mag. Art, NY, 1946-48; art reviewer European edit. N.Y. Herald Tribune, 1954-61; art critic Art Aujourdhui, monthly mag., 1957, 58, 59; dir. Modern Art Munich, 1967-71. Advisor to numerous galleries in Europe and Calif.; dir. New Art Liaison. Author: (autobiography) From Life to Art and Back, 2005, also monographs; contbr. forewords and articles to art mags.; editor catalogs on modern art. Mem. Lindisfarne (assoc.). Democrat. Avocations: enjoy seeing chinese art, travel, chamber music. Home: PO Box 104 329 Sagaponack Rd Sagaponack NY 11962 E-mail: yhagen@btv.net.

HAGENBECK, FRANKLIN LEE, career military officer; b. Rabat, Morocco, Nov. 25, 1949; m. Judy Vaughn; children: Kelly, Leeann. BS, U.S. Mil. Acad., 1971; MS, Fla. State U., 1978; MBA, L.I. U., 1979. Advanced through grades to lt. gen., 2003; brigade comdr. 3rd Tng. Brigade, Ft. Leonard Wood, Mo., 1993—95; chief of staff 10th Mountain Divsn., Ft. Drum, 1995—97; dir., officer pers. mgmt. directorate U.S. Army, Washington, 1997—98; asst. divsn. comdr. ops. 101st Airborne Divsn., Ft. Campbell, Ky., 1998—99; dep. dir, global/multilateral issue/internat. American affs., J-5 Joint Staff, Washington, 1999—2000, dep. dir. ops., J33, 2000—01; commanding gen. 10th Mountain Divsn., Ft. Drum, NY, 2001—03; commdg. gen., coalition task force-mountain Operation Anaconda, Afghanistan, 2001—02; dep. chief of staff for personnel US Army, Washington, 2003—. Decorated Legion of Merit with 3 oak leaf clusters, Bronze Star, numerous others. Mem.: Assn. of U.S. Army, Am. Legion. Office: US Army 300 Army Pentagon Washington DC 20310

HAGENBUCH, JOHN JACOB, investor; b. Park Forest, Ill., May 31, 1951; s. David Brown and Jean Iline (Reeves) H.; m. Kimberly A. Steel, Aug. 20, 2000; children: Henry, Hunter, Hilary, Sydney, John. AB magna cum laude, Princeton U., 1974; MBA, Stanford U., 1978. Assoc. Salomon Bros., N.Y.C., 1978-80, v.p. San Francisco, 1980-85; gen. ptnr. Hellman & Friedman, 1985-93; chmn. M&H Realty Ptnrs., L.P., 1993—. Mem. Burlingame Country Club, Pacific-Union Club, Calif. Tennis Club, Villa Taverna Club, Bohemian Club, Valley Club. Office: M&H Realty Ptnrs 353 Sacramento St Fl 21 San Francisco CA 94111-3620

HAGENBUCH, RODNEY DALE, financial consultant; b. Saxville, Wis. s. Herbert Jenkin and Minnie Leona (Hayward) Hagenbuch; children: Kris, Beth, Patricia; m. LaVerne Julia Scoonover, Sept. 1, 1956. BS, Mich. State U., 1980. Cert. fin. mgr. Designer Olds div. Gen. Motors, Lansing, Mich., 1960-66; institutional account exec. Merrill Lynch, Lansing, 1966-75, institutional mgr., 1975-80, sales mgr. Columbus, Ohio, 1980-82, sr. resident v.p. Tacoma, 1982-93, L.A., 1993-98; ret., 1998; prin. Quantum Group, 1999—; portfolio analyst Affinity Investment Advisors, 2001. Prin. Securities Expert Witness Network, 1999, Quantum Leap Inst., 1999, Quantum Leap Securities, 2001; mem. adv. bd. U. Wash. Sch. Bus., Tacoma, 1998—2002; bd. dirs. Employers Group. Author (with Richard J. Capalbo): Investment Survival: How to Use Investment Research to Create Winning Portfolios, 2002; author: Becoming a Life Advisor (The Ultimate Customer Service Model), 2005. Mem. adv. bd. Charles Wright, 1989—93; mem. econ. devel. bd. City of Tacoma, 1986—93, chmn., 1987—88; pres. Downtown Tacoma Assn., 1986; chmn. Corp. Coun. for the Arts, 1986, L.A. United Way, 1993—2000; pres. Tacoma Symphony, 1988; chmn. human resource commn. Meridian Twp., 1972—74; mem. Meridian Planning Commn., Mich., 1964—70, Meridian Police and Fire Commn., Mich., 1964—70; pres. adv. bd. U. Wash., Tacoma, chmn., 1992; mem. State Wash. Arts Stblzn. Bd.; sec. bd. dirs. Tacoma Art Mus., 1992; legis. chmn. N.W. Securities Industry Assn.; campaign chmn. Pierce County United Way, 1991—92; non-resident dir. Tacoma Art Mus., 1994—2003, Tacoma Urban League, 1983—93; exec. com. fraternity of friends L.A. Music Ctr.; hon. mem. bd. govs. Streetlights L.A., 1998—; vice chair Ingham County Housing Commn., 1978—80; bd. dirs. L.A. Acad. Fin., 1993—98, L.A. United Cerebral Palsy, 1994—; bd. dirs., chmn. L.A. Red Cross, 2002—05; bd. dirs. Forward Wash., New L.A. Mktg. Plan, 1995—97; bd. dirs., mem. dist. 2 com. NASD, 1996—99; bd. govs. L.A. Children's Hosp. Rsch. Inst., 1994—99, mem. fin. com., 1999—2003; bd. govs. L.A. Town Hall, 1996, mem. fin. com., 1999—; bd. govs. L.A. Employers Group. Recipient Outstanding Citizen award Mcpl. League Pierce County, 1988; named Nat. Vol. of Yr., Urban League Western Divsn., 1987. Mem.: Tacoma C. of C., Calif. Club, Tacoma Club (bd. dirs. 1984—93, pres. 1993). Avocations: running, skiing. Home: 16826 Monte Hermoso Dr Pacific Palisades CA 90272-1910 Office Phone: 213-683-4560. Personal E-mail: rdhagen@earthlink.net.

HAGENDORN, WILLIAM HULL, lawyer; b. Bklyn., Sept. 1, 1925; s. William V. and Florence (Hull) H.; m. Patricia Yarvote, Apr. 6, 1974; children: Katherine Florence, Patricia Ann. AB, Princeton U., 1944; JD, Harvard U., 1949; LLM, NYU, 1952. Bar: N.Y. 1949. Practiced in, N.Y.C., 1949—; assoc. firm Debevoise, Plimpton & McLean, N.Y.C., 1953-61, Carter, Ledyard & Milburn, N.Y.C., 1961-65; gen. counsel Am. Express Co., 1965-72, Wells Fargo & Co., 1965-68, Equitable Securities, Morton & Co., N.Y.C., 1966-72; sr. atty. Shearman & Sterling, N.Y.C., 1973-91; ptnr. Burlingham Underwood, N.Y.C., 1991—2002; pvt. practice Bronxville, NY, 2002—. Adviser to com. uniform consumer credit code Nat. Conf. Uniform State Laws, 1966-68; adj. prof. Rutgers Law Sch., Newark, 1991, 93; arbitrator NY Stock Exch., NASD, 1991—. Served with inf. AUS, 1944-46. Mem.: Assn. Bar City NY, NY State Bar Assn. (exec. com. internat. law sect. 1990—, chmn. com. admiralty law, 1990-93 1998—2000, com. banking law 2003—), Univ. Club (NYC). Home and Office: 25 Parkview Ave Apt 3A Bronxville NY 10708-2936 Office Phone: 914-337-5861. E-mail: whagendorn@aol.com.

HAGENLOCKER, EDWARD E., retired automobile company executive; b. 1939; married. BS, MS, Ohio State U., 1962, PhD, 1964; MBA, Mich. State U., 1982. With Ford Motor Co., 1964-98, chief engr., 1973—77, gen. mgr., 1978—80, dir., v.p. ops., 1984-85, dir., pres., 1985-86, v.p., gen. mgr. truck ops. Dearborn, Mich., 1986-92, exec. v.p. N.Am. automative ops., 1992-94, pres. Ford automotive ops., 1994-96, vice chmn., 1996-98. Home: 3707 W Maple Rd Ste 203 Bloomfield Hills MI 48301-3212

HAGENMAN, TERRY G., secondary school educator, music educator; b. Thompson Falls, Mont., Feb. 27, 1951; s. Orval Thomas and Yvonne Marjorie Hagerman; m. Charlotte Lynn Ziegler, Dec. 28, 1999; children: Janaee, Natasha, Katherine, Jaylynn, Jayce, Jealynn. BS in Edn., Western Mont. Coll., 1973. Dir. choir Irving Jr. High Sch., Pocatello, Idaho, 1973—77; pipe fitter Union Pacific Railroad, 1977—82; dir. chorus Hawthrone Jr. High Sch., 1982—87, Highland High Sch., 1987—. Min. music 1st Bapt. Ch., Pocatello, 1977—87; dir. choir United Meth. Ch., 2000—03, Presbyn. Ch., 2004—. Democrat. Baptist. Avocations: restoring old cars, photography.

HAGENSTEIN, WILLIAM DAVID, forester, consultant; b. Seattle, Mar. 8, 1915; s. Charles William and Janet (Finigan) H.; m. Ruth Helen Johnson, Sept. 2, 1940 (dec. 1979); m. Jean Kraemer Edson, June 16, 1980 (dec. 2000). BS in Forestry, U. Wash., 1938; MForestry, Duke, 1941. Registered profl. engr., Wash., Oreg. Field aid in entomology U.S. Dept. Agr., Hat Creek, Calif., 1938; logging supt. and engr. Eagle Logging Co., Sedro-Woolley, Wash., 1939; tech. foreman U.S. Forest Svc., North Bend, Wash., 1940; forester West Coast Lumbermen's Assn., Seattle and Portland, Oreg., 1941-43, 45-49; sr. forester FEA, South and Central Pacific Theaters of War and Costa Rica, 1943-45; mgr. Indsl. Forestry Assn., Portland, 1949-80, exec. v.p., 1956-80, hon. dir., 1980-87; pres. W.D. Hagenstein and Assocs., Inc., Portland, 1980—. H.R. MacMillan lectr. forestry U. B.C., 1952, 77; Benson Meml. lectr. U. Mo., 1966; S.J. Hall lectr. indsl. forestry U. Calif. at Berkeley, 1973; cons. forest engr. USN, Philippines, 1952, Coop. Housing Found., Belize, 1986; mem. U.S. Forest Products Trade Mission, Japan, 1968; del. VII World Forestry Congress, Argentina, 1972, VIII Congress, Indonesia, 1978; mem. U.S. Forestry Study Team, West Germany, 1974; mem. sec. Interior's Oreg. and Calif. Multiple Use Adv. Bd., 1975-76; trustee Wash. State Forestry Conf., 1948-92, Keep Oreg. Green Assn., 1957—, v.p., 1970-71, pres., 1972-73; adv. trustee Keep Wash. Green Assn., 1957-95; co-founder World Forestry Ctr., dir., 1965-89, v.p., 1965-79, hon. dir. for life, 1990. Author: (with Wackerman and Michell) Harvesting Timber Crops, 1966; Assoc. editor: Jour. Forestry, 1946-53; columnist Wood Rev., 1978-82; contbr. numerous articles to profl. jours. Trustee Oreg. Mus. Sci. and Industry, 1968-73. Served with USNR, 1933-37. Recipient Hon. Alumnus award U. Wash. Foresters Alumni Assn., 1965, Dist. Svc. award, 2003, Forest Mgmt. award Nat. Forest Products Assn., 1968, Western Forestry award Western Forestry and Conservation Assn., 1972, 79, Gifford Pinchot medal for 50 yrs. Outstanding Svc., Soc. Am. Foresters, 1987, Charles W. Ralston award Duke Sch. Forestry, 1988, Lifetime Achievement award Oreg. Soc. Am. Foresters, 1995, Centennial Resource Steward award, U.S. Forest Svc., 2005; Honored as only surviving co-founder World Forestry Ctr., 2000, Centennial Resource Stewardshi award, US Forest Svc., 2005. Fellow Soc. Am. Foresters (mem. coun. 1958-63, pres. 1966-69, Golden Membership award 1989); mem. Am. Forestry Assn. (life, hon. v.p. 1966-69, 74-92, William B. Greeley Forestry award 1990), Commonwealth Forestry Assn. (life), Internat. Soc. Tropical Foresters, Portland C. of C. (forestry com. 1949-79, chmn. 1960-62), Nat. Forest Products Assn. (forestry adv. com. 1949-80, chmn. 1972-74, 78-80), West Coast Lumbermen's Assn. (v.p. 1969-79), Forest History Soc. (bd. dirs. 2001-04), David Douglas Soc. Western N. Am., Lang Syne Soc., Hoo Hoo Club, Xi Sigma Pi (outstanding alumnus Alpha chpt. 1973). Republican. Home: 3062 SW Fairmount Blvd Portland OR 97239-1439 Office: 921 SW Washington St Ste 803 Portland OR 97205-2826 Office Phone: 503-223-2012.

HAGER, ANTHONY WOOD, mathematics professor; b. Marshfield, Wis., Dec. 16, 1939; s. Cyril Francis and Margaret Ruth (Wood) H.; 1 child, Amanda D. BS, Pa. State U., 1960, PhD, 1965. Rsch. scientist Leeds & Northrup Co., N. Wales, Pa., 1960-61; instr. U. Rochester, N.Y., 1965-67, asst. prof., 1967-68, Wesleyan U., Middletown, Conn., 1968-69, assoc. prof., 1969-75, prof., 1975—, chmn. dept. math., 1976-77, 88-90, 93, 95-96. Contbr. articles to profl. jours. NAS vis. rschr., Prague, 1973, 75; Italian N.C.R. vis. rschr. Padua, 1978; U. Fla. vis. rschr., Gainesville, 1995. Mem. Am. Math. Soc. Office: Wesleyan U Math Dept Middletown CT 06459-0001 E-mail: ahager@wesleyan.edu.

HAGER, ELIZABETH SEARS, state legislator, social services administrator; b. Washington, Oct. 31, 1944; d. Hess Thatcher and Elizabeth Grace (Harper) Sears; m. Dennis Sterling Hager, Sept. 3, 1966; children: Annie Elizabeth, Lucie Caroline. BA, Wellesley Coll., 1966; MPA, U. N.H., 1979. Prin. Philbrook Ctr., Concord, N.H., 1970-71; rep. N.H. Gen. Ct., Concord, 1973-76, 85-94, 1996—; del. N.H. Constitutional Conv., Concord, 1974, 84; campaign coord. Anderson for Pres. Rep. Primary, N.H., 1980; mem. Concord City Coun., 1982-90; mayor City of Concord, 1988-90; exec. dir. United Way of Merrimack County, Concord, 1996—. Bd. dirs. Jefferson Pilot Funds, Concord, Bank of NH. Pres. Greater Concord United Way, 1980-81; campaign chair United Way of Merrimack County, Concord, 1986. Republican. Episcopalian. Office: 46 N Main St Concord NH 03301-4913 Home: 5 Pleasant View Ave Concord NH 03301-2555

HAGER, GEORGE V., health services executive; BA in Econs., Dickinson Coll., 1978; MBA, Rutgers U. CPA. Ptnr. in charge of health care practice KPMG Peat Marwick LLP, Phila., 1979-92; v.p., CFO Genesis Health Ventures, Inc., Kennett Square, Pa., 1992-94, sr. v.p., CFO, 1994-99, exec. v.p., CFO, 1999, now chmn, CEO. Recipient Cain Bros. award Cain Bros. & Modern Healthcare Mag., 1996. Mem. AICPA, PICPA. Office: Genesis Health Ventures Inc 101 E State St Kennett Square PA 19348*

HAGER, JOHN HENRY, federal official, former lieutenant governor; b. Durham, N.C., Aug. 28, 1936; m. Margaret Dickinson Chase, Feb. 27, 1971; children: John Virgil, Henry Chase. BSME, Purdue U., 1958; MBA, Harvard U., 1960; hon. degree, Averett Coll., 1999, Mary Washington Coll., 1999, U. No. Va., 1999. Various positions Am. Tobacco Co., 1961—74; lt. gov. and pres. State Senate State of Va., Richmond, 1998—2002, asst. to the gov. for Commonwealth preparedness, 2002—04; asst. sec. spl. edn. and rehabilitation svc. US Dept. Edn., Washington, 2004—. Chmn. of Disability Commn.; co-chmn. com. on Ednl. Infrastructure; chmn. Faith Based Cmty. Svcs. Task Force; vice-chmn. Gov.'s Commn. on Transp. Policy; bd. dirs., vice-chair Aerospace State Assn.; trustee, v.p. Jamestown Yorktown Found.; chmn. Greater Richmond Conv. Ctr. Expansion; dir., pres. Sorensen Inst. Polit. Leadership; dir. Ctr. for Politics, U. R.I., Jamestown 2002; past dir. Partnership for Urban Va., past dir. Va. State C of C; trustee, exec. com., fin. com. Va. Mus. Fine Arts; 1st v.p., dir. Va. Pub. Safety Found., Inc.; past pres., trustee, exec. com. Children's Hosp.; Met. Richmond Conv. and Vis. Bur. (past chmn., dir., founding dir.); Va. Health Care Found. (past chmn., dir., exec. com.); 7th Dist. Rep. Party (past vice chmn. 3rd district, exec. com. mem. past precinct, ward and campaign chmn.); Rep. Party of Va. and del./alt. to 4 natl. convs. (past treas., past exec. com. mem., state central com. mem., numerous others); ruling elder 1st Presbyn. Ch., Richmond; mem. drug task force Va. State Crime Commn. 2nd lt. U.S. Army, 1960-61, capt. USAR. 2nd lt. U.S.

Army. Named one of Outstanding Young Men of Am., 1976, Man of Yr., Tobacco Internat. Mag., 1990; recipient Alumni Citizenship award Purdue U., 1987, Svc. award Richmond Rep. Com., 1992, Disting. Alumni award Durham Acad., 1992, Good Govt. award Richmond First Club, 1996, Tourism Leadership award Met. Richmond Convention and Visitors Bur., 1997, Lettie Pate Whitehead Evans award Westminster-Canterbury, 1997, Citizenship award Va. Coun. Indians, 1998. Mem. Am. Legion, Va. C. of C. (dir.), Nat. Assn. Lt. Govs. (mem. exec. com., So. sector chmn.), So. Growth Policies Bd., Adv. Bd. Tobacco History Corp., Jamestown, Richmond Rep. Party Com., Richmond German, Richmond Hundred (past pres., dir.), City of Richmond Electoral Bd. (past chmn.) Pub. Affairs Group (past chmn.), Forum Club (past pres.), Commonwealth Club (past dir.), Custis Fishing and Hunting Club (past dir.), Country Club Va. (past pres. and CEO, past dir.). Republican. Office: Office of Special Edn and Rehab Serv US Dept Edn 550 12th St SW Rm 5107 Washington DC 20065 Office Phone: 202-245-7276. E-mail: john.hager@ed.gov.*

HAGER, MARY HASTINGS, nutritionist, educator, consultant; b. Upland, Calif., Mar. 27, 1948; d. Howard Benjamin and Miriam Agnes Hastings; m. Douglas Francis Hager, Jan. 4, 1982; children: Marghet Janet, Bettina Miriam. BS in Foods and Nutrition, U. Del., 1971; MS in Nutrition and Dietetics, U. Calif., Davis, 1973, PhD in Nutrition, 1978. Registered dietitian. Nutritionist U. Calif. Sch. Medicine, Davis, 1973-74; staff scientist Procter and Gamble Co., Cin., 1978-83, devel. staff, 1986-87; asst. prof. Coll. Mount St. Joseph, Cin., 1983-85, Tex. Christian U., Ft. Worth, 1987-89; vis. lectr. Rutgers U., New Brunswick, N.J., 1989-90; assoc. prof. Coll. of St. Elizabeth, Morristown, N.J., 1991-96, prof., assoc. dean, 1996-2000; scientist Entelos, Inc., Menlo Park, Calif., 2000—03; dir. Hope House, Diver, NJ, 2003; sr. mgr. for regulatory affairs Am. Dietetic Assn., 2004—. Cons. IGA Grocers, Cin., 1984-85, Hoffman-LaRoche Corp., Nutley, N.J., 1989-90, Procter and Gamble Co., Cin., 1990—; dietetic internship site visitor. Contbr. articles and abstracts to profl. publs. Chmn. bd. dirs. Greater Cin. Nutrition Coun., 1985-86; mem. edn. task force Am. Heart Assn., Ft. Worth, 1988-89; pub. edn. com. Am. Cancer Soc., Ft. Worth, 1988-89; mem. Health Care Reform Adv. Bd., 11th Congl. Dist., 1993-94. Grad. fellow Procter and Gamble Co., 1975-78; Amy Rextrew scholar U. Del., 1970; grantee Tex. Christian U. Rsch. Fund, 1988. Fellow Am. Dietetic Assn; mem. Am. Inst. Nutrition (rsch. award 1978), Am. Soc. Enteral Parenteral Nutrition Soc. for Nutrition Edn., N.J. Dietetic Assn. (pres.-elect 1996-97, pres. 1997-98, ho. dels. 1998—), Mortar Bd., Sigma Xi. Democrat. Episcopalian. Avocations: swimming, walking. Home: 12 Kings Ridge Rd Randolph NJ 07869-2743 Office: American Dietetic Assn Ste 480 1120 Connecticut Ave NW Washington DC 20036 Office Phone: 202-775-8277 ext. 13. E-mail: mhager@eatright.org.

HAGER, MICHAEL W., museum director; m. Denise LeAnn Rikansrud; children: Amy, Brian. BA in Biology, Grinnell Coll.; PhD in Geology, U. Wyo. Asst. prof. geology Augustana Coll., 1973-78; dir. Mus. of the Rockies, Mont., 1978-89, Va. Mus. Natural History, Va., 1989-91; exec. dir. San Diego Natural History Mus., Calif., 1991—. Mus. cons. Exec. prodr. film Baja California, 2000. Bd. dirs. Elem. Inst. Sci., Immigration Mus. New Americans. Mem. Assn. Sci. Mus. Dirs. (past pres.). Office: San Diego Natural History Mus PO Box 121390 San Diego CA 92112-1390 Office Phone: 619-232-0248, 619-255-0216. Business E-Mail: mhager@sdnhm.org.

HAGER, ROBERT WORTH, retired aerospace transportation executive; b. Longview, Wash., June 20, 1928; s. Josiah Denver and Merle (Worth) H.; m. Margaret Goodnough, Aug. 25, 1950; children: Stephen M., Sandra Hager Dahl, Shane D. BS in Civil Engring, U. Wash., 1949, MS in Civil Engring, 1950; DSc (hon.), U. Ala., 1995. Rsch. fellow U. Wash., 1949-50; rsch. engr. U.S. Navy Civil Engring. Lab., Port Hueneme, Calif., 1950-53; mem. staff Sandia Corp., Albuquerque, 1953-55; with Boeing Co., Seattle, 1955-93, Minuteman program mgr., 1973-78, v.p., gen. mgr. ballistic missile and space div., 1978-80, v.p. engring., 1980-84, v.p. space sta. Huntsville, Ala., 1984-89, v.p., gen. mgr. Huntsville div. Boeing Aerospace and Electronics, 1989-91, v.p., gen. mgr. Missiles and Space Div. Boeing Def. and Space Group, 1991-93. Past chmn. bd. Univ. Space Rsch. Assn.; past chmn. Bus. Coun. Ala.; mem. Lower Hood Canal Watershed Com.; sec. United Meth. Found. of the N.W.; bd. dir. Hood Canal Salmon Enhancement Group; treas. Pacific N.W. Salmon Ctr. Fellow AIAA, Am. Astron. Soc. Methodist. Home: 51 E Sunset Beach Dr Belfair WA 98528-9534

HAGER, SUSAN KULKA, public relations executive; b. Washington, Oct. 19, 1944; d. Joseph A. and Mary Margaret (Berry) Kulka; m. C. Eric Hager, Nov. 3, 1967; 1 child, Elizabeth Hager Finley. BA in Sociology, Brescia U., 1966. VISTA vol., vol. leader Office Econ. Opportunity, White Mountain, Alaska, 1966—67; VISA and Peace Corps recruiter, cons. Gale Assocs., Washington, 1968; program asst. Office Econ. Opportunity, Washington, 1969—70, program analyst, 1970—71; program dir. Nat. Ctr. for Voluntary Action, Washington, 1971—73; chair, CEO Hager Sharp, Inc., Washington, 1973—. Founder, first pres. Nat. Assn. Women Bus. Owners, Washington, 1974; chmn. U.S. Dept. Trustees Small Bus. Adv. Coun., Washington, 1980—82; pres. Nat. Small Bus. United, Washington, 1992; vis. prof., mentor Brescia U. Editor: (monthly column) Washington Bus. Jour., 1995—97. Bd. dirs. Greater Washington Bd. Trade, Washington, 1990—, Lab Sch. Washington, 1991—95, pres. bd. dirs., 1996—. Named Bus. Woman of the Yr., Nat. Assn. Women Bus. Owners, Washington, 1985, Small Bus. of the Yr., D.C. C. of C., Washington, 1995, Bus. Woman of the Yr., United Cerebral Palsy, Washington, 1998; named one of 25 Heroines and Heroes Whose Actions Over the Last Quarter Century Have Given Women in the Workplace a Better Shot, Working Women mag., 2001. Mem.: Leadership Washington (bd. mem. 1987—), Cosmos Club. Office: Hager Sharp Inc 1090 Vermont Ave NW Washington DC 20005

HAGERMAN, DOUGLAS M., lawyer; b. Dec. 1960; m. Jane Elizabeth Tadych. BA, Drake U., Des Moines, Iowa; JD cum laude, Harvard U. CPA; bar: 1986. Atty. Foley & Lardner LLP, Milw., 1986—95, ptnr., 1995—98, Chgo., 1998—2004; sr. v.p., gen. counsel, sec. Rockwell Automation Inc., Milw., 2004—. Office: Rockwell Automation Inc 777 E Wis Ave Ste 1400 Milwaukee WI 53202

HAGERMAN, JOHN DAVID, lawyer, investment advisor; b. Houston, Aug. 1, 1941; s. David Angle and Noima L. (Clay) H.; m. Linda J. Lambright, June 25, 1975; children: Clayton Robert, Holly Elizabeth. BBA, So. Meth. U., 1963; JD, U. Tex., Austin, 1966. Bar: Tex. 1966, U.S. Ct. Appeals (5th cir.) 1967, U.S. Supreme Ct. 1969; cert. civil trial law, 1980-95; real estate broker Tex. Pres., owner Hagerman & Sereau, Inc., The Woodlands, Tex., 1966—. Condr. bank creditor rights seminars; mem. adv. bd. Amegy Bank. Contbr. articles to profl. jours. Res. dep. sheriff Montgomery County, Tex.; former bd. dirs. 100 club of Montgomery County Fair Assn., 1978—, Montgomery County Hosp. Dist. Found., Seven Coves Homeowners Assn. Mem.: ABA, Houston Philosophy Soc., Comml. Real Estate Assn. Montgomery County, Tex. Assn. Bank Counsel, Tex. Assn. Civil Trial Specialists, Houston Outdoor Advt. Assn., Houston Bar Assn., Tex. Bar Assn., River Oaks Country Club, Briar Club, Woodlands Country Club, Petroleum Club (Houston), Woodlands Rotary Club, Beta Theta Pi. Republican. Avocations: golf, tennis, jogging, shooting. Office: Hagerman & Seureau Inc 24800 I-45 Ste 100 The Woodlands TX 77386-1987 Office Phone: 281-367-8800.

HAGERMAN, KRISTOF, information technology executive; B in Russian and Econ., Dartmouth Coll.; MA in Internat. Rels., Cambridge U.; MBA, Stanford U. Formerly held cons., sales, mktg., bus. devel., and fin. positions Silicon Graphics, Odyssey, Rsch., McKinsey & Co., and others; founder, CEO BigBook Inc., 1995—98, Affinia, 1998—2000; v.p. strategic alliances VERITAS Software Corp., Mountain View, Calif., 2001, v.p. strategic ops., 2001—03, exec. v.p. strategic ops., 2003—. Office: VERITAS Software Corp 350 Ellis St Mountain View CA 94043

HAGERTY, PATRICK K., publishing executive; BA in Fin., U. Ill., 1982. Joined sales staff New Equipment Digest, 1982, Barron's Mag., 1985; sales rep. US News & Report, 1988—89, br. mgr., 1989—94, regional dir., 1994—96, advt. dir., 1996—98, pub., 1998—99; v.p. partnerships Tallan, Inc., 1999—2001; sr. v.p. advt. sales Primedia, Inc., 2001—02; assoc. pub., dir. U.S. sales Newsweek, 2002—03, U.S. pub. N.Y.C., 2003—. Office: Newsweek Mag 251 W 57th St New York NY 10019

HAGERTY, ROBERT E., academic administrator; b. Detroit, Mar. 16, 1937; s. Arthur E. and Paula (Buntrock) H.; m. Barbara Ann Anderson, Aug. 16, 1959; children: Scott Robertson, Mark David. AB, Western Mich. U., 1959; MA, Wayne State U., 1961, EdD, 1971. Tchr. Hazel Park (Mich.) Cmty. Schs., 1959-68, bldg. adminstr., 1968-74, dir. spl. edn., 1974-79, dir. evaluation and pupil svcs., 1979-83; supt. Kokomo (Ind.) N.W. Sch. Corp., 1983-85, Ionia (Mich.) Pub. Schs., 1985-93; head, dept. of ednl. leadership Grand Valley State U., Grand Rapids, Mich., 1993—2003, dean, sch. of edn., 1999—2003; pres. William Tyndale Coll., Farmington Hills, Mich., 2004—. Author: Making Special Education Work, 1978, The Crisis of Confidence in American Education, 1994. Bd. dirs. Royal Oak (Mich.) YMCA, 1976-83, Met. YMCA, Ionia, 1989-93, Boys and Girls Clubs of Oakland, Hazel Park, 1974-83; chair High Hopes Com., Ionia, 1985-87; exec. bd. Hazel Park Youth Protection Com., 1959-83, Hazel Park Youth Aid Found., 1961-83. Recipient Disting. Svc. award Bd. Edn. Ionia, 1993, Disting. Award of Honor, Outstanding Man of Yr., Hazel Park Jaycees, 1970. Mem. Mich. Assn. Profs. of Edn. (past pres., Disting. Leadership award 1993), Am. Assn. Sch. Adminstrs. (Supt. of the Yr. 1989, 90), Nat. Sch. Pub. Rels. Assn. (Award of Honor 1987, Disting. Achievement award 1989), Ionia C. of C. (bd. dirs. 1985-93, exec. bd. 1987-92). Home: 6530 Balsam Dr # D Hudsonville MI 49426-9267 Office: William Tyndale Coll 35700 W Twelve Mile Rd Farmington Hills MI 48331

HAGEWOOD, MARK FREDERICK, music educator, director; s. Ray Harville and Susan Stenberg Hagewood; m. Rachel Claire Britt, Dec. 27, 2003. Ma in Ch. Music, Belmont U., 2003; B in Ch. Music, Martin Meth. Coll., 2000. Dir. student activities Martin Meth. Coll., Pulaski, Tenn., 2003—, asst. dir. choral programs, 2003—. Asst. dir. music First United Meth. Ch., Pulaski, 2004—. Page Southeastern Jurisdictional Conf. of United Meth. Ch., Lake Junaluska, NC, 2004. Mem.: Am. Choral Dirs. Assn. Methodist. Avocation: theater. Office: Martin Meth Coll 433 W Madison St Pulaski TN 38478 Office Phone: 931-424-7354.

HAGGAR, J. M., III, retail executive; s. Isabell Salloum and J.M. Haggar. With Haggar Corp., Dallas, 1969—, dir., 1983—, CEO, 1990—, pres., 1990—94, chmn. bd., 1994—. Office: 11511 Luna RD Dallas TX 75234-6022*

HAGGARD, EDWARD (NED) ROY, writer, consultant; s. Roy Thomas Haggard and Irene Lucille (Kruse) Haggard-Kruse. BA, Ripon Coll., 1968; postgrad., Oxford U., 1968, Harvard U., 1999. Mgr. B. Dalton Bookseller, Mpls., 1974—77, Waldenbooks, Chgo., 1977—78, publ. editor Stamford, Conn., 1978—80; coll. rep. Houghton Mifflin Co., Boston, 1980—83; owner Lakes & Prairies, Inc., Crestwood, Ill., 1983—. Cons. Ebony Energy Publ., Chgo., 2003—; presenter in field. Author: Weave of the Sea, 2005; contbr. articles to profl. jours. Lt. U.S. Army, 1968—71. Recipient 1st pl. poetry, Green River Writers, 1998. Mem.: Riviera Country Club. Avocations: travel, photography, water-skiing, swimming. Office: Lakes and Prairies Inc 13152 S Cicero Ave PMB #110 Crestwood IL 60445

HAGGARD, JOAN CLAIRE, church musician, piano instructor, accompanist, adjudicator; b. Ann Arbor, Mich., July 7, 1932; d. Clifford Buell and Bertha (Woodhurst) Wightman; m. Harold Wallace Haggard, June 30, 1956; children: Alan C., Stephen T., John A., Marian E. BA, Carleton Coll., 1954; postgrad., Ecole des Beaux Arts, Fontainebleau, France, 1954, U. Mich., 1954-55; A., Am. Guild Organists, 1980. Cert. pvt. piano tchr. Organist, choir dir. St. Paul's Episc. Ch., Riverside, Ill., 1955-59; dir. of music St. Andrew's Episc. Ch., Livonia, Mich., 1960-72; organist Christ Episc. Ch., Dearborn, Mich., 1973-83; dir. of music St. Philip's Episc. Ch., Rochester, Mich., 1983-92; organist, music coord. 1st United Meth. Ch., Farmington, Mich., 1992-2000. Pvt. piano tchr., Livonia, 1960—; piano instr. Southfield (Mich.) Sr. Adult Ctr., 1992-99; accompanist Creative and Performing Arts High Sch., Livonia, 1987-90; accompanist many solo instrumental and vocal performances, 1959—; student performance on piano and voice adjudicator Nat. Fedn. Music, Mich. State Band and Orch. Assn. Editor Livonia Youth Symphony Soc. newsletter, 1972-77; contbr. articles to profl. jours. Pres. Livonia Youth Symphony Soc., 1973-76; program dir. Episcopal Diocese Mich. Jr. Choir Camp, 1981-84, 87-89; coord. daily worship Triennial Conv. Episcopal Ch., Detroit, 1988. Mem. Am. Guild Organists (dean Detroit chpt. 1976-79, gen. chmn. nat. conv. 1986, councillor Region V 1986-92), Nat. Guild Piano Tchrs. (judge piano auditions 1987—), Music Tchrs. Nat. Assn., Assn. Anglican Musicians, Hymn Soc. in the U.S. and Can., Assn. Diocesan Liturgy and Music Commns., Music Comm. Episcopal Diocese Mich. (chmn. 1980-81), Mich. Fedn. Music Clubs (pres. eastern dist. 1998-2000), Mich. Music Tchrs. Assn. (local assn. chmn. 1996, student performance on piano and voice adjudicator), The Tuesday Musicale Detroit (pres. 2005—), Piano Tchrs. Forum (Livonia area, pres. 1995-97), The Tuesday Musicale Detroit (pres. 2005—), SAI Friend of Arts, PEO. Avocations: birdwatching, nature, reading. Home: 33974 Hampshire St Livonia MI 48154-2722

HAGGARD, WILLIAM HENRY, meteorologist; b. Woodbridge, Conn., Nov. 20, 1920; s. Howard Wilcox and Josephine Cecelia (Foley) H.; m. Blanche Woolard, Mar. 21, 1944 (div. May 1967); children: William Henry Jr., Robert H.; m. Martina Wadewitz, Oct. 1, 1967. BS in Physics, Yale U., 1942; cert. in profl. meteorology, MIT, 1942; MS in Meteorology, U. Chgo., 1946; postgrad., Fla. State U., 1958-59. Instr. meteorology N.C. State U., Raleigh, 1946-47; rsch. meteorologist U.S. Weather Bur., 1947-48; forecaster USWB Nat. Airport, 1949-50; instr. U.S. AID, Washington, 1950-51; staff weather rsch. project U.S. Navy, Norfolk, Va., 1951-54; chief adv. svcs. br. U.S. Weather Bur., Washington, 1954-59, asst. chief Office of Plans, 1960-61; dep. dir. Nat. Weather Records Ctr., Asheville, N.C., 1961; dir. Nat. Climatic Ctr., Asheville, 1963-75; pres. Climatol. Cons. Corp., Asheville, 1976-97, v.p., 1998; cons., 1999—. Mem. weather com. U.S. Power Squadron, Raleigh, N.C., 1988-98. Contbr. articles to tech. jours., 1947-99. Bd. dirs. ARC, Asheville, 1965-70, United Way, Asheville, 1964-70. Capt. USN, 1942-45, with Res. 1951-54. Recipient Tech. Adminstr. award NOAA, Washington, 1970, Am. Meteor. Soc. award outstanding Contbrns. to Applid Meteorology, 2001. Fellow Am. Meteorol. Soc. (cert. cons. meteorologist, bd. dirs. pvt. sector meteorology sect. 1989-92, mem. cert. cons. meteorologist bd. 1983-88), Nat. Coun. Indsl. Meteorologists (pres. 1988-89, bd. dirs. 1987-90, 94-96, 99-2001, sec., treas. 1994-2002). Republican. Presbyterian. Avocations: sailing, photography. Office: William H Haggard CCM LLC 150 Shope Creek Rd Asheville NC 28805-9795 Office Phone: 828-298-4237. Personal E-mail: cccavl@bellsouth.net.

HAGGERSON, NELSON LIONEL, JR., education educator; b. Silver City, N.Mex., June 11, 1927; s. Nelson L. and Gladys Lenore (Jackson) H.; m. B. Kate Baldwin, June 1, 1949 (dec. 2001); children: Patrick, Frederick, Teresa, Rebecca, Lionel, Mary; m. Catherine Rumsey, Dec. 1, 2001. BA, Vanderbilt U., 1949; MS, Western N.Mex. U., 1952; PhD, Claremont Grad. U., 1960. Cert. secondary tchr.; cert. adminstr. Dir. Exptl. Sch. Webster Coll., Webster Groves, Mo.; asst. prof. edn. Western N.Mex. U., Silver City; prin. Cobre High Sch., Bayard, N.Mex.; prof. emeritus edn. Ariz. State U., Tempe, 1989—. Vis. prof. U. W.I., St. Augustine, Trinidad and Tobago, 1993-99, U. Pitts., 1982, 91, 92, R.I. Coll., 1991, Western N.Mex. U., 1988, 97, 98, 99, 2000, 01. Author: Secondary Education Today, 1967, To Dance With Joy, 1971, Naturalistic Research Paradigms: Theory and Practice, 1983, Informing Educational Policy and Practice Through Interpretive Inquiry, 1992, From Geronimo's Lookout, Growing Up and Living in the Southwest: An Autobiography, 1993, Oh Yes I Can!, A Biography of Arlena Seneca, 1994, A Celebration: The Life of Father Ramon Estivill, Renaissance Man of God, 1999, Expanding Curriculum Research and Understanding, 2000, Stories of the Academy: Learning From the Good Mother, 2002, The Mission of the Scholar: Research and Practice, A Tribute to Nelson Haggerson, 2002, also 12 book chpts.; guest editor: Education in Asia, Silver Ann Edit., World Coun. Curriculum and Instrn., Winter, 1995; contbr. over 50 articles to profl. jours. With USN, 1945-46. Fulbright fellow, 1986; recipient Award in Curriculum, MacDonald, 1986; named Outstanding Researcher, Coll. Edn., 1987, Outstanding Tchr., 1988; rsch. grantee Deakin U., Victoria, Australia, 1988, The Mission of the Scholar, Rsch. and Practice: A Tribute to Nelson Haggerson, 2002; inductee N.Mex. Mil. Inst. Hall of Fame, 2004. Mem. AERA, ASCD, Profs. Curriculum, Soc. for Study of Curriculum History, World Coun. for Curriculum and Instrn. (program chmn. 1989), Order Internat. Fellowship, Phi Delta Kappa, Phi Kappa Phi, Kappa Delta Pi. Home: PO Box 24177 Tempe AZ 85285-4177 Business E-Mail: haggerson@asu.edu.

HAGGERTON, RON C., elementary school educator; b. Lovington, N.Mex., Feb. 13, 1970; s. Ronald G. and Carla F. Haggerton; m. Wendy Dawn George, July 1, 2003; children: Linzy Rae Epperson, Stephanie Michelle. AA, N.Mex Jr. Coll., 1991; BS in Edn., Ea. Mew Mex. U., 1994; MSc, Coll. S.W., 2005. Tchr. Elem. Sch. Hobbs (N.Mex.) Schs., 1994—98, tchr. Jr. H.S., tchr. tech. Mem.: ACTE, Shodin Ji Do Karate (sr. instr. 1997—2005). Home: 815 West Copper Hobbs NM 88240 Personal E-mail: mr.haggerton@excite.com.

HAGGERTY, GRETCHEN R., accounting and finance executive; BS in Acctg., Case Western Reserve U., Cleveland; JD, Duquesne U., Pitts. CPA. V.p. acctg. and fin. U.S. Steel Group, Pitts., tax assist., 1977—80, leasing analyst, 1980—82, sr. financial analyst, 1982—84, corp. finance mgr., 1984—85, dir. plant and gen. acctg. USS Chemicals Div., 1985—86, gen. tax atty., dir. taxes, 1987—88, assist. treasurer corp. finance, 1988—89, assist. comptroller corp. acctg., 1989—91; v.p. and treasurer USX Corp., Pitts., 1991—98; v.p. acctg. and finance U.S. Steel Group, Pitts., 1998—2002, sr. v.p. and controller, 2002, sr. v.p. and treasurer, 2002—03, exec. v.p., treasurer, CFO, 2003—. Chmn. U.S. Steel and Carnegie Pension Fund. Mem.: Allegheny County Bar Assoc. Office: USX Corp 600 Grant St Ste 6100 Pittsburgh PA 15219-2805

HAGGERTY, JAMES JOSEPH, lawyer; b. Scranton, Pa., June 12, 1936; s. James J. Haggerty and Margaret W. Cummings; m. Cecelia Ellen Lynett; children: Jean Margaret McGrath, Mauri Elizabeth Collins, James Joseph Jr., Matthew Edward, Cecelia Ellen, Daniel Patrick, Kathleen Mary. BA in Econs., Holy Cross Coll., Worcester, Mass., 1957; JD, Georgetown U., 1960; LLD (hon.), U. Scranton, 1987; LHD (hon.), Villanova U., 1995. Bar: Pa. 1961, Ct. Common Pleas Lackawanna County 1961, U.S. Dist. Ct. (mid. dist.) Pa. 1961, U.S. Ct. Appeals (3d cir.) 1962, U.S. Ct. Claims 1985. Assoc. Farrell Butler Kearney & Parker, Scranton, 1961-62; law clk. to Hon. William J. Nealon U.S. Dist. Ct. (mid. dist.), Scranton, 1963-64; ptnr. Casey Haggerty and McDonnell, Scranton, 1965-70, Haggerty McDonnell O'Brien, Scranton, 1970-87; former sec. of commonwealth State of Pa., Harrisburg, 1987-89; gen. counsel to gov. Commonwealth of Pa., Harrisburg, 1989-93; ptnr. Haggerty, McDonnell & O'Brien, Scranton, 1993—. Apptd. by U.S. Dist. Ct. trustee in bankruptcy of Blue Coal Corp., 1976-86; mem. hearing com. 3.03 Disciplinary Bd. Pa. Supreme Ct.; permanent mem. Jud. Conf. U.S. 3d Jud. Cir.; mem. Fed. Jud. Screening Com., 1996-2001; chmn. bd. dirs. Shamrock Comm. Corp.; past bd. dirs. Specialty Plastics Products Inc.; past. bd. dirs., solicitor 1st Nat. Community Bank Dunmore. Trustee U. Scranton, 1979—86, chmn. bd., 1982—86, mem.Pres.'s Cir., mem. Pres.'s Club; chmn. Real Bob Casey Com., 1985—86; trustee Scranton Prep. Sch., 1995—2000, chmn. bd., 1999—2000; former bd. dirs. Lackawanna United Way, former chmn. profl. and geog. divsn.; bd. dirs. assocs. Scranton Area Found. With U.S. Army, with Pa. N.G. Mem. ABA, ATLA, Am. Bankers Assn., Pa. Bar Assn. (Spl. Achievement award 1988-89), Pa. Trial Lawyers Assn., Pa. Bankers Assn., Lackawanna Bar Assn. (past pres., bd. dirs.), Greater Scranton C. of C. (bd. dirs., former v.p.), Holy Cross Coll. Alumni Assn. N.E. Pa. (past pres., Outstanding Alumnus award 1982), Scranton Prep. Sch. Alumni Assn. (past mem. bd. govs., T. Donald Reinfret S.J. award Outstanding Alumnus of Yr. 1985), Friendly Sons of St. Patrick Lackawanna County (mem. exec. com., past pres.), Country Club Scranton (bd. dirs.). Roman Catholic. Office: Haggerty McDonnell & O'Brien 203 Franklin Ave Ste 1 Scranton PA 18503-1989 Office Phone: 570-344-9845. Business E-Mail: hmolaw@epix.net.

HAGGERTY, JOSEPH K., lawyer, insurance company executive; b. 1946; AB, Wheeling Jesuit U., 1968; JD, U. Pitts., 1973. Bar: Iowa 1997, Ky. 1994, Pa. 1973. Sr. v.p., dep. gen. counsel ICH Corp.; sr. v.p., gen. counsel AmerUs Group Co., Des Moines, 1994—. Spkr. in field. Office: AmerUs Group Co 699 Walnut PO Box 1555 Des Moines IA 50306 Office Phone: 515-362-3600. Office Fax: 515-362-3652. E-mail: joe.haggerty@amerus.com.

HAGGERTY, MARY ANN, medical educator; b. Jersey City, N.J., Mar. 19, 1948; d. Cornelius Joseph and Catherine Teresa (Mulroy) H.; m. Thomas Gerard Curran, Aug. 7, 1976; children: Catherine, Margaret. BS, Chestnut Hill Coll., 1970; AM, Dartmouth Coll., 1972; MD, U. Medicine & Dentistry N.J., 1979. Tchr. St. Peter's Prep. Sch., Jersey City, 1972-75; sr. pub. health physician N.J. State Dept. Health, Trenton, 1982-83; dir. med. clinic U. Medicine & Dentistry N.J.-Univ. Hosp., Newark, 1983-85; dir. intro. clin. svcs. U. Medicine & Dentistry N.J.-N.J. Med. Sch., Newark, 1985-91, assoc. prof. clin. medicine, 1990—; dir. primary care medicine Newark-Beth Israel Med. Ctr., 1991—2000, interim dir. medicine, 1997-98. Bd. dirs. St. Barnabas Provider Partnership. Mem. AMA, Am. Coll. Physicians, Am. Geriatrics Soc., Am. Med. Women's Assn., Med. Soc. N.J., Essex County Med. Soc. Avocation: walking. Office: 2115 Millburn Ave Maplewood NJ 07040 Office Phone: 973-275-1322. Personal E-mail: mahaggerty@comcast.net.

HAGGERTY, MARY ELIZABETH, retired elementary school educator; b. Little Falls, N.Y., Jan. 15, 1948; d. Edward C. and Margaret (Dise) H. BA, Utica Coll., 1969; MS, Syracuse U., 1971. Cert. elem. tchr., N.Y. Tchr. Little Falls City Schs., Little Falls, 1969—2003, ret., 2003. Active Foothills Girl Scout Coun., Utica, ARC, Herkimer, N.Y.; bd. dirs. Greater Little Falls Community Ch., 1976—, Women's Christian Assn., Little Falls, 1984—. Mem. DAR (registrar 1980—), Little Falls Tchr.'s Assn. (treas. 1976-2003). Roman Catholic.

HAGGERTY, ROBERT HENRY, lawyer; b. N.Y.C., Feb. 25, 1919; s. Daniel A. and Helen Marie (Henry) H.; m. Mary Rita O'Neil, Aug. 28, 1945 (dec. 1990); children: Robert Jr., Daniel J., Nancy D., Thomas H; m. Nadia Ismail, 1991. BBA, Manhattan Coll., 1940; LLB, Harvard U., 1953. Bar: N.Y. 1954, Fla. 1977. Assoc. Root, Ballantine, Harlan, Bushby & Palmer (now Dewey, Ballantine), N.Y.C., 1953—56, 1962—95, ptnr., 1965—; atty. Gen. Electric Co., N.Y.C. and Schenectady, N.Y., 1956-62. Bd. dirs. Ticor Title Guarantee Co., N.Y.C. Editor: PLI Real Estate Construction Current Problems, 1973; editor (vols. 8, 29, 58) PLI Real Estate Construction, 1969-72. Bd. dirs. Plandome (N.Y.) Property Assocs., 1965-76, pres., 1970-76; pres. Plandome Mills Property Owners, 1980-82; village justice of Plandome Manor, 1983-89, mayor, 1989-93. Served to maj. USMC, 1941-45, PTO. Decorated Silver Star, Purple Heart. Mem. Plandome Country Club, Grand Harbor Golf and Country Club. Roman Catholic. Home: 1870 Paseo del Lago Vero Beach FL 32967-7260

HAGGERTY, ROBERT JOHNS, pediatrician, educator; b. Saranac Lake, N.Y., Oct. 20, 1925; s. Gordon Abbott and Nina (Johns) H.; m. Muriel Ethel Protzmann, Oct. 29, 1949; children: Robert, Janet, Richard, John. AB, Cornell U., 1946, MD, 1949; AM (hon.), Harvard U., 1975; DSc (hon.), Ind. U., 1990. Diplomate Am. Bd. Pediat. Intern Strong Meml. Hosp., Rochester, NY, 1949-51; from resident to chief resident pediat. Children's Hosp. Med. Ctr., Boston, 1953-55; med. dir. family health care program, asst. prof. pediat. Harvard Med. Sch., 1953-64; prof. pediat., chmn. dept. U. Rochester Sch. Medicine, 1964-75; Roger I. Lee prof. health svcs., chmn. dept. health svcs. Harvard Sch. Pub. Health, 1975-78; prof. pediat. Harvard Med. Sch., Boston, 1975-78, clin. prof., 1978-80; pres. William T. Grant Found., N.Y.C., 1980-92; clin. prof. pediat. Cornell U. Med. Sch., N.Y.C., 1980-92; prof.

pediat. emeritus U. Rochester Sch. Medicine, 1992—; exec. dir. Internat. Pediatric Assoc., 1993-98. Dir. gen. pediat. acad. devel. program Robert Wood Johnson Found., 1978-88; mem. health svcs. rsch. sect. USPHS, 1964-70, 82-84, chmn., 1968-70, 82-84; mem. N.Y. State Health Planning Adv. Coun., Carnegie Coun. on Children, 1972-77; chmn. panel health scis. rsch., com. on nat. needs for biomed. and behavioral rsch. per. NRC, 1975-78; mem. bd. U.S. Com. on UNICEF, 1981-87; mem. Gov.'s Coun. on Grad. Med. Edn., N.Y. State, 1989-93. Editor: (with M. Green) Ambulatory Pediatrics, 1968, 5th edit., 1999, (with J. Lucey) Pediatrics, 1973-80, Pediatrics in Rev., 1978-2004, Bull. N.Y. Acad. Medicine, 1992-99; assoc. editor New Eng. Jour. Medicine, 1959-64; contbr. articles to med. jours. Mem. vis. com. Grad. Sch. Edn., Harvard U., 1982-88; bd. dirs. Grantmakers in Health, 1985-89; bd. overseers, social scis. dept., Tufts U., 1990-94; bd. visitors U. Okla. Sch. Pub. Health, 1991-94. Capt. USAF, 1951-53. Recipient Martha M. Eliot award Am. Pub. Health Assn., 1976, Disting. Alumni award Cornell U. Med. Coll., 1987, 6 awards various pediatric socs., 1989, Primary Care Achievement award PEW Found. Health Professions Commn., 1994; Markle scholar in acad. medicine, Markle Found., N.Y.C., 1962-67; fellow Ctr. for Advanced Study Behavioral Scis., Stanford, Calif., 1974-75 Mem.: Alliance for Health Care for All (trustee 1991—94), Am. Health Fedn. (trustee 1989—92), NY Acad. Medicine (trustee, sec. 1989—92), Inst. of Medicine (coun. 1974—77, chmn. com. on prevention of mental illness 1992—93, chmn. steering com. nat. study quality assurance programs 1975—76, Gustave Lienhard award 1989), Soc. Pediat. Rsch. (v.p. 1970—71), Internat. Epidemiol. Assn., Assn. Am. Med. Colls., Ambulatory Pediat. Assn. (chmn. 1963—64, George Armstrong award 1969), Am. Pediat. Soc. (Joseph St. Geme award 1989, John Howland award 1998, E.H. Christopherson award for internat. child health 2001, Alfred I. Du Pont award 2004), Am. Acad. Pediat. (v.p., pres. 1983—85, Grulee award 1981, Dale Richmond award 1981, Aldrich award 1986, Job Smith award 1987, Abraham Jacobi award 1996, E.H. Christopherson award for internat. child health 2001, Lifetime Edn. award 2002), Am. Assn. Poison Control Ctrs. (pres. 1962—64), Assn. Med. Sch. Pediat. Dept. Chairmen (pres. 1969—70), Royal Coll. Pediats. and Child Health (hon.), Harvard Club N.Y.C., Alpha Omega Alpha, Phi Beta Kappa. Personal E-mail: robert_haggerty@urmc.rochester.edu.

HAGGETT, ROSEMARY ROMANOWSKI, academic administrator; BA in Biology, U. Bridgeport, 1974; PhD in Physiology, U. Va., 1979. Postdoctoral fellow Northwestern U., Evanston, Ill., 1979-82; asst. prof. biology Loyola U. Chgo., 1982-87; asst. rsch. scientist zoology U. Md., College Park, 1987-88; from program dir. to divsn. dir. animals and nutrition USDA, 1988-94, dep. assoc. adminstr., 1988-94; prof. animal and vet. sci. W.Va. U., Morgantown, 1994—, dean Coll. Agr., Forestry and Consumer Scis., 1994-99, assoc. provost acad. programs, 1999—2003; dir. divsn. undergrad. edn. NSF, 2003—. Office: DUE NSF 4201 Wilson Blvd Ste 835 Arlington VA 22230 Office Phone: 703-292-8670. Business E-Mail: rhaggett@nsf.gov.

HAGGH-HUGLO, BARBARA HELEN, musicologist, educator; b. Memphis, Mar. 18, 1955; d. Raymond Herbert and Hilde Wentzlaff-Eggebert Haggh; m. Michel Victor Huglo, Mar. 4, 1998. AB in German, U. Nebr., Lincoln, 1976; BMus, U. Ill., Urbana, 1978, MMus, 1980, PhD in Musicology, 1988. Instr. Tufts U., Boston, 1987—88; asst. prof., music Baruch Coll., CUNY, N.Y.C., 1988—89, U. Md., Balt., 1989—95; fellow Cath. U. Leuven, Belgium, 1992—94, U. Libre de Bruxelles, Brussels, 1992; fellow, Leverhulme Trust U. London, 1995—97; assoc. prof., music U. N. Tex., Denton, 1998—2000, U. Md., College Park, 2000—. Contbr. articles to profl. jours., chapters to books. Grantee, NEH, 1989, Internat. Rsch. and Exchs. Bd., 1989, The Brit. Acad., 1995, Am. Philos. Soc., 1999. Mem.: Coll. Music Soc. (mem. adv. bd., rep. for musicology 1987—89), Am. Musicological Soc. (coun. mem. 1990—93, mem. editl. bd. 1999), Internat. Musicological Soc. (chair, program com. 1998—2002, Am. dir.-at-large 2002—). Office: Univ Md Sch Music 3110C Clarice Smith Performing Arts Ctr College Park MD 20742

HAGGIS, ARTHUR GEORGE, JR., retired military officer, educator, publisher; b. Youngstown, Ohio, June 3, 1924; s. Arthur George Sr. and Mary Mildred (Campbell) H.; m. Lewanna Evalyn Strom, Apr. 7, 1944; children: Lynda Lee, Arthur George III, Richard Charles, Douglas Hood, Pamela Sue. BS in Edn., Wayne State U., 1957, MEd, 1959, EdD, 1961. Enlisted pvt. U.S. Army, 1943, advanced through enlisted grades to staff sgt., commd. 2d. lt., field artillery/Battle of the Bulge, 1945, advanced through ranks to Brig. Gen., 1964; bn. survey officer field artillery U.S. Army ETO, 1943-46; S-2 475th Field Artillery Battalion and asst. indsl. engr. U.S. Steel Corp., McDonald, Ohio, 1946-51; post dep. comdr., adj. 2d Armored Div. Trains, Bad Kreuznach, Fed. Republic Germany, 1951-54; spl. mil. asst. to Sec. of Army, Chief of Info. U.S. Army, Ft. Wayne, Mich., Detroit Arsenal, Mich. Mil. Dist.; with ordnance tank automotive command Washington and Detroit; mem. gen. staff U.S. Army, Washington, 1954-64; pres., CEO Haggis Assocs. Inc., Washington and Hollywood, D.C. and Fla., 1964-71, Atlantis Pvt. Schs., Inc., Hollywood, 1971—; chmn., CEO The Atlantis-Lewart Group, Inc., Hollywood, 1987—. Pres., CEO Ednl. Cons., Washington and Hollywood, 1966—, Atlantis Pub. Co., Hollywood, 1978—, Atlantis Rsch. Insts., Inc., Hollywood, 1981—, Perfect Body Products, Inc., Hollywood, 1981—; apptd. gubernatorial mem. State of Fla. Bd. Correctional Edn., Correctional Edn. Sch. Authority, term ending 1994; aide-de-camp to Gen. of Army Omar N. Bradley, 1955; negotiator Dept. Def. Armed Forces res. Ann. Unit Tng. Clause, UAW-CIO/GM contract, 1956; comdr. Army Task Force Ground Zero, Operation Plumbbob, atmospheric nuclear exlposion experiment, Frenchman Flat, Nev., 1957; liaison Sec. of Army, 1st U.S. Satellite Explorer I, 1957-58; comdr. U.S. Joint Task Force Mackinac, Mackinac Bridge Dedication Ceremony Mich., 1958; originator Dept. Def. Nat. Com. for Employer Support of Guard and Res., 1955-58; developer Dept. Def. Armed Forces Week, 1955-61. Co-editor, Small Business Library, The Government Market, 1966, Selling to the U.S. Government and its Contractors, vol. I, 1966, Bids, Proposals, Contracts and Contract Administration, vol. II, 1966, Texts of Small Business Enterprise Institute, vol. III, 1966, Bids, Proposals and Contracts for Small Business Enterprise Course Handbook, vol. IV, 1966; author: Educational Evaluation Program: Predicting College Success, 1967; author: (with others) Edu-Care, the New School Concept, 1991, also supporting texts, Atlantis Beginning Language and Number Development Program, Books 1 and 2, 1981, Atlantis Basic Spelling Series, Books A-H, 1981-85, Atlantis Computer Series, Books I-VII, 1982-87, Atlantis Health Series, 1981-87. Sustaining mem. Freedoms Found. at Valley Forge, 1985—, Mus. of Art, 1986—, Opera Soc.; founder Performing Arts Ctr. Pacers, 1985; mem. Opera Guild, Inc., 1986—; pres. Wayne State U. Alumni Club Washington D.C., 1963-69; trustee Philharmonic Orchestra Fla., 1987—; mem. Rep. Presdl. Task Force, 1983—, Rep. Senatorial Inner Circle, Rep. Pres.' Club, 1984—, Mayor's Prayer Breakfast Com., Ft. Lauderdale, 1988—; mem. adv. coun. Broward Community Found., 1987—; sec. of def. appointee nat. com. for employer support of the guard and res. Dept. Def. Decorated Bronze Star, Purple Heart; recipient award City of St. Ignace, 1958, Nat. USO award 1959, citation City of Detroit, 1959, Exceptional Svc. Nat. award Assn. U.S. Army, 1990; decorated Nat. Soc. of SAR, 1985; U.S. Army doctoral scholar Wayne State U., 1960-61; grantee Detroit Edison Co., 1964-65, Litton Industries, 1965-66. Mem. Assn. U.S. Army (state pres., regional v.p. 1984-87, sustaining mem. Landpower Edn. Fund Inc. 1984, chmn. Fla. state exec. coun. 1985-87, bd. dirs. Fla. Gulf Stream chpt. 1984—, nat. adv. bd. dirs. 1990-96), Navy League (bd. dirs. Ft. Lauderdale coun. 1988—), USO (pres. greater Ft. Lauderdale Inc. coun. 1988—, Freedoms Found. at Valley Forge George Washington medal 1991), Nat. Assn. Atomic Vets., Mil. Order of Purple Heart (life), Ret. Officers Assn., Mil. Order of World Wars, Am. Legion, VFW, Disabled Am. Vets., Nat. Sojourners Inc., Nat. Order Battlefield Commns., Nat. Eagle Scout Assn., Vets. of Battle of the Bulge, Greater Ft. Lauderdale C. of C. (founding trustee 1989—), Air Force Assn. (citation 1961), Clan Campbell Soc. of Fla., Inc., Scots-Am. Soc. of Brevard, Army and Navy (Washington), Patrick AFB Officers, K.T., Masons. Republican. Lutheran. Avocations: woodworking, bridge, sailing, water sports. Office: 11911 Snapdragon Rd Tampa FL 33635-6232

HAGGIS, PAUL EDWARD, scriptwriter, television producer, television director; b. London, Ont., Can., Mar. 10, 1953; came to U.S., 1979; s. Edward H. and Mary Yvonne (Metcalf) H.; m. Diane Christine Gettas, Apr. 9, 1977-94; children: Alissa Sullivan, Lauren Kilvington, Katy Elizabeth; m. Deborah Rennard, Jun. 21, 1997; 1 child. Writer (TV series) One Day at a Time, 1975, The Love Boat, 1977, Diff'rent Strokes, 1978, The Facts of Life, 1979, (also prodr. 1984-86), The Tracey Ullman Show, 1987, Thirtysomething, 1987 (Emmy award for Outstanding Drama Series, 1988), Walker, Texas Ranger, 1993 (also creator), (TV films) The Return of the Shaggy Dog, 1987; writer, dir.: (films) Red Hot, 1993; writer, exec. prodr.: (TV films) Due South, 1994, (TV series) Michael Hayes, 1997; writer, prodr. (films) Million Dollar Baby, 2004; writer, exec. prodr., dir. (TV series) EZ Streets, 1996-97, Family Law, 1999, (TV films) Ghost of a Chance, 1998; writer, prodr., dir. (films) Crash, 2004. Trustee Found. for Religious Freedom; mem. adv. bd. Mus. Broadcasting; co-founder Artists for Peace and Justice, bd. dirs. Hollywood Edn. Lteracy Project, For the Arts for Every Child, Environmental Media Assn.; founding mem. Earth Comm. Office; mem. adv. bd. Ctr. Advancement Non-Violence; mem. Pres. Coun. Defenders of Wildlife.*

HAGGLUND, CLARANCE EDWARD, lawyer, publishing executive; b. Omaha, Feb. 17, 1927; s. Clarance Andrew and Esther May (Kelle) H.; m. Dorothy Souser, Mar. 27, 1953 (div. Aug. 1972); children: Laura, Bret, Katherine; m. Merle Patricia Hagglund, Oct. 28, 1972. BA, U. S.D., 1949; JD, William Mitchell Coll. Law, 1953. Bar: Minn. 1955, U.S. Ct. Appeals (8th cir.) 1974, U.S. Supreme Ct. 1963; diplomate Am. Bd. Profl. Liability Attys. Ptnr. Hagglund & Johnson and predecessor firms, Mpls., 1973—; mem. Hagglund, Weimer and Speidel, PA; publ., pres. Common Law Publishing Inc., Golden Valley, Minn., 1991—; mem. Blackwell Igbanogo Attys., Mpls., 2004; with Hagglund Law Offices, 2004—. Pres. Internat. Control Sys., Inc., Mpls., 1979—, Hill River Corp., Mpls., 1976—; gen. counsel Minn. Assn. Profl. Ins. Agts., Inc., Mpls., 1965-86; CFO, Pro-Trac, software for profl. liability ins. industry. Contbr. articles to profl. jours. Served to lt. comdr. USNR, 1945-46, 50-69. Fellow Internat. Soc. Barristers; mem. Lawyers Pilots Bar Assn., U.S. Maritime Law Assn. (proctor), Acad. Cert. Trial Lawyers Minn. (dean 1983-85), Nat. Bd. Trial Advocacy (cert. in civil trial law, bd. dirs.), Douglas Amdahl Inns of Ct. (pres.), Ill. Athletic Club (Chgo.), Edina Country Club (Minn.), Calhoun Beach Club (Mpls.). Roman Catholic. Avocation: flying. Home and Office: Common Law Publishing Inc 3168 Dean Ct Minneapolis MN 55416-4386 Office Phone: 612-926-0210. Personal E-mail: chagglund@mn.rr.com.

HAGIHARA, KENNETH, public relations executive; b. L.A., Sept. 24, 1966; s. stepfather Ralph and Tomi Hagihara; m. Joyce Hagihara, Dec. 16, 1995; 1 child, Nathan. AA, Orange Coast Coll., 1997; BA, Calif. State U., Fullerton, 1999. Electronic technician USAF, 1986-90; satellite comm. technician Dept. USAF, 1990-94, prodn. contr., 1994-97; sr. pub. info. officer U. Calif., Irvine, 1997-98; sr. account exec. GreenLight Comms., 1998-2000. V.p. comms. Air Force Assn., Newport Beach, Calif., 1995-99. With USAF, 1986-90. Mem. Internat. Assn. Bus. Communicators (bd. dirs. 2000—, Helios award of excellence 2000, Helios Award of Merit 1999, Helios Hon. Mentions (2) 2000), Pub. Rels. Soc. Am. (dir. at large 2000—), Am. Legion. Office: Integrity Pub Rels Inc Ste 7- 409 28715 Los Alisos Blvd Mission Viejo CA 92692 E-mail: ken@integritypr.net.

HAGIN, JOSEPH WHITEHOUSE, II, federal official; b. Lexington, Ky., Jan. 6, 1956; s. Joseph Whitehouse and Hannah (Hargett) H. BA, Kenyon Coll., 1979. Personal asst. to v.p. U.S. Office of V.P., Washington, 1981-83, asst. to v.p. for legis. affairs, 1983-85; dir. pub. affairs Federated Dept. Stores, Cin., 1985-87; v.p. pub. affairs Chiquita Brands Ltd., Cin., 1988; dep. asst. to pres. of U.S. for appointments and scheduling The White House, 1989—; dep. campaign mgr. Bush Cheney campaign, 2000; asst. to the Pres. & dep. chief of staff for ops. The White House, 2000—. Govt. affairs com. Cin. C. of C., 1985-88; bd. dirs. Clean Cin., 1986-88, Hamilton County Rep. Fin. Com., 1986—. Mem. Camargo Club, Bankers Club (Cin.). Episcopalian. Office: The White House 1600 Pennsylvania Ave NW W Wing 1st Fl Washington DC 20500*

HAGIN, NANCY, printmaker, painter; b. Elizabeth, NJ, 1940; BFA, Carnegie-Mellon U., 1962; MFA, Yale U., 1964. Prof. Maryland Inst. Coll. Art, Balt., 1964—73, Pratt Inst., NYC, 1973—74, 1985, RI Sch. of Design, 1974, Fashion Inst. Tech., NYC, 1974—, Cooper Union, NY, 1982—92, SUNY Purchase, NY, 1994, U. Arts, Phila., 1999. One-woman shows include Alpha Gallery, Boston, 1972, 1976, 1974, 1979, 1982, 1985, 1992, 1995, 2000, U. Md., 1973, Terry Dintenfass Gallery, NY, 1975, 1978, Fischbach Gallery, NY, 1981, 1982, 1985, 1987, 1989, 1991, 1993, 1995, 1998, 1999, 2002, 2004, exhibited in group shows at Balt. Mus. Ann. Exhbn., 1965—70, IFA Gallery, Washington DC, 1968—73, Allen Frumkin Gallery, NY, 1971, Smithsonian Inst., Washington DC, 1974, Indpls. Mus. Art, 1976, Butler Inst., Ohio, 1977, Lehigh U., Pa., 1979, Nassau County Mus. Art, Roslyn, NY, 1980, New Britain Mus. Am. Art, Conn., 1982, Rahr-West Mus., Wis., 1983, Fitchburg Art Mus., Mass., 1984, William Sawyer Gallery, San Francisco, 1985, C. Grimaldis Gallery, Balt., 1986, Fay Gold Gallery, Atlanta, 1989, Nat. Acad. Design, NY, 1989—90, Rice U., Tex., 1993, NJ Ctr. Visual Arts, 1994, Lizan Tops Gallery, NY, 1995, AAAL, NY, 2001, Doran Gallery, Tulsa, 2002, 323 West Gallery, NY, 2003, DeCordova Mus. & Sculpture Pk., Mass., 2003—04. Recipient Yale/Norfolk award, 1961, Purchase award, Fashion Inst. Tech., 1976, Butler Inst. Tech., 1977, Emil & Dines Carlsen award, Nat. Acad. Design, 1989; Fulbright Grant, Rome, 1966—67, McDowell Colony Fellowship, 1974, 1979, 1982, Creative Artists Pub. Svc. Grant, 1975, Artist in Residence, Palisades Interstate Pk., NY, 1975, NEA Grant, 1982, 1991. Mem.: Nat. Acad. Design, NY, 1992. Mailing: c/o Fischbach Gallery 210 11th Ave New York NY 10001*

HAGMAN, BETTY JO, elementary school educator; b. Tonasket, Wash., Nov. 4, 1937; d. Roy Jilies and Esther Naomi (Juday) VanWoert; m. Karl Robert Hagman, Dec. 28, 1963; children: John Robert, Sandra Gail. BA in Edn., Ea. Wash. U., 1959; postgrad., Western Wash. U., 1963. Cert. tchr. K-12. 2nd grade tchr. Highline Sch. Dist., Burien, Wash., 1959-61; 4th grade tchr. DuPont-Ft. Lewis Sch. Dist., 1962-66; tchr. various grades LaCrosse Sch. Dist., 1976—2003, ret., 2003, substitute tchr., 2003—. Mem. NEA, Nat. Coun. Tchrs. Math., Wash. Edn. Assn., Wash. State Math. Coun., Reading Club (sec., v.p., pres.), Alpha Delta Kappa. Home: PO Box 86 Lacrosse WA 99143-0086

HAGNER, CAROLYN ZEPF, music educator; d. Clifford and Marie Berling Zepf; m. Gerald Lee Hagner; 1 child, Laurel Marie. MusB, Oberlin Conservatory, Oberlin Coll., 1964; Diploma, The Juilliard Sch., 1966; MusM, Manhattan Sch. Music, 1969. Faculty Manhattan Sch. Music, N.Y.C., 1969—74; prof. music No. Ky. U., Highland Heights, 1979—. Founder, dir. No. Ky. U. Summer Piano Inst., 1997—; dir. No. Ky. U. Keyboard Recitals Series, 1980—88. Musician (accompanist): (recitals on piano, harpsichord) Recitals on fortepiano (Harold Bauer award, 1969). Chair, music com. Three Arts Scholarship Fund, Inc, Cin., 1998—. Mem.: Ohio Music Teachers Assn., Music Teachers Nat. Assn., No. Ky. Music Teachers Assn. (co-founder, pres. 1988—93), MacDowell Soc., Pi Kappa Lambda. Achievements include development of Created Certificate in Piano Pedagogy, Northern Kentucky University; Created Bachelor of Music, Accompanying Emphasis degree, Northern Kentucky University; Created Bachelor of Music, Piano Pedagogy Emphasis degree, Northern Kentucky University; Studies in Harpsichord and Women in Music, Northern Kentucky University. Office: Northern Kentucky University Department of Music Highland Heights KY 41099

HAGNER, JOHN D., lawyer; b. Apr. 12, 1945; BS in Mechanical Engring., U. Cin., 1968; JD, Georgetown U. Law Ctr., 1973. Bar: DC 1973, Md. 1973. Founder David, hagner, Kuney & Davidson, Washington, 1977—98; mem. Womble Carlyle Sandridge & Rice, PLLC, Washington. Notary pub., DC, 1973—93, 1994—, Md., 2000—; pro bono atty. Army Retirement Residence Found., Potomac, 1984—; dir., pro bono atty. St. Mark Elderly Housing Corp., 1987—; dir., treas., pro bono atty. George Washington Boyhood Home Found., 1991—97; adj. prof. law, fin. of real & personal property Georgetown U. Law Ctr., 1995—; lectr. in field. Bd. editors Georgetown Law Jour., 1971—73; contbr. articles to profl. jours. Lt., sanitary engr. (bio-medical lab. design & construction) US Pub. Health Svc., NIH, Bethesda, Md. Named 2000 Assoc. Mem. of Yr., Mortgage Bankers Assn. of Metropolitan Washington. Mem.: Am. Coll. of Real Estate Lawyers, DC Bar Assn. (mem., Capital Markets & Edn. & Practice Technology Committees), ABA. Office: Womble Carlyle Sandridge & Rice PLLC 1401 Eye St NW 7th Fl Washington DC 20005 Office Phone: 202-857-4404. Office Fax: 202-261-0004. Business E-Mail: jhagner@wcsr.com.

HAGOOD, JUNE DENIGRIS, pre-school educator, writer; b. Bklyn., Nov. 2, 1958; d. Peter M. and Selma J. (Lieberman) Denigris; life ptnr. William G. Belcher. BA in Elem. and Early Childhood, U. Ctrl. Fla., 1982. Cert. tchr. State of Fla., 1982. Primary math. specialist OCPS-Arbor Ridge Sch., Orlando, Fla., 2004—. Educator, trainer Ctrl. Fla. Writing Project, Orlando, 2000—00, office mgr. & historian, 2000—02; mem. Sch. Adv. Com., 1989—. Contbr. articles to mags. Ctrl. divsn. gov. Greater Orlando Area Toastmasters Internat., 1993—94. Recipient Disting. Toastmaster, Toastmasters Internat., 1993. Mem.: ASCD. Office: Arbor Ridge Sch 2900 Logandale Dr Orlando FL 32817 Office Phone: 407-672-3110. Office Fax: 407-672-1310. Personal E-mail: nycity58@yahoo.com. E-mail: hagoodj@ocps.net.

HAGOOD, MURL FELTON, surgeon; b. Marietta, Ga., Oct. 18, 1941; s. Murl Miller and Mary Evelyn (Jones) H.; m. Martha Addie James, June 20, 1965; children: Gregory Felton, Robert Miller, Richard James. MD, Emory U., 1966. Diplomate Am. Bd. Surgery. Am. Bd. Colon & Rectal Surgery. Intern U. Va. Hosp., Charlottesville, 1966-67, surg. resident, 1967-68; med. officer Charleston Naval Hosp. U.S. Navy, 1968-70; resident gen. surgery Med. U. S.C., 1970-73; fellow colon & rectal surgery Ochsner Found. Hosp., New Orleans, 1973-74; pvt. practice-colon & rectal surgery Kennestone Hosp., Marietta, 1974—. Lt. cmdr. USNR, 1968-70. Mem. Cobb County Med. Soc. (pres. 1993-94), Kiwanis Club, Phi Beta Kappa, Alpha Omega Alpha. Methodist. Avocations: golf, boating. Home: 577 Keeler Woods Dr Marietta GA 30064 Office: Surg Assocs of Marietta 790 Church St NW Ste 570 Marietta GA 30060-8967 Office Phone: 770-428-0462. Personal E-mail: mfhagood@bellsouth.net.

HAGOOD, RICHARD A., academic administrator, educator; b. Ontario, Oreg. m. Junella Hagood; 3 children. BA in History, Northwest Nazarene U.; MA, U. Oreg.; PhD in Educational Policy Studies, U. Ill. With Wash. State U., 1983—93, assoc. provost office of exec. v.p. and provost Pullman, 1990—93; pres. N.W. Nazarene U., 1993—. Spkr. in field. Mem. bd. dirs. Nampa Sch. Dist., Ch. Nazarene, mem. gen. bd.; chmn. bd. dirs. Mercy Med. Ctr. Office: NW Nazarene U 623 Holly St Nampa ID 83686

HAGOOD, THOMAS RICHARD, JR., minister, publisher; b. Charlotte, N.C., Sept. 16, 1954; s. Thomas Richard and Donna Gwendolyn (Williams) H.; m. Susan Stewart Hahn, Nov. 25, 1978; 1 child, Margaret Foster. BA, Davidson Coll., 1976; MDiv, Columbia Theol. Sem., 1996. Ordained to Presbyn. Ch., 1997. Editor Columbia Publ., Inc., Decatur, Ga., 1976—88, publ., 1988—; min. Barnesville Presbyn. Ch., Ga., 1997—2000; sr. min. Columbia Presbyn. Ch., 2000—. Mem. small ch. com., 1997-00, com. preparation ministry Presbytery Greater Atlanta, 1998—, com. World Wide Mins., 1999-2000. Eagle Scout, 1970, Scoutmaster Boy Scouts of Am., Lake City, Fla., 1982-85; pres. Columbian Countians, Lake City, 1982-85; mem. Govt. Study Com., Columbia County, Fla., 1984; elder Presbyn. Ch., Atlanta. Recipient Silver Beaver award North Fla. coun. Boy Scouts Am., 1986. Mem. English Speaking Union, Lake City Rotary (bd. dirs. 1982-85), Woodward Acad. Parent Club. Avocations: backpacking, camping, reading, woodworking. Home: PO Box 982 Decatur GA 30031-0982

HAGOOD, WILLIAM MILLIKEN, III, lawyer; b. Easley, S.C., Dec. 16, 1938; s. George Cleveland and Mary Louise (Smith) H.; m. Virginia Elizabeth Hays, June 10, 1962; children: William Milliken IV (dec.), Virginia Cleveland. BS in Bus. Adminstrn., Presbyn. Coll., Clinton, S.C., 1960; JD, U. S.C., 1963. Bar: S.C. 1963, U.S. Dist. Ct. (we. dist.) S.C. 1963, U.S. Ct. Appeals 1965, U.S. Supreme Ct., 1971. Law clk. Judge Clement F. Haynsworth, Jr., Greenville, S.C., 1964; shareholder Love, Thornton, Arnold & Thomason, P.A., Greenville, 1964—. Mem. faculty Trial Acad., Boulder, Colo., 1988. Author: Physician's Guide to Malpractice Law in South Carolina, 1991. Trustee Presbyn. Coll., 1988-94. Recipient Alumni Svc. award Presbyn. Coll., 1991. Fellow Am. Coll. Trial Lawyers; mem. S.C. Bar Assn., Am. Bd. Trial Advocates, Internat. Assn. Def. Counsel, S.C. Def. Trial Lawyers Assn., Phi Beta Kappa. Presbyn. Avocations: golf, gardening. Office: Love Thornton Arnold & Thomason PA 410 E Washington St Greenville SC 29601-2927 Office Phone: 864-298-2667. E-mail: bhagood@ltatlaw.com.

HAGOORT, THOMAS HENRY, lawyer; b. Paterson, N.J., May 30, 1932; s. Nicholas Hugh and Rae (Sytsma) H.; m. Lois Ann Bennett, Sept. 6, 1954; children: Nancy Hagoort Treuhold, Susan Hagoort Bick. AB cum laude, Harvard U., 1954, LLB magna cum laude, 1957. Bar: N.Y. 1959. Assoc. firm Cleary, Gottlieb, Steen & Hamilton, N.Y.C., 1957-67, ptnr., 1968-90; gen. counsel Albany Internat. Corp., 1991—2002, Sr. V.P., 2002—. Note editor: Harvard Law Rev., 1956—57. Pres. Mountainside Hosp., Montclair, N.J., 1983-85, chmn. bd. trustees, 1985-88; pres. Internat. Baccalaureate of N.Am., N.Y.C., 1980-91, Montclair Bd. Edn. 1966-70; mem., Coun. of Found. Internat. Baccalaureate Orgn., Geneva, 1982-96, pres. and chair exec. com., 1990-96. Mem.: ABA, N.Y. State Bar Assn., Sea Pines Country Club, S.C. Yacht Club, Harvard Club of N.J. (pres. 1977—78). Democrat. Home: PO Box 3229 Hilton Head Island SC 29928-0229

HAGOPIAN, JACOB, federal judge; b. Providence; s. Bedros and Varvar (Leylegian) H.; m. Mary L. Pomoranski; children: Mark Jay, Dana Aquinas, Mary Lou, Jan Christian, Jon Gregory. AB, George Washington U., 1957; JD, Am. U., 1960; grad. thesis in internat. law, Judge Advocate Gen.'s Sch., 1964; postgrad., Indsl. Coll. Armed Forces, 1967. Bar: Va. 1961, R.I. 1964, U.S. Supreme Ct. 1964, U.S. Dist. Ct. R.I., U.S. Dist. Ct. (ea. dist.) Va., U.S. Ct. Appeals (D.C. cir.), U.S. Ct. Customs and Patent Appeals, U.S. Ct. Claims, U.S. Tax Ct. Enlisted U.S. Army, 1944, advanced through grades to 1st sgt. 11th Airborne Divsn., 2d lt. to 1st lt. 82d Airborne Divsn., parachutist, glider pathfinder, & jumpmaster qualified, 1948-50; capt. U.S. Army Security Agency, Washington, 1950-53, 56-60, with 501st Recon group Republic of Korea, 1953, Tokyo, 1954-56; advanced through grades to col. U.S. Army, 1953-68; appellate judge U.S. Ct. Mil. Rev. (U.S. Army Ct. Criminal Appeals), Washington, 1968-70; ret. colonel U.S. Army, 1970; appellate judge U.S. Army Judiciary, Washington, 1968-70; dir. law ctr. Roger Williams Coll., Providence, 1970-71; U.S. magistrate judge U.S. Dist. Ct., Providence, 1971—. Legal advisor to intelligence cmty. Spl. Ops., Berlin, 1960—63; group supr. def. appellate divsn. USA Judiciary, Washington, 1964—66; dep. and chief criminal law divsn. OTJAG dept. of the army The Pentagon, Washington, 1966—68; mem. U.S. Army and U.S. Air Force Clemency and Parole Bd.; lectr. Fed. Jud. Ctr., Washington; adj. prof. Am. U., 1971—, Suffolk U. Law Sch.; vis. prof. Naval War Coll.; mem. hon. faculty fellow AV, 1997—, hon. program U. R.I.; mem. code com. Uniform Code of Mil. Justice, Sec. of Def., 2000—03. Decorated Legion of Merit (2) with first oak leaf cluster; recipient Army Commendation medal with oak leaf cluster. Mem. ABA (former cons. sect. criminal justice, vice chmn. com. on adequate def. and incentives in mil., former sec.-reporter com. mil. law, Houston Justice Assist award 1987), Fed. Bar Assn. (past pres. R.I. chpt., mem. nat. coun., mem. nat. chmn. com. criminal law, chmn. U.S. magistrate judge's com.), Inst. Jud. Adminstrn., U.S. Naval War Coll. Found., Nat. Def. U. Found. Office: US Dist Ct Two Exchange Ter Providence RI 02903 Office Phone: 401-752-7011. Fax: 401-752-7006.

HAGOPIAN, VASKEN, physics educator; b. Beirut, Apr. 21, 1937; s. Bedros and Yeranouni (Kevorkian) H.; m. Sharon Lee Ford, Sept. 4, 1965; 1 child, Ara Peter. BS, Am. U. of Beirut, Lebanon, 1957; PhD, U. Pa., 1963. Rsch. assoc. U. Pa., Phila., 1963—65, asst. prof., 1966—69; vis. asst. prof. U. Calif., Berkeley, 1965—66; assoc. prof. Fla. State U., Tallahassee, 1970—75, prof. physics, 1975—, disting. rsch. prof., 1998, Joseph E. Lannutti prof., 1999—. Contbr. numerous articles to profl. jours. Grantee U.S. Dept. Energy, 1970—, NSF, Tex. Nat. Rsch. Lab. Coun., 1989-93. Fellow Am. Phys. Soc., U.S. CMS Collaboration (elected dep. chmn. 2000-). Office: Fla State U Physics Dept Tallahassee FL 32306-4350 E-mail: vasken@hep.fsu.edu.

HAGSTROM, JACK WALTER CARL KLING, retired pathology educator; b. Rockford, Ill., Dec. 2, 1933; s. Walter Carl Paul Hagstrom and Loretta Christine (Kling) Pearson; life ptnr. Thomas J. Fleming. AB, Amherst Coll., 1955; MD, Cornell U., 1959. Instr. dept. pathology Cornell U. Med. Coll., N.Y.C., 1962-65, asst. prof., 1965-68; assoc. prof. Case We. Res. U., Cleve., 1968-70, Columbia U., N.Y.C., 1970-75, prof. pathology, 1975-91, prof. emeritus, 1991—. Attending pathologist Univ. Hosp., Cleve., 1968—70, Presbyn. Hosp., N.Y.C., 1981—91; dir. dept. pathology Harlem Hosp., N.Y.C., 1981—91; hon. curator modern poetry Amherst Coll. Libr., Amherst, Mass., 1981—. Author: Thom Gunn: A Bibliography, 1979, Dana Gioia: A Descriptive Bibliography with Critical Essays, 2002; contbr. articles to profl. jours. Mem. corporator Holden Arboretum, Mentor, Ohio; chmn. Friends of Amherst Coll. Libr., 1973—90. Fellow: Am. Coll. Cardiology; mem.: Pvt. Librs. Assn., Acad. Am. Poets, Printing History Soc., Bibliograph. Soc. London, Bibliograph. Soc. U. Va., Bibliograph. Soc. Am., Kiambu Club, Northport Yacht Club, Durban Club, Jockey Club, Club Odd Vols., Grolier Club, Pratts Club, Travellers' Club, Garrick Club. Episcopalian. Home: PO Box 105 Seven Ponds Towd Rd Water Mill NY 11976

HAGUE, WILLIAM EDWARD, writer; b. Duquesne, Pa., Feb. 2, 1919; s. William Edward and Edith (Osburn) H.; m. Margaret Cleland Anderson, July 22, 1950 (div.). AB, Princeton U., 1940; postgrad., U. Pitts. Sch. Law, 1940-41. Assoc. editor Tide mag., 1947-49; promotion dir. Living for Young Homemakers mag., 1949-50, copy editor, 1951-54, mng. editor, 1954-61; editor Living's Guide to Home Planning mag., 1958-61; with Conde Nast Publs., N.Y.C.; sr. editor House & Garden, 1961; editor-in-chief House & Garden Guides, 1962-72; asst. account exec. Fitzgerald Advt. Agy., New Orleans, 1950-51. Author: How to Decorate With Color, 1964, What You Should Know About Furniture, 1965, Planning Your Vacation Home, 1968, Plan Your Baths for Beauty and Efficiency, 1969, Plan The Kitchen That Suits You, 1969, Making The Most of The One-Room Apartment, 1969, Your Vacation House, How To Plan It, 1972, Doubleday's Complete Basic Book of Home Decorating, 1976, Know Your America, California, 1978, Remodel, Don't Move, 1981, The New Complete Basic Book of Home Decorating, 1983; editor: Country Kitchens and Baths, 1987; contbg. editor: Reader's Digest's Household Hints, 1987. Lt. USNR, 1942—46. Recipient Dorothy Dawe award for disting. journalistic coverage in home furnishings field, 1969 Mem. Princeton Triangle Club. Home: 49 E 73rd St Apt 5F New York NY 10021-3560

HAGY, JAMES C., lawyer; b. Cleve., 1955; BA Phi Beta Kappa, Case Western Reserve Univ., 1975, JD, 1978. Bar: Ohio 1978, Ill. 1988. Ptnr., co-chair, real estate practice worldwide Jones Day, Chgo. Faculty mem. CoreNet Learning (formerly Inst. of Corp. Real Estate); chair, recruiting com. Jones Day. Editor: Law Rev., 1978; founding mem. (editorial bd.) Journ of Corp. Real Estate, Henry Stewart Publications, London; author: numerous articles in profl. publications. Named one of World's Leading Real Estate Lawyers, Euromoney mag. Mem.: Am. Coll. Real Estate Lawyers, Order of Coif. Office: Jones Day 77 W Wacker Chicago IL 60601-1692 Office Phone: 312-269-4152. Business E-Mail: jchagy@jonesday.com.

HAGY, TERESA JANE, elementary school educator; b. Bristol, Va., Nov. 1, 1950; d. Don Houston and Mary Garnett (Yeatts) Hagy. AA in Pre-Edn., Va. Intermont Coll., 1970, BA in Elem. Edn., 1972; MEd, U. Va., 1976, postgrad., Radford U. Cert. technology cert. U. Va., tchr. Va., Tenn. Tchr. 1st and 4th grades St. Anne's Demonstration Sch., Bristol, Va., 1972-75; tchr. 1st, 3d, 4th, 5th and 6th grades Washington Lee Elem. Sch., Bristol, 1975—. Clin. instr. edn. Va. Intermont Coll., Bristol, 1972-75; coordinator gifted and talented program Bristol Schs., 1980-82; condr. workshops; developer tests to evaluate reading progress. Pres. women's circle Cen. Christian Ch., Bristol, Tenn., also v.p., sec. women's fellowship, libr. chmn., mem. ch. choir, dir. music for Bible Sch., Sunday sch. tchr. 3d and 4th grades, 1979—. Recipient numerous edn. awards; named Tchr. of Yr., S.W. Va. Reading Coun., 1994, Tchr. of Quarter, Bible Sch., 1992, Tchr. of Yr., Rotary, 2000. Mem.: AAUW (sec. 1976—79, v.p. 1981—86), NEA, Va. State Reading Assn., Internat. Reading Assn., Bristol Edn. Assn. (sec. 1978—80, chmn. Am. Edn. Week 1993, v.p. membership chair 1994—95, sch. renewal steering com. 1994—99, chair staff and personal com. 1994—99, comm. rep. 1995—97, faculty rep. 1996—98, comm. rep. 2000—, 2001—), Va. Edn. Assn., Nat. Trust for Hist. Preservation, U. Va. Alumni Assn., Va. Intermont Coll. Alumni Assn. (nat. pres. 1987—89), U. Va. Alumnae Assn., Phi Theta Kappa, Delta Kappa Gamma (chpt. v.p. 1986—88, pres. 1988—90, coordinating coun. chmn. 1990—92). Republican. Avocations: singing, piano, stitchery, walking, reading. Home: 820 Virginia Ave Bristol TN 37620-3935 Office: Washington Lee Elem Sch Washington Lee Dr Bristol VA 24201 Office Phone: 276-821-5800. Business E-Mail: thagy@bristolvaschools.org.

HAH, DOOYOUNG, research scientist; b. Seoul, Republic of Korea, Nov. 19, 1972; s. Jong-Pil Hah and Song-Up Song; m. Induck Lee; 1 child, Heewon. BS, Korea Advanced Inst. Sci. and Tech., Daejeon, Republic of Korea, 1994; MS, Korea Advanced Inst. Sci. and Tech., Daejon, Republic of Korea, 1996; PhD, Korea Advanced Inst. Sci. and Tech., Daejeon, 1990—2000. Postgraduate rschr. UCLA, 2000—01, staff rsch. assoc., 2004—05; sr. mem., rsch. staff Electronics and Telecom. Rsch. Inst., Daejeon, Republic of Korea, 2002—04; asst. prof. La. State U., 2005—. Contbr. articles to profl. jours. Achievements include patents for Optical coupler 2 X 2 optical switch; Optical coupler sensor with movable waveguides; Microwave double-pole double-throw switch; Micro-optical switch using electromagnetic force; Scanning micromirror for optical communication systems. Office Phone: 310-339-9016. Personal E-mail: hady633@yahoo.com. E-mail: dyhah@icsl.ucla.edu.

HAHN, ARTHUR W., lawyer; b. Chgo., July 30, 1944; s. Bernard and Ruth (Fireman) H.; m. Kathy Miller, June 20, 1969; children: Noah, Samuel. Student, London Sch. Econs., 1964-65; BA, Miami U., Oxford, Ohio, 1966; JD, Northwestern U., 1969. Law clk. to presiding judge U.S. Dist. Ct. Ill., Chgo., 1969-71; assoc., then ptnr. Pope, Ballard, Shepard & Fowle, Chgo., 1971-79; ptnr. Katten, Muchin, Zavis, Pearl & Galler, Chgo., 1979-80; dir. Mercantile House Holdings, Chgo., 1980-84; pres., chief exec. officer N.Am. Futures div., Chgo., 1980-84; ptnr. Katten Muchin Zavis Rosenman, Chgo., 1984—. Faculty chmn. Ill. Inst. Tech. Chgo. Kent Coll. Law Grad. Sch. Fin. Svcs. Law, 1987—; mem. Ill. Task Force on Fin. Svcs., Springfield, 1987. Contbr. articles on corp. and commodities law to profl. jours. Mem. Dem. Senatorial Campaign Com., Washington, 1988—; bd. dirs. Spertus Coll. Judaica, Chgo., 1988—. Mem. ABA, Chgo. Bar Assn., Chgo. Bar Assn. (founding chmn. commodities law com.), Futures Industry Assn. (bd. dirs. 1983-84), Futures Industry Inst. (exec. com., trustee 1989—, chmn. internat. div.), Econ. Club, Standard Club, Legal Club, Wigmore Club. Office: Katten Muchin & Zavis 525 W Monroe St Ste 1600 Chicago IL 60661-3693 Office Fax: 312-577-8892. E-mail: arthur.hahn@kmzr.com.

HAHN, BETTY, artist, photographer, educator; b. Chgo., Oct. 11, 1940; d. Eugene Joseph and Esther Josephine (Krueger) H.; widowed. AB, Ind. U., 1963, M.F.A., 1966. Asst. prof. photography Rochester (N.Y.) Inst. Tech., 1969-75; prof. art U. N.Mex., Albuquerque, 1976-97, prof. emeritus, 1997—. One-woman shows include Smithsonian Instn., Washington, 1969, Ctr. Photographic Studies, Louisville, 1971, Focus Gallery, San Francisco, 1974, Sandstone Gallery, Rochester, N.Y., 1978, Blue Sky Gallery, Portland, Oreg., 1978, Susan Spiritus Gallery, Newport Beach, Calif., 1977, 82, Witkin Gallery, N.Y.C., 1973, 79, Washington Project for the Arts, 1980, Ctr. Creative Photography, Tucson, 1981, Columbia Coll. Gallery, Chgo., 1982, Port Washington Pub. Library, N.Y., 1984, Mus. Fine Arts, Mus. N.Mex, Santa Fe, 1986, Lehigh U., 1988, U. Mass., Amherst, 1989, Andrew Smith Gallery, Santa Fe, 1991, U. N.Mex. Art Mus., Albuquerque, 1994. Named Honored Educator, Soc. for Photog. Edn., 1984; Nat. Endowment Arts grantee, 1977-78, 82-83; N.Y. State Council Arts grantee, 1976 Mem. Soc. Photog. Edn., Coll. Art Assn., Evidence Photographers Internat. Council Office: Univ N Mex Art Dept Albuquerque NM 87131-0001

HAHN, DOWON, pharmaceutical researcher, educator; b. Hoo-Chang, Korea, Nov. 20, 1931; came to U.S., 1955; s. Sung-Bum Hahn and Wan-Ok Cho; m. Myung Yun Kim, Aug. 31, 1963; children: Charles, Helen, Anna. BS in Agrl. Mechanics, Mich. State U., 1960, MS in Animal Breeding, 1963; PhD in Endocrinology, U. Mo., 1967. Assoc. scientist Ortho Pharm. Corp., Raritan, N.J., 1968-69, scientist, 1969-70, sr. scientist, 1970-72, group leader, 1973-74, sect. head, 1975-82, asst. dir., 1982-87, dir., 1987-92; Disting. rsch. fellow R.W. Johnson Pharm. Rsch. Inst., Raritan, NJ, 1993—2002; ret., 2002; cons. in field, 2002—. Adj. prof. dept. animal sci. Rutgers U., New Brunswick, N.J., 1982—, dept. ob/gyn. Ea. Va. Med. Sch., Norfolk, 1967—; postdoctoral fellow Worcester Found., 1967-68. Recipient grant Danforth Found., 1958, fellowship Ford Found., 1967, Phillips B. Hoffman Rsch. Scientist award Johnson and Johnson, 1973, 85, Johnson medal Johnson and Johnson, 1990. Mem. Soc. for Study of Reproduction, Soc. for Gynecol. Investigation, The Endocrine Soc., Am. Soc. Reproductive Medicine, Am. Coll. Ob-Gyn., Japan Soc. Ob/gyn. Achievements include discovery of and development of new progestin Norgastimate, the component of birth control pill Ortho-Tri-Cyclin. Home and Office: 9109 Down Crest Way Windermere FL 34786 E-mail: dowon@bellsouth.net.

HAHN, EDWARD KARL, dentist; b. Cleve., June 23, 1930; s. Edward Herman and Pauline Valerie (Zoruba) H.; m. Doris May Monus, June 25, 1956; children: Edward Karl Jr., Sheryl Louise Posey. BS, John Carroll U., 1953; DDS, Case We. Res. U., 1956. Rotating dental intern Brooke Army Hosp., Ft. Sam, Houston and San Antonio, 1956-57; clin. instr. Sch. Dentistry Case We. Res. U., Cleve., 1960-63; pvt. practice North Richland Hills, Tex., 1964-75, 75-96, Grapevine, Tex., 1996—; dentist Dental Implant Restoration, Hurst, Tex., 1997—. Mem. med. edn. com. North Hills Hosp., North Richland Hills, 1984, vice chmn. credentials com., 1989—, chmn. ethics com., 1998—; bd. dirs. dental hygiene program Tarrant County Jr. Coll., advisor and clin. examiner, 1986—; advisor Ft. Worth Dist. Dental Assts. Orgn., 1985—, liaison Tarrant County dental assisting and dental hygiene program, 1986—. Author: The Health of the Dentist, 1957. Mem. zoning bd. adjustment City North Richland Hills, 1968-82. With USAF, 1957-60. Mem. ADA, Tex. Dental Assn., Ft. Worth Dist. Dental Soc. (patient/dentist rev. com. 1976, mem. peer rev. com. 1989, Outstanding Svc. to Dental Profession award 1995), Masons, Mosla Shrine, Lion Heart Lodge, Omicron Kappa Upsilon. Avocations: wwii aircraft, 1930s to 1960s vintage autos. Home: 7500 Windswept Trl Colleyville TX 76034 Office: 230 Park Blvd # 107 Grapevine TX 76051 Office Phone: 817-481-1036. Office Fax: 817-481-5044. E-mail: edandori@earthlink.net.

HAHN, ELLIOTT JULIUS, lawyer; b. San Francisco, Dec. 9, 1949; s. Leo Wolf and Sherry Marion (Portnoy) H.; m. Toby Rose Mallen; children: Kara Rebecca, Brittany Atira Mallen, Michael Mallen, Adam Mallen. BA cum laude, U. Pa., 1971, JD, 1974; LLM, Columbia U., 1980. Bar: N.J. 1974, Calif. 1976, D.C. 1978, U.S. Dist. Ct. N.J. 1974, U.S. Dist. Ct. (cen. dist.) Calif. 1976, U.S. Supreme Ct. 1980. Assoc. von Malitz, Derenberg, Kunin & Janssen, N.Y.C., 1974-75; law clk. L.A. County Superior Ct., 1975-76; atty. Atlantic Richfield Co., L.A., 1976-79; prof. Summer in Tokyo program Santa Clara Law Sch., 1981-83; assoc. prof. law Calif. Western Sch. Law, San Diego, 1980-85; atty. Morgan, Lewis & Bockius, L.A., 1985-87; assoc. Whitman & Ransom, L.A., 1987-88, ptnr., 1989-93, Sonnenschein Nath & Rosenthal, L.A., 1993-97, Hahn & Bolson, LLP, 1997—. Vis. scholar Nihon U., Tokyo, 1982; vis. lectr. Internat. Christian U., Tokyo, 1982; adj. prof. law Southwestern U. Sch. Law, 1986-93, Pepperdine U. law Sch., 1986-93, U. So. Calif. Law Sch., 1997-98; lectr. U. Calif., Davis, Law Sch. Orientation in U.S.A. Law Program, 1994-97. Author: Japanese Business Law and the Legal System, 1984; contbr. chpt. on Japan to The World Legal Ency.; internat. law editor Calif. Bus. Law Reporter. Vice-chmn. San Diego Internat. Affairs Bd., 1981-85; bd. dirs. San Diego-Yokohama Sister City Soc., 1983-85, L.A.-Nagoya Sister City Soc., 1986-1996; mem. master planning com. City of Rancho Palos Verdes, Calif., 1989-91; advisor, exec. com. Calif. Internat. Law Sect., 1990-91, 95, appointee exec. com., 1991-94, vice-chmn., 1992-93, chair, 1993-94; appointee, trustee Palos Verdes Libr. Dist., 1993-94; bd. dirs. Internat. Student Ctr. UCLA, 1996-2004, pres., 2000-01. Fellow Ctr. Internat. Legal Studies; mem. ABA, State Bar Calif., LA County Bar Assn. (bd. dirs. internat. sect., exec. com. Internat. Legal Sec. 1987—, sec. 1995-96, 2d v.p. 1996-97, 1st v.p. 1997-98, chmn. 1998-99, appointee Pacific rim com. 1990-98, chmn. 1991-92, 95-98, trustee 1997-98), Assn. Asian Studies, U. Pa. Alumni Club (pres. San Diego chpt. 1982, pres. coun. Phila. 1983), Anti Defamation League, Japanese-Am. Soc. (book rev. editor Seattle 1983-85). Jewish. Office: Hahn & Bolson LLP 1000 Wilshire Blvd # 1600 Los Angeles CA 90017-2457 Office Phone: 213-630-2620. Business E-Mail: ehahn@hahnbolsonllp.com.

HAHN, ERWIN LOUIS, physicist, researcher; b. Sharon, Pa., June 9, 1921; s. Israel and Mary Hahn; m. Marian Ethel Failing, Apr. 8, 1944 (dec. Sept. 1978); children: David L., Deborah A., Katherine L.; m. Natalie Woodford Hodgson, Apr. 12, 1980. BS, Juniata Coll., 1943, D.Sc., 1966; MS, U. Ill., 1947, PhD, 1949; D.Sc., Purdue U., 1975, U. Stuttgart, Germany, 2001; DrRerNat, U. Stuttgart, 2001. Asst. Purdue U., 1943-44; research assoc. U. Ill., 1950; NRC fellow Stanford, 1950-51, instr., 1951-52; research physicist Watson IBM Lab., N.Y.C., 1952-55; assoc. Columbia U., 1952-55; faculty U. Calif., Berkeley, 1955—, prof. physics, 1961—, assoc. prof., then prof. Miller Inst. for Basic Rsch., 1958-59, 66-67, 85-86. Eastman vis. prof. Balliol Coll., Oxford, Eng., 1988-89; cons. Office Naval Rsch., Stanford, 1950-52, AEC, 1955—; spl. cons. USN, 1959; adv. panel mem. Nat. Bur. Stds., Radio Stds. div., 1961-64; mem. NAS/NRC com. on basic rsch.; advisor to U.S. Army Rsch. Office, 1967-69; faculty rsch. lectr. U. Calif., Berkeley, 1979. Author: (with T.P. Das) Nuclear Quadrupole Resonance Spectroscopy, 1958. Served with USNR, 1944-46. Fellow Guggenheim Found., 1961-62, 69-70, NSF, 1961-62; recipient prize Internat. Soc. Magnetic Resonance, 1971, Humboldt Found. award, 1977, 94, Alumni Achievement award Juniata Coll., 1986, citation U. Calif., Berkeley, 1991, Russell Varian prize Varian Corp., 2004; co-winner prize in physics Wolf Found., 1984; named to Calif. Inventor Hall of Fame, 1984; vis. fellow Brasenose Coll., Oxford U., 1969-70, life hon. fellow, 1984—. Fellow AAAS, Internat. Soc. Electron Paramagnetic Resonance, Am. Phys. Soc. (past mem. exec. com. div. solid state physics, Oliver E. Buckley prize 1971), Soc. Magnetic Resonance in Medicine (hon.); mem. NAS (co-recipient Comstock prize in electricity, magnetism and radiation 1993), Slovenian Acad. Scis. and Arts (fgn.), French Acad. Scis. (fgn. assoc.), Berkeley Fellows, Royal Soc. U.K. (fgn. mem.). Home: 69 Stevenson Ave Berkeley CA 94708-1732 Office: U Calif Dept Physics 367 Birge Berkeley CA 94720-0001

HAHN, FRANK HORACE, economics professor; b. Berlin, Apr. 26, 1925; s. Arnold and Maria (Katz) H.; m. Dorothy Salter, 1946. BSc in Econs., London, 1945, PhD, 1951; MA, Cambridge (Eng.) U., 1960; D in Social Scis. (hon.), Birmingham (Eng.) U., 1981; DLitt (hon.), U. East Anglia, Norwich, 1984; Doctor honoris causa, U. Strasbourg, 1984; DSc in Econs. (hon.), London, 1985; D (hon.), U. York, 1991; LittD (hon.), U. Leicester, 1993; PhD (hon.), U. Athens, 1993; doctor honoris causa, De L'Univ. Paris X, Nanterre, 1999. Lectr., reader math. econs. Birmingham U., 1948-60; lectr. econs. Cambridge U., 1960-66; prof. econs. London Sch. Econs., 1967-72, prof., 1972-92, prof. emeritus, 1992; prof. ordinario U. Siena, 1989—2000; hon. fellow London Sch. Econs., 1989; fellow Churchill Coll., Cambridge, 1960—; emeritus U. Siena, 2000—. Co-author (with Kenneth J. Arrow): General Competitive Analysis, 1971; author: The Share of Wages in the National Income, 1972, Money and Inflation, 1982, Equilibrium and Macroeconomics, 1984, Money, Growth and Stability, 1985; co-author (with Robert Solow): A Critical Essay on Modern Macroeconomic Theory, 1995; editor: The Economics of Missing Markets, Information, and Games, 1989; co-editor (with Ben Friedman): Handbook of Monetary Economics, 1990; co-editor: (with Fabio Petri) General Equilibrium: Problems and Prospects, 2003; mng. editor Rev. Econ. Studies, 1965—68, assoc. editor Jour. Econ. Theory, 1971—76. Recipient Palacky gold medal Czechoslovak Acad. Scis., 1991. Fellow Brit. Acad., Econometric Soc. (pres. 1968-69), NAS (fgn. assoc. 1988), Am. Acad. Arts and Scis. (hon.), Am. Econ. Assn. (hon.), Royal Econ. Soc. (pres. 1986-89), Brit. Assn. Advancement Sci. (pres. sect. F 1990), Italian Assn. History Polit. Economy (hon.).

HAHN, FREDERIC LOUIS, lawyer; b. Chgo., Apr. 28, 1941; s. Max and Margery Ruth (Goodman) H.; m. Susan Firestone, Mar. 26, 1967; 1 child, Frederic Firestone. AB with highest distinction, Cornell U., 1962, MBA with highest distinction, 1963; JD magna cum laude, Harvard U., 1966. Bar: Ill. 1966; CPA, Ill. Assoc. Hopkins & Sutter, Chgo., 1966-72, ptnr., 1973-94, Mayer, Brown & Platt (now Mayer, Brown, Rowe & Maw), Chgo., 1994—. Bd. dirs. Lyric Opera of Chgo., 1988—. Recipient Gold medal (CPA exam) State of Ill., 1963. Mem. Phi Beta Kappa. Home: 1377 Scott Ave Winnetka IL 60093-1444 Office: Mayer Brown Rowe & Maw 171 South Wacker Dr Chicago IL 60606-4637 E-mail: fhahn@mayerbrownrowe.com.

HAHN, GEORGE LEROY, agriculture engineer, biometeorologist; b. Muncie, Kans., Nov. 12, 1934; s. Vernon Leslie and Marguerite Alberta (Breeden) H.; m. Clovice Elaine Christensen, Dec. 3, 1955; children—Valerie, Cecile, Steven, Melanie. BS, U. Mo., Columbia, 1957, PhD, 1971; MS, U. Calif., Davis, 1961. Agrl. engr., project leader and tech. advisor Agrl. Research Service, U.S. Dept. Agr., Columbia, Mo., 1957, Davis, Calif., 1958-61, Columbia, 1961-78, Clay Center, Nebr., 1978—. Contbr. articles to profl. jours. and books on impact of climatic and other environ. factors on livestock prodn., efficiency, and well-being, evaluation of methods of reducing impact and techniques for measuring dynamic responses and characterizing stress in meat animals. Recipient award Am. Soc. Agrl. Engrs.-Metal Bldgs. Mfrs. Assn., 1976 Fellow Am. Soc. Agrl. Engrs. (dir. prof. coun. 1991-93); mem. Am. Meteorol. Soc. (award for outstanding achievement in bioclimatology 1976), Internat. Soc. Biometeorology (treas. 1999—), Am. Soc. Animal Sci. Office: US Meat Animal Rsch Ctr PO Box 166 Clay Center NE 68933-0166 Office Phone: 402-762-4271. Business E-Mail: hahn@email.marc.usda.gov.

HAHN, GEORGE THOMAS, materials engineering educator, researcher; b. Vienna, July 28, 1930; came to U.S., 1938; s. Rudolph and Stella (Honig) H.; m. Charlotte Minovitz, June 10, 1956; children: Claudia Abbott, Elizabeth. BSME, NYU, 1952; MS in Metall. Engring., Columbia U., 1956; ScD in Metall. Engring., MIT, 1959. Rsch. engr. Westinghouse Rsch. Labs., Pitts., 1952; cons. Mfg. Labs., Cambridge, Mass., 1956-60; rsch. assoc. metal sci. sect. Battelle Meml. Inst., Columbus, Ohio, 1960-66, mgr. metal sci. sect., 1966-79; prof. materials sci. and engring. Vanderbilt U., Nashville, 1979-98, prof. materials sci. and engring. emeritus, 1998—, chmn. dept. materials sci. and engring., 1988-93; co-dir. Ctr. Materials Tribology, Nashville, 1987-96; pres. Mechanics & Materials Techs. Inc., Nashville, 1988—. Co-editor: Fracture, 1959, Fast Fracture and Crack Arrest, 1977, Crack Arrest Methods, 1980; contbr. numerous articles to profl. jours. Capt. USAF, 1953-57. Fellow Am. Soc. Metals (Campbell Meml. Lectr. 1981), Metall. Soc., Am. Soc. Lubrication Engrs. Avocation: painting. Office: Vanderbilt U Dept Mech Engring Box 1592 Sta B Nashville TN 37235 E-mail: hahngt@vuse.vanderbilt.edu.

HAHN, GERALD EUGENE, industrial education educator; b. Peoria, Ill., July 15, 1942; s. Earl L. and Clarice A. (Briggs) H. BS, U. Ill., 1965, MEd, 1968. Cert. indsl. edn. tchr., Ill.; ordained deacon 1988. Tchr. Thornton Twp. H.S., Harvey, Ill., 1965—95, chmn. dept. indsl. edn., 1985—90; ret., 1995; tchr. Queen of Apostles Parish Sch., 1998—2003. Mem. Holy Name Soc. Queen of Apostles Parish, PTA (life). Mem. NEA, Ill. Edn. Assn. Lodges: KC. Roman Catholic. Avocations: swimming, stained glass crafting, canoeing, travel, music. Home: 14261 Pennsylvania Ave Apt 11 Dolton IL 60419-1160

HAHN, HELENE B., motion picture company executive; b. N.Y.C. BA, Hofstra U.; JD, Loyola U., Calif., 1975. Bar: Calif. 1975. V.p. bus. affairs Paramount Pictures Corp., L.A., sr. v.p. bus. affairs, 1983-84; sr. v.p. bus. and legal Walt Disney Studios, Burbank, Calif., 1984-87, exec. v.p., 1987-94; co-COO Dreamworks SKG, Glendale, Calif., 1994—2003, COO, 2003—. Recipient Frontrunner award in bus. Sara Lee Corp., 1991, Big Sisters Achievement award, 1992, Clairol Mentor award, 1993, Women in Bus. Magnificent Seven award, 1994. Office: Dreamworks Bungalow 5121 100 Universal Terrace Pkwy Universal City CA 91608-1001

HAHN, JAMES KENNETH, former mayor, lawyer; b. LA, July 3, 1950; s. Kenneth and Ramona Hahn; m. Monica Ann Teson, May 19, 1984; children: Karina Natalie, Jackson Kenneth. BA in English magna cum laude, Pepperdine U., 1972, JD, 1975. Bar: Calif. 1975. Law clk. L.A. County Dist. Atty.'s Office; city pros. L.A. City Atty.'s Office, 1975-79; pvt. practice Marina del Rey, 1979-81; city contr. City of L.A., 1981-85, city atty., 1985—2001, mayor, 2001—05.

HAHN, JOHN WILLIAM, retired insurance company executive; b. N.Y.C., July 12, 1940; s. Ferdinand J. and Evelyn H. H. (Hauser) Hahn; m. L. Dale Mazza, 1963; children: Nancy, John. BA, Queen's Coll, 1962; postgrad., Harvard U., 1973-74. With Atlantic Mut. Cos., N.Y.C., 1963—2002, v.p., adminstrv. svcs., 1963—2002, sr. v.p., adminstrv. svcs. Roanoke, Va., 1978-85, exec. v.p., adminstrn. Madison, NJ, 1985—2002; exec. cons., 2002—. Mem. exec. com., bd. dirs. Ins. Value Added Network Svc., Conn., 1985—92; mem. std. com. Agy. Co. Orgn. R & D; spl. advisor Artbase, N.Y.C., 2003—; bd. dirs. Sun Trust Bank, Luxury Market Coun. With USMC, 1959—66. Mem.: Alliance Productive Tech. (chmn. bd. dirs. 1997—98), Va. Mil. Family Support Ctr., Inc. (exec. v.p.), AGENA Corp. (chmn. bd. dirs. 1993—95), Marines Meml. Assn., Waters Edge Country Club, Piedmont Club, Hidden Valley Country Club (Va.), Roanoke Country Club, Harvard Club (N.Y.C.). Home: 85 Loving Cir Penhook VA 24137-5225 Office Phone: 540-576-1984. Personal E-mail: pmd261@charter.net. E-mail: pmd261@aol.com.

HAHN, JOYCE WEBB, writer; b. Kearney, N.J., Dec. 16, 1925; d. John Glen Webb and Florence Mary Vickers-Webb; m. George Max Hahn, Jan. 22, 1949; children: Peter James, Nina Elizabeth, Jack. BA, U. Calif., Berkeley, 1947; MA, San Francisco State U., 1968. Cert. jr. coll. tchr. Tchr. Cmty. Edn. Ctr., Redwood City, Calif., 1964—75; cons. Head Start, San Francisco, 0745—1980; self-employed writer Monterey, Calif., 1985—. Author: (novel) California Yankee Under Three Flags, 2002; exhibitions include, Stanford and San Francisco, 1970, 1980, 2001. Precinct capt. Dem. Club Berkeley, 1950. Avocations: hiking, travel, archaeology. Home: 93 B Corona Way Carmel CA 93923

HAHN, KARLA LYNN, librarian; b. Champaign, Ill., Aug. 14, 1964; d. William F. and Marilyn E. Hahn; m. Saul Robert Strieb, Nov. 28, 1991. BA, Wittenberg U., 1986; MA, U. Chgo., 1988; MLS, Syracuse U., 1990; PhD, U. Md., 1999. Libr. resident U. Mich. Libr., Ann Arbor, Mich., 1990—92; network based svcs. mgr. Welch Med. Libr., Balt., 1992—95; collection mgmt. team leader U. Md. Libr., Coll. Pk., Md., 1997—2005; dir. office of scholarly comm. Assn. of Rsch. Libr., Wash., DC, 2005—. Contbr. articles various profl. jours. Luth. Office Phone: 202-296-2296.

HAHN, KEITH WORDEN, physiatrist; b. Ft. Lauderdale, Fla., Feb. 11, 1959; s. Theodore Wallace and Virginia (Kennedy) H.; m. Carol Blankenburg, Aug. 8, 1993. BA in Chemistry, Emory U., 1981; MD, U. South Fla., 1985. Diplomate Am. Bd. Physical Medicine and Rehab. Intern The Med. Ctr., Columbus, Ga., 1985-86; resident Univ. Tex., Dallas, 1986-89; med. dir. Bessamer-Carraway Rehab. Hosp., Birmingham, Ala., 1989-90; rehab. physician Tampa VA Hosp., 1990-98, Dallas VA Hosp., 1998—. Active Nature Conservancy, Winter Park, Fla., 1989—, Covenant House, NYC, 1994—. Mem. Am. Acad. Physical Medicine and Rehab. (assoc.). Republican. Episcopalian.

HAHN, KENNETH P., manufacturing executive; b. 1958; Grad., U. Wis., Milw. CPA. Audit mgr. Price Waterhouse; corp. contr. Gehl Co., West Bend, Wis., 1988—, officer, 1994, v.p. fin., treas., 1997—. Office: Gehl Co PO Box 179 143 Water St West Bend WI 53095-3400 Fax: 262-334-6603.

HAHN, LORNA, political organization executive, author; b. Phila., June 16; d. Charles William and Belle Herman; m. Walter F. Hahn; 1 child, Randolph P. BA, Temple U.; MA, U. Pa., PhD in Internat. Rels., 1962. Instr. Temple U., Phila.; researcher Spl. Ops. & Rsch. Office, Washington; rsch. coord. Hist. Evaluation & Rsch. Orgn., Washington; dir. Masters program Am. U., Washington; exec. dir. Assn. Third World Affairs, Washington, 1968—. V.p. Internat. Fedn. for Protection of Religious, Linguistic & Ethnic Minorities, Washington, 1987—; pub. Third World Forum, 1976—; advisor Save Cambodia, Inc.,Washington, 1980—; lectr. Cath. U., Washington, 1965-66, Howard U., Washington, 1971-73, 82-83. Author: North Africa: Nationalism to Nationhood, 1960, Undergrounds in Insurgency, Revolutionary and Resistance Warfare, 1964, Morocco: Old Land, New Nation, 1966, An Historical Dictionary of Libya, 1981; author numerous monographs, articles and reviews; frequent guest on talk shows. Advisor Dem. candidates. Recipient Scholarship medal Phi Gamma Mu. Mem. Dems. 2000. Mem. Unitarian Ch. First woman to lecture at U.S. Nat. War Coll. and other mil. staff colls. Office: Assn Third World Affairs 1629 K St NW Washington DC 20006-1602

HAHN, MARC B., physician; b. Providence, 1958; DO, Des Moines U., 1984. Intern Walter Reed Army Med. Ctr., Washington, 1984-85, resident in anesthesiology, 1985-87; fellow in pain mgmt. Nat. Inst. Health, Bethesda, Md., 1987-88; prof. dept. anesthesiology Pa. State U. Coll. Medicine, Hershey, 1995—2001; dean Texas Coll. of Osteopathic Med., 2001—. Mem. AMA, Am. Osteo. Assn., Am. Pain Soc., Am. Soc. Anesthesiologists, Am. Acad. Pain Medicine, Internat. Assn. Study of Pain. Office: Tex Coll of Osteopathic Med 3500 Camp Bowie Blvd Fort Worth TX 76107-2699

HAHN, MARY DOWNING, writer; b. Washington, Dec. 9, 1937; d. Kenneth Ernest and Anna Elisabeth (Sherwood) Downing; m. William Edward Hahn, Oct. 7, 1961 (div. 1977); children: Katherine Sherwood, Margaret Elizabeth; m. Norman Pearce Jacob, Apr. 24, 1982. BA in Fine Arts and English, U. Md., 1960, MA in English, 1969. Asst. libr. children's sect. Prince George's County (Md.) Meml. Libr. System, 1975-91; instr. English U. Md., College Park, 1970-74; free-lance illustrator PBS/WETA, Arlington, Va., 1973-75. Author: The Sara Summer, 1979, The Time of the Witch, 1982, Daphne's Book, 1983 (William Allen White Children's Choice award 1985-86), The Jellyfish Season, 1985, Wait Till Helen Comes: A Ghost Story, 1980 (11 Children's Choice awards), Tallahassee Higgins, 1987, Following the Mystery Man, 1988, December Stillness, 1988 (Book award Child Study Assn. 1989, Calif. Young Readers' medal 1990-91), The Doll in the Garden, 1989 (Md. Children's Book award 1990-91, 7 Children's Choice awards), The Dead Man in Indian Creek, 1990 (4 Children's Choice awards), The Spanish Kidnapping Disaster, 1991, Stepping on the Cracks, 1991 (Scott O'Dell Hist. Fiction award 1992, ALA notable 1991, Joan G. Sugarman award, Hedda Seisler Mason award, Children's Choice awards), The Wind Blows Backward, 1993 (ALA Best Books for Young Adults), Time for Andrew, 1994 (7 Children's Choice awards), Look for Me by Moonlight, 1995 (Yalsa Quick Picks for Reluctant Readers), The Gentleman Outlaw and Me-Eli, 1996, Following My Own Footsteps, 1996, As Ever, Gordy, 1998, Anna All Year Round, 1999, Promises to the Dead, 2000, Anna on the Farm, 2001, Hear the Wind Blow, 2003, The Old Willis Place, 2004. Recipient Scott O'Dell award for hist. fiction, 1992, author's award Md. Libr. Assn., 1997. Mem. Soc. Children's Book Writers, Washington Children's Book Guild. Personal E-mail: mdh12937@aol.com.

HAHN, ROBERT ALAN, philosophy educator; b. N.Y.C., Aug. 25, 1952; s. Stanley Lawrence and Shirley Laura (Wishner) Hahn; m. Amy Lynn Knoblock; children: Zoë Shirley, Chava Sara. BA summa cum laude, Union Coll., 1973; MA in Philosophy, MPhil, Yale U., 1975, PhD, 1976. Postdoctoral rsch. fellow U. Calif., Berkeley, 1976; lectr. philosophy Yale U., New Haven, 1977; asst. prof. philosophy U. Tex., Arlington, 1977—78; asst. prof. philosophy and history of ideas Brandeis U., Waltham, Mass., 1978—81; asst. prof. Harvard U., Cambridge, Mass., 1979—81; from asst. prof. philosophy to assoc. prof. philosophy So. Ill. U., Carbondale, 1982—, prof. philosophy, 2002—. Vis. prof. Am. Coll. Greece, 1980. Author: Kant's 'Newtonian Revolution' in Philosophy, 1988, Self-Identity and Moral Decisions, 1989, 2nd edit., 1991, Formal Deductive Logic, 1993, 7th edit., 2003, Conduct and Contraints: Testing the Limits of the 'Harm Principle', 1994, 6th edit., 2001, Anaximander and the Architects: The Contribution of Egyptian and Greek Architectural Technologies to the Origins of Greek Philosophy, 2001, Anaximander in Context: New Studies on the Origins of Greek Philosophy, 2003; contbr. articles to profl. jours. including Phronesis, Jour. History of Philosophy, Apeiron, Southwest Jour. Philosophy, Philos. Rsch. Archives, Jour. Chinese Philosophy. Fellow, Yale U., 1974—76; Regents scholar, N.Y. State, Archibald scholar, 1972—73. Mem.: Am. Philol. Assn., Ill. Philos. Soc., N. Am. Kant Soc., Soc. Ancient Greek Philosophy, Archeol. Inst. Am., Am. Philos. Assn., Nat. Classics Honor Soc. (hon.), Phi Beta Kappa. Avocation: semi-profl. tennis player. Office: So Ill U Dept Philosophy Carbondale IL 62901-4505 Business E-Mail: rhahn@jinx.umsl.edu.

HAHN, ROBERT J, lawyer; BA, St. John's Univ., 1979; JD, St. John's Univ. Sch. Law, 1984. Bar: NY 1985, NC 1995. Ptnr. Hunton & Williams LLP, Charlotte, NC. Mem.: ABA. Office: Hunton & Williams LLP Bank of America Plaza Ste 3500 - 101 S Tryon St Charlotte NC 28280*

HAHN, STEVEN, history professor, writer; b. NYC, July 18, 1951; BA, U. Rochester, 1973; MA in History, Yale U., 1975, MPhil. in History, 1976, PhD in History, 1979. Lecturer Yale College, 1976, 1979; assist. prof. history U. Del., 1979—81, U. Calif., San Diego, 1981—83, assoc. prof. history, 1983—87, prof. history, 1987—98, Northwestern U., 1998—2003; Roy F. and Jeannette P. Nichols prof. history U. Pa., 2003—. Author: The Roots of Southern Populism: Yeoman Farmers and the Transformation of the Georgia Upcountry, 1850-1890, 1983 (Frederick Jackson Turner award best first book in American History, 1984, Allan Nevins prize outstanding doctoral diss. in Am. History, 1980), Nation Under Our Feet: Black Political Struggles in the Rural South From Slavery to the Great Migration, 2003 (Pulitzer Prize for History, 2004, Bancroft prize in Am. History, 2004, Merle Curti award best book in Social History, 2004, Lincoln prize finalist, 2004, Mark Lynton History prize finalist, 2004); co-editor: The Countryside in the Age of Capitalist Transformation: Essays in the Social History of Rural America, 1985, Freedom: A Documentary History of Emancipation, Land and Labor in 1865, 2004; contbr. scholarly articles to Am. Hist. Review, Past and Present, Journ. So. Hist. Recipient E. Harold Hugo Meml. Book prize, 1973, ABC Clio Am.: History and Life award, Org. Am. Hist., 1991; fellow, Guggenheim Found., 1989, Am. Coun. Learned Societies and Ctr. Advanced Studies Behavioral Sci., Stanford, 1987, Soc. Am. Historians, 1993. Office: U Pa 218 College Hall Philadelphia PA 19104-6379

HAIBI, ZORAIDA, artist; b. N.Y.C., Apr. 18, 1973; s. Omar and Dora Haibi. AA, Miami Dade C.C., 1994; BFA, Fla. Internat. U., 1996; postgrad. in Fine Arts, Mich. State U. Sub. tchr. Dade County Pub. Schs., Miami, Fla., 1995-97; tchr. art Cath. Sch., Miami, Fla., 1996-97; grad. asst., tchg. asst. Mich. State U., East Lansing, 1997-99. Recipient Pierre Toussaint/Roger Jerome Radloff Found. award, 1997, 98, 99, 2000, Recruitment fellowship Mich. State U., 1997, Equal Opportunity Program fellowship Mich. State U., 1998, award Pitman Photo, 1997. Avocations: painting, photography, reading, writing. Home and Office: 13450 SW 78th St Miami FL 33183-3304 E-mail: chorti@worldnet.att.net.

HAICK, SHANNON MARIE, counseling administrator; b. Niagara Falls, N.Y., Aug. 21, 1972; d. Abraham David and Diane C. Haick. BA in Communication, State U. Coll., Buffalo, 1996, MS in Student Pers., 2000. Acad. advisor Buffalo State Coll.; acad. advisement coord. Pace U., N.Y.C. Pub. rels. specialist Crave Restaurant, Bklyn. Mem.: Assn. Coll. Student Pers. Adminstrs., Nat. Assn. Coll. Acad. Advisors, Nat. Coalition Bldg. Inst. (facilitator 1999—). Avocation: yoga. Office: Pace U 41 Park Row 2d Fl New York NY 10038

HAIDER, PAUL RANDALL, stress management consultant; b. Woodland, Calif., Sept. 10, 1953; s. Ali and Marjorie Haider. AA in Biology, Yuba Coll., Marysville, Calif., 1973; AS in RVT, Cosumnes River Coll., Sacramento, 1979; BA in Psychology and Stress Mgmt., The Union Inst., Sacramento, 1997. Sr. technician x-ray U. Calif., Davis, 1981—88; head of tech. area x-ray U. Wis., Madison, 1988—92; CEO Paul Haider Cons., Pacific Grove, Calif., 1992—. Stress mgmt. cons. Paul Haider Cons., life coach. Contbg. editor: Bus. Mag. P.R., 2001—, San Juan Star, 2001—; assoc. editor: Alternative Mag., 2003—; author: (books) Relax Into Success, 2003, 21 Ways to Live a Stress-Free Life, 2004, (cd) Deep Relaxation, 2000. Mem.: Critical Incident Stress Found., Am. Coun. of Hypnotist Examiners, Am. Assn. of Profl. Hypnotherapists. Avocations: sailing, fishing, camping, photography. Home and Office: Paul Haider Stress Mgmt/Life Coach PO Box 51646 Pacific Grove CA 93950 Office Phone: 831-869-9119. E-mail: relax@paulhaider.com.

HAIDOSTIAN, ALICE BERBERIAN, concert pianist, volunteer, not-for-profit fundraiser; b. Highland Park, Mich., Sept. 21, 1925; d. Harry M. and Siroun Vartabedian Berberian; m. Berj H. Haidostian, Oct. 1, 1949; children: Cynthia Esther Haidostian Wilbanks, Christine Rebecca Haidostian Garry, Dicran Berj. MusB, U. Mich., 1946, MusM, 1949. Pvt. piano tchr., 1946-48; tchr. music Detroit Pub. Sch., 1953; dir. vocal trio The Haidostians, 1959—71; dir. youth choral group Cultural Soc. Armenians from Istanbul, 1965—72. Chmn. adv. coun. Armenian Studies Program, U. Mich., 1984-99. Initiator (Operas) Anoush, Mich. Opera Theatre, 1981—82, 2001—02, Transparent Anatomical Manikin exhibit, Detroit Sci. Ctr., 1976. Initiated Centennial Celebration U. Mich. Sch. Music, Detroit, 1980; mem. Armenian Gen. Benevolent Union Alex Manoogian Sch., 1981—91, Detroit chpt. core group com., 1992—; chmn. Marie Manoogian group Armenian Gen. Benevolent Union Alex Manoogian Sch, 1993—; active Detroit Women's Symphony Orch, Mich. Opera; bd. trustees Mich. Opera Theatre, 1982—; active Oakway Symphony Orch.; mem. Save Orch. Hall women's divsn.Project HOPE, 1964—, pres., 1995—96, Detroit Armenian Women's Club, 1957—; active women's chpt. Armenian Gen. Benevolent Union, Detroit, 1944—93; bd. dirs. Childhelp USA Greater Detroit Aux., 1998—; active Detroit Sci. Ctr., 1976—, bd. trustees, 1999—; organist, choir dir. Armenian Congl. Ch., Detroit, 1946—48; mem. Chancel Choir Westminster Ch. Detroit, 1965—80; bd. dirs. Detroit Symphony Orch., 1986—88. Recipient Spirit of Detroit award, 1980, Heart of Gold award United Found. City Detroit, 1981, Nat. Svc. citation U. Mich. Alumnae Coun., 1980, Disting. Alumni Svc. award U. Mich., 1981, Leadership plaque Detroit Symphony Orch., 1988, Magic Flute award Internat. Found. Mozarteum, Salzburg, Austria, 1989, Lifetime Achievement award Outstanding Woman Mich. Project HOPE, 1998, Cmty. Svc. award Wayne County Med. Soc. Alliance, 2000; named Armenian Mother of Yr., Internat. Inst. Detroit, 1981. Mem. Detroit Assn. Univ. Mich. Women (pres. 1969-71), Mich. Fedn. Music Clubs, Mich. State Med. Soc. Alliance, Wayne County Med. Soc. Aux. (pres. 1975-76), Pro Mozart Soc. Greater Detroit (pres. 1982-02, pres. emeritus 2002-, Cert. Appreciation 2002), Pro Musica Detroit (sec. 1969-90, 1st v.p. 1990—), Tuesday Musicale Detroit (pres. 1970-72), Univ. Mich. Alumni Assn. (chmn. alumnae coun. 1977-79), Univ. Mich. Sch. Music Alumni Soc., Women's Assn. Detroit Symphony Orch. (pres. 1986-88, vol. coun. Detroit Symphony Orch.), U. Mich. Alumni Assn. (bd. dirs.), U. Mich. Emeritus Club (pres. 1997-98). Avocation: piano. Home: 6838 Valley Spring Dr Bloomfield Hills MI 48301-2845

HAIG, ALEXANDER MEIGS, JR., former secretay of state, retired military officer; b. Phila., Dec. 2, 1924; s. Alexander Meigs and Regina Anne (Murphy) H.; m. Patricia Antoinette Fox, May 24, 1950; children: Alexander P., Brian F., Barbara E. Student, U. Notre Dame, 1943; BS, U.S. Mil. Acad., 1947; MA, Georgetown U., 1961; grad., Naval War Coll., 1960, Army War Coll., 1966; grad. hon. law degree, Niagara U.; LL.D. (hon.), U. Utah. Commd. 2d lt. U.S. Army, 1947, advanced through grades to gen., 1973, staff officer Office Chief of Staff for Ops., 1962-64, mil. asst. to sec. of army, 1964, dep. spl. asst. to sec. and dep. sec. of def., 1964-65, bn. and brigade comdr. 1st Inf. Div., 1966-67; regtl. comdr., dep. comdt. U.S. Mil. Acad., 1967-69; mil. asst. to asst. to Pres. for Nat. Security Affairs, Washington, 1969-70; dep. asst. to pres. NSC, Washington, 1970-73; vice chief of staff U.S. Army, Washington, 1973; chief of staff White House, 1973-74; comdr.-in-chief U.S. European Command, 1974-79; supreme allied comdr. Europe SHAPE, 1974-79; ret., 1979; pres., chief oper. officer, dir. United Techs. Corp., Hartford, Conn., 1979-81; sec. state Washington, 1981-82. Chmn., pres. Worldwide Assocs., Inc., 1984, pres., 1984—; bd. dirs. Compuserv Interactive Svcs., Inc., Inc., Interneuron Pharms., Inc., MGM Mirage, Inc., Metro-Goldwyn-Mayer Inc., 506 Internat., Inc. Author: Caveat: Realism, Reagan and Foreign Policy, 1984, Inner Circles: How America Changed the World, A Memoir, 1992; TV host (weekly program) World Bus. Rev. Decorated D.S.C., Silver Star with oak leaf cluster, Legion of Merit with 2 oak leaf clusters, D.F.C. with 2 oak leaf clusters, Bronze Star with oak leaf cluster, Air medal with 23 oak leaf clusters, Army Commendation medal, Purple Heart U.S.; Nat. Order 5th Class; Gallantry Cross with palm; Civil Actions Honor medal 1st Class; grand officer Nat. Order of Vietnam, Republic of Vietnam; medal of King Abdel-Aziz Saudi Arabia; grand cross Order of Merit Fed. Republic Germany; recipient Disting. Svc. medal Dept. of Def.; Disting. Svc. medal U.S. Army; Man of Yr. award Air Force Assn.; James Forrestal Meml. award, Disting. Grad. award West Point. Mem. Soc. of 1st Divsn. Office: Worldwide Assocs Inc 4301 Fairfax Dr Ste 300 Arlington VA 22203-1633 E-mail: ahaig@aol.com.

HAIG, BARBARA FRANCES, elementary school educator; b. Boston, Sept. 26, 1948; d. Harry Michael and Frances V. (Johnson) Tibbetts; m. David Daniel Haig, Jr., May 24, 1981. BS in Edn., State Coll. at Framingham, 1970, MS in Edn., 1974. Cert. in elem. edn., Mass. Tchr. fourth grade Northborough (Mass.) Sch. Dept., 1970—, also K-12 math. coordinating team chair. Cons. Math. Adv. Com. Dept. Edn., Malden, Mass., 1987—; CHIME advocate Nat. Assn. Tchrs. Math., Reston, Va., 1988— Divsn. capt. USCG aux., 1990—. Recipient Anna Seaver Tchr. of Yr. award Northboro Sch. Dept., 1983, Award for Heroism Nat. Safety Coun., 1989. Mem. NEA, ASCD, Mass. Tchrs. Assn. Roman Catholic. Avocations: skiing, boating. Home: 11 Notch Brook Rd Shrewsbury MA 01545-1548

HAIG, DAVID M., diversified financial services company executive; b. New Rochelle, N.Y., May 20, 1951; s. Alexander Salusbury and Joan (Damon) H. Student, Marlboro Coll., 1974. Trustee Estate of S.M. Damon, Honolulu, 1982—, chmn., 1982—. Bd. dirs. BancWest Corp., First Hawaiian Bank, Honolulu. Bd. dirs. YMCA Honolulu, 1985—, chmn., 1999—; dir. Aloha United Way, 1990-94; trustee YMCA Retirement Fund, 1991-99, Hawaii Pacific U., 1988-94; nat. bd. mem. YMCA of U.S.A., 1990-94, bd. dirs. internat. com., 1989-93; chmn. Hawaii Food Bank, 1990-94, dir., 1982-94. Mem. Young Pres.'s Orgn., Oahu Country Club, Waialae Country Club, Rotary, 200 Club, Pacific Club, Honolulu Club. Address: David M Haig Trustee 999 Bishop St Ste 2800 Honolulu HI 96813-4432

HAIG, FRANK RAWLE, physics professor, priest; b. Phila., Sept. 11, 1928; s. Alexander M. and Regina A. (Murphy) H. AB, Woodstock Coll., Md., 1952, S.T.L., 1960; Ph.L., Bellarmine Coll., Plattsburgh, N.Y., 1953; PhD, Catholic U., 1959; LHD honoris causa, SUNY, 1987. Ordained priest Roman Cath. Ch. 1960. Joined S.J., 1946; postdoctoral fellow U. Rochester, N.Y., 1962-63; asst. prof. Wheeling Coll., W.Va., 1963-66, pres., 1966-72; asst. and assoc. prof. Loyola Coll., Balt., 1972-81; pres. Le Moyne Coll., Syracuse, N.Y., 1981-87; prof. physics Loyola Coll., Balt., 1987-2000, emeritus prof., 2000—. Editor Jour. Md. Assn. Higher Edn., 1979-81; contbr. articles on nuclear physics, bibl. theology and internat. politics to profl. publs. Pres., Wheeling C. of C., 1969-71; pres. Syracuse Opera Co., 1983-85, chmn. bd., 1985-87; gen. campaign chmn. United Way Onondaga County, Syracuse, 1985-86 Recipient Mayor's Achievement award Mayor of Syracuse, 1983; Harry J. Carman award Middle States Council for Social Studies, 1985; NSF fellow, 1962-63 Mem.: AAUP (v.p. Md. Conf. 1990—92, 1995, pres. 1995—98, 2005—), Charles Carroll House of Annapolis (chmn. bd. 2001—04), Washington Acad. Scis. (pres. 1993—94, treas. 1999—2005, bd. mgs. at large 2005—), Am. Phys. Soc., Am. Assn. Physics Tchrs. (pres. Chesapeake sect. 1976—77, 1990—92). Republican. Roman Catholic. Office: Loyola Coll Dept Physics 4501 N Charles St Baltimore MD 21210-2699 Office Phone: 410-617-2574.

HAIG, ROBERT LEIGHTON, lawyer; b. Plainfield, N.J., July 30, 1947; s. Richard Randall and Edith (Remington) Haig. AB, Yale U., 1967; JD, Harvard U., 1970. Bar: N.Y. 1971, U.S. Dist. Ct. (so. and ea. dists.) N.Y., U.S. Ct. Appeals (2d cir.). Assoc. Kelley Drye & Warren, N.Y.C., 1970-79, ptnr., 1980—. Mem. bd. advisors Law Dept. Mgmt. Advisor, 1995—. Co-author: Preparing for and Trying the Civil Lawsuit, 1987, 1991, 1994, 1997, 2000, Federal Civil Practice, 1989, 1993, 1997, 2000, Federal Litigation Guide, 1992, 1993, 1994, Corporate Counsel's Guide, 1996, 1997, Products Liability in New York, 1997, 2002; contbr. chpts. in books, articles to profl. jours. Co-chair Comml. Cts. Task Force, 1995—; mem. legis. com. Com. for Modern Cts., N.Y.C., 1986—, bd. dirs., exec. com., 2001—; mem. Am. Law Inst., 1998—; mem. exec. coun. N.Y. State Conf. Bar Leaders, 1988—90, dept. disciplinary com. appellate divsn., 2003—, hearing panel chair, 1999—2001, policy com. mem., 2003—; mem. N.Y. State Jud. Salary Commn., 1997—, policy com., 2003—, Nat. Ctr. State Ct. Lawyers Com., 2002—. Recipient Excellence in CLE award, Assn. CLE Adminstrn., 1991. Fellow: N.Y. Bar Found. (life; v.p. 2002—03, pres. 2003—, bd. dirs.), Am. Bar Found. (life); mem.: ABA (del. 1991—, standing com. on jud. selection, tenure and compensation 1995—96, bus. cts. com. 1996—, chair subcom. on rels between inside and outside counsel 1997—, spl. advisor standing com. fed. judiciary 2002), N.Y. State Bar Assn. (lectr. 1985—, chmn. com. on fed. cts. 1986—88, chmn. comml. and fed. litig. sect. 1988—90, del. 1988—, exec. com. 1991—94, steering com. on commerce and industry 1997—, chair com. on multi-disciplinary practice and legal profession 1998—99, 1st Ann. award for Disting. Pub. Svc. Comml. and Fed. Litig. Sect. 1995), N.Y. County Lawyers Assn. (chmn. com. on supreme ct. 1984—86, lectr. 1984—, v.p. 1986—92, exec. com. 1986—95, chmn. fin. com. 1988—90, pres. 1992—94, pres. Found. 1992—94, dir.), Assn. of Bar of City of N.Y. (jud. com. 1985—88, chmn. 1989—92, coun. on jud. adminstrn. 1989—92, chmn. 1996—99). Office: Kelley Drye & Warren LLP 101 Park Ave Fl 30 New York NY 10178-0062 E-mail: rhaig@kelleydrye.com.

HAIG, SUSAN, conductor; BA in Music Theory and Composition, Princeton U.; DMA in Orchestral Conducting, MM in Orchestral Conducting, MM in Piano, State U. N.Y., Stony Brook; PhD in Humanities (hon.), U. Windsor, 1998. Coaching/conducting fellow Juilliard Am. Opera Centre, 1981—83; assistant conductor Minnesota Opera, 1983—84, New York City Opera, 1984—86, Santa Fe Opera, 1986; resident coach and conducting assistant Canadian Opera Co., 1986—88; resident staff conductor Calgary Philharmonic Orch., 1988—91; artistic dir. and principal conductor Windsor Symphony Orch., 1991—; music dir. designate S.D. Symphony Orch., 2000—. Recipient Heinz Unger Conducting award, 1992, Mayor's award for excellence in the performing arts, 1999. Office: SD Symphony Orch 300 N Dakota Ave Sioux Falls SD 57104

HAIGH, JENNIFER, writer; b. Barnesboro, Pa., Oct. 1968; B, Dickinson Coll.; MFA in Fiction Writing, Iowa Writers' Workshop. Vis. writer Ga. State U., Ohio Wesleyan Univ. Author: Mrs. Kimble, 2003 (PEN/Hemingway award for outstanding first fiction), Baker Towers, 2005, (short stories) Good Housekeeping, Hartford Courant, Alaska Quarterly Rev., Va. Quarterly Rev., others. Fulbright Scholar, James A. Michener Fellowship, 2002. Mailing: c/o Wm Morrow Publishers HarperCollins Inc 10 E 53rd St New York NY 10022

HAIGH, ROBERT WILLIAM, business professor; b. Phila., Aug. 22, 1926; s. Harry E. and Mildred (Elliott) H.; m. Jane Stanton Sheble, June 19, 1948; children: Cynthia Jane, Anne Sheble, Robert William, Barbara Lynne. Student, Muhlenberg Coll., 1944-45; AB cum laude, Bucknell U., 1948; MBA with high distinction, Harvard U., 1950, DCS, 1953. Research and teaching faculty Harvard U. Grad Sch. Bus. Adminstrn., 1950-56, asst. prof., 1953-56; asst. to pres. Helmerich & Payne, Inc., Tulsa, 1956, controller and asst. to pres., 1956-57, fin. v.p., dir., 1957-61, White Eagle Internat. Oil Co., 1957-60; v.p. corp. planning and devel. Standard Oil Co. (Ohio), Cleve., 1963-66; pres. Sohio Chems. & Vistron Corp. Subs., 1966-67, Sohio Chemicals and Vistron Corp. Subs., 1966-67; group v.p., pres. edn. group, dir. Xerox Corp., Stamford, Conn., 1967-72; exec. v.p. Swedlow Corp., 1973-74, pres., chief exec. officer, dir., 1974; pres. Hillsboro Assocs., 1974-75; sr. v.p. Freeport Minerals Co., 1975-76; chmn. bd., chief exec. officer Photo Quest, Inc., Cognitrex, Inc., 1977-78; dir. Wharton Applied Rsch. Ctr., lectr. U. Pa., Phila., 1978-79; Disting. prof. bus. adminstrn. Darden Grad. Sch. Bus. U. Va. Tayloe Murphy Internat. Bus. Studies Ctr., 1979-95; prof. emeritus U. Va., 1995—. Author: (with John G. McLean) The Growth of Integrated Oil Companies, 1954, Leading Virginia Industries series: Textiles and Apparel, A Business Update, 1986, Wood and Paper Products, 1987, Investment Strategies and the Plant-Location Decision: Foreign Companies in the U.S., 1989, Global Markets for Pollution-Control Equipment: An Export Opportunity for Virginia Business, 1991, Medical Products Companies in Virginia: Export Status Report. Served with USNR, 1944-45. Mem. Phi Beta Kappa, Phi Lambda Theta. Home: 404 Ednam Dr Charlottesville VA 22903-4716

HAIGHT, CHARLES SHERMAN, JR., federal judge; b. N.Y.C., Sept. 23, 1930; s. Charles Sherman and Margaret (Edwards) H.; m. Mary Jane Peightal, June 30, 1953; children: Nina E., Susan P. BA, Yale U., 1952, LL.B., 1955. Bar: N.Y. State 1955. Trial atty., admiralty and shipping dept. Dept. Justice, Washington, 1955-57; assoc. firm Haight, Gardner, Poor & Havens, N.Y.C., 1957-68, ptnr., 1968-76; judge U.S. Dist. Ct. (So. Dist. NY), 1976—95, sr. judge, 1995—. Bd. dirs. Kennedy Child Study Ctr.; adv. trustee Am.-Scandinavian Found., chmn., 1970-76; bd. mgrs. Havens Fund. Mem. Maritime Law Assn., U.S., N.Y. State Bar Assn., Bar Assn. City N.Y., Fed. Bar Council. Episcopalian. Office: US Dist Ct US Courthouse 500 Pearl St New York NY 10007-1316*

HAIGHT, DAVID HULEN, ophthalmologist; b. Highland Park, Ill., Mar. 30, 1954; s. Thomas Hulen and Virginia Ellen (Olsson) H. AB in Biochemistry magna cum laude, Brown U., 1976; MD, Johns Hopkins U., 1980. Diplomate Am. Bd. Ophthalmology. Resident ophthalmology Manhattan Eye, Ear and Throat Hosp., N.Y.C., 1981-84, fellow in cornea dept., 1984-85, resident instr., ophthalmology, 1985-87, residency coord., 1989-91, chief Contact Lens Clinic I, 1986—, chief coord. investigator, 1991—, with laser rsch. study, 1991—. Quality assurance com. Manhattan Eye, Ear and Throat Hosp., N.Y.C., 1987—, chmn. ophthalmology credentials com. 1993—; surgeon dir. Manhattan Eye, Ear and Throat Hosp., 1997—, dir. refractive surgery, 1997—; mem. adv. bd. N.Y. Eye Bank for Sight Restoration, N.Y.C., 1992—; sec. med. adv. bd. N.Y. Eye Bank for Sight Restoration, 1995-97; skills transfer adv. com. Am. Acad. Ophthalmology, San Francisco, 1992-96; lectr. ophthalmology Columbia U., N.Y.C., 1997—; clin. asst. prof. ophthalmology N.Y. Weill-Cornell Med. Coll., N.Y.C., clin. prof. ophthalmology NYU Sch. Medicine. Contbg. author: Corneal Surgery, 1986, 2nd edit., 1993, 3d edit., 1999, Color Atlas of Ophthalmology, 1999. Fellow Am. Acad. Ophthalmology (honor award 1993); mem. Med. Soc. of State of N.Y., N.Y. State Ophthalmologic Soc., Internat. Soc. Refractive Surgery, Contact Lens Assn. of Ophthalmologists, Am. Soc. Cataract and Refractive Surgery, Phi Beta Kappa, Sigma Xi (assoc.). Avocations: photography, golf, travel, aviation, birding. Office: 155 E 72nd St New York NY 10021-4371 Office Phone: 212-772-9474. E-mail: dhaight@laserlasik.com.

HAIGHT, JAMES THERON, lawyer; b. Racine, Wis., Dec. 10, 1924; s. Walter Lyman and Geraldine (Foley) H.; m. Patricia Aloe, Apr. 26, 1952; children: Alberta, Barbara, Catherine, Dorothy, Elaine. Student, U. Nebr., 1943—44, U. Bordeaux, France, 1947; diplome d'Etudes, U. Paris, 1948; BA, U. Wis., 1950, LLB, 1951. Bar: D.C. 1952, U.S. Supreme Ct. 1955, Calif.

1968. Atty. Covington & Burling, Washington, 1951-56, Goodyear Tire & Rubber Co., Goodyear Internat. Corp., Akron, Ohio, 1956-61; gen. counsel, sec. George J. Meyer Mfg. Co., Milw., 1961-66; sr. v.p., sec., chief corp. counsel Thrifty Corp., L.A., 1966-92, spl. counsel, 1992-96. Adv. bd. Edward Roybal Inst. Applied Gerontology, Calif. State U., L.A. Fellow: Am. Bar Found. (life); mem.: ABA (chmn. internat. law sect. 1974—75), Am. Soc. Corp. Secs., Pasadena Bar Assn., Calif. Bar Assn., Order of Coif. Home and Office: 1390 Ridge Way Pasadena CA 91106-4514

HAIGHT, WARREN GAZZAM, investor; b. Seattle, Sept. 7, 1929; s. Gilbert Pierce and Ruth (Gazzam) H.; m. Suzanne H., Sept. 1, 1951; children— Paula Lea, Ian Pierce; m. Ottina Mehau, June 25, 1985 AB in Econs, Stanford U., 1951. Asst. Treas. Hawaiian Pineapple Co., Honolulu, 1955-64; v.p., treas. Oceanic Properties, Inc., Honolulu, 1964-67, pres., dir., 1967-85, chmn., 1983-85; pres. Hawaii, Castle & Cooke Inc., 1983-85, Warren G. Haight & Assocs., 1985—; chmn. Molokai Ranch, Ltd., 1996—2002, Pacific Is. Resources, LLC, 2000—03. Bd. dirs. Round Hill Enterprises, Inc., Las Positas Land Co., Inc., Baldwin Pacific Properties, Inc., Hawaii Project Mgmt., Inc., Transamerica Realty Advisors, Inc., Queen Emma Corp., Queens Devel. Corp., Dole Corp., Standard Fruit and Steamship Co., Inc., Bumble Bee Seafoods, Inc. Bd. dirs. Downtown Improvement Assn., Oahu Devel. Conf., Hawaii Island Econ. Devel. Bd., Econ. Devel. Corp. Honolulu, Intellect, Inc., Hawaii Resort Developers Conf., Homeless Solutions, Inc., Mutual Housing of Hawaii, Inc.; mem. Transit Coalition, Honolulu, Govs. Com. on Econ. Futures; pres., bd. dirs. Land Use Rsch. Found. of Hawaii, Pacific Found. for Cancer Rsch., Hawaii Nature Ctr.; mem. policy adv. bd. for elderly affairs State of Hawaii. Lt. USNR, 1951-55. Mem. Housing Coalition, Calif. Coastal Coun., Outrigger Canoe Club, Plaza Club, Pacific Club. Home: 319 Lala Pl Kailua HI 96734-3224 Office: 220 S King St Ste 1465 Honolulu HI 96813-4542 E-mail: haighthawaii@aol.com.

HAILE, ALLEN CLEVELAND, academic administrator; b. Forbes Rd., Pa., Aug. 26, 1930; s. Wesley Matthew and Mary Olivia (Hall) H.; m. Barbara Honey, Dec. 30, 1975; children: Mark, Brice, Scott, Marybeth, Jonathan, Courtney. AB, U. Nebr., Omaha, 1959; MS, U. So. Calif., 1966, MPA, PhD, U. So. Calif., 1971. Commd. 2d lt. USAF, 1953, advanced through grades to lt. col., retired, 1973; v.p. urban affairs Pepperdine U., L.A., 1969-73; sr. rschr. Dept. Info. Scis. Rand Corp., Santa Monica, Calif., 1972-73; regional rep. Pacific Basin U.S. Sec. Commerce, L.A., 1977-81; dept. mgr. human resources devel. Bechtel Civil, Inc., Jubail City, 1981-85, mgr. bus. devel. for bldgs. and infrastructure ops., 1985-87, mgr. mktg., 1987-89, mgr. infrastructure devel. Pacific Rim countries, 1991—; dean Coll. of Bus. Calif. Poly State U., San Luis Obispo, 1993-94, dir. cmty. and govt. rels., 1994—. Adj. prof. Golden Gate Univ., 1992. V.p., bd. dirs. San Luis Obispo ARC, C. of C.; pres. Filipino Am C. of C., 1991; bd. dirs. United Way, San Luis Obispo, Econ. Forecast Project, San Luis Obispo, Larkin St. Youth Ctr., San Francisco Edn. Fund, Ct. Appointed Spl. Advocates for Children, Western Govtl. Rsch. Assn., pres. 1989; pres. San Francisco Social Svcs. Commn. 1989, San Francisco Planning and Urban Rsch. Assn., 1992. Decorated DFC and seven air medals. Mem. Am. Soc. Pub. Adminstrn. (bd. trustees found., chmn. constitution revision com. 1988, 89). Home: 1022 Islay St San Luis Obispo CA 93401-4026 Office: Calif Poly State U Cmty and Govt Rels San Luis Obispo CA 93407

HAILE, BENJAMIN CARROLL, JR., retired chemical engineer, retired mechanical engineer; b. Shanghai, Apr. 6, 1918; arrived in U.S., 1925; s. Benjamin Carroll and Ruth Temple (Shreve) Haile; m. Lola Pauline Lease, Dec. 28, 1957 (dec. Dec. 17, 2002); children: Thomas Benjamin, Ronald Frederick. BS, U. Calif., Berkeley, 1941; cert., Harvard-MIT, 1945; postgrad., U. So. Calif., 1950-51. Registered profl. chem. and mech. engr., Calif. Chem. engr. Std. Oil Calif. (Chevron), San Francisco, El Segundo, 1941-43, 46-48; sr. project chem. engr. C.F. Braun & Co., Alhambra, Calif., 1948-50, 54-56, 67-71, 72; contract chem. and mech. engr. Dow Chem., Stearns-Roger, Fluor et al, Tex., Colo., Ill., 1951-54, 56-57; sr. process engr. Aerojet-Gen. Corp., Sacramento, Covina, Calif., 1957-67; mech. engr. So. Calif. Edison Co., Rosemead, 1972-84; pvt. practice chem. engr. Fontana, Montclair, Calif., 1986, 88, 92; sr. mem. tech. staff Ralph M. Parsons Co., Pasadena, Calif., 1971, 88-91; ret., 1992. 2d lt. USAAF, 1943—46. Mem.: AIChE (mem. emeritus), NSPE (life; pres. Sacramento chpt. 1960—62), Toastmasters Internat. (chpt. v.p. 1979, Outstanding Toastmaster 1984), Psi Upsilon. Republican. Achievements include design of oil refineries, chemical plants, others with estimated cumulative inflation adjusted value of one billion dollars during lifetime; development of new fluid bed adsorption process for air separation; research in economic optimization studies of complete aerospace programs; static electricity protection study for Polaris propellant manufacturing facility; design of one of the world's largest boring machines. Home: 159 N Country Club Rd Glendora CA 91741-3919

HAILE, H. G., German language and literature educator; b. Brownwood, Tex., July 31, 1931; s. Frank and Neil (Goodson) H.; m. Mary Elizabeth Huff, Sept. 1, 1952; children: Jonathan, Christian, Constance Haile Hunsaker. BA, U. Ark., 1952, MA, 1954; student, U. Cologne, Germany, 1955-56; PhD, U. Ill., 1957. Instr. U. Pa., 1956-57; asst. prof., then asso. prof. U. Houston, 1957-63; mem. faculty U. Ill., Urbana, 1963—, prof. German, 1965—, head dept., 1964-73; asso. mem. U. Ill. (Center for Advanced Study), 1969—. Vis. prof. U. Mich., U. Ga. Author: Das Faustbuch nach der Wolfenbuttler Handschrift, 1963, 95, The History of Doctor Johann Faustus, 1965, 1996, Artist in Chrysalis: A Biographical Study of Goethe in Italy, 1973, Invitation to Goethe's Faust, 1978, Luther: An Experiment in Biography, 1983, We Are All Sonsabitches Now, 2000; contbr. numerous articles to profl. and popular jours. Fulbright fellow, 1955; Fellow Am. Coun. Learned Socs., 1961-62. Office: U Ill 3072 Foreign Languages Urbana IL 61801 Personal E-mail: harryhaile@aol.com. *A child of the Dust Bowl who became a foreign language teacher, I was skeptical about America. I have learned to accept skepticism as the American trait which protects us from correctness, collectivism and coercion.*

HAILE, L. JOHN, JR., journalist, publishing executive; b. Cleve., Tenn., Mar. 20, 1945; m. Gwen Marie, 1965; children: Philip Alan, John Christopher. BA, Vanderbilt U., Nashville, 1967; MS in Journalism, Boston U., 1969. Polit. reporter The Nashville Tennessean, 1966-79; dep. mng. editor The Orlando Sentinel, Fla., 1979-81, assoc. editor, 1981-85, editor, 1985—2000; founding ptnr., prin. Inside Out Media Ptnrs., 2000—. Juror Pulitzer Prize Com., 1992—93; former chair New Directions for News; sr. fellow The Media Ctr. at the Am. Press Inst., 2002—; cons. Tribune Co., 2001—, Media Gen., 2003, CCN, Trinidad, 2003, Denver Newspaper Agy., 2005. Nat. Endowment Humanities Profl. Journalism fellow, 1975-76 Mem. Am. Soc. Newspaper Editors. Office Phone: 303-679-3262. E-mail: johnhaile@aol.com.

HAILE, LAWRENCE BARCLAY, lawyer; b. Atlanta, Feb. 19, 1938; m. Ann Leon; children: Gretchen Vanderhoof, Eric McKenzie (dec.), Scott McAllister. BA in Econs, U. Tex., 1958, LLB, 1961. Bar: Tex. 1961, Calif. 1962. Law clk. to U.S. Judge Joseph M. Ingraham, Houston, 1961-62; pvt. practice San Francisco, 1962-67, LA, 1967—. Instr. UCLA Civil Trial Clinics, 1974, 76; lectr. law Calif. Continuing Edn. of Bar, 1973-74, 80-89; nat. panel arbitrators Am. Arbitration Assn., 1965—. Mem. editl. bd. Tex. Law Rev, 1960-61; contbr. articles profl. jours. Mem. State Bar Calif., Tex., U.S. Supreme Ct. Bar Assn., Internat. Assn. Property Ins. Counsel (founding mem., pres. 1980), Vintage Motorsports Coun. (past pres.), Phi Delta Phi, Delta Sigma Rho. Office: 425 E Ocean Blvd Unit 340 Long Beach CA 90802-4951 Office Phone: 562-491-2052. E-mail: lhaile1938@aol.com. *Gold is like brass/Except less crass.*

HAILE, LISA A., lawyer; BA in Biology, Rollins Coll., 1982; PhD in Microbiology & Immunology, Georgetown U. Sch. Medicine, 1987; JD, Calif. Western Sch. Law, 1991. Bar: Calif. 1992, cert.: US Patent and Trademark Office. Postdoctoral fellow La Jolla Cancer Rsch. Found., NIH, 1987—89; ptnr. Gray, Cary, Ware, & Freidenrich, 1999—2004; ptnr., co-chmn. Life Sciences practice group DLA Piper Rudnick Gray Cary, San Diego, 2005—. Adj. prof. patent law Calif. Western Sch. Law; mem. BIOCOM Sci. and Tech. Com., 2004. Bd. mem. Am. Liver Found., Athena; mem. Sci. & Tech. com. BIOCOM. Named one of Top 45 Attorneys Under 45, The Am. Lawyers, 2003. Mem.: ABA, Licensing Exec. Soc., Am. Intellectual Property Law Assn., Calif. Bar Assn., San Diego Bar Assn., San Diego Intellectual Property Law Assn. (pres. 1997—99), Ass. for Women in Sci. Office: DLA Piper Rudnick Gray Cary 4365 Executive Dr San Diego CA 92121 Office Phone: 858-677-1456. Office Fax: 858-677-1401. Business E-Mail: lisa.haile@dlapiper.com.

HAILEY, GARY D., lawyer; b. Joplin, Mo., May 30, 1952; BA cum laude, Rice U., 1974; JD cum laude, Harvard U., 1977. Bar: Tex. 1978, DC 1996. Staff atty. & program advisor, bureau of consumer protection Federal Trade Commn., 1977—85, atty. advisor to Mary L. Azcuenaga, 1985—91; v.p. & gen. counsel, regulatory affairs Nat. Media Corp., 1992—95; assoc. Venable LLP, Washington, 1996—2000, ptnr., advertising, trade regulation, 2000—. Mem.: ABA, DC Bar Assn. Office: Venable LLP 575 7th St NW Washington DC 20004 Office Phone: 202-344-4997. Office Fax: 202-344-8300. Business E-Mail: gdhailey@venable.com.

HAILS, BARBARA GELDERMANN, artist; b. NYC, Mar. 15, 1944; d. Edward Joseph and Helena Monica (McCann) Geldermann; m. Robert Louis Hails Sr., July 2, 1966; children: Robert Louis Jr., Charlotte Lynne. BA, Catholic U. Am., Washington, 1965. Freelance artist Hails Studio, Gathersburg-Olney, Md., 1965—. Speaker Montgomery Coll., Rockville 1987; exhibition juror Md. Fedn. Art, Annapolis 1987. Work exhibited in Capricorn Galleries, Bethesda, Md. 1982—, Cudahy's Gallery, Richmond, Va. 1981—, McBride Gallery, Annapolis, Md. 1985— Hails Fine Art Gallery, Olney, Md., 1994—; one-woman shows include Capricorn Galleries, 1984, 87, Art Expo, NY, 1986-2005, DecorExpo, Atlanta, 1986—; artist in residence City Rockville, Md. 1975; publ. Dimensional Aesthetics Inc., Olney 1985; contbr. articles to profl. jours. Fundraiser Parks and History Assn., Great Falls, Md. 1987, Sandy Spring Mus., Olney 1984. Recipient grant Montgomery County Arts Council, Rockville 1986; named Outstanding Artist Yr. Nat. League Am. Penwomen, Chevy Chase, Md. 1983; invited exhibitor Société Des Patelllistes de France, Lille 1987. Mem. Pastel Soc. Am., Md. Pastel Soc., Artists Equity Assn. Avocations: photography, travel. Office: Dimensional Aesthetics 18319 Georgia Ave Olney MD 20832-1435 Office Phone: 301-774-6249.

HAILS, ROBERT EMMET, aerospace engineer, consultant, manufacturing executive, retired military officer; b. Miami, Fla., Jan. 20, 1923; s. Daniel Troy and Jean (Burke) H.; m. Ethel Fitzgerald Gayle, Mar. 2, 1957; children: Robert Emmet Jr., Merrily Hails Joiner, Florence T. Hails Patton, Laura Hails Smith. BS in Aero. Engring., Auburn U., 1947; MS in Indsl. Engring., Columbia U., 1950; postgrad., C&CS Air U., 1955; postgrad. AMP, Harvard U. Sch. Bus., 1965. Enlisted USAAF, 1942, commd. 2d lt., 1944, advanced through grades to lt. gen., 1974, combat pilot Pacific Theater, 1944-45; assigned to SAC, 1947-48; inspector gen. Hdqrs. USAF, 1950-53; program devel. officer Marcel Dassault Mystere IV Jet Aircraft, French Air Force Am. embassy, Paris, 1953-55; air staff project officer F-104/F-105 aircraft HQ USAF, 1956-60; comdr. procurement dist. USAF, San Francisco, 1960-62; mil. asst. for weapons systems acquisition Office Sec. AF, 1962-66; system program dir. Joint USAF/USN A-7D Aircraft Engring., Devel., Test & Prodn., AF Systems Commd., 1966-68; dep. chief staff maintenance engring. Air Force Logistics Command, 1968-71; comdr. Def. Pers. Support Ctr. Def. Log. Agy., Phila., 1971-72; comdr. Air Logistics Ctr. USAF, Warner Robins AFB, Ga., 1972-74; vice comdr. Tactical Air Command Langley AFB, Va., 1974-75; dep. chief staff systems and logistics Hdqrs. USAF, Washington, 1975-77; ret. USAF, Washington, 1977; mgmt. cons. Atlanta, 1978-80; sr. v.p. internat. ops. LTV Corp., Dallas, 1980-84; pres. Hails Assoc. Inc., Macon, Ga., 1984—. Mem. sci. bd. Loral Corp., Yonkers, NY, 1992-96. Regional exec. Boy Scouts Am.; mem. Auburn U. Alumni Engring. Coun., 1982—; bd. advisors Wesleyan Coll., 1985-90; mem. Found. Bd., Macon State Coll., 1998-2001. Decorated DSM with 2 oak leaf clusters, legion of Merit with 2 oak leaf clusters, Air medal with 2 oak leaf clusters; Order of Nat. Security (Korea); recipient Engring. Achievement award Auburn U., 1998; inducted into State of Ala. Engring. Hall of Fame, 2001, State of Ga. Aviation Hall of Fame, 2001. Mem. AIAA, Air Force Assn., Daedalians, Auburn U. SPADES, Army-Navy Country Club (Arlington, Va.), Idle Hour Golf and Country Club, Omicron Delta Kappa, Sigma Alpha Epsion. Roman Catholic. Achievements include introduction of heads-up-display (HUD) in a US military aircraft. Home: 101 Wolf Creek Dr N Macon GA 31210 Office Phone: 478-474-5588. E-mail: bobehails@cox.net.

HAIMAN, FRANKLYN SAUL, writer, communications educator; b. Cleve., June 23, 1921; s. Alfred Wilfred and Stella (Weiss) H.; m. Louise Goble, June 11, 1955; children— Mark David, Eric Saul. BA, Case Western Res. U., 1942; MA, Northwestern U., 1946, PhD, 1948. Mem. faculty Northwestern U., Evanston, Ill., 1948—, chmn. dept. communication studies, 1964-75, prof. communication studies, 1970-88, John Evans prof. communication studies, 1988-91, John Evans prof. emeritus, 1991—. Adj. prof. U. of San Francisco, 1992—. Author: Group Leadership and Democratic Action, 1951, Freedom of Speech: Issues and Cases, 1965, Freedom of Speech, 1976, Speech and Law in a Free Society, 1981, "Speech Acts" and the First Amendment, 1993, Freedom, Democracy, and Responsibility: The Selected Works of Franklyn S. Haiman, 2000, Religious Expression and the American Constitution, 2003; co-author: The Dynamics of Discussion, 1960, 2d edit., 1980; editor: (book series) To Protect These Rights, 1976-77; contbr. articles to profl. jours. Pres. ACLU of Ill., 1964-75, nat. bd. dirs., 1965-96, nat. corp. sec., 1976-82, nat. v.p., 1987-96, vice chair nat. adv. coun., 1996—. With USAAF, 1942-45. Mem. ACLU, Nat. Comm. Assn., Am. Psychol. Assn., AAUP, Phi Beta Kappa. Home: 5283 Broadway Ter Apt 4-b Oakland CA 94618-1491

HAIMAN, IRWIN SANFORD, lawyer; b. Cleve., Mar. 19, 1916; s. Alfred W. and Stella H. (Weiss) H.; m. Jeanne D. Jaffee, Mar. 8, 1942; children: Karen H. Schenkel, Susan L. Bensoussan. BA, Western Res. U., 1937; LL.B., Cleve. Marshall Law Sch., 1941; JD, Cleve. State U., 1969. Bar: Ohio 1941, U.S. Ct. Appeals (6th cir.) 1961, U.S. Supreme Ct. 1961. Asst. to pres. Tremco Mfg. Co., Cleve., 1936-42; house counsel William Edwards Co., Cleve., 1947-48; pvt. practice Cleve., 1948-68; ptnr. firm Garber, Simon, Haiman, Gutfeld, Friedman & Jacobs, 1968-80; ptnr. McCarthy, Lebit, Crystal & Haiman, 1981—. Lectr. in speech Western Res. U., 1948-70; dir. Washington Fed. Savs. and Loan Assn.; asst. law dir., prosecutor City of Lyndhurst, Ohio, 1965-79, law dir., 1979-84. Trustee Montefiore Home, Cleve., 1974-88 (life trustee 1988—)—, East End Neighborhood House, 1962-68; councilman City of South Euclid, 1948-54, pres., 1952-54; pres. Young People's Congregation, Fairmount Temple, 1951-52; sec., trustee Surburban Temple, 1962-65, trustee, 1983—, pres., 1984-87; chmn. speakers div., bd. dirs. Cleve. chpt. ARC, 1959-62; chmn. speaker and film div. Cleve. United Appeal, 1961-62; chmn. speakers div. Jewish Welfare Fund Cleve., 1973-79. Served as 1st lt. AUS, 1943-47. Mem. Ohio, Cleve. bar assns., Assn. Trial Lawyers Am., Zeta Beta Tau. Clubs: Oakwood Country, Lake Forest Country (pres. 1971-72, 75-79). Home: 20201 N Park Blvd Cleveland OH 44118-5000 Office Phone: 216-696-1422.

HAIMAN, ROBERT JAMES, editor, journalist, educator, media consultant, critic; b. Norwich, Conn., May 6, 1936; s. Albert and Letta (Cone) H.; m. Elizabeth Royce Greenlaw, Sept. 26, 1964 (div. Aug. 1996); 1 child, Robert Greenlaw. Student, U. Conn., 1953-55; BS, U. Fla., 1957. Reporter St. Petersburg (Fla.) Times, 1958-60, copy editor, 1962-63, nat. editor, 1964-66, mng. editor, 1966-76, exec. editor, 1976-83; pres., mng. dir. Poynter Inst. Media Studies, 1983-96, pres. emeritus, disting. editor in residence, 1997—. Bd. dirs. Times Pub. Co., St. Petersburg; trustee Fla. InterAm. Scholarship Found.; mem. minority mgmt. task force Inst. Journalism Edn. Mem. pres. round table Eckerd Coll.; trustee Poynter Inst. Media Studies, St. Petersburg; mem. Pulitzer Prize jury, 1977, 90, 91, 96, 97; internat. adv. bd. Inst. Advancement Journalism, Johannesburg, South Africa; mem. nat. adv. bd. Inst. for Journalists and Pub. Policy Gordon Pub. Policy Ctr. Brandeis U. Mem. bd. advisors U. Fla. Coll. Journalism and Comms.; elder Presbyn. Ch.; trustee Bayfront City Found.; sr. fellow Freedom Forum, Washington, 1998—; mem. Pres.'s coun. U. Fla., U. South Fla., chmn. campus adv. bd., 1989—91; mem. adv. bd. U. Fla. Internat. Ctr.; mem. journalism adv. bd. Knight Found., Inst. Current World Affairs, Hanover, NH, Tampa Bay Com. Coun. on Fgn. Rels. Served with USMC, 1961. Named Disting. Alumnus, U. Fla., 1988. Mem. AP Mng. Editors Assn. (pres. 1982), Am. Soc. Newspaper Editors (dir. 1992-98), Internat. Press Inst. (Vienna), World Editors Forum (Paris), Interam. Press Assn., St. Petersburg Yacht Club, Dragon Club, Quarterback Club, Golden Triangle Club, Soc. Profl. Journalists. Democrat. Home: 5155 Isla Key Blvd S Apt 103 Saint Petersburg FL 33715-1687 Office: 801 3rd St S Saint Petersburg FL 33701-4920

HAIMAN, ZOLTAN, astronomer, educator; BS in Physics, BS in Electrical Engring., MIT, 1993; MA in Astronomy, Harvard U., 1994, PhD in Astronomy, 1998. Teaching fellow MIT, 1993—95, Harvard U., 1993—95; rsch. fellow Harvard-Smithsonian Ctr. for Astrophysics, 1995—98; rsch. assoc. Fermi Nat. Accelerator Lab., 1998—99; Hubble fellow astrophysics Princeton U., 1999—2002; assist. prof. astronomy Columbia U., 2002—. Mem. Sci. Working Group for Next Generation Space Telescope, 1996—97; organizer KIAS World Cup Cosmology Workshop, Republic of Korea, 2001; co-investigator DUO, 2003. Contbtr. numerous articles to profl. jours. including Astrophysical Jour., Physics Rev., Astronomy Jour. Named one of Brilliant 10, Popular Sci. mag., 2002; recipient Isaac Newton Studentship, Cambridge U., 1994—95; grantee Merit Fellowship, Harvard U., 1997—98. Mem.: Hungarian Astronomical Assn. Office: Columbia U Astronomy Dept Mailcode 5246 550 W 120th St New York NY 10027

HAIMBACH, MARJORIE ANNE, music educator; b. Abington, Pa., Feb. 9, 1927; d. Charles Albert and Laura Adeline (Hungerford) Haimbach. BA in Music, Ursinus Coll., Collegeville, Pa., 1948. Pvt. piano tchr., Langhorne, Pa., N.Y.C. Mem.: Soc. of Mayflower Descendants, Am. Coll. Musicians, Pa. State Music Tchrs. Assn., Nat. Guild of Piano Tchrs., Bucks County Assn. of Piano Tchrs. Home: 113 W Maple Ave Langhorne PA 19047

HAIMES, BURTON KENNETH, lawyer; b. N.Y.C., May 22, 1943; s. David and Mildred Florence (Hirscher) H.; m. Elaine Susan Knopping, June 17, 1967; children: Matthew Collins, Spencer Wyatt, Meredith Brooke; m. Monique N.A. Rigon, Nov. 21, 1982; children: Charlotte Elizabeth, Trevor Henry. BA cum laude, Yale U., 1965; LLB, U. Pa., 1968; LLM in Taxation, NYU, 1979. Bar: NY 1968, Tex. 1982. Law clk. to judge U.S. Ct. Appeals (3rd cir.), Wilmington, Del., 1968-69; assoc. Coudert Bros., London, 1969-70; ptnr. Gottesman & Ptnrs., London, 1970-72; assoc. Fried Frank Harris Shriver & Jacobson, N.Y.C., 1972-77; ptnr. Stanley Cohen P.C., N.Y.C., 1977-82; mng. ptnr. Boyle, Vogeler & Haimes, N.Y.C., 1982—; ptnr., bus. dept. Thelen Reid & Priest LLP. Adj. prof. law U. Notre Dame- London Branch, 1969—71. Nat. pres. Am. Youth Soccer Orgn., Hawthorne, Calif., 1985—89, chmn. bd.; bd. dir. US Soccer Hall of Fame; chmn. Action Against Hunger-USA; bd. dir. Yale Alumni Fund, New Haven, 1988—. Fellow: ABA; mem.: State Bar Tex., NY State Bar Assn. Democrat. Jewish. Fluent in French. Office: Thelen Reid & Priest LLP 875 Third Ave New York NY 10022-6225 Office Phone: 212-603-2060. Office Fax: 212-603-2001. Business E-Mail: bhaimes@thelenreid.com.

HAIMES, TODD, artistic director; m. Alison Haimes; children: Hilary, Andrew. Grad., Yale Sch. of Mgmt., U. Pa. Artistic dir. Roundabout Theatre Co., N.Y.C., 1990—. Office: Roundabout Theatre Co 231 W 39th St Ste 1200 New York NY 10018-3109

HAIMM, NEIL KEITH, lawyer; b. Bklyn., Sept. 1, 1955; s. Sydney and Martha (Zimmer) H.; m. Laura Bell, June 29, 1980; children: Caroline Ashley, Ethan Harrison. BA, U. Pa., 1977; JD, NYU, 1980, LLM in Taxation, 1985. Bar: N.J. 1980, N.Y. 1981, Pa. 1984. Assoc. Bondy & Schloss, N.Y.C., 1980-83, Cohen, Shapiro, Polisher, Shiekman and Cohen, Phila., 1983-88, ptnr., 1988—95; joined Drinker Biddle & Reath LLP, Phila., 1995, mng. ptnr., bus. fin. dept., mem., mgmt. com. Bd. dirs., mem. exec. com. Anti-Defemation League, Phila., 1987—; bd. dirs. Golden Slipper Uptown Home, 1988—. Mem. Golden Slipper Club (bd. dirs. 1989—). Democrat. Jewish. Avocations: reading, running, tennis. Office: Drinker Biddle & Reath LLP One Logan Sq 18th & Cherry Sts Philadelphia PA 19103-6996 Office Phone: 215-988-2612. Office Fax: 215-988-2757. Business E-Mail: neil.haimm@dbr.com.

HAIMS, BRUCE DAVID, lawyer; b. NYC, Nov. 25, 1940; s. Samuel Harold and Judith (Feller) H.; m. Judith Jackson; children: Carolyn, Daniel, Nolan. BS in Econs., U. Pa., 1962; LLB magna cum laude, Harvard U., 1965; LLM in Taxation, NYU, 1972. Bar: Conn. 1965, NY 1967, US Ct. Appeals (2d cir.) 1968, US Tax Ct. 1972. Assoc. Debevoise & Plimpton LLP, NYC, 1967-72, ptnr., 1973—, head Tax Dept., 1994—2004. Bd. dirs. The Jeffrey Co., Axe Houghton Found., Brookfield Craft Ctr. Capt. US Army, 1965-67. Mem. N.Y. State Bar Assn., Assn. of Bar of City of N.Y., Internat. Fiscal Assn. Home: 470 W End Ave Apt 14A New York NY 10024-4933 Office: Debevoise & Plimpton 919 3rd Ave Fl 2 New York NY 10022-3904 Office Fax: 202-909-6836. E-mail: bdhaims@debevoise.com.

HAINER, BARRY L., physician; b. Bklyn., Sept. 10, 1951; s. Arthur and Shirley Hainer. BA, Johns Hopkins U., Balt., 1972; MD, Georgetown U., 1976. Diplomate Am. Bd. Family Practice with qualification in geriatrics, Am. Bd. Internal Medicine. Residency in family practice Medical Univ. of SC, 1976—79; dir., residency tng. Dept. Family Medicine, East Carolina U., Greenville, NC, 1985—88; prof., dir. clin. svcs. dept. family medicine Med. U. S.C., rleston, 1988—. Lectr. Am. Acad. Family Physicians, Kansas City, Mo., 1986—2003. Contbr. articles to profl. jours. Fellow: Am. Acad. Family Physicians. Avocations: bicycling, travel. Office: Med Univ South Carolina PO Box 250192 Charleston SC 29425

HAINES, CLIFFORD E., lawyer; b. Phila., Sept. 29, 1944; BA, Muskingum Coll., 1966; JD cum laude, Ohio State U., 1971. Bar: Pa. 1971, US Supreme Ct. 1977, US Dist. Ct., Eastern Dist. Pa. 1981. Asst. dist. atty. City of Phila., 1971—80; shareholder Litvin, Blumberg, Matusow & Young, 1980—2004; principal Haines and Assoc., 2004—. Faculty mem. Acad. Advocacy, 1979—94, Nat. Inst. Trial Advocacy, 1979—, Pa. Def. Inst. Trial Advocacy Tng. Program, 1989—, Phila. Dist. Atty. Tng. Program, 1992, 93, Trial Advocacy Tng. Program for City Solicitors, 1993; lectr. in law Temple U. Sch. Law, 1984—; program planner and faculty mem. Bar Assn. Trial Advocacy Tng. Program, 1988—; mem. Fourth Nat. Inst. Patent Trial Advocacy, Washington; chmn. bd. Pennsylvanians for Modern Cts., 2001—. Editor: Tips from the Trenches, Lit. Section, ABA. Bd. dirs. PILCOP, 1998—; mem. Phila. Vol. Lawyers for Arts Leadership Coun., 2002. With U.S. Army, 1966—68. Named to Top 100 Pa. Super Lawyers, Phila. Mag., 2004; recipient Equal Justice award, Cmty. Legal Svcs., Inc. Phila., 1999, Award for Excellence in Tchg. Trial Advocacy, Roscoe Pound Found., 2000. Fellow: Am. Coll. Trial Lawyers, Pa. Bar Found. (life); mem.: Internat. Acad. Trial Lawyers (fellow 2002), Pa. Futures Comm., Phila. Trial Lawyers Assn. (bd. dirs. 1989—99), Assn. Trial Lawyers Am., Pa. Bar Assn. (co-chair task force legal svcs. to the poor, part II 1998—99, Pres. award 1999), ABA (del. House Del. 1998—2000), Phila. Bar Assn. (mem. medico/legal com. 1982—, chair profl. responsibility com. 1986—87, chair state civil judicial procedures com. 1987—88, mem. prof. guidance com. 1987—, bd. gov. 1989—91, bd. mem. campaign for qualified judges 1990, chair bd. gov. 1991, chair lawyer info. referral svc. 1991, chair evidence code task force 1992—97, mem. Hamilton Cir. 1992—, co-chair by-laws com. 1993, vice-chancellor 1995, chancellor-elect 1996, chancellor 1997, Advocates award Com. Legal Rights Lesbians and Gay Men 1998), Vol. Phila. V.I.P., Tau Epsilon Rho. Achievements include apptd. by Gov. Edward G. Rendell and approved by State Senate to sit on Pa. Coun. Arts, 2004. Office: Haines & Assoc PC 1700 Market St Ste 2710 Philadelphia PA 19103 Office Phone: 215-246-2200.

HAINES, DANIEL WEBSTER, engineering consultant, engineering educator; b. Nashville, Nov. 8, 1937; s. I. Snowden and Elsie (Davis) Haines; m. Brynne Levinson, Nov. 9, 1962; children: Gordon, Laurel. BS, Rutgers U., 1959; MS, Lehigh U., 1961; ScD in Engring., Columbia U., 1968. Registered profl. engr., N.Y., S.C. Rsch. asst. Lehigh U., 1959—61; vol. Peace Corps, Ibadan, Nigeria, 1961—63; trainee NASA, 1964—66; prof. engring. U. SC, Columbia, 1969—77; product engring. mgr. Ciba-Geigy Corp., Ardsley, NY, 1977—81; prin. Midlantic Testing and Cons., White Plains, NY, 1982—87; prof. Manhattan Coll., Riverdale, NY, 1983—, chair mech. engring. dept., 1995—99. Vis. lectr. Yale U., 1975—76; vis. assoc. prof. Stevens Inst., Hoboken, NJ, 1975—76; cons. Institut National de la Recherche Agronomique, Nancy, France, 1999—. Editor (in chief): CAS Jour., 1989—95; mem. editl. adv. bd. CAS Jour., 1999—2003; contbr. articles to profl. jours. Fellow, Sloan Found., Princeton U., 1968—69; grantee, NSF, 1969—77. Mem.: ASME, ASCE, Catgut Acoustical Soc. (treas. 1982—90, trustee 1981—99). Home: 142 Greenridge Ave White Plains NY 10605-3109

HAINES, DENNIS G., military officer; BS in Bus. Adminstrn. and Mgmt., U. Wyo., 1968, MS in Bus. Adminstrn. and Mgmt., 1969; disting. grad., Squadron Officer Sch., 1972; grad., Air Command and Staff Coll., 1978. Commd. 2d lt. USAF, 1968, advanced through grades to maj. gen., 1997; maintenance control officer 19th Tactical Air Support Squadron, 314th Air Divsn., Osan Air Base, South Korea, 1972-73; chief, maintenance control divsn. comdr. 18th Equipment Maintenance Squadron, Kadena Air Base, Japan, 1980-83; dep. dir., dir. for maintenance engring. Hdqs. Pacific Air Forces, Hickam AFB, Hawaii, 1983-87; dep. comdr. for maintenance 37th Tactical Fighter Wing, Nellis AFB, Nev., 1988-90; chief fighter propulsion mgmt. divsn. San Antonio Air Logistics Ctr., Kelly AFB, Tex., 1990-91; dir. aircraft directorate Ogden Air Logistics Ctr., Hill AFB, Utah, 1991-93; dir. logistics Hdqs. Air Edn. and Tng. Command, Randolph AFB, Tex., 1993-95; dir. of supply Hdqs. USAF, Washington, 1995-96; dir. of logistics Hdqs. Air Force Materiel Command, Wright-Patterson AFB, Ohio, 1996-97, Hdqs. Air Combat Command, Langley AFB, Va., 1997-99, dir. combat weapon systems, 1999-2000, comdr. Warner Robins Air Logistics Ctr. Robins AFB, Ga., 2000—. Decorated Legion of Merit with oak leaf cluster, Meritorious Svc. medal with 4 oak leaf clusters.

HAINES, HARRY ALLEN, federal judge; b. Montana, 1939; BA, St. Olaf College, 1961; JD, University of Montana Law School, 1964; LLM Taxation, New York University Law School, 1966. Bar: Montana 1964, U.S. Dist. Ct., Montana 1964. Ptnr. Law Firm of Worden, Thane & Haines, 1966—2003; adjunct prof. law U. Mont., 1967—91; judge US Tax Ct., Washington, 2003—. Office: US Tax Ct 400 Second St NW Washington DC 20217*

HAINES, JAMES, JR., energy executive; JD, Univ. Mo. Columbia Law Sch., 1975. Pres., dir., CEO El Paso Electric Co., 1995—2001, Westar Energy, 2002—. Adj. prof., Skov prof. bus. admin. Univ. Tex. El Paso. Office: Westar Energy PO Box 889 Topeka KS 66601-0889 Office Phone: 785-575-6300.*

HAINES, JOHN MEADE, poet, translator, writer; b. 1924; Homesteader in Alaska, 1947-69; poet-in-residence U. Alaska, Anchorage, 1972-73; vis. prof. English U. Wash., Seattle, 1974; vis. lectr. U. Mont., Missoula, 1974-75; Guggenheim fellowship, 1984-85; disting. vis. lectr. U. Calif., Santa Cruz, 1986; writer-in-residence Montalvo Ctr. for the Arts, 1987-88, Djerassi Found., 1988; vis. prof. Ohio U., Athens, 1989-90. Vis. writer George Washington U., 1991-92; Elliston fellow in poetry U. Cin., 1992; chmn. creative arts Austin Peay State U., Clarksville, Tenn., 1993—; vis. lectr. Ann. Summer Wordsworth Conf., Grasmere, Eng., 1996; writer-in-residence Bellagio Ctr., Italy, 2000; poet-in-residence Bucknell U., 2001; guest poet Internat. Shakespeare Conf, Vladimir U., Russia, 2002. Translator: El Amor Ascendia, 1967; author: Winter News: Poems, 1966, Suite for the Pied Piper, 1967, The Legend of Paper Plates, 1970, The Mirror, 1971, The Stone Harp, 1971, Twenty Poems, 1971, Leaves and Ashes: Poems, 1974, In Five Years Time, 1976; The Sun on Your Shoulder, 1976, Cicada, 1977, In a Dusty Light, 1977, Living Off the Country: Essays on Poetry and Place, 1981, Of Traps and Snares, 1981, Other Days, 1982, News from the Glacier: Selected Poems 1982, Forest Without Leaves, 1984, Stories We Listened To, 1986, The Stars, The Snow, The Fire, 1989, Meditation On a Skull Carved in Crystal, 1989, New Poems, 1980-88, 1990 (Western States Art Fedn. award, Lenore Marshall/Nation award, Poets prize 1990), (poetry) Rain Country, 1990, The Owl in the Mask of the Dreamer, Collected Poems, 1993, A Guide to the Four-Chambered Heart, 1996, At the End of this Summer, 1948-54, 1997, (essay) Fables and Distances, New and Selected Essays, 1996, For the Century's End, Poems 1990-1999, 2001, Of Your Passage, O Summer, Uncollected Poems from the 1960s, 2004, Wartime, A Late Memoir, 2004. Recipient Acad. award in Lit. Am. Acad. of Arts and Letters, 1995; 63d fellow Acad. Am. Poets, 1997; named Alaska Poet Laureate, 1969-73; Gugggenheim fellow, 1965-66, NEA fellow, 1967-68; Amy Lowell traveling scholar, 1976-77; No. Momentum scholar U. Alaska, 2003. Home: 717 Longstaff Missoula MT 59801-3605

HAINES, JOYBELLE, retired elementary school educator; b. Geronomo, Okla., Oct. 20, 1930; d. William Tommie and Ruby Dell Heffington; m. Meredith C. Haines, Aug. 22, 1953; children: Cynthia Elaine, Stephen Michael, Lisa Joy. Grad., Asbury Coll., Wilmore, Ky.; postgrad., Ball State Tchrs. Coll., Calif. State U. Missionary tchr., Seoul, Republic of Korea, 1954—56; tchr. Hartford City, Ind., 1956—65, Muncie, Ind., 1965—66, Stockton (Calif.) Unified Sch. Dist., 1966—2000; ret., 2001. Cons. new tchrs., tutor, Stockton, 1999—. Mem.: AAUW, Rep. Women's Club. Baptist. Home: 9530 Springfield Way Stockton CA 95212

HAINES, KATHLEEN ANN, pediatrician, educator; b. NYC, July 28, 1949; d. George Raymond and Gertrude Ann (Driscoll) H.; m. Emil Claus Gotschlich, May 24, 1975; 1 child, Emily Claire. BA, CUNY, 1971; MD, Albert Einstein Coll. Medicine, 1975. Diplomate Am. Bd. Pediatrics, Am. Bd. Allergy and Immunology. Intern, resident NY Hosp./Cornell U., NYC, 1975-77, fellow in allergy/immunology, 1977-80; from instr. in pediatrics to assoc. prof. Sch. Medicine NYU, NYC, 1980—91, assoc. prof. clin. pediatrics and medicine Sch. Medicine, 1991—2005, adj. assoc. prof. Sch. Medicine, 2005—; dir. pediat. rheumatology Hosp. Joint Diseases/NYU Med. Ctr., 1994—2002; dir. clin. immunology lab. Hosp. Joint Diseases, 1995—2002; sect. chief pediat. immunology Hackensack U. Med. Ctr., NJ, 2002—. Mem. rsch. coun. NY Heart Assn., 1988-90; program com. Am. Coll. Rheumatology, 2000-03, vis. prof., 2001. Contbr. articles to profl. jours., chpts. to books in field. Med. and Scientific Com. N.Y.C. chpt. Arthritis Found., 1993-99. Grantee, N.Y. Arthritis Found., 1990, 1996, NIH, 1993—98. Fellow Am. Acad. Allergy and Immunology, Am. Acad. Pediatrics (mem. exec. com. rheumotology sect., 2003—); mem. Am. Fedn. Med. Rsch., Allergy, Asthma and Immunology Soc. of Greater N.Y. (sec. 1995-97, pres.-elect 1997-98, pres. 1998-99), Harvey Soc., Soc. Pediatric Rsch. Office: Hackensack U Med Ctr 30 Prospect Ave Hackensack NJ 07601 Business E-Mail: khaines@humed.com.

HAINES, KENNETH H., sports television broadcasting and marketing executive; b. Spokane, Sept. 5, 1942; s. Kenneth A. and Helen Elizabeth (Evans) H.; m. Stephanie Marie Phelps, Nov. 23, 1981; 1 child, Avery Jordan. BA, Dakota Wesleyan U., 1964; MA, U. Wyo.; MS, Troy State U., 1970; CAGS, Va. Tech., 1976. News dir. KORN TV, Mitchell, S.D., 1962-64; sta. mgr. KUWR Radio, Laramie, Wyo., 1965-67; gen. mgr. KLME Radio, Laramie, 1967-68; instr. flight ops. U.S. Army, Ft. Rucker, Ala., 1968-70; from dir. radio, tv, film to dir. pub. affairs, univ. rels. Va. Tech., Blacksburg, 1970-81; from exec. v.p., COO to pres., CEO, Raycom Sports, Charlotte, NC, 1981—2002, pres., CEO, 2002—. Bd. dirs. Charlotte Sports Commn., ACC Properties; trustee Dakota Wesleyan U.; exec. dir. Continental Tire Bowl, 2002—. Bd. dirs. Sunshine Football Classic, 1989—, Charlotte Basketball Challenge, 1987—; tournament dir. LPGA Golf, 1997—; exec. dir. Continental Tire Bowl. Named Reporter of Yr., UPI, 1967, Opperman Disting. Lectr., Dakota Wesleyan U., 1998, Outstanding TV Sports Exec., All-Am. Football Found., 1999; recipient golden award Coun. Support Higher Edn., 1978. Mem. Am. Assn. Agr. Writers, Am. Coll. Pub. Rels. Assn. (exceptional achievement award 1974), Va. Press Assn., Coun. for Advancement and Support of Edn. (pres. univ. faculty club 1980-82), Nat. Acad. TV Arts and Scis. (judge), Charlotte C. of C. (bd. dirs.), Phi Kappa Delta, Pi Delta Epsilon, Omicron Delta Kappa. Avocations: sports, photography, television, travel, reading. Home: 1909 Carmel Rd Charlotte NC 28226-5021 Office: Raycom Sports 2815 Coliseum Centre Dr Ste 200 Charlotte NC 28217-1378

HAINES, MARTHA MAHAN, lawyer; b. Detroit, Feb. 4, 1952; d. Albert F. and Martha M. (Sager) Mahan; divorced; children: Ella Catherine, Emily Martha. Student, U. Utah, 1970-72; BA magna cum laude, Wayne State U., 1974; JD, U. Mich., 1977. Bar: Ill. 1978, U.S. Dist. Ct. (no. dist.) Ill. 1982. Assoc. Chapman and Cutler, Chgo., 1978-82, jr. ptnr., 1982-86; of counsel Altheimer & Gray, Chgo., 1986-90, ptnr., 1990-97, Barnes & Thornburg, Chgo., 1997-99; chief Office Mcpl. Securities, SEC, Washington, 1999—; asst. dir. divsn. mkt. regulation SEC, 2000—. Office: Office Mpcl Securities SEC 100 F St NE Washington DC 20549-1001 Office Phone: 202-551-5681. Business E-Mail: hainesm@sec.gov.

HAINES, MICHAEL ROBERT, economist, educator; b. Chgo., Nov. 19, 1944; s. James Joshua and Ann Marie (Welch) H.; m. Patricia Caroline Foster, Aug. 19, 1967 (div. Dec. 1986); children: James, Margaret; m. Eileen Margaret Mulhare, Jan. 5, 1995. BA, Amherst Coll., 1967; MA, U. Pa., 1968, PhD, 1971. Asst. prof. econs. Cornell U., Ithaca, NY, 1972—79; rsch. assoc. prof. Sch. Pub. and Urban Policy, U. Pa., Ithaca, 1979—80; assoc. prof. econs. Wayne U., Detroit, 1980—86, prof. econ., 1986—90; Banfi Vintners Disting. prof. econs. Colgate U., Hamilton, NY, 1990. Vis. lectr. econs. U. Pa., Phila., 1979; cons. NIH, Bethesda Md., 1980-84, 90-91, 93, 95-2003, The World Bank, Washington, 1983, Nat. Rsch. Coun., 1995; rsch. assoc. Nat. Bur. Econ. Rsch., 1987—; rsch. affiliate Population Studies Ctr., U. Mich., Ann Arbor, 1990—. Author: Economic-Demographic Interrelations in Developing Agricultural Regions, 1977, Fertility and Occupation, 1979, Fatal Years, 1991, A Population History of North America, 2000; contbr. articles to profl. jours. Grantee: NIH, 1974-77, 78-82, 89—. Mem. Internat. Union Sci. Study Population, Econ. History Assn. (bd. dirs. 1987-91), Social Sci. History Assn. (bd. dirs. 1983-85, treas. 1985-87, v.p. 1997-98, pres. 1998-99), Am. Econ. Assn., The Cilometrics Soc. (bd. editor 1988-94), Population Assn. Am. Roman Catholic. Avocations: coin collecting/numismatics, wine, book collecting. Office: Colgate Univ Dept Econs 13 Oak Dr Hamilton NY 13346-1338 Business E-Mail: mhaines@mail.colgate.edu.

HAINES, RICHARD FOSTER, retired psychologist; b. Seattle, May 19, 1937; s. Donald Hutchinson and Claudia May (Bennett) H.; m. Carol Taylor, June 17, 1961; children: Cynthia Lynn, Laura Anne. Student, U. Wash., 1955-57; BA, Pacific Luth. Coll., Tacoma, 1960; MA, Mich. State U., 1962, PhD, 1964. Predoctoral rsch. fellow NIH, 1964; Nat. Acad. Sci. postdoctoral resident rsch. assoc. Ames Rsch. Ctr./NASA, Moffett Field, Calif., 1964-67, rsch. scientist, 1967-86, chief of space human factors office, 1987-88, rsch. scientist Rsch. Inst. Advanced Computer Sci., 1988-90; assoc. prof. dept. psychology San Jose State U., 1988-89; computer scientist RECOM Techs., Inc., Moffett Field, Calif., 1993-2000, Raytheon Corp., 2000—01; ret., 2001. Rsch. cons. to NASA Foothill Coll.; cons. Stanford U. Sch. medicine, 1966-67, TRW-Systems Group, 1969-70; mem. adv. com. on vision NRC; founding mem. advanced tech. applications com. Calif. Coun. AIA and NASA, 1975-80; mem. adv. bd. Space Scis. Ctr.-Foothill Coll., 1976-78; bd. advisors Fund for UFO Rsch., Washington; chmn. bd. Novosibirsk Christian Pub.-Calif., 1993—; chief scientist Nat. Aviation Reporting Ctr. on Anomalous Phenomena, 2001—. Author: UFO Phenomena and the Behavioral Scientist, 1979, Observing UFOs, 1980, Melbourne Episode: Case Study of a Missing Pilot, 1987, Advanced Aerial Devices Reported During the Korean War, 1990, Night Flying, 1992, Project Delta, 1994, Close Encounters of the Fifth Kind, 1999, Aviation Safety in America - A Previously Neglected Factor, 2000; mem. editl. and sci. bd. Jour. UFO Studies, Internat. UFO Reporter, Cuadernos de Ufologica; contbr. articles to profl. jours. Mem. Palo Alto (Calif.) Mayor's Com. on Youth Activities, 1967; chmn. adv. coun. Christian Cmty. Progress Corp., Menlo Park, Calif.; v.p., dir. Ctr. Counseling for Drug Abuse, Menlo Park; bd. dirs., chmn. sci. adv. team Threshold Found.; founding co-dir. Joint Am.-Soviet Aerial Anomaly Fedn., 1991—97. Named Alumnus of Yr., Pacific Luth. U., 1972 Fellow Aerospace Med. Assn. (assoc.); mem. Optical Soc. Am., Soc. for Sci. Exploration, Sigma Xi. Achievements include patents for device of advanced detection of glaucoma, optical projector of vision performance data for design engineers, visual simulator optical alignment device, grooming aid for use by astronauts in space.

HAINES, ROBERT L., JR., air transportation executive, educator; b. Springfield, Ill., Sept. 8, 1963; s. Robert L. Haines, Sr. and Edith H. Ginther; m. L. Beverley Hughes, June 28, 1960; children: Adam J. Southard, Bridget C. Southard, Evan R., Catherine E. AAS in Avionics Systems Tech., C.C. of the Air Force, 1988; BA, Governors State U., 2002; MS in Indsl. Orgnl. Psychology, Capella U., 2004. Cert. mechanic, airframe and powerplant FAA, 1992, inspection authorization 2004. Avionics/regional tech. coord. Delta Air Lines, Orlando, Fla., 1996—2000; program mgr., academic support Delta U., Delta Air Lines, Atlanta, 2000—01; mgr., line maintenance ops. Delta Air Lines, Orlando, Fla., 2001—02; chief cons. Pro AMT Services, St. Cloud, Fla., 2002—; dir. maintenance tng. Flight Safety Internat., Little Rock, 2004—. Commr. ex-officio Ctr. for Lifelong Learning, Washington, 2001—03; mem. Olympics planning com. Profl. Aviation Maintenance Assn., Alexandria, Va., 2002—04; mem. industry adv. coun. Embry-Riddle Aero. U., Daytona Beach, Fla., 1999—2001; adj. prof. Northrop Rice Aviation Inst. Tech., 2003. Contbr. articles. Mem., archtl. rev. bd. Ashley Oaks Homeowners Assn., St. Cloud, Fla., 2002—03; mem., athletic boosters St. Cloud H.S., 1998—2003. With USAF, 1982—90. Recipient Award of Merit, Profl. Aviation Maintenance Assn., 2000, Diamond award, FAA Maintenance Technician Awards Program, 2000—04, Ruby award, 1998, 1999, Troubleshooter of the Yr. award, PAMA Aviation Maintenance Olympics, 2002. Mem.: Am. Psychol. Assn., Soc. Human Resource Mgmt., Soc. for Indsl. and Orgnl. Psyhcology, Profl. Aviation Maintenance Assn., Delta Chmn. Club. Office: Pro AMT Services PO Box 3044 Little Rock AR 72203-3044 Personal E-mail: proamt@proamt.com.

HAINES, STEPHEN JOHN, neurosurgeon; b. Burlington, Vt., Sept. 4, 1949; s. Gerald Leon and Frances Mary (Whitcomb) H.; m. Jennifer Lea Plombon; children: Christopher, Jeremy. AB, Dartmouth Coll., 1971; MD, U. Vt., 1975. Diplomate Am. Bd. Neurol. Surgery; diplomate Nat. Bd. Med. Examiners. Intern U. Minn., Mpls., 1975-76; neurol. surgery resident U. Pitts., 1976-81; from asst. prof. to prof. U. Minn., Mpls., 1982—93, prof. neurosurgery, otolaryngology and pediatrics, 1993-97, head divsn. pediatric neurosurgery, 1985-97, chmn. and head dept. neurosurgery, 2003—; prof. neurosurg., Lyle A. French chair, head dept. neurosurg. U. Minn. Med. Sch., 2003—; prof. neurol. surgery, otolaryngology and pediats., chmn. dept. neurol. surgery Med. U. S.C., 1997—2003. Adv. panel FDA Neurologic Devices, 2002—05, chair, 2005; mem. Com. Postmarket Surveillance Pediat Med. Devices, Inst. Medicine, 2004—05. Contbr. articles to profl. jours. Fellow ACS; mem. AMA, Am. Assn. Neurol. Surgeons (Van Wagenen fellow 1981), Congress Neurol. Surgeons (pres. 1996), Soc. Clin. Trials, Neurosurg. Soc. Am., Am. Acad. Neurol. Surgery, Soc. Neurol. Surgeons. Office: Dept Neurosurgery MMC 96 420 Delaware St SE Minneapolis MN 55455 Office Phone: 612-626-5767. Business E-Mail: shaines@umn.edu, headneurosurg@umn.edu.

HAINES, THOMAS HENRY, biochemist, educator, researcher; b. N.Y.C., Aug. 9, 1933; s. Charles and Elizabeth Cubbon Haines; m. Mary Manning Cleveland, Aug. 6, 1986; m. Adrian Sheila Rappaport, Nov. 26, 1960 (dec. May 5, 1985); 1 child, Avril Danica. BS, CUNY, 1957; PhD, Rutgers U., 1965; MS, CUNY, 1999. Rsch. biochemist Boyce Thompson Inst. for Plant Rsch., Yonkers, NY, 1959—62; asst./assoc. prof. chemistry City Coll. CUNY, N.Y.C., 1964—72; prof. chemistry and biochemistry doctoral program CUNY, N.Y.C., 1972—; acting dean, founder Sophie Davis Biomed. Program CUNY Med. Sch., N.Y.C., 1971—73, dir. biochemistry, 1973—. Vis. assoc. prof. U. Calif., Berkeley, 1970—71, vis. rsch. scientist, 1993—94; chair symposium on lipids Internat. Union Pure and Applied Biochemistry, Riga, Latvia, 1970; vis. scholar Nat. Ctr. for Sci. Rsch., Gif-sur-Yvette, France (incl. Monaco), 1970—71; vis. prof. U. Minn., Mpls., 1978—79, Beijing Med. Sch., 1986—87; vis. scientist Mitsubishi-Kasai Inst. for the Life Scis., Machida, Tokyo, Japan, 1986—87; mem., exec. com. Levich Inst. for Hydrodynamics, N.Y.C., 1991—2001; ad hoc mem. biochemistry and cell biology study sect. Nat. Inst. Alcoholism and Alcohol Abuse, Washington, 1992—95; cons. Liposome Tech. Inc., Menlo Park, Calif., 1993—95, Sequus, Inc., Menlo Park, 1995—2000. Co-founder Partnership for Responsible Drug Info., N.Y.C., 1993—2002, Voluntary Com. Lawyers, N.Y.C., 1994—2002. Grantee, NIH, 1972—78, NSF. Mem.: AAAS (life), Assn. Grad. and Med. Schs. Biochemistry Chairs, N.Y. Acad. Scis. (life; chair biophysics sect. 1991—94), City Coll. Sci. Alumni Assn. (pres. 1993—). Achievements include design of model for why animals need cholesterol; research in Lipid Structure and Function. Avocations: gardening, politics, travel. Home: 14 West 68 St New York NY 10023 Office: City Univ New York 139 St at Convent Ave New York NY 10031 Office Phone: 212-873-2982. E-mail: thaines@prdi.org.

HAINES, THOMAS W. W., lawyer; b. Balt., Oct. 10, 1941; s. John Summer and Clara Elizabeth (Ward) H.; m. Vivienne Wilson, Jan. 3, 1981; children: Robert S., Elizabeth E., John M. BA, Cornell U., 1963; LLB, U. Md., 1967. Bar: Md. 1967, U.S. Dist. Ct. Md. 1968, U.S. Ct. Appeals (4th cir.) 1972, U.S. Tax Ct. 1973, U.S. Supreme Ct. 1975. Assoc. Semmes, Bowen & Semmes, Balt., 1968-75, ptnr., 1975—2003, Venable, Baetjer & Howard, LLP, Balt., 1995—2003; pres. Nat. Paving and Contracting Co., Inc., Balt., 2003—. Mem. ABA, Md. Bar Assn., Bar Assn. Balt. City, Gibson Island Club, Md. Club. Office: 6115 Oakleaf Ave Baltimore MD 21215 Personal E-mail: twhaines@comcast.net. E-mail: twhaines@permapatch.com.

HAINES, WALTER WELLS, retired economics professor; b. Stamford, Conn., Dec. 1, 1918; s. Thomas Kelly Peterson and Carrie Hooker (Williams) H.; m. Hazel Ellen Maxwell, Jan. 1, 1945 (div.); children: Jennifer Jean, Deborah Lee, Pamela Ann, Christopher Alan, Liseli Ellen, Timothy Maxwell; m. Mary Lou Peck, Nov. 30, 1991. BA, U. Pa., 1940, MA, 1941, Harvard U., 1942, PhD (Lehman nat. fellow), 1943. Instr. econs. Kenyon Coll., 1946-47; mem. faculty NYU, 1947—, prof. econs., 1960-89, emeritus prof. of econs., 1989—, chmn. dept. Univ. Coll., 1956-68, dir. undergrad. studies, 1983-89; adminstr. Friends Hosp., Tiriki, Kenya, 1969-70. Fulbright prof. econs. U. Peshawar, Pakistan, 1962-63; Fulbright prof. environ. conservation Middle East Tech. U., Ankara, Turkey, 1973-74; lectr. Siena Coll., 1989-92. Author: Money, Prices and Policy, 1961, also articles. Lehman Nat. fellow Harvard U., 1941-43. Fellow Internat. Inst. for Social Econs.; mem. AAAS, World Future Soc., Fulbright Alumni Assn., Cultural Survival, Am. Econ. Assn., Fellowship of Reconciliation, Fedn. Am. Scientists, Assn. for Social Econs., Soc. for Advancement of Socio-Econs., Internat. Soc. Ecol. Econs., Nat. Peace Found., Global Edn. Associates, Amnesty Internat., World Federalists, Parliamentarians for Global Action, Internat. Physicians for the Prevention of Nuclear War, Nat. Wildlife Fedn. Wilderness Soc., Union of Concerned Scientists, Carter Ctr., Albert Einstein Inst., UN Assn. U.S., World Federalists, Habitat for Humanity, Natural Resources Def. Coun., Phi Beta Kappa Mem. Religious Soc. of Friends. Home: 196 Vosburgh Rd Averill Park NY 12018-5710 Personal E-mail: hainesww@earthlink.net. E-mail: peckm@sage.edu. *The wellspring of my life is a belief that there is something of God in every person. From this universality of the divine spark emerge many principles of faith; the brotherhood of man, the importance of the golden rule, the primacy of love. These in turn call for social action to promote civil rights, nondiscrimination, peace, cooperation, democracy, world equality, the preservation of a quality environment, and conservation of resources for future generations. I have no illusion that this belief has brought me "success", but it has contributed much to the richness of life.*

HAINES, WILLIAM JOSEPH, retired pharmaceutical executive; b. Crawfordsville, Ind., Sept. 26, 1919; s. Burt and Lala R. (Luster) Haines; m. Wilma M. Hester, June 6, 1993; 2 children, Paula Sue Haines Curtis-Burn, Eric J. AB summa cum laude, Wabash Coll., 1940, DSc (hon.), 1970; PhD, U. Ill., 1943; grad. exec. program in bus. adminstrn., Columbia Bus. Sch., 1965. Rsch. biochemist Upjohn Co., Kalamazoo, 1943-50, head dept. endocrinology rsch., 1950-54; tech. dir. Armour Labs., Kankakee, Ill., 1954-58; v.p. dir. rsch. Ortho Pharm. Corp., Raritan, N.J., 1958-65, exec. v.p., 1965-67; vice chmn. Johnson & Johnson Internat., 1967-69; dir., mem. exec. com. Johnson & Johnson, New Brunswick, N.J., 1969-79, v.p. corp. office sci. and tech., 1979-82; pres. Bucks-Tech Assocs., Inc. (cons. in mgmt., sci. and tech.), Doylestown, Pa., 1982—. Chmn. sci. adv. com. Alliance Internat. Health Care Trust, 1983-87; former dir. Quidel Corp., La Jolla, Calif.; invited lectr. Laurentian Hormone Conf., 1952, Gordon Rsch. Conf., 1952. Contbr. numerous sci. articles to profl. jours., including pioneer paper on human requirement for essential amino acids, 1942. One of initial investigators to identify essential amino acids for human nutrition; patentee biosynthesis of adrenal cortex hormones, paper chromatography and automatic partition column chromatography of steroids. Trustee Wabash Coll., 1972-93, trustee emeritus, 1993—; trustee Hood Coll., 1975-87, vice chmn. bd., 1982-87, trustee emeritus, 1989—; Joslin Diabetes Found. Inc., Boston, 1974-79; elder Thompson Meml. Presbyn. Ch., New Hope, Pa. Recipient William E. Upjohn prize and medal, 1952, Alumni Merit award Nat. Assn. Wabash Men, 1973. Fellow AAAS, Am. Inst. Chemists; mem. Am. Chem. Soc. (med. cheistry div.), N.Y. Acad. Scis., Endocrine Soc., Am. Soc. Biol. Chemists, Soc. Chem. Industry (former chmn. Am. sect.), Pharm. Mfrs. Assn. (former chmn. R&D sec.), Assn. Rsch. Dirs., Indsl. Rsch. Inst., (dir. emeritus), N.J. Acad. Scis., Soc. Exptl. Biology and Medicine, Pacific Coast Fertility Soc., Am. Fertility Soc., Internat. Soc. Rsch. in Biology Reproduction (charter), Am. Inst. Mgmt. (exec. council), Am. Mgmt. Assn., Am. Found. Pharm. Edn. (Century Club), Ind. Covered Bridge Soc., Sons of Ind. (N.Y.C. chpt.), Chemists Club (N.Y.C.), Masons, Elks, Kiwanis (emeritus), Lake Naomi Club, Phi Beta Kappa, Phi Lambda Upsilon, Phi Kappa Phi, Sigma Xi, Alpha Chi Sigma. Republican. Home: 5 Bedford Dr Doylestown PA 18901-9463 Office: Johnson & Johnson 1 Johnson And Johnson Plz New Brunswick NJ 08933-0002

HAINSWORTH, MELODY MAY, library and information scientist, researcher; b. Vancouver, B.C., Can., May 13, 1946; m. Robert John Hainsworth, Jan. 6, 1968; children: Kaleeg William, Shane Alan. BA with honors, Simon Fraser U., 1968; MLS, Dalhousie U., 1976; PhD, Fla. State U., 1992. Libr. Dept. Edn. of Tanzania, Mbeya, 1969—72, Dept. of Edn. of Zambia, Mwinilunga, 1972—74; law libr., deptl. libr. Dept. of Atty. Gen. of N.S., Halifax, 1975—77; regional libr. Provincial Ct. Librs. Dept. of Atty. Gen. of Alta., Calgary, 1977—80, So. Alta. Law Soc. libr., 1980—89; dir. librs. Keiser Coll., Tallahassee, 1992—93; v.p. info. resources and svcs. Internat. Coll., Naples, Fla., 1993—2005; with HMSMG Mgmt. Group, White Rock, Canada, 2005—. Adj. instr. Sch. Libr. and Info. Studies Fla. State U., Tallahassee, 1990-91, libr. cons., 2004—; spkr. in field; co-founder Naples Free-Net, pres. 1993—; co-founder World Class Acad., rschr. law and info. sci.; mem. faculty Practising Law Inst.; active Women's Polit. Caucus; evaluator SACS/COC, 1999—; mem. external rev. panel ALA/COA, 1999—; spkr. Practising Law Inst. Author monographs; contbr. articles to profl. jours. Co-chair adv. com. edn. and tech. com. Fla. State Bd. Ind. Colls. and Univs., 1993-2001; founding mem. Pub. Access to Law of Fla., 1990—; mem. exec. bd. Calgary Legal Guidance, 1985-89, vice chmn., 1988-89, hon. life mem.; tech. grant com. Collier County Edn. Found., 1994-96, sec./webmaster World Class Collier, supt. search com., 1998; chair edn. com. East Naples Civic Assn., 1998; bd. dirs. Seacrest Country Day Sch., 1996-2002. Student Leader Bursaries Simon Fraser U. scholar, 1966-68; H.W. Wilson scholar Dalhousie U., 1974; recipient Woman of Distinction award AAUW, 1999, Women of Distinction, Tempo Internat., Naples, 2005, Woman of Style, 2005. Mem. Spl. Librs. Assn (pres. 1994-95), Assn. Online Profls., Fla. State Ct. and County Librs. Assn., Tallahassee Law Librs. Assn., Fla. Libr. Assn., Assn. Libr. and Info. Sci. Edn., Alta. Legal Archives Soc. (hon. life), Collier County Bar Assn., Women's Polit. Caucus (webmaster 1999—), Tempo Internat. (bd.

dirs., Named Woman of Distinction 2005), Naples Press Club (bd. dirs.), Women in Bus. Vancouver Avocations: squash, hiking, travel. Office: HMSMG Mgmt Group #501 1225 Merkin St White Rock BC Canada V4B 4B8

HAIR, ROBERT EUGENE, editor, writer, historian; b. Winamac, Ind., Apr. 11, 1921; s. Charles Franklin and Lucy Agnes (Zellers) H.; m. Marian Martha Emerson, Dec. 11, 1949; children: Donald Edward, Martha Anne. AB, DePauw U., Greencastle, Ind., 1942; postgrad., U. Mich., Ann Arbor, 1943-44, 53-56. Newspaper writer and editor; editor Mich. Dept. Health, Lansing, 1956-60; asst. editor Encyclopedia Britannica, Chgo., 1960-64; exec. editor Battelle Rsch. Outlook, Columbus, 1964-69; editor Cordis Corp., Miami, 1969-80. Author: (books) Sturgis, Michigan: Its Story to 1930, 1992, Sturgis, Michigan: 1930-1945, 1996, Sturgis and Its Industrial Growth, 1998, Klinger Lake...Its Origins and Growth, 2001; contbr. articles to profl. jours. Pres. Civic Auditorium Bd., Sturgis, 1994, St. Joseph County Hist. Soc., Centreville, Mich., 1995; v.p. Sturgis Hist. Soc., Mich., 1996, Centennial Celebration Com., Sturgis, 1996. Recipient Award of Merit Hist. Soc. of Mich., 1996, 2001. Mem. Am. Med. Writers Assn., Soc. Profl. Journalists, Masonic Blue Lodge, Sturgis Exchg. Club (pres. 1951-52), Lambda Chi Alpha. Republican. Presbyterian. Avocations: preserving history, stamp collecting/philately, music, photography, collecting antiques. Home: 428 Mortimer St Sturgis MI 49091-2228

HAIRALD, MARY PAYNE, vocational education educator, coordinator; b. Tupelo, Miss., Feb. 25, 1936; d. Will Burney and Ivey Lee (Berryhill) Payne; m. Leroy Utley Hairald, May 31, 1958; 1 child, Burney LeShawn. BS in Commerce, U. Miss., 1957, M in Bus. Edn., 1963; postgrad., Miss. Coll., 1964, Miss. State U., 1970, U. So. Miss., 1986-88, 90, U. Calif., Davis, summer 1997, Babson Coll., summer 1998. Bus. edn. tchr. John Rundle High Sch., Grenada, Miss., 1957-59; youth recreation leader City of Nettleton, Miss., summers 1960-61; tchr. social studies Nettleton Jr. High Sch., 1959-70; tchr.-coord. coop. vocat. edn. program Nettleton High Sch., 1970—; area mgr. World Book, Inc., Chgo., 1972-84; local coord. Am. Inst. for Fgn. Study, Stamford, Conn., 1988—. Instr. bus. Itawamba C.C., Tupelo, 1975-80; with Cmty. Coord. for Program of Acad. Exch. (PAX), 1998—; advisor DECA, Nettleton, 1985—, state officers' advisor, 1995-01; apptd. adv. coord. mem. Miss. Coop. Edn.-State Dept. Edn. Contbr. articles on coop. edn. to newspapers. Co-organizer Nettleton Youth Recreation Booster Club; fund-raiser Muscular Dystrophy Assn.; Sunday sch. tchr. coll. and career class Nettleton United Meth. Ch. Recipient 1st place Nat. Newsletter award Nat. DECA, 1988, 89, 90, 92, Excellence in Supervision award Am. Inst. for Fgn. Study, 1992, Excellence award Pub. Edn. Forum, 1997, Outstanding Tchr. of Yr. award 2005; named Star Tchr., Miss. Econ. Coun., 1978, 95, Tchr. of Yr., Wal-Mart, 1997, Tech. Edn. Air Force award, 2005; finalist award Miss. Mfrs. Assn., 1997, 98, 02. Mem. AAUW (charter), Am. Vocat. Assn. (Region IV New and Related Svcs. Tchr. of Yr. 1986, 96, Region IV Mktg. Edn. Tchr. of Yr. 1988, Region IV Outstanding Vocat. Tchr. of Yr. 1996, Nat. Tchr. of the Yr. 97), Coop. Work Experience Edn. Assn., Miss. Assn. Vocat. Educators (dist. sec., pres. 2001-02), Miss. Assn. Coop. Vocat. Edn. Tchrs. (v.p. 1980-83, pres. 1983-84, Miss. Tchr. of Yr. 1984, 87, 95), Miss. Assn. Mktg. Educators (Dist. II Tchr. of Yr. 1993, 94), Mktg. Edn. Assn., Jim Bowers/DECA Found. (charter, life), Nettleton Ladies Civitan Club (charter), DECA (hon., life, adv. 1985—, adv. state newsletter 1987-92, Nat. Newsletter award 1988-90, 92, named Adv. of Yr. Dist. II Miss. Assn. 1990, 93, 2000, State Adv. of Yr. 2000, Alumni of Yr. 1998, named to Hall Fame 1996), Phi Delta Kappa (Phi Delta Kappa Kappan of Yr. 1998, found. rep., Outstanding Tech. Edn. Tchr. of Yr. 2005) Democrat. Methodist. Home: PO Box 166 Nettleton MS 38858-0166 Office Phone: 662-963-7405. E-mail: teachcoop34@yahoo.com.

HAIRSTON, GEORGE W., lawyer; b. Ironton, Ohio, Aug. 1, 1942; BBA, So. Meth. U., 1965; JD cum laude, Ohio State U., 1968. Bar: Ohio 1968, US Dist. Ct., So. Dist. of Ohio, 1970, US Ct. of Appeals, Sixth Circuit, 1973. Mng. ptnr. Baker & Hostetler, Columbus, Ohio, 1979—, mem. Operating Group & Policy Com. Bd. dirs. Central Benefits Mutual Insurance Co., Dennison Health Providers Assurance Co. Trustee Recreation Unlimited; mem. nat. council Ohio State U. Coll. of Law; bd. dirs. Osteopathic Heritage Found. Mem.: ABA, Columbus Bar Assn., Ohio State Bar Assn. Office: Baker & Hostetler Capitol Sq 65 E State St Ste 2100 Columbus OH 43215-4260 Office Phone: 614-462-2638. Office Fax: 614-462-2616. Business E-Mail: ghairston@bakerlaw.com.

HAIRSTON, HAROLD B., protective services official; m. Anne Hairston; children: Harold, Jr., Jennifer. Student, A&T U., N.C., Pa. State U., Abington; DHL (hon.), Holy Family Coll. With Phila. Fire Dept., 1964—, lt. Ladder Co. # 6, 1971-78, capt., 1978—81, bn. chief, dep. fire marshal, 1981-86, dep. chief, chief divsn. fire prevention, 1986—88, dep. commr., 1988—92, commr., 1992—. Expert witness Mcpl. and Common Pleas Ct.; testifier Consumer Products Safety Commn., Washington. Bd. dirs. Delaware Valley Burn Found., Hero Scholarship Fund, Police Athletic League, Dad Vail Regatta, ARC S.E. Pa. Recipient Outstanding Achievement award, Conf. of Mayors, Excellence in Govt. award, Am. Soc. Pub. Adminstrn., Legion of Honor Gold medallion, The Chapel of the Four Chaplains, 2004. Mem. Nat. Fire Protection Assn., Urban Fire Forum, Bldg. Ofcls. and Code Adminstrs., Internat. Assn. Black Profl. Firefighters, Internat. Assn. Fire Chiefs, Metro Fire Chiefs Assn. (Met. Fire Chief of Yr. 2003), Nat. Burglar and Fire Alarm Assn. (Fire Ofcl. of Yr. 2003). Office: Fire Department Fire Administration Bldg 240 Spring Garden St Fl 2D Philadelphia PA 19123-2923

HAIRSTON, NELSON GEORGE, JR., ecologist, educator; b. Asheville, NC, Sept. 26, 1949; s. Nelson George and Martha Turner (Patton) H.; m. Deborah Susan (Whitaker)Hairston, Nov. 30, 1974; 1 child, Peter Whitaker Hairston. BS, U. Mich., 1971; PhD, U. Wash., 1977. Asst. prof. U. R.I., Kingston, 1977-81, assoc. prof., 1981-85, Cornell U., Ithaca, NY, 1985-87, prof., 1988—, Frank H.T. Rhodes prof. environ. sci., 1996—, chmn. dept. ecology and evolutionary biology, 2001—. Vis. disting. ecologist U. Mich. Biol. Sta., Pelston, 1984; vis. eminent ecologist Mich. State U. Biol. Sta., Hickory Corners, 1989; cons. Westinghouse Savannah River Co., 1990-95, NSF Program in Population Biology and Physiol. Ecology, 1985-87, Swedish Nat. Rsch Coun., 1991, 99, U. Stockholm, 1996, Max Planck Inst. for Limnology, 1997, U. Uppsala, 1998; Douglas Disting. lectr. Rocky Mountain Biol. Lab, Crested Butte, Colo., 1992. Mem. editl. bd. Limnology and Oceanography, 1986-89, 2003-04, Ecology/Ecol. Monographs, 1989-92, 94-96; contbr. more than 80 articles and papers to sci. jours. NSF grantee, 1980, 83, 86, 88-89, 89-90, 91-92, 92-93, 95, 97, 99, 2000; EPA grantee, 1997, 2001; Andrew Mellon Found. grantee, 1997,2003. Mem. Ecol. Soc. Am. (coun. reps. 1990-93, chair awards com. 1992-95, governing bd. 1996-99, 2001-2004), Internat. Assn. Theoretical and Applied Limnology (nat. rep. 1992-95, 2002—). Avocations: boating, skiing, reading. Home: 6125 Perry City Rd Trumansburg NY 14886-9011 Office: Cornell U Dept Ecology and Evolutionary Biology Ithaca NY 14853 Office Phone: 607-254-4231. Business E-Mail: ngh1@cornell.edu.

HAIRSTON, WALTER ALBERT, school system administrator; b. Winston-Salem, NC, Sept. 14, 1928; s. Harvey and Ethel (Marshall) H.; m. Genell Rosella Bright, Mar. 10, 1951 (div. Sept. 12, 1972; m. Jeanette Olivia, Jan. 2, 1979; children: Jacqueline, Walter, Denice, Roslyn, Michael, Linda, Brenda, Telly. BS, Morgan State U., 1959; MEd, Loyola Coll., 1970; graduate, Command and Gen. Staff Coll., 1974, Nat. Def. U., 1979. Commd. U.S. Army, 1955, advanced through grades to col., 1979, ret., 1988; commandant 2071st U.S. Army Sch., 1979; mem. functional area assessment team Transp. Corps, U.S. Army, Fort Eustis, Va., 1984; chief evaluator and dir. Command Gen. Staff Coll., 1979-81; from tchr. to prin. Balt. City Dept. Edn., 1960—. Col. U.S. Army, 1948-85. Mem. Masons, Kappa Alpha Psi, Kappa Delta Pi. Democrat. Presbyterian. Avocations: golf, fishing, boating, woodwork. Home: 14300 Robcaste Rd Phoenix MD 21131-1426 Fax: 410-527-0021. Personal E-mail: walthairst@aol.com.

HAITHCOCK, WILLIAM DANA, JR., physician; b. Bennettsville, S.C., Feb. 19, 1946; s. William Dana and Clarice Anna (Skaggs) H.; m. Nancy Lee, Feb. 10, 1973; children: Judson Legare, Walker Calloway, William Franklin. BS, Wofford Coll., 1968; MD, Med. U. S.C., 1973. Diplomate Am. Bd. Ob-Gyn. Intern William Beaumont Army Med. Ctr., El Paso, 1973-74, resident, 1974-77; practice medicine specializing in ob-gyn. Fayettevill (N.C.) Woman's Clinic, 1980—; med. dir. ob-gyn. svc. line Cape Fear Health System, 2002. Mem. staff Cape Fear Valley Med. Ctr., Highsmith-Rainey Meml. Hosp.; mem. Cumberland County Mental Health Bd., 1980-84 . Trustee Fayetteville Area Health Edn. Found., 1993-99, v.p., mem. exec. com., 1996-99; mem. Fayetteville Regional Airport Commn., 1994-96. Served to maj. U.S. Army, 1973-80. Decorated Army Commendation medal. Fellow Am. Coll. Ob-Gyn.; mem. So. Med. Assn., N.C. Med. Soc., N.C. Ob-Gyn. Soc., So. Clin. Congress Ob-Gyn., Palmetto Soc., Pi Kappa Alpha. Presbyterian.

HAITINK, BERNARD J. H., conductor; b. Amsterdam, Mar. 4, 1929. MusD (hon.), U. of Oxford, 1988, U. of Leeds, 1988. Condr., Netherlands Radio Philharmonic Orch., 1955-61; guest condr. Concertgebouw Orch., Amsterdam, then joint condr., 1956-64, chief condr., music dir., 1964-88; prin. condr. London Philharm. Orch., 1967-79; guest condr. Glyndebourne Festival Opera, 1972-77, music dir. Glyndebourne, 1978-88; music dir. Royal Opera House, Covent Garden, London, 1988-2002; pres. London Philharm. Orch., 1990—; music dir. European Union Youth Orch., 1994-1999; guest condr. Boston Symphony, 1995-; guest condr. Cleve. Philharm., Vienna Philharm., N.Y. Philharm.; chief condr. Dresden Staatskapelle, 2002-; guest condr. Chgo. Symphony, Bayerische Rundfunk Symphony, Munich, Berlin Philharm., Salzburg Festival, London Philharm., Glyndebourne. Recordings include Don Giovanni, Cosa fan Tutte, Figro, Der Rosenkavalier, The Magic Flute, Daphne, Tannhauser, The Ring, Peter Grimes, Fidelio; recorded with Philips, Decca and EMI. Decorated Order Oranje Nassau; chevalier Ordre des Arts et des Lettres; Hon. knight Brit. Empire, 1977; officer Order of Crown (Belgium); recipient Bruckner medal of honor Bruckner Soc., 1970, Gold medal Royal Philharm. Soc., 1991, Erasmus prize The Netherlands, 1991. Fellow Royal Coll. Music; mem. Royal Acad. Music (London) (hon.), Internat. Gustav Mahler Soc. (hon.; gold medal 1970). Office: Sächsische Staatsoper Dresden Orchesterdirektion Theaterplatz 2 Dresden D-01067 Germany*

HAIZLIP, HENRY HARDIN, JR., real estate broker, consultant, retired bank executive; b. Pine Bluff, Ark., Dec. 18, 1913; s. Henry Hardin and Rebecca (Porter) H.; m. Emily Williamson, Feb. 15, 1947; children: Henry Hardin III, Wilson, Jean Hunter, Selden. Student, Tulane U., 1932-33. With W.N. Ballou Cotton Co., Memphis, 1933-36; with First Nat. Bank Memphis, 1936-73, exec. v.p., 1968-70, chmn. exec. com., 1970-73; pres. First Memphis Realty Trust, 1970-73, chmn., 1973-76; pres. First Tenn. Corp., 1973-78; real estate cons. Haizlip/Lovitt, Memphis, 1979—2002. Dir. Mid South Title Co., Union Service Industries Inc.; vice chmn. First Tenn. Nat. Corp., until 1979; ret.; instr. in mortgage financing La. State U., Ohio State U. Pres. Memphis Cotton Carnival Assn., 1966, bd. dirs., 1967—; vice chmn. Shelby United Good Neighbors, 1967-68; mem. Chickasaw coun. Boy Scouts Am.; pres. Future Memphis, Inc., 1974-77; bd. dirs. Memphis and Shelby County unit Am. Cancer Soc., 1967-68; trustee Comty. Found. Greater Memphis, chmn., 1978; mem. pres.'s coun. Tulane U., New Orleans, Rhodes Coll., Memphis; vice-chmn. The Trezevant Manor Episcopal Home. Capt. AUS, 1941-46. Mem. Am. Bankers Assn., Downtown Assn. Memphis (chmn. bd.), Kappa Alpha. Clubs: Memphis Country; Menasha Hunting and Fishing (Turrell, Ark.); Memphis Hunt and Polo. Episcopalian. Home: 965 Audubon Dr Memphis TN 38117-4601 Office: 600 Perkins Memphis TN 38117

HAJARNAVIS, HERAMB R., investment banker; b. Pune, Maharashtra, India, Sept. 13, 1974; s. Ravindra D. and Bhagyashree R. Hajarnavis; m. Tina Hajarnavis, Aug. 20, 2000; 1 child, Kavish H. BS, MIT, 1996; MBA, Harvard Bus. Sch., 2001. Fin. analyst investment banking Goldman, Sachs & Co., N.Y.C., 1996—98, fin. analyst pvt. equity Singapore, 1998—99; v.p. corp. planning Centennial Comm. Corp., Wall, NJ, 2001—03; assoc. investment banking Goldman, Sachs & Co., N.Y.C., 2003—. Avocations: golf, international travel, photography, ethnic cuisine. Office: Goldman Sachs & Co 85 Broad St New York NY 10004 Office Phone: 212-902-1000.

HAJE, PETER ROBERT, lawyer; b. N.Y.C., July 31, 1934; s. Arnold John and Edna Marie (Bossert) H.; m. Helen Heineman, Aug. 13, 1943; children: Michael James, Katherine Joy, Lily Elizabeth. BA, Cornell U., 1955; LLB, Harvard U., 1960. Bar: N.Y. 1961, U.S. Dist. Ct. (so. dist.) N.Y. 1965, U.S. Ct. Appeals (2d cir.) 1965, D.C. 1970, U.S. Ct. Appeals (D.C. cir.) 1981. Assoc. Paul, Weiss, Rifkind, Wharton & Garrison, N.Y.C., 1960-68, ptnr., 1969-90; exec. v.p., gen. counsel Time Warner Inc., N.Y.C., 1990-99, gen. counsel emeritus, 2000—; counselor AOL Time Warner, 2000—02; bus. and legal cons., 2000—. Office: 1790 Broadway New York NY 10019 Office Phone: 212-581-1315. E-mail: prhaje@aol.com.

HAJEK, OTOMAR, mathematician, educator; b. Beograd, Serbia, Dec. 22, 1930; arrived in U.S., 1966, naturalized, 1974; s. Frantisek Josef and Ruzena (Houdekova) Hajek; m. Olga Barbara Nemcova, Feb. 12, 1955; 1 child, Michael. Diploma in math., Caroline U., Prague, Czech. Rep., 1953, candidate sci., 1963; RNDr, Caroline U., Prague, Czech Rep., 1966. Asst. prof. Czech Inst. Tech., Prague, 1953-56, sr. asst. prof., 1956-60; sci. officer Research Inst. Computing Machinery, Prague, 1960-65; sr. sci. officer Caroline U., Prague, 1965-66; assoc. prof. Case Western Res. U., Cleve., 1966-69, prof. math., 1969—, prof. sys. engring., 1988-96, prof. emeritus, 1996—. Author: (book) Dynamical Systems in the Plane, 1968, Pursuit Games, 1975, Control Systems in the Plane, 1991; co-author: Local Semi-Dynamical Systems, 1969; co-editor: Global Differentiable Dynamics, 1970. Recipient von Humboldt award, 1975; Deutsche Forschungsgemeinschaft fellow, Bonn, 1979, 1990, Fulbright fellow, 1990. Mem.: Union Czech Math. and Physicists, Fulbright Assn., von Humboldt Assn., Czechoslavak Soc. Arts and Scis., Am. Math. Soc. Lutheran. Home: 11330 Savannah Dr Fredericksburg VA 22407-9109 Personal E-mail: ohajek@adelphia.net.

HAJEK, ROBERT J., SR., lawyer, real estate broker; b. May 17, 1943; s. James J. Sr. and Rita C. (Kalka) H.; m. Maris Ann Enright, June 19, 1965 (div. Oct. 1991); children: Maris Ann, Robert J., David H., Mandie J. BA, Loras Coll., 1965; JD, U. Ill., 1968; post doctoral studies, Nat. Lewis U., Evanston, Ill., 1985—87. Bar: Ill. 1968, U.S. Tax Ct. 1970, U.S. Dist. Ct. (no. dist.) Ill. 1971, U.S. Ct. Appeals (7th cir.) 1972, U.S. Supreme Ct. 1972; lic. real estate broker, Ill., Nat. Assn. Securities Dealers; registered U.S. Commodities Futures Trading Commn. Ptnr. Hajek & Hajek, Berwyn, Ill., 1968-76; pres., bd. chmn. Hajek, Hajek, Koykar & Heying, Ltd., Westchester, Ill., 1976-85; pres., CEO Land of Lincoln Real Estate, Ltd., Glendale Heights, Ill., 1985-89, also bd. dirs.; ptnr., owner Camelot Manor Nursing Home, Streator, Ill., 1978—, Ottawa (Ill.) Care Ctr., 1981—, Glenwood House Nursing Home, Streator, 1988—, Sullivan House Nursing Home, Ottawa, 1991—, Law Ctr. Bldg., Westchester, 1976-91; pres., CEO, chmn. bd. Rock River Computer Resources, LLC, 1995—. Exec. v.p., gen. counsel Ottawa Long Term Care, Inc.; owner Garfield Ridge Real Estate, Chgo., 1973—78, Centre Realty, Westchester, 1976—85; ptnr. Westbrook Commodities, Chgo., 1983—2005; v.p., bd. mem., gen. counsel DeHart Gas and Oil Devel., Ltd., 1970—73; prin. Northeastern Okla. Oil and Gas Prodn. Venture, Tulsa, 1982—92; exec. v.p., gen. counsel Garrett Plante Corp., 1978—2004; bd. dirs. Ottawa Long Term Care, Inc., 1982—; pres., CEO, bd. chmn. Rock River Computer Resources, LLC, 2005—. Sr. boys' basketball coach Roselle Recreation Assn., Ill., 1981—83. Mem. ABA, Ill. Bar Assn., Nat. Assn. Realtors, Ill. Assn. Realtors, N.W. Suburban Bd. Realtors, Ill. Health Care Assn., Amateur Radio Club, No. Ill. DX Assn., Phi Alpha Delta. Republican. Episcopalian. Personal E-mail: k9ltn@yahoo.com. Business E-Mail: rjhajeksr@wireless.essex1.com.

HAJELA, PRABHAT, engineering educator, researcher; b. Kanpur, India, Dec. 25, 1956; came to U.S., 1977. s. Krishna Prasad and Rajeshwari (Seth) H. B of Tech. Aero. Engring., Indian Inst. Tech., Kanpur, 1977; MS in Aerospace Engring., Iowa State U., 1979; MSME, Stanford (Calif.) U., 1981, PhD in Aeronautics, 1982. Rsch. assoc. U. Calif., L.A., 1982-83; from asst. to assoc. prof. U. Fla., Gainesville, 1983-90; assoc. prof. Rensselaer Poly. Inst., Troy, N.Y., 1990-92, prof., 1993—. Cons. UCLA, 1983-84, Tech. Analysis and Optimization/RCA Astro Electronics, Princeton, N.J., 1983-87, Occidental Petroleum de Colombia, Bogota, 1987-88; program chmn. symposium on Aeroelasticity, Structures & Structural Dynamics, Gainesville, 1986; program chmn. Advances in Aerospace Scis., Stanford, 1993; dir. Emergent Computing Methods in Engring. Design, Greece, 1994. Editor, author: Recent Trends in Aeroelasticity Structures & Structural Dynamics, 1987; assoc. editor, author: Engineering Optimization-Better Results Using OR Methods, 1988; editor: Advances in Aerospace Sciences, 1994; assoc. editor AIAA Jour.; contbr. numerous articles to profl. jours. USAF Rsch. fellow, 1986, NASA-Lewis Rsch. Ctr. fellow, 1989; recipient Tchr. of the Yr. award U. Fla., 1989, Lewis T. Assini Teaching and Counseling award Rensselaer Poly. Inst., 1992. Assoc. fellow AIAA (R.L. Risplinghoff Teaching award 1987, S.E. Faculty Advisor of Yr. 1988), ASME, Soc. Automotive Engrs. (Ralph Teetor award 1987, Am. Soc. Engring. Edn., Am. Helicopter Soc., Sigma Gamma Tau. Hindu. Avocations: skiing, tennis, piano, music. Office: Rensselaer Polytechnic Inst Jonsson Engring Ctr Dept Mech Engring Troy NY 12180

HAKALA, KAREN LOUISE, retired real estate administrator; b. Lansing, Mich., Dec. 8, 1941; d. Herod Maxson and Flora Belle (Barton) Mitchell; m. Paul Kenneth Hakala, June 24, 1959 (div. Nov. 1972); children: Chris, Craig. BS, No. Mich. U., Marquette, 1986. Real estate adminstr. The Cleve.-Cliffs Iron Co., Ishpeming, Mich., 1967-99; ret., 1999. Mediator Cmty. Resolution Resource Ctr., 2002—. Mem. devel. com. Planned Parenthood No. Mich., Marquette, 1996—99; bd. dirs. Marquette Symphony Orch., 1998—2000, treas., 1999—2000; mem. planning commn. City of Negaunee, 2001—, sec., 2001—02, 2005—. Mem. AAUW of Marquette County (pub. policy rep. 1995-99, pres. 1999-2001), LWV Marquette County (bd. dirs. 2002-), Ret. Sr. Vol. Program.

HAKALA, NILA VIRGINIA, primary school educator; b. Manila, Philippines, May 8, 1946; d. Victor George and Nila Dalisay Pryor; m. Daniel Lee Hakala, Mar. 9, 1968; 1 child, Jeffrey Brian. BA, Nat. U., 1991; MEd, Chapman U., 1998. Cert. Reading Specialist Certificate Commn. on Tchr. Credentialing, 2003, Professional Clear Multiple Subject Teaching Credential Commn. on Tchr. Credentialing, 1997, Clear Crosscultural, Language and Academic Development Commn. on Tchr. Credentialing, 1999. Classified staff Los Rios C.C., Sacramento, 1977—97; Miller Unruh reading specialist Wash. Unified Sch. Dist., West Sacramento, 1997—2000; 4th grade tchr. San Juan Sch. Dist., Sacramento, 2000—01; Miller Unruh reading specialist Wash. Unified Sch. Dist., West Sacramento, 2001—03, kindergarten tchr., 2003—. Tchr. rep. Evergreen Site Councill, West Sacramento, 2003—; freelance writer. Mem.: Calif. Tchrs. Assn. Democrat. Roman Catholic. Avocations: writing, photography. Office: Evergreen Elem Sch 919 West Acres Rd West Sacramento CA 95691 Office Phone: 916-375-7680.

HAKALA, REINO WILLIAM, mathematician, educator; b. Albany, NY, Aug. 25, 1923; m. Eunice Irma Kazanowski, June 17, 1950; children: Jonathan, Lisamaria, Christina. AB, Columbia U., 1946, MA, 1947; PhD, Syracuse U., 1965. Chemistry instr. Associated Coll. of Upper NY, Plattsburgh, 1947—48; atomic energy commn. fellow and grad. asst. Syracuse U., 1948—53; adj. prof. chemistry Pa. State U., State College, 1953; assoc. prof. chemistry Fairfield (Conn.) U., 1954—57; asst. prof. chemistry Earlham Coll., Richmond, Ind., 1957—59, Howard U., Washington, 1959—63; NSF sci. faculty fellow Syracuse U., 1963—64; prof. chemistry and math. Mich. Tech. U., 1964—67; chmn. depts. math. and physics Oklahoma City U., 1967—72, pres. faculty senate, 1972; prof. of math. Wash. Tech. Inst., 1972—73; dean of the sch. of sci. and tech. Lake Superior State Coll., Sault Ste Marie, Mich., 1973—77, asst. to v.p. for acad. affairs, 1977, prof. of math., 1978—80, pres. faculty senate, 1978; dean Coll. Arts and Sci. Governors State U., University Park, Ill., 1980—81, spl. asst. to provost, 1982, interim chair divsn. sci., 1983, prof. math., 1984—. Cons. Nat. Bur. Standards, 1962—63; mem. tech. com. pattern recognition IEEE. Contbr. articles to profl. jours. Fellow, Washington (D.C.) Acad. of Scis., 1961, Am. Inst. of Chemists, 1969, fellowships and grants, Atomic Energy Commn., NSF, NATO, Petroleum Rsch. Fund. Mem.: Soc. Ind. and Applied Math., Internat. Assn. Pattern Recognition, Am. Math. Soc., Math. Assn. Am. Home: 2945 Chayes Pk Dr Homewood IL 60430 Office: Governors State University 1 University Pkwy University Park IL 60466 Office Phone: 708-534-4527. E-mail: r-hakala@govst.edu.

HAKALA, THOMAS JOHN, private banker, financial planner, accountant; b. Bayonne, NJ, July 6, 1948; s. John R. and Anna J. (Vida) H.; m. Marilynn Freund, Aug. 15, 1976; children: Lauren V., John C. AB in History, Georgetown U., 1970; JD, St. John's U., 1975; postgrad., NYU, 1975-80. Bar: N.J. 1975, N.Y. 1976; CPA, Tex. Supr. Weeden & Co., NYC, 1970-73; mgr. Coopers & Lybrand, NYC, 1975-87; sr. mgr. KPMG Peat Marwick, NYC, 1987-89, ptnr., 1989-99; exec. dir. fin. planning and wealth mgmt. UBS Warburg, NYC, 1999-2001; dir. UBS Trust Co., NYC, 1999-2001; mng. dir. fin. planning and wealth mgmt. Wilmington Trust, NYC, 2001—. Bd. advisers Jour. Taxation of Estates and Trusts, N.Y.C., 1990-92. Contbr. articles to profl. jours. Mem. Estate Planning Coun. N.Y.C., bd. dirs., 2004—. Mem. AICPA, Finnish Am. Lawyers Assn., Ocean Beach and Yacht Club, Phi Delta Phi. Republican. Roman Catholic. Avocations: reading, history, photography, walking on beaches, swimming. Home: 8 Whitewood Rd Edison NJ 08820-3202 Office: Wilmington Trust FSB 520 Madison Ave New York NY 10022 Office Phone: 212-415-0544. E-mail: thakala@wilmingtontrust.com.

HAKANSSON, NILS HEMMING, economist, educator; b. Marby, Sweden, June 2, 1937; came to U.S., 1956; s. Nils and Anna (Nilsson) H.; m. Joyce Beth Kates, Aug. 28, 1960; children— Carolyn Ann, Nils Alexander BS with honors, U. Oreg., 1958; MBA, UCLA, 1960, PhD, 1966; D. of Econs. (hon.), Stockholm Sch. Econs., 1984. C.P.A., Calif. Staff acct., cons. Arthur Young & Co., L.A., 1960-63; asst. prof. UCLA, 1966-67, Yale U., New Haven, 1967-69; assoc. prof. U. Calif.-Berkeley, 1969-71, prof., 1971-77, Sylvan C. Coleman prof. fin. and acctg., 1977—2003, chmn. fin., 1976-79, 1997—2000. Cons. Rand Corp., Santa Monica, Calif., 1965-71, Bell Labs., Murray Hill, N.J., 1974, 79-81; chmn. bd. dirs. Anna och Nils Hakanssons Stiftelse; bd. dirs. Landus-Rosenberg Mut. Funds. Editorial cons. Acctg. Rev., 1977-80; cons. editor Jour. Acctg. and Econs., 1978-81; contbr. articles to profl. jours. Served with Royal Swedish Corps Engrs., 1956 Recipient Graham and Dodd award Fin. Analysts Fedn., 1976, 82; Ford Found. fellow UCLA, 1963-66; Hoover fellow U. New South Wales, 1975 Fellow Acctg. Rschrs. Internat. Assn.; mem. AICPA (hon. mem.), Fin. Economists Roundtable, Am. Fin. Assn., Western Fin. Assn. (pres. 1983-84), Am. Acctg. Assn., Soc. for Promotion Fin. Studies (founding). Office: U Calif Sch Bus Berkeley CA 94720-1900 E-mail: hakansso@haas-berkeley.edu.

HAKE, RALPH F., appliance manufacturing executive; b. Cin. BBA, U. Cin.; MBA, U. Chgo. V.p. adminstrn.l. Mead Corp., Escababa, Mich., 1980-84, dir. corp. devel. Dayton, Ohio, 1984-87; various fin. and ops. positions including corp. v.p., contr. Whirlpool Corp., Benton Harbor, Mich., from 1987, pres. Bauknecht appliance group, exec. v.p. N.Am. appliance group, sr. exec. v.p. ops., until 1997, sr. exec. v.p., CFO, 1997-1999; exec. v.p., CFO Fluor Corp., Aliso Viejo, Calif., 1999—2001; chmn., CEO Maytag Corp., 2001—. With U.S. Army, 1971-73. Mem. NAM (bd. dirs.).

HAKEL, MILTON DANIEL, JR., psychologist, educator, writer, consultant; b. Hutchinson, Minn., Aug. 1, 1941; s. Milton Daniel and Emily Ann (Kovar) H.; m. Lee Ellen Pervier, Sept. 1, 1962; children: Lane, Jennifer BA, U. Minn., 1963, PhD, 1966. Diplomate in Indsl. and Organizational Psychology Am. Bd. Profl. Psychology. Prof. psychology Ohio State U., Columbus, 1968-85, U. Houston, 1985-91, chmn. dept., 1987-91; Ohio Bd. Regents eminent scholar, prof. Bowling Green State U., 1991—; pres. Organizational Research and Devel., 1977—; ptnr. Applied Research Group, 1984-87. Trustee Am. Bd. Profl. Psychology, 1987-90; mem. com. on assessment and tchr. quality NRC, 1999-2000; mem. bd. testing and assessment NRC, 1999-2005, mem. U.S. nat. com. for Internat. Union for Psychol. Sci.,

1997-2001, chair, 2001-03. Co-author (sr.): Making It Happen: Doing Research with Implementation in Mind, 1982; author: Beyond Multiple Choice: Evaluating Alternatives to Traditional Testing, 1998; editor Current Directions in Psychol. Sci., 1998-99, Personnel Psychology, 1973-84, pub., 1984-2004; co-editor: Applying the Science of Learning to University Teaching and Beyond, 2002; contbr. 40 articles to profl. jours. Chair Human Capital Initiative Coordinating Com., 1991-99, co-chair Applying Sci. Learning to U. Edu. conf. steering com. Recipient James McKeen Cattell award, 1965; Fulbright-Hays Sr. scholar, 1978; NSF grantee, 1966-73; Distng. Svc. Contbrs. award, 1995. Fellow Am. Psychol. Soc. (founding bd. dir.), Soc. Indsl. and Orgnl. Psychology (pres. 1984), Am. Assn. Adv. Sci., Internat. Assn. Applied Psychology (bd. dirs. 2004—), Summit Conf. Presbyterian. Home: 1435 Cedar Ln Bowling Green OH 43402-1476 Office: Bowling Green State U Dept Psychology Bowling Green OH 43403-0001 Business E-Mail: mhakel@bgsu.edu.

HAKIM, FARES SAMIH, physician; b. Damascus, Syria, Nov. 5, 1963; came to U.S., 1989; s. Mohamed Samih and Raja (Abaza) H. BS, French Inst. Syria, Damascus, 1981; MD, Damascus U., 1987. Diplomate Am. Internal Medicine. Resident in internal medicine Cohchin Hosp., Paris, 1988-89; fellow surg. rsch. VA Hosp., Washington, 1990-92; rsch. assoc. Inst. Clin. Rsch., Washington, 1992-94; resident in internal medicine Med. Coll. Ga., Augusta, 1994-97, fellow in gastroenterology, hepatology, 1997-99; fellow in advanced therapeutic endoscopy, hepatology/liver transplantation Konar Ctr. for Digestive and Liver Diseases, U. Rochester Med. Ctr., Rochester, N.Y., 1999—. Contbr. articles to profl. jours. Mem. AMA, ACP, Am. Gastroent. Assn., Am. Coll. Gastroent., Am. Assn. Gastrenterology Endoscopy, Am. Assn. Studies Liver Disease, Am. Digestive Health Found. Avocations: sports, travel, languages. Home: 712 Bay Blvd Pensacola FL 32503-6802 Office: 601 Elmwood Ave # 464 Rochester NY 14642-0001

HAKIM, JOY, writer; b. Forest Hills, NY, Jan. 16, 1931; d. John M. and Ida (Ginsburg) Frisch; m. Sam L. Hakim, Mar. 20, 1955; children: Ellen Hakim Johnson, Jeffrey, Daniel. BA, Smith Coll., 1951; MEd, Goucher Coll., 1954, PhD (hon.), 2003. Tchr. Syracuse (N.Y.) Pub. Schs., 1954-55, Omaha Pub. Schs., 1955-56, Country Day Sch., Virginia Beach, Va., 1960-61; reporter Ledger-Star, Norfolk, Ba., 1961-62; bus. writer, freelance, assoc. editor Va. Pilot, Norfolk, 1963—80; tchr. Tidewater Community Coll., Virginia Beach, Va., 1984-85. Found. bd. mem. Coun. for Am.'s First Freedom, Richmond; mem. Nat. Bd. for Profl. Teaching Stds., Detroit and Washington; mem. review panel Blue Ribbon Schs. Program, Washington, 1992— Author: A History of US, A Young Person's History of the United States, 1995 (10 vols.), Freedom: A History of Us, A Companion to the PBS Series, 2003, The Story of Science, Smithsonian Books, Aristotle Leads the Way, 2004, Newton at the Center, 2005 Trustee Nat. Coun. for History Edn., Inc. Home and Office: 1900 E Girard Pl Apt 400 Englewood CO 80110 E-mail: joyhakim@aol.com.

HAKIMOGLU, AYHAN, electronics company executive; b. Erbaa, Turkey, Aug. 19, 1928; came to U.S., 1955; s. Mekki and Mediha H.; children by previous marriage: Zeynep B., Incigul R. O'Brien, Deborah A. Cueto, Leyla P.; m. Rachida Elmir, July 12, 1997; 1 child, Ayhan, Jr. BSEE, Robert Coll., Istanbul, 1949; MSEE, U. Cin., 1950. Founder, pres., chmn. bd. Dynaplex Corp., Princeton, N.J., 1962-67; gen. mgr. Teledyne Telemetry Co., Los Angeles, 1966-67; founder, chmn. bd., pres. Aydin Corp., Horsham, Pa., 1967-96. Cons. Aydin Corp., Plymouth Meeting, Pa.; investor. Served to lt. Turkish Army, 1951-52. Named Turkish Am. of Yr. Assembly Turkish Am. Assn., 1985; recipient Outstanding Pub. Svc. award, Assembly Turkish Am. Assns., 1988, 89, Disting. Alumni award U. Cin., 1991. Moslem.

HAKKI, AYESHA, editor-in-chief; BA in Journalism & Mass Media, Rutgers U. Asst. editor Men's Club mag., Pakistan; editor NJ Goodlife/Home Design mag., Ladies Home Journal, NYC, photo editor, special interest pub.; art dir. Jupiter Comm., NYC, Compaq Computer Corp., Houston; founder Alias Art, NYC; now editor & publisher Bibi Mag., Hoboken, NJ. Recipient Achievement award, Asia Houston Network, Bronze medal, Art Dirs. Club, Golden Web award, 2003. Office: Bibi Mag 66 Willow Ave Hoboken NJ 07030*

HAKOSHIMA, SHIN-ICHI, publishing executive; b. Dec. 9, 1937; Grad., Kyushu U., 1962. With Asahi Shimbun, 1962—, assoc. editor econ. news dept., 1979-84, econ. editor, Nagoya Head Office, 1985-86, econ. editor Tokyo Head Office, 1987-89, dep. mng. editor Nagoya Head Office, 1990-91, mng. editor Seibu Head Office, 1991, mng. editor Tokyo Head Office, 1992-93, mng dir., adminstrn., 1996-97, mng. dir., CEO, 1998; sr. mng. dir., COO, 1998; pres., CEO, 1999—. Office: The Asahi Shimbun Co 5-3-2 Tsukiji Chuo-ku 104-11 Tokyo Japan

HALABE, UDAYA BHATTA, civil engineering educator, researcher; b. Kathmandu, Nepal, Nov. 19, 1961; came to U.S., 1985; s. Gangadhar Bhatta and Shailaja Bhatta H.; m. Anjali Marathe; children: Esha Bhatta H., Shivali Bhatta H. BE in Civil Engring., U. Roorkee, India, 1984; M in Tech. (Civil Engring.), Indian Inst. Tech., Kanpur, India, 1985; MS in Civil Engring., MIT, 1988, MS in Mgmt., PhD in Civil Engring., MIT, 1990. Registered profl. engr., W. Va. Asst. prof. W.Va. U., Morgantown, 1990-96, assoc. prof., 1996-2001, prof., 2001—. Contbr. numerous articles to profl. jours. and conf. proceedings, over 70 sci. papers, over 30 rsch. reports. Mem. ASCE, Am. Concrete Inst., Am. Soc. for Nondestructive Testing. Avocations: walking, reading, tennis, swimming. Home: 1504 Foxtrot Dr Morgantown WV 26508-9175 Office: W Va U PO Box 6103 Engring Sci Bldg Rm #645 Morgantown WV 26506-6103 Office Phone: 304-293-3031. Business E-Mail: uhalabe@alum.mit.edu.

HALABY, MARGARITA GONZALEZ, marketing professional, communications executive; m. Dominique Halaby; children: Austin C., Cameron R. BJ, U. Tex., 1997. Asst. placement dir., editor, photographer U. Tex. Grad. Sch. Libr. and Info. Sci., Austin, 1993—94; portrait photographer Lifetouch Portrait Studios, Austin, 1995—96; editl. asst. Constrn. Data News Constrn. Data Corp., Austin, 1996—97; staff writer The Brownsville (Tex.) Herald; Freedom Comm. Inc., 1997—98; reporter Valley Morning Star; Freedom Comm. Inc., Harlingen, Tex., 1998—99; mktg. comm. coord. Brownsville Pub. Utilites Bd., 1999—2000; mktg. and comm. mgr. Brownsville Pub. Utilities Bd., 2000—. Mktg. and pub. rels. cons. Importante Inc., Brownsville, 1998—2000. Bd. mem. BBB of South Tex., Weslaco, 2001—, Am. Cancer Soc. - So. Cameron County Chpt., Brownsville, 1999. Recipient Team award for Newspaper Series - Border Govs. Conf., Assn. Profl. Mng. Editors, 1999, Group Study Exch. to Finland, Rotary Internat., 2000, Ann. Report award of merit, Am. Pub. Power Assn., 2000. Mem.: Tex. Assn. Municipal Info. Officers Assn., Am. Mktg. Assn. (assoc.), Pub. Rels. Soc. Am. (assoc.), Tex. Pub. Power Assn. (mktg. and customer svc. com. mem.), Sunrise Rotary Club. Office: Brownsville Public Utilities Board 1425 Robinhood Dr Brownsville TX 78521-4230 E-mail: mhalaby@brownsville-pub.com.

HALABY, SAMIA ASAAD, painter, educator, writer; b. Jerusalem, Palestine, Dec. 12, 1936; s. Asaad Saba and Foutounie Assad (Atallah) H. BS in Design, U. Cin., 1959; MA in Painting, Mich. State U., 1960; MFA in Painting, Ind. U., 1963. Teaching asst. Ind. U., Bloomington, 1962-63, assoc. prof., 1969-72; instr. U. Hawaii, Honolulu, 1963-64, vis. lectr., summer 1966; asst. prof. Kansas City (Mo.) Art Inst., 1964-66, U. Mich., 1967-69; vis. lectr. art Yale U., 1972-73, assoc. prof., 1973-76, adj. assoc. prof., 1976-82. Lectr. in field; vis. prof. U. Hawaii, Honolulu, 1985-86, U. South Fla., 1990; adj. instr. Cooper Union, 1989-92; artist-in-residence Tamarind Lithography Workshop, Albuquerque, 1972; presenter 4th Internat. Symposium on Electronic Art, Mpls., 1993, 7th symposium, Rotterdam, 1996. One-man shows include Gima Gallery, Honolulu, 1964, The Gallery, Bloomington, 1970, Phyllis Kind Gallery, Chgo., 1971, Yale Sch. Art Gallery, 1972, Spectrum Gallery, N.Y.C., 1973, Marilyn Pearl Gallery, N.Y.C., 1978, 22 Wooster Gallery, 1982, 83, Tossan-Tossan Gallery, N.Y.C., 1983, 88, Housatonic Mus., Bridgeport, 1983, Galaria de arte Palace, Granada, Spain, 1986, Gallery II U. Mich., Kalamazoo, 1989, 911 Gallery, Indpls., 1993, Darat Al-Funun, Amman, Jordan, 1995, Galerie Atassi, Damascus, Syria, 1997, Galerie Le Porte, Halab, Syria, 1997, Agial Gallery, Beirut, 1999, 2004, SKOTO Gallery, N.Y.C., 2000, Sakakini Art Ctr., Ramallah, Palestine, 2000, Artim Gallery, Strasbourg, France, 2001, Kahaf Gallery, Internat. Ctr. Bethlehem, 2004, Agiol Gallery, Beirut, 2004; group shows include Solomon R. Guggenheim Mus., N.Y.C., 1975, Susan Caldwell Gallery, N.Y.C., 1977, Iraqi Cultural Ctr., London, 1979, Kunsternes Hus, Oslo, Norway, 1981, U. Art Mus., N.Mex., 1985, Hudson Ctr. Gallery, N.Y.C., 1985, Tercera Bienal de la Habana, Cuba, 1989, Prix Ars Electronica, Linz, Austria, 1990, Art and Algorithm, Mpls. Coll. Art, 1991, Hilo Internat. Exhbn. of Works on Paper, U. Hawaii, 1990, Digitized and Manipulated, Sangre De Cristo Arts Ctr., Pueblo, Colo., 1991, opening exhbn. Darat Al Funun of Shoman Found., Amman, Jordan, 1993, Fourth Internat. Symposium Electronic Art, Mpls., 1993, Arab Women, Nat. Mus. Women in the Arts, Washington, 1994, World Artist at the Millennium, Elizabeth Found., UN Lobby, 1999, Bradley U., Ill., 2001, Musee du Chateau DuFresne, Montreal, 2001, 13th Afro-Asian L.Am. exhbn. Tokyo Met. Mus, 2002, Williamsburg Bridges Palestine, WAH Ctr., Bklyn., 2002, Sta. Mus., Houston, 2003, Chikyudo Gallery, Tokyo, 2004, 4 Walls Gallery, Amman, Jordan, 2005; performance art (computer abstractions) Bklyn. Mus., 1994, Poetry Project, N.Y.C., 1995, Lebanese Am. U., Beirut, 1995, HERE, N.Y.C., 1996; represented in permanent collections Solomon R. Guggenheim Mus., Inst. Du Monde Arab, Paris, Indpls. Mus. Art, Art Inst. Chgo., Nelson Rockhill Gallery Art, Kansas City, Ind. U. Mus., Mich. State U. Mus., Ft. Wayne (Ind.) Mus. Art, Detroit Inst. Art, Cleve. Mus. Art, Cin. Art Mus., Nat. Gallery Jordan, Amman, Yale U. Gallery, Tamarind Inst. Collection, Albuquerque, Alternative Mus., N.Y., Honolulu Acad. Arts, Ind. U. Mus., Bloomington, Mead Art Mus., Amherst, Conn., Palm Springs (Calif.) Desert Mus., Yale U. Gallery, New Haven, The Jane Voorhees Zimmerli Art Museum, New Brunswick, N.J., corp. collections, U.S. Steel, ATT Longlines, First Nat. Chgo, Kemper Ins. Chgo., S.E. Banking Corp. Fla., Witko Chem. Corp., Standard Oil Ohio, IBM, Arab Bank; author: Liberation Art of Palestine, 2003; contbr. articles to profl. jours. Subject of Profl. Publs.; Kansas City Coun. for Faculty Devel. traveling fellow, 1965; Creative Artists Pub. Svc. Program grantee, 1978-79, UN grant UNDP cons., 1999. Studio: PO Box 965 New York NY 10013-0861 Personal E-mail: sahalaby@yahoo.com.

HALABY, THEODORE S., political organization worker, retired lawyer; b. 1940; AB, Harvard U.; LLB, U. Va. Bar: Colo. 1967. Atty. Halaby & Assocs., Englewood, Calif., ret., 2001; chmn. Colo. Rep. Party, Denver, 2003—. Office: Colorado Repulication Committee 1777 S Harrison St Ste 100 Denver CO 80210-3926

HALACKA, KELLY M., biomedical engineer; d. Michael F. and Fanchon P. Halacka. BS, Case Western Res. U., 2003. EIT Ohio. Intern Wyle Lab., Houston, 2000; with NASA Johnson Space Ctr., Houston, 2000—02; engr. NASA Glenn Rsch. Ctr., Cleve., 2003—. Presenter in field. Recipient NASA Flag award. Mem.: Biomed. Engring. Soc., Soc. Women Engrs. Avocations: piano, scuba diving, roller hockey.

HALAMKA, JOHN D., emergency physician, information technology executive; b. Des Moines, Iowa, May 1962; BS in Med. Microbiology, BA in Public Policy, Stanford U., 1984; student Bioengineering grad. program, U. Calif. Berkeley, 1986—89; MD, U. Calif. San Francisco, 1993; MS in Med. Informatics, Harvard/MIT Health Sci. and Tech., 1997; internship in Emergency Med., Harbor-UCLA, 1993—94, residency in Emergency Med., 1994—96; clin. and rsch. fellowship in Informatics, Harvard Med. Sch., 1996—97. CEO Ibis Rsch. Labs, Calif., 1981—92; tech. editor Computer Lang. mag., San Francisco, 1984—87; instr. in Med. Harvard Med. Sch., Boston, 1996—99; attending physician, divsn. Emergency Med. Beth Israel Deaconess Med. Ctr., Boston, 1996—; exec. dir. Ctr. for Quality and Value CareGroup, Boston, 1997—99, chief info. officer, 1998—; co-founder & chmn. New England Health Electronic Data Interchange Network, 1999—; asst. prof. of Med. Harvard Med. Sch., Boston, 2000—, assoc. dean for ednl. tech., 2000—. Recipient Phi Beta Kappa, 1983, Sigma Pi Alpha, 1984, commendation for svc., LA County Bd. of Supervisors, 1996, Martin J. Epstein award, Am. Med. Informatics Assn., 1997, numerous tech. innovation awards, PC Week, Info. Week, Ernst and Young. Mem.: Am. Med. Informatics Assn., Soc. for Acad. Emergency Med., Am. Coll. of Emergency Physicians. Office: Harvard Med Sch CareGroup Health 6th fl 1135 Tremont St Boston MA 02120 also: Harvard Med Sch Gordon Hall 25 Shattuck St Boston MA 02115

HALAS, PAUL ANTHONY, JR., business appraisal and valuation specialist, consultant; b. Chgo., June 27, 1933; s. Paul Aloysius and Elonia Bernidene (Zelinski) H.; m. Shirley Donna Willis, Aug. 17, 1957 (dec.); children: Julie, Vickie, Jon, Carl, Jim; m. Nina Romanenko, Feb. 19, 2000. Student, Columbia Sch. Broadcasting, 1951-53, Northwestern U., 1957-59; MBA, Brunswick U., Laurel, Md., 1983. Cert. mgmt. cons., N.Y. Rep. Solar Chgo. divsn. USI's, 1957-60; rep. J. W. Bolton, Inc., Lawrence, Mass., 1960-62; gen. sales mgr. Schimanek, Internat., Chgo., 1962-63; v.p. mktg. Products Engring. Co., Tinley Park, Ill., 1963-68; gen. sales mgr. Vacudyne Corp., Chicago Heights, Ill., 1968-70; mktg. mgr. Fastron Co., Franklin Park, Ill., 1970-72, Scandura, Inc., Charlotte, N.C., 1972-78; mgmt. cons. Halas & Assocs., Charlotte, 1978-85, valuation specialist, 1985—. Contbr. numerous articles on bus. valuation and appraisal. Recipient Printed award Grain Age Mag., 1976. Mem. BBB, ASME (coord. ANSI A90 com. 1974-77), Nat. Ctr. for Employee Ownership, Inst. Bus. Appraisers, Inst. Mgmt. Cons., Charlotte C. of C. Green Party. Roman Catholic. Avocations: music, photography, travel. Office: Halas & Assocs 425 Roselawn Pl Charlotte NC 28211-4162 Office Phone: 704-364-4440. E-mail: hbvs@halas.com.

HALASKA, TERRELL, federal agency administrator; BA, U. Calif. San Diego; MA, Monterey Inst. Press sec. to Congressman Scott Klug; dir. Washington Office for State of Wis., Office of Gov. Tommy Thompson, Wis.; dep. chief of staff US Dept. Health & Human Svcs., Washington; spl. asst. to Pres. for domestic policy The White House, Washington, 2003—05; asst. sec. edn. for legislation & congl. affairs US Dept. Edn., Washington, 2005—. Office: US Dept Edn 400 Maryland Ave SW Rm 6W315 Washington DC 20202-1510 Office Phone: 202-401-0020. Office Fax: 202-401-1438.*

HALASZ, ISTVAN, chemist; m. Ilona Halasz; children: Susan, Mano. BS in physics and chem., Lajos Kossuth U., Hungary, 1974; D magna cum laude in nat. scis., Lajos Kossuth U., 1983; PhD, Hungarian Acad. Scis., Hungary, 1983. Sr. rsch. fellow Hungarian Hydrocarbon Inst., Szazhalombatta, Hungary, Ctrl. Rsch. Inst. for Chemistry, Hungarian Acad. Scis., Budapest, Hungary, 1986—93; postdoctoral rschr. Wayne State U., Detroit, 1993—96, U. Iowa, Iowa City, 1996—98; sr. chemist PQ Corp., Conshohocken, Pa., 1998—. Arrangement chair; dir. Phila. Catalysis Club, 2001—03; program chair North-East Corridor Zeolite Assn., Phila., 2002—; chair elect Phila. Catalysis Club, 2004—. Contbr. articles various books and profl. jours. Recipient 1st and 2nd prize in Nat. Competition of Student Scientists, Sci. Student Assn. of Hungary, 1971, 1973, Outstanding Young Scientist award, Hungarian Oil Trust, 1979, 1980, 1981, Outstanding Worker, Hungarian Hydrocarbon Inst., 1983; Austrian Sci. Exch. fellow, Hungarian Ministry of Edn., 1982, R. J. Kokes travel grant, North Am. Catalysis Soc., 1995. Mem.: AAAS, North-East Corridor Zeolite Assn. (program chair 2002—04), Phila. Catalysis Club (chair elect 2004), Am. Chem. Soc. Achievements include patents for developing chemical processes, new catalysts, and new methods for fabricating oxide superconductors and zeolites. Avocations: tennis, squash, pin pong/table tennis, board games, theater. Office: PQ Corp 280 Cedar Grove Rd Conshohocken PA PA 19 Office Phone: 610-651-4696. Office Fax: 610-825-1421. E-mail: istvan.halasz@pqcorp.com.

HALASZ, STEPHEN JOSEPH, retired optical engineer; b. Eger-Csehi, Hungary; s. Sandor and Ilona (Huszák) H.; children: Stepehn S., Christopher L. Jacqueline R. BS, Columbia U., 1955. Test engr. J.A. Maurer, Inc., N.Y.C., 1955—56; project engr. GE Co., Utica, NY, 1956—58; sr. physicist Avion divsn. ACF Industries, Paramus, NJ, 1958—65; head IR and Display Lab. Aerojet Gen., 1965—72; sr. specialist Xerox Electro-Optical, Pasadena, Calif., 1972—75, Ford Aeronutronic, Newport Beach, Calif., 1975—83; chief scientist Hughes Aircraft, El Segundo, Calif., 1983—92. Contbg. author: (handbook) IR Handbook, 1969. With U.S. Army, 1945. NRA. Republican. Roman Catholic. Achievements include numerous designs and research projects including optical guidance for satellite interception; IR moving target tracker; handheld thermal imager; scanned matrix for IR pattern recognition; high speed target acquisition with fused sensors; others; patentee in field. Home: 66887 San Carlos Rd Desert Hot Springs CA 92240-2622 E-mail: s_hal@msn.com.

HALASZYNSKI, THOMAS M., anesthesiologist; b. McKeesport, Pa., Mar. 10, 1968; s. Thomas Adam and Eleanor; m. Carolyn A. Sires, Feb. 28, 1998. BA, THBC Coll., 1980; DMD, Temple Dental Sch., 1984; MD, NEOUCOM, 1983; MBA, U. New Haven, 2002. Resident Temple Dental, Phila., Yale New Haven Hosp.; dentist U.S. Pub. Health Svcs., 1980—87; anesthesiologist Yale U. Sch. Medicine, Conn., 1994—. Contbr. articles to profl. jours., chpts. to books. Mem.: AMA, Am. Dental Assn., N.Y. State Dental Soc. Anesthesiology, Am. Soc. Dental Anesthesiology, Pa. Dental Soc. Anesthesiology, Am. Soc. Anesthesiologists, Internat. Anesthesia Rsch. Soc., Am. Soc. Regional Anesthesiology, Conn. State Soc. Anesthesiologists, Soc. Ambulatory Anesthesia, Assn. Clinicians for Underserved, Am. Soc. Critical Care Anesthesiologists, European Soc. Regional Anesthesiology, Wilderness Med. Soc., Conn. State Med. Soc., Am. Coll. Physicians Execs., Am. Acad. Pain Mgmt., Lambda Sigma, Beta Beta Beta. Office: Yale U Sch Medicine 333 Cedar St Branford CT 06405

HALAVAIS, MARY HOYT, history professor, researcher; d. Harold Gavin Hoyt and Evelyn Holland; children: Margaret children: Alexander Campbell, Andrew, Arthur. BA in History, U. Md., 1971; PhD, U. of Calif., San Diego, 1997. Assoc. prof. Calif. State U. - Sonoma, Rohnert Park, Calif., 1999—. Author: Like Wheat to the Miller. Bd. dirs. Interfaith Shelter Network, Santa Rosa, Calif., 2002—05, pres., 2005—; vol. tchr. Prison U. Project, San Quentin, Calif., 2001—05. Fellow, NEH, 2003; Morocco Travel and Rsch. grant, Joint Berkeley-Stanford Ctr. for African Studies, 2001. Mem.: Am. Hist. Assn. (Gutenberg-e prize 2001), Soc. Spanish and Portuguese Hist. Studies (editor bull. 2005—). Office: California State University - Sonoma 1801 East Cotati Ave Rohnert Park CA 94928 Office Phone: 707-664-2489. Office Fax: 707-664-3920. E-mail: halavais@sonoma.edu.

HALBACH, EDWARD CHRISTIAN, JR., law educator; b. Clinton, Iowa, Nov. 8, 1931; s. Edward Christian and Lewella (Sullivan) H.; m. Janet Elizabeth Bridges, July 25, 1953; children: Kristin Lynn, Edward Christian III, Kathleen Ann, Thomas Elliot, Elaine Diane. BA, U. Iowa, 1953, JD, 1958; LLM, Harvard U., 1959; LLD, U. Redlands, 1973. Assoc. prof. Sch. Law, U. Calif., Berkeley, 1959-62, prof., 1963—, dean, 1966-75. Co-author: Materials on Decedents' Estates and Trusts, 1965, 73, 81, 87, 93, 2000, Materials on Future Interests, 1977, Death, Taxes and Family Property, 1977, California Will Drafting, 1965, 77, 92; author: Use of Trusts in Estate Planning, 1975, 81, 84, 86, 91, Fundamentals of Estate Planning, 1983, 86, 87, 89, 91, 93, 95, Summary of the Law of Trusts, 1990, 1998, Principles and Techniques of Estate Planning, 1995; reporter Uniform Probate Code, 1969, Restatement 3d Trusts Prudent Investor Rule, 1992, Restatement of Law of Trusts, vols. 1 and 2, 2003; also articles. 1st lt. USAF, 1954-56. Mem. ABA (chmn. various coms. sect. individual rights and responsibilities and sect. real property probate and trust law, dir. probate and trust divsn., sect. chmn.), Iowa Bar Assn., Am. Law Inst. (reporter Restatement 3d Trusts, advisor Restatement 2d, 3d Property), Am. Acad. Polit. and Social Scis., Am. Bar Found., Am. Coll. Trust and Estate Counsel, Am. Coll. Tax Counsel, Internat. Acad. Estate and Trust Law (v.p., exec. com., pres.). Home: 679 San Luis Rd Berkeley CA 94707-1725 Office: U Calif Sch Law Boalt Hall Berkeley CA 94720 E-mail: bubzed@comcast.net.

HALBACH, VAN VINCENT, neuroradiologist; s. Carl Richard Halbach and Sonya Alycia Leitner, Ted E. Leitner (Stepfather) and Penny Halbach (Stepmother); m. Deborah Ann Foreman, Sept. 9, 1999; children: Daniel Patrick Foreman, Sean Micheal, Kelly Nichole Foreman, Thomas Anthony. BA, Whittier Coll., 1977; MD, UCLA, 1981. Diplomate American Board of Radiology Am. Bd. Radiology. Prof. of radiology, neurol. surgery, neurology, and anesthesia U. Calif., San Francisco, 1986—. Mem.: Am. Soc. Neuroradiology, Soc. Vascular and Interventional Radiologists, World Fedn. Interventional and Therapeutic Neuroradiology (founding mem.), Western Neuroradiology Soc., Radiol. Soc. N.Am., Alpha Omega Alpha. Achievements include first to interventional neuroradiology. Avocations: windsurfing, skiing, mountain biking. Home: 115 Great Circle Dr Mill Valley CA 94941 Office: U Calif San Francisco 505 Parnassus Ave L 352 Dept of Radio San Francisco CA 94143-0628 Office Phone: 415-353-1863. Personal E-mail: van.halbach@radiology.ucsf.edu.

HALBERG, CHARLES JOHN AUGUST, JR., mathematics professor; b. Pasadena, Calif., Sept. 24, 1921; s. Charles John August and Anne Louise (Hansen) Halberg; m. Ariel Arfon Oliver, Nov. 1, 1941 (div. July 1969); children: Ariel Walters, Charles Thomas, Niels Frederick; m. Barbro Linnea Samuelsson, Aug. 18, 1970 (dec. Jan. 1978); 1 stepchild, Ulf Erik Hjelm; m. Betty Reese Zimprich, July 27, 1985. BA summa cum laude, Pomona Coll., 1949; MA (William Lincoln Honnold fellow), UCLA, 1953, PhD, 1955. Instr. math. Pomona Coll., Claremont, Calif., 1949-50; assoc. math. UCLA, 1954-55; instr. math. U. Calif.-Riverside, 1955-56, asst. prof. math., 1956-61, assoc. prof. math., 1961-68, prof. math., 1968—, vice chancellor student affairs, 1964-65. Dir. Scandinavian Study Ctr. Lund (Sweden) U., 1976—78; docent U. Goteborg, Sweden, 1969—70; bd. dirs. Fulbright Commn. Ednl. Exch. between U.S. and Sweden, 1976—79. Author (with John F. Devlin): Elementary Functions, 1967; author: (with Angus E. Taylor) Calculus with Analytic Geometry, 1969; author: Aftermath, 1996. With USAAF, 1945—46. NSF fellow, U. Copenhagen, 1961—62. Mem.: Swedish Math. Soc., Am. Math. Soc., Math. Assn. Am. (chmn. So. Calif. sect. 1964—65, gov. 1968), Phi Beta Kappa, Sigma Xi. Home: 331 Hemlock Ave Carlsbad CA 92008 Business E-Mail: doon@math.ucr.edu.

HALBERSTADT, ROBERT BILHEIMER, optometrist; b. Stockertown, Pa., Feb. 11, 1918; s. Joseph Victor and Lillian (Bilheimer) H.; O.D., No. Ill. Coll. Optometry, 1939; m. Mary Margaret Gassner, Nov. 9, 1940; children: Mary Diane Seip, Victoria Milou Mackenzie. Optometrist, Nazareth, Pa., 1940—; cons. Optometry Whitehall-Coplay Sch. Dist., 1966-78, Pathway Sch., Norristown, Pa. 1966-67, Miller Clinic, Stroudsburg, Pa., 1971-74, Learning Center, Scranton (Pa.) Pub. Schs., 1971-72; staff optometrist, cons. Allentown State Hosp., 1967-68; extern Gesell Inst., New Haven, 1967-68. Active Lehigh Valley Assn. for Brain Damaged Child, 1965-68; 2d Assn. for Brain Damaged Children, 1966-68; program chmn. Lehigh Valley Assn. for Children with Learning Disabilities, 1969-74, bd. dirs., 1971-74, 1st v.p., 1973-74; mem. Council Exceptional Children; with Friendship House, Scranton, 1973-75; mem. pres.'s club Ill. Coll. Optometry, 1973—, Century Club, 1976-88; mem. nat. pilot project team on formation fo spl. edn. model Intermediate Sch. Unit 20 of Pa., 1980-81; mem. Nazareth Area Residents for Clean Air, 1991. With USNR, 1944-46. Mem. Optometric Extension Program (state dir. 1950-58, regional dir. 1958-84, life mem. Pioneer Fund 1987—), Pa. Optometric Assn. (treas. 1948-57). Address: 3205 W Highland St Allentown PA 18104-2668

HALBERSTADTER, DAVID, lawyer; b. Elizabeth, NJ, Sept. 1, 1957; BA, Cornell U., 1979; JD magna cum laude, Georgetown U., 1982. Bar: Calif. 1982. Ptnr., co-chair Entertainment and Media Practice Katten Muchin Zavis Rosenman, LA. Mem.: ABA, LA County Bar Assn., LA Copyright Soc. Office: Katten Muchin Zavis Rosenman Ste 2600 2029 Century Park E Los Angeles CA 90067 Office Phone: 310-788-4408. Office Fax: 310-712-8481. E-mail: david.halberstadter@kmzr.com.

HALBERSTAM, DANIEL, law educator; BA summa cum laude, Columbia Coll.; JD, Yale U. Judicial clk. for Justice David H. Souter US Supreme Ct.; for Judge Patricia M. Wald US Ct. Appeals, DC Cir.; judicial fellow for Judge

Peter Jann Ct. Justice of European Communities; atty.-adv. Office of Legal Counsel, US Dept. Justice; atty.-adv. to Chmn. Robert Pitofsky, FTC; prof. law, founding dir. European Union Ctr. U. Mich. Law Sch., Ann Arbor. Editl. adv. bd. mem. Cambridge Studies in European Law and Policy. Mem.: Phi Beta Kappa. Office: U Mich Law Sch 316 Hutchins Hall 625 S State St Ann Arbor MI 48109-1215 Office Phone: 734-763-4408. Office Fax: 734-763-9375. E-mail: dhalber@umich.edu.*

HALBERSTAM, DAVID, journalist, writer; b. N.Y.C., Apr. 10, 1934; s. Charles A. and Blanche (Levy) H.; m. Elzbieta Tchizevska, June 13, 1965 (div. 1977); m. Jean Sandness Butler, June 29, 1979; 1 dau., Julia Sandness. AB, Harvard U., 1955; degree (hon.), CCNY, Colby Coll., Colorado State, Columbia Coll., Chgo., Dartmouth Coll., Drew Univ., Elizabethtown Coll., Ithaca Coll., Knox Coll., Lake Forest Coll., Lawrence Coll., Mercy Coll., Univ. Mich., Ann Arbor, Univ. New Haven, Niagara Coll., Tufts Univ., Tulane Univ., Univ. South, Sewance, Univ. South Carolina, Spartanburg, Wesleyan Univ. Reporter West Point Daily Times Leader, Miss., 1955—56, Nashville Tennessean, 1956—60; mem. staff N.Y. Times, 1960—67, corr., 1961—62, 1962—63, 1964—65, Warsaw, 1965—66; contbg. editor Harper's mag., 1967—71. Author: The Noblest Roman, 1961, The Making of a Quagmire, 1965, One Very Hot Day, 1968, The Unfinished Odyssey of Robert Kennedy, 1969, Ho (Ho Chi Minh), 1971, The Best and the Brightest, 1972, The Powers That Be, 1979, The Breaks of the Game, 1981, The Amateurs, 1985, The Reckoning, 1986, Summer of '49, 1989, The Next Century, 1991, The Fifties, 1993, October 1964, 1994, Playing for Keeps: Michael Jordan and The World He Made, 1998, The Children, 1998, War In a Time of Peace, 2001, Firehouse, 2002, The Teammates, 2003; co-editor: (with Glenn Stout) The Best American Sports Writing, 1991; editor: (with Glenn Stout) The Best American Sports Writing of the Century, 1999; author intro. for Requiem The Photographs of the Photographers Who Died in the Vietnam War, 1997. Trustee The Brearley Sch., 1993. Recipient Pulitzer prize for internat. reporting, 1964, George Polk Meml. award, 1964, Louis Lyons award, 1964, Page One award for Congo reporting, 1962, Overseas Press Club award, 1973, Elijah Lovejoy award Colby Coll., 1997, Bob Considine award St. Bonaventure Coll., 1999, Robert Kennedy Book award, 1999, Christopher award, 1999, Frederick Melcher Book award Unitarian Ch., 1999, Pres. Award, Trinity Coll., Jean Mayer Award, Tufts Univ., all for The Children, 1999. Mem. Soc. Am. Historians.

HALBERSTAM, HEINI, mathematics professor; b. Most, Czechoslovakia, Sept. 11, 1926; came to Eng., 1939, naturalized, 1998. s. Michael and Judith (Honig) H.; m. Heather M. Peacock, Mar. 11, 1950 (dec. 1971); children: Naomi Deborah, Judith Marion, Lucy Rebecca, Michael Welsford; m. Doreen Bramley, Sept. 28, 1972. BS with honours, Univ. Coll., London U., 1946, MS, 1948, PhD, 1952. Lectr. math. U. Exeter, 1949-57; reader Royal Holloway Coll., London U., 1957-62; Erasmus Smith prof. Trinity Coll., Dublin, Ireland, 1962-64; prof. Nottingham U., England, 1964-80; prof. math. U. Ill., Urbana-Champaign, 1980-96, prof. emeritus, 1996—. Vis. lectr. Brown U., 1955-56; vis. prof. U. Mich., 1966, U. Tel Aviv, 1973, U. Paris-South, 1972 Co-author: Sequences, 1966, 2d edit., 1983, Sieve Methods, 1975; co-editor math. papers of, W.R. Hamilton, H. Davenport; contbr. articles to profl. jours. Mem. London Math. Soc. (v.p. 1962-63, 74-77), Am. Math Soc. Business E-Mail: heini@math.uiuc.edu.

HALBERSTAM, MALVINA, law educator, lawyer; b. Kempno, Poland, May 2, 1937; came to U.S., 1947; d. Marcus and Pearl (Halberstam) H.; m. Wolf Z. Guggenheim (dec. 2002); children: Arye, Achiezer. BA cum laude, Bklyn. Coll., 1957; JD, Columbia U., 1961, MIA, 1964. Bar: N.Y. 1962, U.S. Dist. Ct. (so. dist.) N.Y. 1963, U.S. Ct. Appeals (2d cir.) 1965, U.S. Supreme Ct. 1966, Calif. 1968. Law clk. Judge Edmund L. Palmieri Fed. Dist. Ct. (so. dist.) N.Y., 1961-62; rsch. assoc. Columbia Project on Internat. Procedure, 1962-63; asst. dist. atty. N.Y. County, 1963-67; with Rifkind & Sterling, L.A., 1967-68; sr. atty. Nat. Legal Program on Health Problems of the Poor, L.A., 1969-70; prof. Sch. Law Loyola U., L.A., 1970-76; prof. Benjamin N. Cardozo Sch. Law Yeshiva U., N.Y.C., 1976—. Vis. prof. Gould Law Ctr., U. So. Calif., L.A., 1972-73, U. Va. Sch. Law, 1975-76, U. Tex. Sch. Law, summer 1974, Hebrew U., Jerusalem, 1984-85; counselor on internat. law U.S. State Dept. Office of Legal Adviser, 1985-86; cons., 1986-92. Author (with De Feis): Women's Legal Rights: International Agreements An Alternative to ERA?, 1987; articles and rev. editor Columbia Law Rev., 1960—61, reporter Am. Law Inst. Model Penal Code Commentaries, 1977—81, mem. editl. bd. Jour. Nat. Security Law and Policy, 2005—; contbr. articles, commentary, book revs. to profl. jours. Mem. Bklyn. Coll. Alumni Adv. Bd. on Women's Career Devel. and Leadership Program.; adv. com. to standing com. on law and nat. security, ABA; study group on shape Arab-Israeli settlement, humanitarian, and demographic issues Coun. on Fgn. Rels. Kent scholar (2x); Stone scholar; recipient Jane Marks Murphy prize. Mem.: Am. Assn. Law Schs. (chair sect. internat. law 2002—03, co-vice chmn. sect. nat. security law 2003—04, co-chmn. elect nat. security law sect. 2004—05, mem. exec. com. 2005—), Am. Assn. Jewish Lawyers and Jurists (bd. govs.), Internat. Law Assn. (Am. br. exec. com., human rights com.), Assn. Bar City of N.Y. (coun. on internat. affairs 1998—2004), Am. Soc. Internat. Law, Am. Law Inst. (life), Columbia Law Sch. Alumni Assn., Phi Beta Kappa. Home: 160 Riverside Dr New York NY 10024-2106 Office: Benjamin N Cardozo Sch Law Yeshiva U 55 Fifth Ave New York NY 10003-4391 Office Phone: 212-790-0394. E-mail: halbrstm@yu.edu.

HALBERSTEIN, JOSEPH LEONARD, retired editor; b. Piqua, Ohio, Mar. 10, 1923; s. David and Mollie (Oberferst) H.; m. Lillian Friedman, Aug. 9, 1964; children: Richard Martin, Howard Louis. BA in Journalism, Ohio State U., 1944; postgrad., Pa. State U., 1976. Sportswriter Columbus (Ohio) Citizen, 1943-44; sports editor Lima (Ohio) News, 1944-49; circulation mgr. Town and Village, N.Y.C., 1950-52; sports editor, mng. editor Wilmington (Del.) Sunday Star, 1952-54; wire editor, sports editor Gainesville (Fla.) Sun, 1955-71; mng. editor, assoc. editor Bucks County Courier Times, Levittown, Pa., 1971-93, ret., 1993. Lectr. various univs. Contbr. articles to profl. jours. Bd. dirs. ARC, Langhorne, Pa., 1971-80, Congregation Beth El, Levittown, 1978-85. Recipient 2d Pl. best column Nat. Newspaper Assn., 1961, 1st Pl. best column Keystone Press Assn., 1976, 2d Pl. best game story Basketball Writers Assn. Mem. Fla. Sportswriters Assn. (pres.), Pa. AP Mng. Editors Assn. (pres.), Soc. of Profl. Journalists (greater Phila. chpt. pres. 1981-82), Pa. Soc. of Newspaper Editors, Sigma Delta Chi. Avocations: walking, travel, computer study. Office: Bucks County Courier Times 8400 Route 13 Levittown PA 19057 Personal E-mail: mrslfh@aol.com. *Newspapers bring information to people. Sometimes that information helps people make decisions that affect their lives or the lives of others. In journalism, one has to inform, to help, and, especially to care. Caring is what makes any endeavor a noble one.*

HALBREICH, KATHY, museum director; b. N.Y.C., Apr. 24, 1949; d. Irwin and Betty Ann (Stoll) H.; m. John Kohring; 1 child, Henry. BA, Bennington Coll., 1971; postgrad., Skowhegan Sch. Painting and Sculpture, Maine, 1965, Am. U., Mexico City, 1966. Adminstr. spl. programs Bennington (Vt.) Coll., 1975-766; dir. teaching seminar Assn. Collegiate Schs. Architecture, Washington, 1977; v.p. programs, trustee Artist Found., Boston, 1979-84; dir. com. on visual arts Hayden Gellery, List Visual Arts Ctr., MIT, Cambridge, Mass., 1976-86; ind. curatorial cons., 1986-88; curator contemporary art Mus. Fine Arts, Boston, 1988-90; dir. Walker Art Ctr., Mpls., 1991—. Cons. St. Louis Art Mus., Artists Space, N.Y.C., Capp St. Project, San Francisco, Mus. Modern Art, N.Y.C., Seattle Arts Commn., Southeastern Ctr. for Contemporary Art, Louis Comfort Tiffany Found., Beacon Cos., Frito-Lay Inc., New Eng. Gen. Svcs. Adminstrn. Art-in-Architecture Program, Nat. Endowment for Arts, VA Art-in-Architecture Program; trustee MA Coun. on the arts and Humanities; advisor Pub. Art Policy Project and Publ., Nat. Endowment for Arts, 1987; mem. nat. com. P!ub. Art in Am. Conf., Phila., 1987. Trustee Twin Cities Pub. TV, 1992. Mem. Assn. Art Mus. Dirs., Andy Warhol Found. for Visual Arts Inc. (bd. dirs. 1992), Mpls. Club. Office: Walker Art Ctr 1750 Hennepin Ave Minneapolis MN 55403-1138

HALBREICH, URIEL MORAV, psychiatrist, educator; b. Jerusalem, Nov. 23, 1943; arrived in U.S., 1978, naturalized, 1982; s. Mordechai and Zipora (Tennenbaum) H.; m. Judith Thadine, 1987; children: Jasmine, Bethany. MD, Hebrew U., 1969. Diplomate Tel Aviv U. Psychiatry and Psychotherapy. Intern gen. medicine Hadassah U. Hosp., Jerusalem, 1968; comdr., vice-chief med. officer Israeli Navy, 1970—72, chief psychiatrist, 1977—78; resident, 2d then 1st asst. Hadassah Hosp. Hebrew U., Jerusalem, 1972—78; temp. chief physician Hadassah U. Hosp., Jerusalem, 1978; asst. prof., rsch. psychiatrist Columbia U., N.Y.C., 1978—80; assoc. prof., dir. divsn. biol. psychiatry Albert Einstein Coll. Medicine, N.Y.C., 1982—85; prof. psychiatry, dir. biobehavioral rsch. SUNY, Buffalo, 1985—, prof. ob-gyn., 1988—. Vis. prof. Harvard U., 1996-98, exec. cons. dept. psychiatry; chmn. 1st Internat. Congress on Hormones, Brain and Neuropsychopharmacology, 1993, chmn. sect. on interdisciplinary collaboration World Psychiat. Assn., 1997—, others; chmn. 2d Congress on Hormones, Brain and Neuropsychopharmacology, 2000; chmn. bd. dirs. Internat. Inst. Edn. in Mental Health and Psychopharmacology, 1997—; cons. in field. Editor: Transient Psychosis, 1983, Resistance to Treatment with Antidepressant Drugs, 1986, Hormones and Depression, 1987, Multiple Sclerosis: A Neuropsychiatric Disorder, 1992, Psychopharmacology of Women, 1996, Psychiatric Issues in Women, 1996, Training in Psychiatry and Psychopharmacology, 1998, Psychopharmacology of Mood Anxiety and Cognition, 2000, Psychiatry and the Law in Eastern Europe, 2000, Womens Mental Health, 2002; contbr. articles to profl. jours., chpts. to books. Recipient Ben Gurion award Gen. Fedn. Labor, 1976, Yair Gon award Hebrew U. Hadassah Med. Sch., 1978, Nat. Rsch. Svc. award NIH, 1978, Svc. award Internat. Soc. Psychoneuroendocrinology, 2003; grantee NIMH, 1982—. Fellow: Am. Coll. Psychiatrists, Am. Psychiat. Assn. (disting.), Coll. Internat. Neuropsychopharmacology (co-chmn. edn. com. 1994—96), Am. Coll. Neuropsychopharmacology (chmn. rules and constitution com. 1996), Am. Psychopathology Assn.; mem.: Hormones, Brain and Neuropsychopharmacology (pres.), Endocine Soc., Assn. Med. Psychiatry (chmn. edn. com. 1992—96, councilor 1992—96), Soc. Biol. Psychiatry (chmn. program com. 1992—93), Am. Coll. Psychiatrists, Internat. Assn. Women's Mental Health (pres. 2001—04), Internat. Soc. Psychol. Neurol. Endocrinology (chmn. 21st congress 1990, pres. 1999—2002). Jewish. Office: SUNY Sch Med & Biomed Hayes C Ste 1 3435 Main St Bldg 5 Buffalo NY 14214-3016 Office Phone: 716-829-3808. Business E-Mail: urielh@buffalo.edu.

HALDANE, FREDERICK DUNCAN MICHAEL, physics educator; b. London, Sept. 14, 1951; came to U.S., 1981; BA, Cambridge U., Eng., 1973, PhD in Physics, 1978. Physicist Inst. Laue-Langevin, Grenoble, France, 1977-81; asst. prof. physics U. So. Calif., L.A., 1981-85; mem. tech. staff AT&T Bell Labs., Murray Hill, N.J., 1985-87; prof. physics U. Calif., San Diego, 1987-90, Princeton (N.J.) U., 1990—, Eugene Higgins Prof., 1999—. Trustee Aspen (Colo.) Ctr. for Physics, 1985-90, mem. adv. bd., 1990-1999. Contbr. articles to profl. jours. Alfred P. Sloan Found. fellow, 1984. Fellow AAAS, Am. Phys. Soc. (Oliver E. Buckley prize 1993), Am. Acad. Arts and Scis., Royal Soc. London. Achievements include research in theoretical condensed matter physics; contributions to the understanding of quantum magnetism and the fractional quantum Hall effect. Office: Princeton U Dept of Physics Jadwin Hall Princeton NJ 08544

HALDEMAN, JOE WILLIAM, novelist; b. Okla. City, June 9, 1943; s. Jack Carroll and Lorena (Spivey) H.; m. Mary Gay Potter, Aug. 21, 1965. BS in Physics and Astronomy, U. Md., 1967; MFA in Writing, U. Iowa, 1975. Assoc. prof. writing program MIT, 1983—. Author: War Year, 1972, The Forever War, 1975, Mindbridge, 1976, Planet of Judgment, 1977, All My Sins Remembered, 1977, Infinite Dreams, 1978, World Without End, 1979, Worlds, 1971, (with Jack C. Haldeman II) There Is No Darkness, 1983, Worlds Apart, 1993, Dealing in Futures, 1985, Tool of the Trade, 1987, Buying Time, 1989, The Hemingway Hoax, 1990, Worlds Enough and Time, 1993, 1968, 1995, None So Blind, 1996, Saul's Death and Other Poems, 1997, Forever Peace, 1997, Forever Free, 1999, The Coming, 2000, Guardian, 2002, Camouflage, 2004, Old Twentieth, 2005, War Stories, 2005; editor: (with Martin H. Greenburg and Charles Waugh) Body Armor: 2000, 1986, Supertanks, 11987, Spacefighters, 1988; editor: Cosmic Laughter, 1974, Study War No More, 1977, Nebula Awards 17, 1983. Served with U.S. Army, 1967-69. Decorated Purple Heart; recipient Hugo award World Sci. Fiction Soc., 1976, 77, 91, 95, 98, Nebula award Sci. Fiction Writers Am., 1975, 91, 93, 98, 2001, Rhysling award Sci. Fiction Poetry Assn., 1984, 91, 2001, World Fantasy award, 1993, John W. Campbell award Sci. Fiction Rsch. Assn., 1998, James Tiptree award, 2004. Mem. Sci. Fiction Writers Am. (treas. 1970-73, chmn. grievance com. 1977-79, pres. 1992-94), Authors Guild, Writers Guild, Poets and Writers, Inc., Nat. Space Inst. E-mail: haldeman@mit.edu.

HALE, ALISON EMERY, music educator; b. Summit, N.J., Apr. 25, 1953; d. William Lodge and Carolyn Stevens Hale; m. Christopher George Chapman, May 30, 1982; children: William Chapman-Hale, Emery Chapman-Hale. AB, Mt. Holyoke Coll., 1975; MusM, Manhattan (N.Y.) Sch. Music, 1979, MusD, 1988. Adj. prof. Bater Coll., Lewiston, Maine, 1987—92, Bowden Coll., Brunswick, Maine, 1988—91, Bennington (Vt.) Coll., 1991—2001, Amherst (Mass.) Coll., 1996—, Mt. Holyoke Coll., South Hadley, Mass., 1994—; 2d flute Portland (Maine) Symphony Orch., 1995—; prin. flute Portland (Maine) Opera Repertory Theatre, 1995—. Founder, dir. Music at Orchard Hill, Brattleboro, Vt., 1992—; transcriber op. 20 Ludwig van Beethoven, 1988. Bd. dirs. Friends Music at Guilford, Vt., 1992—. Recipient Mary Lyon award, Mt. Holyoke Coll., 1988. Mem.: Chamber Music Am., Nat. Flute Assn. Independent. Avocations: skiing, singing, travel. Home: 1004 Upper Dummerston Rd Brattleboro VT 05301 Office Phone: 802-579-6401. Personal E-mail: chapman-hale1@juno.com.

HALE, BETHAN KATY, research scientist; b. Pontypridd, Wales, Eng., June 26, 1978; d. Richard John and Ann Hale; life ptnr. John James Watson. BA with honors, U. Oxford, 1999; PhD, U. Birmingham, 2002. Post-doctoral rschr. OARDC/Ohio State U., Wooster, 2003—. Office: OARDC/Ohio State Univ Dept Entomology 1680 Madison Ave Wooster OH 44691 Business E-Mail: bethanhale@yahoo.co.uk.

HALE, BRUCE DONALD, retired marketing professional; b. Oak Park, Ill., Dec. 21, 1933; s. Edward Garden and Mildred Lillian (Pelc) H.; m. Nancy Ann Novotny, July 2, 1955 (div. 1976); children: Jeffrey Bruce, Karen Jill Hale; m. Connie Luella Green Gunderson, Apr. 21, 1979. BA in Econs., Wesleyan U., Middletown, Conn., 1955. Trainee Caterpillar Tractor Co., Peoria, Ill., 1955-56, dealer tng. rep., 1956-59, dist. rep. Albuquerque, 1959-62; asst. sales mgr. Rust Tractor Co., Albuquerque, 1962-65, gen. sales mgr. Albuqerque, 1965-71, v.p. sales, 1971-81, v.p. mktg., 1981-96; ret., 1996. Mem. Am. Mining Congress, Soc. Mining Engrs., Associated Contractors N.Mex., Associated Equipment Distbrs., Rocky Mountain Coal Mining Inst., N.Mex. Mining Assn., Albuquerque Country Club. Avocations: golf, fishing, music, classic cars. Home: 9508 Layton Pl NE Albuquerque NM 87111-1368

HALE, CECIL, communications educator, business educator; b. St. Louis, Aug. 3, 1945; s. Cecil and Allean (Cunningham) H.; m. Brenda Kidd; children: Juanita, Tasha, Cecil-Jamil, Carolyn. Student, So. Ill. U., 1963-66; MA, Internat. U. of Comm., Washington, 1975; PhD, Union Inst., Cin., 1978; MPA, Harvard U., 1995; MBE, Dartmouth Coll., 2004. Lic. by FCC. Announcer, asst. gen. mgr. WMPP Radio, 1966—68; announcer XPRS Radio, L.A., 1972-74; announcer, asst. program/music dir. WNOV Radio, Milw., 1968-70, WVON Radio, Chgo., 1970-77; nat. dir., mgr. Phonogram/Mercury Records, Chgo., 1977-78; v.p. Capitol Records, Inc., Hollywood, Calif., 1978-81; prof. San Francisco State U., 1984-94, City Coll. San Francisco, 1986—; prof. Mass Media Inst. Stanford U., 1987-92; honors examiner Swarthmore Coll., 2004—; CEO Hale Comm., 2005—. Cons. N.T.A., Lagos, Nigeria, 1982-83, Gallo Winery, Inc., Modesto, Calif., 1977, Capitol Records, Inc., Hollywood, 1981-82, Congl. Caucus, Washington, 1975. Author: The Music Industry, 1990; exec. producer phono records. Bd. dirs., pres. Friends of CASA of Alameda County; mem Sickle Cell Cmty. Adv. Bd. Recipient Key to City and City Coun. Resolution, L.A., 1980, Outstanding Tchr. award Acad. Senate, City Coll. San Francisco, 1990, San Francisco State U. Faculty award, 1986; U. Calif. fellow, 1992; honored as Nat. African-Am. History Maker, 2002; fellow NATAS, 2000. Mem.: AFTRA, NEA, NAACP, AAUP, ABA, Am. Political Sci. Assn., Soc. Ethnomusicology, Soc. Values in Higher Edn., Am. Fedn. Tchrs., Am. Fedn. Musicians, Nat. Acad. Recording Arts and Scis., 100 Black Men of Am., Harvard Black Alumni Soc., Harvard Alumni Assn., Stanford Alumni Assn., Coun. Black Am. Affairs, Nat. Eagle Scout Assn., Harvard Club San Francisco (ex-officio bd. mem.), Harvard Club N.Y., Alpha Phi Alpha. Avocations: aviaton, computer science. Home: PO Box 26274 San Francisco CA 94126-2674 Office: City Coll San Francisco 50 Phelan Ave A 6 San Francisco CA 94112-1821 Office Phone: 415-452-5676.

HALE, CHERYL WRIGHT, marketing professional; b. San Jose, Calif., Oct. 1954; d. Edward James Wright, Uva Estelle Wright. BS in Animal Sci., Calif. Poly. State U., San Luis Obispo, 1975; MS in Mass. Comm., San Jose State U., 1978. V.p. Bank of Am., San Francisco, 1985—87; sr. mgr. Deloitte & Touche, San Francisco, 1987—92; mgr. info. resource audit Sun Microsystems, Inc., Palo Alto, Calif., 1992—94, strategic mktg. mgr., 1994—96, profl. svcs. mktg. dir., 1996—99, bus. devel. mgr., 1999—2001; prin. Cheryl Wright Mktg. Consulting, Incline Village, Nev., 2001—02; v.p. mktg. MuseGlobal, Salt Lake City, 2002—. Instr. info. tech. Golden Gate U., San Francisco, 1987—88. Contbr. chapters to books, articles to profl. jours. Vol. Tahoe Women's Svcs., Incline Village, 2001—01. Mem.: Tahoe Rim Trail Assn., AAUW. Avocations: skiing, hiking, kayaking. Personal E-mail: cheryl@cherylhale.net.

HALE, CYNTHIA LYNETTE, religious organization administrator; b. Roanoke, Va., Oct. 27, 1952; BA, Hollins Coll., 1975; MDiv, Duke U., 1979; D in Ministry, United Theol. Sem., Dayton, Ohio, 1991; DD (hon.), Bethany Coll., N.W. Christian Coll. Ordained Disciples of Christ Ch., Va., 1977. Head resident Hollins (Va.) Coll., 1975-76; intern to minister St. Mark's United Meth. Ch., Charlotte, N.C., 1976; undergrad. counselor Office of Minority Affairs Duke U., Durham, N.C., 1976-77; intern to minister Staunton Meml. Ch., Pittsboro, N.C., 1977-78; coordinating counselor summer transitional program Duke U., Durham, N.C., 1978; chaplain Fed. Correctional Instn., Butner, N.C., 1978-83; chaplain, instr. staff tng. acad. Fed. Prison System, Glynco, Ga., 1983-85; pastor, developer Ray of Hope Christian Ch., Decatur, Ga., 1986—; 1st vice moderator Christian Ch. (Disciples of Christ), U.S. and Can., 1993—. Bd. dirs. Coun. on Christian Unity, 1978-81; bd. trustees Disciples Nat. Convocation, 1980-86, pres. 1982-84, pres. ministers' fellowship, 1990—; task force on Renewal and Structural Reform, Disciples of Christ, 1980-87, adminstrv. com. 1982-87, gen. bd., 1982-88; bd. dirs. Disciples Divsn. Higher Edn., St. Louis, 1986-89; bd. trustees Lexington (Ky.) Theol. Sem., 1990—; bd. dirs. Disciples' Nat. Evangelic Assn., 1991—. Mem. Project Impact-Dekalb, South Dekalb Ch. Coalition; bd. dirs. Beulah Heights Bible Coll., Destiny Atlanta.com; mem. governing bd. Nat. Coun. Chs., 1978—83, panel on bio-ethical concerns, 1980—82. Named Outstanding Ga. Citizen and Goodwill Amb., Sec. of State, 2001, Chaplain of the Day, Ho. of Reps., 2004; recipient Liberation award, Disciples Nat. Conv., 1984, Religion award, DeKalb Br. NAACP, 1990, Religious award for dedicated svc., Ninety-Nine Breakfast Club, award, Martin Luther King's Bd. of Preachers, 1993, Chosen award, Atlanta Gospel Choice, 1998, Profiles of Prominence award, Nat. Women Achievement, 2000, Gospel Honor award, 2000, Youth V.I.B.E. award for outstanding contbns. to the cmty., 2003, James H. Costen award in religion, 2004. Mem. Christian Ch. Office: Ray of Hope Christian Ch 2778 Snapfinger Rd Decatur GA 30034-2439 E-mail: kingdominfo@rayofhope.org.

HALE, DANNY LYMAN, diversified financial services company executive; b. Ft. Lauderdale, Fla., Mar. 23, 1944; s. Thomas Hatten and Marion June (Frizzell) H.; m. Reda Fay Kofahl, June 10, 1966; 1 child, Matthew Bryan. BA in Econs., Yale U., 1966. Cons. in fin. planning Gen. Electric Co., Fairfield, Conn., 1977-78, mgr. fin. strategy devel. Louisville, 1978-79, mgr. fin. ops., 1979-80; mgr. divsn. fin. ops. GE Credit Corp., Stamford, Conn., 1980-82, v.p., dept. gen. mgr., 1982-84; mng. dir., mgr. bus. devel. Kidder Peabody Group, N.Y.C., 1987-88; pres. chase Comml. Corp., Chase Manhattan Bank, Paramus, N.J., 1988-91; exec. v.p. U.S.F. & G. Corp., Balt., 1991, exec. v.p., CFO, 1993-98, Promus Hotel Corp., Memphis, 1999; sr. v.p., CFO Allstate Ins. Co., Northbrook, Ill., 2003—. With U.S. Army, 1967-69. Republican. Congregationalist. Office: Allstate Ins Co 2775 Sanders Rd F8 Northbrook IL 60062

HALE, DAVID FREDRICK, biotechnology executive; b. Gadsden, Ala., Jan. 8, 1949; s. Millard and Mildred Earline (McElroy) Hale; m. Linda Carol Sadorski, Mar. 14, 1975; children: Shane Michael, Tara Renee, Erin Nicole, David Garrett. BA, Jacksonville State U. Dir. mktg. Ortho Pharm. Corp. divsn. Johnson & Johnson, Raritan, NJ, 1978—80; v.p. mktg. BBL Microbiology Sys. divsn. Becton Dickinson & Co., Cockeysville, Md., 1980—81, v.p., gen. mgr. BBL Microbiology Sys. divsn., 1981—82; sr. v.p. mktg. and bus. devel. Hybritech, Inc., San Diego, 1982, pres., 1983—86, CEO, 1986—87; pres., CEO, dir. Gensia Sicor, Inc., San Diego, 1987—97; pres., CEO Women First HealthCare, Inc., 1998—2000; pres., CEO, dir. CancerVax Corp., Carlsbad, Calif., 2000—. Bd. dirs. Metabasis Therapeutics, Santarus, Inc., SkinMedica, Somaxon Pharms., Venus Pharms., BIO, Children's Hosp., San Diego Econ. Devel. Corp., BIOCOM San Diego, Calif. HealthCare Inst.; co-founder CONNECT. Mem.: Chief Exec.'s Orgn., World Pres.'s Orgn. Republican. Episcopalian. Home: PO Box 8925 17079 Circa del Sur Rancho Santa Fe CA 92067 Office: CancerVax Corp 2110 Rutherford Rd Carlsbad CA 92008 Office Phone: 760-494-4200.

HALE, DAVID JASON, lawyer; b. Ft. Campbell, Ky., June 30, 1967; s. H. David and Brenda T. Hale; m. Ann F. Hale, Aug. 26, 1989; children: Caroline, John David. BA, Vanderbilt U., 1989; JD, U. Ky., 1992. Bar: Ky. 1992, U.S. Dist. Ct. (ea. and we. dists.) Ky. 1992, U.S. Ct. Appeals (6th cir.) 1992. Assoc. Brown Todd & Heyburn, PLLC, Louisville, 1992-94; asst. U.S. atty. U.S. Atty.'s Office (we. dist.) Ky., Louisville, 1995-99; counsel Reed Weitkamp Schell & Vice, PLLC, Louisville, 1999—. Project coord. (video) What is a Living Will?, 1999. Nat. pres. Coll. Dems. Am., Washington, 1988-89; mem., bd. dirs. State YMCA Ky. Youth Assn., Frankfort, 1996—. Mem. ABA, FBA, Ky. Bar Assn., Louisville Urban League (bd. dirs. 2000), Ky. Ednl. TV. Democrat. Office: Reed Weitkamp Schell & Vice PLLC 500 W Jefferson St Ste 2400 Louisville KY 40202

HALE, DONALD ROY, music educator, musician; b. Watertown, Wis., May 29, 1949; s. Wayne Wilbur and Emmaline Jane Hale; m. Kristine Mary Coughlin, June 27, 1998; children: Eric, Corey. B in Music Edn., Wis. State U., Oshkosh, 1971; MA, U. Wis., Oshkosh, 1983. Band dir. Winneconne HS, Wis., 1971—, wrestling coach, 1971—2004. Recipient Area Coach of Yr., Post-Crescent Newspaper, Appleton, Wis., 2003, Cmty. Leader award, Winneconne Area Edn. Found., 2004. Mem.: Wis. Wrestling Coaches Assn. (exec. com. 1986—, pres. 1995—97, sec. 1989—92, 2001—, Dist. Coach award 2003). Avocations: golf, hunting. Office: Winneconne HS PO Box 5000 Winneconne WI 54986

HALE, HARRY WILLIAM, retired surgeon, educator; b. N.Y.C., Feb. 3, 1917; s. Harry William and Caroline Bridgman (Noyes) H.; m. Mary Augustine Slusher, May 25, 1946 (dec. 2002); children: Nancy D., Harry W. III, Daniel L., Robert H., Alice M. BS in Biology, Rensselaer Poly Inst., 1938; MD, U. Rochester, 1943. Diplomate Am. Bd. Surgery. Intern in surgery Strong Meml. Hosp., Rochester, N.Y., 1943; resident in surgery E.J. Meyer Meml. Hosp., Buffalo, 1946-52; from instr. to prof. surgery SUNY, Buffalo, 1952-69; chmn. dept. surgery Maricopa Med. Ctr., Phoenix, 1969-86, attending surgeon, 1986-95; clin. prof. surgery U. Ariz., Tucson, 1979-92. Chmn. bd. dirs. Ariz. Emergency Med. Services, Phoenix, 1976-81. Contbr. chpts. to books and articles to profl. jours. Served to lt. commdr., USNR, 1944-46, 50-51. Fellow ACS (gov. 1963-69), Am. Assn. for Surgery of Trauma, Soc. Surgery of Alimentary Tract; mem. AMA, Cen. Surg. Assn., Western Surg. Assn., Southwestern Surg. Congress. Avocations: photography, carpentry. Home: 3220 E Stanford Dr Paradise Valley AZ 85253-7525

HALE, JAMES THOMAS, retail executive, lawyer; b. Mpls., May 14, 1940; s. Thomas Taylor and Alice Louise (Mc Connon) H.; m. Sharon Sue Johnson, Aug. 27, 1960; children: David Scott, Eric James, Kristin Lynn. BA, Dartmouth Coll., 1962; LLB, U. Minn., 1965. Bar: Minn. Law clk. Chief Justice Earl Warren, U.S. Supreme Ct., 1965-66; asso. firm Faegre & Benson, Mpls., 1966-73, ptnr., 1973-79; v.p., dir. corp. growth Gen. Mills, Inc., 1979-80, v.p. fin. and control consumer non-foods, 1981; sr. v.p., gen. counsel, corp. sec. Dayton-Hudson Corp., Mpls., 1981-2000; exec. v.p., gen. counsel, corp. sec. Target Corp., 2000—. Adj. prof. U. Minn., 1967-73. Mem. exec. com. Fund Legal Aid Soc., others. Mem. Order of Coif, Phi Beta Kappa. Office: Target Corp 1000 Nicollet Mall Minneapolis MN 55403-2467

HALE, JANE ALISON, literature and language professor; b. Washington, Sept. 29, 1948; BA in French magna cum laude, Coll. William and Mary, 1970; MST in Edn., U. Chgo., 1974; MA in French, Stanford U., 1981; postgrad., Ecole Normale Supérieure de Jeunes Filles, Paris, 1981-82; PhD with distinction, Stanford U., 1984. Student tchg. supr., counselor Peace Corps Tng. Program, Ft. Archambault, Chad, 1971; tchr. French, cross-cultural coord. Peace Corps Tng. Ctr., St. Thomas, V.I., 1972; Peace Corps vol., tchr. English as fgn. lang. Lycée Franco-Arabe, Abéché, Chad, 1970-72; tchr. 2d grade Pleasant Grove Union Elem. Sch., Burlington, N.C., 1974-77; tchg. fellow in French Stanford U., 1982-83; tchr. French Inst. Intensive French, U. Fla., 1986-88; asst. prof. French and comparative lit. Brandeis U., Waltham, Mass., 1985-91, assoc. prof. French and comparative lit., 1991—. Presenter Internat. Conf. on TV Drama at Mich. State U., 1985, Samuel Beckett at 80 at U. Stirling, Scotland, 1986, Internat. Colloquium on Raymond Queneau, Thionville, France, 1990, Internat. Vian-Queneau-Prévert Colloquium at U. Victoria, Can., 1992, Internat. Symposium on Beckett in the 1990s, The Hague, 1992, MLA, N.Y.C., 1992, West Africa Rsch. Assn. Internat. Symposium, Dakar, Senegal, 1997, African Literature Assn., Fès, Morocco, 1999, Internat. Colloquium on Feminist Rsch. in French, Dakar, Senegal, 1999. Author: The Broken Window: Beckett's Dramatic Perspective, 1987, The Lyric Encyclopedia of Raymond Queneau, 1989; contbr. chpts. to books and articles to profl. jours. French Govt. scholar, 1981-82, Fulbright Sr. scholar, Senegal, 1993-94; Whiting fellow in the humanities, 1983-84, Dana faculty fellow Brandeis U., 1985-90, Bernstein faculty fellow Brandeis U., 1989, Marion and Jasper Whiting fellow, 1994-98; NEH travel grantee, 1988, Mazer grantee for faculty rsch. Brandeis U., 1990; recipient Lerman-Neubauer prize for excellence in tchg. and counseling, 2001. Mem. Samuel Beckett Soc. (exec. bd. dirs. 1989-92), Les Amis de Valentin Brû, Phi Beta Kappa. Office: Brandeis U Dept Romance & Comp Lit MS 024 Waltham MA 02454 E-mail: jhale@brandeis.edu.

HALE, JANET, federal agency administrator; b. Buffalo, Apr. 2, 1949; d. Herman Haltom and Rachel (Townes) H. BS, Miami U., Oxford, Ohio, 1971; M.P.A., Harvard U., 1980. Adminstrv. asst. State Rep. Tom Gallagher of Fla., Washington, 1974-76; research asst. House Republican Com., Washington, 1976-77; spl. asst. Senator Edward Brooke, Boston, 1977-79; spl. asst. to sec., dir. exec. secretariat HUD, Washington, 1981-82, dep. asst. sec. for policy, fin. mgmt. and adminstrn., 1982-86; asst. sec. US Dept. Transp., Washington, 1986—89; asst. sec. budget, tech., & fin. US Dept. HHS, Washington, 2002—03; under sec. mgmt. US Dept. Homeland Security, 2003—. Bd. dirs. Big Sisters Boston, 1978-80 Avocation: tennis.

HALE, JERRY B., information technology executive; b. July 1951; B in Math., Berea Coll., Ky.; addition studies, E. Tenn. State and U. Tenn. Dir., global bus. sys. Eastman Chemical Co., Kingsport, Tenn., v.p., e-info. svc. & chief info. officer, 2002—. Named one of top tech. innovators, Info. Week mag., 2004. Office: VP & CIO Eastman Chem 100 North Eastman Rd PO Box 511 Kingsport TN 37662-5075

HALE, JOE (JOSEPH RICE), church organization executive; b. Texarkana, Tex., Mar. 25, 1935; s. Alfred Clay and Bess (Akin) H.; m. Mary Richey, June 2, 1964; 1 son, Jeffrey Glen. BA, Asbury Coll., Wilmore, Ky., 1957; BD, So. Methodist U., 1960; DD, Asbury Theol. Sem., 1978, Asbury Coll., 2005; LHD (hon.), Fla. So. Coll., 1994. Ordained to ministry Meth. Ch., 1958. Pastor Meth. Ch., Sunset, Tex., 1958-60; evangelist, 1960-66; assoc. dir. dept. evangelism Bd. Evangelism, Meth. Ch., 1966-68, dir. ecumenical evangelism, 1968-74; dir. evangelization devel. Bd. Discipleship, United Meth. Ch., 1975; gen. sec. World Meth. Coun., 1976—2001, gen. sec. emeritus, 2001. Exec. com. Key 73, 1970-73; sec. working group evangelism Nat. Coun. Chs., 1972; pres. Comm. Found., Inc., 1974-75; world amb. Internat. Prayer Fellowship, 1974; exec. com. Evangelization Forum, 1973-75; registrar World Meth. Evangelism Convocation, Jerusalem, 1974; mem. Conf. Secs. Christian World Communions, 1976—, chmn. Christian World Communions, 1983-86. Author: Design for Evangelism, 1970, Christ Matters!, 1971, God's Moment, 1972; contbr. articles to profl. jours.; producer: The Spirit is Moving, 1980 (video prodn.) Roots of Faith, 1979, To Live to God, 1984, Nairobi, 1986, Singapore, 1991, Rio de Janeiro,1996, Rio: Walking in the Spirit, 1996, One People In All the World, 1996; editor proc. 13th-17th World Meth. Confs. Decorated Great Cross of Merit, Equestrian Order of the Holy Sepulchre in Jerusalem; recipient Key to City of Daytona Beach Fla., 1963-64, Asbury Coll. Alumni award, 1977, Disting. Svc. award Christian Meth. Episcopal Ch., 1994, Svc. award Gen. Commn. on Archives and History United Meth. Ch., 2002, Philip award Nat. Assn. United Meth. Evangelists, 1998; named Ky. col., 1977, Ecumenical Svc. award Gen. Commn. on Christian Unity United Meth. Ch., 2000, World Meth. Peace award World Meth. Coun., 2001; named Disting. Evangelist, United Meth. Ch., 2001, Disting. Alumnus, Perkins Sch. Theology So. Meth. U., 2002. Methodist. Home and Office: 34 Forest Park Dr Waynesville NC 28785

HALE, JUDSON DRAKE, SR., publishing executive, editor, writer; b. Boston, Mar. 16, 1933; s. Roger Drake and Marian (Sagendorph) H.; m. Sara Huberlie, Sept. 6, 1958; children: Judson Drake, Daniel, Christopher. BA, Dartmouth Coll., 1958; D of Journalism (hon.), New Eng. Coll., 1984; LittD (hon.), Franklin Pierce Coll., 1987; LHD (hon.), Keene State Coll., 1989. Asst. editor Yankee, Inc., Dublin, NH, 1958-61, assoc. editor, 1961-63, mng. editor, 1963-69; editor-in-chief Yankee Mag., Old Farmers Almanac; sr. v.p. Yankee Pub. Inc., Dublin, 1969—, sr. v.p., chmn., 2003—. Editor, v.p. Old Farmers Almanac. Author: Inside New England, 1982, The Education of a Yankee, 1987; editor: That New England, 1968; editor The Best of Yankee mag., 1985, The Best of the Old Farmer's Almanac, 1991, The Old Farmer's Almanac Book of Everyday Advice. Trustee MacDowell Colony. Served with AUS, 1955-57. Mem.: Mass. Hist. Soc., Cheshire County Dartmouth Alumni Club, Phi Kappa Psi. Democrat. Episcopalian. Home: Valley Rd Dublin NH 03444 Office: Yankee Pub Inc Main St Dublin NH 03444-0520 Office Phone: 603-563-8118 x104. Business E-Mail: judh@yankeepub.com.

HALE, LOUIS DEWITT, lawyer; b. Caddo Mills, Tex., June 10, 1917; s. Ernest Louis and Ethel M. (Massay) H.; m. Carol Gene Moore, June 8, 1947; children: Janet Sue Hale Wilde, Nancy Carol Hale (dec.). BA, U. Tex., 1937, MA, 1940. Bar: Tex. 1940, U.S. Supreme Ct. 1946, U.S. Dist. Ct. (so. dist.) Tex. 1947, U.S. Ct. Appeals (5th cir.) 1974. Classification analyst Office Emergency Mgmt., Washington, 1941-42; classification officer Office Def. Transp., Washington, 1942-43; pvt. practice Corpus Christi, Tex., 1946—81, Austin, Tex., 1981—. State rep. Tex. Legislature, 1939-40, 53-62, 65-78, spkr. pro tempore, 1961-62, chmn. jud. com., 1961-62, 69-74; gen. counsel House Gen. Investigating Com., Austin, 1989-92, Tex. Assn. Builders, Austin, 1978-81. Author: Streamlining Texas Judiciary, 1972; contbr. articles to profl. jours. Mem. Tex. Jud. Coun., Austin, 1961-65, 69-81; chmn. jud. com. Tex. Constnl. Conv., Austin, 1974. Served with USAF, 1943-46, res. 1947-73, ret. lt. col. Recipient Disting. Svc. award, Jr. C. of C., 1952. Mem. ABA, State Bar Tex. (Disting. Svc. award 1971, 73, 75), Tex. Assn. Builders (hon. life), Tex. State Tchrs. Assn. (hon. life, Disting. Svc. award 1961). Democrat. Baptist. Avocations: public speaking, historical research, coin collecting/numismatics. Home: 7106 Montana Norte Austin TX 78731-2124 Office: 5808 Balcones Dr Ste 101 Austin TX 78731-4276 Office Phone: 512-452-7817.

HALE, MARGARET SMITH, insurance company executive, educator; b. Browning, Mont., May 10, 1945; d. Stephen Howard and Evelyn Sarah (Beer) Smith; m. Lawrence L. Hale, Apr. 25, 1970 (div. Jan. 1984); children: Katherine Moore, Laura Ellen. BSBA, Boston U., 1967; AS in Risk Mgmt., Ins. Inst. Am., 1986. Underwriter Chubb & Son, Inc., N.Y.C., 1967-70, br. mgr., asst. v.p. Boston, 1970-80; asst. v.p., account exec. Marsh & McLennan Inc., Boston, 1980-84; sr. v.p. Frank B. Hall, Boston, 1984-87; resident v.p. Warwick Ins. Co., Needham, Mass., 1987-90; pres. Smith & Hale Assocs., Inc., South Orleans, Mass., 1990—. Lectr. Risk and Ins. Mgrs. Soc., Boston, 1975—85; mem. fin. divsn. Babson Coll., Wellesley, Mass., 1987—. Bd. dirs. Lupus Erythematosus Assn., Boston, 1975-78, Parker Hill Med. Ctr., Boston, 1978-80; tchr. Congl. Ch. Sch., Needham, Mass., 1982—; chmn. ins. adv. com. Town of Needham, 1982-95; pres. Interfaith Coun. for the Homeless, 1999—. Mem. Ins. Mgrs. Assn. (treas. Boston 1971-80), Ins. Library Assn. (dir. 1980-82). Office: Smith & Hale Assocs PO Box 136 South Orleans MA 02662-0136 Home: 7 Markham RD #20 East Hampton CT 06424-1640 Office Phone: 508-237-3723. Personal E-mail: smithhale@bigplanet.com.

HALE, MARIE STONER, artistic director; b. Greenwood, Miss. Student in Piano, U. Miss., Hattiesburg; studied with Richard Ellis, Christine du Boulay, Jo-Anna Kneeland, David Howard. Tchr. Ellis/du Boulay Sch., Chgo., Jo-Anna Kneeland Imperial Studios, Palm Beach County, Fla.; co-founder Ballet Arts Found., West Palm Beach, Fla., 1973-86; co-founder, artistic dir. Ballet Fla., West Palm Beach, 1986—. Office: Ballet Fla 500 Fern St West Palm Beach FL 33401-5726

HALE, MARNA A., utilities executive; d. Phale D. Hale Sr. and Cleo I. Hale; m. Richard Pace, Sept. 29, 1978 (div.); 1 child, Richard Hale Pace; m. Emanuel Leaks, Oct. 29, 1988 (div.). BA, Spelman Coll., 1973; MA, John Carroll U., 1992. Sect. chief tng. AT&T Techs., 1977—87; sr. instructional devel. Allen-Bradley Co., Inc., 1987—92; tng. cons. Data Corp. Bus. Systems, Inc., 1994—96; software programs tech. editor ABB Automations, 1996—98; profl. & orgnl. devel. cons. Ernst & Young, 1998—2000; program leader Intellinex, 2000—01; cons. Sapphire Techs., 2002—03; project dir. employee tng./devel. City of Cleve. Divsn. Water, 2003—. Author: Take Refuge Under the Halo, 1982, Take Refuge Under the Halo - Princess Diana After Life, 1999, Confessions of A Sister Out of Time, 1999, The Prequel to Confessions of A Sister Out of Time, 2001, How to Get Married: A Strategic and Literary Approach to Wedlock, 2002. Mem. MADD, 1997—. Named Miss Photography, 1969; recipient Foster Parent 10 Yr. award, Beechbrook Treatment Ctr., 2003. Mem.: NAACP, Nat. Writer's Assn., Am. Soc. Tng. and Devel., Internat. Soc. Performance Improvement, Nat. Spelman Alumni Assn. Home: 5455 N Marginal Rd 219 Cleveland OH 44114 Office: Divsn Water 1201 Lakeside Ave Cleveland OH 44114 Office Phone: 216-664-2444 x5829. E-mail: marnahale@yahoo.com.

HALE, NATHAN CABOT, sculptor, artist, poet; b. L.A., July 5, 1925; s. Nathan Cabot Hale, Virginia Markoe Ferris; m. Alison Elizabeth Boothby, Dec. 27, 1964; children: Terri Dean, Lisa Jenny Rose. BS, Empire State Coll., 1973; PhD, The Union Inst., Cin., 1976. Instr. sculpture Pratt Inst., Bklyn., 1960; instr. anatomy and the elements of drawing Art Students League of N.Y., 1975—86; instr. sculpture Nat. Acad. Schulpture, N.Y.C., 1985. Dir. The Ages of Man Found., 1968—; lectr. in field; cons. in field; instr. drawing and anatomy Art Student's League, 1985—90; sr. editor Art World, 1985—89. Author: Creating Welded Sculpture, 1968, 1994, The Embrace of Life, 1969, Abstraction in Art and Nature, 1972, 1993, The Birth of a Family, 1979, The Spirit of Man, 1981, (book of poetry) Fox Tails, 1993, (book of fables) The Elephant's Peaceable Kingdom, On the Perception of Human Form in Sculpture, 2000; contbr. numerous articles to profl. jours.; one-man shows include Felix Landau Gallery, L.A., 1957, Washington Irving Gallery, N.Y., 1960, Feingarten Gallery, Chgo., 1961, N.Y., 1961, Midtown Galleries, 1964, Hazelton Art League, Pa., 1966, Mus. of Ft. Wayne, Ind., 1966, Queens Coll., N.Y., 1966, NYU, 1967, Franklin and Marshall Coll., 1967, Midtown Galleries, N.Y., 1968, Quinata Gallery, Nantucket, 1968, Midtown Galleries, N.Y., 1973, exhibited in group shows at L.A. County Mus., Colo. Springs Fine Art Ctr., Norfolk Mus., Lehigh Univ., Philbrook Art Ctr., Ball State Univ., Hunterdon Art Ctr., Albright-Knox Art Gallery, Herron Mus. of Art, Davenport Mcpl. Art Gallery, Corcoran Gallery, Wayne State U., Pace Coll., Audubon Artists, Nat. Acad. Design, Columbus Gallery of Fine Art, Stamford Mus., Joslyn Mus., Springfield Mus. of Fine Art, Heckscher Mus., The Gallery of Modern Art; author: (novels) The Van Zanzibar Testaments. Dir. Ages of Man Found., 1969—. With USMC, 1941—42, with U.S. Merchant Marine, 1944—45. Recipient Purchase award in sculpture, L.A. County Mus., 1955, Silver medal, Audubon Soc. Sculpture, 1972. Fellow: Nat. Sculpture Soc.; mem.: Nat. Acad. Design (Gold medal in sculpture 1990), Century Assn. Avocations: sailing, fly fishing. Mailing: 57 Sheffield Rd Amenia NY 12501

HALE, RICHARD LEE, magazine editor; b. Formoso, Kans., Jan. 3, 1930; s. Glenn Becton and Ruby Tiarena (Johnson) H.; m. Nancy June Craig, Feb. 22, 1953; children— Steven Craig, Kristin Lee Hale Shurtz, Michael John, Sarah Johanna Hale Wilcher. BS in Journalism, U. Kans., 1952. Editor Bird City (Kans.) Times, 1955-58; editor, pub. St. Francis Herald, Kans., 1958-74; editor Golf Course Mgmt., Lawrence, Kans., 1974-76, PGA Mag., Palm Beach Gardens, Fla., 1976-80; dir. comm. GCSAA, Lawrence, 1980-82; editor Dental Econs., Penn Well Pub. Co., Tulsa, 1982-97, pub., 1989-97. Editor: (ann.) PGA Book of Golf, 1977-80; cons. editor Odontos Pub. Co., 1997-2002. Chmn. local com. Boy Scouts Am., St. Francis, 1970-74; trustee Trinity United Meth. Ch., Palm Beach Gardens, 1979-80, Am. Fund for Dental Health, 1989—. Spl. agt. CIC, U.S. Army, 1952-54. St. Francis Herald named Best Weekly Newspaper Kans. Press Assn., 1962. Mem. Am. Assn. Dental Editors, Am. Fund for Dental Health (trustee, advisor 1989-93), Kans. Press Assn. (bd. dirs. 1973-74), Golf Writers Assn. Am., Riverside Country Club (St. Francis; pres. 1971), Rotary (pres. local chpt. 1970), Alvamar Country Club (pres. 2003-04). Democrat. Mem. United Ch. Of Christ. Avocations: golf, travel, nature walks. Home: 5000 W 18th St Lawrence KS 66047 Personal E-mail: dhale1@juno.com.

HALE, ROBERT FARGO, federal association executive; b. Jan. 21, 1947; s. William David and Elizabeth (Wells) H.; m. Susan Kohn, June 23, 1973; children: Scott, Michael. BS with hons., Stanford U., 1968, MS, 1969; MBA, George Washington U., 1976. Cert. Def. Fin. Mgr., Am. Soc. Mil. Comptrollers. Analyst, study dir. Ctr. for Naval Analysis, Washington, 1972-75; analyst Congl. Budget Office, Washington, 1975-78, dep. asst. dir., 1978-81, asst. dir. def. issues, 1981-94; asst. sec. fin. mgmt. USAF, Washington, 1994-2001; program dir., sr. fellow LMI Gov't Cons., Washington, 2001—05; exec. dir. Am. Soc. Mil. Comptrollers, Alexandria, Va., 2005—. Nat. pres. and v.p. Am. Soc. Mil. Comptrollers; mem. bus. bd. Sec. Def. Served to lt. (j.g.) USNR, 1969-72. Fellow: Nat. Acad. Pub. Adminstrn.; mem.: Nat. Contract Mgmt. Assn., Am. Soc. Mil. Comptrollers, Assn. Govt. Accts., Phi Beta Kappa. Jewish. Home: 3357 Taleen Ct Annandale VA 22003-1161 Office: ASMC 415 N Alfred St Alexandria VA 22314 Office Phone: 703-549-0360. Business E-Mail: hale@asmconline.org.

HALE, ROBERT L., psychologist, educator; b. Bangor, Maine, Jan. 20, 1955; s. Clarence Adalbert and Hughene Ruth (Phillips) Hale; m. Cheryl Ann Goddard, Aug. 26, 1978; children: Lucas Robert, Colleen Claire. BA in Polit. Sci., U. Maine, 1977; BA in Psychology summa cum laude, U. So. Maine, 1979; MS in Exptl. Psychology, Northwestern State U. La., 1985; PhD in Physiol. Psychology, U. Okla., 1988. Grad. rsch. tchg. asst. U. Okla., Psychology Dept., Norman, 1985—87; rsch. asst. U. Okla., Student Devel. Dept., 1986—87; post doctoral fellow Med. U. SC, Psychiatry Dept., Charleston, 1988—90; adj. faculty Coll. of Carleston, SC, 1990—92; rsch assoc., tchg. faculty Med. U. SC, Psychiatry Dept., 1990—92; asst. prof. to assoc. prof. Shippensburg (Pa.) U., Psychology Dept., 1992—. Contbr. articles various profl. jours. and publs., scientific papers., numerous ednl. grants. Mem.: Am. Psycho. Assn., Divsn. 50, Pa. Soc. Biomedical Rsch., Rsch. Soc. on Alcoholism, Pa. Acad. of Sci., Fetal Alcohol Study Group, Ea. Psycho. Assn., Phi Kappa Phi, Psi Chi (life). Avocations: golf, fly fishing, walking. Office: Shippensburg U Pa 1871 Old Main Dr Shippensburg PA 17257-2299 Office Phone: 717-477-1177. Business E-Mail: rlhale@ship.edu.

HALE, ROGER LOUCKS, manufacturing executive, director; b. Plainfield, NJ, Dec. 13, 1934; s. Lloyd and Elizabeth (Adams) H.; m. Sandra Johnston, June 10, 1961 (div.); children: Jocelyn, Leslie, Nina, Deirdre; m. Eleanor L. Hall, Nov. 24, 1989. BA, Brown U., 1956; MBA, Harvard U., 1961. With Tennant Co., Mpls., 1961-99, pres., CEO, 1975-98, chmn., CEO, 1998-99, chmn., 1999, bd. dirs., VisionShare, Inc., 2001—, chmn., 2005—. Bd. dirs. Walker Art Ctr., 1970-2005, pres., 1975-77, 2002-05, chmn. 2005—; bd. dirs. Ploughshares Fund, 1996—, chmn, 2005—; Neighborhood Employment Network, 1980, bd. dirs. Winning Workplaces, 1999-; bd. dirs., chmn. Pub. Radio Internat., 1990, 2003; chmn. Minn. Bus. Partnership, 1993-95; chmn. Gov.'s Workforce Devel. Coun., 1999-2004. Named Exec. of Yr., Corp. Report mag., 1988, One of Minn.'s 5 Outstanding Corp. Dirs., Twin Cities Bus. Monthly, 1996; recipient Mpls. Spl. Recognition award for Svc. to City of Mpls., 1993. Office: Union Plz 333 Washington Ave N Ste 313 Minneapolis MN 55401-1364

HALE, ROGER W., utilities company executive; b. 1943; BA, U. Md., 1965; MS in Management, MIT, 1979. With AT&T, Atlanta, 1966—86, v.p. mktg. southern region, 1983—86; group v.p. BellSouth Corp, 1986-89, exec. v.p. Atlanta, 1988-89; pres., CEO LG&E Energy Corp, Louisville, 1989-92, bd. chmn., CEO, 1992—2001, ret., 2001. Bd. dir. H&R Block, Inc., Kansas City, Mo., Ashland, Inc. With USAF, 1966. Office: LG&E Energy Corp 220 W Main St Louisville KY 40202-1395

HALE, STEPHEN MICHAEL, artist; b. St. Johnsbury, Vt., July 17, 1961; s. Richard Martin and Jeanne Rita (Cormier) H. Student, R.I. Sch. Design, 1979-82. Visual artist, N.Y.C., 1982—. Represented by Bridgewater/Lustberg Gallery, N.Y.C., 1989—, Greathouse Gallery, N.Y.C., 1985-88, Damon Brandt Gallery, N.Y.C., 1983-84; freelance illustrator various mags., 1985-91; represented in permanent collections Ark. Arts Ctr., Little Rock, Mus. Art Carnegie Inst., Pitts. Fellow Nat. Endowment Arts, 1985, N.Y. Found. for Arts, 1988; grantee Pollock-Krasner Found., 1987. Democrat. Roman Catholic. Avocations: photography, film and video. Studio: 185 E 3rd St Apt 3G New York NY 10009-7411

HALE, SUE A., editor; Reporter, metro editor, city editor, news editor Daily Oklahoman, Oklahoma City, asst. mng. editor, 1989—96, gen. mgr. Connect Okla., Inc. subs., 1996—2000, exec. editor, 2000—. Named one of Heroes of the 50 States, State Open Govt. Hall of Fame, Soc. Profl. Journalists/Nat. Freedom of Info. Coalition, 2003. Office: Daily Oklahoman 9000 N Broadway PO Box 25125 Oklahoma City OK 73125

HALE, THOMAS MORGAN, professional services executive; b. Syracuse, N.Y., Nov. 29, 1936; s. Thomas Morgan and Ruth Ingrid (Stangeland) H.; m. Marilyn Johnson, June 12, 1959 (div. Aug. 1980), m. Linda Diana Pappas, Feb. 12, 1981; Children: Rodney, Kenneth, Timothy, Marilee. BS, Fla. State U., 1959; MA, U. Houston, 1967; DPA, George Mason U., 1990; diploma, Nat. War Coll., D.C., 1980. Commd. ensign USN, 1959, advanced through the grades to capt., 1983; served on destroyers, ops. officer USS Sampson, 1963-65; assoc. prof. naval sci. Tex. A&M U., 1965-67; chief staff officer, comdr. Destroyer Squadron Five, 1967-71; with Bur. of Naval Personnel, 1971-74; comdg. officer USS Paul, 1974-76; staff, chief naval ops., chmn. Joint Chiefs of Staff, 1976-83; ret. USN, 1983; sr. mgr. RCI, Vienna, Va., 1983-87, v.p., 1987-96, divsn. gen. mgr., 1992-96, sr. v.p., 1996—2005. Qualified expert witness Federal Dist. Ct. System. Contbr to profl. jours. Recipient Legion of Merit award Sec. of the U.S. Navy, 1983. Mem. U.S. Naval Inst. (life), Assn. Career Mgmt. Firms N. Am. (bd. dirs. 1998-2003), The Retired Officer's Assn. (life), The Tower Club (life), Army Navy Country Club. Methodist. Home: 3783 Center Way Fairfax VA 22033-2602 Office: RCI 2650 Park Tower Dr Vienna VA 22180 Personal E-mail: thomash463@aol.com.

HALE, WESLEY RAYMOND, research scientist, chemical engineer; b. Roanoke, Va., Apr. 20, 1969; s. John Raymond and Bettie Jane Hale; m. Michaela Christina Hale; children: Sarah, Joshua. BS in Chem. Engring. (with honors), Va. Tech., 1993; PhD in Chem. Engring. (with honors), U. Tex., Austin, 1998. Rschr. in polyrotaxanes Va. Tech., 1992—93; grad. internship Acadia Polymers, 1993; grad. rsch., tchg. asst. U. Tex., Austin, 1993—98; advanced rsch. scientist Eastman Chem. Co., Kingsport, Tenn., 1998—2000, sr. rsch. scientist, 2000—02, prin. rsch. scientist, 2002—. Contbr. articles to profl. jours.; reviewer Macromolecules, Polymer Engring. and Sci.; author: Reactive Compatibilization of Poly(butylene terephthalate)/ABS Blends by Methyl Methacrylate, Glycidyl Methacrylate, Ethyl Acrylate Terpolymers, 1993. Active mem. Meals on Wheels, 1994—. Recipient Rhone-Poulenc/Allied Signal Study Abroad Scholarship, 1992, Outstanding Jr. award, DOW Chem. Co., 1992, Rsch. Scholarship, NSF, 1993, Larry Holmes/SPE Endowed Presdl. Scholarship, 1997. Mem.: Soc. Plastics Engrs., Am. Chem. Soc., Omega Chi Epsilon Chem. Engring. Soc., Tau Beta Pi Engring. Honor Soc., Zeta Beta Tau Fraternity (founding father, Va. Tech. chpt., chpt. advisor 1995—96, 1999—2002). Achievements include patents for nylon 6-silicone blends; silicone polymer diol compositions and condensation polymer/silicone polymer blends; amide-type polymer/silicone polymer blends and processes of making the same; polyamide/emulsion polymer blends; diol latex compositions and modified condensation polymers; methods of making modified condensation polymers; modified nylon 6 latex compositions; polyethylene compositions and films formed therefrom having improved moisture vapor transmission rates; multilayer films; research in emulsion chemistry, statistical analysis, polymer thermodynamics, polymer optics, microporous materials and flow dynamics, polymer processing, theoretical modeling of material properties, and others. Avocations: photography, genealogy, gardening, travel, digital technology.

HALE, WILLIAM BRYAN, JR., newspaper editor; b. Stephenville, Tex., Apr. 26, 1933; s. William Bryan and Gladys (Tittle) H.; divorced; children: Shandra Hale Ferguson, Tamara Hale Cameron, Nicholas, Sabrina Hale Park. Student, UCLA, 1953-54. Police beat/courts reporter Santa Monica (Calif.) Outlook, 1953-58; gen. reporter Ontario (Calif.) Daily Report, 1958-59; criminal court writer L.A. City News Service, 1959-60; gen. reporter L.A. Times, 1960-61; reporter Houston Chronicle, 1961-62; news editor Somerset (Pa.) American, 1962-63; night editor Elmira (N.Y.) Star-Gazette, 1963-64; copy editor, investigative reporter Milw. Jour., 1964-70; Tucson corr. Time mag./Time-Life Books, 1970-71; night city editor Tucson Citizen, 1970-71; nat. desk copy editor Los Angeles Times, 1971-90; sr. lectr. U. So. Calif., 1974-88; pres. Nat. Copy Editors Sch., Thousand Oaks, Calif., 1984-90; founder and dir. Australian Sub-Editors Sch., Sydney, Australia, 1989-94. Cpl. USMC, 1951-53. Avocations: horseback riding, hiking. Home: PO Box 35128 Tucson AZ 85740-5128

HALEEM, MOHAMED ABDUL, electrical engineer, researcher; b. Kalmunai, Sri Lanka, Oct. 17, 1963; s. Mohamed Ismail-Lebbe Abdul-Latheef and Kadeeja Ummah; m. Riswana Seeni-Mohamed, Dec. 23, 1991; children: Azamul-Huq Abdul-Haleem, Afra Mizaja Abdul-Haleem. BSEE, U. Peradeniya, 1990; PhD in Elec. Engring., Stevens Inst. Tech., 2005; MPhil in Elec. and Electronic Engring., Hong Kong U. Sci. and Tech., 1996. Asst. lectr. Dept. Elec. and Electronic Engring. U. Peradeniya, Kandy, Sri Lanka, 1990—92, lectr. Dept. Elec. and Electronic Engring., 1992—93; tchg. asst. Hong Kong U. Sci. and Tech., Clear Water Bay, Hong Kong, 1993—94, rsch. asst., 1994—96; cons. Wireless Comm. Rsch. AT&T Rsch., Holmdel, NJ, 1996—97; cons. Wireless Comm. Rsch. Dept., Bell Labs. Lucent Technologies, Inc., Holmdel, 1997—99, mem. of tech. staff Wireless Comm. Rsch. Dept., Bell Labs., 2001—02; rsch. asst. Stevens Inst. Tech., Hoboken, NJ, 2003—. Vis. rsch. scholar Bell Labs., Holmdel, 1996—99. Editor: University of Peradeniya Elec.and Electronic Engring. Students; co-author: Adaptive Resource Assignment in Wireless Communication Network; contbr. articles to profl. jours. Recipient First Pl. Gold medal, Lions Club Sri Lanka, 1978; scholar, Ministry of Edn., Sri Lana, 1983—90. Mem.: IEEE (corr. grantee 1994). Achievements include patents in field. Home: 204 Barnstable Court Freehold NJ 07728 Office: Stevens Institute of Technology 315 Burchards Hoboken NJ 07030 Office Phone: 201-216-8312. Office Fax: 201-216-8246. Personal E-mail: haleem@ieee.org.

HALES, ALFRED WASHINGTON, mathematics professor, consultant; b. Pasadena, Calif., Nov. 30, 1938; s. Raleigh Stanton and Gwendolen (Washington) H.; m. Virginia Dart Greene, July 7, 1962; children— Andrew Stanton, Lisa Ruth, Katherine Washington BS, Calif. Inst. Tech., 1960, PhD, 1962. NSF postdoctoral fellow Cambridge U., Eng., 1962-63; Benjamin Peirce instr. Harvard U., 1963-66; faculty mem. UCLA, 1966-92, prof. math., 1973-92, prof. emeritus, 1992—; dir. IDA Ctr. Comm. Rsch., 1992—2003. Cons. Jet Propulsion Lab., La Canada, Calif., 1966-70, Inst. for Def. Analyses, Princeton, N.J. and LaJolla, Calif., 1964-65, 76, 79-92; vis. lectr. U. Wash., Seattle, 1970-71; vis. mem. U. Warwick Math. Inst., Coventry, Eng., 1977-78, Math. Sci. Rsch. Inst., Berkeley, 1986-87. Co-author: Shift Register Sequences, 1967, 82; contbr. articles to profl. jours. Bd. trustees Math. Sci. Rsch. Inst., Berkeley, 1995—99. Mem. Am. Math. Soc., Math. Assn. Am., Soc. Indsl. and Applied Math. (Polya prize in combinatorics 1972), Pasadena Badminton Club, Sigma Xi. Office: Ctr for Comm Rsch 4320 Westerra Ct San Diego CA 92121-1969 Office Phone: 858-622-5423. Business E-Mail: hales@ccrwest.org.

HALES, DANIEL B., lawyer; b. Oak Park, Ill., Sept. 29, 1941; s. Burton W. and Marion (Jones) Hales; m. Deborah J. Dorr, June 4, 1966 (dec. Nov. 2002); children: Daniel R. J., Marion P., George B. BA in Econs., U. Mich., 1963; JD, Northwestern U., 1966. Bar: Ill. 1966, U.S. Dist. Ct. (no. dist.) Ill. 1967, U.S. Ct. Appeals (7th cir.) 1968, U.S. Supreme Ct. 1977. Gen. counsel Philadelphia Soc., Chgo. Dir. Chgo. Crime Commn.; pres., dir. Ams. for Effective Law Enforcement, Inc., Chgo.; bd. dirs. Duncan YMCA, Chgo.; chmn. Ill. Lawyers for Reagan and Bush, 1980; gen. counsel New Trier Rep. Orgn.; mem. bd. govs., v.p., treas. United Rep. Fund Ill. Mem.: Chgo. Bar Assn. (mem. trust law com. 1975—), Commonwealth Club, Law Club, Federalist Soc. (advisor). Office: 711 Oak St # 102 Winnetka IL 60093 Office Phone: 847-446-6474.

HALES, RALEIGH STANTON, JR., mathematics professor, academic administrator; b. Pasadena, Calif., Mar. 16, 1942; s. Raleigh Stanton and Gwendolen (Washington) Hales; m. Diane Cecilia Moore, July 8, 1967; children: Karen Gwen, Christopher Stanton. BA, Pomona Coll., 1964; MA, Harvard U., 1965, PhD, 1970. Tchg. fellow Harvard U., Cambridge, Mass., 1965—67; instr. math. Pomona Coll., Claremont, Calif., 1967—70, asst. prof., 1970—74, assoc. prof., 1974—85, prof., 1985—90, assoc. dean. coll., 1973—90; pres. Claremont Computations, 1983—90; prof. math. scis., v.p. acad. affairs Coll. Wooster, Ohio, 1990, pres., 1995—. Cons. Calif. Divsn. Savs. and Loan, 1968—70, Econs. Rsch. Assocs., L.A., 1969, Devel. Econs., L.A., 1971, Fed. Home Loan Bank Bd., Washington, 1971—72. Author: computer software; contbr. articles to profl. jours.; patentee calculator. Trustee Polytech. Sch., Pasadena, Calif., 1973—79, Foothill Country Day Sch., Claremont, 1985—90, chmn., 1989—90; coun. Internat. Badminton Fedn., 1989—99; bd. dirs. U.S. Badminton Assn., 1967—73, 1978—89, pres., 1985—88; mem. exec. bd. U.S. Olympic Com., 1989—90. Named Wig Disting. prof., Pomona Coll., 1971. Mem.: Wooster Country Club, Math. Assn. Am., Am. Math. Soc., Univ. Club N.Y., Pasadena Badminton Club (pres. 1978—85). Republican. Episcopalian. Home: 433 E University St Wooster OH 44691-2931 Office: Coll of Wooster 1189 Beall Ave Wooster OH 44691-2393 Office Phone: 330-263-2311. Business E-Mail: shales@wooster.edu.

HALEY, DAVID ALAN, healthcare executive; b. St. Louis, Aug. 29, 1943; s. John David and Helen Ermyl (Richardson) H.; children: Trisha Lynn, Jason Alan, Eric Nathan. BA, So. Ill. U., Edwardsville, 1966; MPH magna cum laude, UCLA, 1971. Adminstrv. asst. Kaiser Found. Hosp., Panorama City, Calif., 1971; assoc. adminstr. Our Lady of Lourdes Hosp., Pasco, Wash., 1971-74, Garfield Hosp., Monterey Park, Calif., 1974-75; assoc. exec. dir. Gen. Hosp., Ft. Walton Beach, Fla., 1976-79; v.p. ops. Our Lady of the Lake Regional Med. Ctr., Baton Rouge, 1979-88; pres. Phoenix Connection, Baton Rouge, 1988-89; CEO Gibson Gen. Hosp., Princeton, Ind., 1989-93; pres., CEO Four States Physicians Assn., Joplin, Mo., 1993-94; exec. dir. MedQuest Health Resources, Inc., 1995-96; pres., CEO The Haley Group, Frankfort, Ill., 1996—2004; CEO St. Anthony's Hospice, Henderson, Ky., 2004—. Mem. Four Rivers Comprehensive Health Planning Agy., Richland, Wash., 1972-74; treas. S.E. Wash. State Hosp. Coun., Pasco, 1973, v.p. 1974; corp. mem. Mid La. Health Systems Agy., Baton Rouge, 1979-82; gubernatorial appointee La. Statewide Health Coord. Coun., Baton Rouge, 1984, Ind. Healthcare Facility Adminstrn. Bd., Indpls., 1991-93; sec.-treas. S.W. Ind. Hosp. Coun., Evansville, 1992-93. Served with USNR, 1967-69. USPHS fellow, 1969-71. Fellow Am. Coll. Healthcare Execs.; mem. Healthcare Fin. Mgmt. Assn., La. Hosp. Assn. (council on planning, 1984-87), Ind. Hosp. Assn. (mem. coun. pub. rels. 1992-93), Vis. Nurse Assn. Southwestern Ind. (bd. dirs. 1992-93), La. Assn. Bus. and Industry (health care council 1987). Lodges: Kiwanis. Republican. Home and Office: The Haley Group 1218 Begonia Ct Evansville IN 47712-4225 Business E-Mail: dhaley@haleygroup.com.

HALEY, GEORGE, Romance languages educator; b. Lorain, Ohio, Oct. 19, 1929; s. George and Mary (Haley). AB, Oberlin Coll., 1948; MA, Brown U., 1951, PhD (Pres.'s fellow), 1956. Prof. U. Chgo., 1968—, chmn. dept. Romance langs., 1970-74. Author: Vicente Espinel and Marcos de Obregón, 1959, The Narrator in Don Quixote, 1965, Diario de un Estudiante de Salamanca, 1977, El Quijote de Cervantes, 1984, Vicente Espinel y Marcos de Obregon: Biografia, Autobiografia y Novela, 1994, En Curso De Lectura, 2005; mem. editl. bd. Modern Philology, 1967-95, Canente, 2004— Guggenheim fellow, 1962-63 Mem. Hispanic Soc. Am., MLA, Phi Beta Kappa. Home: 901 S Plymouth Ct Chicago IL 60605-2059 Office: 1050 E 59th St Chicago IL 60637-1559

HALEY, GEORGE BROCK, JR., retired lawyer; b. Atlanta, Feb. 9, 1926; s. George Brock and Naomi Esther (Alverson) H.; m. Marjorie Elizabeth Griffiths, June 24, 1950; children: Susan Haley Brumfield, Katherine Haley Herman, George Brock III, Victor Pearse. AB, Harvard U., 1948, LLB, 1951. Bar: Ga. 1951, D.C. 1976. Assoc. Kilpatrick & Cody (name changed to Kilpatrick Stockton), Atlanta, 1951-60, ptnr., 1960-93, of counsel, 1994—. Mem. Ga. Gov.'s Jud. Process Rev. Commn., Atlanta, 1988-89; trustee Frances Wood Wilson Found. Staff sgt. AUS, 1944-46, MTO. Mem. ABA, State Bar Ga., Atlanta Bar Assn., Atlanta Lawyers Club, Capital City Club. Methodist. Avocations: boating, travel. Office Phone: 404-815-6370. E-mail: ghaley@kilpatrickstockton.com.

HALEY, GEORGE PATRICK, lawyer; b. Bad Axe, Mich., Sept. 23, 1948; s. Glen Kirk and Bernice (Cooper) H.; m. Theresa L. Thomas, Dec. 24, 1975. BS, U. Mich., 1970; MS, U. Calif., Berkeley, 1971; JD, Harvard U., 1974. Bar: Calif. 1974, U.S. Dist. Ct. (no. dist.) Calif. 1974, U.S. Dist. Ct. (ea. dist.) Calif. 1980. Assoc. Pillsbury Winthrop Shaw Pittman LLP, San Francisco, 1974-81, ptnr., 1982—. Prof. U. Shanghai, Shanghai-San Francisco Sister City Program, 1986-1989. Author numerous articles on uniform comml. code, project fin. Dir. Calif. Shakespeare Festival, Berkeley, 1986-93; dir. Nat. Writing Project, 1996—. Mem. ABA (chmn. com. 1976-93), Am. Coll. Comml. Fin. Lawyers, State Bar Calif. (chmn. fin. instns. com. 1980, comml. code com. 1988). Republican. Methodist. Avocations: tai chi chuan, golf, cooking. Home: 1825 Marin Ave Berkeley CA 94707-2414 Office Phone: 415-983-1272. Business E-Mail: george.haley@pillsburylaw.com.

HALEY, GEORGE THOMAS, marketing educator; b. San Antonio, Tex., Feb. 15, 1952; s. James Bennett and Helen Basila Haley; m. Usha Venkatesan, July 12, 1984. BA, U. Tex., 1972, BBA, 1977, PhD, 1989. Asst. prof. Forham U., N.Y.C., NY, 1989—93; vis. prof. Itesm, Monterrey, Mexico, 1993—94; vis. fellow Nat. U. of Singapore, Singapore, 1994—96; sr. lectr. Queensland U. Tech., Brisbane, Australia, 1996—97; assoc. prof. DePaul U., Chgo., 1997—98; prof. U. New Haven, New Haven, 1998—, dir. Ctr. for Internat. Industry Competitiveness. Author: New Asian Emperors: The Overseas Chinese, Their Strategies and Competitive Advantages, 1998, The Chinese Tao of Business: The Logic of Successful Business Strategy, 2004; contbr. articles various profl. jours.; editor Am. Bus. Rev., mem. editl. bd. Indsl. Mktg. Mgmt., Jour. Bus. and Indsl. Mktg., Internat. Mktg. Rev., Mktg. Intelligence and Planning, Jour. Asia Entrepreneurship and Sustainability. Numerous monetary grants, 1991—93. Mem.: Acad. Internat. Business, Am. Mktg. Assn. Avocations: travel, reading, golf, hiking, swimming. Office: U New Haven Sch of Bus 300 Boston Post Rd West Haven CT 06516 Office Phone: 203-931-6004. Office Fax: 212-208-2468. E-mail: gthaley@sbcglobal.net.

HALEY, JAMES F., JR., lawyer; b. Boston, 1945; BS in chemistry, U. Notre Dame, 1967; MA in chemistry, Brandeis U., 1969, PhD in organic chemistry, 1975; JD magna cum laude, Suffolk U., 1975. Bar: Mass. 1975, NY 1977, U.S. Patent & Trademark Office, US Dist. Ct. So. & Ea. N.Y., US Ct. Appeals 7th & Fed. cir. Ptnr. Fish & Neave, NYC, 1983—2004; ptnr. Fish & Neave IP group & co-head corp. intellectual property practice group Ropes & Gray, N.Y.C., 2005—. Mem. law review Suffolk U., 1973—75. Co-author: (book) From Clones to Claims: European and US Case Law on the Patentability of Biotech. Inventions, 2002. Served to lt. comdr. USN, 1969—71. Named one of Top 10 Patent Lawyers Worldwide, PLC Global Counsel, 2002. Mem.: Fed. Cir. Bar Assn., Internat. Patent and Trademark Assn., NY Intellectual Property Law Assn., Am. Intellectual Property Law Assn. (past chmn., internat. subcom. biotech. com.). Office: Fish & Neave IP Group Ropes & Gray 1251 Ave of the Americas New York NY 10020-1104 Office Phone: 212-596-9034. Office Fax: 212-596-9090. Business E-Mail: james.haley@ropesgray.com.

HALEY, JOHN, risk management consultant; AB in Mathematics, Rutgers U. Global Director of the Benefits Group Watson Wyatt Worldwide, Bethesda, Md., dir., 1992—, pres, CEO, 1999—, chmn., 2002—. Co-author: Fundamentals of Private Pensions. Fellow: Soc. Actuaries. Office: Watson Wyatt 1717 H St W Fl 8 Washington DC 20006-3907*

HALEY, JOHN CHARLES, retired bank executive; b. Akron, Ohio, July 24, 1929; s. Arthur and Katherine (Moore) H.; m. Rheba Hopkins, June 11, 1951; children: Alyson, Susan, John, Thomas. AB, Miami U., Oxford, Ohio, 1950; MS, Columbia Grad. Sch. Bus., 1951; LL.D. (hon.), Pace U., 1984. With Chase Manhattan Bank, N.Y.C., 1953—, asst. treas., 1959-62, asst. v.p., 1962-64, v.p., 1964-70; exec. v.p. Chase Manhattan Corp, 1975-84; dep. chmn. Kissinger Assocs., 1984-85; chmn., chief exec. officer Bus. Internat. Inc., N.Y.C., 1986-87. Group pres. Orion Banking Group, London, 1970-73, dir. Armco Corp., chmn., bd. 1995-96. Trustee Siemens Found.; chmn. emeritus bd. trustees Pace U. Served with AUS, 1951-53. Mem. Beta Theta Pi. Home and Office: 8 Deer Run Path Rutland VT 05701-9654

HALEY, JOHNETTA RANDOLPH, music educator; b. Alton, Ill., Mar. 19; d. John A. and Willye E. (Smith) Randolph; children from previous marriage: Karen, Michael. MusB in Edn., Lincoln U., 1945; MusM, So. Ill. U., 1972. Cert. cons. 1995. Vocal and gen. music tchr. Lincoln H.S., E. St. Louis, Ill., 1945-48; vocal music tchr., choral dir. Turner Sch., Kirkwood, Mo., 1950-55; vocal and gen. music tchr. Nipher Jr. H.S., Kirkwood, 1955-71; prof. music Sch. Fine Arts So. Ill. U., Edwardsville, 1972—, dir. East St. Louis Campus, 1982—. Adjudicator music festivals; area music cons. Ill. Office Edn., 1977-78; program specialist St. Louis Human Devel. Corp., 1968. Interim exec. dir. St. Louis Coun. Black People, summer, 1970; bd. dirs. YWCA, 1975-80, Artist Presentation Soc., St. Louis, 1975, United Negro Coll. Fund, 1976-78; bd. curators Lincoln U., Jefferson City, Mo., 1974-82, pres., 1978-82; chairperson Ill. Com. on Black Concerns in Higher Edn.; mem. Nat. Ministry on Urban Edn. Luth. Ch.-Mo. Synod, 1975-80; bd. dirs. Coun. Luth. Chs. Stillman Coll.; pres. congregation St. Phillips Luth. Ch.; bd. dirs. Girls, Inc.; mem. Ill. Aux. Bd., United Way; v.p. East St. Louis Cmty. Fund, Inc. Recipient Cotillion de Leon award for Outstanding Cmty. Svc., 1977, Disting. Alumnae award Lincoln U., 1977, Disting. Svc. award United Negro Coll. Fund, 1979; SCLC, 1981; recipient Cmty. Svc. award St. Louis Drifters, 1979, Disting. Svc. to Arts award Sigma Gamma Rho, Nat. Negro Musicians award, 1981, Sci. Awareness award, 1984-85, Tri Del Federated award, 1985, Martin Luther King Drum Maj. award, 1985, Bus. and Profl. Women's Club award, 1985-86, Fred L. McDowell award, 1986, Vol. of Yr. award Inroads Inc., 1986, Woman of Achievement in Edn. award Elks, 1987, Woman of Achievement award Suburban Newspaper of Greater St. Louis and Sta. KMOX-Radio, 1988, Love award Greeley Cmty. Ctr., Sammy Davies Jr. award in Edn., 1990, Yes I Can award in Edn., 1990, Merit award Urban League, 1994, Legacy award Nat. Coun. Negro Women, 1995, Diversity award Mo. ARC, 2001; named Disting. Citizen St. Louis Argus Newspaper, 1970, Dutchess of Paducah, 1973; the Johnetta Haley Scholars Acad. minority scholarship named in her honor So. Ill. U. Mem. AAUP, Music Educators Nat. Conf., Nat. Choral Dirs. Assn., Nat. Assn. Negro Musicians, Coll. Music Soc., Coun. Luth. Chs., Ill. Music. Educators, Jack and Jill, Inc., Women of Achievement in Edn., Friends of St. Louis Art Mus., The Links, Inc. (nat. parliamentarian, chair constnl. and by-laws com.), Las Amigas Social Club, Alpha Kappa Alpha (internat. parliamentarian, dir. 17th ctrl. region 1970-74, Golden Soror award 1995, Grad Svcs. award 2001), Mu Phi Epsilon, Pi Kappa Lambda. Lutheran. Home: 1926 Bennington Common Dr Saint Louis MO 63146-2555 Personal E-mail: johnethaley@aol.com.

HALEY, PAUL RICHARD, lawyer, state legislator; b. Boston, June 9, 1953; s. Robert Edward and Mary Louise (Hogan) H.; m. Jacqueline Suzanne Holmes, Oct. 11, 1986. BA in Econs., Harvard U., 1976; JD, Suffolk U., 1986. Bar: Mass., 1986; U.S. Dist. Ct. Mass., 1987; U.S. Supreme Ct., 1993. Asst. dist. atty. Norfolk County, Dedham, Mass., 1986-90; mem. Mass. Ho. of Reps., Boston, 1990—. Overseer South Shore Hosp., Weymouth, Mass. Comdr. USNR, 1977—. Mem. Mass. Bar Assn., Norfolk County Bar Assn., VFW, Elks. Democrat. Roman Catholic. Avocations: flying, athletics. Office: Mass Ho of Reps State House Rm 243 Boston MA 02133

HALEY, PRISCILLA JANE, printmaker; b. Boston, June 22, 1926; d. Arthur Benjamin and Jessamy (Fountain) H.; m. Tadeusz Bilous, May 21, 1961. BA, Oberlin Coll., Ohio, 1948; postgrad., Bklyn. Mus. Sch., 1955. Resident artist Yaddo Found., Saratoga Springs, N.Y., 1957. One-man show Village Art Ctr., N.Y.C., 1960; 3-man show Islip Art Mus., 1975; represented in permanent collection N.Y. Pub. Libr., Nat. Acad. Galleries, Bklyn. Mus., Libr. of Congress, Bowdoin Coll. Art Mus., Oberlin Coll., Addison Gallery art, Wesleyan U. Libr., Portland (Oreg.) Mus. Art, others; portfolio of prints and poems by Maine poets, The Island, 1961. Recipient Medal of Honor Audubon Artists, 1957, 1st prize Bablyon Arts Coun. Juried Exhbn., 1992; Louis Comfort Tiffany Found. grantee, 1959. Mem. Soc. Am. Graphic Artists, York Art Assn. Home: 79 York St York ME 03909

HALEY, RICHARD EDWARD, JR., computer scientist; b. Boston, Nov. 21, 1958; s. Richard Edward, Sr. and Margaret Anne (McLellan) H.; m. Lisa Ann Gillespie, Aug. 13, 1988. Grad. high sch., Plano, Tex. With U. Dallas, Irving, Tex., 1976-84, Dallas Co. Deaf Edn., Tex., 1982-87; dir. transp. Tex. Sch. Deaf, 1987-91; owner Writeswright Word Processing, Dallas, 1986-91; independent game devel., 1987-91; graphics programer Origin Sys., Austin, Tex., 1991-92; network programmer Data Interface, Austin, 1993-94; lan adminstrn. Infinity Group, Albuquerque, N.M., 1994-95; computer tech. Presbyn. Hosp., Albuquerque, 1995—; desktop computer engr. Presbyn. Healthcare, 1995—2002; freelance cons., 2003—. Owner Writch Cons., 2002. Author: (web page) Abraham Gutmann for Senate, 1996, Slugbaby, 1996, Spamless Whitelist Email Filter, 2002; prodr., dir. Roundtable, 1995—96 (Cmty. Impact award, 1995); prodr.: ABQ Pub. Access TV, 1994—, (digital video) HempCar@NM State Fair, 2001—; crew mem. (TV show) Good Health, Good Life, 1995—, Freedom Hour, 1996—. Rep. Green Coun., N.Mex., 1994; vice chmn. Albuquerque Regional Greens, 1994; candidate for Ho. of Reps. from N.Mex. dist. 3, 1997; Green Party candidate for auditor State of N.Mex., 1998; founder Freedom Activist Coalition, 1998; exec. dir. N.Mex. Nat. Orgn. for Reform of Marijuana Laws, 2000—01; founder, primate ZenZion Coptic Orthodox Ch. of Reformed Rastafarianism, 2001. Mem. Delta-9. Avocations: bikes, camping, sailing, hiking. Home and Office: 808 Cagua Dr SE Albuquerque NM 87108-3720 Fax: (505) 268-5710. E-mail: writch@writch.com.

HALEY, ROGER KENDALL, librarian; b. Boston, Oct. 29, 1938; s. John F. and Rose (Walker) Haley; m. Mary Hannon; 1 child, Michael J. AB, Georgetown U., 1960; M.L.S., U. Md., 1976. Reference asst. U.S. Senate Library, Washington, 1964-71, asst. librarian, 1971-73, librarian, 1973-97. Mem. Spl. Librs. Assn. (John Cotton Dana award 1993, Hall of Fame award, 2001). Office: 1243 Independence Ave SE Washington DC 20003-1445

HALEY, ROSLYN TREZEVANT, educational program director; b. Washington, July 23, 1955; d. Morti Trezevant and Sara Roslyn Kebe; m. Darrell D. Haley, July 30, 1988; children: Jessica, Darrell Jr., Donald, Anthony, Krystal. BA in History, S.C. State U., 1976; MPA, Calif. State U., L.A., 1983; EdD, UCLA, 1999. Faculty cert. U. Phoenix, 1996. Admissions evaluator UCLA, 1979-81, counselor Sch. Pub. Health, 1981-83, head counselor dept. theater, 1983-93; dir. student, counseling, and recruitment svcs. UCLA Sch. Theater, Film and TV, 1993—. Adult edn. tchr. L.A. Unified Sch. Dist., 1984-93; lectr. U. Phoenix, Woodland Hills, Calif., 1996—; bd. mem. Palmdale (Calif.) H.S., Visual and Performing Arts Acad., 1999; co-founder, adminstr. Jesus is Lord Christian Ch.; state coord. Calif. March for Jesus, 2005. Author of poetry. March organizer March for Jesus, L.A., 1994, Antelope Valley, 1995-02; adminstr. Command Ctr., Convoy of Hope, Palmdale, 1998; sch. site coun. Palmtree Elem. Sch., Palmdale, 1998-99; recruiter Boy Scouts Am. Western L.A. Coun. Bd., 1998-99; campaign chair Antelope Valley YMCA, 2001; adminstr. Jesus is Lord Christian Ch.; state coord. March of Jesus, Calif. Recipient Outstanding Svc. award March for Jesus, L.A., 1994, Outstanding Svc. award First Missionary Bapt. Ch., Littlerock, Calif., 1997, Outstanding Svc. award Jesus Day, Antelope Valley. Mem. Am. Assn. Ednl. Rsch. Avocations: reading, swimming, horseback riding, bicycling. Home: 37518 Larchwood Dr Palmdale CA 93550-6037 Office: UCLA Sch TFT 405 Hilgard Ave Los Angeles CA 90095-9000 Fax: 310-825-3383. Office Phone: 661-274-0889. Personal E-mail: drrozhaley@yahoo.com. E-mail: rhaley@tft.ucla.edu.

HALEY, ROY W., finance company executive; b. 1947; BS, MIT, 1969. With Arthur Andersen & Co., Houston, 1969-71, 73-88, ptnr., 1980—88; with Ruhmann Mfg. Co., Schulenburg, Tex., 1971-73; pres. Am. Gen. Fin. Inc. (formerly Credithrift Fin. Inc.), 1989-91; also exec. v.p. adminstrn. Am. Gen. Corp., Houston; CEO Am. Gen. Fin. Inc., Evansville, Ind., 1989-91; pres. Am. Gen. Corp., Houston, 1991-93; CEO Wesco Distbn., Pitts., 1994—; chmn., CEO Wesco Internat. Inc., Pitts., 1998—. Chmn. Fed. Res. Bank of Cleve. (Pitts. Branch); dir. United Stationers Inc., Cambrex Corp. Office: Wesco Internat Inc Suite 700 225 W Station Square Dr Pittsburgh PA 15219*

HALEY, SALLY FULTON, artist; b. Bridgeport, Conn., June 29, 1908; d. John Poole and Elizabeth (Akers) H.; m. Michele Russo, June 29, 1935; children: Michael Haley, Gian Donato. BFA, Yale U., 1931. One-woman shows include Marylhurst Coll., 1965, Maryhill Mus. Fine Arts, Washington, 1975, Portland Art Mus., 1960, 75, Woodside Gallery, Seattle, 1971, 76, 79, Gov's. Office, Oreg. State Capitol, 1976, Wentz Gallery, Pacific N.W. Coll. Art, 1984, Fountain Gallery Art, Portland, 1962, 72, 77, 80, 81, 84, 86; exhibited in group shows Stewart Gallery, Boston, 1947, San Francisco Mus. Art, 1949, Walker Art Ctr., Mpls., 1954, Denver Art Mus., 1956, 57, 3d Pacific Coast Biennial Exhbn., 1960, Francis J. Newton's Collection, Bush House, 1964, Seattle Ctr. Art Pavilion, 1976, Womans Bldg., L.A., 1977, Laura Russo Gallery, 1993, 97, Oreg. Group Show, Expn. '86 World's Fair, Vancouver, B.C., Mus. N.W. Art, Conner, Wash., 1998; represented in permanent collections Fred Myer Trust, Wash. State U., State Capitol Bldg., Salem, Portland Art Mus., The Laura Russo Gallery, Portland, Lynn McAllister Gallery, Seattle, Barby Investment Co., AT&T, Kaiser Found., numerous others; retrospective, Marylhurst Coll., 1993, Mus. Northwest Art Ha Conner, Washington, 1998. Named Artist of Yr. Neighbor Newspaper Community, Portland, 1984; recipient Woman of Achievement award YWCA, 1988, Govs. award for the Arts, 1989, Poster award, 1982, Hubbard award Hubbard Mus., Ruidoso Downs, N.Mex., 1990-91.

HALEY, SHIRLEY JEAN, piano educator, photographer; b. Yakima, Wash., Dec. 8, 1932; d. Clayton Emry and Jean Montana (Kimball) Roberts; m. Oliver Louis Kienholz, May 5, 1952 (div. Oct. 1973); children: Clayton Louis Kienholz, Nancy Jean Kienholz, Linda Diane Wilson; m. James William Haley, June 15, 1974. Cert. Nat. Music Tchrs. Assn. Pvt. practice piano tchr., Pullman, Wash., 1946-57, Puyallup, Wash., 1957-71, Burlington, Wash., 1971—. Pvt. practice photographer, Big Lake, Wash. Mem. Skagit Art Assn. (sec. 1994-96, pres. 1996-2000), Tacoma Music Tchrs. Assn. (pres.), Puyallaup Music Tchrs. Assn. (pres.), Mt. Vernon Music Tchrs. Assn. (pres.). Avocations: hiking, mountain climbing, backpacking, botany, writing. E-mail: topshots@valleyint.com.

HALEY, USHA C.V., international business educator; arrived in U.S., 1977; d. Chandrasekara and Nandini Venkatesan; m. George Thomas Haley, June 12, 1984. BA, Elphinstone Coll., Bombay, 1977; MA, U. Ill., 1979; MPhil, NYU, 1987, PhD, 1990. Prof. mgmt. and internat. bus. Inst. Tecnologico y de Estudios Superiores de Monterrey, Mexico, 1993—94, Nat. U. Singapore, 1994—96, Queensland U. Tech., Brisbane, Australia, 1997—98, N.J. Inst. Tech., Newark, 1998—2000, U. Tenn., Knoxville, 2000—03, U. New Haven, West Haven, Conn., 2003—. Rsch. assoc. Australian Nat. U., Canberra, 1998—2000; mem. grad. faculty mgmt. Rutgers U., 1999—2000; vis. prof. internat. bus. Purdue U., Singapore, 1996, Harvard U., Cambridge, Mass., 1999—2000; prin. Haley & Assocs., 1998—; bd. editors Mgmt. Decision, 1996—, Jour. Orgnl. Change Mgmt., 1996—, Jour. Internat. Mgmt., 2002—, Asia Pacific Bus. Review, 2002—, Jour. Bus. Strategy, 2003—, Jour. Leadership and Leaders, 1998; internat. revs. editor Asia Pacific Bus. Review, 2002—; Asia Pacifc regional editor Mgmt. Decision, 1996—, Jour. Orgnl. Change Mgmt., 1996—2003; invited spkr. Successful Women in Business Conference Nat. Assn. Women Bus. Owners, 2004; keynote spkr. Indus Entrepreneurs, Banking in Asia Conf. Trinity Coll. Cambridge U., 2005; mem. internat. adv. bd. Emerald Group Pub., 2004—; mem. adv. bd. Strat. Mgmt. Assn. (ISMA Singapore), 2005—; presenter, cons. in field. Author: New Asian Emperors: The Overseas Chinese, their Strategies and Competitive Advantages, 1998, Strategic Management in the Asia Pacific: Harnessing Regional and Organizational Change for Competitive Advantage, 2000, Multinational Corporations in Political Environments: Ethics, Values and Strategies, 2001, Asian Post-crisis Management: Corporate and Governmental Strategies for Sustainable Competitive Advantage, 2002, The Chinese Tao of Business: The Logic of Successful Business Strategy, 2004; guest editor: Management Decision, 1996, 1997, Jour. Orgnl. Change Mgmt., 1998, author, webmaster: www.asia-pacific.com, 1999—; author, webmaster www.chinestao.com, 2005—; author: behavior simulations; contbr. articles to profl. jours., chapters to books. Recipient Friend of Emerald, Literati Club, 2002, Lifetime achievement award, 2003; grantee, Nat. Ctr. Sci. and Tech., Mexico, 1994, U. Tenn. Dept. Mgmt. and Coll. Bus. Adminstrn., 2001—03; scholar for higher edn., Govt. of India, 1974—77; Charles E. Merriam fellow, U. Ill., 1977—78. Mem.: Acad. Internat. Bus., Inst. Ops. Rsch. and Mgmt. Scis., Strategic Mgmt. Soc., Asia Acad. Mgmt., Acad. Mgmt., Beta Gamma Sigma. Office: U New Haven Sch Bus Dept Internat Bus 300 Boston Post Rd West Haven CT 06516 Office Phone: 212-208-2468. Business E-Mail: uhaley@asia-pacific.com.

HALEY, VINCENT PETER, retired lawyer; b. Phila., Oct. 6, 1931; s. Vincent Paul and Madeline R. (McCrystal) H.; m. Mary Ann Harron, Apr. 14, 1956; children: Paul V., Kevin G., Maureen T., Patricia Ann M., Kathleen A., Brian M., Regina E., Christopher P., Megan A. BS, Villanova U., 1953, JD cum laude, 1959. Bar: Pa. 1960, Fla. 1979. Acct. Arthur Young & Co., CPAs, Phila., 1955-56; assoc. Schnader, Harrison, Segal & Lewis, Phila., 1959-67, ptnr., 1968-99, mem. exec. com., 1985-88, 89-94, sr. counsel, 2000—03; ret. Mem. bd. consultors Law Sch. Villanova U., 1985—95; lectr. in field. Sec. Mercy Health Sys., Bala Cynwyd, Pa., 1969—; mem. Archdiocese of Phila. Bd. Edn., 1973-79, pres., 1977-79; mem., bd. dirs. Police Athletic League of Phila., 1994-2001. With USNR, 1953-55. Mem. Pa. Bar Assn. (chmn. corp., banking and bus. law sect. 1979-81), Phila. Bar Assn., Villanova U. Law Alumni Assn. (pres. 1962-63), Huntingdon Valley Country Club, Roosevelt Racquet Club (Huntingdon Valley, Pa., bd. dirs. 1969-80, 91-94, 97-2000, treas. 1972-80), Order of Coif (chpt. v.p. 1962-63). Home: 305 Madison Rd Huntingdon Valley PA 19006-6713 Office: Schnader Harrison Segal et al 1600 Market St Ste 3600 Philadelphia PA 19103-7287 Personal E-mail: vphaley@verizon.net.

HALFACRE, ROBERT GORDON, ombudsman, landscape architect, horticulturist, educator; b. Newberry, S.C., June 22, 1941; s. Edwin Harvey and Lela (Ruff) H.; m. Carolyn F. Halfacre, Jan. 24, 1963 (div. Jan., 1980); children: Angela, Robert. BS, Clemson U., 1963, MS, 1965; PhD in Horticulture, Va. Poly. Inst., 1968; MLA, N.C. State U., 1973. Registered landscape architect, S.C. Asst. prof. N.C. State U., Raleigh, 1968-71, assoc. prof., 1971-74; assoc. prof. horticulture Clemson (S.C.) U., 1974-79, prof., 1979-90, Alumni disting. prof., 1990—, univ. ombudsman, 1998—. Landscape architect Landscape Archtl. Svcs., Clemson, 1977—; mem. Planning Commn. City of Clemson, 1990-93; pres. faculty senate, Clemson U., 1989-90, bd. visitors, 1992-94, chmn. grievance bd., 1996-98. Author: Carolina Landscape Plants, 1971, Keep 'em Growing, 1972, Fundamentals of Horticulture, 1975, Horticulture, 1979, Plant Science, 1987, Landscape Plants of the Southeast, 5th edit., 1989. Dir. Horticulture Gardens, Clemson U., 1974-77; pres. bd. dirs. Daniel H.S. P.T.A., Clemson, 1985-86; chmn. United Way Campaign, Clemson U., 1996-97. Recipient Silver Seal award Nat. Coun. State Garden Clubs, 1984, Helen S. Hull award, 1979, Sigma Xi Rsch. award, 1968, Outstanding Tchr. award N.C. State U., 1970, Outstanding Faculty award AAUP, 1997. award for Faculty Excellence, Clemson U. Bd. Trustees, 1997. Mem.: U. and Coll. Ombuds Assn. (bd. dirs. 2004—), Am. Soc. Hort. Sci. (Julian C. Miller rsch. award 1968, L.M. Ware Outstanding Tchr. award So. region 1982), Am. Soc. Landscape Archs., Nat. Ombudsman Assn. Republican. Lutheran. Avocations: water-skiing, writing, tennis, travel. Office: Clemson U 101 Clemson House 248 Palmetto Blvd Clemson SC 29631-5107 Fax: 864-656-4373. Office Phone: 864-656-4353. E-mail: ombudsman@clemson.edu.

HALFEN, DAVID, retired publishing executive; b. Newark, July 23, 1924; s. Abraham and Rachael (Sudit) H.; m. Geneviève Alberte Martin, Jan. 15, 1948; children: Daniel William, Alexandre Anthony. BS with high honors, U. Wis., 1948; Diploma in French Civilization with high honors, U. Paris, 1949, PhD with highest honors, 1954. From asst. to chief cost acct. Atlas Constructors, Morocco, 1952-54; from asst. editor to editor-in-chief Hart Pub. Co., N.Y.C., 1954-56, 58-62; fgn. affairs editor Scholastic mag., N.Y.C., 1956-58; from field editor to v.p., gen. mgr. Coll. divsn. Scott, Foresman and Co., Glenview, Ill., 1962-78, v.p., gen. mgr. Lifelong Learning divsn., 1978-87, ret., 1987. Chmn. adv. com. USN Courses at Sea Program, 1987-92; sr. assoc. Middlesex Rsch. Ctr., Bethesda, Md., 1991-93; vol. exec. Internat. Exec. Svc. Corps, Zimbabwe, 1993, cons., 1994-96. Author: La Plume: Revue Symboliste 1889-1899, 1954. With AUS, 1943-46, PTO.

HALFORD, SHARON LEE, academic administrator, advocate, educator; b. Clifton, Colo., July 22, 1946; d. Robert Lee and Florence V. (Kubly) Eighmy; m. Allen A. Dreher, Jan. 29, 1967 (div. Jan. 1979); children: Heidi Ann, Gretchen Christine, Kirsten Beth; m. Donald Gary Halford, May 23, 1986. BS in Edn., U. Colo., 1969; postgrad., U. Denver, 1981-83; M in Criminal Justice, U. Colo., 1987; postgrad., Colo. State U., 2000—. Legal asst. 1st Jud. Dist. Atty., Golden, Colo., 1979-81, legal rschr., 1981-83; victim svcs. dir. 18th Jud. Dist. Atty., Englewood, Colo., 1983-92. Mem. faculty Aurora (Colo.) C.C. Criminal Justice Dept., 1989-95, prof., chair pub. svc. dept., 1995-2001, dir. paralegal studies, 1995-2001, asst. v.p. instrn., 1999-2004, dean academic affairs, 2004-, chair faculty senate, 1997-99, pres. faculty coun., 1997-99; mem. faculty Colo. Faculty Adv. Coun., 1993-99; project coord. Lowry Family Ctr.; cons. Svc. Learning, Colo. Campus Compact, 1997—, faculty devel. trainer, 1999—; lectr. Law Enforcement Tng. Acad., 1994—; cmty. educator Jr. Achievement, 2002--; project cons. WEPIC, U. Pa., 2000--; mem. Oxford (Eng.) 2000 Higher Edn. Law Round Table Contbg. author, editor: Colorado Crime Victims Rights Contitutional Amendment Outreach Manual and Implementation Manual, 1992-93; author: (book) Connecting Colleges, Communities and Careers, 1998. Mem. Domestic Violence Task Force, Douglas County, Colo., 1985-92, Arapahoe County, Colo., 1985-94; trainer Rape Assistance and Awareness Program, Denver, 1985-91, MADD, 1990-92, Colo. Victim Witness Coord. Coalition, 1991; mem. 18th Judicial Dist. Child Advocacy Ctr. Com., 1990-99, Gov.'s Victims' Compensation and Assistance Coord. Com., 1991-95, Colo. Victim Asst. and Law Enforcement Bd., 1991-95, Criminal Justice Educators Task Force, 1992—, chair, 1995-98; mem. Colo. Corrections Consortium, 1992—, officer faculty senate, 1995-99; mem. Colo. Crime Victim Rights Constl. Amendment Com., 1990-99; com. chair Colo. PACT Project, 1993-95; mem. Colo. C.C. Diversity Com., 1997—. Fellow Nat. Orgn. for Victim Assistance, Nat. Victim Ctr.; mem. AAUW, LWV, ACLU, Anti-Defamation League, Colo. Orgn. for Victim Assistance (pres. 1992-95), Colo. Bar Assn. (co-chair paralegal com. 1999—), S.W. Criminal Justice Educators Assn., Acad. Criminal Justice Scis. (com. chair 1999—), Am. Assn. Paralegal Educators, Nat. Fedn. Paralegal Assns., Rocky Mountain Paralegal Assn., Nat. Criminal Justice Assn., So. Poverty Law Ctr., People-to-People Amb. Program, Am. Assn. Higher Edn., Am. Assn. Cmty. Colls.Am. Assn. Women in Cmty. Colls. Democrat. Methodist. Office: Phoenix Coll 1202 W Thomas Rd Phoenix AZ 85013 Office Phone: 602-285-7434. Personal E-mail: dshalford@aol.com. Business E-Mail: sharon.halford@pcmail.maricopa.edu.

HALFVARSON, LUCILLE ROBERTSON, music educator; b. Petersburg, Ill., May 17, 1919; d. Harris Morton and Lucille (Fox) Robertson; m. Sten Gustaf Halfvarson, Aug. 8, 1946; children: Laura, Eric, Linnea, Mary. BA, Knox Coll., 1941; MusM, Am. Conservatory, 1969; DHL (hon.), Aurora U., 2000. Cert. tchr. Ill. Tchr. music and speech Freeman Elem. Sch., Aurora, Ill., 1941-44; choral dir. Galesburg (Ill.) Sr. H.S., 1944-46; dir. of music Our Savior Luth. Ch., Aurora, Ill., 1950-63; oratorio soloist, 1952-67; dir. of music Westminster Presbyn. Ch., Aurora, 1963-84; vocal instr. Merit Music Program, Chgo., 1982-93; ret., 1993. Choir dir. 1st Meth. Ch., Galesburg, 1944-46; choral-vocal instr. Waubonsee C.C., Sugar Grove, Ill., 1967-79; organizer Jr. Coll. Music Festival, Waubonsee Coll., Sugar Grove, 1972-73; pvt. vocal instrn., Aurora, 1979—. Conductor Messiah Concert Waubonsee Coll., Paramount Arts Ctr., 1968—, 25th Concert, 1992. Co-chair Citizens Adv. Com. Paramount Arts. Ctr., Aurora, 1977-78; founder United Arts Bd. Fox Valley, pres., 1977-82, Fox Valley Arts Hall of Fame, 2001; chair Paramount Celebration Arts, 1985-86; residency dir. Met. Life Affiliate Artist, Aurora, 1982-83; bd. dirs. YWCA, 1984-91, chair corp. award com., 1994-95; dir. New Eng. Congl. Ch. Bell Choir, 1997-99. Recipient Disting. Svc. award Cosmopolitan Club, Aurora, Ill., 1983; named Woman of Year YWCA, Aurora, 1976, Disting. Alumni Knox Coll., Galesburg, Ill., 1984; Paul Harris fellow Rotary Found. of Rotary Internat., 1999. Mem. AAUW, DAR, PEO, Music Educators Nat. Conf., Am. Choral Dirs. Assn., Aurora C. of C. (Image Maker 1992), Phi Beta Kappa. Avocations: needlecrafts, gardening, fishing, reading.

HALICZER, JAMES SOLOMON, lawyer; b. Ft. Myers, Fla., Oct. 27, 1952; s. Julian and Margaret (Shepard) H.; m. Paula Fleming, Oct. 3, 1987. BA in English Lit., U. So. Fla., 1976, MA in Polit. Sci., 1978; JD, Stetson U., 1981. Bar: Fla. 1982. Assoc. Conrad, Scherer & James, Ft. Lauderdale, Fla., 1982-86, ptnr., 1988-92; assoc. Bernard & Mauro, Ft. Lauderdale, Fla., 1985-86; shareholder Cooney, Haliczer, Mattson, Lane, Blackburn, Pettis & Richards, Ft. Lauderdale, Fla., 1992-96, Haliczer, Pettis & White, P.A., Ft. Lauderdale, Fla., 1996—2002, Haliczer Pettis, P.A., Ft. Lauderdale, Fla., 2002—. Mem. ABA, Fla. Bar Assn., Broward County Bar Assn., Assn. Trial Lawyers Am., Def. Rsch. Inst., Am. Acad. Healthcare Attys., Phi Kappa Phi, Pi Sigma Alpha, Omicron Delta Kappa. Democrat. Methodist. Avocations: reading, jogging. Office: Haliczer Pettis PA 101 NE 3rd Ave Fort Lauderdale FL 33301-1162 Office Phone: 954-523-9922. Business E-Mail: jhaliczer@haliczerpettis.com.

HALILI, ANTONIO MARQUEZ, facilities maintenance mechanic; b. Caloocan City, Philippines, Jan. 9, 1951; s. Pedro Nosa Halili and Verginia Ileto Marquez; m. Brenda gotay Ferrer, Jan. 22, 1992; children: Jocelyn Jemeno, Anthony Bonifacio, Mark Solomon, Sara Virginia, Celina Marie. *Father graduated from Villamor University in 1937, becoming a physician and doctor of surgical chiropody in 1940. As a World War II rank of major, he was one of ten highest medal recipients in the war, which was given to him by President Manuel Roxas, Philippines, in 1946; a master of surgery on homeopathoc science at Chicago Medical Coll. of Heodeopathology; head of medical indigence of Sen. Eva Estrada Kalaw. Manila Councilman Martin B. Isidro and he were responsible for the re-naming of Magat Salamat Elementary School, from its original name and Bankusay Street. Mother's WWII guerillas participation can be seen on page 201 of Time Life Book, Return to the Philippines, by Raphael Steinberg, 1979.* Diploma, Nat. Tech. Sch., L.A., 1983—85; attended, El Camino C.C., Torrance, Calif., 1986—88. Seafarer AB/QM prodn. elect. tech., merchant marine, Long Beach, Calif., 1971—76; seafarer Domain of Neptunes, 1974. Biographer Cry of the Dying Medicine Man. Vice-chair Asian Pacific Islanders Employee Resource Group/Am. Airlines, 2003; participant, Saving Babies Lives March of Dimes, L.A., 2001—02; relief crew chief and leadman Go for Broke Found.; advocate WW II Filipino Vets.; participant Walk America March of Dimes, 2004; participant Nat. WWII Meml., Washington, 2003—04; lifetime charter mem. WWII Vets. Mem.: Nat. Mgmt. Assn., United Tondo Assn. (assoc.; adviser 2004—05), Knights of Columbus. Achievements include invention of a liquid hose clean up attachment. Home: 1318 E 55th St Long Beach CA 90805 Personal E-mail: tbhalili@hotmail.com.

HALIO, JAY LEON, language educator; b. NYC, July 24, 1928; s. Samuel and Anna (Cohen) H.; children: Brian, Amy; m. Diane S. (Isaacs). BA, Syracuse U., 1950; MA, Yale U., 1951, PhD, 1956. Instr. English U. Calif., Davis, 1955—57, asst. prof., 1957—63, assoc. prof., 1963—68, prof., 1968, U. Del., Newark, 1968—2003, dir. ctr. for tchg. effectiveness, 1975—80, assoc. provost for instrn., 1975—81, dir. humanities semester, 1978—81; chmn. bd. editors U. Del. Press, Newark, 1985—97; dir. ctr. for tchg. effectiveness U. Del., Newark, 1986—87. Central exec. com. Folger Inst. Renaissance Studies, 1975-98; adv. bd. Ctr. for Renaissance and Baroque Studies, U. Md., editl. adv. bd. Coll. Lit., Jour. Theatre and Drama, Text; Fulbright Hays sr. lectr., U. Malaya, 1966-67, Buenos Aires, Argentina, 1974, U. Sofia, Bulgaria, 2004. Author: Angus Wilson, 1964, Understanding Shakespeare's Plays in Performance, 1988, Philip Roth Revisited, 1992, Shakespeare in Performance: A Midsummer Night's Dream, 1994, 2d edit. 2003, Romeo and Juliet: A Guide to the Play, 1998, Understanding the Merchant of Venice, 2000, King Lear: A Guide to the Play, 2001, A Midsummer Night's Dream: A Guide to the Play, 2003; editor: Approaches to Macbeth, 1966, Twentieth Century Interpretations of As You Like It, 1968, Volpone, 1968, Macbeth, 1972, King Lear, 1973, ed edit., 2005; (with David Bevington) Shakespeare: Pattern of Excelling Nature, 1978, Brit. Novelists Since 1960: Dictionary of Lit. Biography, vol. 14, 1983; (with Kenneth Muir, D.J. Palmer) Shakespeare, Man of the Theater, 1983; (with Barbara C. Millard) As You Like It: An Annotated Bibliography, 1985, Critical Essays on Angus Wilson, 1985, King Lear, 1992; (with Jerzy Limon) Shakespeare and His Contemporaries, 1992, The Merchant of Venice, 1993, The First Quarto of King Lear, 1994, Shakespeare's Romeo and Juliet: Texts, Contexts and Interpretation, 1995, Critical Essays on King Lear, 1996, (with Ben Siegel) Daughters of Valor: Contemporary Jewish Am. Women Writers, 1997; (with Hugh Richmond) Shakespearean Illuminations, 1998, Henry VIII, 1999, (with Ben Siegel) Am. Literature Dimensions, 1999, Comparative Literature Dimensions, 2000, Turning Up the Flame: Philip Roth's Later Fiction, 2005. Mem. MLA, Am. Lit. Assn., Assn. Lit. Scholars and Critics, Internat. Shakespeare Assn., Shakespeare Assn. Am., Phi Beta Kappa. Home: 8 Country Hill Dr Newark DE 19711-2526 Office: U Del Dept English Newark DE 19716 Personal E-mail: jlhalio@yahoo.com.

HALITSKY, STEVE, data analyst, statistician, researcher; b. Vinnitsa, Ukraine, Aug. 31, 1943; s. Konstantyn and Olga Halitsky; m. Roxanne Bedzyk, July 8, 1975; children: Andrei, Edward. MS in Applied Stats. and Computers, Cybernetics Inst., Kyiv, Ukraine. C++ cert. Brainbench, 2002. Rschr. Cybernetics Inst., Kyiv, 1972—80; sr. scientist Database Rsch. Inst., Kyiv, 1982—91; translator Bible Socs. Printing Ho., Stockholm and Pasadena, Calif., 1990—93; rschr. Isomedix, Inc., Libertyville, Ill., 1997—98; data analyst SPR, Inc., Oak Brook, Ill., 1998—99, WorldCom, Oak Brook, 2000—01; co-founder, CEO Theta Sys., Skokie, Ill., 1999—. Co-founder Theta Sys. Corp.; co-organizer internat. confs. Ukraine's Univs. Open Sys., Applied Math., Economy and Bus. Translator: The Practical Guide to Splines, 1985; contbr. articles to profl. jours. Humanitarian aid organizer Former GULAG Prisoners Fellowship, Kyiv, 1991—98; organizer Studies Anti-Nazi Resistance and Holocaust in Proximity to Hitler's Werewolf HQ, Podolia, Ukraine, 2001—; translator, interpreter Christian Missions, Kyiv, 1988—91; co-founder Ukraine's Bible Soc. Mem.: Internat. Linear Algebra Soc. (ILAS) (assoc.), Soc. Indsl. Applied Math. (SIAM). Republican. Jewish. Achievements include development, formalization and verification of new and highly efficient methods of analysis of multi-dimensional stochastic dynamic systems; established human rights watch for PhysTech Scientists. Avocations: jazz and classical music, herbal properties and remedies, humanitarian aid, history, reading. Business E-Mail: shalitsky@thetasystems.org.

HALIW, ANDREW JEROME, III, lawyer, electrical engineer; b. Ansbach, Fed. Republic of Germany, Aug. 8, 1946; came to U.S., 1950; s. Ilko and Sophie (Kindrat) H.; children: Larissa Andrea, Andrea Stephanie. BEE, Wayne State U., 1968, JD, 1972; postgrad. in Fin., U. Mich., 1993—. Bar: Mich. 1973, Fla. 1998, N.Y. 2002, U.S. Dist. Ct. (ea. dist.) Mich. 1973, U.S. Supreme Ct. 1982, Mich. (6th cir.) 1986, U.S. Dist. Ct. Wis. 1996, U.S. Tax Ct. 1996; Ct. Appeals Washington 2004; lic. profl. engr., Mich., Fla.; registered patent and trademark atty, mediator 1972. Divisional elec. engr. J & L div. LTV, Warren, Mich., 1968-72; ptr. bd. dirs. Sullivan & Leavitt P.C., Northville, Mich., 1972-79, ptnr., 1979-91, also bd. dirs.; ptnr. Haliw, Siciliano & Mychalowych, P.C., Farmington Hills, Mich., 1991—. Bd. dirs. Am. Supplier Inst., Dearborn Mich.; chmn. Advanced Systems and Designs, Inc., Dearborn; vice chmn. ASI Internat.; commr. SMART, Oakland County. Atty. Ukrainian Cultural Ctr., Warren, 1984; del., dist. dir. Farmington Hills Reps., 1990—; chair Zoning Bd. Appeals, Farmington Hills; bd. dirs. Farmington Area Rep. Club; chmn. Govtl. Affairs Farmington Hills. Mem. ABA, Detroit Bar Assn., Oakland County Bar Assn., Detroit Engring. Soc. (dist. bd. dirs.), Farmington C. of C. (exec. com., bd. dirs., chair), Oakland County Rep. Club (exec. com.). Republican. Ukrainian Catholic. Home: 38250 Nine Mile Rd Northville MI 48167-9014 Office: Haliw Siciliano & Mychalowych PC 37000 Grand River Ave Ste 350 Farmington Hills MI 48335-2812 E-mail: ajhaliw@aol.com, hsmfirm@aol.com.

HALIW, JEROME MICHAEL, civil engineer; s. Harry Jerome and Lillian Haliw; m. Kari Lynn Gagnon, May 20, 1989. BS, Colo. Sch. of Mines, 1991. Design engr. Isbill Associates, Inc., Aurora, Colo., 1992—97; project design engr. Raytheon Infrastructure, Inc., Englewood, Colo., 1997—2000; project mgr. Wash. Infrastructure Services, Inc., Littleton, Colo., 2000—02, chief discipline engr., airport design mgr. Denver, 2002—. Mem.: ASME, Am. Soc. Civil Engrs., Colo. Sch. of Mines Alumni Assn., Order of the Engr. Office: Washington Group International Inc 7800 E Union Ave Ste 100 Denver CO 80237 Office Phone: 303-843-2000. E-mail: jerry.haliw@wgint.com.

HALKETT, ALAN NEILSON, lawyer; b. Chungking, China, Oct. 5, 1931; came to U.S., 1940; s. James and Evelyn Alexandrina (Neilson) H.; m. Mary Lou Hickey, July 30, 1955; children: Kent, James, Kate BS, UCLA, 1953, LL.B., 1961. Bar: Calif. 1962. Mem. firm Latham & Watkins, L.A., 1961-95, mem. exec. com., 1968-72, chmn. litigation dept., 1980-86, chmn. succession com., 1986-87. State chmn. Am. Coll., Calif., 1992-94; designee CPR panel Disting. Neutrals, 1994—. Served to lt. USN, 1954-58 Fellow Am. Coll. Trial Lawyers; mem. Calif. Bar Assn., Nat. Arbitration Forum, Def. Orientation Conf. Assn. (sec.-treas. Nat. Def. Fund 2004—), Chancery Club, UCLA Law Alumni Assn. (pres. 1968), Order of Coif, Palos Verdes Country Club (Palos Verdes Estates, Calif.). Republican. Avocations: golf, old cars. Office: Latham & Watkins 633 W 5th St Ste 4000 Los Angeles CA 90071-2005 Personal E-mail: halkett6@aol.com.

HALKIN, HUBERT, mathematics professor, research mathematician; b. Liege, Belgium, June 5, 1936; came to U.S., 1960; s. Leon E. and Denise H.; m. Carolyn Mulliken, June 22, 1964 (div. 1971); children: Christopher, Sherrill-Anne; m. Katherine Hodges, Dec. 24, 1988 (div. 2001); m. Kathy Ziegler, Oct. 10, 2004. Ingenieur, U. Liège, 1960; PhD, Stanford U., 1963. Tech. staff Bell Telephone Labs., Whippany, N.J., 1963-65; assoc. prof. math. dept. U. Calif., San Diego, 1965-69, prof., 1969—, dept. chmn. San Diego, 1981-87; chief scientist Chrometics Co., 2002—. Editor Jour. Optimization Theory and Applications, 1968—, Revue Française d'Automatique de Recherche Operationnelle, 1973—. Guggenheim fellow, 1971-72. Mem.: Idyllwild, Club Aroma, Sierra Club. Office: U Calif San Diego Dept Math La Jolla CA 92093 E-mail: hhalkin@ucsd.edu.

HALL, ADAM STUART, lawyer; b. Atlanta, June 19, 1971; s. Andrew Clifford Hall and Patricia Ann Bursten. BA with honors, U. Fla., 1993, JD with honors, 1996. Bar: Fla. 1997, U.S. Dist. Ct. (so. dist.) Fla. 1997, U.S. Dist. Ct. (mid. dist.) Fla. 1998. Intern Supreme Ct. Fla., Tallahassee, 1995; assoc. Andrew Hall & Assocs., P.A., Miami, Fla., 1997-98, Hall, David and Joseph, P.A., Miami, 1998—. Chmn. unsecured creditor's com. Inre Telephone Co. Ctrl. Fla., Inc., Orlando, 1998-99. Mem. U. Fla. Coll. Law Alumni Coun., Gainesville, 1997—; mem. young leadership coun. United Way of Dade County, Miami, 1997—. Mem. ABA, ATLA, Acad. Fla. Trial Lawyers, Dade County Bar Assn. Avocations: scuba diving, skiing, football. Office: Hall David and Joseph PA 1428 Brickell Ave Penthouse Miami FL 33131

HALL, ADRIENNE A., international marketing communications executive, consultant; b. L.A. d. Arthur E. and Adelina P. Kosches; m. Maurice Hall; children: Adam, Todd, Stefanie, Victoria, Joe Hibbitt; adopted children: Joe Kwan, Carlos Moreno. BA, UCLA. Founding ptnr. Hall & Levine Advt., L.A., 1970-80; vice chmn. bd. Eisaman, Johns & Laws Advt. Inc., L.A., Houston, Chgo., N.Y.C., 1980-94; pres., CEO The Hall Group, Beverly Hills, Calif., 1994—. Co-founder, chair, bd. dirs. Women, Inc.; chair bd. dirs. Women's Pres. Orgn., 1999—, co-chair, State Econ. Network, 2000—; chmn. Eric Bovy Inc., 1986-89, Hall Partnership, Venture Capital; bd. dirs. Calif. Mfrs. Assn., Calif. Life Corp., Inc.; mem. adv. bd. Global Asset Mgmt., The Edison Co., Sempra Energy, The Gas Co.; mem. devel. bd. Life/Balance. Trustee UCLA; bd. regents Loyola-Marymount U., 1990—, Natl. Bus. Counc., Wash. D.C.; mem. The Founders of Music Ctr., Save the Children, Vietnam and Haiti.; mem., chair women's leadership bd. Kennedy Sch. Govt., Harvard U.; commr. L.A. County Arts Commn.; commr. Calif. Gov.'s Commn. on Econ. Devel., task force Rebuild L.A.; chair, adv. bd. Leading Women Entrepreneurs of the World; bd. dirs. United Way, ARC, Exec. Svc. Corps, The Com. of 200, Shelter Partnership; trustee Nat. Health Found., Women's Enterprise Devel. Corp.; gov. Town Hall; mem. adv. coun. Girls' Clubs Am.; mem. adv. bd. Girl Scouts U.S., Asian Pacific Women's Adv. Bd., Coalition of 100 Black Women, Nat. Network of Hispanic Women, Women of Color, Women in Bus., Downtown Women's Ctr. and residence, Leadership Am., Washington, L.A., Food Bank; mem. exec. bd. Greater L.A. Partnership for Homeless, Recipient Nat. Headliner award Women in Comm., 1982, Profl. Achievement award UCLA Alumni, 1979, Award for Cmty. Svc., 1994, Asian Pacific Network Woman Warrior award, 1994, Woman of the Yr. award Am. Advt. Fedn., 1973, Ad Person of West award Mktg. and Media Decisions, 1982, Bus. Woman of Yr. award Boy Scouts Am., 1983, Women Helping Women award Soroptimists Internat., 1984, 1st ann. portfolio award for exec. women, 1985, Communicator of Yr. award Ad Women, 1986, Leader award YWCA, 1986, L.A. Women's Found. Mentor award, 1997, Leading Women Entrepreneurs of World award, 2003; named Bus. Leader of Yr., L.A. Bus. Coun., 1999, NAW Legal Defense/Edn. Fund. award, 2001; named NAWBO Hall of Fame, 2002, Hall of Fame Enterprising Women Mag., NY, 2004. Mem. Internat. Women's Forum (Woman Who Made a Difference award 1987), Am. Assn. Advt. Agys. (bd. dirs. 1980, chmn. bd. govs. western region), Western States Advt. Agys. Assn. (pres. 1975), Hollywood Radio and TV Soc. (dir.), Nat. Advt. Rev. Bd., Overseas Edn. Fund, Com. 200 (western chmn.), Women in Communications, Orgn. Women Execs., Calif. Women's Forum (founder, chmn. The Trusteeship), Rotary (L.A. 5 chpt.), Internat. Bus. Fellows (mem. adv. bd.), Women's Econ. Alliance, Nat. Assn. Women Bus. Owners (adv. bd.), L.A. Area C. of C. (chmn., alumni dir.). Clubs: Calif. Yacht; Stock Exchange, Los Angeles Advt. (pres.) (Los Angeles). Lodges: Rotary. Achievements include having the Kennedy School Leadership Board establish the Adrienne Hall Women's Mentorship Fund in her honor. Personal E-mail: aahall@earthlink.net.

HALL, ALAN CRAIG, library director; b. Marietta, Ohio, Mar. 9, 1954; s. Harry Edward and Flossie June (Heddleston) H.; m. Barbara Ann Metzger, May 23, 1981; 1 child, Shawn Alan. BS in Edn., W.Va. U., 1976; MLS, Case Western U., 1977. With circulation dept. Washington County Pub. Libr., Marietta, Ohio, 1970-75; with govt. documents dept. Freiberger Libr., Cleve., 1976-77; dir. Delphos (Ohio) Pub. Libr., 1977-83, Pub. Libr. of Steubenville and Jefferson County, 1983—. Cons. Morgan County Libr., McConnellsville, Ohio, 1992-93, Barnesville (Ohio) Pub. Libr., 1991, Reed Meml. Libr., Ravenna, Ohio, 1997-98; chair Ohio Libr. Coun., Columbus, 1994, com. rev. bd. structure, 1999, co-chair Ohio statewide resource sharing com., 1998-99; pres. bd. dirs. SOLO Regional Libr. Sys., Ohio, 2002-2003; historic interpreter Ft. Steuben Project, 2000—. Author: Steubenville: Images of America. 2005, Marietta's Innkeeper, 1991, The Mary Thompson Collection, 1997; editor: The Papers of A.T. Nye, 1975, Abandoned Underground Coal Mines of Jefferson County, 1991, Richmond, Ohio Cemetery Book, 1995; compiler Historic Pages Series, 1975-76; editor: Steubenville (Ohio) Bicentennial History Book, 1996-97; contbr. History of Ohio's Public Libraries, 2003; contbr. articles to profl. publs. Chairperson Ohio Humanities Coun., Steubenville, 1991; pres. Ret. Sr. Vol. Program, Steubenville, 1989-90; ruling elder Starkdale Presbyn. Ch., 1985-88, 94-96, 98-2000, chmn. pastor nominating com., 1996-97; mem. Cmty. Found. Jefferson County, 1999-2003, v.p., 2000—; mem. bicentennial com. Two Ridges Presbyn. Ch., 2002; clerk of session Two Ridges Presbyn. Ch., 2003—. Mem. ALA, Nat. Assn. Rd. Passengers, Jefferson County Hist. Soc., Steubenville Lions Club (pres. 1986-87), Ohio Libr. Assn. (pres. 1992-93, Libr. of Yr. 1989), Steubenville Rotary, SAR. Office: 407 S 4th St Steubenville OH 43952-2942 E-mail: alanh@oplin.org.

HALL, ALMON C., III, investment company executive; s. Almon C. and Norma F. Hall; m. Suzanne Hall. Joined Nortek Holdings, 1977, v.p., treas., 1980, formerly v.p., contr., v.p., contr., CFO Providence, 2002—. Office: Nortek Holdings 50 Kennedy Plaza Providence RI 02903

HALL, ANDREW CLIFFORD, lawyer; b. Warsaw, Sept. 16, 1944; arrived in U.S., 1949, naturalized, 1954; s. Edmund and Maria (Hahn) Hall; m. Gail Meyers, 1993; children: Michael Ian, Adam Stuart, Hilary Meyers Azrael, Katie Meyers. BA, U. Fla., 1965, JD with high honors, 1968. Bar: Fla. 1968, U.S. Dist. Ct. (so. dist.) Fla. 1968, U.S. Dist. Ct. (no. dist.) a. 1971, U.S. Ct. Appeals (5th cir.) 1971, Ga. 1973, U.S. Supreme Ct. 1974, U.S. Ct. Appeals (D.C. cir.) 1974, U.S. Ct. Appeals (11th cir.) 1981. Law clk. to judge U.S. Dist. Ct.; assoc. Haas, Holland, Levison, Gilbert, Atlanta, 1970—72, Frates, Floyd, Pearson, Stewart, Miami, 1972—75; ptnr. Storace, Hall & Hauser, Miami, 1975—79, Hall & Hauser, Miami, 1979—82, Hall, David and Joseph, P.A., 1982—. Instr. bus. law U. Fla. Mem. Coun. of 100 Fla. Internat. U.; trustee U. Fla. Coll. of Law Found.; bd. dirs. Greater Miami Jewish Fedn.; chmn. bd. trustees, bd. dirs. Ctrl. Agy. Jewish Edn., Ash Ha Torah. Mem.: ATLA, ABA, Acad. Fla. Trial Lawyers (diplomate), U. Fla. Coll. Law Alumni (mem. coun.), Am. Judicature Soc., Fla. State Bar Assn., Hebrew Immigrant Aid Assn. (nat. bd. dirs.), Order of Coif, Phi Alpha Delta, Phi Kappa Phi. Democrat. Jewish. Home: 3515 Bayshore Villas Dr Miami FL 33133 Office: Hall David and Joseph PA Att/Karen Fernandez 1428 Brickell Ave Ph Miami FL 33131-3411

HALL, ANTHONY ELMITT, agriculturist, physiologist; b. Tickhill, Yorkshire, Eng., May 6, 1940; came to U.S., 1964; s. Elmitt and Mary Lisca (Schofield) H.; m. Bretta Reed, June 20, 1965; children: Kerry, Gina. Student, Harper Adams Agrl. Coll., Eng., 1958-60; student in agrl. engring., Essex Inst. Agrl. Engring., Eng., 1960-61; BS in Irrigation Sci., U. Calif., Davis,

1966, PhD in Plant Physiology, 1970. Farmer Dyon House, Austerfield, Eng., 1955-58; extension officer Ministry of Agr., Tanzania, 1961-63; research asst. U. Calif., Davis, 1964-70, asst. research scientist, 1971; research fellow Carnegie Inst., Stanford, Calif., 1970; prof. U. Calif., Riverside, 1971—, cons. agrl. devel., 1974—, chmn. dept botany and plant scis., 1994-97; prof. emeritus, 2003. Author: Crop Responses to Environment, 2001; editor: Agriculture in Semi-Arid Environments, 1979, Stable Isotopes and Plant Carbon-Water Relations, 1993; contbr. articles to profl. jours. Recipient BIFAD chair's award for scientific excellence, 2000, USDA Sec.'s Honor award plant breeding rsch., 2001. Fellow: Crop Sci. Soc. Am., Am. Soc. Agronomy; mem.: Phi Kappa Phi, Phi Beta Kappa, Gamma Sigma Delta (Disting. Achievement in Agr. award of merit 1999), Alpha Zeta. Achievements include design (with others) of a steady state porometer for measuring stomatal conductance; research on the physiology and breeding of heat and chilling tolerant, pest resistant and drought adapted cowpea cultivars including developing cowpea varieties CB27 and Ein El Gazal; patents in field, no6,501,006 B1, 2002. Office: U Calif Dept Botany & Plant Scis Riverside CA 92521-0124 Mailing: 2922 Lindsay Lane Quincy CA 95971 Office Phone: 951-236-1580. Business E-Mail: anthony.hall@ucr.edu.

HALL, ANTHONY MICHAEL, actor; b. Boston, Apr. 14, 1968; s. Mercedes Hall. Student, Profl. Children's Sch., N.Y.C. Stage prodns. include The Wake, 1978, St. Joan of the Microphone, Segments of a Contemporary Morning; films include Six Pack, 1982, National Lampoons Vacation, 1983, Sixteen Candles, 1984, The Breakfast Club, 1985, Weird Science, 1985, Out of Bounds, 1986, Johnny Be Good, 1988, Edward Scissorhands, 1990, Whatever Happened to Mason Reese, 1990 (voice), A Gnome Named Gnorm, 1992, Into the Sun, 1992, Who Do I Gotta Kill?, 1992, Six Degrees of Separation, 1993, Hail Caesar, 1994, Ripple, 1995, Exit in Red, 1996, The Grave, 1996, Trojan War, 1997, Cold Night Into Dawn, 1997, The Killing Grounds, 1997, 2 Little, 2 Late, 1999, Revenge, 1999, Dirt Merchant, 1999, Happy Accidents, 2000, The Photographer, 2000, The Caveman's Valentine. 2001, Freddy Got Fingered, 2001, All About the Benjamins, 2002, Funny Valentine, 2005; tv movies include The Gold Bug, 1980, Rascals and Robbers: The Secret Adventures of Tom Sawyer and Huck Finn, 1982, Running Out, 1983, Bucket of Blood, 1995, Hijacked: Flight 285, 1996, Pirates of Silicon Valley, 1999, A Touch of Hope, 1999, 61*, 2001, Hysteria: The Def Leppard Story, 2001, Hitched, 2001; tv series include regular cast mem. NBC's Saturday Night Live, 1985-86, The Dead Zone, 2002. Roman Catholic.*

HALL, ARTHUR RAYMOND, JR., retired minister; b. Danville, Ill., Apr. 16, 1922; s. Arthur Raymond and Hetta Ada (Wheeler) H.; m. Lou Ann Benson, Mar. 16, 1946; children: Janet Marie Hall Graff, Laura Ann Hall Scott Abell, Nancy Marion Hall Berens. AB, U. Ill., 1946, MA, 1948; MDiv cum laude, Union Theol. Sem., N.Y.C., 1951; DD, Hanover Coll., 1961. Ordained to ministry Presbyn. Ch., 1951. Staff asst. McKinley Meml. Ch. and Found., Champaign, Ill., 1946-48; student asst. First Presbyn Ch., N.Y.C., 1948-50; pastor First Presbyn. Ch., Monmouth, Ill., 1951-58, Ctrl. Presbyn. Ch., Louisville, 1958-67, Bradley Hills Presbyn. Ch., Bethesda, Md., 1967-89. Pres. bd. Christian edn. United Presbyn. Ch., 1968-73; sec., bd. dirs. Louisville Presbyn. Sem., 1962-70; chmn. renewal and extension of ministry (United Presbyn. Gen. Assembly), 1965-68; mem. joint com. on Presbyn. Reunion, 1969-83; moderator Synod of Piedmont, 1974-75; trustee U.P. Ch., 1974-83; bd. dirs. U.P. Found., 1974-83; del. Uniting Assembly of World Alliance of Ref. Chs., Nairobi, Kenya, 1970; mem. com. on theol. edn. Presbyn. Ch., U.S.A., 1987, assoc. dir. 1988-90. Contbr. articles to periodicals. Pres. Citizens Met. Planning Coun., Louisville, 1962; chmn. Mayor's Adv. Com. for Cmty. Devel., 1963-67; v.p. Louisville YMCA Downtown Bd., 1963; bd. dirs. Louisville Health and Welfare Coun., 1963-67, Greater Washington Coun. Chs., Johnson C. Smith Theol. Sem., Atlanta, 1973-2000, trustee emeritus, 2000—, Interdenominational Theol. Ctr., Atlanta, 1974-99, trustee emeritus; trustee Centre Coll. Ky., 1959-73, Union Theol. Sem., N.Y.C., 1975-84; trustee Travelers Aid Soc., Louisville, 1959-67, v.p., 1961-67. Lt. (j.g.) USNR, 1943-46. Mem. Am. Guild Organists, Washington Interchurch Club, Rotary, Beta Theta Pi, Phi Delta Phi. Democrat. Home: 580 Russell Ave Gaithersburg MD 20877-2868 E-mail: a3a4hallbenson@starpower.net.

HALL, BARBARA, television producer; b. Danville, Va. d. Ervis and Flo Hall; m. Paul Karon; 1 child, Faith. BA summa cum laude in English, James Madison U., 1982. Author: Skeeball and the Secret of the Universe, 1987, Dixie Storms, 1990, Fool's Hill, 1992, House Across the Cove, 1995, A Better Place, 1994, Close to Home, 1997, Summons to New Orleans, 2000; Writer (TV series) include, Family Ties, Newhart, Anything But Love, Northern Exposure, I'll Fly Away, ER, Chicago Hope, New York News, Writer, prodr. Moonlighting, Writer, exec. prodr., developer Judging Amy, 1999—2002, cons. prodr. Northern Exposure, Chicago Hope, Judging Amy, 2002—, Creator, writer, exec. prodr. Joan of Arcadia, 2003—; singer: (band) The Enablers. Recipient Humanitas award, Golden Laurel, Prodrs. Guild of Am., awards, Am. Libr. Assn., award, Children's Def. Fund. Office: CBS/Sony Productions 10202 W Washington Blvd Tracy West Culver City CA 90232

HALL, BEVERLY BARTON, librarian; b. Cin., July 15, 1918; d. Clarence Earl Barton and Maude Ethel Wedmore; m. Randolph Van Lew Hall, Apr. 26, 1947; children: Barton M., Martha H. Kern, Patricia H. Pellerin. BA, Middlebury Coll., 1940; BS, Columbia U., 1941; MS, So. Conn. State Coll., 1975. Cert. tchr./libr. grades K-12, Conn. Libr. Wellesley (Mass.) Coll., 1941-42, Great Neck (N.Y.) Pub. Libr., 1942-44, Yale U. Sch. Law, New Haven, 1944-50, Amity Regional H.S., Woodbridge, Conn., 1967-80. Author: Secret of the Lion's Head, 1995; also short stories. Founder, bd. dirs. Orange (Conn.) Pub. Libr., 1956-63; founder, head libr. St. John's Ch. Libr., Naples, Fla., 1993—; active Collier County Geneal. Soc., Collier County Hist. Soc., Collier County Friends of the Libr. Mem. Ch. and Synagoge Libr. Assn. (sec. 1999-2000). Republican. Episcopalian. Avocations: reading, water aerobics, counted cross-stitch, crocheting, music. Home: Apt 107 49 High Point Circle South Naples FL 34103

HALL, BEVERLY L., school system administrator; b. Montego Bay, Jamaica; m. Luis Hall, Dec. 22, 1973; 1 child, Jason. BA in English, Bklyn. Coll., 1970, MA in Guidance and counseling, 1973; PhD in Adminstrn., Fordham U., 1990. English tchr. Jr. H.S. 265, Bklyn., 1970—76; asst. prin. Satellite West Jr. H.S., Bklyn., 1977—83; prin. Pub. Sch. 282, Bklyn., 1983—87, Jr. H.S. 113, Bklyn., 1987—92; supt. Cmty. Sch. Dist. 27, Queens, NY, 1992—94; dep. schs. chancellor for instrn. N.Y.C. Pub. Schs., 1994—95; supt. Newark City Schs., 1995—99, Atlanta Pub. Schs., 1999—. Office: Atlanta Pub Schs 130 Trinity Ave SW Atlanta GA 30303 Office Phone: 404-802-2820.

HALL, BLAINE HILL, retired librarian; b. Wellsville, Utah, Dec. 12, 1932; s. James Owen and Agnes Effie (Hill) H.; m. Carol Stokes, 1959; children: Suzanne, Cheryl, Derek. BS, Brigham Young U., 1960, MA, 1965, MLS, 1971. Instr. English, Brigham Young U., Provo, Utah, 1963—72, humanities libr., 1972—96. Book reviewer Am. Reference Book Ann., 1984-2000. Author: Collection Assessment Manual, 1985, Saul Bellow Bibliography, 1987, Jerzy Kosinski Bibliography, 1991, Jewish American Fiction Writers Bibliography, 1991, Conversations with Grace Paley, 1997; editor: Utah Libraries, 1972-77 (periodical award ALA 1977); contbr. articles to profl. jours. Bd. dirs. Orem (Utah) Pub. Libr., 1977-84; mem. Orem Media Rev. Commn., 1984-86; chmn. Utah Adv. Commn. on Librs., 1983-91. With U.S. Army, 1953-54, Korea. Mem. ALA (coun. 1988-92), Utah Libr. Assn. (pres. 1980-81, Disting. Svc. award 1989), Mountain Plains Libr. Assn. (bd. dirs. 1978-83, editor newsletter 1978-83, pres. 1994-96, grantee 1979, 80, Disting. Svc. award 1991), Phi Kappa Phi. Mem. Lds Ch. Avocations: writing, photography, carpentry, family history, reading. Home: 230 E 1910 S Orem UT 84058-8161 Personal E-mail: blainehall@comcast.net.

HALL, BRIAN KEITH, biology professor, writer; b. Port Kembla, N.S.W., Australia, Oct. 28, 1941; s. Harry J. and Doris (Garrad) Hall; m. June Denise Priestley, May 21, 1966; children: Derek Andrew, Imogen Elizabeth. BSc, U. New Eng., Australia, 1963, BSc with honors, 1965; PhD, U. New Eng., 1968, DSc, 1978. Teaching fellow U. New Eng., Armidale, 1965-68; asst. prof. biology Dalhousie U., Halifax, N.S., Can., 1968-72, assoc. prof., 1972-75, prof., 1975—, chmn. dept. biology, 1978-85, Killam rsch. prof., 1990-95, faculty sci., Killam prof. biology, 1996-2001, George S. Campbell prof. of biology, 2001—, univ. rsch. prof., 2002—; Killam rsch. fellow, 2003. Vis. prof. U. Guelph, 1975, U. Queensland, Australia, 1981, Southampton U., England, 1982; Rayne mem. vis. prof. U. Western Australia, 1993; mem. adv. com. on life scis. Natural Scis. and Engring. Rsch. Coun. Can., 1985; Turner-Newall lectr. U. Manchester, England, 1985; Frontiers in Biology lectr. Tex. A&M U., 1992; Von Hofsten lectr. Uppsala U., Sweden, 1993; Plenary lectr. Internat. Congress Vert. Morphol., 1994; Fry lectr. Can. Soc. Zoologists, 1994; Sarnat lectr. UCLA, 1994; Miller vis. res. prof. U. Calif., Berkeley, 1997; Landsdowne vis. prof. U. Victoria, 1998; Glaser Disting. vis. prof. Fla. Internat. U., 2000. Author: (book) Developmental and Cellular Skeletal Biology, 1978; author: (with N. MacLean) Cell Commitment and Differentiation, 1987; author: The Neural Crest, 1988, Evolutionary Developmental Biology, 1992, Evolutionary Developmental Biology, 2d edit., 1998, The Neural Crest in Development and Evolution, 1999; editor: Cartilage, 3 vols., 1983; author: Bones and Cartilage, 2005; editor: Bone, A Treatise, 9 vols., 1990—94; editor: (with S. Newman) (book) Cartilage: Molecular Aspects, 1991; editor: (with J Hanken) The Vertebrate Skull, 3 vols., 1993, Homology: The Hierarchical Basis of Comparative Biology, 1994; editor: (with M. H. Wake) The Origin and Evolution of Larval Forms, 1999; editor: (with W. Olson) Keywords and Concepts in Evolutionary Development Biology, 2003; editor: (with W. R. Pearson and G. Muller) Environment, Development and Evolution, 2003; editor: (with B. Hallgrimsson) Variation, 2005. Recipient Young Scientist of Yr. medal, Atlantic Provinces Interuniv. Com. in Scis., 1974, Fry medal, Can. Soc. Zoologists, 1994, Craniofacial Biology Rsch. award, 1996, Alexander Kowalvsky medal, 2001, award of excellence in rsch., Govt. of Can., 2002, Killam prize, Govt. Can., 2005; fellow, Nuffield Found., 1982, Warwick James, London U., 1989, Ctr. Human Biology, U. Western Australia, 1993—; Killam Rsch. fellow, Govt. Can., 2005—. Fellow: Royal Soc. Can.; mem.: Am. Acad. Arts and Sci. (hon. fgn.). Home: 2384 Armcrescent E Halifax NS Canada B3L 3C7 Office Phone: 902-494-3522. Business E-Mail: bkh@dal.ca.

HALL, BYRON CARLYLE, JR., physics educator, philosopher; b. Cin., Oct. 28, 1937; s. Byron C. Sr. and Mary Alice H. BS in Physics with high honors, U. Cin., 1959; MA in Physics, Johns Hopkins U., 1966; postgrad., Boston U. and St. Louis U., 1970-75. Instr. physics Towson (Md.) State Coll., 1966-69; tchr. physics and chemistry Cardinal Gibbons H.S., Balt., 1969-70; tchr. physics John F. Kennedy H.S., Manchester, Mo., 1975-78; chair dept. math. Louisville Collegiate Sch., 1978-80; instr. physics Talladega (Ala.) Coll., 1980-82; instr. electronics ITT Tech. Inst., Dayton, Ohio, 1983-90; instr. physics Sinclair C.C., Dayton, 1991—. Cons. Higher Edn., Inc., Boston, 1971-72. Editor, pub.: (jour.) Constructive Conservative, 1968-70, author To Save Her Dream: A Mission of Duty Friendship and Justice; contbr. articles to profl. jours. State chmn. Young Ams. for Freedom, Md., 1967-69; bd. dirs. Dayton Right to Life, 1991-94; chmn. Elizabeth C. Smith Found., 1997-99, Blandair Found. (formerly Elizabeth C. Smith Found.), 1999—. Mem. Am. Assn. Physics Tchrs. (mem. So. Ohio sect.), Am. Philos. Assn., Phi Beta Kappa. Avocations: bridge, walking, golf, classical music appreciation.

HALL, CARL WILLIAM, agricultural and mechanical engineer; b. Tiffin, Ohio, Nov. 16, 1924; s. Lester and Irene H.; m. Mildred Evelyn Wagner, Sept. 5, 1949; 1 dau., Claudia Elizabeth. BS, B. in Agrl. Engring. summa cum laude, Ohio State U., 1948; M.M.E., U. Del., 1950; PhD, Mich. State U., 1952. Registered profl. engr., Mich., Ohio. Instr. U. Del., 1948-50, asst. prof., 1950-51, Mich. State U., 1951-53, assoc. prof., 1953-55, prof., 1955-70, chmn. dept. agrl. engring., 1964-70; dean, dir. research (Coll. Engring.); prof. mech. engring. Wash. State U., Pullman, 1970-82, pres. WSU Rsch. Found., 1973-82; dep. asst. dir. Directorate for Engring. NSF, 1982-90; ret., 1990. With ESCOE, Inc., Washington, 1979; dist. vis. prof. Ohio State U., 1991; rsch. con. U. P.R., 1957, 63; del. to USSR, 1958, 87; cons. U. Nacional de Colombia, 1960; cons. dairy engring., India, 1961, food engring., Taiwan, 1961, Mission to Ecuador, 1966, U. Nigeria, 1967, UNDP/SF Project 80 (higher edn. Latin Am.), 1964-70, world food and nutrition study Nat. Acad. Sci., 1976-77; mem. engring. edn. del. to People's Republic of China, 1978, Indonesia, 1978, 93, 94; co-chmn. NRC-India Nat. Sci. Acad. Workshop, New Delhi, 1979; with ACA, Inc. (cons. engring.), 1956-70, pres., 1962-70; chmn. Nat. Dairy Engring. Conf., 1953-66; mem. postgrad. edn. select com. USN, Monterey, Calif., 1975; rsch. fellow Jap. Soc. promotion Sci., 1991. Author: Drying Farm Crops, 1957, Agricultural Engineering Index 1907-60, 1961-70, 71-80, 81-90, (with others) Drying of Milk and Milk Products, 1966, 71, Agricultural Mechanization for Developing Countries, 1973; co-editor: Agricultural Engineers Handbook, 1960, Processing Equipment for Agricultural Products, 1963, 2d edit., 1979, Spanish edit., 1968, Milk Pasteurization, 1968, Ency. of Food Engineering, 1971, 86, Drying Cereal Grains, 1974, 2d edit., 1991, Dairy Technology and Engineering, 1976, Errors in Experimentation, 1977, Dictionary of Drying, 1979, Drying and Storage of Agricultural Products, 1980, Biomass as an Alternative Fuel, 1981, Dictionary of Energy, 1983, Food and Energy, 1984, Food and Natural Resources, 1988, Biomass Handbook, 1989, (with others) Drying and Storage of Grains, 1992, Literature of Agricultural Engineering, 1992, The Age of Synthesis, 1995, Laws and Models, 1999; editor, emeritus: Drying Technology: Marcel Dekker, Inc.; contbr. yearbooks, encys., handbooks, over 400 articles to profl. jours. Staff sgt. infantry U.S. Army, 1943—46, ETO. Decorated Bronze Star and CIB; recipient Disting. Faculty award Mich. State U., 1963, Centennial Achievement award Ohio State U., 1970, Disting. Alumni award Ohio State U., 2003, Mich. State U., 2004, Massey-Ferguson Edn. medal, 1976, Max Eyth medal, Germany, 1979, Medal du Merite, France, 1979, Silver medal, Paris, 1980, Cyrus Hall McCormick medal, 1984, Disting. Svc. award and medal NSF, 1988, Excellence in Drying award IDS, 1990, Food Engring. award and medal, 1993; named Engr. of Yr. D.C. Coun. of Engrs. and Architects, 1999. Fellow AAAS (life), ASME (life, v.p. rsch. 1993-95), ASAE (life, pres. 1974-75), Am. Inst. Med. and Biol. Engring., NAE, Accreditation Bd. Engring. and Tech., Internat. Commn. Agrl. Engrs. (v.p. 1965-74); mem. Am. Soc. Engring. Edn. (life), Am. Inst. Biol. Scis., Wash. Soc. Profl. Engrs. (nat. dir. 1975-79), Va. Soc. Profl. Engrs. (pres. No. Va. chpt. 1987-88), Engrs. Coun. for Profl. Devel. (exec. com., bd. dirs., sec. 1973-74, chmn. engring. accreditation commn. 1979-80), 99th Inf. Divsn. Assn., Nat. Infantry Assn., VFW, Inst. Food Tech., Inst. Biol. Engring., Nat. Inf. Assn., Philos. Soc. Washington (life), U. Club Wash., Sigma Xi, Tau Beta Pi, Phi Kappa Phi, Gamma Sigma Delta, Phi Lambda Tau. Achievements include rsch. in energy, drying, food engring., properties of materials and biomass. Office: Engring Info Svcs 2454 N Rockingham St Arlington VA 22207-1033 Office Phone: 703-534-8321.

HALL, CAROL ANN, music educator; b. Lamar, Colo., Dec. 22, 1952; d. Raymond Dewey and Hazel Vera Morrow; m. Charlie Merle Hall, Apr. 21, 1979 (dec. Oct. 10, 2001); 1 child, Charlie Walter. AA, Lamar C.C., 1972; BA in Elem. Edn., BA in Music Edn. K-12, Adams State Coll., Alamosa, Colo., 1974. 4th grade tchr. Springfield Elem. Sch., 1974—75, tchr. K-6 music, 1990—; tchr. K-6 music Parkview Elem. Sch., Lamar, 1975—78; tchr. K-12 music Vilas Sch., 1986—88. Piano tchr., Vilas, 1986—88; voice tchr., Pritchett, Vilas and Springfield, Colo.; performer, recorded composed song Goldband records, 2002—03. Music leader, mem. Tri Ch. Trio Springfield Bapt. Chapel. Recipient award, Am. Women of Who's Who, 2002—03. Mem.: Springfield Elem. Tchrs. Assn., Music Educators Nat. Conf. Baptist. Avocations: bowling, composing. Home: 429 Monroe Box 85 Pritchett CO 81064

HALL, CATHY JAYNE WRIGHT, psychology educator; b. Rome, Ga., May 11, 1951; d. Hoke S. and Delcia (Gilmore) Wright; m. Thomas Lee Hall, June 6, 1972; 1 child, Chris. BA, Emory U., 1972; MEd, U. Ga., 1974, EdS, 1977, PhD, 1982. Lic. psychologist. Sch. psychologist Oconee County Schs., Watkinsville, Ga., 1974-80; asst. prof. Ft. Hays State U., Hays, Kans., 1983-87, East Carolina U., Greenville, N.C., 1987-99, prof., 1993—. Contbr. articles to profl. jours. Mem. Am. Psychol. Assn., Southeastern Psychol. Assn., Nat. Assn. Sch. Psychologist, Nat. Acad. Neuropsychology. Office: East Carolina Univ Psychology Dept Greenville NC 27858 Office Phone: 252-328-6498. Business E-Mail: hallc@mail.ecu.edu.

HALL, CHARLES WASHINGTON, lawyer; b. Dallas, June 30, 1930; s. Albert Brown and Eleanor Pauline (Hopkins) H.; m. Mary Louise Watkins, Aug. 3, 1957; children: Kathryn Louise, Allison Ash, Charles Washington III. BA, U. of South, 1951; JD, So. Meth. U., 1954, LLM in Taxation, 1959. Bar: Tex. 1954. Ptnr. Storey, Armstrong & Steger, Dallas, 1954-57; sr. ptnr. Fulbright & Jaworski, Houston, 1957—. Mem. adv. com. on tax litigation Dept. Justice, 1979-80; dir. Friedman Ind., Inc., Tex. Med. Ctr., Inc. Houston; mem. Commr. Internal Revenue Adv. Group, 1990-91; mem. adv. coun. U.S. Claims Ct., 1988—. Pres., trustee Sarah Campbell Blaffer Found., Houston; dir. Goodwill Industry, Houston, 1977-84; trustee Inst. Religion, Houston, 1990-2000, Killson Found., Houston, M.D. Anderson Found., Houston, Allbritton Found., Houston, Allbritton Art Inst., Houston, John S. Dunn Rsch. Found., Houston, Houston Child Guidance Ctr., 1984-86, The Howell Family Found., Houston; trustee, treas. Ctr Am. Intrnat. Law (formerly Southwestern Legal Found.), Dallas; S.W. Rsch. Inst., San Antonio; gov. Houston Forum, 1992-95. Recipient Disting. Alumni award, So. Meth. U., 1989. Fellow Am. Bar Found.; mem. ABA (chmn. sect. taxation 1987-88, ho. dels. 1991-95, nat. conf. lawyers and CPAs chmn. 1988-2000), Houston Bar Assn., Dallas Bar Assn., State Bar Tex. (chmn. sect. taxation 1970-71), Internat. Bar Assn., Am. Coll. Tax Counsel (regent 1982-91), Am. Law Inst., River Oaks Country Club, Coronado (pres. 1982-83), Met. Club (Washington), Old Baldy Club, Saratoga, Wyo., Order of St. Lazarus. Episcopalian. Office: Fulbright & Jaworski LLP 1301 Mckinney St Ste 5100 Houston TX 77010-3031

HALL, CHARLES WORTH LEO, college administrator; b. Louisville, Ky., Dec. 18, 1946; s. Worth Leroy and Gertrude Omega (Greenwell) H.; m. Judelyn Lumbab Montebon, Jan. 26, 1990; children: Evelyn, Nghia, Hanh, Wanda, Charlotte, Shenandoah, Michelle, Annamarie, Andre, Angelyn, Bernadette. AA, Hartnell Coll., 1975; BS, U. So. Miss., 1976; MEd, U. Louisville, 1978; EdS, U. So. Miss., 1982; postgrad., Walden U., 1982—, Vanderbilt U., 1984-86. Cert. tchr., Tenn., Ind., Calif., counselor; LPC, Tex., La., Miss., Tenn. Commd. capt. U.S. Army, 1963, tchr. Montrey, Calif., 1972-73, advanced through grades to maj., 1988, career counselor Jackson, Miss., 1976-77; fin. aid counselor Ind. State U., New Albany, 1978; admissions officer Ind. Vocat. Tech. Coll., Sellersburg, 1979-81, asst. dir. student svcs., 1979-81; profl. devel. coord. U. So. Miss., Hattiesburg, 1981-83, asst. registrar, 1981-83; v.p. student affairs Excel Bus. Coll., Madisonville, Tenn., 1984; military personnel officer Camp Shelby, Miss., 1984-86; tng. adminstr. USDA, New Orleans, 1986-92; dir. Internat. Bus. Coll., Agana, Guam, 1992—. Pres. Personnel Svc. Orgn., Jackson, Miss., 1977-78; dir. Marquis Adv. Bd., Hattiesburg, Miss., 1978-82; chmn. Franklin (Tenn.) Battlefield Restoration, 1983-92; exec. dir. New Horizons Devel. Co., Louisville, 1988—. Author: Professional Development, 1981, Needs Assessment for Professional Development, 1982, Professional Development Procedural Guide, 1982, Professional Development Bibliography, 1982. Dist. commr. Pine Burr Coun., Boy Scouts Am., Hattiesburg, 1968-83. Monterey Bay Coun., Salinas Calif., 1972-73; senator U. So. Miss. Student Govt. Assn., Hattiesburg, 1974-75; pres. U. So. Miss. Young Dems., Hattiesburg, 1975-76; SMF social case worker ARC, Hattiesburg, 1975-76; active Foster Parent Plan. Major USAR, 1963-90, major AGC USAR, 1963—. Decorated Army Commendation medal, Army Achievement medal, Army Reserve Achievement medal, Vietnam Cross Gallantry with bronze palm; recipient Scouters Training award, Commissioner's Key award, Order of Arrow; Walden Inst. Advanced Studies fellow, Acad. Mgmt. fellow Pa. State U. Mem. ASTD, AACD, ASPA, KC. (treas. 4th patriotic degree 1975-76), VFW, (surgeon 1991-92), AASECT, AAGC, Philippine-Am. Guardian Assn., Internat. Scout Assn., Ind. Personnel and Guidance Assn. (pres. 1979-80), Order Battle Flag, Am. Assn. Philippines, Children Internat., Confederate Alliance, Friends Confederate Soc., Mensa, Career Coll. Assn., Nat. Bus. End. Assn., Am. Legion, Vets. Vietnam War, Order Vietnam Republic of Cross of Gallantry, Mil. Order World Wars, Reserve Officers Assn., Adjutant Gen. Regimental Assn., Order So. Cross, Hon. Order Ky. Cols., Hub City Kiwanis Club (bd. dirs. 1982-83), Omicron Delta Kappa, Phi Kappa Phi, Alpha Phi Omega (pres. 1976-77, disting. svc. key), Phi Gamma Mu (v.p. 1975-76), Phi Delta Kappa, Phi Tau Chi, Psi Chi, Delta Tau Kappa, Epsilon Delta Chi. Roman Catholic. Avocations internat. youth work, internat. Boy Scout Movement.

HALL, CHARLOTTE HAUCH, editor; b. Washington, Sept. 30, 1945; d. Charles Christian and Ruthadele Bertha (LaTourrette) H.; m. Robert Lindsay Hall, June 8, 1968; 1 child, Benjamin H. BA, Kalamazoo Co., 1966; MA, U. Chgo., 1967. Reporter, news editor The Ridgewood (N.J.) Newspapers, 1971-74; copy editor, news editor The Record, Hackensack, N.J., 1975-76; asst. mng. editor The Boston Herald Am., 1977-78; dep. met. editor The Washington Star, 1979-80; copy chief, met. editor, Nassau editor Newsday, Melville, NY, 1981—86, Washington news editor, 1986—88, asst. mng. editor for Long Island, 1988-94; mktg. dir. Newsday, Inc., Melville, NY, 1994-96, mng. editor, 1997-99, v.p., mng. editor, 1999—2003, v.p. planning, 2003—04; v.p., editor Orlando Sentinel, Fla., 2004—. Trustee Kalamazoo Coll. Recipient Robert G. McGruder Awards for Diversity Leadership award, Am. Soc. Newspaper Editors, 2003. Mem. Am. Soc. Newspaper Editors (bd. dirs.), Newspaper Assn. Am., Phi Beta Kappa. Office: Orlando Sentinel 633 N Orange Ave Orlando FL 32801-1349*

HALL, CHRISTOPHER S., retail executive; Mem. audit staff Arthur Anderson, LLP; v.p. acctg. Ralph's Grocery Co., 1995—98, sr. v.p. fin., 1998—99; exec. v.p., CFO Golden State Foods Corp., 1999—2000; sr. v.p., chief acctg. Rite Aid Corp., 2000—01, exec. v.p. fin. and acctg., 2001—02, exec. v.p., CFO Camp Hill, Pa., 2002—04, exec. v.p., real estate & planning, 2004—. Office: Rite Aid Corp 30 Hunter Ln Camp Hill PA 17011

HALL, CURTIS E., lawyer; b. 1956; BA, U. Va., 1978; JD, Yale U., 1981. Bar: NY 1981, DC 1984, Mich. 1989. Asst. dist. atty. Manhattan, NYC; asst. US atty. Washington; atty. Miller, Canfield, Paddock & Stone, Kalamazoo, ptnr., 1992—94; gen. counsel Stryker Corp., Kalamazoo, 1994—, v.p., 2004—. Office: Stryker Corp 2725 Fairfield Rd Kalamazoo MI 49002

HALL, CYNTHIA HOLCOMB, federal judge; b. LA, Feb. 19, 1929; d. Harold Romeyn and Mildred Gould (Kuck) Holcomb; m. John Harris Hall, June 6, 1970 (dec. Oct. 1980). AB, Stanford U., 1951, JD, 1954; LLM, NYU, 1960. Bar: Ariz. 1954, Calif. 1956. Law clk. to judge U.S. Ct. Appeals 9th Cir., 1954—55; trial atty. tax divsn. Dept. Justice, 1960—64; atty.-adviser Office Tax Legis. Counsel, Treasury Dept., 1964—66; mem. firm Brawerman & Holcomb, Beverly Hills, Calif., 1966—72; judge U.S. Tax Ct., Washington, 1972—81, U.S. Dist. Ct. for Ctrl. Dist. Calif., L.A., 1981—84; cir. judge U.S. Ct. Appeals (9th cir.), Pasadena, Calif., 1984—, sr. judge, 1997—. Lt. (j.g.) USNR, 1951—53. Office: US Ct Appeals 9th Cir 125 S Grand Ave Pasadena CA 91105-1621

HALL, DAVID, retired sound recording engineer, writer; b. New Rochelle, N.Y., Dec. 16, 1916; s. Fairfax and Eleanor Rayburn (Remy) H.; married, June 8, 1940 (widowed Mar. 24, 1992); children: Marion Hall Hunt, Jonathan, Peter, Susannah. BA, Yale U., 1939; postgrad., Columbia U., 1940-41. Advt. copy writer Columbia Records, Bridgeport, Conn., 1940-42; music program annotator NBC, N.Y.C., 1942-48; classics music dir. Mercury Record Corp., N.Y.C., 1948-56; music editor Stereo Rev., N.Y.C., 1957-62, contbg. editor, 1962-98; pres. Composers Rec., Inc., N.Y.C., 1963-67; curator Rodgers and Hammerstein Archives of Recorded Sound., N.Y. Pub. Libr., N.Y.C., 1967-83, cons., 1983-85. Dir. Music Ctr. Am.-Scandinavian Found., N.Y.C., 1950-57; Fulbright vis. scholar Copenhagen U., 1956-57; free-lance writer, lectr.; classical recordings cons., 1967-98; mem. Commn. for the White House Record Libr., 1979. Author: The Record Book, 1940-48. Trustee Wilton Library Assn., Conn., 1975-79. Decorated knight Order of Lion, Finland Mem. Nat. Acad. Rec. Arts and Scis. (trustee 1965-67), Nat. Music Council (dir. 1968-80), Assn. for Recorded Sound Collections (pres. 1980-82) Democrat. Home: PO Box 257 Castine ME 04421-0257 E-mail: dtdh@pretar.com.

HALL, DAVID, newspaper editor; b. Lebanon, Tenn., Mar. 7, 1943; s. Hal Turner Hall and Mildred (Durham) Hall Carson; m. Suzanne Lovell, Sept. 5, 1964; children: Carson, Matthew, Amanda. BS, U. Tenn., 1965, MA in Econs., 1966; postgrad., Northwestern U., 1995. Fin. news reporter, asst. fin. editor, Middle East corr., chief editorial writer, asst. mng. editor Chgo. Daily News, 1966-78; asst. mng. editor Chgo. Sun-Times, 1978; mng. editor St. Paul Pioneer Press, 1978-82; exec. editor St. Paul Pioneer Press and Dispatch, 1982-84; editor, v.p. The Denver Post, 1984-86, editor, sr. v.p., 1986-88; editor, v.p. The Record, Hackensack, N.J., 1988-92; editor The Plain Dealer, Cleve., 1992-99. Bd. dirs. Coun. on World Affairs. With U.S. Army, 1967-69, Vietnam. Recipient Disting. Alumni award Castle Heights Mil. Acad., Lebanon, 1984. Mem. Am. Soc. Newspaper Editors, Cleve. Com. on Fgn. Rels., Soc. Profl. Journalists, Scarabbean Soc.,Phi Gamma Delta. Presbyterian. Home: 426 Anderson St Greencastle IN 46135-1727

HALL, DAVID, law educator, dean, department chairman; b. Savannah, May 26, 1950; s. Levi and Ethel Hall; m. Marilyn Braithwaite-Hall; children: Sakile, Kiamsha, Rahsaan. BS in Polit. Sci., Kans. State U., 1972; MA in Human Rels., U. Okla., 1975, postgrad., 1975—78, JD, 1978; LLM, Harvard U., 1985, Doctor Juridical Scis., 1988. Bar: Ill. 1978, Mass. 1978, Okla. 1978. Profl. basketball player Spaidero Pallacanestro, Inc., Udine, Italy, 1972—74; grad. asst. human rels. dept. U. Okla., Norman, 1974—75; lawyer Chgo. regional office Fed. Trade Commn., 1978—80; assoc. prof. law Sch. Law U. Okla., Norman, 1983—85; asst. prof. law Sch. Law U. Miss., 1980—83; assoc. dean academic affairs Sch. Law Northeastern U., Boston, 1988—92, prof. law, 1985—, dean Sch. Law, 1993—99, provost, 1999—. Instr. ethnic studies dept. and law ctr. U. Okla., Norman, 1975—79; Robert D. Klien U. lectr. Northeasteern U.; co-chair legal edn. forum Law Sch. Harvard U., Cambridge, Mass., 1984—85, co-coord. Nat. Symposium on the Constitution and Race, 1987; coord. law student outreach program Barron Assessment Ctr., Boston. Contbr. articles to profl. jours. Mem. bd. Mass. Civil Liberties Union, 1987—88, Inst. Affirmative action, Boston, TransAfrica Forum Scholars Adv. Coun., Washington, commn. on equal justice Mass. Legal Assistance Corp., 1995—, Nat. Consumer Law Ctr., 1993—; pres. African Cultural Soc. St. Paul A.M.E. Ch., Cambridge, Mass.; bd. dirs. Gang Peace Inc., 1995—. Named Professor of the Yr., NAACP, Outstanding Dean of Yr., Nat. Assn. Pub. Interset Lawyers, 1997; named to Savannah Athletic Hall of Fame; recipient African Am. 1st Oratory Competition, Black Rose award, Sigma Gamma Rho, Humanitarian award, Nat. Conf. Cmty. and Justice. Fellow: Am. Sociol. Assn.; mem.: ABA (standing com. lawyers' pub. svc. responsibility 1995—), Nat. Black Wholistic Soc. (pres. 1993, mem. bd. 1984—), Black Faculty and Staff Orgn., Nat. Conf. Black Lawyers (pres. Mass. chpt. 1986—), Okla. Bar Assn. (Outstanding Sr. award), Mass. Bar Assn. (mem. bd. minorities in the profession 1995—96), Boston Bar Assn., Assn. Law Sch. (diversity in legal edn. 1995—96), Order of the Coif. Office: Northeastern U Office of Provost 112 Hayden Hall 360 Huntington Ave Boston MA 02115-5005 E-mail: d.hall@nunet.neu.edu.

HALL, DAVID WALTER, botanist, consultant; b. New Orleans, Sept. 6, 1940; s. Walter Knowlton and Lenna Anne (Guthrie) H.; m. Tiia Reet Karell, Nov. 25, 1981; children: Alexander, Elizabeth. BS, Ga. So. U., 1965, MS, 1967; PhD, U. Fla., 1978. Cert. Am. Bd. Forensic Examiners, cert. expert in botany; registered profl. wetland scientist. Rsch. assoc. U. Fla., Gainesville, 1971—73, asst. in botany, 1973—81, dir. plant identification and info. svc., 1981—90; sr. scientist KBN Engrng. and Applied Scis., Inc., Gainesville, 1990—96, Golder Assocs. Inc., Gainesville, 1996—97; pres. David W. Hall Cons., Inc., Gainesville, 1997—. Author: Illustrated Plants of Florida and the Coastal Plain, 1993, (with L.B. McCarty, J.W. Everett, J.R. Murphy and F. Yelverton) Color Atlas of Turfgrass Weeds--Golf Courses, Lawns, Roadside, Recreational Areas, Commercial Sod, 2001; co-author spl. publs. Inst. Food and Agrl. Scis., U. Fla., 1987, 88, 89, 92, dept. civil engrng. U. Fla., 1989; contbr. or co-contbr. chpts. to Aquatic Pest Control Applicator Training Manual, 1991, Turf Weeds and Their Control, 1994, Forensic Taphonomy: The Post-Mortem Fate of Human Remains, 1997; contr. to various profl. jours Bd. dirs., v.p. Fla. Tennis Found., 1992—; tennis coach Ga. So. U., 1966-67; profl. racket stringer, 1963-90; pvt. instr. tennis, 1965-90; umpire various tennis tournaments, 1963-85; dir. profl. tennis tournaments, 1964-85; condr. tennis clinics for area high schs. and coll. programs, leagues, underprivileged children; organizer, mem. City of Gainesville Tennis Adv. Bd.; founder U. Fla. Gator Tennis Boosters, 1968; bd. dirs. tennis program 300 Club, Gainesville, 1975-76, organizer, tennis chmn.; organizer, dir. Fla. intercity adult tennis league; mem. dist. 4 Cmty. Devel. Com., 1994-95; commr. tennis Gainesville Sports Coun., 1989-90. Named one of Outstanding Young Men of Am., 1973; NDEA Title IV fellow U. Fla., 1967-70; Mercer Rsch. fellow Harvard U., 1968; recipient Disting. Svc. award Fla. Assn. County Agrl. Agts., 1990, Nat. Assn. County Agrl. Agts., 1990, Disting. Alumni award dept. biology Ga. So. U., 1991, Svc. award Fla. Dept. Environ. Regulation, 1988, Svc. Leadership award Augusta Coll., 1963; ranked in various coll. and other tennis tournaments, 1960-94; named to U.S.A. Tennis Fla. Hall of Fame. Fellow Am. Coll. Forensic Examiners, Am. Acad. Forensic Scis.; mem. Am. Soc. Plant Taxonomists, Exotic Plant Pest Coun., Assn. S.E. Biologists, Soc. Wetland Scientists, Weed Sci. Soc. Am., So. Weed Sci. Soc., Fla. Acad. Scis., Fla. Native Plant Soc. (Green Palmetto Svc. award 1987), Nat. Assn. Environ. Profls., Fla. Assn. Environ. Profls., North Fla. Bot. Soc., Fla. Weed Sci. Soc. (pres. 1987-88, sec., treas. 1984-86, bd. dirs. 1984-90, Outstanding Weed Scientist 1999), Internat. Assn. for Identification (Fla. divsn.), Internat. Weed Sci. Soc., USTA (mem. exec. bd. 1991-93, mem. dels. assembly 1991-93, mem. pres.'s com. 1989-91, active other coms.), Fla. Tennis Assn. (pres. 1989-91, 1st v.p. 1985-87, chmn. adult tennis coun. 1986-89, mem. exec. bd. 1982-95, USTA del. 1991-93, mem. Fla. Tennis Assn./USTA league appeals com. 1985-86, Man of Yr. 1984), Gainesville Area Tennis Orgn. (pres., bd. dirs. 1994-2000), Swannee River Valley Cmty. Tennis Assn. (v.p. bd. dirs. 2000—). Achievements include definition of discipline of forensic botany. Home and Office: 3666 NW 13th Pl Gainesville FL 32605-4823

HALL, DENNIS GENE, optics educator, physics educator, academic administrator; b. Belleville, Ill., Mar. 7, 1948; s. Eugene and Mildred (Klein) H.; m. Rita Mae Winkelmann, June 12, 1970; children: Katherine, Christine, Gregory. BS in Physics, U. Ill., 1970; MS in Physics, So. Ill. U., 1972; PhD in Physics, U. Tenn., 1976. Asst. prof. physics So. Ill. U., Edwardsville, 1976-78; sr. engr. McDonnell Douglas Corp., St. Louis, 1978-80; asst. prof. Inst. Optics U. Rochester, N.Y., 1980-82, assoc. prof., 1982-87, prof., 1987-2001; William F. May prof. Inst. Optics U. Rochester, N.Y., 1995-2001, assoc. dir., 1992-93, dir., 1993-2000; assoc. provost for rsch. Vanderbilt U., Nashville, 2000—, prof. physics, prof. elec. engring., 2000—. Grad. fellow Oak Ridge (Tenn.) Associated Univs., 1975. Contbr. articles to profl. publs., chpts. to books; patentee in field. Capt. USAFR, 1973-89. Fellow Optical Soc. Am. (bd. dirs. 1991-93), Am. Phys. Soc., Internat. Soc. Optical Engring.; mem. Am. Assn. Physics Tchrs. Avocation: tennis. Office: Vanderbilt U 401 Kirkland Hall Nashville TN 37240 E-mail: dennis.g.hall@vanderbilt.edu.

HALL, DON ALAN, editor, writer, educator; b. Indpls., Aug. 7, 1938; s. Oscar B. and Ruth Ann (Leak) H.; m. Roberta Louise Bash, Apr. 30, 1960; children: Alice Leigh, Nancy Elizabeth. BA, Ind. U., 1960, MA, 1968. News editor Rock Springs (Wyo.) Daily Rocket-Miner, 1960-63; mag. editor, picture editor Waukegan (Ill.) News-Sun, 1964-66; reporter, copy editor Salem (Oreg.) Capital Jour., 1966-70; freelance journalist Victoria, Canada, 1970-74; copy editor, sci. writer, music reviewer Corvallis (Oreg.) Gazette-Times, 1974-78, copy desk chief, 1978-82, news editor, 1983-84, author weekly opinion column, 1985-87; author weekly nature column for Oreg. newspapers, 1976-85; instr. dept. journalism Oreg. State U., 1984-87. Author: On Top Of Oregon, 1975, Bird in the Bush, 1986; editor Mammoth Trumpet, Center for the Study of the First Americans, 1991-2001. Recipient Westinghouse-AAAS sci. writing award, 1977 Home and Office: 620 NW Witham Dr Corvallis OR 97330-6535

HALL, DONALD, poet; b. New Haven, Conn., Sept. 20, 1928; s. Donald Andrew and Lucy (Wells) H.; children: Andrew, Philippa; m. Jane Kenyon, Apr. 17, 1972 (dec. Apr. 22, 1995). BA, Harvard U., 1951; B. Litt. (Henry fellow), Oxford U., 1953; postgrad., Stanford U., 1953-54; LHD (hon.), Plymouth State Coll; DLitt (hon.), Presbyn. Coll., Colby-Sawyer Coll., Daniel Webster Coll., Franklin Pierce Coll., New Eng. Coll., Bates Coll., U. N.H., U. Mich. Creative writing fellow Stanford U., 1953; jr. fellow Soc. Fellows, Harvard U., 1954-57; asst. prof. U. Mich., Ann Arbor, 1957-61, assoc. prof., 1961-66, prof., 1966-77; poetry editor Paris Review, 1953-61; mem. poetry bd. Wesleyan U. Press, 1958-64; cons. Harper & Row, 1964-81. Judge Bollingen Prize for Poetry, 1958, 59, Lamont Poetry Competition, 1967-69, Nat. Book Awards, 1968, 92, Edgar Allen Poe and Copernicus awards Acad. Am. Poets, 1975, Nat. Poetry Series, 1979, 93. Author: (poems) Exiles and Marriages, 1955, The Dark Houses, 1958, A Roof of Tiger Lilies, 1963, The Alligator Bride, 1969, The Yellow Room, 1971, The Town of Hill, 1975, A Blue Wing Tilts at the Edge of the Sea, 1975, Kicking the Leaves, 1978, The Toy Bone, 1979, The Happy Man, 1986, The One Day, 1988, Old and New Poems, 1990, The Museum of Clear Ideas, 1993 (National Book award nominee, 1993) The Old Life, 1996, Without, 1998, The Painted Bed, 2002; (essays) Goatfoot, Milktongue, Twinbird, 1978, To Keep Moving, 1980, The Weather for Poetry, 1982, Fathers Playing Catch with Sons: Essays on Sport, 1985, Seasons at Eagle Pond, 1987, Poetry and Ambition, 1988, Here at Eagle Pond, 1988, Life Work, 1993, Death to the Death of Poetry, 1994, Principal Products of Portugal, 1995, Breakfast Served Any Time All Day, 2003; (juvenile) Andrew the Lion Farmer, 1959, Riddle Rat, 1977, Ox Cart Man, 1979, The Man Who Lived Alone, 1985, The Farm Summer, 1992, 94, Lucy's Christmas, 1994, I Am the Dog, I Am the Cat, 1994, Lucy's Summer, 1995; (short stories) The Ideal Bakery, 1987, When Wellard Met Babe Ruth, 1996, Old Home Day, 1996, Willow Temple, 2003; (play) The Bone Ring, 1987, (memoirs) String Too Short to be Saved, 1961, 79, Remembering Poets, 1978, Their Ancient Glittering Eyes, 1992, (biography) Henry Moore, 1966, Dock Ellis in the Country of Baseball, 1976, (with David Finn) As the Eye Moves, 1970, limericks The Gentleman's Alphabet Book, 1972, Writing Well, 1973, 3d edit., 1979, 4th edit., 1982, 5th edit., 1985, 6th edit., 1988, 7th edit., 1991, The One Day, 1988 (Nat. Book Critics award); editor: Harvard Adv. Anthology, 1950, (with L. Simpson and R. Pack) The New Poets of England and America, 1957, (with R. Pack) New Poets of England and America, Second Selection, 1962, A Poetry Sampler, 1962, Contemporary American Poetry, 1962, 2d edit., 1971, (with W. Taylor) Poetry in English, 1963, 2d edit., 1970, (with S. Spender) A Concise Ency. of English and American Poets and Poetry, 1963, 2d edit., 1970, Faber Book of Modern Verse, 1966, The Modern Stylists, 1968, A Choice of Whitman's Verse, 1968, Man and Boy, 1968; Anthology American Poetry, 1969, Pleasures of Poetry, 1971, (with D. Emblen) A Writer's Reader, 1976, 2d edit., 1979, 3d edit., 1982, 85, 4th and 5th edit., 1988, To Read Literature, 1981, rev., 1992, To Read Poetry, 1982, Oxford Book American Literary Anecdotes, 1981, Claims for Poetry, 1982, To Read Fiction, 1987, Oxford Book of Children's Verse in America, 1985, (with Pat Corrington Wykes) Anecdotes of Modern Art, 1990; (memoir) The Best Day The Worst Day: Life with Jane Kenyon, 2005. Deacon South Danbury Ch. Recipient Lloyd McKim Garrison prize for poetry Harvard, 1951, John Osborne Sergeant prize for Latin translation Harvard, 1951, Newdigate prize for poetry Oxford U., 1952, Lamont Poetry Selection Acad. Am. Poets, 1955, Edna St. Vincent Millay Meml. award Poetry Soc. Am., 1955, Longview Found. award, 1960, Sarah Joseph Hale award, 1983, Lenore Marshall award, 1987, Lenore Marshall The Nation award, 1991, Robert Frost Silver medal Poetry Soc. Am., 1991, New Eng. Booksellers Assn. award, 1993, Ruth Lilly prize, 1994; Guggenheim fellow, 1963, 72. Mem. PEN, Authors Guild, Am. Acad. Arts and Letters.*

HALL, DONALD EDISON, minister, writer; b. Winston-Salem, N.C., May 1, 1954; s. Benjamin and Glenola Robinson Hall; m. Susan Williams Hall, Aug. 23, 1975; children: Deborah Lynette, Felicia Rene. BTh, Apostolic Theol. Bible Coll., Tampa, Fla., 2001—04. Full time min. True Deliverance Ch., Thomasville, NC, 1983—. Author: (book) Christians Beware of the Prosperity Gospel. Home: 1143 Charleston Dr Winston-Salem NC 27107 Office: True Deliverance Ch PO Box 2224 Thomasville NC 27361 Office Phone: 336-475-3042. Home Fax: 336-769-9432. Personal E-mail: truedlvr@aol.com.

HALL, DONALD JOYCE, SR., greeting card company executive; b. Kansas City, Mo., July 9, 1928; s. Joyce Clyde and Elizabeth Ann (Dilday) H.; m. Adele Coryell, Nov. 28, 1953; children: Donald Joyce, Margaret Elizabeth, David Earl. AB, Dartmouth, 1950; LL.D., William Jewell Coll., Denver U., 1977. With Hallmark Cards, Inc., Kansas City, Mo., 1953—, adminstrv. v.p., 1958-66, pres., chief exec. officer, 1966-83, chief exec. officer, 1983-86, chmn. bd. only, 1983—. Dir. United Telecommunications, Inc., Dayton-Hudson Corp., William E. Coutts Co., Ltd.; past dir. Fed. Res. Bank Kansas City, Mut. Benefit Life Ins. Co., Business Men's Assurance Co., Commerce Bank Kansas City, 1st Nat. Bank Lawrence. Pres. Civic Council Greater Kansas City; past chmn. bd. Kansas City Assn. Trusts and Founds.; Bd. dirs. Am. Royal Assn., Friends of Art, Eisenhower Found.; bd. dirs. Kansas City Minority Suppliers Devel. Council, Kans. City Minority Suppliers Devel. Council,Kansas City Symphony; past pres. Pembroke Country Day Sch., Civic Council of Greater Kansas City; trustee, past chmn. exec. com. Midwest Research Inst.; trustee Nelson-Atkins Museum of Art. Served to 1st lt. AUS, 1950-53. Recipient Eisenhower Medallion award, 1973; Parsons Sch. Design award, 1977; 3d Ann. Civic Service award Hebrew Acad. Kansas City, 1976; Chancellor's medal U. Mo., Kansas City, 1977; Disting. Service citation U. Kans., 1980 Mem. Kansas City C. of C. (named Mr. Kansas City 1972, dir.), AIA (hon.) Office: Hallmark Cards Inc Office Chmn Bd 2501 Mcgee St Kansas City MO 64108-2600*

HALL, DONALD JOYCE, JR., consumer products company executive; b. Nov. 6, 1955; m. Jill Hall; 2 children. BA in Econs. and Lit., Claremont Coll.; MBA, U. Kans. With Hallmark Cards, Inc., Kansas City, Mo., 1975—, various pos., including dir. splty. store devel., gen. mgr. Keepsake Ornaments, v.p.-creative, v.p. product devel., 1997—99, exec. v.p. strategy and devel., 1999—2002, pres., CEO, 2002—. Bd. dirs. Greater Kansas City Cmty. Found., Civic Coun. Greater Kansas City; chmn. bd. dirs. Heart of Am. United Way; bd. dirs. Midwest Rsch. Inst.; trustee Sci. City at Union Sta. Office: Hallmark Cards Inc 2501 McGee St Kansas City MO 64108

HALL, DORIS SPOONER, music educator; b. New Orleans, Dec. 27, 1949; d. Henry and Geneva (Battley) Spooner; m. Morris D. Hall, Aug. 4, 1973; 1 child, Amy Evon. B of Music Edn., La. State U., 1971, M of Music Edn., 1972, postgrad., ALA A&M U., 1991. Cert. tchr. Ala., La. Band dir. Shreveport (La.) City Schs., 1972-73; asst. band dir. Ala. A&M U., Normal, 1973-74, asst. prof. music, 1974-79, aux. coord. marching units, 1979-87, prof. music, 1980—. Lectr. music U. Ala., Huntsville, 1980-89, Oakwood Coll., Huntsville, 1980-90; clinician Ala. Sch. System, Birmingham, 1989-92; cons. in field. Active Huntsville Sympjony Orch., 1975-79, 86-92; recitals U. Ala. and Ala. A&M U., 1990-92. Named Outstanding Young Women, 1982; recipient Outstanding Achievers awards, 1983. Mem. AAUP, Nat. Flute Assn., Nat. Woodwinds Assn., Music Educators Nat. Conf., Ala. Edn. Assn., Tau Beta Sigma, ALpha Kappa Alpha. Roman Catholic. Avocations: dance, reading, skating. Home: 12000 Bell Mountain Dr SW Huntsville AL 35803-3406 Office: Ala A&M U PO Box 258 Normal AL 35762-0258

HALL, DOUGLAS LEE, computer science educator; b. San Antonio, Feb. 5, 1947; s. Robert Arthur and Thelma (Stischer). AA in Foreign Lang., San Antonio Coll., 1967; BA in Spanish, U. Tex., 1969; MEd in Bilingual Edn., Pan Am. U., 1977; PhD, N. Tex. State U., 1987. Tchr. Edgewood Ind. Sch. Dist., San Antonio, 1969-73, Brownsville (Tex.) Ind. Sch. Dist., 1973-74, 76-78; precious metals specialist Nu-Metals, Inc., Dallas, 1974; tchr. DPC Am. Sch., Dubai, UAE, 1975-76; tng. dir. ABDick, San Antonio, 1978-79; bilingual tchr. Dallas Ind. Sch. Dist., 1979-82; computer cons. Taylor Mgmt. Systems, Dallas, 1982-83; lectr. in field N.Tex. State U., Denton, 1984-86; grad. advisor St. Mary's U., San Antonio, 1986—2004, chair dept. computer sci., 1990—2003, 2005—, pres. faculty senate, 1992-93. Dir. Deutscher Volkstanzverein, San Antonio, 1987—; asst. dir. San Antonio Folk Dance Fest, 1986—; advisor St. Mary's U. Chpt. Assn. for Computing Machinery, 1989—; CEO Athens Solutions, 2000-2004, Xarism Multi Media, 2000—. Contbr. articles to profl. jours. Docent Inst. Texan Cultures, San Antonio, 1989—; pres. Crown Hill Pk. Homeowners, San Antonio, 1986-89; del. 1st U.S.-Japan Grassroots Summit, 1991. Named Tchr. of Yr., Brownsville Ind. Sch. Dist., 1974, 1977, Outstanding Elem. Tchr., 1974, Disting. Grad. Faculty Mem., U. North Tex., 1991—92, Disting. Computer Sci. Alumnus, 1998; recipient Disting. Alumnus award, San Antonio Coll., 2000, Tex. Folk Dance award, 2002. Mem. NEA, IEEE, ACM, Tex. State Tchrs. Assn., Am. Assn. Artificial Intelligence. Avocations: theology, genealogy, foreign languages. Home: 515 Marquis St San Antonio TX 78216-5217 Office: Saint Mary's U One Camino Santa Maria San Antonio TX 78228-8524

HALL, ELEANOR WILLIAMS, public relations executive; b. Boston, 1923; d. James Murray and Julia Eleanor (Williams) Hall. AB cum laude, Radcliffe Coll., 1945. Exec. sec. Am. Express Co., NYC, 1950—62, adminstrv. asst. corp. mktg., 1963—65, mgr. corp. mktg., 1965—69, mgr. corp. pub. rels., 1969—71; mgr. mktg. svcs. Am. Express Internat. Banking Corp. (now Am. Express Bank Ltd.), NYC, 1971—72, asst. treas. advt. and pub. rels., 1972—76, asst. v.p. advt. and pub. rels., 1976—82; pres. Eleanor Hall Assocs., 1982—90. Mem.: Harvard-Radcliffe Club. Address: 342 102d Ave SE Ste 218 Bellevue WA 98004-6165

HALL, ELLIOTT SAWYER, lawyer; b. Detroit, May 1, 1938; s. Otis and Ethel (Burton) H.; m. Shirley Robinson, Oct. 3, 1976; children by previous marriage— Frederick, Lannis; 1 child by present marriage, Tiffany. B.A. in Polit. Sci., Wayne State U., 1962, J.D., 1965; LL.D., Shaw Coll., 1983. Bar: Mich. 1966. Pvt. practice law, Detroit, 1967-74, 75-83; corp. counsel City of Detroit, 1974; chief asst. pros. atty. Wayne County Prosecutor's Office, Detroit, 1983-85, ptnr. Dykenz, Gossett, 1985-87, 2002—, v.p. dealer develop., Ford Motor Co., 1989-2001, v.p. civic and external affairs, 1993-2001. Bd. dirs. Music Hall, Detroit, 1984—, Orch. Hall, Detroit, 1984—, Family Service of Detroit and Wayne County, 1984—, Ford Motor Co., 1987, NC Mutual Life Insurance Co.; mem. pub. safety and justice com. New Detroit, Inc., 1984—, Emergency Transitional Edn. Bd. DC, Detroit/Wayne County Port Authority, Detroit Symphony Orchestra, Mercy Coll. of Detroit, Nat. Rehabilitation Hosp., Marymount Coll., Shakesphere Theatre, Wolf Trap Found., Georgetown U., Clark Atlanta U., Congressional Black Caucus Found.; industry adv. bd., Kennedy Inst.; v.p. Econ. Club Wash., Federal City Coun.; bd. chmn. Joint Ctr. for Polit. and Econ. Studies, Wash., DC, Mt. Carmel Mercy Hosp., Howard U. Hosp., Wash., DC, Wash. Performing Arts Soc.; founding mem. Com. on Pub. Edn.; co-chmn. DC Com. on Pub. Edn.; trustee Wash. Opera, WETA-FM and WETA-TV, Founder's Soc. of Detroit Inst. of Arts, Com. Found. SE Mich., US Capital Hist. Soc., Wash. DC.; treas. Children's Charities Found.; former pres. NAACP, Detroit Branch. Recipient Human Relations Inst. Civic Achievement award, Am. Jewish Com., Disting. Alumni award, Wayne State U. Law Sch., President's award, Nat. Bar Assn., OBA Achievement award, Wayne State U., 1994 Mem. Detroit Bar Assn. (pres-elect), Wolverine Bar Assn. (pres. 1981-82, President's award), Econ. Club Washington (v.p.). Democrat. Office: Dykema Gossett Ste 3800 400 Renaissance Ctr Detroit MI 48243

HALL, FRIEDA ATLAS, history educator; b. Stuttgart, Germany, Feb. 28, 1948; arrived in U.S., 1950; d. David and Sally Atlas; m. Thomas Scott Hall, Jan. 11, 1971; 1 child, Adele Claire Atlas. BA, Washington U., St. Louis, 1970; BS, Bemidji State U., 1977. Rsch. asst. U. Calif. Med. Ctr., San Francisco, 1973—75; social worker Ah-Gwah-Ching Nursing Home, Walker, Minn., 1975—77; tchr. Grand Rapids Mid. Sch., 1977—99, Grand Rapids High Sch., 1999—. Site coun. Grand Rapids High Sch., 2004—05, mem. scholar com., 1999—2005. Bd. dirs. GLBTA Itasca County, Grand Rapids, 2001—04. Recipient Tchr. Recognition award, Initiative Fund, Duluth, Minn., 1992. Mem.: Edn. Minn., Nat. Coun. Social Studies, Amnesty Internat. Freedom Writers. Democrat. Jewish. Avocations: reading, gardening, movies, exercise, travel. Office: Grand Rapids HS 800 NW Conifer Dr Grand Rapids MN 55744

HALL, GARY, JR., Olympic athlete; b. Cin., Sept. 26, 1974; Recipient Gold medal 100 medly relay, Gold medal 100 free relay, Silver medal 50-meter freestyle and Silver 100-meter freestyle Atlanta Olympics, 1996; Gold medal 50-meter freestyle, Gold medal 100 medley relay, Silver medal 100 freestyle relay and Bronze medal 100-meter freestyle Sydney Olympics, 2000, Gold medal, 50-meter freestyle, Athens Olympics, 2004, Bronze medal, 4x100 relay, Athens Olympics, 2004; set Am. record for 50-meter freestyle. Office: USA Swimming 1 Olympic Plz Colorado Springs CO 80909-5746

HALL, GENE E., education educator; PhD, Syracuse U. Faculty mem., project dir. nat. R&D Ctr. for Tchr. Edn. U. Tex., Austin, Tex.; prof. ednl. leadership U. Fla.; dean Coll. Edn. U. N.C., 1988—93; prof. ednl. leadership U. No. Colo., Colo., 1993—98; dean Coll. Edn. U. Nev., Las Vegas, 1999—2004, prof., 2004—. Bd. mem. WestEd Regional Edn. Lab. Author (with S.M. Hord): Implementing Change: Patterns, Principles and Potholes, 2001; author: (with others) Introduction to the Foundations of American Education, 2005; contbr. articles to profl. jours. Office: Univ Nev Las Vegas 4505 Maryland Pkwy Las Vegas NV 89154 Office Phone: 702-895-3441. Business E-Mail: gehall@univ.nevada.edu.

HALL, GUY CHARLES, lawyer; b. Chgo., Aug. 11, 1958; s. Marvin Lester and Lorraine (Sorensen) H.; m. Anne Elizabeth Pollard, july 31, 1982; children: Ryan Charles, Tyler John, Abbey Lorraine BA, U. Ill., 1980; JD, U. Tulsa, 1983. Bar: Ill. 1983, U.S. Dist. Ct. (cen. dist.) Ill. 1984. Prin. Dobbins, Fraker, Tennant, Joy & Perlstein, Champaign, Ill., 1983—. Atty. Village of Pesotum (Ill.), 1984—, Champaign Pk. Dist. Mem. Ill. State Bar Assn. (law office econs. sect. coun. 1995, health care sect. coun. 1998—, sec. 2003-04, vice chair 2004-05), Champaign County Bar Assn. (v.p. 1993-94, Pro Bono Appreciation award 1986), Ill. Assn. Healthcare Attys., Health Care Compliance Assn., Chi Psi. Avocations: racquetball, softball, weight training. Office: Dobbins Fraker Tennant Joy & Perlstein 215 N Neil St Champaign IL 61820-4012 Office Phone: 217-356-7233. E-mail: ghall@dobbinslaw.com.

HALL, HANSEL CRIMIEL, communications executive; b. Gary, Ind., Mar. 12, 1929; s. Alfred McKenzie and Grace Elizabeth (Crimiel) Hall. BS, Ind. U., 1953; LLB, Blackstone Sch. Law, 1982. Officer IRS, 1959-64; gasoline svc. sta. operator, then realtor Chgo., 1964-69; program specialist HUD, Chgo., 1969-73; dir. equal opportunity St. Paul, 1973-75; dir. fair housing Indpls., from 1975; human resource officer U.S. Fish and Wildlife Svc., Twin Cities, Minn. Cons. in civil rights; pres. bd. dirs. Riverview Towers Cooperative Assn., Inc., 1984-87; pres., CEO Crimiel Comms., Inc., 1988-; pres. West Bank Cmty. Coalition, Inc., 2002-03; CFO, treas. Korean War Vets. Edn. Grant Corp., 1996-2001; del. U.S. parliamentarian to Russia and Czechoslovakia, 1992, to Cuba, 1999; bd. dirs. Nat. Korean War Vets. Assn., 1992. With USAF, 1951-53, Korea. Recipient Amb. for Peace cert. Korean Vets. Assn., 1991, Korean Svc. medal Rep. of Korea, 1991. Mem. Res. Officers Assn., Am. Inst. Parliamentarians, Nat. Assn. Parliamentarians, Minn. State Assn. Parliamentarians (pres. 1997-99), Toastmasters DTM, Ind. U. Alumni Assn., Omega Psi Phi. Personal E-mail: crimielhh@hotmail.com.

HALL, HAROLD ROBERT, retired computer engineer; b. Bakersfield, Calif., Feb. 7, 1935; s. Edward Earl and Ethel Mae (Butner) H.; m. Tenniebee May Hall, Feb. 20, 1965. BS, U. Calif., Berkeley, 1956, MS, 1957, PhD, 1966. Chief engr. wave-filter div. Transonic, Inc., Bakersfield, 1957-60; chief design engr. Circuit Dyne Corp., Pasadena and Laguna Beach, Calif., 1960-61; sr. devel. engr. Robertshaw Controls Co., Anaheim, Calif., 1961-63; research engr. Naval Command, Control and Ocean Surveillance Ctr., rsch. and devel. divsn. Navy Research Lab., San Diego, 1966-95. Webmaster for various not-for-profit orgns. including Calif. State Assn. of Parliamentarians, Friends of Ostomates Worldwide-U.S.A. Treas. Pacific Beach Town Coun., San Diego, 1996-98, Friends of Ostomates Worldwide-U.S.A., Akron, Ohio, 1992-2000. Recipient Thomas Clair McFarland award U. Calif., Berkeley, 1956, NSF fellow, 1957. Mem. IEEE, Phi Beta Kappa. Lic. amateur radio extra class. Home: 8585 Via Mallorca Unit 7 La Jolla CA 92037-2585 E-mail: bobn10ab@ieee.org.

HALL, HENRY KINGSTON, JR., chemistry professor; b. N.Y.C., Dec. 7, 1924; s. Henry Kingston and Agnes (Furrer) H.; m. Alene Winifred Brown, Mar. 9, 1951; children: Joan, Douglas, Lillian. BS, Poly. Inst. Bklyn., 1944; MS, Pa. State U., 1946; PhD, U. Ill., 1949. Sr. research chemist textile fibers dept. E.I. DuPont de Nemours & Co., Inc., Wilmington, Del., 1952-65, group leader central research dept., 1965-69; prof. chemistry U. Ariz., Tucson, 1969-96, chmn. dept., 1970-73, emeritus prof., 1996—. Cons. Eastman Kodak Co., Rochester, Ticona Corp., Summit, N.J.; vis. prof. Imperial Coll., London, 1976, Max Planck Inst. for Polymer Rsch., Mainz, Federal Republic of Germany, Jan.-June, 1988; sr. vis. fellow Japan Soc. for Promotion Sci., summer 1981 Contbr. articles profl. jours. Recipient Japan Award for Disting. Svc. in Advancement of Polymer Sci., Soc. Polymer Sci., 1996. Mem. Am. Chem. Soc. (PMSE divsn. award for industry-univ. coop. 1997, Award for Polymer Chemistry 1996, H.F. Mark award 2000). Achievements include research in mechanisms of organic reactions and synthesis of new high polymers. Office: U Ariz Dept Chem PO Box 210041 Tucson AZ 85721-0041 Office Phone: 520-621-6325. E-mail: hkh@u.arizona.edu.

HALL, HENRY LEE, librarian; b. Bladenboro, N.C., Feb. 4, 1949; s. Harry Lee and Annie Carolyn (Hilburn) H.; m. Elisabeth Elmore Hane, Dec. 28, 1971; children: Andrew Ferguson, Patrick Elmore. BA in History, St. Andrews Coll., Laurinburg, N.C., 1971; M.Librarianship, U. S.C., Columbia, 1974. Tchr. Wallace High Sch., S.C., 1971-72, Trexler Sch., Richlands, N.C., 1972-73; librarian Sandhill Reg. Library Sys., Wadesboro, N.C., 1974-76; library dir. Scotland County Meml. Library, Laurinburg, N.C., 1976-80, Stanly County Pub. Library, Albemarle, N.C., 1980-87; media resources coord. Orangeburg-Calhoun Tech. Coll., Orangeburg, S.C., 1987-88, dean learning resource ctr., 1988-89; media specialist Rafting Creek Elem. Sch., Rembert, S.C., 1989-90, R.H. Fulmer Mid. Sch., West Columbia, S.C., 1990—. Adj. faculty U. SC, Columbia, 2005—. Leader Boy Scouts Am., Columbia, S.C., 1987—. Mem. ALA, AASL, S.C. Libr. Assn., S.C. Assn. Sch. Librs. Democrat. Episcopalian. Home: 206 Hounds Run Ln Lexington SC 29072-8703 Office: RH Fulmer Mid Sch 1614 Walterboro St West Columbia SC 29170-2182 E-mail: hlhall@lex2.org.

HALL, HENRY LYON, JR., lawyer; b. Boston, July 23, 1931; s. Henry Lyon and Edith Page (Blanchard) H.; m. Jean Elizabeth Haring, Sept. 13, 1958; children: Henry Lyon, George B. AB, U. Mass., 1953; JD, George Washington U., 1962. Bar: Va. 1963, Mass. 1963. Assoc. Ropes & Gray, Boston, 1963-73, ptnr., 1973-97, of counsel, 1998—. Lectr., panelist seminars Mem. Mass. Gov.'s Commn. Sch. Dist. Orgn., 1971-73; mem. sch. com. Minuteman Reg. Vocat. Sch. Dist., 1971-83, chmn. 1971-75; mem. permanent audit com. town of Belmont, Mass., 1979—, chmn. 1982-92; chmn. by law rev. com. 1979-83, bylaw rev. com., 1983-91; town moderator, Belmont, 1991—; corporator, trustee Belmont Savs. Bank. Served in U.S. Army, 1953-56. Mem. ABA, Mass. Bar Assn., Mass. Moderators Assn. (bd. dirs. 1995—, 1st v.p. 1997-98, pres. 1998-99), Nat. Assn. Bond Lawyers, Va. State Bar, Boston Bar Assn., Mass. Taxpayers Found., Govt. Fin. Officers Assn., Mass. Charitable Soc., Mass. Mcpl. Assn., Order of Coif, Phi Delta Phi. Home: 22 Randolph St Belmont MA 02478-3540 Office: Ropes & Gray One International Place Boston MA 02110-2624 Office Phone: 617-951-7000. Business E-Mail: hhall@ropesgray.com, henry.hall@ropesgray.com.

HALL, HOUGHTON ALEXANDER, electrical engineer, municipal official; b. Kingston, Jamaica, W.I., Aug. 17, 1936; arrived in U.S., 1985; s. James Alexander and Clarice Viola Hall; m. Grace Yvonne Anglin, Feb. 22, 1964; children: Andrew Geoffery, Christine Elizabeth. BS, U. W.I., Kingston, 1958, diploma in chem. tech., 1959, diploma in mgmt., 1977. Registered profl. engr., Fla.; chartered engr. Great Britain. Elec. engr. Jamaica Pub. Svc. Co., Kingston, 1960—84; dir. R&D Ministry of Sci., Tech. and the Environ., Kingston, 1984—85; elec. engr. electric dept. City of Tallahassee, 1985—90, supr., substation engring. electric dept., 1990—. Fellow Fla. Engring. Soc.; mem. IEEE (sr.), NSPE, Inst. Elec. Engrs., Tallahassee Sci. Soc. (charter pres. 1989-97, pres. 2000—04), Fla. Acad. Scis. (chmn. engring. sect. 1994-97, 2000-2004, pres. 1997-99). Baptist. Avocations: electronics, scientific pursuits. Home: 4335 Sherborne Rd Tallahassee FL 32303-7607 Office: City of Tallahassee 2602 Jackson Bluff Rd Tallahassee FL 32304-4408 Office Phone: 850-891-5038. Business E-Mail: halla@talgov.com.

HALL, HOWARD ERNEST, lawyer; b. Cleve., Oct. 4, 1945; s. Howard Leland and Edna Mae (Geiss) H.; m. Jamie L. Sundheimer, Sept. 21, 1968 (div.); children— Matthew Reed, Jennifer Kathleen, Michael John; m. Michelle M. Forne-Karotka, Oct. 22, 1994; stepchildren: Kyle D. Karotko, Desiree N. Karotko. BS, Bowling Green State U., Ohio, 1967; JD, U. Toledo, 1970. Bar: Ohio 1970; U.S. Dist. Ct. (no. dist.) Ohio 1972; U.S. Dist. Ct. (so. dist.) Ohio 1978. Sole practice, Parma, Ohio, 1970-72; assoc. Thomas E. Ray Law Office, Cardington, Ohio, 1972-74; ptnr. Ray & Hall, Cardington, 1974-80, Howard E. Hall Law Office, Cardington, 1980-84, Hall & Elkin, Cardington, 1985—99; asst. prosecutor Morrow County, Ohio, 1977-82, prosecutor, 1985—99; judge Morrow County Common Pleas Ct., 1999—; solicitor Village of Cardington, 1974-77, 83-85. Trustee Morrow County chpt. ARC, Mt. Gilead, Ohio, 1981—; pres. trustees Morrow County Coun. on Alcohol and Drugs, Inc., Mt. Gilead, 1982— . Mem. ATLA, ABA, Ohio State Bar Assn., Ohio Acad. Trial Lawyers, Morrow County Bar Assn. (pres. 1983-85), Rotary, Masons (master 1984-85). Republican. Methodist. Avocations: jogging, sports. Home: 2807 Township Road 167 Cardington OH 43315-9715 Office: Hall & Elkin Law Office Hall Elkin Law Ofc 126 E Cardington OH 43338 Office Phone: 419-947-4515. E-mail: judgehall@rrohio.com.

HALL, HOWARD HARRY, lawyer; b. Syracuse, N.Y., Jan. 9, 1933; s. Harold Gibner and Mildred E. (Way) H. AB, Syracuse U., 1953, JD, 1959. Bar: N.Y. 1960, U.S. Ct. Appeals (2d cir.) 1960, U.S. Dist. Ct. (we., no., so.dists.) N.Y. 1960, U.S. Supreme Ct. 1963, Calif. 1978, U.S. Ct. Appeals (9th cir.) 1978, U.S. Dist. Ct. (we. dist.) N.Y., U.S. Dist. Ct. (cen. and so. dist.) Calif., 1978. Assoc. Hiscock, Cowie, Bruce, Lee and Mawhinney, Syracuse, N.Y., 1959-61; pvt. practice Syracuse, N.Y., 1961-74, Long Beach, Calif., 1978-82, Paramount, Calif., 1982—. Commr. of edn. Syracuse, N.Y., 1968-72. Capt. USMC, 1953-56. Mem. State Bar of Calif., Calif. Trial Lawyers Assn., Bar Register of Preeminent Lawyers. Office: 15559 Paramount Blvd Paramount CA 90723-4330 Office Phone: 562-634-1625. E-mail: info@howard.hallattorney.com.

HALL, HOWARD PICKERING, engineering and mathematics educator; b. Boston, July 8, 1915; s. George Henry and Elizabeth Isabel (McCallum) H.; m. Ellen Marguerite Ide, June 25, 1945 (dec. 1984); children: Charlotte McCallum, Stephanie Wilson, Lindsey Louise, Gretchen Elizabeth. AB, Harvard U., 1936, MS, 1937, DSc, 1951. Registered structural engr., Ill., 1953. Instr., civil engring. Brown U., Providence, 1937-38; structural analyst Mark Linenthal, Engr., Boston, 1938-39; instr., asst. prof., assoc. prof. civil engring. Northwestern U., Evanston, Ill., 1939-56; design engr, field engr. Porter, Urquart, Skidmore, Owings, Merrill, Casablanca, Fr. Morocco, 1951-53; dean, sch. engring., acad. v.p. Robert Coll., Istanbul, Turkey, 1956-68; dir. of studies, acting headmaster St. Stephen's Sch., Rome, 1968-72; prof. math. Iranzamin Internat., Tehran, Iran, 1973-80; math. tchr. Vienna Internat. Sch., 1980-83, Copenhagen Internat. Sch., 1983-86. Cons. S.J. Buchanan, Bryan, Tex., Eng., 1955. Contbr. articles to profl. jours. Served to Capt. U.S. Army, 1942-46, ETO. Recipient Clemens Herschel award Boston Soc. Civil Engrs., 1954. Mem. Sigma Xi. Home: 7733 SW Scholls Ferry Rd Apt 207 Beaverton OR 97008-6592

HALL, HOWARD TRACY, chemist; b. Ogden, Utah, Oct. 20, 1919; s. Howard and Florence (Tracy) H.; m. Ida Rose Langford, Sept. 24, 1941; children— Sherlene, Howard Tracy Jr., David Richard, Elizabeth, Virginia, Charlotte, Nancy. A.S., Weber Coll., 1939; BS, U. Utah, 1942, MS, 1943, PhD, 1948; D.Sc. (hon.), Brigham Young U., 1971; HHD (hon.), Weber State U., 1987. Registered patent agt. Chemist U.S. Bur. Mines, Salt Lake City, 1942-44, 46; research asso. Gen. Electric Research Lab., Schenectady, 1948-55; dir. research, prof. chemistry Brigham Young U., 1955-67, disting. prof. chemistry, 1967-80, disting. prof. emeritus, 1980—. Chmn. Novatek Indsl. Diamond Mfg. Co., Provo. Contbr. articles to profl. jours.; patentee in field. Served as ensign USNR, 1944-46. Co-recipient Research medal Am. Soc. Tool Mfg. Engrs., 1962; Modern Pioneers Creative Industry award NAM, 1965; Engring. Materials Achievement award Am. Soc. Metals, 1973; Man of Yr. award Abrasive Engring. Soc., 1980; Alfred P. Sloan Found. research fellow, 1959-63 Fellow Am. Inst. Chemists (Chem. Pioneer award 1970), AAAS; mem. Am. Chem. Soc. (Creative Invention award 1972), Am. Phys. Soc. (co-winner Internat. Prize for New Materials 1977), Sigma Xi, Phi Kappa Phi. Achievements include pioneering in synthesizing of diamond. Office: Brigham Young Univ Dept Chemistry Provo UT 84602 Home: 1720 Lambert Ln Provo UT 84604-1852

HALL, JAMES CURTIS, economics and business educator; b. Galax, Va., Feb. 12, 1926; s. Alonzo A. and Clara (Crissman) H.; m. Mary Anne Jones, Mar. 13, 1954; children: Michael Crissman, Suzanne King; m. Barbara P. Stamps, May 10, 1985. Student, U. N.C., 1943-44; AB, Duke, 1947; MS, Va. Poly. Inst. and State U., 1952; EdD, Columbia, 1956. Tchr. Galax H.S., 1947-50; instr. Va. Poly. Inst. and State U., 1951-54, Montclair State Coll., 1955; research asst. Columbia, 1955-56; asst. prof. Va. Poly. Inst. and State U., 1956-57; prof. Auburn U., 1957-62; dean Sch. of Bus., Va. Commonwealth U., 1962-88, Univ. prof., 1988-96, prof. emeritus, 1996—. Cons. to So. sch. systems; nat. lectr. econ. edn.; pres. Investment Enterprises, Inc.; dir. Richmond Investment Properties; chmn. adv. coun., divsn. adult and continuing edn., Bluefield Coll., 1998-99. Author: (with E.M. Robinson) College Business Organization and Management, 1964, (with others) General Business for Everyday Living, 3d edit, 1966, 4th edit., 1972, Business and You, 5th edit, 1979. Trustee Nat. Coun. on Econ. Edn., 1972-85, 93-94, mem. bd. founders, 1994—. Recipient John Robert Gregg award McGraw-Hill Co., 1983. Mem. Va. Council Econ. Edn. (exec. com. 1969—, pres. 1971-88, vice chmn. 1988-92, chmn. policies commn. for bus. and econ. edn. 1971-73), Nat. Bus. Edn. Assn. (pres. 1970-71), So. Bus. Edn. Assn. (pres. 1967), So. Bus. Adminstrn. Assn. (v.p. 1987-88), Adminstrv. Mgmt. Soc. (pres. Richmond chpt. 1969-70), Phi Beta Kappa, Phi Kappa Phi, Beta Gamma Sigma, Beta Alpha Psi, Delta Pi Epsilon. Home: 741 Farnham Dr Richmond VA 23236-4108 *Since I can remember, my desire has been to learn something new or to have some new experience every day that I live. I have tried always to treat every other person just as I would want to be treated under the same circumstance. I ask nothing of any person except that he tell the truth and that he treat every other human being with respect.*

HALL, JAMES EVAN, lawyer; m. Anne Stewart Impink; 2 daughters. B, U. Tenn., 1967. Counsel U.S. Senate Subcommittee on Intergovernmental Rels.; staff U.S. Senator Al Gore, Sr.; pvt. practice Chattanooga; mem. cabinet staff Tenn. Gov. Ned McWherter; dir. Tenn. State Planning Office; chief of staff U.S. Senator Harlan Mathews; mem. Nat. Transp. Safety Bd., Washington, 1993—2001, vice-chmn., 1994, chmn., 1994—2001; mng. ptnr. Hall & Assoc. LLC, 2001—. Mem. aviation inst. adv. bd. George Washington U.; com. on combating terrorism Nat. Acad. Engring. Officer U.S. Army, 1967—73, Vietnam. Decorated Bronze Star.

HALL, JAMES FREDERICK, retired college president; b. Detroit, Dec. 30, 1921; s. Cortez Rogers and Bertha Wilhelmina H.; m. Betty Louise Stark, Sept. 17, 1949; children— Kristine Martha, Jay Charles. Student, U. Mich., 1939-41; BA, Wayne State U., 1947, MEd, 1948; Ed.D., Tchrs. Coll., Columbia U., 1954. Instr. Highland Park Jr. Coll., 1948-49; adminstrv. asst., instr. N.Y.C. Community Coll., 1950-51; dir. student personnel services, dept. head Orange County Community Coll., Middletown, N.Y., 1952-55; dean collegiate tech. div., exec. asst. to pres. Ferris State U., Big Rapids, Mich., 1955—57; founding pres. Dutchess Community Coll., Poughkeepsie, NY, 1957—72; pres. Cape Cod Community Coll., 1972-87; pres. emeritus, 1987. Trustee, Mass. rep., Gov.'s appointment New Eng. Bd. Higher Edn., 1975-87; chmn. Pres.'s Council of Regional Community Colls. in Mass., 1976-78; mem. Mass. Postsecondary Edn. Commn., 1978-85; trustee Middle States Assn. Schs. and Colls., 1966-72; mem. mgmt. team Labor Negotiations for Regional Bd. Community Colls., 1978; bd. incorporators Bass River Savs. Bank, 1979-85 Bd. dirs. Cape Cod Conservatory, West Barnstable, Mass., 1973-87, Cape Code YMCA, 1991—, YMCA, 1991-2001; trustee Cape Cod Hosp., Hyannis, Mass., 1978-87; mem. Mass. Health Facilities Appeal Bd., 1988-91; mem. Gov. Oversight Com., Town of Yarmouth, Mass., 1992—; mem. Town of Yarmouth Appeals Bd., 1992-93; apptd. Town of Yarmouth alt. rep. to Steam Ship Authority, 1997-98, 99-2003; trustee Hist. Soc. Old Yarmouth, 1994—. Lt. (j.g.) USNR, 1942-46. Named The James F. Hall Legacy Soc. in his honor, bd. trustees, Dutchess Cmty. Coll., 2004. Mem. New Eng. Assn. Schs. and Colls. (accreditation teams 1975-77), Southeastern Assn. Cooperation in Higher Edn. in Mass. (dir. 1972-79, pres. 1976, treas. 1978), Mass. Adminstrs. in Community Colls. (pres. 1974-75), Associated Colls of Mid-Hudson Area (chmn. bd. trustees 1963-64, 72, trustee 1963-72), Internat. Edn. Consortium (chmn. Coll. Consortium Internat. Studies, bd. dirs. 1985-87), Dutchess County Hist. Soc., South Yarmouth Lawn and Tennis Club (bd. dirs. 1991-93). Home: 29 Liverpool Dr Yarmouth Port MA 02675-1526

HALL, JAMES H(ERRICK), JR., philosophy educator, writer; b. Houston, Oct. 20, 1933; s. James Herrick and Loula Ben (Vining) H.; m. Bonlyn Goodwin, 1957 (div. 1977); children: Christopher Vining, Jonathan Goodwin; m. Myfanwy Seaver Monroe, 1977; 1 child, Charles Trevor. AB, Johns Hopkins U., 1955; BD, Southeastern Sem., Wake Forest, N.C., 1958, ThM, 1960; PhD, U. N.C., Chapel Hill, 1964. Instr. philosophy U. N.C., Chapel Hill, 1960-62; asst. prof. Furman U., Greenville, S.C., 1963-65; assoc. prof. U. Richmond, Va., 1965-74, chmn. dept. philosophy, 1965—89, 1999—2004, prof., 1974—2005, The Thomas chair, 1982—2005, Thomas prof. emeritus, 2005—, quest dir., 1999—2001. Author: Knowledge Belief and Transcendence, 1975, Logic Problems, 1991; (with others) Biblical and Secular Ethics, 1988, Philosophy of Religion, 2003, Practically Profound, 2005, Tools of Thinking, 2005. Mem. vestry St. Paul's Episc. Ch., Richmond, 1988-91, 2004—; profl. ch. musician, Chapel Hill, Raleigh, Balt., Washington, Richmond. Rsch. grantee Duke Found., Durham, 1964, Mednick Trust, 1973-74; named Disting. Educator, U. Richmond, 2001, Outstanding Prof., 2005; Coun. for Philosophic Studies fellow, Grand Rapids, 1973, U. Warwick fellow, Coventry, U.K., 1989-90, Kenan fellow U. NC, 1960-61. Mem. AAUP (chpt. pres. 1991-92), Am. Philos. Assn., Soc. for Philosophy of Religion, So. Soc. for Philosophy and Psychology, Omicron Delta Kappa. Democrat. Episcopalian. Avocations: choral music, camping, computers, travel. Home: 209 Wood Rd Richmond VA 23229-7538 Office: U Richmond Dept Philosophy North Ct Richmond VA 23173 Business E-Mail: jhall@richmond.edu.

HALL, JAMES ROBERT, language educator; b. Rochester, N.Y., Mar. 17, 1946; s. James Robert and Helen Grace (Schauseil) H.; m. Joan Marie Wylie, Aug. 17, 1974; children: Jennifer Joy Wylie Hall, Justin James Wylie Hall. BA, St. John Fisher Coll., 1968; MA, U. Notre Dame, 1970, PhD, 1973. Vis. lectr. U. Ill., Urbana, 1973-74; instr. English St. Mary-of-Woods (Ind.) Coll., 1975; asst. prof. U. Miss., University, 1978-84, assoc. prof., 1984-90, prof., 1990—. Scholarship reviewer Old English Newsletter Western Mich. U., 1976—2001; referee scholarly manuscripts; cons. Nat. Endowment Humanities, Washington, 1990—. Contbr. essays to profl. jours. Adviser Ole Miss Coll. Reps., University, 1995—; mem. exec. com. Lafayette County Rep. Party, Oxford Rep. Party. Am. Coun. Learned Socs. rsch. fellow, 1981-82; Harvard U. tchg.-rsch. Mellon fellow, 1983-84, NEH rsch. fellow, 1993-94; Earhart Found. rsch. fellow, 2000. Mem. Medieval Acad. Am., Internat. Soc. Anglo-Saxonists, Am. Friends Bodleian Libr., Assn. Lit. Scholars and Critics, Nat. Assn. Scholars, Southeastern Medieval Assn. Roman Catholic. Home: 1705 Johnson Ave Oxford MS 38655-4725 Office: U Miss Dept English University MS 38677-1848 Office Phone: 662-915-7145. E-mail: jrhall@olemiss.edu.

HALL, JAMES STANLEY, jazz guitarist, composer; b. Buffalo, Dec. 4, 1930; s. Harold S. and Louella (Cowles) H.; m. Jane Susan Yuckman, Sept. 9, 1965; 1 dau., Debra Jean. MusB, Cleve. Inst. Music, 1955; PhD in Music (hon.), Berklee Sch. Music, Boston, 1995. Author: Exploring Jazz Guitar; joined Chico Hamilton, 1955; mem. Jimmy Giuffre Trio, 1957, tour US and Europe with Jazz at Philharmonic, 1958, 59, Europe and S.A. with Ella Fitzgerald, 1959, 60; featured by Sonny Rollins, 1961-62; formed quartet with Art Farmer, 1962-64; leader own trio and quartet, 1962—; performed at White House, 1969; albums include Jazz Guitar, 1957, Undercurrent, All Across the City, Dedications & Inspirations, Diaglogues, Textures, 1997. By Arrangement, 1998, Jim Hall and Pat Methany, 1999, Grand Slam, 2000, Jim Hall and Basses, 2001, Magic Meeting, 2004; motion picture appearance in Jazz on a Summer's Day, 1958; appearance on Ralph Gleason's TV Show, 1962-63, BBC, 1964, Jim Hall Invitational Concert, 1990, Tonite show, 1992; tour Europe, 1967, 69, 79-82, 86-87, 89—, Japan, 1970, 76, 79, 87, 90—; (documentary film) A Life in Progress. Recipient award Downbeat Critics Poll, 1963-65, 74, 76-80, 82-88, 89-90, 91-93, award Downbeat Readers' Poll, 1965-66, 2001, award Playboy Mag. All-Star Poll for Guitar, 1968-71; named Best Performer Jazz Mag., 1965-66, Best Composer-Arranger, Jazz Critics Cir. NY, 1997; winner Jazz Times poll as Best Guitar, 1991, Jazzpar prize, Denmark, 1998, Disting. Alumni award Cleve. Inst. Music, Jazz Master Nat. Endowment award NEA, 2004. Mem. BMI. Personal E-mail: amsala@aol.com.

HALL, JAMES WILLIAM, university chancellor; b. Chester, Pa., Oct. 14, 1937; s. James William and Margaret (Crothers) H.; children: Laura, Janet, Carol. MusB, Bucknell U., 1959; M of Sacred Music, Union Theol. Sem., 1961; MA, U. Pa., 1964, PhD, 1967; DHL (hon.), Thomas Edison State Coll. N.J., 1992, U. Sys. N.H., 1994, DePaul U., 1996. Instr. Cedar Crest Coll., Allentown, Pa., 1961-66; vis. asst. prof. SUNY, Albany, 1966-71, asst. acad. personnel, sys. adminstrn., 1966-68; assoc. univ. dean univ.-wide activities, 1968-70; asst. vice chancellor policy and planning, 1970-71; pres. Empire State Coll. SUNY, Saratoga Springs, 1971-97; interim pres. SUNY Coll., Old Westbury, N.Y., 1981-82; vice-chancellor for ednl. tech. SUNY System, 1993-95; chancellor Antioch U., Yellow Springs, Ohio, 1998—2002, chancellor emeritus, disting. prof., 2002—. Editor: Am. Problem Series, Forging the American Character, 1971, (with B. Kevles) In Opposition to Core Curriculum: Alternative Models for Undergraduate Education, 1982, Access Through Innovation: New Colleges for New Students, 1991; contbr. articles to profl. jours. Trustee Monmouth Coll., N.J., 1981-93, U.S. Open U., 1999-02, Fielding Inst., Calif., 1990-99, chair 1995-97; bd. dirs. Saratoga Hosp., 1990-93, Nat. Commn. on Coop. Edn., 1999-02; bd. overseers Nelson A. Rockefeller Inst. Govt., SUNY, 1983-95. Danforth fellow, 1959-67 Mem. Am. Studies Assn., Soc. Values in Higher Edn., Am. Assn. Higher Edn., Assn. Am. Colls. (bd. dirs. 1986-89), Coun. for Adult and Experiential Learning (bd. dirs., chmn. 1987-88). E-mail: jhall@antiuch.edu.

HALL, JASON PIERS WILTON, biologist; b. Bristol, Eng., Jan. 23, 1972; s. John Wilton Hall and Tricia Monahan Exdell; m. Alma Maria Solis, May 15, 2003. BA, MA, Oxford U., Eng., 1993; PhD, U. Fla., 1999. Mem. affiliate faculty U. Fla., Gainesville, 1999—2000; rsch. scientist Smithsonian Instn., Washington, 2002—. Designer website www.butterfliesofecuador.com. Author: A Revision of the Genus Theope: Its Systematics and Biology (Lepidoptera: Riodinidae: Nymphidiini), A Phylogenetic Revision of the Napaeina (Lepidoptera: Riodinidae: Mesosemiini); contbr. over 60 articles to profl. jours. (Royal Entomol. Soc. Award for best paper in Systematic Entomology during 2001-2, 2003). Fellow, Smithsonian Instn., 1999—2000, 2001—02; grantee, Nat. Geog. Soc., 1997—2000, NSF, 2001—05. Mem.: Entomol. Soc. Am., Entomol. Soc. Washington (pres. 2005). Achievements include taxonomically described 13 genera and 148 valid new species of butterflies new to science; discovery of over 100 new species of butterflies in Ecuador. Avocations: travel, scuba diving, natural history. Office: Nat Mus Natural History Smithsonian Instn 10th & Constitution Washington DC 20560

HALL, JAY, social psychologist; b. Houston, Oct. 18, 1932; s. Ernest James and Jamie (Clark) H.; m. Missy Hall; children: Kelly, Allison, Jeffrey. BA in Psychology, U. Tex., 1959, MA in Psychology, 1961, PhD in Psychology, 1963. Lectr. dept. psychology U. Tex., Austin, 1961-63, dir. S.W. Ctr. for Law and Behavioral Scis., 1964-66, assoc. prof. Grad. Sch. Bus., 1966-69; assoc. dir. Nat. Parole Insts., Austin, 1963-64; founder, chmn. bd. Telemetrics Internat., The Woodlands, Tex., 1969-93; CEO, chmn. Leadership Systems Internat., The Woodlands, Tex., 1996—. Author: Ponderables: Essays on Managerial Choice-Past and Future, 1982, The Competence Connection: A Blueprint for Excellence, 1988, Models for Management: The Structure of Competence, 1988, The Executive Trap, 1992, Why Some Leaders are Better than Others, 1995, Benchmarks: For a Thoughtful Journey, 2000; co-author: GolfThink: Train Your Mind to Train Your Body, 2004; contbr. numerous articles and psychol. tests to profl. publs. Trustee The Woodlands Med. Ctr., 1980-91, Community Life Found., 1985-88, The John Cooper Sch., The Woodlands, 1986-91; dir. Interfaith, The Woodlands, 1980-88. 1st lt. U.S. Army, 1955-58. Mem. Am. Psychol. Assn., AAAS, N.Y. Acad. Sci., Sigma Xi. Episcopalian. Achievements include invention of swangletrainer for golf; Halford Grip sports/grip prosthesis. Avocation: golf.

HALL, JEFFREY A., lawyer; b. Junction City, Kans., Sept. 4, 1960; BS in Economics, U. Pa. Wharton Sch., 1982; JD magna cum laude, U. Mich., 1988. Bar: Ill. 1989. CPA Price Waterhouse, 1982—85; law clk. to Hon. James L. Ryan US Ct. of Appeals, 6th cir., 1988—89; ptnr. Bartlit, Beck, Herman, Palenchar & Scott LLP, 1993—. Lectr. law, trial advocacy, and tech. U. Chgo. Law Sch. Articles editor: U. Mich. Law Review. Named to The Am. Lawyer's Top 45 Under 45, 2003. Mem.: Order of the Coif. Office: Bartlit Beck Herman Palenchar & Scott Courthouse Place 54 W Hubbard St Chicago IL 60610 Office Phone: 312-494-4400.

HALL, JEROME WILLIAM, research engineering educator; b. Brunswick, Ga., Dec. 1, 1943; s. William L. and Frances K. H.; m. Loretta E. Hood, Aug. 28, 1965; children: Jennifer, Bridget, Bernadette. BS in Physics, Harvey Mudd Coll., 1965; MS in Engring., U. Wash., 1968, PhDCE, 1969. Registered profl. engr., D.C., N.Mex., Va. Asst. prof. civil engring. U. Md., College Park, 1970-73, assoc. prof., 1973-77, U. N.Mex., Albuquerque, 1977-80, prof., 1980—, dir. bur. engring. research, 1981-88, asst. dean engring., 1985-88, chmn. dept. of civil engring., 1990-97. Cons. in field. Contbr. articles to profl. jours. Recipient Teetor award Soc. Automotive Engrs., 1975; Pub. Partnership award Alliance For Transportation Rsch., 1997. Fellow Inst. Transp. Engrs. (pres. N.Mex. sect. 1985, pres. western dist. 1989, internat. bd. dirs. 1993-95); mem. Transp. Rsch. Bd. (chmn. com. 1986-92, chmn. group coun. 1992-95, panel chmn. 1990-2003), Am. Soc. Engring. Edn., Am. Rd. and Transp. Builders Assn. (pres. rsch. and edn. divsn. 2002-03, bd. dirs. 2003-), Nat. Assn. County Engrs. Republican. Roman Catholic. Office: Dept Civil Engring MSC01 1070 UNM Albuquerque NM 87131 Business E-Mail: jerome@unm.edu.

HALL, JESSICA L., music educator; b. Birmingham, Ala., Aug. 6, 1979; d. Thomas F. Hall, II and Janice C. Hall. MusB in Edn., Birmingham-Southern Coll., 2000; MusM, La. State U., 2002. Cert. educator Ala. Dept. of Edn., 2000. Grad. tchg. asst. La. State U., Baton Rouge, 2000—02; part-time music instr. Jefferson State C.C., Birmingham, Ala., 2002—02; youth choir dir. Canterbury United Meth. Ch., 2002—; instr. music, dir. choirs Jefferson State C.C., 2003—, chair concert-lecture com., 2004—, acting chair libreal arts dept., 2005—. Mem. assessment com. Jefferson State C.C., Birmingham, 2003—, mem. profl. pers. policies com., 2003—, mem. grad. com., 2004—, chair, concert-lecture com., 2004—. Youth leadership team Canterbury United Meth. Ch., Birmingham, 2003, youth foundations team, 2003. Mem.: Ala. Music Educators Assn., Am. Musicological Soc., Am. Choral Directors Assn., Music Educators Nat. Conf., Pi Kappa Lambda. Office: Jefferson State Community College 2601 Carson Road Birmingham AL 35215 Office Phone: 205-856-7900. Personal E-mail: jhall@jeffstateonline.com.

HALL, JOAN, artist; b. NYC, Dec. 14, 1939; d. Herbert and Julia Levy. Student, Juilliard Sch. Music, 1954-59, Inst. de Allende, Mexico, 1968-69, Pratt Inst. Dancer, actress, writer Am. Mime Theatre, N.Y.C., 1959-67; mime tchr. Am. Acad. Dramatic Arts, N.Y.C., 1965-67; freelance collage artist, illustrator N.Y.C., 1970—. Instr. Sch. Visual Arts, N.Y.C., 1978—; lectr. in field. Exhibited in group shows at Centre Cultural Georges Pompidou, Paris, 1977, Queens (N.Y.) Mus., 1982, Museo Rufino Tamayo, Mexico City, 1988,

Am. Cultural Ctr., Paris, 1977, U.S. Info. Svc., New Delhi, 1986, Rio de Janeiro, 1987; designed posters for Tokyo Bay Lalaport, 1991. Recipient Citation of Merit, Soc. Publ. Designers, 1972, award Soc. of Illustrators, 1972, 76, 80-81, 87-88, 90. Avocations: yoga, swimming. Home and Office: 155 Bank St # 954H New York NY 10014-2010 Office Phone: 212-243-6059. E-mail: jhcollage@aol.com.

HALL, JOAN B., small business owner; b. Evanston, Ill., July 22, 1926; d. Frederick Joseph and Mona La Mothe (Gunn) Brockhoff; m. Frank Braden Hall, May 11, 1957 (dec. Mar. 23, 2005); children: Braden, Scott. Grad., Northwestern U., 1946. Adminstrv. asst. Walgreen Co., Chgo., 1948-49, NBC, Chgo., 1949-52, A.C. Nielsen Co., Chgo., 1952-57; pres. Joan B. Hall & Assoc., Park Ridge, Ill., 1980—; supr. Maine Twp., Park Ridge, 1989-93. Trustee Oakton C.C., Des Plaines, Ill., 1985-2005, trustee emerita, 2005—; chairwoman bd. trustees, 1993-94, 1997-98, vice-chairwoman, 1996-97; chairwoman Cook County Suburban Rep. Orgn., 1981-90; committeewoman Maine Twp. Rep. Orgn., Des Plaines, 1969-76, 81-90; fundraisesr United Fund Heart Fund, Park Ridge, 1981-92, Cancer Fund, Maine Twp. Recipient Outstanding Govt. Ofcl. award Pvt. Industry Coun., 1991, Rep. Woman of Yr. award, 1993-94, Ray Hartstein Trustee Achievement award, Oakton C.C., 2005, named Outstanding Trustee of Yr., Ill. C.C. Trustees Assn., 2005. Mem.: Internat. Group Agys. and Burs. (bd. govs.), Assn. Women Entrepreneurs, City Club, Chgo. Republican. Home: 2904 Scottlynne Dr Park Ridge IL 60068-2855

HALL, JOAN TORRENS, lawyer; b. Belleville, NJ; d. Alfred and Margaret (Simpson) Torrens;m. John P. Hall Jr.; children: John P. III, James S. AB, Drew U., 1957; JD, Rutgers U., 1990. Bar: N.J. 1991, D.C. 1991. Tchr. Oliphant Sch., Middletown, R.I., 1958-59; psychology rschr. Princeton U., N.J., 1974-98; pvt. practice, 1990—; mediator Mediation Alternative Group, 1998—. Vis. lectr. Rutgers Law Sch., Camden, NJ, 1990; mediator Mercer County Cts. Contbr. articles to profl. jours. Bd. dir. LWV, Hopewell, NJ, 1972-87, 94-97; pres. PTO, Hopewell, 1979-80; chmn. ER Neighborhood Assn., Princeton, 1996-2002; chmn. MasterPlan Com., Hopewell Twp., 1998-2003; mediator PrincetonBoro and Twp. Grantee NSF, 1996-97. Mem. ABA, Princeton Bar Assn. Avocations: tennis, reading.

HALL, JOHN E., medical educator; PhD in Physiology, Mich. State U., 1974. Postdoctoral fellow U. Miss. Med. Ctr., Jackson, Miss., 1974—76, faculty, 1976—82, prof. dept. physiology and biophysics, 1982—, chair dept. physiology and biophysics, 1989—, dir. Ctr. of Excellence in Cardiovascular-Renal Rsch., Guyton prof. Burroughs Wellcome Fund vis. prof. in basic med. scis. Co-author (with Arthur Guyton): Medical Physiology; chief editor Hypertension Physiology: Regulatory, Integrative and Comparative Physiology, author/editor 13 books, mem. editl. bds. several internat. jours.; contbr. over 450 articles to profl. jours. Recipient Merck Sharp and Dohme Internat. Rsch. award, Internat. Soc. Hypertension, Spl. Rsch. Achievement award, Am. Heart Assn.-Miss., NIH Career Devel. award, A.P. Barnard and Billy S. Guyton Disting. Professorships award, U. Miss., Novartis award, AHA; grantee Nat. Heart, Lung and Blood Inst. grantee, 1975—. Fellow: Am. Physiol. Soc. (mem. coun. 1991, mem. strategic planning com. 1992—2000, chair SAC 1997—2000, pres., mem. long range planning com., numerous others, chair, treas. and councillor water and electrolyte homeostasis sect., mem. renal sect., mem. cardiovascular sect., Ernest Starling Lectureship); mem.: Inter-Am. Soc. Hypertension (pres.), Am. Soc. Hypertension (exec. com., Richard Bright award, Marion Young Scholar award), Am. Heart Assn. (past chmn. coun. for high blood pressure rsch., chmn. com. of sci. couns., bd. dirs., Harry Goldblatt award, Lewis Dahl award). Achievements include research in in cardiovascular and renal physiology, mechanisms of hypertension, the renin-angiotensin system, obesity and insulin resistance; also in modeling and computer simulation of the cardiovascular-renal systems. Office: Univ Miss Med Ctr Dept Physiology/Biophysics 2500 N State St Jackson MS 39216-4505

HALL, JOHN FRY, retired psychologist; b. Phila., Apr. 24, 1919; s. Harry R. and Alta (Herner) H.; m. Jean Midlam, May 14, 1943; 1 son, John. BS, Ohio U., 1946; MA, Ohio State U., 1947, PhD, 1949. Mem. faculty Pa. State U., University Park, 1949—, prof. psychology, 1958—; prof. emeritus, 1985—; Program dir. psychobiology NSF, Washington, 1966-67. Vis. prof. U. Va., 1952, U. Wis., 1954, U. Calif. at Berkeley, 1962, U. Hawaii, 1968, Fla. State U., 1975-76 Author: Psychology of Motivation, 1961, Psychology of Learning, 1966, Readings in the Psychology of Learning, 1967, Verbal Learning and Retention, 1971, Classical Conditioning and Instrumental Learning, 1976, An Invitation to Learning and Memory, 1982, Learning and Memory, 1989; contbr. articles to profl. jours. Mem. AAAS, APA, Psychonomics Soc. Home: 237 Courtyard Blvd Sun City Center FL 33573-6938 Personal E-mail: jejohall@aol.com.

HALL, JOHN HENRY, lawyer, historian, educator; b. Mound Bayou, Miss., Nov. 7, 1932; s. John and Icey M. (Roundtree) H.; m. Katie B. Green, Aug. 15, 1957. BS in Social Studies, Ind. U., 1970, MEd, 1971, MS in Secondary Sch. Adminstrn., 1972; JD, Southland U., 1981; EdD, Loyola U., Chgo., 1995; LLM comml. real estate, John Marshall Law Sch., Chgo., 2002. Bar: Ind. 1983, U.S. Supreme Ct. 1987. Foreman U.S. Reduction Co., East Chicago, Ind., 1957-62, shift supt., 1962-68; tchr. Gary (Ind.) Cmty. Schs., 1969-74, asst. prin., 1975—92; sole practice law Gary, 1983—; prof. law, racism and social change Ind. U., Gary, 1984. Legal resource Gary Community Sch. Corp., 1983-84; judge pro tem Lake County (Ind.) Superior Ct., East Chicago and Gary. Article writer Blacks in World History Information Newspaper (edn. and Cmty. Svc. awrd 1983), 1979—. Campaign mgr. Katie Hall State Rep., Indpls., 1976, Katie Hall Congress, Gary, 1984; Sunday sch., BTU tchr., served as chmn. deacon Van Buren (Miss.) Bapt. Ch., Served with USAF, 1952-57. Mem. ABA, Gary Secondary Prins. Assn. (sec./treas., v.p., pres., Outstanding Leadership award 1982), Lake County Bar Assn., Assn. Trial Lawyers Am., Phi Delta Kappa, Phi Alpha Delta. Democrat. Avocations: travel, creative writing, reading, walking, jogging. Office: PO Box 1498 Gary IN 46407-0498

HALL, JOHN HERBERT, lawyer; b. Orange, N.J., Dec. 5, 1942; s. Embert Brown Hall and Elizabeth (Sullivan) Carnahan; m. Suzanne Steeger, Aug. 21, 1965 (div. Apr. 1988); children: Christopher Evan, Jeremy Randall; m. Lisa Gersh, June 19, 1988; children: Samantha Gersh, Madeleine Gersh. BA, Wesleyan U., 1965; MBA, NYU, 1966; JD, Columbia U., 1969. Bar: N.Y. 1970, U.S. Dist. Ct. (so. dist.) N.Y. 1972, (ea. dist.) N.Y. 1981, U.S. Ct. Appeals (2d cir.) 1974, (10th cir.) 1977, (5th cir.) 1980, (11th cir.) 1981, (4th cir.) 1989, (D.C. cir.) 1982, U.S. Supreme Ct. 1981. Assoc. Debevoise, Plimpton, Lyons & Gates, N.Y.C., 1969-72, 73-78; grad. bus. Cmty. Law Offices, N.Y.C., 1972-73; ptnr. Debevoise & Plimpton, N.Y.C., 1979—, chair litig. dept., 1993—2002, mem. mgmt. com., 2003—. Bd. dirs. Cmty. Law Offices, 1974-2000, Legal Aid Soc. N.Y., 1980-88. Co-author: Takeovers-Attack and Survival, 1987, 2d edit., 1993; author: Global Counsel-Dispute Resolution Handbook, 2004-05; panelist in field. Bd. dirs. Vols. Legal Svcs., 1990-96, Welfare Law Ctr. Named a Leading Litigator, Yearbook, 2005. Fellow: N.Y. Bar Found. Bd. Dirs.; mem. ABA (criminal jus. law, litig. sects.), N.Y. Lawyers for Pub. Interest (bd. dirs. 1987-00), Am. Judicature Soc., Supreme Ct. Hist. Soc., Assn. of Bar of City of N.Y. (fed. cts. com. 1981-84), Prep for Prep Inc. (dir. 1984-), U.S. Cycling Fedn., Nat. Legal Aid/Defenders Assn., Law Soc. Eng. and Wales, Global Counsel 3000. Avocations: bicycle racing, tennis. Home: 300 Central Park W Apt 19C New York NY 10024-1513 Office: Debevoise & Plimpton 919 3rd Ave 43rd Floor New York NY 10022-6225 E-mail: Jhhall@debevoise.com.

HALL, JOHN HOPKINS, retired lawyer; b. Dallas, May 10, 1925; s. Albert Brown and Eleanor Pauline (Hopkins) H.; m. Marion Martin, Nov. 23, 1957; children: Ellen Martin, John Hopkins II. Student, U. Tex., 1942, U. of South, Sewanee, Tenn., 1942-43; LL.B., So. Meth. U., 1949. Bar: Tex. 1949. Ptnr. Strasburger & Price, Dallas, 1957-93, ret., 1993. Served with U.S. Army, 1943—45. Fellow Tex. Bar Found., Am. Bar Found., Internat. Acad. Trial Lawyers, Am. Coll. Trial Lawyers; mem. Tex. Bar Assn., Tex. Assn. Def. Counsel, Internat. Assn. Def. Counsel, Fin and Feather Club. Episcopalian.

HALL, JOHN LEWIS, physicist, researcher; b. Denver, Aug. 21, 1934; s. John Ernest and Elizabeth Rae (Long) H.; m. Marilyn Charlene Robinson, Mar. 1, 1958; children: Thomas Charles, Carolyn Gay, Jonathan Lawrence. BS in Physics, Carnegie Mellon U., 1956, MS in Physics, 1958, PhD in Physics, 1961; PhD (hon.), U. Paris XIII, 1989. Postdoctoral rsch. assoc. Nat. Bur. Standards, Washington, 1961-62, physicist Boulder, Colo., 1962-75, sr. scientist, 1975—2004. Cons. Los Alamos (N.Mex.) Sci. Labs., 1963-65; lectr. U. Colo., Boulder, 1977—; cons. numerous firms in laser industry, 1974—. Contbr. articles to profl. jours.; patentee in laser tech.; editor: Laser Spectroscopy 3, 1977. Recipient IR-100 award IR Mag., 1975, 77, Gold medal Nat. Bur. Stds., 1974, Stratton award, 1971, E.U. Condon award, 1979, Gold medal Dept. Commerce, 1969, Presdl. Meritorious Exec. award, 1980, Meritorious Alumnus award Carnegie Mellon U., 1985, Humbolt Sr. Scientist award Munich, 1989, A.V. Astin award NIST, 2000; named French Legion Hon., 2004 knight; Sherman Fairchild Disting. scholar Calif. Tech., 1992. Fellow Optical Soc. Am. (bd. dirs. 1980-82, Charles H. Townes award 1984, Frederic Ives medal 1991, Max Born award, 2002), Am. Phys. Soc. (Davisson-Germer award 1988, Arthur L. Schawlow prize 1993); mem. NAS, Comite Consultatif pour la Definition du Metre. Office: U Colo JILA Boulder CO 80309-0440 Business E-Mail: jhall@jila.colorado.edu.

HALL, JOHN RAYMOND, JR., fire protection executive; b. Washington, Feb. 25, 1948; s. John Raymond and Elizabeth Florence (Lord) H.; m. Jean Baird Horky, Dec. 2, 1972. BA cum laude, Brown U., 1967; PhD, U. Pa., 1972. Rsch. analyst Resource Mgmt. Corp., Bethesda, Md., 1972-73; sr. rsch. assoc. Urban Inst., Washington, 1973-79; ops. rsch. analyst U.S. Fire Adminstrn., within Fed. Emergency Mgmt. Agy., Washington, 1979-82, Ctr. for Fire Rsch., within Nat. Bur. of Stds, Gaithersburg, Md., 1982-84; asst. v.p. fire analysis and rsch. Nat. Fire Protection Assn., Quincy, Mass., 1984—. V.p. mem. activities Inst. of Mgmt. Scis., Providence, 1983-86, sec. 1979-83, mem. at-large of coun., 1977-79, chmn. orgn. and bylaws com., 1979-94, pres. Washington chpt. 1978-79, v.p. for membership coll. on pub. programs and processes, 1982-85; trustee Washington Ops. Rsch./Mgmt. Sci. Coun., 1980-81, 83-84, fellow, 2004-. Author: (with others) Procedures for Improving the Measurement of Local Fire Protection Effectiveness, 1976, How Effective Are Your Community Services?, 1977, 92, The SFPE Handbook of Fire Protection Engineering, 1988, 95, 2002, Fire Protection Handbook, 1986, 97; editor TIMS Chpts. Newsletter, 1976-79; columnist Mgmt. Sci. Update, 1980-81; columnist/editor Applications Rev., 1976-88; contbr. articles to profl. jours. Chmn. Fire Protection Commn., Norwood, Mass., 1986—. Recipient (4) Cert. of Outstanding Performance Fed. Emergency Mgmt. Agy., 1981-83, Cert. of Spl. Achievement, 1982, Cert. of Recognition Nat. Bur. of Stds., 1983-84, Leadership Giving award United Way of Neponset Valley, 1991. Fellow: Inst. Ops. Rsch. and Mgmt. Sci. (mem. fin. com. 1997—99, past pres.); mem.: ASTM (E5 exec. com. 1996—2003, 4th vice chair 1998—2003, Wayne P. Ellis award 2004), AAAS, Nat. Fire Protection Assn. (exec. sec. rsch. sect. 1990—), Combustion Inst., Inst. Mgmt. Scis., Am. Mgmt. Assn., Soc. for Risk Analysis, Ops. Rsch. Soc. Am. (tech. sects. com. 1972—76), Internat. Assn. for Fire Safety Sci. (program com. 1991—, exec. com. 1994—, newsletter editor 1994—, chmn. arrangements com. 2000—02), Sigma Xi, Phi Beta Kappa. Democrat. Achievements include rsch. on the modeling and conceptual framework innovations in fire risk analysis in the USA. Home: 10 Alden Dr Norwood MA 02062-5326 Office: Nat Fire Protection Assn 1 Batterymarch Park Quincy MA 02169-7471

HALL, JOHN ROBERT, psychiatrist; b. Springfield, Mo., Mar. 14, 1959; s. Robert Jean and Martha Weber Hall; m. Sandra Jean Cookson, Aug. 12, 1979; children: Amanda Jean, Crystal Marie. BA, Southwest Bapt. U., 1980; MDiv, Southeastern Bapt. Theol. Sem., 1985; MD, U. Mo., 1996. Resident U. Mo., Columbia, 2001; staff psychiatrist Northland Dist. Health Bd., Whangerei, New Zealand, 2001—02, Arthur Ctr., Mexico, Mo., 2002—. Fellow, U. Mo., 2001. Office Phone: 573-582-1234.

HALL, JOHN THOMAS, lawyer, educator; b. Phila., May 14, 1938; s. John Thomas and Florence Sara (Robinson) H.; m. Carolyn Park Currie, May 26, 1968; children: Daniel Currie, Kathleen Currie. AB, Dickinson Coll., 1960; MA, U. Md., 1963; JD, U. N.C., 1972. Bar: N.C. 1972. Chmn. dept. speech Mercersburg (Pa.) Acad., 1960-63, U. Balt., 1963-69; research asst. N.C. Ct. Appeals, Raleigh, 1972-73, dir. pre-hearing research staff, 1974-75, asst. clk., marshall, librarian, 1980-81; counsel Dorothea Dix Hosp., Raleigh, 1974; asst. dist. atty. State of N.C., Raleigh, 1975-80, 81-83; pvt. practice Raleigh, 1973-74, 83—. Mem. faculty King's Bus. Coll., Raleigh, 1973-75, N.C. Bar Assn., 1987—; undercover inmate Cen. Prison Duke Ctr. on Law and Poverty, Durham, N.C., 1970; lectr. dept. comm. N.C. State U., 2000—. Mem. Raleigh Little Theatre, Theatre in the Park, Raleigh; charter mem. Wake County Dem. Men's Club, 1977—. Named Best Actor, Raleigh Little Theatre, 1975, 77, 80, 82, 85, 86, 93, 98, 2005 Mem.: ABA, Wake County Acad. Criminal Trial Lawyers (v.p. 1986—87), 10th Jud. Dist. Bar Assn. (bd. dirs. 1986—89, chmn. grievance com. 1987—90), Wake County Bar Assn. (bd. dirs. 1986—89, vice chmn. exec. com. 1986—87), N.C. Bar Assn., Scottish Clan Gunn Soc. Avocations: reading, theater. Office: PO Box 1207 Raleigh NC 27602-1207

HALL, JOHN WESLEY, JR., lawyer; b. Watertown, N.Y., Jan. 28, 1948; s. John Wesley and Mary Louise Hall; m. Alison Hall; children: Justin William, Mark Daniel, Juliana Sanchez. BA, Hendrix Coll., 1970; JD, U. Ark., 1973. Bar: Ark. 1973, U.S. Dist. Ct. (ea. and we. dists.) Ark. 1973, U.S. Ct. Appeals (8th cir.) 1973, D.C. 1975, U.S. Ct. Appeals (5th cir.) 1976, U.S. Supreme Ct. 1976, U.S. Ct. Fed. Claims, 1984, Tenn. 1988, U.S. Ct. Appeals (fed. cir.) 1988, U.S. Ct. Appeals (6th cir.) 1991, Nev. 1993, U.S. Ct. Appeals (9th cir.) 1995, N.Y. 1996, U.S. Dist. Ct. N.Y. (So. Dist.) 1999, U.S. Ct. Appeals (2d cir.) 1999, U.S. Dist. Ct. Nev., 2000. Law clk. Ark. Supreme Ct., Little Rock, 1974; dep. pros. atty., Office Pros. Atty., Little Rock, 1973-79, head career criminal divsn., 1978-79; pvt. practice, 1974—. Instr. trial advocacy Ark. Pros. Attys. Assn., 1977-79; adj. prof. Sch. Law, Grad. Sch. Criminal Justice, U. Ark., Little Rock, 1985-88, 91; mem. Ark. adv. com. U.S. Commn. Civil Rights, 2003-04; speaker to lawyer and police groups. Author: Search and Seizure, 3d edit., 2000, Professional Responsibility of the Criminal Lawyer, 2d edit., 1996, 3d edit. 2004, Trial Handbook for Arkansas Lawyers, 4th edit., 2003; editor, author: Arkansas Prosecutor's Trial Manual, 1976-77, Arkansas Extradition Manual, 1978; editor: (with B. Scheck and P. Neufield) DNA: Understanding, Controlling, and Depleting the New Evidence of the 90's, 1990; contbr. articles to law jours. Recipient Robert C. Heeney Meml. award, 2002. Fellow Am. Bd. Criminal Lawyers; mem. NACDL (life, bd. dirs. 1989-95, 97—2003, sec. 2003-04, mem. ethics adv. com. 1990-, lawyer's assistance strike force 1994-97, exec. com. 2000-01), Assn. Responsible Lawyers, Ark. Bar Assn. (ho. of dels. 1976-79), Ark. Assn. Criminal Def. Lawyers (pres. 1987-89, Champion of Justice award 2003), N.Y. State Assn. Criminal Def. Lawyers, First Amendment Lawyers Assn. Episcopalian. Home: 300 Rice St Little Rock AR 72205-6141 Office: John Wesley Hall Jr A Profl Corp 1311 Broadway Little Rock AR 72202 Office Phone: 501-371-9131. Office Fax: 501-378-0888. E-mail: johnwesleyhall@aol.com.

HALL, KATHERINE LEIGH, music educator; b. Salem, Va., Mar. 24, 1977; d. Donald Ray and Shirley Perry Hall. MusB, Carson-Newman Coll., 1999; MSc in Music Edn., Radford U., 2003. Lic. tchr. Tenn., Va. Telephone sales operator Orvis, Roanoke, Va., 1993—99; choir dir., tchr. Franklin County Schs., Rocky Mount, Va., 1999—2003; tchr. Roanoke (Va.) County Schs., 2003—. Camp counselor Camp Little Cross Roads, Lowesville, Va., 1996—98; sec. Carson-Newman Coll. Campus Ministries, Jefferson City, Tenn., 1996—99. Asst. youth coord. dir. First Bapt. Ch., Jefferson City, 1996—99; adult choir dir. Windsor Hills Meth. Ch., Roanoke, 2000—02; dir. adult choir Rocky Mount Christian Ch., 2003. Mem.: NEA, Music Educators Nat. Conf., Va. Choral Dirs. Assn., Va. Music Educators Assn., Kappa Delta Pi, Delta Omicron (publicity dir. 1995—, Outstanding Sr. 1999). Baptist. Avocations: antiques, collecting bears, swimming, piano. Office: Benjamin Franklin Middle Sch 375 Middle School Rd Rocky Mount VA 24151

HALL, KATHRYN H., public relations executive; b. Douglas, Sept. 5, 1944; m. Steve Hall (div. 2003); children: Stephen, Scott, Stuart, Justin. Student, Casper Jr. Coll., Wyo., Nebr. Tchrs. Coll., Mesa State Coll., Grand Junction, Colo. Owner, v.p. Well Servicing Equipment and Supply, Grand Junction, 1979—85; dir. western office U.S. Sen. William Armstrong, Grand Junction, 1985—90, Sen. Hank Brown, Grand Junction, 1990—93; loan officer El Paso Mortgage Co., Grand Junction, 1993—95; br. mgr. Am. Rockies Mortgage Co., Grand Junction, 1995; commr. Mesa County Commn., Grand Junction, 1995—2003; owner Kathy Hall/Pub. Rels., Grand Junction, 2003—. Chair Dept. Human Svcs., Grand Junction, Cmty. Air Svc. Task Force, Grand Junction; chair legis. com. Colo. River Water Conservation Dist. Bd., Grand Junction, 1996—. Contbr. numerous articles to profl. jours. Co-chair United Way, Mesa County, 2003—; mem. Gov.'s Task Force on Welfare Reform, Gov.'s Task Force on Civil Justice Reform, Gov.'s Child Welfare Reform Task Force; chmn. legis. com. Colo. River. Conservation Dist.; mem. Colo. West Mental Health Adv. Com.; steering com. Colo. Benefits Mgmt. System; past chmn., treas. Assoc. Govts. of N.W. Colo.; mem. Riverfront Commn., Pvt. Industry Coun.; pres. Marillac Clinic; mem. Parks Improvement Adv. Bd.; active numerous other civic coms., subcoms., bds.; chmn. bd. Mesa County Commrs., Grand Junction, 1997—99, 2001—02. Recipient Elizabeth Prebich Disting. Leadership award, 2001. Republican. Methodist. Home: 2305 Pheasant Run Grand Junction CO 81506-4877 Office: Kathy Hall Pub Rels 743 Horizon Ct Ste 100C Grand Junction CO 81506

HALL, KATHRYN MARIE, elementary school educator; d. Murray Hall and Mary Nielsen. AS, Snow Coll., 1981; BS, Weber State U., 1997. Cert. tchr. Utah State Bd. Edn., 1997. Tchr. 3d grade Ogden City Sch. Dist., 1999—. Vol. Jordan Sch. Dist., Riverton, Utah, 1992—97; tchr. Utah State U.; profl. devel. trainer Ogden City Sch. Dist.; master tchr., presenter State Office Edn., Utah State U., 2005—; presenter in field. Mem. Cmty. Sch. Council; coach Spl. Olympics, Salt Lake City, 1999—2003. Mem.: Core Acad. (master tchr.), Ogden Edn. Assn. (licentiate), Nat. Coun. Teachers Math. (licentiate). Conservative. Mem. Lds Ch. Avocations: skiing, travel, history, art, music.

HALL, KATHRYN WALT, ambassador; m. Craig Hall; 2 children, 4 stepchildren. AB in Econs., JD, U. Calif., Berkeley. Asst. city atty., Berkeley, Calif.; with Safeway Stores; pres. Kathryn Hall Vineyards, Inc., Walt Mgmt., Inc.; mng. dir., ptnr. Hall Fin. Group, Inc.; amb. to Austria Vienna, 1997—. Mem. hunger adv. com. U.S. Ho. of Reps. Co-founder North Tex. Food Bank; mem. Nat. Adv. Coun. for Violence Against Women; trustee Woodrow Wilson Internat. Ctr. for Scholars; former bd. dirs., v.p. Tex. Mental Health Assn. Mem. Dallas Area C. of C., Comml. Real Estate Women, Tex. Retailers Assn.

HALL, KATHY, health facility administrator; b. Covington, Ky., Feb. 15, 1953; d. Joseph B. and Mary Louise (Weindel) Dusing; m. Harold G. Hall, Oct. 6, 1973; children: Becky, Amy, Sarah. AA, Eastern Ky. U., 1973, BS in Nursing, 1978; MS in Nursing, Bellarmine U., 1999. Med.-surg. staff nurse Good Samaritan Hosp., Lexington, Ky., 1973; infection control nurse Pattie A. Clay Hosp., Richmond, Ky., 1975-93, orientation instr., 1978-82, quality assurance dir., 1982-93; nurse epidemiologist U. Ky. Chandler Med. Ctr., Lexington, 1993—99; edn. dir. Shriners Hosp. for Children, Lexington, 1999—2002; dir. continuing edu. devel. Coll. Health Sci. Ea. KY U. Mem.: NNSDO, KNA, ANA, Ctrl. KY Staff Devel. Group, Sigma Theta Tau. Office: CHS Continuing Edu & Devel 202 Perkins Bldg Ea KY U 521 Lancaster Ave Richmond KY 40475-3102 Office Phone: 859-622-1826. E-mail: Kathy.Hall@eku.edu.

HALL, KENNETH RICHARD, chemical engineering professor, consultant; b. Tulsa, Okla., Nov. 5, 1939; s. Snipes Webster and Selina Rose (Scarpin) H.; m. Janet Beulah Blood, June, 1964 (div. 1975); children: Tara Marie, Deirdre Rene; m. Frieda Maria Karner, Mar. 12, 1976; children: Kent Max, Keith Anton, Krysta Maria. BS ChemE, U. Tulsa, 1962; MS, U. Calif., Berkeley, 1964; PhD, U. Okla., 1967. Registered engr., Tex. Asst. prof. U. Va., Charlottesville, 1967-70, 71-74; asst. to pres. ChemShare Corp., Norman, Okla., 1970; sr. rsch. engr. AMOCO, Tulsa, 1970-71; vis. prof. U. Louvain, Belgium, 1971-72; assoc. prof. Tex. A&M U., College Station, 1974-78, prof., 1978—, dir. Thermodynamics Rsch. Ctr., 1979-85, 97-2000, asst. dir. Tex. Engrng. Experiment Sta., 1985-88, assoc. dean engrng., 1987—94, 2002—03, from assoc. dir. to dep. dir., 1988—94, 2002—03, assoc. dep. chancellor for engrng., 1990—94, 2002—03, interim head petroleum engrng., 1991, interim head chem. engrng., 1994; dir. CTS divsn. NSF, Va., 1994-96; GPSA prof. Tex. A&M U., College Station, 1997-2000, Jack E. and Frances Brown chair, 2001—, head dept. chem. engrng., 2002—. Cons. OPC Engrng., Houston, 1980-85, Quantum Tech., Houston, 1981-85; cons. Precision Measurement Inc., Duncanville, Tex., 1981-90; bd. dirs. Lorax Corp., Syn Fuels. U.S. editor Flow Measurement and Instrumentation; contbr. over 200 articles to profl. jours. Recipient numerous grants for research. Mem.: Am. Inst. Chem. Engrs. (chmn. ctrl. Va. chpt. 1969, chmn. cyrogenics 1977—79, exec. position II South Tex. sect. 1991—92, bd. dirs. fuels and petrochems. divsn. 1992—94), Am. Chem. Soc. Avocations: sports, reading. Home: 1401 Millcreek Ct College Station TX 77845-8352 Office: Tex A&M U Dept Chem Engrng College Station TX 77843

HALL, KERMIT LANCE, academic administrator, historian, educator; b. Akron, Ohio, Aug. 31, 1944; s. Kermit Hall and Katherine Lois Galbraith; m. Phyllis Anne Moke, May 1, 1944. BA, U. Akron, 1966; MA, Syracuse U., 1967; PhD, U. Minn., 1972; MSL, Yale U., 1980. Prof. history Vanderbilt U., Nashville, 1972—76, Wayne State U., Detroit, 1976—81; prof. law and history U. Fla., Gainesville, 1981—92; dean Henry Kendall Coll. Arts and Scis., prof. law and history U. Tulsa, 1992—94; exec. dean Coll. Arts and Scis., dean Coll. Humanities, prof. history and law Ohio State U., Columbus, 1994—99; provost, vice chancellor, prof. history N.C. State U., Raleigh, 1999—2000; pres., prof. history Utah State U., Logan, 2000—04; prof. history U. Albany, NY, 2005—. Dir. Am. Coun. on Edn., Washington, 2000—; adv. dir. Wells Fargo Bank of No. Utah, Salt Lake City, 2002—; mem. exec. adv. com. SCT Corp., Phila., 2001—; dir. Nat. Assn. State Univs. and Land Grant Colls., 2002—, Regence Blue Cross Blue Shield of Utah, 2003—04. Author: (book) The Magic Mirror: Law in American History; editor: The Oxford Companion to the Supreme Court of the United States (Main Selection, History Book Club, 1992), The Oxford Companion to the Supreme Court of the United States, revised 2nd edit., 2005, The Oxford Guide To Supreme Court Decisions (Main Selection, History Book Club, 1999), The Oxford Companion to American Law. Mem. John F. Kennedy Assassination Records Rev. Bd., Washington, 1994—98; dir. Rsch. Triangle Inst., Raleigh, NC, 1999—2000, Utah Festival Opera, Logan, 2000. 1st lt. U.S. Army, 1968—69. Decorated Air Medal; named George E. Knepper Disting. Lectr., U. Akron, 2000, Utah's Best Hands On Leader, Salt Lake Mag., 2001, Simon E. Sobeloff Lectr., U. of Md. Coll. of Law, 1996; recipient James Madison award, ALA, 1996, Outstanding Achievement award, Logan and Cahce Valley, Utah C. of C., 2003, Silver Gavel award, ABA, 1993, Outstanding Reference Work award, ALA, 1992, Hon. Fellow, Ctr. for Gt. Plains Studies, 1992; fellow Earhart Found., 1979—80, Legal History fellow, Am. Bar Found., 1980—81, Lectr. in Finland, Fulbright-Hayes Found., 1987; grantee Minority Scholars in History grantee, Pew Charitable Trust, 1991—94, Rsch. in Selection of Judges grantee, NSF, 1984—86, History Tchg. Alliance grantee, Rockefeller, Exxon, and Hewlett Founds., 1984—87, Defining the Core of Citizenship grantee, NEH, 1993—94, Native Ams. and Higher Edn. grantee, Coca Cola Found., 1994—96; vis. scholar Am. Bar Found., 1986—87, U. No. Iowa, 1996. Fellow: Am. Coun. Learned Socs.; mem.: ABA (com. on pub. edn. about the law 2001—, Silver Gavel award 1993), Am. Hist. Assn., Am. Soc. for Legal History (assoc.; bd. of directors 1994—97), Orgn. of Am. Historians (life), Rotary Internat. (assoc.). Democrat-Npl. Avocations: salt water fishing, hiking, reading, strength conditioning. Office: Univ Adminstrn Bldg Univ Albany Rm 430 Albany NY 12222 Office Phone: 435-797-7172, 518-437-4900. Business E-Mail: khall@uamail.albany.edu.

HALL, LARRY DEAN, utilities executive, lawyer; b. Hastings, Nebr., Nov. 8, 1942; s. Willis E. and Stella W. (Eckoff) H.; m. Jeffe D. Bryant, July 5, 1985; children: Scott, Jeff, Mike, Bryan. BA in Bus., U. Nebr., Kearney; JD,

U. Nebr. Bar: Nebr. 1967, Colo. 1981. Ptnr. Wright, Simmons, Hancock & Hall, Scottsbluff, Nebr., 1967-71; atty., asst. treas. KN Energy Inc., Hastings, 1971-73, dir. regulatory affairs, 1973-76, v.p. law divsn. Lakewood, Colo., 1976-82, sr. v.p., 1982-85, exec. v.p., 1985-88, pres., COO, 1988-94, pres., CEO, 1994—99, also bd. dirs., 1988-94, chmn., CEO, pres., 1996-99; mng. dir. CPS Investments, 1999—; chmn., CEO Guardian Prostar. Bd. dirs. Colo. Assn. Commerce and Industry, Gas Rsch. Inst., Colo. Alliance for Bus., MLA, Magnum Techs., Riverview Tech. Corp.; chmn. Natural Gas Coun., 1998. Bd. dirs. Boy Scouts Am.; active Canyon View Vineyard Ch.; bd. dirs. Denver Police Officers Found. Mem. ABA, Colo. Assn. Commerce and Industry (bd. dirs.), Interstate Natural Gas Assn. Am. (chmn. 1997), RTC (bd. dirs.), Nebr. Bar Assn., Colo. Bar Assn., Midwest Gas Assn. (chmn.). Avocations: skiing, golf, photography. Home: 329 Red Ridge Ct Grand Junction CO 81503 Office: CPS Investments LLC 1400 16th St Ste 400 Denver CO 80202

HALL, LEE, artist, educator, writer; b. Lexington, N.C., Dec. 15, 1934; d. Robert Lee and Florence (Fitzgerald) H. BFA, U. N.C., 1955; MA, N.Y. U., 1959, PhD, 1965; postgrad., Warburg Inst. U. London, 1965; DFA (hon.), U. N.C.-Greensboro, 1976. Asst. prof. N.Y. State U. Coll., Potsdam, 1958-60; assoc. prof., chmn. art dept. Keuka Coll., 1960-62; assoc. prof. art Winthrop Coll., 1962-65; asst. prof., chmn. art dept. Drew U., Madison, N.J., 1965-67, assoc. prof., chmn. art dept., 1967-70, prof., chmn. art dept., 1970-74; dean visual arts State U. N.Y. Coll. at Purchase, 1974-75; pres. R.I. Sch. Design, Providence, 1975-83; sr. v.p., dir. div. arts and communications Acad. for Ednl. Devel., N.Y.C., 1984-92. Dir. rsch. on Pres. Kennedy's image in recent art, John F. Kennedy Meml. Library; panelist NEH, 1972-80. Exhibited in group shows in London, N.Y.C., Winston-Salem, Eugene, Oreg., others; author: Wallace Herndon Smith: Paintings, 1987, Ale Ajay, 1989, Betty Parsons: Artist, Dealer, Collector, 1991; Common Threads: A Parade of American Clothing, 1992; Elaine and Bill (de Kooning), 1993, Olmsted's America, 1994, Athena: A Biography, 1994; contbr. articles to profl. jours. Recipient research grant Am. Philos. Soc., 1965, 68; Childe Hassam Purchase award Am. Acad. Arts and Letters, 1977; RISD Athena medal, 1983 Mem. PEN, Cosmopolitan Club, Nat. Arts Club. Home: 14 Silverwood Ter South Hadley MA 01075-1237 Personal E-mail: lhall8115@aol.com.

HALL, LISA GERSH, broadcast executive, lawyer; m. John Hall; 2 children. JD, Rutgers Law Sch., 1983. Atty. Debevoise & Plimpton, LLP; founding ptnr. Friedman, Kaplan & Seiler, LLP, NYC; co-founder Oxygen Media, Inc., NYC, 1998—, chief adminstrv. officer and gen. counsel, 1998—99, COO, 1999—, pres., 2004—. Office: Oxygen Media Inc 7th Fl 75 9th Ave New York NY 10011

HALL, LOIS BREMER, secondary school educator, educator, volunteer; b. Oak Park, Ill., July 27, 1923; d. Frederick Statler and Mabel (Forbes) Bremer; m. Bruce Hall, Sept. 9, 1955 (dec. Mar. 1981); children: Donald, Richard, Barbara. B in Music Edn., U. Mich., 1946. Cert. elem., secondary tchr. Mich., Ky.; ordained elder Presbyn. Ch. Tchr. handbell ringing Elm St. Recreation Ctr., Atlantic Recreation Ctr. Handbell ringer AARP, Osprey Village and Quality Health, Bapt. Hosp., 1st Presbyn. Ch. Fernandina Beach; dir. Amelia Handbell Choir; singer Amelia Island Chorale, Meml. United Meth. Ch., Amelia Plantation Chapel, Amelia Bapt. Ch., St. Peter's Episcopal Ch., tenor Amelia Island Cmty. Corale. Mem. com. Peck Ctr.; founding mem., vol. coord. CROP Walk, 1989—99; vol. Michah's Place (abused women refuge); player Praise Band, 2000—04; vol. Abused Women Shelter, 2003—04; mem. New Horizon Band, 2004; mem. exec. bd. Meml. United Meth. Ch.; vol. Church World Svc., Fernandina Beach, Synod of South Atlantic Coun., 1989; mem. Presbytery of St. Augustine Coun., 1984—97, music coord. of handbell and choral workshops, 1990—98; mem. hunger com. Presbyn. Gen. Assembly, 1992—96; vol.-in-mission New Hope Meth. Presbyn. Ch., N. Pole, Alaska, 1991—94, 1996; soloist, clarinet Ch. Choirs; mem. Mirth Ch. Handbell Choir, 2002—04; dir., pres. Ch. Handbell Choir, 2004; bd. dirs. Amelia Arts Acad., 1994—2003, Ann. Fernandina Beach Talent Show, 2001—02. Recipient award for cultural enrichment, City of Fernandina Beach, 2001. Mem.: AARP (bd. dirs.), Woman's Club Fernandina Beach (pres. 1983—84, 1991—92, Outstanding New Mem. 1980—81, Cmty. Svc. award 1987—88), Rose Garden Club (treas. 1998—2002), Alpha Omicron Pi, Delta Omicron. Republican. Home: 607 Goldenrod Way Saint Marys GA 31558

HALL, LYDIA JANE, geriatrics nurse; b. Ravenwood, Mo., Mar. 4, 1939; d. George G. and Lydia G. (Lambert) Griffin; m. Clifford Ray Hall, Sept. 18, 1987; children: Ray Ballin, Ronald Ballin, Janet Goad, Julia Newton. Assoc. Nursing, Butler County Community Coll., Eldorado, Kans., 1983; student, Arkansas City Community Coll., 1984, Kans. Newman Coll., Wichita, 1985. Staff nurse Arkansas City Meml. Hosp., 1983-85, St. Joseph Med. Ctr., Wichita, Kans., 1985-86, Heritage House, Winfield, Kans., 1986; evening and night charge nurse Health Concepts IV-Cedar Vale (Kans.) Regional Hosp., 1986-87, 88-89; staff nurse St. Luke's Hosp., Wellington, Kans., 1988, Augusta (Kans.) Med. Complex, Inc., 1989; night charge nurse Cumbernauld Village, Winfield, Kans., 1990; DON Grouse Valley Manor, Dexter, Kans., 1991-97; charge nurse Med. Lodge East, Arkansas City, Kans., 1997-98, Presbyn. Manor, Arkansas City, 1998-2000, Med Lodge Home Health, Arkansas City, 2001, Beverly Healthcare & Rehab, Wellington, Kans., 2001—02; house supr. Kans. Vets. Home, Winfield, Kans., 2002. Mem. sch. bd. Unified Sch. Dist. 462, Burden, Kans., 1975-79; mem., chmn. Cowley County Spl. Edn. Bd., 1975-79. Home: 1021 E 2nd Ave Winfield KS 67156-2302

HALL, LYNDA MARIE, school system administrator, consultant; b. Boise, Feb. 13, 1946; d. Henry William and Betty Marie Miller; m. Ronald Gary Hall, Aug. 26, 1967; children: Ronda Hall Baines, Gary Dean, Celeste Hall Evans. B of Edn., U. N.D., 1968; MA in Edn. Adminstrn., Albertson Coll. Idaho, 1986. Cert. elem. & secondary edn., prin., spl. edn. adminstrn. Tchr. Grand Forks Sch. Dist., ND, 1968—70, Payette Sch. Dist., Idaho, 1975—80; resource tchr. New Plymouth Sch. Dist., 1980—90, dir. title I and migrant edn., 1986—93, vice prin., 1986—, dir. spl. svcs., 1993—. Regional rep. Children's Mental Health/Health & Welfare, New Plymouth, 2002—; sec. Idaho Coun. Children with Behavior Disorders, 2000—. Leader Girl Scouts U.S.A., Fruitland, Idaho, 1986—92; mem. election bd. Payette County, 1990—; tchr. Holy Family Cath. Ch., 1998—2004. Named Tchr. of Yr., Idaho State Det. Edn., Boise, 1985; recipient Nat. award Excellence Title I Edn. Program, U.S. Dept. Edn., New Orleans, 1985, Nat. award, 1986. Mem.: Coun. Exceptional Children, Nat. Assn. Elem. Sch. Prins., Delta Kappa Gamma (2d v.p. 2004—). Republican. Roman Catholic. Avocations: quilting, piano, camping, writing. Office: New Plymouth Sch Dist 204 S Plymouth Ave New Plymouth ID 83655

HALL, MARCIA JOY, non-profit organization administrator; b. Long Beach, Calif., June 24, 1947; d. Royal Waltz and Norine (Parker) Stanton; m. Stephen Christopher Hall, Mar. 29, 1968; children: Geoffrey Michael, Christopher Stanton. AA, Foothill Coll., 1967; student, U. Oreg., 1967-68; BA, U. Washington, Seattle, 1969. Cert. contracts count presenter 2005. Instr. aide Glen Yermo Sch., Mission Viejo, Calif., 1979—80; market rsch. interviewer Rsch. Data, Framingham, Mass., 1982—83; instr. adult edn. Community Sch. Use Program, Milford, Mass., 1982—83; coord. career info. ctr. Milford High Sch., 1983—86; dir. corp. rels. Sch. Vols. for Milford, Inc., 1985—86; coord. N.E. area YWCA of Annapolis and Anne Arundel County, Severna Park, Md., 1987—89; exec. dir. West Anne Arundel County C. of C., Odenton, Md., 1989—2001, also exec. dir. Found., Inc., 1999—2001; coord. bus. and entrepreneurship continuing profl. edn. and outreach Anne Arundel C.C., Arundel Mills, Md., 2001—03, lead instr. nonprofit leadership devel., 2003—; pres., CEO Marcia Hall & Assocs., LLC, Severna Park, Md., 2003—. V.p. Corridor Transp. Corp., 1997-99; bd. dirs. Entrepreneur's Exch.; cert. Contacts Count! presenter, 2005—. Pres. PTO, Mission Viejo, 1979-80, Milford, 1981-84; consumer assistance vol., Calif. Pub. Interest Rsch. Group, 1977-78; chmn. grant com. 21st Century Edn. Found., Ann Arundel Pub. Schs., Leadership Anne Arundel. Mem.: Am. Assn. Women in C.C., Assn. Women in Comm., Md. Assn. C. of C. Execs. (pres. 1999—2000), Toastmasters (treas. 1988—, pres. 1989—). Avocations: piano, music composition, bridge, reading. Home: 507 Devonshire Ln Severna Park MD 21146-1017 Office Phone: 410-987-0857.

HALL, MARY-JO, management consultant; b. Durham, N.C., Jan. 5, 1947; d. Paul Thomas and Miriam Josephine (Burroughs) H.; m. Emmett E. Stobbs, Jr., July 19, 1975. BA in Tchg., High Point U., 1969; MEd, U. Md., 1972; MBA, L.I. U., 1980; PhD in Edn., George Mason U., 1990. Elem. tchr., N.C., Md., Korea, Fed. Republic Germany, 1969-75; adminstr. U.S. Govt., Sacramento, 1976-78; counselor, trainer U.S. Mil. Acad., West Point, N.Y., 1978-81; contracts negotiator USN, Dahlgren, Va., 1981-82; contracts adminstr. USAF, McChord, Wash., 1982-83; leadership and evaluation officer ROTC, U.S. Army, Ft. Lewis, Wash., 1983—87; mgmt. analyst USN, Washington, 1984—89; chief Program Mgmt. Office, dir. combat devel. U.S. Army Engr. Schs., Ft. Leonard Wood, Mo., 1987—89; prof. mgmt. Def. Systems Mgmt. Coll., Ft. Belvoir, Va., 1989-92, spl. asst. to commandant for quality, 1992—96; prof. program mgmt. leadership Def. Acquisition U., 1996—2001, leadership officer Chief Learning Office, 2002—04, prof. Sch. Mgmt., 2005; exec. cons. Fed. Consulting Group, Washington, 2001—02; cons. Cambrough Group, 2005. Vice chair profl. devel. Aerospace and Def. Spl. Interest Group; rsch. fellow ASTD, 2005. Author: Valuing Diversity, Program Manager, 1991, Quality Challenge: To Be Ethical Stewards of the Government's Resources, Defense Technology Information Center, 1992. Recipient achievement award U.S. Army, 1989, Superior Achievement medal Dept. of Def., 1996, Achievement medal Def. Acquisition U., 2004, Exceptional Civilian Performance award Office Sec. of Def., 2005. Mem. Am. Soc. for Quality Control, Am. Soc. Mil. Compts. (edn. award Ozark chpt. 1989), D.C. Profls. in Diversity Work, Acad. Mgmt. Avocations: gardening, jogging, theater. Home: 62 Winding Ridge Rd Durham NC 27713

HALL, MICHAEL C., actor; b. Raleigh, N.C., Feb. 1, 1971; m. Amy Spanger. Grad., Earlham Coll., 1993; MFA, NYU. Actor: (TV series) Six Feet Under, 2001—05; (films) Showboy, 2002, Paycheck, 2003, Bereft, 2004; (plays) Macbeth, Cymbeline, Timon of Athens, Henry V at the Public, The English Teachers, Corpus Christi, Skylight, Cabaret, R Shomon, 2004; TV appearances includ The Tonight Show with Jay Leno, 2003. Office: c/o Don Buchwald & Assocs 10 E 44th St New York NY 10017*

HALL, MICHAEL DAVID, art educator; b. Upland, Calif., May 20, 1941; s. Robert Oscar and Jeanne Lucile Hall; m. Patricia Ann Patterson, Nov. 30, 1991; children: Collin Gabriel, Rane Ivory. BA in sculpture, U. NC, 1962; MFA in sculpture, U. Wash., 1964. Art instr. U. Colo., Boulder, Colo., 1965—66; assoc. prof. U. Ky., Lexington, Ky., 1966—70; resident sculptor, head of sculpture Cranbrook Acad. of Art, Bloomfield Hills, Mich., 1970—90; prof. interdisciplinary studies Miami U., Oxford, Ohio, 1991—. Cons. curator Columbus Mus. of Art, Columbus, Ohio, 1994—2003. Author: Stereoscopic Perspective, 1988; editor: The Artist Outsider, 1994; co-author: North by Midwest: The Paintings of Charles Burchfield, 1997; one-man shows include sculpture Hammarskjold Plaza, N.Y.C., 1972, Detroit Inst. of Arts, Mich., 1973, Scarab Club, 2004, exhibited in group shows at Whitney Mus of Am. Art, N.Y.C., 1968, 1973, one-man shows include sculpture Walker Art Ctr., Mlpls., 1977, exhibited in group shows at Milw. Art Mus., Wis., 1992. Acquisitions bd. mem. Art Gallery of Windsor, Winsor Ontario, Canada, 1992—2002, Detroit Inst. Arts, 2001. Guggenheim fellow, Guggenheim Found., 1973, Nat. Endowment fellowship, Nat. Endowment for the Arts, 1974, Mich. Coun. fellowship, Mich. Coun. for the Arts, 1985—88. Mem.: Intuit: Ctr. for Intuitive and Outsider Art, Internat. Sculpture Ctr. Avocations: art, collecting Am. regionalist painting, Am. Indian art, Am. folk art. Home: 3417 Caniff Ave Hamtramck MI 48212

HALL, MICHAEL DAVIS, principal; b. Dayton, Ohio, Aug. 22, 1938; s. Paul Davis and Anna Rue Hall; m. Ann Gusweiler, June 24, 1960; children: Barbara, Susan, Deborah. BA, Denison U., 1960; MEd, U. Toledo, 1962. Cert. tchr. Ohio. Sci. tchr. Siren Area Schools, Wis., 1977—79; h.s. prin. Wabeno Area Schools, Wis., 1979—82; coord. athletics Forest Hills Schools, Cin., 1982—84; prin. Anderson H.S. Little Miami Schools, Morrow, Ohio, 1984—2003; prin. Miami Valley Christian Acad., Newton, Ohio, 2003—. Bd. mem. Ohio Prevention and Edn. Resource Ctr., Ohio Dept. Edn., 1990—2002, Kids Helping Kids Substance Abuse Treatment Program, Ohio, 1992—2001; bd. mem., mem. exec. com. Coalition for a Drug Free Greater Cin., 1990—2003; Ohio state com. mem. North Ctr. Accrediating Agy., 1998—2001. Contbr. articles to school newsletter. Bd. mem. Ohio H.S. Athletic Assn., Chem. Awareness Com., 1999—2003. Named to Hall of Fame, Nat. Coun. of Sec. Sch. Athletic Dir., 2001; recipient Hamilton County PTA Educator of the Yr., Cin., Ohio, 2003. Mem.: Ohio Assn. Sec. Prins., Nat. Assn. Secondary Prins. Home: 3 Orchard Lane Covington KY 41015 Office: Miami Valley Christian Acad 6830 School St Cincinnati OH 45244 Office Phone: 513-272-6822. Business E-Mail: mike@mikehall.us.

HALL, MILES LEWIS, JR., lawyer; b. Fort Lauderdale, Fla., Aug. 14, 1924; s. Miles Lewis and Mary Frances (Dawson) H.; m. Muriel M. Fisher, Nov. 4, 1950; children: Miles Lewis III, Don Thomas. AB, Princeton U., 1947; JD, Harvard U., 1950. Bar: Fla. 1951, U.S. Supreme Ct., 1972, U.S. Ct. Appeals (11th cir.), U.S. Dist. Ct. (so. and mid. dist.) Fla. Since practiced in, Miami; ptnr. Hall & Hedrick, Miami, 1953—. Dir. Gen. Portland, Inc., 1974-81. Author: Election of Remedies, Vol. VIII, Fla. Law and Practice, 1958. Pres. Orange Bowl Com., 1964-65, dir., 1950—, sec., treas. 1984-86; vice-chmn., dir. Dade County (Fla.) ARC, 1961-62, chmn., 1963-64, dir., 1967-73; nat. fund cons. ARC, 1963, 66-68, trustee, 1985—; pres. Ransom Sch. Parents Assn., 1966; chmn. South Fla. Gov.'s Scholarship Ball, 1966; mem. exec. bd. South Fla. council Boy Scouts Am., 1966-67; citizens bd. U. Miami, 1961-66; mem. Fla. Council of 100, 1961-97, vice chmn., 1961-62; mem. Coral Gables (Fla.) Biltmore Devel. Com., 1972-73; mem. bd. visitors Coll. Law, Fla. State U., 1974-77; bd. dirs. Coral Gables War Meml. Youth Ctr. Assn. Inc., 1967—, pres., 1969-72; bd. dirs. Salvation Army, Miami, 1968-83, Fla. Citizens Against Crime 1984-89; bd. dirs. Bok Tower Gardens Found. Inc., 1987—, sec., 1991—; trustee St. Thomas U., 1990-96, vice chmn., 1993-96; trustee Fla. Supreme Ct. Hist. Soc., 1988—, v.p., 1991-92, pres., 1993-95. 2d lt. USAAF, 1943-45. Fellow Am. Bar Found. (life), Fla. Bar Found. (life); mem. ABA (Fla. co-chmn. membership com. sect. corp. banking and bus. law 1968-72), Dade County Bar Assn. (dir. 1964-65, pres. 1967-68), Fla. Bar Assn., Am. Judicature Soc., Miami-Dade County C. of C. (v.p. 1962-64, dir. 1966-68), Harvard Law Sch. Assn. Fla. (dir. 1964-66), Cottage Club, The Miami Club (v.p., dir. 1989-91, pres. 1990-91), Princeton Club So. Fla. (past pres.), Miami Found. for Cancer Rsch., Inc. (pres. 1998—), Alpha Tau Omega. Methodist. Home: 2707 Alhambra Cir Coral Gables FL 33134 Office: Hall & Hedrick 306 Alcazar Ave Ste 301 Coral Gables FL 33134

HALL, MILTON REESE, retired oil company executive, accountant, controller; b. Vicksburg, Miss., July 5, 1932; s. Alvin Howard and Adelle Vera (McKay) H.; m. Margaret Louise Bailey, Feb. 17, 1957; children: Mark Russell, Stacy Elaine. BS in Acctg., Miss. So. U., 1953; MBA in Acctg., U. Miss., 1956; postgrad., La. State U., 1958-62. CPA, Miss. Trainee, div. contr. Kaiser Aluminum & Chem. Co., various locations, 1956-66; analyst Tex. Instruments, Inc., Dallas, 1966-67; contr., v.p. Koch Industries, Inc., Wichita, Kans., 1967-92; retired, 1993. With U.S. Army, 1953-55. Republican. Baptist. Avocations: music, skiing.

HALL, MONTY, television producer, actor; b. Winnipeg, Man., Can., Aug. 25, 1921; came to U.S., 1955; s. Maurice Harvey and Rose (Rusen) Halparin; m. Marilyn Doreen Plottel, Sept. 28, 1947; children: Joanna, Richard David, Sharon Fay. BS, U. Man., 1945, LLD (hon.), 1987; D Human Scis. (hon.), Hanneman U., 1988; PhD (hon.), Haifa U., 1989. TV personality, emcee, N.Y.C. and Hollywood, Calif., 1955—. Lectr. broadcasting and fund raising various charities. Actor, U. Man., Canadian Army shows; emcee: NBC-Radio, Monitor on NBC-TV, Keep Talking, Byline: Monty Hall, Video Village on CBS-TV, ABC-TV; host Let's Make a Deal, 1964-86, Split Second, 1986-87; Author: Emcee: Monty Hall, 1974; producer (TV show) Your First Impression; guest appearances numerous TV series: starring role (stage prodn.) High Button Shoes, 1978. Bd. dirs. numerous charitable orgns.; bd. govs. Cedars-Sinai Med. Ctr.; active numerous orgns. on behalf of Israel; hon. mayor, Hollywood, 1973-79. Decorated officer Order of Can., Order of Manitoba; recipient star on Hollywood's Walk of Fame, 1973, on Palm Springs Walk of Fame, 1996, on Can. Walk of Fame, 2002; Internat. Humanitarian award Variety Clubs, 1983, over 500 other awards, including Monty Hall floor at U. Calif./L.A. Hosp., Johns Hopkins U., Balt., Mt. Sinai Hosp., Toronto, Hahneman Hosp., Phila. Mem. AFTRA, Screen Actors Guild, Variety Clubs (internat. pres. 1975-77, internat. chmn. 1981—). Clubs: Hillcrest Country. Avocations: golf, tennis. Office Phone: 323-874-3000. Business E-Mail: kelekis@aol.com. *The longer I live, the more I am obsessed with man's inhumanity directed against his fellow man. Is there a basic flaw in man's makeup which prevents the good from overtaking and defeating the evil? I have spent my adult life dedicated to helping children around the world, the diseased, handicapped and underprivileged. The rewards tangible and intangible have shaped my life, have given me an inner peace with myself, and yet a frustration at what could be and is not. The same holds for nation against nation. What could be—and is not. Is this the order of things past and things to come? I pray with all my heart that the teachings of peace shall prevail.*

HALL, NANCY CHRISTENSEN, publishing company executive, author, editor; b. N.Y.C., Nov. 14, 1946; d. Henry Norman and Elvira (Dugan) Christensen; m. John R. Hall Jr., June 12, 1968; children: Jonathan Scott, Kirsten Marie. BA, Manhattanville Coll., 1968; postgrad., Old Dominion U., 1970-71. Sr. assoc. editor Cahners Pub. Co., N.Y.C., 1972-74; freelance editor N.Y.C., 1974-78; sr. editor Grosset and Dunlap, N.Y.C., 1978-81; exec. editor, asst. v.p. Macmillan Pub. Co., N.Y.C., 1981-84; assoc. pub., v.p. Simon & Schuster Pub. Co., N.Y.C., 1984-85; founder, prin. Nancy Hall, Inc., juvenile book devel co., N.Y.C., 1986—; founder, ptnr. Hall Assocs., Inc., 1996—. Author: Monsters: Creatures of Mystery, 1980, Macmillan Fairy Tale Alphabet Book 1983; editor: Platt and Munk Treasury of Stories for Children, 1981, Favorite Tales from Hans Christian Andersen, 1988; prodr. series: Macmillan Jumbo Seasonal Patterns, Macmillan Manipulatives, Sesame Street Early Learning Games, Mickey's Young Readers Libr., Disney's Small World Libr., My First Hello Readers, and others. Office: Nancy Hall Inc 23 E 22nd St New York NY 10010-5304

HALL, NANCY KAY, music educator; b. Texas City, Tex., Mar. 29, 1951; d. Gerald Taylor and Modine (Griffith) Ramsey; m. David Earl Railey, July 20, 1974 (div. Sept. 1983); 1 child, Rachel Michal; m. Michael Mabray Hall, Oct. 13, 1984. BS, Houston Bapt. U., 1973; postgrad., Southwestern Bapt. Theol. Sem., Ft. Worth, 1974. Pvt. piano tchr., Houston, 1970-73, Ft. Smith, Ark., 1977-84, Wharton, Tex., 1984-88, The Woodlands, Tex., 1988—; tchr. Kindermusik of Wharton, Tex., 1987-88, Kindermusik of The Woodlands, 1988—; studio and music store owner Hall's Family Musik, The Woodlands, 1994—. Mem. Nat. Assn. Music Tchrs., Nat. Guild Piano Tchrs. (cert., local chmn. 1997—), Am. Coll. Musicians, Early Childhood Music and Movement Assn. (Level 3 cert.), Kindermusik Educators Assn. (master tchr. cert., maestro 2000-), Conroe Music Tchrs. Assn. (v.p. 1994-96, pres. 1996-98, Tchr. of Yr. 1996). Republican. Avocations: boating, fishing, snorkeling. Home: 64 Eagle Rock Cir The Woodlands TX 77381-4343 Office: Hall's Family Musik and Kindermusik of The Woodlands 25210 Grogans Park Dr The Woodlands TX 77380-2175

HALL, PAMELA S., environmental services administrator; b. Hartford, Conn., Sept. 4, 1944; d. LeRoy Warren and Frances May (Murray) Sheely; m. Stuart R. Hall, July 21, 1967 (dec.). BA in Zoology, U. Conn., 1966; MS in Zoology, U. N.H., 1969, BSBA summa cum laude, 1982; postgrad., Tufts U., 1986-90. Curatorial asst. U. Conn., Storrs, 1966; rsch. asst. Field Mus. Natural History, Chgo., 1966-67; tchg. asst. U. N.H., Durham, 1967-70; program mgr. Normandeau Assocs. Inc., Portsmouth, N.H., 1971-79, marine lab. dir., 1979-81, programs and ops. mgr. Bedford, N.H., 1981-83, v.p., 1983-85, sr. v.p., 1986-87, pres., 1987—. Mem. Conservation Com., Portsmouth, 1977-90, Wells, Estuarine Rsch. Res. Rev.Commn., 1986-88, Great Bay (N.H.) Estuarine Rsch. Res. Tech. Working Group, 1987-89; trustee Trust for N.H. Lands, 1990-93; trustee N.H. chpt. Nature Conservancy, 1991—, chair 1995-99, chair emeritus, 1999, trustee, 2000—, incorporator N.H. Charitable Fund, 1991-99; bd. advisors Vivamos Mejor, USA, 1990—; bd. dirs. Environ. Bus. Coun. New England, 1995—, treas. 1997—; bd. emeritus Ecosystems Inst., 1997—; commr. N.H. Land and Heritage Commn., 1998-99; bd. advisers N.H. Corp. Wetlands Restoration Partnership, 2003—; bd. dirs. Seacoast Sci. Ctr., Rye, N.H., 2004—. Recipient Environ. Leadership award Environ. Bus. Coun. New Eng., 1998; Graham Found. fellow, 1966; NDEA fellow, 1970-71. Mem. Nature Conservancy, Soc. of the Protection NH Forests, Nat. Audubon Soc., Audubon Soc. NH, Am. Mgmt. Assn., Phi Sigma, Sigma Xi. Home: 4 Pleasant Point Dr Portsmouth NH 03801-5275 Office: Normandeau Assocs Inc 25 Nashua Rd Bedford NH 03110-5500 Office Phone: 603-472-5191. E-mail: phall@normandeau.com.

HALL, PENELOPE COKER, writer, magazine editor; b. Charlotte, N.C., Mar. 19, 1932; d. James Lide and Elizabeth (Boatwright) Coker; m. William Parmenter Wilson, Sept. 6, 1964 (div. 1971); 1 child, Eliza Wilson Ingle; m. Mortimer Waddhams Hall, Dec. 8, 1972; stepchildren: Dorothy, Margaret, Mary Howland, Matthew. Student, Sarah Lawrence Coll., Bronxville, N.Y., 1954. Sr. editor, biographer Cleveland Amory's Celebrity Register, N.Y.C.; prodr., commentator Wrap-Up with Mike Wallace, N.Y.C.; co-prodr., interviewer for series of hr. long spls. NBC-TV, N.Y.C.; co-host 10 Around Town Channel 10 TV, Phila.; co-host The New Yorkers Channel 5 TV, N.Y.C., 1968-70; reporter, Sunday anchor 10 O'Clock News, Channel 5, N.Y.C., 1970-73; host cable cooking show Millbrook, NY, 1976—; editor-in-chief Dutchess Mag., N.Y.C., 1993—99, editor-at-large, columnist, 1998—. CEO Alpacalypse Hall LLC, 2005—. Contbr. numerous articles to profl. jours.; author: Fancy and the Cement Patch, 1966, The Wish Bottle, 1967, Riding High, 1990. Bd. trustees Spoleto Festival, Charleston, S.C., 1997—, Coker Coll., Hartsville, S.C., 2000— Mem. Authors League, Nat. Trust for Hist. Preservation Nat. Trust Coun., Sandanona Beagles, Millbrook Hounds, Century Assn., Millbrook Golf and Tennis Club (bd. dirs. 1989-93), Cosmopolitan Club. Democrat. Episcopalian. Avocations: painting, horseback riding, boating. Home: PO Box 516 Millbrook NY 12545-0516

HALL, PETER FRANCIS, physiologist; b. Sydney, Australia, Dec. 12, 1924; s. William and Ruby Alice (Price) H.; m. Helen Ruth Godfrey, Nov. 10, 1968; children: Philip Charles, Warwick David. M.B.BS, U. Sydney, 1947, MD, 1956; PhD, U. Utah, 1962. Sr. med. officer Royal Prince Alfred Hosp., Sydney, 1947-50; registrar Guys Hosp., 1954-59; hon. med. officer Sydney Hosp., 1954-59; NIH fellow U. Utah, 1959-62; asst. prof. dept. physiology U. Pitts., 1962-64; prof. biochemistry Melbourne U., 1964-71; prof., chmn. dept. physiology U. Calif.-Irvine, 1971-78; prin. scientist Worcester Found. Exptl. Biology, Shrewsbury, Mass., 1978-86; chmn. endocrinology U. New South Wales and Prince Henry/Prince of Wales Hosps., Sydney, 1986—; pvt. practice in medicolegal medicine, 1998—. Author: Gynaecomastia, 1959, Function of the Endocrine Glands, 1959; contbr. articles to profl. jours. Recipient Merck prize for chemistry, 1959. Fellow Royal Australian Coll. Physicians, Royal Coll. Physicians (London); mem. Am. Physiol. Soc., Am. Soc. Cell Biology, Am. Soc. Biol. Chemistry, Endocrine Soc. Mem. Ch. Of Eng. Home: 81 Ocean St Woollahra NSW 2025 Australia Office: Prince of Wales Hosp Dept Endocrinology High Street Randwick NSW 2031 Australia

HALL, SIR PETER GEOFFREY, urban and regional planning educator; b. London, Mar. 19, 1932; came to U.S., 1980; s. Arthur Vickers and Bertha (Keefe) H.; m. Carla Maria Wartenberg, Sept. 7, 1962 (div. 1967); m. Magda Mroz, Feb. 13, 1967. BA in Geography, Cambridge (Eng.) U., 1953, PhD, 1959; DDS (hon.), Birmingham (Eng.) U., 1991, 1991; PhD (hon.), Lund (Sweden) U., 1992; DLitt (hon.), Sheffield U., 1995, Newcastle U., 1995; DEng (hon.), Tech. U. Nova Scotia, Can., 1996; ArtsD (hon.), Oxford Brookes U., 1997; LLD (hon.), Reading U., 1999; DSc (hon.), U. West Eng., 2000; D Laws, U. Manchester, 2001; DLitt (hon.), Herriot Watt U., 2002, Guildhall U., London, 2002; DSS (hon.), U. London, 2004; DTech (hon.), U.

Greenwich, 2004. Lectr. Birkbeck Coll., U. London, 1957-65; reader London Sch. Econs., 1966-67; prof. U. Reading, Eng., 1968-89, chmn., 1971-77, dean faculty urban and regional studies, 1975-78, bd. mgmt., 1983-86, prof. emeritus, 1989—; prof. dept. city and regional planning U. Calif., Berkeley, 1980-92, assoc. dir. Inst. Urban and Regional Devel., 1980-88, dir., 1989-92, prof. emeritus, 1993—. Prof. planning The Bartlett, Univ. Coll. London, 1992—, dir. sch. pub. policy, 1996—97; dir. Inst. of Cmty. Studies, 2001—04; spl. advisor Dept. of Environment, London, 1991—94; mem. Urban Task Force, 1998—99. Author: The World Cities, 1966, 3d edit., 1984, Europe 2000, 1977 (Bentinck prize 1979), Great Planning Disasters, 1980, The Inner City in Context, 1981, Silicon Landscapes, 1985, Can Rail Save the City?, 1985, High-Tech America, 1986, Western Sunrise, 1987, Cities of Tomorrow, 1988, London 2001, 1989, Cities and Civilization, 1998; co-author: The Rise of the Gunbelt, 1991, Technopoles of the World, 1994, Sociable Cities, 1998, Cities in Civilization, 1998, Urban Future 21, 2000, Working Capital, 2002. Advisor Social Dem. party, 1983-85; active S.E. Econ. Planning Coun., 1966-79, Social Sci. Rsch. Coun., 1974-79. Fellow Brit. Acad., Royal Geog. Soc. (Gill Meml. prize 1968, Founder's medal 1991), St. Catharine's Coll. (hon.); mem. Royal Town Planning Inst. (hon., Gold medal 2003), Am. Planning Assn., Athenaeum Club, Brit. Acad. Avocations: reading, travel. Office: Young Foundation 18 Victoria Park Sq London E2 9PF England Office Phone: +44 208 709 9263. Business E-Mail: phall@icstudies.ac.uk.

HALL, PETER MICHAEL, physics educator, electronics researcher; b. Belmont, N.Y., July 31, 1934; s. Harris Tremaine and Dorothy Lou (Harris) H.; m. Betty Jane Bressell, Dec. 21, 1956; children: Michael, Ann, Sarah, Philip. BA, Hobart Coll., 1954; MS, Iowa State U., 1956, PhD, 1959. Registered profl. engr., N.C. Mem. tech. staff AT&T Bell Labs., Murray Hill, N.J., 1959-64, fellow Allentown, Pa., 1964-90; Disting. prof. physics Johnson C. Smith U., Charlotte, NC, 1990—2001. Co-author: Thin Film Technology, 1968; contbr. articles to profl. jours., chpt. to book; patentee on fabrication of circuit packages. Recipient award for best paper Electronic Components Conf., 1984. Fellow IEEE (components, hybrids and mfg. tech. group, best paper award 1988); mem. ASME (editor 1989-95), Am. Phys. Soc., Am. Assn. Physics Tchrs., Phi Beta Kappa, Sigma Xi. Democrat. Episcopalian. Avocation: sailing. Home: 140 Lakeside Dr Middletown DE 19709-1372

HALL, PETER W., federal judge, former prosecutor; b. Hartford, Conn., Nov. 9, 1948; BA, U. N.C., 1971, MA, 1974; JD, Cornell U., 1977. Law clk. to Hon. Albert W. Coffrin, 1977—78; asst. US atty, Dist. Vt. US Dept. Justice, 1978—82, 1st asst. US atty., Dist. Vt, 1982—86; ptnr. Reiber, Kenlan, Schwiebert, Hall and Facey, Rutland, Vt., 1986—2001; US atty. ea. dist. US Dept. Justice, Vt., 2001—04; judge US Ct. Appeals (2nd cir.), 2004—. Office: US Ct Appeals 40 Foley Sq New York NY 10007*

HALL, RALPH C., retired architect, mechanical engineer; b. Lowell, Ohio, June 9, 1925; s. Joseph R. and Florence E. (Misel) H.; m. Elizabeth Ruth Lenox, June 28, 1947; children: Nancy Elaine Hall Bell, Stephen Mark. BME, Ohio State U., 1948; MDiv, Grace Theol. Sem., Winona Lake, Ind., 1951; ThD, Christian Bible Coll./Sem., Independence, Mo., 1996. Registered architect, Ohio, 20 other states; registered profl. engr., Ind., Fla., Va. Architect, CEO Brethren Archtl. Svc., Winona Lake, Ind., 1960-74; architect, profl. engr. Ralph C. Hall, P.E., R.A., Winona Lake, 1974-84, Bradenton, Fla., 1984-96; ret., 1996. Chmn. bd. dirs. Brethren Retirement Homes, Winona Lake, 1976-84; chmn. plan commn. Town of Winona Lake, 1976-79. Republican. Grace Brethren Ch. Avocations: photography, travel. Home: 214 Lilys Way Winchester VA 22602-7649 Personal E-mail: ralphchall@verizon.net.

HALL, RALPH MOODY, congressman; b. Fate, Tex., May 3, 1923; s. Hugh O. and Maude Hall; m. Mary Ellen Murphy, Nov. 14, 1944; children: Hampton, Brett, Blakeley. Student, U. Tex., Tex. Christian U., So. Meth. U., LLB, 1951. Bar: Tex. County judge Rockwall County, Tex., 1950-62; mem. Tex. Senate, 1962-72; pres., CEO Tex. Aluminum Corp., 1967—68; past gen. counsel Tex. Extrusion Co., Inc.; past organizer, chmn. bd. Lakeside Nat. Bank of Rockwall; chmn. bd. Bank of Crowley; past chmn. bd. dirs. Lakeside News, Inc.; chmn. bd. Linrock Inc.; pres. Crowley Holding Co.; mem. U.S. Congress from 4th Tex. dist., Washington, 1981—; pres. pro tempore Tex. Senate, 1968—69. Mem. energy and commerce com., mem. sci. com. Served with USNR, 1942-45. Mem. Am. Legion, VFW, Rotary (past pres.). Republican. Methodist. Office: US Ho of Reps 2405 Rayburn Ho Office Bldg Washington DC 20515-4304 E-mail: rmhall@mail.house.gov.*

HALL, RANDY JARVIS, lawyer; b. Ft. Worth, Feb. 24, 1951; s. Benton Garrett Jr. and Janine Hall; m. Gloria Pine, July 18, 1981; children: Randy Jarvis Jr., Matthew Brian. BBA, Tex. Tech U., 1973, JD, 1976. Bar: Tex. 1976, cert.: Nat. Bd. Trial Advocacy (civil trial advocate), Tex. Bd. Legal Specialization (personal injury trial law specialist), Tex. Bd. Legal Specialization (civil trial law specialist), Tex. Bd. Legal Specialization (civil appellate law specialist). Head litig. sect. Decker, Jones, McMackin, McClane, Hall & Bates, Ft. Worth, 1991—. Lectr. continuing legal edn. State Bar Tex., Austin. Named one of Attys. of Excellance, Ft. Worth Bus. Press, 2003, 2004. Fellow: Tex. Bar Found. (life), Tex. Bar Coll. (life); mem.: Am. Bd. Trial Advocates (advocate), Def. Rsch. Inst., Tex. Assn. Def. Counsel. Republican. Avocations: golf, fine dining, travel. Home: 6712 Morning Dew Dr Fort Worth TX 76132-1155 Office: Decker Jones McMackin McClane Hall 801 Cherry St Ste 2000 Fort Worth TX 76102 Office Phone: 817-336-2400. Personal E-mail: bigr817@charter.net. Business E-Mail: rhall@deckerjones.com.

HALL, RAYMOND, social studies educator; b. Marshall, Tex., Feb. 2, 1938; BA, Wiley Coll., 1962; MA, Stephen F. Austin State U., 1968; cert. in Ea. African Studies, Syracuse U., 1971, PhD, 1972; MA (hon.), Dartmouth Coll., 1993. Asst. prof. history and sociology Bishop Coll., Dallas, 1968-69, asst. prof. polit. sci. dept., 1971-72; asst. prof. sociology Dartmouth U., 1972-78, assoc. prof. sociology, 1978-86, prof. sociology, 1986, dir. dept. sociology, 1990, Orvil E. Dryfoos prof. of pub. affairs, 1994. Chmn. polit. sci. dept. Bishop Coll., Dallas, 1971-72; dir. Dartmouth MIT Urban Studies Program, 1975-77; chmn. Dartmouth-Talladega Title III Exch. com., 1973-78; dir. Dartmouth-Boston Urban Studies Program, 1978-80; chmn. urban studies program Dartmouth, 1981-84, acting chmn. dept. sociology, 1984, chmn. dept. sociology, 1985-91, 94-97; faculty adv. bd. The Beacon of Dartmouth, 1990—; cons. P.E.A.C.E., Inc., Syracuse 1969, Dallas Ind. Sch. Dist., 1968, 80, U.S. Dept. of Edn., 1992, field reader, sch. partnership program, 1988, field reader titles III & IX U.S. Dept. Edn., 1982—; field reader and tech. advisor title I and title III programs Dept. of Health, Edn. and Welfare, Dept. Human Svcs., 1975-81; cons. to curriculum com. Dallas Ind. Schs. Dist., 1969; spl. cons. NIH, Harvard Sch. of Pub. Health, 1993. Editl. bd. Gnosis, 1987—; contbr. numerous articles to profl. jours. Bd. trustees Wiley Coll., 1989-91, chair acad. programs com.; bd. dirs. The Forum for U.S.-Soviet Dialogue, 1983-86, A Better Chance, Hanover, N.H., 1973-75, Martin Luther King Recreation Ctr., Dallas, 1968-69, Dallas Opportunities Indsl. Coops., 1968-69. Served U.S. Army, 1962-64. Vis. scholar Social Sci. Rsch. Coun., 1975; Salzburg Seminar Presdl. fellow, 1994, 95; Jr. faculty fellowship Dartmouth Coll., 1977, IBM Faculty fellowship, 1971-73, Richard King Mellon fellowship, The Maxwell Sch., Syracuse U., 1969-70; grantee Spencer Found., Hewlett Found., 1989, Dickey Endowment, 1988-89, Rockefeller Interdisciplinary, 1987-88, Sr. Faculty, Dartmouth Coll., 1981-82, Ford Found. Faculty, 1969-70. Mem. ACLU, Am. Sociol. Assn., Ea. Sociol. Assn., African Heritage Studies Assn., Soc. for the Study of Social Problems, Phi Beta Sigma. Home: 8 Pinewood Vlg West Lebanon NH 03784-3123 Office: Dept of Sociology Dartmouth Coll 106 Silsby Hall Hanover NH 03755 Office Phone: 603-646-2902.

HALL, RICHARD, lawyer; b. Melbourne, Australia, June 23, 1962; B.Comm. with honors, Univ. Melbourne, Australia, 1984; LLB with honors, Univ. Melbourne, 1986; LLM, Harvard Univ., 1988. Bar: Victoria, Australia 1987, NY 1989. Assoc. Cravath Swaine & Moore LLP, NYC, 1988—96, ptnr., corp., 1996—. Mem.: ABA. Office: Cravath Swaine & Moore LLP Worldwide Plz 825 Eighth Ave New York NY 10019-7475 Office Phone: 212-474-1293. Office Fax: 212-474-3700. Business E-Mail: rhall@cravath.com.

HALL, RICHARD CLYDE, JR., retired religious educational administrator; b. Florence, Ala., Apr. 13, 1931; s. Richard Clyde Sr. and Annie Hazel (Darrah) H.; m. Mildred Marie Denham, May 19, 1957; children: Richard Denham, Darralyn Marie, Kevin Clyde, Edward Earnest. AA, U. Fla., 1950, BA, 1953; MRE, Southwestern Bapt. Theol. Sem., 1958, DRE, 1966, EdD, 1975, MA, 1984. Ordained to gospel ministry So. Bapt. Conv., 1955. Youth dir. 1st Bapt. Ch., Miami, Fla., 1953; ednl. sec., youth dir. Ave. J Bapt. Ch., Ft. Worth, 1953-54; dir. Bapt. Student Union Fla. Bapt. Conv., Jacksonville, 1954-57; min. edn. Eastover Bapt. Ch., Ft. Worth, 1957-61; minister edn. 1st Bapt. Ch., Elizabethton, Tenn., 1961-63, Gambrell Street Bapt. Ch., Ft. Worth, 1963-65; assoc. ch. tng. dept. Bapt. Gen. Conv. Tex., Dallas, 1965-72, sec. ch. tng. dept., 1972-73; mgmt. cons. Pro., Inc., San Diego, 1973-74; cons. adult work ch. tng. dept. Bapt. Sunday Sch. Bd., Nashville, 1974-75, cons. gen. adminstrn. ch. tng. dept., 1975-76, mgr. youth sect. discipleship tng. dept., 1976-2000—. Teaching fellow religious psychology and drama Southwestern Bapt. Theol. Sem., Ft. Worth, 1960-61; del. Bapt. World Alliance, Tokyo, 1970; instr. youth edn. Sem. Extension, 1981—; discipleship workshop leader, family group leader Bapt. Youth World Conf., Buenas Aires, 1984; conf. leader, coord. numerous youth confs. Queensland, Australia, New South Wales, Australia, Auckland, New Zealand, Gaza City, Gaza, 1997-98, Victoria, Australia, Windhoek, Namibia, Gaza City, Gaza; conf. leader Caribbean Bapt. Fellowship, Montego Bay, Jamaica, 1986; sem. leader Bapt. Youth World Conf., Glasgow, Scotland, 1988, chaplain, Harare, Zimbabwe, 1993; del. Lausanne II-World Congress on Evangelism, Manila, Philippines, 1989; teaching fellow religious psychology and drama Southwestern Bapt. Theol. Sem., Ft. Worth, 1960-61; guest lectr. Southwestern Bapt. Theol. Sem., New Orleans Bapt. Theol. Sem., So. Bapt. Theol. Sem., Midwestern Bapt. Theol. Sem., Southeastern Bapt. Theol. Sem. and Golden Gate Bapt. Theol. Sem., 1985—; adj. prof. New Orleans Bapt. Theol. Sem., Golden Gate Bapt. Theol. Sem. and Midwestern Bapt. Theol. Sem., 1985—; instr. Okla. Bapt. U., 1991—. Author: Source, 1967-70, Church Training, 1970—; (cassette and workbook) The Work of the Associational Age Group Leader, 1980; (filmstrip) DiscipleLife: Training Youth in Discipleship, 1981, DiscipleLife, 1984; compiler: Youth Leadership Training Pak, 1982, DiscipleHelps: A Daily Quiet Time Guide and Journal, 1985; (with Joe Ford) DiscipleYouth I Kit, 1982, DiscipleYouth I Notebook, 1982, DiscipleYouth II Kit, 1985, DiscipleYouth II Notebook, 1985, DiscipleYouth Library, 1992, (with Dean Finley) The Notebook: A Disciple Youth Experience, 1996; (with Wesley Black) Disciple-Now Manual; (with Valerie Hardy) Mission Trip Administrative Manual. Trauma Center Plus, Handbook for Youth Discipleship, Basic Church Stuff: A Guide for Assimulating New Youth Church Members, Compiler. Recipient Career of Excellence award LifeWay Christian Resources, 1998. Mem. ASTD, Internat. Religious Edn. Assn., So. Bapt. Religious Edn. Assn. (sec.-treas. 1982-83), Ea. Bapt. Religious Edn. Assn. (sec.-treas. 1975-79, pres. 1980), Southwestern Bapt. Religious Edn. Assn., Adult Edn. Assn. Office: LifeWar Christian Resources 2720 Windemere Dr Nashville TN 37214-1733

HALL, RICHARD EDGAR, lawyer; b. Boise, Idaho, Feb. 7, 1944; s. Perce and Orpha Hall; m. Tonya Ann McMurtrey; children: Christine, Tara, Michelle, Erin. BA, U. Idaho, 1966; JD, Harvard U. Law SCh., 1969. Bar: Idaho 1970, U.S. Ct. Appeals (9th cir.) 1971, Washington State Bar, 2004. Ptnr. Moffatt, Thomas, Barrett & Blanton, P.C., Boise, 1969-88; pres. Hall, Farley, Oberrecht & Blanton, Boise, 1988—. Pres. Idaho chpt. Am. Bd. Trial Advs., 1987-89; chmn. bd. dirs. United Heritage Life Ins. Co., United Heritage Fin. Svcs., United Heritage Mut. Holding Co., United Heritage Fin. Group Bd. dirs. Idaho Family Practice Residency, 1981-88; chmn. bd. dirs. United Heritage Fin. Group. Fellow Am. Coll. Trial Lawyers, Am. Bd. Trial Advs.; mem. Idaho Assn. Def. Counsel (pres.), Fedn. Ins. and Corp. Counsel (chmn. med. malpractice com. 1997-99, bd. dirs., exec. com. 2004-05, chmn. corp. counsel initiatives com.), Hillcrest Country Club (pres. 1989), Arid Club, Boise (bd. dirs.), Rotary (pres. Boise 1979) Methodist. Office: Hall Farley Oberrecht & Blanton PO Box 1271 Boise ID 83701-1271 E-mail: reh@hallfarley.com.

HALL, RICHARD MURRAY, JR., finance executive, consultant; b. St. Joseph, Mo., Jan. 1, 1947; s. Richard Murray and Alice Elaine (Huff) H.; m. Joyce Ann Stearns, Mar. 28, 1971 (div. Nov. 1983). BBA in Econs., Wichita State U., 1969, MS in Fin., 1972; Grad. Degree in Banking, So. Meth. U., 1975. Asst. v.p. Fourth Nat. Bank & Trust, Wichita, Kans., 1969-75; v.p. Citizens Frost Bank, San Antonio, 1975-77, United Bank Denver, 1977-84; pres. Am. Nat. Bank/United Bank-City Ctr., Aurora, Colo., 1984-86; sr. v.p. Corp. Fin. Ascs., Denver, 1987-89; dir. Colo. Nat. Leasing, Inc., Denver, 1989-95, pres., 1989-95, chmn. bd. dirs., 1993-95; v.p. and mgr. comml. banking divsn. Colo. Nat. Bank, Denver, 1992-94; pres., chmn. bd. dirs. Colo. Bus. Leasing, Inc., Denver, 1995—2001; pres. Alliance Capital Resources, Inc., 2000—; regional pres. Cache Bank & Trust, Denver, 2003—; dir. Craig Hosp., 2004—. Dir. Am. Heart Assn. Colo., 1980—, pres., 1987-88; emeritus, 1998—; mem. Leadership Denver Assn., 1981, dir., 1990-95, pres. 1994-95; chmn. ArtReach, Inc., Denver, 1988, 89; bd. dirs. Colo. Spl. Olympics, 1994—, vice chmn., 1997, 99, chmn., 2000, dir. emeritus, 2001; bd. dirs. Health Agys. of Colo., 1997—, chmn., 1998-2000; nat. dir. Cmty. Health Charities, 2005— Mem. Denver Athletic Club, Meridian Golf Club. Republican. Avocations: golf, skiing, writing. Office: Cache Bank & Trust 410 Seventeenth St Ste 100 Denver CO 80202 Office Phone: 303-572-8600. Business E-Mail: dhall@cachebankandtrust.com.

HALL, ROBERT ALAN, construction company executive; b. Montgomery, Ala., Oct. 30, 1958; s. Mack Luverne and Miriam (Johnston) H. BS in Commerce and Bus. Adminstrn., U. Ala., 1981. CPA, Ala., cert. internal auditor. Sr. acct. Jackson and Thornton, CPAs, Montgomery, 1981—83; sr. auditor Vulcan Materials Co., Birmingham, Ala., 1983—86, supr. internal audit, 1986—87; mgr., fin. and adminstrn. Saudi Arabian Vulcan Ltd., Jubail, Saudi Arabia, 1987—90; spl. assignments analyst Vulcan Materials Co., 1990—91; contr., treas., asst. sec. Bill Harbert Internat. Constrn. Inc., Birmingham, Ala., 1991—95, v.p., CFO, 1995—2000; sr. v.p., CFO, sec. B.L. Harbert Internat., LLC, 2000—. Presdl. appointee White House Conf. on Small Bus., 1995; mem. Pres.'s Bus. Adv. Coun., Washington, 1995-2001; mem. profl. adv. bd. Sch. Accountancy/U. Ala., 1991—. Charter mem. Rep. Presdl. Task Force, Washington, 1984-86; presdl. appointee White House Conf. Small Bus., 1995. Recipient Presdl. Achievement award Pres. Ronald Reagan, 1983, Cert. of Appreciation, Gov. of Ala., 1988, Sch. of Accountancy U. Ala. Career Achievement award, 2003; named hon. citizen City of L.A., 1984, hon. asst. atty. gen. State of Ala., 1984, hon. gov. of Tex., 1995, hon. lt. gov. of Ala., 1998. hon. col. State of Ala., 2001; named one of Outstanding Young Men of Am., 1986. Mem. AICPA, Ala. Soc. CPAs, Am. Businessmen's Assn. Saudi Arabia (bd. dirs. 1988-90), U. Ala. Sr. Execs. Club., Coll. Commerce, Hon. Order Ky. Cols. Baptist. Home: 416 Old Brook Cir Birmingham AL 35242-2658 Address: PO Box 531390 Birmingham AL 35253-1390 Office Phone: 205-802-2800. E-mail: ahall@bharbert.com.

HALL, ROBERT DALE, mathematician, educator, physicist; b. West Palm Beach, Fla., Mar. 31, 1960; s. Robert Dale Sr. and Eula Katherine (Daniels) H.; m. Joanna Joy Binder, Nov. 23, 1984; children: Charity Ann, Jared Michael. BS in Secondary Edn., Pensacola (Fla.) Christian Coll., 1982. Cert. Fla. Assn. Christian Colls. & Schs. Writer, pub. A Beka Book, Pensacola, 1982-87; chmn. math., physics Grace Christian Sch., Brandon, Fla., 1987—. Coach Fla. Assn. Christian Colls. and Schs., Brainbowl, 1989—, Mathcounts, 1990—, Brandon, Fla. Mem. Nat. Coun. Tchrs. Math. Republican. Avocation: sports. Office: Grace Christian Sch PO Box 843 Brandon FL 33509-0843 E-mail: dhall723@tampabay.rr.com.

HALL, ROBERT EMMETT, JR., investment banker, realtor; b. Sioux City, Iowa, Apr. 28, 1936; s. Robert Emmett and Alvina (Faden) H.; m. De Phan. BA, U. S.D., 1958, MA, 1959; MBA, U. Santa Clara, 1976; grad., Am. Inst. Banking, Realtors Inst. Grad. asst. U. S.D., Vermillion, 1958-59; mgr. ins. dept., asst. mgr. installment loan dept. Northwestern Nat. Bank Sioux Falls, S.D., 1959-61, asst. cashier, 1961-65; asst. mgr. Crocker Nat. Bank, San Francisco, 1965-67, loan officer, 1967-69, asst. v.p., asst. mgr. San Mateo (Calif.) br., 1969-72; v.p., western regional mgr. Internat. Investments & Realty, Inc., Washington, 1972—; owner Hall Enterprises Co., San Jose, Calif., 1976—; pres. Alamaden Oaks Realtors, Inc., 1976—. Instr. West Valley Coll., Saratoga, Calif., 1972-82, Grad. Sch. Bus., U. Santa Clara (Calif.), 1981-82, Evergreen Valley Coll., San Jose, Calif. Treas. Minnehaha Leukemia Soc., 1963, Lake County Heart Fund Assn., 1962, Minnehaha Young Rep. Club, 1963. Mem. Am. Inst. Banking, Calif. Assn. Realtors (vice chmn.), Alamaden Country Club, Elks, Rotary (past pres.), KC, Beta Theta Pi. Home: 6951 Castlerock Dr San Jose CA 95120-4705 Office: Hall Enterprises 100A Crown Blvd San Jose CA 95120-2903 E-mail: rehall5257@aol.com.

HALL, ROBERT ERNEST, economics professor; b. Palo Alto, Calif., Aug. 13, 1943; s. Victor Ernest and Frances Marie (Gould) H.; m. Susan E. Woodward; children: Christopher, Anne, Jonathan, Andrew. BA, U. Calif.-Berkeley, 1964; PhD, MIT, 1967. Asst. prof., acting assoc. prof. U. Calif., Berkeley, 1967-70; from assoc. prof. to prof. MIT, Cambridge, 1970-78; prof., sr. fellow Stanford U. (Calif.), 1978—, Robert and Carole McNeil joint prof. and sr. fellow, 1998. Dir. econ. fluctuation program Nat. Bur. Econ. Research, Cambridge, 1978—; adv. com. Congl. Budget Office, Washington, 1993—. Author: Macroeconomics, 1985, 5th rev. edit., 1997, Booms and Recessions in a Noisy Economy, 1990, The Rational Consumer: Theory and Evidence, 1990, Flat Tax, 1995, Economics, 1997, 2d rev. edit., 2000, Digital Dealing, 2001; editor: Inflation, 1983. Woodrow Wilson fellow, 1964; Ford Found. faculty rsch. fellow, 1969 Fellow Econometric Soc., Am. Acad. Arts and Scis.; mem. Am. Econs. Assn., Am. Statis Assn., NAS. Democrat. Office: Stanford U Hoover Instn Stanford CA 94305 E-mail: hall@hoover.stanford.edu.

HALL, ROBERT JOSEPH, internist, educator; b. Buffalo, June 4, 1926; s. Joseph M. and Florence C. (Kirst) H.; m. Dorothy Nowak, Aug. 28, 1948; children: Thomas R., Kathleen A. Hall Noble, Mary J. Hall Stuart, Michael F., Steven E. Student, Canisius Coll., Buffalo, 1943-45; MD, U. Buffalo, 1948. Diplomate Am. Bd. Internal Medicine, Sub Bd. Cardiovascular Disease (mem. cardiovascular disease sect. 1969-75). Intern Mercy Hosp., Buffalo, 1948-49; commd. 1st lt. M.C. U.S. Army, 1948, advanced through grades to col., 1966; resident in internal medicine Walter Reed Gen. Hosp., Washington, 1949-52, resident in cardiovascular diseases, 1956-57; asst. cardiovascular research Walter Reed Army Inst. Research, 1957-58; service in Korea and Japan, 1952-55; chief cardiology service Brooke Gen. Hosp., Ft. Sam Houston, Tex., 1961-66, Walter Reed Gen. Hosp., 1966-69; ret., 1969; clin. assoc. prof. medicine Georgetown U. Med. Sch., 1967-69; clin. prof. medicine Baylor U. Coll. Medicine, Houston, 1969—, prof. emeritus, 2004—; clin. prof. medicine U. Tex. Med. Sch., Houston, 1977—; med. dir. Tex. Heart Inst., Houston, 1969-93, chmn. exec. com. profl. staff, 1969-93; dir. div. cardiology St. Luke's Episcopal Hosp., Houston, 1969-95, assoc. chief med. service, 1970-83; dir. edn., cardiology Tex. Heart Inst. Tex. Heart Inst. and St. Luke's Episcopal Hosp., 1992—2002, dir. emeritus, 2002—. Cons. Tex. Children's, VA, Brooke Gen. hosps., M.D. Anderson Hosp. and Tumor Inst.; mem. cardiovascular study sect. NIH, 1958-61; mem. phys. evaluation team Gemini project NASA, 1958-61; mem. nat. adv. heart counseil Dept. Def., 1966-69; adv. council Mended Hearts, 1970-78 Contbr. numerous articles med. jours. Mem. President's Adv. Panel Heart Disease. Decorated Legion of Merit; recipient Disting. Alumnus award Canisius Coll., 1995. Fellow A.C.P., Am. Coll. Cardiology (gov. 1968-71-74, chmn. bd. govs. and trustee 1973-74); mem. Am. Heart Assn. (fellow council clin. cardiology; pres. Houston chpt. 1974-75, advisor corp. cabinet 1980-86), Assn. Mil. Surgeons U.S., Assn. Advancement Med. Instrumentation, Pan Am. Med. Assn. (chmn. sect. cardiovascular diseases 1978-81), Assn. Univ. Cardiologists, Tex. Med. Assn., Tex. Cardiology Club, Harris County Med. Soc., Houston Cardiology Soc. (chmn. 1976-77), Houston Soc. Internal Medicine, Alpha Omega Alpha, 1948—. Home: 5504 Sturbridge Dr Houston TX 77056-1623 Office: 6624 Fannin St Ste 2480 Houston TX 77030-2309 Business E-Mail: rjhall@wt.net.

HALL, ROBERT STEVENS, dentist; b. Hartford, Conn., Apr. 19, 1938; s. Llewellyn and Caroline (Doane) Hall; m. Marcia Smith, June 29, 1963; children: Gretchen Ashley, Robert Stevens Jr., Sabra Lee. AB, Middlebury Coll., 1960; DDS, U. Pa., 1964. Pvt. practice dentist, Hartford, 1966—73, Farmington, Conn., 1973—. Instr. U. Conn. Sch. Dental Medicine, 1973—85, 2000—. Capt. U.S. Army, 1964—66. Master: Acad. Gen. Dentistry; fellow: Am. Coll. Dentistry; mem.: Hartford Dental Soc. (dentist peer rev./patient rels. 1980—). Avocations: travel, sports, photography. Home: 53 Sunset Farm Rd West Hartford CT 06107-1332 Office: 291 Farmington Ave Farmington CT 06032

HALL, ROBERT TURNBULL, III, lawyer; b. Norfolk, Va., Aug. 25, 1945; s. Robert Turnbull and Mary Evelyn H.; m. Colleen Coffee, Aug. 17, 1968; children— Meghan, Robert. B.S., Washington and Lee U., 1967; J.D., Georgetown U., 1971. Bar: U.S. Dist. Ct. D.C. 1971, D.C. Ct. Appeals 1971, U.S. Ct. Appeals (D.C. cir.) 1972, U.S. Ct. Appeals (5th cir.) 1972, U.S. Supreme Ct. 1975, U.S. Ct. Appeals (11th cir.) 1981, U.S. Ct. Appeals (9th cir.) 1982, U.S. Ct. Appeals (8th cir.) 1983. Assoc. Thelen, Reid & Priest, N.Y.C., 1971-77, ptnr., 1978— . Mem. ABA, D.C. Bar Assn., Fed. Energy Bar Assn. Home: 162 Mercer St Princeton NJ 08540-6827 Business E-Mail: rhall@thelenreid.com.

HALL, ROBERT WILLIAM, philosophy and religion educator; b. Arlington, Mass., Apr. 6, 1928; s. Samuel Harry and Agness (Babikian) H.; m. Mary Alice Starritt, Oct. 25, 1958; children— Christopher Allen, Jonathan Brooks, Pamela Leigh, Timothy Randall, Jennifer Lane, Nicholas Ramsay. AB, Harvard, 1949, MA, 1951, PhD, 1953. Vis. asst. prof. philosophy Vanderbilt U., 1955-57; asst. prof. philosophy and religion U. Vt., Burlington, 1957-63, assoc. prof., 1963-67, prof., 1967—, Marsh prof. intellectual and moral philosophy, 1985—2002, chmn. dept., 1963-72, prof. emeritus, 2002—. Author: Plato and the Individual, 1963, Studies in Religious Philosophy, 1969, Plato, 1981; editor: APEIRON, 1966-87. Served with CIC AUS, 1953-55. Shedd fellow in religion in higher edn., 1968-69 Mem. Am. Philos. Assn., Soc. Ancient Greek Philosophy (sec.-treas. 1963-72), Am. Soc. Aesthetics, Phi Beta Kappa. Home: 165 N Prospect St Burlington VT 05401-1607 Office: 70 S Williams St Burlington VT 05401-3404

HALL, SHARON GAY, retired language educator, artist; b. Centralia, Ill., Oct. 2, 1942; d. Leon Lucene and Olyve Elizabeth Hall. BS, So. Ill. U., 1966, MS, 1984; postgrad., Ea. Ill. U., 1985—90. Cert. secondary tchr. Ill. English tchr. Webber Twp. H.S., Bluford, Ill., 1966—67, Mt. Vernon (Ill.) H.S., 1967—99, ret., 1999. Artist-in-residence Cedarhurst Art Guild, Cedarhurst Mus., 1974—. Treas. bd. dirs. Bus. and Profl. Women's Club, Mt. Vernon, 1966—76; mem. Jefferson County Hist. Soc., 2000—. Recipient Recognition award, Cedarhurst Mus., 2000. Mem.: NEA, AAUW, Ill. Edn. Assn., Mt. Vernon Edn. Assn. (sec., treas., bd. dirs. 1967—99), Phi Delta Kappa, Phi Theta Kappa, Alpha Delta Kappa. Republican. Avocations: raising exotic animals, handspinner, weaver, fiber artist, seamstress. Home: 11384 E Idlewood Rd Mount Vernon IL 62864

HALL, STEPHANIE MOSKOS, guidance counselor; b. Charleston, S.C., Aug. 31, 1970; d. Steve and Lena E. (Fletcher) Moskos; m. Corey William Hall, July 10, 1999; 1 child, Lena Sophia. MEd, The Citadel, 1997. Cert. secondary edn. counselor S.C. Dept. Edn. Guidance counselor Acad. Magnet H.S., North Charleston, SC, 1997—2004; guidance dir. Charleston County Sch. Dist., North Charleston, 2004—. Grantee, Safe Schs., 1997—2004. Mem.: S.C. DAR (state jr.), TriCounty Counselor's Assn. (corr.; pres. 2000—01). Home: 302 Jennie St Goose Creek SC 29445 Office: Brentwood Mid Sch 2685 Leeds Ave North Charleston SC 29405 Office Phone: 843-745-7094. Office Fax: 843-566-1838. E-mail: stephanie_hall@charleston.k12.sc.us.

HALL, STEPHEN CHARLES, lawyer; b. Carmel, Calif., Sept. 14, 1948; s. Melvin Wiley and Dorothy Louise (Hoyt) H.; m. Kristi Lee Roberts, Feb. 23, 1983; children: Spencer Stephen Rodrigo, Rachel Genevieve Cristina, Trevor Charles. AB, Dickinson Coll., 1971; JD, Vt. Law Sch., 1977. Bar: Pa. 1978, Va. 1979, U.S. Dist. Ct. (ea. dist.) Va. 1982, U.S. Dist. Ct. (we. dist.) Va. 1990, U.S. Ct. Appeals (4th cir.) 1982. Title atty. Chgo. Title Inst. Co., Richmond, 1978-79; assoc. Edward E. Willey Jr., P.C., Richmond, 1979-82; ptnr. Willey & Hall, P.C., Richmond, 1983-88; assoc. Hazel & Thomas, P.C., Richmond, 1988-90, ptnr., 1990-94, Keith & Hall, Richmond, 1994—. Contbr. articles to profl. jours. Past chmn. bd. trustees St. Michael's Episcopal Sch. Mem. Richmond Bar Assn. (past chmn. publs. com.), Chesterfield County Bar Assn. (past pres. 2003—), Bon Air Bus. and Profl. Assn. (past pres.), Salisbury Country Club. Episcopalian. Avocations: golf, photography. Office: Hairfield Morton Watson & Adams PLC 2800 Buford Rd Ste 201 Richmond VA 23235 Office Phone: 804-320-6600. Business E-Mail: shall@hmalaw.com.

HALL, SUSAN LAUREL, artist, educator, writer; b. Point Reyes Station, Calif., Mar. 19, 1943; d. Earl Morris and Avis Mary (Brown) H. BFA, Calif. Coll. Arts and Crafts, Oakland, 1965; MA, U. Calif., Berkeley, 1967. Mem. faculty Sarah Lawrence Coll., Bronxville, NY, 1972—75, Sch. Visual Arts, NYC, 1981—92, Skowhegan Sch. of Painting and Sculpture, Maine, 1981, U. Colo., Boulder, 1981, Art Inst. Chgo., 1981, U. Tex., Austin, 1993, San Antonio, 1995, San Francisco Art Inst., 1996. One-woman shows include San Francisco Mus. Art, 1967, Quay Gallery, San Francisco, 1969, Phillis Kind Gallery, Chgo., 1971, 1998, 98 Greene St. Loft, N.Y.C., Whitney Mus., Henderson Mus. U. Colo., Boulder, 1973, Nancy Hoffman Gallery, N.Y.C., 1975, U. R.I. Gallery, Kingston, 1976, Harcus Krakow Rosen Sonnabend Gallery, Boston, 1976, Hal Bromm and Getler-Pall Galleries, N.Y.C., 1978, Helene Shlien Gallery, Boston, 1978, Hamilton Gallery, N.Y.C., 1978—79, 1981, 1983, Ovsey Gallery, L.A., 1981—82, 1984, 1987, 1989, 1991, Paule Anglim Gallery, San Francisco, 1975—83, Ted Greenwald Gallery, N.Y.C., 1986, Trabia Macafee Gallery, 1988—89, Wyckoff Gallery, Aspen, Colo., 1990—92, Milagros Contemporary Art, San Antonio, 1995, Brendan Walter Gallery, L.A., 1995, U. Tex., San Antonio, 1996, Jan Holloway Gallery, San Francisco, 1997, San Francisco Mus. Art Gallery, 1998, Gail Harvey Gallery, L.A., 1999, 2001, Frank Lloyd Wright Civic Ctr., San Rafael, 1999, Jernigan Wicker Gallery, San Francisco, 1999, Bolinas (Calif.) Mus., 2002, exhibited in group shows at Whitney Mus. Am. Art, San Francisco Mus., Oakland Mus., Balt. Mus., Inst. Contemporary Art, Phila., Hudson River Mus., Bklyn. Mus., Nat. Mus. Women in the Arts, Mus. Fine Arts, Boston, Aldrich Mus. Contemporary Art, G.W. Einstein Gallery, Blum Helman Downtown, Leo Castelli Gallery Uptown, Graham Modern, N.Y.C., Kunstmus., Luzern, Switzerland, Landesmus., Bonn, Ranches and Rolling Hills, Nicasio, Calif., 2001, 2002, 2003, 2004, Represented in permanent collections pub. collections Whitney Mus., San Francisco Mus., Bklyn. Mus., Carnegie Inst., St. Louis Mus., Nat. Mus. Women in the Arts, others; author: Painting Point Reyes, Susan Hall, 2003. Nat. Endowment Arts fellow, 1979-87, Adolph Gottleib Found. fellow, 1995; grantee: Pollack Krasner Found., N.Y. State Coun. on Arts; recipient Marin Arts Coun. Bd. Dirs. award, 1999.

HALL, TEDDY, JR., music educator; b. Birmingham, Ala., Apr. 1, 1975; s. Teddy Hall, Sr. and Therlene Davenport Hall. BS in Music Edn., U. Ala., Birmingham, 1999; MusM, U. Miss., 2003. Music educator Havenview Mid. Sch., Memphis, 1999—2000; prof. Hampton (Va.) U., 2003—. Percussionist Corinth (Miss.) Symphony Orch., 2000—03, Bountiful Blessings Orch., Memphis, 2001—03; music instr. Acad. Performing Arts, Collierville, Tenn., 2001—03; lectr. in field. Musician: (concert) Festival Marimba Orchestra. Minority fellow, U. Miss. Grad. Sch., 2000—03. Mem.: Coll. Band Dirs. Nat. Assn., Music Educators Nat. Conf., Ancient Egyptian Arabic Order of Nobles of Mystic Shrine, Nat. Band Assn., Percussive Arts Soc., Scottish Rite. Avocations: travel, reading. Personal E-mail: teddyhalljr@hotmail.com.

HALL, TERESA JOANNE KEYS, manufacturing engineer, educator; b. Chanute, Kans., 1954; d. William Milton and Mary Joanne (Greve) Keys; m. Douglas Wayne Hall, Jan 31, 1986; 1 child, Benjamin Alan. BA in Industry, U. No. Iowa, 1988, MA in Tech., 1991; PhD in Indsl. Edn. and Tech., Iowa State U., 1997. Cert. mfg. engr. Dept. mgr. Cooks Inc., Waterloo, Iowa, 1974-76; grounds maintenance City of Waterloo, 1976-77; trades mechanic Deere & Co., Waterloo, 1977-79, foundry maintenance planner, 1979-82, metals analyst, 1982-84, sr. maintenance planner, 1984-87; pvt. practice Waterloo, 1988-91; instr. U. Northern Iowa, Cedar Falls, 1992-96, asst. prof., 1997-00, assoc. prof., 2001—03, mfg. program coord., 1998—2003; prof. S.D. State U., Brookings, 2003—, dept. head engring. tech. and mgmt., 2003—, dir. Polytechnic Ctr., 2003—. Expert witness mfg. fabrication and safety issues, 1999—2000; panel reviewer NSF, 1999—2000; dir. Polytech. Ctr. S.D. State U., Brookings, 2003—04. Tech. editor, Am.Jour. Undergrad. Rsch., 2003—;contbr. articles to profl. jours. Grantee NSF, 1996, 98, Tchr. Edn. Alliance, 1997. Mem. AAUW, Soc. Mfg. Engrs. (faculty advisor 1993-2001, Region 9 exec. bd. 1998—, chair chpt.186, 2003, chmn. certification oversight and appeals bd. 2004—, President's award 2000, Internat. award of merit, 2003), Am. Mensa Ltd., Nat. Assn. Indsl. Technologists (Outstanding Prof. of Yr. for Region 2, reviewer Jour. Indsl. Tech.), Epsilon Pi Tau. Avocation: gardening. Office: SD State U Dept Engring Tech & Mgmt Brookings SD 57007-0092

HALL, TERRENCE LYON, lawyer; b. Jackson, Mich., Oct. 24, 1949; s. Kenneth F. and Jean (Lyon) H. B.A., Stanford U., 1972; J.D., Detroit Coll. Law, 1978. Bar: Mich. 1978, U.S. Dist. Ct. (ea. dist.) Mich. 1978, U.S. Ct. Appeals (6th cir.) 1982. Ptnr., Terrence L. Hall & John W. Isgrigg, P.C., Pontiac, Mich., 1978-98; mem. Hall & Doran, P.L.C., Waterford, Mich., 1998- . Vice-chair, Oakland County Br. ACLU Mich., 1982-87, ACLU Mich. Exec. Com., 2000—, Mem. ATLA, Mich. Bar Assn., Mich. Trial Lawyers Assn., Oakland County Bar Assn, Am. Mensa Ltd. Unitarian. Office: 4519 Highland Rd Waterford MI 48328-1132 Office Phone: 248-674-4844.

HALL, THOMAS J., lawyer; b. Elizabeth, NJ, July 25, 1955; BA, Rutgers U., 1977; JD, Fordham U., 1980. Bar: US Dist. Ct. (Dist. NJ) 1980, US Ct. Appeals (3rd Cir.) 1980, NY 1980, US Dist. Ct. (So. Dist.) NY 1981, US Dist. Ct. (Ea. Dist.) NY 1981, NY 1981, US Ct. Appeals (2nd Cir.) 1989, US Dist. Ct. (No. Dist.) NY 1995, US Ct. Appeals (4th Cir.) 1999, US Supreme Ct. 2002. Ptnr., Litig. Chadbourne & Park LLP, NYC, mem. mgmt. com. Mediator, Comml. Divsn. NY Supreme Ct., 1997—. Mng. editor Fordham Law Rev., 1979—80; editor: The Banking Law Jour., 1999—; contbr. articles to profl. jour. Mem.: Fed. Bar Coun., Internat. Litig. Practitioners Forum, ABA (comml. & banking litig. com., internat. litig. com.), NY Bar Assn. Office: Chadbourne& Park LLP 30 Rockefeller Plaza New York NY 10112 Office Phone: 212-408-5487. Office Fax: 212-541-5369. Business E-Mail: thall@chadbourne.com.

HALL, TIMOTHY COUZENS, biology professor, consultant; b. Darlington, Durham, Eng., Aug. 29, 1937; came to U.S., 1965; s. Gilbert Leslie and Dorothea Olive (Lindemann) H.; m. Sandra Severn, Aug. 20, 1960; children: Alexandra Vikki Anna, Liza Bryony, Peter Marcus Jeremy. BSc with honors, U. Nottingham, Eng., 1962, PhD in Plant Physiology, 1965. Louis W. and Maud Hill postdoctoral fellow dept. hort. sci. U. Minn., St. Paul, 1965-66; asst. prof. horticulture U. Wis., Madison, 1966-70, assoc. prof., 1970-75, prof., 1975-82, adj. prof. biophysics and genetics, 1982-84; dir. Agrigenetics Advanced Rsch. Div., Madison, 1980-84, Agrigenetics Rsch. Corp., Boulder, Colo., 1981-84; Disting. prof., head dept. biology Tex. A&M U., College Station, 1984-92, dir. Inst. Devel. and Molecular Biology, 1992-2000. Sr. biotech. cons. Rhône-Poulenc Agrochimie, Lyon, France, 1985-2000; chair, organizer Gordon Conf. on Plant Molecular Biology, 1987; cons. plant biotech. Novartis, 1997-98; mem. sci. adv. bd. Aventis Cropsci., 2000-01; mem. adv. com. Area of Excellence, Chinese U. Hong Kong, 2000—; mem. sci. adv. com. China Nat. Ctr. for Biotech. Devel., 2002—; co-chair, co-organizer Juan March Workshop on Chromatin and DNA Modification, 1998. Editor: (with J.W. Davies) Nucleic Acids in Plants, 2 vols., 1979, (with L. van Vloten-Doting and G.S.P. Groot) Molecular Form and Function of the Plant Genome, 1985; mem. editl. bd. Oxford Surveys Plant Molecular and Cell Biology, 1983-80, Transgenic Rsch., 1991-95, Plant Jour., 1991-99, Jour. Virology, 1996—2001; contbr. numerous articles to profl. jours., book chpts.; patentee in field. Pilot Royal Air Force, 1956-58. Grantee NIH, NSF, USDA, NATO, Dow Agro Scis., Rhône-Poulenc Agrochimie, Internat. Paper Co., Tex. Advanced Tech. Program, Rockefeller Found. Fellow Indian Virol. Soc.; mem. AAAS, Am. Soc. for Biochemistry and Molecular Biology, Am. Soc. Plant Physiologists (organizer Juan March workshop on chromatin and DNA modification Madrid, 1998), Fedn. Am. Socs. Exptl. Biology, Biochem. Soc., Internat. Soc. Plant Molecular Biology, Soc. for In Vitro Biology, RNA Soc., Squash Club Tex. A&M U., Sigma Xi. Avocations: squash, racquetball, bridge, travel. Office: Tex A&M U Inst Devel Molecular Biol College Station TX 77843-3155 Office Phone: 979-845-7728. E-mail: tim@idmb.tamu.edu.

HALL, TOM T., retired country singer, songwriter; b. Olive Hill, Ky., May 25, 1936; s. Virgil Hall; m. Dixie Dean. Student, Roanoke Coll. Founder pub. co. Hallnote Music. With group Tom Hall and the Kentucky Travelers, disc jockey, Sta. WMOR, Morehead, Ky., songwriter with, Newkeys Music, Inc., rec. artist with Mercury Records until 1977, with RCA, Mercury, Polygram records, 1977-2003; performed with band, The Storytellers, Carnegie Hall, N.Y.C., 1973; performed at Smithsonian Instn., 1979, White House, 1980; albums include Magnificent Music Machine, Natural Dreams, 1984, Homecoming, I Witness Life, The Storyteller, Songs of Fox Hollow, Country Classics, Ol' T's in Town, Places I've Done Time, Everything From Jesus to Jack Daniels, many others; songs include Harper Valley P.T.A.; author: Songwriter's Handbook, Laughing Man of Woodmont Coves, Acts of Life, Christmas and the Old House, The Storyteller's Nashville, What a Book! Served in U.S. Army, 1957-61.

HALL, TONY P., ambassador, retired congressman; b. Dayton, Ohio, Jan. 16, 1942; m. Janet Dick, 1973; 2 children. Student, Ohio State U.; AB, Denison U., 1964; LLD (hon.), Asbury Coll., Eastern Coll. Vol. Peace Corps, Thailand, 1966-67; mem. Ohio Ho. of Reps., 1969-72, Ohio Senate, 1973-78, U.S. Congress from 3d Ohio dist., Washington, 1979—2002; mem. rules com., ranking minority mem. subcom. tech. and the house; amb. U.N. Agencies for Food & Agr., 2002—. Founder, steering com. Congl. Friends of Human Rights Monitors; bd. mgrs. Air Force Mus. Found.; trustee Holiday Aid; adv. com. Emergency Resource Bank; chmn. Dem. Caucus Task Force on Hunger; founder Congrl. Hunger Ctr. Recipient Disting. Svc. Against Hunger award Bread for the World, 1984, 87, Tree of Life award Jewish Nat. Fund, 1986, Golden Apple award Nat. Assn. Nutrition and Aging Svcs. Programs, 1986, Freedom award Asian Pacific Am. C. of C., 1986, Presdl. End Hunger award, 1988, Silver Anniversary award NCAA, 1989, Silver World Food Day medal Food and Agriculture Orgn. of UN, Ptnrs. award Oxfam Am., 1992; nominated for Nobel Peace prize, 1998, 99, 2001. Mem. Nat. Assn. Women, Infants & Children (Leadership award 1991). Democrat. Office: US Mission to UN Agencies for Food & Agr via V Veneto 119/A 00187 Rome Italy Office Phone: 39-06-4674-3500. Business E-Mail: halltp@state.gov.

HALL, TRACY LYNN, physician; b. Belleville, Ill., Apr. 28, 1963; d. Norman Keith and Joyce Ann (Greenhill) H. AS, Kaskaskia Coll., Greenville, 1983; BA, Greenville Coll., 1985; DO, Kirksville Coll. Osteo. Med., 1989. Diplomate Am. Bd. Family Practice. Cert. ACLS, BLS, neonatal resucitation. Intern Westview Osteopathic Hosp., Indpls., 1989-90; resident in family practice So. Ill. U., Belleville, 1990-92; physician McCracken-Dawdy-Hall Family Practice, Greenville, Ill., 1992—. Clin. asst. prof. medicine U. Ill., Chgo., clin. prof. Sch. Medicine; clin. asst. prof. medicine, clin. prof. So. Ill. U. Sch. Medicine; sec. Utlant Meml. Med. staff, 1994, v.p., 1995, chief of staff, 1996. Mem. AMA, Am. Osteo. Assn., Am. Assn. Family Practice, Am. Coll. Family Practitioners, Christian Med. and Dental Soc., Am. Acad. Osteo. Sports Medicine, Ind. Assn. Osteo. Physicians, Fellowship Christian Athletes, Bond County Med. Soc. (del. to Il. State Med. Soc. 1997—). Avocations: long and intermediate distance bicycling, art, music. Office: McCracken Dawdy Hall Family Practice 201 Health Care Dr Greenville IL 62246-1155

HALL, WILBUR DALLAS, JR., medical educator; b. Calhoun, Ga., June 22, 1938; m. Marguerite Holt, July 4, 1992; children: Ashley, Brent, Marianne, Tommy. MD, Emory U., 1963. Diplomate Am. Bd. Internal Medicine and Nephrology. Chief med. resident Grady Meml. Hosp., 1966; prof. medicine, dir. div. hypertension Emory U., Atlanta, 1976-97, prof. emeritus, 1997—, program dir. Gen. Clin. Rsch. Ctr., 1988-97. Author 3 books; contbr. 75 chpts. to books, over 100 articles to profl. jours. Master ACP; mem. Ga. Heart Assn. (pres. 1984-85). Home: 1100 Parker Pl NE Atlanta GA 30324-5402

HALL, WILLIAM A., architect; b. 1923; BA, U. Okla.; M in City Planning, Mass. Inst. Tech. Recipient Fulbright Grant, Germany. Fellow: Am. Inst. Architects. Mailing: c/o William A Hall Partnership 42 East 21 St Apt 3 New York NY 10010

HALL, WILLIAM DARLINGTON, lawyer; b. Elkins, W.Va., Jan. 12, 1914; s. Nathan I. and Grace (Darlington) H.; m. Louise Brown, Aug. 3, 1949; children— Carolyn L., Dorothy K., Beverly G. BEE, W.Va. U., 1934, MEE, 1935, EE, 1940; JD, George Washington U., 1946. Bar: DC 1945, D.C. 1945. Engr. GE, Lynn, Mass., 1936-39; radio engr., patent adviser Signal Corps U.S. Army, Washington, 1939-47, chief patent sect., 1946-47; practiced in Washington, 1947-74; ptnr. Hall, Myers and Rose, 1974-89; of counsel Shlesinger & Myers, Bethesda, Md., 1989, Myers, Rose & Liniak, Bethesda, 1990-92, Myers, Liniak and Berenato, Bethesda, 1992-98, Hall, Priddy, Myers and Vande Sande, Potomac, Md., 1998—. Mem. Army-Navy Patent Adv. Bd., 1946-47 Home: 10850 Stanmore Dr Potomac MD 20854-1522 Office: Hall Priddy & Myers 10220 River Rd Potomac MD 20854-4916 E-mail: willdhall@yahoo.com.

HALL, WILLIAM EDWARD, JR., insurance agency executive; b. Roanoke, Va., Oct. 15, 1951; s. William Edward and Virginia (Moomaw) H.; m. Emily Ayers Rierson, May 27, 1972; children: Amanda Marie, John William. BA in Econs., U. N.C., Chapel Hill, 1973, MBA, 1977; MS in Fin. Svcs., Am. Coll., 1989. CPA, CLU, ChFC. Coll. agt. Northwestern Mut. Life, Chapel Hill, 1972-73, 75-77, spl. agt. Greensboro, N.C., 1973-75, 78—; staff acct. Price Waterhouse & Co., Charlotte, N.C., 1977-78; ptnr. Sprinkle & Assocs., Greensboro, 1978-87; sr. v.p., ptnr. Todd Orgn. of the Carolinas, Greensboro, 1987—. Bd. dirs. cen. N.C. chpt. Nat. Multiple Sclerosis Soc.; active Leadership Greensboro Alumni Assn. Bus. Found. fellow, 1977. Mem. AICPA, Nat. Assn. Accts., Estate Planning Coun., Am. Soc. CLUs, Greensboro CLU & ChFC (bd. dirs. 1980-83, sec.-treas. 1988-89, pres. 1990-91), Assn. Advanced Life Underwriters, Todd Nat. (legis. chmn. 1991—), Greensboro Country Club, Kiwanis, Phi Beta Kappa, Beta Gamma Sigma, Beta Theta Pi. Repubican. Presbyterian. Home: 1912 Lafayette Ave Greensboro NC 27408-7204 Office: Todd Orgn of The Carolinas Ste 300 620 Green Valley Rd Greensboro NC 27408-7725 Business E-Mail: hallb@toddorg.com.

HALL, WILLIAM JOEL, retired civil engineer, educator; b. Berkeley, Calif., Apr. 13, 1926; s. Eugene Raymond and Mary (Harkey) H.; m. Elaine Frances Thalman, Dec. 18, 1948; children: Martha Jane, James Frederick, Carolyn Marie. Student, U. Calif., Berkeley, 1943-44, Kings Point, 1944-45; BSCE, U. Kans., 1948; MS, U. Ill., Urbana, 1951, PhD, 1954. Teaching asst. U. Kans., 1947-48; engr. Sohio Pipe Line Co., 1948-49; mem. faculty U. Ill., Urbana, 1954—93, prof. civil engring., 1959-93, head dept. civil engring., 1984-91; prof. emeritus, 1993—. Cons. in structural dynamics, seismic, materials to govts. and industrial orgns. Author books, articles, revs., book chpts. Recipient A. Epstein Meml. award, U. Ill., 1958, Halliburton Engring. Edn. Leadership award, 1980, Disting. Engring. Svc. award, U. Kans., 1985; Univ. scholar, U. Ill., 1986—89. Fellow AAAS; mem. NAE, ASME, ASTM, ASCE (hon., pres. Ctrl. Ill. sect. 1967-68, chmn. structural divsn. exec. com. 1973—, chmn. tech. coun. on lifeline earthquake engring. exec. com. 1982—, Kans. sect. award 1948, Walter L. Huber award 1963, Howard award 1984, Newmark medal 1984, C. Martin Duke award 1990, Norman medal 1992), Am. Concrete Inst., Am. Welding Soc. (Adams Meml. membership award 1967), Earthquake Engring. Rsch. Inst. (Housner medal 1998), Seismol. Soc. Am., Structural Engrs. Assn. Ill. (John Parmer award 1990), Sigma Xi, Tau Beta Pi (Daniel C. Drucker eminent faculty award 1993), Sigma Tau, Chi Epsilon (nat. honor mem. 1998), Phi Kappa Phi. Home: 3105 Valley Brook Dr Champaign IL 61822-6111 Office: U Ill Civil Engring 3103 Newmark Lab 205 N Mathews Ave Urbana IL 61801-2350 Personal E-mail: wj-efhall@worldnet.att.net. Business E-Mail: w-hall3@uiuc.edu.

HALL, WILLIAM N., lawyer; b. Stockholm, Jan. 5, 1953; came to U.S., 1953; s. Goran L. and Virginia (Northrup) H.; m. Melissa A. Montefiore, Nov. 11, 1995. BA in Econs., Bucknell U., 1975; JD, Georgetown U., 1978. Bar: D.C. 1978, U.S. Dist. Ct. D.C. 1979, U.S. Ct. Appeals (D.C. cir.) 1979, U.S. Ct. Appeals (9th cir.) 1988, U.S. Ct. Appeals (5th cir.) 1994, Ind. 1995. Assoc. Cleary Gottlieb Steen & Hamilton, Washington, 1978-84, Breed Abbott & Morgan, Washington, 1984-86, ptnr., 1986-93, Whitman Breed Abbott & Morgan, Washington, 1993-96, Winston & Strawn, Washington, 1996—, head environ. dept. Case and note editor Georgetown Law Jour., 1977-78; contbr. articles to profl. jours. Bd. dirs. Fed. City Coun., D.C. Sports and Entertainment Commn. Mem. Bar Assn. D.C. (chmn. adminstrv. law sect. 1987-88, chmn. environ. law com. 1993—95, Com. Chmn. of Yr. 1994), D.C. Bar Assn. Avocations: reading, travel, golf. Office: Winston & Strawn LLP 1400 L St NW Washington DC 20005-3502 Office Fax: 202-371-5950. E-mail: whall@winston.com.

HALL, ZACH WINTER, academic administrator; b. Atlanta, Sept. 15, 1937; s. Dixon Winter and Marjorie Elizabeth (Owens) H.; m. Anne Browning, June 1958 (div. Aug. 1960); m. Marion Nestle, Dec. 1973 (div. June 1985); m. Julie Ann Giacobassi, Nov. 9, 1987. BA, Yale U., 1958; PhD, Harvard U., 1966. Asst. prof., then assoc. prof. Harvard Med. Sch., Boston, 1968-76; prof. U. Calif., San Francisco, 1976-94; dir. Nat. Inst. Neurol. Disorders and Stroke, Bethesda, Md., 1994-97; assoc. dean for rsch. U. Calif., San Francisco, 1997-98, vice chancellor rsch., 1998-2000, exec. vice chancellor, 2000—01; pres., CEO EnVivo Pharms., Inc., 2001—02; sr. assoc. dean for rsch. Keck Sch. Medicine, U. So. Calif., 2002—. Mem. Med. Adv. Bd., Chevy Chase, Md., 1995-99, Howard Hughes Med. Inst.; Alexander Forbes lectr. Grass Found., 1994; David Nachmanson lectr. Weizmann Inst., Rehovath, Israel, 1996. Author, editor: Molecular Neurobiology, 1992; editor jour. Neuron, 1988-94. Recipient Purkynje medal for sci. achievement, Czech Acad. Sci., 2003. Fellow AAAS; mem. Am. Acad. Arts and Scis., Inst. Medicine. Office Phone: 323-442-1607.

HALLACY, DON, telecommunications industry executive; b. Holland, Mich. BA in Econs. and Computational Math. summa cum laude, Albion Coll. With Arthyr Andersen & Co., 1982—87; mgr. tech. support GC Svcs., Chgo., 1987—88; info. tech. cons. McKinsey & Co., 1988—92, Stuttgart, Germany, 1988—92; various positions Sprint, Atlanta, 1992—99, Dallas, 1992—99, Kansas City, 1992—99; CEO Eltrax Sys., Inc., Atlanta, 1999—2000, Cereus Tech. Ptnrs. (formerly Eltrax, Inc.), 2000—02; chief info. officer domestic ops. Bellsouth Corp., 2002—. Bd. dirs. New Focus, Inc. Office: Bellsouth Corp 1155 Peachtree St NE Atlanta GA 30309-3610

HALLADAY, CRISTEN ROBIN, physical education educator; b. Ogdensburg, N.Y., Nov. 25, 1975; d. Wayne Noel and Cheryl Conant Ladouceur; m. Richard Shane Halladay, July 11, 1998; children: Jackson West, Faith Robin. BS, St. Lawrence U., Canton, N.Y., 1996; MS, Ithaca Coll., N.Y., 1997. Phys. edn. tchr. John F. Kennedy & Sherman Elem. Schs., Ogdensburg, NY, 1997—. Basketball coach Ogdensburg Free Acad., NY, 1997—2000. Democrat. Roman Catholic. Home: 15 Shallow River Ln Massena NY 13662

HALLADAY, LAURIE ANN, public relations consultant, food products executive; b. Monroe, Mich., Aug. 18, 1945; d. Alvin John and Florence (Lowrey) Kohler; m. Edward L. Howell, Aug. 27, 1966; m. 2d Fredric R. Halladay, May 24, 1980. BJ, U. Mo., 1967. Reporter, staff writer Copley Newspapers, L.A., 1967-69; account exec. Furman Assocs., L.A., 1969-71, v.p., 1971-74; account supr. Bob Thomas & Assocs., L.A., 1974-76, v.p., 1976-78; v.p., sr. ptnr. Fleishman-Hillard, Inc., St. Louis, 1980-84; owner, operator McDonald's, Portland, Oreg., 1984-87, McDonald's McStop of Mid.-Mo., Kingdom City, 1988-92. Chmn. press ops. for Budweiser/G.I. Joe's Portland 200 Indy Car Race, 1984-87; mem. advt., promotions com. Hollywood Boosters, 1986. Bd. dirs. Waterman Place Assn., St. Louis, 1983; mem. pub. rels. com. Winston Churchill Meml., Fulton, 1988-92. Recipient Merit award Calif. Press Women, 1969, Lulu award Los Angeles Women's Ad Club, 1976, McDonald's Outstanding Store award, 1985, 86, 89, 90, 91. Mem. PRSA (Prism award 1977), Soc. Am. travel Writers (assoc. 1981-84), Women in Comm. (dir. St. Louis 1980-82), Nat. Tour Assn., Mo. Travel Coun., Delta Delta Delta (alumna adviser 1989, 90, v.p. Delta Xi House Corp. 1991, collegiate dist. officer 1991, 94, regional program chmn. 1994, program resource team pub. rels. specialist 1995-96, nat. chmn. pub. rels. 1996, cons. pub. rels. chpt. 1998-2000). Address: 1602 Alabama Dr 304 Winter Park FL 32789 Personal E-mail: halladayl@yahoo.com.

HALLADAY, ROY, professional baseball player; b. Denver, May 14, 1977; Pitcher Toronto (Can.) Blue Jays, 1998—. Named to All Star Game, 2002, 2003; recipient Cy Young award, Am. League, 2003. Achievements include led Am. League wins in 2003. Office: 1 Blue Jays Way Ste 3200 Toronto ON Canada M5V 1J1

HALLAM, BEVERLY (BEVERLY LINNEY), artist; b. Lynn, Mass., Nov. 22, 1923; d. Edwin Francis and Alice (Linney) Hallam Murphy. BS in Edn, Mass. Coll. Art, 1945; postgrad., Cranbrook Acad. Art, Mich., 1948; MFA, Syracuse U., 1953. Chmn. dept. art Lasell Jr. Coll., Auburndale, Mass., 1945-49; assoc. prof. Mass. Coll. Art, 1949-62. Bd. dirs. Barn Gallery Assocs., Inc., Ogunquit, Maine. One-person shows include Joe and Emily Lowe Art Center, Syracuse U., 1953, DeCordova Mus., Lincoln. Mass., 1954, Shore Galleries, Boston, 1959, 62, 68, 73, 74, Witte Meml. Mus., San Antonio, 1968, U. Maine, 1969, Lamont Gallery, Exeter, N.H., 1969, Addison Gallery, Andover, Mass., 1971, Fitchburg Art Mus., 1972, Fairweather Hardin Gallery, Chgo., 1972, Hobe Sound (Fla.) Galleries, 1973, Inst. Contemporary Art, Boston, 1977, PS Galleries, Maine, 1981, Payson-Weisberg Gallery, N.Y.C., 1984, Farnsworth Mus., Rockland, Maine, 1984, 98, Midtown Galleries, N.Y.C., 1988, Francesca Anderson Gallery, Boston, 1988, Hobe Sound Galleries North, Portland, Maine, 1988, Evansville (Ind.) Mus. Arts and Sci., 1990, Sheldon Swope Mus., Terre Haute, Ind., 1990, Art Mus. S.E. Tex., Beaumont, 1990, Bergen Mus. Art and Sci., Paramus, N.J., 1990, Polk Mus. Art, Lakeland, Fla., 1991, Farnsworth Art Mus., 1998, Ogunquit Art Assn., 1999, Mass. Coll. Art, Boston, 2000, Univ. New England, 2000, Berkshire C.C., Pittsfield, Mass., 2003, River Tree Ctr. for the Arts, Kennebunk, Maine, 2003; two-person show, Inst. Contemporary Art, Boston, 1956, numerous group shows including Barn Gallery, 1954-2005, Busch-Reisinger Mus., Harvard U., 1956, 59, 60, Portland Mus., 1959, 84, 92, 93, 97, 2004, Mus. Fine Arts, Boston, 1960, Inst. Contemporary Art, Boston, 1960, 63, 68, 77, Pace Gallery, Boston, 1962, DeCordova Mus., 1963, 64, 68, 69, 70, 71, 75, Ward-Nasse Gallery, N.Y.C., 1971-72, Ogunquit (Maine) Mus. Am. Art, 1964, 70, 71, 78, 80, 84, 89, 91-93, 95, 98, 2000, 2003, River Tree Ctr. Arts, 2004, R.I. Arts Festival, 1966, Smithsonian Instn., Washington, 1966, Am. Water Color Soc. Traveling Exhibition, 1967, Watercolor U.S.A., Springfield, Mo., 1968, Maine State Mus., 1976, 2004, Maine Coast Artists, 1974, 75, 77, 83, 89, 92, 93, Joan Whitney Payson Gallery of Art, Maine, 1980, Farnsworth Art Mus., 1982, 87, 92, 95, 96, Bowdoin Coll. Mus. Art, 1984, 92, Midtown Payson Galleries, N.Y.C., 1985, 87, 90, 92, Expo '92, Seville, Spain, Barbara Scott Gallery, Bay Harbor Island, Fla., 1993, Fitchburg (Mass.) Art Mus., 1994, Monmouth (N.J.) Mus., 1995, Evansville Mus. Arts and Sci., 1996, U. New England, 2000, Francesca Anderson Fine Art, Lexington, Mass., 2002, River Tree Ctr. for the Arts, Kennebunk, Maine, 2004; represented in permanent collections Rose Art Mus. Brandeis U., Fogg Art Mus., Cambridge, Mass.; Corcoran Gallery Am. Art, Washington, Witte Meml. Mus., San Antonio, DeCordova Mus., Lincoln, Addison Gallery, Andover, Bowdoin Coll. Mus. Art, Fitchburg Art Mus., Ogunquit Mus. Am. Art, Portland Mus., Colby Coll., U. Maine, Currier Gallery Art, Manchester N.H., Farnsworth Library and Art Mus., Rockland, Maine, U. N.H. Art

Galleries, Durham, Everson Mus., Syracuse, First Nat. Bank, Boston, Ernst and Ernst, Chgo., Carnegie Corp., N.Y., Nat. Mus. Women in the Arts, Washington, Gouws Capital Mgmt., Inc., Portland, Maine, Marion Koogler Art Mus., San Antonio, Tex., others, also, pvt. collections, U.S. Can., Paris, Switzerland; Publ. Beverly Hallam, Paintings, Drawings and Monotypes, 1956-71, 1971; subject of book and video Beverly Hallam: The Flower Paintings, 1990, Beverly Hallam: An Odyssey in Art, 1998, (by Carl Little) One Hundred Works From the 20th Century at Colby College Museum of Art, 1996, Maine In America, Farnsworth Art Mus., 2000, On Paper: Masterworks From The Addison Collection, 2003, others. Recipient Pearl Safir award Silvermine Guild Artists, New Canaan, Conn., 1955, Painting prize Boston Arts Festival, 1957, Blanche E. Colman Found. award, 1960, Hatfield awards Boston Soc. Watercolor Painters, 1960, 64, 1st prize Edwin Webster award, 1962, Am. Artist Achievement award, 1993, Disting. Alumna award Mass. Coll. Art, 2000, Maine Coll. Art award for Visual Artist Achievement, 2001. Mem. Ogunquit Art Assn. (past pres.), Archives Am. Art. Avocations: photography, digital abstractions. Home: 30 Surf Point Rd York ME 03909-5053

HALLARD, WAYNE BRUCE, retired economist; b. Plainfield, NJ, Dec. 28, 1951; s. Donald Jay and Patricia (Adelmann) H.; m. Grace Elizabeth Farrell, Apr. 29, 1972 (div. 1979); 1 child, Travis; m. Deborah Jane Russo, Aug. 16, 1987. Student, Brown U., 1970—71; AA in Bus., Union Coll., 1977; BS in Econs., Fairleigh Dickinson U., 1980, MBA in Econs., 1984; postgrad., N.Y.U., 1984—87. Store mgr. Wine Art of NJ, Watchung, 1972; mgr. Verizon, Newark, 1972—2003; ret., 2003. Cons. NJ Coun. Savs. Instns., West Orange, 1987-95, F.A. Russo Assocs., Scotch Plains, NJ, 1989—; ea. conf. organizing com., session chmn. Ctr. Rsch. in Regulated Industries, 1986-2003. Trustee, treas. Lehmen Found., Newark, 1979-84; bd. dirs., treas. Vol. Ctr. of Greater Essex County, 1990-97; mem. Mental Health Assn., East Orange, 1979-80, Newark Mus., 1987—; trustee, past sec., treas. Newark Jaycees Internat. Senators Scholarship Found., 1986-99; umpire Scotch Plains-Fanwood Youth Baseball Assn., 1982—; trustee, past pres. Brotherhood Temple Sharey Tefilo Israel, South Orange, N.J., 1980—; trustee Fairleigh Dickinson U., 2003-2005. With USAFR, 1971-80. Named one of Outstanding Young Men of Am., 1981, 1983, 1985—86, 1988; recipient Cert. of Appreciation, Cts. and Corrections Assn. NJ, 1982. Mem. ACLU, Am. Econ. Assn., Greater Newark C. of C. (bd. dirs. 1980-82), Telephone Pioneers Am., Fairleigh Dickinson U. Alumni Assn. (bd. govs. 1997—, v.p. 1999-2001, pres.-elect 2001-2003, pres. 2003-2005), Am. Dog Show Judges, Ea. Stewards Assn. (treas. 2004—), Am. Sealyham Terrier Club (past bd. dirs.), Garden State All Terrier Club (past treas., past corr. sec.), Mastiff Club Am., Aircraft Owners and Pilots Assn., Stewards Club Am., ARZA, Jewish Chatauqua Soc., Delta Mu Delta. Democrat. Jewish. Avocations: cooking, reading. Home: 518 Jerusalem Rd Scotch Plains NJ 07076-2011 Personal E-mail: wayne.b.hallard@verizon.net.

HALLAUER, ARNEL ROY, geneticist; b. Netawaka, Kans., May 4, 1932; s. Roy Virgil and Mabel Fern (Bohnenkemper) H.; m. Janet Yvonne Goodmanson, Aug. 29, 1964; children: Elizabeth, Paul BS, Kans. State U., 1954; MS, Iowa State U., 1958, PhD, 1960. Rsch. agronomist USDA, Ames, Iowa, 1958-60, geneticist Raleigh, N.C., 1961-62, rsch. geneticist Ames, 1963-89; prof. Iowa State U., 1990—2002, C.F. Curtiss Disting. prof. agr. emeritus, 1991—. Author: (with J.B. Miranda) Quantitative Genetics in Maize Breeding, 1981, 2d edit., 1988; editor: Specialty Corns, 1994, 2d edit., 2000. 1st lt. U.S. Army, 1954-56. Recipient Applied Rsch. and Ext. award 1981, Henry A. Wallace award for disting.svc. to agr., 1992, Disting. Alumni Achievement citation, 1996, Iowa State U., Genetics and Plant Breeding award Nat. Coun. Plant Breeding, 1984, Gov.'s Sci. medal State of Iowa, 1990, Burlington No. Career Rsch. Achievement award Iowa State Found., 1991, Centennial medal Phi Kappa Phi, 1997, Verdent Plant Genetics award Verdent Ptnrs., Chgo., 2001; USDA grantee, 1982, 85, 87, 90; named to USDA/Agrl. Rsch. Sci. Hall of Fame, 1992; honored Inter-Am. Inst. Coop. Agr. significant contbns. to agr., Washington, 2003, Arnel R. Hallaure Internat. Symposium plant breeding, Mexico City, 2003. Fellow Am. Soc. Agronomy (Agronomic Achievement award for crops 1989, Agronomic Rsch. award 1992), Crop Sci. Soc. (Dekalb Pfizer Crop Sci. award 1981, Pres.'s award 2002), Iowa Acad. Sci. (disting. fellow 1985); mem. NAS, Nat. Agri-Mktg. Assn. (nat. award for excellence in rsch. 1993), Am. Genetic Assn., Am. Statis. Assn., Kans. State U. Alumni Assn. (alumni fellow 1997), Iowa State Alumni Assn. (faculty citation 1987, Disting. Achievement Citation 1995), Gamma Sigma Delta (Disting. Svc. to Agr. award 1990, Rsch. Award of Merit 1999). Republican. Lutheran. Home: 516 Luther Dr Ames IA 50010-4735 Office: Iowa State U 1505 Dept Agronomy Ames IA 50010 Office Phone: 515-294-7820. Business E-Mail: hallauer@iastate.edu.

HALLBERG, BENGT O., systems strategy director, fiber optic specialist; b. Stockholm, Dec. 31, 1943; s. Olle E.S. and Anne-Marie K. H.; m. Lena M. Tengelin, June 13, 1975; children: Niklas O., Mattias A., Andreas E. MS in Physics, Royal Inst. Tech., Stockholm, 1978. Constrnl. engr. AB Svenska Bostäder, Stockholm, 1965-76; scientist Inst. of Optical Rsch., Stockholm, 1976-81; pres. Scan Fiber Opto AB, Stockholm, 1988-92, BOH Optical AB, Stockholm, 1981-95; dir. Fiber Network Application Lab, Ericsson, Stockholm, 1995-97; dir. sys. strategy Access Network, Ericsson Inc., N.Y.C., 1997—2000; mgr. BOH Strategy, Stockholm, 2000—. Inventor airborne multispectral radiometer, fiber optic communication system based on WDM; patentee frequency and output regulation in laser diodes. Mem. Optical Soc. Am. Office: Boh Strategy Österbrink SE 130 55 Orno Sweden E-mail: boh@bohstrategy.com.

HALLBERG, BUDD JAYE, management consulting firm executive; b. Ottumwa, Iowa, Oct. 2, 1942; s. Melvin Kenneth and Janet Berina (Dowden) H.; m. Diana May Pierce, Dec. 30, 1962. BA, MA, Goddard Coll., 1980; BS, SUNY, 1981; diploma, Command & Gen. Staff Coll., 1981; cert., Wharton Sch., 1984, Yale U., 1996. Account exec. Francis I. duPont & Co., Moline, Ill., 1966-69, sales mgr. N.Y.C., 1969-70, br. mgr. Toledo, 1970-71; v.p. Dominick & Dominick, Inc., N.Y.C., 1971-72, Hornblower & Weeks, Inc., N.Y.C., 1972-74; mem. N.Y. Mercantile Exchange, N.Y.C., 1974-76; dir. U.S. Commodity Future Trading Commn., Washington, 1976-83; v.p. Heinold Commodities, Inc., N.Y.C., 1983-85; pres. SCAN Mgmt. Inc., Gettysburg, Pa., 1985—. Contbr. articles to profl. jours. Fund raiser Rep. party Old Greenwich, Conn., 1974, Gettysburg, Pa., 1995, St. Saviours Episc. Ch., Old Greenwich, 1975, Prince of Peace Episc. Ch., Gettysburg, 1985—. Lt. col. USAR, ret. Mem.: Swedish Colonial Soc., St. Nicholas Soc. of N.Y., Soc. of Colonial Wars, Friends of The Holland Soc. of N.Y., Sons of Union Vets of Civil War, The William Soc., Pa. Soc. Sons of the Revolution, Colonial Soc. Pa., Rotary, Franklin Inn Club (Phila.), Racquet Club Phila., Army and Navy Club Washington, Scottish Rite, York Rite, Masons (32 deg.). Avocations: fishing, hunting, tennis, jogging, golf. Home: 320 Spangler School Rd Gettysburg PA 17325-8639 Office: SCAN Mgmt Inc PO Box 4835 Gettysburg PA 17325-4835 Office Phone: 717-359-7473. Business E-Mail: scanmngt@supernet.com.

HALLBERG, PARKER FRANKLIN, environmental company executive; b. Detroit, Nov. 21, 1939; s. Franklin Harold and Fae Marie (Parker) H.; m. Jane Birdwell Henderson, Nov. 28, 1964 (div. May 1976); 1 child, Thomas Stalworth Henderson. AB, U. Mich., 1961, MA, 1962. Procurement analyst NASA, Washington, 1964-67; budget officer USIA, Washington, 11967-68, fgn. svc. officer, 1968-92, asst. exec. officer Bangkok, 1968-70, br. pub. affairs officer Davao, The Philippines, 1970-73, pers. officer Washington, 1973-76, exec. officer Bangkok, 1976-78, Jakarta, Indonesia, 1980-82, Paris, 1987-91; ret., 1992; exec. dir. Internat. Vol. Svcs. Inc., Washington, 1996-97, bd. dirs., corp. sec., 1996—; exec. v.p. Enviro Tek Corp., Waterford, Va., 1997—, bd. dirs., corp. sec., 1996—. Bd. dirs. AgriCell.Com.Inc., Waterford. Treas., bd. dirs. Canterbury Sch., Accokeek, Md., 1965-68; vestryman St. Augustine's Episcopal Ch., Washington, 1965-67, Christ Ch., Bangkok, 1970, 78; bd. dirs., mem. exec. com. Episcopal Caring Response to AIDS, Washington, 1993-96; chmn. bd. trustees Internat. Art Found. Former Soviet States, Inc., N.Y.C., 2000—. Mem. Diplomatic and Counselor Officers Ret., Army and Navy Club, Arts Club Washington (bd. govs. 2001—). Democrat. Office: Enviro Tek Corp PO Box 366 Waterford VA 20197 E-mail: pfhallberg@erols.com.

HALLECK, CHARLES WHITE, lawyer, photographer, former judge; b. Rensselaer, Ind., July 6, 1929; s. Charles Abraham and Blanche (White) H.; m. Carolyn L. Wood, Dec. 23, 1950 (div. Oct. 1968); children: Holly Louise, Charles White, Todd Alexander, Heather Leigh, Heidi Lynne, William Hemsley, Hope Leslie; m. Jeanne Wahl, May 16, 1970. AB, Williams Coll., 1951; JD, George Washington U., 1957; LL.D. (hon.), St. Joseph's Coll., 1971; AA in Photography, Foothill Coll., Los Altos Hills, Calif., 1996. Asst. U.S. atty. for D.C., 1957-59; assoc. Hogan and Hartson, Washington, 1959-65; judge Superior Ct. D.C., 1965-77; mem. firm Lamb, Halleck & Keats, Washington, 1977-80; sole practice, 1980-86; photojournalist, 1986-99; fine art photographer, 1999—. Served with USNR, 1951-55; to lt. Res. (ret.). Mem. Beta Theta Pi, Phi Delta Phi.

HALLECK, GEORGE THOMAS, marketing professional; b. Elizabeth, N.J., Mar. 9, 1948; s. Joseph George and Jean Constance Halleck; m. Jacquelyn Ann Halleck, Aug. 23, 1970 (div. Nov. 1994); children: Gregg Christopher, Robert George; m. Judith B. Halleck, Mar. 16, 1995; stepchildren: Vincent James Grillo, Julie Ann Grillo. AA, Union Coll., Cranford, N.J., 1968; BA, Lynchburg Coll., 1970; MS, Va. Commonwealth U., 1972. Tchr. St. Genevieve's Sch., Elizabeth, N.J., 1972-74; sales rep. Parke-Davis, Detroit, 1974-78, Johnson & Johnson, New Brunswick, N.J., 1978-84; sr. group product mgr. Howmedica-Pfizer, Rutherford, NJ, 1984-99; mktg. mgr. Internat. Technidyne Corp., Edison, N.J., 2000—. Roman Catholic. Achievements include patent for surgical instrument. Home: 27 Cornell Rd Cranford NJ 07016 E-mail: halleck3@aol.com.

HALL-ELLIS, SYLVIA DUNN, library and information scientist, educator; b. Kewanee, Ill., June 21, 1949; d. M. Orrill and Elizabeth J. (Boase) Dunn; m. J. Theodore Ellis, Dec. 24, 1989. BA, Rockford (Ill.) Coll., 1971; MLS, U. North Tex., 1972; MA, U. Tex., San Antonio, 1976; PhD, U. Pitts., 1985. Cert. pub. libr. Tex., N.Y., Pa. Sys. coord. San Antonio Pub. Libr., 1973-76; divsn. libr. Corpus Christi Pub. Librs., 1976-78; asst. dir. So. Tier Libr. Sys., Corning, NY, 1978-81; dir. libr. devel. State Libr. Pa., Harrisburg, 1981; devel. officer PRLC, Inc., Pitts., 1981-85; pres., owner Blue Bear Group, Inc., Central City, Colo., 1985-92, 886, Inc., Denver, 1989—; profl. cataloger Arapahoe Libr. Dist., Littleton, Colo., 1991; head libr. Rocky Mountain Coll. Art, Denver, 1992-93; asst. prof. L.S. Sam Houston State U., Huntsville, Tex., 1993-95, adj. prof., 1995—; prof. U. Denver, 1999—. Cons. various state govts., 1981—; devel. officer, grant proposal writer Region One Edn. Svc. Ctr., Edinburg, Tex., 1995—97; adj. prof. libr. sci. U. Ariz., Tucson, 1995, San Jose State U., 2002—; dir. devel. Mid-Continent Regional Ednl. Lab., Aurora, Colo., 1997—98; spl. asst. U.S. Dept. Edn. Region VIII, 2000—01. Author: Grantwriting For School And Small Public Libraries, 1999, Grants for Schools, 2003; contbr. articles to profl. jours. Mem. Gilpin County Econ. Devel. Commn., Central City, 1987—89; cons., treas. Columbine Family Health Ctrs., Inc., Black Hawk, 1988—89; docent Denver Mus. Natural History, 1992—; pres. Rocky Mountain LAN Engrs., Denver, 1993; tech. prep mem. Rio Grande Valley Inc., Tex., 1995—. Mem.: ALA, Colo. Ednl. Media Assn., Colo. Libr. Assn., Tex. Libr. Assn. Office: U Denver Ste 107 2135 E Wesley Ave Denver CO 80208 Office Fax: 303-756-0424. Personal E-mail: shellis@bigplanet.com.

HALLEMANN, JAMES RAYMOND, media specialist; b. Dearborn, Mich., Apr. 19, 1958; s. George Raymond and Lucille Alice Hallemann; m. Kimberlee Dawn Pearson, June 21, 1986. BA in Film Video, U. Mich., 1981; MA in English, Ea. Mich. U., 1991. Media specialist Oakland C.C., Waterford, Mich., 1983—92, instr., 1992—. Office: Oakland C C 7350 Cooley Lake Waterford MI 48327 Office Phone: 249-449-2322.

HALLEN, BARRY, philosopher, educator; b. Chgo., Apr. 5, 1941; s. George and Betty Hallen; m. Carla De Benedetti, Apr. 30, 1986; m. Patricia Slattery, Aug. 5, 1966 (div. Nov. 26, 1974). BA in Philosophy, Carleton Coll., 1963; MA in Philosophy, Boston U., 1968, PhD in Philosophy, 1970. Lectr. in philosophy U. Lagos, Lagos, Nigeria, 1970—75; from lectr. to reader in philosophy U. Ife, Ile-Ife, Nigeria, 1975—83, reader in philosophy, 1983—88; project dir. UNESCO, Milan, 1989—98; vis. prof. philosophy Morehouse Coll., Atlanta, 1997—2000, prof. philosophy, 2000—, chmn. dept. philosophy and Religionr, 2001—. Rschr. W.E.B. DuBois Inst. Harvard U., Cambridge, Mass., 1995—. Co-author: Knowledge, Belief & Witchcraft, 1997; author: The Good, The Bad & the Beautiful, 2000, A Short History of African Philosophy, 2002, African Philosophy: The Analytic Approach, 2005. Borden Parker Bowne fellow, Boston U., 1968—69, Fulbright rsch. grantee, 2003. Mem.: Internat. Soc. African Philosophy and Studies (pres. 2004—), Soc. African Philosophy in N.Am. (gen. sec. 1998—). Avocations: sailing, bicycling, writing detective stories. Office: Morehouse College 830 Westview Drive SW Atlanta GA 30314 Office Phone: 404-215-2607. Business E-Mail: bhallen@morehouse.edu.

HALLENBECK, KENNETH LUSTER, retired numismatist; b. Ann Arbor, Mich., Oct. 20, 1931; s. Kenneth Luster and Ethel (Apfel) Hallenbeck; m. June Eugenia Miekka, July 2, 1955; children: Kevin L., Thomas G., Scott A., Sheryl A. AB in Geography, U. Mich., 1955. Planning analyst Lincoln Nat. Life Ins. Co., Ft. Wayne, Ind., 1957-70, sr. planning analyst, 1970-72, asst. mgr. policy issue, 1972-77; bd. govs. Am. Numismatic Assn., Colorado Springs, Colo., 1971-87, mus. curator, 1977-82, v.p., 1987-89, pres., 1989-91; pres., dir. Hallenbeck Coin Gallery, Inc., Colorado Springs, 1983—; ret. Apptd. by Pres. Nixon to U.S. Assay Commn. 1974; testified before Congl. subcom. on coinage and consumer affairs for commemorative coinage, mem. design selection com. for Olympic coin designs, 1992, Focus group for design of Sacagawea dollar, 1999. Contbr. numerous articles to mags. Mem. Rep. Cen. Com., Ft. Wayne, 1972-77, Better Bus. Bur., Colorado Springs; del. to Rep. County and 5th Congl. Dist. Caucuses; sec. Pioneer Mus. Found. Bd.; mem. focus group Sacajewa Dollar design, 1998. With U.S. Army, 1955-57. Fellow Life Mgmt. Inst.; mem. Colorado Springs C. of C., Tokens and Medals Soc. (past pres.), Pioneer Mus. Found. Bd., Bd. Friends of the Pike's Peak Libr. Dist., Masons, Shriners, also numerous local, regional and nat. coin clubs. Republican. Congregationalist. Avocations: coin collecting/numismatics, western history. Office: Hallenbeck Coin Gallery Inc 711 N Nevada Ave Colorado Springs CO 80903-1007

HALLENBECK, LINDA S., elementary school educator; m. Theodore R. Hallenbeck; 2 children. BS, Kent State U., 1974, MEd, 1976, postgrad. Cert. tchr. K-3, K-8, computer sci., math., Ohio Ohio, Nat. bd. cert. Grad. asst. Kent (Ohio) State U., 1974-76; 3d grade tchr. Hudson (Ohio) Elem. Sch., 1976-77; 1st grade tchr. Evamere Sch., Hudson, 1977-86; 5th grade tchr. J.P. McDowell Elem. Sch., Hudson, 1986-92, East Woods Sch., Hudson, 1992—2001; tchr. Hudson Mid. Sch., 2001—03; rsch. assoc. NSF, 2002—03, Mich. State U., 2003—04. Cons. NSF, Washington, 1989-95, tchr. in residence Office of Gov. Bob Taft, 1999-2001; tchr. Presdl. Acad. for Excellence in Tchg. Math. at Princeton and Northwestern U., Middle Sch. Math. State Trainer, Math Acad., 2001—; mem. exec. bd. Ohio Math./Sci. Coalition. Recipient Presdl. award for excellence in teaching sci. and math. NSF, 1993, Govs. Edn. leadership award, 1998, Ohio Pioneer in Edn award, 2000. Mem. Nat. Coun. Tchrs. Math., Ohio Coun. Tchrs. Math. (pres. 2004—), Ohio Math. Edn. Leadership Coun Avocations: skiing, gardening, sewing, decorating. Home: 7615 Oxgate Ct Hudson OH 44236-1877 Office Phone: 330-650-4912.

HALLENBECK, RACHEL KIRSTEN, music educator, director; b. Jackson, Calif., Nov. 1, 1965; d. Ronald K. and Martha Lou Grabke; children: Kirsten Elizabeth, Brianna Ruth. BSc in Music Edn., Ea. Nazarene Coll., 1989, MEd in Elem. Edn., 1999, MEd in Adminstrn., 2000. Music specialist Braintree (Mass.) Pub. Schs., 1989—2000, dir. music, 2000—. Soloist Boylston Congl. Ch., Boston, 1990—, Town of Braintree, 1990—2003; accompanist Quincy (Mass.) Pub. Schs., 1998—2003, vocal instr. performing arts, 2004—05; condr. Braintree (Mass.) Choral Soc., 2001—02; musical dir. Harmony Youth Chorus and No Place for Hate Project, 2004—05. Singer: Boston (Mass.) Symphony Orch., 1989—; dir.: Quincy (Mass.) Dinner Theater, 1990—93; singer: (albums) The Boston (Mass.) Pops Orch., The Boston (Mass.) Symphony Orch. Republican. Avocations: singing, choreography, piano. Office: Braintree Public Schools 128 Town St Braintree MA 02184

HALLER, ANN CORDWELL, secondary school educator; b. Denver, July 2, 1944; d. Robert William and Dorothy Warne (Dahlberg) Cordwell; m. Frederick Ray Haller, Sept. 18, 1965; children: Michael Frederick, Lori Ann. BA in Pre-Med. Scis., Univ. Montana, 1966; MA in Anatomy, Univ. N.D., 1969; PhD in Anatomy, La. State Univ., 1975. Instr. dept. anatomy, sch. medicine Univ. N.D., Grand Forks, 1969-71; instr. dept. biol. scis. Univ. New Orleans, 1975-76; tchr. Kellogg (Idaho) Joint Sch. Dist. #391, 1980—. Head class adv. Kellogg H.S., 1980—; chmn. faculty coun. Nat. Honor Soc., Kellogg. Bd. dirs. Nat. Sci. Scholars Program, Idaho, other scholarship bds., West Shoshone Hosp., Kellogg, 1977-79; mem. Idaho health Sys. Agy., Boise, 1976-79. Recipient Centennial Tchr. Idaho award NIH, 1987; named Dist. Tchr. of Yr., 2000, Idaho Outstanding Biology Tchr. of Yr., 2003. Mem. NSTA, DAR, Lamaze Internat. (Lamaze childbirth instr. 1978—), Philanthropic Ednl. Orgn., Sigma Xi, Delta Kappa Gamma. Lutheran. Avocations: gardening, reading, classical music, dog training, travel. Home: 804 Country Club Ln PO Box 923 Pinehurst ID 83850-0923 Office: Kellogg Joint Sch Dist 391 Jacobs Gulch Rd Kellogg ID 83837 Office Phone: 208-784-1371.

HALLER, ARCHIBALD ORBEN, sociologist, educator; b. San Diego, Jan. 15, 1926; s. Archie O. and Eleanor (Brizzee) Haller; m. Hazel Laura Zimmermann, Feb. 15, 1947 (dec. 1985); children: Elizabeth Ann, Stephanie Lynn Bylin, William John; m. Maria Camila Omegna Rocha, Apr. 12, 1986 (div. 1987); m. Maria Cristina Del Peloso, Sept. 16, 1989; stepchildren: Graziella, Camila. BA magna cum laude, Hamline U., 1950; MA, U. Minn., 1951; PhD, U. Wis., 1954. Assoc. prof., then prof. sociology Mich. State U., East Lansing, 1956—65; postdoctoral rschr. U. Wis., Madison, 1954—56, vis. prof., 1964, prof. sociology and rural sociology, 1965—94, emeritus prof., 1994—, affiliated faculty Indsl. Rels. Rsch. Inst., 1975—94, faculty in Latin Am., Caribbean and Iberian studies, 1965—94, affiliated faculty Inst. Environ. Studies, Conservation Biology and Sustainable Devel., 1990—94, ind. rsch., writing, lectr., 2002—. Vis. prof. sociology Brigham Young U., Provo, Utah, 1973; Fulbright travel grantee Univ. Sao Paulo, Brasilia, Pernambuco, Paraiba and Ceara, Brazil, 1979; vis. fellow Australian Nat. U., 1981; disting. vis. prof. rural sociology Ohio State U., 1982—83; Fulbright prof. sociology U. Sao Paulo, 1987—90; cons. UNESCO, 1989; cons. on Amazonian rsch. Govt. of Brazil, 1991—95; cons. Fed. U. Pernambuco, 1994; cons. for nat. social change to Pres. of Brazil, 1994—96; cons. on Amazonian rsch. Govt. of Brazil, 1997; cons. Fed. Rural U. Amazonia, 1997—98, others; vis. prof. doctoral program in sociology and polit sci. Fed. U. Minas Gerais, Brazil, 1998; cons. Ind. U., Bangladesh, 1998; organizer symposia on Brazil; cons. on Amazonian rsch. Govt. of Brazil, 1979; fellow Nat. Rsch. Coun. Brazil, 2000—02; vis. prof. doctoral program in sociology and polit sci. Fed. U. Minas Gerais, Brazil, 2000—03; chemistry lab asst. Minn. Mining and Mfg. Co.; vis. rschr. Brazilian Nat. Res. Coun.; Fulbright prof. sociology Rural U. of Brazil, 1962, U. Sao Paulo, 1974, 83, 88, 90. Author: The Occupl. Aspiration Scale: Theory, Structure and Correlates, 1963, 71, The Socioeconomic Macroregions of Brazil-1970, 1983; co-editor (with R.M. Hauser et al) Social Structure and Behavior: Essays in Honor of William Hamilton Sewell, 1982; editor spl. issues Luso-Brazilian Rev.; author rsch. monographs and tech. articles; contbr. articles to profl. jour. Mem. Mich. Com. on Mental Health Policies, 1961-62; Nat. Exec. Res., 1959-66; mem. sociology fellowship panel Coun. on Internat. Exch. Scholars, 1977-81, chmn., 1981. Active duty aviation electronics USNR, 1943—46. Decorated Grand Officer Order of Merit of Labor, Govt. of Brazil, 1981; univ. fellow U. Wis., 1953-1954; recipient John Luddy Phalen award in Latin Am. Studies U. Wis., 2000, Rsch. award Brazilian Sociol. Soc., 2005; Ann. Haller Disting. Lecture Series named in his honor U. Wis., 2000—. Fellow AAAS (consortium affiliates internat. programs 2003-2004), Am. Sociol. Assn.; mem. Internat. Rural Sociol. Assn., Internat. Sociol. Assn., Sociol. Rsch. Assn., Rural Sociol. Soc. (pres. 1970-71, rep. AAAS 1973-86, Disting. Rural Sociologist 1990), Univ. Club, Sigma Xi, Gamma Sigma Delta, Phi Beta Kappa. Achievements include contbr. to theory of societal stratification, to processes of status allocation, to the demographic structure of societal inequality, to identifying the socioeconomic develop. regions of Brazil, and to the measurement of internat. devel. Home and Office: 12928 Salt Cedar Dr Oro Valley AZ 85755 Office: U Wis 350 Agriculture Hall Madison WI 53706 Office Phone: 520-297-2912, 608-262-1510. Business E-Mail: haller@ssc.wisc.edu.

HALLER, CALVIN JOHN, banker; b. Buffalo, July 9, 1925; s. John Martin and and Emelia (George) H.; m. Yvette Ann Hogrewe, June 12, 1948; children: Cary John, Darlene Ann Haller Kalfahs. BS in Bus. Adminstrn. with distinction, U. Buffalo, 1949; DHL (hon.), Keuka Coll., 2005. With Buffalo Savs. Bank (now Goldome), from 1949, now ret. pres. Western N.Y. Bd. dirs. Children's Found., Erie County, Buffalo Fedn. of Neighborhood Ctrs.; trustee Niagara Luth. Health Found., Inc.; trustee, past pres. Met. YMCA Buffalo and Erie County; chmn. bd. trustees YMCA Greater Buffalo; trustee emeritus, past chmn. bd. Keuka Coll. Lt. (j.g.) USNR, 1943-46. Mem. N.Y. Soc. Security Analysts, Newcomen Soc. N.Am., Nat. Assn. Bus. Economists, U. Buffalo Alumni Assn., Beta Gamma Sigma. Clubs: Mason. Clubs (Buffalo), Country (Buffalo), Bond (Buffalo), Buffalo (Buffalo), Equality (Buffalo). Lutheran. Home: 235 Westfall Dr Tonawanda NY 14150-7136 Personal E-mail: calvette@localnet.com.

HALLER, CHARLES EDWARD, engineer, consultant; b. Fairfield, Conn., Sept. 5, 1924; s. William Charles and Gertrude Ida Mae (Belinski) H.; m. Eleanor Margret Hoffman, Oct. 11, 1950 (dec. 2003); children: Carolyn, Debra Lynn, Mark, Charles. Student, Yale U., 1943-44; BEE, Rensselaer Poly. Inst., 1947. Project engr. Western Union Telco., N.Y.C., 1948-56; assoc. lab. dir. ITT Labs., Nutley, N.J., 1956-62; v.p., dir. ops. ITT Worldcom, N.Y.C., 1962-67; pres. ITT Def. Communications, Nutley, N.J., 1967-74; mng. dir. I.O. ITT Telecom N.Am., Nutley, N.J., 1974-83; group gen. mgr., pres. ITT Asia Pacific, N.Y.C., 1983-87; cons. Internat. Enterprises, Kinnelon, N.J., 1987—. Author: Communications Switching Systems, 1964. With USN, 1943-46. Fellow IEEE (life). Republican. Avocations: politics, bowling, golf, reading, travel. Home and Office: 2 Summit Ter N Kinnelon NJ 07405-2436

HALLER, HAL MARTIN, JR., library director; b. Miami, Fla., Jan. 27, 1943; s. Hal Martin and Mary Ann Haller; m. Susanna Elizabeth Houseman, Aug. 6, 1965; children: Hal, Katie, Joy. AA, Miami-Dade C.C., 1963; BA, Fla. Bible Coll., 1966; BD, Luther Rice Sem., 1967; ThM, Dallas Theol. Sem., 1971; Master of Librarianship, Emory U., 1980; postgrad., Reformed Theol. Sem., 1989. Chmn. dept. biblical langs. Fla. Bible Coll., Hollywood, 1971-75, chmn. dept. systematic theology, 1975-79; asst. Pitts Theol. Libr. Emory U., Atlanta, 1980; min. theology Cmty. Bible Ch., Seminole, Fla., 1982-87; acad. dean Fla. Bible Coll., Kissimmee, 1987-96; min. on call First Bapt. Ch., Orlando, Fla., 1996-97; dir. libr. Southeastern Bible Coll., Birmingham, Ala., 1997-2000; asst. prof. Bible and Theology Luther Rice Sem., Lithonia, Ga., 2000—. Asst. libr. Clearwater (Fla.) Christian Coll., 1985-87; asst. prof. Grace Evang. Sch. Theology, Dallas, 1999—; accreditation team evaluator Accrediting Assn. B ible Colls., 2000, Transnat. Assn. Christian Colls. and Schs., 2001-04. Mem. instrnl. materials coun. Sch. Bd. Pinellas County, St. Petersburg, Fla., 1985. Named Alumnus of Yr., Fla. Bible Coll., Kissimmee, 1994. Mem. Assn. Christian Librs., Evang. Theol. Soc., Grace Evang. Soc., Phi Theta Kappa. Republican. Baptist. Avocation: playing guitar. Home: 6526 Stewart Lake Ct Lithonia GA 30038- also: 7301 Aska Rd Blue Ridge GA 30513-5520 Office Phone: 770-484-1204, 770-484-1204. Business E-Mail: hhaller@lrs.edu, hheller@lrs.edu.

HALLER, HERMANN W., romance language educator; b. Aarau, Switzerland, June 2, 1945; s. Walter and Hedi (Arni) H. Student, U. Paris, 1969-70, U. Florence, 1967-68; PhD, U. Berne, 1971. Instr. romance langs. CUNY, 1973-74, from asst. to assoc. prof. romance langs., 1974-83, mem. doctoral faculty, grad. ctr., 1978—, prof., 1984-96, prof. European langs. and lits., 1996—, chmn., 1999—2004. Vis. prof. Italian, Brown U., 1980, Johns Hopkins U., Balt., 1993, 2001, Middlebury Coll., 1994, U. Trent, Italy, 1996, U. Florence, Italy, 2003; dir. Bologna Coop. Studies Program, 1986-87. Author: Il Panfilo Veneziano, 1982, The Hidden Italy, 1986, Una Lingua Perduta e Ritrovata, 1993, The Other Italy: The Literary Canon in Dialect, 1999, La festa delle Lingue. La Letteratura dialettale in Italia, 2002; contbr. articles to profl. jours. Recipient Dino Campana prize Italian Cult Inst., 1991, Premio del Centro Internazionale di Studi Italiani, U. Genoa, 1992; fellow NEH, 1994-95. Mem. MLA (Aldo and Jeanne Scaglione Pub. award 1998), Linguistic Soc. Am., Internat. Linguistic Assn. (pres. 1992-93, 2004-05), Soc. Linguistica Italiana, Soc. de Linguistique Romane, Am. Assn. Italian Studies, Am. Assn. Tchrs. Italian, Assn. Storia Lingua Italiana. Office: Queens Coll CUNY Dept European Langs & Lits Flushing NY 11367-1597 Office Phone: 718-997-5980.

HALLER, ROBERT ANTHONY, art association administrator; b. Pitts., Pa. s. Robert Blum and Catherine B Haller; m. Amy Greenfield. BA in hist., U. Notre Dame, 1965, MA in internat. rels., 1966. Dir. pub. rels. Alliance Coll., Cambridge Springs, Pa., 1967; dir. student publications Bloomsburg State Coll., Pa., 1967—69; mng. editor Jour. of Econ. Lit., Pitts., 1969—73; exec. dir. Pitts. Film Makers, 1973—80, Anthology Film Archives, NYC, 1980—84; dir. of develop. S.I. Inst., 1985—89; dir. collections/spl. projects Anthology Film Archives, NYC, 1990—. Panelist Pa. Council on Arts, 1976—78, Nat. Endowment for Arts, 1980; chmn. Nat. Alliance of Media Arts Ctr., 1980—83. Editor: (book) Brakhage Scrapbook, 1982, Jim Davis-The Flow of Energy, 1992; author: Crossroads- Film in Pittsburgh, 2005; editor: (catalogs) Kenneth Anger, 1980, Ed Emshwiller, 1997, First Light, 1998, Fritz Lang, 2000, Galaxy, 2001, Omer Kavur, 2000, Zeki Demirkubuz, 2003. Rsch. fellowship, Nat. Endowment for Arts, 1981, Rsch. grants, Pa. Coun. on the Arts, 1980. Mem.: Soc. of Cinema Studies. Avocation: photography. Home: 135 St Pauls Ave Staten Island NY 10301 Office: Anthology Film Archives 32 Second Ave New York NY 10003

HALLETT, CHARLES ARTHUR, JR., language educator, humanities educator; b. New Haven, July 19, 1935; s. Charles Arthur and Bridie D. Hallett; m. Elaine Stewartson, Nov. 7, 1958. BA, The New Sch., 1961; MA, Columbia U., 1963; DFA, Yale U., 1967. Mem. faculty Fordham U., Bronx, N.Y., 1967—, assoc. prof. English, 1971-81, prof., 1981—. Asst. project dir. NEH Shakespeare Summerfest, N.Y.C., 1981; vis. prof. U. Warwick, Eng., 1978, Loyola U., New Orleans, 1994, Dartmouth Coll., 2001-. Author: Middleton's Cynics, 1975, The Revenger's Madness, 1981, Analyzing Shakespeare's Action, 1991; (play) Aaron Burr (monograph) Poetry and Reality: The Zetema and Its Significance for Poetics, 1977; contbr. to Ency. Americana; contbr. articles to profl. jours including Studies in Philology, Jour. English and German Philology, Shakespeare Quar., Shakespeare Bull. Fellow Lawrence Langner Theatre Guild Found., 1965-66; Am. Coun. Learned Socs. grantee, 1981. Home: 116 E 91st St Apt 5 New York NY 10128-1667 Office: English Dept Fordham U Bronx NY 10458

HALLETT, JUDITH PELLER, classical studies educator; b. Chgo., Apr. 4, 1944; d. Leonard and Celia (Stern) Peller; m. Mark Hallett, June 26, 1966; children: Nicholas, Victoria. BA, Wellesley (Mass.) Coll., 1966; MA, Harvard U., Cambridge, Mass., 1967, PhD, 1971. Lectr. classics Clark U., Worcester, Mass., 1972-74; asst. prof. classical studies Boston U., 1974-82; Blegen vis. rsch. scholar Vassar Coll., Poughkeepsie, NY, 1980; Mellon vis. asst. prof. Brandeis U., Waltham, Mass., 1982-83; assoc. prof. classics U. Md., College Park, 1983-92, prof. classics, 1993—, acting equity adminstr. Coll. Arts & Humanities, 1988-89, chair classics, 1996—2004. Asst. to assoc. editor The Classical World, 1980—; founder, mem. steering com. Women's Classical Caucus, 1972—. Author: Fathers and Daughters in Roman Society, 1984; co-editor: The Personal Voice in Classical Scholarship and Roman Sexualities, 1997; contbr. more than 50 articles to scholarly jours. Mem. Md. Humanities Coun., 2001—; bd. trustees Balt. Hebrew U., 2002—. Fellow, NEH; grantee. Mem. AAUP (pres. chpt. 1994—), Am. Philol. Assn. (dir. 1997-99), Assn. Ancient Historians, Classical Assn. Atlantic States (2d v.p. 1997-98, pres. 1999-2000), Md. Humanities Coun., Phi Beta Kappa (pres. U. Md. College Park chpt. 1996-98). Democrat. Jewish. Home: 5147 Westbard Ave Bethesda MD 20816-1413 Office: Dept Classics U Md College Park MD 20742-0001 Office Phone: 301-405-2024. Business E-Mail: jeph@umd.edu.

HALLETT, MARK, neurologist, educator, medical researcher, director; b. Phila., Oct. 22, 1943; s. Joseph Woodrow and Estelle (Barg) H.; m. Judith E. Peller, June 26, 1966; children: Nicholas L., Victoria C. BA magna cum laude, Harvard U., 1965, MD cum laude, 1969. Diplomate Am. Bd. Psychiatry and Neurology. Resident in neurology Mass. Gen. Hosp., Boston, 1972-75; Moseley fellow Harvard U., London, 1975-76, lectr., assoc. prof. neurology Boston, 1976-84; head clin. neurophy. lab. Brigham and Women's Hosp., Boston, 1976-84; clin. dir. Nat. Inst. Neurol. Disorders and Stroke NIH, Bethesda, Md., 1984-2000, chief human motor control sect. NINDS, 1984—. Author: (with others) Entrapment Neuropathies, 1990, 3rd edit., 1998; editor: (with M.F. Brin and J. Jankovic) Scientific and Therapeutic Aspects of Botulinum Toxin, 2002; editor-in-chief: Clinical Neurophysiology, 2000—; contbr. numerous articles to profl. jours. Bd. dirs. Easter Seals Rsch. Found., Chgo., 1985-87; mem. med. adv. bd. Nat. Parkinson Found., Miami, 1985—, Dystonia Med. Rsch. Found., Chgo., 1989-93, 2000-03, Benign Essential Blepharospasm Rsch. Found., Beaumont, 1990—, Myoclonus Rsch. Found., Fort Lee, N.J., 1989-2003. Mem. Am. Assn. Electrodiagnostic Medicine (pres. 1991-92), Am. Acad. Neurology (v.p. 2001-05), Am. Neurol. Assn., Am. Clin. Neurophysiology Soc., Soc. for Neurosci., Movement Disorder Soc. (pres. 1999-2000), Phi Beta Kappa, Alpha Omega Alpha. Democrat. Jewish. Home: 5147 Westbard Ave Bethesda MD 20816-1413 Office: NINDS NIH Msc 1428 Bldg 10 Rm 5n226 10 Center Dr Bethesda MD 20892-1428 Office Phone: 301-496-9526. Business E-Mail: hallettm@ninds.nih.gov.

HALLETT, WILLIAM JARED, retired nuclear engineer; b. Rock Springs, Wyo., Apr. 12, 1923; s. William Jared and Florence Myrtle (Miller) H.; m. Marjorie Louise Taylor, Dec. 25, 1942; children— Katherine O. Hallett Rembert (dec.), Carolyn R. Hallett Kortangen, Helen L. Hallett Warren, David William. BS in Chem. Engring., U. Colo., 1944; postgrad., UCLA, 1957-58, 62-70, No. Ill. U., 1973. Registered profl. nuclear engr., Calif. Engr. Tenn. Eastman Corp., Oak Ridge, 1944-47; sect. head Fairchild E & A Corp., Oak Ridge, 1947-50; project mgr. AI Div. Rockwell Internat., Canoga Park, Calif., 1950-66; div. dir., mgr. Argonne Nat. Lab., Ill., 1968-86; ret., 1986. Contbg. author: Nuclear Reactor Engineering, 1963; Nuclear Power and Its Environmental Effects, 1980 Bd. dirs. Simi Valley Unified Sch. Dist., Calif., 1965-68 Republican. Methodist. Avocations: photography, art collecting, travel.

HALLEY, DIANE ESTHER, artist; b. Jasper, Ind., May 14, 1939; d. John and Esther Margaret (Kruse) Darden; m. Norman B. Halley, May 21, 1966; 1 child, William Tull. BS in Elem. Edn., Ind. State U., 1961. Tchr. 4th grade, New Albany, Ind., 1961, Seymour, Ind., 1962-64, Westminster, Colo., 1964-68; portrait artist Arvada, Colo., 1979—. Juror fall exhbn. Colo. Watercolor Soc., 2002. Paintings included in books, Colo., 1990—, Denver Art Mus., Best of Watercolor-Painting Textures, 1997, Splash Six-The Magic of Texture, 2000; one-woman shows include Denver Nat. Bank, 1983, Foothills Art Ctr., Golden, Colo., 1984, Nat. Ctr. Atmospheric Rsch., Boulder, Colo., 1991, Colo. Christian U., 2000, exhibitions include Lincoln Ctr., Ft. Collins, Colo., 2003, Challenge of Champions, Watercolor Art Soc. Houston, 2003, 53rd Nat. Exhibition of Contemporary Realism in Art, Acad. Artists Assn., 2003, Artists Who Happen to be Women, Tex. A&M U., 2004, Watercolor Mo. Nat., Winston Churchill Meml. Libr., 2004 (Bd. Dirs. award, 2004), Great 8 Exhbn., Kans. Watercolor Soc., Wichita Art Mus., 50th Anniversary Mem. Exhbn., Colo. Watercolor Soc., 2004, Small Works Exhbn., Attleboro Art Mus., 2005. Pres. Clear Creek Valley Med. Aux., Lakewood, Colo., 1973—74, 1991—92. Recipient Founder's award, Colo. Watercolor Soc., 1992, Pres.'s award, 1994, Best in Show award, Colo. Watercolor Soc. 50th Ann. Exbn., 2004, Grumbacher award, Pikes Peak Watercolor Soc., 1995, Cash award, Lakewood Arts Coun., 2001, Award of Distinction, Mo. Nat. Watercolor Exhbn., 2003, Westminster Cmty. Artist Series award, 2003. Mem.: Mo. Watercolor Soc. (signature mem.), Kans. Watercolor Soc. (signature mem., Am. artist cash award 1999), Rocky Mountain Nat. Watermedia Soc. (signature mem.), Nat. Watercolor Soc. (signature mem., Del Mar Coll. award 1981), Nat. Assn. Women Artists (signature mem., Cecil Shapiro Meml. award 1998), Catherine Lorillard Wolf Art Club (signature mem., Adriana Zahn award 1985, Cynthia Googal award 1986). Avocations: Bible study, bridge, gardening. Home: 6631 Osceola Ct Arvada CO 80003-6426

HALLEY, GUSTAVO RICARDO, voice educator; b. Santiago, Cuba, Sept. 20, 1940; (parents Am. citizens); s. Gustavo Miguel Halley and Joan Whitehouse; m. Hilda Norbert; m. Sarah Beth Nammock, Nov. 25, 1976; children: Hildi, Gustavo Rafael, Francesca. BA, Jacksonville (Fla.) U.; MusM, MusD, Fla. State U. Interim instr. U. Fla., Gainesville, Fla.; asst. prof. Bethune-Cookman Coll., Daytona Beach, Fla.; pvt. practice profl. singer; assoc. prof. U. Mo., Kans. City, Mo. Prof. voice Am. Inst. Musical Studies, Graz, Austria. Translator: Prollel Voices, 2004; contbr. articles to profl. jours.; author: (albums) Old Cuban Songs, 1995. Named Best Artist in Voice, ACCA, 1985; recipient Accademia Chigiana award, Italian Govt., 1960; grantee, NEH, 1977. Mem.: Phi Iota (life). Democrat. Roman Cath. Avocations: travel, record collecting, Judo. Home: 28 E 69th St Kansas City MO 64113 Office: UMKC Conservatory 4949 Cherry Kansas City MO 64110

HALLEY, JAMES WOODS, physics professor; b. Chgo., Nov. 16, 1938; m. Merile Hobbs (dec. 2001); 2 children. BS, MIT, 1961; PhD, U. Calif., Berkeley, 1965. NSF predoctoral fellow U. Calif., Berkeley, 1963-65; NSF postdoctoral fellow Faculte des Scis., Orsay, France, 1965-66; asst. prof. U. Calif., Berkeley, 1966-68; assoc. prof. U. Minn., Mpls., 1968-77, prof. physics, 1977—, fellow Supercomputer Inst., 1989—, grad. faculty materials sci., 1989—. Vis. prof. Oxford U., 1973, Harwell AERE, 1973, U. Oreg., 1975, Yale U., 1976, Brookhaven N.L., 1976, 79, Harvard U., 1979, Mich. State U., 1980, Argonne, 1981—, Inst. for Theoretical Physics, Santa Barbara, 1983, 97, 98, chemistry dept. U. Calif., Santa Barbara, 1984, U. Calif., Berkeley, 1993; IBM Almaden Rsch. Ctr., 1987, Australian Nat. U., 1988; cons. 3M, 1985-89, UNESCO, 1986, GM Corp., 1989-90, Ednl. Testing Svc., 1989; mem. GRE bd. examiners Ednl. Testing Svc., 1991-96; physics bd. dirs. U.S. Com. for Sci. Coop. with Vietnam, 1985—. Author: Physics of Human Motion, 1981; editor 7 books; contbr. over 180 articles to profl. jours. Recipient George Taylor Tchg. award, 1979, McMillan professorship, 1979; Bush fellow, 1983-84; grantee NSF, 1972-79, 95—, Rsch. Corp., 1970-72, Corrosion Ctr., 1980-92, Ednl. Devel. Program, 1973, 79, 3M, 1982, 2002-05, IBM Advanced Edn. Project, 1985, Dept. Edn., 1986, IBM, 1988-90, Electric Power Rsch. Inst., 1988-90, Dept. Energy, 1990—, Sumitomo Metal Industries, 1992-93, NASA, 1992-95. Fellow Am. Phys. Soc.; mem. AAAS, Am. Chem. Soc., Materials Rsch. Soc. Achievements include research in theory of disorder in condensed matter, statistics and dynamics of polymers, physics of the fluid-solid interface, high temperature superconductivity, condensate fraction in bose superfluids. Office: Univ Minn Sch Physics and Astronomy Minneapolis MN 55455 Office Phone: 612-624-0395. E-mail: woods@woods1.spa.umn.edu.

HALLEY, JANET E., law educator; BA in English Lit., summa cum laude, Princeton U., 1974; PhD in English Lit., UCLA, 1980; JD, Yale U., 1988. Mem. English faculty Hamilton Coll., Clinton, NY, 1980—85; law clk. to Chief Judge Gilbert Merritt US Ct. Appeals 6th Cir., 1988—89; assoc. Skadden, Arps, Slate, Meagher & Flom, Boston, 1989—91; assoc. prof. Stanford Law Sch., 1991—95, prof., 1995—2000; prof. law Harvard Law Sch., Cambridge, Mass., 2000—. Vis. prof. law Harvard Law Sch., 1999. Author: Don't: A Reader's Guide to the Military Anti-Gay Policy, 1999. Named Robert E. Paradise Faculty Scholar for Excellence in Teaching and Rsch., Stanford Law Sch., 1996. Office: Harvard Law Sch 1563 Massachusetts Ave Cambridge MA 02138 Office Phone: 617-496-0182. Office Fax: 617-496-4947.

HALLGREN, RICHARD EDWIN, meteorologist; b. Kersey, Pa., Mar. 15, 1932; s. Edwin Leonard and Edith Marie Hallgren; m. Maxine Hope Anderson, Apr. 17, 1954; children: Scott, Douglas, Lynette. BS, Pa. State U., 1953, PhD, 1960; DSc (hon.), SUNY, 1989. Sys. engr. IBM Corp., 1960-64; sci. adv. to asst. sec. of commerce, 1964-66; dir. world weather sys. ESSA, Rockville, Md., 1966-69, asst. adminstrn., 1969-70; asst. adminstr. NOAA, Rockville, 1970-71, assoc. adminstr. environ. monitoring and prediction, 1971-73, asst. adminstr. for ocean and atmospheric scis., 1977-79; dep. dir. Nat. Weather Svc., Silver Spring, Md., 1973-77, dir., 1979-88; exec. dir. Am. Meteorol. Soc., 1988-99, exec. dir. emeritus, 1999—. Permanent U.S. rep. World Meteorol. Orgn., 1980—88. Contbr. articles to sci. jours. With USAF, 1954—56. Named Meritorious Sr. Exec., 1980, Disting. Sr. Exec., 1986; recipient Arthur S. Flemming award, U.S. C. of C., 1968, Gold medal, Dept. Commerce, 1969, Internat. Meteorol. Orgn. prize, Wold Meteorol. Orgn., 1990, Spl. Achievement award, NOAA, 2001, Charles L. Hosler medal, 2002; Alumni fellow, Pa. State U. Fellow: AAAS, Am. Meteorol. Soc. (hon.; pres., Cleveland Abbe award 2003, C.F. Brooks award 1986); mem.: Am. Geophys. Union, Oceanog. Soc. Lutheran. Home: 11428 Cedar Ridge Dr Potomac MD 20854-3761 Office: Am Meteorol Svc 1120 G St NW Ste 800 Washington DC 20005-6115 Office Phone: 202-737-9006 413. Business E-Mail: hallgren@dc.ametsoc.org.

HALLIBURTON, LLOYD, Romance philology educator; b. Shreveport, La., July 31, 1934; s. Ralph Eloe and Mary Katherine (Smith) H.; m. Donna Lee Cavanagh, May 27, 1965 (div. Sept. 1976); children: Richard Lloyd, William Cavanagh de Tuite, Cristopher Lee, Manon Lee; m. María F. Sánchez, Jan. 6, 1993; children: Carlos David, Lawden Nerea. AB, Centenary Coll., 1955; MA, La. State U., 1961, PhD, 1970; C en F y L, U. de Valladolid, Spain, 1965; LittD (hon.), London Inst. for Applied Rsch., 1993. Instr. Spanish U. Notre Dame, Ind., 1962-63; asst. prof. Spanish Centenary Coll., Shreveport, 1963-66, Va. Mil. Inst., Lexington, 1966-69, assoc. prof. Spanish, 1970-80, asst. commandant, 1971-74; asst. prof. fgn. langs. La. Tech. U., Ruston, 1981-84, assoc. prof., 1984-91, prof., 1991—, dir. grad. program in romance langs., 1992-95. Vis. lectr. Romance langs. U. N.C., 1970; adj. prof. Spanish U. Va., Charlottesville, 1978—80; vis. prof. English Ga. Mil. Coll., Barksdale AFB, La., 1980—81, Grambling State U., 1986, 2001—05, U. Autónoma de Coahuila, Centro de Idiomas, Mexico, 2002; cons. USAF, U.S. Dept. Justice, Mosher Steel Co., Studebaker Internat., Irrigation Internat. de Mex., others; rsch. bd. advisors Am. Biog. Inst. Author: Colombia en la Poesía, 1967, Hendaye, 1990, Saddle Soldiers: General William Stokes and the 4th South Carolina Cavalry, 1993, The Cemaco Seed, 1996, García Lorca and Other Things Spanish: Critical Essays, 2002, John William Corrington: Reflections, 2003, The Duende, 2005; contbr. articles to profl. jours. Mem. State Dem. Com., Lincoln Parish, La., 1984-94. Capt. U.S. Army, 1955-57. NDEA fellow, 1959-62; Fulbright fellow, 1965; NEH fellow, 1971; postdoctoral fellow La. State U., 1992; grantee VMI Found., La. Tech. U., 1967-92, La Tech summer rsch. grantee, Spain, 1998, 2001, 04, 05. Mem. Coun. for Devel. of Spanish in La., Phi Kappa Phi, Phi Sigma Iota, Sigma Tau Delta, Sigma Delta Pi, Alpha Chi, Omicron Delta Kappa. Roman Catholic. Avocations: gardening, hunting, deep-sea fishing. Office: Dept Fgn Langs La Tech U Ruston LA 71272-0001 E-mail: halliburton@garts.latech.edu.

HALLIDAY, IAN, astronomer; b. Lloydminster, Sask., Can., Nov. 10, 1928; s. Clarence Peter and Edith Victoria (Phillips) H.; m. Norma Lillian Mobley, July 7, 1951; children— John Douglas, Janet Elizabeth. BA, U. Toronto, 1949, MA, 1950, PhD, 1954. Sr. sci. officer Dominion Obs., Dept. Energy, Mines and Resources, Ottawa, 1952-70; sr. research officer Herzberg Inst. Astrophysics, Nat. Research Council Can., Ottawa, 1970-90, guest worker, 1990-96. Author research papers in field; editor Jour. Royal Astron. Soc. Can, 1970-75; co-editor: Solid Particles in the Solar System, 1980. Recipient Polish Medal of Merit, 1976, Queen's Silver Jubilee medal, 1977. Fellow Royal Soc. Can.; mem. Internat. Astron. Union (pres. commn. 22 1976-79), Royal Astron. Soc. Can. (pres. 1980-82, hon. pres. 1989-93), Can. Astron. Soc., Am. Astron. Soc., Meteoritical Soc., Planetary Soc., Internat. Halley Watch (chmn. steering group 1985-90). Home: 825 Killeen Ave Ottawa ON Canada K2A 2X8 E-mail: ihalliday@idirect.com.

HALLIDAY, JOHN MEECH, investment company executive; b. St. Louis, Oct. 16, 1936; s. William Norman and Vivian Viola (Meech) Halliday; children: Richard M., Elizabeth. BS, U.S. Naval Acad., 1958; MBA, Harvard U., 1964. Dir. budgeting and planning Automatic Tape Control, Bloomington, Ill., 1964-66; dir. planning Ralston-Purina, St. Louis, 1966-67, v.p. subsidiary, 1967-68, dir. internat. banking, 1967-68; v.p. Servicetime Corp., St. Louis, 1968-70; assoc. R.W. Halliday Assocs., Boise, Idaho, 1970-87. V.p. Sawtooth Comm. Corp., Boise, 1970-73, Comdr. Corp., 1979-81; pres., CEO, bd. dirs. May Lundy Mine, San Francisco, 1979—, H.W.L. Inc., San Francisco, 1985-93; pres. Halliday Labs., Inc., 1980-91; exec. v.p., bd. dirs. Franchise Fin. Corp. Am., Phoenix, 1980-85; bd. dirs., v.p. Harvard Bus. Sch. Assn. No. Calif., 1980-87; pres., CEO, bd. dirs. Cycletrol Diversified Industries, Inc., 1992—; guest lectr. U. Calif. Berkeley, 1991-2000, Calif. Bus.-Higher Edn. Forum, 1995-98; sponsor Halliday lectr. in astronomy, U. Calif. Santa Cruz, 2000—. Pres. Big Bros. San Francisco, 1978-81; trustee, pres. U. Calif.-Santa Cruz Found., 1988—, mem. Pres.Circle, U.S. Naval Acad., Annapolis, 1997—; mem. ad hoc com. on corrections Calif. State Senate, 1995-96; fellow bd. visitors and fellows viticulture and enology U. Calif., Davis, 1999—; sponsor undergrad. rsch. symposium U. Calif. Santa Cruz, 2002—; bd. dirs., charter dir. circle Seymour Marine Discovery Ctr., 2002—. Mem. Restaurant Assn. (v.p. 1969-70), Olympic Club (San Francisco), Scott Valley Tennis Club (Mill Valley, Calif.). Republican. Baptist. Office: 55 New Montgomery St Ste 317 San Francisco CA 94105-3426 Home: Apt 4 190 Miller Ave Mill Valley CA 94941-2779 Personal E-mail: jhalli8835@aol.com.

HALLIDAY, JOSEPH WILLIAM, lawyer; b. NYC, Aug. 9, 1938; s. Joseph John and Marie (Murray) H.; m. Vivian Ross Talbird, July 10, 1960; children: Katherine Ann Langan, Mary Allison Shaw. AB egregia cum laude, Fordham U., 1960, LLB cum laude, 1963. Bar: NY 1964, DC 1965. Assoc. White & Case, NYC, 1965-72, ptnr., 1972-85, Skadden, Arps, Slate, Meagher & Flom, LLP, NYC, 1985—2003, of counsel, 2004—, founder, banking and institutional investing group. Mem. Tribar Legal Opinion Com., lectr. Ctr. for Internat. Banking Studies, U. Va., Banking Law Inst., Inst. Internat. Rsch., Law and Bus., Euromoney, Practicing Law Inst., Law and Business, ABA, NY State Bar Assn. Prog. Editor-in-chief Fordham Law Rev., 1962-63; contbr. author, The Banking Jour. Served to 1st lt. US Army, 1963-65. Mem. ABA, NY State Bar Assn.(banking law com.), Assn. of Bar of City of NY, NY County Lawyers Assn., Larchmont Yacht Club (commodore 1985-86). Republican. Roman Catholic. Avocations: yachting, skiing, golf. Office: Skadden Arps Slate Meagher & Flom LLP 4 Times Sq New York NY 10036 Office Phone: 212-735-3260. Office Fax: 212-917-3260. Business E-Mail: jhallida@skadden.com.

HALLIDAY, WILLIAM ROSS, retired physician, speleologist, writer; b. Atlanta, May 9, 1926; s. William Ross and Jane (Wakefield) H.; m. Eleanore Hartvedt, July 2, 1951 (dec. 1983); children: Marcia Lynn, Patricia Anne, William Ross III; m. Louise Baird Kinnard, May 7, 1988. BA, Swarthmore Coll., 1946; MD, George Washington U., 1948. Diplomate Am. Bd. Vocat. Experts. Intern Huntington Meml. Hosp., Pasadena, Calif., 1948-49; resident King County Hosp., Seattle, Denver Children's Hosp., L.D.S. Hosp., Salt Lake City, 1950-57; pvt. practice Seattle, 1957-65; with Wash. State Dept. Labor and Industries, Olympia, 1965-76; med. dir. Wash. State Div. Vocat. Rehab., 1976-82; staff physican N.W. Occupational Health Ctr., Seattle, 1983-84; med. dir. N.W. Vocat. Rehab. Group, Seattle, 1984, Comprehensive Med. Rehab. Ctr., Brentwood, Tenn., 1984-87. Dep. coroner King County, Wash., 1964—66. Author: Adventure Is Underground, 1959, Depths of the Earth, 1966, 76, American Caves and Caving, 1974, 82, Floyd Collins of Sand Cave, 1998; co-author: (with Robert Nymeyer) Carlsbad Cavern: The Early Years, 1991; editor Jour. Spelean History, 1968-73; contbr. articles to profl. jours. Cons. Egyptian Environ. Affairs Agency; mem. North Cascades Conservation Coun., v.p., 1962—63; pres. Internat. Speleological Found., 1981—87, Internat. Union Speleol. Com. on Volcanic Caves, 1992—98, hon. pres., 1998—; asst. dir. Internat. Glaciospeleological Survey, 1972—76; mem. Gov.'s North Cascades Study Com., 1967—76; chmn. Hawaii Speleol. Survey, 1989—97; dir. We. Speleol. Survey, 1957—83, dir. rsch., 1983—96. Served to lt. USNR, 1949—50, served to lt. comdr USNR, 1955—57. Recipient medal Geol. Soc. China; named Alumnus of Yr., George Sch., 1992. Fellow Am. Coll. Chest Physicians, Nat. Speleological Soc. (hon. mem. 1965, bd. govs. 1950-2001), Explorers Club; mem. AMA, Internat. Assn. Hydrogeologists, Nat. Trust (Scotland), Geol. Soc. Am., Assn. Am. Geographers, Mars Soc., Mountaineers Club (past trustee), Seattle Tennis Club.

HALLIGAN, CHRISTY LYN, music educator; b. Buffalo, N.Y., May 12, 1981; d. William Halligan and Carol Faery. Degree in Music Edn., SUNY, Fredonia, N.Y., 2003. Tchr. music Warwick (N.Y.) Valley Mid. Sch., 2003—. Club advisor Fiddle Club, Warwick; coach Odyssey of the Mind Warwick (N.Y.) Valley Mid. Sch. Mem.: N.Y. State Schs. Music Assn., Am. String Tchrs. Assn., Music Educators Nat. Conf.

HALLIGAN, JAMES EDMUND, academic administrator, chemical engineer; b. Moorland, Iowa, June 23, 1936; s. Raymond Anthony and Margaret Ann Halligan; m. Ann Elizabeth Sorenson, June 29, 1957; children: Michael, Patrick, Christopher. MS in Chem. Engring, Iowa State U., 1962, MS, 1965, PhD, 1968. Registered profl. engr., Okla. Process engr. Humble Oil Co., 1962-64; mem. faculty Tex. Tech U., 1968-77; dean engring. U. Mo., Rolla, 1977-79, U. Ark., Fayetteville, 1979-82, vice chancellor for acad. affairs, 1982-83, interim chancellor, 1983-84; pres. N.Mex. State U., Las Cruces, 1984-94, Okla. State U., Stillwater, 1994—2003, pres. emeritus, 2003—. Mem. Gov. Tex. Energy Adv. Council, 1972-74; prof. achievement citation engr. Iowa State U. Coll. Engring., 1984. Served with USAF, 1954-58. Recipient Disting. Teaching award Tex. Tech U., 1972, Disting. Research award, 1975, 76; Disting. Teaching award U. Mo., Rolla, 1978, Disting. Achievement citation Iowa State U. Alumni Assn., 1996. Mem. AIChE, NSPE, Am. Chem. Soc., Am. Soc. Engring. Edn., Rotary, Tau Beta Pi, Phi Kappa Phi, Pi Mu Epsilon. Roman Catholic. Office: Okla State U 470 SU Stillwater OK 74078-1010 Office Phone: 405-744-2844.

HALLIGAN, JOSEPH WILLIAM, snack food industry executive; b. Boston, Sept. 10, 1944; s. Henry William and Marion (Neaves) H.; m. Nancy Jordan, June 28, 1969; 1 dau., Deborah. BS in Mgmt. and Bus. Adminstrn., Columbia Pacific U., San Rafael, Calif., 1983. Mgr. prodn. line maintenance Union Carbide, San Diego, Calif., 1969, Fotomat Corp., La Jolla, Calif., 1970-74, nat. constrn. dir., 1974-76, v.p. Wilton, Conn., 1976-80, sr. v.p., 1980-83; chief exec. officer Laura Scudder's Inc., Anaheim, Calif., 1983—; pres., dir. Fotomat Video Enterprises, Video Services of Am. Author: Maintenance and Construction Manuel, 1972. Served with USAF, 1965-69. Mem. Nat. Acad. Code Adminstrn., Internat. Conf. Bldg. Ofcls., Bldg. Ofcls. Code Adminstrs., So. Bldg. Code Congress Internat. Office: Laura Scudders Inc 1535 N Raymond Ave Anaheim CA 92801-1112 also: Pres & CEO PharmChem Inc 4600 N Beach St Fort Worth TX 76137

HALLILA, BRUCE ALLAN, welding engineer; b. Washington, Nov. 2, 1950; s. Esko Ensio and Gertrude Naomi (Tilley) H.; m. Pamela Joan Guerin, Dec. 18, 1982; children: Gregory Michael Decedue, April Patrice, Andrew Allan, Joshua Scott. BSME, BS in Welding Engring., LeTourneau U., 1974. Welding engr. Chgo. Bridge & Iron Co., Houston, 1975-77, Avondale Shipyards, Inc., New Orleans, 1977-80, asst. shipbuilding supt., 1980-82; steel supt. Halter Marine, Inc., New Orleans, 1982; welding supt. Bell Halter, Inc., New Orleans, 1982-84; sr. welding engr. Avondale Industries, Inc., New Orleans, 1984-86, chief welding engr., 1986-97; asst. plant sup. Pellerin Milnor Corp., Kenner, La., 1997—. Vice chmn. welding com. Ogden Corp., N.Y.C., 1984-86; welding cons. Gas Tech. Cons., Inc., Metairie, La., 1990—; CWI test proctor Am. Welding Soc., Miami, 1979-97; welding industry cons. State of La VoTech Welding Coun., Metairie, 1982—; panel mem. welding R & D, Maritime Adminstrn.; adv. bd. La. Tech. Coll.-Jefferson Campus, 2002-.

Mem. com. troop 33 Boy Scouts Am., 1991-97. Recipient Gov.'s award State of La., Baton Rouge, 1982. Mem. Am. Welding Soc. (dist. 9 dir. 1994-97, D3 com., 1997, CWI test supr. 1997—, chmn. sect. cert. 1997—, judge regional sci. and engring. fair 1997—, chmn. student scholarship award 1997—, Proposer award 1982, Dist. Meritorious award 1987, 92, named Disting. Mem. 1989, Sect. Educator award 2000, Silver mem. 2000), Am. Bur. Shipping (spl. com. on materials and welding 1997), Delta Sigma Psi. Republican. Avocations: woodworking, welding, photography. Home: 8725 Carriage Rd River Ridge LA 70123-3605 Office: Pellerin Milnor Corp PO Box 400 Kenner LA 70063-0400 E-mail: bahallila@aol.com.

HALLIN, DANIEL CLARK, communications educator; b. Palo Alto, Calif., June 11, 1953; BA in Polit. Sci. with honors, U. Calif., Berkeley, 1973, MA in Polit. Sci., 1974, PhD in Polit. Sci., 1980. Fellow Freedom Forum Media Studies Ctr., Columbia U., N.Y.C., 1991-92; prof. dept. comm., adj. prof. polit. sci. U. Calif., San Diego, 1980—, chairperson, 1994-97. Assoc. Ctr. for War, Peace and News Media; presenter, keynote spkr. various ednl. symposia and confs., most recently at Seoul Nat. U., 1997, Westminster U., London, 1998, Nat. U., Athens, Greece, 1998, Budapest, 2000, U. Leipzig, 2000, U. Munich, 2000, U. Calif. Berkeley, 2000, U. Perugia, 1999; Merkator prof. Inst. Medienwissenschaft U. Dusseldorf, 2000. Author: The "Uncensored War": The Media and Vietnam, 1989, The Presidency, The Press and the People, 1992, We Keep America on Top of the World: Television Journalism and the Public Sphere, 1994; contbr. chpt. to: Critical Theory and Public Life, 1985, Political Communication: Approaches, Studies, Assessments, 1987, Reading the News, 1986, Watching Television, 1986, Is the Cold War Over? Images of the USA and the USSR in Soviet and American Media, 1991, Comparatively Speaking, 1992, Viewing War: How the Media Handled the Persian Gulf, 1994; co-contbr. chpt. to: Taken by Storm: The Media, Public Opinion and U.S. Foreign Policy in the Gulf War, 1994, Mass Media and Society, 1996, Dewesternizing Media Studies, 2000, Tabloid Tales, 2000; mem. editl. bd. Polit. Comm.; contbr. articles and revs. to profl. publs. Pres. Binat. Assn. Schs. of Comm. of the Californias, 1997-99; bd. dirs. Internat. Comm. Assn. Recipient 1st prize media studies project essay contest Woodrow Wilson Internat. Ctr. for Scholars, 1990. Mem. Am. Polit. Sci. Assn., L.Am. Studies Assn., Internat. Comm. Assn., Union for Dem. Comm. Home: 3315 31st St San Diego CA 92104-4619 Office: Univ Calif San Diego Dept Comm 0503 La Jolla CA 92093 E-mail: dhallin@weber.ucsd.edu.

HALLINAN, JOSEPH THOMAS, journalist, reporter; b. Barberton, Ohio, Sept. 3, 1960; s. Neil Patrick and Judith Ann (Tonovitz) H.; m. Pamela L. Taylor, Sept. 10, 2000; children: Jack. BS magna cum laude, Boston U., 1984. Reporter The Indpls. Star, 1984-91; nat. corr. Newhouse News Svc., Washington, 1991-99; reporter Chgo. Tribune, 1999-2000; staff reporter The Wall St. Jour., 2000—. Author: Going Up The River: Travels in a Prison Nation, 2001. Recipient Pulitzer prize for investigative reporting, 1991; named Disting. Alumni, Boston U., 1992; Nieman fellow Harvard U., 1997-98. Roman Catholic. Avocations: fishing, travel. Home: 3750 Lake Shore Dr Chicago IL 60613

HALLINAN, MAUREEN THERESA, sociologist, educator; BA, Marymount Coll., 1961; MS, U. Notre Dame, 1968; PhD, U. Chgo., 1972. Prof. U. Wis., Madison, 1980-84; with U. Notre Dame, 1984—, now William P. and Hazel B. White prof. arts and letters, dept. sociology, dir. Ctr. for Rsch. on Ednl. Opportunity. Assoc. editor Social Forces, 1977-80; assoc. editor Sociology of Edn., 1979-81, 91-2001; editor, 1981-86; author: The Structure of Positive Sentiment, 1974; editor: The Social Organization of Schools: New Conceptualizations of the Learning Process, 1987, Restructuring Schools: Promising Practices and Policies, 1995, Handbook of the Sociology of Education, 2000, Handbook of the Siciology of Education, Chinese edit., 2004; editor: The Social Context of Instruction: Group Organization and Group Processes, 1983, Change in Societal Institutions, 1990; co-editor Stability and Change in American Education: Structure, Process and Outcomes, 2003; contbr. articles to profl. jours. Mem. Am. Sociol. Assn. (session organizer 1980, 84, 89, 92, 96-2001, chmn. sociology of edn. sect. 1991-92, chmn. 1991-92, pres. 1995-96, Willard Waller award 2004), Sociol. Rsch. Assn. (sec.-treas. 1999-2000, pres. 2000-01), Nat. Acad. Edn. (v.p. for fellows 2001-05), Phi Beta Kappa. Office: U Notre Dame Dept Sociology Notre Dame IN 46556

HALLION, RICHARD PAUL, aerospace historian, museum consultant; b. Washington, May 17, 1948; s. Richard Paul and Mary Elizabeth (Flynn) H. BA with high honors in History, U. Md., 1970, PhD, 1975. Curator sci. and tech., curator space sci. & exploration Nat. Air and Space Mus., Smithsonian Instn., 1974-80; prof. history, instr. aerospace engring. U. Md., College Park, 1980-81; assoc. prof. gen. adminstrn. U. Coll., 1980-81; historian Air Force Flight Test Ctr., Edwards AFB, Calif., 1982-86; dir. spl. staff office Aeronautical Systems Divsn., Wright-Patterson AFB, Ohio, 1986-87; exec. staff advanced projects office Air Force Systems Command, Andrews AFB, Md., 1988-90; sr. analyst, sec. Air Force Staff Group, 1990-91. Vis. prof. mil. history U.S. Army War Coll., Carlisle Barracks, Pa., 1987-88; Lindbergh vis. prof. Smithsonian Instn., 1991, chief air force history, 1992—; founder Paralog Assocs.; cons. mus. Author: Supersonic Flight, 1972, Legacy of Flight: The Guggenheim Contribution to American Aviation, 1977, The Wright Brothers: Heirs of Prometheus, 1978, (with Tom D. Crouch) Apollo: Ten Years since Tranquility Base, 1979, Test Polits: The Frontiersmen of Flight, 1981, Designers and Test Polits, 1982, Rise of the fighter, 1984, Naval Air War in Korea, 1986, The Hypersonic Revolution, 1988, Strike from the Sky, 1988, Storm Over Iraq, 1992, Air Power Confronts an Unstable Workd, 1997, The Literature of Aeronautics, Astronautics and Air Power; contbr. articles to profl. jours. Recipient Dr. Robert H. Goddard Hist. Essay award Nat. Space Club, 1980; Daniel and Florance Guggenheim fellow, 1974-75. Mem. AIAA (History Manuscript award 1976, Young Engr./Scientist award NAt. Capitol sect. 1979), Aviation/Space Writers Assn. (Writing citation 1977-78, SpaceLit. award 1979), Internat. Footprinters Assn., Air Force Hist. Found. (mem. editl. adv. bd.), Air Force Assn. (life), U. Md. Alumni Assn. (life), Precision Strike Assoc., Internat. Order of Characters. Office: AF History & Mus Program 1190 Air Force Pentagon Washington DC 20330-1190

HALLISSEY, MICHAEL, retired management consultant; b. Southampton, England, Mar. 6, 1943; s. John Francis and Mary (Kendall) H. Grad., Magdalen Coll., Oxford U., Eng., 1964. Chartered acct., Eng. With Price Waterhouse, 1964-98, asst. mgr. Melbourne, Australia, 1968, Milan, 1969, ptnr. London, 1974-98, head practice devel., 1979-81, head strategic planning, 1981-82, head corp. fin. svcs., 1983-88; dir. strategy Price Waterhouse Europe, 1988-98, PricewaterhouseCoopers (formerly Price Waterhouse), 1998—2003; vis. fellow Imperial Coll. Sci. and Tech., London, 1998—2003; ret., 2003. Contbr. articles to profl. publs. Fellow Royal Soc. of Arts; mem. Inst. Chartered Accts. Eng. and Wales. Mem. Conservative Party. Mem. Ch. of Eng. Avocations: politics, sailing, music, opera. Home: 66 Waterside Point Anhalt Rd London SW11 4PD England

HALLMAN, CATHERINE OWENS, art educator; b. Burlington, NC, Apr. 20, 1962; d. Carlyle Browning and Gale Tapp Owens; m. Richard Rhodes Hallman, Apr. 12, 1986; children: Tapp, Hannah. BFA in Art Edn., U. Cin., 1984. Cert. tchr. Ohio, SC. Art tchr. Bamberg Sch. Dist., Denmark, SC, 1984—91, Orangeburg Sch. Dist., Cordova, SC, 1991—. Mem. bell choir Bethel Park United Meth. Ch., Denmark, 1984—, trustee, 1999—. Mem.: Nat. Art Edn. Assn. Avocations: painting, swimming, organizing children's activities. Office: Carver Edisto Mid Sch Cordova SC

HALLMAN, CECILIA ANN, real estate consultant; d. James Cecil and Lillie Mae Hallman. Certificate in dentistry, Midland Tech. Coll., Columbia, S.C., 1972; student, U. S.C., Aiken, 1993; MBA in Essentials 1 Cert., Tulane U., 2004; Art certificate, Oxford U., 2005. Lic. real estate S.C., Ark. Property mgr. Wyatt Devel. Co., Inc., Aiken, 1987—89, The Keenan Co., Columbia, 1989—90; co-owner, mgr. Aiken Indsl. Supply, Inc., 1990—92; office adminstr. Dr. Rocky L. Napier, Aiken, 1992—96; dir. of mem. svcs. Wyatt Devel./Sage Valley Golf Club, Aiken, SC, 1996—2002; dir. mem. svcs. Stephens Inc./The Alotian Club, Little Rock, 2002—04. Vol. Am. Cancer Soc., Aiken, 1990—92. Mem.: C. of C., Chenal Country Club (assoc.), Country Club of Little Rock (assoc.), Green Boundary Club (assoc.), Rotary. Home and Office: 223 Forest Pines Rd Aiken SC 29803 Office Fax: 803-642-8023. Personal E-mail: chal454@aol.com.

HALLMAN, CINDA A., management consultant; BSc in Math., U. So. Ark. With DuPont, 1981—2001; CEO Spherion Corp., Ft. Lauderdale, Fla., 2001—. Bd. dirs. Toys "R" Us, Catalyst, United Way Am., Christiana Care Health Sys.; bd. trustees Christiana Care. Named CIO of Yr., Info. Week, 1995; named one of Most Influential Info. Tech. Execs. of Decade, CIO Mag., 1997; recipient Visionary award, Comm. Week, 1996.

HALLMAN, GARY L., photographer, educator; b. St. Paul, Aug. 7, 1940; s. Jack J. and Helen A. Hallman; 1 child, Peter J. BA, U. Minn., 1966, MFA, 1971. Mem. faculty dept. studio arts U. Minn., Mpls., 1970—, assoc. prof. photography, 1976—. Vis. adj. prof. R.I. Sch. Design, 1977-78; vis. exchange prof. U. N.Mex., 1984-85; vis. assoc. prof. The Colo. Coll., Colorado Springs, 1990; mem. visual arts adv. bd. Minn. State Arts Coun., 1973-76; bd. dirs. Minn. Artists Exhbn. Program, 1989-91. Exhbns. include Internat. Mus. Photography, George Eastman House, 1974, Light Gallery, N.Y.C., 1975, Balt. Mus., 1975, Mus. Modern Art, N.Y.C., 1978, Mpls. Inst. Arts, 1996, B. Gray Gallery East Carolina U., Greenville, N.C., 1997, Nat. Mus. of Am., Washington, 1984, Frederick R. Weisman Art Mus., Mpls., 1998; Mississippi/Neva curator The State Russian Mus., St. Petersburg, 1998; Barg Gallery/Teheran Mus. Contemporary Art, 2001, Risk/Revisit: The Photography of Gary Hallman, PARTs Gallery, Mpls., 2002, McKnight Found. Open Spaces Project, 2002; co-curator Persian Silver, Tehran Mus. Contemporary Art, 2004; co-curator Persian Silver, Tehran Mus. Contemporary Art, Nash Gallery Mpls., 2004; represented in permanent collections Mus. Modern Art, N.Y.C., Internat. Mus. Photography, Rochester, N.Y., Nat. Gallery Can., Fogg Art Mus., Harvard U., Princeton U. Art Mus., Nat. Mus. Am. Art, Smithsonian Instn., Washington. Served with USN, 1958-61. Nat. Endowment Arts fellow, 1975-76; Bush Found. fellow, 1976-77; McKnight Found. fellow, 1982, 90, Artist Assistance fellowship grant, 1996. Mem. Soc. Photog. Edn., Coll. Art Assn. Am. Office: U Minn Dept Studio Arts Minneapolis MN 55455 Office Phone: 612-625-8096. E-mail: hallm001@tc.umn.edu.

HALLMAN, LINDA D., medical association administrator; b. Wash., DC; BA in Music Education, Indiana U.; MS in Orgnl. Mgmt., George Wash. U. COO Am. Coll. Heathcare Adminstrs., Alexandria, Va.; dir. profl. svcs. Am. Coll. Healthcare Adminstrs., 1989—94, dir. member svcs., 1989—94; pres. Am. Hort. Soc., Alexandria, Va., 1997—2002; exec. dir. Am. Med. Women's Assn., Alexandria, Va., 2002—. Mem.: Assn. Fundraising Professionals, Am. Soc. Assn. Executives. Office: AMWA Ste 400 801 N Fairfax St Alexandria VA 22314

HALLMAN, THOMAS B., finance company executive; BS in Mktg. and Fin., Towson U.; MBA with honors, U. Balt. With Comml. Credit Corp., Citibank, 1st Nationwide Bank; CEO Specialty Fin., 1995—2003; vice chmn. CIT Group, Livingston, NJ, 2003—. Chmn. bd. dirs. CIT Bank; bd. dirs. Dell Fin. Svcs., Snap-On Credit; mem. oper. com. N.J. Bus. Force for Bus. Execs. for Nat. Security. Mem.: Nat. Home Equity Mortgage Assn. (bd. dirs.), Am. Fin. Svcs. Assn. (chair). Office: CIT Group 1 CIT Dr Livingston NJ 07039

HALLMARK, BRUCE CULLEN, JR., lawyer; b. Dallas, Mar. 24, 1958; s. Bruce Cullen and Martha Ann (Rosborough) H.; m. Jone Bergquist, May 10, 1986. BA, St. John's Coll., Santa Fe, 1980; JD, U. Tex., 1984. Bar: N.Mex. 1984, Tex. 1985, U.S. Dist. Ct. N.Mex. 1984, U.S. Ct. Appeals (5th, 10th cirs.) 1985. Assoc. Montgomery & Andrews, Santa Fe, 1984; sole practice Santa Fe, 1985-86; atty. Garber and Hallmark P.C., Santa Fe, 1986—. Mem. Tex. Bar Assn., N.Mex. Bar Assn. Democrat. Methodist. Avocations: skiing, bicycling, mountain climbing, martial arts. Home: 2113 Botulph Rd Santa Fe NM 87505-6974 Office: Garber & Hallmark PC 200 W Marcy St Ste 203 Santa Fe NM 87501-2036

HALLMARK, DONALD PARKER, museum director, educator; b. McPherson, Kans., Feb. 16, 1945; s. Daniel Clell and Esther Ione (Hart) H.; m. Linda Lorraine Lego, June 10, 1967; m. Monica Lynn, Amy Kristen. BFA, U. Ill., 1967; MA, U. Iowa, 1970; PhD, St. Louis U., 1980. From asst. prof. to prof. Greenville (Ill.) Coll., 1970-81, chmn. art dept., 1976-81; dir. Richard W. Bock Sculpture Collection, Greenville, 1975-81, Frank Lloyd Wright's Dana-Thomas House Hist. Site, Springfield, Ill., 1981—. Founding bd. mem. Frank Lloyd Wright Bldg Conservancy, Chgo., 1988-96; adj. prof. Sangamon State U., Springfield, 1986-90; lectr. FLW Bldg. Conservancy, Hollyhock House, L.A., The Gamble House, Pasadena, Calif., The High Mus., Atlanta, Decorative Arts Soc. SAH, Chgo., Indpls. Pub. Libr., The Natural Pattern of Structure Herberger Lectrs., Ariz. State U., Tempe, Art Inst. Chgo., FLW Bldg. Conservancy, Unity Temple, Oak Park, Ill,. FLW Home and Studio Lectrs., Oak Park Pub. Libr., Mus. of Our Nat. Heritage, Lexington, Mass., The Chgo. Arch. Found., Santa Fe Bldg., Chgo., Nat. Bldg. Mus., Washington, Ctrl. Ill. AIA, Decatur. Author: (booklet) The Dana-Thomas House: Its History, Acquisition and Preservation, 1992, (catalogue) Paul Ashbrook, 1990, (illustrated book) Springfield's Lawrence School Memorial Library, 1993, The Natural Pattern of Structure, 1995; TV interview appearances Bob Vila's Guide to Historic Homes, The Dana-Thomas House, 1996, interview Frank Lloyd Wright and the Prairie School, Films for Humanities and Scis., 1999, Home and Garden TV, 2000; editor newsletter Guidelines for the Conservation of Frank Lloyd Wright Decorative Arts, 1996. Cons., sponsor Ill. Govt. Intern Program, Springfield, 1985—; libr. cons., vol. Michael Victor II Libr. Springfield Art Assn., 1988-93. Faculty grantee Shell Found., 1975; Grad. fellow St. Louis U., 1976. Mem.: Nat. Trust for Historic Preservation, The Frank Lloyd Wright Bldg. Conservancy, Am. Assn. Mus. Presbyterian. Avocations: slide library collecting, antique collecting, travel, ground and garden maintenance. Home: 605 W Sheridan Rd Petersburg IL 62675-1359 Office: Ill Hist Preservation Agy 301 E Lawrence Ave Springfield IL 62703-2232 Office Phone: 217-782-6776.

HALLMUNDSSON, HALLBERG, editor; b. Stokkseyri, Iceland, Oct. 29, 1930; came to U.S., 1960; s. Hallmundur Einarsson and Ingibjorg Bjarnadottir; m. May Beatrice Newman Schechner, July 29, 1960. BA, U. Iceland, 1954; postgrad., U. Barcelona, Spain, 1955-56, NYU, 1961. Editor, designer Idunn Publs., Reykjavik, Iceland, 1956-60; from editorial asst. to sr. editor Grolier Inc., N.Y.C., 1961-78; sr. editor history Funk & Wagnall Inc., N.Y.C., 1979-82; prodn. copy editor Bus. Week, N.Y.C., 1984—2001. Publ. Bru Publs., Reykjavik, 1990—. Author: (poetry) Baggar skoplitlir, 2005, Fjadrafok, 2003, Oraeda, 2002, Sneidar-ekki af osti, 2000, Hringferli, 1999, Umhendur, 1997, Vandraedur, 1995, Skyggnur, 1993, Spjaldvisur II, 1991, Thraetubok, 1990, Spjaldvisur, 1985, Neikvaeda, 1977, Haustmal, 1968; author of short stories; editor: Anthology of Scandinavian Literature, 1966; co-editor and translator: Icelandic Folk and Fairy Tales, 1987; translator: Svartir Riddarar (Stephen Crane), 1992, 100 Kvaedi (Emily Dickinson), 1994, Ariel (Sylvia Plath), 1996, Blavindur (Daud Kamal), 1997, Gitarinn (F. Garcia Lorca), 1998, Thad sem eftir er. Valin ljod (Mark Strand), 1998, Thistlar (Ted Hughes), 1999, Adventa (Ylva Eggehorn), 2000, Ordabok Andskotans (Ambrose Bierce), 2000, Littu nidur ljosa tungl (Walt Whitman), 2001, Snjókarlinn (Wallace Stevens), 2001, Rosin fra Lesbos (Henrik Nordbrandt), 2002, Eg er ekki einmana (Nikki Giovanni), 2003, Hugrenningar (Torgeir Schjerven), 2004, Sponsid á tunglinu Valin ljod (Charles Simic), 2004, My Self & I (Thrainn Bertelsson), 2004. Grantee Iceland Ministry of Edn., 1976-79, N.Y. Transl. Ctr., 1975; recipient Achievement award Am.-Scandinavian Soc., 1991, award Icelandic Writers Fund, 1985, Transl. award Minn. Posten, 1966, Short Story prize, 1953, award Icelandic Authors' Libr. Fund, 1998, Translation prize U. Iceland Translation Ctr., 2001, Short Story Prize, 2003; named Scandinavian of Month, 1981. Mem. Am. Literary Translators Assn., Writers' Union of Iceland, Reykjavik Drama Critics' Club (treas. 1957-59). Home: Alftamyri 14 108 Reykjavik Iceland E-mail: haha@simnet.is.

HALLO, WILLIAM WOLFGANG, literature and language professor, writer; b. Kassel, Germany, Mar. 9, 1928; came to U.S., 1940, naturalized, 1946; s. Rudolf and Gertrude (Rubensohn) H.; m. Edith Sylvia Pinto, June 22, 1952 (dec. Oct. 10, 1994); children: Ralph Ethan, Jacqueline Louise; m. Nanette Stahl, Oct. 18, 1998. BA magna cum laude, Harvard U., 1950; candidatus Litterarum Semiticarum, U. Leiden, Netherlands, 1951; MA, U. Chgo., 1953, PhD, 1955; MA (hon.), Yale U., 1965; DHL (hon.), Hebrew Union Coll.-Jewish Inst. Religion, 1986. Rsch. asst. U. Chgo. Oriental Inst., 1954—56; from instr. to asst. prof. Bible and Semitic langs. Hebrew Union Coll.-Jewish Inst. Religion, Cin., 1956-62; asst. prof. Assyriology Yale U., 1962—65, prof. Assyriology, 1965-75, William M. Laffan prof. Assyriology and Babylonian lit., 1976—2002, emeritus prof., 2002—; curator Babylonian collection, 1963-2001; master Morse Coll., 1982-87; chmn. dept. Near Eastern langs. and civilizations, 1975-82, 85-89. Chmn. Univ. (now adv.) com. on Judaic Studies, 1979-84, acting chmn., 1998; vis. prof. Mid. Eastern civilization Columbia U., 1970-71, 80, Jewish Theol. Sem., 1981, 82-83, 2002; Franz Rosenzweig guest prof. U. Kassel, Germany, 1991. Author: Early Mesopotamian Royal Titles, 1957, Sumerian Archival Texts, 1973, The Book of the People, 1991, Origins: The Ancient Near Eastern Background of Some Modern Western Institutions, 1996; (with J.J.A. van Dijk) The Exaltation of Inanna, 1968; (with W.K. Simpson) The Ancient Near East: A History, 1971, 2d edit., 1998; (with Briggs Buchanan) Early Near Eastern Seals in the Yale Babylonian Collection, 1981; co-author: The Torah: A Modern Commentary, 1981, Heritage: Civilization and the Jews, 2 vols., 1984, The Tablets of Ebla, 1984; editor: Essays in Memory of E.A. Speiser, 1968; (with Carl D. Evans and John B. White) Scripture in Context: Essays on the Comparative Method, 1980; (with James C. Moyer and Leo G. Perdue) Scripture in Context II: More Essays on the Comparative Method, 1983; (with Bruce W. Jones and Gerald L. Mattingly) The Bible in Light of Cuneiform Literature: Scripture in Context III, 1990; (with K. Lawson Younger Jr. and Bernard F. Batto) The Biblical Canon in Comparative Perspective: Scripture in Context IV, 1991; (with K. Lawson Younger Jr.) The Context of Scripture, vol. I: Canonical Compositions from the Biblical World, 1997, Vol. II Monumental Inscriptions from the Biblical World, 2000, Vol. III Archival Documents from the Biblical World, 2002; (with Irene J. Winter) Seals and Seal Impressions, 2001; translator: The Star of Redemption, 1971; contbr. articles and book revs. to profl. jours.; mem. editl. bd. Yale Near Eastern Researches, 1967—2002; editor, 1970-2002; mem. editl. bd. Moment Mag., Bible Rev., Archaeology Odyssey. Mem. commn. Jewish edn. Union Am. Hebrew Congregations, 1967-71; co-founder, dir., mem. exec. com. Assn. Jewish Studies, 1970-71, v.p., 1972-74. Fulbright scholar, 1950-51; fellow Guggenheim, 1965-66, Inst. Advanced Studies, Hebrew U., Jerusalem, 1978-79, Nat. Humanities Inst., 1987-88, Shelby Cullom Davis Ctr. for Hist. Studies, Princeton U., 1996-97; honored by an anniversary volume: The Tablet and the Scroll: Near Eastern Studies in Honor of William W. Hallo, 1993. Mem. Am. Oriental Soc. (assoc. editor, 1965-71, chmn. Ancient Near East sect. 1971-78, v.p. 1987-88, pres. 1988-89), World Union Jewish Studies, Fulbright Assn. (v.p. Conn. chpt. 2002-), Harvard Club (So. Conn.), Yale Club (N.Y.C.), Phi Beta Kappa. Home: 245 Blake Rd Hamden CT 06517-3324 Office: Yale Babylonian Collection PO Box 208240 New Haven CT 06520-8240 E-mail: william.hallo@yale.edu.

HALLOCK, ROBERT BRUCE, physics professor; b. Washington, Dec. 9, 1943; s. Robert Frederick and Dorothy Hallock; m. Norma Hallock, Jun 19, 1965; children: Robert William, Kevin Frederick. BS, U. Mass., 1965; MS, Stanford U., 1967, PhD, 1969, postdoctoral, 1969-70. Asst. prof. U. Mass., Amherst, 1970-74, assoc. prof., 1974-79, prof., 1979—2001, disting. prof., 2001—, dir. lab. low temp. physics, 1978—, head dept. physics and astronomy, 1985-93, interim dean Coll. Natural Scis. and Math., 2000—01. Vis. assoc. prof. Brown U., Providence, 1975, Cornell U., Ithaca, NY, 1977—78; co-chair Gordon Rsch. Conf. on Quantum Fluids and Solids, 1982; adj. prof. dept. polymer sci. and engring. U. Mass., 1985—; mem. 5 colls. Radio Astronomy Policy Bd., 1985—87; mem. Rsch. Corp. Grants Adv. Bd., 1989—96; mem. fundamental physics discipline working group NASA, 1997—2001; chair Quantum Fluids and Solids Internat. Conf., 1998—2000; bd. dirs. Rsch. Corp., 2003—. Author, editor: Superfluid Helium, 1983; contbr. articles to profl. jours. Leader Cub Scout Am., Hadley, Mass., 1975-80. Named Disting. Tchr. of Yr., U. Mass., 1998; Woodrow Wilson Found. fellow, 1965, Air Force Office of Sci. Rsch.-NRC fellow, 1969, A.P. Sloan Found. rsch. fellow, 1972-76, U. Mass. fellow, 1974, 93, J.S. Guggenheim Meml. fellow, 1992-93. Fellow Am. Phys. Soc. (exec. coun. New Eng. sect. 1986-89); mem. Phi Beta Kappa, Sigma Xi. Avocation: photography. Office: U Mass/Hasbrouck Lab Dept Physics Amherst MA 01003 Office Phone: 413-545-3529. E-mail: hallock@physics.umass.edu.

HALLORAN, JEAN M., human resources specialist; b. NY; B in History, Princeton U.; MBA, Harvard U. Various positions in human resources, mfg., and strategic planning med. products group Hewlett-Packard, 1980—93, personnel mgr. measurement sys. orgn., 1993—97, dir. corp. edn. and devel., 1997—99; sr. v.p. human resources Agilent Technologies, Palo Alto, Calif., 1999—. Office: Agilent Technologies Inc 395 Page Mill Rd Palo Alto CA 94306 Office Phone: 650-752-5633. Office Fax: 650-752-5633.*

HALLORAN, MICHAEL JAMES, lawyer; b. Berkeley, Calif., May 20, 1941; s. James Joseph and Fern (Ogden) H.; m. Virginia Smedberg, Sept. 6, 1964; children: Pamela, Peter, Shelley. BS, U. Calif., Berkeley, 1962, LLB, 1965. Bar: Calif. 1966, D.C. 1979, Wyo. 1996. Assoc. Keatinge & Sterling, L.A., 1965-67, Pillsbury, Madison & Sutro (now Pillsbury Winthrop Shaw Pittman), San Francisco, 1967-72, ptnr., 1973-90, 97—, mng. ptnr. Washington, 1979-82, sr. ptnr. Corp. & Securities practice San Francisco; exec. v.p., gen. counsel BankAm. Corp. and Bank of Am., San Francisco, 1990-96. Mem. legal adv. com. N.Y. Stock Exch., 1993-96; bd. overseers Inst. Civil Justice, 1994-98. Editor: Venture Capital and Public Offering Negotiation, 1982-2002; mem. bd. adv. Stanford Jour. of Law, Bus. & Fin. Mem. corp. governance, shareholder rights and securities transactions com. Calif. Senate Commn., 1986-98; bd. dirs. Am. Conservatory Theater, 1994-2000; trustee, past bd. pres. Boalt Sch. Law, Univ. Calif. Berkeley. Named one of Top Lawyers in Silicon Valley, San Jose Mag., 2001, 2002, 2004. Mem. ABA (chmn. state regulation of securities com. 1981-84, mem. coun. of sect. of bus. law 1986-90, chmn. banking law com. 1992-96, mem. corp. laws com. 1997—), Bar Assn. San Francisco (bd. dirs. 1993-96). Avocations: skiing, golf, fishing, hiking. Office: Pillsbury Winthrop Shaw Pittman 50 Fremont St San Francisco CA 94105 also: 2475 Hanover St Palo Alto CA 94304-1114 Office Phone: 415-983-1610. Office Fax: 415-983-1200. Business E-Mail: michael.halloran@pillsburylaw.com.

HALLORAN, MIKE, software company executive, music publishing executive; b. Anchorage, May 17, 1954; s. Thomas Orrey and Barbara (Long) H.; m. Sylvia Thayne Edwards, Apr. 28, 1979; children: Marjorie C., Julia C. Student, San Jose State U., 1972-75. Prin. artist/condr. Gilbert & Sullivan Soc., San Jose, Calif., 1973-92; prodr./dir. PFS Prodns., San Jose, Calif., 1974-85; rec. artist MBA Records, San Jose, Calif., 1975-89; owner PF Slow Pub. Co., San Jose, Calif., 1984—; prin. double bass Santa Clara (Calif.) Symphony, 1985-89; owner PPW Wholesale Comms., San Jose, 1986—; sales mgr. Distinct Corp., Saratoga, Calif., 1996—. Cons. vintage/antique musical instruments, San Jose, 1980—. Columnist IAMA Jour., 1990-91; prin. artist San Francisco Lyric Opera, 2000—. Active Santa Clara County Dem. campaign, 1994; music dir. Immanuel Luth. Ch., Los Altos, Calif., 1998—. Mem. Am. Fedn. Musicians, ASCAP. Roman Catholic. Avocations: music, cooking, film, san francisco opera. Home: PO Box 6840 San Jose CA 95150-6840 E-mail: halloranmichael@aol.com.

HALLORAN, RICHARD COLBY, writer, reporter, communications executive, editor; b. Washington, Mar. 2, 1930; s. Paul James and Catherine (Lenihan) H.; m. Carol Prins, June 21, 1958; children: Christopher Paul, Laura Colby, Catherine Anne; m. Fumiko Mori, Nov. 11, 1978. AB with distinction, Dartmouth Coll., 1951; MA, U. Mich., 1957. Staff writer, then asst. fgn. editor Business Week mag., 1957-61; Tokyo bur. chief McGraw-Hill World News, 1962-64; Asia specialist Washington Post, 1965-66, bur. chief Northeast Asia Tokyo, 1966-68, Washington corr., 1968-69; corr. N.Y. Times,

Washington, 1969-72, Tokyo bur. chief, 1972-76, investigative reporter Washington Bur., 1976-78, energy corr., 1978-79, def. corr., 1979-84, mil. corr., 1985—90; dir. comm. and journalism East-West Ctr., Honolulu, 1990-94; ind. writer Honolulu, 1994—2000; editl. dir. Honolulu Star-Bull., 2001—02; columnist The Rising East, 2002—. Adj. fellow Pacific Forum-Ctr. Strategic and Internat. Studies; vis. instr. Asia Pacific Ctr. for Security Studies. Author: Japan: Images and Realities, 196[illegible]nflict and Compromise: The Dynamics of American Foreign Policy, [illegible], To Arm a Nation: Rebuilding America's Endangered Defenses, 1986, Serving America: Prospects for the Volunteer Force, 1988, Sparky: A Portrait of Senator Spark M. Matsunaga of Hawaii, 2002, My Name is Shinseki and I am a Soldier: Brief Biography of Gen. Eric K. Shinseki, U.S. Army. Mem. Honolulu Com. Fgn. Rels., Pacific and Asian Affairs Coun., Japan-Am. Soc. Hawaii. 1st lt. U.S. Army, 1952-55. Recipient citation for interpretation fgn. affairs Overseas Press Club, 1969, George Polk award for nat. reporting L.I. U., 1982, Gerald R. Ford prize for disting. reporting on nat. def. Gerald R. Ford Found., 1988, Outstanding Civilian Svc. medal U.S. Army, 1989, Japan's Order Sacred Treasure, Gold Rays with Rosette, 1998, Lifetime Achievement award Pacific and Asian Affairs Coun., 2000, Fellow of Pacific, Hawaii Pacific U., 2003; Ford Found. fellow Columbia U., 1964-65, Woodrow Wilson nat. fellow Furman U., S.C., Luther Coll., Iowa, Union Coll., N.Y., U. Redlands, Calif., Linfield Coll., Oreg., Goucher Coll., Md., Ohio Wesleyan U., McMurry U., Tex., Trinity Coll., Vt., St. Mary's Coll., Calif., Wabash Coll., Ind., Elon U., N.C. Mem. 100th Infantry Bn. Vet. Assn. (hon.), Fgn. Corrs. Club Japan. Roman Catholic. Home: 1065 Kaoopulu Pl Honolulu HI 96825-1364 Office Phone: 808-395-0511. Personal E-mail: oranhall@hawaii.rr.com.

HALLSTRAND, SARAH LAYMON, denomination executive; b. Nashville, Oct. 25, 1944; d. Charles Martin and Lillian Christina (Stenberg) Laymon; m. John Peter Hallstrand, July 6, 1974; 1 child, Lillian Johanna. BA cum laude, Fla. So. Coll., 1966; ThM, Boston U., 1971; D of Ministry, McCormick Theol. Sem., 1985; grad., Coll. for Fin. Planning, Denver, 1990. Ordained Am. Baptist Ch., 1976; cert. ret. counselor, fin. counselor; CFP. Dir. Christian edn. Trinity United Meth. Ch., Bradenton, Fla., 1968-70, Univ. United Meth. Ch., Syracuse, N.Y., 1971-73; assoc. min. First Bapt. Ch., Syracuse, 1973-78; pastor Oneida (N.Y.) Bapt. Ch., 1978-80; midwest rep. Mins. and Missionaries Benefit Bd., Am. Bapt. Chs., Oak Park, Ill., 1981—2002; pastor First United Meth. Ch., Tellico Plains, Tenn., 2002—03; cons. MMBB, 2002—04; interim exec. min. ABCCONN, 2004, ABC of Greater Indpls., 2005—. Leader ret. planning seminars Am. Bapt. Assembly, Green Lake, Wis., 1985-2002, AutumnQuest Ret. Sems., Midwest Ministry Devel. Svc., 1994—, bd. dirs., 1987-2001, chair, 1993-96; mem. rep. Midwest Ministerial Leadership Commn., Valley Forge, Pa., 1985-2002; adj. prof., pastoral care McCormick Theol. Sem., Chgo., 1986-2001; adj. prof. retirement planning The Divinity Sch., Rochester, N.Y., 1994; vis. scholar Am. Bapt. Bd. Ednl. Ministries, Valley Forge, 1986-87; bd. dirs. The Gathering Place Retreat Ctr., Gosport, Ind., 1988-95; mem. program com. and women in ministry rep. Roger Williams Fellowship, 1988-95; mem. nat. continuing edn. team Am. Bapt. Chs., Valley Forge, Pa., 1991-98; conf. leader for women's spiritual renewal weekends; spkr. in field. Contbg. author: Songs of Miriam: A Women's Book of Devotions, 1994; contbr. articles to profl. jour. including The Inclusive Pulpit Jour., 2003-2004. Mem. Fin. Planning Assn., Alpha Gamma Delta. Democrat. Home and Office: 126 Santee Way Loudon TN 37774 E-mail: sh4406@hotmail.com. *The church has not been called to be successful as measured by the world's standards. It has always been and will always be that the true goal of the church is faithfulness as measured by the liberating and transforming gospel of Jesus Christ.*

HALLSTROM, LASSE, film director; b. Stockholm, June 6, 1946; m. Lena Olin, Mar. 18, 1994; 1 child, Tora; m. Malou Hallstrom (div.); 1 child, Johan. Dir. feature films, including A Lover and His Lass, 1975, Abba: The Movie, 1977, Father to Be, 1979, The Rooster, 1981, Happy We, 1983, My Life as a Dog, 1985, Children of Bullerby Village, 1987, Once Around, 1991, What's Eating Gilbert Grape, 1993, Something To Talk About, 1995, The Cider House Rules, 1999, Chocolat, 2000, The Shipping News, 2001, An Unfinished Life, 2005. Office: ICM 8942 Wilshire Blvd Beverly Hills CA 90211-1934 also: Francis & Assocs 501 S Beverly Dr 3d Fl Beverly Hills CA 90211*

HALLUIN, ALBERT PRICE, lawyer; b. Nov. 8, 1939; children: Russell, Marcus. BA, La. State U., 1964; JD, U. Balt., 1969. Bar: Md. 1970, N.Y. 1985, Calif. 1991. Assoc. Jones, Tullar & Cooper, Arlington, Va., 1969-71; sr. patent atty. CPC Internat. Inc., Englewood Cliffs, N.J., 1971-76; counsel Exxon Rsch. & Engring. Co., Florham Park, N.J., 1976-83; v.p., chief intellectual property counsel Cetus Corp., Emeryville, Calif., 1983-90; ptnr. Fleisler, Dubb, Meyer & Lovejoy, San Francisco, 1990-92, Limbach & Limbach, San Francisco, 1992-94, Pennie & Edmonds, Menlo Park, Calif., 1994-97, Howrey LLP, Menlo Park, 1997—2004; pres., CEO, chmn. Halzyme Tech., Inc., 1995—, Wilson Sonsini Goodrich & Rosati, Palo Alto, Calif., 2004—. Contbr. articles to legal jours. Pres. Belle Roche Homeowners Assn., Redwood City, Calif., 1995-2004. Named One of Top 20 Intellectual Property Lawyers, Calif. Lawyer's mag., 1993. Mem. ABA, Am. Intellectual Property Law Assn. (chmn. chem. practice com. 1981-83, sec. 1984-85, bd. dirs. 1984-89, founding chmn. biotech. com. 1990-92), Licensing Exec. Soc., Assn. Corp. Patent Counsel, Bar Assn. San Francisco, San Francisco Patent Assn. Republican. Episcopalian. Office: WIlson Sonsini Goodrich & Rosati 650 Page Mill Rd Palo Alto CA 94304-1050 Fax: 650-463-8400. Office Phone: 650-565-3585. E-mail: ahalluin@wsgr.com.

HALM, NANCYE STUDD, retired academic administrator; b. Jamestown, N.Y., Mar. 26, 1932; d. Thomas Howerton and Margaret Hazel (LeRoy) Neathery; m. David Philip Mack, Aug. 25, 1951 (div. 1972); children: Margaret, Jennifer, Geoffrey, Peter; m. Loris L. Studd, July 6, 1974; m. James Richard Halm, Aug. 30, 1991. BS in Edn., SUNY, Fredonia, 1954, postgrad., 1954—68, St. Bonaventure U., 1970, postgrad., 1981. Tchr. Morning Sun (Iowa) Consolidated Schs., 1956-57, Panama (N.Y.) Cen. Schs., 1958-65, Jamestown (N.Y.) Pub. Schs., 1967-69, Olean (N.Y.) Pub. Schs., 1969-72, Jamestown Pub. Schs., 1972-73; pers. mgr. F.W. Woolworth Co., Lakewood, N.Y., 1972-79; dir. Nat. Conf. Christians & Jews, Jamestown, 1979-86; counselor N.Y. State Div. for Youth, Jamestown, 1979-89; exec. rep. Am. Bapt. Found., Valley Forge, Pa., 1989-94; adminstr. New Castle Christian Acad., 1996—2002; ret., 2002. Pastor West Pitts. United Meth. Ch., 2003—04, Ellington United Meth. Ch., 2004—. V.p. Chautauqua County Am. Bapt. Women, 1981—90; pres. Falconer Bapt. Women, 1986—90; love gift chmn. Pitts. Bapt. Assn., 1990—91; trustee, chair endowment fund Chautauqua Bapt. Union at Chautauqua Inst., 1982—; pres. ch. coun. Wesley United Meth. Ch., 2001—03; mem. nat. bd. dirs. Am. Bapt. Chs. U.S.A., Valley Forge, Pa., 1988—89. Recipient Cert. of Merit, Cassadaga Job Corp, 1984. Mem. Rebekah. Democrat. Avocations: quilting, reading, crafts. Home: 60 Morgan St Falconer NY 14733

HALMI, ROBERT, SR., film producer, television producer; b. Budapest, Hungary, Jan. 22, 1924; s. Bela and Sarah (Deri) H.; m. Esther Szirmay, Sept. 9, 1980; children: Kevin Gorman, Kim Gorman, Robert, Bill. Grad., U. Budapest, 1946. Mag. photographer, 1946-52; photographer Life mag., 1952-62; documentary producer, 1962-75; chmn. Hallmark Entertainment. Producer over 200 TV movies, miniseries and theatrical features including Nurse, 1980, Wilson's Reward, 1980, Nairobi Affair, 1984, Grand Larceny, 1987, Mayflower Madam, 1987, Pack of Lies, 1987, Best Friends, 1987, Cheetah, 1989, Ivory Hunters, 1990, Call of the Wild, 1993, The Yearling, 1994, Promise Kept: The Oksana Baiul Story, 1994, Getting Out, 1994, The Sunshine Boys, 1995, Kidnapped, 1995, Bye Bye Birdie, 1995, Gulliver's Travells, 1996, Captain Courageous, 1996, 20,000 Leagues Under the Sea, 1997, Moby Dick, 1998, Merlin, 1998, Crime & Punishment, 1998, Rear Window, 1998, Land of Oz, 1999, Don Quixote, 1999, Cleopatra, 1999, Arabian Nights, 1999, Alice in Wonderland, 1999, Noah's Ark, 1999, Mr. & Mrs. Bridge, Gypsy, 1993, The Incident in a Small Town, 1994, Lily in Love, Barnum, Prince Charming, 2001; exec. prodr.: Mother Teresa: In the Name of God's Poor, 1997, Mike Bassett: England Manager, 2001; exec. prodr.(TV): Izzy and Moe, 1985, Cook & Peary: The Race to the Pole, 1983, Spearfield's Daughter, 1986, Spies, Lies & Naked Thighs, 1988, The Josephine Baker Story, 1991, Mrs. Lambert Remembers Love, 1991, An American Story, 1992, Family Torn Apart, 1993, Scarlett, 1994, White Dwarf, 1995, Robinson Crusoe, 1996, Jakes Women, 1996, London Suite, 1996, Mary & Tim, 1996, In Cold Blood, 1996, For Love Alone: The Ivana Trump Story, 1996, Bridge of Time, 1997, Tidal Wave: No Escape, 1997, The Odyssey, 1997, Forbidden Territory: Stanley's Search for Livingstone, 1997, A Christmas Memory, 1997, The Long Way Home, 1998, Moby Dick, 1998, Merlin, 1998, Only Love, 1998, Animal Farm, 1999, Magical Legend of the Leprechauns, 1999, A Christmas Carol, 1999, The 10th Kingdom, 2000, Arabian Nights, 2000, Jason and the Argonauts, 2000, Voyage of the Unicorn, 2001, The Lost Empire, 2001, Infinite Worlds of H.G. WElls, 2001, Snow White, 2001, Stranded, 2002, King of Texas, 2002, Dinotopia, 2002, Mr. St. Nick, 2002, The Snow Queen, 2002, Dreamkeeper, 2003, Prince Charming, 2003, The Lion in Winter, 2004; author: Into Your Hands Are They Delivered, Animals of Africa, Animals of North America, Sports Cars of the World, How To Photograph Women, Zoos of the World, Recipient 15 Emmy awards, Peabody award, Christopher award, Genesis award, CINE Golden Eagle award, numerous Houston Film Festival awards. Address: Hallmark Entertainment 21st Fl 1325 Avenue of the Americas New York NY 10019-6026*

HALMI, ROBERT, JR., television producer; Pres., CEO Hallmark Entertainment, NYC, 1994—; chmn., CEO Crown Media Holdings. Prodr. (or exec. prodr.) of over 150 TV films & miniseries. Office: Hallmark Entertainment 21st Fl 1325 Ave of the Americas New York NY 10019*

HALONEN, JANE SIMMONS, psychology educator, author; b. South Bend, Ind., July 14, 1950; d. Harold Franklin and Dixie Dell (Sewell) Simmons; m. Brian T. Halonen, May 21, 1976. BA, Butler U., Milw., 1972; MS, U. Wis., Milw., 1975, PhD, 1980. Lic. clin. psychologist, Wis. Dir. Shore Sch., Evanston, Ill., 1979-81; prof. Alverno Coll., Milw., 1981-98; therapist Wellspring Com./Assn., Wanwatosa, Wis., 1983-88; therapist, co-founder Phoenix Clinic, Wanwatosa, Wis., 1988-95; prof. James Madison U., Harrisonburg, Va., 1998. Cons. Family Svc. Milw., 1991-96, ETS, Princeton, N.J., 1994-98. Author: (textbooks) Teaching Social Interaction, 1994, Critical Thinking Companion, 1995, Psychology: Contexts of Behavior, 1996, Wadsworth Guide to College Success, 1998. Fellow APA; mem. Am. Assn. Higher Edn., Coun. Tchrs. Undergrad. Psychology (pres. 1990-92), Midwestern Psychol. Assn. Office: Alverno Coll 3401 S 39th St Milwaukee WI 53215-4020

HALPER, EMANUEL B(ARRY), lawyer, real estate developer, consultant, writer; b. Bronx, N.Y., June 24, 1933; s. Nathan N. and Molly (Rabinowitz) H.; m. Ilona Rubinstein, Mar. 5, 1961; children: Eve Brook, Dan Reed. AB, CCNY, 1954; JD, Columbia U., 1957. Bar: N.Y. 1958, Minn. 1982; real estate broker, N.Y. House counsel Howard Stores Corp., Bklyn., 1960; ptnr. Zissu, Berman, Halper & Gumbinger, N.Y.C., 1965-87, of counsel, 1987-97; ptnr. Can. Pacific Realty Co., Fairfield, NJ, 1970—; v.p. devel. Chase Enterprises, Hartford, Conn., 1987-89; pres. Texam. Horizon Ventures, 1989-93, Am. Devel. and Cons. Corp., Greenvale, NY, 1989—. Adj. prof. real estate NYU, 1973-83; spl. prof. law Hofstra U., 1998—. Author: Wonderful World of Real Estate, 1975 (republished as Conversations in Real Estate, 1990), Shopping Center and Store Leases, 1979, Ground Leases and Land Acqusition Contracts, 1988; columnist N.Y. Law Jour., 1982-1992; contbg. editor Real Estate Review, N.Y.C., 1973-99; chmn. editorial policy com. Internat. Property Investment Jour., Hempstead, N.Y., 1982-87. With USAR, 1957-63. Recipient Disting. Teaching award NYU, 1978, Dean's award Hofstra U. Law Sch., 1987. Mem. ABA (chmn. comml. leasing com. 1986-93, chmn. comml. and indsl. leasing group 1993-94, mem. supervisory coun. of real property, probate and trust law sect. 1994-2000, mem. standing com. on CLE, 1994-96, mem. standing com. pubs. 1997-98, mem. standing com. on diversity 1999—, chmn. standing com. cmty. outreach 2004-, Gavel award 1977, Spirit of Excellence award 2005), World Assn. Lawyers (chmn. internat. real estate com. 1982-90), Internat. Inst. for Real Estate Studies (chmn. bd. 1980-87), Am. Coll. Real Estate Lawyers. Jewish. Avocations: writing, painting, gardening, yoga, running. Office: PO Box 261 Greenvale NY 11548-0261 Office Phone: 516-625-8300. Personal E-mail: e1h@aol.com. Business E-Mail: lawezh@hofstra.edu.

HALPER, JUNE, medical center director; Pres. Consortium Multiple Sclerosis Ctrs., 1995—97, exec. dir., 1997—; found exec. dir. Internat. Orgn. Multiple Sclerosis Nurses; founder, exec. dir. Gimbel Multiple Sclerosis Ctr., 1989—. Editor: Comprehensive Nursing Care in Multiple Sclerosis, Advanced Concepts of Nursing Care in Multiple Sclerosis; co-editor: Staying Well with Multiple Sclerosis: A Self-Care Guide. Recipient First June Halper award for Excellence in Nursing Multiple Sclerosis, Inter. Orgn. Multiple Sclerosis Nurses. Fellow: Am. Acad. Nursing; mem.: Am. Acad. Nurse Practitioners. Office: Gimnel Multiple Sclerosis Ctr 718 Teaneck Rd Teaneck NJ 07666

HALPER, THOMAS, political science professor; b. Bklyn., Dec. 1, 1942; s. Albert and Pauline (Friedman) H.; m. Marilyn S. Snyder, Jan. 14, 1979; 1 dau., Pauline. AB, St. Lawrence U., 1963; MA, Vanderbilt U., 1967, PhD, 1970. Instr. Tulane U., 1967-68; asst. prof. polit. sci. Coe Coll., 1968-74, Baruch Coll., 1974-76, prof., chmn. dept., 1976—. Author: Foreign Policy Crises, 1971, Power, Politics and American Democracy, 1981, The Misfortunes of Others, 1989, Positive Rights in a Republic of Talk, 2003; contbr. articles to profl. jours. Mem. Am. Polit. Sci. Assn. Home: 75 Livingston St Brooklyn NY 11201-5054 Office: Baruch Coll Dept Polit Sci 1 Bernard Baruch Way New York NY 10010-5518 Office Phone: 646-312-4413. Business E-Mail: thomas_halper@baruch.cuny.edu.

HALPERIN, BERTRAND ISRAEL, physics professor; b. Bklyn., Dec. 6, 1941; s. Morris and Eva (Teplitsky) H.; m. Helena Stacy French, Sept. 23, 1962; children: Jeffery Arnold, Julia Stacy. AB, Harvard U., 1961; A.M., U. Calif., 1963, PhD, 1965; vis. grad. student, Princeton U., 1964-65. NSF postdoctoral fellow U. Paris, 1965-66; mem. tech. staff Bell Labs., Murray Hill, N.J., 1966-76; lectr. Harvard U., 1969-70, prof. physics, 1976—, chmn. dept. physics, 1988-91, Hollis prof. math. and natural philosophy, 1992—; sci. dir. Ctr. for Imaging and Mesoscale Structures, 1994—2004. Cons. Lucent Technologies, Schlumberger-Doll Rsch. Labs. Assoc. editor: Revs. Modern Physics, 1973-80. Recipient Wolf prize in physics, Wolf Found., Herzlia, Israel, 2003. Fellow Am. Phys. Soc. (Oliver Buckley prize 1982, Lars Onsager prize 2001), Am. Acad. Arts and Scis.; mem. NAS, Am. Philos. Soc. Achievements include rsch. in solid state theory, statis. physics. Office: Harvard U Dept Physics Cambridge MA 02138

HALPERIN, DANIEL I., law educator; b. Bklyn., Jan. 2, 1937; BBA, City Coll. of NY, 1957; JD, Harvard U., 1961. Bar: NY 1962, Pa. 1977, DC 1984. Dep. tax counsel US Dept. Treasury, 1969—70; prof. law U. Pa.; tax legis. counsel US Dept. Treasury, 1977—80; prof. law Georgetown U., 1980—96; Stanley S. Surrey Prof. Law Harvard Law Sch., Cambridge, Mass., 1996—. Vis. prof. law Harvard Law Sch., 1993. Office: Harvard Law Sch 1563 Massachusetts Ave Cambridge MA 02138 Office Phone: 617-496-5505. Office Fax: 617-496-4880. Business E-Mail: halperin@law.harvard.edu.

HALPERIN, DAVID RICHARD, lawyer; b. Bklyn., June 12, 1944; s. David and Mareva (Vinade) H. BA, Columbia U., 1965; MAT, Harvard U., 1966, JD, 1974. Bar: N.Y. 1975. Spl. asst. to Henry Kissinger, asst. to Pres. for Nat. Security Affairs, Washington, 1970-71; assoc. Davis Polk & Wardwell, N.Y.C., 1974-76, Coudert Bros., Hong Kong, 1976—83, ptnr., 1983—. Dir. Altfield Enterprises, Ltd., Staunton Capital, Ltd.; mem. adv. bd. Olympus Capital Ltd., Overlook Investments Ltd.; mem. takeovers and mergers panel Hong Kong Securities and Futures Commn., 1999—2001; mem. disciplinary com. Share Registrars, 2003—. Contbr. articles on internat. banking to legal jours. Served to lt. comdr. USNR, 1965—71, served as aide to dep. comdr. US Naval Forces, 1968—70, Vietnam, spl. asst., chief naval ops., 1970—71. Decorated Bronze Star with combat V. Mem. ABA, Internat. Bar Assn., Assn. Bar City N.Y., Coun. on Fgn. Rels., Knickerbocker Club, Racquet and Tennis Club, Harvard Club of N.Y.C., Univ. Club (Washington), Royal Hong Kong Yacht Club, Hong Kong Club, RBSC Polo Club (Bangkok). Home: 47 Conduit Rd Apt 1A Hong Kong China also: Baan Piyasathorn 5 Soi Suan Plu, S Sathorn Bangkok Thailand Office: Coudert Bros Gloucs Tower 11 Pedder St Ctrl 39th Fl Hong Kong China Office Phone: (852) 2218-9100.

HALPERIN, ERROL R., lawyer; b. Jan. 3, 1941; BS, De Paul U., 1964, JD, 1967; LLM in Taxation, NYU, 1968. Bar: Ill. 1968; U.S. Tax Ct. 1972. Asst. branch chief, legis. and regulations divsn. IRS, 1968-72; legis. atty., joint com. on taxation U.S. Congress, 1977-79; sr. ptnr., Corp. & Securities practices, mem. exec. com. DLA Piper Rudnick Gray Cary, Chgo. Mem.: Nat. Assn. Real Estate Investment Trusts, Nat. Assn. Bond Lawyers, Ill. State Bar Assn., Chgo. Bar Assn. Office: DLA Piper Rudnick Gray Cary Suite 1900 203 N La Salle St Chicago IL 60601-1293 Office Phone: 312-368-4033. Office Fax: 312-236-7516. Business E-Mail: errol.halperin@dlapiper.com.

HALPERIN, GEORGE BENNETT, education educator, retired military officer; b. NYC, Aug. 7, 1926; s. George and Myrual (Lesser) H.; m. Ellen Elizabeth Barber, Dec. 18, 1957 (div. 1988); children: Gail Susan, Thomas Allyn; m. Kathleen Bourdon, Aug. 22, 2000. BS, U.S. Naval Acad., 1950; MBA, Stanford U., 1958; postgrad., Naval War Coll., Newport, R.I., 1965—66; MA in History, U. Vt., 1976; MEd, Harvard U., 1979; postgrad., Oxford U., 1987—88, St. Catherine's Coll., 1987—88. Commd. ensign U.S. Navy, 1950, advanced through grades to comdr., 1965; dir. systems and standards div. Naval Supply Ctr., Oakland, Calif., 1963-65; freight terminal officer Naval Support Activity, Danang, Vietnam, 1966-67; supply officer Naval Air Sta., Barbers Point, Hawaii, 1967-70; ret., 1970; tchr. history Stowe (Vt.) High Sch., 1972-80, asst. prin., 1975-76; tchr. John F. Kennedy Sch., Berlin, 1980-86. Chmn. Lamoille South Dist. Profl. Growth Com., 1977—78. Decorated Navy Commendation medal. Mem. U.S. Naval Acad. Alumni Assn., Army-Navy Country Club, Oxford Soc., Harvard Club Home: # 79 Apple Blossom Dr West Lebanon NH 03784

HALPERIN, HELENA STACY, secondary school educator, writer; b. Mpls., Nov. 16, 1941; d. C. Stacy and Margaret (Coolidge) French; m. Bertrand Israel Halperin, 1962; children: Jeffery Arnold, Julia Stacy. BA in Psychology, U. Calif., Berkeley, 1964; MA in History, Rutgers U., 1976; MA in Tchg. English as a Second Lang., Simmons Coll., 1993; Program dir. North Shore CAP, Peabody, Mass., 1980-81; program assoc. Am. Friends Service Com., Cambridge, 1981-82; dir. fin. planning Citizens for Participation in Polit. Action, Boston, 1983-86; tchr. Phoenix Sch., 1986—, Shamoni Secondary Sch., Kakamega, Kenya, 1989-90, Roxbury C.C., Boston, 1994—; chmn. bd. Jitegemee, Inc., Empowerment Through Edn., 2005; mem. advocates team Nonviolent Peaceforce, 2005. Author: I Laugh so I Won't Cry: Kenya's Women Tell the Stories of Their Lives, 2005. Home: 11 Gray St Arlington MA 02476-6430 Business E-Mail: hhalperin@rcc.mass.edu.

HALPERIN, JEROME ARTHUR, pharmaceutical executive; b. Paterson, N.J., Feb. 21, 1937; s. Harry Nathan and Frieda (Niestat) Halperin; m. Barbara Anne Hott, Sept. 1, 1963; children: Alicia Jennifer Odom, Rachel Elizabeth Halperin Montgomery. BS, Rutgers U., 1958; MPH, Johns Hopkins U., 1962; MS, MIT, 1974; DSc (hon.), Mercer U., 1993, Mass. Coll. Pharmacy, 1995, Phila. Coll. Pharmacy and Sci., 1996; DHL (hon.), Western U. Health Scis., 2000. Commd. officer USPHS, 1958, advanced through grades to rear admiral, 1983; staff pharmacist USPHS Hosps., Dept. HEW, Albuquerque and N.Y.C., 1958-61; radiol. health specialist Calif. Health Dept., Berkeley, 1962-65; agreement states coord. Bur. Radiol. Health, Rockville, Md., 1965-66; dir. indsl. radiation and air hygiene Kans. Dept. Health, Topeka, 1966-68; regional rep. Bur. Radiol. Health, Chgo., 1968-71; dir. Northeastern Radiol. Health Lab., FDA, HEW, Winchester, Mass., 1971-73; dep. assoc. dir. new drug evaluation Bur. Drugs, FDA, HEW, Rockville, 1974-77, dep. dir., 1977-82; acting dir. Office of Drugs Nat. Ctr. Drugs and Biologics FDA, Rockville, 1982-83; v.p. tech. CIBA Consumer Pharms., Edison, NJ, 1983-89; exec. dir. U.S. Pharmacopeial Conv., Inc., Rockville, 1989-95, exec. v.p., CEO, 1995-2000; pres., CEO Food & Drug Law Inst., Washington, 2000—. Chmn. Conf. Pharmacy 21st Century Va., 1984; cons. WHO, 1979—2000; trustee Davis and Elkins Coll., 2003—. Contbr. articles to profl. jours. Mem. Bd. Health, Hoffman Estates, Ill., 1971; bd. dirs. Perspective Woods Citizen Assn., Olney, Md., 1977—80. Named Alumnus of Yr., Rutgers U. Coll. of Pharmacy, 1981, Disting. Person of Yr., Pharmaceutical Planning Svc., Inc., 1998; recipient Outstanding Svc. award, Federally Employed Women's Assn., 1983, Disting. Career award, Drug Info. Assn., 2001, Career Achievement award, Profl. Fraternities Assn., 2001, Disting. Alumni award, FDA, 2002. Fellow: APHA, AAAS, Am. Pharm. Assn. (Remington Honor medal 2001), Am. Assn. Pharm. Scientists; mem.: Food & Drug Adminstrn. Alumni Assn. (treasurer 2004—), Internat. Pharm. Fedn. (expert mem. bd. pharm. scis.). Jewish. Office: FDLI Ste 200 1000 Vermont Ave NW Washington DC 20005 Office Phone: 202-371-1420. Business E-Mail: jah@fdli.org.

HALPERIN, JOHN JACOB, neurology educator, researcher; b. Montreal, Que., Can., Jan. 25, 1950; came to U.S., 1967. s. David M. and Maizie Halperin; m. Toula Jaravinos, June 15, 1975; 1 child, Daniel Mark. SB in Physics, MIT, 1971; MD, Harvard U., 1975. Diplomate Am. Bd. Internal Medicine, Am. Bd. Psychiatry and Neurology, Am. Bd. Electrodiagnostic Medicine added qualifications clin. neurophysiology. Intern, resident in medicine U. Chgo., 1975-77; resident in neurology Mass. Gen. Hosp., Boston, 1977-80, fellow, 1980-83; asst. prof. SUNY, Stony Brook, 1983-89, assoc. prof., vice chmn. dept., 1989-91, acting chmn. dept., 1990-91; chmn. dept. North Shore U. Hosp., Manhasset, NY, 1992—2004. Assoc. prof. Cornell U. Med. Coll., 1992-93, prof. 1993-96; prof. NYU Sch. Medicine, 1996—. Contbr. numerous articles to med. jours., chpts. to books. Fellow Am. Acad. Neurology, Am. Assn. for Electrodiagnostic Medicine (edn. com. 1989-93, examiner 1991—, tng. com. 1995-97); mem. Soc. for Neurosci., Am. Acad. Clin. Neurophysiology (exec. coun. 1993-96), Am. Neurol. Assn. Achievements include research on electrodiagnosis, nervous system Lyme disease. Office: 1000 Northern Blvd Ste 240 Great Neck NY 11021

HALPERIN, JOHN WILLIAM, English literature educator; b. Chgo., Sept. 15, 1941; s. S. William and Elaine P. H. AB, Bowdoin Coll., 1963; MA, U. N.H., 1966, Johns Hopkins U., 1968, PhD, 1969. Asst. prof. English SUNY, Stony Brook, 1969-72, dir. summer session, 1969-72, asst. to acad. v.p., 1971-72; assoc. prof. English U. So. Calif., 1972-77, prof., 1977-83, dir. grad. studies in English, 1973-75; Centennial prof. English Vanderbilt U., Nashville, 1983—. Fellow Wolfson Coll., Oxford U., 1976; vis. prof. U. Sheffield, Eng., 1979-80. Author: The Language of Meditation, 1973, Egoism and Self-Discovery in the Victorian Novel, 1974, (with Janet Kunert) Plots and Characters in the Fiction of Jane Austen, The Brontes and George Eliot, 1976, Trollope and Politics, 1977, Gissing: A Life in Books, 1982, C.P. Snow: An Oral Biography, 1983, The Life of Jane Austen, 1984, reprint, 1996, Jane Austen's Lovers and Other Essays, 1988, Novelists in Their Youth, 1990, Eminent Georgians, 1995, reprinted, 1998; editor: Henry James, The Golden Bowl, 1972, The Theory of the Novel, 1974, Jane Austen: Bicentenary Essays, 1975, George Gissing, Denzil Quarrier, 1979, Anthony Trollope, Lord Palmerston, 1981, Anthony Trollope, Sir Harry Hotspur of Humblethwaite, 1981, Trollope Centenary Essays, 1982, Anthony Trollope, Dr. Wortle's School, 1984, George Meredith, The Ordeal of Richard Feverel, 1984, George Gissing, The Emancipated, 1985, George Gissing, Will Warburton, 1985, Anthony Trollope, The Belton Estate, 1986, Anthony Trollope, The American Senator, 1986, George Gissing, In The Year of Jubilee, 1987, Proust, 1988, Gissing, New Grub Street, 1992, Anthony Trollope, The Vicar of Bullhampton, 1997; contbr. articles and essays to profl. jours. With U.S. Army, 1963-69. NDEA fellow, 1966-69, Rockefeller Found. fellow, 1976, Am. Philos. Soc. fellow, 1978, Guggenheim fellow, 1978-79, 85-86, Am. Coun. Learned Socs. fellow, 1981. Fellow Royal Soc. Lit.; mem. MLA, PEN. Office: Vanderbilt U Dept English Nashville TN 37235

HALPERIN, JONATHAN L., medical school administrator; b. Boston, Jan. 29, 1949; s. Meyer H. and Libby (Shoer) H.; m. Michelle Copeland, June 21, 1970; children: Robert, Libby. AB, Columbia U., 1971; MD, Boston U., 1975.

Diplomate Bd. Cardiovascular Disease. Teaching fellow medicine Boston U. Sch. Medicine, 1976-78, teaching asst. medicine, 1978-80; asst. prof. medicine Mt. Sinai Sch. Medicine, N.Y.C., 1980-85, assoc. prof. clin. medicine, 1985-88, assoc. prof. medicine, 1986—. Assoc. attending physician cardiology Mt. Sinai Hosp., N.Y.C., 1983—; dir. clin. svcs. Mt. Sinai Med. Ctr., N.Y.C., 1983—; cardiology liaison div. cardiothoracic surgery Mt. Sinai Med. Ctr., N.Y.C., 1980-85; staff physician Lynn (Mass.) Hosp., 1978-80. Office: Mt Sinai Med Ctr PO Box 1030 New York NY 10029-0310

HALPERIN, MORTON H., political scientist; b. Bklyn., June 13, 1938; s. Harry and Lillian (Neubert) H.; m. Ina Elaine Weinstein, June 19, 1960 (div. Dec. 1979); children: David, Mark, Gary; m. Carol Pitchersky, Sept. 29, 1991 (dec. Oct. 2004). AB, Columbia U., 1958; MA, Yale U., 1959, PhD, 1961. Rsch. assoc. Harvard U., 1960-66, asst. prof., 1963-66; dep. asst. sec. U.S. Dept. Def., Washington, 1966-69; sr. staff mem. NSC, Washington, 1969; sr. fellow Brookings Instn., Washington, 1969-73; rsch. project dir. Twentieth Century Fund, Washington, 1974-75; dir. Ctr. Nat. Security Studies, Washington, 1975-92; dir. Washington office ACLU, 1985-92; sr. assoc. Carnegie Endowment for Internat. Peace, 1992-94; Barer Prof. Internat. Rels. The George Washington U., Washington, 1992-94; spl. asst. to pres., sr. dir. for democracy NSC, Washington, 1994-96; sr. fellow Coun. Fgn. Rels., Washington, 1996-98; sr. v.p. Twentieth Century Fund/Century Found., Washington, 1997-98; dir. policy planning staff Dept. of State, 1998-2001; sr. fellow Coun. Fgn. Rels., Washington, 2001—03; dir. Washington office Open Soc. Inst., 2002—04; sr. v.p. Ctr. for Am. Progress, 2003—. Dir. US Advocacy Open Soc. Instn., 2005—. Author: Limited War in the Nuclear Age, 1963, Contemporary Military Strategy, 1967, Bureaucratic Politics and Foreign Policy, 1974, Nuclear Fallacy, 1987, Self-Determination in a New World Order, 1992, The Democracy Advantage, 2005. Recipient Meritorious Civilian Svc. award U.S. Dept. Def., 1969; recipient Hugh M. Hefner 1st Amendment Playboy Found., 1981, W. Lucius Cross medal Yale Grad. Sch. Alumni Assn., 1983, John Jay award Columbia Coll., 1986; MacArthur Found. fellow, 1981-85. Mem. ACLU, Coun. Fgn. Rels., Internat. Inst. Strategic Studies. Democrat. Jewish. Home: 3710 McKinley St NW Washington DC 20015 Office Phone: 202-721-5602. Personal E-mail: mortonhalperin@yahoo.com. Business E-Mail: mhalperin@osi.dc.org.

HALPERIN, RICHARD E., lawyer, finance company executive; b. N.Y.C., Dec. 7, 1954; s. Alvin M. and Anne (Beecher) H.; m. Lucy Landesman, Oct. 5, 1980. BS cum laude, Boston U., 1976; JD, New Eng. Sch. of Law, 1979. Bar: N.Y. 1980. Adminstrv. asst. to atty. gen. N.Y. State Exec. Bur., 1979-84; pres. R.O.P. Aviation, Teterboro, N.J., 1984-99; exec. v.p., spl. counsel to the chmn. Revlon Group Inc., N.Y.C., 1985-99, MacAndrews & Forbes Group, Inc., N.Y.C., 1984-99; founder, CEO Velocity Group LLC, N.Y.C., 1999-2000; pres. Quellos Group LLC, N.Y.C. Pres. Revlon Found., 1985-99, MacAndrews & Forbes Found., N.Y.C., 1984-99; prin. Quadra Fin. Group. Address: Quellos Group LLC 667 Madison Ave Fl 25 New York NY 10021-8029 Office Phone: 212-609-4100. E-mail: rhalperin@quellos.com.

HALPERIN, ROBERT MILTON, retired electrical machinery company executive; b. Chgo., June 1, 1928; s. Herman and Edna Pearl (Rosenberg) H.; m. Ruth Levison, June 19, 1955; children: Mark, Margaret, Philip. Ph.B., U. Chgo., 1949; B.Mech. Engring., Cornell U., 1949; MBA, Harvard U., 1952. Locomotive prodn. engr. Electro-Motive divsn. Gen. Motors Corp., La Grange, Ill., 1949—50; trust rep. Bank of Am., San Francisco, 1954—56; adminstr. Dumont Corp., San Rafael, Calif., 1956—57; with Raychem Corp., 1957—94, pres., 1982—90, vice chmn., bd. dirs. Menlo Park, Calif., 1990—94. Chmn. bd. dirs. Avid Tech. Inc., Vitria Tech. Inc. Bd. trustees U. Chgo.; bd. dirs. Harvard Bus. Sch. Pub. Co., Stanford U. Hosp. and Clinics; vice-chair, bd. dirs. Stanford U. Hosp. and Clinics. Lt. USAF, 1952-53. Mem. Harvard Club of N.Y.C. Office: 2121 Sand Hill Rd Menlo Park CA 94025 Office Phone: 650-493-2383. Personal E-mail: rmhalderin@sbcglobal.com.

HALPERIN, SAMUEL, education and training policy analyst; b. Chgo., May 10, 1930; married; 2 children. Student (scholar), Ill. Inst. Tech., 1948-49; AB, A.M. (scholar 1950-52), Washington U., St. Louis, 1952, PhD in Polit. Sci. (fellow 1954-56), 1956; postgrad., Columbia U., 1953-54. Asst. prof. polit. sci. Wayne State U., 1956-60; Am. Polit. Sci. Assn. congl. fellow Com. on Edn. and Labor, U.S. Ho. of Reps., 1960-61; legis. asst. to Hon. Cleveland M. Bailey and Adam C. Powell, 1960-61; cons. to subcom. on edn. and Senator Wayne Morse, Com. on Labor and Public Welfare, U.S. Senate, 1961, subcom. on reorgn., research and internat. orgns., 1970-73; specialist, dir. legis. services br. U.S. Office Edn., Washington, 1961-64; asst. U.S. commr. edn. for legis. and dir. office legis. and congl. relations, 1964-66; dep. asst. sec. for legis. HEW, Washington, 1966-69; founder, dir. Ednl. Staff Seminar, Washington, 1969-73; dir. Inst. for Ednl. Leadership, George Washington U., 1973-81, pres., 1981, sr. fellow, 1981-86; fellow Jerusalem Ctr. Pub. Affairs, 1981-84; coordinator Relief Activities in South Lebanon, Am. Jewish Joint Distbn. Com., 1982; founder, dir. Am. Youth Policy Forum, Washington, 1993—. Professorial lectr. Am. U., 1962-63; adj. prof. Tchrs. Coll. Columbia U., 1966-68; lectr. in edn. policy Duke U. Inst. Policy Scis. and Public Affairs, 1974-75; mem. vis. com. Harvard Grad. Sch. Edn., 1973-79; mem. Urban Edn. Task Force, Nat. Urban Coalition; mem. profl. rev. panels; cons. speaker, guest lectr. in field; mem. nat. adv. bd. U.S. Peace Corps, Exec. High Sch. Internships Am., Nat. Sch. Vol. Program, HEW Steering Com. on Life-Long Learning, Nat. Student Ednl. Fund, Am. Council Edn.'s Nat. Identification Program for Advancement Women in Higher Edn. Adminstrn., United Student Aid Funds; mem. Sec. of Navy's Adv. Bd. on Edn. and Tng.; mem. adv. panel on human resources research Rand Corp. Author: The Political World of American Zionism, 1961, 2d edit., 1985, A University in the Web of Politics, 1960, Essays on Federal Education Policy, 1975, A Guide for the Powerless, 1981, 2d edit. 2000, Any Home a Campus: Open University of Israel, 1984, The forgotten Half Revisited, 1998; co-editor, contbg. author: Perspectives on Federal Educational Policy, 1976, Federalism at the Crossroads, Improving Educational Policymaking, 1977; contbr. numerous articles, revs. to profl. publs.; cons. Change mag.; mem. nat. adv. bd. Crossreference, Jour. Multi-Cultural Edn. Mem. nat. adv. bd. Am. Jewish Com.; founder, sec. D.C. Youth Svc. Corps.; nat. adv. coun. sch.-to-work, D.C. Commn. on Nat. Svc.; exec. bd. Coalition for Nat. And Cmty. Svc.; mem. coun. D.C. Pvt. Industry; bd. dirs. Learning Matters: mem. The Merrow Report on PBS, Ctr. for Youth as Resources, Assocs. for Renewal in Edn., Coun. for Advancement of Adult Lit., Alliance for Excellent Edn.; adv. bd. Gelman Libr., George Washington U.; Maj. ROTC, 1948-52. Recipient Superior Svc. award HEW, 1964, 67, Disting. Svc. award, 1968; award of merit Nat. Assn. Pub. Sch. Adult Edn.; Disting. Svc. awards Nat. Assn. State Bds. Edn., 1977, Nat. Assn. of Svc. and Conservation Corps., 1990, 97, Jobs for the Future, 1994, Pres.'s medal George Washington U., 1994, Harry S. Truman award Am. Assn. C.C., 1995, Lewis Hine award Nat. Child Labor Com., 1999; AFL-CIO rsch. grantee, 1959-60, Wayne State U. faculty rsch. grantee, 1958-59; Rockefeller Found. fellow, Bellagio, 1981, 92. Mem. Phi Beta Kappa, Pi Sigma Alpha (pres.) Home: 3041 Normanstone Ter NW Washington DC 20008-2731 Office: Am Youth Policy Forum 1836 Jefferson Pl NW Washington DC 20036-2505 Office Phone: 202-775-9731. Office Fax: 202-775-9733. Personal E-mail: shalperin18@comcast.net. Business E-Mail: shalperin@aypf.org.

HALPERN, ABRAHAM LEON, psychiatrist; b. Warsaw, Feb. 2, 1925; came to U.S., 1957, naturalized, 1962; s. Rubin M. and Helen (Perelman) H.; m. Marilyn Lois Benjamin; children: Howard, Lon, Marnen, Heather Halpern Schneid, Mark, Emily Halpern Lewis, John. MD, U. Toronto, Ont., Can., 1952. Diplomate Am. Bd. Psychiatry and Neurology with cert. in forensic psychiatry, Am. Bd. Forensic Psychiatry; cert. mental hosp. adminstr.; cert. correctional health profl. Intern Toronto Western Hosp., 1952-53; resident Warren (Pa.) State Hosp., 1957-60, Ea. Pa. Psychiat. Inst., Phila., 1959; assoc. research scientist Mental Health Research Unit, Syracuse, N.Y., 1961-62; commr. mental health Onondaga County, 1962-67; practice medicine specializing in psychiatry Mamaroneck, N.Y., 1967—; dir. psychiatry United Hosp. Med. Ctr., Port Chester, 1967-91; attending psychiatrist Beth Israel Hosp., N.Y.C., 1968-73, Westchester County Med. Ctr., 1971—; cons. forensic psychiatry High Point Hosp., Port Chester, 1969-93; cons. St. Vincent's Hosp., Harrison, N.Y., 1973-93; clin. assoc. prof. psychiatry N.Y. Med. Coll., Valhalla, N.Y., 1973-80, clin. prof. psychiatry, 1980-94, prof. emeritus of psychiatry, 1994—; cons. Rye (N.Y.) Hosp. Ctr., 1994—; attending psychiatrist Kirby Forensic Psychiat. Ctr., Ward's Island, N.Y., 1994-95; attending psychiatrist dept. alcohol/substance abuse treatment Yonkers (N.Y.) Gen. Hosp., 1995-96; clin. dir. mental health svcs. Dept. Correctional Program, Westchester County, N.Y., 1996. Clin. asst. prof. SUNY, Syracuse, 1964-67; asst. clin. prof. Mt. Sinai Sch. Medicine, 1970-74; clin. assoc. prof. N.Y. Med. Coll., 1973-80, clin. prof. psychiatry, 1980-94, prof. emeritus, 1994—; clin. prof. forensic psychiatry, N.Y. Sch. Psychiatry, 1979-82; mem. med. adv. com. Vis. Nurse Assn., Syracuse, 1962-67; mem. N.Y. State Mental Hygiene Med. Rev. Bd., 1982-86; bd. govs. High Point Hosp., 1989-92. Assoc. editor Bull. Am. Acad. Psychiatry and the Law, 1982-88, Jour. Am. Acad. Psychiatry and the Law, 2002—; mem. editorial bd. Psychiat. Jour. of U. Ottawa, 1979-91; mem. exec. editorial com. Psychiat. Quar., 1982-90, assoc. editor, 1990—. Chmn. Syracuse chpt. Com. to Abolish Capital Punishment, 1962-65; mem. profl. adv. com. N.Y. State Assn. for Mental Health, 1964-67; mem. N.Y. State Law Revision Adv. Com. on the Insanity Def., 1979-80; mem. Westchester County Community Mental Health Bd., 1976-78, chmn., 1977-78; mem. Westchester County Hosp. Bd., 1992—; bd. visitors Harlem Valley Psychiat. Center, 1978-82; mem. N.Y. State Correction Med. Rev. Bd., 1980-87, N.Y. State Mental Hygiene Med. Rev. Bd., 1982-85; bd. dirs. Westchester Council on Alcoholism, 1980-85. Served to surgeon lt. comdr. Royal Can. Navy, 1942-45, 53-57. Recipient Citizenship award, NY State Bar Assn., 1966, Liberty Bell award, Onondaga County Bar Assn., 1966, Falun Dafa Appreciation award, 2000. Fellow ACP (William C. Menninger Meml. award for Disting. Contbns. to the Sci. of Mental Health, 2004), Royal Coll. Psychiatrists (hon.), Am. Acad. Forensic Scis., Am. Coll. Psychiatrists, Am. Psychiat. Assn. (com. psychiatry and law 1973-75, com. on abuse and misuse psychiatry and psychiatrists 1993-2003, Human Rights award 2000), Am. Assn. Psychoanalytic Physicians (dir. 1978-84, Sigmund Freud award 2002), Am. Pub. Health Assn., Academia, Medicinae and Psychiatriae Found. (charter); mem. AMA, N.Y. State Med. Soc. (com. on mental health, com. bioethical issues, com. on child abuse and domestic violence, Pres.'s Citizenship award, 2003), Internat. Assn. Forensic Psychotherapy, Soc. Correctional Physicians, Pan Am. Med. Assn. (mem. council sect. on psychiatry 1983-85), Westchester County Med. Soc., Westchester Psychiat. Soc. (pres. 1973-74), Soc. Med. Jurisprudence (trustee 1980-85, 99-), Internat. Acad. Law and Mental Health (pres. 1983-87), Am. Acad. Psychoanalysis (sci. assoc. 1987), Am. Acad. Psychiatry and Law (councilor 1978-81, pres. elect 1981-82, pres. 1982-83, Golden Apple award 1987), Accreditation Coun. on Fellowships in Forensic Psychiatry (pres. 1990-93), Internat. Coun. on Prison Med. Svcs. (v.p. 1991-). Home and Office: 720 The Pky Mamaroneck NY 10543-4227 Office Phone: 914-698-2136. Personal E-mail: ahalpernmd@verizion.net.

HALPERN, ALVIN MICHAEL, retired physicist, educator, consultant; b. N.Y.C., July 17, 1938; s. Bernard and Gilda (Reiss) H.; m. Mariarosa Roffi, Dec. 2, 1966; children: Kenneth, Marc. AB, Columbia U., 1959, MA, 1961, PhD, 1965. Instr. Pratt Inst., N.Y.C., 1964-65; instr. physics Bklyn. Coll., 1965-66, asst. prof., 1966-69, assoc. prof., 1970-74, prof., 1975—, chmn. dept., 1980-90; exec. dir. Applied Scis. Inst., 1990-93; univ. dir. sch. devel., v.p. rsch. found. CUNY, 1993-97, univ. dean rsch., interim pres. rsch. found., 1997-2000; retired. Contbr. articles to profl. jours. Recipient awards CUNY, 1976, 78, 80, 81, 84; Pfister fellow Columbia U., 1961-64, NSF predoctoral fellow Columbia U., 1959-61; NSF grantee, 1970, 72, 73, 78-80, 79-80, 80-82 Mem. AAAS, AAUP, Am. Phys. Soc., N.Y. Acad. Scis. Personal E-mail: alvin_halpern@yahoo.com.

HALPERN, BARRY DAVID, lawyer; b. Champaign, Ill., Feb. 25, 1949; s. I. L. and Trula M. Halpern; m. Cynthia Ann Zedler, Aug. 4, 1972; children: Amanda M., Trevor H. BA, U. Kans., 1971, JD, 1973. Bar: Kans. 1973, U.S. Dist. Ct. Kans. 1973, Fla. 1975, U.S. Supreme Ct. 1976, Ariz. 1978, U.S. Dist. Ct. Ariz. 1978, Colo. 1991. Ptnr. Snell & Wilmer, Phoenix, 1978—. Faculty Ariz. State U., 2002—03. Mem. Gov.'s Task Force Edn. Reform, 1991; judge pro tem Maricopa County Superior Ct.; bd. dirs. Crisis Nursery, Phoenix, 1987, Friends of Foster Children, Phoenix, 1987, Phoenix Symphony, Greater Phoenix Econ. Coun., 2003, Combined Orgn. Met. Phoenix Arts and Scis., 1994—98, pres., 1996—97, mem. exec. com., 1998—2002. Mem.: ABA, Maricopa County Bar Assn. (chmn. med.-legal com. 1995—96), State Bar Colo., State Bar Kans., State Bar Fla., State Bar Ariz., Phoenix C. of C. (health care coun. 1993—96). Office: Snell & Wilmer 1 Arizona Ctr Phoenix AZ 85004-2202 Office Phone: 602-382-6345. Business E-Mail: bhalpern@swlaw.com.

HALPERN, BRUCE PETER, academic administrator, researcher, educator; b. Newark, Aug. 18, 1933; s. Leo and Thelma (Rubin) H.; m. Pauline Touber Anklowitz, June 9, 1956; children: Michael Touber, Stacey Rachael. AB, Rutgers U., 1955; M.Sc., Brown U., 1957, PhD, 1959. Asst. prof. physiology SUNY Upstate Med. U., Syracuse, N.Y., 1961-66; assoc. prof. psychology, neurobiology and behavior Cornell U., Ithaca, N.Y., 1966-73, prof., 1973-95, chmn. dept. psychology, 1974-90, 91-96, Susan Linn Sage prof. psychology, 1995—, prof. neurobiology and behavior, 1974—. Mem. Adv. Panel Sensory Physiology and Perception NSF, 1976-79; mem. adv. com. Nat. Inst. Neurol. and Communicative Disorders and Stroke, NIH, 1978-79, 85-87, Internat. Commn. on Olfaction and Taste, Union of Physiol. Scis., 1986-94; Fogarty sr. internat. fellow, vis. prof. oral physiology Osaka U., 1982-83; chmn. Gordon Conf. on Chem. Senses: Taste and Smell, 1987-90; PHS-NIMH postdoctoral fellow physiology, rsch. assoc., lect. psychology Cornell U., Ithaca, N.Y., 1959-61; vis. scientist Monell Chem. Senses Ctr., 1996-97. Exec. editor Chem. Senses, 1984-88; contbr. articles to profl. jours. NIMH grantee, 1958-62; NIH grantee, 1963-72; NSF grantee, 1972-90. Mem. Am. Physiol. Soc., Assn. Chemoreception Scis. (pres. 1982-83). Office: Cornell U Dept Psychology Dept Neurobiology/Behavior Uris Hall Ithaca NY 14853-7601 Office Phone: 607-255-6433. Business E-Mail: bph1@cornell.edu. *For those with power: As one's ability to influence or control the actions of others increases, one must become increasingly unwilling to use that ability. For scholars: Any generally accepted scientific idea is an ideal area for creative research, since the idea is almost certainly incorrect.*

HALPERN, DIANE F., psychology educator, professional association executive; b. Phila. BA in psychology, U. Penn., 1969; MA in psychology, Temple U., 1973, U. Cin., 1977, PhD in psychology, 1979. Tchg. assistantship U. Cin., 1977—78, cons. behavioral scis. lab., 1978—79; lectr., dept. psychology U. Calif., Riverside, 1979—81; asst. prof. dept. psychology Calif. State U., San Bernardino, 1981—84, assoc. prof. dept. psychology, 1984—86, prof. dept. psychology, 1986—2001, chair, dept. psychology, 1996—99; dir. Berger Inst. for Work, Family, and Children Claremont McKenna Coll., 2001—, prof. psychology, 2001—. Named Scholar-in-Residence, Rockefeller Found., 1995; recipient Prof. Yr. award, C. of C., 1986, Silver Medal, Coun. Advancement and Support Edn. (CASE), 1986, Ednl. Equity award, Assn. Black Faculty and Staff, 1987, Outstanding Alumni award, U. Cin., 1988, Birkett Williams Meml. Lecture award, Ouachita Baptist U., 1992, Fulbright Scholar award, 1994, Arthur Moorefield Meml. award, 1997, Disting. Vis. Scholar award, James Madison U., 1998. Fellow: Western Psychological Assn. (pres. 1999—2000, Outstanding Tchg. award 2002), Am. Psychological Soc. (charter mem.); mem.: APA (pres. 2004, named G. Stanley Hall Lecture 1991, Disting. Career Contbns. to Edn. and Training 1996—97, Eminent Women in Psychology 1998, Am. Psychological Found. award for disting. tchg. 1998—99, fellow divsn. 1, 2, 3, 35 1989), Psychonomic Soc., Am. Assn. Higher Edn. Office: Berger Inst Work, Family, and Children Claremont McKenna Coll Dept Psychology 850 Columbia Ave Claremont CA 91711: APA Pres's Office 750 First St NE Washington DC 20002-4242 Office Phone: 202-336-6074. Office Fax: 909-607-9647, 909-607-9672, 202-336-6157. Business E-Mail: diane.halpern@claremontmckenna.edu.

HALPERN, ERIC FRANKLIN, university publishing director; b. Portsmouth, N.H., Feb. 28, 1952; s. Stephen and Irene Sally (Needle) H.; m. Frances Jane Weatherburn; children: Helen Augusta, Ian Henry. BA, U. Calif., Santa Cruz, 1974, Oxford U., 1977; MA, Stanford U., 1980. Asst. editor acquisitions Cornell Univ. Press., Ithaca, NY, 1981-84; editor humanities Johns Hopkins Univ. Press., Balt., 1984-90, editor-in-chief, 1990-96; dir. Univ. Pa. Press, Phila., 1996—. Trustee Fairmount Park Art Assn. Mem. Assn. Am. Univ. Presses. Office: Univ Pa Press 39055 Spruce Philadelphia PA 19104-4112 E-mail: ehalpern@pobox.upenn.edu.

HALPERN, JACK, chemist, educator; b. Poland, Jan. 19, 1925; came to U.S., 1962, naturalized; s. Philip and Anna (Sass) H.; m. Helen Peritz, June 30, 1949; children: Janice Henry, Nina Phyllis. BS, McGill U., 1946, PhD, 1949, DSc (hon.), 1997, U. B.C., 1986. NRC postdoc. overseas fellow U. Manchester, England, 1949-50; instr. chemistry U. B.C., 1950, prof., 1961-62; Nuffield Found. traveling fellow Cambridge (Eng.) U., 1959-60; prof. chemistry U. Chgo., 1962-71, Louis Block prof. chemistry, 1971-83, Louis Block Disting. Svc. prof., 1983—. Vis. prof. U. Minn., 1962, Harvard, 1966-67, Calif. Inst. Tech., 1968-69, Princeton U., 1970-71, Max. Planck Institut, Mulheim, Fed. Republic Germany, 1983—, U. Copenhagen, 1978; Sherman Fairchild Disting. scholar Calif. Inst. Tech., 1979; guest scholar Kyoto U., 1981; Firth vis. prof. U. Sheffield, 1982, Phi Beta Kappa vis. scholar, 1990; R.B. Woodward vis. prof. Harvard U., 1991; numerous guest lectureships; cons. editor Macmillan Co., 1963-65, Oxford U. Press; cons. Am. Oil Co., Monsanto Co., Argonne Nat. Lab., IBM, Air Products Co., Enimont, Rohm and Haas; mem. adv. panel on chemistry NSF, 1967-70; mem. adv. bd. Am. Chem. Soc. Petroleum Rsch. Fund, 1972-74, Trans Atlantic Sci. and Humanities Program, 2001--; mem. medicinal chemistry sect. NIH, 1975-78, chmn., 1976-78; mem. chemistry adv. coun. Princeton U., 1982—; mem. univ. adv. com. Ency. Brit., 1985—; mem. chemistry vis. com. Calif. Inst. Tech., 1991—; chmn. German-Am. Acad. Coun., 1993-96, chmn. bd. trustees, 1996—. Assoc. editor: Inorganica Chimica Acta, Jour. Am. Chem. Soc.; co-editor: Collected Accounts of Transition Metal Chemistry, vol. 1, 1973, vol. 2, 1977; assoc. editor Procs. NAS; mem. editl. adv. bd. Oxford Univ. Press, Internat. Series Monographs on Chemistry; mem. editl. bd. Jour. Organometallic Chemistry, Accounts Chem. Rsch., Catalysis Revs., Jour. Catalysis, Jour. Molecular Catalysis, Jour. Coord. Chemistry, Gazzetta Chimica Italiana, Organometallics, Catalysis Letters, Kinetics and Catalysis Letters; contbr. articles to Ency. Britannica, rsch. jours. Trustee Gordon Rsch. Confs., 1968-70; bd. govs. David and Arthur Smart Mus., U. Chgo., 1988—; bd. dirs. Ct. Theatre. Recipient Young Author's prize Electrochem. Soc., 1953, award in catalysis Noble Metals Chem. Soc., London, 1976, Humboldt award, 1977, Richard Kokes award Johns Hopkins U., 1978, Willard Gibbs medal, 1986, Bailar medal U. Ill., 1986, Wilhelm von Hoffman medal German Chem. Soc., 1988, Chem. Pioneer's award Am. Inst. Chemists, 1991, Paracelsus prize Swiss Chem. Soc., 1992, Basolo Medal, Northwestern U., 1993, Robert A. Welch award, 1994, Henry J. Albert award Internat. Precious Metals Inst., 1995, award in Organometallic Chem. Am. Chem. Soc., 1995, Order of Merit Federal Republic of Germany, 1996. Fellow AAAS, Royal Soc. London, Royal Soc. Can., Am. Acad. Arts and Scis., Chem. Inst. Can., Royal Soc. Chemistry London (hon.), N.Y. Acad. Scis., Japan Soc. for Promotion Sci.; mem. NAS (fgn. assoc. 1984-85, mem. coun. 1990—, chmn. chemistry sect. 1991-93, v.p. 1993—, assoc. editor Proceedings NAS), Am. Chem. Soc. (editl. bd. Advances in Chemistry series 1963-65, 78-81, chmn. inorganic chemistry 1985, award in inorganic chemistry 1968, award for disting. svc. in advancement of inorganic chemistry 1985, award in organometallic chemistry 1995), Max Planck Soc. (sci. mem. 1983—), Art Inst. Chgo., Renaissance Soc. (bd. dirs.), New Swiss Chem. Soc. (Paracelsus prize 1992), Am. Friends of the Royal Soc. (bd. dirs.), Sigma Xi. Home: 5801 S Dorchester Ave Apt 4A Chicago IL 60637 Office: U Chgo Dept Chemistry Chicago IL 60637 Business E-Mail: jhjh@uchicago.edu.

HALPERN, JAMES BLADEN, lawyer; b. Buffalo, Apr. 20, 1936; s. Philip and Goldene P. (Friedman) H.; m. Jessie Malkoff, July 6, 1958 (div.); 1 child, Jennifer; m. Niesa N. Brateman, Aug. 26, 1979; 1 child, Sheri. BA, Harvard U., 1958, JD, 1961. Bar: D.C. 1970. Atty. corp. fin. div. SEC, Washington, 1961—64; chief counsel-instns., instl. investor study, 1969—70; assoc. firm Proskauer Rose Goetz & Mendelsohn, N.Y.C., 1964—69; assoc. Arent Fox PLLC, Washington, 1971—73, mem., 1974—2003. Mem. Am. Law Inst. Democrat. Jewish.

HALPERN, JOHN HAIM, psychiatrist, researcher; s. Abraham Leon and Marilyn Lois Halpern; m. Mika Nitta. BA, U. Chgo., 1990; MD, SUNY, Bklyn., 1994. Diplomate Nat. Bd. Med. Examiners, Am. Bd. Psychiatry and Neurology. Intern Carney Hosp., Boston, 1994; psychiatry resident Harvard Longwood Psychiatry Residency Tng. Program, Boston, 1994—98; rsch. fellow, clin. neuroendocrinology lab. Alcohol and Drug Abuse Rsch. Ctr., McLean Hosp., Belmont, Mass., 1997—2003, rsch. fellow, biol. psychiatry lab., 1997—2003, assoc. dir. of substance abuse rsch., biol. psychiatry lab., 2003—. Cons. Gershon Leyman Group, N.Y.C., 2002—. Contbr. articles to profl. jours., chapters to books. Mem. Master Plan Com., Stow, Mass., 2004. Recipient Young Investigator award, Am. Psychiat. Assn., 1997, Nat. Rsch. Svc. award, Nat. Inst. on Drug Abuse, 1997, 1999; fellow Ethel Dupont-Warren fellow, Harvard Med. Sch., 1998, Peter Livingston fellow, 1998; grantee, Nat. Inst. on Drug Abuse, 2000—05, 2004—, Rsch. grantee, The Multidisciplinary Assn. for Psychedelic Studies, 2001—; Laughlin fellow, Am. Coll. of Psychiatrists, 1998, Rsch. grantee, The Heffter Rsch. Inst., 1998—2002. Fellow: Boston Med. Libr.; mem.: Am. Coll. of Psychiatrists, Am. Acad. of Psychiatry and the Law, Mass. Med. Soc., Am. Acad. of Forensic Sci. (assoc.; mem., psychiatry & behavioral sci. sect. task force on addiction 2003), Mass. Psychiat. Soc., Am. Psychiat. Assn., AMA, Harvard Club of N.Y.C., Harvard Club of Boston, Sigma Xi. Office: McLean Hospital-ADARC 115 Mill St Belmont MA 02478-9106 Office Phone: 1-617-855-3703. Personal E-mail: john.halpern@gmail.com. E-mail: john_halpern@hms.harvard.edu.

HALPERN, JOSEPH ALAN, physician; b. Bklyn., Feb. 28, 1952; s. Lester A. and Adele Janet (Tax) H.; m. Cynthia Gould, Sept. 1, 1979; 1 child, Elyza. AB, Bard Coll., Annandale on Hudson, N.Y., 1974; MD, N.Y. Med. Coll., Valhalla, 1978. Diplomate ABEM, ABIM. Resident family practice SUNY, Buffalo, 1978-79; resident in medicine Norwalk (Conn.) Hosp., 1979-81, chief resident medicine, 1981-82; emergency physician Kent and Queen Anne Hosp., Chestertown, Md., 1982-83, North Arundel Hosp., Glen Burnie, Md., 1983-85; attending emergency physician Johns Hopkins Hosp., Balt., 1986-87; emergency physician Anne Arundel Med. Ctr., Annapolis, Md., 1987—, assoc. chief emergency medicine, 1994—99. Attending physician Bayview Med. Ctr., Balt., 1992-94. Fellow Am. Coll. Emergency Physicians; mem. ACP, Med. Chi. Md. Avocations: sailing, bicycling. Office: Anne Arundel Med Ctr 2001 Medical Pkwy Annapolis MD 21401 E-mail: jhalp228@aol.com.

HALPERN, MARTIN BRENT, physics professor; b. Newark, Aug. 26, 1939; s. Melvin M. and Blanche B. (Friedman) H.; m. Penelope J. Dutton, June 2, 1988; 1 child, Tamar Lillian. BSc, U. Ariz., 1960; PhD, Harvard U., 1964. Postdoctoral fellow CERN, Geneva, 1964—65, U. Calif., Berkeley, 1965—66, prof. physics, 1967—; postdoctoral fellow Inst. Advanced Study, Princeton, NJ, 1966—67. Office: U Calif 366 Le Conte Hall Berkeley CA 94720-7303

HALPERN, MERRIL MARK, investment banker; b. Bayonne, N.J., May 4, 1934; s. Samuel and Belle (Schwartz) H.; m. Phyllis Goldstein, June 14, 1960 (div.); children: Belle Linda, Jennifer, Samuel, Isaac; m. Dolores M. Eckersley, Aug. 28, 1991. BS, Rutgers U., 1956; MBA, Harvard U., 1962. With Ernst & Ernst, N.Y.C., 1956-60, sr. acct., 1958-60; with McDonnell & Co., Inc., 1962-68, v.p., 1967-68; ptnr., dir. corp. fin. H. Hentz & Co., N.Y.C., 1969-70; prin. Merril M. Halpern & Co., N.Y.C., 1970-73; pres. Charterhouse Group, Inc., N.Y.C., 1973-84, chmn. bd., 1984—. Trustee Nat. Humanities Ctr., 2000—, Continuum Health Ptnrs., 2001—. With U.S. Army, 1957—58. Office: Charterhouse Group Inc 535 Madison Ave New York NY 10022-4212

HALPERN, PAUL G., history educator; b. N.Y.C., Jan. 27, 1937; s. Harry and Teresa (Ritter) H. BA with honors, U. Va., 1958; MA, Harvard U., 1961, PhD, 1966. Instr. Fla. State U., Tallahassee, 1965-66, asst. prof., 1966-70, assoc. prof., 1970-74; prof. dept. history, 1974—2005. Vis. prof. strategy dept. Naval War Coll., Newport, R.I., 1986-87. Author: The Mediterranean Naval Situation, 1908-14, 1971, The Naval War in the Mediterranean, 1914-18 1987, A Naval History of World War I, 1994, Anton Haus: Österreich-Ungarns Grossadmiral, 1998, The Battle of the Otranto Straits, 2004; editor: The Keyes Papers, 3 vols., 1972-81, The Royal Navy in the Mediterranean, 1915-1918, 1987. Mem. Naval Aviation Mus. Found., Pensacola, Fla., Naval War Coll. Found., Newport, R.I. 1st lt. U.S. Army, 1958-60. Fellow Woodrow Wilson Nat. Fellowship Found., 1958. Fellow Royal Hist. Soc.; mem. Am. Hist. Assn., The Navy Records Soc. (coun. 1968-72, 82-86), Naval Rev., U.S. Naval Inst., Royal United Svcs. Inst. Def. Studies, Friends of Imperial War Mus., Friends of Nat. Maritime Mus., Naval Hist. Found., Soc. for Mil. History, Phi Beta Kappa, Phi Eta Sigma. Avocations: model ship collecting, book collecting, model soldier collection. Home: 3103 Brandemere Dr Tallahassee FL 32312-2423

HALPERN, PHILIP MORGAN, lawyer; b. Derby, Conn., Apr. 17, 1956; s. Edwin Vincent and Carol Veronica (Gallagher) H.; m. Carolyn G. McElwreath, Mar. 11, 1989. BS magna cum laude, Fordham U., 1977; JD, Pace U., 1980. Bar: N.Y. 1981, U.S. Dist. Ct. (so. and ea. dists.) N.Y. 1981, U.S. Ct. Appeals (2d cir.) 1982, U.S. Tax Ct. 1984, U.S. Supreme Ct. 1985, U.S. Dist. Ct. Conn. 1989, Conn. 1989, U.S. Ct. Appeals (3d cir.) 1991; cert. trial adv. Nat. Bd. Trial Advocacy, 2002. Law clk. to sr. judge U.S. Dist. Ct. (so. dist.) N.Y., N.Y.C., 1980-82; assoc. litigation dept. Kimmelman, Sexter & Sobel, N.Y.C., 1982-83; ptnr. Collier, Halpern, Newberg, Nolletti & Bock, N.Y.C., 1983—; mng. ptnr. Collier, Haplern, Newberg, Nolletti & Bock LLP, White Plains, N.Y., 1996—. Arbitrator Civil Ct. City N.Y. and Am. Arbitration Assn., 1987-96; adv. coun. Bd. of Judges, So. Dist. of N.Y., 1995-2000; mediator U.S. Dist. (so. dist.) N.Y., 1998—, mem. office ct. adminstrn. adv. com. on civil practice, 1999—. Author: Age Discrimination in Employment Act: Employers Can Enforce Releases Too!, 1992, Fair Value Proceedings: Fixing Fair Value in New York, 1996; author, editor: Civil Pretrial Proceedings in New York, 2 vols., 1999, updated annually through 2004. Chmn. Young Reps., Tuckahoe, N.Y., 1975-77; chmn. taxi commn. Village of Mamaroneck, N.Y., 1986-87, mem. planning bd., 1987-89. Fellow Am. Bar Found. (life); mem. N.Y. State Bar Assn. (com. on lawyer competency, com. on fed. judiciary), Assn. of Bar of City of N.Y., ATLA, N.Y. Trial Lawyers Assn., N.Y. County Lawyers Assn., Fed. Bar Coun., Profl. Golfers Assn. (adv. coun. metro. sect. 1992—), Westchester Country Club. Roman Catholic. Office: Collier Halpern Newberg Nolletti & Bock LLP One N Lexington Ave White Plains NY 10601 also: 99 Park Ave New York NY 10016-1601 Office Phone: 914-684-6800 x120. Business E-Mail: phalpern@chnnb.com.

HALPERN, RALPH LAWRENCE, lawyer; b. Buffalo, May 12, 1929; s. Julius and Mary C. (Kaminker) H.; m. Harriet Chasin, June 29, 1958; children: Eric B., Steven R., Julie B. LL.B. cum laude, U. Buffalo, 1953. Bar: NY 1953. Teaching assoc. Northwestern U. Law Sch., 1953-54; asso. firm Jaeckle, Fleischmann, Kelly, Swart & Augspurger, Buffalo, 1957-58; asso. firm Raichle, Banning, Weiss & Halpern (and predecessors), 1958-59, ptnr., 1959-86, Jaeckle Fleischmann & Mugel LLP, Buffalo, 1986—. Pres. Buffalo Coun. World Affairs, 1972-74, Temple Beth Zion, Buffalo, 1981-83, Bur. Jewish Edn., 2000-02; chmn. Buffalo chpt. Am. Jewish Com., 1975-77; bd. govs. United Jewish Fedn., Buffalo, 1972-78, 91-97, 1999-2004, v.p., 1992-95. Served to capt. JAGC U.S. Army, 1954-57. Recipient Cmty. Svc. award, Am. Jewish Com., Buffalo, N.Y., 2005. Mem. ABA (ho. dels. 1989-95, 97-99), N.Y. State Bar Assn. (chmn. com. profl. ethics 1971-76, chmn. com. jud. election monitoring 1983-86, chmn. spl. com. to consider adoption of ABA model rules of profl. conduct 1983-85, sec. internat. law and practice sect. 1992-93, vice chmn. 1993-95), Erie County Bar Assn., Am. Judicature Soc., Am. Law Inst. Home: 88 Middlesex Rd Buffalo NY 14216-3618 Office: Jaeckle Fleischmann & Mugel LLP 800 Fleet Bank Bldg Buffalo NY 14202-2292 Office Phone: 716-843-3846. Personal E-mail: rlhalpern@adelphia.net. Business E-Mail: rhalpern@jaeckle.com.

HALPERN, RICHARD I., lawyer; b. Pitts., June 10, 1949; BA with distinction, Stanford U., 1971; MBA, U. Pa., 1973; JD, NYU, 1976. Bar: Pa. 1976. Ptnr. Marcus & Shapira, LLC, Pitts. Mem. ABA. Office: Marcus & Shapira LLC 35th Fl One Oxford Ctr Pittsburgh PA 15219 E-mail: halpern@marcus-shapira.com.

HALPERSON, MICHAEL ALLEN, publishing executive; b. Boston, Sept. 11, 1946; s. Bertram David and Rose (Doolan) H. AB, Union Coll., 1968; MA in Teaching, U. Mass., 1970. Asst. to group v.p. Plymouth Rubber Co., Inc., Canton, Mass., 1972-73, corp. dir. pers. and indsl. rels., 1973-79, mgr. mktg., cons. products, 1979-81, dir. sales and mktg., 1981-85, v.p., 1985-92; v.p., gen. mgr. Plymouth Office Products a Hon Industries Co., Pawtucket, R.I., 1992-93; exec. v.p., COO Kryptonite Corp., Canton, Mass., 1994-95; exec. v.p. Dome Pub. Co. Inc., Warwick, R.I., 1995—, Data Binding, Inc., Warwick, R.I., 1995—; v.p. Parkway Realty, Inc., Warwick, R.I., 1995—, Dome Industries, Inc., Warwick, R.I., 1995—. Bd. dirs., v.p. Cape Cod Sea Camps, Inc., Capt. Del Assocs., Inc., Brewster, Mass.; treas. Camp Wono, Inc., Brewster, Mass. Bd. dirs. Canton Assn. Industries, Inc., 1977-92, Neponset Valley Nursing Assn., Inc., 1979-97, Southwood Cmty. Hosp., Norfolk, Mass., 1983-92, Neponset Valley Hospice, 1993-97, Norfolk-Bristol Homemakers Svc., Inc.; bd. dirs. Neponset Valley Health Sys., Inc., Norwood, Mass., 1985-92, chmn., 1990-92; bd. dirs. Norwood Hosp., Inc., 1983-92, chmn., 1988-90; bd. overseers Boston Ballet, 1992-93, Boston Symphony Orch., 1995—; trustee Boston Ballet Ctr. for Dance Edn., 1993-96, Boston Ballet, 1996-2002, sec. 1999-2000, Grant W. Koch Scholarship Trust, 1981—; mem. bd. visitors New Eng. Conservatory of Music, 2003—. With USAF, 1970-72. Mem. Bus. Products Industry Assn., (bd. dirs. 1996-99), Office Products Mfrs. Assn. (bd. dirs. 1985-92, 2000—, pres. 1989, chmn. 1990); St. Botolph Club, Boston, Williams Club, N.Y.C. Avocations: reading, swimming. Home: 78 Cannon Forge Dr Foxboro MA 02035-5217 Office: Dome Pub Co Inc PO Box 1220 Ten New England Way Warwick RI 02887-1220 Office Phone: 401-738-7900.

HALPERT, RICHARD LEE, lawyer; b. Kalamazoo, Mich., Nov. 1, 1947; s. Samuel K. and Rosalie (Zuravel) H.; m. Mary K. Sydlaske, June 24, 1973; children: David, Michael. BA, Kalamazoo Coll., 1969; JD cum laude, Ind. U., 1972. Bar: Mich. 1973, U.S. Dist. Ct. (we. dist.) Mich. 1980, U.S. Supreme Ct. 1985. Trial atty. Van Buren County Pros. Attys. Office, Paw Paw, Mich., 1972-74, Kreis, Enderle, Halpert, Borsos & Ford, Kalamazoo, 1974-82, Halpert & Koning, Kalamazoo, 1982-87, Howard & Howard, Kalamazoo, 1987-95, Halpert, Weston, Wuori & Sawusch, P.C., Kalamazoo, 1996—. Lectr. in field. Co-author over 30 manuals for Inst. Continuing Legal Edn.; note editor Ind. Law Jour., 1971-72. Bd. dirs. YMCA, Kalamazoo, 1989-94, bd. trustees, 1998—, Kalamazoo County Humane Soc.; trustee Ctrl. Mich. U., Mt. Pleasant, 1981-83. Mem. ATLA, Mich. Trial Lawyers Assn., Am. Burn Assn. (spl. mem. 1983—, rehab. com. 1997—), Internat. Soc. for Burn Injuries (spl. mem. 1986—), State Bar Mich. (negligence sect., com. on profl. and jud. ethics 1980-82), Kalamazoo Bar Assn. (chmn. com. on profl. responsibility 1981-83), Phoenix Soc. for Burn Injuries (trustee, 1st v.p.), Am. Arbitration Assn. Avocations: bicycling, nature photography, hiking. Office: Halpert Weston Wuori and Sawusch PC 136 E Michigan Ave Ste 1050 Kalamazoo MI 49007-3917 Home: 3600 Woodcliff Dr Kalamazoo MI 49008-2513

HALPIN, ANNA MARIE, architect, writer; b. Murphysboro, Ill., July 24, 1923; d. John William and Anna Christina (Weilmuenster) H. BS in Architecture, U. Ill., 1948. Designer, project architect various firms, San Francisco, Rome, N.Y.C., 1948-67; editorial dir. Sweet's div. McGraw-Hill, Inc., N.Y.C., 1967-88, ret. Sweet's div.; freelance cons., 1988-98. Rep. to Constrn. Industries Coordination Com., Am. Nat. Metric Council, 1974-80 Mem. AIA (treas., dir. N.Y. chpt. 1974-78, coll. fellows 1976, nat. dir. 1977-79, nat. v.p. 1980, dir. Found. 1980, Richard Upjohn fellow 1991), Women's Equity Action League (pres. N.Y. state orgn. 1976-77), Constrn. Specifications Inst., Alliance Women in Architecture. Home: Apt 401 1404 NW 122nd St Oklahoma City OK 73114-8052

HALPIN, DANIEL WILLIAM, engineering educator, consultant; b. Covington, Ky., Sept. 29, 1938; s. Jordan W. and Gladys E. (Moore) H.; m. Maria Kirchner, Feb. 8, 1963; 1 son, Rainer. BS, U.S. Mil. Acad., 1961; MSCE, U. Ill., 1969, PhD, 1973. Research analyst Constrn. Engring. Research Lab., Champaign, Ill., 1970-72; faculty U. Ill., Urbana, 1972-73; mem. faculty Ga. Inst. Tech., Atlanta, 1973-85, prof., 1981-85; A.J. Clark prof., dir. Constrn. Engring. and Mgmt. U. Md., 1985-87; dir. div. Constrn. Engring. and Mgmt. Purdue U., 1987—, interim head Sch. Civil Engring., 2000—01; head of constrn. engring. Bowen, 2005; cons. constrn. mgmt. Vis. assoc. prof. U. Sydney, Australia, 1981; vis. prof. Swiss Fed. Inst. Tech., 1985, U. Karlsruhe, Germany, 1998; vis. scholar Tech. U., Munich, 1979; vis. lectr. Ctr. Cybernetics in Constrn., Bucharest, Romania, 1973; cons. office tech. assessment U.S. Congress, 1986-87; mem. JTEC Team to evaluate constrn. tech., Japan, 1990; juror emeritus Constrn. Innovation Forum, 1994; mem. rsch. com. Constrn. Industry Inst., 1995—. Author: Design of Construction and Process Operations, 1976, Construction Management, 1980, 3d edit., 2005, Planung und Kontrolle von Bauproduktionsprozessen, 1979, Constructo - A Heuristic Game for Construction Management, 1973, Financial and Cost Control Concepts for Construction Management, 1985, Planning and Analysis of Construction Operations, 1992, Construction Management, 2d edit., 1997. Served with C.E., U.S. Army, 1961-67. Decorated Bronze Star; recipient Lifetime Achievement award INFORMS Constrn. sect., Coll. Simulation, 2004; grantee NSF, Dept. Energy, NIOSH. Mem. ASCE (past sect. pres. 1981-82, chmn. constrn. rsch. coun. 1985-86, Walter L. Huber prize 1979, Peurifoy Constrn. Rsch. award 1992), Am. Soc. Engring. Edn., Nat. Acad. Constrn. (elected 2003), Constrn. Industry Inst. (rsch. com. 1996-2005), Constrn. Innovation Forum (juror emeritus), Sigma Xi. Methodist. Office Phone: 765-494-2244. Business E-Mail: halpin@purdue.edu.

HALPRIN, ANNA SCHUMAN (MRS. LAWRENCE HALPRIN), dancer; b. Wilmette, Ill., July 13, 1920; d. Isadore and Ida (Schiff) Schuman; m. Lawrence Halprin, Sept. 19, 1940; children: Daria, Rana. Student, Bennington Summer Sch. Dance, 1938-39; BS in Dance, U. Wis., 1943; PhD in Human Services (hon.), Sierra U., 1987; PhD (hon.), U. Wis., 1994, Santa Clara U.; student, Calif. Arts Coll., Calif., 2003; PhD (hon.), Art Instit. of San Francisco, Calif., 2003. Presenter opening invocation State of the World Forum by spl. invitation from Mikhail S. Gorbachev. Author: Moving Toward Life, Five Decades of Transformative Dance, Dance as a Healing Art, A Teachers' Guide and Support Manual for People with Cancer; dancer: at Kennedy Ctr., Washington, Yerba Buena Ctr. for Arts, San Francisco, Joyce Theatre, NYC, 2001—, d'Autumne Festival Paris, Pompidou Theatre, 2004, Cowell Theatre, Returning Home, (film) Moving with the Earth Body, Learning Lessons in Life, Loss & Liberation, 2003, Intensive Care, Reflections on Death and Dying, 2003, Jewish Cmty. Ctr., San Francisco, others. Bd. dirs. East West Holistic Healing Inst.; mem. Gov.'s Coun. on Phys. Fitness and Wellness. Recipient award Am. Dance Guild, 1980, Guggenheim award, 1970-71, Woman of Wisdom award Bay Area Profl. Women's Network, Tchr. of Yr. award Calif. Tchrs. Assn., 1988, Lifetime Achievement award in visual and performing arts San Francisco Bay Guardian newspaper, 1990, Women of Achievement, Vision and Excellence award, 1992, Balasaraswati/Joy Ann Dewey Bieneke chair for disting. tchg. Am. Dance Festival, 1996, Lifetime Achievement in Modern Dance award Am. Dance Festival, 1997, Lifetime Achievement award Calif. Arts Coun., 2000, Breast Cancer Watch, 2001, Dance Mag. N.Y.C. award, 2004; Person of Yr. in field of Dance award Ballet-ranz, Berlin; named to Isadora Duncan Hall of Fame, Bay Area Dance Coalition, 1986; Nat. Endowment Arts Choreographers grantee, 1976, NEA choreography grantee, 1977, San Francisco Found. grantee, 1981, Calif. Arts. Coun. grantee, 1990—; inductee Marin Women's Hall of Fame, 1998, lifetime achievement award Marin Arts Coun., Sustained Achieve. award Am. Theatre Edn. Assn., 2005 Fellow Am. Expressive Therapy Assn.; mem. Assn. Am. Dance, Conscientious Artists Am., San Francisco C. of C. Home and Office: 15 Ravine Way Kentfield CA 94904-2713 Office Phone: 415-461-5362. Personal E-mail: anna@annahalprin.org. *Today I am deeply involved in making a contribution as an artist to world peace. I'm interested in the development of public workshops and dance rituals to create harmony and understanding in social and healing interactions in communities. The Planetary takes place around the world and this year 2005 is its 25th anniversary.*

HALPRIN, LAWRENCE, landscape architect, urban planner; b. Bklyn., July 1, 1916; s. Samuel W. and Rose (Luria) H.; m. Ann Schuman, Sept. 19, 1940; children: Daria, Rana. BS in Plant Scis, Cornell U., 1939; MS in Plant Scis, U. Wis., 1941; B.Landscape Architecture, Harvard U., 1942. Sr. assoc. Thomas D. Church & Assos., San Francisco, 1946-49; prin. Lawrence Halprin & Assos., San Francisco, 1949-76; co-founder Round House, San Francisco, 1976-78; founder Lawrence Halprin Studios, 1978—; lectr. U. Calif.-Berkeley, 1960-65, Regents prof., 1982-83. Dir., Halprin Summer Workshop, 1966, 1968; prin. works include Ghirardelli Sq., San Francisco; Sea Ranch, Calif., Nicolett Mall, Mpls., Old Orchard Shopping Center, Skokie, Ill., Lovejoy Fountain, Pettigrove Park, Forecourt Fountain, Portland, Oreg., Market St. reconstrn, San Francisco, Seattle Freeway Park, Rochester Manhattan Park, Franklin Delano Roosevelt Meml, Washington, Levi Park and Plaza, San Francisco, Haas Promenade, Jerusalem, Bunker Hill Stairs, Central Library, Hope St. and Olympic Park, Los Angeles; author: Cities, 1963; rev. edit., 1972, Freeways, 1966, New York, New York, 1968, The RSVP Cycles, 1970, Lawrence Halprin Notebooks, 1959-71, 1972; co-author: The Freeway in the City, 1968, Taking Part: A Workshop Approach to Collective Creativity, 1974, The Sketch Books of Lawrence Halprin, 1981; filmmaker: Le Pink Grapefruit, Franklin Delano Roosevelt Memorial, How Sweet It Is!, Designing Environments for Everyone. Panelist White House Conf. Natural Beauty, 1965; mem. bd. urban cons. Bur. Pub. Roads, 1966-67; design cons. Calif. Div. Hwys., 1963-65; landscape architect, urban cons. San Francisco Bay Area Rapid Transit Dist., 1963-66; mem. Gov.'s Conf. Calif. Beauty, 1966, Nat. Council Arts, 1966—, Adv. Council, Historic Preservation, 1967—; bd. dirs., San Francisco Dancers Workshop Co., 1950— . Served to lt. (j.g.) USN, 1943-46. Named One of Leaders of Tomorrow, Time mag. 1953, recipient awards including Allied Professions Gold medal AIA 1964, Thomas Jefferson award in architecture 1979; Richard J. Neutra award for Excellence, 1986; honored Changing Places Exhbn., San Francisco Mus. Modern Art, 1986. Fellow Am. Soc. Landscape Architects; mem. Am. Acad. Arts and Scis., Sierra Club. Democrat. Jewish. Address: 1160 Battery St Ste 50 San Francisco CA 94111-1215*

HALSBAND, FRANCES, architect; b. N.Y.C., Oct. 30, 1943; d. Samuel and Ruth H.; m. Robert Michael Kliment, May 1, 1971; 1 child, Alexander H. BA, Swarthmore Coll., 1965; MArch, Columbia U., 1968. Registered architect, N.Y., N.J., Mass., Conn., Ohio, Va., N.H., Pa., D.C., N.C., Ill., Miss., La., Fla.; cert. Nat. Coun. Archtl. Reg. Bds. Arch. Mitchell/Giurgola Archs., N.Y.C., 1968-72; ptnr. R.M. Kliment & Frances Halsband Archs., N.Y.C., 1972—. Vis. critic archtl. design Columbia U., 1975-78, 87, N.C. State U., 1978, Rice U., 1979, U. Va., 1980, Harvard U., 1981, U. Pa., 1981, U. Calif., Berkeley, 1997; dean Sch. Architecture, Pratt Inst., 1991-94; Freidman prof. U. Calif., Berkeley, 1997; Emens Disting. prof. Ball State U., 1998; Kea prof. U. Md., 2000; mem. N.Y.C. Landmarks Preservation Commn., 1984-87; lectr. U. So. Calif., U. Va., Temple U., Washington U., Tulane U., Harvard U., U. Oreg., U. Washington. Projects include: computer Sci. Bldg., Columbia U. (AIA Nat. Honor award 1987), Gilmer Hall addition U. Va., Town Hall, Salisbury Conn., Computer Sci. Bldg., Princeton U. (AIA Nat. Honor award 1994), Case Western Res. Adelbert Hall restoration (AIA Nat. Honor award 1994), Alvin Ailey Am. Dance Theater Found., N.Y.C., hdqs. Marsh & McLennan Co., Ind. Bank Hdqs., Bklyn. Coll. Master Plan, Entrance Pavillion L.I. Rail Rd. Penn Sta. (AIA Nat. award), U.S. Courthouse and Post Office, Bklyn., Yale Div. Sch., Dartmouth Roth Ctr. for Jewish Life, U.S. Courthouse, Gulfport, Miss.; works exhibited in Cooper-Hewitt Mus., Bklyn. Mus., Nat. Acad. Design, Deutsches Architekturmuseum, Frankfourt; author: Annotated Bibliography of Technical Resources for Small Museums, 1983. Trustee Nat. Inst. Archtl. Edn., 1988-93; mem. archtl. rev. panel Fed. Res. Sys., 1993—; mem. U.S. Dept. State Office Fgn. Bldgs. Ops. Archtl. Adv. Bd., 1998—; U.S. Gen. Svcs. Adminstrn. Nat. Register Peer Profls., 1998—. Fellow AIA (exec. bd. N.Y.C. chpt. 1979, pres. N.Y.C. chpt. 1991-92), Century Assn.; mem. Archtl. League N.Y. (exec. bd. 1975—, v.p. arch. 1981-85, pres. 1985-89), Assn. Collegiate Schs. Architecture (N.E. regional dir. 1993-95). Office: RM Kliment & Frances Halsband 255 W 26th St New York NY 10001-8001

HALSE, FRANK ADAMS, JR., retired minister; b. Troy, N.Y., May 3, 1927; s. Frank Adams and Anna Evelyn Halse; m. Joyce Holcomb Halse, June 7, 1952; children: Laurie Halse Anderson, Lisa Halse Stevens. AB in Psychology and Religion, Boston U., 1955, MA in Sacred Theology, Psychology and Religion, 1958; MA in Family Studies, Syracuse U., 1972, postgrad., 1972—75. Pastor United Meth. Ch., Parish, NY, 1955—62, exec. dir. Wesley Found. Potsdam, NY, 1962—65, pastor Pulaski, NY, 1965—66, chaplain Syracuse (N.Y.) U., 1966—75; exec. dir. County North Counseling Ctr., Syracuse, 1976—78, N.W. Counseling Ctr., Syracuse, 1978—80; pastor United Meth. Ch., Navarino, NY, 1981—83, Cazenovia, NY, 1984—86; ret. Travelling elder United Meth. Ch.; cons., lectr. in field; specialist adolescent suicide. Author: (newspaper column) Family Talk, 1976—80, (book of poetry) Sidewalks of Fog, 1962, Poems of the Spirit, 1970, A Portable Ark, 1978, The Wreckage of Christianity, 2001, The Lord's Prayer, 2002, The Sadducean Rag and Other Critical Poems, 2004; editor: Stepparents: Living, Loving and Learning, 1977. Del. Dem. Nat. Conv., Miami, Fla., 1972. Cpl. U.S. Army Air Corps, 1945—49, ETO. Mem.: Am. Assn. Marriage and Family Therapists (clin.), Acad. Am. Poets, Poetry Soc. Am. Avocations: poetry, gardening. Home: 506 3rd St Brandon FL 33511

HALSEY, ASHLEY, III, newspaper editor; b. Phila., Aug. 4, 1952; s. Ashley Jr. and Margaret (Woods) H.; m. Laura Jean Ketchum, Apr. 14, 1984; children: Graham Ketchum Halsey, Ellery Ketchum Halsey. BA, Temple U., 1974. Reporter Germantown Courier, Phila., 1972, sports editor, 1973, mng. editor, 1975-77; reporter Phila. Bull., 1977-79, Phila. Inquirer, 1980-81, nat. corr., 1982-85, asst. nat. editor, 1985-86, dep. nat. editor, 1986-88, dep. fgn. editor, 1989-91, nat. editor, 1991-96, travel editor, 1996-97; asst. city editor Washington Post, 1997-98, dep. Md. editor, 1999, Md. editor, 1999—. Avocations: sailing, running. Office: The Washington Post 1150 15th St NW Washington DC 20071-0002 Office Phone: 202-334-6000. Business E-Mail: halseya@washingtonpost.com.

HALSEY, DOUGLAS MARTIN, lawyer; b. Warwick, R.I., 1953; s. Donald Post Jr. and Marita H.; m. Amy Klinow, Sept. 5, 1976; children: Mark, Meredith. BA, Columbia U., 1976; JD cum laude, U. Miami, 1979. Bar: Fla. 1979, U.S. Ct. Appeals (11th cir., 5th cir.), U.S. Dist. Ct. (so. dist., mid. dist.) Fla. Assoc. Paul & Thomson, Miami, Fla., 1979-85; ptnr. Thomson, Bohrer, Werth & Razook, Miami, 1985-88, Douglas M. Halsey, P.A., Miami, 1989-97, Halsey & Burns, P.A., Miami, 1997-2000, White & Case LLP, Miami, 2000—. Rsch. editor U. Miami Law Review, 1978-79. Mem. Alexis de Tocqueville Soc., United Way of Miami-Dade County, 1995—; chmn-.Children's Home Soc. Fla., 2000-2002; chmn. Foster Care Rev., Inc., Miami, Fla., 1998-2000. Mem. Fla. Bar (chmn. environ. and land use law sect. 1993-94, President's Pro Bono Svc. award 1991). Office: Wachovia Fin Ctr 200 S Biscayne Blvd Ste 4900 Miami FL 33131-2352 Office Phone: 305-371-2700. E-mail: dhalsey@whitecase.com.

HALSEY, JAMES ALBERT, entertainer, theater producer; b. Independence, Kans., Oct. 7, 1930; s. Harry Edward and Carrie Lee (Messick) H.; m. Minisa Crumbo; children: Sherman Brooks, Gina, Cris, Woody. Student, Independence Community Coll., 1948-50, U. Kans.; doctorate of Fine Arts honoris causa, Baker Univ., 1992. Pres. Thunderbird Artists, Inc., Independence, from 1950, Jim Halsey Co., Inc., Tulsa, from 1952, Norwood Advt. Agy., James Halsey Property Mgmt. Co., Tulsa Proud Country Entertainment, Stas. KTOW/KGOW, J.H. Radio Mgmt., Cyclone Records, Tulsa Records, J.H. Lighting and Sound Co., Singin' T Prodns.; v.p. Gen. Artists Corp., Beverly Hills, Calif., 1966; chmn., chief exec. officer Century City Artists Corp., Tulsa, Nashville; personal mgr. various entertainment personalities; pres. Internat. Fedn. Festival Orgns.; mgr. Oakridge Boys, 1975. Internat. jurist Golden Orpheus Festival, Bulgaria, 1981-82, 84, 88, 94; ptnr. Billboard Song Contest; cons. William Morris Agy., 1990-95; producer shows for auditoriums, fairs, rodeos, TV, internat. music fests also others in U.S. and internationally including Tulsa Internat. Music Festival, 1977-80, Neewollah Internat. Music Festival, 1981-83; gen. ptnr. Parker Ranch, Tulsa; bd. dirs. Merc. Bank and Trust, Tulsa, Citizens Nat. Bank, Independence, Farmers & Mchts. Bank, Mound City, Kans., Nashville Symphony; chmn. mus. bus. dept. Okla. City U., 1994—; lectr., speaker colls., univs., 1992—. Trustee Philbrook Art Ctr., Tulsa; bd. dirs. Thomas Gilcrease Mus. Assn., Tulsa Philharm. Assn., Roy Clark Celebrity Golf Classic, UNICEF, Nashville Symphony, Nat. Music Coun. Served with U.S. Army, 1954-56. Recipient Disting. Service award U.S. Jr. C. of C., 1959, Ambassador of Country Music award SESAC Corp., 1978, citation Cashbox Mag., 1980, citation Golden Orpheus Festival, 1982, Hubert Long award Wembley Festival, Eng., 1982, commendation Los Angeles Mayor Tom Bradley, Gov.'s medal Kans. Commn., 1986, Frederic Chopin medal Polish Artist Bur., 1987, Lifetime Achievement award Internat. Buyers Assn., 1997, Okla. Govs. award for excellence art and edn., 1998, Cherokee medal of honor Cherokee Hist. Soc., 1999; named Disting. Kansan Topeka Capital Jour.; inductee Okla. Music Hall of Fame, 2000. Mem. Country Music Assn. (bd. dirs. 1963-64, 70-71, v.p. 1979-80, Founding Pres.'s award 1985), Acad. Country Music (bd. dirs. 1969-70, 73-74, v.p. 1975-76, 78-79, 79-80, 88-89, Jim Reeves Meml. award 1977), Internat. Fedn. Festival Orgns. (Am. pres., Oscar Midem award 1982). Home: 720 N 136 Rd Mounds OK 74047-5275

HALSEY, MARTHA TALIAFERRO, Spanish language educator; b. Richmond, Va., May 5, 1932; d. James Dillard and Martha (Taliaferro) H. AB, Goucher Coll., 1954; MA, U. Iowa, 1956; PhD, Ohio State U., 1964. Asst. prof. Spanish Pa. State U., University Park, 1064—1970, assoc. prof., 1970—79, prof., 1979—95, prof. emeritus, 1995—. Vis. Olive B. O'Connor prof. lit. Colgate U., Hamilton, NY, 1983. Author: Antonio Buero Vallejo, 1973, Dictatorship to Democracy: the Recent Plays of Buero Vallejo (La Fundación to Música cercana), 1994; editor: Madrugada, 1969, Hoy es fiesta, 1978, Los inocentes de la Moncloa, 1980, El engañao, Caballos desbocaos, 1981, (with Phyllis Zatlin) The Contemporary Spanish Theater: A Collection of Critical Essays, 1988, Entre actos: Diálogos sobre teatro español entre siglos, 1999, Estreno, 1992-98; gen. editor Estreno Contemporary Spanish Plays, 1992-98, Estreno Studies in Contemporary Spanish Theater, 1998—; mem. editl. bd. Modern Internat. Drama, 1968-75, Ky. Romance Quar., 1970-76, Annals Contemporary Spanish Lit., 1991—, Tesserae: Jour. Iberian and Latin Am. Studies, 1997—; contbr. articles to profl. jours. Grantee Am. Philos. Soc., 1970, 78, Inst. for Arts and Humanistic Studies, 1977, Program Cultural Coop. Between Spanish Ministry Culture and U.S. Univs., 1992, 94-95. Fellow Hispanic Soc. Am. (hon.); mem. MLA, N.E. MLA, Am. Assn. Tchrs. Spanish and Portuguese, Fellowship of Reconciliation, War Resisters League, Phi Beta Kappa, Phi Sigma Iota, Sigma Delta Pi. Democrat. Episcopalian. Home: 500 E Marylyn Ave Apt I-140 State College PA 16801-5248 Office: Pa State U Dept Spanish University Park PA 16802

HALSNE-BAARDA, ALANA MICHELLE, secondary school educator; b. Park Ridge, Ill., Nov. 18, 1971; d. Howard Osmund and Karen Diane Halsne; m. Brent Eric Baarda, May 31, 2002. BS, Ariz. State U., 1993; MA, Northeastern Ill. U., Chgo., 1998; EdD, Loyola U. Chgo., 2002. Cert. tchr., sch. adminstr. Ill. Tchr. Wickenburg H.S., Ariz., 1994—95; summer sch. tchr. Adlai E. Stevenson H.S., Lincolnshire, Ill., 1996—2002, Dist. 211/Palatine H.S., Ill., 2003; adj. prof. Am. Intercontinental U., Hoffman Estates, Ill., 2003—, Coll. of Lake County, Grayslake, Ill., 1997—; tchr. Warren Twp. H.S. #121, Gurnee, Ill., 1995—. Textbook reviewer Thomson Pub., Mason, Ohio, 2002—. Contbr. articles to profl. jours. Dance tchr. Granwood Pk. Dist., Gurnee, 1996—97; swim coach Gurnee Pk. Dist., 1996—; Sun. sch. tchr. St. Gilbert Ch., Grayslake, 2000. Mem.: ASCD, Nat. Bus. Edn. Assn., Phi Delta Kappa. Republican. Roman Catholic. Avocation: scuba diving. Office: Warren Twp High School 500 N O'Plaine Rd Gurnee IL 60031 Office Phone: 847-599-4660. Personal E-mail: abaarda@wths.net.

HALSTEAD, EDWARD ALLEN (TED HALSTEAD), think-tank executive; b. Chgo. Grad., Dartmouth Coll.; Master's Degree, Harvard U. Exec. dir. Redefining Progress, 1993—99; pres., CEO New Am. Found., Washington, 1999—. Spkr. in field; media commentator in field. Co-author (with Michael Lind): The Radical Center: The Future of American Politics; contbr. articles to newspapers. Named Global Leader for Tomorrow, World Econ. Forum, Davos, Switzerland; Montgomery fellow. Mem.: Phi Beta Kappa. Office: New Am Found 7th Fl 1630 Connecticut Ave NW Washington DC 20009

HALSTON, DANIEL WILLIAM, lawyer; b. Mineola, N.Y., Sept. 19, 1960; s. James Matthew and Mary Rita (Magner) H.; m. Liliane Regina Wong, Sept. 27, 1986. BA with honors, Vassar Coll., 1982; JD cum laude, Boston U., 1986. Bar: Mass. 1986, U.S. Dist. Ct. Mass. 1987, U.S. Ct. Appeals (1st cir.) 1987. Law clk. Judge William G. Young, U.S. Dist. Ct. Mass., Boston, 1986-87; assoc. Hale & Dorr, Boston, 1987—91; asst. atty. gen. Office of Mass. Atty. Gen., 1991-94; assoc. Hale & Dorr, Boston, 1994—98, ptnr., 1998—2004; ptnr., Securities dept. & Litigation dept., chmn. Hiring com. Wilmer Cutler Pickering Hale & Dorr, Boston, 2004—. Instr. Boston U. Sch. Law, 1989-90. Contbr. articles to profl. jours. Dir. Mass. Appleseed Ctr. for Law & Justice. Edward G. Hennessey scholar Boston U., 1983-86; named a Mass. Super Lawyer, Boston Mag., 2004. Mem. ABA, Mass. Bar Assn., Boston Bar Assn. (contbr. Boston Bar Assn. Handbook for the Homeless, 1987-88). Democrat. Roman Catholic. Avocations: reading, golf, basketball, travel. Office: Wilmer Cutler Pickering Hale & Dorr 60 State St Boston MA 02109-1816 Office Phone: 617-526-6654. Office Fax: 617-526-5000. Business E-Mail: daniel.halston@wilmerhale.com.

HALSTRÖM, FREDERIC NORMAN, lawyer; b. Boston, Feb. 26, 1944; s. Reginald F. and Margaret M. (Graham) H.; divorced, 1989, m. Lena Strelnikova, 2001; children: Ingrid Alexandra, Reginald Frederic II, Mikhail Strelnikova. Student, Northeastern U., 1961-63, USAF Acad., 1963-65; AB, Georgetown U., 1967; JD, Boston Coll., 1970. Bar: Mass. 1970, U.S. Dist. Ct. Mass., 1971, U.S. Dist. Ct. R.I. 1981, U.S. Tax Ct., 1981, U.S. Ct. Appeals (1st cir.) 1971, U.S. Ct. Appeals (11th cir.) 1991. Assoc. Schneider and Reilly, P.C., Boston, 1970-73; ptnr. Parker, Coolter, Daley and White, Boston, 1973-78; prin. Halström Law Office, Boston, 1978—. Spl. prosecutor Dist. Atty., Norfolk County, 1969-70; spl. asst. city solicitor City of Quincy, 1980. Editor Mass. Law Quar., 1972; contbr. articles to profl. jours. Fellow Boston Coll. Law Sch., v.p. 1988-91, pres. 1991—, benefactor Frederic N. Halström Nat. Moot Ct. Team. Mem. ABA (chmn. products liability com. gen. practice sect. 1980-85, award of achievement young lawyers divsn. 1978, vice chmn. taxation on ins. cos. sect. 1986-88), Assn. Trial Lawyers Am. (gov. 1981-84, 87—), state del. 1976-78, 86-87, chair various coms.), Mass. Acad. Trial Attys. (co-chmn. tort law sect. 1980—, bd. of govs. 1976—, sec. 1987-88, pres.-elect 1995-96, pres. 1996-97), Mass. Bar Assn. (pres. young lawyers divsn. 1977-78, bd. dels. 1978-80), Middlesex County Bar Assn., Mass. Trial Lawyers Assn. (mem/ Bd. of Govs., 2001—), Trial Lawyers Pub. Justice (sustaining founder, v.p. 1989—), Thomas F. Lambert Jr. Endowed Chair Trust), Algonquin Club. Home: 483 River Rd Carlisle MA 01741-1873 Office: 132 Boylston St Boston MA 02116-4616 Fax: 617-426-4791. Office Phone: 800-442-9855. E-mail: FHalstrom@aol.com.

HALTED, MARGO, music educator; b. Bakersfield, Calif., Apr. 24, 1938; d. Anthony Charles and Rose Louise (Buzan) Armbruster; m. A. Stevens Halsted, Sept. 12, 1959 (div. 1987); children: Suzanne, Christopher; m. Peter LeSourd, July 21, 2002. BA, Stanford (Calif.) U., 1960, MA, 1965, U. Calif., Riverdale, 1975; diploma, Netherlands Carillon Sch., 1981. Cert. tchr. Calif. Assoc. carillonneur Stanford (Calif.) U., 1967—77; lectr. U. Calif., Riverside, 1977—87; from asst. to assoc. prof. U. Mich., Ann Arbor, Mich., 1981, assoc. prof. Cons. in field. Musician: various recitals internationally. Recipient Berkeley medal, U. Calif., 1959, Bell and Citation award, World Carillon Fedn., 1986, 2003. Mem.: Guild of Carillonneurs in N.Am. (sec., com. chmn., del., Extraordinary Svc. cert. 1997), American Guild Organists, Coll. Music Soc., Am. Musicological Soc. Achievements include discovery of 2 historic carillon missions in Belgium. Avocations: skiing, languages, hiking. Home: 330 Cordova St # 324 Pasadena CA 91101-3602 Personal E-mail: margo@umich.edu.

HALTER, JON CHARLES, magazine editor, writer; b. Hamilton, Ohio, Nov. 24, 1941; s. Sam Lesher and Helen Louise (Olds) H.; m. Corina Garcia, Feb. 14, 1968; children: Jon Julian, Helen Margaret. BA, Syracuse U., 1964, MA, 1966. Vol. U.S. Peace Corps, Venezuela, 1966-68; asst. editor Nat. Petroleum News mag. McGraw-Hill Inc., N.Y.C., 1968-72; editor, writer Boys' Life mag. Boy Scouts Am., North Brunswick, N.J., 1972-79, Irving, Tex., 1979-90, exec. editor Scouting Mag., 1990-94; editor Scouting Mag., Irving, Tex., 1994—, Exploring Mag., Irving, Tex., 1994—98. Author: Bill Bradley: One to Remember, 1974, Reggie Jackson: All-Star in Right, 1975, Top Secret Projects of World War II, 1978, Their Backs to the Wall: Famous Last Stands, 1980 Mem. Soc. Profl. Journalists, Authors Guild. Democrat. Presbyterian. Avocations: reading, model building, walking. Home: 505 E Huitt Ln Euless TX 76040-5532 Office: Boy Scouts Am Scouting Mag PO Box 152079 1325 W Walnut Hill Ln Irving TX 75015-2079 Office Phone: 972-580-2367. E-mail: jchalter@yahoo.com.

HALTHORE, RANGASAYI NARAYAN, mechanical engineer, atmospheric scientist; b. Bangalore, Karnataka, India; came to U.S., 1977; s. Narayana Iyengar and Alamelu (Narayan) H.; m. Suman Narayan Halthore; children: Aditya, Maya. BE, Bangalore U., 1975; M of Engring with distinction, Indian Inst. Sci., Bangalore, 1977; PhD, Cornell U., 1984. Rsch. assoc. Cornell U., Ithaca, N.Y., 1983-84, SUNY, Stony Brook, 1984-86; scientist Applied Rsch. Corp., Landover, Md., 1986-89; chief scientist Hughes-STX Corp., Lanham, Md., 1989-95; mem. sci. staff Brookhaven Nat. Lab., Upton, N.Y., 1995—. Contbr. articles to profl. jours. Mem. Am. Geophysical Union. Office: Brookhaven Nat Lab DAS/ECD Upton NY 11973

HALTIWANGER, ROBERT SIDNEY, JR., book publishing executive; b. Winston-Salem, N.C., Mar. 15, 1923; s. Robert Sidney and Janie Love (Couch) H.; m. Marguarite C. LaBelle, Aug. 23, 1994. AB, Harvard U., 1947. Coll. field rep. Prentice-Hall Inc., Atlanta, 1947—56, Southeast regional mgr., 1956-65, dir. Two Year div. Englewood Cliffs, N.J., 1965-71; v.p. sales Prentice-Hall Inc, Englewood Cliffs, N.J., 1971-80, exec. v.p. coll. div., 1980-85, pres. sales and mktg. coll. div., 1985—. Cons. Simon & Shuster, 1988-89. Served to 1st lt. USAF, 1943-46, PTO. Recipient Chmn. award Gulf and Western, 1985, Frank Enenbach award Prentice-Hall Coll. Div., 1987. Mem. Am. Assn. Pubs. (liason com. 1975-82), Harvard Club (N.Y.C. chpt.), Knickerbocker Club. Democrat. Presbyterian. Home: 1 Horizon Rd Fort Lee NJ 07024-6502 Office: Prentice Hall Inc Englewood Cliffs NJ 07632 E-mail: bobhalti@aol.com.

HALTOM, MICHAEL FRED, religious studies educator, military officer; b. Dallas, June 22, 1950; s. Aubry Bennie and Margaret Tressie Haltom; m. Jean Anne Pressnall, Aug. 20, 1971; children: Michael David, Andrea Christina McGough. BA, Vennard Coll., 1977; MDiv, Western Evang. Sem., 1984. Ordained Assemblies of God, 1981. Asst. pastor First Evang. Meth. Ch., Duncanville, Tex., 1972—74; pastor Viola Cmty. Ch., Estacada, Oreg., 1974—78; prof. NT greek Eugene Bible Coll., Eugene, Oreg., 1978—85; v.p. World Evangelism Bible Coll. and Sem., Baton Rouge, 1985—88; chair bibl. studies divsn., prof. bibl. langs. Ctrl. Bible Coll., Springfield, Mo., 1988—. Chaplain USAFR, Travis Air Force Base, Calif., 1982—84, Kessler Air Force Base, Miss., 1985—88; wing chaplain Air N.G., Ft. Smith, Ark., 1989—. Editor: (editor) Beginner's New Testament Greek; author: (book) A Second Year Greek Grammar. Lt. col. USAF, 1982—2003. Decorated Meritorious Svc. metal, Air Force Commendation Medal with 3 oak leaf clusters USAF, Air Force Achievement Medal, Reserves Meritorious Svc. Medal with Hourglass and M device, Joint Meritorious Unit award, Armed Forces Svc. Medal USAF; named Outstanding Young Men Am., 1985; recipient Medal of Outstanding Merit, Soc. Mil. Orders World Wars, 1968. Mem.: N.G. Assn. (chaplain 1990—2002), Air Force Assn. (assoc.; chaplain 1982—88), Evang. Theol. Soc. (life). Republican. Mem. Assembly Of God Ch. Achievements include research in Text Types of Ancient Manuscripts. Avocations: travel, gardening, scuba diving. Office: Central Bible College 3000 North Grant Ave Springfield MO 65781 Business E-Mail: fhaltom@cbcag.edu.

HALTOM, WILLIAM H., lawyer; b. Memphis, June 10, 1952; BA, U. Tenn., 1975, JD, 1978. Bar: Tenn. 1978, U.S. Supreme Ct. 1982. Ptnr. Thomason, Hendrix, Harvey, Johnson & Mitchell PLLC, Memphis. Former editor-in-chief of barrister, assoc. editor: Tenn. Bar Jour., humor columnist:. Fellow: Tenn. Bar Found., Am. Bar Found.; mem.: ABA (chmn. bd. editors ABA Jour.), Tenn. Bar Assn. (pres.-elect 2004), Memphis Bar Assn. (pres.), Phi Delta Phi, Omicron Delta Kappa. Office: Thomason Hendrix Harvey Johnson & Mitchell PLLC 29th Fl One Commerce Sq 40 S Main St Memphis TN 38103 Office Phone: 901-577-6128. E-mail: haltom@thomasonlaw.com.

HALVER, JOHN EMIL, nutritional biochemist; b. Woodinville, Wash., Apr. 21, 1922; s. John Emil and Helen Henrietta (Hansen) Halver; m. Jane Loren, July 21, 1944; children: John Emil, Nancylee Halver Hadley, Janet Ann Halver Fix, Peter Loren, Deborah Kay Halver Hanson. BS, Wash. State U., 1944, MS in Organic Chemistry, 1948; PhD in Med. Biochemistry, U. Wash., 1953. Plant chemist Assoc. Frozen Foods, Kent, Wash., 1946-47; asst. chemist Purdue U., 1948—49; instr. U. Wash., Seattle, 1949—50, affiliate prof., 1960—75; prof. U. Wash. Sch. Fisheries, 1978—92; prof. emeritus U. Wash., 1992—. Condr. research on vitamin and amino acid requirements for fish; identified aflatoxin B1 as specific carcinogen for rainbow trout hematoma; identified vitamin C2 for fish; dir. Western Fish Nutrition Lab. U.S. Fish and Wildlife Service, Dept. Interior, Cook, Wash., 1950—75, sr. scientist, nutrition, Seattle, 1975—78; cons. FAO, UNDP, Internat. Union Nutrition Scientists, Nat. Fish Research Inst., Hungary, World Bank, Euroconsult, UNDP, IDRC; affiliate prof. prof. U. Oreg. Med. Sch., 1965—69; vis. prof. Marine Sci. Inst. U. Tex., Port Aransas; pres. Fisheries Devel. Technology, Inc., 1980—90, Halver Corp., 1978—. Lay leader Meth. Ch., 1965—70. Capt. U.S. Army, World War II, col. USAR. Decorated Purple Heart, Bronze Star with oak leaf cluster, Meritorious Service Conduct medal. Fellow: Am. Inst. Nutrition, Am. Inst. Fishery Research Biologists; mem.: NAS, Hungarian Acad. Sci., World Aquaculture Soc., Am. Fishery Soc., Am. Chem. Soc., Am. Sci. Affiliation, Soc. Exptl. Biol. Medicine, Rotary, Alpha Chi Sigma, Pi Mu Epsilon, Phi Lambda Upsilon. Achievements include founder JE Halver Fellowship at University of Washington; founder JE Halver Lecture at Washington State University. Home: 16502 41st Ave NE Seattle WA 98155-5610 Office: U Wash Box 355100 Sch Fisheries and Aquatic Scis Seattle WA 98195-5100 Office Phone: 206-543-9619. Business E-Mail: halver@u.washington.edu.

HALVERSTADT, DONALD BRUCE, urologist, educator; b. Cleveland, July 6, 1934; s. Lauren Oscar and Lillian Frances (Jones) H.; m. Margaret Ann (Marcy), Aug. 4, 1956; children: Donna, Jeffrey, and Amy. BA magna cum laude (hon.), Princeton U., 1956; MD cum laude (hon.), Harvard U., 1960. diplomate Am. Bd. Urology. Intern, then resident in surgery Mass. Gen. Hosp., Boston, 1960—62, resident in urology, 1964—67; pvt. practice medicine specializing in urology Okla City, 1967; chief pediatric urology svc. Okla. Children's Meml. Hosp., Okla. City, 1967; clin. prof. urology and pediat. U. Okla. Med. Sch., 1970; chief staff Okla. Children's Meml. Hosp., Okla. City, 1974—79; interim provost U. Okla. for Health Sci., Okla. City, 1979—80; CEO State of Okla. Tchg. Hosp., 1980—83; spl. asst. to pres. for Hosp. affairs Okla. U., 1980—84; vice chair dept. urology U. Okla. Med. Sch., 1982; bd. dir. State of Okla. Tchg. Hosp.; CEO State Regents for Higher Edn., 1988—93. Mem. U. Okla. Bd. Regents, 1993-2000, (chmn. 1999); founder, vice chmn., dir. Lincoln Nat. Bank, Oklahoma City, 1984-2003; bd. dir. BancFirst of Okla., 2004-. vice chair bd. gov. Okla. Med. Ctr. Hosp. Sys., 1998—; bd. dir. Triad Hosp., Inc., chair compliance com., 2000—, nominating com. Contbr. articles to med. journals. Vice chair bd. gov. Univ. Health Ptnrs.; pres., chmn. bd. Okla. Ind. Phys. Svc. Corp., 1986-96; trustee Columbia Presbyn. Hosp., 1990-96, chmn., 1995-96; bd. dir. Nat. Assn. Basketball Coaches FDTN; athletic dir. adv. coun. U. Okla., 2003. Fellow ACS; mem. AMA (Physicians Recognition Award 1969, 72, 79, 82, 85, 91, 94, 96, 99, 2002), Am. Urol. Assn., Am. Acad. Pediat., Soc. Pediat. Urology, Am. Soc. Nephrology, Soc. Univ. Urologists, So. Med. Assn., Okla. Med. Assn., Okla. County Med. Soc., Okla. State Regents for Higher Edn., Am. Coll. Physician Exec., Assn. Governing Bd. Coll. and Univ. (bd. dir., sec. 1996-97, treas. 1997-98). Presbyterian. Office: 711 Stanton L Young Blvd #707 Oklahoma City OK 73104-5023 Home: 2932 Lamp Post Ln Oklahoma City OK 73120-6105 Business E-Mail: donald-halverstadt@ouhsc.edu.

HALVERSTADT, ROBERT DALE, mechanical engineer, metals manufacturing company; b. Warren, Ohio, Jan. 25, 1920; s. Roscoe B. and Dorothy (Grubbs) Halverstadt; m. Maryella Green, Dec. 31, 1941; children: Marta Jean Halverstadt Carmen, Linda Anne Halverstadt Orelup, Sally Jo Halverstadt Ham. BS in Mech. Engring., Case Inst. Tech., 1951. Registered prof. engr., N.Y., Ohio. Journeyman machinist Republic Steel Corp., Cleve., 1939-51; design engr. GE, Evendale, Ohio, 1951-53; supr. Metalworking Lab., 1953-58; corp. cons. N.Y.C., 1958—59; mgr. Thomson Engring. Lab., Lynn, Mass., 1959—63; gen. mgr. engring. Continental Can Co., N.Y.C., 1963—64; group v.p. Booz, Allen & Hamilton Inc., N.Y.C., 1964-73; CEO Foster D. Snell Inc. subs., N.Y.C., 1964-73; pres. Design and Devel., Inc. subs., N.Y.C., 1966-73; mng. officer BA&H Environ. Resources Group (ERG), 1970—73; v.p. tech. Singer Co., N.Y.C., 1973-74; pres. Spl. Metals Corp. subs. Allegheny Ludlum Industries, Inc., New Hartford, N.Y., 1974-82, Materials Tech. Group, New Hartford, 1980—85; mng. dir. Allegheny Ludlum Industries Ltd., New Hartford; sr. staff v.p. Allegheny Internat., New Hartford, 1983-85; pres. AIMe Assocs., New Canaan, Conn., 1985—. Co-chmn. Titanium Metals Corp. Am., 1980—83; dir. Oneida Nat. Bank, 1979—80, Carus Corp., 1980—, Centrex Lab., 1975—80; mem. adv. bd. Flexmedics, Inc., 1982—92; chmn. bd. Spl. Metals Corp., 1987—2000, chmn. bd. emeritus, 2000—01. Mem. editl. bd.: Internat. Jour. Turbo and Jet Engine Tech. Pres. industry, labor and edn. coun. Mohawk Valley, Inc., 1975—80. Lt (j.g.) USCGR, 1942—45. Recipient Jubilee of Victory medal, Govt. France, 1996, Cert. Recognition, Govt. France & Normandy, 2001. Fellow: Am. Soc. Metals (past treas., bd. dirs., Disting. Life mem. 2002); mem.: ASME, Univ. Club (N.Y.C.), Woodway Country Club, Theta Tau, Tau Beta Pi, Sigma Xi. Mem. United Ch. Of Christ. Achievements include patents in field. Office Phone: 917-816-6468. Office Fax: 203-544-9237.

HALVORSEN, CLAY A., lawyer, construction executive; BA in Economics, Calif. State U., 1982; JD, U. So. Calif., 1985. Bar: Calif. Atty. Gibson, Dunn & Crutcher, 1985—95, ptnr., 1995—97; v.p., gen. counsel, sec. Standard Pacific Corp., Costa Mesa, Calif., 1998—2001, sr. v.p., gen. counsel, sec., 2001—04, exec. v.p., gen. counsel, sec., 2004—. Mem.: Calif. State Bar Assn. Office: Standard Pacific Corp 15326 Alton Pkwy Irvine CA 92618-2338*

HALVORSEN, OLE ANDREAS, financier; b. Apr. 1961; m. Diane Halvorsen; 3 children. Grad., Norwegian Naval Acad., Williams Coll., 1986; MBA, Stanford Grad. Sch. Bus., 1990. Investment banker corp. fin. and merger dept. Morgan Stanley; sr. mng. dir., dir. equities Tiger Mgmt. Corp., 1992—99; co-founding ptnr., mng. dir., chief investment officer Viking Global Investors, LP, 1999—. Mem. Williams Coll. Com. Spl. Strategies. Platoon comdr. Norwegian Navy Seal Team. Office: Viking Capital Ptnrs Inc 133 River Rd Cos Cob CT 06807-2539 Office Phone: 203-861-7300.

HALVORSEN, ROBERT ALFRED, JR., radiologist, educator; b. N.Y.C., Oct. 12, 1948; s. Robert Alfred and Dorothy Deeble (Stalcup) H. BS in Chemistry, U. Miami, 1970, MD, 1974. Rotating intern St. Mary's Med. Ctr., Long Beach, Calif., 1974-75; resident in radiology U. Tex., San Antonio, 1977-80, instr., 1980; fellow ABD imaging Duke U., Durham, N.C., 1980-81, from asst. prof. to assoc. prof., 1981-87; assoc. prof. U. Minn., Mpls., 1987-90; prof., vice-chmn. radiology and medicine U. Calif., San Francisco, 1990—; chief radiology San Francisco Gen. Hosp. Vice chmn. IPA, 1994-98; mem. steering com. County Info. Sys. Network. Contbr. numerous papers to sci. jours., 15 book chpts. Alternate del. Rep. Party, Mpls., 1989. Cadet USCG, 1966-67. Fellow Am. Coll. Radiology, Soc. Emergency Radiologists (chmn. program com. 1995-96, exec. com. 1995-98, 2d v.p., 1997-98); mem. Soc. Computed Body Tomography and Magnetic Resonance (chmn. standards com. 1993-95), Soc. Gastrointestinal Radiology (Roscoe Miller award for best paper 1989), Assn. Univ. Radiologists (exec. com. 1990-95, chmn. Stauffer award com. 1993-95), Calif. Med. Assn. (alt. del. ho. dels. 1998—), San Francisco Med. Assn. (bd. dirs. 1998—). Avocation: sailing. Home: 56 Issaquah Dock Sausalito CA 94965-1325 Office: San Francisco Gen Hosp Dept Radiology 1001 Potrero Ave San Francisco CA 94110-3594

HALVORSON, GEORGE CHARLES, health care insurance company executive; b. Fargo, N.D., Jan. 28, 1947; s. George Charles and Barbara Theone (Johnson) H.; m. Mary Elizabeth Probst, June 27, 1986; children: Jonathan Dale, Seth Gregory, George Charles IV, Michael Thomas. BA, Concordia Coll., Moorhead, Minn., 1968. Cert. health cons., 1981. Successively mgr. market rsch., mgr. corp. planning, dir. planning and budget, v.p. planning and budget, sr. v.p. Blue Cross & Blue Shield, St. Paul, 1968-76; exec. dir. HMO Minn., St. Paul, 1976-83; pres. Sr. Health Plan, St. Paul, 1983-86, Health Accord, Inc., Mpls., 1983-86, Group Health, Inc., Mpls., 1986—2002; chmn., CEO Kaiser Permanent, 2002—. Ops. dir. HMO/Jamaica, Kingston, 1985-86; cons. AIG/Am. Internat. Health, Washington, 1987-88; lectr. in field. Author: How to Cut Your Company's Health Care Costs, 1987; contbr. articles to profl. jours. Chmn. Boy Scout Food Drive, St. Paul, 1988; fund raiser United Way, Mpls., 1987-88. Recipient Internship award Wall St. Jour. Newspaper Fund, 1968. Mem. Nat. Coop. Bus. Assn. (bd. dirs.), Minn. Bus. Partnership (bd. dirs.), Group Health Assn. Am., Minn. Council HMO's (bd. dirs.), Decathlon Club (Bloomington, Minn.), Mpls. Club. Avocations: writing, hunting, chess. Address: Kaiser Permanente Oakland 1 Kaiser Plaza Oakland CA 94612 Office Phone: 510-271-5910.

HALVORSON, NEWMAN THORBUS, JR., lawyer; b. Detroit, Dec. 17, 1936; s. Newman Thorbus and Virginia Westbrook (Markle) H.; m. Sally Clark Stone, May 3, 1969; children: Christina English, Charles Burgess Westbrook. AB, Princeton U., 1958; LLB, Harvard U., 1961. Bar: Ohio 1962, D.C. 1963, U.S. Supreme Ct. 1965. Assoc. Covington & Burling, Washington, 1962-70; asst. U.S. atty. Office of U.S. Atty., Washington, 1983-85; assoc. ind. counsel (spl. prosecutor under Ethics in Govt. Act), 1987-90; ptnr. Covington & Burling, Washington, 1970—83, 1985—2002, sr. counsel, 2002—. Editor, Harvard Law Rev., 1960-61; author: Intermediate Sanctions Regs: Many Questions Remain, Tax Notes, 1998. Sr. warden, Jr. warden, vestryman Christ Ch. Georgetown, Washington, 1983-86, 89-92, chmn. fin. com., 1992-96; bd. dirs. Lupus Found. D.C., 1974-85; mem., bd. dirs. Eugene and Agnes E. Meyer Found., Washington, 1976-91, chmn., 1989-90, asst. sec./treas., 1990—; trustee Hist. Soc. Washington, 1995—2004, chmn. investment com., 1999—2004, chmn. audit comm., 2001—04, vice chmn., 2003-04; bd. dirs. Coun. for Ct. Excellence, Washington; trustee Potomac Sch., McLean, Va., 1980-86, chmn., 1981-83; mem. com. of 100 on Federal City, 1970—, trustee, treas., 1975-79; bd. trustees, mem. exec. com. Greater Washington Rsch. Ctr., 1997-2001; trustee Cleveland Park Hist. Soc., 1997—, pres. 2002-03; dir. Rosedale Conservancy, 2002-03; bd. govs. Coord. Coun. Internat. Univs, 2001—; mem. devel. com. Washington Nat. Cathedral, 2003-. With USMCR, 1961-67. Mem. ABA, D.C. Bar, Met. Club (Washington), Chevy Chase (Md.) Club. Republican. Episcopalian. Home: 3500 Lowell St NW Washington DC 20016-5025 Office: Covington & Burling 1201 Pennsylvania Ave NW Washington DC 20004-2401

HAM, ELDON, lawyer; b. Kewanee, Ill., Feb. 28, 1952; m. Nan Weiss, May 7, 1977; children: Carla, Brandon. BS in Fin., U. Ill., 1974; JD, Chgo.-Kent Coll. Law, 1976. Assoc. Palmer Blackman & Mancini, Park Ridge, Ill., 1976—79; ptnr. Marcus Esses & Ham, Chgo., 1979—84, Ham & Pawlan, Chgo., 1984—89, Zucker & Ham, Northbrook, Ill., 1989—92; pvt. practice Chgo., 1992—. Co-founder Gameplan, Inc., Northbrook, 1992—2002. Author: The 100 Greatest Sports Blunders, 1997, The Playmasters, 2000, Larceny and Old Leather: The Mischievous Legacy of Major League Baseball, 2005. Mem. freshman campus trans. com. New Trier H.S., 2001; founder Loyola Sports Symposium for H.S. Athletics; dir., pres. Ill. Hemophilia Found., Chgo., 1983—89; co-chmn. Attys. for an Unbiased Election Day, Chgo., 1978. Mem.: ABA, Chgo. Bar Assn., Ill. Bar Assn. Avocations: reading, writing. Office: Eldon L Ham PC 30 N LaSalle Ste 2140 Chicago IL 60602

HAM, KAREN, musician, music educator; b. Bklyn., Apr. 13, 1952; d. Irving and Eva (Walker) H. AA, Staten Island Coll., 1974; BA, CUNY, 1978; MA, NYU, 1983; student in piano, French Conservatory Music, N.Y.C., 19905. Tchr. Assn. Black Social Workers, Bklyn., 1978-85, Bklyn. Music Sch., 1985-87; tchr., condr. Holy Innocents Sch., Bklyn., 1985—. Dir. choir and music ensemble, keyboard classes. Roman Catholic. Avocations: research of american songwriters, american musical films. Office: Holy Innocents Sch 249 E 17th St Brooklyn NY 11226-4601 Personal E-mail: kar595@aol.com.

HAM, ROBERT NORRIS, choral director, educator; b. Logansport, Ind., Aug. 27, 1954; s. Robert S. and Lorraine (Broadwater) H.; m. Marilynn Joy McConnell, Aug. 20, 1977; children: Norris Samuel, Meryl Joy. B.M.E., No. Mich. U., 1976, M.M.E., 1978. Music tchr. Brookwood High Sch., Ontario, Wis., 1977-79; asst. prof. music Friends Bible Coll., Haviland, Kans., 1979—, chmn. ch. music dept., 1979—, chmn. faculty, 1982-84, dir. community chorus, 1981-83. Chmn. music com. Haviland Friends Ch., 1979—, minister, 1985—. Named Prof. of Yr., Friends Bible Coll., 1982. Mem. Am. Choral Dirs. Assn. Mem. Soc. of Friends. Avocations: fishing; hunting; swimming; boating; coin collecting. Office: Friends Bible Coll PO Box 288 Haviland KS 67059-0288

HAM, SOMMY L., publisher, writer; b. Houston, Sept. 12, 1953; 5. Robert Steele Jr. and Nellie (McGuinness) Gray; child by previous marriage: Laura Ann; m. Robert E. Ham Jr., Feb. 14, 1986 (div. June 1996); children: Mark, Katie, Jeffrey. AA with honors, Houston C.C., 1994; student, U. Houston, 1994-95. V.p. adminstrn. Cordovan Corp. Pubs., Houston, 1975-82; advt. rep. Golfer Mags., Inc., Houston, 1983-88, gen. mgr., 1996-97, pub., 1997—2001; editor Tomball-Magnolia Tribune, Magnolia, Tex., 2001—03; pres. Sommy's Ink Profl. Comms., 2003—. Editor: Houston Sports Car News, 2004—. Mem. city coun., Magnolia, 2003—05. Houston C.C. scholar, 1993, Alice B. Rogers scholar Advt. Fedn. Houston, 1995-96 Mem. Women in Comms., Exec. Women's Golf Assn., Romance Writers Am. (conf. co-chair N.W. chpt. 1995, treas.), Phi Theta Kappa. Avocation: journalism.

HAMAD, KHALED, research scientist, educator; m. Yasmin Almzainy; 1 child, Noor. BCE, An-Najah Nat. U., Nablus, West Bank, 1996; MCE, U. Del., 2000, PhD in Civil Engring., 2004. Asst. instr. Islamic U. Gaza, Palestine, 1996—98; tchg. and rsch. asst. U. Del., Newark, 1998—2004; asst. rsch. scientist Tex. Transp. Inst., San Antonio, 2004—. Cons. Universal Group for Engring. and Consulting, Gaza, 1996—98; civil engr. Del. Dept. Transp., Dover, 2003—03. Contbr. articles to profl. jours. Pres. Civil Engring. Club, Nablus, Palestine, 1995—96. Fulbright scholar, U.S. Dept. State, 1998—2000, Grad. Assistantship, U. Del., 2000—04. Mem.: ASCE (assoc.), Inst. Transp. Engrs. (assoc.). Achievements include patents pending for new prediction, hybrid method that combines the use of the Empirical Mode Decomposition (EMD) and a multilayer feedforward neural network with backpropagation; development of innovative, simplified methodology for forecasting vehicular traffic demand in Developing Countries; integrated GPS/GIS method for collecting travel time data. Office: Texas Transportation Institute Ste 315 3500 NW Loop 410 San Antonio TX 78229 Office Phone: 210-731-9938. Personal E-mail: k-hamad@tamu.edu.

HAMADA, DUANE TAKUMI, architect; b. Honolulu, Aug. 12, 1954; s. Robert Kensaku and Jean Hakue (Masutani) H.; m. Martha S.P. Lee, Dec. 22, 1991; children: Erin, Robyn, David. BFA in Environ. Design, U. Hawaii, 1977, BArch, 1979. Registered architect, Hawaii, Guam, Florida, Puerto Rico, Saipan. Intern Edward Sullam, FAIA & Assocs., Honolulu, 1979-80; assoc. Design Ptnrs., Inc., Honolulu, 1980-86; prin. AM Ptnrs., Inc., Honolulu, 1986-98, Design Ptnrs. Inc., Honolulu, 1998—. Chmn. 31st Ann. Cherry

Blossom Festival Fashion Show, Honolulu, 1982, 32d Ann. Cherry Blossom Festival Cooking Show, 1983, mem. steering com., 1982, 83. Recipient Gold Key award for Excellence in Interior Design Am. Hotel and Motel Assn., 1990, Renaissance '90 Merit award Nat. Assn. Home Builder's Remodeler Coun., Merit award Honolulu mag., 1990, Cert. of Appreciation PACDIV USN, 1992, Gold Nugget award of Merit, 1997, Design Excellence Concept Design award USAF Hawaii, 2003, Pub. Govt. New Project award NAIOP, 2005 Mem. AIA (jury student awards 1997, 98, jury profl. awards 1999), Constrn. Specifications Inst., Nat. Coun. Archtl. Registration Bds., Colegio de Arcquitectos de P.R Avocations: astronomy, music. Office: Design Ptnrs Inc 1580 Makaloa St Ste 1100 Honolulu HI 96814-3240 E-mail: dhamada@hawaii.rr.com.

HAMADA, RICHARD, computer company executive; B in Fin., San Diego State U. Various positions Avnet Computer, 1983—94; v.p. mktg. Hall-Mark Computer Products (now Avnet Hall-Mark), 1994—97; exec. v.p. Avnet Computer (now Avnet Enterprise Solutions), 1998—99; corp. v.p. Avnet, Inc., 1999, sr. v.p., 2000—; pres. Avnet Hall-Mark, N.Am., 2000—02, Avnet Computer Mktg. (now Avnet Tech. Solutions), 2002—. Named one of Top 25 Most Influential Execs. in Computer Industry, Computer Reseller News mag., 2002. Office: Avnet Inc 2211 South 47th St Phoenix AZ 85034

HAMADA, ROBERT S(EIJI), dean, educator, economist, entrepreneur; b. San Francisco, Aug. 17, 1937; s. Horace T. and Maki G. Hamada; children: Matthew, Janet. BE, Yale U., 1959; SM, MIT, 1961, PhD, 1969. Economist Sun Oil Co., Phila., 1961—63; instr. U. Chgo., 1966—68, asst. prof. fin., 1968—71, assoc. prof., 1971—77, prof., 1977—89, Edward Eagle Brown prof., 1989—93, Edward Eagle Brown Disting. Svc. prof., 1993—2003, Edward Eagle Brown Disting. Svc. prof. emeritus, 2003—, dir. Ctr. for Rsch. in Security Prices, 1980—85, dir. Ctr. Internat. Bus. Edn. and Rsch., 1992—94, dep. dean for faculty Grad Sch. Bus., 1985—90, dean, 1993—2001; CEO, dir. Merchants' Exchange, 2001—02. Vis. prof. univs. including London Bus. Sch., 1973, 79-80, UCLA, 1971, U. Wash., Seattle, 1971-72, U. B.C., Vancouver, Can., 1976; bd. dirs. A.M. Castle & Co., Fleming Cos., Inc., No. Trust Corp., Fed. Signal Corp.; pub. dir. Chgo. Bd. Trade, 1989-2000; cons. numerous fin. instns., banks, mfg., mgmt. cons., acctg. and law firms. Past assoc. editor Jour. Fin., Jour. Fin. and Quantitative Analysis, Jour. Applied Corp. Fin.; cons. editor Scott, Foresman & Co. fin. series; contbr. numerous articles to profl. jours. Bd. dirs. numerous non-profit orgns., including Hyde Park Neighborhood Club, Chgo., Harper Ct. Found., Chgo., Hyde Park Co-op, U. Chgo. Lab. Schs., Window to the World, Inc. (WTTW-TV), Terra Found. for the Arts. Named to 8 Outstanding Bus. Sch. Profs., fortune Mag., 1982; recipient 1st Outstanding Tchr. award, Grad. Sch. Bus., U. Chgo., 1970, McKinsey Tchg. prize, 1981; Sloan Found. fellow, 1959—61, Ford Found. fellow, 1963—65, Standard Oil Found. fellow, 1965—66, MIT scholar, 1959—61, Yale scholar, 1955—59. Mem. Am. Fin. Assn. (bd. dirs. 1982-85), Econometric Soc., Nat. Bur. Econ. Rsch. (bd. dirs., mem. investment and exec. coms.), Am. Econ. Assn. (investment com.), Inst. Mgmt. Scis. (investment com.), Tau Beta Pi. Office: U Chgo Grad Sch Bus 1101 E 58th St Chicago IL 60637-1511 Office Phone: 773-834-1369. Business E-Mail: robert.hamada@gsb.uchicago.edu.

HAMAI, JAMES YUTAKA, manufacturing executive; b. Oct. 14, 1926; s. Seizo and May (Sata) H.; m. Dorothy K. Fukuda, Sept. 10. 1954; children: Wendy A. BS, U. So. Calif., 1952; MS, 1955; postgrad. bus. mgmt. program ind. exec., UCLA, 1963-64. Lectr. chem. engring. dept. U. So. Calif., L.A., 1963—64; process engr., sr. process engr. Fluor Corp., L.A., 1954—64; sr. project mgr. ctrl. rsch. dept. Monsanto Co., St. Louis, 1964—67, mgr. rsch., devel. and engring. graphic sys. dept., 1967—68; mgr. comml. devel. New Enterprise, 1968—69; exec. v.p., dir. Concrete Cutting Industries, Inc., L.A., 1969—72; pres., dir. Concrete Cutting Internat. Inc., L.A., 1972—78, chmn. bd., 1978—; pres., CEO, dir. Techno Enterprises U.S.A., Ltd., L.A., 2000—04, Cons. Fluor Corp., Los Angeles, 1970-72; dir. Intech Systems Co., Ltd., Tokyo, Cutting Industries Co., Ltd., Tokyo; internat. bus. cons. Served with AUS, 1946-48. Mem. AIChE, Am. Mgmt. Assn., Tau Beta Pi, Phi Lambda Upsilon. Club: Rotary (gov. dist. 1982-83). Home: 6600 Via La Paloma Rancho Palos Verdes CA 90275-6449 Office: PO Box 700 Wilmington CA 90748-0700

HAMAMOTO, PATRICIA, school system administrator, educator; b. Honolulu, Sept. 30, 1944; BA in History, profl. tchg. diploma, Calif. State Coll., Long Beach, 1967; education administrator's cert., U. Hawaii M, 1985. Social studies tchr. Fountain Valley H.S., Calif., 1967—72; social studies tchr., dept. chair Iiima Intermediate Sch., Ewa Beach, Hawaii, 1976—81; tchg. grad. asst. geography dept. U. Hawaii at Manoa, 1981—83; tchr. guidance/math. Pearl City H.S., Hawaii, 1985; vice prin. Maui H.S., Kahlui, Hawaii, 1983—85, Nanakul H.S. and Intermediate Sch, Nanakuli, Hawaii, 1985—87; prin. Pearl City Highlands Elem. Sch, Hawaii, 1987—89; pers. specialist ii Office Personnel Svcs. Contract Adminstrn., Honolulu, 1989—91; prin. Pres. William McKinley H.S., Honolulu, 1992—99; dep. supt. Hawaii Dept. Edn., Honolulu, 1999—2001, interim supt., 2001; supt. of edn. Hawaii Dept Edn., Honolulu, 2001—. Mem.: ASCD, Pacific Resources for Edn. and Learning, Coun. of Chief State Sch. Officers, Nat. Assn. Secondary Sch. Prins. Avocations: golf, reading, travel, walking. Home: 1767 Puowaina Dr Honolulu HI 96813 Office: Hawaii Dept Edn PO Box 2360 Honolulu HI 96804-2360 Office Phone: 808-586-3310. E-mail: patricia_hamamoto@notes.k12.hi.us.

HAMAN, RAYMOND WILLIAM, retired lawyer; b. St. Maries, Idaho, Jan. 22, 1927; s. William and Eva Kate (Colliver) H.; m. Phyllis Maxine Garrett, June 24, 1948; children: Lorinda Ann, Bradley Lawrence (dec.). Student, Whitman Coll., 1947-49; JD, Washington and Lee U., 1952. Bar: Wash., 1952, U.S. Dist. Ct. (we. dist.) Wash. 1952, U.S. Ct. Appeals (9th cir.), U.S. Supreme Ct. Assoc. Evans, McLaren, Lane, Powell & Beeks, Seattle, 1952-59, ptnr., 1959-66, Lane Powell, Seattle, 1966-89, 1989-91, of counsel, 1991-2001; ret. Legal counsel Gov. Daniel J. Evans, Olympia, Wash., 1965, 67; mem. statute Law Com., 1966-95, chmn. 1988-95. Trustee, past pres. Lighthouse for the Blind, Inc., Seattle, 1964—; mem. vestry St. Augustine's Episcopal Ch., 1999—2002; bd. dirs. Mercer Island (Wash.) Sch. Dist., 1967—72, Island County (Wash.) United Way, 1993—, pres., 1997—98. With USMC, 1945—46, PTO. Mem. Wash. Bar Assn., Order of the Coif. Republican. Episcopalian. Home: PO Box 926 Langley WA 98260-0926 Office: Lane Powell PC 1420 5th Ave Ste 4100 Seattle WA 98101-2338

HAMAN, SARAH ARMSTRONG, librarian; b. Atlanta, Dec. 25, 1949; d. James Blanding and Margaret Ann (Hill) H.; m. Benjamin M. McKelway III, Mar. 20, 1971 (div. 1974); m. Thomas Harry Clegg, June 24, 1992 (div. 2001); children: Sage Mirrim Clegg-Haman, Heather Anne Clegg-Haman. Student, William & Mary Coll., 1968-70, City Coll. San Francisco, 1974-75; AA, Mendocino Coll., 1990; BA, Sonoma State U., 1999; MLIS, San Jose State Sch. Libr. and Info. Sci., 2001. Libr. clk. Mendocino County Libr., Willits, Calif., 1979-84; instrnl. asst. Sherwood Sch., Willits, 1985-87; elem. libr. Brookside Sch./Baechtel Grove Middle Sch., Willits, 1987—2000; reference libr. Mendocino County Libr., 2000—04; virtual libr., 2001—; trainer/lab. asst. Infopeople, 2004—05; adj. faculty Santa Rosa Jr. Coll., 2005; ref. mgr. Humboldt County Pub. Libr., 2005—. Calif. Sch. Employee's Assn. rep. Willits (Calif.) Unified Sch. Dist. Adv./Budget Com., 1991-93. Bd. mem. Willits (Calif.) Young Actors Theater, 1992-95, sec., 1993-95. Mem.: AAUW, Calif. Libr. Assn., Beta Phi Mu. Democrat. Avocations: reading, bicycling, walking, directing plays. Office Phone: 707-269-1930.

HAMARMAN, STEPHANIE, psychiatrist, educator; b. Phila., Jan. 23, 1964; d. Harry H. and Anne C. H. BA, U. Pa., 1985, MD, 1993. Instr. psychiatry Hosp. U. Pa., 1993-96, Children's Hosp. Phila., 1996-98; med. dir. outpatient child & adolscent psychiatry N.J. Med. Sch., Newark, 1998—2004, asst. prof. psychiatry, 1998—2004; chief psychiatry Lamm Inst., Bklyn., 2004—. Co-author: (chpt.) Child Abuse, 2000; contbr. articles to profl. jours. Recipient Child Psychiatry award Group Advancement Psychiatry, 1997-98. Mem. Am. Acad. Child and Adolscent Psychiatry (prevention com. 2000—, task force child rsch. 1998-2000, Resident Leadership Achievement award 1995, scholar 1997-98, rsch. grantee for child rsch. 2001), Am. Acad. Psychiatry and Law (Rappeport com. 2000-02), Am. Psychiat. Assn., Am. Profl. Soc. on Abuse of Children, Am. Assn. Acad. Psychiatry (Rappeport fellow 1996-97), Nat. Assn. Counsel for Children, N.Y. Psychiat. and Child Psychiatris Assn. Office: Lamm Institute 110 Amity St Brooklyn NY 11201 Office Phone: 718-780-1595. Business E-Mail: shamarman@chpnet.org.

HAMARNEH, SAMI KHALAF, historian, writer; b. Madaba, Jordan, Feb. 2, 1925; came to U.S., 1952, naturalized, 1957; s. Khalaf and Nura A. (Zumut) H.; m. Nazha T. Ajaj, July 4, 1948; 1 son, Faris. BSc in Pharmacy, Syrian U., Damascus, 1948; MSc in Pharm. Chemistry, N.D. State U., Fargo, 1956; PhD in History of Pharmacy and Medicine, U. Wis., 1959; DLitt (hon.), Hamdard U., Karachi, Pakistan, 1998. Curator charge divsn. med. scis. Mus. History and Tech., U.S. Nat. Mus., Smithsonian Instn., Washington, 1959-72; historian dept. sci. and tech. Nat. Mus. Am. History U.S. Nat. Mus., Smithsonian Instn., 1972-77; curator emeritus Mus. History and Tech., U.S. Nat. Mus., Smithsonian Instn., 1977—; prof. history Islamic med. scis. King Fahd Med. Rsch. Ctr./Abdulaziz U., Jeddah, Saudi Arabia, 1982-83; med. historian faculty medicine Allied Sci. Sch. Pub. Health/Yarmouk U., Irbid, Jordan, 1984-86; prof. U. Jordan, Amman, 1987-90; prof. Islamic medicine Internat. Inst. Islamic Thought and Civilization, Kuala Lumpur, Malaysia, 1993-99; ret., 1999. Vis. assoc. prof. George Washington U., 1963-64; vis. prof. history of sci. U. Pa., Phila., 1969; vis. prof. U. Aleppo, Syria, 1977-79; spl. research med. scis., profl. ethics and edn. in medieval Islam. Author: Ward Min Shawk, 1950, Customs and Civilizations in Bible Lands - Genesis, 1960, Bibliography of Medicine and Pharmacy in Medieval Islam, 1964, Index of Arabic Manuscripts on Medicine and Pharmacy at the National Library of Cairo, 1967, Index of Manuscripts on Medicine and Pharmacy in the Zahiriyah Library, 1969, Temples of the Muses and a History of Pharmacy Museums, 1972, Origins of Pharmacy and Therapy in the Near East, 1973, The Physician, Therapist and Surgeon Ibn al-Quff, 1974, Catalogue of Arabic Manuscripts on Medicine and Pharmacy at Brit. Library, 1975, Islamic Bicentennial Exhibition - A Guide Book, 1976, Directory of Historians of Arabic-Islamic Science, 1980, Pharmacy Museums USA, 1981, Health Scis. in Early Islam, Collected Papers, 2 vols., 1983-85, Background of History of Arabic Medicine and Allied Sciences, 1986, Promises, Heritage and Peace, 1986, Introduction on Al-Biruni's Book on Precious Stones, 1988, Ibn al-Quff al-Karaki's Book on the Preservation of Health, 1989, Ibn al-Quff al-Karaki's on Surgery, 1994, Directory of Historians of Islamic Medicine and the Allied Sciences, 1995, Yunani (Greek) Arabic-Islamic Medicine and Pharmacy During the Golden Age, 1997; editor: Jour. History Arabic Sci, 1976-80; mem. adv. bd. Hamdard Medicus, 1980—; contbr. articles to profl. jours. Recipient Star of Jordan medal, 1965; E. Kremers award for distinguished pharmaco-hist. writings, 1966, Citation of Merit, U. Wis., 1997. Mem. Inst. History Arabic Sci. (founding mem. 1976), Am. Inst. History Pharmacy (pres. 1979-81), Arab Soc. for History Pharmacy (Cairo) (founding mem. 1976), Arab Acad. of Damascus (corr. mem.), Al-al-Bayt for Islamic Thought. Home: 4631 Massachusetts Ave NW Washington DC 20016-2361 E-mail: fham@erols.com.

HAMARSTROM, PATRICIA ANN, director, animation/multimedia specialist; b. Kans. City, Mo., Aug. 13, 1952; d. Harold Melchor and Nettie Ann (Wussow) H.; m. John D. Williams, Mar. 10, 1972 (div. 1980): 1 child, Jeffrey D. MFA, U. Mo., Kansas City, Mo., 1981; PhD, U. Tex., Richardson, Tex, 1988. Exec. prodr. video and prodn. mgr. Multi-Image Resources, Inc., Dallas, 1982-85; pres., CEO Hamar Prodns., Inc., Dallas, 1985-97; dir. sch. design & media arts Ill. Inst. Art, Chgo., 1997—. Mem. sr. faculty in computer animation/multimedia Art Inst. Dallas, 1985-97; guest lectr./dramaturg Dallas Theatre Ctr., 1985-91; lectr. U. Tex., Richardson, 1985-88; dir. Playwrighting Program New Arts Theatre, Dallas, 1983-85; founder, pres. Chgo. S.I.G.G.R.A.P.H. Dir. plays, including: The King and I, 1985, Othello, Shakespeare in the Pk., 1988, Long Day's Journey Into Night, Nat. Theatre Yugoslavia, 1988-92; prodr., translator, adapter play: A Tomb for Boris Davidovich, 1986; prodr., dir., screenwriter films: Long Day's Journey Into Night, 1988, Tom, Dick and Harry, 1990, A Tomb for Boris Davidovich, 1991, Dance of the Tigers, 1992, Texas Women, 1992; organizer, artistic dir. Women's Performance and Art Festival, 1991-94. Del. Dem. Nat. Conv., Kansas City, Mo., 1976, Dem. State Conv., Houston, 1992; bd. dirs. Addison Ctr. Theatre, 1984-88; mem. Adv. Bd. Humanities Forum, Dallas Theatre Ctr., 1986-87; chairperson tech. com. Art Inst. Dallas; U.S. cultural rep. to Yugoslavia USIA, 1988. Mem. SIGGRAPH, ACM, AAUW, Internat. TV Assn., Am. Ctr. for Design, Women in Film, Assn. of Theatre In Higher Edn., Am. Film Inst., Women in Animation, Assn. of Multimedia Communicators. Avocations: yoga, computer, music, movies, singing.

HAMAS, ROBERT STEVEN, plastic surgeon; b. Cleve., Mar. 9, 1946; s. Steve and Matilda (Girman) H.; children: Wendy, Kevin, Reagan. BA, Coll. Wooster, Ohio, 1967; MD, Ohio State U., 1971. Diplomate Am. Bd. Plastic Surgery. Surg. intern Mt. Carmel Hosp., Columbus, Ohio, 1971-72; gen. surgery resident U. Tex. Med. Br., Galveston, 1972-73; hand surgery fellow U. N.Mex., Albuquerque, 1974, Grace Hosp., Detroit, 1974-75; resident in plastic surgery U. Pitts., 1977-79; pvt. practice Dallas, 1979—. Faculty U. Tex. Southwestern Med. Ctr., Dallas, 1995—; instr. endoscopic surgery courses (various), 1993—. Contbr. articles to profl. jours.; prodr./writer: Endoscopic Plastic Surgery (videotape), 1995, 97. Bd. dirs. Life Anew Adoption Agy., Paris, Tex., 1987-92. Maj. USAF, 1975-77. Fellow ACS; mem. Am. Soc. Plastic and Reconstructive Surgery, Am. Assn. Accreditation Ambulatory Surgery Facilities (newsletter editor 1995-97), Dallas Soc. Plastic Surgery (pres. 1989-91, sec.-treas. 1986-89), Am. Soc. Aesthetic Plastic Surgery. Avocation: travel. Office: 8345 Walnut Hill Ln Ste 120 Dallas TX 75231-4214 Office Phone: 214-363-1073.*

HAMBARTSOUMIAN, EDOUARD, obstetrician, researcher, embryologist; b. Erevan, Armenia, Sept. 29, 1955; arrived in U.S., 1995; s. Martin Andreas Hambartsoumian and Raya Magaki Stepanian; children: Lily, Vahakn. MD (hon.), Erevan (Armenia) Sch. Medicine, 1981; cert. in fetal medicine, U. Paris, 1994. Chief ob-gyn. dept Aragats Dist. Hosp., Tsakhkahovit, Armenia, 1981—85; chief ob-gyn. dept Erebouni Hosp., Erevan, Armenia, 1985—88, Maternity #3, Erevan, Armenia, 1988—93; scientist Hosp. Antoine Belcere, Paris, 1993—95; sr. scientist Boston U./Fertility Ctr. New England, 1995—. Embryologist Fertility Ctr. New England, Boston, 2000—01. Contbr. articles to profl. jours. Organist local ch. Named Honorary Inventor of USSR, Governement of USSR, 1978; grantee Travel grant, NIH, 1997. Mem.: Soc. Study Reprodn. (assoc.). Avocation: music. Home: 18 Wensley St Boston MA 02120 Office: Fertility Ctr New England 20 Pond Meadow Dr Reading MA 01867 Personal E-mail: hambartsoumian@hotmail.com.

HAMBIDGE, DOUGLAS WALTER, archbishop; b. London, Mar. 6, 1927; emigrated to Can., 1956; s. Douglas and Florence (Driscoll) H.; m. Denise Colvill Lown, June 9, 1956; children: Caryl Denise, Stephen Douglas, Graham Andrew. Assoc. London Coll. Divinity, London U., 1953, BD, 1958, DD, 1969. Ordained deacon Church of England, 1953, priest, 1954, consecrated bishop, 1969; asst. curate St. Mark's Ch., Dalston, London, 1953-55, priest-in-charge, 1955-56; incumbent All Saints Ch., Cassiar, B.C., Can., 1956-58; rector St. James Parish, Smithers, B.C., 1958-64, North Peace Parish, Ft. St. John, B.C., 1964-69; canon St. Andrew's Cathedral, 1965; lord bishop of Caledonia, 1969-80, New Westminster, B.C., 1980-81; lord archbishop of New Westminster and metropolitan of B.C., 1981-93; prin. St. Mark's Theol. Coll., Dar es Salaam, Tanzania, 1993-95; asst. bishop Diocese of Dar es Salaam, Dar es Salaam, 1993-95. Mem. Anglican Consultative Coun., 1985-93; chancellor Vancouver Sch. Theology, 1999. Anglican. E-mail: hambidge@vst.edu.

HAMBLEN, LAPSLEY WALKER, JR., judge; b. Chattanooga, Tenn., Dec. 25, 1926; s. Lapsley Walker Sr. and Libby (Shipley) H.; m. Claudia Royster Terrell, Mar. 20, 1971; children by previous marriage: Lapsley Walker III, Allen M., William Shipley. BA, U. Va., 1949, LLB, 1953. Bar: W.Va. 1954, Ohio 1955, Va. 1957. Trial atty. IRS, Atlanta, 1955; atty. advisor U.S. Tax Ct., 1956; ptnr. Caskie Frost Hobbs & Hamblen and predecessor firms, Lynchburg, Va., 1957-82; dep. asst. atty. gen. tax divsn. U.S. Dept. Justice, 1982; judge U.S. Tax Ct., Washington, 1982-92, chief judge, 1992-94, 94-96, sr. judge, 1996-2000, ret., 2000. Former trustee So. Fed. Tax Inst.; former co-dir. ann. conf. on fed. taxation U. Va. Served with USN, 1945-46. Fellow: Am. Bar Found., Am. Coll. Trust and Estate Counsel, Am. Coll. Tax Counsel; mem.: Raven Soc., Phi Alpha Delta, Omicron Delta Kappa, Order of the Coif. Presbyterian.

HAMBLETON, GEORGE BLOW ELLIOTT, retired management consultant; b. Balt., Dec. 20, 1929; s. John Adams Hambleton and Margaret (Elliott) Carey; m. Janet Findlay MacLaren, Mar. 17, 1962 (dec. 1991); children: Anne Carey, Charles MacLaren, James Elliott; m. Diana Lea Walker, June 29, 1998. AB, Princeton U., 1952; cert. program for mgmt. devel., Harvard U., 1964. Various positions with Latin Am. divsn. Pan Am, 1955—62, asst. mgr. svc. divsn. Miami, Fla., 1963—64, dir. USSR Moscow, 1966—70, dir. internat. affairs Washington, 1971—76, dir. comml. sales N.Y.C., 1977—80; v.p. mktg. N.Y. Airways, N.Y.C., 1976—77; exec. dir., vice chmn. Project Orbis, Inc., N.Y.C., 1980—83; pres. Andrews MacLaren, Inc., N.Y.C., 1983—86; dep. asst. sec., dep. dir. gen. U.S. and fgn. comml. svc. Dept. Commerce, Washington, 1986—88; sr. v.p. Mgmt. Internat. Inc., Westport, Conn., 1988—2001; ret., 2001. Bd. dirs. Flight Found., Inc., Washington, Andrews MacLaren Ltd., Northants, Eng. Dir. Fgn. Policy Discussion Group, Washington, 1975-96; mem. N.J. Conservation Found.; mem. adv. com. East-West Trade, U.S. Dept. Commerce, 1973-79; mem. dist. export coun. U.S. Dept. Commerce, Conn., 1989-93; bd. dirs. River Blindness Found., Houston, 1990-95, Coll. of the Atlantic, Bar Harbor, Maine, 1996—. 1st lt. U.S. Army, 1952-55, Korea. Mem. Upper Raritan Watershed Assn., Brook Club (N.Y.), Met. Club (Washington), Naval and Mil. Club (London), Md. Club (Balt.), Princeton Club (N.Y.), Essex Hunt Club (Far Hills, N.J.), Union Club (N.Y.), Harvard Bus. Sch. Club (Washington, v.p. 1973-76), Wings Club (N.Y.), Soc. Colonial Wars (N.Y.). Republican. Episcopalian. Avocations: flying, fishing, skiing, running, hunting. Home: 280 Pleasant Valley Rd Mendham NJ 07945-2920

HAMBLEY, DOUGLAS FREDERICK, geological and environmental engineer; b. Toronto, Ont., Can., Jan. 14, 1950; s. Fredrick Armstrong and Gwendolyn Shannon (Plant) H.; m. Sherrie Kate Barham Hambley, May 24, 1992 (div. June 2000); m. Paulette Julia Dyon, May 7, 2004. BS in Mining Engring., Queen's U., 1972; MBA, Lewis U., 1986; PhD in Earth Scis., U. Waterloo, Ont., Can., 1991. Registered profl. engr., Can., Ill., Va., Pa., Md., Wis., profl. geologist, Pa., Wis., Ill. Jr. engr. Iron Ore Co. of Can., Schefferville, Que., 1972-73; mining engr. trainee Falconbridge (Ont.) Nickel Mines, Ltd., Can., 1974-75; mining engr. Harrison Bradford & Assocs., Ltd., St. Catharines, Ont., 1975-76; project engr. Denison Mines, Ltd., Elliot Lake, Ont., 1977-80; sr. mining engr. Engrs. Internat., Inc., Westmont, Ill., 1980-84; mining engr. Argonne (Ill.) Nat. Lab., 1984-88; rsch. asst. U. Waterloo, Ontario, 1988; sr. cons. Dunn Geosci. Corp., West Chicago, Ill., 1989; civil/geol. engr. Argonne (Ill) Nat. Lab., 1990-91; mgr., geo-environtl. group Nova, Environtl. Svcs., Des Plaines, 1991; project mgr. Graef, Anhalt, Schloemer and Assocs., Inc., Chgo., Ill., 1992-2000; pvt. practice, 2000—; sr. cons. Practical Environ. Cons., Inc., Schaumburg, Ill., 2000—. Contbr. articles to profl. jours. Recipient Cert. of Appreciation, Office of Geologic Repositories, 1987, Ill. Dept. Profl. Regulation, 2000. Mem. Soc. Mining, Metallurgy and Exploration (chmn. Chgo. sect. 1987-88), Assn. Engring. Geologists (treas. N.C. sect. 1987-88), Can. Inst. Mining and Metallurgy, Assn. Groundwater Scientists and Engrs. (Brownfields task force, 2003—), Soc. Am. Mil. Engrs. (treas. Chgo. post 1996-97, 3rd v.p. 1998, 2d v.p. 1999, pres. 2000), Ill. Engring. Coun (dir. 1998, 2000-03, v.p. 1999), Cornish Am. Heritage Soc. (membership chmn., 2005—). Avocations: travel, cello, guitar, folk music. Home: 1404 Childs St Wheaton IL 60187-4602 Office: Practical Environ Cons 1305 Remington Rd Ste A Schaumburg IL 60173 Office Phone: 847-519-3430. Personal E-mail: dfhambley@comcast.net.

HAMBLIN, TIMOTHY ROBERT, music educator; b. Waterloo, N.Y., Apr. 26, 1966; s. Russel Wilson and Marilyn Jane Hamblin. MusB, Ithaca (N.Y.) Coll., 1988; MS, SUNY, New Paltz,NY, 1993. Cert. tchr. 1993, elem. edn. tchr. 1993. Music tchr. Liberty (N.Y.) Mid. Sch., 1988—. Pres. Liberty Faculty Assn., Liberty, NY, 1996—; music dir. Liberty (N.Y.) Meth. Ch., 1995—; musical dir. Bradstan Country Hotel Cabaret, White Lake, NY, 1998—. Mem.: N.Y. State Sch. Music Assoc. (piano adjucator 1998—), Am. Fedn. of Tchrs., N.Y. State United Tchrs. Avocations: reading, history, running. Home: 255 South Main Street Liberty NY 12754 Office: Liberty Middle School 145 Buckley Street Liberty NY 12754 E-mail: hamblintim@libertyk12.org.

HAMBRECHT, PATRICIA G., retail executive; b. New Orleans; m. George A. Hambrecht; children: Amanda, Elliot. B summa cum laude in History, Yale Coll., 1975; JD, Harvard U., 1978. Assoc. Hughes Hubbard and Reed; gen. counsel Christie's, 1988—95, mng. dir., 1995—97; pres. Christie's North and South Am., 1997—99, Harry Winston Inc., 2000—. Bd. dir. Internat. Found. of Art Rsch. Vol. Lawyers for the Arts; bd. dirs. N.Y.C. Ballet. Avocations: theater, ballet, opera, collecting 19th and 20th century drawings.

HAMBRICK, ERNESTINE, retired colon and rectal surgeon; b. Griffin, Ga., Mar. 31, 1941; d. Jack Daniel and Nannie (Harper) Hambrick Rubens. BS, U. Md., 1963; MD, U. Ill., 1967. Diplomate Am. Bd. Colon and Rectal Surgery, Am. Bd. Surgery. Intern in surgery Cook County Hosp., Chgo., 1967-68, resident in gen. surgery, 1968-72, fellow colon and rectal surgery, 1972-73, attending surgeon, 1973-74, part-time attending surgeon, 1974-80; pvt. practice colon and rectal surgery Chgo., 1974-97; pres. med. staff Michael Reese Hosp., Chgo., 1990-92, chief surgery, 1993-95; founder, chmn. STOP Colon/Rectal Cancer Found., 1997—. Mem. Nat. Colorectal Cancer Round Table, 1997—, steering com. 2000—. Contbr. articles to profl. jours. Trustee Rsch. and Edn. Found., Michael Reese Med. Staff, Chgo., 1994-98, treas., 1994-98. Fellow ACS, Am. Soc. Colon and Rectal Surgeons (v.p. 1992-93, trustee Rsch. Found. 1992-98), Am. Coll. Gastroenterology. Avocations: travel, photography, scuba diving, flying, writing. Office: PMB 133 47 W Division St Chicago IL 60610 Office Phone: 312-944-4636. Personal E-mail: ehcrson@aol.com.

HAMBRICK, GEORGE WALTER, JR., dermatologist, educator; b. Charlottesville, Va., Dec. 4, 1922; s. George W. and Sallie Anna (McCallum) H BS, Concord Coll., 1944; MD, U. Va., 1946. Intern Hosp. U. Iowa, 1946-47; asst. resident dermatology U. Va. Hosp., 1947-48; resident Columbia-Presbyn. Hosp., N.Y.C., 1950-51; fellow dermatology Duke U., Durham, NC, 1951-52, assoc. dermatology, 1953; instr. Columbia U., 1953-55, assoc., 1955-57, asst. prof., 1957-62; assoc. prof. U. Pa., 1962-66, Johns Hopkins U., 1966-69, prof., 1969-76, dir. dermatology Johns Hopkins Med. Inst., 1967-76; prof. U. Cin., 1976-81, dir. dermatology, 1976-81; prof. Cornell U. Coll. Medicine, 1981-96; chief dermatology N.Y. Hosp., 1981-96, prof emeritus, 1996—; sr. lectr. Columbia U., 2001—. Capt. AUS USMC, 1948—50. Fellow ACP; mem. AMA (del. 1981-90), Soc. Investigative Dermatology (pres. 1971-72, hon. mem.), Dermatology Found. (trustee, pres. 1974), Assn. Profs. Dermatology, Am. Dermatol. Assn. (hon.), Am. Acad. Dermatology (dir. 1978), Am. Skin Assn. (pres. 1988-93, 2000-), Alpha Omega Alpha. Office: Am Skin Assn 346 Park Ave S New York NY 10010 Office Phone: 212-889-4858.

HAMBRICK, JAMES L., chemicals executive; BS in Chem. Engring., Tex. A&M U. From various positions to pres. Lubrizol Corp., Houston, 1978—2003, pres. Wickliffe, Ohio, 2003—. Office: Lubrizol Corp 29400 Lakeland Blvd Wickliffe OH 44092

HAMBURG, CHARLES BRUCE, lawyer; b. Bklyn., June 30, 1939; s. Albert and Goldie (Blume) Hamburg; m. Stephanie Barbara Steingesser, June 23, 1962; children: Jeanne M., Louise E. B in Chem. Engring., Poly. Inst. Bklyn., 1960; JD, Geroge Washington U., 1964. Bar: NY 1964. Patent examiner U.S. Patent Office, 1960-63; patent atty. Celanese Corp. Am., NYC, 1963-65, Burns, Lobato & Zelnick, NYC, 1965-67, Nolte & Nolte, NYC, 1967-75; prin. C. Bruce Hamburg, NYC, 1976-79; ptnr. Jordan & Hamburg, L.L.P., NYC, 1979—. U.S. corr. Patents and Licensing, Japan, 1986—. Author: Patent Fraud and Inequitable Conduct, 1972, 78, Patent Law Handbook, 1983-84, 84-85, 85-86, Doctrine of Equivalents in U.S. (in Japanese), 1995, 2d edit. (in Korean), 1998; monthly columnist Patent and Trademark Rev., 1976-85; U.S. corr. Patents and Licensing, 1989—; contbr. chpts. to books. Mem.: ABA, Internat. Fedn. Intellectual Property Attys., Licensing Execs. Soc., Internat. Assn. Protection Intellectual Property, NY Intellectual Property Law Assn., Am. Intellectual Property Law Assn., Masons. Office: 122 E 42nd St New York NY 10168-0002 Office Phone: 212-986-2340. Business E-Mail: jandh@ipattorneys.com.

HAMBURG, DAVID A., psychiatrist, foundation administrator; b. Evansville, Ind., 1925; MD, Ind. U., 1947, D.Sc. (hon.), 1976, Rush U., 1977, Mt. Sinai Sch. Medicine, 1980, U. Rochester, 1981, U. Ill., Chgo., 1984, Albert Einstein Sch. Medicine, 1985, U. Pitts., U. So. Calif., Hahnemann U., 1986; LHD (hon.), Ramapo Coll., 1991, Duke U., 1993, So. Indiana U., 2000. Diplomate Am. Bd. Psychiatry and Neurology. Intern Michael Reese Hosp., Chgo., 1947-48, resident in psychiatry, 1949-50, Yale U.-New Haven Hosp., 1948-49; staff psychiatrist Brooke Army Hosp., San Antonio, 1950-52; practice medicine specializing in psychiatry, 1950-75; research psychiatrist Walter Reed Army Inst. Research, Washington, 1952-53; assoc. dir. Psychosomatic and Psychiat. Inst., Michael Reese Hosp., Chgo., 1954-56; fellow Center for Advanced Study in Behavioral Scis., Palo Alto, Calif., 1957-58, 67-68; chief Adult Psychiat. Br. NIMH, Bethesda, Md., 1958-61; prof., chmn. dept. psychiatry Stanford U. Med. Sch., 1961-72, Reed-Hodgson prof. human biology, 1972-76; Sherman Fairchild Disting. scholar Calif. Inst. Tech., Pasadena, 1974-75; pres. Inst. Medicine Nat. Acad. Scis., Washington, 1975-80; dir. div. health policy research and edn., John D. MacArthur prof. health policy and mgmt. Harvard U., Cambridge, Mass., 1980-82; pres. Carnegie Corp., N.Y.C., 1983-97, pres. emeritus, 1997—. Adv. com. med. rsch. WHO, 1975-86; mem. exec. panel adv. com. Chief of Naval Ops, 1984-92; chmn. sci. adv. bd. NIMH, 1986-87; sec. Energy Adv. Bd., 1990-94; mem. Ctr. for Naval Analysis, 1990-93. Author: No More Killing Fields: Preventing Deadly Conflict, 2002, Learning to Live Together: Preventing Hatred and Violence in Child and Adolescent Development, 2003. Bd. dirs. Rockefeller U., 1979—, Mt. Sinai Med. Ctr., N.Y.C., 1984—; trustee Stanford U., 1988-94, Internat. Devel. Rsch. Ctr., Ottawa, Ont., Can., 1990-94, Am. Mus. Natural History, N.Y.C., 1990—; co-chmn. Carnegie Commn. on Preventing Deadly Conflict, 1994-99; mem. Pres.'s Com. of Advisors on Sci. and Tech., 1994-2001; dep. chmn. Fed. Res. Bank N.Y., Def. Policy Bd., U.S. Dept. Def., 1994-95. Recipient numerous awards including: Pres.'s medal Michael Reese Med. Ctr., 1974, Peace award Cranbrook Found., 2003; A.C.P. award, 1977; MIT Bicentennial medal, 1976, Presdl. Medal of Freedom, 1996; Disting. Presdl. fellow for internat. activities Nat. Acads., 2002. Mem. Am. Psychiat. Assn. (Vestermark award 1977, Disting. Svc. award 1991, Pres.'s medal Bank St. Coll. 1994, Charter medallion Radcliffe Coll. 1994), Nat. Acad. Scis. (com. on internat. security and arms control 1981-86, Pub. Welfare medal 1998, Fgn. Policy Assocs. medal 2004), AAAS (pres. 1984-85, chmn. bd. 1985-86), Assn. Rsch. Nervous and Mental Disease (pres. 1967-68), Am. Philos. Soc., Am. Acad. Arts and Scis., Phi Beta Kappa, Alpha Omega Alpha. Office: NY Presbyterian Hosp Dept Psych 525 E 68th St Box 171 New York NY 10021 Office Phone: 212-746-3750.

HAMBURG, KARIN I., literature and language educator; b. Ludwigsburg, Germany, Jan. 14, 1951; arrived in U.S., 1955; d. Harry Guenther and Hilde Fanny Buehler; m. David Dean Hamburg, July 10, 1982; children: Erin, Alla. B, Augustana Coll., 1973; M, Western Ill. U., 1978; A, Am. Inst. Commerce, 1984. Tchr. English Orion High Sch., Ill., 1973—. Initiater advanced placement programs Orion High Sch., 1995—. Mem.: Iowa County Tchrs. English & Lang. Arts, Nat. Coun. Tchrs. English. Avocations: reading, music, travel. Office: Orion Sch Dist 1100 13 St Orion IL 61273

HAMBURGER, PHILIP ANDREW, law educator; b. 1957; BA in History, summa cum laude, Princeton U., 1979; JD, Yale U., 1982. Bar: Pa. 1982. Assoc. Schnader, Harrison, Segal & Lewis, Phila., 1982—85; assoc. prof. U. Conn. Sch. Law, 1985—88, prof., 1988—92; prof. law & legal history George Washington U. Nat. Law Ctr., 1992—95, Oswald Symister Colclough rsch. prof. law, 1995—2000; John P. Wilson prof. law U. Chgo. Law Sch., 2000—, also Herbert and Marjorie Fried rsch. scholar, dir. legal history program. Vis. assoc. prof. U. Va. Law Sch., 1986; vis. prof. George Washington U. Nat. Law Ctr., 1991—92, U. Chgo. Law Sch., 2000; Jack N. Pritzker disting. vis. prof. law Northwestern U. Sch. Law, 1999. Author: Separation of Church and State, 2002. Mem.: Am. Soc. Legal History (program com. chair 1993—94, mem. nominating com. 1998—2001, bd. dirs. 2004—, Sutherland Prize 1991, 1995), Am. Assn. Law Schools (chair provisional sect. on scholarship 1995). Office: U Chgo Law Sch 1111 E 60th St Chicago IL 60637 Office Phone: 773-834-4162. E-mail: philip_hamburger@law.uchicago.edu.

HAMBURGER, ROBERT N., pediatrician, educator, consultant; b. N.Y.C., Jan. 26, 1923; s. Samuel B. and Harriet (Newfield) H.; m. Sonia Gross, Nov. 9, 1943; children: Hilary, Debre (dec.), Lisa. BA, U. N.C., 1947; MD, Yale U., 1951. Diplomate Am. Bd. Pediatrics, Am. Bd. Allergy and Immunology. Instr., asst. clin. prof. sch. medicine Yale U., New Haven, 1951-60; assoc. prof. biology U. Calif. San Diego, La Jolla, 1960-64, assoc. prof. pediatrics, 1964-67, prof., 1967-90, prof. emeritus, 1990—, asst. dean sch. medicine, 1964-70, lab. dir., 1970-98, head fellows tng. program allergy and immunology divsn., 1970-90; pres., CEO RNA and Co., Inc., 1997—. Chmn., bd. dirs. BioVigilant Sys., Inc., 2002-; cons. various cos., Calif., Sweden, Switzerland, 1986—. Author 1 book; contbr. articles to profl. jours.; patentee allergy peptides, allergen detector. Vol. physician, educator Children of the Californias, Calif. and Baja California, Mex., 1993—, Baker Sch. Free Clinic, 1999—. 1st lt. Air Corps, U.S. Army, 1943-45. Grantee NIH and USPHS, 1960-64, 64-84; Fulbright fellow, 1980, Disting. fellow Am. Coll. Allergy, Asthma, Immunology, 1986. Mem. U. Calif. San Diego Emeriti Assn. (pres. 1992-94). Avocations: flying, skiing, writing. Office: U Calif San Diego Revelle Coll Sch Medicine La Jolla CA 92093-0950 Office Phone: 858-534-7555. E-mail: rhamburger@ucsd.edu.

HAMBURGER, SUSAN, librarian; b. Newark, N.J., Feb. 22, 1949; d. Francis Leo Murphy, Mildred Marie Schultz; m. Joseph Victor Hamburger. AB, Rutgers U., 1975, MLS, 1976; MA, Fla. State U., 1985, PhD, 1994. Cert. archivist. Assoc. univ. libr. Fla. State U., Tallahassee, 1981—89; archivist, head description sect. Va. State Libr. and Archives now Libr. of Va., Richmond, 1989—92; manuscripts cataloger U. Va., Charlottesville, 1992—93, Va. Hist. Soc., Richmond, 1993—94; manuscripts cataloging libr. Pa. State U., University Park, 1994—. Contbr. Book A Guide to the History of Florida, 1989, Book The American Civil War, A Handbook of Research and Literature, 1996 (One of Choice's 625 Outstanding Academic Books of 1997, 1998), Book Encyclopedia of Rural America: The Land and People, 1997 (One of Library Journal's 30 Best Reference Sources 1997, 1998), Book American Book and Magazine Illustrators to 1920 (Dictionary of Literary Biography, vol. 188), 1998, Multi-volume book American National Biography, 1999 (Dartmouth medal, 1999), Book Before the New Deal: Southern Social Welfare History, 1830-1930, 1999, Book Biographical Dictionary of Literary Influences: The Nineteenth Century, 1800-1914, 2001, Book Encyclopedia of New Jersey, 2004, Book Historical African Americans in Sports, 2004, Book Dictionary of Literary Influences: The Twentieth Century, 1914-2000, 2004. Mem.: Fla. Hist. Soc., N.Am. Soc. for Sport History (conf. co-mgr. 1998—99), Soc. Am. Archivists (liaison to ALA com. on cataloging: description and access 2000—04, Am. Archivist editl. bd. 2004—), Mid-Atlantic Regional Archives Conf. (chair publs. com. 1995—99, webmaster 1996—2005, Svc. award 1999, 2000, 2004), Phi Alpha Theta, Alpha Sigma Lambda. Avocations: organic gardening, guitar, selling vintage clothes, reading, cats. Office: Pa State Univ 126 Paterno Libr University Park PA 16802 Office Phone: 814-865-1755. Office Fax: 814-863-7293. Business E-Mail: sxh36@psulias.psu.edu.

HAMBURGER, SYDNEY K., sculptor; d. Sidney and Ruth Kahn; children: Sandy, Marjorie, Isaac, Sidney, Merle. Cert., Oxford U., Eng., 1973; BS in Sculpture, Magdalen Coll. Oxford U., Eng.; MEd, Towson State U., Md., 1973; HDFA, Hood Coll., frederick, Md., 1993. Exhibitions include Shidoni Gallery, Tesuque, N.Mex., 2001, 2002, 2003, 2004, Santa Fe C.C., 1999, 2001, 2002, 2003, 2004, Quietude Garden Gallery, East Brunswick, N.J., 1999, Westbeth Gallery, N.Y.C., 1999, Culture Gallery, 2001, Meguro Mus., Tokyo, 2001, Kapil Jariwala Gallery, London, 2002, 2003, 2004, Govs. Gallery, Santa Fe, 2002, N.Mex. Sculpture Guild, 2003, Bristol-Meyers Squibb, Princeton, N.J., 2003, 2004, Lewallen Gallery, Santa Fe, 2004, Linda Durham Gallery, 2004, James Kelly Gallery, 2004, numerous others, exhibited in group shows at Denise Bibro Fine Art, N.Y.C., 1999, Grounds for Sculpture, Hamilton, N.J., 2000, Chesterwood Mus., Stockbridge, Mass., 2000, numerous others, one-woman shows include Denise Bibro Fine Art, N.Y.C., 2000. Address: PO Box 953 Abiquiu NM 87510-0953

HAMBY, GENE MALCOLM, JR., lawyer; b. Florence, Ala., Mar. 23, 1943; s. Gene Malcolm Sr. and Katherine (Koonce) H.; m. Judy Priscilla Brown, Apr. 10, 1971; children: Mark Clifton, Anne Tyler. BS with great honor, U. North Ala., 1965; JD, U. Ala., Tuscaloosa, 1968. Bar: Ala. 1968, U.S. Dist. Ct. (no. dist.) Ala. 1972, U.S. Ct. Appeals (11th cir.) 1981. Assoc. Heflin & Rosser, Attys., Tuscambia, Ala., 1968-70; ptnr. Pitts & Hamby, Sheffield, Ala., 1970-80; pvt. practice Sheffield, 1981-84; ptnr. Hamby & Baker, Attys., Sheffield, 1984-87, Jones, Hamby & Baker, Attys., Sheffield, 1987-89; pvt. practice, Sheffield, 1989—. Bd. dirs. Shoals Indsl. Devel. Authority, Sheffield, 1985-91, Law Sch. Found., U. Ala. Sch. Law, 1985—, Ala. Archeol. Soc.; past dist. v.p. U. Ala. Alumni, Tuscaloosa; past pres. U. North Ala. Alumni, Florence, Colbert County United Way, Sheffield; chmn. Sheffield Indsl. Devel. Bd., Sheffield, Sheffield Edn. Found., 1992-96; past bd. dirs. United Cerebral Palsy NW Ala., Sheffield, Shoals Indsl. Devel. Authority. With USAR, 1968-74. Recipient Kiwanis Citizen of Yr. award City of Sheffield, 1991, 2001. Mem. ATLA, ABA, Colbert County Bar Assn (past pres.), Ala. State Bar Assn., Ala. Trial Lawyers Assn. (past mem. exec. com.), Sheffield Bus. and Profl. Assn. (pres. 1999-2001), Ala. Archaeol. Soc. (bd. dirs.), Kiwanis Club (past pres. Sheffield chpt.), Colbert County C. of C. (past pres.), Shoals Dem. Club (past pres.), Phi Kappa Phi Democrat. Avocation: indian artifacts. Home: PO Box 328 Sheffield AL 35660-0328 Office: 406 N Nashville Ave Sheffield AL 35660-2938 Office Phone: 205-381-7673. Personal E-mail: ham015@aol.com.

HAMBY, JENNIFER LYNNE, elementary school educator; b. Peoria, Ill., Nov. 4, 1977; BA in Elem. Edn., U. Las Vegas, 2000, MEd in Ednl. Leadership, 2003. Tchr. Clark County Sch. Dist., Las Vegas, 2000—. Mem.: NEA. Home: 2100 Gravel Hill St #106 Las Vegas NV 89117 Personal E-mail: jennifersk@aol.com.

HAMDAN, LAWRENCE ANISE, investment banker, lawyer; b. South Orange, N.J., Aug. 31, 1961; s. Ali A. and Dorothea E. (Nevola) H. AB magna cum laude, Princeton U., 1983; MBA with high distinction, JD magna cum laude, Harvard U., 1989. Bar: N.Y. 1990. Rsch. analyst Brown Bros. Harriman & Co., NYC, 1983-84; pres. FLYERS Svcs. Inc., Cambridge, Mass., 1985-89; assoc. Credit Suisse First Boston (formerly First Boston Corp.), NYC, 1989—98, mng. dir., vice chmn. global mergers & acquisitions, 1998—. Author: F.L.Y.E.R.S., 1985, Youth Trends, 1987. Baker scholar Harvard Bus. Sch., 1989. Mem. Phi Beta Kappa. Roman Catholic. Office: Credit Suisse First Boston Park Avenue Plz New York NY 10055-0002

HAMDI, HAMID S., neurologist and neurorehabilitation specialist, consultant researcher; b. Karachi, Sind, Pakistan, May 5, 1959; s. Mohammad Abul Aas, Habiba Bano Aas; m. Imrana Y. Hamdi, Mar. 26, 1959; children: Mia, Samiha. MBBS, Dow Medical College, Karachi, Pakistan, 1978—84. Medical Officer Civil Hospital and Dow Medical College, Karachi, Pakistan, 1986—88, Saudi Ministry of Health, Riyadh, Saudi Arabia, 1988—93; Resident Lincoln Medical Center, Bronx, NY, 1993—94; Resident in Neurology Nassau County Medical Center, East Meadow, NY, 1994—97; Fellow in Neurorehabilitation Hospital for Joint Diseases, New York, NY, 1997—99; clin. asst. prof. neurology Ind. U., 2003—. Cheif Resident in Neurology Nassau County Medical Center, East Meadow, NY, 1996—97; Faculty Member New York University School of Medicine, New York, NY, 1999—99; Visiting Lecturer Purdue University, West Lafayette, IN, 2000—01; clin. asst. prof. Ind. U. Sch. of Medicine, Ind.; Principal Investigator-KEEPER trial Heartland Neurology Associates, Lafayette, IN, 2000—01, Principal Investigator-Betaserone trial, 2000—01. Author: (Reveiw article) Neurocysticercosis- a reveiw., 1997; editor: (Periodical) NCMC Proceedings, 1996. Speaker National MS Society Indiana Chapter, West Lafayette, IN, 2000—00, Renssalaer, IN, 2001—01, Stroke Support Group, Lafayette, IN, 2001—01. Mem.: American Medical Association. Home: 3137 Covington street West Lafayette IN 47906 Office: Heartland Neurology Assocs 1345 Unity Pl #365 Lafayette IN 47905 Office Phone: 765-445-5300.

HAMDY, RONALD CHARLES, geriatrician; b. Alexandria, Egypt, July 31, 1946; came to U.S., 1985; s. Charles and Mary Hamdy; m. Eleanor Gertrude Hamdy, Aug. 19, 1977; children: Conrad, Gerard, Ronan. MB, ChB with honours, U. Alexandria, 1968, DM, 1971. Rotating intern U. Alexandria, 1968-69; resident in internal medicine Al-Gomhouriya Gen. Hosp., Alexandria, 1969-70; resident registrar internal medicine U. Alexandria Main Tchg. Hosp., 1970-72; sr. ho. officer geriatric and internal medicine Farnborough (Eng.) Hosp., Kent, 1972-73; registrar in geriatric medicine Bromley (Eng.) Group of Hosps., Kent, 1974; sr. registrar in geriatric medicine King's Coll. Group Hosps., London, 1975-77; consulting physician St. John's Hosp. Richmond (Eng.), Twickenham & Roehampton Health Authority, 1977-85, chmn. dept. clin. gerontology, ethics rsch. com., 1981-85; prof. internal medicine, Cecile Cox Quillen prof. geriatric medicine, head divsn. gerontology East Tenn. State U., Mountain Home, 1985—, Cecile Cox Quillen prof. geriatric medicine, head divsn. gerontology, 1990—, dir. osteoporosis ctr., 1997—; chief geriat. VA Med. Ctr., Mountain Home, 1985-88, assoc. chief of staff geriatric and extended care, 1988—2004. Hon. sr. lectr. geriatric medicine St. George's Hosp. Med. Sch., U. London, 1981-85; planning team for elderly Wandsworth Health Care, 1982-85; med. dist. initiated peer rev. orgn. VA Hosps., Dist. 8, 1986-89; vis. prof. Health Care for Elderly, U. London, 1991-93; Burroughs Wellcome vis. prof. geriatric medicine Royal Soc. Medicine, 1994-95; co-chmn. pharmacy and therapeutics com. VA Med. Ctr., Johnson City, Tenn., chmn. adverse drug reaction com.; chmn. program com. Coll. Medicine Continuing Med. Edn., East Tenn. State U.; mem. Gov.'s task force on Alzheimer's Disease, Tenn., task force on edn., prevention and detection of osteoporosis; mem. advisor to pub. guardian 1st Tenn. Devel. Dist.; adv. bd. Colonial Hill Health Care Ctr., Johnson City, Golden J-55, Johnson City Med. Ctr. Hosp., Inc.; sr. health adv. com. 1st Tenn. Regional Health Office; adj. clin. prof. divsn. clin. nutrition and psychiatry East Tenn. State U. Author: Diuretic Therapy in the Older Patient, 1978, Paget's Disease in Bone, Assessment and Management, 1981, Geriatric Medicine: A Problem Oriented Approach, 1984; editor: (with J. Turnbull, M. Lancaster, L. Norman) Alzheimer's Disease: A Handbook for Caregivers, 1990, 3d edit., 1998; mem. editl. adv. bd. Revs. Clin. Gerontology, South Med. Jour., Geriatria; reviewer for med. jours.; contbr. chpts. to books, articles to profl. jours. Fellow ACP (com. geriat. 1987-90, chmn. com. geriat. MKSAP IX 1991-94), Royal Coll. Physicians, Royal Soc. Medicine; mem. Internat. Soc. Clin. Densitometry, Am. Geriat. Soc. (membership com., reviewer jour., ann. meeting planning com. 1993), Gerontol. Soc. Am., Royal Coll. Surgeons, So. Med. Assn. (vice-chmn. coun. 1995-96, chmn. coun. 1996-97, v.p. 1997-98, pres.-elect 1998-99, pres. 1999-2000, editor geriatric medicine sect. Dial-Access program, from assoc. councilor to councilor state Tenn., chmn. adv. com. sci. activities, reviewer jour., assoc. editor So. Med. Jour. 1995-2000, editor 2000—), So. Assn. Geriatric Medicine (pres. 1990-92), So. Assn. for Primary Care (editor clin. revs.), Tenn. Med. Assn. (reviewer jour.), Tenn. Geriat. Soc. (founding), Brit. Med. Assn., Brit. Geriat. Soc., Bone and Mineral Soc., Alzheimer's Assn. (pres. bd. dirs. N.E. Tenn. chpt. 1990-91). Office: Ea Tenn State U Coll Medicine PO Box 70429 Johnson City TN 37614-1704 Business E-Mail: hamdy@etsu.edu.

HAMEKA, HENDRIK FREDERIK, chemist, educator; b. Rotterdam, Netherlands, May 25, 1931; arrived in U.S., 1960, naturalized, 1963; s. Dirk C. and Johanna (Mannebeck) Hameka; m. Charlotte C. Proacci, Aug. 3, 1972. D, U. Leiden, 1953, DSc cum laude, 1956; MA (hon.), U. Pa., 1971. Rsch. assoc. U. Rome, 1956—57; fellow Carnegie Inst. Tech., 1957—58; rsch. physicist N. V. Philips Lamps, Eindhoven, Netherlands, 1958—60; asst. prof. chemistry Johns Hopkins U., Balt., 1960—62; assoc. prof. chemistry U. Pa., Phila., 1962—67, prof. chemistry, 1967—. Disting. vis. rsch. prof. USAF Acad., 1986—87. Author: Advanced Quantum Chemistry, 1965, Introductory Quantum Theory, 1967, Physical Chemistry, 1977, Chemistry, Fundamentals and Applications, 2002, Quantum Mechanics, A Conceptual Approach, 2004; contbr. articles to profl. jours. Recipient Alexander von Humboldt prize, 1981; Alfred P. Sloan Rsch. fellow, 1963—67. Achievements include research on theory of molecular structure and optical and magnetic properties of molecules; calculations of spin-orbit and spin-spin coupling; research on theory of resonance optical rotation, spectral predictions. Home: 1503 Argyle Rd Berwyn PA 19312-1905 Office: U Pa Dept Chemistry Philadelphia PA 19104 Office Phone: 215-898-8303. Business E-Mail: hameka@sas.upenn.edu.

HAMEL, DANA BERTRAND, academic administrator; b. Rumford, Maine, Aug. 9, 1923; s. Donat H. and Louise (Kenison) H.; m. Shirley Elmeree Smith Knavel, Dec. 19, 1945; children— Dana Randolph, Michelle, April. AB, Ashland (Ohio) Coll., 1951; MA, Ohio State U., 1952; EdD, U Cin., 1962; AA in Humanities (hon.), Southside Va. C.C., 2004; AA in Humane Letters (hon.), Va. Western C.C., 2005. Master watchmaker Thomas J. Apryle & Sons, Johnstown, Pa., 1946; owner Hamels, Jewelers, Conemaugh, Pa., 1946-48; mem. mgmt. dept. Gen. Motors Inst., Flint, Mich., 1955-57; dean adminstrv. affairs Ohio Coll. Applied Sci. and Ohio Mechanics Inst., Cin., 1957-63, acting pres., 1961-62, exec. v.p., dean of faculties, 1962-63; dir. Roanoke Tech. Inst., 1963-64; exec. dir. Va. Dept. Tech. Edn., Richmond, 1964-66; founding chancellor Va. Community Coll. System, Richmond, 1966-79, cons., 1979-80; cons. to pres., dir. spl. acad. programs Va. State U., Petersburg, 1980-961980—; exec. dir. Va. Ctr. Pub./Pvt. Initiatives; pres. Hamel & Assocs., Richmond, 1996—. Coord. for offices of Va. Sec. of Edn. and Dept. of Edn. for WorkForce 2000, V-Quest Programs, 1992-96; co-chair Metro Richmond 2000; acting dir. Adminstrv. Affairs, CEBAF. Gov.'s liaison SURA/Continuous Electron Beam Accelerator Facility, 1983—; trustee, v.p. 1983-99, Southeastern Univs. Rsch. Assn., Inc., 1981—; mem. Va. Adv. Coun. Vocat. Edn.; bd. dris. Richmond Eye and Ear Hosp. Authority, 1989—, Ctr. of Excellence, Inc., Richmond Community High Sch., 1981—; chmn. bd. Va. Edn. Rsch. 1981-85, Network for Supercomputers, 1986—; sr. cons. 1986-93, So. Growth Policies Bd. Tech. Coun., 1987-95; Va. coord. Vamanuf Networking, 1990—; exec. dir. Mfg. Networking and Indsl. Modernization Project, 1992—; interim exec. dir. Va. Alliance Mfg. Competitiveness, 1993—; interim dir. Sch. to Work Program, 1994-95. Wth USAAF, 1942-45. Mem. So. Assn. Schs. and Colls. (former pres.), Am. Assn. Jr. Colls. (commn. on legis.), Nat. Coun. State Dirs. (former chmn.), Am. Soc. Engring. Edn., Am. Psychology and Guidance Assn., Nat. Assn. for Gifted Children, Am. Coll. Pers. Assn., Cin. Guidance and Pers. Assn., Va. League Nursing (pres. 1987), Forum Club, Masons, Kiwanians, Phi Delta Kappa, Psi Chi, Iota Lambda Sigma. Home and Office: Hamel & Assocs 300 Coalport Rd Richmond VA 23229-7019

HAMEL, DOUGLAS E., lawyer; b. Anchorage, Feb. 21, 1951; BA, U. Va., 1972, JD, 1976. Bar: Tex. 1976. Ptnr., co-head Employment Litig. and Labor Sect. Vinson & Elkins LLP, Houston. Chmn. Civil Svc. Commn. City of Houston, 1984-87. Office: Vinson & Elkins First City Tower 1001 Fannin St Ste 2300 Houston TX 77002-6706 E-mail: dhamel@velaw.com.

HAMEL, ESTHER VERAMAE, author; b. Circle, Mont., May 20, 1922; d. Frank Max and Catherine (Mahlstedt) Knopp; m. Robert Joseph Hamel, Mar. 16, 1941; children: Kathryn Dee Hamel Kelly, Dennis R. (dec.). Grad. high sch., Ronan, Mont. Co-owner Chalimar Farms, St. Ignatius, Mont., 1942—; lectr. Nat. Coun. State Garden Clubs, 1951—; owner, mgr. Ponderosa Pubrs., St. Ignatius, 1965—; v.p. Rings 'n Things Inc., Missoula, Mont., 1966-72; chief exec. officer, pres. Hamelly Internat., Inc., St. Ignatius and L.A., 1972—. Instr. flower show schs., 1969-80; chmn. landscape licensing bd. State of Mont., 1975-83; dir. fin. orgns. Author: Creative Design with Dried and Contrived Flower, 1971, Gestalt...Flower Show Judging, 1975, Educational Exhibits Explained, 1976, Executive Think Link (TM), 1991; co-author: House of Termites, 1972, Dried Flower Designs, 1973, Feeling Dreams, 1992; editor Mont. Gardens mag., 1956; editor/author newsletters: Judge's Contacts, 1963-65, Nat. Awards News, 1965-69, For Land's Sake, 1971-75; patentee in field. Co-author Bill to Revise Mont. Tax Structure, 1990; bd. dirs. Nat. Teenage Found. Named Golden Poet, Wide World of Poetry, 1990; named Spl. Woman Zonta Internat., 1974, Woman of the Yr. Bus. and Profl. women, 1968, Gardener of the Yr. Mont. Fedn. Garden Clubs, 1958. Mem. Nat. Coun. State Garden Clubs (nat. awards chmn. 1965-69, nat. landscape critics chmn. 1971-75). Office: 1369 Blue Lake Cir Punta Gorda FL 33983-5951

HAMEL, LOUIS REGINALD, systems analysis consultant; b. Lowell, Mass., July 23, 1945; s. Wilfred John and Angelina Lucienne (Paradis) H.; m. Roi Anne Roberts, Mar. 24, 1967 (dec.); 1 child, Felicia Antoinette; m. Anne Louise Staup, July 2, 1972 (div.); children: Shawna Michelle, Louis Reginald III. AA, Kellogg C.C., 1978. Cert. worker's compensation profl. Retail mgr. Marshall Dept. Stores, Beverly, Mass., 1972-73; tech. svc. rep. Monarch Marking Systems, Framingham, Mass., 1973—74; employment specialist Dept. Labor, Battle Creek, Mich., 1977-78; v.p. corp. Keith Polygraph Cons. and Investigative Svc., Inc., Battle Creek, 1978-79; indsl. engr., engine components divsn. Eaton Corp., Battle Creek, 1979-82; tooling and process engr. Kelley Tech. Svcs., Battle Creek, 1983-84, Clark Equipment Inc., 1983-84; tooling and mfg. engr., mfg. mgr. Trans Guard Industries Inc., Angola, Ind., 1983-85; facilitator employee involvement, safety dir. Wohlert Corp., Lansing, Mich., 1985—2004, workers compensation adminstr., tng. dir., 1985—2004, system analysis cons., 1975—. Cons. in field. Mem. Calhoun County Com. on Employment of Handicapped, Battle Creek, Mich., 1977-78; mem. Capital Area Labor Mgmt. Com., 1986-91. With USN, 1963-71, Vietnam. Recipient Svcs. to Handicapped award Internat. Assn. Pers. in Employment Security, Mich. chpt. 1978. Mem. VFW, Nat. Geog. Soc., Mich. Assn. Concerned Vets. (dir. 1974-79), Nat. Assn. Concerned Vets. Democrat. Roman Catholic. E-mail: hamellm@prodigy.net. *Personal philosophy: A warm handshake, with a smile, will give more people a lift than all the elevators in the world.*

HAMEL, MARK EDWIN, lawyer; b. Ontonagon, Mich., Apr. 9, 1953; s. Peter C. and Marian E. (Peterson) H.; m. Pamela Kay Jenkins, May 31, 1975; children: Nathan, Gregory. BA, Carroll Coll., 1975; JD, Harvard U., 1978. Bar: Minn. 1979, U.S. Dist. Ct. Minn. 1979. Law clk. to presiding justice Minn. Supreme Ct., St. Paul, 1978-79; assoc. Dorsey & Whitney LLP, Mpls., 1979-85, ptnr., 1985—, and chmn., real estate practice group. Chmn. bd. dirs. Accessible Space, Inc., bd. dirs. Downtown Coun. Mem. Minn. Bar Assn. (cert. real property law specialist), Hennepin County Bar Assn (real property sect.), Mpls. Athletic Club. Presbyterian. Office: Dorsey & Whitney LLP Ste 1500 50 S 6th St Minneapolis MN 55402-1498 Office Phone: 612-340-8716. Office Fax: 612-340-2868. Business E-Mail: hamel.mark@dorsey.com.

HAMEL, MICHAEL A., career officer; BS in Aero. Engring., USAF Acad., 1972; MBA, Calif. State U., Dominguez Hills, 1974; grad., Squadron Officer Sch., 1975, Air Command and Staff Coll., 1980. Commd. 2d lt. USAF, 1972, advanced through grades to Lt. Gen.; staff devel. planner Space and Missile Sys. Orgn., L.A. AFB, 1972-75; missile analyst fgn. tech. divsn. Lowry AFB, Colo., 1975-77; mission dir. Aerospace Data Facility, Buckley Air N.G. Base, Colo., 1977-79; air staff tng. officer R&D Hdqs. USAf, Washington, 1979-80; project mgr., manned spaceflight engr. Office of Sec. of Air Force for Spl. Projects, L.A. AFB, 1980-86; program element monitor, exec. officer Hdqs. USAF, Washington, 1986-90; chief plans divsn. Hdqs. Air Force Space Command, Peterson AFB, Colo., 1991-94; comdr. 750th Space Group, Onizuka Air Sta., Calif., 1994-95; vice comdr. 21st Space Wing, Peterson AFB, 1995-96; mil. adviser to v.p. The White House, Washington, 1996-98;

vice comdr. Space and Missile Sys. Ctr., L.A. AFB, 1998-99, comdr., 2005—; dir. requirements Air force Space Command HQ, Peterson AFB, Colo., 1999—; dir. space ops. and intergration HQ USAF, Pentagon, 2000—02; comdr. 14th AF Vanderberg AFB, Calif., 2002—05. Decorated Def. Superior Svc. medal, Legion of Merit, Meritorious Svc. medal with 3 oak leaf clusters. Office: 14 AF/CC 747 Nebraska Ave Ste A300-8 Vandenberg Afb CA 93437-6268

HAMEL, RODOLPHE, retired lawyer, pharmaceutical executive; b. Lewiston, Maine, June 3, 1929; s. Rodolphe and Alvina Melanie (Bilodeau) H.; m. Marilyn Vivian Johnsen, June 10, 1957; children: Matthew Edward, Anne Melanie. BA, Yale U., 1950; LLB, Harvard U., 1953. Bar: Maine 1953, D.C. 1953, N.Y. 1957. Assoc. firm Shearman & Sterling, N.Y.C., 1956-66; v.p., corp. sec., gen. counsel Macmillan Inc., N.Y.C., 1972-73; internat. counsel Bristol-Myers Squibb Co. (formerly Bristol-Myers Co.), N.Y.C., 1966-72, 73, v.p., counsel internat. divsn., 1974-81, assoc. gen. counsel, 1978-89, v.p., 1983-92, gen. counsel, 1989-94, sr. v.p., 1992-94, cons., 1995—2005. 1st lt. AUS, 1953-56. Mem. ABA, N.Y. State Bar Assn., Assn. of Bar of City of N.Y., Yale Club.

HAMEL, WILLIAM JOHN, church administrator, minister; b. Marquette, Mich., July 30, 1947; s. John Peter and Jayne B. (Berklund) H.; m. Karen Margaret Holleen, Aug. 10, 1968; children: Krista Joy, Kari Elise. BS, Wheaton Coll., 1969; MDiv, Trinity Evang. Div. Sch., Deerfield, Ill., 1972; DD, Trinity Internat. U., 1998; DCM, Trinity Western U., 1998. Ordained minister Evang. Free Ch. Am., 1978. Pastor West Bloomington (Minn.) Evang. Free Ch., 1972-86; dist. supt. Midwest Dist. Evang. Free Ch. Am., Kearney, Nebr., 1986-90; exec. v.p. Evang. Free Ch. Am., Mpls., 1990-97, pres., 1997—. Mem. Evangelist Free Ch. Am. Office: Evang Free Ch Am 901 E 78th St Minneapolis MN 55420-1334 Office Phone: 952-854-1300. Business E-Mail: president@efca.org.

HAMELIN, MARCEL, historian, educator; b. Saint-Narcisse, Que., Can., Sept. 18, 1937; m. Judy Purcell, Aug. 18, 1962; children— Danielle, Christine, Marc. Doctorat es Lettres, Universite Laval, Can. Faculty U. Ottawa, Ont., Canada, prof. history, 1966—2003, chmn. dept. history, 1968-70, vice dean sch. grad. studies, 1972-74, dean faculty of arts, 1974-90, rector, vice chancellor, 1990—2001, rector emeritus, 2001—; exec. dir. Interamerican Orgn. Higher Edn., 2002—. Chmn. Can.-Africa Cmty. Health Alliance, 2002—. Author: History of the Province of Quebec. Mem. Canadian Hist. Assn., Assn. Canadienne-francaise pour l'avancement des Scis. (pres. 1976-77), Royal Soc. Can. (Chevalier, Légion d'honneur). Business E-Mail: mhamelin@uottawa.ca.

HAMER, DAVIDSON HOWES, infectious diseases specialist; b. Corning, N.Y., Sept. 19, 1958; s. Myron Clifton and Meredith (Rollins) H.; m. Elizabeth Lee Burkhardt, July 27, 1958; children: Cyrus Lyman, Deric Alexander. BA in Biology and French, Amherst Coll., 1981; MD, U. Vt., 1987. Diplomate Am. Bd. Internal Medicine, Am. Bd. Infectious Diseases; cert. in travel and tropical medicine. Immunoassay researcher Ventrex Labs., Inc., Portland, Maine, 1980, 82, Biosystémes, S.A., Montpellier, France, 1980; endorphin researcher Rockefeller U., N.Y.C., 1982-83; intern then resident internal medicine Washington Hosp. Ctr., 1987-90; clin. and rsch. fellow New England Med. Ctr., Boston, 1990-94, asst. dir. travel medicine clinic, 1992-94, dir. traveler's health svc., 1994—; dir. infectious diseases Spaulding Rehab. Hosp., 1995-97. Asst. prof. medicine Tufts U., 1994—; dir. infectious diseases, chmn. infection control Spaulding Rehab. Hosp., 1995-97; project scientist applied rsch. on child health project Harvard Inst. Internat. Devel., 1995—. Contbr. articles to profl. jours. Recipient 1st prize Harry H. Kerr Essay Competition, 1989, award St. Elizabeth's Hosp., Edward Kass award Mass. Infectious Diseases Soc., 1992. Mem. ACP, Infectious Disease Soc. Am., Am. Soc. Travel Medicine and Hygiene, Internat. Soc. Travel Medicine, Mass. Med. Soc. Avocations: cooking, skiing, tennis, travel, wine. Office: New Eng Med Ctr PO Box 7010 Boston MA 02204-7010 Fall: Divsn Geog Medicine ID Box 7010 NEMCH 750 Washington St Boston MA 02111-1526

HAMER, WALTER JAY, chemical consultant, science writer; b. Altoona, Pa., Nov. 5, 1907; s. Jesse James and Naomi Gertrude (Roland) H.; m. Alma Robinson, Mar. 19, 1941; 1 child, Margaret. BS, Juniata Coll., Huntingdon, Pa., 1929, DSc (hon.), 1966; PhD, Yale U., 1932. Asst. instr. Juniata Coll., 1926-29; fellow Yale U., New Haven, 1932-34; rsch. assoc. MIT, Cambridge, 1934-35; rsch. chemist Nat. Bur. Standards, Washington, 1935-50, chief electrochemistry, 1950-70, dir. Electrolyte Ctr., 1968-72; chem. cons. Washington, from 2004. Adj. prof. Georgetown U., Cath. U., govt. agys. commerce and agr., 1940-50; rsch. chemist Manhattan Project, Washington, 1943-45; adj. examiner Civil Svc. Commn., 1948-50; cons. U.S. Dept. Def., 1951-53; mem. electrochem. soc. Internat. Union Pure and Applied Chemistry, 1958-68; U.S. tech. advisor primary cells and batteries Internat. Electrotech. Commn., 1964; mem. vis. panel Electrochemistry Lab., U. Pa., Phila., 1962-63; U.S. tech. advisor primary cells and batteries Internat. Electrotech. Commn., 1964; lectr. in field. Contbr. articles to profl. jours.; editor: Electrochemical Constants, 1953, The Structure of Electrolytic Solutions, 1959. Recipient cert. of merit Manhattan Project, 1945, OSRD, 1945; Superior Accomplishment award U.S. Dept. Commerce, 1954, 62, 65, Disting. Svc. gold medal, 1966; 1st prize for paper IEEE, 1955. Fellow IEEE (life), AAAS (life), Am. Inst. Chemistry (life), N.Y. Acad. Sci. (life), Washington Acad. Sci. (life); mem. Am. Stds. Assn. (mem. com. primary cells and batteries 1952-62), The Electrochem. Soc., Inc. (hon., v.p. 1960-63, pres. 1963-64, Robert T. Foley award Nat. Capital sect. 1991), Yale Chemists Assn. (pres. 1958-61), Eisenhower Commn., Cosmos Club. Republican. Episcopalian. Achievements include discovery of the electromotive series of the elements in Molten Systems, of the primary pH Standard for Aqueous Systems from 0 to 60 degrees Celsius, of the ionization constant of water from 0 to 60 degrees Celsius; research in determining the Faraday Constant, method to set standards for electrolytic conductance, maintenance of U.S. national standard of voltage. Died June 29, 2004.

HAMERLY, MICHAEL T., librarian, historian; b. Seattle, Sept. 23, 1940; s. James Charles Riley and Harriet Elinor (Jackson) H.; m. Carmen Victoria Flores Rosero, Jan. 19, 1963; 1 child, Michael Charles. BA, U. Wash., 1963, MA, 1965, M in Librarianship, 1979; PhD, U. Fla., 1970. From instr. to asst. prof. U. No. Colo., Greeley, 1970-74; dir. Archivo Arzobispal, Ecuador, 1975-78; rschr. Dept. Historia Maritima, Armada del Ecuador, 1975-77; vis. sr. lectr. dept. Spanish and Latin Am. studies Hebrew U., Jerusalem, 1981; cataloguer Pre-Columbian studies Dumbarton Oaks Rsch. Library and Collections, 1983-84; bibliographer/cataloguer Latin Am. Bibliographic Found., Redlands, Calif., 1985—88; catalog librarian, assoc. prof. Pacific collection Micronesian Area Rsch. Ctr., U. Guam, Mangilao, 1988-91; collection devel. lib., assoc. prof. to prof. Robert F. Kennedy Meml. Lib. U. Guam, 1991-98, chmn. press coun., 1990-97, prof., curriculum resources ctr. coord., 1997; spl. project/catalogue libr. John Carter Brown Libr., Providence, 1998—. Andean area editor The Americas; a quar. rev. of Inter-Am. Cultural history, 1974-88; assoc. editor Revista del Archivo Historico del Guayas, 1975-90; contbg. editor Handbook of Latin Am. Studies, 1971—; editor Ecuadorian Studies/Estudios ecuatorianos, 2000—; contbr. articles to profl. jours. NDEA, Title VI, Doherty and Fulbright-Hays grantee, fellow; Am. Coun. Learned Socs. and Social Sci. Rsch. Coun. grantee. Mem. Latin-Am. Studies Assn., Conf. on Latin-Am. History, Centro de Investigaciones Historicas de Guayaquil, Acad. Arquidiocesana de Historia Eclesiastica, Asian-Pacific Am. Librs. Assn., Assn. Historiadores Ecuatorianos, Acad. Nat. Historia, Fulbright Assn., Guam Libr. Assn., Pacific Islands Assn. Librs. and Archives, Beta Phi Mu. Home: 158 Medway St Providence RI 02906 Office: John Carter Brown Libr PO Box 1894 Providence RI 02912-1894 Office Phone: 401-863-3923. Office Fax: 401-863-3477. Business E-Mail: Michael_Hamerly@brown.edu.

HAMERMESH, BERNARD, physicist, researcher; b. Bklyn., Dec. 25, 1919; s. Isidore and Rose (Kornhauser) H.; m. Sylvia Molberger, Sept. 6, 1941; children: Judith Gay Hamermesh Springer, Richard George, Kenneth Scott. BS, CCNY, 1940; MS, NYU, 1942, PhD, 1944. Teaching fellow and tutor CCNY, N.Y.C., 1940-41; from grad. asst. to instr. NYU, N.Y.C., 1941-46; NRC postdoctoral fellow Calif. Inst. Tech., Pasadena, 1946-48; sr. physicist Argonne (Ill.) Nat. Lab., 1948-59; sr. sci. advisor TRW Systems, Redondo Beach, Calif., 1959-68; prof. physics, chmn. dept. Cleve. State U., 1968-85, prof. emeritus, 1985—; vis. prof. physics UCLA, 1987—. Lectr. U. Ill., Chgo., 1956-57, UCLA, 1964. Contbr. over 50 articles to Phys. Rev. Mem. Sch. Bd. Dist. 163, Rich Township Ill., 1949-51; sch. trustee Rich Township, 1951-57. Fellow Am. Phys. Soc.; mem. Phi Beta Kappa. Achievements include research in cosmic ray neutrons; capture gamma rays, 7.7 meter bent crystal gamma spectrometer, micrometeoroid accelerator, high spin states from capture of neutrons by nuclear isomers. E-mail: dr.buddle@gte.net.

HAMERMESH, DANIEL SELIM, economics professor; b. Cambridge, Mass., Oct. 20, 1943; s. Morton and Madeline (Goldberg) H.; m. Frances Witty, Dec. 18, 1966; children: David J., Matthew A. AB, U. Chgo., 1965; PhD, Yale U., 1969. Asst. prof. Princeton (N.J.) U., 1969-73; assoc. prof. Mich. State U., East Lansing, 1973-76, prof., 1976-93, chmn. dept., 1984-88; Edward Everett Hale centennial prof. econs. U. Tex., Austin, 1993—. Rsch. dir. ASPER-U.S. Dept. Labor, Washington, 1974-75, rsch. assoc. Nat. Bur. Econ. Rsch., 1979-; vis. prof. Harvard U., Cambridge, Mass., 1981, Latrobe U., Melbourne, Australia, 1987, Gadjah Mada U., Indonesia, 1990, Australian Nat. U., 1991, Rijksuniversiteit Limburg, The Netherlands, 1992, New Econ. Sch., Moscow, 1993, Hebrew U., Jerusalem, 1995, Erasmus U., The Netherlands, 1997, U. Bristol, Eng., 2000, U. Aberdeen, Scotland, 2002, McMaster U., 2003, U. Mich., 2004; mem. econ. adv. panel NSF, 1995-97; chmn. sci. adv. bd. German Inst. Econ. Rsch., 2003-. Mem. bd. editors Am. Econ. Rev., 1990-94; co-editor Econ. Letters, 1994-98, Labour Econs., 1996-00, Jour. Population Econs., 2001-03, Ind. and Labor Rels. Rev., 2004—. Pres. Congregation Kehillat Israel, Lansing, 1988-90. Recipient Best Article award Western Econ. Assn., 1987, Parents' Assn. Centennial Teaching fellow U. Tex., 1995-96; NSF rsch. grantee, 1980-82, 84-86, 86-91, 95—2003. Fellow Econometric Soc.; mem. Am. Econ. Assn., Midwest Econ. Assn. (pres. 1988-89), Soc. Labor Economists (pres. 2000-01). Jewish. Avocations: running, classical music. Office: U Tex Dept Econs Austin TX 78712 Office Phone: 512-475-8526. Business E-Mail: hamermes@eco.utexas.edu.

HAMEROW, THEODORE STEPHEN, historian, educator; b. Warsaw, Aug. 24, 1920; arrived in U.S.A., 1929, naturalized, 1930; s. Haim Schneyer and Bella (Rubinlicht) H.; m. Margarete Lotter, Aug. 16, 1954 (div. Dec. 27, 1996); children: Judith Margarete, Helena Francisca; m. Diane Franzen, Oct. 4, 1997. BA, CUNY, 1942; MA, Columbia U., 1947; PhD, Yale U., 1951. Instr. Wellesley Coll., 1950-51, U. Md., 1951-52; instr., asst. prof., then asso. prof. U. Ill, 1952-58; mem. faculty U. Wis., 1958-91, prof. history, 1961-91, G. P. Gooch prof. history, 1978-91, chmn. dept. history, 1973-76. Cons. editor Dorsey Press, 1961-71; mem. coun. Internat. Exch. Scholars, 1983-85, Nat. Coun. on Humanities, 1992-2000. Author: Restoration, Revolution, Reaction, 1958, Otto von Bismarck: A Historical Assessment, 1962, The Social Foundations of German Unification 1858-1871, 2 vols, 1969-72, The Birth of a New Europe: State and Society in the Nineteenth Century, 1983, Reflections on History and Historians, 1987, From the Finland Station: The Graying of Revolution in the Twentieth Century, 1990, On the Road to the Wolf's Lair: German Resistance to Hitler, 1997, Remembering a Vanished World: A Jewish Childhood in Interwar Poland, 2001; co-author: History of the World, 1960, A History of the Western World, 1969; editor: Otto von Bismarck, Reflections and Reminiscences, 1962, The Age of Bismarck, 1973; editorial bd.: Jour. Modern History, 1967-70, Central European History, 1968-72, Revs. in European History, 1974-78. Served with inf. AUS, 1943—46. Mem. Am. Hist. Assn., Conf. Group Central European History (sec.-treas. 1960-62, chmn. 1976), Wis. Assn. of Scholars (pres. 1989-91). Home: 885 Terry Pl Madison WI 53711-1956 Office: U Wisc Dept History Madison WI 53711 Office Phone: 608-263-1800. Business E-Mail: dkhamerow@facstaff.wisc.edu.

HAMERS, ROBERT J., chemistry educator, researcher; Prof. chemistry U. Wis., Madison, Evan P. Helfaer chair, 1996—. Recipient Peter Mark Meml. award Am. Vacuum Soc., 1994, IBM Corp. Faculty award, 2002, Arthur Adamson award Am. Chem. Soc., 2005; NSF fellow, 1992-97, John Simon Guggenheim Found. fellow, 2000, S.C. Johnson Co. Disting. fellow, 2000—. Fellow: AAAS, Am. Vacuum Soc. Office: U Wisconsin Dept Chemistry 1101 University Ave Madison WI 53706-1322 Fax: 608-262-0453. Office Phone: 608-262-6371. Business E-Mail: rjhamers@wisc.edu.

HAMER-SMITH, KATHRYN, secondary school educator; b. Billings, Mont., Aug. 26, 1958; d. Roger F. Hamer and Jeanne M. Huntington-Hamer; m. Walter L. Smith, June 24, 1989. BS, U. Wyo., 1981. English tchr. Goshen County Sch. Dist., Torrington, Wyo., head volleyball coach, asst. girls basketball coach, asst. track coach, reading specialist. Presenter in field. Youth coach Goshen County Softball Assn., Torrington, 1995—. Named Wyo. State H.S. Coach of Yr. for volleyball, 1994—96, Wyo. State H.S. Coach of Yr. for asst. basketball, 1996, Wyo. State H.S. Coach of Yr. for asst. track, 1998—2000, Goshen County Tchr. of Yr., Goshen County Edn. Assn., 2001—02, Nat. Assn. Track Coach of Yr., AFLAC, 2002—03; recipient Volleyball Ofcl. of Yr., Wyo. H.S. Activities Assn., 2001—02. Mem.: Wyo. Sports Ofcls. Assn. (state del. 1994—), Nat. Coun. Tchrs. English, Wyo. Coaches Assn. (pres. 2000—02), PEO, Order Ea. Star.

HAMES, MICHAEL J., semiconductor company executive; BS in elec. engring., U. Notre Dame. With Tex. Instruments Inc., 1980—, former v.p. worldwide DSP bus., 1982, DSP mktg. mgr., US DSP product mgr., sr. v.p., mgr. application specific products Dallas. Mem.: IEEE. Office: Tex Instruments Inc 12500 TI Blvd Dallas TX 75243 Office Phone: 972-995-2011. Office Fax: 972-995-4360.

HAMES, WILLIAM LESTER, lawyer; b. Pasco, Wash., June 21, 1947; s. Arlie Franklin and Nina Lee (Ryals) H.; m. Pamella Kay Rust, June 3, 1967; children: Robert Alan, Michael Jonathan. BS in Psychology, U. Wash., 1974; JD, Willamette U., 1981. Bar: Wash. 1981, U.S. Dist. Ct. (ea. dist.) Wash. 1982, U.S. Ct. Appeals (9th cir.) 1985, U.S. Dist. Ct. (we. dist.) Wash. 1985. Counselor Wash. Juvenile Ct., Walla Walla, 1974—76; reactor operator control rm. United Nuc. Inc., Richland, Wash., 1976—77; assoc. Sonderman, Egan & Hames, Kennewick, Wash., 1981—84, Timmons & Hames, Kennewick, 1984—86, Sonderman, Timmons & Hames, Kennewick, 1987—88; ptnr. Hames, Anderson & Whitlow, Kennewick, 1988—. Mem. Wash. State Bar Assn. (chair-elect creditor, debtor sect.), Benton-Franklin County Bar Assn., Bankruptcy Bar Assn. (bd. dirs.), Rotary. Democrat. Methodist. Home: 410 W 21st St Kennewick WA 99337 Office: Hames Anderson & Whitlow PO Box 5498 Kennewick WA 99336-0498 E-mail: billh@hawlaw.com.

HAMID, MICHAEL, electrical engineering educator, consultant; b. Dannaba, Tulkarm, Jordan, June 7, 1934; arrived in Can., 1958; m. Khetam Dahlah; Sept. 1, 1973; children: Rumsey, Sammy, Nady, Reema. BEE, McGill U., 1960, MEE, 1962; PhDEE, U. Toronto, 1966. Registered profl. engr., Ont., Man. Asst., assoc., full prof. U. Man., Winnipeg, Canada, 1965; dean scholar's affairs Universite Internacional, Ann Arbor, Mich., 1972—75; chmn. grad. studies elec. engring dept. U. Man., 1983—88; prof. elec. engring. U. South Ala., Mobile, 1990—, acting chair, 1999—. Mem. Can. Del. to Internat. Union of Radio Sci., 1965; pres., bd. dirs., treas. Internat. Microwave Power inst., 1969-73; adj. prof. Agrl. Engring., U. Man., 1970-77; vis. prof. U. Ctrl. Fla., Orlando, 1987-89; W.W. Clyde chair dept. elec. engring. U. Utah, 1987; mem. Man. Rsch. Coun., Prov. of Man., 1971-75; gen. chmn. Microwave Power Symposium, Monterey, Calif., 1971; vis. prof. Defence Rsch. Establishment, Dept. Nat. Defence Can., Ottawa, 1972; cons. Defence Rsch. Bd. Can., 1971-73; chmn. Internat. Conf. Biol. Effects of Microwaves and Ultrasound, U. Man., 1969; session organizer and chmn., invited speaker, Internat. Union Radio Sci. Gen. Assembly, Commn. VI., Warsaw, Poland, 1972; invited speaker Microwave State-of-the-Art Internat., IEEE Microwave Theory and Techniques Symposium, Chgo., 1972; mem. Man. Rsch. Counc. and chmn. of Elec. and Electronics Products Rsch. Com., 1971-75, Nat. Rsch. Coun. Can. Assoc. Com. on Bird Hazards to Aircraft, 1972-77, Policy Com. and Grants Selection com., Transp. Inst., U. Man., 1972-78; session organizer, invited speaker, Internat. URSI-IEEE-Antennas and Propagation Symposium, U. Colo., 1973; chmn. IEEE edn. activities bd., 1972; invited speaker Brazilian Soc. for Advancement Sci., 25th meeting, Sao Paulo, 1973; invited speaker, mem. Internat. Organizing Com., Colloquium on Microwave Communication, Hungarian Acad. Sci., 1970—; invited speaker NATO Adv. Group for Aerospace R&D E.M. Wave Propagation Panel, The Netherlands, 1974; adj. prof. Naval Postgrad. Sch., Monterey Calif., 1979-81; invited speaker Internat. Conf. on Communications Cirs. and Systems, India, 1981; invited speaker and mem. tech. program com., Internat. Symposium on Microwaves and Communication, Kharagpur, India, 1981; chmn. libr. and fin. coms., U. Man. Transport Inst., 1982-84; mem. Radar Subcom. of Radarsat, Can. Adv. Com. on Remote Sensing, Ottawa, 1983-88; mem. Grad. Studies Awards Com, U. Man., 1984-88; session chmn. URSI/IEEE-Antennas and Propagation Soc. Internat. Symposium, U. B.C., Vancouver, 1985; me. Antenna Tech. and Applied Electromagnetics Conf. Program Com., U. Man., 1986—; expert witness Andrew Antennas vs. Gabriel Electronics, patent infringement litigation, Portland, Maine, 1984-86; expert witness radio interference litigation WKRG, Inc. vs. State of Ala., 1990-91; invited speaker, 78th meeting of N.D. Acad. Sci., U. N.D., Grand Forks, 1986; vis. prof. U. Cen. Fla., dept. elect. engring., 1987—; gen. chmn. Symposium on Electromagnetic Detection of Latent Objects, 1989; me. Internat. Adv. and Tech. Program Com., Internat. Symposium on Recent Advances in Microwave Tech., Beijing, 1989, Reno, 1991, New Delhi, 1993. Author or co-author over 310 tech. articles, 7 monographs and book chpts., over 190 conf. papers, 26 rsch. reports, 25 patents; assoc. editor Jour. Microwave Power, 1969-77; mem. editorial bd. Microwave Jour., Jour. Microwave Power, IEEE Transactions on Microwave Theory and Techniques, 1969—. Fellow IEE, IEEE (life, award for contbns. to electromagnetic scattering and diffraction, devel. dielectric-loaded waveguides, resonators and antennas, life 2000—), Internat. Microwave Power Inst., Electromagnetics Acad. (invited mem.), U. South Ala. Alumni Assn. (Outstanding Scholar award 1998), Am. Assn. Engring Soc., Phi Eta Sigma, Tau Beta Pi, Phi Kappa Phi (scholar 1998). Office: U South Ala Dept Elec Engring Mobile AL 36688-0001 Business E-Mail: mhamid@usouthal.edu.

HAMILL, (WILLIAM) PETE, newspaper columnist, author, editor; b. Bklyn., June 24, 1935; s. William and Anne (Devlin) H.; m. Ramona Negron, Feb. 3, 1962 (div. 1970); children— Adriene, Deirdre; m. Fukiko Aoki, May 23, 1987. Student, Pratt Inst., 1952, Mexico City (Mexico) Coll., 1956-57. Comml. artist, 1957-60; reporter N.Y. Post, later columnist, 1960-74; columnist N.Y. Daily News, 1975-79, 82-84; contbg. editor Saturday Evening Post, 1963-64; contbr. Village Voice, New York Mag., N.Y.C., 1974—; editor Mexico City News, 1986-87; columnist Esquire, 1989-91, N.Y. Post, 1988-93, N.Y. Newsday, 1994—; editor-in-chief N.Y. Daily News, 1997. Author: (novels) A Killing for Christ, 1968, The Gift, 1973, Flesh and Blood, 1977, Loving Women, 1990, Snow in August, 1997, (non-fiction) Irrational Ravings, 1972, A Drinking Life: A Memoir, 1994, Tools as Art, 1995, Piecework, 1996, News is a Verb, 1998, Why Sinatra Matters, 1998, Diego Rivera, 1999, (short stories) The Invisible City: A New York Sketchbook, 1980, Tokyo Sketches, 1993, (screenplays) Doc, 1971, Badge, 373, 1973, Liberty, 1986, Neon Empire, 1987, Downtown: My Manhattan, 2004; contbr. articles to numerous mags. Trustee Mus. City N.Y.; coun. mem. Writers Guild Am. Past. Served with USN, 1952-54. Recipient Meyer Berger award Columbia Sch. Journalism, 1962, award Newspaper Reporters Assn., 1962, 25 Yr. Achievement award Soc. of Silurians, 1989, Peter Kihss award, Silurians, 1992. Mem. PEN, Nat. Assn. Hispanic Journalists, Silurians. Democrat.

HAMILTON, ALLAN CORNING, retired oil company executive; b. Chgo., June 9, 1921; s. Daniel Sprague and Mildred (Corning) H.; m. Edith Johnson, June 3, 1950 (div. 1995); children: Kimball C., Scott W., Dean C., Gail W.; m. Geraldine C. Berndt, Jan. 27, 1996. BS in Econs., Haverford Coll., 1943; LLD (hon.), Union Coll., Schenectady, N.Y., 1979. With Standard Oil Co., N.J., 1946-51, Esso Export Corp., 1951-56; treas. Internat. Petroleum co. Ltd., Coral Gables, Fla., 1956-61, Esso Internat. Inc., 1961-66; with Exxon Corp. (formerly Standard Oil Co., N.J.), N.Y.C., 1966-83, treas., v.p., prin. fin. officer, 1970-83. Lt. USNR, 1943-46. Mem.: Met. Club (N.Y.C.), Explorers Club.

HAMILTON, ANDREW D., chemistry professor, educator; BS, Exeter U., 1974; MS, U. British Columbia, 1976; PhD, Cambridge U., 1980. Asst. prof. chemistry Princeton U., 1981—88; assoc. prof. U. Pitts., 1988—92, prof., 1992—97, chair Dept. Chemistry, 1994—97; Irénée duPont Prof. Chemistry Yale U., New Haven, 1997—, prof. Dept. Molecular Biophysics and Biochemistry, 1998—, chair Dept. Chemistry, 1999—2003, dep. provost Sci. and Tech., 2003—04, provost, 2004—. Arthur C. Cope scholar, Am. Chem. Soc., 1999. Fellow: AAAS. Office: Yale U Dept Chem PO Box 208107 New Haven CT 06520-8107 E-mail: andrew.hamilton@yale.edu.

HAMILTON, BEVERLY LANNQUIST, investment company executive; b. Roxbury, Mass., Oct. 19, 1946; d. Arthur and Nancy Lannquist. BA cum laude, U. Mich., 1968; postgrad., NYU, 1969-70. V.p. Auerbach, Pollak & Richardson, N.Y.C., 1972-75, Morgan Stanley & Co., N.Y.C., 1975-80, United Techs., Hartford, Conn., 1980-87; dep. comptr. City of N.Y., 1987-91; pres., ret. ARCO Investment Mgmt Co, L.A., 1991-2000. Bd. dirs. Oppenheimer Funds, Am. Fund's Emerging Markets Growth Fund; trustee The Calif. Endowment, Monterey Inst. Internat. Studies, Cmty. Hosp. Monterey; investment coms. Rockefeller Found., U. Mich. Trustee Hartford Coll. for Women, 1981-87, Stanford Univ. Mgmt. Co., 1991-99; bd. dirs. Inst. for Living, 1983-87. Mem. NCCJ (bd. dirs. 1987-91), Conn. Natural Gas, 1982-2002, United Asset Mgmt. Corp., 1997-2000. Address: 5485 Quail Meadows Dr Carmel CA 93923-7971

HAMILTON, BOBBY, professional race car driver; b. Nashville, May 29, 1957; m. Debbie Hamilton; 1 child, Bobby Jr. Recipient NASCAR Winston Cup Series Rookie of Yr. award, 1991. Achievements include former Nashville Speedway track champion; NASCAR Winston Cup Series debut 1991; winner Dura-Lube 5000, Phoenix, 1996; 1997 season includes winner Rockingham, AC Delco 400; 1998 season includes winner Goody's 500, 2 top-5s, 8 top-10s, top 15 in points. Mailing: Bobby Hamilton Racing 220 Industrial Dr 37122 PO Box 1708 Mount Juliet TN 37121*

HAMILTON, CANDIS LEE, counselor, director; b. Saratoga, N.Y., Apr. 8, 1942; d. Harry Lee Van Arnam and Lois Carey Pickett; m. Woodbury Rogers Hamilton, Apr. 16, 1963; children: Sonya Ann Thaysen, David Sean, Lise Carey Hamilton-Hall, Paul Tate. Student, Brockport Coll., Tavistock Inst., Harvard U., Moreno Inst., 1976—80, U. Rochester, 1974—78; student (hon.), Sisters of St. Joseph Spirituality Ctr., Rochester, NY, 1986—90; student, St. Bernard's Inst., 1991—. Founder, co-pres. Penfield (NY) Learning Disabilities Assn., 1971—78; program designer, facilitator, instr. Designs for Anti-Racism, Rochester, 1973—81; program facilitator Sisters of St. Joseph Spirituality Ctr., Rochester, 1992—2000, spiritual dir., adj. staff, 1995—. Author: Who am i; Who are U; Who are we?, Woman's Workbook on Mark's Mosaic of Daily Discipleship. Facilitator Wellsprings, Rochester, 1991—96; facilitator, instr. Rochester Jungian Soc., 1990—98; team coord. Sisters of St. Joseph Spirituality Ctr., 1998—2001. Recipient certs. and letters of appreciation, various individuals and local ch. groups, 1971—2003. Democrat. Roman Catholic. Avocations: snorkeling, trampoline, recycling. Home: 844 Whalen Rd Penfield NY 14526

HAMILTON, CARL HULET, retired academic administrator; b. Morris, Okla., Sept. 30, 1934; s. Alva H. and Olah E. (Pryor) H.; m. Gloria Joyce Gore, Sept. 3, 1954; children: Ray, Carla Jo, Deanna Jean. ThB, Southwestern Coll., 1956; BA, Oklahoma City U., 1957; MA, U. Tulsa, 1962; PhD, U. Ark., 1968. English tchr. Southwestern Coll., Oklahoma City, 1957-60; editor Oral Roberts Evangelistic Assn., Tulsa, 1960-62; English tchr., editor Oral Roberts U., Tulsa, 1966-68; acad. dean, 1968-75; provost Oral Roberts U., Tulsa, 1975-84; adminstr. World Evangelism, San Diego, 1984-86; chief of staff Feed the Children, Oklahoma City, 1986-88; provost, chief acad. officer Oral

Roberts U., 1989-98; ret., 2001. Min. of adminstrn. First United Meth. Ch., 1999-2001. Republican. Methodist. Avocations: fishing, water sports, motorcycling. Home: PO Box 488 Disney OK 74340-0488 E-mail: piscatore@brightok.net.

HAMILTON, CARLOS ROBERT, JR., endocrinologist, consultant, academic administrator; b. Houston, June 12, 1939; s. Carlos Robert and Berta (Denman) H.; m. Carolyn Burton, Aug. 12, 1961; children: Carlos R. III, Patricia Frances. BA, U. Tex., 1961; MS, MD with honors, Baylor Coll. Medicine, 1966. Diplomate Am. Bd. Internal Medicine, Am. Bd. Endocrinology and Metabolic Diseases. Intern in internal medicine Johns Hopkins Hosp., Balt., 1966-67, asst. resident in internal medicine, 1967-69, chief resident in medicine, 1970-71; clin. and rsch. fellow Harvard Med. Sch./Mass. Gen. Hosp., Boston, 1969-70; asst. prof. medicine Johns Hopkins U. and Hosp., Balt., 1971-72; staff endocrinologist Wilford Hall USAF Med. Ctr., San Antonio, 1972-74; clin. prof. medicine Baylor Coll. Medicine, Houston, 1974—; clin. prof. medicine Med. Sch. U. Tex., Houston, 1999-2000, prof. internal medicine, 2000—, exec. v.p. for external affairs Health Sci. Ctr., 2002—. Cons. endocrinology and internal medicine Med. Clinic of Houston, L.L.P., 1974—2000; med. advisor employee benefit com. Southwestern Bell Tel. Co., 1975—93; attending physician in endocrinology Ben Taub Gen. Hosp./Baylor Coll. Medicine, 1980—; attending physician, mem. active staff The Meth. Hosp./Meml.-Hermann Hosp., Houston, 1974—; mem. active staff St. Luke's Episcopal Hosp., 2000—, Meml. Hermann Hosp., 2000—; practicing physicians adv. coun. U.S. Dept. HHS, 2003—; mem. health, sci. and rsch. com. World Anti-Doping Agy., Montreal, 2003—. Contbr. articles to profl. jours. Dist. and coun. chair, area pres., regional bd. dirs., v.p. Boy Scouts Am., Houston, Atlanta, Irving, Tex., 1980—; bd. regents Tex. Woman's U., 1999-2001. Recipient Dist. award of merit, Silver Beaver award, Silver Antelope award, Disting. Eagle Scout award, Silver Buffalo award Boy Scouts Am., 1982-99. Fellow ACP (bd. dirs. Tex. chpt., Mead-Johnson Residency scholar 1970, bd. dirs. Tex. Acad. Internal Medicine and ACP-ASIM health and pub. policy com., Tex. Laureate award 2003), Am. Coll. Endocrinology (trustee 1999-2000, sec.-treas. 2001-02, chancellor 2005-); mem. SAR (bd. dirs. Paul Carrington chpt. 1992—, pres. 1993), Am. Soc. Internal Medicine (bd. dirs. polit. action com. 1995-98, Key Congl. Contact of Yr. 1996), Am. Assn. Clin. Endocrinologists (bd. dirs. 1995—, chair legis. and regulatory com. 1998-2000, sec. exec. com. 2000-01, treas. 2001-02, v.p. 2002-2003, pres.-elect 2003-04, pres. 2004-05), Tex. Med. Assn. (exec. com. polit. action com. 1989-01, chair 1995, 96), Harris County Med. Soc. (bd. dirs. 1992-99, pres.-elect 1998, pres. 1999), Kiwanis (bd. dirs. Houston chpt. 1986-95, pres. 1995), Alpha Omega Alpha, Sigma Xi. Office: U Tex Health Sci Ctr 7000 Fannin Rm 1535 Houston TX 77030 Office Phone: 712-500-3825. Business E-Mail: carlos.r.hamilton@uth.tmc.edu.

HAMILTON, CHARLES A., international trade consultant; b. St. Louis, June 1, 1929; s. Alexander and Gertrude (Allan) H.; m. Tanya M. Kellman, May 24, 1970; children: David Edward, Anne Elizabeth. BS in Bus. Adminstrn., Washington U., St. Louis, 1952. Specialist in advt. and sales promotion Gen. Electric Co., San Jose, Calif., 1953-59, cons. govt. rels. Washington, 1959-63; cons. Charles A. Hamilton Assocs., Washington, 1963-69; asst. to sec. of interior Dept. of Interior for Congrl. Liaison, Washington, 1970-71; exec. sec. to chmn. U.S. Internat. Trade Commn., Washington, 1971-81; dep. dir. strategic trade policy Office of Sec. of Def., Washington, 1981-91; pres. Charles A. Hamilton Assocs. LLC, Washington, 1991—. Trade advisor Airbus N.Am.; bd. advisors Ctr. for Strategic Policy, Washington Export Coun., European-Am. Bus. Coun., The European Inst. Writer op-ed articles Jour. of Commerce. Bd. dirs. Neighbors for Livable Cmty., Washington. Capt. USAF, 1951-53. Mem. Army and Navy Club. Republican. Presbyterian. Home: 5025 Overlook Rd NW Washington DC 20016-1911 Office: Charles A Hamilton Assocs LLC 5025 Overlook Rd NW Washington DC 20016-1911 Office Phone: 202-237-8142. E-mail: cahallc@att.net.

HAMILTON, CLYDE HENRY, federal judge; b. Edgefield, S.C., Feb. 8, 1934; s. Clyde H. and Edwina (Odom) Hamilton; children: John C., James W. BS, Wofford Coll., 1956; JD with honors, George Washington U., 1961. Bar: S.C. 1961. Reference asst. U.S. Senate Libr., Washington, 1958—61; assoc. J.R. Folk, Edgefield, 1961—63; assoc., gen. ptnr. Butler, Means, Evins & Browne, Spartanburg, SC, 1963—81; judge U.S. Dist. Ct. S.C., Columbia, 1981—91, U.S. Ct. Appeals (4th cir.), Richmond, Va., 1991—99, sr. judge, 1999—. Gen. counsel Synalloy Corp., Spartanburg, 1969—80. Mem. editl. staff: Cumulative Index of Congl. Com. Hearings, 1935—58, bd. editors: George Washington Law Rev., 1959—60. Pres. Spartanburg County Arts Coun., 1971—73, Spartanburg Day Sch., 1972—74, sustaining trustee, 1975—81; past mem. steering com. undergrad. merit fellowship program and estate planning coun. Converse Coll., Spartanburg; trustee Spartanburg Meth. Coll., 1979—84; mem. S.C. Supreme Ct. Bd. Commrs. on Grievances and Discipline, 1980—81; del. Spartanburg County, 4th Congl. Dist. and S.C. Rep. Convs., 1976, 1980; mem., past chmn. fin. com. and adminstrv. bd. Trinity United Meth. Ch., Spartanburg, trustee, 1980—83. Capt. USAR, 1956—62. Recipient Alumni Disting. Svc. award, Wofford Coll., 1991, The Order of The Palmetto, Gov. Beasley, S.C., 1999. Mem.: S.C. Bar Assn., Piedmont Club (bd. govs. 1979—81). Office: US Ct Appeals 4th Cir 1901 Main St Columbia SC 29201-2443 Office Phone: 803-765-5461.

HAMILTON, D. KIRK, architectural firm executive; MSc in Orgn. Devel., Pepperdine U. Founding prin. Watkins Hamilton Ross Archs., Houston. Pres. Ctr. Innovation in Health Facilities. Fellow: AIA (pres. Acad. Arch.for Health 1999), Am. Coll. Healthcare Archs. Office: Watkins Hamilton Ross Architects Inc 20 Greenway Plaza Ste 450 Houston TX 77046

HAMILTON, DAGMAR STRANDBERG, lawyer, educator; b. Phila., Jan. 10, 1932; d. Eric Wilhelm and Anna Elizabeth (Sjöström) Strandberg; m. Robert W. Hamilton, June 26, 1953; children: Eric Clark, Robert Andrew Hale, Meredith Hope. AB, Swarthmore Coll., 1953; JD, U. Chgo. Law Sch., 1956, Am. U., 1961. Bar: Tex. 1972. Atty. civil rights divsn. U.S. Dept Justice, Washington, 1965-66; asst. instr. govt. U. Tex., Austin, 1966-71; lectr. Law Sch. U. Ariz., Tucson, 1971-72; editor, rschr. Assoc. William O. Douglas U.S. Supreme Ct., Washington, 1962-73, 75-76; editor, rschr. Douglas autobiography Random House Co., 1972-73; staff counsel Judiciary Com. U.S. Ho. of Reps., 1973-74; asst. prof. L.B. Johnson Sch. Pub. Affairs U. Tex., Austin, 1974-77, assoc. prof., 1977-83, prof., 1983—, assoc. dean, 1983-87. Interdisciplinary prof. U. Tex. Law Sch., 1983—; vis. prof. Washington U. Law Sch., St. Louis, 1982, U. Maine, Portland, 1992; Godfrey Disting. vis. prof. U. Maine Law Sch., 2002; vis. fellow U. London, QMW Sch. Law, 1987—88; vis. prof. U. Maine, Portland, 2002; vis. fellow U. Oxford Inst. European & Comparative Law, 1998. Contbr. to various publs. Mem. Tex. State Bar Assn., Am. Law Inst., Assn. Pub. Policy Analysis and Mgmt., Swarthmore Coll. Alumni Coun. (rep.), Kappa Beta Phi (hon.), Phi Kappa Phi (hon.). Democrat. Mem. Soc. Of Friends. Home: 403 Allegro Ln Austin TX 78746-4301 Office: U Tex LBJ Sch Pub Affairs Austin TX 78713 Office Phone: 512-471-4280. Business E-Mail: dagmar.hamilton@mail.utexas.edu.

HAMILTON, DARDEN COLE, construction management company executive; b. Pitts., Nov. 28, 1956; s. Isaac Herman Hamilton and Grace Osborne (Fish) Thorp; m. Linda Susanne Moser, Aug. 7, 1976; children: Christopher Moser, Elijah Cole. BS in Aeronautics, St. Louis U., Cahokia, Ill., 1977; postgrad., Ariz. State U. Lic. pilot, airframe and power mechnic. Engr. McDonnell Douglas Aircraft Co., St. Louis, 1977-80; group leader, engring. Cessna Aircraft Co., Wichita, Kans., 1980-83, sr. flight test engr., 1983-85, Allied-Signal Aerospace (Honeywell) Co., Phoenix, 1986-92, flight test engr. specialist, 1992-98, prin. engr., 1988—2003; mem. Ariz. Senate, Dist. 16, Phoenix, 1998—2003; vice chair transp. com., mem. appropriations com. Ariz. Senate, Phoenix, 1999-2000, chmn. rules com., appropriations edn. sub-com., 2001—02, vice chmn. natural resources, agr. and environ. com., 2001—02, mem. commerce com., 2001—02; corp. pres. CANAMEX, Inc., 2003—05. Editor: Family Proponent Newsletter, 1994—98. Mem. Ariz. Gov.'s Constl. Commemoration Com., 1997—99; bd. dirs. Ariz. Ho. and Senate Chaplaincy, 1997—98, Crisis Pregnancy Ctr. of Greater Phoenix, 2003—; chmn. bd. advisors Ariz. Ho. and Senate Chaplaincy, 1998—2000; mem. resolutions com. Ariz. Gov.'s Mil. Base Retention Task Force, 1999—2003; chmn. domestic violence task force Ariz. Senate, 1999—2003; Desert Sky precinct committeeman Glendale Rep. Com.; vol. coord. legis. dist. 16 campaign John Shadegg for Congress, 1994—96; del. dist. 16 Ariz. Rep. Conv., 1995—98; mem. resolutions com. Ariz. Rep. Com.; mem. adult edn. dept. Rivers Cmty. Ch.; exec. v.p. Marketplace Resources, 2003—. Mem.: NRA (life cert. instr.), Am. Legis. Exch. Coun., Am. Helicopter Soc., Soc. Flight Test Engrs., Ariz. State Rifle and Pistol Assn. (life). Avocations: horses, target shooting, camping. Home: 5533 W Christy Dr Glendale AZ 85304-3889 Personal E-mail: darden@dardenh.com.

HAMILTON, DAVID ARNOLD, retired librarian; b. Grand Rapids, Mich., Aug. 16, 1927; s. Ralph Samuel Hamilton and Margit Agnes Cherny; m. Christine Mary Pearson, Sept. 20, 1956; children: Eric Beth Hamilton Barrett, Mark David. BS in Edn., No. Ill. U., 1960, MS in Edn., 1964. Tchr. English, French Waterman (Ill.) Pub. HS, 1960—62; libr. Simmons Jr. HS, Aurora, Ill., 1962—64; periodical libr. No. Ill. U., DeKalb, 1964—70, cataloging libr., 1970—89, reference libr., 1989—92; dir. Maple Park (Ill.) Pub. Libr., 1990—94; ret., 1994. Archivist advisor George Williams Coll., Williams Bay, Wis., 1999—. Co-author: Ballet Plot Index, 1987, Opera Plot Index, 1990. With U.S. Army, 1950—52. Home: 1227 Gifford St Dekalb IL 60115-4644 E-mail: lshkbibble@aol.com.

HAMILTON, DAVID F., judge; b. 1957; BA magna cum laude, Haverford Coll., 1979; JD, Yale U., 1983. Law clk. to Hon. Richard D. Cudahy U.S. Ct. Appeals (7th cir.), 1983-84; atty. Barnes & Thornburg, Indpls., 1984-88, 91-94; judge U.S. Dist. Ct. (so. dist.) Ind., Indpls., 1994—. Counsel to Gov. of Ind., 1989-91; chair Ind. State Ethics Commn., 1991-94. V.p. for litigation, bd. dirs. Ind. Civil Liberties Union, 1987-88. Fulbright scholar, 1979-80; recipient Sagamore of the Wabash, Gov. Evan Bayh, 1991. Mem.: Am. Inns of Ct. (pres. chpt. 2001—03). Office: US Dist Ct So Dist Ind 46 E Ohio St Rm 330 Indianapolis IN 46204-1921

HAMILTON, DAVID LEE, sports association administrator, retired environmental company executive; b. Pitts., Mar. 26, 1937; s. James Arthur and Margaret (Kennett) H.; m. Molly Anne Wolford, June 27, 1959; children: David Scott, Bryan Lee, Timothy Drew. BSChemE, Bucknell U., 1957; MBA, U. Pitts., 1965. Various positions Exxon Co., USA, 1957-79; exec. asst. to pres. Exxon Corp., N.Y.C., 1979—80, v.p. supply and transp. Exxon Internat. Co., 1980—82, sr. v.p. Exxon Internat. Co., 1982—83, dep. mgr. dept. petroleum products, 1983—85; v.p. Esso Europe, London, 1985-86; v.p. mktg. Exxon Co., Internat., Florham Park, N.J., 1986-88; exec. v.p. OHM Corp., Findlay, Ohio, 1989-92; exec. dir., COO U.S. Tennis Assn., 2003—. Trustee Bucknell U., Lewisburg, Pa., 1984—, chair long-range planning com., 1997—2001, chair Presdl. Search com., 1999, chmn. bd. trustees, 2001—03; pres. Dallas Tennis Assn., 1994—97; treas. Tex. sect. USTA, 1997—99, pres., 1999—2000, chair comm. mktg. coun., 1999—2002, chmn. strategic planning com., 2003, chair blue ribbon commn., 2002; bd. dirs. The Std. Steamship P&I Club, Bermuda, 1982—85, Concord Resource Group, Lawrenceville, NJ, 1989—91. Mem.: Canyon Creek Country Club (Dallas), TBarM Racquet Club (Dallas), Omicron Delta Kappa, Beta Gamma Sigma, Sigma Chi (Significant Sig award 1985). Avocations: grandparenting, tennis, travel, reading. Home: 12115 Elysian Ct Dallas TX 75230-2221 Office Phone: 914-696-7026. E-mail: kelcarchas@aol.com.

HAMILTON, DAVID MIKE, publishing executive; b. Little Rock, 1951; s. Ralph F. and Mickey G. Hamilton; m. Carol N. McKenna, Oct. 25, 1975; children: Elisabeth M., Caroline E. BA, Pitzer Coll., 1973; MLS, UCLA, 1976. Cert. tchr. libr. sci. Calif. Editor Sullivan Assocs., Palo Alto, Calif., 1973-75; curator Henry E. Huntington Library, San Marino, Calif., 1976-80; mgr. prodn., mktg. William Kaufmann Pubs., Los Altos, Calif., 1980-84; pres. Live Oak Press, LLC, Palo Alto, 1984—. Cons., editor, gen. ptnr. Sensitive Expressions Pub. Co., Palo Alto, 1985—98; consulting dir. AAAI Press, 1994—; mng. editor, pub. AI Mag. Author: To the Yukon with Jack London, 1980, The Tools of My Trade, 1986; co-author: Book Club of California Quarterly, 1985, Research Guide to Biography and Criticism, 1986, Making A Digital Book, 1994; contbg. editor, webmaster: AAAI world-wide web site, 1995—; contbr. articles to jours. Trustee Jack London Ednl. Found., San Francisco; bd. dirs. ISYS Forum, Palo Alto, 1987—96; pres. site coun., mem. supt.'s adv. com. Palo Alto Unified Sch. Dist.; bd. dirs. Trinity Parish, Menlo Park, 1985—87, sec. vestry, 1986; mem. parent's coun. Wellesley Coll., 1997—2004. Mem.: ALA, Assn. Computing Machinery (chmn. pub. com. 1984), Soc. Scholarly Pubs. (mem. program com. 1999), Soc. Tech. Comm. (judge 1984), Bookbuilders West (mem. bookshow com. 1983), Author's Guild, Am. Assn. Artificial Intelligence (bd. dirs., dir. publ.), Med. and Ednl. Publs., Coun. Scholarly, Save the Redwoods League (life), Book Club Calif., Commonwealth Club, Sierra Club (life). Democrat. Episcopalian. Avocations: backpacking, camping, hiking, book collecting. Office: The Live Oak Press LLC PO Box 60036 Palo Alto CA 94306-0036

HAMILTON, DOUGLAS WARREN, real estate executive; b. Sacramento, Calif., Feb. 21, 1947; s. Albert James and Maxene Ruth (Gergens) H.; m. Sara Binder, Jan. 19, 1992; children: Ethan A.S.W., Antonia K.R.R. BA in Math., U. Nebr., 1972; MBA, U. Pa., 1977. Asst. v.p. DLJ, N.Y.C., 1977-79; mng. dir. Merrill Lynch & Co., N.Y.C., 1979-93; CEO, chmn. Barker & Little, Inc., Rapid City, S.D., 1993—. With USMC, 1966-69. Office: 816 Saint Joseph St PO Box 2800 Rapid City SD 57709-2800

HAMILTON, ELIZABETH ANN, elementary school educator; m. Jerry L. Hamilton, Dec. 26, 1969; children: Lisa, Alex. Grad., U. North Tex., 1971, U. Tex., 1981. Tchr. kindergarten Richardson Ind. Sch. Dist., Tex., 1981—84; tchr. reading, edn. leader Hutto Elem. Sch., 1984—. Mem. leadership team Hutto Primary Sch., 1994—2005; presenter in field. Sunday sch. tchr., Round Rock, Tex. Mem.: Assn. Tchrs. Pub. Educators, Internat. Reading Assn. Avocation: reading. Office: Hutto Ind Sch Dist 955 Carl Stern Blvd Hutto TX 78634

HAMILTON, FRANK STRAWN, musician, composer, educator; b. N.Y.C., Aug. 3, 1934; s. Frank Strawn and Gladys (Bley) Hamilton; m. Sheila Lofton, Nov. 7, 1957 (div. Nov. 1971); children: Cameron Auguste (dec. 1998), Evan Baird, Liam Christopher (dec. Oct. 2001), Heather Alexa; m. Deeanne Lee Walter, May 5, 1972 (div. Oct. 1980); m. Mary Doyle, Jan. 15, 1983. Student, Los Angeles City Coll., 1952-53, Chgo. Mus. Coll., 1959-62, L.A. Valley Coll., 1963-64. Organizer, head teaching staff, v.p., co-founder Old Town Sch. Folk Music, Chgo., 1957-62; ho. musician Gate of Horn, Chgo., 1959-61; mem. The Weavers, 1962-63. Founder The Hot Club of Atlanta, 1995. Appeared Asheville (N.C.) Folk Festival, 1953, Newport Folk Festival, 1959; motion picture appearance in Subterraneans, 1958; performed with duo Meridian for spl. children's programs Young Audiences in Atlanta Pub. Sch. System, 1987-2003, with wife Mary; rec. artist Folkways, Vanguard records, Long Lonesome Home, ITR records; devel. method annotation folk guitar and 5 string banjo; film score: A Time Out of War, 1952; TV score: Survival; folk singer with wife Mary, The Hamiltons. Mem. Irish Arts Atlanta. Mem. ACLU, Fellowship of Reconciliation, UN Assn., Dramatist Guild, Chgo. Hist. Soc. (hon.), Tai Chi Health and Rsch. Assn. Home: 852 Cinderella Ct Decatur GA 30033-5812 Office Phone: 404-296-1582. E-mail: hamprod@mindspring.com.

HAMILTON, GEORGE DRUMMOND, II, psychotherapist; b. Walterboro, S.C. s. George Drummond and Marianne Fianna Hamilton; m. Charlotte Elizabeth Redden, June 21, 2003. BS in Psychology, Georgetown U., Washington, D.C.; MSW, U. S.C., Columbia. LCSW. Psychotherapist Mental Health Ctr., Lexington, SC, Crossroads Christian Counseling, Columbia, SC; group counselor Domestic Abuse Ctr., Columbia, SC. Author: Chill Out, 2001. Mem.: Am. Assn. Family Counseling.

HAMILTON, GREGORY A., musician, composer; b. Livonia, Mich., Sept. 14, 1959; s. Vogel Wilbur Hamilton and Bernadette Blackburn. MusB, Baldwin-Wallce Coll., 1984; MusM, Royal Coll. Music, 1990; MA, U. Mich., 1994, DA of Music, 2001. Music dir. St. Thomas Apostle Ch., Ann Arbor, Mich., 1999—2005, St. Theresa Ch., Sugar Land, Tex., 2005—. Composer: (music composition) The Breath of the Spirit (Premiered in NYC, and in Notre Dame Cathedral, Paris as part of the), Hymn of Peace, Concerto for cello (Premiered by the Ypsilanti Symphony), (musical composition) O Master walk With Thee (pub. by Morningstar Music, 2005), Shepherds, what is the Lovely Fragance? (pub. by Cantica Nova), (musical comositions) As the Grains of Wheat (pub. by Augsburg Fortress press.). Mem.: Am. Guild Organists, Nat. Pastoral Musicians Assn. (assoc.). Roman Catholic. Achievements include Recitals: New York, Paris, The York Early Music festival, The Boston Early Music festival, Music in Time, Stanford University, radio broadcasts on WFMT, BBC England, Ave Maria National Catholic radio; research in Music Performances; Recitals at The Shrine of the Immaculate Conception, Washington D.C. Avocations: swimming, travel, gardening. Home: 3151 Greenwood Sugar Land TX 77478 Office Phone: 1-283-494-1156 x 261. Personal E-mail: ghmus7@hotmail.com.

HAMILTON, HARRY LEMUEL, JR., academic administrator, science educator; b. Charleston, SC, May 26, 1938; s. Harry Lemuel and Velma Fern (Bell) H.; m. LaVerne McDaniel, June 26, 1965 (div. 1978); children: David M., Lisa L; m. Mary MacIntyre, May 10, 1997. BA in Physics, Beloit Coll., 1960; MS in Meteorology, U. Wis., 1962, PhD in Meteorology, 1965. Asst. prof. atmospheric sci. SUNY, Albany, 1965-71, assoc. prof., 1971-90, dir. ednl. opportunity program, 1968-71, chairperson atmospheric sci., 1976-83, dean undergrad. studies, assoc. v.p. acad. affairs, 1983-88; rsch. scientist GE, Schenectady, N.Y., 1973-75; sr. v.p., provost Chapman U., Orange, Calif., 1990-2000, prof. atmospheric sci., 2000—05, interim provost, 2005—. Trustee Beloit (Wis.) Coll., 1972—, Newport Beach Pub. Libr., 2001—, pres., 2003--; bd. dirs. Albany Med. Ctr., 1988-90, Mohawk Hudson Cmty. Found., 1988-90; pres. Empire State Inst. for Performing Arts, Albany, 1986-90; bd. dirs. world affairs coun. Orange County, 1995-2003; treas. Arts Orange County, 1995-2000; bd. dirs. Discovery Sci. Ctr., 1998-2004. Mem. Am. Meteorol. Soc., Am. Assn. for Higher Edn. Office: Chapman U 1 University Dr Orange CA 92866-1005 Business E-Mail: hamilton@chapman.edu.

HAMILTON, HUGH BASIL, minister; b. Chateaublair, St. Vincent, Sept. 21, 1965; arrived in U.S., 1998; s. Hendrick Lowman and Lyn Grethel Hamilton; m. Diana Clover Coburn, June 26, 1993; children: Joel, Josianne. BA, U. of the W.I., Kingston, Jamaica, 1992; diploma in ministerial studies, United Theol. Coll. of the W.I., Kingston, 1992; MDiv, Drew U., 2002. Cert. ordination Meth. Ch. in Caribbean and Am. Pastor Meth. Ch., Tobago, West Indies, Trinidad, West Indies, 1995—98, St. Paul's/Woodmere United Meth. Ch., L.I., West Indies, 1998—, North United Meth. Ch., Hartford, Conn., 2001—. Dir. N.Y. Meth. Fed. Credit Union, White Plains, 2002—, Coalition for Equity and Justice, Hartford, 2004—. Elder N.Y. Ann. Conf. United Meth. Ch., 2001. Mem.: Tutors Club (bd. dirs. 2002—). Home: 33 Colebrook St Hartford CT 06112 Office: North United Meth Ch PO Box 320255 1205 Albany Ave Hartford CT 06132 Office Phone: 860-525-0573. E-mail: hughlasile@aol.com.

HAMILTON, JACKSON DOUGLAS, lawyer; b. Cleve., Feb. 5, 1949; m. Margaret Lawrence Williams, Dec. 19, 1971; children: Jackson Douglas Jr., William Schuyler Lawrence. BA, Colgate U., 1971; JD, U. Pa., 1974. Bar: Calif. 1974, U.S. Dist. Ct. (cen. dist.) Calif. 1974, U.S. Tax Ct. 1978, U.S. Ct. Claims 1984, U.S. Ct. Appeals (6th and 11th cirs.) 1988, N.C. 1991, U.S. Supreme Ct. 1991, US Ct. Appeals (4th cir.), 2004. Ptnr. Kadison, Pfaelzer, Woodard, Quinn & Rossi, L.A., 1986-87, Spensley, Horn, Jubas & Lubitz, L.A., 1987-91, Roberts & Stevens, Asheville, N.C., 1991—. Adj. prof. law U. San Diego, 1981, Golden Gate U., San Francisco, 1981-85, U. N.C., Asheville, 1994; cons. Calif. Continuing Edn. Bar, 1983-84, select com. on sports Calif. Senate, 1983-85. Editor Entertainment Law Reporter, 1979—; contbr. articles to profl. jours. Mem. ABA (tax sect., internat. law sect.), N.C. Bar Assn. (tax. sect. coun., treas.). Republican. Episcopalian. Office: Roberts & Stevens BB & T Bldg Asheville NC 28802 Office Phone: 828-252-6600.

HAMILTON, JACQUELINE, arts consultant; b. Tulsa, Mar. 28, 1942; d. James Merton and Nina Faye (Andrews) H.; m. Richard Sanford Piper, Jan. 2, 1968 (div. June 1976). BA, Tex. Christian U., 1965; grad., Stockholm U., 1967; postgrad., Harvard U., 1972—73, Tufts U., 1971, Rice U., 1982—83, Houston C.C., 1986—87. Art cons. for corps., pvt. collectors and mus., Houston, 1979—. Expert witness in lawsuits regarding art. Contbr. articles to profl. publs. Bd. dirs. Opera in the Heights. Mem.: AIA (affiliate), Internat. Assn. Profl. Art Advisors, Rice Design Alliance, Assn. Corp. Art Curators, Assn. Fund Raising Professionals, French-Am. C. of C., Norwegian-am. C. of C., Swedish-Am. C. of C., Swedish Club, L'Alliance Francaise, The Forum Club, The Houstonian Club. Presbyterian. Office: PO Box 1483 Houston TX 77251-1483 Personal E-mail: jhamiltonart@sprintmail.com.

HAMILTON, JANE, writer; b. 1957; Author: The Book of Ruth, 1988 (PEN/Ernest Hemingway Found. award, 1989), The Frogs Are Still Singing, 1989, A Map of the World, 1994, The Short History of a Prince, 1998 (Heartland prize for fiction), Disobedience, 2000, short stories. Office: Doubleday Pubs 1540 Broadway New York NY 10036

HAMILTON, JANET RENEE, protective services official; b. Oklahoma City, Sept. 22, 1959; d. Elvert L. Newton and Jelila M. Ramay; m. Jerry A. Hamilton, Oct. 14, 1995; children: Janette M, Sierra L. AA, Rose State Coll., 1985. Emergency Number Professional Nat. Emergency Number Assn., Fla., 2002. Account clk. Okla. Health Dept., Oklahoma City, 1985—88; constrn. sec. T A Forsberg, Punta Gorda, Fla., 88—91; 911 dir. Charlotte County Sheriffs Office, 1992—. Mem. Ams. with Disability Adv. Com., Port Charlotte, Fla., 2001—03, Fla. 911 Legis. Com., 2003—04, Nat. Emergency Number Assn. Pub. Edn., 2003—04. Republican. Presbyterian. Avocations: travel, crafts, boating. Office Phone: 941-575-5339. Office Fax: 941-575-5335. E-mail: hamilton@ccso.org.

HAMILTON, JEAN, finance company executive; BS in Comms., U. Ill.; MBA in Fin. and Acctg., U. Chgo. Sr. v.p., head N.E. banking First Nat. Bank Chgo. (now Bank One Corp.); exec. v.p. Prudential Ins. Co. Am., Newark, 1998—2002, CEO Prudential Instl., 2000—02; CEO Broadstairs Capital. Bd. mem. Renaissance Re Holdings, LTD, First Eagle Funds, Four Nations; coun. Grad. Sch. Bus. U. Chgo.; mem. Women's Forum NY Women's Forum Edn. Fund; bd. mem. Nat. Urban League, The Prudential Found., Prudential Investment & Mgmt. Svcs., Prudential P&C Holdings, Pruco Life, The Prudential Band & Trust Co., The Prudential Savings Bank, The Ind. Coll. Fund NJ, Rewards Plus, The Women's Econ. Roundtable, Standing Tall, Glass Roots, First Eagle Variable Funds. Named one of Bus. Ins. Top 100 Women in Ins., Risk Mgmt. and Employee Benefits, Top 100 Women in Insurance, Risk Mgmt. & Employee Benefits, Bus. News; named to Who's Who in NJ Bus. Leader List, NJ Star Ledger's 10 Most Powerful Women in Bus. List. Mem.: The Econ. Club NY.

HAMILTON, JEAN CONSTANCE, judge; b. St. Louis, Nov. 12, 1945; AB, Wellesley Coll., 1968; JD, Washington U., St. Louis, 1971; LLM, Yale U., 1982. Atty. Dept. of Justice, Washington, 1971-73, asst. U.S. atty. St. Louis, 1973-78; atty. Southwestern Bell Telephone Co., St. Louis, 1978—81; judge 22d Jud. Circuit State of Mo., St. Louis, 1982-88; judge Mo. Ct. Appeals (ea. dist.), 1988-90, U.S. Dist. Ct. (ea. dist.) Mo., 1990—, chief judge, 1995—2002. Office: US Courthouse 111 S 10th St Saint Louis MO 63102

HAMILTON, JERALD, musician; b. Wichita, Kans., Mar. 19, 1927; s. Robert James and Lillie May (Rishel) H.; m. Phyllis Jean Searle, Sept. 8, 1954; children: Barbara Helen, Elizabeth Sarah, Catharine Sandra. MusB, U. Kans., Lawrence, 1948, MusM, 1950; postgrad., Royal Sch. Ch. Music, Croydon, Eng., summer 1955, Union Theol. Sem. Sch. Sacred Music, N.Y.C., summer 1960; studies with, Laurel Everette Anderson, Andre Marchal,

Catharine Crozier, Gustav Leonhardt. From instr. to asst. prof. organ and theory Washburn U., Topeka, 1949-59; dir. Washburn Singers and Choir, 1955-59; asst. prof. organ, dir. univ. singers and chorus Ohio U., Athens, 1959-60; asst. prof. organ and ch. music U. Tex., Austin, 1960-63; lectr. ch. music Episcopal Theol. Sem. S.W., Austin, 1961-63; mem. faculty U. Ill., Urbana-Champaign, 1963-88, prof. music, 1967-88, prof. emeritus, 1988—; organist, choirmaster Grace Cathedral, Topeka, 1949—59, St. David's Ch., Austin, 1960—63, St. John the Divine, Champaign, 1963—88, St. John's Cathedral, Albuquerque, 1988-93, organist-choirmaster emeritus, 1994—. Mem., chmn. commn. ch. music Episc. Diocese Kans., 1951-59; mem. bishop's commn. ch. music Episc. Diocese of Springfield, 1978-80, 82-88; concert organist, 1955-96. Author (with Marilou Kratzenstein) Four Centuries of Organ Music, Detroit Studies in Music Bibliography No. 51, 1984. Fulbright scholar, 1954-55. Mem. Assn. Anglican Musicians, Omicron Delta Kappa, Pi Kappa Lambda, Phi Mu Alpha. Episcopalian. Home: PO Box 3836 Edgewood NM 87015-3836

HAMILTON, JOAN NICE, editor-in-chief; b. Chgo., 1948; d. William and Dorothy Nice. Grad., Pomona Coll., 1970. Former editor High Country News; editor Climbing Mag.; editor-in-chief Sierra Mag., San Francisco. Contbr. articles to Audubon, Defenders, Nat. Wildlife Mags. Office: Sierra Mag 85 2nd St San Francisco CA 94105-3459

HAMILTON, JOE, communications company executive; BA in Math., Fordham U.; MBA in Fin., U. Calif., Berkeley. Numerous positions including sr. v.p. capital markets divsn. Crocker Nat. Bank; chief adminstrv. officer, CFO Grubb & Ellis Co.; exec. dir. Brobeck, Phleger & Harrison Law Firm; C.O.O. and pres. Cunningham Comm., Inc., Palo Alto, Calif. Bd. dirs. Cunningham Comm., Inc.

HAMILTON, JOHN MCFARLAND, plastic surgeon, real estate developer; b. Lebanon, Tenn., July 5, 1925; s. Courtnay Cowper and Sarah Louise (Williamson) H.; m. Imogene Nicholson, Dec. 19, 1951; children: Susan Richards Hamilton Churuti, John McFarland Jr., Courtnay C., Scott Deering. BS, Tulane U., 1946; MD, La. State U., 1949. Diplomate Am. Bd. Plastic Surgery. Inter, resident in gen. surgery George Washington U. Hosp., Washington, 1949-51; resident in gen. and plastic surgery Baylor Med. Sch., Houston, 1953-56, instr. plastic surgery, 1956-57; pvt. practice, St. Petersburg, Fla., 1957—2001. Dir. cleft palate team All Children's Hosp., St. Petersburg, 1957-77; chief staff Children's Hosp., St. Petersburg, 1962-63, Bayfront Med. Ctr., St. Petersburg, 1982-83; lectr. med. jurisprudence Stetson U. Law Coll., St. Petersburg, 1974-80; vice chmn. Bayfront Life Svcs., St. Petersburg, 1985-86, Fla. Med. Polit. Action Com., Tallahassee, 1982-83. Assoc. editor Fla. Med. Jour., 1969-79; contbr. articles to med. jours., including Plastic and Reconstructive Surgery, Fla. Med. Jour., So. Med. Jour., Aesthetic Surgery Jour., Tech. Forum. Founder, treas. Pinellas County Polit. Action Com., St. Petersburg, 1963—; bd. dirs. Fla. Orch., Tampa, 1998-2004; vol. St. Petersburg Clinic, 2003-. Lt. USN, 1943-46; capt. USAF, 1950-53, Korea. Recipient A.J. Gorday award Bayfront Med. Ctr., 1986, Fund Raiser of Yr. award for Fla. West Coast Nat. Soc. Fund Raising Execs., 1987, Golden Baton award Fla. Orch., 1998. Fellow ACS; mem. AMA, Southeastern Soc. Plastic and Reconstructive Surgeons (editor Bull. 1964-68, pres. 1976), Fla. Med. Assn. (del. 1970-78), Fla. Soc. Plastic Surgeons (founding, pres. 1967-68), Pinellas County Med. Soc. (pres. 1975-76, Achievement award 1978, Svc. awards 1988, 2001). Republican. Methodist. Avocations: photography, clarinet, poetry. Home: 430 Brightwaters Blvd NE Saint Petersburg FL 33704-3712

HAMILTON, JOSEPH HANTS, JR., physicist, researcher; b. Ferriday, La., Aug. 14, 1932; s. Joseph Hants and Letha (Gibson) H.; m. Jannelle Jauree Landrum, Aug. 5, 1960; children: Melissa Claire, Christopher Landrum. BS, Miss. Coll., 1954; MS, Ind. U., 1956, PhD, 1958; DSc (hon.), Miss. Coll., 1982; PhD (hon.), Nat. U., Frankfurt, 1992, U. Bucharest, 1999, U. St. Petersburg, 2001, Joint Inst. for Nuc. Rsch., Russia, 2004. Mem. faculty Vanderbilt U., Nashville, 1958—, prof. physics, 1966—, Landon C. Garland prof. physics, 1981-92, Landon C. Garland disting. prof. physics, 1992—, chmn. dept., 1979-85; adj. prof. Tsinghua U., China, 1986—. Hon. adv. prof. Fudan U., People's Republic of China, 1988—; NSF postdoctoral fellow U. Uppsala, Sweden, 1958-59; rsch. fellow Inst. Nuclear Studies, Amsterdam, 1962; vis. prof. U. Frankfurt, 1979-80, 90, 98, U. Louis Pasteur, Strasbourg, France, 1991; mem. adv. panel Nat. Heavy Ion Labs., 1971-73; mem. nat. policy bd. Holifield Heavy Ion Facility, 1974-84; organizer, chmn. exec. com., prin. investigator Univ. Isotope Separator, Oak Ridge, 1970-95; organizer Univ. Radioactive Ion Beam Consortium, 1996; cons. Oak Ridge Nat. Lab., 1972—; mem. coun. Oak Ridge Assoc. Univs., 1974-80, bd. dirs., 1995-97; organizer, dir. Joint Inst. for Heavy Ion Rsch., Oak Ridge, 1980—; mem. Oak Ridge Health Agreement Steering Panel for State of Tenn., 1993-2000; sci. and tech. advisor coun. for State of Tenn., 1994-2001; chmn. Internat. Conf. Internal Conversion Processes, 1965, Internat. Conf. Radioactivity in Nuclear Spectroscopy, 1969, Internat. Conf. Future Directions in Studies Nuclei far from Stability, 1979, Internat. Conf. Dirs. Nuclear Structure Rsch., 1984; co-chmn. Internat. Workshop Physics with a Recoil Mass Spectrometer, 1986; chmn. Internat. Symposium on Reflections and Directions in Low Energy Heavy Ion Physics, 1991, Internat. Conf. on Fission and Properties of Neutron Rich Nuclei, 1997, Internat. Symposium Perspectives in Nuclear Physics, 1998; co-chair Second Internat. Conf. on Fission and Properties of Neutron Rich Nuclei, 1999; chair third Internat. Conf., on fission and properties neutron rich nuclei, 2002; dir. Vanderbilt Summer Sci. Collaborative for High Sch. Students and Tchrs., 1991—; vis. disting. lab. fellow Oak Ridge Nat. Lab., 2000—. Co-author: Science: Faith and Learning, 1972, ORAU from the Beginning, 1980, Graphical Representation of K-shell and Total Internal Conversion Coefficients from Z=30-104, 1984, Modern Atomic and Nuclear Physics, 1996; co-author, editor: Internal Conversion Processes, 1966, Radioactivity in Nuclear Spectroscopy, 1972, Reactions Between Complex Nuclei, 1974, Future Directions in Studies of Nuclear Far from Stability, 1980, Microscopic Models in Nuclear Structure Physics, 1989, Reflections and Directions in Low Energy Heavy Ion Physics, 1993, Structure of the Vacuum and Elementary Matter, 1997, Fission and Properties of Neutron Rich Nuclei, 1998, Perspectives in Nuclear Physics, 1999, Fission and Properties of Neutron Rich Nuclei, 2000; Third Internat. Conf. Fission and properties of Neutron Rich Nuclei, 2003. assoc. editor Jour. Physics G: Nuc. Physics, 1984-87; internat. advisor nuc. physics World Sci. Pub. Corp., 1986-91, Jour. Modern Physics Letters A, 1986-91; mem. editl. bd. Progress in Particle and Nuc. Physics, 1993-98; contbr. articles to profl. jours., chpts. in books. Mem. Mayor Nashville Citizens Adv. Com. Housing, 1970-74; bd. dirs. Vineyard Conf. Center, Louisville, 1972-77, Danforth assoc., 1965-86, So. Bapt. Conv. Hist. Commn., 1983-91. Recipient Harvie Branscomb Disting. Prof. award Vanderbilt U., 1983-84, Humbolt prize W. Germany, 1979, Order Golden Arrow Outstanding Alumni award Miss. Coll., 1985, Sutherland prize for rsch., 1988, Guy and Rebecca Forman award for outstanding physics tchg., 1990, Thomas Jefferson award for svc. in univ. couns., 1995, Jeffrey Nordhaus award for excellence in undergrad. tchg., 1996, Outstanding Sci. Tchr. award, Tenn., 1998, First Outstanding Svc. award Oak Ridge Associated U., 2000, D. Ilkovic Gold medal Slovak Acad. Sci., 2002; Internat. Sci. and Tech. Cooperation award, Peoples Republic China 2002, GN. Flerov Prize Russia 2003; named State of Tenn. Outstanding Prof. of Yr. Coun. Advancement and Support Edn., 1991; grantee NSF, 1959-76, ERDA-Dept. Energy, 1975—. Fellow AAAS (Internat. Cooperation award 1996), Am. Phys. Soc. (vice chmn. Southeastern sect. 1972-73, chmn. 1973-74, mem. coun. 1994-2004, Jesse Beams Gold medal for rsch. 1975, George Peagram Gold medal for tchg. 1988, Francis Slack gold medal for Svc. 2000); mem. Am. Assn. Physics Tchrs., Am. Inst. Physics (governing bd. 2004-), Sigma Xi (chpt. pres. 1970). Home: 305 Mountainside Dr Nashville TN 37215-4324 Office Phone: 615-322-2456. Business E-Mail: j.h.hamilton@vanderbilt.edu.

HAMILTON, JUDITH HALL, computer company executive; b. Washington, June 15, 1944; d. George Woods and Jane Fromm (Brogger) Hall; m. Stephen T. McCellan, Oct. 29, 1988. BA, Ind. U., 1966; postgrad., Boston U., 1966-68, UCLA, 1980-81. Programmer Sys. Devel. Corp., Santa Monica, Calif., 1968-69, dir. programming, 1975-80; sys. analyst Daylin, Inc., Beverly Hills, Calif., 1969-71; sys. mgr. Audio Magnetics, Gardena, Calif., 1971-73; pres. Databasics, Inc., Santa Monica, 1973-75; v.p. Computer Scis. Corp., El Segundo, Calif., 1980-87; ptnr. Ernst & Young, L.A., 1987-89, N.Y.C., 1989-91; sr. v.p., gen. mgr. Locus Computing Corp., L.A., 1991-92; pres., CEO Dataquest, Inc., a Dun & Bradstreet Corp., San Jose, Calif., 1992-95, First Floor Software, Mountain View, Calif., 1996-98, Classrm. Connect, El Segundo, 1999—2002. Dir. Lante Corp. Classroom Connect; bd. dirs. R. R. Donnelley, Software.com, Lante, inc., Evolve, Inc., Artistic Media Ptnrs., Giga Info. Sys., Expression Ctr. for New Media, Com. for Econ. Devel. Bd. dirs. Nat. Pks. Found., 2002—, Wildlife Conservation Soc., 1994—, Com. Breast Helath Project, 1994—99. Recipient Herman Wells Visionary award, Ind. U., 2002. Mem.: Info. Tech. Assn. Am., Assn. Data Processing Svc. Orgns. (bd. dirs., chmn.), Women's Forum West, Com. of 200, Commonwealth Club Silicon Valley (bd. dirs. 1997—99), Kappa Alpha Theta.

HAMILTON, KATHERYNE WORK, secondary school educator; b. Ft Morgan, Colo., Jan. 23, 1908; AB, Sterling Coll., 1929. Tchr. Rural H.S., Rolla, Kans., 1929—31; dir. Christian Edn. First Presbyn. Ch., Hutchinson, Kans., 1960—73. Home: 700 Monterey Pl #524 Hutchinson KS 67502-2266

HAMILTON, KENNETH HAWLEY, surgeon, consultant; b. N.Y.C., Oct. 1, 1933; s. Kenneth and Molly Hamilton; m. Jonna Mariann Hoeg, June 10, 1961; children: Karen Margaret, Ian. BA, Haverford Coll., 1955; MD, McGill U., 1960. Lic. instr. ACLS Am. Heart Assn. Rotating intern Montreal (Que., Can.) Gen. Hosp., 1960—61, asst. resident in medicine, 1961—62; resident in gen. surgery U. Hosps., Iowa City, 1962—66; staff surgeon U.S. Army Hosp., Würzburg, Germany, 1966—70, chief dept. surgery, 1969—70; staff surgeon Stephens Meml. Hosp., Norway, Maine, 1971—88, hon. staff, consulting staff, 1988—95; prin. med. dir. H.O.P.E. Healing of Persons Exceptional. Founder, prin. Healing of Persons Exceptional, South Paris, Maine, 1987—2004; pres. Tri-County Emergency Med. Svcs., Lewiston, Maine, 1974—78; med. dir. outpatient chem. dependency svcs. Stephens Meml. Hosp., Norway, 1990—94. Author: (nonfiction book) SoulCircling: The Journey to the Who, 2002. Mem. Oxford Hills Cmty. Partnership, South Paris, 1990—94. Lt. col. U.S. Army, 1966—70, Germany. Recipient Jefferson award, Am. Inst. for Pub. Svc., 1989. Fellow: ACS (surg. diplomate 1969, instr. ATLS 1980, pres. Maine chpt. 1986—88, mem. Maine chpt.); mem.: Soc. for Healing in Medicine (mem. steering com. Durham U. chpt. 2004—05), Am. Holistic Med. Found. (pres. 1990—92), Maine Med. Assn. (chmn. health care com. 1980—88), Tri-County Emergency Med. Svcs. (pres. 1974—78), John E. Fetzer Inst. Network for Relationship Centered Care, New Eng. Surg. Assn. (life), Network for Attitudinal Healing, Internat. Independent. Quaker. Home: 646 Paris Hill Rd South Paris ME 04281-6318 Office: HOPE Healing of Persons Exceptional PO Box 276 52 High St South Paris ME 04281-0276 Office Phone: 207-743-7458. Business E-Mail: kenhhope@hopehealing.org.

HAMILTON, LAIRD JOHN, professional surfer; b. San Francisco, Mar. 2, 1964; s. Bill and Joann Hamilton; m. Gabrielle Reece, Nov. 30, 1997; 1 child, Reece Viola. Featured on the cover of numerous magazines including Sports Illustrated, People, Life, GQ, L"Uomo Vogue (Italy), High Wind (Japan), Surf (Germany) and Paris Match (France); host The Extremists Outdoor Life Network, 1996—97, host, Fox Sports Net Planet Extreme Championships, 2000. Film appearances include: The Endless Summer 2, 1994; Waterworld, 1995; Die Another Day, 1995; Step into Liquid, 2003; exec. prodr.: (films) Riding Giants, 2004. Recipient Breakout Performance of Yr., Surfer Poll awards, 2000, Rider of Yr. award, France, 2000, ESPN's, Action Sports & Music award for Feat of Yr., 2001. Achievements include invention of the foilboard surfboard which incorporates hydrofoil technology; popularized the tow-in surfing technique.*

HAMILTON, LAURELL K., writer; b. Heber Springs, Ark., 1963; Author: Guilty Pleasures, 1993, The Laughing Corpse, 1994, Circus of the Damned, 1995, The Lunatic Cafe, 1996, Bloody Bones, 1996, The Killing Dance, 1997, Burnt Offerings, 1998, Blue Moon, 1998, Obsidian Butterfly, 2000, A Kiss of Shadows, 2001, Narcissus in Chains, 2002, A Caress of Twilight, 2003, Seduced By Moonlight, 2004, Incubus Dreams, 2004 (Publishers Weekly Bestseller). Office: c/o Author Mail Berkley Pub Penguin Group 375 Hudson New York NY 10014

HAMILTON, LEE HERBERT, educational association administrator; b. Daytona Beach, Fla., Apr. 20, 1931; m. Nancy Ann Nelson, Aug. 21, 1954; children: Tracy Lynn, Deborah Lee, Douglas Nelson. AB, DePauw U., 1952, hon. degree; scholar, Goethe U., Germany, 1952-53; JD, Ind. U., 1956; hon. degree, Hanover Coll., Detroit Coll. Law, Ball State U., U. S. Ind., Wabash Coll., Union Coll., Ind. U., Am. Univ., Marian Coll., Suffolk U. Mem. 89th-105th Congresses from 9th Dist. Ind., Washington, 1965-99; ranking minority mem. House com. internat. rels.; former chmn. select. com. to investigate covert arms transactions with Iran U.S. Congress, mem. joint econ. com., former chmn. fgn. affairs com., former co chair Joint com. Orgn. Congress, former chmn. Ho. intelligence com., former chmn. Ho. com. investigate Oct. surprise; dir. Woodrow Wilson Ctr. Internat. Scholars Smithsonian Instn., Washington, 1999—. Vice chmn., The Nat. Commn. on Terrorist Attacks Upon the U.S. (The 9-11 Commn.), 2002-04. Democrat. Office: Woodrow Wilson Ctr Internat Scholars One Woodrow Wilson Plz 1300 Pennsylvania Ave NW Washington DC 20004-3027

HAMILTON, LEONARD DERWENT, physician, molecular biologist; b. Manchester, Eng., May 7, 1921; came to U.S., 1949, naturalized, 1964; s. Jacob and Sara (Sandelson) H.; m. Ann Twynam Blake, July 20, 1945; children: Jane Derwent, Stephen David, Robin Michael. BA, Balliol Coll., Oxford U., Eng., 1943, BM, 1945, MA, 1946, DM, 1951; MA, Trinity Coll., Cambridge U., Eng., 1948, PhD, 1952. Diplomate Am. Bd. Pathology. USPHS rsch. fellow U. Utah, 1949-50; staff Sloan-Kettering Inst., N.Y.C., 1950-79, head isotope studies sect., 1957-64, assoc. scientist, 1965-79; staff Meml. Hosp., N.Y.C., 1950-65; faculty Sloan-Kettering div. Grad. Sch. Med. Scis. Cornell U., 1956-64; sr. scientist, head divsn. microbiology Med. Research Ctr. Brookhaven Nat. Lab., Upton, N.Y., 1964-76; head biomed. and environ. assessment divsn. Office. Environ. Policy Analysis, 1973-94. Attending physician Hosp. Med. Rsch. Ctr., 1964-85; dir. WHO Collaborating Ctr. for Assessment of Health and Environ. Effects of Energy Systems, 1983-97, WHO focal point on health and environ. effects of energy systems, 1983—, mem. WHO expert adv. panel on environ. hazards, 1983-98; prof. medicine Health Sci. Ctr., SUNY, Stony Brook, 1968—; adj. prof. biometry and epidemiology Med. U. S.C., Charleston, 1996—; cons. HEW, Ctr. Disease Control, Nat. Inst. Occupational Safety and Health, epidemiology study of Portsmouth Naval Shipyard, 1978-88; vis. fellow St. Catherine's Coll., Oxford U., 1972-73; internat. panel experts on fossil fuel UN Environment Programme, 1978, panel on nuclear energy, 1978-79, panel on renewable sources and comparative assessment of different sources, 1980; com. mem. Nat. Acad. Sci.-NRC, Washington, 1975-80; mem. N.Y.C. Mayor's Tech. Adv. Com. on Radiation, 1963-77, N.Y.C. Commr. of Health Tech. Adv. Com. on Radiation, 1978—; energy panel WHO Commn. on Health & Environment, 1990-91; mem. Interant. Expert Group 3, Comparative Environ. and Health Effects of Different Energy Systems for Electricity Generation, 1990-91; sr. expert Symposium on Electricity and the Environ., Helsinki, Finland, 1991. Editor: Gerrard Winstanley, Selections from His Works, 1944; Physical Factors and Modification of Radiation Injury, 1964; The Health and Environmental Effects of Electricity Generation-a Preliminary Report, 1974. Recipient Fed. Lab. Consortium award, 1990; Am. Cancer Soc. scholar, 1953-58; Commonwealth Fund grantee, 1955-62. Mem. AMA, Am. Assn. Cancer Rsch., Am. Soc. Clin. Investigation, Am. Soc. for Investigative Pathology, Soc. for Risk Analysis, Harvey Soc., Cosmos Club (Washington). Office: Brookhaven Nat Lab Upton NY 11973 Office Phone: 631-344-2004. E-mail: vanslyke@bnl.gov.

HAMILTON, LYMAN CRITCHFIELD, JR., telecommunications industry executive; b. L.A., Aug. 29, 1926; s. Lyman Critchfield and Edna Lorraine (Gluck) H.; m. Mary W. Shepard, June 25, 1949 (div. 1984); children: William, Richard, Douglas, David; m. Beverly C. Lannquist, Nov. 17, 1984. Student, U. Redlands, 1944-45; BA, Principia Coll., 1947; MPA, Harvard U., 1949; LLD (hon.), Waynesburg Coll., 1979. Budget examiner U.S. Bur. of Budget, Washington, 1950-56; asst. adminstr. U.S. Civil Adminstrn. of Ryukyu Islands, Okinawa, Japan, 1956-60; investment officer World Bank & IFC, Washington, 1960-62; with Internat. Telephone & Telegraph Corp., N.Y.C., 1962-79, treas., 1967-76, v.p., 1968-73, sr. v.p., 1973-74, exec. v.p., 1974-77, pres., 1977-79, chief oper. officer, 1977, chief exec., 1978-79; chmn., pres. Tamco Enterprises, Inc., N.Y.C., 1980-89; chmn., pres., chief exec. officer Imperial Corp. of Am., 1989-90; pres., chief exec. officer Alpine Polyvision, Inc., 1991-93, chmn., 1993. Chmn. vis. com. Gerald R. Ford Sch. Pub. Policy, U. Mich.; adv. com. Monterey Inst. of Internat. Studies; trustee Monterey (Calif.) Symphony and York Sch., Hartford (Conn.) Symphony. Lt. (j.g.) USNR, 1944—46. Mem. L.A. Country Club, Farmington Woods Country Club, Univ. Club, Old Capital Club (Monterey). Republican. also: 5485 Quail Meadows Dr Carmel CA 93923

HAMILTON, MALCOLM COWAN, retired librarian, personnel director; b. Bath, Maine, Jan. 29, 1938; s. Newell Cowan and Laura Emma (Munro) H. BA, U. Maine, 1961; MS, Simmons Coll., Boston, 1968. Cert. libr., tchr.; sr. profl. human resources cert. Tchr. English, Chelmsford (Mass.) H.S., 1961-67; libr. Harvard U. Grad. Sch. Edn., Cambridge, Mass., 1967-80, Harvard U. John F. Kennedy Sch. Govt., Cambridge, 1980-96, also univ. pers. libr., 1987—2002; project mgr. project adapt Harvard U., Cambridge, 1996-98, sr. cons. Office Human Resources, 1998-99; libr. Harvard U. Div. Sch., Cambridge, 1999—2003, ret., 2003. Author: Travel Index, 1988; editor, indexer: Education Literature, 1907-1932, 11 vols., 1979; compiler: Directory of Educational Statistics; A Guide to Sources, 1974; assoc. editor Jour. Policy Analysis and Mgmt., 1981-87. Mem. ALA, Assn. Coll. and Rsch. Librs., Spl. Librs. Assn. (chmn. ednl. div. 1975-76, chmn. social scis. div. 1985-86, pres. Boston chpt. 1987-88), Soc. for Human Resources Mgmt. Democrat. Anglican. Home: 24 Elmore St Arlington MA 02476-5928 Personal E-mail: mch12938@comcast.net.

HAMILTON, MARK R., academic administrator; BS, U.S. Mil. Acad., 1967; Ma in English lit., Fla. State U., 1973; grad., Armed Forces Staff Coll., U.S. Army War Coll. Comdr. Division Artillery, Fort Richardson, 1988-90; chief staff Alaskan Command, Elmendorf AFB, 1992-93; dep. dir. force structure, resource and analysis Joint Staff, Washington, 1995-97; head recruiting U.S. Army, Fort Knox, Ky., 1997-98; pres. U. Alaska, Fairbanks, 1998—. Office: U Alaska PO Box 755000 Fairbanks AK 99775-5000 Office Phone: 907-450-8000.

HAMILTON, PAT RAY, retired lawyer, state representative; b. Feb. 14, 1923; LLB, W.Va. U., 1949. With FBI, 1949-54; sr. ptnr. Hamilton, Burgess, Young & Pollard, Oak Hill, W.Va., 1954—90, 1997—2002, ret., 2002; mem. W.Va. Senate, 1972-80, W.Va. Ho. of Dels., 1982-86. Address: 10 Arbuckle Rd Oak Hill WV 25901-3109

HAMILTON, PATRICIA ROSE, art dealer; b. Phila., Oct. 21, 1948; d. William Alexis and Lillian Marie (Sloan) Hamilton. BA, Temple U., 1970; MA, Rutgers U., 1971. Sec. to curator Whitney Mus., NYC, 1971-73; sr. editor Art in Am., 1973; curator exhbns. Crispo Gallery, 1974-75; dir. Hamilton Gallery, 1976-84; artist's agt., 1984—2002; art dealer, 2002—. Democrat. Avocations: tennis, swimming, cooking. Home and Office: 6753 Milner Rd Los Angeles CA 90068-3214 Office Phone: 323-512-4737. Personal E-mail: hamiltonpatricia@sbcglobal.net.

HAMILTON, PETER BANNERMAN, manufacturing executive, lawyer; b. Phila., Oct. 22, 1946; s. William George Jr. and Elizabeth Jane (McCullough) H.; m. Elizabeth Anne Arthur, May 8, 1982; children— Peter Bannerman, Jr., Brian Arthur. AB, Princeton U., 1968; JD, Yale U., 1971. Bar: D.C. 1972, Pa. 1972, Ind. 1985. Mem. staff Office Asst. Sec. Def. for Systems Analysis and Office Gen. Counsel, Dept. Def., Washington, 1971-74; mem. firm Williams & Connolly, Washington, 1974-77; gen. counsel Dept. Air Force, Washington, 1977-78; dep. gen. counsel HEW, Washington, 1979, exec. asst. to sec., 1979; spl. asst. to Sec. and Dep. Sec. Def., Washington, 1979-80; ptnr. Califano, Ross & Heineman, Washington, 1980-82; v.p., gen. counsel, sec. Cummins Inc., 1983-86, v.p. law and treasury, 1987-88, v.p., CFO, 1988-95; sr. v.p., CFO, Brunswick Corp., Lake Forest, Ill., 1996-98, exec. v.p., CFO, 1998-99; vice chmn., pres. Brunswick Bowling and Billiards, 2000—04; vice chmn., pres Life Fitness, 2005—. Bd. dirs. Brunswick Corp. Articles editor: Yale Law Jour, 1970-71. Served to lt. USN, 1971-74. Home: 970 E Deerpath Lake Forest IL 60045-2212 Office: Brunswick Corp 1 N Field Ct Lake Forest IL 60045-4811

HAMILTON, RANDY HASKELL, city manager; b. N.Y.C., Dec. 27, 1921; s. Harry and Adelaide Beatrice (Haskell) H.; m. Ruth Manning (div. May 1961); children: Sarah Beth, Leander Munhall III; m. Louanne McKernan, Apr. 29, 1962; children: Jill Katherine, Jennifer Sabrina. BA, U. N.C., 1943, MA in Pub. Adminstrn., 1947, MA in City and Regional Planning, 1949; PhD, U. Zurich, Switzerland, 1963. City mgr. City of Carolina Beach, N.C., 1949-52; dir., assoc. dir. Nat. League Cities, Washington, 1952-56; city mgr., mcpl. adv. Royal Govt. Thailand, Bangkok, 1956-64; dir. comparative urban studies project UN/IPA, N.Y.C., 1964-65; spl. project dir. League Calif. Cities, Berkeley, Calif., 1965-73; dean Grad. Sch. Pub. Adminstrn., Golden Gate U., San Francisco, 1973-90; vis. scholar Inst. Govtl. Studies, U. Calif., Berkeley, 1990—. Mem. editl. bd. Pub. Adminstrn. Rev., 1970-75, Internat. Jour. Pub. Adminstrn., 1977—, State and Local Govt. Rev., 1980-86; editor Western Govtl. Rsch. Jour., 1990-92, Jour. of E Govt., 2003—. Chmn. Gov.'s Adv. Coord. Coun. Pub. Personnel, Sacramento, 1973; chmn. adv. com. Calif. State Welfare Grant, Sacramento, 1972, State Calif., Sacramento, 1975; mem. Calif. Coun. on Criminal Justice, Sacramento, Calif., 1971-73; chmn. Highland Hosp. Found., Oakland, Calif., 1991-93. Capt. USAF, 1943-46. Decorated comdr. Royal Order of Crown (Thailand); named Man of Yr., N.C. Lion's Club, 1950; recipient spl. citation U.S. CSC, 1975. Fellow Nat. Acad. Pub. Adminstrn. (life); mem. Internat. City Mgmt. Assn. (Stephen B. Sweeney award 1980), Am. Soc. for Pub. Adminstrn. (nat. pres. 1976). Republican. Presbyterian. Office: U Calif Inst Govtl Studies 109 Moses Hall Berkeley CA 94720-2370 Office Phone: 510-642-4633.

HAMILTON, RICHARD, Greek language educator; b. Bryn Mawr, Pa., Dec. 19, 1943; s. Charles and Elizabeth Hamilton; m. Lucinda Pantaleoni, Aug. 14, 1965; children: Sarah Elizabeth, Ellen Emma. AB, Harvard U., 1965; PhD, U. Mich., 1971. From asst. prof. to prof. Bryn Mawr Coll., 1971—. Author: Epinikion, 1974, Architecture of Hesiod, 1989, Choes and Anthesteria, 1992, Treasure Map, 2000. Home: 708 Pennstone Rd Bryn Mawr PA 19010-2913 Office: Bryn Mawr Coll Dept Greek 101 N Merion Ave Bryn Mawr PA 19010-2859

HAMILTON, RICHARD ALFRED, academic administrator, finance educator; b. Pitts., Dec. 22, 1941; s. Robert Curtis and Dorothy Katherine (Sexauer) Hamilton. BA, Otterbein Coll., 1965; MBA, Bowling Green State U., 1968; D in Bus. Adminstrn., Kent State U., 1973. Prodn, rate analyst dept. indsl. engring. RCA, Findlay, Ohio, 1966—67; computer sys. analyst dept. market rsch. Marathon Oil Co., Findlay, 1967—68; tchg. fellow Coll. Bus. Adminstrn. Kent State U., 1968—71; assoc. prof. direct mktg. U. Mo., Kansas City, 1971—; pres. Mission Woods Cons., Inc., 1977—. Cons. U.S. Senate Permanent Subcom. on Investigation, 1973—74, Midwest Rsch. Inst. and Office of Tech. Assessment of U.S. Congress, 1974—75; spkr. to profl. orgns. Author (with David R. Bywaters): How to Conduct Association Surveys, 1976; author: Tourism U.S.A.-Marketing Tourism, Vol. 3, 1978, Quantitative Direct Response Market Segmentation, 1989, Readings and Cases in Direct Marketing, NTC Business Books, Helzberg Diamonds-A Retailer's Use of Direct Marketing to Generate Store Traffic, 1995; contbr. articles to profl. jours. Recipient Cray Faculty award, U. Mo., 1987, Robert B. Clarke Outstanding Direct Mktg. Educator award, Direct Mktg. Ednl. Found., 1994, Disting. Rsch. in Mktg. award, Allied Acads., 2001; Univ. fellow, 1968—71, dissertation fellow, Marathon Oil Co., 1972, grant, UNKC, 1982.

Mem.: Direct Mktg. Assn., Am. Mktg. Assn., Beta Gamma Sigma. Methodist. Home: 5306 Mission Woods Rd Shawnee Mission KS 66205-2008 Office: U Mo Bloch Sch Adminstrn Kansas City MO 64110 Office Phone: 816-235-2313. E-mail: hamiltonr@umkc.edu.

HAMILTON, RICHARD CLAY, professional basketball player; b. Coatesville, Pa., Feb. 14, 1978; Student, U. Conn. Profl. basketball player Washington Wizards, 1999—2002, Detroit Pistons, 2002—. Named to USA Basketball Sr. Men's Nat. Team, 1999. Office: Detroit Pistons 4 Championship Dr Auburn Hills MI 48326*

HAMILTON, ROBERT APPLEBY, JR., insurance company executive; b. Boston, Feb. 20, 1940; s. Robert A. and Alice Margaret (Dowdall) H.; m. Ellen Kuhlen, Aug. 13, 1966; children: Jennifer, Robert Appleby III, Elizabeth. Student, Miami U. (Ohio), 1958-62. CLU; chartered fin. cons. With Travelers Ins. Co., various locations, 1962-65, New Eng. Mut. Life Ins. Co., various locations, 1965-90, regional pension rep. Boston, 1968-71, regional mgr. Chgo., 1972-83, sr. pension cons., 1983-90; mktg. and fin. cons. Snowbeck Enterprises, Inc., Geneva, Ill., 1990-97, ret., 1997. Producer Sta. WCTV; mem. Rep. Town Com., Wenham, Mass., 1970-72, Milton Twp., Ill., 1973-75; mem. Wenham Water Commn., 1970-72. Mem. Midwest Pension Conf. (chmn. 1989-90), Am. Soc. Pension Actuaries (assoc.), Am. Soc. CLUs, Am. Assn. Fin. Planners, Profit Sharing Coun. Am., Chgo. Coun. Fgn. Rels., Port Clyde Sailing Club, Alpha Epsilon Rho. Republican. Home: 110 Hamilton Ln Wheaton IL 60187-1807 also: 90 Shumaker Lane Tenants Harbor ME 04860-9709 Personal E-mail: erisabob@aol.com.

HAMILTON, ROBERT D., III, finance educator; b. Phila., Pa., Aug. 8, 1946; s. Robert Devitt Hamilton and Gretchen Longley Leopold; m. Jane Ewen Meier, June 3, 1981; 1 child, Robert Devitt. BS, Cornell U., 1968; MBA, U. Va., 1974; PhD, Northwestern U., 1981. Asst. dir. food svcs. George Washington U. Hosp., 1969—72; exec. dir. Nat. Program for Dermatology, Charlottesville, Va., 1974—75; assoc. exec. dir. Am. Acad. Dermatology, Evanston, 1975—77; lectr. dept. policy and environment Northwestern U., Evanston, Ill., 1981; asst. prof. Temple U., Phila., 1981—87, asst. dean grad. programs, 1989—91, assoc. prof., 1992—97, assoc. prof. dept. gen. and strategic mgmt., 1997—; fin. analyst/planner GM Corp., Detroit, 1983. Instr. evening divsn. Northwestern U., Evanston, 1979—80; spkr. numerous seminars. Contbr. numerous articles to profl. jours., chapters to books. Chair planning and stewardship com. St. Dunstan's Ch., Blue Bell, Pa., 1997—98, mem. vestry, bd. dirs., 1987—91, 1994—95, chair search com. for new rector, 1994—95, cons., co-chair stewardship com., 1987—90. Recipient Lindback Disting. Tchr. award, Temple U., 1993, Great Tchr.'s award, 1994, Asher award for outstanding faculty, 1994; fellow, Northwestern U., 1980; scholar, 1978—79. Mem.: Beta Gamma Sigma, Theta Delta Chi. Episcopalian. Home: 205 Plymouth Rd Gwynedd Valley PA 19437 Office: Temple U Sch Bus and Mgmt Dept Gen and Strategic Mgmt Philadelphia PA 19122

HAMILTON, ROBERT LEE, history educator; b. Shelbyville, Ky., Nov. 3, 1953; s. Lowell Hudson Hamilton and Thelma Doris Rucker; m. Judy Carol Howard, Dec. 15, 1973; children: Charity Elizabeth, Hayley Meredith. AA in gen. edn., Edison Cmty. Coll., 1999; BA in sec. edn., Fla. Gulf Coast U., 2000, MA in curriculum and instrn., 2001. Programmer/analyst Common-Wealth of Ky., Frankfurt, 1975—80; contract programmer Capital Holding Corp., Louisville, 1981—84; sys. analyst Blue Cross Blue Shield, Louisville, 1984—87, Health Mgmt. Assn., Naples, Fla., 1989—2000; history tchr. Collier County Pub. Schools, Naples, Fla., 2001—05. Social studies dept. chair Manatee MS, Naples, 2003—04. Vol. Project Literacy U.S., Shelbyville, 1986—88; pres. PTA Southside Elem., Shelbyville, 1987—88. Recipient Manatee Mid. Sch. Tchr. of the Yr., 2003, Collier County Mid Sch. Social Studies Tchr. of the Yr., Collier County, 2003, Golden Apple Tchr. of Distinction, Edn. Found., 2004. Mem.: Collier County Coun. for Social Studies, Fla. Coun. for Social Studies, Nat. Coun. for Social Studies. Democrat. Bapt. Avocations: gardening, genealogy. Office: Manatee Mid Sch 1920 Manatee Rd Naples FL 34114 Personal E-mail: ky2flbob@aol.com.

HAMILTON, ROBERT WOODRUFF, legal association administrator, retired law educator; b. Syracuse, NY, Mar. 4, 1931; s. Walton Hale and Irene (Till) H.; m. Dagmar S. Strandberg, June 2, 1953; children: Eric Clark, Robert Andrew, Meredith Hope. BA, Swarthmore Coll., 1952; JD, U. Chgo., 1955. Bar: D.C. 1956, U.S. Ct. Appeals (D.C. cir.) 1960, U.S. Supreme Ct. 1965. Law clk. to justice Tom Clark U.S. Supreme Ct., Washington, 1955-56; assoc. Gardner, Morrison & Rogers, Washington, 1956-64; assoc. prof. law U. Tex., Austin, 1964-67, prof., 1967—2004, ret., 2004, prof. emeritus, 2004—05, Minerva House Drysdale Regents chair in law. Rsch. dir. U.S. Admin. Conf., Washington, 1972-73; vis. prof. U. Pa., U. Minn., Washington U., St. Louis, others; Godfrey Disting. prof. law U. Maine Law Sch., 1992, 2003; mem. rev. panel on new drugs HEW, Washington, 1974-77. Author: Texas Practice, vols. 19 and 20, 1973, Cases on Corporations, 1975; author: (with Jonathan Macey) 8th rev. edit., 2003; author: Cases on Contracts, 1984, 2d rev. edit., 1992, Nutshell on Corporations, 1980, 5th rev. edit., 2000, Cases on Corporate Finance, 1984, 2d rev. edit., 1989, Fundamentals of Modern Business, 1990, Money Management for Lawyers and Clients, 1993, Business Organizations: Unincorporated Businesses and Closely Held Corporations, 1996, Business Basics for Law Students, 2d edit., 1998; author: (with Richard Booth) 3d edit., 2002. Chmn. bd. dirs. U. Tex. Coop., 1989-01, U. Coop. Soc., Austin, 1989-02; elected mem. Westlake Hills (Tex.) City Coun., 1969-72; chmn. zoning commn. Westlake Hills, 1983-87. Rsch. grantee U. Tex., 1970, 84, 92, 97. Mem. ABA (reporter), Am. Law Inst., Tex. Bar Assn. (partnership com., corp. laws com.), Tex. Bus. Law Found., Order of Coif. Democrat. Mailing: U Tex Law Sch 727 E Dean Keeton St Austin TX 78705-3224 Office Phone: 512-232-1298. E-mail: rhamilton@mail.law.utexas.edu.

HAMILTON, RONALD RAY, minister; b. Evansville, Ind., May 6, 1932; s. Floyd Ray Hamilton and Ruby Dixon (Chism) Hahn; m. Norma Jean Robertson, Mar. 25, 1956; children: Ronnetta Jean, Andrea, Robert Rae. BA, U. Evansville, 1955; BD, Garrett Theol. Sem., 1958, MDiv, 1972; PhD, Oxford Grad. Sch., Eng., Dayton, Tenn., 1989. Ordained elder United Meth. Ch. Minister Scobey (Mont.) Meth. Ch., 1958-61, St. Andrew Meth. Ch., Littleton, Colo., 1961-67; sr. minister First Meth. Ch., Grand Junction, Colo., 1967-75, Christ United Meth. Ch., Salt Lake City, 1975-80, Littleton United Meth., 1980-86, U. Park United Meth., Denver, 1986-91, First United Meth. Ch., Sun City, Ariz., 1992-98; chaplain Sun Health Corp., Sun City, 1998—. Author: The Way to Success, 1972, The Greatest Prayer, 1983, A Chosen People, 1986; editor jour., 1978. Recipient Spl. award Mental Health Assn., Mesa County, Colo., 1974, Goodwill Rehab. Inc., 1975. Mem. Lions Club, Rotary Club, Civitan (chaplain 1964-67). Republican. Avocations: acting, directing, travel, chess. Home: 20846 N 107th Dr Sun City AZ 85373-2388 Office: Boswell Meml Hosp 10401 W Thunderbird Blvd Sun City AZ 85351

HAMILTON, SAMUEL C., not-for-profit fundraiser; Grad., Clark Coll., 1965. Regional dir. Aetna Life and Casualty Co.; deputy dir. Hartford Econ. Develop. Com., exec. dir. Sr. grand vice polemarch; grand polemarch Kappa Alpha Psi, 2003—. Named one of 100 Most Influential Black Americans, Ebony mag., 2004, 2005; recipient Cmty. Svc. award, United Way Capital Area, 2001. Office: Kappa Alpha Psi 2322-24 N Broad St Philadelphia PA 19132-4590 Office Phone: 215-228-7184. Office Fax: 215-228-7181.*

HAMILTON, STEPHEN DAVID DERWENT, lawyer; b. N.Y.C., Oct. 26, 1952; m. Ona Petra Murdoch, Dec. 1, 1984; 3 children. AB magna cum laude, Princeton U., 1973; JD magna cum laude, Harvard U., 1976. Bar: N.Y. 1977, Pa. 1989. Law clk. to Judge J. Edward Lumbard U.S. Ct. Appeals (2d cir.), N.Y.C., 1976-77; assoc. Paul, Weiss, Rifkind, Wharton & Garrison, N.Y.C., 1977-88, Drinker Biddle & Reath, Phila., 1988-90, ptnr., bus., fin. dept., 1991—, and head, tax practice group. Editor Harvard Law Rev., 1974-76; contbr. articles on fed. income taxation to profl. jours. Mem. ABA (taxation sect.), Phila. Bar Assn. (chmn. fed. tax com. 1992-95), Am. Coll. Tax Counsel Office: Drinker Biddle & Reath LLP One Logan Sq 18th & Cherry Sts Philadelphia PA 19103-6996 Office Phone: 215-988-1990. Office Fax: 215-988-2757. Business E-Mail: stephen.hamilton@dbr.com.

HAMILTON, THOMAS ALLEN, independent insurance agent, securities representative; b. Oklahoma City, July 7, 1947; s. Vernon Carlton and Hazel (Margie) H.; m. Deborah; children: Travis Matthew, Heather Lynne. BBA Mktg. and Mgmt., Okla. U., 1969. Registered securities rep. Mass. Fin. Group, 1984, Sunesco, 1994, LifeMark Securities, Okla. City, 1995, Leonard Securities, Inc., 2003. Dept. mgr. J.C. Penney, Oklahoma City, 1969-71; spl. agt. CNA Ins., Oklahoma City, 1971-74; group cons. Mass. Mut. Ins. Co., Oklahoma City, 1974-79, qualified plan cons.; bus./estate/ins. cons. Mass Mut. Ins. Co., Oklahoma City, 1979-93; ins./investment cons. Sun Fin. Group, Oklahoma City, 1993-95; ind. ins. agt. and fin. advisor Hamilton Ins./Fin. Svs.-licensed in property/casualty, life/health, disability, employee benefit plans, retirement and investment planning, 1996—; registered rep. Leonard Securities, Inc., Oklahoma City, 2003—. Past chmn. troop 177 Boy Scouts Am., Oklahoma City, 1987-88; mem. Crossings Cmty. Ch. Mem. Nat. Assn. Ins. and Fin. Advisors, Nat. Assn. Health Underwriters, Oklahoma City Art Mus., Integris Med. Ctr. Okla. Found., Oklahoma City C. of C., Oklahoma City Ski Club, Oklahoma City Swing Dance Club. Republican. Protestant. Home: 6100 W Gun Hill Way Oklahoma City OK 73132 Office: 4334 NW Expressway St Ste 242 Oklahoma City OK 73116 Office Phone: 405-608-0295. Personal E-mail: tah47@msn.com.

HAMILTON, THOMAS MICHAEL, marketing executive; b. Bronxville, N.Y., Jan. 8, 1947; s. Harold Thomas and Mary Theresa (Byrne) H.; m. Kathryn Borys, May 24, 1984. BS, SUNY, Buffalo. Sales mgr. Herk, Inc., N.Y.C., 1971-73; account exec. William Esty Co., Inc., N.Y.C., 1973-77, account supr., 1977-80, v.p., assoc. dir. sales promotion, 1980-83, sr. v.p., dir. sales promotion, 1983-88; pres. Hamilton Promotions, Inc., Katonah, N.Y., 1988-89; v.p. mktg. Harrington, Righter & Parsons Inc., N.Y.C., 1989-94; prin. The Hamilton Way, Katonah, N.Y., 1994—. Fundraiser United Way of Greater N.Y., 1976-84; council mem. HIP Consumer Council, N.Y.C., 1985; mem. North East Katonah (N.Y.) Community League, 1987—. Served to 1st lt. USAF, 1968-71. Mem. Mktg. Communications Execs. Internat. (bd. dirs. 1983-86), Promotion Mktg. Assn. Am. (bd. dirs. 1986-93, exec. com. 1987-93, vice-chmn. 1989-90, chmn.-elect 1990-91, chmn. bd. 1991-92, chmn. emeritus 1993-94). Avocations: golf, travel.

HAMILTON, TODD, professional golfer; b. Galesburg, Ill., Oct. 18, 1965; m. Jaque Hamilton; 3 children. Grad., U. Okla. Profl. golfer PGA Can. Tour, 1988—89, Nationwide Tour, 1991, PGA Asian Tour, 1992—2002, PGA Tour, 2003—. Recipient Asian Tour Order of Merit champion, 1992. Achievements include 6 Career International Victories; 2 Career PGA Tour Victories; winner British Open, 2004; winner Honda Classic, 2004. Avocations: crossword puzzles, hockey, basketball. Office: c/o PGA Tour PO Box 109601 100 Avenue of Champions Palm Beach Gardens FL 33418

HAMILTON, TYLER, professional cyclist, Olympic athlete; b. Mar. 1, 1971; Profl. Cyclist, 1995—, U.S. Postal Service, 1998—2001, CSC-Tiscali Team, 2001—03, Phonak Team, 2004. Mem. U.S. Olympic Cycling Team, Sydney, 2000, Athens, 04. The Tyler Hamilton Foundation, 2003—. Recipient Coeur de Lion awards, 16 Tour de France, 2003. Achievements include finished 1st, Liege-Bastogne-Liege, 2003; won, Tour of Romandie, 2003. Office: c/o USOC 1 Olympic Plaza Colorado Springs CO 80909

HAMILTON, VIRGINIA MAE, mathematics professor, consultant; b. Winchester, Indiana, Apr. 15, 1946; d. Charles and Mildred Alene (Horseman) Campbell; m. William Earl Hamilton, Dec. 27, 1974; 1 child, Michelle Annette. BS in math., Ball State U., Muncie, Ind., 1968, MA in math., 1974. Math. tchr. Osborn High Sch., Manassas, Va., 1968-71; grad. asst., math. Ball State U., Muncie, Ind., 1971-74; math. tchr. Wes Del High Sch., Gaston, Ind., 1974-76, Ball State U., Muncie, Ind., 1977-87, dir. testing and placement, dir. math learning ctr., 1984-87; math. prof. Shawnee State U., Portsmouth, Ohio, 1987—, dir. assessment, 1995—2004. Cons. assessment, Fla. and Ohio 2000-; faculty devel. mentor, ACCLAIM NSF project 2002-; assessor, Ohio Dept. of Edn.1999-; program assessor/evaluator for Ohio Dept. of Edn., 2001-; cons. placement testing several universities., Calif., Ind., Ohio, 1986—; cons. in svc. Scioto County Schs., Portsmouth, Ohio, 1989—; mentor-tchr. Minority Edn. Advs., Muncie, Ind., 1985-87; presenter, Ohio Acad. Sci., Portsmouth, Ohio, 1988—; assessment chair nat. project to reform Devel. Math., 1992-1998; steering com. Project Discovery South Region, 1994-98; facilitator math. workshop Devel. Edn., 1997; mem. Ohio Faculty Coun., 1998—, exec. bd. dirs., 1999—; coord. gen. edn. conf. Ohio Bd. Regents, 2002-03; mem. oversight bd. Ohio Math. Project, 2004; presenter in field; spkr. in field. Chair, 1999-2002; mem. of a twenty five person people to people math edn. del. to mainland China to advise Chinese Educators on revision of their math edn program in Oct. 2000; author: Testbank for Fundamentals of Mathematics, 1989, Testbank for Elementary Algebra, 1989, Testbank for Intermediate Algebra, 1990, Prepared Tests for Elementary Algebra, 1990, (computer software) Dose Calc, 1984, Arithmetic Skill Builder, 1987, Instructors Manual and Testbank for Intermediate Algebra, 1995; editor: (testbanks) Keedy-Bittinger Worktext Trilogy, 1986, Intermediate Algebra, 1986. Mem. NEA, ASCD, Assn. Appalachian Tchr. Educators, Assn. Tchr. Educators, Nat. Coun. Tchrs. Math., Nat. Assn. Devel. Educators (chmn. com. on math. placement 1990—1998, co-chair math. SPIN 1994-97), Math. Assn. Am., Ohio Coun. Tchrs. Math., South Ctrl. Ohio Coun. Tchrs. Math. (bd. dirs. 1993-97), Ohio Assn. Devel. Educators (chmn. spl. interest group 1989-1999, treas., 1992-97, Svc. award 1992), Ohio Edn. Assn., Am. Math. Assn. 2-Yr. Colls., Am. Assn. Higher Edn., Appalachian Tchrs. Math. Avocations: crochet, plaster craft. Office: Shawnee State U 940 2nd St Portsmouth OH 45662-4347 Office Phone: 740-351-3342. Business E-Mail: ghamilton@shawnee.edu.

HAMILTON, VIRGINIA VAN DER VEER, historian, educator; b. Kansas City, Mo., Sept. 7, 1921; d. McClellan and Dorothy (Rainold) Van der Veer; m. Lowell S. Hamilton, Aug. 4, 1946; children: Carol, David. AB, Birmingham (Ala.)-So. Coll., 1941, MA (Ford Found. Fund Adult Edn. fellow), 1961; PhD, U. Ala., Tuscaloosa, 1968; LittD, U. Ala., 1992. Staff writer AP, Washington, 1942—46, Birmingham News, 1948—50; asst. prof. history U. Montevallo, Ala., 1951—55; asst. prof., asst. to pres. pub. rels. Birmingham-So. Coll., 1955—65; lectr. in history U. Ala., Birmingham, 1965—68, asst. prof., 1968—71, assoc. prof., 1971—75, prof., 1975—87, prof. emerita, 1987—. Author: Hugo Black: The Alabama Years, 1972, Alabama: A History, 1977, The Story of Alabama, 1980, Your Alabama, 1980, Seeing Historic Alabama, 1982, rev. edit., 1996, Lister Hill: Statesman from the South, 1987, Looking For Clark Gable and Other 20th Century Pursuits, 1996; editor: Hugo Black and the Bill of Rights, 1978. Faculty Rsch. grantee U. Ala. at Tuscaloosa, 1969, U. Ala. at Birmingham, 1973-74, 74-75. Mem. So., Am. hist. assns., Orgn. Am. Historians, Soc. Am. Historians, Ala. Assn. Historians, Ala. Hist. Soc. Home: 2350 Montevallo Rd Apt 1602 Birmingham AL 35223-2342

HAMILTON, WARREN BELL, geologist, researcher, geophysicist, educator; b. L.A., May 13, 1925; s. Errett Campbell and Erva Laura (Bell) Hamilton; m. Alicita Victoria Koenig, Dec. 23, 1947; children: Lawrence C., Kathryn E., James D. BA, UCLA, 1945, PhD, 1951; MS, U. So. Calif., 1949. Asst. prof. U. Okla., Norman, 1951-52; from geologist to sr. scientist U.S. Geol. Survey, Denver, 1952-95, Pecora fellow emeritus, 1995-96; Disting. sr. scientist Colo. Sch. Mines, Golden, 1996—. Sr. exch. scientist Acad. Scis., USSR, 1967; vis. prof. Scripps Inst. Oceanography, San Diego, 1968, 79, Calif. Inst. Tech., Pasadena, 1973, Yale U., New Haven, 1980, U. Amsterdam, Netherlands, 1981; mem. plate tectonics del. to China and Tibet, 79; disting. lectr. Am. Assn. Petroleum Geologists, 1983—84; nominator MacArthur Found., 1984—85; vis. scholar We. Mich. U., 1984; Wilbert disting. lectr. La. State U., 1985, adj. prof., 2000—02; regents lectr. U. Calif., Santa Barbara, 1986, San Diego, 90, UCLA, 1988; Hooker disting. lectr. McMaster U., 1990; Ketin lectr. Istanbul (Turkey) Tech. U., 1998; adj. prof. U. Wyo., 2000—; Allday lectr. U. Tex., Austin, 2002; Disting. Alumni lectr. UCLA, 2004. Author: (book) Tectonics of the Indonesian Region, 1979; contbr. articles to profl. jours.; assoc. editor: Geology, 1973—82, Jour. Geophys. Rsch., 1974—76. With USN, 1943—46. Recipient Disting. Svc. award, U.S. Dept. Interior, 1981. Fellow: Geol. Assn. Can., Geol. Soc. Am. (chmn. Cordilleran sect. 1987—88, councilor 1995—98, Penrose medal 1989), Geol. Soc. London (hon.); mem.: NAS, Am. Geophys. Union, Colo. Sci. Soc. (hon.). Office: Colo Sch of Mines Dept of Geophysics Golden CO 80401 Business E-Mail: whamilto@mines.edu.

HAMILTON, WENDY J., foundation administrator; b. N.Y. m. Lawrence Hamilton; children: Kaitlin, Ryan, Greer. Student, Genesee C.C., Batavia. Mem. Ind. chpt. MADD, 1984—, mem. nat. bd. dirs., 1995—, v.p. victim issues, v.p. field issues, nat. pres., 2002—, founder Ill. chpt., founder N.Y. chpt., N.Y. state chair, 1990—94, 1997—98, pub. policy liaison Md. chpt., 1998—2002.

HAMILTON, WILLIAM BERRY, JR., retired transportation executive; b. Birmingham, Ala., Apr. 4, 1929; s. William Berry and Nettie (Whatley) H.; m. Jean Lucile Patteson, Feb. 1, 1951; children: Jean Lucile, Ann Elizabeth, William Berry III. BA, Vanderbilt U., 1951. Accountant Hiwassee Constructors, Chattanooga, 1952; cert. pub. acct. O.E. Johnson & Assocs., Chattanooga, 1952-54; controller, gen. mgr. Spl. Products Co., Inc., Chattanooga, 1954-59; v.p., controller Ryder Truck Lines, Inc., Jacksonville, Fla., 1959-65; v.p. finance Chgo. Rawhide Mfg. Co., 1965-67; v.p., controller-treas. Sea-Land Service Inc., Elizabeth, N.J., 1967-69, exec. v.p. adminstrn., dir., 1969-75; v.p., treas., asst. sec. McLean Industries, Inc., Elizabeth, 1968-74; pres. Monterey Transp. Co., Inc. (subs. R.J. Reynolds Industries, Inc.), Winston-Salem, N.C., 1975-77; pres., dir. Security-First Corp., Jacksonville, Fla., 1977-82; chmn. bd., pres. St. John's Marine Fin. Co. Inc., 1979-95; chmn., chief exec. officer Port of Monmouth Devel. Corp., 1983-87; dir., mem. exec. com. J.J. Henry Co., Inc., N.Y.C., 1981-85; ret. Chmn. bd. Henry Laurel Co. Inc., 1983-87; dir. Henry Properties Ltd., L.I. Devel. Co. Ltd.; instr. acctg. U. Chattanooga, 1953-54 Served with USAF, 1951-52. Recipient Guest Lectr. award U. Fla., 1965 Mem. Am. Bur. Shipping, Soc. Naval Architects and Marine Engrs., Am. Inst. C.P.A.s, Financial Execs. Inst., Am. Trucking Assn. (nat. bd. dirs., chmn. methods and procedures nat. accounting 1959-65), Nat. Def. Transp. Assn., Nat. Assn. Accountants (named most valuable mem. Jacksonville 1959-60, chpt. v.p., bd. dirs. 1960-63), Tenn. Soc. C.P.A.s, Am. Accounting Assn., Nat. Officer Mgmt. Assn., Am. Mgmt. Assn., U.S. Power Squadron, USCG Aux., Propeller Club of U.S., Navy League, Phi Delta Theta, Pi Delta Epsilon. Episcopalian (vestryman). Clubs: Fla. Yacht, River (Jacksonville); Ponte Vedra, Sawgrass (Ponte Vedra Beach, Fla.); Sea Bright (N.J.) Beach; N.Y. Yacht, World Trade Center, Vanderbilt Alumni, Whitehall (N.Y.C.); Twin-City (Winston-Salem); Cat Cay (Bahamas). Lodge: Kiwanis. Home: 695B Ponte Vedra Blvd # 103 Ponte Vedra Beach FL 32082-2783 E-mail: bhamijr@bellsouth.net.

HAMILTON-KEMP, THOMAS ROGERS, organic chemist, educator; b. Lebanon, Ky., May 13, 1942; s. Thomas Rogers and Catherine Rose (Hamilton) K.; m. Lois Ann Groce, Sept. 13, 1980. AA, St. Catharine Coll., 1962; BA, U. Ky., 1964, PhD in Chemistry, 1970. Asst. prof. natural products chemistry U. Ky., Lexington, 1970-75, assoc. prof., 1975-85, prof., 1985—. Contbr. articles to profl. jours. Mem. SAR, Am. Chem. Soc., Am. Soc. Hort. Sci., Sigma Xi, Gamma Sigma Delta Democrat. Roman Catholic. Home: 2025 Williamsburg Rd Lexington KY 40504-3015 Office: U Ky Agrl Sci Ctr N Rm N308 Lexington KY 40546-0001 E-mail: tkemp@uky.edu.

HAMISTER, DONALD BRUCE, retired electronics company executive; b. Cleve., Nov. 29, 1920; s. Victor Carl and Bess Irene (Sutherl) H.; m. Margaret Irene Singiser, Dec. 22, 1946; children: Don Bruce, Tracy. AB cum laude, Kenyon Coll., 1947, LLD (hon.), 1989; postgrad., Stanford U., 1948-49, U. Chgo., 1957; LLD (hon.), Kenyon Coll., 1989. Application engr. S.E. Joslyn Co., Cin., 1947-48; regional sales mgr. Joslyn Mfg. and Supply Co., St. Louis, 1950-52, mktg. mgr. Chgo., 1953-55, asst. to pres., 1956-57, mgr. aircraft arrester dept., 1958-62, gen. mgr. electronic systems div., 1962-71, v.p., gen. mgr., dir. Goleta, Calif., 1973-78, group v.p. indsl. products, 1974-78, pres., chief exec. officer, 1978-85, chmn., 1979-94, ret. chmn., 1994; chmn. Joslyn Mfg. and Supply Co. named changed to Joslyn Corp., 1986; also bd. dirs. Joslyn Corp., 1973—; pres. Joslyn Stainless; chmn. emeritus Joslyn Corp., Goleta, 1995—; pres., dir. Joslyn Stamping Co.; pres., chmn., dir. Joslyn Def. Systems, Inc., 1981—; dir. Brewer Tichener Corp.; chief exec. officer Joslyn Corp., Chgo., 1991-94, ret., 1994. Served to lt. USNR, 1942-46. Mem. IEEE, Airline Avionics Inst. (pres., chmn. 1972-74) Clubs: Univ. (Chgo.). Personal E-mail: dbh1141@aol.com.

HAMKINS, JON, electrical engineer; s. Clark and Monica Hamkins; m. Meera Srinivasan. BS, Calif. Inst. Tech., 1990; MS, U. Ill., 1993, PhD, 1996. Mem. tech. staff Jet Propulsion Lab., Calif. Inst. Tech., Pasadena, 1996—2001, supr., info. processing group, 2001—. Recipient Certificates of Recognition, NASA, 1998, 2003, 2004, NASA award Tech. Excellence, 2002, Level B award, Interplanetary Network Directorate, NASA, 2003. Mem.: IEEE (sr.). Achievements include research in communications technologies used in NASA's robotic deep space exploration. Office: Jet Propulsion Lab Caltech 4800 Oak Grove Dr Mail Stop 238-420 Pasadena CA 91109-8099 Office Phone: 818-354-4764. E-mail: jon.hamkins@jpl.nasa.gov.

HAMLET, RICHARD GRAHAM, education educator, researcher; b. Mpls., Mar. 27, 1938; s. Leon and Charlotte Hamlet; m. Corinne McWilliams, May 9, 1987; m. Sandra Horstman, Jan. 4, 1958 (div.); children: Alan, Rita. BS in Elec. Engring., U. Wis., 1959; MS in Engring. Physics, Cornell U., 1964; PhD in Computer Sci., U. Wash., 1971. Intern in coll. tchg. Shimer Coll., Mt. Carroll, Ill., 1962—64; systems supr. U. Wash., 1968—69; dir. systems programming Computer Ctr. Corp., Seattle, 1968—70; from asst. to assoc. prof. U. Md., College Park, 1971—84; vis. lectr. U. Melbourne, Australia, 1982—83; prof. Oreg. Grad. Ctr., Beaverton, 1984—88; Fulbright scholar U. Coll. Galway, Ireland, 1998—99; E. T. S. Walton fellow Nat. U. Ireland, Galway, 2003—04; prof. Portland State U., Oreg., 1988—, chmn. dept. computer sci., 1997—98. Cons. Naval Rsch. Lab., Washington, 1976—78, IBM Fed. Systems Divsn., Gaithersburg, Md., 1978—83. Author: (textbook) Introduction to Computation Theory, 1974, Principles of Computer Programming: a Mathematical Approach, 1987, The Engineering of Software, 2001; contbr. more than 50 articles to tech. jours. Grantee $683, 000, NSF, 1978-1979, 1988-1993, 2001-2004, $858, 000, Air Force Office of Sci. Rsch., 1979-1985, 1986-1987. Mem.: IEEE, Assn. for Computing Machinery. Achievements include development of major prototype systems for software testing. Office Phone: 503-725-3216. Business E-Mail: hamlet@cs.pdx.edu.

HAMLETT, JAMES GORDON, electronics engineer, management consultant, educator; b. Utica, N.Y. BSEE, Syracuse U., 1947-49; BSBA, SUNY, Syracuse, 1985; MBA, City U., Seattle, 1991. Cert. profl. cons.; chartered cons.; cert. vocat. edn. tchr., N.Y.; 1st class radiotel. lic. with ship radar endorsement, FCC. Engr.-writer Warner, N.Y., Inc., Syracuse, 1952-54; vocation edn. tchr. evenings adult edn. Syracuse Cen. Tech. H.S., 1956-62; project leader GE, Syracuse, 1966-90; mgmt. cons. Syracuse, 1990—. Adj. faculty City U., Seattle; pres., mgmt. cons. IntraGlobal Mgmt., Inc., Syracuse, N.Y., 1994—; lectr. City Univ. Trencin, Slovakia, 1995; steering com. Empire State Coll. SUNY, 1995—; spkr. in field. Author: Your Television Set, 1953, Engineering-Related Abbreviations, 1980-84 (VIP award 1980). Prin. Onondaga (N.Y.) Flood Control Com., 1962; tennis coach U.S. Jaycees, North Syracuse, N.Y., 1968; mem. steering com., sec., mem. exec. com. L.C. Smith Coll. Engring. and Computer Sci., Syracuse U., 1991, founding officer Alumni Assn., 1994—; keynote spkr. VA Regional Hosp., 1995. With U.S. Army, 1942-45, ETO. Recipient Cert. of Appreciation for Outstanding Dedication L.C. Smith Coll. Engring and Computer Sci. Syracuse U., 1993, Testimonial-Belgium Remembers (Battle of the Bulge), Ctr. Rsch. and Info. of Battle of Ardennes, Liége, Belgium, 1996, Citation for disting. svc. during Battle of Bulge, N.Y. State Senate Dist., 1996, N.Y. State Conspicuous Svc. medal, 1997; Bus. and Mgmt. Lectureship Ctrl. European grant, Slovakia, 1994-95. Fellow Soc. for Tech. Commn. (internat. stem mgr., mgmt. theory and practice 1980, exec. com.); mem. IEEE (life sr., exec. com. Cert. 1981, editor Syracuse Scanner 1959-69), VFW, N.Y. Acad. Scis. (cert. 1985), Am. Mgmt. Assn. Internat., Profl. Cons. Assn. Ctrl. N.Y., Am. Cons. League, Internat. Platform Assn., Syracuse GE Engrs. Assn., Greater Syracuse C. of C., Syracuse U. Alumni Assn., Am. Soc. Tng. and Devel., Empire State Coll. Alumni Assn. (pres. Syracuse area alumni/student assn.), City U. Alumni (life), Vets. Battle of the Bulge (life, historian, treas.), Order of the Engr. Avocations: tennis, reading. Home: 850 Vine St Apt 1C Liverpool NY 13088-5234

HAMLIN, DAN WILLIAM, accountant, management consultant; b. Macon, Ga., Oct. 4, 1947; s. Dan William Hamlin and Lillian (Beasley) Moran; m. Sally Johns, June 20, 1970; 1 child, Gwendolyn Breese. AA, Indian River Community Coll., Ft. Pierce, Fla., 1967; BA, U. South Fla., 1969; MS, Johns Hopkins U., 1976. Cert. govt. fin. mgr. Pers. specialist City of Tampa, Fla., 1967-69; mgr. cost analysis U. South Fla., Tampa, 1969-72; asst. contr. Johns Hopkins U., Balt., 1972-76; exec. dir. fin. ops. U. So. Calif., L.A., 1976-81; prin., ptnr. in charge of cons. H.E. and other nonprofits KPMG Peat Marwick, Washington, ptnr.-in-charge pub. svcs. bus. devel., 1998-2000; sr. v.p. bus. devel. pub. sector KPMG Cons., 2000—; v.p. N.Am. Sales, 2000—02, N.Am. Sales Bearing Point, Inc., 2002—04; v.p. edn. Bearing Point, Inc., 2004—05; pres. Higher Edn. Profl. Svcs., LLC, 2005—. Nat. practice dir. Grants Mgmt. Svcs., 1981-98, Inst. Cert. and Evaluation Svcs., 1992-96, Cost Allocation Planning and Performance Svcs., 1992-96, Natural Disaster Adv. Svcs., 1996-98; v.p. sales N.Am. Pub. Svc. Line of Bus., 1998-2004, v.p. edn., 2004-05, ret., 2005; pres. HIgher Edn. Profl. Svcs. LLC, 2005—; spkr. in field of acctg., cost mgmt., univ. student svc. activities and govt. rels.; mng. dir./nat. sales dir. Pub. Svcs., 1994-2000. Contbr. numerous articles on govt. and cost. acctg. to profl. jours. Mem. Indian Bluff Island Civic Assn., Palm Harbor, 1984-95. Mem. Soc. Rsch. Adminstrs., Nat. Assn. Coll. and Univ. Bus. Officers, Coalition Higher Edn. Assistance Orgns., Skull and Dagger, Kappa Sigma, Iron Horse Golf and Country Club. Republican. Episcopalian.

HAMLIN, KENNETH ELDRED, JR., retired pharmaceutical company executive; b. Balt., Mar. 27, 1917; s. Kenneth Eldred and Julia (Gallup) H.; m. Janet Hoy, June 18, 1941; children: Kathleen Ann, Kenneth Thomas. BS, U. Md., 1938, PhD, 1941. Research assoc. U. Ill., Urbana, 1941-42; instr. U. Md., 1942-43; research chemist, asst. head organic research, head organic research, asst. dir. chem. research Abbott Labs., North Chicago, Ill., 1943-61, dir. research, 1961-66; v.p. research and devel. Cutter Labs., Inc., Berkeley, Calif., 1966-73, v.p. research and quality assurance, 1973-74, sr. v.p. sci. ops., 1974-81, vice chmn. bd. dirs., 1980-81, dir., 1968-81. Vol. tchr. gen. sci., computer sci. Author: (with Jenkins, Hartung, Hamlin and Data) The Chemistry of Organic Medicinal Products, 1957. Mem. Am. Pharm. Assn., Am. Chem. Soc., AAAS, Sigma Xi, Rho Chi, Alpha Chi Sigma. Republican. Home: 3270 Terra Granada Dr # 1A Walnut Creek CA 94595-3526 Personal E-mail: kehamlin@comcast.com.

HAMLIN, ROBERT HENRY, public health service officer, educator, management consultant; b. Cambridge, Mass., Apr. 2, 1923; s. Howard E. and Margaret E. (Henry) H.; m. Beate Kraschewski, Dec. 16, 1960; 1 son, Andrew Werner. AB summa cum laude, Ohio State U., 1944; BSM., Northwestern Med. Sch., 1945, B.M., 1946, MD with honors, 1947; M.P.H. magna cum laude, Harvard, 1952, JD, 1953. Diplomate: Am. Bd. Preventive Medicine. Intern Johns Hopkins Hosp., Balt., 1946-47; cons. Mass. commn. reporting, preparing and promulgating legislation on pub. and mental health and pub. welfare, 1950-53; 1st asst. to commnr. pub. health, 1952-53; asst. prof. legal medicine Harvard Law Sch., 1952-57; lectr. pub. health law and adminstrn. Harvard Sch. Pub. Health, 1952-57, asso. prof. pub. health adminstrn., 1959-62, Roger Irving Lee prof. pub. health, 1962-65, chmn. dept. pub. health practice, 1963-65; v.p. Booz, Allen and Hamilton (mgmt. cons.), 1965-67; ind. mgmt. cons., 1968; chmn. bd. MACRO Systems, Inc. (mgmt. cons.), Washington, 1969-80; clin. prof. dept. comprehensive medicine Coll. Medicine, U. South Fla., 1980-83; acting dir., prof. pub. health program Coll. Pub. Health, U. South Fla., 1983; pres. United Health Techs., Inc. (mgmt. cons.), 1981—. Adj. prof. health adminstrn. Columbia U. Sch. Public Health and Adminstrv. Medicine, 1972-80; cons. Rockefeller Found., 1959-61; staff dir. spel. commn. Harvard health services, 1953-54; mem. U.S. Commn. for UNESCO, 1958-60; dir. pub. health, Brookline, Mass., 1953-57; cons. Hoover Commn. II, 1954-55; asst. to sec. health, edn. and welfare, 1957-59; vis. lectr. pub. health adminstrn. and law Harvard, 1957-59 Contbr. articles profl. publs. U.S. del. 10th session gen. conf. UNESCO, Paris, 1958, pub. health adminstrn. cons. to pvt. orgns., state and local govts. Served as apprentice seaman USN, 1943-46; lt. (j.g.) M.C. USNR, 1947-49. Fellow Am. Pub. Health Assn.; mem. Mass. Med. Soc., Phi Beta Kappa, Phi Eta Sigma, Alpha Epsilon Delta, Alpha Omega Alpha, Delta Omega. Office: United Health Techs 13300 Indian Rocks Rd-1904 Largo FL 33774-2010 Fax: 727-595-5581. Office Phone: 727-596-8178.

HAMLIN, SONYA B., communications specialist; b. N.Y.C. d. Julius and Sarah (Saltzman) Borenstein; m. Bruce Hamlin (dec. 1977); children: Ross, Mark (dec. 1992), David. BS, MA, NYU; HLD (hon.), Notre Dame Coll., 1970. Host arts program Sta. WHDH-TV, Boston, 1963-65; host, prodr., writer (syndicated PBS program) Meet the Arts Sta. WGBH-TV, Boston, 1965-68; cultural reporter Sta. WBZ-TV, Boston, 1968-71, TV host, producer The Sonya Hamlin Show, 1970-75; host, producer Sunday Open House program Sta. WCVB-TV, Boston, 1976-80; host, producer, writer Speak Up and Listen program Lifetime Cable Network, N.Y.C., 1982-84; pres. Sonya Hamlin Communications, Boston and N.Y.C., 1977—, Different Drummer Prodns., N.Y.C., 1982-86. Pvt. comm. cons., U.S., Can., and Europe, 1977—; adj. lectr. Harvard Grad. Sch., Edn., Cambridge, Mass., 1974-76, Harvard Law Sch., 1977-81, Kennedy Sch. Govt., Harvard U., 1978-79; adj. asst. prof. Boston U. Med. Sch., 1977-80; mem. faculty Nat. Inst. Trial Advocacy, South Bend, Ind., 1977—, U.S. Dept. Justice, Washington, 1979-87, ABA, Chgo., 1979—; chmn. Law/Video Co., N.Y.C. and Waltham, Mass., 1987-92; comm. cons., weekly and weekend performer Today in NY (NBC), 1995—; daily panelist O.J. Today (Fox), 1995-96. Author: What Makes Juries Listen, 1985, How to Talk So People Listen, 1988, What Makes Juries Listen Today, 1998; prodr., dir., writer (films) China" Different Path, 1979 (Emmy nominee), Paul Revere: What Makes a Hero, 1976, others; contbr. articles to numerous profl. jours. Active Gov. Commn. Status of Women, Mass., 1973-83; campaign co-chair Mass. ERA Campaign, 1975-76; cons. Gov. Michael Dukakis, 1978, Dem. Nat. Party, Washington, 1979; bd. dirs. mem. Nat. Vol. Action com. United Way, Washington, 1986-91; bd. dirs. Taubman Ctr. Kennedy Sch. Harvard U., 1989-95; mem. adv. bd. Martha Graham Dance Co., 1997—, Shakespeare & Co.; mem. Women's Leadership Bd., Kennedy Sch. Govt., Harvard U., 1999—. Recipient Best Program award for Meet the Arts Internat. Ednl. TV Assn., Tokyo, 1969, Ohio State Cultural Reporting award, 1970; named Outstanding Broadcaster New Eng. Broadcasters, Boston, 1973; Sonya Hamlin Day named in her honor Mayor of Boston, 1974.; archive of her works established Boston U. Library, 1983. Mem.: NATAS (two Emmy nominations), Internat. Women's Forum, Am. Fedn. TV and Radio Artists. Avocations: skiing, tennis, piano, dance, museums. E-mail: sonyaham@aol.com.

HAMLISCH, MARVIN, composer, conductor, pianist, entertainer; b. NYC, June 2, 1944; s. Max and Lilly (Schachter) Hamlisch; m. Terre Blair, 1989. Student, Juilliard Sch. Music, 1951—64; BA, Queens Coll., 1967. Prin. Pops condr. Pitts. Symphony, 1994—, Balt. Symphony Orch., 1996—2000, Nat. Symphony Orch., Washington, 2000—. Rehearsal pianist Broadway shows including Funny Girl, Fade Out-Fade In, (TV series) Bell Telephone Hour, early 1960's; composer: (films) The Swimmer, 1968, Take the Money and Run, 1969, Bananas, 1971, Save the Tiger, 1973, Kotch, 1971, The Way We Were, 1974 (Academy Award for best original dramatic score and best title song, 1974), The Sting, 1974 (Academy Award for arranging and playing, 1974), Same Time Next Year, 1979, Ice Castles, 1979, Chapter Two, 1979, Starting Over, 1979, Ordinary People, 1980, Three Men and a Baby, 1987, Sophie's Choice, 1982, Frankie and Johnny, 1991, Switched at Birth, 1991, Seasons of the Heart, 1994, Open Season, 1996, The Mirror Has Two Faces, 1996, (popular songs include) Sunshine, Lollipops and Rainbows, 1960, Nobody Does It Better, 1977, (Broadway Musicals) Minnie's Boys, 1970, Seesaw, 1973, A Chorus Line, 1975 (Pulitzer Prize, Tony award for best musical score, 1976), They're Playing Our Song, 1979, Jean, 1983, Smile, 1986, The Goodbye Girl, 1993, Sweet Smell of Success, 2002, Imaginary Friends, 2002, theme song for Good Morning America, 1975, symphonic work in one movement "Anatomy of Peace" (performed by Dallas Symphony Orch., London Symphony Orch., Symphony for UN at Carnegie Hall), 1991; composer: (lyrics by Alan and Marilyn Bergman) One Song (internat. debut at Barcelona Olympics), 1992; author: The Way I Was, 1992; musical dir. Barbra Streisand: The Concert (Emmy awards for outstanding music direction & achievement in music and lyrics, 1994), Am. Film Inst.'s 100 Years...100 Movies, 1999 (Emmy award for outstanding music and lyrics, 1999), Timeless: Live in Concert, 2001 (Emmy award for outstanding music direction, 2001). Recipient three Oscar awards, four Grammy awards, four Emmy awards, a Tony award and three Golden Globe awards. Office: Nat Symphony Orch 2700 F St NW Washington DC 20566 also: Pitts Symphony Heinz Hall 600 Penn Ave Pittsburgh PA 15222-3259*

HAMM, CLAIRE ROSE, career counselor; b. Trenton, N.J., Aug. 10, 1957; d. Daniel Michael and Rose Mary Serinaldi; m. Kim Edward Hamm, Apr. 25, 1981; children: Dana Rose, Kristopher Edward. Cert. in French, baccalaureate, U. Besançon, France, 1978; BA in French magna cum laude, Rider U., Lawrenceville, N.J., 1979, MA in Ednl. Adminstrn. and Supervision, 1985; MA in Counselor Edn., Coll. N.J., 2003. Cert. prin., supr., N.J.; nat. cert. counselor; lic. assoc. counselor, N.J.; distance credentialed counselor. Office asst. devel. Princeton (N.J.) U., 1979-81, dir. grad. admissions, 1985-87, mgr. grad. programs, 1997-99; dir. rsch. and records Rider U., Lawrenceville, 1981-85; prin. elem. sch. St. Ann Sch., Lawrenceville, 1994-97; founding sch. adminstr. Princeton Acad., 1999-2000; dir. devel. info. svcs., career counselor Rider U., Lawrenceville, NJ, 2001—03, assoc. dir. career svcs., 2003—; founding ptnr. Princeton Ctr. for Career Counseling, 2005—. Recipient award Outstanding Achievement in German Culture Studies, German Consulate, 1979. Mem.: Nat. Career Devel. Assn., N.J. Career Devel. Assn., N.J. Counseling Assn., Am. Counseling Assn., Chi Sigma Iota Internat. (Alpha Epsilon chpt. 2003—), Pi Delta Phi. Roman Catholic. Avocation: exotic birds. Home: 23 Clover Hill Cir Ewing NJ 08638 Office Phone: 609-896-5098. E-mail: careerlady4now@yahoo.com.

HAMM, DAVID BERNARD, lawyer; b. Bklyn., Oct. 6, 1948; s. Isidore I. and Sarah (Lamm) H.; m. Margaret Weiss, June 20, 1971; children: Jennifer A. Maltz, Michael S. BA cum laude, CUNY, Bklyn., 1971; JD magna cum laude, N.Y. Law Sch., 1977. Bar: N.Y. 1978, U.S. Dist. Ct. (no. dist.) N.Y. 1978, U.S. Dist. Ct. (so. and ea. dists.) N.Y. 1979, U.S. Supreme Ct. 1981, U.S. Ct. Appeals (2d cir.) 1982, (3d cir.) 1988. Law clk. to presiding judges N.Y. State Ct. Appeals, Albany, 1977-79; assoc. Herzfeld & Rubin P.C., N.Y.C., 1979-85, mem., 1986—. Mem. Commn. Legis. and Civic Action Agudath Israel of Am., N.Y.C., 1979—. Recipient Cmty. Svc. award Agudath Israel of Am., 1986. Mem. ABA, N.Y. County Lawyers Assn., Jewish Lawyers Guild, N.Y. Law Sch. Alumni Assn. (Prof. Vincent LoLordo award 1977). Democrat. Home: 2015 E 22nd St Brooklyn NY 11229-3615 Office: Herzfeld & Rubin PC 40 Wall St 53d Fl New York NY 10005-2301 Office Phone: 212-471-8542. Office Fax: 212-344-3333. Business E-Mail: dhamm@herzfeld-rubin.com.

HAMM, MIA (MARIEL MARGARET HAMM), retired professional soccer player; b. Selma, Ala., Mar. 17, 1972; m. Christian Corry, 1994 (div. 2001); m. Nomar Garciaparra, Nov. 22, 2003. BS in Polit. Sci., U. NC, 1994. Forward U.S. Women's Nat. Soccer Team, 1987—2004; profl. soccer player Washington Freedom, 2001—03. Mem. US Women's Soccer Team, Athens Olympic Games, 2004. Author: Go for the Goal: A Champions Guide to Winning in Soccer and Life, 1999. Founder Mia Found., 1999. Named US Soccer Female Athlete of Yr., 1994—98, MVP, US Women's Cup, 1995, Best Female Athlete of Yr., ESPY, 1998, 2000, Women's World Player of Yr., FIFA, 2001, 2002; named to Pele's 100 greatest living soccer players list; recipient Soccer Player of Yr. Award, ESPY, 2000, 2001, Best Female Soccer Player, 2004. Achievements include member of U. NC NCAA National Championship teams, 1989-93; number retired, U. NC, 1994; member US Women's Soccer Gold Medal Team, Atlanta Olympics, 1996, Athens Olympic games, 2004; member US Women's Soccer World Cup Championship Team, 1999; mem US Women's Soccer Silver Medal Team, Sydney Olympics, 2000; all-time leading international goal scorer for men and women. Office: US Soccer Fedn US Soccer House 1801 S Prairie Ave Chicago IL 60616-1319

HAMM, MORGAN, Olympic athlete; b. Washburn, Wisconsin, Sept. 24, 1984; s. Sandy and Cecily Hamm. Student, Ohio State U. Mem. U.S. Sr. Nat. Gymnastics team, 2000—, U.S. Gymnastics Team, Sydney Olympics, 2000, U.S. Gymnastics Team, Athens Olympics, 2004. With twin brother Paul, became first set of twins ever to compete in same Olympic games gymnastics competition, Sydney, 2000; 1st prize floor competition, U.S. Championships, 2002, 2003, Silver medal U.S. Team, World Championships, 2003, Silver medal U.S. Gymnastics Team, Athens Olympics, 2004. Office: C/o USOC One Olympic Plaza Colorado Springs CO 80909

HAMM, PAUL, Olympic athlete; b. Washburn, Wis., Sept. 24, 1984; s. Sandy and Cecily Hamm. Student, Ohio State U. Mem. U.S. Sr. Nat. Gymnastics team, 2000—, U.S. Gymnastics Team, Sydney Olympics, 2000, U.S. Gymnastics Team, Athens Olympics, 2004. Named Gymnast of the Year, Internat. Gymnastics Federation, 2003. With twin brother Morgan, became first set of twins ever to compete in same Olympic games gymnastics competition, Sydney, 2000; First U.S. male in history to win a World All-Around championship, 2003; Silver medal U.S. Team, World Championships, 2001, 2003, two Gold medals all-around & floor exercise, World Championships, 2003, 1st prize pommel horse, vault, U.S. Nat. Championships, 2002, 1st prize all-around competition, U.S. Nat. Championships, 2002, 2003, 2004, Silver medal, U.S. Gymnastics Team, Men's High Bar, Athens Olympics, 2004, Gold medal, All-around, Athens Olympic games, 2004. Address: 2747 Marblevista Blvd Columbus OH 43204

HAMM, RICHARD L., church administrator; b. Crawfordsville, Ind., Dec. 21, 1947; m. Melinda Ann Fishbaugh; children: David Lee, Laura Ann. Student, St. Petersburg Jr. Coll., 1966-67; BA in Religion, Butler U., 1970; D of Ministry, Christian Theol. Sem., 1974. Pastor Abington (Ind.) Christian Ch., 1968, Little Eagle Creek Christian Ch., Westfield, Ind., 1970; assoc. pastor Ctrl. Christian ch., Kansas City, Kans., 1974; founding pastor North Oak Christian ch., Kansas City, Mo., 1975-82; sr. pastor 1st Christian Ch., Ft. Wayne, Ind., 1982-90; regional min. Christian Ch. (Disciples of Christ) Tenn., 1990-93; gen. min., pres. Christian Ch. (Disciples of Christ) U.S. and Can., 1993—2003; interim sr. pastor West St. Christian Ch., Tipton, Ind., 2003—. Bd. dirs. mid-Am. region Christian Ch. (Disciples of Christ), 1977-81, bd. dirs. Kans. region, 1980-81, bd. dirs. Ind. region, 1983-90, chair area new ch. com. Ind. region, 1984-87, 89, mem. commn. ministry Ind. region, 1985-87, 89, mem. gen. bd., 1986-90, bd. dirs. divsn. overseas ministries, 1991—, commn. on ministry, 1991—; moderator, Christian Ch. Greater Kansas City, 1980-81; v.p. Nat. Coun. Chs., 1996; mem. ctrl. com. World Coun. Chs., 1998—. Author: From Mainline to Front Line, 1997, 2020 Vision for the Christian Church (Disciples of Christ), 2001. Mem. Mayor's Task Force Domestic Violence, 1990. Recipient Recognition award North Kansas City Edn. Assn., 1979, Recognition award Ft. Wayne, Ind., Edn. Assn. and Ft. Wayne Community Schs., 1984, Ind. Region's Model Ministry award, 1990; named Ecumenist of Yr. of Tenn., 1993. Mem. Tenn. Assn. Chs. (pres.-elect 1992), Clergy United Action (pres. 1984-86), Associated Chs. Ft. Wayne and Allen County (bd. dirs., officer 1982-90), Rotary. Mem. Christian Ch. Office: Christian Church (Disciples of Christ) PO Box 1986 Indianapolis IN 46206-1986

HAMM, SHERYL E., music educator; b. Independence, Mo., Mar. 20, 1966; d. Richard Roland and Gladys Gertrude Boatright; m. David Glen Eaton, Aug. 16, 1986 (div. Dec. 7, 1992); m. Joseph Edward Hamm, Dec. 20, 1997. bachelors in Music Performance, bachelors in Music Edn., U. Mo. Conservatory of Music, Kansas City, 1997. Adj. prof. Penn Valley C.C., Kansas City, 2001—02. Scholar, Federated Music Clubs of Mo., 1995. Baptist. Home: 3900 S Crysler Ave Independence MO 64055-4302

HAMMAKER, ROBERT MICHAEL, chemist, educator; b. Evanston, Ill., Feb. 9, 1934; s. Paul M. and Cordelia Patricia (Curry) H.; m. Geneva Irene Singuefield, Aug. 15, 1959 (div. Nov. 1986); children: Patricia Lucille, Barry Turner. Student, U. Ill., 1952; BS in Chemistry, Trinity Coll., 1956; PhD in Phys. Chemistry, Northwestern U., 1960. Sr. chemist Texaco, Inc., Beacon, N.Y., 1960-61; asst. prof., assoc. prof. Kans. State U., Manhattan, 1961-74, prof., 1974—2004, prof. emeritus, 2004—. Vis. prof. U. East Anglia, Norwich, Eng., 1976-77, U. Calif. Riverside, 1987-88. Contbr. articles to profl. jours. Grantee Dept. Energy, 1985-97, EPA, 1987-94, Dept. Def., 2000-2005. Mem. AAAS, Am. Chem. Soc. (rsch. grant 1965-71), Am. Phys. Soc., Royal Soc. Chemistry, Soc. Applied Spectroscopy, Coblentz Soc., Phi Beta Kappa, Alpha Chi Sigma, Phi Lambda Upsilon, Sigma Pi Sigma, Sigma Xi. Avocations: physical fitness, recreational reading. Home: 3008 Payne Dr Manhattan KS 66503-2450 Office: Kansas State Univ Dept Chemistry Willard Hall Manhattan KS 66506-3701 E-mail: rmh@3008@ksu.edu.

HAMMAM, M. SHAWKY, electrical engineer, educator; b. Aug. 5, 1919; BSc, U. London, Eng., 1943, PhD, 1946. Registered profl. engr., N.Y. Sr. lectr. Alexandria U., Egypt, 1948-55; assoc. prof. Ein Shamus U., Egypt, 1955-63; vis assoc. prof. U. Kans., 1963-64; prof. Clarkson U., Potsdam, N.Y., 1964—. Niagara Mowhawk Power prof. Clarkson U., 1965. Fellow IEEE; mem. Inst. Elec. Engrs. (U.K.), Inst. Physics. E-mail: dmshammam@aol.com.

HAMMANN, GREGG C., fitness equipment executive; b. Ft. Madison, Iowa, Mar. 3, 1963; s. Clifford Carl and Nancy Ann (Schruers) H.; m. Carol Craddock, June 20, 1987;children: Derek Henry, Grant Campbell. BBA, U. Iowa, 1985; MBA, U. Wis., 1997. Sales rep., unit mgr., then oral care brand project mgr. Procter & Gamble, Cin., 1985-91; dir. trade mktg. Rayovac Corp., Madison, 1991-92, pres., gen. mgr. of Can. Toronto, Ont., Can., 1992-94; v.p. mktg. and strategic planning, Famous Footwear, Madison, 1994-96; dir. strategic issues The Coca-Cola Co., Atlanta, 1996, v.p. fountain products divsn., 1997, v.p. nat. chain accounts, 1999; group v.p. bus. devel. McLeodUSA, 2000; sr. v.p., chief customer officer Levi Strauss & Co., 2001—03; pres, CEO The Nautilus Group Inc., 2003—. Active Big Bros./Big Sisters, 1995—, Give Kids the World, 1997—; bd. dirs. Edn. Found., Chgo., 1997—. Avocations: hiking, biking, tennis, golf, running.

HAMMAR, LESTER EVERETT, retired manufacturing executive; b. Tillamook, Oreg., Dec. 15, 1927; s. Leo E. and Harriet L. (Parsons) H.; m. Margrit Steigl, May 9, 1964; children: Lawrence, Thomas, Stephanie. BS, Oreg. State U., 1950; MBA, Washington U., 1964. With Montsanto Co., 1952-69; controller Monsanto-Europe, 1966-69; v.p., controller Smith Kline & French Labs., Phila., 1969-72, Abbott Labs., North Chgo., Ill., 1972-88; ret., 1988. Bd. trustees Asia House Investments; project mgr. Exec. Svc. Corp. Chgo. Mem. audit com. City of Lake Forest; ruling elder, clk. of session 1st Presbyn. Ch. of Lake Forest; bd. dirs. Haven, Clara Abbott Fund; bd. dirs. Teton County Housing Authority. 1st lt. F.A., AUS, 1951-52. Mem. Fin Execs. Inst., Am. Mgmt. Assn. (former chmn. fin. coun., bd. mem.), 100 Club of Lake Country Club. Home: 634 Academy Woods Dr Lake Forest IL 60045 Personal E-mail: leshammar@aol.com.

HAMMAR, SHERREL LEYTON, medical educator; b. Caldwell, Idaho, May 21, 1931; m. Shirley; children: Kathryn M., David Jefferson. BA, Coll. Idaho, 1953; MD, U. Wash., 1957. Intern Mpls. Gen. Hosp., 1957-58; resident U. Wash., Seattle, 1958-60; instr. dept. pediat. U. Wash. Sch. Medicine, Seattle, 1962-64, asst. prof. dept. pediat., 1964-69, assoc. prof. dept. pediat., 1969-71, U. Hawaii, Honolulu, 1971-73; prof. U. Hawaii Sch. Medicine, Honolulu, 1973—2001; interim dean John A. Burns Sch. Medicine U. Hawaii, Honolulu, 1996-99, emeritus prof., 2001—. Chief adolscent clinic U. Wash., 1964-65, acting dir. clin. tng. unit devel. & mental health ctr., 1964, asst., 1965-71, acting dir. clin. tng. unit child devel. and mental retardation ctr., 1970-71; dir. ambulatory pediatric svcs., chief adolescent medicine Kauikeolani Children's Hosp., Honolulu, 1971-72, dir. med. svcs. and tng., 1972-73, chief pediat., 1973—, dir. pediatric med. edn., 1979—; chmn. dept. pediat. U. Hawaii, 1973-97, residency program dir., 1973-97; cons. in field. Contbr. articles to profl. jours. Fellow U. Wash., 1960-62. Fellow APHA, Am. Acad. Pediat. (com. youth 1967-73, 75-81, sect. adolescent health, exec. coun. 1978-80, com. early childhood, adoption and dependent care 1990-92, task force on AIDS 1990-92); mem. AMA (med. sch. sect.), Western Soc. Pediatric Rsch., Hawaii Med. Assn. (pres. 2003-04), Ambulatory Pediatric Assn., Seattle Pediatric Soc., Honolulu County Med. Soc., Alpha Omega Alpha. Office: U Hawaii John A Burns Sch Med Kapiolani Med Ctr 1319 Punahou St Rm 740 Honolulu HI 96826-1001 Personal E-mail: lerram@aol.com.

HAMMER, ALFRED EMIL, artist, educator; b. New Haven, Jan. 11, 1925; s. Forrester L. and Eugenie (Bauer-Enquist) H.; m. Marian Valle, Aug. 14, 1948; children: Alfred Emil, Paul Forrester, Eric Valdemar, Eugenie Bauer; m. Jeanne Baker, Dec. 18, 1966; children: Stephen Drake, Rosamond Swan. BFA, R.I. Sch. Design, 1950, Yale U., 1951, MFA, 1952. From instr. to assoc. prof. painting and drawing R.I. Sch. Design, Providence, 1952-69, chmn. grad. studies, 1958-60, dean students, 1960-61; dean Cleve. Inst. Art, 1969-74; dir., prof. Sch. Art, U. Man., Winnipeg, Can., 1974-82; dir. Pacific N.W. Coll. Art, Portland, Oreg., 1982-83; prof. Hartford Art Sch., U. Hartford, Conn., 1983-88, dean, 1983-86; freelance artist, 1988—. Exhibited in group shows R.I. Ann. (1st prize award 1952), Providence Art Club Ann. (1st prize award 1953, 54, 55, 57), Newport Ann. (1st prize 1959), Boston Arts Festival, 1958, Shippee Gallery, N.Y.C., 1985, Joseloft Gallery U. Hartford, 1992, Conn. Watercolor Soc. (prize 1992, 97), New Britain Mus. Am. Art (1st prize for watercolor 1988); one-man shows include U. Maine, 1954, U. Man., 1980, Thomas Gallery, 1980, Melnyschenko Gallery, Winnipeg, 1981, Movie House Studio Gallery, Millerton, N.Y., 1992; represented in collections Agnes Gund, Jr. C of C., Nat. Mus. Israel, R.I. Sch. Design Mus., Portland Art Mus., Conn. Bank and Trust Co., N.E. Savs., Hartford, Corp. Hdqrs. Otis Elevator Corp., Farmington, Conn., Bank of New Eng., Boston, Shawmut Bank, Hartford, Aenta Ins., Hartford, Govt. of Man., Gov.'s Coll. of Conn. Artists; represented in book Prize Winning Artists, 1960. Mem. Conn. Watercolor Soc., Lyme Art Assn. Home: 55 Bolton St Hartford CT 06114 E-mail: alfredhammer@sbcglobal.net.

HAMMER, BONNIE, broadcast executive; m. Dale Huesner. BA in Edn., MA in Media and New Tech., Boston U. With WGBH, Boston; dir. devel. Dave Bell Associates, LA; programming exec. Lifetime Television Network; v.p. current programs USA Networks, N.Y.C.; sr. v.p. Sci-Fi programming and USA org. productions NBC Universal, 1998—99; exec. v.p., gen. mgr. Sci-Fi Channel (subsidiary of USA Networks), 1999, pres. Universal City, Calif., 2001; pres. USA Network, Sci-Fi Channel NBC Universal, 2004—. Recipient Lillian Gish award, Women in Film. Office: Sci-Fi Channel c/o Vivendi Universal 100 Universal City Plaza Universal City CA 91608-1002

HAMMER, CHARLES F., chemistry professor; b. Fremont, Ohio, July 22, 1933; m. Lois Reel, 1957; 1 child, Laurence N. BA, Bowling Green State U., 1955; PhD in Organic Chemistry, U. Minn., 1959. NIHPD fellow NMR and x-ray crystallography of steroids Brandeis U., 1961—63; from asst. prof. to assoc. prof., 1963-82; dir. Inst. Advanced Analytical Chemistry, 1963-74; prof. chemistry Georgetown U., 1982-95, emeritus prof., 1995—; dir. Hoya/N.Mex. Schs. Chemobile, Santa Fe, 1995—2000. Vis. prof. Dept. Hydrocarbon Chem. Sch. Eng. Kyoto Nat. U., Japan, 1971-72; vis. scholar Dept. Chem. U. Calif., Berkeley, 1978, Nat. Inst. Diabetes, Digestive & Kidney Disease NIH, 1986, Inst. Chemistry, Ljubjana, Slovenia, 1993, Nanjing U., 1994; mem. governing coun. Acad. for Tech. and the Classics Charter Sch., Santa Fe County, 2000—. Recipient Alan Berman Rsch. Publication award NRL, 1987. Mem. AAAS, Am. Chem. Soc. (ChemTec Writing Team 1970-72, Am. Chem. Soc. award for creative invention 1990), Am. Soc. Mass Spectrometry, Soc. Appl. Spectros, Am. Soc. Testing &

Materials, Sigma Xi. Achievements include research in chemistry and mechanisms of nitrogen heterocyclics and steroids; bromination-dehydrobromination reactions; structure elucidation of natural products by instrumental methods; complete structure by 2D-nuclear magnetic resonance; isotope ratio kinetics by mass spectrometry; computer software applications to spectrometric analysis; synthesis of plant growth hormones and antitumor agents. Office: Hoya/NMex Schs Chemobile 2017 Calle Lejano Santa Fe NM 87501-8747 E-mail: cfhammer@cybermesa.com.

HAMMER, DAVID LINDLEY, lawyer, writer; b. Newton, Iowa, June 6, 1929; s. Neal Paul and Agnes Marilyn (Reece) H.; m. Audrey Lowe, June 20, 1953; children: Julie, Lisa, David. BA, Grinnell Coll., 1951; JD, U. Iowa, 1956. Bar: Iowa 1956, U.S. Dist. Ct. (no. dist.) Iowa 1959, U.S. Dist. Ct. (so. dist.) Iowa 1969, U.S. Ct. Appeals (8th cir.) 1996, U.S. Supreme Ct. 1977. Ptnr. Hammer Simon & Jensen, Dubuque, Iowa, Galena, Ill.; mem. grievance commn. Iowa Supreme Ct., 1973—85, mem. adv. rules com., 1986—92. Author: Poems from the Ledge, 1980, The Game is Afoot, 1983, For the Sake of the Game, 1986, To Play the Game, 1986, The 22nd Man, 1989, The Quest, 1993, My Dear Watson, 1994, The Before Breakfast Pipe, 1995, A Dangerous Game, 1997, The Vital Essence, 1999, A Talent for Murder, 2000, Yonder in the Gaslight, 2000, Straight Up with a Twist, 2001, A Deep Game, 2001, The Game is Underfoot, 2002, You Heard What Jesse Said, 2003, O College Fairest of Our Dreams, 2004, A Distinct Touch Watson, 2004, Heaven Will Protect the Working Girl, 2005. Bd. dirs. Linwood Cemetery Assn., 1973—, pres., 1983-84; bd. dirs. Dubuque Mus. Art, 1998-2001, hon. dir.; bd. dirs., past pres. Finley Hosp., hon. dir.; bd. dirs. Finley Found., 1988-95; past campaign chmn., past pres. United Way; past bd. dirs. Carnegie Stout Pub. Libr. With U.S. Army, 1951-53. Named to, Finley Hosp. Hall of Fame, 2004. Fellow Am. Coll. Trial Lawyers; mem. ABA, Young Lawyers Iowa (past pres.), Iowa Def. Counsel Assn. (pres. 1991-92, del. to Def. Rsch. Inst. 1992-93), Assn. Def. Trial Attys. (exec. coun. 1983-86, past chmn. Iowa chpt.), Iowa State Bar Assn. (past chmn. continuing legal edn. com.), Iowa Acad. Trial Lawyers, Dubuque County Bar Assn. (past pres.), Baker St. Irregulars. Republican. Congregationalist. Office: 770 Main St Dubuque IA 52001 Office Phone: 563-583-4010.

HAMMER, DEBORAH MARIE, librarian, paralegal; b. Bronx, N.Y., Nov. 16, 1947; d. Ben and Helen (Lorenz) Halprin; m. Mark Stewart Hammer, May 30, 1976; 1 child, Joshua Robert. BA, CCNY, 1968; MLS, Rutgers U., 1969. Cert. libr. N.Y. Gen. asst. info. tel. ref. divsn. Queens Borough Pub. Libr., Jamaica, NY, 1969-71, gen. asst. popular libr., 1972-80, asst. div. head history, travel & biography, 1972-81, divsn. head history, travel & biography, 1981-92, div. mgr. social scis., 1992-98; fee conciliation coord., computer systems mgr. Nassau County Bar Assn., Mineola, NY, 1999—. Democrat. Avocations: reading, cooking, handcrafts, camping. Office: 15th and West Sts Mineola NY 11501 E-mail: halimer@juno.com.

HAMMER, JACOB MYER, physicist, consultant; b. N.Y.C., Sept. 14, 1927; s. Joseph Israel Hammer and Miriam Silverman; m. Rose Kizner (div. 1975); children: Daniel, Jonathan, Miriam; m. Katrina Schuyler, July 10, 1982; 1 stepson, David Reisberg. BS in Engring. Physics, NYU, 1950, PhD in Physics, 1956; MS in Physics, U. Ill., 1951. Mem. tech. staff Bell Telephone Labs., Murray Hill, N.J., 1956-59, RCA Labs., Princeton, N.J., 1959-68, David Sarnoff Rsch. Ctr., Princeton, 1970-87, photonics cons., 1987—. Sr. visitor Cavendish Lab., Cambridge U., 1968-69. Co-author: Integrated Optics, 1975, Fiber & Integrated Optics, 1979; co-editor: Surface Emitting Semiconductor Lasers and Arrays, 1993; contbr. numerous articles to profl. jours.; patentee in field. With AUS, 1946-47. Fellow IEEE (life, assoc. editor Jour. Quantum Electronics, 1987-90); mem. Am. Phs. Soc., Optical Soc. Am. Office: 42 City Gate Ln Annapolis MD 21401-2736 Office Phone: 410-280-0351. E-mail: jakehammer@ieee.org.

HAMMER, JOYCE MAE, gifted and talented education educator; b. Milw., May 21, 1933; d. George and Sara (Arne) Leviton; children: Deborah, Lori. BS, U. Ill., 1954; MA, Northwestern U., 1958, postgrad., 1974-78, Nat. Coll. Edn., Evanston, Ill., 1986-89, Aurora U., 1990-92, 95. Tchr. math. Fairview Sch., Skokie, Ill., 1957-65, Arie Crown Sch., 1967-72, Fairview South Sch., 1972-77, elem. tchr. gifted math. edn., coord. gifted edn., designer sch. gifted program Skokie, 1978—. Recipient Those Who Excel award; grantee. Mem. Nat. Coun. Tchrs. Math., Phi Delta Kappa.

HAMMER, LINDA See LINDROTH, LINDA

HAMMER, TERENCE MICHAEL, physician; b. Chgo., May 7, 1946; s. Albert S. and Minnetta Elizabeth (Nichols) H.; 1 child, Kathryn Gyo Hammer. BS, U. Ill., 1968; MD, Stanford U., 1973. Diplomate Am. Bd. Family Practice. Intern L.A. County-U. So. Calif. Med. Ctr., 1973-74; med. dir. Long Beach (Calif.) Health Dept. Drug Program, 1974-75; resident in family medicine Contra Costa Med. Svcs., Martinez, Calif., 1975-77; pvt. practice in family medicine Redondo Beach (Calif.) Med. Group, 1977-81, Family Practice Assocs., Torrance, Calif., 1981-96, Med. Inst. Little Co. of Mary Hosp., Torrance, 1996—. Bd. dirs., treas. Med. Inst. of Little Co. of Mary Hosp.; lectr. in field. Bd. trustees Peninsula Edn. Found., Palos Verdes, Calif., 1991-99; bd. examiners Malcolm Baldridge Nat. Quality Awards, 1999, 2001. Named Calif. Rep. of Yr., 2001; named one of America's Top Family Drs., Consumers Rsch. Coun. Am., 2002. Mem. Am. Coll. Physician Execs., Premier Health Med. Group (pres. 1991—), South Bay Ind. Physicians Med. Group (pres. emeritus). Lutheran. Avocations: fresh water fishing, modern art collecting, swimming, writing. Office: Med Inst Little Co Mary Hosp 20911 Earl St Ste 400 Torrance CA 90503-4355 Office Phone: 310-542-0455. Personal E-mail: hefish1@aol.com.

HAMMER, WADE BURKE, retired oral and maxillofacial surgeon, educator; b. Lakeland, Fla., Apr. 21, 1932; s. Orval Seown and Lilly Pearl (Wade) H.; m. Betty Dean Webb, June 22, 1956; children: Robert Burke Hammer, Joanna Wade Hammer Dykes. AA, U. Fla., 1956; D.D.S., Emory U., 1960. Diplomate Am. Bd. Oral and Maxillofacial Surgery. Pvt. practice dentistry, Orange Park, Fla., 1960-61; resident in oral and maxillofacial surgery U. Pa. Grad. Sch. Medicine, Phila., 1961-62, Grady Meml. Hosp., Atlanta and Emory U., 1962-65; practice dentistry specializing in oral and maxillofacial surgery Atlanta, 1965-68; mem. staff Med. Coll. of Ga. Hosp., Augusta; asst. prof. oral and maxillofacial surgery Med. Coll. Ga., Augusta, 1968-71, assoc. prof., 1971-75, prof., 1975-93, prof. emeritus oral and maxillofacial surgery, 1993. Staff VA Hosp. Complex, Augusta, 1969-99; cons. Ft. Gordon Army Med. Ctr., 1970-93, Univ. Hosp., Augusta, 1968-93. Contbr. articles to profl. jours. Chmn. exec. com. Gen. Faculty Orgn. Med. Coll. Ga., 1988; mem. USCG Auxiliary. With USN, 1950-54, col. USAR, 1976-92, ret. Decorated Legion of Merit, Meritorious Svc. medal, Army Commendation medal (5), Knight Hospitalar Order St. John of Jerusalem, Knight Sovereign Mil. Order of the Temple of Jerusalem. Fellow Am. Assn. Oral and Maxillofacial Surgeons (life), Am. Coll. Dentists, Am. Soc. Dental Anesthesiology; mem. ADA (life), Internat. Assn. Dental Rsch., Ga. Dental Assn., Ea. Dist. Dental Assn., Am. Assn. Dental Schs., Augusta Dental Soc., Ga. Soc. Oral and Maxillofacial Surgeons, Southeastern Soc. Oral and Maxillofacial Surgeons (pres. 1984-85), Res. Officers Assn. (Nat. Dental Surgeon 1990-92, Dept. of Ga. Pres. 1998-99), Interallied Confedn. of Res. Officers (US. del. 1992—), Assn. Mil. Surgeons, USCG Aux., Exptl. Aircraft Assn., Am. Legion, VFW, U.S. Army Order Mil. Merit, U.S. Sailing Assn., Boat-U.S., Mil. Officers Assn. Am., Sigma Xi, Omicron Kappa Upsilon (pres. Supreme chpt. 1980-81). Methodist. Personal E-mail: wbhammer@aol.com.

HAMMERGREN, JOHN H., pharmaceutical executive; BBA, U. Minn.; MBA, Xavier U. With Baxter Healthcare Corp./Am. Hosp. Corp. and Lyphomed Inc., 1981-91; pres. med./surgical divsn. Kendall Healthcare Products Co., Mansfield, Mass., 1991-96; corp. exec. v.p., pres., CEO supply mgmt. bus. McKesson HBOC, Inc., 1996-99; group pres. McKesson Health Systems, 1997—99; co-pres, co- CEO McKesson Corp. (formerly McKesson HBOC, Inc.), 1999—2001, pres., CEO, 2001—, chmn. bd., 2002—, dir., 1999—, chief exec. officer supply chain mgmt., 1997—99. Dir. Nadro, S.A. de C.V., Mexico, Verispan LLC. Office: McKesson Corp One Post St San Francisco CA 94104*

HAMMERLE, FREDRIC JOSEPH, metal products executive; b. Newark, Jan. 2, 1944; s. Fredric Frank and Catherine G. (Wankmuller) H.; m. Nancy Elizabeth Looby, June 16, 1979; children: Oliver, Dora. BA, Rutgers U., 1966, MBA, 1967. Prodn. mgr. Engelhard Corp., Plainville, Mass., 1967-72, group v.p., 1978-86; v.p. mfg. Franklin Mint Corp., Franklin Center, Pa., 1972-78; exec. v.p., COO, sr. group exec. Cookson Precious Metals, Providence, 1986—2003; pres., CEO Precision Engineered Products, Inc., Attleboro, Mass., 2003—. Bd. dirs., treas. Internat. Precious Metals Inst. Referee Amateur Hockey Assn. U.S., 1980—; bd. dirs., sec. Sturdy Meml. Hosp., 1989—. Sgt. USMCR, 1966-72. Mem.: Silver Users Assn. (bd. dirs. 1985—, pres.), Gold Filled Assn. (bd. dirs. 1980—, sec., pres.), Mfg. Jewelers Silversmiths of Am. (bd. dirs. 1983—, pres.), Bass Anglers Sportsman Soc. (Montgomery, Ala.), Jewelry Info. Ctr., 24 Karat Club N.Y., Boston Jewelers Club (bd. dirs. 1995—, pres. 2001—). Roman Catholic. Avocations: ice hockey, restoring autos, fishing. Office: Precision Engineered Products Inc 110 Frank Mossberg Dr Attleboro MA 02703 E-mail: fhammerle@pep-corp.com.

HAMMERLING-DIESU, SUSAN, physician assistant; b. Merced, Calif., Jan. 8, 1977; d. John M. and Amy L. Hammerling; m. Patrick John Diesu, Apr. 24, 2002. Degree in Physician Asst. Studies, Nova Southeastern, 2001; M in Physician Asst. Studies, U. Nebr. Cert. Nat. Commn. Physician Assts. Fla., 2001. Physician asst. Watson Clinic, Lakeland, Fla., 2001—. Legis. com. Fla. Acad. Physician Assts., Orlando, Fla. Precinct chair Orange County Rep. Com., Orlando. Fellow: Am. Coll. Phlebology, Am. Acad. Physician Assts.; mem.: Alpha Delta Pi (life). R-Conservative. Methodist. Avocations: swimming, golf, bicycling, reading, travel. Home: 11584 Claymont Cir Windermere FL 34786 Office: Watson Clinic 1600 Lakeland Hills Blvd Lakeland FL 33805 Personal E-mail: diesu2002@yahoo.com.

HAMMERLY, MARY LEVERENZ, lawyer; b. Milw., Apr. 12, 1952; d. Erwin F. and Anna M. (Brehm) Leverenz; children: Aja, Elyse. BM, U. Wis., 1974; JD, U. Puget Sound, 1978. Bar: Wash. 1979, U.S. Dist. Ct. (we. dist.) Wash. 1979, U.S. Ct. of Appeals (9th cir.) 1980. Law clk. to assoc. Johnson & East (now C. Scott East, Inc.), Bellevue, Wash., 1978-82; pvt. practice Redmond, Wash., 1982-83; assoc. Burns & Meyer, Bellevue, 1983-85; ptnr. Burns & Hammerly, Bellevue, 1985-97; pvt. practice Issaquah, Wash., 1997—. Mem. Wash. State Bar Assn. (family law sect.), Seattle King County Bar Assn. (family law sect.). Avocations: downhill skiing, hiking, crafts, wine collecting. Office: 22525 SE 64th Pl STE 118 Issaquah WA 98027-5386

HAMMERMAN, MARC RANDALL, nephrologist, educator; b. St. Louis, Sept. 29, 1947; s. Elmer and Lillian Hammerman; m. Nancy Tutt, Aug. 9, 1974; children: Seth, Megan. AB, Washington U., St. Louis, 1969, MD, 1972. Intern Barnes Hosp., St. Louis, 1972-73, resident, 1973-74, Mass. Gen. Hosp., Boston, 1976-77; instr. Washington U., St. Louis, 1977-78, asst. prof., 1979-84, assoc. prof., 1984-89, prof., 1989—, dir. renal div. Sch. Medicine, 1991—. Mem. study sect. NIH, 1990-95; investigator Am. Heart Assn., 1984. Contbr. over 100 sci. articles, revs. to profl. publs., chpts. to books. Lt. comdr. USPHS, 1974-76. NIH grantee, 1980—. Mem. Am. Fedn. for Clin. Rsch., Am. Soc. Clin. Investigation, Assn. Am. Physicians. Office: Washington U Sch Medicine Renal Div Box 8126 660 S Euclid Ave Saint Louis MO 63110-1010 E-mail: mhammerm@im.wustl.edu.

HAMMERSCHLAG, CARL A, psychiatrist; b. N.Y.C., Apr. 18, 1939; s. Arno Hammerschlag and Hilde Foster; m. Elaine T Tenenbaum, Dec. 26, 1960; children: Tara S. Hammersclag children: Lisa J. Cohen, Amy B. Shapiro. MD, SUNY Upstate Med. Ctr, 1964. Chief of psychiatry Indian Health Svc., Phoenix, 1970—86; psychiatrist in pvt practice, Phoenix, 1986—. Author: The Dancing Healers, 1986, The Theft of the Spirit, 1993, Healing Ceremonies, 1998, The Go-Away Doll, 2001, Sika and the Raven, 2003. Lt. comdr. USPHS, 1970—86, Phoenix Indian Medical Ctr. Named to CPAE- Speakers Hall of Fame, Nat. Speakers Assn. Office: Hammerschlag Ltd 3104 E Camelback Rd #614 Phoenix AZ 85016 E-mail: info@healingdoc.com.

HAMMERSCHMIDT, JOHN PAUL, retired congressman, lumber company executive; b. Harrison, AR, May 4, 1922; s. Arthur Paul and Junie (Taylor) H.; m. Virginia Sharp; 1 child, John Arthur. Student, The Citadel, U. Ark., Okla. State U.; BS in Bus. Mgmt., MA in Philosophy magna cum laude, Canbourne U., London. Chmn. bd. Hammerschmidt Lumber Co., Harrison, 1946-84; mem. 90th-102d Congresses from 3d Ark. Dist., 1967-93. Mem. Pub. Works and Transp. Com., 1967-93, ranking mem., 1987-93; mem. V.A. Com., 1967-93, ranking mem., 1973-86; bd. dirs. 1st Fed. Bank of Ark.; chmn. bd. 1st Fed. Bankshares of Ark.; bd. dirs. Dillard's Dept. Store, Southwestern Energy Co.; chmn. N.W. Ark. Coun.; nat. committeeman Ark. Citizen of Yr. Com.; mem. Presdl. Commn. on Aviation Security and Terrorism; mem. Pres.'s task force on Vets. Health Care; mem. Claude and Mildred Pepper Found., 1989-90 (PVA Speedy award), bd. Met. Washington Airports Authority; chmn. bd., trustee Ark. State U., U. of the Ozarks; committeeman Nat. Rep. Party, 2002. Chmn. Ark. Republican Com., 1964-66; mem. Rep. Nat. Finance Com., 1960-64, nat. Rep. committeeman from, Ark., 1976-80; mem. Harrison City Coun., 1948, 60, 62. Served as pilot USAAF, World War II, CBI. Decorated Air medal with 4 oak leaf clusters, D.F.C. with 3 oak leaf clusters, 3 Battle Stars, The China War Meml. medal, Meritorious Svc. award VFW Congl. award, Silver Helmet award, Nat. Order Trenchrats Legis. Svc. award, Award for Life Svc. to Vets.; named. Ark. Citizen of Yr., 1991, Ark. Aerospace Found. Hall of Fame, 1991. Mem. Ark. Lumber Dealers Assn. (past pres.), Midwest Lumbermens Assn. (past pres.), Harrison C. of C. (named Man of Yr. 1965), Am. Legion, Masons (33 degree-Grand Cross), Scottish Rite, Shriners, Jesters, Elks, Rotary (past pres. Harrison). Republican. Presbyterian (Ordained Elder, Deacon). Office Phone: 870-391-3325. E-mail: jph@northark.edu.

HAMMERSMITH, NITA MARIE, writer; b. Paris, Tex., Aug. 31, 1948; d. Tommie Hugh and Sadie Mae Denson; m. Richard Robert Hammersmith, Nov. 15, 1953; children: Bobby Joe Stamps, Marleen Annette Stamps, Sharon Latrice King. *Husband, Richard Robert Hammersmith, BA 1975, MPA 1981 California State, Fullerton, is currently employed as a Contract Specialist with the United States Government.* AA, Mesa Coll., 2000; student, San Diego State U., 2005—. Waste Water Technology Calif., 1981. Author Nita Hammersmith Ministries, San Diego, 1989—; free lance writer Christian Woman Mag., Phoenix, 2000—; writer Sisterhood Newsletter, Atlanta, 2001—; free lance writer Christian Mirror Internet Mag., Tex., 2002—. Author: (bible study & devotional work book) Lessons To Live By, (bible story for children) Benny & Michael & Jonah & The Big Fish, (biblical book for teenagers) How To Choose A Mate For Life, (bible study) Help Me Lord. Commencement spkr. Mesa Coll. Graduation, San Diego, 2000; keynote spkr. Ch. Christ, 1990—2005, Flint, Mich., 2001, Mpls., 2002, San Diego, 2004, Sisterhood Rally, Atlanta, 2003; facilitator Ch. Christ, 1991—. Recipient Jane Nelson Meml. award, San Diego State U., 2002. Mem.: Phi Theta Kappa (life). Office: Nita Hammersmith Ministries for Women 2196 Fenton Pky #107 San Diego CA 92108 Office Phone: 619-640-2846. Personal E-mail: nitarichnita@san.rr.com.

HAMMERTON-MORRIS, LINDA KAY, language educator; b. Stamford, Conn., Mar. 31, 1962; d. James Cecil and Thelma Ada Hammerton; m. Dean Richard Morris, Aug. 4, 1990; children: Robin Marie, Todd Michel. BA cum laude, Bowling Green State U., 1984; MS with honors, SUNY, Geneseo, 1990. Vol. U.S. Peace Corps, Ecuador, 1984—86; tutor Spanish Waterville Valley Acad., NH, 1986—87; tchr. Spanish Oakfield High Sch., NY, 1987—93, Clarence High Sch., 1993—2003; tchr. Mountain Vista H.S., Highlands Ranch, Colo., 2003—. Tchr. Spanish Erie C.C., Buffalo, 1994—98. Mem.: Western N.Y. Fgn. Lang. Educators Coun., Phi Beta Kappa. Avocations: skiing, bicycling, swimming, reading, camping. Office: Mountain Vista High Sch Highlands Ranch CO 80126 Home: 3868 Miners Candle Pl Castle Rock CO 80109-3565

HAMMES, GORDON G., chemistry professor; b. Fond du Lac, Wis., Aug. 10, 1934; s. Jacob and Betty (Sadoff) H.; m. Judith Ellen Frank, June 14, 1959; children: Laura Anne, Stephen R., Sharon Lyn. AB, Princeton, 1956; PhD, U. Wis., 1959. NSF postdoctoral fellow Max Planck Inst. fur physikalische Chemie, Göttingen, Germany, 1959-60; from instr. to assoc. prof. Mass. Inst. Tech., Cambridge, 1960-65; prof. Cornell U., Ithaca, N.Y., 1965-88, chmn. dept. chemistry, 1970-75, Horace White prof. chemistry and biochemistry, 1975-88, dir. biotech. program, 1983-88; prof. U. Calif., Santa Barbara, 1988-91, vice chancellor, 1988-91; prof. Duke U., Durham, N.C., 1991—; vice chancellor Duke U. Med. Ctr., Durham, N.C., 1991-98; univ. disting. svc. prof. biochemistry Duke U., Durham, N.C., 1996—. Mem. physiol. chemistry sect., phys. biochemistry study sect., Tng. grant com. NIH; bd. counselors Nat. Cancer Inst., 1976-80; mem. adv. coun. chemistry dept., Princeton, 1970-75, Poly. Inst. N.Y., 1977-78, Boston U., 1977-92; mem. NRC, U.S. nat. com. for biochemistry, 1989-95. Author: Principles of Chemical Kinetics, 1978, Enzyme Catalysis and Regulation, 1982; author: (with I. Amdur) Chemical Kinetics: Principles and Selected Topics, 1966, Thermodynamics and Kinetics for the Biological Sciences, 2000, Spectroscopy for the Biological Sciences, 2005; editor: Biochemistry, 1992—2003; contbr. articles to profl. jours. NSF sr. postdoctoral fellow, 1968-69; NIH Fogarty scholar, 1975-76 Mem. NAS, Am. Acad. Arts and Scis., Am. Chem. Soc. (award biol. chemistry 1967, editl. bd. jours., exec. com. div. phys. chemistry 1976-79, exec. com. div. biol. chemistry 1977-88, com. profl. tng. 1985-92, task force on biotech. 1989-90), Am. Soc. Biochemistry and Molecular Biology (coun., editl. bd. jour. pres., William C. Rose award 2002), Phi Beta Kappa, Sigma Xi, Phi Lambda Upsilon. Home: 11 Staley Pl Durham NC 27705-2421 Office Phone: 919-684-8848. Business E-Mail: hamme001@mc.duke.edu.

HAMMES, JEFFREY C., lawyer; BBA, U. Wis., 1980; JD, Northwestern U. Scho. Law, 1985. CPA; bar: Ill. 1985, Calif. 2003. Atty. Arthur Andersen & Co., 1980—82, Kirkland & Ellis LLP, 1985—91, ptnr., mem. firm com., 1991—. Named one of World's Leading Lawyers Corp. M & A, Chambers Global, 2001—. Office: Kirkland & Ellis LLP 200 E Randolph Dr Chicago IL 60601 Office Phone: 312-861-2476. Office Fax: 312-861-2200. Business E-Mail: jhammes@kirkland.com.

HAMMESFAHR, ROBERT WINTER, lawyer; b. Pittsfield, Mass., May 17, 1954; s. Frederick W. and Patricia Lue (Winter) H.; 1 child, Scott Gardner. BA, Colgate U., 1975; JD, Northwestern U., Chgo., 1978. Bar: Ill. 1978, U.S. Dist. Ct. (no. dist.) Ill. 1978, N.Y. 1991, U.S. Supreme Ct. 1989. Mem. Cozen O'Connor, 2001—. Author (with others): Punitive Damages: A Guide to the Insurability of Punitive Damages in the United States and Its Territories, 1988, Punitive Damages: A State-By-State Guide to Law and Practice, 1991, (pocket parts 1993, 96, Japanese edits., 1995, 1999, 2000, 01), 5th edit., 2005, Reinsurance Claims, 2004, The Law of Reinsurance Claims, 1994, supplement, 1997; editor, author (with others): @Risk-Internet and E-commerce Insurance and Reinsurance, 2000, 2.0 version, 2002; contbr. articles to profl. jours. Mem.: ABA, Chgo. Bar Assn. Avocations: skiing, reading. Office: Cozen O'Connor 222 S Riverside Plz Ste 1500 Chicago IL 60606-6000 Office Phone: 312-382-3101. Personal E-mail: rhammesfahr@cozen.com.

HAMMETT, BENJAMIN COWLES, psychologist; b. L.A., Nov. 18, 1931; s. Buell Hammett and Harriet (Cowles) Graham; m. Ruth Finstrom, June 18, 1957; children: Susan Hood, Sarah, Carol Bress, John. BS, Stanford U., 1957; PhD, U. N.C., 1969. Lic. psychologist, Calif. Staff psychologist Children's Psychiat. Ctr., Butner, N.C., 1965-67; sr. psychologist, dir. rsch. VA Treatment Ctr. for Children, Richmond, Va., 1968-71; asst. prof. child psychiatry Va. Commonwealth U., Richmond, 1968-71; instr. psychology Western Grad. Sch. Psychology, 1980-87; pvt. practice clin. psychology Palo Alto, Calif., 1972-92; rsch. psychologist, 1992—; affiliate staff mem. O'Connor Hosp., San Jose, Calif., 1980-84. V.p. bd. dirs. Mental Rsch. Inst., Palo Alto, 1982-83, pres. bd. dirs., 1983-85, treas., 1990-92, mem. staff, 1992—, bd. dirs. emeritus, 1992—, rsch. affiliate, 1992-95, rsch. assoc., 1995—; bd. dirs. Western Grad. Sch. Psychology, 1993-97. Co-author chpts. two books. Scoutmaster Boy Scouts Am., 1952-54; 1st lt. Civil Air Patrol, 1969; vol. Bay Area Action and Peninsula Conservation Ctr., Palo Alto, 1983—, Calif. Acad. Scis., San Francisco, 1987—; treas. John B. Cary Sch. PTA, Richmond, Va., 1969-70; trustee Nat. Parks and Conservation Assn., 1995-98. Named Eagle Scout, 1947; grantee NIMH, 1970. Mem. AAAS, APA, Am. Psychol. Soc., Am. Group Psychotherapy Assn., Internat. Transactional Analysis Assn. (cert. clin. mem.), Assn. Applied Psyehophysiology and Biofeedbck, Biofeedback Soc. Calif., Calif. Psychol. Assn., Assn. for the Advancement of Gestalt Therapy, El Tigre Club Stanford U. (sec. 1954). Democrat. Unitarian Universalist. Avocations: photography, computers, environmental volunteer, international ecological traveler. Home: 301 Lowell Ave Palo Alto CA 94301-3812

HAMMETT, KIRK LEE, musician; b. El Sobrante, Calif., Nov. 18, 1962; m. Rebecca Hammett, Dec. 3, 1987 (div.); m. Lani Hammett, Jan. 31, 1998. Band mem. Exodus, 1981—83; band mem., guitarist Metallica, 1983—. Albums include Kill 'em All, 1983, Ride the Lightning, 1984, Master of Puppets, 1986, ...And Justice For All, 1988, Metallica, 1991, Live Sh*t: Binge and Purge, 1993, Kill 'Em All, 1995, Load, 1996, Reload, 1997, Garage Inc., 1998 (Grammy award), S & M, 1999, St. Anger, 2003 (Grammy award best metal performance, 2003); played on compilation albums including Metal Massacre, 1982, The Good, The Bad and The Live, 1990, Rubaiyant: Elektra's 30th Anniversary, 1990, For Those About To Rock: Moscow, 1992, Woodstock '94, 1994, Spawn: The Album, 1997, Woodstock '99, 2000, WCW: Mayhem The Music, 1999, M:I-2, 2000, NASCAR: Full Throttle, 2001, Swizz Beatz Presents G.H.E.T.T.O. Stories, 2002, Biker Boyz Soundtrack, 2003, We're A Happy Family: Tribute to the Ramones, 2003, I've Always Been Crazy: Tribute to Waylon Jennings, 2003. Recipient Grammy award for Best Metal Performance for One, 1989, Grammy award for Best Metal Performance for Stone Cold Crazy, 1990, Grammy award for Best Metal Performance for Better Than You, 1998, Grammy award for Best Hard Rock Performance for Whiskey in the Jar, 1999, Grammy award for Best Rock Instrumental Peformance for The Call of Ktulu, 2000. Office: Elektra Entertainment Group 75 Rockefeller Plaza New York NY 10019-7284*

HAMMON, JOHN WILLIAM, JR., medical educator, thoracic surgeon; b. Springfield, Mo., Mar. 9, 1942; m. Mary Lisa Hammon; children: Ian, Dudley, James. BA, Drury Coll., 1964; MD, Tulane U., 1968. Diplomate Am. Bd. Surgery, Am. Bd. Thoracic Surgery. Lt. comdr. US Naval Hosp., San Diego, 1970—72; resident Duke U. Med. Ctr., Durham, NC, 1972—77, tchg. scholar cardiac surgery, 1977—78; asst. prof. surgery Vanderbilt U., Nashville, 1978—83, assoc. prof. surgery, 1983—89, prof. dept. cardiac and thoracic surgery, 1989—91; chief cardiac and thoracic surgery VA Hosp., Nashville, 1987—91; Howard Holt Bradshaw prof., chmn. Bowman Gray Sch. Medicine, Winston-Salem, NC, 1991—95; prof. surgery Sch. Medicine Wake Forest U., Winston-Salem, NC, 1995—. Prin. investigator NIH Grants, 1979—2003. Mem. editl. bd. Jour. Surg. Rsch., 1986—91, Cardiac Chronicle, 1986—91, Annals of Thoracic Surgery, 1991—2002, Jour. Cardiac Surgery, 1993—. Recipient Disting. Alumni award, Drury Coll., 1989, 2001; scholar, NIH, 1974. Mem.: ACS (gov. 2002, membership com. 2002—04), Winston-Salem Surg. Assn. (pres. 1999—2000), So. Thoracic Surg. Assn. (v.p. 1999—2000, pres.'s award for best sci. paper 1985), Am. Assn. Thoracic Surgery (residents com. 1999—2003), Omicron Delta Kappa. Avocations: golf, fishing. Office: Dept Cardiothoracic Surgery Medical Ctr Blvd Winston Salem NC 27157-1096 Office Fax: 336-716-3348. E-mail: jhammon@wfubmc.edu.

HAMMOND, BENJAMIN FRANKLIN, microbiologist, educator; b. Austin, Tex., Feb. 28, 1934; s. Virgil Thomas and Helen Marguerite (Smith) H. BA, U. Kans., 1954; D.D.S., Meharry Med. Coll., 1958; PhD, U. Pa., 1962.

Mem. faculty U. Pa. Sch. Dental Medicine, Phila., 1958—, prof. microbiology, 1970—, chmn. dept., 1972-85; Pres.'s lectr. U. Pa., 1981, assoc. dean acad. affairs, 1984, dir. periodontal microbiology lab., 1985—; prof. of medicine, dir. oral microbiology testing svc. lab. Med. Coll. Pa., 1995—; rsch. prof. periodontology Temple U., Phila., 1998—. Mem. oral biology and medicine study sect. NIH, 1972-75, 95-99; mem. Nat. Adv. Dental Rsch. Coun., 1975—; Ralph Metcalf disting. vis. prof. Marquette U., 1986; disting. lectr. U. Paul Sabatier, Toulouse, France, 1991. Trustee Atwater Kent Mus., 1999—, Arthur Ross Gallery, 2001, Brandywine (Pa.) Conservancy, 2004—; bd. dirs. Am. Poetry Soc., 2001, FIRE. Recipient USPHS Research Career Devel. award, 1965, Lindback award U. Pa., 1969; Silver medal City of Paris, 1978; NIH grantee, 1981—. Mem. Am. Soc. Microbiology, Internat. Assn. Dental Rsch. (E.H. Hatton award 1959), Am. Assn. Dental Rsch.(pres. 1978-79), Coll. Physicians of Phila., Phila. Mus. Art (trustee), The Phila. Club. Home: 560 N 23d St Philadelphia PA 19130-3132 Business E-Mail: bhammond@dental.temple.edu.

HAMMOND, BRUCE RAY, academic administrator, consultant; s. Donald Wheeler and Cecilia Margaret Hammond; m. June Hammond, June 17, 1989; children: John Ray, Vanessa Louise. BS, SUNY, Fredonia, 1963; MS, Canisius Coll., Buffalo, 1967; MA, SUNY, Buffalo, 1969, PhD, 1972. Assoc. prof. Canisius Coll., Buffalo, 1966—84; pres. Am. Mgmt. Cons., St. Augustine, Fla., 1984—90; sr. cons. Achieve Global, Tampa, Fla., 1990—2003; assoc. v.p., academic affairs Saint Leo U., Fla., 2003—. Cons. Prudential, London, 1994—96, Time Warner Cable, Cin., 1996—2000, Brit. Telecom, London, 2000—02. Author: Winning the Job Interview Game, 1990; contbr. articles to profl. jours., chapters to books. Project mgr. Fla. Dept. Labor, Tallahassee, 1984—85; pres. Big Brothers/Big Sisters, St. John's County, Fla., 1986—88; task force leader Greater Dade City Chamber, Dade City, Fla., 2004. Sgt. USAR, 1956—64. Mem.: APA, Southern Speech Comm. Assn., Am. Arbitration Assn. (panel mem. 1985). Office: Saint Leo Univ SR 54 Saint Leo FL 33574

HAMMOND, CALEB DEAN, III, publishing executive; b. Orange, N.J., May 11, 1947; s. Caleb Dean Jr. and Patricia Treacy (Ehrgott) H.; m. Stephanie Hoagland, Aug. 9, 1969 (div. Jan. 1978); 1 child, Joshua Dean; m. Kathleen Theresa Doorish, July 8, 1978 (div. Nov. 1998); children: Connor Dean, Kathleen Treacy. BSBA, Susquehanna U., 1970; postgrad., Stetson U. Sch. Law, 1970-72. Pres. Chainwheel Dr., Clearwater, Fla., 1972-74; chmn. Hammond, Inc., Maplewood, NJ, 1974—99; CEO Neighborhood Energy, LLC, Maplewood, NJ, 2002. Mem. Assn. Am. Pubs.

HAMMOND, CHARLES BESSELLIEU, obstetrician, gynecologist, educator; b. Ft. Leavenworth, Kans., July 24, 1936; s. Claude G. and Alice (Sims) H.; m. Peggy A. Hammond, June 21, 1958; children: Sharon L., Charles B. BS, The Citadel, 1957; MD, Duke U., 1961. Diplomate Am. Bd. Ob-Gyn. Intern in surgery Duke U., 1961-62, resident in ob-gyn, 1962-63, 66-69, fellow in reproductive endocrinology, 1963-64, asst. prof. dept. ob-gyn, 1969-73, assoc. prof., 1973-78, prof., 1978-81, E.C. Hamblen prof., 1981—, chmn., 1980—2002. Contbr. in field. Served with USPHS, 1964-66. Fellow Royal Coll. Ob-gyn. (ad eundeum), Soc. Ob-gyn. Can. (hon.); mem. AMA, Am. Fertility Soc. (pres. 1985), ACOG (chmn. dist. IV 1997-2000, pres. 2002), Am. Assn. Ob-Gyn. Found. (pres. 1996-2002), Assn. Profs. Obstetrics and Gynecology, Am. Gynecol. and Obstet. Soc. (pres. 1993-94), Soc. Gynecol. Investigation, Am. Gynecol. Soc., Am. Assn. Obstet. and Gynecology, N.C. Med. Soc., N.C. Soc. Obstetricians and Gynecologists (pres. 1985), Am. Gynecol. Club (pres. 1994), Inst. of Medicine. Presbyterian. Home: 2827 McDowell Rd Durham NC 27705-5604 Office: Duke U Med Ctr PO Box 3853 Durham NC 27710 Office Phone: 919-684-3008. Business E-Mail: hammo005@mc.duke.edu.

HAMMOND, DAVID ALAN, stage director, educator; b. NYC, June 3, 1948; s. Jack and Elizabeth Alida (Furno) H. BA magna cum laude, Harvard U., 1970; MFA, Carnegie-Mellon U., 1972. Mem. faculty Juilliard Theatre Ctr., NYC, 1972-74; asst. conservatory dir. Am. Conservatory Theatre, San Francisco, 1974-81, assoc. stage dir., 1974-78; dir. Summer Tng. Congress, 1976-80, resident stage dir., 1979-81. Adj. assoc. prof. acting and directing Yale Sch. Drama, New Haven, 1981—85; adj. prof. dept. dramatic art U. NC, Chapel Hill, 1985—88, prof., 1988—; artistic dir. PlayMakers Repertory Co., Chapel Hill, 1985—92, 1999—, assoc. producing dir., 1992—99; guest artist Pacific Conservatory Performing Arts, 1976, U. Wash., 1977, SUNY, Purchase, 1979, Tisch Sch. Arts/NYU, N.Y.C., 1999—; guest dir. Aspen (Colo.) Music Festival, 1974—75, San Francisco Opera, 1978, Carmel (Calif.) Bach Festival, 1979—80, Sherwood Shakespeare Festival, Oxnard, Calif., 1981, Roundabout Theatre, NYC, 1983, Valley Shakespeare Festival, Saratoga, Calif., 1984, 86, 88, Shakespeare Festival of Dallas, 1990, Teatro Alianza, Montevideo, 1992, 94, 97, Inst. Teatral El Galpon, Montevideo, 1995, Opera Co. NC, 1998—99; resident dir. Yale Repertory Theatre, New Haven, 1981—85; Arts Am. cultural specialist U.S. Info. Svc., 1992, 94; guest prof. Escuela Mcpl. de Arte Dramatico, 2003, Escuela de Expression Teatral Anglo-o.m.b.u., 2003, El Univ. del Plata, Montevideo, 2003. Recipient Drama-Logue Critics award, LA, 1980, 81, Florencio award, Montevideo, 1992. Mem. Soc. Stage Dirs. and Choreographers, Actors' Equity, Am. Guild Mus. Artists, Dramatists' Guild, Nat. Theater Conf., Assn. for Theatre in Higher Edn. Office: PlayMakers Repertory Co Ctr For Dramatic Art cb 3235 Chapel Hill NC 27599-0001 Office Phone: 919-962-2484. Business E-Mail: dhammond@email.unc.edu.

HAMMOND, DEBORA R., interdisciplinary studies professor; d. Donald L. and Phyllis E. Hammond. BA in History, Stanford U., 1974; MA in History of Sci., U. Calif., Berkeley, 1991, PhD in History of Sci., 1997. Asst. prof. interdisciplinary studies Hutchins Sch. Liberal Studies, Sonoma State U., Rohnert Park, Calif., 1997—2002, assoc. prof. interdisciplinary studies, 2002—. Mem.: Internat. Soc. Systems Scis. (pres. 2005—). Office: Hutchins Sch Sonoma State U 1801 E Cotati Ave Rohnert Park CA 94928 Office Phone: 707-664-3179.

HAMMOND, DEBORAH LYNN, lay worker; b. Olney, Md., Feb. 12, 1958; d. Cornelius Dennis Sr. and Beverly Laura (Dunn) H. AA in Gen. Studies, Catonsville C.C. Sec. Mt. Zion United Meth. Ch., Ellicott City, Md., 1980-95; data entry clerk Balt. Gas Electric Co., Pasadena, Md., 1994-95; sec. The Md. Correctional Instn. for Women, Jessup, Md., 1995-97; instr. computer & typing Milford Mill Acad., Randallstown, Md., 1996—2003; ch. sec. Trinity United Meth. Ch., Catonsville, Md., 1997—2003; adminstrv. ch. office mgr. Falls Rd AME Ch., Balt., 1996—; with Rees Sci. and Tech. Ltd., Balt., 1997—; legal asst. Currant and O'Sullivan P.C., 2003—. Chaplain, vol. activity coord. sec. Md. Correctional Instn. Women, 1995; choir dir. Falls Road AME Ch., 1995—; instr. adult edn. Milford Mill Acad., 1996—; bookkeeper Balt. Subway, 2002. Mem.: Order of the Eastern Star (Myra, Balt. chpt.). Home: 1 Sulky Ct Apt 101 Randallstown MD 21133-3149 Office: Currant and O'Sullivan PC Ste 302 8101 Sandy Spring Rd Laurel MD 20707 also: Falls Rd AME Ch 2145 Pine Ave Baltimore MD 21244-2827 Personal E-mail: deborah5909@aol.com.

HAMMOND, DOUGLAS ALAN, physician; b. Florence, Ala., Jan. 18, 1965; s. Harold Jerry and Peggy Ann (Newbern) Hammond; m. Kathy Dale Belue, Aug. 6, 1988; children: William, John, Christian. BS, U. Ala., 1986; MD, U. Ala. Sch. Medicine, 1991. Cert. Am. Bd. Surgery, 1997, Nat. Bd. Med. Examiners. Surgery resident Meth. Hosps., Memphis, 1991—94, U. Tenn., 1994—96; ptnr. Jackson Surg. Assocs., Montgomery, Ala., 1996—2001, Memphis Surg. Specialists, 2001—. Cons. Wyeth Pharms., 2003. Fellow: Southeastern Surg. Congress, Am. Coll. Surgeons; mem.: AMA. Presbyn. Avocations: reading, travel. Office: Memphis Surg Specialists 1325 Eastmoreland Ste 410 Memphis TN 38104 Office Phone: 901-725-1921.

HAMMOND, GEORGE SIMMS, chemist, consultant; b. Auburn, Maine, May 22, 1921; s. Oswald Kenric and Marjorie (Thomas) Hammond; m. Marian Reese, June 8, 1945 (div. 1977); children: Kenric, Janet, Steven, Barbara, Jeremy; m. Eva L. Menger, May 22, 1977; stepchildren: Kirsten Menger-Anderson, Lenore Menger-Anderson. BS, Bates Coll., 1943; MS, PhD, Harvard U., 1947; DSc (hon.), Wittenberg U., 1972, Bates Coll., 1973; DHC (hon.), U. Ghent, 1973, Georgetown U., 1985, Bowling Green State U., 1990, Weizman Inst. Sci., 1993. Postdoctoral fellow UCLA, 1947—48; mem. faculty Iowa State Coll., 1948—58, prof. chemistry, 1956—58; prof. organic chemistry Calif. Inst. Tech., Pasadena, 1958—72, chmn. divsn. chemistry and chem. engring., 1968—72; Arthur Amos Noyes prof. chemistry; vice chancellor natural scis. U. Calif., Santa Cruz, 1972—74, prof. chemistry, 1972—78; exec. dir. for biosci., metals and ceramics Allied Corp., Morristown, NJ, 1978—88; cons., 1988—. Vis. assoc. prof. U. Ill., 1953; mem. chem. adv. panel NSF, 1962—65; fgn. sec. NAS, 1974—78. Author (with J.s. Fritz): Quantitative Organic Analysis, 1956; author: (with D.J. Cram) Organic Chemistry, 1958; author: (with J. Osteryoung, T. Crawford and H. Gray) Models in Chemical Science, 1971; co-editor: Advances in Photochemistry, 1961; editl. bd. Jour. Am. Chem. Soc., 1967—. Recipient James Flack Norris award, 1968, Nat. medal of sci., 1994, Othmer Gold medal, Chem. Heritage Found., 2003. Mem.: NAS (fgn. sec.), European Photochem. Soc., Inter-Am. Photochem. Soc., Materials Rsch. Soc., Am. Acad. Arts and Scis., Am. Chem. Soc. (award in petroleum chemistry 1960, Priestly medal 1976, Nat. medal of Sci. 1994, Seaborg medal 1994), Sigma Xi, Phi Beta Kappa. Home: Apt 2403 1414 SW 3rd Ave Portland OR 97201 Business E-Mail: george@hammond.name.com. E-mail: meagerhammond@qwest.net.

HAMMOND, GLENN BARRY, SR., lawyer, electrical engineer; b. Roanoke, Va., Sept. 3, 1947; s. Howard Reichard and Billie (Cromer) Hammond; m. Elizabeth Wickham, Aug. 4, 2001; 1 stepchild, T. Rigsby Wickham; 1 child from previous marriage, Glenn Barry. BA, Va. Mil. Inst., 1969; MBA, So. Ill. U., 1974; JD, U. Richmond, 1978; BSEE, Nova Coll., 1995. Bar: Va. 1979, U.S. Dist. Ct. (we. dist.) Va. 1979, U.S. Ct. Appeals (4th cir.) 1981, U.S. Ct. Mil. Appeals 1989, Air Force Ct. Mil. Rev. 1989, U.S. Supreme Ct., 1992. Assoc. Wilson, Hawthorne & Vogel, Roanoke, 1978-79; pvt. practice Roanoke, 1979—80, 1986—2004; atty., advisor to chief adminstrv. law judge Social Security Adminstrn., HHS, Roanoke, 1980-86; ptnr. Wooten & Hart P.C., 1995-98; pres. R.F. Cons., Inc., Roanoke, Va., 1998—2004; fed. adminstrv. law judge Office Of Hearings and Appeals, Social Security Adminstrn., 2004—. Pres., bd. dirs. LCH Broadcasting Group, Inc. Roanoke. Editor: Psychiatry in Military Law, 1988. Sr. vice-comdr. Mil. Order World Wars, Roanoke, 1981. Col. JAGC, USAF, 1969-75, Res. 1975—. Mem. Air Commando Assn. (life), DAV (life), VFW (life), AFA (life), Nat. Mil. Intelligence Assn. (life), Armed Forces Comms. Electronics Assn., Nat. Orgn. Social Security Claimants Reps., Masons. E-mail: bluetig@earthlink.net.

HAMMOND, GRAEME LORD, surgeon, educator; b. NYC, Jan. 30, 1933; married; 2 children. BS, Denison U., Granville, Ohio, 1958; MD, McGill U., Montreal, Can., 1962. Diplomate Am. Bd. Surgery, Am. Bd. Thoracic Surgery; lic. surgeon, N.Y., Mass., Conn. Intern in surgery Royal Victoria Hosp., Montreal, 1962-63; resident in surgery Mass. Gen. Hosp., Boston, 1963-65, 66-68, clin. rsch. fellow in surgery, 1965-66; from asst. prof. to assoc. prof. surgery Sch. Medicine Yale U., 1969-79, prof. New Haven, 1979—; attending surgeon Yale-New Haven Hosp., 1969—, prin. investigator lung transplant program, 1988—. Vis. rsch. scientist dept. biochemistry Hormone Rsch. Lab., U. Calif., San Francisco, 1981-82; mem. examining bd. Nat. Bd. Med. Examiners, 1987-90. Mem. editorial bd. Thoracic and Cardiovascular Surgery, 4th edit., 1982, 5th edit., 1990, 6th edit., 1996. With U.S. Army, 1953-55. Fellow USPHS, 1965-66. Mem. Am. Surg. Assn., Soc. Univ. Surgeons, Am. Assn. Thoracic Surgery, Am. Coll. Surgeons, Am. Heart Assn. (fellow coun. cardiovascular surgery, established investigator 1972-76), Am. Soc. for Biochemistry and Molecular Biology, New England Surg. Soc., Internat. Soc. Cardiovascular Surgery, Internat. Soc. Heart Rsch., Assn. Acad. Surgery, Soc. Thoracic Surgeons, Internat. Soc. for Heart and Lung Transplantation, The Transplantation Soc., The European Assn. for Cardio-Thoracic Surgery, Soc. Vascular Surgery. Office: Yale U Sch Medicine Dept Surgery 333 Cedar St # 121fmb New Haven CT 06510-3289 Office Phone: 203-785-2699. Business E-Mail: graeme.hammond@yale.edu.

HAMMOND, HARMONY, artist, educator; b. Chgo., Feb. 8, 1944; d. William Joseph and Harmony R. (Jensen) H.; m. Stephen Clover, May 1963 (div. 1970); 1 child, Tanya Hammond. BA, U. Minn., 1967. Prof. art dept. U. Ariz., Tucson, 1988—. Vis. artist Phila. Coll. Art, Rutgers U., Art Inst. Chgo., U. N.Mex., Tyler Sch. Fine Art, Santa Fe Art Inst., Anderson Ranch, Vt. Studio Ctr.; co-founder Heresies Mag., A.I.R. Gallery. Author: Wrappings: Essays on Feminism, Art and the Martial Arts, 1984, Lesbian Art in America: A Contemporary History, 2000; one-woman shows include A.I.R. Gallery, N.Y.C., 1973, 1982, 1984, Lerner-Heller Gallery, 1982, Matrix Gallery, Wadsworth Atheneum, Hartford, Conn., 1984, Luise Ross Gallery, N.Y.C., 1984, Bernice Steinbaum Gallery, N.Y.C., 1986, Trabia-MacAffe Gallery, N.Y.C., 1987, Etherton-Stern Gallery, Tucson, 1987, 1994, Linda Durham Gallery, Galisteo, N.Mex., 1988, Tucson Mus. Art, 1993, Linda Durham Gallery, Santa Fe, 1998, Site Santa Fe, 2002, Mus. Contemporary Art, Tucson, 2002, Dwight Hackett Projects, Santa Fe, 2004, Ctr. for Contemporary Arts, 2005, others. Recipient award, Nat. Endowment of Arts-Sculpture, 1979, Nat. Endowment for Arts-Graphics, 1983; grantee, Pollock-Krasner Found., 1989, Guggenheim Found., 1991, Rockefeller Found. Bellagio, 1994, Adolph and Ester Gottlieb Found., 1995, Joan Mitchell Found., 1998, Andrea Frank Found., 2000; CAPS grantee, NY State Coun. of Arts-Sculpture, 1982. Mem. Coll. Art Assn. Avocation: Aikido. Office: U Ariz Sch Art Tucson AZ 85721-0001

HAMMOND, HAROLD LOGAN, pathology educator, oral and maxillofacial pathologist; b. Hillsboro, Ill., Mar. 18, 1934; s. Harold Thomas and Lillian (Carlson) H.; m. Sharon Bunton, Aug. 1, 1954 (dec. 1974); 1 child, Connie; m. Pat J. Palmer, June 3, 1986. Student Millikin U., 1953-57, Roosevelt U., Chgo., 1957-58; DDS, Loyola U., Chgo., 1962; MS, U. Chgo., 1967. Diplomate Am. Bd. Oral and Maxillofacial Pathology. Intern, U. Chgo. Hosps., Chgo., 1962-63, resident, 1963-66, chief resident in oral pathology, 1966-67; asst. prof. oral pathology U. Iowa, Iowa City, 1967-72, assoc. prof., 1972-80, assoc. prof., dir. surg. oral pathology, 1980-83, prof., dir., 1983-2004, prof. emeritus oral pathology, radiology and medicine, 2004-, dir. emeritus, Surg. Oral Pathology Lab., 2004-; cons. pathologist Hosp. Gen. de Managua, Nicaragua, 1970-90, VA Hosp., Iowa City, 1977-2004. Cons. editor: Revista de la Asociation de Nicaragua, 1970-71, Revista de la Federacion Odontologica de Centroamerica y Panama, 1971-77. Contbr. articles to profl. jours. Mosby Pub. Co. scholar, 1962. Fellow AAAS, Am. Acad. Oral and Maxillofacial Pathology; mem. Am. Men and Women of Sci., NY Acad. Scis., AAUP, Internat. Assn. Oral Pathologists, Internat. Assn. Dental Rsch., N.Am. Soc. Head and Neck Pathologists, Am. Dental Assn., Am. Assn. for Dental Rsch. Avocations: collecting antique clocks, collecting gambling paraphernalia, collecting toys. Home: 1732 Brown Deer Rd Coralville IA 52241-1157 Office: U Iowa Dental Sci Bldg Iowa City IA 52242-1001

HAMMOND, HERBERT J., lawyer, arbitrator, mediator; b. Santa Fe, May 19, 1951; m. Myra Hammond; children: Ariel, Jay. BS magna cum laude, U. N.Mex., 1973; JD, NYU, 1976. Bar: Tex. 1977, U.S. Patent and Trademark Office 1977. Sr. ptnr. Thompson & Knight, Dallas, 1994—. Contbr. articles to profl. jours. Mem. State Bar Tex. (vice-chmn. com. on computerization of the profession 1989-92, chair computer sect. 1994-95, newsletter editor computer sect.), Am. Intellectual Property Law Assn., Dallas Bar Assn. (chmn. intellectual property sect. 1998), Phi Beta Kappa, Phi Kappa Phi, Kappa Mu Epsilon. Office: Thompson & Knight 1700 Pacific Ave Ste 3300 Dallas TX 75201-4693 E-mail: hhammond@tklaw.com.

HAMMOND, HOWARD DAVID, retired botanist, editor; b. Phila., Feb. 10, 1924; s. Clarence Elwood Jr. and Myrtle Iva (Sprowles) H.; m. Sarah Lichtenberg, Apr. 30, 1955; 1 child, Julia Ethel. BS, Rutgers U., 1945, MS, 1947; PhD, U. Pa., 1952. Asst. prof. U. Del., Newark, 1957-58, Howard U., Washington, 1958-68; from asst. prof. to assoc. prof. SUNY, Brockport, 1968-83; assoc. editor N.Y. Bot. Garden, Bronx, 1984-92. Co-editor: Floristic Inventory Tropical Countries, 1989, Southwestern Rare and Endangered Plants: Proceedings of the Second Conference/USDA Forest Service, 1996; regional reviewer for Flora of North America, 1997—. Vol. Deaver Herbarium, No. Ariz. U., 1993—; mem. pub. art adv. com. City of Flagstaff, 1996-2002; adj. curator botany Mus. No. Ariz., 1998-2002. Mem. Am. Inst. Biol. Scis., Bot. Soc. Am., Torrey Bot. Soc.(editor 1976-82, 87-92, pres. 1992), Sigma Xi. Home: 4025 Lake Mary Rd Apt 33 Flagstaff AZ 86001-8608 Office Phone: 928-523-7242.

HAMMOND, J. D., retired academic administrator; b. Maitland, Mo., Nov. 14, 1933; s. William Byron and Lillian Irene (Goodpasture) H.; m. Marian Jane Idle, Aug. 20, 1960; children: Nancy Lee, Michael James. AB, N.W. Mo. State U., 1955; PhD, U. Pa., 1961. Asst. prof. econs. Ohio State U., Columbus, 1959-64, assoc. prof. bus. adminstrn., 1964-69, prof. ins., 1969-82, William Elliot prof. ins., 1982-86, William Elliot endowed chairholder, 1986-99; dean Smeal Coll. Bus. Adminstrn. Pa. State U., University Park, 1989-99. Pres. Risk Theory Seminar, 1973-74; bd. dirs. Atlantic Mut. Ins. Co.; disinterested trustee Scudder Kemper Investments, 1985—, Scudder Variable Life Fund, 1985-2000; chmn. workforce diversity task force Am. Assembly Collegiate Schs. of Bus., 1993. Chair campaign Pa. chpt. United Way, 1998. Office: Smeal Coll Bus Adminstrn Pa State U 801 Business Admin Bldg University Park PA 16802-3008 Business E-Mail: jdh9@psu.edu.

HAMMOND, JANE LAURA, retired law librarian, lawyer; b. Nashua, Iowa; d. Frank D. and Pauline Hammond. BA, U. Dubuque, 1950; MS, Columbia U., 1952; JD, Villanova U., 1965, LHD, 1993. Bar: Pa. 1965. Cataloguer Harvard Law Libr., 1952-54; asst. libr. Sch. Law Villanova (Pa.) U., 1954-62; libr. Sch. Law, Villanova (Pa.) U., 1962-76; prof. law Sch. Law Villanova (Pa.) U., 1965-76; law libr., prof. law Cornell U., Ithaca, N.Y., 1976-93. Adj. prof. Drexel U., 1971-74; mem. depository libr. coun. to pub. printer U.S. Govt. Printing Office, 1975-78; cons. Nat. Law Libr., Monrovia, Liberia, 1989. Fellow ALA; mem. ABA (coun. sect. legal edn. 1984-90, com. on accreditation 1982-87, com. on stds. rev. 1987-95), PEO, Coun. Nat. Libr. Assn. (sec.-treas. 1971-72, chmn. 1979-80), Am. Assn. Law Librs. (sec. 1965-70, pres. 1975-76), Assn. Am. Law Schs. (exec. com. 1977). Episcopalian. Office: Cornell U Sch Law Myron Taylor Hall Ithaca NY 14853

HAMMOND, JANE PAMELA, adult education educator; b. Flint, Mich., Aug. 10, 1951; d. Duane Aurther and Norine Janet Moore; m. Larry Duane Hammond, June 22, 1974; children: Jason Duane, Joel Brady. BA in Sociology, Olivet Nazarene U., 1973; postgrad., U. Mich., 1973—74. Lic. real estate Mich. Line supr. Tex. Instruments, Lubbock, Tex., 1976—78; elem. tchr. United Meth. Ch. Sch., Tampa, Fla., 1979—80; adult edn. and substitute tchr. Mt. Morris (Mich.) Consol. Schs., 1981—85, substitute tchr., 1992—99; automobile sales person Hobson Ford Dealership, Clio, Mich., 1985—86; real estate salesperson Century 21, Clio and Flint, Mich., 1987—92; tchr. adult and alternative edn. Clio Area Schs., 1999—. Career pathways rep. Clio Area Schs. Cmty. Edn., 2000—. Mem. exec. com. Genesee County Reps., Flint, 2000—; sustaining mem. Mich. State and Nat. Rep. Coms., 2000—; Sunday sch. tchr. Ch. of the Nazarene, Mt. Morris, Flint, 1986—. Jr. Miss Vocal scholar, House of Harmony, 1967. Mem.: Clio Area C. of C. (Enhancement award 2002), Clio Common Grounds (lifelong learning and arts and recreation com.), Mich. Hist. Soc., Clio Hist. Soc., Mich. Farm Bur., VFW Ladies Aux. Avocations: interior decorating, flower arranging, antiques, camping. Home: 3105 E Dodge Rd Clio MI 48420

HAMMOND, JOHN BAPTISTE, III, academic administrator; b. Baton Rouge, La., Aug. 18, 1962; s. John Batiste Hammond, Jr. and Shirley Jean (Kelly) Hammond; m. Yoko Kusumoto, Mar. 8, 1999; children: Therese Morgan, John Baptiste Hammond, IV. BS, MIT, 1984; MBA, Emory U., 1988; ABD, MIT, 1999. Assoc. dir. of admissions MIT, Cambridge, Mass., 1991—93; asst. dean Goizueta Bus. Sch., Atlanta, 1999—. Orgnl. cons. Hammond Consulting, Atlanta, 1999—; course dir. Goizueta Bus. Sch., 2000—. Author: The Physican Executive. Prin. for a day program Atlanta Pub. Schs., 2001—03; mentor Cambridge Pub. Schs., 1989—92. Mem.: Acad. of Mgmt., Alpha Phi Alpha Frat., Inc. (area dir. 1990—92). Achievements include research in co-author, Dept. of Labor monograph examining the status of african ams. in the workplace. Avocations: reading, travel, movies, bicycling.

HAMMOND, LARRY AUSTIN, lawyer; b. Wichita, Kans., Sept. 17, 1945; BA, U. Tex., 1967, JD, 1970. Bar: Calif. 1971, Ariz. 1975. Law clk. to Hon. Carl McGowan U.S. Ct. Appeals (D.C. cir.), Washington, 1970-71; law clk. to Hon. Hugo L. Black U.S. Supreme Ct., Washington, 1971, law clk. to Hon. Lewis F. Powell Jr., 1971-73; asst. spl. prosecutor Watergate spl. prosecution force U.S. Justice Dept., Washington, 1973-74, dep. asst. atty. gen. office legal counsel, 1977-80; mem. Osborn Maledon P.A., Phoenix, 1995—. Adj. prof. law Ariz. State U., 1977, 85—, U. Ariz., 1983, U. N.Mex., 1983; judge pro tempore Ariz. Ct. Appeals, 1992. Editor-in-chief Tex. Law Rev., 1969-70. Mem. ABA, Am. Judicature Soc. (pres. 2003-05), Order of Coif. Office: Osborn Maledon PO Box 36379 Phoenix AZ 85067-6379 Office Phone: 602-640-9361. Business E-Mail: lhammond@omlaw.com.

HAMMOND, LOU RENA CHARLOTTE, public relations executive; b. Muenster, Tex. d. Louis Martin and Regina L. (Schoech) Wolf; m. Christopher Weymouth Hammond, Sept. 6, 1964; 1 child, Stephen. BA, U. Houston, 1962. Rep. pub. rels. Pan Am. Airways, N.Y.C., 1968-76, mgr. pub. rels., 1977-79, dir. pub. rels., 1980-81, dir. pub. affairs, 1981; pres., ptnr. Taylor and Hammond, N.Y.C., 1981-84; prin., pres. Lou Hammond and Assocs., N.Y.C., 1984—. Editor: (calendar) Avenue mag., 1976-79. Recipient Matrix award in pub. rels., 1992, Winthrop W. Grice award Hotel Sales and Mktg. Assoc. Internat., 1992, Inside PR Mag.'s All-Star award, 1992, Circle of Excellence award Public Relations, Internat. Furnishings and Design Assn (IFDA). Mem. Soc. Am. Travel Writers, Fashion Group, Assn. Better N.Y., Les DAmes de Escoffier, Women's Forum, Women Execs. in Pub. Rels., Doubles Club. Roman Catholic. Avocations: bridge, tennis, 18th century antiques. Office: Lou Hammond & Assocs Inc 39 E 51st St New York NY 10022-5916 Office Phone: 212-308-8880. Personal E-mail: louh@lllammond.com.

HAMMOND, MARIAN CORLEENE, retired literature educator; b. Ramage, W.Va., Dec. 8, 1919; s. Booker Shumate and Sadie Mearl Workman; m. John Elam Moore, July 7, 1942 (annulled Oct. 1945); m. Joseph Hammond, Nov. 17, 1945 (dec. Apr. 1998); children: Terry Colette Humphrey, Lisa Suzanne. AB in English, Berea Coll., 1941; EdM, Mills Coll., 1955; postgrad., Stanford U., 1958—76; adminstrv. credential, Calif. State U., Hayward, 1974; MA in drama, San Francisco State U., 1976. Cert. prin. Calif. Tchr. English and drama Scott H.S., Madison, W.Va., 1941—42; children's libr. N.Y. Pub. Libr., N.Y.C., 1941; sci. tchr. Eccles (W.Va.) Jr. H.S., 1942—43; statistician, speech writer Del Monte Corp., San Francisco, 1946—53; tchr. English and drama San Lorenzo (Calif.) H.S., 1955—57; tchr. drama San Francisco State U., 1958—62; tchr. drama, speech and English Chabot Coll., Hayward, Calif., 1962—70; prin., tchr. grades 7-12 Fremont (Calif.) Unified Sch. Dist., 1968—85; tchr. English, speech and tech. writing Heald Inst. Tech., Hayward, 1992—93; tchr. speech and English Western Career Coll., San Leandro, Calif., 2000—01; ret. Contbr. articles to mags. Active Liberty Counsel, Orlando, Fla., 1999—2005, Am. Ctr. for Law and Justice, Atlanta, 1999—2005, Parents TV Coun., L.A., 2000—05. Mem.: AFTRA, Actors Equity, Hayward Arts Coun., Castro Valley Mineral and Gem Soc. (life; dealer), Alpha Psi Omega (chmn. casting com. Berea Coll. chpt.), Pi Gamma Mu, Tau Kappa Alpha. Republican. Baptist. Avocations: bead stringing and design, writing. Home: 27937 El Portal Dr Hayward CA 94542 Office Phone: 510-886-5095.

HAMMOND, MARK, state official; b. Lancaster, S.C., Nov. 29, 1963; m. Ginny Hammond; children: Matthew, Ross, Grace. BA in Polit. Sci., Newberry Coll., 1986; MEd, Clemson U., 1988. Criminal investigator 7th Cir. Solicitor's Office, 1990—96; clk. of ct. County of Spartanburg, 1996; sec. of state State of S.C., 2002—. Mem. St. Paul United Meth. Ch., Spartanburg. Republican. Office: Edagr Brown Bldg 1205 Pendleton St Ste 525 Columbia SC 29201 Address: PO Box 11350 Columbia SC 29211

HAMMOND, NORMAN DAVID CURLE, archaeology educator, researcher; b. Brighton, Eng., July 10, 1944; BA, U. Cambridge, Eng., 1966, Diploma in Classical Archaeology, 1967, MA, 1970, PhD, 1972, ScD, 1987, DSc (hon.), 1999. Rsch. faculty Cambridge U., Eng., 1967-75; faculty Bradford U., Eng., 1975-77; vis. prof. Rutgers U., 1977-78, faculty, 1978-88, assoc. prof., 1978-84, prof., 1984-88; member staff Peabody Mus., Harvard U., 1988—, Willey lectr., 2000; prof. archaeology Boston U., 1988—, chmn., 2005—. Vis. prof. U. Calif., Berkeley, 1977, Jilin U., China, 1981, Calif. Acad. Sci., 1984-85, U. Paris, 1987, Acad. Scis., USSR, 1991, U. Bonn, 1994; vis. faculty U. Cambridge, 1981-82, 91, 96-97, 2004, U. Oxford, 1989, 2004; archaeology corr. The Times, London (Press award, Brit. Archaeol. Awards 1994, 98), 1967—; field work in North Africa, Afghanistan, Greece, Guatemala, Belize, Ecuador, Spain; disting. lectr. Montana State U., 1996, Bushnell lectr. Cambridge U., 1997, Stone lectr. AIA, 1998, 2004, Brush lectr. AIA, 2001, Armand Brunswick disting. lectr. Met. Mus. Art, 2001. Author: (with F.R. Allchin) The Archaeology of Afghanistan, 1977, (with G.R. Willey) Maya Archaeology and Ethnohistory, 1979, Ancient Maya Civilization, 1982, 5th edit., 1994, various foreign edits., Cuello: An Early Maya Community in Belize, 1991, The Maya, 2000; numerous monographs on excavations in No. Belize, 1973, 75, 76, Lubaantun, 1975, Nohmul, 1985; gen. editor: Procs., 44th Internat. Congress of Americanists, 1982-84. Dumbarton Oaks fellow, 1988; Rockefeller Found. scholar, 1997. Fellow Soc. Antiquaries London (medallist 2001), Brit. Acad Office: Boston Univ Dept Archaeology 675 Commonwealth Ave Boston MA 02215-1406 Office Phone: 617-358-1651.

HAMMOND, PAUL YOUNG, political science professor; b. Salt Lake City, Feb. 24, 1929; s. James Thaddeus and Hortense Clair (Young) H.; m. Merylyn Felt Simmons, Aug. 29, 1950; children: Paul Brett, Wendy Simmons, Robyn Simmons, Spencer Blair, Clifford Simmons. BA, U. Utah, 1949; MA, Harvard U., 1951, PhD, 1953; postgrad. Fulbright scholar, London Sch. Econs., 1952-53. Instr. govt. Harvard U., Cambridge, Mass., 1953—55; lectr. Columbia U., N.Y.C., 1956—57; asst. prof. polit. sci. Yale U., New Haven, 1957—62; rsch. assoc. Washington Ctr. Fgn. Policy Rsch. Johns Hopkins U., 1962—64; mem. rsch. staff Rand Corp., Santa Monica, Calif., 1964—76, head social sci. dept., 1973—76; vis. rsch. polit. scientist U. Calif., Berkeley, 1971—72; Edward R. Weidlein prof. environ. and pub. policy studies U. Pitts., 1976—83, disting. svc. prof. pub. and internat. affairs, 1983—2004, disting. svc. prof. emeritus, 2004—; dir. Ridgway Ctr. of Internat. Security Studies, 1988—91, Energy and Environ. Center, 1979—81; Fulbright rsch. prof. Inst. of S.E. Asian Studies, Singapore, 1993—. Lectr. U. Tex., U. So. Calif., U. Calif., Santa Barbara and L.A.; cons. in field. Author/co-author: Organizing for Defense: The Adminstration of the American Military Establishment, 1961, The Cold War Years: American Foreign Policy Since 1945, 1969, Cold War and Detente: The American Foreign Policy Process Since 1945, 1975, NATO Strategic Planning: Preparations That Do No Harm, 1988, Fulfilling the Promise of the Goldwater-Nichols Act: Operational Planning and Command, 1989, NATO: The Infrastructure of Reassurance, 1989, What Future For the U.S. Military Presence in Europe, 1990, LBJ and the Presidential Management of Foreign Relations, 1992, Towards a Workable European Architecture: Political-Military Problems in the New Europe, 1994, Doing Without America?, 1996, On Taking Peacekeeping Seriously, 1997, Culture Versus Civilization: A Critique of Huntington, 1997; co-author: The American Civil-Military Decisions, 1963, Information System Applications for a High Level Staff, 1972, Social Choice and Soviet Strategic Decision Making, 1977, Regional Energy Policy Alternatives, 1977, Administration of Security Assistance: Systems and Process, 1978, Individual Energy Conservation Behaviors, 1980, The Reluctant Supplier, 1983, Alternative Organizational Structures for NATO, 1992; co-editor: Political Dynamics in the Middle East, 1971. Forrestal fellow in naval history, 1955, Stimson Fund fellow Yale U., 1959, Rockefeller fellow in internat. studies, 1963-64; Fulbright scholar London Sch. Econs., 1952-53. Mem. Am. Polit. Sci. Assn., Internat. Studies Assn., Internat Inst. Strategic Studies. Mem. Lds Ch. Office: Grad Sch Pub & Internat Affairs Posvar Hall University of Pittsburgh Pittsburgh PA 15260

HAMMOND, R. PHILIP, chemical engineer; b. Creston, Iowa, May 28, 1916; s. Robert Hugh and Helen Hammond; m. Amy L. Farmer, Feb. 28, 1941 (div. 1969); children: Allen L., David M., Jean Phyllis, Stanley W.; m. Vivienne Fox, 1972. BSChemE, U. So. Calif., 1938; PhD in Phys. and Inorganic Chemistry, U. Chgo., 1947. Registered profl. engr., Ill., Calif. Chief chemist Lindsay Chem. Co., West Chicago, Ill., 1938-46; group leader Los Alamos (N.Mex.) Sci. Lab., 1947-62, assoc. divsn. leader reactor devel. divsn., 1960-62; dir. nuc. desalination program Oak Ridge Nat. Lab., 1962-73; adj. prof. UCLA, 1972—80; head energy group R & D Assos. Corp., Santa Monica, Calif., 1973-83; desalination cons., 1987—; leader advanced sea water evaporator design Met. Water Dist. of So. Calif., L.A., 1989-98. Author articles on nuc. power reactors, nuc. wastes, reactor safety econs., energy ctrs., metallurgy of plutonium and refractory metals, rare earths, radiation chemistry, remote control engring.; contbr. to Ency. Brit. Mem. U.S. del. Conf. on Peaceful Uses Atomic Energy, Geneva, Switzerland, 1955, 65, 71, IAEA Panel on Desalination, Vienna, Austria, 1964, 65, 66, 71; mem. U.S. team to USSR on desalination, 1964. Naval Rsch. fellow, U. Chgo. Mem. Am. Nuc. Soc. (charter), Am. Chem. Soc., Am. Inst. Chem. Engrs., Sigma Xi, Phi Kappa Phi, Phi Lambda Upsilon. Achievements include patents for improved safety for high speed rail transport, for devices for preventing collisions at sea and for storing nuclear waste; origination of advanced concepts in sea water evaporator construction, and efficient coupling to nuclear energy sources; design (with others) of advanced reactor containment system capable of withstanding melt-down accidents with zero leakage, and of automotive engine using liquid air and liquid natural gas as fuel. Home and Office: PO Box 3971 Laguna Hills CA 92654-3971 *With our achievements in desalination, efficient agriculture, and nuclear power, it is now clear that the food producing ability of the earth is not limited by technology. But our political and social institutions have not kept up. Over a billion people live in hopeless poverty, and without hope, terrorism is an easy choice. Yet small investments by the rich countries in energy supply and clean water will create self-supporting communities with purchasing power. The war on terror is really a war on poverty.*

HAMMOND, RALPH CHARLES, real estate executive; b. Valley Head, Ala., Feb. 1, 1916; s. William Bleve and Alice Corina Jane (Holleman) H.; student Snead Jr. Coll., 1938-39, Berea Coll., 1940-41; AB, U. Ala., 1945; DLitt, Livingston U., 1992; m. Myra Leak, June 20, 1954; children— James, Ben. Press sec. to gov. Ala., Montgomery, 1946-50, exec. sec., 1955-59; gen. rep. ARC, Greensboro, N.C., 1950-54; mayor of Arab (Ala.), 1963-69; pres. City Ctr., Inc., Arab, 1959— . Commr. from Ala., U.S. Study Commn. S.E. River Basins, 1958-64; bd. dirs. Ala. Tb Assn., 1956-83, pres., 1972-74; hon. Christmas Seal chmn., Ala. Served with AUS, 1941-45. Commd. Poet Laureate of Ala., 1991-95; Paul Harris fellow Rotary Internat., 1992. Mem. Ky. Hist. Soc., Phillip Hamman Family Assn. Am. (pres. 1972-78), Ala. Poetry Soc. (pres. 1981-84, Ala. Poet of Yr. 1985), Ala. Writers' Conclave (pres. 1987-89), Nat. Fedn. State Poetry Socs. (treas. 1985-86, 2d v.p. 1990-92, 1st v.p. 1993-94, pres. 1994-96). Democrat. Methodist. Lodge: Masons. Author: My GI Aching Back, 1945; Ante Bellum Mansions of Alabama, 1951; Philip Hamman, Man of Valor, 1976; Song of Appalachia, 1982; How High the Stars, 1982; Upon the Wings of the Wind, 1982; One Golden Apple a Day, 1983; Collected Poems, 1983; Wisdom Is, 1984; Edging Through the Grass (Book of Yr. Ala. Poetry Soc.), 1985; editor: Alabama Poets: A Contemporary Anthology, 1989, A Blossoming of Sonnets, 1990, Upper Alabama-Poems Out of Light (George Washington Honor medal Freedoms Found. Valley Forge 1993, Book of Yr. award Ala. Poetry Soc. 1993), Crossing Many Rivers-Poems Along the Way, 1995 (Book of Yr. award Ala. Poetry Soc. 1995), Vincent Van Gogh--A Narrative Journey, 1997, Personal Encounters, 2001; contbr. short stories and feature articles to jours., mags.; poems pub. in 40 jours. Home: 1280 Guntersville Rd Arab AL 35016-1618 Office: PO Box 486 Arab AL 35016-0486

HAMMOND, ROBIE LEE, health science association administrator; d. Robert Lee Higginbotham and Claudia Elizabeth Elrod; widowed; children: Robby Lee, Gary Joe, Debra Lynn H. Olson. AA, Draughans Bus. Coll., Greenville, S.C., 1946. Cert. med. staff coord. Nat. Assn. of Med. Staff Svcs. Svc. rep. Bell Tel. & Telegraph Co., Greenville, SC, 1946—52, Chesapeake & Potomac Tel. Co., Norfolk, Va., 1953; sec. Portsmouth Psychiat. Ctr., Va., 1976—81; med. libr. Portsmouth Gen. Hosp., Va., 1981—82, med. staff coord., 1983—98; exec. dir. Portsmouth Acad. of Medicine, Va., 1998—, exec. dir. med. found., 1998—. Author. Mem. citizens adv. com. Educare for Seniors, Portsmouth. Mem.: Portsmouth Consortium of Founds., Va. Conf. of Med. Execs. Avocations: golf, gardening, reading, creative writing, decorating.

HAMMOND, ROY JOSEPH, reinsurance company executive; b. St. Louis, Jan. 9, 1929; s. Edward Herman and Alvera Ann (Herzog) H.; m. Donna LaSalle Perkins, Apr. 12, 1951 (div. July 2001); children— Douglas Edward, Donald Erwin, Laura Ann Hammond Budniakiewicz; m. Gloria June Kirkpatrick, Dec. 19, 2001. BS, Northwestern U., 1954; JD, DePaul U., Chgo., 1959. Bar: Ill. bar 1959. With Am. Mut. Reins. Co., Chgo., 1963-91, v.p., then sr. v.p., gen. counsel and sec., 1967-76, pres., chief exec. officer, bd. dirs., 1976-91; pres., chief exec. officer Whitehall Cons., Ltd., Camden, N.C., 1991—; pres. Wheeling (Ill.) Mcpl. Park Dist., 1963-65. Past mem. Reins. Assn. Am., bd. dirs., 1976—86. Served with AUS, 1946-48. Mem. ABA, Ill. State Bar Assn., Internat. Assn. Def. Counsel, Fedn. Ins. and Corp. Counsel, Chgo. Casualty Adjusters Assn. (pres. 1972-73), Chgo. Yacht Club. Republican. Lutheran. Home and Office: Whitehall Shores 201 Azalea Dr Camden NC 27921-6991

HAMMOND, RUSSELL PAUL, music educator; b. Chgo., Oct. 30, 1959; s. John Edgar and Suzanne Louise Hammond; m. Michele Ann Smith. B Music Edn., Bradley U., Peoria, Ill., 1982; MMusic, U. Conns., Storrs, 1996; degree in ednl. leadership, Southern Conn. State U. Chair dept. music Lyme/Old Lyme H.S., Old Lyme, Conn., 1987—2001, dir. choirs and theatre arts, 1987—2001; fine arts chair Ledyard H.S., Conn., 2001—, dir. choirs, 2001—. Recipient Choral Dir. of Yr., Conn., 2003. Mem.: Music Educators Nat. Conf., Am. Choral Dirs. Assn. (state pres. 1993—95, chair repertoire and stds. 1998—2001), Conn. Music Educators Assn. Roman Catholic. Avocations: running, rock-climbing, hiking, reading, acting. Home: 93 Beech Tree Ridge PO Box 878 Killingworth CT 06419 Office: Ledyard High School 24 Gallup Hill Road Ledyard CT E-mail: hammond9@mindspring.com.

HAMMOND, SCOTT ALLEN, minister, counselor; b. Columbus, Ohio, Dec. 5, 1967; s. Richard Dewitt Hammond and Patricia Ann Hoelle; m. Sharon Kay Pulis, Jan. 1, 1990; children: Caleb Zachary, Meagan Grace, Luke Benjamin. BA in Pastoral Ministry, Ctrl. Bible Coll., Springfield, Mo., 1990; MA in Pastoral Counseling, MDiv in Pastoral Ministry, Assembly of God Theol. Sem., Springfield, Mo., 1992; EdD in Counseling Psychology, U. Sarasota, Fla., 2002. Lic. ordained minister Assemblies of God. Pastor 1st Assembly of God, Laurie, Mo., 1989—91; chaplain candidate U.S. Army, 1991—93, chaplain Fort Campbell, Ky., 1993—96, Germany, 1996—2002, Fort Polk, La., 2002—03, Fort Leavenworth, Kans., 2003—04, Fort Campbell, Ky., 2004—; participant Operation Restore Hope, 1995, Operation Joint Endeavor, Bosnia-Herzegovina, 1996, Operation Iraqi Freedom, 2003, Doing Operation Iraq: Freedom Again, 2005—. Maj. U.S. Army. Named one of Outstanding Young Men of Am., 1992; recipient Order of Titus, Office of Chief Army Chaplain. Mem.: APA (assoc.), Am. Assn. Marriage and Family Therapy (assoc.). Home: 3859 Man O War Blvd Clarksville TN 37042-7270

HAMMOND, SHIRLEY HATHAWAY, political scientist; b. Staten Island, N.Y., Aug. 5, 1926; d. Raymond Howell and Mary Frances Hathaway; m. Mansur T. Aftab, Aug. 20, 1947; children: Parry P., Richard E. (dec.), Deanna Aftab Guy; m. Harry H. Hammond, Aug. 18, 1966 (dec.); children: Louise Sharry. BA in S.S., History, MA in Polit. Sci., History, Monmouth U.; PhD candidate, Temple U. RN, N.J. Legis. intern Sen. Thomas Gagliano, Trenton, N.J., 1986, Congressman Chris Smith, Washington, 1985; dir. county ARC, Shewsbury, N.Y., 1981-83; trustee, chair edn. and policy Brookdale Coll., Lincroft, N.J., 1992—. Dir. fin. com. Monmouth County Rep. Party, Holmdel, N.J., 1981—; del. UN Internat. Congress Women, N.Y.C., 1985-89; dep. mayor Twp. Holmdel, 1988-91; rep. county com., 1982-91. Mem. AAUW, Am. Polit. Sci. Assn., Omohundro Inst. Early Am. History, Nat. Mus. Am. Indian. Avocations: writing, publishing, gourmet cooking, charity work. Office: Brookdale CC 765 Newman Springs Rd Lincroft NJ 07738-1543

HAMMOND, THERESA NADINE, art gallery director, educator, curator; b. Bryn Mawr, Pa., Nov. 13, 1959; d. Robert Lyman and Frances Virginia (Newman) Hammond; m. Roy Herman Nydorf, May 12, 1984. BFA, Guilford Coll., 1981; cert. in arts mgmt., U. N.C., 1982. Gallery asst. Greenhill Ctr. N.C. Art, Greensboro, 1981—84; gen. mgr. Antiquities, Ltd., Greensboro, Atlanta, 1984—90; dir., curator Guilford Coll. Art Gallery, Greensboro, 1990—. Freelance curator Triad Stage, Greensboro, 2001—02. Mem. Guildford County Hist. Property Commn., Greensboro, 2002—, Oakridge (N.C.) Planning and Zoning Bd., 2002—; bd. dirs. Greensboro Art Alliance, 2003—. Scholar, Z. Smith Reynolds Found., 1982; Profl. Devel. grantee, N.C. Arts Coun., 1997. Mem.: N.C. Mus. Coun., Southeastern Mus. Conf., Am. Assn. Mus. (Curator's Com. Travel award 1993). Avocations: historic preservation, art conservation. Office: Guilford Coll 5800 W Friendly Ave Greensboro NC 27410

HAMMOND, WILLIAM MICHAEL, historian, educator; b. Pasadena, Calif., Jan. 1, 1943; s. Paul Chester Hammond and Mary Ethel Champieux; m. Lillamaud Munsell Leike, Apr. 28, 1973; children: Michael Anthony, Elizabeth Anne. STB, Cath. U. Am., 1967, MA, 1968, PhD, 1973. Lectr. U. Md., College Park, 1991—; chief gen. histories br. U.S. Army Ctr. Mil. History, Washington, 2001—. Author: The U.S. Army in Vietnam: Public Affairs: The Military and the Media, 1963 - 1968 (Notable Govt. Docs., ALA, 1989), Public Affairs: The Military and the Media, 1968-1973, Reporting Vietnam, Military and Media at War (Richard W. Leopold award, Orgn. Am. Historians, 2000), Black Soldier, White Army: The 24th Infantry in Korea. Editor, web master, bd. dirs. Strathmore - Bel Pre Civic Assn., Silver Spring, Md., 1986—. Rsch. fellow, Joan Shorenstein Ctr. for the Press and Pub. Policy, Harvard U., 1999. Fellow: Interuniv. Seminar on Armed Forces and Soc.; mem.: Orgn. Am. Historians (Disting. Lectr. 2002—), Soc. Mil. History. Roman Catholic. Avocations: photography, watercolor painting, travel. Home: 2604 Bainbridge Ln Silver Spring MD 20906 Office: US Army Ctr Mil History Fort Lesley J McNair Washington DC 20319-5058

HAMMONDS, BRUCE L., bank executive; m. Sandy Hammonds; 2 children. Grad., U. Balt. Branch mgr. Pacific Finance Co.; joined Md. Nat. Bank, Balt., 1978; with Md. Bank N.A. (now MBNA Am. Bank N.A.), 1982, dir., 1986; COO MBNA Corp., Wilmington, Del., 1991—2002, pres., CEO, 2003—; chmn, CEO MBNA Am. Bank N.A., 2002. Bd. dirs. Del. State C. of C., Del. Housing Ptnrship., Del. Bus. Roundtable, Fin. Svcs. Roundtable; trustee Goldey-Beacom Coll.; mem. vis. com. Coll. of Bus. and Econs., U. Del. Office: MBNA Corp 1100 N King St Wilmington DE 19801 Office Phone: 800-441-7048. Office Fax: 302-456-8541.*

HAMMONDS, CARLOS R., secondary school educator; b. Kingsport, Tenn., June 7, 1952; s. Evelyn Hudson; m. Donna M Wright, Aug. 11, 1977; children: Jared C, Audrey F. D, Mid. Tenn. State U., 1979—81. Tchr. Sullivan County Schools, Kingsport, Tenn., 1977—2005. Mem.: TACTE (pres. 1996—97), SCEA, TEA, NEA. Home: 1100 Radcliffe Ave Kingsport TN 37664 Office: Sullivan County Schools 2533 John B Dennis Bypass Kingsport TN 37660 Office Phone: 423-354-1423. Office Fax: 423-354-1406. Personal E-mail: hammondsc@k12tn.net.

HAMMONDS, RICHARD LEE, physician; b. Henry Co., Ga., Apr. 25, 1935; s. Emory H. and Geraldine Hammonds; m. Christine Williams Hammonds, Oct. 11, 1992; children: Terri, Lisa, Tracey, Connie, Jerri, Lee. BS, Auburn U., Mass., 1956; MD, Emory Med. Sch., Atlanta, 1960. Pvt. practice, 1963—92; med. dir. Wellstar Health Sys., 1996—, chmn. bd., 1997—2001. Chief of staff Cobb Hosp., 1967—70; with State Bd. Corrections, Atlanta, 1974—76; health advisor to Pres. Jimmy Carter, Washington, 1976—80. Office: Wellstar Health Sys Austell Rd Austell GA 30106

HAMMONS, ALLEN JAMES, JR., lawyer; b. Houston, Aug. 16, 1958; s. Allen James and Irene Lillian (Harbour) H.; m. Rhonda Kim Welch, Mar. 5, 1983; children: James Richard, LaRhonda Jordan. AA, Brazosport Coll., 1978; BBA, Tex. Tech U., 1979, JD, 1982. Assoc. William A. Dyess, Brownfield, Tex., 1982-84, Hale & Dyess, Brownfield, 1984-85, ptnr., 1986, Hale & Hammons, Brownfield, 1987-92; solo practitioner Brownfield, 1992—. Pres. United Way Terry County, Brownfield, 1986, Terry County Chpt. Am. Cancer Soc., 1988; bd. dirs. Terry County Child Welfare Bd., 1986. Mem. Tex. Bar Assn., Terry County Bar Assn., Tex. Crimminal Def. Lawyers Assn., Brownfield C. of C. (bd. dirs. 1986—, v.p. 1987, pres. 1988), Optimists (sec., treas. 1985-86, pres. 1986—). Methodist. Avocations: tennis, baseball. Home: PO Box 1051 Brownfield TX 79316-1051 Office: 305A W Broadway St Brownfield TX 79316-4311

HAMMONS, BRIAN KENT, lawyer; b. Wurzburg, Federal Republic Germany, Mar. 6, 1958; arrived in U.S., 1958; s. R. Dwain and Donna G. (Carender) H.; m. Kimberly M. Pflumm, July 26, 1980; children: April Michelle, David Dwain, Adam Carender. BS summa cum laude, S.W. Mo. State U., Springfield, 1980; JD cum laude, So. Meth. U., Dallas, 1985. Bar: Mo. 1985. Exec., treas., v.p. Hammons Products Co., Stockton, Mo., 1980-86, exec. v.p., sec., 1987-96, pres., COO, CEO, 1997—; assoc. Stinson, Mag & Fizzell, Kansas City, Mo., 1986-87. Mem. Stockton Airport Bd., 1987-89, Stockton City Coun., 1989-91, Ozark Empire Fair Bd., 2004--; pres. Stockton Cmty. Found., Stockton Cmty. Develop., 2002—; cub scout leader Boy Scouts Am.; Sunday sch. and Bible study tchr.; pres United Meth. Mo. Conf. Fin. and Adminstrn., 2004—; soccer coach. Mem. Mo. Bar Assn., springfield Area C. of C. (bd. dirs. 2003—), Mo. Chamber Commerce and Industry (bd. dirs. 2003—), Masons (sec. 1980-81), Lions (pres. 1990-91), Leadership Mo., Young Presidents Orgn., Phi Delta Phi. Republican. Methodist. Avocations: running, flying, tennis, golf, hunting. Office: Hammons Products Co 105 Hammons Dr PO Box 140 Stockton MO 65785

HAMMOUDI, LAKHDAR, mathematician, educator; PhD, Haute-Alsace U., France, 1996. Adj. asst. prof. U. Haute-Alsace & CNRS, Mulhouse, France, 1995—97; vis. scholar U. Ill., Urbana, Ill., 1997—98; vis. asst. prof. Miami U., Oxford, 1999—2002; asst. prof. Ohio U., Chillicothe, Ohio, 2002—. Achievements include research in research in mathematics solving some open problems. Office: Ohio University 101 University Drive Chillicothe OH 45601 Office Phone: 740-774-7270.

HAMNER, LANCE DALTON, prosecutor; b. Fukuoka, Japan, Sept. 18, 1955; parents Am. citizens; s. Louie D. and Mary Louise (Sloan) H.; m. Karla Jean Cleverly, Sept. 22, 1980; children: Lance Dalton Jr., Nicholas James, Louie Alexander, Samuel Sean, Victoria Jean. BS summa cum laude, Weber State Coll., 1984; JD magna cum laude, Ind. U., 1987. Bar: Ind., US Dist. Ct. (no., so. dist.) Ind. 1988. Atty. Barnes & Thornburg, Indpls., 1988-89; dep. prosecuting atty. Marion County Prosecutor's Office, Indpls., 1989-90; pros. atty. Johnson County, Franklin, Ind., 1991. Legal corr. WGGR Radio News, Indpls., 1995; adj. prof. law Sch. Law Ind. U., Indpls., 1995—96, Bloomington, 1996—98; frequent spkr. on legal topics including search and seizure and interrogation law; lectr. Ind. Continuing Legal Edn. Forum, Indpls., 1992; mem. faculty Newly-Elected Pros. Sch. Ind. Pros. Attys. Coun., 1999; mem. faculty Indpls. Police Acad., 1999, Ind. Police Corps, 2000—. Author: Indiana Search & Seizure Courtroom Manual, 2001, 2002, 2004; editor: Ind. Law Jour., 1987. Scoutmaster Boy Scouts Am., Franklin, Ind., 1999-2003. Mem. Nat. Dist. Attys. Assn., Assn. Govt. Attys. in Capital Litigation, Ind. Prosecuting Atty.'s Coun., Nat. Eagle Scout Assn., Order of the Coif. Republican. Mem. Lds Ch. Avocations: family, exercise, writing. Office: Prosecutor's Office Courthouse Annex N 80 S Jackson St Franklin IN 46131-2353 Office Phone: 317-736-3750. Personal E-mail: lhamner@aol.com.

HAMNER, REGINALD TURNER, lawyer; b. Tuscaloosa, Ala., June 4, 1939; s. Raiford Samuel and Ellie Wells (Turner) Hamner; m. Anne Ellen Young, Nov. 8, 1969; children: Patrick Turner, William Christian. BS, U. Ala., 1961, JD, 1965. Bar: Ala. 1965, U.S. Dist. Ct. (mid. dist.) Ala. 1966, U.S. Ct. Appeals (5th cir.) 1966, U.S. Ct. Mil. Appeals 1968, U.S. Supreme Ct. 1968, U.S. Ct. Appeals (11th and 5th cirs.) 1981. Law clk. Supreme Ct. Ala., Montgomery, 1965; dir. legal-legis. affairs Med. Assn., State of Ala., 1968-69; sec., exec. dir. Ala. State Bar, Montgomery, 1969-94; ct. project coord. U.S. Dist. Ct. (Mid. Dist.) Ala., Montgomery, 1995—. Bd. dirs. S.E. br. YMCA, Montgomery, 1978—81; former legal counsel govtl. adv. panels investigating Ala. Prison Sys.; vice chmn. State Child Welfare Com.; bd. dirs. Attys. Ins. Mut. Ala., Inc.; sec., treas. Ala. Law Found., 1987—93; chmn. Ala. Rhodes Scholarship Com., 1989—94. With JAG USAF, 1965—68, col. USAFR. Named Disting. alumnus, U Ala., 2004. Fellow: Am. Bar Found. (life; state chmn. 1994—95); mem.: ABA (mem. ho. dels. 1972—76, 1985—89, 1993, 1996—), Jud. Conf. U.S. Ct. Appeals (11th cir. 1981—96), Ala. Law Inst. (coun.), Ala. Coun. Assn. Execs. (pres. 1984), Am. Soc. Assn. Execs. (commr. certification com. 1978—79), Nat. Assn. Bar Execs. (pres. 1978—79), Am. Judicature Soc., U. Ala. Nat. Alumni Assn. (pres. 1989—90), Montgomery Country Club, Delta Tau Delta, Phi Alpha Delta, Alpha Epsilon Delta, Omicron Delta Kappa. Episcopalian. Home: 7518 Wynford Cir Montgomery AL 36117-7498 Office: US Courthouse One Church St Ste C-563 Montgomery AL 36104 Office Phone: 334-954-3752.

HAMNER, SUZANNE LEATH, retired history educator; b. Ft. Worth, Feb. 29, 1940; d. Roland Martin and Mabel Lois (Hall) Leath; m. W. Easley Hamner, June 18, 1961; children: Janine Suzanne, Michael Edward. BA summa cum laude, Meredith Coll., Raleigh, N.C., 1961; MA, Tulane U., New Orleans, 1964. Tchg. asst. Tulane U., New Orleans, 1963-66; instr. history Coll. Liberal Arts Northea. U., Boston, 1966-71, lectr. history Univ. Coll., 1972-75; lectr. history Coll. Arts and Scis., Univ. Coll., Boston, 1985—2002, ret., 2002—. Sr. lectr. U. Coll., 1985-2002. Contbg. editor Reclaiming Our Global Heritage, Vol. I and Vol. II, 1990. Mem. adv. com. Follow Through Program, Cambridge (Mass.) Sch. Dept., 1977-79; treas., v.p. adv. bd. Parents Assn., Buckingham Browne and Nichols Sch., Cambridge, 1980-86; clk., bd. dirs., adv. bd. Cambridge Civic Assn., 1976-95; treas. Alice Wolf Election Com., City Coun., Cambridge, 1979-96; advisor Wolf Campaign for State Rep., 1996, 98; overseer Handel and Haydn Soc., Boston, 1989—; trustee Chorus pro Musica, 1993-95; adv. com. Meml. Ch., Harvard U., 1992-94; vice co-chair leadership com. United Way Cambridge, 1997, co-chair, 1998-2001, com. 1997-; incorporator The Cambridge Homes, 1999—, bd. dirs, 2004-, v.p., 2005—; mem. grants com. Meml. Ch., Harvard U., 1998-2000; reader Rec. for the Blind and Dyslexic, 2002—. Woodrow Wilson Found. fellow, Princeton, N.J., 1961-62; Tulane U. scholar, 1962-64. Mem. Am. Hist. Assn., New England Hist. Assn., Mass. Hist. Soc., Cambridge Club (pres. 2005-2006), Phi Alpha Theta. Democrat. Avocations: music, reading, travel, politics. Home: 3 Ellery Sq Cambridge MA 02138-4227

HAMNER, W. EASLEY, architect; b. Altavista, Va., Sept. 22, 1937; s. Robert Wilbourne and Isabelle (Easley) H.; m. Suzanne Leath, June 18, 1961; children: Janine, Michael. Diploma, Ecole de Beaux Arts, Fontainebleau, France, 1959; BArch, N.C. State U., 1960; MArch, Harvard U., 1967. Registered arch. Mass. Assoc. Thompson B. Burk, New Orleans, 1961-66; prin. The Stubbins Assocs., Cambridge, Mass., 1967—2003; founder Boston Internat. Design Collaborative, LLC, 2003—. Architect Citicorp Ctr., 1970-77; bd. dirs. Hyman/Stubbins, Inc.; internat. design juror Jin Mao Bldg., Shanghai, Beijng Olympics, Beihei (China) Beach Resort. Prin. works include Citicorp Ctr., NYC (11 awards), Riverpark, Norwalk, Conn. (award), The MITRE Corp. (award), O'Neill Fed. Bldg., Boston, Bristol-Myers Rsch. Labs, Wallingford, Conn. (award), Suffolk County Jail, Boston (2 awards), Suffolk County House of Corrections, Boston (award), Anhui Internat. Trade Ctr., Hefei, China, Venetian Hotel/Casino, Las Vegas (5 awards), Shezhen City (China) Plz. Pres. Cambridge Cmty. Svcs., 1982-99, Ellery Sq. Owners

Assn., 1983-85; chmn. bd. trustees Pro Arte Chamber Orch., 1993-2004; bd. dirs. Cambridge Cmty. Found., 1993-98; elected mem. Harvard Grad. Sch. Design Alumni Coun., chmn. com. of five, 1983-84; gov. Urban Land Inst. Found. Lt. U.S. Army Intelligence, 1960. Fellow AIA; mem. Boston Soc. Arch., Nat. Assn. Indsl. and Office Properties (mem. nat. mixed-use forum), Urban Land Inst. (mem. internat. coun.), Harvard U. Alumni Assn. (dir. 1984-88), Cambridge Club (pres. 1988-89), Boston Harbor Yacht Club. Democrat. Office: The Stubbins Assocs Inc 1030 Massachusetts Ave Cambridge MA 02138-5388 Office Phone: 617-354-8055. E-mail: wehamner@earthlink.net.

HAMOLSKY, MILTON WILLIAM, physician; b. Lynn, Mass., May 25, 1921; s. Israel and Sophie (Cremer) H.; m. Sandra Oelbaum, Feb. 18, 1979; children: Deborah Lynne, John Stephen, David James, Joy, Robin. AB, Harvard U., 1943, MD, 1946; Ad Eundum, Brown U., 1964. Diplomate Am. Bd. Internal Medicine. Intern Beth Israel Hosp., Boston, 1946-47, resident, 1947-48, 50-51, asst. physician, dir. endocrine clinic, 1957-63; instr. Harvard U. Med. Sch., 1951-55, asst. prof. medicine, 1955-63; prof. med. sci. Brown U., 1963-87, prof. emeritus, 1987—; physician-in-chief R.I. Hosp., Providence, 1963-87, W&I Hosp., Providence, 1981-87, U.S. Vets. Adminstrn. Hosp., 1981-87. Vis. asst. prof. biochemistry Brandeis U., 1958-59; vis. Commonwealth fellow Coll. de France, 1960-62; chief adminstrv. officer R.I. Bd. Med. Licensure and Discipline, 1987-2001; mem. Providence Pub. Sch. Bd., 2003—, v.p., 2004—; bd. govs. Lifespan Hosps., 2003—; exec. com. Diet Counseling Svc. Obstet. Health Care Com.; pres. Zlinkoff Found. Med. Edn. and Rsch., 1989-95; pres. Dolen Found., 1989-95; chmn. adv. com. Comty. Health Ctrs., 1990—; bd. trustees R.I. Hosp., 1986-97, hon. trustee, 2004—; cons. Roger Univ. Bradley Hosps.; acting dir. R.I. Dept. Health, 1995. Author: Thyroid Testing, 1968; contbr. numerous articles on endocrinology to profl. publs. Trustee Planned Parenthood, Providence, R.I. Child Guidance Clinic, Camp Jori, Providence, R.I. Hosp., 1986-97; mem. Bd. Pub. Schs. Edn. Com., 2003-, v.p., bd. 2004-. Served as capt. M.C., U.S. Army, 1948-50. Recipient Henry A. Christian award Harvard U. Med. Sch., 1946, Mallinckrodt award as founder nuclear medicine, 1977, W.W. Keen disting. svc. award Brown U., Am. Heart Assn. Hon. John Chafee award Cmty. Svc., 2002; named to R.I. Heritage Hall of Fame, 1996; Milton Hamolsky Ann. Outstanding Physician of Yr. award named for him, 2001-; tchg. fellow Tufts U., 1950-51, Harvard Univ., 1950-51, rsch. fellow 1951-52, Damon Runyon rsch. fellow 1951-52. Mem. A.C.P. (master gov. R.I. chpt., Milton W. Hamolsky lifetime svc. award 1999), AMA, Am. Thyroid Assn., Endocrine Soc., Am. Physiol. Soc., Soc. Clin. Investigation, Am. Fedn. Clin. Research, R.I. Diabetes Soc. (pres.), R.I. Heart Assn. (pres.) Home: 150 Arlington Ave Providence RI 02906-2330

HAMON, JANICE M., social worker, educator; b. Charleston, W.Va., Mar. 25, 1952; d. Denver Stephens, Jr. and Christine Stephens; m. John Earl Hamon, June 19, 1982; children: J. Eric, Kristen Etta. BS in Social Work, W.Va. U., 1974, MSW, 1979. LCSW. Social worker Brookside Children's Home, Charleston, W.Va., 1975—79; mem. staff behavioral medicine Charleston (W.Va.) Gen. Hosp., 1979; therapist, dir. Step Program Prestera County Mental Health Ctr., Huntington, W.Va., 1980—82; counselor Jackson County Home Health Dept., Ripley, W.Va., 1985—2001; therapist adult mental health Westbrook Health Svcs., Spencer, W.Va., 2001—03; mental health therapist Family Svc. of Kanawha Valley, Charleston, W.Va., 2005—. Instr. sociology and psychology W.Va. U., Ripley, 1987—2001; workship leader in field. Vol. coord. Jackson County Youth Svcs., Ripley, 1974—75; vol. Habitat for Humanity, Inc., Ripley, 1997—2003, chmn. com., 2001—03; choir dir. Fairplain (W.Va.) Union Ch., 1999—2003, tchr. Sunday Sch., 1999—2003; bd. dir. Habitat for Humanity, Inc., 1997—2001. Avocations: writing, sewing, animals, music, camping. Home: Rt 1 Box 133 Given WV 25245 Office: Family Svc of Kanawha Valley 9922 Quarrier St Charleston WV 25301

HAMON, RICHARD GRADY, lawyer; b. Corpus Christi, Tex., Dec. 30, 1937; s. Richard Paul and Dorothy Ileen (Norris) H.; m. Mary Lynn Farmer, Mar. 2, 1963; children: Leigh Ann, Clark Everett. AA, Del Mar Jr. Coll., 1957; BBA, Baylor U., 1959, JD, 1962. Ptnr. Blanchette, Hamon, Tabor & Coke, Dallas, 1962-76; stockholder, v.p. Winstead, Sechrest & Minick, Dallas, 1976-94, of counsel, 1994—. Mem. ABA, State Bar Tex. So. Baptist. Office: Winstead Sechrest & Minick 5400 Renaissance Tower Dallas TX 75270

HAMOY, CAROL, artist; b. N.Y.C., May 22, 1934; d. Morris David and Selma (Essex) Cohen. Student, Newark (N.J.) Sch. Fine Art, 1952-54, Art Students League, N.Y.C., various yrs. Lectr., spkr. in field. Solo exhibitions include USMA/West Point, N.Y., 1978, Katonah (N.Y.) Gallery, 1983, Lower Manhattan Cultural Coun., N.Y.C., 1986, May Mus./Lawrence, N.Y. Ceres, N.Y.C., 1992, MTA-Arts for Transit, N.Y.C., 1993, Robert Kahn Gallery, Houston, 1993, Temple Judea Mus., Elkins Park, Pa., 1993, Univ. Art Ctr., Shreveport, La., 1994, Ceres, N.Y.C., 1995, 98-99, 2001, Goldman Art Gallery, Rockville, Md., 1996, Nat. Mus. Am. Jewish History, Phila., 1996, Broadway Windows, N.Y.C., 1997, Ellis Island Immigration Mus., N.Y.C., 1997, Mizel Mus., Denver, 1997, Breman Heritage Mus., Atlanta, 1998, Eldridge St. Project, N.Y.C., 1998, Inter-Am. Gallery, Miami, Fla., 1998, Skirball Mus., Cincinnati, 1999, Franklin Marshall Coll., Lancaster Pa., 1999, Margolis Gallery, Houston, 1999, Lower East Side Tenement Mus., N.Y., 2000, The Neuberger Mus., Purchase, N.Y., 2000, Ceres, N.Y.C., 2001, Dacotah Prarie Mus., Aberdeen, S.D., 2002, Azarian/McCullough Gallery, Sparkill, N.Y., 2002, Futernick Gallery, Miami, 2003, Longyear Mus., Hamilton, N.Y., 2004, Hebrew Union Coll. Mus., N.Y.C., 2005—, Mizel Mus., Denver, 2005—; exhibited in group shows at Pelham (N.Y.) Art Ctr., 1988, U. Ky., Lexington, 1989, HUC, N.Y.C., 1989, Kentuck Mus., Northport, Ala., 1989, Clough Hansen Gallery, Memphis, 1989, JRC Gallery, Evanston, Ill., 1992, Soho 20, N.Y.C., 1993, Charach-Epstein Mus., West Bloomfield, Mich., 1994, 97, Nat. Jewish Mus., Washington, 1995, Fine Arts Rosen Mus., Boca Raton, Fla., 1995, Right Brain Gallery, Atlanta, 1999, Miss. Univ. for Women, 1999, Skirball Mus., Cin., 1999, Neuberger Mus., Purchase, N.Y., 2000, Ellipse Arts Ctr., Arlington, Va., 2000, Contemporary Crafts, Pitts., 2000, Ceres, 2000, The Joseph Gallery Mus, N.Y.C., 2000-01, Moving On/Frauen Mus., Bonn, Germany, John Jay Coll., 2001—, Joseph Gallery, N.Y., 2000-01, Frauen Mus., Bonn, Germany, 2001-02, Detritus Show John Jay College, N.Y., 2001-02, Judaica Mus., Riverdale, N.Y., 2001-02, Kommunale Galerie Wilmersdorf, Berlin, 2001-02, Ctr. for Visual Art & Culture, Stamford, Conn., 2002, Am. Craft Mus., N.Y., 2002-03, Joseph Gallery, N.Y.C., HUC Mus., N.Y.C., 2003—, Jewish Mus. Md., Balt., 2004, Alper Art Gallery, Miami, Fla., 2004, Wain Ling Art Ctr., Haverford, Pa., 2005, Ruternick Art Gallery, Miami, 2005, Rutgers U., Camden, N.J., 2005, others; permanent collections include Nat. Mus. Women in the Arts, Nat. Jewish Mus., Washington, Frauen Mus., Bonn, others. Nominee, Joan Mitchell Found., 2000; grantee Va. Ctr. for Creative Arts, Sweet Briar, Va., 1980, Artists' Space, N.Y.C., 1981, Hillwood Art Mus., N.Y. State Coun. for Creative Arts, 1992, MTA-Arts for Transit, N.Y.C., 1993, Lucius N. Littauer Found. Bessemere Trust Co. N.A., 1997, Meml. Found./Jewish Culture fellow, Artists' Fellowship, Inc. of N.Y.C., 1999. Studio: 340 E 66th St New York NY 10021-6821 Personal E-mail: hamoycar@aol.com.

HAMPDEN THOMPSON, GILLIAN M.H., research scientist; b. Luton, England, May 5, 1969; d. John H. and Rosemary G. Thompson. BEd with honors, Leeds Metro. U., England, 1992; MSc, Bucknell U., 1999; PhD, Pa. State U., 2004. HS tchr., 1992—97; grad. asst. Bucknell U., 1997—99; tchg. asst Penn. State U., Edn. Policy Dept., 2000—01, rsch. asst., 2001—03, Penn. State U., Ctr. for Work and the Family, 2003—04; rsch. analyst Am. Inst. of Rsch., Wash., DC, 2004—. Contbr. articles various profl. jours. and chpts. to books. Mem.: Comparative and Internat. Edn. Soc., Am. Sociol. Assn., Am. Ednl. Rsch. Assn. Avocations: travel, golf, skiing. Office: Am Inst For Rsch 1990 K St NW Ste 500 Washington DC 20006

HAMPER, ROBERT JOSEPH, marketing executive; b. Chgo., May 20, 1956; s. Robert William and Barbara Jean Hamper. BSBA with honors, Ill. State U., 1977, MBA with honors, 1979; ABD, Northern Ill. U., 1999. Fin. mgr. Ill. Bell, Chgo., 1979-82; staff mgr. AT&T, Basking Ridge, N.J., 1982-84; mem. tech. staff Bell labs., Homedale, N.J., 1983-84; sr. staff. mgr. market analysis Ameritech Svcs., Schaumburg, Ill., 1985-87; dir. strategic planning Ameritech Corp., Chgo., Ill., 1987-90; pres. R.J. Hamper Bus. Cons., River Forest, Ill., 1981—, mgr. investment fund, 1990—. Asst. prof. fin. and mktg. Dominican U., River Forest, 1983-98; adj. prof. fin. Loyola U., Chgo., 1988—; seminar presenter in field; career counselor, 1985—. Author: Developing a Profitable Marketing Plan: Text and Cases, 1987, Marketing and Planning Forms, 1987, Strategic Market Planning, 1990, 92, 94, 97, 99, 2003, Handbook for Proposal Writing, 1995, 97, 2000, 04; contbg. author: College Business Math, 1995, 99, 2003; contbr. articles to profl. jours. Leader Boy Scouts Am., Park Forest, Ill., 1979-83. Mem. Am. Mktg. Assn. (exec.), Am. Mgmt. Assn., Fin. Mgmt. Assn., Am. Fin. Assn., Am. Hosp. Assn. Home and Office: 730 Clinton Pl River Forest IL 60305-1914

HAMPLE, JUDY G., academic administrator; BA in Speech Comm. and Secondary Edn./French, David Lipscomb U.; MA and PhD in Comm., Ohio State U. Univ. fellow, asst. dir. intercollegiate debate Ohio State U.; faculty dept. speech comm. U. Ill., Champaign-Urbana; divsn. dir. dept. comm. arts and scis. Western Ill. U., assoc. dean for budget and pers. Coll. Arts and Scis.; dean Coll. Liberal Arts and Scis. Emporia (Kans.) State U., 1983—86; dean Coll. Arts and Scis. Ind. State U., 1986—93; sr. v.p. acad. affairs U. Toledo, 1993; chancellor Pa. State Sys. of Higher Edn., Harrisburg, 2001—; vice chancellor planning, budget and policy analysis, vice chancellor and chancellor bd. regents State Univ. Sys. Fla., 1998—2001. Cons.-evaluator North Cen. Accreditation Assn.; pub. cons.-evaluator ABA. Co-editor: Teaching in the Middle Ages, 3 vols.; editor: Studies in Medieval and Renaissance Teaching; contbr. articles to profl. jours. Office: Pa State Sys of Higher Edn Dixon Univ Ctr 2986 N 2d St Harrisburg PA 17110 Office Phone: 717-720-4010.

HAMPP, MICHAEL ALLAN, music educator; b. Zanesville, Ohio, Feb. 6, 1952; s. William and Shirley Hampp; m. Shelley A Pritchard, Dec. 18, 1976; children: Andrew M, Emily M. MusB Edn., Kent State U., Kent, Ohio, 1970—74. Ohio teaching certificate Ohio, 2004. Band dir., Tiffin Columbian H.S., Tiffin, Ohio, 1974—, varsity softball coach, 1998—2005. Ch. choir dir. Trinity United Ch. of Christ, Tiffin, Ohio, 1992—2005. Mem.: Music Educator's Nat. Conf. (assoc.). Achievements include state band contest superior rating. Home: 119 N Tecumseh Trail Tiffin OH 44883 Office: Tiffin Columbian H S 300 S Monroe Tiffin 44883 Office Phone: 419 447-6331. Office Fax: 419 447-4600.

HAMPSON, THOMAS MEREDITH, lawyer; b. Ann Arbor, Mich., Feb. 18, 1929; s. Harold Snover and Louise Susan (Goetchius) H.; m. Margaret H. Clark, Nov. 24, 1951 (div. Dec. 1969); children: Melissa Clark, Douglas Meredith; m. Zena Collier, Dec. 30, 1969. BA, Cornell U., 1951, LLB with distinction, 1955. Bar: N.Y. 1955, U.S. Dist. Ct. (we. dist.) N.Y. 1955, U.S. Supreme Ct. 1964. Assoc. Harris, Beach, Wilcox, Rubin & Levey, Rochester, N.Y., 1955-62; ptnr. Harris Beach, LLP, Rochester, 1962—. Vis. instr. Cornell Law Sch., Ithaca, N.Y., 1969-75. Radio broadcaster The Jazz Scene, 1960-80, Jazz Notes, 1979-81, Mostly Jazz, 1985--; newspaper columnist, 1985-88. Chmn. Monroe County Fair Campaign Practices Com., Rochester, 1977-91; trustee Rochester Pub. Libr., 1976-98; dir. Cornell Lab. Ornithology, Ithaca, N.Y., 1984-90, Hawk Mountain Sanctuary Assn., 1990-98, Rundel Libr. Found., 1995—; bd. dirs. N.Y. State Civil Liberties Union, N.Y.C., 1963-69; commr. Rochester Civil Svc. Commn., 1997—, chmn. 2000—. 1st lt. USAF, 1951-53. Recipient Civil Liberties award N.Y. Civil Liberties Union, Genesee Valley chpt., 1987. Mem. ABA, N.Y. State Bar Assn., Monroe County Bar Assn., City Club (pres. 1965-66), Philosophers' Club (pres. 1985-88). Democrat. Unitarian Universalist. Avocations: birding, jazz. Home: 83 Berkeley St Rochester NY 14607-2207 Office: Harris Beach LLP 99 Garnsey Rd Pittsford NY 14534 Office Phone: 585-419-8941.

HAMPTON, BENJAMIN BERTRAM, brokerage house executive; b. N.Y.C., Aug. 3, 1925; s. max and Pauline (Weinberger) H.; m. Elizabeth Golub-Cohen, Oct. 16, 1975; 1 child by previous marriage, Roger Neil; stepchildren: Laurence, James, Lisa. B Aero. Engring., NYU, 1947; cert. in mech. engring., Pa. State Coll., 1945; MBA, Harvard U., 1949. Sales mgr. Carew Products, Inc., N.Y.C., 1949-51; project mgr. Emerson Radio & TV Corp., 1951-52; div. mgr. Paragon Oil Co., Mineola, N.Y., 1952-55; mgmt. cons. E.N. Kagan & co., N.Y.C., 1955-60; exec. asst. to pres. mktg. sect. Fed. Pacific Electric co., Newark, 1960-62; asst. to pres. Seagrave Corp., N.Y.C., 1962-63; v.p. Swingline Inc., Long Island City, N.Y., 1963-68, exec. v.p., 1968-71, bd. dirs., 1970-71; exec. v.p., bd. dirs. Poloron Products Inc., New Rochelle, N.Y., 1971-73, pres., CEO, bd. dirs., 1973-74; exec. v.p., bd. dirs. West Chem. Products, Inc., Long Island City, 1975-78; prin. Hampton Assocs., 1979-82; v.p. Merrill Lynch Pierce Fenner & Smith, Great Neck, N.Y., 1982—. Co-chmn. N.Y. State fin. com. J.F. Kennedy presdl. campaign, 1960. With AUS, 1944-46. Mem. Harvard Club, Pi Lambda Phi. Home: Apt B 6224 Island Bend Boca Raton FL 33496 Office: Merrill Lynch 1010 Northern Blvd Great Neck NY 11021-1134 Office Phone: 800-536-2988. Personal E-mail: ben_hampton@ml.com.

HAMPTON, CAROL MCDONALD, priest, educator, historian; b. Oklahoma City, Sept. 18, 1935; d. Denzil Vincent and Mildred Juanita (Cussen) McDonald; m. James Wilburn Hampton, Feb. 22, 1958; children: Jaime, Clayton, Diana, Neal. BA, U. Okla., 1957, MA, 1973, PhD, 1984; cert. individual theol. study, Episcopal Theol. Sem. of S.W., 1998; MDiv summa cum laude, Phillips Theol. Sem., 1999. Ordained to Episcopal Transitional Diaconate, 1999, ordained priest, 1999. Tchg. asst. U. Okla., Norman, 1976—81; instr. U. Sci. and Arts Okla., Chickasha, 1981—84; coord. Consortium for Grad. Opportunities for Am. Indians U. Calif., Berkeley, 1985—86; trustee Ctr. of Am. Indian, Oklahoma City, 1981. Vice chmn. Nat. Com. on Indian Work, Episc. Ch., 1986; field officer Native Am. Ministry of Episc. Ch. (Nat.), 1986-94, sec., co-chmn., advising elder, prin. elder coun., 1994-96; field officer for Congl. Ministries of Episc. Ch. (Nat.), 1994-97; mem. nat. coun. Chs. Racial Justice Working Group, 1990-97, co-convenor, 1991-93, convenor, 1993-95; officer Multicultural Ministries of Episc. Ch. (Nat.), 1994-97; (hon.) canon of St. Paul's Cath., Oklahoma City, 2001—. Mem. editl. bd.: First Peoples Theology Jour.; contbr. articles to profl. jours. Trustee Western History Collections, U. Okla., Okla. Found. for the Humanities, 1983-86; mem. bd. regents U. Sci. and Arts Okla., 1989-95; bd. dirs. Okla. State Regents for Higher Edn., mem. adv. com. on social justice; mem. World Coun. of Chs. Program to Combat Racism, Geneva, 1985-91; bd. dirs. Caddo Tribal Coun., Okla., 1976-82; accredited observer Anglican Consultative Coun. UN 4th World Conf. on Women, 1995; v.p. Nat. Conf. Cmty. Justice, 1999-2002; bd. dirs. Ctrl. Okla. Human Rights Alliance, 1999—, Planned Parenthood, Oklahoma City, 2002—. Recipient Okla. State Human Rights award, 1987; Francis C. Allen fellow Ctr. for the History of Am. Indian, 1983. Mem.: Okla. Conf. Chs. (bd. dirs. 2000—), Indigenous Theol. Tng. Inst. (bd. dirs. 2000—), Jr. League (Oklahoma City), Am. Assn. Indian Historians (founding mem. 1981—), Okla. Hist. Soc., Am. Hist. Assn., Orgn. Am. Historians, Western Social Sci. Assn., Western History Assn. Democrat. Episcopalian. Avocation: travel. Home: 1414 N Hudson Ave Oklahoma City OK 73103-3721 Office Phone: 405-235-3436. E-mail: cjchampton@sbcglobal.net, champton@stpaulscathedralokc.org.

HAMPTON, CHARLES EDWIN, lawyer, mathematician, computer programmer; b. Oct. 22, 1948; s. Roy Mizell and Hazel Lucretia (Cooper) H.; m. Cynthia Torrance, Sept. 14, 1968; children: Charles Edwin Jr., Adam Ethan. Student, Baylor U., 1967, Rice U., 1967-68; BA with highest honors, U. Tex., 1971, JD with high honors, 1977; MA, U. Calif., Berkeley, 1972, Candidate in Philosophy in Math., 1975. Bar: Tex. 1977, U.S. dist. Ct. (we. dist.) Tex. 1979, U.S. Dist. Ct. (no. dist.) Tex. 1980, U.S. Ct. Appeals (5th cir.) 1986. Rsch. asst. U. Calif., 1974-75; briefing atty. to justice Tex. Supreme Ct., 1977-78; assoc. Law Offices Don L. Baker, PC, Austin, Tex., 1978—81; legal counsel Office Ct. Adminstrn., Tex. Jud. Coun., Austin, 1981; staff atty. Supreme Ct. Tex., Austin, 1981-96; assoc. Rinehart & Nugent, 1984-87. Vis. com. dept. math. U. Tex., Austin, 1987-95. NSF fellow, 1971-74; Moody Found. scholar. Mem. ABA, State Bar Tex., Travis County Bar Assn., Chancellors, Order of Coif, Lions, Phi Beta Kappa, Phi Kappa Phi, Phi Delta Phi. Personal E-mail: hampton-c@sbcglobal.net.

HAMPTON, CYRIL K., counseling administrator; b. New Orleans, June 11, 1957; s. Prince and Julia Sandville Hampton. BS in Bus., So. U., Baton Rouge, 1980, MEd in Counseling, 1988. Cert. sch. counselor Profl. Standards Commn., Ga. Guidance counselor Atlanta Pub. Schs., 1990—; motivational spkr., poet Hampton's Positive Motivations, Decatur, Ga., 1998—2005. Troop com. chmn. Boy Scouts. Am., 1991—96; legis. contact team Ga. Assn. Educators, Atlanta, 1995—2005. Named Sch. Counselor of Yr., Atlanta Sch. Counselors Assn., 1995—96, 2003—04; recipient Dist. award of merit, East Atlanta Boy Scouts Am., 1995. Master: Boy Scouts of Am.; mem.: Atlanta Assn. Educators (pres. 2005—), Ga. PTA-Tull Waters Elem. (hon.; corr. sec. 1991—94), Kappa Alpha Psi (keeper of records 1992—94, vice-polemarch 1994—96, Ednl. Leadership award 1994, Poemarch's Award 1994). Democrat. Baptist. Office: Atlanta Assn Educators 1065 Ralph D Abernathy Ste 204-205 Atlanta GA 30310 E-mail: ckh1957@aol.com.

HAMPTON, JAMES WILBURN, hematologist, oncologist; b. Durant, Okla., Sept. 15, 1931; s. Hollis Eugene and Ouida (Mackey) H.; m. Carol McDonald, Feb. 22, 1958; children: Jaime, Clay, Diana, Neal. BA, U. Oklahoma, 1952, MD, 1956. Int. U. Okla. Hosps., 1956-57, res.; instr. to prof. U. Okla., Oklahoma City, 1959-77; clin. prof. med., 1977—. Mem. admissions bd., 1965—, subcom., 1985-95, bd., 1995-, head hematology/oncology, 1972-77; head hematology, mem. Okla. Med. Rsch. Found., Okla. City 1972-77; dir. cancer prog. and med. oncology Bapt. Med. Ctr., 1977-85; med. dir. Cancer Ctr. S.W., 1985-94; Troy and Dollie Smith Cancer Ctr., 1994—; mem. Internat. Com. on Thrombosis and Hemostasis; cons. NIH, Biomed. and Nat. Cancer Inst., Karolinska Inst., Stockholm; vis. scientist Career Devel. Assn., 1966-67; vis. prof. U. N.C., Chapel Hill, 1966; founder, Stewart Wolf Soc., 1967, pres., 1990-92; founder Robert Montgomery Bird Soc., 1973, pres. 1996-98. Contbr. over 100 articles to profl. jours. Chmn. network Cancer Prevention and Control for Am. Indians/Alaska Natives Nat. Cancer Rsch. Inst., 1990-99; mem. Intercultural Cancer Coun., 1996—, chair-elect 2000-01, chair 2001-02; initiator Hospice of Ctrl. Okla., 1982-89; initiator Hospice of Okla. County, 1990—; bd. dirs. Am. Cancer Soc., mem. at large, nat. bd. dirs., 1990-96, mem. com. task force on Cancer in the Socio-economically Disadvantaged, 1990-2000, chmn. Okla. divsn. svc. and rehab. com., collaborating ptnr. Dialogue on Cancer (Pres. Bush), 1999-2004, chmn., 2004—; chmn. Okla. Pain Initiative, 1996; co-chmn. Save St. Paul's Episcopal Cathedral com., 1983, chmn. bishop's Okla. Com. on Indian work, mem. province VII Indian com., alt del. Diocesan conv. for Okla., 1991-95, mem. adv. com. Office of Minority Health NIH, 1996-99, mem. Coun. on Combating Racism, Epis. Ch. of Am., 1995-97, others. Recipient ACS Humanitarian awd., 1999, NIH Career Devel. awd. 1966-76, Physician of the Yr. (pvt. prac.), Univ. Okla. Alumni Assocs.; honored by Lakota Tribe at Mayo Clinic, 1999. Fellow ACP; mem. AMA (mem. minority affairs consortium, steering com. 1997-2000), Am. Fedn. Clin. Rsch. (pres. midwest sect. 1970-71), Ctrl. Soc. Clin. Rsch. (assoc. editor Jour. Lab. and Clin. Med. 1975-76), Okla. County Med. Soc. (editor bull. 1981—, bd. dirs. 1982-85, 1989-91), Internat. Soc. Thrombosis and Hemostasis, Assn. Am. Indian Physicians (pres. 1978-79, 88-89, Indian Physician of Yr. award 1987, 2000); Am. Physiol. Soc., Assn. Am. Pathologists, Am. Soc. Hematology, Am. Soc. Clin. Oncology, So. Soc. Clin. Investigation, Am. Pscyhosomatic Soc., English Speaking Union, Oklahoma City Golf and Country Club, Blue Cord Club, Faculty House Club, Chaine des Rotisseurs. Home: 1414 N Hudson Ave Oklahoma City OK 73103-3721 Office: US Oncology Lake Hefner Campus 11100 Hefner Pointe Dr Oklahoma City OK 73120-5049

HAMPTON, JOHN JAMES, business educator; b. Jersey City, June 24, 1942; s. John Charles Reilly and Anna Marie (Antonaccio) Hampton; m. Doreen Tango, Oct. 14, 1989. AB in History, Stetson U., 1964; MBA, George Washington U., 1969, D Bus. Adminstrn., 1971. Assoc. prof. Towson State Coll., Md., 1969-75; v.p. Marine Transport Lines, NYC, 1975-77; prof. fin. Seton Hall U., South Orange, NJ, 1977-83, dean Sch. Bus., 1983-87; provost Coll. Ins., NYC, 1987-91; pres. Princeton Cons. Group, Litchfield, Conn., 1991—; dean Sch. Bus., Ctrl. Conn. State U., New Britain, 1995-99; v.p. acad. affairs SUNY Maritime Coll., NYC, 1999—2000; KPMG prof. bus. St. Peter's Coll., Jersey City, 2005—. Author: Fin. Decision Making, 1975, 4th edit., 1986; gen. editor: AMA Mgmt. Handbook, 1993. Capt. US Army, 1964-68. Office: St Peter's Coll Jersey City NJ 07306 E-mail: jackhampton@snet.net.

HAMPTON, JOHN LEWIS, retired newspaper editor; b. Verda, Ky., Jan. 13, 1935; s. John Lewis and Ruby Lillian (Slagle) H.; m. Lillian Valls; children from previous marriage: Rachel, Jessica Hampton Fazio, Jonathan Hugh. AB in Journalism (Outstanding Journalism Grad. award 1959), U. Ky., 1959; MA in Communications and Journalism (grad. fellow 1960), Stanford U., 1960. Staff writer AP, Lexington, Ky., 1960-61; bur. chief Louisville (Ky.) Courier-Jour., 1961-67; staff writer Nat. Observer, Washington, 1967-71, sr. editor, then asst. mng. editor, 1971-77; mem. editorial bd. Miami (Fla.) Herald, 1977, editor, 1978-99; Clendinen prof. journalism U. South Fla., Tampa, 2005—. Served with AUS, 1953-56. Named to Hall Disting. Alumni U. Ky., Ky. Journalism Hall of Fame, 2000; recipient Pulitzer prize in editorial writing, 1983 Mem. Am. Soc. Newspaper Editors, Inter Am. Press Assn. (bd. dirs. 1987-99), Fla. Soc. Newspaper Editors. Office: Miami Herald 1 Herald Plz Miami FL 33132-1693 Personal E-mail: jhampton@herald.com.

HAMPTON, LEROY, retired chemical company executive; b. Ingalls, Ark., Apr. 20, 1927; s. Ed Levi and Kitty Annie (Larry) H.; m. Anne Neris Herndon, July 11, 1954; children: Mary Louise, Gloria, Stanley Lamar, Cedric Leroy, Candice La Neris. BS, U. Colo., 1950; MS, Denver U., 1960. Registered pharmacist, Colo., Mich. Registered pharmacist Rocky Mountain Drug Co., Denver, 1950-53; scientist-chemist Dow Chem. Co., Golden, Colo., 1953-58, profl. scientist-chemist in charge, 1958-61, devel. chemist, 1961-63, devel. leader, 1963-67, recruiting supr. Midland, Mich., 1967-68; recruiting mgr. N.E. Region, 1968-70, mgr. minority employee relations, 1970-75; dir. Dow Chem. Employees Credit Union, 1975-95, pres., 1979, 85, v.p., 1991, pres., chmn., 1992; mgr. issue analysis Dow Chem. Co., 1976-80, rsch. assoc., 1981-86. Owner, operator hardware store, Denver, 1965-67; mem. cmty. adv. panel Do Chem. Co., Mich. Ops. V.p. Midland Bd. Edn., 1981—82, sec., 1979—80; dir.affirmative action Saginaw Valley State U., Univ. Ctr., Mich., 1987—90; v.p. Midland Assn. Retarded Citizens, 1985—86, treas., 1986—87; mem. Midland/Dow Comty. advisory panel, 2001—; deacon Meml. Presbyn. Ch., Midland, 1985—87, 1995—97; Bd. dirs. Midland Kiwanis Club Found., Mich., 1973—74, 1990—95; v.p., 1990—92; pres., 1994—95; bd. dirs. ARC, Midland, 1974—76; mem. Midland Bd. Edn., 1978—82; bd. dirs. Midland Assn. Retarded Citizens, 1982—88. Mem. Am. Chem. Soc., Am. Pharm. Assn., Mich. Pharmacists Assn., Kiwanis (pres. Midland club 1976-77), Alpha Phi Alpha. Democrat. Presbyn. Home: 2206 Burlington Dr Midland MI 48642-3895

HAMPTON, MARGARET ANN BARNES, elementary school educator; b. Blakely, Ga., Aug. 15, 1963; d. Ernest Owen and Jessie Carole (Scarborough) Barnes; m. Kenneth Michael Hampton, June 15, 1984; children: Michael Aaron, Nicholas Edward, Rachel Leigh. BS in Music and Bible, Free Will Bapt. Coll., Nashville, 1986, BS in Elem. Edn., 1996; BS in Music Edn., Free Wil Bapt. Coll., 2002. Asst. tchr. Westminster Mother's Day Out, Nashville, 1987-88; preschool tchr. Clouse Acad., Nashville, 1990-91; substitute tchr. Metro Bd. Edn., Nashville, 1992-96; tchr. kindergarten Woodbine Christian Acad., 1996-98, Tom Joy Elem. Sch., Nashville, 1998—2001, tchr. music, 2001—. Libr. supr. Free Will Bapt. Bible Coll., Nashville, 1987-96. Music grant, VH1, 2002. Republican. Avocations: piano, camping, reading. Home: 1010 Keystone Dr Pleasant View TN 37146-8059 Personal E-mail: margh1@hotmail.com.

HAMPTON, MARK GARRISON, architect; b. Tampa, Fla., July 17, 1923; s. Ham Stonewall and Laura (Bingenheimer) H. BS, B.Arch., Ga. Inst. Tech., 1949. Owner Mark Hampton, Architect, Tampa, 1952-65, Miami, Fla.,

1974—; partner Herbert H. Johnson Assocs., Miami, 1966-73. Prin. works include Chemistry and Life Sci. bldgs, U. So. Fla., Tampa, 1961, First Fed. Office Bldg, Sarasota, 1973. Bd. dirs. Lannan Found., Palm Beach, Fla., 1972-88; pres. Tampa Art Inst., 1958, 64. Served with inf. AUS, 1943-46. Decorated Bronze Star, Purple Heart; recipient award Homes for Better Living competition, 1957, 62; Nat. Design award Horizon Home program, 1963 Fellow AIA (juror Nat. Honor awards 1963, 64, medal of honor for design Fla. Central chpt. 1974, award of honor for design 1987, test of time award 1987). Episcopalian. Office: Mark Hampton Architect FAIA 3900 Loquat Ave Miami FL 33133-5622 Office Phone: 305-443-6946. E-mail: archmark@mac.com.

HAMPTON, PHILIP G., II, lawyer; BS, MS, MIT, 1977; JD, U. Chgo., 1980. Bar: NY, DC, US Patent and Trademark Office, US Ct. Appeals Fed. Circuit, US Claims Ct. Asst. commr. trademarks US Patent and Trademark Office (USPTO), 1994—98; ptnr. Gardner Carton & Douglas, 1998—2004; ptnr., intellectual property group Dickstein Shapiro Morin & Oshinsky LLP, DC, 2004—. Vis. com. U. Chgo. Law Sch., 1995—98; mem. intellectual property adv. bd. DePaul Coll. Law, 1999—2003; trustee Am. Intellectual Property Law Edn. Found. Named a Top Minority IP Ptnr., Diversity & the Bar, 2003; named one of Am. Top Black Lawyers, Black Enterprise Mag., 2003. Master: Giles S. Rich Am. Inn Ct.; mem.: ABA (liaison intellectual property law section, mem. commn. racial and ethnic diversity), Nat. Bar Assn. (mem. exec. com. 1990—93, bd. govs. 1989—94, chair intellectual property section 1989—91, chair budget com. 1992—93), Am. Intellectual Property Law Assn., Internat. Trademark Assn. (mem. classification subcommittee). Office: Dickstein Shapiro Morin & Oshinsky LLP 2101 L St NW Washington DC 20037-1526 Office Phone: 202-572-2664. Business E-Mail: HamptonP@dsmo.com.

HAMPTON, PHILIP MICHAEL, consulting engineering company executive; b. Asheville, N.C., Sept. 5, 1932; s. Boyd Walker and Helen Reba (Smith) H.; m. Wilma Christine Gross, July 7, 1951; children: Philip Michael, Deborah Lynn, Gregg Ashley. AB in Geology, Berea Coll., 1954. Draftsman-designer Johnson & Anderson, Inc., Pontiac, Mich., 1955-57, designer, also project mgr., 1957-59, dir. bus. devel., 1962-76, v.p., 1966-74, exec. v.p., 1974-76; v.p. Spalding G. DeDecker & Assos., Inc., Madison Heights, Mich., 1976-84; founder, pres. Hampton Engring. Assocs., Inc., 1985—; pres. HMA Consultants Inc., 1977—, Geo Internat., Inc., 1978—. V.p. JAVLEN Internat., 1971-73, Micuda-Hampton Assocs., Inc., 1985-86; co-founder, owner My World Shops and Hampton Galleries, Ltd., 1976-90; co-owner Hampton-Tyedten Galleries Ltd., 1979-81; mem. public adv. panel GSA, 1977-78; chmn. task force of com. fed. procurement of architect/engr. svcs. ABA, 1977-79. Editor: Total Scope, 1963-71. Pres. Waterford Bd. Edn., 1969-71; mem. state resolution com. Democratic Conv., 1972; exec. com. Oakland County Dem. Com., 1973-74; precinct del., 1972-76, 80—; trustee Environ. Research Assocs., sec.-treas., 1969-71, pres., 1971-73; chmn. Waterford Cable Communications Commn., 1981-88; mem. Cultural Council Pontiac, 1987-90; bd. dirs. Oakland C. of C., 1972-74, Readings for the Blind, Inc., 2002-; chmn. utilities com. Oakland Bus. Roundtable, 1993—; vice chmn. Pontiac Urban League, 1996—. Named to Honorable Order Ky. Colonels. Fellow Am. Cons. Engrs. Coun. (internat. engring. com. 1971-76, vice chmn. pub. rels. com. 1970-72, chmn. publs. com. 1972-74, chmn. ABA model procurement code com. 1977-79, nat. dir. 1986-89, mem. com. fellows 1988—, Pres. award 1990); ASCE, AAAS, mem. Nat. Water Well Assn. (chmn. tech. div. 1969-71), Cons. Engrs. Coun. Mich. (awards com. 1970-74), Am. Arbitration Assn. (comml. panel 1977—), Pontiac C. of C. (co-founder 1989), Oakland Bus. Roundtable (charter). Clubs: Pontiac Exchange, Pontiac-Detroit Lions Quarterback Club (co-founder). Presbyterian. Home and Office: 2440 Ostrum St Waterford MI 48328-1829 Office: 35 W Huron St Ste 801 Pontiac MI 48342-2128 Office Phone: 243-322-4332. Personal E-mail: heainc35@aol.com. *My first employment, at age 13, was as a janitor. The superintendent of facilities taught me to pay attention to detail. He advised, "clean under the stairwells and the entrance will take care of itself." I understood his meaning and adopted the philosophy as my own in many areas of my life and career.*

HAMPTON, PHILLIP JEWEL, artist, educator; b. Kansas City, Mo., Apr. 23, 1922; s. Cordell Bernard Daniels and Goldie Kelley Powell; m. Dorothy Louise Smith, Sept. 28, 1946 (dec. Oct. 1986); children: Harry James, Robert Keith. Student, Drake U., 1947—48; BFA, Kans. City U., Kan. City Art Inst., 1951; MFA, Kans. City Art Inst., 1952. Dir. art program Savannah State Coll., Ga., 1952-69; prof. art So. Ill. U., Edwardsville, Ill., 1969-92, emeritus prof. fine arts, 1992—; artist, spl. projects Hampton Studio, Edwardsville, Ill., 1992—. Dir. day camp City of Kansas City Recreation, 1952; art cons. US GSA, East St. Louis, Ill., 1995-98; curator 2 spl. exhbns. St. Louis Artists' Guild, 1998—; judge Watercolor Mo. Nat., Winston Churchill Meml., Fulton, Mo., 2001; lectr. St. Louis Ar Mus., 2001. Author: (catalogs) 3d World Drawings, 1979, Schemata of Ethnic Minority Artists, 1980; artist book/promotional materials Symphony Kids, KFUO-99FM, 1996; exhibited in one-man show at So. Ill. U., Edwardsville Gallery, 2000; represented in permanent collection at St. Louis Art Mus. Mem. adv. bd. West Broad YMCA, Savannah, 1966-69; bd. dir. United Fund, Edwardsville, 1971-74; mem. Citizens Adv. Coun. Dist. 7, Edwardsville, 1973-75. Recipient Gov.'s award for best-in-show Ill. State Fair Profl. Art Exhbn., 1990 (Salute to Black Men award, Omicron Eta Omega chpt. 2001), others. Mem. St. Louis Art Mus., Art St. Louis, St. Louis Artists' Guild. Presbyterian. Avocations: reading, writing, chess, market studies. Home: 832 Holyoake Rd Edwardsville IL 62025-2315

HAMPTON, SHELLEY LYNN, hearing impaired educator; b. Muskegon, Mich., Nov. 27, 1951; d. Donald Henry and Ruth Marie (Heinanen) Tamblyn; m. John Pershing Hampton Jr., Aug. 10, 1985; 1 child, Sarah Elizabeth. BA, Mich. State U., 1973, MA, 1978. Cert. tchr., Wash., Mich., N.Y. Tchr. presch. thru 3d grade N.Y. State Sch. for Deaf, Rome, 1973-78; cons. Ingham Intermediate Sch. Dist., Lansing, Mich., 1978-81; hearing impaired coord. Shoreline Sch. Dist., Seattle, 1981—. N.W. rep. Bur. of Edn. Handicapped, N.Y.C., 1978; N.Y. del. Humanities in Edn., 1977; adv. bd. State Libr. for the Blind, Lansing, 1980-81; adj. prof. Mich. State U., 1979-81, Seattle Pacific U., 1984-86; participant World Cong. Edn. and Tech., Vancouver, B.C., 1986; computer resource technician Spl. Programs, 1988-92, collegial team leader, 1992-95; rep. Site-Based Mgmt. Coun., Seattle, 1992-95. Writer: Social/Emotional Aspects of Deafness, 1983-84. Del. N.Y. State Assn. for Edn. of Deaf, N.Y.C., 1974-78; N.Y. del. Humanities in Edn., 1977; mem. bd. Plymouth Congl. Ch., Seattle, 1983-87; coord., Kids on the Block puppet troupe, 1999-2003. Recipient Gov.'s Plaque of Commendable Svc., State of Mich., 1981; grantee State of Wash., 1979, 82, Very Spl. Arts Festival, 1979-81; recipient Outstanding Svc. award Mich. Sch. for the Blind, 1980. Mem. NEA, Wash. State Edn. Assn., Shoreline Edn. Assn., Alexander Graham Bell Assn., Regional Hearing Impaired Coop. for Edn., Internat. Orgn. Educators of the Hearing Impaired, Auditory-Verbal Internat., U.S. Pub. Sch. Caucus, Conf. Edn. Adminstrs. Serving the Deaf. Home: 14723 62nd Dr SE Everett WA 98208-9383 Office: Shoreline Hearing Program 16516 10th Ave NE Seattle WA 98155-5904 Office Phone: 206-361-4271.

HAMPTON, VERNE CHURCHILL, II, lawyer; b. Pontiac, Mich., Jan. 5, 1934; s. Verne Churchill and Mildred (Peck) H.; m. Stephanie Hall, Oct. 5, 1973; children: J. Howard, Timothy H., Julia C. Thibodeau. BA, Mich. State U., 1955; LLB, U. Va., 1958. Bar: Mich. 1958. Since practiced in, Detroit; ptnr. firm Dickinson Wright, 1967—. Bd. dirs., sec. Carhartt, Inc., R & R Radio Corp. Former mem. Mich. Rep. Fin. Com.; bd. dirs. Detroit Bus./Edn. Alliance; corp. mem. Boys' Clubs Met. Detroit. Mem. ABA, State Bar Mich. (chmn. bus. law sect. 1980-84), Detroit Athletic Club, Country Club Detroit, Yondotega Club, Sigma Alpha Epsilon, Phi Alpha Delta. Republican. Episcopalian. Home: 360 Provencal Rd Grosse Pointe Farms MI 48236-2959 Office: Dickinson Wright PLLC 500 Woodward Ave Ste 4000 Detroit MI 48226-3416 Office Phone: 313-223-3546. Business E-Mail: vhampton@dickinson-wright.com.

HAMPTON, VERNETTE EVIELENA, music educator, singer; b. Chgo., Mar. 4, 1946; d. Charles Wesley Cochran and Mattie Nevonia Smith Cochran Young; children: Lester, Jonathan, Shanna. BS in Sci. Edn., Chgo. State U., 1973; MS in Edn., Cambridge Coll., 1997. Cert. in Gifted Edn. Ill. Tchr. Chgo. Bd. Edn., 1973—84, Harvey Dist. 152, Ill., 1985—. Music dir. various chs., Chgo., 1957—; coord. Chgo. Bd. Edn., 1973—, Dist. 152, Harvey, Ill., 1973—; rschr., model, dancer Fabulous Fifty Troupe, 1999—. Mem.: Sigma Gamma Rho (adv. 1999, recording grammeteus 2002—04), Ill. Music Educators Assn., Nat. Edn. Assn. Avocations: dance, ice skating, yoga, bowling. Home: 4582 Provincetown Dr Country Club Hills IL 60478 Personal E-mail: hampton152@yahoo.com.

HAMRAH, PEDRAM, ophthalmologist, researcher; b. Datteln, Germany, Sept. 16, 1971; s. Mahmoud Hamrah and Mansoureh Bagherzadeh-Khorsandi; m. Satgin Seraj. BS in Software Engring., U. Cologne, Germany, 1992, MD, 1999. Tchg. asst. dept. anatomy U. Cologne, Germany, 1993—95, rsch. asst. dept. ophthalmology, 1996—98, rsch. asst. dept. internal medicine, divsn. oncology, 1996—98; rsch. assoc., dept. cell and neurobiology Doheny Eye Inst., U. So. Calif., 1999; postdoctoral fellow dept. ophthalmology Schepens Eye Rsch. Inst., Harvard Med. Sch., Boston, 1999—2001; med. resident dept. internal medicine Good Samaritan Hosp., Cin., 2001—02; vis. scientist dept. ophthalmology Harvard Med. Sch., 2002; postdoc. fellow dept. ophthalmology and visual scis. U. Louisville, 2002—, resident dept. ophthalmology, 2003—, chief resident dept. ophthalmology, 2005—. Mem. internal commn. com. Schepens Eye Rsch. Inst., Harvard Med. Sch., 2001; mem. members-in-training com. Assn. Rsch. in Vision and Ophthalmology, Bethesda, Md., 2003—; presenter in field; organizer clincian, sci. forum Assn. Rsch. vision and Ophthalmology, 2005—. Contbr. chapters to books, articles to profl. jours. including Nature Medicine, Jour. Exptl. Medicine, Am. Jour. Pathology; ad hoc reviewer:; editl. bd. mem. Graefe's Ardives, asst. editor Occular Immunology and Inflammation. Recipient Young Investigator award, 2000, 2001, 2002, Travel award, Nat. Eye Inst., 2001, Young Pathologist fellowship, 2003, Conf. Travel award, 2003, Cornea Rsch. award, 2003, Rsch. award, Assn. U. Profs. Ophthalmology/Rsch. to Prevent Blindness, 2004. Mem.: Am. Soc. Cataract and Reflective Surgeons, Am. Acad. of Ophthalmology, Am. Soc. Investigative Pathology, Fedn. Clin. Immunology Soc., Tearfilm and Ocular Surface Soc. (chair, assoc. adv. bd.), Ocular Microbiology and Immunology Group, Soc. Leukocyte Biology, Assn. Rsch. in Vision. Achievements include discovery of MHC class II-negative population of resident corneal langerhans cell-type dendritic cells in the corneal epithelium; identification of novel resident dendritic cells in the corneal stroma; vascular endothelial growth factor receptor (VEGFR)-3 and VEGF-C on dendritic cells in the cornea; research in draining lymph nodes of corneal transplant hosts exhibit evidence for donor major histocompatibility complex (MHC) class II-positive dendritic cells derived from MHC class II-negative grafts; VEGFR-3 mediates induction of corneal alloimmunity; first to breaking of two dogmas in corneal immunology: namely that immune privilege of the cornea is dependant on the absence of bone marrow-derived cells, and that the cornea does not have any BM derived cell. Office: Univ Louisville Dept Ophthalmology 301 E Mohammad Ali Blvd Louisville KY 40202 Office Phone: 502-345-5679. Business E-Mail: pedram.hamrah@louisville.edu.

HAMRE, JOHN J., think-tank executive; b. Watertown, S.D., July 3, 1950; s. Melvin Sanders and Ruth Lucile (Larson) H.; m. Julia Pfanstiehl, Sept. 4, 1976. BA summa cum laude, Augustana Coll., Sioux Falls, S.D., 1972; MA with highest distinction, Sch. of Internt. Studies, Washington, 1976; PhD, Johns Hopkins U., 1978. Dep. asst. dir. Congl. Budget Office, Washington, 1978-84; profl. staff Senate Armed Svcs. Com., Washington, 1984-94; comtroller, CFO, U.S. Dept. Def., Washington, 1993-97, dep. sec. def., 1997-00; pres., CEO Ctr. for Strategic & Internat. Studies, Washington, 2000—. Office: Ctr for Strategic & Internat Studies 1800 K St NW Washington DC 20006 E-mail: jhamre@csis.org.

HAMRICK, JOSEPH TYSON, elementary school educator; b. Richmond, Va., Feb. 1, 1972; s. Ann and Ronnie Wray (Stepfather); m. Joann Jones, May 23, 1993; children: Joseph Aaron, Sarah Ann. MusB in Edn., Mars Hill (N.C.) Coll., 1994. Dir. band Mullins (S.C.) H.S., 1994—95, Enka Mid. Sch., Candler, NC, 1995—. Cons. TH Svcs., Swannanoa, NC, 2003—. Dir. sunday sch. Swannanoa (N.C.) First Bapt. Ch., 1998—2001, deacon, 2003—05. Mem.: Music Educators Nat. Conf. (assoc.). Democrat. Baptist. Home: 108 Powell Street Swannanoa NC 28778 Office: Enka Middle School 390 Asbury Road Candler NC 28715 Office Phone: 828-670-5010. Personal E-mail: tyson@tysonhamrick.com.

HAMRICK, LESLIE WILFORD, JR., metallurgy supervisor; b. Charleston, W.Va., Dec. 26, 1946; s. Leslie Wilford and Olive Marie (Means) H.; m. Margaret C. Hamrick, Sept. 20, 1970 (div. Jan. 1976); m. Mary Lee Smathers, Aug. 6, 1978; 1 child, Hannah Chance. BA, U. Charleston, 1969. Shift coord. FMC, South Charleston, W.Va., 1973-79; maint. supr. Foote Mineral Co., Graham, W.Va., 1979-86; maint. foreman Century (W.Va.) Aluminum, 1986-92; metallurgy supr. Ravenswood (W.Va.) Aluminum, 1992—. Author: Hating Hugh, 1991 (2d place award 1991), Wozzek's Price, 1990 (2d place award 1992); (short story) Reconciliation, 1992 (3d place award 1993), Roots and Wings - The Family Record of Benjamin Hamrick, 1997. Trustee Point Mountain/Hamrick Reunion, 1995, chmn., 1998. With USN, 1969-73. Republican. Avocation: geneaology. Home: RR 2 Box 157aaa Ravenswood WV 26164-9794

HAN, BERNARD L., air transportation executive; BS, M in Engring., MBA, Cornell U. Various positions Am. Airlines, Northwest Airlines, exec. v.p., CFO Eagan, Minn., 2002—; v.p. fin. planning and analysis Am. West Airlines, sr. v.p. mktg. and planning, exec. v.p., CFO. Office: Northwest Airlines 2700 Lone Oak Pkwy Eagan MN 55121

HAN, BERNARD T., business educator; b. Hsinchu, Taiwan, Nov. 29, 1954; arrived in U.S., 1974; s. Ching Chi Jan and Hsiang Rong Han; m. Jofen Wu Han, Sept. 6, 1986; children: Rachel, Gloria, Samuel. BS, Nat. Chiao-Tung U., 1977; MBA, Ariz. State U., 1981; PhD in Bus. Adminstrn., U. Washington, 1989. Asst. prof. Wash. State U., Pullman, 1988—95, assoc. prof., 1995—98, Western Mich. U., Kalamazoo, 1998—2003, prof., chair, 2003—. Vis. prof. Nat. Chung-Hsin U., Taichung, Taiwan, 1996—97; vis. lectr. Xian U. Tech., China, 2002. 2d ltd. USMC, 1977—79. Grantee, Microsoft Corp., Redmond, Wash., 1997. Mem.: Decision Sci. Inst. Republican. Avocations: reading, music. Home: 3228 Bennington Ct Portage MI 49024 Office: Haworth Coll Bus Dept Bus Info Sys Kalamazoo MI 49008

HAN, BING QIANG, materials scientist; s. Qichao Han and Jingyu Yang; m. Ying Chen, Oct. 30, 1989; children: Frank, Michael. BS in Engring., Beijing (China) U. of Aeronautics and Astronautics, 1985, MS in Engring., 1988; PhD, The Hong Kong Poly. U., 1997. Materials scientist U. Calif., Davis, Calif., 2001—. Mem.: TMS. Office: University of California Davis Chemical Eng & Materials Sci Davis CA 95616 Office Phone: 530-752-9568. Business E-Mail: bqhan@ucdavis.edu.

HAN, CHIEN-PAI, statistics educator; b. Hunan, China, Dec. 17, 1936; came to U.S., 1960; s. Chung-Shih and Pei-Wen Han; m. Maria Han, Aug. 28, 1965; children: Richard, Julie. BA, Nat. Taiwan U., Taipei, 1958; MA, U. Minn., 1962; PhD, Harvard U., 1967. Asst. prof. stats. Iowa State U., Ames, 1967-69, assoc. prof., 1970-75, prof., 1975-82; prof. math. U. Tex.-Arlington, 1982—. Statis. cons. Mus. N.Mex., Santa Fe, 1965; vis. asst. prof. Harvard U., Cambridge, Mass., 1970 Author: (with T.A. Bancroft) Statistical Theory and Inference in Research, 1981; mem. editl. bd. Comms. in Stats. Theory and Methods, 1975-92, Jour. Statis. Rsch., 1994; assoc. editor Comms. in Stats., 1993—. Fellow Am. Statis. Assn. (pres. Iowa chpt. 1971-72); mem. Internat. Statis Inst. (elected), Inst. Math. Stats., Internat. Assn. Survey Statisticians, Internat. Chinese Statis. Assn. (bd. dirs. 1987-92, pres. 2000), Sigma Xi, Mu Sigma Rho. Office: U Tex Dept Math PO Box 19408 Arlington TX 76019-0408

HAN, HAE-RA, medical researcher; BS, Seoul (Korea) Nat. U., 1991, MS, 1994; PhD, U. Md., 2000. Registered Nurse, State Edn. Dept.,New York, 2001, Bd. of Nursing, 2001; Freedom from Smoking facilitator Am. Lung Assn., 2002. Post-doctoral fellow Johns Hopkins U., Balt., 2001—02, instr., 2002—03, asst. prof., 2003—. Recipient D. Jean Wood Nursing Rsch. Award, So. Nursing Rsch. Soc., 2001, Nursing Rsch. award, Sigma Theta Tau Nu Beta Chpt., 2001, Cmty. Based Participatory Rsch. award, Urban Health Inst., 2003; grantee Experiences and Challenges of Informal Caregivers, Agy. for Healthcare Rsch. and Quality, 2003-2005, Devel. of a Tng. Program for Nurse-Community Health Worker Teams, NIH, 2004-2005; scholar Chpt. scholar, Sigma Theta Tau Pi chpt., 1998. Mem.: Oncology Nursing Soc., Coun. for the Advancement of Nursing Sci., Am. Acad. of Nursing, Am. Heart Assn., Am. Stroke Assn., Asian Pacific Islander Caucus of APHA, APHA, So. Nursing Rsch. Soc., Sigma Theta Tau Internat. Achievements include research in Community-based participatory research targeting ethnic minorities. Office: Johns Hopkins Univ 525 N Wolfe St Baltimore MD 21205

HAN, HEE-WON, professional golfer; b. Seoul, South Korea, June 10, 1978; m. Hyuk Son. Attended, Rukoku U. Winner Wendy's Championship for Children at Tartan Fields, 2003, Sybase Big Apple, 2003, Safeway Classic, 2004. 48 victories as amateur; mem. Nat. Conf. Team, 1992—97; silver medallist Hiroshima Asia Games, 1994. Recipient Louise Suggs Rolex Rookie of Yr., 2001. Avocation: quilting. Office: c/o LPGA 100 International Golf Dr Daytona Beach FL 32124-1092

HAN, JIAHUAI, medical researcher; BS in Biochemistry, Beijing U., 1982, MS in Protein Biochemistry, 1988; PhD in Molecular Biology, U. Brussels, 1990. Rsch. fellow Dept. Internal Medicine and Howard Hughes Med. Inst., U. Tex. Southwestern Med. Ctr., Dallas, 1987—92; rsch. assoc. Dept. Immunology, The Scripps Rsch. Inst., La Jolla, Calif., 1992—93, sr. rsch. assoc., 1993—96, asst. mem. to prof., 1996—. Contbr. articles to profl. jours. Recipient Established Investigator award, Am. Heart Assn., 1995. Office: Scripps Rsch Inst IMM-9 10550 N Torrey Pines Rd La Jolla CA 92037-1000*

HAN, MOO-YOUNG, physicist, educator; b. Seoul, Korea, Nov. 30, 1934; came to U.S., 1954; s. Sunghoon and Kiejer (Kim) H.; m. Changki Hong, Aug. 29, 1959; children: Grace, Chris, Tony. BS, Carroll Coll., Waukesha, Wis., 1957; PhD, U. Rochester, 1964. Research assoc. Syracuse U., 1964-65; asst. prof. U. Pitts., 1965-67; asst. prof. physics Duke U., Durham, N.C., 1967-71, assoc. prof., 1971-77, prof., 1977—. Vis. prof. Kyoto U., 1974, Korea Advanced Inst. of Sci., 1982 Author: The Secret Life of Quanta, 1990, The Probable Universe, 1992, Quarks and Gluons, 1999, A Story of Light, 2005, Quantum Field Theory of Quarks and Leptons, 2005; editor-in-chief Korean Am. Sci. and Tech. News, 1995—. Recipient Outstanding Prof. award Duke U., 1971, Disting. Tchg. award Duke U., 1972, Disting. Fgn. Scholar award Kyoto U., 1974, Global Korea award Mich. State U., 1998. Mem. Soc. Korean-Am. Scholars, Golden Key (hon.). Home: 615 Duluth St Durham NC 27705-1824 Office: Duke U Dept Physics Durham NC 27708 E-mail: myhan@phy.duke.edu.

HAN, NONG, artist, sculptor, painter; b. Seoul, Korea, Oct. 10, 1930; arrived in U.S.A., 1952, naturalized, 1958. Commr. Asian Art Commn. Asian Art Mus. San Francisco, The Avery Brundage Collection, city and county of San Francisco, 1981—84. One-man exhbns. paintings and or sculpture include Ft. Lauderdale, Fla. Mus. Arts, Santa Barbara,Calif. Mus. Art, Crocker Art Mus., Sacramento, 1965, Ga. Mus. Art, Athens, 1967, El Paso, Tex. Mus. Art, 1967, Nat. Mus. History, Taiwan, 1971, Nihonbashi Gallery, Tokyo, Japan, 1971, Shinsegye Gallery, Seoul, Korea, 1975, Nat. Mus. Modern Art, Seoul, 1975, San Francisco Zool. Garden, 1975, Tongin Art Gallery, Seoul, 1978, Consulate Gen. Republic of Korea, L.A., 1982, Choon Chu Gallery, Seoul, 1982, Mee Gallery, Seoul, 1984, 86, Leema Art Mus., Seoul, 1985, Tong A Dept. Store, Taegu, Korea, 1986, Tongso Gallery, Masan, Korea, 1986, Han Kwang Art Mus., Pusan, Korea, 1986, Union de Arte, Barcelona, Spain, 1987, Acad. de Belles Arts, Sabadell, Spain, 1987, Nong Hyup Art Mus., Ft. Lee, N.J., 1995, The Info. Ctr. Korean Embassy, Washington, 1997; Gallery Art Exchange, N.Y.C., 1998, Korean Cultural Ctr., Annandale, Va., 1999, Paeksang Meml. Hall The Korea Times, Seoul, 2000, The Korea Central Daily, Vienna, Va., 2001, YTN, 24 hour news channel Seoul, Korea, 2004, KM Art Ctr., Sandy Spring, Md., 2005, Visitor's Ctr. Mormon Ch., Kensington, Md., 2005; numerous group exhibits including most recently Taipei Gallery Taiwanese Cultural Ctr., N.Y.C., 1998, Fisher Gallery U. So. Calif., L.A., 1998, Japanese Am. Nat. Mus., L.A., 1998, Bedford Gallery, Dean Lesker Regl. Ctr. for the Arts, Walnut Creek, 1998, The Kaohsing Museum of Fine Art, 1998, Taipei Mus. of Fine Arts, 1998, Marugame Genichiro Inokuma Mus. of Contemporary Art, Japan, 1999, Fukuoka Asian Art Mus., Fukuoka City, 1999, Akita Senshu Mus. Art, Akita City, 1999; represented in numerous permanent collections including, Santa Barbara Mus. Art, Anchorage Alaska Hist. and Fine Art Mus., Museo de Arte, Lima, Peru, Govt. Peru, Nat. Mus. History, Govt. of Republic of China, Oakland, Calif. Art Mus., Ga. Mus. Art, Athens, Korean Embassy, Lima, Peru, Nat. Mus. of Modern Art, Nat. Mus. Korea, Govt. of Republic of Korea, Seoul, Nat. Gallery of Modern Art, New Delhi, India, Asian Art Mus. San Francisco, Govt. of People's Republic China, Beijing and Shanghai, Palacio de la Zarzuela, Madrid, Palacio de la Moncloa, Madrid, The Korean Embassy, Madrid, Mus. Art de Sabadell, Spain, Mus. Nat. des Beaux-Arts, Monte Carlo, Monaco, The Philatelic Mus. Palais des Nations, Geneva, Korean Embassy, Wash., Nat. Mus., Manila, Philippines, others; author: Nong Questions, 1982. Chmn. San Francisco, Seoul Sister City Com., city and county San Francisco, 1981-84. Served in U.S. Army, 1956-59; USAF, 1959-60. Recipient numerous awards including citations from Republic of Korea; Cert. Disting. Achievement, State of Calif., 1982, Proclamation City and County of San Francisco, 1982; Nong Stamp issued in his honor UNISEF, 1996. Office: Nong Gallery 7057 N Seminole Trl Leon VA 22725 *Beauty and ugliness, good and bad, right and wrong. Which test should I choose to measure these? Then, how long can I rely on the test I choose?.*

HAN, OKSOO, musician, music educator; b. Seoul, Korea, June 18, 1938; d. Kyung-Seok H. and Young-Hwan Kim; m. Won-Hoon Park, Sept. 25, 1971; children: Suzanne, Thomas. BA, Ewha Women's U., Seoul, Korea, 1960; MA, Cin. Conservatory Music, 1962; DMA, William Penn Coll., 1983. Artist Eric Semon Mgmt., N.Y.C., 1965-72; prof. L.I. U., 1966-75, Kyunghee U., Seoul, Korea, 1976-78, Dankook U., Seoul, Korea, 1983—; dir. Korean chpt. World Piano Competition, Cin., 1987—; chmn. Han Romanson Internat. Piano Competition, Seoul, 1994—. Jury Tchaikovsky, Prokofiev, Cin. Internat. Competitions, others, 1987—. Musician (soloist): Carnegie Recital Hall, 1964, European Debut Recitals, 1964; musician: (recording) My Favorite Chopin, 1991, Beethoven Piano Concerto No. 5, 2003; author: Chopin Etudes, 1983, Chopin Preludes, 1984, Rachmaninoff Etudes-Tableaux, 2000. Recipient Cultural Merit citation Korean Govt., 1967; named Musician of Yr., Seoul, 1982. Mem. Am. Music Scholarship Assn. (bd. dirs. 1987—), Kawon Internat. Piano Soc. (chair 1994-). Home: 17-29 Kookee-Dong Chongroku Seoul 110-011 Republic of Korea Office: Dankook U San 8 Hannam-Dong Seoul 140-210 Republic of Korea Office Phone: 011-354-6072. E-mail: hanoksoo@kornet.net.

HAN, RUNLIN, biochemist, researcher; b. Huhhot, Neimongol, China, Aug. 10, 1966; arrived in U.S., 2002; s. Gaohuai Han and Erhua Zhang; m. Zhihong Zhao, Oct. 15, 1992; 1 child, Zhengyang. BSc, Jilin Agrl. U., China, 1987; MS, Hebei Agrl. U., China, 1990; PhD, Chinese Acad. of Sci., Beijing, China, 2001. Postdoctoral rsch. assoc. U. Toledo, 2002—03; chief engr. Fangzhou Sino-USA Biopharmaceutical Co., Suzhou, China, 2003—04; rsch. assoc. W.Va. U., Morgantown, W.Va., 2004—. Contbr. scientific papers pub. to profl. jour. Recipient Outstanding Dissertation, Inst. of Process Engring., Chinese Acad. of Sciences, 2001. U.S. Taxpayers. Christian. Avocations: travel, music. Office: W Va U 1 Med Ctr Dr Morgantown WV 26506 Office Phone: 304-293-2474. Personal E-mail: runlinhan@yahoo.com.

HAN, SHIN-CHAN, geophysicist, researcher; s. Beom-Yeol Han and In-Soon Cho; m. In-Young Yeo, June 22, 2002. PhD, Ohio State U., Columbus, Ohio, 2003. Rschr. Ohio State U., Columbus, Ohio, 2003—.

Recipient Karrina and Weikko A. Heiskanen Jr. Award, Ohio State U., 2001, Am. Assn. for Geod. Surveying Award, Am. Congress on Surveying and Mapping, 2002, 1st Pl. Winner, Student Paper Competition, Inst. of Nav., 2002. Mem.: Inst. of Nav., Am. Geophys. Union. Achievements include research in Earth's Gravity Field. Office: Ohio State Univ 2070 Neil Ave Columbus OH 43210 Office Phone: 1-614-292-2269.

HAN, SHUFENG, agricultural engineer, researcher; b. Zhejiang, China, Dec. 3, 1960; s. Guoquan Han and Xiuzhen Wu; m. Min Zhu, July 25, 1961; 1 child, Kevin. BS, Zhejiang U., China, 1982; MS, Zhejiang U., 1985; PhD, U. Of Ill., 1992. Registered profl. engr., Wash., 1997. Lectr. Zhejiang U., Zhejiang, China, 1985—89; agrl. engr. Wash. State U., Prosser, 1993—97; sr. engr. Case Corp., Burr Ridge, Ill., 1997—2000; asst. prof. U. Of Ill., Urbana, 2000—02; scientist Deere & Co., Urbandale, Iowa, 2002—. Contbr. articles to profl. jours. Scholar Bao Yugang Scholar, Bao Yugang Found., 1989. Mem.: ASAE (vice chair ctrl. Ill. sect. 2001—02, chair PM-58 com. 2002—03, sec. PNW sect. 1996—97), SAE (assoc.). Achievements include patents for Vision guidance systems, sensing of crop health; research in off-road vehicle automation; precision agriculture; precision application technology. Home: 9015 Telford Cir Johnston IA 50131-2747 Office: Deere & Company 4140 114th St Urbandale IA 50322-2064 Office Phone: 515-331-4675. Personal E-mail: hanshufeng@johndeere.com.

HAN, TIMOTHY WAYNE, drug abuse professional, public health educator; b. Seoul, Korea, Aug. 31, 1953; came to U.S., 1977; s. Ki Cho and Man (Soo) H.; m. Kimmy Jin Sook, Apr. 14, 1991; 1 child, Paige Yuri. BS, Mercy Coll., 1982; BA, CUNY, 1986, MEd, MS, 1987. Health resource coord. N.Y.C. Dept. Health, 1987-91, AIDS tng. specialist, pub. health adviser Bur. AIDS, 1989—, substance abuse prevention specialist, 1991—. Lectr., educator Asian-Am. communication Columbia U., N.Y.C., 1993—; cons. N.Y.C. Bd. Edn., Bronx, 1991—, child crisis intervention team, 1987—. Teen columnist: N.Y. Korea Times, 1989—; weekly radio talk show host: (Korean Christian Broadcasting Network) The Parade of Youth, 1993—; contbr. articles to profl. jours. Counselor YWCA, 1989, teen dir., 1986-90; youth leader Greater N.Y. Conf., 1992, youth dir., 1984—. Mem. APHA, AMA. Avocations: camping, music, playing piano and guitar, travel, climbing.

HAN, WENLI, research scientist; b. Chongqing, Sichuan, China, July 4, 1966; s. Ziqing Han and Yirong Sun; m. Yi Lu, Apr. 18, 1993; 1 child, Kevin. PhD, Poly. U., Bklyn., 1998. Sr. rsch. assoc. Baxter Healthcare Corp, Miami Lakes, Fla.; rsch. scientist Kos Pharm., Inc., Hollywood, Fla., 2002—. Achievements include invention of melt-spun polysulfone semipermeable membranes and methods for making the same. Office: Kos Pharm Inc 2 Oakwood Blvd Suite 140 Hollywood FL 33020 Office Phone: 954-924-5043. E-mail: whan@kospharm.com.

HAN, ZHAOHONG, linguist, education educator; b. Hubei, China, June 5, 1962; d. Bingzhang Han and Guohuang Wu; m. Gang Bao, Sept. 2, 1985; 1 child, Amy BaoHan. PhD, U. London, 1998. Asst. prof. linguistics and edn. Tchrs. Coll., Columbia U., N.Y.C., 1999—2001, assoc. prof. linguistics and edn., 2002—. Contbr. articles to profl. jours. Recipient Outstanding Tchg. award, Tchrs. Coll., Columbia U., 2001—04. Mem.: Internat. TESOL Assn. (chair rsch. interest sect. 2003—04, Cert. of Appreciation 2004, Heinle and Heinle Disting. Rsch. award 2003), Am. Assn. for Applied Linguistics. Achievements include research in fossilization in adult second language acquisition. Office: Teachers College Columbia University 525 W 120th St New York NY 10027 Office Phone: 212-678-4051.

HANAHAN, DONALD JAMES, biochemist, educator; b. Springfield, Ill., May 13, 1919; s. James Francis and Clara (Schiller) H.; m. Lillian Marie Larsen, June 21, 1947; children: Douglas A., Laura J., Timothy J., Colleen J., Carolyn M. BS, U. Ill., 1941, PhD, 1944. Rsch. assoc. Manhattan Project, 1944-45; fellow U. Calif., Berkeley, 1945-47; faculty U. Wash., Seattle, 1948-67, prof. biochemistry, 1958-67; prof., head dept. biochemistry U. Ariz., Tucson, 1967-76; prof. biochemistry U. Tex. Health Sci. Center, San Antonio, 1976—, chmn. dept., 1976-84, prof. emeritus San Antonio, 1994-98. Author: Lipid Chemistry, 1960, A Guide to Phospholipid Chemistry, 1997; contbr. articles to profl. jours. Guggenheim Found. fellow, 1955; NIH spl. fellow, 1965-66; Macy faculty scholar, 1974 Mem. Am. Chem. Soc., Am. Soc. Biol. Chemists. Home: 25 Arroyo Ln Novato CA 94947 E-mail: d.hanahan@sonic.net.

HANAHAN, JAMES LAKE, retired insurance executive; b. Burlington, Iowa, Aug. 27, 1932; s. Thomas J. and Clarice P. (Lorey) Hanahan; m. Marilyn R. Lowe, Dec. 27, 1952; children: Bridget Sue Bahlke, Erin Hoff-Hanahan. BS, Drake U., 1955; postgrad., George Williams Coll., 1956. Phys dir. Monmouth (Ill.) YMCA, 1955-56; cmty. rels. staff Caterpillar Tractor Co., Peoria, Ill., 1956-57; rep. Conn. Gen. Life Ins. Co., Des Moines, 1957-59, asst. mgr., 1959-63, mgr. group ins. ops. Tampa, Fla., 1963-80; pres., chief exec. officer WHP, First In Employee Benefits Inc., 1980-91, J&H Cons. Group Inc., 1980-91; v.p. AON Cons., 1991-2000; ret., 2000. Instr. C.P.C.U. courses; seminar leader C.L.U. workshop; cons. ins. seminar Fla. State U.; guest instr. U. South Fla., Hillsborough County Schs. Great Am. Teach-In. Bd. dirs. West Coast Employee Benefit Coun., Tampa Sports Found., Jr. Achievement, Tampa Bay Acad.; chmn. joint bd. trustees Town and Country Hosp. and Meml. Hosp, Tampa; past pres. Pinellas Emergency Mental Health Svcs.; mem. Hillsborough County Health Coun. Recipient Double D award, Drake U., PEMHS Cmty. Svc. award. Mem. Sales Mktg. Execs. Tampa (past pres., Exec. of Yr. 1982), Nat. Risk Mgmt. Soc., Greater Tampa C. of C., Mineret Soc. Tampa U., Tampa Sports and Recreation Coun. (bd. dirs.), Self Ins. Assn. Am., Pinellas Econ. Devel. Coun. (chmn.), Health Ins. Inst. Am., Profl. Benefit Adminstrs. Assn., Com. of 100, Nat. D Club (Drake U.; dir.), Timber Greens Country Club, Pres.'s Assn., Phi Sigma. Democrat. Roman Catholic. Home: 6659 Garden Palm Ct New Port Richey FL 34655-5117 Office Phone: 813-636-3046. E-mail: jim_l_hanahan@aoncons.com.

HANAMEY, ROSEMARY T., nursing educator; b. Detroit, May 16, 1937; d. Albert Edward and Catherine Margaret (Shaheen) Hanamey. BSN, Mercy Coll., Detroit, 1959; MS, Boston Coll., 1963; postgrad., U. Mich., 1982. RN Mich., 1959. Staff nurse Mt. Carmel Mercy Hosp., Detroit, 1959—60, Mass. Gen. Hosp., Boston, 1960—63; instr. nursing Mercy Coll., Detroit, 1963—65, asst. prof., 1967—69; asst. exec. sec. Mich. Nurses Assn., Lansing, 1965—67; exec. sec. Mich. Conf. AAUP, Detroit, 1969—70; instr. nursing Madonna Coll., Livonia, Mich., 1972—76; asst. prof. nursing Ea. Mich. U., Ypsilanti, 1976—80; vol. parish nurse St. Joseph Cath. Ch., Dexter, Mich., 1997—. Mem. careers com. Mich. League Nursing, Detroit, 1977—97; cons. Detroit Practical Nurse Ctr., 1980—85; mem. parish nurse partnership St. Joseph Mercy Health Sys., Ann Arbor, Mich., 1997—. Author: (videotape) Intravenous Therapy: Monitoring and Problem Solving, 1977 (2nd place, 1978), Intravenous Therapy: Basic Concepts, 1977 (3rd place, 1978). Precinct del. Dem. Party, Detroit, 1966—69. Grantee, USPHS, 1961—62; scholar, Marygrove Coll., Detroit, 1955—56. Mem.: AAUP, Cath. Med. Assn. Avocations: swimming, walking. Home: 8074 Huron St Unit I Dexter MI 48130-1053

HANAN, PATRICK DEWES, foreign language professional, educator; b. New Zealand, Jan. 4, 1927; s. Frederick Arthur and Ida Helen (Dewes) H.; m. Anneliese Drube, July 1951; 1 son, Rupert Guy. BA, Auckland U., 1948, MA, 1949; BA, U. London, 1953, PhD, 1960. Lectr. Sch. Oriental and African Studies, 1954-63; assoc. prof., then prof. Stanford U., 1963-68; from prof. Chinese lit. to prof. emeritus Harvard U., Cambridge, Mass., 1968—2003, prof. emeritus, 2003—. Dir. Harvard-Yenching Inst., 1987-95. Author: The Chinese Short Story, 1973, The Chinese Vernacular Story, 1981, The Invention of Li Yu, 1988; transl.: The Carnal Prayer Mat, 1990, Silent Operas, 1990, A Tower for the Summer Heat, 1995, The Sea of Regret, 1995, The Money Demon, 1999, Chinese Fiction, 2004. Named Officer of New Zealand Order of Merit. Fellow Am. Council Learned Socs., Guggenheim Found.; Mem. Am. Acad. Arts and Scis. Office: 2 Divinity Ave Cambridge MA 02138-2020

HANAS, STEPHEN MICHAEL, lawyer; b. Hammond, Ind., June 1, 1954; s. Eugene Edward and Laverne Theresa (Carson) H.; m. Carol J. Wedding, Oct. 16, 1976; 1 child, Wesley Preston. BS in Bus Adminstrn., St. Joseph's Coll., 1976; JD, John Marshall Law Sch., 1983. Bar: Ill. 1983, Tex. 1986, U.S. Dist. Ct (no. dist.) Ill., 1983, U.S. Dist. Ct. (so. dist.) Tex. 1987; U.S. Supreme Ct. 1998. Fin. analyst Dun & Bradstreet, Chgo., 1976-78; supr. adminstrn. svcs. E.J. Brach & Sons, Chgo., 1978-79; contracts mgr. Clow Corp., Oakbrook, Ill., 1979-83, corp. counsel, 1983-86; pvt. practice Oak Brook, Ill., 1985-86; managing ptnr. Brooks, Hyatt & Willis, Houston, 1986-89; asst. gen. counsel legal divsn. FDIC, Washington, 1989—. Chmn. adminstrv. coun. United Meth., Fairfax Station, 1993—. Trustee archtl. bd. Homeowners Assn., Fairfax Station, Va., 1991—. Mem. ABA (vice chmn. real property 1995—), Ill. State Bar Assn., Water Equipment Mfrs. Assn. (chmn. 1984-85). Republican. Methodist. Home: 11351 Andrew Ln Fairfax VA 22030 Office: FDIC Legal Divsn 550 17th St NW Rm H-3131 Washington DC 20429-0001 Office Phone: 202-736-0353. Business E-Mail: shanas@fdic.gov.

HANAUER, JOE FRANKLIN, real estate executive; b. Stuttgart, Fed. Republic Germany, July 8, 1937; came to U.S., 1938; s. Otto and Betty (Zurndorfer) H.; m. Jane Boyle, Oct. 20, 1972; children: Jill, Jason, Elizabeth. BS, Roosevelt U., 1963. Pres. Thorsen Realty, Oak Brook, Ill., 1974-80; sr. v.p. Coldwell Banker, Newport Beach, Calif., 1980-83, pres., 1984, chmn. bd., CEO, 1984-88; prin. Combined Investments LP, Laguna Beach, Calif., 1989—; chmn. bd. dirs. Grubb & Ellis Co., San Francisco, 1993-97. Bd. dirs. MAF Bancorp, Chgo.; chmn. bd. Homestore.com., Calamos Mutual Funds; chmn. policy adv. bd. Joint Ctr. for Housing Studies Harvard U., 1995-96. Bd. dirs. Chgo. Chamber Orch., 1976—; trustee Roosevelt U. Home: 179 E Lake Shore Drive Chicago IL 60611 Office: Combined Investments LP 361 Forest Ave Ste 200 Laguna Beach CA 92651-2146

HANAWALT, PHILIP COURTLAND, biology professor, researcher; b. Akron, Ohio, Aug. 25, 1931; s. Joseph Donald and Lenore (Smith) H.; m. Joanna Thomas, Nov. 2, 1957 (div. Oct. 1977); children: David, Steven; m. Graciela Spivak, Sept. 10, 1978; children: Alex, Lisa. Student, Deep Springs Coll., 1949-50; BA, Oberlin Coll., 1954; MS, Yale U., 1955, PhD, 1959; ScD (hon.), Oberlin Coll., 1997. Postdoctoral fellow U. Copenhagen, Denmark, 1958-60, Calif. Inst. Tech., Pasadena, 1960-61; rsch. biophysicist, lectr. Stanford U., Calif., 1961-65, assoc. prof., 1965-70, prof., 1970—, Howard H. and Jessie T. Watkins univ. prof., 1997—, chmn. dept. biol. scis., 1982-89; faculty dept. dermatology Stanford Med. Sch., 1979—. Mem. physiol. chemistry study sect. NIH, Bethesda, Md., 1966—70, mem. chem. pathology study sect., 1981—84; mem. sci. adv. com. Am. Cancer Soc., N.Y.C., 1972—76, Coun. for Extramural Grants, 1998—2001; chmn. 2d ad hoc senate com. on professoriate Stanford U., 1985—90; mem. NSF fellowship rev. panel, 1985; mem. carcinogen identification com. Calif. EPA, 1995—98; mem. toxicology adv. com. Burroughs-Welcome Fund, 1995—2001, chmn., 1997—2000; mem. sci. adv. bd. Fogarty Internat. Ctr., NIH, 1995—99; chmn. Gordon Conf. on Mutagenesis, 1996, Gordon Conf. on Mammalian DNA Repair, 1999; mem. bd. on radiation effects rschr. NAS Commn. on Life Scis., 1996—98; trustee Oberlin Coll., 1998—; lectr. Curie Inst., Paris, 2003; pres., chair organizing com. 9th Internat. Conf. on Environ. Mutagens, San Francisco, 2005. Author: Molecular Photobiology, 1969; author, editor: DNA Repair: Techniques, 1981, 83, 88, Molecular Basis of Life, 1968, Molecules to Living Cells, 1980; mng. editor DNA Repair Jour., 1982-93; sr. editor Jour. Cancer Rsch., 2003—; assoc. editor Jour. DNA Repair, Molecular Carcinogenesis, Environ. Health Perspectives, Biotechniques; bd. rev. editors Sci.; mem. editl. bd. Procs. of NAS, 2003—; contbr. more than 400 articles to profl. jours. Recipient Outstanding Investigator award Nat. Cancer Inst., 1987-2001, Excellence in Tchg. award No. Calif. Phi Beta Kappa, 1991, Environ. Mutagen Soc. Ann. Rsch. award, 1992, Peter and Helen Bing award for Disting. Tchg., 1992, Am. Soc. for Photobiology Rsch. award, 1996, Internat. Mutation Rsch. award, 1997, Ellison Found. Sr. scholar award, 2001—, John B. Little award in radiation scis. Harvard Sch. Pub. Health, 2002; Hans Falk lectr. Nat. Inst. Environ. Health Scis., 1990, Severo Ochoa Meml. Hons. lectr. NYU, 1996, IBM-Princess Takamatsu lectr. Japan, 1999, Sonnebonn lectr. Ind. U., 2002; Fogarty sr. rsch. fellow, 1993. Fellow: AAAS, Am. Acad. Microbiology; mem.: NAS, European Molecular Biology Orgn. (fgn. assoc.), Radiation Rsch. Soc., Environ. Mutagen Soc. (pres. 1993—94, Student Mentoring award 2001), Am. Soc. Biochemistry and Molecular Biology, German DNA Repair Network (hon.), Biophys. Soc. (exec. bd. 1969—71), Genetics Soc., Am. Soc. for Photobiology, Am. Assn. Cancer Rsch. (bd. dirs. 1994—97), Radiation Rsch. Soc. Achievements include co-discovery of DNA excision-repair and transcription-coupled DNA repair; research in role of DNA change in human genetic disease and aging. Home: 317 Shasta Dr Palo Alto CA 94306-4542 Office: Stanford U Dept Biol Scis Herrin Biology Labs 371 Serra Mall Stanford CA 94305-5020 Office Phone: 650-723-2424. Business E-Mail: hanawalt@stanford.edu.

HANAWAY, CATHERINE L., state representative, prosecutor; b. Schuyler, Nebr., Nov. 8, 1963; m. Christopher; children: Lucy, Jack. BA, Creighton U., 1987; JD, The Catholic U. of Am., 1990. Owner, atty. Hanamore Solutions, LLC; atty. Peper, Martin, St. Louis, 1990—93; campaign mgr. Bredemeier for Atty. Gen., 1996; dist. dir. Senator Kit Bond, 1993—96, 1996—98; polit. advisor Missourians for Kit Bond, 1998; mem. Mo. State Ho. of Reps., 1998—, spkr., 2002—; exec. dir. Mo. Bush/Cheney, 2002; US atty. (Ea. dist.) Mo US Dept. State, 2005—. Mem. Housing Adv. Bd.; bd. dirs. Hope House, Foster and Adoptive Care Coalition. Mem.: Mo. Bar Assn., St. Louis Junior League, St. Louis Jaycees (past pres.). Roman Catholic. Office: State Capital, Rm 308 201 W Capitol Ave Jefferson City MO 65101*

HANBALI, FADI, neurosurgeon, educator; b. Beirut, July 12, 1967; s. Samir Hanbali and Dunia Ghossayni; m. Rana N Kronfol. BS, Am. U. of Beirut, Lebanon, 1988. MD Am. U. of Beirut Med. Ctr., 1988—92; resident in neurol. surgery Am. U. Beirut Med. Ctr., 1992—98; fellow in complex spine surgery Cleve. Clinic Foun., 1998—99; fellow in neurosurgery and oncology MD Anderson Cancer Ctr., Houston, 1999—2001; asst. prof. of neurosurgery and orthop. surgery U. Tex. Med. Br., Galveston, 2001—04, assoc. prof. of neurosurgery and orthop. surgery, 2005—. Contbr. articles to profl. jours., chapters to books. Grantee Rsch. grantee, NIH, 2004. Mem.: AMA, World Assn. of Lebanese Neurosurgeons, Singleton Surg. Soc., Congress of Neurol. Surgeons. Office: University of Texas Medical Branch 301 University Blvd Galveston TX 77555-0517 Office Fax: 409-772-6352.

HANBERRY, MELODY A., music educator; b. Hattiesburg, Miss., Oct. 31, 1975; d. Jerry M. and Linda (Fillingane) Hanberry. BMus in Piano Performance, William Carey Coll., Hattiesburg, 1998; MMus in Piano Pedagogy, La. State U., Baton Rouge, 2000, PhD in music edn. and piano pedagogy, 2004—. Piano instr. La. State U. Acad. Sch. Music, Baton Rouge, 1998—, coord., 2000—02; prof. of music Sterling Coll., Kans., 2002—. Mem.: Baton Rouge Music Tchrs. Assn., La. Music Tchrs. Assn., Music Tchrs. Nat. Assn. (presenter poster session 2001—02, 2004), MENC, Delta Omicron (Omicron Sigma chpt.). Achievements include poster session presenter at Nat. Conf. on Keyboard Pedagogy, 2001. Personal E-mail: melhanberry@hotmail.com.

HANBURY, GEORGE LAFAYETTE, II, academic administrator; b. Norfolk, Va., Sept. 20, 1943; s. Emmette Cecil and Adah Christine (Nelligar) H.; m. Jana Hanbury; 1 stepchild, Jia; children from previous marriage: George Lafayette III, Melissa Lee. BS in Pub. Adminstrn, Va. Poly. Inst., 1965; MPA, Old Dominion U., 1977; postgrad., Sr. Exec. Inst. Govt., U. Va., 1985; PhD, Fla. Atlantic U., 2001. Asst. to city mgr., Norfolk, 1967-70; asst. city mgr. Virginia Beach, Va., 1970-74; city mgr., 1974-82, Portsmouth, Va., 1982-90, Ft. Lauderdale, Fla., 1990-98; exec. v.p. Nova Southeastern U., Ft. Lauderdale, 1998—. Mem. Internat. City Mgmt. Assn., Am. Soc. Pub. Adminstrs., Pi Alpha Alpha. Home: The Four Seasons 333 Sunset Dr Apt 807 Fort Lauderdale FL 33301-2655 Office: Nova Southeastern Univ 3301 College Ave Fort Lauderdale FL 33314-7796 Office Phone: 954-262-7555. E-mail: hanbury@nova.edu.

HANBURY, KEVIN M., dean, priest; b. Jersey City, N.J., June 25, 1946; s. Raymond F. and Roseann Hanbury. BA, Seton Hall U., 1968; MDiv, Immaculate Conception Seminary, 1976; MA, Forham U., 1978; EDS, Seton Hall U., 1979, EdD, 1985. Priest Holy Family Parish, Nutley, NJ, 1972—75; H.S. tchr. Seton Hall Prep. Sch., West Orange, NJ, 1975—85; from asst. dean for enrollment to assoc. dean Seton Hall U., South Orange, NJ, 1987—97, assoc. dean for coll. human svcs., 1997—. Asst. dir. campus ministry Seton Hall U., 1958—87; rep. Resources in Christian Living, Allen, Tex., 1998—2001; cons. Silver-Burdett Pub. Co., 1985—90, Tabor Pub. co., 1982—97; dir. retreat Newark Archdiocese, Newark, 1995—2000; dir. master degree program Cath. Sch. Leadership, 1998, Edn. Ptnrs. in Cath. Schs., 2000. Contbr. articles to mags. and profl. jours. Grantee, RASKOB Found. for Cath. Activities, 2001, Alliance in Cath. Edn. grant, Notre Dame U., 2000—06, Our Sunday Visitor grant, Our Sunday Visitor Pub. Inc., 2001, 2002. Mem.: Kappa Delta Pi. Roman Catholic. Home and Office: Seton Hall University 400 South Orange Ave South Orange NJ 07079 E-mail: hanburke@shu.edu.

HANCE, JAMES HENRY, JR., bank executive; b. St. Joseph, Mo., Sept. 16, 1944; s. James Henry Sr. and Kathryn (Lichty) H.; m. Beverly Vaughan Smith, May 20, 1960; children: Samantha, Lindsay, Meredith, Blair. BA in Econs., Westminster Coll., 1966; MBA in Fin., Washington U., 1968. CPA. Ptnr. Price Waterhouse, Phila. and Charlotte, NC, 1968-85; chmn. bd. Consolidated Coin Caterers Corp., Charlotte, 1985-86; exec. v.p., chief acctg. officer NCNB Corp., Charlotte, 1987-88; CFO Bank Am. (formerly NationalBank), Charlotte, 1988—2004; co-vice chmn. Bank Am., Chalotte, NC, 1988—. Bd. dirs. Nationsbank, Tenn., D.C., Md., Charlotte. Bd. dirs. Microelectronis Ctr., NC, Rsch. Triangle Pk., 1988; trustee Presbyn. Hosp. and Presbyn. Hosp. Health Svcs. Corp., Charlotte, 1989, Charlotte Country Day Sch., 1990; mem. acctg. and fin. commn. Bank Adminstrn. Inst., Rolling Meadows, Ill., 1989. Fellow Soc. Internat. Bus. Fellows. Republican. Presbyterian. Office: Bank Am 100 N Tryon St Fl 58 Charlotte NC 28202-4000

HANCOCK, BEVERLY J., retired counseling consultant, secondary school educator; b. Bridgeton, N.J., Dec. 16, 1943; m. J. Everett Hancock, Jr., Aug. 9, 1969; children: J. Michael, Faith Lynn. BE, Montclair (N.J.) State U., 1966; MEd in counseling, Temple U., Phila., 1972. Cert. Social Studies Tchr. N.J. Dept. Edn., 1966, Sch. Counselor N.J. Dept. Edn., 1972, Nat. Bd. Cert. Counselors, 1983, lic. Profl. Counselor Bd. of Marriage and Family Therapy Examiners of N.J., 1999, nat. cert. counselor, nat. cert. sch. psychologist. Tchr. English and social studies Burlington Twp. (N.J.) HS, 1966—69, Burlington County Inst. Tech., Westhampton, NJ, 1969—72, guidance counselor, 1972—93, student resource ctr. counselor, 1993—98, guidance counselor, 1998—2002, cons. counselor, English instr., 2002—04; ret., 2004. Staff coord. Student-Supr. Liason Com., 1988—90; cons. N.J. Statewide Non-Traditional Career Assistance Ctr., 1992—. Author: Work Resource Handbook, 1986, Student Leadership Handbook, 1989; editor: The Source Guidance Bull. Co-developer Burlington County Job Fair for HS Srs. Mem.: NEA, N.J. Sch. Counselors Assn. (Counselor of Yr. 1990), N.J. Edn. Assn., Burlington County Sch. Counselors Assn., Am. Sch. Counselor Assn., Delta Kappa Gamma, Chi Sigma Iota. Episcopalian. Achievements include created and distributed wallet size Human Services CARE (help number) Cards to county schools and organizations. Avocations: crafts, carpentry, reading. Home: 1419 Noreen Dr Burlington NJ 08016

HANCOCK, CAMILLA ANN, pharmacist; b. St. Louis, Mo., May 1962; d. Harold and Violet Boone Hancock. BS in Pharmacy, St. Louis Coll. of Pharmacy, 1980—85. Registered pharmacist Ill. Dept. of Registration and Edn., 1985, Mo. Bd. of Pharmacy, 1986, lic. real estate salesperson Mo. Real Estate Commn., 1985, real estate broker Mo. Real Estate Commn., 1989. Staff pharmacist Madigan Army Hosp., Ft. Lewis, Wash., 1990—92, VA Hosp., St. Louis, 1992—93, Fitsimmons Army Med. Ctr., Aurora, Colo., 1993—95, Brooke Army Med. Ctr., Ft. Sam Houston, Tex., 1995—2001, VA Hosp., Kerrville, Tex., 2002—03, Tenet, St. Louis, 2003—05, Spectrum Healthcare, St. Louis, 2005—. Poet/ writer (poem collection) Poem Collection #1; singer: (cd) Vocal Collection #1. Recipient Cert. for Exceptional Performance in Pharmacy, Dept. of the Army, 1995, Cert. for Superior Performance, 1997, Cert. for being Instrumental in initiating Pharmacy Interventions in the Pharmacy's Care Plan, 1999. Mem.: So. Poverty Law Center-Supporter, NAACP (life). Achievements include invention of Camilla's Safety Ware; donating to various humanitarian causes. Home: 11561 Francetta Lane Saint Louis MO 63138

HANCOCK, CHARLES R., education educator; BA in Edn., MA in Secondary Edn., La. State U.; attended, Fondation Franco-Américaine, Paris; PhD, Ohio State U. Assoc. supt. divsn. secondary, vocation, adult and community edn. Balt. City Pub. Schs.; coord. of foreign lang. Montgomery County Pub. Schs., 1984-85; prof. edn., assoc. dean Coll. Edn. Ohio State Univ., 1986—. Pres. Am. Coun. Tchg. Fgn. Lang., 1984-85, Md. Fgn. Lang. Assn., 1990-91, Ohio Fgn. Lang. Assn., 1990-91. Recipient Anthony Papalia award for Excellence in Tchr. Edn., 1992, Florence Steiner award for Leadership in Foreign Lang., 1980. Office Phone: 614-292-7231.

HANCOCK, DAVID CARL, artist, educator; b. Winfield, Ill., Sept. 19, 1981; s. Don Edward and Beth Elaine Hancock; m. Cynthia Marie Chizmar, June 28, 2003. Diploma in Painting, Angel Acad. of Art, Florence, Italy and Toronto, Canada, 2001; BA in Philosophy cum laude, Wheaton Coll., 2002. One-man shows include Wheaton (Ill.) Conservatory of Music, exhibited in group shows at Palazzetto Cenci, Rome, Gallery 37, Chgo., Water Street Gallery, Providence, Westbeth Arts Gallery, N.Y.C., Non-Word & Upward Annual Juried Exhbn., Wheaton, Ill., Angel Acad. of Art End of Year Exhbn., Florence, Italy, Hilligoss Galleries, Chgo., 2004, Chiesa dell'Educatorio de Fuligno, Florence, Italy, 2004, Florence Biennale, 2004, Oil Painters Am. Nat. Exhbn., represented in numerous pub. and pvt. collections, portrait commd., Jessica Simpson, Nick Lachey, Lt. Govt. Loren Leman. Finalist Internat. Salon Competition, Art Renewal Ctr., 2004, Artist's Mag. Competition, The Artist' Mag., 2004; recipient Blue Ribbon award for Excellence in Journalism, Ill. Sch. Press Assn., 1999, 1st pl. award, Mr. Natural Classic Bodybuilding Championship, Teen Divsn., 2000, 2d pl., Mr. Natural Classic Bodybuilding Championship, Adult Divsn., 2000, 1st pl., Non-Word & Upward Ann. Juried Competition, Wheaton Ill., 2003, Hon. Mention, Art Renewal Ctr. Internat. Salon Competition, 2005, award, Francis and Leslie T. Posey Found., 2005, Hon. Mention, Angelico Religious Arts Exhbn., Gallery 66, Chgo., 2003; grantee, Wheaton Coll., 1999-2001; Merit scholarship, Saks, Inc., 1999, President's award, Wheaton Coll., 1999-2001. Mem.: Fellowship of Christians in Portraiture, Chgo. Artists' Coalition, Oil Painters of Am., Palette & Chisel Acad. of Fine Arts (Chgo.). Office: David C Hancock World Class Fine Art 4940 Spaulding 2d Fl Chicago IL 60625 Office Phone: 773-989-7434. E-mail: info@davidchancock.com.

HANCOCK, GERRE EDWARD, musician, educator; b. Lubbock, Tex., Feb. 21, 1934; s. Ervin Edward and Flake (Steger) H.; m. Judith Duffield Eckerman, July 22, 1961; children: Deborah, Lisa. MusB, U. Tex., 1955; diploma, U. Sorbonne, Paris, 1956; M in Sacred Music, Union Theol. Sem., N.Y.C., 1961; MusD, Nashotah House Episcopal Sem., 1986, U. South, 1999; DD, Gen. Theol. Sem., 2004. Asst. organist St. Bartholomew's Ch., N.Y.C., 1960-62; organist, choirmaster Christ Ch. Cathedral, Cin., 1962-71; mem. artist faculty Coll.-Conservatory Music, U. Cin., 1964-71; organist, master choristers St. Thomas Ch., N.Y.C., 1971—2004; faculty Juilliard Sch., N.Y.C., 1971—2004, Inst. Sacred Music, Yale U., New Haven, 1974—2002, Eastman Sch. Music, U. Rochester, NY, 1995—2000, Sch. of Music, U. Tex. Austin, 2004—. Concert organist McFarlane Mgmt., Cleve., 1964—; condr. choral festivals, U.S. and Europe, 1964—; clinician organ and choral workshops, Australia, Korea, and Republic of South Africa, 1964—. Author: Organ Improvisations, 1976, Improvising: How to Master the Art, 1994; composer: (cantata) Plum Line and City, 1967, (choral works) Missa

Resurrectionis, 1979; performer concerts throughout U.S., Can., Europe, South Africa, Australia, Japan. Served with U.S. Army, 1956-58. Recipient The Cross of St. Augustine, Archbiship Canterbury, 2004. Fellow Royal Sch. Ch. Music, Am. Guild Organists (past mem. coun.), Royal Coll. Organists (hon.); mem. Assn. Anglican Musicians (founder, past pres.), Phi Mu Alpha Sinfonia (past pres.), Pi Kappa Lambda. Clubs: St. Wilfrid (N.Y.C.) (pres. 1973-74). Independent. Episcopalian. Avocation: tennis. Office: U Tex Austin School Music 1 Univ Sta E 3100 Austin TX 78712-0435 Office Phone: 512-471-6711.

HANCOCK, HERBERT JEFFREY (HERBIE HANCOCK), composer, pianist, publisher; b. Chgo., Apr. 12, 1940; s. Wayman Edward and Winnie (Griffin) Hancock; m. Gudrun Meixner, Aug. 31, 1968. Student, Grinnell (Iowa) Coll., 1956-60, Roosevelt U., Chgo., 1960, Manhattan Sch. Music, 1962, New Sch. Social Research, 1967. Owner-pub. Hancock Music Co., 1962—; founder Hancock and Joe Prodns., 1989—; pres. Harlem Jazz Music Center, Inc. Performer: Chgo. Symphony Orch., 1982, Coleman Hawkins, 1960, Donald Byrd, 1960—63, Miles Davis Quintet, 1963—68; recorded with Chick Corea, scored (films) The Spook Who Sat By the Door, 1973, Death Wish, 1974, A Soldier's Story, 1984, Jo Jo Dancer, Your Life is Calling, 1986, Action Jackson, Colors, 1988, Harlem Nights, 1989, Livin' Large, 1991, scored and appeared 'Round Midnight, 1986 (Academy award best original score, 1986), albums Takin' Off, 1963, Succotash, Speak Like a Child, 1968, Fat Albert Rotunda, 1969, Mwandishi, 1971, Crossings, Sextant, 1972, Headhunters, 1973, Thrust, The Best of Herbie Hancock, 1974, Man-Child, 1975, The Quintet, V.S.O.P., 1977, Sunlight, 1978, An Evening with Herbie Hancock and Chick Corea in Concert, Feets Don't Fail Me Now, 1979, Monster, Greatest Hits, 1980, Lite Me Up, 1982, Future Shock, 1983, (with Foday Musa Suso albums) Village Life, 1985, (with Dexter Gordon albums) The Other Side of 'Round Midnight, 1987, Perfect Machine, 1988, Jamming, 1992, Cantaloupe Island, Tribute to Miles, 1994, Dis Is Da Drum, 1995, The New Standard, 1996, 1 + 1, 1997, Gershwin's World, 1998 (3 Grammy awards), (albums) Future 2 Future, 2001. Named top jazz artist Black Music mag., 1974; recipient citation of achievement Broadcast Music, Inc., 1963, Jay award Jazz mag., 1964, critics poll for talent deserving wider recognition Down Beat mag., 1967, 1st place piano category, 1968, 1969, 1970, composer award, 1971, All-Star Band New Artist award Record World, 1968, Grammy award for best rhythm and blues instrumental performance, 1983, 1984, Grammy award for best jazz instrumental composition (co-composer), 1987, Grammy award best jazz instrumental performance, 1995. Mem.: Nat. Acad. TV Arts and Scis., Nat. Acad. Rec. Arts and Scis., Broadcast Music, Jazz Musicians Assn., Pioneer (Grinnell Coll.). Address: Hancock Music # 1600 1880 Century Park E Ste 1600 Los Angeles CA 90067-1661

HANCOCK, JAMES BEATY, interior designer; b. Hartford, Ky. s. James Winfield Scott and Hettie Frances (Meadows) H. BA, Hardin-Simmons U., 1948, MA, 1952. Head interior design dept. Thornton's, Abilene, Tex., 1945-54; interior designer The Halle Bros. Co., Cleve., 1954-55; v.p. Olympic Products, Cleve., 1955-56; mgr., interior designer Bell Drapery Shops of Ohio, Inc., Shaker Heights, 1957-78, v.p., 1979—. Lectr. interior design; works include 6 original murals Broadway Theater, Abilene, 1940, mural Skyline Outdoor Theatre, Abilene, 1950, cover designs for Isotopics mag., 1958-60. With AUS, 1942-46. Recipient 2d place award of oil painting West Tex. Expn., 1940, honorable mention, 1940, Diploma for being an Am. vet. of WWII who liberated France, Govt. of France. Mem. Abilene Mus. Fine Arts (charter), Western Res. Hist. Soc., Cleve. Cir. of the Decorative Arts Trust (charter), Trideca Soc. Cleve Mus. Art, English Speaking Union. Home and Office: 1 Bratenahl Pl Apt 103 Cleveland OH 44108-1152 Personal E-mail: hancockjb@aol.com.

HANCOCK, JOHN WALKER, III, banker; b. Long Beach, Calif., Mar. 8, 1937; s. John Walker and Bernice H.; m. Elizabeth Hoien, June 20, 1959; children: Suzanne, Donna, Randy, David. BA in Econs, Stanford U., 1958, MBA, 1960. With Security Pacific Nat. Bank, L.A., 1960-92, v.p., 1968-77, sr. v.p., 1977-84, exec. v.p., 1984-92; pres. Bancap Investment Group, Long Beach, Calif., 1992—. Bd. dirs. Harbor Bank; chmn. Meml. Med. Ctr.; pres. Port of Long Beach. Bd. dirs. Long Beach Symphony, Meml. Hosp., Long Beach City Coll. Found. Mem. Stanford U. Alumni Assn., Calif. Club (L.A.), Va. Country Club, Balboa Bay Club, Pacific Club, Bohemian Club, Thunderbird Country Club. Republican. Home: 258 Roycroft Ave Long Beach CA 90803-1717 Office: Bancap Investment Group 192 Marina Dr Long Beach CA 90803-4613

HANCOCK, M(ARION) DONALD, political science professor; b. McAllen, Tex., Aug. 20, 1939; s. Robert Nicklas and Florence Olive (Norquest) H.; children: Erik Lorans, Kendra Lee. BA, U. Tex., 1961; postgrad., U. Bonn, Germany, 1959-60; MA, Columbia U., 1962, PhD, 1966; postgrad., U. Stockholm, 1963-64. Instr. Columbia U., spring 1965; asst. prof. polit. sci. U. Tex., Austin, 1965-69, assoc. prof., 1969-75, prof., 1975—79, dir. Center for European Studies, 1970-79, assoc. dean, Coll. Social and Behavioral Scis., 1976-79; prof. Vanderbilt U., Nashville, 1979—, dir. Title VI Nat. Resource Ctr. on Western Europe, 1992-95; dir. Center for European Studies, 1981—90; co-chmn. Coun. for European Studies, 1981-85. Vis. prof. Columbia U., 1967, U. Bielefeld, 1973, U. Mannheim, 1977, U. Regensburg, 1986-87; Washington del. representing Commn. of the European Cmty. (Team Europe); lectr. in field. Author: Sweden: The Politics of Postindustrial Change, 1972, West Germany: Politics of Democratic Corporatism, 1989; co-author: Managing Modern Capitalism, 1991, German Unification: Process and Outcomes, 1994; editor: Politics in Europe, 3d edit., 2003; co-author: Transitions to Capitalism and Democracy in Russia and Central Europe, 2000; editor, co-author: Politics in the Post-Welfare State: Repsonses to the New Individualism, 1972, co-author: Comparative Politics, 1978. Woodrow Wilson fellow, 1961-62; Dept. State Internat. Affairs fellow, summer 1962; Council Fgn. Relations internat. affairs fellow, 1972-73 Mem.: Conf. Group on German Politics (pres. 1990—92), European U. Studies Assn. (exec. com. 1999—), Coun. European Studies Soc. Advancement Scandinavian Studies, Soc. Polit Sci. Assn., Am. Polit. Sci. Assn. Democrat. Episcopalian. Office: Vanderbilt U Dept Polit Sci Nashville TN 37235 Office Phone: 615-322-6234. Business E-Mail: donald.hancock@vanderbilt.edu.

HANCOCK, RANDY A., safety engineer; s. E. E. and Ruth M. Hancock; m. Lila J. Jurado, Sept. 25, 1982; children: Bethany A., Kristen, Patricia. BA in Psychology, U. NC, Charlotte, 1982; MS, Ctrl. Mo. State U., 1985; student, Ind. State U., 2004—. Cert. Bd. Cert. Safety Profls. Safety engring. lead Jacobs-Sverdrup, Cape Canaveral Air Force Sta., Fla., 2002—04; sr. safety engr. Sci. Applications Internat. Corp., Kennedy Space Center, Fla., 2004—. Contbr. articles to profl. jours. Deacon Destiny Christian Ch., Merritt Island, Fla., 2001. Capt. USAF, 1983—87. Mem.: Am. Soc. Safety Engrs. (assoc.). Home: 5555 Fraley Ct Merritt Island FL 32953 Office: SAIC Sa-B2 Kennedy Space Center FL 32899 Personal E-mail: daddy2004@mail.com.

HANCOCK, TAPP, elementary school educator; b. Sept. 17, 1958; d. Alexander Hamilton and Tapp Latta Hancock. BA in Elem. and Spl. Edn., Converse Coll., 1980, M Elem. Edn., 1981; specialist in early childhood edn., U. SC, Spartanburg, 1985; MA in Counseling, Calif. Luth. U., 1990. Cert. tchr., counselor Calif. Elem. tchr. Spartanburg City Schs., 1981—86, Granville County Schs., Creedmoor, NC, 1986—87, Bakersfield (Calif.) City Schs., 1987—. Cons. Han-5 Math., Bakersfield, 1995—2002; presenter, spkr. in field. Mem. adv. bd.: McGraw Hill 2002 Math Textbook, 2002, adv. chmn.: Standards for Excellence in Math. and Language Arts, 1997, contbg. editor: C.M.C. Jour., 1999, inventor: math. kits, books/manipulatives Han-5, An Innovative System Teaching Mathematics, 2000. Regional coord. San Joaquiin Valley Math. Project, Bakersfield, 1996—2001; chmn. elem. math. events Bakersfield Math. Coun., 1996—2000; mem. Calif. History-Social Sci. Project, Santa Barbara, 2000—02; master tchr. CBET, Bakersfield, 2001—02. Named Outstanding Tchr. for Kern County, Bakersfield Math. Coun., 1999; recipient regional Presdl. Excellence award in math., NSF, Washington, 1997; scholar, Fulbright Found., 2000—01. Mem.: Nat. Coun. Tchg. Math., Calif. Math. Coun. Avocations: sailing, reading, travel, wine. Office: Han5 Math 8000 Kroll Way Condo # 2 Bakersfield CA 93311

HANCOCK, WILLIAM FRANK, JR., management consultant; b. Richmond, Va., Jan. 4, 1942; s. William Frank and Gladys Elizabeth (George) H.; m. Donna G. Hosmer, May 18, 1968; children: Peter James, Jeffrey William, Jennifer Beth. BBA, U. Iowa, 1964; MBA, U. Pa., 1966; postgrad., Capella U. CPA, CLU, CPCU, CMA, CDP. Exec. asst. to exec. v.p. John Hancock Mutual Life Ins. Co., Boston, 1966-69; mgmt. cons. Keane Assocs., Boston, 1969-74, regional mgr., 1974-75; v.p., gen. mgr. comml. sys. SofTech, Inc., Waltham, Mass., 1975-79; dir. internat. sales and field ops. Nixdorf Computer Co., Burlington, Mass., 1979-80; mgr. mktg. Digital Equipment Corp., 1980-84, electronic commerce mgr., 1984-97; mgmt. cons. electronic commerce Grant Thornton LLP, 1997—98; mgmt. cons., nat. electronic commerce practice Ernst & Young, LLP, 1998—2000; prin. IBM, 2000—02; mng. dir. 3 Rivers Assocs., Sherborn, Mass., 2002—. Adj. prof. acctg. and fin. Grad. Sch. Bus., Northeastern U., Boston, 1966—, sr. instr. acctg. Grad. Sch. Bus. Babson Coll., Wellesley, Mass, 1985—; assoc. dean Sch. Mgmt., Cambridge Coll., 2002—. Treas. Pilgrim Ch.; trustee Sherborn Libr.; chmn. Sherborn coun. Boy Scouts Am. With U.S. Army, 1967-72. Recipient Outstanding Teacher of Yr. Awd., Northeastern Univ., 1989. Mem. AICPA, Data Processing Mgmt., Nat. Assn. Accts., Assn. Computing Machinery, Boston C. of C., Exec. Club Boston, Wharton Alumni Club, U. Iowa Alumni Assn. Congregationalist. Home and Office: 3 Rivers Assocs 24 Dexter Dr Sherborn MA 01770-1124 Office Phone: 508-653-9939. Personal E-mail: william.hancock@comcast.net.

HANCOX, DAVID R(OBERT), audit administrator, educator; b. Albany, NY, Aug. 1, 1951; s. Robert F. and Elaine C. (Morgart) H.; m. Judith A. Gaylord, Jan. 17, 1975; children: Robert, Bradford, Ryan D. AS, Hudson Valley Community Coll., 1973; BBA, Siena Coll., 1975. Cert. internal auditor; cert. govt. fin. mgr. State auditor N.Y. State Comptr., Albany, 1974—; lectr. Albany Bus. Coll., 1982-83, Schenectady (N.Y.) Community Coll., 1988, Siena Coll., Loudonville, N.Y., 1991—, Sage Coll., Albany, 1992-97; dir. state audits N.Y. State Comptr., 1989—. Co-author: State and Local Government, Program Control and Audit: Handbook for Managers and Auditors, 1997, Small Government Finance Library: Accounting, Reporting, Auditing, 1999, Government Performance Audit in Action, 2001, 2d edit., 2004. Chair adminstrn. com., v.p. parish coun. St. James Ch., 1994-98, pres. parish coun., 1998-99; cluster leader Albany Diocese, 1995-96; bd. dirs. Homeless and Travelers Aid Soc., 1999. Mem. Assn. Govt. Accts. (pres. N.Y. Capital chpt. 1986-87, bd. dirs. 1987-89, Arlington, Va. regional v.p. 1990—, Gold award 1991, Educator of Yr. 2005), Inst. Internal Auditors (Albany chpt. bd. govs. 1988-90, 93-96, pres. 1996-97). Roman Catholic. Avocations: reading, computers, exercising. Office: N Y State Comptr 110 State St Albany NY 12236-0001 Home: 57 Maxwell St Albany NY 12208-1638 E-mail: dhancox@nycap.rr.com, dhancox@osc.state.ny.us.

HAND, ANGELA RENE, singer; b. Springfield, Mo., June 26, 1960; d. Charles Eugene and Nieta Lee (Routh) Hand. B Music Edn., S.W. Bapt. U., 1982; MusM in Vocal performance, Memphis State U., 1987; DMA in Vocal performance, U. Tex., 2000. Cert. level I Orff Schulwerk music specialist. Orff music specialist Memphis City Schs., 1988—90; tchr. music Walter Sundling Jr. H.S., Palatine, Ill., 1990—94; tchr. pvt. voice Westlake H.S., Austin, Tex., 1995—99; tchg. asst. voice U. Tex., Austin, 1995—99, asst. instr. voice, 1998—99; asst. prof. Augustana Coll., Rock Island, Ill., 1999—2005. Co. mgr. City Opera of Quad Cities, Davenport, Iowa, 2005—. Singer: (Operas) (various roles) Opera@Augustana, 1999—2004, Genisius Guild, Lincoln Park Series, 2003, Opera Theatre, 1994—99, So. Opera Theatre, 1984—89, Opera Memphis, 1986, So. Ohio Light Opera, 1990—94; soprano soloist Handel Oratorio Soc., 2001—02; soprano soloist: Tarrytown United Meth. Ch., 1996—99, Chy. of Good Shepherd, 1994—96, Buntyn Presbhn. Ch., 1984—90, various area chs., chief writer, contbr.: Pop Hits tchg. guides, 1992—96. Judge musical convs., competitions in field; mem. Rep. Nat. Com., 1985—, Bettendorf Mission, Iowa, 2000—. Scholar, Getty Found., 1998; Annie Giles Barnhart scholar, 1994. Mem.: NRA, Coll. Music Soc., Nat. Assn. Tchrs. Singing, Nat. Opera Assn., Tau Beta Sigma. So. Baptist. Avocations: target shooting, writing science fiction, gardening, riding. Office: Augustana Coll Bergendoff Fine Arts 639 38th St Rock Island IL 61201 Office Phone: 309-794-7425. Business E-Mail: muhand@augustana.edu.

HAND, ANTOINETTE MARIE, accountant; b. St. Louis, Mo., Mar. 1, 1962; d. John Anthony and Patricia Ann Garanzini; m. William David Hand II, June 16, 1989; children: Gabriella Michelle, Krystal Alishia, Avery Tygre, Casey Orion. BS in Acctg. summa cum laude, Strayer U., 1999. Fin. officer Dept. State, Washington, 1989-98, CIA, Washington, 1983—88, 1998—, budget officer, dep. CFO, 1999-2000, CFO, 2000—04, sys. acct., 2004—. Mem., troop leader Girl Scouts Am., 1998—. Mem. Phi Beta Lambda (pres. Sierra Vista Chpt. 1981-82, state v.p. Ariz., 1982). Avocations: reading, needlecraft, walking, travel. Home: 14529 William Carr Ln Centreville VA 20120

HAND, CADET HAMMOND, JR., retired marine biologist; b. Patchogue, NY, Apr. 23, 1920; s. Cadet Hammond and Myra (Wells) H.; m. Winifred Werdelin, June 6, 1942; children: Cadet Hammond III, Gary Alan. BS, U. Conn., 1946; MA, U. Calif. at Berkeley, 1948, PhD, 1951. Instr. Mills Coll., 1948-50, asst. prof., 1950-51; rsch. biologist Scripps Inst. Oceanography, 1951-53; mem. faculty U. Calif. at Berkeley, 1953—, prof. zoology, 1963-85, prof. emeritus, 1985—; dir. Bodega Marine Lab., 1961-85; Cons. NIH, 1964-66, NSF, 1964-69; mem. atomic safety and licensing bd. panel Nuc. Regulatory Commn., 1971-92, adminstrv. judge atomic safety and licensing bd. panel, 1980-92; rsch. Bodega Marine-Lab., 1992—2003; ret., 2003. NSF sr. postdoctoral fellow, 1959-60; Guggenheim fellow, 1967-68 Contbr. articles to profl. jours. Fellow Calif. Acad. Scis.; mem. No. Calif. Malacozool. Soc. (pres. 1963-87), Soc. Systematic Zoology, Ecol. Soc. Am., Ray Soc. (Gt. Britain), Am. Soc. Zoologists (chmn. div. invertebrate zoology 1977-78), Am. Soc. Limnology and Oceanography. Home: PO Box 1016 Bodega Bay CA 94923-9769

HAND, HERBERT HENSLEY, finance educator, writer, entrepreneur; b. Hamilton, Ohio, July 11, 1931; s. Herbert Lawrence and Berta Elizabeth (Hensley) H.; m. Katharine Harris Gucker, July 26, 1952; children: Stephen Harris, Herbert Gucker. BS, Ind. U., 1953; MSEE, ABT, MIT, 1955; MBA, U. Miami, 1966; PhD, Pa. State U., 1969. V.p. Hand Oil Co., 1955—65; instr. Pa. State U., 1968—69; asst. and assoc. prof. Ind. U., Bloomington, 1969—73, assoc. prof., 1973—76; disting. prof. entrepreneurship U. S.C. Coll. Bus. Adminstrn., Columbia, 1976—95. State dir. Small Bus. Devel. Ctr. S.C., 1968-69; exec. v.p. Carter-Miot Engring. Co., Columbia, S.C., 1981, also bd. dirs.; pres. Carolina Consultants, 1973-84; chmn., CEO, pres. Phronesis, Inc., 1985-92, Alternative Control Sys. Corp., 1993-99; cons. to numerous cos., 1973—. Author: (with H.P. Sims, Jr.) Managerial Decision Making in the Business Firm-A Systems Approach, 1972, The Profit Center Simulation, 1975; (with A.T. Hollingsworth) A Guide to Small Business Management, 1979, Practical Readings in Small Business, 1979; contbr. over 90 research articles and papers in field to profl. jours.; mem. editorial bd. Bus. Horizons, 1971-73, Acad. of Mgmt. Review, 1975-79; holder numerous U.S. and fgn. patents in field of biotech. Served to 1st lt. USAF, 1953-55. Recipient Western Electric award for most innovative bus. course, 1971, 23 other teaching awards; Small Bus. Inst. Regional award SBA, 1976, 80, 81, Small Bus. Inst. Nat. award, 1980; Office Naval Research grantee, 1976, 77, 78. Mem. Acad. Mgmt., So. Mgmt. Assn., Am. Inst. Decision Scis., Internat. Coun. for Small Bus., Rotary. Presbyterian. Personal E-mail: hekat@msn.com.

HAND, JOHN OLIVER, museum curator; b. N.Y.C., Aug. 17, 1941; s. John Osborn and LaBelle (Bridges) H. BA, Denison U., Granville, Ohio, 1963; MA, U. Chgo., 1967; M.F.A. (Samuel Kress Found. fellow 1969-72), Princeton U., 1971, PhD (Belgian Am. Found. fellow 1972-73), 1978. With edn. dept. Nat. Gallery Art, Washington, 1965-69, curator No. Renaissance painting, 1973—. Preceptor Princeton U., 1971 Author papers in field. Office: Nat Gallery Art Washington DC 20565-0001 Address: 2000B S Club Dr Landover MD 20785 Office Phone: 202-842-6145. Business E-Mail: j-hand@nga.org.

HAND, LLOYD N., lawyer; BA, Univ. Tex., 1952, LLB, JD, Univ. Tex., 1957. Bar: Tex. 1957, DC 1970, US Supreme Ct. Asst. to U. S. Senate Majority Leader Lyndon B. Johnson, Washington, 1957—61; U.S. Chief of Protocol, with rank of ambassador for Pres. Johnson, 1965—66; ptnr. Allbritton McGee & Hand, Washington; sr. v.p. & asst. to bd. chmn. TRW; sr. ptnr. Verner Liipfert Bernhard McPherson & Hand, Washington, 1984—2002; sr. ptnr., Energy, Federal Affairs & Legis. practices DLA Piper Rudnick Gray & Cary, Washington, 2002—. Bd. mem. & gen. counsel Congl. Econ. Leadership Inst. Mem. Chief of Naval Ops. Exec. Panel; vice chmn. Washington Roundtable, Ctr. for Strategic & Internat. Studies; mem. Exec. Council on Diplomacy; mem. bd. dir., treas. Blair House; mem. Council of Am. Ambassadors. Officer USN, 1951—55, Korean War. Mem.: ABA, DC Bar Assn., Tex. Bar Assn., Phi Alpha Delta. Office: DLA Piper Rudnick Gray Cary 1200 19th St NW Washington DC 20036-2412 Office Phone: 202-861-3434. Office Fax: 202-689-8555. Business E-Mail: lloyd.hand@dlapiper.com.

HAND, MARYANNE KELLY, artist, educator; b. Augusta, Ga., Apr. 15, 1955; d. Issac Marvin and Dorothy Whaley Kelly; children: Jill Estes Tatum, Micah Kelly. AA in Graphic Design/Visual Comm., Art Inst. Atlanta, 1974; postgrad., Ga. So. U., Ga. State U. Tchr. Episcopal Day Sch., Augusta, 1984—91; tchr. art Augusta State U., 1993—2000; pvt. tchr. sales and design Transatlantic Antiques, Augusta, 2002—; freelance artist. Exhibitions include Phipps Plz., Atlanta, The Historic Cotton Exch., Augusta Mus. History, Ga. Welcome Ctr., Augusta Mayor's Office, Barnes and Noble, Augusta, Sacred Heart Cath. Ctr., Hawg Wild and Big Iron Saloon, Snug, Vallarte Restaurant, Augusta, Shapers Hair and Nail Salon, Salon Denovo, Villa Design Trans Atlantic and Gifts, Atlanta, Cottage Collection, The Blue Door, Pastel, The Blue Door, Bailies Art Ctr., Represented in permanent collections Augusta Mus. History, coverpiece, SASS mag. Named to Nat. Archives Women Artists; recipient Hon. Mention, Manhattan Arts. Mem.: S. Ea. Pastel Soc. Avocations: interior decorating, painting, dance, woodcarving. Office: Transatlantic Antiques 3309 Washington Rd Augusta GA 30904 Office Phone: 706-339-5916. E-mail: makart@comcast.net.

HAND, PETER JAMES, neurobiologist, educator; b. Oak Park, Ill., Jan. 5, 1937; s. James Harold and Edna Mae (Watson) H.; m. Mary Minnis, Sept. 16, 1958; children: Katherine Patricia, Carol Jane, Margaret Anne, Robin Lynn, Stephen Douglas, Peter James; m. Carol Louise Corson, Oct. 23, 1976; m. Christine L. Arnold, Sept. 19, 1986. VMD, U. Pa., 1961, PhD, 1964. Mem. faculty U. Pa., Phila., 1964—, prof. anatomy, 1979-99, head dept. anatomy, 1980-87, 91-97, emeritus prof., 1999—. Mem. NIH rev. com. Regional Primate Ctrs., 1985-89; mem. nominating com. Lifu Acad. award in Chinese Medicine; adj. faculty Indian River C.C., 2003-; COO Hand Wine Cons., Inc. Contbr. articles to profl. jours.; columnist: Hometown News, 2005—. Pres. coun. USO, Cape May, NJ, 1972—73, nat. del.; wine columnist Hometown News, 2005—; mem. ch. coun. Jupiter First Ch., 2002—05; trustee Mid-Atlantic Ctr. for Arts, Cape May, NJ, 1973—74; bd. dirs. Cape May Taxpayers Assn., 1972—74, University City Hist. Soc., Phila., 1978—80; v.p. bd. dirs. Arbors Village Assn., 2002—03, chmn. environ. com., 2003—04. NIH grantee, 1970-82, 86-92, 95—2003. Mem. Am. Assn. Anatomists, Am. Assn. Vet. Anatomists, Soc. Neurosci. (pres. Phila. chpt. 1984-85), Internat. Brain Rsch. Orgn., World Assn. Vet. Anatomists, Internat. Assn. for Study of Pain, Am. Coll. Acupuncture (pres. 1997-98), Internat. Coll. Acupuncture and Electro-Therapeutics, Sigma Xi, Alpha Psi (trustee 1965-87). Republican. Office: Hand Wine Cons Inc 5290 SE Joshua Tree Ter Hobe Sound FL 33455-7891 E-mail: handpain@adelphia.net.

HAND, ROGER, physician, educator; b. Bklyn., Sept. 25, 1938; s. Morton and Angela (Belvedere) H.; m. Susan Hand; children: Christopher, Jessica. BS, NYU, 1959, MD, 1962. Intern, then resident in internal medicine NYU Med. Ctr., 1962-68; postdoctoral fellow, asst. prof. Rockefeller U., N.Y.C., 1968-73; clin. asst. prof. medicine Cornell U. Med. Coll., N.Y.C., 1970-73; asst. prof., then assoc. prof. medicine McGill U., Montreal, Que., Can., 1973-80; prof. medicine, dir. McGill Cancer Ctr., 1980-84; sr. physician Royal Victoria Hosp., Montreal, 1980-84; chmn. internal medicine Ill. Masonic Ctr., Chgo., 1984-88; prof. medicine U. Ill., Chgo., 1984—, chief sect. gen. internal medicine, 1988-95, prof. health policy and adminstrn. Sch. Pub. Health, 1995—2002. Prin. clin. coord. Ill. Found. Quality Health Care, Chgo., 1996-00; physician advisor OLR Med. Ctr., Chgo., 2000-01, ret., 2001-. Contbr. articles to profl. jours. Brig. gen. USAR, 1963-71, 85-03, ret.; diaster relief-search-and-rescue pilot auxs. USCG, USAF; vol. disaster relief programs ARC, FEMA. Decorated Air medal, Meritorious Svc. medal, Army Commendation medal, Legion of Merit; med. rsch. grantee. Fellow ACP, Royal Coll. Physicians and Surgeons, Am. Coll. Med. Quality; mem. Am. Soc. Clin. Investigation, Am. Soc. Biol. Chemists, Am. Assn. Cancer Research, Am. Soc. Clin. Oncology, Infectious Disease Soc., Can. Soc. Clin. Investigation, Cen. Soc. Clin. Rsch., Am. Cancer Soc.(bd. dirs. Ill. div.), Am. Health Quality Assn. E-mail: buckgeneral@ameritech.net.

HAND, SHIRLEY ANN, music educator, director; b. Nashua, N.H., Nov. 17, 1941; d. Malcom Armstrong (Stepfather) and Pearl Haven Taylor; m. Donald Lewis Hand, Oct. 28, 1978; children: Karen Ann Carrigan, Kimberly Pearl Pearce. BS in Edn., Lowell U., Mass., 1963; MusM, Hartt Coll. Music U. Hartford, Conn., 1966. Cert. tchr. music Conn., 1966, Fla., 1966. Music educator Oak Hill Sch. Blind, Hartford, Conn., 1965—66, Mansfield State Tng. Sch., Mansfield, 1966—75; substitute tchr. music Fla. Pub. Schools, Pinellas County, 1977—78; pvt. music educator Clearwater, 1978—; organist and choir dir. Rogate Luth. Ch., 1989—. Music dir. Suzuki Players Pinellas County, Clearwater, 1979—. Performer piano and cello Clearwater Symphony Orch., Clearwater, Fla., 1978—79; performer Tropical Strings, 1979—83; music dir. string groups Bay Area Renaissance Festival, Largo, 1983—94; music therapy The Palms of Largo, 1995—; music tutor First Luth. Sch., Clearwater, 2001—; nursing home ministries Rogate Luth. Ch., 1990—2005. Recipient Young Artist Music award, Music Tchrs. Assn. Western Mass., 1959; Music assistantship, U. Hartford, 1963. Mem.: Nat. Guild Piano Tchrs. (life; faculty mem. 1964—, adjudicator 1980—, diplomate 1964). Lutheran. Achievements include Music Education for Handicapped. Avocations: bowling, camping, music concerts, swimming. Home: 1780 Suffolk Dr Clearwater FL 33756 E-mail: playtoccata@yahoo.com.

HANDA, RUMIKO, architect, educator; d. Ichio and Tatsuko Handa; children: Maya, Ami. BArch, U. Tokyo, 1979; MArch, U. Pa., Phila., 1983, MS, 1985, PhD, 1992. Arch. Arcom Archs. & Planners, Tokyo, 1979—82; adj. asst. prof. U. Mich., Ann Arbor, 1991—92; asst. prof. Tex. Tech. U., Lubbock, 1992—96, U. Nebr., Lincoln, 1996—2000, assoc. prof., 2000—. Com. for female archs. Tokyo Soc. of Archs. & Bldg. Engrs., 1990—92; internat. fellowship panel AAUW, Washington, 1995—98. Contbr. articles to profl. jours. Recipient Nat. Educator Hon. Award, Am. Inst. Arch. Students, 2001—02; Farfel fellow, Huntington Libr., 2002. Mem.: Soc. of Archtl. Historians. Office: Univ Nebr Room 237 Arch Hall West Lincoln NE 68588 Business E-Mail: rhanda1@unl.edu.

HANDAL, KENNETH V., lawyer; b. N.Y.C., Feb. 7, 1949; AB, Georgetown U., 1970; JD, U. Chgo., 1973. Bar: N.Y. 1974, D.C. 1975. Law clk. to Hon. Robert A. Ainsworth Jr. U.S. Ct. Appeals 5th Cir., New Orleans, 1973-74; asst. U.S. atty. Criminal Divsn., Southern Dist. N.Y., 1977-82; atty. Arnold & Porter, N.Y.C., 1982—96; counsel in-house compliance & ethics Altria, 1996—2004; v.p., gen. counsel Computer Associates Internat., 2004—. Dir. Legal Aid Soc., Assn. of Bar of NY Fund, Inc. Mng. editor: U. Chgo. Law Review, 1972-73. Bd. dirs. Brooklyn Acad. of Music, Internat. League for Human Rights. Office: Computer Associates Internat One Computer Assocs Plaza Islandia NY 11749

HANDEL, DAVID JONATHAN, health facility administrator; b. NYC, Jan. 2, 1946; s. Milton M. and Ruth (Stamer) H.; m. Julia Elizabeth Noll, June 26, 1971; chldren: Daniel, Jennifer. BS, Cornell U., 1966; MBA, U. Chgo., 1968. Assoc. planning coordinator for health scis. Northwestern U., Chgo., 1970-73, adminstr. Northwestern U. Med. Clinics and Med. Assocs., 1973-76; dir. planning and implementation Mid-Ohio Health Planning Fedn., Columbus, Ohio, 1976-79; assoc. hosp. adminstr. Vanderbilt U. Hosps., Nashville, 1979-82, assoc. dir. ops., 1982-85; dir. Ind. U. Hosps., Indpls., 1985-96; exec. v.p., COO Clarian Health Ptnrs., Inc., Indpls., 1997—2004; dir. MHA program Ind. U., 2004—. V.p. United Hosp. Svcs., Indpls., 1986-88, pres., 1989-90, Bedford Reg. Med. Ctr., 1997-2004, La Porte Regional Health Sys., Inc., 1998-2004; chmn. Rehab. Hosp. Ind., 2002—; with Goshen Health Sys., 2000-2004; bd. dirs. Ruth Lilly Health Edn. Ctr., Indpls. Contbr. articles to profl. jours. Sr. asst. health svcs. officer USPHS, 1968-70. Fellow Am. Coll. Health Care Execs.; mem. Ind. Hosp. Assn. (bd. dirs. 1994-97). Office: Ind U BS4085 801 W Michigan St Indianapolis IN 46202 Business E-Mail: dhandel@iupui.edu.

HANDEL, MORTON EMANUEL, film company executive, management consultant; b. NYC, Apr. 12, 1935; s. Benjamin and Mollie (Heller) H.; m. Irma Ruby, Aug. 5, 1956; children: Mark, Gary, Karen. BA, U. Pa., 1956; postgrad., NYU, 1957-59; DHum (hon.), U. Hartford, 2002. V.p. Dale Plastic Playing Card Corp., N.Y.C., 1955-57; gen. mgr. Handel Nets & Fabrics Corp., N.Y.C., 1957-62; pres. A.M. Industries, Inc., Farmingdale, N.Y., 1962-68, Allan Marine, Inc., Deer Park, N.Y., 1969-71; chmn. bd. Marlow Yacht Corp., Deer Park, 1969-71; v.p. fin., sec.-treas. Aurora Products Corp. (subs. Nabisco Inc.), 1971-73, sr. v.p., CFO, 1973—74; v.p. fin., CFO Coleco Industries Inc., 1974—78, sr. v.p., CFO, 1978—82, exec. v.p. fin. and adminstrn., 1982-83, exec. v.p. corp. com., 1983-85, exec. v.p. corp. devel., 1985-88, chmn., dir., CEO, 1988—90; pres., dir. Morton Handel Co., Inc., Bloomfield, Conn., 1990—. Bd. dirs. Linens 'N Things, Clifton, N.J., Trump Entertainment & Resorts; pres. and dir. Ranger Industries, Inc., Bloomfield, Conn., 1997-2001; chmn. bd. dirs. Marvel Enterprises, Inc., N.Y.C., 1997— Pres. Rochdale Village Civic Assn., 1964-65; pres. bd. dirs. Hartford Symphony Orch., 1976—; bd. dirs. Jewish Children's Svc. Corp., 1976-78; corporator St. Francis Hosp., 1982—; bd. dirs. One Thousand Corp., 1983-95, Greater Hartford Arts Coun., Inc., 1987-89, Hebrew Home for the Aged, 1989—; regent U. Hartford, 1990—; vice chmn. bd. regents U. Hartford, 1992-2000; trustee, vice chmn. Hartt Sch. Music, 1991—; bd. dirs. Jewish Fedn. of Greater Hartford, 1996-2000, Hartford Dispensary Inc., 1996-2002; bd. overseers Bushnell Ctr. for Performing Arts, 2002—. Mem. Am. Mgmt. Assn., Fin. Execs. Inst., Alpha Epsilon Pi. Office: Morton Handel Co Inc One Regency Dr Bloomfield CT 06002-2404 Office Phone: 860-726-9006. Personal E-mail: morthandel@aol.com.

HANDEL, PETER H., physics professor; b. Hermannstadt, Siebenbuergen, Transylvania, Oct. 16, 1937; came to U.S., 1969; s. Peter and Anna (Broneske) H.; children: Susanne C., Christine D., Peter F. MS in Physics, U. Bucharest, Romania, 1959; PhD in Physics, U. Bucharest, 1965. Scientist Hydroetechnic Rsch. Inst., Bucharest, 1959; rsch. scientist Physics Inst. of Romanian Acad., Bucharest, 1960-66, Physics Inst. Max von Laue-Paul Langevin, Munich, Fed. Republic Germany, 1967-69; assoc. prof. physics dept. U. Mo., St. Louis, 1969-72, prof. physics, 1972—. Cons. Emerson Electric Co., St. Louis, 1975-81; sr. scientist, cons. McDonnell Douglas Rsch. Labs., St. Louis, 1982-83; 16 prestigious vis. prof. appointments, various univs. in Europe, Australia, Japan, and U.S., 1970—; mem. internat. program com. of conf. series on noise in phys. systems and head conf. series on quantum 1/f noise. Contbr. over 190 articles to profl. jours. Grantee NSF, 1971-77, 90—; rsch. grantee USAF, 1984—, USN, 1978-82, 90—, Ultra-low Phase Noise MURI, 2001—. Achievements include research in quantum 1/f noise theory; phase noise; polarization catastrophe theory of cloud electrification; identified origin of excess heat in electrolysis; patents in field. Office: U Mo Dept Physics 8001 Natural Bridge Rd Saint Louis MO 63121-4901 Office Phone: 314-516-5021. Business E-Mail: handel@umsl.edu.

HANDEL, RICHARD CRAIG, lawyer; b. Hamilton, Ohio, Aug. 11, 1945; s. Alexander F. and Marguerite (Wilks) H.; m. Katharine Jean Carter, Jan. 10, 1970. AB, U. Mich., 1967; MA, Mich. State U., 1968; JD summa cum laude, Ohio State U., 1974; LLM in Taxation, NYU, 1978. Bar: Ohio 1974, S.C. 1983, U.S. Dist. Ct. (so. dist.) Ohio 1975, U.S. Dist. Ct. S.C. 1979, U.S. Tax Ct. 1977, U.S. Ct. Appeals (4th cir.) 1979, U.S. Supreme Ct. 1979; cert. tax specialist. Assoc. Smith & Schnacke, Dayton, Ohio, 1974—77; asst. prof. U. S.C. Sch. Law, Columbia, 1978—83; ptnr. Nexsen, Pruet, Jacobs & Pollard, Columbia, 1983—87, Moore & Van Allen, Columbia, 1987—88, Nexsen Pruet Jacobs & Pollard, Columbia, 1988—89; chief tax policy and appeals S.C. Tax Commn., Columbia, 1989—95; chief coun. Policy S.C. Dept. Revenue, Columbia, 1995—2003, sr. adminstr., gen. counsel, 2003—. Adj. prof. U. S.C. Sch. Law, 1990—2001. Contbr. articles to legal jours. Bd. dirs. Friends of Richland County Pub. Libr., 1993-99. With U.S. Army, 1969-70, Vietnam. Recipient Outstanding Law Prof. award, 1980—81; Gerald L. Wallace scholar, 1977—78. Mem.: ABA (vice-chmn. com. tax procedures 1993—94, chmn. membership com. 1997—2005, sec. 2003—05, vice chmn. state and local taxes com., com. stds. tax practice, vice chair 2005—), Order of Coif., S.C. Bar Assn. Office: SC Dept Revenue PO Box 12265 301 Gervais St Columbia SC 29211 Office Phone: 803-898-5132. Personal E-mail: rickch@aol.com. Business E-Mail: handelr@sctax.org.

HANDEL, YITZCHAK S., psychologist, educator; b. Bklyn., Aug. 7, 1940; s. Sol and Pauline (Kreisel) H.; m. Noemi Lowinger, Nov. 18, 1967; children: Eliezer Tzvi, Sara Leah, Devorah Yehudit, Raphael Alexander, Ben-Tzion Yaacov. BA, Yeshiva U., 1962, MS, 1965, City Coll. N.Y., 1970; PhD, Yeshiva U., 1977. Cert. profl. psychologist, sch. psychologsit. Tchr. Talmud, bible, law Yeshiva of Hartford (Conn.), 1965-67, Yeshiva U. High Sch., N.Y.C., 1967—; assoc. prof. psychology and Jewish edn. Yeshiva U., N.Y.C., 1988—; pvt. practice psychologist N.Y.C., 1980—. Asst. dir. grad. Jewish edn. Ferkauf Grad. Sch., NYC, 1977-83; ednl. adv., cons. Yeshiv and U. Students for the Spritual Survival of Soviet Jewry, 1992; founding dir. Azrieli Grad. Sch., NYC, 1980-2003; presenter in field Author: Educational Principles of the Haggada, 1984; contbr. articles to profl. jours. Recipient Bernard Revel Meml. award Yeshiva Coll. Alumni Assn., NYC, 1990, Excellent Tchr. award Gruss Found., NYC, 1999 Mem. Am. Psychol. Assn., Assn. Orthodox Jewish Scientists. Jewish. Office: Yeshiva Univ 245 Lexington Ave New York NY 10016-4699 Business E-Mail: handel@yu.edu.

HANDELMAN, ALICE SAMUELS, public relations professional, writer; b. Bklyn., Mar. 17, 1943; d. Ned Harlan and Margaret (Isaacs) Samuels; m. Howard Talbot Handelman, Aug. 29, 1965; children: Karen, Patricia Handelman Bloom, Marjorie Lynn. BJ, U. Mo., 1965. Intern reporter Miami (Fla.) News, summer 1964; staff feature writer St. Louis Blues hockey club, 1968-77; freelance writer St. Louis, 1967—; cmty. rels. assoc. Jewish Ctr. for Aged of Greater St. Louis, Chesterfield, Mo., 1981-85, dir. cmty. rels., 1985-2000. Pub. rels. cons. Jewish Family and Children's Svc., St. Louis, 1983, 89; guest lectr. Maryville U., 1997. Author, photographer: LaSalle Street--A History of the St. Louis Wholesale Flower market, 1987; freelance writer, contbr. to St. Louis Globe-Dem., St. Louis Post-Dispatch, N.Y. Times, St. Louis Jewish Light, St. Louis Blues Goal Mag., Hockey News, Hockey World, Ladue News, Sporting News, Nat. Hockey League, Hockey Pictorial, Suburban Jour. Newspapers; writer copy for Knight's Catalogue, 1983. Instr. hockey for women Meramec C.C., St. Louis, 1976—77; adv. com. vis. prof. program JCA Assocs., 1981—83, Gerontol. Inst., St. Louis, 1981—83; pres. Weber Sch. PTA, Creve Coeur, Mo., 1982; mem. Women's Am. ORT, 1965; mem. ctrl. advancement team Pkwy. Ctrl. H.S., 1985—89; photographer Tour de Cure bicycle ride to benefit Am. Diabetes Assn., 1992, 1993; sec., bd. dirs. Gateway Elder Svcs., 1998—, pres., 1999—; chair devel. com. Mideast Area Agy. on Aging, 2001—03; mem. adult days svcs. adv. com. Jewish Cmty. Ctr., 2001—, strategic planning comm. com.; mem. Shofar Soc. Congregation Temple Israel, 2000—; mem. gala com. Reform Jewish Academy St. Louis; co-chair 50th ann. celebration Women of Achievement; pub. rels. chmn. Nat. Coun. Jewish Women, 1981—83, publicity chmn. fashion sale, 1985; life mem. Jewish Hosp. Aux., 1965—, Jewish Ctr. for Aged Aux., 1986—, Nat. Coun. Jewish Women; pres. Young Women's Coun. on Edn. of Jewish Fedn. St. Louis, 1969; mktg./pub. rels. com. Reform Jewish Acad. St. Louis, 2000—01, Jewish Family and Children's Svc., 2000; mem. pub. rels. com. Temple Israel, 2000, 2001; bd. dirs. Am. Jewish Com., 2001—03; bd. dirs. women's divsn. Jewish Fedn. St. Louis; bd. dirs. Mideast Area Agy. on Aging, 1997—2003; strategic planning comms. com. Jewish Cmty. Ctr., 2004. Recipient William Randolph Hearst award Hearst Found., Columbia, Mo., 1965, United Way Graphic Design award, 1986, United Way Photography award, 1987, 89, 2d place award Guide to Jewish Life in St. Louis photo contest, 1989, 2d place award Jewish Hosp. St. Louis Generations of Women photo contest, 1989, Star Communicator comm. program award United Way Greater St. Louis, 1990, Bronze Photography award, 1995, 15 Yr. Svc. award Jewish Ctr. for Aged, 1997, Fred Goldstein Communal Svc. award Jewish Fedn. St. Louis, 1998; named St. Louis Woman of Achievement, 2002, co-chair 50th Anniversary com., bd. dirs., 2004—; Besse Marks Meml. scholar, 1964-65. Mem. Nat. Fedn. Press Women (1st place award comm. contest, 3d place photo feature 1989, 3d place award advt. photography 1993, hon. mention advt. photo, 2d place mktg. new svc. award, 2d place mag. advt., 1996, 3d place direct mail mktg. fundraising lit., 2d place direct mail advt.-fund raising Ann. NFPW Comm. Contest 1996, 3d place Color mag. advt. 1996, 1st place feature article 2003, St. Louis chpt. Quest award for disting. achievement in comm. 2000, 1st place award for personality profile 2002), Jewish Ctr. for Aged Aux., Fellows of Jewish Hosp., Mo. Press Women (1st place corp. newsletter category state feature writing comm. contest 1988, 93, 1st place advt. photography, 2d place feature article, 3 1st place awards 1994, 1st place not for profit newsletter 1994, 5 1st place comm. awards 1995, 2d pl. feature writing, 1st place newsletter award Mo. Assn. of Homes for the Aging 1994, planning com. Fair St. Louis Srs. Day 1995-98, planning com. Srs. Day VP Fair 1994), Mo. Assn. Homes for the Aging (publicity com., Outstanding 1st Place Newsletter award), Mo. Press Women (pub. chmn. 1994, 2000—), Women in Comm. (Ruth Philpott Collins award 1984, Best in the Midwest 2d place feature writing 1992), Press Club Met. St. Louis (bd. dirs. 2002, 1st v.p. 2003—), Westwood Country Club. Jewish. Home: 12 Terry Hill Ln Saint Louis MO 63131-2422 Personal E-mail: alicehandel@charter.net.

HANDELMAN, WALTER JOSEPH, lawyer; b. New Rochelle, N.Y., Sept. 8, 1931; s. Edward and Blanche Edith (Berman) Handelman; m. Judith Helen Ashe, Oct. 12, 1958; children: David, Daniel, Matthew. AB magna cum laude, Harvard U., 1953, LLB, 1958. Bar: N.Y. 1959, U.S. Dist. Ct. (so dist.) N.Y. 1962, U.S. Dist. Ct. (ea. dist.) N.Y. 1962. Assoc. Edward Handelman, N.Y.C., 1958—71; prin. Walter J. Handelman, N.Y.C., 1971—84, White Plains, NY, 1985—. Mem. bd. archtl. rev. Village of Scarsdale, NY, 1965—68; pres. East Scarsdale Assn., 1969—71; mayor Village of Scarsdale, 1993—95, mem. bd. appeals, 1980—87, mem. bd. ethics, 1988—90, 2005—; trustee Scarsdale Pub. Libr., 1974—77, Preservation League N.Y. State, 1986—92, Jay Heritage Ctr., 1989—, Westchester Reform Temple, 1995—2001, Ptnrs. for Sacred Places, 1993—, Scarsdale Found., 1996—, pres., 2003—05; mem. coun. Nat. Trust for Historic Preservation, 1986—. LT. USNR, 1953—55. Mem.: Westchester County Bar Assn., N.Y. County Lawyers Assn., Town Club (pres. 0198—1979). Republican. Jewish. Home: 260 Mamaroneck Rd Scarsdale NY 10583-7240 Office: 1 N Broadway White Plains NY 10601-2310 Office Phone: 914-428-9305. Business E-Mail: handelaw@hotmail.com.

HANDELMAN, WILLIAM ALAN, physician; b. Bronx, N.Y., Feb. 15, 1948; s. Herbert and Yetta (Aniess) H.; m. Leslie Ann Scott, May 17, 1981; children: Scott Alexander, Benjamin Isaac, Sarah Kim. AB, Columbia Coll., 1969; MD, SUNY, Bklyn., 1973. Diplomate Am. Bd. Internal Medicine, Am. Bd. Nephrology, Am. Bd. Med. Examiners. Resident Bronx (N.Y.) Mcpl. Hosp. Ctr., 1973-76; fellowship in nephrology U. Colo. Med. Ctr., Denver, 1976-79, asst. prof. med., 1979-80; pvt. practice Torrington, Conn., 1980—. Co-dir. dialysis unit Charlotte Hungerford Hosp., Torrington, 1981—, chmn. dept. medicine, 1985-95; pres. med. staff Charlotte Hungerford Hosp., 2002—; clin. asst. prof. medicine U. Conn. Med. Ctr., Farmington, 1982—; med. adv. bd. Qualadigm Co-author: (book chpts.) Antimicrobial Therapy, 1980, Clinical Pharmacology and Therapeutics In Nursing, 1979, Textbook of Infectious Disease, 1982; editorial bd. Conn. Medicine Jour., New Haven, 1986—. Recipient advanced attainment in internal medicine, Am. Bd. Internal Medicine, Phila., 1988. Mem. ACP, Litchfield County Med. Soc. (exec. com. 1980—, pres. 1994-96), Conn. Med. Soc., Ind. Practice Assn. (bd. dirs. 1988—), Am. Soc. Internal Medicine, Renal Physicians Assn. Ind. Jewish. Avocations: skiing, tennis, stamp collecting/philately. Home: 89 East St Morris CT 06763-1802 Office: 538 Litchfield St Ste 201 Torrington CT 06790-6669

HANDELSMAN, JO, plant pathologist, educator; BS in agronomy, Cornell Univ., Ithaca, NY; PhD in molecular biology, U. Wis.-Madison. Asst. prof. to prof. U. Wis.-Madison, 1985—, dir. Inst. Pest & Pathogen Mgmt., 1997—99, Clark Lectr. Soil Biology, 2002—. Co-author: Biology Brought to Life, 1997. Grantee professorship, Howard Hughes Med. Inst., 2002—. Achievements include establishing Women in Sci. & Engring. Leadership Inst. Office: Dept Plant Pathology U Wisconsin-Madison 1630 Linden Dr Madison WI 53706 Office Phone: 608-263-8783. Office Fax: 608-265-5289.

HANDELSMAN, LAWRENCE MARC, lawyer; b. N.Y.C., Jan. 17, 1945; s. David and Ruth (Litner) H.; m. Sara Pruzan, June 10, 1967; children: Sharon, Carolyn. BBA, CCNY, 1965; JD, NYU, 1968. Bar: N.Y. 1968, U.S. Ct. Mil. Appeals 1969, U.S. Dist. Ct. (so. and ea. dists.) N.Y. 1973, U.S. Ct. Appeals (2d cir.) 1973, Fla. 1978. Assoc. Stroock & Stroock & Lavan, N.Y.C., 1973-78, ptnr., 1979—. Served to capt. JAGC U.S. Army, 1969—73. Mem. ABA (bus. bankruptcy com. 1969—), Assn. of Bar of City of N.Y. (bankruptcy com. 1974-77, 1985—). Home: 22 Scarsdale Farm Rd Scarsdale NY 10583-1919 Office: Stroock & Stroock & Lavan 180 Maiden Ln Fl 36 New York NY 10038-4937 Office Phone: 212-806-5426. E-mail: lhandelsman@stroock.com.

HANDELSMAN, YEHUDA, endocrinologist, preventive medicine physician; b. Tel Aviv, Aug. 22, 1947; came to U.S., 1969; s. Jacob and Zahava (Lewin) H.; m. Nava Dina Pedazur, Feb. 22, 1986; children: Tomer Lee, Roy Gil. AA with honors, San Joaquin Delta Coll., Stockton, Calif., 1973; BA summa cum laude, U. of the Pacific, Stockton, Calif., 1975; MD, Tel Aviv U., 1984; postdoctoral fellow, U. So. Calif., 1988-89. Diplomate Am. Bd. Internal Medicine. Intern Beekman Downtown Hosp., N.Y.C., 1985-86, resident in internal medicine, 1986-88; clin. fellow in diabetes and endocrinology L.A. County-U. So. Calif. Med. Ctr., L.A., 1988-89; attending physician Midway Hosp., L.A., 1990-93, Granada Hills (Calif.) Cmty. Hosp., 1991—, Encino-Tarzana (Calif.) Med. Ctr., 1991—, head sect. endocrinology, dir. med. edn. Diabetes Care Ctr.; med. dir. The Metabolic Inst. of Am., Tarzana, 2001—. Cons., bd. dirs. Dynamic Home Care, L.A., Las Vegas, 1991—; cons. Yad B'yad-Human Saving Fund, L.A., 1991—; sr. sci. cons. Metabolic Endocrine Edn. Found., 2002—; clin. instr. medicine U. So. Calif. Med. Sch., 1988-90; dir. endocrine quar. conf. Encino-Tarzana Med. Ctr., dir. monthly diabetes edn. seminars, 1995—, head of sect. 1998—; mem. diabetes edn. faculty Bristol Myers Squibb, 1997—; mem. spkrs. bur. Parke-Davis, 1997—; co-chmn. Internat. Com. for Insulin Resistance, 2003, clair program dir. World Congress on Insulin Resistance, pres. Calif. AACE, 2004, trustee Am. Coll. Endocrinologist, 2004. Med. columnist Israel Shelanu, 1992-94, L.A. News, 1989-91, L.A. Health News, 2001-03. Bd. dirs. Diabetes Care Ctr. Encino-Tarzana Hosp., 1994—; dir. Israeli Spl. Olympic Games, 1968-82. Fellow ACP, Am. Coll. Endocrinology (co-chmn. nat. task force for insulin resistance 2001-02); mem. AMA (Physician Recognition award 1988, 95, 98), Am. Assn. Clin. Endocrinologists (bd. dirs. 2002—), Calif. Med. Assn. (Physician Recognition award 1995, 98), N.Am. Menopause Soc., Nat. Osteoporosis Found., Am. Diabetes Assn., Am. Israeli Med. Soc., L.A. County Med. Assn., Calif. Med. House Staff Assn., Am. Med. Student Assn., Coun. Israel Cmty. (pres.), Phi Kappa Phi, Theta Alpha Phi, Alpha Gamma Sigma, Delta Psi Omega. Avocations: talk show host, theater, basketball, politics, music. Office: 18372 Clark St #212 Tarzana CA 91356-2804 Office Phone: 818-708-9944. Business E-Mail: yhadelsman@pol.net.

HANDFORD, H. ALLEN, retired psychiatrist, educator; b. Des Moines, July 1, 1930; s. Harvey Eugene and Lenore (Allen) H.; m. Sandra Lee Betz, Sept. 3, 1955 (div.); children: Lee Allen, Christiana Lenore, Jennifer Miriam, Alice Faith; m. Laura Jane Diller, May 2, 1970 (div). AB, Harvard U., 1953; MD, State U. Iowa, 1957. Intern Broadlawns, Des Moines, 1957-58; fellow in psychiatry Pa. Hosp. Inst., 1958-60; fellow child psychiatry St. Christopher's Hosp., Phila., 1960-62; pvt. practice Villanova, Pa., 1962—78; dir. rsch. unit autistic children Ea. State Sch. and Hosp., Phila., 1962-73; dir. children's unit Haverford (Pa.) State Hosp., 1973-74; dir. children and youth programs mental Pa. Dept. Pub. Welfare, 1976-79; clin. asst. prof. psychiatry and human behavior Jefferson Med. Coll., Phila., 1974-78; assoc. prof. psychiatry Coll. Medicine, Pa. State U., Hershey, 1978—2000, also co-founder, past dir. divsn. child psychiatry residency tng.; ret., 2000. Dir. psychiatry/psychology Univ. Hosp. Rehab. Ctr., 1979-84; dir. psychosocial program Hemophilia Ctr. Cen. Pa., 1979-96; past mem. mental health com. Nat. Hemophilia Found. Contbr. articles to med. jours. Bd. dirs. Dauphin County Mental Health/Mental Retardation. Mem. AMA, Am. Psychiat. Assn., Am. Acad. Child and Adolescent Psychiatry, Pa. Med. Soc., Pa. Psychiat. Soc., Ctrl. Pa. Regional Coun. Child Psychiatry (founder), Coll. Physicians Phila. Rsch. on childhood autism, psychosocial aspects of hemophilia, childhood depression, child and parent reaction to Three Mile Island nuclear accident, sleep disorders of childhood, eating disorders of childhood. E-mail: hhandford@aol.com.

HANDFORTH, MARK, artist; b. Hong Kong, China, 1969; One-man shows include, Mus. Contemporary Art, North Miami, 1996, Gavin Brown's Enterprise, NY, 2002, Galleria Franco Noero, Italy, 2002, Lamppost, Pub. Art Fund, NY, 2003, exhibited in group shows, Gavin Brown Enterprise, 1998, Mus. Contemporary Art, North Miami, 1999, 2000, Johanniterbrucke, Beasel, 2001, Charlottenborg Exhbn. Hall, Copenhagen, 2002, It Happened Tomorrow, La Biennale d'art contemporain de Lyon, 2003, Mark Handforth, Modern Inst., Glasglow, 2004, Its All An Illusion. A Sculpture Project, Migros Mus. fur Gegenwartskunst, Zurich, 2004, Whitney Biennial, Whitney Mus. Am. Art, 2004. Mailing: c/o Gavin Browns Enterprise 436 West 15th St New York NY 10011*

HANDLEMAN, AARON L., lawyer; b. Bridgeport, Conn., Mar. 31, 1946; s. Howard W. and Beatrice (Kaplan) H.; m. Sandra R. Landow, Aug. 31, 1969; children: Michelle, Jessica. BA, Marietta Coll., 1968; JD, George Washington U., 1971. Bar: D.C. 1971, U.S. Dist. Ct. D.C. 1971, Md. 1972, U.S. Supreme Ct. 1978. Ptnr. Danzansky, Dickey, Tydings et al, Washington, 1971-81, Finley, Kumble, Wagner, Heine, Underberg, Manley & Casey, Washington, 1981-87, Laxalt, Washington, Perito & Dubuc, 1988-90, Eccleston & Wolf, Washington, 1990—. Gen. counsel, bd. dirs. Cultural Alliance Greater Washington, 1981-89; trustee Marietta Coll., Ohio, 1985-90, 92—. Named Outstanding Young Alumni Marietta Coll., 1981. Mem. Marietta Coll. Alumni Assn. (pres. 1990-92). Democrat. Jewish. Home: 11713 Le Havre Dr Potomac MD 20854-3175 Office: Eccleston & Wolf 2001 S St NW Washington DC 20009

HANDLER, ARTHUR M., lawyer; b. N.Y.C., Feb. 16, 1937; BS, Queens Coll., 1957; LLB, Columbia U., 1960. Bar: N.Y. 1960, U.S. Dist. Ct. (ea. dist.) N.Y. 1960, U.S. Dist. Ct. (so. dist.) N.Y. 1963, U.S. Tax Ct. 1971, U.S. Ct. Appeals (2d cir.) 1971, U.S. Supreme Ct. 1965. Staff counsel SEC, Washington, 1960-61; law clk. to Judge Richard H. Levet, U.S. Dist. Ct. for So. Dist.N.Y., N.Y.C., 1961-62; asst. U.S. atty. So. Dist. N.Y., N.Y.C., 1962-65; assoc. Proskauer, Rose, Goetz & Mendelsohn, N.Y.C., 1965-67, Golenbock and Barell, N.Y.C., 1967-70, ptnr., 1970-89, Whitman & Ransom, N.Y.C., 1990-93, Burns Handler & Burns, N.Y.C., 1993-99, Handler & Goodman, N.Y.C., 1999—. Arbitrator NASD and Am. Stock Exchange, N.Y.C, 1986—. Vol. atty. Pres.'s Com. for Civil Rights under Law, Jackson, Miss., 1966. Mem. ABA, N.Y. State Bar Assn., Bar Assn. of City of N.Y., Fed. Bar Council, Am. Arbitration Assn. (arbitrator 1969—). Clubs: University (N.Y.C.); Lords Valley Country (Hawley, Pa.) (bd. govs. 1977-80). Avocations: golf, skiing, theater, travel. Office: Handler & Goodman LLP 805 3d Ave New York NY 10022 Office Phone: 646-282-1900. Business E-Mail: amhandler@handlergoodman.com.

HANDLER, CAROLE ENID, lawyer, city planner; b. N.Y.C., Dec. 23, 1945; d. Milton and Marion Winter (Kahn) Handler; m. Peter U. Schoenbach, May 30, 1965 (div. Sept. 1979); children: Alisa, Ilana. AB, Radcliffe Coll., 1957; MS, U. Pa., 1963, JD, 1975. Bar: Pa. 1975; Calif. 1987; U.S. Dist Ct. Ea. Pa. 1976, N.J. 1979, Ctrl. Calif. 1987, So. Calif. 1990, So. N.Y. 1990, No. Calif. 1991, Ea. Calif. 1993, Mid. & So. Fla. 1994; U.S. Ct. Appeals 3d cir. 1976, 9th cir. 1988, 2d cir. 1989, 11th cir. 1992; Pa. Supreme Ct.; U.S. Supreme Ct. Planner Boston Redevel. Authority, 1959-61; head gen. plans sect. Phila. City Planning Commn., 1963-66; ednl. facilities planning cons. Phila. Sch. Dist., 1966-67, coordinator and dir. policy planning, 1967-69; instr. U. Sao Paulo, Rio de Janeiro, 1970-71, Cath. U., Rio de Janeiro, 1970-71; law clk. presiding judge Pa. Superior Ct., Phila., 1975-76; assoc. Goodman & Ewing, Phila., 1976-78, Schnader, Harrison, Segal & Lewis, Phila., 1978—; sr. v.p., gen. counsel MGM/UA Distbn. Co., Los Angeles, 1985-87; ptnr. Le Boeuf, Lamb, Leiby & MacRae, L.A., 1987-89, Proskauer Rose Goetz & Mendelsohn, L.A., Alschuler Grossman Pines, L.A., Kaye Scholer Fierman Hays & Handler, L.A., 1997—2000, O'Donnell & Shaeffer, L.A., 2000—04, Thelen Reid & Priest, L.A., 2004—. Adj. prof. Univ. So. Calif. Bd. dirs. St. Peter's Sch., Society Hill Synagogue, L.A. Chamber Orch., 1990—, Public Counsel 1999-; exec. bd. Am. Jewish Congress 2004-; mem Bet Tzedek Legal Svcs. Named one of Top 50 Women Litigators in Calif., Daily Journal Extra, 2002—04. Mem. Phila. Vol. Lawyers for the Arts (v.p.), ABA, Fed. Bar Assn., Pa. Bar Assn., N.Y. Bar Assn., Beverly Hills Bar Assn., L.A. County Bar Assn. (chair antitrust sect. 1992-93), Assn. Bus. Trial Lawyers, Copyright Soc., Internat. Monitor Inst., Calif. Women's Law Ctr. Jewish. Office: Thelen Reid & Priest LLP Suite 2900 333 S Hope St Los Angeles CA 90071-3048 Business E-Mail: chandler@thelenreid.com.

HANDLER, DANIEL (LEMONY SNICKET), writer; b. San Francisco, Feb. 28, 1970; s. Louis and Sandra Handler; m. Lisa Brown, 1998; 1 child. BA in English and Am. Studies, Wesleyan U., 1992. Author: The Basic Eight, 1999, Watch Your Mouth, 2000; author: (under pen name Lemony Snicket) The Bad Beginning, 1999, The Reptile Room, 1999, The Wide Window, 2000, The Miserable Mill, 2000, The Austere Academy, 2000, The Ersatz Elevator, 2001, The Vile Village, 2001, The Hostile Hospital, 2001, The Carnivorous Carnival, 2002, The Slippery Slope, 2003, The Grim Grotto, 2004, Lemony Snicket: The Unauthorized Biography, 2002; writer (films) Kill the Poor, 2003, Lemony Snicket's A Series of Unfortunate Events, 2004, actor, writer Rick, 2003. Recipient prize, Acad. Am. Poets, 1990; Olin fellow, 1992. Office: c/o HarperCollins Childrens Books 1350 Avenue of the Americas New York NY 10019*

HANDLER, ENID IRENE, health care administrator, consultant; b. N.Y.C., Oct. 17, 1932; d. Solomon and Fran S. (Bernstein) Ostrov; m. Murry Raymond Handler, Nov. 22, 1952; children: Lowell S., Lillian Handler Koch, Evan Elliott. BS, Queens Coll., 1968; MS in Adminstrv. Medicine, Columbia U., 1973. Adminstrv. dir. Phelps Mental Health Ctr., North Tarrytown, N.Y., 1973-85; cons. to health and human service agencies, 1986—. Bd. dirs. Orange County (N.C.) AIDS Svc. Agy., 1992-94, Inst. for Parapsychology; presenter to profl. orgns. Contbr. articles and book revs. to profl. jours. Mem. adv. bd. Marymount Coll., North Tarrytown, N.Y., 1983, Iona Coll., New Rochelle, N.Y., 1983; mem. adv. bd.; numerous bds. dir. in N.Y. and N.C.; pres. Westchester Assn. Vol. Agys., 1981-82; mem. Westchester County Community Svcs. Bd., 1980-86. NIH fellow Columbia U., N.Y.C., 1971-72. Fellow Am. Orthopsychiat. Assn.; mem. Columbia U. Alumni Assn., N.C. Soc. for Ethical Culture (bd. dirs.). Avocations: music, travel. Home and Office: Enid Handler Cons 433 Fearrington Post Pittsboro NC 27312-8519

HANDLER, HAROLD ROBERT, lawyer; b. Jersey City, Aug. 24, 1935; s. Morris Sidney and Fan (Krieger) Handler; m. Lynne Tishman Handler; children from previous marriage: Maren, Jeremy, Jolyon. BS, Lehigh U., 1957; LLM, Columbia U., 1961. Bar: N.Y. 1961, U.S. Tax Ct. 1963, U.S. Ct.

Appeals (2d cir.) 1980. Atty., advisor U.S. Tax Ct., Washington, 1961-63; assoc. Simpson Thacher & Bartlett, N.Y.C., 1963-69, ptnr., 1970-97, of counsel, 1998—. Adj. assoc. prof. law NYU, 1978-80. Chmn. fin. com., citizens adv. com. Met. Transp. Authority, N.Y.C., 1975—79; trustee Citizens Budget Commn.; pres., chmn. exec. com. Jewish Cmty. Ctr. in Manhattan, N.Y.C., 1992—2001; trustee Jewish Communal Fund, 1997—, pres., 2005—. Fellow Am. Coll. Tax Counsel; mem. ABA, N.Y. State Bar Assn. (chmn. subcom. tax sect. 1979-83, mem. exec. com. tax sect. 1990—, officer 1996-2000, chair 1999-20000), Assn. of Bar of City of N.Y. (chmn. tax com. 1983-86, mem. tax coun. 1990-98), Am. Law Inst., Inst. Fed. Taxation (panelist), Inst. Securities Regulation (panelist).

HANDLER, JEROME SIDNEY, anthropology educator; b. N.Y.C., Sept. 3, 1933; s. Sam and Sara (Wieder) H.; children: Joshua Martin, Lisa Frances. BA, UCLA, 1956, MA, 1959; PhD, Brandeis U., 1965. From asst. prof. to prof. anthropology So. Ill. U., Carbondale, 1964-93, prof. Black Am. studies, 1993-95, prof. emeritus, 1995—. Olive B. O'Connor vis. prof. Am. instns. Colgate U., Hamilton, N.Y., 1971-72; hon. rsch. asst. Univ. Coll., London, 1966-67; staff archaeologist New World Archaeol. Found., Chiapas, Mex., 1957; cons. AID, fall, 1964, Peace Corps, summer 1969; cons. Libr. of Congress, 1998, 99, 2000, 01, panelist NEH, 1977-79, 82, NSF, 2004; mem. adv. com. African Burial Ground, N.Y.C., GSA, 1991-93. Author: A Guide to Source Materials for the Study of Barbados History, 1627-1834, 1971, The Unappropriated People: Freedmen in the Slave Society of Barbados, 1974, Supplement to A Guide to Source Materials for the Study of Barbados History, 1991; co-author: Plantation Slavery in Barbados: An Archaeological and Historical Investigation, 1978, Searching for a Slave Cemetery in Barbados: A Bioarcheological and Ethnohistorical Investigation, 1989 Vis. rsch. fellow U. W.I., Jamaica, 1969-70, Barbados, 1983; rsch. assoc. Rsch. Inst. for Study of Man, N.Y.C., 1978-79; vis. scholar Ctr. for Afro-Am. Studies, UCLA, 1980, dept. Afro-Am. Studies, Harvard U., summer 1992; Rsch. grantee NSF, 1966-67, 71-73, Wenner-Gren Found. Anthrop. Rsch., 1971-72, 87, Rsch. Inst. Study Man, 1962, 70, NIH, 1965, Am. Philos. Soc., 1968, Nat. Geographic Soc., 1987, NEH Inst. for Coll. Tchrs., 1997-98; NEH fellow, 1969-70, 75-76, 79; Travel grant Am. Coun. Learned Socs., 1977, grantee Social Sci. Rsch. Coun. and Am. Coun. Learned Socs. Joint Com. on Latin Am. Studies, 1983; Nat. Humanities Ctr. fellow, 1982-83, John Carter Brown Libr. fellow, 1985, 88, 2002, DuBois Inst. Afro-Am. Rsch. fellow Harvard, 1989-90; fellow Va. Found. Humanities, 1995-99, sr. fellow, 2002; Va. Found. sr. fellow, 2002—; fellow Libr. Co. Phila., 2002; Sch. Am. Rsch. fellow, Santa Fe, summer 2004. Fellow Am. Anthrop. Assn. (rep. to Am. Coun. Learned Socs. 1985-90); mem. Caribbean Studies Assn. (past mem. exec. council) Home: 120 Blithe Ct Charlottesville VA 22901 Office: Va Found Humanities 145 Ednam Dr Charlottesville VA 22903-4629 Office Phone: 434-924-3296.

HANDLER, JOEL F., law educator; b. 1932; AB, Princeton U., 1954; JD, Harvard U., 1957. Asst. prof. Vanderbilt U., 1961-62, U. Ill., 1962-64; prof. U. Wis., 1965-80, George A. Wiley prof., 1980-82; vilas rsch. prof., 1982-85; vis. prof. UCLA, 1984-85, prof., 1985—. Vis. prof. Stanford, 1969-70. Fellow John Simon Guggenheim, 1974-75, German Marshall Fund, 1978. Mem. Law and Soc. Assn., Nat. Res. Coun. Status of Black Am; fellow, Am. Acad. of Arts and Sci. Office: UCLA Law Sch 405 Hilgard Ave Los Angeles CA 90095-9000*

HANDLEY, LEON HUNTER, lawyer; b. Lakeland, Fla., Sept. 9, 1927; s. Driskle Hubert and Mamie (Denmark) H.; m. Mary Virginia Wolfe, May 2, 1953; children: Leon Hunter, Mary Ellen, Laura Catherine, Leann Virginia. BSBA with honors, U. Fla., 1949, JD, 1951. Bar: Fla. 1951, U.S. Dist. Ct. (so. dist.) Fla. 1952, U.S. Dist. Ct. (mid. dist.) Fla. 1962, U.S. Supreme Ct. 1956, U.S. Ct. Appeals (5th cir.) 1960, U.S. Ct. Appeals (11th cir.) 1981. Pres. Gurney & Handley, Orlando, Fla., 1951—; ptnr. Rumberger, Kirk & Caldwell, P.A., Orlando, 2005—. Bd. dirs. Orlando/Tampa Cracker Groves, Inc., Orlando, 1964—; v.p., bd. dirs. So. Indsl. Savs. Bank, Orlando, Claude H. Wolfe, Inc., Orlando, 1969—; pres., chmn. bd. dirs. Mine & Mill Supply Co., Lakeland, 1966—; gen. counsel, life dir., past pres. Cen. Fla. Fair; chmn. bd. trustees Sta. WMFE-TV. Pres. Chesley Magruder Charitable Trust; elder Presbyn. Ch.; trustee Lake Highland Prep. Sch., Orlando. Warrant officer U.S. Maritime Svc., 1945-46, ETO; sgt. U.S. Army, 1946-48, Korea; capt. USAFR, 1949-59. Named one of Best Lawyers in Am.; named to U. Fla. Hall of Fame. Fellow Am. Coll. Trial Lawyers; mem. ABA, Am. Bd. Trial Advocates (Fla. Trial Lawyer of Yr. 1966, advocate), Orange County Bar Assn. (past pres.), Fla. Bar Assn. (past pres. sta. jr. bar sect., bd. govs. 1959-60), Fedn. Ins. and Corp. Counsel, Internat. Assn. Def. Counsel, Assn. Def. Trial Attys., Trial Attys. Am., Am. Judicature Soc., Pres.'s Coun. (founder U. Fla. chpt.), Citrus Club, Orlando Country Club, Univ. Club, Masons (grand orator Fla. 1982, 86), K.T., Shriners, Scottish Rite (33d degree, insp. gen. hon. 1979), Rotary (pres. Orlando chpt. 1984, Paul Harris fellow), Travelers' Century Club, Fla. Blue Key (pres. 1951), Phi Delta Phi, Alpha Tau Omega (pres. U. of Fla. chpt. 1951), Phi Kappa Phi, Alpha Kappa Psi, Beta Gamma Sigma. Republican. Avocations: jogging, handball. Home: 1800 Turnberry Ter Orlando FL 32804-6015 Office: Rumberger Kirk & Caldwell PA PO Box 1873 Orlando FL 32801 Office Phone: 407-872-7300. Office Fax: 407-841-2133.

HANDLEY, ROBERT, lawyer; b. Chgo., 1952; married; 4 children. BA, U. Ill., 1975; JD, No. Ill. U., 1978. Bar: Ill. 1979. Ptnr. Moroni & Handley, Carol Stream, Ill. Adj. prof. Aurora U., 1979-81; mem. inquiry panel and hearing bd. Atty. Registration and Disciplinary Commn. of Supreme Ct. of Ill., 1986-94. Pres. Pre du Chevaux Homeowners Assn., 1989-96; treas. Wayne Cmty. Assn., 1992—; mem. Village of Wayne Plan Commn., 1994—, chair, 1996—; mem. Village of Wayne Zoning Bd. Appeals, 1994, Village of Roselle Zoning Bd. Appeals, 1988-90; mem. St. Patrick Sch. Edn. Commn., 1998—. Mem. Ill. State Bar Assn. (newsletter editor tort law sect. coun. 1995—, Assembly rep. 1983-89, 92-94, chair civil practice and procedure sect. coun. 1993, ins. standing com. 1980-86, pub. rels. com. 1986-90, chair ARDC liaison com. 1998—, com. on membership and bar activities 1994—, seminar spkr./panelist 1986, 89, 92, 94, contbr. trial briefs), Ill. Trial Lawyers Assn. (pub. rels. com. 1984, chair 1986, young lawyers com. 1984, legis. com. 1986-89) Office: Moroni & Handley 373 S Schmale Rd Ste 203 Carol Stream IL 60188-2773

HANDLEY, SIOBHAN A., lawyer; BA cum laude, Coll. of the Holy Cross, 1990; JD, NYU Sch. Law, 1994. Bar: NY, US Dist. Ct., NY (Ea. & So. Dist.). Assoc. Orrick, Herrington & Sutcliffe LLP, NYC, ptnr., product liability litigation, 2003—. Mem.: NY State Bar Assn. Office: Orrick, Herrington & Sutcliffe LLP 666 Fifth Ave New York NY 10103-0001 Office Phone: 212-506-5000. Office Fax: 212-506-5151. Business E-Mail: shandley@orrick.com.

HANDLIN, DANITA L., lawyer; b. Ft. Ord, Calif., Oct. 25, 1963; d. Harry G. Jones Jr. and Joanne M. Jones; m. Dale L. Handlin Jr., May 11, 1997; 1 child, Alexandra Dayle. BBA, U. Houston, 1991, JD, 1998. Bar: Tex. 1999. Assoc. Allison Jones & Assocs., Houston, 1999—2000; atty. pvt. practice, 2000—. Mem.: ABA (mem. family sect.), Coll. of State Bar Tex., Houston Bar Assn. (mem. family sect.). Avocations: travel, scuba diving, reading. Office: 11511 Katy Fwy Ste 540 Houston TX 77079 Office Phone: 281-752-8150. Fax: 281-752-8160. E-mail: dlhandlin@hotmail.com.

HANDS, ERIC WILLIAM, civil engineer, researcher; b. Oakland, Calif., Sept. 27, 1943; s. Richard Ford Hands and Esther Mae (Larson) Hazelet; m. Monica Louise Ulery, 1968 (div. 1973); 1 child, Lars Michael Foxen; m. Sherrill Ann Gardner, 1977 (div. 1985); 1 child, Lief Forrest. Student, U. Calif., Davis, 1975-80, U. Wash., DC, 1981-82, 84, Griffin Bus. Coll., 1983; BS, Regents Coll., SUNY (now Excelsior Coll.), Albany, 1984; student, West Coast U., 1988. Engr.-in-tng., Calif., 1985, EPA universal type, Rule 608, 2001; lic. med. provider 2004; cert. advanced marine firefighter 2002, lic. Mcht. Marine officer, 2004. Engring. technician, software developer Naval Undersea Warfare Engring. Sta., Keyport, Wash., 1980-81; engr., carpenter, marine electrician, mariner, sales profl. various orgns., 1984—; real estate/ins. sales staff Channel Islands Real Estate/Met. Ins., Port Hueneme, Camarillo, Calif., 1985; civil engr. Martin, Northart & Spencer, Santa Barbara, Calif., 1985-86, Dept. Pub. Works, County of Santa Barbara, Santa Barbara, Calif., 1986-87; owner, tech. cons. Winters Soldiers Cons., Seattle, 2001—; vendor Eagle-1 Mfg. Cons./logistics support Operation Enduring Freedom, 2001—05, Operation Iraqi Freedom, 2003—05. Author, editor: Energy and Resources, 1976. Sr. team leader, sustaining mem. Rep. Nat. Com., 2000—; contbg. mem. Dem. Nat. Com., 1993; hon. mem. Rep. Nat. Com., 1992; sr. team leader Nat. Rep. Congl. Com., 2001, sr. del., mem. bus. adv. coun., 2002—03; active Citizens Against Govt. Waste; founding mem. Rep. Leadership Found.; platinum mem. Rep. Presdl. Task Force; active New Rep. Majority Fund. Named one of 2000 Outstanding Scientists of 20th Century, 2001, 2000 Outstanding Scientists of 21st Century, 2002; recipient Cert. of Appreciation, Nuc. and Plasma Sci. Soc., 2000. Mem.: NSPE, ASCE, IEEE (cons. AICN 2000 database), Internat. Brotherhood of Elec. Workers, Sailors Union of the Pacific, NY Acad. Sci., Wash. Soc. Profl. Engr. (rec. sec. Seattle chpt. 1998—2001), United Brotherhood Carpenters and Joiners (Shipwrights and Joiners), Congl. Legion of Merit, Am. Legion (asst. adj. Queen Anne Post 170) (Winter Soldier Cons., 2001) (op. Iraqi Freedom 2003). Address: Winter Soldier Cons PO Box 95462 Seattle WA 98145 Office Phone: 206-527-0643. E-mail: eds2@seanet.com.

HANDS, TERENCE DAVID (TERRY HANDS), theater and opera director; b. Jan. 9, 1941; s. Joseph Ronald and Luise Berthe (Kohler) H.; m. Josephine Barstow, 1964 (div. 1967); m. Ludmila Mikaël, 1974 (div. 1980); 1 child; ptnr. Julia Lintott, 1988-1996; 2 children; m. Emma Lucia, 2002. BA in English Lang. and Lit. with honors, Birmingham (Eng.) U., 1962, DLitt (hon.), 1988; diploma with honors, Royal Acad. Dramatic Art, 1964; DLitt (hon.), Middlesex U., 1997. Founder, artistic dir. Liverpool (Eng.) Everyman Theatre, 1964-66; artistic dir. RSC Theatreground, 1966-67; from assoc. dir. to artistic dir. Royal Shakespeare Co., England, 1967-91, dir. emeritus, 1991—. Cons. Comedie Francaise, 1975-80, Clwyd Theatr Cymru, dir., 1997— contbr. to Theatre 72, Playback pubs.; translator of plays. Dir.: (plays) Hamlet, 1994, Merry Wives of Windsor, 1995, The Pretenders, 1996, The Royal Hunt of The Sun, 1996, The Importance of Being Ernest, 1997, A Christmas Carol, 1997, Equus, 1997, The Journey of Mary Kelly, 1998, The Seagull, 1998, The Norman Conquests, 1998, Macbeth, 1999, 12th Night, 1999, Under Milk Wood, 1999, Macbeth (Broadway), 2000, Private Lives, 2001, King Lear, 2001, Bedrom Farce, 2001, The Rabbit, 2001, Rosencrantz and Guildenstern Are Dead, 2002, Betrayal, 2002, Romeo and Juliet, 2002, The Four Seasons, 2002, Blithe Spirit, 2003, Crucible, 2003, Pleasure and Repentance, 2003, One Flew Over the Cuckoo's Nest, 2004, Brassed Off, 2004, Troilus and Cressida, 2005. Decorated chevalier des Arts et des Lettres; recipient Pragnell Shakespeare award 1991. Fellow Shakespeare Inst. (hon.), Royal Welsh Coll. Music and Drama, North East Wales Inst. Office: Clwyd Theatr Cymru Mold Flintshire North Wales CH7 1YA England

HANDSAKER, JUDITH ANN, elementary school educator; b. Iowa City, Apr. 11, 1953; d. Leonard Aaron and Shirley Jean Larson; m. James Eugene Handsaker, July 19, 1980; children: Jacob William, Brett Aaron, Brian James. BA in Edn., Iowa State U., 1975. Tchr. 6th grade English West Liberty Cmty. Schs., Iowa, 1975—79; tchr. 4th grade Nevada Cmty. Schs., 1979—2000, substitute tchr., 2000—02, Hubbard-Radcliffe Schs., 1988—98, tchr. 4th grade, 1998—. Sec. Uniserv Unit II ISEA, Hampton, Iowa, 2001—. Sec. Hubbard-Radcliffe Music Parents Assn., 2001—04; mem. Rebel Spirit, 2001—05; chmn. Women's Mission Fedn., Radcliffe, 1986—. Mem.: Hubbard-Radcliffe Edn. Assn. (pres. 2001—02, 2005—, sec., v.p.), Beta Sigma Phi (pres. 1990—91). Republican. Lutheran. Avocations: gardening, walking. Home: 12676 290th St Radcliffe IA 50230

HANDSCHU, BARBARA ELLEN, lawyer; b. Buffalo, June 28, 1942; d. Joseph and Rose H. BA, NYU, 1963; JD, U. Mich., 1966. Bar: N.Y. 1967, U.S. Dist. Ct. (ea., so. and we. dists.) N.Y., U.S. Supreme Ct. Hearing examiner Erie County Family Ct., Buffalo, 1981-82; lectr. SUNY, Buffalo, 1983; pvt. practice Buffalo; spl. counsel Mayerson Stutman, N.Y.C. Contbr. articles to legal pubs. Mem. Buffalo Housing Ct. Adv. Bd., 1981-84; pres., bd. dirs. Neighborhood Legal Svcs., Buffalo, 1981-85. Recipient proclamation Buffalo City Coun., 1983, Women Helping Women award NOW, Buffalo, 1986. Fellow Internat. Acad. Matrimonial Lawyers; mem. ABA (co-chmn. custody com. 1987—), NY State Bar Assn. (chair family law sect. 1990-92), Am. Acad. Matrimonial Attys. (pres. 2004-05, v.p. 1997-2003, pres. NY chpt. 1995-97, bd. mgr. NY State chpt. 1986—, editor-in-chief jour. 1995-97), Phi Beta Kappa. Democrat. Jewish. Office Phone: 716-885-8005. E-mail: bhandschu@mayersonstutman.com.

HANDSCHUMACHER, ROBERT EDMUND, biochemistry professor; b. Abington, Pa., Oct. 16, 1927; m. Joan A. Goddard; children: Kurt, Mark. BSChemE, Drexel Inst., 1949; MS in Biochemistry, U. Wis., 1951, PhD in Biochemistry, 1953. Postdoctoral fellow Lister Inst., 1953-54; postdoctoral fellow pharm. Yale U. Sch. Medicine, New Haven, 1955-56, asst. prof. pharm., 1956-60, assoc. prof. pharm., 1960-64, dir. div. biol. scis., 1969-72, chmn. dept. pharm., 1974-77, prof. pharm., 1964-95, prof. emeritus, 1996—. Chmn. Eleanor Roosevelt Internat. Fellowship Com., 1966-73, Am. Cancer Soc. Coun. Rsch. Grants, 1977-78, sci. rev. com. Ludwig Cancer Unit, Brussels, 1980-84, health and med. care com. Conn. Acad. Sci., 1984—; sec., treas. Am. Assn. Cancer Rsch., Phila., 1982-88; rsch. prof. Am. Cancer Soc., 1977-95; Philips Meml. lectr. Meml. Sloan-Kettering, N.Y.C., 1985; chmn. exp. therap. adv. bd. B-W Fund, 1990-93; coun. mem. Nat. Inst. Environ. Health Scis., 1987-91. Author 250 articles, book chpts., etc. Sci. dir. Anna Fuller Fund, Yale U. Sch. Medicine, 1973-88; chmn. Samuel Roberts Noble Found. Adv. Bd., Okla., 1982-90; mem. bd. govs. Yale U. Press, New Haven, 1989-93; bd. dirs., v.p. Lutherans in Mission, 1999—. Fellow AAAS; mem. Conn. Acad. Sci. & Engring. (charter). Democrat. Lutheran. Achievements include development of new cancer treatments involving Asparaginase, 5-Fluorouracil; initial purification of the Lymphokine IL-1; discovery of receptor for the transplantation drug Cyclosporin. Home: 97 Great Harbor Rd Guilford CT 06437-3036 Personal E-mail: handschumacher@comcast.net.

HANDY, DENISE ANN, nurse practitioner; b. Belleville, NJ, Mar. 27, 1965; d. Richard Thomas and Joan Audrey Handy; m. Emil Jared Burnham, May 24, 2003. BS, U. S.C., 1987; MSN, advanced cert. nurse practitioner, Columbia U., 1995. RN NJ, cert. nurse practitioner, ANCC, NJ. Nurse Monmouth Med. Ctr., Long Branch, NJ, 1987—98; surg. nurse practitioner Atlantic Surg. Group, Oakhurst, NJ, 1998—. Surg. coord. Monmouth Med. Ctr., 1991—98, nurse mgr. of emergency rm., 1995—97; dir. bariatric program Atlantic Surg. Group, 2003—. Mem. Riverview Med. Team, Rio Vista Equipo Medico Team, Guatemala, 1998. Mem.: Sigma Theta Tau. Avocations: golf, triathlons. Home: 580 Patten Ave Marina Bay Club # 5 Long Branch NJ 07740 Office: Atlantic Surg Group 255 Monmouth RD Oakhurst NJ 07755 E-mail: nursehandee@aol.com.

HANDY, EDWARD OTIS, JR., retired diversified financial services company executive; b. Akron, Ohio, Jan. 9, 1929; s. Edward Otis and Alice (Saalfield) H.; m. Susan Eastabrooks, May 12, 1951; children: Susan Littlefield, John E., Edward O. III, Seth H. AB, Harvard U., 1951, LLB, 1956. Bar: R.I. 1956, U.S. Dist. Ct. R.I. 1956. Assoc. Edwards & Angell, Providence, 1956-59; staff atty. Textron Inc., Providence, 1960-74, asst. gen. counsel, 1974-76, v.p. employee benefits, 1976-87, v.p., sec., 1987-91; ret., 1991. Bd. dirs. ERISA Industries Com., 1982-91, vice chmn., 1990-91; pres., bd. dirs. Providence Athenaeum, 1972-78; trustee various orgns. Capt. USMC, 1951-53, Korea. Mem. Providence Art Club, Hyannisport Club. Republican. Unitarian Universalist.

HANDY, JOHN W., career military officer; b. Raleigh, NC, Apr. 29, 1944; BS in History, Meth. Coll., 1966; Diploma, Squadron Officer Sch., 1972, Air Command and Staff Coll., 1979; MS in Systems Mgmt., U. So. Calif., 1979; Diploma, Air War Coll., 1982, Nat. War Coll., 1984; postgrad., Harvard U., 1993. Commd. 2d lt. USAF, 1967, advanced through ranks to gen., 2000; various assignments to dir. of programs and evaluations Hdqtrs. USAF, Washington, 1995-97; comdr. 21st Air Force, McGuire AFB, N.J., 1997-98; dep. chief of staff for installations and logistics Hdqtrs. USAF/The Pentagon, Washington, 1998-2000; vice chief of staff USAF/The Pentagon, Washington, 2000—01; comdr. U.S. Transportation Command, Scott AFB, Ill., 2001—. Decorated Def. Disting. Svc. medal, Disting. Svc. medal, Legion of Merit with oak leaf cluster, Meritorious Svc. medal with three oak leaf clusters, Air medal with oak leaf cluster, Antarctica Svc. medal, Vietnam Svc. medal with three svc. stars, Republic of Vietnam Gallery Cross with Palm, others. E-mail: ustcpa@hq.transcom.mil.

HANDY, MARY THOMAS, retired elementary school educator; b. Marion, Md., Apr. 9, 1936; d. Monroe Henry Thomas and Agnes Elizabeth Mack; m. William Thomas Handy, Dec. 23, 1961 (div. Feb. 1972); children: Andrew Eltonio Thomas, William Thomas Jr. BS, Bowie State U., 1958; MEd, U. Va., 1971; AGS, U. Md., 1988. Tchr. elem. sch. Withams Elem. Sch., Va., 1963—64, North Accomack Elem. Sch., Mappsville, Va., 1964—70, Prince St Elem Sch, Saisbury, Md., 1970—85; tchr. mid. sch. Wicomico Mid. Sch., Salisbury, 1985—98; ret., 1998. Counselor dormitory U. Va., Charlottesville, 1971—. Mem. prin. adv. bd. Carter G. Woodson Mid. Sch., Crisfield, 2003—; adv. bd. Somerset County Pub. Charter Sch.; discipline com. Somerset County Bd. Edn.; bd. dirs. United Cmty. Ministries. Recipient Cert. of Appreciation, Wicomico County Bd. Edn., Salisbury, Md., 1995, McCready Found., Inc. Jr. Aux. Bd., Crisfield, Md., 2000, Letter of Appreciation dedication, Wicomico County Bd. Edn., Salisbury, 1998, Ret. Tchr. award, Crisfield-Woodson Alumni Assn., 1999, Top Vol. award, 2004. Mem.: AARP, NAACP (life; sec. edn. com. 2001, bd. dirs. Somerset County chpt., by-laws com., strategy team), Wicomico County Ret. Tchr.'s Assn. (Top Vol. award 2004), Md. Ret. Tchr.'s Assn., Crisfield-Woodson Alumni Assn. (sec. Ea. Shore chpt. 1997—), Bowie Alumni Assn. (life), Somerset County Democratic Club. Avocations: bicycling, exercising, walking, singing, travel. Home: 28152 Holland Crossing Rd Marion Station MD 21838

HANDY, RICHARD LINCOLN, civil engineer, educator; b. Chariton, Iowa, Feb. 12, 1929; s. Walter Newton and Florence Elizabeth (Shoemaker) H.; married, Apr. 18, 1964 (div. 1980); 1 child, Beth Susan.; m. Kathryn Etona Claussen, Feb. 13, 1982. BS in Geology, Iowa State U., 1951, MS, 1953, PhD in Soil Engring. and Geology, 1956. Asst. prof. civil engring. Iowa State U., Ames, 1956-59, assoc. prof., 1959-63, prof., 1963-87, disting. prof., 1987-91, disting. prof. emeritus, 1991—; prof.-in-charge Spangler Geotech. Lab., 1963-91; cons. in soil engring., soil and rock testing, landslide stabilization; v.p. research W.N. Handy Co., 1958-91, chmn. bd., 1986-90; pres. Handy Geotech. Instruments, Inc., 1980-93, 1999—, chmn. bd. dirs., 1993—; mem., chmn. bd. dirs. Geopier Found. Co., L.C., 1993-95. Author: The Day the House Fell, 1995; co-author: (with M.G. Spangler) Soil Engineering 3rd edit., 1972, 4th edit. 1983; contbr. articles to profl. jours. Recipient faculty citation Iowa State U., 1976; named Anson Marston Disting. Prof. Engring., Iowa State U., 1987. Fellow AAAS, Geol. Soc. Am., Iowa Acad. Sci.; mem. ASCE (Thomas A. Middlebrooks award 1986), Soil Sci. Soc. Am., Internat. Soc. Soil Mech. and Found. Engrs. Achievements include patents for soils and rock testing instruments. Home and Office: 1502 270th St Madrid IA 50156-7522 Office Phone: 515-795-3355. Business E-Mail: rlhandy@iowatelecom.net.

HANDY, ROLLO LEROY, philosopher, researcher; b. Kenyon, Minn., Feb. 20, 1927; s. John R. and Alice (Kispert) H.; m. Toni Scheiner, Sept. 17, 1950 (dec. July 1997); children: Jonathan, Ellen, Benjamin. BA, Carleton Coll., Northfield, Minn., 1950; MA, Sarah Lawrence Coll., 1951; postgrad., U. Minn., 1951-52; PhD, U. Buffalo, 1954. Mem. faculty U. S.D., 1954-60, prof. philosophy, head dept., 1959-60; assoc. prof. Union Coll., Schenectady, N.Y., 1960-61; mem. faculty SUNY, Buffalo, 1961-76, prof. philosophy, 1964-76, chmn. dept., 1961-67, chmn. divsn. philosophy and social scis., 1965-67, provost faculty ednl. studies, 1967-76; pres. Behavioral Rsch. Coun., Great Barrington, Mass., 1976-84, Am. Inst. Econ. Rsch., Great Barrington, Mass., 1977-91, pres. emeritus, 1991—; ret. Author: Methodology of the Behavioral Sciences, 1964, Value Theory and the Behavioral Sciences, 1969, The Measurement of Values, 1970, (with Paul Kurtz) A Current Appraisal of the Behavioral Sciences, 1964; (with E.C. Harwood) rev. edit., 1973, (with E.C. Harwood) Useful Procedures of Inquiry, 1973; co-editor: Philosophical Perspectives on Punishment, 1968, The Behavioral Sciences, 1968, The Idea of God, 1968. With USNR, 1945-46. Mem. AAUP (chpt. pres. 1964-65), Am. Anthrop. Assn., Am. Philos. Assn. E-mail: rhandy4728@aol.com.

HANDY, VIRGINIA MAE, writer; b. Benton Harbor, Mich., July 21, 1935; d. C. Russell and Mary Charlotte Edwards Handy. AA, Benton Harbor Jr. Coll., 1954; BA cum laude, Western Mich. U., 1956. Cert. libr. Mich. Bd. Librs. Cataloger Detroit Pub. Libr., 1956—62, Lakehead U. Libr., Thunder Bay, Canada, 1964—67, Sodus Twp. Libr., Sodus, Mich., 1968—72; med. records abstractor Mercy-Meml. Med. Ctr., Benton Harbor and St. Joseph, Mich., 1972—91; Log Cabin Day coord., editor Log Cabin Soc. Mich., Sodus, 1987—; fiber arts instr. Salvation Army Ctr. for the Arts, Benton Harbor, 1997—. Spinning and weaving demonstrator, 1975—; profl. cons. for log cabins Mich. Humanities Coun., East Lansing, 2002—; columnist Mich. Mag., 1992—. Photographs in: Life's Canvas, Internat. Soc. Photographers, 2000, Best Photos of 2000, 2001, Best Photos of 2003; author: The Palmer Park Log Cabin: A Souvenir History, 2001, Flax Craft, a Collection of Newsletters, 1993-1999, 2002, From the Little Log Cabin in the Lane, 2004, The Log Cabins of Michigan, a Pictorial Survey, 2005; editor: Log Cabin News, the Quar. Newsletter of the Log Cabin Soc. Mich., 1989—, The Memoirs of John Handy, Sodus Farmer, 2005; contbr. articles to jours. in field. Founder Log Cabin Day in Mich., 1987; leader 4-H, 1975—85; mem. Blossomland Arts and Cultural Coun., St. Joseph, Mich., 1993—94; organizer Detroit 300 Event and Log Cabin Day, 2001; lobbyist for Log Cabin Day bill Mich. Legis., Lansing, 1988—89. Recipient Award of Merit for founding Log Cabin Soc. Mich., Hist. Soc. Mich., 1991, 1st place for linen curtain, Fiberfest, 1992, Silverbowl award for outstanding achievement, Internat. Soc. of Photographers, 2004; Artist-in-Residence grantee, Arts Coun. of Greater Kalamazoo, 2003. Mem.: Mich. League of Handweavers, Mich. Festivals and Events Assn., Mich. Centennial Farm Assn., Pioneer Am. Soc., Log Cabin Soc. Mich. (co-founder 1988, sec.-treas. 1988—, 10th Log Cabin Day plaque 1996), Mich. Archival Assn., Hist. Soc. Mich., Mich. Barn Preservation Network. Achievements include gave the Dr. Frank Bicknell lecture to the Grosse Pointe Historical Society for February, 1999; gave a paper "From the Michigan Frontier to the City Beautiful" to the Pioneer America Society in Richmond, Va., 2000. Avocations: photography, piano, genealogy, restoring old garden and farm buildings, book collecting. Home: 3503 Rock Edwards Dr Sodus MI 49126-8700 Office Phone: 269-925-3836. Business E-Mail: logcabincrafts@qtm.net.

HANDZLIK, JAN LAWRENCE, lawyer; b. N.Y.C., Sept. 21, 1945; s. Felix Munso and Anna Jean Handzlik; children: Grant, Craig, Anna. BA, U. So. Calif., 1967; JD, UCLA, 1970. Bar: Calif. 1971, U.S. Dist. Ct. (ctrl. dist.) Calif. 1971, U.S. Ct. Appeals (9th cir.) 1971, U.S. Supreme Ct. 1975, U.S. Dist. Ct. (no. dist.) Calif. 1979, U.S. Tax Ct. 1979, U.S. Dist. Ct. (ea. dist.) Calif. 1981, U.S. Dist. Ct. (so. dist.) Calif. 1982, U.S. Ct. Internat. Trade 1984, U.S. Ct. Appeals (2d cir.) 1984. Law clk. to Hon. Francis C. Whelan, U.S. Dist. Ct. (ctrl. dist.) Calif., L.A., 1970-71; asst. U.S. atty. fraud and spl. prosecutions section criminal divsn. U.S. Dept. Justice, L.A., 1971-76; assoc. Greenberg & Glusker, L.A., 1976-78; ptnr., prin. Stilz, Boyd, Levine & Handzlik, P.C., L.A., 1978-84; prin. Jan Lawrence Handzlik, P.C., L.A., 1984-91; ptnr. Kirkland & Ellis, LLP, L.A., 1991—2004, Howrey LLP, L.A., 2004—. Counsel to Ind. Christopher Commn. Investigation regarding racism and brutality L.A. Police Dept., 1991; dep. gen. counsel to Webster commn. L.A. Police Dept. response to urban disorders, 1992; mem. adv. com. Office Los Angeles County Dist. Atty., 1994—96; mem. standing com. on atty. discipline U.S. Dist. Ct. (ctrl. dist.) Calif., 1997—2001; dep. gen. counsel ind. rev. panel Rampart investigation police corruption L.A. Police Commn., 2000; blue ribbon rev. panel for investigation of L.A. Police Dept. handling of corruption incident, 2003—05. Mem. editl. adv. bd. DOJ Alert, 1994—95. Bd. dirs. Friends Child Advs., L.A., 1987—91, Inner City Law Ctr., L.A., 1995—2002; mem. bd. judges Nat. and Calif. Moot Ct. Competition Teams, UCLA Moot Ct. honors program. Mem.: ABA (mem. litigation sect. 1990—, vice chair west coast white collar crime com. 1994—96, chair west coast white collar crime com. 1996—98, vice chmn. nat. com. white collar crime 1998—2000, chair nat. com. white collar crime 2000—02, mem. task force on implementation of sect. 307 of Sarbomos-Oxley Act 2002, mem. criminal justice sect. governing coun. 2002—, chair criminal justice sect. working group on atty.-client rels. 2003—04, mem. anti-terrorism and money laundering working group 2003—04, mem. pres.'s task force on atty.-client privilege 2004—), L.A. County Bar Assn. (coms. on fed. cts. 1988—2001, chair criminal practice subcom. 1989—90, fed. appts. evaluation 1989—93, white collar crime com. 1991—97, exec. com. criminal justice sect. 1997—2002, fed. cts. coord. com. 2001—), State Bar Calif. (sects. on criminal law and litigation), Fed. Bar Assn. (exec. com. 1997—), Chancery Club. Office: Howrey LLP Ste 1100 550 S Hope St Los Angeles CA 90071-2627 Office Phone: 213-892-1802. Office Fax: 213-892-2300. Business E-Mail: handzlikj@howrey.com.

HANE, AMIE ASHLEY, psychology professor, researcher; b. Baltimore, Md., Nov. 8, 1974; d. James M. and Marian Michelle Ashley; m. Matthew L. Hane, Jan. 10, 1997; children: Jacob Robert, Jonah Matthew. PhD, U. Md., 2002. Rsch. asst. prof. U. Md., College Park, Md., 2002—, faculty rsch. assoc., 2004—. Mental health assoc. U. Md. Med. Sys., 1995—2000; pediatric neuropsychology extern Mt. Wash. Pediatric Hosp., Baltimore, Md., 1999—2000; course instr. U. Md. Balt. County, Baltimore, Md., 2001—02. Recipient Outstanding Grad. Student fellowship, Dept. of Psychology, U. Md., Balt. County, 2000-2001; Dissertation fellowship, U. Md. Balt. County, 2001. Mem.: Soc. for Rsch. in Child Devel., Internat. Soc. on Infant Studies. D-Liberal. Roman Catholic. Achievements include research in record of publication in various scientific journals and books; presentations at international conferences, including invited talks, symposia participation (organizer and presenter), and more than a dozen poster presentations. Office Phone: 301-405-2834.

HANEKE, DIANNE MYERS, retired education educator; b. San Francisco, Feb. 23, 1941; d. Wayne and Dorothy (Johnson) Myers; m. John Paul Haneke, Apr. 10, 1965; children: Mark, Debra, Julie. BA in Social Sci., Edn., So. Calif. Coll., 1964; MS in Edn., SUNY, Albany, 1971, cert. in advanced studies, 1990, PhD in Reading, 1998. Cert. elem., social studies and reading tchr. N.Y. Reading specialist Greenville (N.Y.) Elem. Sch., 1971-72, 84-85, Durham (N.Y.) Elem. Sch., 1972-74, Cairo (N.Y.) Durham Schs., 1979-82, 86-89; counselor Capital Area Christian Counseling, Delmar, NY, 1980-81; instr. psychology Columbia Greene CC, Hudson, NY, 1982-83; reading specialist Hunter (N.Y.)-Tannersville Schs., 1985-86; instr. edn. and reading Mt. St. Mary Coll., Newburgh, NY, 1990-92; assoc. prof. reading edn. Concordia U., Austin, Tex., 1993—2001, dir. field work experiences, 1993—2001, prof. emeritus, 2001—. Author: A Woman After God's Own Heart, 1982, A View From the Inside: An Action Plan for Gender Equity in New York State Educational Administration, 1990, Improve Your Writing: A Workshop and Desktop Reference, 2001. Instr. water safety ARC, 1978—91; host parents Youth for Understanding, 1984—85, 1988—89; leader, resource person Girl Scouts U.S., 1978—90. Recipient Alumnus of the Yr. award, So. Calif. Coll., 1979, Disting. Contbr. award, 1988, Disting. Svc. award, So. Calif. Coll. Alumni Assn., 1994; Myers-Haneke Edn. endowed scholar. So. Calif. Coll., 1971—. Mem.: ASCD, Tex. State Reading Assn., Internat. Coun. Tchrs. English, Nat. Reading Conf., Coll. Reading Assn., Christian Educators Assn. Internat., Capital Area Reading Coun., Assn. Tchr. Educators, Am. Ednl. Rsch. Assn., Phi Delta Kappa, Delta Kappa Gamma. Republican. Avocations: swimming, tennis, music, travel, Special Olympics. Personal E-mail: d.haneke@prodigy.net.

HANELINE, DOUGLAS LATHAM, literature educator; b. Greenwich, Conn., Sept. 14, 1948; m. Ellen J. Bilstein, Sept. 2, 1983; children: Joellen, Elizabeth. AB, Middlebury Coll., 1970; MA, U. Del., 1972; PhD, Ohio State U., 1978. Assoc. prof. English Dakota State U., Madison, SD, 1979—84; prof. English Ferris State U., Big Rapids, Mich., 1984—, asst. v.p. for acad. affairs, 1999—2001. Dir. Mich. Humanities Coun., Lansing, 1996-2000. Fellow Am. Med. Writers Assn. (editl. rev. bd. AMWA Jour. 1997—, awards adminstr. 1998-2000). Home: 20182 12 Mile Rd Big Rapids MI 49307-8805 Office: Ferris State U Languages and Literature 820 Campus Dr Big Rapids MI 49307-2281 Office Phone: 231-591-2525. E-mail: douglas_haneline@ferris.edu.

HANELY, ALLISON ANNE, federal agency administrator; b. Glenridge, N.J., Oct. 31, 1964; d. Michael Joseph Hanley and Carole Helen Matosin. AA in Bus., Abraham Baldwin U., 1984; BSc in Edn., Western Ill. U., 1989; MA, Seton Hall U., 2000. Mil. police sgt. U.S. Army, 1990—96; canine enforcement officer U.S. Customs, Newark, 1997—2001, supr. canine officer Washington, 2001—02; program mgr. Anti-Terrorism Divsn. Customs and Border Protection Dept. Homeland Security, Washington, 2002—05, program mgr. Anti-Terrorism Divsn. Customs and Border Protection, 2005—. Nat. recruiter U.S. Customs, Newark, 1998—2001, Washington, 1998—2001; nat. K-9 evaluator Customs and Border Protection, mem. def. tactics and baton. Sgt. U.S. Army, 1991—96, discharged U.S. Army, 1996. Decorated NATO medal U.S. Army, Expeditionary award. Mem.: Women in Fed. Law Enforcement, Nat. Women's History Mus., Seton Hall U. Hon. Soc. Republican. Roman Cath. Avocations: sports, reading, fishing. Office: Dept Homeland Security Customs and Border Protection 1300 Penn Ave Office Tng and Devel Washington DC 20229

HANEMAN, VINCENT SIERING, JR., consulting engineer, educator, dean; b. Orange, N.J., Feb. 19, 1924; s. Vincent Siering and Helen (Harris) H.; m. Adelaide Russell, Oct. 3, 1961 (dec.); children: Vincent Siering III, Charles Frederick, Rosalyn Tullos, Kaye Kavísic; m. Barbara Gilliam, June 1, 2002. S.B., MIT, 1947; MS in Aero. Engring, U. Mich., 1950, PhD, 1956. Registered profl. engr., Ohio, Okla., Tex., Ala., Alaska. Asst. head flight research Project Meteor, Mass. Inst. Tech., 1947-49; project head automatic wind tunnel data reduction U. Mich., 1949-51; project officer analogue computer research Wright Air Devel. Center, Ohio, 1951-52; assoc. prof., asst. dept. head aero. engring. Air Force Inst. Tech., Wright Patterson AFB, Ohio, 1955-59; chief spl. projects div. guidance and control directorate Air Force Ballistic Missile Div., 1959-60; pres., sr. asso. Haneman Assos., Richardson, Tex., 1960-66, Stillwater, Okla., 1967-72, Auburn, Ala., 1972-73; chmn. bd. Haneman Assos., Inc., Richardson, Stillwater and Auburn, 1961-73, exec. v.p. Stillwater, 1966-67; prof. mech. engring., dir. engring. research, asso. dean Coll. Engring., Okla. State U., 1966-72; prof. aeros. engring., dean Sch. Engring., Auburn U., 1972-80; prof. mech. engring., dean sch. engring. U. Alaska, Fairbanks, 1980-91, prof. emeritus, dean emeritus sch. engring., 1991—. Cons. flight simulator project U. Mich., 1952-55, Gen. Electric Co., Gen. Dynamics, Space Tech. Labs., Chance Vought Corp., Ling Temco-Vought, Nat. Acad. Scis., Union Carbide, Auburn U., State of Ark., U. Tex. Pan-Am., Brownsville, others. Contbr. articles on instrumentation, control and guidance, aircraft performance, engring. edn. to tech. jours. Mem. Army Sci. Adv. Panel, 1967-77; chmn. night low level com. Project Master, Point of Contact Airmobile. Served to 1st lt. USAAF, 1943-45, MTO; to maj. USAF, 1951-60; to maj. gen. Res., moblzn. asst. to dep. chief staff for research and devel. Decorated D.S.M., Legion of Merit with oak leaf cluster, D.F.C. with oak leaf cluster, Air medal with 7 oak leaf clusters, Air Force Commendation medal. Assoc. fellow Am. Inst. Aeros. and Astronautics; fellow Am. Soc. Engring. Edn. (past sec. mech. and aero. divs., past nat. chmn. aero. div., past mem. gen. council, past mem. exec. com., past chmn. engring. research council, past 1st v.p., chmn. dean's inst. 1978, chmn. planning factors com. Engring. Coll. Council 1976-80, pres. 1980-81), Am. Astronautical Soc. (sr.), Am. Helicopter Soc., IEEE, Nat. Soc. Profl. Engrs. (ethics com. 1974-75, nat. chmn. Engring. Week 1977, 78, chmn. cost of engring. edn. com., nat. dir. 1979-80), Ala. Soc. Profl. Engrs. (state chmn. Engring. Week 1973-76), Alaska Soc. Profl. Engrs. (pres. 1985-86, pres. Fairbanks chpt. 1982-83, gov. 1974—, exec. com. Sustaining U. Program com.), Nat. Conf. Advancement Research (ad hoc mem. exec. com. 1977-79), Sigma Xi, Tau Beta Pi, Sigma Tau, Phi Kappa Phi, Pi Epsilon Gamma, Sigma Nu. Address: 1906 Leonard St #4 Columbus GA 31906

HANES, BARBARA D., artist; b. Des Moines, Iowa, Sept. 27, 1949; d. John Fredrick and Betty Ruth Erquist; m. Brad C. Hanes, May 26, 1972; children: Brooks, Nathan, Rachel. BA, U. No. Iowa, 1972. Guest instr. Waterloo (Iowa) Center for Arts, 2004. One-man shows include Ctr. for Arts, Waterloo, Iowa, 2004, exhibitions include Laredo Ctr. for the Arts, Laredo, Tex., 2001, Ottumwa Area Arts Coun./Smithsonian Inst. Traveling Exhbns., 2001, St. Louis Artists' Guild, 2001, La. State U., Baton Rouge, 2002, New Visions Gallery, Marshfield, Wis., 2002, Mill Atelier Gallery, Santa Fe, 2002, Franklin Sq. Gallery, Southport, N.C., 2003, Wind River Valley Artists Guild, Dubois, N.Y., 2003, Pastel Soc. Am., NYC, 2003, Catharine Loralberd Wolf, 2003, Women Artists in West, Dubois, Wyo., 2003, Represented in permanent collections Northeast Iowa Med. Edn. Found., Waterloo, work in numerous pvt. collections, Krizek and Assocs., Pc., Waterloo; featured artist: various jour. and publs. Guest artist N.E. Iowa Med. Edn. Found., Waterloo, 2000; artist of note Waterloo/Cedar Falls Symphony Orch., 2002; artists Friends of Waterloo Ctr. for the Arts Silent Auction, 2000—02. Recipient Marion Scott Meml. prize, St. Louis Artists' Guild, 2001, Acrylic award, Hilton Head Art League's Nat. Juried Exhbn., S.C., 2000, Leo award, Past Soc. of Southwest, 2000, First Pl. Mixed Media award for Women Artists in West, various hon. mention awards in field. Mem.: Pastel Soc. Am. (Uschi Grueterich Meml. award 1999), Knickerbocker Artists (N.Y.) (bd. dirs. 1997, sec. 1997, amb. at large 1997).

HANES, FRANK BORDEN, writer, former business executive, farmer; b. Winston-Salem, NC, Jan. 21, 1920; s. Robert March and Mildred (Borden) H.; m. Barbara Mildred Lasater, Dec. 3, 1942 (dec. Feb. 1990); children: Frank Borden, Nancy Hanes White, Robin March; m. Jane Craig, July 3, 1991. BA, U. NC, 1942, DHL, 2005, St. Andrew's Presbyn. Coll., 1992. Columnist, feature writer, reporter, copy editor Winston-Salem Jour. and Sentinel, 1946—49; vice chmn., dir. Mchts. Devel. Co., shopping center, Winston-Salem, 1956—64. Dir. Chatham Mfg. Co., Elkin, N.C., Hanes Cos., Winston-Salem. Author: Abel Anders, 1951, The Bat Brothers, 1953, The Fleet Rabble, 1961, Journey's Journal, 1958, Jackknife John, 1964, The Seeds of Ares, 1977, The Garden of Nonentities, 1983. Chmn. com. for endowed professorships U. N.C., 1965-67; chmn. Friends of U. N.C. Libr., 1966-68, Old Salem, Inc., 1968-70, Summit Sch., 1959-62; pres. Winston-Salem Operetta Assn., 1949-50, Winston-Salem Arts Coun., 1955-56, N.C. Lit. and Hist. Assn., 1973-74; mem. bd. visitors U. N.C., 1980-86; chmn. Arts and Sci. Found., 1976-90; vice chmn., trustee John Motley Morehead Found.; chmn. John W. and Anna Hodgin Hanes Found.; bd. govs. U. N.C. Press; mem. bd. N.C. Soc.; bd. dirs. N.C. Children's Home Soc., N.C. Zool. Soc. With USNR, 1942-45 Recipient Roanoke Chowan award for poetry N.C. Lit. and Hist. Assn., 1953, award Winston-Salem Arts Coun., 1957, Cum Laude Soc. award Woodberry Forest Sch., 1961, Sir Walter Raleigh award for fiction, 1961, Disting. Alumnus award U. N.C., 1975, Disting. Svc. medal U. N.C., Alumni Assn., 1978, Ragan award for contbns. to fine arts, 1985, William R. Davie award U. N.C. Bd. Trustees, 1989, Fortner award for contbns. to writers and cmty. St. Andrew's Presbyn. Coll., 1995, Frederic W. Marshall disting. svc. award, 2002, N.C. Soc. award for contbns. to N.C. culture, 2002, N.C. award pub. svc., 2003. Mem. PEN, NC Writers Conf. (chmn. 1951-52), NC Quarter Horse Assn. (pres. 1963-64), Order of Gimghoul (pres. 1940-42), Order of Minotaur (pres. 1940-41), Rotary (pres. Winston-Salem chpt. 1961), Old Town Club (Winston-Salem), Rancheros Visitadores Club (Santa Barbara, Calif.), Roaring Gap Club (pres. NC 1976-78), Rainbow Springs Club (Macon County, NC), Sigma Alpha Epsilon Home: 1057 W Kent Rd Winston Salem NC 27104-1131

HANES, JOHN WARD, civil engineer, sculptor, rancher, director; b. San Francisco, June 5, 1936; s. Ward Herbert and Ruth Florence (Jacks) H.; m. Virginia Rae Meadows, Nov. 27, 1957 (div. Feb. 1966); children: Derek S., Kim R., Mark A.; m. Meda Lee Walter, June 29, 1968; 1 child, Ward W. BS in Engring., U. Calif., Davis, 1979. Registered civil engr., Calif. From engr. technician to civil engr. Soil Conservation Svc., USDA, Berkeley, Calif., 1960-79, civil engr. Davis, 1979-83, hydraulic engr., 1983-90; sculptor, consulting civil engr. Boonville, Calif., 1990—; CEO Hanes Ranch, Inc., Boonville, 1999—. Pres. Santa Rosa (Calif.) Ski Club, 1971. Mem. Gualala Arts Ctr., Mendocino Arts Ctr., Nat. Sculpture Soc. Avocations: multi media art, hunting, fishing. Home: Box 510 29000 Mountain View Rd Boonville CA 95415

HANES, LEIGH B., JR., lawyer; b. Roanoke, Va., Apr. 4, 1918; s. Leigh Buckner and Lillian Lee (Thompson) H.; m. Frances Hulda Hilton, Nov. 1, 1945; children: Katherine W. Hanes Feldman, Leigh Thompson, David Hilton. BA cum laude, Hampden-Sydney Coll., 1940; LLB, U. Md., 1948. Bar: Va. 1951, U.S. Supreme Ct. 1970. Spl. agt. FBI, 1943-49; ptnr. Hanes & Hanes, Roanoke, Va., 1951-56; asst. U.S. atty. Western Dist. Va., 1956-59; U.S. atty., 1969-75; commonwealth atty. Botetourt County, Va., 1976-79; town atty. Troutville, Va., 1983—86. Mem. jud. conf. 4th Cir. Ct. Appeals, 1969-95; mem. City Council Roanoke, 1953-56; vice mayor, Roanoke, 1953-56. Mem. State Scenic River adv. bd.; co-founder Conflict Resolution Ctr., Roanoke, Va.; mem. arbitration panel BBB, Western Va. Served with AUS, 1944-46. Mem. Fed. Bar Assn., Roanoke Bar Assn., Botetourt County Bar Assn., Masons, Rotary, Omicron Delta Kappa, Tau Kappa Alpha, Chi Beta Phi, Sigma Upsilon, Shenandoah Club. Republican. Presbyterian.

HANES, MICHAEL L., dean, educator, educational administrator, researcher; b. Bremen, Ind., Sept. 27, 1947; s. Charles E. and E. Kathleen (Kirby) H.; m. Madlyn A. Levine, July 22, 1977; children— Cara, Jena, Michael Ross. B.S., Ind. U., 1970, M.S. (univ. fellow), 1972, Ph.D. (univ. fellow), 1973. Asst. prof. Coll. Edn., U. Fla., Gainesville, 1973-76, assoc. prof., 1977, research assoc. Inst. for Devel. of Human Resources, 1973-77; dir. High/Scope Ednl. Research Found., Ypsilanti, Mich., 1977-80; prof., asst. dean adminstrv. and acad. affairs Coll. Edn., U. S.C., Columbia, 1980-84, exec. dir. presdl. commn., 1984-86; dir. Booker T. Washington Ctr., 1986-87; dean Sch. Edn., West Chester (Pa.) U., 1987—. Recipient Grad. Research awards U. Fla., 1974-75; numerous grants U.S. Dept. Edn., 1977-80; Southeastern Council for Ednl. Improvement grantee, 1981. Mem. Am. Ednl. Research Assn., Am. Assn. Colls. Tchr. Edn. Author: (with N. Anastasiow) Language Patterns of Poverty Children, 1976; (with N. Anastasiow and M. Levine Hanes) Language and Reading Strategies for Poverty Children, 1982; (with I. Flores and J. Rosario) Un Marco Abierto, 1979; Directions for Academic Excellence, 1985; editor: (with I. Gordon and B. Brievogel) Update: The First Ten Years of Life, 1977. Office: West Chester U Office Of Dean West Chester PA 19382

HANES, RALPH PHILIP, JR., retired textiles executive, horse breeder; b. Winston-Salem, N.C., Feb. 25, 1926; s. Ralph Phillip and Dewitt H (Chathan); m. Joan Audrey Humpstone, Jan. 14, 1950 (dec. Jan. 1983); m. Mary Charlotte Metz, Dec. 23, 1984. Grad., Woodberry Forest Sch., 1944; student, U. N.C., 1944-46; BA, Yale U., 1949; L.H.D. (hon.), St. Andrews Coll., Laurinburg, N.C., 1981; DFA (hon.), N.C. Sch. of Arts, 1987; HHD (hon.), Wake Forest U., 1990. With Hanes Cos., Inc. (formerly Hanes Dye and Finishing Co.), Winston-Salem, N.C., 1950-93; pres. Hanes Dye and Finishing Co., 1965-68, chmn. bd., 1968-88, chmn. emeritus, 1988-93; chmn. bd. Ampersand, Inc., 1976-85. Mem. coun. of sr. fellows Salzburg Seminars in Am. Studies. Editor (cons. editor): (other) Performing Arts Rev., 1981—85, Jour. Arts Mgmt. and Law, 1981-86; editorial adv. bd. Art Economist, 1982-86., 1981—86, editorial adv. bd. Art Economist, 1982—86. Mem. (appt. by Pres. L. B. Johnson) Nat. Coun. Arts, 1965—70; mem. Moravian Music Found., 1963—65; founder/mem. bd. visitors N.C. Sch. Arts, 1985—; bd. visitors Barter Theatre State Theatre of Va., 1967—75; trustee exec. com. N.C. Sch. Arts, 1966—78; assoc. fellow Jonathan Edward Coll., Yale U., 1971—74; mem. Spoleto Festival, 1979—86, Nat. Mus. Am. Art, Renwick Gallery, 1976—89, Alliance for Arts Edn., 1976—79; mem. exec. com. Nat. Coun. for Arts and Edn., 1976—79; mem. adv. coun. for arts Fed Res. Bank of Richmond, 1977—78; mem. Bus. Com. for Arts Arena Stage, Washington, 1980—86; mem. Gov.'s Coun. Bus., Arts and Humanities, 1977—85; mem. fine arts com. Fed. Res. Bank of Washington, 1979—81; mem. adv. bd. Pauline Koner Dance Consort, 1977—80; mem. Arts Resources Corp., 1981—83; chmn. Am. Art Forum, 1986—87, bd. dirs., 1986—90, Arena Stage, 1990—92; com. mem. State of N.C. award, 1993; Yr. of Mountains Commn. N.C., 1995—96; corp. mem. Woods Hole Oceanog. Inst., 1994—98; mem. coun. advisors Blue Ridge Pky., 1998—; exec. com. Ambs. for the Arts, NEA, 1999—; mem. Art Based Elem. Schs., 2000; founder/commr. Winston-Salem Commn. Cultural Affairs, 2001—; co-chair Artsignite Fest., 2002; initiator New River Blue Way, N.C., Va., W.Va., 2002; mem. adv. bd. Blue Ridge Rural Land Trust, 2003—; craft adv. com. Mint Mus., Charlotte, 2004—; mem. Winston-Salem Commr. Cultural Affairs, 2001—; mem. coun. of advisors Blue Ridge Pkwy, 2002—; initiator New River VA Blueway, 2002, H. John Heinz III Ctr. for Sci., Econs. and the Environment, 2004—; arts cons. Govt. of Austria, 1978; bd. dirs. Nat. Coun. Friends of Kennedy Ctr., 1975—80; mem. founding com. Agri-Rsch. Extension Network of N. Am., 1995—97; chmn. cabinet Spl. Olympics World Games, 1999; bd. dirs. (appt. by Pres. J.F. Kennedy) Nat. Cultural Ctr. for Performing Arts, 1962—65; bd. dirs. Am. Symphony Orch. League, 1958—61; trustee Salem Coll., 1961—64; bd. dirs. Jargon Soc. Inc., 1968—69, pres., 1968—75; founder N.C. State Arts Coun., chmn., 1964—66; founder/bd. dirs. Ams. for the Arts (formerly Am Coun. Arts), 1960—69; pres. Ams. for the Arts, 1964—66, vice chmn., 1967—69; mem. nat. adv. com. Brevard Sch. Music, 1969—74, Am. Crafts Coun., 1970—72, Appalachian Trail Conf., 1973—76; chmn. Yale U. Coun. com. on Music, 1970—73; bd. dirs. Nat. Audubon Soc., 1972—78, John. W. and Anna H. Hanes Found., 1974—, So. Appalachian Highlands Conservancy, 1974—78, Old Salem Inc., 1974—77, Isaak Walton League Am., 1974—78, Nature Conservancy, 1975—79; bd. dirs. (apptd. by Pres. Gerald Ford) Kennedy Ctr. for the Performing Arts, 1975—80; bd. dirs. Salzburg Seminar of Am. Studies, 1978—82, Am. Land Trust, 1976—93, Arts Internat., 1981—85; adv. com. Am. Farmland Trust, 1983—97; mem. internat. coun. N.Y.C. Ballet, 1984—86; trustee emeritus Kennedy Ctr. for the Arts, DC, 1999—; bd. govs. Nat. Com. for the New River, N.C., Va., W. Va., 1999—2001; commissioner of cultural affairs Nat. Com. for the New River, N.C., Va., W. Va., 2001—; mem. internat. coun. Mus. Modern Art, 1978—83. Named Young Man of Yr. Winston-Salem Jaycees, 1958, Young Man of Yr. N.C. Jaycees, 1958, Hon. Comdr., USS N.C., 1998; recipient Chmn.'s award NEA, 1966, Gov.'s award for preservation of natural area, 1969, pub. svc. award State of N.C., 1976, Morrison award for the Arts, 1977, Swan award, Tenn., 1970, N.C. Soc. of N.Y.C. award, 1979, Cmty. Svc. award Winston-Salem Urban League, 1979, Conservation award Isaac Walton League Am., 1982, award for disting. svc. to arts Nat. Gov.'s Assn., 1982, N.C. Gov.'s award in fine arts, 1982, awards Winston-Salem chpt. NAACP, 1983, Nat. Medal of Arts Amb. for the Arts presented by Pres. George Bush, 1991, award Piedmont Opera Theatre, 1992, tribute Nat. Arts Club, N.Y.C., 1995, Southeastern Ctr. for Contemporary Arts Leadership award, 1998, Winston-Salem Arts Coun. Young Leadership award, 2000, Charlotte & Philip Hanes Art Gallery award, Wake Forest U., 2001, Excellence award, Downtown Winston-Salem, 2003, award, Phil and Charlotte Hanes Student Commons Bldg., NCSA, 2003, Winston-Salem Found. award, 2003, Founder award, Nat. Assn. of State Arts Agencies, 2005. Mem.: Nat. Assn. of State Arts Agencies (Founder award, 2005), Piedmont Triad Entrepeneurs Network, Piedmont Triad Partnership Bd., Century Assn. (N.Y.C.), Walpole Soc., Wilderness Soc., Royal Soc. Arts, Ut Prosim Soc., Pa. Acad. Fine Arts, N.Am. Mycological Assn., Nat. Wildlife Fedn., East African Wildlife Soc., Appalachian Consortium, World Bus. Coun., Trout Unltd., S.E. Coun. on Founds., Peale for Visual Arts (Phila.), Potomac Appalachian Mountain Club, Am. League Anglers, Isaac Walton League, Appalachian Trail Conf., Currituck, Bohemian Club, Cane River Club, Twin City Club, Piedmont Club, Met. Club (Washington), Lotos Club (N.Y.C.), Yale Club (N.Y.C.). Home and Office: PO Box 1704 Winston Salem NC 27102-1704 Office Phone: 336-761-0570.

HANESIAN, DERAN, chemistry professor, chemical engineer, environmental scientist, consultant; b. Niagara Falls, Sept. 26, 1927; s. Vahan and Anna (Kabasakallian) H.; m. Eva Hanesian. BChE, Cornell U., 1952, PhD, 1961. Registered profl. engr., N.Y., N.J. Prodn. engr. E.I. duPont de Nemours, Niagara Falls, 1952—57, rsch. engr. Deepwater, NJ, 1960—63, E.I. duPont, 1964—66; prof. and master tchr. Otto H. York dept. chem. engring. N.J. Inst. Tech., 1963—, chmn. Otto H. York dept. chem. engring., 1975—88. Rsch. engr. Exxon, Florham Park, N.J., 1967-70; tchr. Celanese, 1977, 80, Algerian Petroleum Inst., 1978; vis. prof. U. Edinburgh, 1981, Yerevan Poly. Inst., Armenia, USSR, 1982, 83; acting dep. dir., vis. prof. Ctr. for Plastics Recycling Rsch., Rutgers U., Piscataway, N.J., 1989-93. Served with U.S. Army, 1945-46. Recipient Robert Van Houten award N.J. Inst. Tech., 1977, 2001, Outstanding Profl. Devel. by Tenured Faculty Mem. award, 1994, Excellence in Tchg. (lower divsn. undergrad.) award, 1998, 2004, Engring. Excellence in Tchg. award Newark Coll., 2004, Bd. Overseers Pub. and Inst. Svc. award, 1999, Newark Coll. Engring. Innovation in Engring. award, 2000, Newark Coll. Engring. Excellence in Tchg. award, 2004; grantee NSF, 1967, 72, 91, German Acad. Exch. Svc., 1982, Fulbright grantee Yerevan Poly. Inst., 1982. Fellow: AIChE (emeritus), Am. Chem. Soc., Am. Soc. Engring. Edn. (life), Mid-Atlantic AT& T Found. (award 1986, Centennial cert. award 1993, John Fluke award 1994, Mid Atlantic Disting. Tchg. award 1997, Mid Atlantic Outstanding Campus Rep. award 1999, Zone 1 Outstanding Campus Rep. award 1999, Mid Atlantic Outstanding Campus Rep. award 2001, Outstanding US Campus Rep. award 2001, Chester F. Carlson award 2003); mem.: AAUP, Armenian Students Assn. Am. (Prof. Dicran H. Kabakjian award 1998), Sigma Xi, Alpha Chi Sigma, Omega Chi Epsilon, Omicron Delta Kappa, Tau Beta Pi, Order of Engrs., Fulbright Assn. Armenian Apostolic. Home: 51 Shepard Pl Nutley NJ 07110-2730 Office: NJ Inst Tech 323 Dr ML King Blvd Newark NJ 07102 Office Phone: 973-596-3597. E-mail: hanesian@adm.njit.edu.

HANESSIAN, GRANT ARAM, lawyer, educator; b. Rochester, N.Y., Jan. 9, 1954; s. Haig John and Ann (Mangurian) H.; m. Anne Schwartz, June 15, 1985; children: Aram, Molly. BA, U. Pa., 1975; JD, NYU, 1980; LLM, Columbia U., 1985. Bar: Fla. 1981, N.Y. 1986. Staff atty. Internat. Human Rights Law Group, Washington, 1982-83; law clk. to Hon. Dominick DiCarlo, U.S. Ct. Internat. Trade, N.Y.C., 1984-86; ptnr. Duane Morris & Heckscher, N.Y.C., 1998-2000; atty. Baker & McKenzie, N.Y.C., 1986-98, ptnr., 2000—. Adj. prof. law N.Y. Law Sch., N.Y.C., 1990-96; spl. prof. law Hofstra U. Law Sch., Hempstead, N.Y., 1993—. Author: Gulf War Claims Reporter, 1997; contbr. articles to law jours. Mem. ABA, Am. Soc. Internat. Law, Assn. Bar City N.Y. Office: Baker & McKenzie 805 3d Ave New York NY 10022 E-mail: grant.hanessian@bakernet.com.

HANES-STEVENS, LAVERNE E., minister, social services administrator; b. Pitts., Apr. 22, 1959; m. Stephen A. Stevens, July 3, 1982. BS, Syracuse U.; MSEd, Duquesne U.; PhD, South Fla. Bible Coll. and Theol. Sem., 2001. Nat. bd. cert. counselor, cert. master addictions counselor 1999. Exec. dir. Lydia's Pl., Pitts., 1996—98; women's substance abuse clin. supr. Chesterfield (Va.) County Mental Health Svcs., 1998—2000; dir. Renewal Ministries, Midlothian, Va., 2000—; substance abuse grants mgr. Richmond (Va.) Behavioral Health Authority. Elder Remnant of Faith Worship Ctr., Midlothian, 2000—. Author: (book) The Fruit of Your Pain: Experiencing Spiritual Renewal Through Seasons of Struggle, 2002. Mem.: Am. Assn. Christian Counselors. Office: Renewal Ministries P O Box 4874 Midlothian VA 23112 E-mail: lhs@renewalmin.com.

HANEY, J. TERRENCE, retired insurance consultant; b. Omaha, Nov. 26, 1933; s. James Cletus and Claire (Wilson) H.; m. Joanne M. Beach, Feb. 12, 1966 (div. Nov. 1971); children: Terrence L., Kim Marie, Robert R., J. Stephen, Patrick M., Amy Liz; m. Judy Lynch, May 27, 1989. Student, Creighton U., 1952; BS, U. Nebr., Omaha, 1991, MA, 1998. CLU. Salesman, unit mgr., div. mgr., dir. mass mktg. R.D. Marcotte & Assocs., Omaha, 1958-64; exec. v.p., gen. mgr. Ins. Cons., Inc., Omaha, 1964-85, pres., CEO, 1985-99. Former pres. St. Margaret Mary Bd. Edn.; former chmn. bd. dir. Roncalli High Sch.; former bd. dir. Creighton Prep H.S.; bd. dirs., mem. fin. com. Omaha Cmty. Found.; bd. dir., chmn. Cmty. Found; trustee U. Nebr. Found. Named to Order of the Tower, U. Nebr. at Omaha, 2003; recipient Herber Locke Disting. Svc. award, 2005. Mem. Nebr. Assn. Health Underwriters (past pres.), Internat. Assn. Health Underwriters (former bd. dir.), Soc. CLUs (past pres. Omaha chpt.), Omaha Assn. Life Underwriters, Edward & Maria Lucretia Creighton Soc. (chmn.), Creighton U. Alumni Assn. (past pres. Omaha chpt.), Golden Key. Clubs: Plaza, Plains Track, Toastmasters (past pres.), Internat. Order of Rocky Mountain Goats. Republican. Roman Catholic. Avocations: bicycling, physical fitness. Home: 407 N Elmwood Rd Omaha NE 68132-2602 Office: 2301 Kiewit Plz Omaha NE 68131-3376

HANEY, RANDY GAYLE, philosopher, educator; s. Henry Kramer Haney, Sr. and Rossie Lee Haney; m. Chung Sup Yoon, Dec. 22, 1979; 1 child, Abigail Lee. BA with hons. in Theology, Pacific Bapt. Coll., 1982; MDiv with hons., Biola U., 1985; MA with hons. in Theology, Fuller Theol. Sem., 1987; PhD with hons. in Religion, MA with hons. in Religion, Claremont Grad. U., 1999; MA with hons. in Korean Studies, Korea U., 2004. Instr. philosophy & religion Mt. San Antonio Coll., Walnut, Calif., 1988—2000; vis. prof. philosophy & religion Kyung Hee U., Seoul, Republic of Korea, 2000—, vis. prof. internat. mgmt. & rels. Suwon, Republic of Korea, 2001—; adj. prof. internat. studies Korea U., Seoul, 2003—. Author: (book on interpreting hebrew poetry) Text and Concept Analysis in Royal Psalms, (essay in a book (compendium) of essays) Divided Korea: Longing for Reunification, Reading the Hebrew Bible for a New Millennium. Ordained pastor for internat. ministry Good Shepherd Meth. Ch., Seong Nam City, Republic of Korea, 2001—05; ordained pastor for youth ministry Orange County Korean Presbyn. Ch., Garden Grove, Calif., 1995—2000, Hanmi Korean Presbyn. Ch., LA, 1990—95. Fellow, Claremont Grad. U., 1992; grantee Asia Rsch. Fund, Yonsei U., Seoul, 2004; scholar Korea U., Freeman Found., 2002—04. Mem.: Am. Polit. Sci. Assn. (corr.), Colloquium on Violence and Religion (corr.), Assn. Asian Studies (corr.), Peace History Soc. (corr.), Cath. Bibl. Assn. (corr.), Am. Acad. Religion (corr.). Avocations: photography, mountain hiking, swimming, reading american ethnic fiction, watching korean history films. Home: 129 E Colorado Blvd #407 Monrovia CA 91016 Office Phone: 011-8231-201-2064. Personal E-mail: rg_haney@yahoo.com.

HANEY, ROBERT LOCKE, retired insurance company executive; b. Morgantown, W.Va., June 14, 1928; s. John Ward and Katherine Eugenia (Locke) H. BA, U. Calif., Berkeley, 1949. Sr. engr. Pacific Telephone Co., San Francisco, 1952-58; mgmt. analyst Lockheed Missiles & Space Co., Sunnyvale, Calif., 1958-64; sr. cons. John Diebold, N.Y.C., 1964-65; sr. indsl. economist Mgmt. & Econs. Research, Inc., Palo Alto, Calif., 1965-67; prin. economist Midwest Research Inst., Kansas City, Mo., 1967-69; dir. mktg. coordination Transam. Corp., San Francisco, 1969-73; staff exec. Transam. Ins. Corp., L.A., 1974-82; 2d v.p. Transam. Life Cos., L.A., 1982-93; ret., 1993. Cons. in field. Co-author: Creating the Human Environment, 1970. Lt. (j.g.) USN, 1949-52. Mem. Scabbard & Blade. Republican. Episcopalian. Avocations: photography, gardening, bicycling. Home: The Ariz Sr Acad Village 7709 S Vivaldi Ct Tucson AZ 85747 E-mail: Bhan83@cs.com.

HANFORD, AGNES RUTLEDGE, retired investment advisor; d. Warren Day and Agnes Beatrice (Kane) H. Grad., Convent of Sacred Heart Prep. Sch., N.Y.C.; BA in English, French, Newton Coll., 1950. Asst. clk. rules com U.S. Ho. of Reps., Washington, 1953-56; account exec. W.E. Hutton & Co., N.Y.C., 1956-74; fin. cons. Thomson McKinnon Securities, N.Y.C., 1974-80, Tampa, Fla., 1980-89; fin. adviser Prudential Securities, Inc., Tampa, 1989-94; ret., 1994. Mem. Hillsborough County Rep. Exec. Com., Tampa, 1980-93, Women's Econ. Coun., N.Y., 1979-80, Tampa Mus. Art, 1980—, Tampa Bay History Ctr., 1995—; mem. Friends of Plant Park, 1995—, bd. dirs., 1997—; mem. adv. coun. U. South Fla. Contemporary Art Mus., 1996—. Mem. Women's Nat. Rep. Club (mem. bd. govs. 1970-75, v.p. 1975-76), Tampa Yacht and Country Club, Lawrence Beach Club. Roman Catholic. Home: 4141 Bayshore Blvd No 301 Tampa FL 33611-1803

HANFORD, GEORGE HYDE, retired educational association administrator; b. Cambridge, Mass., July 29, 1920; s. Alfred Chester and Ruth Hyde H.; m. Elaine Halstead, Sept. 15, 1942; children: Anne Catherine, Mary Lee Hanford Wile. BA, Harvard U., 1941, MBA, 1943; L.L.D. (hon.), W.Va. Wesleyan Coll.; EdD (hon.), Thomas Edison State Coll. Asst. dean Harvard Grad. Sch. Bus. Adminstrn., 1946-48; treas., bus. mgr., tchr., coach N. Shore Country Day Sch., Winnetka, Ill., 1948-55; treas., then v.p., exec. v.p. Coll. Entrance Exam. Bd., N.Y.C., 1955-79, pres., 1979-86, pres. emeritus, 1987—. Author: Life with the SAT, 1991, A Tale of Three Cities in One, 1996, For the Entertainment of Strangers, 1997. Former trustee Nat. Scholarship Svc. and Fund Negro Students, Dwight Sch., Ednl. Testing Svc., Am. Coun. on Edn., Ea. Ednl. Consortium, United Bd. Coll. Devel., Thomas A. Edison State Coll., N.J. Inst. Collegiate Tchg. and Learning, Nat. Coun. for Excellence in Critical Thinking; bd. overseers Mt. Auburn Hosp. With USNR, 1943-46. Recipient disting. or spl. svc. awards Am. Sch. Counselors Assn., Nat. Assn. Coll. Admissions Counselors, Nat. Assn. Secondary Sch. Prins., Nat. Assn. Student Fin. Aid Adminstrs., Johnson C. Smith Univ.; inducted into Harvard Varsity Club Hall of Fame, 1997. Mem. Exec. Svc. Corps of New Eng., Hawaiian Mission Children's Soc., Cambridge Hist. Soc. (pres. 1995-97), Canterbury Soc. (symposiarch 1993-2004, symposiarch emeritus, 2004-), Belmont Hill Club, Cambridge Boat Club, Tenafly Tennis Club. Episcopalian. E-mail: symposiarch@earthlink.net.

HANFORD, GRAIL STEVENSON, writer; b. Far Rockaway, NY, Apr. 10, 1932; d. Warren Day and Agnes Beatrice (Kane) Hanford. BA, Smith Coll., 1954. Reporter Tustin (Calif.) News, 1955; newspaper editorial asst. The Register, Santa Ana, Calif., 1955; assoc. editor Am. Mercury Mag., N.Y.C., 1956-59; freelance writer N.Y.C., 1959-60; editor Royal Ins. Cos., N.Y.C., 1960-62; book editor/copy editor Am. Legion Mag., N.Y.C., 1962-75, sr. editor Washington and Indpls., 1976-82, asst. editor Indpls., 1982-83; sr. writer Writers For Bus., Indpls., 1983-88, Tampa, Fla., 1988—. Contbr. articles to profl. jours. Bd. dirs. Cathedral Sch. of St. Mary, Garden City, N.Y., 1967-71, pres. Alumna Assn., 1967-69; bd. dirs. Hort. Soc. Indpls. Mus. of Art, 1981-86; pres. Smith Coll. Club Indpls., 1982-84. Mem. Fla. Motion Picture and TV Assn., Nat. Book Critics Cir., Indpls. Press Club (bd. dirs. 1980), Am. News Women's Club, West Fla. Smith Coll. Club (v.p. 1992-94. pres. 1996-99), Ivy League Club of Tampa Bay (bd. dirs. 1989-96, sec. 1990, v.p. 1991). Republican. Roman Catholic. Home and Office: Writers For Bus 4141 Bayshore Blvd Tampa FL 33611-1803

HANFT, NOAH JONATHAN, lawyer; b. N.Y.C., Jan. 12, 1953; s. Edwin and Gladys (Potash) H.; m. Dora Barlaz Hanft, May 31, 2004; children: Alexandra Julia, Elizabeth Anna, Genevieve Suzanne. BA in Govt. and Pub. Adminstrn., Am. U., 1973; JD, Bklyn. Law Sch., 1976; LLM in Trade Regulations, NYU, 1982. Sr. trial atty. Legal Aid Soc., N.Y.C., 1977-81; assoc. Ladas & Parry, N.Y.C., 1982-84; sr. atty. Mastercard Internat., N.Y.C., 1984-87, v.p., counsel, 1987-90; sr. v.p., asst. gen. counsel AT&T Universal Card Svcs. Corp., Jacksonville, Fla., 1990—93; from sr. v.p., asst. gen counsel to gen. counsel, corp. sec. Mastercard Internat., Purchase, NY, 1993—. Instr. Cordoza Inst. of Trial Advocacy, N.Y.C., 1982—. Office: Mastercard Internat 2000 Purchase St Purchase NY 10577

HANFT, RUTH S. SAMUELS, health science association administrator, consultant, economist; b. N.Y.C., July 12, 1929; d. Max Joseph and Ethel (Schechter) Samuels; m. Herbert Hanft, June 17, 1951; children: Marjorie Jane, Jonathan Mark. BS, Cornell U., 1949; MA, Hunter Coll., 1963; PhD, George Washington U., 1989; ScD (hon.), U. Osteo. Med & Health Scis., 1993. Cons. Urban Med. Econs. Project, Hunter Coll., N.Y.C. and D.C. Dept. Health, 1962—63; health economist Office of Rsch. and Stats., Social Security Adminstrn., Washington, 1964—66; chief grants mgmt. health div. Office Econ. Opportunity, Washington, 1966—68; sr. health analyst Office of Asst. Sec. Planning and Evaluation HEW, Washington, 1968—71, spl. asst., asst. sec. health, 1971—72, dep. asst. sec. for health policy, rsch. and stats. Office of Asst. Sec. for Health, 1977—79, dep. asst. sec. for health rsch., stats. and tech., 1979—81; health care cons., 1981—88; cons., rsch. prof. dept. health svcs. mgmt. and policy George Washington U., Washington, 1988—91, prof., 1991—95; cons., 1995—. Vis. prof. Dartmouth Med. Sch., 1976—; sr. rsch. assoc. Inst. Medicine NAS, Washington, 1972—76; adj. Ctr. for Bioethics, U. Va., 1999—; mem. exec. adv. coun., adj. prof. James Madison U., 2004—. Contbr. articles to profl. jours. Mem. Med. Assistance Svc. Bd. Commonwealth Va., 1984—89; trustee Meharry Med. Coll., 1989—94; mem. adv. bd. Inst. on Innovation in Health and Human Svcs., James Madison U., 2004—; bd. dirs. N.W. Va. Health Sys., 2003—. Fellow: Acad. Health Svcs. Rsch., Hastings Ctr., Nat. Acad. of Social Ins. (charter mem.); mem.: NAS, Inst. Medicine, Cosmos Club. Jewish. Home: 3340 Brookside Dr Charlottesville VA 22901-9566 Personal E-mail: hrhanft@aol.com.

HANG, BO, biochemist; b. Nanjing, Jiangsu, China, May 28, 1961; s. Zhengming Hang and Qumei Lu; m. Xiaoyan Chen, Aug. 14, 1988; 1 child, Michael C. MD, Nanjing Med. U., China, 1982; MS, Shanghai Med. U., China, 1988; PhD, U. Medicine & Dentistry N.J., 1994. Postdoctoral fellow Lawrence Berkeley Nat. Lab., Berkeley, Calif., 1994—96, scientist, 1996—2000, staff scientist, 2000—. Rev. panel mem. NIH, Bethesda, Md., 2003. Co-author: Exocyclic DNA Adducts in Mutagenesis and Carcinogenesis; contbr. articles various rsch. papers. R01 Rsch. grant, NIH, 1996-2006. Mem.: Am. Assoc. for Cancer Res., Sigma Xi. Avocations: art, photography, reading, writing. Office: Donner Lab Lawrence Berkeley Natl Lab U Calif Berkeley CA 94720 Office Phone: 510-495-2537. E-mail: bo_hang@lbl.gov.

HANGLEY, WILLIAM THOMAS, lawyer; b. Long Beach, N.Y., Mar. 11, 1941; s. Charles Augustus and Faustine Charmillot H.; m. Mary Dupree Hangley, July 24, 1965; children: Michele Dupree, William Thomas, Katherine Charmillot. BS in Music, SUNY-Coll. at Fredonia, 1963; LLB cum laude, U. Pa., 1966. Bar: Pa. 1966, U.S. Ct. Appeals (3d cir.) 1966, U.S. Dist. Ct. (ea. dist.) Pa. 1966. Assoc. Schnader, Harrison, Segal & Lewis, Phila., 1966-69; mem., CEO, Hangley Connolly Epstein Chicco Foxman & Ewing, Phila, 1969-94, CEO Hangley Aronchick Segal & Pudlin, 1994—; judge protem Phila. Ct. of Common Pleas, 1991—; mem. adv. bd. Pub. Interest Law Ctr. Phila. Contbr. articles to profl. publs. Bd. dirs. Ams. for Dem. Action, 1972-81. Fellow Am. Coll. Trial Lawyers (chmn. Com. on Fed. Rules of Evidence, 2001-02, mem. Pa. state com. 1999—, comms. com. 2002—), Am. Bar Found.; mem. ABA (co-chmn. litigation sect. com. on fed. procedure 1990-95—, co-chair task force on merit selection of judges 1995-97, mem. task force on discovery 1997-98, task force on judiciary 1998—), Pa. Bar Assn. (ho. of dels. 1989-92), Am. Law Inst., Phila. Bar Assn., Legal Club (v.p. 2001—), Jr. Legal Club, Order of Coif, U. Pa. Inns of Ct. (master of the bench). Roman Catholic. Office: Hangley Aronchick Segal & Pudlin 1 Logan Sq Fl 27 Philadelphia PA 19103-6995 E-mail: whangley@hangley.com.

HANI, ANTOINE GEORGE, psychiatrist, researcher; b. Beirut, May 1, 1925; came to U.S., 1953; s. George Antoine Hani and Marie Haddad; m. Virginia Helen Ahlstrom; children: George, Valerie; m. Théa Jeitani Hani, Oct. 6, 1984; 1 child, Stéphanie. MD, St. Joseph U., Beirut, 1953. Bd. cert. Adult Psychoanalysis and Child and Adolescent Psychoanalysis. Tchg. analyst Washington Psychanalytic Inst., 1969, supervising and tng. analyst, 1981—, dir., 1996-99; pvt. practice Chevy Chase, Md., 1958—. Contbr. articles to profl. jours. Cross fertilizing rels. Fedn. European Psychoanalysts, Fedn. Latin Am. Psychoanalysts. Recipient cert., Washington Psychoanalytic Soc., Inst. and Found., 2002. Fellow: Am. Coll. Psychoanalysts (honor 1999), APA (disting. life, honor 1973); mem.: Washington Psychoanalytic Soc. (pres. 1987—89, honor and recognition for disting. career in psychoanalysis), Am. Psychoanalytic Assn. (fellow bd. on profl. stds. 1993—99), Internat. Psychoanalytic Assn. (mem. new groups com. 1995—, chmn. com. to develop psychoanalysis in Mid. East 1995—). Roman Catholic. Home: 8501 Thornden Ter Bethesda MD 20817 Office: 5480 Wisconsin Ave # 1619 Chevy Chase MD 20815 E-mail: antoinehani@aol.com.

HANIGAN, LAWRENCE, retired rail transportation executive; b. Notre-Dame-de, Stanbridge, Can., Apr. 3, 1925; s. John Henry and Alice (Lareau) H.; m. Anita Martin, July 20, 1946; children: Carmen, Doris, Guy, Patricia, Michael. Sales mgr. Boisse Lumber Co., Montreal, 1950-52; regional mgr. Cooper-Widman Ltd., Montreal, 1952-70; mem. City of Montreal Exec. Com., 1970-78; chmn. Montreal Urban Community Exec. Com., 1972-78; chmn., gen. mgr. Montreal Urban Community Transit Commn., 1974-85; chmn. VIA Rail Canada Inc., 1985-93. Home: 358 du Baron St Saint-Sauveur PQ Canada J0R IR4

HANIN, ISRAEL, pharmacologist, educator; b. Shanghai, Mar. 29, 1937; s. Arie and Rebecca (Lubarsky) Hanin; m. Leda Toni, June 12, 1960; children: Adam, Dahlia. BS, UCLA, 1962, MS, 1965, PhD in Pharmacology, 1968. Vis. scientist dept. toxicology Karolinska Inst., Stockholm, 1968; staff pharmacologist Lab. Preclin. Pharmacology, NIMH, Washington, 1969-73; from asst. prof. to assoc. prof. psychiatry and pharmacology U. Pitts. Sch. Medicine, 1973-81, prof., 1981-86; prof., chmn. dept. pharmacology and exptl. therapeutics Loyola U. Chgo. Stritch Sch. Medicine, Maywood, Ill., 1986—2003, dir. Inst. Neurosci. and Aging, 1986—2000, dir. MD/PhD program, 1992—2003, prof. emeritus, 2004—; pres. IQL Initiatives, Inc., 2004—. Rsch. grant rev. com. NIMH, 1979—82, Nat. Inst. Aging, 1987—92, NIH Res., 1991—95; pharmacology test com. Nat. Bd. Med. Examiners, 1987—90; sci. adv. bd. Interneuron Pharms., Inc., Lexington, Mass., 1991—2000; cons. UCB Pharm., Brussels, 1981—98; Alzheimer's disease rsch. fund panel Ill. Dept. Pub. Health, 1995—2000; AMVETS rsch. initiative com. Hines VA Hosp., 1996—2003. Editor 16 books; contbr. articles to profl. jours. Served to 2d lt. Armored Corps, Israeli Army, 1955-58 NIMH, NIH, Nat. Inst. Aging grantee, 1965—2003. Mem.: Assn. Med. Sch. Pharmacology Chairs (treas. 1998—2002, pres. 2002—04), Am. Coll. Neuropsychopharmacology, Am. Soc. Neurochemistry, Am. Soc. Pharmacology and Exptl. Therapeutics (co-founder Great Lakes chpt. 1987, pres. 1990—92), Am. Chem. Soc., Neurosci. Soc. (pres. Pitts. chpt. 1982—83, pres. Chgo. chpt. 1990—91). Address: Loyola U Chgo Stritch Sch Medicine Pharmacol Rm 3621 Bldg 102 Maywood IL 60153 E-mail: ihanin@lumc.edu.

HANING, WILLIAM FREES, III, health facility administrator, academic administrator; m. Elizabeth Char. AB, Princeton U., 1971; MD, U. Hawaii, 1975. Bd. cert. gen. psychiatry Am. Bd. Psychiatry and Neurology, bd. cert. addiction psychiatry Am. Bd. Psychiatry and Neurology, lic. med. rev. officer Am. Soc. Addiction Medicine, cert. addiction medicine Am. Soc. Addiction Medicine. Program dir. addiction psychiatry/addiction medicine John A. Burns Sch. of Medicine, U. of Hawaii, Honolulu, 1996—, assoc. dean, 2000—; dir. Pacific Addictions Rsch. Ctr., Honolulu, 2000—; res. force surgeon U.S.Marine Forces Pacific, Camp H.M. Smith, Hawaii, 2001—. Past pres. Life Found., Honolulu, 1992—2003; oral bd. examiner, mem. exams. com. for addiction psychiatry Am. Bd. of Psychiatry and Neurology, Deerfield, Ill., 1999—2003. Capt. USNR, 1972—. Fellow: Am. Soc. of Addiction Medicine (pres. Hawaii chpt. 1989—2003); mem.: Assn. for Continuing Med. Edn., Assn. of Am. Med. Colls., Am. Psychiat. Assn. (Nancy C.A. Roeske, MD, Award for Excellence in Tchg.), Assn. of Mil. Surgeons of the U.S., Assn. for Med. Edn. and Rsch. in Substance Abuse, Am. Acad. of Addiction Psychiatry. Avocations: companion to wife, running, weightlifting. Office: U Hawaii John A Burns Sch Medicine Dept Psychiatry 4th Fl 1356 Lusitana St Honolulu HI 96813 Office Phone: 808-586-2900.

HANKENSON, E(DWARD) CRAIG, JR., performing arts executive; b. Mankato, Minn., Apr. 12, 1935; s. Edward Craig and Ethel Irene (Favre) H.; m. Francis Joyce Hall, Mar. 23, 1957 (div. 1978); 1 child, Meridith Joyce.; m. Catherine Ann Donaldson, 1981; 1 child, Jennifer Leigh. MusB, Eastman Sch. Music, 1957, MusM, 1959. Head voice and opera dept. Auburn U., Ala., 1959-62; bus. mgr. Chautauqua Opera Assn., N.Y., 1958-61, stage mgr., 1957-59, stage dir., 1962; mgmt. intern San Francisco Opera Co., 1962-65; assoc. dir. Brevard Mus. Center, N.C., 1965-68; gen. mgr. Saratoga Performing Arts Ctr., N.Y., 1968-75, dir., 1975—78; exec. dir. Wolf Trap Found. Performing Arts, Vienna, Va., 1978-81; pres. Producers, Inc., 1980; dir., chmn. dept. arts mgmt. and events U. South Fla., Tampa, 1983-86; pres. KiddyCart Inc., 1987—, Producers, Inc., 1981—; chmn. bd. PICASTAR, 1985—. Dir. Rochester Comty. Opera, N.Y., 1957-59; mem. Title III adv. coun. N.Y. Dept. Edn., 1969-75, N.Y. Gov.'s Commn. on Arts in Edn., 1978; cons. N.Y. Coun. on Arts; coun. bd. Rensselaer Poly. Inst.; cons. theater constrn. and mgmt. Concord Pavillion, Calif., Blossom Music Ctr., Cleve., Art Park, Buffalo, Mud Island, Memphis, Tampa Bay Performing Arts Ctr., Tampa, Robin Hood Dell, Phila.; ops. cons. Worcester Ctr. Performing Arts. Prodr.: (TV spls.) Snow White, PBS, 1973, Al Hirt and Pete Fountain Together, PBS, 1979, Great Jazz Pianists, PBS, 1979-81, Brigadoon, Majestic Theatre, N.Y.C., 1980-81, Lionel Hampton's Return to the Paradise, PBS, 1988, Thames Live Cinema, Radio City Music Hall, 1988; nat. tour of Show Boat, 1980, Kiss Me Kate and Taming of the Shrew, Washington Internat. Jazz Festival, 1980, nat. tour Pete Fountain, Jerry Mulligan and Al Hirt, 1982, 83, Tom Paxton, Dab O' Dixie, 1987, translator: Haydn's Lo Speziale, 1958, Smetana's Bartered Bride, 1964; creator Ticket Reservation Systems, 1968, prodr. of Glenn Miller, Artie Shaw, Woodie Herman, Helen O'Connell, Warren Covington, Don Cornell, Pied Pipers BigBand Nat. Tour Show, 1993; prodr.: (tours) Midnight in the Garden of Good and Evil, 1999, Last Swing of the Century, 1999, Irish Christmas, 1999. Bd. dirs. Capitol Area Resident Opera Co., 1969-71; mem. alumni adv. bd. Eastman Sch. Music, 1974-78; mem. com. performing arts Leukemia Soc. Am., Inc.; mem. spl. adv. com. on spl. projects and presenting orgns. Nat. Endowment for the Arts, 1979-80; elder, mem. ruling session Temple Ter. Presbyn. Ch., 1990—, chmn. rsch. and planning, 1992—; bd. dirs., sec. Ter. Landings Assn.; youth group leader H.S., 1996—, Terrace Presbyn. Ch., 1996—; small group leader, Montreat, NC, Youth Conf., 2000, 01, leader 12-step program, 2001; pres. Univ. Cmty. Civic Assn., 1997—; mem. adv. bd. Tampa Habitat for Humanity, 2000—, mem. com., 2001; bd. dirs. Parents Coun. Hollins U., 2001-, vice chmn., 2003—; co-chair Hollins U. Parents Coun., 2003-04, chair, 2004—. Recipient citation Ctrl. Theaters, Moscow, 1973. Mem. Internat. Assn. Concert and Festival Mgrs. (dir.), Performing Arts Assn. N.Y. (pres. 1972-78), Orgn. Summer Festival Mgrs. (moderator 1971-79, dir), N.Y. Fedn. Music Clubs (dir.), Saratoga Springs C. of C. (dir. 1969-72, chmn. promotion com. 1970-72), Council of Pres.'s, Albany League Arts, Saratoga Springs PTA (pres. 1972-73), Temple Terrace C. of C. (spl. events com., bd. dirs., bd. dirs. Farmer's Market), Univ. Cmty. Civic Assn. (pres.), Rotary (chair programming com.), Hollins U. Parents' Coun. Bd., Temple Terrace Police (adv. coun., 2000, 01), Temple Terrace Rotary (bd. dirs. 2003—), Rotary Found. (bd. dirs. 2003-). Achievements include conceiving process of computerized event tickets and consulted for Ticketron ticket system. Office: Producers Inc 11806 N 56th St Ste B Tampa FL 33617-1652 Office Phone: 813-988-8333. Personal E-mail: chanken1@tampabay.rr.com. Business E-Mail: craigh@producersinc.com.

HANKES, MARGARET ELLEN, literature and language professor, consultant; b. Hastings, Minn., Nov. 3, 1945; d. Paul Roy and Margaret Ann (Beard) Hankes. BS in English Edn., Winona State U., Minn., 1967; MA in Edn., St. Mary's U., Winona, 1995. Lic. tchr. State of Minn. Tchr. English Battle Creek Pub. Sch., Mich., 1967—69, Presentation of BVM, Maplewood, Minn., 1970—79, St. Jerome's Sch., Maplewood, 1980—86, St. John the Baptist Sch., New Brighton, Minn., 1986—. Cons. facilitator C.R.E.A.T.E. Chem. Health Orgn., Mpls., 1984—. Named Local Tchr. of Yr., Wal-mart, 2000; recipient Carnegie Hero Medal, Carnegie Orgn., 1999. Mem.: Nat. Cath. Edn. Assn., Nat. Coun. Tchrs. of English. Roman Catholic. Avocations: theater, travel. Home: 1000 Thomas Ave Saint Paul MN 55104 Office: St John the Baptist Sch 845 2nd Ave NW New Brighton MN 55112

HANKET, MARK JOHN, lawyer; b. Jan. 28, 1943; s. Laddie W. and Florence J. (Kubat) H.; m. Carole A. Dalpiaz, Sept. 14, 1968; children: Gregory, Jennifer, Sarah. AB magna cum laude, John Carroll U., 1965; JD cum laude, Ohio State U., 1968; MBA, Xavier U., 1977. Bar: Ohio 1968, Mich. 1993. Atty. Chemed Corp., Cin., 1973-77, asst. sec., 1977-82, sec., 1982-84, v.p., sec., 1984-86; v.p., gen counsel DuBois Chems. Divsn., 1986-87; v.p., sec. gen. counsel DuBois Chems., Inc., 1987-91; sec. gen. counsel Diversey Corp., 1991-94, v.p., sec. gen. counsel, 1994-96; v.p. law and people excellence, sec. Americlean Sys., Inc., 1996-99; asst. gen. counsel Diversey Lever, Inc., 1999—2002; sr. counsel JohnsonDiversey, Inc., Southfield, Mich., 2002—. Capt. U.S. Army, 1968—73. Decorated Meritorious Svc. medal, Army Commendation medal with oak leaf cluster. Mem. ABA, Mich. Bar Assn., Am. Corp. Counsel Assn., Ohio Bar Assn. Office Phone: 248-304-3439. E-mail: mark.hanket@johnsondiversity.com.

HANKIN, JOSEPH NATHAN, college president; b. N.Y.C., Apr. 6, 1940; s. Harry and Beatrice H.; m. Carole G. Hankin, Aug. 20, 1960; children—Marc, Laura, Brian. BA in Social Scis. (N.Y. State Regents scholar), CCNY, 1961; MA in History, Columbia U., 1962, Ed.D. in Adminstrn. Higher Edn. (Kellogg fellow), 1967; postgrad. seminar, Harvard U. Grad. Sch. Bus., 1979; Litt.D. (hon.), Mercy Coll., 1979; DHL (hon.), Coll. New Rochelle, 1996; D Pedagogy (hon.), Manhattan Coll., 2000; DHL (hon.), Lehman Coll., 2002. Cert. large complex case arbitrator Am. Arbitration Assn. N.Y. State Regents coll. teaching fellow, 1961-63; fellow dept. history CCNY, 1962-63, lectr., 1963-65; lectr. history Bklyn. Coll. CUNY, summer 1963, lectr. history Queens Coll., summer 1964; course asst. dept. higher and adult edn. Tchrs. Coll., Columbia U., spring 1965, occasional lectr., 1965—, adj. prof. higher and adult edn., 1976—; dir. evening div. and summer session Harford Jr. Coll., Bel Air, Md., 1965-66, dean continuing edn. and summer session, 1966-67, pres., 1967-71, Westchester C.C., Valhalla, N.Y., 1971—. Mem. vis. team Md. State Bd. Cmty. Colls., Annapolis, 1976; bd. dirs. Mut. Funds Trust, 1988—; mem. task force on study higher edn. in D.C., 1966-67; spkr., panelist and cons. in field; condr. workshops and seminars. Contbr. articles and revs. to profl. publs. and newspapers. Mem. adv. com. Columbia U. Tchrs. Coll. C.C. Ctr., 1970—; bd. dirs., mem. exec. com. Westchester C.C. Found., 1971—; mem. Tri-State Coll. Consortium (now Eastern Ednl. Consortium), 1975—, pres., 1977-89, fin. com., 1982-87; mem. adv. com. SUNY Ednl. Opportunity Ctr., 1975—; mem. Coun. for Arts in Westchester, N.Y., 1971—, mem. coll. adv. com., 1971, mem. arts action plan for Westchester com., 1974-75, mem. Friends of Arts, 1976—, mem. benefit com., 1983-86, trustee, 1983-85; mem. Westchester Rockland Newspapers Lend-A-Hand Adv. Bd., 1974-90; mem. Friends Harrison Pub. Libr., 1980—, Friends Neuberger Mus., 1979—; bd. advisors Hudson River Mus., 1985—; mem. adv. bd. Westchester County Hist. Soc., 1981-84; trustee Westchester Econ. Understanding Found., 1979, Hartford Family Found., 1984—. Recipient Disting. Service award Bel Air (Md.) Jaycees, 1968, Brotherhood award Westchester region NCCJ, 1975, Arabic Soc. plaque, 1977, Plaque Pres. Ea. Ednl. Consortium, 1978, Championship of Youth award Youth Services div. B'nai B'rith, 1978, Community Svc. award Soc. Italian-Am. Orgns., 1986, plaque Alpha Beta Gamma and Drucker Mgmt. Soc., 1983, plaque Italian Club, 1984, plaque French Club, 1977, Honor award AIA, 1983, Cert. Vol. Services United Way Westchester, 1986, Cert. Appreciation Westchester 2000, 1988; Kellog fellow in C.C. adminstrn. Columbia U., 1965. Mem. Am. Assn. Jr. Colls. (v.p. 1971-74, bd. dirs. 1971-74, pres.'s acad. 1976—, various coms., Cert. Recognition 1981), Am. Assn. Higher Edn. (charter life), Assn. Pres.'s Public C.C.s (legis. com. 1974-76, 86—, exec. com., mem.-at-large 1987-88), Faculty Student Assn. Westchester C.C. (dir. 1971—), Coll. Consortium for Internat. Studies (exec. com. 1974-88, sec.-treas. 1984-88, mem. ad hoc com. on by-laws 1983), Middle States Assn. Colls. and Schs. (ad hoc com. centennial celebration 1985—, pres. 1999) N.Y. State Assn. Jr. Colls., Young Presidents Orgn. (pres.'s forum 1979-90, founding dir. 1979-80, 84-85, day chairperson 1977-89), CEO Orgn., World Pres. Orgn., Westchester County C. of C. (bd. dirs. 1981-85, chmn. 1988, reaccreditation task force com. on staff 1982-83, chmn. nomination com. 1983-85), Phi Delta Kappa, Alpha Beta Gamma (hon.), Phi Theta Kappa. Home: 4 Merion Dr Purchase NY 10577-1302 Office: Westchester Community Coll 75 Grasslands Rd Valhalla NY 10595-1636 Office Phone: 914-606-6707. Business E-Mail: joseph.hankin@sunywcc.edu. *In order to succeed, to do the best we can at whatever level on whatever path we choose, we do not need brilliance, nor money, nor luck, nor successful parents, nor benign climate, nor even perfect health. We do need belief and hope, imagination and inventiveness, foresight, preparation, and also motivation and perseverance, as well as hard work.*

HANKINS, IRVIN W., III, lawyer; b. Charlotte, N.C., Sept. 1, 1946; AB, U. N.C., 1968, JD with honors, 1975. Bar: N.C. 1975, US Dist. Ct. (NC), US Ct. Appeals (4th cir.), US Supreme Ct. Ptnr., litig. & gen. counsel Parker Poe Adams & Bernstein LLP, Charlotte, NC, mng. ptnr., 1987—2002. Adminstrv. editor N.C. Law Rev., 1974-75. Trustee & mem. pres. adv. council Queens Univ., Charlotte; past gen. counsel Charlotte C. of C. Served to Lt. USN, 1968—72. Mem. NC State Bar Council (mem. exec. com., grievance com.), NC Assn. Def. Attys., Order of the Coif. Office: Parker Poe Adams &

Bernstein LLP Ste 3000 3 Wachovia Ctr 401 S Tryon St Charlotte NC 28202-1935 Office Phone: 704-335-9016. Office Fax: 704-335-9667. Business E-Mail: iwhankins@parkerpoe.com.

HANKINS, MICHAEL JAMES-EDWIN, broadcast executive; b. Metropolis, Ill., July 7, 1933; s. Addison Bernard Michael and Maude Isabele Hankins; m. Patricia Mae Courtney, June 25, 1960; children: Denise Michelle Hankins-Overton, Michelle Kristine. Grad. with honors, Non Commd. Officers Sch., 1953; BS, So. Ill. U., 1959; MBA, Pepperdine U., 1977. Ops. and program mgr. KOIL & KICN(FM)/Star Stas., Omaha, 1964—67; ops. mgr. KQV & WDVE(FM)/ABC Radio, Pittsburgh, 1967—70; sta. ops. mgr. WLS/ABC Radio, Chicago, Ill., 1970—73; v.p. and gen. mgr. KAUM(FM), Houston, 1973—77; founder, pres., CEO PGM/Programation, Inc., Houston, Austin, Tex., 1978—, MCCRadio, Inc., Houston, Austin, Tex., 1979—, 1RADIOnly.com, Austin, 2004—. Team leader N. Harris County Rep. Men's Club, Houston, Tex., 1974—79. Cpl. U.S. Army VII Corps HQ&HQ Co., 1953—55, Mohringen (Stuttgart), Germany. Mem.: Nebr. Radio Hall of Fame (hon.), MBA Execs. Assn. (assoc.), Broadcast Pioneers Assn. (life). R-Conservative. Protestant. Avocations: jogging, hiking, writing, reading. Office: MCCRadio/PGM 13021 Amarillo Ave/Ste 202 Austin TX 78729-7538 Office Phone: 512-335-1907. Office Fax: 512-249-8808. E-mail: mccradio@swbell.net.

HANKINS, PHILLIP R., music educator; b. Ironton, Ohio, June 22, 1945; s. Carl Wilson and Nellie Marie Hankins; m. Deidre May, June 14, 1973; 1 child, Sean. MusB in Edn., U. Tampa, 1972. Cert. Tchr. Music K-12 1972. Dir. band Hillsborough County Sch. Sys., Tampa, Fla., 1972—. Music dir. Keystone United Meth. Ch., Odessa, Fla., 1995—. Staff sgt. USAF, 1967—71. Mem.: Fla. Band Master Assn. (n/a). Democrat-Npl. Methodist. Avocation: tournament bass fishing. Home: 604 Speck Ct Tampa FL 33613 Personal E-mail: hankins604@aol.com.

HANKINS, STEVEN G., food company executive; Grad., Harding Univ.; M.B.A, Univ. of Arkansas; CPA. With Tyson Foods, Inc., Springdale, Ark., 1983—, sr. v.p., financial planning and shared services, exec. v.p., CFO, 1998—. Mem.: Arkansas Society of CPA's, American Institute of CPA's. Office: Tyson Foods 2210 Oaklawn Dr Springdale AR 72762-6999

HANKINSON, DEBORAH G., former state supreme court justice; BS with distinction, Purdue U.; MS, U. Tex., Dallas; JD, So. Meth. U. Bar: Tex., U.S. Ct. Appeals (5th cir.) 1995; cert. civil appellate law Tex. Bd. Legal Specialization. Spl. edn. tchr. Plano (Tex.) Ind. Sch. Dist.; assoc. Thompson and Knight, Dallas, 1983-95; judge U.S. Ct. Appeals (5th cir.), Dallas, 1996, Tex. Supreme Ct., Dallas, 1997—2003. Liaison Gender Bias Reform Implementation Com., family law sect. Dallas Bar. Editor-in-chief Southwestern Law Jour. Fellow Tex. Bar Found., Dallas Bar Found. Mem. ABA (litigation sect., com. appellate practice, judicial sect.), State Bar Tex. (judicial, litigation, appellate sects.), Dallas Bar Assn. (apellate law sect.), 5th Cir. Bar Assn., Coll. of State Bar Tex., Order of the Coif. Home: Apt 2F 3510 Turtle Creek Blvd Dallas TX 75219-5543

HANKINSON, TIM, soccer coach; b. NYC, Feb. 18, 1955; BS in Athletic Adminstrn., U. S.C., 1977. Lic. coach U.S. Soccer Fedn. Head coach Oglethorpe U., Atlanta, 1978-80, Ala. A&M, 1980-81, De Paul U., 1982, Datagraphic Soccer Club, 1984, Syracuse U., 1985-90, UMF Tindastol, Iceland 2nd Divsn., 1991; head coach, gen. mgr., owner Charleston Battery, USISL, 1992-94; gen. mgr. Raleigh Flyers, USISL, 1995; dir. player devel. Maj. League Soccer, 1996-98; head coach Tampa Bay Mutiny, 1998—2000, Colorado Rapids, 2000—. Former coach U.S. Pro-40 Select team; former chmn. mktg. com. USISL. Named Big East Conf. Coach of Yr., 1986, Nat. Coach of Yr., USISL, 1994. Achievements include leading Ala. A&M to NCAA Final Four, 1980, 81, Datagraphic Soccer Club to U.S. Amateur Cup semifinals, 1984, Syracuse U. to Big East Conf. Tournament Championship, 1985. Office: Colorado Rapids MLS Pepsi Ctr 1000 Chopper Cir Denver CO 80204

HANKOWSKY, WILLIAM P., real estate company executive; Degree, Brown U. With Office Econ. Devel. City Camden, NJ; with Reading Corp.; dir. commerce City Phila.; pres. Phila. (Pa.) Indsl. Devel. Corp., 1989—2000; from exec. v.p., CIO to chmn., pres., CEO Liberty Property Trust, Malvern, Pa., 2001—03, chmn., 2003—, pres., 2003—, CEO, 2003—. Vice chmn. Kimmel Ctr. Inc., 2003—; bd.dir. North Phila. (Pa.) Health Sys., Phila. (Pa.) Shipyard Devel. Corp., U. City Sci. Ctr. Mem. transition team Gov. Rendell, Pa.; bd. dirs. Phila. (Pa.) Orch., Phila. (Pa.) Convention and Visitors Bur., Kimmel Ctr. Performing Arts.

HANKS, ALAN R., chemistry professor; b. Balt., Nov. 30, 1939; s. Raymond Hanks and Lillian (Simon) Miller; m. Beverly Jean Hinson, Jan. 17, 1961; children: Craig, Denise, Leta. BS in Physics, West Tex. State U., 1962; MS in Biophys. Chemistry, N. Mex. Highlands U., 1964; PhD in Biophysics, Pa. State U., 1967. Nuclear med. sci. officer Armed Forces Inst. Pathology, Washington, 1967-69; from asst. to prof. biochemistry, biophysics Tex. A&M U., Coll. Sta., Tex., 1969-82; state chemist, seed commnr., prof. Purdue U., West Lafayette, Ind., 1982—. Corr. mem., liaison Collaborative Internat. Pesticide Analytical Coun., 1988—; mem. FAO panel on pesticides UN, 1991—, mem. WHO panel on pesticides, 2001—. Contbr. articles to profl. jours. Fellow Assn. Ofcl. Analytical Chemists (chmn. methods bd. 1986-89, bd. dirs. 1990-96, sec.-treas. 1992-93, pres.-elect 1993-94, pres. 1994-95, chmn. liaison com. 1997-2001); mem. Assn. Am. Feed Control Ofcls. (chmn. minerals com. 1985-96, pres. 1999-2000, lab. methods and svc. com. 1988-93, bd. dirs. 1996-2001, codex observer mem. to codex com. on methods of analysis and sampling 2000—), Assn. Am. Plant Food Control Ofcls. (chmn. Magruder check sample com. 1988-90, bd. dirs. 1989-94, chmn. environ. affairs com. 1990-99, pres.-elect 1991-92, pres. 1992-93). Avocations: fishing, gardening, sports, travel. Home: PO Box 2627 West Lafayette IN 47996-2627 E-mail: hanksa@purdue.edu.

HANKS, CLAY DAVID, academic administrator; b. Luling, Tex., Oct. 27, 1959; s. Edgar Earl and Laura Ann Hanks, Laura Ann Hanks; m. Cheryl Lynn Otte; children: Clayton, Cole. BA, Tex. A&M U., 1988, MPA, 1989, PhD, 2000. Sr. acad. bus. adminstr. Tex. A&M Sys. Health Sci. Ctr., College Station, 1999—2001, dir. adminstrn., 2001—02. Survey coord. Tex. schs. Pub. Policy Rsch. Inst., College Station, 1993—96. Author: (instr. manual) An Introduction to Political Science Metholds, 1992; contbr. articles to profl. jours. Mem. Easterwood Airport Zoning Bd., College Station, 1992—93. Home: 711 Honeysuckle College Station TX 77845 Office: Tex A&M Sys Health Sci Ctr 1716 Briarcrest Dr Bryan TX 77802 Personal E-mail: brazosinvest1@hotmail.com. Business E-Mail: chanks@medicine.tamu.edu.

HANKS, EUGENE RALPH, real estate developer, rancher, forester, retired military officer, investor; b. Corning, Calif., Dec. 11, 1918; s. Eugene and Lorena B. Hanks; m. Frances Elliot Herrick, Mar. 4, 1945; children: Herrick, Russell, Stephen, Nina. Student, Calif. Poly. Coll., 1939—41, U. So. Calif., 1949—50, Am. U., 1958—59; grad., Command and Staff Coll., Norfolk, Va., 1960. With Naval Aviation Flight Tng.,V-5 Program USN, 1941-42, commd. ensign, 1942, advanced through ranks to capt., 1963; carrier fighter pilot, Am. Ace, six victories, 1942-45; test pilot Naval Air Test Ctr., 1946-48; mem. Navy Flight Exhbn. Team Blue Angels, 1950; commdg. officer 3 jet fighter squadrons including Navy's 1st squadron of F4 Phantoms, Mach II Missile Fighters, Miramar, Calif., 1952-61; 1st ops. officer U.S.S. Constellation, 1961-62; dir. ops. Naval Air Missile Test Ctr., 1963—66; test dir. Joint Task Force Two, Albuquerque, 1966-69; ret., 1969; owner, mgr., developer Christmas Tree Canyon, Cebolla Springs and Mountain River subdivsns., Mora, N.Mex., 1967—. Decorated Navy Cross, DFC with star (2), Air medal (7), Legion of merit; named Citizen of Yr., Citizen's Com. for Right to Bear Arms, 1987, 93—. Mem.: NRA, Am. Forestry Assn., Naval Aviation Assn., Am. Air Mus. Gt. Britian, Am. Air Mus. U.S., Mora C. of C., Combat Pilots Assn., Ret. Officers Assn., Am. Fighter Aces Assn., Blue Angels Assn., Am. Aviation Mus., Naval Aviation Mus. Found., Dun and Bradstreet's Million Dollar Club, Oxford Club (chmns. cir.), Am. Legion, Legion of Valor. Republican. Home and Office: Christmas Tree Canyon Box 239 Mora NM 87732-0239 Business E-Mail: rhanks@nnmt.net.

HANKS, GEORGE CAROL, JR., state judge; b. Breaux Bridge, La., Sept. 25, 1964; s. George Carol and Quenola Reese Hanks; m. Stacey L. Hanks, Apr. 29, 1995. JD, Harvard U., 1989; BA summa cum laude, La. State U., 1986. Bar: Tex. 1989, U. S. Dist. Ct. (so. dist.) Tex. 1992, U.S. Ct. Appeals (5th cir.) 1993, U.S. Dist. Ct. Ariz. 1994, U.S. Supreme Ct. 2003, U.S. Ct. Internat. Trade 2003, D.C. 2003. Jud. law clk., Houston, 1989-91; assoc. atty. Fulbright & Jaworski, Houston, 1991-96; shareholder Wickliff & Hall PC, Houston, 1996-2001; judge 157th Dist. Ct., State of Tex., 2001—02; justice Tex. Ct. Appeals (1st cir.), Houston, 2003—. Panel chmn. grievance com., spl. disciplinary counsel State Bar Tex., Houston, 1993—99. Contbr. articles to profl. jours. Bd. dirs. Big Bros. and Big Sisters, Houston, 1995—97, Houston chpt. ARC, 2001—. Fellow Houston Bar Assn.; mem. Fed. Bar Assn., Nat. Bar Assn., Am. Judges Assn., Houston Bar Assn. Avocations: aviation, scuba diving. Home: 12035 Circle Dr E Houston TX 77071 Office: 1037 San Jacinto Fl 10 Houston TX 77002 Office Phone: 713-655-2708. Personal E-mail: georgehanks@sbcglobal.net. Business E-Mail: george.hanks@1stcoa.courts.state.tx.us.

HANKS, JAMES JUDGE, JR., lawyer; b. Washington, Jan. 31, 1943; s. James Judge and Dorothy (Teeple) H. AB, Princeton U., 1964; LLB, U. Md., 1967; LLM, Harvard U., 1969. Bar: Md. 1967. Law clk. to judge U.S. Ct. Appeals (D.C. cir.), 1967—68; assoc. Weinberg and Green Law Firm, Balt., 1969—74; ptnr. Weinberg and Green, Balt., 1975—93, Ballard Spahr Andrews & Ingersoll, LLP, Balt., 1993—2003, Venable, LLP, Baltimore, 2003—. Vis. prof. of law Cornell Law Sch., 1993,2005, adj. prof. law 1994—, adj. prof. mgmt., Cornell Bus. Sch., 1999—; adj. prof. law Northwestern Law Sch., 1997, 2002-; lectr. various profl. orgns. and law schs.; Commerzbank vis. prof. law Bucerius Law Sch., 2003. Author: Maryland Corporation Law; co-author: Legal Capital, 3d edit.; contbr. articles to profl. jours. Fellow Am. Bar Found.; mem. ABA, Am. Law Inst., Md. State Bar Assn. (chmn. bus. law sect. 1982-83), Md. Club. Democrat. Episcopalian. Home: 1159 Riverside Ave Baltimore MD 21230-4119 Office: Venable LLP Two Hopkins Plz Ste 1800 Baltimore MD 21201 Office Phone: 410-244-7500. E-mail: jhanks@venable.com.

HANKS, N(ORMAN) LINCOLN, music educator, composer; b. Douglas, Ariz., Mar. 5, 1969; s. Glyn Dale and Audrey Anne Hanks. BA, Lipscomb U., 1991; MusM, Ind. U., 1995, Mus D, 2000. Assoc. prof. Pepperdine U., Malibu, Calif., 1998—. Composer: Tota Pulchra, 1998, Thus I Create the Dance, 2000, Prayer, 2005. Named Disting. Alumnusn, Lipscomb U., 2004. Mem.: Am. Music Ctr., Soc. Composers, Am. Composers Forum. Office: Pepperdine U Seaver Coll 24255 PCH Malibu CA 90263

HANKS, STEPHEN GRANT, lawyer, construction executive; b. Rexburg, Idaho, June 7, 1950; s. Grant E. and Elaine (Stephens) H.; m. Debra Joan Dyrr, Aug. 6, 1975; children: Adrianne, Brandon, Tiffany, Lindsey. BS, Brigham Young U., 1974; MBA, U. Utah, 1975; JD, U. Idaho, 1978. Bar: Idaho 1978, U.S. Dist. Ct. Idaho 1978. Corp. atty. Morrison-Knudsen Co., Inc., Boise, Idaho, 1978-82, asst. gen. counsel, 1982-85, Morrison Knudsen Corp., Boise, 1985-86, assoc. gen. counsel, 1986-90, sec., assoc. gen. counsel, 1990—, v.p., corp. sec., gen. counsel, 1991—92, sr. v.p., gen. counsel, 1992—95, exec. v.p., chief legal officer, 1995—2000; pres. Washington Group Internat. (formerly Morrison Knudsen Corp.), Boise, Idaho, 2000—, CEO, bd. dir., 2001—, chmn. Bd. dir. Danny Thompson Memorial Leukemia Found., Inc., U. Idaho President's Spl. Adv. Group; bd. dir., pres. Boise Pub. Schs. Edu. Found., Discovery Ctr. Idaho, Ore-Idaho Coun. of Boy Scouts of Am., St. Alphonsus Reg. Med. Ctr. Found.; adv. bd. U. Idaho Coll. Bus. and Econs., U. Idaho Found.; chmn. Character and Fitness Com. of Idaho State Bar. Mem. ABA, AICPA, Idaho Soc. CPAs. Home: 3130 Terra Dr Boise ID 83709-3860 Office: Washington Group International PO Box 73 720 Park Blvd Boise ID 83729-0073

HANKS, TOM, actor, producer, director; b. Concord, Calif., July 9, 1956; m. Samantha Lewes, Jan. 24, 1978 (div. Mar. 19, 1987); 2 children; m. Rita Wilson, Apr. 1988; children: Chester, Truman Theodore. Student, Calif. State U., Sacramento. V.p., Am. Acad. of Motion Picture Arts & Sciences, 2005-Motion picture appearances include He Knows You're Alone, 1980, Splash, 1984, Bachelor Party, 1984, Volunteers, 1985, The Man with One Red Shoe, 1985, The Money Pit, 1986, Nothing in Common, 1986, Every Time We Say Goodbye, 1986, Dragnet, 1987, Big, 1988, Punchline, 1988, Turner and Hooch, 1989, The 'Burbs, 1989, Joe Versus the Volcano, 1990, Bonfire of the Vanities, 1990, Radio Flyer, 1992, A League of Their Own, 1992, Sleepless in Seattle, 1993, Philadelphia, 1993 (Golden Globe for Best Actor - Drama 1994, Academy Award for Best Actor 1994), Forrest Gump, 1994 (Academy Award for Best Actor 1995), Apollo 13, 1995, Celluloid Closet, 1995, Toy Story (voice), 1995, Saving Private Ryan, 1998 (nominated Acad. awards), You've Got Mail, 1998, Toy Story 2 (voice), 1999, The Green Mile, 1999, Cast Away, 2000 (also prodr.) (Golden Globe for Best Actor 2001), Road to Perdition, 2002, Catch Me If You Can, 2002, The LadyKillers, 2004, The Terminal, 2004, The Polar Express, 2004 (also exec. prodr.); actor, dir., writer That Thing You Do!, 1996; prodr. My Big Fat Greek Wedding, 2002; exec. prodr.: (TV films) We Stand Alone Together, 2001, (TV series) West Point, 2000, My Big Fat Greek Life, 2003; TV movie appearances include Mazes and Monsters, 1982, I Am Your Child, 1997, (TV series) Bosom Buddies, 1980-82, (TV mini-series) dir., prodr., writer From the Earth to the Moon, 1998 (Emmy award for best mini-series, 1999), Band of Brothers, 2001 (Emmy awards for best directing and best mini-series, 2002). Recipient Louella O. Parsons Awd., Hollywood Women's Press Club, 1994, Golden Globe award, 1995, People's Choice award, 1995, 99; named Man of the Yr., Harvard's Hasty Pudding Theater Club, 1995; named one of 50 Most Powerful People in Hollywood Premiere mag., 2004, 2005. Mem. Actors' Equity Assn., Screen Actors Guild, AFTRA. Office: Creative Artists Agy c/o Richard Lovett 9830 Wilshire Blvd Beverly Hills CA 90212-1804*

HANLEY, DEBORAH ELIZABETH, meteorologist, wildland firefighter; b. Liverpool, NS, Canada, Nov. 5, 1967; d. Richard Joseph and Nancy Elizabeth (Payzant) Hanley; m. Philip Cunningham, Dec. 30, 1994; children: Catherine Elizabeth Cunningham, Victoria Anne Cunningham. BSc with honors, Dalhousie U., Halifax, NS, 1990, diploma in Meteorology, 1991, MS, 1993; PhD, SUNY, Albany, 1999. Cert. wildland firefighter Fla. Postdoctoral rsch. assoc. Fla. State U., Tallahassee, 2000—02; meteorologist Fla. Divsn. Forestry, Tallahassee, 2002—. Reviewer Holt, Rinehart and Winston, Austin, Tex., 2003—04. Contbr. articles to profl. jours. Mem.: Internat. Assn. Wildland Fire, Am. Geophys. Soc., Am. Meteorol. Soc., Big Bend Parents of Twins Club. Roman Catholic. Achievements include research in effect of upper-tropospheric troughs on the intensification of hurricanes in the Atlantic basin. Avocations: racquetball, golf, sewing, reading. Office: Florida Divsn Forestry 3125 Conner Blvd Tallahassee FL 32399 Office Phone: 850-413-7172. E-mail: hanleyd@doacs.state.fl.us.

HANLEY, FRANK LOUIS, surgeon, educator; MD, Tufts U. Sch. Medicine, 1978. Diplomate Am. Bd. Surgery, Am. Bd. Thoracic Surgery. Resident in general and cardiothoracic surgery U. Calif., San Francisco, prof., chief cardiothoracic surgery, 1993—2001; asst. prof. Harvard Med. Sch., Boston Children's Hosp., 1989—92; prof., cardiothoracic surgery, dir. heart ctr. Stanford U. Med. Ctr., Calif., 2001—. Editor: (books) Cardiac Surgery in the Neonate and Infant, Cardiac Surgery, Pediatric Cardiac Intensive Care, Infant-Annals of Thoracic Surgery; contbr. several articles to profl. publs. Mem. Am. Assn. for Thoracic Surgery (adv. editl. bd.), Congenital Heart Surgeons' Soc. Data Ctr., Soc. of Thoracic Surgeons, Thoracic Surgery Dirs. Assn., Howard C. Naffziger Surgical Soc., Western Thoracic Surgical Assn. Office: Stanford U Sch Medicine Falk Cardiovasc Rsch Bldg 300 Pasteur Dr Falk CVRC Stanford CA 94305-5407 Office Phone: 650-723-0190. Office Fax: 415-476-9678, 650-725-0707. Business E-Mail: frannk.hanley@stanford.edu, fhanley@stanford.edu.

HANLEY, HENRY GORMAN, cardiologist; b. Providence, Feb. 11, 1941; s. James Lawrence and Mary Rose (Gorman) H.; m. Linda Ellis, June 20, 1970 (div. Jan. 1989); children: Tara, April; m. Kathy Davis, Nov. 18, 1989; children: Eric, Alan. AB, Harvard U., 1962; MD, Yale U., 1966. Diplomate in internal medicine and cardiovascular diseases Am. Bd. Internal Medicine. Asst. prof. Baylor Coll. Medicine, Houston, 1971-76, asst. prof. dept. cell biophysics, 1974-76; assoc. prof. medicine U. Ky. Coll. Medicine, Lexington, 1976-80; prof. medicine, chief sect. cardiology La. State U. Med. Ctr., Shreveport, 1980—2002; cardiologist Freedman Meml. Cardiology LLC, Alexandria, La., 2002—. Contbr. articles to profl. jours. Fellow: Am. Coll. Cardiology (mem. exec. coun. La. chpt. 1997—98, gov. La. chpt. 2000—03); mem.: Am. Heart Assn. (pres. La. chpt. 1988—90), Shreveport Country Club. Roman Catholic. Avocations: golf, travel. Office: Freedman Meml Cardiology LLC Doctors Bldg Ste 112 3311 Prescott Rd Alexandria LA 71301 Home: 6400 Genevieve Alexandria LA 71303 Office Phone: 318-767-0960. E-mail: hghanley@aol.com.

HANLEY, KEVIN LANCE, maintenance company executive; b. Oil City, Pa., Nov. 25, 1961; s. Harold Edward and Helen Louise (Banta) H.; m. Patricia Yolanda DeLeon, Sept. 29, 1984 (div. Feb. 2001); children: Jennifer Jessica, Kevin Lance Jr; m. Carolyn Jean Rydman, May. 18, 2002; 1 adopted child, Jessica Joy Rydman Grad. high sch., Titusville, Pa.; diploma, McDonald's Regional Hdqs., L.A., 1986. Maintenance supr. Paschen Mgmt. Corp. McDonald's, Camarillo, Calif., 1980-86, asst. mgr., 1986-88, 95, maintenance cons., 1988-89; apartment mgr. Bartlein & Co., Ventura, Calif., 1990-97; mgr. phys. plant Westmont Coll., Santa Barbara, Calif., 1988—2004; gen. cons. "R" Cleaning Maintenance, Santa Paula, Calif., 1989—91; owner Custodial-Plus Svcs., Montecito, Calif., 1996—. Veteran Operation Iraqi Freedom, 2004. Sec.-treas. Ch. of God of Prophecy, Carpinteria, Calif., 1987—95, 1997—2000, co-pastor, 1988—95. 1st class petty officer USNR, 1994—. Decorated 6 Navy and Marine Corps Achievement medals, Global War on Terrorism Expeditionary medal, Nat. Def. medal, , Republican. Avocations: backpacking, bowling, camping. Office: Custodial Plus Svcs PO Box 5304 Montecito CA 93150 Office Phone: 805-455-0310. Business E-Mail: khanley@custodialplus.com.

HANLEY, MARK YOUNG, historian, educator, researcher; b. Pueblo, Colo., Oct. 18, 1953; s. Harold Gordon Hanley and Winifred Haskell Snyder; m. Janet Susan McCormick, Aug. 7, 1976; children: Matthew Mark, Kelly Suzanne. BA, Western State Coll., 1976; MA, U. Ill., 1984; PhD, Purdue U., 1989. Vis. asst. prof. history Ind. U.-Purdue U., Indpls., 1991—91; asst. prof. history N.E. Mo. State U., Kirksville, 1991—96; assoc. prof. history Truman State U., Kirksville, Mo., 1997—2004, prof. history, 2004—. Chmn. editl. bd. Truman State U. Press, Kirksville, 2000—03. Author: (book) Beyond a Christian Commonwealth: The Protestant Quarrel with the American Republic, 1830-1860; contbr. book The Foreign Missionary Enterprise at Home: Explorations in North American Cultural History, reference book Encyclopedia of American Cultural and Intellectual History. Grantee, Pew Charitable Trust and Nat. Assn. for the Study Am. Evangelicals, 1997. Mem.: Nat. Assn. for the Study Am. Evangelicals, Soc. for Historians the Early Am. Republic, Am. Soc. Ch. History, Orgn. Am. Historians, Rotary Internat. Avocations: antiques, skiing. Home: 22535 Harrison Trail Kirksville MO 63501 Office: Truman State Univ 100 E Normal St Kirksville MO 63501 Office Phone: 660-785-4098. E-mail: ss04@truman.edu.

HANLEY, THOMAS PATRICK, obstetrician, gynecologist; b. St. Louis, Apr. 16, 1951; s. Thomas P. and Virginia Barbara (Lydon) H.; m. Patricia Ann McHargue, Dec. 27, 1975; children: Colleen, Thomas III, Timothy, Matthew. BA, St. Louis U., 1973, MD, 1977. Diplomate Am. Bd. Ob-gyn. Intern St. Louis U., 1977-78, resident, 1978-81; practice medicine specializing in ob-gyn St. Louis, 1981—; pres. med. staff St. Mary's Health Ctr., 1993; mem. staff Mo. Bapt. Hosp., St. Luke's Hosp., sSt. Joseph's Hosp., Kirkwood, Mo.; clin. prof. St. Louis U. Med. Sch., 1983—. Mem. AMA (Physicians Recognition award 1981—), Am. Coll. Ob-Gyn. (Physicians Excellence award 1986—), Mo. State Med. Soc., St. Louis Gynecol. Soc. (pres. 1989-90), St. Louis Met. Med. Soc. Independent. Roman Catholic. Avocation: golf. Office: 1035 Bellevue Ave Ste 208 Saint Louis MO 63117-1846 Office Phone: 314-238-9000.

HANLEY, THOMAS RICHARD, engineering educator; s. Thomas Jesse and Dorothy Louise (Hay) H.; m. Norma Kathryn Decker, Dec. 27, 1979; children: Thomas Jeffrey, Alan Michael, Andrew Richard, Caitlin Marisa. BSChemE, Va. Poly. Inst., 1967; MSChemE, Va. Poly. Inst. & State U., 1971, PhDChemE, 1972; MBA in Mgmt., Wright State U., 1975. Registered profl. engr., Ky. Devel. engr. AF Materials Lab., Wright Patterson AFB, Ohio, 1972-75; asst. prof. Tulane U., New Orleans, 1975-79; assoc. prof. Rose-Hulman Inst. Tech., 1979-83; prof., dept. head La. Tech. U., Ruston, 1983-85; prof., chmn. dept. Fla. State U., Fla. A&M U., Tallahassee, 1985-91; dean Speed Sci. Sch. U. Louisville, 1991—2003; provost Auburn U., Ala., 2003—05. Bd. dirs. Plasticolors, Ashtabula, Ohio; divsn. advisor NSF, Washington, 1987-93; presenter at numerous nat. and internat. profl. confs. Contbr. articles to profl. jours. Capt. USAF, 1972-75. Recipient award Soc. Am. Mil. Engrs., 1966, 67, Acad. award Am. Legion, 1967, Ralph R. Teetor Ednl. award SAE, 1989, Outstanding Engr. in Edn. award Ky. Soc. Profl. Engrs., 1994; grantee NSF, Nat. Renewable Energy Lab., GE, Colgate-Palmolive, United Catalysts, IKA Works, Swan Biomass, Toro, Olin, Stone and Webster. Fellow AIChE (profl. devel. recognition cert. 1980, student chpt. advisor award 1979); mem. Am. Soc. Engring. Edn., Nat. Assn. Basketball Coaches, Sigma Xi, Phi Kappa Phi, Tau Beta Pi, Phi Lambda Upsilon, Omega Chi Epsilon. Office: Auburn Univ 114 OD Smith Hall Auburn AL 36849 Office Phone: 334-844-7773. Business E-Mail: hanley@auburn.edu.

HANLON, DONALD, architecture educator; BArch, Cornell U., 1972; MArch, U. Wash., 1979, MBA, 1981. Registered arch., Wis., NCARB. Vis. lectr. U. Wash., 1978—83; asst. prof. Tex. Tech. U., 1984—87, U. Wis., 1987—91; assoc. prof. dept. arch. U. Wis. Sch. Arch. and Urban Planning, Milw., 1991—. Active Cold Spring Pk. Assn. Cudahy Pub. Libr. Esperanza Unida, Friendship Inc. Guest House Shelter, Harambee Ombudsman, Hmong-Am. Friendship Assn. Ctr. Hope House Homeless Shelter, Imani Cmty. Family Resource Ctr. Inner City Redevelopment Corp., Guadalupana Making a Difference Partnership, Met. Milw. Sewerage Dist., Walker's Point Devel. Corp. West Side Conservation Corp. Westside Housing Cooperative. Recipient Pres. medal for tchg. excellence, Tex. Tech. U., 1987, Cmty. Partnership award, U. Wis., Milw., 1994, Merit award, AIA-Wis. chpt., 1995, Educator award, AIA-U. Wis. Milw. Student Chpt., 2001, Alumni award for tchg. excellence, U. Wis. Milw., 2001. Office: U Wis Milw Sch Arch and Urban Planning PO Box 413 Milwaukee WI 53201

HANLON, FRANCIS X., lawyer; b. Aug. 27, 1941; BA, Dartmouth Coll., 1964; LLB, Univ. N.C., 1967. Bar: Mass. 1967. Assoc. Ropes & Gray, Boston, 1967—76, ptnr. corp. dept., 1976—, head real estate practice group. Order of the Coif Office: Ropes & Gray 1 Internat Pl Boston MA 02110-2624 Office Phone: 617-951-7232. Office Fax: 617-951-7050. Business E-Mail: francis.hanlon@ropesgray.com.

HANLON, GLEN, professional athletics coach; Goaltender Vancouver (Can.) Canucks, 1978—82, St. Louis (Mo.) Blues, 1982—83, N.Y. Rangers, 1983—86, Detroit (Mich.) Red Wings, 1986—91; asst. coach Vancouver (Can.) Canucks, 1992—99; head coach Portland (Oreg.) Pirates, 1999—2002; asst. coach Washington (D.C.) Capitals, 2002—03, head coach, 2003—. Office: Washington Capitals 401 9th St NW Ste 750 Washington DC 20004

HANLON, JAMES ALLISON, confectionery company executive; b. Oak Park, Ill., Nov. 27, 1937; s. James Graves and Frances (Allison) H.; m. June Weiland, May 30, 1959; children: Perian, Loretta, Jill, James. BA, U. Notre Dame, 1959; postgrad., U. London, 1979, U. Pa., 1980. Mgr. accounts Needham Harper Steers Advt., Chgo., 1959-67; mgr. mktg. L.S. Heath & Co., Inc., Robinson, Ill., 1967-70; v.p. mktg. Peter Paul Cadbury, Naugatuck, Conn., 1970-79, pres., chief exec. officer, 1983-86; pres. Cadbury Can.,

Toronto, Ont., 1979-83, also bd. dirs.; pres., chief exec. officer Leaf N.Am., Bannockburn, Ill., 1988-95; chmn., CEO, pres. Harmony Foods, Santa Cruz, Calif., 1996—2004. Nat. trustee Boy's Clubs of Am. With USMCR, 1956-59. Named Mktg. Warrior of Yr., AMR, Inc., 1979, Most Motivated Exec., 1992; recipient Kettle award Confectionary Industry, 1992, Lifetime Achievement award Nat. Confectionary Assn., 2002. Mem. New Haven Country Club. Roman Catholic. Home: 403 Estancia Ct Monterey CA 93940 Office Phone: 831-656-9961. *Life unfolds itself at it's own pace...Any grand plans should be tempered by the unaticipated events.*

HANLON, MICHAEL GREGORY, lawyer; b. Palo Alto, Calif., May 7, 1953; s. Paul David and Carol Claire (Crowley) H. BA, U. Oreg., 1975; JD, Lewis & Clark Coll., Portland, 1979. Bar: Oreg. 1979, U.S. Dist Ct. Oreg. 1979, U.S. Ct. Appeals (9th cir.) 1979, U.S. Supreme Ct. 1995. Assoc. Law Offices Henry A. Carey, Portland, 1979, 81-83; asst. atty. gen. Antitrust div. State of Oreg. Dept. Justice, Salem, 1980; pvt. practice Portland, 1983—. Mem. ABA, Oreg. State Bar Assn. (chair antitrust sect. 1999-2000, chair fed. practice and procedure com. 2004), Multnomah County Bar Assn. (mem. MBA legis. com., chair professionalism com. 2000-01, Award of Merit 2001), U.S. Dist. Ct. (Oreg.) Hist. Soc., Univ. Club, Multnomah Athletic Club, Columbia-Edgewater Country Club. Democrat. Roman Catholic. Office: Law Offices Michael G Hanlon 1300 Congress Ctr 1001 SW 5th Ave Portland OR 97204-1020 Office Phone: 503-228-9787. Business E-Mail: mgh@hanlonlaw.com.

HANLON, STEPHEN F., lawyer; b. St. Louis, Mo., Dec. 1, 1941; BS in English and History, St. Louis U., 1963; JD, U. Mo. Sch. Law, 1966. Bar: Mo. 1966, Fla. 1976, DC 2003. Ptnr. pro bono Holland & Knight LLP, Washington. Past pres. Fla. Legal Svcs., Inc. Named Boss of Yr., Tampa Legal Secretaries Assn.; recipient Nelson Poynter award, ACLU Fla., 1996, Steven M. Goldstein Criminal Justice award, Fla. Assn. of Criminal Lawyers, 2000, Equal Justice award, So. Ctr. for Human Rights, 2001, Award for Human Rights Advocacy, Tampa Urban League, Award for Betterment of Race Rels., Office of Cmty. Rels. for the City of Tampa, Achievement award for Meritorious Svc. in the Field of Edn., Fla. Edn. Assn./United, "Keep the Dream Alive" award, Dr. Martin Luther King Commemorative Com. in Hillsborough County. Mem.: Fla. Bar Found. (dir. 1995—96), ABA (chair exec. coun. individual rights and responsibilities sect., mem. commn. on legal problems of the elderly 1991—93, past mem. coordinating group on bioethics and the law), DC Bar, Mo. Bar, Fla. Bar (chmn. pub. interest law sect. 1992—93). Office: Holland & Knight LLP 2099 Pennsylvania Ave NW Ste 100 Washington DC 20006 Office Phone: 202-828-1871. Business E-Mail: shanlon@hklaw.com.

HANLON, WILLIAM R., lawyer; BA, Coll. William and Mary, 1975; BA in Jurisprudence with honors, St. John's Coll., Oxford Univ., 1977; JD cum laude, Univ. Pa., 1979. Bar: DC 1981. Law clerk, Hon. Arlin M. Adams US Ct. Appeals (3rd cir.), 1979—80; adminstrv. ptnr., mem. exec. com. Shea & Gardner (merged with Goodwin Procter, 2004); ptnr., co-leader, litig. dept., mem. exec. com. Goodwin Procter LLP, Washington, 2004—. Spl. counsel Ctr. for Claims Resolution. Assoc. editor Univ. Pa. Law Rev. Office: Goodwin Procter LLP 901 New York Ave NW Washington DC 20001 Office Phone: 202-346-4239. Office Fax: 203-346-4444. Business E-Mail: whanlon@goodwinprocter.com.

HANMER, STEPHEN READ, JR., retired federal official; b. Denver, Aug. 15, 1933; s. Stephen Read and Mary Virginia (Marchant) H.; m. Lois Eileen Boteler, June 25, 1955; children: Susan Eileen Hanmer Alexander, Stephen Read III, Sara Lynn. BS in Phys., Va. Mil. Inst., Lexington, 1955; MS in Aerospace Engring., MSME, U. So. Calif., 1964. Commd. 2d lt. U.S. Army, 1956, major, 1965, lt. col., 1968, comdg. 6th bn., 32d Artillery, 1968, col., 1975, retired, 1977; assoc. prof. dept. mechanics U.S. Mil. Acad., 1964-67; def. plans div. staff mem. U.S. Mission to NATO, Brussels, 1978-81; dir. theater nuclear force policy Office of Sec., Dept. Def., Washington, 1981-84; prin. dep. asst. sec. Internat. Security Policy Dept. Def., Washington, 1984-85; amb., dep. head U.S. del. Strategic Arms Reduction Talks, 1985-87, amb., chief U.S. del., 1988-89; dep. dir. ACDA, 1989-93; asst. to pres. Kaman Scis. Corp., Alexandria, Va., 1993-98; ret., 1998. Mary Moody Northen chair dept. internat. studies Va. Mil. Inst., 2002. Decorated Legion of Merit, Bronze Star; recipient Meritorious Civilian Svc. medal U.S. Dept. Def., 1981, Sec. of Def. medal, 1987, Sr. Exec. Svc. Disting. Exec. award, 1988, Sec. State Superior Honor award, 1993, Disting. Honor award ACDA, 1993. Mem. St. Andrews Soc. Washington (sec. 1995-96, v.p. 1997, 2004), Sertoma Club (bd. dirs. 1977), Internat. Inst. for Strategic Studies, Am. Def. Preparedness Assn. Republican. Episcopalian.

HANN, LUCY E., radiologist, educator; b. 1946; MD, Harvard Med. Sch., 1971. Cert. diagnostic radiology 1977. Resident U. Pa. Hosp., Mass. Gen. Hosp.; assoc. prof. radiology Cornell U.; radiologist, dir. ultrasound Meml. Sloan-Kettering Cancer Ctr., N.Y.C.; prof. radiology Weill Med. Coll., Cornell U. Office: Meml Sloan-Kettering Cancer Ctr 1275 York Ave Rm C278 New York NY 10021

HANN, ROY WILLIAM, JR., civil engineer, educator; b. Oklahoma City, Mar. 21, 1934; s. Roy W. and Irene (Billups) H.; m. Ann Mullman, Dec. 27, 1960 (div. Apr. 1983); children: Kimberly Anne, Sharon Irene, Roy Lee, Karen Bea; m. Martha D'Anne Metting, June 23, 1984; children: Tyson Orion, Heather Eileen. BS, U. Okla., 1956, M.C.E., 1957, PhD, 1963. Registered profl. engr., Okla., Tex. lic. real estate broker, Tex. lic. comml. pilot. Engr. C.H. Guernsey and Assos., Oklahoma City, 1959-60; asst. prof. civil engring U. S.C., Columbia, 1962-64; asst. prof. civil engring. dept. environ. engring. div. Tex. A&M U., College Station, 1965-67, assoc. prof., 1967-71, prof., rsch. engr., 1971—, head environ. engring. div., 1970-75, 81-86, dir. sea grant program, 1976-77; dir. Inst. for Oil Spill Tech. Tex. Engring. Experiment Sta., 1991—. Pres. Civil Engring. Systems, Inc., Internat. Spill Tech. Corp., Hann Investments; owner, operator Spring Valley Ranches; cons. in field. Author: Fundamental Aspects of Water Quality Management, 1972; contbr. articles to profl. jours. With USPHS, 1957-59. Recipient Palladium medal Nat. Audubon Soc. and Am. Assn. Engring. Socs., 1983. Mem. ASCE (Paper award 1970-72), Am. Soc. Engring. Edn., Tex. Soc. Profl. Engrs. (Named Outstanding Young Engr. Brazos chpt. 1969), Am. Water Works Assn. (Outstanding Paper award 1969), Sigma Xi, Sigma Chi, Chi Epsilon, Bryan-College Station Apt. Assn. (pres. 1975-76, dir. 1977-84), Omicron Delta Kappa, Tau Beta Pi. Achievements include research in computer methods, oil pollution control and water supply, water pollution. Home: 1300 Walton Dr College Station TX 77840-2529 Office: Tex A&M Univ Dept Civil Engring College Station TX 77843-3136 Office Phone: 979-845-3012. Business E-Mail: r-hann@civil.tamu.edu.

HANNA, ANNE MARIE, artist; b. Bloomington, Ind., Mar. 16, 1938; d. August de Belmont Hollingshead and Carol Evaleen Dempsey; m. Gary E. Hanna, June 10, 1961; children: Haldee Calore, Mark H., Scot E. Student, Cen. Sch. Art, London, 1958—59; BA, BS, Ind. U., 1961. Mgr. art dept. Curry's Coll. Bookstore, Ind. U., Bloomington, Ind., 1961—65; nursery sch. tchr. Powder Mill Village, Beltsville, Md., 1965—67; art tchr. Prince Georges County Schs., Laurel, Md., 1973—89; dir. Savage Mill Galleries Savage Mill Corp., Savage, Md., 1989—96; artist Mid-Atlantic region, 1980—. Pres. Laurel Art Guild, 1973—74; lectr. art film series South Coastal Lab., Bethany Beach, Del., 2003—; grad. sculpture instr. Ind. U., 1960; chair vol. program JHES/Prince Georges County Schs., 1972—86; docent Rehobeth Art League, 1998—. Represented in permanent collections Am. Founders of Scouting, portaits, Boy Scouts Am., Qoro LLC, Internat. Art Expo NY Javits Ctr., 2004. U.S. rep. Citizen Amb. Program to China, 1993; ofcl. portrait artist Nat. Capital Area Coun. Boy Scouts Am., Washington, 1984—2000; leader Girl Scouts Am., Prince Georges County, Md., 1968—76, Boy Scouts Am., Washington, 1974—94, leader Sea Scout, 1986—94, dist. tng. chair Patuxent dist., 1984—89, woodbadge instr., 1984—94. Recipient Best in Show award, Rehobeth Art League, 2002, 2004, Zwanfendael Art Gallery, Nat. Landscape Show, 2003, Silver Beaver award, Boy Scouts Am., 1986, Sea Badge award, 1992, Best in Show award, Rehoboth Art League, 2002, 2004, 2005; Individual Artist Opportunity grantee, Del. State Arts Divsn. Mem.: Nat. League Am. Pen Women, Nat. Portrait Soc., Potomac Valley Watercolorists, Balt. Watercolor Soc. (life), DAR (historian Laurel chpt. 1981—95). Home: 143 Riverview Dr Dagsboro DE 19939 Personal E-mail: artfoxag@msn.com.

HANNA, COLIN ARTHUR, municipal official, management consultant, computer consultant; b. Abington, Pa., Dec. 3, 1946; s. Arthur and Jean Victoria (McClure) H.; m. Anne Price Hemphill, Dec. 28, 1967; children: Jean Price, Colin Alexander. AB, U. Pa., 1968. With CBS, Inc., 1969-76; account exec. CBS Radio Spot Sales, N.Y.C., 1969-70, 71-72, sales mgr. Phila., 1974-76; mgr. creative svcs. CBS-Viacom Group, N.Y.C., 1970-71; acct. exec. WCAU Radio, Phila., 1972-74; dir. sales devel. WCAU-TV, Phila., 1976; pres. Hanna & Wile Advt., Wayne, Pa., 1976-77, Tri-State Trade Exch., Inc., West Chester, Pa., 1978-80, Hanna Enterprises Ltd., 1980—. Prin. Whittlesey and Assocs., West Chester, 1980-85; pres. The Cheshire Group, West Chester, 1985-91, The Bank Execs. Network, Inc., 1988-90, PC Helper, 1991-95 Vestryman Ch. of Good Samaritan, Paoli, Pa.; mem. bd. overseers Sch. Arts and Scis. U. Pa.; elected mem. Chester County Rep. Com.; county commr. Chester County, 1995-2003, chmn. bd. commrs., 1998, 99, 2001, 03; bd. mem. Delaware Valley Regional Planning Commn., 1996—, chmn., 1996-97, 98—; apptd. co-chmn. Pa. Census 2000 advisory panel; apptd. mem. Human Resources Investment Coun., Sound Land Use Adv. Panel; pres. Let Freedom Ring, Inc., 2004—. With USNR, 1968-69. Mem. Shakespear Soc. Phila., Newcomen Soc. N.Am., Coll. Alumni Soc. U. Pa. (pres.), Gen. Alumni Soc. U. Pa. (v.p.), Alumni Assn. U. Pa. (pres.), County Commrs. Assn. Pa., Mensa, Racquet (Phila.), Radley Run Country (West Chester), Tred Avon Yacht (Oxford, Md.). Republican. Episcopalian. Home and Office: 603 Fairway Dr West Chester PA 19382-2013

HANNA, DUKE ELLSWORTH, retired neurological surgeon; b. Indpls., July 24, 1923; s. Duke Ellsworth and Alice Roosevelt (Morehouse) H.; m. Eleanor Jane Myron, Mar. 10, 1945; children: Anita, Cheryl, Robert. BS, Ind. U., 1944, MD, 1946. Diplomate Am. Bd. Neurol. Surgery. Resident neurol. surgery U. Chgo., 1951-54, instr. neurol. surgery, 1954-55; asst. clin. prof. neurol. surgery UCLA, 1972-83, assoc. clin. prof. neurosurgery, 1983—2004. Chief neurol. surgery St. John's Hosp., Santa Monica, Calif., 1976-79, Santa Monica, UCLA Med. Ctr., 1965-75. Author: Illustrative Cranial Neuroradiology, 1967; contbr. articles to profl. jours. Coroner Jay County Ind., Redkey, 1950-51. Lt. (j.g.) USN, 1946-48. Mem. AMA, Calif. Med. Assn., Am. Soc. of Neuroimaging, Congress of Neurol. Surgery, Calif. Assn. Neurol. Surgery, Am. Assn. Neurol. Surgery. Republican. Avocations: aviation, photography. Personal E-mail: DukeHanna@cs.com.

HANNA, FAHED ESSA, music educator; b. Corpus Christi, Tex., July 9, 1937; s. Fahed Essa Hanna Sr. and Sarah Louise Ezar Hanna. B in Music Edn., U. N.Tex., 1961, M in Music Edn., 1970. Music educator, 1956—58, 1971—2005, Corpus Christi Ind. Sch. Dist., 1961—68, 1971—94, Dept. Def. Ind. Sch. Dist., 1968—71. Music educator Dept. Def., Zama, Japan, 1968—71. Musician (soloist): Corpus Christin Chorale, 1992—2001. Soloist Good Shepherd Ch., Corpus Christi, 1954—2005; bd. dirs. Bethune Day Care, Corpus Christi, 1995—2005. Mem.: Tex. Choral Dir., Am. Choral Dir., Lebanese Heritage Soc. Democrat. Episcopalian. Avocations: travel, singing. Home: 1400 Ocean Dr #603C Corpus Christi TX 78404 Office Phone: 361-887-7555.

HANNA, FRANK JOSEPH, JR., credit company executive; b. Apr. 20, 1939; s. Frank Joseph and Josephine (Nahoom) Hanna; m. Vail Deadwyler, Sept. 15, 1960; children: Frank, Lisa, David. BBA, U. Ga., 1961. Credit mgr. Sears, Roebuck & Co., Atlanta, 1961—63, GM, Atlanta, 1963—65; gen. mgr. Rollins Acceptance Corp., Atlanta, 1965—81; with Credit Claims & Collections, 1981—90, First Fin. Mgmt. Corp., 1990—93, Worldwide, Inc., Atlanta, 1993—. Real estate investor, 1968. Office: 245 Perimeter Center Pky Ste 300 Atlanta GA 30346

HANNA, GEORGE VERNER, III, lawyer; b. Shelby, N.C., Mar. 2, 1943; s. George and Mildred Mae (McSwain) H.; m. Linda Faye Tyndall, May 4, 1982 (div.); children: George Verner IV, Mark W., Elizabeth P.; m. Deborah Henson Hannon, Apr. 14, 1984. AB, U. N.C., 1965, JD, 1968. Bar: N.C. 1968, U.S. Dist. Ct. (we. dist.) N.C. 1969, U.S. Dist. Ct. (ea. dist.) N.C. 1972, U.S. Dist. Ct. (mid. dist.) 1974, U.S. Ct. Appeals (4th cir.) 1976, U.S. Supreme Ct. 1976; cert. mediator N.C. Dispute Resolution Commn. Law clk. N.C. Supreme Ct., Raleigh, 1968-69; assoc. Moore & Van Allen, PLLC, Charlotte, N.C., 1969-73, ptnr., 1974—. Arbitrator Am. Arbitration Assn. Former com. chmn. Mecklenburg Coun. Boy Scouts Am.; past vice-chair bd. mgrs. Harris YMCA, Charlotte; past chmn. bd. mgrs. McCrorey YMCA, Charlotte; past pres., bd. dirs. So. Piedmont Legal Svcs., Charlotte, Children's Law Ctr., Charlotte. Fellow: Am. Bar Found.; mem.: ABA, Mecklenburg Bar Found. (past pres.), Mecklenburg County Bar (past pres.), N.C. Bar Assn. (past bd. govs.), Quail Hollow Club. Methodist. Home: 244 Hempstead Pl Charlotte NC 28207-1922 Office: Moore & Van Allen PLLC Bank of Am Corp Ctr 100 N Tryon St Ste 4700 Charlotte NC 28202-4003 Fax: 704-378-2030. Office Phone: 704-331-1030. E-mail: georgehanna@mvalaw.com.

HANNA, JOAN C., music educator; b. Nov. 5, 1953; BME, U. Ctrl. Ark., Conway, 1975, MME, 1979. Music specialist Alma (Ark.) Pub. Schs., 1975-79; assoc. prof., chmn. dept. music edn. Ctrl. Bapt. Coll., Conway, Ark., 1979—. Mem. Music Tchrs. Nat. Assn. Office: 1501 College Ave Conway AR 72034-6404

HANNA, KATHRYN LURA, university administrator; b. Fairmont, Minn., Jan. 23, 1947; d. Russell George and Dorothy Jane (Buchner) Hanna; m. Jeffrey R. Hoelmer, June 10, 1968 (div. Dec. 1980). BA, Hamline U., 1969; MA, Mankato State U., 1971; PhD, U. Minn., 1999. Instr. biology U. Minn., Waseca, 1971-77, asst. prof., 1977-86, assoc. prof., 1986—, dir. arts & scis., 1990, vice chancellor acad. affairs, 1990-93, asst. dean Coll. Biol. Scis. St. Paul, 1993—99, assoc. dean Coll. Biol. Scis., 2000—01, dir. biology colloquium program, 2001—. V.p. membership Grad. Women in Sci., Mpls., 1993-97; mem. Commn. on Women, U. Minn., Mpls., 1988-97. Author: The New Bio Book, 1984; co-author: The Bio Book Too, 1984. Bd. dirs. Mpls. Coll. of Art and Design Assocs., 1991—, Minn. Acad. Sci., 2001--. Recipient Svc. award Sigma Delta Epsilon, 1989; named Outstanding Educator Adminstr. South Cen. Edn. Assn., 1991. Mem. AAAS, Assn. for Study of Higher Edn. Office: U Minn Coll Biol Scis 123 Synder Hall 1475 Gortner Ave Saint Paul MN 55108-6172 Home: 1816 Commerce Blvd Mound MN 55364-1127

HANNA, MARSHA L., artistic director; b. Tiffin, Ohio, Nov. 27, 1951; d. Willis Leondadis and Frances Lucille (Neeley) H. BS, Bowling Green State U., 1980. Drama specialist City of Dayton, Ohio, 1975-80; gen. mgr. Illumination Theatre, 1978-85; product analyst Lexis/Nexis, 1980—86; instr. Sinclair C.C., 1986—; freelance stage dir., 1986—; resident dir. Human Race Theatre Co., 1986—, artistic dir., 1990—. Dir.: Equus, 1981, Beyond Therapy, 1983, The Diviners, 1984, Amadeus, 1985, The Fantasticks, 1986, Getting Out, 1987, Orphans, 1988, Fool for Love, 1989, A Shayna Maidel, 1990, A Christmas Carol, 1991, Steel Magnolias, 1992, The Elephant Man, 1993, Closer Than Ever, 1993, The Good Times Are Killing Me, 1994, Cloud Nine, 1995, Three Tall Women, 1996, The Cherry Orchard, 1996, Quilters, 1997, Taking Sides, Stonewall Jackson's House, 1998, On Golden Pond, 1999, Three Days of Rain, 1999, Art, 2000, Resident Alien, 2001, I Hate Hamlet, 2002, The Dazzle, 2003, Odd Couple, 2004, Every Good Boy Deserves Favour (with Dayton Philharmonic), Johnny Appleseed, 2005. Office: The Human Race Theatre Co 126 N Main St Ste 300 Dayton OH 45402-1766 E-mail: Marsha@humanracetheatre.org.

HANNA, MARTIN SHAD, lawyer; b. Bowling Green, Ohio, Aug. 4, 1940; s. Martin Lester and Julia Loyal (Moor) H.; m. Ann I. Amos; children: Jennifer Lynn, Jonathan Moor, Katharine Anne. Student, Bowling Green State U.; BS, Purdue U., 1962; JD, Am. U., 1965. Bar: Ohio 1965, D.C. 1967, U.S. Supreme Ct. 1969. Ptnr. Hanna, Middleton & Roebke, 1965-70; ptnr. Hanna & Hanna, Bowling Green, 1971—. Spl. counsel for atty. gen. Ohio, 1969-71, 82-85, Ohio Bd. Regents, 1974; instr. Bowling Green State U., 1970, Ohio Div. Vocat. Edn., 1970—, Ohio Peace Officer Tng. Council, 1968; legal adviser NW Ohio Vol. Firemen's Assn., 1970— Contbr. articles to profl. publs. Elder, lay minister Presbyn. Ch.; state chmn. Ohio League Young Republican Clubs, 1972-73; nat. vice chmn. Young Rep. Nat. Fedn., 1973-75, counselor to chmn., 1975-77; cive chmn. Wood County Rep. Exec. Com., Ohio, 1972-80, precinct committeeman, 1968-80; trustee Bowling Green State U., 1976-86; mem. Ohio State Fire Commn., 1979-87; mem. Ohio Rural Fire coun., 1993—. Recipient George Washington honor medal award Freedoms Found. at Valley Forge, 1969, award of merit Ohio Legal Ctr. Inst., 1973, Robert A. Taft Disting. Service award, 1974, James A. Rhodes Leadership award, 1975; named one of 10 Outstanding Young Men, Ohio Jaycees, 1968. Mem. ABA, D.C. Bar Assn., Ohio Bar Assn., Northwest Ohio Bar Assn., Wood County Bar Assn., Toledo Bar Assn., Am. Trauma Soc. (trauma and law com.), Phi Delta Phi, Pi Kappa Delta, Omicron Delta Kappa Home: PO Box 1137 Bowling Green OH 43402-1137 Office: Hanna & Hanna 700 N Main St Bowling Green OH 43402-1815

HANNA, MICHAEL GEORGE, JR., immunologist, pharmaceutical executive; b. Cleve., July 7, 1936; s. Michael George and Camella (Karem) Hanna; m. Barbara Ann Pearson, Sept. 6, 1958; children: Michael George, Christina Louise, Suzanne Kathleen. BS in Biology, Baldwin-Wallace Coll., 1958; MS in Biology, Notre Dame U., 1960; PhD, U. Tenn., 1964; DSc (hon.), Baldwin-Wallace Coll., 2000. Rsch. biologist biology div. Oak Ridge Nat. Lab., 1964-68, dir. immunology carcinogenesis group, 1968-75; dir. cancer biology, head host tumor interaction sect. cancer biology program Nat. Cancer Inst. Frederick (Md.) Cancer Rsch. Facility, 1975-79, dir., 1979-82, Litton Inst. Applied Biotech., Rockville, Md., 1982-85; sr. v.p., COO Biotech. Rsch. Inst., Rockville, Md., 1985-94; pres., CEO PerImmune, Inc., Rockville, Md., 1994-98; chmn., pres., chief sci. officer Intracel, Frederick, 1998—2002; chmn. emeritus, chief sci. officer Intracel Resources, Frederick, Md., 2002—. Cons. NASA Lunar Receiver Lab., 1968—70; chmn. tech. adv. com. biotech. U.S. Dept. Commerce, 1985—90; mem. working group biotech. U.S. Dept. Def., 1985—90; mem. bd. overseers Ctr. Advanced Rsch. Biotech., 1984—88; commencement spkr. Baldwin-Wallace Coll., 2000. Gen. editor: Contemporary Topics in Immunobiology, 1971—85, Vaccine Rsch., 1991—96, mem. editl. bd.: Immunopharmacology, 1978—2003, Cancer Rsch., 1978—92, Jour. Biol. Response Modifiers, 1982—2002, Cancer Metastasis, 1984—; contbr. articles of 300 to profl. jours. Chmn. local emergency planning com. homeland security Frederick County, 2002—04; trustee Baldwin-Wallace Coll., 1998—. Recipient Charles Thornton award, Litton Industries, 1984, Ohio Found. Ind. Colls. Career Excellence award, 2005. Mem.: Internat. Soc. Imunopharmacology (coun. 1991—), Am. Assn. Immunologists, Am. Assn. Cancer Rsch., Soc. Exptl. Pathology. Achievements include patents for (with others) for Tumor Specific Monoclonal Antibodies; (with others) Tumor Associated Monoclonal Antibodies Derived from Human B-Cell Line; (with others) Active Specific Immunotherapy of Carcinomas. Office: 93 Monocacy Blvd Frederick MD 21701 Office Phone: 301-668-8400. Business E-Mail: hannam@intracel.com.

HANNA, NESSIM, marketing educator; b. Assiut, Egypt, Apr. 30, 1938; came to U.S., 1961, naturalized, 1973; s. Yanni and Lulu Shehata (Oweda) H.; m. Dana Lascu, Aug. 28, 1987 (div. 1988); m. Margaret Ann Curzan, 1996. BS in Commerce, Cairo U., 1958; MS in Mktg., U. Ill., 1964, PhD in Mktg, 1969. Asst. prof., chmn. dept. mktg. W.Va. Inst. Tech., Montgomery, 1968-69; asso. prof. bus. adminstrn. Mid. Tenn. State U., Murfreesboro, 1969-70; prof. mktg. No. Ill. U., De Kalb, 1970—98; mktg. cons. Arab Rsch. and Adminstrn. Ctr., 1975-77, Investments Cons. Internat., 1974-77; with Roosevelt U., Schaumburg, Ill., 2001—. Vis. prof. mktg. U. Petroleum and Minirals, Dharan, Saudi Arabia, 1980-81, Norwegian Sch. Mgmt., Oslo, 1988; chmn. dept. mktg., dir. research inst. King Saud U., Kassim, Saudi Arabia, 1983-84; vis. scholar Hong Kong Bapt. U., fall 1991. Author: Marketing Opportunities in Egypt: A Business Guide, 1977, Principles of Marketing, 1985, Pricing Policies and Procedures, 1995, Winning Strategies, 1991, Consumer Behavior: An Applied Approach, 2001; contbr. articles to profl. jours. Named Outstanding Citizen Citizenship Council Met. Chgo., 1974 Mem. Southwestern Social Sci. Assn., Am. Mktg. Assn., Midwest Bus. Adminstrn. Assn., Assn. Egyptian-Am. Scholars (treas.), Acad. Mktg. Sci., Am. Inst. Decision Scis., Phi Beta Lambda, Beta Gamma Sigma, Phi Kappa Phi, Alpha Mu Alpha. Republican. Christian Orthodox. Avocation: overseas travel. Home: Ste 2402 5415 N Sheridan Rd Chicago IL 60640-1939 Office: Roosevelt Univ Dept Bus Schaumburg IL 60173 Office Phone: 773-769-3488. E-mail: nessimh@aol.com.

HANNA, NOREEN ANELDA, retired adult education administrator, consultant; b. Napa, Calif., Nov. 28, 1939; d. Thomas James and Eileen Anelda (Jordan) H.; m. Leon O'bine Gotcher, Aug. 14, 1971 (div. Nov. 1980); children: John Allen, Tamara Kay. BA, San Francisco State U., 1963; postgrad., Sonoma State U., 1974-81, Ctr. for Leadership Devel., 1982-83; MA, U. San Francisco, 1989. Cert. gen. elem., specialist in reading, gen. adminstrv. svcs. Classroom tchr. Ullom Elem. Sch., Las Vegas, Nev., 1963, J. L. Shearer Elem. Sch., Napa, 1963-78, reading resource tchr., 1978-80; asst. prin. Napa Valley Adult Sch., Napa, 1980-81, acting prin., 1981-82; prin. El Centro Elem. Sch., Napa, 1982-83; adminstr. J.T.P.A./Gain Programs, Napa, 1983-90; prin. Napa Valley Adult Sch., Napa, 1983-99, retired, 1999; inst., curriculum for adult learners U.C. Berkley, 2001—. Commn. mem. Calif. Post Secondary Edn., 1987-89; cons. Calif. Dept. Edn., Sacramento, 1988-2002, Staff Devel. Inst., Sacramento, 1990-2001; adv. bd. dir. Ctr. for Adult Edn., San Francisco (Calif.) State U., 1988-95; adv. bd. mem. Immigration Reform & Control Act, Sacramento, 1989-92; presenter and cons. in field, cons. Am. Inst. Rsch., 2002. Exec. bd. dir. Leadership Napa Valley, 1985-93; sec. Leadership Napa Valley Found., 1988-99. State Edn. scholar Calif. PTA, 1976, Grad. Edn. scholar Delta Kappa Gamma, Napa, 1977; recipient Cmty. Leadership award Napa Valley Unified Sch. Dist., 1988, George C. Mann Discing. Svc. award Calif. Coun. for Adult Edn., 1994; named Outstanding Adult Edn. Adminstr., Calif. Adult Edn. Adminstrs. Assn., 1998. Mem. ASCD, Am. Assn. Adult and Continuing Edn., Assn. Calif. Sch. Adminstrs. (chair to state adult edn. com. 1988-1991, 93—95, state rep. assembly del. 1989-92, state adult edn. com. chairperson 1989-92, Adult Edn. Adminstr. of Yr. award 1992), Calif. Coun. Adult Edn. (North Coast chpt. bd. dir. 1988-99), Napa C. of C. (bd. dir. 1985-88, edn./bus. com. 1985-99, others), Correctional Educators Assn., Soroptimist Internat. of Napa, Napa Valley Historical Soc. (pres. 1999-01), Napa Valley Geneological and Bio. Soc. (chart. mem.), Phi Delta Kappa, Delta Kappa Gamma. Democrat. Roman Catholic. Avocations: needlepoint, reading, sailing, swimming, hot air ballooning. Office Phone: 707-252-7433. E-mail: nahanna@interx.net.

HANNA, SAMI A., education educator; b. Fayoum, Egypt, Oct. 3, 1927; s. Ayad and Balsam H.; m. Nadia Ayad, Dec. 29, 1981; children: Lisa, Mark, Michael. BA, Cairo U., 1948; Higher Diploma of Edn., Ein Shaws U., Cairo, 1950; MS, Hunter Coll., 1956; MA, Columbia U., 1958; PhD, U. Utah, 1964. Asst. dir. Mid. East Ctr., U. Utah, Salt Lake City, 1969-73; prof. U. Bahrain, 1983-93; dean Senior Univ., B.C., Can., 1993—; pres., founder Am. Coptic Studies Assn., Portland, 1996—. Vis. prof. coptic studies Pa. State U., 1993—. Author: Dictionary of Modern Linguistics, 1997; contbr. articles to profl. jours.; editor-in-chief Am. Jour. Arabic Studies, Am. Jour. Coptic Studies. Fulbright award Washington, 1997-98. Mem. Mid. East Studies Assoc., Brit. Mid. East Studies Assn., Am. Bahrain Friendship Assoc., Arab Gulf Studies Soc., Phi Delta Kappa, Phi Kappa Phi. Avocations: fishing, painting, cinematography, music, writing. Home: 41725 N Rolling Green Way Anthem AZ 85086-1154 E-mail: cfsh@pdx.edu.

HANNA, TERRY ROSS, lawyer, small business owner; b. Wadsworth, Ohio, May 17, 1947; s. Harry Ross and Geraldine (Frensley) H.; m. Max Anna Hindes, Jan. 20, 1968; children: Travis, Taylor, Molly. BBA, U. Okla., 1968, JD, 1972; LLM, NYU, 1973; MA in Bibl Studies, Dallas Theol. Sem., 1988. Bar: Okla. 1972, U.S. Tax Ct. 1974, U.S. Ct. Appeals (10th cir.) 1979, U.S. Supreme Ct. 1989; CPA, Okla. Mem. McAfee & Taft, Oklahoma City, 1972-80; pres. P 356 Inc., Oklahoma City, 1980—; of counsel Crowe & Dunlevy, Oklahoma City, 1987—. Owner Mo Jo Video, 1995—; spl. lectr.

Oklahoma City U. Sch. Law, 1974-75. Editor Okla. U. Law Rev., 1970-72. Mem. internat. com. Boy Scouts Am., 1988—; dir. U.S. Found. for Internat. Scouting, Irving, 1989—. Baden-Powell fellow World Scout Found., 1988—; recipient Silver Beaver award Boy Scouts Am., 1988. Mem.: Sports Lawyers Assn., Okla. Bar Assn. (pres. taxation sect. 1978—79), Order of Arrow (lodge advisor 1989—2003), Phi Delta Phi (magister 1972), Kappa Sigma (chpt. advisor 1974—75). Republican. Mem. Christian Ch. Avocations: coach, patch collector, fishing, golf, computers. Home: 2600 W Coffee Creek Rd Edmond OK 73003-3326 Office: Crowe & Dunlevy 1800 Mid America Towers Oklahoma City OK 73102 E-mail: HANNAT@crowedunlevy.com, terryhanna@aol.com.

HANNA, WILLIAM BROOKS, publishing executive, literary agent; b. Montreal, Can., Feb. 22, 1936; s. George Spencer and Phyllis Edith (Brooks) H.; children: Catherine Frances, Philip Spencer; m. Frances Ann Gerhardt, Nov. 20, 1982. Grad., Upper Can. Coll., 1954; BA in Modern History, U. Toronto, 1958. Successively coll. sales mgr., sch. sales mgr., editor-in-chief Collier-Macmillan-Can., Ltd., 1958-65; pres. Pergamon of Can., Ltd., also dep. chmn. bd. Toronto, 1967-68; exec. v.p., dir. Pergamon Press, Inc., 1966-68; v.p., dir. Burns & MacEachern, Ltd., Toronto, 1968-70; pres., dir. GLC Pubs., Toronto, 1970-75; pres., chief exec. officer, dir. Holt Rinehart & Winston of Can., Ltd., Toronto, 1975-78; pub. joint UNICEF/Red Cross Com. for 1979 Internat. Yr. of Child, 1978-79; v.p. Gen. Pub. Co. Ltd., Toronto, 1979—84, Stoddart Pub. Co. Ltd., Toronto, 1984—2000, Acacia House Pub. Svcs. Ltd., 2001—. Chmn. convocation Trinity Coll., U. Toronto, 1994-96, trustee 1996-2002; chmn. export com. Can. Book Publ. Coun., 1993-95. Mem. Assn. Can. Pubs. (rep. to 25th Congress of Internat. Assn. Publs. (dir. CANCOPY 1997-98), co-chmn. copyright com. 1998-2000, Arbor award U. Toronto 1998), Faculty Club U. Toronto. Home and Office: 51 Acacia Rd Toronto ON Canada M4S 2K6 Business E-Mail: bhanna.acacia@rogers.com.

HANNA, WILLIAM JOHNSON, electrical engineering educator; b. Longmont, Colo., Feb. 7, 1922; s. William Grant and Anna Christina (Johnson) H.; m. Katherine Fagan, Apr. 25, 1944 (dec. 1993); children: Daniel August, Paul William; m. Helen Yeager McCarty, Sept. 19, 1996. BSEE, U. Colo., 1943, MS, 1948, D in Elec. Engring., 1951. Registered profl. engr., Colo., Kans. Mem. faculty U. Colo., 1946-91, prof. elec. engring., 1962-91, prof. emeritus, 1991—; ret., 1991. Cons. in field; mem. Colo. Bd. Engring. Examiners, 1973-85; with Ponderosa Assocs., Lafayette, Colo. Author articles, reports. Served to 1st lt. AUS, 1943-46. Recipient Faculty Recognition award Students Assn. U. Colo., 1956, 61, Alfred J. Ryan award, 1978, Archimedes award Calif. Soc. Profl. Engrs., 1978, Outstanding Engring. Alumnus award U. Colo., 1983, Faculty Service award, 1983; named Colo. Engr. of Yr. Profl. Engrs. Colo., 1968; named to Hon. Order of Ky. Cols. Mem. IEEE, Am. Soc. Engring. Edn., Nat. Soc. Profl. Engrs. (pres. Colo. 1967-68), Nat. Coun. Engring. Examiners (pres. 1977-78, Disting. Svc. award with spl. commendation 1990), AIEE (chmn. Denver 1961-62) Clubs: Masons. Republican. Presbyterian. Home and Office: 27 Silver Spruce Nederland Star Rt Boulder CO 80302-9604 Office Phone: 307-666-8112. *Honors and awards I have received are but a reflection of the character of my friends and associates. To them and my family go the accolades.*

HANNAFORD, PETER DOR, public relations executive, writer; b. Glendale, Calif., Sept. 21, 1932; s. Donald R. and Elinor (Nielsen) H.; m. Irene Dorothy Harville, Aug. 14, 1954; children: Richard H., Donald R. II. AB, U. Calif. Acct. exec. Helen A. Kennedy Advt., 1957; v.p. Kennedy-Hannaford, Inc., San Francisco and Oakland, Calif., 1957-62, pres., 1962-67, Pettler & Hannaford, Inc., Oakland, Calif., 1967-69; v.p. Wilton, Coombs & Colnett, Inc., 1969-72; pres. Hannaford & Assoc., Oakland, Calif., 1973; asst. to Gov. of Calif., Calif.; dir. pub. affairs Gov. Office, Calif., 1974; chmn. bd. Hannaford Co., Inc. (formerly Deaver & Hannaford, Inc.), 1975-95; pub. Ferndale Enterprise, Calif., 1996-98; pres. Hannaford Enterprises Inc., 1998—; sr. counselor APCO Worldwide, 2001—. Vice chmn. Calif. Gov. Consumer Fraud Task Force, 1972—73; bd. dirs. Eberle Comms. Group Inc. Author: The Reagans: A Political Portrait, 1983, Talking Back to the Media, 1986 (Japanese edit. 1990); co-author: Remembering Reagan, 1994, Recollections of Reagan, 1997, My Heart Goes Home: A Hudson Valley Memoir, 1997, The Quotable Ronald Reagan, 1998, The Essential George Washington, 1999, The Quotable Calvin Coolidge, 2000, Ronald Reagan and His Ranch, 2002. Mem. Alameda County Rep. Ctrl. Com., Rep. State Ctrl. Com. Calif., 1968-74, The Commonwealth Fund's Commn. on Elderly People Living Alone, 1986-91; Rep. nominee for U.S. Congress, 1972; governing bd. Tahoe Regional Planning Agy., 1973-74; trustee White House Preservation Fund, 1981-89, pub. rels. adv. com. USIA, 1981-92; mem. adv. com. Mt. Vernon 1991-96; 1st lt. Signal Corps, U.S. Army, 1954-56. Shapiro fellow, George Washington U. Sch. Media and pub. affairs, 2002. Mem.: Author's Guild, Potomac Polo Club, Cosmos Club, U. Club (N.Y.), Theta Xi. Presbyterian. Office: Ste 800 700 12th St NW Washington DC 20005-3949 Office Phone: 202-659-7922.

HANNAH, DARYL, actress; b. Chgo., Dec. 3, 1960; d. Don and Sue Hannah. Student, U. So. Calif., Goodman Theater Co., Chgo. Ind. actress, 1978—. Films include The Fury, 1978, The Final Terror, 1981, Hard Country, 1981, Summer Lovers, 1982, Blade Runner, 1982, Reckless, 1984, Splash, 1984, The Pope of Greenwich Village, 1984, The Clan of the Cave Bear, 1986, Legal Eagles, 1986, Roxanne, 1987, Wall Street, 1988, High Spirits, 1988, Steel Magnolias, 1989, Crimes and Misdemeanors, 1989, Crazy People, 1990, At Play in the Fields of the Lord, 1991, Memoirs of an Invisible Man, 1992, Grumpy Old Men, 1993, The Little Rascals, 1994, A Hundred and One Nights, 1995, The Tie that Binds, 1995, Grumpier Old Men, 1995, Two Much, 1996, The Last Days of Frankie the Fly, 1996, the Real Blonde, 1997, Gun, 1997, The Gingerbread Man, 1998, Hi-Life, 1998, Tripwire, 1999, Wild Flowers, 1999, Hearts and Bones, 1999, Speedway Junky, 1999, My Favorite Martian, 1999, Enemy of My Enemy, 1999, Dancing at the Blue Iguand, 2000, Diplomatic Siege, 1999, Cord, 2000, Cowboy Up, 2001, Jackpot, 2001, A Walk to Remember, 2002, Run for the Money, 2002, Bank, 2002, Northfork, 2003, The Job, 2003, The Big Empty, 2003, Casa de los babys, 2003, Kill Bill: Volume 1, 2003, Kill Bill: Volume 2, 2004, Silver City, 2004; (TV films) Paper Dolls, 1982, Attack of the 50 Foot Woman, 1993, The Last Don, 1997, The Last Don II, 1998, Rescuers: Stories of Courage: Two Families, 1998, Addams Family Reunion (voice), 1998, Rear Window, 1998, Hard Target, 2000, Jack and the Beanstalk: The Real Story, 2001; prodr, dir.(feature films), Strip Notes, 2001; (short films) The Last Supper (Jury award for Best Short, Berlin Internat. Film Festival, 1994), 1994. Office: c/o UTA 9560 Wilshire Blvd #500 Beverly Hills CA 90212

HANNAH, DAVID H., metal products executive; BSBA, U. So. Calif. CPA. Mgr. audit divsn. Ernst & Whinney, L.A., 1973-81; CFO Reliance Steel & Aluminum, L.A., 1981-87, v.p., 1987-92, dir., exec. v.p., CFO, 1992-95, pres., 1995—, CEO, 1998—. Office: Reliance Steel & Aluminum Ste 5100 350 S Grand Ave Los Angeles CA 90071 Office Phone: 213-687-7700. Office Fax: 213-687-8792.*

HANNAH, JAMES, state supreme court justice; b. Dec. 26, 1944; BSBA in Acctg., JD, U. Ark. Pvt. practice Lightle, Tedder, Hannah & Beebe; city atty. City of Searcy, Ark., 1969—78; juvenile judge White County, 1976—78; chancery,probate judge 17th Jud. Dist., 1979—99; assoc. justice Supreme Ct. Ark., 2001—04, chief justice, 2004—. Faculty adv. Nat. Jud. Coll. Former chmn. of bd. of adv. Wilbur Mills Alcoholism Treatment Ctr. Mem.: Ark. Bar Assn., Ark. Jud. Coun., Ark. Bd. of Pardons and Paroles (sec. 1972—79), White County Bar Assn. (former pres., treas., sec.), Am. Judges Assn. Office: Ark Supreme Ct Justice Bldg Rm 230 625 Marshall St Little Rock AR 72201 Business E-Mail: jim.hannah@arkansas.gov.

HANNAH, JAN STERLING, elementary school educator; b. Royal Oak, Mich, June 30, 1959; d. John A. and Carol Mae (Heyn) Savage; m. Steven James Hannah, May 24, 1986; 2 children, Zachary Steven and Luke Andrew. AS, Washtenaw C.C., 1982; BS, Ea. Mich. U., 1988; MS, Ea. Mich. U, 1998. Substitute tchr. Washtenaw County, Mich., 1988-90; tchr. summer porgram Michelle Norris Montessori Sch., Ann Arbor, Mich., 1990; tchr. TRI-HOPE Rehab. Svc., Ypsilanti, Mich., 1990-91; reading specialist St. Francis Elem. Sch., 1998—2003; lectr. Ea. Mich. U, 2000—01. Avocations: camping, bike riding, photography.

HANNAH, LAWRENCE BURLISON, lawyer; b. Urbana, Ill., Aug. 5, 1943; s. Lawrence Hugh and Margaret Alene (Burlison) H.; 1 child, Scott David. BA, Dartmouth Coll., 1965; JD cum laude, U. Pa., 1968. Bar: Wash. 1971, U.S. Dist. Ct. (we. dist.) Wash. 1971, Ct. of Appeals (9th cir.) 1971, U.S. Supreme Ct. 1990. Analyst U.S. Central Intelligence Agency, Langley, Va., 1969-71; ptnr. Perkins Coie, Bellevue, Wash., 1971—. Contbr. articles to profl. jours. Mem. King County Personnel Bd., Wash., 1984-90; mem. fin. com. Mcpl. Gov. Candidates, King County, 1972—. 1st lt. USAF, 1968-69. Mem. ABA, Wash. State Bar Assn., Seattle-King County Bar Assn. Methodist. Avocations: jogging, boating, tennis. Home: 1611 103rd Ave SE Bellevue WA 98004-7002 Office: 10885 NE 4th St Ste 700 Bellevue WA 98004 Office Phone: 425-635-1401. Business E-Mail: hannl@perkinscoie.com.

HANNAH, MELODY LORRAINE, music educator, elementary school educator; b. Jefferson City, Mo., Sept. 26, 1956; d. Dale and Pauline Currence; m. Robert Kent Hannah, June 11, 1977; children: Korin Robert, Ethan Raine. MusB, Central Mo. State U., 1979. Music tchr. Clarksburg (Mo.) C-II Sch., 1979—80; day care dir. Someplace Special, Holts Summit, Mo., 1980—82; activities dir. Beverley Enterprises, Jefferson City, 1982—83; Eldon music tchr. Eldon (Mo.) R-1 Sch. Dist., 1983—. Music min. First Bapt. Ch., Eldon, Mo., 1992—; sec. Friends of Music, Eldon, 1996—; associational music dir. Miller County Bapt. Ch., Eldon, 1998—2002. Named Part-Time Music Minister of Yr., Mo. Bapt. Ch. by Southwest Bapt. U., 2001. Mem.: Am. Choral Dirs. Assn., Music Edn. Nat. Conf., Greater Lake Area Choral, Eldon Friends of Music, Beta Sigma Phi. Southern Baptist. Home: 3 Rosewood Dr Eldon MO 65026 Office: Eldon R-1 Sch Dist South Maple Eldon MO 65026 E-mail: khannah@socket.net.

HANNAH, WAYNE ROBERTSON, JR., lawyer; b. Freeport, Ill., Aug. 18, 1931; s. Wayne Robertson and Edith (Biene) H.; m. Patricia Anne Matthews, June 1, 1957; children— Tamara Lee, Wendy, Wayne Robertson III BA, Ill. Coll., 1953; JD, NYU, 1957. Bar: Ill. 1957, U.S. Dist. Ct. (no. dist.) Ill., U.S. Supreme Ct. Ptnr. Sonnenschein, Nath & Rosenthal, Chgo., 1965—. Dir. Checker Motors Corp., N.Y.C. and Kalamazoo, 1982-86; lectr. Ill. Inst. Continuing Edn. Sec. 7th cir. Root-Tilden Scholarship Program NYU, 1967-94; chmn. Root-Tilden-Kern scholarship com., 1981-86, trustee law ctr., 1985—; pres. bd. Firman Cmty. Svcs, Chgo., 1972-75; trustee, pres., chmn. bd. Chgo. City Ballet, 1982-86. 2d lt. USMC, 1951-54. Root-Tilden scholar NYU, 1954-57; Fulbright scholar, 1953-54 Mem. ABA (real estate com.), Chgo. Bar Assn. (chmn. condominium subcom. real estate com. 1977-78, sec., dir. condominium assn. 1991—), Ill. Bar Assn. (real estate com.), Econ. Club (Chgo.), Skokie Country Club (Glencoe, Ill.). Presbyterian. Avocations: tennis, golf. Office: Sonnenschein Nath and Rosenthal 233 S Wacker Dr Ste 8000 Chicago IL 60606-6491 Office Phone: 312-876-8045. Business E-Mail: whannah@sonnenschein.com.

HANNAMAN, ALBERTA ANNA, artist; b. Passaic, N.J., Dec. 11, 1932; d. Henry George and Alice Edith Hannaman. Student, Newark Sch. Fine & Indsl. Art, 1950-53. Offset stripper Screenline Photo, N.Y.C., 1956-84, Verilen Graphics, N.Y.C., 1984-87; offset stripper inhouse printing dept. DDB Needham Worldwide, N.Y.C., 1987-88, Screen Images, N.Y.C., 1988-91. Poet, artist: Prince of Flowers, 1987; contbr. articles to poetry anthologies; exhibited in group shows at Del Bello Gallery, Toronto, Ont., Can., 1988-91, The Miniature Painters, Sculptors and Gravers Soc., Washington, 1990, 91, 98-2004, Long Beach Island Art Gallery, Surf City, N.J., 1990, 91, 98, 2003-04.

HANNAM-OOSTERBAAN, MARIA GERTRUDE, secondary school educator; b. The Netherlands, July 28, 1916; U.S., 1948, arrived in U.S., 1948; d. Jan and Anna Geertruida (Vanderweg) O.; m. Aug 12, 1940. Tchr. Degree, Christian Coll., Amsterdam, 1936; Bachelor, Whittier Coll., 1953. Elem. tchr. Batavia Christian Sch. Dist., Java, Indonesia, 1937-38; tchr. Palembang, Sumatra, Indonesia, 1938-41; clandestine tchr. Concentration Camp, Semarang, Indonesia, 1942—46; tchr. Ranchito Sch. Dist., Pico., Calif., 1953—55, L.A. City Sch. Dist., 1955-77. Mem. Westminster Presbyn. Ch. Mem. AAUW, Calif. Ret. Tchrs. Assn., Order Eastern Star. Presbyn. Home: # G222 710 W 13th Ave Escondido CA 92025-5511

HANNAN, EDWARD LEES, secondary school educator; b. Troy, N.Y., Aug. 21, 1943; s. Edward J. and Marian (Cooper) H.; m. Maryanne Casey, Mar. 25, 1983; children: Elizabeth, Kathleen. BS, Union Coll., 1964, MS, 1970, Syracuse U., 1966; PhD, U. Mass., 1973. Instr. math. SUNY-Albany, 1966-68; sr. statistician N.Y. State Dept. Transp., Albany, 1968-70; asst. prof. Inst. Adminstrn. & Mgmt., Union Coll., Schenectady, 1973-78; assoc. prof. Sch. Bus. Fla. Internat. U. Miami, 1978-80; dir. Bur. Health Care Rsch. and Info. Svcs. N.Y. State Dept. Health, Albany, 1980-90; prof. sch. pub. health SUNY, 1990—. Cons. U.S. Coast Guard, 1978-80, Am. Lung Assn., 1972-73. Mem. planning com. Albany area chpt. ARC, 1982-83. Mem. Ops. Rsch. Soc. Am., Am. Pub. Health Assn., Am. Statis. Assn., Inst. Mgmt. Scis., Am. Inst. for Decision Scis., Sigma Xi, Kappa Mu Epsilon, Alpha Pi Mu. Home: 7 Locust Ave Troy NY 12180-5123 E-mail: eh03@health.state.ny.us.

HANNA-WEIR, SCOT ALAN, music educator, conductor; b. Boston, Oct. 23, 1981; s. Frank Richard Weir, Jr. and Denise Croteau Weir; m. Mary Elizabeth Hanna, May 22, 2004. MusB in Edn., U. N.C., 2003; MusM, U. Wis., 2005. Dir., founder Madrigal Singers U. N.C., Greenboro, NC, 2002—03; tchg. asst. U. Wis., Madison, 2003—05. Scholar, U. N.C., Greensboro, N.C., 1999—2003; Warzyn-Thorpe scholarship, 2003. Mem.: Am. Choral Dirs. Assn. (pres. U. N.C. student chpt. 2002—03). Democrat. Lutheran. Avocations: piano, singing. Personal E-mail: scothanna-weir@hotmail.com.

HANNAY, JANNEKA EVANS, artist; b. Orange, N.J., Aug. 16, 1933; d. David Philip and Cornelia (Irons) Evans; m. Gerald White Hannay (div. 1983); children: James, David, Jeffrey; m. Rodney Baird. BFA, Miami of Ohio U., 1955; MA, Kean Coll. of N.J., 1978; M Profl. Studies, Pratt Inst., 1989. Registered art therapist. Chairperson art dept., gallery dir. Kent Pl. Sch., Summit, N.J., 1974-82; artist Vorpal Gallery, N.Y.C., 1988—2003; art therapist Carrier Found., Belle Mead, N.J., 1986—. Vol. art workshops, Runnels Hosp., Overlook Hosp., Carrier Found., N.J., 1987-2005. Recipient Best in Show award, N.J. Ctr. for Visual Arts, Summit, 1978. Mem. Delta Phi Delta. Home: 183 Buttermilk Bridge Rd Asbury NJ 08802

HANNAY, WILLIAM MOUAT, III, lawyer; b. Kansas City, Mo., Dec. 3, 1944; s. William Mouat and Gladys (Capron) H.; m. Donna Jean Harkins, Sept. 30, 1978; children: Capron Grace, Blaike Ann, William Mouat IV. BA, Yale U., 1966; JD, Georgetown U., 1973. Bar: Mo. 1973, D.C. 1974, N.Y. 1975, Ill. 1980. Law clk. to Judge Myron Bright, U.S. Ct. Appeals, 8th Cir., St. Louis, 1973-74; law clk. to Justice Tom Clark U.S. Supreme Ct., Washington, 1974-75; assoc. Weil Gotshal & Manges, N.Y.C., 1975-77; asst. dist. atty. New York County Dist. Atty.'s Office, N.Y.C., 1977-79; ptnr. Schiff Hardin LLP, Chgo., 1979—. Adj. prof. IIT/Chgo.-Kent Law Sch., 1983—. Author: International Trade: Avoiding Criminal Risks, 1994, Designing an Effective Antitrust Compliance Program, rev. 2004, Tying Arrangements, rev. 2004, International Antitrust Enforcement, rev. 2004; contbr. articles to profl. jours. Chmn. bd. dirs. Gilbert and Sullivan Soc. Chgo., 1984-87, Served with U.S. Army, 1967-68, Vietnam. Mem. ABA (chair sect. internat. law and practice 1998-99, chair Africa law initiative coun. 2000-02, mem. ho. of dels. 2002-), Chgo Bar Assn. (chmn. antitrust com. 1986-87), Yale Club (pres. 1987-89), Chgo. Yacht Club, Union League Club (Chgo.). Democrat. Episcopalian. Home: 591 Plum Tree Rd Barrington IL 60010-2329 Office: Schiff Hardin LLP 7200 Sears Tower Chicago IL 60606 Office Phone: 312-258-5617. Business E-Mail: whannay@schiffhardin.com.

HANNEMAN, LEROY C., JR., real estate executive; married; 2 children. BS in Construction Engring., Ariz. State U. Estimator Del Webb Corp., Sun City, 1972, v.p. housing, 1984, exec. v.p., 1996, pres., COO, Phoenix, 1998—2001, CEO, 1999—2001; co-founder, CEO Element Homes, 2003—. Office: Element Homes One Gateway 426 N 44th St Ste 204 Phoenix AZ 85008*

HANNEMAN, RODNEY ELTON, metallurgical engineer; b. Spokane, Wash., Mar. 14, 1936; s. Christie Luther and Viva Helen (Sugrue) H.; married; 3 children. BS in Phys. Metallurgy, Wash. State U., 1959; MS in Metallurgy, MIT, 1961, PhD, 1964; grad., GE Mgmt. Devel. Inst., 1979. With GE Co., Schenectady, 1963-81, mgr. materials characterization lab., 1977-80, mgr. materials programs, 1980-81; v.p. research, devel. and energy resources Reynolds Metals Co., Richmond, Va., 1981-85, v.p. quality assurance and tech. op., 1985-98; dir. Face Internat., 1988—97; pres. Mgmt. and Tech. Consultants, Richmond, Va., 1998—2002; chmn. Aluminum Assn. Tech. Comm., 1998—2002. Mem. vis. com. dept. materials sci. and engring. MIT, 1975—80, mem. adv. bd. Materials Processing Ctr, 1980—97; mem. adv. bd. U. Va., 1982—87, chmn. indsl. adv. bd. grad. engring. program, 1983—86; chmn. rsch. coordinating coun. Gas Rsch. Inst., 1985—87, adv. coun., 1988—2001; bd. dirs. Materials Properties Coun., 1982—90; mem. adv. com. Va. Ctr. for Innovative Tech., 1999—2002; adv. bd. Commonealth Grad. Enging., Richmond, 2003—. Exec. v.p. found. bd. Sci. Mus. Va., 1989—; v.p. Civic Assn., 1990-92. Recipient Alumni Achievement award Wash. State U., 1978; Joint Engring. Council award, 1984 Mem. AIME, MAPI, SAE, Am. Soc. Metals (Geisler award 1971, Engring. Materials Achievement award 1973), Am. Chem. Soc. (Chem. Innovator award 1970, Edison medallion 1979), Indsl. Rsch. Inst., Aluminum Assn. (chmn. tech. com. 1989-97), Sigma Xi. Achievements include patents in field.

HANNEMANN, MUFI, mayor; b. Honolulu; s. Gustav and Faiaso Hannemann; m. Gail Hannemann. BA with honors, Harvard Univ.; graduate degree, Victoria Univ., New Zealand. Chmn. City Coun., Honolulu, 1995—2000; mayor City of Honolulu, Hawaii, 2005—. Office: Office of the Mayor 530 S King St Honolulu HI 96813 E-mail: mayor@honolulu.gov.*

HANNER, KARL TIGER, lawyer; b. Austin, Tex., Dec. 27, 1964; s. Karl Marion and Lenesse (Harper) Hanner; m. Amy Michelle Anderson, Oct. 16, 1993; children: Alexandra Marie, Kendall Taylor. Student, Yale U., 1984-86; BA with spl. honors, U. Tex., JD, 1991. Bar: Tex. 1991, U.S. Dist. Ct. (we. dist.) Tex. 1991. Assoc. atty. Mullen, MacInnes, Redding & Grove, Austin, 1991-95, Maroney, Crowley & Bankston, Austin, 1995, Brim, Arnett and Robinett, PC, Austin, 1995—. Mem.: Travis County Bar Assn., Austin Young Lawyers Assn., Tex. Relays Ofcls. Assn., Tex. Bar Found. Democrat. Roman Catholic. Avocations: athletics, running, gardening. Office: Brim Arnett and Robinett PC 2525 Wallingwood Dr Bldg 14 Austin TX 78746-6900 Business E-Mail: thanner@brimarnett.com.

HANNES, MARTIN ROY, telecommunications company executive; b. Sydney, NSW, Australia, Mar. 10, 1950; s. Jack Dieter and Morna Jean (Houghton) H.; m. Diana Elizabeth Sutton, Jan. 21, 1989; children: William, Amelia. B in Engring., Sydney U., 1973; MBA, Harvard U., 1978. Exec. v.p. Baia Corp., Jackson, Mich., 1979-86; mng. dir. Hanimex Corp., Sydney, 1984-86; CEO Palcolor Ltd., Sydney, 1985-86, 91-93; sr. v.p. Continental Cablevision Asia Pacific, 1996-99; mng. dir. USWest Asia Pacific, 1999—. Dir. Singapore Cablevision Ltd., Trans Nat. Investments Ltd., Hong Kong, Hanset Pty. Ltd., Road Runner Internat. Fellow Australian Inst. Dirs., Australian Inst. Mgmt.; mem. Inst. Engrs. Australia, Australian Inst. Mgmt., Harvard Club (Boston), Royal Prince Alfred Club (Newport, Australia), Yacht Club. Avocations: skiing, yachting, tennis, golf. Home: 4520 Foxhall Crescent Washington DC 20007 Office: 13241 Woodland Park Dr Round Hill VA 20141 E-mail: mhannes@attglobal.net.

HANNETT, FREDERICK JAMES, healthcare consulting company executive; b. Seattle, Sept. 12, 1950; m. JoAnne Thompson, May 10, 1980; children: Tom, Emily. Pres., COO The Jefferson Group, Washington, 1987-96; mng. prin. The Capitol Alliance, Washington, 1997—. Mem. Va. Bd. Health; bd. advisors Dem. Leadership Coun., Washington. Avocations: tennis, skiing, golf. Home: 4949 Rock Spring Rd Arlington VA 22207-2705

HANNIFAN, PATRICIA G., musician, educator; b. The Dalles, Oreg., Dec. 27, 1957; d. James Edward Hannifan and Margaret Jean Miller. BA, Calif. State U., Northridge, CA, 1992; MusM, U. So. Calif., 2002; MusD, U. Calif., L.A., Calif., 2003. Pvt. instructor-piano/organ/voice Self-Employed, Van Nuys, Calif., 1978—. Instr. East L.A. Coll., Monterey Park, Calif., 1990—2004, L.A. Valley Coll., Valley Glen, Calif., 1997—. Musician: (albums) Music of Scandinavia, Claude Grodon Internat. Brass Workshop, 1988—93, San Gabriel Valley Choral Co., 1995—99; dir.(music): Woodland Hills Cmty. Theatre, 1997—. Musician benefit concert for homeless Frontline Found., Northridge, Calif., 1993—93, L.A. (Calif.) Cath. Worker, 1992; organist Our Saviour's Luth. Ch., 1994—, benefit concert for victims of 9/11, 2001—01. Recipient Artistic Dirs. Achievement award, Valley Theater League, 1998, 2001. Mem.: Nat. Fedn. Music Clubs, Music Tchrs. Assn. of Calif., Am. Guild Organists (chmn. program com. 2005—), Music Assn. Calif. C.C.s. Democrat. Avocations: horseback riding, gardening, travel, swimming, bicycling. Home: 14121 Sylvan St Van Nuys CA 91401 Office: Los Angeles Valley College 5800 Fulton Valley Glen CA Office Phone: 818-947-2347. Personal E-mail: patricia.hannifan@gmail.com.

HANNIG, GARY L., state representative; b. Litchfield, Ill., July 22, 1952; m. Elizabeth Hannig. BS, U. Ill., 1974. CPA. Mem. Ill. Ho. of Reps., 1978—, asst. majority leader, 1997—2005, dep. majority leader, 2005—. Mem. Holy Family Cath. Ch. Mem.: Nat. Rifle Assn., Wolfpack Antique Car Club, Macoupin County Hist. Soc., K. of C., Benld Croation Lodge. Democrat. Office: 300 Capitol Bldg Springfield IL 62706 Address: 218 S Macoupin St Gillespie IL 62033

HANNIGAN, PATRICIA C., prosecutor; b. July 1949; BA, U. Mass.; JD, Rutgers U. Bar: Del. 1982. With U.S. Atty. Office, Wilmington, Del. Mem.: Del. State Bar Assn. (pres. 2002). Office: US Attys Office Ste 1100 1201 Market St PO Box 2046 Wilmington DE 19899-2046

HANNIGAN, WILLIAM J., telecommunications industry executive; MBA U. Colo., 1996. From field engr. to v.p. engring. and applications support Sprint, 1983—96; v.p., bus. sales Pacific Bell Bus. Comm. Svc., 1996—97; pres., global markets SBC Communications Inc., 1998—99; pres. Sabre, Southlake, Tex., 1999—2000, CEO, chmn., 2000—03; pres. AT&T Corp., Bedminster, NJ, 2003—. Mem. President's Info. Tech. Advisory Com. Bd. dirs. Dallas Citizens Coun., Cotton Bowl Athletic Assn.; tech. adv. com. Bush-Cheney 2000 Campaign. Served in submarine svc. USN. Office: AT&T Corp One AT&T Way Bedminster NJ 07921

HANNING, GARY WILLIAM, utilities executive, consultant, water transportation executive; b. Sherman, Tex., Aug. 30, 1942; s. William Homer and Mary Maxine (Harshbarger) H.; m. Robin Dale Smith, June 8, 1974; children: TJ, Lorissa Diane. BS, Rollins Coll., 1974; MBA, Stetson U., 1976. Mgr., co-owner Hanning Water Systems, Denison, Tex., 1963-66; engring. technician Gen. Dynamics, Ft. Worth, 1966-67; engr. supr. Bendix Field, Pasadena, Calif., 1967-70; engr. Philco-Ford Corp., Cape Kennedy, Fla., 1970-73, Jet Propulsion Lab., Pasadena, 1973-74; sect. mgr. Planning Rsch. Corp., Kennedy Space Ctr., 1974-77; pres. S.S.S. Water Systems, Inc., Denison, 1978-83, Texoma Svcs. Corp., Pottsboro, Tex., 1980-99, Tanglewood Water Co., 1994-99; exec. Tecon Water Cos. Inc., 1999—2004. Bd. dirs. Boy Scouts Am., Circle Ten, Dallas; entrepreneur Bells Discount Supply, Tex., 1983-87; adv. bd. Expresiv Techs., Austin, 2000-03. Contbr. articles to profl. jours. Mem. City Coun., Pottsboro, Tex., 1992-98. With USN, 1960-63. Mem. State

Bar Tex. (grievance com. 2000-02), Tanglewood Golf Assn. (sec.-treas. 1992-96), Am. Legion, C. of C. Mem. Ch. of Christ. Avocations: inventing, camping, reading, golf, boating, hunting. Home and Office: 27 Ellen Dr Pottsboro TX 75076-3305

HANNON, BETTIE BENVENUTA, retired elementary school educator; b. N.Y., June 8, 1930; d. Andrew Carlino and Rose LaTorre; m. Lawrence E. Hannon, May 7, 1956; children: Lauren Marci, Andrea Lynn. Student, Glassboro Rowan Coll/, Glassboro, N.J., Trenton State Coll., Trenton, N.J. Kindergarten tchr. Middlesex Sch. Sys., Middlesex, NJ, Brigewatter Raritan, Bridgewater, NJ; 1st dir. head start Somerset County, Somerville, NJ; freelance writer The Beachcomer News, Long Island Beach. Home theatrical dir. Martinsville Cmty. Ctr., Somerville, NJ. Mem.: NJEA, Ret. Nat. Found. Independent. Protestant. Avocations: theater, writing.

HANNON, BRENDA ANN MARIE, psychology professor, researcher; d. Willard James and Mary Ellenor Kelly. BA Honours, York U., Can., 1994; MA, U. Toronto, 1994—95, PhD, 1995—2001. Lectr. U. Toronto, Canada, 2000—02; asst. prof. U. Tex., San Antonio, 2003—. Contbr. articles to profl. jours. Fellow, NSERC, 2001. Achievements include development of the task for measuring component processes of reading comprehension ability. Office: Univ Texas 6900 N Loop 1604 W San Antonio TX 78249 Business E-Mail: bhannon@utsa.edu.

HANNON, BRUCE MICHAEL, engineering educator; b. Champaign, Ill., Aug. 14, 1934; s. Walter Leo and Kathleen Rose (Phalen) H.; m. Patricia Claire Coffey, Aug. 11, 1956; children: Claire, Laura, Brian. BSCE, U. Ill., 1956, MS in Engring. Mechanics, 1966, PhD in Engring. Mechanics, 1970. Engr. with chem. industry, 1957-66; instr. U. Ill., Urbana, 1966-71, assoc. prof. energy rsch., 1974-83, prof. regional sci., 1983—, Jubilee prof. liberal arts and scis., 1991—. Vis. prof. Nat. Ctr. for Supercomputing Applications; cons. NSF, NAS, NAE, chem. industry, various fed. energy agys; patentee in field. Contbr. articles to profl. jours. 1st lt. C.E. AUS, 1956-57. Named Engring. Tchr. of Yr., U. Ill., 1970, Man of Yr., Sierra Club, 1971; recipient 1st prize Mitchell Award Club of Rome, 1975. Home: 1208 W Union St Champaign IL 61821-3229 Office: U Ill 220 Daven Hall Urbana IL 61801 Office Phone: 217-333-0348. Business E-Mail: bhannon@uiuc.edu.

HANNON, SHERRILL ANN, artist; d. Helen Lorraine Hartley and Frederick Henry White; m. Frederick Daniel Hannon Jr., July 21, 1973; 1 child, F. Daniel III. BA, U. N.H., 1972; student, Paul Ingbretson Studio of Drawing and Painting, Manchester, N.H., 1995—99. RN Mass. RN Newton-Wellesley Hosp., Newton Lower Falls, Mass., 1978—83; real estate salesperson Prudential, DeWolfe and Delta Real Estate, Westwood/Medfield, Mass., 1983—95; fine artist Tripp St. Studios, Framingham, Mass., 2000—. Artist demonstrator Everett (Mass.) Art Assn., 2003—. Exhibited in group shows at Salmagundi Club Grand Nat. Exhbn., 2000, Am. Artists Profl. League 73d Grand Nat. Exhbn., 2001, Am. Artists Profl. League 75th Grand Nat. Exhbn., 2003, Acad. Artists Assn. 52d Nat. Exhbn., 2002, Harvard Club, 2002, 2004, Boston Guild Artists Exhbn., 2002, 2004, Rockport Art Assn., 2003, 2004, 2005, Powers Gallery, 2004, 2005. Housing adv. mem. Greater Boston Interfaith Orgn., Boston, 2001, nursing home advocate mem., 2004—; v.p. LWV, Westwood, 1986—87; local coord. Bread for the World, 1985—87. Recipient Ampersand Art award, Copley Art Soc., Boston, 1999, 1st prize, Neponset River Watershed Assn. Canton, Mass., 2000. Mem.: Nat. Academic Artists Assn., Portrait Soc. Am., Rockport Art Assn. (Francis S. Butler Meml. award 1998), Am. Artists Profl. League, Catharine Lorillard Wolfe Art Club (assoc.). Avocations: skiing, reading, gardening. E-mail: sherrillhannon@hotmail.com.

HANNULA, ELIZABETH ANN, professional society administrator, consultant; b. Gardner, Mass., Nov. 17, 1945; d. Wilho S. and Lempi H. (Tuomi) Aalto; m. Edward A. Hannula, Aug. 24, 1968; children: Sadie Ann, Eric Axel. BSc in Elem. Edn., Bridgewater State Coll., Mass., 1967; MA Studies of Am. Civilization, Fitchburg State Coll., Mass., 1973. Tchr. Norwell Schs., Westminster Schs., Mass., 1967—68, 1968—76; substitute tchr. Westminster Schs., Mass., 1982—84; visitor svcs. supr. Gardner Heritage State Pk., Mass., 1984—92; exec. dir. Greater Gardner Cmty. Devel. Corp., Gardner, Mass., 1992—94; small bus. devel. dir. Twin Cities Cmty. Devel. Corp., Fitchburg, Mass., 1994—99; exec. dir. Fitchburg Hist. Soc., Mass., 2000—. Bd. dirs. Greater Gardner C. of C., Mass., 1987—92, Square Two of Garener, Mass., 1988—92, Worcester County Conv. and Visitors Bureau, Mass., 1988—90; cons. in field, 1994—2000. Vol. Westminster Hist. Soc., Mass., 1974—, Westminster Hist. Commn., Mass., 1974—, vice chmn., 1974—; host family ctrl. Mass. rep. Fresh Air Fund, NYC, 1969—84; bd. dirs. Finnish Cultural Ctr., Fitchburg, Mass., 1991—93. Recipient Pres.'s award, Greater Gardner C. of C., Mass., 1991, Woman of Achievement award, Bus. & Profl. Women's Club, 1991, Pub. Svc. award, Square Two Gardner, Mass., 1992. Mem.: Westminster Historical Soc. (curator, pres., v.p. 1974—), Nat. Trust Hist. Preservation, Preservation Mass. (regional adv. coun. 2004—). First Congl. United Ch. Christ. Avocations: genealogy, photography, painting, singing. Home: 68 Harrington Rd Westminster MA 01473 Office: Fitchburg Historical Society 50 Grove St Fitchburg MA 01420

HANNUM, TERENCE J., artist, director, art critic; Attended projects in Painting, NYU, 2000; BA in Religion/Philosophy & studio Art, Fla. Southern Coll., Lakeland, Fla., 2001; post-baccalaureate cert. in Painting and Drawing, Sch. of Art Inst. Chgo., 2002, MFA in Painting and Drawing, 2004. Graphic designer Steppendwarf Theatre Comp., Lakeland, Fla., 2000; gallery asst. Harmon-Meeks Gallery, Naples, Fla., 2001; painting and drawing instr. The VonLiebig Art Ctr., Naples, Fla., 2002; tchr. asst. for Anatomy II, painting and drawing dept. Sch. of Art Inst. Chgo., 2003, office asst., painting and drawing dept., 2003; dir. Panel-House.com, Chgo. Writer (articles) Regulator, F News, Bridge Online, (art reviews) panel-house.com; one-man shows include New Work, Small Gallery, Lakeland, Fla., 2000, New Paintings, Liquid, Naples, Fla., 2001, exhibitions include Valentine's Day Peep Show, Hyde Park Fine Arts, Tampa, Fla., 2000, Sr. Thesis Exhbn., Melvin Gallery, Fla. So. Coll., Lakeland, Fla., 2001, Identities and Autobiographies, VonLiebig Art Ctr., Naples, Fla., 2002, The Pick-Up, 1926, Chgo., Ill., 2002, Faculty Biennial, VonLiebig Art Ctr., Naples, Fla., 2002, MFA Post-Baccalaureate Exhbn., G2, Chgo., Ill., 2002, Brilliant, Zolla/Lieberman Gallery, 2003, Song Lyrics, So-and-So Gallery, 2003, ArtHotel 2003, Embassy Suites, 2003, Stray Show, Zeek & Neen/Municipal, 2003, Modest Contempory Art Projects. Mem.: Chgo. Art Critics Assn. Office: Panel-House c/o Terence Hannum PO Box 220651 Chicago IL 60622 Address: 1046 N Honore St 1F Chicago IL 60622 Business E-Mail: terence@panel-house.com. E-mail: thannu@artic.edu.*

HANOVER, DONNA ANN (DONNA ANN KOFNOVEC), actress; b. Oakland, Calif., Feb. 3, 1950; d. Bob and Gwen Kofnovec; m. Stanley Hanover (div.); m. Rudolph Guilani, Apr. 15, 1984 (div. July 10, 2002); children: Caroline, Andrew; m. Edwin Oster, Aug. 3, 2003. BA in Polit. Sci., Stanford U.; MA in Journalism, Grad. Sch. Journalism, Columbia U. Former radio and television journalist, Pa.; former anchor WPIX Channel 11, NYC; former first lady of NYC. Host (TV series) House Beautiful; actor: (films) Power, 1986, Running on Empty, 1988, The Dream Team, 1989, The People vs. Larry Flynt, 1996, Ransom, 1996, Night Falls on Manhattan, 1997, Celebrity, 1998, The Siege, 1999, Just the Ticket, 1999, Superstar, 1999, Light it Up, 1999, The Intern, 2000, Keeping the Faith, 2000, Series 7: The Contenders, 2001, Someone Like You, 2001, Just a Kiss, 2002; (TV films) Another Woman's Husband, 2000, Jenifer, 2001; (TV series) Another World, 1997, As the World Turns, 1999, All My Children, 1999, One Life to Live, 2000, (guest appearances) Law & Order, The Practice, Ally McBeal, Family Law, Sex and the City; author: (books) My Boyfriend's Back, 2005; actor: (plays) The Vagina Monologues, 2000.*

HANOWER, LEE DAVID, lawyer; b. NYC, June 13, 1959; s. Lee and Gloria Jane (Frankel) Hanower; m. Sandra L. Chamberlin, Sept. 26, 1992. AB, Harvard U., 1981; JD, U. Chgo., 1985. Bar: Wash. 1985, Tex. 1995. Assoc. Perkins Coie, Seattle, 1985-89; asst. v.p. law Burlington Resources Inc., Houston, 1989-91, v.p. law, 1991—96, sr. v.p. law, 1996—98, sr. v.p. law and adminstrn., 1998—. Bd. visitors U. Cancer Found. U. Tex. M.D. Anderson Cancer Ctr., Houston. Mem.: Wash. State Bar Assn., Tex. State Bar Assn., ABA. Office: Burlington Resources Inc 717 Tex Ave Ste 2100 Houston TX 77002

HANRAHAN, LAWRENCE MARTIN, healthcare consultant; b. Cin., Mar. 9, 1961; s. Robert Donald and Mary Francis (Doran) Hanrahan, Barry Wright and Kathryn Regina Kinkaid; m. Madeleine Carol Routon. AB in Chemistry, Miami U., 1983; MD, U. Cin. Coll. Medicine, 1988; MBA, U. Tex. Grad. Sch. Bus., 1992. Founder, owner Landscaping group, Cin., 1975—85; chief ultrasound tech., instr., rsch. assoc. Good Samaritan Hosp. Peripheral Vascular Lab., Cin., 1983—84; instr., technologist Clin. Vascular Lab. Christ Hosp., Cin., 1986; tech. cons., instr. Biosound, Inc., Indpls., 1983—89; surg. rsch. fellow divsn. surgery Boston U. Sch. Medicine; instr. peripheral vascular technologist Seton Med. Ctr., Austin, 1991; summer assoc. health care ops. Deloitte & Touche, Houston, 1991, cons. health care ops., 1991—92, sr. cons., 1992—94, mgr. health care ops., 1994—; sr. assoc. healthcare provider cons. William M. Mercer, Inc., Houston, 1995—97; co-founder Hanrahan Williams LLC, Houston, 1997—2000; dir. Genesis Healthcare Internat., Inc., Houston, 2000—; co-founder, chmn. IQHPC, L.P., Houston, 2001—; sr. mgr. Capgemini US LLC, 2004—05, Accenture, 2005—. Founder, chmn., pres. CORE Med. Techs., Inc., Houston, 1992—; sr. mgr., treas. Miami Med. Edn. and Devel., Miami U., 1975-79; com. mem. Disting. Lecture Series, U. Tex. Sch. Bus., Austin; founding pres. Tex. Bus. Hall of Fame Found. Scholarship Alumni Assn., 1992-93; bd. dirs., exec. com., 1992-93; mem. adv. bd. Healthcorp MBA, Owen Sch., Vanderbilt U., 2005-2006. Contbr. articles to profl. jours. Finalist ACS resident competition, 1990, San Diego State U. Entrepreneurship competition; winner New Eng. Surg. Soc. resident competition, 1990; Tex. Bus. Hall of Fame Found. scholar, 1991, Abell-Hanger Endowed presdl. scholar, 1991. Mem. AMA, Soc. for Vascular Tech., Mass. Med. Soc., Harris County Med. Soc., Med. Student Surg. Soc., Tex. Med. Assn. (com. on physician access 1999—, alt. del. 2003-2006, chmn. 2005-2006), Harris County Med. Soc., Beta Theta Pi. Achievements include patents in field. Avocation: jazz music. Office: 1401 McKinney St Ste 900 Houston TX 77010 Office Phone: 281-610-6258. E-mail: lawrence.m.hanrahan@accenture.com.

HANRAHAN, PAUL THADDEUS, utilities executive; b. Phila., Nov. 10, 1957; s. Paul and Mary (Walsh) H.; m. Rodanthe Nichols, July 30, 1988; two children. BS in Mech. Engring., U.S. Naval Acad., 1979; MBA, Harvard Bus. Sch., 1986. Submarine officer USS Parche, San Francisco, 1979-84; project dir. AES Corp., Washington, 1986-89, pres., CEO, 2002—; mng. dir. AES Transpower, London, 1990-93; pres., CEO AES China, Hong Kong, 1993—2002. Office: AES Corporation 11th Fl 4300 Wilson Blvd Arlington VA 22203

HANRAHAN, ROBERT JOSEPH, chemist, educator; b. Chgo., Jan. 7, 1932; s. James Richard and Lucille Florence (Granger) H.; m. Mary Ellen Hogan, Oct. 28, 1957; children: Ann Marie, Sheila Frances, Robert Joseph, Margaret Evyleen. BS, Loyola U., Chgo., 1953; PhD, U. Wis., Madison, 1957. Research chemist Pure Oil Co., Crystal Lake, Ill., 1953; teaching asst., research asst. Monsanto research fellow U. Wis., Madison, 1953-57; NSF postdoctoral fellow Leeds (Eng.) U., 1957-58; asst. prof. phys. chemistry U. Fla., 1958-64, assoc. prof., 1964-71, prof., 1971—, chmn. phys. chemistry div., 1977-86. Vis. sci. Hahn-Meitner Inst. Nuclear Research, Berlin, 1976; cons. in field. Patentee in field; contbr. articles to profl. jours. AEC rsch. grantee, 1963-74; ERDA grantee, 1975-77; Dept. Energy grantee, 1977-88, 2001—; Dreyfus Found. grantee, 1983. Mem. Am. Chem. Soc., Am. Phys. Soc., Radiation Research Soc., AAAS, Am. Soc. Mass Spectrometry, Inter-Am. Photochem. Soc. Democrat. Roman Catholic. Achievements include rsch. in chem. effects of nuclear radiation and on solar energy systems. Home: 3730 NW 16th Pl Gainesville FL 32605-4848 Office: U Fla Dept Chemistry Gainesville FL 32611 Office Phone: 352-392-1442. Business E-Mail: hanrahan@chem.ufl.edu.

HANRATH, LINDA CAROL, librarian, archivist; b. Chgo., Aug. 22, 1949; d. John Stanley and Victoria (Fraint) Grzesiakowski; m. Richard Alan Hanrath, Nov. 1, 1980; 1 child, Emily. BA in History, Rosary Coll., 1971, MA in Library Sci., 1974. Tchr. social studies Notre Dame High Sch., Chgo., 1971-75; outreach libr. Indian Trails Pub. Libr., Wheeling, Ill., 1975-76, Arlington Heights (Ill.) Meml. Libr., 1976-78; corp. libr. William Wrigley Jr. Co., Chgo., 1978—. Mem. Spl. Librs. Assn. (chmn. libr. jobline com. 1981-83, 86-87, food agrl. and nutrition divsn. 1988-89, sec. Ill. chpt. 1984-86, pres.-elect 1993-94, pres. Ill. chpt. 1994-95, conf. bd. info. svcs. adv. coun. 1990—, winner outstanding achievement award 1997), Assn. Records Mgrs. and Adminstrs., Soc. Am. Archivists, Midwest Archives Conf., Beta Phi Mu. Avocations: needlecrafts, skiing, reading, gourmet cooking. Home: 715 E Devon Ave Roselle IL 60172-1461 Office: William Wrigley Jr Co 410 N Michigan Ave Chicago IL 60611-4213 Office Phone: 312-644-2121. E-mail: lhanrath@wrigley.com.

HANSCH, CORWIN HERMAN, chemistry professor; b. Kenmare, N.D., Oct. 6, 1918; s. Herman William and Rachel (Corwine) H.; m. Gloria J. Tomasulo, Jan. 8, 1944; children: Clifford, Carol. BS, U. Ill., 1940; PhD, N.Y.U., 1944; honoris causa, U. Torino, 2004. Research chemist Manhattan project E.I. du Pont de Nemours & Co., Inc., 1944-45, research chemist, 1945-46; prof. chemistry Pomona Coll., 1946—. Spl. research relationship chem. structure and drug action. Guggenheim fellow Fed. Inst. Tech., Zurich, Switzerland, 1952-53, Pomona Coll., 1966-67, Petroleum Rsch. Fund fellow U. Munich, 1959-60; recipient medal Italian Soc. Pharm. Sci., 1967, Coll. Chemistry Teaching award Mfg. Chemists Assn., 1969, Rsch. Achievement award Am. Pharm. Assn., 1969, E.A. Smissman award Medicinal Chemistry Am. Chem. Soc., 1975, Undergrad. Rsch. award, 1986, Tolman award Los Angeles sect., 1976, award for computers in chem. and pharm. rsch. ACS, 1999, Pratesi Medal, Soc. Chem. Italiana, 2003; named hon. prof. Beijing Med. U., 1990. Fellow Royal Soc. Chemistry (London, hon.); mem. L'Istituto Lombardo Accademiadi Scienze E Letters (Milan, hon.), L'Istituto Lombardo (hon.), Italian Soc. Pharm. Sci. (hon.). Home: 4070 Olive Knoll Pl Claremont CA 91711-1411 Office Phone: 909-621-8445.

HANSCHEN, PETER WALTER, lawyer; b. San Francisco, July 7, 1945; s. Walter A. and Dorothy E. (Watkins) H.; m. Brenda C. Hanschen, Feb. 7, 1987. BA, San Francisco State U., 1967; JD, U. Calif.-Berkeley, 1971. Bar: Calif. 1972, U.S. Supreme Ct. 1985, U.S. Ct. Appeals D.C. Cir. 1975. Assoc. Lawler, Felix & Hall, L.A., 1971-73; atty. Pacific Gas Transmission Co., San Francisco, 1973-76, Pacific Gas & Elec. Co., San Francisco, 1976-79; gen. counsel Pacific Gas Transmission, San Francisco, 1979-83; asst. gen. counsel Pacific Gas & Elec. Co., San Francisco, 1983-88; ptnr. Graham & James, San Francisco, 1988-99, Morrison & Foerster, San Francisco, 1999—. Mem. ABA, Internat. Bar Assn., Fed. Energy Bar Assn., Counsel of Calif. Pub. Utilities. Avocations: golf, gardening, sports. Office: Morrison & Foerster LLP Ste 450 101 Ygnacio Valley Rd PO Box 8130 Walnut Creek CA 94563-8130 Office Phone: 925-295-3450. Personal E-mail: phanschen@mofo.com.

HANSE, JOEL G., research and development company executive, engineer; b. Morris, Minn., Feb. 6, 1944; s. Walter and Pearl Hanse; m. Diane Brandt, Sept. 4, 1965; children: Deborah Eilers, Eric, Kristin Bowie. PhD, Colo. State U., 1972. Engr. Honeywell, Mpls., 1973—78, rsch. scientist, 1978—81, rsch. mgr., 1981—87, program mgr., 1987—96, engring. fellow, 1996—2000, chief scientist, 2000—. Achievements include patents for dual-polarization interferometer with single-mode waveguide; apparatus for interference fringe shift sensing; dither suspension mechanism for ring laser angular rate sensor; cluster dither apparatus; self-calibrating inertial measurement system method and apparatus. Office: Honeywell DSES 2600 Ridgway Pky Minneapolis MN 55413 Office Phone: 612-951-5114.

HANSEL, JAMES GORDON, engineer, educator; b. NYC, Oct. 17, 1937; s. Gordon Franklin and Edith (Bradshaw) H.; m. Sarah Elizabeth Martin, Dec. 27, 1964 (dec. Mar. 2003); 1 child, Claire E.; m. Joan Nancy Lasko, Jan. 3, 2004. BS in Engring. with high honors, Stevens Inst. Tech., 1959, MSME, 1960, ScD, 1964. Mem. rsch. faculty Princeton (N.J.) U., Guggenheim Labs., 1964-69; rsch. engr. Exxon Rsch., Linden, N.J., 1969-72; mgr. new catalyst devel. Engelhard Corp., Menlo Park, N.J., 1972-81; sr. engring. assoc. Air Products and Chems., Inc., Allentown, Pa., 1981—. Adj. assoc. prof. Columbia U., N.Y.C., 1976-80; vis. lectr. mech. engring. Stevens Inst. Tech. Hoboken, N.J., 1970-76; cons. on engring. safety to major corps., 1987—; adj. prof. chem./mech. engring. Pa. State U., State Coll., 1992-2000. Author: Theory of Experiments, 1967; contbg. author Book of Knowledge ency., 1979, Encyclopedia of Chemical Technology, 1994; contbr. articles to profl. jours. Bd. dirs. Am. on Wheels Mus., 1998—; indsl. and profl. adv. coun. Pa. State U., Coll. of Engring., 1998—. Mem. Am. Inst. Chem. Engrs. (tech. com. on reactive chems.), Internat. Standards Orgn. (tech. com. on hydrogen vehicles), N.Y. Acad. Sci., Sigma Xi, Tau Beta Pi. Achievements include patents for on applications of oxygen; development of Three Way Conversion catalyst and automotive engine control system used in over 400 million automobiles worldwide; first to apply hydrogen industry safety practices to hydrogen powered vehicles. Home: 829 Frank Dr Emmaus PA 18049-1505 Office: Air Products & Chems Inc 7201 Hamilton Blvd Allentown PA 18195-1526 Business E-Mail: hanseljg@airproducts.com.

HANSEL, WILLIAM, biology professor; b. Vale Summit, Md., Sept. 16, 1918; s. John W. and Helen M. (Sperlein) H.; m. Milbrey Downey, Aug. 16, 1942; children: Barbara, Kay. MS, Cornell U., 1947, PhD, 1949. Asst. prof. Cornell U., Ithaca, N.Y., 1949-52, assoc. prof., 1952-61, prof., 1961-90, Liberty Hyde Bailey prof., 1983-90, chmn. physiology dept., 1978-83; Gordon D. Cain prof. La. State U., Baton Rouge, 1990—. Scientific adv. Merck, Sharp and Dohme, Rahway, 1980-85, Smith, Kline, Beecham, Westchester, Pa., 1986-91. Author: Genetic Engineering of Animals, 1990, Nutrition and Reproduction, 1998; contbr. over 300 articles to profl. jours. Maj. U.S. Army, 1941-46, ETO. Recipient 13 nat. or internat. rsch. and svc. awards including first Pharmacia and Upjohn Internat. award for life time rsch. in ruminant reproduction, 1998. Fellow AAAS; mem. Soc. Study Reprodn. (pres. 1976), Am. Physiol. Soc., Endocrine Soc., Soc. Exptl. Biology and Medicine (treas. 1975), Gamma Sigma Delta, Sigma Xi, Phi Kappa Phi. Achievements include isolation and identification of cusative agent of bovine x-disease; development of successful technique for estrous cycle regulation in cattle; pioneered development of assays for hormones in blood of animals; discovery of control mechanisms for corpus luteum function in cattle; demonstrated the relationships between nutrition and reproduction in cattle; development of successful targeted treatment for human prostate, breast, ovarian and testes cell tumors grown in test mice. Office: Pennington Biomed Rsch Ctr 6400 Perkins Rd # B1047 Baton Rouge LA 70808-4124 Office Phone: 225-763-3198. Business E-Mail: hanselw@pbrc.edu.

HANSELL, DEAN, lawyer; b. Bridgeport, Conn., Mar. 24, 1952; BA, Denison U., 1974; JD, Northwestern U., 1977. Bar: Ill. 1977, US Dist. Ct. (no. dist.) Ill. 1977, US Ct. Appeals (7th cir.) 1978, US Ct. Appeals (DC cir.) 1978, US Ct. Appeals (9th cir.) 1979, Calif. 1980, US Dist. Ct. (ctrl. dist.) Calif. 1981, US Dist. Ct. (so. dist.) Calif. 1989, US Supreme Ct. 1998, US Ct. Appeals (8th cir.) 2001. Asst. atty. gen. for environ. control State of Ill., Chgo., 1977-80; atty. FTC, LA, 1980-83; assoc. Donovan Leisure Newton & Irvine, LA, 1984-86; ptnr. LeBoeuf, Lamb, Greene & MacRae, LA, 1986—2001, co-mng. ptnr. LA office, 2001—. Mem. Ill. Solar Resources Adv. Panel, 1978—80; adj. assoc. prof. Southwestern Univ. Sch. Law, LA, 1982—86; judge pro tem LA County Mcpl. Ct., 1987—97, LA County Superior Ct., 1989—; mem. adv. bd. Fayette Haywood Legal Svcs., Tenn., 1979—83, Nat. Inst. Citizen Edn. in Law, 1989—94, Asian Pacific Am. Legal Ctr., 1996—. Mem. editl. bd.: Los Angeles Lawyer Mag., 1995—2005, Internat. Reins. Dispute Reporter, 1996—2001; contbr. articles to profl. jours. V.p., commr. LA Bd. Police Commrs., 1997—2001, v.p., 2001; commr. LA Bd. Info. Tech., 2001—, v.p., 2003—04, pres., 2004—; bd. dirs. Jewish Fedn. Coun. Met. LA Region, 1984—87, Project LEAP, Legal Elections All Precincts, Chgo., 1976—80, Martin Luther King Jr. Ctr. Nonviolence, LA, 1991—95, LA Pub. Libr. Found., 1997—2005. Mem.: ABA, Calif. Bar Assn., LA County Bar Assn. (mem. exec. com. antitrust sect. 1982—92, chair 1989—90), Phi Beta Kappa, Omicron Delta Kappa. Office: LeBoeuf Lamb Greene & MacRae 725 S Figueroa St Ste 3100 Los Angeles CA 90017-5404 Office Phone: 213-955-7331. Office Fax: 213-955-7399. Business E-Mail: dhansell@llgm.com.

HANSELL, DENNIS A., oceanography educator; b. Palo Alto, Calif., Nov. 6, 1954; s. Paul E. and Rose Marie Hansell; m. Paula K. Parero, Mar. 15, 1986; children: Allison K., Rachel M. PhD, U. Alaska, 1989. Sr. rsch. scientist Bermuda Biol. Sta. for Rsch., Inc., St. Georges, Bermuda, 1992—2000; prof. U. Miami Rosenstiel Sch. Marine and Atmospheric Sci., Miami, 2001—, divsn. chmn., 2002—. Vice chmn. sci. steering com. Integrated Marine Biogeochemistry and Ecosys.Rsch., Brest, 2004—. Editor: Biogeochemistry of Marine Dissolved Organic Matter, (sci. jour.) Continental Shelf Rsch.; contbr. articles to sci. jours. Mem. sci. steering com. U.S. Joint Global Ocean Flux Study, Woods Hole, Mass., 1996—99; coun. mem. Univ.-Nat. Oceanog. Lab. Sys., Narragansett, RI, 1996—2002. Mem.: AAAS, Am. Soc. Limnology and Oceanography, Am. Geophys. Union (mem. ocean scis. meeting program com. 2001—02). Office: U Miami RSMAS/MAC 4600 Rickenbacker Causeway Miami FL 33149 Office Phone: 305-421-4078.

HANSELL, DOUGLAS M., physician, anesthesiologist, educator, researcher; b. Springfield, Mass., Aug. 6, 1959; s. William Edward Hansell and Winona Margaret Milo; m. Jan L. Cook, Sept. 16, 1989; 1 child, Alexander C. BS in Chemistry, U. Ill., 1981; MD, U. Ill., Chgo., 1985; MPH, Harvard U., 1994. Diplomate Am. Bd. Internal Medicine, Am. Bd. Anesthesiology. Resident internal medicine Washington U., St. Louis, 1985-88; attending physician Mo. Bapt. Hosp., St. Louis, 1988-89; resident anesthesia Harvard U./Mass. Gen. Hosp., Boston, 1989-91, fellow cardiovascular anesthesia, 1991-92; attending physician Mass. Gen. Hosp., Boston, 1992—. Instr. anesthesia Harvard U., Cambridge, 1992—; adv. bd. mem. Santi, Tucson, 1995. Co-author: Clinical Anesthesia Practices, 1993. Mem. AMA, ACP, Am. Soc. Anesthesiology, Am. Soc. Echocardiography, Mass. Med. Soc., Soc. Cardiovascular Anesthesia, Alpha Omega Alpha, Phi Beta Kappa. Office: Mass Gen Hosp 32 Fruit St Boston MA 02114-2620

HANSELL, EDGAR FRANK, lawyer; b. Leon, Iowa, Oct. 12, 1937; s. Edgar Noble and Celestia Delphine (Skinner) H.; m. Phyllis Wray Silvey, June 24, 1961; children: John Joseph, Jordan Burke. AA, Graceland Coll., 1957; BBA, U. Iowa, 1959, JD, 1961. Bar: Iowa 1961. Assoc. Nyemaster, Goode, West, Hansell & O'Brien, P.C., Des Moines, 1964-68, ptnr., shareholder, 1968—. Bd. dirs. The Vernon Co., Greater Des Moines Partnership, Downtown Cmty. Alliance, Inc., Des Moines Internat. Airport; mem. adv. com. to bd. dirs. The Lauridson Group, Inc.; adj. prof. law Drake U., Des Moines, 1990—98. Mem. editorial adv. bd. Jour. Corp. Law, 1985—. Bd. dirs. Des Moines Child Guidance Ctr., 1972-78, 81-87, pres., 1977-78; trustee Iowa Law Sch. Found., 1975-90, pres., 1983-87, bd. dirs. Iowa Natural Heritage Found., 1988-93, Iowa Sports Found., 1986-97; bd. dirs. Iowa State Bar Found., 1991-2000, pres., 1996-98. With USAF, 1961-64. Mem. ABA, Iowa Bar Assn. (pres. young lawyers sect. 1971-72, bd. govs. 1971-72, 85-87, mem. grievance commn. 1973-78, Merit award young lawyers sect. 1977, 98, chmn. corp. and bus. law com. 1979-85, pres. 1989-90), Polk County Bar Assn., Des Moines Club (pres. 1979-80). Home: 139-37th Des Moines IA 50312-4303 Office: Nyemaster Goode West Hansell & O'Brien PC 700 Walnut St Ste 1600 Des Moines IA 50309-3800 Office Phone: 515-283-3150. Business E-Mail: efh@nyemaster.com.

HANSELL, JOHN ROYER, retired pathologist; b. Phila., June 30, 1931; s. Henry Lewis and Elizabeth (Campbell) H. AB, U. Pa., 1953; MD, Jefferson Med. Coll., 1957. Diplomate Am. Bd. Pathology, Am. Bd. Nuclear Medicine (chmn. 1988-89). Intern Germantown Hosp., Phila., 1957-58, resident, pathologist, 1956-61, Bryn Mawr (Pa.) Hosp., 1961-62; pathology fellow New Eng. Deaconess Hosp., Boston, 1962-63; resident Mayo Clinic, Rochester, Minn., 1966-67; chief nuclear medicine VA Med Ctr., Phila., 1967-93. Contbr. chpts. to books and articles to profl. jours. Comdr. USPHS, 1963-66. Fellow Soc. Nuclear Medicine, Coll. Am. Pathologists. Republican. Avocations: antiques, gardening.

HANSELL, PHYLLIS SHANLEY, nursing educator, administrator, researcher, consultant; b. NYC, Jan. 3, 1947; s. Peter James and Jewell Mae (Altis) S.; m. Robert Lewis Hansell, June 16, 1984; children: Benjamin, Christopher. BS, Fairleigh Dickinson U., 1972; MEd, Columbia U., 1975, EdD, 1981. RN. Staff nurse Mountainside Hosp., Montclair, NJ, 1967-69; head nurse NY Med. Coll., NYC, 1970-72, clin. instr., 1972-75; instr. Seton Hall U., South Orange, NJ, 1975-77, asst. prof., 1977-79, prof. nursing, 1986-94, 96—, dir. nursing rsch., 1986-94, dept. chair, 1996-99, acting dean, 1999-2000, dean Coll. Nursing, 2000—, dean, prof. Coll. Nursing, 2000; dir. nursing rsch. Meml. Sloan-Kettering, NYC, 1984-86. Chair NJ Assn. of Baccalaureate and Higher Degree Programs in Nursing; commr. Nat. Commn. for VA Nursing, 2002—04; mem. adv. coun. Future of Nursing in NJ, 2002—04. Contbr. articles to profl. jours., chpt. to book. Bd. dirs. Jr. League, Montclair, 1992-94, chair grants and corp. devel., chair Newark Teen Arts Festival, Montclair and Newark, 1994-95. Recipient Gov.'s merit award Gov. NJ, 1994. Fellow: Am. Acad. Nursing; mem.: ANA (chair rsch., Gov.'s award 1994), NJ State Nurses Assn. (mem. coun., Rsch. award 1994), Am. Acad. Practice (Disting. Practitioner 2000), Sigma Theta Tau (v.p. Gamma Nu chpt. 1994—96, Rsch. award 1983). Avocations: opera, ballet, skiing, tennis, golf. Office: Seton Hall U 400 S Orange Ave South Orange NJ 07079-2697

HANSELL, RICHARD STANLEY, obstetrician, educator, gynecologist, educator; b. Indpls., Nov. 18, 1950; s. Robert Mathey and Jewell (Martin) H.; m. Cathy C., Oct. 7, 1995; children: Elizabeth, Victoria. BA, DePauw U., 1972; MD, Ind. U., 1976. Cert. Am. Bd. Obstetrics and Gynecology. Practice medicine specializing in ob-gyn. Cedarwood Med. Ctr., St. Joseph, Mich., 1980-86; asst. prof. ob-gyn. Ind. U., Indpls., 1986-93, assoc. prof., 1993—2002, prof., 2002—. Instr. Western Mich. U., Kalamazoo, 1980-86; med. bd. Planned Parenthood, Benton Harbor, Mich., 1980-86; med. dir. Planned Parenthood of Ctrl. Ind., 1991-95; examiner Am. Bd. Ob-gyn., 1994—. Mem. AMA, Am. Coll. Ob-gyn., Assn. of Profs. of Gynecology and Obstetrics, Ind. State Med. Soc., Ctrl. Assn. Ob-gyn., Indpls. Med. Soc. Presbyterian. Avocations: golf, fishing. Office: Ind U Med Sch Dept Ob-Gyn 1001 W 10th St Indianapolis IN 46202-2859 Business E-Mail: rhansell@iupui.edu.

HANSELMAN, RICHARD WILSON, entrepreneur; b. Cin., Oct. 8, 1927; s. Wendell Forest and Helen E. (Beiderwelle) H.; m. Beverly Baker White, Oct. 16, 1954; children: Charles Fielding, II, Jane White. BA in Econs, Dartmouth Coll., 1949. V.p. merchandising RCA Sales Corp., Indpls., 1964-66, v.p. product planning, 1966-69, v.p. product mgmt., 1969-70; pres. luggage divsn. Samsonite Corp., Denver, 1970-73, pres. luggage group, 1973-74, exec. v.p. ops., 1974-75, pres., 1975-77; sr. v.p. Beatrice Foods Co., Chgo., 1976-77, exec. v.p., 1977-80; pres., COO, dir. Genesco Inc., Nashville, 1980-86, CEO, 1981-86, pvt. investor, corp. dir., 1986—. Chmn. Forward Air. Hon. trustee Com. for Econ. Devel. Served with U.S. Army, 1950-52. Mem. Belle Meade Country Club, Union League, Chgo. Club, Phi Kappa Psi. Office: 104 Westhampton Pl Nashville TN 37205

HANSEN, ALEXANDER E., advertising agency executive; BA, Williams Coll.; MDiv, Princeton Theol. Seminary; studied, Cal State LA bus. program. CPA Lic., Calif. Fin. exec. with DS Waters of Am. LP, Groupe Danone, J. Walter Thompson; pres., CEO Bravant LLC, L.A.; fin. leadership (CFO) ptnr. Tatum CFO Ptnrs., LLP, L.A.; CFO Adchek, Ventura, Calif. Mem.: Calif. Soc. CPA, AICPA. Office: Tatum CFO Ptnrs LLP 11755 Wilshire Blvd Ste 1100 Los Angeles CA 90025 also: Adchek 2225 Sperry Ave Ste 2000 Ventura CA 93003*

HANSEN, ANDREW MARIUS, retired library director; b. Storm Lake, Iowa, Mar. 25, 1929; s. Andrew Marius and Margaret Mary (Van Wagenen) H.; m. Rina M. Smith, Feb. 24, 1967; 1 child, Neil S. BA, U. Omaha, 1951; postgrad., U. Md., 1955; MA, U. Minn., 1962; postgrad. U. Iowa, 1968-71. Librarian Bismarck (N.D.) Public Library, 1957-63, Sioux City (Iowa) Public Library, 1963-67; instr. Sch. of Library Sci., U. Iowa, Iowa City, 1967-71; exec. sec. ALA, Chgo., 1971-80, exec. dir. reference and adult services div., 1980-94. Vis. asst. prof. Ind. State U., Terre Haute, 1966; adj. faculty Dominican U., River Forest, Ill., 2001. Pres. Friends of Wilmette Pub. Libr., 1984-85; mem. Village of Wilmette Transp. Commn., 1995—2003; bd. dirs. United Way of Wilmette, 2004-05. Served with USAF, 1951-55. Mem. ALA (Mudge-Bowker award 1993), N.D. Libr. Assn. (pres. 1958-59, sec.-treas. 1962-63), Iowa Libr. Assn. (pres. 1967-68), Coalition Adult Edn. Orgns. (bd. dirs. 1972-93), Ch. and Synagogue Libr. Assn. (treas. Northeastern Ill. chpt. 1985-91), Chgo. Libr. Club (sec. 1983-84), Rotary. Presbyterian. Home: 314 Skokie Blvd Wilmette IL 60091-3002 E-mail: andy_hansen@msn.com.

HANSEN, ARTHUR GENE, former academic administrator, consultant; b. Sturgeon Bay, Wis., Feb. 28, 1925; s. Henry A. and Ruth (Anderson) H. BSEE, Purdue U., 1946, MS in Math., 1948, DEng (hon.), 1971; PhD in Math., Case Inst. Tech., 1958; DSc (hon.), Ind. U., 1982. Rsch. scientist NASA, 1948-49, 50-58; tchr. U. Md., 1949-50; sect. head Cornell Aero. Lab., Buffalo, 1958-59; faculty mech. engring. U. Mich., 1959-66; dean Ga. Inst. Tech., 1966-69, pres., 1969-71, Purdue U., 1971-82; chancellor Tex. A&M U. System, 1982-86; dir. rsch. Hudson Inst., 1987-88. Prof. mech. engring. Tuskegee Inst., 1965; sr. rsch. engr. Douglas Aircraft Co., 1964; cons. to industry, 1961-70; chmn. bd. Corp. for Edn. Tech., 1992-94; chmn. Atlanta Civic Design Commn., 1968-79, Ga. Sci. and Tech. Commn., 1968-71, Ga. Ocean Sci. Ctr. of Atlantic Commn., Atlanta, 1968-71; adv. coun. Skidaway Oceanographic Inst. for Univ. System Ga., 1968-71; pres. Ind. Conf. Higher Edn., 1975; chmn. com. on minorities in engring. NRC, 1974-76; energy rsch. adv. bd. Dept. Energy; chmn. adv. coun. Electric Power Rsch. Inst., 1973-79; chmn. bd. Ind. State Symphony Soc., 1989-91. Author: Similarity Analyses of Boundary Value Problems in Engineering, 1964, Fluid Mechanics, 1967. Chmn. bd. visitors Air U., 1974-77; bd. visitors Air Force Inst. Tech., 1987-89; trustee Nat. Fund Minority Engring. Students, 1980-81; mem. acad. adv. bd. U.S. Naval Acad., 1975-79; past chmn. Tex. Com. Employer Support of Guard and Res., Tex. Sci. and Tech. Coun.; chmn. Ind. Commn. for Higher Edn., 1994—; bd. dirs. CUNY Rsch. Found., 1994-97. With USMCR, 1943-46. Recipient Leather medal Sigma Delta Chi, Disting. Svc. medal Dept. Def., 1985; named Ind. Engr. of Yr., 1979, Purdue Disting. Alumnus, 1979. Fellow AAAS; mem. NAE, Gas Rsch. Inst. (chmn. adv. coun. 1976-79), Sigma Xi, Eta Kappa Nu, Pi Tau Sigma, Tau Beta Pi, Phi Kappa Phi, Omicron Delta Kappa, Phi Eta Sigma, Kappa Kappa Psi. Home: 815 Sugarbush Rdg Zionsville IN 46077-1911

HANSEN, BARBARA CALEEN, physiologist, science educator; b. Boston, Nov. 24, 1941; d. Reynold L. and Dorothy (Richardson) Caleen; m. Kenneth Dale Hansen, Oct. 8, 1976; 1 child, David Scott. BS, UCLA, 1964, MS, 1965; PhD, U. Wash., 1971. Asst. prof. then assoc. prof. U. Wash., Seattle, 1971—76; prof., assoc. dean U. Mich., Ann Arbor, 1977—82; assoc. v.p. acad. affairs and research, dean grad. sch. So. Ill. U., Carbondale, 1982—85; v.p. for grad. studies and research U. Md., Balt. and Balt. County, 1985—90, prof. physiology, dir. obesity and diabetes rsch. ctr., 1990—. Mem. adv. com. to dir. NIH, Washington, 1979—83; mem. joint health policy com. Assn. Am. U., Washington, 1982—86, Nat. Assn. State U. and Land-Grant Colls., Washington, 1982—86, Am. Coun. on Edn., Washington, 1982—86; mem. nutrition study sect. NIH, 1979—83; mem. program com. Inst. Medicine-NAS, Washington, 1982—84; mem. Armed Forces Epidemiology Bd., 1991—95; mem. bd. sci. counselors NIEHS, 1992—94, NIH, 1992—94, mem. nat. toxicology bd., 1992—94, NIEHS, 1992—94; mem. search com. Office of Rsch. Integrity, NIH, 1992—93. Author: The Commonsense Guide to Weight Loss for People with Diabetes, 1998, The Metabolic Syndrome X, 1999; co-editor: Controversies in Obesity, 1983, editor chpts. on physiology; contbr. articles to profl. jours.; co-editor: Insulin Resistance and Insulin Resistance Syndrome, 2002. Mem. adv. com. Am. Bur. Med. Advancement China, NYC, 1982—85; mem. adv. bd. African-Am. Inst., 1987—91; mem. adv. com. Robert Wood Johnson Found., Princeton, NJ, 1982—91. Fellow Nueroscis. fellow, U. Pa., 1966—68. Mem.: Internat. Assn. Study of Obesity (pres. 1986—90), Nat. Assn. State U. and Land Grant Colls. (chmn. coun. on rsch. policy and grad. edn. 1986—87), N.Am. Assn. Study of Obesity (pres. 1984—85, 1986—), Am. Soc. for Clin. Nutrition (pres.-elect 1994—95, pres. 1995—96, v.p.), Am. Soc. for Nutritional Scis., Inst. Medicine of NAS, Am. Physiol. Soc., Phi Beta Kappa (Arthur Patch McKinley scholar 1964). Republican. Presbyterian. Achievements include discovery of of periodic (10-14 min.) cycling pattern of pancreas insulin secretion; identification of the pattern of progressive defects in insulin secretion and insulin action preceeding overt clinical type 2 diabetes mellitus; showed prevention of obesity prevents most type 2 diabetes. Office: U Md-Balt Sch Medicine Obesity-Diabetes Rsch Ctr 10 S Pine St MSTF 600 Baltimore MD 21201-1116

HANSEN, BRUCE D., mining executive; BS in Mining Engring., Colo. Sch. Mines; MBA, U. N.Mex. Sr. v.p. corp. devel. Santa Fe (N.Mex.) Pacific Gold, 1994—97; v.p. project devel. Newmont Mining Corp., Denver, 1997—99, sr. v.p., 1999—, CFO, 1999—. Office: Newmont Mining Corp 1700 Lincoln St Denver CO 80203*

HANSEN, BRUCE LYNN, retired music educator; b. Brigham City, Utah, Oct. 17, 1951; s. Rulon Han and Edith Irene Hansen; m. Dora Marie Jones, Aug. 28, 1976; children: Nicole Irene, Joelyn Marie, Donnelle Caroline, Bruce Robert, Taylor Ashley. BA, Utah State U., 1973; MA, U. Wash., 1980. Cert. tchr. Wash., 1974. Tchr. music St. John Sch. Dist., Wash., 1973—76, Napavine Sch. Dist., Napavine, 1976—77, Port Townsend Sch. Dist., 1977—83, Centralia Sch. Dist., 1983—2003; ret., 2003. Priesthood leader Ch. of Jesus Christ of Latter-day Saints, Centralia, 1983—2003. Conservative. Achievements include Centralia MS Band selected to participate in Washington DC Independence Day Parade; The band was selected in 1986. Avocations: travel, backpacking, music. Office: Centralia School District 901 Johnson Rd Centralia WA 98531

HANSEN, CARL R., management consultant; b. Chgo., May 2, 1926; s. Carl M. and Anna C. (Roge) Hansen; m. Christia Marie Loeser, Dec. 31, 1952; 1 child, Lothar. MBA, U. Chgo., 1954. Dir. mkt. rsch. Kitchens of Sara Lee, Deerfield, Ill., Earle Ludgin & Co., Chgo.; svc. v.p. Mkt. Rsch. Corp. Am., 1956—67; pres. Chgo. Assoc., Inc., 1967—. Chmn. Ill. adv. coun. SBA, 1973—74; exec. com. Ill. Gov.'s Adv. Coun., 1969—72; resident officer U.S. High Commn., Germany, 1949—52; chmn. Viking Ship Restoration Com.; mem. Cook County Bd. Commrs., 1970, 1974—, chmn. legis. com., adminstrn. com.; active Am. Scandinavian Found.; vice chmn. Rep. Ctrl. Com. Cook County; chmn. Cook County Young Reps., 1957—58, 12th Congl. Dist. Rep. Orgn., 1971—74, 1978—82, Suburban Rep. Orgn., 1974—78, 1982—86; del. Rep. Nat. Conv., 1968, 1984, 1992; chmn. Legis. Dist. Ill., 1964—; del. Rep. State Conv., 1962—96; committeeman Elk Grove Twp. Rep., 1962—2002; pres. John Ericsson Rep. League of Ill., 1975—76; Rep. presdl. elector State of Ill., 1972; bd. dir. Nat. Assn. Counties. 1st lt. U.S. Army, 1948, maj. USAR. Mem.: VFW, Planning Forum, Nat. Assn. Counties, Am. Statis. Assn., Am. Mktg. Assn., Swedish Am. Hist. Soc., Dania Soc., Chgo. Hist. Soc., Lions, Am. Legion, Res. Officers Assn., Shriners, Masons, Sons of Norway. Home: 110 S Edward St Mount Prospect IL 60056-3414 Office: 118 N Clark St Chicago IL 60602-1304 Office Phone: 847-818-0200.

HANSEN, CAROL LOUISE, literature and language professor; b. San Jose, Calif., July 17, 1938; d. Hans Eskelsen and Thelma Josephine (Brooks) Hansen; m. Merrill Chris Davis, July 17, 1975 (div.). BA in English, San Jose State U., 1960; MA in English Lit., U. Calif., Berkeley, 1968; PhD in English Lit., Ariz. State U., 1975. Asst. prof. English City Coll. San Francisco, Calif., 1985—, Coll. San Mateo, Calif., 1987—, De Anza Coll., 1998-99; lectr. expository writing U. San Francisco, 2001; prof., dean of journalism Olivet U., San Francisco, 2005—. Writing coord. Calif. State U., Monterey Bay, 1996; mem. rsch. com. Conf. on Coll. Composition and comm., 2001; presenter in field. Author: Woman as Individual in English Renaissance Drama, 1993, 2d edit., 1995, 3d edit., 2000, The Life and Death of Asham: Leonard and Virginia Woolf's Haunted House, 2000, Beyond Evil: Cathy and Cal in East of Eden, 2002; contbr. articles to profl. jours. Active Grace Cathedral, San Francisco. Fellow NDEA. Mem.: MLA (chair exec. com. discussion group on two-yr. colls. 1999), Virginia Woolf Soc. Episcopalian. Avocation: animal welfare. Office: City Coll San Francisco 50 Phelan Ave San Francisco CA 94112-1821 Office Phone: 415-452-7068. Personal E-mail: carhansen@sbcglobal.net.

HANSEN, CHARLES, lawyer; b. Jersey City, May 23, 1926; s. Charles Henry and Katherine (Bensch) H.; m. Carolyn P. Smith, Sept. 26, 1953; children: Mark, Melissa. BS, U. Mich., 1946; JD, Mich. Law Sch., 1950. Bar: N.Y. 1951, Wis. 1961, Mo. 1980. Engr. Westinghouse Electric Co., 1946; assoc. Mudge, Stern, Williams & Tucker, 1950-53; chief labor counsel, div. counsel Sylvania Electric Products, 1953-61; sec., gen. counsel Trane Co., La Crosse, Wis., 1961-69, exec. v.p., 1968-73; pres. Cutler-Hammer World Trade, Inc., 1973-77; v.p. Cutler-Hammer, Inc., 1973-77, exec. v.p., 1977-79; sr. v.p. law Emerson Electric Co., 1979-84, sr. v.p., sec., gen. counsel, 1984-89; ptnr. Bryan Cave, 1989-95, of counsel, 1995—. Adj. prof. Sch. Law St. Louis U., 1987-99. Served to lt. (j.g.) USNR, 1943-46. Mem. ABA, Wis., Mo. bar assns., Am. Law Inst., Order of Coif, Tau Beta Pi. Home: 8 Wydown Ter Saint Louis MO 63105-2217 Office: 211 N Broadway 1 Metropolitan Sq Ste 3600 Saint Louis MO 63102-2750 Office Phone: 314-259-2676. Personal E-mail: hansenc1h@aol.com. Business E-Mail: chansen@bryancave.com.

HANSEN, CHARLES JAMES, lawyer; b. Boston, Dec. 26, 1947; m. Margaret Hansen; children: Christine R., Caroline M. BA, U. Kansas, 1970; JD, Boston Collge, 1974. Assoc. Lord Bissell & Brook, Chgo., 1974—77, Shearman & Sterling, N.Y.C., 1977—82; asst. gen. counsel Am. Hospital Supply Co., Evanston, Ill., 1982—85; assoc. gen. counsel Baxter Internat., Deerfield, Ill., 1985—87; v.p., gen. counsel, sec. Carson Pirie Scott & Co., Milw., 1987—98; sr. v.p., dep. gen. counsel Saks Inc., Birmingham, Ala., 1998—2003, exec. v.p.-law, gen. counsel, 2003—. Mem.: Chgo. Bar Assn., NY State Bar Assn., State Bar Wis. Office: Saks Inc 750 Lakeshore Pky Birmingham AL 35211 Home: 3187 Overhill Rd Birmingham AL 35223-1247 Office Phone: 205-940-4000. Office Fax: 205-940-4987.

HANSEN, CHARLES MARTIN, III, lobbyist; s. Charles Martin Hansen, Jr. and Sheila Anne Madigan; m. Anjali Hansen; children: Charles Martin Hansen, IV, Katarina Genevieve, Alexander Keegan. BA, Vanderbilt U., 1985; MPA, U. Tex., 1995. Legislative staff Office of U.S. Senator Lloyd Bentsen, Washington, 1985—89; assoc. dir. State of Tex. Washington Office, 1991; dir. congl. liaison U.S. Internat. Trade Commn., Washington, 1992—94; mng. ptnr. Podesta Assoc., Washington, 1994—2001; pres. Hansen Govt. Rels., Washington, 2001—. Contbr. articles to profl. jours. D-Liberal. Roman Catholic. Office: Hansen Govt Rels 2600 Virginia Ave NW Ste 505 Washington DC 20037 Office Phone: 202-333-2524. E-mail: hansen@hansen-gr.com.

HANSEN, CHARLES MORTON, editor, retired military officer; b. Huntington Park, Calif., Sept. 27, 1933; s. Andrew Hansen and Lena S. Andrew. BA in History, UCLA, 1955; MA in History, San Francisco State U., 1985. Commd. 2d lt. U.S. Army, 1955, platoon leader, 1957-59, co-comdr., 1962—63, sr. adv., 1965-66, bn. comdr., 1969-70, advanced through grades to col., 1977, ret., 1982; contbg. editor Am. Genealogist, 1988—; editor The Genealogist, 1996—. Contbr. articles to profl. jours. Decorated Legion of Merit, Bronze Star, Combat Infantry Badge, Cross of Gallantry Republic of Vietnam; recipient Coddington award for Merit, New Eng. Hist. Geneal. Soc., 1995. Fellow: Am. Soc. Genealogists; mem.: Soc. Heraldica Scandinavia (Denmark), Heraldry Soc. (London), Soc. Genealogists (London), Ninth Infantry Rgt. Assn., Harbor Point Racquet Club. Methodist. Avocation: tennis. Home: 25 Rodeo Ave Apt 22 Sausalito CA 94965-1783

HANSEN, CHRISTIAN ANDREAS, JR., plastics and chemical company executive; b. New Braunfels, Tex., Sept. 12, 1926; s. Christian Andreas and Velma Arbeda (Ivy) Hansen; m. Emily Dann. BS, Rice U., 1948. Dir. mfg. chem. div. G.A.F. Corp., N.Y.C., 1969—71; chmn. bd., CEO, pres., founder Hanlin Group, Inc., Linden Chlorine Products, Inc., 1971—93, LCP/Nat. Plastics, Inc., 1977—93; retired, 1993. With Exxon 21 years, last position gen. mgr., Linden, N.J.; founder, chmn., CEO, pres. Pathways, Inc., 1994-98, Hansen Plastics, Inc., 1994-98; co-founder Ultrapure Products, Inc., 2000-; real estate agt. Weichert Realtors, N.J. Pub.: God's Bible and Jesus' Papers, 1994; patentee in field. Councilman City of Baytown, Tex., 1961—63; pres. Union County United Fund, N.J., 1967—69; chmn. Chem. Industry Coun., Trenton, N.J., 1977—82; mem. Gov.'s Commn. on Hazardous Waste Disposal; leader Boy Scouts, Sea Scouts; mem. Eastern Union County C. of C., v.p., 1968—69. Lt. USNR, 1943—46. Named Man of Yr., Union County United Fund, 1970. Mem.: Chlorine Inst. (past. pres., past bd. dirs.), Am. Inst. Chem. Engrs. Home and Office: 1 Scenic Dr Highlands NJ 07732-1329

HANSEN, CHRISTINE MERRI, music educator; b. Inglewood, Calif., Dec. 26, 1954; d. Oluf Steffen and Betty Jane (Henderson) H. PharmD, U. So. Calif., L.A., 1979; AA in Music, piano tchg. cert., Golden West Coll., 1993. Cert. pharmacist; cert. piano tchr. Clin. pharmacist, lectr. pharmacology Cottage Hosp., Santa Barbara, Calif., 1979-87; pvt. math and sci. tutor Calif., 1987—; math. and sci. tutor Golden West Coll. Tutoring Ctr., Huntington Beach, Calif., 1991-93; model La Belle Agy., 1990-91, John Robert Powers Agy., 1991-93. Pvt. piano tchr. Writer, pub.: (newsletter) Our Generation. City of Huntington Beach and Mercury Savs. scholar Golden West Coll., 1975, Gift of Music scholar Golden West Coll., Huntington Beach, 1993. Avocations: poetry, songwriting, singing, watercolors.

HANSEN, CLAIRE V., financial executive; b. Thornton, Iowa, June 3, 1925; s. Charles F. and Grace B. (Miller) H.; m. Renee C. Hansen, Aug. 17, 1946; children: Charles James, Christopher David, Peter Chrissis. BSc, U. Notre Dame, 1947; MBA, Harvard U., 1948. Chartered fin. analyst. With Salk, Ward & Salk, Inc.; v.p. Salk Inst. Agency, 1954-59; with Duff, Anderson & Clark, Chgo., 1959-67, v.p., dir., 1967-71; dir. Duff and Phelps, Inc., 1972-88; exec. v.p. Duff & Phelps, 1973-75, pres., chief exec. officer, 1975-84, chmn. and CEO, 1984—87; chmn. bd. dir. Duff & Phelps Utilities Income, Inc., Chgo., 1987—2001, CEO, 2000—01; chmn. bd. dir. DNP Select Income Fund, Inc., 2002—05. Bd. dir. Chgo. Lung Assn., 1962-80, pres. 1973-75; bd. dir. Am. Lung Assn., 1971-83, Ctr. Religion and Psychotherapy in Chgo., 1979-83; trustee Glenwood Sch., 1974-95, chmn., 1983-87; bd. dirs. Auditorium Theatre Coun., 1983-88, treas., 1987-88; bd. dir. Schwab Rehab. Hosp., 1978-82, pres., 1980-82; bd. dir. Pelican Bay Found. Inc., 1993-99, treas., 1993-96, pres., 1996-97. Mem. Inst. Chartered Fin. Analysts, Univ. Club, Chgo. (Ill.) Club, Olympia Fields Country Club, Club Pelican Bay, Hole-in-the-Wall Golf Club. Republican. Episcopalian. Home: 5601 Turtle Bay Dr Apt 2001 Naples FL 34108-2703 Office: 5601 Turtle Bay Dr # 2001-02 Naples FL 34108 E-mail: verdelle@msn.com.

HANSEN, CURTIS LEROY, federal judge; b. 1933; BS, U. Iowa, 1956; JD, U. N.Mex., 1961. Bar: N.Mex. Law clk. to Hon. Irwin S. Moise N.Mex. Supreme Ct., 1961-62; ptnr. Snead & Hansen, Albuquerque, 1962-64, Civerolo, Hansen & Wolf, P.A., 1964—92; dist. judge U.S. Dist. Ct., N.Mex., 1992—2003, sr. dist. judge, 2003—. Mem. State Bar N.Mex., Albuquerque Bar Assn., Am. Coll. Trial Lawyers, Am. Bd. Trial Advocates, Albuquerque Country Club. Mailing: PO Box 669 Albuquerque NM 87103 Office: US Courthouse 421 Gold Ave SW 5th Fl Albuquerque NM 87102

HANSEN, DAVID RASMUSSEN, federal judge; b. Exira, Iowa, 1938; BA, N.W. Mo. State U., 1960; JD, George Washington U., 1963. Asst. clk. to minority House Appropriations Com. Ho. of Reps., 1960—61; adminstrv. aide 7th Dist. Iowa, 1962—63; law clerk, assoc. atty. Jones, Cambridge & Carl, Atlantic, Iowa, 1963—64; capt., judge advocate General's Corps US Army, 1964—68; pvt. practice Barker, Hansen & McNeal, Iowa Falls, Iowa, 1968—76; ptnr. Win-Gin Farms, Iowa Falls, 1971—; judge Police Ct., Iowa, 1969—73, 2d Jud. Dist. Ct., Iowa, 1976—86, US Dist. Ct. (no. dist.), Cedar Rapids, Iowa, 1986—91, US Ct. Appeals (8th cir.), Cedar Rapids, 1991—2002, chief judge, 2002—03, sr. judge, 2003—. Chmn. Hardin County Rep. Central Com., 1975—76; mem. Jud. Conf. of US, 2002—03. Mem.: Dean Mason Ladd Inn of Ct., Iowa State Bar Assn. Office: US Courthouse Rm 304 101 1st St SE Cedar Rapids IA 52401-1202*

HANSEN, DONALD MARTY, journalist, retired accountant; b. Elmhurst, Ill., July 6, 1935; s. Donald Joseph Hansen and Vivian Leona (Bourgart) Guthrie; m. Rose Ann Baumeister, Aug. 12, 1961 (div.); children: Teresa Lynn, Donna Louise, David Lawrence, Daniel Leonard. Assoc. in Acctg., Racine Tech., 1970. Drill press operator J.I. Case Co., Racine, Wis., 1964-70; acct. Scott Petersen Meat Co., Chgo., 1974-95, Crosby Freezer, Inc., Chgo., 1995-2000; editor, pub. Don Hansen's Nat. Weekly Football and Basketball Gazettes, Westmont, Ill., 1987—; columnist USA Today Online, 1998—; editor, pub. Don Hansen's Ann. 52-page Football Schedules Booklet, 2000—. Stringer Football News, Miami, 1981—, The Sporting News, St. Louis, 1987—, USA Today, Arlington, Va., 1987—; mem. Melberger award selection com. Downtown Wilkes-Barre Touchtown Club, 1993—; mem. com. for NCAA Divsn. III Player of the Yr., John Gagliardi award, 1993—. Editor, pub. Don Hansen's Annual 52-Page Football Schedules Booklet, 2000—; contbr. articles to profl. jours. Originator, promoter, operator annual summer wrestling tournament Oak Park-River Forest (Ill.) H.S., 1978-80; mem. selection com. Farm All-Am. Football Team, 1999—; mem. selection com. NCAA Divsn. II Hall of Fame Football, 1999—. With USN, 1952-54. Recipient Leadership trophy Chase Park (Chgo.), 1947, Celebrity Cert. of Appreciation ARC, 1992, Statistician of the Yr. Oak Park-River Forest H.S., 1981. Mem. CO-SIDA Coll. Sports Info. Dirs. Am., Knucklers Card Club (sgt. at arms and host 2001). Republican. Mem. Assembly of God Ch. Home: Apt 10 5613 King Arthur Ct Westmont IL 60559-2269 Office: Don Hansen's Nat Weekly Football Gazette PO Box 305 Westmont IL 60559-0305 E-mail: fbgazette@thc.to, don@donhansen.com.

HANSEN, DONALD W., diversified financial services company executive, consultant; b. Chgo., June 9, 1924; s. Chris M. and Violet Louise (Anderson) H.; m. Nancy SanRoman, Dec. 21, 1944; children: Donald W. II, Scott D., Debra Anne. BS in Bus. and Econs, Ill. Inst. Tech., 1948; postgrad., U. Chgo. Grad. Sch. Bus., 1957. Fin. rep., mgr. bank relations Comml. Credit Co., Chgo., 1948-57; pres. Sears Roebuck Acceptance Co., Wilmington, Del., 1957-63; v.p. fin. services Allstate Ins. Co., 1963-75, v.p. money center and banking adminstrn., 1971-76; pres. Allstate Fin. Corp., 1964-74; chmn. bd. Allstate Savs. & Loan Assn., 1963-66; pres., chief exec. officer Allstate Enterprises Mortgage Corp., Anaheim, Calif., 1972-74, First Farwest Corp., Portland, Oreg., 1976-78, Midwestern United Life Ins. Co., Ft. Wayne, Ind., 1978-83, United Equitable Corp., Lincolnwood, Ill., 1983-86, Am. Warranty Corp., 1983-86. Active Young Pres. Orgn., 1959-73. Served to 1st lt. AUS, 1943-46, aide-de-camp to Brig. Gen. W. A. Biederlinden 44th Div. Mem. Scottsdale Country Club. Republican. Presbyterian. Home: Apt 166 14500 N Frank Lloyd Wright Scottsdale AZ 85260 E-mail: hansen069@webtv.net.

HANSEN, ELAINE TUTTLE, academic administrator; m. Stanley Hansen; children: Emma, Isla. AB with greatest distinction cum laude, Mt. Holyoke Coll., 1969; MA, U. Minn., 1972; PhD, U. Wash., 1975. Asst. editor Mid. English dictionary U. Mich., 1975-77, assoc. rsch. editor, 1977—78; asst. prof. dept. English Hamilton Coll., NY, 1978—80, Haverford (Pa.) Coll., 1980—86, assoc. prof., 1986—90, chair, 1989—92, prof., 1991—2002, provost, 1995—2002; pres. Bates Coll., Lewiston, Maine, 2002—. Lectr. in field. Author: The Solomon Complex: Reading Wisdom in Old English Poetry, 1988, Chaucer and the Fictions of Gender, 1992, Mother Without Child: Contemporary Fiction and the Crisis of Motherhood, 1997; mem. editl. bd. Coll. Lit.; reader manuscripts for jours. and univ. presses; contbr. articles to profl. jours., also revs. and papers. NEH Summer stipendee, 1981; Mellon grantee for faculty devel. in humanities, 1983-84, Whitehead grantee for faculty in the humanities, 1987-88; Am. Coun. Learned Socs. fellow, 1993-94. Mem. MLA (mem. Chaucer divsn. exec. com. 1995-99, divsn. rep.

to del. assembly 1996-99, com. on acad. freedom and profl. rights and responsibilities 1997-2000), Am. Coun. Learned Socs. (prescreener Cen. Fellowship Program), Medieval Acad., New Chaucer Soc., Nat. Women's Studies Assn., Soc. for Feminist Medieval Scholarship (pres. 1993-95). Office: Bates College Office of the Pres Lane Hall Rm 204 Lewiston ME 04240 E-mail: president@bates.edu.

HANSEN, ELIZABETH, lawyer; b. San Francisco, 1964; d. Mary-Helen (Duffy) Hansen. BA in Econ., U. Washington, 1985; student, London Sch. Econ., 1988-89; JD, George Washington U., 1990. Bar: Md. 1991, Calif. 1992, cert. specialist estate planning, probate and trust adminstrn, State Bar Calif. Bd. Legal Specialization. Pvt. practice, San Francisco, Calif., 1992—. Contbr. article to profl. jours. Recipient Atty. of Yr. award AIDS Legal Referral Pane., 1994. Mem. State Bar Calif. (estate planning, trust and probate sect., Wiley W. Manuel award for pro bono legal svc. 1992, 93, 94, 95, 96), Bar Assn. San Francisco (Outstanding Vol. Pub. Svc. award 1993, 94, chair barristers club, profl. devel. com., Barrister of Yr. 1998). Democrat. Episcopal. Office: 220 Montgomery St Ste 1200 San Francisco CA 94101-3549 Office Phone: 415-986-7500. Business E-Mail: elizabeth_hansen@juno.com.

HANSEN, FLORENCE MARIE CONGIOLOSI (MRS. JAMES S. HANSEN), social worker; b. Middletown, NY, Jan. 7, 1934; d. Joseph James and Florence (Harrigan) Congiolosi; m. James S. Hansen, June 16, 1959 (dec. Nov. 1989); 1 child, Florence M. BA, Coll. of New Rochelle, 1955; MSW, Fla. State U., 1960; PhD, Union Inst., 1992. Caseworker Orange County Dept. Pub. Welfare, N.Y., 1955-57, Cath. Welfare Bur., Miami, Fla., 1957-58, supr. Spokane, Wash., 1960, Cuban Children's Program, Spokane, 1962-66; founder, dir. social svc. dept. sacred Heart Med. Ctr., Spokane, 1968-85, dir. Kidney Ctr., 1967-91; caseworker Cath. Welfare Bur., Miami, Fla., 1957-58. Asst. in program devel. St. Margaret's Hall, Spokane, 1961-62; trustee Family Service Spokane, 1981—, also bd. dirs.; mem. budget allocation panel United Way, 1964-76, mem. planning com., 1968-77, mem. admissions com., 1969-70, chmn. projects com. 1972-73; mem. kidney disease adv. com. Wash.-Alaska Regional Med. Program, 1970-73. Mem. Spokane Quality of Life Commn., 1974-75; vol. primary health care Nangoma Mission Hosp., Mumbwa Dist., Zambia, 1992—; cons. CARE Internat., Zambia, 1993-95. Recipient Ursula Laurus citation Coll. of New Rochelle, 1990, Angela Merici medal, 1995. Mem. NASW (pres. Wash. chpt. 1972-74, Wash. State Social Worker of Yr. award 1991, Nat. Social Worker of Yr. award 1991), Acad. Cert. Social Workers (charter). Roman Catholic. Home: 5609 W Northwest Blvd Spokane WA 99205-2039 Office: Nangoma Mission Hosp Mumbwa Dist PO Box 1 Nangoma Zambia

HANSEN, GEORGE ERIC, political scientist, educator; b. Milw., Nov. 25, 1938; s. A. (Andrew) Eric and Kathleen Hearty Hansen. BA summa cum laude, Lawrence Coll., 1961; MA, Fletcher Sch., Tufts U., 1962, MALD, 1963, PhD, 1966. Instr. polit. sci. Wellesley Coll., Mass., 1963—64; asst. prof. polit. sci. MIT, Cambridge, 1964—69, Haverford Coll., Pa., 1969—73; lectr. internat. rels. San Francisco State U., 1974—76; prof. internat. polit. econ. St. Mary's Coll. Calif., Moraga, 1977—. Author: The Culture of Strangers: Globalization, Localization, and the Phenomenon of Exchange; contbr. articles to profl. jours. Fellow, Ford Found., 1960, Nat. Def. Found., 1961—64; Younger Humanist fellow, NEH, 1971—72. Mem.: AAUP, Phi Beta Kappa. Avocations: travel, architecture, museums, theater. Home: 250 B Red Rock Way San Francisco CA 94131 Office: Saint Mary's College of California 1928 Saint Mary's Road Moraga CA 94575 Personal E-mail: ehansen@stmarys-ca.edu.

HANSEN, GLORIA JEAN, choral director, singer; b. Port Washington, Wis., Nov. 9, 1954; d. Willard Herman and Elsie May Berndt; m. James Hansen, July 4, 1990. AA, Concordia Coll., 1974; BFA in Music, U. Wis., Milw., 1979, MusM, 1997. Asst. dir. of choirs U. Wis., Milw., 1997—; min. of music Trinity Luth. Ch., Cedarburg, Wis., 1997—2003; dir. of music North Shore Presbyn. Ch., Milw., 2003—04; choral dir. Beautiful Savior Luth. Ch., Mequon, Wis., 2005—. Pres., bd. dirs. Milw. Choral Artists, 1998—2002; fin. chair Wis. Choral Dirs. Assn., Waldo; singer Milw. Choral Artists, 1998—. Singer: (CD) Exultate!. Mem.: Assn. Luth. Ch. Musicians, VoiceCare Network, Music Educators Nat. Conv., Am. Choral Dirs. Assn. Lutheran. Avocations: gardening, hiking, travel. Office: Univ Wis 3223 N Downer Ave Milwaukee WI 53211 Business E-Mail: gloriajh@uwm.edu.

HANSEN, GRANT LEWIS, retired air transportation executive; b. Bancroft, Idaho, Nov. 5, 1921; s. Paul Ezra and Leona Sarah (Lewis) H.; m. Iris Rose Heyden, Apr. 21, 1945; children: Alan Lee, Brian Craig, Carol Margaret, David James, Ellen Diane. BS in Elec. Engring., Ill. Inst. Tech., 1948; postgrad. engring. and mgmt., UCLA, Calif. Inst. Tech.; D.Sc., Nat. U., 1978. With Douglas Aircraft Co., 1948-60; v.p., program dir. for Centaur (Convair div.), 1960-65; v.p. launch vehicle programs Convair div. Gen. Dynamics Corp., 1965-69, v.p., gen. mgr., 1973-78; asst. sec. air force for research and devel., 1969-73; v.p. Gen. Dynamics Corp., San Diego, 1974-78; exec. v.p. System Devel. Corp., Santa Monica, Calif., 1978-86; also pres. SDC Systems Group, 1978-84. U.S. del. NATO (Adv. Group for Aerospace Research and Devel.), 1969-73; U.S. mem. sci. com. for nat. reps. SHAPE Tech. Center, The Hague, Netherlands, 1969-73; mem. research and tech. adv. council NASA, 1971-73; mem. sci. adv. bd. Dept. Air Force, 1976-86. Served with USNR, World War II Decorated Purple Heart; recipient Pub. Service award NASA, 1966, Disting. Pub. Service award NASA, 1975, Alumni Recognition award Ill. Inst. Tech., 1967, USAF Exceptional Civilian Service medal, 1973, 83; inducted Ill. Inst. Tech. Hall of Fame, 1984. Fellow AIAA (nat. pres. 1975), Am. Astronautical Soc., AAAS, Internat. Acad. Astronautics; mem. IEEE (sr.), German Soc. Air and Space Travel (corr.), Nat. Acad. Engring., NR, Eta Kappa Nu, Tau Beta Pi. Home: 10737 Fuerte Dr La Mesa CA 91941-5740 *I've given my whole self to each challenge I've accepted, believing that what's best for my future is an honest day's effort today. I have great faith in my God and my country.*

HANSEN, H. JACK, management consultant; b. Chgo., Mar. 28, 1922; s. Herbert Christian John and Laura Elizabeth (Osterman) Hansen; m. Joan Dorothy Norum, Nov. 28, 1980; children: Marilyn Joan, Gail Jean(dec.), Mark John, Jacquelyn Lee. BSME, Ill. Inst. Tech., 1944. Cert. mgmt. cons. Mech. and indsl. engr. Harper Wyman Co., Chgo., 1944-51; chief indsl. engr. Shakeproof divsn. Ill. Tool Works, Des Plaines, 1951-53; cons., prin. A.T. Kearney & Co., Chgo. and N.Y.C., 1953-71; pres. H.J. Hansen Co., Elburn, Ill., 1971—2000. Acting mfg. engring. mgr. European Ops., Hobart Corp., 1974—78; owner, mgmt. cons. Hansen Mgmt. Search Co., Mt. Prospect, Ill., 1980—93; active turnaround cons., 1992—2000; apptd. by Kane County States Atty. Second Chance Panel, 2001—; apptd. to Kane County Chronicle's Readers adv. bd., 2002—04; rsch. participant shingles prevention study, 2000—. Mem. Planning Commn. Village of Elburn, 1995—97, trustee, 1997—2001, chmn. Pers. Commn., mem. Fin. Commn., mem. Pub. Works Commn.; pres. Men's Club, 1987—90, Good Shepherd Luth. Ch., Des Plaines, Ill., 1988—90; active mem. mcpl. legis. com. DuKane Valley Coun., 1997—2001; rsch. participant Shingles Prevention Study, 2000—. With U.S. Army, 1945—46. Named to Tilden Tech. Alumni Assn. Hall of Fame, 2000. Mem. Inst. Mgmt. Cons. (founding), Methods-Time Measurement Assn. (bd. dirs. 1964-70, pres. 1967-68), Am. Arbitartion Assn., Soc. Advancement Mgmt. (past bd. dirs.), coun. for Internat. Progress in Mgmt. (past bd. dirs.), Found. Internat. Progress in Mgmt. (past bd. dirs.), Econ. Devel. Com. (tech. com., membership com.), Elburn C. of C. Achievements include research in shingles prevention. Office: H J Hansen Co 317 Prairie Valley St Elburn IL 60119-8977

HANSEN, H. REESE, law educator, former dean; b. Logan, Utah, Apr. 8, 1942; s. Howard F. and Loila Gayle (Reese) H.; m. Kathryn Traveller, June 8, 1962; children: Brian T., Mark T., Dale T., Curtis T. BS, Utah State U., 1964; JD, U. Utah, 1972. Bar: Utah, 1974. Atty. Strong, Poelman & Fox, Salt Lake City, 1972-74; from asst. prof. to assoc. prof. Brigham Young U., Provo, Utah, 1974-79, prof. law, 1979—, from asst. dean to assoc. dean, 1974-89, dean, 1989—2004. Commr. ex officio Utah State Bar, Salt Lake City, 1989-2004; commr. Nat. Conf. Commrs. on Uniform State Laws, 1988-95. Co-author: Idaho Probate System, 1977, Utah Probate System, 2nd edit., 2005, Cases and Text on Laws of Trusts, 7th edit., 2001; editor: Manual for Justices of Peace--Utah, 1978; contbr. articles to profl. jours. Mem. Lds Ch. Office: Brigham Young U 536 JRCB Provo UT 84602-1029 Office Phone: 801-422-3616.

HANSEN, HAROLD B., JR., elementary school educator; b. Sewickley, Pa., July 3, 1955; s. Harold B. and Mary Clara (VanderVort) Hansen; m. Patty Jo Gabhart, Sept. 19, 1976; children: Jeremiah James, Joshua Andrew, Esther Beth, Christopher Seth. BA in Elem. Edn., Purdue U., 1980; MA in Sch. Adminstrn., Western N.Mex. U., 1987. Cert. secondary lang. arts and spl. edn. tchr., TESL tchr., instrnl. leader, sch. adminstr., elem. tchr., coach N.Mex. Resource rm. tchr. Flossmoor/Homewood (Ill.) Pub. Schs., 1981, Newcomb (N.Mex.) H.S., 1981—82; tchr. self-contained spl. edn. Chester (Mont.) Pub. Schs., 1982—84; adminstr., prin., tchr. Bennett (Colo.) Bapt. Ch. Sch., 1984; propr., tutor Hemispheric Learning Tutorial Svcs., 1982—; tchr. resource room, coach cross county, wrestling, track and field Gallup-McKinley County Pub. Schs., Tohatchi/Navajo Reserv., N.Mex., 1985—90, elem. tchr. phys. edn. and health, at-risk tchr. Tohatchi Elem. Sch. Tohatchi, 1990—98, 5th grade track & field head coach, 1991—98, 5th grade boys' and girls' basketball asst. coach, 1995—98; prin. Smith Lake Elem. Sch., Gallup-McKinley County Pub. Schs., 1998—2003; tchr. APS: Mission Ave. Elem. Sch., Albuquerque Pub. Schs., 2003—. Mem. various sch. coms. Gallup-McKinley County Pub. Schs., 1990—98, 2001—03; seminar leader on hemispherecity; dep. registration officer McKinley County, N.Mex., 1986—98; mem. Prins.' Leadership Inst. with RE: Learning NM, Prins.' Leadership Acad. with Success for All Found. Past pres. Village of Hope, substance abuse tng. ctr.; co-founder, past bd. dirs. Christian Home Educators Assn.; dir. Approved Workmen Are Not Ashamed; past coord. Jump Rope for Heart, Am. Heart Assn.; past mem. Coun. for Curricular Excellence, McKinley County; pst TESOL rep. for Western N.Mex. U.'s Gallup Grad. Ctr.'s Advd. Coun., 1997—99. Named one of Outstanding Young Men of Am., 1987. Mem.: Aesthetic Realism Found., Christian Home Educators Assn., N.Mex Assn. Health, Phys. Edn., Recreation and Dance. Home: 631 Sienna St NW Albuquerque NM 87120-5921 Office Phone: 505-344-5269 ext. 57305. Personal E-mail: hbchansen@yahoo.com. Business E-Mail: hansen_ch@aps.edu.

HANSEN, HEIDI NEUMANN, marketing consultant; b. N.Y.C., Feb. 2, 1955; d. Roy G. and Carolyn (Holmes) Neumann; m. Bruce Alan Hansen, Sept. 1, 1984. Student, MIT, 1975-76; AB, Colby Coll., 1977. Benefits adminstr. Gen. Host Corp., Stamford, Conn., 1977-78; pres. Letterworks Internat., Portland, Maine, 1981-97, H.N. Hansen & Co., Portland, 1998—2000, 2004—; v.p. sales& mktg. N.H. Hansen & Co., Portland, 2004—; v.p. sales and mktg. BlueTarp, Inc., Portland, 2000—03. Bd. dirs. SALT Ctr. Documentary Studies, 1993-95; bd. advisors Docktrap River Fish Farm, 1992-97. Mem. editl. bd. AudioFile mag., 1997-2000. Dir. Maine Handicapped Skiing, Portland, 1984-92, 98-99; vol. Maine Med. Ctr., Portland, 1982-97, corporator, 1993—, trustee, 1998-; audit com. Mainet Health, 2000—; bd. dirs. Portland Concert Assn., 1992-2000; trustee Portland Mus. Art, 1993-2000. Mem. Ad Club Greater Portland (bd. dirs. 1983-85, v.p. 1985-87, pres. 1987-88), Portland C. of C. (bd. dirs. 1990-92). Avocations: travel, hiking, sailing. Home: 313 Fowler Rd Cape Eliz ME 04107-2501 Office: HN Hansen & Co 111 Commercial St Portland ME 04101-3427

HANSEN, HERBERT W., management consultant; b. June 16, 1935; s. Olive Anita (Read) French; m. Susan Lockwood Develin; children: Mary, Kathryn. AB, Dartmouth Coll., 1957; MBA, U. New Haven, 1973. Gen. mgr. clay pipe divsn. Interpace Corp., L.A., 1974-75, v.p., gen. mgr. structural products divsn. Seattle, 1975-77, pres. retail dinnerware and tile divsn., 1977-79, pres., gen. mgr. Tuttle & Bailey divsn. New Britain, Conn., 1979-81; pres. Greater Hartford C. of C., Conn., 1981-86, Hartford Mgmt. Group, Inc., 1986-90; chmn. Hi-Speed Machine Products, 1990; pres. No. R.I. C. of C., Lincoln, 1991-92, Hansen Assocs., 1992—. Bd. dirs. Downtown Coun., Hartford, 1981-87, Hartford Area Pvt. Industry Coun., 1981-87, BBB, 1981-85, World Trade Ctr. of Conn., 1987-90; pres. Greater Hartford Corp., 1981-84; treas. Greater Hartford Arts Coun., 1981-87, exec, com., 1986, arts coun. dir., 1987-88; corporator Wadsworth Atheneum, 1985-91, Hartford Hosp., 1982-81, Mt. Sinai Hosp., 1981-90; overseer Dartmouth Hitchcock Med. Ctr., 1993—; chmn. Hartford Sem., 1987-90, trustee, 1990-92, pres. coun., 1992—; sec. bd. visitors Mortensen Libr.; dir. Riverfront Recapture, 1981-91; chmn. Episc. Charities Found., Hartford, 1985-87, dir., 1987-88; pres. Episc. Bishop's Fund, 1983-91; mem. Fellow-Am. Leadership Forum, audit com. Op. Fuel, 1986-88. Lt. comdr. USN, 1957-68. Episcopalian. Home: Box 917 13 Fernwood Ln Grantham NH 03753 Office: Hansen Assoc PO Box 917 Grantham NH 03753-0917 Office Phone: 866-238-7976. E-mail: hansen@adelphia.net.

HANSEN, JACK WINSOR, musician, educator; b. Seward County, Nebr., Dec. 5, 1927; s. Grant Elbert Hansen and Ruby Gertrude Winsor. MusB, Roosevelt U., 1950, MusM cum laude, 1952; studied with, Rudolph Ganz and Mollie Margolies; pvt. studies with Marguerite Long, Paris; pvt. studies with Maurice Dumesnil, pvt. studies with Sir William Walton. Mem. piano faculty Chgo. Mus. Coll., 1952—54; tchr. piano Sherwood Sch. Music, Chgo., 1954—56; instr. piano and composition N.D. State Coll., Minot, 1956—57; concert pianist various U.S. cities, 1957—87. Musician: NBC Artist Showcase Symphony, WGN Symphony, CBS Beethoven Bicentennial celebration with Chgo. Chamber Orch., numerous radio shows throughout U.S.; contbr. articles to profl. publs.; musician (soloist): Am. premiere of Haydn G Major Concerto, 1955, Can. premiere of Haydn G Major Concerto, 1968, world premiere of Markaitis Concerto for piano and woodwinds, 1966, Am. TV premiere of Beethoven post. Rondo for piano and orch., 1970; author: Sibyl Sanderson - Requiem for a Diva, 2004. Recipient Richard Strauss award, 1949, Midwest Young Artists award, Soc. Am. Musicians, 1949, Allied Arts award, 1956—57. Mem.: N.W. Ind. Music Tchr.'s Assn., South Suburban Music Tchr.'s Assn., Chgo. Area Music Tchr.'s Assn., Nat. Music Tchr.'s Assn., Massenet Soc. (former bd. dirs.). Avocations: writing, poetry, collecting antiques, Egyptology. Home: 6346 Hohman Ave Hammond IN 46324

HANSEN, JAMES ALLEN, state agency administrator; b. West Point, Nebr., Jan. 10, 1939; s. Walter J. and Dorothy (Kay) H.; m. Janice A. Wenke, June 27, 1964 (div. 1975); m. Rebecca A. Bayer, Nov. 28, 1975. BA, Wayne State Coll., 1965. Pres. Farmers State Bank, Lexington, Nebr., 1972-80, No. Bank, Omaha, 1980-86, 1st Nat. Bank, Fremont, Nebr., 1986-87; regional v.p. Am. First Co., Omaha, 1987-90; mng. agt. FDIC/RTC, Burnsville, Minn., 1990; dir. Nebr. Dept. Banking & Fin., Lincoln, 1991-98; chmn., CEO Centennial Bank, Omaha, 1999—. Chmn. Conf. State Bank Suprs., Washington, 1992-97, vice-chmn. adv. bd., 2002—. Group study exch. team to Australia, Rotary Internat., 1970. 1st lt. U.S. Army N.G., 1960-66. Home: 18109 Mayberry St Omaha NE 68022 Office: Centennial Bank 9003 S 145th St Omaha NE 68138-3636

HANSEN, JAMES E., physicist, meteorologist, federal agency administrator; b. Mar. 29, 1941; BA in Physics and Math. with highest distinction, U. Iowa, 1963, MS in Astronomy, 1965; postgrad., U. Kyoto and Tokyo U., 1965-66; PhD in Physics, U. Iowa, 1967. NAS-NRC resident rsch. assoc. Goddard Inst. for Space Studies, N.Y.C., 1967-69; NSF postdoctoral fellow Leiden Observatory, Netherlands, 1969; rsch. assoc. Columbia U., 1969-72; mem. staff, space scientist, mgr. planetary and climate programs Goddard Inst. for Space Studies, 1972-81, head, 1981—. Adj. assoc. prof. dept. geol. scis. Columbia U., 1978-85, adj. prof., 1985—; co-prin. investigator AEROPOL Project, 1971-74; co-investigator Voyager Photopolarimeter Experiment, 1972-85; prin. investigator Pioneer Venus Orbiter Cloud-Photopolarimeter Experiment, 1974-78, co-investigator, 1978—; prin. investigator Galileo Photopolarimeter Radiometer Experiment, 1977—, Earth Observing System Interdisciplinary Investigation, 1989—. Author: (with others) Radiation in the Atmosphere, 1978, Carbon Dioxide Review, 1982. Recipient Goddard Spl. Achievement award, 1977, Group Achievement award NASA, 1982, 93, Exceptional Svc. medal NASA, 1984, Presdl. Rank award NASA, 1990, Heinz Environ. award, 2001; nominee Rave award in Science, WIRED, 2005. Fellow: Am. Geophys. Union (Roger Revelle Medal 2001); mem.: NAS. Achievements include research in radiative transfer in planetary atmospheres, interpretation of remote sounding of planetary atmospheres, the properties of the clouds of Venus leading to their identification as sulfuric acid; development of simplified climate models and 3-D global climate models, climate mechanisms such as the role of clouds in climate, current climate trends from observational data and projections of man's impact on climate. Known for his testimony on climate change to congressional committees in the 1980s that helped raise awareness to the global warming issue. Office: Goddard Inst Space Studies 2880 Broadway New York NY 10025-7886 Office Phone: 212-678-5500. Business E-Mail: jhansen@giss.nasa.gov.

HANSEN, JAMES EDWARD, medical educator, researcher; b. Green Bay, Wis., Sept. 4, 1926; s. James Christian and Helen Dorothy (Terp) H.; m. Beverly May Kapke, June 5, 1948; children: Barbara Parry, Patricia Begley, Linda DeGroot, James H. Student, St. Norbert's Coll., 1942-43, U. Wis., 1943-44, Marquette U., 1944-45; MD, Johns Hopkins U., 1945-49. Diplomate Am. Bd. Internal Medicine. Intern, then resident Letterman Army Med. Ctr., San Francisco, 1949-53; commd. 1st lt. U.S. Army, 1949, advanced through grades to col., 1975, physician, 1950-62; chief physiology div. U.S. Army Med. Rsch. and Nutrition Lab., Denver, 1962-65; sci. dir. U.S. Army Rsch. Inst. Environ. Medicine, Natick, Mass., 1965-71; chief clin. investigation svcs. Tripler Army Med. Ctr., Honolulu, 1971-75; assoc. prof. dept. medicine UCLA, Torrance, 1976-78, prof. dept. medicine, 1978-86, emeritus prof. dept. medicine, 1986—. Instr., asst. prof. U. Colo., 1961-65; liaison mem. applied physiology study sect. NIH, 1965-71; cons. environ. medicine U.S. Army Surgeon Gen., Washington, 1965-73; lectr. environ. medicine Johns Hopkins U., Balt., 1966-71; clin. prof. physiology U. Hawaii, 1972-75. Co-author: Principles of Exercise Testing and Interpretation, 1986, 4th rev. edit., 2005; contbr. numerous articles to profl. jours. Chmn. congregation St. Matthew's Luth. Ch., Aurora, Colo., 1962-64, Gloria Dei Luth. Ch., Pearl City, Hawaii, 1972-74; sch. supt. Luth. Ch., Natick, 1967-69; elder, mission com. chmn. St. Peter's By the Sea Presbyn. Ch., Rancho Palos Verdes, Calif., 1992-95. Pulmonary fellow Fitzsimons Army Med. Ctr., 1960, UCLA Ctr. Health Scis., 1975-76; recipient Sustaining Membership award Assn. Mil. Surgeons, 1970, Calif. medal Am. Lung Assn., 1996; named Layperson of Yr., South Coast Interfaith Coun., 2004. Fellow ACP, Am. Coll. Chest Physicians; mem. Am. Physiol. Soc., Am. Thoracic Soc. (sci. adv. bd. 1983-2000), Calif. Thoracic Soc. (pulmonary chmn. 1980-83, physiology com). Avocations: piano, tennis. Home: 1692 Morse Dr San Pedro CA 90732-4336 Office: Harbor-UCLA Med Ctr PO Box 405 1000 W Carson St Torrance CA 90502-2004 Office Phone: 310-222-3803. E-mail: jimandbev@cox.net.

HANSEN, JAMES LEE, sculptor; b. Tacoma, June 13, 1925; s. Hildreth Justine and Mary Elizabeth Hansen; m. Annabelle Hair, Aug. 31, 1946 (dec. Sept. 1993); children: Valinda Jean, Yauna Marie; m. Jane Lucas, May 13, 1994. Grad., Portland Art Mus. Sch. Faculty Oreg. State U., Corvallis, 1957-58, U. Calif., Berkeley, 1958, Portland (Oreg) State U., 1964-90. One-man shows include Fountain Gallery, Portland, 1966, 69, 77-81, U. Oreg. Art Mus., Eugene, 1970, Seligman (Seders Gallery), Seattle, 1970, Portland Art Mus., 1971, Cheney Cowles Meml. Mus., Spokane, Wash., 1972, Polly Freidlander Gallery, Seattle, 1973, 75-76, Smithsonian Instn., Washington, 1974, Hodges/Banks Gallery (now Linda Hodges Gallery), Seattle, 1983, Abanté Gallery, Portland, 1986, 88, 92, Maryhill Mus. of Art, Goldendale, Wash., 1997-98, Bryan Ohno Gallery, Seattle, 1997, 99, 2002, 04, Mus. Northwest Art, La Conner, Wash., 1999; exhibited in group shows at N.W. Ann. Painters and Sculptors, Seattle, 1952-73, Oreg. Ann. Painters and Sculptors, Portland Art Mus., 1952-75, Whitney Mus. Am. Art, NYC, 1953, Santa Barbara (Calif.) Mus. Art, 1959-60, Denver Art Mus., 1960, San Francisco Art Mus., 1960, Smithsonian Instn., Washington, 1974, Wash. State U., Pullman, 1975, Benton County Hist. Mus., 1998; represented in permanent collections Graphic Arts Ctr., State Capitol, Olympia, Wash., U. Oreg., Eugene, Salem (Oreg.) Civic Ctr., Clark Coll., Vancouver, Wash., Portland Art Mus., Transit Mall, Portland, Seattle Art Mus., Gresham Town Fair (Oreg.), Oreg. Health Scis. U., Portland, Vancouver Sculpture Park, others; represented by Hansen Studio, Battle Ground, Wash., Peter Bartlow Gallery, Chgo., Bryan Ohno Gallery, Seattle. Address: 28219 NE 63rd Ave Battle Ground WA 98604-7107 Office Phone: 360-687-4627. Business E-Mail: info@jamesleehansen.com.

HANSEN, JOHN PAUL, retired metallurgical engineer; b. Bain, Minn., Feb. 11, 1928; s. Charles George and Henrietta Eva (Taylor) H.; m. Doris Alma Dropps, Sept. 9, 1950; children: Steven Michael, Bradley Paul, Kurt Lewis. BS, U. Minn., 1954, MS, 1955, PhD, 1958. Registered profl. engr., Ala. Metall. engr. U.S. Bur. Mines, Mpls., 1958-63, chief Tuscaloosa Metallurgy Rsch. Lab. Tuscaloosa, 1967-70; prof. metall. engring. U. Ala., University, 1963-87, head chem. and metall. engring. dept., 1970-73, prof. emeritus metall. engring. Tuscaloosa, from 1988. Lectr. U. Ala.; cons. Army Missile Command, Ala. Geol. Survey. Served with AUS, 1946-49, 50-52. Mem. AIME, Sigma Xi, Tau Beta Pi, Alpha Sigma Mu, Omega Chi Epsilon. Clubs: University Faculty (pres. 1973). Lutheran. Achievements include research in reduction of iron ores and prereduced iron ore pellets. Home: Dallas, Tex. Died May 15, 2005.

HANSEN, JO-IDA CHARLOTTE, psychology professor, researcher; b. Washington, Oct. 2, 1947; d. Gordon Henry and Charlotte Lorraine (Helgeson) H.; m. John Paul Campbell. BA, U. Minn., 1969, MA, 1971, PhD, 1974. Asst. prof. psychology U. Minn., Mpls., 1974-78, assoc. prof., 1978-84, prof., 1984—, dir. Ctr. for Interest Measurement Rsch., 1974—, dir. counseling psychology program, 1987—, dir. Vocat. Assessment Clinic, 1997—, prof. human resources and indsl. rels., 1997—, assoc. dean for grad. studies Coll. Liberal Arts, 2005—. Author: User's Guide for the SII, 1984, 2d edit., 1992, Manual for the SII, 1985 2d edit. 1994; editor: Measurement and Evaluation in Counseling and Development, 1993-2000; editor Jour. Counseling Psychology, 1999-2005; contbr. over 150 articles to profl. jours., chpts. to books. Recipient early career award U. Minn., 1982, E.K. Strong, Jr. gold medal, 1984. Fellow APA (coun. reps. 1990-93, 97-99, pres. divsn. counseling psychology 1993-94, chmn. joint com. testing practices 1989-93, com. to revise APA/Am. Ednl. Rsch. Assn. nat. coun. measurement evalation testing stds. 1993-99, exam. com. Assn. State Provincial Psychology Bds. 1996-99, bd. sci. affairs, 2003-05, chair coun. of editors 2003-04; Leona Tyler award for rsch. and profl. svc. 1996); mem. ACA (extended rsch. award 1990, disting. rsch. award 1996), Assn. for Measurement and Evaluation (pres. 1988-89, Exemplary Practice award 1987, 90). Avocations: golf, theater, music, water and downhill skiing, spectator sports. Office: U Minn Dept Psychology Ctr Interest Measurement 75 E River Rd Minneapolis MN 55455-0280 Business E-Mail: hanse004@umn.edu.

HANSEN, JOSEPH T., labor union administrator; Organizer, rep., regional dir. United Food & Comml. Workers Internat. Union, dir. food processing, packing and mfg., sec.-treas., 1997—2004, internat. pres., 2004—. Mem. com. on immigrant workers AFL-CIO; pres.-elect Union Network Internat. Office: UFCW Internat Union 1775 K St NW Washington DC 20006 Office Phone: 202-223-3111.

HANSEN, KATHRYN GERTRUDE, editor, former state official; b. Gardner, Ill., May 24, 1912; d. Harry J. and Marguerite (Gaston) Hansen. BS with honors, U. Ill., 1934, MS, 1936. Sec. U. N.C., Chapel Hill, 1936—37; sec. Univ. H.S. U. Ill., Urbana, 1937—44, pers. asst., 1944—46, supr. tng. and activities, 1946—47, pers. officer, instr. psychology, 1947—52; exec. sec. U. Civil Svc. Sys., Ill., also sec. for merit bd., 1952—61, adminstrv. officer, sec. merit bd., 1961—68, dir. sys., 1968—72; law asst. Webber, Balbach, Theis and Follmer, P.C., Urbana, 1972—74. Author: (with others) A Plan of Position Classification for Colleges and Universities: A Classification Plan for Staff Positions at Colleges and Universities, Grundy-Corners, 1982, Sarah, A Documentary of Her Life and Times, 1984, Ninety Years with Fortnightly, Vols. I and II, an historical compilation, 1986, Vol. III, 1995, Whispers of Yesterday, 1989, Through the Years with the Champaign-Urbana Business and Professional Women's Club, 1912-33, 1993, My Heritage, 1995, Presbyterian Women of First Presbyterian Church, Champaign, Illinois, An Historical Documentary, 1870-1995, 1996, (with Patricia Phillips) Fifty Golden Years, Altrusa International of Champaign-Urbana, Illinois, 1950-2000, 2001, Heritage, Vision and Mission: The First Prebyterian Church, Champaign, Illinois, 1850-2000, 2005; editor: The Illini Worker, 1946-52, Campus Pathways, 1952-61, This is Your Civil Service Handbook, 1960-67; author, cons., editor publs. on personnel practices. Bd. dirs. U. YWCA, 1952-55, chmn., 1954-55; bd. dirs. Champaign-Urbana Symphony, 1978-81; mem., sec. Presbyn. Women 1st Presbyn Ch., Champaign, 1986-90, mem. coordinating team, 1986-91, hon. life mem., 1999. Mem. Coll. and Univ. Pers. Assn. for Human Resources (hon., life, editor jour. 1955-73, newsletter, internat. pres. 1967-68, nat. publs. award named in her honor 1987, Ill. State award 1996), Annuitants Assn. State Univs. Retirement Sys. Ill. (state sec.-treas. 1974-75), U. Ill. Found., Pres.'s Coun. (life), Laureate Cir., U. Ill. Alumni Assn. (life), Friends of U. Ill. Libr. (bd. dirs. 1987-91), Nat. League Am. Pen Women, AAUW (state 1st v.p. 1958-60, hon., life), Secretariat U. Ill. (life, named scholarship 1972—), Grundy County Hist. Soc. (life), Altrusa Internat., Fortnightly Club (Champaign-Urbana), Eastern Star, Delta Kappa Gamma (state pres. 1961-63), Phi Mu (life), Kappa Delta Pi, Kappa Tau Alpha. Home: 3602 Brook Ridge Cir Champaign IL 61822

HANSEN, KENNETH, lawyer; b. Columbus, Ohio, Jan. 27, 1951; AB cum laude, Harvard Coll., 1974; MA, Yale U., 1976; MPA, Harvard U., 1979; JD cum laude, U. Pa., 1983. Bar: Mass. 1984, DC 2002. Counsel, sr. comml. counsel, asst. gen. counsel, assoc. gen. counsel Overseas Pvt. Investment Corp., Washington, 1986—95; counsel Baker & Botts, 1995; gen. counsel Export-Import Bank, Washington, 1995—99; ptnr., Fin. Chadbourne & Parke, LLP, Washington, 1999—, hiring ptnr. Washington Office. Adj. prof. Georgetown U., 1991—, Boston U., 1992—99, George Washington U., 1992—94, Tufts U., 1993; professorial lectr. John Hopkins U., 2000—. Contbr. articles to profl. jour.; spkr. in field. Mem.: Washington Fgn. Law Soc. (pres.-elect 2005), Am. Soc. Internat. Law, ABA. Office: Chadbourne & Parke LLP 1200 New Hampshire Ave NW Washington DC 20036-6802 Office Phone: 202-974-5600. Office Fax: 202-974-5602. Business E-Mail: khansen@chadbourne.com.

HANSEN, KENT FORREST, nuclear engineering educator; b. Chgo., Aug. 10, 1931; s. Kay Frost and Mary (Cummins) H.; m. Katherine Elizabeth Kavanagh, June 13, 1959 (dec. Dec. 1975); children: Thomas Kay, Katherine Mary; m. Deborah Lea Hill, June 26, 1977, (div. Aug. 1991); 1 child, Gordon Benedict; m. Léonie Andrews Work, June 11, 1992. S.B., Mass. Inst. Tech., 1953, Sc.D., 1959. Sr. engr. Sylvania Electric Products, Waltham, Mass., 1957-58; asst. prof. nuclear engring. MIT, Cambridge, Mass., 1960-64, assoc. prof., 1964-68, prof., 1968—, assoc. dean engring., 1979-81, assoc. dir. energy lab., 1984-90. Bd. dirs. EG&G, Inc., Stone & Webster, Inc.; cons. to industry. Co-author: Numerical Methods of Reactor Analysis, 1964, Advances in Nuclear Science and Technology, Vol. 8, 1975. Ford postdoctoral fellow, 1960-61 Fellow Am. Nuclear Soc. (dir., Arthur Holly Compton award 1978); mem. Am. Nuclear Soc., Nat. Acad. Engring., Sigma Xi, Sigma Chi. Home: 23 Phillips Pond Rd Natick MA 01760-5643 Office: MIT Cambridge MA 02139-4325 Office Phone: 617-253-7384. Business E-Mail: kfhansen@mit.edu.

HANSEN, KRISTOPHER M., lawyer; b. 1970; BS, Fordham Univ., 1992, JD, 1995. Bar: NY 1996. Adminstrv. ptnr., fin. restructuring practice Stroock & Stroock & Lavan LLP, NYC, 2004—. Office: Stroock & Stroock & Lavan LLP 180 Maiden Ln New York NY 10038-4982 Office Phone: 212-806-6056. Office Fax: 212-806-9056. Business E-Mail: khansen@stroock.com.

HANSEN, LAUREL D., biology professor; b. Davenport, Iowa, June 2, 1940; d. Laurence A. and Lucille E. Reinbold; children: Devorah Meyer, Darren. BA, Ea. Wash. U., 1962; MS, Wash. State U., 1968, PhD, 1985. Tchr. Cheney (Wash.) Pub. Sch., 1962—65, West Valley Sch., Spokane, Wash., 1965—68; rsch. tec. Wash State U., Pullman, Wash., 1980; rsch. asst. Wash. State U., 1965—67; instr. Wash. CC Dist., Spokane, 1965—. Rsch. project dir. Spokane Falls CC, 1994—2005. Co-author: Carpenter Ants of United States and Canada, 2005; contbr. articles various profl. jours. Mem.: Entomological Soc. of Am., Internat. Union Study Social Insects, Oregon Pest Control Assn. (hon.), Was. State Pest Control Assn. (hon.), Pi Chi Omega. Avocations: travel, reading. Office: Spokane Falls CC 3410 W Ft Wright Dr Spokane WA 99224 Office Phone: 509-533-3666. Office Fax: 509-533-3856. E-mail: laurelh@spokanefalls.edu.

HANSEN, LEONARD JOSEPH, writer, journalist, editor, communications executive; b. Aug. 4, 1932; s. Elnar L. and Margie A. (Wilder) Hansen; m. Marcia Ann Rasmussen, Mar. 18, 1966 (div.); children: Barron Richard, Trevor Wilder. AB in Radio-TV Prodn. and Mgmt., San Francisco State U., 1956, postgrad., 1956—57; cert., IBM Mgmt. Sch., 1967. Jr. writer Sta. KCBS, San Francisco, 1952—54; assoc. prodr., dir. Ford Found. TV Rsch. Project San Francisco State U., 1955—57; crew chief live and remote broadcasts Sta. KPIX-TV, San Francisco, 1957—59, dir. air promotion, writer, 1959—60; pub. rels. mgr. Sta. KNTV-TV, San Jose, Calif., 1961; mgr. radio and TV promotion Seattle World's Fair, 1962; mgr. pub. rels. and promotion Seattle Ctr., Seattle, 1963—64; dir. pub. rels. Dan Evans for Gov. Com., Seattle, 1964; propr., mgr. Leonard J. Hansen Pub. Rels., Seattle, 1965—67; campaign mgr. Walter J. Hickel for Gov. Com., Anchorage, 1966; exec. cons. Gov. Alaska, Juneau, 1967; gen. mgr. No. TV Inc., Anchorage, 1967—69; v.p. mktg. Sea World, Inc., San Diego, 1969—71; editor, pub. Sr. World Publs., inc., San Diego, 1973—84; chmn. Sr. Pubs. Group, 1977—89; pres., editor-in-chief WriteRight, Inc., 1999—. Panelist pub. affairs radio programs, 1971—92; lectr. journalism San Diego State U., 1975—76; spkr., mktg. cons. to sr. citizens, 1984—92; chmn. Mature Market Seminars, 1987—90; pres., pub. Mature Market Editl. Svcs., 1991—98. Columnist: Mainly for Srs., 1984—99, Travel for Mature Adults, 1984—99, writer, journalist: Mature Market; contbg. editor: Mature Life Features, 1987—90; author: Life Begins at 50 - The Handbook for Creative Retirement Planning, 1989. Del. White House Conf. Aging, 1981; mem. Mayor's Ad Hoc Adv. Com. Aging, San Diego, 1976—79; founding mem. Housing Elderly and Low Income Persons, San Diego, 1977—78; vice chmn. Housing Task Force, San Diego, 1977—78; bd. dirs. Crime Control Commn., San Diego, 1980. With U.S. Army, 1953—55. Recipient numerous svc. and citizen awards, Long Term Achievement in Nat. Media award, Am. Soc. Aging, 1999; fellow, Alicia Patterson Found., 1999; Nat. Press Found. fellow, 1994, 1997, 1998. Mem.: Am. Soc. Aging, Nat. Soc. Newspaper Columnists, Am. Soc. Journalists and Authors, Nat. Press Club, San Diego Press Club (Best Newswriting award 1976—77, Headliner of the Yr. award 1980), Soc. Profl. Journalists (Best Investigative Reporting award 1979). Home and Office: Ste E-11 1901 18th St Bellingham WA 98225-8033 Office Phone: 360-752-1772. E-mail: len@lenhansen.com.

HANSEN, LOUISE HILL, music educator, retired application developer; b. Claudville, Va., Oct. 28, 1936; d. James Hobert Hil and Ruth Hubbard Hill; m. Gary George Hansen, Mar. 2, 1958; 1 child, Ricky Allen. AA, Sandhill C.C., 1969; BA in History, West Chester (Pa.) State U., 1971; cert., Assumption Montessori Tchrs. Sch., 1972; student in Music, Lincoln U., 1977—95; MPA, U. Mo., 1984. Cert. tchr. 1996. Clk. The Pentagon USAF, Washington, 1955—57; tchr. Libertyville (Ill.) Montessori Sch., 1972—75; adminstrv. asst. Office Gov. Joseph Teasdale, Jefferson City, Mo., 1977—81; programmer analyst Dept. Social Svcs., Jefferson City, 1981—96; prin., owner Hansen Music Studio, Waupaca, Wis., 1997—. Organist Crystal Lake Ch., Waupaca, 2000—. Mem.: DAR, Nat. Guild Piano Tchrs., Wis. Music Tchrs. Assn., Suzuki Assn. Am. (tchr. tng. 1996, 1997, 1999—2001, 2003—04). Democrat. Avocations: exercise, travel. Home and Office: Hansen Music Studio N2237 Smith Rd Waupaca WI 54981

HANSEN, MARCIA LINN POTTS, music educator, musician; b. Kansas City, Mo., June 13, 1956; d. Earl F. and Meta Ardell Wall Potts; m. Craig William Hansen, Feb. 21, 1981; children: Michael W.F., Katherine G. B of Choral Music Edn., U. Mo., Kansas City, 1977; MA in Tchg., Webster U., 1992. Cert. choral music tchr. Mo. Choral music educator Pky. Sch. Dist., St. Louis, 1977—82, Webster Groves Sch. Dist., St. Louis, 1991—2000; organist, assoc. dir. music Kirkwood United Meth. Ch., St. Louis, 1996—; choral music educator Kirkwood Sch. Dist., St. Louis, 2000—. Artistic dir. Bel Canto Chorus, St. Louis, 1996—99; accompanist Kirkwood Children's Chorale, St. Louis, 1998—; freelance accompanist, St. Louis, 1977—. Officer NW Webster Groves (Mo.) Assn., 1986—89. Named Outstanding Woman Educator, State of Mo., 2004. Mem.: Am. Guild Organists, Am. Choral Directors Assn., Music Educators Nat. Conf. Office Phone: 314-213-6130. Business E-Mail: hansenm@gw.kirkwood.k12.mo.us.

HANSEN, MARK R., music educator; b. Salt Lake City, Utah, Oct. 11, 1952; s. Jay Russell and Marilyn Hendricks Hansen; m. Lise Haymond, Nov. 23, 1981; 1 child, Alicia Gayle. MusB, U. of Utah, 1971—77; MusM, Brigham Young U., 1977—80; D, U. of North Tex., 1982—88. Founding dir., sunderman conservatory of music Gettysburg Coll., Pa., 2004—; chair, dept. of music Western Ill. U., 1998—2004; dir. of gen. edn. Ill. Wesleyan U., 1995—98, assoc. prof. of music, 1989—98; asst. prof. of music U. of Ctrl. Ark., 1983—89; spl. instr. of piano Brigham Young U., Provo, Utah, 1980—82. Contbr. music performance reference. Recipient membership, Phi Kappa Phi, 1976, Pi Kappa Lambda, 1989. Mem.: Music Teachers Nat. Assn., Assn. of Ill. Music Schools (pres. elect 2004—04), Nat. Assn. of Schools of Music. Office: Gettysburg Coll 300 North Washington St Gettysburg PA 17325 Office Phone: 717-337-6814. E-mail: mhansen@gettysburg.edu.

HANSEN, MATILDA, former state legislator; b. Paullina, Iowa, Sept. 4, 1929; d. Arthur J. and Sada G. (Thompson) Henderson; m. Robert B. Michener, 1950 (div. 1963); children: Eric J., Douglas E.; m. Hugh G. Hansen (dec.). BA, U. Colo., 1963; MA, U. Wyo., 1970. Tchr. history Englewood (Colo.) Sr. H.S., 1963-65; dir. Albany County Adult Learning Ctr., Laramie, Wyo., 1966-78, Laramie Plains Civic Ctr., 1979-83; treas. Wyo. Territorial Prison Corp., Laramie, 1988-93, also bd. dirs. Bd. dirs. Wyo. Territorial Pk. Author: (textbooks) To Help Adults Learn, 1975, Let's Play Together, 1978, Clear Use of Power, A Slice of Wyoming Political History, 2002. Legislator Wyo. Ho. of Reps., Cheyenne, 1975-95, minority whip, 1987-88, asst. minority leader, 1991-92, 93-94; mem. mgmt. coun. Wyo. State Legislature, Cheyenne, 1983-84; chair Com. for Dem. Legislature, Cheyenne, 1990-94, Wyo. State Dems., 1995-99; clk. Wyo. Soc. of Friends meeting, 2003-. GE fellow in econs. for high sch. tchrs., 1963; named Pub. Citizen of Yr., Wyo. Assn. Social Workers, 1980-81. Mem. LWV Wyo. (v.p. 1966-68), LWV Laramie (bd. dirs. 1966-72, Nat. Conf. State Legislators (vice chair human resources 1983, nat. exec. com. 1990-94), Laramie Area C. of C., Laramie Women's Club, Faculty Women's Club. Democrat. Avocations: gardening, quilting, mountain climbing. Home and Office: 1306 E Kearney St Laramie WY 82070-4142

HANSEN, NICK DANE, lawyer; b. Detroit, June 19, 1938; s. Nick F. and Ellen (Adelorn) H.; m. Susan Fox Cohee, Aug. 23, 1963; children: Todd Erik, Dana E. BA, Albion Coll., 1960; JD, Wayne State U., 1964; LLM, Georgetown U., 1970. Bar: Mich. 1964, Ill. 1970, Wis. 1975, Tex. 1985. Law clk. to assoc. justice Mich. Supreme Ct., Lansing, 1964-66; atty. Office of Chief Counsel IRS, Washington, 1966-70; ptnr. McDermott, Will & Emery, Chgo., 1970-74; sr. tax atty. Kimberly-Clark Corp., Neenah, Wis., 1975, tax counsel, 1975-76, staff v.p., 1976-80, v.p., tax counsel Dallas, 1980-98; cons., 1998—2001. Bd. dirs. ithought.com Mem. bd. advisor Jour. Internat. Taxation. Sec., bd. dirs. Bergstrom-Mahler Mus., Neenah, 1982-85. Mem. ABA (chmn. com. fgn. activities tax sect. 1991-92, article editor The Tax Lawyer), Tex. Bar Assn., Wis. Bar Assn., Tax Execs. Inst. E-mail: ndhans2000@aol.com.

HANSEN, PER BRINCH, computer scientist, researcher; b. Copenhagen, Nov. 13, 1938; came to U.S., 1970, naturalized, 1992; s. Jorgen Brinch and Elsebeth (Ring) H.; m. Milena Marija Hrastar, Mar. 27, 1965; children: Mette, Thomas. MS, Tech. U. Denmark, Copenhagen, 1963, Dr.techn., 1978. Sys. programmer Regnecentralen, Copenhagen, 1963-70, mgr. software devel., 1967-70; rsch. assoc. Carnegie-Mellon U., Pitts., 1970-72; assoc. prof. Calif. Inst. Tech., Pasadena, 1972-76; chmn. dept. computer sci. U. So. Calif., L.A., 1976-77, prof., 1976-84, Henry Salvatori prof., 1982-84; prof. U. Copenhagen, 1984-87; disting. prof. Syracuse (N.Y.) U., 1987—. Cons. Burroughs, Honeywell, IBM, JPL, Mostek, TRW, others. Author: Operating System Principles, 1973, The Architecture of Concurrent Programs, 1977, Programming a Personal Computer, 1982, On Pascal Compilers, 1985, Studies in Computational Science, 1995, The Search for Simplicity, 1996, Programming for Everyone, 1999, Classic Operating Systems, 2001, The Origin of Concurrent Programming, 2002, A Programmer's Story, 2005; mem. editl. bd. Acta Informatica, Annals of the History of Computing, Concurrency, Software, Lecture Notes in Computer Sci.; contbr. articles to profl. jours.; inventor programming langs. Concurrent Pascal, Edison, Joyce, SuperPascal. Recipient Chancellor's medal Syracuse U., 1989; grantee NSF, Army Rsch. Office, Office Naval Rsch., Rome Air Devel. Ctr. Fellow IEEE (Computer Pioneer award 2002). Avocations: history, photography, jazz. Home: 5070 Pine Valley Dr Fayetteville NY 13066-9723 Office: Syracuse U 2-175 CST Syracuse NY 13244-0001 Business E-Mail: pbh@ecs.syr.edu.

HANSEN, PETER, international organization executive; b. Aalborg, Denmark, June 2, 1941; Degree, Arhus University, 1966. Asst. prof., internat. rels. Arhus Univ., 1966, chmn., dept. polit. sci.; prof., polit. Odense Univ.; asst. sec.-gen., programme planning and coordination. UN; exec. dir., Geneva UN Comm, on Global Governance, Geneva, 1992—94; asst. sec.-gen and exec. dir. UN Ctr. on Transnational Corps., 1985—92; under sec.-gen. for humanitarian affairs and UN emergency relief coordinator, 1994—96; under sec.-gen. Commr.-Gen. of UNRWA, NYC, 1996—. Address: PO Box 338 78100 Ashqelon Israel E-mail: p.hansen@unrwa.org.

HANSEN, REX COSSEY, mechanical engineer; b. Salt Lake City, Dec. 23, 1952; s. Alvin Leo and Norma Dean (Cossey) H.; m. Gloria Lyn Haslam, May 18, 1978; children: Karen, Angela, Staci, Kayla. AA, Snow Coll., 1975; BS, Brigham Young U., 1977. Mech. engr., gas res. engr. Pacific Gas & Electric Co., San Francisco, 1977-81; sr. reservoir engr. Northwest Pipeline Corp., Salt Lake City, 1981-93; sr. petroleum engr. Williams Prodn. Co., Salt Lake City, 1993-95; compression engr. Northwest Pipeline Co., Salt Lake City, 1995-98; sr. petroleum engr. Wexpro Co., Salt Lake City, 1998—. Mem. gas storage steering com. Gas Rsch. Inst., Chgo., 1990-98; mem. natural gas res. com. Am. Gas Assn., Chgo., 1979-88. Mem. Soc. Petroleum Engrs. (tech. com. chair 1993-94, sect. chair 1990-91). Avocations: sailing, skiing, gardening.

HANSEN, RICHARD EMORY, psychologist; b. Pierre, S. D., Mar. 31, 1948; s. Hugo Ferdinand and Betty Louise Hansen; m. Kyle Patrick Back, Jan. 1, 1983; 1 child, Steven. BA, Pacific Lutheran Coll., Tacoma, Wash., 1971; MS, City U., L.A., 1994; PhD, U.Wash., Seattle, 2000. Psychologist Highline Sch. Dist. Seattle, 1987—90, Pacific Luth. Coll., Tacoma, 1990—93, U. Wash. Med. Ctr., Seattle, 1993—95, Capitol Hill Counseling, 1995—. Cons. King County Prosecutor's Office, Seattle, 1987—91. Mem. City Coun., Berrien, Wash., 2000. Home: 2020 S 320th K84 Federal Way WA 98003 Office: Capitol Hill Counseling 1011 Boren Ave Seattle WA 98104 Office Phone: 206-279-0279. E-mail: phill71@yahoo.com.

HANSEN, RICHARD OLAF, geophysicist, educator; b. Ottawa, Ont., Can., Oct. 4, 1946; came to U.S., 1968; s. Hyllard Olaf and Muriel Lenora (Helson) H.; m. Kathleen Jean Thoms, June 15, 1968. BSc with honors, Carleton U., 1968; MS, U. Chgo., 1969, PhD, 1973. Research assoc. U. Pitts., 1973-75; postdoctoral research asst. U. Oxford, Oxford, Great Britian, 1975-76; lectr. U. Calif., Berkeley, Calif., 1976-78; staff scientist EG&G Geometrics, Sunnyvale, Calif., 1979-85; prof. Colo. Sch. of Mines, Golden, Colo., 1985-95; prin. geophysicist Pearson, de Ridder and Johnson, Inc., Lakewood, Colo., 1995—2002, pres., 2003—. Assoc. editor Geophysics, 1987-91, 95-99. Mem. Soc. Exploration Geophysicists (hon.), Am. Geophys. Union, Am. Phys. Soc., European Assn. Geoscientists and Engrs., Sigma Xi. Office: PRJ Inc Ste 100 12640 W Cedar Dr Lakewood CO 80228-2032 Office Phone: 303-987-1114. E-mail: rohansen@prj.com.

HANSEN, ROBERT CLINTON, electrical engineer, consultant; b. St. Louis, 1926; married, 1952; 2 children. BS, U. Mo., 1949, DEng (hon.), 1975; MS, U. Ill., 1950, PhD, 1955. Rsch. assoc. antenna lab. U. Ill., 1950-55; sr. staff engr. microwave lab. Hughes Aircraft Co., 1955-59; sr. staff engr. telecomm. lab. Space Technol. Labs., 1959-60; dir. test mission analysis office Aerospace Corp., Calif., 1960-67; head electronics divsn. KMS Technol. Ctr., 1967-71; pres., cons. R.C. Hansen, Inc., Tarzana, Calif., 1971—. Mem. commn. B Internat. Sci. Radio Union. Editor: Microwave Scanning Antennas, 1964—65, Significant Phased Array Papers, 1973, Geometric Theory of Diffraction, 1981, Moment Methods in Antennas and Scattering, 1990; author: Phased Array Antennas, 1998. Recipient Disting. Alumnus award, U. Ill. Elec. Engring. Dept., 1981, Disting. Alumnus Svc. medal, 1986. Fellow: IEEE (pres. antennas and propagation soc. 1964, 1980), Inst. Elec. Engrs. (London), Aerospace & Electronic Sys. Soc. (Barry Carlton award 1991, AP Disting. Achievement award 1994, Electromagnetics award 2002); mem.: NAE, Am. Phys. Soc. Office: RC Hansen Inc PO Box 570215 Tarzana CA 91357 Office Phone: 818-345-0770.

HANSEN, ROBERT JOSEPH, civil engineer; b. Tacoma, May 27, 1918; s. Joseph and Olaug (Axness) H.; m. Eleanor Swaim Welch, Dec. 26, 1948; children: Eric Charles, Karen Welch. BS, U. Wash., 1940; Sc.D., MIT, 1948. Research engr. NRC, 1940-43; Princeton U., 1943-45; Arthur D. Little Co., Cambridge, Mass., 1945; NRC predoctoral fellow, 1946-47; research asso. MIT, 1947-48, mem. faculty, 1948—, prof. civil engring., 1957—, dep. dir. Project Transp., 1964-67. Ptnr. Hansen, Holley & Biggs, Inc. (cons. engrs.), Cambridge, 1955-88, prin., 1975-88; ptnr. Newmark, Hansen & Assos., Cambridge and Urbana, Ill., 1958-68; cons. biomechanics Mass. Gen. Hosp., 1956-60; mem. security resources panel Exec. Office of Pres., 1957; mem. sr. adv. panel Air Force Ballistic Div., USAF, 1958-60; mem. exec. com. Adv. Com. CD, Nat. Acad. Scis., 1959— Author: (with others) Structural Design for Dynamic Loads, 1959; also articles, chpts. in books.; editor: Seismic Design for Nuclear Power Plants, 1970. Recipient Army-Navy cert. of appreciation, 1948; Disting. Service citation Dept. Def., 1969 Fellow ASCE (Moisseiff award 1974, Raymond C. Reese research prize 1975, Innovation Civil Engring award 1989); mem. Boston Soc. Civil Engrs., Sigma Xi, Tau Beta Pi. Home: 25 Cambridge St Winchester MA 01890-3703

HANSEN, ROBYN L., lawyer; b. Terre Haute, Ind., Dec. 2, 1949; d. Robert Louis and Shirley (Nagel) Wieman; m. Gary Hansen, Aug. 21, 1971 (div. 1985); children: Nathan Ross Hansen, Brian Michael Hansen; m. John Marley Clarey, Jan. 1, 1986; 1 child, John Zender Clarey. BA, Gustavus Adolphus, 1971; JD cum laude, William Mitchell Coll. Law, 1977. Bar: Minn. 1977, U.S. Dist. Ct. Minn. 1977. Atty. Briggs and Morgan P.A., St. Paul, 1977-93, Leonard, Street and Deinard, St. Paul, 1993—. Trustee Actors Theatre, St. Paul, 1980—88, Minn. Mus. Am. Art, 1994—97; active Minn. Inst. Pub. Fin., 1987—93, bd. dirs., 1993—95, pres., 1995; bd. dirs. St. Paul Downtown Coun., 1985—93, St. Paul Area Conv. and Vis. Bur., 1995—2005, chair, 1999—2001; trustee Met. State U. Found., 1993—2005, chair, 2000—02; bd. dirs. Capital City Partnership, 1997—, Pk. Sq. Theatre, 2003—, St. Paul Found., 2005—. Mem. ABA, Minn. Bar Assn., Ramsey County Bar Assn., Nat. Assn. Bond Lawyers, St. Paul Area C. of C. (bd. dirs., exec. com. 1997-99). Office: Leonard Street and Deinard 380 St Peter St Ste 500 Saint Paul MN 55102 Office Phone: 651-291-3506. Business E-Mail: robyn.hansen@leonard.com.

HANSEN, RON, writer, language educator; b. Omaha, Nebr., Dec. 8, 1947; s. Frank L. and Marvyl M. H.; m. Bo Caldwell, July 4, 1996; stepchildren: Kate Arnold, Scotty Arnold. BA, Creighton U., 1970; MFA, U. Iowa, 1974; MA, Santa Clara (Calif.) U., 1995. Author: (novel) Desperadoes, 1979, The Assassination of Jesse James by the Coward Robert Ford, 1983, Mariette in Ecstasy, 1991, Atticus, 1995, Hitler's Niece, 1999, (collection of essays) A Stay Against Confusion, 2001 (children's books) The Shadowmaker, 1987 (short stories) Nebraska, 1989. 1st lt. U.S. Army, 1970-72. Roman Catholic. Avocations: golf, film, painting. Office: Dept of English Santa Clara U Santa Clara CA 95053 E-mail: RHansen@scu.edu.

HANSEN, SAM, cardiologist; b. Jenin, Jordan, Aug. 1, 1956; MBChB, Mosul U., Iraq, 1983. Physician Oak Hill Med., Lake Isabella, Calif., 1997—2001; cardiologist Care Group LLC, Lafayette, Ind., 2001—. Office: The Care Group LLC 1116 N 16th St Ste B Lafayette IN 47904 Home: 3221 Covington St West Lafayette IN 47906 Office Phone: 765-428-2500. E-mail: shansen@thecaregroup.com.

HANSEN, STEPHEN CHRISTIAN, banker; b. N.Y.C., July 3, 1940; s. Norbert C. and Harriet C. H.; m. Ethel Olmsted, June 12, 1971; 1 son, Lee Christian. AB, Princeton U., 1962; LL.B., U. Va., 1966; postgrad., Brown U. Grad. Sch. Banking. Bar: N.Y. 1966. Assoc. Alexander & Green, N.Y.C., 1966-68; mem. N.Y. State Legislature, 1968-70; spl. asst. to undersec. HUD, Washington, 1970-73; spl. asst. to chmn. FDIC, Washington, 1973-76; sr. v.p. Dollar Bank, Pitts., 1976-78, pres., 1978—, pres., CEO, 1982—. Chmn. Regional Indsl. Devel. Corp. Bd. dirs. Pitts. Regional Alliance; trustee Carnegie Inst.; bd. dirs. Carnegie Sci. Ctr.; bd. dir. Cleve. Dist. Pitts. Fed. Res. Mem. N.Y. State Bar Assn. Office: Dollar Bank PO Box 987 Pittsburgh PA 15230-0987

HANSEN, THOMAS NANASTAD, pediatrician, health facility administrator; b. Neenah, Wis., Oct. 11, 1947; m. Cheryl Bailey, June 9, 1979; children: Elaine Christ, William Thomas. BS in Physics summa cum laude, Tex. Christian U., 1970; MD, Baylor Coll. Medicine, 1973. Diplomate Am. Bd. Pediatrics. Intern in pediatrics Baylor Coll. Medicine, Houston, 1973-74, resident in pediatrics, 1974-76, postdoctoral fellow in neonatal perinatal medicine, 1976-78; postdoctoral fellow in pediatric pulmonary disease U. Calif., San Francisco, 1978-81; asst. prof. pediatrics Baylor Coll. Medicine, 1978-84, assoc. prof. pediatrics, 1984-89; prof. pediatrics and cell biology Tex. Children's Hosp. Found., Houston, 1989-95; head sect. on neonatology Baylor Coll. of Medicine, 1987-95, vice-chmn. rsch. dept. pediatrics, 1994-95, dir. child health rsch. ctr., 1994-95, co-dir. ctr. for tng. in molecular medicine, 1994-95; chmn. pediat., CEO Children's Hosp., Columbus, Ohio, 1995—. Mem. exam com. Am. Bd. Pediatrics, 1982—, sub-bd. neonatal-perinatal medicine, 1992—, chmn. credentials com., 1993—, chmn.-elect sub-bd. neonaatal perinatal medicine, 1994. Contbr. numerous articles to profl. jours. Trustee Tex. Women's Hosp., 1988-91. Mem. Western Soc. for Pediatric Rsch., So. Soc. for Pediaatric Rsch., Soc. for Pediatric Rsch. (sec.-treas. 1986-91, chmn. student rsch. com. 1990—, trustee internat. chpt. 1992—), Am. Physiol. Soc., Am. Pediatric Soc., Am. Fedn. for Clin. Rsch., Am. Thoracic Soc., Am. Acad. of Pediatrics, N.Y. Acad. of Scis., Am. Soc. for Cell Biology, Assn. of Med. Sch. Pediatric Dept. Chmn., Sigma Xi. Home: 4328 Vaux Link New Albany OH 43054-9681 Office: Med Dir's Office Childrens Hosp 700 Childrens Dr Columbus OH 43205-2664

HANSEN, VAGN KEITH, political science educator, college administrator; b. Jackson, Miss., Jan. 24, 1944; s. Vagn Aage and Elizabeth Eleanor (Keith) H.; m. Marleen Kibler Berry, June 7, 1969; 1 child, Vagn Keith II. BA cum laude, Tulane U., 1966; MA, U. Va., 1969, PhD, 1971. Asst. prof. history and polit. sci. Va. Mil. Inst., Lexington, 1971-74; with Delta State U., Cleveland, Miss., 1974-85, prof. polit. sci., 1979-85, chmn. div. social scis., 1981-85; Jefferson-Pilot prof. polit. sci. High Point U., NC, 1985—2000; provost, v.p. acad. affairs Miss. U. for Women, Columbus, 2000—03, acting pres., 2001; coord. acad. rsch. and svc. Miss. Instns. Higher Learning, Jackson, 2003—04; dean Coll. Arts and Scis. U. N. Ala., Florence, 2004—. Author: Mississippi State and Local Government, 1988; contbr. articles to profl. jours. Pres. Community Concert Assn., High Point, 1990-92; bd. dirs. Community Action Program, Cleveland, 1976-80; chair govtl. affairs com. High Point C. of C.,

1998-2000; mem. Leadership Shoals, Florence, 2004-. Mem. Phi Beta Kappa, Omicron Delta Kappa. Avocations: travel, running, music. Home: 408 7th St S Columbus MS 39701-5752 Office: UNA Box 5021 Florence AL 35632

HANSEN, VICKI D. (VICTORIA ROBERTS), writer; b. Miami, Okla., May 17, 1961; d. Elmer Dewitt and Wanda Jean (Stanley) Wynn; m. Richard Kent Hansen, May 27, 2001; 1 child: Joseph. AA, Northeastern Okla. A&M U., 1981; BA, Okla. Bapt. U., 1984. Vol. Bapt. Student Union dir. Mission Svc. Corps. So. Bapts., San Francisco, 1984-86; pharmacy technician St. Francis Hosp., Tulsa, Okla., 1986—96; exec. asst. The Williams Cos., Tulsa, Okla., 1988-98. Active Chinese children's ministry Nichols Hills Bapt. Ch., Oklahoma City, 1982; Sunday sch. tchr., summer camp tchr. First Assembly, Miami, Okla., 1994; asst. Acteens leader First Bapt. Ch., Miami, 1983-84; hosp. and deaf ministry Victory Christian Ctr., Tulsa, 1990-92; notary pub. Tulsa County, 1998; fund raising vol. United Way, Tulsa, 1992-94, Muscular Dystrophy Assn., Tulsa, 1995-96. Mem. Ministerial Alliance, Phi Theta Kappa. Avocations: photography, growing orchids and violets, scuba diving, tropical vacations. Home and Office: 2314 W Atlanta Court Broken Arrow OK 74012

HANSEN, W. LEE, economics professor; b. Racine, Wis., Nov. 8, 1928; s. William R. and Gertrude M. (Spillum) H.; m. Sally Ann Porch, Dec. 26, 1955; children— Ellen J., Martha L. BA, U. Wis., Madison, 1950, MA, 1955; PhD, Johns Hopkins U., 1958. Asst. prof. econs. UCLA, from 1958, assoc. prof., to 1965; assoc. prof. econs. U. Wis., Madison, from 1965, prof., prof. emeritus, 1996—. Sr. staff economist Pres.'s Coun. Econ. Advisers, Washington, 1964-65; trustee Nat. Coun. on Econ. Edn., N.Y.C., 1976-2000, sec., 1996-2000; mem. bd. founders NCEE, 2000—. Author: Benefits, Costs, and Finance of Public Higher Education, 1969, Education, Income, and Human Capital, 1970, The Labor Market for Scientists and Engineers, 1973, Perspectives on Economic Education, 1977, A Framework for Teaching Basic Economic Concepts, 1984, The End of Mandatory Retirement, 1989, Unemployment Insurance: The Second Half-Century, 1990, Academic Freedom on Trial: 100 Years of Sifting and Winnowing at the University of Wisconsin, 1998, Discussing Economics, 2005, Discussing Economics, 2005; contbr. articles to profl. jours. Sgt. U.S. Army, 1951-53. Recipient Amoco Disting. Tchg. award U. Wis., 1982, Hilldale award, 1988, Disting. Svc. award Nat. Coun. on Econs. Edn., 1991, Marvin Bower award, 1994, Henry H. Villard Rsch. award, 2000, Tchr. Acad. U. Wis., 1994, Outstanding Postsecondary Educator award nat. Fedn. Ind. Bus. Found., 1992, Leavey award for excellence in pvt. enterprise edn. Freedoms Found., 1996; Guggenheim fellow, 1969-70; Fulbright sr. scholar, Australia, 1988. Mem. AAUP (chair com. on the econ. status of the profession 1979-86, mem. nat. coun. 1980-82, retirement com. 1985-95), Am. Econ. Assn. (chmn. com. on econ. edn. 1983-88, exec. sec. commn. grad. edn. econs. 1988-91), Indsl. Rels. Rsch. Assn., Midwest Econs. Assn. (pres. 1987), Phi Beta Kappa. Unitarian Universalist. Office: U Wis Dept Econs 1180 Observatory Dr Madison WI 53706-1320 Business E-Mail: wlhansen@wisc.edu.

HANSEN, WAYNE W., lawyer; b. Clintonville, Wis., June 7, 1942; s. William W. and Berniece M. (Kuehn) H.; m. Carolyn M. Lemke, Dec. 21, 1969; children: Drew D., Janna J. BBA, U. Wis., 1965, JD, 1967. Bar: Wis. 1967, U.S. Dist. Ct. (we. dist.) Wis. 1971, U.S. Ct. Appeals (7th cir.) 1972, U.S. Dist. Ct. (ea. dist.) Wis. 1975, Wash. 1979, U.S. Dist. Ct. (we. dist.) Wash. 1979, U.S. Ct. Appeals (9th cir.) 1982, U.S. Dist. Ct. (ea. dist.) Wash. 1986. Atty. NLRB, Mpls., 1967-70, Schmitt Nolan Hansen & Hartley, Merrill, Wis., 1970-79; ptnr. Lane Powell Spears Lubersky, Seattle, 1979-98; mng. ptnr. Seattle office Jackson Lewis LLP, 1998—. Contbg. author: Developing Labor Law, 1971, Doing Business in Washington State*Guide for Foreign Business, 1989. Office: Jackson Lewis LLP 600 University St Ste 2900 Seattle WA 98101-4174 Office Phone: 206-626-6400. E-mail: hansenw@jackson.law.com.

HANSEN, WIDMER CASE, retired engineer; b. Aug. 1, 1913; s. William Carl and Ada Margaret (Nelson Borg) Hansen; m. Blanche Davis, July 13, 1946 (div. 1981); children: June Hansen Butkas, Jacqueline Hansen Conlon, Widmer Case Jr.(dec.); m. Colombe Martha Schultz, Dec. 28, 1983 (dec. 1995); 1 stepchild, Carol Colombe Schultz Cross. BSEE, U.S. Naval Acad., 1937; postgrad., Naval Postgrad. Sch., 1946—47, Indsl. Coll. of Armed Forces, 1956—57; MEngring., Johns Hopkins U., 1949. Cert. naval ordnance engr. Commd. ens. U.S. Navy, 1937, advanced through grades to capt., 1963, ret., various assignments, 1937—52; comdr. and capt. Bur. Ordnance, Bur. Naval Weapons, Washington, 1952—60; capt. Spl. Projects Office Tech. Rep., Syosset, NY, 1960—63; weapons sys. analyst Air-Air Grumman Corp., Bethpage, NY, 1963—76; ret. Mem. human investigations subcom., R&D com. VA Med. Ctr., Canandaigua, NY, 1985—97. Mem.: NRA, Sigma Xi. Republican. Achievements include first to prodn. of naval missiles for service use. Avocations: travel, photography, marksmanship. Home: 4477 County Rd 32 #1 Bloomfield NY 14469-9731

HANSEN-FLASCHEN, JOHN HYMAN, medical educator, researcher; b. Hamilton, Ohio, June 25, 1950; s. Steward Samuel and Joyce (Davies) Flaschen; m. Susan Lauretta Hansen, Aug. 22, 1951; children: Lynn, Lauren. AB, Brown U., 1972; MD, NYU, 1976. Diplomate in internal medicine, pulmonary medicine, critical care medicine Am. Bd. Internal Medicine. Resident in medicine U. Pa., Phila., 1976-79, chief resident in medicine, 1980-81, pulmonary fellow, 1979-80, 81-82, attending physician, 1982—, asst. prof. medicine, 1982-87, assoc. prof., 1988-98, prof., 1999—, dir. edn. and tng. programs in pulmonary and critical care, 1983-90, dir. pulmonary and critical care divsn., 1990-98, chief pulmonary, allergy and critical care divsn., 1998—, dir. Penn Lung Ctr., 1996—. Mem. editl. bd. Clin. Pulmonary Medicine, Respiratory Medicine, UpToDate; editor Pulmonary and Critical Care MKSAP 13, ACP; contbr. articles to profl. jours. Steering com. Nat. Emphysema Treatment Trial, 1997—2003. Recipient Spl. Investigator award Am. Heart Assn., 1982-84, Lindback Tchg. award U. Pa., 1999, others; Measey Found. fellow, 1982-83. Fellow ACP, Am. Coll. Chest Physicians, Coll. Physicians Phila.; mem. Am. Thoracic Soc. (chmn. postgrad. edn. com. 1995—, clin. problems long range planning com. 1997-99, Clinician Educator award 2004), Soc. for Critical Care Medicine, Soc. for Bioethics Consultation, Laennec Soc. Phila. (pres. 1990-91), Drinker Soc. for Critical Care in Phila. (founder, 1st pres. 1988-90), Sigma Xi, Alpha Omega Alpha. Democrat. Home: 365 Penn Rd Wynnewood PA 19096-1401 Office: Hosp U Pa 873 Mahoney Bldg 3400 Spruce St Philadelphia PA 19104-4206

HANSEN-KYLE, LINDA L, counselor, nursing educator; b. Selma, Calif, Aug. 24, 1947; d. Ernest L. and Mary Hansen; m. Kenton L. Kyle, Feb. 16, 1974. BA in History summa cum laude, Humboldt State, 1969, MA in Psychology, 1972; ASN, Saddleback Coll., 1976; MS in Human Resources and Mgmt. Devel., Chapman U., 1993; MSN, Calif. State U., Dominguez Hills, 2000; postgrad. in nursing, U. San Diego, 2001—. Cert. case mgr.; RN Calif. ICU nurse supr. Scripps Clinic and Rsch., San Diego, 1978-81; asst. dir. nursing Mary Knoll Coll., San Diego, 1980-85; mgr. of ops. United Healthcare, San Diego, 1985—97; adj. instr. nursing Grossmont CC, 1999—. Adj. instr. U. San Diego, 2003—. Mem.: ANA, Case Mgmt. Soc. Am., Western Inst. Nursing Rsch., Phi Kappa Phi, Sigma Theta Tau.

HANSEN-THOMAS, HOLLY HARBOUR, language educator; b. San Antonio, Sept. 18, 1969; d. Alton Arthur and Sheila Eileen Lovell Hansen; m. William Howard Thomas, Aug. 19, 1995. B.A. in Art History, U. Tex., Austin; M.A. in Bicultural/Bilingual Studies with emphasis in ESL, U. Tex., San Antonio, 1999, Ph.D., 2005. Tchg. cert. Tex., 1995. English tchr., Dresden, Germany; ESL and spanish tchr. Eisenhower Mid. Sch., San Antonio, 1995—98; vis. prof. in applied linguistics and second lang. tchg. Eotvos Lorand U., Budapest, Hungary, 2000—01; undergraduate instr. ESL and applied linguistics U. Tex., San Antonio, 2001—. Bd. dirs. Tex. TESOL San Antonio. Contbr. articles to profl. jours. Mem. Tex. TESOL, San Antonio, 2002—05; conf. com. chairperson TESOL, Va., 2005. Scholar Deborah Partridge Wolfe Laureate scholar, Kappa Delta Pi, 2005, Women's Studies Inst., U. of Tex. at San Antonio, 2004-2005; Profl. Devel. scholar, TESOL, 1998, grad. scholar, AAUW, 1999, 2004, Fulbright fellow, 2002. Mem.: AAAL, AERA (AERA/IES dissertation fellow), TESOL.

HANSHAW, JAMES BARRY, pediatrician, educator; b. Scarsdale, N.Y., Dec. 23, 1928; s. George Lee and Kathryn Frances (Reilly) H.; m. Marian Christine Kernan, Aug. 14, 1954; children: Thomas, Lee, Elizabeth, John, Margaret. AB, Syracuse U., 1950; MD, SUNY, Syracuse, 1953, DSc (hon.), 1991. Intern Cin. Gen. Hosp., 1953-54; resident pediatrics U. Rochester Med. Center, 1956-58; Nat. Found. postdoctoral fellow virology Harvard U. Sch. Pub. Health, 1958-60; academic medicine, specializing in pediatrics Rochester, N.Y., 1960-75; instr. to prof. pediatrics and microbiology U. Rochester Sch. Medicine, 1960-75; prof., chmn. dept. pediatrics U. Mass., Worcester, 1975-85, interim vice chancellor, acad. dean, 1985-86; interim chancellor, 1987; provost, dean U. Mass., 1986-89, dean and provost emeritus, prof. pediatrics, 1989—, interim chmn. dept. pediatrics, 1997-98; chmn. dept. pediatrics Meml. Health Care, 1993-98. Lectr. pediatrics Harvard U. Med. Sch., 1975-2002; vis. prof. Inst. Child Health, London U. and Hosp. for Sick Children, London, 1971-72; coll. health physician WPI, 1990—. Author: (with J.A. Dudgeon) Viral Infections Fetus and Newborn, 1978, 2d edit. (with Dudgeon and W.C. Marshall), 1985. Served with USAF, 1953-56. Recipient Disting. Alumnus award Upstate Med. U., 2003, Career Achievement award Worcester Dist. Med. Soc., 2004; Buswell fellow U. Rochester, 1960-62; NIH grantee, 1962-75. Mem. AMA, Am. Pediatric Soc., Soc. Pediatric Research, Am. Acad. Pediatrics, Infectious Diseases Soc. Am., New Eng. Pediatric Soc., Sigma Xi, Alpha Omega Alpha. Home: 18 Baypath Dr Boylston MA 01505-1427 Office Phone: 508-869-6038. E-mail: jhans76271@aol.com.

HANSMAN, ROBERT G., art educator, artist; BFA, U. Kans., 1970. Asst. prof. Washington U., St. Louis. Instr. dept. parts and recreation Project Artspark, 1993, Arts Connection/City Faces, 1994—; instr. juvenile detention program Children's Art Ctr., 1995; established Jermaine Lamond Roberts Meml. Art Studio, clinton-Peabody Pub. Housing, 1997. One-man shows include St. Louis C.C. at Forest Park, 1988, MJF Arts Studio Gallery, 1990, University City Pub. Libr., 1992, 1995, Bonsack Gallery, 1995. Mem. pub. housing revitalization focus group Darst-Webbe, 1995. Named Reader's Poll Best Local Artist, The Riverfront Times, 1995; recipient First Pl. award/Best of Show, St. Louis Artists Guild, 1988, 1992, Componere Gallery, 1990, Not Just An Art Dirs. Club, 1990, The Gallery Connection, 1991, Art St. Louis Gallery, 1991, World of Difference award City Faces, 1996, Mo. Arts award, Mo. Arts Coun., 1997, Excellence in Tchg. award, Emerson Electric, 2000, Disting. Faculty award, 2001, honoree, Colin Powell's Am. Promise, 1999, Mo. Ho. of Reps., 1997; grantee, Bi-State Arts in Transit Project, 1995, 1996, 1999. Office: Washington U Sch Arch Campus Box 1079 One Brookings Dr Saint Louis MO 63130 E-mail: hansman@architecture.wustl.edu.

HANSMANN, HENRY BAETHKE, law educator; b. Highland Park, Ill., Oct. 5, 1945; s. Elwood Hansmann and Louise Frances (Baethke) Moore; m. Marina Santilli, 1992; 1 child, Lisa Santilli. BA, Brown U., 1967; JD, Yale U., 1974, PhD, 1978. Asst. prof. law U. Pa. Law Sch., Phila., 1975-81, assoc. prof. law, econs. and pub. policy, 1981-83; prof. law Yale U., New Haven, 1983—2003, Augustus E. Lines prof. law, 2004—; George T. Lowy prof. law NYU, 2003—04. Author: The Ownership of Enterprise, 1996. John Simon Guggenheim Found. fellow, 1985-86. Mem. Am. Econs. Assn., Am. Law and Econ. Assn. Home: 26 E 81st St Apt 4S New York NY 10028-0219 Office: Yale Law Sch PO Box 208215 New Haven CT 06511 Office Phone: 203-432-4966. Business E-Mail: henry.hansmann@yale.edu.

HANSMANN, RALPH EMIL, investment executive, director; b. Utica, NY, May 25, 1918; s. Emil C. and Friedericka (Fuchs) H.; m. Doris Macdonald, Oct. 16, 1943; children: Robert E., Jane C. AB, Hamilton Coll., 1940, LLD, 1992; MBA, Harvard, 1942. Investment assoc. Harold F. Linder, William T. Golden, N.Y.C., 1945-48, 53—; staff Gen. Am. Investors Co., Inc., 1949-52. Emeritus trustee Inst. Advanced Study, Princeton, N.J.; life trustee Hamilton Coll., Clinton, N.Y., N.Y. Pub. Libr. Served as lt. USNR, 1942-45. Mem. Ridgewood (N.J.) Country Club, Harvard Club (N.Y.C.), Phi Beta Kappa. Home: 385 Manchester Rd Ridgewood NJ 07450-1212 Office: 500 Fifth Ave New York NY 10110 Office Phone: 212-391-8960.

HANSON, ARNOLD PHILIP, retired lawyer; b. Berlin, NH, July 11, 1924; s. Arnold H. and Evelyn (Renaud) H.; m. Della Ann Lavernoich, June 26, 1948; children: Arnold Philip, Caryl Hanson Brensinger, Julie E. Hanson Mook. BA, U. N.H., 1948; JD, Boston, 1951. Bar: N.H. 1951. Pvt. practice, Berlin, N.H., 1951-60; ptnr. Bergeron & Hanson, Berlin, 1960-80, Bergeron & Hanson, P.A., Berlin, 1980-87, Bergeron, Hanson & Bornstein, P.A., Berlin, 1988-91; county atty. Coos County, N.H., 1952-56; ret. Mem. ct. accreditation com. State of N.H., 1970-77, Regional Criminal Justice Planning Coun., 1978-88; ptnr. North Country TV Cable Co., Groveton, N.H., 1962-89; chmn. bd., chmn. exec. com. Berlin City Bank, 1975-87. Chmn. city Republican Conv., Berlin, 1952-54; bd. dirs. Rep. State Com., 1958-60; del. Rep. Nat Com., 1964; trustee A.V. Hosp., 1976-85, mem. coms., 1976-86; area chmn. fundraising campaigns including ARC, U. N.H. Centennial Fund, Crippled Children, N.H. Children's Aid Soc., Boy Scouts Am., Boston U. Law Sch. Centennial Fund, St. Paul's Sch. Advanced Studies Program, A.V. Hosp. Bldg. Fund maj. gifts program, Frank Kenison Fund Boston U. Law Sch.; mem. U. N.H. 50th Reunion Fund Raising Class of 1948, 1996-98. Served with USN, 1943-46. Recipient Silver Shingle award Boston U. Sch. Law, 1977, Alumni Meritorius award U. N.H., 1986, U. N.H. Hubbard Family award for svc. to philanthropy, 2004. Fellow Am. Bar Found.; mem. N.H. Bar Assn. (pres. 1974-75, bd. govs. 1973-76), Coos County Bar Assn. (pres. various yrs.), Tri-Legal County Svcs., N.H. Alumni Assn. (bd. dirs. 1974-77), Boston U. Alumni Assn., Am. Legion (post judge adv. 1952-64), VFW (post judge adv. 1952-93), Nashua Country Club (Nashua, N.H.), Seven Lakes Country Club (Ft. Myers, Fla.), Kiwanis (pres. 1966). Lutheran. Home: 55 Hawthorne Village Rd Nashua NH 03062-2271 also: 13190 Oakmont Drive #8 Fort Myers FL 33907-8020

HANSON, ARTHUR STUART, physician, consultant; b. Mpls., Mar. 10, 1937; s. Arthur Emanuel and Frances Elenor (Larson) H.; m. Gail Joan Taylor, June 16, 1963; children: Marta Eileen, Peter Arthur. BA, Dartmouth Coll., 1959; MD, U. Minn., 1963. Diplomate Am. Bd. Internal Medicine, Am. Bd. Pulmonary Disease. Intern Hennipen County Med. Ctr., 1963-64; resident in internal medicine U. Minn., 1964-65, 68-70, fellow pulmonary disease, 1970-71; cons. in pulmonary and critical care medicine Park Nicollet Clinic, Mpls., 1971—, med. dir., 1975-82, v.p. legis. and cmty. affairs, 1982-86; dir. med. edn. Park Nicollet Med. Found., Mpls., 1982-86; pres., CEO Park Nicollet Inst., Mpls., 1986—2002. Bd. dirs. Minn. Health Data Inst., 1993-03. Pres., bd. chair Minn. Smoke Free Coalition, 1985-88, 96-98, 2005—; vice chair Minn. Partnership for Action Against Tobacco, 1998-2003; chmn. bd. Smoke Free Generation Minn., 1984-90. Recipient Cmty. Leadership award, Am. Lung Assn. Hennepin County, 1987, Harvey H. Rogers Meml. award, Minn. Pub. Health Assn., 1988, award for excellence in health promotion, Minn. Health Commr., 1989, Physician of Excellence award, Park Nicollet Health Svcs., 2000, Lynn Smith 25-Yr. award, Am. Cancer Soc., 2001. Fellow ACP, AMA (del., chmn.), Am. Coll. Chest Physicians; mem. Minn. Med. Assn. (pres. 1992-93, Stop the Violence award 1994, Disting. Svc. award 1998), Minn. Healthcare Coalition on Violence, Hennepin County Med. Soc. (pres. 1990-91, Charles Bolles Bolles-Rogers award 1998). Unitarian Universalist. Avocations: birding, gardening, physical fitness, reading, travel. Office: Park Nicollet Clinic Ste 300 6490 Excelsior Blvd Minneapolis MN 55426 Office Phone: 952-993-3242. Business E-Mail: astuart.hanson@parknicollet.com.

HANSON, COOPER, artist; b. Jan. 27, 1965; Grad., Interlochen Arts Acad. H.S., 1983. Dir. Resurgam Gallery, Balt., 1994-95. One-woman show paintings Sheldon Knorr Gallery, Balt., 1997, Corcoran Mus., 2002, U. Md., 2002, Craig Flinner Gallery, 2002; artist work on loan U.S. Ambassadorial Residence, Bucharest, Romania, 1998—. Exhibit and event dir. Under 100 Balt., 1994. Mem. Md. Art Pl., Sch. 33 Art Ctr. Office: 700 Park Ave Baltimore MD 21201-4741

HANSON, CURTIS, film director, scriptwriter; b. Mar. 24, 1945; Dir., screenwriter (film) Sweet Kill, 1972, The Bedroom Window, 1988; dir., co-producer (film) The Little Dragons, 1977; dir. (film) The Arousers, 1970, Losin' It, 1983, Bad Influence, 1990, The Hand That Rocks the Cradle, 1992, The River Wild, 1994; dir., prodr., screenwriter (film) L.A. Confidential, 1997; dir., prodr. (film) Wonder Boys, 1999, 8 mile, 2002, In Her Shoes, 2005; screenwriter: The Dunwich Horror, 1970, The Silent Partner, 1978, White Dog, 1982, Never Cry Wolf, 1983; actor (TV) Hitchcock: Shadow of a Genius, 1999; (film) Adaptation, 2002. Office: United Talent Agy 9560 Wilshire Blvd Fl 5 Beverly Hills CA 90212-2400*

HANSON, DALE S., retired bank executive; b. Milw., Nov. 11, 1938; s. Yngve Holger and Evelyn (Johnson) H.; m. Joan Benton, July 15, 1961; children— Thomas S., Tim B. BA in Econs., Carlton Coll., 1960; postgrad. Exec. Program, Credit and Fin. Mgmt. Stanford U., 1966-67. Asst. cashier First Bank, St. Paul, 1964-66, asst. v.p., 1966-68, v.p., 1968-82, sr. v.p., 1982-83, exec. v.p., 1983-84, pres., 1984-88; pres., mng. ptnr. FBS Mcht. Banking Group, 1987-90; mng. ptnr. Matrix Leasing Internat., 1989-90; exec. v.p. 1st Bank System, Mpls., 1984-91; v.p., treas., chief fin. officer C.H. Robinson Co., Mpls., 1991-98, also bd. dirs.; ret., 1998. Bd. dirs. W.A. Lang Co., Edwards Mfg. Co. Mem. Corp. Health One, Inc.; bd. dirs. St. Paul Chamber Orch., Twin City Pub. TV, St. Paul Riverfront Devel. Corp., 1985-91. 1st lt. USNG, 1961-67. Mem. Robert Morris Assocs. (pres. 1982-83), Fin. Execs. Inst. (bd. dirs. Twin Cities chpt.), Somerset Golf Club, Mpls. Club, Minn. Club (St. Paul). Republican. Presbyterian. Avocations: skiing, sailing, golf, photography. Office: care C H Robinson Co 8100 Mitchell Rd Ste 200 Eden Prairie MN 55344-2178

HANSON, DAN LEWIS, music educator, composer; b. Lamesa, Tex., Mar. 28, 1953; s. Harvey James and Jerri Hanson; m. Judy Fawn Leatherwood, June 28, 2001; children: Erin Taylor, Kim Aline Zahn, Mallory Jaymes. MusB, Tex. Tech U., 1975, MusM, 1981; MusD, U. North Tex., 1987. Asst. prof. music South Plains Coll., Levelland, Okla., 1977—84; prof. music U. Sci. and Arts Okla., Chickasha, Okla., 1987—. Composer: (songs) A Triumphal Procession, (plays) The History of American Education in Song, 2002. Recipient Faculty Superior Tchg. award, U. Sci. and Arts Okla., 2005. Mem.: Okla. Music Theory Roundtable (pres. 2002—03), Okla. Music Educators Assn., Lions Club (v.p. 2000—05), Phi Mu Alpha Sinfonia. Democrat. Avocations: reading, travel. Home: 7 Misty Glenn Dr Chickasha OK 73018 Office: Univ of Science and Arts of Oklahoma 1727 West Alabama Chickasha OK 73018 Personal E-mail: dhanson3@cox.net. E-mail: dhanson@usao.edu.

HANSON, DAVID ALAN, music educator; b. Bryan, OH, Dec. 6, 1945; s. Chester Adams and Mary Adele (Daenitz) Hanson; m. Lori Ray Stelzer, Aug. 16, 1960. MusB, Bowling Green State Univ., Bowling Green, OH, 1968; MusM, Univ. of Mich., Ann Arbor, Mich., 1972. Cert. Permanent Tchng. Certificate Ohio. Music ed. Findlay City Sch., Findlay, Ohio, 1968—2003, Heidelberg Coll., Tiffin, Ohio, 1974—2005, Bluffton Coll., Bluffton, Ohio, 2000—05. Prin. double Bass Lima Symphony, Lima, Ohio, 1968—74. Author: (7 music articles) Triad, (4 music articles) The Instrumentalist; composer: (compositions) 18 for brass, full orchestra, choir, guitar, double Bass- two publ. Recipient Outstanding Young Educator Award, Findlay Jaycees/ Findlay, OH, 1977, Tchr. Golden Apple Award, Findlay Rotary Club/Findlay, OH, 1996, D. Robert Baker Award, Findlay City Sch./Findlay, OH, 1999, Tchr. of Yr. award, Ohio String Tchrs. Assn., 1995. Mem.: Am. String Tchr. Assoc., Ohio Music Ed. Assoc. (NW Region Chair), Music Ed. Nat. Conf., Findlay Arts Coun. Avocations: lepidoptera study, reading, photography, bicycling. Home: 1709 Forest Park Findlay OH 45840

HANSON, DAVID JAMES, lawyer; b. Neenah, Wis., July 20, 1943; s. Vernon James and Dorothy O. Hanson; m. Diana G. Severson, Aug. 25, 1965 (div. Sept. 1982); children: Matthew Vernon, Maja Kirsten, Brian Edward; m. Linda Hughes Bochert, May 28, 1983; children: Scott Charles, Sarah Katherine. BS, U. Wis., 1965, JD, 1968. Bar: Wis. 1968, U.S. Dist. Ct. (we. dist.) Wis. 1968, U.S. Dist. Ct. (ea. dist.) Wis. 1969, U.S. Ct. Appeals (7th cir.) 1970, U.S. Supreme Ct. 1971. Asst. atty. gen. State of Wis. Dept. of Justice, Madison, 1968-71, dep. atty. gen., 1976-81; asst. chancellor, chief legal counsel U. Wis., Madison, 1971-76; ptnr. Michael, Best & Friedrich LLP, Madison, 1981—. Lectr. Law Sch., U. Wis., Madison, 1972-75; bd. dirs., chair govt. law sect. State Bar Wis., Madison, 1979-88. Contbr. articles to profl. jours. Bd. dirs. Sand County Found., Madison, 1988—, Wis. Ctr. for Academically Talented Youth, Madison, 1991-94, Access Cmty. Health Ctrs., 2004—, Wis. Law Alumni Assn., 2000—, chair 2004—, trustee Edgewood Coll., Madison, 1997—, chair 2003-05, Great Lakes Higher Edn. Corp. and affiliates, 2000—. Mem. ABA, Madison Club, Blackhawk Country Club. Democrat. Unitarian Universalist. Avocations: canoeing, skiing, golf, biking, hunting. Office: Michael Best & Friedrich PO Box 1806 Madison WI 53701-1806 Office Phone: 603-257-3501. E-mail: djhanson@michaelbest.com.

HANSON, DENNIS MICHAEL, retired health facility administrator; b. Cleve., Aug. 20, 1943; s. John Joseph and Victoria (Tucholski) H. BBA, Cleve. State U., 1971; MPH, U. Pitts., 1974. Asst. adminstr. Huron Rd. Hosp., Cleve., 1974-76; adminstr. asst. Mt. Sinai Med. Ctr., Cleve., 1976-80; dir. radiology U. Louisville, Ky., 1980-84, assoc. prof., 1982-86; sr. cons. Honeywell, Mpls., 1986-87; mgr. radiology U. N.C., Chapel Hill, 1987-90; mgr. diagnostic imaging Kaiser Hosp., Honolulu, 1990-97; cons. Dowdy Mgmt. and Consulting, Cocoa Beach, Fla., 1999—2000; with Norton Healthcare, 2000—04; ret., 2005. Cons. Dowdy Mgmt. and Consulting, Cocoa Beach, Fla., 1999-2000; radiol. tech. Norton Healthcare, Louisville, Ky. Councilman City of Meadowbrook Farm, Ky., 1982-86. With USAF, 1961-65. Named Ky. Colonel, 1984. Fellow Am. Coll. Healthcare Execs.; mem. Am. Hosp. Radiology Adminstrs. Home: Unit 103 3901 Yardley Ct Louisville KY 40299-7355 E-mail: dmhansonmph@aol.com.

HANSON, FLOYD BLISS, mathematician; b. Bklyn., Mar. 9, 1939; s. Charles Keld and Violet Ellen (Bliss) H.; m. Ethel Louisa Hutchins, July 27, 1962; 1 child, Lisa Kirsten BS, Antioch Coll., 1962; MS, Brown U., 1964, PhD, 1968. Space technician Convair Astronautics, San Diego, 1961; applied mathematician Arthur D. Little, Inc., Cambridge, Mass., 1961; physicist Wright-Patterson AFB, Dayton, Ohio, 1962; assoc. research scientist Courant Inst., N.Y.C., 1967-68; asst. prof. U. Ill., Chgo., 1969-75, assoc. prof., 1975-83, prof., 1983—, assoc. dir. Lab. for Advanced Computing, 1990—, assoc. dir. Lab. for Control & Info., 1993—. Faculty rsch. participant Argonne (Ill.) Nat. Lab., 1985-87, faculty rsch. leave, 1987-88, rsch. assoc., 1988—; vis. prof., divsn. applied math. Brown U., 1994; mem. vis. faculty Sch. Civil and Environ. Engring., Cornell U., 1995. Assoc. editor-in-chief Applied and Computational Control Signals and Circuits, 1996—; contbr. articles in field to profl. jours., chpt. to book. Recipient Tchr. Recognition award, UIC CETL, 1999, Excellence in Tchg. award, Premier UIC, 2001—02; grantee, NSF, 1970—83, 1988—, 1973, Nat. Ctr. Supercomputer Applications, 1986—2004, Los. Alamos Nat. Lab., 1990—97, Cornell Theory Ctr., 1993—96, Pitts. Supercomputer Ctr., 1993—98, 2003—04, San Diego Supercomputer Ctr., 1998—2002. Mem. IEEE (tech. com. on control edn. appointment, 2002), Soc. Indsl. and Applied Math., Computer Soc. of IEEE, Control Sys. Soc. of IEEE, Resource Modeling Assn. Home: 5435 S East View Park Chicago IL 60615-5915 Office: U Ill Dept Math Stats and Computer Sci M/C 249 851 S Morgan St Rm 322 Chicago IL 60607-7042 Business E-Mail: hanson@uic.edu.

HANSON, GAIL G., physicist, researcher; b. Dayton, Ohio, Feb. 22, 1947; married 1968 (div. 1998); 2 children. BS in Physics, MIT, 1968, PhD in Exptl. High Energy Physics, 1973. Rsch. assoc. Stanford Linear Accelerator Ctr., 1973-76, physicist, continuing staff mem., 1976-84, physicist, permanent staff mem., 1984-89; prof. physics Ind. U., Bloomington, 1989-97, disting. prof., 1997—. Mem. subpanel High Energy Physics Adv. Panel, 1989-90; mem. physics adv. com. Univs. Rsch. Assn. Fermilab, 1990-94, mem. bd. overseers, 1991-97, dir. rev. panel, 1993-94, mem. vis. com., 1995-97; mem. com. examiners GRE Physics Test, 1992-2000; mem. collaboration exec. com. U.S.

ATLAS, 1994-95. Guggenheim fellow, 1995. Fellow AAAS (mem. electorate nominating com. physics sect. 1996—), Am. Phys. Soc. (W.K.H. Panofsky prize 1996). Office: Ind U Dept Physics Bloomington IN 47405 E-mail: gail@indiana.edu.

HANSON, GERALD WARNER, retired county official; b. Alexandria, Minn., Dec. 25, 1938; s. Lewis Lincoln and Dorothy Hazel (Warner) H.; m. Sandra June Wheeler, July 9, 1960; 1 child, Cynthia R. AA, San Bernardino Valley (Calif.) Coll., 1959; BA, U. Redlands (Calif.), 1979; MA, U. Redlands, 1981; EdD, Pepperdine U., 1995. Cert. advanced metrication specialist. Dep. sealer San Bernardino (Calif.) County, 1964-80, div. chief, 1980-85, dir. weights and measures, 1985-94; CATV cons. City of Redlands, 1996—2004, City of Yucaipa, 1998-99, ret., 1994. Substitute tchr. Redlands Unified Sch. Dist., 2003-04. Chmn. Redlands Rent Rev. Bd., 1985-99; bd. dirs. House Neighborly Svc., Redlands, 1972-73, Boys Club, Redlands, 1985-86; mem. Redlands Planning commn., 1990-98. With USN. Fellow U.S. Metric Assn. (treas. 1986-88, 92—); mem. NRA (life), Nat. Conf. on Weights and Measures (life, asst. treas. 1986-94), Western Weights and Measures Assn. (life, pres. 1987-88), Calif. Assn. Weights and Measures Ofcls. (life, 1st v.p. 1987), Calif. Rifle and Pistol Assn. (life), Masons, Shriners, Kiwanis (treas. Redlands club 1983-95), Over the Hill Gang (San Bernardino, newsletter editor 1998-2000). Avocations: golf, digital photography, mechanics, microcomputers. Home: 225 E Palm Ave Redlands CA 92373-6131 Personal E-mail: doctorjer@hotmail.com.

HANSON, GLEN R., pharmacologist, educator; DDS, UCLA, 1973; PhD, U. Utah, 1978. Fellow Nat. Inst. Health Pharmacology Rsch. Assocs. Tng. Program, 1978—80; dir., divsn. neuroscience and behavioral rsch. Nat. Inst. Drug Abuse, Bethesda, Md., 2000—01, acting dir., 2001—02; assoc. prof. pharmacology and toxicology U. Utah, Salt Lake City, 2003—. Mem. editl. bd. Jour. Pharmacology and Experimental Therapeutics. Office: 6001 Executive Blvd Rm 5274 Bethesda MD 20892-9581

HANSON, HAROLD PALMER, physicist, editor, academic administrator, government official; b. Virginia, Minn., Dec. 27, 1921; s. Martin Bernhard and Elvida Elaine (Paulsen) H.; m. Mary Jean Stevenson, June 22, 1944; children: Steven Bernard, Barbara Jean. BS, Superior (Wis.) State Coll., 1942; MS, U. Wis., 1944, PhD, 1948. Mem. faculty U. Fla., 1948-54, dean grad. sch., 1969-71, v.p. acad. affairs, 1971-74, exec. v.p., 1974-78, exec. v.p. emeritus, 1990—; mem. faculty U. Tex., Austin, 1954-69, prof. physics, 1961-69, chmn. dept., 1962-69; provost Boston U., 1978-79; exec. dir. Com. on Sci. and Tech., U.S. Ho. of Reps., Washington, 1979-82, 84-90; provost Wayne State U., Detroit, 1982-84. Summer rsch. physicist Lincoln Labs., MIT, 1953, Gen. Atomic Co., San Diego, 1964; summer vis. lectr. U. Wis., 1957; Fulbright rsch. scholar, Norway, 1960-61. Editor DELOS, 1991—. Bd. dirs. N. Central Fla. Health Planning Coun.; mem. steering com. Fla. Ednl. Computer Network. With USNR, 1944-46. Decorated St. Olav's medal Norway, Order of North Star 1st class Sweden; U. Fla. presdl. scholar, 1976 Fellow Am. Phys. Soc.; mem. Sigma Xi, Sigma Pi Sigma, Omicron Delta Kappa. Clubs: Town and Gown (Austin); Rotary. Business E-Mail: hanson@phys.ufl.edu.

HANSON, HEIDI ELIZABETH, lawyer; b. Portsmouth, Ohio, Nov. 13, 1954; BS, U. Ill., 1975, JD, 1978. Bar: Ill. 1978, U.S. Dist. Ct. (no. dist.) Ill., U.S. Ct. Appeals (7th cir.). Atty. water, air and land pollution divs. Ill. EPA, Springfield, Ill., 1978-85, atty. water pollution div. Maywood, Ill., 1985-86; assoc. Ross & Hardies, Chgo., 1987-89, ptnr., 1990-94; founder H.E. Hanson Law Offices, Western Springs, Ill., 1994—. Named hon. Ky. Col., 2000. Mem.: Indsl. Water, Waste and Sewer Group, Air and Waste Mgmt. Assn., Chgo. Bar Assn., Chicagoland C. of C. Avocation: gardening. Office: 4721 Franklin Ave Ste 1500 Western Springs IL 60558-1720 Personal E-mail: heh70@hotmail.com.

HANSON, JANE, newscaster; married; 1 child. BA in Broadcast Journalism, U. Minn. Reporter Sta. KSFY-TV, Sioux Falls, Iowa; from gen. assignment reporter to anchor Sta. WMT-TV, Cedar Rapids, Iowa; corr., anchor WNBC, N.Y.C., 1979—, co-anchor Today in New York, 1988—2003, host Jane's New York, 2003—. Adj. prof. Stern Coll., L.I. Chmn. March of Dimes Walk-Am.; hon. chair Susan B. Koman Found.'s Race for the Cure, N.Y.C.; bd. dirs. Graham Windham, N.Y.C., NY. Named Corr. of the Yr., N.Y. Police Detectives, N.Y. Firefighters, Outstanding Mother of the Yr., Nat. Mother's Day Com., 1995; recipient Emmy Outstanding Morning News Program, 1996, 1997, 2000. Mem.: NATAS (trustee, bd. govs. N.Y. chpt.). Office: WNBC 30 Rockefeller Plz New York NY 10112

HANSON, JEAN ELIZABETH, lawyer; b. Alexandria, Minn., June 28, 1949; d. Carroll Melvin and Alice Clarissa (Frykman) Hanson; children: Catherine Jean, Benjamin Colman (twins). BA, Luther Coll., 1971; JD, U. Minn., 1976. Bar: NY 1977, U.S. Dist. Ct. (so. dist.) 1977. Probation officer Hennepin County, Mpls., 1972-73; law clk. Minn. State Pub. Defender, Mpls., 1975-76; assoc. Fried, Frank, Harris, Shriver & Jacobson, N.Y.C., 1976-83, ptnr., 1983-93, 94—. Gen. counsel U.S. Treasury, Washington, 1993—94; mem. bd. regents Luther Coll., Concordia Coll.; mem. bd. visitors Law Sch. U. Minn. Recipient Disting. Svc. award Luther Coll., 1991, Outstanding Achievement award U. Minn., 1999. Mem. ABA, N.Y. State Bar Assn., Assn. of Bar of City of N.Y. (securities regulation com. 1991-98, mem. task force women in the profession 1995-98), U. Minn. Law Alumni Assn. Democrat. Lutheran. Office: Fried Frank Harris Shriver & Jacobson One New York Plaza New York NY 10004 Office Phone: 212-859-8198. E-mail: jean.hanson@friedfrank.com.

HANSON, JERRY CLINTON, lawyer; b. Freeport, Tex., Aug. 6, 1939; s. C. C. and M. Frances (Richardson) H.; m. Susan S. Hanson, Mar. 27, 1971 (div. 1984); children: Melanie Joy, Blair Clinton. BS with honors, Stephen F. Austin U., 1963; JD with highest honors, South Tex. Coll. of Law, 1969. Bar: Tex. Ptnr. Hanson, Most & Lamson, Houston, 1970-83, Jerry C. Hanson & Assocs., Houston, 1984—. Bd. chmn. H.A.S.P., Inc., Houston, 1981-83. Chmn. deed restrictions com. Lakewood Forest Civic Assn., Houston, 1980-82; mem., dir. Simon for Pres. Com., Houston, 1988; mem. Clinton for Pres. Com., Houston, 1992. Mem. ABA, Assn. Trial Lawyers Am., State Bar Tex., Tex. Trial Lawyers Assn., Delta Theta Phi. Democrat. Avocations: tennis, hunting, fishing. Office: 901 N Perry St Palestine TX 75801-7749

HANSON, JO, artist, educator, writer; b. Carbondale, Ill. d. Thomas A. and Carrie M. H. MA in Art, San Francisco State U.; MA in Edn, U. Ill. Past instr. sculpture U. Calif., Berkeley, Calif. Coll. Arts and Crafts, Oakland. Participant art panels Women's Caucus for Art and Coll. Art Assn., 1979, 81, 89, 91, 93, 99, Exploratorium Symposium, "Rising Above Our Garbage", San Francisco, 1994; co-curator Living in Balance, San Francisco Internat. Airport and Richmond Art Ctr., 1993, 94, Dear Mother Earth, Marin County Civic Ctr., 1998; moderator Bioneers Conf. panels on art and ecology, 1999—; presenter Soc. for Ecol. Restoration, 1999; subject of "Life Messages" book by Josephine Carleton, Andreus McMeel, 2002. Author: Artists' Taxes, The Hands-on Guide, 1987; co-prodr. Women Environment Artists Directory, 1996—; contbr.: Women, Art and Technology, 2003; one-woman shows of sculpture and installations include, Corcoran Gallery Art, Washington, 1974, Pa. Acad. Fine Arts, Phila., 1976, Utah Mus. Fine Arts, Salt Lake City, 1977, San Francisco Mus. Modern Art, 1976, 80, Internat. Sculpture Conf., San Francisco, 1982, Internat. Conf. Healthy Cities, San Francisco, 1993, Dublin (Calif.) Civic Ctr., 1994, Fresno Art Mus., 1998; exhibited in group shows at San Francisco Mus. Modern Art, 1978, Museau de Arte Contemporanea da U. de São Paulo, Brazil, 1980, Pratt Manhattan Center, N.Y.C., 1981, Auckland City Art Gallery, N.Z., 1985, Municipal Art Soc., N.Y. 1990, John F. Kennedy U., San Francisco, 2001, Yerba Buena Ctr., San Francisco, 2002; represented in permanent collections including Herbert F. Johnson Mus. Cornell U., Fresno (Calif.) Art Mus., Mills Coll., Oakland, Calif., Oakland Mus. of Art, San Francisco Arts Commn., San Francisco Mus. Modern Art, numerous pvt. collections; contbg. San Francisco Arts commr., 1982-89; adv. bd. artist-in-residence Exploratorium, San Francisco, 1983-91; originator, advisor artist-in-residence program San. Fill Co., San Francisco, 1989—; advisor art and ecology Bioneers Conf., 1999—, EarthLight Mag., 1999—. Recipient citation San Francisco Bd. Suprs., 1980, San Francisco mayor, 1989, Honor award Bioneers Conf., 2000, Honor award Calif. Lawyers for the Arts, 2004; named Disting. Woman Artist of Yr., Fresno (Calif.) Art Mus., 1998; Nat. Endowment for Arts fellow, 1977, grantee, 1980. Mem. Coll. Art Assn. (co-chair panel art and ecology 1999), Women's Caucus for Art (Regional Lifetime Achievement award 1992, Nat. Lifetime Achievement award 1997), Pacific Rim Sculptors Group. Office Phone: 415-864-7139.

HANSON, JOHN J., retired lawyer; b. Aurora, Nebr., Oct. 22, 1922; s. Peter E. and Hazel Marion (Lounsbury) H.; m. Elizabeth Anne Moss, July 1, 1973; children from their previous marriages— Mark, Eric, Gregory. AB, U. Denver, 1948; LL.B. cum laude, Harvard U., 1951. Bar: N.Y. bar 1952, Calif. bar 1955. Asso. firm Dewey, Ballantine, Bushby, Palmer & Wood, N.Y.C., 1951-54; ptnr. firm Gibson, Dunn & Crutcher, L.A, 1954—, mem. exec. com., 1978-87, adv. ptnr., 1991—2004, ret., 2004. Contbr. articles to profl. jours. Trustee Palos Verdes (Calif.) Sch. Dist., 1969-73. Served with U.S. Navy, 1942-45. Fellow Am. Coll. Trial Lawyers; mem. Am. Bar Assn., Los Angeles County Bar Assn. (chmn. antitrust sect. 1979-80), Bel Air Country Club. Home: 953 Linda Flora Dr Los Angeles CA 90049-1630 Office: Gibson Dunn & Crutcher 333 S Grand Ave Ste 4400 Los Angeles CA 90071-3197

HANSON, JOHN M., civil engineering and construction educator; b. Brookings, S.D., Nov. 16, 1932; m. Mary Josephson, Jan. 16, 1960 (dec. 1999); m. Mary Jayne Skau, May 19, 2004. BSCE, S.D. State U., 1949; MS in Structural Engring., Iowa State U., 1957; PhD in Civil Engring., Lehigh U., 1964. Profl. engr. Ill., N.C., Colo., Oreg., Mich. Structural engr. J.T. Banner & Assoc., Laramie, Wyo., 1957-58, Phillips, Carter, Osborn, Denver, 1958-60; research inst. prof. Lehigh U., Bethlehem, Pa., 1960-65; engr., asst. mgr. structural devel. Portland Cement Assn., Skokie, Ill., 1965-72; rsch. dir., v.p., pres. Wiss, Janney, Elstner Assocs., Northbrook, Ill., 1972-92; disting. prof. civil engring. and constrn. N.C. State U., Raleigh, 1993-2000, cons. engr., 2000—. Contbr. articles to profl. jours. Served to lt. USAF, 1953-55, Korea Recipient Disting. Engr. award, S.D. State U., 1979, Profl. Achievement citation, Iowa State U., 1980, Parmer award, Structural Engring. Assn. Ill., 2005. Fellow Prestressed Concrete Inst. (bd. dirs. 1977-80, 93-95, Korn award 1978); mem. ASCE (hon., State of Art award 1974, Reese award 1976, 88, T.Y. Lin award 1979, Boase award 1995, Forensic Engring. award 1999), Am. Concrete Inst. (hon., bd. dirs. 1981-84, 88-94, v.p. 1988-89, pres. 1990, Bloem award 1976, Henry Crown award Ill. chpt. 1993), Internat. Assn. Bridge and Structural Engring. (hon., pres. 1993-97), Internat. Concrete Repair Inst. Lutheran. Office Phone: 919-637-0839. E-mail: jmhanson@nc.rr.com.

HANSON, JOHN NILS, industrial high technology manufacturing company executive; b. Berwyn, Ill., Jan. 22, 1942; s. Robert and Stephanie Ann (Kazluskas) H.; m. Stephanie Morgan, June 5, 1965; children: Laurel, Mark Nils. BS in Chem. Engring., MIT, 1964, MS in Nuclear Engring., 1965; PhD in Nuclear Sci. and Engring., Carnegie-Mellon U., 1969. Sr. scientist Westinghouse Electric Corp., Bettis Atomic Power Labs., West Mifflin, Pa., 1965-70, asst. to gen. mgr. advanced test core, 1971-73; fellow White House, Washington, 1970-71; asst. to pres. Gould Inc., Rolling Meadows, Ill., 1973-74, pres., gen. mgr. electric motor div. St. Louis, 1974-78, group v.p. elec. products Rolling Meadows, 1978-80; v.p. Internat. Harvester, 1980-81; pres. Solar Turbines Internat., San Diego, 1980—; v.p. Caterpillar Tractor Co., Peoria, Ill., 1981—; chmn., CEO Joy Global. Contbr. articles on indsl. tech. to profl. jours. Vice chmn. Friends of Scouting Fundraising-Boy Scouts Am., San Diego council, 1983—; mem. Judge Wallace Longrange planning com., 1983—, vice chmn. fin. adv. com., 1983—; mem. cabinet fund drive United Way, San Diego County Chpt., 1982—; mem. exec. fin. com. Pete Wilson for Senate campaign, San Diego, 1982; vice chmn. Children's Hosp. Research Ctr., 1983—; mem. vis. com. sponsored research MIT, Cambridge, 1978—; mem. Pvt. Industry Council, 1983. Mem. White House Fellows Assn., Greater San Diego C. of C. (bd. dirs.) Office: Solar Turbines Inc PO Box 85376 San Diego CA 92186-5376 also: Caterpillar Inc 100 NE Adams St Peoria IL 61629-0001*

HANSON, JON D., law educator; b. Houston, Dec. 24, 1960; BA in Economics & Pub. Policy, Rice U., 1986; JD, Yale U., 1990. Law clk. to US Dist. Judge Jose A. Cabranes; asst. prof. law Harvard Law Sch., Cambridge, Mass., 1992—97, prof., 1997—. Office: Harvard Law Sch 1563 Massachusetts Ave Cambridge MA 02138 Office Phone: 617-496-5207. Office Fax: 617-496-5156. Business E-Mail: hanson@law.harvard.edu.

HANSON, KAREN, philosopher, educator; b. Lincoln, Nebr., Apr. 11, 1947; d. Lester Eugene and Gladys (Diessner) H.; m. Dennis Michael Senchuk, Aug. 22, 1970; children: Tia Elizabeth, Chloe Miranda. BA summa cum laude, U. Minn., 1970; MA, PhD, Harvard U., 1980. Lectr. to assoc. prof. Ind. U., Bloomington, 1976-91, prof. philosophy, 1991—, Rudy prof., 2001—, adj. prof. Am. studies, gender studies and comparative lit., 1991—, chair philosophy, 1997—2002, dean E. L. Hutton Honors Coll., 2002—. Mem. governing bd. Ind. U. Inst. for Advanced Study, Bloomington, 1992-95, Ind. U. Soc. for Advanced Study, 2001-02; mem. editl. bd. Peirce Edition Project, Indpls., 1982-89, 90—. Author: The Self Imagined, 1986; co-editor: Romantic Revolutions, 1990; assoc. editor Jour. Social Philosophy, 1982-86; mem. editl. bd. Philosophy of Music Edn. Rev., 1992—, Notre Dame Philosophical Reviews, 2001-, Essays in Philosophy, 2000-, Symploke, 1998-; editl. cons. Am. Philos. Quar., 1995-99; contbr. articles to profl. books and jours. Del. Am. Coun. Learned Socs., 1993-98 (exec. com., 1994-98); officer John Dewey Found., 1989—. Recipient Disting. scholar award, Office Women's Affairs, 1995. Mem. Am. Philos. Assn. (exec. officer 1986-91, 2000-03, program com. 1984-91, nominating com. 1993-94, 95-96, chair com. priorities and problems 1998-2000, acting chair bd. officers 2004—), Am. Soc. Aesthetics (program com. 1989-90, 98-2000, trustee 1997-2000), Soc. Women in Philosophy, Phi Beta Kappa (exec. com. Gamma Ind. chpt. 1993-97, 2002—, officer 1995-97, 2002—, pres. 1996-97, 2004-2005). Home: 3678 Sterling Ave Bloomington IN 47401-4448 Office: Ind U Dept of Philosophy Sycamore 026 Bloomington IN 47405 also: Honors Coll 324 N Jordan Bloomington IN 47405 Office Phone: 812-855-3550. E-mail: hansonk@indiana.edu.

HANSON, KENT BRYAN, lawyer; b. Litchfield, Minn., Sept. 17, 1954; s. Calvin Bryan and Muriel (Wessman) H.; m. Barbara Jane Elenbaas, Aug. 24, 1974; children: Lindsay Michal, Taylor Jordan, Chase Philip. AA with high honors, Trinity Western Coll., 1974; BA, U. B.C., Vancouver, 1976; JD magna cum laude, U. Minn., 1979. Bar: Minn. 1979, U.S. Dist. Ct. Minn. 1980, U.S. Ct. Appeals (8th cir.) 1980, U.S. Dist. Ct. (we. dist.) Wis. 1983, Wis. 1985, U.S. Ct. Appeals (9th cir.) 1989, U.S. Dist. Ct. Ariz. 1992, Ohio 1993, Calif. 1994. Assoc. Grossman, Karlins, Siegel & Brill, Mpls., 1979-81, Gray, Plant, Mooty, Mooty & Bennett, Mpls., 1981-85; ptnr. Bowman & Brooke, Mpls., 1986-95; CEO Hanson, Marek, Bolkcom & Greene, Ltd., Mpls., 1996—. Bd. dirs. Inner City Boys Club, Ctrl. Free Ch., Mpls., 1979-81; 12th ward del. Mpls. Dem. Farmer Labor Com. Conv., 1982; mem. exec. bd. Ctrl. Free Ch., Mpls., 1986; chair exec. bd. Ctrl. Community Ch., 1993-96. Mem. ABA, State Bar Assn. Wis., Minn. Def. Lawyers Assn., Minn. State Bar Assn., Hennepin County Bar Assn., Calif. State Bar Assn., State Bar of Ohio, Def. Rsch. Inst. Avocations: classical music, golf, tennis, computers, motorcycles. Office: Hanson Marek Bolkcom & Greene Ltd 2200 Rand Tower 527 Marquette Ave Minneapolis MN 55402-1302 Office Phone: 612-342-2880. Business E-Mail: khanson@hmbglaw.com.

HANSON, KERMIT OSMOND, business administration educator, retired dean; b. Troy Twp., Iowa, May 14, 1916; s. Gerhard Severin and Sunniva Fosmark (Borge) H.; m. Jane Elizabeth Haugen, Aug. 17, 1940; children: James Stephen, Katherine Jane, Paul Richard, Daniel Gerhard. AB cum laude, Luther Coll., Decorah, Iowa, 1938; MS, Iowa State U., 1940, PhD, 1950; D.Sc. (hon.), Luther Coll., 1981. Ops. analyst Fed. Land Bank, Omaha, 1941-43; chief statis. service sect. VA br. office, Seattle, 1946-47; mem. faculty Sch. Bus. Adminstrn., U. Wash., Seattle, 1948-81, prof. acctg., finance and statistics, 1954-81, chmn. dept. accounting, finance and statistics, 1955-60, assoc. dean, 1959-64; dean Sch. Bus. Adminstrn., U. Wash. (Grad. Sch. Bus. Adminstrn.), 1964-81, dean emeritus, 1981—; John F. Mee Disting. prof. Sch. Bus. Adminstrn. Pacific Luth. U., 1985-86. Instr., ednl. dir. Pacific Coast Banking Sch., 1948-81, also mem. bd. dirs.; exec. dir Pacific Rim Bankers Program, 1977-89, vice chmn. bd. dirs., 1979-98, chmn. emeritus, 1998—; bd. dirs. Pacific Horizon Funds, Inc., 1982-98, Wash. Fed. Savs. & Loan Assn., 1966-2004, Seafirst Retirement trust, 1993-97, Safeco Corp., 1976-81; cons. GAO, 1970-78; chmn. Wash. Gov.'s Adv. Coun. on Productivity, 1974-75; mem. bd. adv. Naval Postgrad. Sch., Monterey, Calif., 1976-84. Author: Managerial Statistics, 1955, 2d edit. (with G. Brabb), 1961, (with M. Tomich) (monograph) Pacific Rim Bankers Program—A Brief History—The First Ten Years 1977-1986, 1987, The Pacific Coast Banking School—The First 50 Years, 1988. Mem. adv. com. Chief Seattle coun. Boy Scouts Am., 1958-2004, pres., 1967-69; bd. trustees Horizon House, 1990-96, pres., 1994-96; mem. adv. bd. U. Miami (Fla.) Sch. Bus., 1983-88, Pacific Luth. U. Sch. Bus., Tacoma, 1987-90, Seattle Pacific U. Sch. Bus., 1985-90; bd. dirs. Journey for Perspective Found., 1964-76. Lt. USNR, 1943-46. Recipient Silver Beaver award Seattle Coun. Boy Scouts Am., 1963, Disting. Svc. award U. Wash., 1981, Pioneer Meml. award Luther Coll., 1997. Mem. Am. Assn. Collegiate Schs. Bus. (pres. 1971-72), Am. Accounting Assn., Am. Finance Assn., Financial Execs. Inst., Beta Gamma Sigma, Beta Alpha Psi, Alpha Kappa Psi. Lutheran. Home: 17760 14th Ave NW Shoreline WA 98177-3207

HANSON, MARK S., bishop; b. Mpls., Dec. 2, 1946; m. Ione Agrimson; children: Aaron Hanson, Alyssa, Rachel, Ezra, Isaac, Elizabeth. Grad., Minnehaha Acad., 1964; B Sociology, Augsburg Coll., 1968; Rockefeller fellow, Union Theol. Sem., 1969, MDiv, 1972; attended, Luther Sem., 1973—74; Merrill fellow, Harvard U., 1979. Ordained 1974. Pastor Prince of Glory Luth. Ch., Mpls., 1973—79, Edina Cmty. Luth. Ch., Edina, Minn., 1979—88, U. Luth. Ch., Hope, Mpls., 1988—95; bishop St. Paul Area Synod Evang. Luth. Ch. Am., 1995, presiding bishop, 2001—. Pres. Minn. Coun. Chs., 1998—2000. Author: Faithful Yet Changing: The Church in Challenging Times. Office: Evang Luth Ch Am Office of Bishop 8765 W Higgins Rd Chicago IL 60631 E-mail: bishop@elca.org.

HANSON, MARTIN PHILIP, mechanical engineer, farmer; b. Watseka, Ill., Feb. 4, 1937; s. Philip Andrew and Mary Jane (Martin) Hanson; m. Virginia Ann Garfield, Jan. 2, 1960; children: Martin Philip Jr., Adam Gunnar. BS, US Naval Acad., 1959. Registered profl. engr., Mich., Ill. Commd. ensign USN, 1959, advanced through grades to lt. comdr., 1968; reactor mech. asst. USS Enterprise (CVAN-65), Alameda, Calif., 1968-69; resigned, 1969; project engr. Consumers Power Co., Jackson, Mich., 1969-74; project engring. mgr. United Engrs. and Constructors Inc., Phila., 1974-77, Seabrook, N.H., 1977-82, Glen Rose, Tex., 1982-83, Washington, 1983-87; project control specialist Systematic Mgmt. Svcs., Argonne, Ill., 1987-92; project engr. Mac Tech. Svcs. Co., Argonne, 1992-95; sr. project mgmt. specialist Aguirre Engrs., Inc., Argonne, 1995-97; v.p. RERC Environ., Inc., Chgo., 1997-99. Sec. repository coordination group Dept. Energy, Washington, 1983—85, sec. repository change control, 1985—87. Capt. USNR, 1969—92, comdr. res. regts. USNR. Mem.: SAR, ASME (past chmn. New Eng. sect.), Organ Transplant Support (past dir.-at-large). Achievements include organizing new programs for continuous fiber ceramic composites and other technologies. Avocations: automobiles, opera, classical music. Home: 1009 Troutlilly Ln Darien IL 60561-8819 Personal E-mail: navy59@comcast.net.

HANSON, MATTHEW, scriptwriter, educator, consultant; b. Madison, Wis., Oct. 22, 1969; s. David Hanson and Diana; m. Sophie Hanson, Feb. 21, 1995; 1 child, Paul. Student, Boston U., 1988—90; AB, Harvard Coll., 1992; D, Boston U., 2000. Prof. Swiss Hotel Assn. Hotel Mgmt. Sch., Bluche, Switzerland, 1996—96; intern, writer's asst., writer Renaissance Pictures, Universal City, Calif., 1998—98; writer Am. TV Ventures, Newport Beach, 1998—2000; tchr. Met. Coll., Boston U., 2000—00; sys. designer Panther Project Trading Systems, Madison, Wis., 2002—04; tchr. Madison Area Tech. Coll., 2002—04; v.p. Travel Mgmt. Consultants, Inc., 2002—04; tchr. Am. Sch. Switzerland, Montagnola, 2004—. Sled dog handler Silver Creek Kennels, Grand Rapids, Minn., 1994; adj. prof. Am. Coll. Switzerland, Leysin, 1995; cons. Weathervane Investments, SITE Capital Mgmt. LLC, Greenwich, Conn., 1998—2002. Vol. New Eng. Aquarium, Boston, 1990—92. Recipient Bowdoin prize Best Undergraduate Essay, Harvard Coll., 1991. Mem.: MLA. Democrat. Avocations: writing, rowing. Home Fax: 206-289-2692. Personal E-mail: matt_hanson@post.harvard.edu.

HANSON, PAUL W., band director; b. Sacramento, May 10, 1947; s. Marlo and Norma Jane Hanson; m. Jolayne Hanson, June 7, 1969; children: Cornie Jo, Mary Jane, Todd. BA, Augustana Coll., 1969. Band dir. Dawson-Boyd P.S., Minn., 1969—2003, Whittier Mid. Sch., Sioux Falls, SD, 2003—. Mem. bd. Minn. Music Educators Assn.; mem. Sioux Empire Brass, 2003—. Recipient Exemplary Music Dept. award, Minn. Music Educators Assn. Mem.: NEA, Music Educators Nat. Conf. Lutheran. Home: 2004 S Willow Ave Sioux Falls SD 57105

HANSON, PAULA, sports association executive; B.Journalism, U. Colo. Dir. promotions Denver Nuggets, v.p. mktg., v.p., asst. gen. mgr.; v.p. team svcs. NBA, 1985—96, sr. v.p. team ops., 1996—99; sr. v.p., COO WNBA, N.Y.C., 1999—2003, sr. v.p. Team Business Operations, 2003—.

HANSON, RANDALL A., lawyer; b. Charleston, W.Va., Dec. 18, 1960; s. William F. and Lilly Sue Hanson; m. Cynthia Brann, May 22, 1982; 1 child, Alexander Trent. AB, U. NC, 1983, JD with honors, 1985. Bar: DC 1985, NC 1993. Assoc. Winston & Strawn, Washington, 1985-88, Piper & Marbury, Washington, 1988-93, Womble Carlyle Sandridge & Rice PLLC, Winston-Salem, NC, 1993-95, mem., 2000—01, Greensboro, NC, 2001—, mng. mem. Greensboro office; assoc. gen. counsel, corp. sec., gen. counsel Mexican ops. Burlington Industries, Inc., Greensboro, NC, 1995—2000. Bd. dirs. Cmty. Theatre of Greensboro, The Nussbaum Ctr. for Entrepreneurship. Mem.: ABA (bus. law sect. com. negotiated acquisitions), Internat. Bar Assn., NC Bar Assn. (bus. law sect.). Democrat. Avocations: college basketball, tv and radio production, travel. Office: Womble Carlyle Sandridge & Rice PLLC PO Box 21104 Greensboro NC 27402-6025 Office Phone: 336-574-8070. Office Fax: 336-574-4515. Business E-Mail: rhanson@wcsr.com.

HANSON, RICHARD E., paper company executive; BS in Indsl. Mgmt., U. Oreg., 1965. With Weyerhaeuser Co., Tacoma, 1969—, v.p., western timberlands, 1996—98, sr. v.p., timberlands, 1998—2002, exec. v.p., timberlands and international, 2002—03, exec. v.p., COO, 2003—. Bd. dirs. Oreg. Forest Industries Coun., also operating com.; adv. com. Oreg. State U. Forest Rsch. Lab. Trustee Oreg. Zoo; mem. founder's cir. Stop Oreg. Litter & Vandalism. Office: Weyerhaeuser PO Box 9777 Federal Way WA 98063-9777

HANSON, ROBERT DELOLLE, retired lawyer; b. Harrisburg, Pa., Dec. 13, 1916; s. Henry W. A. and Elizabeth (Painter) H.; m. Barbara Esmer, Apr. 22, 1949 (dec. Mar. 2000). BA, Gettysburg Coll., 1939; LLB, Dickinson Law Sch., 1942. Bar: Pa. 1942. Pvt. practice, Harrisburg, 1946-98; solicitor Dauphin County, 1958-76, Dauphin County Redevel. Authority, 1959-98; ret. Pres. coun. of congregation Luth. Ch., 1953-55, 57-59; pres. Family and Children's Svc. of Harrisburg, 1956-57; mem. Harrisburg Sch. Bd., 1952-57, Dauphin County Housing Authority, 1960-98; gen. chmn. Tri-County United Fund, 1969, pres., 1971-72; trustee Gettysburg Coll., 1974—, sec., 1980, vice chmn., 1983-86; pres. Keystone area coun. Boy Scouts Am., 1980-82. Maj. inf. AUS, 1942-46, ETO. Decorated Bronze Star, Purple Heart; recipient Silver Beaver award Boy Scouts Am., 1980, Eagle award Boy Scouts Am., 1990, Alexis de Tocqueville award United Way of Am., 1991, Others award Salvation Army, 1992, Lavern Brenneman award Gettysburg Coll., 1996, Wisdom award of honor The Wisdom Soc. for the Advancement of Knowledge, Learning and Rsch. in Edn., 1999. Mem. ABA, Pa. Bar Assn. (sec., treas. taxation sect. 1948-59), Dauphin County Bar Assn. (dir. 1958-59),

Gettysburg Coll. Alumni Assn. (treas. 1958-59, v.p. 1968-71, pres. 1971-72), Masons (33d degree, past master, pres. bd. trustees 1982-85), Execs. Club (pres. 1953), Harrisburg Rotary (pres. 1979). Lutheran. Home: c/o Homeland Ctr 1901 N 5th St Rm 3-M-7 Harrisburg PA 17102-1510

HANSON, ROBERT DUANE, engineering educator; b. Albert Lea., Minn., July 27, 1935; s. James Edwin and Gertie Hanson; m. Kaye Lynn Nielsen, June 7, 1959; children: Craig Robert, Eric Neil. Student, St. Olaf Coll., Northfield, Minn., 1953-54; BSE, U. Minn., 1957, MS in Civil Engring., 1958; PhD, Calif. Inst. Tech., Pasadena, 1965. Registered profl. engr., Mich., N.D. Design engr. Pitts.-Des Moines Stel, Des Moines, 1958-59; asst. prof. U. N.D., Grand Forks, 1959-61; rsch. engr. Calif. Inst. Tech., 1965; asst. prof. U. Calif.-Davis, 1965-66; from asst. prof. to prof. civil engring. U. Mich., Ann Arbor, 1966—2001, prof. emeritus, 2001—, chmn. dept. civil engring., 1976-84; sr. earthquake engr. Fed. Emergency Mgmt. Agy., 1994-2000. Vis. prof., dir. Earthquake Engring. Rsch. Ctr., U. Calif., Berkeley, 1991; dir. BCS divsn. NSF, Washington, 1989-90; cons. NSF, 1979-88, 92-94; cons. Bechtel Corp., Ann Arbor, 1976-87, Sensei Engrs., Ann Arbor, 1977-90, Bldg. Seismic Safety Coun., 1988-94, Fed. Emergency Mgmt. Agy., 1992-94, 2000—. Contbr. articles to profl. jours. Recipient Reese Rsch. award ASCE, 1980; recipient Disting. Svc. award U. Mich., 1969; tchg. award Chi Epsilon, 1985, Attwood Engr. Excellence award, 1986. Fellow ASCE (life; com. chmn. 1975-94); mem. NAE, Earthquake Engring. Rsch. Inst. (hon., v.p. 1977-79, bd. dirs. 1976-79, 88-92, pres.-elect 1988, pres. 1989-91, past pres. 1991-92). Lutheran. Home: 2926 Saklan Indian Dr Walnut Creek CA 94595-3911 Personal E-mail: rdhanson2@aol.com.

HANSON, RONALD WILLIAM, lawyer; b. Aug. 3, 1950; s. Orlin Eugene and Irene Agnes Hanson; m. Sandra Kay Cook, Aug. 21, 1971; children: Alec Evan, Corinn Michele. BA summa cum laude, St. Olaf Coll., 1972; JD cum laude, U. Chgo., 1975. Bar: Ill. 1975, U.S. Dist. Ct. (no. dist.) Ill. 1975, U.S. Ct. Appeals (7th cir.) 1978, U.S. Ct. Appeals (10th cir.) 1989. Assoc. Sidley & Austin, Chgo., 1975-83, ptnr., 1983-88, Latham & Watkins, Chgo., 1988—, chmn. audit com., 1998—2005. Ofcl. advisor to Nat. Conf. of Commrs. on Uniform State Laws; lectr. Ill. Inst. Continuing Legal Edn., Springfield, Am. Bankruptcy Inst., Washington, Banking Law Inst., Practicing Law Inst., Am. Law Inst. Contbr. articles to profl. jours. Mem. ABA, Ill. Bar Assn., Chgo. Bar Assn., Order of Coif, Met. Club, Phi Beta Kappa. Republican. Lutheran. Home: 664 W 58th St Hinsdale IL 60521-5104 Office: Latham & Watkins Sears Tower Ste 5800 Chicago IL 60606-6306 Office Phone: 312-876-7700. Business E-Mail: ronald.hanson@lw.com.

HANSON, SAMUEL LEE, state supreme court justice; b. Mankato, Minn., Aug. 26, 1939; s. Lester Kenneth and Margaret Dorothy (Brockmeyer) H.; m. Beret Elizabeth Brown, July 28, 1962 (div. Apr. 1976); children: Greta E., Chrystina E., Benjamin D.; m. Mirja Pirkko Karikosky, Sept. 23, 1977; children: Leif O., Luke A., Jai N. BA, St. Olaf Coll., 1961; LLB, William Mitchell Coll. Law, 1965. Bar: Minn. 1965, U.S. Dist. Ct. Minn. 1966, U.S. Ct. Appeals (8th cir.) 1966, U.S. Supreme Ct. 1971. Law clk. to hon. Douglas K. Amdahl Hennepin County Dist. Ct., Mpls., 1965; law clk. to hon. Robert J. Sheran Minn. Supreme Ct., St. Paul, 1966; assoc., shareholder Briggs and Morgan, St. Paul, Mpls., 1966—2000, pres., 1988-93; appt. Ct. of Appeals, Minn., 2000—02; justice Minn. Supreme Ct., Minn., 2002—. Mem. adv. com. Minn. Supreme Ct., St. Paul, 1984-86; adj. prof. William Mitchell Coll. Law, St. Paul, 1966-71; co-chair Minn. Legal Services State Planning Commn., 2002-; chair supreme ct. Gender Fairness Implementation Com., 2002-; liaison supreme ct. Advisory Com. Gen. Rules of Practice, 2002-, supreme ct. Bd. of Legal Certification, 2002-. Contbr. articles to profl. jours. Bd. dirs. Rural Ventures Inc., Mpls., 1981-87, Rural Tech. Partnership, St. Paul, 1987—, Global Vols., St. Paul, 1984—. Fellow Am. Coll. Trial Lawyers (chair Minn. chpt. 1991), Am. Bd. Trial Advocates, Crossroads, Inc. Avocations: rural development, organizational development. Home: 5510 Edgewater Blvd Minneapolis MN 55417-2605 Office: Minn Supreme Ct 305 Minn Jud Ctr 25 Rev Martin Luther King Jr Blvd Saint Paul MN 55155 Office Phone: 651-297-7676. Business E-Mail: sam.hanson@courts.state.mn.us.

HANSON, TAMARA W., accountant; b. Lewiston, Idaho, Oct. 23, 1948; d. Brooks E. and Dona J. (Rogers) O'Kelley; m. Thomas J. Hanson Jr., 1 son, Stewart Alan. BBA cum laude, North Tex. State U., 1976. Securities lic., ins. lic.; CPA, Tex. Staff acct. James C. Beach CPA, Carrollton, Tex., 1972-76, Deloitte, Haskins & Sells, CPA, 1976-77; CFO Comm. Sys., Inc. (name changed to Scott Cable Comm. 1983), Irving, Tex., 1977-84; pvt. practice acctg. Dallas, 1984-93; treas., v.p. FTS Life Ins. Agy., Inc., 1993—. Author: Mastering the Dance, 2004. Active St. Andrews United Meth. Ch. Mem. AICPA, Tex. Soc. CPA (former Dallas chpt. ethics com.), Beta Alpha Psi.

HANSON, THOR, retired health agency executive, retired naval officer; b. Amarillo, Tex., May 7, 1928; s. Carl Joseph Emanuel and Lillian (Nelson) H.; m. Charlotte Ann Edens, Oct. 6, 1956; children: Inge Rew, Erica Karen, Ivor Carl, Lars Jon, Ursula Edens. BS, U.S. Naval Acad., 1950; MA, Oxford U., Eng., 1954. Commd. ensign U.S. Navy, 1950, advanced through grades to vice adm., 1979, service in Korea and Vietnam, naval aide, exec. asst. to sec. Navy, 1970-72, comdg. officer Naval Sta. Pearl Harbor, 1973-74; chief U.S. Naval Mission to Brazil, 1974-76; comdr. Cruiser-Destroyer Group 8; also comdr. Attack Carrier Striking Group 2, U.S. 6th Fleet, 1976-77; mil. asst. to Sec. of Def., 1977-79; dir. joint staff Office Joint Chiefs Staff, 1979-82, ret., 1982; mil. analyst Cable News Network, 1982; pres., CEO Nat. Multiple Sclerosis Soc., 1982-92, pres. emeritus, 1992—. Chmn. Nat. Health Coun., 1991-93; hon. bd. dirs. Rsch.! Am. Bd. dirs. Empires Ranch Found., Tucson Boys Chorus; pres. Southold Citizens for Safe Roads, 1995-2005. Decorated Def. D.S.M. with oak leaf cluster, Legion of Merit, Bronze Star with combat V, Meritorious Service medal, Joint Service Commendation medal; Vietnam Navy Distinguished Service medal; Brazilian Naval Order of Merit; Rhodes scholar, 1951-54 Mem. Am. Assn. Rhodes Scholars, Coun. on Fgn. Rels., U.S. Naval Inst., U.S. Naval Acad. Alumni Assn., Am. Fedn. Musicians (hon. life), Century Assn., N.Y. Yacht Club, Leander Rowing Club (England), Ends of the Earth Club, Digressionists Club. Episcopalian. Home: 249 Windmill Rd Tunnel Springs Ranch PO Box 1201 Sonoita AZ 85637 E-mail: vadmthor@direcway.com.

HANSON, VICTOR HENRY, II, newspaper publisher; b. Augusta, Ga., Aug. 17, 1930; s. Clarence Bloodworth, Jr. and Elizabeth (Fletcher) H.; m. Elizabeth Stallworth, Dec. 29, 1953; children: Clarence Bloodworth III, Victor Henry III, Elizabeth Mickel, Mary Fletcher, Robert Stallworth. Grad., Choate Sch., 1949; student, U. Va., 1949-51; BA, U. Ala., 1954. With Birmingham (Ala.) News & Post Herald, 1946-54, 57—, gen. mgr., 1963-83; with advt. and prodn. dept. WAPI-TV, Birmingham, 1954-55; v.p. Birmingham News Co., 1960-79, pres., 1979-2000, pub., 1983-2000. Trustee Birmingham Mus. of Art; bd. dirs. Grace House Ministries; elder Presbyn. Ch. Served to capt. USAF, 1955-57. Recipient Tree of Life award, Nat. Jewish Fund, 1991. Mem. SAR, Birmingham C. of C., Soc. of Cincinnati, N.C. Soc. of Cincinnati, Birmingham Country Club, Mountain Brook Club, Kappa Alpha. Home: 3910 Hunters Ln Birmingham AL 35243-5920 Office: 402 Office Park Dr Ste 100 Birmingham AL 35223 Office Phone: 205-879-8562. Personal E-mail: vhii@bellsouth.net.

HANSON, VIRGINIA A., activities director; b. Mpls., Apr. 26, 1935; d. Edwin Fred Wahl, Elsie (Johnson) Wahl; m. Marshall Richard Hanson, Mar. 10, 1956; children: Bruce M., Christopher, Brian(dec.). Student, St. Olaf Coll., 1953—55, Mpls. Sch. Art, 1955—56, U. Cin., 1974. Cert. activity dir. Nat. Certification Coun. for Activity Profls. Fashion artist Daytons, Mpls., 1956—57, Maurice L. Rothchild-Young Quinlan, Mpls., 1957—58; activity dir. Beechknoll Woods, Cin., 1975—81; tchr. art, recreational counselor New Horizons for Developmentally Disabled, Millbrook, NY, 1983—91; tchr. therapeutic recreation art Waterside Retirement Estates, Sarasota, Fla., 1996—2001, Sarasota Bay Club, 2002—. Developed unique style archtl. gouache painting, 1984—. Recipient 1st pl. in Watercolor, Kent Art Assn., 2001, Critics Choice award, Pindar Art Gallery, 1990. Mem.: Womens Resource Ctr., Therapeutic Recreation Assn. (v.p. 1976—80), Women Contemporary Artists (Merit award 1982). Home: 5172 Marshfield Ln Sarasota FL 34235

HANSON, WENDY KAREN, retired chemical engineer; b. Mpls., May 29, 1954; d. Curtis Harley Hanson and Patricia Lou (Vogler) Schweiger. BS, U. Minn., 1976; BA, U. Colo., Denver, 1984; postgrad., U. Calif., La Jolla, 1984—87. Chem. technician Shasta Beverages, Mpls., 1977-78, Conwed, Roseville, Minn., 1978-80; geologist Century Geophys. Corp., Grand Junction, Colo., 1980, Tooke Engring., Grand Junction, 1980-82; sr. scientist Sci. Ventures, San Diego, 1987-96; engr. Parker-Hannifin Corp., San Diego, 1996-97; ret., 1997. Judge San Diego Sci. and Engring. Fair, 1987—96; leader, publs. editor San Diego Wilderness Assn., 1989—97. Achievements include patents for magnesium separation from Dolomitic phosphate by sulfuric acid leaching. Avocations: backpacking, gardening, spitoon collecting.

HANSRAJ, KENNETH KARAMCHAND, surgeon, research scientist; b. Georgetown, Guyana, Oct. 28, 1961; arrived in U.S., 1974; s. Augustus and Anjanie Hansraj; m. Marcia Dee Griffin, Aug. 1, 1998; 1 child, Jonathan. BS, Fairleigh Dickinson U., 1982; grad., Columbia U. Sch. General Studies; MD, Hahnemann U., 1987. Cert. Am. Bd. Minimally Invasive Spinal Medicine and Surgery, 1999, Am. Bd. Orthopedic Surgeons, 2001, Nat. Bd. Med. Examiners, 1989, lic. N.Y., 1996, Calif., 1991. Fellow in biomechanics Hosp. for Special Surgery, N.Y.C., 1987—88; gen. surgery tng. Mt. Sinai Hosp., N.Y.C., 1988—90; resident orthopaedic surgery King/Drew Med. Ctr., L.A., 1990—95; fellow in minimally invasive spinal surgery Calif. Ctr. for Minimally Invasive Spine Surgery, Thousand Oaks, Calif., 1995; fellow in scoliosis and spinal surgery Hosp. for Special Surgery, N.Y.C., 1995—96; spinal surgeon, dir. The Special Spine Inst., Poughkeepsie, NY, 1997—. Attending orthopaedic surgeon St. Francis Hosp., Poughkeepsie, NY, 1997—, St. Vincent's Hosp., Staten Island, NY, 1997—, Bailey Seton Hosp., Staten Island, NY, 1997—; jr. attending orthop. surgeon Hosp. for Special Surgery, N.Y.C., 1995—96, New York Hosp., N.Y.C., 1995—96, Meml.-Sloan Kettering Med. Ctr., N.Y.C., 1995—96; presenter in field. Editor: Surgical Techniques International; contbr. articles to profl. and med. jours. Fellow: Am. Acad. Orthopaedic Surgeons. Office: The Spl Spine Inst Ste 202 243 North Rd Poughkeepsie NY 12601 Office Phone: 845-471-9200. Office Fax: 845-471-1551. Personal E-mail: specialspine@aol.com.

HANSSEN, SHIRLEY MAE, retired librarian; b. Faber, Va., July 2, 1935; d. Leonard Walker and Charlotte Jane (Kidd) Mawyer; m. Norman Wilton Toms, Nov. 7, 1953 (div. 1965); children: N. Wayne Toms, Debra M. Helm, Mark A. Toms; m. Christian Ingvald Hanssen, Aug. 16, 1973 (dec.). AS magna cum laude, Piedmont CC, Charlottesville, Va., 1991. Payroll supr. State Farm Ins. Co., Charlottesville, 1952-54; libr. clk. Alderman Libr. U. Va., Charlottesville, 1964-68, libr. clk. Darden Grad. Sch. Bus. Adminstrn., 1968-76, libr. asst. McIntire Sch. Commerce Libr., 1976-94, libr. asst. Clemons Libr., 1994—2000; ret., 2000. Mem. consumer adv. panel Giant Foods, Charlottesville, 1986; mem. panel Home Testing Inst., Palatine, Ill., 1990—, Consumers Mail, Port Washington, NY, 1992—. Vol. tax aide Am. Assn. Ret. People, 2004—; vol. adminstrv. asst. Sr. Ctr. of Charlottesville; election ofcl. City of Charlottesville, 2001—. Mem.: Va. Libr. Assn. Paraprofl. Forum. Home: 105 Camellia Dr Charlottesville VA 22903-4206

HANTHORN, DENNIS WAYNE, performing arts association administrator; b. Lima, Ohio, Dec. 21, 1951; s. Floyd Wilber and June J. (Rummel) H.; m. Rebecca R. Hackler, Aug. 2, 1975; children: Rachel R., Micah A, Hanna. BS in Music Edn., Southwest Mo. State, Springfield, 1975; MusM in French Horn, U. Wis., 1977. Instr. U. Ala., 1978-79; founder, dir. Queen City Brass, 1979-83; gen. mgr. Cin. Chamber Orch., 1980-82; mng. dir. Dayton (Ohio) Opera, 1982-89; gen. dir. Florentine Opera Co., Milw., 1989—2004, The Atlanta Opera, 2004—. Office: The Atlanta Opera Ctr 728 W Peachtree St NW Atlanta GA 30308-1139

HANTMAN, BARRY G., software engineer; b. Boston, May 22, 1962; s. Leonard M. and Barbara R.; m. Susan Chapman, June 2, 1985; 1 child, Noam Seth. BA, Brandeis U., 1984; postgrad., Fitchburg State Coll., 1984-86. Cons. Wicat Sys., Waltham, Mass., 1982-84; mgr. validation and BMC3I software Raytheon Co., Tewksbury, Mass., 1984—. Open Software Found. primary rep. Raytheon Co., Tewksbury, 1991-93, CAD Framework Initiative primary rep., 1993-94, program mgr. Dept. Def. Microwave/Millimeter Advanced Computational Environ. Program, 1992-97, Dept. Def. Mfg. Automation and Design Engring. Program, 1996. Lodge chief Order of Arrow, Stoneham, Mass., 1979-81; chmn. Town of Danville (N.H.) Planning Bd.; chmn. Cable TV Com., Rockingham County (N.H.) Planning Commn. Mem. IEEE Computer Soc., U.S. Holocaust Meml. Coun., African Wildlife Found., World Wildlife Fund, Wildlife Conservation Soc., Assn. Computing Machinery, Mentor Graphics User Group (pres. 1988-90, v.p. 1987-88, mem. steering com. 1985-87, 90-92). Avocations: foreign travel, video editing.

HANTON, E. MICHAEL, public information officer, consultant; b. Gary, Ind. s. Zachary and Maria (Suciu) H. AB, Ind. U., 1951, MA, 1955; grad., USAF Air War Coll., 1968. Various prodn. positions U.S. Steel Corp., Gary, 1940-41, 50; prodn. contr. Douglas Aircraft Corp., Santa Monica, Calif., 1946-47; classified advt. mgr Weaver Pub. Co., Santa Monica, 1947-48; reporter Muncie (Ind.) Evening Press, 1952, Gary Post-Tribune, 1952-53; head cashier Office Lake County Treas., Gary, 1955-60; pub. and pers. rels. cons. Gary, 1960—, Plattsburgh, N.Y., 1968—. Asst. prof. State U. Coll. Arts & Scis., Plattsburgh, 1966-67; cons. community rels. and fund raising. Author: The New Nurse, 1973. With USAAF, 1941-45, USAF active res. 1945-69, ret. Decorated Air medal, Purple Heart. Mem. Am. Med. Writers Assn., Assn. Edn. in Journalism and Mass Communications, Health Scis. Comm. Assn., Am. Acad. Advt., Nat. League Nursing, Gary C. of C., Plattsburgh C. of C., Air Force Assn., Res. Officers Assn., Nat. Arts Club, Steel Club, Caterpillar Club, Flying Boot Club. Office: PO Box 872 Chico CA 95927

HANUS, JEROME GEORGE, archbishop; b. Brainard, N.E., May 26, 1940; Student, Conception Sem., Mo., St. Anselm U., Rome, Princeton Theol. Sem., Princeton U. Ordained priest Roman Cath. Ch., 1966. Abbot Conception Abbey, 1977—87; pres. Swiss Am. Benedictine Congregation, 1984—87; bishop Diocese of St. Cloud, Minn., 1987—94; co-adjutor archbishop Dubuque, Iowa, 1994—95; archbishop, 1995—. Office: Archdiocese of Dubuque 1229 Mt Loretta Ave Dubuque IA 52004*

HANUSHEK, ERIC ALAN, economics professor; b. Lakewood, Ohio, May 22, 1943; s. Vernon F. and Ruth (Hostetler) H.; m. Nancy L. Keleher, June 11, 1965 (div.); children: Eric Alan, Megan E.; m. Margaret E. Raymond, Oct. 10, 2003. BS, U.S. Air Force Acad., 1965; PhD in Econs., MIT, 1968. Sr. staff economist Coun. Econ. Advisers, Washington, 1971-72; assoc. prof. USAF Acad., Colo., 1972-73; sr. economist Cost of Living Coun., Washington, 1973-74; assoc. prof. econs. Yale U., New Haven, 1975-78; dir. pub. policy analysis U. Rochester, N.Y., 1978-83, prof. econs. and polit. sci., 1978-2000, chmn. dept. econs., 1982-87, 88-90, dir. W. Allen Wallis Inst. Polit. Economy, 1992-99; rsch. assoc. Nat. Bur. Econ. Rsch., 1996—; Hanna sr. fellow Hoover Instn. Stanford (Calif.) U., 2000—; sr. rsch. fellow Green Ctr. U. Tex., Dallas, 2000—; sr. fellow Stanford Inst. for Econ. Policy Rsch., 2003—. Dep. dir. Congl. Budget Office, Washington, 1984-85; mem. com. nat. stats. Nat. Rsch. Coun., 1992-98, adv. coun. on Edn. Statistics, 2002; cons. World Bank 1984-95, U.S. Com. on Civil Rights, 1986-89; chair exec. bd. Tex. Schs. Project, U. Tex., Dallas, 2003—; mem nat. bd. for edn. scis. U.S. Dept. Edn., 2005—. Author: Education and Race, 1972, (with J. Jackson) Statistical Methods for Social Scientists 1977, (with C. Citro) Improving Information for Social Policy Decisions, 1991, (with R. Harbison) Education Performance of the Poor, 1992, Making Schools Work, 1994, (with J. Banks) Modern Political Economy, 1995, (with N. Maritato) Assessing Knowledge of Retirement Behavior, 1996, (with Dale W. Jorgenson) Improving America's Schools, 1996, (with Constance F. Citro) Assessing Policies for Retirement Income, 1997, The Economics of Schooling and School Quality, 2003. Served to capt. USAF, 1965-74. Disting. vis. fellow Hoover Instn., Stanford U., 1999-2000. Fellow Internat. Acad. Edn. (bd. dirs. 2002—), Assn. Pub. Policy Analysis and Mgmt. (v.p. 1986-87, pres. 1988-89), Am. Econ. Assn., Econometric Soc., Soc. Labor Economists. Office Phone: 650-736-0942. Business E-Mail: hanushek@stanford.edu.

HANWAY, DONALD GRANT, retired agronomist, educator; b. Broadwater, Nebr., Aug. 6, 1918; s. Frank Pierce and Emma Terrissa (Twist) H.; m. Blanche Elizabeth Larson, Sept. 26, 1942 (dec. Aug. 1996); children: Donald Grant, Wayne Edward, Janice Kay; m. Susanne Ruth Pennington, Apr. 10, 1999 (dec. Sept. 2004). BS, U. Nebr., 1942, MS, 1948; PhD, Iowa State Coll., 1954. Tchr. rural schs., Morrill County, Nebr., 1936-40; mem. faculty dept. agronomy U. Nebr., Lincoln, 1947-84, chmn. faculty dept. agronomy, 1955-76, prof. emeritus, 1984—, also extension agronomist, chief of party univ. mission to Ataturk U. Erzurum, Turkey, 1965-67. Agronomic cons., Nigeria, Columbia, Morocco, Tunisia; mem. Plant Variety Protection Adv. Bd., 1987-90. Contbr. articles to profl. jours. Mem. Nebr. Commn. on Status of Women, 1986-89. With USAAF, 1942-46. Honoree Nebr. Hall of Agrl. Achievement, 1988. Fellow AAAS, Am. Soc. Agronomy, Crop Sci. Soc.; mem. Soil Sci. Soc. Am., Soil and Water Conservation Soc., Am. Inst. Biol. Scis., Phi Beta Kappa, Sigma Xi, Alpha Zeta, Gamma Sigma Delta. Episcopalian. Home: 5600 Pioneers Blvd Apt 214 Lincoln NE 68506-5175

HANWAY, H. EDWARD, insurance company executive; m. Ellen Hanway. BA, Loyola Coll., Balt., 1974; MBA, Widener U., 1984. CPA Pa. With CIGNA and predecessor companies, 1978—; v.p. opers. CIGNA Corp., 1986-88; pres. CIGNA Internat., 1989—96, CIGNA Healthcare, Phila., 1996—99; pres., COO CIGNA Corp., Phila., 1999—2000, chmn., CEO, 2000—. Chmn. bd. dirs. MedUnite; past chmn. Coun. Affordable Quality Healthcare. Bd. trustees Loyola Coll. Balt., Eisenhower Exch. Fellowships; bd. advisors March of Dimes Found.; bd. dirs. Phila. Orch. Mem.: Bus. Roundtable, Pa. Inst. CPAs, AICPA. Office: Cigna Corp 1 Liberty Place Philadelphia PA 19192*

HANZALEK, ASTRID TEICHER, public information officer, consultant; b. N.Y.C., Jan. 6, 1928; d. Arthur Albin and Luise Gertrude (Funke) Teicher; m. Frederick J. Hanzalek, Nov. 11, 1955. A, Concordia Coll., 1947; BA, U. Pa., 1949. Cons., Suffield, Conn., 1960—; state rep. Conn. Gen. Assembly, Hartford, 1970-80, asst. majority leader, 1973-74, asst. minority leader, 1975-80. Corporator Conn. Childrens Med. Ctr., 1986—95; bd. dirs. Conn. Water Co., Clinton; mem. Conn. Nitrogen Credit Adv. Bd., 2001—. Contbr. articles to profl. jours. Mem. Conn. State Coun. Environ. Quality, Hartford, 1980—93; chmn. Conn. State Ethics Commn., Hartford, 1985—93; commr. New Eng. Interstate Water Pollution Control Commn., 1993—; mem. Conn. Greenways Commn., 1992—; mem., chair history com. Conn. Commn. on Culture and Tourism, 2003—; trustee Priscilla Maxwell Endicott Scholarship Fund, 1972—; vice chmn. Bd. State Acad. awards, 1996—; chmn. Conn. Energy Found., Hartford, 1986—96; vice-chmn. Bradley Internat. Airport Commn., 1972—2002, Greater Hartford chpt. ARC, 1975—82; mem. Conn. Inter Agy. Libr. Planning Com., Hartford, 1975—85; bd. dirs. Riverfront Recapture, Inc., 1986—; chmn. Conn. River Watershed Coun., Greenfield, Mass., 1980—92; pres. Conn. Sr. Intern Program, Bridgeport, 1980—90; sec. Conn. Humanities Coun., Middletown, 1980—92. Named Panelist of the Yr., Auto. Consumer Action Panel, 1975—85; recipient Man of the Yr. award, Conn. Jaycees, 1972, Suffield Citizenship award, 1996. Mem.: Nat. Order Woman Legislators, Suffield Land Conservancy (bd. dirs. 1965—98, founder), Conn. Coun. Environ. Quality, Conn. Forest and Pk. Assn. (v.p., bd. dirs. 1975—), Antiquarian and Landmarks Soc. (v.p. 1974—95, pres. 1996—2002, bd. dirs.). Republican. Lutheran. Avocations: musical activities, sports, culinary arts. Home: 31 Abraham Ter Suffield CT 06078-2167

HANZEL, MIMI S., psychotherapist; b. Asheville, N.C., Aug. 28, 1941; d. James Andrew and Mary Athalinda (Wilmerding) Sutton; m. Charles J. Hanzel, June 1, 1963; children: Charles J., Mary Athalinda. BA, Calif. State U. L.A., 1984, MS, 1987; PhD, The Fielding Inst., 1995. Dual diagnosis coord. Pacific Clinics-El Camino, Santa Fe Springs, Calif., 1995—. Vol. Nat. Charity League, 1982-88, Assistance League of Pasadena, Calif., 1980-88. Recipient Outstanding Student Yr., The Fielding Inst., 1990-91; grantee L.A. Dept. Mental Health, 1997. Mem. San Gabriel Valley Psychol. Assn. (gov. affairs chair 1997), Am. Psychol. Assn., Calif. Psychol. Assn., Calif. Assn. Marriage and Family Therapists. Episcopal. Avocations: walking, reading, travel. Office: Pacific Clins-El Camino 11721 Telegraph Rd Ste A Santa Fe Springs CA 90670-6835

HANZELKA, RICHARD LOUIS, education educator; b. Belle Plaine, Iowa, Aug. 8, 1939; s. Louis Bernard and Agnes Lucille (Stoklas) H.; m. Mylene Glee Millhollin, Aug. 8, 1964; children: Kristine Marie, Susan Lynette, Marci Joelle, Amy Katherine. BA, U. Iowa, 1961, MA, 1964, PhD, 1974. Permanent profl. cert., Iowa; cert. supt., Iowa. Tchr. jr. h.s. lang. arts Cedar Rapids (Iowa) Comty. Schs., 1961-64; asst. prof. SUNY, New Paltz, 1964-69; cons. K-12 lang. arts Muscatine-Scott Co. Sch. Sys., Davenport, Iowa, 1969-74; staff devel. coord. K-12 lang. arts Miss. Bend Area Edn. Agy., Davenport, 1974-88, acting dir. edn. svcs. Bettendorf, Iowa, 1988-89, dir. gen. edn., 1989—99, dir. orgnl. strategic planning, 1999—2001; head edn. dept. Marycrest Internat. U., Davenport, Iowa, 2001—02; dir. Ea. Iowa Writing Project St. Ambrose U., Davenport, Iowa, 2002—. Mem. steering com., co-dir. Iowa Writing Project, Cedar Rapids, 1978—; dir. orgnl., strategic planning Miss. Bend Area Edn. Agy., Bettendorf, 1992—; Franklin Flex Trainer instr. Franklin Quest, Salt Lake City, 1994—. Contbr. articles to profl. jours. Coord. pre-Cana program Diocese of Davenport, 1979-82, deacon evaluation team, 1990-92; bd. dirs. 90 Miles Off Broadway, New Paltz, N.Y., 1968-69; pres. parish coun. St. John Vianney Ch., Bettendorf, 1989-91. Recipient Disting. Svc. award Miss. Valley Coun. Tchrs. of English, 1981; Drew Meml. scholar U. Iowa, 1957-60; NDEA Title IV fellow U. Iowa, 1972-73. Mem. ASCD (bd. dirs. 1991-99, nominating com. 1996, exec. coun. 2000—), Nat. Coun. Tchrs. of English (State Lit. Mag. leader 1984-87), Ednl. Svcs. Dirs. (chmn. 1991-92), Sch. Adminstrs. Iowa, Iowa Coun. Tchrs. of English (pres. 1979-81, disting. svc. award 1984), Iowa Assn. for Supervision and Curriculum Devel. (pres. 1991-92, exec. dir. 1995—). Roman Catholic. Avocations: singing, acting, woodworking, walking, reading. Home and Office: 2580 New Lexington Dr Bettendorf IA 52722-2115

HANZLIK, RAYBURN DEMARA, lawyer; b. LA, June 7, 1938; s. Rayburn Otto and Ethel Winifred (Membery) H.; m. Marilyn Burnap; children: Kristina, Rayburn N., Alexander, Geoffrey. BS, Principia Coll., 1960; MA, Woodrow Wilson Sch. Fgn. Affairs, U. Va., 1968; JD, U. Va., 1974. Bar: Va. 1975, D.C. 1977. Staff asst. to Pres. U.S., Washington, 1971-73; assoc. dir. White House Domestic Council, 1975-77; atty. Danzansky Dickey Tydings Quint & Gordon, Washington, 1977-78, Akin Gump Strauss Hauer & Feld, Washington, 1978-79, Darling, Rae & Gute, L.A., 1979-81; adminstr. Econ. Regulatory Adminstrn., Dept. Energy, Washington, 1981-85; ptnr. Heidrick and Struggles, Inc., 1985-91, McKenna & Hanzlik, Irvine, Calif., 1991-92; chmn. Lanxide Sports Internat., Inc., San Diego, 1992-95, Stealth Propulsion Internat., Ltd., San Diego, Calif. and, Melbourne, Australia, 1994-97; exec. v.p. Commodore Corp., N.Y.C. and McLean, Va., 1997-98; atty. Trainum, Snowdon & Deane, Washington, 1999—; mng. dir. Washington Technology Strategies, 2002—. Contbg. author: Global Politics and Nuclear Energy, 1971, Soviet Foreign Relations and World Communism, 1965. Alt. del. Republican Nat. Conv., 1980; dir. Calif. Rep. Victory Fund, 1980; candidate U.S. Senate, 1980. Served to lt. USN, 1963-68, Vietnam. Republican. Christian Scientist. Office Phone: 202-783-4350. Personal E-mail: rayburn.hanzlik@verizon.net.

HAO, TIAN, physical chemist, materials scientist; b. Sept. 19, 1967; 1 child, Taige. BS, Northwestern U., 1987; MS, Chinese Acad. Sci., 1992; PhD, Inst. Chemistry, Chinese Acad. Scis., Beijing, 1995. Rschr. Nat. Inst. Materials and Chem. Rsch., Tsukuba, Japan, 1997—99; rsch. assoc. Rutgers U., Piscataway, NJ, 1999—2003; sr. scientist E Ink, Cambridge, Mass., 2004—. Fellow, Japen

Sci. and Tech. Agy., 1997. Mem.: Am. Physics Inst. Achievements include development of a theory accounting for the electrorheological effect. Office: E INK Co 733 Concord Ave Cambridge MA 02138 Office Phone: 617-499-6183.

HAOUDI, ABDELALI, science educator; b. Casablanca, Morocco, July 19, 1966; s. Hassan Haoudi and Zoubida Moumen; m. Halima Bensmail, Feb. 14, 2003; children: Elias Nabel children: William Mehdi, Kevin Hassan. PhD, Pierre and Marie Curie U., Paris, 1992—96. Vis. scientist NIH, Research Triangle Park, NC, 1997—2000; rschr., prof. Ea. Va. Med. Sch., Norfolk, 2000—. Founder, pres. Internat. Coun. Biomedicine and Biotechnology, Va., 2003—. Exec. editor Jour. Biomedicine and Biotechnology. Recipient Fogarty Internat. award, NIH, 1997—2000, Biosafety Conf. award, Ministry of Environ. and Water Resources, Sultanate of Oman, Soc. Photochemistry and Photobiology, 2005; grantee, Commonwealth Health Rsch. Bd. Va., 2001—02, Elsa U. Pardee Found., 2004—05. Mem.: AAAS, European Assn. Cancer Rsch., Am. Assn. Cancer Rsch. Office: Ea Virginia Med Sch 700 W Olney Rd Norfolk VA 23507 Office Phone: 757-446-5682. Personal E-mail: haoudi@i-council-biomed-biotech.org. Business E-Mail: haoudia@evms.edu.

HAPGOOD, ROBERT DERRY, language educator; b. Lompoc, Calif., Dec. 11, 1928; s. Arthur Richard and Elsie Rachel (Brown) H.; m. Marilyn Janelle Oliver, July 16, 1950; children— Miranda Kristin, Susanna Elizabeth. BA with highest honors, U. Calif., Berkeley, 1950, MA, 1951, PhD, 1955. Instr. English Ind. U., 1955-57; vis. prof. Am. lit. and civilization Dijon (France) U., 1957-58; instr. U. Calif., Berkeley, 1958-59, asst. prof. Riverside, 1959-65; mem. faculty U. N.H., Durham, 1965—, prof. English, 1969-95; prof. emeritus English, 1996—; chmn. dept. U. N.H., 1972-75, dir. London program, 1986-89; dir. U. N.H./Cambridge U. summer program, 1982-85; exchange prof. Osaka (Japan) U., 1977-79. Vis. prof. Shoin Women's U., Japan, 1992; dir. Shakespeare Workshop, Bowdoin Coll., summers 1972-75. Author: Shakespeare the Theatre-poet, 1988; editor: Hamlet - Shakespeare in Production, 1999; mem. editorial bd. Univ. Press New Eng., 1975-77. Served with AUS, 1953-55. Recipient essay prize English Inst., 1968, Lindberg award for Outstanding Scholar-Tchr., 1990; fellow Inst. Renaissance Studies, Ashland, Oreg., 1961; Mellon postdoctoral fellow, 1964-65; fellow Southeastern Inst. Medieval and Renaissance Studies, Chapel Hill, N.C., 1969; Am. Coun. Learned Socs. fellow, 1979-80, Folger Inst. fellow, 1987, NEH summer fellow, 1994. Mem. MLA. Home: 1730 Traver Rd Ann Arbor MI 48105 Office: U NH English Dept Hamilton Smith Hall Durham NH 03824 Personal E-mail: HapgoodR@aol.com.

HAPNER, MARY LOU, securities trader and dealer, writer; b. Ft. Wayne, Ind., Nov. 9, 1937; d. Paul Kenneth Brooks and Eileen (Summers) H. BS with honors, Ariz. State U., 1966, MS, 1967. Stockbroker Young, Smith & Peacock, Phoenix, 1971-76, v.p., 1976-89, Peacock, Hislop, Staley & Given, Phoenix, 1989-90, 1st v.p., 1990—. Author: Career Courage, 1984; (poems) The Power of Forgiveness, 1995, Take Someone's Hand, 1997, Cherubs, 1997, Self Portrait, 1998, Vision, 1999, Millenium, 2000, Walk with Me, 2001, Lullabies at Night, 2004. Chmn. March of Dimes, Sun City, Ariz., 1983; trustee St. Lukes, Phoenix, 1978; mem. fin. com. YWCA, Phoenix, 1975; mem. dean's coun. of 100, Ariz. State U. Coll. Bus., 2000-03; chair budget com. Ch. of Beatitudes, Phoenix, mem. exec. coun., 1991; bd. dirs. Ariz.'s Children Found., 1998; founder Ariz. Biltmore Country Club Women's Orgn., 1976, champion 1976-83. Recipient Spirit of Philanthropy award, 1997, Impact award for Enterprising Women, 2001, Arthritis Angel award, 2002, Rookie of Yr. award Arthritis Found., 2003. Mem. Charter 100 (chair membership 1979-81, pres. 1980, pres. 1982, v.p. 1981, treas., membership chair 1995, v.p. 2003—, chair 25th Anniversary 2004). Republican. Lutheran. Avocations: golf, singing with concert choirs, poetry. Business E-Mail: mlhapner@phs&g.com.

HAPP, HARVEY HEINZ, electrical engineer, educator; b. Berlin, June 27, 1928; came to U.S., 1947, naturalized, 1953; s. Harry and Hertha (Friedmann) H.; m. Ruth Hollander, Nov. 17, 1951; children: Deborah Ann, Sandra Eva. BS in Elec. Engring, Ill. Inst. Tech., 1954; M.E.E., Rensselaer Poly. Inst., Troy, N.Y., 1958; D.Sc., U. Belgrade, Yugoslavia, 1962. Registered profl. engr., N.Y. With Gen. Electric Co., 1954-88, sr. application engr. Schenectady, 1968-72, mgr. analytical engring. services, 1972-77, mgr. advanced system tech., 1977-82, mgr. system analysis, 1982-87, cons., 1987-88, also mem. faculty power system engring. course; with N.Y. State Dept. Pub. Service, 1988—. Lectr. colls. Author: Diakoptics and Networks (translated into Russian and Romanian), 1971, Piecewise Methods and Applications to Power Systems (translated into Chinese), 1980; editor: Gabriel Kron and Systems Theory, 1973; mem. editorial bd. Procs. IEEE, 1979-84; contbr. numerous articles and book revs. to profl. jours., chpts. to tech. books. Fellow IEEE (life; Prize Paper award Region 5 1962, power sys. engring. com. 1977, Region 1 award 1980); mem. Tensor Soc. Gt. Britain (v.p. 1972-82), Conf. Internat. des Grands Reseaux Electrique a Haute Tension, Internat. Power Sys. Computations Conf. (co-founder 1962), Gen. Electric Co. Engrs. and Scientists Assn. (chmn. policy com. 1968-70), Ill. Inst. Tech. Alumni Assn., Sigma Xi, Tau Beta Pi, Eta Kappa Nu. Home: 2211 Webster Dr Niskayuna NY 12309-3930 Office: NY State Dept Pub Svc 3 Empire State Plz Albany NY 12223-1000 E-mail: harvey_happ@dps.state.ny.us.

HAPPER, WILLIAM, JR., physicist, researcher; b. Vellore, India, July 27, 1939; came to U.S., 1941, naturalized, 1961; s. William and Gladys (Morgan) H.; m. Barbara Jean Baker, June 10, 1967; children: James William, Gladys Anne. BS, U. N.C., 1960; PhD, Princeton U., 1964. Rsch. assoc. Radiation Lab., Columbia U., N.Y.C., 1964, asst. prof. physics, 1967-70, assoc. prof., 1970-74, prof., 1974-80; dir. Radiation Lab., Columbia U. (Radiation Lab.), 1976-79; prof. Princeton (N.J.) U., 1980-91, 93—; dir. office energy rsch. U.S. Dept. Energy, Washington, D.C., 1991-93. Chmn. Jason/Mitre, 1987-90; trustee Mitre Corp., Lounsbery Found.; cons. in field. Alfred P. Sloan fellow, 1967; recipient Alexander von Humboldt award Germany, 1976. Fellow NAS, Am. Phys. Soc. (Herbert Broida prize 1997, Davisson Germer prize 2000), Am. Acad. Arts and Scis., Am. Philos. Soc. Note, only current corporate directorships are listed and they are not dated, per style. Home: 559 Riverside Dr Princeton NJ 08540-4007 Office: Princeton U Dept Physics Princeton NJ 08544-0001

HAQUE, MALIKA HAKIM, pediatrician; b. Madras, India; arrived in US, 1967; d. Syed Abdul and Rahimunisa (Hussain) Hakim; m. C. Azeez Haque, Feb. 5, 1967; children: Kifizeba Haque Akbar, Masarath Haque Khan, Asim Zayd Haque. MBBS, Madras Med. Coll., 1967. Diplomate Am. Bd. Pediatrics. Rotating intern Miriam Hosp. Brown U., Providence, 1967-68; resident in pediatrics N.J. Coll. Medicine Childrens Hosp., 1968-70; fellow in devel. disabilities Ohio State U., 1970-71; acting chief pediat. Nisonger Ctr., 1973-74; staff pediatrician Children and Youth Project Children's Hosp., Columbus, Ohio; clin. asst. prof. pediatrics Ohio State U., 1974-80, clin. assoc. prof. pediatrics, 1981-99, clin. assoc. prof. dept. internat. health Coll. Medicine, 1993-99, clin. prof. pediatrics and internat. health Coll. Medicine, 1999—. Pediatrician Children's Hosp. Physician Health Ctrs. Children's Hosp., Columbus, 1982—; dir. Pediat. Academic Assn., 1992-2002; cons. Ctrl. Ohio Head Start Program, 1974-79; med. cons. Bur. Rehab. and Devel. Disabilities for State of Ohio, 1990—. Contbr. articles to profl. jours. and newspapers. Charter founder Ronald Reagan Rep. Ctr.; trustee Asian Am. Health Alliance Network, Columbus, 1994-2001. Recipient Physician Recognition award, AMA, 1971—86, 1988—99, 2002—05, Gold medals in surgery, radiology, pediat. and ob-gyn., Presdl. medal of Merit, Pres. Ronald Reagan, 1982, Nat. Leadership award, Nat. Rep. Congl. Com., 2001, Physician of the Yr. award, 2003. Fellow Am. Acad. Pediatrics; mem. Islamic Med. Assn., Am. Assn. of Physicians of Indian Origin, Pediat. Acad. Assn. (dir. 1992-2002), Ambulatory Pediat. Assn., Ctrl. Ohio Pediatric Soc. Achievements include research on enuresis and tumors caused by human papilloma viruses. Home: 5995 Forestview Dr Columbus OH 43213-2114 Office: 700 Childrens Dr Columbus OH 43205-2664 Office Phone: 614-722-4957.

HAQUE, PROMOD, venture capitalist; b. Shimla, India, Apr. 28, 1948; s. Alexander and Phulwanti (Gangaram) Haque; m. Dorcas Haque. BSEE, U. Delhi; PhD in Electrical Engring., Northwestern U.; MBA, Northwestern Kellog Sch. Mgmt. Sales exec. Seimens, New Delhi, 1969—72; prod. devel. mgr. Thornton EMI, 1976—81; COO Emergent Corp., 1981—83; CEO Dimensional Medicine, Inc., Twin Cities, Minn., 1983—88; cons. Norwest Venture Partners, Minneapolis, 1989, mng. ptnr., 1990—95, Menlo Park, Calif., 1995—. Bd. dirs. Veraz Networks. Advisory bd. Northwestern U. Sch. Mgmt. Office: NVP 525 University Ave Palo Alto CA 94301-1922 Office Phone: 650-321-8000. Office Fax: 650-321-8010.

HARA, GEORGE, computer company executive; b. Osaka, Japan, Oct. 10, 1952; s. Nobutaro and Mitsuko (Kuroda) H.; m. Junko Yamada, Oct. 8, 1988. LLB, Keio U., Tokyo, 1975; MS in Engring., Stanford U., 1981, MBA in Bus. Fin. officer UN Capital Devel. Fund, N.Y.C., 1980-81; founder, pres. Gekee Fiberoptics Inc., Palo Alto, Calif., 1981-83; pres. Data Control Ltd., Osaka, 1984-85; v.p. Pacific Catalyst Group, L.A., 1984—; gen. ptnr. Japan Incubation Capital, Tokyo, 1985-88; pres., chief exec. officer Data Control Ltd., Osaka, Tokyo and Palo Alto, 1985—; founder, mng. ptnr. DEFTA, Palo Alto and San Francisco, 1986—. Founder, advisor Control Tech. Ltd., Osaka, 1986—; bd. dirs. Wollongong Group Inc., Palo Alto, IDA Bldg. (USA) Corp., San Francisco, Plantec Inc., Tokyo, Borland Internat.; chief exec. advisor Hankyo Corp., Osaka., 1989—. Advisor coll. bus. U. San Francisco, 1987—, advisor to pres., 1988—; advisor to gov. Prefecture of Osaka, 1986-88; active task force for econ. devel. Osaka Kansai Keizaidoyukai, 1981; bd. dirs. Metadigm Found., Calif. Mem. Archaeol. Inst. Am., Japan-Cen. Am. Soc. (pres. 1976-78), Shotosha Found. (chmn. 1977—), Japan Software Rsch. Found. (bd. dirs. 1988—), Networking Japan (pres. 1985), Alliance Japan (pres. 1986, chmn. 1989), Alliance 90 (chmn. 1990), Smithsonian Inst., Calif. Acad. Sci., Stanford Assn. Japan, U.S.-Japan High Tech. Trade and Strategic Alliance Com. (pres. 1989—) Cen. Am. Mita Assn., Kansai Stanford Assn. (mus. soc. officer), Nat. Venture Capital Assn. Office: DEFTA Ptnrs 111 Pine St Ste 1410 San Francisco CA 94111-5616 also: One Embarcadero Ctr San Francisco CA 94111 Office Phone: 415-433-2262. Business E-Mail: ghara@deftapartners.com.

HARA, TADAO, educational administrator; b. Shimonoseki, Japan, Oct. 21, 1926; s. Ikuhisa and Chitose Hara; m. Suzuko Hara, May 12; children: Nobumichi, Izumi. BA, Tamagawa U., Machida, Japan, 1952; MA in Bibl. Theology, N.W. Coll., 1958; MA in Ednl. Psychology, Calif. State U., Long Beach, 1965; HHD (hon.), Newport Asi Pacific U., 2001; LittD (hon.), Northwest Coll., 1990. Ordained to ministry Assembly of God Ch. Fgn. student counselor Calif. State U., Long Beach, 1965-68; prof. edn. Tamagawa U., 1969-79, dean students, 1973-77, dir. internat. edn., 1976-79; founder, chmn. bd., pres. emeritus Internat. Bilingual Sch., Palos Verdes Estates, Calif., 1979—2003; dir. Mesa Verde United Meth. Ch., Japanese Lang. Fellowship, Costa Mesa, 2003—. Mem. adv. bd. Calif. State U. Long Beach Coll. Edn., 1985-88. Recipient Disting. Alumnus award Edn., Calif. State U., Long Beach, 1994. Mem. Delta Upsilon Chi. Home: 3992 Toland Cir Los Alamitos CA 90720-2261 Office: Mesa Verde UMC 1701 Baker St Costa Mesa CA 92626-3645

HARACZ, STEPHEN M., lawyer; BS, MS, Fordham U., 1980; JD cum laude, NY Law Sch., 1985. Bar: NY 1986. Ptnr., group co-leader Intellectual Property Bryan Cave LLP, NYC. Office: Bryan Cave LLP 1290 Ave of the Americas New York NY 10104 Office Phone: 212-541-1271, 212-904-0511. E-mail: smharacz@bryancave.com.

HARAD, GEORGE JAY, retired manufacturing executive; b. Newark, Apr. 24, 1944; m. Beverly Marcia Harad, June 12, 1966; children: Alyssa Dawn, Matthew Corde. BA, Franklin and Marshall Coll., 1965; MBA with high distinction, Harvard Bus. Sch., 1971. Staff cons. Boston Cons. Group, 1970-71; asst. to sr. v.p. housing Boise Cascade Corp., 1971, asst. to v.p. Palo Alto, Calif., 1971; fin. mgr. Boise Cascade Realty Group, Palo Alto, Calif., 1972-76; mgr. corp. devel. Boise Cascade Corp., Boise, Idaho, 1976—80, dir. retirement funds, risk mgmt., 1980—82, v.p., contr., 1982—84, sr. v.p., CFO, 1984—89, exec. v.p., CFO, 1989—90, exec. v.p. paper, 1990—91, pres., COO, 1991—94, pres., CEO, 1994—95, chmn., bd. dirs., 1995, CEO, chmn., 1995—2002; exec. chmn. OfficeMax Inc., Itasca, Ill., 2004—05, interim pres., CEO, 2005. Bd. dirs. FmGlobal Ins. Co., U.S. West, 1997—2000, Dial Corp., 2003; bd. govs. Nat. Coun. for Air and Stream Improvement Inc. Founder, pres. Boise Coun. for Gifted and Talented Students, 1977—79; bd. dirs. Boise Philharm. Assn., 1983—84; dir. bd. trustees Coll. Idaho, 1986—91. Recipient George F. Baker scholar, 1970—71; Grad. Prize fellow, Harvard Grad. Sch. Arts and Scis., 1965—69, Frederick Roe fellow, Harvard U. Sch. Bus., 1971. Mem.: Am. Forest and Paper Assn. (bd. dirs., mem. exec. com. 1984—94), NAM (bd. dirs), Century Club (Boston), Arid Club, Crane Creek Country Club.

HARADA, NORIO, software engineer, researcher, educator; b. Aichi, Japan, Feb. 12, 1945; s. Iwao and Tomiko Harada; m. Reiko Harada, Oct. 31, 1971; children: Shin, Satoshi. BS, Nagoya U., Nagoya-Shi, Japan, 1967, MS, 1969; DEng, Kyoto U., Kyoto-Shi, Japan, 1979. Rschr. Nippon Electric Co. Ltd., Kawasaki-Shi, Kanagawa, Japan, 1969-82, rsch. supr., 1982-84; rsch. mgr. NEC Corp., Kawasaki-Shi, 1984-87, mgr. Minato-Ku, Tokyo, 1987-91, chief engr., 1991-96; prof. computer sci. Takushoku U., Tokyo, 1996—. Contbr. articles to profl. jours. Recipient Yonezawa Meml. Paper award, 1985. Mem. IEEE, AAAS, Assn. Computing Machinery, Math. Soc. Japan, Inst. Electronics, Info. and Comm. Engrs. Japan (Excellent Paper award 1985, 88), Info. Processing Soc. Japan, NY Acad. Scis. Buddhist. Avocations: mathematics, tennis, reading, research. Home: 18-5 Yokoyamadai 1-Chome Sagamihara-Shi Kanagawa 229-1121 Japan Office: Takushoku U 815-1 Tatemachi Hachioji-Shi Tokyo 193-0985 Japan Business E-Mail: nharada@cs.takushoku-u.ac.jp.

HARAGAN, DONALD ROBERT, academic administrator, geologist, educator; b. Houston, Apr. 15, 1936; s. Donald William and Mary (Thompson) H.; m. Willie Mae O'Berry, July 2, 1966; children— Shannon Lea, Shelley Jo. BS, U. Tex., 1959, PhD, 1969; MS, Tex. A & M U., 1960. Registered profl. engr., Tex. Research asst. Tex. A & M U., College Station, 1959-60; research scientist U. Tex., Austin, 1960-66, instr., 1966-69; asst. prof. Tex. Tech. U., Lubbock, 1969-72; assoc. prof. Tex. Tech U., Lubbock, 1972-78, prof. geosci., 1978—, dept. chmn., 1972-77, 80-83, interim dean, 1985, interim v.p., 1985-86, v.p. for acad. affairs and research, 1986-88, exec. v.p., provost, 1988—; interim pres. Tex. Tech. U., Lubbock, 1996, pres., 1996-2000, pres. emeritus, 2000—. Contbr. articles in field to profl. jours. Mem. Am. Soc. Civil Engrs., AAAS, Am. Meteorol. Soc., Am. Water Resources Assn., Tex. Acad. Sci. Home: 6914 Nashville Dr Lubbock TX 79413-6002 Office: Tex Tech U Honors Coll Lubbock TX 79409 Office Phone: 806-742-0031.

HARALICK, ROBERT MARTIN, electrical engineering educator; b. N.Y.C., Sept. 30, 1943; s. David and Yetta (Stier) H.; m. Joy Gold, Aug. 20, 1967 (div. July 1977); 1 child, Tammy-Beth; m. Linda G. Shapiro, Feb. 12, 1978 (div. Aug. 1992); 1 child, Michael Aaron; m. Ihsin T. Phillips, Dec. 1993. BA, U. Kans., 1964, BS, 1966, MS, 1967, PhD, 1969. Asst. prof. elec. engring. U. Kans., Lawrence, 1969-71, assoc. prof., 1971-75, prof., 1975-78, Va. Poly. Inst. and State U., 1979-84; v.p. rsch. Machine Vision Internat., Ann Arbor, Mich., 1984-86; Boeing Clairmont Egtvedt prof. elec. engring., adj. prof. computer sci. U. Wash., Seattle, 1986-2000; pres. Mnemonics Inc., 1979—; disting. prof. computer sci. Grad. Ctr. CUNY, 2001—. Co-dir. NATO Advanced Study Inst. Image Processing, 1978; co-chmn. NATO Advanced Study Inst. on Image Processing, 1980, Robust Computer Vision Workshop, 1990, 92, 94; vice chmn. 5th Internat. Conf. on Pattern Recognition, Miami, 1980; dir. NATO Advanced Study Inst. on Pictorial Data Analysis, 1982; adj. prof. Ctr. Bioengring. U. Wash., Seattle, 1988—; program chmn. 10th annual ICPR Conf. on Pattern Recognition Systems and Applications, 1990; program co-chmn. Internat. Conf. on Document Analysis and Recognition, 1991, vice chmn., 1997; co-chmn. Evaluation and Validation of Computer Vision Algorithm, 1998, chmn., 2001. Author: (with T. Creese) Differential Equations for Engineers, 1977; Pictorial Data Analysis, 1983, (with L. Shapiro) Computer and Robost Vision, Vol I and II, 1992, The Inner Meaning of Hebrew Letters, 1995, (with M. Glazerson) The Torah Codes and Israel Today, 1996, (with M. Glazerson, Joel Gallis and Robert Wolf) Light Out of Darkness, 2005; editor: (with J. C. Simon) Issues in Digital Image Processing, 1980, Digital Image Processing, 1981; assoc. editor Computer Vision, Graphics and Image Processing, 1975-93, Pattern Recognition, 1977-93, Communication of the ACM, Image Processing, 1982-92, IEEE Transactions on Systems, Man and Cybernetics, 1979-88, IEEE Transactions on Image Processing, 1992-96, Jour. of Electronic Imaging, 1994—; mem. editl. bd. IEEE Transactions on Pattern Analysis and Machine Intelligence, 1981-84, IEEE Expert, 1986-90, Machine Vision and Applications, 1987—, Real Time Imaging, 1994—, mem. adv. bd.; mem. adv. program com. Structural & Syntactic Pattern Recognition, 1990; contbr. over 525 articles to profl. jours.; digital computer art exhbns. include William Rockhill Nelson Gallery, Kansas City, Mo., 1971, Nat. History Mus., U. Kans., 1971, Dulin Gallery Art, 1971 (2 purchase awards), Nat. Invitational Print Show, U. R.I., 1972, Fla. State U., 1972, San Diego State Coll., 1972; author of over 550 books, book chpts., others. Recipient Dow Chem. Young Outstanding Faculty award Am. Soc. Engring. Educators, 1975, Outstanding Young Elec. Engrs. Honorable Mention award Eta Kappa Nu, 1975, Best Paper award 5th Ann. Symposium on Automatic Imagery Pattern Recognition, 1975, Best Paper award Pattern Recognition Soc., 1989; NSF faculty fellow, 1977-79. Fellow IEEE, IAPR; mem. IEEE Computer Soc. (chmn. pattern analysis and machine intelligence tech. com. 1975-82, acoustics, signal and speech processing, sys., man and cybernetics, pattern recognition tech. subcom. 1975-81, data structures and pattern recognition subcom. 1975-81, biomed. pattern recognition subcom. 1975-81, internat. assn. for pattern recognition gov. bd. 1986-2000, pres. 1996-98, program com. pattern and image processing conf. 1978, 4th internat. joint conf. on pattern recognition 1978, conf. B-pattern recognition methods and sys. program com. 11th internat. conf. on pattern recognition 1992, structural and syntactic pattern recognition 1992, 2d internat. conf. on document analysis and recognition 1993, chairperson various workshops and confs., Cert. Appreciation award 1978, 84), Pattern Recognition Soc., Internat. Assn. for Pattern Recognition (pres. 1996-98), Am. Assn. Artificial Intelligence, Assn. Computing Machinery. Avocation: hammered dulcimer. Home: 1500 Ocean Pky Apt 2k Brooklyn NY 11230 Office Phone: 212-817-8192. Business E-Mail: haralick@ptah.gc.cuny.edu. E-mail: haralick@netscape.net.

HARARI, ELI, computer company executive; BS in Physics with honors, Manchester Univ.; MA, PhD in Solid State Scis., Princeton Univ. Technical mgmt. positions Hughes Aircraft, Honeywell; co-founder, pres., CEO Wafer Scale integration; founder, pres., CEO SanDisk Corp., Sunnyvale, Calif., 1988—. Patentee in field. Office: 140 Caspian Ct Sunnyvale CA 94089-1000*

HARARI, GUY, chemicals executive; b. Sao Paulo, Brazil, Sept. 4, 1960; s. Ezra Selim and Regina Harari; m. Elena Berger Harari, Dec. 10, 1987; children: Cesar, Daniel, Melissa. Degree in mech. engring., U. São Paulo, 1982; postgrad. in mgmt., Fundacao Dom Cabral/Northwestern U., 1995, INSEAD, France, 1989. Fibers BU comml. mgr. Rhodia SA, São Paulo, 1990—92, textile Fibers BU mgr., 1992—93, new bus. devel. mgr., 1993—94, gen. mgr. pet resin bus. unit, 1994—96; sr. bus. analyst Aventis SA, Paris, 1997—98; strategic bus. mgr. Aventis Animal Nutrition France, Antony, 1998—99; pres. Aventis Animal Nutrition USA, Inc., Alpharetta, Ga., 1999—2002, Adisseo USA Inc, Alpharetta, 2002—. Achievements include patent for production of animal feed. Personal E-mail: guyharari@comcast.net.

HARASZTHY, VIOLET IBOLYA, dentist, researcher; b. Palic, Serbia-Montenegro, May 29, 1960; d. Vilmos and Rozsa Farkas; m. Gary Geza Haraszthy, Jan. 23, 1987. DDS, Szegedi Orvostudomanji Egjetem, Szeged, Hungary, 1984; MS, SUNY, Buffalo, 1993, DDS, 2001, PhD, 1999. Cert. Prosthodontist SUNY, Buffalo, 1998, Periodontist SUNY, Buffalo, 1994; RN Nursing Sch. Subotica, Yugoslavia, 1979. Dentist Mezohegyes (Hungary) Hosp.; clin. asst. prof. SUNY, Buffalo, 1993—99, asst. prof., 1999—. Lab. dir. SUNY, Buffalo, 2001—. Contbr. articles to profl. jours. Grantee Colgate, 2002—03; Rsch. grantee, Am. Acad. of Dentistry, 2001. Republican. Achievements include research in Heart Disease And Periodontal Disease Connection; Identifing the role of iron in Actinobacillus actinomycetemcomitans; Studying the distribution of highly toxic Actinobacillus actinomycetemcomitans; Identifying bacteria associated with periodontal disease and their geographycal distribution. Office: SUNY 3435 Main St Buffalo NY 14214 E-mail: vh1@acsu.buffalo.edu.

HARATANI, JOAN MEI, lawyer; b. Redwood City, Calif., Aug. 2, 1957; d. Donald R. Chambers and Claire Meiko Haratani Chambers; m. Ralph Gregory Latza, Jan. 6, 2002. BA in Philosophy, St. John's Coll., 1979; JD, U. Calif.-Davis, 1984. Bar: all Calif. state cts., no. and ctrl. fed. cts. 1985. Assoc. Crosby Heafey Roach & May, Oakland, Calif., 1984—90, ptnr., 1990—2002, Shook Hardy & Bacon, San Francisco, 2002—05, Morgan, Lewis & Bockius, 2005—. Sec. The Asian Pacific Fund, San Francisco, 1999—, Lawyers Commn. of Civil Rights, 2004—; mem. bd. Leukemia & Lymphoma Soc., 2001—; pres.-elect Bar Assn. of San Francisco, 2004—; past pres. Asian Am. Bar Assn. of the Greater Bay Area, 2000; mem. Claremont Resort. Named a Super Lawyer of No. Calif., San Francisco mag., 2004, 2005; named one of 500 Most Influential Asians in Am., Ave. Asia mag., 2003; recipient Top Rainmaker, Calif. Law Bus., 1996—97, 1999, Advocate of Yr. Joe Morozumi award, Asian Am. Bar Assn of No. Calif., 2001, Female Litigator on the Rise, Diversity & the Bar (publ. of Minority Corp. Counsel Assn.), 2004. Mem.: Nat. Asian Pacific Am. Bar Assn., Assn. Managing Counsel. Achievements include completing Iron Man triathlon race, 2000. Avocations: triathlete, wine, cooking, reading. Office: Morgan Lewis & Bockius 1 Market Spear St Tower San Francisco CA 94105 Office Phone: 415-442-1000. Office Fax: 415-442-1001. Business E-Mail: jharatani@morganlewis.com.

HARB, MAC, Canadian government official; BS, U. Ottawa, Ont., Can., 1979, M in Elec. Engring., 1983. Alderman City of Ottawa, 1985-88, dep. mayor, 1987-88; mem. of parliment Ho. of Commons, Ottawa, 1988—, sec. to min. for internat. trade, 1993-95, chmn. internat. trade com., vice chair pub. account com. Former vice-chmn. Ottawa Non-Profit Housing Corp, Ottawa Econ. Affairs Com.; bd. mgmt. Preston St. bus. improvement bd. Mem. Assn. Profl. Engrs. on Ont. Avocations: cooking, gardening, travel. Office: Ho of Commons Ctr Block Rm 552D Ottawa ON Canada K1A 0A6

HARBATER, DAVID, mathematician; b. N.Y.C., Dec. 19, 1952; s. Maurice and Marilyn (Haber) H. AB summa cum laude, Harvard U., 1974; MS in Math., Brandeis U., 1975; PhD in Math., MIT, 1978; MA (hon.), U. Pa., 1984. Asst. prof. U. Pa., Phila., 1978-83, assoc. prof., 1983-91, prof., 1991-96, E. Otis Kendall prof. math., 1996—. Contbr. articles to profl. jours. Fellow NSF, 1975-78, 82-83, Sloan Found., 1984-87, Lindback award for disting. tchg. U. Pa., 1995. Mem. Am. Math. Soc. (postdoctoral fellow 1978-79, Frank Nelson Cole Prize in Algebra, 1995), Phi Beta Kappa, Sigma Xi. Democrat. Jewish. Home: 1711 Lombard St Philadelphia PA 19146 Office: U Pa Dept Math 209 S 33rd St Dept Math Philadelphia PA 19104-6317 E-mail: harbater@math.upenn.edu.

HARBAUGH, DANIEL PAUL, lawyer; b. Wendell, Idaho, May 18, 1948; s. Myron and Manuelita (Garcia) Harbaugh. BA, Gonzaga U., 1970, JD, 1974. Bar: Wash. 1974, U.S. Dist. Ct. (ea. dist.) Wash. 1977, U.S. Ct. Appeals (9th cir.) 1978. Asst. atty. gen. State of Wash., Spokane, 1974-77; ptnr. Richter, Wimberley & Ericson, Spokane, 1977-83, Harbaugh & Bloom, P.S., Spokane, 1983—. Bd. dirs. Spokane Legal Svcs., 1982—86; bd. govs. LAWPAC, Seattle, 1980—92. Bd. dirs. Spokane Ballet, 1983-88; chpt. dir. Les Amis du Vin, Spokane, 1985-88; mem. Spokane County Civil Svc. Commn., 1991-2003, chmn., 1999-2003, Gonzaga U. Pres.' Coun., 1991-2000. Mem. ATLA, Wash. State Bar Assn. (spl. dist. counsel 1982-95, mem. com. rules for profl. conduct 1989-92, mem. legis. com. 1995-96), Spokane County Bar Assn. (chair med.-legal com. 1991), Wash. State Trial Lawyers Assn. (v.p. 1988-89, co-chair worker's compensation sect. 1992, 93, spl. select. com. on workers' corp. 1990—, forum 1994—, vice-chmn. 1994-97, mem. legis. com. 1995-98), Nat. Orgn. Social Security Claimants Reps., Internat. Wine and Food Soc. (pres. local chpt. 1989-91, cellar master 1994-96, 2004-, cellar com. 2001—), Spokane Enol. Soc., Spokane Club, Spokane Country Club (adminstrv. com. 1995-98, chmn. 1997-98, trustee 1996-99, sec.-treas. 1997-98, pres. 1998-99, ex-officio 1999-2000, long range planning com. 1999-2001), Alpha Sigma Nu, Phi Alpha Delta. Roman Catholic. Office: Harbaugh & Bloom PS PO Box 1461 Spokane WA 99210-1461 Business E-Mail: dan@hblaw2.com.

HARBAUGH, JOHN WARVELLE, geologist, educator; b. Madison, Wis., Aug. 6, 1926; s. Marion Dwight and Marjorie (Warvelle) H.; m. Josephine Taylor, Nov. 24, 1951 (dec. Dec. 25, 1985); children: Robert, Dwight, Richard; m. Audrey Wegst, Oct. 21, 2000. BS, U. Kans., 1948, MS, 1950; PhD, U. Wis., 1955. Prodn. geologist Carter Oil Co., Tulsa, 1951-53; prof. geol. sci. Stanford (Calif.) U., 1955-99, prof. emeritus, 1999—. Author: (with G. Bonham Carter) Computer Simulation in Geology, 1970, (with D.M. Tezlaff) Simulating Clastic Sedimentation, 1989, (with P. Martinez) Simulating Nearshore Environments, 1993, (with R. Slingerland and K. Furlong) Simulating Clastic Sedimentary Basins, 1994, (with J.C. Davis and J. Wendebourg) Computing Risk for Oil Prospects: Principles and Programs, 1995, (with J. Wendebourg) Simulating Oil Entrapment in Clastic Sequences, 1997. Recipient Haworth Disting. Alumni award U. Kans., 1968, Krumbein medal Internat. Assn. Math. Geologists, 1986, U. Wis.-Madison Disting. Alumni award, 2003. Fellow Geol. Soc. Am.; mem. Am. Assn. Petroleum Geologists (Levorsen award 1970, Disting. Svc. award 1987, Disting. Edn. award Pacific sect. 1999, 2001). Republican. Home: 683 Salvatierra St Stanford CA 94305-8539 Office Phone: 650-723-3365. Business E-Mail: harbaugh@pangea.stanford.edu.

HARBER, M(ICHAEL) ERIC, manager, management consultant; b. Tulsa, Okla., Nov. 14, 1965; s. Charles C. and Joyce F. (Allen) H.; m. Alyson Kelley, Sept. 1, 1990. Student, Oxford U., 1987; BS in Indsl. Engring. and Mgmt., Stanford U., 1988; postgrad., Duke U. Cert. in systems integration. Rsch. asst. Amoco Rsch. Ctr., Tulsa, 1985; quality control and design asst. Nutter engring. divsn. Patterson-Kelly, Tulsa, 1986; indsl. engring. coop. intern space systems divsn. Gen. Dynamics, San Diego, 1987; indsl. engring. cons. Hewlett-Packard, Cupertino, Calif., 1988; mgmt. assoc., asst. mgr. backcards divsn. Citicorp, San Mateo, Calif., 1988-90; sr. mgmt. analyst El Camino Healthcare System, Mountain View, Calif., 1990-94; mgr. consulting divsn. Arthur Andersen, 1994—. Co-chmn., mentor program adv. bd. Silicon Valley Indsl. Engring., Sunnyvale, Calif., 1993-94; spkr., lectr., author in field. Recipient Engr.'s ring Order of Engr., 1993. Mem. NSPE, Inst. Indsl. Engrs. (sr., chpt. pres. 1992-93), Am. Mgmt. Assn., Am. Soc. Quality Control (sr.), Soc. Health Sys., Healthcare Fin. Mgmt. Assn., Soc. Engring. Mgmt. Sys., Calif. Soc. Profl. Engrs., Inst. Mgmt. Cons. Avocations: scuba diving, volleyball, teaching, travel, poetry. Home: 207 Haley House Ln Apex NC 27502-4508

HARBERGER, ARNOLD CARL, economist, educator; b. Newark, July 27, 1924; s. Ferdinand C. and Martha (Bucher) H.; m. Ana Beatriz Valjalo, Mar. 15, 1958; children: Paul Vincent, Carl David. Student, Johns Hopkins U., 1941-43; MA, U. Chgo., 1947, PhD, 1950; Doctor honoris causa, U. Tucuman, 1979, Cath. U. Chile, 1988, Tech. U. Cen. Am., 1989, U. Francisco Marroquin, 2004. Asst. prof. polit. economy Johns Hopkins U., 1949-53; asso. prof. econs. U. Chgo., 1953-59, prof., 1959—, chmn. dept., 1964-71, 75-80, Gustavus F. and Ann M. Swift disting. svc. prof., 1977-91, prof. emeritus, 1991—, dir. Ctr. Latin Am. Econ. Studies, 1965-92. Vis. prof. MIT (Ctr. Internat. Studies), New Delhi, 1961-62, Econ. Devel. Inst., IBRD, 1965, Harvard U., 1971-72, Princeton U., 1973-74, UCLA, 1983, 84, U. Paris, 1986; prof. econs. UCLA, 1984—; cons. IMF, 1950, 89, 2002-05, U.S. Pres.'s Materials Policy Commn., 1951-52, U.S. Treasury Dept., 1961-75, Com. Econ. devel., 1961-78, Planning Commn., India, 1961-62, 73, Pan Am. Union, 1962-76, Dept. State, 1962-76, Cen. Bank, Chile, 1965-70, Dominican Republic, 1989, China, 1995, Ecuador, 1996, Planning Dept., Panama, 1963-77, Colombia, 1969-71, Nicaragua, 1990, Indonesia, 1997—2001; cons. Ford Found., 1967-77, Planning Commn., El Salvador, 1973-75, Budget and Planning Office, Uruguay, 1974-75, Can. Dept. Regional Econ. Expansion, 1975-77, Econ. Min. Argentina, 1994-2000, Fin. Ministry, Bolivia, 1976, Mex., 1976—; cons. Can. Dept. Employment and Migration, 1980-82, Indonesian Ministry Fin., 1981-82, 86, 97-2000, Can. Dept. Fin., 1982-88, Can. Dept. Industry, Sci. and Tech., 1991-99, Chinese Ministry Fin., 1983; ministry fin., Malawi, 1988, Venezuela, 1989, Colombia, 1991, 94, 2002, Dominican Republic, 1996, 97, Egypt, 2002; mem. internat. adv. coun. Inst. Internat. Studies, Stanford U., 1991-99; v.p., chmn. adv. coun. Inst. for Policy Reform; cons. Office Econ. Adviser to the Pres. Russia, 2000-04. *In 2005 he completed 56 years of graduate teaching in economics. His students have made notable contributions both in the academic world and in public policy formation. Over a dozen have been rectors or presidents of universities, and literally scores have been economics deans or department heads. In economic policymaking, over a dozen have been heads of their countries central banks, and over thirty have been cabinet ministers (secretaries). In Latin America, and especially in Chile, Argentina and Mexico, his former students have been important leaders in the liberalization and modernization of economic policy.* Author: Project Evaluation, 1972, Taxation and Welfare, 1974; editor: Demand for Durable Goods, 1960, The Taxation of Income from Capital, 1968, Key Problems of Economic Policy In Latin America, 1970, World Economic Growth, 1985, (with Glenn P. Jenkins) Cost-Benefit Analysis, 2002; contbr. sci. papers to profl. jours. and govt. publs. With AUS, 1943-46. Guggenheim fellow; Fulbright scholar; faculty rsch. fellow Social Sci. Rsch. Coun.; Ford Found. faculty rsch. fellow, 1968-69. Fellow Econometric Soc., Am. Acad. Arts and Scis., Am. Econ. Assn. (mem. exec. com. 1970-72, v.p. 1992, pres.-elect 1996, pres. 1997, disting. fellow 1999), Western Econ. Assn. (v.p. 1987-88, pres. 1989-90), Royal Econ. Soc., Nat. Tax Assn. (Holland medal 2001), NAS, Phi Beta Kappa. Home: 136 Buckskin Rd Bell Canyon CA 91307-1125 Office: UCLA PO Box 951477 405 Hilgard Ave Los Angeles CA 90095-1477 Office Phone: 310-825-1011. Business E-Mail: harberger@econ.ucla.edu.

HARBERT, BILL LEBOLD, retired construction corporation executive; b. Indianola, Miss., July 21, 1923; s. John Murdock and Mae (Schooling) H.; m. Mary Joyce Patrick, June 28, 1952; children: Anne Harbert Moulton, Elizabeth Harbert Cornay, Billy L., Jr. BS, Auburn U., 1948; Advanced Mgmt. Program, Harvard U., 1966. Lic. profl. engr. and land surveyor, Ala. Exec. v.p. Harbert Constrn. Corp., Birmingham, Ala., 1948-79, pres., 1979-81; pres., COO Harbert Internat., Inc., Birmingham, 1981-90, vice-chmn., 1990-91, pres., chmn. bd., 1991-98; pres., chmn. bd. dirs. Bill Harbert Internat. Constrn., Inc., 1992—, chmn., CEO, 1998-99; ret., 1999. Trustee, co-chmn. Laborers Nat. Pension Fund, Dallas, 1968-2001; bd. dirs. U. Ala. Health Svc. Found., Birmingham, 1983-95, Met. Devel. Bd. of Birmingham, 1980-83, AMI Brookwood Med. Ctr., 1990—, Internat. Pipe Line Contractors Assn., 1980, 88, 93-94, 98, 2d v.p., 1999-2000, Comprehensive Cancer Ctr.-U. Ala., Birmingham, 1999-2000, SouthTrust Corp., 1979-1996. Sgt. U.S. Army, 1943-46. Mem. Birmingham Area C. of C., Vestavia Country Club (pres. 1971), Riverchase Country Club (pres. 1980). Methodist. Home: 205 Vestavia Cir Birmingham AL 35216-1351

HARBERT, CHARLES ARMON, retired pharmaceutical executive, chemist, writer; b. Indpls., Apr. 7, 1940; s. Charles Homer and Ruth Laura (Griffey) H.; m. Kay Louise Strode, Sept. 9, 1961; children: Kelle Harbert Moley, Jennifer Ruth. BS, U. Colo., 1962; PhD, U. Mo., 1967. NIH postdoctoral fellow Stanford U., 1967—69; rsch. scientist Pfizer Ctrl. Rsch., Groton, Conn., 1969-72, project leader, 1972-76, mgr., 1976-81, dir., 1981-84, exec. dir., 1984-91, sr. exec. dir., 1991-93, v.p., 1993—99; ret., 1999. Co-chair Keystone Symposium, 1995; mem. adv. com. U. Mo. Chemistry Dept., Columbia, Mo., 1992-99; mem. vis. com. Conn. Coll., New London, 1986, 93; chair medicinal chemistry Gordon Rsch. Conf., New London, 1990. Mem. Bd. Edn., Waterford, Conn., 1979-81, Bd. Fin. Waterford, 1977-78, Bd. Tax Review, Waterford, 1975-77. NIH Postdoctoral fellow NIH, Stanford, 1967-69; recipient Disting. Alumni award U. Mo., 1993. Mem. Am. Chem. Soc. (awards com. med. chem. divsn. 1994-99, Team Innovation award 2005), Phi Lambda. Achievements include inventor/patents including conformational mapping of dopmaine receptor for antagonists; co-inventor Zoloft.

HARBERT, GUY MORLEY, JR., retired obstetrician, gynecologist; b. Fredericksburg, Va., Dec. 19, 1929; s. Guy Morley and Hannah (Turman) H.; m. Peggy Ann Simpson, Sept. 8, 1951; children— Lucille Hannah, Guy Morley, III, Michael Simpson. BA, U. Va., 1952, MD, 1956. Diplomate: Am. Bd. Ob-Gyn (maternal-fetal medicine). Intern Barnes Hosp., St. Louis, 1956-57; resident in ob-gyn U. Va. Hosp., 1959-63; med. faculty U. Va. Med. Sch., 1963—, prof. ob-gyn, 1976-95, prof. emeritus, 1995. Mem. human embryology and devel. study sect. NIH, 1975-79 Author articles in profl. jours., chpts. in books. Served as officer M.C. USAF, 1957-59. Mem. Soc. Gynecol. Investigation (exec. council 1973-76), Perinatal Research Soc. (exec. council 1977-79), So. Perinatal Assn. (exec. council 1974-77), Am. Gynecol. Soc., Am. Assn. Obstetricians and Gynecologists, N.Y. Acad. Scis., Am. Coll. Obstetricians and Gynecologists, Assn. Profs. Ob-Gyn, S. Atlantic Assn. Obstetricians and Gynecologists, Sigma Xi. Presbyterian. Office: U Va Hosps Jefferson Park Ave Charlottesville VA 22908-0001

HARBERT, TED (EDWARD W. HARBERT III), broadcast executive; m. Susan Harbert; children: Emily, William. Degree in comm., Boston U., 1977. Prodr. news dept. WHDH Radio, Boston, 1976—77; feature film coord. ABC Entertainment, 1977—79, feature film and late night programming supr., 1979, asst. to v.p. of program planning and scheduling, 1979—81, dir. program planning and scheduling, 1981—83, v.p. program planning and scheduling, 1983, v.p. of motion pictures, 1986—87, v.p. of motion pictures and scheduling, 1987—88, v.p. prime time, 1988—89, exec. v.p. prime time, 1989—93, pres., 1993—96, chmn., 1996—97; prodr. DreamWorks TV, 1997—99; pres. NBC Studios, 1999—2003; prodr. 20th Century Fox TV, 2003—04; pres., CEO E!Networks, 2004—. Mem. dean's adv. bd. U. So. Calif. Sch. of Theater, Film and TV; mem. TV adv. coun. U. So. Calif. Sch. of Cinema-TV; exec. com. Boston U. Sch. Comm.; bd. govs. UCLA Ctr. for Comm. Policy; bd. dirs. Friends of the LA Free Clinic. Recipient Disting. Alumni Award, Boston U., 1999. Office: E!Networks 5670 Wilshire Blvd Los Angeles CA 90036

HARBIN, CALVIN EDWARD, retired educator; b. Puxico, Mo., Mar. 26, 1916; s. Samuel Wesley and Ada Maria (Shelton) H.; m. Dorothy Comoh, June 26, 1947; chilren: Maria, Ruth, Charles. BS, S.E. Mo. State U., 1949; MA, Peabody-Vanderbilt U., 1949; EdD, U. Mo., 1952; LLD (hon.), Rio Grande Coll., 1976. Prof., dean Ft. Hays State U., Hays, Kans., 1952-81; cons. faculty mem. U.S. Army Command and Gen. Staff Coll., Ft. Leavenworth, Kans., 1968-72. Counselor Hansen Found., Logan, Kans., 1981—. Author: Teaching Power, 1967; co-author (with Dane and Polly Bales): Kate Hansen, Beloved Teacher, America's Cultural Ambassador to Japan, 1999, Grandest Mission on Earth, 2000; contbr. articles to profl. jours.; composer hymns. Col. U.S. Army, 1941-76, ETO. Mem. SAR. Republican. Presbyterian. Avocations: gardening, writing, senior citizen's organizations. Home: 303 W 19th St Hays KS 67601-3116

HARBISON, ED, state legislator, broadcast journalist, motivational speaker; b. Prattville, Ala., Aug. 25, 1941; m. Cecilia Harbison; children: Edward, Ladena. Grad., Career Acad. Sch. Broadcasting, 1969, Troy (Ala.) State U. Broadcast journalist, pub. rels. cons., Columbus, Ga., 1994—; mem. Ga. Senate, Atlanta, 1993—, also mem. def. and vets. affairs com., mem. ethics com., mem. reapportionment com., mem. ethics and corrections coms., banking and fin. instns. com., health and human svcs. com. Ins. and Label Panel in Senate, Second v.p. Muscogee County Sch. Bd., Columbus, 1985—; former mem. Columbus Charter Rev. Commn., Mayor's Com. for Drug-Free Columbus, Community Task Force on Gangs, Columbus Cable TV Study Commn.; grad. Leadership Columbus, 1990; bd. dirs. A.J. McClung YMCA; chmn. Ga. Legis. Black Caucus, 2003—. Sgt. USMC, 1963-67. Recipient numerous awards for profl. accomplishments and community svc., including Dr. John W. Townsend award, ann. award for best regularly scheduled TV newscast AP, PUSH Excellence award, award of support Bambino League, honored by Alpha Kappa Alpha, citation NAACP, 1989, award for outstanding contbns. to African-Ams., Columbus Times, Outstanding Man of Yr. award Men's Progressive Club, 1994; named One of 50 Most Influential African-Ams. in Columbus, Phenix City, Ft. Benning, Ga., Among 50 Most Influential African Am. in Ga., Ga. Forum Newspaper, 2004. Mem. Ga. Assn. Newscasters (former officer). Democrat. Mem. African-Methodist-Episcopal Ch. Home: PO Box 1292 Columbus GA 31902-1292 Office Phone: 706-571-0400.

HARBISON, JAMES WESLEY, JR., lawyer; b. Mooresville, N.C., Aug. 30, 1934; s. James Wesley and Ola Mae (Bonney) H.; m. Margaret Geddes Morgan, Apr. 15, 1961; children: Anne, James. AB, Duke U., 1956; LLB, Yale U., 1959. Bar: N.C. 1959, N.Y. 1960, U.S. Dist. Ct. (so. and ea. dists.) N.Y. 1961, U.S. Ct. Appeals (2d cir.) 1962, U.S. Supreme Ct. 1968, U.S. Ct. Appeals (7th cir.) 1970, U.S. Ct. Appeals (5th cir.) 1975. Assoc. Simpson, Thacher & Bartlett, N.Y.C., 1960-73; ptnr. Wickes, Riddell, Bloomer, Jacobi & McGuire, N.Y.C., 1973-78, Morgan, Lewis & Bockius LLP, N.Y.C., 1979—. Served to capt. USAF, 1959-60, N.Y. A.N.G., 1960-68. Mem. ABA, N.C. Bar Assn., N.Y. State Bar Assn., Assn. of Bar of City of N.Y., Fed. Bar Council, Am. Judicature Soc. Clubs: Met., Yale (N.Y.C.). Democrat. Methodist. Home: 30 E End Ave New York NY 10028-7053 Office: Morgan Lewis & Bockius LLP 101 Park Ave Fl 44 New York NY 10178-0060 Office Phone: 212-309-6090.

HARBISON, JOHN, composer; b. Orange, N.J., Dec. 20, 1938; m. Mary Rose Harbison. BA, Harvard U., 1960; MFA, Princeton U., 1963; studied composition with Boris Blacher, Berlin; Roger Sessions and Earl Kim Choth, Princeton U.; hon. degree, New Eng. Conservatory, 1995. Instr. MIT, 1969-82; condr. Cantata Singers, 1969-73, 80-82, L.A. Philharm., The Boston Symphony, Speculum Musicae; creative chair St. Paul Chamber Orch., 1990—92. Composer-in-residence Pitts. Sympnony, L.A. Philharmonic, The Tanglewood, Santa Fe Chamber Festivals, Am. Acad., Rome., Aspen Music Festival, Ojai Music Festival, Calif., 1991; former music dir. Cantata Singers, Boston; instr. CalArts, Boston U.; prin. guest condr. Emmanuel Music; guest condr. Seattle Symphony, 2003. Composer: (operas) The Winter's Tale, 1974, Full Moon in March, 1977; (ballets) Ulysses' Raft, 1983, Ulysses' Bow, 1983; (symphonies/orchestral) Sinfonia, 1963, Diotima, 1976, Descant-Nocturne, 1976, Piano Concerto, 1978, Violin Concerto, 1978-80, Snow Country, 1979, Symphony No. 1, 1981, Deep Potomac Bells, 1983, Concerto for Clarinet, Oboe, and Strings, 1985, Remembering Gatsby: A Foxtrot for Orchestra, 1986, Symphony No. 2, 1987, Concerto for Double Brass Choir and Orchestra, 1988, Concerto for Viola and Orchestra, 1989, Symphony No. 3, 1990; (chamber/instrumental) Duo, 1961, Verses, 1964, Confinement, 1965, Four Preludes, 1967, Serenade, 1968, Parody-Fantasia, 1968, Piano Trio, 1969, Bermuda Triangle, 1970, Die kurze, 1970, Amazing Grace, 1972, Quintet for Woodwinds, 1979, Organum for Paul Fromm, 1981, Piano Quintet, 1981, Variations, 1982, Exequiem for Calvin Simmons, 1982, Overture: Michael Kohlhaas, 1982, String Quartet No. 1, 1985, Twlight Music, 1985, Four Songs of Solitude, 1985, Music for Eighteen Winds, 1986, Christmas Concerto, 1987, String Quartet No. 2, 1987, Piano Sonata, 1987, Magnum mysterium, 1988, Two Choral Preludes, 1988, Fantasy Duo, 1988, November 19, 1828, 1989; (vocal/choral) Autumnal, 1965, Shakespeare Series, 1965, Music, 1966, Five Songs of Experience on Poems of William Blake, 1971, Elegiac Songs, 1974, Book of Hours and Seasons, 1975, Moments of Vision, 1975, Three Harp Songs, 1975, The Flower-fed Buffaloes, 1976, Samuel Chapter, 1978, Nunc dimittis, 1980, Motetti di Montale, 1980, Mirabai Songs, 1982, The Flight into Egypt, 1986 (Pulitzer Prize for music 1988), The Natural World, 1987, The Three Wise Men, 1988, Simple Daylight, 1988, Words from Paterson, 1989; commissions include Balt. Symphony, the Juilliard String Quartet, The Met. Opera, 1999. Paine travelling fellow Harvard U., Guggenheim fellow, 1978, MacArthur fellow, 1989; recipient Kennedy Ctr. Friedheim award, 1980, Heinz award for the arts and humanities, 1998, Harvard Arts medal, 2000, Letter of Distinction, Am. Music Ctr., 2000, Disting. Composer award Am. Composer's Orch., 2002. Mem. Am. Acad. and Inst. of Arts and Letters, 1992. Office: 479 Franklin St Cambridge MA 02139-3115

HARBISON, STEVEN KENT, communications executive, consultant; b. Fayetteville, NC, July 16, 1956; s. James Albert and Billie Jean (Mason) Harbison; m. Sarah Ingles Jones, June 29, 1985; children: Annie O'Keefe, Quincy Marshall, John Mason. AA in Social Sci., Hiawassee Coll., Madisonville, Tenn., 1976; BS in Mass Media, Mid-Tenn. State U., 1979; degree in newspaper mgmt., Northwestern U., 1992. Photographer, reporter Monroe County Observer, Madisonville, 1974-77; campus police patrolman Mid-Tenn. State U., Murfreesboro, 1978-79; owner Harbison Comml. Photography, Nashville, 1979-85; mgr. prodn., press quality Greeneville (Tenn.) Sun, 1985-87, v.p., gen. mgr., 2002—; dir. mktg. Bus. Jour. Upper East Tenn. and S.W. Va., Johnson City, Tenn., 1987-88, publ., gen. mgr., 1988-93; v.p. spl. projects Jones Media, Inc., Greeneville, 1993—. Mem. gov.'s adv. coun. Tenn. Film Establishment, Nashville, 1998—. Active Greeneville Leadership, 1996—97; bd. dirs. N.E. Tenn. Twp., Tri-Cities, 1996—97; mem. E. Tenn. State U. Found.; bd. dirs. Greene County Partnership, mem. presdl. search com.; jr. warden St. James Episc. Ch., Greeneville, 1997—98, sr. warden, 1999—2000; trustee E. Tenn. State U., 1992—95. Mem.: Link Hills Country Club (bd. dirs.), Tri-City Advt. Club (treas. 1990—92), Pioneer Club, Rotary. Avocations: fishing, hiking, reading, piano, photography. Office: Jones Media Inc 121 W Summit St Greeneville TN 37744

HARBORDT, CHARLES MICHAEL, forest products executive; b. Houston, Apr. 8, 1942; s. Charles and Mary Lydia (Shumard) H.; m. Jackie Ward, June 23, 1960; children: Michelle, Katherine, Julie. BS, Stephen F. Austin U., Nacogdoches, Tex., 1963; MS, So. Meth. U., 1965; PhD, Tex. A&M U., 1970. Cert. environ. profl., Nat. Assn. Environ. Profls., Nat. Registry Environ. Profls. Assoc. chemist Texaco, Inc., Bellaire, Tex., 1965-67, sr. chemist, 1970-71; environ. dir. Temple Industries, Diboll, Tex., 1971-75, Temple-Eastex Inc., Diboll, 1975-80, energy, environ. and individual hygiene dir., 1980-90; v.p. Temple-Inland Forest Products Corp., Diboll, 1990—, Temple-Inland, Diboll, 1996-2000. Mem. oper. com. Nat. Coun. Air and Stream Improvement, 1994-2000, chmn. chem. health effects and mgmt., 1994-97; mem. sr. adv. coun. Global Environ. Mgmt. Inst., 1998—. Apptd. Tex. Regional Water Devel. Bd., 1998; v.p. United Fund, Lufkin, Tex., 1976; mem. adminstrn. bd. Lufkin Meth. Ch., chmn. bd. trustees, 1989-91, trustee, 1996—; chmn. career edn. com. Lufkin H.S., 1980-86; trustee Stephen F. Austin U. Found., 1996-99—; bd. dirs. Stephen F. Austin U. Real Estate Found., 1997-99, Bus. Coun. for Sustainable Devel., Gulf of Mexico, 1993—. Robert A. Welch Found. fellow, 1963-65, Stephen F. Austin U. Disting. alumnus, 1994. Fellow Am. Inst. Chemists; mem. Am. Hardboard Assn. (chmn. environ. com. 1982-85, chmn. environ. com. 1983-85), TAPPI, Air Pollution Control Assn., Water Pollution Control Fedn., Diboll Jaycees, Angelina County (Tex.) C. of C. (bus. com. 1979, mem. edn. coun. 1984), Phi Kappa Phi, Phi Lambda Upsilon. Avocations: hunting, photography, reading, travel. Office: Temple Inland Inc PO Drawer N Diboll TX 75941

HARBOUR, PAMELA JONES, lawyer; m. John Harbour; 3 children. BMus, Ind. U., Bloomington, 1981; JD, Ind. U., 1984. Asst. counsel N.Y. State Dept. Trans., Albany, NY; atty. antitrust bur. N.Y. State Atty. Gen., 1987—96, dep. atty. gen. pub. advocacy, 1997—99; ptnr. litig. dept. Kaye Scholer LLP, NY, 1999—2003; commr. Fed. Trade Commn., Washington, 2003—. Recipient Antitrust Section Svc. award, NY State Bar Assn., 2005. Office: Fed Trade Commn 600 Penn Ave NW Washington DC 20580

HARBOUR, TED IRA, lawyer; b. 1957; BS, JD, Tex. Tech. U. Sr. v.p. D.R. Horton, Arlington, Tex., chief legal officer. Mem.: Tex. Bar 1982. Office: DR Horton 1901 Ascension Blvd Ste 100 Arlington TX 76006

HARBUCK, EDWIN CHARLES, insurance agent; b. Shreveport, La., Mar. 5, 1934; s. Charles Adam and Elsie (Owens) H.; m. Delores Threlkeld, June 10, 1955; children: Jonathan S., Edwin Seth, Christopher L., Charles Adam II. BS, Centenary Coll., 1956. CLU. Vice pres., gen. mgr. Harbuck Sporting Goods, Inc., Shreveport, 1958-63; agt. Prudential Ins. Co. of Am., Shreveport, 1963—. Chmn. bd. trustees First Bapt. Ch. Sch., Shreveport, 1978, 98-99; mem. La. State Civil Svc. Commn., 1981-93; chmn. Centenary Coll. Gt. Tchrs. Scholar Campaign, Shreveport, 1992-93; campaign chmn. United Way N.W. La., Shreveport, 1989, pres., 1993; trustee Centenary Coll. La., 1990, vice chmn. bd. trustees, 1999—; v.p. La. Civil Svc. League, 1994—. Recipient Monte M. Lemann Pub. Svc. award La. Civil Svc. League, New Orleans, 1985, Clyde E. Fant Meml. award for Cmty. Svc., 1994; named Shreveport Outstanding Young Man, Jaycees, 1962, Outstanding Young Men in Am., U.S. Jaycees, Washington, 1970. Mem. Chartered Life Underwriters (pres. Shreveport chpt. 1976), Tax Inst. Arklatex, Estate Planning Coun., Million Dollar Roundtable (life), Shreveport Club, Pierremont Oaks Tennis Club. Methodist. Avocations: tennis, hunting, fishing, scuba diving. Home: 4364 Richmond Ave Shreveport LA 71106-1418 Office: Harbuck & Ridley LLC 400 Travis St Ste 808 Shreveport LA 71101-3112 Business E-Mail: edharbuck@harbuckridley.com.

HARCOURT, BERNARD E., law educator; b. NYC, Jan. 28, 1963; AB in Politics, Princeton U., 1984; JD cum laude, Harvard U., 1989, PhD in Polit. Sci., 2000. Bar: NY 1989, DC 1990, Ala. 1991, Mass. 1996. Law clk. to Hon. Charles S. Haight, Jr. US Dist. Ct. So. Dist. NY, 1989—90; trial and appellate atty. Equal Justice Initiative, Montgomery, Ala., 1990—94; sr. fellow grad. program Harvard U., 1995—97; assoc. prof. law U. Ariz., 1998—2003, assoc. prof. philosophy, 1998—2003, dir. Rogers Program on Law, Philosophy and Social Inquiry, 1998—2003; prof. law U. Chgo. Law Sch., 2003—, faculty dir. academic affairs, 2003—. Vis. prof. law Harvard U., 2001—02, NYU, 2002—03. Author: Illusion of Order: The False Promise of Broken-Windows Policing, 2001, Language of the Gun: Youth, Crime, and Public Policy, 2005; editor, contbg. author Guns, Crime and Punishment in America, 2003. Office: U Chgo Law Sch 1111 E 60th St Chicago IL 60637 Office Phone: 773-834-4068. E-mail: bharcour@law.uchicago.edu.

HARCOURT, ROBERT NEFF, educational administrator, genealogist, journalist; b. East Orange, NJ, Oct. 19, 1932; s. Stanton Hinde and Mary Elizabeth (Neff) H. BA, Gettysburg Coll., 1958; MA, Columbia U., 1961. Cert guidance, secondary edn., career and vocational guidance, N.Mex. Social case worker N.J. State Bd. Child Welfare, Newark and Morristown, 1958-61; asst. registrar Hofstra U., 1961-62; asst. to evening dean of students CCNY, 1961-62; housing staff U. Denver, 1962-64; fin. aid and placement dir. Inst. Am. Indian Arts, Santa Fe, 1965-95, contract cons., 1999, apptd. by coll. pres. to steering com., 2000, nat. capital campaign; appointed by corp. pres. to adv. bd. Genre Ltd. Art Pubs., L.A., 1986—; nat. color ad participant The Bradford Exchange, Chgo., 1986—. Truman scholar coord. Donor Am. Indian Libr. collection Gettysburg (Pa.) Coll.; active Santa Fe Civic Chorus, 1977-78, art judge Aspen Fundraiser Nat. Mus. Am. Indian, 1993-94, vol. Inst. for Preservation Original Langs. Am. With U.S. Army, 1954-56. Decorated Nat. Def. medal, 1970; named Hon. Okie, Gov. Dewey F. Bartlett; postmasters fellow U. Denver, 1962-64, col. a.d.c. to N.Mex. Gov. David F. Cargo, 1970; recipient disting. Alumni award Gettysburg Coll. Alumni Assn., 1995. Mem. Am. Contract Bridge League (exec. bd., Santa Fe unit, silver life master, former dist. 17 rep., video presenter 2004-05), SAR, Santa Fe Coun. Internat. Rels., Am. Assn. Counseling and Devel., New England Historic Geneal. Soc., Assn. Specialists in Group Work, Adult Student Pers. Assn., Southwestern Assn. Indian Affairs, Neff Family Hist. Soc., Gen. Soc. Mayflower Descs. (bd. assts. N.Mex. chpt.), Pilgrim John Howland Soc., Upson Family Assn., Order of the Founders and Patriots of Am. (regional counselor), Mil. Order of the Loyal Legion of the U.S., Mil. Order Fgn. Wars of U.S., Gen. Soc. of War of 1812, Nat. Soc. Sons and Daus. of the Pilgrims, Soc. Descs. Washington's Army at Valley Forge, Presdl. Families Am. (N.Mex. regent), Order of the Families of the Pres.'s and First Ladies of Am., Soc. of Des. of the Colonial Clergy through Rev. John Lathropp, Decs. Colonial Physicians and Chirurgiens, The Winthrop Soc., First Families Conn., Frontier Families Conn., Phi Delta Kappa (past mem. exec. bd. local chpt.), Alpha Tau Omega, Alpha Phi Omega, Safari Club Internat Home: 2980 Viaje Pavo Real Santa Fe NM 87505-5344

HARCROW, E. EARL, lawyer; b. Carrizozo, N.Mex., Mar. 4, 1954; s. James Earl and Nettie (McInnes) H.; m. Julie A., Apr. 16, 1987; children: Ashley Nicole, James Earl. BS, Tex. Tech. U., 1976, JD, 1979. Bar: Tex. 1979, U.S. Dist. Ct. (no. dist.) Tex., U.S. Ct. Appeals (5th cir.) 1979. Asst. dist. atty. Lubbock (Tex.) Dist. Atty. Office, 1979-80, Tarrant Dist. Atty. Office, Ft. Worth, 1980-83; ptnr. Shannon, Gracey, Ratliff & Miller, Ft. Worth, 1985-99, mng. ptnr., 1995-96, ptnr. in charge of tech., 1996-99; ptnr. Haynes & Boone, Ft. Worth, 1999—; gen. counsel Dallas Ft. Worth Med. Ctr., 1990—99. Bd. dirs. Planned Parenthood North Tex., 1987-92; fellow Tex. Bar Found., 1991—. Office: Haynes and Boone LLP 201 Main St Ste 2200 Fort Worth TX 76102-3126 Office Phone: 817-346-6646. Business E-Mail: earl.harcrow@haynesboone.com.

HARDAGE, PAGE TAYLOR, elementary school educator; b. Richmond, Va., June 27, 1944; d. George Peterson and Gladys Odell (Gordon) Taylor; 1 child, Taylor Brantley. AA, Va. Intermont Coll., Bristol, 1964; BS, Richmond Profl. Inst., 1966; MPA, Va. Commonwealth U., Richmond, 1982. Cert. tchr., Va. Competent toastmaster, dir. play therapy svcs. Med. Coll. Va. Hosps., Va. Commonwealth U., Richmond, 1970-90; dir. Inst. Women's Issues, Va. Commonwealth U., U. Va., Richmond, 1986-91; adminstr. Scottish Rite Childhood Lang. Ctr. at Richmond, Inc., 1991-99. Bd. dirs. Richmond Bus. Coun. Math. and Sci. Ctr. Found., Richmond, Emergency Med. Svcs. Adv. Bd., Richmond. Treas. Richmond Black Student Found., 1989—90, Leadership Metro Richmond Alumni Assn.; group chmn. United Way Greater Richmond, 1987; bd. dirs. Maggie L. Walker Hist. Found., Richmond YWCA, 1989—91, Capital Area Health Adv. Coun.; commr. Mayors Commn. of Concerns of Women, City of Richmond. Mem.: ASPA, NAFE, Va. Assn. Fund Raising Execs., Va. Recreation and Park Soc. (bd. dirs.), Internat. Mgmt. Coun. (exec. com.), Adminstrv. Mgmt. Soc., Rotary Club of Hanover. Unitarian Universalist. Avocations: bridge, target shooting, aerobics.

HARDAWAY, ERNEST, II, oral and maxillofacial surgeon, public health service officer; BS, Howard U., 1957, DDS, 1966, cert. in oral and maxillofacial surgery, 1972; MPH, Johns Hopkins U., 1973. Intern, then chief resident oral and maxillofacial surgery Howard U. Med. Ctr., Washington, 1969-72; asst. prof., mem. attending staff Howard U. Coll. Medicine and Med. Ctr., Washington, 1974—; with Bur. Quality Assurance, HHS, Washington, 1974-77; various adminstrv. positions Bur. Med. Services and Health Services Adminstrn., USPHS, 1977-80; dep. commr., then commr. pub. health City of Washington, 1982-84; acting v.p. fin. and adminstrv. affairs Mile Sq. Health Ctr., Inc., 1984; asst. to regional health adminstr. Fed. Employee Occupl. Health Program, 1985, dir., 1986—89, Chgo. and Kansas City, 1989—90; mem. CFO coun. com. on entrepreneurial govt. Office Mgmt. and Budget, Washington, 1991—2001; chmn. com. on acad. affairs Coll. Bus. U. Ill., 2001—. Profl. staff Com. on Ways and Means, U.S. Ho. of Reps., 1972; spl. asst. to dir. Office Policy Planning and Evaluation, HEW, 1973; presenter in field. Contbr. articles to profl. jours. Mem. D.C. Emergency Med. Care Adv. Com., D.C. Long-Term Planning Group, 1983, D.C. Health Coordinating Council, D.C. Commn. on Homelessness, 1984; mem. adv. bd. Rosemont Health Ctr., 1984; sec. D.C. Commn. on Licensure to Practice Healing Art, 1983; bd. dirs. United Black Fund, 1984, Potomac Valley Myastenia Gravis Found., 1984; mem. com. human rsch. Instnl. Rev. Bd., Chgo., 1994-2001; chmn. com. acad. affairs U. Ill., 2002. Global Community Health fellow HEW, 1971, Louise C. Ball fellow, 1969; recipient Meritorious Service award USPHS, 1982, J.B. Johnson Nursing Ctr. award, 1983, Outstanding Service placque D.C. Village Choir, 1984, Disting. Service cert. Concerned Citizens for Alcohol Abuse, 1984, Whitman-Walker award for AIDS effort, 1984, Exceptional Accomplishment award Regional Health Adminstr., 1987. Fellow Am. Assn. Oral and Maxillofacial Surgeons (ho. of dels. 1977-80), Internat. Coll. Dentistry, Royal Soc. Health, Acad. Dentistry Internat., Am. Coll. Dentistry; mem. ADA (cons. council hosp. dental care 1976-77), D.C. Soc. Oral and Maxillofacial Surgeons (sec.-treas. 1979-81), Nat. Dental Assn. (Dentist of Yr. 1983, 1st ann. Disting. Service award 1984), Omicron Kappa Upsilon, Chi Delta Mu, Sigma Pi Phi. Home: 88 W Schiller St Apt 1204 Chicago IL 60610-2037 Office Phone: 312-213-1265.

HARDAWAY, PENNY (ANFERNEE DEON HARDAWAY), professional basketball player; b. Memphis, July 18, 1972; Grad., Memphis State U. Guard, forward Orlando Magic, Fla., 1993—99, Phoenix Suns, 1999—2004, N.Y. Knicks, 2004—. Mem. Ea. Conf. Champions Orlando Magic, 1994—95, Dream Team III, 1996. Actor: (films) Blue Chips, 1994. Named to 1st team, All Am. Memphis State U., 1992—93, Newcomer of Yr. in the BMC, 1992—93, NBA All-Rookie 1st team, 1993, All-Star team, Ea. Conf., 1994—95, 1995—96, All-NBA 1st team, 1995; recipient Nat. H.S. Player of Yr. award, Paracle Mag., 1990—91. Achievements include being honored by retiring of Jersey at Memphis State U., 1994. Office: c/o New York Knickerbockers 2 Pennsylvanyia Plaza New York NY 10121

HARDAWAY, ROBERT MORRIS, III, retired surgeon; b. Camp John Hay, The Philippines, Jan. 9, 1916; s. Robert Morris and Olive (Gray) Hardaway; m. Lee H. Harkey, June 12, 1939; children: Robert Morris IV, Elizabeth J., Thomas G. II, Christopher L. AB, U. Denver, 1936; postgrad., U. Colo. Med. Sch., 1935-37; MD, Washington U., St. Louis, 1939. Diplomate Am. Bd. Surgery. Commd. 1st lt., M.C. U.S. Army, 1939, advanced through grades to brig. gen., 1970; ward officer, surg. svc. Fitzsimons Gen. Hosp., Denver, 1940-41, resident surgery, 1949-50; ward officer, surg. svc. N. Sector Gen. Hosp., Hawaii, 1941-43; tchr. Med. Field Service Sch., Carlysle Barracks, Pa., 1943-45; surg. trainee Nichols Gen. Hosp., Louisville, 1945-46; resident surgery Madigan Gen. Hosp., Tacoma, 1946-47; chief surg. service 34th Gen. Hosp., Republic of Korea, 1947-49, Sta. Hosp., Ft. Belvoir, Va., 1950-54; chief surg. svc. 97th Gen. Hosp., Frankfurt, Germany, 1954-58, comdg. officer, 1967-70; chief surg. service Martin Army Hosp., Ft. Benning, Ga., 1958-60; dir. divsn. surgery Walter Reed Army Inst. Rsch., Washington, 1960-67; comdg. gen. William Beaumont Army Med. Ctr., El Paso, 1970-75; prof. surgery Tex. Tech U. Sch. Medicine, El Paso, 1976—2002; staff R.E. Thomason Gen. Hosp., El Paso, 1975—2002; ret., 2002. Author: Syndromes of Disseminated Intravascular Coagulation, 1966, Clinical Management of Shock, Surgical and Medical, 1968, Capillary Perfusion in Health and Disease, 1981, Shock-the Reversible Stage of Dying, 1988, Treatment of Wounded in Vietnam, 1988, Blood Problems in Critical Care, 1989; contbr. articles to profl. jours. Decorated Legion of Merit with oak leaf cluster, DSM; recipient 2d prize for exhbn., AMA, 1964, Silver award exhibit, Am. Soc. Clin. Pathologists-Coll. Am. Pathologists, 1964, cert. of Outstanding Achievement, U.S. Army Sci. Conf., 1964. Fellow: ACS, Microcirculation Assn., Am. Assn. Surgery Trauma, Am. Coll. Angiology; mem.: AMA, Assn. Mil. Surgeons U.S., Alpha Omega Alpha. Episcopalian. Achievements include research in intravascular coagulation and hemorrhagic shock. Personal E-mail: hardawayiii@juno.com. *Nothing we know, (or think we know) is the ultimate truth.*

HARDBERGER, PHILLIP DUANE, mayor, judge, lawyer, journalist; b. Morton, Tex., July 27, 1934; s. Homer Reeves and Bess (Scott) H.; m. Linda Morgan, May 1968; children: Amy, Kimberlea Jones BA, Baylor U., 1955; MS, Columbia U., 1960; LL.B., Georgetown U., 1965. Reporter Waco (Tex.) News Tribune, 1952-54; press rep. Tex. Baptist Conv., 1958-59; assoc. editor Mil. Pub. Inst., N.Y.C., 1961; exec. sec. Peace Corps, 1962-66; spl. asst. to dir. OEO, 1967-68; trial lawyer, 1968-94; chief justice Fourth Ct. of Appeals, State of Tex., San Antonio, 1994—2003; mayor City of San Antonio, San Antonio, 2005—. Author: Texas Courtroom Evidence, Texas Workers' Compensation Trial Manual; contbr. articles to profl. jours. Served to capt. USAF, 1955-58. Home: 319 W Hollywood Ave San Antonio TX 78212-2211 Office: City Hall Office PO Boc 839966 San Antonio TX 78283-3966 Business E-Mail: phardberger@wt.net.

HARDEN, ANITA JOYCE, nurse; b. Jackson, Tenn., May 17, 1947; d. Percy Lawrence and Marjorie (Robinson) H.; 1 child, Brian Robinson Weir. BSN, Ind. U., 1968, MBA, 1989; MSN, Ind. U.-Purdue U., Indpls., 1973. Staff nurse Indpls. Hosps., 1968-71; instr. Ind. U. Sch. Nursing, 1973-75; dir. continuing care Gallahue Mental Health Ctr., Indpls., 1975-80; mgr. psychiatry Cmty. Hosp., Indpls., 1980-87, product line mgr. for psychiat. and mental health svcs., 1986—; dir. psychiat. svcs. Cmty. Hosp. North, 1987-89, v.p., 1990-94; exec. dir. mental health svcs. Cmty. Hosps. of Ind., Inc., 1989-90; exec. dir. mental health St. Vincent-Cmty. Health Network, 1994-96; exec. dir. behavioral care svcs. Cmty. Hosps. Indpls., 1996-2001, v.p. behavioral health, 2001—03; pres. Cmty. Hosp. East, 2003—. Clin. asst. prof. Ind. U., 1977-82, clin. assoc. prof., 1982—; clin. assoc., trainer Suicide Prevention Svc., Indpls., 1974-77; chmn. adv. bd. de-institutionalization project Cen. State Hosp., Indpls., 1978-79; bd. dirs. Safe Sitter, Behavioral Sys. LLC, InteCare Contbr. articles to profl. jours. Mem. Ind. County Cmty. Mental Health Ctr., 1979-80; bd. dirs. Marion County Mental Health Assn., Indpls. Zoo; bd. dirs. Alternatives in Madison County, Jackson-Peoples Living Ctr. Recipient Outstanding Achievement in Professions award Ctr. Leadership Devel., 1981, Clin. Excellence award Ind. U. Sch. Nursing, 1989. Mem. Ind. U. Alumni Assn., Christian Women's Fellowship, 500 Festival Assocs., Greater Indpls. Orgn. Nurse Execs. (v.p.), Coalition 100 Black Women (bd. dirs.), Neal-Marshall Aumni Club, Alpha Kappa Alpha, Sigma Theta Tau, Chi Eta Phi. Mem. Christian Ch. Home: 7607 Newport Bay Dr Indianapolis IN 46240-3370 Office: 7150 Clearvista Dr Indianapolis IN 46256-1695 Office Phone: 317-355-5526. Business E-Mail: aharden@ecommunity.com.

HARDEN, BLAINE CHARLES, journalist; b. Moses Lake, Wash., Apr. 4, 1952; s. Arno E. and Betty (Thoe) H. BA in Polit. Sci. and Philosophy, Gonzaga U., 1974; MA in Journalism, Syracuse U., 1976. Reporter Trenton (N.J.) Times, 1976-78, The Washington Post, 1979-83, Africa corr., 1985-89, Ea. Europe corr., 1989-93, investigative staff, 1994-95, nat. polit. reporter, 1995-96, N.Y. bur. chief, 1997-98; reporter N.Y. Times, N.Y.C., 1999—. Author: Africa: Dispatches from a Fragile Continent, 1990, A River Lost: The Life and Death of the Columbia, 1996. Recipient Livingston award, 1986, non-deadline writing writing award Am. Soc. Newspapers Editors, Washington, 1988, Ernie Pyle award for human interest, 1993; Alicia Patterson rsch. fellow, 1993. Office: NY Times 229 W 43d St New York NY 10036

HARDEN, DANIEL R., secondary school educator; b. L.A., Oct. 18, 1948; s. John P. and Harriett E. Harden; m. Reba Pearl Harden, Oct. 18, 1992; children: Erica Middleton, Kyle John. EdD, Nova Southeastern, Fla., 2004; postgrad., Armstrong Atlantic, Savannah, Georgia, 1995. Tchr. Effingham Co. Schs., Springfield, Ga., 1995—. Cons. in field. Mem.: ASCD. R-Liberal. Personal E-mail: dharden@nova.edu.

HARDEN, JON BIXBY, publishing executive; b. Fitzgerald, Ga., Mar. 7, 1944; s. William Harmon and Mary Bixby (Brewster) H.; m. Lynne Ann Lumsden, May 3, 1986; children: Gregory Ross, Heather Lynne. AAS, Rochester Inst. Tech., 1965; BS, Univ. Rochester, 1967; MBA, U Pa., 1969. Research analyst Doubleday & Co., Inc., N.Y.C., 1969-72, mgr. corp. research, 1972-74, pub. group mgr., 1974-77; dir. bus. devel. McGraw-Hill Book Co., N.Y.C., 1977-80, dir. planning and devel. Internat. div., 1980-84; v.p. corp. devel. and strategic planning Simon & Schuster, Inc., N.Y.C., 1984-85; pres. Dodd, Mead & Co., Inc., N.Y.C., 1985-88; gen. mgr. Romaine Pierson Pubs., Inc., Port Washington, 1988-89; pres. JBH Communications, Inc., 1989—; editor, pub. The Hartford News, Conn., 1989—; pub. Greater Hartford mag., 1996—. Bd. dirs. SCAN Vol. Parents Aids Assn., Inc., 1980—89, v.p., 1985—89; treas. Ancient Burying Ground Assn., 2000—02, v.p., 2002—; bd. dirs. Cmty. Ptnrs. in Action, 2000—; bd. mgrs. West Side YMCA, 1985—89, vice-chmn., 1987—89. Mem. The Hartford Club, The Hartford Golf Club. Home: 16 Oak Ridge Ln West Hartford CT 06107-3505 Office: JBH Comms Inc 99 Hanmer St Ste A Hartford CT 06114-3071 Office Phone: 860-296-6128. Personal E-mail: jonh1@aol.com.

HARDEN, MARCIA GAY, actress; b. LaJolla, Calif., Aug. 14, 1959; m. Thaddaeus D. Scheel, 1996; children: Eulala Grace Scheel, Hudson Harden Scheel, Julitta Dee Harden Scheel. BA in Theatre, U. Tex., 1980; MFA, NYU. Actor: (plays) Simpatico, 1994, Angels in America: Millennium Approaches/A Gay Fantasia on National Themes, 1993 (Tony nomination); (films) The Imagemaker, 1986, Miller's Crossing, 1990, Crush, 1992, Used People, 1992, Safe Passage, 1994, The Spitfire Grill, 1996, The Daytrippers, 1996, Spy Hard, 1996, The First Wives Club, 1996, Far Harbor, 1996, Flubber, 1997, Desperate Measures, 1998, Meet Joe Black, 1998, Curtain Call, 1999, Space Cowboys, 2000, Pollock, 2000 (Acad. award for best supporting actress, N.Y. Film Critics Circle award for best supporting actress), Gaudi Afternoon, 2001, Mystic River, 2003 (Acad. Award nomination for best supporting actress, 2004), Casa de los babys, 2003, Mona Lisa Smile, 2003, Just Like Mona, 2003, Welcome to Mooseport, 2004, Bad News Bears, 2005; (TV films) Kojak: None So Blind, 1990, In Broad Daylight, 1991, Fever, 1991, Sinatra, 1992, Talking with, 1995, Convict Cowboy, 1995, Path to Paradise: The Untold Story of the World Trade Center Bombing, 1997, Labor of Love, 1998, Spenser: Small Vices, 1999, Thin Air, 2000, See You In My Dreams, 2000, From Where I Sit, 2000, Walking Shadow, 2001, King of Texas, 2002, She's Too Young, 2003; (TV series) The Education of Max Bickford, 2001; (TV miniseries) Guilty Hearts, 2002. Office: Creative Artists Agy 9830 Wilshire Blvd Beverly Hills CA 90212-1825*

HARDEN, MARVIN, artist, educator; b. Austin, Tex. s. Theodore R. and Ethel (Sneed) H. BA in Fine Arts, UCLA, 1959, MA in Creative Painting, 1963. Prof. art Calif. State U., Northridge, 1967-97, prof. emeritus, 1997—; Tchr. art Santa Monica City Coll., Calif., 1968; mem. art faculty UCLA Extension, 1964-68; instr. art LA Harbor Coll., Calif., 1965—68. Mem. visual arts fellowship, painting panel NEA, 1985. One-man shows include Ceeje Galleries, LA, 1964, 66, 67, LA City Coll., 1968, Occidental Coll., LA, 1969, Whitney Mus. Am. Art, NYC, 1971, Eugenia Butler Gallery, LA, 1971, Rath Mus., Geneva, Switzerland, 1971, Irving Blum Gallery, LA, 1972, LA Harbor Coll., 1972, David Stuart Galleries, LA, 1975, Coll. Creative Studies, U. Calif., Santa Barbara, 1976, James Corcoran Gallery, LA, 1978, Newport Harbor Art Mus., Survey, 1979, LA Mcpl. Art Gallery, Major Retrospective, 1982, Conejo Valley Art Mus., 1983, Simard Gallery, LA, 1985, The Armory Ctr. for the Arts, Pasadena, Calif., 1994, Ventura (Calif.) Coll. Art Gallery, 1997, Louis Stern Gallery, LA, 1998; group shows include US State Dept. Touring Exhbn., USSR, 1966, Oakland (Calif.) Mus. Art, 1966, UCLA, 1966, Mpls. Inst. Art, 1968, San Francisco Mus. Art, 1969, Phila. Civic Ctr. Mus., 1969, Mus. Art, RI Sch. Design, 1969, NJ State Mus., 1969, Everson Mus. Art, Syracuse, 1969, La Jolla (Calif.) Mus., 1969, 70, High Mus. Art, Atlanta, 1969, Flint (Mich.) Inst. Arts, 1969, Ft. Worth Art Center Mus., 1969, Contemporary Arts Assn., Houston, 1970, U. N.Mex., 1974, U. So. Calif., 1975, Bklyn. Mus., 1977, LA County Mus. Art, 1977, 95, Newport Harbor Art Mus., 1977, Frederick S. Wight Gallery, UCLA, 1978, Cirrus Editions, Ltd., LA, 1979, 81, 82, Franklin Furnace, NYC, 1980, Art Ctr. Coll. Design, LA, 1981, Alternative Mus., NYC, 1981, Laguna Beach Mus. (Calif.), 1982, Cirrus, 1982, LA Inst. Contemporary Art, 1983, Mus. Contemporary Art, Chgo., 1983, Mint Mus., Charlotte, NC, 1983, DeCordova and Dana Mus. and Park, Lincoln, Mass., 1983, Equitable Gallery, NYC, 1984, LA Municipal Art Gallery, 1984, 1985, Cirrus, LA, 1986, 1990, Heal the Bay, Surfboard Art Invitational, 1990, Pasadena Armory Ctr. for the Arts, 1992, Claremont Coll. West Gallery, LA, 1992, Grolier Club, NYC, 1993, Calif. State U., San Luis Obispo, 1994, Cheney Cowles Mus., Spokane, Wash., 1995, Louis Stern Fine Art, LA, 1995, Porter Troup Gallery, San Diego, 1995, Armory Ctr. for the Arts, Pasadena, 1996, 97, Tel Aviv Mus. Art, 1998, Gail Harvey Gallery, Santa Monica, Calif., 1998, Palos Verdes Art Ctr., 1999, LA City Coll., 1999, Davis and Cline Gallery, Ashland, Oreg., 2002, Hunsaker/Schlesinger Fine Art, Santa Monica, 2002, Glendale Coll. Art Gallery, 2002, Davis and Cline, Ashland, Oreg., 2003, Harriet and Charles Luckman Fine Arts Complex, L.A., 2004, Schneider Mus. Art, Ashland, Oreg., 2004; others; represented in permanent collections include Whitney Mus. Am. Art, NYC, Mus. Modern Art, NYC, NY Pub. Libr. Spence Collection, Getty Ctr. for Arts and Humanities, LA County Mus. Art, Atlantic Richfield Co. Corp. Art Coll., Grunwald Ctr. Graphic Arts UCLA, City of LA, Metromedia, Inc., LA, San Diego Jewish Cmty. Ctr., Berkeley (Calif.) U. Mus., Home Savs. & Loan Assn., LA, also pvt. collections. Bd. dir. Images & Issues, 1980-86; mem. artists adv. bd. LA Mcpl. Art Gallery Assn., 1983-86. Recipient UCLA Art Coun. award, 1963, Disting. Prof. award Calif. State U. Northridge, 1984, Exceptional Merit Svc. award Calif. State U. Northridge, 1984; Nat. Endowment Arts fellow, 1972; Awards in Visual Arts fellow, 1983; Guggenheim fellow, 1983. Mem. LA Inst. Contemporary Art (co-founder 1973). Home: Inwardness Ranch PO Box 1793 Cambria CA 93428-1793 Office Phone: 805-238-9163.

HARDEN, MARY LOUISE, human resources consultant, real estate broker, real estate appraiser; b. Natchez, Miss., Mar. 27, 1942; d. John Charles and Dorothy Louise (Reynolds) Brown; m. Billy Gene Redd, Mar. 12, 1957 (div. 1961); children: Andre Ranier, Allison Lawanda, Robin Yvette; m. Percy Lawrence Harden Jr., Aug. 31, 1968; children: Darrell Lawrence, Craig Robison. Student, Ball State U., 1975—76, Ind. U., Purdue U., 1983—88; BSBA, Ind. Wesleyan U., 1989; postgrad., U. S.C., 1990; MA, Ball State U., 1995; grad. in Diversity Leadership, Acad. Greater Indpls., 2003. Editor-in-chief U.S. Army Fin. and Acctg. Ctr., Indpls., 1974-81, pers. mgmt. specialist, 1981-87, pub. affairs officer, 1987-91; pers. mgmt. specialist Def. Fin. and Acctg. Svc., 1991-99; fed. women's program mgr. U.S. Army Fin. and Acctg. Ctr., Indpls., 1981-85; appraiser OAS Land Acquisition Group, Carmel, Ind., 1999—. Minority advisor United Way of Ctrl. Ind., Indpls., 1985—2000; active Ind. Fever Adv. Team, 2001—, Ind. Consortium to Eliminate Achievement Gaps, 2003; bd. dirs. Nat. Coalition of 100 Black Women, Indpls., 1986—, pres., 2002—03, chair nat. program com., 2004—05; bd. dirs. Urban Mission YMCA, 2002—, C.J. Walker Theatre Ctr., 2001—, Madame C.J. Walker, YMCA Greater Indpls., 2005—; exec. bd. Pres.'s Roundtable, 2004—. Named Madame C.J. Walker Outstanding Woman of Yr., Ctr. for Leadership Devel. and Indpls. C. of C., 1988, Sarah Lewis Lifetime Achievement award, United Way Ctrl. Ind., 2003. Fellow: Dept. Def. Exec. Leadership Program; mem.: AARP, Nat. Assn. Ret. Fed. Employees, Am. Soc. Mil. Comptrs., Federally Employed Women. Presbyterian. Avocations: photography, real estate, flea markets, reading.

HARDEN, OLETA ELIZABETH, literature educator, academic administrator; b. Jamestown, Ky., Nov. 22, 1935; d. Stanley Virgil and Myrtie Alice (Stearns) McWhorter; m. Dennis Clarence Harden, July 23, 1966. BA, Western Ky. U., 1956; MA in English, U. Ark., 1958, PhD, 1965. Teaching asst. U. Ark., Fayetteville, 1956-57, 58-59, 61-63; instr. S.W. Mo. State Coll., Springfield, 1957-58, Murray (Ky.) U., 1959-61; asst. prof. English Northeastern State Coll., Tahlequah, Okla., 1963-65; asst. prof. Wichita (Kans.) State U., 1965-66; asst. prof. English Wright State U., Dayton, Ohio, 1966-68, assoc. prof., 1968-72, prof., 1972-93, asst. chmn. English dept., 1967-70, asst. dean, 1971-73, assoc. dean, 1973-74, exec. dir. gen. univ. services, 1974-76, pres. of faculty, 1984-85, prof. emerita, 1993—. Author: Maria Edgeworth's Art of Prose Fiction, 1971, Maria Edgeworth, 1984; editor: The Extension, 1999—. Grantee, Ford Found., 1971. Mem. MLA, AARP (impact alliance leader Ohio, 2001—), AAUP, Coll. English Assn., Women's Caucus for Modern Langs., Am. Conf. for Irish Studies (presenter 1989, 91, 94, 95), Wright State U. Retiree Assn. (pres. 1995-96), Elizabeth McWhorter Harden Forensics Alumni Assn. (founder, pres. We. Ky. U. chpt. 2004—). Office: Wright State U Dept English 7751 Colonel Glenn Hwy Dayton OH 45431-1674 Home: 2618 Big Woods Trl Dayton OH 45431-8704 Office Phone: 937-775-3136. Personal E-mail: oharden@aol.com.

HARDEN, PATRICK ALAN, journalist; b. Twickenham, Eng., Aug. 13, 1936; s. Ernest William and Annie Ceridwen (Jones) H.; m. Connie Marie Graham, Nov. 2, 1963; children: Marc Graham, Ceri Marie. Cert. in journalism, Ealing (Eng.) Tech. Coll., 1957. With UPI, 1960-78, regional exec. London, 1968-69, European picture mgr. London and Brussels, 1969-72, regional exec. Detroit, 1973-75; gen. mgr. UPI Can. Ltd., Montreal, 1976-78, UP Can., Toronto, 1979-82, dir., sec., 1979-82; treas. UPI Can. Ltd.; gen. mgr. Edmonton (Alta.) Sun, 1982-84, pub., 1984-92; v.p. Toronto Sun Pub. Corp., 1989-94; v.p., bur. chief Washington, 1992-94; Washington columnist Toronto Sun Pub. Corp., 1994-97; freelance writer, 1997-98; Washington bur. chief LRP Pubs., Arlington, Va., 1998—. Office Phone: 703-516-7002. E-mail: pharden@lrp.com.

HARDEN, PRESTON LEWIS, computer company executive; b. Atlanta, Feb. 11, 1969; s. Charles Lewis and Sarah Frances Harden. BS in Bus. Mgmt., Clayton State U., 1992. Cons. Parson's Group, Atlanta, 1996—98; from sr. cons. to svcs. exec. Microsoft Corp., Alpharetta, Ga., 1998—2005, svcs. exec., 2005—. Mem.: PMP (assoc.). Home: 3815 Pleasant Oaks Drive Lawrenceville GA 30044 Office: Microsoft Corporation 1125 Sanctuary Parkway - Suite#300 Alpharetta GA 30044 Personal E-mail: prestonharden@hotmail.com.

HARDER, GLENN E., utilities, energy company executive; BS in Mathematics, MBA, Tulane U. CPA. With Arthur Young & Co., New Orleans, 1976—78; various fin. positions including v.p., fin. strategies and treas. Entergy Corp., New Orleans, 1978—94; sr. v.p. fin. services Carolina Power & Light Co., 1994, CFO, exec. v.p. fin. Raleigh, NC, 1995—2000; exec. v.p., CFO Coventor, 2000—02; pres. GEH Advisory Services LLC, 2002—. Bd. dirs. DPL Inc., 2004—. Recipient CFO Excellence award, 1999. Office: DPL 1065 Woodman Dr Dayton OH 45432

HARDER, KELSIE BROWN, retired language educator; b. Pope, Tenn., Aug. 23, 1922; s. Prince William and Belle (MaGee) H.; m. Louise Maron, Oct. 9, 1960; children: Kelsie Terry, Gerald William, Dennis Prince, Frank Maron, Thomas Brown, Ann Leslie, Marcia Louise. BA magna cum laude, Vanderbilt U., 1950, MA, 1951; PhD, U. Fla., 1954. Asst. prof. English Youngstown U., 1954-58, assoc. prof., 1958-60, prof., 1960-64; Fulbright lectr. India, 1962-63; prof. English SUNY, Potsdam, 1964-89, chmn. English and drama depts., 1964-78, chmn. faculty, 1985-89, chmn. governance com. SUNY faculty senate, 1988-91, Disting. Teaching prof., 1989-94, Disting. Prof. English Emeritus, 1994—. Chair Symposium on Contemporary American Fiction, 1995; Fulbright vis. prof. U. Lodz, Poland, 1971-72; cons. Office Edn., Washington, summers 1966, 67, Random House Dictionary of the English Lang., Dictionary of American Reg. English; mem. Com. on Place Name Survey of U.S., SUNY Awards Com., 1976-81; dir. Place Name Survey of U.S., 1988-91. Guest appearances: Cable News Network, stas. WXYZ, WEWS.; Editor: Names, 1966-68, 81-87, Illustrated Dictionary of Place Names: Canada and the United States, 1976, 2d edit., 1985, Favorite Baby Names, 1985, Names and Their Varieties: A Collection of Essays in Onomastics, 1986; mem. adv. bd.: American Speech, 1960-61, 80-81, Unusual and Most Popular Baby Names, 1988; co-editor: A Dictionary of Am. Proverbs, 1992; co-author: Claims to Name, 1993; contbr. articles to profl. jours. Served with AUS, 1944-46. Recipient SUNY Best award, 1989. Mem.: MLA, Eta Sigma Phi, Am. Dialect Soc. (proverbs chmn., usage com.), Internat. Ctr. Onomastics (Belgium), N.Y. Folklore Soc. (exec. com.), Miss. Folklore Soc., Tenn. Folklore Soc., Ohio Folklore Soc. (past pres.), Am. Name Soc. (past exec. sec.-treas., v.p., pres.), Publ. MLA, St. Lawrence County Hist. Assn. (past pres., trustee), Milton Soc. (life), Spenser Soc. (life), Phi Kappa Sigma (counselor), Phi Kappa Phi (chpt. pres. 1993), Sigma Delta Pi, Sigma Phi Epsilon (counselor, dist. gov. 1965—66, chpt. pres. alumni bd. 2000—02), Phi Beta Kappa. Home: 5 Lawrence Ave Potsdam NY 13676-1815 Office Phone: 315-265-8644.

HARDER, KELSIE T., artist, educator; b. Trenton, Tenn., Mar. 8, 1942; s. Kelsie Brown Harder and Geneva Lee (Tomlin) Carlson; m. Kumiko Tanaka, Oct. 2, 1991; children: Tyler B., Michon Skyler, Samuel Armstrong (dec.), Tsunami Tomlin and Tanaka Solomon (twins) Student, Claremont (Calif.) Men's Coll., 1960-61, Escuela de Bellas Artes, Morelia, Mex., 1961, Ventura (Calif.) Coll., 1961-62; BA, U. Nev., 1973-75, candidate Masters of Edn., 1977—78. Cert. inventory mgmt. specialist USAF, illustrator technician USAF. Artist self-employed, 1957—; prof. Truckee Meadows C.C., Reno, 1978—. Chmn. art dept. Truckee Meadows C.C., 1982—91; art exhibit judge 35 regional exhbns. Contbr. art and articles to profl. jours., mags., textbooks; 31 one-man shows, including, Sierra Nev. Mus. Art, 1969, 1981, 1991,

Rush-Presbyn.-St. Luke's Art Gallery, Chgo., 1973, Blue Cross Art Corp., Oakland, Calif., 1982, Alan Short Gallery, Stockton, Calif., 1991, Elizabeth Sturm Libr. Gallery, Reno, 2004, represented in over 150 collections. Recipient numerous regional and nat. awards including Nev. Centennial Eight Western State Drawing and Painting Competition, 1st Pl. award for drawing and 1st Pl. award for painting Nev. Mus. Art, 1964, YWCA Silver cert. for Outstanding Cmty. Svc., No. Nev., 1972, 88. Office: Truckee Meadows CC 7000 Dandini Blvd Reno NV 89512-3901 Office Phone: 715-673-7000. Business E-Mail: kharder@tmcc.edu.

HARDER, ROBERT CLARENCE, state official; b. Horton, Kans., June 4, 1929; s. Clarence L. and Olympia E. (Kubik) H.; m. Dorothy Lou Welty, July 31, 1953; children: Anne, James David. AB, Baker U., Baldwin, Kans., 1951; MTh, So. Meth. U., 1954; ThD in Social Ethics, Boston U., 1958; LHD (hon.), Baker U., 1983, Ottawa U., 1991. Ordained to ministry Meth. Ch., 1959; pastor East Topeka Meth. Ch., 1958-64; mem. Kans. Ho. of Reps., 1961-67; rsch. assoc. Menninger Found., Topeka, 1964-65; instr. Washburn U., Topeka, 1964, 68, 69; dir. Topeka Office of Econ. Opportunity, 1965-67; tech. asst. coordinator Office of Gov. of Kans., 1967-68; dir. community resources devel. League of Kans. Municipalities, 1968-69; dir. Kans. Dept. Social Welfare, Topeka, 1969-73, sec., 1973-87; projects adminstr. Topeka State Hosp., 1987-89. Adj. prof. pub. adminstrn. Kans. U., 1987-95, instr. Sch. Social Welfare, 1971-87; cons. Menninger Topeka, 1991-92; sec. Kans. Dept. Health and Environment, 1992-95. Contbr. articles to profl. jours. Recipient Disting. Svc. award East Topeka Civic Assn., 1963, Romana Hood award, 1965, Cert. of Recognition, State of Kans., 1979, 87, Spl. Commendation award Kans. Senate, 1987, Spl. Commendation, Kans. Ho. of Reps., 1987, Outstanding Alumnus award Perkins Sch. Theology, So. Meth. U., 1994, M. L. King Jr. Living the Dream Humanitarian award, 1997, Disting. Svc. award Kans. Children's Svc. League, 1998, Grant award for Exceptional Volunteerism, 1999, Advocacy award Disability Caucus, 2003, cert. appreciation Scott Sch., 2003, award of excellence Friends Edn. Award, 2004, Cmty. Leader award Topeka Pub. Schs., 2004, others; named Outstanding Pub. Ofcl. of the Yr., 1987. Mem. Am. Soc. Public Adminstrs. (Public Adminstr. of Yr. Kans. chpt. 1980), Am. Public Welfare Assn., Kans. Health Care Commn., Kans. Conf. Social Welfare (Outstanding Person of Yr. 1987). Democrat. E-mail: rharder6@cox.net.

HARDER, ROLF PETER, graphic designer, painter; b. Hamburg, Germany, July 10, 1929; came to Can., 1955; s. Henry and Henriette (Loeffler) H.; m. Maria-Inger Rumberg, May 3, 1958; children— Christopher, Vivian Student, State Art Sch. (Acad. Fine Arts), Hamburg, 1948-52. Designer Rolf Ruehle Werbung, Hamburg, 1952-55; designer Schneider Cardon Ltd, Montreal, Que, Can, 1955-56; art dir. George Ferguson Assocs., Montreal, 1956-57; visualizer Lintas GmbH, Hamburg, 1957-59; designer, owner Rolf Harder Design, Montreal, 1959-65; co-founder, designer Design Collaborative, Montreal, 1965-77; pres., designer Rolf Harder & Assocs., Montreal, 1977—. Mem. internat. adv. bd. Typos Mag., London, 1979—; co-organizer exhibition The Visual Image of the Munich Games, Mus. Fine Arts, Montreal, 1972 Published: works and exhibited in U.S., Can., Europe, Japan, South Korea, S. Am, USSR; Represented in permanent collections Nat. Archives of Can., Ottawa, Libr. of Congress, Washington, Musee de La Publicité, Palais du Louvre, Paris, Die Neue Sammlung, Munich, AGI Archives, Essen, Germany, Mus. Arts and Crafts, Hamburg, Germany, Mus. Modern Art, N.Y.C., San Francisco, Design Austria, Vienna, U. Reading, Eng., U. Que., Musee De Quebec, The Montreal Mus. Fine Arts, McGill U., Rare Books Dept. Coach Beaconsfield Soccer Assn., Montreal, 1966-70. Recipient over 100 nat. and internat. design awards, including World Logo Design award, Internat. Trademark Ctr., Belgium, 1998. Fellow Soc. Graphic Designers of Can.; mem. Royal Canadian Acad. Arts, Alliance Graphique Internationale (past pres. Can. group). Clubs: Clearpoint Tennis, West-Island Tennis (Montreal). Avocations: tennis, music. Home: 43 Lakeshore Rd Beaconsfield PQ Canada H9W 4H6 E-mail: rolf@rolfharder.ca.

HARDER, VIRGIL EUGENE, business administration educator; b. Ness City, Kans., July 19, 1923; s. Walter J. and Fern B. (Pausch) H.; m. Dona Maurine Dobson, Feb. 4, 1951; children— Christine Elaine, Donald Walter. BS, MA, U. Iowa, 1950; PhD, U. Ill., 1958. Instr. bus. adminstrn. U. Ill., Urbana, 1950-55; asst. prof. U. Wash., Seattle, 1955-59, assoc. prof., 1959-67, prof., 1967-86, prof. emeritus, 1986—, asso. dean sch. bus. adminstrn., 1966-74; dir. Inst. Fin. Edn. Sch. for Exec. Devel., Seattle, 1974-83. Served with AUS, 1943—45. Fellow: Am. Bus. Communications Assn. (pres. 1965); mem.: Trail Blazers Club. Office: U Wash Sch Bus Adminstrn Seattle WA 98195-0001

HARDESTY, DAVID CARTER, JR., university president; b. Philadelphia, Miss., Sept. 20, 1945; m. Susan B. Hardesty, 1968; children: Ashley, D(avid) Carter III. AB, W.Va. U., 1967; MA, Oxford (Eng.) U., 1969; JD, Harvard U., 1973. Bar: W.Va. 1973. Tax commr., sec. Econ. Devel. Authority, State of W.Va., Charleston, 1977-80, chmn. Mcpl. Bond Commn., 1977-80; assoc. Bowles Rice McDavid Graff & Love, Charleston, 1973-77, ptnr., 1981-95; pres. W.Va. U., Morgantown, 1995—. Chmn. W.Va. Tax Study Commn., 1982-84; mem. W.Va. Asian Trade Missions, 1978-79, 95; chmn. W.Va. Roundtable, Inc., 1994-95; frequent spkr. at govt., edn. and bus. group meetings. Chancellor United Meth. Ch., W.Va., 1986-95; trustee Univ. Sys., 1989-95, 1st chmn., 1989-91; trustee W.Va. Wesleyan Coll., 1986-94, Nat. 4-H Coun., 2000—, chmn. 2004—; mem. Gov.'s Energy Task Force, 2001—; mem. W.Va. Rhodes Scholar Selection Com., 1980-2000, sec., 1991-98; bd. advisors W.Va. U., 1980-89, chmn. bd. advisors, 1987-89; bd. dirs. United Meth. Charities W.Va., 1978-94; bd. dirs. Greater Kanawha Valley Found., 1980-89, chmn., 1988-90. Rhodes scholar, 1969. Mem.: ABA, Nat. Assn. State Univs. and Land Grant Colls., Nat. Assn. Coll. and Univ. Attys., Am. Coun. on Edn., 4th Cir. Jud. Conf., W.Va. Bar Assn. Office: WVa U Office of Pres PO Box 6201 Morgantown WV 26506-6201 Office Phone: 304-293-5531. Business E-Mail: david.hardesty@mail.wvu.edu.

HARDESTY, JAMES, state supreme court justice; b. Reno, Nev., Nov. 28, 1948; m. Sandy Hardesty, 1971; 2 children. BS in Acctg., U. Nevada, Reno, 1970; JD, U. Pacific McGeorge Sch. of Law, 1975. Bar: Nev. 1975, U.S. Dist. Ct. Nev. 1975, U.S. Tax Ct. 1976, U.S. Ct. of Appeals, Ninth Circuit 1980. Atty. priv. practice, 1978—80; prtnr. Breen, Young, Whitehead, Belding & Hardesty, 1980—84, Anderson, Pearl, Hardesty, Lyle and Murphy, 1991—95; judge Nev. Second Jud. Dist. Ct., 1999—2001, chief judge, 2001—04; justice Nev. Supreme Ct., 2005—. Prof. Nat. Jud. Coll., 2002—; lecturer media law U. Nev. Donald Reynolds Sch. of Journalism; co-chair Nev. Supreme Ct. Task Force to Create Bus. Ct., 2000; mem. Nev. Supreme Ct. Task Force Multi-Jurisdictional Practice of Law, 2001, Nev. Supreme Ct. Commn. on Jud. Funding, 2003—, Nev. State Bd. of Ed., 1983—84. Mem.: ABA, Am. Inns of Ct., Assn. of Trial Lawyers of Am., Nev. Dist. Judges Assn. (bd. trustees pres. 2000, bd. trustees 2000—04), Washoe County Bar Assn. Office: Nev Supreme Ct 201 S Carson St Carson City NV 89701

HARDESTY, LARRY LYNN, librarian; b. Hyannis, Nebr., Aug. 8, 1947; s. George Kenton and Enid LaVon (Cotton) H.; m. Carol Jean Weaver, June 6, 1970. BA in Edn., Kearney State Coll., 1969, MS in Edn., 1971; MLS, U. Wis., 1974; MS in Edn., Ind. U., 1978, PhD, 1982. Tchr. Cen. Cath. High Sch., Grand Island, Nebr., 1969-70; social worker Adams County Welfare Office, Hastings, Nebr., 1971, Hall County Welfare Office, Grand Island, 1972; reference libr. Kearney State Coll., 1973-75; head reference dept. DePauw U., Greencastle, Ind., 1975-83; dir. of libr. svcs. Eckerd Coll., St. Petersburg, Fla., 1983-95; coll. libr. Austin Coll., Sherman, Tex., 1995—; dean libr. U. Nebr. Kearney, 2004—. Cons. Office of Mgmt. Studies, Washington, 1979-81; organizer libr. confs. Eckerd Coll., 1984-92; spkr. in field. Author: Faculty and the Library, 1991; editor: Book, Bytes and Bridges, 2000; co-editor: User Instruction in Academic Libraries, 1986, Bibliographic Instruction in Practice, 1993; mem. several editl. bds. profl. jours.; contbr. numerous articles to profl. jours. With USAR, 1970-76. Recipient Disting. Alumnus award Ind. U.-Bloomington, Sch. Libr. and Info. Sci., 2000, Disting. Alumnus award U. Wis.-Madison, 2002, U. Nebr., Kearney, 2002; Coun. on Libr. Resources grantee, 1975-77, 84, 88, 92, 94. Mem. ALA (life, chairperson coll. librs. sect. 1995-96, coun. mem. 2003-), Assn. Coll. and Rsch. Librs. (bd. dirs. 1987-91, 1999-2001, chair bd. dirs. Fla. chpt. 1986-87, pres. 1999-2000, chair nat. conf. 2003, Acad./Rsch. Libr. of Yr. 2001), So. Accreditation Assn. (reaffirmation team 1991-2002), Fla. Libr. Assn. (bd. dirs 1988-1990), Beta Phi Mu, Phi Alpha Theta Democrat. Methodist. Avocations: antique collector, model and full size farm tractor collector. Home: 7240 West 87th St Kearney NE 68845 Office Phone: 308-865-8535. E-mail: hardestyll@unk.edu.

HARDESTY, ROBERT LYNCH, surgeon, educator; b. New Brighton, Pa., Sept. 12, 1940; s. Robert and Cora Belva (Cable) H.; m. Catherine Ann Steward, Oct. 3, 1965; children: Lara Ann, Derek John, Kieran Steward. Student, U. Pitts., 1958-59, MD, 1966; BS, Allegheny Coll., 1962. Diplomate Am. Bd. Surgery, Am. Bd. Thoracic Surgery. Resident in surgery U. Pitts., 1966-71, resident in cardiothoracic surgery, 1971-72, asst. prof. surgery, 1974-80, assoc. prof., 1980-86, prof., 1986—. Author: Extracorporeal Membrane Oxygenation (ECMO) for Neonatal Pulmonary Insufficiency, 1974, Cardiac Transplantation, 1981, Cardiac and Pulmonary Transplantation, 1982. Maj. USAF, 1972-74. Recipient Man of Yr. award Pitts. Acad. Medicine, 1986, Man of Yr. award in sci. vectors Alpha Omega Alpha, 1987. Fellow Am. Soc. for Artificial Internal Organs; mem. Am. Surg. Assn., Am. Assn. Thoracic Surgery, Soc. Univ. Surgeons, Transplantation Soc., Phi Eta Sigma. Republican. Roman Catholic. Avocation: woodworking. Home: 1050 Fox Chapel Rd Pittsburgh PA 15238-2014 Office: U Pitts Med Ctr Dept Surgery C-700 Presbyn U Hosp Pittsburgh PA 15213

HARDESTY, W. MARC, lawyer, educator; b. Daytona Beach, Fla., Sept. 3, 1960; s. Henry Haines and Janet W. H.; m. Margie Gail Boyd; children: Meredith Janet, Marcus Clay. BA in Polit. Sci., Furman U., 1982; student, U. London, 1981; JD, Mercer U., 1989. Bar: Fla. 1990, U.S. Ct. Appeals (11th cir.) 1990, U.S. Dist. Ct. (mid. dist.) Fla. 1990, U.S. Supreme Ct. 1997, U.S. Ct. Mil. Appeals 1997. Comd. 2d lt. U.S. Army, 1982, various positions, 1982-89, co. comdr. 345th Combat Support Hosp. Desert Storm Jacksonville, 1990-93, adminstrv. officer, 1994-95; staff judge adv. officer 143rd Transp. Brigade, Orlando, Fla., 1995-96; maj., staff JAG USAR, 174th LSO, Jacksonville, Fla., 1996—; asst. state atty. State Attys. Office 4th Jud. Cir., Jacksonville, Fla., 1989-94; ptnr. Hardesty & Tyde, P.A., Jacksonville, 1994—. Sales mgr. beauty care divsn. Procter & Gamble Co., 1982-86; instr. criminal law Am. Inst. Paralegal Studies, Jacksonville U., 1992-93; instr. legal case analysis, criminal law, workers' compensation U. N. Fla., 1993—. Mem. adv. coun. bd. U. Fla., 1994—; explorer post adv. trial team coach Boy Scouts Am.; mem. S. Jacksonville Presbyn. Ch.; bd. dirs. Boys Home Assn., 1999—. Decorated Bronze Star; Army ROTC scholar, Rotary scholar. Mem. Fla. Bar Assn. (mem. mil. affairs com. 1998—, mem. jud. evaluation com. 1998—), Jacksonville Bar Assn. (chmn. law explorers com. 1992, 93, bd. dirs., numerous others), Acad. Fla. Trial Lawyers, Jacksonville Trial Lawyers Assn., N. Fla. Criminal Def. Lawyers Assn., Rotary (bd. dirs. Arlington 2000—), Phi Delta Phi, Alpha Tau Omega. Avocation: offshore sport fishing. Office: Hardesty & Tyde PA 4004 Atlantic Blvd Jacksonville FL 32207-2037

HARDGROVE, JAMES ALAN, lawyer; b. Chgo., Feb. 20, 1945; s. Albert John and Ruth (Noonen) H.; m. Kathleen M. Peterson, June 15, 1968; children: Jennifer Anne, Amy Kristine, Michael Sheridan. BA, U. Notre Dame, 1967; cert. English law, U. Coll. Law, 1969; JD, U. Notre Dame, 1970. Bar: Ill. 1970, U.S. Ct. Appeals (7th cir.) 1970, U.S. Dist. Ct. (no. dist.) Ill. 1970, U.S. Dist. Ct. (cen. dist.) Ill. 1978, U.S. Supreme Ct. 1980. Law clk. to presiding justice U.S. Ct. Appeals (7th cir.), Chgo., 1970-71; assoc. Sidley Austin Brown & Wood LLP, Chgo., 1971-76, ptnr., 1977—. Mem. ABA, Ill. Bar Assn., Chgo. Bar Assn., Legal Club. Home: 948 Ridge Ave Evanston IL 60202-1720 Office: Sidley Austin Brown & Wood LLP Bank One Plz 10 S Dearborn St Chicago IL 60603-2000 Office Phone: 312-853-7464. E-mail: jhardgrove@sidley.com.

HARDIE, GEORGE GRAHAM, hotel executive; b. Cleve., Aug. 19, 1933; s. William M. and Helen (Graham) H.; children: George Graham Jr., Jennifer. With sales dept. Hardie Bros., Pitts., later various mgmt. positions, operator dist. sales agys.; owner, driver, trainer, racer standardbred horses, 1963—; owner, mgr. Profile, Inc., Las Vegas, 1973—; founder, mng. ptnr. Bell Gardens Bicycle Club Casino, 1984-94; mayor City of Cathedral City, Calif., 1988-90, mayor pro tem, 1990-92; owner, mgr. Profile Comm. Inc., 1990—, Hardie's Korn Kettle Inc., 1990—, Hardie's Korn Kettle Gold, 2003. Owner, mgr. investment and acquisitions co. Lodestar Internat. Inc. (formerly The Hardie Group), 1990—; owner Emerald Meadows Ranch, 1989—. Active cmty. and civic affairs. Recipient Congl. award, 1987; commendation L.A. County Suprs., 1987, L.A. County Office Dist. Atty., 1987; resolution Calif. Senate, 1987, cert. of recognition City of Bell Gardens, 1987; named Man of Yr. Variety Boys & Girls Club of the Desert, 1996. Mem. Calif. Harness Drivers Guild (past pres.), Western Standardbred Assn. (past bd. dirs.), Golden State Greyhound Assn. (organizer, pres. 1973), Bell Gardens C. of C. (pres. 1986). Achievements include oepning of largest casino in Central America. Office: Lodestar Internat Inc 1350 E Flamingo Rd # 347 Las Vegas NV 89119 Office Phone: 702-891-5252. E-mail: gghardie@aol.com.

HARDIE, JAMES CARL, academic administrator, consultant; b. Pitts., June 10, 1922; s. Stanley Frank and Helen Katherine (Wassel) H.; m. Emma Kathryn Cepko, Jan. 28, 1956; children: James Matthew, Lynn Anne. BA, U. Pitts., 1943, ML, 1948. Counselor U. Pitts., 1946, dir. athletic publicity, 1947-48; dir. housing, head men's dormitories Carnegie Inst. Tech., Pitts., 1946-47; dir. campaign Ketchum, Inc., Pitts., 1948-57; dir. devel., v.p. Case Inst. Tech., Cleve., 1957-67; v.p. Case We. Res. U., Cleve., 1967-69; cons. to more than 60 non-profit instns. Cleve., 1969—. Author: Fred Crawford and Fifty Golden Years of Philanthropy, 2005. Chmn. bd. Jennings Found. Yardstick Project, 1968-81; founder Corp. 1% Program for Higher Edn., 1961-69; trustee George S. Dively Found., 1985-97. Lt. U.S. Army, 1943-45. Decorated Purple Heart; recipient Disting. Svc. award Ohio Coun. Fund-Raising Execs., 1988, Citation Coun. Fin. Aid to Edn., 1979; named Outstanding Profl. Nat. Soc. Fund-Raising Profls., 1991. Mem. Union Club Cleve., Grand Harbor (Fla.) Country Club, Grenelefe (Fla.) Country Club, Omicron Delta Kappa, Delta Sigma Rho. Republican. Avocations: golf, reading, gardening, piano, writing. also: 1508 Ocean Dr Apt 103 Vero Beach FL 32963-5346 Office Phone: 216-831-2488.

HARDIE, JAMES HILLER, lawyer; b. Pitts., Dec. 1, 1929; s. James H. and Elizabeth Gillespie (Alcorn) H.; m. Frances P. Curtis, Dec. 5, 1953; children: J. Hiller, Janet Hardie Harvey, Andrew G., Michael C., Rachel Hardie Share. AB, Princeton U., 1951; LL.B., Harvard U., 1954. Bar: Pa. 1955. Assoc. Reed Smith LLP, Pitts., 1954-62, ptnr., 1962-99, of counsel, 1999—. Mem. ABA, Am. Law Inst., Pa. Bar Assn. Office: Reed Smith LLP PO Box 2009 Pittsburgh PA 15230-2009 E-mail: jhardie@reedsmith.com.

HARDIE, MICHAEL HOWARD, mathematician, educator; b. Marysville, Calif., Sept. 4, 1949; s. Howard Keith and Barbara Jane Hardie; m. Lynda Lee Morrison, Sept. 26, 1970 (div. Sept. 1996); children: Stephanie Rebecca, Virginia Catherine; m. Joseph Henry Edson, June 17, 2000. BS in Math., U. Santa Clara, 1971; EdM, U. Idaho, 1976, MS in Math., 1977; EdD, U. Nev., 1990. Tchr. Prairie H.S., Cottonwood, Idaho, 1972—74, Pullman (Wash.) H.S., 1976—81; prof. Western Nev. C.C., Carson City, 1981—. Recipient Horizon award, Phi Theta Kappa, 1992; Brown fellow, U. Santa Clara, 1971—72. Mem.: Nev. Math. Assn. Two-Yr. Colls. (pres. 2003—04).

HARDIE, RUSSELL CRAIG, electrical engineer, educator; b. Balt., Oct. 31, 1966; BS in Engring. sci., Loyola Coll., Balt., 1984—88; MS in Elec. Engring., U. Del., Newark, 1988—90, PhD in Elec. Engring., 1990—92. Sr. scientist Earth Satellite Corp., Rockville, Md., 1992—93; asst. prof. U. Dayton, Ohio, 1993—98, assoc. prof., 1998—. Cons. iCAD, Beavercreek, Ohio, 2002—. Contbr. articles to profl. jours. Recipient Rudolf Kingslake Medal and Prize, SPIE, 1998. Mem.: IEEE. Office: Univ Dayton 300 College Park Dayton OH 45459-0226 Office Phone: 937-229-3611. Office Fax: 937-229-2097. E-mail: rhardie@udayton.edu.

HARDIGAN, PATRICK CHARLES, director, researcher; b. East Lansing, Mich., Mar. 12, 1963; s. William David and Janet Louise Hardigan; m. Pamela Jean Sax, June 4, 1994; children: Seamus Patrick, Liam Edward. BS, Ferris State U., 1987; MBA, U. Wyo., 1991, PhD, 1996. Assoc. dean Coll. Allied Health and Nursing Nova Southeastern U., Ft. Lauderdale, Fla., 2001—03, exec. dir. assessment, evaluation and faculty devel., 2003—, dir. Statis. Consulting Ctr., 2004—05. Mem.: Assn. Behavioral Scis. and Med. Edn. (bd. dirs. 2004—). Office: Nova Southeastern U 3200 South University Dr Fort Lauderdale FL 33328 Home Fax: 954-262-1522; Office Fax: 954-262-2252. Personal E-mail: patrick@nova.edu.

HARDIMAN, JOSEPH RAYMOND, security firm executive; b. Salisbury, Md., May 27, 1937; s. Leonard Roy and Virginia Mildred (Darden) H.; m. Katherine McCampbell, Mar. 23, 1963; children: Katherine Hughes, Elizabeth Gore. BA, U. Md., 1959, LLB, 1962. Bar: Md. 1962. Law clk. to Hon. Hall Hammond Md. Ct. of Appeals, 1962-63; assoc. Miles & Stockbridge, Balt., 1963-68; exec. v.p., sec., dir. Robert Garrett & Sons, Inc., Balt., 1968-75; gen. ptnr. Alex. Brown & Sons, 1975-87, mng. dir., COO, 1984-87; pres., CEO, dir. Nat. Assn. Securities Dealers, Inc., 1987-97, Nasdaq Stock Market, Inc., 1987-97. Bd. dirs. Broadwing Corp., Deutsche Scudder Funds, ISI Funds, Nevis Fund, Brown Investment Adv. and Trust Co. Bd. dirs. Arthritis Found., Md., 1975-79, pres., 1976-78; bd. dirs. Balt. Urban Coalition, 1975-78, U. Md. Med. Sys., 1980-86, Fund for Ednl. Excellence, 1984-91, Ctr. for the Study of the Presidency, 1992-97, U. Md. Found., 1992-2000, U. Md. Balt. Found., 2000—; steering com. Baltimore County Charter Rev. Commn., 1977-78; trustee St. Paul's Sch. for Girls, 1978-86, Securities Industry Found. Econ. Edn., 1988-96; adv. bd. U. Calif. Securities Regulation Inst., 1988-97; bd. visitors U. Md. Sch. Law, 1990—; active Am. Bus. Conf., Con. on Competitiveness, 1994-97. Mem. Md. Club, Elkridge Club (Balt.), Links Club (N.Y.C.), Gulfstream Club (Fla.), Order of Coif, Phi Delta Theta, Omicron Delta Kappa. Home: 8 Bowen Mill Rd Baltimore MD 21212-1053

HARDIN, ADLAI STEVENSON, JR., judge; b. Norwalk, Conn., Sept. 20, 1937; s. Adlai S. and Carol H. BA, Princeton U., 1959; LLB, Columbia U., 1962. Bar: N.Y. 1963, U.S. Dist. Ct. (so. and ea. dists.) N.Y. 1965, U.S. Supreme Ct. 1967, U.S. Ct. Appeals (2d cir.) 1965, U.S. Ct. Appeals (5th cir.) 1974, U.S. Ct. Appeals (3d cir.) 1977, U.S. Ct. Appeals (9th cir.) 1982, U.S. Ct. Appeals (4th and D.C. cirs.) 1985, U.S. Ct. Appeals (7th cir.) 1988. Assoc. Milbank, Tweed, Hadley & McCloy, N.Y.C., 1963, ptnr., 1971; judge U.S. Bankruptcy Ct., 1995—. Judge Bankruptcy Appellate Panel for 2d Circuit, 1996-2000. Trustee Spence Sch., 1981-87; former elder, trustee Madison Ave. Presbyn. Ch. With USAR, 1962-68. Mem. ABA (past chmn. N.Y. State membership com., antitrust sect., litigation sect.), Fed. Bar Coun. (trustee 1983-92, v.p. 1986-88, chmn. bd. dirs. 1990-92), Fed. Bar Found. (pres. 1992-94), N.Y. State Bar Assn. (mem. com. on profl. ethics, mem. jud. election monitoring com., mem. internat. litigation com.), Assn. of Bar of City of N.Y. (sec. 1979-82, chmn. com. on profl. and jud. ethics 1970-73, mem. spl. com. on lawyers role in securities transactions, mem. spl. com. to cooperate with ABA in revision of Canons of Ethics, mem. nominating com., mem. com. on membership, mem. com. on profl. discipline), Nat. Conf. Bankruptcy Judges, Am. Bankruptcy Inst., Westchester County Bar Assn. Office: US Bankruptcy Ct US Courthouse 300 Quarropas St White Plains NY 10601-4150

HARDIN, CHRISTOPHER DEMAREST, medical educator; b. Syracuse, N.Y., July 31, 1961; BS in Biology, Cornell U., 1983; MS in Physiology, U. Rochester, 1986; PhD in Physiology and Biophysics, U. Cin., 1989. Sr. fellow Dept. Radiology U. Wash., Seattle, 1989-91, rsch. asst. prof. dept. radiology, 1991—93; asst. prof. physiology U. Mo., Columbia, 1993—99, assoc. prof. physiology, 1999—. Tutor, mentor, spkr. in field; guest reviewer for 29 jours. in field. Mem. internat. advisory bd. Physiological Research, 1997-; contbr. articles to profl. jours; chpts. to books. Albert J. Ryan fellow, 1986-89, tng. grant fellow U. Cin.,. 1985-86, univ. grad. fellow U. Rochester, 1983-85; recipient Jeffrey D. Doane Meml. award, 1987, Nat. Rsch. Svc. award, 1989-92, Dorsett L. Spurgeon Disting. Med. Rsch. award, 1999. Mem. AAAS, Internat. Soc. Heart Rsch. (N.Am. sect), Am. Heart Assn. Sci. Coun. (basic sci.), Am. Physiol. Soc., Harold Lamport award Outstanding Young Invesitgator 1995), Biophysical Soc., Am. Physiological Soc. (elected fellow 2002, awards com. 2005-), Am. Assn. Advancement Sci., Am. Heart Assn. (sci. coun.). Home: 4480 Roemer Rd Columbia MO 65202-7060 Office: Univ Mo Dept Physiology MA415 Med Sci Bldg Columbia MO 65212-0001 Business E-Mail: harding@missouri.edu.

HARDIN, DALE WAYNE, political science professor; b. Peoria, Ill., Sept. 9, 1922; s. James P. and Lucille Maureen (Elgin) H.; m. Sandra L. Gorzen, July 3, 1939; children: Bradley J., Stacy Keaton, Rebecca M., J. Scott Keaton. AB in Polit. Sci., George Washington U., 1949, JD, 1951. Bar: Va. 1951, D.C. 1951, U.S. Dist. D.C. 1951, U.S. Ct. Appeals (D.C. cir.) 1951. Assoc. Mills & Partridge, Washington, 1951; spl. agent FBI, Washington, 1951-54; fin. counsel ICC, Washington, 1954-55, legis. counsel, 1955-64, presdl. appointee as commr., 1967-77, vice chmn., acting chmn. agy., 1971-73, chmn. rates divsn., 1975-77; Presdl. appointee, mem. Adminstrv. Conf. U.S., 1969-72; dir. dept. transp. and comm. U.S. C. of C., Washington, 1964-66; v.p. govt. affairs Overmeyer Co., Washington, 1966-67; spl. counsel Am. Trucking Assn., Washington, 1967; assoc. prof. polit sci. S.W. Tex. State U. (now Tex. State U.), San Marcos, Tex., 1977—, assoc. prof. emeritus, 1989-00, acting dean sch. liberal arts., 1986-87, chmn. dept. home econs., 1990-92; ret. law educator, 2000. Gen. counsel Transp. Assn. Am., Washington, 1959; exec. v.p. GC Wheaton Van Lines, Indpls., 1981-82; moderator 14th Ann. Seminar, State Bar Tex., 1982, moderator profl. devel. program gen. paralegal skills, 1988, standing com. on legal assts., 1988-00; chmn. Tex. forum IV Conf. Legal Asst. Educators, 1985, chair forum VII, 1988; presenter papers in field. Bus. sec. George Washington U. Sch. Law Rev., 1951. With USMC, 1942—46, PTO. Mem. Soc. Former Spl. Agents FBI. Fed. Bar Assn., Va. State Bar., D.C. Bar, Phi Delta Phi. Avocation: golf. Home: 10829 River Plantation Dr Austin TX 78747-1490

HARDIN, EDWARD LESTER, JR., lawyer; b. Wetumpka, Ala., Mar. 29, 1940; s. Edward Lester and Katherine (Williams) H.; m. Lila Manor, June 10, 1962; children: Leigh Hardin Hancock, Caroline Hardin Butler, Laura Elizabeth, Edward Lester III. BA, Birmingham So. Coll., 1962; JD, U. Ala., 1965. Bar: Ala. 1965, U.S. Dist. Ct. (no., mid. and so. dists.) Ala. 1965, U.S. Ct. Appeals (11th cir.), U.S. Supreme Ct. Pvt. law practice, 1965—98; exec. v.p., gen. counsel, bd. dirs. Caremark Rx, Inc., Nashville, 1998—. Mem. editl. bd. U. Ala. Law Rev., 1964-65; contbr. to profl. publs. Mem. ABA, Am. Bd. Trial Advocates, Assn. Trial Lawyers Am. (bd. govs. 1976), Ala. Bar Assn., Ala. Trial Lawyers Assn. (exec. com., pres. 1975-76), Omicron Delta Kappa, Phi Alpha Delta. Methodist. Avocations: marlin fishing, golf, hunting. Office: Caremark Rx Inc 211 Commerce St Nashville TN 37201 Office Phone: 615-743-6615. Business E-Mail: ed.hardin@caremarkrx.com.

HARDIN, ELIZABETH CRAWFORD, commercial display artist, interior designer; b. Lumberton, S.C., Sept. 16, 1942; d. Theodore McLellan and Elizabeth (McAshan) Crawford; m. Edward Reel Hardin, JUly 1, 1967 (div. Apr. 1985); 1 child, Edward Reel. AA, Peace Coll., 1962; BA, U. N.C., 1964, MS, 1967; accreditation des etudes artistiques, Sorbonne U., Paris, 1965. Interior designer The Alderman Co., High Point, N.C., 1967-74; show rm. designer Singer Furniture Co., Roanoke, Va., 1975-81; freelance designer Elizabeth C. Hardin ASID, High Point, 1981—. Cons. showroom displays, photography cons. Pilliod Cabinet Co., 1982-84, Wesley Allen Co., 1983-88, Webb Furniture Enterprises, 1984—, Baldwin Furniture, 1985-86; photography designer The John Henry Co., Norling Studios, High Point, Tatum, Toomey & Whicker Agy., High Point; Carter Mfg. Co., 1987, Home Furnishings Market, High Point; author, editor teaching kit on design; design lectr. Guilford County Community Coll., High Point, 1974, 85. U. N.C. teaching fellow, 1966-67; drafting workshop tchr., developed cirriculum High Point Design Inst.; display dir. Klaussner Furniture Industries, 1990; studio display designer The Alderman Co., Omega Studios; set designer for location footage Bernhardt Furniture Co. Recipient Excellence in Design award,

Interior Design Soc., 1990. Mem. Am. Soc. Interior Designers, Nat. Homes Furnishings, Interior Design Soc. (exec. dir. 1988-90, Excellence in Design award 1990), Hardin Ednl. and Advanced Design Systems 1990, cons., tng. seminar svcs. for retailers), Assn. of Jr. League. Methodist. Avocations: tennis, skiing. Home: 1014 N Rotary Dr High Point NC 27262-3610

HARDIN, EUGENE BROOKS, JR., bank executive; b. Wilmington, N.C., Oct. 18, 1930; s. Eugene Brooks Hardin and Roberta Gilmour (Sterling) Demme; m. Olivia Lynch, Aug. 16, 1958; children: John Haywood II, Olivia Cary. BS, U. N.C., 1952. With Wachovia Bank & Trust Co., Wilmington, 1956—, asst. v.p., 1957-60, v.p., 1962-68, sr. v.p., 1969-72, sr. v.p., regional exec. Raleigh, 1972-79, regional v.p., 1979-95; cashier Burlington, N.C., 1961-62; ret., 1995. Bd. dirs. Wachovia Bank, Raleigh, N.C. Pres., bd. dirs. Babies Hosp., Wilmington, 1968-72; pres. United Fund, 1970; treas., trustee Episcopalian Diocese East Carolina, 1965-72; chmn. Raleigh Civic Center Authority, 1978-81; chmn. Raleigh-Durham Airport Authority, 1981-82; chmn. bd. trustees St. Mary's Coll., 1979-85; bd. dirs. Children's Home Soc. N.C. Served with USNR, 1948-49; to lst lt. USAF, 1952-56. Mem. Robert Morris Assos. Clubs: Civitan (pres. Wilmington 1971-72); Carolina Yacht (Wrightsville Beach); Carolina Country (Raleigh); Cape Fear Country (Wilmington); Land Fall (Wilmington). Home: 404 Drummond Dr Raleigh NC 27609-7006

HARDIN, HAL D., lawyer, judge, former US attorney; BA, Middle Tenn. State U.; JD, Vanderbilt U., 1968. Bar: Tenn., D.C., Tex., Ky., U.S. Ct. Claims, U.S. Tax. Ct., U.S. Ct. Mil. Appeals, U.S. Supreme Ct. Dir. St. Louis Job Corps Ctr.; vol. Peace Corps; asst. dist. atty.; pvt. practice; presiding judge Nashville Trial Cts., 1976-77; spl. judge Ct. of Appeals, 1977; U.S. atty. Middle Dist. Tenn., 1977-81; practice law Nashville, 1981—. Adj. prof. Aquinas Coll., Tenn. State U., 1975—76, Nashville Sch. Law, 1993—. Bd. dirs. Nat. Assn. Former U.S. Atty., 1993—96, Leadership Nashville, 1983, Capital Case Resource Ctr., 1988—95, Leadership Alumni Assn., 1985. Master: Inns of Ct.; fellow: Tenn. Bar Found.; mem.: Washington D.C. Bar Assn., Ky. Bar Assn., Nat. Peace Corps Assn. (bd. dirs. 2001—04), Am. Bd. Trial Advs. (sec. Tenn. chpt. 1987, nat. bd. dirs. 1988—89, pres. Tenn. chpt. 1990), 6th Cir. Jud. Coun. (life), Tenn. Criminal Def. Attys. Assn., Nat. Criminal Def. Attys. Assn., Tex. Bar Assn., Tenn. Bar Assn. (gen. counsel 1982—90), Nashville Bar Assn. (bd. dirs. 1983—85, v.p. 1985). Office Phone: 615-369-3377.

HARDIN, JAMES CARLISLE, III, lawyer, educator; b. Charlotte, N.C., Sept. 12, 1948; s. James Carlisle Jr. and Mary Gene (Roberts) H.; m. Sally M. Drennan, June 6, 1968 (div. Dec. 1973); 1 child, Christine M.; m. Caryle Wilson (dec. June 1986); 1 child, James Carlisle IV; m. Katharine C. Harrison, May 2, 1992. AB, Wofford Coll., 1969; MA in History, U. Va., 1970, postgrad., 1970-71; JD, Duke U., 1974. Bar: S.C. 1974, U.S. Dist. Ct. S.C. 1976, N.C. 1989; U.S. Dist. Ct. (we. dist.) N.C. 1989; cert. legal specialist in estate planning and probate law, SC, NC. Ptnr. Roddey, Carpenter & White, P.A., Rock Hill, S.C., 1974-86, Kennedy Covington Lobdell & Hickman, Charlotte & Rock Hill, SC, 1986—2005; atty. James C. Hardin III and Assocs., PLLC, 2005—. Chmn. specialization adv. bd. S.C. Supreme Ct., 1988-90; mem. S.C. Commn. on Continuing Lawyer Competence and Specialization, 1990-97; instr. Winthrop Univ., Rock Hill, 1979-91; mem. sect. coun. Probate Estate Planning and Trust Sect. S.C. Bar, 1997—, chmn., 1981, 91, 2003; bd. dirs. Rock Hill Econ. Devel. Corp., chmn. 1998-2000. Mem. bd. dirs. Rock Hill YMCA, 1986-89, S.C. Meth. Found., 1986—; bd. dirs. St. John's United Meth. Ch., Rock Hill, 1997—; bd. dirs. Piedmount Med. Ctr., 1994—2000, chmn., 1996. Fellow Am. Coll. Trust and Estate Coun. (state chmn. 1991-); mem. Rock Hill C. of C. (bd. dirs. 1991-95), Kiwanis (bd. dirs. Rock Hill 1978-80), Rock Hill Country Club, Phi Beta Kappa. Avocations: golf, swimming. Office: James C Hardin III & Assocs PLLC 113 E Main St Rock Hill SC 29730 Office Phone: 803-329-7601.

HARDIN, JAMES NEAL, language educator, writer; b. Nashville, Feb. 17, 1939; s. James N. and Ina M. (Anderson) H.; m. Anne Farr. AB, Washington and Lee U., 1960; postgrad., U. Berlin, 1960-61; PhD, U. N.C., 1967. Prof. German lit. U. S.C., Columbia, 1969—98. Pres. Hardin Pub. Inc. Author: Co-founder, Camden House, imprint published by Boydell & Brewer Ltd., Johann Beer, 1983, Johann Beer Bibliographie, 1984, Christian Gryphius Bibliographie, 1985, J.C. Ettner Bibliographie, 1988; editor: Der Verliebte Oesterreicher, 1977; editor/co-editor: Dictionary of Lit. Biography, Vols. 59, 66, 69, 81, 85, 90, 94, 97, 118, 124, 129, 133, 138, 148, 194 and 168, Goethe's Wilhelm Meister's Travels, 1991; founder, co-editor: Studies in German Language, Literature and Linguistics, Works of Christian Gryphius, 2 vols., 1985; contbr. articles to profl. jours. and mags. Capt. U.S. Army, 1967-69. Decorated Army Commendation medal; recipient Alexander von Humbolt award, 1974-75, Russell award for scholarship, 1979, German-Am. Friendship award, 2004; Fulbright scholar, 1960-61 Mem. MLA, South Atlantic MLA. Office: 4088 Spring Island Okatie SC 29909 Business E-Mail: jameshardin@direcway.com.

HARDIN, JAMES W., botanist, educator, aquarium administrator; b. Mar. 31, 1929; BS, Fla. So. Coll., 1950; MS, U. Tenn., 1951; PhD, U. Mich., 1957. Instr. U. Mich., 1956-57; from asst. prof. to prof. N.C. State U., Raleigh, 1957-68, prof., 1968-96, emeritus prof., 1996—, curator herbarium, 1957-96. Vis. prof. Mountain Lake Biological Sta. U.Va., summers 1962, 64, 83, U. Okla. Biological Sta., summers 1967, 70; mem. exec. com. Flora Southeastern U.S., 1966-97; endangered species com. N.C. Dept. Natural & Econ. Resources, 1973-74, natural areas adv. com., 1973-79; mem. plant conservation sci. com. N.C. Dept. Agriculture, 1980-97, chmn. 1987-97; mem. endangered species com. N.C. Wildlife Resources Commn., 1976-78, N.C. State Mus. Natural Hist., 1975-78; pres. Highlands Biological Station, Inc., 1963-69, trustee, 1958-69, sec., 1960-63; invited symposium speaker. Author: Human Poisoning, 1974, Textbook of Dendrology, 2001; editor ASB Bull., 1980-86; mem. editorial com. Am. Jour. Botany, 1964-66; mem. editorial bd. Brittonia, 1964-67, Brimleyana, 1975-97; reviewer jours. in field. Trustee Highlands Biol. Found., 1976-. Recipient Outstanding Tchr. award, NC State U., 1966—67, 1969—70. Mem. Am. Soc. Plant Taxonomists (pub. policy com. 1976-78, editorial bd. 1964-67, editor-in-chief Systematic Botany 1985-91, pres. elect 1991-92, pres. 1992-93, past pres. 1993-94, Cooley award 1958), Southern Appalachian Botanical Club (v.p. 1959-60, pres. 1964-65, Bartholomew award 1994), Botanical Soc. Am. (editorial com. 1964-66, chair southeastern sect. 1968-69), Assn. Southeastern Biologists (Meritorious Teaching award 1991, chmn. local arrangements 1966, 77, v.p. 1968-69, pres. 1979-80, editor 1980-86), Soc. Economic Botany (chmn. local arrangements 1979), Phi Kappa Phi, Sigma Xi (exec. com. N.C. chpt. 1962-63, sec. 1965-66, treas. 1966-67, v.p. 1967-68, program chmn. 1968-69, pres. 1969-70). Home: 204 Furches St Raleigh NC 27607-4056 Office: 204 Furches St Raleigh NC 27607 E-mail: jwhardin@mindspring.com.

HARDIN, LOWELL STEWART, retired economics professor; b. nr. Knightstown, Ind., Nov. 16, 1917; s. J. Fred and Mildred (Stewart) H.; m. Mary J. Cooley, Sept. 21, 1940; children: Thomas Stewart, Joyce Ann, Peter Lowell. BS, Purdue U., 1939, DAgr (hon.), 1990; PhD, Cornell U., 1943. Grad. asst., instr. Cornell U., 1939-43; instr., asst. and assoc. prof., prof. Purdue U., 1943-65, adj. prof. agrl. econs., 1965-66, prof., 1981-84, emeritus prof., asst. dir. internat. programs, 1984—, acting head dept. agrl. econs., 1954-57, head dept., 1957-65; also dir. Purdue Work Simplification Lab. Program adviser agr. Ford Found., 1965-66, program officer agr., 1966-81; former trustee Internat. Food Policy Rsch. Inst., Washington, Internat. Ctr. for Agrl. Rsch. in Dry Areas, Aleppo, Syria, Internat. Svc. for Nat. Agrl. Rsch., The Hague, The Netherlands, Winrock Internat. Inst. for Agrl. Devel., Little Rock, Ark. Author: (with L.M. Vaughan) Farm Work Simplification, 1949. Fellow AAAS, Am. Agrl. Econ. Assn. (pres. 1963-64); mem. Internat. Assn. Agrl. Economists, Sigma Xi, Alpha Gamma Rho, Phi Kappa Phi, Alpha Zeta, Sigma Delta Chi. Federated Church. Home: 2628 Calvin Ct W Lafayette IN 47906-1402 Office Phone: 765-494-8460.

HARDIN, MARTHA LOVE WOOD, civic leader; b. Muncie, Ind., Aug. 13, 1918; d. Lawrence Anselm and Bonny Blossom (Williams) Wood; m. Clifford Morris Hardin, June 28, 1939; children: Susan Hardin Wood, Clifford Wood, Cynthia Hardin Milligan, Nancy Hardin Rogers, James Alvin. Librarian U. Chgo., 1939-40. Co-author Genealogy: Ancestors of Lawrence Anselm Wood, Genealogy Ancestors of Bonny Williams Wood; contbr. articles to profl. jours. Chair Nebr. Heart Fund, 1967; vol. worker Lincoln Gen. Hosp., 1965, Clarkson Hosp., 1966; hon. chair Symphony Ball, Washington, 1970; met. bd. YWCA, Washington, 1969-71, St. Louis, 1973-95; women's com. Pres.'s Com. on Employment of Handicapped, 1970-91, bd. dirs., 1970—; co-chmn. nat. fund-raising campaign U. Nebr. Found., 1977-80. Mem. DAR, PEO, Soc. Mortar Bd., Lincoln Country Club, Wednesday Club, Phi Beta Kappa, Pi Beta Phi. Home: 6525 Lone Tree Dr Lincoln NE 68512-2405

HARDIN, PAUL, III, law educator; b. Charlotte, NC, June 11, 1931; s. Paul and Dorothy (Reel) Hardin; m. Barbara Russell, June 8, 1954; children: Paul Russell, Sandra Mikush, Dorothy Holmes. AB, Duke U., 1952, JD, 1954; LHD (hon.), Clemson U., 1970, Coker Coll., 1972; LittD (hon.), Nebr. Wesleyan U., 1978; LLD (hon.), Adrian Coll., 1987, Monmouth Coll., 1988; HHD (hon.), Wofford Coll., 1989; LLD (hon.), Rider Coll., 1990; LHD (hon.), Duke U., 1994. Bar: Ala. 1954. Practiced in, Birmingham, 1954, 1956—58; asst. prof. Duke Law Sch., 1958—61, assoc. prof., 1961—63, prof., 1963—68, univ. trustee, 1969—74, 1995—2001; pres. Wofford Coll., Spartanburg, SC, 1968—72, So. Methodist U., Dallas, 1972—74, Drew U., Madison, NJ, 1975—88; chancellor U. NC, Chapel Hill, NC, 1988—95, chancellor emeritus, prof. law, 1995—; interim pres. U. Ala., Birmingham, Ala., 1997. Vis. prof. U. Tex., 1960, U. Pa., 1962—63, U. Va., 1974; dir. Smith Barney mut. funds. Author (with Sullivan, others): The Administration of Criminal Justice, 1966; author: (with Sullivan) Evidence, Cases and Materials, 1968; contbr. articles to profl. jours., law revs. Chmn. Human Rels. Com., Durham, NC, 1961—62; pres. Nat. Assn. Schs. and Coll. of United Meth. Ch., 1984; mem. gen. conf. United Meth. Ch., 1968, 1976, 1980, 1984; chmn. Nat. Commn. on United Meth. Higher Edn., 1975—77. Served with CIC U.S. Army, 1954—56. Mem.: Order of Coif, Carnegie Found. for Advancement Tchg. (bd. dirs. 1990—98), Phi Beta Kappa.

HARDIN, STEVE, librarian; m. Debra M. Moore; 1 child, Lynne M. McCown. BS in Radio-TV, U. Ill., 1976, MS in Libr. and Info. Sci., 1989. Prodr./announcer Sta. WILL Radio, Urbana, Ill., 1976—89; libr. Ind. State U., Terre Haute, 1989—. Lay leader Centenary United Meth. Ch., Terre Haute, 2000—03. Mem.: ALA, Am. Soc. Info. Sci. and Tech. (dir.-at-large 1995—98), Phi Kappa Phi (life). Office: Ind State U 650 Sycamore St Terre Haute IN 47809 Office Phone: 812-237-7685. Business E-Mail: shardin@indstate.edu.

HARDIN, TERRENCE ARMSTRONG, former radio broadcasting manager; b. Cin., Sept. 10, 1961; s. Oliver Wendell and Carol Lockwood H.; m. Dayna Lynn Glasson, Oct. 8, 1994. BFA in Radio, TV Comms., So. Meth. U., 1985. Cert. radio mktg. cons. Nat. sales mgr. Sta. WBAP and Sta. KSCS-FM, Dallas, 1986-88; gen. sales mgr. Sta. WMJI-FM, Cleve., 1988-90, Stas. KCBQ-AM-FM and Sta. KIHI-FM, Denver and San Diego, 1990-92, Sta. WPNT-FM, Chgo., 1992-95; v.p., gen. mgr. Stas. KYOT-FM, KZON-FM, KOY and KISO, Phoenix, 1995-99; gen. mgr. WLIT, 1999—. Guest speaker Ariz. State U., Tempe, 1995; advisor Glaser Capital, Cin., 1990—. Mem. awards com. Medallion of Merit Scholarship Found., Ariz. State U., Tempe, 1995-96; fund raiser Children's Cancer Ctr., Phoenix, 1995-96; exec. coun. Boys and Girls Club of Met. Phoenix. Mem. Am. Diabetes Assn. Avocations: travel, golf, mountain biking. Office: WLIT Sta Mgr 150 N Michigan Ave Ste 1135 Chicago IL 60601-7524

HARDIN, WILLIAM DOWNER, retired lawyer; b. Newark, Sept. 27, 1926; s. Charles R. and Emma (Downer) H.; m. Rosemarie Koellhoffer, Jan. 19, 1952 (dec. Mar. 1996); m. Ruth M. Johnson, May 29, 1999; children: William Downer, David Gerth, Peter Roe. AB, Princeton, 1948; LL.B., Columbia, 1951. Bar: N.J. 1951. Law clk. N.J. Superior Ct., 1951-52; assoc. firm Pitney, Hardin, Kipp & Szuch, Newark and Morristown, 1952—57, mem. firm, 1957—96. Mem. N.J. Bd. Bar Examiners, 1964-68, chmn., 1968; mem. local draft bd. SSS, 1953-74, chmn., 1970-74; mem. Family Svc. Bur., Newark, 1953-75, pres., 1960-66; mem. Family Svc. Morris County, 1976-85, 87-98, pres., 1979-82, 95-97, v.p., 1992-95; mem. membership com. Family Svc. Assn. Am., 1965-78, dir., 1971-79, 89-95; mem. Nat. Budget and Consultation Com., 1966-71, Coun. on Accreditation Svcs. for Families and Children, 1978-80. Trustee Newark Acad., 1952-85, pres., 1969-72, chmn., 1976-78; mem. Legal Svcs. of N.J., 1983-2002, chmn., 1990-96; mem. Legal Aid Soc. of Morris County, N.J., 1984-93, pres., 1989-90. With USNR, 1944-46. Mem. ABA, Fed. Bar Assn., N.J. Bar Assn., Essex County Bar Assn., Morris County Bar Assn., Morristown Club, Nassau Club, Coral Beach and Tennis Club, Short Hills Club, Princeton Club of N.Y., Morris County Golf Club. Episcopalian. Home: 15 Gapview Rd Short Hills NJ 07078-2077 Office: 200 Campus Dr Florham Park NJ 07932-1007 Office Phone: 973-966-8100.

HARDING, CLIFFORD VINCENT, III, medical educator; b. Arlington, Va., Jan. 31, 1957; s. Clifford Vincent Harding, Jr. and Drusilla Ruth (Van Hoesen) Harding; m. Mina Kay Chung, May 7, 1983; children: Clifford Vincent IV, Andrew Richard. BA magna cum laude, Harvard U., 1979; MD, PhD, Washington U., 1985. Diplomate Nat. Bd. Med. Examiners. Resident in pathology Washington U., St. Louis, 1985—89, chief resident in pathology, 1989—90, instr. pathology, 1989—90, asst. prof. pathology, 1990—93, Case Western Res. U., Cleve., 1993—96, assoc. prof. pathology, 1996—99, prof. pathology, 1999—, dir. med. scientist tng. program, 2001—; med. staff physician U. Hosps. Cleve., Cleve., 1993—2003; adj. staff Cleve. Clinic Found., 2004—. Reviewer NIH study sects. NIH, Bethesda, Md., 1996—, chmn. AITC study sect., 1999—2001. Mem. editl. bd.: Advances in Anatomic Pathology, 1994—2000, Traffic, 1998—2001, Cellular Microbiology, 1998—. Recipient Jr. Faculty Rsch. Award, Am. Cancer Soc., 1991; grantee, NIH, 1994—; scholar, Pfizer, Inc, 1991. Mem.: AAAS, Am. Soc. Microbiology, Am. Soc. for Investigative Pathology (Am. Assn. Pathologists Exptl. Pathology-in-Tng. award 1989), Am. Soc. for Cell Biology, Am. Assn. Immunologists, Phi Beta Kappa. Achievements include research in immunology and cell biology. Office: Case Western Reserve Univ Pathology Wolstein 5534 2103 Cornell Rd Cleveland OH 44106-7288 E-mail: cvh3@cwru.edu.

HARDING, COURTENAY MAIN, medical educator; d. Robert C. and Eleanor E. Main; children: Robert H., Ashley K., Brooke W. BA in Psychology, U. Vt., 1976, PhD, 1984, MA in Psychology, 1981. Assoc. rsch. scientist Sch. Medicine Yale U., New Haven, 1884—1986, asst. prof. Sch. Medicine, 1986—89; assoc. prof. psychiatry Sch. Medicine U. Colo., Denver, 1996—2000; prof. Boston (Mass.) U., 2001—. Assoc. dir. Ctr. Studies Prolonged Psychiat. Disorders Sch. Medicine Yale U., 1985—89; assoc. dir. Programs Pub. Psychiatry Sch. Medicine U. Colo., 1989—2000; dir Mental Health Program Western Interstate Commn. Higher Edn., Boulder, Colo., 1996—2000; sr. dir. Ctr. Psychiat. Rehab. Boston (Mass.) U., 2002—, dir. Inst. Study Human Resilience, 2001—; The Catherine Garwood-Jones lectr. McMaster U., 1987. Contbr. articles to profl. jours. and books. Recipient Young Scientist award, Internat. Congress Schizophrenia Rsch., 1990, Armin Loeb award, Internat. Assn. Psychosocial Rehab., 1990; grantee, NIMH, 1979—92; Ebaugh scholar, U. Colo. Sch. of Medicine, 1990—91. Mem.: APA (task force serious mental illness 1999—2001, Rsch. award 2005, Gralnido award 2004—05), Am. Pub. Health Assn., Soc. Rsch. in Psychopathology, Am. Psychopathological Assn., Internat. Soc. Psychol. Treatments Schizophrenia and Other Psychoses (internat. exec. com. 1998—2003). Avocations: skiing, sailing, travel, antiques. Office: Boston University 940 Commonwealth Ave - 2nd Floor Boston MA 02215 Office Phone: 617-353-3549.

HARDING, FANN, retired science administrator; b. Henderson, Ky., Jan. 29, 1930; d. James Hilary and Lucy (Caldwell) H. Student, Western Coll., Oxford Ohio, 1947-48; AB in Biology, Coker Coll., Hartsville, S.C., 1951; MS in Anatomy, Med. U. S.C., Charleston, 1954, PhD, 1958. Research and teaching asst. dept. anatomy Med. U. S.C., 1951-53, teaching fellow, 1953-55, research fellow, 1955-58; analyst pub. health research program, research and tng. grants br. Nat. Heart Inst., Bethesda, Md., 1958-61, scientist adminstr. research and tng. grants br., 1961-64, chmn. nat. adv. heart council statements com., 1961-64, sr. health scientist adminstr. research grants br. (sect. chief), 1964-69, sr. health scientist adminstr. thrombosis and hemorrhagic diseases br. (acting chief), extramural program, also arteriosclerosis program, 1969-72; mem. Nat. Heart Inst. (Fellowship Bd.), 1966-68; sr. health scientist adminstr. thrombosis and hemorrhagic diseases program (acting chief), div. blood diseases and resources Nat. Heart and Lung Inst. (name changed to Nat. Heart, Lung and Blood Inst. 1976), Bethesda, 1972-74; asst. to dir. div. blood diseases and resources Nat. Heart, Lung and Blood Inst., 1974—, program dir. extramural research tng. and career devel. in blood diseases and transfusion medicine, exec. sec. blood diseases and resources adv. com., 1974-95; asst. coordinator U.S.-USSR Health Exchange Program, 1974-95; ret., 1996; sculptor, 1996—. Women's Action Program adv. coun. HEW, 1971-72; cons. James H. Mitchell Found., Washington, 1962-67, Washington VA Hosp., 1968-70; environ. cons. Henderson (Ky.) Citizens Com., 1974-76; initiated and implemented concept of transfusion medicine, 1982—; adv. bd. Psychoceramic Found., 2001—. Editorial bd.: Lupus News, 1988—. Organizer NIH Orgn. for Women, 1970; bd. dir. Assn. Women in Sci. Edn. Found., 1973-77, Lupus Found. Am., 1985-88; bd. visitors Coker Coll., 1974-78; bd. dir., sec., treas. Nat. Children's Choir, Washington, 1981-91; bd. advisors Psychoceramie Found., 2002; mem. Women's Nat. Dem. Club, 2004. Recipient Ruth Patrick award, 1951, NIH sustained performance award, 1973, Nat. award Fedn. Orgns. for Profl. Women, 1977, Disting. Svc. award Transfusion Medicine Acad. Award Program, Am. Assn. Blood Banks, 1990, Disting. Alumni award Coker Coll., 1992, award of Merit, NIH, 1993, Founder's award, Fedn. Orgns. for Profl. Women, 1995, Foremother award, Nat. Rsch. Ctr. Women and Children, 2005. Fellow Sigma Delta Epsilon; mem. AAAS (panel on women in sci. 1973-77), Nat. Women's Polit. Caucus (charter), Assn. Women in Sci. (founding mem. 1971, exec. bd. 1973-75), Fedn. Orgn. Profl. Women (founding pres., exec. bd. 1972—), Nat. Microcirculatory Soc. (charter), Reticuloendothelial Soc. (charter), Am. Assn. Blood Banks, Internat. Soc. Thrombosis & Haemostasis, Internat. Soc. Blood Transfusion, Internat. Soc. Lymphology, Womans Party Sewell-Belmont Ho. and Mus. (bd. dir. 1981-2005, corr. sec. 1989-91, rec. sec. 1991-96, chair audit com. 2005), Woman's Nat. Dem. Club. Home: 1661 Crescent Pl NW Apt 305 Washington DC 20009-4066 Home Fax: 202-265-3267. Personal E-mail: ffharding@aol.com.

HARDING, JOHN EDWARD, lawyer; b. San Francisco, Sept. 5, 1963; s. Merle Lewis and Trudy (Evertz) H.; m. Lisa Elliott; children: Jack Joseph, Ryan Elise. BA, St. Mary's Coll., Moraga, Calif., 1986; JD, Golden Gate U., 1989. Bar: Calif. 1989, U.S. Dist. Ct. (no. dist.) Calif. 1989, U.S. Ct. Appeals (9th cir.) 1989, D.C. 1991, Wyo. 1996, U.S. Dist. Ct. (ctrl. dist.) Calif. 1997. Assoc. Law Offices of Merle L. Harding, Pleasanton, Calif., 1989; ptnr. Harding & Harding, Pleasanton, 1990-2000, Harding & Assocs., Pleasanton, 2000—. Bd. dirs. Tri-Valley br. Am. Heart Assn., Oakland, Calif., 1992-93, Valley Community Health Ctr., Pleasanton, 1992-96. Mem. ABA, ATLA, Consumer Atty. Calif., State Bar Calif., D.C. Bar Assn., Wyo. Bar Assn., Pleasanton C. of C. (bd. dirs. 1993-96, v.p. pub. affairs 1994). Avocations: golf, softball, backpacking, fishing, spectator sports, reading, travel. Office: Harding & Assocs 78 Mission Dr Ste B Pleasanton CA 94566-7683 E-mail: jharding@hardinglaw.com.

HARDING, JOHN HIBBARD, retired insurance company executive; b. Plainfield, N.J., Jan. 12, 1936; s. Ernest Reginald and Emily (Hibbard) H.; m. Joan Edith Tarro, Nov. 29, 1973; children— David, Philip, Robert, Brooke, Ashley. BA, Princeton U., 1958. Asst. actuary Nat. Life Ins. Co., Montpelier, Vt., 1965-67, assoc. actuary, 1967-69, actuary R&D, 1969-72, v.p., actuary, 1972-80, sr. v.p., chief actuary, 1980-83, exec. v.p., 1983-85, vice chmn. bd., dir., 1985-87, pres., COO, 1987-96; v.p., chief actuary Blue Cross-Blue Shield of Vt., 1997-2000. Chmn., CEO Adminstrv. Svcs., Inc.; dir. Equity Svcs., Inc., Nat. Life Investment Mgmt. Co., Sentinel Advisors, Inc., 1987-96. Fellow Soc. Actuaries (bd. govs. 1993-95); mem. Am. Acad. Actuaries (bd. dirs. 1982-85, v.p. 1988-90, pres.-elect 1991-92, pres. 1992-93, immediate past pres. 1993-94). Home: PO Box 180 East Calais VT 05650-0180 E-mail: hardingcalais@aol.com.

HARDING, MAJOR BEST, former state supreme court chief justice; b. Charlotte, N.C., Oct. 13, 1935; m. Jane Lewis, Dec., 1958; children: Major B. Jr., David L., Alice Harding Sanderson. BS, Wake Forest U., 1957, JD, 1959; LLM in Jud. Process, U. Va., 1995; LLD, Stetson U., 1991, Fla. Coastal Sch. Law, 1999. Bar: N.C. 1959, Fla. 1960. Staff judge adv. hdqrs., Ft. Gordon, Ga., 1960-62; asst. county solicitor Criminal Ct. of Record, Duval County, Fla., 1962-63; pvt. practice law, 1964-68; judge Juvenile Ct., Duval County, 1968-70, 4th Jud. Cir. of Fla., 1970—91, chief judge, 1974-77; justice Supreme Ct. of Fla., Tallahassee, 1991—2002, chief justice, 1998-2000; shareholder Ausley and McMullen, Tallahassee, 2003. Supervisory judge Family Mediation Unit, 1984-90; mem. Matrimonial Law Commn. and Gender Bias Study Commn.; chair Fla. Ct. Edn. Coun., past mem. Jud. Conf.; 1st dean New Judges Coll., 1975, faculty mem. in probate and juvenile areas, until 1979; dean Fla. Jud. Coll., 1984-92, faculty mem., 1984-2003, mem. bench-bar commn.; chmn. Supreme Ct. com. on law-related edn., 1997—. Former bd. dirs. Legal Aid Assn., Family Consultation Svc., Daniel Meml. Home; mem. bd. visitors Wake Forest Sch. Law, Winston-Salem, N.C., Reformed Theol. Sem., Orlando, Fla.; past pres. Rotary Club of Riverside, Jacksonville, Fla., Rotary Club of Tallahasee; chmn. U.S. Constn. Bicentennial Commn., Jacksonville; past mem., deacon, elder St. John's Presbyn. Ch.; commr. Gen. Assembly Presbyn. Ch. U.S., 1971; mem. vestry St. John's Episcopal Ch., Tallahassee. Recipient Award for Outstanding Contbn. to Field of Matrimonial Law Am. Acad. Matrimonial Lawyers, 1986, Disting. Svc. award Nat. Ctr. State Cts., 2001, William A. Dugger Profl. Integrity award Capital Rotary Club. Mem. ABA (Commn. Lawyer Assistance Programs Jud. Recognition award), Am. Bd. Trial Advocates (Jurist of Yr. Jacksonville chpt. 2000), The Fla. Bar, N.C. State Bar Assn., Chester Bedell Inn of Ct. (past pres., ex-officio bd. mem., master emeritus Chester Bedell), Dade County Trial Lawyers Assn. (Justice Harry Lee Anstead professionalism award 1998), Scabbard and Blade, Tallahassee Am. Inn of Ct. (ex officio trustee), Tallahassee Bar Assn., Econ. Club of Fla. (v.p.), Sigma Chi (Significant Sig award 1997), Phi Delta Phi. Episcopalian. Office: Ausley and McMullen 227 S Calhoun St Tallahassee FL 32301 Office Phone: 850-224-9115. Business E-Mail: mharding@ausley.com.

HARDING, MARC STEVEN, lawyer; b. Des Moines, Nov. 8, 1947; s. John Henry and Marilyn Gloria (Anderson) H.; married. BS, U. Iowa, 1970, JD, 1973; DO, U. Osteopathic Medicine, 1996, M in Healthcare Adminstrn., 1996. Bar: Iowa 1973, US Dist. Ct. (no. and so. dists.) Iowa 1973, US Ct. Appeals (8th cir.) 1974, US Ct. Claims 1976, US Tax Ct. 1976, US Supreme Ct. 1976. Pvt. practice, Des Moines, 1973—. Mem.: Iowa Trial Lawyers Assn., Assn. Trial Lawyers Am., Iowa State Bar Assn., Nat. Bd. Trial Advocacy, Am. Coll. Legal Medicine. Office Phone: 515-287-1454.

HARDING, MARGARET TYREE, minister; b. Lynchburg, Va., May 28, 1951; d. Aubrey Nathaniel and Audrey (Riley) Tyree; m. William R. Harding, Sep. 11, 1993. BA, Averett Coll., 1978; MDiv, Southeastern Bapt. Theol. Sem., Wake Forest, N.C., 1981. Min. youth Moffett Meml. Bapt. Ch., Danville, Va., 1976-78, West Main Bapt. Ch., Danville, 1979-81; min. edn. and youth North Run Bapt. Ch., Richmond, Va., 1981-84; min. edn., youth and adminstrn. Grandin Ct. Bapt. Ch., Roanoke, Va., 1984-99; adult specialist Woman's Missionary Union Bapt. State Conv. N.C., 1999—. Contbr. articles to profl. jours. Devotional officer Jr. Women's Club, Madison Heights, Va., 1971-75; alumni rep. Averett Coll., Danville, 1984—, mem. mins. adv. com., 1991; usher Mill Mountain Theater, Roanoke, Va., 1990—. Mem. Religious Edn. Assn. U.S. and Can. (bd. dirs. 1991), Va. Bapt. Gen. Assn. (gen. bd. 1989—), Va. Bapt. Religious Assn. (pres. 1989), So. Bapt. Religious Edn. Assn. (asst. sec. 1994-95), Roanoke Area Religious Edn. Assn. (pres. 1991). Home: 201 Tapestry Ter Cary NC 27511-7259 Office: NC Woman's Missionary Union PO Box 1107 Cary NC 27512 Business E-Mail: mharding@bscnc.org. *Make the most of every momement of your life. It is given to you by God to be enjoyed and lived to the fullest.*

HARDING, MARIE, ecological executive, artist; b. Glen Cove, NY, Nov. 13, 1941; d. Charles Lewis and Marie (Parish) H.; m. John P. Allen, Jan. 29, 1965 (div. Oct., 1991); 1 child, Eden A. Harding. BA, Sarah Lawrence Coll., 1964; postgrad., Arts Students League, N.Y.C., 1965. Founder Synergia Ranch Ctr. for Innovation, Retreats and Confs., Santa Fe, 1969; founding mem., actress Theater of All Possibilities, Santa Fe, 1971-86; founding mem., dir. Inst. Ecotechnics, Santa Fe, also London, 1974—; bd. dirs., founding mem. Savannah Systems Pty., Ltd., Kimberly region, Australia, 1976—, Outback Sta. Pty. Ltd., Kimberly region, Australia, 1976-94; chair, dir. EcoWorld, Inc., Santa Fe, 1982-94; dir., founding mem., CFO Space Biospheres Ventures, Biosphere 2, Ariz., 1984-94; chair, CEO Oceans Expdns., Inc., 1986-92; pres. ecol. and biosphere R&D/implementation project Global Ecotechnics Corp., Santa Fe, 1994—; pres. Decisions Team, Inc. Ecol. Project Mgmt., Ariz., 1994—; pres., mng. mem. Synergia Ranch, LLC, Santa Fe. Particpant in constrn. and fin. Capt. R. Heraclitus rsch. vessel, Oakland, Calif., 1974; bd. dirs. Synergetic Press, London and Ariz.; mem. San Marcos Dist. Planning Com., 2004- Exhibitions include Biosphere 2, Ariz., 1979-93, Biosphere 2, October Gallery, London, 1996, 2003-04, Berlin, 2003, Peoples Bank N.Mex., 2003; project dir., artist mural project History of Jazz, Dance, Theater, Ft. Worth, 1982-83, San Marcos Studio Tours, 1999-2004; prodr., dir. (films) Bryon Gysin Loves ya, Project Charlie, The Search, Planet Earth Conf Vol. Swallows, Madras, India, 1964, Project Concern, Vietnam, Hong Kong, 1964-65; artist, founder, trustee October Gallery Trust, London, 1979; planning com. San Marcos Dist., 2004 Avocations: ecological project implementation, endangered lifestyles/cultures, painting, landscape gardening, retreat facilitation. Home and Office: 26 Synergia Rd Santa Fe NM 87508-4438 Office Phone: 505-471-2573.

HARDING, STEVE, real estate company executive; BBA in Acctg. and Mgmt., Tex. A&M U. CPA Tex., cert. fin. planner. Various positions KPMG Peat Marwick, Houston; asst. contr. Ayrshire/Eland Corp., Houston; sr. contr. Hines Interests, Dallas; CFO Transwestern Comml. Svcs., Inc., Houston, also bd. dirs. Mem.: AICPA, Tex. Soc. CPAs, Nat. Assn. Real Estate Cos. Office: Transwestern Comm Svcs Ste 1300 1900 W Loop S Houston TX 77027

HARDIS, STEPHEN ROGER, retired manufacturing company executive; b. N.Y.C., July 13, 1935; s. Abraham I. and Ethel (Krinsky) H; m. Sondra Joyce Rolbin, Sept. 15, 1957; children: Julia Faye, Andrew Martin, Joanna Halley. BA with distinction, Cornell U., 1956; M.P.A. in Econs., Woodrow Wilson Sch. of Pub. and Internat. Affairs Princeton U., 1960. Asst. to controller Gen. Dynamics, 1960-61; fin. analyst Pfaudler Permutit Inc., 1961-64; staff asst. to controller, 1964; mgr. corp. long-range planning Ritter Pfaudler Corp., 1965-68, dir. corporate planning, 1968; treas. Sybron Corp., Rochester, N.Y., 1969—, v.p. fin., 1970-77, exec. v.p. fin. and planning, 1977-79; vice chmn., chief fin. and adminstrv. officer Eaton Corp., Cleve., 1979—, vice chmn., CEO, 1995, chmn., CEO, 1996-2000; ret., 2000; chmn. Axcelis Techs., 2000—. Bd. dirs. Progressive, Nordson Corp., Lexmark Corp., Marsh & McLennan Past mem. Gov.'s Task Force on High Tech. Industry; past mem. bd. dirs. Rochester Area Hosp. Corp., Rochester Area Ednl. TV Sta., Genesee Hosp.; trustee Cleve. Clinic, Inc. With USNR, 1956-58. Mem. Phi Beta Kappa.

HARDISON, DONALD LEIGH, retired architect; b. Fillmore, Calif., Mar. 23, 1916; s. Leigh Winter and Myrtle Glenn (Thorpe) H.; m. Betty Jane Decker, June 14, 1942; children: Stephen Decker, Janet Leigh Hardison Brown AB, U. Calif.-Berkeley, 1938. Lic. architect, Calif. Prin. Hardison & Assocs., Richmond, Calif., 1948-56; ptnr. Hardison & Komatsu, Richmond, 1956-64, pres. San Francisco, 1965-78; chmn. bd. Hardison Komatsu Ivelich & Tucker, San Francisco, 1978-87, ret., 1987. Prin. works include Sonoma State Coll. Residence Hall, 1972 (AIA award 1977), Chevron Cafeteria-Tech. Ctr., Richmond, 1981, McAllister Tower, San Francisco, 1982, (co-architect) U. Calif.-Berkeley Student Ctr. Complex, 1970 (AIA award 1970) Mem. Richmond Planning Commn., 1952-55; mem. Calif. Commn. on Housing and Cmty. Devel., 1969-74; bd. dirs. Art Ctr., Richmond, 1965-70, Richmond Mus. of History, 1990-2003. Fellow AIA (bd. dirs. 1978-80, chancellor Coll. Fellows 1985, pres. East Bay chpt. 1954, pres. Calif. council 1965, Calif. council Disting. Service citation 1984) . Clubs: Commonwealth (San Francisco). Lodges: Rotary (pres. Richmond, Calif. 1986-87). Republican. Presbyterian.

HARDISTY, WILLIAM LEE, English language educator; b. Creston, Iowa, Feb. 14, 1946; s. Ernest Dale and Velda Marie (Schaffer) H.; m. Bernadine Maxine Reimers, July 30, 1967; children: Lance William, Chad Eugene. AA, Creston (Iowa) C.C., 1965; BS, N.W. Mo. State U., Maryville, 1967, MA, 1972; postgrad., U. No. Iowa, Cedar Falls, 2004. Cert. tchr., Iowa, Mo. Instr. Iowa Western Coll., Council Bluffs, 1987—; chmn. lang. arts A-H-S-T H.S., Avoca, Iowa, 1967—2005, drama dir., 1967-92; instr. U. No. Iowa Workshops. Presenter Iowa Tchrs. English, Des Moines, 1991—95, Iowa Conservation Edn. Coun., Ames, 1995, Iowa State Edn. Assn., 1982—99, Iowa Sci. Tchrs., 1996—2004, others. Contbr. articles to profl. and popular publs. Dist. chmn. Mid-Am. coun. Boy Scouts Am., 1984—2005, trustee; pres. Iowa Assn. County Conservation Bds., Des Moines, 1990, Pott count R.E.A.P. Bd., Council Bluffs, 1992; mem. Sheriff's Dept. Citizens Adv. Bd., 1994—; chmn. Rep. party Knox Twp., Avoca, 1988—; elder Presbyn. Ch., 1969—. Mem. NRA (life), NEA (life), Nat. Coun. Tchrs. English (life), Pheasants Forever (bd. dirs. 1990-91), Iowa State Edn. Assn., Southwest Uniserv Unit (exec. bd. 1994—, UNIeiicadre 1998—), Nat. Elk Fedn. (life), Phi Delta Kappa. Avocations: writing, hunting, hiking, canoeing, travel. Home: 317 E Jaycee St Avoca IA 51521-5104 Office: Hardisty's 317 E Jaycee St Avoca IA 51521 Office Phone: 712-343-6665. Personal E-mail: hardisys@walnutel.net.

HARDMAN, HAROLD FRANCIS, pharmacology educator; b. East Orange, N.J., Aug. 2, 1927; s. Harold Maine and Agnes Lillian (McGovern) H.; m. Jean Ely Dettmer, June 27, 1950; children— David, Timothy, John, Susan. B.Sc. (Am. Found. Pharm. Edn. scholar), Rutgers U., 1949; M.Sc. (Am. Found. Pharm. Edn. fellow), U. Ill. at Chgo., 1951; PhD (Am. Found. Pharm. Edn. fellow), U. Mich., 1954, MD, 1958. Asst. prof. pharmacology U. Mich., 1958-60; assoc. prof. pharmacology Marquette U., Milw., 1960-62; prof. pharmacology, chmn. dept. Med. Coll. of Wis. at Milw., 1962—, chmn. dept., 1962-88, assoc. dean basic scis., 1968-70; prof. emeritus, 1992—; chmn. retirees, 1993-95. Bd. dirs. Med. Coll. Wis., 1980-82; trustee Biosis, 1988-91 Served to sgt. AUS, 1946-47. John and Mary Markle scholar acad. medicine, 1958-62; recipient Outstanding Alumni award U. Mich., 1989, Disting. Svc. award Med. Coll. Wis., 1985, Med. Alumni recognition award, 1995, Pharmacology Grad. Student Recognition award, 1995; Citation Esteem, Dean and Bd. Dirs. Med. Coll. Wis., 1988. Mem. Am. Soc. Pharmacology and Exptl. Therapeutics (chmn. program com. 1973-76, councillor 1976-79, pres.-elect 1981-82, pres. 1982-83), Fedn. Am. Socs. Exptl. Biology (pres. 1983-84), Assn. Med. Sch. Pharmacology Chairmen (sec. 1970-72, pres. 1978-80), Milw. Acad. Medicine (pres. 1974-75) Achievements include rsch. in cardiovascular pharmacology with continuous support from NIH for 32 yrs. Studied the effect of drug and receptor ionization upon pharmacological activity with emphasis upon beta adrenergic receptor agonists and antagonists. Also conducted studies on the behavioral and cardiovascular actions of marijuana and derivatives. Home: 1120 Indianwood Dr Brookfield WI 53005-5705 Personal E-mail: jhardman7@worldnet.att.net.

HARDMAN, JAMES CHARLES, lawyer, transportation executive; b. Chgo., Sept. 22, 1931; s. William Pryor and Mary Margaret (O'Donnell) H.; children: James Pryor, Katie Maura. BS in Bus., Quincy Coll., 1953; MBA, Northwestern U., 1958, JD, 1961. Bar: Ill. 1961, Minn. 1984, U.S. Dist. Ct. (no. dist.) Ill. 1962, U.S. Ct. Appeals (7th cir.) 1968, U.S. Dist. Ct. D.C. 1971, U.S. Supreme Ct. 1971, U.S. Ct. Appeals D.C. Cir. 1978, U.S. Dist. Ct. Minn. 1984. Gen. atty. Swift & Co., Chgo., 1961-62; sole practice Chgo., 1962-83; v.p. adminstrn., gen. counsel Dart Transit Co., St. Paul, 1984-94; atty. Law Offices James C. Harman, St. Paul, 1994—. Vis. prof. law U. Denver, 1978-79; lectr. small bus. mgmt. Northeastern Ill. U., Chgo., 1982 Author: Fair Labor Standard Act and Motor Carrier Operations, 1974, Motor Carriage: The Interstate Commerce Commission, 1976, Welcome to the Wonderful World of Political Action, 1990; contbr. articles to profl. jours. V.p. Sauganash Cmty. Assn., Chgo., 1980-83; chmn. bd. govs. Transp. Law Jour., Denver, 1976-78, 2004—. Served to lt. (j.g.) USN, 1953-55 Recipient Am. Jurisprudence Labor Law award, 1961, award of Merit Transp. Law Inst., 1968, 72, Lifetime Achievement Award, Transportation Lawyers Assn., 1999, Minnesota Trucking Assn., 2001, Truckload Carrier Assn., 2003. Mem. Transp. Lawyers Assn. (pres. 1980, chmn. 1982, Lifetime Achievement award 1999, 2001), Minn. Trucking Assn. (chmn., Disting. Svc. award 1998), Minn. Bar Assn., Ill. State Bar Assn., Chgo. Bar Assn. (Legal Writing award 1970), Elks. Roman Catholic. Home: 753 Carla Ln Saint Paul MN 55109-1925 Office: Law Offices James C Hardman 753 Carla Ln Little Canada MN 55109-1925 Office Phone: 651-483-5560. E-mail: jhardman5560@comcast.net.

HARDMAN, JOHN B., psychiatrist, director; m. Laura Hardman. Med. dir. Charter Peachford Hosp., Atlanta, 1980—88; from dir. anti-tobacco initiatives to exec. dir. Carter Presdl. Ctr., Atlanta, 1989—2004, exec. dir., 2004—. Adj. prof. Emory U.; pres. Ga. Coun. Child and Adolescent Psychiatry. Pres. Leadership Ga. Mem.: Ga. Psychiatric Physicians Assn. (pres.), Atlanta (Ga.) Hist. Soc. (pres.). Office: The Carter Ctr One Copenhill 453 Freedom Pkwy Atlanta GA 30307

HARDMON, FRANK, artist, educator; b. Vance, Miss., Apr. 2, 1941; s. McKinley and Clottell Hardmon; m. Earnestine Armstrong Hardmon, Aug. 21, 1966; children: Trenita Fay, Elanda Vonsha. AA, Coahoma Jr. Coll., 1964; BS, Miss. Valley State U., 1966; MFA, Inst. Allende, Mexico, 1972. Tchr. art Nugent Ctr. H.S., Benoit, Miss., 1966—72; assoc. prof. art Miss. Valley State U., Ittabena, Miss., 1972—. Chmn. state art exhbn. Nat. Conf. Arts, Greenville, 1973; cons. in field. Works of Artists, Smith Robertson Cultural Ctr., 1992, Represented in permanent collections Five Out Of One Links, Inc. Bd. dirs. Arts for Success, Greenwood, Miss., 1993. Named one of Outstanding Educators Am., 1974; recipient Advocacy award, Gov.'s Office Human Devel., Jackson, Miss., 1985, Appreciation cert., Mike Espy 2d Dist Art Contest, 1989, Headwae award, Miss. Legis. Work in Art, 2000. Mem.: Internat. Soc. Artists, Nat. Art Ednl. Assn., Shad Club (sec. 2002—). Home: 1574 Northview Dr Mc Kenzie TN 38201 Office: Mississippi Valley State U 14000 Hwy 82 7255 Itta Bena MS 38941

HARDWAY, WENDELL GARY, retired academic administrator; b. Bolair, W.Va., Mar. 5, 1927; s. Ressie Bruce and Elsie Clennen (Miller) H.; m. Hannah Lou Garrett, July 12, 1950. BS, W.Va. U., 1949, MS, 1953; PhD, Ohio State U., 1959. Tchr. Troy (W.Va.) High Sch., 1949-54; asst. prof. sci. Glenville (W.Va.) State Coll., 1954-57, assoc. prof. edn., 1959-61, prof., chmn. div. edn., dir. student teaching, 1961-66; pres. Bluefield (W.Va.) State Coll., 1966-73, Fairmont (W.Va.) State Coll., 1973-88, ret., 1988. Pres. United Way, Fairmont, 1976; mem. Glenville City Council, 1958-64; pres. W.Va. Intercollegiate Athletic Conf., 1977-78. Served with AUS, 1945-46. Named Man of Yr., Bluefield Jaycees, 1969, Disting. Pioneer, Glenville State Coll., 1985, Outstanding Alumnus, W.Va. U. Coll. Agr., 1987. Hardway Libr. at Bluefield State Coll. and Hardway Hall (adminstrn. bldg.) at Fairmont State Coll. named in his honor. Mem. Phi Delta Theta, Gamma Sigma Delta, Phi Delta Kappa, Kappa Delta Pi. Methodist. Home: 4 Bel Manor Dr Fairmont WV 26554

HARDWICK, CHARLES LEIGHTON, pharmaceutical executive, former state legislator; b. Somerset, Ky., Nov. 8, 1941; s. Joseph Fulton and Lucy Belle (Simpson) H.; m. Patricia Ruth Johnson, Mar. 30, 1959 (div. July 1993); children: Virginia Lee, Charles Jr; m. Sheilagh Mylott, Aug. 10, 2002. BS, Fla. State U., 1962, MBA, 1964. Sales supr. Continental Baking Co., Detroit, 1964-66; sales rep. Pfizer, Inc., N.Y.C., 1966-70, regional mgr., 1970-73, dir. mktg., 1973-77, dir. civic info., 1977—; v.p. govt. and pub. affairs Pfizer Inc., N.Y.C., 1977—2002, sr. v.p. worldwide govt. and pub. affairs, 2002—, mem. Pfizer Leadership Team; state rep. State of N.J., 1978—92, Rep. Assembly minority leader, Gen. Assembly, 1985-87, speaker of assembly, 1986-89, N.J. Assembly minority leader emeritus, 1989-91. Pres., exec. dir. Pfizer Found.; vice chmn. U.S. Trade Adv. Commn., Washington, 1983-85; mem. Presdl. Federalism Adv. Commn., Washington, 1981-83. Mem. Am. Legis. Exchange Coun. (past bd. dirs., named Legislator of Yr. 1986), Nat. Rep. Legislators Assn. (pres. 1982-84). Avocation: tennis. Office: 235 E 42d St New York NY 10017 Office Phone: 212-573-7833. E-mail: chuck.hardwick@pfizer.com.

HARDWICK, DAVID FRANCIS, pathologist; b. Vancouver, B.C., Can., Jan. 24, 1934; s. Walter H. W. and Iris L. (Hyndman) H.; m. Margaret M. Lang, Aug. 22, 1956; children: Margaret F., Heather I., David J. MD, U. B.C., 1957, LLD (hon.), 2001. Intern Montreal (Que., Can.) Gen. Hosp., 1957-58; resident Vancouver Gen. Hosp., 1958-59, Children's Hosp., Los Angeles, 1959-62; research assoc. U. So. Calif., 1961-62; clin. instr. U. B.C., Vancouver, 1963-65, asst. prof. pathology, 1965-69, assoc. prof., 1969-74, prof., 1974—, head dept. pathology, 1976-90, assoc. dean rsch. and planning, 1990-96; dir. labs. Children's Hosp., Vancouver, 1969-92, Vancouver Gen. Hosp., 1976-90; chmn. M.A.C., Children's Hosp., 1970-87; interinstitutional planning U. B.C. Medicine, 1996-98, spl. advisor on planning, 1999—. Adj. prof. Chinese U. Hong Kong; mem. U. B.C. Senate, 1966-71. Author: Acid Base Balance and Blood Gas Studies, 1968, Intermediary Metabolism of Liver, 1971, Directing the Clinical Laboratory, 1990, Laboratory Supervision and Management, 2d edit., 2002; contbr. numerous articles to profl. publs. Bd. dirs. Children's and Women's Rsch. Inst., B.C., 1998—, Women's Hosp. Found., 1997-2000, B.C. Transplant Found., 1993—. Recipient Queen's Centennial medal Govt. Can., 1978, U. B.C. Faculty Citation Teaching award, 1987, Wallace Wilson Leadership award, 1990, William Boyd Lectureship award Canadian Assn. Path, 1994, Sydney Israels Founders award B.C. Rsch. Inst. Children and Family, 1997, Univ. medal for Outstanding Svc., U. B.C., 1997; Sydney Farber lectr., Soc. Ped. Path., 1998. Fellow Royal Coll. Physicians (Can.), Coll. Am. Pathologists; mem. Internat. Acad. Pathology (pres. 1996, v.p. N.Am. 1998—, Gold medal 2002), Can. Med. Assn., B.C. Assn. Lab. Medicine, B.C. Med. Assn., N.Y. Acad. Sci., Soc. Pediat. Pathology, Internat. Acad. Pathology (Disting. Svc. award 1994), U.S. and Can. Acad. Pathology (Pres.'s award 2004), B.C. Transplant Found. (chmn. bd. 2000—), Med. Student and Alumni Ctr. Soc. (chair 2001—), Alpha Omega Alpha. Home: 727 W 23rd Ave Vancouver BC Canada V5Z 2A7 Office: U BC Dept Pathology 2211 Wesbrook Mall Vancouver BC Canada V6T 1W5 Business E-Mail: david.f.hardwick@ubc.ca.

HARDWICK, ELIZABETH, writer; b. Lexington, Ky., July 27, 1916; d. Eugene Allen and Mary (Ramsey) H.; m. Robert Lowell, July 28, 1949 (div. Oct. 1972); 1 child, Harriet. AB, U. Ky., 1938, MA, 1939; postgrad., Columbia U., 1939-41. Adj. assoc. prof. Barnard Coll. Author: (novels) The Ghostly Lover, 1945, The Simple Truth, 1955, Sleepless Nights, 1979, (essays) A View of My Own, 1962, Seduction and Betrayal, 1974, Bartleby in Manhattan, 1983, Sight Readings, 1998, Herman Melville, A Life, 2000; editor: The Selected Letters of William James, 1960; adv. editor: N.Y. Rev. Books. Recipient George Jean Nathan award for dramatic criticism, 1966, Gold medal for criticism, Am. Acad. Arts and Letters, 1993; Guggenheim fellow, 1947. Mem. Am. Acad. and Inst. Arts and Letters, Acad. Arts and Scis. Home: 15 W 67th St New York NY 10023-6226

HARDWICKE, CATHERINE HELEN, film director, set designer; b. McAllen, Tex., 1955; d. John Benjamin III and Jamee Alberta (Bennett) H. BArch with highest honors, U. Tex., 1979; postgrad., UCLA. Prodn. designer: (films) Tapeheads, 1988, I'm Gonna Git You Sucka, 1988, Martins Go Home, 1990, Passed Away, 1992, Posse, 1993, Freaked, 1993, Tombstone, 1993, Car 54, Where Are You, 1994, Tank Girl, 1995, 2 Days in the Valley, 1996, SubUrbia, 1996, Mad City, 1997, The Newton Boys, 1998, Three Kings, 1999, Antitrust, 2001, Vanilla Sky, 2001, Laurel Canyon, 2002, (theatre) Carnage, Methusalem, Alagazam--After the Dog Wars; dir.: (films) Thirteen, 2003 (also writer), Lords of Dogtown, 2005; art dir.: (films) Hunk, 1987, Mr. Destiny, 1990 Recipient Card Walker Animation award Disney Studios, 1984, Nissan Focus award, 1984, Joseph Jefferson award Chgo. Non-Equity Theatre, 1990, others.*

HARDY, BEATRIZ BETANCOURT, historian; b. Washington, Sept. 1961; d. Ernesto Francisco and Raquel (Prieto) Betancourt; m. Stephen Gregg Hardy, June 23, 1990. BA, Goucher Coll., 1983; MA, U. Va., 1984; PhD, U. Md., 1993. Instr. history Univ. Coll., Adelphi, Md., 1991; lectr. history George Washington U., Washington, 1991-93; asst. prof. history Coastal Carolina U., Conway, SC, 1993—98; outreach program mgr. Nat. History Day, College Park, Md., 1998—2002; libr. dir. Md. Hist. Soc., Balt., 2002—. Contbr. articles to profl. jours. Class agt. Goucher Coll. Alumni Assn., Towson, Md., 1986-1998; listserv editor, H-History Day, 1999-2003; book review editor, 4-Maryland, 2001-04. Philip Francis Dupont fellow U. Va., Charlottesville, 1983-84, Md. history fellow Md. State Archives, Md. Hist. Soc., 1989-90, dissertation fellow U. Md., College Park, 1990-91, minority dissertation rsch. fellow George Washington U., Washington, 1991-93; recipient Colonial Essay Prize, Colonial Soc. Pa., Phila. Ctr. Early Am. History, 1991. Mem. Am. Hist. Assn., Orgn. Am. Historians, Phi Beta Kappa, Phi Alpha Theta, Southern Hist. Assn., Inst. Early Am. Hist. & Culture. Home: 9508 Clock Tower Ln Columbia MD 21046-1876 Office: Maryland Hist Soc 201 W Monument St Baltimore MD 21201

HARDY, BEN (BENSON B. HARDY), orchid nursery executive; b. Oakland, Calif., Nov. 22, 1920; s. Lester William and Irene Isabell (Bliss) H. Student pub. schs., Oakland, Calif., Concord, Calif.; grad. photo, Intelligence Sch., Denver, 1949. Served as enlisted man U.S. Navy, 1942-48; joined USAF, 1948; advanced through grades to capt., 1957; with 67th Reconnaissance Squadron, 1951-52; Hdqrs. Squadron Thule AFB, 1956; resigned, 1957; material requirements analyst-coord. Teledyne Ryan Aero. Co., San Diego, 1958-73, 83-98, ret., 1998. Dispatcher-coord. Cubic Western Data Co., San Diego, 1977-80; owner-ptnr. orchid nursery. Pres. Exotic Plant Soc., 1976-78, 81-84, San Diego Gesneriad Soc., 1978; dir. 23d Western Orchid Congress, 1979. Author: (with John Klemme) The Orchid Badge Collector's Guide, 1993, (with Duane Hall) Photographic Aerial Reconnaissance and Interpretation Korea 1950-1952, 2004. Decorated Bronze Star; recipient Letter of Commendation NASA, also others. Mem. Am. Orchid Soc. (life), N.Z. Orchid Soc., San Diego County Orchid Soc. (life, pres. 1972-73, 75-76), Hoya Soc. Internat. (pres. 1981-83, 95-2002), Orchid Digest Corp., Auckland Orchid Club, Orchid Badge Club Internat. (found. 1988, pres. 1991—), Dirs. Club, San Diego Zool. Soc., Korean War Vets. Assn. (life), VFW (life). Home: 9443 E Heaney Cir Santee CA 92071-2919 Personal E-mail: Cptdltl@aol.com.

HARDY, CHARLOTTE B., insurance agent; b. Springhill, La., Sept. 23, 1943; d. Willis Bevil and Vivian Ernestine (Britt) Burns; m. Barry Wayne Hardy, Aug. 18, 1963; children: Pamela H. Davis, Jason W. AA, So. Ark. U., 1978, BS, 1980. Mem. office staff Nickerson Ins. Agy., Springhill, La., 1961-62; exec. sec. Berry Petroleum, Magnolia, Ark., 1963-66; piano tchr. El Dorado, Ark., 1969-79; tchr. El Dorado Pub. Schs., 1980-85; ins. agt. State Farm Ins., El Dorado, 1985—. Recipient Pub. Rels. award NALU, 1995, 97, Nat. Sales Achievement award, 1995-2001, Nat. Multiline Sales award, 1997, 99-2001. Mem. Nat. Assn. Ins. Fin. Advisors, Ark. State Life Underwriters (Pub. Rels. award 1994, 95), El Dorado Life Underwriters Assn. (sec.-treas. 1988-89, v.p. 1989-90, Pres.'s Leadership award 1998), El Dorado-Camden Life Underwriters Assn. (pres.-elect 1992-93, pres. 1993-94), Golden Triangle Life Underwriters Assn., El Dorado C. of C. (bd. dirs. 1990-93). Baptist. Avocations: music, fishing. Home: 200 Meadow Hills Dr El Dorado AR 71730 Office: State Farm Ins Cos 600 W Main El Dorado AR 71730 E-mail: hardy.b3ep@statefarm.com.

HARDY, CHERRYL, artist; b. Jackson, Miss., Mar. 7, 1952; d. Thomas G. Jr. and Jo Anne (Parker) H.; m. John L. Hawkins, Mar. 20, 1987. BA, U. Ala., Birmingham, 1979. One-man shows include White House Gallery, Williams Bay, Wis., 1988; represented in permanent collection at The Parthenon, Nashville. Recipient Disting. award U. Ala., 1978, 80. Avocations: piano, flute.

HARDY, CHESTER ALFRED, engineer; b. El Paso, Tex., Nov. 17, 1929; m. Evelyn Anne Moore, June 22, 1955; 1 child, Clinton Alfred (dec.). BS in Engring., U. Tex., El Paso, 1955; MS in Engring., So. Meth. U., 1959, MS in Engring. Adminstrn., 1961. Registered profl. engr., Tex. Mgr. Gen. Dynamics, Fort Worth, Tex., 1980-87; dir. Lockheed Martin, Fort Worth, 1987—. Chmn. corp. R&M panel Gen. Dynamics, 1976; lectr. Agard Nato, Munich, London, N.Y., 1976; tchr. bus. sch. Tex. Christian U., Ft. Worth, 1968. Contbr. articles to profl. jours. With USN, 1948-52. Named to, Lockheed Martin Aero. Hall of Fame. Mem. Tex. Soc. Profl. Engrs., Moslah Shrine, Colonial Country Club, Petroleum Club, Soc. of the Cincinnati, Sco. Sons of Bench and Bar, Soc. Mayflower Descs., Jamestowne Soc., Ancient and Hon. Arty. Co. of Mass., SAR, Flagon and Trencher, Colonial Order of the Crown, Magna Charta Barons, Soc. Knights of the Garter, Soc. Descs. of Colonial Clergy, Nat. Huguenot Soc., Nat. Soc. Sons and Daus. of Pilgrims, Plantagenet Soc. Episcopalian. Avocations: tennis, skiing.

HARDY, CLARENCE EARL, JR., government, nonprofit and corporate sector executive; b. Edenton, N.C., July 2, 1944; m. Mae A. Brewer; children: Clarence, Melva. BA in Polit. Sci. and Econs., N.C. Ctrl. U., 1967; MPA in Pub. Adminstrn., Syracuse U., 1969; diploma in sr. mgrs. in govt. program, Harvard U., 1990. Pers. mgmt. analyst Atomic Energy Commn., 1971-73; pers. officer, mgmt. analyst Atomic Energy Commn. Energy Rsch. and Devel. Adminstrn., 1973-75, sr. mgmt. analyst, program evaluation officer, 1975-76, chief hqrs. pers. ops. br., 1976-77; pers. officer Fed. Energy Regulatory Commn., 1978; chief pers. mgmt. svcs. Dept. Energy Hqrs., 1977-78, dep. dir. hqrs. pers. ops. divsn., 1978-79; chief pers. divsn. Nat. Bur. Standards, 1979; dir. pers. mgmt. EPA, 1979-88, dep. dir. Office of Human Resources Mgmt., 1988-97; dir. Office Cooperative Environ. Mgmt., 1997—2001; exec. dir. Combined Fed. Campaign of Nat. Capital Area, 2001—03; pres. & CEO DQC Consultants, 1994—. Prof. George Mason U., 1998—99. Recipient Disting. Fed. Career award, 2001; N.C. Ctrl U. Polit. Sci. scholar, 1966, 67, Presdl. rank award, 1998; Maxwell fellow, 1968, 69, Congl. fellow Brookings Instn., 1996. Mem. Internat. Pers. Mgmt. Assn., Internat. Platform Assn., Am. Soc. Pub. Adminstrn., Am. Mgmt. Assn., Am. Judicature Soc., Acad. Polit. and Social Sci., Am. Polit. Sci. Assn., World Future Soc., Acad. Mgmt., Nat. Assn. Environ. Profls. Office Phone: 301-869-2909. Personal E-mail: cehardy44@aol.com.

HARDY, DEBORAH LEWIS, dean, educator, dental hygienist; b. Nov. 11, 1963; Student, Christopher Newport Coll., 1982-84; BS in Dental Hygiene, Old Dominion U., 1989, cert. in gerontol. studies, MS in Dental Hygiene, Old Dominion U., 1991; postgrad., U. Tex., Dallas, 1993. Cert. ADA Joint Commn. on Nat. Dental Exam.; lic. S.E. Regional Va., Tex., Va.; cert. in cardiopulmonary resuscitation. Assoc. prof. Caruth Sch. Dental Hygiene Baylor Coll., Dallas, 1991-95; assoc. dean health occupations-dental N.E. Wis. Tech. Coll., Green Bay, 1995-97, assoc. dean health and cmty. svc., 1997—. Dental asst. Dr. William Griffin, Newport News, Va., 1989; dental asst., dental hygienist Dental Power, Inc., Newport News, 1988-90; dental hygienist Dr. John Caudill, Virginia Beach, 1990-91, Drs. Cash and Weisburg, Norfolk, Va., 1990-91; dental hygienist, educator Riverside Regional Convalescent Ctr., Newport News, 1991; part-time dental hygienist East Dallas Clinic, 1992-95, Nelson-Tebedo Dental Clinic, Dallas, 1995, Oneida (Wis.) Dental Clinic, 1997; cons., educator Skilled Nursing Facility, Collins Hosp., Baylor U. Med. Ctr., Dallas, 1992; lectr. and spkr. in field. Author: (book) Preventive Oral Health Services Provided by Nurses' Aides to Nursing Home Residents, 1991, (book chpt.) Oral Health and the Older Adult, 1995; editor: (newsletter) Oral Examiner, 1993-95; mem. editl. bd. Profl. Devel. Quar. PDQ, 1994-95; contbr. numerous articles and abstracts to profl. jours. Dental hygienist, educator Operation Smile Internat., Ghana Med. Mission, Accra, 1989; vol. Ea. Va. Med. Sch.-Ea. Shore, 1988, Girls Inc., Dallas, 1992; coord. Spirit of Christmas Program, Caruth Sch. Dental Hygiene, 1991, Sr. Student

Oral Health Edn., St. Philip's Episcopal Sch. and Comty. Ctr., Dallas, 1993, Health Fair, Dallas Marriott Quorum Hotel, 1993. Recipient Acad. Dentistry for the Handicapped award, 1989, award for phenomenal achievement and leadership Women Dentists' Awards Luncheon, 1993; fellow Old Dominion U., 1990; also numerous rsch. grants in field. Mem. Am. Vocat. Assn., Nat. Dental Hygienists' Assn., Am. Dental Hygienists' Assn., Am. Assn. Dental Schs., Student Nat. Dental Assn. (faculty facilitator 1992-95), N.E. Wis. African Am. Assn. (membership chair 1997), Dallas Dental Hygienists' Soc. (Mem. of Month 1993, 95), Sigma Phi Alpha. Office: NE Wis Tech Coll PO Box 19042 2740 W Mason St Green Bay WI 54303-4966

HARDY, DORCAS RUTH, business and government relations executive; b. Newark, N.J., July 18, 1946; d. C. Colburn and Ruth (Hart) H.; m. Samuel V. Spagnolo. BA, Conn. Coll., 1964-68; MBA, Pepperdine U., 1976. cert. sr. advisor. Legis. rsch. asst. U.S. Senator Clifford P. Case, Washington, 1970; spl. asst. White House Conf. Children and Youth, Washington, 1970-71; exec. dir. Health Svcs. Industry Commn., Cost of Living Coun., Washington, 1971-73; asst. sec. Calif. Dept. Health, Sacramento, 1973-74; assoc. dir. U. So. Calif. Ctr. Health Svcs. Rsch., 1974-81; asst. sec. human devel. svcs. HHS, Washington, 1981-86; commr. Social Security Washington, 1986-89; pres. Dorcas R. Hardy & Assocs., Spotsylvania, Va., 1989—; exec. v.p. Pub. Issue Mgmt., Washington, 2001—03. Chmn. bd. dirs., and CEO Work Recovery, Inc., Tucson, 1996-98; bd. dirs. First Coast Svc. Options, Inc., Options Clearing Corp., Wright Investors Svc. Managed Funds; Social Security Advisory Bd.; chmn. vocat. rehab. and employment task force VA, 2003-04; chmn. com. 2005 White House Conf. on Aging Policy, 2004—. Author: Social Insecurity: The Crisis in America's Social Security System and How to Plan Now for Your Own Financial Survival, 1992. Mem. Girl Scouts USA, Va. Bd. Rehab. Svcs.; bd. dirs. Com. on Developing Am. Capitalism; former chmn. Pres.'s Task Force on Legal Equity for Women. Mem. Soc. Cert. Sr. Advisors. Office: Washington Metro Office 11407 Stonewall Jackson Dr Spotsylvania VA 22553-4608

HARDY, DOROTHY CARROLL, dean, consultant; b. Town Creek, Ala.; d. Odis Cal; divorced, 1956; 1 child, Althea J. Mootry. B.S., Ala. State U., 1956; M.Ed., Xavier U., 1960; Ed.D., U. Cin., 1976. Cert. tchr., Ohio. Asst. dean U. Cin., 1973-77; asst. prof. Kans. State U., Manhattan, 1979-80; pres. Cin. Life Adj. Inst., 1980-83, also dir.; commr. Ohio Dept. Mental Health, Columbus, 1983-84; dir. student devel. services Southeast Mo. State U., Cape Girardeau, 1985— . Author: (poems) Pebbles in the Pond, Under the Cranberry Tree, 1986 (Golden Poet award); editor Neighborhood Youth Corps News; contbr. biog. sketches, articles to local newspapers, mags. Fundraiser Ohio Democratic party Citizens for Ohio, 1983; minority coordinator Citizens for Ohio for Issues 2 and 3; tng. vol. Gov. Richard F. Celeste campaign, Cin., 1982; tng. dir. Mondale/Ferraro presdl. campaign, 1984. Recipient Brodie Research award U. Cin., 1975, Outstanding Woman of 1981 Community Service award, NAACP, 1981, Cert. Merit for fiction Writer's Digest, Cert. Merit for poetry Creative Enterprise; grantee U. Cin., 1974. Mem. Nat. Assn. Student Personnel Adminstrs. (chmn. 1981-83), Am. Assn. Counseling and Devel. (chmn. multicultural com. Nat. Conf. 1983), Omega Phi Psi. Baptist. Avocation: writing poetry, novels and articles. Home: 517 North St Cape Girardeau MO 63701-4843

HARDY, HARVEY LOUCHARD, retired lawyer; b. Dallas, Dec. 2, 1914; s. Nat L. and Winifred F. (Fouraker) H.; m. Edna Vivian Bedell, Feb. 14, 1948; children: Victoria Elizabeth Hardy Pursch, Alice Anne Hardy Gannon. Bar: Tex. 1936, U.S. Dist. Ct. (so. and we. dists.) Tex. 1946, U.S. Ct. Appeals (5th cir.) 1946, U.S. Supreme Ct. 1949. First asst. dist. atty. Bexar County, San Antonio, 1947-50, acting dist. atty., 1950-51; city atty. San Antonio, 1952—53, Castle Hills, Tex., 1967—96, Helotes, Tex., 1984-96, Fair Oaks Ranch, Tex., 1973-96; legal adviser bd. trustees Fireman and Policemen's Pension Fund of San Antonio, 1956-96; ret. Legal advisor Grey Forest Utilities, 1986-96. Author: A Lifetime at the Bar: A Lawyer's Memoir, 1999. 1st lt. inf. U.S. Army, 1941-45. Decorated Bronze Star with cluster. Fellow Tex. Bar Found.; mem. Tex. Bar Assn., San Antonio Bar Found., Tex. Assn. City Atts., San Antonio Bar Assn. Methodist. Home: 215 Atwater Dr San Antonio TX 78213

HARDY, HUGH, architect; b. Mallorca, Spain, July 26, 1932; s. Gelston Hardy and Barbara Hardy LaVenture; m. Tiziana Spadea, Jan. 29, 1966; children: Sebastian, Penelope. B.Arch., Princeton U., 1954, M.F.A. in Architecture, 1956. Archtl. asst. to Jo Mielziner, N.Y.C., 1958-62; founder Hugh Hardy & Assocs., N.Y.C., 1962-67; ptnr., owner Hardy Holzman Pfeiffer Assocs., N.Y.C. and L.A., 1967—. Davenport vis. prof. archtl. design Yale U., 1976; Saarinen vis. prof. Yale U., 1987; past chmn. Design Arts Adv. Panel Nat. Endowment for the Arts; apptd. to Nat. Council on the Arts by Pres. of U.S., 1992; cons., lectr. in field. Designer: Orchestra Hall, Mpls., 1974, Cooper-Hewitt Mus., N.Y.C., 1976, St. Louis Art Mus., 1977, The Joyce Theater, N.Y.C., 1982, Rizzoli Bookstore, N.Y.C., New Victory Theater, 1995, Bryant Park Restaurant, 1995, Windows in the World, 1996, New Amsterdam Theater, 1997, U.S. Customs and Immigration Ctr. Rainbow Bridge, Niagara Falls, N.Y., 1998, Radio City Music Hall, N.Y.C., 1999, Bridgemarket, N.Y.C., 2000. Bd. dirs. Isamu Noguchi Found., Mcpl. Art Soc. N.Y., N.Y.C., 1976—, v.p., 1981—, lifetime dir., 1992—; bd. mem. N.Y.C. Hist. House Trust, 1989—. Recipient D'Amato prize Princeton U., 1954, Brunner prize in architecture Nat. Inst. Arts and Letters, 1974, Benjamin West Clinedinst medal Artists' Fellowship Inc., 1988. Fellow AIA (N.Y. chpt. medal of honor 1978, Archtl. Firm award 1981, several honor awards); mem. Archtl. League N.Y. (v.p. for architecture 1977-81, bd. dirs. 1987—), Nat. Acad. Design (assoc.), Am. Acad. Arts and Letters, Century Assn. Office: Hardy Holzman Pfeiffer Assocs 902 Broadway Fl 19 New York NY 10010-6082*

HARDY, JOHN CHRISTOPHER, physicist, researcher, educator; b. Montreal, Que., Can., July 10, 1941; s. Noel Woodburn and Ethel May (Collins) H.; m. Lynn Helen Frederick, June 3, 1964 (div.); children: Ericka, Kirsten, Bruce, Alana; m. June Dennie, July 5, 1997; stepchildren: Benjamin, Samantha. BSc, McGill U., Montreal, 1961, MSc, 1963, PhD, 1965. NRC Can. postdoctoral fellow Oxford (Eng.) Nuc. Physics Lab., 1965—67; Miller rsch. fellow Lawrence Radiation Lab., Berkeley, Calif., 1967—69, staff physicist, 1969—70; assoc. rsch. officer Atomic Energy Can. Ltd., Chalk River, 1970—74, sr. rsch. officer, 1975—83, head nuc. physics br., 1983—86, asst. v.p., 1986—89, dir. tandem accelerator superconducting cyclotron divsn., 1989—97; prof. physics Tex. A&M U., College Station, 1997—. Sci. assoc. CERN, Geneva, 1976-77; program adv. coms. Oak Ridge Nat. Lab., UNISOR, 1979-85, HHIRL, 1991-92, HRIBF, 1999—, chmn., 2000—; program adv. coms. Lawrence Berkeley Lab., Super HILAC, 1983-86, Cyclotron, 1994-99, chmn., 1995-99; program adv. com. Nat. Superconducting Cyclotron Lab., 1990-93; mem. adv. bd. TRIUMF, 1992-98, U. Chgo. rev. com. for physics divsn. Argonne Nat. Lab., 1999; mem. sci. policy com. HRIBF, Oak Ridge Nat. Lab., 2002—. Contbr. articles to profl. jours. and books; editor North Renfrew Times, 1972-97; mem. editl. bd. Nuc. Physics News Internat., 1995-97, Phys. Rev. C. Jour., 1980-82, 95-97. Chmn. bd. dirs. Deep River Sci. Acad., 1986-97, trustee 1997—. Recipient D.W. Ambridge prize, McGill U., 1965. Fellow: Am. Phys. Soc. (DNP program com. 1999—2001, exec. com. DNP 2002—04, chair DNP publs. com. 2003—04), Royal Soc. Can. (v.p. acad. III 1992—95, chmn. fundraising com. 1994—97, Rutherford medal in physics 1981); mem.: Can. Assn. Physicists (Herzberg medal 1976). Office: Tex A&M U Cyclotron Inst College Station TX 77843-3366 Office Phone: 979-845-1411. E-mail: hardy@comp.tamu.edu.

HARDY, JOHN EDWARD, language educator, writer; b. Baton Rouge, Apr. 3, 1922; s. Roger Barlow and Mary (McCoy) H.; m. Marie Elam, Dec. 30, 1942 (div.); children: Margot (Mrs. Timm Ferguson), Leonore (Mrs. David Dvorkin), Catherine, Laura, Anne, Eve; m. Willene Schaefer, June 25, 1969. BA, La. State U., 1944; MA, State U. Iowa, 1946; PhD, Johns Hopkins U., 1956. Mem. English faculties U. Detroit, 1945-46, Yale U., 1946-48, U. Okla., 1948-52, Johns Hopkins U., 1952-54; mem. faculty U. Notre Dame, 1954-66, prof. English, 1964-66, mem. acad. council, 1963-66, grad. council, 1963-66; prof. English, chmn. dept. U. South Ala., 1966-69; prof. English U. Colo., Boulder, 1969-70; prof. English, chmn. dept. U. Mo., St. Louis, 1970-72; dir. grad. studies in English U. Ill.-Chgo., 1972-75, prof. English, 1972-92; prof. emeritus, 1992—; head dept. English U. Ill.-Chgo., 1984-89, mem. grad. coll. exec. com., 1974-76, 81-82. Author: (with Cleanth Brooks) Poems of Mr. John Milton, 1951, The Curious Frame, 1962, Man in the Modern Novel, 1964, Katherine Anne Porter, 1973, Certain Poems, 1958, The Fiction of Walker Percy, 1987; Editor: The Modern Talent, 1964, (with Seymour L. Gross) Images of the Negro in American Literature, 1966. Fulbright prof. Am. lit. U. Munich, Germany, 1959-61; Ford Faculty Study fellow, 1952-53; Rockefeller fellow poetry, 1954; fellow Inst. for Humanities U. Ill. Chgo., 1989-90. Mem. MLA, Phi Beta Kappa. Home: 6033 Riverbend Lakes Dr Baton Rouge LA 70820-5050

HARDY, JOSEPH A., SR., wholesale distribution executive; b. 1923; BS in Engring., U. Pitts. Retail jeweler Hardy & Hayes Corp., Pitts., 1946—52; founder Green Hills Lumber, 1952—56; founder, chmn., CEO 84 Cash & Carry Inc. (now 84 Lumber Co.), Eighty Four, Pa., 1956—; pres. 84 Lumber Co., 1956-93. Vice chmn. Fayette County Bd. Commissioners. With U.S. Army, 1942-46. Recipient Philanthropist of the Year award, Assn. Fundraising Professionals, 2004, Golden Hammer award, Home Channel News, 2004. Office: 84 Lumber Co 1019 Rt 519 Eighty Four PA 15330*

HARDY, JULIA IRENE, elementary school educator; b. Montrose, Iowa, Aug. 11, 1917; d. Carl Alfred Peterson, Achsa Leah LaDuke; m. Francis William Hardy, Oct. 12, 1940; children: Judith (Jeudi) Kay Vitale Eblin, Bruce William. BS in Edn., We. Ill. U., 1965, MS in Edn., 1970; postgrad., Colo. State U., Nat. Coll. Edn., U.S. Internat. U., U. Hawaii. Cert. Permanent profl. cert. Iowa, 1976. Clk. - typist Burlington Ordnance Plant, Iowa, 1941—45; tchr., counselor, reading specialist Keokuk Cmty. Sch. Dist., Keokuk, Iowa, 1957—81. Tchr. Lee County Pub. Schs., Montrose, Iowa, 1936—48; grad. asst. We. Ill. U., Macomb, 1967—68; bd. dirs., chmn. credit com. Keokuk Cmty. Sch. Employees Credit Union, 1986—2001; pvt. tutor, Keokuk, Iowa, 1969—89; presenter poetry programs and readings Christvision, Keokuk, Iowa, 1993—98; presenter poetry symposiums and convs., 1985—2003. Author: Theatre of the Wind, 2003—04, Colours of the Heart, 2003—04, (inspirational poetry) The Wonder of It All, 1996; composer: poems set to music for Emerald Records, 2000—. Tchr. Bethel Bible, 1970. Mem.: Internat. Soc. Poets (life Internat. Poetry Hall of Fame 1997), Internat. Reading Assn. (life Outstanding Achievement in Poetry award), Am. Legion Aux., Order Ea. Star (past matron, Grand page 1952), Kappa Delta Pi, Delta Kappa Gamma (com. mem. Alpha Epsilon chpt., Scholarship 1960), Internat. Beta Sigma Phi. Democrat. Lutheran. Avocations: art, reading, poetry, dramatics, family. Home: 2720 McKinley Ave Keokuk IA 52632-2250

HARDY, MICHAEL C., performing arts administrator; b. Durham, N.C., July 14, 1945; s. William Marion Hardy and Eloise Frances (Carrington) Schipke; children: Miranda, Christopher. AB, Duke U., 1966; MA, U. N.C., 1968; PhD, U. Mich., 1971. Gen. mgr. drama dept. East Carolina U., 1971-73; prodr. Krannert Ctr. Performing Arts at U. Ill., 1973-79, dir., 1979-83; pres., CEO, Snug Harbor Cultural Ctr., Inc., N.Y.C., 1983-88; ind. cons., 1988-91; exec. dir. Internat. Soc. for the Performing Arts, Grand Rapids, Mich., 1991-98; pres. Ky. Ctr. for the Arts, Louisville, 1998—2002, Miami Performing Arts Ctr., 2002—. Contbr. articles to profl. jours. With N.Y. Cultural Inst. Group, 1984-88; CIG chair Mayor Ed Koch's Commn. Cultural Affairs, N.Y.C., 1987-88; bd. dirs. Leadership Louisville, 1999-2002, Regional Leadership Coalition, 2001-02, Louisville Bach Soc., 2001-02; vice chair Collaborative for Tchg. and Learning, 1998-2002 Recipient Carolina Playmaker's Mask award U. N.C., 1968, Commendation for Achievement award N.Y. State Legis., 1988, Dept. Parks and Recreation citation N.Y.C., 1988. Mem.: Internat. Soc. for Performing Arts, Miami C. of C. (bd. govs. 2005—). Office: Miami Performing Arts Ctr 1444 Biscayne Blvd Ste 202 Miami FL 33132 Office Phone: 305-372-7894. Business E-Mail: mhardy@miamipac.org.

HARDY, MICHAEL JOHN, statistician, educator; s. Nigel Robert and Adeline Elizabeth (Gerszewski) Hardy; m. Barbara Jo Short, Oct. 10, 1993. PhD, U. Minn., Mpls., 1997. Vis. lectr. U. N.C., Chapel Hill, 1997—98, asst. prof. Pembroke, 1998—99; lectr. applied math. MIT, Cambridge, Mass., 1999—2002; lectr. joint program MIT/Woods Hole Oceanog. Instn., Woods Hole, Mass., 2000—02; vis. asst. prof. U. Toledo. Contbr. textbook, articles to profl. jours. Mem.: Am. Statis. Assn. Achievements include research in scaled Boolean algebras and application to epistemic probability theory. Personal E-mail: hardy@math.umn.edu.

HARDY, PAUL DUANE, lawyer; b. N.Y.C., Nov. 7, 1936; s. Reginald Sayre and Mae Estelle (Sculthorp) Hardy; m. Jacqueline Hardy, June 8, 1971; children: Valerie, Christopher. BA, U. Pa., 1958; LLB, U. Va., 1961. Bar: Pa. 1963, DC 1972, Fla. 1974. Ptnr. Rawle & Henderson Law Firm, Phila., 1963-70, Holland & Knight Law Firm, Tampa, Fla., 1973-86, Stagg Hardy Law Firm, Tampa, 1986-93, Akerman Senterfett Law Firm, Tampa, 1993—. Chief trial counsel U.S. Maritime Adminstrn., Washington, 1970—73. With U.S. Army, 1961—63. Mem.: Maritime Law Assn. U.S. (bd. dirs. 1983—86). Office: Akerman Senterfett Law Firm 100 S Ashley Dr Tampa FL 33602-5360 E-mail: PaulHardy1617@aol.com.

HARDY, RALPH W. F., biochemist; b. Lindsay, Ont., Can., July 27, 1934; s. Wilbur and Elsie Hardy; m. Jacqueline M. Thayer, Dec. 26, 1954; children: Steven, Chris, Barbara, Ralph(dec.), Jon. BSA, U. Toronto, 1956; MS, U. Wis.-Madison, 1958, PhD, 1959; DSc (hon.), U. Guelph, 1997. Asst. prof. U. Guelph, Ont., Can., 1960-63; research biochemist DuPont deNemours & Co., Wilmington, Del., 1963-67, research supr., 1967-74, assoc. dir., 1974-79, dir. life scis., 1979-84; pres. Bio Technica Internat., Inc., Cambridge, Mass., 1984-86; pres., CEO Boyce Thompson Inst., Inc., Ithaca, NY, 1986-95, pres. emeritus, 2000—; dep. chmn. Bio Technica Internat., Inc., 1986-90, cons., bd. dirs., 1990-99; pres. Nat. Agrl. Biotech. Coun., Ithaca, 1996—. Mem. exec. com. bd. agr. NRC, 1982—88, mem. commn. life scis., 1984—90, bd. biology, 1984—90, mem. com. on biotech., 1988—95, chmn. com., 1993—94, bd. sci. technol. internat. devel., 1990—93, chmn. com. on biol. control, 1992—95, chmn. com. on biol. nitrogen fixation, 1992—94, chmn. com. on natural products, 1996—97; mem. com. genetic experimentation Internat. Coun. Sci. Union, 1981—95; chmn., founder Nat. Agrl. Biotech. Coun., 1988—93; mem. sci. adv. com. U.S. Dept. Energy, 1991—95; mem. alt. agr. rsch. comml. bd. USDA, 1992—96, mem. and corp. sec. alt. agrl. rsch. comml. corp., 1996—2000; mem. Can. reallocations com. NSERC, 1997—98; mem. sci. adv. bd. Foragen, Guelph, Ont., Canada, 1999—; bd. dirs. BioCap, Canada, BioProducts, Can. Author: Nitrogen Fixation, 1975, A Treatise on Dinitrogen Fixation, 3 vols., 1977—79; contbr. articles to profl. jours. Mem. biotechnology exec. bd. Cornell U., 1986—95, mem. adv. coun. Vet. Coll., 1989—96; mem. gov. bd. Cornell Ctr. Environment, 1991—95. Recipient Gov. Gen.'s Silver medal, 1956, Sterling Henricks award, 1986; WARF fellow, 1956—58, DuPont fellow, 1958—59. Mem.: Am. Soc. Microbiology, Am. Soc. Agronomy, Am. Soc. Plant Biology (mem. exec. com., treas. 1974—77), Am. Soc. Biol. Chemists and Molecular Biologists, Am. Chem. Soc. (mem. exec. com. biol. chemisty divsn. 1978—81, Del. award 1969), Agr. Rsch. Inst. (bd. govs. 1988—91), Indsl. Biotechnology Assn. (bd. dirs. 1986—89). Episcopalian.

HARDY, RICHARD ALLEN, mechanical engineer, engineering executive; b. Cleve., Sept. 16, 1928; s. Harry and Mae Hardy; m. Lois L. Fawcett, May 16, 1953 (dec. Dec. 1990); children: Pamela, Richard, James, Thomas. BSME, Case Inst. Tech., 1952. Founder, CEO Fluid Mechanics Inc., Cleve., 1957—. Cpl. U.S. Army, 1946-48. Recipient Weatherhead 100 award Cleve., 1989. Mem. Assn. of Diesel Specialists (various coms. 1960—). Roman Catholic. Achievements include helped design and build largest dynamic fuel-injection pump test stand in Western hemisphere. Avocations: racquetball, scuba. Home: 26875 Hilliard Blvd Cleveland OH 44145-3213

HARDY, RICHARD EARL, rehabilitation counseling educator; b. Victoria, Va., Oct. 11, 1938; s. Clifford E. and Louise (Hamilton) H.; 1 son, Jason Elliott. BS, Va. Poly. Inst. and State U., 1960, MS, 1962, EdD, 1966. Rehab. counselor State of Va., Richmond, 1961-63; rehab. advisor HHS, Washington, 1964-66; chief psychologist S.C. Dept. Rehab., Columbia, 1966-68; prof. chmn. dept. rehab. counseling Med. Coll. Va., Richmond, 1968-96, chmn., prof. emeritus, 1996—. Former bd. mem. S.C. State Bd. Psychology, former ABPP candidate examiner; internat. cons. to numerous countries including Turkey, Iraq, Peru, Uruguay, South Africa, Brazil, Thailand Author, editor: International Rehabilitation: Approaches and Programs, Hemingway: A Psychological Portrait, 1988, Gestalt Psychotherapy, 1991, Hispaniola Episode: A Mental Health Allegory, 1992, (with J.G. Cull) The Brass Chalice: Drug Prevention Stories and Information for Children and Youth, 1994, Counseling in the Rehabilitation Process, 1999, Woodpeckers Don't Get Headaches: The Psychology of Stress, Relationships, and Addiction, 2001, numerous others. Recipient Nat. award Nat. Rehab. Assn., 1976; recipient Nat. award Am. Assn. Workers for Blind, 1976, Outstanding Grad. award Med. Coll. Va./Va. Commonwealth U., Dept. Rehab. Counseling, 1997, Richard E. Hardy endowed scholarship Med. Coll. Va., 1998. Fellow Am. Psychol. Soc., Assn. Allied & Preventive Psychology; mem. Am. Assn. Vol. Action Scholars, Phi Kappa Phi. Office: Va Commonwealth U 6962 Forest Hill Ave Richmond VA 23225 E-mail: richardehardy@cs.com.

HARDY, SARALYN REECE, museum director; b. m. Randall Hardy; children: Stephen, Thomas, William. BA, U. Kans., 1976, MA in Am. studies, 1994. Project coord. Helen Foresman Spencer Mus. Art, U. Kans., Lawrence, 1977—79, dir., 2005—, Salina Art Ctr., Kans., 1986—2002; dir. mus. and visual arts Nat. Endowment for Arts, Washington, DC, 1999—2002. Recipient Women of Achievement award, Salina YWCA, Kansas Gov.'s Art Award, 1995. Mem.: Inst. Mus. and Libr. Svcs., Mus. Trustee Assn., Am. Assn. Mus., Am. Fedn. of Arts Mus. Dirs., Getty Leadership Inst. Office: Spencer Mus Art U Kans 1301 Mississippi St Lawrence KS 66045-7500

HARDY, VICTORIA ELIZABETH, finance educator; b. Marion, N.C., Feb. 26, 1947; d. Milton Victor Roth and Bertha Jean (Norris) R.; m. Michael Carrington Hardy, June 19, 1983 (div. 1993); 1 child, Christopher. BS in Edn., U. Mo., 1970; postgrad., So. Ill. U., 1974-75; postgrad. Mgmt. Devel. Program, Stanford U., 1980-81; MA in Mgmt., Aquinas Coll., 1999. Cert. facility mgr. Pub. sch. tchr. English and Theater, 1970-75; gen. mgr. Miss. River Festival, Edwardsville, Ill., 1975-77; dir. events and svcs. Stanford (Calif.) U., 1977-83; exec. dir. Meadowlands Ctr. for the Arts, Rutherford, N.J., 1983-87; pres., chief exec. officer Music Hall Ctr. for the Arts, Detroit, 1987-89; prin. AMS Planning & Rsch., Conn., 1989-94; prof. facility mgmt. Ferris State U., Big Rapids, Mich., 1994—2003; acad. dept. head Wentworth Inst. Tech., Boston, 2003—. Contbr. to various publs. Mem. USICA study team to China, 1981; bd. dirs. Internat. Facility Mgmt. Assn., 1994-97, standing coms. recognition and profl. devel.; mem. People to People facilities del. to Australia and New Zealand, 1996; bd. dirs., chair IFMA Found., 1998-2004. Named Disting. Educator of Yr., IFMA, 2001, Educator of Yr., Boston IFMA, 2005; named to Creativity in Business Doubleday, 1986; recipient Gold medal for Cmty. Programs, Coun. for Advancement and Support of Edn., Stanford, 1985. Mem. League of Hist. Am. Theaters (pres. bd. dirs. 1987-89). Democrat. Avocations: skiing, gardening. Office: Acad Dept Head Design & Facilities Wentworth Inst Tech 550 Hungtington Ave Boston MA 02115 Office Phone: 617-989-4050.

HARDY, VOLEEN LAURIE, dentist; b. Southfield, Mich., Jan. 19, 1972; d. Henry Paul and Martha Mary Isonik; m. Jeffrey Joseph Hardy, Jan. 27, 2000 (div.); 1 child, Jamie Lynn; 1 child, Frankin. BS, Villanova, 1994, MD, 1999. Lic. oral surgeon NY, 1999, cert. Mo., 1999. Intern U. Va. Health Sys., Charlottesville, 1999—2001; residency oral surgery Sunnybrook Health Sci. Ctr., Northville, Va., 2001—04; oral surgeon Meriks, Jobesburg, Weinburg & Franfurs, DDS, Southfield, 2004—. Contbr. articles to profl. jours. Lay worker 1st Baptist Ch., Florencetown, Mich., 2005—. Named Best New Surgeon, Meriks, Jobesburg, Weinburg & Franfurs, DDS, 2005. Mem.: ADA (sec. 2000—01, Outstanding New Dentist Adminstr. 2001). Reform. Baptist. Avocations: sports, art. Home: 52 Brown Dock Rd Southfield MI 48034 Office: Meriks Jobesburg Weinburg Franfurs DDS 29209 Northwestern Hwy #501 Southfield MI 48034-1023 Office Phone: 326-654-9893. Office Fax: 326-654-9894. Business E-Mail: vhardy@mjwf.com.

HARDY, WALTER NEWBOLD, physics professor, researcher; b. Vancouver, B.C., Mar. 25, 1940; s. Walter Thomas and Julia Marguerite (Mulroy) H.; m. Sheila Lorraine Hughes, July 10, 1959; children: Kevin James, Steven Wayne. BSc in Math and Physics with honors, U. B.C., 1961; PhD in Physics, Univ. B.C., 1965. Postdoctral fellow Centre d'Etudes Nucleaires de Saclay, France, 1964-66; mem. tech. staff N.Am. Rockwell, Thousand Oaks, Calif., 1966-71; assoc. prof. physics U. B.C., 1971-76, prof., 1976—. Vis. scientist Ecole Normale Superieure, Paris, 1980-81, 85, 95. Contbr. articles to sci. jours.; patentee precision microwave instrumentation. Recipient Stacie prize NRC of Can., 1978, Gold medal B.C. Sci. Coun., 1989, Killam prize Can. Coun., 1999, Fritz London Prize, 2002; Rutherford Meml. scholar, 1964; Alfred P. Sloan fellow, 1972-74; Can. Coun. Rsch. fellow, 1984-86. Mem. Can. Assn. Physicists (Herzberg medal 1978, gold medal for achievement in physics, 1993, Brockhouse medal 1999), Am. Phys. Soc. Office: U BC Dept Physics Astronomy Vancouver BC Canada V6T 1Z1

HARDY, WAYNE RUSSELL, insurance and investment broker; b. Denver, Sept. 5, 1931; s. Russell Hinton and Victoria Katherine (Anderson) H.; m. Carolyn Lucille Carvell, Aug. 1, 1958 (July 1977); children: James Russell Hardy, Jann Miller Hardy. BSCE, U. Colo., 1954; MS in Fin. Svcs., Am. Coll., 1989. CLU; chartered fin. cons. Mgr. we. dist. Fenestra, Inc., San Francisco, 1956—63; ins. and investment broker John Hancock Fin. Svs., Denver, 1963—, Wayne R. Hardy Assocs., Denver, 1963—. Speaker convs. and sales seminars, 1977, 81, 84, 85, 89; v.p. CLU assn. John Hancock, 1979-80, chmn. agt.'s adv. com., 1983-84; active State of Colo. Ins. Adv. Bd., 1991-93; profl. model, actor J.F. Images Agy., Denver, 1964-89. Chmn. Colo. Coun. Camera Clubs, Denver, 1962; bd. dirs. Porter Charitable Found., Denver, 1983-85; deacon, class pres. South Broadway Christian Ch., 1961-65; mem. Denver Art Mus., Denver Botanic Gardens, Rocky Mountain Estate Planning Coun., Mensa, Alliance Francaise. Capt. U.S. Army, 1954-56, Korea, USAR, 1956-80. Mem. Am. Soc. CLU and ChFC (pres. Rocky Mountain chpt. 1990-91), Nat. Assn. Life Underwriters (pres. Denver chpt. 1983-84, Nat. Quality award 1968—, expert witness ins. litigation, Disting. Life Underwriters award 1970-83), Screen Actors Guild, Million Dollar Round Table (life), U. Colo. Alumni (bd. dirs. 1990-92), U. Colo. Alumni C Club (bd. dirs. 1972-74), Univ. Club, Greenwood Athletic Club, Village Tennis Club, Rocky Mountain Optimist Club (pres. 1984-85). Republican. Avocations: tennis, photography, foreign languages, art, travel. Home and Office: PO Box 2837 Toluca Lake CA 91610-0837 Office Phone: 303-292-6402.

HARDY, WILLIAM ROBINSON, lawyer; b. Cin., June 14, 1934; s. William B. and Chastine M. (Sprague) H.; m. Leslie Warrington Bailey, Apr. 16, 1999; children from previous marriage: Anita Christina, William Robinson Jr. AB magna cum laude, Princeton U., 1956; JD, Harvard U., 1963. Bar: Ohio 1963, U.S. Supreme Ct. 1975. Life underwriter New Eng. Mut. Life Ins. Co., 1956-63; assoc. Graydon, Head & Ritchey, Cin., 1963-68, ptnr., 1968-98. Mem. panel comml. and constrn. industry arbitrators Am. Arbitration Assn., 1972—, mem. panel large complex case program, 1993—, panel of mediators, 1993—, comml. arbitrator tng. faculty, 1998—; reporter joint com. for revision of rules of U.S. Dist. Ct. for So. Dist. Ohio, 1975, 80, 83, mem., 1990—2003. Bd. dirs. Cin. Union Bethel, 1968-82, pres., 1977-82, emeritus, 1982—; bd. dirs. Ohio Valley Goodwill Industries Rehab. Ctr., Cin., 1970—, pres., 1981-92; mem. Cin. Bd. Bldg. Appeals, 1976-2001, vice chmn., 1983, chmn., 1983-2001; pres. Hamilton County (Ohio) Alcohol and Drug Addiction Svcs. Bd., 1990-92; trustee Substance Abuse Mgmt. and Devel. Inc., 1998-99. Capt. USAR, 1956-68; maj. gen. Ohio Mil. Res., comdr., 1996-2001. Recipient award of merit Ohio Legal Ctr. Inst., 1975, 76, Ohio Commendation medal, 1999. Mem. ABA, AAAS, Ohio Bar Assn., Cin. Bar

Assn., Ohio Acad. Trial Lawyers, Am. Arbitration Assn., Assn. for Conflict Resolution, 6th Cir. Jud. Conf. (life), Soc. Lees Va., Assn. Former Intelligence Officers, Diplomatic and Consular Ret. Officers, Ohio Soc. Colonial Wars (gov. 1979), Princeton (N.Y.C.) Club, Interlachen Country Club (Winter Park, Fla.), Edgartown (Mass.) Yacht Club, Phi Beta Kappa. Mem. Ch. Of Redeemer. Office: 432 Walnut St Ste 206 Cincinnati OH 45202-3909 Office Phone: 513-621-4220. Personal E-mail: wmrhardy@earthlink.net.

HARDYMAN, LISA W., music educator, elementary school educator; b. Rigby, Idaho, Apr. 27, 1957; d. B. Wayne and Delores E. (Labrum) Wood; m. Paul B. Hardyman, June 6, 1986; children: Nathan, Megan. BA, Brigham Young U., 1979, MusM, 1987. Tchr. Sch. Dist. #251, Rigby, Idaho; music specialist Provo (Utah) Sch. Dist.; grad. asst. music Brigham Young U., Provo; tchr. Provo Sch. Dist.; music tchr. Rigby HS. Mem.: Music Tchrs. Nat. Assn. Home: 134 S 3rd W Rigby ID 83442-1343

HARDYMON, DAVID WAYNE, lawyer; b. Columbus, Ohio, Aug. 22, 1949; s. Philip Barbour and Margaret Evelyn (Bowers) H.; m. Monica Ella Sleep, Mar. 13, 1982; children: Philip Garnet, Teresa Jeanette. BA in History, Bowling Green State U., 1971; JD, Capital U., Columbus, Ohio, 1976. Bar: Ohio 1976, U.S. Dist. Ct. (so. dist.) Ohio 1976; U.S. Supreme Ct. 1980, U.S. Ct. Appeals (6th cir.) 1982, Ky. 1999, U.S. Dist. Ct. (no. dist.) Ohio 1999, W.Va. 2000, U.S. Dist. Ct. (so. dist.) W.Va. 2000. Asst. prosecuting atty. Franklin County Prosecuter's Office, Columbus, Ohio, 1976-81; assoc. Vorys, Sater, Seymour & Pease, Columbus, 1981-86, ptnr., 1987—. Mem. Chmn's. Club Franklin Country Rep. Orgn., 1983. Fellow Columbus Bar Found.; mem. Ohio State Bar Assn., Columbus Bar Assn. Avocations: sailing, archery. Office: Vorys Sater Seymour & Pease LLP PO Box 1008 52 E Gay St Columbus OH 43215-3161 Office Phone: 614-464-5651.

HARDY-PARCELL, CATHY KAY, music educator, department chairman; d. R. Keith and Beverly Louise Hardy; m. John Cleo Parcell, Sept. 30, 1990. MusB Edn., Wheaton Coll., Ill., 1980; MM in Vocal performance, U. of Mo., 1987. Opera express dir. Lyric Opera of Kans. City, Kans .City, Mo.; voice instr. U. of Mo., Kans. City, 1983—93, Mo. Western State Coll., St. Joseph, 1986—89; role singer Lyric Opera, Kans. City, Mo., 1986—89; music dept. head Longview C.C., Lee's Summit, Mo., 1989—. Guest conductor-choral festival Ctr. Pl. Restoration Sch., Independence, Mo., 2003. Singer: (competition) Operatic Arias (Competions Winner, 1984). Keyboard player Various Bapt. Chs., Kans. City, Mo., 2000—03. Mem.: Mo. Chpt. of Music Educators Nat. Conf., Music Educators Nat. Conf., Coll. Music Soc., Am. Coral Dirs. Assn. Conservative. Avocations: computer technology, carpentry, sewing. Office: Longview C C 500 SW Longview Rd Lees Summit MO 64081-2100 E-mail: hardy@kcmetro.edu.

HARE, CLARE KEAN, aeronautical and aerospace engineer, consultant; b. N.Y.C., July 10, 1962; s. Peter Hewitt and Daphne Joan Hare. BS in Math., BS in Engring., Harvey Mudd Coll., 1984; MS in Aero. and Astronaut. Engring., Stanford U., 1985. Engr. mission engring. Hughes Aircraft, El Segundo, Calif., 1985-87, engr. sys. test, 1987-88, lead sys. engr., 1988-90, controls engr. Reston, Va., 1990, mgr. El Segundo, 1991-95; cons. on software and comm., Manhattan Beach, Calif., 1995-99; payload operation mgr. Astrolink Internat., Manhattan Beach, 1999—. Contbr. articles to Am. Jour. Econs. and Sociology. Mem. AAAS. Home and Office: 4312 Glencoe Ave Apt 6 Marina Del Rey CA 90292-7611 E-mail: clarksterh@earthlink.net.

HARE, DAVID, playwright; b. St. Leonards, Sussex, Eng., June 5, 1947; s. Clifford Theodore and Agnes (Gilmour) H.; m. Margaret Matheson, Aug. 1970 (div. 1980); children: Joe, Lewis, Darcy; m. Nicole Farhi, 1992. MA, Cambridge U., 1968. Founder Portable Theatre, 1968, Joint Stock Theatre Group, 1974, Greenpoint Films, 1983; assoc. dir. Royal Nat. Theatre, London, 1984-88, 89-97. Author: (plays) Slag, 1970 (Evening Standard Drama award 1970), The Great Exhibition, 1972, (with Howard Brenton) Brassneck, 1973, Knuckle, 1974 (John Llewlyn Rhys award 1975), Teeth 'n' Smiles, 1975, (with others) Deeds, 1978, Plenty, 1978 (N.Y. Drama Critics Circle Best Fgn. Play award 1983, Best Play Tony award nominee 1983), A Map of the World, 1982 (Dramalogue award), (with Brenton) Pravda, 1985 (Evening Standard Drama award 1985, Plays and Players best play award 1985, City Limits best play award 1985), The Bay at Nice, 1986, Wrecked Eggs, 1986, The Knife, 1987, The Secret Rapture, 1988 (Plays and Players Best Play award 1988, Drama mag. Best Play award 1988, Drama Desk Best Play award nominee 1990), Racing Demon, 1990, 93, 95 (Olivier Best Play award 1990, Time Out (Theatre award 1990, Plays and Players best play award 1990, London Critics Circle Best Play award 1990, Tony award nominee 1996), Murmuring Judges, 1991, 92, 93, The Absence of War, 1993, Skylight, 1995, 96, 97 (Olivier Best Play award), Amy's View, 1996, 97, 98, 99, The Judas Kiss, 1997, 98, Via Dolorosa, 98, 99, The Breath of Life, 2002, The Permanent Way, 2003, Stuff Happens, 2004; (adaptations) Fanshen (William Hinton), 1975, Rules of the Game (Luigi Pirandello), 1971, 92, The Life of Galileo (Bertolt Brecht), 1994, Mother Courage and Her Children (Brecht), 1995, Ivanov (Anton Chekhov), 1997, The Blue Room (Schnitzler), 1998, The House of Bernarda Alba (Lorca), 2005; plays performed U.S.-Broadway, Pub. Theatre, N.Y.C., Goodman Theatre, Chgo., Arena Theatre, Washington, Lincoln Ctr., and other places; (TV films) Man Above Men, 1973, Licking Hitler (Brit. Acad. Film and TV Arts Best Play award 1978), Dreams of Leaving, 1980, Saigon: Year of the Cat, 1983, Heading Home, 1990, The Absence of War, 1995; (screenplays) Plenty, 1985, Wetherby, 1985 (Golden Bear award best film Berlin Film Festival 1985), Paris By Night, 1988, Strapless, 1989, Damage, 1992, The Secret Rapture, 1993, Feasting with Panthers, 1995; (essays) Writing Lefthanded, 1991, Asking Around, 1993, The Hours, 2003; dir: (theatre) Inside Out, 1968, Christie in Love, 1969, Purity, 1969, Fruit, 1970, Blow Job, 1971, England's Ireland, 1972, Brassneck, 1973, The Pleasure Principle, 1973, The Provoked Wife, 1973, The Party, 1974, Teeth 'n' Smiles, 1975, Weapons of Happiness, 1976, Devil's Island, 1977, Plenty, 1978, Total Eclipse, 1981, A Map of the World, 1983, Pravda, 1985-86, King Lear, 1986, The Bay at Nice and Wrecked Eggs, 1986-87, The Knife, 1987, The Secret Rapture, 1989, The Designated Mourner, 1996; (films) Wetherby, 1985, Paris by Night, 1989, Strapless, 1989, (TV) Licking Hitler, 1978, Dreams of Leaving, 1980, Heading Home, 1992, The Designated Mourner, 1996, Heartbreak House. 1997; (opera libretto) The Knife, 1988; author: (books) Writing Left-handed, 1991, Asking Around, 1993, Acting Up, 1999; plays, dir. include include Slag, Hampstead, 1970, Royal Court and N.Y. Shakespeare Festival, 1971, The Great Exhibition, Hampstead, 1972, Brassneck, Nottingham Playhouse (with Howard Brenton), Knyuckle, Comedy Theatre, 1974, Fanshen, ICA and Hampstead, 1975, Nat. Theatre, 1992, Teeth 'n' Smiles, Royal Court, 1975, Wyndhams, 1976, Plenty, 1978, 1982, 1999, A Map of the World, 1983, 85, Pravda, 1985, others; screenplays, actor, and dir. include Wetherby, 1985, Paris by Night, 1989, Strapless, 1990, Plenty, 1985, Lee Miller, 2001, Via Dolorosa, 2000, The Secret Rapture, 1993, others; films, dir. assoc. producer for TV include Licking Hitler (BBC), 1978, Dreams of Leaving (BBC), 1979, Saigon: Year of the Cat (Thames), 1983, Heading Home (BBC), 1991, The Absence of War (BBC), 1995; adaptations include The Rules of the Game-Pirandello, 1992, The Life of Galileo, 1994, Mother Courage and Her Children, 1995, Ivanov, 1997, 98, others; opera libretto, dir. include The Knife, 1988; author: Writing Lefthanded, 1991, Asking Around, 1993, Acting Up, 1999; dir. plays include Christie in Love (by Howard Brenton), 1969, Fruit (by Howard Brenton), 1970, Blowjob, 1971, England's Ireland (by seven writers, co-dir.), 1972,The Provoked Wife (by John Vanburgh), 1973, The Pleasure Principle (by Snoo Wilson), 1973, The Party (by Trevor Griffiths), 1974; dir. films, producer include The Designated Mourner (by Wallace Shawn), 1996. Fellow Royal Soc. Lit.; mem. Officiers de l"ordre des Artes et Lettres, Dramatists Club. Office: c/o Casarotto Ramsay 60 Wardour St London W1 England

HARE, JERRY WAYNE, communications executive; b. Claremore, Okla., Nov. 16, 1937; s. Curb and Metheta Evelyn (Doss) H.; m. Mary Jo Sellers, Nov. 15, 1956; children: Pamela S., Anthony W., Rhonda S. Calhoun, LaDonna E. Girdner. Indstl. elec. technician, Okla. State U., 1960. Founder, owner Sooner TV, Tahlequah, Okla., 1963—. Founder, owner Crystal Creek Ranch, Tahlequah, 1968—, Bird-Link Sys., Tahlequah, 1984—, Crystal Creek Dairy, Tahlequah, 1990—. Mem. Profl. Svc. Assn. Inc., Nat. Fedn. Ind. Businessman, Nat. Write Your Congressman, Tahlequah Area C. of C., U.S. C. of C., Masons (32nd degree award 1968), Okla. Cattlemen Assn. Democrat. Avocations: fishing, hunting, family activities. Office: Sooner TV Bird Link Sys 405 E Downing St Tahlequah OK 74464-3015

HARE, PETER HEWITT, philosophy educator; b. N.Y.C., Mar. 12, 1935; s. Michael Meredith and Jane Perry (Jopling) H.; m. Daphne Joan Kean, May 30, 1959 (dec. Aug. 1995); children: Clare Kean, Gwendolyn Meigs; m. Susan Howe, Nov. 1, 2000. BA, Yale U., 1957; MA, Columbia U., 1962, PhD, 1965. Lectr. philosophy SUNY, Buffalo, 1962-65, from asst. prof. to prof., 1965-97, disting. svc. prof., 1997—, asst. chmn. dept., 1965-68, chmn. dept., 1971-75, 85-94, assoc. dean divsn. undergrad. edn., 1980-82, prof. emeritus, 2001—. Vis. prof. Moscow State U., 1989; bd. advisors, Peirce Edition Project, Ind. U./Purdue U., 1998—. Author: A Woman's Quest for Science, 1985; (with others) Evil and the Concept of God, 1968, Causing, Perceiving and Believing, 1975; editor: Doing Philosophy Historically, 1988, (with others) History, Religion and Spiritual Democacy, 1980, Naturalism and Rationality, 1986, (series) Frontiers of Philosophy, Prometheus Books, 1986—; photo illustrations in Susan Howe, Kidnapped, 2002, The Midnight, 2003; mem. editl. bd. Am. Philos. Quar., 1978-87, Jour. Speculative Philosophy, 1987—, Streams of William James, 1999-2005, William James Studies, 2005—. Fellow Ctr. for Inquiry; mem. Am. Philos. Assn. (nominating com. ea. divsn. 1990-92, program com. 1993-95, chmn. program com. 1994-95, mem. nat. bd. officers 1996-99, chmn. com. career opportunities, 1996-99, ombudsman 1996-99, chair Romanell lectr. com. 2000-01), Peirce Soc. (editor Transactions 1974—), pres. 1975-76), N.Y. State Philos. Assn. (pres. 1975-77), Soc. for Advancement Am. Philosophy (exec. com. 1977-80, pres. 1988-90, Herbert W. Schneider award 1996), Josiah Royce Soc. (mem. exec. com. 2003—), William James Soc. (v.p. 2005), Elizabethan Club. Home and Office: 115 New Quarry Rd Guilford CT 06437-1621 Office Phone: 716-645-2444. E-mail: phhare@buffalo.edu.

HARE, ROBERT YATES, musicologist, educator; b. McGrann, Pa., June 14, 1921; s. Robert Deemar and Beulah (Yates) H.; m. Constance King Rutherford, Mar. 31, 1948; children: Stephen, Beverly, Madeleine. MusB, U. Detroit, 1948; MA, Wayne State U., 1950; PhD, U. Iowa, 1959. Instr. Marietta (Ohio) Coll., 1949-51, Del Mar Coll., Corpus Christi, Tex., 1951-55; adj. instr. U. Tex., 1953—55; prof., chmn. grad. studies San Jose (Calif.) State U., 1956-65; prof., dean Eastern Ill. U. Music, 1965-74; prof. music history and lit. Ohio State U., Columbus, 1974-86, prof. emeritus, 1986—, dir. Sch. Music, 1974-78, dir. audio-rec. engring., 1979-82, arts adminstr. rsch. and faculty devel., 1982-86. Cons. in field; mem. coun. music edn. in higher edn. Ill. Music Educators Assn., 1969-74. Condr. coll. symphony band, 1956-63, San Jose Youth Symphony, 1957-59, univ. symphony, 1968-74, Ea. Ill. U. Symphony, 1968-74; French horn recitals, Carnegie Music Hall, Pitts., 1940, 42; French hornist, Pitts. Symphony Orch., 1941-44, Buffalo Philharm., 1943-44, Cin. Summer Opera Co., 1945, Indpls. Symphony Orch., 1945-46, San Antonio Symphony Orch., 1947-49; orchestrator, San Antonio Symphony Orch., 1947-49; recs. include Pitts. Symphony Orch., Indpls. Symphony Orch. (as French hornist), San Jose State U. Symphonic Band (as condr.); contbr. articles to profl. jours. Mem. com. grad. and profl. edn. in arts and humanities Ill. Bd. Higher Edn., 1969-70; mem. performing arts commn. Ill. Sesquicentennial, 1967; mem. exec. bd. Greater Columbus Arts Coun., 1974-76, Ohio Alliance for Arts in Edn., 1974-76; trustee Columbus Symphony Orch., 1975-79. Profl. Promise scholar Carnegie-Mellon U., 1939. Mem. Music Educators Nat. Conf. (publs. planning com. 1970-76), Am. Musicol. Soc., Coll. Music Soc., Masons, Shriners, Phi Mu Alpha, Sinfonia (hon.), Pi Kappa Lambda (hon.), Delta Omicron (hon.). Home: 2624 SW Ashworth Pl Topeka KS 66614-2507 Office: Ohio State U Coll Arts 305 Mershon Auditorium Columbus OH 43210 E-mail: rhare4@cox.net.

HAREYAN, ARMEN, religious organization administrator; b. Yerevan, Armenia, Dec. 13, 1973; s. Harut Hareyan and Gohar Simonyan; m. Lilit Alikhanyan, July 26, 2003; 1 child, Harutiun. U. Degree in music composition, Yerevan State Conservatory, 1992—98; MA in religious studies, Ctrl. Bapt. Theol. Sem., 1999—2001; MBA, Lenoir Rhyne Coll., 2001—03; BA in musicology, R. Melikyan Music Coll., 1988—2002. Organist St. Etchmiadzin Cathedral, Etchmiadzin, Armenia, 1993—95; music dir. Armenian Patriarchate in Jerusalem, Jerusalem, Israel, 1994—95. Dir. of music ministry St. Aloysius Cath. Ch., Hickory, NC, 2000—05. Composer: (music composition) Alaba, Alma Mia Al Senior; dir.(choir conductor): 16th Concorso Internationale do Canto Corale, 2005 (Bronze award in the 16th Verona Internat. Choir Festival, Italy). Achievements include development of http:/www.eMaxHealth.com- a free portal of health information freely available for consumers worldwide. Office: St Aloysius Cath Ch 921 Second St NE Hickory NC 28601 Office Phone: 828-327-2341.

HAREZI, ILONKA JO, medical technology research executive; b. Princeton, Ind., Jan. 17, 1949; d. Joseph and Helen Marie Fullop; m. John O. Schofield, Dec. 14, 1971 (div. Dec. 1982); 1 child, Franceska; m. Courtland Reeves, Nov. 26, 1986; children: Bryan, Katharine. PhD, Chgo. Sch. Design, 1969. Mktg. ptnr. Fullop and Assocs., 1983-85; founder, sec., treas. Kinetic Energy Ltd., 1985-90; freelance set designer Ilonka Creative Environments, 1974-84; founder, v.p. Harezi Internat., 1980-84; founder, sec., treas. Elf Cocoon Corp., 1984-86; founder, pres., chmn. Elf Cocoon Internat. Ltd., 1985-92; founder, pres. Elfworks, Inc., 1991-94, Elfworks, Nev., 1994-96; pres., dir. Allied Fund for Capital Appreciation, Inc., 1994—98; v.p. Phillip Stein Teslar, 2001—; pres. Nanogy, Inc., 2003—, Biotelemetric Signaling, Inc., 2004—. Interviewed by radio, TV, and newspapers on design and extremely low frequency electromagnetic tech.; presenter tech. sems. on ELF, the Quantum and scalar phenomena. Author: The Resonance in Residence; contbr. articles to profl. jours. Bd. dirs. Inst. for Higher Human Learning Potential, Phila., 1979. Fellow N.Y. Acad. of Sci.; mem. NAFE, ACLU, AAAS, Am. Inst. Interior Designers, Women's Internat. League for Peace and Freedom, Nat. Assn. Against Health Fraud, Nat. Narcotics Officers Assns. Coalition, N.Y. Acad. Sci., UN-USA Bus. Coun., Knights of Malta (dame), Knights of Africa (dame), U.S. Acad. Polit. Sci., Am. Craft Coun. Achievements include patents pending for transdermal pump and teslar chip. Office: ELF Tesler St Rt 1 Saint Francisville IL 62460 Office Phone: 618-948-2393, 305-398-7690. Personal E-mail: ilonkaharezi@aol.com.

HARFF, CHARLES HENRY, retired lawyer, retired diversified financial services company executive; b. Wesel, Germany, Sept. 27, 1929; s. Philip and Stephanie (Dreyfuss) H.; m. Marion Haines MacAfee, July 19, 1958; children— Pamela Haines, John Blair, Todd Philip BA, Colgate U., 1951; LL.B., Harvard U., 1954; postgrad., U. Bonn, Fed. Republic Germany, 1955. Bar: N.Y. 1955. Assoc. Chadbourne & Parke, N.Y.C., 1955-64, ptnr., 1964-84; sr. v.p., gen. counsel, sec. Rockwell Internat. Corp., Pitts., 1984-94, sr. v.p., spl. counsel, 1994-96, ret., 1996. Cons., 1996—2001; bd. dirs. Arvin Meritor, Inc., 1997—. Trustee Christian A. Johnson Endeavor Found., N.Y.C., 1984-2001; bd. dirs. Atlantic Legal Found., 1989-98, Fulbright Assn., 1995-2002, pres., 2001. Fulbright scholar U. Bonn, Germany, 1954-55. Mem. ABA, N.Y. State Bar Assn., The Assn. Gen. Counsel, Harvard Club of N.Y.C., Duquesne Club, Allegheny Country Club, Farm Neck Golf Club (Martha's Vineyard, Mass.)(founder, pres.).

HARFORD, JAMES, writer; b. Jersey City, Aug. 19, 1924; s. Thomas William and Jane Hume (Henderson) H.; m. Mildred Rita Waters, Apr. 19, 1952; children: Susan Gately, James Joseph, Peter Benedict (dec.), Jennifer, Christopher. BSME, Yale U. 1945W. Sales engr. Worthington Corp., 1946-49; assoc. editor Modern Industry, 1950-52; free-lance writer Europe, 1952-53; exec. sec. Am. Rocket Soc., 1953-63; exec. dir. Am. Inst. Aeros. and Astronautics, 1963-88, exec. dir. emeritus, 1988—. V.p. Internat. Astronautical Fedn., 1988—90. Author: Korolev (How One Man Masterminded the Soviet Drive to Beat America to the Moon), 1997, (with others) China Space Report, 1979. Mem. 1945W class coun. Yale U.; trustee Friends of Princeton Pub. Libr., 1996—2002. Lt. (j.g.) USNR, 1945—46. Recipient NASA Pub. Svc. award, 1985, Air Force Exceptional Svc. award, 1987, Nat. Space Club Robert Goddard Hist. Essay prize, 1995, Internat. Astron. Fedn. award, 1997; Verville fellow Nat. Air and Space Mus., 1989-92. Fellow AIAA (Disting. Svc. award 1988, Internat. Coop. Aerospace award 1995), AAAS, Brit. Interplanetary Soc., Royal Aero. Soc. (assoc.); mem. Internat. Acad. Astronautics, Cosmos Club, Nassau Club. Home and Office: 601 Lake Dr Princeton NJ 08540-5634 E-mail: j.harford@att.net.

HARGADON, BERNARD JOSEPH, JR., retired consumer goods company executive; b. Ardmore, Pa., Dec. 27, 1927; s. Bernard Joseph and Anna Mendenhall (Lancaster) H.; m. Jill Dinwiddie, Dec. 15, 1990; children from previous marriage: Geoffrey, Robert, Louise, Lawrence (dec.), David. BS, Drexel U., 1952, MBA, 1959; PhD (hon.), Golden Gate U., 1995. Auditor Gen. Motors Corp., 1955-57; prof. acctg. Drexel U., 1957-59; with AID, Colombia, 1960-63, McKesson, San Francisco, 1964—; pres. McKesson Internat., 1980-95, ret., 1995. Adj. prof. internat. bus. Golden Gate U. Author: in Spanish Principles of Accounting, 1964, Principles of Cost Accounting, 1971. Bd. dirs. World Affairs Coun. No. Calif., Opera Carolina, Charlotte, N.C., WDAV, Davidson, N.C.; mem. Pacific Coun. Internat. Policy. With USN, 1945-48 E-mail: bhargadon@aol.com.

HARGAN, CHARLES JAMES, retired lithographer, village official; b. Clarion, Iowa, June 24, 1941; s. Vernon Garney and Olive Lucile (Tourtelotte) H.; m. Carol Ann Moze, Nov. 25, 1961 (div. June 1981); children: Robert, James, Susan; m. Inga Lynn Johnson, Oct. 6, 1984 (dec. July 2002); 1 child, David. Lithographer W.A. Krueger Co. (now Quebecor World Inc.), Brookfield, Wis., 1962—2001, ret., 2001—. Pres. Village of Germantown, wis., 1993—, trustee, 1986-93. With U.S. Army, 1958-62. Mem. Am. Legion. Republican. Lutheran. Avocations: bowling, fishing, writing, travel, history. Office: Village of Germantown PO Box 337 Germantown WI 53022-0337

HARGENS, CHARLES WILLIAM, III, electrical engineer, consultant; b. Phila., Oct. 21, 1918; s. Charles William Jr. and Marjorie (Garman) H.; m. Mary K. Johnson, June 14, 1941; children: William Garman, Mary Van Deusen, Roger Snow. SB, MIT, 1941. Registered profl. engr., Pa. Design engr. Lockheed Aircraft, Burbank, Calif., 1941-42; group engr. Gilfillan Bros., L.A., 1942-43; vis. staff mem. MIT Radiation Labs., Cambridge, 1942-44; group engr. RCA, Camden, N.J., 1945-47; sr. engr., tech. dir., inst. fellow Franklin Inst. Labs., Phila., 1947-88; assoc. prof. Temple U., Phila., 1976-77, Drexel U., Phila., 1978-87; noise control cons. air mgmt. div. City of Phila., 1978—. Rsch. assoc. Wills Eye Hosp., 1970; cons., prof. acoustics; invited lectr. U. Wis., 1962, 63, 64. Co-author: Studies in Medicine, Physics and Voice, 1968, (chpts.) Bioengineering and the Skin, 1981, Handbook of Noninvasive Methods and the Skin, 1994; contbr. articles to Jour. Ophthalmic Surgery, Jour. Acoustical Soc. Am., Investigative Dermatology, Indsl. Rsch., Electronics Jour. Instrument Soc. Am., Jour. Franklin Inst., IEEE Transactions. Mem. adv. com. Spring Garden Coll., Phila., 1972-76; rsch. assoc. Bd. of City Trusts, 1970. Recipient Diploma, War Manpower Commn., 1944, Citation Mayor City of Phila., 1974. Fellow IEEE (Phila. Sect. Appreciation award 1972, Benjamin Franklin Key award 2003); mem. ASTM (Citation 1982), Franklin Inst. (com. sci. and arts 1981-99), MIT Alumni Assn. (life, Bronze Beaver award 1976), Numerical Control Soc. (founder), Sigma Xi. Episcopalian. Achievements include 12 patents for radio, electronics, computation, instrumentation optics and measurement; development of specialized instruments for dermatologists, brain tissue and other researchers. Home and Office: 718 Radcliff Ct Lansdale PA 19446-5895 *Never retire completely from your profession, unless health forces it upon you. It is foolish to give up all the experience, knowledge, and associations acquired over a productive lifetime.*

HARGIS, DAVID MICHAEL, lawyer, writer; b. Warren, Ark., Feb. 10, 1948; s. James Von Hargis and Noma Lee (Anderson) Watkins; m. Carolyn Jane Sangster (div. 1981); children— Michelle Leigh, Michael Bradley; m. Linda Jane Huckelbury, Jan. 8, 1981; 1 child, Christopher Key. B.S.B.A. with honors, U. Ark., 1970, J.D., 1973. Bar: Ark. 1973, U.S. Dist. Ct. (ea. and we. dists.) Ark. 1974. Assoc. Williamson Law Firm, Monticello, Ark., 1973-74; asst. U.S. atty. Eastern Dist. Ark., Little Rock, 1974-75; assoc. House, Holmes & Jewell, Little Rock, 1975-79; ptnr. House, Holmes & Jewell, P.A., Little Rock, 1979-85; founder Wilson, Wood & Hargis, 1985—; atty. Legal Services Corp., Little Rock, 1977; county atty. Pulaski County, Ark., 1980-82; atty. Pulaski County Quorum Ct., 1980-82; spl. circuit judge Pulaski County Circuit Ct., 1982; atty. Office of Spl. Prosecutor, Pulaski County Grand Jury, 1983-84; spl. counsel Ark.Ins. Dept., 1984. Editor-in-chief Ark. Law Rev., 1972-73; guest columnist Ark. Gazette, 1984. Contbr. articles to legal jours. Co-author: Quality Assurance in Health Test, American College of Pathologists, 1986. Recipient spl. commendation Legal Services Corp., 1977, Ark. Edn. Assn., 1984. Mem. ABA (legal edn. sect., corp. sect.), Ark. Bar Assn., Omicron Delta Kappa, Beta Gamma Sigma. Methodist. Home: 10 Durance Dr Little Rock AR 72223-9106 Office: 807 W 3rd St Little Rock AR 72201-2103

HARGIS, V. BURNS, lawyer; b. Victoria, Tex., Oct. 29, 1945; s. A.V. and Rosalie (Burns) H.; m. Ann Whiting, June 8, 1969; children: Matthew Burns, Kathryn Ann. BS, Okla. State U., 1967; JD, U. Okla., 1970. Bar: Okla. 1970. Pvt. practice law, Okla. City, 1970-75; ptnr. Reynolds, Ridings & Hargis, Okla. City, 1975-89; dir. Hartzog, Conger, Cason & Hargis, Okla. City, 1989-94; shareholder McAfee & Taft, Oklahoma City, 1994-97; vice chmn. Bank of Okla., Oklahoma City, 1997—. Pres., bd. dirs. Neighborhood Homes, Inc., 1973. Vice chmn. Okla. State Election Bd., 1975-80; legal counsel Okla. State Rep. Com., 1971-73; bd. dirs. Neighborhood Services Orgn.; pres., bd. dirs. Oklahoma City Community Food Bank, 1978-87; exec. com. Last Frontier Council, 1988—; chmn. Mayor's Econ. Devel. Com., Oklahoma City, 1986; chmn. Okla. Commn. Human Services, 1987; sr. warden All Souls Episcopal Ch., 1974-78; bd. regents, chair Okla. State U., 2005. Served to capt. U.S. Army, 1970-76. Fellow Am. Bar Found., Okla. Bar Found. (trustee, pres. 1987); mem. ABA, Okla. Bar Assn. (outstanding cmty. svc. award 1986), Okla. County Bar Assn. (pres. 1982, leadership award 1986), Oklahoma City Golf and Country Club, Rotary (pres., bd. dirs. Oklahoma City 1986), Greater Okla. City C. of C., United Way Ctrl. Okla (chair, 2005—). Republican. Avocations: golf, tennis, squash.

HARGITAY, MARISKA MAGDOLINA, actress; b. LA, Jan. 23, 1964; d. Mickey Hargitay and Jayne Mansfield; m. Peter Hermann, Aug. 28, 2004. Student, UCLA. Actor: (films) Ghoulies, 1985, Welcome to 18, 1986, Jocks, 1987, Mr. Universe, 1988, The Perfect Weapon, 1991, Strawberry Road, 1991, Hard Time Romance, 1991, Bank Robber, 1993, Leaving Las Vegas, 1995, Lake Placid, 1999, Perfume, 2001; (TV films) Finish Line, 1989, Blind Side, 1993, Gambler V: Playing for Keeps, 1994, The Advocate's Devil, 1997, Plain Truth, 2004; (TV series) Downtown, 1986—87, Falcon Crest, 1988, Tequila and Bonetti, 1992, Can't Hurry Love, 1995—96, Prince Street, 1997, Law & Order: Special Victims Unit, 1999— (Golden Globe award for best actress TV series - drama, 2005); (TV miniseries) Night Sins, 1997, (TV appearances include) Falcon Crest, 1984, In the Heat of the Night, 1988, Freddy's Nightmares, 1988, Baywatch, 1989, Wiseguy, 1990, Thirtysomething, 1990, Booker, 1990, Gabriel's Fire, 1990, Key West, 1993, Seinfeld, 1993, Hotel Room, 1993, All-American Girl, 1995, Ellen, 1996, The Single Guy, 1996, Cracker, 1997, ER, 1997—98. Office: Law and Order SVU NBC 30 Rockefeller Plaza New York NY 10112*

HARGRAVE, RUDOLPH, state supreme court justice; b. Shawnee, Okla., Feb. 15, 1925; s. John Hubert and Daisy (Holmes) H.; m. Madeline Hargrave, May 29, 1949; children: Cindy Lu, John Robert, Jana Sue. LLB, U. Okla., 1949. Bar: Okla. 1949. Pvt. practice, Wewoka, Okla., 1949—64; asst. county atty. Seminole County, 1951-55; judge Seminole County Ct., 1964-67, Seminole County Superior Ct., 1967-69; dist. judge Okla. Dist. Ct., Dist. 22, 1969—78; justice Okla. Supreme Ct., Oklahoma City, 1978—, former vice chief justice then chief justice. Former v.p. Nat. Conference of Chief Justices; mem. Okla. Jud. Conference. Mem. Seminole County Bar Assn., Okla. Bar Assn., ABA Lodges: Lions; Masons. Democrat. Methodist. Office: Okla Supreme Ct State Capitol Bldg Room 202 Oklahoma City OK 73105

HARGRAVE, SARAH QUESENBERRY, consulting company executive, public relations executive; b. Mt. Airy, N.C., Dec. 11, 1944; d. Teddie W. and Lois Knight (Slusher) Quesenberry. Student, Radford Coll., 1963-64, Va. Poly. Inst. and State U., 1964-67. Mgmt. trainee Thalhimer Bros. Dept. Store, Richmond, Va., 1967-68; Cen. Va. fashion and publicity dir. Sears Roebuck & Co., Richmond, 1968-73, nat. decorating sch. coord. Chgo., 1973-74, nat. dir. bus. and profl. women's programs, 1974-76; v.p., treas., program dir. Sears-Roebuck Found., Chgo., 1976-87, program mgr. corp. contbns. and memberships, 1981-84, dir. corp. mktg. and pub. affairs, 1984-87; v.p. personal fin. svcs. and mktg. Northern Trust Co., Chgo., 1987-89; pres. Hargrave Consulting, 1989—. Spkr., seminar leader in field. Bd. dirs. Am. Assembly Collegiate Schs. Bus., 1979-82, mem. vis. com., 1979-82, mem. fin. and audit com., 1980-82, mem. task force on doctoral supply and demand, 1980-82; mem. Com. for Equal Opportunity for Women, 1976-81; chmn., 1978-79, 80-81; mem. bus. adv. coun. Walter E. Heller Coll. Bus. Adminstrn., Roosevelt U., 1979-89; co-dir. Ill. Internat. Women's Yr. Ctr., 1975. Named Outstanding Young Women of Yr. Ill., 1976; named Women of Achievement State Street Bus. and Profl. Woman's Club, 1978 Mem. ASTD, Profl. Women's Network, Profl. Coaches & Mentors Assn. Home and Office: 34 Fairlawn Ave Daly City CA 94015-3425 Personal E-mail: shargrave@earthlink.net.

HARGRAVE, VICTORIA ELIZABETH, librarian; b. Ripon, Wis., Aug. 22, 1913; d. Alexander Walter and Estelle Winifred (Swanson) H. AB, Ripon Coll., 1934; library diploma, U. Wis., 1938; MA, U. Chgo., 1947; postgrad., U. Cal. at Los Angeles, 1970. Tchr. Brandon (Wis.) High Sch., 1934-37; extension librarian Ia. State Coll. Library, 1938-44; librarian Ripon Coll., 1944-46, MacMurray Coll., 1947-78. Mem. adv. council librarians U. Ill. Grad. Sch. Library Sci., 1962-64 Mem. A.L.A., AAUW. Home: 4650 54th Ave S Apt 416 Saint Petersburg FL 33711-4637

HARGRAVES, J. LEE, sociologist, researcher; b. Winshire, Tex., July 28, 1956; s. Johnnie Lee Hargraves and Barbara Jones Currie; m. Linda Carol Phalen, Oct. 3, 1992; children: Erik Phalen, Emma Phalen. BS, U. Gt. Falls, 1982; MA, U. Mont., 1985; PhD, Boston (Mass.) Coll., 1994. Sr. project dir. Sch. Pub. Health Harvard U., Boston, 1989—94; sr. survey scientist Picker Inst., Boston, 1994—99; sr. health rschr. Ctr. Studying Health Sys. Change, Washington, 1999—2004; rsch. assoc. prof. Med. Sch. U. Mass., Worcester, Mass., 2004—. Contbr. articles to profl. jours. Sgt. USAF, 1976—80. Decorated Air Force Commendation Medal USAF. Office: U of Massachusetts Medical School 55 Lake Avenue North Worcester MA 01655 Personal E-mail: lhargraves@hotmail.com.

HARGRAVES, MARTHA ANN, health services administrator, researcher; b. Mexia, Tex., July 24, 1945; d. Willie Henry and Luerean (Edmond) Houston; m. Archie Lee Hargraves, June 10, 1965 (div. 1975); 1 child, Sharon Denise. BSBA, Jarvis Christian Coll., 1967; M in Pub. Health, U. Tex., 1975, PhD in Mgmt./Policy Scis., 1992. Chief interagy. coordination Dept. of Health and Human Svcs., Washington, 1975-77, spl. asst. Office of Sec., 1977-79; dep. asst. sec. licensing and regulation Dept. of Health and Human Svcs., State of La., 1979-81; program mgmt. officer Ctrs. for Disease Control USPHS, Atlanta, 1981-88; faculty assoc., rsch. assoc. U. Tex. Sch. of Pub. Health Ctr. for Health Policy, Houston, 1988-92, postdoctoral fellow Office of the Pres., 1992-93, asst. prof., dir. health policy and health svcs. rsch. Galveston, 1993—. Com. mem. osteoporosis adv. com. Tex. Dept. of Health, Austin, Tex., 1996-98; com. mem. mayor's com. for the advancement of families and children, Galveston, 1998—; mem. panel of experts U.S. Dept. Health and Human Svcs., USPHS, 1997—. Contbr. articles to profl. jours. Bd. dirs. YMCA, Galveston, 1994-98, San Jacinto Girl Scouts, Houston, 1990-93. Recipient Disting. Alumni Citation of Yr. Nat. Assn. for Equal Opportunity in Higher Edn., 1997. Mem. Soc. for the Study of Social Problems (com. of budget and fin. 1999—, chair minority grad. scholarship com. 1998), Chauncey Leake History of Medicine Soc., Consortium of Doctors, Ltd., Phi Kappa Phi. Avocations: cooking, walking, travel. Office: U Tex Med Br at Galveston 301 University Blvd Galveston TX 77555-5302 Fax: 409-747-4991. E-mail: mhargrav@utmb.edu.

HARGRAVES, WILLIAM FREDERICK, II, mathematics professor, computer science educator; b. Cin., Aug. 18, 1932; s. William Frederick and Annie Leona (Thomas) H.; m. Maurine Collins, July 5, 1957; children: William Frederick III, Jock Frederick, Charles Frederick. BS in Edn. with honors, Miami U., Oxford, Ohio, 1954, MA in Physics, 1961. Commd. 2d lt. USAF, 1954, advanced through grades to col., ret., 1982, comdr. 20th mil. airlift squadron, 1955-59, air liaison officer Wright-patterson AFB, Ohio, 1959-61; rsch. scientist USAF, Weapons Rsch. Ctr., Kirtland AFB, N.Mex., 1961—65; aircraft comdr., instr. pilot 22 mil. airlift command USAF, Tachikawa, Japan, 1965-70, air liaison officer 1st ARVAN Divsn. Vietnam, 1970-71, asst. prof. air sci., AFROTC program, Miami U. Oxford, Ohio, 1971-74, chief flight deck devel., R&D Wright Patterson AFB, 1978, dep. divsn. chief, US Pentagon Washington, 1978-82, ret., 1982; asst. prof., asst. dean arts and scis. Cen. State U., Wilberforce, Ohio, 1982—. Asst. track and field coach Cen. State U., 1993—. Founder Pilgrim Bapt. Chr. Men's Choir, Hamilton, Ohio, 1980, Grant Chapel Ave. Ch., Albuquerque, 1962; trustee Bethel AME Ch., 2002—. Decorated Dist. Flying Cross 72, Air medal, Air Force commendation medal with 2 oak leaf clusters, Vietnam Service medal with 5 bronze stars, Nat. Def. Svc. medal; named to Covington (Ky.) Black Hall of Fame, 1992; Rhodes scholar candidate, Ky., 1950. Mem. Am. Registry of Outstanding Profls. (life; honors), Phi Beta Kappa, Omicron Delta Kappa, Kappa Delta Pi, Pi Mu Epsilon, Sigma Pi Sigma. Methodist. Home: 123 W Walnut St Oxford OH 45056-1721 Office: Cen State U 1400 Brush Row Rd Wilberforce OH 45384 Office Phone: 937-376-6179. Business E-Mail: whargraves@centralstate.edu.

HARGREAVES, DAVID R., toy company executive; Mem., fin. dept. Ford Motor Co.; head, fin., U.S. toy, internat. and opers. groups Hasbro, Inc., Pawtucket, RI, sr. v.p., fin. and adminstrn., domestic toy opers., sr. v.p., fin. and planning, global opers., 1996—97, sr. v.p., fin. and planning, global mktg., 1997—99, sr. v.p., fin., 1999, dep. CFO, 1999—2001, CFO, sr. v.p., 2001—. Office: Hasbro Inc 1027 Newport Ave Pawtucket RI 02862

HARGREAVES, DAVID WILLIAM, retired communications company executive; b. Akron, Ohio, May 4, 1943; s. William B. and Helen Grace (Slusser) H.; m. Sandra Jean Tessier, Sept. 4, 1965; children: Kristen Elizabeth, Cinda Anne, Gregory David. BSEE, U. Maine, Orono, 1965; MBA, U. Rochester, 1967. Sales engr. Mobile Communications div. Gen. Electric, Lynchburg, Va., 1970-74, mgr. systems projects, 1974-75, mgr. systems bids/proposals, 1975-78; mgr. internat. mktg. Gen. Electric Powerline Carrier Bus., Lynchburg, 1978-80; gen. mgr. Gen. Electric Microwave Link Operation, Owensboro, Ky., 1980-84; mng. dir. Alpha Telecom div. Alpha Industries, Methuen, Mass., 1984-86; pres. Dynatech Tactical Comms. Inc. (formerly Controlonics Corp.), Nashua, N.H., 1986-97; pres., CEO DTC Comms. Inc., Nashua, 1997—2004. Condr. seminars in field. Contbr. articles to profl. jours. Chmn. bd. Gen. Electric United Way Pacesetter campaign, Lynchburg, 1978; advisor Jr. Achievement project bus., Owensboro, 1982, 83. Served to capt. U.S. Army, 1968-70, Vietnam. Decorated Bronze Star, D.S.C.; named N.H. High Tech. Coun. Entrepreneur of Yr., 2003. Mem.: Am. Mktg. Pres.'s Assn., Massibesic Yacht Club, Tau Beta Pi, Eta Kappa Nu. Republican. Avocations: sailing, skiing, amateur radio. Home: 191 Buttrick Rd Hampstead NH 03841-2183 Personal E-mail: david.hargreaves@comcast.net.

HARGREAVES, GEORGE HENRY, civil and agricultural engineer, researcher; b. Chico, Calif., Apr. 2, 1916; s. Carey and Luella May (Raymond) H.; m. Elizabeth Ann Gardner, Aug. 9, 1941 (dec. Dec. 1948); 1 child, Margaret Ann Hargreaves Stolpmann; m. Sara Etna Romero, Jan 6, 1951; children: Mark Romero, Sonia Maria Hargreaves Hart, George Leo. BS in Soils, U. Calif., Berkeley, 1939; BSCE, U. Wyo., 1943. Civil engr. U.S. Bur. Reclamation, Sacramento, 1946-48; reclamation engr. U.S. Army C.E., Greece, 1948-49; engr. AID, Greece, Peru, Haiti, Philippines, Brazil and Colombia, 1950-68; chief civil engr. engring. br. Natural Resources divsn. Inter-Am. Geodetic Survey, Ft. Clayton, 1968-70; rsch. engr. in irrigation Utah State. U., Logan, 1970-86; rsch. Internat. Irrigation Ctr., 1980-86, rsch. prof. emeritus, 1986—. Author: World Water for Agriculture, 1977; co-author: Irrigation Fundamentals, 1998, Fundamentos Del Riego, 2000; contbr. numerous articles to profl. jours. Lt. (j.g.) USNR, 1943-46, PTO. Recipient Royce J. Tipton award, 1997. Fellow: ASCE; mem.: Internat. Commn. Irrigation and Drainage (chmn. U.S. Com. on crops and water use 1992—96, drainage and flood control 1999—2003, chmn. U.S. com. on history of irrigation), Am. Soc. Agrl. Engrs. (chmn. Rocky Mountain sect. 1974). Achievements include development of methodology used by the International Water Management Institute in the IWMI World Water and Climate Atlas, providing worldwide climate data and an index of rainfall adequacy for agricultural production. Home: 1660 E 1220 N Logan UT 84341-3040 Office: Utah State U Internat Irrigation Ctr Dept Biol Irrigation Engring Logan UT 84322-4150

HARGREAVES, MARY-WILMA MASSEY, retired history educator; b. Erie, Pa., Mar. 1, 1914; d. Albert Edward and Bess (Childs) Massey; m. Herbert Walter Hargreaves, Aug. 24, 1940 (dec. July 1998). BA, Bucknell U., 1935; MA, Radcliffe Coll./Harvard U., 1936, PhD, 1951. Rsch. editor Harvard U. Grad. Sch. Bus. Adminstrn., Cambridge, Mass., 1937-39; fellow Brookings Inst., Washington, 1939-40; assoc. editor Clay Papers U. Ky., Lexington, 1952-74, co-editor, project dir. Clay Papers, 1974-79, asst. prof. history, 1964-69, assoc. prof., 1969-73, prof., 1973-84, Hallam prof. history, 1973-75, prof. emerita, 1984—. Mem. adv. bd. Henry Clay Found., 1995—. Author: Dry Farming in the Northern Great Plains, 1900-1925, 1957, Presidency of John Quincy Adams, 1985, Dry Farming in the Northern Great Plains, Years of Readjustment, 1920-1990, 1993; assoc. editor, co-editor: The Papers of Henry Clay, 6 vols., 1959-81; mem. editl. bd. Great Plains Quar., 1986-88; contbg. editor Miller Ctr. of Pub. Affairs, U. Va., 2003. Recipient Saloutos Book award in Agrl. History, 1994. Mem. Am. Hist. Assn. (com. chmn.), Orgn. of Am. Historians (com. chmn.), Agrl. History Soc. (pres. 1975-76, com. chmn.), So. Hist. Assn. (com. chmn.), Econ. History Assn., Ky. Hist. Soc., Mont. Hist. Soc., Phi Beta Kappa, Sigma Tau Delta, Phi Alpha Theta Democrat. Methodist. Avocations: reading, gardening, classical music. Home: 237 Cassidy Ave Lexington KY 40502-2303 Office: U Ky History Dept 1715 Patterson Office Tower Lexington KY 40506-0027 Personal E-mail: marywilma237@yahopo.com.

HARGREAVES-FITZSIMMONS, KAREN ANN, painter, illustrator; b. Highland Park, Mich., July 19, 1945; d. Richard Hollowell and Belle Helen (Edson) Hargreaves; m. Thomas Fitzsimmons, Mar. 20, 1978. BA, Oakland U., 1967; MA, U. Mich., 1971. Counselor Mich. State Employment Commn., Detroit, 1969-73; art dir. Katydid Prodns., Santa Fe, 1973—. Instr. Ann. Sumi-e Lecture/demonstrations, Oakland U., Mich., 1984-88, Corpus Christi Coll., Oxford U., Eng., 1985, Ctr. for Creative Studies, Detroit, 1986. Two-woman show includes Hakumon Internat. Festival of Arts, Toyko, 1974, Laurel Seth Gallery, Santa Fe, 1994; one-woman shows include Am. Cultural Ctr., Tokyo, 1974, Tokyodo Bunka Salon, 1983, Genkan Gallery, Toyko, 1984, USIS Am. Cultural Ctr. Gallery, Tokyo, 1985, Komaba Garden Gallery, Tokyo, 1985, William Pelletier Gallery, Ann Arbor, Mich., 1986, Aura Gallery, Santa Fe, 1993, Randall Davey Audubon Ctr., Santa Fe, 1995, St. John's Coll. Art Gallery, Santa Fe, 1998, Laurel Seth Gallery, Santa Fe, 1999, Jean Cocteau Therter, Santa Fe, 2000; open studio shows include West Bloomfield, Mich., 1987, 88, Kamakura, Japan, 1989, Peymeinade (Cannes), France, 1990, 91, Santa Fe, 1992, 93, 94-2004; group exhbns. include 18th Ann. Oakland County Art Show, 1980, 8th Mich. Ann. Juried Show, 1980, Southfield Civic Ctr., 1980, Ann Arbor Art Assn. Show, 1980, Birmingham-Bloomfield Art Assn. Gallery, 1980-82, Ann Arbor Art Assn. Gallery, 1980-82, Detroit Inst. Arts Rental Gallery, 1980-88, Laurel Seth Gallery, Santa Fe, 1993, 94—, Santa Fe Studios Ann. Show, 2002, Coll. Santa Fe Monoprint Monothon, 1995-2001, Hand Artes Gallery, Truchas, N.Mex., 1995-98; author: (with Thomas Fitzsimmons) Water Ground Stone, 1994, Is Two Becomes One, 2005; designer, illustrator 40 books of Japanese, European, Bengali and Am. poetry. Home: 1 Balsa Rd Santa Fe NM 87508-8319

HARGROVE, ERWIN CHARLES, JR., political science professor; b. St. Joseph, Mo., Oct. 11, 1930; s. Erwin Charles and Gladys Lenore (France) H.; m. Lynne Douglas, Apr. 10, 1961 (div. Jan., 1991); children: John, Amy, Sarah; m. Julia Mosher, Sept. 21, 1991. BA, Yale U., 1953, PhD, 1963. From asst. prof. to prof. polit. sci. Brown U., Providence, 1960—76, prof., dept. chair polit. sci., 1973—75; sr. fellow Urban Inst., Washington, 1976—85; prof. polit. sci., dir. Inst. for Pub. Policy Studies Vanderbilt U., Nashville, 1976-85, chmn. dept. polit. sci., 1992-96, prof. polit. sci. emeritus, 2000—, lectr. dept. history, 2003—. Author: Presidential Leadership, Personality and Political Style, 1966, Professional Roles in Society and Government: The English Case, 1972, The Power of the Modern Presidency, 1974, The Missing Link: The Study of Implementation of Social Policy, 1975, Jimmy Carter as President, Leadership and the Politics of the Public Good, 1988 (Richard E. Neustadt award, 1988), Prisoners of Myth: Leadership of the Tennessee Valley Authority, 1933-1990, 1994, The President as Leader: Appealing to the Better Angels of Our Nature, 1998; co-author (with Michael Nelson): Presidents, Politics and Policy, 1984; editor: The Future of the Democratic Left in Industrial Democracies, 2003; co-editor (with Paul Conkin): TVA, Fifty Years of Grass Roots Bureaucracy, 1983; co-editor: (with Samuel Morley) The President and the Council of Economic Advisers: Interviews with CEA Chairmen, 1984; co-editor: (with Jameson Doig) Leadership and Innovation: A Biographical Perspective on Entrepreneurs in Government, 1987; co-editor: (with John Glidewell) Impossible Jobs in Public Management, 1990; co-editor: (with John E. Owens) Leadership in Context, 2003. With U.S. Army, 1954-56. Democrat. Episcopalian. Home: 662 Timber Ln Nashville TN 37215-1120 E-mail: Erwin.C.Hargrove@Vanderbilt.edu.

HARGROVE, JOHN RUSSELL, lawyer; b. Chgo., Jan. 20, 1947; s. John Francis and Dolly (Arzich) H.; m. Mary Cheryl Fuller, Feb. 12, 1972; children: John Ashby, James Fuller. BS, Butler U., 1969; JD magna cum laude, Ind. U., 1972. Bar: Ind. 1972, Fla. 1974, U.S. Tax Ct. 1975, U.S. Supreme Ct. 1976. Law clk. to Hon Roy L. Stephenson U.S. Ct. Appeals Ind., 1971-72, U.S. Ct. Appeals (8th cir.), 1972-74; mng. dir. and shareholder Heinrich, Gordon, Hargrove, Weihe & James, P.A., Ft. Lauderdale, Fla., 1985-91. Lead articles and book rev. editor Ind. Law Rev., 1971-72. Bd. visitors Ind. U. Sch. Law, 1995—; bd. dirs. EV Ready Broward, 1996-98; nat. co-chair Franciscan Games, 1996. Schofield scholar. Recipient Faculty award Ind. U. Sch. of Law, 1972. Fellow Fla. Acad. Probate and Trust Litigation; mem. ABA, Fed. Bar Assn. (Broward County Fla. chpt., exec. com. 1979-80, v.p. 1980-81, pres. 1981-82), Fla. Bar Assn., Ind. Bar Assn. (mem. bd. vis. Sch. of Law 1995—). Roman Catholic. Office: 500 E Broward Blvd Ste 1000 Fort Lauderdale FL 33394-3087 Home: 338 Royal Palm Way Boca Raton FL 33432-7944

HARGROVE, MIKE (DUDLEY MICHAEL HARGROVE), former professional baseball team manager; b. Perryton, Tex., Oct. 26, 1949; m. Sharon Rupprecht, Dec. 12, 1970; children: Kimberly Denise, Melissa Kathryn, Pamela Christine, Andrew Michael, Cynthia Michelle. BS in Phys. Edn. and Social Scis., Northwestern Okla. State U. Baseball player Tex. Rangers, 1974-78, San Diego Padres, 1979, Cleve. Indians, 1979-85, coach minor league team, 1986, mgr. minor league team, 1987-89, coach, 1990-91, mgr., 1991-99; mgr. Am. League championship team, 1995, 97; mgr., coach Balt. Orioles, 1999—2003; sr. adviser, baseball ops. dept. Cleve. Indians, 2003—. Named Am. League Rookie of Yr. Baseball Writers' Assn. Am., 1974, Am. League Rookie Player of Yr. Sporting News, 1974; named to All-Star team, 1975, Am. League Mgr. of Yr. Sporting News, 1995. Office: Cleveland Indians 2401 Ontario St Cleveland OH 44115

HARGROVE, ROY BELMONT, III, stockbroker; b. Farmville, Va., Sept. 2, 1958; s. Roy Belmont Jr. and Margaret Ann (Heaton) H.; children: Roy B. IV, Katherine Allyn. BS, Lynchburg Coll., 1980, MBA, 1985. CFP. Account exec. Wheat First Securities, Williamsburg, Va., 1980-86, investment officer, 1986-88, v.p., investment officer, 1988-94; sr. v.p. Wheat First Butcher Singer, Williamsburg, 1994—; br. mgr. Williamsburg office Wachovia Securities, Williamsburg, 1996—. Trustee Endowment, Williamsburg Bapt. Ch., 1990-99, chmn. ofcl. bd., 1988, Sunday sch. tchr., 1990-98; founding bd. dirs., past chmn. Hospice Support Care of Williamsburg, 1982-91, 95—; fundraiser Am. Cancer Soc., Williamsburg, 1992—; mem. local com. Kingsmill chpt. Ducks Unltd., 1982-90; coach Williamsburg Recreation Jr. Basketball Program, 1994-2000; bd. dirs. Williamsburg Landing Retirement Cmty., 1996-2002; mem. budget and fin. com. Kingsmill Comty. Svc. Assn., 1996-2000; bd. dirs. Hampton Roads Acad., 1999—, chmn. bd. trustees, 2004-. Recipient Disting. Alumni award Prince Edward Acad., 1998. Mem. Kiwanis. Avocations: golf, skiing, fishing. Office: Wachovia Securites 275 Mclaws Cir Williamsburg VA 23185-5649 Home: 101 Sheriffs Pl Williamsburg VA 23185 Office Phone: 757-258-1664. Business E-Mail: rhargrove@wachoviasec.com.

HARGROVE, SANDRA LEIGH, financial planner; b. Hillsboro, Oreg., Dec. 1, 1946; d. William Paul and Hazel Hannah Burgher; m. Larry Burke Hargrove, Nov. 25, 1977; m. John Anthony Coleman, July 13, 1964 (div. May 0, 1977); children: Tereasa Kay Taylor, Deborah Leigh Coleman. Student, Clatsop County C.C., Astoria, Oreg., 1983—85. Mgr. Columbia Ins., Knappa, Oreg., 1973—75; office supply and mail rm. staff Crown Zellerbach Corp Wauna Mill, Clatskanie, Oreg., 1975—76; switchboard operator/receptionist Crown Zellerbach Wauna Mill, Clatskanie, 1976—78, acct. #1 & 2 paper machines, 1978—80; gen. ledger acct. Crown Zellerbach/James River Corp. Wauna Mill, Clatskanie, 1980—84; fin. mgr. James River Corp. Wauna Mill, Clatskanie, 1984—89; co-owner S & K Images, Svenson, Oreg., 1996—98; relief postmaster USPS Oysterville (Wash.) Post Office, 2002—. Originator of project concept & manager (historical/genealogical research) The Lewis & Clark Descendant Project. Treas. Immanuel Luth. Ch., Knappa, 1996—98. Mem.: Pacific County Wash. Geneal. Soc. (pres. 1999—2001), Clatsop County Oreg. Geneal. Soc. (pres. 1998—2001). Democrat. Lutheran. Avocations: walking, genealogy. Personal E-mail: shargrov@pacifier.com.

HARGROVE, WADE HAMPTON, lawyer; b. Clinton, N.C., Mar. 6, 1940; s. Wade Hampton and Susan (Baker) H.; m. Sandra Dunaway, June 7, 1969; children: Wade Hampton III, Andrew D. AB with honors, U. N.C., 1962, JD, 1965. Bar: N.C. 1965, D.C. 1967. Ptnr. Brooks, Pierce, McLendon, Humphrey, Leonard, Raleigh, NC, 1995—; gen. counsel, exec. dir. N.C. Assn. Broadcasters, 1970—, N.C. CATV Assn., 1980—; chmn. bd. dirs. 1st Union Nat. Bank, Raleigh, 1989-93. Mem. N.C. Gov.'s Coun. on State Policy, 1974—79; chmn. N.C. News Media Adminstrn. Justice Coun., 1976; commr. N.C. Milk Commn., 1976—78, chmn., 1988—2000; commr. N.C. Agy. Pub. Telecom.; spl. advisor to U.S. at Internat. Conf. on Direct Satellite Broadcasts, Geneva, 1983; mem. legis. study Commn. on Open Govt., 1993; chair N.C. Ctr. Pub. Policy Rsch., 1994—; bd. visitors U. N.C., 1991—, U. N.C. Sch. Journalism, 1993—. Trustee Peace Coll., 2003. Named to N.C. Assn. Broadcasters Hall of Fame, 1998; recipient Disting. Svc., N.C. Assn. Broadcasters, 1973, N.C. CATV Assn., 1985. Mem. ABA, N.C. State Bar, D.C. Bar, Fed. Comms. Bar Assn., U. N.C. Law Alumni Assn. (pres. 1991-94), Capital City Club (bd. govs. 1983-91), Figure Eight Yacht Club, Cardinal Club (bd. govs. 1992—), Order of the Long Leaf Pine. Presbyterian. Home: 1005 Marlowe Rd Raleigh NC 27609-6971 Office: Brooks Pierce McLendon Humphrey Leonard 1600 First Union Bank Capitol Ctr Raleigh NC 27601-1309

HARGROVE, WALTER CLARK, III, cardiothoracic surgeon; b. Greenville, N.C., May 24, 1947; s. Walter Clark, Jr. and Alice Leigh (Blow) H.; m. Claudia Liane Ludwig, Aug. 20, 1991; children: Nelson, Nicholas, Saskia. BS, U. N.C., 1969; MD, Bowman Gray Sch. Medicine, 1973. Resident in surgery Hosp. U. Pa., Phila., 1974-75, fellow in vascular surgery, 1981, resident in thoracic surgery, 1982-83; from asst. prof. to assoc. prof. surgery U. Pa., Phila., 1984-96, clin. prof. surgery, 1998—; prof. cardiothoracic surgery Allegheny U. Health Scis., Phila., 1996-98. Maj. U.S. Army, 1979-81. Fellow ACS; mem. Am. Assn. Thoracic Surgery, Soc. Thoracic Surgery. Episcopalian. Avocation: golf. Office: Phila Heart Inst Ste 2 D 39th and Market St Philadelphia PA 19104 Office Phone: 215-662-9595. Business E-Mail: clark.hargrove@uphs.upenn.edu.

HARI, KENNETH STEPHEN, painter, sculptor, writer; b. Perth Amboy, N.J., Mar. 31, 1947; s. Stephen John and Jeannette Anna (Matuszewsky) H. Diploma, Newark Sch. Fine and Indsl. Arts, 1966; BFA, Md. Inst. Art, 1968, Yale U., 1970; postgrad., NYU, 1988. Cons. various cos. One man exhbns. include ctrl. Ala., 1996, Beijing, 1996; group exhbns. include Trave Exhibit, 2004, Beijing Mus. Fine Art, 2004, Md. State Mus., 1967, Union Coll., Schenectady, 1969, Monmouth (N.J.) Coll., 1970, Newark Mus., 1971, Trenton State Coll., 1972, one-man exhbns. include C.C. Price Gallery, N.Y.C., H.S. Graphics, Ltd., Keasbey, N.J.; represented in permanent collections of over 390 mus. throughout world, including Vatican, Lincoln Ctr. Gallery for Performing Arts, N.Y.C., Va. Poly. Inst., Blacksburg, N.J. State Mus., Trenton, Grand Ole Opry House, Nashville, Xiaoyi Liu collection, Met. Mus. Art, N.Y.C., Mus. Kenneth Hari, Beijing, China, established 1991, other pub. and pvt. collections; important works include portraits of W.H. Auden, N.Y.C., 1969, M. Moore, N.Y.C., 1969, Pablo Casals, Marlboro, Vt., 1970, Andres Segovia, N.Y.C., 1972, James Michener, Piperville, Pa., 1973, Marcel Marceau, N.Y.C., 1973, Donald Delue, N.Y.C., 1973, Dr. Allan Callow, Boston, 1973, Kurt Vonnegut, Jr., 1973, Buckminster Fuller, 1973, Lord Hailsham, London, 1978, Dr. Linus Pauling for Pauling Inst., Menlo Park, Calif., 1979, Paul Robeson for Paul Robeson Ctr., Rutgers U., Newark, 1979 (Hay award recipients.); Zhao Peng Fei, Beijing, Philip Johnson, N.Y.C., Paul Roache, Spain, Chen Chi, N.Y.C., Liu Zongyu, Beijing, Zhongguo Shengj, Living Treasure of China, 1999, Hiroko Seta, Tokyo, Japan, 1999, Rosemary Clooney, Beverly Hills, Calif., 1999, Paul Robeson exhbn. Rutgers U., 2003; exhibited at Johnson & Johnson, New Brunswick Travel Exhbn., The Angel of Revelation Mural, N.J., 1990; Original lithographs pub. Prophet, 1971, Lovers of Our Time, 1971, Vermont, 1972, Folk Singer, Marcel Marceau, 1973, Abraham, 1973, Ernest Hemingway, 1978, Homage to Virginia, 1980, Tropical Ladies, 1981, The Pearl, 1999, Lorin Pierucci Collection, 2004, Xiaoyi Liu Collection, Beijing Mus. Fine Arts, 2004, Ajeenah Collection of Paintings and Drawings, 2004, Lorin Piervcci Collection, Art Is the Soul of Man, and Without It He Is Lost. Bd. dirs. N.J. Art Festival, 1973-. Office: Eastman & John Watson Art Galleries Care John Eastman PO Box 243 Keasbey NJ 08832-0243 Office Phone: 732-442-8031. Personal E-mail: kennethhari@msn.com. *Art is the soul of man, and without it he is lost.*

HARIJAN, RAM, technology transfer researcher; b. Keecheri, Kerala, India, June 3, 1938; s. Narayanan and Devaki (Amma) Nambiar; m. Lakshmi VP, Aug. 19, 1977; 1 child, Pooja Devi. BA with honors, Madras U., India; MA with award, Southampton U., Eng.; PhD, Reading U., Eng. Lectr. Kerala (India) U.; mining officer Singareni Collieries, India; sch. tchr. Barnstaple Grammar Sch., Eng.; lectr. Bosworth Coll., Eng.; tutor cons. Open U., Eng.; researcher Centre for Studies in Tech. Transfer, Eng. Involved in rsch. which influenced the computerisation policies of Indian Govt., 1982-96; vis. prof. U. Madras, 1982, Calicut U., 1985. Chmn. North Devon Dist. Labour Party, 1972-77, North Devon Assn. Racial Equality, 1978-80; vol. social worker Helping the Disabled and Disadvantaged. Avocations: bridge, chess. Home: 30 Norfolk Rd Desford Leicester LE9 9HR England Personal E-mail: drramofindia@yahoo.com.

HARIK, SAMI ISKANDAR, neurologist, educator; b. Beirut, July 27, 1941; came to U.S., 1968; s. Iskandar M. and Georgette (Moubarak) H.; m. Wafa Bashir, June 2, 1968; children: Nahla, Nada, Hala. BS, Am. U. Beirut, 1961, MD, 1965. Diplomate Am. Bd. Psychiatry and Neurology. Asst. prof. Neurology Am. Univ. Beirut, Lebanon, 1973-76; asst. prof., assoc. prof. Neurology U. Miami (Fla.) Sch. Medicine, 1976-81; prof. Neurology, Pharmacology, Neurosci. Case We. Res. U., Cleve., 1981-94; prof., chmn. Neurology U. Ark., Little Rock, 1994—. Assoc. editor Neurology; mem. editl. bd. Jour. Neurochemistry, Neurology, Neurochem. Rsch.; contbr. chpts. to books, articles to profl. jours. Grantee Cerebral Vascular Disease Rsch. Ctr., 1979-81, 82-84, Nat. Parkinson Found., 1980-81, Cleve. Found., 1982-84, USPHS, 1983-86, 85-88, 86-89, 88-93, Alzheimer's Disease Rsch. Ctr., 1988-93. Fellow Am. Acad. Neurology (mem. sci. issues com.); mem. Internat. Brain Rsch. Orgn., Am. Neurol. Assn. (mem. membership com., councilor), Microcirculatory Soc., Internat. Soc. for Neurochemistry, Am. Soc. for Neurochemistry, Ark. Med. Soc. Office: Univ Ark Med Scis 4301 W Markham St # 500 Little Rock AR 72205-7101 Office Phone: 501-686-7236. E-mail: harikcamii@uams.edu.

HARING, ELLEN STONE (MRS. E. S. HARING), philosophy educator; b. L.A., 1921; d. Earl E. and Eleanor (Pritchard) Stone; m. Philip S. Haring, Dec. 1942 (div. June 1951). BA, Bryn Mawr Coll., 1942; MA, Radcliffe Coll., 1943, PhD (AAUW fellow), 1959. Adminstrv. worker ARC, Boston, 1943; mem. faculty Wheaton Coll., Norton, Mass., 1944-45, Wellesley Coll., 1945-72, assoc. prof., 1958-64, prof. philosophy, 1964-72, U. Fla., Gainesville, 1972-93, prof. emerita, 1993—, chmn. dept., 1972-80. Mem.: Am. Philos. Assn., Metaphys. Soc. Am. E-mail: ellenharing@netzero.net.

HARING, EUGENE MILLER, lawyer; b. Washington, May 16, 1927; s. Horace E. and Edith (Miller) H.; m. Janet K. Marshall, Apr. 10, 1971. AB summa cum laude, Princeton U., 1949, A.M. (Woodrow Wilson fellow), 1951; LL.B., Harvard U., 1955. Bar: N.J. 1955, U.S. Dist. Ct. N.J. 1955, U.S. Ct. Appeals (3d cir.) 1962, U.S. Supreme Ct. 1969, N.Y. 1983, U.S. Dist. Ct. (so. and ea. dists.) N.Y. 1992. Asst. in instrn. Princeton U., 1950-52; assoc. McCarter & English, Newark, 1955-61, ptnr., 1961-97, chmn. exec. com., 1982-97, of counsel, 1997—. Cert. mediator U.S. Dist. Ct., 1994—; mediator CPR Inst. for Dispute Resolution, N.J. Panel, 1994—; mem. roster of mediators Judiciary of State of N.J; mem. civil justice reform act adv. com. U.S. Dist. Ct. N.J., 1997—2000. Contbr. articles to profl. jours. Chmn. Princeton Twp. Zoning Bd. Adjustment, 1979-80, mem. bd., 1975-79; vestryman Trinity Episc. Ch., Princeton, 1975-79, 97-2000, warden, 1980-84; mem. com. on constn. and canons Episc. Diocese of N.J., 1980-87, chancellor, 1983-94, 99—, hon. canon (life), 2001—; trustee Gen. Theol. Sem., N.Y., 1987-90; mem. vis. com. Rutgers U. Law Sch., 1994-2000; trustee N.J. Jersey Shore Found., 1988-92. Served with USNR, 1945-46. Fellow Am. Bar Found. (life), Lawyers Adv. Com. (U.S. Ct. Appeals 3d cir. 1990-93, U.S. Dist. Ct. N.J. 1997—); mem. ABA, N.J. State Bar Assn. (emeritus), N.J. State Bar Found. (trustee 1986-87, v.p. 1987-88, chmn. 1988-90), Essex County Bar Assn. (Spl. Merit award 1998), Mercer County Bar Assn., Am. Law Inst. (life), Harvard Law Sch. Assn. N.J. (pres. 1971-72, nat. v.p. 1972-73), Hist. Soc. U.S. Dist. Ct. for Dist. N.J. (trustee 1987-90, 97—), Hist. Soc. 3d Cir. Ct. Appeals (bd., dirs. 1993-2000), Nassau Club, Princeton, Springdale Golf Club, Princeton, Monmouth Hunt Club, Phi Beta Kappa. Avocation: golf. Home: 75 Rosedale Ln Princeton NJ 08540-2417 Office: McCarter & English Gateway 4 100 Mulberry St Newark NJ 07102-4004 Business E-Mail: eharing@mccarter.com.

HARING, KATHRYN ANN, special education educator, research scientist; b. Syracuse, N.Y., Oct. 1, 1955; d. Norris G. and Dorothy M. (Borgens) H.; m. David L. Lovett, Nov. 11, 1950; children: Momaur, Bastick, Kokopellie. BS, U. Western Wash., 1977; PhD, U. N.Mex., 1987. Tchr., coach Federal Way (Wash.) Schs., 1979-82; clin. supr. U. N.Mex., Albuquerque, 1983-84; tchr. Albuquerque Pub. Schs., 1985-86; asst. prof. Utah State U., Logan, 1986-90; coord. rsch. scientist San Francisco State U., 1987-90; prin. investigator, assoc. prof. spl. edn. U. Okla., Norman, 1990—. Adv., expert N.Mex. Protection and Advocacy, Albuquerque, 1983-86; witness for people with disabilities and their families ACLU, San Francisco, 1987-90, Okla. Indigent Def. Fund, 1996—. Author, editor: Integrated Lifecycle Services for People with Disabilities, 1992. Faculty advisor Students for Exceptional Children, Norman, Okla., 1990-97, Habitat for Humanity, Norman, 1996—; mem. exec. bd., treas. Assn. for People with Severe Disabilities, 1994-96. Mem. Am. Assn. Learning Disabilities (pres. 1984-86), Coun. Exceptional Children (divsn. rsch. treas 1986-88, divsn. early childhood editl. bd. 1992—), Grad. Student Assn. U. N.Mex. (pres. 1983-86). Democrat. Unitarian Universalist. Avocations: running, hiking, vegetarian cooking, dance, gardening. Home: 4612 Crystal Lake Rd Norman OK 73072-9739 Office: Univ Okla 820 Van Vleet Oval # 321 Norman OK 73019-2040

HARING, ROBERT WESTING, newspaper editor; b. Salem, Mo., Nov. 13, 1932; s. Arthur S. and Martha I. (Westing) H.; m. Jo M. Houser, June 1, 1957 (dec. Nov. 1991); children: Robert A., Joel B., Jon G.; m. Carolyn Scudder, May 20, 1995. AA, Kansas City (Mo.) Jr. Coll., 1951; BJ, BA in History, U. Mo., 1954. Reporter So. Illinoisan, Carbondale, Ill., 1954-55, city editor, 1957-59; writer AP, Little Rock, 1959-61, corr. Tulsa, 1961-64, asst. bur. chief Columbus, Ohio, 1964-67, bur. chief Newark, 1967-71, exec. N.Y.C., 1971-75; Sunday editor Tulsa World, 1975-81, exec. editor, 1981-95; ret., 1998. Chmn. Goodwill Industries, Tulsa, 1990-94; bd. dirs. River Parks Authority, Tulsa, 1985-93; pres. Tulsa Zoofriends, 1994-96; chmn. Tulsa Mentoring Coun., Tulsa Lit. Coalition, 1996-98; initiated price earnings ratio in newspaper stock tables, 1973. With U.S. Army, 1955-57. Avocations: running, tennis, bicycling. Home: 1620 S Detroit Ave Tulsa OK 74120-6214 Personal E-mail: harings@msn.com.

HARING-SMITH, TORI, academic administrator; b. Chgo., Jan. 1, 1953; d. Philip Smyth and Jacqueline (Kolle) Haring; m. Robert Henry Smith, June 1, 1974; 1 child, Whitney Patrick Haring-Smith. BA, Swarthmore Coll., 1974; MA, U. Ill., 1977, PhD, 1980. Tchg. asst. U. Ill., Urbana, 1975-80; asst. prof. Brown U., Providence, 1980-86, assoc. prof. English, 1986—96, assoc. prof. theatre, 1987—96, dir. writing fellows program, 1980—90; prof. theatre Am. U., Cairo, 1996—99, chair dept. performing and visual arts, 1996—99; exec. dir. Thomas J. Watson Found., 1999—2001; dean Coll. Liberal Arts Willamette U., 2001—02, v.p. ednl. affairs, 2002—04; pres. Washington & Jefferson Coll., Pa., 2005—. Freelance ednl. cons., Providence, 1981—; theatre dir., Providence, 1986—; artistic dir. Wallace Theatre, Cairo, 1996—99. Author: A.A. Milne, 1982, A Guide to Writing Programs, 1984, From Farce to Melodrama, 1985, Learning Together, 1992, Writing Together, 1993, Monologues for Women by Women, 1994, (translation) Napoli Milionaria, 1995, More Monologues for Women by Women, 1996, Scenes for Women by Women, 1998, also numerous on pedagogy, lit. and theatre, (book) New Monologues for Women by Women, 2004. Recipient sr. class citation Brown U., 1984, 85, 86; fellow Watson Found., 1974, Lilly Found., 1981, Wriston fellow Brown U., 1984. Mem.: Assn. Am. Colls. and Univs., Am. Coun. Acad. Deans., Assn. for Theatre in Higher Edn. Office: Washington & Jefferson Coll 60 S Lincoln St Washington PA 15301 Business E-Mail: tharingsmith@washjeff.edu.

HARINGTON, CHARLES RICHARD, vertebrate paleontologist; b. Calgary, Alta., Can., May 22, 1933; s. Charles Frederic and Florence Katherine (Shillington) H.; m. Gail Doreen Rice, Sept. 15, 1994. BA, U. Alta., 1954, BSc, 1957, PhD, 1977, DSc (hon.), 2004; MSc, McGill U., 1961. Wildlife biologist Can. Wildlife Svc., Ottawa, Ont., 1960-65; vertebrate paleontologist Can. Mus. Nature, Ottawa, 1965—98; coord. climatic change in Can. program Nat. Mus. Natural Scis., Ottawa, 1977—92; curator quaternary zoology emeritus, rsch. assoc. Can. Mus. Nature, Ottawa, 1998—. Chmn. Can. Com. on Climatic Fluctuations and Man, Ottawa, 1985-90. Author: Quaternary Vertebrate Faunas of Canada and Alaska, 1978; editor: Climatic Change in Canada, 5 vols., 1980-85, Canada's Missing Dimension: Science and History in the Canadian Arctic Islands, 1990, The Year Without a Summer?: World Climate in 1816, 1992, Annotated Bibliography of Quaternary Vertebrates of Northern North America, 2003; contbr. articles to profl. jours., popular publs. and revs. Decorated officer Order of Can.; recipient Can. Assn. Geographers prize, 1957, Meritorious Svc. award, Yukon Govt., 1998, Lifetime Achievement Heritage award, Yukon Hist. and Mus. Assn., 2002, The Queen's Golden Jubilee medal, 2002. Fellow Royal Geog. Soc. (Eng.), Royal Can. Geog. Soc. (Massey medal 1987), Arctic Inst. N.Am., Soc. Vertebrate Paleontology (hon.). Avocations: travel, camping, reading, canoeing, bicycling. Office: Paleobiology Can Mus of Nature Ottawa ON Canada K1P 6P4 Office Phone: 613-364-4052. E-mail: dharington@mus-nature.ca.

HARIPRAKASHA, HUMCHA KRISHNAMURTHY, research scientist; MSc Ed, Regional Coll. of Edn., Mysore, India, 1990; PhD, Indian Inst.Sci., Bangalore, India, 1997—2007. Sr. rsch. fellow Coun. of Sci. and Indsl. Rsch., Bangalore, India, 1992—95; charge du rsch. associe of cnrs Centre Nat. de la Recherche Scientifique, Rennes, France, 1998—99; robert a. welch postdoctoral fellow U. North Tex., Denton, Tex., 1999—2000; rsch. fellow Nat. Cancer Inst., NIH, Frederick, Md., 2001—. Contbr. articles pub. to profl. jour., abstracts of conference. Recipient Best Outgoing Student Award, Regional Coll. of Edn., Mysore, India, 1990; fellow Robert A. Welch Postdoctoral Fellow, U. North Tex., 1999-2000, Charge de Recherche Associe, Centre Nat. de la Recherche Scientifique, France, 1998-1999; scholar Jr. Rsch. Fellow, Coun. of Sci. and Indsl. Rsch., India, 1990-1992, Sr. Rsch. Fellow, 1992-1995. Mem.: Am. Chem. Soc. Achievements include patents pending for Internat. Publ. No. WO 03/072058 A2, Title: DNA-Binding Polyamide Drug Conjugates, 2003; Internat. Application No. 60/508, 543. Title: Building Blocks for DNA Binding Agents, 2003. Home: 621 Biggs Ave #1 Frederick MD 21702

HARIRI, GISUE, architect, educator; b. Abadan, Iran, May 16, 1956; came to U.S., 1974; d. Karim Hariri and Behjat (Isphahani) Saboonchi. BArch, Cornell U., 1980. Apprentice Jennings and Stout, San Francisco, 1980-82; Paolo Soleri, Arcosanti, Ariz., 1982-83; apprentice Paul Segal Assocs. Architects, N.Y.C., 1983-85; ptnr. Hariri & Hariri, N.Y.C., 1986—. Lighting and furniture designer, 1993—; participant in Urban Housing Festival, The Hague, The Netherlands, 1991; lectr. in field. Work exhibited in Mus. Modern Art, 1999, Storefront for Art and Architecture, N.Y.C., 1988, Parson Sch. Design, N.Y.C., 1988, Princeton (N.J.) U., 1988, Archtl. League N.Y., 1990, Kent (Ohio) State U., 1991, Richard Anderson Gallery, N.Y.C., 1993, Cornell U., Ithaca, N.Y., 1993, Contemporary Arts Ctr., Cin., 1993, others, also in various profl. publs.; Monograph: Hariri & Hariri Work in Progress, 1996, Kliczkowski Casas Internat., 1997. Recipient Young Architects Forum award Archtl. League N.Y., 1990. Mem. Internat. Interior Design Assn. Media Stars, 1998. Office: Hariri & Hariri 18 E 12th St New York NY 10003-4458

HARISH, ZIV, allergist, immunologist; b. Jerusalem, July 2, 1954; MD, Ben-Gurion U. Med. Sch., Israel, 1983. Diplomate Am. Bd. Allergy and Immunology, Am. Bd. Pediat. Intern Morristown (N.J.) Meml. Hosp., 1985—86; resident in pediat. Albert Einstein Coll. Medicine, Bronx, NY, 1986—88, fellow, 1988—91, asst. prof., 1991—; pvt. practice Englewood, NJ. Mem. staff Englewood Hosp., 1993—, Bronx-Lebanon Hosp., 1993—; attending physician Pascack Valley Hosp., Westwood, NJ, 1996—. Named one of Top Drs. in N.Y. Metro Area, Castle Connolly, 2003, Top Drs. 2003, N.J. Monthly Mag. Mem.: Am. Acad. Asthma, Allergy and Immunology, Am. Coll. Asthma, Allergy and Immunology. Office: Englewood Hosp and Med Ctr 200 Engle St Ste 18 Englewood NJ 07631

HARITON, JO ROSENBERG, psychotherapist, educator; b. Albany, N.Y., June 12, 1948; d. Irving H. and Madeline P. Rosenberg; m. Frank J. Hariton; 2 children. BA, Goucher Coll., Towson, Md., 1970; MS, Columbia U., 1973; PhD, NYU, 1992; postgrad., Postgrad. Ctr. Mental Health, N.Y.C., 1979. Cert. psychoanalyst. With maternal and child health dept. Bronx (N.Y.) Mcpl. Hosp. Ctr., 1973-76, coord. emergency svcs. children's dept. child psychiatry, 1976-79; field work instr. NYU Sch. Social Work, 1977-79; sr. psychiat social worker divsn. child and adol. psychiatry Westchester divsn. N.Y. Hosp.-Cornell Med. Ctr., White Plains, N.Y., 1979-82, social work coord., 1982-98; mem. faculty Cornell U. Med. Sch., 1982—; pvt. practice psychoanalysis and psychotherapy N.Y.C. Co-head ADHD Svc. Line, 1996—. Contbr. articles on group therapy to profl. jours. Fellow N.Y. State Soc. Clin. Social Work Psychotherapists; mem. NASW, Acad. Cert. Social Workers, Am. Orthopsychiat. Assn., Am. Group Psychotherapy Assn. Home: 1065 Dobbs Ferry Rd White Plains NY 10607-2212 Office: NY Presby Hosp Westchester Divsn 21 Bloomingdale Rd White Plains NY 10605-1596 Office Phone: 914-997-5957. E-mail: jhariton@med.cornell.edu.

HARITON, LORRAINE JILL, information technology executive; b. N.Y.C., Nov. 7, 1954; d. Martin and Barbara (Jaffee) H.; m. Stephen Alan Weyl June 17, 1979; children: Eric, Laura. BS in Math Sci., Stanford U., 1976; MBA, Harvard U., 1982. Sales rep. IBM, N.Y.C., 1977-80, regional rep. San Francisco, 1982-84, sales mgr. Oakland, Calif., 1984-86; mgr. pricing Rolm, Santa Clara, Calif., 1986-87, adminstrv. asst. to v.p. sales, 1987-88, br. mgr., 1988-90, product line mgr., 1990-92; dir. mktg. Verifone, Inc., Redwood City, Calif., 1992-93; v.p. mktg. Network Computing Devices, Mountain View, Calif., 1993—99; pres., CEO Beatnik Inc., San Mateo, Calif., 1999—2003, chmn., 2003—; pres., CEO Apptera, Inc., San Bruno, Calif., 2003—05. Office: Apptera Inc 1150 Bayhill Dr Ste 203 San Bruno CA 94066 Business E-Mail: chariton@applera.com.

HARITOS, MARY J., language educator, interpreter; b. Chgo., May 9, 1948; d. Victor and Eileen Martell; m. George K. Haritos, June 20, 1971; children: Konstantinos G, Marika G. BA with honors, U. Ill., Chgo., 1970; MA, U. Ill., 1973; PhD, Northwestern U., 1985. Tchr. Bennet Hill Acad., Colorado Springs, Colo., 1978-79; adj. prof. Wright State U., Dayton, Ohio, 1984-85, Am. U., Washington, Va., 1986-88, George Mason U., Fairfax, Va., 1987-92; tenured lectr. Wright State U., Dayton, Ohio, 1992—. Author: Las Novelas de Pedro Jorge Vera, 1989. Mem. ch. coun. The Annunciation Greek Orthodox Ch., Dayton, 1999—. Mem.: Wright-Patterson AFB Officers Wives' Club (advisor 1999—2002, bd. govs. 1999—2002). Avocations: musician (piano), choir, rollerblading, gourmet cooking. E-mail: maryharitos@wright.edu.

HARJUNG, KURT STEPHEN, management consultant; b. Trenton, N.J., Sept. 21, 1950; s. Stephen Edward and Alice Ann Marie (Audren) H.; m. Anita B. Moyle, Mar. 31, 2001. BA in Govt., Otterbein Coll., 1972. Material control mgr. Dow Jones, Princeton, N.J., 1972-75; sr. buyer RCA Corp., Moorestown, N.J., 1975-76; material specialist Dataram Corp., Cranbury, N.J., 1976-79; operations analyst Warner Lambert Co., Morris Plains, N.J., 1979-84; pres. The Phoenix Group, Princeton, NJ, 1984—2004; real estate sales assoc. South Seas, Sanibel & Captiva Properties, Captiva, Fla., 2004—. Hunter edn. instr. State of N.J., 1992-1995. Mem. Nat. Assn. Purchasing Mgmt., Am. Prodn. Inventory Control Soc., Am. Orchid Soc., NRA. Republican. Methodist. Avocations: raising hybrid orchids, skin diving. Office: The Phoenix Group 1826 Farm Trail Sanibel FL 33957 Home: 1826 Farm Trl Sanibel FL 33957-4118 Office Phone: 239-395-6128. E-mail: kurtshomes@earthlink.net.

HARK, WILLIAM HENRY, federal and medical administrator, military officer; b. Charleston, W.Va., Nov. 1, 1932; s. Zundel and Esther Sylvia (Henry) H.; m. Claudette Berkley Watson, Apr. 14, 1961; 1 child, William Tucker. AB, W.Va. U., 1954, BS, 1955; MD, Med. Coll. Va., 1957; MPH, Harvard U., 1963. Diplomate Am. Bd. Preventive Medicine. Intern Walter Reed Gen. Hosp., Washington, 1957-58; resident in aerospace medicine U.S. Army, 1962-65, advanced through grades to col., physician, aviation med. cons., 1957-76, ret., 1976; mgr. med. specialties divsn. FAA, Washington, 1980-92, dep. fed. air surgeon, 1992-99. Adv. group for aerospace R&D, NATO, Brussels, 1969-71; mem. joint com. on aviation pathology Dept. of Def., Washington, 1969-71. Decorated Legion of Merit, Air medal, Bronze Star, Vietnam Campaign medal U.S. Army, 1968. Fellow Am. Coll. Preventive Medicine, Aerospace Med. Assn.; mem. Assn. Mil. Surgeons U.S. Avocations: photography, computers. Home: 4317 Southwood Dr Alexandria VA 22309-2822

HARKAVY-FRIEDMAN, JILL MARTINE, psychologist; BA, U. Pa., Phila., 1978; PhD, U. Fla., 1984. Assoc. prof. clin. psychology in psychiatry Columbia U., N.Y.C., 1989—; rsch. scientist N.Y. State Psychiat. Inst., N.Y.C., 1989—. Mem. bus. adv. bd. League for the Hard of Hearing, N.Y.C., 2000, co-chair comedy night, 1994. Fellow, USPHS, 1980—83; grantee, NIMH, 1997—2002, Am. Found. for Suicide Prevention. Mem.: APA, Am. Found. for Suicide Prevention (mem. rsch. adv. coun. 1999). Achievements include research in suicidal behavior, schizophrenia and psychiatric diagnosis and assessment. Office: NYSPI/ Columbia Univ 1051 Riverside Dr New York NY 10032 E-mail: jmf6@columbia.edu.

HARKEN, SHELBY ELAINE, librarian; b. Minot, N.D., May 6, 1947; d. Albert Strand, Elaine Genevieve Strand; m. Stephen John Harken, Aug. 14, 1971; 1 child, Stephanie. MLS, U. N.D., 1971. Head cataloger Chester Fritz Libr., Grand Forks, ND, 1971—, head acquisitions, bibliographic control, 1991—. Author: (journal) Cataloging & Classification Quarterly, 1996, North Dakota Division of the American Association of University Women, 1964—, 1984, (newsletter) ODIN Information Notes, 1990, So This is How You Run a Media Center! Organizing, Administering, and Developing an Instructional Media Center - An Annotated Bibliography., 1971. Music leader Newman Cath. Ch., Grand Forks, 1980—99; sec. Red River Valley Gymnastics, Grand Forks, ND, 1985—97, Roy Lake Assn., Mahnomen, 1989—. Grantee, LSTA, 1999—2000, N.D. Dept. Pub. Instrn., 2000—01. Mem.: AAUW, ALA (subject analysis com. 1998—), Assn. Coll. and Rsch. Libr. (univ. sect. comm. com. 1991—93, SAC subcom. metadata 1998—2001, subject analysis com. 2001—, SAC subcom. semantic interoperability 2002—), Assn. Libr. Collections and Tech. Svcs. (MARBI com. 1991—96), Libr. and Info. Tech. Assn. (TESLA mem. 1996—98, com. cataloging and description and access liaison 2001—), Mountain Plains Libr. Assn. (tech. svc. sect. chair 1997—98), N.D. Libr. Assn. (tech. svc. roundtable 1991—92, govt. documents roundtable chair 1997—98), World-wide PALS Users Group (sec. 1996—2001). Roman Catholic. Avocations: swimming, crafts, gardening. Home: 1679 River Cove Manvel ND 58256-9789 Office: Univ ND Chester Fritz Libr Box 9000 Grand Forks ND 58202-9000 Office Phone: 701-777-4634. Office Fax: 701-777-3319. Business E-Mail: shelby_harken@und.nodak.edu.

HARKER, BRIAN, tobacco company executive; b. Kabwe, Zambia, Apr. 30, 1950; MBA, Cranfield (Eng.) Sch. Mgmt., 1981. Chartered acct., 1974. V.p. Monk-Austin Inc., sr. v.p. internat. ops., 1991-95; sr. v.p. DIMON Inc., Danville, Va., 1995-96, exec. v.p., CFO, 1996-99, pres., COO, 1999—2003, pres., CEO, 2003—, chmn. bd. dirs., 2003—. Office: 512 Bridge St Danville VA 24541-1406

HARKER, JOHN V., information technology executive; b. Denison, Iowa; m. Judith Skelley; children: Julie, John Jr., Jam. BS in Mktg., U. Colo. Mgr. IBM Corp., 1963—79; v.p., ptnr. Booz Allen & Hamilton, 1979—82; pres. mktg. & corp. devel. Data Products, Inc., 1982—84; exec. v.p. Genicom Corp., 1984—92; pres., CEO InFocus Corp., Wilsonville, Oreg., 1992—2004, chmn. bd., 1994—. Bus. adv. coun. Coll. Bus. Adminstrn. U. Colo., Sch. Bus. Adminstrn. Portland State U.; exec. adv. & review com. Alexander Hutton Venture Ptnr., L.P.; chmn. exec. com. Oreg. Coun. Am. Electronics Assn. Bd. trustees Oreg. Mus. Sci. & Industry. Avocations: golf, skiing, mountain climbing. Office: InFocus Corporations 27700B SW Parkway Ave Wilsonville OR 97070-9215

HARKEY, CECILIA CLEMMER, gifted and talented educator; b. Mount Holly, NC, Apr. 10, 1957; d. Coit Javen and Virginia Davis Clemmer; m. Bobby Lee Harkey, Aug. 11, 1979; children: Jason Coit, Justin Lee. AA, Gaston Coll., 1975—77; BS, Appalachina State U., 1977—79; MA, Gardner Webb Coll., 1980—83. Elementary Education 4-9 NC, 1979, Gifted Education Specialist U. of NC at Charlotte, 1988, Reading K-12 NC, 1983, Academically Gifted NC, 1993, Middle Grades Mathematics NC, 1983, Middle Grades Science NC, 1979, nat. bd. cert. middle childhood generalist 2001. Tchr. Lincoln County Schools, Lincolnton, NC, 1979—. Presentor Lincoln County School's Parent Forum, NC, 1999—2001; state academcially/intellectually gifted rev. team Lincoln County Schools, 1999—2000, presentor at gifted and talented ann. conf., 1998—99, tech. mentor, 1997—98; grant reviewer in field. Coord. for cmty. svc. Iron Sta. Angel Tree, Lincolnton, NC, 2002—04; coord. cmty. svc. project Rock Springs Elem. Sch./Hospice, Denver, NC, 2002—03; united meth. women v.p. Rhyne Heights UMC, Lincolnton, NC, 1998—2005. Mem.: N.C. Assn. Educators (assoc. Outstanding Math. Educator 2005), N.C. Academically Gifted and Talented (assoc. grantee Edn. Found.), N.C. Tchr. Math. (assoc. Bright Ideas grantee). Methodist. Avocations: camping, reading, boating, bicycling. Office Phone: 704-483-2281.

HARKEY, JOHN NORMAN, judge; b. Russellville, Ark., Feb. 25, 1933; s. Olga John and Margaret (Fleming) H.; m. Willa Moreau Charlton, May 24, 1959; children— John Adam, Sarah Leigh. AS, Marion (Ala.) Inst., 1952; LLB, BS, BSL, U. Ark., 1959, JD, 1969. Bar: Ark. 1959. Since practiced in, Batesville; pros. atty. 3d Jud. Dist. Ark., 1961-65; ins. commr. Ark., 1967-68; chmn. Ark. Commerce Commn., 1968-69; spl. justice Ark. Supreme Ct., 1988; judge juvenile divsn. Ark. 16th Dist., 1989-90; sr. ptnr. Harkey, Walmsley and related firms, Batesville, 1970-92; chancery and probate judge 16th Jud. Dist., Batesville, Ark., 1993-98, circuit and chancery judge, 1999-2001, circuit judge, 2001—. 1st lt. USMCR, Korea. Mem. Ark. Bar Assn., Am. Bar Register, U.S. Marine Corps League. Home: 490 Harkey Rd Batesville AR 72501-9294 Office: PO Box 2656 Batesville AR 72503-2656 Office Phone: 870-793-8890.

HARKEY, ROBERT SHELTON, retired lawyer; b. Charlotte, NC, Dec. 22, 1940; s. Charles Nathan and Josephine Lenora (McKenzie) H.; m. Barbara Carole Payne, Apr. 2, 1983; 1 child, Elizabeth McKenzie. BA, Emory U., 1963, LLB, 1965. Bar: Ga. 1964, U.S. Dist. Ct. (no. dist.) Ga. 1964, U.S. Ct. Appeals (1st, 5th, 7th, 9th and 11th cirs.) 1964-86, U.S. Supreme Ct. Assoc. Swift, Currie, McGhee & Hiers, Atlanta, 1965-68; atty. Delta Air Lines, Atlanta, 1968-74, gen. atty., 1974-79, asst. v.p. law, 1979-85, assoc. gen. counsel, v.p., 1985-88, gen counsel, v.p., 1988—90, gen. counsel, sr. v.p., 1990-94, gen. counsel, sr. v.p., sec., 1994—2004; ret., 2004. Coun. mem. Emory U. Law Sch., 1997—; bd. adv. Emory U. Med. Sch., 2004. Unit chmn. United Way, Atlanta, 1985; trustee Woodruff Arts Ctr., 1995-2001; bd. vis. Emory U., 1996-99. Mem. ABA (chmn. gen. counsels), Air Transport Assn. (chmn. law coun. 1996-98), State Bar Ga. (chmn. corp. counsel sect. 1992-93), Atlanta Bar Assn., Corp. Counsel Assn. Greater Atlanta (bd. dirs. 1990), Commerce Club, Cherokee Town and Country Club. Presbyterian. Avocations: tennis, reading. Office: Ford and Harrison 1275 Peachtree St Atlanta GA 30329 Personal E-mail: bobharkey@comcast.net.

HARKIN, DANIEL JOHN, controller; b. Bradenton, Fla., Mar. 29, 1955; s. John Lewis and Stella Marie H.; m. Theresa Ann Ford; children: Erin Kathleen, Shaun Ford. BBA, Fla. Atlantic U., 1975. CPA, Fla. Controller Vis. Home Health Svc., Boca Raton, Fla., 1975-78; CPA Cherry Bekaert & Holland, Ft. Lauderdale, Fla., 1978-85; controller Griffin Bros. Co., Inc., Davie, Fla., 1985-90, L.W. Rozzo, Inc., Pembroke Pines, Fla., 1990—. Contbr. articles to profl. jours. Fla. univ. faculty scholar Fla. Atlantic U., 1972-75. Mem. AICPA, Fla. Inst. CPAs (mem. com. 1980-91, adv. com. MAS 1990-91, speaker 1984), Nat. Inst. Tax Profls., Inst. Mgmt. Accts., Rosicrucian Order AMORC. Roman Catholic. Avocations: computer systems and programming, gardening, boating, philosophy, teaching. Home: 1834 SW 21st St Fort Lauderdale FL 33315-1833 Office: L W Rozzo Inc 17200 Pines Blvd Hollywood FL 33029-1505

HARKIN, RUTH R., lawyer; b. Vesta, Minn. d. Walter Herman and Virginia (Coull) Raduenz; m. Tom Harkin, July 6, 1968; children: Amy, Jenny. BA in English, U. Minn., 1966; JD, Cath. U., 1972. With Dept. Army, Korea, 1966-67, Polk County Social Svcs., Des Moines, 1968; clk. Lawyers Com. Civil Rights under Law; elected county atty. Story County, Iowa, 1972-76; spl. prosecutor Polk County, 1977-78; dep. gen. counsel Dept. Agriculture, Washington, 1979-81, Akin, Gump, Strauss, Hauer & Feld, LLP, Washington, 1983-93; pres., chief exec. officer Overseas Pvt. Investment Corp., Washington, 1993—97; sr. v.p. internat. affairs, gov. relations United Tech. Corp., Hartford, Conn., 1997—; chair United Tech. Internat., 1997—. Bd. mem. ConocoPhillips, Nat. Assoc. of Mfr., U.S.-Russia Bus. Council. Mem. Iowa Bar Assn., D.C. Bar Assn. Democrat. Lutheran. Office: United Tech Corp One Financial Plz Hartford CT 06101

HARKIN, THOMAS RICHARD, senator; b. Cumming, Iowa, Nov. 19, 1939; s. Patrick and Frances H.; m. Ruth Raduenz, 1968; children: Amy, Jenny. BS, Iowa State U., 1962; JD, Cath. U. Am., 1972. Mem. staff Ho. of Reps. Select Com. U.S. Involvement in S.E. Asia, 1970; mem. 94th-98th

Congresses from 5th Iowa Dist., mem. sci. and tech. com., mem. agr., nutrition and forestry coms.; U.S. Senator from Iowa, 1984—. Mem. Dem. Steering Com., com. labor and human resources; chmn. Appropriations Subcom. on Labor, Health and Human Svcs and Edn.; chmn. Agr., Nutrition, and Forestry subcom. on Rsch., Nutrition, and Gen. Legis.; mem. Small Bus. Com.; prin. author Ams. with Disabilities Act. Co-author: (with C.E. Thomas) Five Minutes to Midnight: Why the Nuclear Threat is Growing Faster than Ever, 1990. Dem. candidate for Presidency of U.S., 1992. Served with USN, 1962-67. Named Outstanding Young Alumnus Iowa State U. Alumni Assn., 1974 Democrat. Office: US Senate 731 Hart Senate Bldg Washington DC 20510-0001*

HARKINS, DANIEL CONGER, lawyer; b. Akron, Ohio, Aug. 9, 1960; s. Daniel Drury and Marjorie Helen (Conger) H. BA in Econs., Coll. of Wooster, 1982; JD, Case Western Res. U., 1985; LLM in Taxation, NYU, 1986. Bar: Ohio 1985, D.C. 1986. Assoc. Williams, Zumkehr & Welser, Kent, Ohio, 1985-88; assoc. Martin, Browne, Hull & Harper, Springfield, Ohio, 1988-93, ptnr., 1993-96; pvt. practice Springfield, 1996-98; prin. Harkins & Assocs., 1998—. Mem. Bd. Bldg. Appeals, Springfield, 1990-98, vice chmn., 1991-92, chmn., 1995-97,; trustee Springfield Family YMCA, 1991-95, treas., 1991-94, pres., 1994-96; v.p., sec. Jr. Achievement, 1991-94; trustee Clark County Mental Health Found., 1991-98; chmn. fin. com., mem. ctrl. and exec. coms. Clark County Rep. Com., 1992-97; vice chmn. Clark County Rep. Ctrl. Com., 1994-97; chmn. Clark County Rep. Party, 1997—; coach wrestling team Cath. Ctrl. H.S., Springfield, 1992-93; pres. elect Tecumseh Coun., Boy Scouts Am., 1996—, pres. 1998-2000, pres.-elect 1996-98, pres. & v.p., area 5; mem. Clark County Bd. of Elections, 1998—; bd. dirs. Clark State Cmty. Coll. Found., 1999—; mem Florida Presidential Vote Recount Team, 2000. Mem. Ohio State Bar Assn. (chmn. mcpl. income tax com., taxation com. 1995—), D.C. Bar Assn., Clark County Bar Assn. (exec. com. 1991—, treas. 1993—), Clark County Law Libr. Assn. (treas. 1996—). Congregationalist. Avocations: running, swimming, skiing, amateur wrestling. Office: 333 N Limestone St Ste 104 Springfield OH 45503-4250

HARKINS, EDWIN L., musician, educator; b. Decatur, Ill., Nov. 20, 1940; s. Hoyle Edward and Lucile (McBride) H.; m. Bonnie Lu Turpin, June 17, 1962. BM in Trumpet, Ill. Wesleyan U., 1963; MusM in Trumpet, Yale U., 1965; postgrad., U. Chgo., 1965-66; PhD in Composition, U. Iowa, 1968. Instr. New. England Conservatory of Music, Boston, 1968-70, Neighborhood Sch. Music, New Haven, Conn., 1970-72, U. Calif., San Diego, 1972-76, asst. prof., 1976-78, assoc. prof., 1980-84, prof., 1984—. Trumpeter with SONOR, La Jolla, Calif., 1976—; mem. N.H. Symphony, 1963-65, 20th Century music ensembles U. Chgo., 1965-66, U. Iowa, 1966-68, U. Calif., San Diego, 1972-76, appears on 24 records; guest soloist Hartford Symphony, 1963, Arch Ensemble, 1981, CONTINUUM, 1985; as vocalist mem. Extended Vocal Techniques Ensemble, 1975-85, appears on 3 records; as composer, performer co-founder (with Philip Larson) of (THE); composer Vis-à-Vis, 1986; author: (book) Maynard Ferguson: A Jazz Discography, 1976; contbr. articles to profl. jours.; designed and built programmable rhythm sequencer (with Rob Gross), 1975; designed computer program LASAR, 1978. Grantee Calif. Arts Council, 1984, 85, Nat. Endowment Arts, 1986, 87; Calif. Arts Council fellow, 1976, U. Calif. fellow, 1973-76. Mem. Soc. Music Theory, Internat. Trumpet Guild. Democrat. Avocations: golf, baseball statistics. Business E-Mail: eharkins@ucsd.edu.

HARKINS, HERBERT PERRIN, otolaryngologist, educator; b. Aug. 13, 1912; s. Percy Stoner and Myra (Perrin) H.; Anna Catherine Shepler, July 16, 1938; children: Herbert P., Sally Anne, Nancy Shepler. BS, Lafayette Coll., 1934; MD, Hahnemann Med. Coll., 1937; MSc, U. Pa., 1942. Res. Diplomate Am. Ba. Otolaryngology. Lectr. otolaryngology Hahnemann Med. Coll., 1939-44; assoc. prof., 1944-51; prof. head dept. otolaryngology, 1951; asst. prof. otolaryngology Grad. Sch. Medicine, U. Pa., 1951—. Sr. staff otolaryngology Lankenau Hosp. Bd,. Studies in Higher Edn. Contbr. numerous articles on ear, nose and throat to med. jours. Trustee Lafayette Coll. Comdr. USN, 1945—48. Fellow ACS, Am. Otolaryngology Soc. Plastic Surgery; mem. Am. Soc. Ophthalmic and Otolaryngologic Allergy (pres.), Am. Pa. acads. ophthalmology and otolaryngology, Coll. Physicians Phila., Phila. Laryngol. Soc., Phila. County Med. Soc., AMA, Am. Laryngol., Rhinol. and Otol. Soc. Clubs: Union League, Phila. Country Bachelors Barge. Home: 1400 Waverly Rd A220 Gladwyne PA 19035

HARKINS, JOHN EDWARD, social studies educator, historian; b. Memphis, Nov. 25, 1938; s. Charles Joseph and Mary Helen (Fay) Harkins; m. Georgia Saxby Strain, Dec. 18, 1965. BS, Univ. Memphis, Tenn., 1967; MA, La. State Univ., Baton Rouge, La., 1971; PhD, Univ. Memphis, Tenn., 1976. Cert. Nat. Archives Inst., Washington, 1980. City-county archivist Memphis/Shelby County, Tenn., 1979—85; tchr. dept. chair Memphis Univ. Sch., 1986—. Mem. Nat. Coun. for History Edn., 1999—. Author: Metropolis of the American Nile, 1982, 1991, The MUS Century Book, 1993, The MUS Century Book, 2d edit., 2003, The New Orleans Cabildo: Colonial Lousiana 's First City Government 1769-1803, 1996; contbr. articles pub. to prof. jour.; prodr.(host): (local cable TV show), 1983—85; contbr. columns in newspapers. Mem. Tenn. Hist. Records Commn., Nashville, 1981—88, Shelby County Hist. Com., Memphis, 1993—2002, Tenn. Archivists, Nashville, 1979—85, Memphis Internat. Heritage Com., Memphis, 1985—92; bd. mem. Davies Manor Assn., 1996—. With USN, 1956—65. Recipient CBHS Hall of Fame, 1995, Tenn. Outstanding Am. History Tchr. award, DAR, 1997, Medal of Honor, 1996. Mem.: Nat. Coun. for History Edn., So. Hist. Assn., Tenn. Hist. Soc., West Tenn. Hist. Soc. (pres. 1990—94, 2004—05). Office: Memphis Univ Sch 6191 Pk Ave Memphis TN 38119 Office Fax: 901-260-1325. Business E-Mail: john.harkins@musowls.org.

HARKINS, JOHN GRAHAM, JR., lawyer; b. Phila., May 9, 1931; s. John Graham and Elizabeth Taylor (Bowers) H.; m. Beatrice Gibson McIlvain, June 30, 1955 (dec. Aug. 4, 2002); children: John Graham III, Alida McIlvain. BA cum laude, U. Pa., 1953, LL.B. summa cum laude, 1958. Bar: Pa. 1959, U.S. Supreme Ct. 1971. Assoc. firm Pepper, Hamilton & Scheetz, Phila., 1958-63, partner, 1963-92, co-chmn., 1982-86, chmn., 1986-92; ptnr. Harkins Cunningham, Phila., 1992—. Instr. U. Pa., 1956-58, lectr. Law Sch., former bd. overseers-law, 1981-95; mem. adv. com. Inst. Law and Econs., 1981—, com. chmn., 1981-91. Editor-in-chief: U. Pa. Law Rev, 1957-58. Supr. Easttown Twp., Pa., 1972-77; past bd. dirs. Chester County Hosp.; past trustee Curtis Inst. Music; trustee U. Pa., 1987-97, trustee emeritus, 1998—; trustee U. Pa. Health Sys., 1988-2001, vice chmn., 1991-2001; mem. bd. overseers U. Pa. Med. Sch., 1990-2001, chmn., 1991-2001; dir. Citizens for Pa.'s Future, 2001-. With U.S. Army, 1953-55. Fellow Salzburg Seminar in Am. Studies, 1961 Fellow Am. Coll. Trial Lawyers; mem. Am. Law Inst., Am. Bar Assn., Pa. Bar Assn., Phila. Bar Assn., Jud. Conf. U.S. Ct. of Appeals for 3d Circuit, Order of Coif, Phi Beta Kappa. Clubs: Merion Cricket, Radnor Hunt. Home: Lowbrook PO Box 813 Devon PA 19333-0813 Office: Harkins Cunningham 2800 One Commerce Sq 2005 Market St Philadelphia PA 19103-7075 Office Phone: 215-851-6701. Office Fax: 215-851-6710. Business E-Mail: jharkins@harkinscunningham.com.

HARKLEROAD, JO-ANN DECKER, special education educator; b. Wilkes-Barre, Pa., Oct. 22, 1936; d. Leon Joseph Sr. and Beatrice Catherine (Wright) Decker; m. A. Dwayne Harkleroad; 1 child, Leon Wade. AS, George Washington U., 1960, BS in Health, Phys. Edn. and Recreation, minor in Spl. Edn., 1968, MA in Spl. Edn. and Ednl. Diagnosis and Prescription, 1969, postgrad., 1997-99. Recipient Appreciation cert. Fairfax County (Va.) Police Dept., 1987, Meritorious Svc. medal Pres. Com. on Employment of People with Disabilities, 1988. Instr. Cath. U. Am., Washington, 1960-61; tchr. Bush Hill Day Sch., Franconia, Va., 1961-63; ednl. diagnostician Prince William County Schs., Manassas, Va., 1969-71, supr. title I, 1971-72; writer, editor Sta. WNVT-TV, Fairfax, Va., 1980-82; dir. spl. edn. Highland County Schs., Monterey, Va., 1987-90. Author: (novels) Horse Thief Trail, 1981, 3d edit., 1986, Blood Atonement, 2004, Ketch Colt, 2005; columnist op-ed page The Recorder; radio broadcaster Sta. WVMR, Frost, W.Va. Ruling elder Presbyn. Ch., McDowell, Va., Clifton, Va.; mem. divsn. of Faith in Action Hunger com. Shenandoah Presbytery; dir. McDowell Presbyn. Ch. Choir; rotating dir. Highland County Cmty. Choir; past pres. Highland County Pub. Libr. Bd. Avocations: hiking, camping, rifleshooting, reading, gardening. Home: Windy Ridge Farm HC 33 Box 60 Mc Dowell VA 24458-9704

HARKNA, ERIC, advertising executive; b. Tallinn, Estonia, June 24, 1940; came to U.S., 1947; s. Erich K. Harkna and Adelaide Mender; children: Britt, Kristiana, Christian Erik; m. Tonise Paul. BA, Colgate U., 1962; MBA, Columbia U., 1964. Account exec. Benton & Bowles, N.Y.C., 1965-68; v.p., account supr. Kenyon & Eckhart, N.Y.C., 1969-71, BBDO, Inc., N.Y.C., 1973-74, v.p., mgmt. supr., 1974-76, sr. v.p., dir., 1977-82; exec. v.p., dir., 1979-82; pres., dir. BBDO, Inc., Chgo., 1982-84, pres., chief exec. officer, 1984-93; sr. v.p. BBDO Worldwide, Chgo., 1993—. Chmn. ann. awards dinner Advt. Age, 1987; chmn. Media Subcom., Chgo.; guest lectr. Chgo. Coun. Fgn. Rels., World Econ. Forum. Bd. dirs. United Cerebral Palsy Found., Chgo., 1982-94, Friends of Prentice Hosp.; v.p. nat. fund raising exec. com. Juvenile Diabetes Found. Internat., 1987-95, bd. dirs., 1990-96, internat. long range planning com. 1995-98; bd. dirs. Chgo. Coun. Profl. Psychology, 1991-96, Mus. Broadcast Commn., 1992—, U.S. Baltic Found., 1996—, Del. Place Bank. Colgate U. Norwegian Study grantee, 1961; recipient Internat. Bus. award Columbia U., 1964 Mem. Am. Assn. Advt. Agys. (reginal bd. govs. 1994), Am. Mktg. Assn., Chgo. Coun. Fgn. Rels., Chgo. Advt. Club, Chgo. Econs. Club, Lake Shore Soc. Clubs, Execs. Club Chgo., N.Y. Athletic Club (N.Y.C.), N.Y. A.C. Yacht Club (Pelham), Chgo. Estonia House, Chgo. Yacht Club, 410 Club (founder, chmn., bd. dirs., bd. govs.). Office: BBDO Worldwide Inc 410 N Michigan Ave Ste 8 Chicago IL 60611-4273

HARKNESS, ERIK A., historical fiction novelist; b. St. Paul, Sept. 21, 1970; s. Ward Allen and June Evelyn (Dahlquist) H. Grad., Highland Park Sr. H.S., St. paul, 1989. Mem. Work In Progress. Lutheran. Avocations: writing, movies. Home: 2835 Pascal St # 7G Roseville MN 55113-1791

HARKNESS, JOHN CHEESMAN, architect; b. N.Y.C., Nov. 30, 1916; s. Albert and Sara Arden (Cheesman) H.; m. Sarah Pillsbury, June 14, 1941 (separated); children: Sara Harkness Super, Joan Harkness Hantz, Nell, Timothy (dec.), Alice, Frederick, John Pillsbury. BFA cum laude, Harvard U., 1938, BArch, MArch, 1941. Registered architect Maine, Mass., R.I. Architect Saarinen and Swanson, Birmingham, Mich., Harrison, Fouilhoux and Abramovitz, N.Y.C., Skidmore, Owings and Merrill, N.Y.C., prior to 1945; prin. The Architects Collaborative, Cambridge, Mass., 1945-95, pres., 1966-67, 77-84, also bd. dirs., chmn. bd. prins., 1984-86. Mem. design faculty Harvard Grad. Sch. Design, 1946-50, mem. vis. com.; mem. vis. com. R.I. Sch. Design; mem. capitol area planning bd., Minn. State; archtl. advisor Boston Redevel. Authority for Park Pla., Mass. Design Competition. Author: Encyclopedia of Architecture, 1989; prin.-in-charge projects Martin County Libr., Fla., Creative Arts Ctr., master plan, Squires addition Student Activities Ctr., Biology Bldg., all at Va. Poly. Inst. and State U., Blacksburg, Univ. Ctrs., Coll. William and Mary, Va., Sci. Bldg. Middlebury (Vt.) Coll., Hillside Office Bldg., Waltham, Mass., CBS Office Bldg., Mt. Pleasant, N.Y., master plan and 6 med. bldgs. Children's Hosp. Med. Ctr., Boston (Harleston Parker medal Boston Soc. Architects, Honor award AIA), hdqrs. CIGNA, Bloomfield, Conn. (award N.Eng. Regional Coun. AIA, award excellence Am. Inst. Steel Constrn. 1985), Hoffman Lab. Exptl. Geology (Boston Arts Festival award 1964), athletic facilities, addition Mus. Comparative Zoology, med. sch. Lab. Reprodn. and Reproductive Biology, all at Harvard U., master plan indsl. complex, Jubail, Saudi Arabia, master plan and office bldg. Summit at Westchester, Mt. Pleasant, Cen. Nat. Mus., Riyadh, Saudia Arabia, hdqrs. Shawmut Bank Boston, Amoskeag Bank, Manchester, N.H., Montego Bay (Jamaica) Hosp., Ainsworth Gymnasium Smith Coll., Northampton, Mass. (honor award N.Eng. Regional Coun. AIA), U. Tunis Libr. and Sch. Law, Econs., and Bus. Adminstrn., Tunisia, James L. Hanley Edn. Ctr., Providence (award), New Trier Twp. High Sch., Winnetka, Ill, Blue Hills Regional Vocat. Sch., Canton, Mass., Wayland (Mass.) High Sch. Ambulance driver Am. Field Svc., 1943-44. Pvt. U.S. Army, 1945, ETO, NATOUSA, bronze cross of merit with swords from Polish Rep. for action at the Battle of Casino, Italy. Recipient various competition and archtl. design awards including 6 awards Am. Assn. Sch. Adminstrs., 1960-67, William Ware award, Boston Soc. Architects honor award, 1993; named Harvard Athletic Hall of Fame, NCAA Wrestling champion, 1938, lifetime svc. to wrestling award Mass. and Nat. Wresting Hall of Fame, 1999. Fellow AIA (archtl. juror various design programs, 2d award alt. to Appleton Travelling fellowship); mem. NAD, Boston Soc. Architects (past pres., 1st prize 1940), Mass. State Assn. Architects (past pres.), Archtl. League N.Y., Harvard Grad. Sch. Design Alumni Assn. (past pres.), Harvard U. Alumni Assn. (former dir. 1988), Phi Beta Kappa. Office: Fletcher Harkness Cohen Moneyhun Inc 46 Waltham St Boston MA 02118-2436

HARKNESS, LAURA S., dietician, educator; b. Lansing, Mich., Apr. 4, 1964; PhD, Case Western Res. U., 2003. Registered dietitian Am. Dietetic Assn. Instr. Kent (Ohio) State U., 2000—02; asst. prof. pediat. and nutrition MetroHealth Med. Ctr., Cleve., 2002—. Office: MetroHealth Med Ctr 2500 MetroHealth Dr Cleveland OH 44109 Office Phone: 216-778-2643.

HARKNESS, MARY LOU, librarian; b. Denby, SD, Aug. 19, 1925; d. Raleigh Everette and Mary Jane (Boyd) Barker; m. Donald R. Harkness, Sept. 2, 1967. BA, Nebr. Wesleyan U., 1947; AB in L.S, U. Mich., 1948; MS, Columbia U., 1958. Jr. cataloger U. Mich. Law Library, 1948-50; asst. cataloger Calif. Poly. Coll., 1950-52; asst. cataloger, then head cataloger Ga. Inst. Tech., 1952-57; head cataloger U. South Fla., Tampa, 1958-67, dir. libraries, 1967-87, dir. emeritus, 1987—. Cons. Nat. Library Nigeria, 1962—63. Bd. dirs. Southeastern Library Network, 1977—80. Recipient Alumni Achievement award Nebr. Wesleyan U., 1972 Mem. ALA, Fla. Library Assn., Athena Soc. Democrat. Presbyterian. Home: 13511 Palmwood Ln Tampa FL 33618-8409 E-mail: marylouh@tampabay.rr.com.

HARKNESS, NANCY P., lawyer; b. 1959; BA in Economics, Cornell U., 1980; JD, Fordham U., 1985. Bar: NY, Calif. With Internat. Broadcasting, LA; cons. Olympic Regional Devel. Authority, Lake Placid; head bus. & legal affairs dept. Motown Record Co. LP, 1995—97; named v.p. bus. & legal affairs Universal Studios Consumer Products Group, 1997; sr. v.p. bus. affairs Digital Entertainment Network Inc.; sr. counsel Akin, Gump, Strauss, Hauer & Feld, LLP; of counsel Sonnenschein Nath & Rosenthal, LA. Office: Sonnenschein Nath & Rosenthal LLP 601 S Figueroa St, Ste 1500 Los Angeles CA 90017 Office Phone: 213-892-5151. Office Fax: 213-623-9924. Business E-Mail: nharkness@sonnenschein.com.

HARL, NEIL EUGENE, economist, educator, lawyer, writer; b. Appanoose County, Iowa, Oct. 9, 1933; s. Herbert Peter and Bertha Catherine (Bonner) H.; m. Darlene Ramona Harris, Sept. 7, 1952; children: James Brent, Rodney Scott. BS, Iowa State U., 1955, PhD, 1965; JD, U. Iowa, 1961. Bar: Iowa 1961. Field editor Wallace's Farmer, 1957-58; research assoc. U.S. Dept. Agr., Iowa City and Ames, Iowa, 1958-64; assoc. prof. Iowa State U., Ames, 1964—67, prof., 1967—2004, prof. emeritus, 2004—, dir. Ctr. Internat. Agrl. Fin., 1990—2004. Mem. adv. group to commr. IRS, 1979-80; mem. adv. com. Heckerling Inst. on Estate Planning, Miami, Fla., 1983-96; mem. adv. com. Office Tech. Assessment, U.S. Congress, 1988-95, vice chair, 1992-93, chair, 1993-94; mem. exec. bd. U.S. West Comms., Iowa, 1989-90; mem. adv. com. on agrl. biotech. USDA, 2000-02; mem. Fed. Commn. on Payment Limitations in Agr., 2002-03; lectr. in field. Author: Farm Estate and Business Planning, 1973, Farm Estate and Business Planning, 15th edit., 2001, Legal and Tax Guide for Agricultural Lenders, 1984, Legal and Tax Guide for Agricultural Lenders, supplement, 1987, Agricultural Law, 15 vols., 1980—81, revised edit., 2005, Agricultural Law Manual, 1985, The Farm Debt Crisis of the 1980s, 1990, Arrogance and Power: The Saga of WOI-TV, 2001; co-author: Farmland, 1982, Principles of Agricultural Law, 1997, Taxation of Cooperatives, 1999, Reporting Farm Income, 2000;: rev. edit., 2005, Family Owned Business Deduction, 2001, The Law of the Land, 2002; author, actor films and videotape programs; contbr. articles to profl. jours. Trustee Iowa State U. Agrl. Found., 1969-85. 1st lt. AUS, 1955—57. Recipient Outstanding Tchr. award Iowa State U., 1973, Disting Svc. to Agr. award Am. Soc. Farm Mgrs. and Rural Appraisers, 1977, Iowa sect. 1996, Faculty Svc. award Nat. Univ. Ext. Assn., 1980, Disting. Svc. award Am. Agrl. Editors Assn., 1984, Disting. Achievement citation Iowa State U., 1985, Disting. Svc. to State Govt. award Nat. Gov.'s Assn., 1986, Disting. Svc. award Iowa State U., 1986, Farm Leader of Yr. award Des Moines Register, 1986, Henry A. Wallace award, 1987, Superior Svc. award USDA, 1987, Disting. Svc. to Iowa Agr. award Iowa Farm Bur., 1992, Faculty Excellence award, Iowa Bd. Regents, 1993, Charles A. Black award Coun. Agrl. Sci. Tech., 1997, Excellence in Internat. Agr. award Iowa State U., 1999, Disting. Svc. to Agr. award Chgo. Farmers Club, 1999, Exceptional Svc. to Agr. award Iowa Master Farmers, Wallaces Farmer, 2000, Pres.'s award for disting. svc. Iowa State U., 2002, Lifetime Achievement award Iowa Farmers Union, 2003; named Seminar Leader of Yr. Nat. Assn. Accts., 2000. Fellow: Iowa State Bar Found., ABA Rsch. Found., Am. Coll. Trusts and Estates Counsel, Am. Agrl. Econs. Assn. (exec. bd. 1979—85, pres. 1983—84, Am. Agrl. Econs. Found. pres. 1993—94, Outstanding Ext. Program award 1970, Excellence in Communicating Rsch. Results award 1975, Disting. Undergrad. Tchr. award 1976); mem.: ABA, Iowa Bar Found. (bd. dirs. 1997—2005, v.p. 1999—2001), Am. Agrl. Law Assn. (pres. 1980—81, Disting. Svc. award 1984), Iowa Bar Assn. (Pres. award 1991), Golden Key. Home: 2821 Duff Ave Ames IA 50010 Home (Winter): 78-261 Manukai St # 3001 Kailua Kona HI 96740 Office: Iowa State U Dept Econs 381 Heady Hall Ames IA 50011-1070 Office Phone: 515-294-6354. Business E-Mail: harl@iastate.edu.

HARLAN, JANE ANN, lawyer; b. Newton, Iowa, Oct. 8, 1947; d. Ellis and Julia (Blount) H.; m. Adel Zahian Hanna, 1971 (div. 1981); children: Samuel, Laura, Magda. BA, Drake U., 1969; JD, DePaul U., 1974. Bar: Ill. 1975, Wis. 1978, Iowa 1984. Pvt. practice, Chgo., 1975-78, Greendale, Wis., 1978-84, Newton, Iowa, 1984-94; adminstrv. asst. Office of State Pub. Defender, Racine, Wis., 1994-95, Milw., 1995-99; atty. Appalachian Rsch. and Defense Fund, Somerset, Ky., 1999—. Cooperating atty. Wis. Civil Liberties Union, Milw., 1978-84; chairperson S.W. Suburban Dems., Milwaukee County, Wis., 1982-83. Recipient Outstanding Svc. plaque, Milw. Dems., 1983, citation for outstanding contbns. Wis. State Assembly, 1984. Mem. NOW, ACLU, Ky. Bar Assn., Wis. Bar Assn., Assn. for Retarded Citizens. Avocations: band music, pipe organ. Office: Appalachian Rsch and Def Fund PO Box 1334 Somerset KY 42502-1334

HARLAN, LEONARD MORTON, merchant banker; b. Newark, June 1, 1936; s. Harold Robinson and Doris Harriet (Siegler) H.; children: Joshua, Noah. BME, Cornell U., 1959; MBA with distinction, Harvard U., 1961, DBA, 1965. Lic. real estate broker, N.Y., N.J. V.p. Donaldson, Lufkin & Jenrette, Inc., 1968-69; founder, chmn. bd. The Harlan Co., Inc., N.Y.C., 1969-96; bd. dirs. Ryland Group, Inc., 1984—; pres. Castle Harlan, Inc., 1987—; gen. ptr. Legend Capital Group, 1987—; pres. Castle Harlan Ptnrs. II, 1992—, Castle Harlan Ptnrs. III, 1997—. Bd. dirs. Tradesco Molding, Inc., Matrix Global Investments, Inc.; guest lectr. Harvard U. and Columbia U. Grad. Schs. Bus. Adminstrn., 1968—; adj. prof. banking and real estate NYU Real Estate Inst., 1968-93, Grad. Sch. Bus. Adminstrn., 1976-80; adj. prof. bus. adminstrn. Columbia U. Grad. Sch. Bus. Adminstrn., 1980-93; trustee North Country Sch./CTT, 1989-95. Mem. editl. bd. Real Estate Rev. Jour., 1971-84; mem. bd. advisors Jour. Pvt. Equity, 1997—; contbr. articles to profl. jours. Mem. Pres.'s Com. on Indsl. Innovation, 1978; mem. Urban Devel. Action Grant Task Force, HUD, 1984; mem. nat. leadership coun. Am. Jewish Com., 1993—, mem. exec. com. Ctrl. N.J. chpt., 1980—, treas., 1988-96, bd. govs., 1996—, nat. budget com., 1986-87; trustee N.Y.C. Citizens Budget Commn., 1988—; mem. Cranbury (N.J.) Mcpl. Planning Bd., 1987-93; mem. vis. com. Harvard Bus. Sch., 1992—. Recipient Charles B. Shatuck Meml. award Am. Inst. Real Estate Appraisers, 1967, 72; Disting. Tchr. award NYU, 1979; Ford Found. fellow, 1964-65; Zurn fellow, 1962-63. Mem. Harvard Bus. Sch. Alumni Assn. (v.p. 1991-93, bd. dirs. 1989-93), Harvard Club N.Y. (admissions com. 1973-75), Harvard Bus. Sch. Club Greater N.Y. (v.p. N.Y.C. chpt. 1977-79, bd. dirs. 1989-98), Harvard Club of Princeton, Cornell Club of Princeton. Office: Castle Harlan Inc 150 E 58th St Fl 37 New York NY 10155-3799

HARLAN, LINDA CAROL, epidemiologist; b. Glasgow, Mont., Feb. 24, 1950; d. Norman Joseph Mavencamp and Bernice Audrene Klingler; m. William Robert Harlan, Aug. 23, 1980; 1 child, Nicole Porter. BSN, Mont. State U., 1972; MPH, U. Mich., 1981, PhD, 1985. RN Calif., 1972. Project coord. U. Calif., Davis, 1973—80; sr. rsch. analyst Westat, Inc., Rockville, Md., 1981—82; rsch./tchg. asst. U. Mich., Ann Arbor, 1983—84, post-doctoral fellow, 1985—87; biostatistician, epidemiologist Henry Ford Hosp., Detroit, 1984—85; cancer epidemiologist Nat. Cancer Inst., Bethesda, Md., 1987—; mem. Am. Coll. Sugeons Commn. on Cancer, 2005. Mem. editl. bd.: Jour. Clin. Oncology, 2003—; contbr. articles to profl. jours. Mem.: ACS (Commn. on Cancer 2005—). Office: Nat Cancer Inst Ste 4005 6130 Executive Blvd Bethesda MD 20892-7344 Business E-Mail: lh50w@nih.gov.

HARLAN, M. ANN, lawyer; BA, Skidmore Coll.; JD, Case Western Reserve U. Ptnr. Calfee, Halter & Griswold LLP; asst. gen. counsel J.M. Smucker Co., gen. counsel, asst. sec., 2002—. Office: JM Smucker Co 1 Strawberry Lane Orrville OH 44667

HARLAN, MEGAN, journalist, poet; b. Burlington, Vt., Jan. 1, 1970; d. Neal MacLaren and Sherry (Yandle) Harlan; m. Matthew Thomas Culligan, July 28, 2001. BA, Tufts U., 1991; MFA, NYU, 1993. Freelance book critic The N.Y. Times, N.Y.C., 1996—; freelance journalist Elle mag., N.Y.C., 1997—2000; freelance travel writer The N.Y. Times, N.Y.C., 1999—; freelance book critic The San Francisco Chronicle, 2001—. Contbg. writer, book critic Entertainment Weekly, NYC, 1995—2003. Author short stories, numerous poems. Recipient Writers fellowship, NYU GSAS, 1991—93. Mem.: PEN West (assoc.), Nat. Book Critics Cir. (assoc.). Liberal. Personal E-mail: meg@meganharlan.com.

HARLAN, NEIL EUGENE, retired healthcare company executive; b. Cherry Valley, Ark., June 2, 1921; s. William and Mary Nina (Ellis) H.; m. Martha Almlov, Sept. 27, 1952; children: Lindsey Beth, Neil Eugene, Sarah Ellis. Student, U. Edinburgh, Scotland, 1946; BS, U. Ark., 1947, LLD, 1969; MBA, Harvard U., 1950, DBA, 1956. Mem. faculty Grad. Sch. Bus. Adminstrn. Harvard U., 1951-62, asst. prof., 1954-58, assoc. prof., 1958-61, prof., 1962; asst. sec. Air Force Washington, 1962-64; exec. v.p. Anderson, Clayton & Co., 1964-67; dir. McKinsey & Co., Inc., 1967-74, McKesson Corp., San Francisco, 1974-93, chmn., CEO. Author: Management Control in Air Frame Subcontracting, 1956, Managerial Economics, 1962. Chmn. San Francisco Ballet, 1982-85; trustee exec. com. World Affairs Coun. No. Calif., 1983—; vice-chmn., dir. Nat. Park Found., 1986-92; bd. govs. San Francisco Symphony, 1985-88; mem. Calif. Com. on Campaign Fin., Calif. Bus. Roundtable, 1984-87; pres. San Francisco Pvt. Industry Coun.; mem. vis. com. Harvard Bus. Sch., 1984-87. Served with AUS, 1943-46. Mem. Webhannet Golf Club, Bohemian Club, Pacific Union Club. Office: McKesson Corp One Post St San Francisco CA 94104-5292 Home: 21 Admirals Way Kennebunk ME 04043

HARLAN, NORMAN RALPH, construction executive; b. Dayton, Ohio, Dec. 21, 1914; s. Joseph and Anna (Kaplan) H.; m. Thelma Katz, Sept. 4, 1955; children: Leslie, Todd. Indsl. Engring. degree, U. Cin., 1937. Chmn. Am. Constrn. Corp., Dayton, 1949, Harlan, Inc., realtors. Mem. Dayton Real Estate Bd., Ohio Real Estate Assn., Nat. Assn. Real Estate Bds., C. of C., Pi Lambda Phi. Home: 303 Glenridge Rd Kettering OH 45429-1631 Office: Am Constrn Corp 2451 S Dixie Dr Dayton OH 45409-1861 Office Phone: 937-294-1426.

HARLAN, RAYMOND CARTER, special investigator, writer, retired communication executive, educator, and military officer; b. Shreveport, La., Nov. 13, 1943; s. Ross E. and Margaret (Burns) H.; m. Nancy K. Munson, 1966 (div. 1978); children: Kathleen Marie, Patrick Raymond; m. Sarah J. Kinzel, 1979 (div. 1982); m. Linda Frances Gerdes, Mar. 30, 1985; stepchildren: Kimberly Jo Gillis, Kellie Leigh Raffa, Ryan William Gerdes. BA in Speech and Drama cum laude, Southwestern U., 1966; MA in English, U.

Tex., 1968; MA in Speech & Theatre Arts, Bradley U., 1976. Commd. 2d lt. USAF, 1968, advanced through grades to maj., 1980, ret., 1988, missile launch officer, instr. Malmstrom AFB, Mont., 1968—72. Asst. prof. Bradley U., Peoria, Ill., 1972-76, Air Force Inst. Tech., Gayton, Ohio, 1985-88; mgr. Minuteman Edn. Program; instr., asst. prof., course dir. Air Force Acad., Colorado Springs, 1976-81; pres. ComSkills Tng., Aurora, Colo., 1988-2000; internat. trainer Inst. for Internat. Rsch., London, 1990-92; mgr. doc and tng. AT&T Broadband, 2000-01; program instr. Afloat Coll. Edn., 2002-03; spl. investigator U.S. Investigations Svcs., 2003—; scriptwriter Progressive Lang., Inc., 2002—. Author: The Confident Speaker, 1993; co-author: Telemarketing That Works, 1991, Interactive Telemarketing, 1995; contbr. articles and revs. to profl. jours. Decorated Air Force Commendation medal with three oak leaf clusters, Air Force Meritorious Svc. medal with one oak leaf cluster; recipient George Washington Honor Medal Freedom Found., 1983, Leo A. Codd award Am. Def. Preparedness Assn., 1975, 1st prize Ariz. State Poetry Soc., 1979. Mem.: Soc. Children's Book Writers and Illustrators, Assn. Air Force Missileers. Lutheran. Avocations: writing, skiing, bicycling, gardening. E-mail: rayha2@comcast.net.

HARLAN, ROBERT DALE, library and information scientist, educator, academic administrator; b. Hastings, Nebr., Aug. 4, 1929; s. Hugh Allan and Madge Keister (Newmyer) H. BA, Hastings Coll., 1950; MA in Library Sci., U. Mich., 1956, MA, 1958, PhD, 1960. Head book order sect. Library U. Mich., Ann Arbor, 1956-58, lectr., 1960; asst. prof. Sch. Library Sci. U. So. Calif., Los Angeles, 1960-63; asst. prof. library and info. studies U. Calif., Berkeley, 1963-70, assoc. prof., 1970-76, prof., 1976-94, prof. emeritus, 1994—; assoc. dean Sch. Library and Info. Studies, 1971-74, 77-82; acting dean Sch. Library and Info. Studies U. Calif., Berkeley, 1985-86. Vis. assoc. prof. Sch. Libr. Sci. UCLA, summer 1973; cons. NEH, Washington; proprietor Park Hills Press. Author: John Henry Nash, 1970, Bibliography of the Grabhorn and Grabhorn-Hoyem Presses, 1977, George L. Harding, 1978, The Colonial Printer: Two Views, 1978, Chapter Nine, 1982, William Doxey's Publishing Venture: At the Sign of the Lark, 1983, The Two Hundredth Book, 1993; chmn. edit. bd. catalogues and bibliographies series U. Calif. Press, 1982-99; contbr. numerous articles and revs. to profl. jours. Rackham pre-doctoral fellow, U. Mich., 1958-60, summer faculty fellow U. Calif., Berkeley, 1964; grantee Assn. Coll. and Research Libraries, 1960, 63. Mem. Bibliog. Soc. Am., Bibliog. Soc. U. Va., Am. Soc. 18th Century Studies, Will Cather Pioneer Meml. Soc., Fine Press Book Assn., Book of Calif. Club (bd. dirs. 1982-88, sec. bd. 1987-88). Office: U Calif Sch Info Mgmt Berkeley CA 94720-0001 Office Phone: 415-642-4375.

HARLAN, ROBERT ERNEST, professional football team executive; b. Des Moines, Sept. 9, 1936; m. Madeline Harlan; children: Kevin, Bryan, Michael. BJ, Marquette U., 1958. Former gen. reporter UPI, Milw.; sports info. dir. Marquette U., Milw., 1959; dir. community rels. St. Louis Cardinals baseball team, 1966-68, dir. pub. rels., 1968-71; asst. gen. mgr. Green Bay (Wis.) Packers, 1971-75, corp. gen. mgr., 1975-81, corp. asst. to pres., 1981-88, exec. v.p. adminstrn., 1988-89, pres., chief exec. officer, 1989—. Bd. dirs. Firstar Bank, Green Bay. Mem. exec. bd. Packer 65 Roses Sports Club. Served with U.S. Army. Mem. bd. of trustees, St. Norbert Coll., Wis. Avocation: golf. Office: Green Bay Packers 1265 Lombardi Ave Green Bay WI 54304-3997 also: Green Bay Packers Lambeau Field PO Box 10628 Green Bay WI 54307-0628*

HARLAN, ROSS EDGAR, retired utility company executive, writer, lecturer, consultant; b. Poteau, Okla., July 11, 1919; s. Edgar Leslie and Leola (Carter) H.; m. Margaret Burns, May 31, 1942; children: Raymond Carter, Rosemary, Marvin Allen, Scott Lee. Student, Southeastern Okla. State U., 1937-38, Eastern Okla. State Coll., 1938-39; BSBA, Okla. State U., 1941; postgrad., Harvard U., 1942. Mem. faculty, coach Poteau High Sch., 1945-46, Poteau Jr. Coll., 1945-46; with Okla. Gas & Electric Co., Oklahoma City, 1946-85, mgr. rates and contracts dept., 1954-64, v.p., 1964-78, sr. v.p. div. mgmt., 1978-80, sr. v.p. adminstrn. and public affairs, 1980-85; ret.; ind. cons., writer Oklahoma City, 1985—. Cons. spl. books div. Reader's Digest, 1985—. Author: Strikes, 1946, Frontier Oklahoma-The Twin Territories, 1994. Pres. Okla. Council on Econ. Edn., 1977-79; pres. alumni bd. Ea. Okla. State Coll., 2000-03; bd. govs. Nat. Wrestling Hall of Fame, 1977-85; pres. adv. bd. Okla. State U. Coll. Bus. Assos.; adv. bd. Okla. State U. Tech. Inst.; bd. govs. Okla. State U. Found., bd. govs. Ea. Okla. State Coll. Devel. Found. With Army N.G., 1937-38; to lt. col. USAAF, 1941-46, Res. 1946-79. Named to Okla. State U. Coll. Bus. Hall of Fame, 1980, Ea. Okla. State Coll. Hall of Fame, 1992; recipient George Washington Honor medal Freedoms Found. Am., 1970, 2002, Disting. Alumnus award Okla. State U., 1979; named Boss of Yr., Nat. Secs. Assn., 1977; charter mem. Poteau (Okla.) Athletic Hall of Fame. Mem. Oklahoma City C. of C., Ea. Okla. State Coll. Alumni Assn. (pres. 2001-03), Toastmasters Internat. (comm. and leadership award 1985), Am. Legion, VFW, Mil. Order of World Wars (Silver Patrick Henry medallion 2000), Disabled Am. Vets Methodist. Home and Office: 2639 N Eagle Ln Oklahoma City OK 73127-1166

HARLAN, WILLIAM ROBERT, JR., internist, educator, researcher; b. Richmond, Va., Nov. 1, 1930; s. William Robert and Helen J. (Weaver) H.; m. Linda Carol Mavencamp, Aug. 23, 1980; children: Elizabeth, William, Christopher, Nicole. BA, U. Va., 1951; MD magna cum laude, Med. Coll. Va., 1955. Diplomate Am. Bd. Internal Medicine, Am. Bd. Family Practice. Intern U. Wis., Madison, 1955-56; resident in medicine Duke U. Hosp., Durham, N.C., 1958-62; dir. Clin. Research Center, Med. Coll. Va., 1963-70; asso. dean U. Ala. Med. Sch., 1970-72; prof. medicine and community health scis. Duke U., 1972-74; prof. medicine and postgrad. medicine U. Mich., Ann Arbor, 1974-88, asst. dean Med. Sch.; dir. div. epidemology and clin. applications Nat. Heart, Lung and Blood Inst., 1988-91; assoc. dir. for disease prevention NIH, Bethesda, 1991—2002; expert NIMH, 2001—, sr. advisor, 2001—. Cons. World Bank; mem. sci. adv. bd. U.S. Air Force; mem. Armed Forces Epidemiology Bd., NIH study sects. and adv. councils. Contbr. articles to med. jours. Lt. USMC, 1956—58, US Naval Sch. Aerospace Medicine. Fellow ACP, Am. Coll. Preventive Medicine, Am. Acad. Family Practice, Am. Heart Assn.; mem. N.Y. Acad. Sci., Sigma Xi, Alpha Omega Alpha (Markle Scholar in Acad. Medicine). Democrat. Episcopalian. Avocations: tennis, golf, skiing. Home: 3503 Windsor Pl Chevy Chase MD 20815-4001 also: 155 N Sea Pines Dr Hilton Head Island SC 29928-5804 Personal E-mail: wharlan@starpower.net.

HARLASS, FREDERICK E., obstetrician, gynecologist; b. Butte, Mont., Feb. 14, 1947; s. June Rena and Edward Gustave Harlass; m. Penny M. Wylie, Feb. 22, 1952; children: Steven Bruce, Scott Alexander, Sarah Lynn. MD, U. of Wash., 1980. Maternal-Fetal Medicine Am. Bd. of Obstetrics & Gynecology, 1996. Obstetrician, gynecologist U.S. Army, Ft. Wainwright, Alaska, 1984—86, chief, ambulatory care Ft. Lewis, Wash., 1986—87, fellow perinatal medicine, 1987—89, chief divsn. of obstetrics El Paso, 1989—91; residency dir. Tex. Tech U., El Paso, 1991—95, chmn., dept. of obstetrics & gynecology, 1995—2000, prof., 2000—. Chief dept. obstetrics, and gynecology, med. dir. for labor and delivery Del Sol Med. Ctr., El Paso, 2000—. Author numerous textbooks. Bd. mem. Lay Midwifery Commn., El Paso, 1993—97. Lt. col. U.S. Army and USN, 1966—99. Decorated 14 awards U.S. Army and USN. Fellow: FACOG (assoc.). Achievements include research in Diabetes in pregnancy. Avocations: golf, travel. Home: 5637 Buckley Dr El Paso TX 79912 Office: Tex Tech U 4800 Alberta El Paso TX 79912 Personal E-mail: frederick.harlass@ttuhsc.edu.

HARLE, THOMAS STANLEY, radiologist; b. Detroit, Aug. 17, 1932; s. Edward John and Daisy Odell (Bacon) H.; m. Barbara Janette Chrestman, Oct. 15, 1960; children: Blair Thomas, Timothy John. Student, Mich. State U., 1950-53; BS, Northwestern U., 1954; MD, Northwestern U., Chgo., 1957. Diplomate Am. Bd. Radiology (trustee 1987-99). Intern Passavant Meml. Hosp., Chgo., 1957-58; radiology resident Brooke Army Med. Ctr., San Antonio, 1958-61, asst. chief radiology, 1964-65; radiologist Ft. Detrick, Frederick, Md., 1961-62, Kelsey Seybold Clinic, Houston, 1965-66; chief of radiology Irwin Army Hosp., Ft. Riley, Kans., 1962-64; asst. prof., then assoc. prof. Baylor Coll. Medicine, Houston, 1966-69; assoc. prof. Duke U. Med. Ctr., Durham, N.C., 1969-71; prof. U. Tex. Med. Sch., Houston, 1975-78, 80-82, chmn. dept. radiology, 1975-78; prof. Mich. State U., East Lansing, 1978-80, U. Tex. M.D. Anderson Cancer Ctr., Houston, 1982-1997, asst. v.p. acad. affairs, 1982-90, assoc. v.p. acad. affairs, 1990-94; prof. dept. radiology Wake Forest U., Winston Salem, N.C., 1997—. Contbr. articles to profl. jours., chpts. to books. Maj. U.S. Army, 1958-65. Fellow Am. Coll. Radiology; mem. Assn. Univ. Radiologists (pres. 1983-84), Radiol. Soc. N.Am. (pres. 1993), European Assn. Radiologists (hon.), Faculty of Radiologists, Royal Coll. Surgeons in Ireland (hon.), Brit. Inst. Radiology (hon.). Republican. Baptist. Avocation: architecture. Office: Wake Forest U Medical Center Blvd Winston Salem NC 27157-0001 Office Phone: 336-716-4316. Business E-Mail: tharle@wfuamc.edu.

HARLEM, SUSAN LYNN, librarian; b. L.A., Oct. 1, 1950; d. Frank Joseph and Esther Frances (Bomell) H.; m. Anthony Stephen Hacsi, Aug. 31, 1990. BA, UCLA, 1972, MLS, 1976. Libr. U. Md., College Park, 1976-79, U.S. Dept. Edn., Washington, 1979-82, GSA, Washington, 1982-87, NLRB, Washington, 1988—. Tutor Washington Lit. Coun., 1992—. Co-author: Washington on Foot, 1984. Office: NLRB Libr 1099 14th St NW Washington DC 20570-0001 Business E-Mail: susan.harlem@nlrb.gov.

HARLEMAN, ANN, literature educator, writer; BA in English, Douglass Coll., 1967; PhD in Linguistics, Princeton U., 1972; MFA in Creative Writing, Brown U., 1988. Asst. prof. dept. English, Rutgers U., New Brunswick, N.J., 1973-74, U. Wash., Seattle, 1974-79, assoc. prof., 1979-84; vis. assoc. prof., rsch. affiliate writing program MIT, Cambridge, 1984-86; vis. scholar program in Am. civilization Brown U., Providence, 1986—; Cole disting. prof. Wheaton (Mass.) Coll., 1992-93; prof. English, RISD, Providence, 1994—. Fulbright-Hays lectr., 1980-81. Author: Graphic Representation of Models in Linguistic Theory, 1976, (with Bruce A. Rosenberg) Ian Fleming: A Critical Biograhy, 1989, Happiness, 1994, Bitter Lake, 1996; translator: Mute Phone Calls, 1992; contbr. over 50 articles to scholarly publs., transls. and revs., poems and short stories to lit. mags. Recipient Raymond Carver prize, 1986, Nelson Algren runner-up award Chgo. Tribune, 1987, 3d prize Judith Siegal Pearson award, 1988, Chris O'Malley fiction prize Madison Rev., 1990, Judith Siegal Pearson award, 1991, syndicated fiction award PEN, 1991, Iowa short fiction award, 1993, spl. mention, Pushcart prize, 1998, Zoetrope Fiction award, 2002, O'Henry prize, 2003, Goodheart prize, 2004, Rona Jaffe Writer's award, 2004; Guggenheim fellow, 1976-77, fellow Huntington Libr., 1979-80, MacDowell Colony, 1988, 99, 2004, Am. Coun. Learned Socs., 1992, Wurlitzer Found., 1992, R.I. Coun. Arts, 1989, 97, Berlin fellowship in Lit., 2000; sr. scholar Am. Coun. Learned Socs./IREX, 1976-77; grantee NEH, 1988, Rockefeller Found., 1989, Bogliasco Found., 1998, 2004. Mem. PEN Am. Ctr. Address: 18 Imperial Pl #5 Providence RI 02903 Office Phone: 401-272-7987. E-mail: ann_harleman@brown.edu.

HARLEY, COLIN EMILE, lawyer; b. Columbia, S.C., Mar. 27, 1940; s. William Hummel and Caroline (Monteith) H.; m. Emilia Saint Amand, June 5, 1965; children: Emile, Gray; m. Anita H. Laudone, May 20, 1978; children: Clayton, Victoria. AB, Dartmouth Coll., 1962; LLB, U. S.C., 1965; LLM in taxation, NYU, 1967. Bar: S.C. 1965, N.Y. 1968. Sole practice, Laurens, S.C., 1965; assoc. Davis Polk & Wardwell, N.Y.C., 1967-72, ptnr., 1973—, head equipment fin. practice group; adj. asst. prof. taxation NYU Sch Law, 1970-75. Trustee Greenwich (Conn.) Country Day Sch., 1987-96, pres., 1994-96. With USMCR, 1961-67. Office: Davis Polk & Wardwell 450 Lexington Ave 21st Fl New York NY 10017-3982 Office Phone: 212-450-4600. Office Fax: 212-450-3600. Business E-Mail: colin.harley@dpw.com.*

HARLEY, NAOMI HALLDEN, radiologist, educator, environmental scientist; b. N.Y.C., Aug. 4, 1932; d. Carl Edward and Ida Wilson (Palmer) Hallden; m. John Henry Harley, Sept. 11, 1964. BS, Cooper Union U., N.Y.C., 1959; MS, NYU, 1967, PhD, 1971, Advanced Profl. Cert., 1983. Phys. scientist U.S. AEC, N.Y.C., 1951-65; rsch. prof. environ. medicine NYU, 1965—; coun. mem., sci. com. chmn. Nat. Coun. on Radiation Protection and Measurement, Washington, 1982—. Contbr. articles to profl. jours. Adviser to UN Sci. Com. on Effects of Atomic Radiation (UNSCEAR), 1989—. USPHS fellow, 1988. Fellow: AAAS, Health Physics Soc. Democrat. Office: NYU Sch of Medicine Dept Environ Medicine 550 1st Ave New York NY 10016-6402 Office Phone: 212-263-5287. E-mail: naomi.harley@med.nyu.edu.

HARLEY, ROBISON DOOLING, ophthalmologist, educator; b. Pleasantville, N.J., Feb. 27, 1911; s. Halvor L. and Alice (Robison) H.; children—Robison Dooling, Ardee R., Heather L., Halvor L. II, William W. B.Sc., Rutgers U., 1932; MD, U. Pa., 1936; PhD, U. Minn., 1949. Diplomate Am. Bd. Ophthalmology. Intern Phila. Gen. Hosp., 1936-38; fellowship Mayo Clinic, Rochester, Minn., 1938-41, jr. staff cons., 1941-42; pvt. practice as ophthalmologist and ophthalmic surgeon Atlantic City and Phila., 1947-67; attending surgeon, dir. ophthalmology St. Christopher's Hosp. for Children, Phila., 1958-70; chief surgeon Atlantic City Hosp., 1950-67; cons. Shore Meml. Hosp., Somers Point, 1958-67; attending surgeon Temple U. Hosp., Phila., 1947-87; also Wills Eye Hosp. and Research Inst. Cons. Betty Bacharach Home for Children; cons. surgeon Wills Eye Hosp.; attending surgeon, dir. dept. pediatrics and motility; formerly prof., chmn. ophthalmology, prof. pediatrics Temple U. Health Sci. Ctr., Phila.; now prof. emeritus; dir. Overseas Eye Programs: Project Hope, Care-Medico, Internat. Eye Surgeons, Project Orbis; adj. prof. Thomas Jefferson U.; A.L. Morgan lectr., Toronto, 1972, Antonio Navas lectr., P.R., 1979, Frank Costenbader lectr., Washington., 1979; vol. over 20 countries Author 152 med. publs. indluding book chpts. and 4 textbooks; contbg. author: Textbook of Pediatrics, 1975, 77, 79, 98; contbr. chpt. Pediatric Ophthalmological Surgery; editor: Pediatric Ophthalmology, 1975, Pediatric Opthalmology textbook, 2 vols., 1983, 5th edit., 2005; contbr. articles to profl. jours., chpts. to books; mem. editorial bd.: Jour. Pediatric Ophthalmology and Strabismus. Mem. exec. bd. Atlantic area coun. Boy Scouts Am., 1949—; mem. Fight for Signt Inc., N.Y.C., Retinitis Pigmentosa Found. Served to lt. col. AUS, 1942-47. Decorated Legion of Merit from Panama (Vasco Nunez de Balboa); recipient Outstanding Humanitarian award Am. Acad. Ophthalmology, Dallas, 2000, Hero of Medicine, Pride of the Profession award AMA, 2001. Fellow ACS (gov. 1959-62), Am. Acad. Ophthalmology (assoc. sec. continuing edn., Outstanding Humanitarian award 2000); mem. Assn. Rsch. Ophthalmology, Pan-Am. Congress Ophthalmology, Am. Ophthal. Soc., Del. Assn. Blind. (pres.), Phi Beta Kappa, Sigma Xi. Clubs: Explorers N.Y.C., Brigantine (N.J.) Yacht (commodore); Union League (Phila.); Corinthian Yacht (Cape May, N.J.). Home: 2401 Pennsylvania Ave Apt 704 Wilmington DE 19806-1410

HARLEY, ROBISON DOOLING, JR., lawyer, educator; b. Ancon, Panama, July 6, 1946; s. Robison Dooling and Loyde Hazel (Goehenauer) Harley; m. Suzanne Purviance Bendel, Aug. 9, 1975; children: Arianne Erin, Lauren Loyde. BA, Brown U., 1968; JD, Temple U., 1971; LLM, U. San Diego, 1985. Cert.: Calif. Bd. Legal Specialization (criminal law specialist since 1981), Nat. Bd. Trial Advocacy (criminal trial adv. since 1982), bar: Pa. 1971, Calif. 1976, NJ 1977, DC 1981, US Dist. Ct. (cen. and so. dists.) Calif. 1976, US Dist. Ct. NJ 1977, US Dist. Ct. (ea. dist.) Pa. 1987, US Ct. Appeals (9th cir.) 1982, US Ct. Appeals (3rd cir.) 1986, US Supreme Ct. 1980, US Ct. Mil. Appeals 1972. Asst. agy. dir. Safeco Title Ins. Co., LA, 1975—77; ptnr. Cohen, Stokke & Davis, Santa Ana, Calif., 1977—85; prin. Harley Law Offices, Santa Ana, 1985—. Adj. prof. Orange County Coll. Trial Advocacy; adj. prof. paralegal program U. Calif.; instr. trial adv. programs US Army, USN, USAF, USMC; judge pro-tem Orange County Cts. Author: Orange County Trial Lawyers Drunk Driving Syllabus; contbr. articles to profl. jours. Trial counsel, def. counsel, mil. judge, asst. staff judge adv. USMC, 1971—75, regional def. counsel Western Region, 1986—90; bd. dirs. Orange County Legal Aid Soc. Lt. col. JAGC USMCR. Decorated Nat. Def. Svc. medal, Res. medal, Navy Commendation medal; named Super Lawyer, So. Calif., 2004, 2005. Mem.: ATLA, ABA, Orange County Criminal Lawyers Assn. (found. com.), Orange County Trial Lawyers Assn., Orange County Bar Assn. (judiciary com., criminal law sect., adminstrn. of justice com.), Assn. Specialized Criminal Def. Advs., Nat. Assn. for Criminal Def. Attys., Calif. Pub. Defenders Assn., Calif. Attys. for Criminal Justice, Calif. Trial Lawyers Assn., Marine Corps Assn., Marine Corps Res. Officers Assn., Res. Officers Assn. Republican. Avocations: sports, physical fitness, reading. Home: 31211 Paseo Miraloma San Juan Capistrano CA 92675-5505 Office: Harley Law Offices 825 N Ross St Santa Ana CA 92701-3419 Office Phone: 714-972-8141. Business E-Mail: robharley@earthlink.net.

HARLEY, RUTH, artist, educator; b. Phila. children: Peter W. Bressler, Victoria Angela. Student, Pa. State U., 1941; BFA, Phila. Coll. Art, 1945; postgrad., U. N.H., 1971, Hampshire Coll., 1970. Instr. Phila. Mus. Art, 1946-59; art supt. Ventnor (N.J.) City Bd. Edn., 1959-61. Art tchr. Print Club, Phila., Allens Ln. Art Ctr., Phila., Suburban Ctr. Arts, Lower Merion, Pa., Radner (Pa.) Twp. Adult Ctr., 1949—59, Atlantic City Adult Ctr., 1959—60. One-woman shows include Dubin-Lush Galleries, Phila., 1956, Contemporary Art Assn., 1957, Vernon Art Exhbns., Germantown, Pa., 1958, Detroit Inst. Arts, 1958, Phila. Mus. Art, 1957, 1959, Moore Inst., Phila., 1962—68, Greenhill Galleries, 1974, Phila. Civic Ctr., 1978, Natal Rio Grande du Norte, Brazil, 1979, Galerie Novel Esprit, Tampa, Fla., 1992—95, Mind's Eye Gallery, St. Petersburg, Fla., 1993, Ga. Tech. Art Ctr., 1998, Robert Ferst Ctr. for Arts Ga. Inst. Tech., 1998—99, exhibited in group shows at Group 55, Phila., 1955, Print Club, 1955, Nat. Tours, 1956—59, Pa. Acad. Fine Arts, 1957, Vernon Art Exhbns., 1958, Detroit Inst. Arts, 1958, Phila. Mus. Art, 1959, Moore Inst., 1962, Phila. Civic Ctr. Mus., 1975, Galerie Novel Esprit Assemblage Russe, 1992, Kenneth Raymond Gallery, Boca Raton, 1992—93, Mind's Eye Gallery, 1993, Polk Mus. Art, Lakeland, Fla., 1993, Don Roll Gallery, Sarasota, Fla., 1994—95, Las Vegas (Nev.) Internat. Art Expo, 1994, Heim Am. Gallery, Fisher Island, Fla., 1996, McLean Gallery, Malibu, Calif., 1997—99, Robert Ferst Ctr. for Arts Ga. Inst. Tech., 1998—99, Christina Gallery, Atlanta, 1999, Adrian Howard Gallery, St. Petersburg, 2000—02, 2004, Melrose (Fla.) Bay Art Gallery, 2001, Red River Valley Mus., Vernon, Tex., 2001, Kirkpatrick Mus., Okla., 2001, Airport, Gainesville, Fla., 2001, In Celebration of Art, 2004, Represented in permanent collections U. Villanova (Pa.) Mus., Temple U. Law Sch., Pa., Woodmere Mus., Phila.; included in Art in Am. Ann. Guide, 2000—01, 2002; commd. sculpture, Phila. Re-Devel. Authority. Contbr. art prize Ventnor N.J. Sch. Sys. Home and Office: PO Box 433 Melrose FL 32666-0433 Office Phone: 352-475-2881. Personal E-mail: harleyruth@aol.com.

HARLIN, MARILYN MILER, marine botany educator, researcher, consultant; b. Oakland, Calif., May 30, 1934; d. George T. and Gertrude (Turula) Miler; m. John E. Harlin II, Oct. 25, 1955 (dec. Feb. 1966); children: John E. III, Andrea M. Harlin Cilento. AB, Stanford U., 1955, MA, 1956; PhD, U. Wash., 1971. Instr. Am. Coll. Switzerland and Leysin, 1964-66; asst. prof. Pacific Marine Sta., Dillon Beach, Calif., 1969; asst. prof. marine biology U. R.I., Kingston, 1971-75, assoc. prof., 1975-83, prof., 1983-2000, prof. emerita, 2000—, chair botany dept., chair dept. biol. scis. Guest scientist Atlantic Regional Lab., Halifax, N.S., Can., 1973-78; hon. vis.prof. LaTrobe U., Bundoora, Victoria, Australia, 1984; resource person R.I. Coastal Resource Mgmt. Coun., 1980-2000, R.I. Dept. Environ. Mgmt., 1980; cons. Applied Sci. Assocs., Narragansett, R.I., 1988-98, Western Australia Water Authority, Perth, 1994; rsch. assoc. U. Calif., Santa Cruz, 1993. Co-editor: Marine Ecology, 1976, Freshwater and Marine Plants of Rhode Island, 1988. Bd. dirs. Westminster Unitarian Ch., East Greenwich, R.I., 1987; bd. govs. Women's Ctr., Kingston, 1989-90. Grantee NOAA, 1975-81, Dept. Environ. Mgmt./EPA, 1989-91, U.S. Fish and Wildlife, 1995. Mem. Internat. Phycological Soc., Phycological Soc. Am. (editor newsletter 1982-84, editorial bd. 1988-90), Union Concerned Scientists (nat. adv. bd. 2004—), N.E. Algal Soc. (exec. com.), Sigma Xi (pres., sec. 1979-82). Avocations: yoga, hiking, reading, writing, gardening. E-mail: mharlinor@earthlink.net.

HARLIN, RAY M., trucking executive; b. 1951; BS in Bus. Admin., U. Tenn., Knoxville. Various positions Arthur Andersen LLP, 1972—97; exec. v.p. fin. U.S. Xpress Enterprises, Chattanooga, 1997—, CFO, 1997—, dir. Office: US Xpress Enterprises Inc 4080 Jenkins Rd Chattanooga TN 37421

HARLIN, RENNY (RENNY LAURI MAURITZ HARJOLA), film director; b. Riihimaki, Finland, Mar. 15, 1959; m. Geena Davis, Sept. 18, 1993 (div. Jun. 21, 1998); 1 child. Dir. (films) A Nightmare on Elm Street 4: The Dream Master, 1988, Deep Blue Sea, 1999, Exorcist: The Beginning, 2004, (TV films) T.R.A.X., 2000; dir., writer: (films) Huostaanotto, 1980, Born American, 1986, Prison 1988, Die Hard 2, 1990, The Adventures of Ford Fairlane, 1990; dir., prodr.: (films) Cliffhanger, 1993, Cutthroat Island, 1995, Long Kiss Goodnight, 1996, Deep Blue Sea, 1999, Driven, 2001; prodr.: (films) Rambling Rose, 1991, Speechless, 1994, Blast From the Past, 1999; dir., prodr., writer: (TV series) Gladiaattorit, 1993; exec. prodr.: (TV films) Mistrial, 1996; exec. prodr., dir: (TV films) Mindhunters, 2004.*

HARLOW, BARBARA JEAN, publishing executive; d. Robert and Beatrice Swedenborg; m. Fred C. Harlow, Aug. 17, 1957; children: Michael, Douglas, David. MusB, U. So. Calif., 1956; MusM, Calif. State U., Fullerton, 1971. Prof. music Santa Barbara City Coll., 1975—89; pres. Santa Barbara Music Pub., Inc., 1990—. Author: You, The Singer, 1985, How to Get Your Choral Composition Published, 1995. Mem.: Pi Kappa Lambda. Office Phone: 805-962-5800. Office Fax: 805-966-7711.

HARLOW, CAROL JEAN, prospect researcher; b. New Haven, Conn., Apr. 12, 1952; d. Frank J. and Aileen W. H.; children: Anna, Lydia. BA, U. Conn., Storrs, 1974; MS, Southern Conn. State U., New Haven, 1978. Circulation librarian Atlanta Coll. of Art, Atlanta, 1980-83; registrar, 1983-85; admissions coord. Emory Univ. Sch. of Nursing, Atlanta, 1985-88; tech. writer TechData, Clearwater, FL, 1995-96; dir. prospect rsch. Univ. Tampa, Tampa, FL, 1996—. Mem.: Downtown Tampa Bus. and Profl. Women, Assn. Profl. Rschrs. for Advancement (track co-chmn. 16th ann. internat. conf.). Democrat. Avocations: reading, opera. Office: University of Tampa 401 W Kennedy Blvd Tampa FL 33606-1450 Office Fax: 813-258-7297.

HARMAN, BRENDA KAY, writer, researcher; b. Sutton, W.Va., June 19, 1953; d. Chester Harley and Louella Jane Bishop; m. Timothy Jon Harman, June 13, 1971; children: Timothy Jon II, Kimberly Jane, Gwendolyn Sue, Benjamin Sean. A in Adminstrv. Office Support Systems, Glenville State Coll., 1998. Author: Visions, Feathers and Sandstones, 1999 (Bearded Wolf's award of Excellence, 1998, award of Excellence, 1999). Tchr., rschr. AAIWV, Little Birch, W.Va., 1998—2004. Recipient Beareded Wolf's award of Excellence, 1999. Mem.: DAR (life), Appalachian Am. Indians of W. Va. (life). Home: 1987 Old Turnpike Rd Little Birch WV 26629 Personal E-mail: windsongb@peoplepc.com. E-mail: wnosn@writeme.com.

HARMAN, GEORGE GIBSON, physicist, consultant; b. Norfolk, Va., Dec. 7, 1924; s. George Gibson and Annie Wall (Baldwin) Harman; m. Ann Worischek, Jan. 31, 1953 (div. 1985); children: Joyce Catherine, Arthur Lawrence, Stewart Thomas; m. Donna K. Williamson, 1986. BS in Physics, Va. Poly. Inst., 1949; MS in Physics, U. Md., 1959. With Nat. Inst. Stds. and Tech. (formerly Nat. Bur. Stds.), Washington, 1950—, sr. rsch. scientist, 1976-93, fellow, 1993—2003, dean of staff, 2001—. Rsch. fellow Reading U., England, 1962—63. Author: 2 books; contbr. articles to profl. jours. With U.S. Army, 1943—46. Recipient Silver medal, U.S. Dept. Commerce, 1973, Gold medal, 1979, Achievement award, Internat. Electronics Packaging Soc., 1988. Fellow: IEEE (chmn. fellows and awards com. 1989—, Centennial medal 1984, Outstanding Contbns. award 1992, 1993, 15-Yr. Outstanding Contbns. to ECT Conf. 1993, Harry Diamond Meml. award 1996, Third Millennium medal 2000, Outstanding Sustained Tech. Contbns. award 2001), Soc. Mfg. Engrs. (Excellence in Electronic Mfg. award 2001), Internat. Microelectronics Packaging Soc. (chpt. pres. 1980—82, regional dir. 1698—1987, chmn. found. grants com., chmn. nat. tech. program com. 1990—92, nat. pres. 1995, Tech. Achievement award 1981, Lewis F. Miller award 1984, Disting. Svc. award 1986, 1987, Daniel C. Hughes award 1989, DVS European Electronic Packaging award 1998); mem.: ASTM, Am. Phys. Soc., Cosmos Club Washington, Sigma Pi Sigma, Sigma Xi. Achievements include patents in field. Home: 4719 Dorset Ave Bethesda MD 20815-5445 Office: Nat Inst Standards and Tech Div # 812 Gaithersburg MD 20899-0001

HARMAN, GILBERT HELMS, philosophy educator; b. East Orange, NJ, May 26, 1938; s. William Henry and Marguerite Variel (Page) H.; m. Lucy Newman, Aug. 14, 1970; children: Elizabeth, Olivia. BA, Swarthmore Coll., 1960; PhD, Harvard U., 1964. With dept. philosophy Princeton (N.J.) U., 1963—, prof., 1971—, acting chair, 2001—02, chair cognitive studies program, 1992-97. Author: Thought, 1973, The Nature of Morality, 1977, Change in View, 1986, Skepticism and the Definition of Knowledge, 1990, (with Judith Jarvis Thomson) Moral Relativism and Moral Objectivity, 1996, Reasoning, Meaning, and Mind, 1999, Explaining Value and Other Essays in Moral Philosophy, 2000; editor: On Noam Chomsky, 1974, (with Donald Davidson) Semantics of Natural Language, 1971, (with Donald Davidson) The Logic of Grammar, 1975, Conceptions of the Human Mind, 1993. Recipient Jean Nicol prize, 2005. Fellow: Cognitive Sci. Soc.; mem.: AAAS, Am. Acad. Arts & Scis., Linguistic Soc. Am., Philosophy Sci. Soc., Am. Psychol. Soc., Am. Philos. Assn. Home: 106 Broadmead St Princeton NJ 08540-7216 Office: Princeton Univ Dept Philosophy Princeton NJ 08544-1006 Business E-Mail: harman@princeton.edu.

HARMAN, JANE, congresswoman; b. N.Y.C., June 28, 1945; d. A. N. and Lucille (Geier) Lakes; m. Sidney Harman, Aug. 30, 1980; children: Brian Lakes, Hilary Lakes, Daniel Geier, Justine Leigh. BA, Smith Coll., 1966; JD, Harvard U., 1969. Bar: D.C. 1969, U.S. Ct. Appeals (D.C. cir.) 1972, U.S. Supreme Ct. 1975. Spl. asst. Commn. of Chs. on Internat. Affairs, Geneva, 1969-70; assoc. Surrey & Morse, Washington, 1970-72; chief legis. asst. Senator John V. Tunney, Washington, 1972-73; chief counsel, staff dir. Subcom. on Rep. Citizen Interests, Com. on Judiciary, Washington, 1973-75; adj. prof. Georgetown Law Ctr., Washington, 1974-75; chief counsel, staff dir. Subcom. on Constl. Rights, Com. on Judiciary, Washington, 1975-77; dep. sec. to cabinet The White House, Washington, 1977-78; spl. counsel Dept. Def., Washington, 1979; ptnr. Manatt, Phelps, Rothenberg & Tunney, Washington, 1979-82, Surrey & Morse, Washington, 1982-86; of counsel Jones, Day, Reavis & Pogue, Washington, 1987-92; mem. U.S. Ho. of Reps., 36th Calif. dist., 1993—99, 2001—; mem. nat. security com., intelligence com. 103rd-105th Congresses; mem. energy and commerce com., intelligence com. 107th Congress, 2001—; mem. Nat. Commn. on Terrorism, 1999—2000. Regents prof. UCLA, 1999-2000; mem. vis. coms. Harvard Law Sch., 1976-82, Kennedy Sch. Govt., 1990-96. Vice-chmn. Ctr. for Nat. Policy, Washington, 1981—90; trustee Smith Coll.; counsel Dem. Platform Com., Washington, 1984; chmn. Dem. Nat. Com. Nat. Lawyers' Coun., Washington, 1986—90; bd. dirs. Planned Parenthood, 1998—2000, Venice (Calif.) Family Clinic, 1998—2000. Mem. Phi Beta Kappa. Democrat. Office: 2400 Rayburn HOB Washington DC 20515-0536 also: 2321 Rosecrans Ave #3270 El Segundo CA 90245-4932

HARMAN, JOHN ROYDEN, retired lawyer; b. Elkhart, Ind., June 30, 1921; s. James Lewis and Bessie Bell (Mountjoy) H.; m. Elizabeth Rae Crosier, Dec. 12, 1943 (dec. May 1995); 1 child, James Richard. BS, U. Ill., 1943; JD, Ind. U., 1949. Bar: Ind. 1949. Assoc. Proctor & Proctor, Elkhart, 1949-51; pvt. practice, Elkhart, 1952-60; ptnr. Cawley & Harman, 1960-65, Thornburg, McGill, Deahl, Harman, Carey & Murray, 1965-82, Barnes & Thornburg, Elkhart, 1982-89; ret., 1989. Atty. City of Elkhart, 1952-60. State del. Ind. Republican Com., 1962-70; pres., bd. dirs. Crippled Childrens Soc.; bd. dirs. United Community Services Elkhart County. 1st lt., F.A.,AUS, 1943-46, PTO. Fellow Ind. Bar Found; mem. ABA, Ind. Bar Assn., Elkhart County Bar Assn. (pres. 1977), Elkhart City Bar Assn. (pres. 1970), Elkhart C. of C. (pres. 1977, bd. dirs. 1972-75), Elcona Country Club (bd. dirs.), Phi Kappa Psi, Alpha Kappa Psi, Phi Delta Phi. Republican. Presbyterian. Avocation: golf. Office: NBD Bank Bldg 121 W Franklin St Ste 200 Elkhart IN 46516-3200 *Be honest and forthright— think positively— continually try to enhance the cause of mankind.*

HARMAN, MARYANN WHITTEMORE, artist, educator; b. Roanoke, Va., Sept. 13, 1935; d. John Weed and Clifford Kelly Whittemore; m. Roger Walke, Aug. 25, 1984; children: Mary Kelly, John Whittemore, Phillip Mears. BA, Mary Washington Coll., 1955; MA, Va. Poly. Inst., 1974. Faculty Va. Poly. Inst., Blacksburg, 1963—, prof. art, 1981—. Guest artist Emma Lake Art Workshop, U. Sask., 1985. One-woman shows include Andre Emmerich Gallery, N.Y.C., 1976, 78, Rubiner Gallery, Detroit, 1977-78, 90, Meredith Long Gallery, N.Y.C., 1980, Theodore Haber Gallery, N.Y.C., 1981-82, 84-85, Osuna Gallery, Washington, 1982, 84, 87, Wade Gallery, L.A., 1986-87, 89, 91, Ulysses Gallery, 1990, 94, Osuma Gallery, 1993, Martha Mabey Gallery, 1994, Gallery K, Washington, 1996, Armory Art Gallery VATECH, Va., 1997, 2002, Art Pannonia, Va., 2003, Va. Commonwealth U. Anderson Gallery, 2004; exhibited in group shows at Va. Mus. Art, Richmond, 1973-75, 80-81, Southeastern Ctr. for Contemporary Art, Winston Salem, N.C., 1963, 65, 67, 71, 76, Boston Mus. Fine Arts, 1981, 84, Roanoke (Va.) Mus., 1963-79, Butler Inst. Contemporary Art, Youngstown, Ohio, 1969, 72, Anita Shapolsky Gallery, N.Y.C., 1988, Wade Gallery, 1989, Rubiner Gallery, 1990, C.S. Schulte Gallery, East Orange, NJ, 1998-2004, Lee Hausley Gallery, NC, 2001-2004, Sandy Carson Gallery, Col., 2001-2004, Gallery One, Toronto, 1990-2004, Studios in the Square, Va., 2000-2004, Peter Alpers Gallery, Ma., 2001-2004, Les Yeux du Monde, Va., 2003-04; represented in permanent collections Boston Mus., Gen. Motors, Detroit, Hunter Mus., Chattanooga, Roanoke Mus., Phillip Morris Corp., Richmond and N.Y.C., Mfrs. Hanover Trust, N.Y.C., Am. Can Corp., N.Y.C., Shawmut Bank of Boston, Mint Mus., CSX Corp., Ethyl Corp, Capital One, others. Mem. Coll. Art Assn., Nat. Hon. Art and Architecture Soc., Tau Sigma Delta. Episcopalian. Home: 22 Boardwalk 1 Larkspur CA 94939

HARMAN, RAEJEAN ANN, music educator; b. Belleville, Ill., Dec. 20, 1954; d. Kenneth Dick and Dorothy Dean Ward; children: Justin Adam, Alisyn Leigh. BS in Art Edn., S.W. Va. C.C., Wardell, 1996; BS in Music Edn., Concord Coll., 1977. Cert. optician Va. Sec., optician J.J. Auville & Assocs., Bluefield, W.Va., 1977—79; optician Taylor Optical Co., Bluefield, 1979—80; instnl. aide Graham Intermediate Sch., Bluefield, 1990—91; art resource tchr. Tazewell (Va.) County Schs., 1991—93; choral dir., asst. band dir. Tazewell H.S., 1993—2005, art tchr., 1997—2002; choral dir. Virginia H.S., Bristol, 2005—. Murals, Tazewell County Schs., 1991—96, Boissevain Miners Mus., 1995, Bluefield Profl. Group, 1995—96. Sunday sch. tchr. Ch. of Christ, Bluefield, 1974—; coach Odyssey of the Mind, Bluefield, 1989—91. Named to Pres.'s Club for Outstanding Sales, Avon Co., 1987; recipient award, Va. Blue Ribbon Sch. Music, 2003—04, Pres.'s Club for Outstanding Sales, Avon Co., 1988. Mem.: NEA, Va. Edn. Assn., Music Educators Nat. Conf., Va. Congress Parents and Tchrs. (life), Kappa Delta Pi. Republican. Mem. Ch. Of Christ. Avocations: sewing, drawing, crafts. Office: Bristol Pub Schs 1200 Long Crescent Dr Bristol VA 24201

HARMAN, SIDNEY, audio and video company executive; b. 1918; BS, CCNY, 1939; PhD, Union Inst., 1973. Co-founder Harman-Kardon Inc. (now div. of Harman Internat. Industries), 1952; dep. sec. U.S. Dept. Commerce, 1977—80; chmn. bd., CEO Harman Internat. Industries, 1980—2000, exec. chmn., 2000—. Co-author (with Daniel Yankelovich): Starting With the People, 1988; author: Mind Your Own Business, 2003; contbr. articles to newspapers & magazines. Mem. adv. com. John F. Kennedy Sch. Govt., Harvard Univ.; chmn. prog. com. Aspen Inst.; chmn. exec. com. Pub. Agenda Found.; trustee Carter Ctr., Emory Univ.; bd. mem. Leadership Inst., Univ. So. Calif. Fellow: Am. Acad. Arts & Sciences; mem.: Council on Competitiveness, Council on Fgn. Rels., Bus. Executives for Nat. Security (chmn. exec. com.). Office: Harman International Industries Ste 1010 1101 Pennsylvania Ave NW Washington DC 20004*

HARMAN, WILLARD NELSON, malacologist, educator; b. Geneva, NY, Apr. 20, 1937; s. Samuel Willard and Mary Nelson (Covert) H.; m. Susan Beth Mead, June 12, 1968 (div. 1980); children: Rebecca Mary, Willard Wade; m. Barbara Ann Stong, June 8, 1981; children: Jessica Mary, Samuel Willard. Student, Hobart Coll., 1954—55; BS, Coll. Environ. Sci. and Forestry, SUNY, 1965; PhD, Cornell U., 1968; postgrad., Marine Biol. Lab., Woods Hole, Mass., 1968. Asst. prof. SUNY, Oneonta, 1968-69, assoc. prof., 1969-76, prof. biology, 1976—2002, chmn. dept. biology, 1981-89, dir. Biol. Field Sta., 1989—, disting. svc. prof., 2002—. Resource advisor N.Y. State Dept. Environ. Conservation, Albany, 1980—. Contbr. articles to profl. jours. Rep. Otsego County Rep. Com., N.Y., 1973-76; chmn. planning bd., Springfield, N.Y., 1984-96. Served with USN, 1956-61. Recipient Chancellor's award SUNY, 1974-75, Quality award EPA, 1989, Excellence award SUNY, 1990. Mem. Soc. Limnology and Oceanography, N.Am. Benthological Soc., Soc. for Exptl. and Descriptive Malacology, Am. Malocological Union, Otsego County Conservation Assn. (bd. dirs. 1970—, pres. 1974-78, 80-81, chmn. lake com. 1981—). Episcopalian. Avocations: sailing, fishing, scuba diving, skiing. Home: RR 2 Box 829 Cooperstown NY 13326-9327 Office: Biol Field Sta 5838 St Hwy 80 Cooperstown NY 13326-9330 Office Phone: 607-547-8778. Business E-Mail: harmanwn@oneonta.edu.

HARMAN, WILLIAM BOYS, JR., lawyer; b. Newport News, Va., June 5, 1930; s. William Boys and Helen (Conner) H.; children: Susan Carol, Thomas Scott, Ann Carrington. AB, Coll. William and Mary, 1951, JD, 1956; LLM, Georgetown U., 1960. Bar: Va. 1956, D.C. 1961. Tax atty. Gen. Motors Corp., Detroit, 1956-58; atty. Office Chief Counsel, IRS, Washington, 1958-59, Office of Tax Legis. Counsel, U.S. Treasury Dept., Washington, 1959-61; atty. firm Cummings & Sellers, Washington, 1961-62; asso. gen. counsel Am. Life Conv., Washington, 1962-67, gen. counsel, 1968-72; v.p. law Am. Life Ins. Assn., 1973-75; exec. v.p. Am. Council Life Ins., 1976-78; partner firm Sutherland, Asbill & Brennan, Washington, 1978-85, Davis & Harman, Washington, 1985—. Served with USCGR, 1952-54. Mem. ABA, Va. State Bar, D.C. Bar Assn., Assn. Life Ins. Counsel, Am. Law Inst., SAR, William and Mary Law Sch. Assn., Order of Coif, Washington Golf and Country Club, Metropolitan Club, Phi Beta Kappa, Phi Alpha Delta, Sigma Alpha Epsilon. Home: 3839 N Tazewell St Arlington VA 22207-4568 Office: Davis & Harman Ste 1200 1455 Pennsylvania Ave NW Washington DC 20004-1008 E-mail: wbharman@davis-harman.com.

HARMEL, HILDA HERTA See PIERCE, HILDA

HARMEL, MEREL HILBER, anesthesiologist, educator; b. Cleve., May 19, 1917; s. Louis and Hermine (Greenbaum) H.; m. Armide Chilcoat, July 2, 1944 (dec. 1988); children: Nancy Armide, Ruth Courtney, Priscilla Gover, Mary Louise; m. Ernestine Friedl Levy, Dec. 27, 1990. BA, Johns Hopkins U., 1938, MD, 1943. Diplomate Am. Bd. Anesthesiology. Fellow in anesthesiology NRC; anesthesiologist-in-chief Albany Med. Ctr., 1948-52, Kings County Med. Ctr., Bklyn., 1952-68, pres. med. bd., 1958-62, chmn. exec. com., 1964-65; cons. L.I. Jewish, St. Albans Naval, Maimonides, St. John's Episcopal, VA hosps., N.C. Eye and Ear Hosp., Durham; assoc. prof. anesthesiology (surgery) Albany Med. Coll., 1948-52; prof., chmn. dept. anesthesiology SUNY Downstate Med. Ctr., 1952-68, Pritzker Sch. Medicine, U. Chgo., 1968-71; prof. anesthesiology Duke Med. Ctr., Durham, NC, 1971—, chmn. dept. anesthesiology ctr., 1971-83, prof. anesthesiology, 1983-87, Merel H. Harmel prof. anesthesiology, 2002, prof. emeritus, 1987—; prof. anesthesiology Duke U. Med. Ctr., Durham, 2002—. Vis. prof. dept. anesthesiology Sch. Medicine, Johns Hopkins U., 1985—. Contbr. articles to profl. jours. Named Disting. alumnus, Johns Hopkins Sch. Medicine, 2003; Commonwealth fellow Oxford U., 1961-62, hon. mem. Sr. Common Rm., Pembroke Coll., 1961, Disting. Alumnus award Johns Hopkins Sch. Medicine, 2004; Merel Harmel vis. lectureship established Duke U. Med. Ctr., 1983, Merel H. Harmel chair dept. anesthesiology established, 2003. Fellow Am. Coll. Anesthesiology (bd. govs.), Royal Coll. Anaesthesia Faculty; mem. AMA, Am. Soc. Anesthesiologists (Living History Series), Assn. Univ. Anesthetists, Duke U. Med. Ctr. Founders Soc., Johns Hopkins U. Soc. Scholars, Japan Soc. Anesthesiologists (hon.), Assn. Anesthesiologists Français (hon.), Oxford Soc. Carolinas (hon. sec. 1990—, W.G. Anlyan Lifetime Achievement award 1999). Business E-Mail: harme001@mc.duke.edu.

HARMEL, WARREN, marketing professional; married; 3 children. Degree in bus. adminstrn., mktg. cum laude, U. Cape Town, South Africa. Founding ptnr., gen. mgr. Mortimer Tiley/BBDO, 1979; dir. Phillips Petroleum Acct. Tracy-Locke, Dallas, 1986, promoted to v.p. strategic planning; sr. v.p. bus. devel. and strategy Orneles & Assocs., 1990—95; founder, mng. ptnr. Dieste Harmel & Partners, Dallas, 2002—. Recipient 4 Effie awards, David Ogilvy Rsch. award, Adv. Rsch. Found. Mem.: Assn. Hispanic Adv. Agys. (founder). Office: Dieste Harmel & Partners 3102 Oak Lawn Ste 109 Dallas TX 75219

HARMELIN, STEPHEN JOSEPH, lawyer; b. Phila., May 7, 1939; s. Louis M. and Ethel (Katz) H.; m. Julia Tose, June 18, 1995; children: Alison Kate, Melina Alexis. BA cum laude, U. Pa., 1960; LLB, Harvard U., 1963. Bar: Pa. 1964, U.S. Supreme Ct. 1968. Atty. broadcast bur. FCC, Washington, 1964; aide White House, Washington, 1964-65; assoc. Dilworth, Paxson, Kalish & Dilks (name now Dilworth Paxson LLP), Phila., 1965-70; ptnr. Dilworth, Paxson, Kalish & Dilks, Phila., 1970-86; co-chmn. corp. dept. Dilworth, Paxson, Kalish & Dilks (now Dilworth Paxson LLP), Phila., 1986-91; mng. ptnr. Dilworth Paxson LLP, Phila., 1991—. Bd. dirs., chmn. CONFAB, Inc., King of Prussia, Pa., 1996-97; chmn. Publicker Industries, Greenwich, Conn., 1980-84; lectr. Phila. Coll. Art, 1970-72. Spl. asst. dist. atty. City of Phila., 1970; commr. Pa. Conv. Ctr. Authority, Phila., 1989-2002; gen. counsel Pa. Legis. Reapportionment Commn., 1982-98; chmn. Thomas Skelton Harrison Found., sec., gen. counsel Nat. Constitution Ctr., Phila., 1982, Found. of the Phila. Heart Inst., 1988; trustee The Barnes Found., 2002; dir. Greater Phila. First Found., 2002; bd. dirs. Phila. divsn. Am. Cancer Soc., 1986, crusade chmn., 1987-88. With USCGR, 1963-69. Mem. ABA, Phila. Bar Assn., Union League Club. Republican. Jewish. Office: Dilworth Paxson LLP 1735 Market St Philadelphia PA 19103-7501 Office Phone: 215-575-7060. Business E-Mail: sharmelin@dilworthlaw.com.

HARMELINK, HERMAN, III, minister, writer, religious studies educator; b. Sheldon, Pa., Dec. 26, 1933; s. Herman II, and Thyrza (Eringa) H.; m. Barbara Mary Conibear, Aug. 11, 1959; children: Herman IV Alan, Lindsay Alexandra (Mrs. Richard L. LeMay, Jr.). BA cum laude, Central Coll., 1954; MA, Columbia U., 1955; postgrad., U. London, 1955; MDiv, New Brunswick Theol. Sem., 1958; World Coun. Chs. scholar, U. Heidelberg, 1959; STM magna cum laude, Union Theol. Sem., N.Y.C., 1964, MPhil, 1978. Ordained to ministry Reformed Ch. Am., 1959. Min. Cmty. Ch., Glen Rock, N.J., 1959-64, Woodcliff Cmty. Ch., Woodcliff-on-Hudson, N.J., 1964-71, Reformed Ch., Poughkeepsie, N.Y., 1971—; ecumenical officer Internat. Coun. Cmty. Chs., 2000—. Adj. faculty in philosophy SUNY, Marist Coll.; chaplain Holland-Am. Line; mem. faith and order commn. Nat. Coun. Chs., 2000—, vice chmn., 1976-79, mem. commn. on regional and local ecumenism, 1981-84, mem. exec. bd., 2000—, del. Gen. Assembly, 1999—; pres. Synod of N.J., 1969; chmn. interch. rels. Ref. Ch. Am., 1964-71; chmn. Ecumenical Rels. Commn. Internat. Coun. of Cmty. Chs., 1994—; del. 18th Plenary Consultation on Ch. Union, St. Louis, 1999; mem. steering com. Reconciliation of Ministries task force Chs. Uniting in Christ, 2002—; pres. Dutchess Interfaith Coun., 1977-78, devel. retirement cmty. com., 1989—, bd. dirs.; del. gen. coun. World Alliance Ref. Chs., Frankfurt, 1964, Nairobi, 1970; adv. Gen. Assembly World Coun. Chs., Uppsala, Sweden, 1968; U.S. del. 50th Anniversary Faith and Order Commn., Lausanne, Switzerland, 1977. Author: Ecumenism and the Reformed Church, 1968, The Reformed Church in New Jersey, 1969, Another Look at Frelinghuysen and His Awakening, 1969; contbg. author: Concord Makes Strength, 2002, Piety and Patriotism, 1976, Vision from the Hill, 1984, The Livingston Legacy, 1987. Trustee Peter A. Lindsay Trust Imperial Coll. U. London; trustee St. Francis Hosp., exec. com. of bd., joint conf. com., chmn. planning com.; bd. dirs. Dutchess County Arts Coun., 1976-80, Bardavon 1869 Opera House, 1978-79; mem. allocation and planning divsn. United Way of Dutchess County; mem. Dutchess County Execs. Com. on Med. Ethics; sec. bd. dirs. Rehab. Programs, Inc., 1977-79; bd. dirs. Anderson Ednl. Found., Collingwood Repertory Theatre, 1978-80, Mid-Hudson Meml. Soc., 1981-84; pres. Poughkeepsie Generating Cmty., 1974—; bd. dirs. Literacy Vol. of Dutchess County, pres. 1987-89; bd. dirs. Literacy Vols. Am., N.Y., chmn. pers. comm., mem. program com., pres.-elect, 1992-93, pres. 1993-96, bd. dirs. nat. bd. Lit. Vols. Am.; Poughkeepsie Rural Cemetery, chmn. fin. com.; pres. Ranfurly Library Svc. of N.Y. Inc., Town of Poughkeepsie Dem. Com., Dutchess County Dem. Com.; participant U.S.-S. African Leader Exchange Program, 1971; adv. bd. Wartburg Luth. Svcs., 1993—; chmn. Anderson Sch. Wine Showcase; ecumenical adv. del. Presbyn. Ch. Gen. Assembly, Long Beach, Calif., 2000, Episc. Gen. Conv., Mpls., 2003, United Meth. Gen. Conf., 2004. Lt. USNR, 1957-61. Decorated knight Order of the Temple of Jerusalem; Fulbright Travel grant, Germany, 1958—59. Mem. N.Am. Acad. Ecumenists, Am. Soc. Ch. History, Presbyn. Hist. Soc., Poughkeepsie C. of C., Dutchess Interfaith Coun., Dutchess County Clergy Club, Dutchess County Hist. Soc. (life, bd. dirs. 1974-78), Poughkeepsie Rotary (pres. 1977-79, sec. 1979—, sec. Dist. 721, 1980-81, gov. 1982-83, chmn. World Community Svc., Rotary Internat. Coun. on Legis., Monte Carlo, 1983, Rotary Internat. pres.'s rep. to dist. confs. 1984, 88, Paul Harris fellow, sect. leader internat. conv., Portland, 1990), Lumanites (sec.-treas.), 251, Poughkeepsie Social Reading Club (past pres.), Circumnavigators Club (NYC), The Club, Travelers Century Club (life), Fjord Club, Mil Order Fgn. Wars of U.S. (life vet. companion, chaplain, coun. NY commandery), Fulbright Assn. (life), St. George's Soc. N.Y. (life), Chevalier du Tastevin (France), Royal Overseas League (London), Friends of St. George's and Descendants of the Knights of the Garter (life, Windsor), English Speaking Union, Co. of Pastors, Witherspoon Soc., Ctr. for Lifetime Study. Office: 70 Hooker Ave Poughkeepsie NY 12601 *In the words of John Bunyan, "He who would valiant be 'gainst all disaster, let him in constancy follow the Master. There's no discouragement shall make him once relent his first avowed intent to be a pilgrim.".*

HARMELINK, RUTH IRENE, marriage and family therapist, writer; b. Rock Valley, Iowa, Aug. 22, 1945; d. Gerritt Harmelink and Rena Miedema; m. John Bruce Kragt, Aug. 14, 1964 (div. June 1980); children: Daniel John, Thomas Dean, Michele Renae Kersten; m. Dennis Oliver Kaldenberg, May 23, 1982; 1 child, Sarah Ruth. AA, Iowa Lakes C.C., 1976; BA magna cum laude, Buena Vista Coll., Storm Lake, Iowa, 1978; MA, Drake U., Des Moines, 1983; PhD, Iowa U., 1985. Extension specialist Iowa State U., Ames, 1985—86; asst. prof. S.D. State U., Brookings, 1986—87, Oreg. State U., Corvallis, 1987—89; pvt. practice Corvallis, 1985—86, 1989—96; prof., dir. marriage & family therapy masters program Northwest Christian Coll., Eugene, Oreg., 1991—96; therapist pvt. practice Ind., 1997—2000; adjunct prof. Notre Dame U., South Bend, 2000—01. Approved supr. Lutheran Family Svc., Portland, Oreg.; organizational cons. Tng. Inst., South Bend, 1997—; therapist Chapin Street Clinic, South Bend, 2000—. Author (and editor): (videotape) Lenders: Working Through the Farmer and Lender Crisis!, 1986. Elder Presbyn. Ch., Corvallis. Oreg. and South Bend, Ind., 1989—; bd. dirs., counselor Story County Sexual Assault and Care Ctr., Ames, Iowa, 1983—85. Recipient Pearl S. Swanson fellowship, Coll. Home Econs, Iowa State U., 1983. Mem.: Am. Assn. Marriage and Family Therapists. Democrat. Presbyterian. Avocations: gardening, knitting, reading, sewing, quilting. Home: 52471 Sunfield Loop Granger IN 46530 Personal E-mail: rihdok@comcast.net.

HARMON, ANGIE (ANGIE SEHORN), actress; b. Dallas, Aug. 10, 1972; d. Larry and Daphne Harmon; m. Jason Sehorn, 2001; children: Finley Faith, Avery Grace. Actor: (TV series) Baywatch Nights, 1995-97, C-16: FBI, 1997-98, Law & Order, 1998-2001, Inconceivable, 2005- (TV films) Video Voyeur: The Susan Wilson Story, 2002, Sudden Fear, 2002, (films) Lawn Dogs, 1997, Good Advice, 2001, Agent Cody Banks, 2003, The Deal, 2005. Office: c/o CAA 9830 Wilshire Blvd Beverly Hills CA 90212*

HARMON, BARBARA SAYRE, artist; b. Yerington, Nev., Aug. 8, 1927; d. Ruth (Barker) and Fred Grayson Sayre; m. Cliff Franklin Harmon, July 7, 1948; 1 child, Jonathan Henry. Student, Bisttram Sch. Fine Art, 1945—48, Black Mountain Coll., 1950; studied bookbinding with Johanna Jalowitz, studied etching with Lawton Parker, 1951. Founder, mgr. Children's Gallery, Taos, N.Mex., 1963—, Children's Gallery Press, 1967—; co-dir. Torreon Gallery, Taos, 1980—. Exhibitions include paintings, graphics and book art Southwestern galleries, 1963—; author, illustrator Tabbigail's Garden, 1967, Little People's Counting Book, 1968, This Little Pixie, 1969, Monday's Mouse, 1970, The Tumpfee Wood Acorn Book, 1977, Thimbly Hill, 1980, cover designer, illus. N.Mex. mag. Christmas story, 1981; Represented in permanent collections Harwood Mus., U. N.Mex., Stanford U. Libr., Palo Alto, U. N. Mex. Libr., Taos Pub. Libr., Taos Art Mus., numerous pvt. collections; works appear in numerous mags. and books. Home: PO Box 202 6584NDCBU Taos NM 87571-0202

HARMON, CLARA CHOKENEA, public relations/marketing executive; b. Cleve., Feb. 5, 1953; d. Arthur Charles and Clara Ann (Sinagra) Chokenea; m. John Clifford Harmon, July 21, 1979; children: Anna Grace, Gail Frances. BS in Journalism, Bowling Green State U., 1975; MBA, Rochester Inst. Tech., 1979. Employee info. editor, news svcs. editor, sales rep. Eastman Kodak Co., Rochester, N.Y., 1975-79; mgmt. asst. South Ctrl. Bell/AT&T, Louisville, 1979-81; account exec. Caldwell Van Riper Inc., Indpls., 1981-82; editl. staff writer Sherman-Eckert Visual and Verbal Comms., Webster, N.Y., 1993; dir. comms. Pers. Works Inc., Pittsford, N.Y., 1993-95, dir. mktg., 1995-96; group leader corp. comm. Vis. nurse svc. Rochester and Monroe Coutny, 1996—98; dir. mktg. and pub. rels. U. New Haven, 1999—2000; dir. mktg. comms. Pitney Bowes Office Systems (spin-off Imagistics Internat.), 2000—02; mgr. mktg. comms., property and casualty The Hartford, 2002—. Loaned exec. United Way, Rochester, 1979; chair cmty. rels. com., bd. dirs. Girls Clubs of Greater Indpls., 1982-84; mem. mktg./publ rels. com. ARC, Rochester, 1984-86; mem. bldg. mgmt. team, parent rep. shared decision-making team Thornell Rd. Elem. Sch., Pittsford, 1993-95; various com. chair positions Plank South Sch. PTSA, Webster, N.Y., 1991-92, chair family to family program, 1990-92; founder Plank Rd. South Pub. Ctr., Webster, 1991-92; dir. sch. program Mt. Rise United Ch. Christ, 1996-98; mem. bd. child and youth edn., Sunday sch. tchr. kindergarten First Ch. Congl., Fairfield, Conn., 2003—. Mem. Pub. Rels. Soc. Am. (bd. dirs. health acad.), Women in Comms. (pres. Rochester chpt. 1978-79, membership v.p. 1994-95, nat. nominations chair 1982-82), Soc. for Human Resource Mgmt. (newsletter editor 1994-96), Chi Omega. Mem. United Ch. of Christ. Avocations: crafts, quilting, sewing, gardening. Home: 66 Under Cliff Rd Trumbull CT 06611-2547 Office: The Hartford Hartford Plz 690 Asylum Ave Hartford CT E-mail: clara.harmon@sbcglobal.net.

HARMON, DANIEL PATRICK, classics educator; b. Chgo., May 3, 1938; s. Bernard Leonard and Dorothy Mildred (Lesser) H. AB, Loyola U., Chgo., 1962; MA, Northwestern U., 1965, PhD, 1968; postgrad., Am. Sch. Classical Studies, Athens, Greece, 1975. Acting asst. prof. U. Wash., Seattle, 1967-68, asst. prof. classics, 1968-75, assoc. prof., 1975-76, assoc. prof. classics and comparative lit., 1976-84, prof. classics, 1984—2004, prof. emeritus, 2004—, chmn. classics, 1976-91; dir. U. Wash. Rome Ctr., 1992-2000. Contbr. articles and revs. to profl. jours. Mem. Am. Philol. Assn., Archaeol. Inst. Am., Société des Études Latines, County Louth (Ireland) Archaeol. and Hist. Soc., Classical Assn. Pacific Northwest (pres. 1974-75). Avocations: painting, photography, music. Home: 3149 NE 83rd St Seattle WA 98115-4751 Office: U Wash Dept Classics PO Box 353110 Seattle WA 98195-3110 Business E-Mail: dph@u.washington.edu.

HARMON, DAVID EDWARD, education educator, artist; b. St. Louis, May 30, 1953; s. Dewey Edward and Lorraine Irma Harmon; m. Susan Lee Nusbaum-Harmon, Nov. 21, 1981; children: James, Stephen, Daniel, Michael. BFA, Webster U., 1977; MFA, Pa. State U., 1982. Grad. tchg. asst. Pa. State U., 1979—82; vis. prof. of art U. of So. Miss., 1982—83; vis. asst. prof. of art and lectr. U. Ariz., 1984—85; asst. prof. of art Potsdam Coll. (SUNY), 1985—89; vis. lectr. Liverpool Inst. of Higher Edn., 1988; vis. painter Keystone Jr. Coll., La Plume, Pa., 1989—90; assoc. prof. of art Bethel Coll., 1990—; assoc. faculty Ind. U. at South Bend., 1998—, Ball State U., 2003—05; prof. art Savannah Coll. Art and Design, Ga., 2005—. Vis. artist Jentel Artist Residency Program (summer), Banner, Wyo., 2003; juror South Bend Regional Mus. of Art, 2001; panel chair Mid-Am. Southeast Coll. Art Assn. Conf., Louisville, 2000; panel moderator Mid-Am. Coll. Art Assn. Conf., Lexington, Ky., 1998; juror Art Festival, Plymouth, Ind., 1998, No. Ind. Artists Assn., 1997. One-man shows include Huntington Coll., Ind., 2004, Bachman Gallery, Ctr. for Visual Arts, Munster, Ind., 2004, Colfax Cultural Ctr., South Bend, Ind., 2003, Harbor Inn Gallery, New Buffalo,

Mich., 2003, So. Suburban Coll., Chgo., 2003, Andrews U., Berrien Springs, Mich., 2002, Fernwood Gallery, Niles, Mich., 2002, Pa. State U. at Altoona, 2001, West Valley Art Mus., Surprise, Ariz., 2001, Elgin Cmty. Coll., Ind., 2000, UP Gallery, U. Wyo., 1999, one-man shows include U. of Gt. Falls., Mont., 1999, Kishwaukee Coll., Malta, Ill., 1999, Spring Arbor Coll., 1998, U.S. Airforce Acad., Colo. Springs., 1997, South Bend Art Ctr., Ind., 1992—93, Contemporary Artlink Artspace, Ft. Wayne, Ind., 1992—93, Adams Hall Gallery, Art Dept. Wheaton Coll., 1991, Asbury Coll. Gallery, Wilmore, Ky., 1991, Napa Valley Coll., Calif., 1990, Reed Cultural Ctr., Las Vegas, 1989, Wilson Art Gallery, LeMoyne Coll., Syracuse, NY, 1989, Rockwell Kent Gallery, SUNY at Plattsburg, 1989, One-one Eight Gallery, Ann Arbor, Mich., 1988, Armstrong Gallery of Armstrong State Coll., U. Ga., 1987, Brainerd Hall Gallery, Potsdam Coll., 1986, Union Gallery, U. Ariz., 1985, Gallery One, Ohio State U., 1981, Jackson Hall Gallery, Ky. State U., 1981, Pa. State U., Ogontz Campus, 1980, exhibited in group shows at Period Gallery, Omaha, Neb., 2003, Am. Dream Exhbn., Ladover, Md., 2002, 8th Biennial Juried Fine Arts Exhbn., LaPorte, Ind., 2001, Stanley Clark Sch., South Bend, Ind., Allen R. Hite Art Inst., U. of Louisville, Ky., 2000, Burnell R. Roberts Gallery, Dayton, Ohio, 2000, Lawton Gallery, U. of Wis., 2000, Concordia U., Austin, Tex., 1998, Reconstruction Gallery, Santa Ana, Calif., 1997, Elder Gallery, Neb. Wesleyan U., 1997, Gallery One, New Buffalo, Mich., 1997, Weaver Gallery, Everest-Rohrer Chapel Fine Arts Ctr., Bethel Coll., Dunes Show, Gallery No., New Buffalo, Mich., 1996, Lake St. Gallery, Gary, Ind., 1995, Southwestern Mich. Coll., 1994, Buckham Gallery, Flint, Mich., 1993, Trinity Luth. Ch., 1993, Eleven East Ashland Gallery, Phoenix, 1991, Represented in permanent collections Jentel Artists Residency, Banner, Wyo., Munson-Williams Proctor Inst., Utica, NY, Mr. Gary Mason, Liverpool, Eng., Ms. Allison Alice, Potsdam, NY, Mr. Johan Parks, Stockton, Calif., The Jewish Mus. of Highland Pk., Chgo., U. of Mo., Bethel Coll., U. of So. Miss., SUNY Potsdam, Emmanuel Bapt. Ch., U. of Scranton, Pa., Environ. Health Labs, South Bend, Ind., Sanctuary River Pk. United Meth. Ch. and others. Recipient Outstanding Artists and Designers of the 20th Century, Cambridge, Eng., 2002, 2d Pl. award, 8th Biennial Juried Fine Arts Competition, LaPorte, Ind., 2001, Hon. Mention, Sacred Arts Exhbn., 1992, Best of Show award, 3d Biennial Exhbn., LaPorte, Ind., 1991, Merit award, Heartland Artist's Regional Exhbn., Plymouth, Ind., 1990, 1st Pl. Painting award, Sacred Arts Exhbn., Wheaton Coll., 1990, Best Landscape award, No. Country Regional Show, Gibson Gallery, 1987, Purchase award, U. of Mo. at St. Louis, 1976; fellowship, Jentel Artist Residency, 2003, Miss. Arts Commn. grant, 1984, Ford Found. grant, 1981. Mem.: Found. in Art Theory and Edn., Cooperstown Art Assn., Mid-Am. Coll. Art Assn., Coll. Art Assn., Nat. Coun. of Art Administrators. Office: Art Ctr Bethel Coll 1001 W McKinley Ave Mishawaka IN 46545 Home: 56521 Lake St Osceola IN 46561 Office Phone: 574-257-2670.

HARMON, DAVID EUGENE, optometrist, geneticist; b. Greeneville, Tenn., July 27, 1951; s. Carl Eugene and Kathryn Elizabeth (Colyer) H. BS, U. Tenn., 1973, MS, 1975; PhD, U. Ga., 1978; OD, New Eng. Coll. Optometry, 1989; computer cert., Carson-Newman Coll., 2000. Fellow U. Ga., Athens, 1978, U. Fla., Gainesville, 1979; vis. asst. prof. So. Ill. U., Carbondale, 1980-82; asst. prof. Clemson (S.C.) U., 1982-85, assoc. prof., 1985; internist VA Hosp., Boston, 1988, Children's Hosp., Boston, 1988-89, Dimock Community Health Ctr., Boston, 1989; eye specialist Morristown, Tenn., 1989—; geneticist, 1989—. Genetic cons. Nigerian Govt., 1980—. Contbr. articles to profl. jours. Mem. Sunday sch. Trinity United Meth. Ch., Greeneville, 1954—; sch. rep. New Eng. Coll. Optometry, 1987; coach nat. winning dairy cattle judging team, 1980, 81. Recipient Breeder All-Am. Dairy Animal award Am. Guernsey Cattle Club, 1973, Nat. 4-H Pub. Speaking award, 1969, Nat. 4-H Leadership award, 1970. Mem. Am. Optometric Assn., Am. Dairy Assn., Am. Soc. Animal Sci., Tenn. Optometric Assn., So. Coun. Optometrists, Am. Holstein Assn., Morristown C. of C., New Eng. Coll. Optometry Alumni Assn. (life), Lions Club Morristown, Sigma Xi, Alpha Zeta. Avocations: camping, hiking, ping pong/table tennis. Home and Office: 131 N Henry St Morristown TN 37814-4626

HARMON, FOSTER (LOREN FOSTER HARMON), arts consultant; b. Judsonia, Ark., Nov. 5, 1912; s. Alfred Roscoe and Mae (Foster) H.; m. Martha Rowles Foster, July 25, 1943. Student, Ind. U., 1930-32, Ohio U., 1932-33, DFA (hon.), 1993; BA, U. Iowa, 1935; MFA, 1936. Dir. Univ. and Exptl. Theatre, Ind. U., Bloomington, 1936-42; mgr. pub. rels. Sta. WKBN Broadcasting Corp., Youngstown, Ohio, 1943-48; owner, developer, dir. Pine Shores Park, Sarasota, Fla., 1950-54; v.p., dir. Players, Sarasota, 1955-57; dir. pub. rels. Ringling Mus. Art, Sarasota, 1958-59; dir. Oehlschlaeger Galleries, Sarasota, 1961-70; founder, owner, dir. Harmon Gallery, Naples, Fla., 1964-79; owner, dir. Foster Harmon Galleries Am. Art, Sarasota, 1979-93. V.p. Vandium Tool Co., Athens, Ohio, 1954-64; trustee, advisor Ohio U. Mus. Am. Art, Fla. Artists Group Mus. and Gallery, 1974-87; founder Foster and Martha Harmon Am. Art Study Ctr. and Archives Ohio U., 1995. Active Ringling Mus. Coun., 1957—; trustee Ringling Sch. Art, Sarasota, 1981—; bd. dirs. Asolo State Theater, 1982-89, Sarasota Opera Assn., 1983—, Van Wezel Performing Arts Hall Found., 1987—, Players, 1989-94. Recipient cert. of merit Ohio U., 1970. Mem. Am. Ednl. Theatre Assn. (founder), Am. Fedn. Arts, Sarasota Art Assn. (pres. 1959-60), Fla. League Arts, Smithsonian Instn., Archives Am. Art, Sarasota Arts Coun., St. Armands Assn. (pres. 1957-58), Internat. Platform Assn., Sarasota Yacht Club, Univ. Club. Home: 1255 N Gulfstream Ave Apt 1102 Sarasota FL 34236-8932

HARMON, GAIL MCGREEVY, lawyer; b. Kansas City, Kans., Mar. 15, 1943; d. Milton and Barbara (James) McGreevy; m. John W. Harmon, June 11, 1966; children: James, Eve. BA cum laude, Radcliffe Coll., 1965; JD cum laude, Columbia U., 1969. Bar: Mass. 1970, D.C. 1976, U.S. Dist. Ct. D.C. Assoc. Gaston Snow & Ely Bartlett, Boston, 1970-75, Steptoe & Johnson, Washington, 1975-76, Roisman, Kessler & Cashdan, Washington, 1976-77; ptnr. Harmon, Curran & Tousley, Washington, 1977-90, Harmon, Curran, Spielberg & Eisenberg, Washington, 1990—. Pres. Women's Legal Def. Fund, 1982-84; steering com. Emily's List, 1985—; bd. dirs. Population Svcs. Internat., 1998—. Mem. Population Svcs. Internat. (bd. dirs.) Democrat. Episcopalian. Office Phone: 202-328-3500. E-mail: gharmon@harmoncurran.com.

HARMON, GEORGE MARION, academic administrator; b. Memphis, Aug. 12, 1934; s. George Marion and Madie P. (Foster) H.; m. Bessie W. Porter, Dec. 27, 1958; children: Nancy R., Mary K., Elizabeth T., George Marion III. BA, Rhodes Coll., 1956; MBA, Emory U., 1957; DBA, Harvard U., 1963. Market rsch. analyst Continental Oil Co., Houston, 1957; rsch. assoc. Harvard U., 1960-63; asst. prof. Coll. Bus. Adminstrn., dir. Salzberg Meml. Transp. Program Syracuse U., N.Y., 1963-66; sr. assoc. sys. econs. divsn. Planning Rsch. Corp., Washington, 1966-67; prof., chmn. dept econs. and bus. adminstrn., dir. continuing edn. program in econs. and bus. adminstrn. Rhodes Coll. (formerly Southwestern at Memphis), Memphis, 1967-74; prof., dean divsn. bus. and mgmt. W.Va. Coll. Grad. Studies, Charleston, 1974-75; prof., dean Sch. Bus. and Mgmt. Saginaw Valley State Coll., University Center, Mich., 1975-78; pres. Millsaps Coll., Jackson, Miss., 1978-2000, pres. emeritus, sr. counsel spl. projects, 2000—; mem. faculty fin. Sch. Banking of the South, La. State U., 1968-72; dir. Audio Visual Sys., Inc., Tenn., 1970-72; v.p., treas. Allen Industries, Inc., Tenn., 1970-72; co-founder, v.p. Computer Survey Sys., Inc., Tenn., 1972-73. Bd. dirs., chmn. exec. compensation com. MacCarty Farms, Inc., Magee, Miss., 1982-95; bd. dirs. Entex, Inc., Houston, 1981-99; mem. So. Regional Edn. Bd., Atlanta, 1994-98; bd. dirs. Union Planters Bank of Miss. Contbr. articles on bus. adminstrn. to profl. jours. Bd. dirs. Fayetteville-Manlius (N.Y.) Ctrl. Sch. Dist., 1961—63, John Houston Wear Found., Jackson, 1979—2000, Eudora Welty Found., 1999—2003, Jackson Symphony Orch. Assn., 1981—85, Miss. Opera Assn., 1981—86, Cath. Charities of Miss., 2002—, Madison County Libr. Found., 2002—04, St. Catherine's Village Retirement Ctr. Found., 2002—; trustee, chmn. pers. and labor rels. com. Saginaw Osteo. Hosp., 1977—78; chmn. So. Colls. and Univs. Union, 1983—86, Miss. Found. Ind. Colls., 1982; com. and sec. Jackson Internat. Airport Authority, 1991—97; chmn., bd. dirs. Jackson Med. Edn. Dist., 1998—2000; univ. senate United Meth. Ch., 1990—2000; bd. dirs., mem. exec. com. he Cath. Found., Diocese of Miss., 2005—. Mem. NCAA (coun. 1986-92), Jackson C. of C. (bd. dirs. 1981-84), Newcomen Soc. Miss. (pres. 2001-, chmn. 2001-), Soc. Internat. Bus. Fellows, Jackson Country Club, Univ. Club, Capitol City Club, Harvard Club (N.Y.C.), Rotary, Phi Beta Kappa, Beta Gamma Sigma, Omicron Delta Kappa, Kappa Sigma (Pres.'s Commn. 2000—). Roman Catholic. Home and Office: 104 Adderbury Ct Ridgeland MS 39157-8709 Office Phone: 601-898-1800. Home Fax: 601-898-1801. Business E-Mail: harmon@millsaps.edu.

HARMON, HARRY WILLIAM, architect, former university administrator; b. San Francisco, Feb. 8, 1918; s. Harry A. and Isabel (Quagelli) A.; m. Lois Anna Holtin, July 28, 1953; children: Bruce Gregory, Mark Brian, Patricia Andree. B.Arch., U. So. Calif., 1941. Draftsman Kaufmann, Lippincott & Eggers (architects), Los Angeles, 1945-48; project architect UCLA, 1948-50, sr. architect, 1952-62; chief coll. facilities planning Calif. State Colls., Inglewood, Calif., 1962-67, asst. vice chancellor Los Angeles, 1967-69; vice chancellor phys. planning, devel. Calif. State Univs., 1969-75, exec. vice chancellor, 1975—83, exec. vice chancellor emeritus, 1983—. Spl. cons. FAO; mem. Nat. Panel Arbitrators. Chmn. bd. visitors USAF Installation Devel. for USAF Directorate of Engring. Svcs., 1989—. Lt. USNR, 1942-45; lt. comdr. 1950-51; capt. Res. ret. Fellow AIA (nat. dir. 1977-80, sec. 1981-85, Disting. Svc. award Calif. coun. 1985, Edward C. Kemper award 1986, chair nat. jud. coun. 1986-88, mem. coun. 1986-93), Assn. Univ. Architects; mem. Coun. Ednl. Facility Planners Internat., Soc. Coll. and U. Planners, Am. Arbitration Assn., U. So. Calif. Alumni Assn., Blue Key, Alpha Rho Chi. Home: 1410 La Plaza Dr San Marcos CA 92078-4712 E-mail: hharmon@owl.csusm.edu.

HARMON, JANE, theater producer; With Jane Harmon Assocs., N.Y.C. Prodr. The Last Night of Ballyhoo (by Alfred Uhry), Tony award Best Play, Driving Miss Daisy (by Alfred Uhry, Pulitzer prize), also nat. and internat. tours and Broadway, Buried Child (by Sam Shepard), A Life in the Theatre (by David Mamet), The Robber Bridegroom (by Waldman/Uhry); co-prodr. Asinamali!, Beloved Friend. Bd. dirs. Young Playwrights Inc.; mem. League of Am. Theatres and Prodrs. Inc., Off Broadway Theatre League, League of Profl. Theatre Women. Office: Jane Harmon Assocs One Lincoln Plaza Ste 280 New York NY 10023 Office Phone: 212-362-6836.

HARMON, LYNN ASTRID, broadcaster, writer; b. Wenatchee, Wash., Jan. 19, 1947; d. Maurice A and Betty Tipler Harmon; m. Bruce K Lumpkin, Feb. 17, 1973 (dec. May 1999); children: Tad W Lumpkin, Elin L Griffin. BA in radio, TV, film, U. Ky., 1969. Program coord. Internat. Telecable Productions, Balt., 1970—71; prod., show hostess WBKY-FM, Lexington, Ky., 1966—70; instr. Broadcasting Inst. of Md., 1971—88; sales promotion mgr. WBFF-TV, Balt., 1971—76; pub. rels., mktg. dir. Chattanooga Theatre Ctr., 1995—98; dir. underwriting and partnership develop. Thurston Cmty. TV, Olympia, Wash., 2002—, comty. rels. and outreach dir., 2004—. Freelance writer, 2001—; freelance broadcast talent, 1970—; performing arts reporter, critic The Sitting Duck, Olympia, 2003; bd. dirs. Capital Playhouse, Olympia, Wash., 2005—. Author: Two Rings Around the Moon, 2000, Notes on Parenting, 2001, (plays) All for One: A Forum, 2004. Publicist Concert Artists of Balt., 1990—91; pres., gen. mgr. Harmony Unlimited, 1985—86; mem. Balt. Symphony Chorus, Chattanooga Theatre Ctr. Mem.: South Sound Partners in Philanthropy. Democrat. Avocations: theater, films, skiing, music. Office: Thurston Cmty TV 440 C Yauger Way Olympia WA 98502

HARMON, MARY FRANCES, principal; b. Sevierville, Tenn., Aug. 15, 1952; d. James Vincent and Veryl Alice Turner; m. Marvin D. Harmon, Dec. 16, 1972; children: Brad M., Michael T., Melissa A. BS, U. Tenn., 1975; Master's degree, Union Coll., Barbourville, Ky., 1978; EdS, Lincoln Meml. U., Harrogate, Tenn., 1995; EdD, East Tenn. State U., 2001. Cert. sch. adminstr. Tenn. Tchr. Pigeon Forge (Tenn.) Elem., 1976—86, Pigeon Forge (Tenn.) Mid., 1986—97; asst. prin. Sevierville Primary, 1997—2000; asst. supr. Sevier County Schs. Spl. Edn., Sevierville, 2000—01; prin. Trula Lawson Early Childhood Ctr., Sevierville, 2001—. Named Tchr. of Yr., Pigeon Forge Mid., 1997, Sevier County Schs., 1997, East Tenn. Tchr. of Yr., Tenn. Assn. Mid. Schs., 1997. Republican. Baptist. Avocations: reading, exercise, U. of Tenn. football, Tenn. Titans football. Office: Trula Lawson Early Childhood Ctr 550 Eastgate Rd Sevierville TN 37862

HARMON, MONICA RENEE, music educator; b. Greenville, Ohio, June 3, 1960; d. William Neil Harmon and Julie Ann Erk; m. Ronald Burk Lummis, Apr. 3, 1999. MusB magna cum laude, Morehead State U., 1983; BS, W.Va. State Coll., 1986; MusM, U. Miami, 1996. Profl. Tchr. Cert. Nat. Bd. for Profl. Tchg. Stds., 2002. Permanent substitute tchr. South Charleston (W.Va.) Jr. High, 1987—88; music tchr. Coconut Grove (Fla.) Elem., 1988—90; music dir. George Wash. Carver Mid. Sch., Miami, Fla., 1990—, dept. head electives, 1996—. Children's choir dir. Coral Gables (Fla.) Congl. Ch., 1991—94, Plymouth Congl. Ch., Coconut Grove, 1995—96; vocalist Coral Gables Chamber Symphony and Opera Co., 2003—, Polyphony, Renaissance Ensemble, 2004—. Choir mem. St. Thomas Episc. Parish, 2002—. Mem.: Am. Choral Dirs. Assn., Fla. Orch. Assn., Fla. Vocal Assn., Fla. Bandmasters Assn., Music Educators Nat. Conf. Home: 9720 SW 146th St Miami FL 33176 Office: George Washington Carver Middle School 4901 Lincoln Dr Miami FL 33133 Office Phone: 305-444-7388. Personal E-mail: harmonlummis@yahoo.com. E-mail: harmonm@gwcm.dadeschools.net.

HARMON, PATRICK, historian, retired editor, retired commentator; b. St. Louis, Sept. 2, 1916; s. Jack and Laura (Duchesne) H.; m. Anne M. Worland, Aug. 31, 1940; children— Michael, Timothy, Kathleen, Daniel, John, Sheila, Peggy, Brigid, Kevin, Teresa, Christopher. AB, U. Ill., 1939. Sports editor News-Gazette, Champaign, Ill., 1942-47, Gazette, Cedar Rapids, Iowa, 1947-51, Post, Cin., 1951-85; ret., 1985; sports commentator Sta. WCPO-TV, 1953-56, Sta. WKRC, 1958, Sta. WLW-TV, 1958-68; curator, historian Coll. Football Hall of Fame, Kings Island, Ohio, 1986-95; historian Nat. Football Found., Morristown, NJ, 1994—2005; ret., 2005. Contbg. sports editor: World Book, 1959—2004. Recipient Fred Hutchinson Meml. award for community service, 1969; named Internat. Churchmen's Sports Writer of Year, 1973 Mem. Sigma Chi. Home and Office: 608 Maple Trace Cincinnati OH 45246 Office Phone: 513-782-6457.

HARMON, PEALINE PALMER, librarian; b. Macon, N.C., Mar. 14, 1942; d. Richard E. Palmer, Carrie B. Palmer; m. Roosevelt Harmon; children: Jewelle Lynnette, Joycelyn Rosetta. BS, N.C. Ctrl. U., 1964; MLS, Atlanta U., 1971. Cert. Cert. libr. Va. Sch. libr. Portsmouth Sch. Sys., Portsmouth, Va., 1966—73; acad. libr. Norfolk State U., Norfolk, Va., 1973—74; libr. J. Sargent Reynolds C.C., Richmond, Va., 1974—79, Weeks Mid. Sch., Newton Centre, Mass., 1980—81, Portsmouth City Sch., 1981—90; reference libr. Norfolk State U., 1990—2000; acad. libr. Tidewater C.C., Virginia Beach, Va., 2001—. Active Portsmouth Libr. Bd., Hampton Rds. chpt. Va. Breast Cancer Found. Mem.: ALA, AAUW, Va. Libr. Assn., Las Amigas, Inc. (v.p. 2000—01), Delta Sigma Theta. Avocations: gardening, collecting recipes. Office: Tidewater Cmty Coll College Way Virginia Beach VA 23456 Home: PO Box 6630 Portsmouth VA 23703-0630

HARMON, RENATE MARIA, special education educator; b. Balt., Md., Oct. 14, 1954; d. Glenn Walcott and Margareta Eizabet Harmon. BS, Plymouth State Coll., 1978; M, Notre Dame Coll., 1995. Cert. experienced educator NH, 1978, elem. tchr. K-8 NH, general spl. edn., learning disabilities, emotionally disturbed NH. Sci. tchr., administr. asst. Spaulding Youth Ctr., Tilton, NH, 1978—84; asst. dir. Lakes Region Day Care, Laconia, NH; administr. asst. Rundlett Mid. Sch., Concord Sch. Dist., Concord, NH, 1982—87; tchr. Pittsfield Elem. Sch., Pittsfield, NH, 1987—89; spl. edn. tchr. Merrimack Valley Sch., Penacook, NH, 1989—. Head coach NH Spl. Olympics Blazing Colors Team, Penacook, NH, 1995—. Bldg. rep. Merrimack Valley Edn., NH, 2003—; mem. chmn. Assn. NEA-NH, NH, 2003—; justice of the peace Justice of the Peace State of NH, Penacook, NH, 1997—. Mem.: Coun. for Exceptional Children, Am. Legion Auxiliary State of NH (pres. 1999—). Independent. Cath. Avocations: travel, camping, gardening. Office: Penacook Elem Sch 60 Village St Concord NH 03301 Office Phone: 603-753-4891.

HARMON, TERESA WILTON, lawyer; b. 1968; BS, U. Ala., 1990, MBA, 1991; JD, U. Chgo., 1994. Bar: Ill. 1994. Clk. for Hon. Phyllis Kravitch, U.S. Ct. Appeals (11th cir.), 1994; with Sidley Austin Brown & Wood LLP, Chgo., 1995—, ptnr., 2003—. Adj. prof. U. Ill. Coll. Law. Mem.: ABA (sect. bus. law and uniform comml. code com.), Chgo. Bar Assn. (co-chair comml. fin. and transactions com.). Office: Sidley Austin Brown and Wood LLP Bank One Plz 10 S Dearborn St Chicago IL 60603

HARMON BROWN, VALARIE JEAN, hospital laboratory director, information systems executive; b. Peoria, Ill., June 21, 1948; d. Donald Joseph and Frances Elizabeth (Classen) Harmon; m. James Roger Brown, Aug. 21, 1982 (dec. May 1994). BSMT, Northwestern U., Chgo., 1970. Med. tech. Evanston (Ill.) Hosp., 1970-71, chief tech., 1971-75; med. tech. II M.D. Anderson Hosp., Houston, 1975-76; dir. lab. Physicians Ref. Lab., Houston, 1978-81, Med. Ctr. Hosp., Conroe, Tex., 1981-91, Palo Pinto Gen. Hosp., Mineral Wells, Tex., 1993-94; sales mgr. Long Beach (Calif.) Meml. Med. Ctr., 1995-96; quality assurance/regulatory affairs mgr. Consol. Med. Labs., Lake Bluff, Ill., 1996-97; adminstrv. dir. Bio-Diagnostics Labs., Torrance, Calif., 1997-2000; asst. dir. lab. Parkview Cmty. Hosp. Med. Ctr., Riverside, Calif., 2000—01; regional mgr. Memphis Antech Diagnostics, Southaven, Miss., 2001—03; lab. mgr. Doctor's Data, Inc., St. Charles, Ill., 2003—04, Idexx Labs., Elmhurst, Ill., 2004—. Lab. cons. Texaco Chem. Wellness Program, Conroe, 1989; health career sponsor Willis Ind. Sch. Dist., Tex., 1989, 90; mem. adv. bd. Med. Lab. Technician program Weatherford Coll., 1994. Coord. blood drive Gulf Coast Region Blood Ctr., 1986-91; sponsor colon cancer screening Montgomery County Health Fair, 1986; sponsor Camp Sunshine/Lions Club, 1988; sponsor cholesterol screening Med. Ctr. Hosp. Health Fair, 1989. Mem. NAFE, Am. Soc. Clin. Pathologists, Am. Soc. Med. Technologists, Clin. Lab. Mgmt. Assn. Republican. Roman Catholic. Avocations: embroidery, reading, antiques. Home: 313 Larsdotter Ln Geneva IL 60134 Office Phone: 630-516-7966. Business E-Mail: valarie-brown@idexx.com.

HARMOND, RICHARD PETER, historian, educator; b. NYC, Mar. 19, 1929; s. William and Violet (Makein) H. BA, Fordham U., 1951; MA, Columbia U., 1954, PhD, 1966. Assoc. prof. history St. John's U., N.Y.C., 1957—. Co-author: Long Island as America, 1977, A History of Memorial Day: Unity, Discord and the Pursuit of Happiness, 2002; co-editor: Technology in the 20th Century, 1983, Biographical Dictionary of American and Canadian Naturalists and Environmentalists, 1997; assoc. editor L.I. Hist. Jour., 1989—2003, mem. editl. bd., 2003—; contbr. articles to profl. jours. With U.S. Army, 1951-53. Mem. Orgn. Am. Historians, Soc. History of Tech., Theodore Roosevelt Assn. (trustee 1994-97), Phi Alpha Theta (paper prize com. 1994-97). Office: St John's U Hist Dept Jamaica NY 11439-0001

HARMONY, MARLIN DALE, chemistry professor; b. Lincoln, Nebr., Mar. 2, 1936; s. Philip and Helen Irene (Michal) H. AA, Kansas City (Mo.) Jr. Coll., 1956; BS in Chem. Engring., U. Kans., 1958; PhD in Chemistry, U. Calif.-Berkeley, 1961. Asst. prof. U. Kans., Lawrence, 1962-67, assoc. prof., 1967-71, prof., 1971-98, chmn., 1980-88, prof. emeritus, 1998—. Panel mem. NRC-Nat. Bur. Standards., 1969-78; mem. review panel NSF, 1977, 92. Author: Introduction to Molecular Energies and Spectra, 1972; contbg. editor: Physics Vade Mecum, 1981; mem. editorial bd. Structural Chemistry, 1989-98; contbr. articles to profl. jours.; patentee in field. Postdoctoral fellow NSF Harvard U., 1961-62. Fellow AAAS; mem. Am. Chem. Soc., Am. Phys. Soc., Sigma Xi, Alpha Chi Sigma, Phi Lambda Upsilon, Tau Beta Pi Democrat. Home: 1033 Avalon Rd Lawrence KS 66044-2505 Office: U Kans Dept Chemistry Lawrence KS 66045-0001 Business E-Mail: harmony@ku.edu.

HARMS, DAVID B., lawyer; b. Whittier, Calif., 1954; BA, SUNY, Purchase, 1978; JD, NYU, 1984. Bar: NY 1985. Law clk. Judge Edward Weinfeld US Dist. Ct. (so. dist.) NY, 1984—85; assoc. Sullivan & Cromwell, NYC, now ptnr., and coord. broker/dealer regulation practice area. Office: Sullivan & Cromwell 125 Broad St Fl 28 New York NY 10004-2489 Office Phone: 212-558-4000. Office Fax: 212-558-3588. Business E-Mail: harmsd@sullcrom.com.

HARMS, ELIZABETH LOUISE, artist; b. Milw., May 26, 1924; d. Frederick George and Veva (Sanderson) H.; m. Douglas Derwood Craft, Sept. 8, 1951. Diploma, Sch. Art Inst. Chgo., 1950, BFA, 1963, MFA, 1964. One-man shows: 55 Mercer St., N.Y.C., 1980, Fischbach Gallery, N.Y.C., 1975, Carnegie Inst. Mus. Art, 1969, Condeso/Lawler, 1982, 84, 85, 86, 90, 93, Gallery Jupiter, Little Silver, N.J., 1987, Jersey City Mus., 1988, Paul McCarron, N.Y.C., 2001, DVA, Narrowsburg, N.Y., 1996, 2002; group shows include Moravian Coll., Bethlehem, Pa., 1978, Jersey City Mus., 1980, 86, North of New Brunswick, South of N.Y., Rutgers-Newark, 1981, Coll. of New Rochelle, 1982, T. Bell Invitational, Condeso/Lawler, 1985, Montclair (N.J.) Art Mus., 1984, 86, Robeson Mus., Rutgers, Newark, 1988, Invitational Acad. & Inst. for Arts & Scis., N.Y.C., 1992, Skidmore Coll., Saratoga Springs, N.Y., 1993, So. Allegheny Mus. Art, Loretto, Pa., 1994, NAD Invitational, N.Y.C., 2004. Recipient Armstrong prize, Art Inst. Chgo., 1962; grantee, Tiffany Found., 1977. Home: PO Box 245 Jeffersonville NY 12748-0245

HARMS, JOHN KEVIN, lawyer; b. Bitburg Air Base, Germany, Oct. 19, 1960; s. William Robert and Catherine Dorothy (Heslin) H.; m. Pamela Tinkham, 1988; children: William Cameron Harms, Wade Devlin Harms. Student Wash. Seminar in Econ. Policy, Am. U., 1981; BPA magna cum laude, Loyola U., New Orleans, 1982; JD, Northwestern U., 1985; MBA, Western New Eng. Coll., 1989; postgrad., U.S. Army Command and Gen. Staff Coll., 1997, USAF Air War Coll., 1997, U.S. Navy Coll. Continuing Edn. Bar: Ill. 1985, U.S. Army Ct. Mil. Review 1986, U.S. Ct. Mil. Appeals 1991, Mass. 1994. Commd. 2d lt. USAR, 1982, advance through grades to lt. col., 2001; aide-de-camp to comdg. gen. 33d Inf. Brigade, Ill. Army Nat. Guard, 1983-85; rsch. asst. Am. Bar Found., Chgo., 1985; legal assistance atty. Office of Staff Judge Advocate, Ft. Devens, Mass., 1986; trial def. counsel U.S. Army Trial Def. Svc., Ft. Devens, Mass., 1986-87, sr. def. counsel, 1987-90; deputy staff judge adv. Office of Staff Judge Adv. Mil. Traffic Mgmt. Command Ea. Area, Bayonne, N.J., 1990-92; internat. ops. law atty. Third Mil. Law Ctr., U.S. Army Res., Boston, 1992-95; atty.-advisor, environ. law specialist Office of the Staff Judge Adv., Fort Devens, 1992-95; chief counsel Devens Res. Forces Tng. Area, Devens, Mass., 1995-96; atty., advisor govt. contracts and chief environ. law Electronic Sys. Ctr., Hanscom AFB, Mass., 1996—2003; adminstrv. and contract law atty. 94th Regional Support Command, USAR, Devens, 1996—2000; dep. staff judge adv. 94th Regional Support Command, Ft. Devens, 2000—; assoc. gen. counsel environment, installations & logistics Defense Logistics Agency, Fort Belvoir, Va., 2003—. Mem. North Western Law Review, 1985; mem. 1st del. of Am. criminal lawyers to the Peoples Rep. of China as part of Citizen Amb. Program, People to People Internat., 1987. Cubmaster Cub Scout Pack 50, Boy Scouts Am., 1999—2001; leader den Weblos/Boy Scouts Am., 2001—03; mem. sixth ring U.S. Olympic Com., 2003; bd. trustee North Ctrl. Charter Essential Sch., Fitchburg, Mass., 2002—, sec., 2003—. Named Outstanding Young Man Am., 1988. Mem. ABA, Fed. Bar Assn., Assn. U.S. Army, Navy League U.S., Boston Bar Assn. (mem. environ. law sect.), Bluekey Nat. Honor Fraternity, Alpha Sigma Nu, Delta Sigma Pi, Beta Gamma Sigma. Avocations: racewalking, novel writing, Kindai Inazuma Ryu karate (green belt). Office: Office Gen Counsel Defense Logistics Agency 8725 John J Kingman Rd Ste 1644 Fort Belvoir VA 22060 E-mail: john.harms@us.army.mil.

HARMS, NANCY ANN, nursing educator; d. Orval M. and Ruth Marie (Nelson) H.; m. Gerhart J. Wehrbein. Diploma, Bryan Meml. Hosp., 1971; BS in Natural Sci., Nebr. Wesleyan U., 1971; BSN, U. Nebr., 1975, MSN, 1977, PhD, 1988. RN, Nebr. Staff nurse, asst. supr., ins. coord. Brewster Hosp., Holdrege, Nebr., 1971-72; instr. Immanuel Sch. Nursing, Omaha, 1972-75; coord. nursing care plan devel. Hosp. Info. Sys. U. Nebr. Med. Ctr., Omaha, 1975; asst. chair dept. Coll. St. Mary, Omaha, 1975-80; curriculum coord. Midland Luth. Coll., Fremont, Nebr., 1980-88, chair nursing divsn., 1988—. Mem. ANA (mem. Ho. of Dels.), Nebr. Nurses' Assn. (Nurse Excellence award, Excellence in Writing award jour., adv. Nebr. Student Nurses Assn., mem. various coms.), Nat. League Nursing, Sigma Theta Tau (theta omega, gamma pi chpts.).

HARMS, ROBERT THOMAS, linguist, educator; b. Peoria, Ill., Apr. 12, 1932; s. Wilbert Erwin and Mildred Matilda (Thomas) H.; m. Sirpa Helina Aaltonen, July 1, 1956; children: Kirsti Maria, Ritva Helena, Eerik Thomas, Timo Kalevi. AB, U. Chgo., 1952, A.M. in Slavic Langs, 1956, PhD in Linguistics, 1960; postgrad. (Fulbright scholar), U. Helsinki, Finland, 1954-56; U.S.-Soviet exchange, Leningrad State U., 1962-63. Instr. U. Tex., Austin, 1958-61, asst. prof. linguistics, 1961-64, asso. prof., 1965-67, prof., 1967—, chmn. dept. linguistics, 1973-77. Vis. asst. prof. Columbia U., 1960, vis. asso. prof., 1965; vis. asso. prof. Ohio State U., 1964; U.S.-Hungary exchange prof. U. Szeged (Hungarian Acad. Scis.), Budapest, 1967-68 Author: Estonian Grammar, 1962, Finnish Structural Sketch, 1964, Introduction to Phonological Theory, 1968; Editor: (with Emmon Bach) Universals in Linguistic Theory, 1968. Fulbright research grantee Finland, 1968; Nat. Acad. Scis. exchange prof. Acad. Scis. USSR and Estonian Acad. Scis. Mem. Linguistic Soc. Am., Finno-Ugrian Soc., Phi Beta Kappa. Lutheran. Home: 2609 Deerfoot Trl Austin TX 78704-2715 Office: U Tex Dept Linguistics Austin TX 78712

HARMS, ROBERT WAYNE, lawyer; b. Stanley, N.D., Aug. 3, 1955; s. Penn Baldwin and Eva Frances (Frisinger) H.; m. Cherie D. Olson, Oct. 11, 1986. BS in Polit. Sci., N.D. State U., 1977; JD, U. N.D., 1980. Bar: N.D. 1980, U.S. Dist. Ct. N.D. 1982, U.S. Ct. Appeals (8th cir.) 1984. Founding ptnr. Harms Law Offices and predecessor firms, Williston, N.D., 1980-92; counsel Gov.'s Office, Bismarck, 1992—2003; gov. rels. cons. The Harms Group, 2003—. Mem. Ethics Com., Bismarck, 1984-85, Legal Counsel for Indigents, Bismarck, 1985-89, Law Sch. Com., Grand Forks, N.D., 1989-91. Vice chmn. Rep. Party Dists. 1 and 2, Williston, 1986-91; bd. dirs. Crime Stoppers, Williston, 1989-92; legis. candidate N.D. Rep. Party, Williston, 1988. Scholar Burtness Found., 1978, Blikre scholar Clare T. Blikre, 1976, scholar Nat. Inst. Trial Advocates, 1990; recipient Allan Smith award Allan Smith Co., Grand Forks, 1980. Mem. ABA, ATLA, N.D. Trial Lawyers Assn., Williston Area C. of C. (bd. dirs. 1990-93), Lions, Blue Key Nat. Honor Frat. Avocations: sailing, landscaping, hiking, woodwork. Home: 815 N Mandan St Bismarck ND 58501-3618 Office: The Harms Group 815 Maddau Rd Bismarck ND 58501

HARMS, STEVEN ALAN, lawyer; b. Detroit, Feb. 15, 1949; s. Herbert Rudolph and Elsa Jane (McClelland) H.; m. Nancy Gayle Banta, June 26, 1971; children: Jennifer Elizabeth, Heather Lynn, Robin Ann. BA, Hope Coll., 1970; JD, Detroit Coll. Law, 1975. Bar: Mich. 1975, U.S. Dist. Ct. (so. dist.) Mich. 1975, U.S. Ct. Appeals (6th cir.) 1982; bd. cert. creditors rights specialist. Ptnr. Muller, Muller, Richmond, Harms, Myers & Sgroi, P.C., Birmingham, Mich.; sec. gen. practice session State Bar Mich., 1982-83; mediator Oakland County Cir. Ct., 1990—. Lectr. in field; adj. prof. Bus. Law Walsh Coll., Troy, Mich., 1990—. Author: Successful Collection of a Judgement, 1981, Post Judgement Collection, 1988, Handling the Collection Case in Michigan, 1989, rev. edit., 2003, Collection Law, 2003, A Credit Manager's Guide to Collection Law, 2003; co-author: Attorney Fee Agreements, 1995; contbg. editor: Michigan Civil Procedure, 1997, rev. edit., 2002. Bd. dirs. fin. com. YMCA, North Oakland County, Mich., 1987-2004, chmn. bd., 1990-91. Mem.: Pearson Yacht Owners Assn. (commodore 1988-90), Hunter Sailing Assn. (vice commodore 1985-86, commodore 1987-88). Republican. Office: Muller Muller Richmond Harms Myers & Sgroi PC 33233 Woodward Ave Birmingham MI 48009-0903 Office Phone: 248-645-2440. Business E-Mail: steve@mullerfirm.com.

HARMSEN, DOROTHY, food products executive; b. Minneapolis; m. William Harmsen, 1939; children: William Jr., Robert, Michael. Student, U. Minn. Co-founder Jolly Rancher Candies, Wheatridge, Colo., 1942. Author: Two Comprehensive Western Art Volumes, 1972-79. Bd. dirs. Denver Art Mus., Arthritis Found., Salvation Army, Harmsen Mus. Art, Habitat for Humanity. Home: 3131 E Alameda Ave Denver CO 80209-3409

HARMSEN, TYRUS GEORGE, librarian; b. Pomona, Calif., July 24, 1924; s. Fred H. and Hazel H.; m. Lois Spaulding, Apr. 15, 1955; children: Mark Spaulding, Caroline Lora. AB, Stanford, 1947, MA, 1950; AB in L.S, U. Mich., 1948. Cataloguer dept. manuscripts Henry E. Huntington Libr., San Marino, Calif., 1948—49, 1950—59; coll. librarian Occidental Coll., L.A., 1959—86, dir. book arts program, prof. bibliography, 1986—91. Vis. lectr. Sch. Library Sci., U. So. Calif., 1958, 68. Author: The Plantin Press of Saul and Lillian Marks, 1960, Joseph Arnold Foster, Printer, 1998. Served with AUS, 1943-46. Council on Library Resources fellow, 1969 Mem.: Zamorano, Rounce and Coffin (Los Angeles) (treas. 1956-91). Presbyterian. Home: 1300 Medford Rd Pasadena CA 91107-1603

HARMUTH, HENNING F., electrical engineer, educator; b. Vienna, July 27, 1928; arrived in U.S., 1969; s. Adolf Alois Harmuth and Margarete Beckert; m. Anna Elisabeth Hoene-Harmuth, June 21, 1957 (div. 1978); 1 child, Ursula; m. Anne Blackshear Spragins-Harmuth, June 27, 1979. Diploma in Engring., Tech. U., Vienna, Austria, 1951; D of Tech. Scis., Tech. U., 1953. Registered engr., Md., 1980. Cons. engr. pvt. practice, Karlsruhe, Germany, 1965—71; prof. Cath. U. Am., Washington, 1971—96; ret., 1996. Cons. UN/UNESCO, Warangal, India, 1972. Author: Transmission of Information by Orthogonal Functions, 1969, Transmission of Information by Orthogonal Functions, 2d edit., 1972, Sequency Theory - Foundations and Applications, 1977, Acoustic Imaging with Electronic Circuits, 1981, Autennas and Waveguides for Nonsinusoidal Waves, 1984, Propagation of Nonsinusoidal Electromagnetic Waves, 1986, Information Theory Applied to Space-Time Physics, 1989, Radiation of Nonsimusoidal Electromagnetic Waves, 1990, Propagation of Electromagnetic Signals, 1994, Electromagnetic Signals - Reflection, Focusing, Distortion, and Their Applications, 1999, Interstellar Propagation of Electromagnetic Signals, 2000, Modified Maxwell Eduations in Quantum Electrodynamics, 2001, Calculus of Finite Differences in Quantum Electrodynamics, 2003, Dogma of the Continuum and the Calculus of Finite Differences in Quantum Physics, 2005; contbr. articles to profl. jours. Mem.: IEEE (life). Home: 757 Bayou Dr Destin FL 32541

HARNACK, DON STEGER, retired lawyer; b. Milw., June 19, 1928; s. Benjamin John and Katherine (Steger) H.; m. Rosemarie Ball, Oct. 17, 1959; children: Christopher Wallen, Gretchen Marie, Pamela Ann. BS, U. Wis., 1950; LLB, Harvard U., 1953. Bar: Wis. 1953, U.S. Dist. Ct. (ea. dist.) Wis. 1955, U.S. Tax Ct. 1957, Ill. 1959, U.S. Dist. Ct. (no. dist.) Ill. 1962, U.S. Ct. Appeals (6th and 7th cirs.) 1963, U.S. Ct. Claims 1966, U.S. Ct. Appeals (8th cir.) 1971, U.S. Supreme Ct. 1972. Assoc. Quarles, Spence & Quarles, Milw., 1955-57; trial atty. regional counsel IRS, Chgo., 1957-61; assoc. Dixon, Todhunter, Knouf & Holmes, Chgo., 1961-65; ptnr. McDermott, Will & Emery, Chgo., 1965-96, of counsel, 1997-98; ret., 2001. Contbr. articles to profl. jours. Active Winnetka (Ill.) Zoning Bd., 1971-75; park bd. atty. Winnetka Park Dist., 1978-83; pres. N.E. Ill. coun. Boy Scouts Am., 1982-83; life trustee ULC Boys and Girls Club, Chgo., UL Civic and Arts Found.; trustee Village of Winnetka, 1984-88. Served with U.S. Army, 1953-55, USNR, 1959-69. Recipient Silver Beaver award Boy Scouts Am., 1984, named distinguished Eagle Scout, 1996. Mem. ABA, Ill. Bar Assn., Wis. Bar Assn., Union League Club (bd. dirs., officer, v.p. 1981-87, pres. 1987-88). Republican. Avocations: fishing, golf, reading. E-mail: bigcoho2@aol.com.

HARNDEN, EDWIN A., lawyer; BA Columbia U., 1969, JD Columbia U., 1972. Mng. ptnr. Barran Liebman LLP, Portland, Oreg.; pres. Oreg. State Bar, 2001—02. Past pres. Profl. Liability Fund. Fellow: Am. Coll. of Labor and Employment Lawyers, Am. Bar Found. (life). Office: ODS Tower 601 SW 2d Ave Ste 2300 Portland OR 97204-3159 Office Phone: 503-276-2101. E-mail: eharnden@barran.com.

HARNEDY, JOAN CATHERINE HOLLAND, retired systems analyst; b. Hackensack, N.J., May 31, 1936; d. John Joseph and Marion Rita (Sexton) Holland; m. Edmund Richard Harnedy, Dec. 29, 1962; children: Richard J., Julia Ann. BS, Coll. New Rochelle, 1957. Adminstrv. asst. Ford Found. funded, Rockefeller Found. funded, 1957—59; sys. analyst IBM, White Plains, NY, 1960—65; publicity chairperson YWCA, White Plains, NY, 1966—69; ret., 1969. Travel cons., photographer, White Plains, 1970—92. Supporter Am. Heart Assn., Am. Cancer Soc., Nat. Children's Cancer Fund, Children's Cancer Rsch. Found., Nature Conservancy. Mem.: NAFE, Phi Chi. Avocations: writing, gardening, art history, photography, gourmet cooking.

HARNER, JAMES LOWELL, language educator; b. Washington, Ind., Mar. 24, 1946; s. Thomas Lloyd and Ruth Ellen (Clark) H.; m. Darinda Jane Wilson, Aug. 26, 1967; 1 child, Lenée Francais. BS magna cum laude, Ind. State U., 1968; MA, U. Ill., 1970, PhD, 1972. Prof. English Bowling Green (Ohio) State U., 1971-88, Tex. A&M U., College Station, 1988—. Author: Literary research Guide, 1989 (Choice Mag. Outstanding Acad. Book 1990), 4th edit., 2002, English Renaissance Prose Fiction, 1978, 3d edit., 1992, On Compiling an Annotated Bibliography, 1983-2000, Samuel Daniel and Michael Drayton, 1980, Directory of Scholarly Presses, 1991, (online database) World Shakespeare Bibliography Online, 1996—, (Besterman medal 1997, Besterman/McColvin medal, 2001); editor World Shakespeare Bibliography, 1988—, Essential Bibliographies Series, 1985-96; mem. editl. bd. Seventeenth-Century News, 1973—, Lit. Rsch., 1984—, Shakespeare Yearbook, 1992—, Shakespeare Quar., 1993—. Mem. MLA, The Bibliog. Soc., Shakespeare Assn. of Am., Internat. Shakespeare Assn., Bibliog. Soc. of Am. Democrat. Presbyterian. Avocations: book collecting, travel, manuscript collecting. Home: 4736 Stonebriar Cir College Station TX 77845 Office: World Shakespeare Bibliog Tex A&m U Dept English College Station TX 77843-4227 Office Phone: 979-845-3400. Business E-Mail: j-harner@tamu.edu.

HARNER, MICHAEL JAMES, anthropologist, educator; b. Washington, Apr. 27, 1929; s. Charles Emory and Virginia (Paxton) H.; m. June Knight (Kocher), 1951; children: Teresa J., James E.; m. Sandra Ferial (Dickey), 1966. AB, U. Calif., Berkeley, 1953, PhD, 1963; PhD (hon.), Calif. Inst. of Integral Studies, 2003. Asst. prof. Ariz. State U., 1958—61; from sr. mus. anthropologist to assoc. rsch. anthropologist and asst. dir., Hearst Mus. Anthropology U. Calif., Berkeley, 1961—66; from vis. assoc. prof. to assoc. prof. Columbia U., N.Y.C., 1966—70; from assoc. prof. to prof. grad. faculty New Sch. Social Rsch., N.Y.C., 1970—87, chmn. dept. anthropology, 1973—77; internat. tchr. shamanism, 1977—; founder, dir. Ctr. for Shamanic Studies, Norwalk, Conn., 1980—87; founder, pres., trustee Found. for Shamanic Studies, Mill Valley, Calif., 1985—. Field rsch. Harvard U. Upper Gila expdn., 1948, Upper Amazon Basin, 1956-57, 60-61, 64, 69, 73, Western North Am., 1951-53, 59, 65, 76, 78, Lapland, 1983, 84, Can. Arctic, 1987; vis. assoc. prof. U. Calif., Berkeley, 1971, 72, vis. prof., 1975; vis. assoc. prof. Yale U., 1970; co-organizer first Internat. Congress on Shamanism, Moscow, 1999. Author: Population Pressure and the Social Evolution of Agriculturalists, 1970, The Jivaro: People of the Sacred Waterfalls, 1972, 2d edit., 1984, The Ecological Basis for Aztec Sacrifice, 1977, The Way of the Shaman, 1980, 3d edit., 1990; co-author: Cannibal, 1979, Core Practices in the Shamanic Treatment of Illness, 1999; editor: Hallucinogens and Shamanism, 1973. Fellow Social Sci. Rsch. Coun., Doherty Found., Am. Mus. Nat. History fellow. Fellow Am. Anthrop. Assn., Royal Anthrop. Inst. G.B. and Ireland, NY Acad. Scis.; mem. Am. Ethnol. Soc., Soc. Ethnohistory, Internat. Transpersonal Assn. (bd. dirs. 1982-85, 89-91), Assn. for the Anthropology of Consciousness, Inst. Andean Studies, Internat. Soc. Shamanistic Rsch., Soc. for Anthropology of Lowland South America. Office: Found Shamanic Studies PO Box 1939 Mill Valley CA 94942-1939 E-mail: michaelharner@shamanism.org.

HARNER, WILLIAM BERKELEY, III, music educator; s. William Berkeley Jr. and Vanessa Jean Harner. B of Music Edn., Shanandoah U. Band dir. Madison (Va.) County HS, 2002—. Mem.: Music Educators Nat. Conf., Va. Music Educators Assn.

HARNESS, WILLIAM EDWARD, tenor; b. Pendleton, Oreg., Nov. 26, 1940; s. Edward Cleo and Edna Margaret (Senn) H.; m. Anna Marie Ward, Jan. 11, 1964; children— Janine Kay, Heidi Maurine, William Edward, Shaana Marie, Shane Michael. Student pub. schs., Spokane, Wash. Gen. carpenter Rainway Mfg. Co., Spokane, 1958-61; with Wash. Water Power Co., Spokane, 1961-62; tech. service rep. Nat. Cash Register Co., Seattle, 1962-73. Concert and opera tenor various opera cos. and symphonies, 1973—; released e secular rec., 13 sacred recs., U.S. and Can.; profl. debut, San Francisco Opera Co., 1973, debut with N.Y.C. Opera, 1976, Met. Opera, N.Y.C., 1977, Hamberg (West Germany) Opera, 1978, maj. symphony debuts include Vancouver (B.C., Can.), Seattle, Los Angeles Philharm., San Francisco, Minn., Milw. Symphonies, sacred concert artist, 1978—; roles include: Edmondo in Manon Lescaut, Tonio in Daughter of the Regiment, Alfredo in La Traviata, Rodolfo in La Boheme, Count Almaviva in The Barber of Seville, Tamino in The Magic Flute, Faust in Faust, Cauaradossi in Tosca, Prince Calof in Turandot, Riccardo in Un Ballo in Maschera; sacred concert artist, U.S. and Can., South Africa, Latvia, Romania, Croatia. Recipient V.I.P. award Nat. Cash Register Co., 1970; Florence Bruce award San Francisco Opera, 1972; Enrico Caruso award, 1973; Cecilia Schultz award Seattle Opera, 1972; Distinguished Citizen award State of Wash., 1974; Nat. Opera Inst. fellow, 1973-74; Martha Baird Rockefeller grantee, 1974-76 Address: PO Box 328 Washougal WA 98671-0328 Business E-Mail: whsc@pobox.com.

HARNETT, JOSEPH DURHAM, oil industry executive; b. Paterson, N.J., Aug. 23, 1917; s. James Harold and EMily (Steele) H.; m. Wilhelmina Nordstrom, June 21, 1941 (dec. July 1958); children: Gordon D., Linda C., Ralph H., David S.; m. Nancy Beam. BS, Purdue U., 1939. With Consol. Edison Co., N.Y.C., 1939, Worthington Pump & Machinery Corp., 1940, Standard Oil Co., Cleve., 1941-80, v.p., 1957-68, sr. v.p., 1968-70, exec. v.p., 1970-77, pres., 1977-80. Mem. Am. Petroleum Inst. (bd. dirs.), Country Club Cleve., Pepper Pike Club, Everglades Club, Lost Tree Club. Presbyterian. Home: 11090 Turtle Beach Rd # 204 North Palm Beach FL 33408-3423 Office: Moore and Ellrich 4400 P G A Blvd Ste 400 Palm Beach Gardens FL 33410-6557

HARNEY, KATHRYN ANN, opera singer; b. Lincoln, Nebr., Sept. 8, 1955; d. Herman and Sylvia (Korbel) H. Fellowship Artist, Hochschule fur Musik, Munich, 1979; Diploma in Opera, Hartt Coll. of Music, Hartford, Conn., 1975; BMus, U. Nebr., 1972, MMus, 1973. Faculty U. So. Miss., Hattiesburg, 1975-77, Shepherd Sch. of Music/Rice U., Houston, 1977; opera singer/mezzo-soprano various roles in Europe, 1977—; opera singer/debut Conn. Opera, Hartford, 1974. Opera roles include: Charlotte in Werther, Baba the Turk in Rakes Progress, La Principessa di Bouillon in Adriana Lecouvreur, Der Komponist in Ariadne Auf Naxos, Venus in Tannhausser, Dorabella in Cosi Fan Tutte. Mem. Sigma Alpha Iota. Methodist. Avocations: cooking, interior decorating. Home: PO Box 15374 Hattiesburg MS 39404-5374 Office: Artist Mgmt Owen-Evans Ltd London England

HARNSBERGER, RICHARD STEPHEN, law educator; b. Omaha, Dec. 14, 1921; s. Carl Wesley Harnsberger and Lillian Lucille Coppersmith; children: Richard Stephen, Robert Scott. BS, U. Nebr., 1943, MA, 1951, JD cum laude, 1949; D in Juridicial Sci., U. Wis., 1959. Bar: Nebr. 1949. Assoc. Stewart and Stewart, Lincoln, Nebr., 1949—55; dep. county atty. Lancaster County, Lincoln, 1955—56; faculty U. Nebr. Coll. Law, Lincoln, 1956—. Mem. adv. bd. Nebr. State Dept. Environ. Control, Lincoln, 1973—77; trustee Groundwater Found., Lincoln, 1983—96, Govs. Water Coun., Lincoln, 1996; spkr. in field. Co-author: Nebraska Water Law, 1984; contbr. articles to profl. jours. Trustee Family Svcs. Assn., Lincoln, 1952—58; mem. citizens adv. group City of Lincoln Street Action Plan, 1976—78; bd. dirs. Legal Svcs. S.E. Nebr., Lincoln, 1982—86, Water Com. Nebr. Legis., Lincoln, 1998. Capt. U.S. Army, 1943—46, ETO. Recipient Maurice Kremer Groundwater Achievement award, Groundwater Found., 1999, Outstanding Educator award, Nebr. State Bar Found., 2002. Mem.: ABA (mem. standing com. on environ. law 1973—79), Nebr. State Bar Assn., Order of the Coif, Beta Gamma Sigma. Avocation: reading. Home: 1919 S 48th St Lincoln NE 68606 Office: U Nebr Coll of Law Lincoln NE 68583-0902

HARON, DAVID LAWRENCE, lawyer; b. Detroit, Sept. 24, 1944; s. Percy and Bess (Holland) H.; m. Pamela Kay Colburn, May 25, 1969; children: Eric, Andrea. BA, U. Mich., 1966, JD, 1969. Bar: Mich. 1969, U.S. Dist. Ct. (ea. dist.) Mich., 1969, U.S. Supreme Ct. 1974, U.S. Ct. of Appeals (6th cir.) 1996. Law clk. to chief judge Mich. Ct. Appeals, Detroit, 1969-70; assoc. Barris, Sott, Denn & Driker, Detroit, 1970-74; sr. ptnr. Josephson, Tennen, Haron, Weiner and Navarro, Southfield, Mich., 1974-90; prin., shareholder, sr. v.p. Frank, Haron, Weiner and Navarro, Troy, Mich., 1990—; arbitrator Mich. Prudential Securities, Inc. Expedited Arbitrations, 1994-96. Cons. Universe Computer Software, 1985; pres., bd. dirs. S&H Licensing Corp., Southfield; panelist Ct. TV Law Ctr. Bar Assn.; spkr. in field. Mem. editl. bd. Prospectus Jour. Law Reform, 1969, (newsletter) Atty.'s Mktg. Report, 1986-88; contbr. articles to profl. jours. Active Farmington Hills Planning Commn., 1996—, vice-chair, 2000-01, chair, 2001—03; vol. handicap parking enforcement officer Farmington Hills Police Dept., 1990-93; bd. dirs. Forest Elem. Sch. PTO, 1983, 87-88; v.p. North Farmington Baseball for Youth, 1984; active Sta. WTVS Auction, Detroit, 1985-88; trustee C.A.T.C.H., 1996—, Temple Israel, West Bloomfield, Mich., 1987-93, tchr. Sunday Sch., 1986-88, chmn. Ritual com., 1988-93, advisor youth group, 1987-90; chmn. Farmington Hills Com. to Increase Voter Participation, 1987-89; bd. dirs. Met. Detroit chpt. Zionist Orgn. Am., 1987-90; pres. North Farmington H.S. Parent Club, 1989-95; bd. advisors Farmington Hills Corps.-Salvation Army, 1997-2000; site selection com. South Oakland County Habitat for Humanity; chair Cardozo Law Soc. of the Jewish Fedn. Met. Detroit, 1999-2002; bd. dirs., treas. Mich. Psychoanalytic Found., 2003-04, pres., 2004—. Recipient Outstanding Alumnus award Mumford H.S., Detroit, 1985, Cert. recognition City of Farmington Hills, 1986. Fellow Roscoe Pound Found., Mich. State Bar Found.; mem. ABA (com. on comml. leasing 1987-94, real property, probate and trust law sect., bus. law sect. com. on fed. regulation of securities, subcom. on alternative dispute resolution, SEC enforcement matters), ASTM (com. on environ. assessment 1992—), ATLA, Nat. Arbitration Forum (arbitrator), Assn. Health Lawyers Am. (co-chmn. fraud & abuse SISLC false claims/qui tam working group), Mich. Trial Lawyers Assn., Am. Soc. Writers on Legal Subjects, Internat. Assn. Jewish Lawyers and Jurists, Million Dollar Advocates Forum, State Bar Mich. (pro bono com. real property sect. 1996-98, professionalism com. 1994-2002, chmn. professionalism com. 1996-98, chmn. unauthorized practice of law com. 1990-92, unauthorized practice of law com. 1999-2002, chmn. Ct. Appeals com. 1977-78, mem. rep. assembly 1999—), Nat. Assn. Securities Dealers (mediator), Am. Arbitration Assn. (arbitrator, mediator), Comml. Law League Am., Detroit Bar Assn., Jewish Fedn., Oakland County Bar Assn. (participant Mich. law-related edn. project 1988-89, real estate com. 1990—, environ. law com. 1992-95, lawyer dispute conciliator, chmn. professionalism com. 1995-97, Cir. Ct. facilitator, master Inn of Ct. 1997—, Professionalism award, 2003), Oakland County Bar Found. (trustee, treas. 2003-04, v.p. 2004-05), U. Mich. Alumni Assn., U. Mich. Victor's Club, Zionist Orgn. (bd. dirs. Detroit 1987-90), Tau Epsilon Rho Legal Soc., Tau Delta Phi. Jewish. Home: 34685 Old Timber Rd Farmington Hills MI 48331-1436 Office: Frank Haron Weiner and Navarro 5435 Corporate Dr Ste 225 Troy MI 48098-2624 Office Phone: 248-952-0400. Office Fax: 248-952-0890. Business E-Mail: dharon@fhwnlaw.com.

HAROON, NASREEN, artist; b. Karachi, Pakistan, Dec. 10, 1952; arrived in U.S., 1980; d. Ahmad and Amina (Dada) Adaya; m. Haroon Haji Husein, Apr. 29, 1972; children: Omar, Sana. BA in Psychology, Philosophy and History, St. Josephs Coll., Karachi, 1972. Design cons. Shangri-La Hotel, Santa Monica, Calif., 1983—; spkr. on cultural, ethnic, religous diversity, 1991—. Exhibited oil paintings in numerous exhbns., 1992—; featured in premier issue Zarposh Mag., 1997; appeared regularly on Adelphia Cable TV program God Squad; participant Muslim Jewish Dialogue; paintings selected for Art In Embassies program, displayed at U.S. Embassy, Pakistan, Senegal and United Arab Emirates. Bd. dirs. Islamic Ctr. So. Calif., 1999-2002, pres. women's assn., 1991, Pakistan Arts Coun. of Pacific Asia Mus., Pasadena, Calif., 1994-96, v.p., 1997-99, Devel. in Literacy, L.A., 1996-97, Santa Monica (Calif.) Bay Interfaith Coun., 1994—; co-chmn. Muslim Jewish Dialogue; bd. dirs. Cornerstone Theater Prodns. Co. Recipient award for planning Youth Day, Westside Interfaith Coun., 1998. Democrat. Moslem. Avocations: reading, gardening, jewelry design, photography, travel. Office: Shangri-La Hotel 1301 Ocean Ave Santa Monica CA 90401-1010

HAROUCHE, ÉLIE FRÉDÉRIC, plastic surgeon; BS in Engring., NYU, 1966—70; MD, U. Paris, 1977. Cert. Am. Bd. Plastic Surgery, 1985, Am. Bd. Otolaryngology Head & Neck Surgery, 1982. Chief, facial plastic surgery Lenox Hill Hosp., N.Y.C. Fellow: ACS, Am. Acad. Facial Plastic Surgery, Am. Soc. Plastic Surgeons. Office: FACS 903 Park Ave New York NY 10021

HARP, LINDA LINDER, elementary school educator; b. Winter Haven, Fla., Jan. 24, 1948; d. Charles F. and Nan L. (Russ) Linder; m. D. James Harp Jr., Mar. 20, 1971; children: Tiffany Nicole, D. James III. AA, AS in Libr. Sci., Polk Jr. Coll., 1968; BA in Elem. edn., U. South Fla., 1970. Tchr. Auburndale (Fla.) Kindergarten, 1970-72; tchr. kindergarten Cypress Park Elem. Sch., Orlando, Fla., 1972-73, Croissant Park Elem. Sch., Ft. Lauderdale, Fla., 1973-87, Lancaster Elem. Sch., Orlando, 1987-91; tchr. Hidden Oaks Elem. Sch., Orlando, 1991—. Active Pine Castle Little League, Orlando, 1987-98, Grace Covenant Presbyn. Ch., Orlando, 1990— Named Tchr. of Yr., Lancaster Elem. Sch., 1989. Mem. NEA, Fla. Edn. Assn., Orange County Tchrs. Assn. Democrat.

HARP, LOWELL ERICSON, psychologist; s. Carl Jason and Viola Harp; m. Sandra Jean McAvoy, Aug. 30, 1969; children: Jennifer Louise Shower, Sarah Elizabeth Krup, Dylan Robert. BS in edn., Ill. State U., 1970, MS in edn., 1977. Tchr. Newburg H.S., Mo., 1972—75; sch. psychologist Drew Edn. Agy., Siqua Ctr., Iowa, 1977—87, Ogle County Ednl. Cooperative, Byron, Ill., 1987—. Contbg. editor: (quarterly newsletter) Sch. Psychology in Ill. Mem.: Ill. Sch. Psychologist Assn., Nat. Assn. Sch. Psychologists. Avocations: running, exercise, bicycling, singing, writing. Office: Ogle County Ednl Coop Oregon IL 61061

HARPER, A(LFRED) J(OHN), II, lawyer; b. El Paso, Tex., Aug. 11, 1942; s. Mosely Lloyd and Marion M. (McClintock) H.; m. Cynthia Newkam; children— A. John, Leslie J. BA, North Tex. State U., 1964; LLB cum laude, So. Meth. U., 1967. Bar: Tex. 1967, U.S. Dist. Ct. (so. dist.) Tex. 1967, U.S. Dist. Ct. (no. dist.) Tex. 1975, U.S. Dist. Ct. (we. dist.) Tex. 1976, U.S. Dist. Ct. (ea. dist.) Tex. 1995, U.S. Ct. Appeals (5th cir.) 1968, U.S. Ct. Appeals (9th cir.) 1976, U.S. Ct. Appeals (11th cir.) 1982, U.S. Ct. Appeals (10th cir.) 1984, U.S. Ct. Appeals (6th cir.) 1990, U.S. Ct. Appeals (1st cir.) 1991, U.S. Ct. Appeals (2d cir.) 1995, U.S. Ct. Appeals (8th cir.) 2002, U.S. Supreme Ct. 1971. Assoc. Fulbright & Jaworski, LLP, Houston, 1967-74, ptnr., 1975—, and head, labor and employment law dept. Cert. labor and employment law specialist State Bar Tex. bd. legal specialization. Editor Jour. Air Law and Commerce, 1966-67; contbr. articles to profl. jours. With USMCR, 1960-66. Named a Texas Super Lawyer, Tex. Monthly Mag., 2003, 2005. Fellow Coll. Labor and Employment Lawyers; mem. ABA (past coun., labor and employment law sect., past mgmt. co-chmn. com. on devel. law under Nat. Labor Rels. Act, past mgmt. co-chmn. meetings and insts. com., labor law sect.),

Tex. Bar Assn., Order of Coif, Houston Country Club. Republican. Methodist. Office: Fulbright & Jaworski LLP Ste 5100 1301 McKinney St Houston TX 77010-3031 Office Phone: 713-651-5151. Office Fax: 713-651-5246. E-mail: ajharper@fulbright.com.

HARPER, ARTHUR H., manufacturing executive; B in chem. engring., Stevens Inst. Tech., 1978. Tech. sales rep. chem. div. Conoco, Inc., Houston, 1978; mktg. rep. polymer products dept. DuPont Corp., 1983—84; market devel. specialist ULTEM bus. GE Plastics, 1984, aerospace application field programs specialist, mgr. aircraft application program; dist. sales mgr. GE Silicones, Brea, Calif., 1987; plant mgr. GE Plastics, Oxnard, Calif., 1991, bus. leader crystalline materials Pittsfield, Mass., 1992, bus. leader LEXAN Bus., 1994; pres. GE Plastics Greater China, 1996; v.p. global mfg. GE Plastics, Bergen op Zoom, Netherlands, 1998—2000; pres., sr. mng. dir. GE Plastics Europe, Bergen op Zoom, 2000; exec. v.p., mem. office of CEO GE Capital, 2001—02; pres., CEO GE Equipment Mgmt., Stamford, Conn., 2002—; mem. corp. exec. coun. GE. Exec. com. GE African Am. Fourm; chair Stanford Commn. Edn. Achievement; bd. mem. Yerwood Ctr., Stamford. Recipient Black Achievers in Industry Award, 1984, Career Achievement Award, Stevens Inst. Tech., 1998, Social Justice Hero award, Fairfield County Region Nat. Conf. for Cmty. and Justice, 2004, Whitney M. Young, Jr. Svc. award, Boy Scouts Am. Greater NY Coun., 2004. Avocations: golf, collecting jazz recordings, African Am. art. Office: General Electric Co GE Equipment Svcs 120 Long Ridge Rd Stamford CT 06927

HARPER, BARBARA CLARA, educational program administrator, counselor; b. NYC, Aug. 9, 1932; d. James Gullins and Irene Christine (Robinson) H.; m. William C. Booth, Apr. 24, 1951 (div. 1958); 1 child, James Alan; m. Washington Mays, Jan. 1, 1959 (div. 1987). AA, Mattaluck Community Coll., 1978; BS, N.H. Coll., 1987, MS, 1989. Cert. profl. counselors inc. Conn. Bd., lic. profl. counselor, foster mother. Gen. office staff Avnet Electronics, Bronx, NY, 1955-59; sec., gen office staff PHA, Waterbury, Conn., 1959-64; pers. interviewer Scovill Mfg. Co., Waterbury, 1964-66; caseworker, ctr. dir. New Opportunities for Waterbury, 1966-68; coord. Waterbury Cmty. Sch., 1969-94; clinician Child Guidance Clinic Greater Waterbury, Inc., 1963—. Part-time instr. Displaced Housewives and Work Incentive Programs, 1975-80; mem. clerical staff Mattaluck C.C., Waterbury, 1974-80. Mem. Drug Free Sch., 1984; vol. leader Coop. Ext. Svc., USDA 4-H, 1984-91; com. leader Boy Scouts Am., 1974-76, Girl Scouts, 1962; sec. Northeastern Heights Coun., 1971, The Promoters Club of Wilson Sch., 1980; bd. dir. NOW Inc., 1964; vol. organist, choir dir. St. Cecilia's Ch., 1960. With USAF, 1950-52. Recipient Silver Clover award Coop. Extension Svc., U. Conn. 1989, Cert. of Appreciation award Youth Svc. Bur., Dedicated Svc. Appreciation award Boy Scouts of Am. Troop 223, 1975. Mem.: Conn. Assn. Marriage and Family Counselors (sec. 1998—99, pres. 2001—02), Nat. Polit. Congress of Black Women (sec. 1998—99, pres.-elect 1999—2001, pres. 2001—02), Long Hill Cmty. Club (sec.), Waterbury Black Dem. Club. Democrat. Home and Office: 165 Traverse St Waterbury CT 06704-3229

HARPER, CARRIE LYNN, school counselor; b. Milw., Nov. 18, 1952; d. Ludie and Beverly Harper. BA in Psychology, U. Wis. Eau Claire, 1975; MEd Counseling, U. Wis. River Falls, 1978. Cert. profl. sch. counselor K-8 Dept. of Pub. Instrn./Wis., 1978. Music/recreation therapy aide Sacred Heart Hosp., Eau Claire, 1972—74; juvenile correctional counselor Minn. State Tng. Sch., Red Wing, 1975—77; student assisting student program coord. River Falls Sch. Dist., 1976—77; k-8 sch. counselor Elkhart Lake-Glenbeulah Sch. Dist., Wis., 1978—, coord. student assistance program, 1988—. Coord. peer mediator program Elkhart Lake-Glenbeulah Sch. Dist., 1990—93. Crisis response team mem. Sheboygan County Mental Health Assn., Sheboygan, Wis., 1994—; mem. Psi Chi, Nat. Psychology Honor Soc., 1974—75. Recipient Sch. Award for Youth Suicide Prevention, Wis. Chpt. on Youth Suicide, 1989, 25 Years of Svc., Elkhart Lake-Glenbeulah Sch. Dist., 2003, Selected as an Outstanding Young Woman of Am., Outstanding Young Women of Am., Inc., 1984. Mem.: NEA (licentiate), Elkhart Lake-Glenbeulah Edn. Assn. (licentiate; pres., chief negotiator, profl. com. chairperson), Wis. Sch. Counselor Assn. (licentiate), Wis. Edn. Assn. Coun. (licentiate), Am. Sch. Counselor Assn. (licentiate), PTA (licentiate), Psi Chi. Office: Elkhart Lake-Glenbeulah Sch Dist 251 E Maple St Elkhart Lake WI 53020 Office Phone: 920-876-3307. Business E-Mail: charper@elgs.k12.wi.us.

HARPER, CATHERINE B., primary school educator; d. William Joseph and Mariam Bradley; m. Robert T. Harper, July 4, 1982. BS in Elem. Edn. summa cum laude, L.I. U., 1974; MS in Edn., Hofstra U., 1975. Educator educably mentally retarded William Floyd UFSD, Beach, NY, 1975—86, 2nd grade educator, 1986—. Presenter in field. Contbr. chapters to books. Vol. Bellport (N.Y.) Housing Alliance, 1993—97; organizer, coord. North Fork (N.Y.) Parish Outreach, 1991—. Named torchbearer, 2002 Olympic Winter Games, 2002; recipient Am. Tchr. award, Walt Disney Co., 1996; scholar, Fulbright Meml. Fund, Japan, 2002. Roman Catholic. Avocations: preservation, restoring 19th century textiles, reed organ. Office: Woodhull Elem Landau Pl Shirley NY 11967

HARPER, CATHERINE MARIE, lawyer, state official; b. Phila., Apr. 5, 1956; d. Thomas Buckman and Frances (McCarron) Harper; m. Paul J. Kelly III, Oct. 3, 1981; children: Paul J. IV, Thomas Harper. BA, LaSalle U., Phila., 1978; JD, Villanova U., 1981. Bar: Pa. 1981, U.S. Dist. Ct. (ea. dist.) Pa. 1982, U.S. Ct. Appeals (3rd cir.) 1982, U.S. Supreme Ct. 1986. Assoc. McAllister & Gallagher, Phila., 1981-85; ptnr. Hamburg, Rubin, Mullin & Maxwell, Lansdale, Pa., 1985-90, Hepburn Willcox Hamilton & Putnam, Blue Bell, Pa., 1990-93, DelRicci, Harper, Zentgraf & Czaplicki, PC, 1993—97, Timoney Knox, LLP, Fort Washington, Pa., 1997—; state rep. Pa. House 61st Dist., Montgomery County, 2000—. V.p. Horseways Conservation Group, Montgomery County, Pa., 1984-86; chmn. bd. suprs. Lower Gwynedd Twp. Montgomery County, 1987-91, 94-95. Mem. ABA, Gwynedd Mercy Acad. (elem. bd. dirs.), 10,000 Friends of Pa. (bd. dirs.), Mongomery County Planning Commn. (vice chair 1994-2000), Montgomery Conty Township Officials Assn. (past pres.), Statewide Water Resources Planning Com., Montgomery County Open Space Planning Bd. (chair), Montgomery County Lands Trust (chair). Republican. Roman Catholic. Office: Timoney Knox LLP 400 Maryland Dr PO Box 7544 Fort Washington PA 19034-7544 Office Phone: 215-540-2622. Business E-Mail: charper@timoneyknox.com. E-mail: kharper@pahousegop.com.

HARPER, CHARLES MICHEL, food company executive; b. Lansing, Mich., Sept. 26, 1927; s. Charles Frost and Alma (Michel) Harper; m. Joan Frances Bruggema, June 24, 1950; children: Kathleen Harper Wenngatz, Carolyn, Charles Michel, Elizabeth Harper Murphy. BS in Mech. Engring, Purdue U., 1949; MBA, U. Chgo., 1950; LHD (hon.), U. Nebr., 1986; hon. (hon.), Coll. St. Mary, 1986; JD (hon.), Law Coll. of St. Mary, 1986; DEng (hon.), Purdue U., 1989; LHD (hon.), Kearney State U., 1990, Bellevue Coll., 1993, Creighton U., 1993. Supr. methods enging. Oldsmobile divsn. Gen. Motors Corp., Detroit, 1950—54; indsl. engr. Pillsbury Co., Mpls., 1954—55, dir. indsl. engring., 1955—60, dir. engring., 1961—66, v.p. rsch., devel. and new products, 1965—70, group v.p.-poultry, food svc. and venture bus., 1970—74; exec. v.p., COO, dir. ConAgra Inc., Omaha, 1974—76, pres., CEO, 1976—81, chmn. bd., CEO, dir., 1981—93; chmn. bd., CEO RJR Nabisco Holdings Corp., N.Y.C., 1993—95, chmn. bd., 1995—96, ret., 1996. Mem. exec. com. Nat. Commn. on Agrl., Trade and Export Policy, 1984—86; bd. dirs. Burlington Northern Inc., 1985—91, Norwest Bank Holding Co., 1987—97, DuPont, 1992—98, Valmont Industries, Inc., Peter Kiewit Sons, Inc., ConAgra, Inc. Pres. Mid-Am. Coun. Boy Scouts Am., 1983—84; mem. coun. Village of Excelsior, Minn., 1965—70, mayor, 1974. Served U.S. Army, 1946—48. Named Alumnus of Yr., U. Chgo. Grad. Sch. Bus., 1991. Mem.: U. Nebr. Lincoln Coll. Bus. Adminstrn. Alumni Assn. (hon. life mem.), Ak-Sar-Ben (gov.), Omaha C. of C. (chmn. 1979), U.S. C. of C. (bd. dirs., chmn. food and agrl. com.), Beta Theta Pi. Office Phone: 402-571-6612. Personal E-mail: 14041.2015@compuserve.com.

HARPER, CONRAD KENNETH, lawyer, former federal official; b. Detroit, Dec. 2, 1940; s. Archibald Leonard and Georgia Florence (Hall) H.; m. Marsha Louise Wilson, July 17, 1965; children: Warren Wilson, Adam Woodburn. BA, Howard U., 1962; LLB, Harvard U., 1965; LLD (hon.), CUNY, 1990, Vt. Law Sch., 1994. Bar: NY 1966. Law clk. NAACP Legal Def. and Ednl. Fund, N.Y.C., 1965-66, staff lawyer, 1966-70; assoc. Simpson Thacher & Bartlett, N.Y.C., 1971-74, ptnr., 1974—93, 1996—2002, of counsel, 2003—; legal adviser U.S. Dept. of State, Washington, 1993-96. Lectr. law Rutgers U., 1969-70; vis. lectr. law Yale U., 1977-81; cons. HEW, 1977; chmn. admissions and grievances com. U.S. Ct. Appeals, 2d cir., 1987-93; co-chmn. Lawyers' Com. for Civil Rights Under Law, 1987-89; mem. Permanent Ct. of Arbitration, The Hague, 1993-96, 1998—2004, Adminstrv. Conf. U.S., 1993-95, Harvard Corp., 2000-05; bd. dirs. N.Y. Life Ins. Co., Pub. Svc. Enterprise Group. Trustee Inst. Internat. Edn., 1992-93, N.Y. Pub. Libr., chmn. exec. com., 1990-93, vice-chmn. bd. trustees, 1991-93; trustee William Nelson Cromwell Found., 1990—, Met. Mus. of Art, 1996—; bd. mgrs. Lewis Walpole Libr., 1989-93; bd. visitors Fordham Law Sch., 1990-93, CUNY, 1989-93; vestryman Ch. of St. Barnabas, Irvington, N.Y., 1982-85; bd. dirs. Phi Beta Kappa Assocs., 1992-93; chancellor The Episc. Diocese of N.Y., 1987-92; bd. legal advisors Martindale-Hubbell, 1990-93. Fellow Am. Bar Found., N.Y. Bar Found., Am. Coll. Trial Lawyers, Am. Acad. Arts and Scis.; mem. Am Philos. Soc. (v.p. 2005-), ABA (bd. editors jour. 1980-86), Nat. Bar Assn., N.Y. State Bar Assn., Assn. Bar City N.Y. (chmn. exec. com. 1979-80, pres. 1990-92), Am. Law Inst. (mem. coun. 1985—, 2d v.p. 1998-2000, 1st v.p. 2000-04), Am. Assn. for Internat. Commn. Jurists (bd. dirs. 1988-93), Am. Soc. Internat. Law (mem. exec. coun. 1997-2000, exec. com. 1998-2000, counselor 2000—), Met. Black Bar Assn., Acad. Polit. Sci. (bd. dirs. 1998—), Coun. Fgn. Rels., Grolier Club (coun. mem. 1993, 1997—2004), Century Assn., Harvard Club (mem. bd. mgrs. 1993-05), Phi Beta Kappa. Democrat. Episcopalian.

HARPER, DAVID TAYLOR, civilian military employee; b. L.A., Feb. 3, 1959; s. Clarence Bluford Harper and Myrtle Marie Sparks, Dwain Sparks (Stepfather); m. Joyce Lee Van Leuvan, Jan. 15, 1996 (dec. Aug. 2004); m. Barbara Christine Jecz, Aug. 13, 1982 (div. Sept. 1, 1990); 1 child, Benjamin; stepchildren: Donald Drorbaugh, Deborah Drorbaugh. AAS, C.C. of the Air Force, Maxwell AFB, Ala., 1984; AA, U. Md., 1985; BS with honors, Calif. State U., Sacramento, 1988; MPA, Calif. State U., Carson, 1999. Spl. agt. Air Force Office Spl. Investigations, N.Y.C., 1988—89, El Segundo, Calif., 1989—2005, spl. agent-in-charge Hanscom AFB, Mass., 2004—. Instr. criminal justice U. Phoenix, 2002—04. Tech., sgt. USAF, 1976—85. Mem.: ASPA, Acad. Polit. Sci., Am. Polit. Sci. Assn. (assoc.), Pi Alpha Alpha. Avocations: computers, writing, travel. Office: USAF Office Spl Investigations Detachment 102 Hanscom Afb MA 01731 Office Phone: 781-377-4607. Personal E-mail: dtharper@verizon.net.

HARPER, DONALD VICTOR, retired transportation and logistics educator, consultant; b. Chgo., Mar. 27, 1927; s. Victor Rudolph and Mildred Victoria (Safbom) H.; children: Christine Ann, Diane Elizabeth, David Victor. Student, Wright Jr. Coll., 1945, 46-47; BS in Journalism, U. Ill., Urbana, 1950, PhD in Econs., 1957. Instr. Coll. Commerce and Bus. adminstrn. U. Ill., Urbana, 1953-56; lectr. Carlson Sch. Mgmt. U. Minn., Mpls., 1956, asst. prof. Carlson Sch. Mgmt., 1956-59, assoc. prof., 1959-65, prof. transp. and logistics, 1965-97, chmn. dept. mgmt. and transp., 1967-70, dir. MBA and PhD programs, 1970-79, dir. PhD program, 1979-80, chmn. dept. mktg. and logistics mgmt., 1991-96; prof. emeritus, 1997—; cons. to bus. and govt. agys. Author: Economic Regulation of the Motor Trucking Industry by the States, 1959, Price Policy and Procedure, 1966, Transportation in America: Users, Carriers, Government, 2d edit, 1982; contbr. articles to profl. jours. Served with USN, 1945-46. Mem. Am. Econ. Assn. (Disting. Mem. award transp. and pub. utilities group 1988), Am. Mktg. Assn., Transp. Research Forum, Am. Soc. Transp. and Logistics, Transp. Club Mpls. and St. Paul, Assn. Transp. Law, Logistics and Policy. Home: 2451 Sheldon St Saint Paul MN 55113-3138 Office: U Minn Carlson Sch Mgmt 321 19th Ave S Minneapolis MN 55455-0438 Business E-Mail: dharper@csom.umn.edu.

HARPER, DOREEN C., nursing educator; Student, Albertus Magnus Coll., 1966-68; BSN, Cornell U., 1971; MSN, Catholic U., 1974; PhD in Human Devel., U. Md., 1980. Cert. adult nurse practitioner ANA. Home care nurse Child Devel. Ctr. R.I. Hosp., Providence, 1971; pub. health nurse Fairfax County Health Dept., Fairfax, Va., 1971-72; charge nurse adolescent mental health unit The Bancroft Inst., Falls Church, Va., 1973; college health nurse Trinity Coll., Washington, 1973-84; asst. prof. nursing dept. nursing George Mason U., Fairfax, Va., 1974-77, assoc. prof. nursing dept. nursing, 1980-82, 1987—, project dir. adult and gerontological nurse practitioner trg. grant, 1988-91, adult nurse practitioner student health svcs., 1990—, coord. nurse practitioner program Coll. Nursing and Health Scis., 1991—; adult nurse practioner Kaiser/Georgetown Cmty. Health Plan, Springfield, 1979-81; chair RN to BSN program, asst. prof.Sch. Nursing U. Md., Catonsville, 1982-86; adult nurse practitioner OB-GYN Assocs., Alexandria, Va., 1987-1990; dir. nurse practitioner program Sch. Medicine and Health Scis. George Washington U., Washington, 1994—; prof. nurse practitioner Univ. Mass. Med. Sch. Cons. in field; principal investigator Nat. Ctr. Nursing Rsch. NIH, 1989-92; presenter in field; mem. nursing task force Va. Area Health Edn. Ctrs., 1993—. Editor: Nursing Connections, 1987-89; editl. review bd. Advances in Nursing Sci., 1989-93; contbr. numerous chpts., articles to profl. jours. and books. Predoctoral rsch. fellow Nursing Rsch. Svcs. Adminstrn.U. Md., 1977-80; recipient: Nat. Inst. Mental Health traineeship award Dept. Health, Edn. and Welfare Catholic U. Am., 1972-74. Fellow Am. Acad. Nursing (nat. peer review com. 1980-88); mem. Va. Nurses Assn. (dist. VIII Outstanding Nurse of the Year award 1975, del. 1976, 81 conv., mem. joint med./nursing practice com. 1976-78, dist. 8 chmn. nominating com. 1981-82), Sigma Theta Tau (Kappa chpt. nominating com. 1978-79, Epsilon Zeta chpt. 1987—, nominating com. 1989-91). Home: 159 Robbins Rd Thompson CT 06277-2846 Office: Univ Mass Worcester 55 Lake Ave N Worcester MA 01655*

HARPER, EMERY WALTER, lawyer; b. Hackensack, NJ, Feb. 25, 1936; s. Walter Van Saun and Dorothy Charlotte (Schmidt) H.; m. Judith Van Nest Hover, Sept. 9, 1961 (div. 1991); 1 child, Caroline Curry BA cum laude, Amherst Coll., 1958; LLB, Yale U., 1961. Bar: N.Y. 1962. Assoc. Lord Day & Lord, Barrett Smith, N.Y.C., 1961-69, ptnr., 1970-93, Schnader, Harrison, Segal & Lewis, N.Y.C., 1993-96, chmn. internat. maritime group, 1993-95; pres. Harper Cons., Inc., N.Y.C., 1997—; of counsel Inman Deming LLP, 1998—2003, Law Offices Harry A. Inman, 2003—. Bd. dirs. The Shipping Network, Inc.; bd. dirs., founding mem. The Admiralty/Fin. Forum, Inc.; lectr. on maritime law Dalian, PRC, 1984; advisor U.S. del. to joint working group on liens and mortgages Internat. Maritime Orgn., 1st, 2d, 5th and 6th sessions UN Conf. on Trade and Devel., 1986-89; lectr. on admiralty and maritime financing; lectr. on ship fin. topics, Mex., Panama, Chile, Thailand, 1993-95; course dir. practice and techniques Financing Marine Assets and Ops., N.Y., 1995; organizer, pres. Am. Corps. in Coastwise Trade; participant U.S. Delegation to IMO/UNCTAD Joint Diplomatic Conf. on Maritime Liens and Mortgages, Geneva, 1993; cons. Inman Deming Internat., LLC, Washington, 1998—2003; del. to diplomatic conf. arrest of ships Internat. C. of C., 1999. Co-author: Essays on Maritime Liens and Mortgages and on Arrest of Ships, 1985; contbr. articles to profl. publs. Trustee The Gateway Sch., N.Y., 1975-83; deacon Brick Presbyn. Ch., 1970-76, elder, 1976-82, trustee, corp. sec., 1982-88; mem. legal adv. com. Liberian Shipowners Coun., 1988-2000; chmn. Subcom. on Liberian Maritime Law Revision, 1993-99; chmn. Marshall Islands Roundtable, 1999-2001; mem. Seatransport com. U.S. Coun. for Internat. Bus., 1987-91; dir. Cmty. Living Corp. Found., Inc., 2002—; bd. dirs. CLC Found., Inc., 2002—. With USAFR, 1961-67. Mem. ABA (chmn. admiralty and maritime law com., sect. internat. law), Assn. of Bar of City of N.Y. (mem. admiralty com. 1974-80, 90-93, 98-2000, chmn: 1977-80), Maritime Law Assn. (founding chmn. com. on Marine financing 1978—), Com. Maritime Internat. (internat. subcom. on maritime liens and mortgages), N.Y. Amherst Alumni Assn. (pres. 1975-77), Pilgrims Soc., Union Club, Down Town Club. Office: 18 E 48th St Fl 10 New York NY 10017 also: East Tower 1301 K St NW Ste 800 Washington DC 20005-3373 Office Phone: 212-317-0686. Personal E-mail: eharper974@aol.com.

HARPER, GERARD EDWARD, lawyer; b. N.Y.C., Feb. 2, 1953; s. Eugene Walter and Muriel (Drumgoole) H.; children: Amanda, Julia. BA, Rutgers U., 1975; JD, NYU, 1978. Bar: N.Y. 1980, U.S. Supreme Ct. 1986, D.C. 1989, U.S. Ct. Appeals (9th cir.) 1988), U.S. Ct. Appeals (2d cir.) 1991, U.S. Dist. Ct. (so. and ea. dists.) 1980, N.Y. 1985, U.S. Dist. Ct. (no. dist.) Calif., U.S. Dist. Ct. (D.C. cir.). Law clk. to Justice George MacKinnon U.S. Cir. Ct., Washington, 1978-79; assoc. Paul, Weiss, Rifkind, Wharton & Garrison, LLP, N.Y.C., 1979-86, ptnr., 1986—. Editor-in-chief NYU Law Rev., 1977-78. Gen. counsel, chmn. law com., mem. exec. com. N.Y. Dem. State Com., N.Y.C., 1987—. Mem. ABA, N.Y. State Bar Assn., N.Y. County Lawyers' Assn., Assn. of Bar of City of N.Y., Order of Coif. Roman Catholic. Office: Paul Weiss Rifkind Wharton & Garrison LLP 1285 Avenue Of The Americas Fl 21 New York NY 10019-6028 Office Phone: 212-373-3000. E-mail: gharper@paulweiss.com.

HARPER, HENRY H., retired military officer; b. Ft. Benning, Ga., Aug. 24, 1934; s. H.M. and Frances Louise (Hearn) Harper; m. Helen Harpe, Apr. 2, 1960; children: Cynthia Jane, Linda Leigh BS, U. Md., 1964; MA, George Washington U., 1965; Disting. grad., Indsl. Coll. Armed Forces, 1973. Commd. officer U.S. Army, 1954, advanced through grades to maj. gen., 1980, dep. comdg. gen. Armaments Command Rock Island, Ill., 1977-79, dir. logistics U.S. European Command Stuttgart, Fed. Republic Germany, 1979-82, comdg. gen. Depot System Command Chambersburg, Pa., 1982-86, ret., 1986; corp. sr. v.p. Synovus Fin. Corp., Columbus, Ga., 1986-95; ret., 1995. Dir. Ga. State Golf Assn., 1999—. Chmn. bd. dirs. Easter Seals West Ga., Inc.; chmn., bd. dirs. Goodwill Industries, Springer Opera House; bd. dirs. Universal Bank. Mem. Assn. U.S. Army (bd. govs., dir. Chambers Fort chpt. 1982-85), Columbus C. of C. (bd. dirs.). Episcopalian. Avocations: golf, jogging. Personal E-mail: g2mmhm@knology.net.

HARPER, JEWEL BENTON, pharmacist; b. Springfield, Tenn., Nov. 14, 1925; s. William Henry and Violet Irene (Benton) H.; m. Josephine Cook, Feb. 12, 1953; children: Pamela Jewel, Karen Jo. BS, Austin Peay State U., 1948, Samford U., 1950; diploma, U.S. Army Med. Field Svc. Sch., 1964, U.S. Army Command and Gen. Staff Coll., 1968, U.S. Army Logistics Mgmt. Ctr., 1977, Indsl. Coll. Armed Forces, Nat. Def. U., 1977, Air War Coll, Air U., 1977. Pharmacist Battlefield Pharmacy, Nashville, 1950-52, VA Hosp., Nashville, 1952-63, Lexington, Ky., 1963-67, Durham, N.C., 1967-76, Manchester, N.H., 1976-82, Vanderbilt U., Nashville, 1982-86, Nashville Meml. Hosp., 1986-91. Served to col. Med. Svc. Corps, USAR, 1944-85. Fellow Am. Coll. Apothecaries (emeritus); mem. Assn. Mil. Surgeons U.S., Am. Pharm. Assn., Tenn. Pharmacists Assn., Res. Officers Assn. U.S. (pres. chpt. 1962-63, sec. 1970-73, dept. surgeon 1977-82), Mil. Order of the World Wars (mem. in perpetuity, charter Screaming Eagles chpt. 2003), Mil. Officers Assn. Am., Assn. U.S. Army, Am. Legion, VFW, The Gideons Internat., Lambda Chi Alpha, Kappa Psi. Republican. Baptist. Avocations: country music, deep sea fishing, horticulture. Home and Office: 503 Cunniff Ct Goodlettsville TN 37072-3003

HARPER, JUDSON MORSE, retired university administrator, consultant, educator; b. Lincoln, Nebr., Aug. 25, 1936; s. Floyd Sprague and Eda Elizabeth (Kelley) H.; m. Patricia Ann Kennedy, June 15, 1958; children: Jayson K., Stuart H., Neal K. BS, Iowa State U., 1958, MS, 1960, PhD, 1963. Registered profl. engr., Minn. Instr. Iowa State U., Ames, 1958-63; dept. head Gen. Mills, Inc., Mpls., 1964-69, venture mgr., 1969-70; prof., dept. head agrl. and chem. engring. Colo. State U., Ft. Collins, 1970-82, v.p. rsch. and info. tech., 1982-2000, interim pres., 1989-90, spl. asst. to the pres., 2000—04. Cons. USAID, Washington, 1972-74, various comml. firms., 1975—; Lady Davis scholar Technion, Haifa, Israel, 1978-79. Author: Extrusion of Foods, 1982, Extrusion Cooking, 1989; editor newsletter Food, Pharm. & Bioengring. News, 1979-83, LEC Newsletter, 1976-89; contbr. articles to profl. publs.; patentee. Mem. sch. bd. St. Louis Park, Minn., 1968-70. Recipient Disting. Svc. award Colo. State U., 1977, Fulbright-Hayes scholar, 1978, Svc. award Centro de Investigaviones y Asistencia Technologica de Estado de Chihuahua, Chichuahua, Mex., 1980, Food Engring. award Dairy and Food Industry Supply Assn. and Am. Soc. Agrl. Engrs., 1983, Cert. of Merit, USDA Office Internat. Coop. and Devel., 1983, Cert. of Merit, Consejo Nacional de Ciencia y Technologie en Mexico, Mexico City, 1984, Profl. Achievement Citation Iowa State U., 1986, Cert. Appreciation Chinese Inst. of Food Tech., 1987, Charles Lory Pub. Svc. award, 1993, Hammer award The Nat. Performance Rev., 1994. Fellow Inst. Food Technologists (Internat. award 1990), AAAS; mem. Am. Inst. Chem. Engring. (dir. 1981-84), Am. Soc. Agrl. Engrs. (com. chmn. 1973-78, hon. engr. Rocky Mountain region), Am. Chem. Soc., Am. Soc. Engring. Edn. (com. chmn. 1976-77). Mem. Ind. United Methodist Ch. Home: 1818 Westview Rd Fort Collins CO 80524-1891 Business E-Mail: judson.harper@colostate.edu.

HARPER, KENNETH FRANKLIN, retired state legislator, real estate broker; b. Covington, Ky., Jan. 15, 1931; s. Kenneth Wellington and Elizabeth Mary (Brickler) H.; m. Eileen Ann Kathman, May 16, 1953; children: Gregory, Scott, Glenn, Bryan, Lesley. Student, U. Ky. Mem. Ky. Ho. of Reps., 1964-68; asst. commr. Ky. Dept. Child Welfare, 1969-70; commr. Ky. Dept. Pub. Info., 1970; sec. of state Commonwealth of Ky., 1971; broker, owner, pres. Harper Realty, 1986—; mem. from 63d dist. Ky. Ho. of Reps., 1963-68, 82-94, minority caucus chmn., 1989—92, vice-chmn. tourism and energy com. Adv. bd. U.S. Bank, No. Ky.; bd. dirs. Harper Group LLC. Exec. com. Kenton County Rep. Party, No. Ky.; chmn. emeritus No. Ky. Univ. Found.; past mem. Rep. State Ctrl. com.; commr. emeritus No. Ky. Conv. and Visitors Bur., chmn., 1991-92; mem. Southbank Ptnrs.; past state co-chmn. Am. Legis. Exch. Coun.; mem. No. Ky. Assn. for the Retarded; past mem. Exec. Task Force on Hist. Preservation; mem. Greater Cin. Tall Stacks Commn.; past mem. No. Ky. U. Small Bus. Incubator; v.p. The Southbank Fund. Recipient numerous Jaycee awards, Boss of Yr. award Nat. Secs. Assn., 1971, Walter L. Pieschel award No. Ky. C. of C., 1980, KMI Alumni Spirit of Excellence award, 1993, others; Paul Harris fellow Rotary Internat., 1989; named one of Outstanding Young Men of Am., 1964. Mem. Nat. Assn. Realtors, Ky. Assn. Realtors, No. Ky. Assn. Realtors (life), Nat. Rep. Legislators Assn. (pres. 1991-92), Pi Kappa Alpha (Omega Chpt. Outstanding Alumni). Roman Catholic. Home and Office: Harper Group LLC PO Box 17717 2700 Main Chase Ln Crestview Hills KY 41017-4707 E-mail: kfh@fuse.net.

HARPER, LYNN D., biologist; BA, MS in Cell and Molecular Biology, U. Bridgeport. Tech. writer, asst. mgr. Bionetics Corp., Washington, 1982—83; tech. dir. space sys. divsn. Gen. Electric Mgmt. and Tech. Svcs. Co., Washington, 1983—86; program mgr. advanced missions and spl. projects space life scis. divsn. NASA, 1986—89; chief advanced life support divsn. NASA Ames Rsch. Ctr., 1990—93, acting chief advanced life support divsn., 1993—94, sr. sys. engr. space scis. divsn., 1994—96, lead, integrative studies. Office: NASA Ames Rsch Ctr MS 239-15 Bldg 244 Rm 148 Moffett Field CA 94035

HARPER, MARY SADLER, financial advisor; b. Farmville, Va., June 15, 1941; d. Edward Henry and Vivien Morris (Garrett) Sadler; m. Joseph Taylor Harper, Dec. 21, 1968; children by previous marriage: James E. Hatch III, Mary Ann Hatch Czajka. Cert., Fla. Trust Sch., U. Fla., 1976. Registered securities rep., Fla., gen. securities prin., fin. and ops. prin., options prin., mcpl. securities prin., investment mgmt. advisor, wealth adv. specialist. Dep. clk. Polk County Cts., Bartow, Fla., 1964-67; rep. Allen & Co., Lakeland, Fla., 1967-71; with First Nat. Bank, Palm Beach, Fla., 1971-89, sr. v.p., 1984-86, S.E. Bank N.A., Palm Beach, 1986-89, 1st United Bank, 1997-98; pres., CEO Palm Beach Capital Svcs., Inc., 1986-88; mng. dir. Investment Svcs., Palm Beach Capital Svcs. Divsn., 1988; v.p. investments, trustee J.M. Rubin Found, Palm Beach, 1983—; v.p. sec., sr. v.p. investment divsn. Island Nat. Bank & Trust Co., 1989-97; chair, dir., pres., CEO Island Investment Svcs., Inc. (A Wachovia Co.), Palm Beach, 1989-98; also bd. dirs., mng. exec., sr. v.p. Wachovia Investments, Palm Beach, 1998-2000; sr. v.p. Wachovia Bank N.A., 1999-2000; sr. v.p., investment mgmt. advisor Wachovia Securities, Inc., 2000—; sr. v.p. investments, wealth adv. specialist Legg Mason, Wood, Walker, Inc., 2000—. Adv. coun. Nuveen, 1987-99, pres.'s coun., 2001, chmn.'s coun., 2002—; adv. bd. Kidsanctuary, Inc. Adv. panel

Palm Beach County YWCA, 1985, mem. endowment com., 1990—93; mem. pres.'s club Jupiter Med. Ctr. Found., 1989—; life mem. Juno Beach Civic Assn.; profl. endowment com. Rehab. Ctr. for Children and Adults, 1998—2002; chmn. Palm Beach adv. bd. Palm Beach Nat. Bank & Trust Co., 2000—01; dir., v.p. Friends of Abused Children, 2001—03; mem. Fla. History Mus.; dir. Ctr. for Family Svcs., 2003—; bd. dirs. Biomotion Found., 2002—05, pres., 2004—05; mem. Palm Beach Hist. Soc., 2004—. Mem. Inst. CFPs (assoc.), Nat. Assn. Securities Dealers (dist. com. mem. 1995-98), Fin. Planners Assn., Fin. Women Internat., Fla. Securities Dealers Assn., Exec. Women of Palm Beaches (fin. com. 1985-92), Internat. Soc. Palm Beach (treas., trustee 1986—), Jupiter Med. Ctr. Found. (pres.'s club 1989—), Loxahatchee Hist. Soc. (bd. dirs. 1991-93, chair devel. com. 1992-93), Sebring, Fla. Hist. Soc. (life), Jupiter/Tequesta C. of C. (assoc.), United Daus. of Confederacy, Gov.'s Club, Pub. Securities Assn. (exec. rep.), Jonathans Golf Club, Rotary (Palm Beach Found. com. 1990—, bd. dirs. 1992-94, co-chair, 1997, bd. dirs. 2000—, chair Rotary Internat. Found., Palm Beach 1998-2004, Paul Harris fellow 1992), Lighthouse Ctr. for the Arts (life), Norton Art Mus. (patron), Palm Beach Yacht Club, Ritz Carlton Spa and Club (Jupiter), Palm Beach County Hist. Soc. Democrat. Baptist. Avocations: reading, history. Home: 800 Ocean Dr PH 4 Juno Beach FL 33408-1730 Office: Legg Mason 324 Royal Palm Way Ste 100 Palm Beach FL 33480 Fax: 561-626-7978. Business E-Mail: msharper@leggmason.com.

HARPER, MICHAEL CHRISTOPHER, music educator; s. Michael W. and Lee Harper. MusB Edn., Valdosta State U., 2001. Cert. music edn. tchr. Ga. Asst. band dir. Cook County H.S., Adel, Ga., 2000—01; dir. bands Screven County H.S., Sylvania, Ga., 2001—. Instrument repair tech. M&M Music, Sandy Campbell Music, Valdosta, Ga., 1998—2000; clinician and adjudicator Mid. H.S. Bands. Musician: Valdosia Symphony Orch., Albany Symphony Orch., Statesboro Symphony Orch. Mem.: Prof. Assn. Ga. Educators, Nat. Band Assn., Music Educators Nat. Conf., Ga. Music Educators Assn. (assoc.). Republican. Avocations: music research, travel. Home: PO Box 3107 Statesboro GA 30459 Office: Screven County HS PO Box 1688 Sylvania GA 30467 Personal E-mail: harperatl@yahoo.com. E-mail: charper@screven.k12.ga.us.

HARPER, OLIVER WILLIAM, III, investment company executive, consultant; b. Chgo., Nov. 25, 1953; s. Oliver William and Pauline W. (Simpson) H.; children: Oliver W., Julia D. BA, U. Ill.-Chgo., 1978, MBA U. Chgo., 1993. Agt., Occidental Life of Calif., 1979; registered rep. Lincoln Nat. Life Ins. Co., Ft. Wayne, Ind., 1979-80, 93—; agt., registered rep. Penn Mut. Life Ins. Co., Phila., 1980-85; dir. employee benefit div. Penn Fin. Group, Chgo., 1981-85; CEO, exec. v.p. Corp. Plan Cons., Inc., 1985-95, pres., 1995—; pres. Benefit Premium Claims Admins., Inc., 1993-2003, Oliver W. Harper, Ltd., 2003—; v.p. Manage Care Mktg., 1996-97. Pres., trustee Employers Svc. Assn.; mng. adminstr.; Mem. Internat. Soc. Cert. Employee Benefit Specialists, Profl. Assn. Diving Instr., Chgo. Assn. Life Underwriters, Nat. Assn. Life Underwriters, Notaries Assn. Ill., U. Ill. Alumni Assn., Underwater Explorers Soc. Episcopalian. Club: Masons. E-mail: oliverharper@allstate.com.

HARPER, PATRICIA LOUISE, music educator; b. Flushing, N.Y., Aug. 21, 1942; d. Harold Louis Hornberger and Virginia Lee Sellers; m. Robert Leslie Harper, Aug. 29, 1964; children: Ian Leslie, Mary Alice. BA cum laude, Smith Coll., 1964; postgrad., Royal Scottish Acad. Music, 1965; MusM, Yale U., 1967. Flutist New Haven Symphony Orch., 1965—70, USCG Band, New London, 1975; prof. Conn. Coll., 1975—, So. Conn. State U., New Haven, 1996—. Guest lectr. Cin. Conservatory, 2001, Stanford U., Palo Alto, Calif., 2001, Rice U., Houston, 2003; tchr. residency flute master classes, Brownsville, Vt., 2000—, Greensville, SC, 2004—. Author, narrator: CD The Remarkable Career of Flutist, Julius Barker; editor: reconstructed flute duets by Kuhlau; editor: (cons.) Poulenc's Sonata for Flute and Piano; co-editor (with Paula Robison): The Lanier Collection. Jury Ea. Conn. Symphony Orch. Competition, 2002—05; coord. bi-lingual music/theatre Conn. Coll., 2000. Mem.: N.Y. Flute Club (life), Brit. Flute Soc. (life), Nat. Flute Assn. (life; exec. bd. 2002—04). Avocations: hiking, travel, birdwatching. Home: 38 Oak Dr Centerbrook CT 06409 Office: Conn Coll 270 Mohegan Ave New London CT 06320 Office Phone: 860-439-2719. E-mail: patricia@patriciaharper.com.

HARPER, PATRICIA NELSEN, psychiatrist; b. Omaha, July 25, 1944; d. Eddie R. and Marjorie L. (Williams) Nelsen. BS, Antioch Coll., Yellow Springs, Ohio, 1966; MD, U. Nebr., 1975; grad., Topeka Inst. Psychoanalysis, 1997. Cert. psychiatrist. Psychiatric residency Karl Menninger Sch. of Psychiatry, Topeka, 1975-78; staff psychiatrist The Menninger Clinic, Topeka, 1978-98; chmn. dept. mental health Park Nicollet Clinic, 2004—. Faculty mem. Karl Menninger Sch. of Psychiatry, Topeka, 1982-98. Program dir. Addictions Recovery Program C.F. Menninger Meml. Hosp., Topeka, 1987-98. Mem. Am. Psychiatric Assn., Am. Med Women Assn., Am. Psychoanalytic Assn. Office: Pk Nicollet Clinic 3800 Park Nicollet Blvd Minneapolis MN 55416-2527 Office Phone: 952-993-3307.

HARPER, RICHARD HENRY, film producer, film director; b. San Jose, Calif., Sept. 15, 1950; s. Walter Henry and Priscilla Alden H.; m. Ann Marie Morgan, June 19, 1976; children: Christine Ann, Paul Richard, James Richard. Show designer Walt Disney Imagineering, Glendale, Calif., 1971-76; motion picture producer, dir. Harper Films, Inc., La Canada, Calif., 1976—. Producer, dir. (films) Impressions de France, Disney World, Fla., 1982, Magic Carpet Round the World, Disneyland, Tokyo, 1983, American Journeys, Disneyland, Calif., 1985, Collecting America, Nat. Gallery Art, Washington, 1988, Hillwood Mus., Washington, 1989, Journey Into the 4th Dimension for Sanrio World, Journey Into Nature for Sanrio World, Japan, 1990, Masters of Illusion, Nat. Gallery of Art, Washington, 1992. Recipient more than 150 awards world-wide for outstanding motion picture prodn. including Silver trophy Cannes Internat. Film Festival, 2 Gold awards Internat. Festival of the Ams., 1981, 82, 14 Golden Eagle C.I.N.E. awards, 1977-92, Emmy award Nat. Acad. TV Arts and Scis., 1993-. Mem. Acad. of Motion Picture Arts and Scis.

HARPER, ROBBIE JANE, critical care nurse, nursing administrator; b. Midwest City, Okla., Sept. 14, 1967; d. Billey Kent and Robbie Jo (McGruder; m. Danny Scott Harper I, June 19, 1987; children: Christina Krichelle, Danny Scott II. BSN, U. Okla., 1990. CCRN; CMC. NICU nurse Children's Hosp., Oklahoma City, 1990-91; charge nurse Marshall County Hosp., Madill, Okla., 1991-92; MICU nurse VA Hosp., Oklahoma City, 1992-97, case mgr., 1997-99, utilization rev. coord., 1999—2001, quality improvement specialist, 2001—. Named Critical Care Nurse of the Yr., Am. Assn. Critical Care Nurses, 1996. Mem.: Am. Inst. Outcomes-Case Mgmt. Presbyterian. Avocations: swimming, sewing.

HARPER, ROBERT, actor; b. N.Y.C., May 19, 1951; BA in English with high distinction, Rutgers Coll., 1974. Mem. repertory co. Arena Stage, Washington, 1974-76. Guest artist Rutgers U., New Brunswick, N.J., 1977, 84. Actor: Long Wharf Theater, 1978, 1984, Theater for a New City, 1981; (Broadway plays) Once in a Lifetime, 1978, The Inspector General, 1978, The American Clock, 1980; (TV films) J. Edgar Hoover, The Wrong Man, Not Quite Human, Payoff, Running Mates, The Story of Bill W, Paper Angels, Ruby Ridge; (TV series) Newhart, Roseanne, Murphy Brown, Wiseguy, L.A. Law, NYPD Blue, Law and Order, Philly, Frank's Place; (films) Creepshow, 1982, Once Upon a Time in America, 1984, Amazing Grace and Chuck, 1987, Twins, 1989, Final Analysis, 1992, Deconstructing Harry, 1997, The Insider, 1999. Advisor charity events The Laugh Factory, Hollywood, 1981—. Regents fellow U. Calif., 1974, Kennedy Ctr. award Am. Coll. Theater Festival, 1974. Mem. MLA (spkr. conv. 1996), ACLU (sponsor Garden Event 1994), Acad. Motion Picture Arts and Scis., Acad. TV Arts and Scis., Am. Soc. Aesthetics, Screen Actor's Guild, Actor's Equity Assn. Office: 8721 Santa Monica Blvd West Hollywood CA 90069-4507

HARPER, ROBERT AUGUSTUS, lawyer; b. Fla., Aug. 15, 1946; s. Robert Augustus Sr. and Ida Frances (Allen) H.; m. Jill Beth Levin, June 2, 1977; children: Robert Augustus III, Myriah Beth, Alexandra Rose. BA, U. Fla., 1968, JD, 1970. Bar: Fla. 1970, U.S. Ct. Appeals (5th cir.) 1973, U.S. Dist. Ct. (no., mid. and so. dists.) 1973, U.S. Supreme Ct. 1976, U.S. Dist. Ct. (so. dist.) Tex. 1977, U.S. Ct. Appeals (2d cir.) 1978, U.S. Ct. Appeals (3d cir.) 1980, U.S. Ct. Appeals (11th cir.) 1981, U.S. Dist. Ct. (so. dist.) Ala. 1983, U.S. Dist. Ct. (ea. dist.) Mich. 1987, U.S. Ct. Appeals (1st cir.) 1987, U.S. Ct. Appeals (9th cir.) 1987, U.S. Dist. Ct. (no. dist.) Ga. 1988, U.S. Ct. Appeals (7th cir.) 1988, Ga. 1988, U.S. Ct. Appeals (6th and 4th cirs.) 1989, U.S. Dist. Ct. (so. dist.) Ill. 1990, U.S. Tax Ct. 1994, U.S. Dist. Ct. (mid. dist.) Ga. 1996. Pvt. practice, Tallahassee, Fla. Expert witness Fla. Legislature, 1996—2000; chmn. jud. nominating commn., First Dist. Ct. Appeal, Fla., 1999-2000; guest lectr. U. Fla., Fla. State U.; moot ct. judge Contbr. articles to profl. publs. Ret. capt. USAR. Mem. Fla. Bar (appellate rules com. 1994—), Fla. Assn. Criminal Def. Lawyers (pres. Tallahassee chpt. 1992-93, bd. dirs. 1990-97, Pres.' award 1992-94), Am. Inns of Ct. (master lawyer), Alpha Tau Omega (pres.). Democrat. Presbyterian. Avocations: gardening, law. Office: Robert Augustus Harper Law Firm PA 325 W Park Ave Tallahassee FL 32301-1413 Office Fax: 850-224-9800. E-mail: harperlaw@harperlawfirm.com.

HARPER, ROBERT LESLIE, architect, educator; b. Rochester, N.Y., July 2, 1939; BA, Amherst Coll., 1961; MArch, Columbia U., 1964. Registered architect, Conn., Mass., N.Y., R.I. Dir. Moore Grover Harper, P.C., Essex, 1975-85; ptnr. Centerbrook, Essex, 1985-97; architect pvt. practice, Centerbrook, Conn., 1997—. Vis. critic in archtl. design R.I. Sch. Design, Providence, 1975-89, Yale U., New Haven, 1983-84. Author mag. articles; contbr. to exhbn. Speaking a New Classicism, 1981-82. Chmn. Bldg. Code Bd. Appeals 6 town region Conn., 1974—. Scholar Ecole des Beaux Arts, Fontainebleau, France, 1963; recipient Lowenfish prize Columbia U., 1964, Archtl. record interior, 1976, Conn. AIA award, 1980, honor award AIA, 1981, Red Cedar Shingle Bur. award, 1981, Builders Choice award Builder Mag., 1984; William K. Fellows fellow Columbia U., 1964-65. Fellow AIA, Conn. Soc. Architects. Office: 38 Oak Dr Centerbrook CT 06409-1041 Business E-Mail: bob@robertlharper.com.

HARPER, SHIRLEY FAY, nutritionist, educator, consultant, lecturer; b. Auburn, Ky., Apr. 23, 1943; d. Charles Henry and Annabelle (Gregory) Belcher; m. Robert Vance Harper, May 19, 1973 (dec. Mar. 2000); children: Glenda, Debra, Teresa, Suzanna, Cynthia. BS, Western Ky. U., 1966, MS, 1982. Cert. nutritionist and lic. dietitian, Ky. Dir. dietetics Logan County Hosp., Russellville, Ky., 1965-80; cons. Western State Hosp., Hopkinsville, Ky., 1983-84, instnl. dietetic adminstr., 1984-88; dietitian Rivendell Children's Psychiat. Hosp., Bowling Green, Ky., 1988-90; instr. nutrition Western Ky. U., Bowling Green, 1990-92. Cons. Auburn (Ky.) Nursing Ctr., 1976-95, Belle Meade Home, Greenville, Ky., 1980—, Brookfield Manor, Hopkinsville, 1983—, Sparks Nursing Ctr., Ctrl. City, Ky., 1983—, Muhlenberg Cmty. Hosp., Greenville, 1989-2000, Russellville Health Care Manor, 1978-83, 92-, Westlake Cumberland Hosp., Columbia, Ky., 1993-, Franklin-Simpson Meml. Hosp., Franklin, Ky., 1993-2003, Lakeview Health Care Ctr., Morgantown, Ky., 2001-03, Morgantown Care and Rehab. Ctr., 2003-, Trigg County Personal Care Home, Cadiz, 2002-, Gainsville Manor, Hopkinsville, 2002-; nutrition instr. Madisonville (Ky.) C.C., 1995-98. Mem. regional bd. dirs. ARC of Ky., Frankfort, 1990-96; vice chair ARC of Logan County, 1992-93, chmn., 1993-96, 97—; bd. dirs. Logan County ARC United Way, 1993—; co-chair adv. coun. devel. disabilities Lifeskills, 1992-93, adv. coun. Lifeskills Residential Living Group Home, 1993-2000, human rights adv. coun., 1994-2000; chair Let's Build our Future Campaign; nutrition del. Citizen Am. Program to USSR, 1990; adv. chair for vocat. edn., Russellville; mem. adv. coun. for home econs. and family living, We. Ky. U., 1990-93; bd. dirs. ARC of Logan County for United Way, 1993—; del. 24th Internat. Congress on Arts and Comm., Oxford (Eng.) U., 1997. Recipient Outstanding Svc. award Am. Dietetic Assn. Found., 1993, Outstanding Svc. award Barren River Mental Health-Mental Retardation Bd., 1987, Svc. Appreciation award Logan-Russellville Assn. for Retarded Citizens, 1987, Internat. Woman of Yr. award for contbn. to Nutrition and Humanity, Internat. Biog. Assn., 1993-94, World Lifetime Achievement award Am. Biog. Inst., 1995; inaugurated Lifetime Dep. Gov., Am. Biog. Rsch. Bd., 1995, Pres.'s award ARC of Logan County, 1996, award of excellence Oxford, Eng. Internat. Congress on Arts and Comm., Internat. Sash of Acad., Am. Biog. Inst., 1997. Mem. Am. Dietetic Assn., Nat. Nutrition Network, Ky. Dietetic Assn. (pres. Western dist. 1976-77, Outstanding Dietitian award 1984), Bowling Green-Warren County Nutrition Coun., Nat. Ctr. for Nutrition and Dietetics (charter), Ky. Nutrition Coun., Logan County Home Economist Club (sec. 1994-95, 1999-2000, v.p. 1995-96, 2000-01, pres. 1996-97, 2001—), Internat. Biog. Assn., Internat. Platform Assn., Diabetes Care and Edn., Dietitians in Nutrition Support, Cons. Dietitians in Health Care, Phi Upsilon Omicron (pres. Beta Delta alumni chpt. 1994-96, Outstanding Alumni award 1997). Avocations: music, drawing and art, poetry, reading, cake decorating. Home and Office: 443 Hopkinsville Rd Russellville KY 42276-1286

HARPER, SPENCER E., III, business consultant, lawyer; b. Louisville, Dec. 31, 1956; s. Spencer E. Jr. and Clarice Carol (Sharpe) H. AB cum laude, Princeton U., 1978; JD, Columbia U., 1981. Bar: N.Y. 1981. Assoc. atty. Christy & Viener, N.Y.C., 1981-82; cons. Harper, Ferguson & Davis, Louisville, 1978-86; real estate developer Hoboken, N.J., 1981-86; spl. outside counsel Internat. Paper Realty Corp., Park Ridge, N.J., 1987-89, v.p., gen. counsel, 1989-93; bus. cons., pvt. legal counsel N.Y.C., 1993—. Arts. mgmt. cons., N.Y.C., 1983—. Bd. dirs. Ascension Music Chorus and Orch., Inc., N.Y.C., 1990-99, pres. bd. dirs., 1997-99. Mem. N.Y. State Bar Assn., Print Club of N.Y., J.B. Speed Art Mus. (life), SAR, Soc. Colonial Wars. Presbyterian. Office: 470 W 24th St New York NY 10011-1205

HARPER, STEVEN JAMES, lawyer; b. Mpls., Apr. 25, 1954; s. James Henry and Mary Margaret H.; m. Kathy Joseph Loeb, Aug. 21, 1976; children: Benjamin James, Peter William, Emma Suzanne. BA with distinction, MA in Econs., Northwestern U., 1976; JD magna cum laude, Harvard U., 1979. Bar: Ill. 1979, U.S. Dist. Ct. (no. dist.) Ill. 1979, U.S. Dist. Ct. (we. dist.) Wisc. 1988, U.S. Ct. Appeals (10th Cir.) 1989, U.S. Dist. Ct. (ea. dist.) Mich. 1997, U.S. Ct. Appeals (5th Cir.) 2001, U.S. Ct. Appeals (3rd Cir.) 2002, U.S. Ct. Appeals (7th Cir.) 2002. Assoc. Kirkland & Ellis LLP, Chgo., 1979-85, ptnr., 1985—; adj. prof. of law Northwestern U., Evanston, Ill., 1997—. Mem. ABA, Bd. of Visitors Northwestern U. 1999-; fellow Am. Coll. of Trial Lawyers 1999-. Office: Kirkland & Ellis LLP 200 E Randolph Dr Fl 54 Chicago IL 60601-6636

HARPER, TONI JANE, secondary school educator; b. Lancaster, Pa., Oct. 17, 1945; d. George Howard and Zella M. Rehrer; 1 child, Joni. BA, Indiana U. Pa., 1969, BS, 1980; MEd, Ohio U., 1985, U. Wis., Whitewater. Cert. English and humanities tchr. Ohio. Tchr. Donegal Sch. Dist., Mt. Joy, Pa., 1968-69, numerous sch. dists., Ohio, 1971-77; tchr. English New Lexington (Ohio) City Schs., 1980—2002, libr. specialist Mid. Sch., 2002—. Mem. continuous improvement com. New Lexington City Schs., chairperson local profl. devel. com. Former program dir. Supplemental Rec. Activities Overseas ARC, Washington; mem. coun. Bremen (Ohio) Village, 1991—96, mayor, 1996—2002. Recipient Tchr. award, Ohio Ednl. Media Assn., 1989; grantee, New Lexington City Schs. Mem.: New Lexington Edn. Assn. (past treas., v.p.), Ohio Fedn. Tchrs. (mem. retirement com.), Am. Fedn. Tchrs., Ohio Accountability Task Force, Phi Delta Kappa. Office: New Lexington City Schs 2550 Panther Dr NE New Lexington OH 43764-2303 Office Phone: 740-342-4128. Business E-Mail: nl_tharper@seovec.org.

HARPER, WILLIAM THOMAS, III, psychologist, educator; b. Newport News, Va., Sept. 10, 1956; s. William Thomas Jr. and Queen Vastie (Wilson) H. BS in Psychology, Va. State U., 1978, MEd in Counseling, 1980; cert. in teaching, Coll. William and Mary, 1987; postgrad., Old Dominion U., 1990—; MAT in Urban Counseling, Norfolf State U., 1995. Cert. tchr., Va.; cert. substance abuse and alcoholism counselor, addiction counselor, rehab. technician, substance abuse prevention specialist. Edn. specialist, counselor U.S. Army, Arlington, Va., 1984-85; counselor Dept. Vets. Affairs Med. Ctr., Hampton, Va., 1980-82, mental health technician, 1995-97; asst. supr. testing, dir. student support svcs. Hampton U., 1982—88; asst. to prin., home sch. coord. Hampton City Schs., 1988—89; dir. transition programs Norfolk (Va.) State U., 1989—; v.p. devel. AmChest Diversified Inc., Hampton, 1990—. Crisis counselor Va. State U., Petersburg, 1978-80; counselor ManPower Tng. Svcs., Newport News, Va., 1980; rsch. assoc. Ea. Va. Med. Sch.-The Med. Coll. of Hampton Roads, Norfolk, Va.; rsch assoc. Health Promotions 1st Med. Group, USAF, Langley AFB, Hampton, Va.; exec. v.p. rsch. grants and devel. Lott Cary Hist. Found. Inc.; rsch. bd. advisors Am. Biog. Inst.; mental health technician, counselor Vets. Adminstrn. Med. Ctr., Hampton, Va.; tchr. Christopher Newport U. Excel Program. Spl. Olympic vol. Sarah Boswell Hudgins Regional Ctr., Hampton, 1983—; advisor Psi Chi Nat. Honor Soc., Hampton, 1986; v.p. rsch., grants and devel. Lott Cary Hist. Soc. Exec. Bd.; v.p. r&d The Lott Cary Hist. Found. Recipient Disting. Svc. award peer counselors Hampton U., 1982, U.S. Army Svc. award, 1985, Va. Coll. Pers. Assn. award, 1981, 85, Community Svc. award Kappa Alpha Psi, 1986, Edn. Achievement award, 1986, Va. State U. Alumni award, 1985, Historically Black Coll. Program Counselor Achievement award, 1985, Psi Chi Honor Soc. Achievement award, 1986, Leadership Devel. Tng. Achievement award Howard U., 1983, 85, 86, Hampton VA Med. Ctr. award, 1990, 91, Nat. Black Male Conf. Achievement award, 1990, 91, Black Am. Doctoral Rsch. award, 1991-92, Recognition awards Christopher Newport Coll., 1985-86, Boys Club of Greater Hampton Roads, 1987, 88, 89, 90, City of Alexandria Dept. Human Svcs., 1987, 88, Fraternal Order Police Hampton, Mayor of City of Newport News, 1990, 91, Bd. Govs. Coll. of William and Mary/Internat. Platform Assn., 1990, 4th Nat. Black Student Leadership Devel. 1990-91, Va. Alcohol Safety Action Program, 1990, 91, Commonwealth of Va. Ho. of Dels., 1991, Commonwealth Va. Dept. Mental Health Mental Retardation Substance Abuse Svcs. scholarship, 1995, 96, others; Old Dominion U. grad. scholar, 1983, 85, Hampton U. Mobile Oil scholar, 1985, Va. Dept. Mental Health, Mental Retardation and Substance Abuse Svcs., 1995-98, Am. Cancer Soc. scholar, 1997, Va. Assn. Drug and Alcohol Program scholar, 1998. Mem. AACD, Nat. Assn. Black Psychologist, Nat. Assn. Alcoholism & Drug Abuse Counselors, Va. Assn. Alcoholism & Drug Abuse Counselors, Va. Assn. Adminstrs. in Higher Edn., Va. Assn. Black Psychologists (chmn. com.), Va. Assn. Black Psychologists, Assn. for Prevention of Nicotine Addiction, Peninsula Literacy Coun. (counselor), Internat. Platform Assn. (bd. govs. 1990), Southea. Testing Assn., Alliance Prevention and Treatment Nicotine Addiction, Sci. Soc. of Beta Kappa Chi, Alpha Kappa Mu, Beta Kappa Chi, Kappa Alpha Psi. Democrat. Baptist. Avocations: swimming, bowling, basketball, football skating. Home: 1042 44th St Newport News VA 23607-2313 Office: Norfolk State U 2401 Corprew Ave Norfolk VA 23504-3993

HARPER, WILLIARD FLEMMETT, language educator; b. Cleve., Aug. 1, 1924; s. Huel and Annie Mae (Benton) H. BA, Morehouse Coll., 1947; MA in Langs., Case Western Res. U., 1948; cert. d'etudes, McGill U., Montreal, Can., 1949; PhD, Sorbonne, Paris, 1954. Prof. French and Spanish Wiley Coll., Marshall, Tex., 1948-50; prof., chmn. humanities Dillard U., New Orleans, 1950-54, Albany (Ga.) State Coll., 1954-59; Smith-Mundt and Fulbright scholar U.S. Govt., 1959-65; UNESCO expert Kinshasa, Zaire, 1965-68, Institut Pedagogique, Butare, Rwanda, 1968-70; staff devel. program UN, N.Y.C., 1970-84; cons. UN Devel. Program, N.Y.C., 1984—; U.S. lang. escort, UN resident coord., UNOP resident rep. U.S. Dept. State, Washington, 1987—. Adj. prof. Cuyahoga Community Coll., Cleve., 1989—. Mem. adv. com. Notre Dame Coll., Cleve., 1989; apptd. humanities coun., Gov. Ohio; bd. trustees Cleve. Mus. Nat. History; bd. dirs. Am. Sickle Cell Anemia Assn. Staff sgt. U.S. Army, 1941-43. Ford Found. fellow, 1951-52. Mem. Huachucans (treas. 1987-90). Baptist. Avocations: bridge, chess, reading, classical music. Home: 2202 Acacia Park Dr Cleveland OH 44124-3858

HARPER HAINES, JAN FRANCES, writer, educator; b. Sitka, Alaska, Feb. 9, 1943; d. Walter A. and Flora Jane (Harper) Petri; m. Lawrence W. Haines, Aug. 12, 1977. BS, U. Alaska, 1965. Tchr. Orion Jr. H.S., Anchorage, 1966—67; advt. asst. Milici Valenti, Honolulu, 1971—74; advt. Crocker Bank, San Francisco, 1975—77, stats. analyst, ad mgr., 1977—86; mkt. mgr. 1st Nationwide Bank, San Francisco, 1987—88; spkr., guest lectr. U. Alaska, Juneau, Anchorage and Fairbanks, 1998—2003, panel spkr. Anchorage and Fairbanks, 2003. Author: Cold River Spirits, The Legacy of An Athabascan-Irish Family from Alaska's Yukon River, 2000; contbr. reviews to Whole Earth Pub., Alaskan Embers. Bd. dirs. San Anselmo Libr., Calif., 1994—2004. Grantee, Cook Inlet Region Inc, Anchorage and Doyon Corp., Fairbanks, 1994. Mem.: Sisters In Crime. Home: 66 Tamalpais Ave San Anselmo CA 94960 Office Phone: 415-459-1789.

HARPHAM, VIRGINIA RUTH, violinist; b. Huntington, Ind., Dec. 10, 1917; d. Pyrl John and Nellie Grace (Whitaker) Harpham); m. Dale Lamar Harpham, Dec. 25, 1938; children: Evelyn, George. AB, Morehead State U., 1939. Violinist Nat. Symphony Orch., Washington, 1955-90, prin. of second violin sect., 1964-90; mem. Lywen String Quartet, 1960-69, Nat. Symphony String Quartet, 1973-82. Named to Hall of Fame, Morehead State U., 2003. Episcopalian. Home: 5354 43d St NW Washington DC 20015-2008 E-mail: veeharp@tidalwave.net.

HARR, JOSHUA, information technology executive; PhD in Computational Chemistry, B in Molecular Biology, Brigham Young U. Chief tech. officer Linux Networx, Bluffdale, Utah. Cons. in the field; lectr. in field. Achievements include laying the technical roadmap for Linux Networx and leading the team that is developing cluster management tools. Office: Linux Networx 14944 Pony Express Rd Bluffdale UT 84065 Office Phone: 877-505-5694. Office Fax: 801-568-1010.

HARR, LUCY LORAINE, public relations executive; b. Sparta, Wis., Dec. 2, 1951; d. Ernest Donald Harr and Dorothy Catherine (Heintz) Harr Vetter BS, U. Wis., Madison, 1976, MS, 1978. Lectr. U. Wis., Madison, 1977-82; from asst. editor to editor Everybody's Money Everybody's Money Credit Union Nat. Assn., Madison, 1979-84, mgr. ann. report, 1984-92, v.p. pub. rels., 1984-93, sr. v.p. credit union devel., 1993-96, sr. v.p. consumer rels. and corp. responsibility, 1996-97; owner Providing Solutions, Stoughton, Wis., 1997—; ptnr. Fourth Lake Comm., LLP. Dir. consumer appeals bd. Ford Motor Co., Milw., 1983-87. Author: Credit Union Basic Guide to Retirement Planning, 1998. Bd. dirs. Madison Area Crimestoppers, 1982-84; Midwest coord. of ofcls. USA Triathlon, 2003. Recipient Clarion award, 1982. Mem. Women in Comm. (pres. Madison profl. chpt. 1982-83, nat. v.p. programs 1986-87, vice-chair/sec. nat. interim bd. 1996-97, chair nat. bd. dirs. 1997-2001), Internat. Assn. Bus. Communicators (program chair dist. meeting 1981), Am. Soc. Assn. Execs. (Gold Circle award 1984) Avocations: bicycling, reading. E-mail: lharr@providing-solutions.com.

HARRELD, JAMES BRUCE, information technology executive; b. Gallipolis, Ohio, Dec. 12, 1950; s. James Baldwin and Ann Elizabeth (Lascu) Harreld; m. Mary E. Gillilan; children: Sara Elisabeth, Kelly Lynn, James Christopher, Matthew Parker. BS, Purdue U., 1972; MBA, Harvard U., 1975. Asst. to exec. sec. Sigma Chi, Evanston, Ill., 1972—73; asst. to pres. Epsilon Data Mgmt., Boston, 1973—74; v.p., dir. Boston Cons. Group, Boston, Munich, Chgo., 1975—82; v.p. Dart & Kraft, Northbrook, Ill., 1982—84; sr. v.p. strategy and devel. Kraft, Inc., Glenview, Ill., 1984—89, sr. v.p., chief info. officer, 1988—89, Kraft Gen. Foods, Glenview, 1989—92, sr. v.p. mktg. svcs. and info. systems, 1992—93; pres. and dir. Boston Chicken, Inc., Golden, Colo., 1993—95; sr. v.p., chief strategist IBM, Armonk, NY, 1995—. Adj. prof. mgmt. Kellogg Grad. Sch. Bus. Adminstrn. Northwestern U., 1993—95. Co-author: Survival Manual, 1973. Recipient Balfour Province award, Sigma Chi, 1972, Significant Sig award, 1989, recipient Disting. Engring. Alumnus award, Purdue U., 1991. Mem.: Bachelor Coach Club, Stanwich Club, Amelia Island Plantation Club, Amelia Island Club, Hot Springs Club, Harvard Club (Boston), Denver Country Club, Alpha Pi Mu, Tau Beta Pi. Republican. Presbyterian. Avocations: reading, golf. Office: IBM New Orchard Rd Armonk NY 10504 Office Phone: 914-499-5443. Business E-Mail: harreld@us.ibm.com.

HARRELD, MICHAEL N., bank executive; b. 1944; BA, U. Louisville, 1966, JD, 1969. Joined Citizens Fidelity Bank (now PNC Bank), Louisville, 1969; pres. Citizens Fidelity Corp., 1986, pres., CEO, 1989; regional pres. Ky. and Indiana PNC Bank, 1989—2005, regional pres. Greater Washington D.C., 2005—. Chmn. bd. Louisville Cmty. Found. Bd. dirs. J. B. Speed Art Mus., Norton Healthcare Inc., The Muhammad Ali Ctr. Recipient Louisvillian of the Year award, Advertising Club of Louisville, Disting. Alumnus award, U. of Louisville Law Sch., U. of Louisville Coll. Arts and Sciences, Gold Cup award, Greater Louisville Inc., Different Hero award, Metropolitan Housing Coalition. Mem.: The Ky. Bankers Assn., C. of C., Bd. Greater Louisville Inc.*

HARRELL, CARLTON (BENJAMIN CARLTON HARRELL), writer, retired editor; b. Mamie, NC, Oct. 1, 1929; s. Taylor Smith Jr and Nellie Augusta (Gallop) Harrell; m. Audrey Jeanine Tarkenton, Apr. 26, 1952; children: Melissa Ann, Sheila Lynn. Student, U. N.C., 1947-49. Reporter Daily Advance, Elizabeth City, N.C., 1950-52, 53-56, Goldsboro (N.C.) News-Argus, 1956-57, Durham (N.C.) Sun, 1957-64, state editor, 1964-65, asst. city editor, 1965-69, city editor, 1969-72, mng. editor, 1972-90; assoc. editor Herald-Sun, Durham, 1991-96, editor emeritus, columnist, 1996—. 2d lt U.S. Army, 1952—53. Mem.: Hist Preservation Soc Durham, Res Officers Asn, Am Soc Newspaper Eds. Home and Office: 410 Argonne Dr Durham NC 27704-1428

HARRELL, CAROLYN HARDISON, nursing home administrator; b. Feb. 25, 1942; d. Dewey Jasper and Emma Blanche (Lilley) Hardison; m. Jerry W. Harrell, Apr. 18, 1979; children from previous marriage: Natalie Dawn, John Michael Cameron. B in Nursing, Pacific Western U., 1981, DSc in Health Care Adminstrn., 1982. RN Va. Staff nurse Petersburg Gen. Hosp., 1963—66; staff nurse, supr., insvc. dir. Cen. State Hosp., Petersburg, 1963—73; owner, oper. Cameron's Day Care Ctr., Colonial Heights, Va., 1973—74; dir. nurses Guardian Corp., Petersburg, 1974—76; adminstr. Am. Health Care Corp., Richmond, Va., 1976—77, Beverly Enterprises, Greenville, NC, 1977—83, Pitt County Meml. Hosp., 1983—85, Britthaven, Inc., Kinston, NC, 1985—86, regional dir., 1986—94, v.p. ops., 1994—2001; ret., 2001. Vocat. adv. com. Martin C.C., 1979. Recipient Citizenship award, 1960. Mem.: N.C. Health Care Facilities Assn., Va. Health Care Facilities Assn., Am. Coll. Nursing Home Adminstrs., Bus. and Profl. Women Club. Republican. Office Phone: 252-217-5669. Personal E-mail: harrel6614@earthlink.net.

HARRELL, CHARLES LYDON, JR., lawyer; b. Norfolk, Va., Oct. 22, 1916; s. Charles Lydon Sr. and Ethel Theresa (Toone) H.; m. Martha de Weese Guild, Feb. 5, 1943 (dec. March 1991); children: Charles Lydon III, John Morgan, Marshall Guild, deWeese Toone; m. Lynn Aikens Johnson, July 13, 1993. BA, Randolph-Macon Coll., 1938; LLB, U. Richmond, 1941. Bar: Va. 1940, U.S. Dist. Ct. (ea. dist.) Va. 1946, U.S. Bankruptcy Ct. (ea. and we. dist.) Va. 1946, U.S. Ct. Appeals (4th cir.) 1947, U.S. Ct. Internat. Trade 1950, U.S. Supreme Ct. 1952. Ptnr. Harrell & Landrum, Norfolk, 1947-76; pvt. practice, Norfolk, 1987—. Commr. in chancery Cir. Ct. Princess Anne County, 1950—76; commr. in chancery City of Norfolk, 1955—57; spl. justice Princess Anne County, 1952—65. Mem. health care consumer coun. Naval Hosp., Portsmouth, 1980-90; mem. coun. of ch. Ghent United Meth. Ch., 1950—, tchr. Bible class, 1966—, master, mem. com. Boy Scouts of Am., Sea Scouts; mem. Coun. of Ministries, 1955-88, chmn. commn. on Christian concerns Meth. Ch., 1971-76; co-founder, chmn., pres. bd. dirs. Ghent Venture, Inc.; v.p. Norfolk Seaman's Soc., 1970-80, bd. dirs., 1990—, v.p.; bd. dirs. Handicaps Unltd. of Va., legis. chmn., legal advisor; vol. prayer counsellor Christian Broadcast Network, 1977-93; co-founder, bd. dirs. Va. Assn. of Blind, 1981—; dir. Norfolk Interfaith Coalition for the Elderly, Tidewater Christian Outreach Project; pres. Mobility on Wheels, Inc., 1980-83, bd. dirs., 1977—, v.p. 2000—; mem. com. for therapeutic recreation of handicapped people City of Norfolk, 1991-98; co-founder, v.p., dir. New Life Devel.; pro bono counsel Tidewater Legal Aid Soc., 1989—. Comdr. USN, to 1962. Decorated 9 campaign medals, 4 combat stars; recipient Cross Mil. Svc., UDC. Mem. ABA, Norfolk-Portsmouth Bar Assn., Va. State Bar Assn. (Lawyers Helping Lawyers), Va. Bar Assn., Jud. Soc., Christian Legal Soc., Am. Legion, VFW (past comdr.), Jr. C. of C., Jesus to the World Evangelistic Assn. (co-founder, bd. dirs., v.p., chmn. bd.), Christian Legal Soc., Gideons, Masons, Shriners, Kiwanis, Ret. Officers Assn., The Fleet Res., Tin Can Sailors Assn., Mine Warfare Assn., The Caine Mutineers, McNeil Law Soc., Phi Beta Kappa, Omicron Delta Kappa (sec. Tidewater Alumni chpt.), Tau Kappa Alpha. Avocations: swimming, scuba diving, spear fishing. Home and Office: 4464 Ocean View Ave Virginia Beach VA 23455

HARRELL, EDWARD HARDING, newspaper executive; b. Richmond, Va., Dec. 1, 1939; s. Emmett Livingston Harrell and Martha Mason (Harding) Harrell Owen; m. Diane Greer Dickerson, July 18, 1965 (dec.); children: Sara Wesley, Katherine Harding Cole. BA, U. Va., 1962. Advt. salesman Richmond Newspapers, 1963-68, asst. advt. dir., 1975-82; gen. mgr. Westover Pub., Richmond, 1968-71; mktg. dir. Media Gen. Fin., Richmond, 1971-74; asst. gen. mgr. Pitts. Press, 1982-86; pres. Harrell Assocs., 1986-89, Tribune Rev., 1989—. Bd. dirs. Conv. and Vis. Bur., Pitts., 1985—87, Pitts. Dance Coun., 1985—2000; pres., bd. dirs. Sweetwater Arts Ctr., Sewickley, Pa., 1985—94, Va. Mus. Natural Hist., 1987—94, Pitts. Downtown Partnership, 1994—2004, Pitts. Cultural Trust Bd., 1994—, Phipps Conservatory, 1997—2004, Opportunities Made Equal Bd., 1997—99, Press Club Western Pa., 1995—; pres. City Theatre, 1994—. Capt. U.S. Army, 1962—66. Mem. Newspaper Assn. Am., Duquesne Club (Pitts.), Pitts. Athletic Assn., Edgeworth Club (Sewickley). Democrat. Episcopalian. Avocations: sailing, reading. Office: 503 Martindale St Pittsburgh PA 15212-5746 Office Phone: 412-320-7856. Personal E-mail: edharrell@triweb.com.

HARRELL, GARY PAUL, lawyer; b. Texas City, Tex., July 8, 1952; s. James Eugene Jr. and Mary Alice Harrell; m. Leigh Evans, May 27, 1978. BS, U. Tex., 1977, MA, 1979; cert. mgmt. healthcare facilities, UCLA, 1984; JD cum laude, Lewis & Clark Coll., 1991. Bar: Oreg. 1991, U.S. Dist. Ct. (fed. dist.) Oreg. 1991; diplomate Am. Coll. Healthcare Execs. Staff/charge nurse Healthcare Facilties, Austin, Tex., 1972-78; gen. mgr. Nursing Support Svcs., Austin, 1978-80; dir. edn. Downey (Calif.) Cmty. Hosp., 1980-84; v.p. patient care Grande Ronde Hosp., La Grande, Oreg., 1984-88; assoc. Lane Powell Spears Lubersky, Portland, Oreg., 1990-94; ptnr. Harrell & Nester, LLP, Portland, 1994—. Adj. prof., asst. prof. Calif. State U., Long Beach, 1980-84; pres. Oreg. State Bd. Nursing, Portland, 1987-90. Contbr. chapters to books. With USNR, 1970-74. Recipient Am. Jurisprudence award, 1989. Fellow: Am. Coll. Health Care Adminstrs. (past pres. Oreg. chpt.), Healthcare Fin. Mgmt. Assn. (past pres. Oreg. chpt.); mem.: Oreg. Health Care Assn., Oreg. Health Lawyers Assn. (sec.), Am. Health Lawyers Assn., Oreg. Assn. Nurse Attys. (sec., past pres.), Oreg. State Bar (chair, health law section). Avocations: flying, sailing, motorcycling. Office: Harrell & Nester LLP 1515 SW 5th Ave Ste 1022 Portland OR 97201-5445

HARRELL, GLENN T., JR., judge; BA, U. Md., 1967, JD, 1970. Bar: Md. 1970. Assoc. O'Malley, Miles & Harrell, 1973-76, ptnr., 1977-91; assoc. county atty. Prince George's County, 1971-73; judge at large Ct. Spl. Appeals, 1991-99; judge Ms. Ct. Appeals, Prince George's County, Md., 1999—. Chair Commn. on Jud. Disabilities, 1996-98; mem. exec. com. Md. Jud. Conf., 1997-99; adj. prof. legal writing Sch. Law U. Balt., 1997-; lectr. in field. Mem. Md. Bar Assn., Prince George's County Bar Assn., Md. Bar Found., J. Franklyn Bourne Bar Assn. Office: Ct Appeals PO Box 209 Upper Marlboro MD 20773-0209 Office Phone: 301-952-2716. Business E-Mail: glenn.harrell@courts.state.md.us.

HARRELL, HENRY HOWZE, tobacco company executive; b. Richmond, Va., Sept. 18, 1939; s. Theron Rice and Susan Howze (Haskell) H.; m. Jean Covington Camp, Feb. 7, 1970; children— Susan Hampton, Shelby Madison AB, Washington and Lee U. V.p. Universal Leaf Tobacco Co., Inc., Richmond, 1974-81, sr. v.p., 1981-82, exec. v.p., 1982-86, pres., 1986-88, pres., chief exec. officer, 1988-91; chmn., chief exec. officer Universal Corp. (formerly Universal Leaf Tobacco Co., Inc.), 1991—2002; chmn., dir. Universal Corp. Bd. dirs. Jefferson Bankshares Inc., Charlottesville, Va.; mem. bd. visitors James Madison U., Harrisonburg, Va. Mem. Forum Club, Commonwealth Club, Phi Beta Kappa, Omicron Delta Kappa. Clubs: Country of Va., Deep Run Hunt (bd. dirs. 1981-83), Ocean First Golf, Sunningdale Golf, Kinloch, Foundry Golf. Republican. Episcopalian. Avocations: fishing, gardening.

HARRELL, JERRY DEWITT, ophthalmologist, director; b. Port Arthur, Tex., Sept. 13, 1930; s. Jerry DeWitt and Carrie Belle (Sterrett) Harrell; m. Elizabeth Jane Cooke, Aug. 29, 1952; children: Kathleen Harrell Storm, Deborah Harrell Reining, David DeWitt. BA, Wheaton Coll., 1952; MA, U. Pa., 1957; MD, Jefferson Med. Coll., 1961; DTM & H, London Sch. Hygiene and Tropical Medicine, 1990. Diplomate Am. Bd. Ophthalmology. Fellow Mayo Clinic, Rochester, Minn., 1966—68; med. missionary Wycliffe Bible Translators, Yarinacocha, Peru, 1968—71, Bolivia, 1974—75; resident in ophthalmology Gorgas Army Hosp., Balboa, Panama, 1971—74; col., chief surgery US Army Hosps., 1975—90; med. dir. Lighthouse For Christ Eye Ctr., Mombasa, Kenya, 1990—. Contbr. articles to profl. jours. Med. officer U.S. Army, 1961—65. Decorated Legion of Merit; recipient Hon. Pub. Svc. award, Panama Canal Co., 1985, Humanitarian award, Soc. Mil. Ophthalmologists, 1998. Fellow: ACS, Royal Soc. Tropical Medicine and Hygiene, Am. Acad. Ophthalmology. Republican. Presbyterian. Avocations: tennis, target shooting, reading. Home: 411 Whitefield Ave Saint Simons Island GA 31522 Office: Lighthouse for Christ Eye Ctr Abdel Nasser Rd Mombasa Kenya

HARRELL, KYLE ALEXANDER, lawyer; b. Durham, N.C., Jan. 18, 1960; s. Robert Lewis and Alice Jamison Harrell; m. Shirley Ruth Skyers, May 30, 1998; children: Skye Alexandra, Vanessa Faith, Kyle Alexander II. BSCE, N.C. State U., 1984; JD, N.C. Ctrl. U., 1997. Bar: N.C. 1997, Conn. 2000, U.S. Dist. Ct. Conn. 2002. Design engr. Charlotte-Mecklenburg Utility Dept., Charlotte, NC, 1984—94; assoc. Micheaux and Micheaux, Durham, 1997; asst. pub. defender N.C. Dist. 26 Pub. Defender, Charlotte, 1997—99; ptnr. Skyers and Skyers, Bridgeport, 2000—02; mng. ptnr. The Barrister Law Group, 2002—. Bd. dirs., treas. Brooklawn Acad., Fairfield, Conn., 2001—; mem. Bd. Tax Assessment Appeals, Bridgeport, 2001, chmn., 2002. Mem.: ABA, Conn. Bar Assn., N.C. Bar Assn. (Pro Bono Student Year 1997). Office: The Barrister Law Group 211 State 2d Fl Bridgeport CT 06604 Office Phone: 203-334-4800. Business E-Mail: kaharrell@barristerlawgroup.com.

HARRELL, MARGARET ANN, writer, editor, researcher, photographer; b. Greenville, NC, Sept. 25, 1940; d. John Henry and Rosa Lee Harrell; m. Jean-Marie Mensaert, Feb. 25, 1970 (dec. 1990). BA in History with honors and distinction, magna cum laude, Duke U., 1962; MA in Contemporary Brit. and Am. Lit., Columbia U., 1964; postgrad., U. N.C., 1976, Carl Jung Inst., Zurich, Switzerland, 1984-87; cert. practitioner of basic applications of psycho-dynamic systems, Inst. Human Devel., Ghent, 1992; tchg. diploma, Light Body Internat., Ter Duinen, Belgium, 1999. Moderator Ford Found. summer courses in Greek classics Columbia U., N.Y.C., 1963; copy editor, asst. editor Random House Pubs., N.Y.C., 1965-68; dance instr., 1969; sec. Euro-clear, Brussels, 1972-75; asst. to psychologist, dream rschr., 1983-84; co-organizer US and Indian workshops and lectrs., 1993—; editor, 1968—. Contbr. poetry reading Am. Book Week, Leuven, Belgium, 1992; participant Internat. Poetry Festival, Belgium and Romania, 1992; del. Culture Building Stone for Europe, 2002, Brugge, Belgium, 1993, Athens, 1994; mem. computer parapsychology project U. Amsterdam, 1994, 2000-01; contbr. Internat. Drama Festival, Sibiu, Romania, 1995-96; guest lectr. Sibiu U., 1995; editing coord. internat. Mus. Exhbn. on Life of Jan Mensaert, 1995-2001; pvt. tchr. LuminEssence, Awakening Your Light Body, 2002—. Radiance: Self Exciting, 2004-, Filling in the Frequencies, 2005; presenter, panelist Internat. Parapsychol. Assn., 1995; writer in residence C. Peter McGrath Ctr., Sibiu, Romania, 2005, nat. radio interviewer, Radiance: Filling in the Frequencies, 2005—, Faulkner Fulbright Conf., 2005; presenter in field *"A thoughtful and thought-provoking text illustrating a powerful and extended journey into a higher consciousness...An enthusiastically recommended reading experience, ...a seminal work of wit, wisdom, and imagination." Midwest Book Review, "Reviewer's Choice, " Small Press Bookwatch. "According to Harrell, meditative encounters with remarkable individuals provide the means for tapping into the hidden wellspring of collective worldwide consciousness, as well as the basis of transcending boundaries of time and space and actualizing the latent potential of mankind. She describes in detail her psychic encounters with New York City luminary and poet, Milton Klonsky, and influential Indian Yoga master and saint, Shri Dhyanyogi Madhusudandasji...nuggests of brilliant insight into life, death and the collective unconsciousness." Kirkus Discoveries.* Author: Marking Time with Faulkner: A Study of the Symbolic Importance of the Mark and of Related Actions, 1999, Love in Transition: Vol. I: Voyage of Ulysses: Letters to Penelope, 1996, Vol. II: Voyage of Ulysses: Letters to Penelope, 1996, Vol. III: The Christ State, 1996, Vol. IV: The Bedtime Tales of Jesus, 1998, Space Encounters: Chunking Down the 21st Century (Love in Transition Vol. VI), 2002, Space Encounters II: Chunking Down the 21st Century (Love in Transition Vol. VII), 2002, Space Encounters III:Inserting Consciousness into Collisions (Love in Transition Vol. VIII), 2003, Toward a Philosophy of Perception: The Magnitude of Human Potential: Cloud Optics, 2005; author numerous poems; internat. editing coord. Life, Page One (mus. e-book and 2 music CD-roms), 2001, solo photgraphy exhibit Sun in Profile- So Bright it's Dark, C. Peter McGrathh Ctr., Sibiu,Romania, 2005; contbr. articles to profl. jours. Sponsor Save the Children, 1985—; co-organizer Introduction of South Indian Tamil Siddha tradition into Belgium. Fellow MacDowell Colony, 1969, 1970, 1973. Mem. Publishers Mktg. Assn., Am. Soc. for Psychical Rsch., Romanian Cure Hist. Archeological Soc. (hon.), writer in residence C. Peter McGrath Ctr. (hon.), 2005, Kayumari (co-founder), various wildlife orgns, Am. Assn. Advancement Sci Avocations: t'ai chi, energy studies, art, computers. Office Phone: 919-782-9257. Personal E-mail: marharr@bellsouth.net.

HARRELL, RAY EVANS, performing company executive, conductor, educator; b. Ada, Okla., Dec. 3, 1941; s. Ray E. and Cleo Mae Harrell, William O.A. Rockko; m. Stephanie Rose Weems, June 27, 2005; 1 child, Jane Angela. BA, U. Tulsa, 1964; MM, Manhattan Sch. Music, 1973. Cert. in Rubenfeld synergy method Rubenfeld Ctr., NYC, 1979. Commd. piano tchr. Tulsa (Okla.) U., 1962—64; vocal soloist U.S. Army Field Band, Fort George G. Meade, Md., 1964—66, US Army Chorus, Washington, 1966—70; tchr. voice, performance, opera and vocal anatomy Manhattan Sch. Music, NYC, 1978—86; founder, artistic dir. Magic Cir. Opera Repertory Ensemble Inc., NYC, 1978—; master voice tchr. Magic Cir. Tng., NYC, 1978—; summer opera dir. Mannes Coll. Music, NYC, 1987—89; artistic dir., prodr. Am. Masters Arts Festival Biennial, NYC, 2003—. Lectr. on Donald Schoen Tchrs. Coll., Columbia U., NYC, 1988—89; co-leader MCORE Florentine Conf. on Arts and Econs. in Am., Washington, 2004; singer Miramax Films - Naqoyqatsi, 2001—02; rec. prodr. Magic Cir. Opera Repertory Ensemble, NYC, 1990—; dir. Magic Cir. Awards. Singer: (movie) Pocahontas, 1994 (Oscar, Grammy, Golden Globe awards, 1995); author: (libretto) A Gypsy Carmen. Lectr., panel mem. non-govtl. orgns. UN, NYC, 2000; Cherokee priest Nuyagi Keetoowah Soc., Inc., NYC, 1988—2005. Served with U.S. Army, 1964—70. Regional Finalist, Met. Opera, 1969. Mem.: The Rec. Acad. (life mem.), Phi Mu Alpha. Liberal. Traditional Cherokee Keetoowah. Achievements include design of Magic Circle American Arts centers; Magic Circle training for chamber opera; America's first traditional Cherokee University; Cirque du Soleil approved artist listing. Office: Magic Circle Opera Repertory Ensemble 200 W 70th St Ste 6-C New York NY 10023 Office Phone: 212-724-2398. Personal E-mail: mcore@nyc.rr.com.

HARRELL, SAMUEL MACY, agribusiness executive; b. Indpls., Jan. 4, 1931; s. Samuel Runnels and Mary (Evans) H.; m. Sally Bowers, Sept. 2, 1958 (div.); children: Samuel D., Holly Evans, Kevin Bowers, Karen Susan, Donald Runnels, Kenneth Macy. BS in Econs., Wharton Sch., U. Pa., 1953. Pres., chmn. bd., chief exec. officer, chmn., exec. com. Early & Daniel Industries, Cin., 1971—; chmn. bd., chmn. exec. com. Early & Daniel Co., Cin., 1971—; chmn. bd., chief exec. officer, chmn. exec. com. Tidewater Grain Co., Phila., 1971—. Dir. Harriman Inst. Columbia U.; bd. dirs. Wainwright Bank & Trust Co., Wainright Abstract Co., Nat. Grain Trade Council, U.S. Feed Grains Council; mem. Chgo. bd. Trade Contbg. author: The Status of Agribusiness in Russia and the CIS. Dir. Harriman Inst., Columbia U. With AUS, 1953-55. Mem. Nat. Assn. Cert. Valuation Analysts, Inst. Bus. Appraisers, Am. Soc. Farm Mgrs. & Rural Appraisers, Am. Soc. Agrl. Cons., Internat. Bus. Brokers Assn., Young Pres.'s Orgn., U. Pa. Alumni Assn. (past pres.), Terminal Elevator Grain Mchts. Assn. (dir.), Millers Nat. Fedn. (dir.), Assn. Operative Millers, Am. Soc. Bakery Engrs., Am. Fin. Assn., Council on Fgn. Relations, Fin. Exec. Inst., N.Am. Grain Export Assn. (dir.), Mpls. Grain Exchange, St. Louis Mchts. Grain Exchange, Buffalo Corn Exchange, Delta Tau Delta (Past prs. Ind. alumni) Clubs: Columbia, Indpls. Athletic, Woodstock, Traders Point Hunt, Dramatic, Players, Lambs (Indpls.); Racquet (Phila.); University (Washington and N.Y.C.). Lodges: Masons, Rotary. Presbyterian. Office: EDI Internat Inc 3200 Teton Pines Dr Wilson WY 83014 Home: 15787 Imperial Point Ln Wellington FL 33414-7114 Office Phone: 307-734-6504. E-mail: samharrell@hotmail.com.

HARRELL, TAMARA SUE, music educator; b. Elmhurst, Ill., June 11, 1980; d. Scott Bruce and Cynthia Ann Harrell. B in Music Edn., Valparaiso (Ind.) U., 2002. Music dir. South Ctrl. Schs., Union Mills, Ind., 2002—. Oboe player Windiana, 2002—. Lutheran. Avocations: music, reading, walking, planning events. Home: 1903 Wood St Valparaiso IN 46383-6671

HARRELSON, CLYDE LEE, retired secondary school educator; b. Baton Rouge, Nov. 20, 1946; s. Hezzie Clyde and Marguerite Lucille (Tucker) Harrelson. BA, Southeastern La. U., 1968; MA, La. State U., 1974, EdS, 1980, postgrad., 1981, So. U., 1982. Cert. social studies and English tchr., prin., supr. La. Tchr. English East Baton Rouge Parish Sch. Bd., 1970—2003, McKinley Mid. Magnet Sch., Baton Rouge, 1982—2001, dean of students, 1998—2001; tchr. social studies Ctrl. HS, 2002—03; ret., 2003; tchr. practitioner advisor/mentor Teach La. Consortium/La. Resource Ctr. for Educators, 2003—. Mem. Arts Coun. Greater Baton Rouge, Found. Hist. La., La. Preservation Alliance, Nat. Trust Hist. Preservation, Colonial Williamsburg Found., NCCJ, La. Dem. Com., Nat. Dem. Com.; mem. exec. com. East Baton Rouge Parish Dems., 1981—85, 1996—2004. Mem.: Smithsonian Instn., Mus. Modern Art, Met. Mus. Art, New Orleans Mus. Art, Baton Rouge Gallery, La. Endowment for the Humanities, Old State Capitol Assocs., La. Arts and Sci. Ctr., La. State U. Mus. Art, Kiwanis, Phi Delta Kappa. Episcopalian. Home: 3101 Highland Rd #109 Baton Rouge LA 70802-7814

HARRELSON, F(REDERICK) DANIEL, lawyer; b. Wynne, Ark., Feb. 23, 1942; s. Frederick Crippen and Martha (Proctor) H.;m. Kathryn Plummer, Aug. 23, 1964; children: Kimberly Anne, Mary Elizabeth. BSBA in Acctg., U. Ark., 1964, LLB, 1967. Bar: Ark. 1967, U.S. Dist. Ct. (ea. dist.) Ark. 1969, U.S. Tax Ct. 1979. Law clk. Ark. Supreme Ct., Little Rock, 1967-68; ptnr. Ramsay, Bridgforth, Harrelson & Starling, Pine Bluff, Ark., 1968—. Mem. Ark. Bar Assn. (chair probate com. 1975), Jefferson County (Ark.) Bar Assn. (pres. 1985). Episcopalian. Avocations: general aviation, golf, fishing. Home: 108 Park Pl Pine Bluff AR 71601-6635 Office: Ramsay Bridgforth Harrelson & Starling PO Box 8509 Pine Bluff AR 71611-8509

HARRELSON, WALTER JOSEPH, minister, educator; b. Winnabow, N.C., Nov. 28, 1919; s. Isham Danvis and Mabel (Rich) H.; m. Idella Aydlett, Sept. 20, 1942; children: Marianne McIver, David Aydlett, Robert Joseph. Student, Mars Hill (N.C.) Coll., 1940-41, Litt.D. (hon.), 1977; AB, U. N.C., 1947, Litt.D. (hon.), 1994; B.D., Union Theol. Sem., 1949, Th.D., 1953; postgrad., U. Basel, Switzerland, 1950-51, Harvard, 1951-53; D.D. (hon.), U. of South, 1974, Christian Theol. Sem., 1992. Instr. philosophy U. N.C., 1947; ordained to ministry Baptist Ch., 1949; tutor asst. Union Theol. Sem., 1949-50; prof. Old Testament Andover Newton Theol. Sch., 1951-55; dean, assoc. prof. Old Testament U. Chgo. Div. Sch., 1955-60; prof. Old Testament Div. Sch., Vanderbilt U., Nashville, 1960-75, chmn. grad. dept. religion, 1962-67, dean, 1967-75, Disting. prof. Hebrew Bible, 1975-90, prof. emeritus, 1990—, dir. Lilly Ministry Project, 1990-94; interim dean Disciples Div. House, 1993-94; prof. Wake Forest U., 1994-96, adj. univ. prof. Divinity Sch., 1996—. Dir. Ecumenical Inst. Advanced Theol. Studies, Jerusalem, 1977-78, 78-79; chmn. transl. com. New Rev. Standard Version of the Bible, 2000; vis. prof. Brite Div. Sch. Tex. Christian U., 1992, Boston Coll., 1991, 93; mem. ch. rels. com. U.S. Holocause Meml. Mus. Author: Jeremiah, Prophet to the Nations, 1959, Interpreting the Old Testament, 1964, From Fertility Cult to Worship, 1969, 80, The Ten Commandments and Human Rights, 1980, rev. edit., 1997, (with Rabbi R.M. Falk) Jews and Christians: A Troubled Family, 1990, (with Bruce M. Metzger and Robert C. Dentan) The Making of the New Revised Standard Version of the Bible, 1991, (with Rabbi R.M. Falk) Jews and Christians: In Pursuit of Social Justice, 1996, Festschrift, Passion, Vitality, and Foment: The Dynamics of Second Temple Judaism, 2001; co-author, editor: Teaching the Biblical Languages, 1967, New Interpreter's Study Bible, 2003; editor, contbr.: Israel's Prophetic Heritage, 1962; editl. chmn. Religious Studies Rev., 1974-80; assoc. editor Mercer Dictionary of the Bible, 1990; assoc. editor Mercer Commentary on the Bible, 1995. Dir. project to film Ethiopian Manuscripts, NEH, 1972-84; bd. dirs. Dead Sea Scrolls Found., 1991—, Planned Parenthood Assn., Nashville; active ch. rels. com. U.S. Holocaust Meml. Coun. Traveling fellow Union Theol. Sem., 1949; Am. Coun. Learned Socs. fellow, 1950-51, 70; exch. fellow U. Basel, 1950-51; fellow Inst. Internat. Edn., 1950-51; Fulbright rsch. scholar, Rome, 1962-63; Harvie Branscomb Disting. prof. Vanderbilt U., 1977-78, Alexander Heard Disting. Svc. prof., 1985-86; NEH fellow, Rome, 1983-84; recipient Thomas Jefferson prize, 1987-88, Alumni/ae award Vanderbilt U., 1989, Festschrift, Justice and the Holy, 1989, Union Theol. Sem., N.Y.C., 2003, NC award for Literature, 2004. Mem. NAS (mem. ethics com. Inst. Medicine), Soc. for Values in Higher Edn. (pres. 1972-74), Soc. Bibl. Lit. (pres. 1972), Am. Acad. Religion, Cath. Bibl. Assn., Phi Beta Kappa. Home and Office: 3605 Bechler Ln Winston Salem NC 27106 Office Phone: 336-744-4409. Personal E-mail: walterharrelson@bellsouth.net.

HARRELSON, WOODY, actor; b. Midland, Tex., July 23, 1961; s. Charles V. Harrelson; m. Nancy Simon, 1985 (div. 1986);m. Larua Louie, 1998; children: Deni Montana, Zoe. BA in Theater Arts and English, Hanover Coll., Ind. Appearances include (TV series) Cheers, 1985-93 (Emmy nomination 1986, 87, 89, 91, Emmy award 1988), Will & Grace, 2001, (TV movies) Bay Coven, 1987, Killer Instinct, 1988, Mother Goose Rock 'n' Rhyme, 1990; (feature films) Wildcats, 1986, Eye of the Demon, 1987, Casualties of War, 1989, Cool Blue, 1990, Doc Hollywood, 1991, Ted and Venus, 1991, L.A. Story, 1991, White Men Can't Jump, 1992, Indecent Proposal, 1993, The Cowboy Way, 1994, I'll Do Anything, 1994, Natural Born Killers, 1994, The Sunchaser, 1996, The People vs. Larry Flynt, 1996, Kingpin, 1996, Wag the Dog, 1997, The Thin Red Line, 1998, The Hi-Lo Country, 1998, Edtv, 1999, Austin Powers: The Spy Who Snagged Me, 1999, Grass (voice), 1999, Play It to the Bone, 1999, American Saint, 2000, Scorched, 2002, Anger Management, 2003, She Hate Me, 2004, After the Sunset, 2004; (TV host) Comedy Club All-Star IV, 1990; understudy Broadway prodn. Biloxi Blues; starred in Off-Broadway prodns. The Boys Next Door, 1987, The Zoo Story; actor, playwright Two on Two, Furthest From the Sun, 1993. Avocations: sports, writing, juggling, chess, playing guitar, Elvis Presley, playing piano. Office: Creative Artists Agy 9830 Wilshire Blvd Beverly Hills CA 90212-1825

HARRIBANCE, SEAN LALSINGH, parapsychologist; b. Fyzabad, Trinidad and Tobago, Nov. 11, 1939; arrived in U.S., 1969; s. Harribance Singh and Sampatia Batchasingh; m. Christine Ann Comyn, Feb. 28, 1971; children: Linnea Christine, Sean Lalsingh Jr. Cashier Trinidad Bus Svc., San Fernando, 1959—69; part-time rsch. subject Parapsychology Lab., Dr. Hamlyn Dukhan, Trinidad, 1966—69; parapsychol. rsch. subject Found. for Rsch. on Nature of Man, Durham, NC, 1969—73; part-time rsch. subject Psychical Rsch. Found., Durham, NC, 1969—73, 1980; pres. Sean Harribance Inst. for Parapsychology, Inc., 1980—. Part-time parapsychology rsch. subject Laurentian U., Sudbury, Ont., Can., 1996, 97, 2000; hon. dir. Sean Harribance Inst. for Parapsychology Rsch., Inc., Tex., Sean Harribance Inst. Parapsychology Found., Trinidad; affiliated with engring. dept. Duke U., 1975. Co-author: This Man Knows You, 1976; contbr. articles to profl. jours. including Internat. Jour. Psychophysiology, Internat. Jour. Neuroscience,

Perceptual and Motor Skills, Jour. Parapsychology, Jour. Am. Soc. for Psychical Rsch., Jour. Neuropsychiatry and Clin. Neuroscience, Procs. Parapsychol. Assn., Rsch. in Parapsychology. Named Hon. Citizen, recipient key to city, City of Baton Rouge, 1975; named hon. lt. col. aide-de-camp Ala. State Militia, 1975. Home: PO Box 908 Sugar Land TX 77487-0908 Office Phone: 281-980-3860. Personal E-mail: harribance@yahoo.com.

HARRICE, CY (NICHOLAS PSIHARIS), announcer; b. Chgo., Mar. 1, 1915; s. Peter and Vasiliki (Anargyros) Psiharis; child by previous marriage, Lincoln Peter; m. 2d, Helena Seroy, Dec. 12, 1959; 1 child, Melanie Samantha. Student Sch. Commerce, Northwestern U., 1934-38. Concession barker Chgo. World's Fair, 1934; with Samuel Insull ABC Network, 1935; announcer, copywriter, newsman, programmer Sta. WLS, Chgo., 1936-42; news broadcaster Sta. WGN, Chgo., 1942-45; freelance comml. announcer NBC, CBS, ABC and Mutual, N.Y.C., 1945—. Contract comml. announcer "and, they are mild!" segment Pall Mall cigarette advt. campaign for radio and TV, 1946-70; product spokesman for GM, Proctor & Gamble, DuPont Co., Miller Brewing Co., Alka-Seltzer, Kaiser-Fraser; host Adventures Sherlock Holmes, 1947-49; announcer radio programs for Walter Winchell, Grand Cen. Sta., Cavalcade of Am., The Big Story, H.V. Kaltenborn, Wednesday Night Fights, William L. Shirer, RCA Victor Show, The Thin Man, Quick as a Flash; producer What's the Good Word; co-starred with Ginger Rogers in Seven Hundred Boiled Shirts, Cavalcade of Am., NBC, 1951; pres. Stair Mountain Prodns. Recipient Sargent Oratorical award, 1935; Clio award, 1962; 1st place Gold medal sabres Ill. Fencers League, 1936, Advt. Fedn. Am. medal; mem. champion sabre team Amateur Fencers League Am., 1935. Mem. SAG (bd. dirs. 1966-69), AFTRA (bd. dirs. 1956-60), Friars Club, Lambs Club, Deru Club, Lynx Club. Address: PO Box 189 Kelly WY 83011-0189 Office Phone: 307-733-9705.

HARRIES, JAMES THEODORE, psychologist; b. Buffalo, N.Y., June 25, 1930; s. James Theodore Harries and Lula Anna Willer-Harries; m. Karen Louise Davies, June 27, 1964 (dec. June 1997). Student, Art Inst. Buffalo, 1948-50, Albright-Knox Art Sch., 1955-58; BFA, U. Buffalo, 1958; MEd, SUNY, Buffalo, 1960, PhD, 1970. Lic. psychologist, ednl. psychology, Mass.; health svc. provider cert. Mass. Bd. Registration Psychologists. Cert. sch. psychologist Amherst (N.Y.) Sch. Sys., 1966-67; adj. prof. Canisius Coll. Grad. Sch., Buffalo, 1968-69; dir. doctoral program sch. psychology Boston U., 1969-73; dir. Mental Health Ctr. Salem (Mass.) Coll., 1973-77, coord. grad. studies in counseling, 1977; pres. Behaviorl Devel. Assocs., P.C., Brookline, Boston, 1977—. Pres. Western N.Y. Pers. and Guidance Assn., Buffalo, N.Y., 1966-68; vis. prof. U. Heidelberg, Germany, 1971; resident prof. U.S. Dept. Def., Boston U., Karlsruhe, Germany, 1971. Author: Psychological Dimensions of Prostate Cancer, 1999; editor: 38 Psychological Measures: A Reference for Counselors, 1969; editor The Counselor, 1964-65, Jour. N.Y. State Counselors Assn., 1967-68. Active Buffalo Soc. Artists, 1954-69; bd. mem. Mental Health Assn. Erie County, Buffalo, 1966; co-founder N.Y. State Sch. Counselors Assn., 1966. Recipient George E. Hutcherson Hon. award State N.Y. Counselors Assn., 1968. Mem. APA, Am. Coll. Forensic Examiners, Inc., Am. Assn. Clin. Counselors, Nat. Assn. Sch. Psychologists (nat. dir. New Eng. region 1975-77, nat. bd. mem. 1975-77), Prescribing Psychologists' Register Inc. (charter), Mass. Sch. Psychologists Assn. (pres. 1974-76, Presdl. award 1976), Phi Delta Kappa (life). Avocations: organizational structure, anxiety research, watercolor painting, travel, architecture. Home: Sea Cliff Walk Folly Point Rd Gloucester MA 01930 Office: Behavioral Devel Assocs PO Box 389 Rockport MA 01966-0489

HARRIES, KARSTEN, philosophy educator, researcher; b. Jena, Thuringia, Germany, Jan. 25, 1937; came to U.S., 1951; s. Wolfgang and Ilse (Grossmann) H.; m. Elizabeth Wanning, July 4, 1959; children: Lisa, Peter, Martin; 2d m., Elizabeth L. Langhorne, Mar. 14, 1991. BA, Yale U., 1958, PhD, 1962. Instr. Yale U., New Haven, 1961-63, asst. prof. philosophy, 1965-66, assoc. prof., 1966-70, prof., 1970—, Mellon prof., 1986-91; asst. prof. U. Tex., Austin, 1963-65. Lectr. U. Bonn, Fed. Republic Germany, winters 1965-66, 68-69. Author: The Meaning of Modern Art, 1967, The Bavarian Rococo Church, 1983, The Broken Frame, 1989, The Ethical Function of Architecture, 1996 (Winner of 8th Ann. AIA Internat. Architecture Book award for criticism), Infinity and Perspective, 2001; editor: (with Christoph Jamme) Martin Heidegger: Kunst, Politik, Technik, 1992, Martin Heidegger: Politics, Art, and Technology, 1994; contbr. numerous articles and revs. to profl. jours. Recipient Disting. Teaching Effectiveness award U. Tex., 1964; Morse fellow Yale U., 1965-66, Guggenheim fellow, N.Y.C., 1971-72. Mem. Am. Philos. Assn., Soc. for Eighteenth Century Studies, Renaissance Soc. Am., Cusanus Soc. Home: 16 Morris St Hamden CT 06517-3423 Office: Yale U Dept Philosophy New Haven CT 06520 E-mail: karsten.harries@yale.edu.

HARRIFF, SUZANNA ELIZABETH BAHNER, media consultant; b. Vicksburg, Miss., Dec. 30, 1953; d. David S. and F. Suzanne (McElwee) Bahner; m. James R. Harriff, Sept. 10, 1977; 1 child, Michael James. BA summa cum laude, SUNY-Fredonia, 1976; postgrad., Cornell U. Law Sch., 1981; MDiv with distinction, Colgate Rochester Div. Sch., 1995. Ordained to ministry Am. Bapt. Chs. USA, 1995. Media asst. Comstock Advt., Syracuse, N.Y., Buffalo, 1976-77; media buyer/planner G. Andre Delporte, Syracuse, 1979-81; media dir. Roberts Advt., Syracuse, 1982; dir. media svcs. Signet Advt., Syracuse, 1982-84; owner, pres. MediaMarCon, Syracuse, 1984—. Interim dir. mktg. and comm. Onondaga CC, 1998—99; adj. prof. Newhouse Sch. Syracuse U., 2001—02; pub. rels. cons. Syracuse Symphony Orch., 2000—01, 2005. Vol. pub. TV auction drive, chair media divsn. Sta. WCNY-TV, 1986—97, 2004, gen chair, 1994, chair media divsn., 1986—97, 2004—; Pheresis donor ARC, 1987—; accompanist musicals and chorus Manlius-Pebble Hill Sch., 1991—96; resource devel. chair Winterfest, Syracuse, 1992; lead female vocalist Aspen Dreams, 1996—; cmty. liason Cmty. United Way, 2000—01; media panelist Hugh O'Brien Youth Leadership Conf., 2003, 2004; bd. dirs. Westminster Manor, 2004—; music dir., pianist Manlius (N.Y.) United Meth. Ch., 1983—92, youth dir., 1983—85; co-chair St. Nicholas Ecumenical Festival, 1992—98, Am. Bapt. Ch. Nat. Biennial Conf., 1995; dir. music First Bapt. Ch., Manlius, 1993—96; assoc. pastor Andrews Meml. United Meth. Ch., 1996—99; workshop leader United Meth. Ch., 1997—; interim pastor Oswego First United Meth. Ch., 2000; pastor Apulia and Onativia United Meth. Chs., 2000—02; interim pastor Hannibal (N.Y.) Cmty. Ch., 2003—04; tchr. Am. Bapt. Chs. N.Y. state lay studies program Bethel Bible Inst., Syracuse. Recipient 500 Hour Svc. pin, WCNY, 1996, Gold Medallion of Excellence, Upstate N.Y. Dist., 1999, Bronze and Silver Paragon awards, Nat. Coun. Mktg. and Pub. Rels., 2000, Women in Bus. award, 2001. Mem.: NAFE, Irish-Am. Cultural Inst. Syracuse, Syracuse Advt. Club (bd. dirs. 1985—88, program chair 1986—88, pres. 1988—89), Phi Beta Kappa. Democrat. Avocations: music, theater. Home: 8180 Bluffview Dr Manlius NY 13104-9740 Office Phone: 315-423-0226. Business E-Mail: sharriff@mediamarcon.com.

HARRIGAN, ANTHONY HART, author; b. N.Y.C., Oct. 27, 1925; s. Anthony Hart and Elizabeth Elliott (Hutson) H.; m. Elizabeth McP. Ravenel, Aug. 16, 1950; children: Anthony Hart, Elizabeth Chardon, Elliott McP., Mary Ravenel. Student, Bard Coll., Kenyon Coll., Gambier, Ohio, U. Va. Reporter Virginian-Pilot, Norfolk, 1953-55, Charleston (S.C.) News & Courier, assoc. editor, 1957-70; exec. v.p. U.S. Indsl. Coun., Nashville, 1970-78, pres., 1978-90. Pres. U.S. Bus. and Indsl. Coun. Ednl. Found., 1978-90; trustee, rsch. fellow Nat. Humanities Inst.; lectr. Harvard U., Nat. War Coll., Vanderbilt U., U. Colo.; past mem. rsch. com. S.C. Commn. Higher Edn. Author: Ten Poets Anthology, 1947, The Editor and the Republic, 1952, Red Star Over Africa, 1964, The New Republic, 1965, Defense Against Total Attack, 1966, A Guide to the War in Vietnam, 1965, American Perspectives, 1974, American Perspectives II, 1977; co-author: The Indian Ocean and the Threat to the West, 1976, The Southern Oceans and the Security of the Free World, 1978, Putting America First, 1987, American Economic Pre-eminence, 1989; co-author or editor other works, 1978; editl. adv. bd. Modern Age, 1955—; author newspaper column, 1970-90, also numerous articles in nat. jours. Trustee Nat. Humanities Inst. Served with USMCR, World War II. Recipient Mil. Rev. award U.S. Army Command and Gen. Staff Coll., 1965; grantee Relm Found., 1966, Wilbur Found., 1992, 95, Earhart Found., 1993. Mem. Soc. Colonial Wars in S.C., Carolina Yacht Club. Anglican. Home: 46 Eugenia Ave Kiawah Island SC 29455-5609

HARRIGAN, DANIEL JOSEPH, lawyer; b. Indpls., Oct. 30, 1937; m. Ann Boersig. BS, Ind. U., 1959, JD, 1962. Bar: Ind. 1963, U.S. Dist. Ct. (so. dist.) Ind., 1963, cert. in civil law Nat. Bd. Trial Advocacy., U. S. Dist. Ct. (no. dist.) Ind., 1965, U.S. Supreme Ct., 1970. Law clk. to Hon. Dewey Kelley Ind. Appellate Ct., Indpls., 1963; ptnr. Bayliff, Harrigan, Cord & Maugans, Kokomo, Ind., 1966—. Sr. counsel Am. Coll. Barristers; lectr. in field. Note editor Ind. Law Jour., 1962. Mem. ATLA (state committeeman 1980-81,chair RR law sect. 1996, bd. govs. 1992-97), Ind. Bar Found., Ind. Bar Assn., Ind. Trial Lawyers Assn. (bd. dirs. 1977—, exec. com, 1977-86, treas. 1978-82, 1st v.p. 1982, 1st v.p. 1983, pres. 1984-85, coll. of fellows 1986—, pres. 1995), Howard County Bar Assn. (pres. 1987), Phi Alpha Delta. Office: Bayliff Harrigan Cord & Maugans PO Box 2249 Kokomo IN 46904-2249 Office Phone: 765-459-3941. Business E-Mail: dan.harrigan@bhcmlaw.com.

HARRIGAN, EDMUND PATRICK, physician, researcher; b. Springfield, Mass., Jan. 31, 1953; s. Edmund Lawrence and Kathleen Marie (Griffin) H.; m. Julie Marie Burghardt, Apr. 22, 1950; children: Eamon Patrick, David Russell, Jeffrey Conor, Paul William. BA in Chemistry magna cum laude, St. Anselm Coll., Manchester, N.H., 1974; postgrad., UCLA, 1975; MD, U. Mass., 1979. Diplomate Am. Bd. Psychiatry and Neurology. Intern in internal medicine Berkshire Med. Ctr., Pittsfield, Mass., 1979-80; resident in neurology Boston U., 1980-83, teaching fellow in neurology, 1980-83; pres. Coastal Neurology Svcs., Inc., Somersworth, N.H., 1985-90; with CIBA Geigy Pharm., Summit, N.J., 1990-92, Pfizer Ctrl. Rsch., Groton, Conn., 1992—. Contbr. articles to profl. jours., chpt. to book. Mem. AMA, Am. Acad. Neurology, Am. Soc. Exptl. Neuro-Therapeutics (mem. exec. com.). Office: Pfizer Ctrl Rsch Eastern Point Rd Groton CT 06340

HARRIGAN, JOHN THOMAS, JR., physician, obstetrician, gynecologist; b. Perth Amboy, N.J., Apr. 20, 1929; s. John T. and Mary E. (Czapp) H.; m. Marlene Lulka, Apr. 14, 1961 (div.); children: John, Alisa, Edmund; m. Karen Tiejen, Aug. 23, 1992. Student, U. Va., 1946-49; MD, George Washington U., 1953. Diplomate Am. Bd. Ob-Gyn. Intern Doctors Hosp., Washington, 1953-54; resident in ob-gyn Luth. Hosp., Balt., 1954-55, Providence Hosp., Washington, 1957-58, Free Hosp. for Women, Boston, 1958-59; practice medicine specializing in ob-gyn, sub specialist in maternal-fetal medicine Jersey City, 1960-65, Colonia, N.J., 1962-70, Madison Twp., N.J., 1965-70; asst. attending in ob-gyn Margaret Hague Hosp., Jersey City, 1960-65; attending physician in ob-gyn Rahway Hosp., N.J., 1962-70, South Amboy Hosp., N.J., 1965-73, sec. to med. staff, 1970; attending in ob-gyn Martland Hosp. Unit, Newark, 1970-74; dir. dept. ob-gyn Monmouth Med. Ctr., Long Branch, N.J., 1974-76, dir. regional perinatal edn. program, 1975-78; dir. Monmouth Perinatal Ctr., Long Branch, 1975-78; sr. attending in ob-gyn St. Peter's Med. Ctr., 1978—; assoc. prof. ob-gyn Hahnemann Med. Coll., Phila., 1975-78; prof. dir. div. maternal-fetal medicine Rutgers Med. Sch., Piscataway, N.J., 1978—, prof. ob-gyn., dir. div. maternal-fetal medicine, 1978-86, U. Medicine and Dentistry N.J., Robert Wood Med. Sch., 1986—. Cons. in maternal-fetal medicine to physicians, Eastern N.J.; mem. maternal and infant care services com. N.J. Dept. Health, 1975—; dir. statewide premature delivery prevention project; med.-legal expert cons.; tech. adv. panel Healthstart program, N.J. Health Dept. Contbr. articles to med. jours.; reviewer med. jours. Mem. task force on biomed. causes and pub. rels. Gov.'s Coun. on Prevention Mental Retardation, N.J., task force on genetics and fetal defects, 1984—; mem. pub. affairs com. MOD Birth Defects Found.; pres. Perinatal Assn. N.J., 1991-93; mem. N.J. Commn. of Health and Parental and Child Health adv. Com., 1993—, vice chair, 1995—. Capt. M.C. U.S. Army, 1955-57. Fellow ACOG (vice chmn. N.J. sect. 1979-82, chmn. N.J. sect. 1982—, nat. adv. coun. 1982—, legis. rep., treas. dist. III 1986); mem. AMA, Med. Soc. N.J. (maternal infant care com. 1988—), Am. Inst. Ultrasound in Medicine (legis. com. 1994), Am. Fertility Soc., N.J. Perinatal Assn. (v.p. 1980-90, pres. 1990), N.J. Perinatal Tech. adv. Com. Baker channing Soc., N.J. Ob-gyn. Soc. (coun.), N.J. Maternal Fetal Medicine Soc. (pres. 1994-95). Democrat. Roman Catholic. Home: 301 Sussex Ave Spring Lake NJ 07762-1231 Office: Jersey Shore Med Ctr Perinatal Inst 301 Sussex Ave Spring Lake NJ 07762-1231 Personal E-mail: j.harrigan@verizon.net.

HARRIGAN, LORI, Olympic athlete; b. Las Vegas, Nevada, Sept. 5, 1970; Student, U. Nevada, Las Vegas. Motivational speaker; mem. USA Women's Softball Team, Athens Olympics, 2004. Named 2 time All-Am. Achievements include number retired at U. Nevada, Las Vegas, February 26, 1998; mem. USA Women's Softball Gold medal Teams, ISF World Championships, 1994, 98, 2002; mem. USA Women's Softball Gold medal Team, Atlanta Olympics, 1996; mem. USA Women's Softball Gold medal Team, Sydney Olympics, 2000, Athens Olympics, 2004; mem. Calif. Commotion ASA Championship Team, 1999; first individual pitcher to throw an Olympic no-hitter.

HARRIGAN, ROSANNE CAROL, medical educator; b. Miami, Feb. 24, 1945; d. John H. and Rose (Hnatow) Harrigan; children: Dennis, Michael, John. BS, St. Xavier Coll., 1965; MSN, Ind. Univ., 1974, EdD in Nursing and Edn., 1979. Staff nurse, recovery rm. Mercy Hosp., Chgo., 1965, evening charge nurse, 1965—66; head nurse Chgo. State Hosp., 1966—67; nurse practitioner Health and Hosp. Corp. Marion County, Indpls., 1975—80; assoc. prof. Ind. U. Sch. Nursing, Indpls., 1978—82; nurse practitioner devel. follow up program Riley Hosp. for Children, Indpls., 1980—85; prof. Ind. U. Sch. Nursing, Indpls., 1982—85; chief nursing sect. Riley Hosp. Child Devel. Ctr., Indpls., 1982—85; chmn., prof. maternal child health Loyola U., Niehoff Sch. Nursing, Chgo., 1985—92; dean sch. nursing U. Hawaii, Honolulu, 1992—2002; nurse practitioner Waimanalo Health Ctr., Hawaii, 1998—; Frances A. Matsuda chair women's health John A. Burns Sch. Medicine, Honolulu, 2000—, assoc. dean, 2002—, chair complementary and alternative medicine dept., 2002—, prof. pediat., 2003—. Lectr. Ind. U. Sch. Nursing, 1974-75, chmn. dept. pediat., family and women's health, 1980-85; adj. prof. of pediat. Ind. U. Sch. Med., 1982-85; editl. bd. Jour. Maternal Child Health Nursing, 1984-86, Jour. Perinatal Neo-natal, 1985—, Jour. Perinatology, 1989—, Loyola U. Press, 1988-92; adv. bd. Symposia Medicus, 1982-84, Proctor and Gamble Rsch. Adv. Com. Blue Ribbon Panel; sci. rev. panel NIH, 1985; mem. NIH nat. adv. coun. nursing rsch., 2000-; cons. in field. Contbr. articles to profl. journals. Bd. dir. March of Dimes Ctrl. Ind. Chpt., 1974-76, med. adv., 1979-85; med. and rsch. adv. March of Dimes Nat. Found., 1985—, chmn. Task Force on Rsch. Named Nat. Nurse of Yr. March of Dimes, 1983; faculty rsch. grantee Ind. U., 1978, Pediatric Pulmonary Nursing Tng. grant Am. Lung Assn., 1982-85, Attitudes, Interests, and Competence of Ob-Gyn. Nurses Rsch. grant Nurses Assn. Am. Coll. Ob-Gyn., 1986, Attitudes, Interests, and Priorities of Neo-natal Nurses Rsch. grant Nat. Assn. Neonatal Nurses, 1987, Biomedical Rsch. Support grant, 1988; Doctoral fellow Am. Lung Assn. Ind. Tng. Program, 1981-86. Mem. AAAS, ANA (Maternal Child Nurse of Yr. 1983), Assn. Women's Health, Obstetrical and Neonatal Nursing (chmn. com. on rsch. 1983-86), Am. Nurses Found., Nat. Assn. Neo-natal Nurses, Nat. Perinatal Assn. (bd. dir. 1978-85, rsch. com. 1986), Midwest Nursing Rsch. Soc. (theory devel. sect.), Ill. Nurses Assn. (commn. rsch. chmn. 1990-91), Ind. Nurses Assn., Hawaii Nurses Assn., Ind. Perinatal Assn. (pres. 1981-83), N.Y. Acad. Sci., Ind U. Alumni Assn. (Disting. Alumni 1985), Sigma Xi, Pi Lambda Theta, Sigma Theta Tau (chpt. pres. 1988-90). Office Phone: 808-692-0909. Business E-Mail: harrigan@hawaii.edu.

HARRILL, S. KENT, management consultant; BA in Tech. Writing and Editing, NC State U., 1986; MA in Drama Studies with honors, Johns Hopkins U., 1994; MBA in Strategy and Fin., Cornell U., 1996. Tech. writer Northern Telecom (now Nortel), Raleigh, NC, 1984—86, Hekimian Labs., Gaithersburg, Md., 1986—87; from tng. writer, trainer to proposal mgr. Weber and Assoc., Reston, Va., 1987—89; founder, lead cons. Harrill and Assoc., Alexandria, Va., 1989—94; assoc. cons. APM (now CSC Healthcare), Atlanta, 1996—97; from assoc. cons. to cons. Wilkerson Group (now IBM, NYC, 1997—99; from sr. cons. to dir. Adv. Bd. Co., Washington, 1999—2001; prin. PA Cons. Group, Cambridge, Mass., 2001—03; founder, lead cons. Harrill and Assoc., Clearwater, Fla., 2003—. Avocations: tennis, weightlifting, soccer, swimming, piano. Mailing: 2757 Via Cipriani Ste 1135 Clearwater FL 33764

HARRILL, WILLIAM DAVIS, SR., retired principal; b. Bostic, NC, Sept. 22, 1922; s. Grover Bryan and Judie Clara (Davis) Harrill; m. Elizabeth Hopper; children: William Davis Jr., Gloria Dee. MA in hist. and bus. edn., Peabody U., 1950. Cert. sch. prin. NC. Prin. Pub. Sch. Greco Creek, Columbus, NC, Pub. Sch., Lake Luke, NC, 1997—2003; ret., 2003. NC state legislator NC, Raleigh, NC. Pvt. army signal corps, 0940—1947, NC. Mem.: Forest City NC C. of C. (pres.). Democrat. Bapt. Avocations: writing spiritual humor, radio talk shows. Home: 105 Maple St Apt 3 Spindale NC 28160

HARRIMAN, GERALD EUGENE, retired business administrator, retired economics professor; b. Dell Rapids, S.D., May 30, 1924; s. Roy L. and Margaret (Schrantz) H.; m. Eileen Bernadine Bensman, June 10, 1950; children— G. Peter, Mary K., Margaret C., Elizabeth A. BS, U. Notre Dame, 1947; A.M., U. S.D., 1949; PhD, U. Cin., 1957. Expediter Minn. Mining & Mfg. Co., 1947-48; from instr. to asst. dean, chmn. dept. bus. adminstrn. and finance Xavier U., 1949-66; prof. bus. adminstrn., chmn. div. bus. and econs. Ind. U., South Bend, 1966-75, prof. bus. adminstrn. and econs., 1975-89, prof. emeritus, 1989—, dean faculties, 1975-87, acting chancellor, 1979, vice chancellor acad. affairs, 1987-89; ret., 1989. Vis. prof. fin. U. S.D., 1962; chmn. acad. deans Ind. Conf. Higher Edn., 1981-82; cons. in field. Mem. citizens adv. coun. long range fin. planning Coun. of City of Cin., 1963; mem. Community Edn. Roundtable, 1984—; mem. Scholarship Found. of St. Joseph County, Inc., 1992. Served with USNR, 1942-45. Mem.: Am. Econs. Assn., Am. Fin. Assn., Beta Gamma Sigma. Home: 16600 Gerald St Granger IN 46530-9579 Office: 1700 Mishawaka Ave South Bend IN 46615-1408

HARRIMAN, JOHN, music educator; b. Greensboro, NC, Oct. 18, 1952; s. Joseph Kimball and Mary Ann Harriman; m. Monica Sorrells, Aug. 16, 1975; children: Carr, Drew. MusB, U. of Ga., 1975, M Mus. Edn., 1991. Itinerant strings specialist Clarke County Schs., Athens, Ga.; lead tchr. strings specialist Dougherty Pub. Schs., Albany, Ga., 1976—79; pub. and co-owner Halo Corp., Inc. d/b/a Homes and Land Of North Atlanta, and d/b/a Auto Showcase of Atlanta, Dunwoody, 1979—82; itinerant strings specialist Gwinnett County Schools, Lawrenceville, Ga., 1982—92; strings specialist Lilburn Mid. Sch., Ga., 1992—94; orch. dir., strings specialist Collins Hill H.S., Suwanee, Ga., 1994—. Fine arts leadership team Gwinnett County Schools, 1992—94; adjudicator GMEA Large Group Festivals, Ga., 1976—, GMEA Solo/Ensemble Festivals, Ga., 1975—, Georgia's Gov. Honors Program; chmn. GMEA 9th Dist., Ga.; founder/dir. Albany Youth Symphony, Ga., 1977—79, Lilburn MS Chamber Players, 1990—94, Lawrenceville MS Chamber Players, 1994—97; cellist Gainesville Symphony Orch., Ga., 1984—, Toccoa Symphony Orch., Ga., 1982—94; bassist Perimeter Coll. Jazz Ensemble, Clarkston, Ga., 1986—, Jazzlites, Footnotes Jazz Quartet. Performer Dept. Interior Johnny Horizon's Cleanup Am. Campaign for 1976, Washington, 1973—75; organizer Musicians for area performances, Atlanta, 1982—2002. Mem.: Nat. Sch. Orch. Assn., Am. Strings Teachers Assn., Music Educators Nat. Conv., Ga. Music Educators Assn. (9th dist. chmn. 1994—96), Phi Mu Alpha (v.p. 1974—75). Methodist. Avocation: carpentry, performing big band/jazz, performing classical music, composing and arranging music. Office: Collins Hill HS 50 Taylor Rd Suwanee GA 30024 E-mail: john_harriman@gwinnett.k12.ga.us.

HARRIMAN, JOHN HOWLAND, retired lawyer; b. Buffalo, Apr. 14, 1920; s. Lewis Gildersleeve and Grace (Bastine) H.; m. Barbara Ann Brunmark, June 12, 1943; children— Walter Brunmark, Constance Bastine, John Howland. AB summa cum laude, Dartmouth, 1942; JD, Stanford U., 1949. Bar: Calif. 1949. Assoc. firm Lawler, Felix & Hall, L.A., 1949-55; asst. v.p., then v.p. Security Pacific Nat. Bank, L.A., 1955-72, sr. v.p., 1972-85; ret., 1985. Sec. Security Pacific Corp., 1971-85; dir. Master Metal Works; mem. nat. adv. coun. The Pub. Svc., 1992-93. Mem. L.A. adv. coun. Episcopal Ch. Found., 1977-79; mem. Republican Assocs., 1951-72, trustee, 1962-72; mem. Calif. Rep. Central Com., 1956-69, 81—, exec. com., 1960-62, 81-84; mem. L.A. County Rep. Central Com., 1958-70, exec. com., 1960-62, vice chmn., 1962; chmn. Calif. 15th Congl. Dist. Rep. Central Com., 1960-62, Calif. 30th Congl. Dist. Rep. Central Com., 1962; treas. United Rep. Fin. Com. L.A. County, 1969-70; chmn. L.A. County Reagan-Bush campaign, 1980, co-chmn., 1984; exec. dir. Calif. Rep. Party, 1985-86. With USAAF, 1943-46. Mem. Am. Bar Assn., State Bar Calif., Phi Beta Kappa, Theta Delta Chi, Phi Alpha Delta. Clubs: California (Los Angeles); Lincoln, Breakfast Panel (pres. 1970-71).

HARRIMAN, RICHARD LEE, performing arts association administrator, educator; b. Independence, Mo., Sept. 10, 1932; s. Walter S. and M. Eloise (Faulkner) Harriman. AB, William Jewell Coll., 1953, LittD (hon.), 1983; MA, Stanford U., 1959. Instr., asst. prof. English U. Dubuque, Iowa, 1960—62; asst. prof. English William Jewell Coll., Liberty, Mo., 1962, acting head English dept., 1965—69, dir. fine arts program, 1965—2003, assoc. prof., 1966—. Artistic dir. Harriman Arts Program, Liberty, 2003—. Treas. Kansas City Arts Coun., 1980, sec, 1981, Kansas City Am. Arts Festival, 1988—89. With AUS, 1953—55. Woodrow Wilson fellow, 1957. Mem.: AAUP, MLA, Assn. Performing Arts Presenters (nat. exec. bd. 1975—78), Shakespeare Assn. Am., Internat. Soc. Performing Arts, Alpha Psi Omega, Sigma Tau Delta, Lambda Chi Alpha. Methodist. Home: 1043 E Hwy H Liberty MO 64068-4303

HARRINGER, OLAF CARL, architect, museum administrator; b. Hamburg, Germany, Apr. 29, 1919; came to U.S., 1927; s. Henry Theodore and Anke (Berger) H.; m. Helen Ehrat Hedges, Dec. 20, 1975; children— Carla, Brita, Eric. Student, Evanston Acad. Fine Arts, The New Bauhaus, 1937-38, Ill. Inst. Tech., 1942-45. Designer Raymond Loewy Assos., Chgo., 1946-49, H. Allan Majestic Assos., Chgo., 1949-51, Dickens, Inc., Chgo., 1951-52, Olaf Harringer and Assos. (architects/designers), Chgo., 1952-62; account exec. several exhibit firms Chgo., 1962-68; dir. exhibits Mus. Sci. and Industry, Chgo., 1957-60, 68-80; prin. Olaf Harringer Assos., Chgo., 1981-95. Mem. AIA (emeritus). Home: 3650 N 36th Ave # Villa5 Hollywood FL 33021-2543 E-mail: hharringer@aol.com.

HARRINGTON, ANTHONY STEPHEN, lawyer, diplomat; b. Taylorsville, N.C., Mar. 9, 1941; s. Atwell Lee and Louise (Chapman) H.; m. Hope Reynolds, Sept. 25, 1971; children: Adam Reynolds, Michael Addison. AB, U. N.C., 1963; LLB, Duke U., 1966. Asst. dean Duke Law Sch., Durham, N.C., 1966-68; assoc. Hogan & Hartson, Washington, 1968-73, ptnr., 1974-99; U.S. amb. to Brazil, 2000-01; pres. Stonebridge Internat. LCC, 2001—. Bd. dirs. Ovation, Inc., Ctr. for Democracy, SouthernNet Inc., Southeastern Metal Products, Rosemount Ctr., PRE Holdings Inc., Kenan Inst. Pvt. Enterprise; co-chair Nat. Alliance to End Homelessness; vice-chmn. Pres. Fgn. Intelligence Adv. Bd., 1993-99; mem. Commn. on Roles and Capabilities of Intelligence Cmty., 1995; chmn. Pres. Intelligence Oversight Bd., 1994-99. Gen. Counsel Dem. Nat. Com., Washington, 1981-85. Episcopal. Club: Met. Avocations: politics, reading, gardening, tennis. Home: Ratcliffe Manor 7768 Ratcliffe Manor Ln Easton MD 21601-7432 also: 701 Pennsylvania Ave NW Washington DC 20004-2608 Office: Stonebridge Internat 555 13th St NW Washington DC 20004-1109

HARRINGTON, BRUCE MICHAEL, lawyer, investor; b. Houston, Mar. 12, 1933; s. George Haymond Harrington and Doris (Gladden) Maginnis; m. Anne Griffith Lawhon, Feb. 15, 1958; children: Julia Griffith, Martha Gladden, Susan McIver BA, U. Tex., 1960, JD with honors, 1961. Bar: Tex. 1961, U.S. Dist. Ct. (so. dist.) Tex. 1962, U.S. Ct. Appeals (5th cir.) 1962, U.S. Supreme Ct. 1973. Assoc. Andrews & Kurth and predecessor firm, Houston, 1961-73, ptnr., 1973-84. Dir. Offenhauser Co., Houston, Allied Metals, Inc., Houston Trustee St. John's Sch., Houston, 1981-92, chmn. bd., CEO, 1986-92; chmn. bd. Covenant House, Tex., 1991-95; trustee St. Luke's Episcopal Hosp., Tex. Med. Ctr., Houston, 1983-86; bd. dirs. YMCA Bd.

Mgmt., Am. Cancer Soc., 1992-94, Ctr. for Hearing and Speech, 1993, chmn. bd., 1995-98; vice chmn. Gateway Found., 1993-95; mem. adv. com. Assn. Governing Bds. of Colls. and Univs. Mem. ABA, Nat. Assn. Ind. Schs. (chmn. trustee com.), Ind. Schs. Assn. S.W. (chmn. trustee com., bd. exec. com.), Tex. Bar Assn., Houston Bar Assn., The Mil. and Hosp. Order of St. Lazarus (grand chancellor), The Venerable Order of St. John (U.K.), The Order of Saints Maurice and Lazarus (Savoy), Houston Country Club, Petroleum Club, Houston Club, Phi Delta Phi, Order of Coif. Republican. Episcopalian. Home: 3608 Overbrook Ln Houston TX 77027-4128

HARRINGTON, CAROL A., lawyer; b. Geneva, Ill., Feb. 13, 1953; d. Eugene P. and M. Ruth (Bowersox) Kloubec; m. Warren J. Harrington, Aug. 19, 1972; children: Jennifer Ruth, Carrie Anne. BS summa cum laude, U. Ill., 1974, JD magna cum laude, 1977. Bar: Ill. 1977, U.S. Dist. Ct. (no. dist.) Ill. 1977, U.S. Tax Ct. 1979. Assoc. Winston & Strawn, Chgo., 1977-84, ptnr., 1984-88, McDermott, Will & Emery, 1988—. Adv. com. Heckerling Inst. Estate Planning; speaker in field. Co-author: Generation-Skipping Tax, 1996, Generation-Skipping Transfer Tax, Warren, Gorham & Lamont, 2000. Fellow Am. Coll. Trusts and Estate Coun. (bd. regents 1999-2005); mem. ABA (chmn. B-1 generation skipping transfer com. 1987-92, coun. real property, probate and trust law sect. 1992-98), Ill. State Bar Assn., Chgo. Bar Assn., Chgo. Estate Planning Coun. Office: McDermott Will & Emery 227 W Monroe St Ste 3100 Chicago IL 60606-5096 Office Phone: 312-984-7794.

HARRINGTON, CLIFFORD M., lawyer; b. Lafayette, La., Nov. 20, 1947; BA with distinction, Univ. Southwest La., 1969; JD, Univ. Colo., 1972. Bar: Colo. 1972, DC 1975, US Ct. Appeals (DC cir.), US Supreme Ct. Atty., Office of Opinions & Review FCC, 1972—74; ptnr., chmn. Comm. group Pillsbury Winthrop Shaw Pittman, Washington. Mem.: ABA, Fed. Comm. Bar Assn., DC Bar Assn. Office: Pillsbury Winthrop Shaw Pittman 2300 N St NW Washington DC 20037-1128 Office Phone: 202-663-8525. Office Fax: 202-663-8007. Business E-Mail: clifford.harrington@pillsburylaw.com.

HARRINGTON, DAN WILLIAM, state senator; b. Butte, Mont., Feb. 12, 1938; m. Pat Harrington; children: Kathleen, Dan, Kevin. BS, Western Mont. Coll., 1960. Cert. tchr., Mont. Tchr. Sch. Dist. No. 1, Butte, 1961-97; Dem. rep. dist. 38 Mont. Ho. of Reps., 1976-2000; Dem. senator dist. 38 Mont. State Senate, 2000—. Majority whip Mont. Ho. of Reps., 1983, minority whip, 1995-99; pres. pro-tem. Mont. Senate, 2005-. Pres. Silver Bow Young Dems., 1960-62; del. Mont. Constl. Conv., 1971-72; chair Silver Bow County Dem. Com., 1970-90; pres. Silver Bow Dem. Burrows Club, 1997-01. Mem. Butte Tchrs. Union. Roman Catholic. Office: 1201 N Excelsior Ave Butte MT 59701-8505 also: Mont State Senate Capitol Station Helena MT 59620 Business E-Mail: dznwharrington@in-tch.com.

HARRINGTON, REV. DONALD JAMES, university president; b. Bklyn., Oct. 2, 1945; s. John Joseph and Ruth Mary (Cummings) H. BA, Mary Immaculate Sem., Northampton, Pa., 1969, MDiv, 1972, ThM, 1973; LLD (hon.), St. John's U., 1985; postgrad., U. Toronto, 1980—82; PhD (hon.), Fu Jen U., Taipei, Taiwan, 1994; HHD (hon.), Am. U. Rome, 1994, Dowling Coll., 1996; D of Pedagogy (hon.), St. Thomas Aquinas Coll., Sparkhill, N.Y.; STD (hon.), Niagara U., 2000; STD, Kokushikan U., 2002. Ordained priest Roman Catholic Ch., 1973. Instr. Niagara U., NY, 1973-80, dir. student activities, 1974-77, dean student activities, 1977-80, exec. v.p., 1981-84, pres., 1984-89, St. John's U., Jamaica, NY, 1989—. Bd. dirs. The Bear Stearns Cos., Inc., 1993—, Commn. Ind. Colls. and Univs., Albany, N.Y., 1987-89, 91-94, 2003-; mem. bd. Cath. edn. Diocese of Buffalo, 1987-89. Trustee Niagara U., 1984-89, emeritus bd. mem., 2002-, St. John's U., 1986—, DePaul U., 1988-91, Sem. Immaculate Conception, 1990-97, Res. Group, 1988—, Sisters Hosp., Buffalo, 1988-89; chair adv. com. Love Canal Land Use, 1988-89; chair Big East Athletic Conf., 1994-97; mem. sanctity of life com. Diocese of Bklyn., 1990-96; chair Western N.Y. Consortium for Higher Edn., 1988-89, mem. exec. com., 1985-89; mem. adv. bd. New Yorkers Caring for N.Y.-N.Y. Med. Coll., 1998- . Recipient Pro Ecclesia et Pontifice, Pope John Paul II, 1989. Mem. Assn. Cath. Colls. and Univs. (bd. dirs. 1997-2003). Office: St John's U Office of Pres 8000 Utopia Pkway, Newman Hall Rm 318 Jamaica NY 11439-0001

HARRINGTON, ELLIS JACKSON, JR., lawyer; b. Barnesville, Ga., Aug. 10, 1944; s. Ellis Jackson Sr. and Inez (Dixon) H.; m. Elizabeth Gray, Dec. 23, 1965; children: Lisa Jackson, Sara Christine. AB, U. N.C., 1966, JD, 1969. Bar: N.C. 1969, U.S. Ct. Mil. Appeals 1970, U.S. Dist. Ct. (mid. dist.) N.C. 1976. Asst. pub. defender 18th Jud. Dist. of N.C., Greensboro, 1973-75; ptnr. Booth, Fish, Simpson & Harrison, Greensboro, 1975-79, Booth, Harrington Johns & Campbell, Greensboro, 1979-95, Booth, Harrington Johns & Toman, L.L.P., Greensboro, 1995—2002, Booth Harrington & Johns LLP, Greensboro, 2002—. Bd. dirs. Child Care Ministries, Greensboro, 1980-86, Greensboro Commn. of Status of Women, 1992-97. Recipient Cert. of Appreciation, ARC, 1987. Mem. ABA, Am. Bd. Trial Advocates, N.C. Bar Assn., Assn. Trial Lawyers Am., N.C. Acad. Trial Lawyers, 18th Jud. Dist. Bar Assn. (pres. 1986-87), Phi Beta Kappa, Phi Delta Phi. Democrat. Presbyterian. Avocations: travel, fishing, photography. Office: Booth Harrington & Johns LLP 239 N Edgeworth St Greensboro NC 27401-2217 Office Phone: 336-275-9567. Business E-Mail: JHarrington@nc-law.com.

HARRINGTON, GEORGE FRED, aviation consultant; b. Killingly, Conn., July 29, 1923; s. George Whitman and Beatrice Evelyn (Sheldon) H.; m. Ruth Lydia Saarinen, June 7, 1947; children: Joanne Ruth, George Lauri, Julie Ann. BS, U.S. Mil. Acad., 1947; MBA, Harvard U., 1957; grad., Armed Forces Staff Coll., 1961, Indsl. Coll. of Armed Forces, 1967. Commd. 2d lt. USAF, 1947, advanced through grades to col., 1968, ret., 1977; mgr. market devel. Beech Aircraft, Washington, 1978-81, gen. mgr. internat. div. Wichita, 1981-82, v.p., 1982-85; cons. Gen. Aviation, Arlington, Va., 1986—. Cons. in field. Pres. Collingwood Libr. and Mus. on Americanism, Alexandria, Va.; overseer Plimoth (Mass.) Plantation; trustee US Mil. Acad. Assn. Grads Decorated D.S.M., Legion of Merit with oak leaf cluster. Mem. Air Force Assn., Ret. Officers Assn., Harvard Bus. Sch. Club of Washington (pres. 1988-89), Masons, Shriners, Nat. Sojourners (past nat. pres.). Republican. Methodist. Avocations: gardening, music. Home and Office: 1300 Crystal Dr # 304 Arlington VA 22202-3234

HARRINGTON, HERBERT H., accountant; b. Meadville, Pa., Sept. 19, 1946; s. Herbert H. and Sara R. (Rogers) H. BA, Kent State U., 1969; postgrad., Memphis State U., 1975; MS in Criminal Justice, Dyersburg State U., 1977. CPA, Tenn. Transp. dir. West Tenn. Easter Seal Soc., 1972-75; compt. So. Trucking, Inc., 1976-77; acct. Cen. So., Inc., 1978-79; compt. Wonder div. ITT Baking Corp., 1980-84; contr. N. Fla. Transport, 1985-86; fin. con. Computa-Tax, Inc., 1986—; pres. H&H Enterprises, Inc., Covington, 1989—; CEO Tenco, Inc., Burlison, Tenn., 1995—. Cons. computer and accting. software, Covington, 1973—. Author 3 textbooks on acctg. procedures and practice. Served with USN, 1963-81. Mem. Covington C. of C. Lodges: Lions, Good Fellows, Optimists, Rotary. Episcopalian. Home and Office: PO Box O Munford TN 38058-1914

HARRINGTON, JAMES TIMOTHY, lawyer; b. Chgo., Sept. 4, 1942; s. John Paul and Margaret Rita (Cunneen) H.; m. Roseanne Strupeck, Sept. 4, 1965; children: James Timothy, Roseanne, Maris Zajdela. BA, U. Notre Dame, 1964, JD, 1967; MS in Environ. Mgmt., Ill. Inst. Tech., 2004. Bar: Ill. 1967, Ind. 1968, U.S. Dist. Ct. (no. dist.) Ill. 1967, U.S. Dist. Ct. (no. and so. dists.) Ind. 1968, U.S. Ct. Appeals (7th cir.) 1969, U.S. Ct. Appeals (4th cir.) 1977, U.S. Ct. Appeals (8th cir.) 1979, U.S. Ct. Appeals (3d cir.) 1981, U.S. Supreme Ct. 1979, U.S. Ct. Appeals (D.C. cir.) 1993. Law clk. U.S. Dist. Ct. (no. dist.) Ind., 1967-69; assoc. Rooks, Pitts & Poust, Chgo., 1969-75, ptnr., 1976-87, Ross & Hardies, Chgo., 1987—2003; ptnr., chmn. bd. of adv. McGuireWoods, LLP, 2003—. Adj. prof. environ. mgmt. Ill. Inst. Tech., 2004—, Stuart Grad. Sch. Bus.; lectr. environ. law and mgmt., fed. procedures, adminstrv. law, 1960—. Vice chmn. Mid Am. Legal Found., 1998—; chmn., bd. dirs. Ill. Safety Coun., 2002-05; chmn., bd. adv. Ill. Inst. Tech. Sch. Bus. Fellow Am. Bar Found.; mem. Ill. Bar Assn., Ind. Bar Assn., Chgo. Bar Assn. (environ. law com., real estate com.), Indsl. Water Waste and Sewer Group (past chmn.), Air and Waste Mgmt. Assn. (sec. Lake Mich. sect.), Assn. Environ. Law Inst., Lawyers Club Chgo., Union League Club Chgo. Roman Catholic. Home: 746 Foxdale Ave Winnetka IL 60093-1908 Office: McGuire-Woods LLP 77 W Wacker Dr Ste 4400 Chicago IL 60601 Office Phone: 312-849-8252. Business E-Mail: jharrington@mcguirewoods.com.

HARRINGTON, JEAN PATRICE, academic administrator; b. Denver; d. James Michael and Katherine Ann (Holl) H. BA, Coll. Mt. St. Joseph, 1953; MA, Creighton U., 1958; PhD, U. Colo., 1967; LHD (hon.), Xavier U., 1983, Ohio Dominican Coll., 1988; LLD (hon.), St. Thomas Inst., Cin., 1985, Coll. Mt. St. Joseph, 1988, Hebrew Union Coll., 1990; D. Tech. Studies (hon.), Cin. Tech., 1988; LLD (hon.), No. Ky. U., 1996, U. Dayton, 1999. Joined Sisters of Charity of Cin., 1940; prin. St. Rose of Lima, Denver, 1953-56; tchr. Cathedral H.S., Denver, 1956-58, prin., 1958-68; dir. instl. rsch. Coll. Mt. St. Joseph, Cin., 1968-69, pres., 1977-87; exec. dir. Cin. Youth Collaborative, 1988-90; interim pres. Cin. State Coll., 1997. Bd. dirs. Penrose Hosp., Colorado Springs, 1976-86, St. Mary Corwin Hosp., Pueblo, Colo., 1972-80, Cin. Bicentennial Commn., 1982-89, Samaritan Health Resources, Inc., 1983-96, St. Rita Sch. for Deaf, 1983-86, United Appeal Cabinet, 1983, Cin. Cmty. Chest, 1988-95, Dan Beard coun. Boy Scouts Am., 1988-91; trustee Good Samaritan Hosp. and Health Ctr., Dayton, Ohio, 1978-80, 89-97, bd. dirs., 1989-96; trustee Miami U., 1989-97, chmn. 1994-97; bd. dirs. Coll. of Mt. St. Joseph, 1995-2002; trustee U. Dayton, 1999-2002. Recipient Disting. Svc. citation NCCJ, 1987, Women Helping Women award Soroptimist Internat., 1990, Statesman award Cin. Assn. Execs., 1988, St. Francis award Friars Club, 1994, Daniel Ransahoff Initiative award, 1994, Lincoln award No. Ky. U., 1994, Gt. Living Cincinnatian award C. of C., 1996, Svc. to Edn. award Ohiana Libr. Assn., 1998, Children's Advocate award Beech Acres; named Career Woman of Achievement YWCA, 1981, Disting. Bus. and Profl. Woman of Yr., 1982; inductee Hall of Excellence of Ohio Fedn. of Ind. Colls., 1990, Ohio Women's Hall of Fame, 2000, Pres.' award Children's Def. Fund, 2003. Mem. Nat. Assn. Ind. Colls. and Univs., Assn. Cath. Colls. and Univs. (bd. dirs.), Ohio Found. Ind. Colls., Greater Cin. Consortium Colls. and Univs. (vice chmn. 1980-82), Coun. Ind. Colls. (bd. dirs. 1981-85), Cin. C. of C. (bd. dirs. 1978-84, trustee 1981-85, sec. 1979-85, named Great Living Cincinnatian 1996). Roman Catholic. E-mail: jphsc@juno.com.

HARRINGTON, JEFFREY MICHAEL, military officer; b. Mansfield, Ohio, Sept. 26, 1962; s. Paul Owen and Lois Ruth Harrington; m. Susan Marie Pangrass, May 11, 1960; children: Elizabeth, Meghan, Patric. BS, U. of State of N.Y., 1994; MPA, U. Okla., 1995; postgrad., Nova Southeastern U., 1999—. Cert. journeyman legal sec., shorthand legal reporter. Commd. 2d. lt. USMC, advanced through grades to capt., 1980—, adj. Quantico, Va., 1998—. Adj. prof. Strayer U., Washington, 1996—. Trustee KC, Quantio, 1997-98. Mem. ASCD, Am. Soc. Pub. Adminstrn. (Eastern N.C. chpt. 1996-97), Nat. Assn. Scholars, Am. Statis. Assn., Acad. Polit. Sci., Army-Navy Club, Quantico Sharks Swim Club (pres. 2000-02). Democrat. Roman Catholic. E-mail: ssgt4429@comcast.net.

HARRINGTON, JEREMY THOMAS, priest, publishing executive; b. Lafayette, Ind., Oct. 7, 1932; s. William and Ellen (Cain) H. BA, Duns Scotus Coll., 1955; postgrad., U. Detroit, 1955, Marquette U., 1961; MA, Xavier U., Cin., 1965; MS in Journalism, Northwestern U., 1967; LHD (hon.), St. Bonaventure U., 1999. Ordained priest Roman Cath. Ch., 1959. Joined Order Friars Minor, 1950; tchr. Roger Bacon High Sch., Cin., 1960-64; assoc. editor St. Anthony Messenger, Cin., 1964-66, editor, 1966-81, pub., 1975-81, pub., CEO, 1991—; mem. bd. Franciscan Province Cin., 1969-72, 75-81, chief exec. bd., 1981-90. Author: Your Wedding: Planning Your Own Ceremony, 1974; Editor: Conscience in Today's World, 1970, Jesus: Superstar or Savior?, 1972. Mem. Catholic Press Assn. (pres. 1975-77, dir.), Kappa Tau Alpha. Home: 1615 Vine St Cincinnati OH 45202 Office: St Anthony Messenger 28 W Liberty St Cincinnati OH 45202 Business E-Mail: JeremyH@AmericanCatholic.org. *My success has been made by others. As a priest, as well as an editor and publisher, my challenge is to discover, recognize, encourage and make available to others the talents of authors and artists. To me, that's a parable of life. The more we can discover, appreciate and foster the good qualities and strengths of others, the more "successful" we are. Success in life is realizing how many gifts are made available to us by God and our fellow human beings.*

HARRINGTON, JOHN MICHAEL, JR., lawyer; b. Boston, July 5, 1921; s. John Michael and Marie Bernadine (Ratchford) H.; m. Ellen Patricia White, May 12, 1951; children— John Michael III, Marc W., Francis X. B., Ellen M., Matthew J., Patrick W. AB, Harvard U., 1943, LL.B., 1949. Bar: Mass. 1949, U.S. Dist. Ct. (Mass.) 1950, U.S. Ct. Appeals (1st cir.) 1956, U.S. Supreme Ct. 1968. Law clk. Supreme Jud. Ct. Mass., Boston, 1949-50; assoc. Ropes & Gray LLP, Boston, 1950-55, 57-61, ptnr., 1961-93, counsel, 1994—; asst. U.S. atty. Dist. of Mass., Boston, 1955-57. Trustee Winchester Sav. Bank, Mass., 1966-91; mem. Mass. Jud. Conduct Commn., Boston, 1978-81. Trustee Roxbury Latin Sch., Boston, 1962-67, St. Sebastian's County Day Sch., Needham, Mass., 1973-86; mem. fin. com. Town of Winchester, 1959-62. Served to capt. field arty. U.S. Army, 1943-46, ETO. Fellow Am. Coll. Trial Lawyers, Am. Bar Found.; mem. ABA (standing com. on fed. judiciary 1st cir. 1978-84), Boston Bar Assn. Clubs: Union (v.p. 1982-86, pres. 1986-88), Curtis, Harvard (Boston). Democrat. Roman Catholic. Home: 19 Cabot St Winchester MA 01890-3501 Office: Ropes & Gray LLP One International Pl Boston MA 02110-2624 Office Phone: 617-951-7612.

HARRINGTON, JOHN TIMOTHY, retired lawyer; b. Madison, Wis., May 26, 1921; s. Cornelius Louis and Emily (Chisholm) H.; m. Deborah Reynolds, May 23, 1948; children— Elizabeth Chisholm, Samuel Parker, Hannah Quincy, Jane McRae BS, Harvard U., 1942, LL.B., 1948. Bar: Wis. 1949. Assoc. Quarles & Brady and predecessor firms, Milw., 1948-58, ptnr., 1958-91; ret., 1991—. Served to lt. comdr. USNR, 1942-46, PTO Home: 924 E Juneau Ave Milwaukee WI 53202-2748 Office: Quarles & Brady 411 E Wisconsin Ave Ste 2550 Milwaukee WI 53202-4497 Personal E-mail: jtharrington_4@msn.com.

HARRINGTON, JOHN TOLAN, medical educator, internist, nephrologist, dean emeritus; b. Fall River, Mass., Dec. 30, 1936; s. John J. and Elizabeth C. (Tolan) Harrington; m. Gertrude Rose Hargraves, Aug. 27, 1960; children: Gertrude, Kathleen, Daniel, Ann, John, Mark, Timothy. BA magna cum laude, Coll. of the Holy Cross, 1958; MD cum laude, Yale U., 1962. Diplomate Am. Bd. Internal Medicine. Intern, resident in internal medicine N.C. Meml. Hosp., Chapel Hill, 1962-65; clin. and rsch. fellow in nephrology New Eng. Med. Ctr., Boston, 1965-68, nephrologist, dir. hemodialysis unit, 1971-81, chief gen. medicine divsn., 1981-86, sr. nephrologist, 2003—; chmn. dept. medicine Newton (Mass.)-Wellesley Hosp., 1986-94; dean academic affairs Tufts U. Sch. Medicine, Boston, 1994-95, asst. prof. medicine, 1971-75, assoc. prof. medicine, 1975-79, prof. medicine, 1979—, dean ad interim, 1995-96, dean, 1996—2002, dean emeritus, 2003—. Author: Acid-Base, 1982; editor: Nephrology Forum Kidney Internat., 1979—2005; contbr. articles to profl. jours. Pres. Hummocks Cmty. Orgn., Portsmouth, RI, 1978—80, Nat. Kidney Found., Mass., 1988. Master: ACP (gov. Mass. chpt. 1989—93); fellow: Royal Irish Coll. Physicians (hon.); mem.: Am. Soc. Nephrology, Internat. Soc. Nephrology, Holy Name Soc. Democrat. Roman Catholic. Avocations: sailing, swimming, Irish poetry and drama, baseball. Office Phone: 617-636-9439. Personal E-mail: Trudy1@verizon.net. Business E-Mail: jharrington@tufts-nemc.org.

HARRINGTON, JOHN VINCENT, retired communications executive, engineer, educator; b. N.Y.C., May 9, 1919; s. John Joseph and Dorothy (Neisel) H.; m. Frances Cullinane, Jan. 23, 1943; children: John F., Nancy Harrington Higgins, Jeffrey, Richard, Brian. B.E.E., Cooper Union, 1940; M.E.E., Poly. Inst. Bklyn., 1948; Sc.D., Mass. Inst. Tech., 1957. Research engr. U.S. Air Force Cambridge Research Lab., Mass., 1946-51; leader data transmission group Lincoln Lab., M.I.T., Cambridge, 1951-56, asso. div. head aircraft control and warning, 1956-58, head radio physics div., 1958-63; prof. aeros., astronautics and elec. engring., 1st dir. Center Space Research, M.I.T., 1963-73; v.p. research and engring. Communications Satellite Corp., Washington, 1973-79; sr. v.p. research and devel., dir. COMSAT Labs., Clarksburg, Md., 1979-84. Dir. Epsco, Inc., 1964-72, Shawmut County Bank, Cambridge, 1964-73, COMSAT Gen. Telesystems, Inc., Washington, 1973-81, Environ. Research and Tech., Inc., Concord, Mass., 1981-82; mem. Space Applications Bd., NRC, 1975-81 Contbr. articles to profl. jours. Lt. USNR, 1942-46. Recipient Exceptional Civilian Service medal U.S. Air Force, 1952, Exceptional Profl. Achievement citation Cooper Union, 1965, Gano Dunn award Cooper Union, 1983. Fellow IEEE, AAAS, AIAA. Home: 11657 Asbury Cir Solomons MD 20688

HARRINGTON, JOHN WALTER, pediatrician, medical researcher; s. William J. and Joan Frances Harrington; m. Chifumi Usui, Jan. 16, 1993; children: Claire Royelle, Sean Usui, Maya Therese. MD, N.Y. Med. Coll., Valhalla, 1992. Diplomate Am. Acad. of Pediat., 1995. Assoc. prof. pediats. N.Y. Med. Coll., Valhalla, 1997—. Unit dir. Maria Farari Children's Hosp., Valhalla, NY, 1998—; primary care rsch. adv. N.Y. Med. Coll., Valhalla, 2001—. Delivered internat. lecture Child Abuse in America; contbr. articles to profl. jours. Robert Wood Johnson Primary Care Rsch. fellow, 1997-1998, Health and Rsch. Svcs. grantee, 2001-2005. Fellow: Am. Acad. Pediats. Roman Catholic. Achievements include research in diagnosis of autism. Avocations: basketball, juggling, poetry.

HARRINGTON, JOSEPH FRANCIS, educational company executive, history educator; b. Boston, Oct. 24, 1938; s. Joseph Francis and Mary Virginia (Lynch) H.; m. Brenda Marie Crowley, Sept. 3, 1966; children: Megan Marie, Christopher Joseph John. BS, Boston Coll., 1960; MA, Georgetown U., 1963, PhD, 1971. Instr. Framingham State Coll., Mass., 1966-68, asst. prof., 1968-70, assoc. prof., 1970-72, prof., 1972—2003, chmn. dept. history, 1972—82, prof. emeritus, 2004—; pres. Learning, Inc., Stoughton, 1979—2003, bd. dirs.; pres. J.C. Enrichment. Program, 2003—. Treas. The East European Rsch. Ctr., 1990—. Author: Masters of War, Makers of Peace, 1985, Powers, Pawns and Parleys, 1978, Tweaking the Nose of the Russians: American-Romanian Relations, 1940-90; American-Romanian Relations: From Pariah to Partner, 1989-2004; editorial bd. dirs. New England Jour. of History, 1991—, editor, 1995-2004; editor: The Creative Child and Adult Quarterly, 1991-94; contbr. articles to profl. jours. Mem. Stoughton, Mass. Sch. Com., 1971-77, 82-87, 91-94. With U.S. Army, 1962-65. Tchg. fellow Georgetown U., Washington, 1960-62, 65-66, hon. fellow Kennedy Presdl. Libr., 1986-93. Mem. Mass. Assn. for Advancement of Individual Potential (bd. dirs., pres. 1987-89, 90-92, v.p. for R&D 1989), Nat. Assn. Creative Children and Adults (bd. dirs. 1985-92, editor The Creative Child and Adult Quar. 1991-93), New Eng. Slavic Assn. (v.p. 1990-91, treas. 1991-98), Soc. for Romanian Studies (pres. 1994-97, bd. dirs. 1997-2000), Kennedy Libr. Acad. Adv. Coun. Roman Catholic. Avocations: reading, racquetball. Home: 119 Holmes Ave Stoughton MA 02072-1926 Office: Framingham State Coll State St Framingham MA 01701 Office Phone: 781-344-7174. Personal E-mail: cacg1@aol.com.

HARRINGTON, KATHLEEN M., public relations company executive, former federal agency administrator; BA, Colgate U., 1972; MA in Psychology, The Cath. U. Am., 1977. Adminstrv. asst. to Rep. Jim Dunn US Ho. Reps., Washington, 1981—83, 1983—87; asst. adminstr. pub. affairs FAA, Washington; asst. sec. congrl. and intergovtl. affairs US Dept. Labor, Washington, 1989—93; v.p. govt. rels. Aetna, Inc.; dir. Office of Elizabeth Dole Dole-Kemp Campaign, 1996; sr. v.p. pub. affairs and advocacy Health Ins. Assn. Am.; asst. sec. pub. affairs US Dept. Labor, Washington, 2002—03; sr. v.p. pub. affairs, dir. policy outreach Porter Novelli, Washington, 2003—. Office: Porter Novelli 1909 K St NW Washington DC 20006

HARRINGTON, MARY EVELINA PAULSON (POLLY HARRINGTON), writer, educator; b. Chgo. d. Henry Thomas and Evelina (Belden) Paulson; m. Gordon Keith Harrington, Sept. 7, 1957; children: Jonathan Henry, Charles Scranton. BA, Oberlin Coll., 1946; postgrad., Northwestern U., Evanston, Ill., Chgo., 1946-49, Weber State U., Ogden, Utah, 1970s, 80s; MA, U. Chgo.-Chgo. Theol. Sem., 1956. Publicist Nat. Coun. Chs., N.Y.C., 1950-51; mem. press staff 2d assembly World Coun. Chs., Evanston, Chgo., 1954; mgr. Midwest Office Communication, United Ch. of Christ, Chgo., 1955-59; staff writer United Ch. Herald, N.Y.C., St. Louis, 1959-61; affiliate missionary to Asia, United Ch. Bd. for World Ministries, N.Y.C., 1978-79; freelance writer and lectr., 1961—; corr. Religious News Svc., 1962—. Prin. lectr. Women & Family Life in Asia series to numerous librs., Utah, 1981, 1981—82; pub. rels. coord. Utah Energy Conservation/Energy Mgmt. Program, 1984—85; tchr. writing Ogden Cmty. Schs., 1985—89; adj. instr. writing for publs. Weber State U., 1986—; instr. Acad. Lifelong Learning, Ogden, 1992—95, Eccles Cmty. Art Ctr., Ogden, 1993—94; dir. comm. Shared Ministry, Salt Lake City, 1983—97; chmn. comm. Intermountain Conf., Rocky Mountain Conf. Utah Assn. United Ch. of Christ, 1970—78, 1982—, Ind. Coun. Chs., 1960—63, United Ch. of Christ, Ogden, 1971—; dir. comm. United Chs., 1971—78, Christ Congl., Ogden, 1980—; chmn. comm. Ch. Women United Utah, 1974—78, Ogden rep., 1980—, hostess Northern Utah, 1998. Editor: Sunshine and Moonscapes: An Anthology of Essays, Poems, Short Stories, 1994, (booklet) Family Counseling Service: Thirty Years of Service to Northern Utah, 1996; contbr. numerous articles and essays to religious and other publs. Pres. T.O. Smith Sch. PTA, 1976-78, Ogden City Coun. PTA, 1983-85; assoc. dir. Region II, Utah PTA, Salt Lake City, 1981-83, mem. State Edn. Commn., 1982-87; chmn. state internat. hospitality and aid Utah Fedn. Women's Clubs, 1982-86; v.p. Ogden dist., 1990-92, pres. Ogden dist., 1992-96, state resolutions com., 1996—; trustee Family Counseling Svc. No. Utah, Ogden, 1983-95, emeritus trustee, 1995—; Utah rep. to nat. bd. Challenger Films, Inc., 1986—; state pres. Rocky Mountain Conf. Women in Mission, United Ch. of Christ, 1974-77, sec., 1981-84, vice moderator Utah Assn., 1992-94; chair pastor-parish rels. com. United Ch. of Christ Congl., Ogden, 1999-03, chmn. search com., 1995-96, Mission com., 2002-, Interfaith Works!, rep. Interfaith Cmty., North Utah. Recipient Ecumenical Svc. citation Ind. Coun. Chs., 1962, Outstanding Local Pres. award Utah PTA, 1978, Outstanding Latchkey Child Project award, 1985, Cmty. Svc. award City of Ogden, 1980, 81, 82, Celebration of Gifts of Lay Woman Nat. award United Ch. of Christ, 1987, Excellence in the Arts in Art Edn. award Ogden City Arts Commn., 1993, Spirit of Am. Woman in Arts and Humanities award Your Cmty. Connection, Ogden, 1994, Heart and Hand award United Ch. of Christ, Ogden, 2001; Utah Endowment for Humanities grantee, 1981, 81-82. Mem. Nat. League Am. Penwomen (chmn. Utah conv. 1973, 11 awards for articles and essays 1987-95, 1st pl. news award 1992, 1st pl. short stories 1997, 3d pl. articles 1997), AAUW (state edn. rep. 1982-86, parliamentarian Ogden br. 1997—, membership v.p. Ogden br. 2003—), League of Utah Writers (Publ. Quill award 1998). Democrat. Home and Office: 722 Boughton St Ogden UT 84403-1152 E-mail: gkharrington1@comcast.net.

HARRINGTON, PATTI, school system administrator; BA, MEd, Brigham Young U.; PhD in Edn. Adminstrn., U. Utah. Prin. Provo HS, Utah; asst. supt. Provo; supt., 2001; assoc. supt. State of Utah, 2002—04, supt. of pub. instrn., 2004—. Recipient Secondary Sch. Prin. of Yr., 1997. Office: Utah Office of Edn 250 E 500 S PO Box 144200 Salt Lake City UT 84114-4200 Office Phone: 802-538-7500. Office Fax: 801-538-7768.*

HARRINGTON, PETER TYRUS, emergency management company executive, public relations consultant, author, photographer; b. N.Y.C., Aug. 28, 1951; s. Don and Gerry S. Harrington. BA, Union Coll., 1973, MA in Am. Labor, 1975. Lic. pvt. investigator. Spl. investigator U.S. Dept. of Commerce, 1970; staff dir. N.Y. State Assembly, N.Y.C., 1971-73; editl. staff mem., writer, photographer Nat. Geographic Mag., Washington, 1974-76; ptnr. Don Harrington Assocs., Wilton, Conn., 1977—; pres. Harrington Comm., Wilton, 1980—; pub. affairs officer Fed. Emergency-Mgmt. Agy., Washington, 1983—, Fed. Catastrophic "Red" Team, 1996-97; exec. officer Hurricane Andrew recovery, 1992-94; chief-of-staff to chmn. County Bd. Commrs., Dade County, Fla., 1994-95; founding mem. U.S. Dept. Homeland Security, 2003—. Cons. IBM, Armonk, N.Y., 1984-85, Expdns. Inc., New Canaan, Conn., 1987-88, Sony Corp., 1991, Pitney Bowes, 1992; contbr. GE Capitol

Corp.; contbg. editor Travel Mktg. Mag., 1985—; spl. cons. So. Conn. Newspaper Syndicate (Greenwich Time, Stamford Advocate); contbg. corr. L.A. Times, Washington Post Syndicate. Author: The Last Cathedral, 1979 (Book of Yr. award 1979), Never Too Old, 1981; author and photographer, The Sailing Chef, 1978, Maine, 1989; contbr. Murdock, Travel Marketing, Intrepid, Discovery, People, Yankee, Video and TV Guide mags., Smithsonian, Arizona Republic, Chicago Tribune, N.Y. Times, Wall Street Journal, Miami Herald, Boston Herald; contbr. and photographer of many articles with expertise in Amazon and Polar Region. Scoutmaster troop, Boy Scouts Am., Albany, N.Y., 1971-73; exec. dir. ACLU, Albany, 1972-73; mem. bd. Annapolis Youth Ctr., Md., 1978; past pres. Wilton Summer Playshop, 1972—; mem. adv. bd. ARC, Conn. Recipient Pub. Svc. Citation, Fed. Govt., 1985, Metro-Dade (Fla.), 1993. Fellow Author's Guild, Nat. Press Found., Soros Found.; mem. Writers Union, Nat. Press Club, Legis. Councils Assn., Nat. Press Photographers Assn., Am. Soc. Media Photographers. Office: Don Harrington Assocs 271 Wilson Ave Melbourne Beach FL 32937-2933 Home: 213 Birch Ave Melbourne Beach FL 32951

HARRINGTON, RICHARD J., information business executive; b. 1947; BS in Acctg., U. R.I. CPA R.I. Pres., CEO, Thomson Profl. Pub., Mitchell Internat.; pres., CEO Thomson Newspapers, Inc., Des Plaines, Ill., 1993—; now pres., CEO The Thomson Corp., Stamford, Conn., 1997—. Bd. dirs. Xerox Corp.; mem. internat. adv. coun. Citigroup. Mem. adv. bd. William F. Achtmeyer Ctr. Global Leadership; mem. bus. adv. coun. U. R.I.; bd. dirs. Norwalk C.C. Found. Office: Thomson Corp The Metro Center One Station Pl Stamford CT 06902

HARRINGTON, ROBERT DUDLEY, JR., retired printing company executive; b. Worcester, Mass., Dec. 19, 1932; s. Robert Dudley and Anne Victoria Harrington; m. Melissa Banks Hubner, Mar. 25, 1978 (div.). AB, Brown U., 1955; MBA, Columbia U., 1957. With Morgan Guaranty Trust Co., N.Y.C., 1957-59; v.p. Faulkner, Dawkins & Sullivan, N.Y.C., 1959-69; pres. Printers Express Co., Inc., Greenwich, Conn., 1976—99, ret., 1999. Hon. trustee, hon. mem. Woods Hole Oceanographic Instn. Corp. Mem.: Edgartown Reading Rm., Sail Newport (bd. dirs.), Round Hill Club, Edgartown Yacht Club, N.Y. Yacht Club, Guiding Lights Lodge, Pilgrims, Holland Lodge.

HARRINGTON, ROGER FULLER, electrical engineering educator, consultant; b. Buffalo, Dec. 24, 1925; s. Henry Bassett and Emilie (Fuller) H.; m. Juanita L. Crawford, Aug. 7, 1954; m. Sandra, Judith, Alan, Laura. BS, Syracuse U., 1948, MS, 1950; PhD, Ohio State U., 1952. Instr. Syracuse U., N.Y., 1948-50, asst. prof., 1952-56, assoc. prof., 1956-60, prof., 1960-94, dir. Electromagnetics Ctr., 1982-94. Vis. prof. U. Ill., Urbana, 1959-60, U. Calif., Berkeley, 1964, E. China Normal U., 1983, Ecole Poly. Fédéral de Lausanne, Switzerland, 1991; guest prof. Tech. U. Denmark, Lyngby, 1969; cons. in field. Author: Introduction to EM Engineering, 1956, Time-Harmonic EM Fields, 1961, Field Computation by Moment Methods, 1968. Served with USN, 1944-46. Rsch. fellow Ohio State U., Columbus, 1950-52; Fulbright lectr., Denmark, eng., 1969; named Disting. Alumni Ohio State U., 1970; recipient Chancellor's Citation Syracuse U., 1984, URSI van der Pol Gold medal, 1996, jubilee medal Nicola Tesla Found., 1998. Mem. IEEE (Centennial medal 1984, Disting. Achievement award 1989, Electromagnetics award 2000, Third Millennium medal 2000), AAUP, Sigma Xi, Sigma Nu. Home: 5424 N Strada De Rubino Tucson AZ 85750-6061 Office: U Ariz Dept Elec Computer Engring Tucson AZ 85721-0001

HARRINGTON, ROY EDWARDS, agricultural engineer, author; b. Atlanta, Mo., Oct. 23, 1925; s. Quincy K. and Sally Ethel (Edwards) H.; m. Dorose Oleta Zink, Sept. 6, 1953; children: Ellen Joyce Thompson, Janet Lisa Fish, Linda Carol Timmons. BS in Agrl. Engring., U. Mo., 1950. Registered profl. engr., Ill. Product devel. mgr. Deere & Co., Moline, Ill., 1950-66, mgr. product planning, 1971-86, ret., 1986; agrl. engr. Ford Found., New Delhi, 1966-71. Cons. farm mechanization Winrock Internat., Ill., 1992, New Delhi, 1987, Vols. in Tech. Asst., Peshawar, Pakistan, 1989, World Bank, Hungary, 1986; spkr. in field. Author: A Tractor Goes Farming, 1995, Grandpa's John Deere tractors, 1996, How John Deere Tractors & Implements Work, 1997; co-author: John Deere Tractors and Equipment, 1991; author: (booklet) Agricultural Mechanization in India, 1973; contbr. Genuine Value, The John Deere Journey, 2000 (Timeline Products); holder 21 tractor and farm implement patents, 1953-68; contbr. articles to profl. jours. Pres. Quad Cities World Affairs Coun., Moline, 1981-82; farm equipment mgr. Great Collections of Quad Cities, Moline, 1993; vol. exec. Internat. Exec. Svcs. Corps., Ludhiana, India, 1997. Served to sgt. inf. U.S. Army, 1944-46. Fellow Am. Soc. Agrl. Engrs. (v.p. 1987-90), Indian Soc. Agrl. Engrs.; mem. Soc. Automotive Engrs. Baptist. Avocation: photography. Home: 3500 27th Avenue Ct Moline IL 61265-5366

HARRIS, AARON, management consultant; b. Birmingham, Ala., Oct. 27, 1930; s. Moses and Fannie (Williams) H.; m. Edna Mabel Turner, May 13, 1954; children: Kevin Brian, Edwin Maurice. BA, Talladega Coll., 1952; MS, Columbia U., 1959; postgrad., Princeton U., 1961. Trainee Bklyn. Pub. Library, 1956-59; asst. librarian Burroughs Wellcome Co., Tuckahoe, N.Y., 1959-64; assoc. librarian IBM Corp., East Fishkill, N.Y., 1964-66; library mgr. IBM Research Lab., San Jose, Calif., 1966-73; personnel exec. IBM Corp., San Jose, 1973-77; v.p. Discovery Sys., Inc., 1974—; data processing mgr. IBM, 1977-80, mgr. tng. and devel., 1980-84, mgr. human resources info. systems, 1985-88; program mgr. mgmt. devel. Rolm Systems, Santa Clara, Calif., 1988-91. Adv. instr. IBM Mgmt. Inst., 1992; cons.; pres. Amistad Assocs. Gen. chmn. Citizens Com. on Schs., San Jose, 1969-71; mem. San Jose CSC, 1974-78; foreman pro tem Santa Clara County Grand Jury, 1979-80; candidate San Jose Sch. Bd., 1969, 73; past bd. dirs. Santa Clara chpt. ARC, Mus. Art, San Jose; bd. dirs. Opera San Jose, 1986-92, Santa Clara County Urban League, 1984-87; San Jose Planning Commr., 1989-92; bd. dirs. Am. Civil Liberties Union Ala., 1996-99; conf. pres. laymen's coun. AME Zion Ch. With AUS, 1952-55. Recipient Citizen of Year award Omega Psi Phi, 1970, Outstanding Contbn. award Omega Psi Phi, 1991. Mem. Talladega Coll. Alumni Assn. (pres. Birmingham chpt. 1995-2000, Outstanding Contbn. award 2000, Outstanding Alumnus award Talladege Coll. 2005). Mem. AME Zion Ch. Home and Office: 341 Turnberry Rd Birmingham AL 35244-3291 E-mail: aaron_harris@prodigy.net. *Those who have presented obstacles for failure have been overwhelmed by my confidence. Those who longed for my success have been supportive with encouragement and opportunity. The principles embodied in the golden rule are my constant aim.*

HARRIS, ADAM C., lawyer; b. East Orange, NJ, 1960; BA, Emory U., 1982; JD magna cum laude, Georgetown U., 1986. Bar: NY 1987, US Dist. Ct. (So. and Ea. Districts of NY) 1987, US Ct. Appeals (2nd Cir.). Ptnr. O'Melveny & Myers LLP, NYC, mem. policy com. Mem.: Assn. Bar City of NY. Office: O'Melveny & Myers LLP Times Square Tower 7 Times Square New York NY 10036 Office Phone: 212-326-2182. Office Fax: 212-326-2061. Business E-Mail: aharris@omm.com.

HARRIS, ALICE, linguist, educator; b. Columbus, Ga., Nov. 23, 1947; d. Joseph Clarence and Georgia (Walker) H.; m. James Vaughan Staros, Aug. 7, 1976; children: Joseph Vaughan, Alice Carmichael. BA, Randolph-Macon Woman's Coll., 1969; MA, U. Essex (Eng.), 1972; PhD, Harvard U., 1976. Tchg. fellow linguistics Harvard U., Cambridge, Mass., 1972-74, 75-76, lectr. linguistics, 1976-77, rsch. fellow linguistics, 1977-79; rsch. asst. prof. linguistics Vanderbilt U., Nashville, 1979-84, assoc. prof. linguistics, 1985-91, assoc. prof. anthropology, 1986-92, prof. linguistics, 1991—2002, prof. anthropology, 1992—2002, chair dept. Germanic, Slavic langs., 1993—2002; prof. linguistics SUNY, Stony Brook, 2002—. Chair faculty coun. Coll. Arts and Scis., 1995-96; vice chair grad. faculty coun., 1993-94, sec. faculty senate, 1993-94; assoc. rsch. U. Tbilisi, USSR, 1974-75; tutor linguistics Dunster House, Harvard U., Cambridge, 1975-77; cons. to Simon and Schuster; Erskine vis. prof. U. of Canterbury, Christchurch, New Zealand, 1999; adv. bd. Pubs. MLA, 1995-98. Author: (book) Georgian Syntax, 1981, Diachronic Syntax, 1985, The Indigenous Languages of the Caucasus, 1991, Endoclitics and the Origins of Udi Morphosyntax, 2002; co-author: Historical Syntax in Cross-Linguistic Perspective, 1995 (Leonard Bloomfield book award, 1998); assoc. editor (jour.) Language, 1988—89, mem. editl. bd. Diachronica, 1994—2002, Natural Language and Linguistic Theory, 1987—90, Linguistic Typology, 2003—; contbr. articles to profl. jours. Sinclair Kennedy fellow Harvard U., 1974-75, NSF Nat. Needs Postdoctoral fellow, 1978-79; grantee Internat. Rsch. and Exch. Bd., 1973, 74-75, 77, 81, 89, 92, Linguistic Soc. Am., 1981, NSF 1980-83, 81-83, 83-85, 85-89, 97-99, 2001-03, 2003-06, NEH, 1990-91, Deutscher Adademischer Austausch Dienst, 1994; scholar Harvard U. 1972-73, Georgetown U., 1973; recipient Mellon Found. Regional Faculty Devel. award 1981, ACLS travel award, 1988, venture fund Vanderbilt U., 1987, 92, 94, Earl Sutherland prize for rsch. Vanderbilt U., 1998. Mem. Internat. Soc. Hist. Linguistics (mem. exec. com. 1995-01), Linguistic Soc. Am. (cons., com. status women in linguistics, nominating com.), Southeastern Conf. Linguistics, Soc. for Study of Caucasia (exec. coun. 1990-98), Societas Caucasologica Europaea (v.p. 1990-92, exec. com. 1992-94, 1994-2000), Phi Beta Kappa. Office: SUNY Dept Linguistics Stony Brook NY 11794-4376 Office Phone: 631-632-7758. Business E-Mail: alice.harris@stonybrook.edu.

HARRIS, ALVIN LOUIS, lawyer; b. Boston, Jan. 27, 1959; s. Morton Allen and Judye Rose Harris; m. Kathy Lynn Howerton, June 19, 1982; children: Jeffrey Louis, Natalie Rosemary. BA, Vanderbilt U., 1981, JD, 1985. Bar: U.S. Dist. Ct. (mid. dist.) Tenn. 1986, U.S. Ct. Appeals (11th cir.) 1986, U.S. Dist. Ct. (mid. dist.) Ga. 1990. Law clk. hon. R. Lanier Anderson 11th Cir. Ct. Appeals, Macon, Ga., 1985-86; atty. O'Hare, Sherrard & Roe, Nashville, 1986-89, Page, Scrantom, Harris & Chapman, Columbus, Ga., 1990-93, Greene & Greene, Nashville, 1993-97; ptnr. Weed, Hubbard, Berry & Doughty PLLC, Nashville, 1997—. Adj. bus. law instr. Columbus (Ga.) Coll., 1990-91. Pres. Nashville Chess Ctr., 1996-2000. Mem. ABA, Tenn. Bar Assn., Cmty. Assn. Inst., Phi Beta Kappa, Order of the Coif. Avocations: chess, running. Office: Weed Hubbard Berry & Doughty PLLC 201 4th Ave N Ste 1420 Nashville TN 37219-2089 E-mail: alvinharris@home.com, aharris@whbdlaw.com.

HARRIS, ANDREW MICHAEL, director; b. Olean, NY, Jan. 10, 1967; s. David Joseph and Yvonne Anne H. BS in Bus. Adminstrn., Boston U., 1989, MBA, 1995. Commd. U.S. Army, 1989, advanced through grades to maj.; asst. to the sr. v.p. Boston U., 1991—94, mgr. of fin. and adminstrn., 1994—96, dir. fin. planning and budget, 1998—2003, assoc. dir. analytical svcs., 1998—. Cmty. task force mem. Boston U. Cmty. Task Force, Boston, 2002—03; philanthropic support Boston Briefing Series, Boston, 2002—03. Decorated Army Commendation Medal US Army, Overseas Svc. Ribbon, Army Achievement Medal; recipient Pi Lambda Phi Alumni award, Pi Lambda Phi Nat. Hdqs., 1989-1998, Hon. Scarlet Keyaward, Boston University Alumni Assn., 2002; ROTC 4 Yr. Academic Scholarship, US Army, 1985. Mem.: N.G. Assn. U.S., Boston Briefing Series (life; founder and bd. mem. 2002—03), Soc. Preservation Audubon Circle, Algonquin Club of Boston (com. mem. 1999—2003), Army and Navy Club, Pi Lambda Phi Alumni Assn. (life). Republican. Roman Catholic. Avocations: travel, book collecting, politics, wine, exercise. Office: Boston U Med Campus 715 Albany St 560 Boston MA 02118 Personal E-mail: amh@bu.edu.

HARRIS, ANN BIRGITTA SUTHERLAND, art historian; b. Cambridge, Eng., Nov. 4, 1937; came to U.S., 1965, naturalized, 1996; d. Gordon B.B.M. and Gunborg Elizabeth (Wahlström) Sutherland; m. William Vernon Harris, July 13, 1965 (div. Oct. 1999); 1 son, Neil William Orlando Sutherland. BA with 1st class honours, Courtauld Inst., U. London, 1961, PhD, 1965. Asst. lectr. U. Leeds (Eng.), 1964-65; asst. prof. art history Columbia U., N.Y.C., 1965-71, Hunter Coll., N.Y.C., 1971-73; assoc. prof. SUNY, Albany, 1973-77; chmn. for acad. affairs Met. Mus. Art, N.Y.C., 1977-80; part-time faculty Juilliard Sch., N.Y.C., 1978-84; prof. U. Pitts., 1984—. Founder, 1st pres. Women's Caucus for Art, 1973-76; disting. vis. prof. U. Tex.-Arlington, fall 1982; Mellon prof. history of art U. Pitts., spring 1984; vis. prof. history of art So. Meth. U., Dallas, fall 1993. Author: Andrea Sacchi, 1977, Selected Drawings of Gian Lorenzo Bernini, 1977, Seventeenth Century Art and Architecture, 2004; co-author: Die Zeichnungen von Andrea Sacchi und Carlo Maratta, 1967, Women Artists: 1550-1950, exhbn. catalogue, 1977, Landscape Painting in Rome, 1575-1675, exhbn. catalogue, 1985, Italian, French, English and Spanish Drawings and Watercolors in the Detroit Institute of Arts, 1992. Fellow Guggenheim Found., 1971, Ford Found., 1975-76, NEH, 1981-82, rsch. fellow Getty Mus. Art, 1988. Mem. Coll. Art Assn., Women's Caucus for Art. Office: U Pittsburgh Dept History of Art Pittsburgh PA 15260 Office Phone: 412-648-2408.

HARRIS, ANN MARIE, mathematician, educator; b. Cambridge, Cambridgeshire, Eng., Apr. 30, 1956; d. Drew Warren Tomberlin and Jeanne Esther Britney; m. Laurence Earl Harris, May 30, 1980 (div.); children: Britney Jeanne, David Earl, Christen Marie. BA, Miss. U. for Women, Columbus, 1978; MS, Utah State U., 1996. Tchg. asst. U. of Mo., Rolla, 1978—79; h.s. math tchr. Cuba Sch. Dist., Cuba, Mo., 1979—80; jr. high math tchr. Edinburg Sch. Dist., 1980—81; tchg. asst. Utah State U., Logan, 1993—96; instr. Idaho State U., Pocatello, 1996—99; prof. math. Brigham Young U. - Idaho, Rexburg, 1999—. Contbr. articles to profl. jours. Recipient Achievement in Writing award, Nat. Coun. of Tchrs. of English, 1974, Rollins award, Utah State U., 1996; scholar Nat. Merit scholar, Miss. U. for Women, 1974—78. Mem.: Math. Assn. of Am. (sec.-treas. Intermountain sect. 2000—). Avocations: reading, sewing, cooking, snowboarding, biking. Home: 152 South 2nd East Rexburg ID 83440 Office: Brigham Young U Idaho RKS 232J Rexburg ID 83460 Office Phone: 208-496-1405. Business E-Mail: harrisa@byui.edu.

HARRIS, ANN TALT, protective services official, educator; b. Flint, Mich., Oct. 17, 1951; d. Matthew Talt and Susanne Marie O'Sullivan; children: Ryan Matthew, Amy Nicole. Student, Hott C.C., U. Tex. Cert. pvt. detective Mich. Police officer Flint Police Dept., Mich.; tchr., coach Flint Bd. Edn., social svcs. field worker; families first specialist Inter Tribal Coun., Mt. Pleasant. Site dir. Genesee County Youth Athletic Assn., Flint; track coach McKinley Jr. High Sch.; cheer leading coach Beaverton Rural Schs. Actor: (books); contbr. articles to profl. jours. Pres. Gladwin County Hist. Soc., Mich., 2004—05; bd. dirs. Gladwin Area Artists Guild, 2003—, Mich. State U. Gladwin County, 2002—05, Cmty. Action Agy., 2002—05. Named Best of Show Photography, Gladwin County; recipient, Saginaw, Midland. Mem.: Am. Bus. Women's Assn. Avocations: photography, boating, travel.

HARRIS, ARLENE, lawyer; b. Buffalo, Dec. 29, 1944; d. Yetta (Kerner) Cramer; m. Ira S. Harris, Dec. 25, 1971; children: Elliot, David, Sara. BA cum laude, Bklyn. Coll., 1965; JD, NYU, 1968. Bar: NY 1969. Assoc. trusts and estates dept. Paul, Weiss, Rifkind, Wharton & Garrison, 1968-75; asst. atty. gen. NY State Dept. Law, 1975-76; law asst.-referee NY County Surrogate's Ct., 1976-78, chief law asst., 1978-90; ptnr. trusts and estates dept. Shea & Gould, NYC, 1990-93; spl. counsel, chair Wills & Estates Dept. Kaye, Scholer LLP, NYC, 1993—. Mem. Internat. Acad. of Estate and Trust Law, Estate's Discussion Groups; bd. dirs. Estate Planning Coun.; adj. prof. law St. John's U. Sch. Law, 1984-92; instr. NYU Sch. Continuing Edn., 1991—; lectr. on estate planning, trusts and estates ABA Nat. Inst., World Trade Inst., NY County Lawyer's Assn., Acad. Trial Lawyers, United Jewish Appeal Ann. Estates Conf., Practising Law Inst. Contbr. chpt. to book, articles to legal publs. and procs. Bd. dirs. East Bay Civic Assn., Inc., 1974-87. John Norton Pomeroy scholar NYU, 1968. Fellow Am. Coll. Trusts and Estate Counsel; mem. NY State Bar Assn. (chmn. legislation com., former mem.-at-large trusts and estates sect., lectr. trusts and estates law sect.), Assn. of Bar of City of NY (mem. trusts, estates and surrogate's cts. com. 1979-81), Order of Coif. Avocations: gardening, reading, boating. Office: Kaye Scholer LLP 425 Park Ave New York NY 10022-3506 E-mail: aharris@kayescholer.com.

HARRIS, BARBARA CLEMENTINE, bishop; b. Phila., 1930; Grad., Charles Morris Price Sch. Advt. and Journalism, Phila.; student, Villanova U., Urban Theology Unit, Sheffield, Eng.; D in Sacred Theology (hon.), Hobart and William Smith Colls., 1981; DD (hon.), Gen. Theol. Sem., 1989, Episc. Div. Sch., 1989, Amherst Coll., 1989. Ordained to ministry Episcopal Ch. as deacon, 1979, as priest, 1980. Pres. Joseph V. Baker Assocs., Phila., 1958-68; sr. staff cons., mem. community rels. dept. Sun Oil Co.; priest-in-charge St. Augustine of Hippo, Norristown, Pa.; interim rector Ch. of the Advocate, Phila.; exec. dir. Episc. Ch. Pub. Co., 1984-88; suffragan bishop Episcopal Diocese of Mass., Boston, 1989—. Trustee Episc. Div. Sch. Address: Episc Diocese of Mass 138 Tremont St Boston MA 02111-1318

HARRIS, BARBARA MCDANIEL-WOLFE, retired elementary school educator; b. Richmond, Va., May 7, 1928; d. Leonard Eugene and Lillian Beatrice (Ward) McDaniel; children: Traci Gaye Wolfe Hood, Troy Guy Wolfe. Student, Howard U., 1946—48; BS, Va. Union U., 1950; MA in Devel. Psychology, Columbia U., 1956. Tchr. grade 3 John M. Gandy Sch., Ashland, Va., 1952—55; tchr. grade 3-4 Woodville Sch., Richmond, Va., 1955—58; tchr. grade 4 Cedarbrook Sch., Plainfield, NJ, 1968—69; innovative tchr. grade 4-5 Westhampton Learning Ctr., Richmond, 1970—71; tchr., summer sch. prin. Bellevue Sch., Richmond, 1971—83; tchr. grade 2-3 A.V. Norrell Sch., Richmond, 1983—86; tchr. grade 2 Ginter Park Sch., Richmond, 1986—93. Pres. state club Va. Columbia U., N.Y.C., 1955—56; facilitator Project Teach U. Richmond, 1986; curriculum writer grade 3 Va. Commonwealth U., 1985. Prodr.: (slide/tape) Historic Church Hill, 1981. Organizer, founder Belle Ringers of Richmond, 1992; mem. scholarship benefit com. Richmond br. Nat. Assn. Univ. Women; team mem. Piano Keys Internat. Congress of Women Grads., Va. Union U.-Coburn Hall, 1992; organizer, sponsor Black History Mus. and Cultural Ctr. Youth Guild. Named Outstanding Vol. of Yr., Chandler Mid. Sch., 1996—98; recipient Vol. Cmty. Svc. award, 47th Mid-Atlantic Regional Conf., 2000. Mem.: LWV (mem. voter registration com., youth hostess coord.), Va. Found. for Women (mem. poster project com.), Alpha Kappa Alpha, Pi Lambda Theta (past pres. 1994—97, mem. history com.). Democrat. Baptist. Avocations: travel, computers, creative writing, collecting family documents. Home: 417 S Davis Ave Richmond VA 23220

HARRIS, BARBARA S., publishing executive; BS in Phys. Edn., Fla. State U., 1978; Masters, N.E. Mo. State U. Editl. dir. Weider Publ., Woodland Hills, Calif., 1986—2003; exec. v.p. Am. Media, Woodlands Hills, Calif., 2003—. Past adviser Calif. Gov.'s Coun. on Phys. Fitness and Sports; past chmn. bd. dirs. Am. Coun. Exercise; mem. adv. bd. L.A. Commn. on Assaults Against Women, Melpomene Inst.; mem. adv. bd. Fitness Cert. program U. Calif., L.A.; instr. Omega Inst.; presenter in field. Appearances on Oprah, Today Show, CNN, MSNBC, Access Hollywood, Entertainment Tonight. Achievements include climbing 20,000 foot mountain in the Bolivian Andes, Mt. Rainier and Mt Kilimanjaro. Avocations: running, weightlifting, kayaking, photography, rock climbing. Office: Am Media 21100 Erwin St Woodland Hills CA 91367-3712 Business E-Mail: bharris@weiderpub.com.

HARRIS, BEN M., education educator; b. Chgo., Feb. 8, 1923; s. Eva Mae (Barber) Sands; m. Mary Lee Christian, Sept. 28, 1948; children: Kim Christian, Tamara Lee. AA, Glendale Coll., 1943; BA, UCLA, 1948, MEd, 1951; EdD, U. Calif., Berkeley, 1958. Cert. elem. tchr., secondary tchr., prin., sch. adminstr., Calif. Chemist Desert Chem. Co., Twenty Nine Palms, Calif., 1943-44; tchr. Burbank (Calif.) Jr. High Sch., 1948-51; curriculum coordinator Inyo County Schs., Independence, Calif., 1951-54; tchr. Lafayette (Calif.) Elem. Sch., 1954-55; dir. curriculum Lafayette Sch. Dist., 1955-56, dir. pers., 1956-57; acad. asst. dept. edn. U. Calif., Berkeley, 1957-58; asst., then assoc. prof. U. Tex., Austin, 1958-68, prof. edn. adminstrn., 1968-87, M.K. Hage Centennial prof. edn., 1987, prof. emeritus, 1988—. Cons. Ministry Edn., Venezuela, 1973, Bahrain, 1985, Effective Border Schs. R&D Initiative, 1995-96, U. Sch. Collaborative project, Austin Pub. Schs., 1995-97; vis. prof. U. Wash., Seattle, 1976, U. Tex., San Antonio, 1989, U. Tex. Pan Am., Edinburg, 1992, 1997-2002; planning cons. Ministry of Edn., Egypt, 1987, Venezuela, 1973, 75, Malaysia, 1989, 91; UNESCO advisor U. Cordoba, Spain, 1971, U. Petroleum and Minerals, Dharan, 1979; advisor Lagoven, S.A. Venezuela Petroleum, 1991-92, Am. 2000 New Generation Schs. Project, Austin, 1991-92; vis. lectr. Taiwan Tchrs. Coll., Taichung/Kaochsfungand, 1994; dir. evaluation effective schs. border project, Edinburgh, 1995-97; co-dir. Visioning the Future Project Austin (Tex.) Ind. Sch. Dist., 2004. Author: Supervisory Behavior in Education, 1963, 3d edit., 1985, Developmental Teacher Evaluation, 1986, Inservice Education for Staff Development, 1980, 2d edit., 1989; (with others) Inservice Education: A Guide to Better Practice, 1969, Personnel Administration in Education, 1980, 3d edit., 1992, Invention*Developmental Teacher Evaluation Kit; co-developer Diagnostic Executive Competency Assessment System, 1988, Performance Criteria for School Executives, 1991, Summary Report on Formative Evaluation of Partner School Progress, 1997; mem. editl. bd. Handbook of Rsch. on School Supervision, 1998; co-author: Visioning the Future for for Austin Senior High Schools, 2004. Served with USNR, 1944-46. Fulbright scholar U. Teheran, Iran, 1962-63, Bahrain, 1985. Mem. ASCD (nat. bd. dirs. 1973-75, 80-82), Am. Edn. Rsch. Assn., Coun. Profs. of Instrnl. Supervision (pres. 1976-77), Sam Bass Theatre Assn., Trad. Jazz Club, Fulbright Alumni Assn., Phi Delta Kappa. Avocations: country and western dancing, singing, gardening. Office: U Tex Austin Dept Ednl Adminstrn 05400 George Sanchez Bldg 310 Austin TX 78712 Fax: 512-471-5975. Office Phone: 512-475-8585.

HARRIS, BENJAMIN HARTE, JR., lawyer; b. Sept. 12, 1937; s. Ben H. and Mary Cade (Aldridge) H.; m. Martha Elliott Lambeth, Aug. 26, 1961; children: Benjamin Harte, Wayt. AB, Davidson Coll., 1959; JD, U. Ala., 1962. Bar: Ala. 1964, U.S. Dist. Ct. (so. dist.) Ala. 1965, U.S. Ct. Appeals (5th cir.) 1981, U.S. Supreme Ct. 1971, U.S. Ct. Appeals (11th cir.) 1981. Assoc. Johnstone, Adams, Bailey, Gordon & Harris (formerly Johnstone, Adams, May, Howard & Hill, LLC), Mobile, Ala., 1964-70; mem. Johnstone, Adams, Bailey, Gordon & Harris, Mobile, 1971. Chmn. Atty's Ins. Mut. Ala., bd. dirs. Past bd. dirs., past pres. Boys' Club, 1989-95; past chmn., past trustee UMS Prep Sch.; v.p., bd. dirs. Gordon Smith Ctr.; mem. stds. com. United Way. Fellow: Ala. Bar Found. (past. pres., past trustee, past pres.), Am. Bar Found. (life); mem.: Nat. Conf. Bar Pres. (past exec. coun.), 11th Cir. Ct. Appeals Hist. Soc. (trustee, v.p.), Ala. Jud. Commn., Am. Arbitration Assn., Am. Judicature Soc., Ala. Def. Lawyers Assn., Ala. Law Sch. Found. (past pres., trustee, Pipes Disting. Alumnus award 2003), Ala. Law Inst., Ala. State Bar (bd. commrs. 1978—87, mem. exec. com., trustee bar found., past chmn. disciplinary commn., past pres.), Mobile County Bar Assn. (exec. com. 1980—87), ABA (past ho. of dels., past bd. govs.), Athelstan Club, Murray House (pres. 2003—, dir.), Mobile Rotary Club (Paul Harris fellow), Brock Inn of Ct. (pres. 1996—98). Episcopalian. Office: PO Box 1988 Mobile AL 36633-1988 Office Phone: 251-441-9205. Business E-Mail: bhh@johnstoneadams.com.

HARRIS, BERNARD, statistician, mathematician, educator; b. N.Y.C., N.Y., June 20, 1926; s. Samuel S. and Ella L. Harris; m. Anita Belle Greenberg, May 19, 1929 (dec. Sept. 2, 1977); children: Shelley Anne, Mark Bruce, David Brian, Susan Elizabeth; m. Susan Stephens Burns, Sept. 24, 1983; stepchildren: Laura Burns, Erin Burns. BBA, CCNY, 1946; MA, George Washington U., 1953; PhD, Stanford U., 1958. Statistician U.S. Census Bur., Suitland, Md., 1950—52; mathematician Nat. Security Agy., Ft. Meade, Md., 1952—58; assoc. prof. U. Nebr., Lincoln, 1958—64; prof. Math. Rsch. Ctr. U. Wis., Madison, 1964—85, prof. stats. dept., 1966—. Chmn. stats. task force FAA/DOD Com. on Material Properties, 1986—90, 1981—82; mem. PRA Procedures Rev. Bd., 1981—82, PRA Rev. Bd., U.S. Nuclear Regulatory Commn., 1992—95; lectr. in field; vis. prof. U. Lund, Lund, Sweden, 1990, U. So. Calif., 1992; vis. rsch. prof. Math. Inst. Steklova, Moscow, 1991, Moscow, 92, Moscow, 96, U. Muenster, Germany, 1993, Heinrich Heine U., Duesseldorf, Germany, 1994, Duesseldorf, 95, Duesseldorf, 96, Kungliska Techniska Hogskolan, 1998, 99; cons. to various govt. and indsl. orgns., 1958—63. Mem. editl. bd.: Statistics and Decisions, 1983—2002; author: (books) Theory of Probability, 1966; editor: Spectral Analysis of Time Series, 1967, Graph Theory and Its Applications, 1970; contbr. articles and revs. to profl. pubs. Fellow: Am. Statis. Assn. (bd. dirs. 1978—80, mem. coun. 1996—, pres. Nebr. chpt. 1958—60, chmn. sect. risk analysis 1994—95), Inst. Math. Stats. (program chair 1996); mem.: AAAS, Classification Soc. N.Am. (bd. dirs. 1991—2001, Univ. Faculty award 1999), Math. Assn. Am., Am. Math. Soc., Internat. Statis. Inst. Office: U Nebras Math Dept Lincoln NE 68588-0323

HARRIS, BRECK ANTHONY, business educator, writer, researcher; b. Denver, Aug. 2, 1953; s. Bobby Elywn Harris and Patricia Rosebrook (Stepmother), Joyce Schroeder; m. Dora Argyropoulos, Sept. 15, 1984; children: Jason John, Nikolas Bobby. AA, Coll. Alameda, 1978; BS, San Francisco State U., 1980, MBA, 1982; cert., Boeke Kenshu Ctr., Inst. Internat. Studies and Tng., Fujinomiya Shi, Japan, 1981; Ed. D., U. La Verne, 2000. Elec. engring. sales rep. Sq. D. Corp., Pleasanton, Calif., 1988—92. Cons. Internat. Exch. Corp., Oakland, Calif., 1982; spkr., presenter in field. Contbr.: college textbook Great Ideas for Teaching Marketing; musician (percussionist): (CD) Let Your Spirit Fall. Amb. Chamber of Commerce, Fresno, Calif.; bd. of trustees mem. Fresno Pacific U., 2003—04. With USN, 1972—76. Recipient Bus. award, Bank of Am., 1978, Alameda First Nat. Bank, 1978, Internat. Studies Grad. Fellowship award, San Francisco State U., 1981, Sigma Phi Award for Scholastic Achievement award in field of fgn. trade, San Francisco Propeller Club. Mem.: Nat. Soc. Exptl. Edn., Coun. Adult and Exptl. Learning, Adult Higher Edn. Alliance, Christian Adult Higher Edn. Assn., Beta Gamma Sigma. Avocations: travel, backpacking, running, music. Office: Fresno Pacific U 1717 S Chestnut Ave Fresno CA 93702 Office Phone: 559-453-2288. E-mail: baharris@fresno.edu.

HARRIS, BRIAN CRAIG, lawyer; b. Newark, Sept. 8, 1941; s. Louis W. and Lillian (Frankel) H.; m. Ellen M. Davis, Aug. 20, 1978; children; Andrea, Keith. BS, boston U., 1963; JD, Rutgers U., 1966. Bar: N.J. 1968, D.C. 1968, U.S. Ct. Appeals (3d cir.) 1968, N.Y. 1984, U.S. Ct. Appeals (2d cir.) 1985. Asst. corp. counsel, Newark, 1968-70; assoc. Braff, Litvak & Ertag, East Orange, N.J., 1970-72; ptnr. Braff, Litvak, Ertag, Wortmann & Harris, East Orange, 1972-85, Braff, Ertag, wortmann, Harris & Sukoneck, Livingston, N.J., 1985-91, Braff, Harris & Sukoneck, 1991—. Adj. lectr. law and medicine Seton Hall U., South Orange, N.J., 1982-83, trial preparation Rutgers U. Law Sch., 1983, strategy of def. United Tech. Corp., Chgo., 1986. Sustaining mem. Product Liability Adv. Coun., Inc.; contbg. mem. Nat. Ileitis found., N.Y.C., 1983—. Named Master of Inns. of Ct., Arthur J. Vanderbilt Sect., 1988. Mem. ABA (employment law sect., tort and ins. sect.), Internat. Assn. Def. Counsel, Profl. Liability Underwriters Soc., N.Y. State Bar Assn., N.Y. Trial Lawyers Assn., Essex County Trial Lawyers Assn., Middlesex County Trial Lawyers Assn., Def. Rsch. Inst. (mem. com. employment law, mem. com. profl. liability, trustee Hamonie Group), N.J. Trial Lawyers Assn., N.J. Def. Assn., East Hampton Indoor Outdoor Tennis Club, Orange Lawn Tennis Club. Jewish. Avocations: running, basketball, theater, tennis, study of military strategy of land forces in world war ii. Home: Llewellyn Pk West Orange NJ 07052-5402 Office: Braff Harris & Sukoneck 570 W Mount Pleasant Ave Ste 18 Livingston NJ 07039-1688 also: 305 Broadway Fl 7 New York NY 10007-1109

HARRIS, CARL G., music educator; b. Fayette, Mo., Jan. 14, 1935; s. Carl G. Harris Sr. and Frances M. (Harris) Harris. BA, Philander Smith Coll., 1956; MA, U. Mo., 1964; Mus D, U. Mo., Conservatory of Music, 1972. Dir. of choirs Philander Smith Coll., Little Rock, 1959—69; prof., chair, dir. of choirs Va. State U., Petersburg, Va., 1971—84, Norfolk State U., Norfolk, Va., 1984—97; prof. of music, organist Hampton U., Hampton, Va., 1997—. Min. of music Bank St. Meml. Bapt. Ch., Norfolk, 1984—2004; min. of music emeritus bank St. Meml. Bapt. Ch., Norfolk, 2005—; organist Gillfield Bapt. Ch., Petersburg, Va., 1971—84, Centennial United Meth. Ch., Kans. City, Mo., 1968—71. Contbr. articles various profl. jours. Recipient Disting. Alumnus award, U. Mo., 1980, Alumnus award, Philander Smith Coll., 1975. Mem.: Lions, Kappa Delta Pi in Edn., Alpha Kappa Mu Nat., Tau Beta Sigma Hon. Band Soc., Phi Delta Kappa Edn., Kappa Kappa Psi Hon. Band, Phi Mu Alpha Sinfonia Music, Omega Psi Phi Fraternity, Inc. Democrat. Episcopal. Home: 171 Atlantic Ave A Hampton VA 23664 Office: Hampton U Dept of Music Hampton VA 23668 Office Phone: 757-727-5702. Personal E-mail: charris54@cox.net.

HARRIS, CARLA ANN, investment company executive; m. Victor Adrian Franklin, Aug. 11, 2001. BA in economics, Harvard U., 1984, MBA, 1987. Joined Morgan Stanley, N.Y.C., 1987, mergers, acquisitions, and restructuring dept., 1987—91, joined equity capital markets dept., 1991, mng. dir., head equity pvt. placements and retail capital markets. Singer: (albums) Carla's First Christmas, 2000, Joy is Waiting, 2005. Funded Carla Harris Scholarship at Harvard U. and Bishop Kenny H.S., Jacksonville, Fla.; exec. bd. Food for Survival, N.Y.C. Food Bank, St. Charles Borromeo Cath. Sch., Sponsors for Ednl. Opportunities, A Better Chance Inc.; bd. dirs. Boy Scouts Am., Manhattan; bd. mem. Apollo theater. Named Most Powerful African Am., Fortune Mag.; recipient Bethune Award, Nat. Coun. Negro Women, Ron Brown Trailblazer Award, St. John's U. Sch. Law, Women of Distinction Award, Girl Scouts of Greater Essex and Hudson Counties, Frederick Douglass Award, NY Urban League, 2003. Office: Morgan Stanley 1585 Broadway New York NY 10036 Office Phone: 212-761-5375. Business E-Mail: carla.harris@morganstanley.com.

HARRIS, CHARLES DAVID, music educator; b. Mpls., Jan. 6, 1939; children: Laura Kathleen, Mary Louise, Caroline Ruth. MusB, Northwestern U., 1960, MusM, 1961; PhD, U. Mich., 1967. Levitt prof. music history and harpsichord Drake U., Des Moines, 1965—2003. Editl. bd. Early Keyboard Journal, 2000—03. Editor: (critical editions) Johann Caspar Kerll: The Collected Works for Keyboard, Johann Friedrich Doles, Jr., Johann Kuhnau; contbr. articles to profl. jours. Grantee, Fulbright Commn., 1964—65, 1971—72. Mem.: Midwestern His. Keyboard Soc. (founding mem.), Am. Musicological Soc., Pi Kappa Lambda (assoc. regent 1990—93). Democrat. Avocation: hiking. Home: 1536 SE 74th Ave Portland OR 97215 Personal E-mail: dh1376@comcast.net.

HARRIS, CHARLES E., venture capital investment executive; b. 1943; m. Susan Harris; children: Elizabeth, David. BA, Princeton U., 1964; MBA, Columbia U. Grad. Sch. Bus., 1967. Chmn. Wood, Struthers and Winthrop Mgmt. Corp. (investment adv. subs. of Donaldson, Lufkin & Jenrette), 1966—84; chmn. bd., CEO Harris & Harris Group, Inc., NY, 1984—, chief compliance officer, 1997—2001, mng. dir., 2004—; dir. NBX Corp., Calif., 1996—, NeuroMetrix, Inc., Waltham, Mass., 1996—. Mem. NY Soc. Security Analysts; life-sustaining fellow Entrepreneurship Ctr., MIT, mem. Pres. coun., shareholder; mem. Pres. coun. Cold Spring Harbor Lab., trustee, Nidus Ctr., head audit com.; mem. adv. panel Congl. Office Tech. Assessment; judge Lemelson-MIT Inventor Awards Program, 2002—; spkr. in field. Mem.: Thoroughbred Club Am., Saratoga Reading Rooms, Jupiter Hills Golf Club, Princeton Club NY, Creek. Office: Harris & Harris Group Inc 111 W 57th St Ste 1100 New York NY 10019 also: Harris & Harris Group Inc 11150 Santa Monica Blvd Ste 1200 Los Angeles CA 90025 Office Phone: 212-582-0900, 310-479-2595. Office Fax: 212-582-9563, 310-312-1868. Business E-Mail: admin@tinytechvc.com.

HARRIS, CHARLES EDGAR, retired wholesale distribution company executive; b. Englewood, Tenn., Nov. 6, 1915; s. Charles Leonard and Minnie Beatrice (Borin) H.; m. Dorothy Sarah Wilson, Aug. 20, 1938; children: Charles Edgar, William John. Pres., chmn., CEO H.T. Hackney Co., Knoxville, Tenn., 1972-83; ret. Former chmn. bd., chief exec. officer, dir. various corps. in Tenn., Ky., N.C., and Ga.; former bd. dirs. Park Nat. Bank, 1st Am. Nat. Bank Knoxville; dir. U.S. Indsl. Coun. Former bd. dirs. Downtown Knoxville Assn., Greater Knoxville Smoky Mountain coun. Bou Scouts Am., Met. YMCA, Knoxville, United Way Knoxville; mem. budget com. 1982 World's Fair, Knoxville; deacon, trustee Ctrl. Bapt. Ch., Knox County Assn. Bapt.; mem. exec. bd. Tenn. Bapt. Conv., Nashville; assoc. chmn. Layman's Nat. Bible Week, Washington; trustee Carson Newman Coll., Jefferson City, Tenn.; dir. Tenn. Taxpayers Assn.; dir. Religious Heritage of Am., St. Louis; bd. dirs. Tenn. Bapt. Children's Homes. Recipient Outstanding Community Leadership award Religious Heritage Am., Red Triangle award and Silver Triangle award YMCA. Mem. Greater Knoxville C. of C. (bd. dirs., Outstanding Corp. Citizenship award), Nat. Assn. Wholesalers-Distbrs., LeConte Club (charter), Knoxville Execs. Club (bd. dirs.), Rotary (officer, bd. dirs.). Home: #202 7350 Middlebrook Pike Knoxville TN 37909-3138

HARRIS, CHARLES ELMER, retired lawyer; b. Williamsburg, Iowa, Nov. 26, 1922; s. Charles Elmer and Loretto (Judge) H.; m. Marjorie Clark, Jul. 9, 1949 (div. June. 1969); m. Linda Rae Slaymaker, Nov. 25, 1992; children: Martha Ann, Julie Ann, Charles Elmer III. Student, St. Ambrose Coll., 1940-42; BSC., U. Iowa, 1946, JD, 1949. Bar: Iowa 1949. Mem. firm Brody, Parker, Roberts, Thoma & Harris, Des Moines, 1949-66, Herrick, Langdon, Belin Harris, Langdon & Helmick, Des Moines, 1966-78, Belin Harris Helmick, P.C., Des Moines, 1978-91, Belin, Harris, Lamson, McCormick, P.C., Des Moines, 1991-96; pvt. practice, Des Moines, 1997-99; ret., 1999. Lectr. tax schs., meetings, 1951, 55, 67, 69, 77-84, 90, 91. Comments editor: Iowa Law Rev., 1948-49. Bd. dirs. NCCJ, 1964-67, Iowa Bar Found., 1977-92, Iowa Law Sch. Found., 1977-90, United Way Found., 1981-89. Lt. (j.g.) USNR, 1943-46. Fellow Am. Coll. Trust and Estate Counsel; mem. ABA, Iowa Bar Assn. (bd. govs. 1973-80, Merit award 1980), Polk County Bar Assn. (pres. 1972-73), Polk County Jr. Bar Assn. (pres. 1952-53), Order of Coif, Sigma Chi, Delta Theta Phi. Roman Catholic. Home: 5141 Robertson Dr Des Moines IA 50312-2170 Personal E-mail: Harris5141@aol.com.

HARRIS, CHARLES GEORGE, research scientist, consultant; b. Indpls., Ind., Aug. 17, 1955; s. Charles George and Frances Barge Harris; m. Mary Louise Smith, Nov. 24, 1989; children: Nicholas Lawrence, Jeremy Francis Harrissmith. Field svcs. mgr. Hydropro, Inc., Lake Park, Fla., 1984—99; tech. mgr. Energy Recovery, Inc., Chesapeake, Va., 1999—2000; sys. mgr. Advanced Membrane Sys., Newport News, Va., 2000—. Contbr. articles to profl. jours. Actor ArtsEnter of Cape Charles, Va., 2001—03. Mem.: S.E. Desalting Assn., Internat. Desalination Assn., Am. Membrane Tech. Assn., Am. Water Works Assn. Avocations: motor racing, acting. Home: PO Box 1064 Cheriton VA 23316 Office: Advanced Membrane Sys 9286A Warwick Blvd Newport News VA 23607 Personal E-mail: chipdad@aol.com. E-mail: charris@amswater.com.

HARRIS, CHRISTINE, dance company executive; b. Milw. Mktg. dir. Milw. Symphony Orch., 1984-90, head Arts in Cmty. Edn. program, 1990-95; with Inst. Music, Health and Edn., Mpls., 1996-97; exec. dir. Milw. Ballet, 1997—2002; pres. United Performing Arts Fund, 2002—. Office: United Performing Arts Fund 929 N Water St Milwaukee WI 53202

HARRIS, CHRISTOPHER, publishing executive, product designer, editor; b. Plainfield, N.J., June 7, 1933; s. Maynard Lawrence and Edith Johnson (Bushnell) H.; m. Linda Martin Robinson, Oct. 8, 1955 (dec. 1967); children— Katherine Hamilton, Stephen Christopher, Andrea Lawrence; m. Sarah Pickett Hargrove Sullivan, Aug. 18, 1977. BA, Yale U., 1955. Book mfg. coordinator Rand McNally & Co., Hammond, Ind., and N.Y.C., 1955-60; mng. editor Studio Books div. Viking Press, N.Y.C., 1960-70; editor, pres. Chatham Press, Riverside and Old Greenwich, Conn., 1970-76; dir. design and prodn. Yale U. Press, New Haven, 1977-88; dir. Summer Hill Books, 1978—; editor Proctor Libr. Newsletter, Weathersfield, Vt., 1996—; auditor Town of Weathersfield, 1996-97. Chmn., Weathersfield Dem. Town Com., 2000-03; trustee Proctor Libr., 2003—; mem. Weathersfield Conservation Commn. Democrat. Home and Office: 304 Beaver Pond Rd Weathersfield VT 05151-9558

HARRIS, CHRISTY FRANKLIN, lawyer; b. Greensboro, N.C., Dec. 8, 1945; s. Luther Franklin and Rebecca Ann (Bluster) H.; children: Stacey Lynn, Aubrey Leigh. AA, Oxford Coll., Emory U.; BA, U. Fla., 1967, JD with honors, 1970. Bar: Fla. 1970, U.S. Dist. Ct. (mid. dist.) Fla. 1970, U.S. Ct. Mil. Appeals 1971, U.S. Ct. Appeals (11th cir.) 1984. Assoc. Holland & Knight, Lakeland, Fla., 1970, 1973-74; pres. Canan & Harris P.A., Lakeland, Fla., 1974-76; pres., sr. atty. Harris, Midyette & Clements P.A., Lakeland, Fla., 1976-89, Harris & Midyette, P.A., Lakeland, Fla., 1989-91, Harris, Midyette, Geary, Darby & Morrell, P.A., Lakeland, Fla., 1991-98, Harris, Midyette & Darby, P.A., Lakeland, Fla., 1998-2000; shareholder Peterson & Myers, P.A., Lakeland, Fla., 2000—03; of counsel Kinsey, Vincent, Pyle, L.C., Daytona Beach, Fla. Mem. 10th cir. Grievance Com., Lakeland, 1976—79, Lakeland, 1983—86, vice chmn., 1979, chmn., 86; mem. Unauthorized Practice of Law Com., 1983—86; bd. dirs. Internat. Speedway Corp., 1984—. Bd. dirs. Program to Aid Drug Abusers, Lakeland, 1975-76, Campfire, 1979-85. Served to capt. USMCR, 1968-73, mil. judge, 1972-73. Named to Hon. Order of Ky. Cols., 1974. Mem. Volusia County Bar Assn., Attys. Title Ins. Fund, Grand Am. Rd. Racing Assn., LLC (founding mem.), Order of Coif, Phi Beta Kappa, Phi Kappa Phi. Republican. Avocations: motor sports, sport fishing. Home: 6022 S Williamson Blvd Port Orange FL 32128 Office: Kinsey Vincent Pyle LC 150 S Palmetto Ave Box A Daytona Beach FL 32114 Office Phone: 386-252-1561. Business E-Mail: cfh@kvplaw.com.

HARRIS, CURTIS C., physician; MD, U. Kans. Intern and resident in internal medicine and oncology; chief Lab. Human Carcinogenesis Nat. Cancer Inst., NIH, Bethesda, Md., also head molecular genetics and carcinogenesis sect. Deichmann lectr. VII Internat. Congress of Toxicology, 1995. Editor: 10 books; exec. editor Carcinogenesis; contbr. articles and revs. to profl. jours. Recipient Alton Ochsner Relating Smoking and Health award, 1993, Walter Hubert award lectr., Brit. Assn. Cancer Rsch., 1995. Mem.: Am. Assn. Cancer Rsch., Chem. Industry Inst. Toxicology (mem. sci. adv. panel, chmn. 1989—94, Founder's award 1995), Internat. Soc. Gastroentergol. Carcinogenesis (Charles Heidelberger award 1999). Office: NIH Nat Cancer Inst Lab Carcinogenesis Rm 3068 37 Convent Dr Bldg 37 Bethesda MD 20892-0001

HARRIS, CYRIL MANTON, physicist, educator, acoustical engineer, engineering and architecture educator; b. Detroit; s. Bernard O. and Ida (Moss) H.; m. Ann Schakne; children: Nicholas Bennett, Katherine Anne. BA, UCLA, 1938, MA, 1940; PhD, MIT, 1945; Sc.D. (hon.), N.J. Inst. Tech., 1981, Northwestern U., 1989. Rsch. asst. Carnegie Instn. Washington, 1941; mem. staff Bell Telephone Labs., 1945-51; cons. Office Naval Research, London, Eng., 1951; Fulbright lectr. Tech. U., Delft, Holland, 1951-52; Charles Batchelor prof. elec. engring., prof. architecture and past chmn. div. archtl. tech. Columbia U.; now prof. emeritus. Vis. Fulbright prof. U. Tokyo, 1960; acoustical cons. Met. Opera House, N.Y.C., John F. Kennedy Ctr. Performing Arts, Washington, Krannert Ctr. Performing Arts, U. Ill., Powell Symphony Hall, St. Louis, Nat. Acad. Scis. Auditorium, Washington, Minn. Orch. Hall, Mpls., Nat. Ctr. Performing Arts, Bombay, Symphony Hall, Salt Lake City, Benaroya Hall, Seattle; past dir. Inst. Theatre Tech.; mem. noise control group, mem. com. on undersea warfare NRC, 1955-57, mem. bldg. adv. bd., 1977-79; mem. coun. hearing and bio-acoustics Armed Forces-NRC, 1953-55; mem. adv. panel 213 to Nat. Bur. Standards, 1966-69, chmn., 1969-71. Author: (with V.O. Knudsen) Acoustical Designing in Architecture, 1950, rev., 1980, Handbook of Noise Control, 1957, 2d edit., 1979, 3d edit retitled Handbook of Acoustical Measurements and Noise Control, 1991, Dictionary of Architecture and Construction; Historic Architecture Sourcebook, 1977, Illustrated Dictionary of Historic Architecture, 1983; Handbook of Utilities and Services for Buildings, 1990, Noise Control in Buildings, 1993, American Architecture: An Illustrated Encyclopedia, 1998, Shock and Vibration Handbook 5th edit., 2002; mem. editl. adv. bd.: Physics Today, 1955-66; contbr. articles to profl. jours. Hon. trustee St. Louis Symphony Soc., 1977—; mem. nat. adv. bd. Utah Symphony Orch., 1976-85. Recipient Franklin medal, 1977; Emile Berliner award, 1977; Hon. award U.S. ITT, 1977; Wallace Clement Sabine medal, 1979; AIA medal, 1980; Gold Medal Audio Engring. Soc., 1984; award of honor for sci. and tech. City of N.Y., 1985; Alumni award UCLA, 1989, Pupin medal Columbia U., 1998. Fellow IEEE, Acoustical Soc. Am. (pres. 1964-65, assoc. editor jour. 1959-70, Gold medal), Audio Engring. Soc. (hon.); mem. NAS, NAE, Am. Inst. Physics (governing bd. 1965-66), N.Y. Acad. Scis. (pres. 1991-93, chmn. bd. 1992-94), Am. Philos. Soc., Century Assn., Sigma Xi, Tau Beta Pi. Office: Columbia U Mudd Bldg New York NY 10027

HARRIS, D. ALAN, lawyer; b. Oak Park, Ill., Mar. 4, 1949; s. E.B. and M.A. (Solberg) H.; m. Marcella Ruble, July 13, 1985. AB, U. Ill., Urbana, 1970, JD, 1973. Bar: Ill. 1974, U.S. Dist. Ct. (no. dist.) Ill. 1974, U.S. Ct. Appeals (7th cir.) 1975, U.S. Ct. Appeals (3rd cir.) 1984, Calif. 1990. From assoc. to ptnr. Freeman, Freeman & Salzman, Chgo., 1974-81; sole practice Chgo., 1981-89; ptnr. Harris & Ruble, Chgo., 1990—, L.A., 1997—. Spl. dep. atty. gen. Commonwealth of Pa., 1981-97. Mem. ABA, Ill. Bar Assn., Chgo. Bar Assn. Clubs: Union League (Chgo.). Office: 1625 Woods Dr Los Angeles CA 90069-1633 E-mail: law@harrisandruble.com.

HARRIS, DALE BENNER, psychologist, educator; b. Elkhart, Ind., June 28, 1914; s. Ward Manning and Lillian (Benner) H.; m. Elizabeth Saltmarsh, July 17, 1935; children— Ruthann E., James S., David B., Geoffrey M. AB with high distinction (Rector scholar), DePauw U., 1935; MA, U. Minn., 1937, PhD, 1941. Ednl. dir. Minn. Tng. Sch. for Boys, 1936-38; staff Inst. Child Welfare U. Minn., 1939-59, prof., 1948-59, dir., 1954-59; prof. psychology Pa. State U., 1959-79, prof. emeritus, 1979—, chmn. dept. psychology, 1962-67. Fulbright vis. prof. Ochanomizu U., Tokyo, 1968-69 Author: Children's Drawings as Measures of Intellectual Maturity, 1963; co-author: Child Care and Training, 8th edit, 1958; Editor: The Concept of Development, 1957, Child Development Abstracts, 1964-71; editorial com.: Ann. Rev. of Psychology, 1956-62; Contbr. articles to profl. jours. Mem. Mpls. Citizens Com. on Pub. Edn., 1946-59, Gov.'s Adv. Com. on Children and Youth, 1950-55, on Exceptional Children, 1956-59; mem. bd. Children's Home Soc. Minn., 1954-59; mem. adv. com. young workers Bur. Labor Standards, Dept. Labor, 1955-59; mem. adv. com. Clearing House for Research Relating to Children, U.S. Children's Bur., 1962-68; mem. exec. bd. Joint Commn. Correctional Manpower and Tng., 1965-69; mem. task force Joint Commn. Mental Health Children, 1966-69; research adv. com. Commonwealth Mental Health Research Found.; Mem. bd. Pa. Mental Health Assn., 1970-76. Fellow Am. Psychol. Assn. (past pres. div. developmental psychology), A.A.A.S. (governing council 1962-72, v.p., sect. I chmn. 1972), Soc. for Research in Child Devel. (sec., mem. governing council 1957-61, cons. editor monographs); mem. Nat. Soc. Study Edn., AAUP, Am. Edn. Research Assn. (v.p. 1964), Phi Beta Kappa, Sigma Xi, Psi Chi, Phi Sigma, Phi Delta Kappa. Home: 38 Boston Rd Apt 321 Middletown CT 06457-3565

HARRIS, DALE HUTTER, retired judge; b. Lynchburg, Va., July 10, 1932; d. Quintus and Agnes (Adams) Hutter; m. Edward Richmond Harris Jr., July 24, 1954; children: Mary Fontaine, Frances Harris Russell, Jennifer Harris Haynie, Timothy Edward. BA, Sweet Briar Coll., 1953; MEd in Counseling and Guidance, Lynchburg Coll., 1970; JD, U. Va., 1978; LLD (hon.), Wilson Coll., 1988; LHD (hon.), Lynchburg Coll., 2002. Bar: Va. 1978, U.S. Dist. Ct. (we. dist.) Va. 1978, U.S. Ct. Appeals (4th cir.) 1978. Admissions asst. Sweet Briar Coll. (Va.), 1953-54; caseworker Winchester/Frederick Dept. Welfare, Va., 1954-55; vis. lectr. Lynchburg Coll., Va., 1971; assoc. Davies & Peters, Lynchburg, 1978-82; substitute judge 24th Dist. Gen. Dist., Juvenile and Domestic Rels. Dist. Ct., Va., 1980-82; judge Juvenile and Domestic Rels. Dist. Ct., Lynchburg, 1982—2003. Judge Family Ct. Pilot Project, Va., 1990—91; lectr. law U. Va. Law Sch., 1986—98; pres. Va. Coun. Juvenile and Family Ct. Judges, 1994—96; mem. panel of experts and adv. com. Child Protection and Custody Resource Ctr., 1994—2001; mem. Commn. on Future of Va.'s Jud. Sys., 1987—89; mem. adv. bd. Hilton Project on Model State Laws about Family Violence. Vice chmn. bd. dirs. Sweet Briar Coll., 1976-86; vol. coord. vols. in probation with Juvenile and Domestic Ct., 1971-73; chmn. steering com. for establishment Youth Svc. Bur., Lynchburg, 1972-73; chmn. bd. dirs. Lynchburg Youth Svcs., 1973-75; mem. adv. bd. Juvenile Ct., 1957-60, 62-68, sec., 1966-68; bd. dirs. Family Svc. Lynchburg, 1967-69; Lynchburg Fine Arts Ctr., 1965-67, Seven Hills Sch., 1966-73, Greater Lynchburg United Fund, 1963-65, Lynchburg Assn. Mental Health, 1960-61, Miller Home, 1980-82, Lynchburg Gen.-Marshall Lodge Hosps., Inc., 1980-82; v.p. Lynchburg Mental Health Study Commn., 1966; bd. dirs. Lynchburg Sheltered Workshop for Mentally Retarded Young Adults, 1965-69; bd. dirs. Lynchburg Guidance Ctr., 1959-61, v.p., 1970, pres., 1961; bd. dirs. Hist. Rev. Bd. Lynchburg, 1978-82; adv. bd. study of effectiveness of civil protection orders Nat. Ctr. State Cts., 1994-97. Mem.: ABA, Am. Prosecutors Rsch. Inst., Nat. Coun. Juvenile and Family Ct. Judges (mem. child custody edn. com. 1993—98, chair family violence commn. 1998—2000, trustee 1998—2001, chair custody com. 1999—2001), Lynchburg Bar Assn., Va. State Bar (bd. govs. criminal law sect. 1988—90, bd. govs. family law sect. 1989—91), Va. Bar Assn., Phi Beta Kappa. Office: Juvenile and Domestic Relations Dist Ct PO Box 757 Lynchburg VA 24505-0757

HARRIS, DALE RAY, lawyer; b. Crab Orchard, Ill., May 11, 1937; s. Ray B. and Aurelia M. (Davis) H.; m. Toni K. Shapkoff, June 26, 1960; children: Kristen Dee, Julie Diane. BA in Math., U. Colo., 1959; LLB, Harvard U., 1962. Bar: Colo. 1962, U.S. Dist. Ct. Colo. 1962, U.S. Ct. Appeals (10th cir.) 1962, U.S. Supreme Ct. 1981. Assoc. Davis, Graham & Stubbs, Denver, 1962-67, ptnr., 1967—, chmn. mgmt. com., 1982-85. Spkr. instr. in field; civil litigation editl. adv. bd. Bradford Pub. Co., 2005—. Mem. campaign cabinet Mile High United Way, 1986—87, chmn., atty. adv. com., 1988, sec., legal counsel, trustee, 1989—94, 1996—2001, mem. exec. com., 1989—2001, chmn. bd. trustees, 1996, 1997; trustee The Spaceship Earth Fund, 1986—89, Legal Aid Found. Colo., 1989—95, 2000—01; mem. devel. coun. U. Colo. Arts and Scis. dept., 1985—93; area chmn. law sch. fund Harvard U., 1978—81; bd. dirs. Colo. Jud. Inst., 1994—2003, vice chair, 1998; bd. dir. Colo. Lawyers Trust Account Found., 1996—2001; steering com. Youth-At-Work, 1994, School-To-Work, 1995; mem. jud. adv. coun. Colo. Supreme Ct., 2001—; bd. dirs. Rocky Mountain Arthritis Found., 2002—, Qualife Wellness City, 2002—. With reserves USAR, 1962—68. Recipient Williams award Rocky Mountain Arthritis Found., 1999. Fellow: Am. Coll. Trial Lawyers, Am. Bar Found. (Colo. state chmn. 1998—2005); mem.: ABA (antitrust and litigation sects.), Colo. Assn. Corp. Counsel (pres. 1973—74), Denver Bar Assn. (chmn. centennial com. 1990—91, bd. trustees 1992—95, pres. 1993—94, Merit award 1997), Colo. Bar Assn. (coun. corp. banking and bus. law sect. 1978—83, chmn. antitrust com. 1980—84, bd. govs. 1991—95, chmn. family violence task force 1996—2000, pres.-elect 1999—2000, co-chair multi-disciplinary practice task force 1999—2000, bd. govs. 1999—2002, pres. 2000—01, chmn. transitions com. 2001—03, chmn. profl. reform initiative task force 2001—), Colo. Bar Found. (award of merit 2002), Rotary (Denver), Denver Law Club (pres. 1976—77, Lifetime Achievement award 1997), Univ. Club, Colo. Forum, The Two Percent Club (exec. com. 1994—), Citizens Against Amendment 12 Com. (exec. com. 1994), Phi Beta Kappa. Home: 2032 Bellaire St Denver CO 80207-3722 Office: Davis Graham & Stubbs 1550 17th St Ste 500 Denver CO 80202-1202 Office Phone: 303-892-9400. Business E-Mail: dale.harris@dgslaw.com.

HARRIS, DANIEL Y., private school educator, poet, artist; b. Paris, July 1962; s. Donald Harris and Nadine Bicher. BA in Philosophy & Religious Studies, U. Denver, Denver, Colo., 1984; MDiv, U. Chgo., Chgo., Ill., 1985. Dir. comm. MesArt.com, San Francisco, 2002—; faculty mem. Lehrhaus Judaica, Berkeley, Calif., 2002—. Co-dir. art ArtShip Found., Oakland, Calif., 1998—2002; co-founder, prin. author Sparks Project, Oakland, Calif., 2001—. Prin. works include Euphrat Mus.; contbr. poetry pub. to profl. jour., academic essays. Mem. adv. com. Metapolitical Inst., Oakland, Calif., 2003—04; co-author of essay presented at the vienna peace summit Internat. Peace U., Vienna, 2001; panelist & artist Jewish Cmty. Libr., San Francisco, 2004—04; sec. bd. ArtShip Found., Oakland, Calif., 2000—02, mem. bd., 1998—2002. Grantee Artist Showcase Project Support & Adancement, City of Oakland, Crafts & Cultural Arts Commn., 1998-2002. Jewish. Achievements include development of MesArt.com, an Internet art gallery. Avocations: tennis, guitar. Home: 457 Taylor Ave Apt B Alameda CA 94501 Office: MesArtcom PO Box 31804 San Francisco CA 94131-0804 Personal E-mail: danielyharris@sbcglobal.net. Business E-Mail: daniel@mesart.com.

HARRIS, DARRYL WAYNE, publishing executive; b. Emmett, Idaho, July 29, 1941; s. Reed Ingval and Evelyn Faye (Wengreen) H.; m. Christine Sorenson, Sept. 10, 1965; children: Charles Reed, Michael Wayne, Jason Darryl, Stephanie, Ryan Joseph. BA, Brigham Young U., 1966. Staff writer Deseret News, Salt Lake City, 1965, Post-Register, Idaho Falls, 1966-67;

tech. editor Idaho Nuc. Corp., Idaho Falls, 1967-68; account exec. David W. Evans & Assocs. Advt., Salt Lake City, 1968-71; pres. Harris Pub., Inc., Idaho Falls, 1971—; pub. Potato Grower of Idaho mag., 1972—, SnoWest Mag., 1974—, Sugar Prodr. mag., 1974—, Blue Ribbon mag., 1987-90, Modstock mag., 1992—, SnowAction mag., 1987—2000, Western Guide to Snowmobiling, 1988—, Houseboat Mag., 1990—, Pontoon and Deck Boat Mag., 1995—, Mountain Turf mag., 2001—, Idaho Falls mag., 2001—, SnoWest Canada mag., 2001—, Today's Playground mag., 2001—, SkatePark Mag., 2001—, Sledheads Mag., 2001—, River Jet Mag., 2004—. Campaign mgr. George Hansen for Congress Com., 1974, 76; campaign chmn. Mel Richardson for Congress Com., 1986; 1st counselor to pres. Korean Mission, Ch. Jesus Christ of Latter-day Saints, Seoul, Korea, 1963, area pub. comm. dir., Ea. Idaho, 1976-86; pres. Korea Seoul Mission, 1997-2000; High Priest, LDS Ch., 1987-2002, Bishop BYU, Idaho 27th Ward, 2003—, high coun. Idaho Falls Ammon Stake, 1987-91, Ammon 8th Ward Bishopric, 1991-96; founder Blue Ribbon Coalition, 1987; v.p. Teton Peaks coun. Boy Scouts Am., 1987-92; publicity chmn. Upper Snake River Scout Encampment, 1988; founder, pres. Our Land Soc., 1989-92. Mem. Agr. Editors Assn., Internat. Snowmobile Industry Assn. (Best Overall Reporting journalism award 1979, 80), Western Publs. Assn., World Champion Cutter and Chariot Racing Assn. (historian 1966-80), Nat. Snowmobile Found. (founder 1988), Kappa Tau Alpha, Pres. Club (award 1978), Idaho Falls Kiwanis (Disting., pres. 1978). Office: Harris Pub Inc 360 B St Idaho Falls ID 83402

HARRIS, DAVID ALAN, not-for-profit organization executive; b. Santa Monica, Calif., Sept. 23, 1949; s. Eric Albert and Nelly (Chender) H.; m. Giulia Boukhobza, Jan. 14, 1979; children: Daniel, Michael, Joshua. BA, U. Pa., 1971; MS, London Sch. Econs., 1972, student, 1975-77, Oxford (Eng.) U., 1977-78; PhD (hon.), Hebrew Union Coll., 2003. Dir. govt. and internat. affairs Am. Jewish Com., N.Y.C., 1987-90, exec. dir., 1990—. Nat. coord. Freedom Sunday for Soviet Jewry rally, Washington, 1987; pub. mem. U.S. Del. to Conf. on Security and Coop. in Europe; vis. scholar Johns Hopkins U., 2000-02. Author: The Jokes of Oppression, 1988, Entering a New Culture, 5th edit., 1989, The Jewish World, 1989, In The Trenches, Vol. 1, 1999, Vol. 3, 2004; contbr. over 100 articles to mags. and newspapers. Trustee Conn. Coll., 1999-2002. Cited by Lifestyles mag., Avenue mag., and Jewish monthly as Jewish leader; honored by govts. of Bulgaria, Germany and Poland. Mem.: Coun. Fgn. Rels. Office: Am Jewish Com 165 E 56th St New York NY 10022-2709 E-mail: harrisd@ajc.org.

HARRIS, DAVID FORD, management consultant, retired federal official; b. Hillsboro, Mo., Feb. 14, 1931; s. Walter Dunklin and Nelle (Landrigan) H.; m. Erna Beckmann, Mar. 5, 1964; children: Christopher Beckmann, Stefanie Ford. BS, U.S. Mil. Acad., West Point, 1954; MBA, Stanford U., 1961. Budget officer Post Office Dept., Washington, 1964-68, spl. asst. postmaster gen., 1968-70; chief adminstrv. officer, sec. Postal Rate Commn., Washington, 1970-83; sec. to bd. govs. U.S. Postal Svc., Washington, 1983-95; ret., 1995; mgmt. cons. representing N.Am. for CB Group, Santiago, Chile, 1996—. Capt. U.S. Army, 1954-64. Mem. West Point Alumni Assn., Stanford Alumni Assn., Alexandria Sportsman's Club. Roman Catholic. Home and Office: 3643 Trinity Dr Alexandria VA 22304-1840 Office Phone: 703-751-6945.

HARRIS, DAVID HENRY, retired life insurance company executive; b. N.Y.C., May 7, 1924; s. Julian A. and May L. (Wilenski) H.; 1 child, Jean Harris Haig; m. Cassandra Sturman, Feb. 20, 1987. Student, Sherborne (Eng.) Sch., 1937-40. With Prudential Ins. Co. Am., 1940-43, Equitable Life Assurance Soc. U.S., N.Y.C., 1946-86, exec. v.p., 1973-77, exec. v.p., chief adminstrv. officer, 1977-80, exec. v.p., chief staff, 1981-86, bd. dirs., 1977-86; pres. Equitable Found., 1986-88. Chmn. bd. Equimatics, Inc., 1971-73, Informatics, Inc., 1974-75; vice chmn. Equitable Variable Life Ins. Co., 1975-76, chmn., 1976-77. Bd. dirs. Can. Life of Am. Series Fund, 1989-2000; trustee Chappaqua Libr., 1991-94. With AUS, 1943-46. Fellow Soc. Actuaries. Home: 130 E 67th St New York NY 10021-6136

HARRIS, DAVID PHILIP, crisis management executive; b. Boston, June 23, 1937; s. David Henry and Edith Endicott (Young) Harris; m. Judith Ann Brown, Oct. 23, 1999; children from previous marriage: Kristian Alexander, Thomas Cameron. BS in Sci., U. Rochester (N.Y.), 1959; MBA, U. Pa., 1963. Auditor Touche, Ross et al, Boston, 1960-61; asst. contr. Kendall Co., Chgo., Charlotte, N.C., 1963-65; mgr. internal cons. Dart Industries, Stamford, Conn., 1965-67; asst. contr. Achushnet Co., New Bedford, Mass., 1967-70; asst. treas. Bell & Howell Co., Chgo., 1970-73; v.p., treas. CFS Continental, Inc., Chgo., 1973-78; pres., chief exec. officer Harris Devel. Co., Lake Forest, Ill., 1975—. Chmn., CEO Amtec Devel. Co., Highland Park, Ill., 1978—83; affiliate Morris Andersen & Assocs., Glenview, Ill., 1984—93; bd. dirs. Juvenile Shoe Corp., Intellimedia Corp.; exec. v.p., dir., STS Cons. Ltd., Deerfield, Ill., 1995—98. Treas., dir. Lake Forest Symphony Assn., 1983—88, Touchstone Theatre, Chgo., 1987—90; mem. engring. com. Beach Restoration Project, Lake Forest, 1987—88, mem. long term plan com., 1991—; bd. dirs. Zoning Bd. Appeals, Lake Forest, 1988—93; bd. mem. ARS Viva Symphony Orch., 1998—; fin. planning advisor bd. edn. Lake Forest (Ill.) Sch. Dist. 67, 1992—99, mem. sch. bd. edn., 2001—, pres., 2005—, sec., 2003—05, pres., 2005—; dir. rsch. Lake Forest (Ill.) Civic Fedn., 1992—98; trustee adv. coun. U. Rochester, 2002—. With U.S. Army, with USAR, 1959—65. Mem.: Fin. Mgrs. Assn. Chgo. (sec. 1972—91, pres. 1988—89), Tower Club. Republican. Presbyterian. Avocation: sailing. Office Phone: 847-615-0200. Business E-Mail: dharris@harden.com.

HARRIS, DAVID THOMAS, immunology educator; b. Jonesboro, Ark, May 9, 1956; s. Marm Melton and Lucille Luretha (Buck) Harris; m. Francoise Jacqueline Besencon, June 24, 1989; children: Alexandre M., Stefanie L., Leticia M. BS in Biology, Math. and Psychology, Wake Forest U., 1978, MS, 1980, PhD in Microbiology and Immunology, 1982. Fellow Ludwig Inst. Cancer Rsch., Lausanne, Switzerland, 1982-85; rsch. asst. prof. U. N.C., Chapel Hill, 1985-89; assoc. prof. U. Ariz., Tucson, 1989—2004, prof., 1996—. Cons. Teltech, Inc. Mpls., 1990—, Advanced Biosci. Resources, 1994-95; bd. sci. advisors Cryo-Cell Internat., 1992-95; bd. dir. Ageria, Inc., Tuscon; dir. Cord Blood Stem Cell Bank, 1992—; mem. Ariz. Cancer Ctr., Steele Meml. Children's Rsch. Ctr., Ariz. Arthritis Ctr. Program, sci. adv. bd. Cord Blood Registry, Inc., chief sci. dir. Cord Blood Registry, Inc.; founder ImmuneRegen BioScis., Inc., 2002, Advanced Genetic Tools (Quregen, Inc.), 2004. Co-author chpts. to sci. books, articles to profls. jour.; reviewer sci. jour.; co-holder 7 scientific patents. Grantee numerous grants, 1988—. Mem. AAAS, Am. Assn. Immunologists, Reticuloendothelial Soc., Internat. Soc. Hematotherapy and Graft Engring., Internat. Soc. Devel. and Comparative Immunology, Scandanavian Soc. Immunology, Sigma Xi, Democrat. Church Of Christ. Avocations: tennis, hiking, jogging, skiing, travel. Office: U Ariz Dept Immunology Life Sci North 1501 N Campbell Ave Tucson AZ 85724 Office Phone: 520-626-5127. Business E-Mail: davidh@U.Arizona.edu.

HARRIS, DEANNA LYNN, special education educator, writer; b. Granite City, Ill., Feb. 25, 1948; d. Robert Eugene and Emma Lee Harris; m. George Thomas Aebel, May 6, 1967 (div. Apr. 28, 1983). BS. So. Ill. U., 1973, MS, 1986; degree, Inst. of Children's Lit., 1989. Cert. tchr. Madison County, Ill., 1973, Camden County, Mo., 1985. Adminstrv. sec. So. Ill. U., Edwardsville, Ill., 1966—69; elem. tchr. St. Boniface Sch., Edwardsville, 1973—77, Wolf Ridge Edn. Ctr., Bunker Hill, Ill., 1977—85; spl. edn. tchr. Camdenton (Mo.) R-III Sch. Dist., 1985—; propr. Heron Ho. Pub. Co., Linn Creek, Mo., 1996—. Pvt. tutor, Camdenton, 1985—. Author: God's Gift, 1995 (Editor's Choice award The Nat. Libr. of Poetry, 1995), Taters of the Ozarks, The Feud, 1996, 101+ Tater Jokes, 1996, The Man, 1998; editor: (newsletter) Foxtales, 1986—88. Recipient English award, St. Elizabeth Sch., 1962, Presdl. Sports award, President's Coun. on Phys. Fitness, 1988, 1993, 1996; grantee, State of Ill., 1972—73; scholar, 1969—73. Master: Red Hat Soc. (queen mother 2003); mem.: Coun. for Exceptional Children (assoc.), Learning Disabilities Assn. (assoc.), Mo. State Tchrs. Assn. (assoc.), Nat. Honor Soc., Quill and Scroll Journalism, Holy Childhood Assn. Republican. Roman Catholic. Avocations: travel, gardening, water sports, pets, reading. Home: 22 Old Mine Drive Linn Creek MO 65052 Office: Camdenton R-III School District Township Rd Camdenton MO 65020 Business E-Mail: dharris@mail.camdenton.k12.mo.us.

HARRIS, DENISE MICHELLE, advertising account executive; b. Stockton, Calif., Sept. 7, 1970; d. Overton Thomas Harris Sr. and Evelyn Jean Harris. BA, CSU Hayward, Hayward, CA, 1998. Advt. account exec. ANG Newspapers, Hayward, Calif., 1996—98, The San Jose Mercury News, San Jose, Calif., 1998—99; advt. account mgr. The Weather Channel, Atlanta, Ga., 1999—2001. Recipient Academic Senate's Student of the Month, San Joaquin County Academic Senate, 1993, Advt. Excellence Tng. Award, Knight Ridder, Effective Presentation Tng., Mandel Comm., Profl. Selling Skills Tng., Achieve Global. Mem.: Alpha Kappa Alpha Sorority Inc. (connection chair 1999—2001). Avocations: skiing, reading, writing, travel, yoga.

HARRIS, DIANA KOFFMAN, sociologist, educator; b. Memphis, Aug. 11, 1929; d. David Nathan and Helen Ethel (Rotter) Koffman; m. Lawrence A. Harris, June 24, 1951; children: Marla, Jennifer. Student, U. Miami, 1947-48; BS, U. Wis., 1951; postgrad., U. Oxford (Eng.), 1968-69. Advt. and sales promotion mgr. Wallace Johnston Distbg. Co., Memphis, 1952-54; welfare worker Tenn. Dept. Pub. Welfare, Knoxville, Tenn., 1954-56; instr. sociology Maryville (Tenn.) Coll., 1972-75, Fort Sanders Sch. Nursing, Knoxville, 1971-78, U. Tenn., Knoxville, 1967—; series editor Garland Pub., Inc., 1989—. Author: Readings in Social Gerontology, 1975, (with Cole) The Elderly in America, 1977, The Sociology of Aging, 1980, 2d edit., 1990; co-author: Sociology, 1984, Annotated Bibliography and Sourcebook: Sociology of Aging, 1985, Dictionary of Gerontology, 1988, Teaching Sociology of Aging, 1991, 4th edit., 1996, 5th edit., 2000; co-editor: Encyclopedia of Ageism, 2005; aging series editor Garland Pub., Inc., 1989—; contbr. articles to profl. jours. Chmn. U. Tenn. Coun. on Aging, 1979—; organizer Knoxville chpt. Gray Panthers, 1978; mem. Govnr.'s Task Force on Preretirement Programs for State Employers, 1973, White Ho. Conf. on Aging, 1981; bd. mem. Knoxville-Knox County Coun. on Aging, 1976, Sr. Citizens Info. and Referral, 1979, Sr. Citizens Home-Aide Svc., 1977; del. E. Tenn. Coun. on Aging, 1977. Recipient Meritorious award Nat. U. Continuing Edn. Assn., 1982, Pub. Svc. award Nat. Alumni Assn., 1992, Appreciation award Assn. Gerontology in Higher Edn., 1994, Appreciation award for excellent scholarly contbn. to ednl. gerontology lit. Ednl. Gerontology jour., 1996; grantee Retirement Rsch. Found., 1997—. Mem. Am. Sociol. Assn., AAAS, Gerontol. Soc. Am., Popular Culture Assn., So. Sociol. Soc., So. Gerontol. Soc. (pres.'s award 1984), N. Central Sociol. Assn., London Competitor's Club, Nat. Contest Assn., Knoxville Kontestars. Home and Office: U Tenn Dept Sociology PO Box 50546 Knoxville TN 37950-0546 Business E-Mail: dharris@utk.edu.

HARRIS, DIANE CAROL, merger and acquisition consulting firm executive; b. Rockville Centre, NY, Dec. 25, 1942; d. Daniel Christopher and Laura Louise (Schmitt) Quigley; m. Wayne Manley Harris, Sept. 30, 1978. BA, Cath. U. Am., 1964; MS, Rensselaer Poly. Inst., 1967. With Bausch & Lomb, Rochester, N.Y., 1967-96, dir. applications lab., 1972-74, dir. tech. mktg. analytical systems divsn., 1974-76, bus. line mgr., 1976-77, v.p. planning and bus. programs, 1977-78, v.p. planning and bus. devel. Soflens divsn., 1978-80, corp. dir. planning, 1980-81, v.p. corp. devel., 1981-96; v.p. RID-N.Y. State, 1980-83; pres. Hypotenuse Enterprises, Inc., 1994—. Mem. adv. bd. Merger Mgmt. Report, 1986—92; internat. bd. dirs. Assn. Corp. Growth, v.p. corp. mem. affairs, 1993—94, v.p. internat. expansion, 1994—95, pres.-elect, 1996—97, pres., 1997—98, immediate past pres., 1998—99; bd. dirs. Flowserve Corp., chmn. audit com., 2001—04; bd. dirs. Monroe Fund, Venture Capital Group. Contbr. articles to profl jours. Pres Rochester Against Intoxicated Driving, 1979—83, chmn polit action comt, 1983, 1986; bd dirs, chmn long range planning comt Rochester area Nat Coun Alcoholism, 1980—84; mem Stop DWI Adv Panel to Monroe County Legis, 1982—87, NY State Coalition for Safety Belt Use, 1984—85; mem. key exec. group Rensselaer Poly. Inst., 1993—96; mem. Com. 200, 1993—2002; mem ACG Speakers Bur, 1993—; mem adv comt Catalyst, 1995; bd dirs Rochester Rehab Ctr, 1982—84, Friends of Bristol Valley Playhouse Found, 1983—87. Named one of 50 Women to Watch in Corp Am, Bus Week Mag, 1987, 1992, 100 Women to Watch, Duns Bus Rev, 1988; recipient Distinguished Citizen's Award, Monroe County, 1979, Tribute to Women in Indust and Serv Award, YWCA, 1983, Pres's 21st Century Leadership Award, Women's Hall of Fame, 1995; grantee NSF, 1963. Mem.: Assn. Corp. Growth (Meritorious Svc. award 1995), Internat. Alliance Com. and Rochester Women's Network (com. of 200 1993—2002), Nat. Assn. Women Bus. Owners, Fin. Execs. Inst., Am. Mgmt. Assn., C. of C. (pub safety com. Rochester area chpt, task force on hwy. safety 1981—86, High Tech. Rochester adv. panel 1989—91, high technology Rochester adv. panel 1999—2000), Phi Beta Kappa, Delta Epsilon Sigma, Sigma Xi. Home: 60 Mendon Center Rd Honeoye Falls NY 14472-9363 Office: Hypotenuse Enterprises Inc 1545 East Ave Rochester NY 14610-1614 Office Phone: 585-473-7799. E-mail: harris@hypot.com.

HARRIS, DOLORES M., retired academic administrator, adult education educator; b. Camden, NJ, Aug. 5, 1930; d. Roland Henry, Sr. and Frances Anna (Gatewood) Ellis; m. Morris E. Harris, Sr., 1948 (div. 1987); children: Morris E. Jr., Sheila Davis, Gregory M. Sr. BS, Glassboro (NJ) State Coll., 1959, MA, 1966; EdD, Rutgers U., 1983. Tchr., reading specialist Glassboro Bd. Edn., 1958-68, dir. aux. svcs., 1968-70; supr. adult edn. Camden Welfare Bd., summer 1968; head state dir. Glassboro SCOPE, summer 1969-70; assoc. dir. Jersey City State Coll., summer 1971; dir. adult edn. Glassboro State Coll., 1970-74, dir. continuing edn. dept., 1989-90, acting assoc. v.p. acad. affairs, 1989-91; ret., 1991. Cons. Mich. State Dept. Edn., Lansing, 1973; examiner N.Y. State Civil Svc. Commn., 1976—; chmn. adv. bd. Women's Ednl. Equity Comm. Network Project, San Francisco, 1977—78; cons. crossroads project Temple U., Phila., 1977; bd. dirs. Glassboro State Coll. Mgmt. Inst.; cons. corrections project Va. Commonwealth U., Richmond; vice-chmn. comm. Accrediting Coun. Continuing Edn. and Tng., Richmond, 1985—89, chmn., 1989—. Author: (book) How to Establish ABE Programs, 1972; author: (with others) Black Studies for ABE and GED Programs in Correction, 1975; founding editor: newsletter For Adults Only, 1970; contbr. articles to profl. jours. Founder, trustee, chair bd. trustees Glassboro Child Devel. Ctr., 1974—87; bd. dirs. Gloucester County United Way, NJ, 1977—, sec. bd. dirs., 1980, pres. bd. dirs., 1983—85; charter mem., bd. dirs. Glassboro Glass Mus., 1979—87; vice chair, chair, mem. Gloucester County Commn. Women, NJ, 1983—87; trustee Frederick Douglas Meml. and Hist. Assn., 2000—. Named Woman of the Yr., Gloucester County Bus. and Profl. Women's Club, 1985, Woman of Achievement, Gloucester County Commn. Women, 1987, Counselor of Yr., Svc. Corps Ret. Execs., 2003; named one of Outstanding Citizens, Holly Shores Girl Scouts U.S., 1987, 100 Most Influential Black Ams., Ebony Mag., 1989—92; named to Legion of Honor, Chapel of Four Chaplains, 1983; recipient Disting. Alumnae award, Glassboro State Coll., 1971, Disting. Svc. award, Camden County, 1974, Holly Shores Girl Scouts U.S., 1979, N.J. Woman of Achievement award, 1991. Mem.: AAUW (v.p. membership com. Gloucester County chpt. 1986—87), NEA, Ea. Montgomery County Svc. Corps Ret. Execs. (chair seminars, workshop programs 2001—, Counselor of Yr. 2003), NJ Edn. Assn., Women Greater Phila. (bd. dirs.), Soc. Docta (bd. dirs. 1987—), N.J. Adult Edn. Assn. (life; pres. 1973—74), Links Club, Nat. Assn. Colored Women's Clubs, Inc. (pres. 1988—92), Northeastern Fedn. Women's Clubs (v.p.-at-large 1983—85, parliamentarian 1985—), NJ State Fedn. Colored Women's Clubs (pres. 1976—80). Presbyterian. Avocations: reading, fitness exercises.

HARRIS, DON VICTOR, JR., lawyer; b. Nottingham Twp., Ind., Jan. 16, 1921; s. Don Victor and Nellie Florence (Dukes) H.; m. Joan Elliott Haffler, Aug. 15, 1959; children: Leigh Elliott Hay, Meghan St. Clair Zeisser. AB, DePauw U., 1943; JD, Harvard U., 1945. Bar: DC 1947. Law clk. to judge U.S. Ct. Appeals 2d Cir., 1945-46; assoc. firm Covington & Burling, Washington, 1946-57, ptnr., 1957—. Lectr. in law George Washington U., 1963-64; lectr. tax insts.; mem. IRS Commr.'s Adv. Group, 1976. Contbr. articles to law jours.; case editor: Harvard Law Rev. Bd. dirs. Oak Hill Cemetery Co., Found. for Preservation Hist. Georgetown. Fellow Am. Coll. Tax Counsel, Am. Bar Found. (life); mem. Am. Law Inst. (life), ABA (chmn. sect. taxation 1976-77), DC Bar Assn., Fed. Bar Assn., Phi Beta Kappa, Beta Theta Pi, Am. Cathedral Soc. (judge), Met. Club, Chevy Chase Club, John's Island Club (Fla.). Episcopalian. Home: 2803 P St NW Washington DC 20007-3067 also: John's Island 777 Sea Oak Dr No 715 Vero Beach FL 32963-3541 Office: Covington & Burling 1043-C 1201 Pennsylvania Ave NW Washington DC 20004-2401 Office Phone: 202-662-5330. Personal E-mail: ursa1921@aol.com. Business E-Mail: dharris@cov.com.

HARRIS, DONALD, composer; b. St. Paul, Apr. 7, 1931; s. Barney William and Hattie (Paper) H.; m. Marilyn Hackett, 1983; children: Daniel, Jeremy. Mus.B., U. Mich., 1952, Mus.M., 1954. Music cons. Am. Cultural Center, USIS, Paris, 1965-67; asst. to pres. for acad. affairs New Eng. Conservatory Music, Boston, 1967-71, v.p., 1971-74, exec. v.p., 1974-77, mem. teaching faculty depts. composition and music lit., 1967-77; composer-in-residence, prof. music, chmn. composition and theory Hartt Sch. of Music, U. Hartford, Conn., 1977-80, dean, 1981-88; dean Coll. of the Arts The Ohio State U., 1988-97, prof. composition, 1997—. Vis. prof. music George Washington U., 1998; pres. Internat. Coun. Fine Arts Deans, 1994-96. Composer: Piano Sonata, 1956, Fantasy for Violin and Piano, 1957, Symphony in Two Movements, 1961, String Quartet, 1965, Ludus for 10 Instruments, 1966, Ludus II for 5 Instruments, 1973, Charmes for Voice and Orchestra, 1977, On Variations, 1976, For the Night to Wear (Hortense Flexner), mezzo-soprano and 7 instruments, 1978, Balladen for solo piano, 1979, Of Hartford in a Purple Light (Wallace Stevens) for soprano and piano, 1979, Prelude to a Concert in Connecticut, 1981, Les Mains (Marguerite Yourcenar) for mezzo-soprano and piano, 1983, Meditations for Solo Organ, 1984, Three Fanfares for Four Horns, 1984, Canzona & Carol for Double Brass Quintet and Timpani, 1986, Pierrot Lieder (soprano & 5 instruments), 1988, Mermaid Variations (chamber orch.), 1993, Second String Quartet, 2002, Five Tempi, 2004; recs., CRI, Delos, Golden Crest Records; co-editor: The Correspondence Between Arnold Schoenberg and Alban Berg, 1986. Recipient commns. from Serge Koussevitzky Music Found., 1977, Elizabeth Sprague Coolidge Found., 1977, Goethe Inst., 1978, Conn. Commn. Arts, 1979, French Nat. Radio, 1972, Festival Contemporary Am. Music at Tanglewood, 1965, Boston Musica Viva, 1973, Cleve. Orch., 1975, Arnold Schoenberg Inst., 1988, Cleve. Chamber Orchestra, 1991, Jefferson Acad., 2001; recipient Louisville Orch. award, 1954, Prince Rainier of Monaco Composition prize, 1960, award Am. Acad. and Inst. Arts and Letters, 1991; grantee-in-aid Rockefeller Found., 1969; grantee-in-aid Chapelbrook Found., 1970; fellowship grantee Nat. Endowment for Arts, 1974; Fulbright scholar, 1956; Guggenheim fellow, 1965. Mem. ASCAP (Deems Taylor award 1989, others 1973—). Address: 5257 Courtney Pl Columbus OH 43235-3474 E-mail: harris.27@osu.edu.

HARRIS, DONALD RAY, lawyer; b. Lake Preston, S.D., Apr. 21, 1938; s. Raymond H. and Nona (Trousdale) H.; children: Beverly, Scott, Bradley, Lindi; m. Sharon K. Brown, Sept. 4, 1982. BA, State U. Iowa, 1959; JD, U. Iowa, 1961. Bar: Ill. 1963, U.S. Dist. Ct. (no. dist.) Ill. 1963, U.S. Ct. Appeals (3d, 4th, 6th, 7th, 9th and fed. cirs.) 1966-95, U.S. Dist. Ct. (we. dist.) Tex. 1989, U.S. Supreme Ct. 1977, U.S. Ct. Fed. Claims 1995, U.S. Dist. Ct. (ea. dist.) Wis. 1997. Assoc. Jenner & Block, Chgo., 1963-70, ptnr., 1970—. Lt. inf. U.S. Army, 1961-63. Mem. ABA, Ill. Bar Assn., Chgo. Bar Assn., Bar Assn. 7th Cir., Chgo. Coun. Lawyers, Am. Coll. Trial Lawyers, ITC Trail Lawyers Assn., Lawyers Club of Chgo. Office: Jenner & Block One IBM Plz Chicago IL 60611-3586 E-mail: dharris@jenner.com.

HARRIS, DONNA, elementary school educator; b. Salem, N.J., July 5, 1950; d. Donald and June (Holt) Dawson; m. Donn Harris, June 10, 1972; children: Timothy Ryan, Lindsay Rebecca. BA, Glassboro (N.J.) State Coll., 1973. Tchr. grades 1-3 John Fenwick Sch., Salem, N.J.; tchr. 6th grade Neuse Christian Sch., Raleigh; dir., tchr. Raleigh's Children Ctr.; tchr. kindergarden and 1st grade Wake Christian Acad., Raleigh. Staff dir. Presch. dept. Midway Bapt. Ch.; layout designer, advts. and billboards; caterer. Avocation: country crafts. Home: 2301 Huntsbridge Dr Clayton NC 27520-8630

HARRIS, DOUGLAS CLAY, retired newspaper executive; b. Owensboro, Ky., Oct. 9, 1939; s. Marvin Dudley and Elizabeth (Adelman) H. BS, Murray State U., 1961; MS, Ind. U., 1964, EdD, 1968; grad. advanced mgmt. program, Harvard U., 1987. Counselor, asst. to dean of students Ind. U., Bloomington, 1965-68; mgmt. appraisal specialist United Air Lines, Elk Grove Village, Ill., 1968-69; dir. manpower div. Computer Age Industries, Washington, 1969; area personnel dir. Peat Marwick Mitchell & Co., N.Y.C., 1969-72; v.p. personnel Knight-Ridder, Inc., Miami, Fla., 1972-85, v.p., sec., 1986-98. Served to capt. U.S. Army, 1961-62. Republican. Home and Office: 218 Fairchild Dr Highlands Ranch CO 80126-4751

HARRIS, DUDLEY MICHAEL, film producer, film director, writer; b. Tampa, Fla., Jan. 2, 1936; s. Dudley Raw Harris and Madalene Lois Mosher; m. Evelyn Claire Clack, July 3, 1971; 1 child, Madalene Elizabeth;children from previous marriage: Lisa Gael, John Michael, Gerald Michael, Stephen Herschel. BS in Advt., U. Fla., Gainesville, 1957; grad., Naval Flight Tng., Pensacola, Fla., 1960. Copy writer Henry Quednau Advt., Tampa, Fla., 1960—63; regional sales mgr. Jim Walter Corp., 1963—65; asst. advt. mgr. Mary Carter Paint Co., 1965—70; exec. dir. Am. Bowl RMS Sports, 1971—76; pres., prodr./dir./writer HMS Films, Fla., 1977—79; pres., expdn. leader Internat. Expdns., 1980—94; pres. and CEO San Bao Enterprises, Inc., 1995—. Writer, lectr. Titanic expdns., Orlando, Fla., 1983; writer, lectr. Dead Sea Scrolls, Qumran, Israel, 1994—95; writer, lectr. Ming treasure ships, Beijing, 1995—96; contr. In Search of... ABC TV, United States, 1982, Germany, 83, Philippines, 83. Author: The Sun Rose Late, 1975; dir., writer: (TV films) Deadly Fathoms with Rod Serling, 1972 (Silver medal, Atlanta Internat. Film Festival, 1973); dir.(author): Search for the Titanic with Orson Welles, 1980; co-author: Search for the Titanic with James Drury, 1981; author: (screenplays) Expdn. to Noah's Ark with Joseph Cotten, 1977, Pancho Villa's Treasure with Cesar Romero, 1978. 1st lt. Reserves USMC, 1957—60. Recipient ADDY award, Fla. Advertisers, 1979. Fellow: Royal Geog. Soc.; mem.: The Explorer's Club (spkr. ann. banquet 1981). Republican. Christian Scientist. Achievements include having led first expdns. to search for Titanic. Avocations: flying, skin diving, travel, history, exploring. Fax: 813-962-1328.

HARRIS, E. LYNN See HARRIS, ELEANOR

HARRIS, ED (EDWARD ALLEN HARRIS), actor; b. Englewood, N.J., Nov. 28, 1950; s. Bob L. and Margaret Harris; m. Amy Madigan, 1983; 1 child, Lilly. Student, Columbia U., 1969-71, U. Okla., Norman, 1972-73; BFA, Calif. Inst. of Arts, Valencia, 1975. Appeared in plays A Streetcar Named Desire, Sweet Bird of Youth, Julius Caesar, Hamlet, Camelot, Are You Lookin?, Time of Your Life, Learned Ladies, Kingdom of Earth, Grapes of Wrath, Present Laughter, Balaam, Killers' Head, Fool for Love (Obie award 1983), Prairie Avenue (L.A. Drama Critics Circle award 1981), Scar, 1985 (San Francisco Critics award), Precious Sons, 1986 (Theater World award), Simpatico, 1994, 95, Taking Sides, 1996; (repertory plays) Servant of Two Masters, Ohio, Claptrap, Cambridge, Mass., 1985, Pirates of Penzance at N.Y. Shakespeare Festival, Glass Menagerie, Long Wharf, New Haven, 1986, Bobby Gould in Hell, 1989; appeared in films including Coma, 1978, Borderline, 1978, Knightriders, 1980, Dream On, 1980, Creepshow, 1981, The Right Stuff, 1982, Swing Shift, 1982, Under Fire, 1982, Places in the Heart, 1983, A Flash of Green, 1984, Alamo Bay, 1984, Sweet Dreams, 1985, Code Name: Emerald, 1985, Walker, 1987, To Kill a Priest, 1988, Jacknife, 1989, The Abyss, 1989, State of Grace, 1990, Glengarry Glen Ross, 1992, Needful Things, 1993, The Firm, 1993, China Moon, 1994, Milk Money, 1994, Apollo 13, 1995 (Acad. award nominee for best supporting actor 1996, SAG award 1996), Just Cause, 1995, Eye for an Eye, 1995, Nixon, 1995, The Rock, 1996, Absolute Power, 1997, Stepmom, 1998, The Truman Show, 1998 (Golden Globe award, 1999), The Third Miracle, 1999, Waking the Dead, 2000, The Prime Gig, 2000, Enemy at the Gates, 2001, Buffalo Soldiers, 2001, A Beautiful Mind, 2001, Just a Dream, 2002, The Hours, 2002, Masked and Anonymous, 2003, The Human Stain, 2003, Radio, 2003, A History of Violence, 2005, Winter Passing, 2005; acted, dir., prodr., Pollock, 2000; TV movies include The Amazing Howard Hughes, 1977, The Seekers, 1979, The Aliens Are Coming, 1980, The Last Innocent Man, 1987, Paris Trout, 1991, Running Mates, 1992, The Stand, 1994 (unbilled cameo), Riders of the Purple Sage (also exec. prodr), 1997; TV miniseries Empire Falls, 2005; TV appearances The Rockford Files, 1978, Lou Grant, 1979, 80, 81, Barnaby Jones, 1979, CHiPs, 1981, Hart to Hart, 1981, Cassie and Co., 1982, Frasier, 1995. Trustee Calif. Inst. of Arts, Valencia, 1985—. Mem. Screen Actors Guild, Equity. Address: 22031 Carbon Mesa Rd Malibu CA 90265-5008*

HARRIS, EDWARD DAY, JR., physician; b. Phila., July 7, 1937; children: Ned, Tom, Chandler. AB, Dartmouth Coll., 1958, grad. with honors, 1960; MD cum laude, Harvard U., 1962. Diplomate Am. Bd. Internal Medicine and Rheumatology (chmn. subsplty. bd. in rheumatology 1986-88). Intern Mass. Gen. Hosp., Boston, 1962-63, asst. resident, 1963-64, sr. resident, 1966-67, clin. research fellow arthritis unit, 1967-69; asst. prof. Harvard Med. Sch., Boston, 1970; from asst. prof. to prof. Dartmouth Med. Sch., Hanover, N.H., 1970-83, Eugene W. Leonard prof., 1979-83, chief connective tissue disease sect., 1970-83; mem. staff Mary Hitchcock Meml. Hosp., 1970-83; chief med. service Middlesex Gen. U. Hosp., New Brunswick, NJ, 1983—; asst. prof. Harvard U. Med. Sch., Boston, 1970; prof., chmn. medicine U. Medicine and Dentistry N.J.-Rutgers U. Med. Sch., New Brunswick, 1983-88; Arthur L. Bloomfield prof. medicine Stanford U. Sch. Medicine, 1988-95, chmn. dept. medicine, 1988-95, George DeForest Barnett prof. medicine, 1988—; acad. sec. to Stanford U., 2002—. Chief med. svc. Stanford U. Hosp., 1988-95; dir. Ctr. for Musculoskeletal Diseases, Stanford, 1996-99, emeritus, 2003—; pres. med. staff, Stanford U. Hosp., 1997-99; med. dir. Internat. Med. Svc., 1997—2002. Master: Am. Rheumatism Assn. (numerous coms. 1967—, pres. 1985—86); fellow: ACP (gov. No. Calif. chpt. 2000—), Royal Soc. Medicine; mem.: Alpha Omega Alpha (exec. sec. 1997—, editor The Pharos 1997—). Office: Alpha Omega Alpha 525 Middlefield Rd Ste 130 Menlo Park CA 94025 Business E-Mail: e.harris@alphaomegaalpha.org.

HARRIS, EDWARD FREDERICK, orthodontics educator; b. San Jose, Calif., Oct. 2, 1947; s. Roy Hayward and Bonnie (Keeble) H.; m. Karen J. Morse, May 29, 1970 (div. July 1983); children: Jeremy T., Emily J.; m. Betsy D. Barcroft, Jan. 24, 1990. BA, San Jose State U., 1969; MA, Ariz. State U., 1972, PhD, 1977. Asst. prof. orthodontics U. Conn., Farmington, 1978-80; prof. orthodontics Coll. Dentistry U. Tenn. Ctr. for Health Scis., Memphis, 1980—. Contbr. articles to profl. jours. NIH fellow, 1973-80. Mem. Am. Assn. Phys. Anthropologists, Internat. Assn. Dental Rsch., Sigma Xi. Republican. Methodist. Office: 875 Union Ave # 301S Memphis TN 38163-0001 Office Phone: 901-448-6265. Business E-Mail: eharris@utmem.edu.

HARRIS, ELAINE K., medical consultant; b. N.Y.C., Mar. 17, 1924; d. Julius and Bertha (Wecker) Kirschbaum; m. Herbert Harris, Aug. 1, 1948; children: Gail, Linda, Geoffrey. AB Bus. Economics cum laude, Hunter Coll.; AM Bus. Edn., Columbia U. Lic. tchr. bus. NY. Founder, pres. Sjogren's Syndrome Found., 1983-91, exec. dir., 1991-94. Cons. in field; v.p. exec. bd. Nat. Alliance for Oral Health; developer Sjogren's Syndrome Ednl. Symposia for lay and profls., nat. and internat. support group network. Editor: Moisture Seekers Newsletter, 1984-94, Sjogren's Syndrome Handbook: An Authoritative Guide for Patients, 1989; editor: The New Sjogren's Syndrome Handbook, 1998; contbg. author: Sjogren's Syndrome: Clinical and Immunologic Aspects, 1987, Self-Help, Concepts and Applications, 1992; contbr. articles to profl. jours. Founded Nassau-Suffolk Chpt. Hunter Coll. Alumni Assn., 1949; treas. Youth Employment Svc., Great Neck (N.Y.) Pub. Schs., former chair of Broader Horizons Com., PTA, Great Neck Pub. Sch., others; active Jewish communal field. Recipient Women's Living Legacy, Women's Internat. Ctr., 1994, Third Internat. Conf. on Sjogren's Syndrome, Greece, 1991; elected to Hunter Coll. Hall of Fame, 1989. Mem. Pi Lambda Theta. Avocations: gardening, baking, photography, duplicate bridge.

HARRIS, ELEANOR LYNNE K. (E. LYNN HARRIS), religious studies educator, literature educator, minister, writer; b. Villa Park, Ill., July 07; d. Robert Carl and Karin Elizabeth (Peterson) Karlström. BA, MA, U. Chgo.; MDiv, No. Bapt. Theol. Sem., 1975; D of Ministry, Chgo. Theol. Sem., 1980; PhD, NYU, 1980. Ordained min. United Ch. of Christ, 1987. Prof. U. Ill., Chgo., 1970—. Interim min. Union Congl. Ch., Moline, Ill., 1997; min. Glen Ellyn (Ill.) Congl. Ch., 1987-89; night ministry, Chgo., 1999, 2000, 01; adj. faculty religious studies Loyola U., Chgo., U. St. Francis; adj. faculty English Ind. U. Northwest, DePaul U., Ill. Benedictine U.; sec. Bd. Christian Witness in Soc., 1984-88; mem. seminaries com. Chgo. Met. Assn., United Ch. Christ, 2000-03; active Night Ministry, Chgo., summers 1999-2001; presenter, cons. adult edn. St. Pauls Ch., 2002; contbr. poetry to Kavya Bharati; presenter in field. Author: The Mystic Spirituality of A.W. Tozer, A Twentieth Century American Protestant, 1992; contbr. poems and articles to profl. jours. Recipient Lucia Queen of Light award City of Chgo., 1970. Mem. MLA, Am. Acad. Religion, Soc. Sci. Study Religion, Am.-Scandinavian Found., Chgo. Metro. Assn. (seminaries com.), Mensa. Avocations: art, music, travel, folk dancing, camping. Home: PO Box 412 Wheaton IL 60189-0412

HARRIS, EMILY LOUISE, special education educator; b. New London, Conn., Nov. 16, 1932; d. Frank Sr. and Tanzatter (McCleese) Brown; m. John Everett Harris Sr., Sept. 10, 1955; children: John Everett Jr., Jocelyn E. (dec.). BS, U. Conn., 1955; MEd, Northeastern U., 1969. Cert. tchr. elem. spl. subject sci., Mass., spl. subject reading, secondary prin., elem. prin. Tchr. New Haven Sch. Dept., 1957-59, Boston Sch. Dept., 1966-68, Natick (Mass.) Sch. Dept., 1969-72; cert. nurse's asst. The Hebrew Rehab. Ctr., Roslindale, Mass., 1973-75; spl. edn. educator Boston Sch. Dept., 1975-76, 78—, support tchr., 1976-78. Site coord. Tchr. Corps., 1977-81; leader, co-leader Harvard U. Student Tchrs. at Dorchester H.S. Sem., 1995—; tchr. adviser Future Educators Am. Dorchester H.S. Editor, compiler: Cooking With the Stars, 1989. Mem.-del. Mass. Fedn. Tchrs., Boston, 1993-96; elected rep. AFL-CIO (Boston Tchrs. Union), 1986-96; registrar of voters Dorchester (Mass.) H.S., 1986—; adv. bd. New England Assn. Schs. and Colls., 1980-93; 1st v.p., bd. dirs. League of Women for Comty. Svcs., Boston, 1976-80, Cynthia Sickle-Cell Anemia Fund, Boston, 1976-80. Recipient Tchg. award Urban League Guild Mass., 1993. Mem. AAUW, Zeta Phi Beta (Zeta of Yr. 1994), Alpha Delta Kappa, Kappa Delta Pi, Order Ea. Star (past worthy matron Prince Hall chpt. 1983-84), Delta Omicron Zeta, Phi Delta Kappa. Baptist. Avocations: reading, sewing. Home: 36 Dietz Rd Hyde Park MA 02136-1134

HARRIS, EMMYLOU, singer; b. Birmingham, Ala., Apr. 2, 1947; d. Walter and Eugenia; children: Hallie, Meghann. Student, U.N.C.-Greensboro. Singer, 1967; assisted Gram Parsons on album GP, Grievous Angel, 1973; toured with Fallen Angels Band, performed across Europe and U.S.; recording artist on albums for Reprise Records, Warner Bros. Records., Electra/Asylum Records; appeared in rock documentary The Last Waltz, 1978; albums include The Gliding Bird, 1969, Pieces of the Sky, 1975, Elite Hotel, 1976 (Grammy award), Luxury Liner, 1977, Quarter Moon In A Ten Cent Town, 1978, Profile: Best of Emmylou Harris, 1978, Blue Kentucky Girl, 1979, Light of the Stable, 1979, Evangeline, 1981, Last Date, 1982, White Shoes, 1983, Profile II: Best of Emmylou Harris, 1984, The Ballad of Sally Rose, 1985, Thirteen, 1986, Trio (with Dolly Parton, Linda Ronstadt), 1987 (Grammy award), Angel Band, 1987, Bluebird, 1988, Duets, 1990, Cowgirl's Prayer, 1993, Songs Of The West, 1994, Wrecking Ball, 1995 (Grammy award 1996), Spyboy, 1998, The Horse Whisperer, 1998, Singin' with Emmy Lou Harris, Vol. 1, 2000, Vol. 2, 2003, Red Dirt Girl, 2000, Anthology: The Warner-Reprise Years, 2001, Nobody's Darling But Mine, 2002, Stumble Into Grace, 2003; co-writer, co-prodr.: (with Paul Kennerley) The Ballad of Sally Rose, 185. Pres. Country Music Found., 1983. Recipient of 11 Grammy awards, 1979, 80, 81, 84, 87, 92, 96, 98, 99, 2000, 2001, Orville H. Gibson Lifetime Achievement award, 1996, Patrick J. Leahy Humanitarian award-Americana Music awards Lifetime Achievement Performer, 2002; named Female Vocalist of Yr., Country Music Assn., 1980; co-recipient (with Dolly Parton and Linda Ronstadt) Album of Yr. award Acad. Country Music, 1987; named to Ala. Music Hall of Fame, 2003. Office: Vector Management 1607 17th Ave S Nashville TN 37212-2875

HARRIS, EON NIGEL, dean, rheumatologist, internist; b. Georgetown, Guyana, S.Am. came to U.S., 1987; s. T. Wilson and Cicely H.; m. Yvette Williams, 1981; children: Zaman Rashid, Tamia Alisha, Sandhya Caroline. BS, Howard U., 1968; MPhil, Yale U., 1970; MD, U. Pa., 1976; PhD in Medicine, U. West Indies, Kingston, Jamaica, 1982. Diplomate Am. Bd. Internal Medicine, Am. Bd. Rheumatology. Intern U. of the West Indies, Kingston, Jamaica, 1977, resident, 1978-81; lectr. U. West Indies, Kingston, 1981-83; rheumatology fellow Hammersmith Hosp., London, 1983-85; dir. Lupus rsch. lab. St. Thomas Hosp., London, 1985-87; asst. prof. U. Louisville, Ky., 1987-91, assoc. prof., 1991—93, prof., 1993—96; dean, sr. v.p. acad. affairs Morehouse Sch. of Medicine, Atlanta, prof. dept. medicine, 1996—. Chief div. rheumatology U. Louisville; med. adv. bd. Lupus Found. Am.; sci. adv. bd. Alliance for Lupus Rsch. Editor: Phospholipid Binding Antibodies, 1991; contbr. articles to profl. jours. Recipient Internat. League Against Rheumatism prize Ciba-Geigy, 1993. Fellow Am. Coll. Rheumatology (chmn. antiphospholipid study group 1993—); mem. Phi Beta Kappa, Alpha Omega Alpha. Office: Morehouse Sch Medicine 720 Westview Dr SW Atlanta GA 30310-1458 Office Phone: 404-752-1727.

HARRIS, ETHAN S., diversified financial services company executive; married; 2 children. BA, Clark U.; PhD in Econs., Columbia U. Internat. polit. economist JP Morgan; sr. economist, mgr. domestic rsch. div. Fed. Res. Bank N.Y., 1990—96; mng. dir, deputy chief economist Lehman Bros., Inc., N.Y., 1996, chief U.S. economist, 2003—. Avocations: history, Boston Red Sox. Office: Lehman Brothers Inc 745 Seventh Ave New York NY 10019*

HARRIS, F. CHANDLER, retired director; b. Neligh, Nebr., Nov. 5, 1914; s. James Carlton and Helen Ayres (Boyd) Harris; m. Barbara Ann Hull, Aug. 10, 1946; children: Victoria Williams, Randolph Boyd. AB, UCLA, 1936. Assoc. editor Telegraph Delivery Spirit, L.A., 1937—39; writer, pub. svc. network radio programs Univ. Explorer, Sci. Editor, U. Calif., 1939—61; pub. info. mgr. UCLA, 1961—75, dir., 1975—82, dir. emeritus, 1982—. Editor: Interfraternity Rsch. Adv. Coun. Bull., 1949—50, Carnation, 1969—80, Royce Hall, 1985. Mem. pub. rels. com. western region United Way, 1972—75; bd. dirs. Am. Youth Symphony, L.A., 1978—98, v.p., 1983—98; bd. dirs. Hathaway Home Children, 1982—88, Western L.A. Region C. of C., 1976—80. Recipient 1st prize, NBC Radio Inst., 1944, Adam award, Assistance League Mannequins, 1980, Univ. Svc. award, UCLA Alumni Assn., 1986. Mem.: U. Calif. Retirees Assn. L.A. (pres. 1985—87), UCLA Faculty Club (sec. bd. govs. 1968—72), Delta Sigma Phi (nat. pres. 1959—63, Harvey Hebert medal 1947, Mr. Delta Sig award 1972), Sigma Delta Chi. Home: 7774 Skyhill Dr Los Angeles CA 90068-1232

HARRIS, FRED R., political scientist, educator, retired senator; b. Walters, Okla., Nov. 13, 1930; s. Fred Byron and Alene (Person) Harris; m. LaDonna Crawford, Apr. 8, 1949 (div. 1981); children: Kathryn, Byron, Laura; m. Margaret S. Elliston, Sept. 5, 1982. BA, U. Okla., 1952, JD, 1954. Bar: Okla. 1954. Founder, sr. partner firm Harris, Newcombe, Redman & Doolin, Lawton, Okla., 1954-64; mem. Okla Senate, 1956-64, U.S. Senate from Okla., Washington, 1964-73; prof. polit. sci. U. N.Mex., Albuquerque, 1976—. Author: (book) Alarms and Hopes, 1969, Now is the Time, 1971, The State of the Cities: Report of the Commission on Cities in the 70's, 1972, Social Science and National Policy, The New Populism, 1973, Potomac Fever, 1977, America's Democracy, 1980, America's Democracy, 3d edit., 1985, Readings on the Body Politic, 1987, Deadlock or Decision, 1993, In Defense of Congress, 1994, Coyote Revenge, 1999, Easy Pickin's, 2001; co-author: America's Legislative Processes, 1983, Understanding American Government, 1988, Quiet Riots, 1988, America's Government, 1990, Locked in the Poor House, 1998;: Following the Harvest, 2004. Mem. Nat. Adv. Commn. Civil Disorders, 1967—68; chmn. Dem. Nat. Com., 1969—70. Mem.: Order of Coif, Phi Beta Kappa. Office: U New Mexico Dept Polit Sci Albuquerque NM 87131-0001 E-mail: fharris@unm.edu.

HARRIS, FREDERICK JOHN, foreign language and literature educator; b. N.Y.C., July 29, 1943; s. Frederick and Anna (Guttmann) H. BA, Fordham U., 1965; MA, Columbia U., 1966, PhD, 1969. Asst. prof. Fordham U., N.Y.C., 1970—79, assoc. prof., 1979—84, prof. French and comparative lit., 1984—, chmn. divsn. humanities, 1979—85, chmn. dept. modern langs. and lits. (bi-campus), 1995—99. Bd. dirs. Fordham U. Press, NYC; mem. adv. com. Krieg und Literatur/War and Literature. Author: André Gide-Romain Rolland: Two Men Divided, 1973, Encounters with Darkness: French and German Writers on World War II, 1983, Friend and Foe: Marcel Proust and André Gide, 2002; contbr. articles to profl. jours. Mem. MLA, PEN Am. Ctr. (translation com. 1999-2004), Am. Assn. Tchrs. French, Internat. Comparative Lit. Assn., Am. Comparative Lit. Assn., Coll. English Assn., Assn. des Amis d'André Gide, Société des Professeurs Français et Francophones d'Amérique (bd. dirs. 1995-98), Stewart Hall (v.p. 1989-90, bd. dirs.). Roman Catholic. Office: Rose Hill Campus Lincoln Center Campus Fordham U New York NY 10023 Office Phone: 212-636-6790. E-mail: fharris@fordham.edu.

HARRIS, GAYLE ELIZABETH, bishop; b. Cleve., Feb. 12, 1951; m. Peter W. Peters; 3 children. BA in history, Lewis and Clark Coll., Portland, 1978; MDiv, Ch. Div. Sch. of the Pacific, Berkeley, Calif., 1981. Ordained deacon, 1981, priest, 1982; priest-in-charge Holy Communion Ch., Washington, 1984—92; rector St. Luke and Simon Cyrene, Rochester, NY, 1992—2002; consecrated bishop, 2003; bishop suffragen Episcopal Diocese of Mass., Boston, 2003—. Episcopalian. Office: Episcopal Diocese of Mass 138 Tremont St Boston MA 02111*

HARRIS, GREGORY K., credit manager, information technology manager; BS in Bus. Adminstrn. and Acctg., Morris Brown Coll., Atlanta, 1980; grad. Corp. Credit course, Dun & Bradstreet, 1982. Corp. credit and collection mgr. Health Ins. Plan of Greater N.Y., N.Y.C., 1982—93; mgr. customer accounts Nat. Assn. Security Dealers, Rockville, Md., 1994—95; accounts receivable and collections manager NOS Comms., Bethesda, 1995—96; mgr. risk credit and collection policy Verizon Internet Solutions and Verizon Video Svcs., Reston, Va., 1996—99; risk mgr. and sys. design cons. Resources Connection, McLean, Va., 2000; sr. billing mgr. spl. projects and exec. escalations MCI, Ashburn, 2000—03; sr. project manager internat. inmerstat satellite telecomm. settlements FCC, Washington, 2003—05. Mem.: Omega Psi Phi. Address: 5608 Oakham Pl Centreville VA 20120

HARRIS, GREGORY SCOTT, municipal official; b. Denver, June 5, 1955; s. Herbert E. and Marcia Jean (Raabe) H. BS in Journalism with honors, U. Colo., 1977; MBA, Loyola U., Chgo., 1981. Dir. public relations IMPACT Internat., Inc., Chgo., 1977-78; dir. edn. Nat. Home Furnishings Assn. (NHFA), Chgo., 1978-79, v.p. industry affairs, 1981-87, exec. v.p., chief operating officer, 1987-88; exec. dir. Interior Design Soc., Chgo., 1979-82; sec. NHFA Service Corp., 1986-87, v.p., 1986-87, pres., 1987-91, also bd. dirs.; pres. Open Hand: Chgo. Found., 1988-91; chief of staff Chgo. City Coun., 1992—. Mem. Devel. Adv. Coun. City of Chgo., 1990-92; bd. dirs. Nonprofit Fin. Ctr.; mem. advocacy and pub. policy com. AFC, Ctr. Halsted Fin. com., 2003—. Trustee Design Found., Chgo., 1980-88; chmn. bd. dirs. AIDS Walk Found., 1990-91; bd. dirs. AIDS Legal Coun., 1992-94, Heartland Alliance for Human Needs and Human Rights; fin. dir. Simpson for Congress Com., 1991-92; mem. adv. bd. The Neofuturists, 2000. Recipient Leadership in Mktg. award Newspaper Pubs. Assn., 1983, Outstanding Young Chicagoan award Chgo. Jaycees, 1992, Outstanding Svc. to Immigrant and Refugee Cmty. award, 1996, Uptown C. of C. Ann. award, 1996, Voice of People Cmty. award, 1994, Equality award Human Rights Campaign, 1997, W. Clement Stone award, 1998, Biggest Heart award Hearts Found., 1999, Food For Life award, Florence Bezazian Citizenship award, 1999, Greater Chgo. Com. Humanitarian Efforts award, 2000, Inst. Cultural Affairs USA cert. of appreciation, 2000, Svc. award Cambodian Buddhist Assn., 2002, Chgo. House Pub. Svc. award, 2002, Hopeful Spirit award Names Project, 2005; named to City of Chgo. Hall of Fame, 1996. Office: Chgo City Coun City Hall 121 N La Salle St Chicago IL 60602-1202 Office Phone: 312-744-6860.

HARRIS, HAROLD STEPHEN, JR., lawyer; b. Nashville, June 9, 1955; s. Harold Stephen Sr. and Aline (Broadway) H.; m. Shigeko Ikeda, May 20, 1989; 1 child, Lee Ikeda. AB, Cornell U., 1977; JD with honors, Columbia U., 1982, cert. with honors. Bar: Ga. 1982, U.S. Dist. Ct. (no., so. and mid. dists.) Ga. 1982, U.S. Ct. Appeals (11th, 4th, 5th cirs.) 1982. Ptnr. Alston & Bird LLP, Atlanta, 1982—, chmn., antitrust group and global svcs. task force. Mem. ABA (antitrust law sect., internat. law sect.), Japan-Am. Soc. Ga., Internat. Bar Assn. (competition and trade com.). Office: Alston & Bird LLP 1 Atlantic Ctr 1201 W Peachtree St NW Ste 4200 Atlanta GA 30309-3449 Office Phone: 404-881-7197. Office Fax: 404-881-7777. Business E-Mail: sharris@alston.com.

HARRIS, HARRIET, actress; b. Ft. Worth, Tex., Jan. 8, 1955; Grad., Juilliard. Actor: (TV series) The Five Mrs. Buchanans, 1994, Union Square, 1997—98, Stark Raving Mad, 1999, The Beast, 2001, It's All Relative, 2003, Desperate Housewives, 2005; (plays) Hamlet, 1986—, Four Baboons Adoring the Sun, 1992, Jeffrey, 1993—, The Man Who Came to Dinner, 2000, The Dining Room, 2005, (Broadway musical) Thoroughly Modern Millie, 2002— (Tony award, 2002); (films) Memento, 2000, Nurse Betty, 2000.*

HARRIS, HENRY WILLIAM, physician; b. Catawba, N.C., Jan. 6, 1919; s. Henry William and Katie (Coulter) H.; m. Margaret Ann Roberts, Nov. 29, 1950; children: Henry William, John R., James P. BA, U.N.C., 1940; MD cum laude, Harvard U., 1943. Diplomate: in pulmonary disease Am. Bd. Internal Medicine. Intern Harvard Med. Service, Boston City Hosp., 1944-45, asst. resident medicine, 1945-46; resident fellow Thorndike Meml. Lab., 1944, 46; resident chest service Bellevue Hosp., N.Y.C., 1947; staff physician Gundersen Clinic, LaCrosse, Wis., 1948-53; asst. prof. medicine U. Utah Coll. Medicine, 1955-59, asso. prof., 1959-60; chief pulmonary disease service VA Hosp., Salt Lake City, 1955-60; prof. chmn. dept. medicine Woman's Med. Coll. of Pa., 1960-67; chmn. dept. medicine Catholic Med. Center Bklyn. and Queens, 1967-70; asso. prof. clin. medicine N.Y.U. Sch. Medicine, 1969-70, prof., 1970—. Adj. staff chest svc. Bellevue Hosp., N.Y.C.; hon. staff Tisch Hosp., N.Y.C.; sr. coms. Bur. Tb, Dept. of Health, N.Y.C. Mem. editorial bd.: Annals of Internal Medicine, 1976-80; Contbr. articles to profl. publs. Bd. dirs. Am. Lung Assn., 1961-79, v.p., 1972-73; bd. dirs. N.Y. Lung Assn., 1974-95, v.p., 1983—, pres. 1987-90; bd. dirs. Am. Bur. Med. Advancement in China., 1978—, v.p., 1983-87, pres. 1987-92, chmn. H. Wm. Harris vis. prof. com., 1986-96. Served to capt., M.C. AUS, 1953-55. Fellow ACP; mem. Am. Thoracic Soc. (pres. 1962-63). Home: 4 Birchwood Ct Apt 3L Mineola NY 11501-4513 Office: Chest Service Bellevue Hosp 1st Ave New York NY 10016

HARRIS, HOLTON EDWIN, plastics machinery manufacturing executive; b. NYC, Aug. 24, 1923; s. David William and Mildred (Stoutenborough) H.; m. Jeanne Deming, Feb. 22, 1963; children: Walter Deming, Dorothy Stoutenborough. *Grandfather, Nathaniel E. Harris, founder of the Georgia Institute of Technology in Atlanta, and later Governor of Georgia. Father, David W. Harris, was president of the Universal Oil Products Company and a prime mover in the petroleum industry. Uncle was General Walter A. Harris, World War II General, and one of the founders of the Ocmulgee National Monument in Macon, Georgia commemorating the Creek Indians.* BSEE, MIT, 1947, MSEE, 1948. Engr. GE, Syracuse, N.Y., 1948-49, sect. sales mgr. Schenectady, N.Y., 1949-52; asst. to pres. R.W. Cramer Co., Centerbrook, Conn., 1952-53; sales mgr. Ea. Air Devices, Dover, N.H., 1953-54; mgr. comml. products Reeves Instrument Corp., Carle Place, N.Y., 1954-58; pres. Harrel, Inc., Norwalk, Conn., 1958—. Lectr. in field. Author: Extrusion Control; contbg. author: Modern Plastics Ency., 1990, Blow Molding Handbook, 1989; patentee in field; contbr. numerous articles to profl. jours. Mem. Representative Town Meeting, Westport, Conn., 1965-75, 93-97, 99-2001, dep. moderator, 1973-75, chmn. fin. com.; chmn. Rep. Town. Com., Westport; mem. Charter Revision Com., Westport. 1st lt. U.S. Army Signal Corp., 1943-46, South Pacific. Recipient award in recognition of meritorious svc., Town of Westport, Conn. Mem. IEEE (life), Soc. Plastics Engrs. (sr.), Instrument Soc. Am. (sr.). Avocation: amateur radio. Home: 5 Newtown Tpke Westport CT 06880-1802 Office: Harrel Inc 16 Fitch St Norwalk CT 06855-1392 E-mail: info@harrel.com, harrish@harrel.com.

HARRIS, HOWARD HUNTER, retired oil industry executive; b. Cushing, Okla., Dec. 7, 1924; s. Oscar Hunter and Gertie Lee (Stark) H.; m. Gwendolyne J. Moyers (died July 26, 2003), Dec. 31, 1945; children: Howard Sidney, Rodney Craig. BS in Bus. Adminstrn., JD, U. Okla., 1949; postgrad. in advt. mgmt., Stanford U., 1971. Atty. Emery & Harris, Cushing and Stillwater, Okla., 1949-50; staff atty. Sun Oil Co., Tulsa, 1950-54; div. atty. Marathon Oil Co., Tulsa, 1954-63; staff atty Marathon Internat. Oil Co., Findlay, Ohio, 1963-65; mgr. legal affairs Deutsche Marathon Petroleum Gmbh., Frankfurt and Munich, 1965-70; mktg. aty. and assoc. gen. counsel Marathon Oil Co., Findlay, Ohio, 1970-74, v.p. corp. external affairs, 1974-86, ret., 1986. Pres. Gainey Ranch Cmty. Assn., 1995-98. Served with AUS, 1943-45. Decorated Bronze Star Mem. Am. Petroleum Inst., ABA, Ohio Bar Assn., Okla. Bar Assn., Order of Coif, Beta Gamma Sigma. Lodges: Masons. Republican. Episcopalian.

HARRIS, HUGH STANLEY, JR., lawyer; b. Savannah, Ga., Aug. 6, 1957; s. Hugh Stanley and Nancy Jane (Anderson) H.; m. Stephanie Helen Webster, Aug. 14, 1982 (div. Aug. 1990), m. Nancy Lea Winstead, Aug. 2, 1991; children: Carter Winstead, Alexandra Elizabeth. AB, U. Ga., 1979; JD, U. Tenn., 1982. Bar: Tenn. 1983, N.C. 1984. Assoc. Guess and English, Knoxville, Tenn., 1983, Myers, Hulse & Brown, Charlotte, N.C., 1984-89; ptnr. Myers, Hulse & Harris, Charlotte, 1989-94; pvt. practice Charlotte, 1994—. Chmn. fin. com. Meml. United Meth. Ch. Mem. ATLA, N.C. Acad. Trial Lawyers, Providence Country Club. Democrat. Avocations: scuba diving, skiing, running, hunting, golf. Office: 130 N Mcdowell St Ste A Charlotte NC 28204-2268

HARRIS, IRVING, lawyer; b. Cin., May 23, 1927; s. Albert and Sadye H.; m. Selma Schottenstein, June 18, 1950; children: Jeffrey Philip, Jonathan Lindley (dec.), Lisa Ann Hollister. Undergrad. degree, U. Cin., 1948, LLB, 1951. Bar: Ohio 1951, U.S. Dist. Ct. Ohio 1952, U.S. Ct. Appeals (6th cir.) 1952, U.S. Supreme Ct. 1960. Ptnr. Cors, Hair & Hartsock, 1954-81, Hartsock, Harris & Schneider, Cin., 1981-82, Porter, Wright, Morris & Arthur, Cin., 1982-89; ptnr. firm Harris, Harris, Field Schacter & Bardach Ltd., Cin., 1989-2000. Mem. Ohio Trade Mission to Orient, 1973, to Eng. and Germany, 1974; spl. counsel to Atty. Gen. Ohio, 1963-71; life mem. 6th Cir. Jud. Conf.; lectr. Advising, Oper. and Rebuilding the Financially Distressed Co., 1991; bd. dirs. Bank One, Cin., 1993-2000, HRC Ltd. Partnership (Hyatt Regency (Cin.) Cin. Mem. Ohio Devel. Financing Commn., 1974—84, vice-chmn., 1978—79; spl. counsel Ohio Atty. Gen.'s Office for the Police and Firemen's Disability and Pension Fund, 1994—97; trustee Skidmore Coll., 1976—90, trustee emeritus, 1991—, Big Bros.; trustee Cin. Symphony Orch., 1989—96; bd. overseers U. Cin. Law Sch., 1998—; arbitrator Ct. of Common Pleas of Hamilton County, 2001—; mediator U.S. Dist. Ct. (so. dist.) Ohio Western divsn., 1999—2000. Mem. ABA (Sherman act com., sect. on antitrust and bus. law 1969-2000, subcoms. on derivative actions, bankruptcy, litigation of bus. and corp. litigation 1992-2000), Ohio Bar Assn., Cin. Bar Assn., Am. Judicature Soc., Potter Stewart Inn of Ct. (master of the bench), Queen City Club, Univ. Club, Camargo Hunt Club, Cin. Tennis Club, Roaring Fork Country Club, Ocean Reef Club. Home: 18 Grandin Ln Cincinnati OH 45208-3365 Office: 3801 Carew Tower 441 Vine St Cincinnati OH 45202-2806

HARRIS, ISIAH, JR., telecommunications industry executive; BS, Iowa State U.; MBA, U. Minn. CPA. Profl. football player St. Louis Cardinals, New Orleans Saints; with KPMG Peat Marwick; v.p., corp. controller Supervalu, Inc., Mpls.; chief fin. officer Bellsouth Telecomm., corp. v.p. fin.; pres. comsumer svcs. Bellsouth Corp., Atlanta, 2000—. Bd. dirs. Internat. Multi-Foods, Inc., Atlanta Lofe Fin. Group; bd. govs. Iowa State U. Found. Mem. fin. com. United Way, Atlanta, Prevent Child Abuse, chair major gifts com. Mem.: AICPA, Minn. Soc. CPA's. Office: Bellsouth Corp 1155 Peachtree St NE Atlanta GA 30309-3610

HARRIS, JACK F., police chief; b. 1950; m. Connie Harris. BA in polit. sci., Ariz. State U., 1977, grad. cert. pub. mgr. program; M in human resources, Ottawa U., 2000; grad., FBI Nat. Acad. Patrol officer Phoenix Police Dept., 1972, spl. investigations, undercover, vice and narcotics, 1981—84, sgt. patrol divsn., 1984—88, sgt. tng. acad. and street crimes, 1985—88, lt. patrol and motorcycle divsn., 1988—89, unit comdr. spl. assignments unit (SWAT team), 1989—95, city mgr. liaison, 1996—97, comdr. Desert Horizon Police Precinct, 1997—99, comdr. profl. standards divsn. (internal affairs), 1999—2000, asst. police chief North Divsn., 2000—04, interim police chief, 2004, chief of police, 2004—. Achievements include spearheaded Safe City Task Force; development of first cmty.-policing station in Palomino area in northeast Phoenix. Office: 620 W Washington St Phoenix AZ 85003 Office Phone: 602-262-7626. Business E-Mail: jack.harris@phoenix.gov.

HARRIS, JACK HOWARD, II, financial consultant, director; b. Chgo., Mar. 22, 1945; s. Jack Howard and Myrtice Geneva (Dickson) Harris; m. Barbara Beck Czika, Jan. 1, 1983; children: Jack, William, Thomas P. stepchildren: Joseph C Czika, Brad D. Czika. AB, U. Chgo., 1966; MPh, George Washington U., 1984. Chief China desk Air Force Intelligence, USAF, Washington, 1971—74; dir. policy studies BDM Corp., Washington, 1974—78; sr. assoc. Booz-Allen and Hamilton, Washington, 1979; corp. v.p. govt. ops. Sci. Applications, Inc., Washington, 1980—85; exec. v.p., CFO The Harris Group, Inc., Washington, 1985—95; with Ctr. for Nat. Program Evaluation, Washington, 1988—94; v.p. Corp. and Polit. Comms., Inc., Melbourne Beach, Fla., 1995—. With USAF, 1967—71. Mem.: VFW, DAV, Internat. Platform Assn., Air Force Assn., Mensa, Am. Legion, Triple Nine Soc., Phi Gamma Delta. Home and Office: 2009 Neptune Dr Melbourne Beach FL 32951-2707 E-mail: jack@theharrises.cc.

HARRIS, J(ACOB) GEORGE, health products executive; b. Kings Mountain, N.C., Sept. 5, 1938; s. James A. and Carolyn (Hord) H.; m. Sondra Gilbert, Mar. 29, 1959; children: Cynthia, Susan, David. BA in Math., Duke U., 1960. With Am. Hosp. Supply Corp., 1960-84, region mgr. South San Francisco, 1964-67, pres. Port Credit, Ont., Can., 1967-70, v.p. ops. Evanston, Ill., 1970-71, pres. dietary products div. McGaw Park, Ill., 1971-74, corp. v.p. Evanston, 1974-78, exec. v.p., 1978-84; chmn., chief exec. officer Health Group Inc., Nashville, 1984-85; founder, pres., CEO Pinnacle Care Corp. (merged Mariner Health Group), 1985-94; pres., COO Mariner Health Group, 1994; ret., 1994; formerly bd. dirs. Mariner Health Group. Bd. dirs. Union Spl. Corp., Chgo., Monoclonal Antibodies, Inc., Mountain View, Calif., Electro Neucleonics Inc., Health Group, Electro-Biology Inc., Dialogic Comm. Corp. Bd. dirs. Highland Park (Ill.) Hosp., 1981-84; trustee McCormick Sem., Chgo. Mem. Scientific Apparatus Mfrs. Assn. (bd. dirs.), Richland Country Club. Home: 1204 Beddington Park Nashville TN 37215-5810 Office Phone: 615-340-9191. Personal E-mail: bocaj1938@aol.com.

HARRIS, JAMES BRAXTON, retired humanities educator, freelance/self-employed writer; b. Reidsville, NC, Apr. 30, 1929; s. Whitelaw Reid and Willie Zoie (Kelly) Harris; m. Gertrude Lawrence, Dec. 24, 1950; children: Lorraine, Helen, Joseph, Kelene, Lawrence. BA, Lenoir-Rhyne Coll., 1949; MA, Appalachian State U., 1956; EdD, Ind. U., 1960. Tchr. English and history Pub. Schs., Hildebran, Francisco and Hickory, NC, 1949—50, 1953—57; prof., vice chancellor Appalachian State U., Boone, NC, 1958—64, 1970—90, prof. emeritus, 1991—; dean Brevard (NC) Coll., 1964—68; dir. pre-svc. tchr. edn. NC Dept. Pub. Instrn., Raleigh, 1968—70; freelance writer Hendersonville, NC, 1991—. Tech. tng. cons. Naval Sea Sys. Command USN, Washington, 1985—89; cons. to colls., univs. and profl. orgns. Author: Lyrics for Three Julies: Song Lyrics for Three Musical Plays, 1992, Lyrics for Three Lovers: Song Lyrics for Three Musical Plays, 1993, Bittersweet Lyrics: Song Lyrics for Three Musical Plays, 1994, The Bolejack Chronicle, 2000, The Stokesburg Trilogy, 2000, The Dorian Chronicle, 2000, The Boldorian Chronicle, 2000, The Trinity Trilogy, 2000, The Chronicle of Scale, 2000, The Technics Trilogy, 2000, The C (sic) cycle: Precis and Personae, 2000, Dalton's Folly, 2003, Bay's Book: Being Benign Bagatelles Befitting Beneficent Bards, 2003, Lyrical Eyes: Song Lyrics for Three Musical Plays, 2004, Ray's Way, 2004; contbr. articles to profl. jours.; author: Brooke Lyrics: Song Lyrics For Three Musical Plays, 2004. Bd. dirs. Western Carolina Cmty. Action, Hendersonville and Brevard, 1966—68. 1st lt. USAF, 1950—53, Capt. USAFR, 1953—61. Grantee, Appalachian State U., 1972—73. Avocation: designing houses and small buildings. Home: 37 Jeter Mountain Rd Hendersonville NC 28739

HARRIS, JAMES CAROL OVERTON, JR., psychiatrist, pediatrician; b. Birmingham, Ala., Nov. 6, 1940; s. James Carol and Mary Virginia (Respess) H. BS, Univ. Md., 1962; MD, George Washington U., 1966. Cert. Am. Bd. Pediat., Am. Bd. Psychiatry, Am. Bd. Child Psychiatry. With Peace Corps, Thailand, 1967-70; dir. devel. neuropsychiatry Johns Hopkins U., Balt., 1976—; pres. med. staff Kennedy Krieger Inst., Johns Hopkins U., Balt., 1986-88; asst. prof. Johns Hopkins U., Balt., 1976-82, interim dir. divsn. of child and adolescence psychiatry, 1978-82, dir. consultation/ liason svc., 1978-82, dir. edn. divsn. of child and adolescence psychiatry, 1982-89, assoc. prof. psychiatry, mental hygiene, pediat., 1982—97, prof., 1997—, co-dir. autism clinic, 1983—, co-dir. sleep disorder clinic, 1983—, joint appointment dept. of mental hygiene, 1985—. Adj. scientist Ctr. for Brain Evolution and Behavior, Poolesville, Md., 1978—84, Lab. Comparative Ethology, 1984—93; mem. White House conf. on Mental Health, 1999; cons. Joseph P. Kennedy Jr. Found., 2000—; mem. Pres.'s Com. on Mental Retardation, 2001—02; vis. scholar dept. psychiatry U. Chgo., 2001—02, vis. rsch. scientist Inst. for Mind and Biology, 2001—02; cons. U of Ill, Brain and Body Inst., 2003—. Author: Developmental Neuropsychiatry Fundamentals, 1995, Developmental Neuropsychiatry: Assessment, Diagnosis and Treatment, 1995 (Med. Book of Yr. award 1995), Intellectual Disability, 2005; mem. editl. bd. Jour. Child Neurology, 2001—; art and cover editor Archives of Gen. Psychiatry, 2002—; contbr. more than 100 articles and abstracts to profl. jours. Recipient NIMH Trainee award, 1964—65, Pollen award, 1965—66, R-01 Rsch. award, Nat. Inst. Child Health and Human Devel.; Fgn. fellow, Assn. Am. Med. Colls.-Smith Kline & French, 1965. Fellow: Am. Acad. Child and Adolescent Psychiatry, Am. Psychiat. Assn. (Disting.); mem.: Am. Coll. Psychiatry, Soc. Profs. Child and Adolescent Psychiatry (pres. 1998—2000), Soc. Study Behavioral Phenotypes, Am. Assn. Psychiatry and the Law, Soc. Neurosci., Am. Assn. Dirs. Psychiat. Residency Tng., Md. Psychiat. Soc., Am. Coll. Neuropsychopharmacology. Avocation: foreign travel. Home: 3704 N Charles St Apt 105 Baltimore MD 21218 Office: Johns Hopkins U Sch Medicine CMSC 371 600 N Wolfe St Baltimore MD 21287-0005: 505 N Lakeshore Dr Apt 416 Chicago IL 60611 Office Phone: 410-955-6181. Personal E-mail: jamesharris@erols.com. Business E-Mail: jharrisor@jhmi.edu.

HARRIS, JAMES HAROLD, minister; b. Cullowhee, NC, Sept. 7, 1939; s. James Albert and Lucille (Wiggins) Harris; m. Judith Ann Harris, Aug. 28, 1959; children: Janalce, Jeffery, James Jr. BA, Bryan Coll., 1972; D in bible, Theological Seminary, 1979; PhD, Am. Coll. Theology, 1999. Minister Popular Springs Bapt. Ch., Bonn, NC, Symna Bapt. Ch., Dayton, Tenn., Lake Drive Bapt. Ch., Sale Creek, Tenn., 1st Bapt. Rosewood, Goldesboro, NC, Salem Bapt., Elizabeth City, NC, Rock Ch., Elizabeth City. Chaplan McKee Baking Co., Chattanooga, 1990, E. Ridge Hosp., E. Ridge, Tenn., 1995, Christian Network Internat., Nashville, 2001; cert. master life leader Southern Bapt. Conv., 1990. With U.S. Army, 1967—69. Republican. Bapt. Home: 103 Hull Ln Hendersonville TN 37075 E-mail: jhh9739@aol.com.

HARRIS, JAMES HERMAN, pathologist, neuropathologist, consultant, educator; b. Fayetteville, Ga., Oct. 19, 1942; s. Frank J. and Gladys N. (White) H.; m. Judy K. Hutchinson, Jan. 30, 1965; children: Jeffrey William, John Michael, James Herman. BS, Carson-Newman Coll., 1964; PhD, U. Tenn.-Memphis, 1969, MD, 1972. Diplomate Am. Bd. Pathology; sub-cert. in anatomic pathology and neuropathology. Resident, fellow NYU-Bellevue Med. Ctr., N.Y.C., 1973-75; adj. asst. prof. pathology NYU, N.Y.C., 1975-83; asst. prof. pathology and neuroscis. Med. Coll. Ohio, Toledo, 1975-78, assoc. prof., 1978-82, dir. neuropathology and electron microscopy lab., 1975-82; cons. Toledo Hosp., 1979-82, assoc. pathologist/neuropathologist, dir. electron microscopy pathology lab., 1983-91, mem. courtesy staff, 1991—, mem. overview com., credentials com., appropriations subcom. medisgroup, interqual task force. Chmn. clin. support svcs. com., vice chmn. med. staff quality rev. com. Toledo Hosp.; cons. neuropathologist Mercy Hosp., 1976—93, mem. courtesy staff, 1993—; cons. neuropathologist U. Mich. Dept. Pathology, 1984—93; cons. med. malpractice in pathology and neuropathology; mem. AMA Physician Rsch. and Evaluation panel; mem. edtl. and profl. affairs commn., exec. coun. Acad. Medicine; mem. children's cancer study group Ohio State U. Satellite; chmn. tech. and issues subcom. of adv. com. Blue Cross; mem. Task Force on Cost Effectiveness N.W. Ohio; chmn. med. necessity appeals com. Blue Cross/Blue Shield; adv. bd. PIE Mut. Ins. Co. Author med., sci. papers; reviewer Jour. Neuropathology and Exptl. Neurology. Chmn. fin. com., dir. bldg. fund campaign First Bapt. Ch., Perrysburg, Ohio; chmn. steering com. Pack 198 Boy Scouts Am.; faculty chmn. Med. Col. Ohio United Way Campaign; mem. adv. com. Multiple Sclerosis Soc. N.W. Ohio; chmn. alumni scholarship fund Carson-Newman Coll., 1994—95; alumni exec. com. Truett McConnell Coll., 1995—2003, pres. alumni assocs., 1998—2002, capital campaign steering com., 1998—2000; chmn. Loyalty Fund Campaign for 50th Ann., 1996—98. Recipient Outstanding Tchr. award Med. Coll. Ohio, 1980; named to Outstanding Young Men Am., U.S. Jaycees, 1973; USPHS trainee, 1964-69, postdoctoral trainee, 1973-75; grantee Am. Cancer Soc., 1977-78, Warner Lambert Pharm. Co., 1978-79, Miniger Found., 1980, Toledo Hosp. Found., 1985, Promedica Health Care Found., 1986. Mem. Am. Profl. Practice Assn., Am. Pathology Found., Am. Soc. Law and Medicine, Am. Coll. Physician Execs., Lucas County Acad. Medicine (bar acad. liaison com.), Ohio State Med. Assn. (fed. key contact), Med. Assn. Ga., Am. Asn. Neuropathologists (profl. affairs com., awards com., program com., constn. com.), Internat. Acad. Pathologists, Ohio Soc. Pathologists, EM Soc. Am., Sigma Xi. Republican. Avocations: tennis, real estate rehabilitation, building developer, gardening, white water rafting. Home and Office: 9105 Nesbit Lakes Dr Alpharetta GA 30022-4028

HARRIS, JAMES THOMAS, III, college administrator, educator; b. Findlay, Ohio, July 31, 1958; s. James Thomas II (dec.) and Carolyn Sue (Cairns) H.; m. Mary Catherine Kurdila, June 27, 1981; children: Zachary James, Braden Gerald. BE in Secondary Edn., U. Toledo, 1980; MEd in Ednl. Adminstrn., Edinboro U., 1983; D in Edn., Pa. State U., 1988; postgrad. Inst. Ednl. Mgmt., Harvard U., 1993. Pres. Defiance (Ohio) Coll., 1994—2002; pres., prof. Widener U., Chester, Pa., 2002—. Chmn. bd. dirs. Pa. Campus Compact; bd. dirs. NAICU, AICUP. Contbr. articles to profl. jours. Chair Vol. Connection of Defiance County, 1995-2002; vol. Leadership Defiance, Defiance, Ohio, chair, 1992-94; bd. dirs. Defiance County United Way, 1998-2001; vol. ARC, Cin., 1988-91; bd. trustees Ohio Found. of Indep. Colls., 1994-2002; exec. com. Ohio Campus Compact, 1998-2002. Recipient Excellence in Edn. award Pa. State U., 2000, Alumni Leadershiip and Svc. award Pa. State U., 1996, Disting. Alumni award U. Toledo, 1999, Cmty. Leadership award NAACP N.W. Ohio Chpt., 1999, Bud Williams Humanitarian award NAACP N.W. Ohio Chpt., 2003, CASE Stueben Apple award, 2004; named to Top 50 Coll. and Univ. Presidents Templeton Found, 1999; Alumni Fellow, Pa. State U., 2003. Mem. NAACP, Am. Assn. Higher Edn., Pa. Assn. of Indep. Colls. and Univs., Delaware County C. of C. (bd. dirs. 2003—), Rotary, Young President's Orgn., Alpha Kappa Delta, Pi Lambda Theta. Roman Catholic. Avocations: reading, blues music, walking. Office: Widener Univ 1 University Pl Chester PA 19013 Office Phone: 610-499-4100.

HARRIS, JAY TERRENCE, communications educator; b. Washington, Dec. 3, 1948; s. Richard James and Margaret Estelle (Burr) H.; m. Eliza Melinda Dowell, June 14, 1969 (div.); 1 child, Taifa Akida; m. Anna Christine Harris, Oct. 25, 1980; children: Jamarah Kai, Shala Marie. BA, Lincoln U., 1970, LHD (hon.), 1988. Reporter Wilmington (Del.) News-Jour., 1970-73, spl. project editor, 1974-75; instr. journalism and urban affairs Medill Sch. Journalism, Northwestern U., Evanston, Ill., 1973-75, asst. prof., 1975-82, asst. dean, 1977-82; nat. corr. Gannett News Service, Washington, 1982-84, columnist Gannet newspapers and USA Today, 1984-85; exec. editor Phila. Daily News, 1985—88; v.p. Phila. Newspapers, Inc., 1987—94; chmn., pub. San Jose Mercury News, 1995—2001; Annenberg prof. journalism & comm. Annenberg Sch. for Comm., USC, 2001—. Asst. dir. Frank E. Gannett Urban Journalism Ctr., Northwestern U., 1977-82; founder, exec. dir. Consortium for Advancement of Minorities in Journalism Edn., Evanston, 1978-81; dir. Dow Jones Newspaper Fund, Princeton, N.J., 1980—; bd. visitors John S. Knight Profl. Journalism Fellowships, Palo Alto, Calif., 1982—; head Minorities and Communication Div. Assn. for Edn. in Journalism, 1982-83; journalist in residence Notre Dame, 2002-03; bd. mem. Deep River Assocs., 2002—. Author: (annual census) Minority Employment in Daily Newspapers, 1978-82; co-author series articles on drug trafficking in Wilmington, 1972 (Pub. Service awards AP Mng. Editors Assn. 1972, Greater Phila. chpt. Sigma Delta Chi 1973) Past mem. bd. advisors Sch. Journalism U. Mo. Frank E. Gannett Urban Journalism fellow, 1973-74; recipient Pub. Service award Greater Phila. chpt. Sigma Delta Chi, 1973; Pub. Service award AP Mng. Editors Assn., 1972; Spl. Citation Nat. Urban Coalition, 1979; Par Excellence Disting. Service in Journalism award Operation PUSH, 1984; Drum Maj. for Justice award Southern Christian Leadership Conf., 1985; Robert C. Maynard Fellow, 2001—. Mem. Am. Soc. Newspaper Editors (chmn. readership and rsch. com.), Women in Communication, Nat. Assn. Black Journalists, Omega Psi Phi Office: San Jose Mercury News 750 Ridder Park Dr San Jose CA 95190-0001*

HARRIS, JEFFREY, lawyer; b. Bklyn., Mar. 20, 1944; s. Herman and Pearl (Herman) H.; m. Joyce Rosa Meckler, June 22, 1975; 1 child, Daniela Rose. BS, NYU, 1965; JD, Syracuse U., 1968. Bar: N.Y. 1969, U.S. Supreme Ct. 1976, D.C. 1977, Va., 1990. Asst. U.S. atty. So. Dist. N.Y., U.S. Dept. Justice, N.Y.C., 1972-76; chief investigation rev. unit. U.S. Dept. Justice, Washington, 1976-77; dep. chief counsel U.S. Ho. of Reps., Korean Investigation, Washington, 1977-79; asst. dir. FTC, Washington, 1979-81; exec. dir. Atty. Gen.'s Task Force on Violent Crime, U.S. Dept. Justice, Washington, 1981; dep. assoc. atty. gen. U.S., Washington, 1981-83; sr. v.p. Capital Bank N.A., Washington, 1983-85; sr. v.p., counsel Capital Bancorp, Miami, Fla., 1983-85; ptnr. Sachs, Greenebaum & Tayler, Washington, 1985-90, Rubin, Winston, Diercks, Harris & Cooke, LLP, Washington, 1990—. Instr. Advocacy Inst., U. Calif. Hastings Coll. Law, San Francisco, 1979-83; adj. asst. prof. George Washington U., Washington, 1980 Lt. (j.g.) USN, 1968-71. Named Meritorious Exec. Pres. of U.S.; recipient Spl. Commendation, Att. Gen. of U.S.; decorated Navy Commendation medal, Vietnam Cross of Gallantry. Mem. ABA Office: Rubin Winston Diercks Harris & Cooke LLP 6th Fl 1155 Connecticut Ave NW Washington DC 20036-4306 Office Phone: 202-861-0870. E-mail: jharris@rwdhc.com.

HARRIS, JEFFREY SAUL, physician, consultant, health facility administrator; b. Pitts., Mar. 13, 1949; s. Aaron Wexler and Janet Mary (Wexler) Harris; m. Mary V. Anderson, Jan. 2, 1981; children: Sarah Ariel, Noah Aaron, Susannah Leia. BS in Molecular Biophysics/Biochemistry, Yale U., 1971; MD, U. N.Mex., 1975; MPH, U. Mich., 1982; MBA, Vanderbilt U., 1988. Diplomate Am. Bd. Preventive Medicine in Occupl. Medicine and Gen. Preventive Medicine, Am. Bd. Emergency Medicine, Am. Bd. Medicine Quality, Am. Bd. Ind. Med. Exam. Gen. med. officer USPHS, Juneau, Alaska, 1976-78; clin. dir. S.E. Alaska Native Health Corp, Juneau, 1978-79; asst. to commr. Tenn. Dept. Health and Environ., Nashville, 1980-83; dir. health care mgmt. Northern Telecom Inc., Nashville, 1983-88; pres. HDM, Inc., Nashville, 1988-90; med. dir. Aetna Health Plans of Tenn., Nashville, 1990-91; nat. practice leader, health strategy Alexander & Alexander Cons. Group, San Francisco, 1991-94; chief prevention, health and disability officer Indsl. Indemnity, San Francisco, 1994-97; pres. J. Harris Assocs., Inc., Mill Valley, Calif., 1979—; CEO Med-Fx, Inc., 1999—2004; physician The Permanente Med. Group, San Rafael, Petaluma, Calif., 2000—. Author: Best Practices in Occupational Medicine, 2005—; author, co-editor Occupational Medicine Practice Guidelines: Evaluation and Management of Common Health Problems and Functional Recovery in Workers, 1997, 2004; author, co-editor: Integrated Health Management, 1998; author, editor Managed Care in Occupational Medicine, 1998, Quick Reference to Practice Guidelines in Occupational Medicine, 1999, author, co-editor Managing Employee Health Care Costs, 1992, Manual of Occupational Health and Safety, 1992, 1996, 2004—, Health Promotion in the Work Place, 1994, 2001, 2003; author: Strategic Health Management, 1994; mem. editl. bd. Am. Jour. Health Promotion, 1985—, Occupl. Environ. Med. Report, 1988—; contbg. editor: JAMA, Am. Jour. Public Health, Internat. Jour. Occupl. Environ. Health; contbr. articles to profl. jours., chapters to books. Fellow Am. Coll. Occupl. Environ. Medicine (dir., chmn. practice guidelines com. 1992-98, Presdl. award 1996, achievement award, 2004), Am. Coll. Preventive Medicine, Am. Coll. Med. Quality, Am. Bd. Ind. Med. Examiners. Avocations: skiing, running, playing music, painting, writing. Home: 386 Richardson Way Mill Valley CA 94941-4053 E-mail: jharrismvl@aol.com.

HARRIS, JEREMY, former mayor; b. Wilmington, Del., Dec. 7, 1950; s. Ann Harris; m. Ramona Sachiko Akui. BA, BS in Biology, U. Hawaii, 1972; MS in Population and Environ. Biology, U. Calif., Irvine, 1973. Lectr. oceanography, biology Kauai C.C.; marine advisor Sea Grant Program, U. Hawaii; del. Hawaii Constl. Conv., 1978; chmn. Kauai County Council, 1979—81; exec. asst. to mayor City and County of Honolulu, 1984—86, dep. mng. dir. of Honolulu, 1986-94, mng. dir., 1986—94, acting mayor, 1994, mayor, 1994—2004. Founder, chair Mayors' Asia-Pacific Environ. Summit, 1999; established Pacific Islands Environmental Symposium, China-US Conf. of Mayors and Bus. Leaders, Asia-Pacific Urban Tech. Inst. Am.-Nat. chair Japan-Am. Conf. of Mayors and C. of C. Presidents, 1996—. Mem.: Am. Planning Assn. (Disting. Leadership award 2002), Internat. Downtown Assn. (Merit award), Am. Soc. Pub. Adminstrn. (Pub. Adminstr. of Yr. 1993, 1994), Am. Inst. Archs. (hon.). Office: Office Mayor Honolulu Hale 530 S King St Honolulu HI 96813

HARRIS, JOE FRANK, former governor; b. Cartersville, Ga., Feb. 16, 1936; s. Grover Franklin and Frances (Morrow) H.; m. Elizabeth Carlock Harris, June 25, 1961; 1 son. Joe Frank, Jr. BBA, U. Ga., 1958; LLD (hon.), Woodrow Wilson Coll. Law, 1981, Asbury Coll., 1983, Morris Brown Coll., 1983, LaGrange Coll., 1987, Mercer U., 1987. Sec.-treas. Harris Cement Products, Inc., Cartersville, 1958-79; pres. Harris Georgia Corp., Cartersville, 1979-83; mem. Ga. Gen. Assembly, 1965-83; gov. State of Ga., 1983-91; prof., Disting. Exec. fellow Ga. State U., Atlanta, 1993—. Bd. regents Univ. Sys. Ga., 1999—. Served with U.S. Army, 1958. Democrat. Methodist.

HARRIS, JOEL B. (JOEL BRUCE HARRIS), lawyer; b. N.Y.C., Oct. 15, 1941; s. Raymond S. and Laura (Greene) H.; m. Barbara J. Rous, June 13, 1965 (div.); 1 child, Clifford S.; m. Deborah Sherman, Apr. 1, 1986 (div.); children: Sydney Anne, Cassidy Raye; m. Marcia E. Haddad, Aug. 18, 1999. AB, Columbia U., 1963; LLB, Harvard U., 1966; LLM, U. London, 1967. Bar: N.Y. 1968, U.S. Dist. Ct. (so. dist.) N.Y. 1970, U.S. Ct. Appeals (2d cir.) 1970, U.S. Dist. Ct. (ea. dist.) N.Y. 1975, U.S. Supreme Ct. 1976, U.S. Ct. Appeals (3d cir.) 1980, U.S. Dist. Ct. (we. dist.) N.Y. 1981. Assoc. Simpson, Thacher & Bartlett, N.Y.C., 1967-70; asst. U.S. atty. So. Dist. N.Y., 1970-74, chief civil rights unit, 1973-74; assoc. Weil, Gotshal & Manges, N.Y.C., 1974-76, ptnr., 1976-86, Thacher, Proffitt & Wood, N.Y.C., 1986—; chmn. litigation dept., Latin Am. practice group. Speaker, panelist, moderator confs. Contbr. articles to profl. jours. Knox Meml. fellow, 1966-67. Fellow Am. Bar Found.; mem. ABA (chmn. com. internat. litigation 1981-84, chmn. com. personal rights litigation 1984-87), N.Y. State Bar Assn. (mem. internat. law and practice sect., sect. chair 1997-98, mem. exec. com. 1990—, chmn. internat. dispute resolution com. 1990-93, chmn. seasonal meeting 1993, 2001), Assn. Bar City N.Y., Inter-Am. Bar Assn., N.Y. County Lawyers Assn. (bd. dirs. 2004-, treas. 2005-, mem. exec. com. 2005-), Fed. Bar Coun., Am. Soc. Internat. Law, Internat. Law Assn., Am. Judicature Soc. Home: 40 Prince St New York NY 10012-3426 Office: Thacher Proffitt & Wood Two World Fin Ctr New York NY 10281 Office Phone: 212-912-7785. Business E-Mail: jharris@tpw.com.

HARRIS, JOHN, chef; b. Chgo. With Cafe Allegro, Pitts., Spiaggia, Chgo.; sous chef Bayona Restaurant, New Orleans, 1994; apprentice Amphyclese, France, Le Pre Catalin, France; exec. chef Gautreau's Restaurant; with Gerard's Downtown; owner, chef Lilette, New Orleans, 2000—. Named Chef of Yr., New Orleans Mag., 2001; named one of Am.'s Top Ten Best New Chefs, Food and Wine, 2002, Top Ten Restaurants in New Orleans, Times Picayung, 2004; named to The Next Generation of Chefs, Bon Appetit, 2000; recipient Four Beans, S.M. Hahn, Times Picayune. Office: 3637 Magazine St New Orleans LA 70115 Office Phone: 504-895-1636. E-mail: liletterestaurant@yahoo.com.

HARRIS, JOHN EDWARD, lawyer; b. Mpls., Nov. 16, 1936; s. John Law and Harriet Comilla (Hunt) H.; m. Ruth Wilder Esty, Aug. 26, 1958; children— Jeffery Langdon, Stowe John Wilder, Benjamin Wood BA summa cum laude, Lawrence Coll., 1959; JD, Harvard U., 1962. Bar: Minn. 1962, U.S. Dist. Ct. Minn. 1962, U.S. Tax Ct. 1963. Assoc. Faegre & Benson, Mpls., 1962-69, ptnr., 1970-2000, head, trusts, estates and found. group, 1974-97. Trustee Ucross Found., Wyo., 1981-93, 97— Contbr. articles to Notre Dame Planning Inst., 1976, 78 Bd. dirs. Meth. Health Care Minn., 1986-93; chmn. Meth. Hosp., St. Louis Park, Minn., 1979-81, bd. dirs., 1993-94; pres. West Met. Hosp. trustee Coun., Mpls., 1980-81; chmn. Minn. Coun. on Founds., Mpls., 1985-88; bd. dirs. Twin Cities RISE!, 1995—. Mem. ABA (chmn. com. on charitable trusts, real property and trust law sect. 1973-77, exempt orgns. com., tax section 1991—), Minn. Bar Assn. (chmn. probate and trust law sect. 1979-80, mem. study com. Minn. Nonprofit Corps. 1986-91, mem. nonprofit corps. com. 1998—), Phi Beta Kappa Home: 713 Coventry Ln Minneapolis MN 55435-5653 Office: Faegre & Benson 2200 Wells Fargo Ctr 90 S 7th St Ste 2200 Minneapolis MN 55402-3901 E-mail: jharris@faegre.com, jharris331@excite.com.

HARRIS, JOHN W., real estate company executive; BA, U. N.C.; postgrad., Am. U. Lic. real estate broker N.C., S.C., Tenn., Ga., Va. Bldg. mgr. The Bissell Cos., Inc., v.p., pres., Lincoln Harris, LLC (formerly The Harris Group), Charlotte, NC, 1992—. Dir. emeritus USAir, Inc.; bd. dirs. Dominion Resource, Inc., Richmond, Va., Piedmont Natural Gas. Mayoral appointee Airport Adv. Com.; past chmn. bd. trustees U. N.C., Chapel Hill; past chmn. Charlotte organizing com. NCAA Final Four; active Charlotte Regional Partnership; dir. Charlotte-Mecklenburg Hosp. Authority. Recipient Man of Yr. award, Charlotte News, 1984, Cornerstone award, Charlotte Region Comml. Bd. Realtors, 1994. Mem.: Charlotte C. of C. (chmn. 1990), Urban Land Inst., Charlotte Regional Comml. Bd. Realtors, Nat. Collegiate Athletic Found. Office: Lincoln Harris 100 N Tryon St Charlotte NC 28202

HARRIS, JOSEPH MCALLISTER, retired chemist; b. Pontiac, Ill., July 27, 1929; s. Fred Gilbert and Catherine Marguerite (McAllister) H.; m. Margot Jeanette L'Hommedieu, Feb. 17, 1952; children: Timothy, Kaye, Paula, Bruce, Anne, Martha, Rebecca. BA, Blackburn Coll., Carlinville, Ill., 1952; postgrad., So. Ill. U., 1953-54, U. Ill., 1956-61. Technician Olin Ind., Inc., Energy, Ill., 1953-54; quality control staff Union Starch and Refining Co., Granite City, Ill., 1954; rsch. asst. Ill. State Geol. Survey, Urbana, 1954-61; chemist II Water Pollution Control Bd., Annapolis, Md., 1961-63; phys. chemist Ball Bros. Rsch., Inc., Muncie, Ind., 1963-66; engr. Radio Corp. Am., Marion, Ind., 1966-70; chemist OA Labs., Inc., Indpls., 1973-86, OA Labs. & Rsch., Inc., Indpls., 1986-93, cons., 1993—. Bd. dirs. Tri-County Hearing Assn. for Children, Muncie, 1967-70. Mem. Am. Chem. Soc., AAAS, Soc. Applied Spectroscopy. Republican. Presbyterian. Avocations: gardening, camping. Home: 800 E Washington St Muncie IN 47305-2533 Personal E-mail: berrijoe@aol.com.

HARRIS, JUDITH ANN WHITE, occupational health nurse, educator; b. Springfield, Ohio, Mar. 6, 1939; d. Willis and Tennessee Belle (Poole) Martin; m. Allen G. Harris, Mar. 21, 1986; 1 child by previous marriage, Denise Marian Womble. Student, U. South Fla., 1978-85, BS/MS in Psychology, 2000. RN, Fla.; cert. tchr., Fla. Nurse Dr. Robert Tapogna, Springfield, Ohio, 1960-62, Springfield City Hosp., 1962-65, Dr. Robert Beam, Springfield, 1965-75; ednl. coord., instr. med. assisting Sarasota Vocat. Ctr., Fla., 1977-82, instr. med. assisting program, chmn. dept., 1982-84, 89-91, instr. health svc.

occupations, placement coord. health occu, 1985-88; dept. chmn. Allied Health, 1989-95. Bd. dirs. Fla. Bd. Inc.; pres. J.W. Harris Pub. Co.; cruise ship lectr. for Princess, Royal Caribbean and Celebrity Cruise Lines; v.p., sec. Al Harris Pest Control, Inc. 1996-; dir. adv. & mktg., 2000-. Author: J.W. Harris Medical Assisting Review Manual, 1995, Templin, 2002; contbr. articles to profl. jours. Vol. Children's Breath Clinic, Sarasota, 1977-79, Kidney Found., Sarasota, 1982, ARC, Sarasota, 1976-88; dir. Spl. Care Unit, 1984-88; v.p. Sons of Norway, 1993-95; choir soloist Beneva Christian Ch., 1989—, deaconess, 1993-96, elder 1997—, chmn. Health Care Svcs. Dept., 1996—, vice chmn. bd. dirs., 2001-02, chmn. bd., 2002—; asst. state dir. Fla. Good Sons, 1993-94; bd. dirs. Fla. Bd. Camping Assn., Inc., sec., 1999--, newsletter editor, 1996—; chmn. FVA Leadership Forum, 1992—; parish nurse and chmn. health svcs. dept. Beneva Christian Ch., 1995—; pres. FVA Post Pres.'s Club, 1999—; 1st v.p. Sarasota Bay Republican Women's Club Federated, 1998-2001; mem. Sarasota Tiger Bay Club, 1999—, Sarasota Homebuilders Assn., 1999—; sec. Acorn Glass Bowling League, 2000—. Named Outstanding Vocat. Tchr. Sarasota County Sch. Bd., 1985, Woman of Impact for Edn., Sarasota County Commn. on the Status of Women, 1995. Mem. Am. Vocat. Assn. (Outstanding Vocat. Tchr. region II 1985, Vocat. Tchr. Yr. 1987), Health Occupations Educators (vice chmn. policy com. 1985-86), Nat. Assn. Health Occupations Tchrs. (v.p. region II 1984-86, pres. elect 1988, pres. 1989-91), Fla. Vocat. Assn. (bd. dirs. 1983-85, pres. 1987-88, Pres. award 1984, Outstanding Vocat. Educator region 23 award 1982, Sarasota Mayors award 1984, Gov.'s Proclamation for Outstanding Tchg. 1987, chmn. leadership forum 1993—), Health Occupations Educators Assn. Fla. (pres. 1983-84, chmn. legis. com. 1985-93, Outstanding Tchr. 1983), Sarasota County Vocat. and Adult Edn. Assn. (pres. 1978-80, editor newsletter 1978-83), Am. Assn. Med. Assts., Good Sams Inc. Fla. (asst. state dir. dist. 12 1993-95), Fraternal Order of Eagles Aux. (dist. 3 auditor 1995-96, eagle nurse 1995-97, chair health care dept. 1995—, condr. 1996—), Sarasota Bay Republican Women's Club (life; v.p. 1998—), Women's Coun. Realtors (ways and means chair 2002-, corr. sec. 2003, rec. sec. 2004), Sarasota Assn. Realtors, Sunrise Rotary Club (Paul Harris fellow, 2002-, Rotary Internat. Sustaining Mem. 2002-), Tiger Bay Club, Delta Kappa Gamma, Phi Kappa Phi. Avocations: swimming, camping, knitting, sewing, biking. Home: PO Box 7278 Sarasota FL 34278 Office: 6100 Palmer Blvd Sarasota FL 34232 E-mail: alharrispestcontrol@netzero.net.

HARRIS, JUDITH E., lawyer; b. Apr. 28, 1945; AB, Mount Holyoke Coll., 1967; JD, Howard U., 1970. Bar: Pa. 1971. City solicitor City of Phila., 1992-93; ptnr. Morgan, Lewis & Bockius LLP, Phila. Office: Morgan Lewis & Bockius LLP 1701 Market St Philadelphia PA 19103-2903 Office Phone: 215-963-5028. Business E-Mail: jeharris@morganlewis.com.

HARRIS, JULIE (JULIE ANN HARRIS), actress; b. Grosse Pointe Park, Mich., Dec. 2, 1925; d. William Pickett and Elsie (Smith) H.; m. Jay I. Julien, Aug. 12, 1946 (div. 1954); m. Manning Gurian, Oct. 21, 1954 (div. 1967); 1 child, Peter; m. Erwin Carroll, Apr. 1977, (div. 1982). Student, Perry Mansfield Theatre Work Shop, 1941-43, Yale Drama Sch., 1944-45. Theater debut in It's a Gift, N.Y.C., 1945; appeared in plays Playboy of the Western World, 1946, Oedipus, 1946, Henry IV-Part II, 1946, Alice in Wonderland, 1947, We Love A Lassie, 1947, Macbeth, 1948, Sundown Beach, 1948 (Theatre World award 1949), The Young and Fair, 1948-49, Magnolia Alley, 1949, Montserrat, 1949, The Member of the Wedding, 1950-51 (Donaldson award 1950), I Am a Camera, 1951-52 (Tony award 1952, Donaldson award 1952, Variety-N.Y. Drama Critics Poll 1952), Mademoiselle Colombe, 1954, The Lark, 1955 (Tony award 1956), The Country Wife, 1957, The Warm Peninsula, 1959, Little Moon of Alban, 1960, Romeo and Juliet, 1960, King John, 1960, A Shot in the Dark, 1961, Marathon 33, 1964 (Tony nomination 1964), Hamlet, 1964, Ready When You Are, C.B, 1964, The Hostage, 1965, Skyscraper, 1965 (Tony nomination 1969), A Streetcar Named Desire, 1967, Forty Carats, 1968 (Tony award 1969), The Women, 1970, And Miss Reardon Drinks A Little, 1971-72, Voices, 1972, The Last of Mrs. Lincoln, 1972 (Tony award 1973), The Au Pair Man, 1973 (Tony nomination 1974), In Praise of Love, 1974, Break a Leg, 1979, On Golden Pond, 1980, Mixed Couples, 1980, Under the Ilex, 1983, Tusitala, 1988, (nat. co.) Driving Miss Daisy, Love Letters, 1989, The Belle of Amherst, 1977 (Grammy award 1977, Tony award 1977), Currier Bell, Glass Menagerie, 1994, Ellen Foster, 1997, Love is Strange, 1999, Fossils, 2001; one-woman theater presentations include Lucifer's Child, 1991; film debut in The Member of the Wedding, 1952 (Acad. award nomination); other films include The East of Eden, 1955, I Am A Camera, 1955, The Truth About Women, 1958, Poacher's Daughter, 1960, Requiem for a Heavyweight, 1962, The Haunting, 1963, The Moving Target, 1966, You're a Big Boy Now, 1966, Reflections in a Golden Eye, 1967, The Split, 1968, Journey into Midnight, 1968, The People Next Door, 1970, The Hiding Place, 1975, Voyage of the Damned, 1976, The Bell Jar, 1979, The Prostitute, 1980, The Nutcracker: The Motion Picture, 1986, Gorillas in the Mist, 1988, Housesitter, 1992, The Dark Half, 1993, Little Surprises, 1995, Carried Away, 1996; TV series include Thicker Than Water, 1973, The Family Holvak, 1975, Knots Landing, 1979-87; TV movies include Wind From the South, 1955, The Good Fairy, 1956, The Lark, 1957, Johnny Belinda, 1968, Little Moon of Alban, 1958 (Emmy award 1959), A Doll's House, 1959, Victoria Regina, 1961 (Emmy award 1962), The Power and the Glory, 1961, Pygmalian, 1964, Hamlet, 1964, The Holy Terror, 1965, Anastasia, 1967, The House on Green Apple Road, 1970, How Awful About Alan, 1970, Home for the Holidays, 1972, The Greatest Gift, 1974, Backstairs at the White House, 1979, The Gift, 1979, The Christmas Wife, 1979, Too Good To Be True, 1988, Single Women, Married Men, 1989, They've Taken Our Children: The Chowchilla Kidnapping Story, 1993, When Love Kills: The Seduction of John Nearn, 1993, One Christmas, 1994, Scarlett, 1994, The Christmas Tree, 1996, James Dean: A Portrait, 1996, Carried Away, 1996, Bad Manners, 1997, Ellen Foster, 1997, The First of May, 1998, (voice) Frank Lloyd Wright, 1998; author: (with Barry Tarshis) Julie Harris Talks to Young Actors, 1971. Recipient Antoinette Perry award for best actress in Forty Carats, 1969, The Last of Mrs. Lincoln, 1973; Nat. Medal of the Arts, 1994, Tony award for lifetime achievement in Theater, 2002, Drama Desk Career Achievement award for commitment to excellence in theatre, 2005. Office: William Morris Agy c/o Samuel Liff 1325 Avenue of the Americas New York NY 10019*

HARRIS, K. DAVID, senior state supreme court justice; b. Jefferson, Iowa, July 29, 1927; s. Orville William and Jessie Heloise (Smart) H.; m. Madonna Theresa Coyne, Sept. 4, 1948; children: Jane, Julia, Frederick. BA, U. Iowa, 1949, JD, 1951. Bar: Iowa 1951, U.S. Dist. Ct (so. dist.) Iowa, 1958. Sole practice Harris & Harris, Jefferson, 1951-62; dist. judge 16th Judicial Dist., Iowa, 1962-72; justice Iowa Supreme Ct., Des Moines, 1972-99, sr. justice, 1999—; ret., 2005. Served with U.S. Army, 1944-46, PTO. Mem. VFW, Am. Legion, Rotary. Roman Catholic. Avocation: poetry. Office: Iowa Supreme Ct State Capitol Bldg Des Moines IA 50319-0001 Office Phone: 515-386-4321.

HARRIS, KATHERINE, congresswoman; b. Key West, Fla., Apr. 5, 1957; m. Anders Ebbeson. Student, U. Madrid, 1978; BA in History, Agnes Scott Coll., 1979; MPA in Internat. Trade, Harvard U., 1996. Senator 24th dist. Fla. State Legislature, 1994—98; sec. of state State of Fla., 1999—2002; mem. U.S. Ho. of Reps from 13th Fla. dist., 2003—. Vice chmn. banking and ins. com. Fla. State Senate, vice chmn. govtl. reform and oversight com., chmn. commerce and econ. opportunities com. Congl. intern U.S. Senate and U.S. Ho. of Reps., 1978; vice chmn. Sarasota County Legis. Del.; mem. Supreme Ct. Gender Bias Commn.; vice chmn. Fla. Am. Legis. Exch. Coun.; mem. arts and tourism com. Nat. Conf. State Legislators; former mem. adv. coun. Mote Marine Lab., Women's Resource Ctr., Sarasota County Arts Coun.; mem. Leadership Sarasota, Leadership Tampa; former vice chmn. bd. trustees Ringling Mus.; mem. nominating com. Pub. Svc. Commn.; active Habitat for Humanity, New Coll., Fla. Rep. Exec. Com. Recipient Disting. Leadership Alumni award, Leadership Sarasota, 1994, Arts Advocacy award, Sarasota County Arts Coun., 1995, Best Govt. Ofcl. award, Sarasota Mag., 1995—2002, Legislator of Yr. award, Sarasota Opera, 1996, Ind. Funeral Dirs. of Fla., 1996, Fla. Optometric Assn., 1996, Legis. Appreciation award, Dept. Labor and Employment Security, 1996. Mem. Sarasota C. of C. (Disting. Leadership Alumni award 1994), Englewood C. of C., Charlotte C. of C., Venice C. of C., Jaycees. Republican. Presbyterian. Avocations: reading, sailing, painting, skiing, skeet shooting. Office: 116 Cannon Ho Office Bldg Washington DC 20515-0913

HARRIS, KATHERINE SAFFORD, speech and hearing educator; b. Lowell, Mass., Sept. 3, 1925; d. Truman Henry and Katherine (Wardwell) Safford; m. George Harris, Oct. 2, 1952; children: Maud White, Louise. BA, Radcliffe Coll., 1947; PhD, Harvard U., 1954. Rsch. assoc. Haskins Labs., New Haven, 1952-85, v.p., 1985—; prof. CUNY, N.Y.C., 1970—, disting. prof., 1982—. Active U.S./Israeli Speech Program Littauer Found., N.Y.C., 1986. Author: (with Borden and Raphael) Speech Science Primer, 1970, 4th edit., 2002, (with Baer and Sasaki) Phonatory Control, 1986. Active U.S./Israeli Speech Program Littauer Found., N.Y.C., 1986. Nat. Inst. Deafness and Other Comm. Disorders grantee. Fellow AAAS, Acoustical Soc. Am. (pres. 2000-01), Am. Speech Hearing Assn., N.Y. Acad. Scis. Office: CUNY Grad Sch 415 5th Ave New York NY 10016 E-mail: loumau2003@yahoo.com.

HARRIS, KATHLEEN RENEE, marketing professional; b. LA, Nov. 30, 1954; d. William Rogiere Harris and IdaBelle (Norman) Rivers. AA in Data Processing, Chabot Coll., 1980; BS in Bus. Mgmt., U. Phoenix, 2001. Gen. clk. sec. Western Girl Temp. Agy., San Leandro, Calif., 1973-75; mag card II operator Bechtel Inc., San Francisco, 1975-76, data entry operator, 1976-79, office asst., 1979-80; adminstrv. asst. II Bechtel Power Corp., Walnut Creek, Calif., 1980-82; computer programmer I Bechtel Corp., San Francisco, 1982-86; ind. programmer/analyst, 1987—; project mgr. Clorox Co., 1998-99, info. systems super., 1999—. Database analyst Wollborg-Michelson; sys. support analyst Kraft Foods, 1990-92; LAN adminstr. So. Pacific Lines, 1992-93; sr. help desk specialist Triad Sys/Geoworks/Concord Gen., 1994-95; PC support tech. EDS/Blue Shield, 1995-96; LAN support mgr., Pacific Bell, 1996-97; project coord. Charles Schwab, 1997-98; project mgr., Clorox Co., 1998-99, info. tech. mgr. Clorox Svcs. Co., 1999-03; regional dir. First Class Benefits, Inc., 2003-; designer, seamstress, owner Feline Fit, Etc., Calif.; co-owner Next Generation Model Mgmt. Co., 1984. Mem. Better Bus. Bur. Avocation: licensed private pilot. Home: 894 Shelborne Dr Tracy CA 95377-8228 Office Phone: 209-304-3278.

HARRIS, KEVIN L., art educator, artist; b. Louisville, Feb. 25, 1961; s. Richard H. and Consuelo W. Harris; m. P.D. Edwards-Harris, Sept. 7, 1994. BA, Hampton Inst., 1983; MFA, U. Cin., 1988. Lectr. No. Ky. U., Highland Heights, Ky., 1989—95; asst. prof. Lincoln U., Pa., 1995—2000; assoc. prof. Sinclair C.C., Dayton, Ohio, 2004—, asst. prof., 2000—05. One-man shows include NET, Washington, 2000, Dadian Gallery, Cin., 2002, Upstairs at the Greenwich, Dayton, 2003, Riverbend Arts Ctr., 2003. Recipient Candle of Creativity award, Dayton Found., 2002. Avocations: chess, martial arts, gardening, astronomy. Home: 3121 Patrick Ct Franklin OH 45005 Office: Sinclair C C 444 W 3d St Dayton OH 45402 Business E-Mail: kevin.harris@sinclair.edu.

HARRIS, KIM A., elementary school educator; b. Ada, Okla., Aug. 9, 1965; d. Mary Magdalene and Glen Stanley Fulton; m. Kevin L. Harris, Apr. 16, 1991. BS, East Ctrl. U., 1983—87, EdB, 1991—92, MS, 1989—90, Med, 1993—96. Cert. Nat. Bd. Cert. Tchr. (Early Adolescent English Language Arts). Tchr. Ada City Schools, Ada, Okla., 2000—, Roff Pub. Schools, Roff, Okla., 1992—2000. Mem. NEA, 2001—, Okla. Edn. Assn., 2001—, Ada Edn. Assn., 2001—. Author: (educational book review) Writing Through Childhood: Rethinking Process and Product. Office: Ada Junior High School 223 W 18th St Ada OK 74820 Office Phone: 580-310-7260.

HARRIS, LANI M., theater educator; b. LA, June 8, 1951; d. Charles Edward and Lucy Rosetta McDonald; m. Thomas Lee Langkau, Sept. 30, 1980; children: Aeryn Paige Howard, Joseph Thomas Travis Langkau. AA, Coll. of the Redwoods, 1972; BA, Humboldt State U., 1976; MFA, U. So. Calif., L.A., 1980. Instr. Shasta Coll., Redding, Calif., 1983—90; lectr. Calif. State U., Chico, 1990—93, guest artist lectr. Bakersfield, 1993; asst. prof. U. Ala., Tuscaloosa, 1994—97; assoc. prof. U. Ctrl. Fla., Orlando, 1997—. Artistic dir. RCT Theatre, Redding, 1983—91. Contbr. chapters to books Stage Directions Guide to Auditions, 1998, 50 Great Directors of the Twentieth Century, 2003; prodr.: Air Born, 1995. V.p. Shasta County Arts Coun., Redding, 1986—91; chair coll. univ. divsn. Southeastern Theatre Conf., Greensboro, NC, 2001—04; bd. dirs. ACLU, Orlando, 1999—2002. Recipient Women's Rsch. award, U. Ctrl. Fla., 2005; grantee, Fulbright-Hays Grant Program, 2003; Sr. fellow, U. Ctrl. Fla. Mem.: Kennedy Ctr. Am. Coll. Theatre Festival (dir. of plays 1991—). Avocations: horseback riding, constitutional law. Office: U Ctrl Fla PO Box 162372 Orlando FL 32816-2372 E-mail: lharris@mail.ucf.edu.

HARRIS, LARRY B., academic administrator, dean; b. Kingman, Kans., May 25, 1947; s. Loren M. and Beatrice A. (Reinoldt) H.; m. Carmen E. Glidewell, June 15, 1968; children: Todd J., Ryan M., Kelly R., Kyle D. BA, Friends U., 1969; MEd, Wichita State U., 1977; PhD, Kans. State U., 1985. English/reading tchr. Wichita Pub. Schs., 1970-77, Haven (Kans.) Pub. Schs., 1977-78; instr. Wichita State U., 1978-83; asst. prof. Mount Marty Coll., Yankton, S.D., 1985-87; assoc. prof., prof., divsn. head Wayne (Nebr.) State Coll., 1987-93; dean Sch. Edn. U. Ark., Monticello, 1993-97; dean Coll. Edn. Idaho State U., Pocatello, 1997—. Active Boy Scouts Am., Yankton, 1987. Mem. Phi Delta Kappa (pres. 1992-93), Kappa Delta Pi, Phi Kappa Phi. Avocations: fishing, reading, travel, gardening. Home: 140 N 19th Ave Pocatello ID 83201-3311 Office: Idaho State Univ PO Box 8059 Pocatello ID 83209-0001 Office Phone: 208-282-3259. Fax: 208-235-4697. E-mail: harris@isu.edu.

HARRIS, LESTER EARLE, JR., biology professor; b. Washington, June 4, 1922; s. Lester Earle and Irene Malvina Harris; m. Marjorie Louise Schultz, Sept. 8, 1946; children: Lester III, Deborah, Charlie, Julia. BA, Columbia Union Coll., Takoma Park, Md., 1949; D of Pedagogy (hon.), Columbia Union Coll., 1970; MS, U. Md., 1951; postgrad., Cornell U., 1952—54. Grad. asst. instr. Columbia Union Coll., 1949—50, 1951—52, asst. prof., 1952—56, assoc. prof., 1956—60, prof., 1960—73; chmn. sci. dept. Middlesex H.S., 1973—76, 1980—81; prof. Loma Linda U., 1976—79, 1981—87, contract tchr., 1989, Riverside C.C., 1989—96, La Sierra U., 1990—97. Founder, educator biol. sta. Columbia Union Coll., Headwaters, Va., 1956—73, Loma Linda U., Galapagos, Ecuador, 1968—87; co-founder, bd. dirs. Ea. Seabord Herpetologists League, 1972—82; bd. dirs. Va. Herpetologists Soc., 1974—82, Jurupa Mt. Cultural Ctr., 1985—87, chmn. bd. dirs., 1986—87. Author: Galapagos, 1975, also Dutch and Swedish edits., The Frog-Eating Electric Light Bug, 1978; assoc. editor Outdoor World mag., 1968—71, editl. asst. Herpetol. Natural History, 1994—. Cpl. combat medics U.S. Army, 1942—46. Decorated Asiatic Pacific Campaign award with 2 stars, G.C. medal; named Tchr. of Yr., Columbia Union Coll., 1955, 1970, Riverside C.C., 1996. Mem.: N.Y. Acad. Sci., Md. Acad. Sci., Phi Delta Kappa. Republican. Seventh Day Adventist. Avocations: writing, raising cactuses and rare plants. Home: PO Box 1077 985 Virginia St Urbanna VA 23175

HARRIS, LIONEL, writer, educator; b. Cin., Jan. 25, 1967; s. Simmie and Louise Harris; children: Gabrielle, Launa, Eric, Ashley. A of Sociology, Shawne State C.C., Portsmouth, Ohio, 1993; BBA, Columbus State CC, 2003. Welding engr. Trinity Industries, Cin., 1985—91; CFO The Economics Club, Lebanon, Ohio, 1993—96, CEO, 1996—. Cons. Laubach Literacy Found., Lebanon, 1994—95. Author: Young In the Game, 2004 (Best New Author, 2004); contributing author: Chicken Soup for the Soul; author: Founder Lebanon Literacy Program, 1993; sec. Seventh Step Orgn., Lebanon, 1996; facilitator Madison Literacy Program, London, Ohio, 2001. Mem.: United Chess Fedn., Greater Cin. Christian Writers Fellowship, Cin. Writers Project (advisor 1996—99). Democrat. Achievements include chess Grandmaster ranking 2004; Runner-up in Mr. Cincinnati bodybuilding contest 1985; Four-time winner of Madison Chess Tournament; Adams Charlie Chess Tournament Champion 2001-2004. Avocation: chess. Home: PO Box 740-252066 London OH 43140

HARRIS, MARCELITE JORDAN, retired career officer; b. Houston, Jan. 16, 1943; d. Cecil Oneal and Marcelite Elizabeth (Terrell) Jordan; m. Maurice Anthony Harris, Nov. 29, 1980 (dec. Jan. 1996); children: Steven Eric, Tenecia Marcelite. BA, Spelman Coll., 1964; postgrad., Ctrl. Mich. U., 1973-75, crwa. State U., 1975-76, Chapman Coll., 1979-80; BS, U. Md., Okinawa, Japan, 1986. Tchr. Head Start, Houston, 1964-65; commd. 2d lt. USAF, 1965, advanced through grades to maj. gen., 1965-97; student Squadron officers Sch., 1975; with Hdqrs. USAF, Pentagon, 1975; comdr. 39 Cadet Squadron, USAF Acad., Colorado Springs, Colo., 1978, Air Refueling Wing, McConnell AFB, Kans., 1980, Avionics Maintenance Squadron, McConnell AFB, 1981, Field Maintenance Squadron, McConnell AFB, 1982; dir. maintenance Pacific Air Forces Logistics Support Ctr., Kadena Air Base, Japan, 1982; student Air War Coll., 1983; dep. chief maintenance Tech. Tng. Ctr., Keesler AFB, Miss., 1986, wing comdr., 1988; student Harvard U.Sr. Officers Course, 1988, Capstone Flag and Gen. Officers Course, 1990; vice comdr. Oklahoma City Air Logistics Ctr., Tinker AFB, 1990-97; dir. tech. tng. USAF, Randolph AFB, Tex., 1993-97, dir. of maintenance, 1994, ret., 1997. Cabinet mem. United Way, Oklahoma City, 1991; mem. adv. bd. Salvation Army, Oklahoma City, 1991—; bd. dirs. U.S. Automobile Assn., 1993—, 5 Who Care, 1992, Urban League. Decorated Bronze star, D.S.M.; named one of Top 100 Afro-Am. Bus. and Profl. Women, Dollars and $ense Mag., 1989, named Most Prestigious Individual, 1991, One of Top 100 Most Influencial People, City News, N.J., 1997; recipient Ellis Island Medal of Honor award, 1996, Living Legacy award 1998. Mem. AAUW, Air Force Assn. (life), Tuskegee Airmen Inc. (life), Maintenance Officer Assn., Retired Officer Assn., Ret. Officer Assn., Delta Sigma Theta. *Life is a miracle, but you have to give it meaning, shape and value. Choose what you can contribute to make society better. My sister and I got our strength from our parents. We learned to keep trying until we succeeded. That's perseverance.*

HARRIS, MARIAN S., social work educator; b. Tallahassee; d. Leo and Ida Mae Hoskin; 1 child, Trina S. Madison. BA, Fla. A&M U., 1964; MSW, Fla. State U., 1977; PhD, Smith Coll., 1997. Cert. social worker, diplomate in clin. social work, lic. ind. clin. social worker Wash., lic. clin. social worker Ill. Program dir. Ctrl. Bapt. Family Svcs., Chgo., 1990—93; postdoctoral fellow U. Wis.-Madison, 1997—99; rsch. adv. Smith Coll. Sch. for Social Work, Northampton, Mass., 1996—, adj. asst. prof., 1997—; asst. prof. U. Ill., Chgo., 1999—2002; faculty assoc. Chapin Hall Ctr. for Children U., Chgo., 2002—; asst. prof. U. Wash., Tacoma, 2002—; pvt. practice Tacoma, 2004—. Cons. reviewer U.S. Children's Bur., Washington, 2002—; expert witness O'Callaghan & Colleagues, PC, Chgo., 2002—05; cons. FAST Program, Madison, 2003; commr. Coun. Social Work Edn., Alexandria, Va., 1999—2005; pvt. practice social work, 2004—. Cons. editor: AFFILIA Jour. Women and Social Work, 2003—08. Chair Children's Alliance Pub. Policy Coun., Seattle, 2005—; bd. dirs. Children's Alliance, Seattle, 2005—. Recipient SAMHSA Clin. Tng. award, Coun. Social Work Edn., 1994—97, Social Work Educator of Yr., Wash. State Chpt., Nat. Assn. Social Workers, 2004; postdoctoral fellow, NIMH, 1997—99, Founder's Endowment grantee, U. Wash., 2003. Mem.: Pub. Policy Coun., Soc. Social Work and Rsch., Coun. Social Work Edn. (commn. role and status of women 1994—2005), Children's Home Soc. West Ctrl. Region, Alpha Kappa Alpha. Democrat. Roman Catholic. Avocations: tennis, swimming, jogging, travel, music. Office: U Wash 1900 Commerce St Tacoma WA 98402-3100 also: 2412 N 30th St Ste 102 Tacoma WA 98407 Business E-Mail: mh24@u.washington.edu.

HARRIS, MARILYN JUNE, music educator; d. Barbara Harris Polome and Donald Penn Harris. MusB, Mannes Coll. of Music, N.Y.C., 1986; MusM, SUNY, Stony Brook, 1988; D of Mus. Arts, U. So. Calif., 1992. Profl. musician Harris Enterprises, South Pasadena, Calif., 1992—2004, music tchr. Pasadena, Calif., 1992—2004; quartet cellist Nidom Hotel, Tomokomai City, Japan, 1994; orchestral musician Long Beach Symphony, Calif., 1994—2004; solo cellist Mu Phi Epsilon, Cin., 1995—97; cello instr. Pasadena City Coll., Calif., 1996—99; orchestral cellist New West Symphony, Thousand Oaks, Calif., 1997—2004, Santa Barbara Symphony, Calif., 1997—2004; music tchr. Anita Oaks Sch., Duarte, Calif., 1998—99; solo cellist Arch Angel Prodns., L.A., 2001—02. Music advisor and arts presenter Harris Enterprises, South Pasadena, Calif., 1992—2004. Vol. Jaycees, Pasadena, Calif., 2000—04; big sister Big Brother/Big Sister, L.A., 2003—04; activist Act, Dnc, Phila., 2004, Santa Fe, 2004—04; sec., contract negotiator Long Beach Symphony Orch. Com., Calif., 2002—04. Recipient Concerto Competition winner, Dept. Music, U. Tex., 1983, Techniques of Music, Acad. Achievement award, Mannes Coll. of Music, 1986, Concerto Competition winner, 1986, Outstanding Doctoral Student award, U. So. Calif., 1992, Internat. Competition winner, Mu Phi Epsilon, 1995; Tchg. Assistantship, Dept. Music, SUNY, Stony Brook, 1987-88, Dept. Music Edn., U. So. Calif., 1989-91, Competition grant, Alpha Delta Kappa, 1996. Mem.: Am. Fedn. of Musicians, Mu Phi Epsilon. Avocations: travel, hiking, swimming, dancing, volunteering.

HARRIS, MARK W., mayor, lawyer; b. Evanston, Wyo., May 17, 1957; m. Diane Harris; children: Bryan, Cameron. BS, U. Wyo., 1979, JD, 1982. Bar: Wyo. 1982. Atty. Harris Law Firm PC, Evanston, Wyo.; city atty. Evanston, Wyo., 1983—87; spl. asst. atty. gen. Wyo.; ct. commr. and magistrate Uinta County Circuit Ct., Wyo., Third Jud. Dist. Ct., Wyo.; mayor City of Evanston, 2003—. Adj. instr. We. Wyo. CC, Evanston. Past chmn. Evanston Urban Renewal Agency; past pres. Uinta Med. Found. Bd. Mem.: Wyo. State Bar (sec., treas. 1997—2002, commr. 1994—97, pres. 2004—). Office: Evanston City Hall 1200 Main St Evanston WY 82930 E-mail: mayor@allwest.net.

HARRIS, MARTHA JANE, retired librarian; b. Milton, W.Va., Dec. 29, 1926; d. Dolphus Marshall and Julia Esther (Seabright) Martin; m. Byron Stanley Harris Sr., Dec. 1, 1944; 1 child, Byron Stanley. Student, Indian River Community Coll., Ft. Pierce, Fla., 1972-73; BS, Fla. State U., 1974, MA, 1975. Cert. tchr., Fla. Libr. Henrico County Sch. Bd., Richmond, Va., 1959-64; children's libr. Martin County Pub. Libr., Stuart, Fla., 1964-65, St. Lucie-Okeechobee Regional Libr. System, Ft. Pierce, 1965-70; dir. youth svcs. St. Lucie County Libr., Ft. Pierce, 1975-76; high sch. libr. Sch. Bd. St. Lucie County, Ft. Pierce, 1976-90. Mem. AAUW (br. pres. 1982-84), ALA, Fla. Libr. Assn., Order Ea. Star (chaplain 1957-58), Beta Phi Mu. Methodist. Avocations: writing, collecting, geology, travel, gardening. Home: 6710 Samba St Fort Pierce FL 34945-3069 E-mail: mhj6710@aol.com.

HARRIS, MAURICE DANIEL, internist; b. N.Y.C., Feb. 3, 1950; MD, SUNY, 1977. Diplomate Am. Bd. Internal Medicine. Intern Emory U. Affiliated Hosps., Atlanta, 1977-78, resident in internal medicine, 1978-80, fellow in cardiology, 1980-82; staff DeKalb Med. Ctr., Decatur, Ga., Rockdale Hosp., Decatur, Piedmont Hosp., Decatur. Mem. Am. Coll. Cardiology. Office: 2675 N Decatur Rd Ste 200 Decatur GA 30033-6132 Office Phone: 404-296-1256.

HARRIS, MEL, broadcast executive; b. Arkansas City, Kans., 1942; married; 1 child. PhD in Mass Comm., Ohio U. Pres. TV Group Paramount Pictures, 1978—92, Sony Pictures Entertainment, Culver City, Calif., 1992—95, co-pres., COO, 1999—. Former radio announcer; formerly with Kaiser and Metromedia broadcast groups; co-founder Paramount Home Video, CIC Home Video. With U.S. Army, Vietnam. Decorated Bronze Star; named one of 20 most influential studio execs., Video Store mag., 1999; named to Video Hall of Fame, 1986. Mem.: Acad. TV Arts and Scis., Motion Picture Assn. Am. (bd. dirs.).*

HARRIS, MERLE WIENER, college administrator, educator; b. Hartford, Conn., July 25, 1942; d. Irving and Leah (Glasser) Wiener; m. David R. Harris, June 23, 1963; children: Jonathan, Rebecca. BS, Ctrl. Conn. State U., 1964, MS, 1973; EdD, U. Mass., 1988. Clk., edn. com. Conn. Gen. Assembly, Hartford, 1971-72; career edn. coordinator Bloomfield (Conn.) Pub. Schs., 1973-78; asst. to commr. Dept. of Higher Edn., Hartford, Conn., 1978-82, asst. commr., 1982-88, deputy commr., 1988-89; pres. Charter Oak State Coll., New Britain, Conn., 1989—; exec. dir. Bd. for State Acad. Awards, New Britain, Conn., 1989—; interim pres. Cen. Conn. State U., 1995-96. Cons.on career edn. U.S. Dept. Edn., Washington, 1974; fellow Inst. for Ednl. Leadership, 1980; bd. dirs. Old State House, 1996—2003, Conn. Hist. Soc.,

2003—, Conn. Literacy Vols., 1991—98, Conn. Humanities Coun., 1991—97, Conn. Acad. for Edn. in Math., Sci. and Tech., 2000—, vice chmn., 2002—; chmn. Joint Com. Ednl. Tech., 1991—98; mem. Conn. Commn. Ednl. Tech., 2000—. Mem. New Eng. Assn. Schs. and Colls. (bd. dirs. 1997-2003), Am. Coun. on Edn. (commr. on ednl. credit and credentials 1995-98). Democrat. Jewish. Avocations: gardening, cooking, teaching. Office Phone: 860-832-3875. Business E-Mail: mharris@charteroak.edu.

HARRIS, MICALYN SHAFER, lawyer, educator, arbitrator, consultant, mediator; b. Chgo., Oct. 31, 1941; d. Erwin and Dorothy (Sampson) Shafer. AB, Wellesley Coll., 1963; JD, U. Chgo., 1966. Bar: Ill. 1966, Mo. 1967, US Dist. Ct. (ea. dist.) Mo. 1967, US Supreme Ct. 1972, US Ct. Appeals (8th cir.), 1974, NY 1981, NJ 1988, US Dist. Ct. NJ, US Ct. Appeals (3d cir.) 1993. Law clk. US Dist. Ct., Mo., 1967-68; atty. May Dept. Stores, St. Louis, 1968-70, Ralston-Purina Co., St. Louis, 1970-72; atty., asst. sec. Chromalloy Am. Corp., St. Louis, 1972-76; pvt. practice St. Louis, 1976-78; atty. CPC Internat., Inc., 1978-80; divsn. counsel CPC N.Am., 1980-84, asst. sec., 1981-88; gen. counsel S.B. Thomas, Inc., 1983-87; corp. counsel CPC Internat., Englewood Cliffs, NJ, 1984-88; assoc. counsel Weil, Gotshal & Manges, NYC, 1988-90; pvt. practice, 1991; v.p., sec., gen. counsel Winpro, Inc., 1991—. Arbitrator Am., Arbitration Assn., NYSE, NASD; adj. prof. Lubin Sch. Bus. Pace U.; expert cons., mediator. Mem.: ABA (Ctr. Profl. Responsibility, bus. law sect., past chair corp. counsel com., past chair subcom. counseling mktg. function, mem. securities law com., tender offers proxy statements subcom., chair task force e-mail privacy, task force electronic contracting, task force conflicts interest, ad hoc com. tech., profl. responsibility com., task force on the revised jud. code of conduct, profl. conduct com. task force on revised code of jud. conduct), Am. Law Inst. (mem. consultative group for restatement of agy., mem. consultative group for internat. enforcement of judgments, intellectual property sect.), Assn. Bar City NY (mediation coach), NJ Bar Assn. (computer law com.), NY State Bar Assn. (securities regulation com., past chair internet technology law com., past chair subcom. on licensing, task force shrink-wrap licensing, electronic comm. task force). Mailing: 625 N Monroe St Ridgewood NJ 07450-1206

HARRIS, MICHAEL GENE, optometrist, educator, lawyer; b. San Francisco, Calif., Sept. 20, 1942; s. Morry and Gertrude Alice (Epstein) H.; m. Dawn Block; children: Matthew Benjamin, Daniel Evan, Ashley Beth, Lindsay Meredith. BS, U. Calif., 1964, M in Optometry, 1965, D in Optometry, 1966, MS, 1968; JD, John F. Kennedy U., 1985. Bar: Calif., U.S. Dist. Ct. (no. dist.) Calif. Assoc. practice optometry, Oakland, Calif., 1965-66, San Francisco, 1966-68; instr., coord. contact lens clinic Ohio State U., 1968-69; asst. clin. prof. optometry U. Calif., Berkeley, 1969-73, dir. contact lens extended care clinic, 1969-83, chief contact lens clinic, 1983—, assoc. clin. prof., 1973-76, from asst. chief to assoc. chief contact lens svc., 1970—, from lectr. to sr. lectr., 1978—, vice chmn. faculty Sch. Optometry, 1983-85, 95—, prof. clin. optometry, 1984-86, clin. prof., 1986—, dir. residency program, 1993-95, asst. dean, 1994-95, assoc. dean, 1995—, acting dean, 2000, dir. policy and planning, 2003—; lectr. Peter's Meml. U. Calif. Sch. Optometry, 2000. Peter's Meml. lectr. U. Calif. Sch. Optometry, 2000; vis. prof. City U., London, 1984; vis. rsch. fellow U. NSW, Sydney, Australia, 1989; sr. vis. rsch. scholar U. Melbourne, Victoria, Australia, 1989, Victoria, 92; mem. ophthalmic devices panel med. device adv. com. FDA, 1990—, interim chmn., 1994; lectr., cons. in field; mem. regulation rev. com. Calif. Bd. Optometry; cons. hypnosis Calif. Optometric Assn., Am. Optometric Assn.; cons. Nat. Bd. Examiners in Optometry, Soflens divsn. Bausch & Lomb, 1973—, Barnes-Hind Hydrocurve Soft Lenses, Inc., 1974—87, Pilkinton-Barnes Hind, 1987—94, Contact Lens Co., 1977—2001, Palo Alto, Va., 1980, Primarius Corp., Cooper Vision Optics, 1979—, Alcon, 1980—, CIBA, 1976—, Vistakon, 1980—2000; co-founder Morton D. Sarver Rsch. Lab., 1986. Editor current comments sect. Am. Jour. Optometry, 1974-77; editor Eye Contact, 1984-86; assoc. editor The Video Jour. Clin. Optometry, 1988-92; cons. editor Contact Lens Spectrum, 1988—; author: Contact Lenses: Treatment Options for Ocular Disease, Contact Lenses for Pre & Post-Surgery; editor: Problems in Optometry, Special Contact Lens Procedures; Contact Lenses in Ocular Disease, 1990; mem. editl. bd. Contact Lens and Anterior Eye Jour.; contbr. chpts. to books, articles to profl. jours. Planning commnr. Town of Moraga, Calif., 1986, vice-chmn., 1987—88, chmn., 1988—90; mem. Town Coun., Moraga, 1992—96; mem. adv. planning commn. Medi-Cal., 1993—95, chmn., 1994—96, with managed care commn., 1995—, chmn. managed care commn., 1996—98; life mem. Bay Area Coun. for Rescue & Recovery, 1976—; grantor Michael G. Harris Family Endowment Fund U. Calif., Dr. Michael G. Harris Tchg. award U. Calif.; commr. Sunday Football League Contra Costa County, 1974—78; planner, fin. advisor College Pk. HS Track Project; mem. Pleasant Hill C. of C., Friends of Rodgers Ranch, Friends of Libr.; mem. adv. bd. Mt. Diablo Regional YMCA, 2003—; vice-mayor Town Coun., Moraga, 1994—95, mayor, 2004—05; city county rels. com. Contra Costa County, Calif.; planning commr. City of Pleasant Hill, Calif., 1999—2002, coun. mem., 2002—; vice chair Redevel. Agy., Pleasant Hill, 2002—, vice mayor, 2003—, mayor, 2004—05; founding mem. Young Adults divsn. Jewish Welfare Fedn., 1965—69, chmn., 1967—68; charter mem. Jewish Cmty. Ctr. Contra Costa County; founding mem. Jewish Cmty. Mus. San Francisco, 1984; pararabinnic Temple Isaiah, Lafayette, Calif., 1987, bd. dirs., 1990, Jewish Cmty. Rels. Coun. Greater East Bay, 1979—83, Campolindo Homeowners Assn., 1981—85, League of Calif. Cities East Bay Divsn., 2002—; bd. dirs. East Bay divsn. League of Calif. Cities. Named Alumnus of Yr., U. Calif. Sch. Optometry, 1999; recipient Eminent Svc. award, Am. Acad. Opometry, 2003; U. Calif. fellow, 1971, Calif. Optometric Assn. scholar, 1965, George Schneider meml. scholar, 1964, Disting. scholar, Nat. Acad. Practice in Optometry, 2004. Fellow: Prentice Soc. (pres.-elect 1994—96, pres. 1996—98), Assn. Schs. and Colls. Optometry (coun. on acad. affairs), British Contact Lens Assn., Am. Acad. Optometry (diplomate cornea and contact lens sect., chmn. contact lens papers, mem. contact lens com. 1974—, vice-chmn. contact lens sect. 1980—82, chmn. sect. 1982—84, immediate past chmn. 1984—86, chmn.jud. com. 1989—2001, chmn. bylaws com. 1989—, ethics taskforce 1999—, Eminent Svc. award 2003); mem.: ABA, Nat. Acads. of Practice (Distin: Scholar 2004—), Contra Costa Bar Assn., Calif. Acad. Sci., Calif. State Bd. Optometry (regulation rev. com.), Internat. Soc. Contact Lens Rsch., Mex. Soc. Contactology (hon.), Nat. Coun. on Contact Lens Compliance, Am. Optometric Found., Internat. Assn. Contact Lens Educators, Assn. Optometric Contact Lens Educators, Calif. Optometric Assn., Am. Optometric Assn. (proctor 1969—79, cons. on hypnosis, mem. contact lens sect., position papers com., mem. com. on opthalmic stds., subcom. on testing and certification, cons. editor Jour.), Internat. Assn. Contact Lens Educators, Robert Gordon Sproul Assn. U. Calif., Mensa, Benjamin Ide Wheeler Soc. U. Calif., JFK U. Sch. Law Alumni Assn., U. Calif. Optometry Alumni Assn. (life), Pleasant Hill C. of C. Democrat. Office: U Calif Sch Optometry Berkeley CA 94720-2020 E-mail: mharris@berkeley.edu.

HARRIS, NEIL, historian, educator; b. Bklyn., 1938; s. Harold and Irene Harris. AB, Columbia U., N.Y.C., 1958; BA, Cambridge U., Eng., 1960; PhD, Harvard U., 1965. From instr. to asst. prof. history Harvard U., Cambridge, Mass., 1965-69; assoc. prof. U. Chgo., 1969-72, prof., 1972-90, Preston and Sterling Morton prof. of history, 1990—, dir. Nat. Humanities Inst., 1975-77, chmn. dept. history, 1985-88. Mem. adv. bd. Temple Hoyne Buell Ctr., Columbia, 1984-89; mem. adv. com. dept. architecture Art Inst. Chgo., 1982—; mem. Smithsonian Council, 1978-84, chmn. 1984-92; visiting prof. Yale U., 1974; dir. d'etudes Ecole des Hautes Etudes en Sci. Sociales, Paris, 1985. Author: Artist in American Society, 1966, Humbug: The Art of P.T. Barnum, 1970, Cultural Excursions, 1990, Building Lives, 1999, Chicago Apartments, 2004; editor: Land of Contrasts, 1970, the WPA Guide to Illinois, 1983; bd. editors New Eng. Quar., 1982—, Winterthur Portfolio, 1978-80, 85-88, Frederick Law Olmsted Papers, 1973, Am. Scholar, 1994-2000; mem. editorial adv. bd. History Today, 1978-86. Trustee H.F. DuPont Winterthur (Del.) Mus., 1978-87, Newberry Libr.; mem. Nat. Mus. Svcs. Bd., Washington, 1977-84; vis. com. J. Paul Getty Mus., 1995—; bd. dirs. Nat. Mus. Am. History, 1997-2000, Terra Found. for Arts, 2002—. Am. Coun. Learned Socs. fellow, 1972-73, NEH fellow, 1980-81, Guggenheim fellow, 1999-2000; Getty scholar, 1991, Nat. Mus. Am. Art scholar, 1995-96; Boucher lectr. Johns Hopkins U., 1971, Cardozo lectr. Yale U., 1974, Tandy lectr. Whitney Mus. Am. Art, 1982, Kemper lectr. Pitzer Coll., 1980, Buell lectr. Columbia U., 1993; recipient Joseph Henry medal Smithsonian Instn., 1991. Fellow Am. Acad. Arts and Scis.; mem. Am. Antiquarian Soc., Am. Coun. Learned Socs. (vice chmn. N.Y. 1978-89, chmn. 1989-93), Phi Beta Kappa (senator united chpts. 1985-97, vis. lectr. 1985-86). Home: 4950 S Chicago Beach Dr Chicago IL 60615-3207 Office: U Chgo Dept History 1126 E 59th St Chicago IL 60637-1580 Business E-Mail: nh16@uchicago.edu.

HARRIS, NICHOLAS GEORGE, publisher; b. Salisbury, Eng., Sept. 8, 1939; s. George Ivan and Phyllis Dorothy (Porter) H.; m. Margaret Jane Darling, Feb. 3, 1968; children: Nicola, Gregory. Sales rep. Collins Pubs., London, 1963-67, Montreal, 1967-72, sales dir. Toronto, 1972, exec. v.p., 1973; pres. William Collins Sons & Co., Can. Ltd., 1974-87; chmn., pres. Collins Pubs. N.Am., 1986-87; mng. dir. McClelland & Stewart, 1988-89; pres. Wright Harris, Inc., 1990; v.p., gen. mgr. Grolier, Ltd., 1990-92; pres. Nick Harris Assocs., 1993—, Harris Sorensen Internat. Inc., 2003—. Trustee Markham Pub. Lib., 1994-2000. Served to 1st lt. Brit. Army, 1958-63. Mem.: Donalda Club (Toronto). Anglican. E-mail: nickharris@sympatico.ca.

HARRIS, NORMAN EDWIN, food scientist, consultant; b. Riverside, NJ, Oct. 20, 1929; s. George Martin and Hilda Edith Harris; m. Patricia Ann Stiles, Sept. 15, 1956; children: Steven, Christopher, Juli, Jeffrey. BS, Mich. State U., East Lansing, 1957, MS, 1960. Food technologist Lever Bros. Rsch. & Devel., Edgewater, NJ, 1960—62; rsch. asst. Union Carbide Devel. Co., Tarrytown, NY, 1962—64; food technologist Corn Products, Waltham, Mass., 1964—68, U.S. Army Rsch. & Devel. Ctr., Natick, Mass., 1968—93. Bd. dirs. Piscataquis Golf Course, Guilford, Mass., 2000—, pesticide mgr., 2000—. Co-author: Formulary of Candy Products, 1991, 1998; contbr. over 30 sci. jour. food articles to profl. jours., chapters to books. Mem. Hist. Soc., Riverton, NJ, 2000. Airman 1st class USAF, 1950—54. Mem.: Svc. Corps. of Retired Execs. (chair 2000—02), Sigma Xi. Achievements include patents in field; fortified Tang with calcium used in NASA moon landing, July 1969; discovery in sensory taste tests that sucrose was sweeter than fructose in many food applications, contradicting establised literature values. Avocations: walking, reading, gardening, golf. Home: 83 Douty Hill Rd Sangerville ME 04479-3103 Office: Harris Consulting 83 Douty Hill Rd Sangerville ME 04479-3103 Office Phone: 207-876-4166.

HARRIS, PAUL, sculptor; b. Orlando, Fla., Nov. 5, 1925; Student, U. N.Mex., New Sch. Social Research, Hans Hofmann Sch. Fine Arts. Fulbright prof. sculpture Universidad Catolica de Chile, 1961-62; later faculty San Francisco Art Inst., Calif. Coll. Arts and Crafts, Oakland; artist-in-residence Rinehart Sch. Sculpture, Md. Inst. Art, 1981, U. Ariz., Tucson, 1986. Vis. critic, lectr. U.S.F.S. Ctrs., Valparaiso and Concepcion, Chile, 1962, Rinehart Sch. Sculpture, spring 1981, Md. Inst. Art, (9 times) 1963-86, U. Oreg., Eugene, 1968, Newark (N.J.) State U., 1970, Mont. State U., Bozeman, 1970, 74, State U. N.Mex., Las Cruces, 1971, Montclair (N.J.) State U., 1973, Commonwealth U. Va., 1975, 76, 95, Clemson U., 1975, Haverford Coll., 1977, Phila. Coll. Art, 1977, R.I. Sch. Design, 1977, U. Ariz., Tucson, 1986. One-man shows include Poindexter Gallery, N.Y.C., 1957, 1960, 1963, 1967, 1970, Lanyon Gallery, 1965, Berkeley Gallery, 1965, William Sawyer Gallery, San Francisco, 1969, 1971, 1986, 1987, Galerie Thelen, Essen, 1970, San Francisco Mus. Art, 1972, U. Calif., Santa Barbara, 1972, U. N.Mex., 1973, Ark. Arts Ctr., 1973, Loch Haven Art Ctr., Orlando, 1981, Stanford U. Art Mus., Calif., 1982, Greenville County Mus. Art, S.C., 1982, Iannetti-Lanzone Gallery, San Francisco, 1989, Fuller Goldeen Gallery, 1983, C. Grimaldis Gallery, Balt., 1989, Galerie Redmann, Berlin, 1990, 1995, Michael Himowitz Gallery, Sacramento, 1993, Bolinas (Calif.) Mus., 1999, Fresno (Calif.) Art Mus., 1999, 2003, The Coll. of Marin Gallery, Kentfield, Calif., 2000, Yellowstone Art Mus., Billings, Mont., 2001, Holter Mus. Art, Helena, Mont, 2003, Wiegand Gallery, Notre Dame de Namur U., Belmont, Calif., 2004, exhibited in group shows at Mus. Modern Art, N.Y.C., 1958, 1963, N.Y. World's Fair, 1965, Art Inst. Chgo., 1965, Md. Inst. Art, 1966, Mus. Contemporary Crafts, 1966, 1973, São Paulo Bienal, 1967, Crocker Art Gallery Assn., Sacramento, 1968, Smithsonian Instn. Traveling Exhibn., 1969, Phila. Inst. Art., San Francisco Mus. Art, N.J. State Mus., L.A. County Mus., 1973, Brandeis U., A.C.A. Gallery, 1972, Contemporary Art Ctr. Cin., 1973, Coll. Marin Galleries, 1974, JPL Gallery, London, 1975, Yellowstone Art Ctr., Billings, Mont., 1976, Renwick Gallery, Nat. Coll. Fine Arts, Washington, 1976—77, Falkirk Ctr., San Rafael, Calif., 1980, Transam. Bldg. Gallery, San Francisco, 1982, San Francisco Mus. Modern Art, 1983, Otis Art Inst. Parsons Sch. Design, 1984, Fendrick Gallery, 1984, William Sawyer Gallery, San Francisco, 1985, 1993, Iannetti Lanzone Gallery, 1987, Meml. Union Art Gallery, U. Calif., Davis, 1988, Civic Arts Gallery, Walnut Creek, Calif., 1988, Constantine Grimaldis Gallery, Balt., 1988, Gallery, San Francisco, 1989, Cologne (Germany) Art Fair, 1989, 1992, 1995, 1997, Galerie Redmann, Berlin, 1990, 1993, 1994, Bolinas Mus., Calif., 1990, Wolk Gallery, St. Helena, Calif., 1993, 1994, Oliver Art Ctr., Calif. Coll. Arts and Crafts, Oakland, Calif., 1993, Orlando (Fla.) History Mus., 1994, Sheldon Meml. Art Gallery, U. Nebr., 1996, Western Book Exhibit, San Francisco, 1996, The Woodson Art Mus., Wausaw, Wis., 1997—98, others, Wrongtree Press, 1973, on aspects of ballet A False Alarm on the Nightbell Once Answered-It Cannot Be Made Good, Not Ever, Art in Am. Illus. Torso (Dorothy Schmidt), 1974, Paul Harris (Dennis Leon, Harry Abrams), 1975, drawings, for Pas d'Une, 1979; writer, artist (drawings) Phases of the Moon, 1995, designer (book) Motives and Cues by Marguerite Harris, 1993; lithographs, Paradise: Variations, 1996, Paul Harris, drawings, 1998, sculpture, 1999. Recipient Longview Found. grant, 1960, Neallie Sullivan award, 1967; Tamarind fellow, 1969-70; named Miembro Academico de la Facultad de Bellas Artes Universidad Catolica de Chile, 1962; resident Macdowell Colony, 1977; grantee Lebovitz Fund, 1978; Guggenheim fellow 1979. Address: PO Box 930 Bolinas CA 94924-0930

HARRIS, PAUL LYNWOOD, retired aerospace transportation executive; b. Richmond, Va., May 30, 1945; s. Paul Lynwood Sr. and Marjorie (Southward) H.; m. Susan Lee, Sept. 20, 1969; children: Meredith Lynn, Joanna Lee. AA, Ferrum Coll., 1965; BS, U. Richmond, 1967. CPA, Va. Staff acct. Price Waterhouse & Co., Washington, 1967-71, sr. acct., 1971-73; v.p. fin. Universal Restoration Inc., Washington, 1973-76; treas. Hawker Siddely Aviation Inc., Washington, 1976-78, Brit. Aerospace Inc., Herndon, Va., 1978-81, v.p. fin., 1981-86, sr. v.p. fin., 1986-88; fin. dir. Brit. Aerospace Comml. Aircraft, Hatfield, Eng., 1988-92; sr. v.p. adminstrn. Brit. Aerospace, Inc., Herndon, Va., 1992-93; sr. v.p., gen. mgr. Brit. Aerospace N.Am., Inc., Herndon, Va., 1993-99; ret., 2000; chmn. Ferrum Coll., 2002—. Bd. trustees Ferrum Coll., 1999-2000. Bd. dirs. Reflectone, Inc., Cheshire Homes No. Va., Arlington, 1986, Washington Dulles Task Force, 1993-2001, Dulles Area Transport Assn., 1993-95; chmn. fin. com. United Christian Parish, Reston, Va., 1979. Mem. AICPA, Nat. Aviation Club (pres. 1995-96), Fin. Execs. Inst. Methodist. Home: 2525 Heath Pl Reston VA 20191-4224 E-mail: paulsusan2000@yahoo.com.

HARRIS, PAUL N, lawyer; BA, U. Chgo., 1980; JD, Stanford Law Sch., 1983. Ptnr. in charge Thompson Hine LLP, Cleve., 1983—88; sr. counsel Revco DS Inc. (now CVS), 1988—97; with Thompson Hill LLP, 1997; exec. v.p., sec., gen. counsel Keycorp, Cleve., 2003—. Mem.: Am. Soc. Corp. Sec., Cleve. Bar Assn. Office: Keycorp 127 Public Sq Cleveland OH 44114-1306 Office Phone: 216-689-6300. Office Fax: 216-689-7009.

HARRIS, PAUL SMITH, human resources professional; b. Santa Monica, Calif., Nov. 29, 1935; s. Wallace Albert and Henrietta (Smith) H.; m. Jill B. Hall, Sept. 15, 1956 (div. June 1974); children: Gregory A., Geoffrey A.; m. Nancy Lynn Cherry, Sept. 9, 1975; 1 child, Doug B. BA in Psychology, U. Utah, 1958; postgrad., UCLA, 1961-63. Mgr. employment Western Airlines Inc., L.A., 1956-64; mgr. selection Am. Airlines Inc., N.Y.C., 1964-66; mgr. adminstrn. IBM, Princeton, N.J., 1966-72; dir. orgn. planning and devel. CNA Fin. Corp., Chgo., 1972-76; v.p. human rsch. developer W.E. Walker Stores Inc., Jackson, Miss., 1976-80; pres. Harris Cons., Inc., Salt Lake City, 1980-83; dir. pers. Americas divsn. Intercontinental Hotels, Washington, 1983-88; v.p. human rsch. devel. Showboat Casino and Hotel, Atlantic City, 1988-93; exec. v.p. Showboat Devel. Co., Atlantic City, 1993-98; ret., 1998. Bd. dirs. C. of C., Middlesex County, N.J., 1970-71, Chgo. Alliance of Businessman, 1974-75. Mem. Masons (master mason Mt. Moriah # 2 Utah, 32 degree). Republican. Christian Scientist. Avocations: tennis, skiing, flying.

HARRIS, PENNY SMITH, fundraising consultant; b. Old Town, Maine, Apr. 6, 1941; d. Owen Halbert and Louise Marion (Whitten) Smith; m. Parker Fred Harris, June 22, 1963 (div. 1992); children: Susan Leslie, Nancy Lynne. BS in Sociology, U. Maine, 1963; MS in Bus. Mgmt., Husson Coll., 1984. Cert. fund raising exec. Social worker Elizabeth Lund Home, Burlington, Vt., 1964—65; pub. sch. tchr. Essex Junction, Vt.; asst. dir. devel., corp. support mgr. Maine Pub. Broadcasting Network, Bangor, 1985—89; dir. devel. Ea. Maine Healthcare, Bangor, 1989—94; dir. healthcare campaign N.E. Health, Rockland, Maine, 1994—97; sr. assoc. Copley Davenport Co., Inc., Wenham, Mass., 1997—98, M. Davenport Assocs., 1998—; pres. PS Harris Assocs., Portland, Maine, 2001—. Trustee Maine Pub. Broadcasting Corp., 1991—95, Ctr. for Maine Contemporary Art, 1993—, U. Maine Sys., 1991—2001; mem. task force on campaign fin. Senator George Mitchell, Augusta, Maine, 1983; mem. All Am. City selection award jury, Nat. Civil League, N.Y.C., 1987; chmn. bd. dirs. Ctr. for Maine Contemporary Art, 2003—; bd. dirs. Greater Bangor United Way, 1990—93. Mem. LWV (pres. Bangor-Brewer chpt. 1979-81, state pres. 1982-85, nat. bd. dirs. 1986-88, sec. nat. bd. dirs. 1988-90, project dir. TV polit. debates Bangor 1982, project dir. Nat. Security and You Conf., Portland, Maine 1983), U. Maine Alumni Assn. (v.p. bd. dirs. 1991-93), Greater Portland C. of C. Democrat. Methodist. Avocations: skiing, travel, hiking, bicycling. Home and Office: PO Box 2862 South Portland ME 04116 Office Phone: 207-741-9086. Personal E-mail: penny.harris2@verizon.net. Business E-Mail: penny@harrisfundraising.com.

HARRIS, PHILIP JOHN, engineering educator; b. Montreal, Que., Can., Mar. 22, 1926; s. Thomas Percival and Gladys Marion (Gillett) H.; m. Norma Joyce Maynard, May 23, 1953; children: Elizabeth Joyce Harris Richardson, Janet Constance. B.Sc., U. Man., 1948; M.Eng., McGill U., 1949, PhD, 1964. Structural designer Dominion Bridge Co. Ltd., Lachine, Que., 1949-51; chief civil engr. C.D. Howe Co., Ltd., Montreal, 1951-58; asst. prof. dept. civil engring. McGill U., Montreal, 1958-59, assoc. prof., 1959-73, prof. dept. civil engring., 1973-91, chmn. dept., 1977-84, bd. govs., 1975-82, prof. emeritus, 1993—; prof. dept. civil engring. McMaster U., Hamilton, Ont., 1991-95. Cons. structural and found. engring., 1958-91; cons. engr., 1991-99. Contbr. articles to profl. jours. NRC Can. grantee, 1965-79; Natural Scis. and Engring. Research Council grantee, 1979-87. Fellow Can. Soc. Civil Engring., Engring. Inst. Can.; mem. ASCE (life). Anglican. Home: 408 Swanson Ct Burlington ON Canada L7R 4G6

HARRIS, PHILIP ROBERT, management and space psychologist; b. Bklyn., Jan. 22, 1926; s. Gordon Roger and Esther Elizabeth (Delahanty) H.; m. Dorothy Lipp, July 3, 1965 (dec. 1997); m. Janet Belport, Feb. 14, 2001. BBA, St. John's U., 1949; MS in Psychology, Fordham U., 1952, PhD, 1956; spl. student, NYU, 1948-49, Syracuse U., 1961. Lic. psychologist U. of State of N.Y., 1959, N.Y. Dir. guidance St. Francis Prep. Sch., N.Y.C., 1952-56; dir. student personnel, v.p. St. Francis Coll., N.Y.C., 1956-63; exec. dir. Assn. Human Emergency-Thomas Murray Tng. Program, 1964-66; vis. prof. Pa. State U., 1965-66; vis. prof., cons. Temple U.; sr. assoc. Leadership Resources Inc., 1966-69; v.p. Copley Internat. Corp., La Jolla, Calif., 1970-71; pres. Mgmt. and Orgn. Devel. Inc. (now Harris Internat. Ltd.), La Jolla, 1971—; edn. dir. Air/Space Am., 1988; sr. scientist Netrologic, Inc., La Jolla, Calif., 1990-93; prof. Calif. Sch. Internat. Mgmt., 2005—. Rsch. assoc. Calif. Space Inst., U. Calif., San Diego, 1984-90; adj. prof. Pepperdine U., U. No. Colo.; acad. adv. Command Coll., Commn. on Peace Officers Stds. and Tng. State of Calif., Dept. Justice, 1986-94; past cons. Westinghouse, N.V. Philips, I.B.M., Computer Sci. Corp. Control Data, govt. agys.; chmn. bd. dirs. United Socs. in Space, Inc., 1993-97 Author: Effective Management of Change, 1976, Improving Management Communication Skills, 1978, Managing Cultural Differences, 1979, 6th edit., 2004, New Worlds, New Ways, New Management, 1983, Managing Cultural Synergy, 1982, Management in Transition, 1985, Living and Working in Space, 1992, 2d edit., 1996, High Performance Leadership, 2d edit., 1994, New Work Culture, 1998, Launch Out, 2003; co-author: Transcultural Leadership, 1993, Developing Global Organizations, 1993, 2d edit., 2001, Multicultural Management 2000, 1998, Multicultural Law Enforcement, 1995, 3d edit., 2004, Managing the Knowledge Culture, 2005; editor: Innovations in Global Consultation, 1980, Global Strategies in Human Resource Development, 1983; author (series) New Work Culture, 3 vols., 1994-98; co-editor Manging Cultural Differences Series Butterworth-Heinemann/Elsevier Sci., 1979—; mem. editl. bd. European Bus. Rev.; founding editor emeritus Space Governance Jour., 1993-98; contbr. 225 articles to profl. jours. V.p. Bklyn. Downtown Renewal Effort, 1957-59. Recipient Literati Club award for excellence, 2005; named to Gulf Pub. Author Hall of Fame, 1999; Fulbright prof. to India U.S. State Dept., 1962; NASA faculty fellow, 1984. Fellow AIAA (assoc.); mem. ASTD (Torch award 1975), Aviation Space Writers Assn. (journalism awards 1986, 88, 89, 93), World Bar Assn. (Space Humanitarian award1992), Nat. Space Soc., United Socs. in Space (dir. emeritus), Soc. for Human Performance in Extreme Environments, La Jolla Beach and Tennis Club, Literati Club (Excellence award 2005) Independent. Home and Office: 2702 Costebelle Dr La Jolla CA 92037-3524 E-mail: philharris@aol.com.

HARRIS, R. STEVEN (RICHARD STEVEN HARRIS), data processing executive, consultant, educator; b. Kansas City, Kans., Aug. 3, 1949; s. George Joseph and Bonnie Jean (Knecht) H.; m. Phyllis Lea Stopp, Aug. 29, 1970 (div. Nov. 2000); children: April Lea, Steven Erhardt; m. Bonnie Jean (Ter Veen) Baker, Aug. 25, 2001. BA magna cum laude, Knox Coll.; MS in Edn., Western Ill. U.; postgrad., Columbia Pacific U. Cert. secondary tchr., sch. guidance counselor, Ill.; cert. vocat. and tech. adult edn. tchr., Wis. Sci. tchr., counselor Brimfield (Ill.) High Sch., 1972-74, grad. of five factories, Galesburg, Ill., 1971-72, 74-80; plant mgr. Jacobson Barrel Corp., Milw., 1980-82; ind. systems cons. Milw. area, 1982-84; programmer Effective Mgmt. Systems, Milw., 1984-85; systems and programming tchr. Milw. Bus. Tng. Inst., 1985-86; programmer, customer support analyst, software package quality assurance specialist Systems For Profit, Inc., Milw., 1986-89; MIS mgr. Gendex Corp., Milw., 1989; ind. cons./contract programmer Milw., 1989-90, 91-92; staff analyst, cons. CAP Gemini Am., Milw., 1990-91; sr. sys. and tech. cons. Chaney Systems, Inc., New Berlin, 1992—95; sr. cons. and founder JoB Sys. LLC, Oak Creek, 1996—2000; application devel. team leader Priority Health, Grand Rapids, Mich., 2002; foundation specialist and sales rep. Everdry of Greater Grand Rapids, 2002—04; sr. health and life ins. agt. Small Bus. Ins. Specialists, 2002—04; sales lighted electric signage ind. bus. owners Signtronix Corp., 2004—. Bus. math. systems and programming tchr. Milw. Area Tech. Coll., 1987—91; ind. rep. Excel Comm., regional dir., regional tng. dir., 1999—; networking and programming cons. ITT Tech. Inst., Milw. and Grand Rapids, 2001. Founding Pastor Covenant Apostolic Ch. Greater Milw. area, 1991-2000. Fellow Am. Prodn. and Inventory Control Soc. (fellow cert. 1985—, inst. Milw. 1985-87); mem. Creation Sci. Soc. Milw. (program chmn. 1985-86), Creation Rsch. Soc. (life), Creation Social Sci. and Humanities Soc. (charter, voting), Inst. Cert. Computer Profls. (cert. computer profl. with six specializations, cert. data processor, cert. bus., sci. and operating systems computer programmer, charter mem., voting mem.), Assn. Systems Mgmt. (cert. systems profl.), Soc. Data Educators (cert.), Phi Beta Kappa. Mem. Christian Ref. Ch. Avocations: swimming, bicycling, home bible study, research activities, teaching and pastoring ministry. Home and Office: 875 Quintara Ct NE Comstock Park MI 49321-8379 Office Phone: 616-706-2023. E-mail: rsharris@myexcel.com. *Personal philosophy: I believe in the Lord Jesus Christ as my Creator-God, Savior, Lord, and King. In all things we should prayerfully ask, "What would Jesus do?".*

HARRIS, RANDALL DUANE, management consultant, educator; BA, U. Tex., 1986, MBA, 1989; PhD, U. Fla., 1995. Asst. prof., mgmt. Calif. State U., Turlock, Calif., 1996—2002, assoc. prof., mgmt., 2002—. Dir., MBA program Calif. State U., MBA Program, 2001. Contbr. articles various profl. jours. Impact coun. chair United Way of Stanislaus County, Modesto, Calif., 2000—04. Recipient Chair's award, United Way of Stanislaus County, 2003.

Mem.: Western Casewriters Assn. (v.p. 2003—04), Acad. of Mgmt. Office: Calif State U Stanislaus 801 W Monte Vista Ave Turlock CA 95382 Office Phone: 209-667-3723. Office Fax: 209-667-3210.

HARRIS, RAYMOND JESSE, retired federal official; b. Van Buren, N.Y., Dec. 28, 1916; s. Francis Elbert and Anna Marie (Selinsky) H.; m. Rosalba Emilia Prestianni, Jan. 7, 1950 (dec. 1989). AB, Harvard U., 1940, postgrad., 1940-42, U. Pa., 1952-54, 59-60. Corr. drafter U.S. State Dept., Washington, 1947; vice consul Am. consulate palermo, Italy, 1947-50, Munich, Germany, 1950-51; personnel technician, information officer City of Phila., 1952-59, administrv. asst. to water commr., 1959-79; ret., 1979; Republican committeeman 59th ward City of Phila., 1986-98. Served with USAAF, 1942-45; ETO. Named Water Dept. Supr. of Year, 1971, 72, 73, 76; recipient Ted Moses award Pa. Water Pollution Control Assn., 1978. Mem. Am. Water Works Assn., Archeol. Inst. Am., Amnesty Internat. USA, Nat. Trust Historic Preservation, Pa. Hist. Soc., Acad. Polit. Sci., Am. Anti-Vivisection Soc., Planetary Soc., Harvard of Phila. Club, Germantown Rep., Preservation Alliance Greater Phila. Home: 275 W Tulpehocken St Philadelphia PA 19144-3209

HARRIS, REUBEN, wholesale distribution executive; BS in Mech. Engring., Antioch Coll., 1969; MBA, U. Rochester, 1972; PhD, Stanford U., 1972. V.p. R&D Tom Peters Group, 1985—91; cons. C&S, 1988—2001; vice chmn. C&S Wholesale, Brattleboro, Vt., 2001—; dir. C&S Holdings, 1992—. Bd. dirs. Bulab Holdings, Inc., 1997—; mem. mgmt. faculty Naval Postgrad. Sch., Monterey, Calif., 1978—2001, dean Grad. Sch. Bus. and Pub. Policy, 1995—2001; faculty mem. Coll. Bus. Adminstrn. U. Calif., Berkeley; faculty mem. Alfred P. Sloan Sch. Mgmt., MIT, Irish Mgmt. Inst., Dublin. Author 2 books; contbr. articles to profl. jours. Trustee Antioch U. Office: C&S Wholesale 7 Corporate Dr Keene NH 03431

HARRIS, RICHARD EUGENE VASSAU, lawyer; b. Detroit, Mar. 16, 1945; s. Joseph S. and Helen Harris; m. Milagros A. Brito; children: Catherine, Byron. AB, Albion Coll., 1967; JD, Harvard U., 1970; postdoctoral, Inst. Advanced Legal Studies, London, 1970-71. Bar: Calif. 1972. Assoc. Orrick, Herrington, Rowley & Sutcliffe, San Francisco, 1972-77; ptnr. Orrick, Herrington & Sutcliffe, San Francisco, 1978-98; pvt. practice Richard E. V. Harris Law Office, Oakland, Calif., 1998—. Faculty Calif. Tax Policy Conf., 1987, 95; spkr. univ., govtl. and profl. groups. Knox fellow, Harvard U., 1970—71. Mem.: ABA (litig. sect. corp. counsel com., subcom. chmn. 1980—82, antitrust law sect. state action com. 1981—, vice chmn. 1982—83, vice chmn. govt. liability com. 1982—84, co-chmn. Nat. Insts. Antitrust Liability 1983, Boulder task force 1983—84, coun. urban state and local govt. sect. 1983—88, litig. sect. corp. counsel com., subcom. chmn. 1983—, co-chmn. Nat. Insts. Antitrust Liability 1985, bus. law sect., SEC investigation atty.-client privilege waiver task f 1988, profl. conduct com., tax sect., state and local taxes com. 1989—, tax litig. com. 1992—, conflicts of interest task force 1993—96, internat. com. 1994—, corp. counsel com. 1995—, conflicts of interest com. 1996—2000, ad hoc com. on ethics 2000, com. profl. conduct 2001—, Ctr. Profl. Responsibility, ABA Ethics 2000 adv. group), Bar Assn. San Francisco (ethics com. 1980—, state bar conf. del. 2003), Am. Law Inst. (cons. restatements of law unfair competition 1991—94, governing lawyers com. 1991—2000, torts com. 1993—, agy. com. 1996—2005, trusts com. 1996—). E-mail: richardevh@aol.com.

HARRIS, RICHARD FOSTER, JR., insurance company executive; b. Athens, Ga., Feb. 8, 1918; s. Richard Foster and Mai Audli (Chandler) H.; m. Virginia McCurdy, Aug. 21, 1937 (div.); children: Richard Foster (dec.), Gaye Karyl Harris Law; m. Kari Melandso, Dec. 29, 1962. BCS, U. Ga., 1939. Bookkeeper, salesman 1st Nat. Bank, Atlanta, 1936-40; agt. Vol. state Life Ins. Co., Atlanta, 1940-41; asst. mgr. N.Y. Life Ins. Co., Atlanta and Charlotte, N.C., 1941-44; mgr., agt. Pilot Life Ins. Co., Charlotte and Houston, 1944-63; mgr., agt. bus. planning divsn., city agy. Am. Gen. Life Ins. Co., Houston, 1963—. Bd. dirs. Fidelity Bank & Trust Co., Houston, 1965-66, mem. bd. bus. devel. Sterling Bank, Upper Kirby Br., 1996. Chmn. fund dr. Am. Heart Assn., Charlotte, Mecklenburg County, 1958-59, chmn. bd., 1959-61; gen. chmn. Shrine Bowl Promotion, Charlotte Shriners, 1955; v.p., bd. dirs. Myers Park Meth. Ch. Men's Class, 1956-59, bd. stewards, Charlotte, 1959-61; bd. dirs. Houston Polit. Action Com., 1982—; charter mem. Rep. Presdl. Task Force, pres., 1981-90; at large del. Rep. Nat. Conv. Planning Platform, Houston, 1992; co-chmn. Christian Cmty. Svc. Ctr., 1984-90; mem. 1st Tuesday Group, Houston, 1985—; tchr. Men's Bible class St. John the Divine Ch., 1963-93; founder Episcopal H.S., Houston, 1984. Recipient Pres.'s Cabinet award Am. Gen. Life Ins. Co., 1964-67, 69, 71, 77-83, Disting. Salesman award Charlotte Sales Exec. Club, 1955, 57-59, Bronze Medallion award Am. Heart Assn., 1959, Nat. Quality awards, 1965-92, The Rep. Presdl. Legion of Merit award, 1992; named Adm. of Tex. Nav. Gov. of Tex., 1989. Mem. Assn. Advanced Life Underwriters, Am. Soc. CLUs, Nat. Assn. Life Underwriters, SAR (Good Citizenship award 1991), Life Underwriters Polit. Action Com. (life), Houston Estate and Fin. Forum, English Speaking Union, Mensa Internat., Houston Assn. Life Underwriters, Lone Star Leaders Club, Tex. Leader's Round Table (life), Million Dollar Round Table (life), Tex. Assn. Life Underwriters, Am. Security Coun. (nat. adv. bd. 1979—), Houston Intown C. of C. (charter mem.), Houston Club, 100 Club, Forum Club of Houston, Pachyderm Club, Houston Intown C. of C., Kiwanis (bd. dirs. 1979—), Masons (32 degree), Shriners, Sertoma (life, v.p. bd. dirs. Charlotte chpt.), Royal Order Jesters. Episcopalian. Home and Office: 2701 Westheimer Rd Houston TX 77098-1243 Office: Am Gen Life Ins Co Wortham Tower 2727 Allen Pkwy Ste 104 Houston TX 77019-2100

HARRIS, RICHARD LEE, engineering executive, retired military officer; b. Bellevue, Pa., Dec. 26, 1928; s. Everett Lee and Marjorie Anna (Messer) H.; m. Patricia Ann Walton, Dec. 12, 1953; children: Sandra Jo, Carole Jill, William Walton, Robert Lee. BS, U.S. Mil. Acad., West Point, N.Y., 1951; student, Army Engr. Sch., 1951, 59; MS, MIT, 1956; grad., Oak Ridge Sch. Reactor Tech., 1957, Command and Gen. Staff Coll., 1963, Nat. War Coll., 1967. Designated sr. parachutist, nuclear reactor comdr. registered profl. engr., Pa., Tex. Commd. 2d lt. U.S. Army, 1951, advanced through grades to maj. gen., 1973; with (32d Engrs. Combat Bn.), 1951; co-comdr. (13th Engrs. Combat Bn., 7th Inf. Divsn.), Korea, 1952-53; res. engr. (Phila. Engrs. Dist.), 1953-54; engrs. supply officer Columbus Depot, 1954-55; tech. ops. officer AEC, N.Y.C., 1957-59; officer in charge (SM-1A Nuclear Power Plant), Alaska, 1960-62; with (U.S. STRIKE Command), 1963-65; bn. comdr. (20th Engrs. Combat Bn.), Vietnam, 1965-66; with Office Chief of Staff, U.S. Army, 1967-68, Hdqrs. U.S. Army Pacific, 1968-70; comdr. divsn. support command (1st Cav. Divsn.), Vietnam, 1970-71; asst. comdt. Army Engrs. Sch., 1971-73; dir. mgmt. info. sys. Office Chief Staff Army, Hdqrs. Dept. Army, 1973-76; comdr. U.S. Army Tng. Ctr.-Engr. and Ft. Leonard Wood, Mo., 1976-78; divsn. engr. North Ctrl. Engr. Divsn., 1978-80; ret., 1980; v.p. Radian Corp., Austin, 1980-93; ret., 1993. Decorated D.S.M., Legion of Merit with 4 oak leaf clusters, Bronze Star with 2 oak leaf clusters, Air medal with 4 numerals, Joint Services Commendation medal, Purple Heart. Fellow: Soc. Am. Mil. Engrs.; mem.: Mil. Officers Assn., Assn. U. S. Army, Phi Kappa Phi. Home: 8817 Balcones Club Dr Austin TX 78750-3042

HARRIS, RICHARD W., law educator, lawyer, accountant; b. Arlington, Va., Aug. 4, 1952; s. Glendal W. and Jean K. Harris; m. Deborah Lynn Weber, Nov. 22, 1987; children: Lindsey, Taylor, Cameron. BS in acctg., U. Md., Coll. Pk., 1974, MBA, 1976; JD with honors, U. Md., Balt., 1981; LLM tax, Georgetown Law Ctr., Washington, 1989. CPA Md., 1975; bar: Md. 1982, U.S. Supreme Ct. 1984. Assoc. Levitan, Ezrin, West & Kerxton, Bethesda, Md., 1981—84; pvt. practice Lanham, Md., 1984—89; asst. prof. taxation Am. U., Washington, 1989—95; prof. taxation Grand Valley State U., Grand Rapids, Mich., 1995—. Dir. grad. tax program Grand Valley State U., 1995—2002, L. William Seidman chair of acctg. and taxation, 1995—, chair MST adv. bd., 1995—2002; chair West Mich. Tax Symposium, Grand Rapids, Mich., 1995—; adj. instr. Mich. State U., Lansing, 2004—. Contbr. articles to profl. jours. Co-founder and dir. Grand Rapids Vol. Income Tax Assistance Program, 1997—. Mem.: ABA, Mich. Assn. of CPA's, Md. State Bar Assn. Avocations: pvt. pilot, basketball coach, motorhome travel. Home: 3751 Oak Creek Ct Grand Rapids MI 49546 Office: Grand Valley State Univ 401 W Fulton Grand Rapids MI 49504 Office Phone: 616-331-7399. Business E-Mail: harrisr@gvsu.edu.

HARRIS, ROBERT A., retired music educator; b. Rich Hill, Mo., May 8, 1928; s. Archie L. and Edith Jeannette (Bailey) H. AA in Music, Joplin Jr. Coll., 1948; MusB, Kans. State Tchrs. Coll., 1950, MS in Edn., 1953; student, Rosina Lhevinne. Pianist, organist 1st United Meth. Ch., Carthage, 1946—; pvt. tchr. piano Carthage, Mo., 1947—; tchr. music, choir dir. Coll. Our Lady of the Ozarks, Carthage, 1949-53, 55-57; prof. music Mo. So. State U., Joplin, 1971-95. Piano adjudicator; presenter piano and organ recitals. Cpl., chaplain's asst. US Army, 1953-55. Mem. Nat. Guild Piano Tchrs., Nat. Fedn. Music Clubs (local v.p.), Fellowship of United Meths. in Music and Worship Arts, Music Tchrs. Nat. Assn. (permanent profl. piano cert.), Am. Coll. Musicians, Mo. State Tchrs. Assn., Mo. Federated Music Club (ch. musician yr. 1993). Avocation: collectibles. Personal E-mail: rharris@joplin.com.

HARRIS, ROBERT DALTON, history professor, researcher, writer; b. Jamieson, Oreg., Dec. 24, 1921; s. Charles Sinclair and Dorothy (Cleveland) H.; m. Ethel Imus, June 26, 1971. BA, Whitman Coll., Walla Walla, Wash., 1951; MA, U. Calif., Berkeley, 1953, PhD, 1959. Tchg. asst. U. Calif., Berkeley, 1956-59; instr. history U. Idaho, Moscow, 1959-61, asst. prof., 1961-68, assoc. prof., 1968-74, prof. history, 1974-86, prof. emeritus, 1986—. Author: (Book) Necker, Reform Statesman of Ancient Regime, 1979, Necker & Revolution of 1789, 1986. 1st lt., U.S. Army, 1942-46; Ballet Folk of Moscow, Idaho, (bd. dirs., 1971-73), Historian, First United Methodist Church, Moscow, Idaho, 1989—. Mem. Am. Hist. Assn., Am. Assn. of U. Prof. Democrat. Methodist. Avocations: social dancing, violinist. Home: Apt 318 640 N Eisenhower St Moscow ID 83843-9588

HARRIS, ROBERT GAYLEN, art director, small business owner; b. Tacoma, Nov. 29, 1960; s. Gaylen Amon and Janelle Lee (Hinton) H.; m. Chelene Hope Ward, Sept. 24, 1988 (div. Nov. 1995). AD, Tacoma C.C., 1981; student, Brigham Young U., 1981-84. Graphic artist Phone Directories, Provo, Utah, 1983-84; graphic designer Clark Pub., Tacoma, 1984-89; art dir. Bringhurst Corp., Tacoma, 1989-98; owner Images, Tacoma, 1987—, Art Haus Harris Gallery, Tacoma, 1997—; art dir. Web-X, Tacoma, 1998—; pres. Art Haus, Inc., Tacoma. Curator The Pierce County Playwrights Festival, Tacoma, 1995-97; cons. in field. Designer holiday poster Tacoma C. of C., 1991-97; designer fire safety poster Tacoma Fire Dept., 1992; designer food safety awareness posters Domani Labs., Tacoma, 1997; mem. Tacoma Art Mus., Seattle Art Mus., Bellevue Mus. Art. Named regional winner Corel/Egghead Software Nat. Design Contest, 1995, 2nd place original concept-digital PIP Corp. Masters Competition, 1998; winner Corp. Identification Corel World Design Contest, 1996, 2001, Grand prize winner abstract category Dec.-Jan. Corel 10th World Design Contest, 2000, cover art/article Corel User, May 2000; featured artist Reader Gallery, Corel Mag., Mar. 1996, June 1998. Mem. Allied Artists Am. Avocations: painting, writing, reading, computing, travel. Home and Office: 1119 E 53d St Apt D Tacoma WA 98404-2720 Personal E-mail: arthausharris@hotmail.com.

HARRIS, ROBERT LAIRD, minister, theology educator emeritus; b. Brownsburg, Pa., Mar. 10, 1911; s. Walter William and Ella Pearl (Graves) H.; m. Elizabeth Krugar Nelson, Sept. 11, 1937 (dec. 1980); children: Grace Sears, Allegra Smick, Robert Laird; m. Anne Paxson Krauss, Aug. 1, 1981. BSChemE, U. Del., Newark, 1931; postgrad, Washington U., 1931-32; ThB, Westminster Theol. Sem., 1935, ThM, 1937; MA in Oriental Studies, U. Pa., 1941; PhD, Dropsie Coll., 1947. Ordained to ministry Presbyn. Ch. Am., 1936; instr. Faith Theol. Sem., Phila., 1937-43, asst. prof. Bibl. Exegesis, 1943-47, prof. Bibl. Exegesis, 1947-56; prof. Covenant Theol. Sem., St. Louis, 1956-81, dean, 1964-71, prof. emeritus, 1981—; prof. Winona Lake Summer Sch. of Theology, 1964, 66-67, Near East Sch. Archaeology and Bible, Jerusalem, 1962; vis. prof. China Grad. Sch. Theology, Hong Kong, 1981, Freie Theologische Akademie, Giessen, Fed. Republic Germany, 1982-85, Tyndale Theol. Sem., Amsterdam, The Netherlands, 1986-2000, Bibl. Theol. Sem., Hatfield, Pa., 1992, J. Manoel Conceicao Presbyn. Sem., Sao Paulo, Brazil, 1995. Vis. lectr. Wheaton Coll., Ill., 1957-61; lectr. Japan, Korea, 1965, India, 1981, Australia, 1989; moderator Presbyn. Ch. in Am., 1982. Author: Introductory Hebrew Grammar, 1950, Inspiration and Canonicity of the Bible, 1957, 2d edit., 1995, Man-God's Eternal Creation, 1971, You and Your Bible, 1990; editor: Theological Wordbook of the Old Testament, 2 vols., 1981, Leviticus in Expositor's Bible Commentary, Vol. 2, 1990; mem. editorial bd. New Internat. Version of Bible, 1965-2000, chmn., 1970-74; contbg. author various books. Trustee Bibl. Theol. Sem., Hatfield, Pa., 1985-2000. DuPont fellow U. Del., 1930-31; recipient first prize Zondervan Textbook Contest, 1955; Foxwell Lecture lectureship Tokyo Christian Theol. Sem., 1981. Mem. Evang. Theol. Soc. (pres. 1961), Tau Beta Pi, Phi Kappa Phi Republican. Home: 625 Robert Fulton Hwy Quarryville PA 17566 *In my ministry of over 60 years I have seen a distressing erosion of national morals and decency. But there has also been a counter-resurgence of evangelical faith. As part of this movement, I am gratified to have had a part in producing the New International Version of the Bible.*

HARRIS, ROBERT L(EE), judge; b. Spokane, Wash., Oct. 3, 1934; s. Roy L Harris, Celia A Reed; m. Mary Jo Bourke; children: Joanna, Marie, Robert. BA, Wash. State U., 1954; JD, U. Wash., 1958. Bar: Wash. 1958. Judge Superior Ct. of Wash., Vancouver, 1979—. Mem. Project 2001, Supreme Ct. Task Force, Bd. Jud. Adminstrn., trial ct. funding Supreme Ct. Task Force 2003, chmn. Pres. St. Joseph Cmty. Hosp., Vancouver, 1967—74. Mem.: Superior Ct. Judges Assn. (pres. 2001—02). Achievements include one of first judges to use therapists to debrief jurors following their trial to help provide psychological assistance in gruesome trials. Avocation: youth sports. Office: Superior Court PO Box 5000 Vancouver WA 98666 Office Phone: 360-397-2017. Business E-Mail: robert.harris@clark.wa.gov.

HARRIS, ROBERT LEE, JR., history professor; b. Chgo., Apr. 23, 1943; s. Robert L. Sr. and Ruby L. (Watkins) H.; m. Anita B. Campbell, Nov. 14, 1964; children: Lisa M., Leslie S., Lauren Y. BA, Roosevelt U., 1966, MA, 1968; PhD, Northwestern U., 1974. Tchr. 6th grade St. Rita Elem. Sch., Chgo., 1965-68; instr. Miles Coll., Birmingham, Ala., 1968-69; asst. prof. U. Ill., Urbana, 1972-75, Cornell U., Ithaca, NY, 1975-82, assoc. prof. history, 1982—2004, dir. Africana studies, 1986-91, vice provost, 2000—, prof., 2004—. Mem. tech. adv. com. Grad. Record Exam., Princeton, N.J., 1988-94; cons. Cicada Films, N.Y.C., 1988-89, Cin. Pub. Sch. System, 1990-91; chair adv. com. for U.S. history Coun. for Internat. Exch. of Scholars, Washington, 1992-94; mem. N.Y. State adv. com. U.S. Commn. on Civil Rights, 1999-2002. Author: Black Studies in the United States, 1990, Teaching African-American History, 1992; also articles. Bd. dirs. N.Y. Coun. for the Humanities, N.Y.C., 1983-87; trustee DeWitt Hist. Soc., Ithaca, 1994-99. NEH fellow, 1974-75, Ford Found. fellow, 1983-84; W.E.B. DuBois Inst. fellow Harvard U., 1983-84; Rockefeller Humanities fellow SUNY, Buffalo, 1991-92. Mem. Am. Hist. Assn. (life, chmn. program com. 1995), Assn. for Study of Afro-Am. Life and History (life, pres. 1991-92), Orgn. Am. Historians (life, chair com. on minority history and historians 1999)), Soc. for History of Edn. (bd. dirs. 1996—), Alpha Phi Alpha (nat. historian 1999—). Avocations: music, gardening, jogging, basketball. Office: Cornell U Africana Studies Rsch Ctr Ithaca NY 14850 Office Phone: 607-255-5358.

HARRIS, ROBERT NORMAN, advertising executive, educator; b. St. Paul, Feb. 11, 1920; s. Nathan and Esther (Roberts) H.; m. Paula Nidorf, May 2, 1992; children: Claudia, Robert Norman, Randolph B. BA, U. Minn., 1940. A founder Toni Co., div. Gillette Co., 1940-55; exec. v.p. Lee King & Ptnrs., Chgo., 1955-60, Allen B. Wrisley Co., Chgo., 1960-62, North Advt., Chgo., 1962-72; pres. Robert Piguet, Ltd., Chgo., 1972-73, Westbrook/Harris, Inc., Chgo., 1973-77; exec. v.p., gen. mgr. Creamer Inc., Chgo., 1977-81; pres. The Harris Creative Group, Inc., 1981—; prof. advt. and mass communications San Jose State U. (Calif.), 1983-92. Bd. dirs. KTEH Pub. Broadcasting Sys. Found., San Jose, 1987-99, CHM Villages Golf and Country Club CATV Sys., 1995-99. Mem. NATAS, Am. Mktg. Assn., Am. Advt. Fedn., Am. Assn. Advt. Agys., Sons in Retirement (bd. dirs. 1986-90). Office Phone: 310-474-0302. Personal E-mail: zugmir11@aol.com.

HARRIS, ROBERT SHIELDS, dean; b. Eden, N.C., Nov. 6, 1949; married; 2 children. BA in econs. summa cum laude, Davidson Coll., 1971; PhD in econs., Princeton U., 1977. Faculty Wharton Sch. Bus., U. Pa., 1975-78, Kenan-Flagler Bus. Sch., U. NC, Chapel Hill, 1978—88, Darden Grad. Sch. Bus. Adminstrn., U. Va., Charlottesville, 1988—, Charles C. Abbott prof. bus. adminstrn. and C. Stewart Sheppard prof. bus. adminstrn., assoc. dean faculty Charlottesville, 1990—93, dean, 2001—; v.p., chief learning officer United Tech. Corp., 1998—2001. Vis. prof. London Grad. Sch. Bus., 1984. Assoc. editor: Fin. Mgmt., 1984—93, Jour. Fin. Rsch., 1984—90, Fin. Review, 1992—98; co-author (with John Pringle): (textbooks) Introductory Corporate Finance, 1989, Essentials of Managerial Finance, 1984, 1987; co-author: (with R. Bruner and K. Eades) (CD/ROM Tutorial) Finance Interactive, 1997. Mem.: Fin. Mgmt. Assn. (v.p. fin. edn.). Office: Darden Grad Sch Bus Adminstrn U Va PO Box 6550 Charlottesville VA 22906-6550 Office Phone: 434-924-7481. Business E-Mail: HarrisR@darden.virginia.edu.

HARRIS, ROGER CLARK, psychiatrist, consultant; b. Washington, Aug. 27, 1938; s. Lester Wilbur and Margaret Elizabeth (Gilligan) H.; m. Ann Marie Dorman, Sept. 22, 1962; children: Laura Colleen, Gregory Scott Henry. BS, U. Md., 1961, postgrad., 1961—62, MD, 1968. Diplomate Am. Bd. Med. Examiners, Am. Bd. Psychiatry and Neurology. Intern Washington Hosp. Ctr., 1968—69; resident in psychiatry U. Md. Med. Sch., 1969—72; staff psychiatrist Portsmouth Psychiat. Ctr., Va., 1972—73, Larry H. Dizmang and Assoc., Annapolis, Md., 1973—74; pvt. practice Annapolis, 1974—75; prin. Roger C. Harris Group Practice of Psychiatry and Assocs., Annapolis, 1975—; pres. Chesapeake Comprehensive Counseling Ctrs., Inc., Washington and Balt., 1988—96. Co-founder Psychiatry Consultation Svc. of Baltimore City Police Dept., 1970-72; chief psychiatry svc. Anne Arundel Gen. Hosp., Annapolis, 1978-81; asst. clin. prof. psychiatry U. Md. Sch. Medicine, 1973—; acting dir. of outpatient clinic U. Md. Emergency Psychiat. Svcs., 1971-72, chief resident, 1971-72; primary founder psychiatry dept. Anne Arundel Gen. Hosp. Mem. Disability Rev. Bd. for Anne Arundel County, 1985-87, Orgn. of Physicians for Social Responsiblity, 1985—. Recipient Cert. Appreciation Arundel Lodge, Inc., Annapolis, 1988, Mitchell Scholarship, Alpha Tau Omega Social Fraternity, College Park, Md., 1960. Mem. Chesapeake Bay Psychiat. Soc., Am. Psychiat. Assn., Md. Psychiat. Soc., Anne Arundel County Med. Soc., Am. Group Psychotherapy Assn., Orthopsychiat. Assn., Epping Forest Boat Club, Young Foresters Orgn., Alpha Tau Omega (sec. 1958-60). Democrat. Presbyterian. Avocations: boating, swimming, body surfing, bodyboard surfing, classical music. Home: 212 Eareckson Ln Stevensville MD 21666-3040 Office: 1511 Ritchie Hwy Ste 201 Arnold MD 21012-2410 Office Phone: 410-757-1511.

HARRIS, ROGERS SANDERS, bishop; b. Anderson, S.C., Feb. 22, 1930; s. Wilmot Louis and Sarah Elizabeth (Sanders) H.; m. Anne Marshall Stewart, Mar. 28, 1953; children: Katherine Anne, Frances Elizabeth, Rebecca Susan. BA, U. of South, 1952, MDiv, 1957, DD (hon.), 1986; D Ministry, Va. Theol. Sem., 1977, DD (hon.), 1986. Ordained deacon Episcopal Ch., 1957, priest, 1958, bishop, 1985. Vicar Grace Episcopal Ch., Ridge Spring, S.C., 1957-59, St. Paul's Episcopal Ch., Batesburg, S.C., 1957-59; rector Ch. of Good Shepherd, Greer, S.C., 1959-69, St. Christopher's Ch., Spartanburg, S.C., 1969-85; suffragan bishop Diocese of Upper S.C., Columbia, S.C., 1985-89; bishop Diocese of S.W. Fla., St. Petersburg, 1989-97. V.p. Province IV of Episcopal Ch., 1991-94, pres., 1994-97; mem. Presiding Bishop's Coun. of Advice, N.Y.C., 1994-97. Trustee U. of South, Sewanee, Tenn., 1985—; trustee, v.p. Bishop Gray Inn, Davenport, Fla., 1989-97. 1st lt. USMC, 1952-54, Korea. Mem. Order of Holy Cross (assoc.). Episcopalian.

HARRIS, RONALD DAVID, chemical engineer; b. Norman, Okla., Apr. 9, 1938; s. Loyd Ervin and Maurine Cora (Dill) H.; m. Judith Anne Wright, July 28, 1962 (div.); children: Todd David (dec.), Scott Howard, Susanna Katherine. B.Chem. Engring., M.Sc., Ohio State U., 1961; MBA, U. Cin., 1970; student, Chase Law Sch., Cin., 1970-71. Chem. engr. Procter & Gamble Co., Cin., 1961-62, process devel. group leader, 1964-71; mgr. food product devel. Clorox Co., Oakland, Calif., 1971-73, dir. R & D Pleasanton, Calif., 1973-77; v.p. R & D Anderson Clayton Foods, Dallas, 1977-87; v.p. tech. Kraft Inc., Glenview, Ill., 1987-90; v.p. Kraft U.S.A. Tech., 1990-94; v.p. sci. rels. Kraft Foods, Inc., 1994-96; exec. v.p. R & D, Nabisco, Inc., Hanover, N.J., 1999-2001; mng. gen. ptnr. Harris Mgmt. LLC, 1998—. Instr. Keller Grad. Sch. Mgmt., 1995—; assoc. dir. exec. edn., sr. lectr. Ohio State U., 1996-99, 2001—; adj. prof. food sci., lectr. mgmtm. sci. Ohio State U., 1996—. Patentee process for adsorbent bleaching oils, dry prepared fluffy frosting mixes. Trustee San Ramon Valley Unified Sch. Dist., 1977; mem. Richardson City Planning Commn., 1980-83, Richardson City Coun., 1983-87, Lake Forest Bldg. Rev. Bd., 1993-99; bd. dirs. Richardson Symphony Orch., 1982-85, Heard Natural Sci. Mus., 1985-87, Richardson br. YMCA, 1984-87, 1st United Meth. Ch., Richardson, 1986-87, Chilled Foods Assn., 1988-94, 1st Presbyn. Ch., Lake Forest, 1988—; bd. dirs. Hull House Assn., 1988-96, vice chmn., 1993-96; mem. citizens adv. com. North Tex. Mcpl. Water Dist., 1980; mem. adv. com. doctorate in chemistry program U. Tex., Dallas, 1983-89; mem. adv. bd. dept. food sci. U. Minn., 1984-96; mem. adv. bd. dept. chem. engring. Ohio State U., 1991—, pres. Chem. Engring. Alumni Soc., 1998-99, alumni assn. adv. coun. Ohio State U., 2000—, mem. Pres.' Club; mem. adv. bd. Masters in Ops. and Tech. Ill. Inst. Tech., 1995-99; mem. Leadership Richardson, 1984-87; life mem. Julian C. Hyer Youth Camp; mem. Littlefield Soc., U. Tex., Austin, 1991—. Officer U.S. Army, 1962-64. Named Disting. Alumnus, Ohio State U., 1992, Meritorious Svc. award, 2000. Mem. Am. Chem. Soc., Inst. Food Technologists, Am. Oil Chemists Soc., Richardson C. of C. (1st v.p., dir., pres. 1982), Richardson Hist. Soc., Tex. Mcpl. League, Columbus Athletic Club, Lake Forest Club, Lions (bd. dirs., pres. 1982-83), Columbus Rotary, Symposiarchs, Tau Beta Pi, Phi Eta Sigma (past chpt. pres.), Phi Lambda Upsilon, Delta Mu Delta, Kappa Sigma (past chpt. pres., alumnus advisor 1996-99, house corp. 2001—). Home: 1051 Urlin Ave Columbus OH 43212 E-mail: hiyoron@aol.com.

HARRIS, RONNA S., artist, educator; b. L.A., July 25, 1952; d. James and Janet (Marcuson) H.; m.; 1 child, Claire Morgan. Student, San Francisco Art Inst., 1973; BA in Drawing, Calif. State U., Northridge, 1974; MFA in Painting, U. Calif., Santa Barbara, 1977. Tchg. asst. U. Calif., Santa Barbara, 1976-77; instr. art Humboldt State U., Arcata, Calif., 1977-78; asst. prof. Saddleback Coll., Mission Viejo, Calif., 1978; asst. prof. dept. art and art history U. Miami, Coral Gables, Fla., 1985-89; asst. prof. dept. art Newcomb Coll., Tulane U., New Orleans, 1989-92, assoc. prof., 1992—. Scenic artist ABC-TV, NBC-TV, Universal Studios, L.A., Disney Studios, L.A., 1979-85; dir. vis. artist program Humboldt State U., 1977-78; undergrad. advisor, grad. advisor U. Miami, 1985-89, coord. found. drawing program dept. art and art history, 1988-89; grad. advisor Tulane U., 1989-91, freshman advisor art dept. Newcomb Coll., 1990-91, 92, 93, grad. coord. dept. art Newcomb Coll., 1993-94; juror art exhbns. at Miami-Dade County Pub. Schs., 1986, Fla. Internat. U., Miami, 1987, Royal Poinciana Fiesta, City of Miami, 1988, Broward Art Guild, 1988, Plantation Jr. Woman's Club, 1988, Ann. Deerfield Beach Festival of Arts, 1989; lectr., slide presenter Fla. Internat. U., 1987, U. Mass., Amherst, U. Colo., 1991; mem. panel, slide presenter Slidell Cultural Ctr., Calif., 1991. One-woman shows include U. Calif., Santa Barbara, 1977, Herbert Palmer Gallery, Beverly Hills, Calif., 1979, 84, New Gallery, Coral Gables, 1985, O.K. South Gallery, Miami Beach, Fla., 1987, Sculpture Space Gallery, South Miami, Fla., 1987, Gellert Fine Arts Gallery, Bay Harbor Islands, Miami, 1988, Phyllis Morris Gallery, L.A., 1989, Newcomb Gallery, Tulane U., 1990, Still-Zinsel Gallery, New Orleans, 1990, 92, 94, 96; exhibited in group shows at numerous galleries and mus., most recently Still-Zinsel Gallery, 1990, 91, 92, 93, 94, 95, 96, Alexander F. Milliken Gallery, N.Y.C., 1990, U. Colo., 1991, Capricorn Gallery, Bethesda, Md., 1991, Contemporary Art Ctr., New Orleans, 1992, Newcomb Gallery, 1990, 93, 94, Pensacola (Fla.) Art Mus., 1993, Louisiana Women Artists, Baton Rouge, 1994; represented in permanent collections at New Orleans Arts Coun., S.E. Bank, Fla., Interloom, Inc., Atlanta, Jacksonville (Fla.) Art Mus., various individuals; contbr. revs., articles and works to publs. in field. Recipient Anna Arnold Bing award UCLA, 1975, 1st pl., Best of Show award Santa Barbara County Fair, 1977, finalist Am. Acad. in Rome, 1977, Cert. of Excellence, Internat. Art Competition, Scarsdale (N.Y.) Art Soc., 1987, many others. Home: 4111 Vincennes Pl New Orleans LA 70125-2742 Office: Tulane Univ Newcomb Art Dept New Orleans LA 70118

HARRIS, ROY JAY, JR., editor, business journalist; b. St. Louis, Oct. 2, 1946; s. Roy Jay and Ruth Dorothy (Schofer) H.; m. Andrea McKenna (dec.); children: David McKenna Harris, Roy Jay Harris III; m. Eileen Carol McIntyre. BS in Journalism, Northwestern U., 1968, MS in Journalism, 1971. Staff reporter The Wall Street Jour., Pitts., 1971-74, L.A., 1974-88, dep. bur. chief, 1988—94; sr. editor CFO Mag., Boston, 1996—. James C. Millstone Meml. lectr. Emerson Coll., 2002, adj. prof., 04. Contbg. author: Best Practices of the Business Press, 2004. With U.S. Army, 1969-70. Mem. Am. Soc. Bus. Publ. Editors (nat. v.p. 2003-04, nat. pres. 2005—), Soc. Am. Bus. Editors and Writers, Soc. Profl. Journalists. Office: CFO Mag 253 Summer St Fl 3 Boston MA 02210-1118 E-mail: royharris@cfo.com.

HARRIS, S. BUDDY, architect, interior designer; b. N.Y.C., Jan. 4, 1927; s. Edward and Lola Taylor; m. Phyllis Frank, July 8, 1951; children: Robert I., Richard Craig. BBA, CCNY, 1948. Exec. dir. Redevel. Agy., Woodbridge, N.J., 1960-64; dir. dept. planning and devel. City of Woodbridge, 1964-66; v.p. and mng. dir. Gruen Assocs., Washington, 1966-84, ptnr., 1984-86, pres., 1986-88, ret., 1988. Guest lectr. Sch. of Architecture, Va. Poly. Inst., 1978, Sch. Arch., Cath. U., 1979; founder Inst. for Econ. and Environ. Balance, 1976-84; dir. Greater Washington Bd. of Trade, 1980-86, vice chmn. Cmty. Devel. Bur., 1979-84. Editor, pub.: U.S. Air Force Aux.Fla. Facts Mag., 1995—. Chmn. D.C. Met. Planning Com., 1975-79, D.C. Water Resources Com., 1977-84; v.p. Washington Bldg. Congress, 1978; mem. house com., chmn. design com. Jewish Ctr. of Marco Island, 1989; vice chmn. We The People, Inc.; active Collier County Beach Renourishment Adv. Com., 1990, Collier County Commrs. Adv. Com., 1990-92; chief of staff Marco Island CAP Squadron, 1990, Fla. wing staff officer, 1997-2001; mem. residents bd., treas. Residents Assn. Fund. Lt. col. USAF Aux., 2001—. Mem.: EPE Computer Club (chmn., 2002—). Home: Apt B509 23343 Blue Water Cir Boca Raton FL 33433-7025 E-mail: sbharris@att.net.

HARRIS, SCOTT BLAKE, lawyer; b. N.Y.C., June 18, 1951; s. Stanley Robert and Adele Jean (Ganger) Harris; m. Barbara Straughn, Aug. 5, 1978. AB magna cum laude, Brown U., 1973; JD magna cum laude, Harvard U., 1976. Bar: DC 1977, U.S. Ct. Appeals (DC cir.) 1978, U.S. Supreme Ct. 1983. Law clk. to presiding justice U.S. Dist. Ct., Washington, 1976-77; assoc. Williams & Connolly, Washington, 1977-84, ptnr., 1984-93; chief counsel Bur. Export Adminstrn., U.S. Dept. Commerce, Washington, 1993-94; chief internat. bur. FCC, 1994-96; ptnr. Gibson, Dunn & Crutcher, Washington, 1996-98; mng. ptnr. Harris, Wiltshire & Grannis LLP, Washington, 1998—. Mem. adv. bd. Ctr. Wireless Tech., Va. Tech. U., 1996—2004, Satellite Comm. Mag., 1996—2000, Critical Infrastructure Fund, LLP, 1999—2000, Telecom. Reports Internat., 2000—02, Morphics Tech., Inc., 2000—02; adj. prof. Georgetown U. Law Ctr., 1996, 2001—02. Columnist: Aviation Week, 2000—01, Space News, 2001—. Trustee Fed. Comm. Bar Assn. Found., 1997—2000. Recipient Marconi-Bell award, Nat. Assn. Radio and TV Engrs., 2004. Mem.: ABA (co-chair telecom. com., sect. internat. law 1999—2002), US ITU Assn. (bd. dirs. 1999—2003), Fed. Comm. Bar Assn. (co-chair online comm. com. 2000—02, co-chair legislation com. 2004—), Phi Beta Kappa. Home: 3409 Fulton St NW Washington DC 20007-1436 Office: Harris Wiltshire & Grannis LLP 1200 18th St NW Washington DC 20036-2506 Office Phone: 202-730-1330. Business E-Mail: sharris@harriswiltshire.com.

HARRIS, SKILA, government agency administrator; b. Bowling Green, Ky. d. Skiles Browning and Dorothy (Lester) Harris; m. Fred Graham. BS in Polit. Sci., Western Ky. U.; MS in Legis. Affairs, George Washington U. V.p. devel. and compliance Steiner-Liff Iron and Metal Co., Nashville, 1989—92; spl. asst. V.P. Al Gore, 1993—97; chief of staff Tipper Gore, 1993—97; with U.S. Dept. Energy, Washington, U.S. Synthetic Fuels Corp.; exec. dir. U.S. Sec. of Energy Adv. Bd., 1997—99; dir. TVA, Knoxville, 1999—. Bd. dirs. Nuclear Elec. Ins. Ltd.; vice chair2002 Consumer Energy Coun. Am.'s Forum on Energy Security and Electric Industry Restructuring. Grad. Leadership Knoxville, 2001. Office: TVA 400 W Summit Hill Dr Knoxville TN 37902-1499 Office Phone: 865-632-3871.

HARRIS, STANLEY S., retired judge, arbitrator, mediator; b. Washington, Oct. 19, 1927; s. Stanley Raymond and Elizabeth (Sutherland) H.; m. Rebecca Ashley, Aug. 1, 1964; children: Scott Sutherland, Todd Ashley, Mark Ashley. BS, U. Va., 1951, JD, 1953. Bar: D.C. 1953, U.S. Supreme Ct. 1964. Assoc., then ptnr. Hogan & Hartson, Washington, 1953-70; judge Superior Ct. D.C., 1971-72, D.C. Ct. Appeals, 1972-82; U.S. atty. for D.C. Dept. Justice, 1982-83; judge U.S. Dist. Ct. D.C., 1983—, sr. judge, 1996—2001; ret., 2001; arbitrator, mediator. Mem. com. on criminal law Jud. Conf. U.S., 1988-94, chmn. com. intercircuit assignments, 1994-2000. Served with U.S. Army, 1945-47. Recipient Judiciary award Assn. Fed. Investigators, 1982. Mem. Bar Assn. D.C. (bd. dirs. 1970-72, Lawyer of Yr. award 1982, Disting. Career award 1996), Lawyers' Club of Washington (pres. 1998-99). Republican. Home: 4982 Sentinel Dr Apt 406 Bethesda MD 20816-3579 Personal E-mail: stanley.s.harris@verizon.net.

HARRIS, STEVEN MICHAEL, lawyer, accountant; b. Miami, Fla., Feb. 27, 1952; s. Joseph Herbert and Mollye (Rinzler) H. BBA, U. Ga., 1973, M in Acctg., 1974; JD, U. Miami, 1979. Bar: Fla. 1979, U.S. Dist. Ct. (so. dist.) Fla. 1979, U.S. Claims Ct. 1979, U.S. Tax Ct. 1979, U.S. Ct. Appeals (11th cir.) 1982, U.S. Dist. Ct. (mid. dist.) Fla. 1980, U.S. Dist. Ct. (no. dist.) Fla. 1989; CPA, Fla.; pvt. practice, Miami; adj. lectr. tax course Fla. Internat. U., 1976, U. Miami Grad. Sch. Bus., 1978-83; lectr. in field. Mem. ABA (chair civil and criminal tax penalties, sect. taxation 1992—). Contbr. numerous articles to profl. jours. Office: 1000 Brickell Ave Ste 1140 Miami FL 33131-3014

HARRIS, STUART INNES, construction equipment engineer, marketing professional; b. NYC, Feb. 2, 1928; s. John David and Rose Marie (Fatt) H.; m. Susan Margiotta, Dec. 4, 1954 (div. Feb. 1971); children: Douglas Keith, Gail Harris Nichols, Patricia Ann. BS in Mining Engring., Lehigh U., 1951; MS in Orgnl. Dynamics, U. Pa., 1984. Registered profl. engr., NJ, Ala. Projects engr. N.Y. Trap Rock Corp., West Nyack, 1951-52; line officer USN, 1952-55; sales engr. Keasbey & Mattison, Ambler, Pa., 1955-58; v.p. Vacuum Concrete Corp. of Am., Phila., 1958-60; engring. control analyst RCA, Moorestown, N.J., 1960-62; sales engr. COMAD Equipment Corp., Moorestown, 1962-63, State Equipment Corp., Phila., 1963-65; CEO, owner Stuart I. Harris Constrn. Equipment, Haddonfield, N.J., 1965—; mgr. ea. distbn. ctr. Clark Equipment Co., Benton Harbor, Mich., 1970-74; sr. crane engr. Phila. Naval Shipyard, 1980-90; sales rep. Alex Lyon & Son, Bridgeport, N.Y., 1992—. Heavy equipment expert cons. Tech. Adv. Svc. for Attys., Blue Bell, Pa., 1973—. Mem. Friends Hosp. Corp., Phila., 1978—; mem. property com. Haddonfield Friends Meeting, 1995-2000; charter mem. Charles Custis Harrison Soc., U. Pa., 1995—. Lt. comdr. USNR, 1951-54, Korea. Recipient Legion of Honor award The Chapel of Four Chaplains, Valley Forge, Pa., 1980. Mem. ASME, Soc. of Mining, Metallurg., and Petroleum Engrs., Cooper River Yacht Club (over 100 racing trophies). Republican. Mem. Soc. Of Friends. Office: Stuart I Harris Constrn Equipment PO Box 255 Haddonfield NJ 08033-0217 Office Phone: 856-429-9149. Personal E-mail: stuharris50@hotmail.com.

HARRIS, SUSAN V., lawyer; b. 1961; BA, Oberlin Coll., 1983; JD, U. Chgo., 1992. Bar: Ill. 1992. With Sidley Austin Brown & Wood, Chgo., ptnr., 2000—. Mem.: ABA. Office: Sidley Austin Brown and Wood Bank One Plz 10 S Dearborn St Chicago IL 60603

HARRIS, SYDNEY MALCOLM, retired judge; b. Toronto, Ont., Can., June 23, 1917; s. Samuel Aaron and Rose (Geldzaeler) H.; m. Enid Harriet Perlman, Nov. 9, 1949; children: Mark, David. BA, U. Toronto, 1939; Barrister-at-Law, Osgoode Hall, Toronto, 1942; LLB, York U., Toronto, 1991. Bar: Ont. 1942, created Queen's Counsel 1962. Barrister, solicitor firm Harris & Rubenstein, Toronto, 1950-76; judge criminal div. Ont. Provincial Ct., Toronto, 1976-90; judge provincial divsn. Ont. Ct., Toronto, 1990-92. Mem. Assessment Rev. Bd., 1993-99; dep. judge Small Claims Ct., 1993-99. Pres. Canadian Jewish Congress, 1974-77. Recipient Centennial medal, 1967, Queen's Jubilee medal, 1977 Mem. Am. Judges assn., Can. Bar Assn., Ont. Conf. Judges, Assn. of Ont. Land Surveyors (hon.; exec. com. coun. and complaints rev. councillor 1995-2001). Home: 3303 Don Mills Rd Apt 2006 Toronto ON Canada M2J 4T6

HARRIS, T. GEORGE, editor; b. Hillsdale, Ky., Oct. 4, 1924; s. Garland and Luna (Byrum) Harris; m. Sheila Hawkins, Oct. 31, 1952 (dec. Jan. 1977); children: Amos, Anne, Crane, Gardiner; m. Ann Rockefeller Roberts, Mar. 3, 1979 (div. Apr. 1993); children: Clare, Joseph, Mary Louise, Rachel Pierson; m. Jeannie Pinkerton, Sept. 12, 1998; 1 child, A. J. Clancy. Student, U. Ky., 1946; BA, Yale U., 1949. Reporter Clarksville (Tenn.) Leaf-Chronicle, 1942; corr. Time, Dallas, Atlanta and Washington, 1949—55; Chgo. bur. chief Time-Life-Fortune, 1955-58, San Francisco bur. chief, 1960-62; sr. editor Look mag., 1962-68; editor in chief Psychology Today mag., 1969-76, 88-90, US, 1977; founding editor Am. Health mag., Behavior Today, AH Fitness Bull., Spirituality & Health, Beliefnet.com, 1980-90; exec. editor Harvard Bus. Rev., Boston, 1992-93; cons. P&G Creative Svcs. Group, 1993—; editor UCSD-Connect Hi-tech. Weekly Online, 2000—03. Sci. adv. ABC's 20/20 Program, Inst. Advancement of Health. Editor: WGBH Bodywatch on PBS. Bd. dirs. Am. Health Found., Ch. Soc. for Coll. Work, Nat. Vol. Ctrs., Rockefeller Bros. Fund, Go Code Corp.; med. adv. com. Nat. YMCA; regent Cathedral of St. John the Divine, NYC. Staff sgt., 1st lt. battlefield Commn. at Bastogne, F.A. AUS, WWII. Mem.: Time-Life Alumni, Century Assn., Yale Club N.Y.C., UCSD Faculty Club, La Jolla Beach and Tennis Club, Phi Beta Kappa. Episcopalian. Home and Office: 8115 Paseo Del Ocaso La Jolla CA 92037-3140 Fax: 858-459-0838. Office Phone: 858-459-5694. Personal E-mail: tgeorgeh@aol.com.

HARRIS, TERESA MARIA, visual artist; b. St. Louis, Dec. 20, 1957; d. Singleton Levi and Josie Bernice (Watkins) H. BFA, Washington U., St. Louis, 1975; MA, Fontbonne Coll., 1981; MFA, Pratt Inst., 1991. Cert. elem. and secondary sch. tchr., Mo. Art tchr. Christensted Bd. of Edn., St. Croix, V.I., 1975-76, St. Louis Bd. of Edn., 1976-87, 88-89; art tcht. Newark Mus./Rutgers U., 1995—96; prof. art N.J. City U., 1995—97, Passaic County Cmty. Coll., Paterson, NJ, 1996—2000, Katharine Gibbs Coll., 1999—2000, Jefferson Coll., Hillsboro, Mo., 2003—. Art tchr., cons. Jamaica Arts Ctr., 1992-95, Bronx Coun. on the Arts, 1992-94, Children's Arts Carnival, N.Y.C., 1991-92, Bklyn. Arts and Cultural Assn., Bklyn., 1990-91. One-woman shows include Sunshine Inn Restaurant, 1980, Vaughn Cultural Ctr., 1989, Teahouse Gallery at the N.Y. Open Ctr., N.Y.C., 1998; exhibited in group shows at Kimberly Gallery, 1976, Fontbonne Coll., 1981, U. Mo., 1982, Webster Coll., 1984, Florissant Valley Cmty. Coll., 1984, Ridge Street Gallery, 1991, L.I. City Artlofts, 1992, Citicorp Bldg., Cmty Showcase Gallery, 1992, Art in General, 1994, Serengeti Plains, 1999; contbr. articles to profl. jours. Individual artist grant N.Y. Dept. of Cultural Affairs, 1995; fellowship Nat. Endowment for the Humanities, 1980. Mem. Jamaica Co-op, Coll. Art Assn. Avocations: dance, reading, travel, walking, researching and practicing natural living and eating methods. Home: 3543 Saint Henry Ln Saint Louis MO 63121-4135

HARRIS, TERRELL LEE, prosecutor; b. 1961; BA, Rhodes Coll.; JD, U. Miss. Assoc. Kirkpatrick, Kirkpatrick and Efird, Memphis, 1986—87; asst. dist. atty. gen. Shelby County Dist. Atty.'s Office, 1987—2001; U.S. atty. (we. dist.) Tenn. U.S. Dept. Justice, 2001—. Office: 800 Clifford Davis Fed Office Bldg 167 N Main St Memphis TN 38103-1898

HARRIS, THERESA, lawyer; b. Bronx, NY, July 25, 1957; BSN, Coll. Mt. St. Vincent, Riverdale, NY, 1979; JD, Pace U., 1995. Bar: NY 1995, NJ 1995, US Dist. Ct. Ea. Dist. NY, US Dist. Ct. So. Dist. NY. Ptnr. Wilson, Elser, Moskowitz, Edelman & Dicker LLP, NYC. Mem.: ABA, NY State Bar Assn. Office: Wilson Elser Moskowitz Edelman & Dicker LLP 23rd Fl 150 E 42nd St New York NY 10017-5639 Office Phone: 212-490-3000 ext. 2776. Office Fax: 212-490-3038. Business E-Mail: harrist@wemed.com.

HARRIS, THOMAS L., public relations executive; b. Dayton, Ohio, Apr. 18, 1931; s. James and Leona (Blum) H.; m. JoAnn K. Karch, Apr. 14, 1957; children: James Harris, Theodore Harris. BA, U. Mich., 1953; MA, U. Chgo., 1956. Exec. v.p. Daniel J. Edelman Inc., Chgo., 1957-67; v.p. pub. rels. Needham Harper & Steers, Chgo., 1967-72; pres. Foote Cone & Belding Pub. Rels., Chgo., 1973-78, Golin-Harris Communications Inc., Chgo., 1978-89, also vice chmn.; adj. prof. Medill Sch. Journalism, Northwestern U., Evanston, Ill., 1987—; mng. ptnr. Thomas L. Harris & Co., Highland Pk., Ill., 1992—. Served with U.S. Army, 1953-55. Mem. Public Relations Soc. Am. (Gold Anvil award 2000). Office: Thomas L Harris & Co 600 Central Ave Highland Park IL 60035-3211 E-mail: ttlhco@aol.com.

HARRIS, THOMAS RAYMOND, biomedical engineer, educator; b. San Angelo, Tex., Feb. 19, 1937; s. Loyd Franklin and Rubye Harris; m. Alene Blythe Hawes; children: Calvin Thomas, Andrew Mitchell. BS, Tex. A&M U., 1958, MS, 1962; PhD, Tulane U., 1964; MD, Vanderbilt U., 1974. Design engr. Standard Oil Co. Calif., 1958-60; mem. faculty Vanderbilt U., Nashville, 1964—, prof. biomed. engring. and chem. engring., 1976—; assoc. prof. medicine Vanderbilt U. Sch. Medicine, 1980-85, prof. medicine, 1985—; dir. biomed. engring. program Vanderbilt U. Sch. Engring., 1977-88, chair dept. biomed. engring., 1988—, Orrin Henry Ingram Disting. prof. engring., 2002—. Cons. in field. Author articles in field; mem. editorial bds. profl. jours. Served as 2d lt. AUS, 1958-59. Grantee Nat. Heart, Lung and Blood Inst., NSF. Mem. Am. Physiol. Soc., Am. Inst. Chem. Engrs., Am. Soc. Engring. Edn., Am. Heart Assn. (sci. councils), Biomed. Engring. Soc. (pres. 1985-86), Soc. Engring. in Medicine and Biology, Microcirculatory Soc. Baptist. Office: Vanderbilt U Dept of Biomed Engring PO Box 1724 Nashville TN 37235 Business E-Mail: thomas.r.harris@vanderbilt.edu.

HARRIS, VENITA VAN CASPEL, retired financial planner; b. Sweetwater, Okla. d. Leonard Rankin and Ella Belle (Jarnagin) Walker; m. Lyttleton T. Harris IV, Dec. 26, 1987. Student, Duke, 1944-46; BA, U. Colo., 1948, postgrad., 1949-51, N.Y. Inst. Fin., 1962. CFP. Stockbroker Rauscher Pierce & Co., Houston, 1962-65, A.G. Edwards & Sons, Houston, 1965-68; founder, pres., owner Van Caspel & Co., Inc., Houston, 1968—87, Van Caspel Wealth Mgmt.; owner, mgr. Van Caspel Planning Svc., Van Caspel Advt. Agy.; sr. v.p. investments Raymond James and Assocs., 1987-95; ret., 1995. Moderator PBS TV show The Money Makers and Profiles of Success, 1980; 1st women mem. Pacific Stock Exchange. Author: Money Dynamics, 1978, Money Dynamics of the 1980's, 1980, The Power of Money Dynamics, Money Dynamics for the 1990's, 1988; editor: Money Dynamics Letter. Bd. dirs. Horatio Alger Assn.; trustee Northwood U.; founding mem. Com. of 200. Recipient Matrix award Theta Sigma Phi, 1969, Horatio Alger award for Disting. Americans, 1982, Disting. Woman's medal, Northwood Univ., 1988, George Norlin award U. Colo. Alumni Assn., 1987. Mem. Internat. Assn. Fin. Planners, Inst. Cert. Fin. Planners, Phi Gamma Mu, Phi Beta Kappa. Methodist. Home: 4 Saddlewood Estates Dr Houston TX 77024-6841 Office: 6524 San Felipe St Ste 102 Houston TX 77057-2611

HARRIS, VIRGINIA SYDNESS, religious organization administrator, publisher; m. G. Reed Harris; children: G. Richard, Donald Thomas, Steven Jeffrey. Student, Mills Coll., 1964—66; BA in Polit. Sci. and Edn., Moorhead State U., 1967; C.S.B., Mass. Metaphys. Coll., 1982. Asst. to presdl. interpreter U.S. Dept. State, Washington, 1967-68; sec. sch. tchr. Fargo (N.D.) Pub. Schs., 1968-70; TV host, prodr. Pub. Broadcast Sys., Fargo, 1968-70; Christian Sci. practitioner, 1979—; Christian Sci. tchr., 1982—; Christian Sci. lectr., 1983-89. Bd. dirs. LWV, 1969-74; faculty mem. Healing & Spirituality Symposium Harvard Med. Sch. and Mind/Body Inst., Boston, 1995—; clk. The First Ch. of Christ Scientist, 1986-90; bd. dirs. The Christian Sci., 1990—, chmn. bd. dirs., 1992—. Pub. The Writings of Mary Baker Eddy, 1992—. Mem., treas., bd. dirs. Nat. Found. Women Legislators, Inc., Washington, 1994-2001; fellow George H. Gallup Internat. Inst., 1998-; chmn bd. trustees The Mary Baker Eddy Libr. for the Betterment of Humanity, 2000—, Dr.'s Coun. Harvard Divine Sch.'s women's studies in religion program, 2000—; adv. bd. Drucker Found., 2001-; bd. overseers Boston Symphony Orch., 2003-. Mem. Coun. Women World Leaders Founders Fund Inaugural Cir., City Club Washington, Internat. Women's Forum (lectr., spkr., contbr. to profl. jours.). Avocations: skiing, reading, golf. Office: The First Ch of Christ Scientist 175 Huntington Ave # A253 Boston MA 02115-3117

HARRIS, WALTER EDGAR, chemistry professor; b. Wetaskiwin, Alta., Can., June 9, 1915; s. William Ernest and Emma Louise (Humbke) H.; m. Phyllis Pangburn, June 14, 1942; children: Margaret Anne, William Edgar. BS, U. Alta., 1938, MS, 1939; PhD, U. Minn., 1944; DSc (hon.), U. Waterloo, 1987, U. Alta., 1991. Research fellow U. Minn., 1943-46; prof. analytical chemistry U. Alta., Edmonton, 1946-80, chmn. dept. chemistry, 1974-79, chmn. Pres.'s Adv. Com. on Campus Revs., 1980-90. Author: (with H.W. Habgood) Programmed Temperature Gas Chromatography, 1965, (with B. Kratchovil) Chemical Separations and Measurements, 1974, Teaching Introductory Analytical Chemistry, 1974, An Introduction to Chemical Analysis, 1981, Risk Assessment, 1997, (with H.A. Laitinen) Chemical Analysis, 1975; contbr. numerous articles to profl. jours. Decorated Order of Can.; recipient Outstanding Achievement award U. Minn., 1973; Govt. Alta. Achievement award, 1974, Associated Honor award U. Alta. Alumni, 2003. Fellow AAAS, Royal Soc. Can., Chem. Inst. Can. (hon., Fisher Sci. Lecture award 1969, Chem. Edn. award 1975, hon. fellow, 2001); mem. Am. Chem. Soc., Sigma Xi. Home: Ste 515 11148-84 Ave Edmonton AB Canada T6G 0V8 Office: U Alta Dept Chem Edmonton AB Canada T6G 2G2 Office Phone: 780-492-3252. E-mail: Walter.Harris@ualberta.ca.

HARRIS, WARREN LYNN, computer engineer; b. Albuquerque, May 8, 1966; s. Jerry Dale and Viola Guadalupe (Gutierrez) H., m. Clarissa Cosgrove, Apr. 1, 1998, 1 child: Tiffany Bellan. BS, Ariz. State U., 1988. Programming mgr. I.P.C. Computer Svcs., Inc., Tempe, Ariz., 1985-89; software sys. engr. Intel Corp., Chandler, Ariz., 1990; dir. software R & D Pics, Inc., Tempe, 1990-91; dir. software R & D parics divsn. Ansoft Corp., Tempe, 1991-94, devel. engr. Phoenix, 1994—2002; software engr. Neolinear, Inc., Tempe, 2002—04; mem. cons. staff Cadence Design Systems, Tempe, 2004—. Contbr. articles to profl. jours. Mem. IEEE, Assn. for Computing Machinery, Mortar Bd., Golden Key, Upsilon Pi Epsilon. Avocations: racquetball, model building, chess, pool, star trek collecting. Office: Cadence Design Sys Inc 1620 W Fountainhead Pkwy Ste 250 Tempe AZ 85282

HARRIS, WARREN WAYNE, lawyer; b. Houston, Nov. 5, 1962; BBA, U. Houston, 1985, JD, 1988. Bar: Tex. 1988, U.S. Ct. Appeals (5th cir.) 1989, U.S. Ct. Appeals (fed. cir.) 1995, U.S. Ct. Appeals (8th, 10th and 11th cirs.) 1996, U.S. Ct. Appeals (9th cir.) 2004, U.S. Dist. Ct. (so., no., ea. and we. dists.) Tex. 1990, U.S. Supreme Ct. 1991; bd. cert. civil appellate law Tex. Bd. Legal Specialization. Briefing atty. Tex. Supreme Ct., Austin, 1988-89; ptnr. Bracewell & Giuliani LLP, Houston, 1996—. Adj. prof. U. Houston Law Ctr., 2001—. Editor-in-chief: Houston Lawyer mag., 1991-92; assoc. editor: The Appellate Advocate, 1992-97; editor: The Appellate Lawyer, 1994-96; chair editl. bd. Tex. Bar Jour., 2002—. Fellow: Houston Bar Found., Tex. Bar Found. (co-chair dist. 4 nominating com. 1994—2000); mem.: ABA (tort and ins. practice sect. appellate advocacy com. 1990—, chair litigation sect. appellate practice com. 2000—01), Houston Lawyer Referral Svc. (trustee 1994—95), Houston Young Lawyers Assn. (pres. 1999—2000), Houston Bar Assn. (coun. appellate practice sect. 1993—, chair appellate practice sect. 1998—99, Pres.'s award 1993—94), Tex. Young Lawyers Assn. (bd. dirs. 1994—98, outstanding dir. 1995—96, Pres.'s award 1996—97), State Bar Pro Bono Coll., State Bar Coll. (bd. dirs. 1994—95), State Bar Tex. (appellate sect. 1988—, coun. 1997—2000, chmn. 2005—), Houston Livestock Show and Rodeo (steer auction com. 2001—, capt. 2003—), Stages Repertory Theatre (pres., chmn. 1994—95, bd. dirs., WineFest com. chair 1994—96), Order of Barons, Order of Barristers, Phi Delta Phi. Republican. Office: Bracewell & Patterson LLP 711 Louisiana St Ste 2100 Houston TX 77002-2781 Office Phone: 713-221-1490. Business E-Mail: warren.harris@bracewellgiuliani.com.

HARRIS, WAYNE, retail executive; Various positions Kroger Co., 1962—92; chmn., CEO Grand Union Co., 1997—2000, Can. Co. GAP, divsn. of the Gt. Atlantic and Pacific Tea Co.; sr. v.p. GAP (Northeast divsn.); exec. v.p., COO GAP (US ops.); exec. v.p. JC Penney Corp., 2000—; chmn., CEO Eckerd Corp., 2000—. Office: J C Penney Corp 6501 Legacy Dr Plano TX 75024-3698

HARRIS, WAYNE MANLEY, lawyer; b. Dec. 28, 1925; s. George H. and Constance M. Harris; children: Wayne, Constance, Karen, Duncan, Claire. LLB, U. Rochester, 1951. Bar: N.Y. 1952, U.S. Supreme Ct. 1958. Ptnr. Harris, Chesworth & O'Brien (and predecessor firms), Rochester, NY, 1958—. Drafter 5 laws passed in State of N.Y. Pres. Adopt-A-Stream program Delta Labs, Inc., 1971—; pres. Friends Bristol Valley Playhouse Found., 1984—87, Monroe County Conservation Coun., Inc., 1956—61, v.p., 1984—87, Powder Mills Pk. Hatchery Preservation, Inc., 1993—95, pres., 1995—2002. With U.S. Army, 1944—46, Germany. Decorated Bronze Star; named Vol. Conservationist of the Yr., N.Y. State Conservation Coun. Inc., 2000; recipient Sportsman of the Yr. award, Genesee Conservation League, Inc., 1960, Conservationist of the Yr. award, Monroe County Conservation Coun., Inc., 1961, N.Y. State Conservation Coun. Nat. Wildlife Fedn. Water Conservation, 1967, Kiwanian of the Yr. award, Kiwanis Club, 1965, Livingston County Fedn. Sportsmen award, 1967, Hon. Fellowship award, Rochester Acad. Sci., 1970, Meritorious Leadership in Civic Devel. award, Rochester C. of C., 1972, Svc. award, Rochester Against Intoxicated Drivers, 1989, Conspicuous Svc. cross, N.Y. State, 2000, N.Y. State Senate Resolution 241 award, 2001. Mem.: ATLA, Indsl. Mgmt. Coun., AIDA Reins. and Arbitration Soc., N.Y. State Trial Lawyers Assn., Wild Turkey Fedn. Home: 60 Mendon Center Rd Honeoye Falls NY 14472-9363 Office: Harris Chesworth et al 300 Linden Oaks Ste 100 Rochester NY 14625

HARRIS, WESLEY L., aeronautical engineer, educator; b. Richmond, Va., Oct. 29, 1941; s. William M. and Rosa P. (Minor) Harris; m. Myrtle Ann Satterwhite, June 14, 1960 (div. Mar. 1985); children: Wesley Jr., Zelda, Marcus, Kamau, Kalomo, Eletha; m. Sandra Maria Butler, Sept. 21, 1985; 1 child, Tosha. B in Aeronautical Engring. with honors, U. Va., 1964; MA in Aeronautical Scis., Princeton U., 1966, PhD in Aeronautical Scis., 1968; LHD (hon.), Lane Coll., 1994; DEng (hon.), Milw. Sch. Engring., 1994; DSc (hon.), Old Dominion U., 1995. Asst. prof. aerospace engring. U. Va., 1968-70, assoc. prof., 1971-72; assoc. prof. physics Southern U., 1970-71; dir. office min. edn., 1975—78; assoc. prof. aeronautics & astronautics/ocean engring. MIT, Cambridge, 1973-79, assoc. prof. aeronautics and astronautics, 1980-81, prof., 1981-85, 1996—2001, Charles Stark Draper prof. of aeronautics and astronautics, 2001—, head dept. aeronautics and astronautics, 2003—; mgr. computational methods Office Aeronautics & Space Tech. NASA Hdqs., Washington, 1979-80, assoc. administr. Office of Aeronautics, 1993-96; dean sch. engring. U. Conn., Storrs, 1985-90; v.p. U. Tenn. Space Inst., Tullahoma, 1990-93. Mem. adv. groups Nat. Rsch. Coun. Commn. Engring. and Tech. Sys., Bd. Engring. Edn., Bd. Army Sci. and Tech., Air Force Studies Bd., Com. Aero. Techs.; mem. adv. com. NSF, U.S. Army Sci. Bd.; advisor univs.; nat. adv. com. dept. engring. Hampton U., 1989—96. Contbr. scientific papers to profl. jours. Trustee Sci. Mus. Conn., 1985—90, Princeton (N.J.) U., 2001—05; adv. bd. dirs. Am. City Bank, Tullahoma, 1990—93; bd. vis. sch. engring. Duke U., 1991—99; vis. com. dept. aeronautics and astronautics MIT, 1988—95. Named Milton Pikarsky Meml. lectr., CCNY Sch. Engring., 1990, Barry Goldwater chair, Am. Instns. Ariz. State U., 2000—01; recipient Herbert S. and Jane Gregory Disting. Lectr.

award, Coll. Engring. U. Fla., 1992, Dr. Martin Luther King Leadership award, MIT, 2001. Fellow: AIAA, Am. Helicopter Soc.; mem.: NAE, AAAS, Nat. Tech. Assn., Math. Assn. Am., Am. Phys. Soc. Democrat. Avocation: squash. Office: MIT Dept Aeronautics 33-207 77 Mass Ave Cambridge MA 02139-4307 Business E-Mail: weslhar@mit.edu.

HARRIS, WHITNEY ROBSON, lawyer, educator, military officer, volunteer; b. Seattle, Aug. 12, 1912; s. Olin Whitney and Lily Harris; m. Jane Freund Foster, Feb. 14, 1964 (dec.); 1 child, Eugene Whitney; m. Anna Galakatos, Jan. 8, 2000. AB magna cum laude, U. Wash., 1933; JD, U. Calif., 1936; LHD (hon.), McKendree Coll., 1999; LHD (hon.), U. Mo., 2001. Bar: Calif. 1936, U.S. Supreme Ct. 1945, Tex. 1953, U.S. Ct. Mil. Appeals 1955, Mo. 1964. Pvt. practice, L.A., 1936-42; trial counsel at trial of maj. German war criminals, Nuremberg, Germany, 1945-46; chief legal advice br. U.S. Mil. Govt. for Germany, 1946-48; prof. law So. Meth. U., 1948-54; staff dir. legal service and proc. Com. Orgn. Exec. Br. Govt., 1954; exec. dir. ABA, 1954-55; solicitor for Tex. Southwestern Bell Telephone Co., Dallas, 1955-63, gen. solicitor St. Louis, 1963-65; pvt. practice St. Louis, 1965-89; arbitration judge, 1993—. Sr. counselor Mo. Bar Assn., 1987—; lectr. UCLA, Stanford U., Washington U., Wellesley Coll., U. Denver, Reed Coll., U. Wash., Claremont Coll., Boston Coll., Williams Coll., So. Meth. U., U. Mo., McKendree Coll., Ga. State Coll., Slippery Rock U., others; trustee McKendree Coll. Author: Family Law, 1953, Tyranny On Trial, 1954, 3rd. edit., 1999, Legal Services and Procedure, 1955, The Tragedy of War, 2004; author: (with others) Law, Culture and Values, 1989; contbr. articles to profl. jours., Ency. Brit., 1954, Whitney Robson Harris collection on Third Reich Washington U., 1980. Capt. USN, 1942—46, WWII. Decorated Legion of Merit, Order of Merit Officer's Class (Germany), Medal of the War Crimes Commn. (Poland); named nat. outstanding fund raising vol. Nat. Soc. Fund Raising Execs., 1985, Disting. Lawyer St. Louis Bar Assn., 2005. Mem. ABA (chmn. internat. law sect. 1953-54, chmn. adminstrv. law sect. 1960-61), Naval War Coll. Found. (grad. level), Order of Coif, Phi Beta Kappa, Phi Kappa Psi, Delta Theta Phi. Achievements include establishment of Whitney Robson Harris Collection on Third Reich of Germany, Washington U., 1980; Whitney R. Harris Inst. Global Legal Studies, Wash. U., 2002; establishment of Whitney and Anna Harris Conservation Forum at U. Mo., St. Louis. Home: 2818 Stonington Pl Saint Louis MO 63131-3417 Personal E-mail: whitneyharris@msn.com. *Tyranny leads to inhumanity, and inhumanity is death. Let us resolve that tyranny shall not extend its sway, nor war become its game— placing our faith in the cause of justice, in the freedom of man, and in the mercy of God.*

HARRIS, WILLIAM JAMES, JR., retired science administrator; b. South Bend, Ind., June 17, 1918; s. William James and Elizabeth M. (Scott) H.; m. Ruth Laubinger, Aug. 26, 1944 (dec. 1977); children: June Elizabeth Sherren, William James III, Debbie Shafer Hayden, Britta Shafer Kreuger, Barkley Shafer.; m. Elizabeth Dotten Shafer, June 24, 1978. BS in Chem. Engring; MS in Engring, Purdue U., 1940, D.Engring. (hon.), 1978; Sc.D., M.I.T., 1948. Head ferrous alloys br. metallurgy div. Naval Research Lab., 1947-51; exec. sec. materials adv. bd. Nat. Acad. Sci.-NRC, 1951-54, exec. dir., 1957-60, asst. sec., planning div. engring., 1960-62; asst. to dir. Battelle Meml. Inst., 1954-57, asst. to v.p., 1962-67; asst. dir. tech. Columbus Labs., 1967-69; v.p. research and test dept. Assn. Am. Railroads, 1970-85; E.B. Snead and Disting. prof. transp. engring. Tex. A&M U., 1985-95; assoc. dir. Tex. Transp. Inst., 1987-95, sr. rsch. engr., 1995—97; disting. prof. emeritus/Snead prof. emeritus Tex. A&M U., 1995-97; commr. Pres.'s Commn. on Critical Infrastructure Protection, 1997-98, sr. exec., 1998-99; cons. CIAO, 1999—2002. Hon. prof. China Acad. Ry. Scis., 1987; pres. W. J. Harris, Inc., 1985-98; pres., chmn. bd. Piscataway Co., Accokeek, Md., 1958-63; mem. Nat. Exec. Res. Dept. Transp., 1983—; sr. tech. advisor UN Devel. Orgn., 1987-91. Editor: (with others) Perspectives in Materials Research, 1963; co-author: Guildelines for Best Heavy Haul Practices, 2002; contbr. (with others) articles to tech. publs. Mem. nat. materials adv. bd. Nat. Acad. Sci., 1967—, chmn., 1969-70; sec. Pres.'s Com. on Hwy. Safety, 1969; mem. high speed ground transp. adv. com. U.S. Dept. Transp., 1972-74, Md. Gov.'s Sci. Adv. Com., 1972-76, Md. Gov.'s Energy Council, 1974-76; pres. Moyoane Assn., 1951-53, 58; pres., chmn. bd. Alice Ferguson Found., 1966-68; chmn. exec. com., disting. profs. Tex. A&M U. Served to lt. comdr. USNR, 1941-45. Decorated Naval letter of commendation; recipient Disting. Svc. award (Carey award) Transp. Rsch. Bd., NRC, 1977, Roy Crum award for disting. rsch., 1989; Disting. Rsch. award Transp. Rsch. Forum, 1986; named R.R. Man of Yr., 1976; inducted into Cooperstown Conf. R.R. Hall of Fame, 1993, Batteile Meml. Inst. Transp. Hall of Fame, 1994, Internat. Heavy Haul of Fame, 1999. Fellow Am. Soc. Metals, ASME, Metall. Soc. (pres. 1970), Nat. Acad. Engring., elected 1977, (chair program com. 1995-98, chmn. audit com. 1982, fin. com. 1995-98); mem. Intelligent Transp. Soc. Am. (hon. mem., coord. coun. 1990-97, bd. dirs. 1997—, chmn. N.Am. steering com. 1993-95, chmn. clearinghouse and publ. speech com., world congress bd. dirs., Spl. award for Internat. Congress Leadership 1995), Am. Inst. Mining, Metall., and Petroleum Engrs. (dir. 1964-69, v.p. 1964-67, chmn. inst. metals divsn. 1960, Mathewson medal 1950), Engrs. Joint Coun. (bd. dirs. 1965-70, pres. 1968-70), Engring. Found. (chmn. rsch. conf. com. 1964-67, bd. dirs. 1968-70), Am. Ordnance Assn. (chmn. materials divsn. 1966-68), Nat. Security Indsl. Assn. (chmn. exec. planning com. 1965-67, chmn. rsch. and devel. adv. com. 1967-69), Transp. Rsch. Bd. (exec. com. 1977-85, 87-90, chmn. coun. 1989-95, emeritus internat. transp. sys. com. of transp. rsch. bd. com.), Nat. Def. Transp. Assn. (life, chmn. com. on engring. tech.), Found. on Engring. Techs. (chmn. 1990-97), Internat. Heavy Haul Assn. (chmn. 1982-89), Alice Ferguson Found. (hon. life mem.), Sigma Xi, Alpha Sigma Mu, Tau Beta Pi, Phi Lambda Upsilon, Sigma Delta Chi. Home: 1200 N Nash St Apt 1140 Arlington VA 22209-3682

HARRIS, WILLIAM VERNON, history professor; b. Nottingham, Eng., Sept. 13, 1938; naturalized; 1982; s. K. W. F. and Elizabeth H.; m. Silvana Patriarca; 1 child, Neil BA, Oxford U., 1961, MA, 1964, D.Phil., 1968. Instr. history Columbia U., N.Y.C., 1965-68, asst. prof., 1968-71, assoc. prof., 1971-76, prof., 1976—, William R. Shepherd prof. history, 1995—, chmn. history dept., 1988-94, acting chair, 2005. Mem. adv. council Am. acad. in Rome, 1976—, resident, 1978, 82; dir. NEH summer seminars, 1979, 81; mem. Inst. Advanced Study, Princeton, N.J., 1970-71, 78; Gray lectr. Cambridge U., 1998. Author: Rome in Etruria and Umbria, 1971, War and Imperialism in Republican Rome, 1979, Ancient Literacy, 1989, Restraining Rage: The Ideology of Anger-Control in Classic Antiquity, 2002 (James Henry Breasted prize Am. Hist. Assn.); editor: (series) Columbia Studies in the Classical Tradition, 1976—, The Imperialism of Mid-Republican Rome, 1984, The Inscribed Economy, 1993, The Transformations of Urbs Roma in Late Antiquity, 1999, Rethinking the Mediterranean, 2005; co-editor (with G. Ruffini): Ancient Alexandria between Egypt and Greece, 2004. Fellow, NEH, 1978, Guggenheim Found., 1982—83, Nat. Humanities Ctr., 1998, vis. fellow, All Souls Coll., Oxford U., Eng., 1983, St. John's Coll., Oxford U., 2002; fellow, Am. Coun. of Learned Soc., 1970—71, 2005—. Fellow AAAS, Soc. Antiquaries (London), Finnish Soc. Scis.; mem. Academia Europaea (fgn.), Archaeol. Inst. Am., Am. Philol. Assn., Am. Hist. Assn., Assn. Ancient Historians, Century Assn. Office: Columbia U 624 Fayerweather Hall New York NY 10027 E-mail: wvh1@columbia.edu.

HARRIS, WILLIAM WOLPERT, foundation administrator; b. St. Paul, Mar. 11, 1940; s. Irving Brooks and Rosetta (Wolpert) H.; m. Robie Heilbrun, 1968; 2 children. BA, Wesleyan U., 1961; PhD, MIT, 1977; DHL (hon.), Lesley Coll., 1988. Exec. Conley Electronics, 1961-63; exec. v.p. G. Barr Co., div. Pittway Corp., 1963-66; asst. to pres. North Advt., Inc., 1966; dir. Janus Films, Inc., 1966-77; asst. to dir. Fordham U. Ctr. for Communications, 1967-68. Founder, exec. dir. Pub. Interest Communication Svcs., Inc., 1976-88; instr. urban media MIT, 1977; lectr. urban media Boston U. Met. Coll., 1974, 75, 78; adj. assoc. prof. media and communications policy Tufts U., 1981-82; vis. prof. sociology Wesleyan U., 1993; vis. prof. Brandeis U., 1997-98; sr. fellow Tufts U. Coll. Citizenship and Pub. Svc., 2000—; founder, treas. KIDSPAC, 1981—; founder, chmn. Children's Rsch. and Edn. Inst., Inc., 1984—; mem. Presdl. Mission on AIDS to Africa, 1999. Ind. prodr. documentaries; contbr. articles to profl. jours. Pres. Coydog Found. Recipient Outstanding Children's Leader award Statewide Adv. Coun., Office for Children, Commonwealth of Mass., 1992, Spl. Pub. Recognition award, Mass. Psychol. Assn., 1990, Award for Disting. Contbn. to Child Advocacy, Am. Psychol. Assn., 1989, Dale Richmond award Am. Acad. Pediats., 1997, Leadership award for pub. svc. Zero to Three, 2000, Disting. Alumnus award Wesleyan U., 2001, Pub. Advocacy award Internat. Soc. for Traumatic Stress Studies, 2002. Office: 2 Brighton St 2d Fl Belmont MA 02478

HARRIS, YOLANDA, newscaster; b. Columbus, Ohio; married. BS in Broadcast Journalism, Bowling Green U. Reporter Call & Post Newspaper, Columbus, Ohio; with promotions, Kids Club dept. Sta. WSYX/WTTE-TV, reporter, 1996—99, weekend anchor, 1999—2002, main anchor, 2002—. Office: WSYX/WTTE-TV 1261 Dublin Rd Columbus OH 43215 E-mail: yharris@sbgnet.com.

HARRIS-OFFUTT, ROSALYN MARIE, counselor, consultant, mental health nurse, writer; b. Memphis; d. Roscoe Henry and Irene Elnora (Blake) Harris; 1 child, Christopher Joseph. RN, St. Joseph Cath. Sch. Nursing, Flint, Mich., 1965; student, Hurley Med. Ctr. Sch. of Anesthesia, 1970; BS in Wholistic Health Scis., Columbia-Pacific U., 1984, postgrad., 1985—. RN; cert. registered nurse in anesthesia; nat. bd. cert. addiction counselor; cert. psychiat. nursing Kalamazoo State Hosp.; lic. profl. counselor, N.C.; cert. detoxification acupuncturist; bd. cert. med.-legal nurse cons. Staff nurse anesthetist, clin. instr. Cleve. Clinic Found., 1981-82; pvt. practice psychiat. nursing and counseling; assoc. counselor human svcs. Shaker Heights, Ohio, 1982-84; ind. contractor anesthesia Paul Scott & Assocs., Cleve., 1984, Via Triad Anesthesia Assocs., Thomasville, N.C., 1984-85; sec. Cons. Psychology Counseling, P.A., 1984-86; pvt. practice psychiat. nursing and counseling Greensboro, N.C., 1984-86; pvt. practice psychiat. nursing, counseling, psychotherapy UNA Psychol. Assocs., 1986—; staff cons. Charter Hills Psychiat. Hosp. in Addictive Disease, 1991—98. Nat. resource cons. Am. Assn. Nurse Anesthetists on Addictive Disease; cons. Ctr. for Substance Abuse Prevention, also advisor to assoc. and clin. med. dir. Ctr. Substance Abuse Prevention. Contbr. chpt. to book, also articles and columns in health field. Co-sponsor adolescent group Jack and Jills of Am., Inc., Bloomfield Hills, Mich., 1975; co-sponsor Youth of Unity Ctr., Clevelend Heights, Ohio, 1981-84; vol. chmn. hospitality Old Greensboro Preservation Soc., 1985; bd. dirs. Urban League, Pontiac, Mich., 1972; apptd. mem. gov's. coun. on alcohol and other drug abuse State of N.C., 1989—, gov's. coun. women's issues of addiction, 1991—; apptd. advisor to assoc. clin., med. dir. Ctr. for Substance Abuse Prevention, Dept. Health and Human Svcs. U.S., 1991—, nat. spkrs. bur., 1991—, cons.; apptd. legis. com., mental health study commn. on child and adolescent substance abuse State of N.C., 1992—; lay speaking min. United Meth. Ch.; mem. Triad United Meth. Native Am. Ch. Mission. Columbia-Pacific U. scholar, 1983. Fellow Soc. Prevention Nutritionists; mem. Am. Assn. Profl. Hypnotherapists (registered profl. hypnotherapists, adv. bd.), Am. Assn. Nurse Anesthetists (cert.), Nat. Alaska Native Am. Indian Nurses Assn., Assn. Med. Educators and Rsch. in Substance Abuse, Nat. Acupuncture Detoxification Assn., Am. Assn. Counseling and Devel., Assn. for Med. Edn. and Rsch. in Substance Abuse, Am. Assn. Clin. Hypnotists, Am. Assn. Wholistic Practitioners, Am. Acad. Experts Traumatic Stress, Am. Nurse Hypnotheray Assn. (state pres. 1992-93), Am. Nurse Assn., Am. Holistic Nurses Assn. (charter mem.), Guilford Native Am. Assn., Negro Bus. and Profl. Women Inc. (v.p., parliamentarian 1961-83, 2001-03), Oakland County Coun. Black Nurses (v.p. 1970-74), Assn. Med. Educators (rschr. substance abuse, ad hoc com. mem. cultural diversity 1994—), Zeta Phi Beta (Nu Xi Zeta chpt. 2d anti-basilevs 1992-93, Beta Nu Zeta chpt. Greensboro). Republican. Avocations: music, nature, reading, egyptian history, metaphysics. Office: UNA Psychol Assocs and Prima Med-Legal Nurse Cons 620 S Elm St Ste 371 Greensboro NC 27406-1398 E-mail: rharrisoffutt@cs.com.

HARRISON, ANGELA EVE, manufacturing executive; b. Little Rock, Apr. 9, 1967; d. Stephen E. and Donie E. (Brown) H.; m. Petey King, Sept. 19, 1998; children: Haven Harrison King, Ashton Harrison King. BA in Psychology, U. Ark., 1989. Clin. specialist Nutri-Sys., Little Rock, 1990-91; sec., trea. Welsco, Inc., Maumelle, Ark., 1991-94, pres., CEO, 1994—. Co-chairperson Humane Soc., Pulaski County, Ark., 1996-98. Recipient Ark. Bus. Exec. Yr. Ark. Bus., 1997, named Top 100 Women Ark., 1996, 97, 98, 99, Top 500 Women Owned Cos. Working Women Mag., 1998, 99, 2000, 2001. Mem.: Internat. Oxygen Mfg. Assn. (bd. dirs. 1996—2000), Nat. Welding Supply Assn. (regional chmn. 1996—2000), Nat. Assn. Women Bus. Owners (Woman Bus. Owner of Yr., Ark. chpt. 1998), Young Pres.'s Assn. Avocation: golf. Office: Welsco Inc 9006 Crystal Hill Rd North Little Rock AR 72113-6693 Business E-Mail: mail@welsco.com.

HARRISON, ANN TUKEY, foreign language educator; b. Geneva, N.Y., Apr. 19, 1938; d. Harold Bradford and Ruth (Schweigert) Tukey; m. Michael J. Harrison, Sept. 1, 1970. BA, Mich. State U., 1957; MA, U. Mich., 1958, PhD, 1962. Instr. NDEA Summer Inst., East Lansing, Mich., 1961, U. Wis., Madison, 1961-63, asst. prof., 1963-65, Mich. State U., East Lansing, 1965-66, assoc. prof., 1966-73, prof., 1973—99; ret., 1999. Author: Charles d'Orleans and the Allegorical Mode, 1975; editor: Danse Macabre of Women, 1994. Woodrow Wilson Fellow, 1957-58; recipient Disting. Alumni award Mich. State U., 1970; named Ruth Dean lectr. in medieval studies, Mt. Holyoke Coll., 1975-76, Mich. Fgn. Lang. Tchr. of Yr., 1991. Mem. Am. Assn. Tchrs. of French (v.p. 1985-90). Home: 277 Maplewood Dr East Lansing MI 48823-4746

HARRISON, BETTY CAROLYN COOK, education educator, administrator; b. Cale, Ark., Jan. 11, 1939; d. Denver G. and Minnie (Haddox) Cook; m. David B. Harrison, Dec. 31, 1956; children: Jerry David, Phyllis Lynley. BSE, Henderson State Tchrs. Coll., Arkadelphia, Ark., 1961; MS, U. Ark., 1971; PhD, Tex. A&M U., 1975. Tchr. secondary schs., McCrory, Ark., 1962-64, Taylor, Ark., 1964069, Shongaloo, La., 1969-73, Minden, La., 1974-76, 77-80; adminstrv. intern La. Dept. Edn., 1974; cooperating tchr., supr. student tchrs. Grambling (La.) State U., 1974-76, La. Tech. U., Ruston, 1974-76, 78-80; asst. prof. vocat. edn. Va. Poly. Inst. and State U., Blacksburg, 1976-77; asst. prof. vocat. edn. Coll. Agr., La. State U., Baton Rouge, 1980-85, assoc. prof. Sch. Vocat. Edn., 1985-90, prov. vocat. edn., 1990—. Prof. career devel. specializing in instrnl. methodologies, edn. educator, sect. leader home econs. edn. La. State U., 1982-85, head dept. home econs. edn.and bus. edn., 1985-87, dir. La. Job Link Ctr., 1988-91; mem. La. State U. Grad. Coun., 1990-96, courses and curriculum sch. and coll., 1989-92. Contbr. articles to profl. jours. HEW fellow, 1973; grantee Future Homemakers Am., 1956, Coll. Acads., 1956, Ark. Edn. Assn., 1966-69, Internat. Paper Co., 1966-68, La. Dept. Edn., 1972, others. Mem. NEA (nat. assembly del.), ASTD (v.p. comm. 1991-92, sec. 1993-94), Am Vocat. Assn., Nat. Assn. Vocat. Spl. Needs Pers., Am. Vocat. Edn. Rsch. Assn., Am. Home Econs. Assn., La Home Econs. Assn. (bd. dirs., pres.-elect), La. Vocat. Assn. (bd. dirs.), La. Assn. Vocat. Home Econs. Tchrs. (pres.), Nat. Assn. Vocat. Home Econs. Tchrs., Nat. Assn. Vocat. Home Econs. Tchr. Educators, (newsletter editor), Home Econs. Edn. Assn. (regional dir., nat. v.p., editor and chair publs. 1987-93), Family Rels. Coun. La. (edn. chmn. officer) Phi Delta Kappa, Delta Kappa Gamma (chpt. v.p., rsch. chair 1978-86), Gamma Sigma Delta (historian, sec., treas. 1984-93). Democrat. Baptist. Home: 2100 College Dr Apt 157 Baton Rouge LA 70808-1810 Office: La State U Sch Vocat Edn Baton Rouge LA 70803-0001 E-mail: bcharrison@worldnett.att.net.

HARRISON, BLAIR, information technology executive; Grad. with honors, U. Bristol. Architect 2G Mobile Telephony Group for Cable and Wireless PLC; CEO, founder of computer animation software co. London; founding exec., chief tech. officer FasTV (online video libr.); exec. v.p., chief tech. officer iFilm, Hollywood, 2001—. Recipient Rave award, Wired mag., 2005. Office: iFilm 1024 N Orange Dr Los Angeles CA 90038*

HARRISON, BROOKS TALTON, law firm official; b. Pasadena, Tex., Sept. 5, 1971; s. Ben Talton and Suzanne Marie (Brannon) H. BS in Polit. Sci., U. Houston, 1999. Environmentalist Environomentalist, Inc., Pasadena, 1994-96; client coord. Foster and Sear, LLP, Pasadena, 1996-2000; adminstr. Internat. Union Oper. Engrs. 347, Texas City, Tex., 2000-01; exec. adminstr. Harrison and Assocs., Pasadena, 2001—. Dir. BTH Consulting, Deer Park, Tex., 1996—. Writer/cons. Dem. Party of Tex., 1993—. Mem. Harris County Labor Coun. (del.), Galveston County Labor Coun. (del.). Judaism. Avocations: fast pitch softball, reading, volunteering. Home: 2007 Fir Springs Dr Humble TX 77339-1701 E-mail: brooksharrison@hotmail.com.

HARRISON, BRYAN GUY, lawyer; b. Norman, Okla., Nov. 22, 1963; s. Danny Guy and Judith Kay (Dalke) H.; m. Kathleen Hazel Cody, May 8, 1993. BS, Lehigh U., 1986; JD, Emory U., 1989. Bar: Tex. 1989, Ga. 1991. Assoc. Shank, Irwin, Conant, Lipshy & Casterline, Dallas, 1989-90; trial atty. antitrust div. U.S. Dept. Justice, Dallas, 1990-91; assoc. Morris, Manning & Martin, Atlanta, 1991-97, ptnr., 1998—. Office: Morris Manning & Martin 3343 Peachtree Rd NE Ste 1600 Atlanta GA 30326-1044

HARRISON, CECIL W., JR., lawyer; b. New Bern, NC, July 29, 1947; BA, Univ. NC, 1969, JD, 1973. Bar: NC 1973, US Supreme Ct. 1979. Mng. ptnr., comml. & appellate litigation, employment law, mem. mgmt. com. Poyner & Spruill LLP, Raleigh, NC. Mem.: ABA, NC Bar Assn., Wake County Bar Assn. Office: Poyner & Spruill LLP 3600 Glenwood Ave Raleigh NC 27612 Office Phone: 919-783-2814. Office Fax: 919-783-1075. Business E-Mail: cwharrison@poynerspruill.com.

HARRISON, CHARLES MAURICE, retired lawyer, retired communications executive; b. Anderson, SC, Aug. 30, 1927; s. Emmitte Smallwood and Jessie Maysel (Hawkins) H.; m. Lorna Jean Tomalty, June 27, 1970; children: Suzanne Elizabeth, Linda Jean. AB, Marshall U., 1949; JD, W.Va. U., 1952. Bar: W.Va. 1952, D.C. 1958, N.Y. 1965, N.J. 1972. Legal asst. W.Va. Dept. Ins., Charleston, 1952-54; hearing examiner Pub. Svc. Commn., Charleston, 1954-57; atty. Chesapeake and Potomac Tel. Co., Washington and Charleston, 1957-64, Western Electric Co., N.Y.C., 1964-69; gen. atty., sec., treas. Bellcomm, Inc., Washington, 1969-71; asst. gen. counsel, asst. sec. Bell Tel. Labs., Murray Hill, N.J., 1971-75, gen. atty., sec., 1975-76, sec., gen. counsel corp. matters, 1976-84; asst. sec., asst. gen. counsel AT&T Bell Labs, 1985-87; gen. atty. AT&T, Berkeley Heights, N.J., 1987-89; of counsel Ventantonio & Wildenhain, Warren, NJ, ret., 2004. Bd. dirs. Somerset County C. of C. (chmn. 1990-92). Trustee Family Counseling Svcs. Somerset County, N.J., 1976-94, pres., 1978-81; chmn. R&D Coun. N.J., 1985-87, Bridgewater (N.J.) Commn. Substance Abuse, 1986-89, Bridgewater Mcpl. Facilities Commn., 1988-89, Bridgewater Twp. Alliance Com. on Alcoholism, 1989-99; bd. dirs. Martin Luther King Youth Ctr., 1984-90, Somerset Alliance for Future, 1992, N.J. affiliate Am. Heart Assn., 1991-94, Somerset County Coalition on Affordable Housing, 1995—; bd. dirs., pres. Somerset Treatment Svcs., 1992-99, bd. dirs., 2002—; mem. Bridgewater-Raritan Youth Svcs. Commn., chmn., 1989-90; mem. Bridgewater Planning Bd., 1989-94, chmn., 1992-94; mgmt. com. Ridewise Traffic Mgmt. Assn., 1992-96; mem. Somerset County Local Adv. Com. on Alcohol and Drug Abuse, 1992-99, Bridgewater Twp. Operation (police-pub.) Cooperation, 1992—, 200 Club of Somerset County, 1990—; trustee Henderson Meml. Scholarship Fund, 1993-99; mem. Twp. Coun., 1994-2001, coun. pres., 1996, 2000; mem. Bridgewater Zoning Bd. of Adjustment, 2002-, Bridgewater Econ. Devel. Adv. Com., 2005-. With AC, U.S. Army, 1945-46, W.Va. Air N.G., 1955-57, UsAFR, 1955-62. Named Somerset County Citizen of Yr., 1996. Mem. Rotary (pres. Somerville and Bridgewater, 2000-01, treas. 2005-06), Somerville Elks, Am. Legion. Republican. *Regardless of profession, career, occupation, or trade, success in life can only be achieved if a significant part of one's effort includes the gift of one's personal talent, energy, and time to his or her community. In this part of one's life, financial reward, public recognition, or even results, do not count as much as dedication and sincerity, but the opportunities for creativity and personal satisfaction are enormous.*

HARRISON, CHARLES WAGNER, JR., applied physicist; s. Charles Wagner and Etta Earl (Smith) H.; m. Fern F. Perry, Dec. 28, 1940; children: Martha R., Charlotte J. Student, U.S. Naval Acad. Prep. Sch., 1933-34, U.S. Coast Guard Acad., 1934-36; BS in Engring., U. Va., 1939, EE, 1940; SM, Harvard U., 1942, M of Engring., 1952, PhD in Applied Physics, 1954; postgrad., MIT, 1942, 52. Registered profl. engr., Va. Engr. Sta. WCHV, Charlottesville, Va., 1937-40; commd. ensign U.S. Navy, 1939, advanced through grades to comdr., 1948; research staff Bur. Ships, 1939-41, asst. dir. electronics design and devel. div., 1948-50; research staff U.S. Naval Research Lab., 1944-45, dir.'s staff, 1950-51; liaison officer Evans Signal Lab., 1945-46; electronics officer Phila. Naval Shipyard, 1946-48; mem. USN Operational Devel. Force Staff, 1953-55; staff Comdg. Gen. Armed Forces Spl. Weapons project, 1955-57; ret. U.S. Navy, 1957; cons. electromagnetics Sandia Nat. Lab., Albuquerque, 1957-73. Instr. U. Va., 1939-40; lectr. Harvard U., 1942-43, Princeton U., 1943-44; vis. prof. Christian Heritage Coll., El Cajon, Calif., 1976. Author: (with R.W.P. King) Antennas and Waves: A Modern Approach, 1969; contbr. numerous articles to profl. jours. Fellow IEEE (Electronics Achievement award 1966, best paper award electromagnetic compatibility group 1972); mem. Internat. Union Radio Sci. (commn. B), Electromagnetics Acad., Famous Families Va., Sigma Xi. Home: 2808 Alcazar St NE Albuquerque NM 87110-3516 *Research is like saving - if postponed until needed, it is too late to start. One should keep expanding his mind.*

HARRISON, CLIFFORD, chef, small business owner; Grad., Calif. Culinary Inst., San Francisco, 1987; postgrad, U. Hawaii. Chef, co-owner Bacchanalia, Atlanta, Float Away Cafe, Ga.; chef with Judy Rogers Zuni Cafe, San Francisco; chef with Bob Kinkead 21 Federal, Nantucket Island, Mass.; chef Bimini Twist, NY, La Petite Ferme, NY, Grolier Club, NY. Elected mem. James Beard Found.

HARRISON, CLIFFORD JOY, JR., banker; b. Nashville, Feb. 21, 1925; s. Clifford Joy and Rosa Lee (Bennett) H.; m. Saralu Fondren, May 3, 1957; children: Julia Lee, Clifford Joy III, John Fondren. BA, Vanderbilt U., 1949; postgrad., Law Sch., 1949-50, Nashville Sch. Law, 1950-53; LLB, Stonier Grad. Sch. Banking, Rutgers, 1963; student, Advanced Mgmt. Program, Harvard U., 1975. With 3d Nat. Bank, Nashville, 1950-88, ret. vice chmn. in charge trust divsn., retail divsn. and mktg., 1988. Past pres. Estate Planning Coun.; past pres. trust divns. Tenn. Bankers Assn. Past pres. YMCA Found. Bd.; past chmn. bd. trustees Tenn. Nature Conservacy. 1st lt. USAAF, 1943-46. Decorated Air medal with oak leaf cluster. Mem. Exch. Club, City Club (past pres.), Belle Meade Country Club, Beta Theta Pi, Phi Alpha Delta. Episcopalian. Home: 102 Abbottsford Nashville TN 37215-2437 E-mail: cjharrison@mindspring.com.

HARRISON, DANIEL E., elementary school educator; b. Aurora, Ill., June 29, 1965; s. Richard E. and Lynn Harrison; m. Sherri Ann Lyons, June 21, 1997; children: Kelsey Malynn, Kendall Ann. BS in Edn., No. Ill. U., 1988; MusM, Ea. Ill. U., 1991. Band dir. East Richland HS, Olney, Ill., 1991—95, West Chicago (Ill.) HS, 1995—97, Thompson Jr. High, Oswego, Ill., 1997—. Named Chicagoland Outstanding Music Educator, Quinlan and Fabish Music Co., 2002, Most Influential Music Educator, Oswego Sch. Dist., 2004. Mem.: Nat. Band Assn., Music Educators Nat. Conf., Nat. Educators Assn. Office: Thompson Jr High 440 Boulder Hill Pass Oswego IL 60543

HARRISON, DAVID D., corporate financial executive; BA, Marietta Coll., Ohio; MBA in Fin. Mgmt., Ohio U., Athens. CMA. With Borg-Warner, Gen. Elec.; CFO Coltec Industries, Pentair, Inc., 1994—96, exec. v.p. and CFO, 1996—. Office: Pentair Inc Ste 800 5500 Wayzata Blvd Golden Valley MN 55416

HARRISON, DONALD CAREY, academic administrator, cardiologist, educator; b. Blount County, Ala., Feb. 24, 1934; s. Walter Carey and Sovola (Thompson) H.; m. Laura Jane McAnnally, July 24, 1955; children: Douglas, Elizabeth, Donna Marie. BS in Chemistry, Birmingham So. Coll., 1954; MD, U. Ala., 1958. Diplomate Am. Bd. Internal Medicine (cardiovascular disease). Intern, asst. resident Peter Bent Brigham Hosp., 1958-60; fellow in cardiology

Harvard U., 1961, NIH, 1961-63; mem. faculty Stanford U. Med. Sch., 1963-86, chief div. cardiology, 1967-86, prof. medicine, 1971-86; chief cardiology Stanford U. Hosp., 1967-86, William G. Irwin prof. cardiology, 1972-86; sr. v.p., provost for health affairs U Cin. Med. Ctr., 1986—2003; sr. v.p., provost for health affairs, emeritis U. Cin. Med. Ctr.; prof. medicine, cardiology U. Cin. Coll. Medicine; CEO U. Cin. Med. Ctr., 1987—2003. Cons. to local hosps., industry and govt.; mng. dir. Charter Life Sci. Venture Fund; bd. dir. Med. Edn. and Consultation, AtriCure Med., Venturi, LLP, Uterine Muscle Dysfunction, Inc., Kendle Industries, Entero Medics, Inc., Am. Heart Assn., U. Cin. Physicians. Mem. editorial bd. Brit. Jour. Clin. Practice, 1993—; mem. editorial bd. Drugs, 1980—, Am. Jour. Cardiology, 1984—; contbr. articles to med. jours., chpts. to books. Served with USPHS, 1961-63. Fellow Interam. Soc. Cardiology (v.p. 1980-86), Am. Coll. Cardiology (mem. chmn., v.p. 1972-73, sec. 1969-70, trustee 1972-78), Am. Heart Assn. (fellow coun. circulation, clin. cardiology and basic sci., chmn. program com. 1972-76, nat. chmn. publs. com. 1976-81, pres.-elect 1980-81, pres. 1982-83); mem. ACP, Am. Soc. Clin. Investigation, Am. Fedn. Clin. Rsch., Am. Assn. Physicians, Assn. U. Cardiologists, Am. Clin. and Climatol Assn., Brit. Cardiac Soc., Acad. Medicine Cin., Assn. Acad. Health Ctrs. (past chmn.). Home: 9250 Old Indian Hill Rd Cincinnati OH 45243-3438 Office: U Cin Med Ctr ML 0669 G11 Wherry Hall Cincinnati OH 45267-0669 Office Phone: 513-558-6397. Business E-Mail: don.harrison@uc.edu.

HARRISON, EARL DAVID, lawyer, real estate company officer; b. Bryn Mawr, Pa., Aug. 25, 1932; 1 child. BA, Harvard U., 1954; JD, U. Pa., 1960. Bar: DC 1960. Pvt. practice, Washington; exec. v.p. Washington Real Estate Corp., Washington, 1986-94; pres. EDH Assocs., Inc., 1994—. Capt. U.S. Army, 1954—57. Decorated Order of Rio Branco Brazil, Order of Merit Italy. Mem.: ABA, Coun. Internat. Restaurant Real Estate Brokers Ltd., Met. Washington Restaurant Assn., Nat. Restaurant Assn., Nat. Assn. Realtors, Greater Washington Comml. Assn. Realtors, Washington Assn. Realtors, DC Bar Assn., Internat. Coun. Shopping Ctrs., U. Pa. Club, Nat. Press Club, Harvard Club. Office: 1077 30th St NW Ste 706 Washington DC 20007-3834 Office Phone: 202-333-6776. Business E-Mail: david@edhlaw.com, david@edhassoc.com.

HARRISON, ELLA GUIDRY, writer; d. Timothy and Leola Watkins; m. Bernard Harrison; 1 child, Bernard Jr. AA, San Jose (Calif.) City Coll., 1981; BA, San Jose State U., 1983. Lic. social worker Md. Author: An Unholy Alliance, Deadly Roses (submitted for a Pulitzer Prize). Co-founder Black Writers Guild of Md., Inc., Balt., 1998; organizer Santa Clara County Food Pantry, Milpitas, Calif., 1982—83, Save the Children, Knaresborough, England, 1984. Named Cmty. Svc. award, Menwith Hill Women's Club, Harrogate, Eng., 1985; recipient proclamation, Mayor Julian E. Dufreche, 1996. Mem.: Nat. Coalition 100 Black Women, Zeta Phi Beta Sorority, Inc. Avocations: speed walking, gardening. Office Phone: 410-518-6166. Home Fax: 410-518-6166. Personal E-mail: ellaguidry@aunthagarschaps.com.

HARRISON, EMMETT BRUCE, JR., public relations counselor; b. Lanett, Ala., Apr. 3, 1932; s. Emmett Bruce and JeNelle (Williams) H.; m. Patricia DeStacy, Aug. 26, 1973; children by previous marriage: Susan, Emmett, Joe. AB, U. Ala., 1954; postgrad., Cath. U. Am., 1966-67. Mng. editor Talladega (Ala.) News, 1955; polit. reporter Columbus (Ga.) Ledger, 1956; adminstrv. asst. to U.S. Rep. K.A. Roberts Washington, 1957-61; pub. rels. dir. Mfg. Chemists' Assn., Washington, 1961-69; v.p. Freeport Minerals Co., N.Y.C., 1969-73; pres. Harrison Assocs., Washington, 1973-77; pres., chmn. E. Bruce Harrison Co., Inc., Washington, 1978—. Instr. bus. studies George Washington U.; bd. dirs. PR News. Author: Going Green: How to Communicate Your Company's Environmental Commitment, 1993; prodr. plays at Dramarena, N.Y.C., and Washington Theatre Club, Arena Stage, 1966-69. Asst. press mgr. J.F. Kennedy campaign Ala., 1960; mem. U.S. Coun. Internat. Bus. Named Outstanding Journalism Grad., U. Ala., 1954; recipient AP Radio award, 1956, Nat. Endowment of Arts Play award, 1969. Fellow Pub. Rels. Soc. Am., Counselors Acad. (chair 1990—), Arthur W. Page Soc. (pub. rels. seminar), Nat. Press Club, Senate Press Secs. Club, Chemists Club N.Y., Soc. Profl. Journalists (bd. 2003-), Guest Svcs. Inc. (bd. 1998-2001), Univ. Club (Washington), Capitol Hill Club, Washington Golf and Country Club, Sigma Delta Chi (bd. com. 1991-93), Omicron Delta Kappa, Pi Kappa Phi. Methodist. Home: 3201 N Vermont St Arlington VA 22207-4480

HARRISON, ERIC JAY, construction executive, consultant; b. Pitts., Mar. 8, 1936; s. Max Clark and Helen Rigg Harrison; m. Sharon Stricker Hamburg, Sept. 1, 1962 (div. Dec. 16, 1977); children: Todd, Mark; m. Judith Lee Casteel, Sept. 22, 1984; children: Todd, David. BA, Haverford Coll., 1958; MA, Columbia U., 1961; cert., East Asian Inst., 1961, Wayne State U., 1968. Constrn. mgr. St. Marys (Pa.) Area Sch. Dist., 1991—95, CCI Constrn., Mechanicsburg, Pa., 1995—96, Slippery Rock (Pa.) Area Sch. Dist., 1996—97, City of Pitts. Sch. Dist., 1997—98, Hayes Large Architects, Altoona, Pa., 1998, N.J. Cunzolo and Assocs., Bellevue, Pa., 1998—99, STV Inc., Douglassville, Pa., 1999—2003; program mgr. Winchester Thurston Sch., Pitts., 2003. Founder Citizens E. Credit Union, Pitts., 2000—04. Exhibitions include Pitts. Opera Verbena Gala; author: (poetry) The Marginal Review, 1980. Founder Greentree Hist. Soc., Pa., Fishers of Men, Upper St. Clair, Pa., 1997; pres. synod coun. for Presbyn. Men Synod of the Trinity, 2003—; elder Westminster Presbyn. Ch., Upper St. Clair, mem. Christian formation seminars com., adult spiritual devel. commn. and evangelism com.; elder Adult Spiritual Devel. Commn. With USCG, 1961—62. Named Bus. Man of the Yr., 2003. Mem.: AIA (profl. affiliate), Pitts. History and Landmarks. Presbyterian. Avocation: photography. Home and Office: 1591 Pinehurst Dr Pittsburgh PA 15241-3201 Office Phone: 412-325-6713.

HARRISON, FRANK, former university president; b. Dallas, Nov. 21, 1913; s. Frank and Ruby (Davison) H.; m. Elsie Claire Redfearn, June 26, 1946; children— Frank, Susan Claire, James Redfearn. BS, So. Methodist U., 1935; MS, Northwestern U., 1936, PhD, 1938; MD, U. Tex. Southwestern Med. Sch., 1956. Mem. faculty U. Tenn. med. units, Memphis, 1938-51, prof., 1946-51, chief divsn. anatomy, 1946-51; prof. anatomy U. Tex. Southwestern Med. Sch., Dallas, 1952-68, assoc. dean, 1956-68; assoc. dean grad. studies U. Tex. at Arlington, 1965-68, acting pres., 1968-69, pres., 1969-72, Health Sci. Ctr., San Antonio, 1972-85, dir. Inst. Biotech., 1985, pres. emeritus. Named Distinguished Alumnus So. Meth. U., 1971 Mem. Am. Assn. Anatomists, Am. Physiol. Soc., Tex. Philos. Soc., Biophys. Soc., IEEE, Soc. Exptl. Biology and Medicine, Phi Beta Kappa, Alpha Omega Alpha, Kappa Sigma, Alpha Kappa Kappa. Home: 4168 Valley Ridge Rd Dallas TX 75220-1924 E-mail: lsfh@msn.com.

HARRISON, GAIL G., public health educator; M in Nutritional Scis., Cornell U.; PhD in Biol. Anthropology, U. Ariz. Mem. faculty Coll. Medicine, founding dir. program in internat. health, prof. family and cmty. medicine U. Ariz., 1976—92; chair, prof. dept. cmty. health scis. UCLA Sch. Pub. Health; asst. program dir. program for health and at-risk populations UCLA/Jonsson Comprehensive Cancer Ctr. Mem. Food and Nutrition Bd., Nat. Acad. Scis./Inst. Medicine; cons. WHO, UNICEF. Mem.: Inst. Medicine, 2004. Office: UCLA Ctr for Health Policy Rsch 10911 Weyburn Ave Ste 300 Los Angeles CA 90024 Business E-Mail: gailh@ucla.edu.

HARRISON, GEORGE BROOKS, engineer, researcher, retired military officer; b. Greenville, S.C., July 30, 1940; s. William Henry and Mary Carter (Ogburn) Harrison; m. Pennie Maria Jenkins, Nov. 29, 1963; children: Taylor Leigh, Todd Henry, Tracy Elizabeth. BS in Pub. Policy, USAF Acad., 1962; MBA, U. Pa., 1970. Cert. flight instr. single and multi-engine instrument glider, lic. airline transport pilot. Commd. 2d lt. USAF, 1962, advanced through grades to maj. gen., 1989; fighter pilot, forward air contr. and instr. 557th and 436th Tactical Fighter Squadron, Fla., 1963—69; joint exercise planner U.S. Readiness Command, MacDill AFB, Fla., 1971-74; grad. Armed Forces Staff Coll., Norfolk, Va., 1974; ops. officer 13th and 25th Tactical Fighter Squadron, Udorn, Thailand, 1974-75; comdr. 4485th Test Squadron, Eglin AFB, Fla., 1975-78; grad. Air War Coll., Montgomery, Ala., 1979; wing comdr. 479th Tactical Tng. Wing, Holloman AFB, N.Mex., 1982-86; chief joint ops. divsn. Orgn. of Joint Chiefs of Staff, Washington, 1984-86; dept. chief staff plans USAF Europe, Ramstein AFB, Germany, 1986-89, dep. chief staff ops., 1991-92; asst. chief staff studies and analyses Hdqrs. USAF, Washington, 1989-91; comdr. Air Warfare Ctr., Eglin AFB, Fla., 1992-93; comdr. combined/joint task force USAF, S.W. Asia, 1993; comdr. Air Force Operational Test and Evaluation Ctr., Kirtland AFB, N.Mex., 1994-97; prin. rsch. engr., dir. rsch. ops. Ga. Tech Rsch. Inst., 1997—; mil. affairs cons. CNN, 1997—. Mem. sci. adv. bd. USAF, Washington, 1998—; sponsor Mil. Ops. Rsch. Soc., 1989—91; U.S. del. NATO Adv. Group Aerospace R & D, Paris, 1989—91; lectr. to mil., tech. and civic groups, 1982—2005. Contbr. articles to mil. jours. Mem., lt. col. CAP, SC, 1978—; dist. commr. Boy Scouts Am., Germany, 1986—89, coun. commr., 1991—92, exec. coun., 1995—97; exec. v.p., bd. dirs. Air Warrior Courage Found., 1998—; bd. dirs. Nat. Mus. Aviation, 1998—; Ga. Aviation Hall of Fame, 2005. Decorated DSM with oak leaf cluster, DFC, Air medal with eleven oak leaf clusters, Legion of Merit with one oak leaf cluster, Def. Superior Svc. medal; recipient Lt. Gen. Glen Kent Leadership award, USAF, 2005. Fellow: Beta Gamma Sigma; mem.: Air Force Assn., Quiet Birdmen, Order of Daedalians (flight capt. 1987—89, 2003—05). Baptist. Avocation: aviation. Office: Ga Tech Rsch Inst 400 10th St CRB 225 Atlanta GA 30318-5712 Office Phone: 404-358-8120. E-mail: george.harrison@gtri.gatech.edu.

HARRISON, GEORGE HARRY, III, (HANK HARRISON), publishing executive, author; b. Monterey, Calif., June 17, 1940; s. Edith Cooke; 1 child, Courtney Love. BA in Psychology, San Francisco State Univ., 1965; postgrad., Univ. London, 1978-81. Mgr. Grateful Dead (formerly Warlocks), Palo Alto, Calif., 1965-66, 70-73; founder, counselor LSD rescue founder Inst. Contemporary Studies, San Francisco, 1967; pvt. practice counselor San Francisco, 1967-78; pub., founder Arkives Press, San Francisco, 1979—. Writer-in-residence Montalvo Ctr. Arts, Saratoga, Calif., 1974; founder Media Assocs., Los Altos, Calif., 1991—; presenter, expert witness, lectr. in field; co-owner Sacramento Equestrian Ctr., Riverglades, 1998; story cons., contbg. editor NBC prodn. The Search for the Unicorn Killer, 1999; co-developer Adobe Acrobat, Irish Govt.; cons. in field; lectr. in field. Author: The Dead Trilogy, 1972-97, Quest for Flight, 1975, 2nd edit., 1995, The Cauldron and the Grail, 1992, The Stones of Ancient Europe, 1996, Ace of Cups: The Grail in Tarot, 1998, Hamburger Zen, 2001, Crown of Stars, 2003; co-author Courtney Love Biography, 2004, Kurt Cobain: Beyond Nirvana, 2003; contbr. VSD (Paris), San Francisco Oracle, The Berkeley Barb, The Ga. Straight and L.A. Free Press, Dragon's Quest, E Channel, Court TV, True Hollywood Story: Courtney Love, 2003; editor emeritus Doctor Dobb's Jour.; tech., staff writer Info World Apple Plus Mag., radio, TV guest including Geraldo, Am. Jour., Inside Edition, Hard Copy, Maury Povitch Show, America's Most Wanted, Fox News Contribution, 1998; editor: Vancouver Mag., 1974-75, Las Vegas Sun, 1976-77, Jour. Psychedelic Drugs, 1967; contbg. editor High Times, 1996-97; prodr. (CD) Garcia: The Lost Concert, 1999; commentator Mystery of the Holy Grail Sacred Mysteries (The Learning Channel), Crown of Stars: The Grail in the Troubadour World, 2004; editor: (book and CD) A Guide to Fractional and Civil War Currency, 2003; editor, co-author Kravitz Guide to Fractional Currency, 2003; contbr. Dateline Feature: Was Kurt Coban Murdered?, 2004. With M.C., USN, 1958-61. Rocky Mountain Writers Conf. scholar, 1968, Frances Yates scholar Warburg Inst. U. London, 1978-80. Mem. Press Club, Ind. Pub. Assn., San Francisco Press Club, Las Vegas Press Club, Sacramento Press Club, Masons. Democrat. Avocations: horse breeding, dog breeding, animal rescue. Home and Office: PO Box 46 Wilton CA 95693-0046 Office Phone: 800-373-1897. Office Fax: 800-748-1913. Personal E-mail: riverglade@hotmail.com, hankharrison@hotmail.com.

HARRISON, GILBERT WARNER, investment banker; b. N.Y.C., Dec. 25, 1940; s. Daniel and Trese (Warner) Harrison; m. Shelley Danien, Dec. 18, 1965; children: Edward D., Robin G. Kaplan, Nancy L. Lascher. BS, U. Pa., 1962, JD, 1965. Bar: Pa. 1968, N.Y. 1965, Conn. 1965, Fla. 1969. Practice law, N.Y.C. and Phila., 1965—71; dir., fin. officer Precision Plastics Co., Phila., 1965—71; mng. dir. Shearson Lehman Bros Inc., N.Y.C. and Phila., 1985—89; chmn. Financo, Inc., N.Y.C. and Phila., 1971—; founding ptnr. Mercantile Capital Ptnrs., LLC, N.Y.C., 2000—. Mng. ptnr. Financo Investor's Fund L.P.; gen. ptnr. Financo Investors Mgmt. Partnership L.P.; mem. undergrad. bd. The Wharton Sch., U. Pa., 1984—; bd. dirs. Fashion Inst. Tech. Ednl. Found., N.Y.C., 1995—, Peggy Guggenheim Collection, Venice, 1996—, Penn Club N.Y.C., 1995—; cons., lectr. in field. Mem.: ABA, Am. Arbitration Assn., Fla. Bar, Phila. Bar Assn., Pa. Bar Assn., Assn. Corp. Growth, Wharton Entrepreneurial Ctr., Am. Mgmt. Assn., Trump Internat. Golf Club (Fla.), Breakers Club (Fla.), Noyac Golf Club (N.Y.), Harmonie Club (N.Y.C.), Locust Club (dir., Phila.), Philmont Country Club (Huntingdon Valley, Pa., dir.). Office: Financo Inc 535 Madison Ave 3rd Fl New York NY 10022-4212 E-mail: gharrison@financo.com.

HARRISON, GORDON RAY, engineering executive, consultant, research scientist; b. Wister, Okla., Dec. 14, 1931; s. Trannie Gordon and Isah Lee (Ray) H.; m. Barbara Ann Herndon, June 22, 1957; children: William Andrew, Melissa Leigh, Lori Jeanne, Amanda Ray. BS in Physics, U. Central Ark., 1952; MS, Vanderbilt U., 1954, PhD, 1958. Sr. staff engr. and engring. mgr. Sperry Microwave, Clearwater, Fla., 1957-71; prin. research scientist to lab. dir. Engring. Expt. Sta., Ga. Inst. Tech., Atlanta, 1971-83; v.p. Electromagnetic Scis., Inc., Atlanta, 1983-91; ind. cons. tech., bus., 1991—. Contbr. chpt. to book, numerous articles to profl. jours.; patentee microwave ferrimagnetic garnets. Fellow IEEE; mem. Soc. Microwave Theory and Techniques, Magnetics Soc., Mustang Club Am., Sigma Xi. Democrat. Methodist. Office: Electromagnetic Scis Inc PO Box 7700 Norcross GA 30091-7700

HARRISON, GUY NEWELL, lawyer; b. Longview, Tex., Dec. 14, 1946; s. Guy Franklin and Margaret Louise (Newell) H.; m. Lucinda Dodson, July 5, 1969; children: Parker Trigg Harrison, Worth McKinley Harrison. BBA, So. Meth. U., 1968, JD, 1974. Bar: Tex., U.S. Dist. Ct. Tex., U.S. Supreme Ct. Ptnr. Green & Harrison, Longview, Tex., 1974—. Pres. Longview YMCA, 1976-78; bd. dirs. YMCA of the USA, 1990-91, Good Shepherd Hosp. Found., Longview, 1989-91. Sgt. U.S. Army, 1968-70, Vietnam. Recipient Lowell Linnes award YMCA of the Midwest, 1979; named Atty. of Yr. Longview Legal Secs. Mem. Gregg Bar Assn., Tex. Trial Lawyers Assn., Tex. State Bar Assn. (bd. dirs. 1995-, chmn. 1997-98, pres.-elect 2001-02, pres. 2002-03); fellow (life) Tex. Bar Found. (trustee 1998-). Office: 100 W Methvin Longview TX 75601

HARRISON, HENRY STARIN, real estate appraiser, educator, entrepreneur; b. New Haven, June 19, 1930; s. Julius and Helen (Starin) H.; m. Minna Snyder, Apr. 16, 1960 (div. 1970); children: Julie, Eve; m. Ruth Lambert, May 30, 1976; children: Kate, H. Alex. BS in Econs., U. Pa., 1952; MA, Goddard Coll., 1974. Asst. to pres. Charlton Press, Derby, Conn., 1954-56; assoc. Harris Weissbuck Co., New Haven, 1956-57; pres. Harrison Appraisal Co., New Haven, 1958-90, H & R Ins. Agy., 1975-88, Health Care Mmgt. Co., 1964-86, The H2 Co., New Haven, 1986-95, H Squared Co., 1995—, A&A World Travel, New Haven, 1989-94; treas., v.p. Forms & Worms, Inc., 1989-97; pub. NAFFA, Inc., New Haven, 1985—. Appraisal cons. Nat. Assn. Environ. Risk Auditors, Bloomington, Ind., 1989-94. Author: Houses, Houses, Houses, 1974, URAR-Illustrated Guide, 1975, Appraising Single Family Residences, 1978, Home Buying-The Complete Illustrated Guide, 1980, Small Income Property-Illustrated Guide, 1980, Dictionary of Real Estate Appraisal, 1982, Condominium-Illustrated Guide, 1984, Review Appraisers Handbook, 1987, Appraising Residences and Income Properties, 1989, ARIP Student Workbook, 1989, NAERA Environmental Manual, 1989, Environmental Risk Screening, 1990, 1001 Q & A Appraisal Exam Preparation, 1990, Standards of Professional Appraisal Practice and Ethics, 1991, ARIP General Property Supplement, Real Estate 2055 Evaluation Illustrated Guide, 2005, Real Estate Principles and Practices Plus, 1994, Russian Appraisal Textbook, 1994, Advanced Appraisal Methods, 1994, Guide to New Haven, Connecticut, 1995, How To Make an FHA Single Family Appraisal, 1999, How To Pass the HUD/FHA Appraisal Qualification Examination, 1999, Spanish and English Dictionary of Real Estate and Appraisal, 2000, Hopkins History and Chronicles (1660-2000), 2004, Small Residential Income Property Appraisal Report-Mini Guide, 2005, Uniform Residential URAR Appraisal Report-Mini Guide, 2005, others; pub.: Real Estate Valuation Mag., 1985—; contbr. articles, chapters to books, audio-visual materials; patentee: Perpetual Birthday and Anniversary Reminder Calendar, —. Alderman City of New Haven, 1961-63; pres. Young GOP, New Haven, 1960, Real Estate Edn. Found., 1980—, Greater New Haven Arts Coun., 1989-91; trustee Goddard Coll., 1976-78. 1st lt. USAF, 1952-54. Recipient Real Estate Educators Assn. award, 1995. Fellow Am. Coll. Health Care Adminstrs. (award 1984); mem. Am. Inst. Real Estate Appraisers (pres. Conn. chpt. 1975-76, Profl. recognition award 1976, 78, MAI award 1980), Am. Soc. Appraisers (award 1987), Soc. Real Estate Appraisers (nat. vice gov. 1980), Columbia Soc. Appraisers (award 1959), Greater New Haven Real Estate Bd. (Realtor of Yr. award 1976, Educator of Yr. 1992), Lawn Club. Jewish. Avocations: water sports, travel. Home: Carriage House 315 Whitney Ave New Haven CT 06511-3715 Office: Harrison Cos Carriage House 315 Whitney Ave New Haven CT 06511-3772 Office Phone: 203-562-3159. E-mail: henryhsq@aol.com.

HARRISON, HOLLY A., lawyer; b. 1958; BA, U. Denver, 1981; JD, Boston U., 1984. Bar: Mass. 1984, Ill. 1985. Law clk. to Hon. Raymond J. Pettine, U.S. Dist. Judge Dist. R.I., 1984—85; with Sidley Austin Brown & Wood, Chgo., 1985—, ptnr., 1992—. Office: Sidley Austin Brown and Wood Bank One Plz 10 S Dearborn St Chicago IL 60603

HARRISON, JACK WAYNE, speech professional, minister; b. Crawfordsville, Ind., Oct. 18, 1932; s. Eddie Wayne and Gladys Marie Harrison; m. Patricia Lee Quisenberry, May 7, 1953; children: Gale Lynn Darnieder, Vickie Lee, Gary Wayne. BS, Johnson Bible Coll., Knoxville, Tenn., 1969. Cameraman R.R. Donnelly, Crawfordsville, 1953—65; CEO Creative Programs Svc., Lafayette, Ind., 1969—71; assoc. min. Broadway Christian Ch., Lexington, Ky., 1971—73; pastor Merritt Island (Fla.) Ch., 1973—76; prin. Merritt Island (Fla.) Ch. Sch., 1973—76; cons. H and H Enterprises, Cinn., Ohio, 1977—85, profl. spktr., trainer Cicero, Ind., 1985—2004. Dir. devel. Myler Ch. Builders, Crawfordsville, 1977—78; dir., trainer USAF, Patrick AFB, Fla., 1990—91; gen. asst. Dale Carnegie Leadership. Editor: (jour.) Christianity in Action, 1972—75. Dir., trainer Rep. Party, Cocoa Beach, Fla., 1988. 2d lt. U.S. Army, 1947—59. Mem.: Pro Golf Orgn., Kiwanis (chaplin 1972—76). Republican. Avocations: golf, swimming, jogging, walking, reading. Home: 329 Iron Bridge Rd Cicero IN 46034 Office: H and H Enterprises 329 Iron Bridge Rd Cicero IN 46034 Office Phone: 317-626-5015. Office Fax: 317-984-6014. Personal E-mail: jackharrison46034@yahoo.com.

HARRISON, JAMES WILBURN, gynecologist; b. Martin, Tenn., Mar. 23, 1918; s. Woodie and Georgia Harrison; m. Babs Wise Dudley, Jan. 29, 1948; children: James Wilburn Jr., James Michael, Babs Suzanne, Linda Denise. Student, U. Tenn., Martin, 1936-37, U. Tenn., Knoxville, 1937-38; MD, U. Tenn., Memphis, 1941; grad., U.S. Army Command and Gen. Staff Coll., Ft. Leavenworth, Kans., 1952; grad. in Med. Svcs. Officers Advanced Course, U.S. Army, 1952. Diplomate Am. Bd. Ob-gyn. Asst. resident Brooke Gen. Hosp., Ft. Sam Houston, Tex., 1947; chief surgery Station Hosp., Clark AFB, Philippines, 1948-49; resident, sr. resident Letterman Gen. Hosp., San Francisco, 1949-51; advanced through grades to col. U.S. Army; ret., 1954; chief staff St. Michael Hosp., Texarkana, Ark., Wadley Regional Med. Ctr., Texarkana, Tex., So. Clinic, Texarkana, Ark.; chief ob-gyn. Ft. Polk, La., 1953—54. Asst. clin. prof. ob-gyn. U. Ark. Coll. Medicine, Little Rock. Chmn. Bowie County Child Welfare Bd.; mem. NE Tex. Mental Health Bd. With USAR, 1955—78, ret. USAR, 1978. Decorated Legion of Merit U.S. Army, Commendation medal. Fellow: VFW (life), ACOG (life), ACS (life), Tex. Soc. Ob-gyn. (life), Assn. Mil. Surgeons U.S. (life), Internat. Coll. Surgeons (life); mem.: AMA (life), AMA Sr. Physicians, Tri-State Med. Soc. (pres. 1960), Tex. Med. Assn., Mil. Officers Assn. Am., Alumni Assn. U.S. Army Command and Gen. Staff Coll. (founding mem.), Tex. 50 Yr. Club, Northridge Country Club (founding mem.), Am. Legion. Methodist. Avocations: collecting, travel, military history. Home: 4009 Pecos St Texarkana TX 75503-2857

HARRISON, JEREMY THOMAS, dean, law educator; b. San Francisco, Dec. 23, 1935; s. James Gregory and Agnes Johanna (Patrick) H.; m. Roseanne E. Thomas, Dec. 29, 1962 (dec. Oct. 1983); children: James, Amelia, Roseanne, Jeremy, Alexandra, Nadya, Rachel; m. Laura Ellen Marrack, Apr. 28, 1990; children: Robert, Peter, Paul, Philip, John. BS, U. San Francisco, 1957, JD, 1960; LLM, Harvard U., 1962. Bar: Calif. 1961, Hawaii 1987. Assoc. Brobeck, Phleger & Harrison, San Francisco, 1960-61; law clk. to assoc. justice U.S. Ct. Claims, Washington, 1962-63; lectr. law U. Ghana, Accra, 1963-64, U. Ife, Ibadan, Nigeria, 1964-66; prof. law U. San. Francisco, 1966-85; dean Sch. Law U. Hawaii, Honolulu, 1985-94; dean Mich. State U. Coll. Law, East Lansing, 1996-98, prof. law, 1998—. Vis. prof. law Haile Sellassie I U., Addis Ababa, Ethiopia, 1971-74, U. Hawaii, 1977-79; Elips Disting. prof. law Gadjah Mada U., Yogyakarta, Indonesia, 1995-96. Author: Cases and Materials on Evidence, Africa, 1967, Cases and Materials on Ethiopian Civil Procedure, 1974. Counsel citizen's panel Hawaii's Jud. Adminstrn., Honolulu, 1985-86; bd. dirs. Straub Found., Honolulu; pres. Pacific Health Rsch. Inst., Honolulu, 1993-95. Mem. ABA, Am. Bar Found., Calif Bar Assn., Hawaii Bar Assn. Office: Mich State U Coll Law 465 Law College Bldg East Lansing MI 48824-1300

HARRISON, JOHN COLLIER, law educator; b. Columbus, Ohio, July 9, 1956; s. James Collier and Margaret Eva (Bradenburgh) H. BA, U. Va., 1977; JD, Yale U., 1980. Bar: DC 1980. Assoc. Patton, Boggs & Blow, Washington, 1980-82; law clk. to Hon. Robert H. Bork US Ct. Appeals DC Cir., Washington, 1982-83; with US Dept. Justice, Washington, 1983—93, dep. asst. atty. gen. Office Legal Counsel, 1990—93; assoc. prof. U. Va. Sch. Law, 1993—98, prof., 1998—, now David Lurton Massee, Jr. prof. law, Horace W. Goldsmith rsch. prof. Mem. Soc. for Am. Baseball Research. Office: U Va Sch Law 580 Massie Rd Charlottesville VA 22903-1789 Office Phone: 434-924-3093. E-mail: jh8m@virginia.edu.*

HARRISON, JOHN CONWAY, retired state supreme court justice; b. Grand Rapids, Minn., Apr. 28, 1913; s. Francis Randall and Ethlyn (Conway) H.; m. Ethel M. Strict; children: Nina Lyn, Robert Charles, Molly M., Frank R., Virginia Lee. LLD, George Washington U., 1940. Bar: Mont. 1947, U.S. Dist. Ct. 1947. County atty. Lewis and Clark County, Helena, Mont., 1934-60; justice Mont. Supreme Ct., Helena, 1961-98, ret., 1998. Pres. Mont. TB Assn., Helena, 1951-54, Am. Lung Assn., N.Y.C., 1972-73, Mont. coun. Boy Scouts Am., Great Falls, Mont., 1976-78. Col. U.S. Army Mem. ABA, Mont. Bar Assn., Kiwanis (pres. 1953), Sigma Chi. Home: 215 S Cooke St Helena MT 59601-5143 Office Phone: 404-442-5833.

HARRISON, JOHN RAYMOND, foundation administrator, retired publishing executive; b. Des Moines, June 8, 1933; s. Raymond Harrison and Dorothy (Stout) Harrison Cohen; m. Lois Cowles, June 24, 1955 (div. Apr. 1981); children: Gardner Mark, Kent Alfred (dec.), John Patrick, Lois Eleanor; m. Mary Gee MacQueen, Sept. 5, 1981 (div. 2000); m. Bonnie Lynne Anderson, Aug. 26, 2000; stepchildren: Jennifer Alicia Anderson, Michael Christopher Anderson. Grad., Phillips Exeter Acad., 1951; AB, Harvard U., 1955, postgrad. Sch. Bus., 1955-56; DHL (hon.), Fla. So. Coll. With various papers throughout the U.S.; vice pres. N.Y. Times Co., ret.; chmn. Harrison Charitable Found., Sarasota, Fla. Dir. Internat. Herald-Tribune, Paris, 1974-91. Bd. dirs. Ft. Pierce (Fla.)-St. Lucie County Indsl. Devel. Coun., 1959-62, Ft. Pierce Meml. Hosp., 1959-62, Lincoln Pk. Child Care Ctr., Ft. Pierce, 1959-62, Gainesville United Fund, 1965, Boys Club Gainesville, 1965, U. Fla. Found., 1967, YMCA Greater Lakeland, 1967-69, Human Rels. Coun. Lakeland, 1967-69, Boys Club Lakeland, ARC, 1967-69; trustee Robert H. Anderson Found., Ridge Sch., Bartow, Fla., High Mus., 1988-94; mem. Pres.'s Resources Coun. Wellesly (Mass.) Coll.; mem. bd. counsellors Fla. So. Coll., 1974; mem. bd. visitors Emory U., 1984, pres., 1986; trustee Westminster Schs., 1989-92, Kennesaw State Coll. Found.; mem. bd. councillors Carter Presdl. Ctr.; mem. bd. overseers Harvard U., 1995-2001; bd. trustees Ringing Sch. Art and Design, 2003. Recipient Pulitzer Prize for editl. writing, 1965, Nat Headliners award for pub. svc.

editl. writing, Nat. Headliners Club, 1972, Walker Stone award for editl. writing Scripps-Howard Found., 1974, 76, Silver Gavel award for pub. svc. editls. ABA, 1977, Sigma Delta Chi Bronze medal, 1970, 73. Mem. Greater Lakeland C. of C. (dir. 1966-67), Associated Harvard Alumni (dir. 1979-82), Spee Club, Hasty Pudding Inst. 1770 (grad. dir.), Harvard Club (N.Y.C., Boston, Ga. bd. dirs.), Oaks Club-Sarasota, Fla.

HARRISON, JOHNNIE SHEPPARD, religious organization administrator; b. Jacksonville, Fla., Oct. 16, 1947; d. John and Sarah Sheppard; m. Augustine Richard Harrison, Sr., Aug. 11, 1969; children: Rezella Delourse, Augustine Richard Harrison, Jr.; children: Kyle Harold Taylor, Deltris Quinn Sheppard. AA, Brevard C.C., Melbourne/Cocoa, Fla., 1983; AS, BA, Living Word Bible Coll. & Sem., Maryland Heights, MO, 1986; BS, Orlando Coll., 1996; MBA, Nova Southeastern U., 1999; postgrad. Nova Southeastern U., 2003—. Title clk. Dept. of Interior, Big Cypress, Naples, Fla., 1977—78; resources control clk. NASA, Kennedy Space Ctr., Fla., 1978—85; postal worker USPS, Melbourne, Fla., 1985—90; dir. Kids at Risk Programs and Svcs. ministry Outreach, Melbourne, Fla., 2002—; pres., CEO Outreach Mission Internat., Melbourne. Author: InnerCity Ministry (Cert. of Appreciation, 1997), (poem) I Am A Woman; composer: (peom) Celebration; author: (poem) Life is a Celebration, Strategies for Constructive Leadership (Cert. of Achievement, 2001). Supr. of women Ch. of God in Christ, Inc., Memphis, 1998. Mem.: So. Brevard Ministerial Alliance, Inc. (assoc.; parliamentarian 2002—03). Home: 626 Reddick St Melbourne FL 32901-7112 Office: Ch of God In Christ Inc PO Box SS 6281 Np Nassau The Bahamas also: Outreach Mission Internat 2712 S Main St Melbourne FL 32901 Office Fax: 484-231-3400. E-mail: johnnie_harrison714@hotmail.com.

HARRISON, JOSEPH HEAVRIN, lawyer; b. Evansville, Ind., July 23, 1929; s. Homer William and Lillie Isabelle (Heavrin) H.; m. Sharon Jeanene Miller, June 30, 1957 (div. 1976); children: Joseph Heavrin, Sara Ann; m. Julie Anne Gerard, Dec. 10, 1976; 1 child, Meghann. BA in Econs., U. Notre Dame, Ind., 1952; JD cum laude, U. Notre Dame, 1953. Bar: Ind. 1953, U.S. Dist. Ct. D.C. 1953, U.S. Dist. Ct. (so. dist.) Ind. 1953, U.S. Ct. Appeals (7th cir.) 1968, U.S. Tax Ct. 1984. Mng. ptnr. Bowers Harrison and predecessors, Evansville, Ind., 1955. Pres. Sandy's Assocs., Inc. (18 Hardee's franchised restaurants). Dir. Vanderburgh County Legal Aid Soc., Evansville, 1958—68, pres., 1964—65; Ind. counsel Bush Presdl. campaign, 1988; co-chair Ind. Lawyers for G.W. Bush, 2000—; chmn. Vanderburgh County Election Bd., 1979—90, Vanderburgh Rep. Fin. Com., 1982—89; mem. Evansville Econ. Devel. Commn., 1991—2002, pres., 1995—2001; Ind. commr. Ohio River Valley Water Sanitation Commn., 1982—, chmn., 1987; commr. Vanderburgh County Conv. & Vis. Bur., 1997—2001; bd. dirs. Arbor Hosp., 1991—94. With U.S. Army, 1953—55. Fellow Ind. Bar Found.; mem. ABA, Evansville Bar Assn., Ind. Bar Assn., Am. Judicature Soc., Evansville Country Club (pres. 1976), Oak Meadow Country Club. Republican. Roman Catholic. Avocations: golf, flying. Office: Bowers Harrison LLP PO Box 1287 25 NW Riverside Dr Evansville IN 47708-1255 Office Phone: 812-426-1231. Business E-Mail: jhh@bowersharrison.com.

HARRISON, LARRY J., health facility administrator; BS in Microbiology, Mich. State U.; MHS, Johns Hopkins U.; MBA, U. So. Calif. Exec. v.p., opers. Health Ptnrs., Inc., Norwalk, Conn.; exec. dir. Cleve. Clinic Fla. Health Network; pres., health plan svcs. Scripps Clinic Found., La Jolla, Calif., exec. dir., physicians med. group, exec. dir., med. found., COO, 2001—03, clinic adminstr., 2003—. Office: Scripps Clinic Found 1066 N Torrey Pines Rd La Jolla CA 92037-1027

HARRISON, LOIS SMITH, hospital executive, educator; b. Frederick, Md., May 13, 1924; d. Richard Paul and Henrietta Foust (Menges) Smith; m. Richard Lee Harrison, June 23, 1951; children: Elizabeth Lee Boyce, Margaret Louise Wade, Richard Paul. BA, Hood Coll., 1945, MA, 1993, Columbia U.; LHD (hon.), Hood Coll., 1993. Counselor CCNY, 1945-46; founding adminstr., counselor, instr. psychology and sociology Hagerstown (Md.) Jr. Coll., 1946-51, registrar, 1946-51, 53-54, instr. psychology and orienta, 1954-56; registrar, instr. psychology Balt. Jr. Coll., 1951-54; bus. mgr., acct. for pvt. med. practice Hagerstown, 1953-2000; trustee Washington County Hosp., Hagerstown, 1975-97, chmn. bd., 1986-88, 95—; mem. bd. Washington County Health Sys. Inc., 1997—. Chmn. Home Fed. Savs. Bank, Hagerstown, 1997-99; chmn. acute care Health Sys. Bd., 1997—; chmn. bd. dirs. Home Fed. Savs. Bank, 1998-2000, emeritus, 2001—; spkr. ednl. panels, convs. hosp. panels and seminars Author: The Church Woman, 1960-65, With Courage and Vision: Christ's Reformed Church Celebrate 150 Years, 2004. Trustee Hood Coll., Frederick, 1972—, chmn. bd., 1979-95; mem. Md. Gov.'s Commn. to Study Structure and Ednl. Devel. Commn., 1971-75; pres. Washington County Coun. Ch. Women, 1970-72; appointee Econ. Devel. Commn., County Impact Study Commn. Bd.; bd. dirs. Md. Hosp. Assn., 1988-98, Md. Chs. United, 1975—; chmn. bd. dirs. Md. Hosp. Edn. Inst., 1978-98; mem. Christ's Reformed Ch., 1935—; pres. Ch. Consistory; chmn. Chesapeake Healthcare Forum, 1995-97; chmn. Centennial Celebration, Washington County Hosp. Bd. Recipient Alumnae Achievement award Hood Coll., 1975, Washington County Woman of Yr. award, AAUW, 1984, Md. Woman of Yr. award, 1984, Md. Woman of Yr. award Francis Scott Key Commn. for Md.'s 350th Anniversary, 1984; named one of top 10 women Tri-State area, Herald-Mail Tri-State newspaper, 1990, Zonta Internat. Woman of Yr., 1994, Outstanding Woman of the Yr., Woman At the Table award, 2002. Mem. Hagerstown C. of C. Republican. Home: 12835 Fountain Head Rd Hagerstown MD 21742-2748 Office: Washington Cty Hosp Off Chmn Bd Hagerstown MD 21740 Office Phone: 301-790-8107. Personal E-mail: lorichco@aol.com.

HARRISON, LYNN HENRY, JR., cardiovascular surgeon; b. Oklahoma City, Jan. 8, 1944; s. Lynn Henry and Vera Alice (Pritchett) H.; m. Lura Ann Wright, June 21, 1969; children: Parker, Tyler. BA, Yale U., 1966; MD, U. Okla., 1970. Diplomate Am. Bd. Surgery, Am. Bd. Thoracic Surgery. Clin. assoc. surgery Nat. Heart and Lung Inst., Bethesda, Md., 1972-74; resident surgery Duke U., Durham, N.C., 1970-72, 74-78, teaching scholar surgery, 1978-79; asst. prof. surgery U. Okla. Sch. Medicine, Oklahoma City, 1979-84; clin. asst. prof. La. State U. Sch. Medicine, New Orleans, 1986-89, clin. assoc. prof., 1989, assoc. prof. surgery, chief sect. cardiovascular surgery, 1993-98, prof. surgery, 1998—, Craighead chair surgery, 2002; ptnr. The O'Neill Surg. Group, New Orleans, 1984-91; pres. Crescent Surgical Assocs., Marrero, La., 1991-93. Bd. dirs. Ballet Okla., Oklahoma City, 1983-85. Fellow ACS (counselor La. chpt. 1988—, pres. 1995, gov. 1998-2004); mem. Assn. Acad. Surgery, Soc. Thoracic Surgeons, Am. Assn. Thoracic Surgery, So. Surg. Assn., Surg. Assn. of La. (pres. 1996), Andrew G. Morrow Soc., David C. Sabiston Jr. Surg. Soc., Timberlane Country Club (bd. dirs.). Avocations: golf, hunting. Office: LSU Sch of Medicine Dept of Surgery 1542 Tulane Ave New Orleans LA 70112-2825 Business E-Mail: lharri@lsuhsc.edu.

HARRISON, MARION EDWYN, lawyer; b. Phila., Sept. 17, 1931; s. Marion Edwyn and Jessye Beatrice (Cilles) H.; m. Carmelita Ruth Deimel, Sept. 6, 1952; children: Angelique Marie (Mrs. Kevin B. Bounds), Marion Edwyn III, Henry Deimel. BA, U. Va., 1951; LLB, George Washington U., 1954, LLM, 1959. Bar: Va. 1954, DC 1958, US Supreme Ct. 1958. Spl. asst. to gen. counsel PO Dept., 1958-60, mem. bd. contract appeals, 1958-61, assoc. gen. counsel, 1960-61; ptnr. firm Harrison, Lucey & Sagle (and predecessors), Washington, 1961-78, Barnett & Alagia, 1978-84; ptnr. Scott, Harrison & McLeod, 1984-86, Law Offices Marion Edwyn Harrison, Washington, 1986—; pres. Free Congress Rsch. and Edn. Found., Inc., 2002—. Mem. coun. Adminstrv. Conf. US, 1971—78, sr. conf. fellow, 1984—88; mem. DC Law Revision Commn., 1975—92; adv. dir. NationsBank, N.A., 1987—93; lectr. Nat. Jud. Coll., Reno, 1979, La. State U. Law Sch., Aix-en-Provence, 1987, Aix-en-Provence, 89, Tulane U. Law Sch., Crete, 1997, Thessaloniki, 2001, Rhodes, 04, Hofstra U. Law Sch., Nice, France, 1999, Nice, 2003, Pa. State U. Dickinson Law Sch., Vienna, 2000, St. Mary's U. Law Sch., Innsbruck, Austria, 2002, U. Kans. Law Sch., Istanbul, 2005. Contbr. articles to profl. publs.; editor-in-chief Fed. Bar News, 1960-63; mem. editl. bd. Adminstrv. Law Rev., 1976-89. Trustee AEFC Pension Fund, Chgo., 1986-92; pres. Young Rep. Fedn. Va., 1954-55; mem. Va. Rep. Ctrl. Com., 1954-55; bd. visitors Judge Adv. Gen. Sch., Charlottesville, Va., 1976-78; chmn. Wolf Trap Assn., 1984-87; bd. dirs. Wolf Trap Found., 1984-88; pub. mem. USIA Mission, Argentina, 1971. Officer AUS, 1955-58. Decorated Commendation medal. Fellow: Am. Bar Found. (life); mem.: ABA (chmn. sect. adminstrv. and reg. law 1974—75, ho. of dels. 1978—88, chmn. lawyers in govt. com. 1980—82, bd. govs. 1982—86, chmn. com. on fgn. and internat. orgns. 1986—87), Bar Assn. DC (chmn. adminstrv. law sect. 1970—71, bd. dirs. 1971—72), Inter-Am. Bar Assn., Fed. Bar Assn. (nat. coun. 1966—82), Coun. for Nat. Policy, Supreme Ct. Hist. Soc., Federalist Soc., George Washington U. Law Assn. (pres. 1974—77), Smithsonian Instn. (nat. bd. dirs. 1991—97), Soc. Mayflower Desc., Farmington Country Club (Charlottesville, Va.), Gainey Ranch Golf Club (Scottsdale, Ariz.), Met. Club, Washington Golf and Country Club, Knight of Malta. Republican. Roman Catholic. Home: 4111 N Ridgeview Rd Arlington VA 22207-4617 Address: 7222 E Gainey Ranch Rd Scottsdale AZ 85258-1529 Office: 717 Second St NE Washington DC 20002 Address: Dufourstrasse 32 8008 Zurich Switzerland

HARRISON, MARK B., lawyer; b. Bronx, NY, Feb. 20, 1953; BA, SUNY, 1973; JD, Rutgers U., 1977. Bar: Pa. 1977, US Ct. of Customs and Patent Appeals 1977, DC 1982, US Dist. Ct., DC, US Patent and Trademark Office. Former examining atty. US Patent and Trademark Office, 1977—81; ptnr., chair trademark group Venable LLP, Washington, 1982—. Mem.: ABA, Pa. Bar Assn., DC Bar Assn. Office: Venable LLP 575 7th St NW Washington DC 20004 Office Phone: 202-344-4019. Office Fax: 202-344-8300. Business E-Mail: mbharrison@venable.com.

HARRISON, MARK ISAAC, lawyer; b. Pitts., Oct. 17, 1934; s. Coleman and Myrtle (Seidenman) H.; m. Ellen R. Gier, June 15, 1958; children: Lisa, Jill. AB, Antioch Coll., 1957; LLB, Harvard U., 1960. Bar: Ariz. 1961, Colo. 1991. Law clk. to justices Ariz. Supreme Ct., 1960-61; ptnr. Harrison, Harper, Christian & Dichter, Phoenix, 1966-93, Bryan Cave, LLP, Phoenix, 1993—2003, Osborn Maledon, P.A., Phoenix, 2004—. Adj. prof. U. Ariz. Coll. Law, 1995-97, Ariz. State Coll. Law, 2001—; nat. bd. visitors, 1996—. Co-author: Arizona Appellate Practice, 1966; editorial bd. ABA/BNA Lawyers Manual on Profl. Conduct, 1983-86; contbr. articles to profl. jours. Chmn. Phoenix City bond Adv. Commn., 1976—79; pres. Valley Commerce Assn., 1978, Ariz. Friends of Talking Books, Inc., 2000—01; vice chmn. Maricopa County Dem. Cen. Com., 1967—68, Ariz. Dem. Com, 1969—70, legal counsel, 1970—72; del. Dem. Nat. Conv., 1968; bd. dir. Careers for Youth, 1963—67, pres., 1966—67; bd. dir. Planned Parenthood of Cen. and No. Ariz., 1992—98, pres., 1995; bd. dir. Ariz. Policy Forum, 2000—03. Recipient Peggy Goldwater award, Planned Parenthood, 2003, Planned Parenthood of Ctrl. and No. Ariz., 2003, Good Guys award, Ariz. Women's Polit. Caucus, 2004, Learned Hand Cmty. Svc. award, Am. Jewish Com., 2005. Fellow: Am. Acad. Appellate Lawyers (pres. 1993—94), Am. Bar Found.; mem.: ABA (standing com. profl. discipline 1976—84, chmn. 1982—84, chmn. commn. pub. understanding law 1984—87, chmn. coord. com. on professionalism 1987—89, com. on women in the profession, 1996-98, ethics com. 1999—2002, commn. Brown v. Bd. of Edn. 2003—04, chmn. joint com. Code of Judicial Conduct 2003—, Michael Franck Profl. Responsibility award 1996, Disting. Hon. Alumnus award), Lawyers Com. for Civil Rights Under Law (bd. dirs.), Law Coll. Assn. U. Ariz. (bd. dir. 1999—, pres. 2002—), Am. Law Inst. (lawyers com. for human rights nat. coun. 1995—), Harvard Law Sch. Assn. (nat. exec. coun. 1980—84), Ariz. Civil Liberties Union, Am. Judicature Soc. (exec. com. 1983—86, bd. dir. 1983—87), Western States Bar Conf. (pres. 1978—79), Nat. Conf. Bar Pres. (pres. 1976—77), Am. Inns of Ct. (master, pres. Sandra Day O'Connor chpt. 1993—94), Ariz. Bar Found. (pres. 1991, Walter E. Craig Disting. Svc. award 2002), State Bar Ariz. (bd. govs. 1971—77, pres. 1975—76), Am. Bd. Trial Advocates, Maricopa County Bar Assn. (pres. 1970), Assn. Profl. Responsibility Lawyers (pres. 1992—93). Office: Osborn Maledon PA 2929 N Central Ave Ste 2100 Phoenix AZ 85012 Office Phone: 602-640-9324. Personal E-mail: ellenmark1@cox.net. Business E-Mail: mharrison@omlaw.com.

HARRISON, MARVIN, professional football player; b. Phila., Aug. 25, 1972; Degree in Retailing, Syracuse U. Wide receiver Indpls. Colts, 1996—. Named to Am. Football Conf. Pro Bowl Team, 1999—2004. Achievements include holding NFL record for receptions in one season (147); led NFL in receptions, 2000, 2002, recieving yards, 1999, 2002. Office: Indpls Colts 7001 W 56th St Indianapolis IN 46254*

HARRISON, MICHAEL, opera company director; b. Augusta, Ga., June 22, 1940; s. Oscar T. and Helen (Harrison) Smith. BA, Vanderbilt U., 1962; postgrad., Yale U., 1962-64. Actor, singer Broadway, Regional Opera and Theatres, 1964-80; gen. dir. Providence Opera Theatre, 1979-81, Opera/Columbus, Columbus, Ohio, 1983-89, Balt. Opera Co., 1989—. Pres. Harrison/Connor Consultants, L.A., 1981—83. Mem.: Md. Club, Rotary, Ctr. Club. Episcopalian. Office: Balt Opera Co Inc 110 W Mount Royal Ave Ste 306 Baltimore MD 21201-5732*

HARRISON, MICHAEL ALLEN, healthcare marketing executive, consultant; b. West Islip, N.Y., Mar. 9, 1960; s. Hugh Allen and Theresa Ann (Filippelli) H.; m. Gabriella Sue Goldberg, 1991. BBA, Hofstra U., 1982, MBA, 1993. Acct. McCall Pub. Co., N.Y.C., 1982-84; dir. ops. Hofstra Health Dome, Hempstead, N.Y., 1984-88, dir. mktg., 1988-92; dir. pub. health policy, 1993—; pres. Turnstyles, U.S.A., L.I. Lectr., nat. panelist Mktg. Health Promotion Series, 1991. Editor: Hints for Health, Enlightened Eating for Better Health, 1988; pub. Health Promotion as Corporate Strategy, 1992. Cons. L.I. Heart Coun. Mem. L.I. Assn. (health svcs. com., nat. health care reform subcom., chmn. subcom. on health promotion and disease prevention), Assn. for Worksite Health Promotion. Avocations: songwriting, hockey, softball, chess. Office: PO Box 1253 North Massapequa NY 11758-0905

HARRISON, MICHAEL JAY, physicist, researcher; b. Chgo., Aug. 20, 1932; s. Nathan J. and Mae (Nathan) H.; m. Ann Tukey, Sept. 1, 1970. AB, Harvard, 1954; MS, U. Chgo., 1956, PhD, 1960. Fulbright fellow and H. Van Loon fellow in theoretical physics U. Leiden, Netherlands, 1954-55; NSF fellow U. Chgo., 1957-59; research fellow math. physics U. Birmingham, Eng., 1959-61; asst. prof. Mich. State U., East Lansing, 1961-63, assoc. prof., 1963-68, prof., 1968—, faculty grievance officer, 1972-73, dean Lyman Briggs Coll., 1973-81, adj. prof. epidemiology, 1993—, adj. prof. pediatrics and human devel., 2004—. Vis. research physicist Inst. Theoretical Physics, U. Calif., Santa Barbara, 1980-81; with Air Force Cambridge Research Center, summer 1953, M.I.T. Lincoln Lab., summer 1954, RCA Sarnoff Lab., summers 1961-63; physicist Westinghouse Labs., summer 1956; cons. RCA Lab., 1961-64, United Aircraft Co., 1964-66, U.K. Atomic Energy Authority, Harwell Lab., summer 1960, Thailand project in Bangkok, Mich. State U.-AID, summer 1968; vis. research affiliate theoretical biology and biophysics, Los Alamos Nat. Lab., 1987-88. Contbr. articles to U.S., fgn. profl. jours. Am. Council on Edn. fellow U. Calif., Los Angeles, 1970-71. Fellow Am. Phys. Soc.; mem. AAUP (chpt. treas. 1966-67), N.Y. Acad. Scis., Harvard Club of Ctrl. Mich. (pres. 1988-93), Rotary, B'nai B'rith, Phi Beta Kappa, Sigma Xi. Jewish. Avocations: hiking, travel, photography. Home: 277 Maplewood Dr East Lansing MI 48823-4746 Office: Mich State U Physics Dept East Lansing MI 48824 Office Phone: 517-355-9200 x2205. Business E-Mail: harrison@pa.msu.edu.

HARRISON, NEDRA JOYCE, surgeon; b. Buffalo, Apr. 16, 1951; d. Herman Lloyde and Gertrude (Newsom) H. BS, Rosary Hill Coll., 1973; MD, SUNY, Buffalo, 1977. Diplomate Am. Bd. Surgery. Resident in surgery Millard Fillmore Hosps., Buffalo, 1977-82, mem. active attending staff in gen. surgery, 1983—2000; practice medicine specializing in gen. surgery Buffalo, 1982—2000; courtesy staff Scottsdale (Ariz.) Healthcare, 2000—. Cons. staff Bry-Lyn Hosp., 1986-89; provisional staff in gen. surgery St. Joseph Intercommunity Hosp., 1986-87, active staff, 1995-2000; courtesy staff Scottsdale (Ariz.) Healthcare, Shea, Ariz., 2001—, Osborn, Ariz., 2001—. Chmn. United Thank Offering, Episcopal Ch., Buffalo, 1982; bd. dirs. Niagara Luth. Home, 1987-2000; mem. alumni bd. dirs. SUNY at Buffalo Sch. Medicine, 1986-92. Recipient Best Rsch. Paper in Gen. Surgery award Millard Fillmore Hosps., 1978, 81. Fellow ACS; mem. AMA, Am. Med. Women's Assn., Maricopa County Med. Soc., Christian Med. Soc., Delta Epsilon Sigma. Episcopalian. Office: 10210 N 92nd St Scottsdale AZ 85258 Office Phone: 480-551-2528.

HARRISON, PATRICIA DE STACY, broadcast executive, former federal agemcy administrator; b. N.Y.C. m. Emmett Bruce Harrison; 3 children. BA, Am. U., 1968; MA, George Mason U.; PhD (hon.), Am. U., 2002. V.p. Holly Realty Co., Arlington, Va., 1965-69; co-founder, ptnr. E. Bruce Harrison Co., Washington, 1973—96; former pres. AEF/Harrison Internat., Washington; asst. sec. edn. & cultural affairs U.S. Dept. State, Washington, 2001—05, acting sec. pub. diplomacy & pub. affairs, 2004; pres., CEO Corp. for Pub. Broadcasting, Washington, 2005—. Keynote spkr. U.S. Dept. Labor del. to Israel and Greece, Indsl. Devel. Authority of Ireland Conf./Women Execs. in Mgmt., U.S. Info. Agy./WorldNET program for entrepreneurs via satellite to 7 countries, Export Expo '90, Seattle, Nat. Govs. Conf., U.S. SBA Fin. Mgmt. Conf. in 9 states, mgmt. and tng. program for women entrepreneurs Budapest, Hungary (Alliance Decade for Democracy series); guest lect. Thomas Colloquium on Free Enterprise, 1989; trustee Guest Svcs., Inc.; mem. adv. coun. Avon Products, Inc. Author: Inside and Out: The Story of a Hostage, 1981, (with Margaret Mason, editor) The Washington Post Pocket Style Plus, 1983-84, America's New Women Entrepreneurs, 1986. Bd. dirs. Med. Coll. Pa. Recipient Librs.' and Tchrs.' award for play produced at Kennedy Ctr., 1980, Del. award Insieme per La Pace, Rome, 1988, Disting. Woman award Northwood Inst., 1991; named Washington Woman of Yr., Washington Women Mag., 1985, Entrepreneur of Yr., Washington, Arthur Young Co. and Venture mag., 1988, Women of Enterprise award. Mem. Nat. Women's Econ. Alliance Found., Pres.'s Export Coun., SBA Nat. Adv. Coun. (co-chmn., exec. com.), SBA Women's Network for Entrepreneurial Tng. (adv. coun.), Nat. Coal Coun. (exec. com.), Women in Internat. Trade, Nat. Fedn. Press Women (ex-officio, communication award 1979, bus. communicator of yr. 1988), Capital Press Women (ex-officio, named bus communicator of yr. 1988, journalist award for non-fiction 1988), Pub. Rels. Soc. Am. (counsellors acad.), Internat. Pub. Rels. Assn. Office: Corporation Public Broadcasting 401 Ninth St NW Washington DC 20004-2129 Office Phone: 202-879-9600.*

HARRISON, PATRICK WOODS, lawyer; b. St. Louis, July 14, 1946; s. Charles William and Carolyn (Woods) Harrison; m. Rebecca Tout, Dec. 23, 1967; children: Heather Ann, Heath Aaron. BS, Ind. U., 1968, JD, 1972. Bar: Ind. 1973, U.S. Dist. Ct. (so. dist.) Ind. 1973, U.S. Supreme Ct. 1977, U.S. Dist. Ct. Nebr. 1982. Assoc. Goltra, Cline, King & Beck, Columbus, Ind., 1972-73; ptnr. Goltra & Harrison, Columbus, 1973-78; pvt. practice Columbus, 1979-80; ptnr. Cline, King, Beck and Harrison, Columbus, 1980-85, Beck, Harrison & Dalmbert, Columbus, 1985—. Ind. Nominating Commn. nominee Ind. Supreme Ct., 1984. With U.S. Army, 1968—70. Fellow: Ind. Trial Lawyers Assn. (bd. dirs. 1984, emertitus dir. 1999, Co-Trial Lawyer of the Yr. 1999); mem.: Am. Trial Lawyers Assn. Republican. Baptist. Avocation: golf. Home: 14250 W Mount Healthy Rd Columbus IN 47201-9309 Office: Beck Harrison & Dalmbert 320 Franklin St Columbus IN 47201-6732 Office Phone: 812-372-8858. Personal E-mail: pharrison@direcway.com. Business E-Mail: woodyh@bhdatty.com.

HARRISON, PAULA JEAN, church musician; b. Kansas City, Mo., May 9, 1949; d. Lester Irving and Isabelle Marie (Entsminger) Mast; m. Gerald Wayne Waltz, Aug. 23, 1970 (div. Nov. 1992); children: Matthew Amos Waltz, Amy Elizabeth Waltz; m. Paul Douglas Harrison, Dec. 20, 1997. Student, Ind. U., 1970, Perkins Sch. Theology, 2004, Our Lady of Lake U., 2005—. Cert. ordained min. candidate 2005. Tchr. piano, flute Paula Waltz Music Studio, Houston, 1982—92; tchr. music The Kinkaid Sch., Houston, 1983—89; accompanist Houston Bapt. U., 1989—90; dir. music Richmond Plaza Bapt. Ch., Bellaire, Tex., 1990—92; accompanist Tex. Music Educators Assn. Dist. IX Honor Choir, 1994—97; choir accompanist Conroe H.S., Tex., 1992—98; tchr. piano Paula Harrison's Music Studio, Conroe, 1992—2004; organist, chirldrens choir dir. First United Meth. Ch., Conroe, 1996—2004; rehearsal pianist Montgomery County Choir Soc., Conroe, 1996—2004; dir. music and fine arts Cedar Bayou United Meth. Ch., Baytown, Tex., 2004—05. Flutist Webster Groves Symphony Orch., 1966—67, performer, flutist St. Louis All-County Double Woodwind Quintet, 1966—67, performer, accompanist Annie - Class Act Productions, 1998, performer, flutist Gypsy - Crighton Theater, 1996, Nunsense - Crighton Theater, 1995. Fl. gov. Ind. U. Wilkie Dorm, 1968—69, female v.p., 1969—70; mem. childrens and dirs. workshop planning com. An August Adventure; active Baytown Area Missionary Alliance; chaplain Sigma Alpha Iota, Ind. U., 1968—69; organist Grace Luth. Ch., Conroe, Tex., 1992—95; bd. dirs. Tex. Conf. Choir Clinic, Baytown Interfaith Hospitality Network. Recipient Am. Band Master's award, Phi Beta Mu-Lambda Chpt., 1966. Mem.: Tex. Music Educators Assn., Jr. Music Club, Tex. Fedn. of Music Clubs, Houston Chorister Guild (pres. 2004—), Huntsville Music Tchrs Assn. (pres. 2001—04), Am. Assn. of English Handball Ringers, Sigma Alpha Iota, Ind. U. (pres. 1969—70). Republican. Methodist. Avocations: reading, needlecrafts, walking, swimming. Home: 2205 French Pl Baytown TX 77520 Office Phone: 281-427-4754 215.

HARRISON, RACHEL, artist; b. NYC, 1966; One-woman shows include Posh Floored as Ali G Tackles Beck, Galerie Arndt & Ptnr., 2004, Brides & Bases, Oakville Galleries, Can., 2002, Look of Dress-Separates, Greene Naftali Gallery, NYC, 1997, Should Home Windows, Arena Gallery, Bklyn., 1996, exhibited in group shows at Dreams & Conflicts: Dictatorship of Viewer, La Biennale di Venezia, Venice, 2003, Experimenters, Lombard-Freid Fine Arts, NYC, 1997, Rachel Harrison & Michael Lazarus, Feature, NYC, 1996, Space, Mind, Place, Andrea Rosen Gallery, NY, 1996, Summer Exhbn., Greene Naftali Gallery, NY, 1996, Sex, Drugs & Explosives, New London Art Forms, London, 1996, Sculpture Incorporating Photog., Feature Gallery, NY, 1996, Post Hoc, Stark Gallery, NY, 1996, Facing the Millennium: The Song Remains the Same, Arlington Mus., Tex., 1996, Oy, 121 Greene St., NY, 1995, High Anxiety, 66 Crosby, NY, 1995, Looky Loo, Sculpture Ctr., NY, 1995, Dark Room, Stark Gallery, NY, 1995, Unsuccess, 479 Broome St., NY, 1994, Tight, Tannery Gallery, London, 1994, Dirty, John Good Gallery, NY, 1994, I Could Do That, 109 Spring St., NY, 1994, Poverty Pop: Aesthetics of Necessity, Exit Art, NY, 1993, Resurrections, William Benton Mus. Art, U. Conn., 1993, Benefits for Four Walls Gallery, David Zwirner Gallery, NY, 1993, Shooting Blanks, 81 Greene St., NY, 1993, 1920: Subtlety of Subversion, Continuity of Intervention, Exit Art, NY, 1993, Simply Made in Am., Aldrich Mus. Contemporary Art, 1993, I Was Born Like This, Mulberry St. Gallery, NY, 1993, Morality Cafe, Postmasters Gallery, NY, 1993, Unlearning, 142 Greene St., NY, 1991, Open Bar, Flamingo East, NY, 1991. Mailing: c/o Greene Naftali Gallery 526 West 26th St New York NY 10001*

HARRISON, RICHARD DEAN, minister, counselor; b. Gaffney, S.C., Oct. 15, 1952; s. Wiley H. and Georgia Ann (Earwood) H.; m. Sandra Kay Parris, Oct. 16, 1970; children: Kathryn Hope, Richard Dean Jr. BA, U. S.C., 1973, MAT, 1975; MDiv, So. Bapt. Theol. Sem., 1986, DMin, 1990. Ordained to ministry So. Bapt. Conv., 1985. Pastor English Bapt. Ch., Stephensport, Ky., 1985-87, Rehoboth Bapt. Ch., Gaffney, 1987-92; counselor Cherokee Mental Health and Counseling Ctr., Gaffney, S.C., 1992—; pastor Lando (S.C.) Bapt. Ch., 1997—. Singer, songwriter, 1999—. Chaplain Gaffney Jaycees, 1977-79, Asbury-Rehoboth Vol. Fire Dept., Gaffney, 1989—; bd. dirs. Piedmont Community Action Agy., Spartanburg, S.C., 1979-81. Mem. Breckinridge Bapt. Assn. (exec. com. 1985-87), Broad River Bapt. Assn. (exec. com., dir. Sunday sch. 1987-92). Home: 117 Stacy Dr Gaffney SC 29341-1433 Office: Cherokee Mental Health and Counseling Ctr 125 E Robinson St Gaffney SC 29340-2444

HARRISON, RICHARD WAYNE, lawyer; b. Marfa, Tex., June 23, 1944; AA, Schreiner U., 1964; BBA, U. Tex. Austin, 1966; JD, U. Tex. Sch. Law, 1968. Ptnr. Florence & Harrison, Hughes Springs, Tex., 1968-69; pvt. practice Hughes Springs, Tex., 1969-73; asst. atty. gen. Atty. Gen.'s Office of Tex., Austin, 1973-74, chief tax divsn., 1974-76, spl. asst. atty. gen., 1976-78; ptnr. McGinnis, Lochridge & Kilgore, Austin, 1978-87, Jones, Day, Reavis &

Pogue, Austin, 1987-94; mng. ptnr. Harrison & Rial LLP, Austin, 1994—2000; owner Rick Harrison & Assocs., Austin, 2000—02; ptnr. Fritz, Byrne, Head & Harrison LLP, Austin, 2002—. Pres. Hughes Springs Indsl. Found., 1970; Cass County chmn. Salvation Army, 1970—72; chmn. Hughes Springs United Fund Drive, 1972; mem. Austin Convocation Cursillo Steering Com., 1983—86, chmn., 1985—86; precinct chmn. Cass County Dem. Com., 1969—73; area coord. Lloyd Bentsen for Senate Com., 1970; trustee, treas. St. Andrew's Episcopal Sch., Austin; sr. warden St. Luke's-on-the-Lake Episcopal Ch., 1984. Fellow: Tex. Bar Found. (life); mem.: Schreiner Coll. Former Student Assn. (bd. dirs. 1984—88), Cass County Bar Assn. (past pres.), Travis County Bar Assn., State Bar of Tex. (fed. jud. com. 1980—83, bar jour. com. 1980—83), Barton Creek Country Club, Masons. Democrat. Home: 1730 Camp Craft Rd Austin TX 78746-7317 Office: Fritz Byrne Head & Harrison LLP 98 San Jacinto Blvd Ste 2000 Austin TX 78701 Office Phone: 512-476-2020.

HARRISON, ROBERT ALLEN, retired aerospace executive; b. Omaha, Sept. 15, 1929; m. Joyce Eleanor Amirikian, Sept. 9, 1961; children: Lynda Joy, Robert Amirikian. AB, Harvard U., 1951; MS, George Washington U., Washington, 1982. Pres. Harrison and Co., Fairfax, Va., 1990—97, Harrison Aerospace Corp., Fairfax, 1997—2001. Dir. Am.-Russian Tech. Exch. Ctr., Moscow, 1991—93. Editor: (book) Handbook of Reliability Engineering. Mem.: Inst. for Ops. Rsch. and Mgmt. Sci., Cavalier Golf and Yacht Club, Harvard Club of Washington (vice-president 1994—95). Home: 8909 Glenbrook Rd Fairfax VA 22031 Home (Summer): 303 Atlantic Ave Virginia Beach VA 23451 Office Phone: 703-280-2202. Personal E-mail: rharrison25@cox.net. E-mail: raharrison@starpower.net.

HARRISON, ROBERT L., photographer, writer, retired transportation executive, poet, playwright; s. William Henry Harrison and Roberta Louise Clark; m. Dorothy E. Vokoun, July 28, 1973; children: Roger, Kevin. AA, Nassau C.C., Garden City, NY, 1969; BA, Stony Brook U., 1971; ASD, Hofstra U., 1975. Tchr. spl. edn. Suffolk BOCES, Lindenhurst, NY, 1972—73; pers. asst. MTA L.I. Bus, Garden City, 1973—75, transp. dispatcher, 1975—79, mgr. command ctr., 1979—99; writer, photographer, 1999—. Photographer Animal People Mag., 1993—, Suffolk Sports Hall of Fame, 2001—, L.I. Press, 2003—; photography judge East Meadow Pub. Libr., 2002, 04. Photo contbr. (children's book) Way to Go: Sports Poems, 2001, Bridgeport Baseball, 2003, New York State Encyclopedia, 2005, photographer (one-man shows), Hofstra U. Law Libr., 1995—2003, Poly. U., Farmingdale, 1995—98, African Am. Mus., 2001, Adelphi U. Swirbul Libr., 2004, Hofstra Mus., 2004, (group shows), Brookhaven Coun. of Arts, 1996—2000, 2002, (group shows), Firehouse Gallery, Garden City, 1999—2000, 2005, Mills Pond House, Smithtown Coun. of Arts, 2000, numerous others; prodr.(writer): (plays) Bloom & O'Hara, 1998, Confessions of a Shakespeare Addict, 2004;, author of poems. Airman 1st class USAF, 1961—65. Named Best of Show, New Eng. Wildlife Expn., 1995, Wildlife Assn. Expn., 1995; recipient cert. of recognition, South Nassau Communities Hosp., 1995—96, Town of Hempstead Calendar Contest, 1998—2005, Town of Hempstead, 2001, South Nassau Communities Hosp., 2000—02, African Am. Mus., Hempstead, 2001, Nassau County Legislature, 2001, Village of Hempstead, 2001, cert. of appreciation, Poly. U., Farmingdale, NY, 1996—97, Brookhaven Arts Coun., 2002, award cert., Winter Arts Festival, L.I. State Pk. Region, 1997—99, Pall Corp. award, Art League L.I., 2000, cert. of achievement, Nassau County Exec., 2001, Folio award, L.I. Coalition for Fair Broadcasting, 2004, citation for photography, Nassau County Exec., 2004; grantee, NY Coun. Arts at Freeport, 2001. Mem.: Soc. Children's Book Writers and Illustrators, Hofstra George Estabrook Alumni Assn. (v.p. 2003—), L.I. Arts Coun. at Freeport (panelist 2001—). Home: 2447 Fifth Ave East Meadow NY 11554

HARRISON, RUSSELL SAGE, political science professor, consultant, social studies educator; b. Southport, N.C., Feb. 24, 1944; s. Russell S. and Julia (Grayson) H. BA, Duke U., 1966; PhD, U. N.C., 1971. Asst. prof. polit. sci. Rutgers U., Camden, N.J., 1971-77, assoc. prof. polit. sci., 1977—, chmn. dept. polit. sci., 1997-99. Project dir. Camden County Mgmt. Audit, 1995-96, Professionalization of County Govt., Camden, 1991-92. Author: Inequality of Public School Finance, 1977. Cons. South Jersey Port Authority, Salem (N.J.) Port Authority, N.J. Dept. Transp., Fed. Econ. Devel. Adminstrn., N.J.; trustee Cadbury Retirement Cmty., Camden, 1995-98, asst. sec., 1995-98; active Soc. of Friends, clk., 1998—. Mem. Am. Polit. Sci. Assn., Am. Soc. Pub. Adminstrn., Northeastern Polit. Sci. Home: 301 Plantation Dr Cinnaminson NJ 08077-4308 Office: Rutgers U Dept Political Sci Camden NJ 08101-0020

HARRISON, S. DAVID, lawyer; b. N.Y.C., Jan. 29, 1930; s. Louis and Molly (Ginsburg) Harrison; m. Joan S. Horowitz, Mar. 23, 1958 (dec. May 1993); children: Andrew L., Rachel E.; m. Roberta S. Karmel, Oct. 29, 1995. AB, Harvard U., 1951, LLB, 1954; LLM, NYU, 1959. Bar: NJ 1955, NY 1968. Law sec. to Hon. William J. Brennan, Jr. N.J. Supreme Ct., 1954-55; from assoc. to ptnr. Platoff, Platoff & Heftler, Union City, NJ, 1955-65; corp. counsel Beaunit Corp., N.Y.C., 1965-71, corp. sec., 1966-71; asst. sec. Tyrex, Inc., 1969-71; dir. Man-Made Fibers Prodrs. Assn., 1970-71; pvt. practice law N.Y.C., 1971—; of counsel Rosen & Livingston. Bd. dirs. various corps.; mem. panel arbitrators N.Y. Stock Exch. Chmn. zoning bd. Village Hastings-on-Hudson, 1988—98; bd. dirs. Am. Friends Sarah Herzog Hosp. Jerusalem, 1992—; trustee Gallery at Hastings, NY, 1993—97. Mem.: ABA, Am. Arbitrators Assn., Nat. Panel Arbitrators, N.Y. State Bar Assn., Harvard Club Westchester, Harvard Club N.Y., Masons. Home: 66 Summit Dr Hastings On Hudson NY 10706-1215 Office: 275 Madison Ave New York NY 10016

HARRISON, STANLEY L., editor, educator, writer, communications educator; s. Frank Imwold Harrison and Thelma Emma Baer; m. Frances Keane, Nov. 22, 1956. BA, U. Md., 1955, MA, 1962; PhD, Am. U., 1967. Sr. leader Inst. Def. Analyses, DC, 1960—63; sr. analyst Rsch. Analysis Corp., Chevy Chase, Md., 1963—70; legis. asst. Ho. of Reps., 1971—73; assoc. editor Nat. Jour., 1973—76; dir., corp. comm. Corp. for Pub. Broadcasting, 1976—85; assoc. prof. comms. U. Miami, Coral Gables, Fla., 1986—; editor Enoch Pratt Free Libr., Balt., 1999—. Author: (book) Cavalcade of Journalists 1900-2000, Mencken Revisited: Author, Editor & Newspaperman, Editorial Art of Edmund Duffy, Florida's Editorial Cartoonists; editor: a.k.a. H.L. Mencken: Selected Pseudonymous Writings, Editorial Puffy, 1998, Mencken Revisited, 1999, Menckeniana, 2002. Chmn. Dem. State Ctrl. Com., Howard County, 1960—63. Airman 1st class USAF, 1950—53. Decorated Silver Medal award US Naval Inst.; recipient Writer of Merit, Mil. Rev., 1965, Gov.'s Citizenship award, Gov. of Md., 1974; Wilton Pk. Fellow, Fgn. Office, 1969, Pub. Affairs Fellowship, Stanford U., 1970-72. Mem.: Internat. Inst. for Strategic Studies, Nat. Press Club, Mencken Soc., Pi Sigma Alpha, Pi Delta Epsilon, Pi Alpha Theta, Omicron Delta Kappa, Sigma Delta Chi. Protestant. Avocation: reading. Home: 5783 SW 40th St 221 Miami FL 33155 Personal E-mail: menckeniana@earthlink.net.

HARRISON, THOMAS FLATLEY, lawyer; b. N.Y.C., Jan. 11, 1942; s. John P. and Mary F. (Flatley) H.; m. Lorraine Brereton, Aug. 16, 1969; children: John J., Jane C., Ann B., Peter T. AB, Holy Cross Coll., 1963; JD, Fordham U., 1966. Bar: N.Y. 1967, Ill. 1979, Ohio 1981, D.C. 1988, Conn. 1989. Asst. counsel N.Y.C. Dept. Rent and Housing, 1966-69; asst. atty. gen. N.Y. State Dept. Law, 1969-74; chief enforcement N.Y. region U.S. EPA, 1974-76, regional counsel Chgo., 1976-80; sr. corp. counsel B.F. Goodrich Co., Akron, Ohio, 1980-87; ptnr. Manatt, Phelps, Rothenberg & Evans, Washington, 1987-88; ptnr., co-chmn. environ. and land use dept. Day, Berry & Howard LLP, Hartford, Conn., 1988—. Faculty Practising Law Inst. Contbr. articles to profl. jours. Mem. 49th Assembly Dist. Rep. Orgn., N.Y.C., 1963-73, bd. govs., 1969-73; active Silver Lake, Ohio, Rep. Orgn., 1981-87; mem. Rep. Town Com., Avon, Conn., 1991—, Inland Wetlands Commn., Avon, 1992-95; mem. Bd. Fin. 1995—, chmn., 2002—; mem. Conn. Coun. on Environ. Quality, 1997—, chmn., 2004—; mem. Conn. Small Bus. Compliance Adv. Panel, 1996—; bd. dirs. Conn. League of Conservation Voters, 2000—, Nat. Audubon Conn. 2001—. Recipient Outstanding Performance award EPA, 1976. Mem. Conn. Bar Assn. (exec. com. environ. law sect. 1989—, sect. chair 1998-99). Roman Catholic. Home: 51 Briar Hill Rd Avon CT 06001-4007 Office: Day Berry & Howard LLP City Place Hartford CT 06103-3499 Office Phone: 860-275-0480. Business E-Mail: tfharrison@dbh.com.

HARRISON, TODD A., lawyer; b. Duarte, Calif., Apr. 16, 1962; BS magna cum laude, U. Houston, Clear Lake, 1989; JD with honors, U. Tulsa Coll., 1993. Bar: Tex. 1993, Md. 1994, DC 1999. Ptnr. Buchanan Ingersoll PC, Washington; ptnr., food and drug group Venable LLP, Washington, 2004—. Author: (articles) Introducing New Dietary Ingredients, 2002, The Cholestin Case: The Ongoing Saga, 2002, FDA's Proposed Rule for Dietary Supplement cGMPs, 2003. Recipient Am. Jurisprudence award. Office: Venable LLP 575 7th St NW Washington DC 20004 Office Phone: 202-344-4724. Office Fax: 202-344-8300. Business E-Mail: taharrison@venable.com.

HARRISON, WALTER ASHLEY, physicist, researcher; b. Flushing, NY, Apr. 26, 1930; s. Charles Allison and Gertrude (Ashley) H.; m. Lucille Prince Carley, July 17, 1954; children: Richard Knight, John Carley, William Ashley, Robert Walter. B. Engring. Physics, Cornell U., 1953; MS, U. Ill., 1954, PhD, 1956. Physicist Gen. Elec. Research Labs., Schenectady, 1956-65; prof. applied physics Stanford (Calif.) U., 1965-2001, prof. emeritus, 2001—, chmn. applied physics dept., 1989-93, prof. emeritus, 2001—. Scientific adv. bd. Max Planck Inst., Stuttgart, Germany, 1989-92. Author: Pseudopotentials in the Theory of Metals, 1966, Solid State Theory, 1970, Electronic Structure and the Properties of Solids, 1980, Elementary Electronic Structure, 1999, revised edit., 2004, Applied Quantum Mechanics, 2000; editor: the Fermi Surface, 1960, Proceedings of the International Conference on the Physics of Semiconductors, 1985, Proceedings of the International Conference on Materials and Mechanisms of High-Temperature Superconductivity, 1989. Guggenheim fellow, 1970-71; recipient von Humboldt sr. U.S. scientist award, 1981, 89, 94; vis. fellow Clare Hall, Cambridge U., 1970-71. Fellow Am. Phys. Soc.; mem. European Phys. Soc. Home: 817 San Francisco Ct Stanford CA 94305-1021 Office: Stanford U Dept Applied Physics Stanford CA 94305-4045 Office Phone: 650-723-4224. E-mail: walt@stanford.edu.

HARRISON, WALTER LEE, university president; b. Pitts., May 15, 1946; s. Lester Maurice and Alice Hagedorn (Cohen) H.; m. Dianne Ellen Mintz, June 22, 1970. BA, Trinity Coll., 1968; MA, U. Mich., 1969; PhD, U. Calif., Davis, 1980. Lectr. Johannes Gutenberg U., Mainz, Fed. Republic of Germany, 1976-77; instr. Iowa State U., Ames, 1978-80, Colo. Coll., Colorado Springs, 1980-82, dir. coll. rels., 1982-85; pres. Gehrung Assocs., Keene, N.H., 1985-89; exec. dir., v.p. univ. rels. U. Mich., Ann Arbor, 1989-98; pres. U. Hartford, West Hartford, 1998—. Vis. prof. Colo. Coll., 1988-91; adj. prof. U. Mich., 1991-98. Contbr. articles to profl. jours. Trustee Fountain Valley Sch., 1990-99; bd. dirs. Univ. Musical Soc., 1990-98, Mich. Journalism Fellow Program, 1991-98; dir. St. Francis Hosp. and Med. Ctr., 1998—, Hartford Stage Co., 2000-, Hartford Symphony Orch. 1998-; trustee Suffield Acad., 2002-; bd. dirs. divsn. I, NCAA, 2002-, chair com. on acad. performance, 2004-, chair exec. com., 2005-. Mem. Phi Kappa Phi. Avocations: baseball, recreational sports. Office: Univ of Hartford 200 Bloomfield Ave West Hartford CT 06117-1599 Office Phone: 860-768-4417. Business E-Mail: horky@hartford.edu.

HARRISON, WENDELL RICHARD, musician, composer; b. Detroit, Oct. 1, 1942; s. Walter R. Harrison and Ossalee (Punche) Lockett; m. Pamela Wise, May 1995. Grad. HS, Detroit. Musician, composer Wenha Music/Rebirth Inc., Detroit; artistic dir. Rebirth Inc., Detroit. Author: Be Boppers Method Books, I, 1999, II, 2000. Recipient Compositions award, Arts Serve Mich., 1998, Creative Works award, Chamber Music Am., 2003, Residency Partnership Program award, 2004. Mem.: Am. Fedn. Musicians.

HARRISON, WILLIAM A., lawyer; b. Beppu, Japan, Oct. 13, 1953; arrived in U.S., 1955; s. Henry and Machiko Levy; m. Erika Pang Harrison, Aug. 6, 1985; children: Jamaal, Jordan, Kiira. BA, U. Hawaii, 1976, MA, 1981; JD, William Richardson, 1981. Bar: Hawaii 1981, N.J. 1982, U.S. Ct. Appeals (9th cir.) 1982, U.S. Supreme Ct. 1985, U.S. Ct. Appeals (fed. cir.) 1993. Ptnr. Harrison & Matsuoka, Attys. at Law, Honolulu. Chairperson litigation com. ACLU of Hawaii, Honolulu, 1982—84; lawyer select State Jud. Conf., Honolulu, 1991—94; pres. bd. Domestic Violence Clearing House, Honolulu, 1991—92; chairperson Jud. Selection Com., Honolulu, 1995—97. Del. Hawaii Dem. Party State Conv., Honolulu, 1988, 1990, 1992, 1994, 1996, 1998, 2000, 2002. Named Outstanding Young Man of Am., 1979, Newsmaker, Star Bull. Newspaper, Honolulu, 1990, Coach of Yr., Interscholastic League Honolulu, 1990. Mem.: Nat. Assn. Criminal Def. Lawyers (life). Lutheran. Avocations: surfing, golf. Office: Harrison & Matsuoka Ste 800 841 Bishop St Honolulu HI 96813

HARRISON, WILLIAM BURWELL, JR., bank executive; b. Rocky Mount, N.C., Aug. 12, 1943; s. William Burwell and Katherine (Spruill) H.; m. Anne MacDonald Stpehens, Dec. 7, 1985; children Katherine Adams, Anne Stephens. AB in Econs., U. N.C., Chapel Hill, 1966, spl. student in bus. adminstrn., 1966-67; Sr. Mgmt. Program, Harvard Bus. Sch., Vevey, Switzerland, 1979. Trainee Chem. Bank, N.Y.C., 1967-69, Mid-South corp. and corr. banking group, 1969-74, West Coast corp. and corr. banking group, 1974-76, dist. head, Western regional coord. San Francisco, 1976-78, regional coord., sr. v.p. London, 1978-82, sr. v.p., divsn. head Europe, 1982-83, exec. v.p. U.S. corp. divsn. N.Y.C., 1983-87, group exec. banking and corp. fin. group, 1987-90, vice chmn. instl. banking, 1990—94; vice chmn. Global Bank, N.Y.C., 1992—99, Chase Manhattan Corp., N.Y.C., 1995—99, pres., CEO, 1999, chmn., CEO, 2000; pres., CEO J.P. Morgan Chase & Co., N.Y.C., 2000—01, chmn., CEO, 2001—. Bd. dirs. Merck & Co., Inc., Whitehouse Station, NJ; mem. bd. advisors N.C. Outward Bound Sch., Asheville; mem. Bretton Woods Com. Mem. bd. visitors Kenan Flagler Bus. Sch.; mem. bd. overseers Sloan-Kettering Cancer Ctr., 1999—. Mem.: Nat. Golf Links Am., Golf Club Purchase, Field Club Greenwich, Links Club, Racquet Club, Bus. Coun., Bus. Roundtable, Fin. Svcs. Roundtable, Augusta Nat. Golf Club, Blind Brook Club, Round Hill Club. Episcopalian. Avocations: athletics, travel.

HARRISON, WILLIAM HENRY, retired medical educator; b. Aberdeen, SD, Feb. 24, 1924; s. William Henry Sr. and Catherine Marie (McMasters) Harrison; m. Mary Anne Peavy (div.); children: Karen, William, Thomas, Kenneth. Student, Washington U., St. Louis, 1943—44, Harvard U., 1944—45; BA in Chemistry, U. Minn., 1948, MS in Biochemistry, 1952, PhD in Biochemistry, 1954; postgrad., Columbia U., 1958—62. Sr. biochemist Eli Lilly Rsch. Lab., Indpls., 1954—58; neurochemistry rschr. NIH, Bethesda, Md., 1963—64; asst. prof. Chgo. Med. Sch., 1963—64, U. Ill., Chgo., 1964—68; assoc. prof. Rush Med. Ctr., Chgo., 1968—71, Rush. Med. Coll., Chgo., 1971—73, prof., 1973—98, prof. emeritus, 1998—. Assoc. dir. minority med. edn. programs Chgo.-Rush-Robert Wood Johnson Ill. Inst. Tech., 1987—96. Contbr. chapters to books, articles to profl. jours. With USAAF, 1943—46. Recipient Rsch. award, Chgo. Heart Assn., 1963—69, Mark Lepper MD Soc. Tchrs. award, Rush Med. Coll., 1986, James Campbell MD Disting. Svc. Alumni award, 1997; Rsch. grantee, NIH, 1963—88. Avocations: camping, fishing, dance, reading, writing. Home: 1783 Jonathan Way Apt D Reston VA 20190

HARRISON, (HILDE), artist; b. Wallduern, Baden, Germany, Mar. 16, 1936; came to U.S., 1953; d. Heinz Lennartz and Hilde Lennartz-Klein; m. Charles E. Harrison Jr., Jan. 31, 1959; children: Charles, Marianne, Andrea, Pete, Bianca. Assoc. BS, Lord Fairfax Coll., 1989; BFA, Shepherd U., 1994; MA, NYU, Venice, 2001. Tchr. Pavan, Winchester, Va., 1998; pvt. lessons Front Royal, Va., 1999—; lectr. Frederick County Sch. Sys., Va., 1999—. Lectr. Culpeper (Va.) Art League, Manasas (Va.) Art League, Lurray (Va.) Art League. One-woman shows include Blue Ridge Arts Coun., Front Royal, 1984, Wallduern, Germany, 1992, Presina, Italy 1999, Venice, Italy, 1999, 2000, N.Y.C., 2001. Pres. Assn. for Children with Learning Disability, West Chester, Pa., 1972; founder, pres. Warren County Assn. for Children with Learning Disability, Front Royal, 1975; chair Warren County Sch. Bd. Spl. Edn., Front Royal, 1980, Vacation Bible Sch., Front Royal. Recipient Corning Glass award, 1980, Wheat Security award, 1984, 1st pl. Regional Show, Blue Ridge Arts Gallery, 2002, 2d pl., 2003. Mem. Women Arts, Va. Watercolor Assn., Blud Ridge Arts Coun. (docent), Shenandoah Valley Art Assn., Shenandoah Arts Coun. Avocations: reading, hiking, cooking, swimming, crafts. Home: 381 Windy Ridge Rd Front Royal VA 22630-7207

HARRISON-JERVAY, EVELYN YVONNE, publishing executive; b. Macon, NC, Mar. 7, 1945; d. John Andrew and Sallie Elizabeth (Somerville) Harrison; m. Paul Reginald Jervay, July 24, 1989; children: Nikki, Shenay, Adria, Kelvin; m. Roy Dunston, Jan. 28, 1961 (div. Apr. 1980); children: Sylvia, Sharon, Kerry, Sonja. AA, Am. Coll., 1972, AA survey of adv. sales, 1974, AA bus. taxation, 1976; div. requirement, Shaw Div. Sch., 1985. Supr. First Nat. City Bank, NY, 1963—72; ins. agt. Mut. of NY, 1972—76; self employed Evelyn's, Raleigh, NC, 1977—80; founder Nay-Kel Edn. Ctr., Raleigh, NC, 1980—, Nay-Kel Ministries, Warrenton, NC, 2001—; co-pub. Carolinian Newspaper, Raleigh, 1997—; pub. The Carolina Call, Raleigh, NC, 1994—. Recipient Trailblazer in Media award, 2d Dist. Ch., Va., 2003, Outstanding Media award, Am. Minority Media, 1998. Avocations: reading, tennis, art, thrift shopping. Office: The Carolinian, Nay-Kel Ministries 610 Maywood Ave Raleigh NC 27603 Office Phone: 919-834-5558. Office Fax: 919-832-3243. Personal E-mail: carolinian@mindspring.com.

HARRISS, ELAINE ATKINS, music educator; b. Springfield, Tenn., Oct. 20, 1945; d. I.L. (Jack) Jr. and Mildred (Coke) Atkins; m. Ernest Charles Harriss II, Aug. 29, 1965; children: Edward, Ernest. MusB, Vanderbilt U., 1966, MusM, 1967; PhD, U. Mich., 1981. Studio tchr. piano, flute, and Kindermusik, Martin, Tenn., 1970—; prin. flute Jackson (Tenn.) Symphony Orch., 1971-83, Paducah (Ky.) Symphony Orch., 1985—2001; duo-pianist Allison Nelson-Elaine Harriss Duo, Martin, 1986—; prof. music U. Tenn., Martin, 2001—. Faculty mem. Kindermusik Internat., Greensboro, N.C., 1987-2001; dir. Kindermusik of Martin, 1986-2004, dir. ednl. standards and profl. devel. Kindermusik Internat., Greensboro, 1993-2001. Contbr. articles to profl. jours. Elder Trinity Presbyn. Ch., Martin, Tenn., 1980, 86, 93, 2001; pres. U. Tenn. Faculty Womens Club, Martin, 1984-85. Recipient Algernon Sidney Sullivan award George Peabody Coll. Tchrs., 1967, Rho Province Leadership award Sigma Alpha Iota, 1967. Mem. Nat. Kindermusik Educators Assn. (pres. 1999-2003), West Tenn. Music Tchrs. (pres. 1986-90), Martin Area Music Tchrs. Assn. (pres. 2001-05), Philharm. Music Guild (pres. 1971-73, 84-86, 92-93). Avocations: gardening, reading. Home: 205 University St Martin TN 38237-2434 Office: 211 Fine Arts Bldg U Tenn Martin Martin TN 38237-2434 Office Phone: 731-881-7411. E-mail: elaineh@utm.edu.

HARRIS-STOKES, JOYCE A., secondary school educator; b. Detroit, Dec. 22, 1954; d. Willie L. Sr. and Mary L. (Hightower) H.; m. Daniel T. Taylor, July 17, 1980 (div.); m. Vernon L. Stokes, July 11, 2002. BS in Math., Columbus State U., 1977, BS in Edn. and Math., 1979. Cert. math. tchr., Ga. Pvt. practice math. tutor, Columbus, Ga., 1974-78; news and sports editor The Saber, Columbus, 1975-77; math. tchr. Russell County Bd. Edn., Phenix City, Ala., 1979—, math. chairperson, 1981—. Adv. Jr. Honor Soc., 1980—84; dist. dir. SECME, 2000—; del. Ala. Edn. Assn., 2004—. Storyteller:; author: Zap Pow Pop-An Interdisciplinary Unit on Energy; co-author (with Mary L. Highwater-Harris): Tales and Poems from Grandma Tempie-Angels. Mem. Juvenile Justice Com., Russell County Com. for Change; vol. United Hospice. Mem.: ASCD, NEA, Russell County Edn. Assn., Ga. Edn. Environ. Coun., Environ. Edn. Assn. Ala., Ala. Edn. Assn., Am. Math. Soc., Math. Assn. Am., Chattahoochee Coun. Tchrs. of Math., Ala. Coun. Tchrs. of Math., Nat. Fedn. State Poetry Socs. (legislature contact team), Ga. Poetry Soc. Baptist. Avocations: designing, photography, basketball, sewing, writing. Office: Russell County HS 4699 Old Seale Hwy Seale AL 36875-4006

HARRIS-WARRICK, RONALD MORGAN, education educator; b. Berkeley, Calif., July 28, 1949; s. Morgan and Marjorie Ruth (Mason) H.; m. Rebecca Lamar Warrick, Apr. 5, 1975; children: Sheridan, Thomas. BA, Stanford U., 1970, PhD, 1976, Postdoctoral fellow, 1978, Harvard Med. Sch., Boston, 1980. Asst. prof. Cornell U., Ithaca, N.Y., 1980-86, assoc. prof., 1986-92, prof., 1992—. Vis. scientist Ecole Normale Superieure, Paris, 1986-87; vis. prof. Stanford Med. Sch., 1994, Karolinska Inst., Stockholm, Sweden, 2001-02; chmn. dept. neurobiology and behavior Cornell U., 2002—. Editor: Dynamic Biological Networks, 1992; assoc. editor Jour. Neurophysiology; contbr. articles to profl. jours; assoc. editor Jour. Neurophysiology. Asst. scoutmaster Boy Scouts of Am., Ithaca, N.Y., 1992—. Recipient Stephen Fox Meml. award Stanford U., 1970, Guggenheim fellowship, 1985. Mem. AAAS, Internat. Soc. for Neuroethology, Soc. for Neurosci., Phi Beta Kappa. Avocations: skiing, camping, hiking, music. Office: Cornell U Sect Neurobiology/Behavior Seeley G Muld Hall Ithaca NY 14853 Office Phone: 607-254-4355. E-mail: rmh4@cornell.edu.

HARROLD, BERNARD, lawyer; b. Wells County, Ind., Feb. 5, 1925; s. James Delmer and Marie (Mounsey) H.; m. Kathleen Walker, Nov. 26, 1952; children— Bernard James, Camilla Ruth, Renata Jane. Student, Biarritz Am. U., 1945; AB, Ind. U., 1949, LLB, 1951. Bar: Ill. 1951. Since practiced in, Chgo.; assoc., then mem. firm Kirkland, Ellis, Hodson, Chaffetz & Masters, 1951-67; sr. ptnr. Wildman, Harrold, Allen & Dixon, 1967—. Note editor: Ind. Law Jour, 1950-51; contbr. articles to profl. jours. Served with AUS, 1944-46, ETO. Fellow Am. Coll. Trial Lawyers, Acad. Law Alumni Fellows Ind. U. Sch. Law; mem. ABA, Ill. Bar Assn. (chmn. evidence program 1970), Chgo. Bar Assn, Lawyers Club, Univ. Club, Order of Coif, Phi Beta Kappa, Phi Eta Sigma. Home: 809 Locust St Winnetka IL 60093-1821 Office: Wildman Harrold Allen & Dixon 225 W Wacker Dr Fl 28 Chicago IL 60606-1229 *I try to see people and events for what they really are, apply my talents, work hard, and pay good attention to fairness.*

HARROLD, JOHN ANDREW, education educator, consultant; b. Ft. Wayne, Ind., July 11, 1937; s. Virgil Odell and Naomi Roth Harrold; m. Anna Margaret Kaserman; children: John Andrew Jr., Rebekah Ann Overbey. BS in Edn., Ind. U., 1961, MA in Geography & Sociology, 1967, MA in Polit. Sci., 1971; diploma in Civil Affairs, Civil Affairs Sch., US Army, 1966. Instr. and evaluation officer U. S. Army Q.m. Sch., Petersburg, Va., 1962—63; social studies tchr. Martinsville (Ind.) H.S., 1964—67; tchr. and dept. chair MSD of Lawrence Twp., Indpls., 1967—72; state social studies cons. Ind. Dept. Edn., Indpls., 1972—76, dir. of curriculum, 1976—85, spl. asst. for long-range planning, 1985—91, performance-based edn. cons., 1991—98; pres. 21st Century Learning Cmtys., Indpls., 1998—. Fellow social studies field agt. tng. program Ind. U., Bloomington, 1970—72; instr. Ind. U., Purdue U., Indpls., 1973—74; co-dir. Egypt studies program Ind. Consortium for Internat. Programs, Terre Haute, 1973—75; chairperson textbook adoptions Ind. State Bd. Edn., Indpls., 1984—90, exec. dir. 21st century schooling, 1984—91; prin. Gary (Ind.) Consulting Group, 1994—98; mgr. fwy. sch. program Ind. Dept. Edn., Indpls., 1996—98; edn. chairperson Indpls. Regional Transp. Coun., 1998—; dir. learning systems and techs. Keyway Assocs., Inc., Indpls., 1999—; bd. mem. East Ctrl. Ind. Chambers Partnership, Greenfield, 2000—; dir., cmtys. and new econs. Am.'s Nat. Rd. Corridors of Learning, Indpls., 2003—. Councilman, coun. pres., utilities bd. chair Cumberland (Ind.) Town Coun., 1995—2002; bd. mem. Hancock Econ. Devel. Coun., Greenfield, 1999—; candidate state supt. pub. instrn. Rep. Party, Ind., 1991—92. Maj. USAR, 1962—81. Named to Sagamore of the Wabash, Gov. State of Ind., 1998; recipient Exceptional Svc. award, Ind. Coun. Social Studies, 1977, Outstanding Leadership award, Gov. State of Ind., 1987, Outstanding Svc. award, Ind. State Bd. Edn., 1990, Outstanding Contbns. award, Ind. Coun. Econ. Edn., 1998. Home: 12256 Dunbar Cir S Indianapolis IN 46229-3262 Office: 21st Century Learning Cmtys LLC 10535 E Washington St Ste 177 Indianapolis IN 46229-2609 Office Phone: 317-894-3595. Office Fax: 317-894-7743. Personal E-mail: learning21stclc@aol.com.

HARROLD, RONALD THOMAS, research scientist; b. Fulham, London, Eng., Apr. 4, 1933; arrived in U.S., 1963; s. John and Cicely Helen (Eddenden) H.; m. Ann Marie Whitley, Dec. 3, 1955; children: Lesley Ann,

Linda Jane. BS, Chelmsford Coll. Tech., Eng., 1962, Twickenham Coll. Tech., 1955. Student apprentice Brit. Thomson-Houston Co., Willesden, London, Eng., 1950-55; lectr. radar tech. Army Sch. Electronics, Arborfield, Berkshire, Eng., 1955-57; devel. engr. English Electric Valve Co., Chelmsford, Essex, Eng., 1957-61; rsch. engr. Sylvania-Thorn Color TV Labs., Enfield, Middlesex, Eng., 1961-63; adv. rsch. scientist Westinghouse Sci. and Tech. Ctr., Pitts., 1963-96, cons., 1996—. Contbr. articles to profl. jours. Fellow IEEE (life); mem. Instn. Elec. Engrs., Oxford Athletic Club. Republican. Episcopalian. Achievements include 30 U.S. patents in field of vapour mist dielectrics, acoustic waveguide monitoring. Home: 4052 Benden Cir Murrysville PA 15668-1336 Office: George Westinghouse Rsch and Tech Park 1310 Beulah Rd Pittsburgh PA 15235-5098 E-mail: marieron@adelphia.net.

HARROLD, THOMAS J., JR., lawyer; b. Athens, Ga., July 22, 1944; s. Thomas J. and Virginia Harris Harrold; m. Constance P. Harrold, May 1, 1971; 1 child, Elizabeth Virginia. BA in History, Columbia U., 1966; JD, U. Ga., 1969. Bar: Ga. 1969, U.S. Dist. Ct. (no. dist.) Ga. 1969. From assoc. to ptnr. Fortson, Bentley, Griffin, Athens, Ga., 1969—76; dep. commr. Ga. Dept. Revenue, Atlanta, 1976—78; ptnr. Cofer, Beauchamp, Hanes & Harris, Atlanta, 1978—85, Glass, McCullough, Sherrill & Harrold, Atlanta, 1985—97, Miller & Martin, LLP, Atlanta, 1997—. Author: Starting and Operating a Business in Georgia, 1986. Pres. World Law Group, 1995—97; bd. trustees Ga. Econ. Devel. Found., Atlanta, 1988—; bd. dirs. German Am. C. of C., Atlanta, 1995—, Japan Am. Soc., Atlanta, 1992—. Capt. Ga. Air NG, 1969—75. Democrat. Methodist. Avocations: reading, jogging, travel. Office: Miller & Martin LLP 1275 Peachtree St Atlanta GA 30309 E-mail: tharrold@millermartin.com.

HARRON-HORIATES, COLLEEN MARY, health service professional; b. Camden, N.J., Aug. 18, 1964; d. Robert Ernest and Kathryn Augustine Harron; m. Nicholas George Horiates, June 10, 1989; children: Kathryn Patricia Horiates, Zachary Nicholas Horiates. BA, Trenton State Coll., Ewing, N.J., 1986, MS in Mgmt., 1987; PhD, Century U., N.Mex., 2001. Tech. specialist Travelers Ins. Co., Voorhees, NJ, 1989—93; network devel. specialist MetraComp, Cherry Hill, NJ, 1993—97; PPO adminstr. MetraComp/Nat. Healthcare Resoures, N.Y.C., 1997—2000; regional dir., Provider Networks Nat. Healthcare Resources/Focus, Cherry Hill, NJ, 2000—04. Mem.: Bus. Coun. of N.J., Nat. Assn. Rehab. Profls. in Pvt. Sector, Pa. Workers' Compensation Assn. Avocations: antiques, reading, running. Office: MedRisk Inc PO Box 61570 2701 Renaissance Blvd King Of Prussia PA 19401 Office Phone: 610-768-5812. E-mail: charron-horiates@medrisknet.com.

HARROP, DANIEL SMITH, III, psychiatrist; b. Warwick, RI, June 15, 1954; s. Daniel Smith and Dorothy Jane (Hickey) H. *The family descends from ancestor James Harrop of Ridge Hill, Ashton-under-Lyne, Lancashire, England, who died in 1608, through George Harrop, who lived from 1797-1859, and emigrated to Rhode Island around 1840. Ancestors through other lines include members of the Rittenhouse, Arner and Kester families. Dr. Harrop is recognized by the Lord Lyons King of Arms of Scotland as the Feudal Baron of Cambusnethan, Wishaw, Scotland.* BA, Brown U., 1976, MD, 1979; MBA, Edinburgh Bus. Sch., Scotland, 1997. Diplomate Am. Bd. Med. Examiners, Am. Bd. Psychiatry and Neurology, Am. Bd. Geriatrics, Am. Bd. Forensic Examiners. Resident in psychiatry Brown U., Providence, 1983; med. dir. East Bay Cmty. Mental Health Ctr., Barrington, R.I., 1983-87; asst. unit chief Butler Hosp., Providence, 1988-89, chief gen. treatment unit, 1989-93; clin. asst. prof. psychiatry Brown U., Providence, 1985—; physician advisor Magellan Behavioral Health, Balt., 1991-2000, 2003—; collaborator lab. for clin. and exptl. psychopathology Harvard Med. Sch., Fall River, Mass., 2000—02. Med. dir. United Behavioral Sys., Warwick, RI, 1993-96; med. dir. The Corrigan Ctr., Fall River, Mass., 1996-2002; cons. Harvard Pilgrim Healthcare, 2004—; chmn. utilization rev. Butler Hosp., Providence, 1985-93; instr. dept. psychiatry Harvard U., 1997-2003; physician advisor Value Options, Reston, Va., 2003—, Am. PsychSystems, Bethesda, Md. Pres. parish coun. St. Joseph's Ch., Providence, 1987-91, trustee, 1991—; bd. gov.'s Associated Alumni Brown U., Providence, 1988-92; pres. Assn. Class Officers Brown U., Providence, 1988-92; chair Libertarian Party of RI, 2000—05; alumni assn. pres., bd. dirs. Hendicken HS, Warwick, RI, 04—. Fellow: Am. Assn. Integrative Medicine; mem.: SAR, KC (grand knight 1998, 2002, faithful navigator 2004), AMA (life), Brown Club of RI (v.p. 2005—), Mass. Med. Soc. (med. edn. com. 1999—), Am. Group Psychotherapy (Assembly 1989—97), R.I. Group Psychotherapy Soc. (pres. 1989—91), R.I. Psychiat. Soc. (pres. 1989—90), R.I. Med. Soc. (med. edn. com. 1989—), Am. Psychiat. Assn. (com. on quality care 2003—), Mil. Order Fgn. Wars U.S., Roman Cath. Alumni Assn. Brown U. (pres. 1982—83, 1993—97), R.I. Hist. Soc. (life), Soc. Sons & Daus. The Pilgrims, Ancient Order of Hibernians, Sons of Union Vets. of Civil War, Serra Internat., Sierra Club, Providence Art Club, Galilee Beach Club (Narragansett, R.I.) (pres. 1995—98), Faculty Club of Brown U. (pres. 1994—95), Internat. Order of Odd Fellows, Masons (worshipful master 2001—03), Sigma Chi (grand coun. 1981—), Sigma Xi. Roman Catholic. Office Phone: 401-331-7778. Personal E-mail: danharrop@hotmail.com.

HARROP, WILLIAM CALDWELL, retired ambassador; b. Balt., Feb. 19, 1929; s. George A. and Esther (Caldwell) H.; m. Ann G. Delavan, Aug. 22, 1953; children— Mark D., Caldwell, Scott N., George H. AB, Harvard U., 1950; postgrad., Grad. Sch. Journalism U. Mo., 1953-54; fellow, Woodrow Wilson Sch., Princeton U., 1968-69. Fgn. Service officer, 1954-93; vice consul Palermo, 1954-55; 2d sec. Rome, 1955-58; internat. relations officer Dept. State, 1958-63; 1st sec. Brussels, 1963-66; consul Lubumbashi, Congo, 1966-68; dir. Office Research for Africa, Dept. State, Washington, 1969; dep. chief mission Am. embassy, Canberra, Australia, 1973-75; U.S. ambassador to Guinea, 1975-77; dep. asst. sec. of state for Africa, 1977-80; ambassador to Kenya and Seychelles, 1980-83; insp. gen. Dept. State and Fgn. Service, 1983-86; ambassador to Zaire, 1987-91; ambassador to Israel, 1992-93; ret., 1994. Bd. dirs. Am. Fgn. Svc. Assn., 1970-73, Assn. for Diplomatic Studies and Tng. Chmn., bd. dirs. Population Svcs. Internat. Humane Soc. Washington D.C., Henry L. Stimson Ctr. Served with USMCR, 1951-52. Recipient Dept. State Merit Service award, 1968, Presdl. Disting. Service award, 1985, State Dept. Disting. Service award, 1987. Mem.: Chevy Chase (Md.) Club, Met. Club (Washington), Fly Club (Cambridge, Mass.). Address: 3615 49th St NW Washington DC 20016-3214 E-mail: HarropBill@mac.com.

HARROUN, DOROTHY SUMNER, artist; b. El Paso, Tex., Nov. 29, 1935; d. Daniel Stuart and Eleanor (Flowers) H. BFA, U. N.Mex., 1957; postgrad., U. Paris Sorbonne, 1957—58; MFA, U. Colo., 1960. Art dir. Wood-Reich Advt. Agy., Boulder, 1960—61; lectr. U. Colo., Boulder, 1961—62; art tchr. Langley-Porter Neuropsychiat. Inst. U. Calif., 1963; lectr. San Francisco State Coll., 1964—65; tchr. Art Ctr. Sch., Albuquerque, 1975—79; tchr. watercolor, drawing U. N.Mex., 1980—81. One-woman shows include The Gondolier Gallery, Boulder, Colo., 1961—62, Sta. KAFE-FM Gallery, San Francisco, 1963—64, Lovelace-Bataan Hosp., Albuquerque, 1976, 1979, Ea. N.Mex. U., 1981, Rathaus, Kelkheim, Germany, N.Mex. State U., United World Coll., Montezuma, N.Mex., 2002, exhibited in group shows at Whitte Mus., San Antonio, 1960, Hyannis, Mass., Waterbury, Conn., Newport, R.I., 1964—65, Mus. N.Mex., Santa Fe, 1966, Ogunguit (Maine) Art Ctr., 1977, Am. Watercolor Soc., NYC, 1979, Coos Art Mus., Coos Bay, Oreg., 1980, We. Slope Show, Montrose, Colo., 1981—82, Ga. Watercolor Soc. Open, 1983, We. Fedn. Watercolor Socs., 1984—88, Sun Carnival Art Show, El Paso, 1984, El Paso Mus. Art, 1987, Gov.'s Gallery, N.Mex., 1988, State Fair Fine Arts Gallery, Albuquerque, 1988, Ch. Farm House Mus., London, 1988—89, St. John's Coll., Santa Fe, 1991, Gallery of the Rep., 1993, On Water, 1994, Fuller Lodges, Los Alamo, N. Mex., 2003, Carlsbad Mus. Fine Arts, 2004 (award), Represented in permanent collections U. N.Mex., U. Colo., Fine Arts Mus., Carlsbad, N.Mex., N.Mex. State Capitol, Santa Fe, also pvt. collections, U.S., France, Italy, Germany; author, illustrator Take Time to Play and Listen, 1963, Phun-y Physics, 1975, illustrator Mini Walks on the Mesa, 1989. Pres. fine arts alumni bd. U. N.Mex., 1989—; bd. dirs. Santa Fe Desert Chorale, 1986—92. Recipient Lobo award, U. N. Mex., 2000; Fulbright scholar. Mem.: AAUW (state cultural dir.), Santa Fe Concert Assn. (bd. dirs. 1996—2004), N.Mex. Watercolor Soc. (v.p. 1984, pres. 1985), Nat. League Am. Pen Women (pres. Albuquerque br. 1982—83), Artist Equity Assn. (pres. Albuquerque chpt. 1977—79). Home: 1365 Thunder Rdg Santa Fe NM 87501-8875

HARROW, MARTIN, psychologist, educator; b. N.Y.C., Aug. 22, 1933; s. Morris Harrow and Thelma Black; m. Helen M. Kramer, Aug. 19, 1956; children: Jean Libera, Wendy Donovan, Barbara Perez, Ellen. BA, CUNY, 1955; PhD, Ind. U., 1960. Lic. psychologist Ill., diplomate in clin. psychology. Asst. prof. Yale U., New Haven, 1964—69, assoc. prof., 1969—73; chief psychologist Yale-New Haven Hosp., New Haven, 1968—73; prof. U. Chgo., 1973—89; chief psychologist Michael Reese Med. Ctr., Chgo., 1973—95; prof. U. Ill., Chgo., 1989—. Dir. psychology, dept. psychiatry U. Ill., Chgo., 1989—; mem. sci. adv. bd. Schizophrenia Bull., 1995—. Mem. editl. bd.: Jour. Abnormal Psychology, 1979—89, Clin. Psychology Rev., 1985—; author (with J.F. Goldberg): Bipolar Disorders: Clinical Course and Outcome, 1999; contbr. more than 230 articles to profl. jours. Recipient Outstanding Contbn. to Psychology awaard, Ill. Psychol. Assn., 1990, Gralnick award, Am. Assn. Suicidology, 1998, Merit award, Nat. Inst. Mental Health, 1997, Zublin Award for Lifetime Contributions to the Understanding of Psychopathology, Soc. for Rsch. Psychopathology, 2005; grantee, Nat. Inst. Mental Health, 1975—2002, 2004—. Fellow: APA; mem.: Soc. for Rsch. in Psychopathology, Midwestern Psychol. Assn. Achievements include former U.S. chess master placed in top 7 in U.S. Open Chess Championship three times; two draws in tournament chess game against Bobby Fischer. Office: U Ill Coll Medicine Dept Psychiatry 1601 W Taylor St MC 912 Chicago IL 60612 Office Phone: 312-996-3585. Business E-Mail: mharrow@psych.uic.edu.

HARROW, NANCY (MRS. JAN KRUKOWSKI), singer, lyricist; b. NYC, Oct. 03; d. Benjamin and Frances (Kirschenbaum) H.; m. Jan Krukowski; children: Damon, Anton. BA, Bennington Coll. From copy editor to editor William Morrow & Co., NYC; editor Am. Jour., NYC, 1972-73, editor-at-large, 1974—. Vocalist Tommy Dorsey Orch., 1958; singer Jazz Gallery, Café Au Gogo, Mars Club, N.Y.C. and Paris, 1961-64, Cookery, Plaza Hotel, Upstairs at Cecil's, NYC, 1975-76, Rachel's, Lush Life, Freddy's, Blues Alley, NYC and Washington, 1984-85; singer WDR Big Band, Cologne, Brussels, Holland, NYU Highlights in Jazz, Mazur Theatre, 1986; singer Jan Wallman's NYC, 1987, 89, Stockholm Jazz Festival, 1988, Michael's Pub, 1990, Judy's Supper Club, The Salon, NYC, 1995-96; The Marble Faun, 1999, The Salon, NYC, Maya the Bee Puppet Show, 2000, 45 Bleecker Theater, N.Y.C. Recording artist (albums) Wild Women Don't Have the Blues, 1961, You Never Know, 1963, Anything Goes, 1979, The John Lewis Album for Nancy Harrow, 1981, Two's Company: Nancy Harrow with Jack Wilkins, 1984, You're Nearer, 1986, Street of Dreams, 1990, The Beatles and Other Standards, 1990, Two's Company: Nancy Harrow with Jack Wilkins, 1991, Secrets, 1992, Lost Lady, 1994, You're Nearer, 1998, The Marble Faun, 1999, Maya the Bee, 2000, Winter Dreams, 2003, The Cat Who Went to Heaven, 2005; songwriter: (John Lewis music) As Long As It's About Love, Distant Lover, 1981; composer: (Nancy Harrow music and lyrics) 5 songs for Secrets album, 1992, 12 songs for the Lost Lady album, 1994, (Raymond Patterson lyrics) A Little Blue, 1990, (Nancy Harrow music and lyrics) 21 songs for Maya the Bee, 2000, 13 songs for The Marble Faun, 1999, 11 Songs for Winter Dreams, 2003, (16 songs) The Cat Who Went to Heaven, 2004, 2005. Mem.: Century Assn. Address: 130 E End Ave New York NY 10028-7553 Office Phone: 212-249-4376. E-mail: nancyjazz@aol.com.

HARRYMAN, RHONDA L., special education educator; b. Perry, Okla., Apr. 1, 1954; d. Otis Issac Jr. and Jeanette Roberta (Creacy) Shelley; m. Gilbert Wayne Harryman, Mar. 19, 1978. BS in Edn. cum laude, U. Ctrl. Okla., 1975, M in Spl. Edn., 1979; postgrad., Okla. State U., 1992—. Cert. learning disabilities, mentally handicapped, physically handicapped, emotional disturbance, elem. sch. adminstrs., Okla. Asst. workshop coord. for trainable mentally handicapped, physically handicapped Edmond (Okla.) ARC, 1974-76; instr. educable mentally handicapped, physically handicapped, emotionally disabled Edmond Pub. Schs., 1976-77, instr. spl. edn., emotionally disabled, educable mentally handicapped, physically handicapped, visually and hearing impaired, 1977-91; univ. coord., supr. practicums, instr. spl. edn. U. Ctrl. Okla., Edmond, 1992—. Edn. advisor tchrs. undrepresented populations in Shawnee, Okla. Three Feathers Assn., Norman, Okla. 1983; pvt. teaching, parent counseling learning disabilities, 1982-87; instr. spl. edn. Okla. Christian U., 1992—, mem. tchr. edn. adv. coun.; co-moderator New Eng. Joint Conf. Specific Learning Disabilities, Boston, 1991; edn. rep. Okla. Joint Conf. Juvenile Justice; edn. del. Okla. Japan-Am. Grassroots Coun., Tokyo, 1991; conducted workshops, presented insvcs., speaker in field. Editorial rev. bd. Teaching Resources, Dayton, Ohio. Counselor Edmond Youth Advocacy Bd.; mem. Gov.'s Round Table on Edn. and Bus., Edmond Juvenile Crime Commn.; sponsor Ala-Teen, Boys Ranch Town. Named Okla. Tchr. of Yr. by Okla. State Dept. Edn., 1992. Mem. Orton Dyslexia Soc., Coun. Exceptional Child, Kappa Delta Pi. Home: 3816 Deason Dr Edmond OK 73013-7742 Office: U Ctrl Okla Dept Spl Svcs 100 N University Dr Edmond OK 73034-5207

HARSANYI, JANICE, retired soprano, educator; b. Arlington, Mass., July 15, 1929; d. Edward and Thelma (Jacobs) Morris; m. Nicholas Harsanyi, Apr. 19, 1952; 1 son, Peter Michael. BMus, Westminster Choir Coll., 1951; postgrad., Phila. Acad. Vocal Arts, 1952-54. Voice tchr. Westminster Choir Coll., Princeton, N.J., 1951-63, chmn. voice dept., 1963-65; lectr. music Princeton Theol. Sem., 1956-63; voice tchr. summer sessions U. Mich., 1965-70; artist-in-residence Interlochen Arts Acad., 1967-70; voice tchr. N.C. Sch. Arts, Winston-Salem, 1971-78; music faculty Salem Coll., 1973-76; condr. voice master classes, choral clinics various colls., 1954—; prof. voice Fla. State U., Tallahassee, 1978—, chmn. dept., 1979-83; ret., 2005. Concert singer, 1954—, debut, Phila. Orch., 1958; appearances with, Am., Detroit, Houston, Minn., Nat., Symphony of Air orchs., Bach Aria Group, 1967-68, maj. music festivals, U.S., 1960—; toured with, Piedmont Chamber Orch., 1971-78, concerts and recitals, in major U.S. cities, also in Belgium, Eng., Ger., Italy, Switzerland and Sweden; rec. artist, Columbia, Decca, CRI records. Mem. Nat. Assn. Tchrs. Singing, Music Tchrs. Nat. Assn., Coll. Music Soc., Riemenschneider Bach Inst., Sigma Alpha Iota, Pi Kappa Lambda. Home: 2116 Trescott Dr Tallahassee FL 32308-0732 Office: Florida State Univ Sch Music Tallahassee FL 32306 Office Phone: 850-644-5432.

HARSH, GRIFFITH R., IV, neurosurgeon, educator; AB, Harvard Coll., 1975; MA, Oxford U., 1978; MBA, Boston U., 1999; MD, Harvard U., 1980. Resident neurosurgery U. Calif., San Francisco, 1980—86; prof. neurosurgery Stanford Med. Sch., Calif., 1998—. Dir. neurosurg. oncology Stanford Med. Ctr., 1998—. Author: Molecular Biology of Neurosurgical Disease, 1996, Cerebral Metastases, 1996, Chordomas and Chondrosarcomas, 2003. Scholar, Rhodes Trust, Oxford, Eng. Office: Stanford Med Ctr CC2222 875 Blake Wilbur Dr MC 5826 Stanford CA 94305-0701 Office Phone: 650-725-0701. Business E-Mail: gharsh@stanford.edu.

HARSHA, PHILIP THOMAS, retired aerospace engineer; b. N.Y.C., Feb. 22, 1942; s. Palmer and Catherine (Redinger) H.; m. Jean Ann Quinn, Oct. 23, 1965; children: Peter Charles, Evan Michael. BS in Engring. Sci., SUNY, Stony Brook, 1962, MS in Engring. Sci., 1964; PhD in Aerospace Engring., U. Tenn., 1970. Combustion rsch. engr. GE, Cin., 1964—67; lead rsch. engr. Aro, Inc., Arnold Engring. Devel. Ctr., Tenn., 1969—74; rsch. specialist R & D Assoc., Marina Del Rey, Calif., 1974—76; divsn. mgr. Sci. Applications Internat. Corp., Chatsworth, Calif., 1976—85; chief aero. scientist Lockheed Aero. Sys. Group, Burbank, Calif., 1985—88; chief project engr. Rocketdyne divsn. Rockwell Internat., Canoga Park, Calif., 1988—90; dep. program dir. Nat. Aero-Space Plane Program, 1990—95; program mgr. The Boeing Co., Huntington Beach, Calif., 1994—2004, Boeing Tech. fellow, 2002—. Contbr. articles to profl. jours. Recipient Disting. Alumnus award U. Tenn. Space Inst., 1984. Mem. AIAA, ASME, N.Y. Acad. Sci., Sigma Xi. Republican. Methodist. Home: 677 Oak Glade Dr Fallbrook CA 92028-3693 E-mail: harsha322@adelphia.net.

HARSHBARGER, RICHARD B., retired economics professor; b. Lafayette, Ind., May 6, 1934; s. Albert E. and Olive M. (Shambaugh) M.; m. Jane L. Newcomer, Aug. 24, 1958; children: Lisa, Jon. BS, Manchester Coll., 1956; MA, Ind. U., 1958, PhD, 1964. Fuels economist Tenn. Valley Authority, Chattanooga, 1958; econ. prof. Manchester Coll., North Manchester, Ind., 1960-99, ret., 1999. Vis. prof. Pasadena (Calif.) Coll., 1968-69, Eastern Nazarene Coll., Quincy, Mass, 1977-78. Active Manchester (Ind.) Park Bd., 1972—76, Manchester Sch. Bd., 1972—76, Town Forum, 1986—2004, Indsl. Policy Com., North Manchester, 1990—; pres. Shepherd Ctr., 2002—04; fin. com. Cmty. Svcs. North Manchester, 2005—; active Meals on Wheels, North Manchester, 2002; bd. dirs. Bethany Theol. Sem., Oak Brook, Ill., 1987—92, Camp Mack, Milford, Inc., 1986—92, 2001—; fin. com. Wabash County Found., 1997—. Fellow NSF, 1958-59, grad. fellow Ind. U., 1956-58. Mem. Am. Econ. Assn., Midwest Econ. Assn., Ind. Acad. Social Sci. (dir. 1965-66), Ind. Econ. Forum (pres. 1973-74), Rotary (pres. 1979-80). Democrat. Mem. Ch. of Brethren.

HARSHMAN, DALE RICHARD, physicist; b. Honolulu, Aug. 13, 1956; s. Richard Eugene and LaVonne Olive (Berg) H.; m. Sandra Joan Vecchione, Feb. 2, 1985; 1 child, Joshua Dale. BSc, Pacific Lutheran U., 1978; MSc, Western Wash. U., 1980; PhD, U. B.C., Vancouver, Can., 1986. Rsch. assoc. U. B.C., 1980-86, postdoctoral fellow, 1986, Bell Labs., Murray Hill, N.J., 1986-88, mem. tech. staff., 1988-97; exec. v.p., dir. sci. rsch. Physikon Rsch. Corp., Lynden, Wash., 1997—. Vis. prof. U. Notre Dame, Ind., 1999—2004, adj. prof., 2004—; vis. prof. Ariz. State U., Tempe, 1999—2002, adj. prof., 2002—; cons. U.S. Dept. Energy, Arlington, Va., 1992, Argonne, Ill., 93; spkr. in field. Contbr. numerous articles to profl. jours. Recipient William Cochrane prize for physics, Inst. for Postdoc. Studies, Scottsdale, Ariz., 2002; grantee, U.S. Dept. Energy, 1995—98. Mem.: Am. Phys. Soc. Avocations: robotics, bike riding, poetry, music, fishing. Office: Physikon Rsch Corp PO Box 1014 Lynden WA 98264 Business E-Mail: drh@physikon.net.

HARSHMAN, MILTON MOORE, retired marketing professional; b. Sullivan, Ill., July 30, 1936; s. Paul Irving and Gladys Leland (Moore) H.; m. Marsha Sue Minor, July 23, 1965; children: Hilary A. Harshman-Short, Stacy A. Harshman. Grad. H.S., Sullivan. Sr. v.p. AGRI-FAB, Inc., Sullivan, ret. Office: AGRI-FAB Inc 303 W Raymond St Sullivan IL 61951-1823

HARSHMAN, RICHARD J., metal products executive; BS, Robert Morris U. From mem. Corp. Internal Audit Dept. to CFO Allegheny Technologies Inc., Pitts., 1978—2000, CFO, 2000—, sr. v.p. fin., 2001—03, exec. v.p. fin., 2003—. Bd. trustees Robert Morris U. Office: Allegheny Technologies Inc 100 Six PPG Pl Pittsburgh PA 15222

HARSHMAN, RICHARD R., manufacturing executive; b. Apr. 22, 1947; BS, Fordham U, Bronx, N.Y. Lucy Ellen/F & F Labs.; v.p. sales, mktg. Tootsie Roll; CEO, pres. Storck USA, Storck North America, 1985-98; CEO Favorite Brands Internat., Lincolnshire, Ill., 1998—. Office: Favorite Brands Intl 100 Deforest Ave East Hanover NJ 07936-2813

HART, ANN WEAVER, academic administrator; b. Salt Lake City, Nov. 6, 1948; d. Ted Lionel and Sylvia (Moray) Weaver; m. Randy Bret Hart, Sept. 12, 1968; children: Kimberly, Liza, Emily, Allyson. BS in History, U. Utah, 1970, MA in History, 1981, PhD in Ednl. Adminstrn., 1983. Tchr. pub. schs., Salt Lake City, 1970-73, 80-81; jr. high sch. prin. Provo (Utah) Pub. Schs., 1983-84; prof. ednl. adminstrn. U. Utah, Salt Lake City, 1984—98, assoc. dean Grad. Sch. Edn., 1991-93, dean Grad. Sch., 1993—98; provost, v.p. acad. affairs Claremont Grad. U., Calif., 1998—2002; pres. U. N.H., Durham, 2002—. Bd. dirs. Citizens Bank N.H. Author: Principal Succession: Establishing Leadership in Schools, 1993, The Principalship, 1996, Designing and Conducting Research, 1996; editor: Ednl. Adminstrn. Quar., 1990-92; contbr. articles to profl. jours. Grantee U. Utah, State of Utah, U.S. Dept. Edn. Mem. Am. Ednl. Rsch. Assn., Am. Coun. on Edn., Phi Beta Kappa, Phi Kappa Phi. Avocations: skiing, backpacking, hiking, kayaking, bicycling. Office: Univ of New Hampshire Pres Office 201 Thompson Hall Durham NH 03824 Office Phone: 603-862-2450. Business E-Mail: presidentsoffice@unh.edu.

HART, ARTHUR ALVIN, historian, author; b. Tacoma, Feb. 13, 1921; s. Albert Arthur and Erma Lola (Maltby) H.; m. Novella D. Cochran, Feb. 26, 1944; children: Susanna, Robin, Catherine, Allison. BA, MFA, U. Wash., Seattle, 1948; postgrad., Biarritz Am. U., Hans Hofmann Sch. Fine Arts, U. Calif., Berkeley; HHD (hon.), Coll. Idaho, 1985. Head art dept., chmn. divsn. fine arts Coll. Idaho, 1948-53; instr. art Colby Jr. Coll. Women, New London, N.H., 1953-54; head art dept., dir. adult edn. Bay Path Jr. Coll., Longmeadow, Mass., 1955-69; dir. Idaho Hist. Mus., Boise, 1969-75, Idaho Hist. Soc., 1975-86. Lectr. Am. architecture Boise State U., 1970-86; mem. Boise Allied Arts Council, 1970-78, Idaho Historic Preservation Coun., 1971-87, Boise Bicentennial Commn., 1975-76, Idaho Centennial Commn., 1985-90, Idaho Humanities Coun., 1985-86; mem. adv. bd. Snake River Regional Studies Ctr., 1969—, Boise Redevel. Agy., 1986-87, Basque Mus. and Cultural Ctr., 1985—, Idaho Aviation Hall of Fame, 1990—. Author: Steam Trains in Idaho, 1971, Space, Style and Structure: Building in Northwest America, 1974, Fighting Fire on the Frontier, 1976, Historic Boise, 1979, The Boiseans: At Home, 1984, Idaho, Gem of the Mountains, 1985, Basin of Gold, 1986, Life in Old Boise, 1989, Camera Eye on Idaho: Pioneer Photography 1863-1913, 1990, Wings Over Idaho: An Aviation History, 1991, Boise Baseball: The First 125 Years, 1994, The Boise Children's Home, 1996, Barns of the West: A Vanishing Legacy, 1996, The Arid Club, Its Life and Times, 1997, Centennial History of the Western Idaho Fair, 1897-1997, 1997, To Protect and To Serve: Law Enforcement in Boise, Idaho, 1863-2000, 2000, Boise: An Illustrated History, 2000, Chinatown: Boise, Idaho, 1870-1970, 2002, Echoes from the Ada County Courthouse, 1928-2001, 2005; contbg. author: Encyclopedia of American Forest and Conservation History, 1983, Dictionary of American Medical Biography, 1984; weekly columnist (newspaper) Idaho Statesman, 1970-95, Boise Weekly, 1995-97, Idaho Mag., 2002—. Mem. Mayor's Boise 2000 Com. Recipient Idaho Statesman Disting. Citizen award, 1973, Allied Arts Coun. award for hist. writing, 1972, Phoenix award for leadership in conservation Soc. Am. Travel Writers, 1982, Idaho Bar Assn. award, 1985, James C. Howland Urban Enrichment award, 1990, Preservationist award Idaho Hist. Preservation Coun., 1999, Disting. Achievement in the Humanities award Idaho Humanities Coun., 2000, Esto Perpetua award Idaho State Hist. Soc., 2003. Mem. AIA (hon.), AAUP, Coll. Art Assn., Soc. Archtl. Historians (pres. No. Pacific Coast chpt. 1974-76), Am. Assn. Museums (mem. council 1980-82, pres. Western regional conf. 1979-81)

HART, BRENDA GAIL, academic administrator; b. Williamstown, Mass., July 8, 1949; d. Thomas Alexander and Adalyne Monroe Hart; children: Patrick L. McAnulty, Katheryn G. McAnulty. BA, Boston U., 1970; MEd, U. Louisville, 1972. Asst. dir. pub. svc. careers Jefferson County Govt., Louisville, 1972—73; asst. dir. coop. edn. and placement U. Louisville Speed Sch., 1973—77, asst. prof., asst. dir. gen. engring. studies, 1977—82, 1982—89, dir. gen. engring. studies, 1989—94, prof., dir. minority and women in engring. programs, 1994—2002; dir. student affairs J.B. Speed Sch. Engrs., 2002—. Cons. NSF, Washington, 1991—94. Contbr. articles to profl. jours. Mem. steering com. Black Achievers Program, Louisville, 1997—. Recipient Trustees award, U. Louisville, 1997, Bethune Svc. award, Nat. Coun. Negro Women, 1996. Mem.: U. Louisville Alumni Assn. (bd. dirs. 1998—2002), Nat. Acad. Advising Assn. (newsletter editor 2000—02), Women in Engring. Program Advocates Network (adv. bd. 1998—2002). Office: Univ of Louisville Speed Sch 3d and Eastern Pkwy Louisville KY Office Phone: 502-852-0440. Business E-Mail: brenda@louisville.edu.

HART, BROOK, lawyer; b. N.Y.C., Aug. 24, 1941; s. Walter and Julie H.; divorced; children: Morgan M., Leilani L., Ashley I., Ariel I. BA, Johns Hopkins U., 1963; LL.B., Columbia U., 1966. Bar: N.Y. 1966, U.S. Ct. Appeals (9th cir.) 1967, Hawaii 1968, U.S. Supreme Ct. 1972, Calif. 1973. Law clk. to chief judge U.S. Dist. Ct. Hawaii, 1966-67; chief pub. defender Legal Aid Soc. Hawaii, 1970—72; assoc. Greenstein and Cowan, Honolulu, 1968-70; co-founder, ptnr. Hart, Leavitt, Hall and Hunt, Honolulu, 1972-80,

Hart and Wolff, Honolulu, 1980-96; sr. ptnr. Law Offices of Brook Hart; pvt. practice. Instr. course U. Hawaii, 1972-73, lectr. Sch. Law, 1974—; apptd. Nat. Commn. to Study Def. Svcs., 1974, Planning Group for U.S. Dist. Ct. Hawaii, 1975; spl. counsel City Coun. of City and County of Honolulu, 1976-77, spl. investigative counsel to trustee in bankruptcy THC Fin. Corp., 1977; mem. Jud. Coun. State of Hawaii com. on revision state penal codes, 1984—; lectr. schs., profl., civic groups; mem. com. to select Fed. Pub. Defender Dist. Hawaii, 1981, 95; guest commentator Court TV, 1995, 99, 2002, 03, 04; with faculty Hawaii Inst. Continuing Legal Edn., 1988, Hawaii Pub. Defender Advocacy Inst., 1993-. Contbr. chpts. to books, articles to profl. publs. Named Bencher, Am. Inn of Ct., Hawaii, 1982—. Fellow Am. Bd. Criminal Lawyers; mem. ABA, Hawaii Bar Assn., State Bar Calif., Am. Judicature Soc., Nat. Legal Aid and Defender Assn. (Reginald Herber Smith award Outstanding Pub. Defender in Nation, 1971), Nat. Assn. Criminal Def. Lawyers, Calif. Attys. for Criminal Justice. Office: Ste 610 Melim Bldg 333 Queen St Honolulu HI 96813-4726 Office Phone: 808-526-0811. Office Fax: 808-531-2677. E-mail: hartlaw@hawaii.rr.com.

HART, BUSTER CLARENCE, lawyer; b. Promise City, Iowa, Mar. 19, 1923; s. Harry H. and Alfreda (DeBolt) H.; m. Jean E. Hart, July 7, 1933; children: Nannette, Kyle, Charles, Charlotte. AB, U. Iowa, 1947; JD, Harvard U., 1950. Bar: Minn. 1951, U.S. Ct. Mil. Appeals 1956, U.S. Supreme Ct. 1956. Ptnr. Briggs and Morgan, P.C., St. Paul, 1951-76, pres., 1976-83, Hart, Bruner, O'Brien & Thornton and predecessors, Mpls., 1983—; ptnr. Fabyanske, Westre & Hart, 1983—. V.p. Downtown St. Paul, 1956—59; bd. dirs. Lakewood Coll. Found., 1974—76; mem. Minn. Citizens Com. for Voyageurs Nat. Park, 1975—; co. chmn. United Fund, bd. dirs., 1958—61, 1981—; mem. midwest regional adv. com. Nat. Park Svc. Lt. col. USAR. Fellow: Am. Bar Found.; mem.: ABA (chmn. tort and ins. practice sect. 1980—81, Martin J. Andrew Lifetime Achievement award, Tips Andrew Hecker Lifetime Achievement award), ATLA, Forum on the Constrn. Industry (Cornerstone award), Harvard Law Sch. Assn. (state pres. Minn., nat. v.p.), Am. Coll. Constrn. Lawyers (past pres.), Am. Bd. Trial Advocates (state pres. 1973), Am. Coll. Trial Lawyers, Internat. Assn. Ins. Counsel, Ramsey County Bar Assn., Fed. Bar Assn., Minn. Bar Assn. (chmn. ct. rules com. 1973—77), Minn. Club (bd. dirs. 1980—86), St. Paul Athletic Club, Phi Beta Kappa. Office: Fabyanske Westra & Hart Ste 1900 800 LaSalle Ave Minneapolis MN 55402 E-mail: bchart@minnlaw.com.

HART, CECIL WILLIAM JOSEPH, otolaryngologist, surgeon; b. Bath, Somerset, Eng., May 27, 1931; came to U.S., 1957. s. William Theodore Hart and Paulina Olive (Adams) Gilmer; m. Brigid Frances Molloy, June 15, 1957 (dec. Nov. 1984); children: Geoffrey Arthur, Paula Mary, John Adams; m. Doris Crystel Katharina Alm, Mar. 14, 1987; children: Kristen-Linnea Alm, Erik Alm, Britt-Marie Alm. BA, Trinity Coll., Dublin, Ireland, 1952, MB, BCH, BAO, 1955, MA, 1958. Diplomate Am. Bd. Otolaryngology. Intern Dr. Steevens Hosp., Dublin, Ireland, 1956, Little Co. Mary Hosp., Evergreen Park, Ill., 1957, mem. staff, 1958-59; resident in otolaryngology U. Chgo. Hosp. and clinic, 1959-62; instr. U. Chgo. Med. Sch., 1962-64, asst. prof., 1964-65; practice medicine specializing in otolaryngology Chgo., 1958—; mem. staff Northwestern Meml. Hosp., 1972-97, Rehab. Inst. Chgo., 1965-97, Children's Meml. Hosp., 1972-97, Little Co. of Mary Hosp., 1977-94, LaGrange (Ill.) Comty. Meml. Hosp., 1977-94, Loyola U. Med. Ctr., 1997—. Tchg. assoc. Cleft Palate Inst., 1968, dir. otolaryngology, 1969-92; asst. prof. dept. otolaryngology-head and neck surgery Northwestern U. Med. Sch., 1965-75, assoc. prof., 1975-92, prof., 1992-97, prof. emeritus, 1997—; lectr. dept. otorhinolaryngology Loyola U., 1972, prof. otolaryngology, head and neck surgery, 1997-2001; med. adv. bd. So. Hearing and Speech Found., Nat. Inst. of Deafness and Other Communicative Disorders, 1989-95. Producer videos, movie; contbr. numerous articles to profl. jours. and mags.; also guest appearances various radio and TV talk shows. NIH fellow U. Chgo., 1962-63; NIH grantee, 1985-88. Fellow Am. Neurotology Soc. (pres. 1974-75, chmn. editorial review & publ. com. 1978-79, constn. and bylaws com. 1979-97), Am. Acad. Otolaryngology-Head and Neck Surgery (chmn. subcom. on Equilibrium 1980-86, computer com. 1987-90), ACS, Inst. Medicine Chgo., Soc. for Ear, Nose and Throat Advances in Children; mem. AMA, Brit. Med. Assn., Ill. State Med. Soc., Chgo. Med. Soc., Am. Cleft Palate Assn., Am. Council Otolaryngology, Am. Otological Soc., Chgo. Laryngological and Otological Soc. (v.p. 1975-76), Northwestern Clin. Faculty Med. Assn. (vice chmn. 1976-78, pres. 1979-81), Barany Soc., Royal Soc. Medicine, Irish Otolaryngological Soc., So. Hearing and Speech Found (med. adv. bd.), Chgo. Hearing and Balance Assn. (pres.), Sigma Xi. Roman Catholic. Avocations: travel, baroque music, symphony, opera, tennis. E-mail: cwjhart@aol.com.

HART, C(HARLES) W(ILLARD), JR., zoologist, curator; b. Farmville, Va., Jan. 30, 1928; s. Charles Willard and Etta Catharine (Sawyer) H.; m. Margaret Waddell Gordon, Sept. 17, 1957 (div. Jan. 1958); m. Nancy Dabney Gardner, June 9, 1962. BA, Hampden-Sydney (Va.) Coll., 1949, BS, 1950; postgrad., Fla. State U., 1950-52, 53-54; MA, U. Va., 1951. Instr. biology Washington Coll., Chestertown, Md., 1954-55, Randolph Macon Woman's Coll., Lynchburg, Va., 1955-56; med. editor Smith, Kline & French Labs., Phila., 1956-58; editor sci. publs. Acad. Natural Scis., Phila., 1958-70, dir. water pollution studies, 1968-74; asst. to dir. Natural History Mus., Smithsonian Instn., Washington, 1974-79, curator dept. invertebrate zoology, 1979-92, chmn. dept., 1988-91, rsch. scientist, curator, 1992-96, rsch. scientist emeritus, 1996—. Author: A Dictionary of the Non-Scientific Names of Freshwater Crayfishes, 1994; (with Janice Clark) An Interdisciplinary Bibliography of Freshwater Crayfishes from Aristotle Through 1987, 1989; editor: (with P. Holt and R. Hoffmann) The Distributional History of the Biota of the Southern Appalachians, Part I: Invertebrates, 1969, (with S.L.H. Fuller) Pollution Ecology of Freshwater Invertebrates, 1974, Pollution Ecology of Estuarine Invertebrates, 1979, (with Dabney G. Hart) The Ostracod Family Entocytheridae, 1974; contbr. numerous articles to profl. jours. Mem. Phila. Rep. City Com., 1966-68; bd. dirs. Archbold Ctr. for Tropical Rsch., Dominica, 1987-96. Fellow AAAS; mem. Am. Soc. Zoologists (com. on rsch. in systematic biology 1974-78), Crustacean Soc. (treas. 1981-85), Biol. Soc. Washington (editor Procs. Biol. Soc. Washington 1978-80, sec. 1986-88), Assn. Southeastern Biologists (editor ASB Bull. 1961-72, pres. 1970-71), Coun. Biology Editors (treas. 1968-71), Explorers Club, Cosmos Club Washington (mem., chair, program com. 1996-98), Cosmos Club Found. (trustee 1998-2005, advisor 2005-), Phi Beta Kappa, Sigma Xi. Episcopalian. Avocations: web page design and maintenance, flying (private pilot instrument and glider ratings), sailing, jewelry design and fabrication, cartography of Bermuda. Home: 6449 Walters Woods Dr Falls Church VA 22044-1424 E-mail: winston@patriot.net.

HART, CHRISTOPHER ALVIN, lawyer; b. Denver, June 18, 1947; s. Judson Duncan and M. Murlee (Shaw) H.; children: Adam Christopher, Brooke Corinne; m. Leeann Moore, 2002; B.S. in Aerospace Engring., Princeton U., 1969, M.S. in Aerospace Engring., 1971; J.D., Harvard U., 1973. Bar: D.C. 1973, U.S. Dist. Ct. D.C. 1973, U.S. Ct. Appeals (D.C. cir.) 1973, U.S. Ct. Appeals (8th cir.) 1981, U.S. Supreme Ct. 1985. Assoc. Peabody, Rivlin & Lambert, Washington, 1973-76, Dickstein, Shapiro & Marin, Washington, 1979-81; gen. atty. Air Transport Assn., Washington, 1976-77; dep. asst. gen. counsel U.S. Dept. Transp., Washington, 1977-79; charter, prin. firm Hart & Chavers, Washington, 1981-90; mem. Nat. Transp. Safety Bd., 1990-93; dep. adminstr. Nat. Highway Traffic Safety Adminstrn., 1993-94; assoc. adminstr. for system safety Fed. Aviation Adminstrn., 1994—. Bd. dirs. Howard U. Hosp. Cancer Ctr., Washington, 1983-88, WPFW (Pacific Found.)-FM, 1984-90, Nat. Sleep Found., 1997—. Recipient Superior Performance award U.S. Dept. Transp., 1979. Mem. D.C. Bar (com. ethics 1983-89, mem. bd. profl. responsibility 1989-94), Washington Bar Assn., Fed. Bar Assn., Fed. Communications Bar Assn., Lawyer-Pilots Bar Assn., Black Princeton Alumni (dir. N.Y.C. 1981-87). Democrat. Episcopalian. Home: 1612 Crittenden St NW Washington DC 20011-4218 Office: Fed Aviation Adminstrn 800 Independence Ave SW Washington DC 20591-0001 Office Phone: 202-267-3611. Business E-Mail: chris.hart@faa.gov.

HART, DABNEY GARDNER, retired environmental scientist; b. Jackson, Miss., Dec. 3, 1940; d. Malcolm Everett and Nancy Elizabeth (Parrish) Gardner; m. Charles Willard Hart, Jr., June 9, 1962. AB, Bryn Mawr (Pa.) Coll., 1962, MA, 1970; MS, Am. U., 1984, PhD, 1989. Biologist Acad. of Natural Scis., Phila., 1962-73, spl. projects editor, 1973-75; sr. writer/editor Mitre Corp., McLean, Va., 1975-76, tech. staff, 1976-80, group leader, 1980-98; ret. Participant Breeden-Archibold-Smithsonian Biol. Survey of Dominica, 1963, 65; mem. sci. adv. com. EPA, 1978-82. Author: The Ostracod Family Entocytheridae, 1974; contbr. numerous articles to profl. jours. Mem. Jr. League, Phila., Washington. Rsch. grantee NSF, 1962-73. Mem. AAAS (sr. scientist and engr.), Bryn Mawr Coll. Alumnae Assn., Cosmos Club (Washington, bd. of mgmt. 2002-2005, admissions com. 1996-2001, chmn. 1999-2001), Explorers Club, Sigma Xi. Avocations: travel, needlecrafts. E-mail: winston@patriot.net.

HART, DANIEL ANTHONY, bishop; b. Lawrence, Mass., Aug. 24, 1927; s. John J. and Susan M. (Tierney) H. BSBA, Boston Coll., 1956; MEd, Boston State Coll., 1972; MDiv, St. John's Sem., Brighton, Mass., 1974. Priest Roman Cath. Ch., 1953. Asst. pastor, Lynnfield, Mass., 1953—54, Wellesley, Mass., 1954—56, Malden, Mass., 1956—64; vice-chancellor Archdiocese of Boston, 1964—70; asst. pastor Peabody, Mass., 1970—76; titular bishop of Tepelta, aux. bishop of Boston, 1976—95; regional bishop S. region, 1976—95; archdiocesan vicar for pastoral devel., 1976—85; bishop of Norwich Conn., 1995—2003; bishop emeritus of Norwich, 2003—. Pres. Boston Senate of Priests, 1972—74; mem. exec. bd. Nat. Fedn. Priests' Couns., 1973—75. Roman Catholic. Address: 213 Broadway Norwich CT 06360-4307 E-mail: dahart@sbcglobal.net.

HART, DON LEE, academic administrator, writer; b. Vinita, Okla., Mar. 11, 1953; s. Roy Junior and Iona Mae Hart; m. Lisa Anne Hilburn, Apr. 21, 1961; children: Nicholle Michelle, Matthew Sterling, Katharine Elizabeth. BA, U. N.Mex, 1979, MA, 1984. Cert. distance learning adminstr. Teletraining Inst./Stillwater, Okla., 2000. Libr. U. N.Mex, Albuquerque, 1983—85; dir. Woolworth Pub. Libr., Jal, 1985—86; libr. Nickerson H.S., Nickerson, Kans., 1986—93; tchr. Reno County Edn. Coop, Hutchinson, 1993—94; reporter Sterling Bull., 1994—94, Hutchinson News, 1994—97; dir. learning resources Pratt C.C., 1997—. Presenter League Innovation C.C., Orlando, 2000—00, Mpls., 2001—01. Author: Year of the Rat, (short stories) Smith Magazine; contbr. articles in Vietnam magazine. With USN, 1971—73. Mem.: U.S. Distance Learning Assn., Phi Alpha Theta. Avocations: creative writing, photography, fishing. Office: Pratt Community College 348 Northeast State Road 61 Pratt KS 67124 E-mail: donh@prattcc.edu.

HART, EDWARD LEROY, poet, educator; b. Bloomington, Idaho, Dec. 28, 1916; s. Alfred Augustus and Sarah Cecilia (Patterson) H.; m. Eleanor May Coleman, Dec. 15, 1944 (dec. Dec. 1990); children: Edward Richard, Paul LeRoy, Barbara, Patricia; m. Leah Yates Bryson, Apr. 30, 1993 (dec. Aug. 2001); m. Frances Cannon Lee, June 7, 2002. BS, U. Utah, 1939; MA, U. Mich., 1941; DPhil (Rhodes scholar), Oxford (Eng.) U., 1950. Instr. U. Utah, Salt Lake City, 1946; asst. prof. U. Wash., Seattle, 1949-52, Brigham Young U., Provo, Utah, 1952-55, assoc. prof., 1955-59, prof., 1959-82, prof. emeritus, 1982—. Vis. prof. U. Calif., Berkeley, 1959-60, Ariz. State U., summer 1968. Author: Minor Lives, 1971, Instruction and Delight, 1976, Mormon in Motion, 1978; (poems) To Utah, 1979, Poems of Praise, 1980; More Than Nature Needs, 1982, God's Spies, 1983; contbr. articles to profl. jours. Lt. USNR, 1942-46. Am. Philos. Soc. grantee, 1964; First prize in poetry and biography Utah State Arts Coun., 1973, 75; Fulbright-Hays sr. lectr. Pakistan, 1973-74; recipient Charles Redd award Utah Acad., 1976, Coll. Humanities Disting. Faculty award Brigham Young U., 1977, presdl. citation Brigham Young U. Commencement, 1998. Fellow Am. Coun. Learned Socs., Found. Econ. Edn.; mem. Phi Beta Kappa, Phi Kappa Phi. Democrat. Mem. Lds Ch. Home: 1401 Cherry Ln Provo UT 84604-2848 Office: Brigham Young U Dept English Provo UT 84602 *As a young writer in graduate school, I made the shocking discovery one day that I had written some things I did not really believe. I wanted to be a writer, but I made a vow in my journal that I would not do so at the expense of my integrity: that I would never write anything again that I did not believe and accept with all my being. I have kept that promise, and at the same time have tried to be creative and resourceful. I do not believe that my writing has suffered from the attempt to be honest, but if it has, that is a small price to pay for self-respect.*

HART, ELIZABETH ANN, foundation administrator; b. Moulton, Ala., Sept. 14, 1942; d. Maburn L. Bertie Hale and Julia Mae Evans; m. Bruce Burleson Hart, Dec. 19, 1964; 1 child, Alexandra Natasha Burleson Hart. Diploma in Nursing, Brigham & Women's Hosp., Boston, 1963; BA in Psychology and English, George Washington U., Washington, 1971; postgrad. in business, Le Tourneau U., Longview, Tex., 1999—. RN, N.Y. Co-therapist Psychiatric Inst., Washington, 1969—72; staff nurse NIMH, Bethesda, Md., 1966—67; instr. biology Vernon Ct. Jr. Coll., Newport, RI, 1965—66; chmn., CEO Susan G. Komen Breast Cancer Found., Dallas, 1994—95; pres., CEO Hart Internat., Dallas, 1995—, Easter Seals Rehab. Svcs., Dallas, 1999—, Easter Seals Greater Dallas, 2002. Instr. biology and gen. sci. Miramar Sch. Girls, Newport, R.I., 1965-66; cons. Nat. Cancer Inst., Bethesda, 1993—, Ctr. Non-Profit Mgmt., Dallas, 1995—, Cancer Cube, 1996—, Dept. Defense, Washington, 1997-99; cons. U.S. Army Breast Cancer Rsch. Program, 1993-97, consumer evaluation subcom., writing group, 1994, exec. com. integration panel, 1994-95, exec. com. liaison subcom., 1995-96; adv. coun. sch. nursing U. Tex., Austin, 1994-99; patient adv. com. NSABP/BCPT, 1995, subcom. clin. ctr. performance evaluation, 1995; bd. dirs. Nat. Cancer Policy Bd., Bethesda, 1997-99; data safety and monitoring com. Internat. Breast MRI Consortium. Exec. prodr. (film) Women's Lives Dialogues on Breast Cancer, 1996; prodr. (video) Building for the Future, 2001. Pres. Women's Guild United Cerebral Palsy, 1985, Presbyn. Women, 1994-99; active Nat. Plan on Breast Cancer, Washington, 1995-2000; v.p. devel. Yellow Rose Found., 1996, v.p. cmty. outreach, 1997, Dallas Action Symphony Orch. League, Friends of Timberlawn. Recipient Vol. of Yr. award United Cerebral Palsy Assn. Met. Dallas, 1983, 101% Vol. award, 1983. Mem. Dallas-Ft. Worth Internat. Soc. Republican. Avocations: music, reading, mountain climbing, painting. Home: 9051 Oak Path Ln Dallas TX 75243 Office: Easter Seals Rehab Svcs 4443 N Josey Ln Carrollton TX 75010 E-mail: hart.elizabeth@worldnet.att.net, ehart@easterseals.com.

HART, ERIC MULLINS, consumer products company executive; b. Clanton, Ala., Aug. 6, 1925; s. Eric and Myrtle (Mullins) H.; m. Joy Porter, May 16, 1953; children: Anne Porter, Eric Mullins. BS, U. Ala., 1946; grad., Harvard Advanced Mgmt. Program, 1970. With Internat. Paper Co., 1946-69, asst. to v.p.-treas., 1962-64, comptroller, 1964-69; treas. Red River Paper Mill, Inc., 1964-69; fin. v.p. Lever Bros. Co., 1969-83, dir., 1969-83, Unilever U.S. Inc., 1981-83, Macmillan, Inc., 1975-88; exec. in residence Columbia U. Bus. Sch., 1983-88. Trustee King Sch., Stamford, Conn., 1970-76. Mem. Union League Club (N.Y.C.), Lakewood Golf Club, Fairhope Yacht Club, Sigma Alpha Epsilon. Home: 106 Oak Bend Ct Fairhope AL 36532

HART, FREDERICK MICHAEL, law educator; b. Flushing, N.Y., Dec. 5, 1929; s. Frederick Joseph and Doris (Laurian) H.; m. Joan Marie Monaghan, Feb. 13, 1956; children: Joan Marie, Ellen, Christiane, F. Michael, Margaret, Andrew, Brigid, Patrick. BS, Georgetown U., 1951, JD, 1955; LL.M., N.Y. U., 1956; postgrad., U. Frankfurt, Germany, 1956-57. Lectr., dir. food law program N.Y. U., N.Y.C., 1957-58, asst. prof., 1958-59; prof. law Albany Law Sch., Union U., 1959-61, Boston Coll., 1961-66, Law Sch., U. N.Mex., Albuquerque, 1966—, dean, 1971-79, acting dean, 1985-86; dir. Law Sch., U. N.Mex. (Indian Law Center), 1967-69; vis. prof. U. Calif., Davis, spring 1981. Pres., chmn. bd. trustees Law Sch. Admission Test Council, 1974-76 Author: Forms and Procedures Under the Uniform Commercial Code, 1963, Uniform Commercial Code Reporter-Digest, 1965, Handbook on Truth in Lending, 1969, Commercial Paper Under the U.C.C, 1972, Student Guide to Secured Transactions, 1985, Student Guide to Sales, 1987; editor: Am. Indian Law Newsletter, 1968-70. Served to lt. USAF, 1951-53. Mem. ABA (law sch. accreditation com. 1986-93, skills tng. com. 1995-98, nominating com. 1987), Order of Coif, Phi Delta Phi. Roman Catholic. Home: 1505 Cornell Dr NE Albuquerque NM 87106-3703 Office: U NMex Sch Law 1117 Stanford Dr NE Albuquerque NM 87131-1431 Office Phone: 505-277-4737. Business E-Mail: hart@law.unm.edu.

HART, GARY W., retired senator, lawyer; b. Ottawa, Kans., Nov. 28, 1936; m. Lee Ludwig, 1958; children: Andrea, John. BA, Bethany Nazarene Coll., Okla., 1958; BD, Divinity Sch. Yale U., 1961; JD, Yale U., 1964; D.Phil. in Politics, Oxford U., 2001. Bar: Colo. 1964. Began career as atty. U.S. Dept. Justice, Washington; then spl. asst. to sec. U.S. Dept. Interior; practiced in Denver, 1967-70, 72-74; nat. campaign dir. Senator George McGovern Democratic Presdl. Campaign, 1970-72; U.S. senator from Colo., 1976-84; of counsel Davis, Graham & Stubbs, Denver, 1985; of counsel, strategic and legal advisor, internat. law Coudert Brothers, San Francisco, 1988—; co-chmn. US Commn. Nat. Security/21st Century Dept. of Def., 1998—2001. Founder, 1st chmn. Environ. Study Conf., 1975; congl. adviser Salt II Talks, 1977; adviser UN Spl. Session on Disarmament, 1978; chmn. Nat. Commn. on Air Quality, 1978-81; founder Congl. Mil. Reform Caucus, 1981 Author: Right From the Start, 1973, A New Democracy, 1983, America Can Win, 1986, The Strategies of Zeus, 1987, Russia Shakes the World, 1991, The Good Fight: The Education of an American Reformer, 1993, The Patriot, 1996, The Minuteman, 1998, Restoration of the Republic, 2002; co-author: The Double Man, 1985. Student vol. John F. Kennedy Presdl. Campaign, 1960; vol. organizer Robert F. Kennedy Presdl. Campaign, 1968; bd. visitors U.S. Air Force Acad., 1975—, chmn., 1978-80; nat. co-chmn. Share Our Strength, 1985; candidate for Democratic presdl. nomination, 1983-84, 87-88. Office: Coudert Brothers LLP One Market Spear St Tower Ste 2100 San Francisco CA 94105-1126*

HART, GURNEE FELLOWS, investment counselor; b. Chgo., Apr. 26, 1929; s. Percival Gray and Marguerite May (Fellows) H.; m. Marjorie Walker Leigh, Apr. 23, 1966. BA cum laude, Pomona Coll., 1951; MBA, Stanford U., 1955; vis. scholar, Jesus Coll., Cambridge, Eng., 1994-95. With Willis & Christy, L.A., 1955-65; investment counsel Scudder, Stevens & Clark, Inc., L.A., 1965-67; with Scudder, Stevens & Clark, N.Y.C., 1967—, ptnr., 1972-85, mng. dir., 1985-94, adv. mng. dir., 1994—2002. Bd. dirs. Lincoln Ctr. for the Performing Arts, Inc., 1981-86, 2004—, NY Philharmonic, 1974—, vice-chmn., exec. com., 1976-96, trustee, 1988-2005; chmn. Friends of NY Philharm., 1975-82; bd. dirs., v.p. Berkshire Farm Ctr. and Svcs. for Youth, 1972-83; trustee Pomona Coll., 1982-2000, trustee emeritus, 2000—; bd. dirs., treas. Am. Friends of Cambridge U., 1997-2000; bd. dirs. Cambridge U. Devel. Office in U.S., Inc., 1998-2000; chmn. Cambridge in Am., 2000-04; trustee The Cambridge Found., U.K., 2001-05; adv. bd. Yale Ctr. Parliamentary Hist., 2003-. 1st lt. inf. USAR, 1951—53, Korea. Decorated Bronze Star. Mem. St. Andrew's Soc. State of N.Y., Soc. Mayflower Desc., Century Assn., Univ. Club, Knickerbocker Club, Indian Harbor Yacht Club (Greenwich, Conn.), Phi Beta Kappa. Republican. Episcopalian. Home: 133 E 64th St New York NY 10021-7045

HART, HERBERT MICHAEL, military officer; b. St. Louis, Oct. 19, 1928; s. Herbert Malcom and Helen Genevieve (Quigley) Hart; m. Teresa Keating, Oct. 13, 1958 (dec. Sept. 11, 2002); children: Bridget, Erin, Bret, Tracy, Megan, Michael, Patrick. BS in Journalism, Northwestern U., 1951. Commd. 2d lt. USMC, 1951, advanced through grades to col., 1972, infantry platoon, co. and bn. comdg. officer, 1952—53, 1957—60, 1969-70; Arab, Israeli, Persian plans officer U.S. Strike Command, Mid. East and Tampa, Fla., 1967-69; head profl. edn. Dept. Navy, Washington, 1977-78; head hist. br. Marine Corps. Hqrs., Washington, 1973-77, dep. dir. pub. affairs, 1978-80, dir. pub. affairs, 1980-81, ret., 1981—99; dir. pub. affairs Res. Officers Assn. of U.S., Washington, 1982-94. Cons. office of History U.S. Army Corps Engrs., 1981-94; mem. adv. bd. ad hoc com. Nat. Park Svc., 1985-94; mem. com. on Cemeteries and Memls. VA, 1987-92; mem. coun. advisors Nat. Park Conservation Assn., 1992-99. Author 9 mil. history books; editor ROA Nat. Security Report, 1983-94; mem. editl. bd. Mil. History mag., 1983-95; asst. editor Leatherneck Mag., Washington, 1946-47; editor-in-chief Daily Northwestern, Evanston, Ill., 1949-51. Decorated 2 Purple Heart medals, 2 Legion of Merit medals; recipient Award of Merit Am. Assn. State and Local History, 1976, Cultural Achievement award Sec. of Interior, 1979, Conservation Svc. award Sec. Interior, 1986, named Hon. Ky. Col. by Gov. of Ky. Fellow Co. Mil. Historians; mem. Potomac Westeners (pres. 1974-75, 84-85), Res. Officers Assn. U.S. (life), Marine Corps Res. Assn. (life), Marine Corps Combat Corres. Assn. (life), Marine Corps Hist. Found. (charter, bd. dirs. 1983-87), Assn. U.S. Army, Army. Hist. Found. (charter), Nat. Pk. Svc. Employee and Alumni Assn. (life), VFW (life), Am. Legion (life), Mil. Order Purple Heart (life), Civil War Preservation Trust (charter mem.), Mil. Officers Assn. (life), 1st Marine Divsn. Assn. (life), 3rd Marine Divsn. Assn. (life), Coun. Am. Mil. Past (co-founder 1966, exec. dir. 1971—), Western History Assn. (charter), Nat. Assn. Uniformed Svcs. (life), Coast Def. Study Group, Naval and Maritime Corrs. Circle, State Hist. Soc. S.D. (life), Ft. Adams, R.I. Trust (charter), Ft. Douglas, Utah, Mus. Assn. (life), Civil War Fortifications Study Group (charter), Friends of Ft. Davis, Tex. (life), Battlefield Preservation Coalition (dir. 1991-2003), Friends of Ft. Ward, Va. (charter), Friends of Manassas Battlefield, Va. (charter), Nat. Trust Hist. Preservation, Theodore Roosevelt Assn., Va. Hist. Soc., Order of Indian Wars (companion), Apollo Soc. (bd. dirs. 1983-87), Am. Civil Def. Assn. (bd. advisors 1991-2000), Soc. Mil. History (trustee 1978-83), Ft. Phil Kearny/Bozeman Trl. Assn. (life), Ft. DeRussy La. Friends, Ft. Point and Presidio Assn. (life), Mil. Order of Carabao, U.S. Cavalry Assn. (life), K.C., Soc. Profl. Journalists, Theta Xi (life). Republican. Roman Catholic. Avocation: photography. Office: PO Box 1151 Fort Myer VA 22211-0151 Home: 7510 Gambrill Rd Springfield VA 22153-1809 Office Phone: 703-912-6124.

HART, HOWARD ROSCOE, JR., retired physicist; b. Fayetteville, N.C., Dec. 6, 1929; s. Howard Roscoe and Elisabeth Grattan (Stover) H.; m. Emily Sawyer, Mar. 1, 1958; children: Evelyn, Alice, Susan. B of Engring. Physics, Cornell U., 1952; MS, U. Ill., 1955, PhD, 1960. Engring. physicist E.I. duPont de Nemours & Co. Inc., Wilmington, Del., 1952-54; rsch. assoc. U. Ill., Urbana, 1960; physicist corp. R & D GE, Schenectady, N.Y., 1960-94, ret., 1995, cons., 1995—. Contbr. over 100 articles to jours. in field; patentee in field. Named Inventor of Yr., Intellectual Property Owners Assn., Washington, 1991. Fellow Am. Physical Soc. (sec.-treas. divsn. condensed matter physics 1981-85); mem. NAE, Am. Geophys. Union.

HART, JAMES WARREN, retired academic administrator, retired professional football player; b. Evanston, Ill., Apr. 29, 1944; s. George Ezrie and Marjorie Helen (Karsten) H.; m. Mary Elizabeth Mueller, June 17, 1967; children: Bradley James and Suzanne Elizabeth (twins), Kathryn Anne. BS, So. Ill. U., 1967. Quarterback St. Louis Cardinals Profl. Football Team, 1966—83, Washington Redskins Profl. Football Team, 1984; radio sports personality Sta. KMOX, 1975—84, Sta. KXOK, 1985—86; sports analyst Sta. WGN Radio, Chgo., 1985—89; athletics dir. So. Ill. U., Carbondale, 1988—99, assoc. chancellor for external affairs, 1999—2000; head coach So. Ill. Spl. Olympics, 1973—90, Mo. Spl. Olympics, 1976—78; co-owner Dierdorf & Hart's Steak House (2 locations), St. Louis; spl. asst. to vice chancellor for instnl. devel. So. Ill. U., 1999—2002. Co-author: The Jim Hart Story, 1977. Gen. campaign chmn. St. Louis Heart Assn., 1974-88; hon. chmn. St. Louis Sr. Olympics, 1986-88. Named Most Valuable Player in Nat. Football Conf., 1974, Most Valuable Player with St. Louis Cardinals, 1973, 1975, 1978, Man of Yr., St. Louis Dodge Dealers, 1975—76, Miller High Life, 1980; named to So. Ill. U. Sports Hall of Fame, 1978, Mo. Sports Hall of Fame, 1998, Mo. Valley Conf. Hall of Fame, 2001, Chicagoland Sports Hall of Fame, 2003; recipient Brian Piccolo Nat. YMCA award for most civic minded profl. athlete, 1980. Mem.: AFTRA, NFL Players Assn. (Byron Whizzer White award 1976, Most Civic Minded Profl. Athlete 1980, Brian Piccolo Nat. YMCA award 1980), Fellowship Christian Athletes. Republican.

HART, JAMES WHITFIELD, JR., retired public relations executive, lawyer; b. Greenwood, Fla., Dec. 20, 1935; s. James Whitfield Sr. and Lela (Cox) H.; m. Patricia Ann Landrum, Mar. 11, 1961; children: William Gordon, Melanie Ann. AA, Chipola Jr. Coll., 1956; JD, U. Ala., 1973; MBA,

MIT, 1982. Bar: Ala. 1974, Colo. 1976; cert. flight instr. News dir., anchorman Sta. WTVY-TV, Dothan, Ala., 1958-60, Sta. WSFA-TV, Montgomery, Ala., 1960-62; exec. dir. Am. Petroleum Inst., Montgomery, 1962-75; mgr. pub. affairs Gulf Oil Corp., Atlanta, 1975-76, dir. pub. affairs Denver, 1976-81, sr. dir. pub. affairs Pitts., 1981-85; sr. v.p. Blue Cross/Blue Shield, Jacksonville, Fla., 1985-86; sr. v.p., gen. mgr. Hill & Knowlton, Denver, 1986-88; v.p. pub. affairs PanEnergy Corp., Houston, 1988-97; v.p. Duke Energy Corp., 1997-99; ret. Res. dir. pub. affairs Office Sec. Air Force, 1988-95; bd. dirs. Vita-Living, Inc.; chmn. interstate natural gas Am. Pub. Affairs Com., 1994. Mem. adv. bd. City of Sugar Land Airport; former pres. Ala. N.G. Assn.; bd. dirs. Opportunity Fla., Boy Scouts; pres. Chipola Jr. Coll. Found. Brig. gen. USAFR, 1990-95. Decorated Disting. Svc. medal, Legion of Merit, Meritorious Svc. medal, Air Force Commendation medal; recipient Meritorious Svc. award and Disting. Svc. award State of Ala., Outstanding Young Man of Am. award U.S. Jaycees, 1965, Outstanding Pub. Rels. Practitioner award, 1991, Pub. Rels. Practitioner of Yr., 1996. Mem. ABA, Pub. Rels. Soc. Am., Tex. Pub. Rels. Assn. (bd. dirs., chmn. pub. affairs coun. 1996, pres. 1996, Gold Spur award 1999), Coun. Assn. Execs. (former pres.), Am. Petroleum Inst., Am. Gas Assn., Pub. Affairs Coun. (past chmn.), Res. Officers Assn. (life), Air Force Assn. (life), Tex. Coun. Econ. Edn. (bd. dirs.), Tex. Rsch. League (bd. dirs.), Forum Club Houston, Houston Club, Univ. Club Houston, Rotary, Sigma Delta Kappa (former chancellor). Baptist. Home: 7371 Cox Rd Bascom FL 32423-9411 Office Phone: 850-592-4740. E-mail: jimwhart@digitalexp.com.

HART, JANET MARILYN, writer, lecturer; b. Dublin, Tex., Sept. 13, 1940; d. Nathan L. and Minnie (Novit) Siegel; m. Charles Benjamin Hart, June 4, 1961; children: Deborah Leigh, Katherine Helaine, David Wolf. AA, Lon Morris Jr. Coll., Jacksonville, Tex., 1973. Lic. in real estate, Tex. With Beall's Dept. Store, Jacksonville, 1972-73, Jacksonville Pub. Libr., 1974-76, Rippon Middle Sch., Woodbridge, Va., 1976-77; sec. Camp Fire, Inc., Temple, Tex., 1978-80; sec./adminstrv. asst. Scott & White Hosp., Temple, 1980-82; salesperson Century 21, Temple, 1984-86, Charles B. Hart, Broker, Temple, 1986—. Author: (children's books) Hanna, the Immigrant, 1991, The Many Adventures of Minnie, 1992. Active Jr. League, Temple, Contemporaries, Temple, Aggie Mother's Club, 1979-91, visual arts, Friends of the Cultural Activities Ctr., Temple Tex. Jewish Hist. Soc.; bd. dirs. Chisholm Trail Chorus of Sweet Adelines, Inc., 1980-91, Harmony Internat. 1980—, Temple Civic Theatre, 1988-91. Avocations: acting, singing, walking, bridge, travel.

HART, JEREMY MICHAEL, lawyer; b. Yuma, Ariz., Aug. 29, 1975; s. George Robert and Catherine Claire Moore; m. Shawna Melia Hart, Feb. 17, 2001; 1 child, Andrew Joseph. BA in Criminal Justice, Washburn U.; JD, U. Mo., Kansas City, 2001. Bar: Mo. 01, U.S. Dist. Ct. (we. dist.) Mo. 01, Kans. 02, U.S. Dist. Ct. Kans. 02. Assoc. Wonder Law Offices, Kansas City, Mo., 1998—. Mem.: ATLA, ABA, Kansas City Met. Bar Assn. (mem. mcpl. ct. com. 2001—), Kans. bar Assn., Mo. Bar Assn., KC (4th degree mem., advocate). Republican. Roman Catholic. Avocations: golf, reading, writing music. Office: Wonder Law Office 404 E Bannister Rd Ste F Kansas City MO 64131-3020 E-mail: jeremyhart@kc.rr.com.

HART, JOHN, professional sports team executive; b. Tampa, Fla., July 21, 1948; m. Sandi DeVorak; 1 child, Shannon. Degree in History and Phys. Edn., U. Ctrl. Fla., 1973. Minor league mgr. Montreal Expos, 1969-75, Balt. Orioles, 1975-88, third base coach, 1988; spl. assignment scout, interim mgr. Cleve. Indians, 1989-91, exec. v.p. and gen. mgr., 1991—2001; gen. mgr. Texas Rangers, Arlington, Tex., 2001—. Named Major League Baseball Exec. of the Yr., The Sporting News, 1994, 1995. Office: Texas Rangers Ballpark at Arlington #400 1000 Ballpark Way Arlington TX 76011*

HART, JOHN, writer; b. Berkeley, Calif., June 18, 1948; s. Lawrence and Jeanne McGahey Hart; m. Helen Schoenhals, 2004. BA, Princeton U., 1970. Dir. Lawrence Hart Inst., San Rafael, Calif., 1983—; co-editor Blue Unicorn, A Tri-Quarterly of Poetry, Kensington, Calif., 2002—. Author: San Francisco Bay: Portrait of an Estuary (Carla Bard Bay Edn. Award, 2003), Walking Softly in the Wilderness: The Sierra Club Guide to Backpacking (4th edit.), 2005 (Work of Significance, Nat. Outdoor Book Awards, 1999), Storm Over Mono: The Mono Lake Battle and the California Water Future (Commonwealth Club Medal in Californiana, 1997), Farming on the Edge: Saving Family Farms in Marin County, California (Commonwealth Club Medal in Californiana, 1992), Hiking the Great Basin: The High Desert Country of California, Nevada, Oregon, and Utah (second edition), San Francisco's Wilderness Next Door, The Climbers, Hiking the Bigfoot Country: The Wildlands of Northern California and Southern Oregon, Legacy: Portraits of 50 Bay Are Environmental Elders, 2005; editor: The New Book of California Tomorrow: Reflections and Projections from the Golden State; contbr. Yosemite Once Removed: Portraits of the Backcountry, Gardens of Alcatraz; contbr. articles various jours. Recipient James D. Phelan award, San Francisco Found., 1970, David R. Brower award for Outstanding Svc. in the Field of Conservation, Am. Alpine Club, 1992. Mem.: Authors Guild, Assn. of Lit. Scholars and Critics, Cragmont Climbing Club, Am. Alpine Club (co-chair, conservation com. 1989—91). Avocations: climbing, backpacking, opera, travel. Office: PO Box 4262 San Rafael CA 94903 Office Phone: 415-507-9230. Office Fax: 415-479-9502. E-mail: jh@johnhart.com.

HART, JOHN CLIFTON, lawyer; b. Chgo., Apr. 29, 1945; s. Clifton Edwin and Eleanor (Zielinski) H.; m. Dianne Lynn Wenzel, Jan. 18, 1969; children: David Clifton, Steven Philip, Kristin Dianne. BS, Loyola U., 1967; postgrad., Northwestern U., 1967—69; JD, U. N.D., 1972. Bar: Minn. 1973, U.S. Dist. Ct. Minn. 1973, Tex. 1979, U.S. Dist. Ct. (no. dist.) Tex. 1979, U.S. Dist. Ct. (we dist.) Tex. 1981, U.S. Dist. Ct. (ea. dist.) Okla. 1981, U.S. Dist. Ct. (ea. dist.) Tex. 1984, U.S. Dist. Ct. (no. dist.) Okla. 1999, U.S. Ct. Appeals (5th and 8th cirs.) 1980, U.S. Supreme Ct., 1997. Ptnr. Robins, Zelle, Larson & Kaplan, Mpls., 1973-81; v.p. Gollaher & Hart, Dallas, 1981-84; pres. Hart & Engen, Dallas, 1984-87, Hart & Assocs., Dallas, 1987-88; mng. ptnr. S.W. regional office Robins, Kaplan, Miller & Ciresi, 1988-93; ptnr. Cantey & Hanger L.L.P., 1993-98, Brown, Dean, Wiseman, Liser, Proctor & Hart, LLP, 1998—. Contbr. articles to profl. jours. Maj. USAF, 1969-73. Mem. ABA, State Bar Tex., Tarrant County Bar Assn., Fedn. Ins. and Corp. Counsel, Loss Exec. Assn. Republican. Lutheran. Office: Brown Dean Wiseman Liser Proctor & Hart LLP 306 W 7th St Ste 200 Fort Worth TX 76102-4905 Office Phone: 817-820-1112. Business E-Mail: jhart@browndean.com.

HART, JOHN EDWARD, lawyer; b. Portland, Oreg., Nov. 21, 1946; s. Wilbur Elmore and Daisy Elizabeth (Bowen) H.; m. Bianca Mannheimer, Mar. 29, 1968 (div. 1985); children: Ashley Rebecca, Rachel Bianca, Eli Jacob; m. Serena Callahan, Nov. 9, 1991; 1 child, Katelyn Elizabeth. Student, Oreg. State U., 1965-66; BS, Portland State U., 1971; JD, Lewis and Clark Coll., 1974. Bar: Oreg. 1974, U.S. Dist. Ct. Oreg. 1974, U.S. Ct. Appeals (9th cir.) 1975. Ptnr. Schwabe, Williamson and Wyatt, Portland, 1973-92, Hoffman, Hart & Wagner, Portland, 1992—. Adj. faculty U. Oreg. Dental Sch., 1987—; legal cons. Oreg. Chpt. Obstetricians, Gynecologists, Portland, 1985—, Am. Cancer Soc. Mammography Project, 1987—. Contbr. articles to profl. jours. Co-chmn. Alameda Sch. Fair, Portland, 1983. With U.S. Army, 1967-68. Mem. ABA, Am. Coll. Trial Lawyers, Am. Bd. Trial Advocates (pres. 1995) Am., Inns of Ct., Oreg. State Bar Assn., Oreg. Assn. Def. Counsel (pres. 1989), Multnomah Athletic Club. Democrat. Presbyterian. Avocations: jogging, weightlifting, outdoor activities. Office: Hoffman Hart & Wagner 1000 SW Broadway Ste 2000 Portland OR 97205-3072

HART, JOSEPH THOMAS CAMPBELL, lawyer; b. Orange, N.J., May 23, 1936; s. Maurice I. and Anne G. (Campbell) H. AB, Fordham U., 1958, JD, 1961. Bar: N.Y. 1962, U.S. Dist. Ct. (so. and ea. dists.) N.Y. 1966, U.S. Ct. Appeals (2d cir.) 1974, U.S. Ct. Appeals (5th cir.) 1983. Assoc. Dewey, Ballatine, Bushby, Palmer & Wood, N.Y.C., 1962-65, Fulton, Rowe, Hart & Coon, N.Y.C., 1965-71, ptnr., 1971—. Sec. The G. Unger Vetlesen Found., N.Y.C., 1987, The Ambrose Monell Found., N.Y.C., 1994. Mem. Assn. of the Bar of the City of N.Y. Office: Fulton Rowe Hart & Coon One Rockefeller Plaza New York NY 10020

HART, KITTY CARLISLE, performing arts association administrator; b. New Orleans, Sept. 3, 1910; d. Joseph and Hortense (Holtzman) Conn; m. Moss Hart, Aug. 10, 1946 (dec. 1961); children: Christopher, Cathy. Ed., London Sch. Econs., Royal Acad. Dramatic Arts; DFA (hon.), Coll. New Rochelle; DHL (hon.), Hartwick Coll.; LHD (hon.), Manhattan Coll., Amherst Coll., Curtis Inst. Music. Chmn. emeritus N.Y. State Council on the Arts. Former panelist: TV show To Tell the Truth; actress on stage and in films including The Marx Brothers A Night at the Opera, 1936; Broadway theatre appearance in On Your Toes, 1983-84; singer, Met. Opera; one woman show on Great Performances My Broadway Memories, 1999; TV moderator and interviewer; author: (autobiography) Kitty, 1988; contbr. book revs. to jours. Assoc. fellow Timothy Dwight Coll. of Yale U., NYU, Skidmore Coll.; bd. dirs. Empire State Coll.; formerly spl. cons. to N.Y. Gov. on women's opportunities; mem. vis. com. for the arts MIT Recipient Nat. medal of Arts from Pres. Bush, 1991.

HART, LORING EDWARD, academic administrator; b. Bath, Maine, Sept. 22, 1924; s. Joseph Edward and Elizabeth (Hayes) H.; m. Marilyn Louise Cummings, Jan. 7, 1950; children: Ellen Louise, Matthew Cummings. BA, Bowdoin Coll., 1948; MA, U. Miami, 1951; PhD, Harvard U., 1961; degree (hon.), Bowdoin Coll., Norwich U., St. Joseph's Coll., Maine. Teaching fellow Harvard U., 1954-56; instr. English U. Ky., 1956-57; from asst. prof. to prof. Norwich U., Northfield, Vt., 1957-83, head dept. English, 1961-68, dean of faculty, 1968-69, v.p., dean, 1969-72, pres., 1972-82; assoc. dir. devel. campaign Bowdoin Coll., Brunswick, Maine, 1983-86; pres. St. Joseph's Coll., Standish, Maine, 1987-95. With armored inf. AUS, World War II, ETO. Decorated Bronze Star, Combat Inf. badge; recipient Outstanding Civilian Svc. award Air Force, Army. Mem. SAR, Sons of Colonial Wars, 4th Armored Divsn. Assn., Phi Beta Kappa, Sigma Nu. Address: PO Box 13 Yarmouth ME 04096-0013 Personal E-mail: blanding@aol.com.

HART, MARA KIRK, librarian; b. N.Y.C., Dec. 25, 1933; d. George W. and Lucile D. (Dvorak) Kirk; BA, Miami U., Oxford, Ohio, 1955; MA, NYU, 1957; MA, U. Minn., 1973; m. Robert C. Hart, Aug. 1983; children by previous marriage— Steve Bauer, Jenny Bauer. Teenage dir. Central Br. YWCA, N.Y.C., 1957-58; tchr. English, Cleve., Mpls., 1958-61; dir. bibliography rm. U. Minn. Library, Mpls., 1964-65, Portuguese, Latin Am., Spanish bibliographer, 1965-69, acquisitions librarian, Duluth campus, 1973-84, head reference dept., 1985—; humanities bibliographer Claremont Colls., 1969-71; pub., editor Kirk Press Books. Manor Club scholar, 1956-57; Wis. Arts Bd. awardee, 1979. Democrat. Unitarian. Editor: Corn Village, 1971; poetry editor Plainsong, 1967-69, N. Country Anvil, 1971-77; translator various books from Spanish; author: (poetry) Some Yellow Flowers, 1979; pub.: Second Pond, 1980; Till Hope Creates, 1981; contbr. articles to profl. jours. Home: 205 W Kent Rd Duluth MN 55812-1101

HART, MARIAN GRIFFITH, retired reading educator; b. Bates City, Mo., Feb. 5, 1929; d. George Thomas Leon and Beulah Winiferd (Hackley) Griffith; m. Ashley Bruce Hart, Dec. 23, 1951; children: Ashley Bruce Hart II, Pamela Cherie Hart Gates. BS, Ctrl. Mo. State Coll., 1951; MA, No. Ariz. U., 1976. Title I-chpt. I reading dir. Page (Ariz.) Sch. Dist.; Title I dir. Johnson O'Malley Preschool; dist. reading dir. Page Sch. Dist.; ret. Bd. dirs. Lake Powell Inst. Behavioral Health Svcs., sec., 1993-95, chmn. fin. com., 1995-96. Contbr. articles to profl. jours., childrens mags. Vol., organizer, mgr., instr. Page Cmty. Adult Literacy Program, 1986-91, Marian's Literacy Program, 1991-95; lifetime mem. Friends of Page Pub. Libr., sec. bd., 1990-91. Mem. Delta Kappa Gamma (pres. chpt. 1986-90, historian 1990-92, Omicron state coms., scholarship 1988-89, nominations 1991, Omicron State Comms. com. 1995-99, Tau chpt. nominations com. chair 1998), Beta Sigma Phi (pres. chpt., v.p. chpt., pvt. reading tutor 1997-2000). Home and Office: 66 S Navajo Dr PO Box 763 Page AZ 86040-0763 Office Phone: 928-645-2239. Personal E-mail: marian@pageamerica.net.

HART, MARY T., lawyer; BA, Georgetown U., 1991; JD, Fordham U., 1995. Bar: NY, US Dist. Ct. So. Dist. NY, US Dist. Ct. Ea. Dist. NY. Ptnr. Wilson, Elser, Moskowitz, Edelman & Dicker LLP, NYC. Mem.: Assn. of the Bar of the City of NY. Office: Wilson Elser Moskowitz Edelman & Dicker LLP 23rd Fl 150 E 42nd St New York NY 10017-5639 Office Phone: 212-490-3000 ext. 2113. Office Fax: 212-490-3038. Business E-Mail: hartm@wemed.com.

HART, MATTHEW AARON, music educator; b. Latrobe, Pa., Dec. 27, 1976; s. Jane Elizabeth Hart. MusB in Music Edn., Shenandoah U., 2000. Dir. music, organist Ephesus Christian Ch., Foneswood, Va., 1996—2000; min. music Carmel United Meth. Ch., Kinsale, Va., 2000—03; music tchr. Pennington Traditional Sch., Manassas, Va., 2001—03, Tyler Elem. Sch., Gainesville, Va., 2003—, Signal Hill Elem. Sch., Manassas, Va., 2003—. Dir. Signal Hill Singing Sensations, Manassas, Pennington Premiers Show Choir, Woodbridge (Va.) Youth Chorale, 2005—; prodn. assoc. TV series The Joy of Music, 2000—03. Assoc. organist, song leader Trinity United Meth. Ch., McLean, Va., 2004—; choir dir., organist Covenant Presbyn. Ch., Woodbridge, Va., 2004—. Mem.: Music Educators Nat. Conf., Am. Guild Organists. Avocations: auto detailing, auto repair, exercise. Personal E-mail: matthewhrt@hotmail.com. E-mail: hartma@pwcs.edu.

HART, MATTHEW J., hotel and recreation executive; married; 3 children. BA cum laude, Vanderbilt U., 1974; MBA, Columbia U., 1976. Mktg. rsch. assoc. Merrill Lynch; lending officer Bankers Trust Co., N.Y.; from mgr. project fin. to exec. v.p., CFO Marriott Corp., 1981—92; exec. v.p., CFO Host Marriot Corp., 1992—95; sr. v.p., treas. Walt Disney Co., 1995—96; CFO, exec. v.p. Hilton Hotels Corp., Beverly Hills, Calif., 1996—2004, pres., 2004—, COO, 2004—. Bd. dirs. Kilroy Realty Co., First Washington Realty Trust, Inc., Kilroy Realty Corp. Bd. dirs. Heal the Bay, Westside Breakers. Office: Hilton Hotels Corp PO Box 5567 9336 Civic Center Dr Beverly Hills CA 90210-3604

HART, MELISSA ANNE, congresswoman; b. Pitts., Apr. 4, 1962; d. Donald P. and Albina Simone Hart. BA, Washington and Jefferson Coll., 1984; JD, U. Pitts., 1987. Pa. state senator, 1990-2000; mem. U.S. Congress from 4th Pa. dist., 2001—; mem. fin. svcs. com., judiciary com., sci. com. Chmn. Sen. Fin. Com.; vice chmn. Sen. Urban Affairs & Housing Com.; bd. dirs. C.C. Allegheny County, Pitts. Cancer Inst., SWPA Vets. Home Adv. Coun. Bd. dirs. Vietnam Vets. Leadership Program; bd. trustees U. Pitts. Mem.: North Suburban Builders Assn., Allegheny County Bar Assn., Pa. Bar Assn. Republican. Office: 1508 Longworth Ho Office Bldg Washington DC 20515-3804 also: 2525 Rochester Rd Ste 202 Cranberry Township PA 16066*

HART, MELISSA JOAN CATHERINE, actress; b. Smithtown, N.Y., Apr. 18, 1976; m. Mark Wilkerson, July 19, 2003. Appeared in TV series, including Clarissa Explains It All, Sabrina The Teenage Witch; appeared in TV movies, including Kane and Able, Christmas Show, The Tale of the Frozen Ghost, Family Reunion, Twisted Desire, Sabrina The Teenage Witch, Two Came Back, Sabrina Goes to Rome, Silencing Mary; appeared in feature film Can't Hardly Wait, Drive Me Crazy, 1999, Recess: School's Out (voice), 2001, Hold On, 2002, Rent Control, 2002, Jesus, Mary and Joey, 2003; appeared in plays, including Besides Herself, Imagining Brad, The Crucible; actress (TV movie) The Voyage to Atlantis: The Lost Empire, 2001; actress, prodr. (TV movie) Sabrina, Down Under, 1999. Office: Creative Artists Agy 9830 Wilshire Bvd Beverly Hills CA 90212

HART, OLIVER D'ARCY, economics professor; b. London, Oct. 9, 1948; came to U.S., 1984; s. Philip D'Arcy and Ruth D'Arcy (Meyer) H.; m. Rita B. Goldberg, June 9, 1974; children: Daniel S., Benjamin P. BA, Cambridge U., 1969; MA, U. Warwick (Eng.), 1972; PhD, Princeton U., 1974; PhD (hon.), Free U. Brussels, 1992, U. Basel, Switzerland, 1994. Lectr. econs. U. Essex (Eng.), 1974-75, Cambridge (Eng.) U., 1975-81; prof. econs. London Sch. Econs., 1981-85, MIT, Cambridge, 1984-93, Harvard U., Cambridge, 1993—, Andrew E. Furer prof. econs., 1997—. Marvin Bower fellow Harvard U. Bus. Sch., Boston, 1988-89; Centennial vis. prof. London Sch. Econ., 1997—. Author: Firms, Contracts, and Financial Structure, 1995; editor Rev. Econ. Studies, 1979-83; contbr. articles to profl. jours. Guggenheim fellow, 1987-88. Fellow Econometric Soc. (coun. 1983—, Fisher-Schultze lectr 1988), Am. Acad. Arts. and Scis., Brit. Acad. (corr.); mem. Am. Law and Econ. Assn. (v.p., pres. elect). Avocation: listening to music. Office: Harvard U Dept Econs Cambridge MA 02138 Office Phone: 617-496-3461. Business E-Mail: ohart@harvard.edu.

HART, PAUL VINCENT, JR., emergency and acute care physician, inventor; b. Estherville, Iowa, Sept. 28, 1950; s. Paul Vincent and Florence Mary (Gehringer) H.; m. Susan Murphey, Sept. 27, 1989. BS, Iowa State U., 1972; MD, Creighton U., 1976. Diplomate Am. Bd. Emergency Medicine. Resident in gen. surgery U. Minn., Mpls., 1976-77; emergency physician Wheeling (W.Va.) Med. Ctr., 1977-79; pvt. practice Kansas City, Kans., 1979-84, Westwood, Kans., 1985—. V.p. Organ Design & Mfg., Westwood, 1989—; cons. Hepatocyte Transformation Lab. Hannover (Germany) U. Med. Sch., 2000—. Mem. Am. Acad. Family Physicians. Republican. Roman Catholic. Achievements include patents for transformed kidney cells for renal assist device; patents pending for bioartifical kidney; co-patentee liver assist devices. Office: 17416 158th St Bonner Springs KS 66012 Office Phone: 913-728-2408.

HART, RICHARD BANNER, lawyer; b. Winston-Salem, NC, Apr. 9, 1932; s. Samuel Bruce and Cordia M. (Lamb) H.; m. Jean Elizabeth Shinn, Apr. 28, 1956; 1 dau., Fabra. AB in Polit. Sci, U. NC, 1957, JD, 1959. Bar: N.C. 1959, Tenn. 1970, U.S. Supreme Ct. 1991; CLU. Assoc. counsel Jefferson Standard Life Ins. Co., Greensboro, N.C., 1959-70; with NLT Corp. and Nat. Life and Accident Ins. Co., Nashville, 1970-73, asst. v.p., counsel, 1973-75, sec., counsel, 1975-84; v.p., sec., assoc. gen. counsel Am. Gen. Ins. Cos., Nashville, 1982-88; v.p., sec., gen. counsel Intereal Co., 1984-85; spl. counsel Bowne of Nashville, Inc., 1988-94, Richard B. Hart & Assocs., 1988—; judge City of Belle Meade, Nashville. Lectr. in field; adv. com. U.S. Dist. Ct. (mid. dist.) Tenn. Civil Justice Reform Act 1990. Bd. editors U. N.C. Law Rev., 1958-59. Budget com. Guilford County United Fund, N.C., 1968-69; bd. dirs. Guilford County Mental Health Assn., 1968-69; nat. bd. dirs. Joint Action in Cmty. Svc., 2005—; treas. Nashville Exch. Club Charities, 1987-88; trustee West End United Meth. Ch., 1998-2000; vol. The Talking Libr.; bd. govs. Shakespeare on the Cumberland. With U.S. Army, 1953-55. Mem. Assn. Life Ins. Counsel, Am. Corp. Counsel Assn. (pres., chmn. bd. dirs. Tenn. chpt. 1990-92), Am. Soc. Corp. Secs. (exec. com., pres. S.E. region 1979-81), Tenn. Mcpl. Judges Assn., Nashville Com. Fgn. Rels., English Speaking Union U.S. (bd. dirs. 1998—, pres. Nashville br. 1999-01), Phi Delta Phi, Phi Kappa Sigma (nat. officer, exec. bd. 1971-77), Phi Kappa Sigma Ednl. Fund, Inc. (trustee 1997-00), Exch. Club (Nashville) (bd. dirs. 1984-85), Univ. Club Nashville (bd. dirs.). Home: 2815 Kenway Rd Nashville TN 37215-1903

HART, ROBERT M., lawyer; b. N.Y.C., Nov. 7, 1944; s. Charles John and Helen Ann (Hammond) H.; m. Dale Elizabeth McConaughy, Nov. 21, 1970; children: Michael, Jonathan, Bryan. BA, Marist Coll., 1966; JD, Duke U., 1969. Bar: N.Y. 1969, U.S. Ct. Appeals (2d cir.) 1970, U.S. Dist. Ct. (so. dist.) N.Y. 1979. Assoc. Donovan Leisure Newton & Irvine, N.Y.C., 1969-71, 74-77, London, 1972-73, ptnr. N.Y.C., 1977-84, 88-94, Dorsey & Whitney, N.Y.C., 1984-88; sr. v.p., gen. counsel, sec. Alleghany Corp., N.Y.C., 1994—; dir., chmn. comp.com. Chgo. Title Corp., 1998-2000. Sr. lectr. law Duke U., Durham, NC, 1986—. Contbr. articles to profl. jours. Sr. fellow, Duke U., 1983—. Mem. ABA (securities regulation com. 1981—), N.Y. State Bar Assn., Assn. Bar City N.Y. (securities regulation com. 1979-82), Am. Law Inst. Office: 7 Times Sq Tower 17th Flr New York NY 10036 Office Phone: 212-752-1556. Personal E-mail: rhart@alleghany.com.

HART, RONALD WILSON, radiobiologist, educator, toxicologist, business adviser; b. Syracuse, N.Y., Mar. 23, 1942; s. Wilson and Annabell Hart. BS, Syracuse U., 1967; MS, U. Ill., 1970, PhD, 1971; postgrad. (Nat. Cancer Inst. trainee), Oak Ridge Nat. Lab., 1973. USPHS trainee, 1970-71; asst. prof. dept. radiology Ohio State U., Columbus, 1971-75, dir. radiation biology rsch. divsn., 1971-82, assoc. prof. depts. biology, biophysics, preventive medicine, 1976-78, assoc. prof. pharmacology, medicinal chemistry dept. preventive medicine, 1977-78, dir. chem., biomed. environ. rsch. group dept. preventive medicine, 1977-82, prof. depts. radiology, preventive medicine, pharmacology, medicinal chemistry, vet. pathobiology, 1978-82; dir. Nat. Ctr. for Toxicological Rsch., Jefferson, Ark., 1980-92, Disting. scientist in residence, 1992-2000; rsch. prof. Strang Cancer Prevention Rsch. Ctr. Rockefeller U., 2000—04. Disting. prof. U. Poona, India, 1978-2004, Cairo U., 1989—; disting. prof. carcinogenesis Guang Zhou Med. Coll., China, 1988—; adj. prof. U. Ark. for Med. Sci., 1980-, U. Tenn. Health Scis., 1983-; adj. prof. pharmacology Coll. Pharmacy, U. Ark., 1997—; cons. Oak Ridge Nat. Lab., 1971-75, Brookhaven Nat. Lab., 1975-78, Argonne Nat. Lab., 1975-78, EPA, 1976, 78, Am. Indsl. Health Coun., 1978, PPG Industries, 1978, Informatics, 1978-80, FDA, 1980; mem. NAS/NRC Bd. on Toxicology and Environ. Health Hazards, 1976-82; mem. interagy. staff group Office Sci. and Tech. Policy Exec. Office of Pres., 1982-85, chmn., 1983-85; chmn. bd. dirs. Ark. Sci. and Tech. Authority, 1983-84, mem., 1985-88; bd. dirs. Chem. Overseas Link, 2000-04, Microgen, Inc., 2001-03, Whole Hog Cafes, LLC, 2005-, Miltos Pharms., 2005—; mem. adv. bd. Petrotech, 1991-92, VoiceNet, 1998-99, Waterchef Inc., 2001-03, Micromed Labs., 2002-04, Biomed, 2002—, Applied DNA Scis., Inc., 2003-05, Fla. A&M U. Rsch. Ctr., 1985-2004, Omega Foods, 2004-, Met. Area Networks, 2004-, Ship OK, LLC, 2004-, Biophora, Inc. 2005-, Gulided Theraputics, 2005-; bd. visitors Memphis State U., 1984-90; mem. adv. bd. Miss. State U., 1987-96; chair task force on risk assessment/risk mgmt. HHS, 1985, chmn. com. to coordinate environ., health and related programs, 1985-88, chmn. sci. panel Agent Orange working group, 1986-88, mem. USAF toxicology rev. panel, 1987; chmn. Intergovtl. Task Force on Tech. Transfer, 1987-88, DHHS Task Force on Tech. Transfer, 1987-88; mem. Inter Govt. Commn. on Competitiveness, 1987-94; apptd. del. to U.S.-USSR Emerging Leaders Summit, chmn. Sci. and Tech. Commn., 1988; disting. adj. prof. Moscow State U., 1989—, Guanzou (China) Med. U., 1988—, U. Udina, Italy, 1999-2002; chmn. Ark. Sch. for Math. and Sci. Found., 1997-2003. Contbr. chpts. to books, numerous articles to profl. jours. Recipient Hopkins award for grad. rsch., 1971; recipient Japanese Med. Assn. award, 1978; Karl-August-Forester award W. Germany, 1980, award of merit FDA, 1982, 85, 86, Sr. Exec. Svc. award, 1982, 84, 85; Superior Svc. award USPHS, 1983, Gov.'s Award Outstanding Svc., State of Ark., 1985, Letter of Commendation, Pres. of U.S., 1985, Commr's Spl. Citation, FDA, 1987, Pres. Rank award for Meritorious Svc., 1987, Superior Svc. award outstanding accomplishment Guangzhou Med. Coll., 1988, Bose medal Bose Inst., 1994; Internat. Union Against Cancer; named Syracuse U. Outstanding Alumnus, 1976; Ednl. medal, U. Ark., 2005. Fellow Gerontol. Soc., Am. Coll. Toxicology (past pres.), Risk Anal Soc., Am. Assn. Clin. Chemistry, AAAS; mem. Radiation Rsch. Soc., Biophys. Soc., Photochem. and Photobiol. Soc., Sr. Execs. Assn., Sigma Xi. Office: 4821 Crestwood Little Rock AR 72207 Personal E-mail: rhart99@comcast.net.

HART, RUSSELL HOLIDAY, retired lawyer; b. Chgo., May 1, 1928; s. Russell Holiday and Allegra (Prince) H.; m. Mary Gehres, June 16, 1951; children: Holiday Hart McKiernan, Robert Russell, Andrew Richard. AB, DePauw U., 1950; JD, Ind. U., 1956. Bar: Ind. 1956, U.S. Dist. Ct. (no. and so. dists.) Ind. 1956, U.S. Ct. Appeals (7th cir.) 1965, U.S. Supreme Ct. 1973. Assoc. Stuart & Branigin, Lafayette, Ind., 1956-61, ptnr., 1961-99; ret., 1999. Lectr. Ind. Continuing Legal Edn. Forum; tchr. trial lawyers Nat. Inst. for Trial Advocacy. Served with U.S. Army, 1951-53. Fellow: Acad. Law Alumni Ind. U. Sch. Law, Ind. Bar Found. (sec., v.p. 1985), Internat. Acad. Trial Lawyers, Am. Coll. Trial Lawyers, Am. Bar Found., Internat. Soc. Barristers; mem.: ABA (del.), Nat. Assn. Railroad Trial Counsel (past pres.), Def. Trial Counsel of Ind. (past pres.), Ind. Def. Trial Counsel (diplomate), Tippecanoe County Bar Assn. (past pres.), Ind. Bar Assn. (pres.-elect 1986—87, pres. 1987—88, bd. mgrs., former treas., chmn. trial lawyers sect.). Office: Stuart & Branigin PO Box 1010 Lafayette IN 47902-1010 Office Phone: 765-423-1561.

HART, SARAH V., federal agency administrator; BS in Criminal Justice, U. Del.; JD, Rutgers U. Asst. dist. atty. appeals unit Phila. Dist. Attys. Office, 1979—86, chief civil litigation unit, 1986—95; chief counsel Pa. Dept. Corrections, 1995—2001; dir. Nat. Inst. Justice U.S. Dept. Justice, Washington, 2001—. Vice chair legal affairs com. Am. Correctional Assn.; chmn. sentencing and corrections subcom. Federalist Soc.; bd. dirs. Crime Victims Law Inst.; mem. appellate procedural rules com. Pa. Supreme Ct.; trainer in field. Contbr. articles to profl. jours. Office: US Dept Justice Nat Inst Justice 810 7th St NW Washington DC 20531

HART, STANLEY ROBERT, geochemist, educator; b. Swampscott, Mass., June 20, 1935; s. Robert Winfield and Ruth Mildred (Standley) H.; m. Joanna Smith, Sept. 1, 1956 (div. Dec. 1978); 1 dau., Jolene Kaweah; m. Pamela Coulouras Shepherd, Nov. 4, 1980; children: Elizabeth Ann, Nathaniel Charles. BS, MIT, 1956, PhD, 1960; MS, Calif. Inst. Tech., 1957. Staff mem. Carnegie Instn., Washington, 1960-75; prof. dept. earth and planetary sci. Mass. Inst. Tech., Cambridge, 1975-89; sr. scientist Woods Hole (Mass.) Oceanographic Instn., 1989—, C.O. Iselin chair; mem. U.S. Nat. Com. for Geochemistry, 1973-76, chmn., 1975; mem. ocean crust panel Internat. Phase of Ocean Drilling, 1974-76; mem. U.S. nat. com. Internat. Geol. Correlations Program, 1974-76. Assoc. editor: Jour. Geophys. Rsch., 1966-68, Revs. of Geophysics, 1970-72, Geochimica et Cosmochimica Acta, 1970-76; editorial bd.: Physics of the Earth and Planetary Interiors, 1977-92, Earth and Planetary Sci. Letters, 1977-87, Chem. Geology, 1985—; contbr. articles in field to profl. jours. Fellow Am. Acad. Arts and Scis., Geol. Soc. Am., Am. Geophys. Union (Harry H. Hess medal 1997), Geochem. Soc. (councillor 1981-83, v.p. 1983-85, pres. 1985-87, V.M. Goldschmidt award 1992), European Assn. Geochemistry; mem. NAS. Home: 53 Quonset Rd Falmouth MA 02540-1656 Office: Woods Hole Oceanographic Inst Dept Geology & Geophysics Woods Hole MA 02543 *I view science, the search for truth and understanding, as an infinitely long road; getting to the end is not as important as how we get there.*

HART, TERRY JONATHAN, communications executive; b. Pitts., Oct. 27, 1946; s. Jonathan Smith Hart and Lillian Dorothy (Zugates) Hart Pierson; m. Mary Jane McKeever, Aug. 13, 1999; children: Amy, Lori. B of Mech. Engrng., Lehigh U., 1968, DEng (hon.), 1988; MS, MIT, 1969; MEE, Rutgers U., 1978. Mem. tech. staff AT&T Bell Labs., Whippany, N.J., 1968-69, 73-78, supr., 1984—, head cellular systems strategic planning, 1989—; astronaut NASA Johnson Space Ctr., Houston, 1978-84, captured solar maximum satellite, 1984, div. mgr. Telstar 4 Satellite Program; pres. Loral Skynet, Bedminster, N.J., 1997—. Patentee in field. Served to lt. col. USAF Air N.G., 1969-90. Recipient N.J. Disting. Service medal, NASA Space Flight medal, Pride of Pa. medal; named N.J. Aviation Hall Fame. Mem. IEEE, Sigma Xi, Tau Beta Pi. Avocations: skiing, golf. Office: Loral Skynet 500 Hills Dr 3rd Fl Bedminster NJ 07921-1538

HART, THOMAS HUGHSON, III, lawyer; b. Montgomery, Ala., Aug. 19, 1955; s. Thomas H. and Nora A. (McDonald) H.; m. Jane Elizabeth Morgan, Aug. 4, 1979; children: Morgan Elizabeth, Katherine MacDonald, Mary MacQuarrie, Teresa Jane. BA in Polit. Sci., Furman U., 1977; JD, U. S.C., 1980. Bar: S.C. 1980, U.S. Dist. Ct. S.C. 1981, U.S. Ct. Appeals (4th cir.) 1981, U.S. Ct. Appeals (11th cir.) 1982, u.S. Ct. Appeals (10th cir.) 1985, U.S. Surpeme Ct. 1987, U.S. Ct. Appeals (8th cir.) 1990, U.S. Ct. Appeals (3d cir.) 1991, V.I. 1991. Assoc. Blatt and Fales, Barnwell, S.C., 1980-83; ptnr. Ness, Motley, Loadholt, Richardson & Poole, Barnwell, S.C., 1983-90, Brady, Hart & JAcobs, Christiansted, V.I., 1990-93, Alkon, Rhea & Hart, Christiansted, V.I., 1993—. Articles editor S.C. Law Rev., 1978-80. Baruch scholar Furman U., Greenville, S.C., 1973-77, Jamer Verner scholar U. S.C. Law Sch., 1978, Paul Cooper scholar, 1979. Mem. ABA, S.C. Trial Lawyers Assn. (bd. govs.), Assn. Trial Lawyers Am., S.C. Bar Assn., V.I. Bar Assn., Barnwell County C. of C. (bd. dirs.). Roman Catholic. Home: 2 Boetzburg Christiansted VI 00820-4516 Office: 2212 Queen Cross St Christiansted VI 00820-4835 Business E-Mail: tom@thhpc.com.

HART, THOMAS J., music educator, choral conductor; b. Centerville, Iowa, Jan. 8, 1956; s. James M. and Mary Louise Hart; m. Martha J. Hart, Sept. 1, 1979; 1 child, Christopher James. BA, Olivet Coll., 1978; MusM, Mich. State U., 1983, DMA, 1989. Intern Mich. Coun. for Arts, Detroit, 1978; asst. to chmn. performing arts dept. Olivet (Mich.) Coll., 1979-82; tchg. asst. Mich. State U., East Lansing, 1983-86; music prof. Graceland U., Lamoni, Iowa, 1986—, chmn. fine arts divsn., 1997—2002, Vredenburg prof. of music, 2001—04. Chmn. dept. vocal music Blue Lake Fine Arts Camp, Twin Lake, Mich., 1986-2000; dir. Bay View (Mich.) Music Festival, 2000-2001. Mem. Am. Choral Dirs. Assn. (chmn. collegiate repertoire and stds. 1997-99). Office: Graceland U Dept Music 1 University Pl Lamoni MI 50140

HART, TIMOTHY RAY, lawyer, dean; b. Portland, Jan. 5, 1942; s. Eldon V. and Wanda J. (Hillyer) H.; m. Mary F. Barlow, Aug. 31, 1964 (div. Dec. 1975); children: Mark, Matthew, Marisa, Martin; m. Annette Bryant, Aug. 8, 1981. AA, San Jose City Coll., 1968; BA, San Jose State U., 1970; MA, Wash. State U., 1973; JD, San Joaquin Coll. Law, Fresno, Calif., 1983. Bar: Calif. 1983, U.S. Dist. Ct. (ea. dist.) Calif. 1983. Police officer City of Santa Clara, Calif., 1965-71; chief of police U. Idaho, Moscow, 1971-73; crime prevention officer City of Albany, Oreg., 1973-75; instr. criminal justice Coll. of Sequoias, Visalia, Calif., 1975-81, dir. paralegal dept., 1982-83, chmn., dir. adminstrn. justice divsn., 1983-88, assoc. dean instrn., 1988—; sole practice law Visalia, 1983—. Apptd. dep. chief police City of Sanger (Calif.), 1995, apptd. chief of police, 2001-02. Parliamentarian Interagy. Youth and Cmty. Svcs., Inc. With USAF, 1960-63. Mem. ABA, ATLA, Calif. Bar Assn., Assn. Criminal Justice Educators, Am. Criminal Justice Assn., Delta Phi. Mennonite. Home: 1012 W Hemlock Ave Visalia CA 93277-7435 Office: Coll Sequoias 915 S Mooney Blvd Visalia CA 93277-2214 Office Phone: 559-737-4878. Personal E-mail: tim95law@juno.com. Business E-Mail: timothyh@cos.edu.

HART, TRIP, lawyer; BS, U. Pa., 1975; JD, U. Miami, 1978. Bar: Wash. 1979, U.S. Dist. Ct. (we. dist.) Wash. 1979. Office: 1224 Griffin Enumclaw WA 98022 E-mail: trip@tx3.net.

HART, WILLIAM C., underwriter, educator, writer; b. Orange, N.J., Jan. 6, 1947; s. William Gerard and Etchen (Alsberg) Hart; m. Wendy Clarkson, Oct. 14, 1978 (div.); m. Charlotte R. Wagner, Oct. 7, 1989. AB, Fla. So. Coll., 1969; MBA, Ashbourne U., 1973; diploma in real estate fin., NYU, 1975; profl. garden tng. program, Longwood Garden, Kennett Sq., Pa., 1976; postgrad., Dale Carnegie Inst., 1994. Cert. land title profl. Land Title Inst. Va. Regional underwriter Chgo. Title Ins. Co., Dallas, 1980—83; sr. adv. title officer Lawyers Title Ins. Corp., New Brunswick, NJ, 1983—85; chief title officer Am. Title Ins. Co., Miami, Fla., 1985—92; chief title underwriter emeritus T. A. Title Ins. Co., Media, Pa., 1993—; prin. Title Law Assocs., Phila., 1999—; editor in chief Title Mgmt. Today, 2003—. Lectr. N.J. Land Title Sch., Upsala Coll., East Orange, NJ, 1972, Land Title Sch., Austin, 1982, N.J. Lawyers Title Inst., Summit, 1984—85, Land Title Inst. Va., 1990, 91; instr. Neumann Coll. CLE Cert., 1995—97, NBI, Inc., 2003—. Author: (book) Standard Title Underwriting Practices, 1991, Creditors Rights and Title Insurance, Questionable Title, Remedies & Extra-Hazardous Risks, 1991, Title Insurance Underwriting Principles and Exception Language, 1992, Instructions as the Use of Title Insurance Endorsements, 1992, Title Insurance Underwriting Process, 1994, The Law of Titles in Florida, 1996, The Law of Titles in New York, 1996, The Law Titles in Pennsylvania, 1998; editor: New Jersey Titles Annotated, 1986, Alta Title Counsel, 1989—, Title Law Annotated, 2000—, The Law of Titles, 2002, Title Management Today, 2003—; contbg. editor: book Patton & Palomar on Land Titles, 2003, contbg. author: Thompson/Westgroup. Mem.: USGA (assoc.), Internat. Platform Assn., Internat. Platform Assn., Pa. Land Title Assn. (mem. forms com. 1989—92, 1994), N.J. Land Title Assn. (chmn. title officers com. 1987—88), Pa. Sheriffs Assn., Fraternal Order Police (assoc.), World Affairs Coun. Phila., Golden Horshoe Golf & Country Club, Ashbourne Country Club, Sigma Phi Epsilon. Republican. Avocations: martial arts (black belt), golf, stamp collecting/philately, gardening. Home: 612 Boyer Rd Cheltenham PA 19012-1610 Office: Ttle Law Assocs PO Box 7137 Elkins Park PA 19027-0137 Office Phone: 800-220-3901 132. Personal E-mail: TitleLaw@comcast.net. Business E-Mail: whart@tatitle.com.

HART, WILLIAM THOMAS, federal judge; b. Joliet, Ill., Feb. 4, 1929; s. William Michael and Geraldine (Archambeault) H.; m. Catherine Motta, Nov. 27, 1954; children: Catherine Hart Maher, Susan Hart DaMario, Julie Hart Boesen, Sally Hart Collins, Nancy Hart McLaughlin. JD, Loyola U., Chgo., 1951. Bar: Ill. 1951, U.S. Dist. Ct. 1951, U.S. Ct. Appeals (7th cir.) 1954, U.S. Ct. Appeals (D.C. cir.) 1977. Asst. U.S. atty. U.S. Dist. Ct. (no. dist.) Ill., Chgo., 1954-56; assoc. Defrees & Fiske, 1956-59; spl. asst. atty. gen. State of Ill., 1957-58; assoc. then ptnr. Schiff, Hardin & Waite, 1959-82; spl. asst. state's atty. Cook County, Ill., 1960; judge U.S. Dist. Ct. Ill., 1982—; now sr. judge. Mem. exec. com. U.S. Dist. Ct. (no. dist.) Ill., 1988-92; mem. com. on adminstrn. fed. magistrates sys., Jud. Conf. U.S., 1987-92, 7th cir. Jud. Coun., 1990-92; mem. edn. com. Fed. Jud. Ctr., 1994-99; chair No. Dist. Ill. Ct. Hist. Assoc., 1998—. Pres. adv. bd. Mercy Med. Ctr., Aurora, Ill., 1980-81; v.p. Aurora Blood Bank, 1972-77; trustee Rosary H.S., 1981-82, 93-98; bd. dirs. Chgo. Legal Asst. Found., 1974-76. Served with U.S. Army, 1951-53. Decorated Bronze Starl named to Joliet/Will County Hall of Pride, 1992. Mem. 7th Cir. Bar Assn., Law Club, Legal Club, Soc. Trial Lawyers, Union League Club of Aurora, Ill. (hon.), Inn of Ct., Serra Club of Aurora (v.p. 2000). Office: US Dist Ct No Dist Ill US Courthouse Rm 2246 219 S Dearborn St Chicago IL 60604-1702

HART-DULING, JEAN MACAULAY, clinical social worker; b. Bellingham, Wash. d. Murry Donald and Pearl N. (McLeod) Macaulay; m. Richard D. Hart, Feb. 3, 1940 (dec. Mar. 1973); children: Margaret Hart Morrison, Pamela Hart Horton, Patricia L. Hart-Jewell; m. Lawrence Duling, Jan. 20, 1979 (dec. May 1992); children: Lenora Daniel, Jayne Munch. BA, Wash. State U., 1938; MSW, U. So. Calif., 1961. Lic. clin. social worker, Calif.; accredited counselor, Wash. Social worker Los Angeles County, 1957-58; children's svc. worker Dept. Children's Svcs., L.A., 1958-59; program developer homemakers svcs. project Calif. Dept. Children's Svcs., L.A., 1962-64; developer homemaker cons. position State of Calif., L.A., 1964-66; supr. protective svcs. Dept. Children's Svcs., L.A., 1966-67; dep. regional svc. adminstrn. Dept. Los Angeles County Children's Svcs., 1967-76; adminstr. Melton Home for Developmental Disability, 1985-86; pvt. practice pro bono therapy Calif. and Wash. Therapist various pro bono cases. Mem. Portals Com., L.A., 1974, Travelers Aid Bd., Long Beach, Calif. 1969. Recipient Nat. award work in cmty., spl. award for work with emotionally disturbed Com. for Los Angeles, 1974. Mem. AAUW, NASW, Acad. Cert. Social Workers, Calif. Lic. Clin. Soc. Workers, Wing Point Golf and Country Club (Bainbridge Island, Wash.), Los Angeles County Retirement Assn. Republican. Congregationalist. Avocations: golf, bridge. E-mail: hart4942@aol.com.

HARTE, CHRISTOPHER MCCUTCHEON, investment manager; b. Hanover, NH, Nov. 20, 1947; s. Edward Holmead and Janet (Frey) H.; m. Kay Marie Wagenknecht, Feb. 11, 1984 (dec.); 1 child, William; m. Katherine Stoddard Pope, June 10, 1999. BA, Stanford U., 1969; MBA, U. Tex., 1974. Assoc. McKinsey and Co., Inc., Dallas, 1974-76; dir. rsch. and promotion Austin Am. Statesman, Tex., 1976-79; pvt. practice pub., comm., 1979-83; mem. advanced mgmt. devel. program Miami Herald, Fla., 1983-85; asst. to pres. newspaper div. Knight-Ridder Inc., Miami, Fla., 1985-86; pres., pub. Ctr. Daily Times, State Coll., Pa., 1986-89, Akron Beacon Jour., Ohio, 1989-92; pres. Portland Press-Herald and Maine Sunday Telegram, 1992-94; ptnr. Cerrito Ptnr. Bd. dir. Harte-Hanks, Inc., Geokinetics, Inc., Crown Resources, Mincron Inc.

HARTELIUS, CHANNING JULIUS, lawyer; b. Gt. Falls, Mont., Oct. 2, 1946; s. Chester Werner and Hildegarde Margaret (Kelm) Hartelius; children: Rhonda, Kerry, Chanin, Courtney. BA with honors, U. Mont., 1968; JD with honors, George Washington U., 1971. Bar: Va. 1971, Mont. 1971. Asst. atty. gen., Mont., 1971; ptnr. Wuerthner & Hartelius, Gt. Falls, 1972—73, Hartelius & Lewin, Gt. Falls, 1973—78, Hartelius & Assocs., P.C., Gt. Falls, 1978—87, Hartelius, Ferguson, Baker and Kazda, P.C., 1987—. Asst. city atty., Gt. Falls, 1972—76; instr. Coll. Gt. Falls, 1980. Author: Understanding Bankruptcy, A Guide, 1981, Montana Handbook on Contract for Deeds, 1982; co-author: Law and the Municipal Ecology, 1971; contbr. articles to legal jours. Participant Leadership Gt. Falls, 1983; bd. dirs. Selective Svc., 1995—. Served to capt. USAR, 1971—82. Recipient Presdl. award of excellence, U.S. Jaycees, 1976. Mem.: ATLA, ABA, Cascade County Bar Assn. (pres. 1997), Mont. Bar Assn., Mont. Hist. Soc. Lutheran (pres. Ch. 1996, 1997), Gt. Falls Jaycees (pres. 1976), Meadow Lark Country Club, Toastmasters (pres. 1975, 1997). Home: 825 4th Ave N Great Falls MT 59401-1511 Office: PO Box 1629 Great Falls MT 59403-1629

HARTEN, ANN M., relocation services executive; married; 1 child. BA in Indsl. Psychology, Indiana U. of Pa. With Boise Cascade, 1987—2000, dir. integrated supply, 1999—2000; v.p., chief info. officer US ops. SIRVA, Westmont, Ill., 2000—. Office: SIRVA 700 Oakmont Ln Westmont IL 60559

HARTER, DAVID HOUSTON, pediatric neurosurgeon, educator; b. NYC, Apr. 29, 1968; s. Donald Harry Harter and Lee Kimmel; m. Amy Beth Goldman, Oct. 28, 1965; children: Emily Elizabeth, Charlotte Isabelle. MD, Georgetown U., 1994. Lic. Am. Bd. Neurol. Surgery. Fellow in pediatric neurosurgery Children's Meml. Hosp., Chgo., 2000—01; asst. prof. neurosurgery NY Med. Coll., Valhalla, 2001—. Dir. pediat. neurosurgery Westchester Med. Ctr., Valhalla, 2001—. Mem.: Internat. Soc. Pediat. Neurosurgery. Office: NY Med Coll Dept Neurosurgery Munger Pavilion Scarsdale NY 10583 Office Phone: 914-594-7195. Personal E-mail: david_harter@nymc.edu.

HARTER, DONALD HARRY, neurologist, medical educator; b. Breslau, Germany, May 16, 1933; came to U.S., 1940; naturalized, 1945; s. Harry Morton and Leonor Evelyne (Goldmann) H.; m. Lee Grossman, Dec. 18, 1960 (div. 1976); children: Kathryne, Jennifer, Amy, David; m. Rikki Horne, May 18, 1985 (div. 1986); m. Marjorie Brandt Dahlin, Oct. 12, 1990. AB, U. Pa., 1953; MD, Columbia U., 1957. Diplomate Am. Bd. Psychiatry and Neurology. Intern in medicine Yale-New Haven Med. Center, 1957-58; asst. resident, then resident neurology N.Y. Neurol. Inst., 1958-61; guest investigator Rockefeller U., 1963-66; mem. faculty Columbia Coll. Physicians and Surgeons, 1960-75, prof. neurology and microbiology, 1973-75; vis. fellow Clare Hall, Cambridge, England, 1973-74; attending neurologist N.Y. Neurol. Inst., Presbyn. Hosp., 1973-75; Charles L. Mix prof. Northwestern U., 1975-85, Benjamin and Virginia T. Boshes prof. neurology, 1985-87, chmn. dept. neurology, 1975-87, Northwestern Meml. Hosp., Chgo., 1975-87; dir. rsch. scholars program Howard Hughes Med. Inst./NIH, Bethesda, 1989-2000; with dept. neurology George Washington U. Med. Ctr., Washington, 1987—. Vis. sci. officer Howard Hughes Med. Inst., 1986—87, sr. sci. officer, 1987—2000; clin. prof. neurology George Washington U. Sch. Medicine and Health Scis., 1987—2001, prof. emeritus clin. neurology, 2001—03; prof. emeritus neurology in residence George Washington U., 2004—; vis. rsch. fellow Dept. Pathology U. Cambridge, England, 1973—74, 2000—01; vis. life mem. Clare Hall, 2000—01; mem. adv. com. on fellowships Nat. Multiple Sclerosis Soc., 1976—79, chmn., 1977—79, rsch. programs adv. com., 1989—94; mem. Nat. Commn. on Venereal Disease, HEW, 1970—72; mem. med. adv. bd. Am. Parkinson Disease Assn., 1976—90, Myasthenia Gravis Found., 1980—87; mem. sci. adv. coun. Nat. Amyotrophic Lateral Sclerosis Found., 1978—85; mem. bd. sci. counselors Nat. Inst. Dental Rsch. NIH, 1990—95; sr. sci. advisor Amyotrophic Lateral Sclerosis Assn., 1992—2000. Mem. editorial bd. Neurology, 1976-82, Anns. of Neurology, 1983-89; mem. adv. bd. Archives of Virology, 1975-81. Recipient Joseph Mather Smith prize Columbia U., 1970, Lucy G. Moses award, 1970, 72, Donald W. Mulder award The ALS Assn., 1998; Am. Cancer Soc. scholar, 1973-74; USPHS spl. fellow, 1963-66, Guggenheim fellow, 1973. Fellow: AAAS, Am. Acad. Neurology, Infectious Diseases Soc. Am.; mem.: Am. Soc. Virology, Am. Soc. Microbiology, Deutsche Gesellschaft fur Neurologie (corr.), Am. Neurol. Assn., Am. Soc. Clin. Investigation, Univ. Club Washington, Yale Club N.Y.C., Cosmos Club, Phi Beta Kappa, Sigma Xi. Office: George Washington U Med Ctr Ste 7-404 2150 Pennsylvania Ave NW Washington DC 20037-3201

HARTER, HUGH ANTHONY, foreign language educator; b. Columbus, Ohio, Dec. 13, 1922; s. Anthony Hugh and Georgiana (Hayes) H.; m. Driscilla Escher, Aug. 31, 1959 (div. 1961); m. Frances D. Reichman, Oct. 7, 1970; stepchildren: Ellen Berliner, Andrew Berliner, Nancy Berliner Rudolph. Student, Ohio Wesleyan U., 1940-41, Hamilton Coll., 1943, Ecole du Syndicat de la Haute Couture, Paris, 1947, NYU, 1975, New Sch. Social Research, 1975; BA cum laude, Ohio State U., 1947, PhD, 1959; MA cum laude, Mexico City Coll., U. Ams., 1951. Student teaching asst. Ohio State U., 1946-47, grad. teaching asst., 1951-53; asst. to prof. French Mexico City Coll., U. Ams., 1951; instr., asst. prof. Romance langs. Wesleyan U., Middletown, Conn., 1953-59; assoc. prof. Elmira Coll., 1959-60; Andrew Mellon postdoctoral fellow U. Pitts., 1960-61, spl. lectr., 1963-64, NDEA Insts. fellow, 1962, 63; assoc. prof. Chatham Coll., 1961-64, Loyola U., Chgo., 1964-66; prof. Ohio Wesleyan U., Delaware, 1966-84; chmn. dept. Romance langs. Ohio Wesleyan U., Delaware, 1966-80, Robert Hayward prof. modern fgn. langs., 1976-84, dir. Internat. Inst. of Spain, 1984-87, prof. emeritus. Pres. Vitalicio, Fundacion Juan Ruiz, Segovia, Spain, 1971-86, Horizons for Learning, Delaware, Ohio, 1974—, Cursos Americanos e Internacionales, Segovia, 1986-1998; acct. Columbus Coated Fabrics Corp., Columbus, 1941-42; auditor European Post Exchange System, Bad Nauheim, Germany, 1948; co-owner John Anthony Studios, Columbus, 1954-64; v.p., dir. Von Mock Assocs., N.Y.C., 1969-70; spl. lectr. U. Catolica de Santa Maria, Arequipa, Peru, 1969; dir. Acad. Program in Segovia, 1969-1998. Author: Gertrudis Gomez de Avellaneda, 1981, Tangier and All That, 1993, reissue, 1997, D'Utah Beach aux Ardennes: Itiéraires 1944-1994, 1996, Return to Patton's France 1944's Odyssey Retraced, 1999, The Countess, 2004, Juan Ramon Jiminez's Diary of a Newlywed Past, 2004; co-author (with J. D. Mitchell): Staging a Spanish Classic: El hospital de los locos, 1990; translator, author The Scavenger, 1962, Femmes/Hommes, 1977, The Butts (Driss Chraïbi), 1983, Mother Comes of Age (Driss Chraïbi), 1983, Mother Spring (Driss Chraïbi), 1989, Past Tense (Driss Chraïbi), 1990, The Distant Friend (Claude Roy), 1990, Shadow of Paradise: Vicente Aleixandre, 1987, Remembrance of a Time Just Past, 1993, Shattered Vision (Rabah Belamri), 1994, translator, editor A History of Spanish Literature, 1971; co-editor (with Willis Barnstone): Riconocete y Cortadillo, 1960; co-editor: (with R.C. Allen, Jr.) A First Spanish Handbook for Teachers in Elementary Schools, 1961; co-editor: A Second Spanish Handbook for Teachers in Elementary Schools, 1963; lyricist More About the Pear Tree, The Death of the Soldier Guard, 1976; translator: Diary of a Newlywed Poet, 2004. Bd. dirs. Centro Segovia, 1971-80; v.p. Delaware (Ohio) Heritage Inc., 1973-75, bd. dirs., 1975-78, pres., 1978-80; pres. Delaware Shakespeare Soc., 1980-81. Served with M.I. 3d Army, Normandy, No. France, then Air Transport Command, U.S. Army, ETO. Recipient medals of St. Calais, Vendome, Blois, Dombasle, Utah Beach, Avranches, Blois, St. Calais, Ouzouer, 1994, medaille d'Honneur of Confedn. Europeene des Anciens Combattants, 1992, 93; named Hon. Citizen City of Segovia, 1976; summer rsch. grantee Andrew Mellon Found., Morocco, 1973; spl. grantee Govt. of Morocco, 1975; spl. langs. grantee Mellon Mediterranean Studies, Algeria and Tunisia, 1977. Mem.: AAUP, MLA, ASCAP, Am. Assn. Tchrs. Spanish and Portuguese, Authors' Guild, Coll. Lang. Assn., La Academia de San Quirce (Segovia corr.). Home: 135 Bow St #8 Portsmouth NH 03801 Office Phone: 603-373-8000. Personal E-mail: hharter@comcast.net.

HARTER, JAMES LESTER, academic administrator, consultant; b. Lima, Ohio, Feb. 2, 1959; s. Lester Rudolph and Patricia Lou (Pryer) Harter; m. Cynthia Ann Whitaker, Dec. 18, 1981; children: Joshua James, Jennifer Leigh, Jonah Reed. BS in Edn., Bowling Green (Ohio) State U., 1981, MA in Coll. Student Pers., 1982. Head resident Bluffton (Ohio) Coll., 1981—82; hall dir., complex coord. Bowling Green (Ohio) State U., 1982—84; dir. student life SUNY, Purchase, NY, 1984—85; dir. residence life Franklin (Ind.) Coll., 1985—89; v.p. student affairs, dean students Defiance (Ohio) Coll., 1989—94; tchr. Paulding (Ohio) H.S., 1994—95; dean student affairs Mercy Coll. N.W. Ohio, Toledo, 1995—2004, v.p. adminstrv. svcs., 2004—. Cons. Partners in Planning, Grand Rapids, Ohio, 1996—2002. Mem. adv. com. Toledo (Ohio) Housing Ct., 2004—05; pres. bd. edn. Otsego Local Schs., Tontogany, Ohio, 1999—2005; bd. dirs. Nieghborhoods in Partnership, Toledo, 2004—05, UpTown Assn., Toledo, 2002—05; chmn. devel. com. Habitat for Humanity Wood County, Bowling Green, 2005. Mem.: Am. Coll. Pers. Assn. (assoc.), Mercy Children's Hosp. Kiwanis (assoc.; pres. 2003—05). Republican. Avocations: travel, walking, reading. Home: 17090 Wapakoneta Road Grand Rapids OH 43522 Office: Mercy College of Northwest Ohio 2221 Madison Avenue Toledo OH 43624-1132 Office Phone: 419-251-1786. Office Fax: 419-251-1570. E-mail: james.harter@mercycollege.edu.

HARTER, JOHN J., economic analyst; b. Canyon, Tex., Jan. 31, 1926; s. Ralph E. and Grace S. Harter; m. Irene T. Harter, May 25, 1957 (dec. Feb. 2002); children: Tian, Tonia, Lal; m. Evelyn Bland Harter, Sept. 19, 2004. BA, U. So. Calif., 1948, MA, 1953; M of Econs., Harvard U., 1963. Lectr. in history U. So. Calif., L.A., 1948-53; fgn. svc. officer, various fgn. assignments Geneva, South Africa, Chile, Thailand, Dept. of State, Washington, 1954-83; oral historian Washington, 1983—2005; conf. affairs officer Am. Fgn. Svc. Assn., Washington, 1989-96; freelance writer, cons. Washington, 1983—; declassifier Agy. for Internat. Devel., Washington, 1998—. Author: The Language of Trade, 1984. Sec., mem. vestry Am. Ch., Geneva, 1969-70. Mem. Diplomatic and Consular Officers Ret., Am. Fgn. Svc. Assn. Democrat. Episcopalian. Home: 12109 Kershaw Pl Glen Allen VA 23059-6978 Office Phone: 202-712-0286. E-mail: jjitharter@aol.com.

HARTER, LAFAYETTE GEORGE, JR., retired economics professor; b. Des Moines, May 28, 1918; s. Lafayette George and Helen Elizabeth (Ives) H.; m. Charlotte Mary Toshach, Aug. 23, 1950; children— Lafayette George III, James Toshach, Charlotte Helen. BA in Bus. Adminstrn, Antioch Coll., 1941; MA in Econs, Stanford, 1948, PhD, 1960. Instr. Menlo Coll., Menlo Park, Calif., 1948-50; instr. Coll. of Marin, Kentfield, Calif., 1950-60; prof. econs. dept. Oreg. State U., 1960-85, prof. emeritus, 1985—, chmn. dept., 1967-71. Mem. panel arbitrators Fed. Mediation and Conciliation Svc., 1965-84, Oreg. Conciliation Svc., 1967-84; mem. Univ. Ctrs. for Rational Alternatives. Author: John R. Commons: His Assault on Laissez-faire, 1962, Labor in America, 1957, Economic Responses to a Changing World, 1972; editorial bd. Jour. Econ. Issues, 1981-84. Assoc. campaign chmn. Benton United Good Neighbor Fund, 1970-72, campaign chmn., v.p., 1972-73, pres., 1973-74, vice chmn.; pub. mem. Adv. Commn. on Unemployment Compensation, 1972, 73, chmn., 1974-78; Bd. dirs. Oreg. Coun. Econ. Edn., 1971-89; pub. mem. local profl. responsibilities Oreg. State Bar Assn., 1980-83; pub. mem. Oreg. Coun. on Ct. Procedures, 1985-93, bd. mem. Community Econs. of Corp., Community Econ. Stabilization Corp. Lt. comdr. USNR, 1941-46. Mem. AAUP, Am. Arbitration Assn. (pub. employment disputes panel 1970-92), Am. Western Econ. Assns., Indsl. Rels. Rsch. Assn., Am. Assn. for Evolutionary Econs., Oreg. State Employees Assn. (v.p. faculty chpt. 1972, pres. 1973), Am. Assn. Ret. Persons (pres. local chpt. 1992-93), Corvallis Retirement Village (fin. com., bd. dirs.). Democrat. Mem. United Ch. of Christ (moderator 1972, 73; mem. fin. com. Oreg. conf. 1974-82, dir. 1978-81, mem. personnel com. 1983-85). Home: 4700 SW Hollyhock Cir Apt 233 Corvallis OR 97333-1486

HARTER, PHILIP J., lawyer, educator; b. Columbus, Ohio, Apr. 14, 1942; s. Joseph M and Edith R. Harter; m. Nancy B. Gammel, Aug. 22, 1964; 1 child, Alexa. AB, Kenyon Coll., 1960—64; MA in Math., U. Mich., Ann Arbor, 1965—66, JD, 1966—69. Bar: D.C. 1971, Supreme Ct. U.S. 1979. Vis. prof. of law Vt. Law Sch., South Royalton, Vt., 1999—2003; dir. program on democracy and governance; mediator The Mediation Inst., Washington, 1998—2003; Earl F. Nelson prof. law U. Mo., Columbia, 2003—. Author: Negotiating Regulations: A Cure for Malaise, 1981. Recipient Gellhorn award, Federal Bar Assn., 1998, award for Outstanding

Contribution to the Pub. Policy of fostering the use of ADR, Soc. of Profls. in Dispute Resolution, 1992, award for Outstanding Achievement for Excellence and Innovation in Alternative Dispute Resolution, Ctr. for Pub. Resources, 1992. Mem.: ABA (chmn. sect. adminstrv. law and regulatory practice 1995—96, chmn. working group on regulatory reform 1995—98). Avocation: bicycling. Address: 201 S Glenwood Ave Columbia MO 65211 Office: U Missouri Hulston Hall Columbia MO 65211 Office Phone: 573-884-3614. Business E-Mail: harterpj@missouri.edu.

HARTER, RALPH MILLARD PETER, lawyer, educator; b. Auburn, N.Y., Mar. 15, 1946; s. Donald Robert and Ruth (Ashdown) H.; m. Robin Ann Bampton, June 29, 1968 (div. Oct. 1994); m. Leslie J. Teague, Sept. 13, 1997; children: Robin Brooke, Donald Bampton. BA, Hobart Coll., 1968; JD, Cornell U., 1972; postgrad., Colgate Rochester Divinity Sch., 2001—, Bexley Hall Episcopal Sem. Bar: Pa. 1972, U.S. Dist. Ct. (ea. dist.) Pa. 1972, N.Y. 1981, U.S. Dist. Ct. (we. dist.) N.Y. 1981. Assoc. Duane, Morris & Heckscher, Phila., 1972-81, Harter, Secrest & Emery, Rochester, N.Y., 1981-83; ptnr. Goldstein, Goldman, Kessler & Underberg, Rochester, 1983-91, Sutton, DeLeeuw, Clark & Darcy, Rochester, 1991-94; mng. ptnr. Burke, Albright, Harter & Reddy, LLP, Rochester, 1994—2003. Educator elder law issues, right to die, ethics, trusts and estates issues. V.p., gen. counsel, bd. dirs. Otetiana council Inc., Boy Scouts Am., Rochester, 1982-2000; mem. various coms. Episcopal Diocese and Ch., Phila. and Rochester, 1972—; chair bd. dirs. Episcopal Sr. Life Cmtys., 1997-99, bd. dirs., 1995—; trustee Colls. of Seneca (Hobart & William Smith Colls.), 1987-96; bd. dirs. Allendale Columbia Sch., 1991-96; trustee Sigma Phi Ednl. Found., N.Y.C., 1990—; pres., gen. coun., bd. dirs. Rochester chpt. Alzheimer's Assn., 1981-2003. Served with USAR, 1969-75. Mem. ABA, N.Y. State Bar Assn. (various sects., lectr.), Pa. Bar Assn., Phila. Bar Assn., Monroe County Bar Assn., Nat. Acad. Elder Law Attys., Rochester Area C. of C. (United Way coms. 1984-96), Alzheimer's Disease and Related Disorders Assn. Inc. (pres., gen. counsel, bd. dirs. 1981—), Assn. of Adirondack Scout Camps (bd. dirs. 1986-93), Cornell U. Law Sch. Assn., Hobart Coll. Alumni Assn. and Alumni Council (pres. 1984-86), Hobart Coll. Statesmen Athletic Assn. (gen. counsel, bd. dirs. 1983-2003), Hobart Coll. Club of Rochester (pres. 1984-86), The Genesse Valley Club (Rochester), Webhannet Golf Club (Kennebunkport, Maine), Delta chpt. Sigma Phi. Republican. Avocations: flyfishing, duck decoy carving, white water rafting, canoeing, golf. Home: Tuckaway Farm 98 Canfield Rd Pittsford NY 14534-9709 Office: 1800 Hudson Ave Rochester NY 14617-5128 E-mail: harter@rochesterlawyer.com.

HARTFORD, MAUREEN A., academic administrator; m. Jay Hartford. BA in French and History, MA in coll. tchg., U. N.C., Chapel Hill; EdD in higher edn. adminstrn., U. Ark. Dean of student affairs Case Western Res. U., Cleve., 1982—86; vice provost student affairs Wash. State U., 1986—92; v.p. student affairs U. Mich., Ann Arbor, 1992—99; pres. Meredith Coll., Raleigh, NC, 1999—. Faculty Ctr. Study of Higher and Post-Secondary Edn., Ann Arbor, Mich., 1992—99. Mem. governing bd. LeaderShape; bd. trustees Wake Edn. Partnership; bd. dir. Greater Raleigh C. of C., N.C. Triangle United Way; bd. of governors Capital City Club. Recipient Women in Bus., Bus. Jour., 2002, Dist. Scholar award, N.C. Coll. Pers. Assn., 2002. Office: Meredith Coll 3800 Hillsborough St Raleigh NC 27607

HARTH, SIDNEY, musician, educator; b. Cleve., Oct. 5, 1929; s. Leonard and Anne (Dunnire) H.; m. Teresa Testa, July 7, 1949; children: Laura, Robert. Mus.B., Cleve. Inst. Music, 1947; studied with, Joseph Knitzer, Mishel Piastro, Georges Enesco. Assoc. prof. U. Louisville, 1953-58; faculty DePaul U., 1959-62; chmn. dept. music, A.W. Mellon disting. prof. Carnegie-Mellon U., Pitts., 1963-73; mem. faculty Aspen (Colo.) Music Festival, 1963-74; exchange artist Les Jeunesses Musicales de France, 1952; with Mrs. Harth nat. tour, 1952; concertmaster Louisville Orch., 1953-58, Chgo. Symphony, 1959-62; condr. Evanston (Ill.) Orch., 1960-62; assoc. condr., concertmaster Los Angeles Philharm., 1973-79; chief guest condr. Jerusalem Symphony, 1975-77; music dir. Puerto Rican Symphony, 1977-79; condr. Can. Nat. Chamber Orch., 1979, 80; concertmaster N.Y. Philharm., 1980-81; orch. dir. Mannes Coll. of Music, 1981-84; prof. SUNY, Stony Brook, 1981-82, Yale U., 1982-99; prin. condr. Natal Symphony Orch., Durban, South Africa, 1994-99. Dir. orchestral activities Hartt Sch. Music, U. Hartford, 1991-93; violin Wieniawski competition laureate, Poland, 1957; orch. dir., vis. prof. U. Houston, 1985; dir. orchestral studies Carnegie-Mellon U., Pitts., 1989-90; faculty, Carnegie-Mellon U., 2000—, dir. Orchestral Sch. Music and condr. orch., Duquesne U., Pitts., 2001—. Extern. internat. tours including Yugoslavia, Poland, Belgium, Austria, Eng., USSR, Poland, Czechoslovakia, Romania, Switzerland, Holland., Vanguard, Iramac, Concert Hall Soc., Stradivari Records; contbr. articles to nat. mags. Recipient Ysaye medal; Wieniawski medal. Home: 135 Westland Dr Pittsburgh PA 15217-2538 Office Phone: 412-396-6079.

HARTH-BEDOYA, MIGUEL, conductor; b. Lima, Peru, 1968; Degree, Curtis Inst. Music, Juilliard Sch. Music dir. Eugene (Oreg.) Symphony Orch.; now music dir. Ft. Worth Symphony Orch.; assoc. dir. L.A. Philharmonic Orch. Music dir., condr. N.Y. Youth Symphony Carnegie Hall; guest condr. N.Y. Philharm., L.A. Philharm., Fla. Orch., Seattle Symphony, Colo. Symphony, Que. Symphony, Auckland Philharm., New Zealand, Puerto Rico Symphony, Buenos Aires Philharmonia, Evansville Philharm. Orch., Ind.; condr. Juilliard Orch. tour, France, 1993, Japan, 95, St. Luke's Orch., 1995; founder, artistic dir. New Opera Co. Peru, Orquestra Filarmonica de Lima; mem. conducting faculty Juilliard Sch. Office: Fort Worth Symphony Orch 330 E 4th St Ste 200 Fort Worth TX 76102-4019

HARTIGAN, JOHN FRANCIS, lawyer; b. Abington, Pa., June 16, 1950; s. James Joseph and Ann Patricia (O'Neill) H.; m. Laurie Kirkwood, Sept. 6, 1980; children: Erin, Caitlin, Tess. BS in Fin., U. Ill., 1972; JD, Georgetown U., 1975. Bar: D.C. 1975, Calif. 1984. Atty. Div. of Enforcement, SEC, Washington, 1975-78, br. chief, 1978-81, asst. dir., 1981-84; sr. ptnr. Morgan, Lewis & Bockius LLP, L.A., 1984—, mng. ptnr.-LA Office. Case and notes editor The Tax Lawyer, 1974-75, mem. exec. bd. editors, 1975. Mem. State Bar Calif. (chmn. edn. com. bus. law sect. 1989-90, treas. exec. com. bus. law sect. 1992, vice chmn. exec. com. bus. law sect. 1993), Los Angeles County Bar Assn. (mem. exec. com.), Fin. Instns. Ins. Assn. (bd. dirs., gen. counsel), Jonathan Club, L.A. Country Club. Avocation: golf. Office: Morgan Lewis & Bockius LLP 300 S Grand Ave Ste 2200 Los Angeles CA 90071-3132 Office Phone: 213-612-2630. Office Fax: 213-612-2554. Business E-Mail: jhartigan@morganlewis.com.

HARTIGAN, KARELISA VOELKER, classics educator; b. Stillwater, Okla., Mar. 5, 1943; d. Charles Henry and Elsie Florence Voelker; m. Barry Hartigan, Apr. 21, 1966 (div. Feb. 1978); 1 child, Timothy Lawrence; m. Kevin Michael McCarthy, Dec. 22, 1992. BA in Classics, Coll. of Wooster, 1965; AM in Classics, U. Chgo., 1966, PhD in Classics, 1970. Asst. prof. St. Olaf Coll., Northfield, Minn., 1969-73; asst. prof., assoc. prof. Greek studies U. Fla., Gainesville, from 1973, prof., 1991—, co-dir. Ctr. for Greek Studies, 1980—, assoc. dir. honors program, 1989-95. Author: The Poets and the Cities, 1979, Ambiguity and Self-Deception, 1991, Greek Tragedy on the American Stage, 1995, Myths Behind Our Words, 1998, Muse on Madison Avenue, 2001; editor Text and Presentation jour., 1983-94; editor spl. issues Classical and Modern Lit.; Classical Reflections, 1980. Recipient Excellence in Tchg. award Am. Philol. Assn., 1985; Disting. Alumni Prof. award U. Fla., 1987-89, Univ.-Wide Tchg. award, 1990, Tchg. award, 1994, Disting. Prof. award, 2001. Mem. Modern Greek Studies Assn. (sec. 1983-1986), Classical Assn. Mid. West and South (pres. so. sect. 1986-88, nat. pres. 1992-93). Avocations: bicycling, swimming, travel, cooking, dogs. Office: University of Florida Ctr Greek Studies PO Box 117435 Gainesville FL 32611-7435 E-mail: kvhrtgn@classics.ufl.edu.

HARTLAND, JAMES ROBERT, retired minister; b. Johnstown, Pa., June 21, 1920; s. Walter Daniel Hartland and Alice Maude Wilson; m. Helen Jane Croft, Sept. 7, 1947 (dec. 1997). AB, Mt. Union Coll., 1947; MST, Boston U. Sch. Theology, 1950; MEd, U. Pitts., 1958. Ordained to ministry Meth. Ch., 1950. Student pastor Meth. Ch., Winona, Ohio, 1945—47, Aqawm, Mass., 1947—50; pastor Irwin, Pa., 1950—52, Concord Ch., Beaver Falls, Pa., 1952—54, Whitaker Cmty. Ch., Pa., 1954—57, 1st Meth. Ch., Rochester, Pa., 1957—58; min. of edn. Lakewood Meth. Ch., Ohio, 1958—61; pastor 1st Sylvania Meth. Ch., Ohio, 1961—66, 1st Sidney Meth. Ch., Ohio, 1966—70, Christ Columbus Ch., Ohio, 1970—75, United Meth. Ch., Tipp City, Ohio, 1975—82, First Urbana United Meth. Ch., Ohio, 1982—86; ret., 1986. Contbr. articles to profl. jours. Mem. Rotary Internat., Sidney, Ohio, 1966—86; aux. Sch. Bd., Sidney, Ohio; chair bd. edn. West Ohio Conf., 1970—80; chaplain Civil Air Patrol, 1972—; mem. Libr. Bd., Sylvania, Ohio. Mem.: Ret. Pastors West Ohio Conf., Psi Kappa Omega, Pi Gamma Nu. Avocations: travel, workshop leader. Home: 61 Brookhill Woods Ln Tipp City OH 45371

HARTLAND, SARAH C., music educator; b. Abington, Pa., Nov. 9, 1980; d. John W and Deborah J Bowen; m. Nathanael D. Hartland, June 8, 2002. MusB, BS, Phila. (Pa.) Biblical U., 2002. Mgr. and cellist Madison String Quartet, Warminster, Pa., 1996—2001, pvt. music tchr., 1996—2004; instrumental music tchr. Phil-Mont Christian Acad., Erdenheim, Pa., 2002—04, pvt. music tchr. Towson, Md., 2004—; freelance musician Towson, Md., 2004—. Faculty/dir. sponsor MENC/PMEA, Erdenheim, Pa., 2003—04. Composer: (songs) The King Adored, 2002. Mem.: Alpha Chi Epsilon. Avocation: cooking.

HARTLE, ROBERT WYMAN, retired literature and language professor; b. Kongmoon, China, Sept. 1, 1921; s. Jacob Everett and Margaret (Wyman) H.; m. Ann Dorothy Mordhorst, Jan. 5, 1980; 1 son, Robert Wyman, Jr.; children by previous marriage: Shirley Ann (Mrs. Jan McDaniel), John Wyman. BA, MA, U. Tex., 1947; AM, Princeton U., 1949, PhD, 1951. Instr. French Princeton U., 1950-53, asst. prof., 1953-60; assoc. prof. modern langs. U. Oreg., 1961-63; asst. prof. Romance langs. Queens Coll. (now CUNY-Queens Coll.), N.Y.C., 1960-61, prof., chmn. dept. Romance and Slavic langs., 1963-65, assoc. dean faculty, 1964-65, dean faculty, 1965-70, prof., 1972-87, prof. emeritus, 1987—, chmn. ad hoc legal affairs com., mem. univ. acad. senate, 1979-81, dir. PhD program in France, 1970-72, mem. senate. Founder, dir. programs of study abroad, 1963-70; vis. prof. Inst. Liberal Arts, Emory U., 1985-93. Author: Index du vocabulaire du théâtre classique: Racine, 8 vols, 1956-64; transl. Tartuffe (Molière), 1963; contbr. articles on the iconography of Alexander the Great, 17th century French art and architecture, Hellenistic Art, 1955—; French translator Papers of Robert Morris, 1973-84; French cons. Papers of Thomas Jefferson, Princeton U. Press, 1986—. Bd. dirs. Am. Ctr. for Students and Artists, Paris, 1970-78. Decorated officer Ordre des Palmes Académiques (France), knight Order of Merit (Italy), officer's cross Order of Merit (Germany). Mem. MLA, AAUP (pres. chpt. 1975-80) Home: 1803 Westminster Way NE Atlanta GA 30307-1134 E-mail: rwhartle@comcast.net.

HARTLEY, CELIA LOVE, nursing consultant, writer, retired nursing educator, nursing administrator; b. Colfax, Wash., Oct. 25, 1935; d. Thomas Warren and Ella Marie (Kerkman) Love; m. Lawrence Dosser (div.); children: Laurie Denise Draper, Byron Garth Dosser; m. Gordon E. Hartley, Dec. 17, 1972. Diploma, Deaconess Hosp. Sch. Nursing, Spokane, 1956; BSN, U. Wash., 1965, MSN, 1968. RN, Wash., Calif. Staff nurse Deaconess Hosp., Spokane, 1956-62; charge nurse Northgate Gen. Hosp., Seattle, 1963-65; hosp. supr. Stevens Meml. Hosp., Edmonds, Wash., 1965-66; prof. nursing Shoreline C.C., Seattle, 1967-73, dir. nursing edn., asst. div. chmn. health occupations, 1973-92; chair health sci. divsn. Coll. of the Desert, Palm Desert, Calif., 1992-99, prof. emerita, 1999—; nursing curriculum cons. Pres. Coun. on Nursing Edn. in Wash. State, 1992; adv. com. Antioch West and Seattle U., 1979-81, Nursing Edn. Com. Higher Edn. Coordinating Bd., 1990, Western Wash. U. Nursing, 1984, Seattle Pacific U. Nursing, 1992; other coms. various orgns., 1979—; presenter in field. Author: (with Janice Ellis) Nursing in Today's World; Challenges, Issues, and Trends, 1980, 8th rev. edit., 2004, Managing and Coordinating Patient Care, 1991, 4th edit., 2005, Fundamentals of Nursing, 1992; mem. editl. bd. Assoc. Degree Nurse, 1987-91, Jour. Nursing Edn., 1991—; contbr. articles to profl. jours. Mem. Nat. League of Nursing (bd. dirs. 1981-84, appeal panel Coun. AD Programs 1988-91, 95-98, chmn.-vice chmn. various coms.), Wash. Constituent League (v.p. 1986-87, chmn. nominating com. 1984-85, chmn. membership com. 1985-86), Sigma Theta Tau. Methodist. Home: 3234 Mabana Rd Camano Island WA 98282 Office Phone: 360-387-0822. Personal E-mail: cegohart@aol.com.

HARTLEY, DUNCAN, fundraising executive; b. Sept. 27, 1941; s. Harold Shephard and Catherine Carmichael (Hursley) H.; m. Adrienne Ashley, Aug. 19, 1971. BA, U. Mich., 1964; MA, Wayne State U., Detroit, 1966, PhD. Instr. English dept. Wayne State U., 1969-71; asst. prof. William Paterson Coll., 1971-74; adminstr. ednl. resources, chpt. liaison Young Pres.'s Orgn., N.Y.C., 1974-78; dir. planned giving Carroll Coll., Waukesha, Wis., 1978-80; dir. capital gifts Greater N.Y. Coun. Boy Scouts Am., N.Y.C., 1980-84; dir. individual giving, exec. dir. pres.'s coun. Meml. Sloan-Kettering Cancer Ctr., N.Y.C., 1984-96; assoc. dean of devel. and alumni affairs Sch. Medicine Case Western Res. U., Cleve., 1996—. Co-editor, author: The Sociology of the Arts, 1974. Mem. Princeton Club of N.Y., Audiophile Soc. Presbyterian. Avocation: audio equipment reviewing. Office: Case Western Res U Sch Medicine 10900 Euclid Ave Cleveland OH 44106-1712 Home: 212 Via Emilia Palm Beach Gardens FL 33418-1724

HARTLEY, HAL, film director; b. Islip, N.Y., Nov. 3, 1959; BA with honors in Film, SUNY, Purchase, 1984. Writer, dir.: (feature films) The Unbelievable Truth, 1990, Trust, 1991, Simple Men, 1992, Amateur, 1994, Flirt, 1995 (short films) Dogs, The Cartographer's Girlfriend, (TV films) Surviving Desire, 1989, Theory of Achievement, 1991, Ambition, 1991, Henry Fool, 1997, The Book of Life, 1998, Monster, 2000, Kimono, 2000. Office: Possible Films Inc 302A W 12th St 334 New York NY 10014-1947

HARTLEY, HELEN ROSANNA, business educator; b. Hannibal, Mo., May 6, 1947; d. Roger Chase and Rose Evelyn (Peterson) Higgins; m. William Clarence Hartley, Aug. 17, 1969; children: Nathan William, Andrew Chase. BS in Edn., Ctrl. Mo. State U., 1969; MA, Appalachian State U., 1988. Cert. tchr., N.C., Mo. Instr. Spanish, Ctrl. H.S., Argyle, Iowa, 1969-70; tchr. modern langs. Burke County Pub. Schs., Morganton, N.C., 1974-81; instr. ednl. computing Appalachian State U., Boone, N.C., 1988-91; instr. info. sys./internet techs. Western Piedmont C.C., Morganton, 1990—, chmn. faculty and staff coun., 1998-99, Sterling R. Collett endowed tchg. chair, 2000. Mem. N.C. Virtual Learning Cmty., 1999-2001; mem. tech. adv. com. Burke County, N.C., 1991-93, mem. chpt. II adv. com., 1992-94; sponsor computer club Salem Elem. Sch., Burke County, 1989-91; mem. Info. Tech. Task Force, 1995—, N.C. Curriculum Improvement Project, 1994-96. Contbr. articles to profl. jours. Mem., NC Tech. Prep. Articulation Com., 2003-2004; mem. past officer Morgan Jr. Woman's Club, 1975-86; advisor Explorer Scout Post, Morganton, 1990-93. Mem. State Employees Assn. N.C., Computer Instrs. Assn. (treas. 1998-2002). Avocations: hiking, sewing, painting, reading. Office: Western Piedmont CC 1001 Burkemont Ave Morganton NC 28655-4504 E-mail: rhartley@wpcc.edu.

HARTLEY, JAMES EDWARD, lawyer; b. Orange, N.J., Nov. 4, 1949; s. George and Carolyn (Stewart) H.; m. Judy Franklin, Mar. 1, 1986; 1 child, Jonathan. BA, U. Calif., Berkeley, 1971, JD, 1974. Bar: Colo. 1974, U.S. Dist. Ct. Colo. 1974, U.S. Ct. Appeals (10th cir.) 1975, U.S. Supreme Ct. 1981, U.S. Ct. Appeals (Fed. cir.) 1993. Assoc. Holland & Hart, Denver, 1974-80, ptnr., 1980—. Adj. prof. Denver U. Law Sch., 1985-86. Co-author: Private Litigation Under Section 7 of the Clayton Act: Law and Policy, 1989, Antitrust Pitfalls in Outpatient Services, 1992, Rule of Reason Monograph, 1999, State Antitrust Practice and Procedure, 1999; asst. editor: ABA Antitrust Law Jour., 1994-98. Mem. ABA (coun. antitrust law sect. 2003—), Colo. Bar Assn., Denver Bar Assn., Order of Coif, Phi Beta Kappa (named one of Best Lawyers in Am. 2004). Home: 2540 Briarwood Dr Boulder CO 80305-6804 Office: Holland & Hart LLP 555 17th St Ste 3200 Denver CO 80202-3950

HARTLEY, JAMES R., musician, writer; b. Wash., Dec. 23, 1948; s. James Aaron Hartley and Ruth Virginia Pope; m. Carol Ann Creed, Apr. 14, 1994 (div. Dec. 18, 2001). AA TV, Radio, Montgomery Coll., 1981. Tech. asst. Montgomery County Pub. Schs., Rockville, Md., 1968—84; musician self-employed, Md., 1980—, 1980—. Newsletter editor / pub. Wash. Baseball Hist. Soc., Germantown, Md., 2001—. Author (pub.): Washington's Expansion Senators (1961-1971), 1998. Recipient award, Phi Theta Kappa, 1981. Mem.: Soc. Am. Baseball Rsch., Washington Baseball Hist. Soc. (newsletter editor, pub. 2001—). Democrat. Christian. Achievements include authored and published the first extensive history of the Washington senators expansion baseball team from 1961-71. Avocations: baseball history, golf. Office: Corduroy Press PO Box 2248 Germantown MD 20875 E-mail: natnative7@aol.com.

HARTLEY, MICHAEL J., online travel executive; CEO Cheap Tickets, Inc., Honolulu, 1986—. Recipient Hawaii Ernst & Young Entrepreneur of Yr. award, 2000. Office: Cheap Tickets Inc Po Box 291987 Nashville TN 37229-1987

HARTLEY, PHILIP. L., academic administrator, psychologist, educator; b. Eureka, Calif., Apr. 13, 1946; s. Duane D. and Katherine M. Hartley; m. Donna R. Hartley, Aug. 1, 1970; 1 child, Stephanie. BA, Humboldt State U., 1969; MA, U. Calif., Riverside, 1971, PhD, 1976. Psychology lectr. Calif. State U., San Bernardino, 1985-90; prof. psychology Chaffey Coll., Alta Loma, Calif., 1973-83, divsn. chair, 1983-92; dean instrn. Mendocino Coll., Ukiah, Calif., 1992-98; v.p. Coll. of the Canyons, Santa Clarita, Calif., 1998—2004; pres. West Valley Coll., Saratoga, 2004—. Contbr. articles to profl. jours. Mem. Rotary. Avocations: scuba diving, photography, wine growing and making. E-mail: fillhart@comcst.net.

HARTLYN, JONATHAN, political scientist, educator; BA magna cum laude, Clark U., 1974; MPhil, Yale U., 1976, PhD, 1981. Asst. prof. Vanderbilt U., Nashville, 1981-87, assoc. prof., 1987-88, U. N.C., Chapel Hill, 1988-97, prof., 1997—, chair dept. polit. sci., 2000—, dir. Inst. Latin Am. Studies, 1997—2000. Author: The Politics of Coalition Rule in Colombia, 1988, The Struggle for Democratic Politics in the Dominican Republic, 1998; co-author: Latin America in the Twenty-First Century,2003; co-editor: Latin American Political Economy, 1986, The United States and Latin America in the 1990s, 1992, Democracy in Developing Countries: Latin America, 2d edit., 1999; contbr. articles to profl. jours. Tinker Found. fellow, 1985-86. Mem. Am. Polit. Sci. Assn., Latin Am. Studies Assn., Phi Beta Kappa. Office: U NC Dept Polit Sci Cb 3265 Hamilton Hl Chapel Hill NC 27599-3265 Office Phone: 919-962-3041. E-mail: hartlyn@unc.edu.

HARTMAN, BRUCE, writer; b. Passaic, N.J., Dec. 7, 1948; s. Paul and Billye Hartman; m. Martha G. Hartman; children: Fred, Tom, Jack. BA, Wesleyan U., 1969. Author: (novels) The Great Leap Forward, 1980, The Unexamined Life, 1986, (screenplays) Judgment, 1993, Accidents Waiting to Happen, 1996; composer: (songs) In My Next Lifetime, Fifteen Minutes of Fame, In a Perfect World, Ask a Country Girl.

HARTMAN, BRUCE L., apparel executive; BA, Suffolk U., 1975. CFO Robinson'd May Dept. Stores, 1990—93, CFO Famous Barr, 1993—94, CFO Filene's Basement, 1994—96; from v.p., controller to CFO Foot Locker, Inc., N.Y., 1996—99, CFO, 1999—, sr. v.p., 1999—2002, exec. v.p., 2002—. Office: Foot Locker Inc 112 West 34th St New York NY 10120

HARTMAN, CARL (HOWARD CARL HARTMAN), reporter; b. Morris Twp., N.J., Jan. 9, 1917; s. Dennis and Ruth (Shavelson) H.; m. Josephine M. Troxell, Aug. 25, 1942; 1 dau., Jessica A. Student, George Washington U., 1932-33; AB, Princeton, 1936; MS in Journalism, Columbia, 1942. Engaged in gold mining, Calif., 1936-37; translator, publicity, copy boy, reporter various newspapers, 1937-40; fgn. editor Puerto Rico World-Jour., San Juan, P.R., 1940-41; reporter, rewrite man N.Y.C. News Assn., 1941; Washington corr. Jewish Telegraphic Agy., also Overseas News Agy., 1942-44; city editor Puerto Rico World-Jour., 1944; various assignments internationally AP, 1944-57, corr. Budapest, Hungary, 1957-59, staff mem. Frankfurt, 1959, corr. Berlin, 1959-63, Bonn and European Econ. Affairs, 1963-67, Common Market and NATO, Brussels, 1967-78; European editor N.Y.C., 1978; reporter internat. econ. affairs AP World Svcs., Washington, 1978-96; arts and humanities, 1997—. Alternate Pulitzer travelling fellow, 1942 Mem. Berlin Fgn. Press Assn. (pres. 1960-61), Anglo-Am. Press Assn. Paris (dir. 1951, 56), Overseas Writers Club, Nat. Press Club, Phi Beta Kappa. Home: 1066 Thomas Jefferson St NW Washington DC 20007-3832 Office: Associated Press 2021 K St NW Fl 6 Washington DC 20006-1082 E-mail: chartman@ap.org.

HARTMAN, CARMEN TERESA, language educator; b. Velez, Colombia, Sept. 18, 1954; arrived in US, 1986; d. Roque Julio Ortiz and Librada Nieves; m. William N. Hartman, Feb. 15, 1986; 1 child, Sarah P.; 1 child from previous marriage, Daniel Ortiz. BA, U. La Gran Colombia, 1977; cert. in Applied Linguistics, U. Essex, 1979; MA, SUNY, Albany, 1992, PhD with hons., 2000. Asst. to project mgr. GE, Maracaibo, Venezuela, 1978—85; tchr. pub., pvt. high sch., Albany, Schenectady, NY, 1986—92; educator, lectr., tchg. asst. SUNY, Albany, 1993—99; labor svc. rep. Dept. Labor, Albany, 1999—2000; educator Union Coll., Schenectady, 2000, Schenectady C.C., 2001—. Tutor Spanish Shenendehowa Sch. Dist., Clifton Park, NY, 1995—. Author: The Trapping Effect of the Signifier Over Subject and Text, 2003. Mem.: MLA, Soc. Hispanistas (spkr.). Avocations: travel, book collecting, reading. Office: Schenectady Couny Cmty Coll Washington Ave Schenectady NY 12305

HARTMAN, CHARLES HENRY, transportation executive, educator, not-for-profit developer; b. Red Lion, Pa., Feb. 1, 1933; s. Earl Eugene and Jeannette (Kline) Hartman; m. Patricia A. Cooper, Aug. 3, 1956 (div. May 1974); children: Elizabeth Jean, Amy Joan; m. Catherine M. Wheeler, June 7, 1975 (div. Apr. 1994); children: Eric Michael, Jennifer Leigh, David Wheeler, Scott Andrew; m. Andrea S. Anderson, July 8, 2000. BS, Millersville U., 1954; MA, Mich. State U., 1958, EdD, 1962. Tchr. Hollidaysburg Pub. Schs., Pa., 1956-57; assoc. prof. Ill. State U., Normal, 1959-62; vis. lectr. edn. U. Wis., Madison, 1962-63, Milw., 1963-64; dir. edn. Automotive Safety Found./Hwy. Users Fedn., Washington, 1964-70; dep. adminstr. Nat. Hwy. Traffic Safety Adminstrn., U.S. Dept. Transp., Washington, 1970-73; pres. Motorcycle Safety Found., Irvine, Calif., 1973-84; also pres. Touchstone Mgmt. Svcs., Delta, Pa., 1984-88; exec. v.p. AAHPERD, Reston, Va., 1988-90; exec. dir. Am. Coll. Health Assn., Balt., 1990-98; pres. Nonprofit Orgn. Mgmt. and Consultation, 1998—2002; dir. transp. and support svcs. Red Lion Area Sch Dist., Red Lion, Pa., 2003—04; office mgr. Andrea S. Anderson Law Offices, 2004—. Cons. Nat. Assn. Women Hwy. Safety Leaders, Md. State Dept. Edn., 1969—70; dir. Nat. Safety Coun., Chgo., 1976—79; vice chmn. traffic conf., 1976—78; presdl. appointee Nat. Hwy. Safety Adv. Commn., Washington, 1977—80; gov.'s appointee Pa. Task Force Alcohol and Hwy. Safety, 1981—82; vice chmn. Alliance Traffic Safety, 1981—83, chmn., 1983—85; mem. policy com. Hwy. Users Fedn.; lectr. bus. adminstrn. Capitol Campus Pa. State U., Middletown, 1987—88; bd. dirs. Lincoln Intermediate Unit # 12, 1987—89, 1991—93; sr. cons. York Nonprofit Mgmt. Devel. Ctr., 1998—2000; spkr. in field. Sch. dir. Red Lion (Pa.) Area Schs., 1986—2003, pres. sch. bd., 1988, 1996—2003, v.p., 1989—95; mem. York 2000 Commn.; trustee Nat. Motorcycle Fund; pres. Howard County C. of C., Columbia, Md., 1985—87. With U.S. Army, 1954—56. Named to Hall of Fame, Red Lion Area Sch. Dist., 1993; recipient Traffic Safety Educator of the Yr. award, Wis. Traffic Edn. Assn., 1972, Sec.'s award, U.S. Dept. Transp., 1973. Fellow: Am. Acad. Safety Edn.; mem.: NEA, Pa. Sch. Bds. Assn., Assn. Advancement Automotive Medicine, Am. Driver and Traffic Safety Edn. Assn., Pres. Assn./Am. Mgmt. Assn., Soc. Automotive Engrs., Am. Soc. Assn. Execs. (vice-chmn. evaluation com. 1984—85, chmn. 1985—86). Phi Delta Kappa. Republican. Home: 122 E McKinley Rd Delta PA 17314 Office: 901 Delta Rd Red Lion PA 17356-9179 Business E-Mail: charley@asa-law.com.

HARTMAN, DAVID G., actuary; b. Evanston, Ill., July 10, 1942; s. Fred E. and Martha Hartman; m. Katherine A. Holmes; children: Timothy, Andrew. Student, Ripon Coll., 1960-62; BBA, U. Mich., 1964, M in Actuarial Sci., 1965. Various positions Kemper Ins. Co., Chgo., 1966-71; mng. dir., sr. v.p., chief actuary Chubb & Son, Warren, N.J., 1971—. Trustee Overlook Hosp., Summit, NJ, 1993—2002, Overlook Hosp. Found., Summit, 1999—; elder New Providence Presbyn. Ch., NJ, 1973—75, 1986—88. Fellow: Casualty Actuarial Soc. (pres. 1987—88, v.p. 1985—86, cert.), Can. Inst. Actuaries; mem.: ASTIN (chair 2003—), Actuarial Stds. Bd. (bd. dirs. 1996—2001, chmn. 1998—99), Internat. Actuarial Assn. (coun. 1996—), Am. Acad. Actuaries (v.p. 1983—85, pres.-elect 1992—93, pres. 1993—94, cert.). Office: Chubb Group of Ins Cos 15 Mountain View Rd Warren NJ 07059-6795

HARTMAN, DEANNA MEARS, retired family counselor, addiction counselor; b. Norfolk, Va., Aug. 11, 1937; d. James Gordon Jr. and Sarah Talmadge (Johnson) Mears; m. David Luther Brinkley Jr. (div.); children: Kim Brinkley Hebebrand, David III, Jeffrey Lawrence Brinkley; m. Shirish Ramachandra Pandya, June 7, 1978 (dec.). AA, U. Akron, 1980; BA, Va. Wesleyan, 1983; MA, Antioch U., 1994. Cert. cognitive behavioral therapist; nat. cert. counselor. Dir. edn. svcs. Va. Coun. on Alcoholism, Drugs, Norfolk, 1985-87, exec. dir., 1990-93; outpatient program specialist Maryview Psychiat. Hosp., Portsmouth, Va., 1988-89; clin. therapist City of Portsmouth, 1988-89; educator, therapist City of Va. Beach, 1984-86, 93-95; mental health counselor Glasgow High Wellness Ctr., Newark, Del., 1995; family counselor, addiction specialist Williamsburg Pl., Farley Ctr., Williamsburg, Va., 1997—. Founder Survivors of Suicide, Virginia Beach, 1982-86, vol. educator AARP Bear, Del., 1995. Contbr. articles to profl. jours., various presentations. Bd. dirs. Hospice of Virginia Beach, 1983-85, Safe Place, 1988-90, Civitan Internat., 1990-92, comty. adv. coun. for curriculum Coll. of Edn., Old Dominion U., Norfolk, 1991-92. Named Rookie of Yr., Civitan Internat., 1991; recipient Disting. Svc. award Va. Alcohol and Drug Abuse Counselors, 1992. Avocations: reading, writing, walking, birdwatching. Home: 932 Anna St Norfolk VA 23502-3314 E-mail: deannahartman@aol.com.

HARTMAN, EARL KENNETH, writer; b. Chgo., Jan. 31, 1943; s. Ferdinand Frederick and Betty Marie (Sjerslee) H.; m. Linda Lee Griffin, July 10, 1981 (div. June 1988); m. Beatrice Gail Adams, Mar. 11, 1989. BA, Fla. Atlantic U., 1980, B of Edn., 1981. Promotion mgr., spl. issues editor Asheville (N.C.) Citizen-Times, 1966—67; reporter Shelby (N.C.) Daily Star, 1967; copy editor Palm Beach Post-Times, West Palm Beach, Fla., 1968—69; dist. exec. Boy Scouts Am., West Palm Beach, Fla., 1973—76, Albany, Ga., 1983—84; tchr., asst. dir. Unity Sch., Delray Beach, Fla., 1981—83; tchr. Tift County (Ga.) Bd. Edn., 1984—85; sr. reporter Island Reporter, Sanibel Island, Fla., 1985—87; free-lance writer Fort Myers, Fla., 1987—; creator, developer Family Choice Game Series, Wider Etonah, NC, 2000—05; prin., owner Family Choice Game website, 2005—. Mem. Nat. Eagle Scout Assn.

HARTMAN, FREDERICK COOPER, retired biochemist; b. Memphis, Aug. 17, 1939; s. Fred Francis and Raymie Constance (Cooper) H.; m. Patricia Jean Ballard, Sept. 7, 1961; children: Patricia Suzanne, Sheila Katherine. BS in Chemistry, Memphis State U., 1960; MS in Biochemistry, U. Tenn., 1962, PhD in Biochemistry, 1964; postgrad., U. Ill., 1964-66. Sr. rsch. biochemist Oak Ridge (Tenn.) Nat. Lab., 1966—99; group leader protein chemistry Oak Ridge Nat. Lab., 1972-99, sect. head molecular and cellular scis., 1975-88, dir. biology divsn., 1988-97; prof. dept. biochemistry U. Tenn., Knoxville, 1999—2004; ret., 2004. Mem. editl. bd. Jour. Biol. Chemistry, BioSci., Jour. Protein Chemistry; contbr. numerous articles to profl. jours. Grantee Dept. Agr., 1978—. NSF, 1980-87; fellow USPHS, 1962-64, NIH, 1963, 65. Fellow AAAS; mem. Am. Chem. Soc. (Pfizer award 1979, nominating com. 1982), Am. Soc. Biol. Chemists (nominating com. 1979, 81), Am. Soc. Plant Physiologists, Protein Soc., Sigma Xi. Home: 103 Dansworth Ln Oak Ridge TN 37830-8754 Office: Biology Div Oak Ridge Nat Lab Oak Nat Lab Oak Ridge TN 37830

HARTMAN, GARY E., pediatric surgeon; b. Wisconsin, Feb. 10, 1948; MD, U. Wisconsin Med. Sch., 1974. Intern Highland Gen. Hospital, Oakland, 1974—75, surgery resident, 1975—79; pediatric surgery fellow Stanford U. Hospital, Stanford, 1979—81; pediatric surgery resident U. Okla., Oklahoma City, 1981—83; assoc. prof. pediatric surgery Stanford U. Hospital, Stanford, 1983—93; chmn. pediatric surgery Children's Nat. Med. Ctr., Wash., DC, 1993—. Achievements include leading team of surgeons to successfully separate conjoined twins in 2004. Office: Childrens Nat Med Ctr 111 Michigan Ave NW Washington DC 20010

HARTMAN, GEORGE EITEL, architect; b. Ft. Hancock, N.J., May 7, 1936; s. George Eitel and Evelyn (Ritchie) H.; m. Ann Burdick, May 22, 1965 (div. Oct. 2000); children— Sarah, Joshua; m. Jan Cigliano, Jan. 21, 2001. BA, Princeton, 1957, M.F.A., 1960. Registered arch., Md., Washington, Va. Pvt. practice architecture, 1964-65; ptnr. Hartman-Cox Architects, Washington, 1965—; Design critic Cath. U. Am., 1964-69, U. Md.; Kea Disting. prof. architecture N.C. State U., 1973-74, prof. architecture, 1977. Chmn. adv. coun. Princeton U. Sch. Architecture, 1985-87; mem. architecture rev. panel Fgn. Bldg. Office, Dept. State, 1991—, mem. architecture adv. bd. Works include EURAM office bldg, Washington, Waterfront Center, Washington; Brewer residence, Chevy Chase, Md., Conant residence, Potomac, Md., Nat. Humanities Center, Raleigh, N.C., Nat. Permanent Bldg., Washington, 1001 Pennsylvania Ave, Washington; Folger Shakespeare Library, Washington, Immanuel Presbyn. Ch., McLean, Va., Sumner Sch., Washington, H.E.B. hdqrs., San Antonio, Market Square, Washington, Franklin Sq., Washington, Pa. Plaza, Washington, U.S. Embassy, Kuala Lumpur, Malaysia, Chrysler Mus., Norfolk, Va., 555 11th St., Washington. Served to 2d Lt., F.A. AUS, 1957. Recipient Louis Sullivan award arch., 1972, 100 Nat., State and Local Design awards, 1967—; fellow Am. Acad. Rome, 1977-78. Fellow AIA (pres. Washington chpt. 1975, chmn. nat. capitol com. 1976, chmn. nat. com. on design 1977, AIA Nat. Honor award 1970, 71, 81, 83, 89, 94, AIA Firm award 1988, fellow 1975); mem. U.S. Commn. Fine Arts, Cosmos Club (pres. 1985). Office: Hartman Cox Architects 1074 Thomas Jefferson St NW Washington DC 20007-3832

HARTMAN, JAMES AUSTIN, retired geologist; b. Lanark, Ill., Jan. 29, 1928; s. Llewelyn John and Gladys Mae (Doyle) Hartman; m. Zoe Marie Wiley (dec. Dec. 1996); children: Victoria Lynn, Lester James;. BS, Beloit (Wis.) Coll., 1951; MS, U. Wis., 1955, PhD, 1957. Geologist Reynolds Jamaica (W.I.) Mines, Jamaica, W.I., 1951-53, Union Carbide Ore Co., Parimaribo, Surinam, 1956-57; various positions Shell Oil Co., New Orleans, 1957-86; cons. New Orleans, 1986-94; ret., 1994. Bd. mgmt. YMCA, Metairie, 1972-74; pres. Jefferson Com. for Better Schs., Metairie, 1961-63, pres. Westgate PTA, Kenner, La., 1964-65. With U.S. Army, 1946-47. Union Carbide Rsch. fellowship U. Wis., 1954-56. Mem. Am. Assn. Petroleum Geologists (hon., sec. 1981-83, Disting. Svc. award 1985), New Orleans Geol. Soc. (hon., 2d v.p. 1975-76, pres.-elect 1984-85, pres. 1985-86, Outstanding Mem. 1977), Gulf Coast Assn. Geol. Socs. (hon., v.p. 1987, pres. 1988), Sigma Xi. Republican. Episcopalian. Achievements include research in heavy minerals in Jamaican Bauxite, titanium mineralogy of Bauxites, petroleum geology. Home: 4512 Newlands St Metairie LA 70006-4138

HARTMAN, JAMES MATTHEW, lawyer; b. Bklyn., May 28, 1928; s. Irving I. and Esther (Kramer) H.; m. Alys Florence Moses, Sept. 18, 1949 (div. Aug. 1963); children— Victoria I., Elizabeth A., Sarah M.; m. 2d Frances June Ouweleen, Feb. 29, 1964. B.A., NYU, 1950; LL.B., Columbia U., 1953. Bar: N.Y. 1954, U.S. Dist. Ct. (so. and ea. dists.) N.Y. 1957, U.S. Dist. Ct. (we. dist.) N.Y. 1964, U.S. Supreme Ct. 1964, U.S. Ct. Claims 1964, U.S. Ct. Appeals (2d cir.) 1969, U.S. Dist. Ct. (no. dist.) N.Y. 1976, D.C. 1980, Fla. 1982, U.S. Ct. Appeals (6th and 11th cirs.) 1982. Assoc. firm Swain & Moore, N.Y.C., 1954-55; sole practice N.Y.C., 1955-60; assoc. Fellner & Rovins, N.Y.C., 1960-61; ptnr. Harris Beach, Wilcox, Rochester, N.Y., 1962—; adj. assoc. prof. Cornell U. Law Sch., 1973-77; instr. trial advocacy N.E. Region, Nat. Inst. Trial Advocacy, 1976—, nat. instr., 1981; instr. Hofstra Law Sch., 1978-81, Harvard Law Sch., 1979, Emory Law Sch., 1983, also various bar assns.; mem. Monroe County Med. Malpractice Arbitration Panels. Chmn. com. on health care for elderly Monroe County Health Planning Council, 1971-73; mem. health services and legal services coms. Human Resource Task Force; mem. pres.'s adv. bd., bd. regents McQuaid Jesuit High Sch., 1973-75; mem. Rochester Meml. Art Gallery, Rochester Mus. and Sci. Ctr.; bd. dirs. Rochester Eye Inst.; bd. dirs., mem. fin. com., mem. planning and coordinating com. St. Ann's Home for Aged; nat. bd. dirs. Abota Found. Served with AUS, 1946-48. Mem. ABA, Am. Bd. Trial Advocates (past pres. Rochester chpt., mem. nat. bd. dirs.), N.Y. State Bar Assn. (mem. ho. dels. 1973-76, chmn. trial lawyers sect. 1973-74, various other coms.), Monroe County Bar Assn. (past pres.), Am. Bd. Trial Advocates (Rochester chpt. past pres.), N.Y. Bar Found., Am. Bar Found. Clubs: Oak Hill Country, Hunt Hollow Ski. Home: 15 Oakfield Way Pittsford NY 14534-1886

HARTMAN, JOAN EDNA, retired literature educator, provost; b. Bklyn., Oct. 5, 1930; d. H. Graham and Edna (Kuebler) H. BA, Mt. Holyoke Coll., 1951; MA, Duke U., 1952; postgrad., Oxford U., 1958-59; PhD, Radcliffe Coll., 1960. Instr. Washington Coll., Chestertown, Md., 1952-54, Wellesley Coll., 1959-62, asst. prof., 1962-63, Conn. Coll., New London, 1963-66, CUNY-Queens Coll., Flushing, 1967-70, CUNY-S.I. C.C., 1970-72, assoc. prof., 1972-76; prof. CUNY-Coll. S.I., 1976-98, acting dean humanities and social scis., 1995-98; ret., 1998. Vis. prof. Am. U. of Rome, 1991, 99, 2001, 03, acting provost, 2005—. Editor: Women in Print I, II, 1982, (En)Gendering Knowledge, 1991, The Norton Reader, 2000; contbr. articles to profl. jours. Fellow, AAUW, NEH, Mellon Found., Folger Shakespeare Libr. Mem.: MLA, Women's Caucus for the Modern Langs., Soc. Study of Early Modern Women, Nat. Arts Club. Home: 201 E 21st St Apt 17C New York NY 10010-6423 Personal E-mail: hartman@mail.csi.cuny.edu.

HARTMAN, JOHN JORGEN, music educator; b. Arcata, Calif., Mar. 18, 1954; s. Jack and Iona Jencina Hartman; m. Gayla Ann Johnson, Aug. 7, 1976; 1 child, Daniel Fletcher. B in Music Edn., U. Oreg., 1976, MusM in Music Edn., 1982. Cert. music educator Oreg. Tchrs. Stds. and Practices Commn. Band dir. North Bend (Oreg.) Sch. Dist. #13, 1976—. Coun. mem. Bay Area Foursquare Ch., Coos Bay, 1983—86, 1993—94, 2001—04; bd. dirs. Coos Bay (Oreg.) Seaman's Ctr., 1982—85, Coos Bay Caring Pregnancy Ctr., 2000—05. Mem.: Oreg. Music Educators Assn. (Dist. 7 v.p. 2001—02), Music Educators Nat. Conf., Masons (life). Avocations: collecting and operating Lionel trains, hunting, geology, paleontology. Office: North Bend Mid Sch 1500 16th St North Bend OR 97459 Office Phone: 541-756-8341. E-mail: jhartman@nbms.nbend.k12.or.us.

HARTMAN, LORIL JANE, music educator; b. Fort Wayne, Ind., Sept. 1930; d. David Baxter and Esther Heine; m. Wilbur E. Hartman, May 20, 1950 (dec. July 19, 1998); children: Max D., Cheryl A. Vassiliadis, Michael A., Jeffrey D., Loril J. Cert. Tchr. St. Louis Inst. Music, 1949. Piano tchr. Castle Studios, Ft. Wayne, Ind., 1948—51, Loril Hartman Piano Studio, Ft. Wayne, Ind., 1951—. Ballet, dance accompanist Ft. Wayne Ballet Sch., 1960—2005; organist Gethsemane Luth. Ch., Ft. Wayne, 1977—97, choir dir., 1977—97; profl. ballet accompanist Am. Ballet Theatre Tour, Chgo., 1983. Singer: Six Weeks Every Summer / What A Way To Waste My Mind; composer: (albums) With Feeling, 1988; musician (video, TV soundtrack). Mem.: Am. Music Scholarship Assn., Nat. Guild of Piano Tchrs. (chmn. 1975—95, local overseer 1975—95, adjudicator). D-Conservative. Lutheran. Avocations: swimming, sewing, theater, movies, dance. Home: 6604 Bittersweet Dr Fort Wayne IN 46825 Office: Themalloftheworld 9758 Old Leo Rd Fort Wayne IN 46825 Personal E-mail: lorilhartmanmusic@yahoo.com, je123sus76@hotmail.com.

HARTMAN, MARY S., historian, educator; b. Mpls., June 25, 1941; married. BA, Swarthmore Coll., 1963; MA, Columbia U., 1964, PhD, 1970. From instr. to asst. prof. Rutgers U., 1968-75; from assoc. prof. to prof. history Douglass Coll., Rutgers U., 1975—; dean Douglas Coll. Rutgers U., 1982-94; dir. Inst. for Women's Leadership Douglass Coll., 1994—; prof. Rutgers U., 1994—. Author: Clio's Consciousness Raised, 1974, Victorian Murderesses, 1978; editor: Talking Leadership: Conversations with Powerful Women, 1999, The Household and the Making of History: A Subversive View of the Western Past, 2004. Office: 162 Ryders Ln New Brunswick NJ 08901-8555 Office Phone: 732-932-1463 ext. 648.

HARTMAN, MATTHEW TURNER, music educator; b. Norwalk, Ohio, Dec. 19, 1975; s. Bernard Michael and Karen Rose Hartman. MusB, Heidelberg Coll., 2000. Cert. music tchr. Ohio, 2004. Security staff Heidelberg Coll., Tiffin, Ohio, 1997—2000; choral dir. Seneca East Local Schs., Attica, Ohio, 2000—01. Mem.: Ohio Music Collegiate Educators Assn. (pres., v.p. 1996—2000), Ohio Music Educators Assn., Tau Mu Sigma. Roman Catholic. Avocations: poetry, music composition, French horn, rollerblading. Home: 12498 E Township Rd 178 Bellevue OH 44811

HARTMAN, ROBERT CARL, retired lithographer, researcher, writer; b. Chgo., Sept. 30, 1935; s. John Theodore Hartman and Verona Larson Hartman; m. Carol Janeen Johnson Larson Hartman, May 27, 1978; stepchildren: Janeen Lynn, David Robert, Susan Joan; m. Mary Carol McCants (div. 1962); children: Robert Joseph, Christie Marie, Kathryn Mary(dec.), John Patrick, Patricia Ann; m. Mary Ann Hart (div. 1975); children: Mary Ellen, Carl Robert. Lithographer, Chgo., 1954—96. Book reviewer; bass player; spkr. Harp Guitar Gathering, Williamsburg, Va., 2003, 04; contr. author Blue Book of Acoustic Guitars, 1996—; author Harp Guitars.com, 2003—. Author: Guitars and Mandolins in America Featuring the Larsons' Creations, 1984, rev. edition, 1988, The Larsons' Creations Guitars and Mandolins, 1996, The Larsons' Creations Guitars and Mandolins Centennial Edition, 2005; contbr. articles to musical periodicals; prodr.: (CD recordings). Mem. Trinity Luth. Ch., Durand, Ill., 1997—. Mem.: Chamber Music Assn. Avocations: fishing, camping, travel, ping pong/table tennis, ballroom dancing.

HARTMAN, ROBERT LEROY, artist, educator; b. Sharon, Pa., Dec. 17, 1926; s. George Otto and Grace Arvada (Radabaugh) H.; m. Charlotte Ann Johnson, Dec. 30, 1951; children: Mark Allen, James Robert. BFA, U. Ariz., 1951, MA, 1952; postgrad., Colo. Springs Fine Arts Ctr., 1947, postgrad., 1951, Bklyn. Mus. Art Sch., 1953—54. Instr. architecture, allied arts Tex. Tech. Coll., 1955-58; asst. prof. art U. Nev., Reno, 1958-61; mem. faculty dept. art U. Calif., Berkeley, 1961—, prof., 1972-91, prof. emeritus, 1991—, chmn. dept., 1974-76. Mem. Inst. for Creative Arts, U. Calif., 1967-68. One-man shows include Bertha Schafer Gallery, N.Y.C., 1966, 69, 74, Santa Barbara Mus. Art, 1973, Cin. Art Acad., 1975, Hank Baum Gallery, San Francisco, 1973, 75, 78, San Jose Mus. Art, 1983, Bluxome Gallery, San Francisco, 1984, 86, U. Art Mus., Berkeley, 1986, Instituto D'Arte Dosso Dossi, Ferrara, Italy, 1989, Victor Fischer Galleries, San Francisco, 1991, Triangle Gallery, San Francisco, 1992, 93, 95, 97, 99- 2002, 04, Augusta State U., 1998, Mary Pauline Gallery, Augusta, Ga., 2001, Oakland Mus., 2002; group exhbns. include Richmond Mus., 1966, Whitney Mus. Biennial, 1973, Oakland Mus., 1976, San Francisco Arts Commn. Gallery, 1985 (award), Earthscape Expo '90 Photo Mus., Osaka, Japan, 1990, In Close Quarters, American Landscape Photography Since 1968, Princeton Art Mus., 1993, Facing Eden: 100 Years of Landscape Art in The Bay Area, San Francisco, 1995, Colorado Springs Fine Arts Ctr., 1998; represented in permanent collections, Nat. Collections Fine Arts, Colorado Springs Fine Arts Ctr., Corcoran Gallery, Roswell Mus., Princeton Art Mus. U. Calif. humanities rsch. fellow, 1980. Office: U Calif Dept Art Berkeley CA 94720-0001

HARTMAN, ROBERT S., retired paper company executive; b. Chgo., Oct. 7, 1914; s. Edward A. and Blanche S. (Straus) H.; m. Betty Regenstein, Oct. 25, 1941; children; Ann, Ruth. Student, Northwestern U., 1933-34. Br. mgr. Draper & Kramer, Inc., 1937-41; pres. Arvey Corp., Chgo., 1957-85. Vice pres., bd. dirs. Chgo. Boys Clubs. Served with AUS, 1943-46. Mem. Chgo. Envelope Mfg. Assn. (pres. 1949-51), Envelope Mfg. Assn. Am. (dir. 1950-54) Clubs: Lake Shore Country (Glencoe, Ill.), Mayacoo Lakes (W. Palm Beach, Fla.). Home: 220 Woodley Rd Winnetka IL 60093-3739

HARTMAN, RONALD G., lawyer; b. Harrisburg, Pa., Aug. 13, 1950; s. Manny and Helene (Levine) H.; m. Leslie Ann Golomb, May 31, 1980; children: Molly, Samuel. BA, U. Pitts., 1972, JD, 1975. Bar: Pa. 1975, U.S. Dist. Ct. (we. dist.) Pa. 1975. Assoc. Baskin & Sears, Pitts., 1975-84; ptnr. Reed Smith LLP, Pitts., 1985—. Bd. dirs. Citizens League Southwestern Pa., Pitts., 1988; bd. dirs. Am. Cancer Soc.-Greater Pitts. Unit, exec. com., 1990—, chair, 2003-; bd. dirs. Jewish Family and Children's Svc. of Pitts., pres. 1995-97; bd. dirs. United Jewish Fedn. Greater Pitts., 1995-97, 98-2000, co-chmn. bus. and profl. divsn., 1989-91, mem. steering com. atty. divsn., 1992—; chair Cardoza Soc., 1999-2001; bd. dirs. Jewish Chronicle, 1997-2000. Mem.: ABA, Pa. Bar Assn., Allegheny County Bar Assn. Jewish. Avocations: jogging, reading. Home: 500 Glen Arden Dr Pittsburgh PA 15208-2809 Office: Reed Smith LLP 435 6th Ave Pittsburgh PA 15219-1886

HARTMAN, ROSEMARY JANE, retired special education educator; b. Gainesville, Fla., Aug. 24, 1944; d. John Leslie and Irene (Bowen) Goddard; m. Alan Lynn Gerber, Feb. 1, 1964 (div. 1982); children: Sean Alan, Dawn Julianne Silva, Lance Goddard; m. Perry Hartman, June 27, 1992. BA, Immaculate Heart Coll., 1967; MA, Loyola U., 1974. Cert. resource specialist. Tchr. L.A. Unified Schs., 1968-78; resource specialist Desert Sands Unified Sch. Dist., Palm Desert, 1978-83, Palm Springs Unified Schs., 1983-99, ret., 1999. Facilitator Phobics Anonymous World Svc. Ctr. Author: Jesus, My Higher Power, 2005; co-author: The Twelve Steps of Phobics Anonymous, 1989, One Day At A Time in Phobics Victorious, 1992, The Twelve Steps of Phobics Victorious, 1993; founder Phobics Victorious, 1992. Mem. Anxiety Disorders Assn. Am. Office: Phobics Victorious PO Box 695 Palm Springs CA 92263-0695 Business E-Mail: rosemaryjane@dc.rr.com.

HARTMAN, RUTH CAMPBELL, director, educator; b. Galion, Ohio, Aug. 18, 1938; d. Richard Lewis and Florence Evelyn (Ireland) Campbell; m. Richard Louis Hartman, Jan. 14, 1956; children: Jeffery Lee, Marsha Elaine, Jerry Steven. BS, Ohio State U., 1970; MEd, U. LaVerne, 1976, postgrad., 1985, U. Akron, 1977—85. cert. tchr., Ohio. Tchr. Willard City Schs., Ohio, 1964—65; educator Mansfield City Schs., Ohio, 1966—, home tutor, 1971—81, faculty advisory com., 1990—2001, young authors coord., 1991—92, co-coord. career edn., 1991—97; owner, dir. Hope Sch., Plymouth, Ohio, 2002—. Cons. Ohio State U., Ashland (Ohio) Coll., Mt. Vernon (Ohio) Nazarene Coll., 1976—. Co-author: Handbook for Student Teachers, 1983; contbr. to Norde News. Dir. constrn. Hope Sch. Mem NEA, Ohio Edn. Assn., North Ctrl. Ohio Tchrs. Assn., Mansfield Edn. Assn. Republican. Methodist. Avocations: reading, travel, tennis, music. Home: RR 1 Plymouth OH 44865-9801 Office: Hope School 4200 Opdyke Rd Plymouth OH 44865- Office Phone: 419-687-6707.

HARTMANIS, JURIS, computer scientist, educator; b. Riga, Latvia, July 5, 1928; arrived in U.S., 1950, naturalized, 1956; s. Martins and Irma (Liepins) Hartmanis; m. Ellymaria Rehwald, May 16, 1959; children: Reneta, Martin, Audrey. Student, U. Marburg, 1947-49; MA, U. Kansas City, 1951; PhD, Calif. Inst. Tech., 1955; LHD (hon.), U. Dortmund, Germany, 1995; D, DHL, U. Mo., 1999. Instr. Cornell U., Ithaca, NY, 1955-57, prof., 1965—. Walter R. Read prof. engring., 1980—, chmn. dept. computer sci., 1965-71, 77-82, 92-94. Asst. prof. Ohio State U., 1957—58; rsch. mathematician GE R&D Ctr., Schenectady, 1957—65; asst. dir. NSF Computer and Info. Sci. & Engring., Arlington, Va., 1996—99. Author (with R. E. Stearns): (book) Algebraic Structure Theory for Sequential Machines, 1966; author: Feasible computations and Provable Complexity Properties, 1978; editor: SIAM Jour. Computing; assoc. editor: Jour. Computer and Sys. Scis., 1966—, Jour. Math. Sys. Theory, 1966—89; co-editor: Springer-Verlag Lecture Notes in Computer Sci., 1973—2004. Recipient Turing award, 1992, B. Bolzano Gold medal, Acad. Scis. Czech Republic, 1995, Grand medal, Latvian Acad. of Sci., 2001. Fellow: AAAS, Computing Machinery, Am. Acad. Arts and Scis.; mem.: NAE, Latvian Acad. Sci. (fgn., Grand medal 2001), Assn. N.Y. Acad. Scis., Am. Math. Soc., Sigma Xi. Home: 324 Brookfield Rd Ithaca NY 14850-2008 Office: Cornell Univ Upson Hall Ithaca NY 14853 Office Phone: 607-255-9208. Business E-Mail: jh@cs.cornell.edu, jh111@cornell.edu.

HARTMANN, FREDERICK HOWARD, retired political science professor; b. N.Y.C., July 6, 1922; s. Frederick Herman and Grace (MacNamara) H.; m. Regina Lou Kiracofe, Dec. 26, 1943; children: Lynne Merry, Vicky Carol, Peter Howard. AB, U. Calif. at Berkeley, 1943; MA, Princeton, 1948, PhD, 1949; student, Grad. Inst. Internat. Studies, U. Geneva, Switzerland, 1947. Instr. politics Princeton, 1947; from asst. prof. to prof. polit. sci. U. Fla., 1948-66; dir. Inst. Internat. Relations, 1963-66; Alfred Thayer Mahan prof. maritime strategy U.S. Naval War Coll., 1966-88, prof. emeritus, 1988—, spl. acad. advisor, 1966-86. Vis. prof. Wheaton (Mass.) Coll., part-time, 1966-69, Brown U., part-time, 1968-69, U. R.I., part-time, 1970-71, Tex. Tech U., 1974-75; vis. prof. polit. sci. U. Calif., Berkeley, 1979-80, Middle East Tech. U., Ankara, Turkey, 1988. Author: The Relations of Nations, 4th edit., 1973, 5th edit., 1978, 6th edit., 1983, Spanish edit., 1986, The Swiss Press and Swiss Foreign Affairs, 1960, Germany Between East and West, 1965, The New Age of American Foreign Policy, 1970, Naval Renaissance: The U.S. Navy in the 1980s, 1990, (Chinese transl. 1994), America Under Threat, 2002; (with Robert L. Wendzel) To Preserve the Republic, 1985, Defending America's Security, 1988, America's Foreign Policy in a Changing World, 1994; editor: Basic Documents of International Relations, 1951, Readings in International Relations, 1952, World in Crisis, 4th edit., 1973; contbr. to: System for Educating Military Officers in the U.S., 1976, The Conservation of Enemies, 1981. U. Fla. rep. Fla. Bd. Control Com. Acad. Freedom, 1961-62; mem. Fulbright Nat. Selection Com., 1954-56; U.S. del. 4th Conf. Naval War Colls. Am., 1966, 6th Conf., 1970, 10th Conf., 1980, 12th Conf., 1985. Served to lt. (j.g.) USNR, 1943-46; capt. Res. Recipient Meritorious Civilian Service medal Dept. Navy, 1985; Fulbright research prof. U. Bonn, Germany, 1953-54; Rockefeller grantee, 1959; Exxon Corp. grantee, 1973 Mem. AAUP (pres. U. Fla. chpt. 1959-60, mem. nat. council 1963-66), Am. Polit. Sci. Assn., Internat. Studies Assn. (pres. New Eng. div. 1971-72), New Eng. Polit. Sci. Assn. (exec. com. 1982-84), Fla. Blue Key, Pi Sigma Alpha, Delta Phi Epsilon. Home: 8457 Twin Rocks Rd Granite Bay CA 95746-8123

HARTMANN, FREDERICK WILLIAM, newspaper editor; b. Wilmington, Del., Feb. 3, 1928; s. William and Louise (Askani) H.; m. Mary Lucille Nelson, Oct. 16, 1954; children: Michele Mary, Randi Lucille, Frederick Andrew, Eric William, Adam Nelson. BA, U. Del., 1951; postgrad., Am. U., 1952; MS, Columbia U. Grad. Sch. Journalism, 1953. Reporter AP, N.Y.C., 1954; dir. news and sports WDEL Radio, Wilmington, 1954-56; reporter Morning News, News-Jour. Co., Wilmington, 1956-60, asst. city editor, 1961-62, city editor, 1962-64, Morning and Evening Jour., 1964-67, met. editor, 1967-72, asst. to pres., 1972-74, dir. corp. mktg., 1974-75, exec. editor, 1975-80, v.p., 1977-80; mng. editor Fla. Times-Union, Jacksonville, 1980-83; exec. editor Times-Union/Jacksonville Jour., Jacksonville, 1983-88, Times-Union, Jacksonville, 1988-98, ret., 1998. Lectr. U. Del., 1971, 72; Pulitzer prize juror, 1981, 82. Mem. budget com. United Way of Del., 1973, 74; v.p. Brandywine Little League, 1973; bd. dirs. United Cerebral Palsy Assn. of Del., 1970-72. Served with AUS, 1946-48. Mem. Theta Chi. Home: 3852 Mcgirts Blvd Jacksonville FL 32210-4337 Personal E-mail: freditor39@bellsouth.net.

HARTMANN, GEORGE HERMAN, retired manufacturing company executive; b. N.Y.C., Nov. 6, 1927; s. Herman George Dietrich and Margaret Bertha (Winkler) H.; m. Anne Katharine Martin, July 9, 1960; children: Michael George, Steven Herman, Katharine Margaret, Elizabeth Anne. AB cum laude, Dartmouth Coll., 1949, MS in Mech. Engring, 1950. With Gen. Electric Co., 1950-70; v.p. mfg. Gen. Signal Corp., 1970-71; exec. v.p., then pres. GE Espanola, 1971-74; pres. Davol Co. (subs. Internat. Paper Co.), 1975-78, corp. v.p. human resources, then v.p. materials, 1979-80; pvt. investor, 1980-81; group v.p. Textron Inc., Providence, 1981-92; ret., 1992. Trustee R.I. Coun. Econ. Edn., 1977, vice chmn. 1983-92; trustee Am. Sch., Bilbao, Spain, 1972-74, chmn., 1973-74; trustee Joint Coun. Econ. Edn., 1986-91, Nat. Security Indsl. Assn., 1988-92, Calvin K. Kazanjian Econs. Found., Inc., 1996-; zoning bd. mem. Lyme, NH, 2002-, chmn. 2004-; U.S. del. NATO Indsl. Adv. Group, 1989-92; mem. adv. com. Lebanon (N.H.)

Airport, 2000-, vice chmn., 2005-. Served to lt. USNR, 1955-60. Mem. NAM (dir. 1977-80), R.I. C. of C. (dir. 1977-78), Greater Providence C. of C. (dir. 1976-78), N.Y. Yacht Club, Cruising Club Am. (Parkinson Meml. Trophy for Transoceanic Passage 1993, 97), Ocean Cruising Club. Independent.

HARTMANN, JAMES M., lawyer; b. N.Y.C., Mar. 8, 1946; s. Morton Woodrow and Miriam Rose H.; m. Nancy K. Deming, May 20, 1988. BA, St. Lawrence U., 1967; MA, U. Wis., 1968; JD, Bklyn. Law Sch., 1974. Bar: N.Y. 1975, U.S. Dist. Ct. (so. and ea. dists.) N.Y. 1975, U.S. Ct. Appeals (2d cir.) 1975, U.S. Dist. Ct. (no. and we. dists.) N.Y. 1989, U.S. Supreme Ct. 1991. Gen. atty. U.S. Dept. Justice, N.Y.C., 1975-76, trial atty., 1976-79; pvt. practice N.Y.C., 1979-86, Delhi, N.Y., 1989—; head dept. litig. Frenkel & Hershkowitz, N.Y.C., 1986-89. Spl. dist. atty. Del. County, Delhi; mem. libr. com. Supreme Ct., Delhi, 1992—. Mem. N.Y. State Bar Assn., N.Y. Trial Lawyers Assn., N.Y. State Criminal Def. Lawyers Assn., Del. County Bar Assn. (mem. grievance com. 1994—), Pi Sigma Alpha. Office: PO Box 206 Rte 10 Delhi NY 13753

HARTMANN, ROBERT ELLIOTT, retired manufacturing executive; b. Bklyn., Apr. 10, 1926; s. James and Edna Mae (Schroeder) H.; m. Anne Marie Mongiello, Feb. 15, 1948; children: Barbara Hartmann Kaszor, Donna Hartmann Dow. BS, Miami U., Oxford, Ohio, 1946. CPA, N.Y. Acct. Price, Waterhouse & Co., N.Y.C., 1948-57; mgr. fin. acctg. Air Products & Chems., Allentown, Pa., 1957-58; v.p. Alpha Portland Cement Co. divsn. Alpha Portland Industries, Inc., Easton, Pa., 1958-82. Sec. Slattery Group, Inc. (formely Alpha Portland Industries, Inc.), Easton, 1962-89; sec., treas. Energy and Resource Recovery Corp., until 1982; sec., treas., dir. H.O.H. Corp., until 1982; past pres. Moravian Book Shop, Inc. Bd. dirs. Bethlehem Area Moravians. Served to lt. Supply Corps USNR, World War II. Mem. Inst. Mgmt. Accts. (pres. Lehigh Valley chpt. 1973-74), Financial Execs. Inst. (treas. N.E. Pa. chpt. 1972-74), Am. Inst. C.P.A.s. Mem. Moravian Ch. Home: 285 Bridle Path Rd Bethlehem PA 18017-3867

HARTMANN, ROBERT SANKEY, health facility administrator, not-for-profit fundraiser; b. June 9, 1948; s. Robert Trowbridge and Roberta (Sankey) H.; m. Ruth Eva Satterthwaite, Dec. 2, 1978; children: Daniel Satterthwaite, David Trowbridge. BA in Speech/Drama cum laude, Occidental Coll., 1969, MA in Speech/Drama, 1971; student, Guildhall Sch. Music & Drama, 1970; mgmt. devel. course, Harvard Bus. Sch., 1974. Spl. asst. to chmn. Nat. Endowment for Arts, Washington, 1973—78; lobbyist for Daniel J. Edelman Washington, 1978; creative dir., lobbyist Hill and Knowlton, Washington, 1978—81; sr. v.p. Ruder Finn & Rotman, Washington, 1981—84; dir. pub. rels. World Wildlife Fund, Washington, 1984—86; sr. v.p. and dir. pub. rels. Abramson Assocs., Inc., 1986—90; v.p. pub. affairs, mktg. and devel. Nat. Rehab. Hosp., Washington, 1990—. Chmn. bd. dirs. Met. Meth. Nursery Sch., 1989—94. Named Outstanding Young Man Am., 1983. Mem. Pub. Rels. Soc. Am. (Thoth award 1984), Internat. Assn. Bus. Communicators (Gold Quill award 1984), Westmoreland Citizens Assn. (pres. 1992-93), Nat. Press Club, Capitol Hill Club, Silver Owl Club. Home: 5023 Worthington Dr Bethesda MD 20816-2748 Office: Nat Rehab Hosp 102 Irving St NW Washington DC 20010-2949 Office Phone: 202-877-1776. Business E-Mail: robert.s.hartmann@medstar.net.

HARTMANN, ROBERT TROWBRIDGE, newspaperman, presidential counselor; b. Rapid City, SD, Apr. 8, 1917; s. Miner Louis and Elizabeth (Trowbridge) H.; m. Roberta Sankey, Jan. 17, 1943; children: Roberta H. Brake, Robert S. AB, Stanford U., 1938. Reporter Los Angeles Times, 1939-41, 45-48, editorial writer, 1948-54, chief Washington bur., 1954-63; chief (Mediterranean and Middle East Bur.), 1963-64; FAO info. adviser Washington, 1964-65; editor Republican Conf. U.S. Ho. Reps., 1966-69; minority sgt.-at-arms U.S. Ho. Reps., 1969-73; chief staff to the Vice Pres., 1973-74; counsellor (with cabinet rank) to Pres. Gerald R. Ford, 1974-77; sr. research fellow Hoover Instn., Stanford U., 1977—; trustee Gerald R. Ford Found., 1981—. Mem. U.S. Ho. of Reps. Mission to Peoples' Republic of China, 1972. Author: Palace Politics, An Inside Account of the Ford Years, 1980. Asst. to permanent chmn. Rep. Nat. Conv., 1968, 72; bd. visitors U.S. Naval Acad., 1977-80. Served from ensign to capt. USN, 1941-45, PTO; ret. Recipient Sigma Delta Chi Distinguished Service award for Washington Corrs., 1957; Better Understanding citation English Speaking Union of U.S., 1958; Overseas Press Club citation, 1961; Freedoms Found. citation, 1963; Distinguished Eagle Scout award Boy Scouts Am., 1975; Reid Found. fellow, 1951 Mem. Navy League, Hammer and Coffin Soc., Delta Chi, Sigma Delta Chi, Delta Sigma Rho. Mem. Ch. of Christ. Clubs: Nat. Press (Washington), Army and Navy (Washington), Capitol Hill (Washington); Mil. Order of the Carabao, Chevaliers du Tastevin; Country Club of St. Croix (V.I.). *I'm not sure I have "achieved success" but I have had a very good life so far. The greatest evil in life is a lie, and the greatest blessings are love and laughter.*

HARTMANN SIANTAR, CHRISTINE LOUISE, physicist; b. Sauk City, Wis., Dec. 9, 1965; d. Gordon Leonard and Mary Ann Hartmann; m. Darsa Purnama Siantar, Dec. 15, 1990; children: Benjamin Alamsjah Siantar, Maxwell Gordon Siantar. BS, U. Wis., 1982, MS, PhD, 1991. Dir. Glenn T. Seaborg Inst. Lawrence Livermore (Calif.) Nat. Lab., 2001—04, dep. program leader Nuc. and Radiol. Countermeasures Program, 2004—. Tchr. faith formation St. Michael's Roman Cath. Ch., Livermore, 2003—05. Recipient Presdl. Early Career award, White Ho., 1996, Young Ind. Scientist award, U.S. Dept. of Energy, 1996, R&D 100 award, R&D Mag., 1999; Edward Teller fellow, Lawrence Livermore Nat. Lab., 2000. Achievements include first to led the development of the PEREGRINE system, which uses radiation transport technology developed in the nuclear weapons program to improve the accuracy of radiation treatment of cancer patients. Office: Lawrence Livermore National Laboratory PO Box 808 Livermore CA 94550 Office Phone: 925-422-4619. Office Fax: 925-422-4100. E-mail: chs@llnl.gov.

HARTNER, JOHN GEORGE, language educator; b. Pitts., June 11, 1955; B, Carnegie-Mellon U., 1979; M, Duquesne U., 1983. Instr. Cmty. Coll. Allegheny County, Pitts., 1982—. Instr. Point Park Coll., Pitts., 1983—2002, Art Inst. Pitts., 2002—. Author (poetry): Spectral Countenance, 1982, Horrorshow Up Ahead, 1983, Whitman Visits Bard's Dairyland, 1984, Proteus, 1987, Renaming Orion, 1996. Republican. Avocations: films, Boston Terriers, history. Home: 327 Caperton St Pittsburgh PA 15210

HARTNESS, DIANNE, literature and language educator; b. Ridgeland, SC, Sept. 14, 1977; d. Robert Eugene and Deborah Evans Hartness. BA, U. SC, 2000; MEd, Columbia coll., 2003. Tchr. Newberry HS, SC, 2000—. Literacy team mem. Newberry County Schs., 2004—. Named Tchr. of Month, Newberry HS, 2001, 2003. Mem.: Carolina Alumni Assn. (com. mem. 2004—05, young alumni coun. mem. 2005), Delta Zeta. Methodist. Avocations: reading, painting, exercise.

HARTNETT, JAMES PATRICK, engineering educator; b. Lynn, Mass., Mar. 19, 1924; s. James Patrick and Anna Elizabeth (Ryan) H.; m. Shirley Germaine Carlson, July 14, 1945 (div. 1969); children: James, David, Paul, Carla, Dennis; m. Edith Zubrin, Sept. 10, 1971. BS in Mech. Engring, Ill. Inst. Tech., 1947; MS, MIT, 1948; PhD, U. Calif., Berkeley, 1954. Engr. gas turbine div. Gen. Electric Co., 1948-49; rsch. engr. U. Calif., Berkeley, 1949-54; asst. prof. to prof. mech. engring. U. Minn., 1954-61; Guggenheim fellow, vis. prof. U. Tokyo, Japan, 1960; cons. ICA, Seoul, Korea, 1960; Fulbright lectr., cons. mech. engring. U. Alexandria, Egypt, 1961; H. Fletcher Brown prof. mech. engring., chmn. dept. U. Del., 1961-65; engring. cons., 1954-74; prof., head dept. energy engring. U. Ill., Chgo., 1965-74; dir. Energy Resources Ctr., 1974-98. Sci. exch. visitor, Romania, 1969; vis. prof. Israel Inst. Tech., 1971; cons. Asian Inst. Tech., Bangkok 1977; 1st Dr. Arcot Ramachandran prof. heat transfer Indian Inst. Tech., Madras, 1995-96. Editor: Recent Advances in Heat and Mass Transfer, 1961; co-editor: Internat. Jour. Heat and Mass Transfer, 1960—, (with T.F. Irvine, Jr.) Advances in Heat Transfer, 1963—, Heat Transfer-Japanese Research, Soviet Research, 1971, Fluid Mechanics-Soviet Research, 1971; contbr. articles on heat transfer, fluid mechanics, energy to tech. jours. Mem. organizing com. and sci. coun. Internat. Centre Heat and Mass Transfer, Ankara, Turkey, 1969—; mem., sec. Ill. Energy Resources Commn., 1974-85; mem. sci. coun. Regional Center for Energy, Heat and Mass Transfer for Asia and Pacific, 1976—; sec. Midwest Univs. Energy Consortium, 1980—. Recipient Profl. Achievement award Ill. Inst. Tech. Alumni Assn., 1977; recipient Luikov medal Internat. Ctr. Heat and Mass Transfer, 1981; Japan Soc. for Promotion of Sci. fellow, 1987. Fellow ASME (Meml. award heat transfer divsn. 1969, 40th Anniversary award 1989, AIChE-ASME Max Jakob Meml. award 1989), Indian Nat. Acad. Engring., Japanese Soc. Mech. Engrs. (hon.); mem. Internat. Higher Edn. Acad. of Scis./Moscow (Disting. prof. 1997), Sigma Xi, Tau Beta Pi, Pi Tau Sigma. Address: Univ of Ill 1919 W Taylor St Chicago IL 60612-7246

HARTNETT, JOSH, actor; b. San Francisco, July 21, 1978; s. Daniel and Molly Hartnett (Stepmother). Student, SUNY, Purchase. Actor: (films) Halloween: H2O, 1998, The Faculty, 1998, The Virgin Suicides, 1999, Here on Earth, 2000, Blow Dry, 2001, Member, 2001, Town & Country, 2001, Pearl Harbor, 2001, O, 2001, Black Hawk Down, 2001, The Same, 2001, 40 Days and 40 Nights, 2002, Hollywood Homicide, 2003, Wicker Park, 2004, Sin City, 2005, Mozart and the Whale, 2005; (TV films) Debutante, 1998; (TV series) Cracker, 1997—98. Named ShoWest Male Star of Tomorrow, 2002. Office: Patricola Lust Pub Relatiolns Inc 8383 Wilshire Blvd Ste 530 Beverly Hills CA 90211-2404*

HARTNETT, THOMAS ROBERT, III, retired lawyer, writer; b. Sioux City, Iowa, July 19, 1920; s. Thomas and Florence Mary (Graves) H.; m. Betty Jeanne Dobbins, Mar. 3, 1943; children: Thomas Robert Joseph, Jeanine Elizabeth, Dennis Edward, Glenn Michael. Student, Trinity Coll., 1937-39; LLB, U. So. Calif., 1948. Bar: Tex. 1948, U.S. Dist. Ct. (no. dist.) Tex., 1949, U.S. Ct. Appeasl (5th cir.) 1954, (10th cir.) 1955, (11th cir.) 1983, U.S. Supreme Ct., 1957. Pvt. practice, Dallas, 1948-88; of counsel Hartnett Law Firm, Dallas, 1988—2005; ret. Author: The Root of the Whys, 1998. With USAAF, 1939-45. Mem. State Bar Tex., Dallas Bar Assn. Republican. Roman Catholic. Home: 5074 Matilda St Apt 224 Dallas TX 75206-4268

HARTNETT, WILL FORD, lawyer; b. Austin, Tex., June 3, 1956; s. James Joseph and Emily (High) Hartnett; m. Tammy Lynn Cotton, Dec. 7, 1996; children: Will, Winston, Warner. BA, Harvard U., 1978; JD, U. Tex., 1981. Bar: Tex. 1981, U.S. Ct. Appeals (5th cir.) 1985, U.S. Supreme Ct. 1985; cert. in Estate Planning and Probate Law Tex. Bd. Legal Specialization. Assoc. Turner & Hitchins, Dallas, 1981-82; ptnr. The Hartnett Law Firm, Dallas, 1982—. Bd. dirs. Tex. Guaranteed Student Loan Corp., Austin, 1987-90. Co-author: Annual Survey of Wills and Trusts, 1986. Mem. Tex. Ho. of Reps., 1991—. Tex. Jud. Coun.; vice chmn. Ho. Judiciary Com., 1995-02, chmn., 2003-. Fellow: Tex. Bar Found., Am. Coll. Trust and Estate Coun.; mem.: SAR, Dallas Bar Assn., Mensa, St. Nicholas Soc., Harvard Club Dallas (bd. dirs., treas. 1983—95). Republican. Roman Catholic. Home: 4722 Walnut Hill Ln Dallas TX 75229-6354 Office: The Hartnett Law Firm 1717 Main St Ste 5350 Dallas TX 75201 Office Phone: 214-742-4655. Business E-Mail: will@hartnettlawfirm.com.

HARTNETT, WILLIAM M., lawyer; b. NYC, Feb. 23, 1954; BA cum laude, Rider U., 1976; JD cum laude, Fordham U., 1979. Bar: NY 1980. Ptnr., Corp. Fin and Mergers & Acquisitions Practice Areas Cahill Gordon & Reindel LLP, NYC, mem. exec. com. Mem. Fordham Law Rev., 1978—79. Office: Cahill Gordon & Reindle LLP 80 Pine St New York NY 10005-1702 Office Phone: 212-701-3847. Office Fax: 212-378-2198. Business E-Mail: whartnett@cahill.com.

HARTNICK, ALAN JAY, lawyer, educator; b. N.Y.C., Feb. 27, 1930; s. Saul and Sally Hartnick; m. Karen L. Hartnick; children: Jonathan (dec.), Kate, Christopher, Maggie. AB magna cum laude, Syracuse U., 1950; JD cum laude, Harvard U., 1953. Bar: N.Y. 1953. Ptnr. Abelman, Frayne and Schwab, N.Y.C. Adj. prof. Seton Hall U. Sch. Law, Newark, 1976—79, NYU Sch. Law, 1978—2001, Fordham Law Sch., 2003—; vis. lectr. Yale Law Sch., 1979; mem. copyright office adv. com. Libr. Congress, Washington, 1981—84; cons. Register of Copyright, 1989; U.S. del. Com. Govt. Experts on the Printed Wk. World Intellectual Property Orgn., Geneva, 1987. Editor-in-chief Jour. Copyright Soc., 1984-87; contbr. articles to profl. jours. Lt. USNR, 1953-56. Mem. Copyright Soc. USA (pres. 1982-84, hon. trustee 1984-2004), Mag. Pubs. Assn. (legal affairs com. 1983—), N.Y. State Bar Assn. (com. chair copyright and trademark 1988-2004), Assn. of the Bar of the City of N.Y. (copyright and literary property com. 1964-67, 78-81, 91-94, 98-04, entertainment law com. 1994-97, ad hoc info. superhighway com. 1994-95), Phi Beta Kappa. Home: 168 E 74th St New York NY 10021-3561 Office: Abelman Frayne & Schwab 666 Third Ave 10th Fl New York NY 10017-5621 Office Phone: 212-949-9022. E-mail: ajhartnick@lawabel.com.

HARTOUGH, HOWARD DALE, JR., pharmaceutical company executive; b. Phila., Dec. 10, 1943; s. Howard Dale and Cornelia (Tysse) H.; m. Pamela Hibbitt, June 9, 1969; children: Hugh, Lynn. BChemE, Ga. Inst. of Tech., 1966; MBA, U. Utah, 1975. Plant engr. Degussa, Frankfurt, Germany, 1966-70; sr. cons. Divo Inmar GmbH, Frankfurt, 1971-75; comml. devel. specialist Dart Industries Inc., Paramus, N.J., 1975-79; mgr. worldwide mktg. rsch. Borg Warner Chems., Parkersburg, W.Va., 1979-88; dir. bus. devel. Chemfirst Inc., Jackson, Miss., 1988-92; mgr. bus. devel. Catalytica Inc., Mountain View, Calif., 1992-97; dir. purchasing DSM Catalytica Pharms., Greenville, N.C., 1997—. Mem. Town coun., North Hills, W.Va., 1988; chmn. Friends of W.Va. Pub. Radio, Charleston, 1988; founder, chmn. Artsbridge Inc., Parkersburg, 1986; pres., founder East Carolina Jr. Volleyball Club, Greenville, 1999. Mem. Nat. Assn. Purchasing Mgmt., Comml. Devel. and Mktg. Assn., Lic. Exec. Soc. Episcopalian. Avocations: genealogy, coin collecting/numismatics, golf. Office: Catalytica Pharmas Inc Intersection of US 264 and US 13 Greenville NC 27834

HARTRICK, JANICE KAY, lawyer; b. Baytown, Tex., Oct. 15, 1952; BA, Rice U., 1974; JD, U. Houston, 1976. Bar: Tex. 1977, La. 1980. With contracts sect. Texaco Corp., Houston, 1977-78; asst. gen. counsel Cities Exploration Co., Watson Oil Corp., Houston, 1978-79; sr. atty. Coastal Corp., Houston, 1979-87; chief counsel, v.p. Seagull Energy Corp., Houston, 1987-97; gen. counsel, sr. v.p. EEX Corp., Houston, 1997-2000; v.p., assoc. counsel Apache Corp., 2000—. Coun. Thompson and Knight, LLP, Houston. Contbg. editor Regulation of the Natural Gas Industry, 1980-84. Vice chair adv. bd. Internat. Oil and Gas Ednl. Ctr., Southwestern Legal Found.; trustee Rocky Mountain Mineral Law Found. Mem. ABA (chair oil and gas exploration and prodn. 2000-2002), Tex. Bar Assn., State Bar of Tex. (oil, gas and mineral law sect. chair 1999), La. Bar Assn. Avocation: track. Office: Apache Corp 2000 Post Oak Blvd Ste 100 Houston TX 77056-4400

HARTSFIELD, HENRY WARREN, JR., electronics executive, retired astronaut; b. Birmingham, Ala., Nov. 21, 1933; s. Henry Warren and Alice Norma (Sorrell) H.; m. Judy Frances Massey, June 30, 1957; children: Judy Lynn, Keely Warren. BS, Auburn U., 1954; postgrad., Duke U., 1954-55, Air Force Inst. Tech., 1960-61; MS, U. Tenn., 1970; DSc (hon.), Auburn U., 1986. Commd. 2d lt. USAF, 1955, advanced through grades to col., 1974, assigned to tour with 53d Tactical Fighter Squadron Bitburg, Fed. Republic Germany, 1961-64; instr. USAF Test Pilot Sch., Edwards AFB, Calif., 1965-66; assigned to Manned Orbiting Lab. USAF, 1966-69; astronaut, NASA Lyndon B. Johnson Space Ctr., 1969-97, mem. support crew Apollo 16, Skylabs 2, 3, 4 missions, pilot STS-4; comdr. STS-41D, STS-61A; ret., 1977; civilian astronaut NASA; dep. dir. Flight Crew Ops. Directorate, 1987-89; dir. tech. integration and analysis Office Space Flight, NASA Hqrs., 1989-90; dep. dir. ops. space sta. projects Marshall Space Flight Ctr. NASA, 1990-91; mgr. man-tended capability phase Space Sta. Freedom Program, 1991-94; mgr. Internat. Space Sta. Ind. Assessment at Johnson Space Ctr., 1994-97; ret., 1998; dir. Houston ops. Raytheon Sys. Co., 1998-99; v.p. aerospace engring. svcs. Raytheon Tech. Svcs. Co., 1999—. In space: 483 hours. Decorated Meritorious Service medal, D.S.M. NASA, 1982, 88, Space Flight medal NASA, 1982, 84, 85; recipient Nat. Geog. White Space Trophy, 1973 Mem. Soc. Exptl. Test Pilots, Air Force Assn., Sigma Pi Sigma Office: Raytheon 2224 Bay Area Blvd Houston TX 77058-2008 E-mail: henry_w_hartsfield@raytheon.com, hhartsfield@raytheon.com.

HARTSFIELD, JAMES KENNEDY, JR., orthodontist, geneticist; b. Decatur, Ala., Feb. 12, 1955; s. James Kennedy and Shirley Joann (Bridwell) H.; m. Karen Lee Whitaker, May 8, 1977; 1 child, Kennedy Whitaker. BS, U. S.C., 1977; DMD, Med. U. S.C., 1981; MS, Ind. U., 1983; M in Med. Sci., Harvard U., 1987; PhD, U. South Fla., 1993. Diplomate Am. Bd. Med. Genetics., Am. Bd. Orthodotnics. Intern Hillsborough Dental Rsch. Clinic, Tampa, Fla., 1981-82; clin. fellow Ind. U., Indpls., 1982-83; rsch. fellow Harvard U., Boston, 1983-86, Mass. Gen. Hosp., Boston, 1984-86; clin. fellow U. South Fla., Tampa, 1986-87, asst. prof., 1987-93; assoc. prof. Sch. Dentistry and Medicine Ind. U., Indpls., 1993—99, prof. Sch. Dentistry and Medicine, 1999—2002; pres. Meridian Orthodontics, 2003—. Dir. Teratogen Info. Svc., U. South Fla., 1987-93; dir. oral facial genetics divsn. Sch. Dentistry Ind. U., 1993-, acting chmn. oral facial devel., 1998-99, chmn., 1999-2002; pres. Meridian Orthodontics, P.C., 2003-. Contbr. articles to profl. jours. Recipient Physician-Scientist award NIH, 1989, 1st Ind. Rsch. Support and Transition award, 1996, B.F. Dewell Meml. Biomed. Rsch. award Am. Assn. Orthodontists Found., 2001. Fellow Am. Coll. Med. Genetics (founding), Am. Coll. Dentists, Coll. of Diplomates of Am. Bd. Orthodontics; mem. ADA, Am. Soc. Human Genetics, Am. Assn. for Dental Rsch., Internat. Assn. Dental Rsch. (v.p. craniofacial biology group 2003-04, pres.-elect 2004-, pres. 2005—), Soc. Craniofacial Genetics (pres. 1989-90), Am. Dental Edn. Assn., Am. Cleft Palate Assn., Am. Assn. Orthodontists. Presbyterian. Avocations: music, boating. Home: 8095 Sunfish Ct Indianapolis IN 46236-8887 Office: Ind U Schs Dentistry and Medicine 1121 W Michigan St Indianapolis IN 46202-5186 Also: 8801 N Meridian St Ste 313 Indianapolis IN 46260-5316 Office Phone: 317-278-1148.

HARTSFIELD, PAULA KINDRICK, vocational educator; b. Springfield, Mo., Apr. 12, 1954; d. Clarence Mitchell and Hilda N. (Nichols) Kindrick; m. George Thomas Hartsfield, May 1, 1982. B.S. in Edn., S.W. Mo. State U., 1976; M.S., Kans. State U., 1978. Cert. vocat. home econs. tchr., gen sci. tchr., vocat. dir. Sec. Ozark Empire Fair, Springfield, Mo., 1972-77; piano and flute tchr., Springfield, 1972-76; vocat. home econs. tchr. Monett Sch. Dist., Mo., 1976-78; consumer protection paralegal intern Mo. Atty. Gen., Jefferson City, Mo., 1978; Supr. home econs. edn. Mo. Dept. Elem. and Secondary Edn., Jefferson City, 1979-83, state dir. home econs. edn., 1983-88; asst. dir. Nichols Career Ctr. Area Vocat. Tech. Sch., Jefferson City, 1988-94; coord. A+ schs. Jefferson City Sch. Dist., Mo., 1997-97, dir. planning and at schs. coord., 1997-98, dir. of curriculum and staff devel., 1998-02, dir. planning and assessment, 2002—; mem. home econs. adv. bd. Favorite Recipes Press, Nashville, 1983-88; proposal reader and ranker U.S. Office Consumer Edn., Washington, 1981; nat. bd. dirs. Future Homemakers Am., Washington, 1977-78, 86-88. Contbr. articles to profl. jours. Treas. Capitol Area Chpt. March of Dimes, Jefferson City, 1982-83, exec. com. 1981-83, leader Mother's March, 1983-84; membership chairperson Capitol Women's Polit. Caucus, Jefferson City, 1982; trustee Caroline B. Ullman Student and Scholarship Fund Mo. PTA, 1983-88. Recipient family econs. research assistantship Kans. State U., 1978, Disting. Service award Mo. Assn. Future Homemakers Am., 1984, Woman of Achievement in Pub. Affairs AAUW, Jefferson chpt., 1986. Mem. Mo. Home Econs. Assn. (state v.p. 1986-88, dist. H. pres. elect 1984-85, pres. 1985-86), Nat. Assn. Vocat. Home Econs. Tchrs. (state legis. contact person 1983-84), Am. Council Consumer Interests (state membership chmn. 1984-86), Am. Vocat. Assn., Nat. Coun. for Local Adminstrs., Nat. Employment Tng. Assn., Mo. Vocat. Assn. (state bd. dirs. 1983-88), Mo. Coun. of Vocat. Adminstrs. (co-chair vocat. leadership acad. com. 1991-93), Bus. and Profl. Women's Club (1st v.p. Jefferson City chpt. 1983-84), Rotary Club (found. chair, 2004—), Kappa Omicron Phi (nat. v.p. program 1984-86, workshop leader Nat. Conclave, 1980, 86). Democrat. Episcopalian. Club: Zonta (Jefferson City program com. mem. 1984-85, chmn. membership com. 1985-86), Rotary (chmn. found. Jefferson City 2004—). Avocations: walking, entertaining, travel, reading. Home: 1909 Sarah Ln Jefferson City MO 65101-2356 Office: Jefferson City Sch Dist 315 East Dunklin Jefferson City MO 65101-2814 Office Phone: 573-659-3043.

HARTSOCK, LINDA SUE, management consultant; b. St. Joseph, Mo., Feb. 20, 1940; d. Waldo Emerson and Martha (Skelkop) H. BS, Ctrl. Meth. Coll., Fayette, Mo., 1962; EdM, Pa. State U., 1965, EdD, 1971. Cert. assn. exec. Am. Soc. Assn. Execs. Tchr. Jr. High Sch. (North Kansas City (Mo.) Pub. Sch. Sys.), 1962; sr. resident Pa. State U., 1963—64, asst. coord. residence halls, 1964—65, residence hall coord., 1965—66, asst. dean women, 1966—68, asst. dean students, 1968—71; rschr. Ctr. for Study Higher Edn., 1971, dir. new student programs, 1971—72; nat. dir. program AAUW, 1972—76; exec. dir. Adult Edn. Assn., 1976—80; now ret. CEO Integrated Options, Inc., assn., edn. and mgmt. svcs., Greenbackville, Va.; designer tng. and ednl. programs for various orgns. and assns. V.p. fin. Com. for Full Finding Edn., 1979; mem. first adv. panel convened future directions of a learning soc. project Coll. Entrance Exam. Bd., 1978, mem. planning group for Course-By-Newspaper exam. project, 1979; bd. dirs. Coalition Adult Edn. Orgns., 1976; mem. White House Conf. on Aging Com., 1979; mem. nat. adv. bd. Nat. Ctr. Higher Edn. Mgmt. Sys. Project to Develop a Taxonomy for the Field of Adult Edn., 1978; nat. adv. coun. on adult edn. Futures and Amendments Project, 1977; adv. Collection of Census Data, Nat. Ctr. Ednl. Stats., 1977; mem. pub. policy com., program com. chmn. Adv. Coun. Nat. Orgns. to Corp. for Pub. Broadcasting, 1976; adv. devel. New Mediated Programs, Office Instructional Resources, Miami Dade C.C., 1976; mem. innovative awards com. Nat. Univ. Ext. Assn., 1977; field reader U.S. Dept. Edn. Title III Grants, 1981-83. Mem. editl. bd. Off to Coll. mag, 1972-74; contbr. articles to profl. jours. Mem. Greenbackville Va. Fire Dept. Women's Aux., 2000—02; instr. water exercise Lower Shore YMCA, Pocomoke City, Md., 2002—; guide Chincoteague Nat. Wildlife Refuge, 2002—; chair family coun. Hartley Hall Nursing Home; bd. mgrs. Lower Shore YMCA, 2004—, chair fin. devel. com., 2005—. Recipient Disting. Alumni award Ctrl. Meth. Coll., 1978. Mem. Am. Soc. Assn. Execs. (individual membership coun. 1979-81, edn. com. 1985-88, 92-94, univ. affairs commn. 1989-92, awards com. 1991), Washington Women's Forum (budget, program and exec. coms. 1978-82), Alumni Soc. Coll. Edn. Pa. State U. (bd. dirs., chairperson strategic planning com. 1986, Outstanding Alumni award). E-mail: ioinc@dmv.com.

HARTSOE, ROBERT JONES, lawyer; b. Washington, Feb. 26, 1962; s. Joseph Della and Hazel May (Jones) H.; m. Kimberly Ann Barcroft, Sept. 23, 1987; children: Lee, Kate. BA, Coll. William and Mary, 1984; JD, U. Richmond, 1987. Bar Va., U.S. Dist. Ct. (ea. dist., we. dist.) Va., U.S. Ct. Appeals (4th cir.), U.S. Supreme Ct. Assoc. Hugh A. West, Inc., Suffolk, Va., 1987-90, Katz & Stone, Vienna, Va., 1990-91, Law Offices of James A. Franca, Fairfax, Va., 1990-93; pvt. practice Fairfax, 1993-96; ptnr. Hartsoe & Brown PLLC, Fairfax, 1996-98, Hartsoe, Brown & Mansfield, PLLC, Fairfax, 1998-2000, Hartsoe & Mansfield, PLLC, Fairfax, 2000—04, Hartsoe & Mansfield and Morgan, PLLC, Fairfax, 2005—. Mem. Fairfax Bar Assn., Loudoun Bar Assn. Democrat. Methodist. Avocation: civil war. Office: 10621 Jones St Ste 201B Fairfax VA 22030-7511 also: 208 S King St Ste 203 Leesburg VA 20175-3018

HARTSOUGH, GAYLA ANNE KRAETSCH, management consultant; b. Lakewood, Ohio, Sept. 16, 1949; d. Vernon W. and Mildred E. (Austin) Kraetsch; m. James N. Heller, Aug. 20, 1972 (div. 1977); m. Jeffrey W. Hartsough, Mar. 12, 1983; 1 child, Jeffrey Hunter Kraetsch Hartsough. BS, Northwestern U., 1971; EdM, Tufts U., 1973; MEd, PhD, U. Va., 1978. Vol. VISTA, Tenn., 1970-71; asst. tchr. Perkins Sch. for the Blind, Watertown, Mass., 1971-72; resource tchr. Fairfax (Va.) County Pub. Schs., 1972-76; asst. dir. ctr. U. Va., Charlottesville, 1976-78; sr. program officer Acad. for Edn. Devel., Washington, 1978-80; mng. cons. Cresap/Towers Perrin, Washington and L.A., 1980-86; pres. KH Consulting Group, L.A., 1986—. Mem. nat. adv. coun. Northwestern U. Sch. Speech, Evanston, Ill., 1992—; bd. dirs. BTW; cons. in field. Contbr. more than 20 articles to profl. jours. Co-founder L.A. Higher Edn. Roundtable, L.A., 1987-94; mem. nat. adv. coun., coun. 100, Northwestern U., 1999-. Recipient Outstanding Woman of Achievement award Century City C. of C., 1991. Mem. BTW (bd. mem.), Orgn. Women Execs. (previous pres., bd. dirs. L.A. 1986-95). Home: 15624 Royal Ridge Rd Sherman Oaks CA 91403-4207 Office: KH Consulting Group 1901 Ave Of Stars Ste 1900 Los Angeles CA 90067-6020 Office Phone: 310-203-5419. Office Fax: 310-203-5417. Personal E-mail: khcggak@aol.com.

HARTT, GROVER, III, lawyer; b. Dallas, Apr. 12, 1948; s. Grover Jr. and Dorothy June (Wilkins) H. BA with high honors, So. Meth. U., 1970, LLM in Tax, 1986; JD with high honors, Tex. Tech U., 1973. Bar: Tex. 1973, U.S. Dist. Ct. (no. dist.) Tex. 1974, U.S. Dist. Ct. (we. dist.) Tex. 1975, U.S. Ct. Appeals (5th cir.) 1975, U.S. Dist. Ct. (ea. dist.) Tex. 1999, U.S. Ct. Fed. Claims, 2005, U.S. Supreme Ct. 1976. Law clk. to presiding justice Ct. Criminal Appeals Tex., Austin, 1973-75; atty. Hartt and Hartt, Dallas, 1975-79; atty., advisor Office Spl. Counsel U.S. Dept. Energy, Dallas, 1979-80, dep. chief counsel, 1981-83; trial atty. tax divsn. U.S. Dept. Justice, Dallas, 1983-86, dep. atty.-in-charge tax divsn., 1986-95, asst. chief southwestern region civil trial sect. tax divsn., 1995—. Nat. spkr. on taxation, bankruptcy and litig. Contbg. author: Collier on Bankruptcy; contbr. articles to profl. jours. Recipient Atty. Gen's award for disting. svc., 1996. Fellow Am. Coll. Bankruptcy; mem. ABA (mem. ct. procedure com. tax sect., chmn. bankruptcy litig. subcom. 1995-2003, mem. bus. bankruptcy com. bus. law sect., vice chmn. tax and fed. claims subcom. 1996-2000, chmn. 2000—, Dept. of Justice liaison 2003—), Tex. Bar Assn., Dallas Bar Assn., Am. Bankruptcy Inst., Coll. of State Bar of Tex., John C. Ford Am. Inn of Ct. (master of the bench 2000—). Office: US Dept Justice Tax Divsn 717 N Harwood St Ste 400 Dallas TX 75201-6506 Office Phone: 214-880-9733. Business E-Mail: grover.hartt@usdoj.gov.

HARTWELL, CAROL L., Spanish language educator, technical recruiter; b. Fargo, ND, Jan. 6, 1948; d. Edward Everett and Alaine C. (Meyer) H.; m. Howard M. Hammer, May 25, 1974 (div. Mar. 1995); children: Laura Elizabeth, Stephanie Lynn. BA magna cum laude, U. Utah, 1970; MA, Ind. U., 1971; MBA, Ball State U., 1978. Pers. dir. Pacemaker Driver Svc., Indpls., 1973-74; mgr. acctg. dept. Rex Bus. Machines (now Minolta), Indpls., 1974-76; br. mgr. Flexible Pers., Muncie, Ind., 1993-95; pres. Metro. Tech., Inc., Muncie, 1995—; instr. bus. mgmt. Ball State U., Muncie, 1978-79; instr. fin. dept., 1992; instr. Spanish, Ind. Acad., 1996—. Cons. in field. Mem.: Am. Assn. Tchrs. Spanish and Portuguese, Am. Contract Bridge League, Phi Kappa Phi. Democrat. Unitarian Universalist. Avocations: duplicate bridge, Go, chess, Scrabble, miscellaneous card games. Office Phone: 765-285-7366. Business E-Mail: clhartwell@bsu.edu.

HARTWELL, LELAND HARRISON (LEE HARTWELL), geneticist, educator; b. Los Angeles, Oct. 30, 1939; s. Majorie (Taylor) H.; m. Theresa Naujack. BS, Calif. Inst. Tech., 1961; PhD, MIT, 1964. Postdoctoral fellow Salk Inst., 1964-65; asst. prof. U. Calif., Irvine, 1965-67, assoc. prof., 1967-68, U. Washington, Seattle, 1968-73, prof. genome sciences, 1973—, adj. prof. of medicine, 2003; pres., dir. Fred Hutchison Cancer Rsch. Ctr., Seattle, 1997—. Rsch. prof. Am. Cancer Soc., 1990—. Recipient Eli Lilly award, 1973, NIH Merit award, 1990, GM Sloan award, 1991, Hoffman LaRoche Mattia award, 1991, Gairdner Found. Internat. award, 1992, Simon Shubitz award U. Chgo., 1992, Brandeis U. Rosenstiel award, 1993, Sloan Kettering Cancer Ctr. Katherine Berkan Judd award, 1994, Genetics Soc. of Am. medal, 1994, MGH Warren Triennial prize, 1995, Keith Porter award Am. Soc. Cell Biology, 1995, Carnegie Mellon Dickson award, 1996, Louisa Gross Horwitz prize Columbia U., 1995, Albert Lasker Basic Med. Rsch. award Albert and Mary Lasker Found., 1998, Brinker Internat. award for basic sci. Susan G. Komen Breast Cancer Found., 1998, Disting. Alumni award Calif. Inst. Tech., 1999, City of Medicine award, 1999, medal of honor Am. Cancer Soc., 1999, Léopold Giffuel prize Assn. pour la Recherche sur le Cancer, France, 2000, The Massry prize The Meira and Shaul G. Massry Found., Nobel prize in Physiology or Medicine, 2001; Guggenheim fellow, 1983-84; Am. Bus. Cancer Rsch. grantee, 1983—; Am. Cancer Soc. scholar; laureate Passano Found., 1996. Mem. NAS, AAAS, Am. Soc. Microbiology, Am. Soc. Cell Biology, Genetics Soc. Am. (pres. 1990). Office: Hutchinson Cancer Rsch Ctr D1-060 1100 Fairview Ave N PO Box 19024 Seattle WA 98109-1024*

HARTWELL, STEPHEN, investment company executive; b. Phila., Apr. 10, 1915; s. Stephen Warren and Elizabeth (Thompson) H.; m. Elizabeth van Laer Speer, Feb. 21, 1946 (div. 1973); children: Stephen Warren II, Robert van Laer; m. Norma Bostick, Dec. 9, 1978. BS in Adminstrv. Engring., Lafayette Coll., 1936. Investment analyst Pa. Co. Banking & Trusts, 1936-41; procurement officer electronic equipment CAA, 1947-48; indsl. specialist AEC, 1948-49, chief progress and stats. sect., prodn. div., 1949-51, chief constr. engring. reports br., 1951-54; exec. v.p. Atomic Devel. Securities Co. (and successor cos.), 1954-68; v.p. Washington Mut. Investors Fund, Inc., 1968-81, pres., 1981-85, chmn., 1985—2001, chmn. emeritus, 2001—. Pres. Washington Investment Advisers Inc., 1992-2001; chmn. emritus Tax Exempt Bond Fund Md., 2001, Tax Exempt Fund Va., 1986-97, chmn. emeritus, 1997—; pres., bd. dirs. Colchester Corp., Woodbridge, Va., 1971—; chmn. WMIF Mgmt. Corp., Washington, 1986— Hartick LLC, 1997—; bd. dirs. Wentz Corp., Wilmington, Del., Johnston Lemon Group Inc.; trustee Ameribanc Investors Group, 1985-95. Mem. Fairfax County (Va.) Planning Commn., 1961-67, chmn., 196466; mem. No. Va. Regional Planning and Econ. Devel. Commn., 1963-64, Fairfax County Rep. Com., 1955-61, 66-70, 79-81; bd. govs. Gunston Hall Sch., Va.; active Mt. Vernon Life Guards, 1992—, chmn., 1998—; trustee Am. U., 1983-88, trustee emeritus, 1990—; trustee Woodlawn Found., 1983-89; trustee, treas. Found. for Middle East Peace, 1993—, Fairfax Hosp. Assn., 1986-93; trustee, treas. Inova Health Systems, 1987-96, chmn. investment and pension com., 1997-2002; chmn. Jefferson Hosp., Alexandria, Va., 1986-92; chmn. Virginia Coll. Bldg. Authority, Richmond, Va., 1994-2001; mem. Commonwealth Coun. Richmond, Va., 1998-2002. Maj. AUS, 1941—45. Mem.: NASD (Dist. 10 com. 1968—71), SAR, Nat. Economists Club, Washington Soc. Investment Analysts, Met. Club, Mt. Vernon Country Club, Phi Alpha (pres.), Zeta Psi (trustee Ednl. Found. 1997—, pres. 1999—2000). Home: Riversedge PO Box 33 Mount Vernon VA 22121-0033 Office: AMA Bldg 1101 Vermont Ave NW Fl 12 Washington DC 20005-3583 Office Phone: 202-842-5670. Personal E-mail: stephcom@msn.com.

HARTWELL, WILLIAM GERSHAM, III, retired music educator; s. William Gersham Hartwell Jr. and Barbara Lillian Parker Hartwell; m. Janis Louese Quier, Jan. 15, 1982; children: Ted, Susanne, John Harrison, Brian Harrison, Mark Harrison. BA in Music, Whitman Coll., 1961; MMus in Voice and Pedagogy, Ind. U., 1964. Instr. music Ea. Wash. State, Cheney, 1963—66; asst. prof. music Whitworth Coll., Spokane, 1967—68; assoc. instr. music Ind. U., Bloomington, 1969—71; asst. prof. music Alma (Mich.) Coll., 1971—72; assoc. prof. music Tex. Tech U., Lubbock, 1973—2004. Dirigent Spokane German Chorale, 1964—69; dir. Sweet Adelines Chorus, Spokane, 1968—69; dir. music Ch. of the Cross, Bloomington, 1970—71, St. John's United Meth. Ch., Lubbock, 1974—82, Asbury Meth. Ch., Lubbock, 1996—. Contbr. (CD-ROM) Liberty, Equality, Fraternity, 2001; numerous vocal performances in recitals, musicals, operas. Mem.: Nat. Assn. Tchrs. of Singing, Beta Theta Pi, Phi Mu Alpha, Phi Delta Kappa, Pi Kappa Lambda. Republican. Avocations: fishing, hunting, golf, bowling, reading. Home: 3204 68th St Lubbock TX 79413 Office: Tex Tech Sch Music PO Box 42033 Lubbock TX 79409 Office Phone: 806-799-2034. E-mail: wghartwell@sbcglobal.net.

HARTWICK, GARY GLENN, entertainment company executive; b. New Orleans, Jan. 8, 1943; s. Glenn Edwin and Viola Rita Hartwick; m. Patricia Jean Brown, 1968 (dec. 1979); m. Nancy Allen Kelly, Feb. 16, 1980; children Timothy T., Jeffrey J. Student, U. Rochester, 1961-69, MBA, 1982; postgrad., U. Denver, 2000—. Sr. engring. programmer Rochester (N.Y.) Applied Sci. Assocs., 1969-71; v.p. software engring. Pi-Rad, Inc., Rochester, 1972-82; mgr. electronics products engring. Scientifa-Atlanta, 1982-87; dir. residental video applications Bellcore, Red Bank, N.J., 1987-93; sr. dir. strategic mktg. DSC Comm., Petaluma, Calif., 1993-94; v.p. tech. and ops. Viacom Inc., N.Y.C., 1994—. Vice chmn. tech. security com. Davic, 1995-98; inst. dir. Nat. Comm. Forum, 1995. Trustee Natural History Mus. of Adirondacks, Tupper Lake, N.Y., 2000—; adviser Paul Smiths (N.Y.) Coll. With USN, USNR, 1961-63. Mem. IEEE, Soc. Motion Picture and TV Engrs. (bd. editors 1989—), Saranac Lake Fish and Game Club, Rochester Yacht Club. Democrat. Episcopalian. Avocations: yacht racing, model railroading, pilot. Home: PO Box 1368 Lake Placid NY 12946 Office: Viacom 1515 Broadway New York NY 10036 E-mail: gary.hartwick@viacom.com.

HARTWICK, THOMAS STANLEY, technical management consultant; b. Vandalia, Ill., Mar. 19, 1934; s. William Arthur and Bernice Elizabeth (Daniels) H.; m. Alberta Elaine Lind, June 10, 1961; children: Glynis Anne, Jeffrey Andrew, Thomas Arthur. BS, U. Ill., 1956; MS, UCLA, 1958; PhD, U. So. Calif., 1969. Mgr. quantum electronics dept. Aerospace Corp., El Segundo, Calif., 1973-75, asst. dir. electonics research lab., 1975-79; mgr. electro-optical devel. lab. Hughes Aircraft Co. subs. Gen. Motors Corp., El Segundo, 1979-82, chief sci. advanced tactical programs, 1982-83; mgr. electro-optics research ctr. TRW Corp., Redondo Beach, Calif., 1983-86, mgr. microelectrics ctr., 1986-90, program mgr., 1990-96. Chmn., bd. dirs. Laser Tech., Inc., Hollywood, Calif., 1990-94; cons. mem. U.S. Dept. Def. Adv. Group on Electronic Devices, Washington, 1977—, group C chmn., 1988-94, main group chmn., 1998-04, chmn. emeritus, 2004-05; mem. Japan/U.S. Tech. Assessment Team, Washington, 1984; mem. Army Rsch. Labs. Adv. Bd., 1993-95; bd. dirs. 3D Tech. labs., Inc., IMEC, Inc.; chmn. FAA security Nat. Rsch. Coun., 1997-2002, chmn. trans. sec. adminstrn., 2002-05, bd. mfg. and engring. design, 2005—, mem. nat. nanotechnology com., 2005—; mem. adv. bd. Continuum Ventures, 2000-04; chmn. bd. dirs. Cystal Rsch.; mem. tech. adv. bd. Corvis Inc. Contbr. articles to profl. jours.; inventor FAR Infrared Laser, 1975. Mem. Am. Phys. Soc., Optical Soc. Am., (com. mem. 1976-79), Am. Def. Preparedness Assn. (dep. chmn. West Coast seminar 1987-88), mem. Nat. Res. Coun. Comm. Optical Sci and Engring., 1995-99, mem. NAS (nat. assoc. 2002), Nat. Res. Coun. Nat. Materials Adv. Bd. 2000—). Avocations: piano, sports.

HARTY, JAMES D., former manufacturing company executive; b. Bridgeport, Conn., Oct. 5, 1929; s. John S. and Catherine (Lee) H.; m. Margaret O'Connor, June 4, 1955; children: Shaun, Kevin, Maura, Megan. Grad., U.S. Army Officer Candidate Sch., Ft. Bliss, Tex., 1952; degree in indsl. engring, U. Bridgeport, 1962. Analyst E.I. DuPont, 1947-51; prodn. control mgr. Sikorsky Aircraft, 1954-62; plant mgr. Stanley Works, 1962-68; corp. mgr. prodn. and inventory control ITT, 1968-70; corp. dir. mfg. projects Singer Co., N.Y.C., 1970-74; pres., chief operating officer Raymond Corp., Greene, N.Y., 1974-84, also dir., now ret.; owner, cons. J.D. Harty Assocs., Hilton Head Island, S.C., 1984-94. Mem. engring. tech. adv. com. and M.B.A. adv. bd. SUNY-Binghamton, mem. found.; mem. Sch. Bd. Found., Hilton Head Island, S.C. 1st lt. U.S. Army, 1951-53, Korea. Recipient Corp. Leadership award MIT, 1987. Mem. Am. Mgmt. Assn. (Internat. Svc. award), Am. Prodn. and Inventory Control Soc. (past internat. v.p. edn. and rsch., Disting. Svc. award), Hilton Head Island Computer Club, Country Club of Hilton Head. Home: 4 Herring Gull Ln Hilton Head Island SC 29926-2655 Personal E-mail: jdharty@adelphia.net.

HARTY, JAMES QUINN, lawyer; b. Phila., Dec. 10, 1925; s. William Lawrence and Marie Sarita (Quinn) H.; m. Ann Elizabeth McGeeney, July 23, 1955; children: Michael, Martha Harty Scheines, Christopher, Patrick, Mark, Paul. AB, LaSalle Coll., 1949; MBA, U. Pa., Phila., 1952, LLB, 1959. Bar: Pa. 1961. Personnel mgr. Corning (N.Y.) Glass Works, 1952-56; lectr. Wharton Sch. U. Pa., Phila., 1956-59; assoc. Reed, Smith, Shaw & McClay, Pitts., 1961-70, ptnr., 1971-95, Plummer DeWalt & Linn, Pitts., 1995—. Research editor: Office Management Handbook, 1958. Mem. Thornburg Zoning Rev. Bd., Thornburg Borough Coun., Pitts., 1968-76. With USN, 1943-46, PTO, CBI. Fulbright lectr. U. Kanazawa, Japan, 1959-60. Mem. Pa. Bar Assn. (chmn. labor sect. 1982), Allegheny Bar Assn., Pitts. Athletic Assn. Clubs: Pitts. (gov. 1986-87), Chartiers Country (Pitts.). Roman Catholic. Avocation: golf. Office: DKW Law Group LLC US Steel Tower 58th Fl 600 Grant St Pittsburgh PA 15219-1912 Office Phone: 412-355-8152. Business E-Mail: jharty@dkwlaw.com.

HARTY, THOMAS H., publishing executive; Advt. dir. Reader's Digest; assoc. pub. TV Guide, N.Y.C., 1998—99, v.p., publisher, 1999—2001; sr. v.p., gen. mgr. Golf Digest Cos., Trumbull, Conn., 2002—. Office: Golf Digest PO Box 850 Wilton CT 06897-0850

HARTZ, ARTHUR J., medical researcher; b. Balt., Md., June 21, 1944; s. Alvin Sidney and Muriel Abrams Hartz; m. Ellen Louise Vastine, June 11, 1968; children: Alisa Louise, Sarah McConnell. BA, Swarthmore Coll., 1966; PhD, John Hopkins Sch. of Hygiene, 1974; MD, Med. Coll. of Wis., 1982. MD State of Iowa, 1998. Asst. prof. Med. Coll. of Wis., 1974—79, assoc. prof., 1983—85; asst. prof. Milton S. Hershey Med. Ctr., Hershey, Pa., 1985—87; assoc. prof. Med. Coll. of Wis., 1987—93, prof., 1994—97; prof. and rsch. dir. U. Iowa, 1997—, endowed prof. for quality in family medicine, 2002—. Cons. Nat. Adv. Com. for Rsch., Balt., 1988—92, Agy. for Healthcare Policy and Rsch., Silver Springs, Md., 1989—93, NIH CFS Spl. Emphasis Panel, Bethesda, Md., 1999—2003. Bd. mem. Congregation Sinai, Milw., 1992—95, Agudas Achim, Iowa City, 2002—. Achievements include introduced the waist hip ratio as a measure of body fat distribution and risk factor for disease; found that smoking was a risk factor for cardiomyopathy; identified the characteristics of hospitals that provide the best medical care; explored the value and validity of observational studies for the assessment of medical treatments. Avocations: travel, bicycling, square dancing. Office: U Iowa Dept Family Medicine 200 Hawkins Dr 01292-DPFP Iowa City IA 52242 Office Phone: 319-384-7765. Office Fax: 319-384-7822. Business E-Mail: arthur-hartz@uiowa.edu.

HARTZ, BRIAN DAVID, physical therapist, educator, small business owner; b. Lancaster, Pa., Dec. 15, 1972; s. John F. and Nancy K. Hartz; m. Amy M. Walker, June 9, 2001; 1 child, Zachary W. BSc in Biology, Rider U., 1995; MPT, Hahnemann U., 1998; DPT, Temple U., 2003. Cert. clin. specialist ortho. physican therapy 2004. Owner/ pres. HARTZ Phys. Therapy, Lititz, Pa., 2000—; adj. prof. Rider U., Lawrenceville, NJ, 1999—2001, Franklin and Marshall Coll., Lancaster, Pa., 2002—. Named Phys. Therapist of the Yr., Lancaster AMBUCS, 2003; recipient AMBUCS Phys. Therapy Scholarship, AMBUCS - Lititz Chpt., 1996—98. Mem.: Pa. Phys. Therapy Assn., Am. Phys. Therapy Assn. Home: 164 Riveredge Dr Leola PA 17540 Office: HARTZ Physical Therapy 100 Highlands Dr Ste 100 Lititz PA 17543

HARTZ, DEBORAH SOPHIA, editor, writer; b. Plainfield, N.J., July 11, 1951; d. Sylvester and Margaret (Buschart) H.; m. Thomas McDonald July 24, 1971 (div. Dec. 1976). BA, U. Pa., 1973; MS, U. Wis., 1977. Asst. editor Whitney Communications Corp., N.Y.C., 1978-79; lifestyles editor News Dispatch, Michigan City, Ind., 1979-80; food editor, restaurant critic Daily Herald, Arlington Heights, Ill., 1980-88; editor in chief Cook's mag., Bridgeport, Conn., 88-90; food Editor Sun-Sentinel, Ft Lauderdale, Fla., 1990—. Cons. newsletter, Cuisinart Corp., Greenwich Conn., 1985-88. Recipient Golden Carnation award, 1986, James Beard Journalism award. Mem. Am. Inst. of Wine and Food, Assoc. of Food Journalists, Les Dames d'Escoffier. Office: Sun-Sentinel 200 E Las Olas Blvd Ste 1000 Fort Lauderdale FL 33301-2293

HARTZ, HARRIS L, judge; b. Balt., Jan. 20, 1947; s. Alvin Sidney and Muriel (Abrams) H.; children: Jacob Cameron, Andrew Samuel. A.B. summa cum laude, Harvard U., 1967, J.D. magna cum laude, 1972. Bar: N. Mex. 1972, U.S. Dist. Ct. N.Mex. 1972, U.S. Ct. Appeals (10th cir.) 1973. Asst. U.S. atty. Dept. Justice, Albuquerque, 1972-75; asst. prof. Coll. Law, U. Ill., Champaign, 1976; atty., exec. dir. Gov.'s Organized Crime Prevention Commn., Albuquerque, 1976-79; assoc. Poole, Tinnin & Martin, P.A., Albuquerque, 1979-82; assoc. Miller, Stratvert, Torgerson & Brandt, Albuquerque, 1982-83, ptnr., dir., 1983-88; judge N. Mex. Ct. Appeals, 1988-99; judge U.S. Court Appeals (10th cir.) Albuquerque, 2001-. Case and devels. editor Harvard Law Rev., 1971-72, editor 1970-71; bd. editors Litigation Mag., 1983-86. Mem. exec. com. Bernalillo County Republican Party, Albuquerque, 1982-83; Rep. nominee for N.Mex. Supreme Ct. elections, 1986, 92, 96; chmn. N.Mex. Racing Commn., 1987-88; bd. dirs. Appellate Judges Edn. Inst., 2003-; mem. com. on rules of practice and procedure U.S. Jud. Conf., 2003-. Recipient Founders' award Nat. Kidney Found., N.Mex., 1997; nominee Joan Pew award Nat. Assn. State Racing Commrs., 1988. Mem. ABA (mem. adv. com. standing com. law and nat. security 1995-97, chmn. appellate judges conf. 2004—), Am. Law Inst. (advisor restatement law agy. 1996—), Albuquerque Com. on Fgn. Rels. (chmn. 1981-82), Am. Judicature Soc., Rotary Club of Albuquerque (pres. 1996-97), Phi Beta Kappa. Office: 201 3d St NW # 1870 Albuquerque NM 87102-4391 Office Phone: 505-843-6196. Business E-Mail: judgeharrishartz@ca10.uscourts.gov.

HARTZ, JILL, museum director; b. Montreal, Que., Can., July 25, 1950; Undergrad. study, Oberlin U., 1969-71; MA in English Lang. and Lit. with honors, U. St. Andrews, Scotland, 1973; student, Cornell U., 1989-94. Mgr. Tompkins County Arts Coun., Ithaca, 1981-82, Grapevine Graphics, Ithaca, 1982-83; co-editor Grapevine Weekly Mag., Ithaca, 1983-84, Living Publs., Ithaca, 1984-86; coord. exhbns., asst. to dir. Herbert F. Johnson Mus. of Art, Cornell U., 1976-81, dir. pub. rels. and publs. Ithaca, 1986-93; asst. to chair, dept. of art Cornell U., Ithaca, 1993-94; coord. pub. rels. and spl. programs Coun. for the Arts, Cornell U., Ithaca, 1993-94; dir. comm. Arts & Scis. Devel. Office, U. Va., Charlottesville, 1994-97; interim dir. U. Va. Mus. Art (Bayly Art Mus.), Charlottesville, 1997, dir., 1997—. Co-curator Agnes Denes exhbn., 1991-92, editor monograph; co-founder, ptnr. LunaMedia pub. rels. co., Ithaca, 1993-94. Mem. Am. Assn. Museums, Nat. Cultural Alliance. Office: U Va Mus Art 155 Rugby Rd Charlottesville VA 22903 Fax: 804-924-6321.*

HARTZ, MICHAEL O., lawyer; b. Flint, Mich., July 24, 1953; BA, Kalamazoo Coll, 1975; JD, U. Detroit, 1978; LLM in Taxation, U. Fla., 1979. Bar: Mich. 1978, Fla. 1979, Ill. 1980. Ptnr. estate planning Katten Muchin Zavis Rosenman, Chgo. Fellow: Am. Coll. of Trusts and Estates Counsel. Office: Katten Muchin Zavis Rosenman 525 W Monroe St, Ste 1600 Chicago IL 60661 Office Phone: 312-902-5279. Office Fax: 312-577-8789. E-mail: michael.hartz@kmzr.com.

HARTZ, RICHARD ALLEN, research scientist; s. Jacob Allen and Fannie Mae Hartz. BS in chemistry, Eastern Mennonite U., 1988; PhD in organic chemistry, U. Pa., 1996. Postdoctoral fellow Ind. U., Bloomington, Ind., 1996—97, U. Mich., Ann Arbor, Mich., 1997—98; sr. rsch. scientist DuPont Pharm. Co., Wilmington, Del., 1998—2001; sr. rsch. investigator Bristol-Myers Squibb Co., Wallingford, Conn., 2001—. Contbr. articles various profl. jours. Mem.: NY Acad. Sci, Am. Chem. Soc. Avocations: bicycling, skiing. Office: Bristol-Myers Squibb Co 5 Rsch Pkwy Wallingford CT 06492 E-mail: richard.hartz@bms.com.

HARTZ, STEVEN EDWARD MARSHALL, lawyer, educator; b. Cambridge, Mass., July 11, 1948; s. Louis and Stella (Feinberg) H.; m. Janice Lindsay, June 12, 1976. AB magna cum laude, Harvard Coll., 1970; JD, U. Chgo., 1974. Bar: N.Y. 1975, U.S. Dist. Ct. (so. and ea. dists.) N.Y. 1975, U.S. Ct. Appeals (2d cir.) 1975, Fla. 1979, U.S. Dist. Ct. (so. dist.) Fla. 1979, U.S. Tax Ct. 1979, U.S. Ct. Appeals (5th cir.) 1979, U.S. Supreme Ct. 1979, U.S. Ct. Appeals (11th cir.) 1981, U.S. Dist. Ct. (mid. dist.) Fla. 1984. Assoc. Cleary, Gottlieb, Steen & Hamilton, N.Y.C., 1974-79; asst. U.S. atty. U.S. Dept. Justice, Miami, Fla., 1979-82, dep. chief criminal divsn., chief fraud and pub. corruption sect., 1981-82; sole practice Miami, Fla., 1982-90; of counsel Akerman, Senterfitt & Eidson, P.A., Miami, 1980, ptnr., shareholder, 1991—. Lectr. dept. English, U. English, U. Miami, 1984, adj. assoc. prof., 1985-86. Co-author: Housing, A Community Handbook, 1973. Vol. atty. Mobilization for Youth Legal Svcs., N.Y.C., 1978. Recipient Dirs.' award U.S. Dept. Justice, 1981; Fulbright Hays scholar, 1970. Mem. ABA, FBA, Fla. Bar Assn., N.Y. State Bar Assn., Dade County Bar Assn., Assn. Bar City N.Y., Phi Beta Kappa. Office: One Southeast 3rd Ave 28th Fl Miami FL 33131-4943 Office Phone: 305-982-5639. Business E-Mail: steven.hartz@akerman.com.

HARTZELL, ANDREW CORNELIUS, JR., retired lawyer; b. Balt., Nov. 5, 1927; s. Andrew Cornelius and Mary Frances (Milholland) H.; m. Mary Leontine McPhillips, July 31, 1954; children: Andrew Cornelius III, Stephen Carroll, Mary Leontine, James Francis, John Michael, Peter Milholland. BA, Yale U., 1950, LL.B., 1953. Bar: N.Y. 1953, Ohio 1955, U.S. Supreme Ct. Law clk. Fed. Judge Irving R. Kaufman, N.Y.C., 1953-54; assoc. Thompson, Hine & Flory, Cleve., 1954-63, Debevoise, Plimpton, Lyons & Gates, N.Y.C., 1963-65; ptnr. Debevoise & Plimpton and predecessor firms, 1966-96, chmn. litigation dept., 1989-92, of counsel, 1996-98. Author: The Treacherous Snows, 1993; contbr. articles to legal jours. and to Antitrust Advisor, McGraw-Hill Pub. Co., 1971, 78; Note and Comment editor Yale Law Jour, 1952-53. Mem. bd. archtl. rev. Village of Scarsdale, N.Y., 1965-67; mem. Adv. Coun. on Environ. Conservation, 1986-90, chmn., 1987-89; mem. Sch. Facilities Adv. Com., 1988-90; bd. dirs. Friends of Scarsdale Parks, 1991-2000; mem. Scarsdale Bowl com., 2001-02; Bd. Assessment Review, 1998-2003; Rep. candidate for Congress 18th dist. N.Y., 1994. With U.S. Army, 1946-48. Fellow Am. Coll. Trial Lawyers; mem. ABA, Union Internat. des Avocats, Scarsdale Golf Club, Yale Club N.Y., Town and Village Club (Scarsdale), Am. Alpine Club. Roman Catholic. Home: 7 Eastwoods Ln Scarsdale NY 10583-6401 Office: Debevoise & Plimpton LLP 919 Third Ave New York NY 10022-3904 Office Phone: 212-909-6397.

HARTZELL, CHARLES R., science foundation director, cell biologist, biochemist; b. Butler, Pa., Aug. 12, 1941; s. Charles R. and Ada Grace (Giles) H.; m. Marguerite K. Getty; children: Scott David, Amy Lynette. BS, Geneva Coll., 1963; PhD, Indiana U., 1967; MDiv, Union Theol. Sem., 2002. Post-doctoral fellow Ind. U., Bloomington, 1967; rsch. fellow Commonwealth Sci, and Industry Rsch. Orgn., Melbourne, Australia, 1967-68; rsch. fellow, asst. rsch. prof. U. Wis., Madison, 1968-71; asst. prof. Pa. State U., University Park, 1971-75, assoc. prof., 1975-78; sr. rsch. scientist Alfred I. DuPont Inst., Wilmington, Del., 1978-80, dir. rsch., 1981-97, Nemours Children's Clinics, Fla., 1987—2001; rsch. mgr. The Nemours Found., Jacksonville, 1987—2001; prof. pediat. Jefferson Med. Coll., Phila., 1989—; dir. Cross Heart Ministries, Inc., Wilmington, 2002—. Contbr. articles to profl. jours. NIH fellow, 1968-70; established investigator Am. Heart Assn., 1970-75. Republican. Presbyterian. Avocations: ballroom dancing, music, carpentry, exercise. Office: Cross-Heart Ministries Inc 34 Colefax Ct Wilmington DE 19804-2950 Personal E-mail: chartzell@juno.com.

HARTZELL, KARL DREW, retired university dean, historian; b. Chgo., Jan. 17, 1906; s. Morton C. and Bertha V. (Drew) H.; m. Anne Lomas, Sept. 7, 1935; children: Karl Drew, Richard Lomas, Julian Crane; m. Elizabeth Farnum Guibord, Oct. 2, 1993. PhB cum laude, Wesleyan U., 1927; AM, Harvard U., 1928, PhD, 1934. Mem. faculty European history and Western civilization Carleton Coll., 1930-31; mem. faculty European history and western civilization dept. Ga. Sch. Tech., 1935-40; with SUNY, Geneseo, 1940-47; historian N.Y. State War Coun., 1945-46; adminstrv. officer Brookhaven Nat. lab., 1947-52; dean Cornell Coll., Iowa, 1952-56, Bucknell U., 1956-62; acting chief adminstrv. officer SUNY, Stony Brook, 1962-65, adminstrv. officer, 1965-71; libr. Inst. Advanced Studies of World Religions, cons. Author: The Empire State at War: World War II, 1949, Opportunities in Atomic Energy, 1950, A Philosophy for Science Teaching, 1957, The Laws of the Living: American Values in Action, 2005; editor: The Upperclass Student and His Curriculum, 1955; co-editor: The Study of Religion on the Campus of Today, 1967. Wilbur Fisk scholar, Wesleyan U. Fellow Soc. for Values in Higher Edn. (sr. mem.); mem. Soc. Christian Ethics, Phi Beta Kappa. Republican. Home (Summer): PO Box 166 Shelter Island Heights NY 11965-0166 Home (Winter): 1000 Vicar's Landing Way 210 Ponte Vedra Beach FL 32082 Office Phone: 904-980-9730. E-mail: kdh27@comcast.net.

HARTZFELD, HOWARD ALEXANDER, JR., lawyer; b. Bartlesville, Okla., July 18, 1966; s. Howard Alexander Sr. and Pearly Faye H. BA in Journalism, U. Okla., 1988; JD, Pepperdine U., 1991; LLM in Transnational bus., McGeorge Sch. Law, 1993. Bar: Calif. 1992, Ariz. 1995, U.S. Dist. Ct. Ariz. 1995. Pvt. practice, Washington, 1992, 94-95; stagrere Loeff Claeys Verbeke, Rotterdam, The Netherlands, 1993; pvt. practice Phoenix, 1995-99, Tobin & Louie, 1999-2000, Louie, Almeida & Stettler, 2000—05, Louie Stettler & Liebherr, Burbank, Calif., 2005—. Mem. Ariz. State Bar Assn. (exec. bd. young lawyers divsn. 1998-99), Maricopa County Bar (bd. dirs. internat. law sect. 1997-99, treas. 1998-99, chmn. domestic violence necessities drive 1997). Office: Louie Stettler & Liebherr 4th Fl 303 N Glenoaks Blvd Burbank CA 91502 Office Phone: 818-461-9559. Business E-Mail: hhartzfeld@laslaw.net.

HARTZLER, GENEVIEVE LUCILLE, physical education educator; b. Hammond, Ind., June 19, 1921; d. Lewis Garvin and Effie May (Orton) H. BS in Edn., Ind. U., 1944; MEd, U. Minn., 1948. Tchr. phys. edn. Griffith (Ind.) Pub. Schs., 1944-45, Northrup Collegiate Sch., Mpls., 1945-47; supr. student tchrs., 1947-79; tchr. phys. edn. Marquette (Mich.) Pub. Schs., 1948-50, Albion (Mich.) Pub. Schs., 1951-56, Jackson (Mich.) Pub. Schs., 1957-79, coord., project dir., tchr., coach, 1979-83. Chair equity workshop Jackson Pub. Schs., 1979-83; chair various convs., 1964-70. Mem. Am. Heart Assn., Jackson, 1977-83; mem., chair Women in Mgmt., Jackson, 1981-83; mem. Bus. and Profl. Women, Jackson, 1980-90. Recipient Honor awards Young Woman's Christian Assn. and Mich. Divsn. Girls and Women's Sports. Mem. AAHPERD, NEA, Mich. Assn. Health, Phys. Edn. and Recreation (Honor award), Mich. Edn. Assn. (Women's Cultural award), Delta Kappa Gamma (Woman of Distinction award). Avocations: golf, swimming, travel, reading. Home: 703 Bay Meadows Cir Lady Lake FL 32159-2285 E-mail: genhar621@webtv.net.

HARTZLER, GEOFFREY OLIVER, retired cardiologist; b. Goshen, Ind., Nov. 6, 1946; s. Robert Willis and Emma Irene (Blosser) H.; m. Lois Anne Kauffman, June 1967 (div. May 1983); children: Abigail, Christine, Amanda; m. Dorothy Eloise Arnn, July 1985. BA, Goshen Coll., 1968; MD with honors, Ind. U., 1972. Diplomate Am. Bd. Internal Medicine, Bd. in Cardiovascular Disease. Intern Mayo Grad. Sch. Medicine, Rochester, Minn., 1972—73, fellow in medicine, 1973—74, fellow in cardiology, 1974—76; assoc. cons. internal medicine and cardiovascular disease Mayo Clinic, Rochester, 1976—77; instr. medicine Mayo Med. Sch. and Grad. Sch. Medicine, Rochester, 1976—79; cons. cardiovasc. disease and internal medicine Mayo Clinic and Mayo Found., Rochester, 1977—80; dir. invasive diagnostic electrophysiology Mayo Clinic, Rochester, 1979—80; cardiologist Cardiovasc. Cons., Inc., Kansas City, Mo., 1980—93; clin. prof. medicine U. Mo., Kansas City, 1985—95. Cons. cardiologist Mid-Am. Heart Inst., Kansas City, 1980-95; dir. advanced angioplasty fellowship program St. Luke's Hosp., Kansas City, 1985-92, med. dir. cardiovasc. clin. rsch. ctr. Mid-Am. Heart Inst., 1993-95; cons. Advanced Cardiovasc. Sys., Inc., Santa Clara, Calif., 1983-95; past mem. editl. or rev. bd. Am. Jour. Cardiology, Jour. Am. Coll. Cardiology, Cath. and CV Diagnosis, others; co-founder Ventritex, Inc., Sunnyvale, Calif., 1985-88, Triax Internat., Inc., Lenexa, Kans., 1989-96; prin., bd. dirs. Kustom Signals, Inc., Lenexa, 1990-96, LMP Steel & Wire Co., Maryville, Mo., Hartz Properties, Inc., Prairie Village, Kans., Lett Electronics, Inc., Topeka, 1995-98, Intraluminal Therapeutics, Inc., Kansas City, Kans., Cardiovasc. Sys., Mpls., 2002—. Contbr. articles to profl. jours., chpts. to books; made TV presentations to lay people on aspects of cardiology. Recipient K.K. Chen award, 1970, E.V. Allen scholarship, 1971, Osler award U. Miami, 1986, 1st Ann. Career Achievement award Cardiol. Rsch. Found., 1994. Fellow Am. Coll. Cardiology, Coun. on Clin. Cardiology of Am. Heart Assn., Soc. for Cardiac Angiography; mem. AMA, Mo. State Med. Assn., Jackson County Med. Assn., Am. Heart Assn., Alpha Omega Alpha. Avocations: music, motorcycling, reading, travel, business. Office: 2600 Verona Rd Shawnee Mission KS 66208-1266

HARTZOG, ELIZABETH WINDHAM, music educator; b. Bartlesville, Okla., Oct. 23, 1951; d. Malcolm Virgil and Betty Garig Windham; m. H. Miller Hartzog, Sept. 4, 1982; children: Katherine Elizabeth, Anna Karen, Mary Carole, Nathan, Andrew. MusB magna cum laude, U. Tex., 1974; MusM high honors, Eastman Sch. Music, 1976; MusB in Edn., cum laude, La. State U., 1982. Music copyist U.S. Army Band, Ft. Myer, Va., 1977—80; choir dir. Trafton Acad., Baton Rouge, 1982—83; piano tchr. Chapel Sch., Baton Rouge, 1984—85; pvt. practice piano tchr. Baton Rouge, 1985—. Dir. Merry Hearts Music Ensemble, Baton Rouge, 1988—2003; music dir. Crossroads Cmty. Ch., Baton Rouge, 2003—; conversational English volunteer tchr. La. State U.; piano tchr., 1991—; conversational English tchr. La. State U., 2004—05. Composer: (songs) Trio for Winds, 1974 (2d Pl. award Aspen (Colo.) Music Contest, 1974), And When Spring Comes, 1976 (1st Pl. award Mich. State Contest, 1976). English tchr. La. State U., Baton Rouge, 1984—89. With U.S. Army, 1977—80. Recipient Am. Spirit award, US Army-Women's Army Corps. basic training, 1977. Mem.: Music Tchrs. Nat. Assn., La. Music Tchrs. Assn., Nat. Fedn. Music Clubs. Republican. Avocations: sewing, playing recorder, hosting international students. Home: 10338 Hackberry Baton Rouge LA 70809 Personal E-mail: millerhartzeg@juno.com. E-mail: millerhartzog@eatel.net.

HARTZOG, IRA BARNES, air transportation executive; b. Hobart, Okla., July 15, 1918; s. Ira Barnes, Sr. and May Bentley (Arnold) H.; m. Ruth Jane Thompson; children: Ira B. III, Clarice Mears, Betty Roth, Nancy Anderson. Cert. airline transport pilot FAA, flight instr. Flt. instr. Coleman (Tex.) Flying Sch., 1941-42; pilot Air Transport Command, worldwide, 1943-46; tng. capt. Pan Am. Airways, Latin Am., 1946-48; pilot Irvin Air Chute, Inc., Buffalo, N.Y., 1949-52; chief divsn. mgr. Butler Corp., Dallas, 1952-55; founder Flt. Proficiency Svc., Inc., Ft. Worth, Tex., 1954-55; divsn. mgr. Butler Co., Chgo., 1955-60. Founder, CEO Hartzog Aviation, Inc., Rockford, Ill., 1960-84, Airmanship, Inc., Ill., Calif. and Ariz., 1978-99; adv. bd. Beech Aircraft Corp., Wichita, 1960-64, So. Ill. Univ., Carbondale, 1980-84. Prodr.: (video tapes) Aviation Safety Tng. Video Tapes (24 titles), 1980-97; contbr. articles to profl. jours. Active Quiet Bird Men, 1957-2002. Lt. col. USNG, ret. Decorated Disting. Flying Cross, U.S. Army Air Forces, Air medals, Theater ribbons, others. Mem. Nat. Bus. Aircraft Assn. (disting., bd. dirs. 1962-63). Avocations: reading, travel, video production, writing. Home: 13840 W Elmbrook Dr Sun City West AZ 85375-5427 E-mail: iragoz@aol.com.

HARUTUNIAN, ALBERT T(HEODORE), III, judge; b. San Diego, May 15, 1955; s. Albert Theodore Jr. and Elsie Ruth H.; m. Rebecca Blair, 1999. BA, Claremont McKenna Coll., 1977; JD, U. Calif., Berkeley, 1980. Bar: Calif. 1980, U.S. Dist. Ct. (so. dist.) Calif. 1980, U.S. Ct. Apppeals (9th cir.) 1982, U.S. Supreme Ct. 1984. Law clk. to Hon. Howard B. Turrentine U.S. Dist. Ct., San Diego, 1980-81; assoc. Luce, Forward, Hamilton & Scripps, San Diego, 1982-87, ptnr., 1988-95; judge San Diego Mcpl. Ct., 1995-98, San Diego Superior Ct., 1998—. Spl. counsel standing com. on discipline U.S. Dist. Ct. Calif., San Diego, 1983-85; chmn. San Diego Bar Labor and Employment Sect., 1988-89; chmn. fed. cts. com. Calif. State Bar, 1989-90. Bd. dirs. ARC San Diego chpt., 1992-2002, Crime Victims Fund, 1995-97; bd. govs. Muscular Dystrophy Assn., San Diego, 1985; grad. LEAD Inc., San Diego, 1986; planning com. San Diego United Way, 1986-92. Named one of Outstanding Young Men of Am., 1983; recipient Outstanding Service award 9th Cir. Jud. Conf., 1986. Mem. ABA, Calif. State Bar Ct. (referee 1985-88), Am. Arbitration Assn. (arbitrator 1986-95), Calif. Judges Assn. (mem. criminal law and procedure com. 1997-2000), Boalt Hall Alumni Assn. (bd. dirs. 1994-97), Claremont McKenna Coll. Alumni Assn. (founding dir. San Diego chpt. 1984-2000), Rotary (bd. dirs. San Diego club 1995—). Republican. Avocations: music, golf. Office: San Diego Superior Ct PO Box 122724 San Diego CA 92112-2724

HARVEL, TRACY DAWN, music educator; b. Wilmington, NC, Jan. 9, 1980; d. Dorothy Jackson and J. C. Wilkes (Stepfather). BS in Music Edn., Western Carolina U., 2002; MusM, U. NC, 2005. NC Tchg. Lic. NC State Bd. Edn., 2002. Gen. music tchr. Montgomery County Schs., Star, NC, 2002—. Mem.: Music Educators Nat. Conf. (assoc.; treas. 2000—02), Sigma Alpha Iota (life; editor 2000—01). Personal E-mail: tracy_harvel@hotmail.com.

HARVER, ANDREW ROBERT, psychology professor; b. Youngstown, Ohio, Oct. 29, 1955; s. Andrew and Eleanor Dzuracky H.; m. Nancy Hall Harver, June 30, 1984; children: Philip, Emma. BS, U. Wash., 1979; MS, Ohio U., 1982, PhD, 1984. Postdoct. fellow Dartmouth Med. Sch., 1984-87; rsch. asst. prof. SUNY, Stony Brook, 1987-91; asst. prof. to prof. U. N.C., Charlotte, 1991—, interim assoc. dean the grad. sch., 2001—02, chair dept. health behavior and adminstrn., 2002—. Editl. bd. Chest, 1999—; co-editor: Self-Management of Asthma, 1998; contbr. articles to profl. jours. including Psychophysiology, Biological Psychology, Am. Jour. of Respiratory and Critical Care Medicine. Mem. Am. Thoracic Soc. (program chair BS assembly 1999-2000), Internat. Soc. for the Advancement of Respiratory Psychophysiology (pres. 1999-2000). Avocations: camping, gardening, travel, antiques. Office: UNC Charlotte 9201 University City Blvd Charlotte NC 28223-0001 E-mail: aharver@carolina.rr.com, arharver@email.uncc.edu.

HARVEY, ALBERT C., lawyer; b. Knoxville, Tenn., June 30, 1939; m. Nancy Rutherford; children: Anne, Elizabeth. BS, U. Tenn., 1961, JD, 1967. Law clk. Tenn. Supreme Ct.; asst. to pub. defender Shelby County, 1969-71; ptnr. Thomason, Hendrix, Harvey, Johnson & Mitchell, Memphis. Instr. med. and dental jurisprudence U. Tenn., Memphis. Bd. editors Tenn. Law Rev. Pres. Goodwill Boys Club, 1983-85; active YMCA, Arthritis Found., Citizens Assn. Memphis and Shelby County, Shelby County War Memls.; sr. warden of vestry Calvary Episcopal Ch. Maj. gen. USMCR, comdg. gen. 4th Marine divsn. Recipient Sam A. Myar, Jr. award Tenn. Bd. Law Examiners, 1978. Fellow: Tenn. Bar Found. (pres. 1993—94), Am. Bar Found. (life); mem.: Memphis Area C. of C. (pres. mil. affairs coun.), Am. Inns. of Ct., Memphis Bar Assn. (v.p. 1989, pres. elect 1990, pres. 1991, pres. young lawyers divsn.), Tenn. Bar Assn. (pres. 2002—03), Am. Bd. Trial Advocates (adv.), Am. Judicature Soc. (nat. bd. dirs.), ABA (bd. govs., ho. dels. charter mem. and coun. sect. litigation, young lawyers sect., fellow young lawyers divsn., com. on ethics and profl. responsibility, ethics 2000 spl. com.), Ctrl. Garden Area Assn. (pres.), Memphis Rotary Club, Univ. Club Memphis (pres.), Kiwanis, Phoenix Club (1st v.p.), Navy League, U. Tenn. Nat. Alumni Assn. (pres. Memphis chpt., nat. bd. govs.). Office: Thomason Hendrix Harvey Johnson & Mitchell 29th Fl 1 Commerce Sq Memphis TN 38103 Office Phone: 901-525-8721. Business E-Mail: Harveya@ThomasonLaw.com.

HARVEY, ALEXANDER, II, retired federal judge; b. Balt., May 3, 1923; s. Fred B. and Rose (Hopkins) H.; m. Mary E. Williams, Feb. 24, 1951; children: Elizabeth H., Alexander IV. BA, Yale U., 1947; LLB, Columbia U., 1950. Bar: Md. 1950. Assoc. Ober, William, Grimes & Stinson, Balt., 1950-66, ptnr., 1953-66; asst. atty. gen. Md., 1957-58; judge U.S. Dist. Ct. Md., 1966-86, chief judge, 1986-91, sr. judge Balt., 1991—2004. Mem. Gov.'s Com. To Study Blue Sky Law of Md., 1961; mem. character com. Ct. Appeals Md. for 8th Jud. Cir. Bd. dirs. Balt. Symphony Assn., 1966-68; pres., dir. Balt. Opera Guild, 1960; bd. dirs. Balt. Coun. Social Agys., 1957-63; trustee Ch. Home and Hosp., Balt., 1952-71. 1st lt. AUS, World War II, ETO. Mem. Am., Md., Balt. bar assns., Phi Beta Kappa. Episcopalian (vestry 1967-70). Home: 7300 Brightside Rd Baltimore MD 21212-1011 Office: US Dist Ct 101 W Lombard St Ste 404 Baltimore MD 21201-2605

HARVEY, BIRT, retired pediatrician, educator; b. Teheran, Iran, Nov. 24, 1928; five children. BA, Johns Hopkins U., 1948; MD, N.Y.U., 1952. Pvt. practice, 1958-88; prof. pediat. emeritus Stanford U., Palo Alto, Calif., 1995—. Past sr. fellow Inst. Health, Policy Studies, U. Calif., San Francisco. Mem. Inst. Med. Nat. Acad. Scis. (emeritus), Am. Acad. Pediatrics (past pres.), Am. Pediat. Soc. (emeritus).

HARVEY, CATHERINE D., health services administrator, consultant; b. Charlotte, N.C., Nov. 27, 1950; children: Lance I. Anthony, Allison M. BSN, U. N.C., Charlotte, 1970; MSN, U. N.C., Chapel Hill, 1973; Dr.PH, U. S.C., Columbia, 1991. Cert. health exec. Am. Coll. of Healthcare Execs., 1994; RN NC, 1970, cert. mental health specialist, ANA, 1980, advanced oncology nurse, Oncology Nursing Soc., 2003. Adminstrv. dir. cancer ctr. CCTR, Richland Meml. Hosp., Columbia, SC, 1984—89, Grossmont Hosp., La Mesa, Calif., 1989—91; assoc. dir. for adminstrn., asst. prof. Hollings Cancer Ctr., MUSC, Charleston, SC, 1991—94; exec. dir., COO, Nat. Comprehensive Cancer Network, Huntingdon, Pa., 1994—96; v.p., patient rels. and pub. policy OnCare Inc., San Bruno, Calif., 1996—2000; ptnr. Oncology Assocs., Victoria, Va., 2000—. Founding pres. Am. Coll. of Oncology Adminstrs., Southfield, Mich., 1991—95; chair Cancer Control Adv. Com., Dept. of Health, Columbia, SC, 1994—2001; chair bd. dirs. Nat. Coalition for Cancer Survivorship, Silver Spring, Md., 2003—. Contbr. articles to profl. jours. Orgnl. dir. Hospice of Charleston, Charleston, SC, 1994—2000. Recipient Vis. Professorship, Samaritan Health Sys., 1988; scholar, NIMH, 1971-1973. Mem.: Assn. Cancer Execs. (bd. dirs. 1995—98), Am. Soc. Clin. Oncology, Oncology Nursing Soc. (clin. practice com. 1986—91), Sigma Theta Tau. Avocations: cooking, writing. Office: Oncology Assocs 655 Cain Dr Mount Pleasant SC 29464 E-mail: oncologyassociates@comcast.net, catherineharvey@comcast.net.

HARVEY, CHARLES ALBERT, JR., lawyer; b. Beverly, Mass., Sept. 28, 1949; s. Charles A. and Phyllis B. (O'Rourke) H.; m. Whitney Ann Neville, Sept. 21, 1985; children: John Whitney, Charlotte Baird. AB, Assumption Coll., 1971; JD, U. Maine, 1974. Bar: Maine 1974, Mass. 1974, U.S. Supreme Ct. 1979. Assoc. Verrill & Dana, Portland, Maine, 1974-79, ptnr., 1979-95, Harvey & Frank, Portland, 1995—. Assoc. chief counsel President's Commn. on Accident at Three Mile Island, Washington, 1979; mem. adv. com. on civil rules Maine Supreme Jud. Ct., 1978-91, chmn. adv. com. on cameras in trial cts., 1991-93, cons. on civil rules, 1996—, chmn. adv. com. on civil rules, 1987-91; chmn. adv. com. on local rules U.S. Dist. Ct. Maine, 1985—, mem. civil justice adv. com., 1992-97; chmn. Maine Gov.'s Select Com. on Jud. Appointments, 1987-91; mem. Senator Olympia J. Snowe's adv. com. on appointment of U.S. Dist. Judge, U.S. Atty. and U.S. Marshal, 2001-02; chmn. grievance commn. Maine Bd. Overseers of the Bar, 1996-97. Contbr. articles to profl. jours. Trustee Portland Sympnony Orch., 1980-89, pres., 1987-89, adv. trustee, 1989—; trustee Portland Stage Co., 1984-87, adv. trustee, 1987—; trustee Waynflete Sch., 1990-96; adv. trustee Maine Childrens Mus., 1992-1999, Maine Vol. Lawyers for the Arts, 1994-1999. Fellow Portland Mus. of Art, 1993—. Fellow Am. Coll. Trial Lawyers, Maine Bar Found.; mem. Am. Law Inst. Republican. Office: 2 City Ctr Portland ME 04101-4010

HARVEY, CHRISTINE LYNN, publishing executive; b. Bklyn., Dec. 7, 1962; AS in Liberal Arts, Nassau C.C., 1982; BA in Comm. Arts, Adelphi U., 1985. Cert. EMT, 1983-86. Franchise mgr. N.Y. Daily News, Mineola, 1981-84; copywriter, vido prodr., 1984-85; pub. rels. assoc. King Features Syndicate, N.Y.C., 1986; account exec. Promotional Broadcasting Svc., Babylon, N.Y., 1986-87; sr. account mgr. L.I. Bus. News, Ronkonkoma, N.Y., 1987-91; sr. ptnr. Karen Saeger Assocs., Stony Brook, N.Y., 1990—; editor The Steuben News, Ridgewood, N.Y., 1992—; founder, pub., editor-in-chief New Living, Stony Brook, 1991—; pub. rels. cons. Am. Health Found., Valhalla, NY, 1994—96; radio prodr./dir./host New Living Prodns., Stony Brook, 1997—98. Clin. hypnotherapist, Reiki master, 1999; TV prodr. Outlook Mag., 1985; TV news reporter, field prodr. LI News Tonite, 1984. Avocations: running, swimming, bicycling, hiking, golf. Office: New Living 1212 Route 25A Ste 1B Stony Brook NY 11790-1919

HARVEY, CHRISTOPHER P., lawyer; b. 1961; BA summa cum laude, Boston Coll., 1983, JD magna cum laude, 1986. Bar: Mass. 1986. Ptnr., co-chmn. Investment Mgmt. group Wilmer Cutler Pickering Hale & Dorr, Boston. Editor: Boston Coll. Law Rev. Mem.: Mass. Bar Assn., Boston Bar Assn., Phi Beta Kappa. Office: Wilmer Cutler Pickering Hale & Dorr 60 State St Boston MA 02109 Office Phone: 617-526-6532. Office Fax: 617-526-5000. Business E-Mail: christopher.harvey@wilmerhale.com.

HARVEY, CYRIL LESLIE, education educator; b. Bagotville, Demerara, Aug. 5, 1950; arrived in U.S., 1971; s. Cyril Leslie Vernon and Lucille Emelda Harvey. BS in Biology and Econs., U. Miami, Fla., 1979; M. Environment Study, Dalhousie U., Halifax, N.S., Can., 1987; MA in Multiculture Edn., Calif. State U. Dominguez, Carson, 1997; MA in Ednl. Curriculum, Calif. State U. Dominguez, 1997; postgrad., Calif. Coast U., Santa Ana, 2000—, Dalhousie U. Lic. life sci. tchr. Calif. Tchr. Ministry of Edn., Upper Dem Rio, Guyana, 1969—71, West Dem Rio, Guyana, 1975; fisheries officer Ministry of Agr., Georgetown, Guyana, 1980—83; tchr. L.A. Unified Sch. Dist., 1989—. Mem. student ct. judiciary U. V.I., St. Thomas, 1972—73; mem. tchg./coaching team nat. athletics champions Ministry of Edn., Upper Demerara, 1970—71; mem. sch. improvement coun. Henry Clay Mid. Sch./L.A. Unified Sch. Dist., 2000—01; proof reader Jour. of Caribbean Studies, 1987; participating scientistJoint Shrimp Tagging cruise, Western and Caribbean Fisheries Ctr. Brazil, French Guyana, Suriname and Guyana Food and Agr. Orgn., UN. Contbr. articles to profl. jours. Recipient Grad. Fellow award, Dalhousie U., 1985—87, Cert. of Achievement for Application and Diffusion of Rsch., U.S. Dept. Agr., 1982. Mem.: AAAS, Phi Kappa Phi. Avocations: tennis, cricket, bicycling, chess, running. Home: 12920 S Manhattan Pl Gardena CA 90249-1905

HARVEY, DANIEL RICHARD, retired minister; b. Franklin, Pa., Aug. 27, 1930; s. Richard H. and Dorothy E. (Winder) H.; m. Lois V. Meyers, Mar. 7, 1953; children: Deborah, Stephen, Rebecca, Timothy, Rachel. BA, John Brown U., 1952; postgrad., Moody Bible Inst., 1953-54, Burnside-Ott Aviation, 1970-71. Ordained to ministry Trans World Radio Ch., 1956. Pastor Christian and Missionary Alliance, Siloam Springs, Ark., 1949-52, Urbana, Ill., 1953-55; missionary Trans World Radio, various locations, 1956—; evangelist, 1992—2002; ret., 2002. Chaplain Guam Dept. Pub. Safety, Agana, 1975-82, Lakeland, Fla. Police Dept., 1991—; chmn. bd. dirs. Chaplaincy Corps, 1991-93; civilian chaplain USN, Agana, 1975-82; pres. adv. coun. Taccoa Falls (Ga.) Coll., 1996—. Bd. dirs. ARC, Agana, 1976-82. Named to Ancient Order of Chammori, Govt. of Guam, 1982; recipient citation Comdr. Naval Forces Marianas, USN, 1982. Mem.: Internat. Conf. Police Chaplains (Fla. regional dir. 2003—05). Home: 4818 Leisurewood Ln Lakeland FL 33811-1592 Office Phone: 863-660-3709.

HARVEY, DAVID R., chemical company executive; With Sigma-Aldrich Corp., St. Louis, 1981—, pres., COO, 1995—, pres., CEO, 2000—, also bd. dirs. Office: Sigma-Aldrich Corp 3050 Spruce St Saint Louis MO 63103

HARVEY, DONALD, artist, educator; b. Walthamston, Eng., June 14, 1930; s. Henry and Annie Dorothy (Sawell) H.; m. Elizabeth Clark, Aug. 9, 1952; children— Shan Mary, David Jonathan. Art tchrs. diploma, Brighton Coll. Art, 1951. Art master Ardwyn Grammar Sch., Wales, 1952-56; mem. faculty dept. art U. Victoria, B.C., Can., 1961-95, now prof. emeritus painting. One man exhbns. include, Albert White Gallery, Toronto, 1968, retrospective, Art Gallery of Victoria, 1968; represented in permanent collections, Nat. Gallery Can., Montreal Mus., Albright-Knox Mus., Seattle Art Mus. Mem. accessions com. Art Gallery of Victoria, 1969-72. Can. Council fellow, 1966 Mem. Royal Can. Acad. of Arts (full academician), Can. Group Painters, Can. Painters and Etchers. Home: 1025 Joan Crescent Victoria BC Canada V8S 3L3 E-mail: doharvey@telus.net.

HARVEY, DONALD JOSEPH, historian, educator; b. N.Y.C., Oct. 4, 1922; s. William Harold and Helen (Chiampou) Harvey; m. Jacqueline Rozendaal, June 11, 1955; 1 child, Nanette. BA cum laude, Princeton U., 1943; MA, Columbia U., 1948, PhD, 1953; postgrad., U. Paris, 1950-51. Instr. history Hunter Coll., CUNY, N.Y.C., 1951-56, asst. prof., 1956-60, asso. prof., 1960-67, prof., 1967—84, prof. emeritus, 1984—, chmn. dept. history, 1968-71. Reader, cons. Yale U. Press, Cornell U. Press, SUNY Univ. Press; cons. humanities fellowship program Rockefeller Found., 1974—78, NEH, 1977—85, Funk & Wagnall's, 1989—91; cons. hist. TV series STa. WGBH-TV, Boston, 1987. Author (with E. M. Earle): Modern France, 1951; author: France Since the Revolution, 1968; author: (with W. O. Shanahan) Nationalism: Essays in Honor of Louis Snyder, 1981; author: Murder in Dreyfus Days, 2005; assoc. editor (with H. Rowen): Reviews in Europen History, 1973—79; contbr. articles to profl. jours. Served to capt. arty. U.S. Army, 1943—46, ETO. Ford Found. fellow, 1954—55, Fulbright alt., 1959—60. Mem.: AAUP, Soc. French Hist. Studies, Am. Hist. Assn., Phi Alpha Theta. Home: 666 Main St Apt 404 Winchester MA 01890-1959

HARVEY, DONALD LEROY, secondary school educator; b. Ashland, Ky., Oct. 5, 1950; s. George Leroy and Ruby Jean (Sparks) H.; m. Shirley Dawn Habada, Sept. 6, 1970; children: Tammra Michelle, Kevin Michael, Ana Maria, Juliana. AS, Kettering Coll. Med. Arts, 1970; BS, Walla Walla Coll., 1973; MS, Andrews U., 1982. Sci./math. tchr. Reading (Pa.) Jr. Acad., 1973-77, Greater Balt. (Md.) Jr. Acad., 1977-83; sci. dept. chmn. Bass Meml. Acad., Lumberton, Miss., 1983—2001, Madison (Tenn.) Acad., 2001—. Mem. curriculum com., acad. standards com., libr. com. Bass Meml. Acad., Lumberton, 1985—; tchr., facilitator Miss. Literacy Program, Lumberton, 1988. Recipient Thomas and Violet Zapara Award of Recognition for Excellence in Tchg., Office of Edn. of the Gen. Conf. of Seventh-day Adventists, 1989, Star Tchr. award Miss. Econ. Coun., Jackson, 1989-90. Mem. AAAS, Nat. Sci. Tchrs. Assn. (tchr. cert. in biology 1993), Nat. Assn. Biology Tchrs. Avocations: sports, scuba diving, flying, photography. Home: 625 Vanoke Drive Madison TN 37115 Office: Madison Academy 100 Academy Drive Madison TN 37115

HARVEY, DOUGLASS COATE, retired photographic company executive; b. Batavia, N.Y., Aug. 28, 1917; s. Homer A. and Della S. Harvey; m. Elizabeth Kellas, June 27, 1942; children: Robert, Anne, Katharine, Douglass Coate Jr. BSME with highest distinction, Purdue U., 1939, DEng (hon.), 1982. With Eastman Kodak Co., Rochester, N.Y., 1939-82, dir. corp. product devel., 1970-73, v.p., gen. mgr. apparatus divsn., 1973-77; exec. v.p., gen. mgr. Eastman Kodak Co. (mgr. U.S. and Canadian photog. divns.), 1977-82; ret., 1982. Commr. Monroe Co. Case Commn. Former trustee Alfred (N.Y.) U.; former exec. bd. Otetiana (N.Y.) coun. Boy Scouts Am.; former chmn. bd. dirs. Rochester and Monroe County YMCA, nat. bd. dirs., 1979-81; ret. chmn. engring. adv. coun. Clarkson U., Potsdam, N.Y.; former bd. mgrs. Meml. Art Gallery; trustee Internat. former Mus. Photography, Adirondack Pk. Inst., Inc., former bd. dirs. George Eastman Ho. Mus. Photography. Named Outstanding Mech. Engr., Purdue U., 1991. Mem. Nat. Acad. Engring., Optical Soc. Am., Photog. Soc. Am., Soc. Photog. Scientists and Engrs., Rochester Engring. Soc., Rochester C. of C., Nat. Security Indsl. Assn. (ret., trustee 1973-78), Rochester Country Club (former mem. bd. stewards), Genesee Valley Club, Lake George Club (Diamond Point, N.Y.), Rotary, Tau Beta Pi, Pi Tau Sigma. Republican. Home: 3155 East Ave Rochester NY 14618-3427 E-mail: dch25@juno.com.

HARVEY, EDWIN GORDON, lawyer; b. Muscatine, Iowa, June 4, 1958; B.A. in Polit. Sci. and Philosophy, N.E. Mo. State U., 1979; J.D., Washington U., St. Louis, 1982. Bar: Mo. 1982, Ill. 1983, U.S. Dist. Ct. (we. dist.) Mo. 1982, U.S. Dist. Ct. (ea. dist.) Mo. 1983, U.S. Ct. Appeals (8th cir.) 1983, U.S. Ct. Appeals (9th cir.). Assoc. Coburn, Croft & Putzell, St. Louis, 1982-88; ptnr. Alderman, Lakeshire, Mo., 1983-85, Coban & Cright, 1999-96, Thompson Coburn, 1996—. Mem. Mo. Bar Assn., Bar Assn. Met. St. Louis, Ill. Bar Assn. Office: Thompson Coburn First Star Plaza Saint Louis MO 63101

HARVEY, ELEANOR JONES, museum curator; b. Washington, Sept. 20, 1960; d. Charles Roy Jr. and Margaret McChesney (Jeffries) Jones; m. Stephen Jay Harvey, Oct. 10, 1992. BA with distinction summa cum laude, U. Va., 1983; MA, Yale U., 1985, MPhil, 1987, PhD, 1998. Asst. curator Am. paintings Mus. Fine Arts, Boston, 1989-91; assoc. curator Am. art Dallas Mus. Art, 1992-98, cons. curator Am. art, 1996—99, curator Am. art, 1999—2002; cons. curator Nat. Mus. Wildlife Art, 1996—99; curator Luce Foundation Center for American Art, Washington, 2003; chief curator Smithsonian American Art Museum, Washington, 2003—. Lectr. in field. Author: The Painted Sketch: American Impressions from Nature, 1830-1880,

1998, In Context: Painting in Dallas 1889-1945, 1999, Thomas Moran and the Spirit of Place, 2001, The Voyage of the Icebergs: Frederic Church's Arctic Masterpiece, 2002; co-author: Albert Pinkham Ryder, 1990, The Lure of Italy, 1992, Dallas Museum of Art: A Guide to the Collection, 1996, Cosmos: From Romanticism to the Avant Garde 1801-2001, 1999, Hudson River School Visions Landscapes of Sanford R. Gifford, 2003; contbr. articles to profl. jours. Bd. dirs. Wood Turning Ctr., Phila., 1998—; mem. ann. giving adv. coun. U. Va.; mem. U. Va. Assocs. of Libr., 1998—. Henry S. McNeill fellow in Am. decorative arts Yale U., 1985-87, Smithsonian predoctoral fellow Nat. Mus. Am. Art, 1988-89; Henry Luce Found. grantee, 1987-88. Mem. Am. Assn. Mus., Am. Craft Guild, Coll. Art Assn. Avocation: dressage. Office: Smithsonian American Art Museum MRC 970 PO Box 37012 Washington DC 20013-7012 Office Phone: 202-275-1503. Business E-Mail: harveye@si.edu.

HARVEY, FRANCIS J., civilian military employee; m. Mary Harvey; 2 children. BS, U. Notre Dame, 1965; PhD in Metallurgy and Material Scis., U. Pa., 1969. Joined Sci. & Tech. Ctr. Westinghouse Electric Corp., 1969, Westinghouse Defense Group, 1979, engring. mgr. Marine Div., gen. mgr. Electrical Sys. Div., gen. mgr. Marine Div., v.p. Sci. & Tech., 1993—94, pres. Govt. & Environ. Svcs. Co., 1994—95, pres. Electronics Sys. Group, 1995—96, chmn., CEO Industry & Tech. Group, 1996—99; dir., vice chmn. Duratek Inc., Md., 1999—2004; spl. asst. to sec. U.S. Dept. Defense, 1978, sec. U.S. Army, 2004—. Dir. IT Group, Inc., Gardner Technologies, Inc., Bridge Bank, Kulman Electric Corp.; mem. Army Sci. Bd., 1999—2001. Mem. bd. regents Santa Clara U.; co-chair Campaign for Santa Clara. Named White House Fellow, 1978—79. Office: US Army 101 Army Pentagon Washington DC 20310-0101

HARVEY, GLENN FRANCIS, association manager; b. Tarentum, Pa., May 10, 1940; s. Howard F. and Evelyn H.; m. Linda M. Herr, Mar. 19, 1960; children: Jeffrey Howard, Lisa Anne. BSEd., Slippery Rock State Coll., 1961; M.Ed., Duquesne U., 1964; MBA, U. Pitts., 1975. Tchr. Fox Chapel Area Schs., Pitts., 1961-67; exec. dir. Instrument Soc. Am., Research Triangle Park, NC, 1967-99; cons., 1999—2003; exec. dir. Am. Ceramic Soc., Westerville, Ohio, 2003—. Mem. Am. Soc. of Assn. Execs., Coun. Engring. and Sci. Soc. Execs. Republican. Personal E-mail: glennharvey@worldnet.att.net.

HARVEY, GREGORY MERRILL, lawyer; b. Morris Twp., N.J., Jan. 6, 1937; s. Merrill Piercy and Dorothy Ceola (Gregory) H.; m. Emily Mitchell Wallace, June 14, 1969. AB, Harvard U., 1959; JD, Harvard Law Sch., 1962. Bar: Pa. 1963. Assoc. Morgan, Lewis & Bockius, Phila., 1962-69, ptnr., 1969-99, Montgomery, McCracken, Walker & Rhoads, Phila., 1999—. Chmn. City of Phila. Bd. Ethics, 1984-91; trustee Fairmount Park Art Assn., Phila., 1981—; co-chmn. 8th Ward Dem. Exec. Com., Phila., 1984—; bd. dirs. Ams. for Dem. Action Southeastern Pa. chpt., 1966-, bd. dirs. Conservation Ctr. Art and Historic Artifacts, Phila., 1995-. Recipient James Madison award Soc. Profl. Journalists, 1986, Judge Learned Hand Human Rels. award Am. Jewish Com., 1991. Fellow Am. Coll. Trial Lawyers; mem. ABA, Pa. Bar Assn., Phila. Bar Assn., Phila. Club, Franklin Inn (Phila.), Merion Cricket Club (Haverford, Pa.), Racquet Club (Phila.), Phi Beta Kappa. Home: 1939 Panama St Philadelphia PA 19103-6609 Office: Montgomery McCracken et al 123 S Broad St Philadelphia PA 19109-1099 Office Phone: 215-772-7684. Business E-Mail: gharvey@mmwr.com.

HARVEY, IAN, artist, educator; b. Weston, Mass., Nov. 20, 1953; s. Earl Miners and Aileen Harvey; m. Kyung-Sook Koo, July 16, 2004; 1 child, Ki-Sung Yun. BA, Wesleyan U., Middletown, Conn., 1977; MFA, Columbia U. Sch. Arts, N.Y.C., 1980. Asst. prof. art Wesleyan U., Middletown, Conn., 1980—89, Calif. State U., Sacramento, 2005—. Vis. artist Bemis Ctr. for Contemporary Art, Omaha, 2003—03, Triangle Artists' Workshop, Monroe, NY, 1997—97; artist resident Vt. Studio Ctr., Johnson, Vt., 1996—96. Exhibitions include New Paintings created at Bemis Center for Contemporary Art. Grantee, The Pollock Krasner Found., 2002, The Artist Resource Trust, 2001. Mem.: Coll. Art Assn., Phi Beta Kappa. Office: Calif State U Art Dept 6000 J St Sacramento CA 95819-6061

HARVEY, J. BRETT, energy executive; With Kaiser Steel Corp.; vice-pres. mining, CEO PacifiCorp Energy Inc.; pres., CEO CONSOL Energy Corp. Vice-chmn. World Coal Inst. Mem.: Assn. Devel. Inland Nav. in America's Ohio Valley (chmn.), Nat. Mining Assn. (chmn.). Office: CONSOL Energy 1800 Washington Rd Pittsburgh PA 15241-1421

HARVEY, JAMES A., lawyer; b. Heidelburg, Germany, Sept. 18, 1961; BA in Econ., Univ. Ark., 1983; JD with honors, Univ. NC, 1988. Bar: Ga. 1988. Ptnr., tech. group Alston & Bird LLP, Atlanta. Editl. bd. Internet & Computer Lawyer, GigaLaw.com; contbr. articles to profl. jours. Mem.: Computer Law Assn., Phi Beta Kappa. Office: Alston & Bird LLP One Atlantic Ctr 1201 W Peachtree St NW Atlanta GA 30309-3424 Office Phone: 404-881-7328. Office Fax: 404-881-7777. Business E-Mail: jharvey@alston.com.

HARVEY, JAMES CLEMENT, lawyer; b. Shattuck, Okla., June 8, 1941; s. T.C. Jr. and Loucille (Miller) H.; m. Sue Simmons White, Aug. 11, 1962 (div. Feb. 1970); 1 child, Shannon Suzanne; m. Sherry L. Grant, Sept. 24, 1979. BBA, So. Meth. U., 1963, JD, 1966. Bar: Tex., 1966; U.S. Dist. Ct. (no. dist.) Tex. 1968. Pvt. practice, Dallas, 1966. Methodist. Home: 4129 Bowser Ave Dallas TX 75219-3719 Office: 3811 Turtle Creek Blvd Ste 350 Dallas TX 75219-4450

HARVEY, JAMES GERALD, educational consultant, researcher; b. Calif., Mo., July 15, 1934; s. William Walter and Exie Marie (Lindley) Harvey. BA, Amherst Coll., 1956; MAT (fellow), Harvard U., 1958, MEd, 1962. Asst. to dean grad. sch. edn. Harvard U., Cambridge, Mass., 1962—66, dir. admissions, fin. aid, 1966—69; dir. counseling svc. U. Calif., Irvine, 1970—72; ednl. cons. LA, 1972—; v.p. CraniaMania.com, 2000—02. Author: (ednl. materials) HARVOCAB Vocabulary Program, 1985—. 1st lt. USAF, 1958—61. Recipient Amherst Mayo-Smith grant, 1956—57; UCLA Adminstrn. fellow, 1969—70. Mem.: Internat. Reading Assn., Nat. Coun. Measurement in Edn., Am. Ednl. Rsch. Assn. Achievements include Champion of "Jeopardy" in 2004. Address: 1845 Glendon Ave Los Angeles CA 90025-4653

HARVEY, JAMES MATHEWS, JR., communications specialist; b. Detroit, Dec. 5, 1964; s. James M. and Leotha (Frazier) Harvey; m. Leesa Ann Hatch, June 10, 2000; 1 child, James (Trey) III. BS, Troy State U., 1987. Media assoc. Ctr. for Environ. Rsch., Troy, Ala., 1987-88; prodr., dir. Coop. Ext. Svc. (became Coop. Ext. Sys. 1995), Auburn, Ala., 1988—99; media coord. Ala. Indsl. Devel. Tng., Montgomery, 1999—2001; pub. comms. specialist Shelby County Ala. Govt., Columbiana, 2001—. Dir. videos including: Nature's Way, 1988, Red Drum: A Struggle for Survival, 1989, Pond Management, 1991; slide series including: Nature's Way, 1988, Beach Mice and Their Habitat, 1989; dir., editor Safety in the Logging Woods series, 1989-95, Forestry in Alabama, 1993, Small Business Resources Series, 1995, Adult Education Principles for Loggers, 1996, Multiple Use Management, 1996; assoc. producer, dir. Extension Today, 1990; assoc. producer satellite programs Principles of Parenting and State of Our Environment, 1991, White-Tailed Deer Management, 1991-92, Residential Landscaping, 1992, Small Business Resources, 1994, Wildlife Damage Management, 1995, Alabama Forest Resources Today, 1996; creator, prodr. Ala. 4-H Congress Video, 1990-99, 4-H Performing Arts Video, 1993-99; prodr., dir. Street Trees and Sewing Update for Entrepreneurs, 1994, Tax Fraud Prevention, 1995, AU Presents, 1998; guest columnist The Messenger, 1993-94. Mem. agrl. adv. com. Pike County H.S., Brundidge, Ala., 1983-95, pres. 1995-2000; bd. dirs. Pike County Agrl. Complex Bd., 1996. Mem. Nat. Assn. County Info. Officers, Troy State U. Journalism Alumni Assn. Baptist. Avocations: music, movies, tennis, model trains. Home: 1332 Waxwing Trl Alabaster AL 35007-9027 Office: Shelby County Planning 115 County Svcs Dr Pelham AL 35124-6128

HARVEY, JEFFREY A., physics professor; b. San Antonio, Texas, Feb. 15, 1955; BS in Physics, U. Minnesota, 1977; PhD in Physics, Calif. Inst. Tech., 1981. Rsch. assoc. Princeton U., Princeton, NJ, 1981—83, asst. prof., 1983—87, assoc. prof., 1987—90, prof., 1990—91, U. Chicago, 1991—. Mem. Aspen Ctr. for Physics, 1986—97; editorial bd. mem. Physical Review, 1989—91; dir. Theoretical Advanced Study Inst., 1992, 99; mem. ITP Advisory Bd., 1993—97, chair, 1995—96; mem. TASI Advisory Bd., 1997—2003; chair UCSB Physics External Review Com., 1997—98; editorial bd. mem. Classical & Quantum Gravity, 1998—; mem. physics advisory council Princeton U., 1998—2002. Recipient Presidential Young Investigator award, NSF, 1987; grantee Earl C. Anthony Fellowship, 1977—78, A. P. Sloan Fellowship, 1986—90. Fellow: Am. Acad. Arts & Sciences, Am. Physical Soc. Office: Enrico Fermi Inst U Chicago 5640 Ellis Ave Chicago IL 60637*

HARVEY, JOHN ADRIANCE, psychologist, educator, pharmacologist, researcher; b. N.Y.C., Oct. 14, 1930; s. John Adriance Harvey and Paula Ann (Truhar) Oestreich; m. Rhoda S. Sadigur, Dec. 20, 1958; children: David Alexander, Andrew Martin, Michael Allen. AB, U. Chgo., 1955, PhD, 1959. Research assoc. U. Chgo., 1959-61, asst. prof., 1961-67, assoc. prof., 1967-68; prof. psychology and pharmacology U. Iowa, Iowa City, 1968-88; prof. pharmacology and physiology, chief div. behavioral neurobiology Drexel U. Coll. Medicine, Phila., 1988—. Guest worker Maudsley Hosp., London, 1966-67; chmn. biopsychology rsch. rev. com. NIH, 1983-85; chmn. behavioral neurobiology rsch. rev. com. NIMH, 1986-90, mem. adv. panel; mem. extramural sci. adv. bd. Nat. Inst. on Drug Abuse, 1990—. Author: Behavioral Analysis of Drug Action, 1971, (with Barry Kosofsky) Cocaine: Effects on the Developing Brain; editor Jour. Pharmacology and Exptl. Therapeutics, 1990-98; contbr. numerous articles to profl. jours. Recipient Rsch. Devel. award, NIMH, 1963—68, Rsch. Scientist award, 1969—74. Fellow APA (pres. divsn. 28 1984-85), Am. Coll. Neuropsychopharmacology; mem. Am. Soc. for Pharmacology and Exptl. Therapeutics (editl. adv. bd.), Soc. for Neurosci. (fin. com.), Soc. for Neurochemistry, European Soc. for Neurochemistry, Pavlovian Soc., Soc. for Biol. Psychiatry, Behavioral Pharmacol. Soc. (pres. 1996-98). Home: 1 Druim Moir Ct Philadelphia PA 19118 Office: Drexel U Coll Medicine Dept Pharmacology/Physiol 245 N 15th St Mail Stop 488 Philadelphia PA 19102 Office Phone: 215-762-2369. Business E-Mail: john.harvey@drexel.edu.

HARVEY, JOHN ARTHUR, nuclear physicist; b. Saskatoon, Sask., Can., Dec. 14, 1921; naturalized U.S. citizen; married; 2 children. BSc, Queen's U., Ont., Can., 1945; PhD in Physics, MIT, 1950. Physicist Atomic Energy Can., Ltd., 1945-46; rsch. asst. MIT, 1946-50; assoc. physicist Brookhaven Nat. Lab., 1951-55; physicist Oak Ridge Nat. Lab., 1955-93, dir. linear accelerator, 1965-93, retired, 1993, cons., 1993—. Rsch. prof. U. Tenn., 1995—. Fellow Am. Phys. Soc. (sec.-treas. divsn. nuc. physics 1966-86). Home: 108 Ogontz Ln Oak Ridge TN 37830-3905 Office: Oak Ridge Nat Lab PO Box 2008 Oak Ridge TN 37831-6354 E-mail: harveyjm@icx.net.

HARVEY, JOHN COLLINS, internist, educator; b. Youngstown, Ohio, Sept. 11, 1923; s. J. Paul and Mary J. (Collins) H.; m. Adele Dillon, Nov. 26, 1949; children: Elizabeth V.R. (Mrs. Charles Yon), John Collins Jr., William Charles II, Amy L.R. (Mrs. L. F. Reese), Margaret J.B. (Mrs. Gregory Granitto). Grad., Phillips Exeter Acad., 1941; BS, Yale U., 1944; MD, Johns Hopkins U., 1947, MLA, 1968; MAS, Johns Hopkins, 1974; MA, St. Mary's U., 1975, PhD in Theology, 1988; DSc (hon.), Barry U., 1992. Diplomate: Am. Bd. Internal Medicine. Successively house officer, asst. resident, resident Osler Med. Service, Johns Hopkins Hosp., 1947-53, physician, 1953-73; successively instr., asst. prof., asso. prof., prof. medicine Johns Hopkins, 1953-73; prof. medicine Georgetown U., Washington, 1973-89, prof. medicine emeritus, 1989—; sr. rsch. scholar Kennedy Inst. of Ethics, Georgetown U., Washington, 1989—, Ctr. for Clin. Bioethics, Georgetown Med. Ctr., 1993—. Vis. prof. medicine U. Ibadan, Nigeria, 1964; hon. assoc. prof. medicine Guy's Hosp., London, 1973 Co-editor: Catholic Perspectives on Medical Morals, Catholic Studies in Bioethics; Contbr. articles to profl. publs. Mem. various local, state and nat. govt. med. adv. coms.; trustee emeritus Washington Home for Incurables; mem. emeritus med. adv. com. Sacred Congregation for Causes of Saints, Holy See, Vatican City. Col. (ret.) M.C., USAR. A. Blaine Brower Traveling fellow ACP to Guy's Hosp. London, 1956; sr. scholar Kennedy Inst. Ethics, Georgetown U., 1973-89. Fellow ACP (master), APHA; mem. AAAS, AMA, Am. Clin. and Climatol. Assn., Biophys. Soc., Johns Hopkins Soc. Scholars, Tudor and Stuart Club (Balt.), Cosmos Club, Knights of St. Gregory, Knights of Malta, Phi Beta Kappa, Sigma Xi, Alpha Omega Alpha. Republican. Roman Catholic. Home: 12610 Three Sisters Rd Potomac MD 20854-6359 Office Phone: 202-687-1160. Office Fax: 202-687-8955. E-mail: jcviola@aol.com.

HARVEY, JOHN GROVER, mathematics professor, information scientist; b. Waco, Tex., Aug. 10, 1934; s. John Grover and Mary Inez (Davidson) H. AA, Navarro Jr. Coll., Corsicana, Tex., 1953; BS, Baylor U., 1955; MS, Fla. State U., 1957; PhD, Tulane U., 1961. Instr. math. U. Ill., Urbana, 1961-63, asst. prof., 1963-66; assoc. prof. math. U. Wis., Madison, 1966-75, prof., 1975-2001, prof. emeritus, 2001—. Prin. investigator Wis. R & D Ctr. for Cognitive Learning, Madison, 1968—78; co-dir. Computer Placement Test Project, 2005—. Editor: Matching High School Preparation to College Needs: Prognostic and Diagnostic Testing, 1996.; editor, contbg. author: Models for Technology Teacher Education in Mathematics, 1997; contbr. chpts. to books. Mem. Math. Assn. Am. (assoc. editor 1969-74, chmn. com. on testing 1988-93), Am. Ednl. Rsch. Assn., Nat. Coun. Tchrs. of Math., Am. Math. Soc. Episcopalian. Home: 330 Morgan St # 506 New Orleans LA 70114-1070 E-mail: jgharvey2@cox.net.

HARVEY, JOHN HERTFORD, academic and athletics administrator, consultant; b. The Hague, The Netherlands, Nov. 9, 1935; came to U.S., 1939; s. Frederick Sailor and Alexandria Commins H.; m. Lois Anderson, Dec. 20, 1971 (div. 1995). BA in Philosophy, Coll. William and Mary, 1957, MEd in History, 1969; PhD in Higher Edn., Boston Coll., 1971. Tchr., coach Coll. William and Mary, Williamsburg, Va., 1964-69; acad. adminstr., coach Harvard U., Cambridge, Mass., 1970-80; tchr., coach., adminstr. Grinnell (Iowa) Coll., 1980-83; asst. prof., dir. athletics St. Mary's (Md.) Coll., 1983-89; dir. athletics Carnegie Mellon U., Pittsburgh, Pa., 1989—2004, ret., 2004; cons. athletic dept. Harvard Univ., 2004—. Cons. in field. Author: (with others) Organizational Management for Athletics, 1998; contbr. articles to publs. Active Big Bros. Assn., Boston, 1970-80, Nantucket (Mass.) Libr. Assn., 1992-99. Recipient So. Fellowship award Coll. William and Mary, 1957-58. Mem. NCAA (v.p. divsn. III, 1992-94, exec. com. 1992-95, chmn. com. 1992-96, chmn. governance com. 1995-97), Nat. Assn. Basketball Coaches, Am. Assn. Health Phys. Edn. Recreation, Athletic Dirs. Assn. (divsn. III), Phi Beta Kappa, Omicron Delta Kappa. Episcopalian. Avocations: white water rafting, sports, music, exercise.

HARVEY, JONATHAN MATTHEW, lawyer; b. Worcester, Mass., July 6, 1955; s. Irwin and Hannah H.; m. Lyssa Lynn Kligman, Dec. 17, 1977; children: Laurel Eden, Jordane Mills, Kyle Michael. BA cum laude, U. Ga., 1977; JD, U. S.C., 1981. Bar: S.C. 1981, U.S. Dist. Ct. S.C. 1982, U.S. Ct. Appeals (4th cir.) 1992. Asst. solicitor Fifth Judicial Circuit Solicitor's Office, Columbia, S.C., 1982-83; asst. atty. gen. Office of the Atty. Gen., Columbia, S.C., 1983-86; lawyer pvt. practice, Columbia, 1986—. Vice chair Richland Sch. Dist. Ednl. Found., 2001—02; fin. dir. Richland County Dems., Columbia, SC, 1987—88, mem. exec. com., 1987—90, 1998—2000; commr. East Richland County Pub. Svc. Dist., 1990—99, chmn., 1999—2000. Mem.: ATLA, S.C. Trial Lawyers Assn., S.C. Assn. Criminal Def. Lawyers (bd. dirs. 5th jud. cir. 1998—2001, treas. 2002—), S.C. Bar Assn., Richland County Bar Assn. Democrat. Avocations: tennis, outdoor activities. Office: 1804 Bull St Columbia SC 29201-2506 Office Phone: 803-779-3363.

HARVEY, JOSEPH PAUL, JR., orthopedist, educator; b. Youngstown, Ohio, Feb. 28, 1922; s. Joseph Paul and Mary Justinian (Collins) H.; m. Martha Elizabeth Toole, Apr. 12, 1958; children: Maryalice, Martha Jane, Frances Susan, Helen Lucy, Laura Andre. Student, Dartmouth Coll., 1939-42; MD, Harvard U., 1945. Diplomate: Nat. Bd. Med. Examiners. Intern Peter Bent Brigham Hosp., Boston, 1945-46; resident Univ. Hosp., Cleve., 1951-53, Hosp. Spl. Surgery, N.Y.C., 1953-54; instr. orthopedics Cornell Med. Coll., N.Y.C., 1954-62; mem. faculty Sch. Medicine, U. So. Calif., Los Angeles, 1962-69; prof. orthopedic surgery U. So. Calif., 1966-92, prof. emeritus, 1992—; chmn. sect. orthopedics Keck Sch. Medicine, U. So. Calif., 1964-78. Dir. dept. orthopedics U. So. Calif.-Los Angeles County Med. Center, 1964-79, mem. staff, 1979— Editor-in-chief: Contemporary Orthopedics, 1978-96. Served to capt. AUS, 1946-48. Exchange orthopedic fellow Royal Acad. Hosp., Upsala, Sweden, 1957 Fellow Western Orthop. Assn., Am. Acad. Orthop. Surgery, A.C.S., Am. Soc. Testing Materials; mem. AMA, Calif. Med. Assn., Los Angeles County Med. Assn., Am. Rheumatism Assn., Am. Orthop. Assn., Internat. Soc. Orthopedics and Traumatology. Clubs: Boston Harvard. Home: 432 Arlington Dr Pasadena CA 91105-2850 Address: The Athenaeum 551 South Hill Ave Pasadena CA 91106 Office Phone: 626-441-0554. Business E-Mail: harvey@usc.edu.

HARVEY, KENNETH M, corporate financial executive; married; 3 children. BSc in fin., DePaul U., 1981. With Household Internat., 1989—; mng. dir., CIO Household Internat. Inc., 1999—2002; group exec., CIO Household Internat., Inc., 2002—. Mem. bd. dirs. Vertical Networks, Kanbay Inc. Recipient 2000 CIO 100 award, CIO Mag., Innovation award, Information Week. Office: Household Internat Inc 2700 Sanders Rd Prospect Heights IL 60070

HARVEY, LA VERNE DEBORAH, writer, theater producer, educator; b. N.Y.C. d. Oliver and Janie Williams; 1 child, Yannick. BA in English cum laude, CCNY, 1989; M.Ednl. Theatre, NYU, 1997. Asst. producer, writer, stage mgr. Sta. WABC-TV, N.Y.C., 1969-80. Adj. prof. basic writing CCNY, 1990-91, tutor basic writing, 1990-91. Recipient The Goodman Fund Film and TV award, 1988, Minashaughnessy Oxford U. Press award, award Nat. Assn. of Media Women's Ann. N.Y. Black Film Festival for Producing and Writing Documentaries; semi-finalist Writers Guild of Am.; East Found. fellowship, 1987. Mem. Dirs. Guild Am., Alpha Sigma Lambda. Democrat. Avocations: tennis, writing, reading, movies, family outings. Office: PO Box 382 New York NY 10037-0382

HARVEY, LISA MARIE, physiologist; b. Phila., Dec. 26, 1960; d. Frederick Chambers and Sarah Evelyn (Gorman) Batten; m. Jeffrey Warren Harvey, Oct. 25, 1980; children: Tashelle, Serina, Stephanie. BA, Point Loma Coll., San Diego, 1984; PhD, Loma Linda (Calif.) U., 1992. Rschr. Loma Linda U., 1984-92; sci. tchr. Rialto (Calif.) Elem. Schs., 1992-94; postdoctoral fellow San Diego State U., 1993-94; prof. Riverside (Calif.) C.C., 1994—. Contbr. articles to profl. jours. Tchr. ch. Sunday sch., San Bernardino, Calif.; sch. site coun. Bemis Elem. Sch., Rialto. Grantee Loma Linda U., 1988. Mem. Soc. for Study of Fetal Physiology (Best oral presentation 1992), Sigma Xi. Achievements include research on changes in the hypothalamic-pituitary-adrenal axis following exposure to long-term hypoxemia at high altitute in the ovine fetus.

HARVEY, LOUIS-CHARLES, minister, seminary president, religion educator; b. Memphis, May 5, 1945; s. Willie Miles Harvey and Mary Elizabeth Jones: married, July 10, 1976 (div. Dec. 1993); children: Marcus-Louis, Melanee-Charles. BS, LeMoyne-Owen Coll., 1967; MDiv, Colgate Rochester Theol. Sem., 1971; MPhil, Union Sem., N.Y.C., 1977, Phd, 1978. Ordained to ministry A.M.E. Ch. as elder, 1971. Asst. prof. theology Colgate Rochester (N.Y.) Theol. Sem., 1974-78; prof., acad. dean Payne Theol. Sem., Wilberforce, Ohio, 1978-79, pres., 1989-96; mem. faculty United Theol. Sem., Dayton, Ohio, 1979-89, prof., 1985-89; pastor Met. A.M.E. Ch., Washington, 1996—2001; presiding elder Potomac Dist. A.M.E. Ch. Washington Ann. Conf., 2001—; faculty mem. Ebenezer Bible Inst., Ft. Washington, Md., 2002—. Contbr. articles to religious jours. Mem. Challenge 95 Leadership Com., Dayton, 1991. Mem. Soc. Study Black Religion (sec. 1988, treas. 1992-98), Alpha Phi Alpha (sec. 1989-90, Alpha Excellence award 1995).

HARVEY, LYNNE COOPER, broadcast executive, civic worker; b. near St. Louis; d. William A. and Mattie (Kehr) Cooper; m. Paul Harvey, June 4, 1940; 1 child, Paul Harvey Aurandt. DHL (hon.), Rosary Coll., 1996; D (hon.), Washington U., 1988. Broadcaster ednl. program KXOX, St. Louis, 1940; broadcaster-writer women's news WAC Variety Show, Ft. Custer, Mich., 1941-43; gen. mgr. Paul Harvey News ABC, 1944—. Pres. Paulynne Prodn., Ltd., Chgo., 1968—, exec. prodr. Paul Harvey Comments, 1968—; pres. Trots Corp., 1989—; editor, compiler The Rest of the Story. Pres. women's bd. Mental Health Assn. Greater Chgo., 1967-71, v.p. bd. dirs., 1966—; pres. woman's aux. Infant Welfare Soc. Chgo., 1969-71, bd. dirs., 1969—, benefits hon. chmn., 1994, 96; mem. Salvation Army Woman's Adv. Bd., 1967; reception chmn. Cmty. Lectures; women's com. Chgo. Symphony, 1972—; pres. Mothers Coun., River Forest, 1961-62; charter bd. mem. Gottlieb Meml. Hosp., Melrose Park, Ill.; mem. adv. bd. Nat. Christian Heritage Found., 1964—; mem. USO woman's bd., 1983, woman's bd. Ravinia Festival, 1972—; trustee John Brown U., 1980—; bd. dirs. Mus. Broadcast Comms., 1987—; adv. coun. Charitable Trusts, 1989—; mem. Joffrey Ballet Com.; chmn. Brookfield Zoo Whirl, 2000. Named to, Mus. Broadcast Comm.-Radio Hall of Fame; recipient Heritage of Am. award, 1974, Little City Spirit of Love award, 1987, Salvation Army Others award, 1989, disting. friend award, NCPCA, disting. alumni award, Washington U., Friske Meml. award, USO, 2000, Lynne Harvey scholarship named in her honor, Musicians Club of Women.

HARVEY, MARC S(AN), lawyer, historian, law educator; b. NYC, May 4, 1960; s. M. Eugene and Coleen (Jones) H. BA with highest honors, So. Ill. U., 1980; Pre-Law, Wash. U., 1980; JD, Southwestern U., 1983; MBA, Loyola Marymount U., L.A., 1984-86; postgrad., Oxford U., Christ Ch. Coll., 1994—97. Bar: Calif., U.S. Supreme Ct. Counsel U.S. SBA, L.A., 1982-83; counsel enforcement div. U.S. SEC, L.A., 1983-84; counsel State Farm Ins. Co., L.A., 1984-85, 20th Century Ins. Co., Woodland Hills, Calif., 1985-86; pvt. practice Encino, Calif., 1986—. Lectr. in field. Contbr. articles to profl. jours. Judge pro tem Culver Mcpl. Ct.; charter mem., trustee Rep. Presdl. Task Force, Washington, 1981—; mem. Nat. Rep. Senatorial Com., Washington, 1983—, Rep. Congl. Leadership Coun., Washington, 1987—, Rep. Senatorial Inner Cir., Washington, 1988—. Named Vol. of Yr., L.A. County, 1992; recipient 1st pl. essay award, VFW, 1976, Judge Pro Tem of Yr. award, Culver Mcpl. Ct., 1991. Mem.: SAG, AFTRA, ATLA, ABA, L.A. Trial Lawyers Assn., Calif. Trial Lawyers Assn., Nat. Thespian Soc., Themis Soc., U.S. Supreme Ct. Hist. Soc. Office Phone: 818-990-3990.

HARVEY, MARK SUMNER, composer, educator, minister, musician; b. Binghamton, N.Y., July 4, 1946; s. Robert Mark and Marjorie Grace (Tolley) H.; m. Kate Matson, Aug. 14, 1983. AB, Syracuse U., 1968; ThM, Boston U., 1971, PhD, 1983. Ordained to ministry United Meth. Ch. as deacon, 1970, as elder, 1975. Intern min. Old West United Meth. Ch., Boston, 1969-71, staff mem., assoc. min., 1971-73; min. with jazz and arts community Emmanuel Ch., Boston, 1974—93; with Harvard-Epworth United Meth. Ch., 1993—2003. Mem. music faculty MIT, Cambridge, Mass., 1981—; founder, music dir. Aardvark Jazz Orch., 1973—, New Am. Music Ensemble, 1969— Composer chamber, choral, jazz orch. pieces; 7 CD recs. of original compositions; contbr. articles to profl. jours. Pres., founder The Jazz Coalition, inc., Boston, 1971-83; trustee Mass. Cultural Alliance, Boston, 1971-73, 81-87; mem. music adv. panel Mass. Coun. on the Arts and Humanities, Boston, 1971-75, 79-82, Meet the Composer/Reader's Digest Commissioning Program, 1989; mem. arts adv. com. Harvard U. Ctr. for Study of World Religions, 1994-97. Fellow NEH, 1987, The Whiting Found., 1986; recipient Contbn. to Cultural Activity award Mass. Cultural Alliance, 1987, City of Boston, 1980. Fellow Soc. for the Arts, Religion, and Contemporary Culture (chmn. 1991-95, bd. dirs. 1986—); mem. ASCAP, Am. Acad. Religion, Soc. for Am. Music, Duke Ellington Soc., Am. Studies Assn., Theta Chi Beta. Office: PO Box 8721 JFK Sta Boston MA 02114 Office Phone: 617-452-3205. Business E-Mail: mharvey@mit.edu.

HARVEY, MORRIS LANE, lawyer; b. Madisonville, Ky., Apr. 22, 1950; s. Morris Lee and Margie Lou (Wallace) H.; m. Mary Topel Harvey; children: Morris Lane Jr., John French, Laura Kathleen. BS, Murray State U., 1972; JD, U. Ky., 1974. Bar: Ill. 1975, U.S. Dist. Ct. (so. dist.) 1979. Assoc. Hanagan & Dousman, Mt. Vernon, Ill., 1975-77; ptnr. Feiger, Quindry, Molt & Harvey and successor firms, Fairfield, Ill., 1977-85; sole practice Fairfield, 1986-97, Mt. Vernon, 1997—2003; assoc. Harvey and Bradley, Mount Vernon, 2004—. Instr. Frontier C.C., Fairfield, 1977-79; spl. asst. atty. gen. State of Ill., Fairfield, 1977-82; Ill. pres. Woodman of World Life Ins. Soc., 1985-87; mem. nat. fraternal com., 1987-89, 2000-2002, nat. legis. com., 1989-93, nat. jud. com., 1993-97. Recipient Outstanding Young Man Am. U.S. Jaycees, 1978, 81, 89. Mem. ABA, Ill. Bar Assn., Assn. Trial Lawyers Am., Ill. Trial Lawyers Assn. Home: 5 Webster Hill Est Mount Vernon IL 62864-2346 Office: 2029 Broadway St Mount Vernon IL 62864-2910 Office Phone: 618-244-9544.

HARVEY, NORMAN RONALD, retired finance company executive; b. Rahway, N.J., Aug. 17, 1933; s. George Henry and Jennie Louise (Proudfoot) H.; m. Gail Molitor, May 26, 1962 (dec.); 1 dau., Anne. BA in Econs., Cornell U., 1955; MBA in Investments, NYU, 1962. Security analyst Bankers Trust Co., N.Y.C., 1958-61, Anchor Corp., Elizabeth, N.J., 1961-64; dir. research Auerbach, Pollak & Richardson, N.Y.C., 1964-75; chief investment officer E.W. Axe & Co., Inc., Tarrytown, N.Y., 1975-82; sr. v.p., equity funds investment officer Merrill Lynch Asset Mgmt., Princeton, N.J., 1982-99; ret. Served to 1st lt. USAR, 1957-58. Corson Meml. scholar, 1951 Mem. NY Soc. Security Analysts, The Union League NY, Edgcomb Tennis Club,Eagle Rock Yacht Club. Republican. Home: 39 Florence Ln Princeton NJ 08540-2631 also: 27 Woodland Ave Kennebunk ME 04043-7528

HARVEY, PATRICIA A., school system administrator; BS in elem. edn., Lincoln U.; MA in sch. admin., Roosevelet U. Prin. Hefferan Elem. Sch., Chgo., Idaho; exec. asst. to gen. supt. Chgo. Schs., 1994—95, chief accountability officer, 1995—97; sr. fellow dir. urban edn. Nat. Ctr. Edn. and Econ., Wash., DC, 1997—99; supt. Saint Paul Pub. Schs., Saint Paul, Minn., 1999—. Office: Saint Paul Pub Sch 360 Colborne St Saint Paul MN 55102

HARVEY, PAUL, commentator, writer, columnist; b. Tulsa, Sept. 4, 1918; s. Harry Harrison and Anna Dagmar (Christensen) Aurandt; m. Lynne Cooper, June 4, 1940; 1 child, Paul Harvey. LittD (hon.), Culver-Stockton Coll., 1952, St. Bonaventure U., 1953; LLD, John Brown U., Ark., 1959, Mont. Sch. Mines, 1961, Trinity Coll. Fla., 1963, Parsons Coll., 1968; HHD, Wayland Bapt. Coll., 1960, Union Coll., 1962, Samford U., 1970, Howard Payne U., Tex., 1978, Sterling Coll., 1982; Degree (hon.), Rosary Coll., 1996; LHD (hon.), Hillsdale Coll., Mich., 2000. Announcer radio sta. KVOO, Tulsa; sta. mgr. Salina, Kans.; spl. events dir. radio sta. KXOK, St. Louis; program dir. radio sta. WKZO, Kalamazoo, 1941-43; dir. news and information OWI, Mich., Ind., 1941-43; news commentator, analyst ABC, 1944—; syndicated columnist Los Angeles Times Syndicate (formerly Gen. Features Corp.), 1954—; TV commentator, 1968. Author: Remember These Things, 1952, Autumn of Liberty, 1954, The Rest of the Story, 1956, You Said It, Paul Harvey, 1969, Our Lives, Our Fortunes, Our Sacred Honor; Album rec. Yesterday's Voices, 1959, Testing Time, 1960, Uncommon Man, 1962. Bd. dirs. John D. and Catherine T. MacArthur Found.; mem. bd. govs. Orchestral Assn. Chgo. Symphony Orch. Recipient citation DAV, 1949, 11 Freedoms Found. awards, 1952-76, radio award Am. Legion, 1952, citation of merit, 1955, 57, Cert. of merit VFW, 1953, Bronze Christopher's award, 1953, award of honor Sumter Guards, 1955, nat. pub. welfare services trophy Colo. Am. Legion, 1957,Great Am. KSEL award, 1962, Spl. ABC award, 1973, Ill. Broadcaster award, 1974, John Peter Zenger Freedom award Eagles, 1975, Am. of Year award Lions Internat., 1975, Outstanding Broadcast Journalism award, 1980, Gen. Omar N. Bradley Spirit of Independence trophy, 1980, Man of Yr. award Chgo. Broadcast Advt. Club, 1981, Golden Radio award Nat. Radio Broadcasters Assn., 1982, Best Speaking Voice award Am. Speech, Lang. and Hearing Assn., 1982, Horatio Alger award, 1983, Outstanding Broadcast Personality award Advt. Club Balt., 1984, Meritorius Svc. award Am. Acad. Family Physicians, 1984, Cert. of Appreciation Humane Soc. of U.S., 1985, Genesis award The Fund for Animals, 1986, Okla. Assn. Broadcasters award, 1987, Henry G. Bennett Disting. Svc. award Okla. State U., 1987, James Herriot award Humane Soc. U.S., 1987, Lowell Thomas award, 1989, Gold medal Internat. Radio & TV Soc., 1989, Others award Salvation Army, 1989, Journalism award Internat. Radio Festival, 1989, 5 Marconi awards Network Personality of Yr., 1989, 91, 96, 98, 2002, Dante award, 1990, William Booth award Salvation Army, 1990, Journalism award Chgo. Hall of Fame, 1990, Bd. of Dirs. award Nat. Religious Broadcasters, 1991, Great Am. Race Legend's award Interstate, 1991, Good Guy award Am. Legion, 1992, Outstanding Pub. Spkr. award Toastmasters Internat., 1992, Paul White award Radio T.V. News Dirs., 1992, Peabody award 1993, 94, Spirit of Broadcasting award NAB, 1994, Silver award Am. Advertising Fedn., 1994, Hall of Fame award Broadcasting & Cable Mag., 1995, Am. Spirit award USAF, 1996, Lifetime Achievement award Radio Mercury, 1997, Lifetime Achievement award Gold Angel, 1998, Lifetime Achievement award Radio Mercury, 1997, Tex McCrary award Journalism from Congl. Medal Honor Soc., 2000, Lifetime Achievement A.I.R. award Radio Broadcasters Chgo., 2001, R&R News/Talk Radio Lifetime Achievement award, 2003, NY Festivals World Gold Medal award best personality network/syndicated, 2004; elected to Okla. Hall of Fame, 1955, Nat. Assn. Broadcasters Hall of Fame, 1979; named Top Commentator of Yr. Radio-TV Daily, 1962, Father of Yr. Father's Day Coun., 1980, Laureate Lincoln Acad. of Ill., 1987 (Ill. highest honor); to Emerson Radio Hall of Fame, 1990; one of The Men of the Century Broadcast and Cable Mag., 1999; among 20th Century's Most Significant Americans George Mag., 1998. Mem. Washington Radio and Television Corrs. Assn., Aircraft Owners and Pilots Assn. Clubs: Chicago Press. Achievements include having broadcasts and columns reprinted in Congressional Record 102 times. Office: 333 N Michigan Ave Ste 1600 Chicago IL 60601-4005 Office Phone: 312-899-4085.

HARVEY, PETER C., state attorney general; BA in Polit. Sci., Morgan State U., 1979; JD, Columbia U., 1982. Bar: N.Y. 1984, D.C. 1985, N.J. 1989. Asst. U.S. atty. Dist. N.J., 1986—89; spl. asst. to N.J. Atty. Gen., 1989—90; law clk. for Hon. Dickinson R. Debevoise US Dist. Ct. NJ; ptnr. Riker, Danzig, Scherer, Hyland and Perretti LLP, Morristown, NJ; 1st asst. atty. gen., dir. divsn. criminal justice State of N.J., 2002—03, acting atty. gen., atty. gen., 2003—. Mediator U.S. Dist. Ct., NJ, N.J. Supreme Ct.; mem. lawyers' adv. com. U.S. Dist. Ct. for the Dist. N.J., U.S. Ct. of Appeals (3d cir.). Named Lawyer of the Year, NJ State Law Jour., 2003. Office: Richard J Hughes Justice Complex 25 Market St PO Box 080 Trenton NJ 08625

HARVEY, RICHARD DUDLEY, marketing consultant; b. Atlanta, Sept. 24, 1923; s. Robert Emmett and June (Dudley) H.; m. Donna Helen Smith, Oct. 12, 1944 (dec. Mar. 1990); 1 child, Louise Dudley; m. Catherine M. McFarland, Nov. 13, 1993. BA, U. Denver, 1947; postgrad., Harvard U., Stanford U. Various positions in sales, sales promotion & mktg. The Coca-Cola Co., St. Louis, Denver, Atlanta, 1948-60, v.p., brand mgr., mktg. mgr., mktg. dir. Atlanta, 1965-70, v.p. orgn. & mktg. devel., 1970-75; sr. v.p. mktg. Olympia (Wash.) Brewing Co., 1975-78; pres. Sound Mktg. Svcs., Inc., Seattle, 1978-93, Harvey Mktg. Corp., Upper Montclair, N.J., 1994—. Vice chmn. bd. Roman Meal Co., Tacoma, Washington, 1990—; dir. Lone Star Brewing Co., San Antonio, 1976-78. Trustee Episcopal Radio-TV Found., Atlanta, 1961-88, vice chmn., 1975-84, emeritus trustee, 1988—; bd. dirs. Oreg. Shakespearean Festival Assn., 1982-86; vol. Nat. Exec. Svc. Corps., N.J., N.Y.C., 1997—; chmn. mktg. com., trustee Seattle Symphony, 1983-88; mem. gov.'s adv. com. bus. devel. and job retention, State of Wash., 1988-92; mem. Montclair HIst. Preservation Commn., 1998-2000; mem. cmty. adv. bd. Montclair State U., 2002—03. Served with USAAF, 1942-45. Mem. Am. Mktg. Assn. (pres. Seattle chpt. 1983-84), Arc of NJ (bd. dirs. 1997-98, exec. com. 1998-99), Mktg. Comm. Execs. Internat. (pres. Seattle chpt. 1984-85), Inst. Mgmt. Cons. (pres. NJ chpt. 1995-96), Seattle Tennis Club, Glen Ridge Country Club, Phi Beta Kappa, Omicron Delta Kappa; fellow Inst. of Mgmt. Cons. Home and Office: 28 Robinhood Dr Mountain Lakes NJ 07046 E-mail: dickharvey@earthlink.net.

HARVEY, RONALD GILBERT, research chemist; b. Ottawa, Ont., Can., Sept. 9, 1927; arrived in U.S., 1948; s. Gilbert and Adeline (LeClair) H.; m. Helene H. Szpara, May 18, 1952; 1 child, Ronald Edward. BS in Biology, UCLA, 1952; MS in Chemistry, U. Chgo., 1956, PhD in Chemistry, 1960. Project leader Sinclair Rsch. Labs., Harvey, Ill., 1956-58; instr. U. Chgo., 1960-63, asst.prof., 1964-68, assoc. prof., 1968-75, prof., 1975-97, prof. emeritus, 1997—; postdoctoral fellow Imperial Coll., London, Eng., 1963-64. Cons. Nat. Cancer Inst., Washington, Farmacon Corp., Oakbrook, Ill., CIDAC, Palo Alto, Calif., 1978-80; OMNI Research Mayaguex, P.R., 1973-74, Nat. Inst. Environ. Health Sci., Washington, Am. Cancer Soc., Atlanta, U.S.-Israel Binational Sci. Found. Author: Polycyclic Aromatic Hydrocarbons Chemistry and Carcinogenesis, 1991, Polycyclic Aromatic Hydrocarbons, 1997; editor: Polycyclic Hydrocarbons and Carcinogenesis; mem. editl. bd. Polycyclic Aromatic Compounds (1990-), Mini Reviews in Organic Chemistry (2003-); contbr. more than 440 articles to profl. jours. Recipient ISPAC award for rsch. in polycyclic hydrocarbon chemistry, 1995. Fellow Royal Chem. Soc., Am. Inst. Chemists; mem. AAAS, Am. Chem. Soc., Am. Assn. Cancer Rsch., Sigma Xi. Achievements include patents for synthesis of alpha-olefins, anti-androgen compounds. Home: 10550 Golf Rd Orland Park IL 60462-7420 Office: U Chgo Ben May Inst 5841 S Maryland Ave Chicago IL 60637-1463 Business E-Mail: rharvey@huggins.bsd.uchicago.edu.

HARVEY, SHEILA MCCAFFERTY, lawyer; b. Ridgewood, NJ, June 28, 1954; AB summa cum laude, Bryn Mawr Coll., 1976; JD, Univ. Mich., 1979. Bar: DC 1979. Ptnr., co-chmn. Environ. Land Use & Natural Resources practice Pillsbury Winthrop Shaw Pittman, Washington. Mem.: ABA, Environ. Law Inst. Office: Pillsbury Winthrop Shaw Pittman 2300 N St NW Washington DC 20037-1128 Office Phone: 202-663-8224. Office Fax: 202-663-8007. Business E-Mail: sheila.harvey@pillsburylaw.com.

HARVEY, STEVEN PATRICK (STEVE HARVEY), comedian, actor; b. Welch, W.Va., Nov. 23, 1956; s. Jesse and Eloise Harvey; m. Mary Lee Harvey, 1999; children: Wynton, Brandi, Karli 1 stepchild, Steven. Student, Kent State U., 1977—80. Assembly line worker Ford Motor Co.; life ins. rep.; salesperson cleaning supplies and pet products; first appeared on stage at club Cleve.; performer various clubs; owner Steve Harvey Comedy House, Dallas, 1993—. Actor: (films) The Fighting Temptations, 2003, Love Don't Cost a Thing, 2003, Johnson Family Vacation, 2004, You Got Served, 2004, (voice) Racing Stripes, 2005,; (TV series) Me and the Boys, 1994, The Steve Harvey Show, 1996—2002 (Image award for outstanding lead actor in comedy series, 1998, 1999, Image award for outstanding actor in comedy series, 2001, 2002); host: It's Showtime at the Apollo, 1994—2000 (Image award for outstanding performance in variety series, 1999); (radio shows) WGCI-FM morning radio show, 1996—97; The Beat, 2000—; exec. prodr.: (TV series) Big Time, 2003—, Pulled Over, 2004, (CD) Signs of Things to Come, 2002—; TV appearances include: Comedy Concert Hour, Nashville Network, 1990; Comedy from the Caribbean, Arts and Entertainment, 1992; Diamonds in the Rough, Black Entertainment TV, 1994; Cohost from Fla., Dick Clark's New Year's Rockin' Eve, 1994; HBO Comedy Half-Hour: Steve Harvey, 1995; Steve Harvey: One Man, HBO Comedy Hour, 1997; All-New All-Star TV Censored When Bloopers Attack!, 1997; lead actor (DVD) Def Comedy Jam--Best of Steve Harvey, 2002; performer: Kings of Comedy tour, 1997—2000. Founder King Love Ctr.; co-founder Mary L. Harvey Found. Recipient Image award for Entertainer of Yr., 2001.*

HARVEY, WILLIAM ARTHUR, III, aerospace material development chemist; b. Phila., Sept. 27, 1955; s. William A. Jr. and Mary Kathryn (Ostenfeld) H. BS in Chemistry, Villanova (Pa.) U., 1980; BBA in Fin., U. Pa., Phila., 1984. Jr. chemist Rohm and Haas Co., Springhouse, Pa., 1980-81; staff chemist Quaker Chem. Co., Conshohacken, Pa., 1981-82; chemist M.A. Bruder & Sons Inc., Phila., 1984-86; aerospace chemist Teleflex, Inc., Limerick, Pa., 1986-90; devel. chemist Colorcon, Inc., West Point, Pa., 1991-92; environ. chemist Gov.'s Office Commonwealth Pa., Pa. Dept. Transp., Harrisburg, 1993-94. Campaign worker Joe Hoeffel for U.S. Congress Orgn., Norristown, Pa., 1998; vol. Homework Helpline, 1999-2001. Mem. Am. Chem. Soc. Achievements include patents representing significant development in the use of ion reactive pigments with organic polymers for use to protect active metals. Home: 208 Meadowview Ln Mont Clare PA 19453-5131

HARVEY, WILLIAM BRANTLEY, JR., lawyer, retired lieutenant governor; b. Walterboro, S.C., Aug. 14, 1930; s. William Brantley and Thelma (Lightsey) H.; m. Helen Coggeshall, Dec. 30, 1952; children: Eileen L., William Brantley, III, Helen C., Margaret D., Warren C. AB in Polit. Sci., The Citadel, 1951, LLD (hon.), 1978; JD magna cum laude, U. S.C., 1955. Bar: S.C. 1955. Since practiced in, Beaufort, S.C.; sr. ptnr. Harvey & Battey; mem. S.C. Ho. of Reps. from Beaufort County, 1958-74, chmn. rules com., mem. constl. revision com.; lt. gov. State of S.C., 1974-78. Bd. dirs., past chmn. Carolina Motor Club (AAA); mem. exec. com. Assoc. Marine Inst., past chmn.; bd. dirs., sec. Beaufort Marine Inst.; past chmn. Beaufort County Transp. Com.; pres. S.C. Bar, 1986—87; mem., vice chmn. S.C. State Bd. for Tech. and Comprehensive Edn.; chmn. AMI Found. Former commr. S.C. Dept. Hwys. and Pub. transp.; former commr., vice chmn. S.C. Parks, Recreation and Tourism Commn.; mem. Coastal Caroline coun. Boy Scouts Am.; mem. adv. bd. The Salvation Army Beaufort Unit; pres. Beaufort Indsl. Park, Beaufort County Devel. Corp.; bd. dirs. The Citadel Found.; Lowcountry Habitat for Humanity, Mustard Seed Found. Mem. ABA, S.C. Bar Assn., Beaufort County Bar Assn., Rotary, Phi Beta Kappa, Kappa Alpha, Phi Delta Phi, Omicron Delta Kappa. Presbyterian (elder). Home: 501 Pinckney St Beaufort SC 29902-4739 Office: Harvey & Battey Attys PO Box 1107 1001 Craven St Beaufort SC 29902-5577 Office Phone: 843-524-3109. Business E-Mail: wbharvey@islc.net.

HARVEY, WILLIAM D., utilities executive, lawyer; BA in Econs., U. Wis., Madison, 1971, JD, 1974. Solo practice, 1974—76; prin. Wheeler, Van Sickle, Anderson, Norman & Harvey, S.C., 1976—86; v.p. and assoc. gen. counsel Wis. Power & Light (now Alliant Energy Corp.), 1986—89, v.p and gen. counsel, 1989—92, v.p. natural gas and gen. counsel, 1992—93, sr. v.p., 1993—98; exec. v.p. generation Alliant Energy-Wis. Power & Light Co. (now Alliant Energy Corp.), 1998—2004; pres. and COO Alliant Energy Corp., Madison, Wis., 2004—05, now pres., CEO. Bd. dir. Am. Transmission Co.; chair bd. dir. Wis. Utilities Assn. Bd. dir. United Way of Dane County, 1993—2001, campaign chair, 2001, mem. cmty. bldg. com., 1996—2000; bd. dir. Greater Madison C. of C., 1993—, Madison Symphony Orch., 1998—2001; exec. com. Dane County Econ. Summit Coun.; bd. dir. Wis. Botechnology Assn., 1998—2001, Riverlands Conservancy, Inc. Office: Alliant Energy Corp 4902 N Biltmore Ln Madison WI 53718

HARVEY, WILLIAM ROBERT, university president; b. Brewton, Ala., Jan. 29, 1941; s. Willie D. C. and Mamie Claudis (Parker) H.; m. Norma Baker, Aug. 13, 1966; children: Kelly Renee, William Christopher, Leslie Denise. BA, Talladega Coll., 1961; EdD, Harvard U., 1972. Asst. govt. affairs to dean Harvard U. Grad. Sch. Edn., 1969-70; adminstrv. asst. to pres. Fisk U., Nashville, 1970-72; v.p. student affairs/dir. planning Tuskegee (Ala.) Inst., 1972-76, v.p. adminstrv. services, 1976-78; pres. Hampton (Va.) U., 1978—; owner Pepsi-Cola Bottling Co., Houghton, Mich., 1986—. Chmn., bd. dirs. Fund for the Improvement of Post Secondary Edn.; mem. Coun. Presidents, Assn. Gov. Bds. of Univs. and Colleges; former bd. mem. Trigon Blue Cross Blue Shield Va., Newport News Shipbuilding, Fannie Mae. Contbr. articles to profl. jours. Bd. dirs. United Way, Peninsula Econ. Devel. Council; vice-chmn. President's nat. adv. council ESEA; mem. Harvard U. Alumni Council; mem. nat. adv. com. Woodrow Wilson Nat. Fellowship Found. Served with U.S. Army, 1962-65. Woodrow Wilson Martin Luther King fellow, 1968-70; Woodrow Wilson Found. intern fellow, 1970-72; Harvard U. Higher Edn. Adminstrv. fellow, 1968-70 Mem. Am. Coun. Edn., Am. Assn. Higher Edn., Nat. Assn. Equal Opportunity in Higher Edn. (chmn., bd. dirs.), Va. Assn. Higher Edn., 100 Black Men (charter mem. Newport News chpt.), Nat. Guardsmen (Norfolk chpt.), Peninsula C. of C. (dir.), Coun. Ind. Colls. in Va., Omega Psi Phi, Phi Delta Kappa, Sigma Pi Phi. Baptist. Office: Hampton U Office of Pres Hampton VA 23668 E-mail: presidentsoffice@hamptonu.edu. *It is very important today for people to have the opportunity to do some thinking about ethics and morals. It is my firm belief that decency is as important as degrees and this means not only being good doctors, lawyers, professors, engineers and nurses, but good moral leaders who have a sense of community and service as well.*

HARVIE, CRAWFORD THOMAS, lawyer; b. NYC, Mar. 28, 1943; s. William Mead and Barbara Adele (Johnson) H.; m. Iris Ruth Alofsin, June 10, 1972; children: Katherine, Edward. AB, Stanford U., 1965; LLB, Yale U., 1968; cert. advanced mgmt. program, Harvard U., 1992. Bar: N.Y. 1969. Assoc. Debevoise & Plimpton, N.Y.C., 1971-75; counsel TRW, Inc., Cleve., 1976-77, sr. counsel, 1978-79, asst. gen. counsel, v.p., 1980-83; v.p. law TRW Automotive, Cleve., 1983-90; v.p., assoc. gen. counsel TRW Inc., 1990-95; sr. v.p., gen. counsel, sec. Goodyear Tire and Rubber Co., Akron, Ohio, 1995—. Trustee Cleve. Inst. of Music, 1989—; bd. overseers Blossom Music Ctr. Mem. Am. Corp. Counsel Assn., Assn. of Gen. Counsel, Chief Legal Officer Roundtable-U.S. Home: 6537 Thornbrook Cir Hudson OH 44236-3552 Office: Goodyear Tire and Rubber Co 1144 E Market St Akron OH 44316-0001

HARVILL, MELBA SHERWOOD, retired school librarian; b. Bryson, Tex., Jan. 22, 1933; d. William Henry and Delta Verlin (Brawner) Sherwood; m. L. E. Harvill, Jr., Feb. 2, 1968; children: Sherman T., Mark Rolling. BA, North Tex. State Coll., 1954; MA, North Tex. State U., 1968, MLS, 1973, PhD, 1984. Tchr. Graham (Tex.) Ind. Sch. Dist., 1966-68; reference libr. Midwestern U., Wichita Falls, Tex., 1968—73; dir. librs. Midwestern State U., Wichita Falls, 1973-2000; ret., 2000. Presenter in field. Vol. Boy Scouts Am., Wichita Falls, 1969—74, Wichita Falls Sr.-Jr. Forum, 1978—2000, mem. exec. bd. girls club, ways and means com., sec., asst. treas.; chmn. United Way Midwestern State U., 1975—76; mem. talent coordinating com. Wichita Falls Centennial Celebration; vol. Conv. and Vis. Bur., Lone Stars, 1993—; grad. Leadership Wichita Falls, 1990; pres. Southside Girls Club, 1997—98; auditor, budget com. chair Woman's Forum, 1997—99; ednl. programming chair Wichita Falls Arts Coun., 2001—04, bd. dirs., 2004—07; former mem. ALA Tex. Coun. State U. Librs., sec., treas., 1990—92; mem. U. North Tex. Advancement Adv. Coun.; bd. dirs. YWCA Wichita Falls, 1987—94, pres. bd. dirs., 1989—91, 1994—95; bd. dirs. River Bend Nature Works. Named Met. BPW Woman of the Yr., 1980; recipient Svc. award., Sr.-Jr. Forum, Cmty. Svc. award, Wichita Falls United Way, 1975, Svc. award, YWCA Bd. Dirs., 1991. Democrat. Avocations: sports, swimming, music, reading, travel. Home: 4428 BUS 287J Iowa Park TX 76367 E-mail: mharvill@msn.com.

HARVIN, CHARLES ALEXANDER, III, state legislator, lawyer; b. Sumter, S.C., Feb. 7, 1950; s. Charles Alexander Harvin, Jr. m. Cathy Jane Brand; 1 child, Mary Franklin; Grad. in history and polit. sci. Baptist Coll., Charleston, S.C., 1972, Augusta Law Sch., 1976; hon. degree Sherman Chiropractic Coll., Spartanburg, S.C., 1979, Francis Marion Coll., 1986; LLD (hon.) Charleston So. Univ., 1988. Mem. S.C. Ho. of Reps., 1976—, asst. majority leader, majority whip, 1978-82, majority leader, 1982—, mem. ways and means com., vice chmn. rules com., majority leader Emeritus Ho. of Reps., S.C., 1987—. Pres. Bapt. Coll. Young Dems., 1970-72; officer Charleston County Young Dems., 1971-72; chmn. 6th Congl. Dist. Young Dems., 1975-76; life mem. S.C. Young Dems.; chmn. Clarendon County Dem. Com.; vice chmn. S.C. Dem. Com., 1976-78, also mem. exec. com.; del. Dem. Nat. Conv., 1984; mem. S.C. Gov.'s Agr. Study Com.; U.S. Constn. Bicentennial Commn., 1985—; trustee S.C. Hall of Fame; vice chmn. alumni bd. Bapt. Coll., 1975-76; bd. visitors Clemson U., 1977-78,.Med. Univ. S.C., 1986-87, Charleston So. Univ., 1988-90. Maj. USNG. Recipient Outstanding Service award Charleston County Young Dems., 1972, S.C. Young Dems., 1977; Disting. Service award S.C. Dem. Com., 1981; appreciation award S.C. Tech. Edn. Colls., 1981; Legislator of Yr. award S.C. Young Dems., 1982, S.C. Student Legislature, 1981, S.C. State Library Bd., 1982, S.C. Assn. for Deaf, 1985; award S.C. Coun. for Exceptional Children, 1982, S.C. Agrl. Cmty., 1982; Outstanding Legislator Service award United Parcel Svc., 1984; Disting. Svc. award Bapt. Coll. of Charleston Alumni Assn., 1984, also numerous other awards and commendations. Mem. ABA, Am. Judicature Soc., S.C. Trial Lawyers Assn., Clarendon County Farm Bur., Clarendon County Hist. Soc. (v.p. 1983-84, pres. 1985-86), S.C. State Employees Assn., NAACP, Huguenot Soc. of S.C., First Families of S.C., Alpha Phi Omega (life). Lodges: Masons, Shriners. Office: South Carolina Ho of Reps PO Box 11867 Columbia SC 29211-1867

HARVIN, DAVID TARLETON, lawyer; b. Houston, Feb. 15, 1945; s. William Charles and Ruth Helen (Beck) H.; m. Sarah Ann Hartman, Apr. 21, 1973; children: Kimberly Kate, William Hartman, John Andrew. BA, Yale U., 1967; JD, U. Tex., 1970. Bar: Tex. 1970, U.S. Dist. Ct. (so. dist.) Tex. 1972, U.S. Dist. Ct. (ea. dist.) Tex. 1977, U.S. Dist. Ct. (no. dist.) Tex. 1979, U.S. Dist. Ct. (we. dist.) Tex. 1988, U.S. Ct. Appeals (5th cir.) 1971, U.S. Supreme Ct. 1977. Law clk. U.S. Ct. Appeals (5th cir.), 1970-71; assoc. Vinson & Elkins L.L.P, Houston, 1971-77, ptnr., 1977—, mgmt. com., 2000—. Trustee Episcopal Theol. Sem. of S.W., 1995-2002, Stehlin Found. for Cancer Rsch., 1986-96, Kinkaid Sch., 1997-2003; vice-chancellor Episcopal Diocese of Tex. Fellow Am. Coll. Trial Lawyers, Tex. Bar Found., Houston Bar Found.; mem. ABA, Houston Country Club, The Downtown Club, Old Baldy Club. Home: 111 Maple Valley Rd Houston TX 77056-1007 Office: Vinson & Elkins LLP 1001 Fannin St Ste 2300 Houston TX 77002-6706 Office Phone: 713-758-2368. E-mail: dharvin@velaw.com.

HARVIN, KAY KERCE, elementary school educator; b. Arcadia, Fla., Mar. 9, 1947; d. Woodrow and Mary Lillian (Durrance) Kerce; m. Wesley Reid Harvin Sr., Aug. 22, 1964; 1 child, Wesley Reid II. BA, Fla. State U., 1967; MA, U. South Fla., 1974, EdS, 2001. Tchr. Hillsborough County, Tampa, Fla., 1967-71, Leon County, Tallahassee, Fla., 1971-73, Pinellas County, St. Petersburg, Fla., 1973-76, Martin County, Stuart, Fla., 1977—. ESOL trainer, 1996—; adj. instr. Indian River C.C., 1996—; presenter in field Author: Janet the Spider; Contbr. to Anthology of Treasured Poems, 1995, 96, 97, 98. Mem. Jr. Women's Club, 1969-80; mem. Rep. Exec. Com., Martin County, 1979-81; vol. Polit. Campaigns, Martin County, 1978, 80, 82, 84, 92, 94. Methodist. Avocations: reading, writing. Home: 3959 SW Marlin Dr Palm City FL 34990-3817 Office: Martin County Schs 500 E Ocean Bvld Stuart FL 34994

HARWARD, DONALD WEST, retired academic administrator; m. Ann Harward; 2 children. B, Maryville Coll.; M, Am. U.; PhD, U. Md. Prof. U. Del., 1968—82; v.p. acad. affairs Coll. Wooster, Ohio, until 1989; pres. Bates Coll., Lewiston, Maine, 1989—2002, pres. emeritus, 2002—. Chmn. and co-founder LA Excels. Fellow: Assn. of Am. Colleges and Universities (sr.). Office: PO Box 152 Corea ME 04624-0152

HARWELL, DAVID WALKER, retired state supreme court chief justice; b. Florence, S.C., Jan. 8, 1932; s. Baxter Hicks and Lacy (Rankin) H.; married; children: Robert Bryan, William Baxter. LL.B., JD, U. S.C., 1958; HHD (hon.), Frances Marion U., 1987. Bar: S.C. 1958, U.S. Dist. Ct. S.C. 1958, U.S. Ct. Appeals 1964, U.S. Supreme Ct. 1961. Circuit judge 12th Jud. Ct. S.C., 1973-80; justice S.C. Supreme Ct., 1980-91, chief justice, 1991-94; ret., 1994; spl. counsel Nelson, Mullins, Riley and Scarborough. Mem. S.C. Ho. of Reps., 1962-73. Served with USNR, 1952-54. Mem. Am. Bar Assn., Am. Trial Lawyers Assn., S.C. Bar Assn., S.C. Trial Lawyers Assn. (Portrait and Scholarship award 1986). Presbyterian. Office: PO Box 2459 Myrtle Beach SC 29578-2459 Office Phone: 843-448-3500. Business E-Mail: david.harwell@nelsonmullins.com.

HARWELL, KENNETH E., chemist, researcher, consultant; b. Bell Springs, Tex., Sept. 11, 1921; s. Samuel Franklin and Hettie Mae (King) H.; m. Joye Murphy, Dec. 19, 1961. BS in Chemistry, Baylor U., 1945; MA in Organic Chemistry, U. Tex., 1947, PhD in Organic Chemistry, 1952. Spl. problems chemist Union Carbide Chems. Co., Texas City, Tex., 1947-48; rsch. scientist Cotton Rsch. Com. of Tex., Austin, 1948-50; rsch. chemist

Celanese Corp. of Am., Clarkwood, Tex., 1951; project supr., rsch. chemist, electronics engr. Tex. A&M Rsch. Found., College Station, 1952-54; asst. prof., assoc. mem. grad. faculty Tex. A&M Coll., College Station, 1952-54; sr. rsch. chemist Jefferson Chem. Co., Austin, 1954-58; owner, mgr. Tex. Fine Chems. Co., Austin, 1958-59; dir., mgr., treas. Quality Chems. Corp., Austin, 1960; rsch. chemist, exploratory rsch. sect. petrochems. divsn. Continental Oil Co., Ponca City, Okla., 1961-65; sr. rsch. chemist plastics divsn. Gulf R & D Corp., Merriam, Kans., 1965-72; rsch. chemist R&D dept. Cook Paint and Varnish Co., Kansas City, Mo., 1972-79; owner, mgr. Merriam Chem. Devel. Co., Edwardsville, Kans., 1979-89; cons. Skiatook, Okla., 1989—. R & D cons. Nalle Plastics, Inc., Austin, 1958-59. Author 1 book; contbr. articles to profl. jours.; patentee in field. Mem. AAAS, AIChE, NRA, Am. Chem. Soc., Sigma Xi, Phi Lambda Upsilon. Avocations: photography, writing, travel. Home: PO Box 158 Skiatook OK 74070-0158

HARWELL, WILLIAM EARNEST (ERNIE HARWELL), retired commentator; b. Washington, Ga., Jan. 25, 1918; s. Davis Gray Harwell; m. Lula Tankersley, Aug. 30, 1941; children: William Earnest, Jr., Gray Neville, Julie, Carolyn. AB, Emory U., 1940; LittD (hon.), Adrian Coll., 1985; LHD (hon.), No. Mich. Coll., 1990. Sports dir. Sta. WSB, Atlanta, 1940-43; announcer Atlanta Crackers, 1946-48, Bklyn. Dodgers, 1948-49, N.Y. Giants, 1950-53, Balt. Orioles, 1954-59, Detroit Tigers, 1960—91, 1993—2002; ret., 2002. Announcer All-Star games, World Series, NBC, CBS Radio, pro football Balt. Colts, N.Y. Giants; broadcaster Master's golf tournament, NBC, 1942, 46. Author: Tuned to Baseball, 1985, Diamond Gems, 1991, The Babe Signed My Shoe, 1994, Stories From My Life in Baseball, 2001, Life After Baseball, 2004; composer songs including I Don't Know Any Better, Move over Babe, Only a Fool, One-Room World, One Dream, Sing Every Song. With USMC, 1942-46. Recipient Lowell Thomas Broadcast award, 1985, Alvin Foon award Mich. Jewish Sports Hall of Fame, 1988, 90, Big Mac award Detroit News, 1989, Golden Compass award Campfire Inc., 1989, Life Directions Enrichment award, 1989, Nat. Lifetime Nat. Achievement award March of Dimes, 1991, Joe Louis award, 1991, Ken Hubbs Meml. award, 1991, Stanley Kresge award, 1994, U. Detroit Jesuit Magis award, 1995; named Most Durable Baseball Announcer, Guinness Book Records, 2003; inducted Baseball Hall of Fame, Cooperstown, 1981, Mich. Sports Hall of Fame, Emory U. Hall of Fame, Nat. Sportscasters and Sportswriters Hall of Fame, Am. Sportscasters Hall of Fame, Catch Hall of Fame, Ga. Broadcasters Hall of Fame, Nat. Radio Hall of Fame, 1998, SAE Leadership Hall of Fame, 2001. Mem. ASCAP, Sigma Alpha Epsilon.

HARWIT, MARTIN OTTO, astrophysicist, writer, educator, museum director; b. Prague, Czechoslovakia, Mar. 9, 1931; came to U.S., 1946, naturalized, 1953; s. Felix Michael and Regina Hedwig (Perutz) Haurowitz; m. Marianne Mark, Feb. 1, 1957; children: Alexander, Eric, Emily. BA in Physics, Oberlin Coll., 1951; MA in Physics, U. Mich., Ann Arbor, 1953; PhD in Physics, Mass. Inst. Tech., 1960. NATO postdoctoral fellow Cambridge (Eng.) U., 1960-61; NSF fellow Cornell U., Ithaca, N.Y., 1961-62, asst. prof. astronomy, 1962-64, asso. prof., 1964-68, prof., 1968-87, prof. emeritus, 1988—, chmn. dept. astronomy, 1971-76, co-dir. program for history and philosophy of sci. and tech., 1985-87; dir. Nat. Air and Space Mus. Smithsonian Instn., Washington, 1987-95. E.O. Hulburt fellow Naval Rsch. Lab., Washington, 1963-64; Nat. Acad. Sci. exch. visitor Czechoslovak Acad. Sci., Prague, 1969-70; v.p., dir. Spectral Imaging Inc., Concord, Mass., 1971-77; external mem. Max Planck Soc., Inst. Radioastronomy, Bonn., West Germany, 1979—; cons. NASA.; chair for space history Nat. Air and Space Mus., Smithsonian Instn., 1983; chmn. astrophysics mgmt. ops. working group, NASA, 1985-87; Adriaan Blaauw prof. U. Groningen, The Netherlands, 2002. Author: Astrophysical Concepts, 1973, 3d edit., 1998 (transl. into Chinese 1981), (with N.J.A. Sloan) Hadamard Transform Optics, 1979, Cosmic Discovery-The Search, Scope and Heritage of Astronomy, 1981 (transl. into German and French 1982), (with the mus. staff) Treasures of the National Air and Space Museum, 1995, An Exhibit Denied: Lobbying the History of Enola Gay, 1996 (transl. into Japanese 1997): editor: (with M. G. Hauser) The Extragalactic Infrared Background and its Cosmological Implications, International Astronomical Union Symposium 204, 2001. With U.S. Army, 1955-57. Recipient Alexander von Humboldt Found. sr. U.S. scientist award Max Planck Inst. Radioastronomy, 1976-77; NSF grantee, 1963-68; Research Corp. grantee, 1970-75; NASA grantee, 1965—; Air Force Cambridge (Mass.) Research Labs. grantee, 1969-74. Fellow AAAS (chmn. sect. on astronomy, 2001-02, coun. mem. 2002-03), Am. Phys. Soc. (chmn. div. history of physics 1986-87, chmn. astrophysics div. 1988-89), Royal Astron. Soc.; mem. Soc. for History of Tech., Am. Astron. Soc. Home: 511 H St SW Washington DC 20024-2725

HARWOOD, DAVID M., geologist, educator; b. Dayton, Ohio, June 6, 1958; s. Harold James and Gloria Maxine Harwood; m. Cari Rose Dicks, July 8, 1967; children: Cara Lynne, Kelsey Rae, Cabe Makon, Kalea Rose. BS, U. of Akron, 1980; MS, Fla. State U., 1982; PhD, The Ohio State U., 1986. Sr. rsch. assoc. Byrd Polar Rsch. Ctr., Ohio State Univ., Columbus, 1987—90; prof. dept. geosci. Univ. Nebraska-Lincoln, 1990—, T.M. and E.E. Stout chair of stratigraphy, 1994—. Dir. ANDRILL Sci. Mgmt. Office, Univ. Nebraska-Lincoln, Lincoln, Nebr., 2001—. Recipient Presdl. Young Investigator award, NSF, 1992—97, Disting. Dissertation award, Ohio State U., 1997, Grad. Leadership award, 1996. Office: Univ of Nebraska-Lincoln 214 Bessey Hall - Geosciences Lincoln NE 68588-0340 Office Fax: 402-472-4917.

HARWOOD, ELEANOR CASH, retired librarian; b. Buckfield, Maine, May 29, 1921; d. Leon Eugene and Ruth (Chick) Cash; m. Burton H. Harwood, Jr., June 21, 1944 (div. 1953); children: Ruth (Mrs. Wiliam R. Cline), Eleanor, James Burton. BA, Am. Internat. Coll., 1943; BS in Libr. Sci., New Haven State Tchrs. Coll., 1955. Libr. Rathbun Meml. Libr., East Haddam, Conn., 1955-56; asst. libr. Kent (Conn.) Sch., 1956-63; cons. Chester (Conn.) Pub. Libr., 1965-71. Author: (with John G. Park) The Independent School Library and the Gifted Child, 1956, The Age of Samuel Johnson, LLD, Remember When, 1987, (essay) Growing Up in Chester, 1993, Moosley Yours, 1996, Chester, Years Ago, 2002. Mem. United Ch. Lt. (j.g.) USNR, 1944—46, WWII. Named Eleanor C. Harwood prize in her honor, Rev. Jacob Meml. Christian Coll., India, libr. named in her honor, 2003; recipient medal, Am. Theater-Victory. Mem. ALA, Conn. Libr. Assn., Chester Hist. Soc. (trustee 1970-72), DAV, Am. Legion, Am. Legion Aux., Soc. Mayflower Descs., Appalachian Mountain Club. Home: 10 Maple St Chester CT 06412-0255

HARWOOD, HAROLD JAMES, JR., biochemist; b. New Haven, July 27, 1954; s. Harold James and Gloria Maxine (Rogers) H.; m. Janice Kay Gill, Mar. 19, 1977; children: Katryn Renee, William Bradley. BS in Chemistry, U. Akron, 1976, BS in Biology, 1977; PhD in Biochemistry, Purdue U., 1982. Lab. asst. Inst. Polymer Sci., Akron (Ohio) U., 1971-72, rsch. assoc. applied rsch. divsn., 1976-77; demonstration rm. technician Monsanto Chem. Co., 1973-76; grad. rsch. assoc. dept. biochemistry Purdue U., West Lafayette, Ind., 1977-82; postdoctoral fellow in medicine U. Fla., Gainesville, 1982-84, rsch. asst. prof. dept. medicine, 1984-86; from rsch. scientist dept. metabolic diseases to prin. investigator Pfizer Cen. Rsch., Groton, Conn., 1986—97, prin. rsch. investigator, 1997—. Music programmer Conn. Coll. Broadcasting Assn., 1997—. Musician: Pfizer Chamber Orch., 1999—. Coach Ledyard (Conn.) Soccer Club, 1990-97, Gainesville Youth Soccer Orgn., 1984-86; USSF Referee, 1996-, referee assignor, 1996-2004; mem. coun. on basic scis. Am. Heart Assn.; projectionist Akron Inst. Civic Edn., 1974-77; guitarist Prophet's Town Band, Battleground, Ind., 1981-82; referee USSF, 1996—. David Ross fellow Purdue U., 1979-81; recipient New Investigator Rsch. award Nat. Cancer Inst., 1985-88. Mem. Am. Chem. Soc., Am. Fedn. Clin. Rsch., Am. Soc. Biochemistry, Assn. Molecular Biology, Am. Diabetes Assn., Am. Heart Assn. (peer rev. com. 1989-2002, rsch. com. 2002—), Purdue Alumni Assn., Alpha Chi Sigma. Avocations: music, soccer, camping, hiking, gardening. Home: 10 Eska Dr Ledyard CT 06339-1344 Office: Pfizer Global R&D MS 820-3190 Eastern Point Rd Groton CT 06340 Office Phone: 860-441-3090. Business E-Mail: h.james.harwood@pfizer.com.

HARWOOD, JERRY, market research executive; b. Jersey City, June 19, 1926; s. Louis and Dorothy (Cohen) Horowitz; m. Ruthella Zimmerman, June 25, 1950; children: Robin Jill, Dean Brook. BA cum laude, L.I. U., 1949; MA, NYU, 1953. Tech. instr. U.S. Bur. Census, 1950-51; v.p., assoc. research dir. Kenyon & Eckhardt Advt., N.Y.C., 1962-66; sr. v.p., dir. research Needham, Harper & Steers Advt., N.Y.C., 1966-73; sr. v.p., group research dir. Benton & Bowles Advt., N.Y.C., 1975-88; mktg. cons. Short Hills, NJ, 1988—; mem. Census Adv. Com., 1976-83. Adj. assoc. prof. NYU Grad. Sch. Bus., 1984-85 Pres. Temple B'nai Jeshurun, 1980-82, Jewish Family Svc. of MetroWest, 1984-87, N.J. Jewish News, 1992-95; v.p. Mental Health Assn. Essex County, 1992-99; mem. Essex County Child Placement Rev. Bd., 1988—; bd. dirs. Am. Jewish Com., 1996—, v.p., 2005; trustee Hebrew Immigrant Aid Soc., 1997-98. Mem. Am. Mktg. Assn. (pres. N.Y.C. chpt. 1970-71, nat. v.p. pub. policy and issues 1973, nat. v.p. mktg. rsch. 1981-82, mem. editl. bd. 1992-98, chmn. Marketing Hall of Fame 1995-98), Nat. Assn. Jewish Family and Children Agys. (pres. 1997-99). Home and Office: 22 Athens Rd Short Hills NJ 07078-1312 E-mail: jandrharwood@comcast.net. *The individual who respects the rights, opinions and needs of others is the individual who manages his own life most productively and successfully.*

HARWOOD, JOHN H., II, lawyer; b. Sept. 20, 1945; BA, Harvard Univ., 1967; JD, Columbia Univ., 1973; LLM, Georgetown Univ., 1974. Bar: DC 1973. Ptnr., chmn. Comm. & E-Commerce dept. Wilmer Cutler Pickering Hale & Dorr, Washington. Adj. prof. Georgetown Univ. Law Ctr., 1978; past fellow & acting dep. dir. Inst. for Pub. Interest Representation. Contbr. articles to profl. jours. Served USMC, 1967—70. Mem.: ABA, Fed. Comm. Bar Assn., DC Bar. Office: Wilmer Cutler Pickering Hale & Dorr 1801 Pennsylvania Ave NW Washington DC 20006 Mailing: Wilmer Cutler Pickering Hale & Dorr 2445 M St NW Washington DC 20037 Office Phone: 202-663-6333. Office Fax: 202-663-6363. Business E-Mail: john.harwood@wilmerhale.com.

HARWOOD, JULIUS J., metallurgist, educator; b. N.Y.C., Dec. 3, 1918; m. Naomi Beitner, 1983; children: Dane L., Gail A., Caren L., Rochelle. BS, CCNY, 1939; MS, U. Md., 1953; D of Engring. (hon.), Mich. Tech. U., 1986. Materials engr. U.S. Naval Gun Factory, 1940-46; metall. Off Naval Rsch., 1946-60; mgr. metall. sci. lab. Ford Motor Co., Dearborn, Mich., 1960-69, mgr. rsch. planning engring. and rsch. staff, 1969-71, dir. Material Sci. Lab, engring. and rsch. staff, 1971-83; prof. engring. Wayne State U., Detroit, 1984; pres. Ovonic Synthetic Material Co., Troy, Mich., 1984-87, Harwood Cons., Orchard Lake, Mich., 1987—, West Bloomfield, Mich. Adj. prof. Wayne State U., Detroit, 1975. Editor 5 books on materials; contbr. articles to profl. jours. Fellow AAAS, Metall. Soc. (pres. 1973), Am. Soc. Metals (John H. Shoemaker award 1977), Engring. Soc. of Detroit (Gold Medal award 1983); mem. Am. Inst. Mining, Metall. and Petroleum Engrs. (pres. 1976, hon.), Am. Ceramic Soc. (Orton lectr. 1978), Nat. Acad. Engrs. (life). Office: 5023 Pheasant Cv West Bloomfield MI 48323-2093

HARWOOD, LYNNE, artist, book designer; b. Boston, Nov. 16, 1944; d. Reed and Faith (Garrison) H.; m. Roland Louis Gilbert, Aug. 1, 1979 (div. Aug. 1982); children: Curtis Gilbert, Sarah Gilbert. BA, Sarah Lawrence Coll., 1968. Self-employed artist, Anson, Maine, 1972—; pres. Union of Maine Visual Artists, 1988. Author, illustrator: Honeybees at Home, 1994. Maine Green Party. Avocations: gardening, beekeeping. Home: 608 Pease Hill Rd Anson ME 04911-9742

HARWOOD, ROBERT BERNARD, JR., state supreme court justice; b. Oct. 17, 1939; Student, U. of the South, 1958—59; BS in Commerce and Bus. Adminstrn., U. Ala., 1962, JD, 1963. Spl. asst. atty. gen. State of Ala., 1969—75; dep. city judge City of Tuscaloosa, Ala., 1975—80; cir. judge Tuscaloosa County, 1991—2001; assoc. justice Ala. Supreme Ct., 2001—. Lectr. law and trial advocacy U. Ala., 1979—83, 1989—99. Mem. exec. bd. Black Warrior coun. Boy Scouts Am., 1976—, pres., 1993; mem. leadership assn. United Way Tuscaloosa County; mem. Carroll Creek Vol. Fire Dept.; bd. dirs. FOCUS on Sr. Citizens of Tuscaloosa County. Recipient Silver Beaver award, Black Warrior Coun. Boy Scouts Am., 1994. Mem.: ABA, Am. Coll. Trial Lawyers, Am. Bd. Trial Advocates, Am. Bar Found., Am. Judges Assn., Tuscaloosa County Bar Assn. (pres. 1978—79), Tuscaloosa Inn of Ct. (pres. 1991—92), Ala. Bar Assn., Tuscaloosa County Cattlemen's Assn., Ala. Cattlemen's Assn., Order of the Coif. Republican. Episcopalian. Office: Ala Supreme Ct 300 Dexter Ave Montgomery AL 36104-3741 E-mail: bernarwood@comcast.net.

HARWOOD, SANDRA STABILE, lawyer, state representative; b. June 25, 1950; BBA, Kent State U., 1988; JD, Univ. Akon Sch. of Law, 1991. State rep. dist. 65 Ohio Ho. of Reps., Columbus, 2002—, mem. judiciary, ranking minority mem. civil and comml. law, econ. devel. and environ, health. Democrat. Office: 77 S High St Columbus OH 43215-6111 Office Phone: 614-466-3488.

HARWOOD, STANLEY, retired judge, lawyer, arbitrator, mediator; b. N.Y.C., June 23, 1926; s. Benjamin and Hannah (Schwartz) H.; m. Deborah Weinerman, June 18, 1950 (dec. 1995); children: Richard, Ellen Harwood Jacobs, Michael, Jonathan; m. Cathleen Hamilton, May 25, 1997. AB, Columbia U., 1949, LLB, 1952. Bar: N.Y. 1954, U.S. Dist. Ct. (ea. and so. dists.) N.Y. 1956, U.S. Supreme Ct. 1960. Atty. Dept. of Navy, Washington, 1952—53; assoc. Benjamin Harwood, Bklyn., 1953—56; pvt. practice Levittown, NY, 1956—61; law clk. to justice N.Y. Supreme Ct., Mineola, 1961—65, justice, 1982—92, judge appellate divsn., 1987—92; ptnr. Mishkin, Miner, Harwood & Semel, Mineola, 1965—69, Shayne, Dachs, Stanisci & Harwood, Mineola, 1969—81, Bower & Gardner, N.Y.C., 1992—94; counsel Jaspan, Schlesinger & Hoffman, 1994—. Mem. N.Y. State Assembly, 1966-72; chmn. Nassau County Dem. Com., 1973-81; commr. elections Nassau County Bd. Elections, 1976-81; bd. dirs. Nat. Conf. Christians and Jews, 1993-98. With USNR, 1944-46, U.S. Merchant Marines. Mem. N.Y. State Bar Assn., Nassau County Bar Assn. (chmn. cts. com. 1971-73, chmn. pro bono com. 1988-90, bd. dirs. 1997-2000, Nassau-Suffolk Law Svs. Committment to Justice medal 2002), Mill River Club. Jewish. Home: 2 Bull Calf Ln Centerport NY 11721-1669 Office: Jaspan Schlesinger & Hoffman 300 Garden City Plz Garden City NY 11530-3324 Fax: 516-393-8282. Office Phone: 516-746-8000. Business E-Mail: sharwood@jshllp.com.

HARWOOD, WILLIAM SCOTT, science educator; b. Clearwater, Fla., Nov. 1, 1958; s. Daniel Irving and Shirley Klein Harwood; m. Diana L. Morgan, Oct. 6, 1965; children: Seth Franklin, Nathaniel Isaac, Amanda Beth. BS, U. Mass., 1980; PhD, Purdue U., 1986. Dir., chemsitry and biochemistry undergrad. program U. Md., College Park, 1989—96, asst. dean undergrad. studies, 1996—98; dean Ind. U., Bloomington, 1998—2000, exec. dir., 21st century tchrs. project, 2000—05, assoc. prof., 1998—. Vis. asst. prof. Wittenberg U., Springfield, Ohio, 1987—89. Author: (songs) General Chemistry, 6th through 9th edits., (website development and design) Common Molecules (Sci./Tech. award Sci. Am., 2004), (online tutorial) Symmetry. Grantee, NSDL, 2001—03, Transforming Undergrad. Biology and Biochemistry, Howard Hughes Med. Inst., 2002—06. Mem.: AAAS (edn. sect. nominations com. 2000—03), Internat. Ctr. First Yr. Undergrad. Chemistry (membership com. 2003—), Divsn. Chem. Edn. (18th bcce program co-chair 2000—04, biennial conf. com. 2005—), Am. Chemistry Soc. Achievements include research in Activity Model for the Process of Scientific Inquiry; invention of Inquiry Teaching Belief Instrument. Office: Indiana U 201 N Rose Ave ED 3068 Bloomington IN 47405 Office Phone: 812-856-8164. Office Fax: 812-856-8116. Personal E-mail: wharwood@indiana.edu.

HARYONO, IGNATIUS WIBISONO, writer; s. Henricus Harjono Martodirjo and Anastasia Kusmaria Soemodirjo; m. Wijakti Karlina Harlim, Dec. 24, 1943. PhD, Rosevelt U., Brussels, 1980; DD, Rosevelt U. Belgium, Brussels, 1981. Philosophy docent Pajajaran State U., Bandung, Indonesia, 1968—73; u. prof. Parahyangan Cath. U., Bandung, 1972—79; prof. State and Cath. U., Bandung, 1972—78; asst. to provincial Order of the Holy Cross, Bandung, 1975—79; asst. to bishop Diocese of Bandung, 1978—80; asst. to chaplain Cath. Ch., L.A., 1990—. Dir. USA Today, Glendale, 1985—90; postal worker Burbank Post Office, Calif., 1989—90; religious cons. (prvt.), 2000—. Author: (book) Was Mary Also Redeemed, 1989, poems in Nat. Libr. of Poetry; contbr. articles to religious publs. Dir. religious edn. Indonesian Cath. Cmty. of Archdiocese, L.A., Calif., 1994—2000; dir., leader Bible Readers Club, 1995; mem. Lumen Christi Indonesian Cath. Bible Study. Lt. col. titular chaplaincy Indonesian Army, 1972—79. Recipient Presdl. award, W. Java Cath. Youth Orgn., 1973, 1979, Moderator award, Cathedral Youth Orgn., 1978, 1979, Indonesian Cath. Cmty. award, 2001, award, KKIA Inc., 2001. Master: Iggy LLC (immigrants helper 2000—01, pres., owner). Populist. Roman Catholic. Avocation: travel. Personal E-mail: yhwhwibi@worldnet.att.net. E-mail: yhwh1100@webtv.com.

HARZMAN, BRADLEY EARL, music educator; b. Osborne, Kans., Apr. 2, 1962; s. Donald Earl and Nancy Mae Harzman. BA, Music Edn., Kans. Wesleyan U., Salina, KS, 1985; MusM Edn., Emporia (Kans.) State U., 2002. Cert. Tchr.K-12 Vocal and Instrumental Music Kans., 1985. Tchr. 5-12 vocal & instrumental music Oswego (Kans.) Pub. Schools, Ala., 1990—93; tchr. 5-12 vocal & instrumental music United Sch. Dist. 251/North Lyon County, Americus, Kans., 1993—. Ch. choir dir. St. Marks' Luth. Ch., Emporia, Kans., 1997—. Staff sgt. Kans. Army N.G., 1996—, Olathe, KS. Mem.: Music Educators Nat. Conf. Liberal. Lutheran. Avocations: trumpet, French horn, reading, working on house. Home: 525 Exchange St Emporia KS 66801 Office: North Lyon County Schs 1208 Rd 345 Allen KS 66833 Office Phone: 620-528-3521. Personal E-mail: mr_holland66801@yahoo.com.

HASALONE EVE, ANNETTE LEONA, research and development company executive; d. Glenn Allen Greene and Betty Leona Palmer; m. Mark Joseph Eve, Sept. 24, 2002; m. Cipriano Ramirez, May 24, 1977 (div. Sept. 0, 1985); children: Elizabeth Leona Ramirez, Dominic Earl Ramirez, Jerrod Emmett Ramirez. D in Naturopathy, Trinity Coll. Natural Healing, Warsaw, Ind.ana, 2003. Pres. Elemental Rsch., LLC, Post Falls, Idaho, 1999—; R&D cons. Eniva Corp., Blaine, Minn., 1999—2003. Case mgr. Homeless Mental Health Program, Oroville, Calif., 1984—86; account clk. I GAIN, Woodland, Calif., 1986—88; drug and alcohol specialist Health and Human Svcs., Woodland, 1988—89; DUI edn. counselor AK Bean Found., Fairfield, Calif., 1988—89; mgr./cons. WaterOz, Grangeville, Idaho, 1997—99; radio talk show host WGTG, Ga., 1998—2000, WHJM, Knoxville, Tenn., 1998—2000; product knowlege liaison Shagoi/Lanea Rx Larrea Corp., 2005. Author: (educational book) Mono-Atomic Minerals Information and Reference Guide, 1999, Off Balance, 2003, (educational booklet) Essential Information Booklet, (audio tape) Naturally Healthy With Mono-Atomic Minerals, (protocols for natural healing) Protocols Booklet. Campaign mgr. Ted Gunderson for Pres., Las Vegas, Nev., 1996—96. Recipient Outstanding Achievement in Poetry award, Internat. Libr. Poetry and Poetry.com, 2001, Outstanding Contbn. award, Enira Corp., 2001. Mem.: NAFE (assoc.), Internat. Ozone Soc. (assoc.). Republican. Achievements include invention of proprietary process for cell ready, ionic, liquid, water-soluble mineral supplements. Avocations: skiing, art, research and development, guitar, poetry. Office: Elemental Research LLC 4353 E Poleline Ave Post Falls ID 83854 Office Phone: 208-773-5264. Business E-Mail: annette@elementalresearchllc.com.

HASAN, SYED HAMIDDUDDIN, medical researcher, consultant; b. Hyderabad, India, Nov. 2, 1935; arrived in U.S., 1995; s. Syed Samiullah and Zohra Khatoon; m. Amina H. Rasul, Oct. 15, 1960; children: Roomana, Afzia, Humaira, Syed Fareed. BSc in Chemistry, Botany and Zoology, Osmania U., Hyderabad, 1956; PhD in Pharmacology, Bristol (Eng.) U., 1968. Lectr. Bristol U., 1966—68, U. Ibadan, Nigeria, 1968—69; sr. rsch. assoc. Schering AG, Berlin, 1969—95. Vis. scientist Worcester (Mass.) Found., 1969—70, Cornell U., NYC, 1973, Ohio State U., Columbus, 1974, U. Man., Winnipeg, Canada, 1976; cons. UN devel. programme U. Karachi, Pakistan, 1983; cons. Ohio State U., Columbus, 1984—95. Contbr. articles to profl. jours. Mem.: Pharmacol. Soc. Pakistan, Am. Chem. Soc., Am. Endocrine Soc., Brit. Endocrine Soc., German Endocrine Soc. Achievements include patents pending for antiprogestinins; research in pharmacological studies and effects of progesterone-antagonists, clinical and pharmacological properites of cyproterone acetate. Avocations: gardening, photography, reading, travel, cooking. Home: 1671 Orchard Ln Northfield IL 60093

HASDAY, ROBERT JOEL, lawyer; b. NYC, Apr. 30, 1949; s. Isaac and Dora (Ariewitz) Hasday; m. Carol Minette Rosenfelt, June 18, 1970; children: Jill Elaine, Michael Jonathan, Lisa Robin. BA magna cum laude, Brandeis U., 1970; MBA, U. Chgo., 1972; JD, Yale U., 1975. Bar: NY 1976. Assoc. Shea & Gould, NYC, 1975-83, ptnr., 1984-94, Duane Morris LLP, NYC, 1994—, mng. ptnr. NY office, 1994—, mem. partners bd., 1998—. Bd. dirs. Apple Bank for Savings, NYC, 1991—. Mem. Assn. Bar City of NY (com. securities regulation 1987-90), Phi Beta Kappa, Beta Gamma Sigma. Office: Duane Morris LLP 380 Lexington Ave New York NY 10168 Office Phone: 212-692-1010. Office Fax: 212-692-1020. Business E-Mail: rjhasday@duanemorris.com.

HASE, DAVID JOHN, lawyer; b. Milw., Feb. 27, 1940; s. John Henry and Catherine Charlotte (Leekley) H.; m. Penelope Sue Pritchard, Sept. 2, 1964; children: Jeffrey David, Jennifer Anne, John Paul. AB, Dartmouth Coll., 1962; LLB, U. Wis., 1965. Bar: Wis. 1965, U.S. Dist. Ct. (ea. dist.) Wis. 1965, U.S. Ct. Appeals (7th cir.) 1971, U.S. Ct. Appeals (D.C. cir.) 1975, U.S. Ct. Appeals (9th cir.) 1989, U.S. Supreme Ct. 1975. Assoc. Grootemaat, Cook & Franke, Milw., 1965-67, ptnr., shareholder Milw., 1968-70; shareholder Cook & Franke S.C., Milw., 1970-73; legal counsel to gov. Wis., Madison, 1973-74; dep. atty. gen. State of Wis., Madison, 1974-76; assoc. Foley & Lardner, Milw., 1976-77, ptnr., 1977-94; shareholder Cook & Franke S.C., Milw., 1994—. Mem. Sch. Bd., Mequon, Wis., 1971-94, treas., 1973-75, pres., 1975-94. Mem. ABA. Democrat. Home: 2108 W Raleigh Ct Mequon WI 53092-5416 Office: Cook & Franke SC 660 E Mason St Ste 401 Milwaukee WI 53202-3877 Office Phone: 414-227-1281. E-mail: hase@cf-law.com.

HASEGAWA, TOMOHIRO, marketing manager; b. San Francisco, Nov. 26, 1962; s. Akira and Miyoko (Okada) H.; 1 child, Audrey Kei Hueymiin. BSEE, MSEE, MIT, 1985. Data clk. Bell Labs., Murray Hill, N.J., 1979-80; computer programmer Ctr. for Space Rsch., MIT, Cambridge, Mass., 1981-82; coop. engring. intern Hewlett Packard Co., Andover, Mass., 1982-85, rsch. and design engr., 1985-92; sales devel. mktg. mgr. Hewlett Packard/Agilent Techs., 1992-2001; mktg. mgr. Imaging Sys. Divsn. Agilent Techs., Japan, 2001—. Coll. recruiter Hewlett Packard Co., Andover, 1987-92. Inventee (with others) pulsed doppler flow mapping apparatus, method and apparatus for elimination of mirroring in signal processing system; contbr. articles to profl. jours. Recipient Raymond Freany Meml. award Town of New Providence (N.J.), 1980; MIT scholar, 1984-85. Mem. Straight Down & Spare Parts Volleyball Clubs, Eta Kappa Nu, Tau Beta Pi. Avocations: travel, music, competative sports. Office: Hewlett Packard Co 3000 Minuteman Rd Andover MA 01810-1099 E-mail: tomo_hasegawa@agilent.com, tho1845@yahoo.com.

HASEK, DOMINIK, professional hockey player; b. Pardubice, Czech Republic, Jan. 29, 1965; Goaltender Chicago Blackhawks, 1990—92, Buffalo Sabres, 1992—2001, Detroit Red Wings, 2001—02, 2003—04, Ottawa Senators, 2004—. Goaltender Czech Republic, Nagano Olympics, 1998, Czech Republic, Salt Lake City Olympics, 2002. Named Best Goaltender, Nagano Olympic Games, 1998; named to NHL All-Star Game, 1996—99, 2001—02, NHL First All-Star Team, 1994, 1995, 1997—99, 2001; recipient Vezina Trophy, 1994, 1995, 1996, 1997, 1998, 2001, Hart Trophy, 1997, 1998, Lester B. Pearson, 1997, 1998, William M. Jennings Trophy, 2001. Achievements include mem. of Stanley Cup Championship Team, 2002; mem. of Gold Medal Czech Republic Team, Nagano Olympics, 1998. Office: c/o Ottawa Senators Corel Center 1000 Palladium Dr K2V 1A5 Kanata ON Canada

HASELDEN, GREGORY W., accountant, educator; BA summa cum laude, Furman U., Greenville, S.C., 1990—94. CPA S.C. Dept. Labor, Licensing, and Regulation, 1997. Sr. acct. Deloitte & Touche LLP, Greenville, SC, 1994—98; dir. of fin. & bus. ops. St. Joseph's Cath. Sch., Greenville, SC, 1998—2004. V.p. for fin. and ops. Erskine Coll. & Theol. Sem., Due West, SC, 2004—. Eucharistic min. St. Anthony's Cath. Ch., Greenville, SC, 1992—; v.p., fundraising The Greenville Chorale, SC, 2003—; mem., past pres. Mardi Gras Charity Ball, Greenville, SC, 1994—2005; treas. St. Joseph's H.S., Greenville, SC, 1995—98. Mem.: S.C. Assn. Cert. Pub. Accts., AICPA. Office: Erskine Coll PO Box 338 Due West SC 29639 Office Phone: 864-379-8812. Office Fax: 864-379-6547. E-mail: haselden@erskine.edu.

HASELL, MARY JOYCE (JO), architecture educator; BS in Interior Design, U. N.C., Greensboro, 1967, MS in Interior Design, 1971; DArch, U. Mich., 1983. Registered interior designer, Fla. Interior design faculty U. Fla., Gainesville, 1988—, dir. PhD program, prof. Coll. Design, Constrn. and Planning, grad. coord. Master of Interior Design. Co-author: Accessible Design Review Guide: ADAAG Compliance in Building and Site Plans and Specifications; chair publ. bd.: Jour. Interior Design, mem. editl. rev. bd.: Named Tchr. of Yr., 1992; recipient Tchg. Improvement award, 1994. Office: Univ Fla Coll Design Constrn and Planning 362 Architecture PO Box 115705 Gainesville FL 32611-5701

HASELMANN, JOHN PHILIP, management consultant; b. Summit, N.J., Feb. 25, 1940; s. John and Elizabeth Haselmann; divorced; children— Terri Lee, Karen Lynn, Guy Philip BSEE, N.J. Inst. Tech., 1961; MBA in Indsl. Mgmt., Ops. Research and Mgmt. Sci., U. Pa., 1963. Asst. dir. Behavior Systems, Phila., 1961-63; prof. econs. Union Coll., 1964-66; mgr. mgmt. sci. divsn. Western Electric Co., Princeton, NJ, 1970-73; mgr. mktg. sci. div. AT&T Long Lines, Bedminster, NJ, 1974-78; pres., founder, chmn. of bd. Info. Mgmt. Group, Morristown, NJ, 1978-83; pres. Trinet Inc., Morristown, NJ, 1984-85; pres., founder, chmn. of bd. Entity Advt. and Graphics, Inc., Florham Park, NJ, 1986-88, Integrated Mktg. Svcs., Inc., Parsippany, NJ, 1989—; founder and exec. dir. Am. Employers Assn., Washington, 1989—95; co-founder, vice chmn., exec. v.p., bd. dirs. TCI Comm. Mgmt. Corp., Parsippany, NJ, 1991-95; pres., founder, chmn. bd. Computer Tech. Integration, 1995—; founder, exec. dir. Assn. for the Adv. Knowledge-Mgmt., Morristown, NJ, 2001—. Guest lectr. on application of sci. to problems in mtkg. Columbia Grad. Sch. Bus., Sloan Sch. MIT, Wharton Grad. Sch. U. Pa. Author: Computers and Data Processing Applied to a Personnel Processing System as a Management Tool, 1963, How to Improve the Effectiveness of Your Advertising/Marketing/Sales Investment, 1987, How to Lower the Cost of Getting an Order and Increase Revenues through Improved Market Analysis and Sales Management, 1990. Mem. Am. Mgmt. Assn., Am. Soc. Assn. Execs., Am. Soc. Profl. Cons. Republican. Lutheran. Avocations: golf, sailing. Office: PO Box 339 Morristown NJ 07963-0339 Office Phone: 973-715-7771. Personal E-mail: jhaselmann@rcn.com.

HASELTINE, FLORENCE PAT, obstetrician, gynecologist, research administrator; b. Phila., Aug. 17, 1942; d. William R. and Jean Adele Haseltine; m. Frederick Cahn, Mar. 12, 1964 (div. 1969); m. Alan Chodos, Apr. 18, 1970; children: Anna, Elizabeth. BA in Biophysics, U. Calif., Berkeley, 1964; PhD in Biophysics, MIT, 1969; MD, Albert Einstein Coll. of Medicine, 1972. Diplomate Am. Bd. Ob-Gyn., Am. Bd. Reproductive Endocrinology. Asst. prof. dept. ob-gyn. and pediatrics Yale U., New Haven, 1976—82, assoc. prof. dept. ob-gyn. and pediatrics, 1982—85; dir. Ctr. for Population Research, Nat. Inst. Child Health and Human Devel. NIH, Bethesda, Md., 1985—; founder Haseltine System, Inc., Products for the Disabled, 1995—. Co-author: Woman Doctor, 1976, Magnetic Resonance of the Reproductive System, 1987; co-editor: 25 books on reproductive scis. Bd. dirs. Older Women's League, 1998—. Am. Women in Sci., 1998—. Fellow: AAAS (bd. dirs.); mem.: Soc. Cell Biology, Soc. for Advancement Women's Health Rsch. (founder, bd. dirs.), Soc. Gynecol. Investigation, Inst. of Medicine. Office: NIH/NICHD Ctr Population Rsch 6100 Executive Blvd Rm 8b07 Bethesda MD 20892-0001

HASELTINE, JAMES LEWIS, artist, consultant; b. Portland, Oreg., Nov. 7, 1924; s. William Ambrose and Clara Thusnelda (Scharpf) H.; m. Jane Winsberg, Nov. 14, 1948 (div. 1953); m. Margaret Ann Wilson, Aug. 15, 1955; children: Thomas, Jean, Kay, Suzanne, Angela. Student, Ark. State Coll., 1943-44, Reed Coll., 1946-47, Mus. Art Sch., 1947, 49, Art Inst. Chgo., 1947-48, Bklyn. Mus. Sch., 1950-51. Dir. Salt Lake Art Ctr., Salt Lake City, 1961-67; exec. dir. Wash. State Arts Commn., Olympia, Wash., 1967-80; prof. artist, 1950—. Vis. lectr. art history U. Utah, Salt Lake City, 1964-65; panel mem. Nat. Endowment for the Arts, Washington, 1969-80; various art cons. positions, 1980—. Author: 100 Years of Utah Painting, 1965 (Mormon History Assn. award 1965); paintings and prints represented in permanent collections Portland Art Mus., Oakland Art Mus., Mus. Art U. Oreg., Mus. Fine Arts U. Utah, Tacoma Art Mus., Willamette U., Salem, Oreg. Mem. search com. for pres. Evergreen State Coll., Olympia, 1984; trustee Portland Art Mus., 1953-55. With U.S. Army, 1942-46, ETO. Mem. Western Assn. Art Mus. (pres. 1964-66), Artists Equity Assn. (nat. dir. 1955-58, chmn. Oreg. chpt. 1953-55), Western States Arts Found. (bd. dirs. 1975-77), Brit.-Am. Art Assn. (trustee 1980-84). Home and Office: 3820 Sunset Beach Dr NW Olympia WA 98502-3542

HASELTINE, WILLIAM ALAN, virology educator, former biopharmaceutical company executive; b. St. Louis, Oct. 17, 1944; s. William R. and Jean (Ellsberg) H.; m. Patricia Gercik; children: Mara, Alexander; m. Gale Hayman, Feb. 16, 1991. BA, U. Calif., Berkeley, 1966; PhD, Harvard U., 1973. Fellow MIT, Cambridge, 1973-74; asst. prof. Harvard Med. Sch., Dana Farber Cancer Inst., Cambridge, 1975-78, assoc. prof., 1979-88, prof. Boston, 1988-95; assoc. prof. Harvard Sch. Pub. Health, Boston, 1979-88, chief, prof. divsn. human retrovirology, 1988, prof., 1988; founder, former chmn. bd., CEO Human Genome Scis., Inc., Rockville, Md., 1992—2004. AIDS exec. com. NIH, 1986. Assoc. editor Cancer Rsch., 1985-93, Leukemia Rsch., 1986; editor in chief Jour. AIDS, 1987—; contbg. author: The Microverse: The Genetic Code, 1989; contbr. articles to Sci. Am., Jour. AIDS. Trustee Leukemia Soc. Am. (Disting. svc. award 1987). Recipient Faculty Rsch. award Am. Cancer Soc., 1978-82, AIDS Recognition award Goiv. of Mass., 1986; grantee Bristol-Myers Squibb Co., 1991. Mem. Am. Fedn. AIDS Rsch., Coun. Nat. Inst. Allergy and Infectious Diseases. Office: Harvard Med Sch Dana Farber Cancer Inst 44 Binney St Boston MA 02115-6013

HASELTON, MARY MICHELSON, retired foreign service officer, artist; b. Kansas City, Mo., May 15, 1920; d. Michael A. and Jeannette (MacFarlane) Michelson; m. George Harry Haselton, Sept. 4, 1964 (dec. Jan. 1995). Student, Washburn U., 1939-41, U. Tex., 1947-52; B in Liberal Arts, Harvard U., 2001. Rsch. sec. Mil. Intelligence U.S. Army, Econ. Def. Bd., Washington, 1941-43; statis. analyst Quartermaster U.S. Army Depot, San Antonio, 1943-44; office mgr. physicians San Antonio, 1944-46; sec. to dir. rsch. IMF, Washington, 1946-47; legis. asst. U.S. Senate, Washington, 1954-59; internat. rels. tchr. Simons Rock Coll., Great Barrington, Mass., 1966-72; fgn. svc. officer Dept. State, Washington, 1960-64, 74-79. Sr. assoc. mem. St. Antony's Coll., Oxford (Eng.) U., 1972—. Exhbns. include Tex. Watercolor Soc., Delgado Mus., New Orleans. Bd. dirs., exec. com. Austin Symphony Orch., 1947-53; mem. various coms. Tex. Fine Arts Assn., Austin, 1947-53; U.S. del. to world population conf. UN, Bucharest, Romania, 1974, Mexico City, 1975. Recipient numerous awards for paintings. Avocations: painting, music, philosophy, science, religion. Home: 85 S Main St Hanover NH 03755 E-mail: mhaselton@valley.net.

HASELTON, RICK THOMAS, lawyer; b. Albany, Oreg., Nov. 5, 1953; s. Shirley (Schantz) H. AB, Stanford U., 1976; JD, Yale U., 1979. Chair Oreg. State Bd. Bar Examiners, 1988-89, bd. dirs., 1986-88; mem. adv. com. on rules of practice 9th Cir. Ct., 1991-93. Law clk. U.S. Ct. Appeals (9th cir.) Oreg., Portland, 1979-80; from assoc. to ptnr. Lindsay, Hart, Neil & Weigler, Portland, 1979-93; sole practice Portland, 1993-94; assoc. judge Oreg. Ct. Appeals, Salem, 1994—. Chair Multnomah County Legal Aid, Portland, 1985-86, bd. dirs., 1982-87. Mem. ABA, Oreg. Bar Assn., ACLU (cooperating atty. 1982-94), Phi Beta Kappa. Jewish. Office: 300 Justice Blvd Salem OR 97310-0001

HASELWOOD, ELDON LAVERNE, retired education educator; b. Barnard, Mo., July 19, 1933; m. Joan Haselwood; children: Ann, Karen, Polly, Amy. BS in Edn., U. Omaha, 1960; MA in Libr. Sci., U. Denver, 1963; PhD, U. Nebr., 1972. Libr. Omaha Pub. Schs., 1960-61, Lewis Cen. Community Schs., Council Bluffs, Iowa, 1961-63; documents libr. U. Omaha, 1963-66; prof. dept. tchr. edn. U. Nebr., Omaha, 1966—99, coord. ednl. tech. Coll. Edn., 1993—2002, ret., 2002. Cons. Nat. Park Svc., Omaha, 1978—. Commr. Nebr. Libr. Commn., 1981—86; bd. dirs. U. Nebr. at Omaha Libr. Friends, 1980—. Cpl. U.S. Army, 1953—55. Mem.: ALA (councilor 1988—91, excellence in tchg. award 1987), Nebr. Ednl. Media Assn. (disting. svc. award 1993), Nebr. Libr. Assn. (pres. 1981, meritorious svc. award 1983, Mad Hatter award 1998), Mountain Plains Libr. Assn. (rep. 1999—2001), Am. Assn. Sch. Librs. Home: 615 S 122nd St Omaha NE 68154-3015 Personal E-mail: hasel@alltel.net.

HASEN, BURTON STANLEY, painter; b. N.Y.C., Dec. 19, 1921; s. Herman Harold and Mina (Leibowitz) H. Student, Art Students League, 1940-42, 46, H. Hoffmann Sch. Fine Arts, 1947-48, Acad. dela Grande-Chaumiere, Paris, 1948-50; student (Fulbright grantee), Acad. delle Belle-Arti, 1959-60. Tchr. Sch. Visual Arts, N.Y.C., 1953-2000, Mpls. Sch. Art and Design, 1966 One-man shows include T'Pandje Gallerie, Belgium, 1981, Anita Shapolsky Gallery, 1987, 1992, 94, Gallery 1100-Niagara, Buffalo, 1993, Staller Ctr. for Arts, SUNY, Stony Brook, 1995, Hamilton Coll., Clinton, N.Y., 1996, Hugode Pagano gallery, N.Y.C., 1997, Nat. Jewish Mus., Washington, 1997, Islip Art Mus., N.Y., 2003, Retrospective Southeast Mo. State, Cape Girardeau, 2005; group shows include Mus. Modern Art, Paris, 1951, Whitney Mus. Am. Art, N.Y.C., 1964, Corcoran Gallery Art, Washington, 1959, Kresge Art Center, U. So. Ill., 1961, Krannert Art Mus.-U. Ill., Urbana, Am. Acad. Arts and Letters, N.Y.C., 1965, Berlin Acad. Arts, 1956, W.G. Picker Gallery, 1969, Colgate U., Hamilton, N.Y., 1969, Mus. Modern Art, N.Y.C., 1966, Met. Mus. Art, N.Y.C., 1952, Worcester (Mass.) Art Mus., 1968, Walker Art Center, Mpls., 1966, Bklyn. Mus., 1954, Artist Choice Mus., N.Y.C., NAD, N.Y.C., 1985, Anita Shapolsky Gallery, 1989, 90, 92, 2000, Neo Persona Gallery, 1989, 90, Rider Coll., 1992, Albright-Knox Mus., 1992, Islip Art Mus., 1992, Cleve. Inst. Art, 1993, Swiss Cultural Inst., 1993, David Anderson Gallery, Buffalo, 1993, Henry St. Settlement, N.Y.C., 1993, Sordoni Art Gallery, Wilkes-Barre, Pa., 1994, Nat. Acad., 1995, 96, 97, 99, 2000, 01, 03, 05, Alysia Duckler Gallery, Portland, 1996, Pagano Gallery, N.Y.C., 1997, 98, Studio 18 Gallery N.Y.C, 2002, Sheldon Meml. Art Gallery, U. Nebr., Lincoln, 2003, Brooms Street Gallery, N.Y.C., Denise Bibro Gallery, N.Y., 2004, Lohin Geduld Gallery, N.Y., 2005, NY Soc. Etchers, Studio 12N, N.Y.C., NAD, N.Y.C., Terrain Gallery, N.Y.C., Artist's Equity Gallery, N.Y.C.; represented in permanent collections Walker Art Center, Worcester Art Mus., Hampton Inst., CIBA-GEIGY Co., Bibliotheque Nationale, Paris, N.Y. Pub. Library, Princeton U., Columbia U., Mus. Fine Art, Portland, Maine, N.Y. Crestview Coll., Muhlenberg, Fine Prints Dept., SUNY, Buffalo, 1989, CCNY, Rider U., Lawrenceville, N.J., 1993, Islip Mus., East Islip, N.Y., Hamilton Coll., Clinton, N.Y., Nat. Jewish Mus., Washington, Southeast Mo. State U., Cape Giradeau, Mo., Birmingham, Southern Coll., Ala., Hudgens Ctr. Arts, Duluth, Ga., Savannah Coll. Art and Design, Birmingham Mus. Art, Ala., High Mus., Miami, Fla., Newberger Mus. Art, Purchase, N.Y., Libr. Congress, Fine Print Collection, Smithsonian, Washington, Jules Shermaw Collection, N.Y., Robert Blackburn Collection, N.Y., The Lowe Art Mus., U. Miami, The U. Chgo.; illustrator books, 1959-89, Beyond the Furies, 1985, Franklin Mint, Phila., 1991, The Flame Charts, 2002; archives include Smithsonian Mus. Am. Art, Centre Georges Pompidou, Musée d'Art Moderne, Paris. With AUS, 1942—46. Recipient Emily Lowe Found. Purchase prize, 1955; N.Y. Found. Arts grantee, 1990, Nat. Acad. Design, 2001; Richard Florsheim Art Fund Grant 1993, 1996, 1997; Pollack Krasner fellow 1995-96, 1999-2000, 2003, 04, Am. Acad. Arts & Letters, 2000, 01, 02, 03. Mem. Nat. Acad. Design, Fulbright Alumni Assn., N.Y. Artists Equity. Office Phone: 212-962-3865. Personal E-mail: burthasen@aol.com. *The motivating force of my life has been the desire to paint meaningful paintings that express my innermost feelings. Art for me is the exhilarating experience of discovering new worlds. Each work is a projection of myself into the cosmic universe. This compulsion to paint my fantasy has never faltered or been self-deceptive.*

HASENFUS, HAROLD JOSEPH, retired mechanical engineer, naval technical director; b. NYC, Apr. 9, 1921; s. Joseph Vincent and Ethel Elizabeth (Galvan) Hasenfus; m. Mary Margaret Boone, Nov. 7, 1945; children: James Joseph, Stephen Francis, Jean Marie, Edward Harold. BSME, CCNY, 1943; MSEE, Va. Tech., 1981, MS in physics, 1986. Cert. Vatican's Cert. of Recognition St. Joan of Arc's Roman Cath. /MD, 1959. Rsch. asst.-Manhattan Project U of Chgo., Chgo., 1944; project engr., Manhattan Project Fercleve Corp., Oak Ridge, Tenn., 1945; ordnance engr. Ballistic Rsch. Lab., Aberdeen Proving Ground, Md., 1946—52; chief Ballistic Rsch. Lab., rocket br., Aberdeen Proving Ground, Md., 1952—60; head,satellite applications div. Naval Weapons Lab., Dahlgren, Va., 1960—61; tech. dir. Naval Space Surveillance Sys., Dahlgren, Va., 1961—86, tech. dir. emeritus, 1986—. Cons. Nat. Def. Indsl. Assoc., 1955—60; cons., satellite detection Naval Space Surveillance Sys., Dahlgren, Va., 1986—88; del., Tripartite Conf. on armaments U.S. Army, Quebec, Canada, 1959; del., Tripartite Conf. on artificial Earth satellites U.S. Navy, 1971. Author: (poem) John Adams' Reward, 2002. Chmn., Cub Scout Com. Boy Scouts of Am., Dahlgren, Va., 1971—86. Decorated Group Achievement Dept. of the Navy; recipient Tech. Dir. emeritus, Naval Space Surveillance Sys. Mem.: ASME (life), AIAA (sr.), Am Inst. for Aeronautics and Astron. (Dir. 1960—62), Am. Rocket Soc., MD Sect. (Pres. 1959), Com. on Guidance for MD, Am. Math. Soc. (hon.), Res. Officers Assoc. (life), Nat. Def. Indus. Assoc. (life), Am. Assoc. for the Advancement of Sci. (life). Democrat. Roman Catholic. Achievements include development of rocket weapons, oversaw advances in the understanding of rockets as artillery weapons. Avocations: singing, languages, acting, poetry, pen and ink drawing. Home: 311 Ingleside Drive, Fredericksburg VA 22405-2344

HASER, WILLIAM H., automotive executive; BS in chem. engring., Cornell U.; grad., Northwestern U., Kellogg Sch. Mgmt. Bus. analyst Tenneco Automotive, 1983; asst. to CEO Tenneco Packaging; prod. mfg. mgr. Tenneco Specialty Packaging; plant gen. mgr., molded fiber Tenneco Automotive, contr., paperboard; v.p., chief info. officer Tenneco Packaging, 1995—98, Tenneco Automotive, Am. Bus., 1998—2002, Tenneco Automotive, Lake Forest, Ill., 2002—. Office: Tenneco Automotive 500 N Field Dr Lake Forest IL 60045

HASERICK, JOHN ROGER, retired dermatologist; b. Mpls., Sept. 23, 1915; s. Ernest B. and Addie (Swanson) H.; m. Jane Margaret Fleckenstein, May 10, 1941; children: John Roger, Jane. BA, Macalester Coll., 1937; MD, U. Minn., 1941, MS in Dermatology, 1946. Diplomate: Am. Bd. Dermatology (pres. 1975). Intern Ancker Hosp., St. Paul, 1940-41; resident in medicine Univ. Hosps., Mpls., 1941—42, resident in dermatology, 1945-46; med. svc. 26th Gen. Hosp., 1943—45; pvt. practice Pinehurst, N.C., 1970-87; head dept. dermatology Cleve. Clinic, 1948-67; prof. Case Western Res. U., Cleve., 1967-70; clin. prof. medicine and dermatology Duke U., Durham, N.C., 1970-85; with Pinehurst Dermatology Clinic, 1970-87; clin. prof. dermatology U. Minn., 1997—. Author: LE Primer, 1972, The Wolves Club, 2002; contbr. 75 articles to med. jours.; author: (CD-ROM) Consultations in Lupus Erythematosus, 2003. Mem. Vols. in Medicine, Martin County Med. Soc., Stuart, Fla., 1997—; bd. dirs. Moore County Free Care Clinic, 2004—. Recipient Discovery award Dermatology Found., 1999. Fellow ACP; mem. AMA (Hektoen Silver award 1952), Am. Acad. Dermatology (pres. 1974), Am. Soc. Dermatopathology (pres. 1975, Founder's award 1996), N.C. Med. Assn., Am. Soc. Investigative Dermatology, Am. Dermatol. Assn., Country Club of N.C. (Pinehurst), Wolves Club (Pinehurst, pres. 1983). Achievements include discovering LE factor (antinuclear) in blood of patients wih lupus erythematosus. Home: 52 Middleton Pl Southern Pines NC 28387 E-mail: haserick@juno.com.

HASHIMOTO, KEN, dermatologist, educator; b. Niigata City, Japan, June 19, 1931; came to U.S., 1956; m. Noriko Sakai, Oct. 3, 1961; children: Naomi, Martha, Eugene, Amy. MD, Niigata U., 1955. Cert. Am. Bd. Dermatology, 1968, Dermatopathology, 1972. Asst. prof. dermatology Tufts U. Sch. Medicine, Boston, 1965-68; assoc. prof. medicine, anatomy U. Tenn., Memphis, 1968-70, prof. medicine, assoc. prof. anatomy, 1970-77, dir., dermatopathology, prof., 1975-77; prof., dir. dermatology, prof. anatomy Wright State U., Dayton, Ohio, 1977-80; chief, dermatology sect., dir. elec. microscopy lab. VA Med. Ctr., Dayton, 1977-80; dermatologist in chief Detroit Med. Ctr., 1987—; prof., chmn. dermatology Wayne State U., Detroit, 1980-99, prof. emeritus, 1999—. Mem. dermatol. drugs adv. com. FDA. Fulbright scholar, 1956-59; participant med. investigatorship career devel. program VA, 1969-77. Mem. Am. Soc. Dermatopathology (pres. 1986-87), Nat. Bd. Med. Examiners, Japanese Soc. Investigative Dermatology (hon.), Memphis Dermatological Soc. (pres. 1973-74), Soc. Investigative Dermatology (v.p. 1980-81, chmn. program com. 1985-86), Soc. Francaise de Dermatologie et de Syphilographie (corr. 1989), Japanese Assn. Dermatology (hon.). Office: Wayne State U Sch Medicine Dept Dermatology 540 E Canfield St Detroit MI 48201-1928

HASHMI, SAJJAD AHMAD, finance educator, dean; b. India, Dec. 20, 1933; m. Monica Ruggiero; children: Serena, Jason, Shawn, Michelle. BA, U. Karachi, 1953, MA, 1956; PhD in Ins., U. Pa., 1962. Lectr. Ohio State U., Columbus, 1962-64; asst. prof. Roosevelt U., Chgo., 1964-66; prof. Ball State U., Muncie, Ind., 1966-83, chmn. dept. fin., 1973-83; Jones disting. prof., dean emeritus Sch. Bus. Emporia (Kans.) State U., 1983—. Cons. and speaker to profl. ins. agts., Indpls., Louisville, Springfield, Ill.; tech. advisor Ind. Arts Commn.; vice chmn. bd. trustees Kans. Ins. Edn. Found.; appeared on TV and radio programs, testified before N.Y., Kans. and Ind. legis. coms. Author: Insurance is a Funny Business, 1972, Automobile Insurance, 1973, Contemporary Personal Finance, 1985, Make Every Second Count, 1989, Strategies for The Future, 1990; contbr. articles, revs., monographs to profl. publs. Named Prof. of Yr., Ball State U. Students, 1971, Outstanding Tchr. of Yr., Ball State U., 1970. Mem. Am. Risk and Ins. Assn., Midwest Fin. Assn., Fin. Mgmt. Assn., Emporia C. of C., Emporia Country Club, Rotary, Beta Gamma Sigma, Sigma Iota Epsilon, Alpha Kappa Psi, Gamma Iota Epsilon, Phi Kappa Phi. Home: 7187 Boca Grove Pl # 204 Bradenton FL 34202 E-mail: shashmi1@tampabay.rr.com.

HASIOTIS, STEPHEN T., geologist, educator; s. Christos S and Andronicki Hasiotis; m. Carol E. Hasiotis; children: Christina, Stephanie. PhD, U. Colo. Prof. U. Kans., Lawrence, Kans., 2001—; courtesy faculty KU Natural History Mus. and Biodiversity Rsch. Ctr., Lawrence, Kans., 2002—. Assoc. editor, palaios SEPM, Tulsa, Okla., 2002—; nominating com. Paleontol. Soc., Lawrence, Kans., 2003—; rsch. grant com. Geol. Soc. of Am., Boulder, Colo., 2003—. Author: Continental Trace Fossils; contbr. articles numerous profl. jours. Grantee Office of Polar Programs, NSF, 1997-1998; Geology and Paleontology Rsch. grant, 2002-2006, Post-doctoral fellowship, Exxon Prodn. Rsch. Co., 1998-1999. Mem.: Am. Assn. of Petroleum Geologists, Paleontol. Soc. (nominating com. 2003), Geol. Soc. of Am. Achievements include research in defining the field of continental ichnology. Office: U Kansas Dept Geology 1475 Jayhawk Blvd Lindley Hall rm 120 Lawrence KS 66045-7613 Office Phone: 785-864-4941. Office Fax: 785-864-5276. E-mail: hasiotis@ku.edu.

HASKAYNE, RICHARD FRANCIS, retired petroleum company executive; b. Calgary, Alta., Can., Dec. 18, 1934; s. Robert Stanley and Bertha (Hesketh) H.; m. Lee Mary Murray, 1958 (dec. 1993); m. Lois P. Heard, 1995. B.Comm., U. Alta., 1956; postgrad., U. Western Ont., 1968, LLD, U. Calgary, U. Alta. Chartered acct., Alta. With Riddell, Stead & Co., chartered accts., Calgary, 1956-60; corp. acctg. supr. to v.p. fin. Hudson's Bay Oil & Gas Co., Ltd., Calgary, 1960-73; compt. Canadian Arctic Gas Study Ltd., 1973-75; sr. v.p. to pres. Hudson's Bay Oil & Gas Co. Ltd., Calgary, 1975-81; pres., CEO Home Oil Co., Ltd., Calgary, 1981-91; chmn. bd. NOVA Corp., Calgary, 1992-98; ret., 1998. Pres., CEO Interprovencial Pipe Line Co., 1987—91, Interhome Energy, 1989—91; bd. dirs. Fording Inc., chmn. bd., 2001—03; past chmn. bd. dirs. TransCanada Corp.; chmn. bd. TransAlta Corp., 1996—98, TransCan Corp., 1998—2005, MacMillan Bloedel Ltd., 1996—99; dir. emeritus CIBC. Chmn. emeritus bd. govs. U. Calgary. Recipient award Officer of the Order of Can., 1997. Fellow Fin. Execs. Inst., Inst. Corp. Dirs.; mem. Calgary Petroleum Club (past pres.), Calgary Golf and Country Club, Earl Grey Golf Club, Ranchmen's Club, U. Calgary Chancellor's Club, The York Club, Libr. Club, Commerce Club, Alta Inst. Chartered Accts., Kappa Sigma Office: 2030 Bankers Hall 855 2d St SW Calgary AB Canada T2P 4J8 Office Phone: 403-265-5931.

HASKELL, ARTHUR JACOB, retired water transportation executive; b. Newark, Apr. 16, 1926; s. Isidore David and Elena (Greenbaum) H.; m. Amparo Serrano, Dec. 31, 1958 (div.); children: Amparo Rocio, Vincent Isidore, Joaquin Arthur; m. Marge Gibson, June 8, 1986. BS, U.S. Naval Acad., 1947; profl. naval engr., MIT, 1953. Sr. procurement engr. Nat. Bulk Carriers, N.Y.C., 1956-62; asst. plant mgr. Western Gear Corp., Belmont, Calif., 1962-64; project engr. Matson Nav. Co., San Francisco., 1964-70, v.p., 1970-73, sr. v.p., 1973-91, ret., 1991. Mem. marine bd. NRC, 1981-85; bd. mgrs. Am. Bur. Shipping, 1988-92; bd. dirs., budget officer Nat. Liberty Ship Meml. Bd. dirs. San Francisco Marine Exchange, 1975-78, v.p., 1976-77, pres., 1977-78. Served to comd. USN, 1947-56. Mem. Soc. Naval Architects and Marine Engrs. (chmn. No. Calif. sect. 1971-72, v.p. 1973-83, exec. com. 1977-80, 83-96, hon. v.p. for life 1983—, pres. 1989-91), Assn. for Preservation of Presdl. Yacht Potomac (bd. govs. 1984—, co-pres. 1993-99). Home: 287 Sheridan Rd Oakland CA 94618-2717 Personal E-mail: arthur.haskell@alum.mit.edu.

HASKELL, BARBARA, curator; b. San Diego, Nov. 13, 1946; d. John N. and Barbara (Freeman) H.; m. Leon Botstein; children: Clara Haskell Botstein, Maxim Haskell Botstein. BA, UCLA, 1969. Asst. registrar Pasadena (Calif.) Art Mus., 1969, curatorial asst., 1970, asst. curator, 1970, assoc. curator, 1970-72, curator painting and sculpture, 1972-74, Whitney Mus. Am. Art, N.Y.C., 1975—. Author: Arthur Dove, 1974, Marsden Hartley, 1980, Milton Avery, 1982, Blam! The Explosion of Pop, Minimalism and Performance 1958-64, 1984, Georgia O'Keefe: Works on Paper, 1985, Ralston Crawford, 1985, Charles Demuth, 1987, Red Grooms, 1987, Donald Judd, 1988, Burgoyne Diller, 1990, Agnes Martin, 1992, Joseph Stella, 1994, The Am. Century: Art and Culture 1900-1950, 1999, Edward Steichen, 2000, Elie Nadelman, 2002. Named Woman of Yr., Mademoiselle mag., 1973. Office: Whitney Mus Am Art 945 Madison Ave New York NY 10021-2701 Office Phone: 212-570-3606. E-mail: barbara_haskell@whitney.org.

HASKELL, BARRY GEOFFRY, computer engineer, researcher; b. Lewiston, Maine, 1941; s. George Raymond and Dorothy H.; m. Ann Kantrow, Sept. 13, 1964; children: Paul Eric, Andrew. AA, Pasadena City Coll., 1962; BSEE, U. Calif., Berkeley, 1964, MSEE, 1965, PhD, 1968. Electronics engr. Lawrence Livermore (Calif.) Lab., 1965; rsch. asst. Electronics Rsch. Lab. U. Calif., Berkeley, 1965-68; mem. tech. staff AT&T Bell Labs., Holmdel, N.J., 1968-76, head radio comm. rsch. dept., 1976-83, visual comm. cons., 1984-86, head visual comm. rsch. dept., 1987-95; head image processing rsch. dept. AT&T Labs., Middletown, N.J., 1996-99; sr. scientist Apple Computer, Inc., Cupertino, Calif., 2002—. Adj. prof. Rutgers U., New Brunswick, N.J., 1976-79, CCNY, 1983-84, Columbia U., N.Y.C., 1987, 93; negotiator Internat. Stds. Orgn., Am. Nat. Stds. Inst., Internat. Telecom. Union - Telecom Sector. Co-author: Image Transmission Tech., 1979, Digital Pictures, 1988, 2d edit., 1995, Digital Video—An Introduction to MPEG-2, 1996; contbr. articles to profl. jours.; patentee in field. Recipient Elec. Engring. Dept. Outstanding Alumnus award U. Calif., Berkeley, 1998; co-recipient Japan's Computer and Comm. prize, 1997, N.J. Inventor Hall of

Fame Inventor of Yr., 2000; AT&T fellow, 1998. Fellow IEEE, Phi Beta Kappa; mem. Sigma Xi. Avocations: sailing, skiing, guitar playing. Office: Apple Computer 302-3KS 2 Infinite Loop Cupertino CA 95014

HASKELL, JOHN HENRY FARRELL, JR., investment company executive; b. N.Y.C., Jan. 24, 1932; s. John Henry Farrell and Paulette (Heger) H.; m. Francine G. Le Roux, June 30, 1955; children: Michael J., Christopher E., Diana F. T. BS, U.S. Mil. Acad., 1953; MBA with distinction, Harvard U., 1958. Assoc. Dillon, Read & Co., N.Y.C., 1958-61, mgr. European office Paris, 1961-66; v.p Dillon, Read & Co. (now UBS Securities, LLC), N.Y.C., 1964-75, mng. dir., 1975-99, sr. advisor, 2000—04. Pres., CEO The France Fund, Inc., 1986—89; bd. dirs. Pall Corp., Security Capital Corp.; mem. adv. coun. Overseas Pvt. Investment Corp., 1972—75. Bd. dirs. Belgian-Am. Ednl. Found.; co-chmn. bd. trustees French Inst./Alliance Francaise; mem. adv. coun. Lycee Francais de N.Y.; bd. trustees St. Paul's Sch., Concord, N.H. Decorated Legion of Honor, Ordre National du Merite France; recipient Presdl. Recognition award For Cmty. Svc., 1986. Mem. Coun. Fgn. Rels., French-Am. C. of C. (councillor), Assn. Grads. of U.S. Mil. Acad. (trustee 1984-87), Am. Soc. French Legion of Honor (bd. dirs., v.p.), Links Club, Univ. Club, Meadow Brook Club (Jericho, N.Y.), Bohemian Club (San Francisco), Eagle Springs Golf Club (Wolcott, Colo.). Home: 120 East End Ave New York NY 10028-7552 Office: 4th Fl 535 Madison Ave New York NY 10022 Office Phone: 212-906-7810. Business E-Mail: jhaskell05@yahoo.com.

HASKELL, MOLLY, writer; b. Charlotte, N.C., Sept. 29, 1939; d. John Haskell and Mary Clark; m. Andrew Sarris, May 31, 1969. BA, Sweet Briar Coll.; student, U. London, England, Sorbonne, Paris. Pub. rels. assoc. Sperry Rand; writer, editor French Film Office, N.Y.C.; film critic Village Voice, Viva, New York Magazine, Vogue, 1969-74, 74-80; film reviewer "Special Edition" Pub. TV; film reviewer "All Things Considered" Nat. Pub. Radio; assoc. prof. film Barnard Coll., N.Y.C., 1990; adj. prof. film Columbia U., N.Y.C., 1992—95, Sarah Lawrence Coll., 2004; writer. Artistic dir. Sarasota French Film Festival. Author: From Reverence to Rape: The Treatment of Women in the Movies, 1973, rev. edit., 1987, Love and Other Infectious Diseases: A Memoir, 1990, Holding My Own in No Man's Land, 1997; (plays) The Last Anniversary, 1990; contbr. articles and essays to jours. Decorated chevalier Order Arts and Letters (France); recipient Nat. Bd. Review of Motion Pictures award, 1989, Disting. Alumna award Sweet Briar Coll., 1994. Mem. N.Y. Inst. for the Humanities, Authors Guild (coun. 2000-03), The Century Club, Phi Beta Kappa.

HASKELL, PAUL GERSHON, retired law educator; b. Boston, Mar. 31, 1927; s. David Israel and Leah (Paris) H.; m. Sarah Potter Evarts, Jan. 22, 1955; children: Peter, Thomas, John. AB, Harvard U., 1948, LLB, 1951. Bar: N.Y. 1952. Assoc. Kelley, Drye, Newhall & Maginnes, N.Y.C., 1951-56, White & Case, N.Y.C., 1956-59; asst. gen. counsel The Houston Corp., St. Petersburg, Fla., 1959-60; resident counsel, asst. treas. Ednl. Testing Service, Princeton, N.J., 1960-62; prof. law Georgetown U., Washington, 1962-67, Case Western Res. U., Cleve., 1967-79, U. N.C., Chapel Hill, 1979-83, Graham Kenan prof. law, 1983-91, William R. Kenan prof. law, 1991-98; ret., 1998. Co-author: Preface to Estates In Land and Future Interests, 1966, 2d edit., 1984; author: Preface to the Law of Trusts, 1975, Preface to Wills, Trusts and Adminstration, 1987, 2d edit. 1994, Why Lawyers Behave As They Do, 1998; contbr. articles to profl. jours. Bd. dirs. Cleve. Fair Housing Inc., 1967-70; trustee Harvard Club of Cleve., 1976-79. Served with USN, 1945-46. Mem. ABA (spl. com. to revise standards for legal edn. 1970-73, coun., sect. on legal edn. and admissions to bar 1973-76, standing com. on legal assts. 1976-80). Republican. Home: 1805 Rolling Rd Chapel Hill NC 27514-7505 Office: U NC Sch Of Law Chapel Hill NC 27599-3380 Business E-Mail: phaskell@email.unc.edu.

HASKELL, PETER ABRAHAM, actor, director; b. Boston, Oct. 15, 1934; s. Norman Abraham and Rose Veronica (Golden) H.; m. Ann Compton, Feb. 27, 1960 (div. 1974); m. Dianne Tolmich, Oct. 26, 1974; children: Audra Rosemary, Jason Abraham. BA, Harvard U., 1962; student, N.Y. Law Sch., 1982-83. Actor (films) Finnegans Wake, 1965, Legend of Earl Durand, 1972, Christina, 1974, Forty Days of Musa Dagh, 1982, Riding the Edge, 1987, Child's Play II, 1990, Child's Play III, 1991, Robot Wars, 1993; (TV series) Bracken's World, NBC, 1969-71, Rich Man Poor Man, Book II, ABC, 1976-77, Ryan's Hope, ABC, 1982-83, Search for Tomorrow, NBC, 1983-85, Rituals, Metromedia, 1985, The Law and Harry McGraw, CBS, 1987-88; (TV films) Love, Hate, Love, 1970, The Eyes of Charles Sand, 1972, Mandrake, 1977, The Cracker Factory, 1979, Christine Cromwell, 1990, Columbo, 1991, Maid for Each Other, 1992, Faces of Deception, 1993, Never Talk to Strangers, 1997; dir. (plays) Nightgames, 2000, Mrs. Warren's Profession, 2004. Wwith U.S. Army, 1954-56. Mem. SAG, AFTRA, Actors Equity. Democrat. Avocations: photography, skiing. Office: care Eric Klass 139 S Beverly Dr Ste 331 Beverly Hills CA 90212-3020 Office Phone: 310-274-9169. E-mail: peterhaskell@aol.com.

HASKELL, WYATT RUSHTON, lawyer; b. Birmingham, Ala., May 15, 1940; s. Preston Hampton and Mary Wyatt (Rushton) H.; m. Susan Porter Nabers, June 1, 1968; children: John Howze, Henry Devereux, Samuel Drayton. AB, Amherst Coll., 1961; LLB, Yale U., 1965. Bar: Ala. 1965. Assoc. Bradley, Arant, Rose & White, Birmingham, 1966-71; staff atty. So. Natural Gas Co., Birmingham, 1971-73; ptnr. Haskell, Slaughter, Young & Rediker, LLC, Birmingham, 1973—. Vis. rsch. asst. U. Muenster, Germany, 1965—66; vis. prof. U. Ala. Law Sch., 1970—73; bd. dirs. Bio Horizons Implant Systems, Inc. Contbr. articles to profl. jours. Bd. dirs. Ala. Shakespeare Fest, Montgomery, Folger Shakespeare Libr., Washington. Thomas Pope fellow Trinity Coll., Oxford. Mem. ABA, Ala. Bar Assn., Birmingham Bar Assn., Mountain Brook Club. Presbyterian. Home: 2964 Cherokee Rd Birmingham AL 35223-2609 Office: Haskell Slaughter et al 1400 Park Place Tower 2001 Park Place North Birmingham AL 35203 Office Phone: 205-254-1415. Business E-Mail: wrh@hsy.com.

HASKETT, DIANNE LOUISE, retired mayor, lawyer, consultant; b. London, Ont., Can., Mar. 4, 1955; d. Allan Douglas and Frances Shirley (Crone) H.; m. Jack Kotowicz; 1 child, Annie. BA, U. Waterloo, Ont., 1974; LLD, U. Western Ont., 1977; LLM, London Sch. Econs., 1979. Lawyer Law Soc. of Upper Can., Canada, 1980—; founding ptnr. Haskett, Menear Assoc., Law Firm, 1980—94; speechwriter, internat. cons., and pub. rels. advisor Washington Contact, 2001—; estate and bus. coord. Living Trust Atty. Ltd., Fairfax, Va.; Senate and Congl. campaign advisor. V.p. London Urban Alliance on Race Rels. Contbr. articles to profl. jours. City councillor London City Coun., 1991-94; mayor, 1994-2000; founder Open Homes Can., London, Ont., 1992; founding mem. London Citizens Com., 1980-84; v.p. Ark Aid Street Mission Inc., London, On., 1986-88. Recipient Pericles award Am. Hellenic Ednl. Progressive Assn., 1999; Grad. scholar Rotary Internat., 1978-79; Paul Harris fellow Rotary Clubs London, 1998. Mem. Law Soc. of Upper Can. Avocations: journalism, collecting antiques and rare books, reading, speech making. Home: 2970 Kildare Ln Fairfax VA 22031

HASKINS, CHARLES GREGORY, JR., lawyer; b. Chgo., Jan. 27, 1951; s. Charles G. and Ellen Barbara (Essman) H.; m. Gail Beaubien Ferbend, June 14, 1987; 1 child, Charles Robert. BA, U. Ill., 1972; JD, John Marshall Law Sch., 1976. Bar: Ill. 1976, U.S. Dist. Ct. (no. dist.) Ill. 1976. Assoc. George J. Cullen, Ltd., Chgo., 1976-82; shareholder George J. Cullen & Assoc., Ltd., Chgo., 1982-89, Cullen, Haskins, Nicholson & Menchetti, Chgo., 1989—. Mem.: ATLA, Workers Injury Law and Advocacy Group (bd. dirs. 1997—, sec. 2001—04), Chgo. Bar Assn. (chmn. indsl. commn. com. 1987—88), Ill. Trial Lawyers Assn. (bd. mgrs. 1989—, co-chmn. workers compensation com. 1991—2001, co-editor Case Notebook 1992—, treas. 1997, 2004—05, parliamentarian 2005—), Ill. Bar Assn., Workers Compensation Lawyers Assn. (bd. dirs. 1986—96, pres. 1989). Democrat. Roman Catholic. Avocations: golf, water-skiing, skiing. Office: Cullen Haskins Nicholson & Menchetti 35 E Wacker Dr Ste 1760 Chicago IL 60601-2271 Office Phone: 312-332-2545. E-mail: chaskins@chnm-law.com.

HASKINS, DEBRA MAY, academic administrator, educator; d. John Albert and Norma W. Haskins; m. Lee Mead; children: Julia, Kerry, Donna, Gavin, Jacqueline. BA, SUC Cortland, NY, 1975; MA, SUNY, Stony Brook, 1991; student, Coll. New Rochelle, NY, 1992—94, St. John's U., Jamaica, NY, 1995—2005. Cert. social studies educator, grades 7-12, sch. dist. adminstr. Pub. rels. position Taylor Wine Co., Hammondsport, NY, 1973—75; realtor Carriage Home Realty, Smithtown, NY, 1979—81; social studies tchr. Baldwinsville Acad., NY, 1975—79, Sachem Schs., Holbrook, NY, 1983—84, Huntington Unified Sch. Dist., NY, 1981—83, 1984—98, chairperson social studies, 1998—. Exec. bd. tchr. ctr. Huntington Tchr. Ctr., 1999—; exec. bd. mem. Long Island Coun. Social Studies, NY, 2001—03. Women's advocate Chosin Few, L.I., 1996—2003. Mentoring Grant for Tchrs., Huntington, NY, 1999—2002, Art and Architecture grant, NEA, 2002—04. Mem.: Nat. Coun. Social Studies, Long Island Coun. Social Studies (exec. bd. 2001—03), Assn. Curriculum Develop. Independent. Avocations: painting, writing, reading, travel, dream interpretation. Home: 96 Summit Dr Smithtown NY 11787

HASKINS, LINDA L., language educator; b. Beaver Falls, Pa., Aug. 31, 1947; d. Henry Griffin and H. Elizabeth Haskins. BA in English, Del. State U., 1969; MA in English, Seton Hall U., 1971; MA in Film, West Chester State U., 1983; postgrad., U. Del., 1988-91. Instr. Capitol Sch. Dist., Dover, Del., 1971-72, U. Del., Newark, 1972-75; asst. prof. Del. State U., Dover, 1975—. Contbg. editor: Succeeding Despite the Odds; editor Tangled Roots. Recipient NEH award, 1983. Mem. AAUP, AAUW, Nat. Coun. Tchrs. of English, NAACP, Alpha Kappa Mu, Alpha Kappa Alpha. Avocations: reading, gardening, singing, collecting african-americana. Office: Del State U 1200 N Dupont Hwy Dover DE 19901-2277 Office Phone: 302-857-6575.

HASKINS, ROBERT, musicologist, performing artist, music critic; b. Roanoke, Va., June 24, 1960; s. J.J. and Verna H. BM in Piano, Peabody Inst. Johns Hopkins, Balt., 1982; Concert Recital Diploma, Guildhall Sch. Music and Drama, London, 1985; MM in Music History and Piano, Peabody Inst. Johns Hopkins, Balt., 1984, 92; doctoral studies, Eastman Sch. of Music, 1993—. Keyboard performer, 1984—; composer, 1986—; classical music critic Columbia (Md.) Flier, 1990-93; contbg. writer Balt. Sun, 1990-93, Chorus!, Duluth, Ga., 1992-93; critic Am. Record Guide, Cin., 1993—. Guest panelist WBJC-FM Radio, Balt., 1990-93; panelist Internat. Brass Festival, Balt., 1991; assoc. Arthur Friedheim Libr. Peabody Inst., Balt., 1991—; program advisor Peabody Computer Music Consort, Balt., 1992-93; guest writer Rochester Dem. and Chronicle, 1994—. Contbr. 210 reviews and articles to profl. jours., 1988—. Grantee Composers Performance Meet the Composer, N.Y.C., 1988-90, Md. State Arts Coun., Balt., 1989; fellow Andrew F. Mellon in Humnanistic Studies, Woodrow Wilson Found., Princeton, N.J., 1993; recipient Sproull fellowship U. Rochester, N.Y., 1993. Mem. Broadcast Music Inc., Am. Musicological Soc. (participant nat. meeting 1994), Phi Mu Alpha Sinfonia. Avocations: electronic mail, chess, cats, recordings, video. Home: 40 Stewart St Rochester NY 14620-2823 Office: Eastman Sch Music Dept Musicology 26 Gibbs St Dept Rochester NY 14604-2599

HASKO, JUDITH ANN, lawyer; b. Waterbury, Conn., Feb. 11, 1964; BA, Vassar Coll., 1986; MPhil, U. Sussex, Brighton, Eng., 1988; JD, U. Wis., 1994. Bar: Wis. 1995, Calif. 1995, U.S. Patent and Trademark Office 1998. Rsch. assoc. Genentech Inc., South San Francisco, Calif., 1988-92; ptnr. Cooley Godward, Palo Alto, Calif., 1994—. Articles editor Wis. Law Rev., 1993-94. Mem. ABA. Office: Cooley Godward 5 Palo Alto Sq Palo Alto CA 94306-2122 Office Phone: 650-843-5065. E-mail: haskoja@cooley.com.

HASKVITZ, ALAN PAUL, elementary education educator, consultant; b. Mpls., Sept. 7, 1942; s. Harry and Rose (Portugal) H.; married, Apr. 1, 1970; children: Anna, Maxwell Harry. AA, Chaffey Coll., 1963; MS, Calif. State U., 1965; BE, Meml. Coll., St. John's, Newfoundland, 1972; MA, Calif. State U., L.A., 1970. Cert. secondary tchr., adminstr., Calif.; cert. tchr., Ont., Newfoundland, N.Y.; cert. cmty. coll. instr., Calif.; cert. audio-visual. Tchr. Cornwall (Ont.) Sch. Bd., Can., 1970-78; vice prin. Quest School for the Gifted, Oshawa, Ont., 1978-80; tchr. Corono (Calif.) Sch. Sys., 1980-81, Walnut (Calif.) Sch. Dist., 1987—; cons. Edn. Strategies, Alta Loma, Calif., 1981—. Lectr. U. Calif., 1970—89, Calif. Poly., 1970—89, Western Wash. U., 2000; pres.-elect Nat. Coun. for the Social Scis.; mem. Nat. Critical Thinking Com., Coun. of Chief State Sch. Officers, Nat. Assessment of Ednl. Progress, Nat. Responder Com. on Tchrs. and Schs., Constl. Rights Found., Western States Accreditation Commn., Cal Poly Master Tchr. Com. on Student Tng. Programs; evaluator Nat. Coun. for Accreditation of Tchr. Edn.; spkr. to numerous orgns., meetings and confs.; sr. Olympian weightlifter. Author: Resources for Social Studies Educators; syndicated automobile journalist: The Car Family; contbr. numerous articles to profl. jours.; features in: Futures videos, Project citizen video, Time, Newsweek, CNN, ABC, CBS, NBC, NPR, numerous textbooks. Commr. City of Rancho Cucamonga, 1986—; pres. United Counties Sports, Cornwall, 1980-84; bd. advisors Americans All. Named USA Today All Am. Educator, 2000; named one of 100 Most Influential Educators in Am.; named to Nat. Tchrs. Hall of Fame, 1997; recipient Am.'s Profl. Best Tchr. award, Learning mag., 1989, Heroes in Edn. award, Reader's Digest, George Washington medal, Freedom Found., 1992, Spirit of Edn. award, NBC, 1997, Nat. Bicentennial Tchg. award, Bicentennial Com., 1993, Presdl. award for environ. edn., 1988, Calif. Dept. Water Agencies, Cmty. award, Walnut Valley Water Dist., 1989, Outstanding Citizen award, L.A. County Supr., 1994, Outstanding Tchr. award, Christa McAuliffe award, 1996, Nat. Coun. for Social Studies, 1992, Nation's Best Program, 1994, Nation's Outstanding Mid. Sch. Tchr., 1996, Agr. Tchr. of Yr., Nat. Coun. for Social Studies, 1995, Baylor U., Calif. Agr. in Classroom, Robert Cherry Internat. Tchr. of Yr., 1997, Campbell's Tchrs. in Am. award, Disney Regional Winner, Busch Environ. award, 1996, Nat. Garden award, Leavey award for pvt. enterprise edn., 1998, Freedom Found., Calif. Water Environ. Edn. award, Calif., 1995, Agy. for Water Edn., Calif. History Tchrs. of Yr., Daus. of Am. Colonies, 1999, Crystal Apple award, NBC, 1998, Bell award, Calif. Sch. Bd. Assn., 1987, 1997, numerous awards for sch. programs. Achievements include devel. of Reach Every Child and the Children's Speed Reading Record Holders. Home: 9655 Carrari Ct Alta Loma CA 91737-1653 E-mail: freealan@yahoo.com.

HASL, RUDOLPH CARL, dean, law educator; b. Aug. 30, 1942; BA, Xavier U., 1964; JD, St. Louis U., 1967; LLM, NYU, 1973. Bar: Ill. 1967. Law clk. 5th Dist. Appellate Ct., Ill., 1966—67, 1971; teaching fellow NYU, 1967—68; asst. prof. St. Louis U., 1971—73, assoc. prof., 1973—77, asst. dean Sch. Law, 1973—76, acting dean, 1976, prof., 1977—91, assoc. dean, 1976—78, dean, 1979—91; prof. St. John's U. Sch. Law, 1991—2000, dean, 1991—98, Seattle U. Sch. Law, 2000—05. Co-author: Missouri Law of Evidence, 1984; author: The Internationalization of Law Practice: Issues of Access and Education, 1994. Capt. U.S. Army, 1968—71. Mem.: ABA, Alpha Sigma Nu. Home: 4643 NE 89th St Seattle WA 98115-4975 Office: Seattle U Sch Law Room 210J 900 Broadway Seattle WA 98122 E-mail: hasl@seattleu.edu.

HASLAM, EDWARD T., finance company executive; BA in Bus. Adminstrn., MBA, Temple U. CPA. Fin. mgr. Mfrs. Hanover Fin. Svcs., Inc.; fin. mgmr. SEI Corp.; COO Electronic Payment Svcs., Inc., 1994—99; with Concord EFS, Inc., Memphis, 1999—2000, CFO, 2000—, sr. v.p., 2001—, treas., 2001—. Office: Concord EFS Inc 2525 Horizon Lake Dr Ste 120 Memphis TN 38133

HASLAM, GERALD WILLIAM, writer, educator; b. Bakersfield, Calif., Mar. 18, 1937; s. Fredrick Martin and Lorraine Hope (Johnson) H.; m. Janice Eileen Pettichord, July 1, 1961; children: Frederick W., Alexandra R., Garth C., Simone B., Carlos V. BA, San Francisco State U., 1963, MA, 1965; PhD, Union Grad. Sch., 1980. Instr. English San Francisco State U., San Francisco, 1966-67; asst. prof. English Sonoma State U., Rohnert Park, Calif., 1967-70, assoc. prof. English, 1970-74, prof. English, 1971-97, emeritus prof. English, 1997—; prof. Fromm Inst./U. San Francisco, 2001—. Adj. prof. Union Grad. Sch., Cin., 1984—, The Nat. Faculty, Atlanta, 1984—; prof. Usher Lifelong Learning Inst., Sonoma State U., 2003—, U. Calif., Berkeley, 2005-. Editor various anthologies; author various booklets, monographs, film scripts, (fiction) Okies: Selected Stories, 1973, Masks: A Novel, 1976, The Wages of Sin: Collected Stories, 1980, Hawk Flights: Visions of the West, 1983, Snapshots: Glimpses of the Other California, 1985, The Man Who Cultivated Fire and Other Stories, 1987, That Constant Coyote: California Stories, 1990, Condor Dreams and Other Fictions, 1994, The Great Tejon Club Jubilee, 1996, Manuel and the Madman, 1999, Straight White Male, 2000, Haslam's Valley, 2005, (non-fiction) Voices of a Place, 1987, Coming of Age in California, 1990, The Other California, 1990, The Great Central Valley: California's Heartland, 1993, Workin' Man Blues: Country Music in California, 1999, Coming of Age in California, 2d enlarged edit., 2000; contbg. writer LA Times Mag., 2005. With U.S. Army, 1958-60. Creative Writing fellow Calif. Arts Coun., 1989; recipient Benjamin Franklin award, 1993, Bay Area Book Reviewers' Non-fiction award, 1994, Commonwealth Club medal for Calif., 1994, Merit award Assn. State & Local History, 1994, Commendation citation, 2001; Fulbright sr. lectr., 1986-87, Josephine Miles award, 1990, Ralph J. Gleason award, 2000, Carey McWilliams award, 2001, Western States Book Fiction award, 2001, Sequoia - Giant of the Valley award, 2003, Cert. of Commendation, Calif. Arts Coun., 2004. Mem. NAACP, Great Valley Ctr. (adv. bd.), Western Lit. Assn. (bd. dirs., past pres., Disting. Achievment award 1999), Calif. Studies Assn. (steering com., founding mem.), Calif. Hist. Assn., Calif. Tchrs. Assn., San Francisco State U. Alumni Assn. (life), Union Inst. Alumni Assn., Multi-Ethnic Lit. of U.S. (founding mem.), Robinson Jeffers Assn. (founding mem.), Sierra Club, The Nature Conservancy, Calif. Trout (founding mem.), Tulare Basin Archeology Group, Defenders of Wildlife, Common Cause, Soc. of the Third Infantry Divsn., Yosemite Assn. (bd. dirs.). Roman Catholic. Avocations: bicycling, hiking, fishing. Office: Sonoma State U 1801 E Cotati Ave Rohnert Park CA 94928-3609 Office Phone: 707-792-2944. Personal E-mail: ghaslam@sonic.net.

HASLAM, ROBERT THOMAS, III, lawyer; b. Taunton, Mass., May 4, 1946; s. Robert Thomas and Marcella Neale (Compton) H.; children: Laurel Ashley, Julia Compton; m. Molly Haslam. BS Aeronautics and Astronautics, MIT, 1968; JD, Hastings Coll., 1976. Bar: Calif., 1976. Atty., ptnr. Heller, Ehrman, Menlo Park, Calif., 1976—. Capt. USAF 1969-73. Mem. ABA (co-chair litigation, intellectual property sect. 1993—). Avocations: tennis, soccer. Office: Heller Ehrman 275 Middlefield Rd Menlo Park CA 94025-3506 Home: 1410 Enchanted W San Mateo CA 94402 Office Phone: 650-324-7073.

HASLANGER, PHILIP CHARLES, journalist; b. Menominee, Mich., May 11, 1949; s. Harry LeRoy and Agnes Gertrude (Seidl) H.; m. Rosemary Ann Raasch Carta, May 27, 1972 (div.); children: Brian David, Sarah Marie; m. Ellen Jean Reuter, Apr. 9, 1983; children: Michael Kenneth, Julia Jane. BA in Sociology, U. Wis., 1971, MA in Journalism, 1973. With The Capital Times, Madison, Wis., 1973—, mng. editor, 1998—. Author: Stories of Call, 1998. Authorized lay pastor United Ch. of Christ, 2004—. Mem. Nat. Conf. Editl. Writers (bd. dirs. 1993, 94, 97, 2003, officer 1999-2002), New Media Fedn. Avocations: reading, music, hiking, theology. Home: 5409 Vicar Ln Madison WI 53714-3443 Office: The Capital Times 1901 Fish Hatchery Rd Madison WI 53713-1248 E-mail: phaslanger@madison.com.

HASLER, WILLIAM ALBERT, electronics executive; b. Los Angeles, Nov. 22, 1941; s. Albert Ernst and LaDella (Stewart) H.; m. Janet Louise Kindstrom, June 10, 1963; children— Claire, Laura, James BA, Pomona Coll., 1963; MBA, Harvard U., 1967. C.P.A., Calif. Ptnr. Peat, Marwick, Mitchell & Co., Los Angeles, 1972-76, ptnr.-in-charge, 1976-81, N.Y.C., 1981-84; vice chmn., dir., mem. operating com. Peat, Marwick, Main & Co., San Francisco and N.Y.C., 1984-91; dean Haas Sch. Bus., U. Calif., Berkeley, 1991-98; co-CEO Aphton Corp., Miami, 1998—2003, vice chmn., 2003—; chmn. Solectron, 2003—. Mem. council KPMG Internat., 1985— Mem. editorial adv. bd. Jour. Accountancy Fellow Huntington Library, San Marino, Calif.; treas. Harvard U. Bus. Sch. Alumni Bd.; trustee Pomona Coll.; bd. dirs. Nat. Ctr. Fin. Services; mem. Pacific Basin Econ. Council Mem. Am. Inst. C.P.A.s, Calif. Soc. C.P.A.s, Calif. C. of C. Clubs: Calif. (Los Angeles); Union League (N.Y.C.); University (bd. dirs.); St. Francis Yacht. Avocations: sailing, skiing, diving. Office: Solectron 847 Gibraltar Dr Milpitas CA 95035 also: Aphton Corp 444 Brickell Ave Ste 51-507 Miami FL 33131-2403*

HASLETT, JARED WOODDELL, physicist, researcher; b. Akron, Ohio, Oct. 11, 1930; s. George William and Mildred W. H.; m. Winona Rose Goss, 1954 (div.); children: Jonathan, Joel, Jeanne; m. Diane Margaret Crowley, Sept. 4, 1965; children: Ethan, Benjamin. MS, Ill. Inst. of Tech., 1955. Physicist U. Chgo., 1956-57; educator U. Ill., Chgo., 1959-94. Dir. undergrad. studies dept. physics U. Ill., Chgo.; resident rsch. assoc. Argonne (Ill.) Nat. Labs., 1959—65; rsch. physicist Chgo. Wesley Meml. Hosp., 1966; cons. physicist Michael Reese Hosp., Chgo., 1966—67; cons. on Rudolf Steiner's works to various libraries, 1998—. Author: Works of Rudolf Steiner in English Translation, 1998. Treas. Waldorf Sch. of Chgo., 1975-77; libr. Rudolf Steiner Group Anthroposophical Soc. in Am., 1971-75. Faculty fellowship NSF, 1988, 89. Mem. AAAS (life), Anthroposophical Soc., Bioelectromagnetics Soc., Am. Mensa Ltd.(life), Am. Radio Relay League, Agni Yoga Soc., Moose (life), Sigma Pi Sigma, Sigma Xi (life). Espicopalian. Avocations: chess, tennis, bicycling, amateur radio. E-mail: JHaslett@uic.edu.

HASLETT, JIM, professional football coach; b. Pittsburgh, Pa., Dec. 9, 1955; BA in Elem. Edn., Ind. U. of Pa., 1978. Profl. football player Buffalo Bills and NY Nets, 1979-87; asst. football coach U. Buffalo, 1988-89; asst. coach Los Angeles Raiders, 1993-94, Pittsburgh Steelers, 1996-99; head coach New Orleans Saints, 2000—; mem. College Football Hall of Fame, 2001. Named NFL Coach of the Yr., 2000. Office: New Orleans Saints 5800 Airline Dr Metairie LA 70003-3876

HASNAIN, MEMOONA, medical educator, researcher; b. Karachi, Sindh, Pakistan, May 2, 1966; arrived in U.S., 1998; d. Syed Hazur and Shirin Hasnain; m. Ehsan Ullah, Oct. 6, 1988; children: Hassan Nawaz Janjua, Farooq Nawaz Janjua. MD, U. Karachi, 1989; M Health Professions Edn., U. Ill., Chgo., 2000, PhD, 2001. House officer dept. ob-gyn. Dist. Hdqrs. Hosp., Mardan, Pakistan, 1990—91; house officer dept. internal medicine Fauji Found. Med. Ctr., Rawalpindi, Pakistan, 1992—93; med. officer Hearts Internat. Hosp., Internat. Islamic U., Rawalpindi, 1993—94; med. officer dept. ob-gyn. Kamal Hosp., Karachi, Pakistan, 1994—95; med. educator WHO Ctr. Rsch. and Tng. of Health Profls., Coll. Physicians and Surgeons, Pakistan, 1995—98; from rsch. asst. med. decision making Dept. Med. Edn. Coll. Medicine to dir. rsch. U. Ill., Chgo., 1998—2002, dir. rsch., 2002—, interim dir. rsch., 2002. Adj. asst. prof. U. Ill., 2004—. Contbr. articles to profl. jours. Recipient Chgo. Bar Assn. Pub. Health award, U. Ill. Chgo. Scholarship Assn., 2001, Ray E. Helfer Award for Innovation in Pediatric Edn., Ambulatory Pediatric Assn., 2001; Internat. fellow, Coll. Physicians and Surgeons, Pakistan, 1998—99, AAUW Ednl. Found., 2000—01. Mem.: APHA, Soc. Med. Decision Making (Outstanding Paper award 2003), Pakistan Med. and Dental Coun., Soc. for Tchrs. Family Medicine, Assn. Med. Edn. in Pakistan (life), Phi Kappa Phi, Delta Omega (Lambda chpt.). Moslem. Office: Univ Ill Chgo Dept Family Medicine 1919 W Taylor St Chicago IL 60612

HASS, LAWRENCE JOEL, lawyer; b. NYC, Dec. 1, 1946; s. Nathan Harold and Helen Bernice (Goldin) H.; children: Joanna Sheri, David Brian, Lindsay Jill. BA, U. Pa., 1967; JD, Bklyn. Law Sch., 1971. Bar: NY 1972, DC 1977. Atty. SEC, Washington, 1971-75, U.S. Dept. Labor, Washington, 1975-76; spl. asst. to adminstr. Pension & Welfare Benefit Program, Washington, 1976-77; prin. Groom & Norberg, Chartered, Washington, 1977—87; ptnr. Akin, Gump, Strauss, Hauer & Feld, Washington, 1987—92, Paul Hastings Janofsky & Walker, NYC, 1992—, mem. policy com. Bd. dirs., gen. counsel Pension Real Estate Assn., Hartford, 1985—; chmn. Broadcast Capital Fund, Washington, 1995-2002. Author: The Annotated Fiduciary,

1981. Mem. ABA, DC Bar Assn. Avocations: tennis, jogging. Office: Paul Hastings Janofsky & Walker LLP 75 E 55th St First Floor New York NY 10022 Office Phone: 212-318-6401. Business E-Mail: larryhass@paulhastings.com.

HASS, ROBERT L., writer, literature educator; b. San Francisco, 1941; Prof. Dept. English U. Calif., Berkeley. Author: (books of poetry) Sun Under Wood: New Poems, 1996, Human Wishes, 1989, Praise, 1979, Field Guide, 1973; co-translator vols. of poetry with Czeslaw Milosz including: Facing the river, 1995; author/editor essays and translation including: The Essential Haiku: Versions of Basho, Buson, and Issa, 1994, Twentieth Century Pleasures: Prose on Poetry, 1984 (Nat. Book Critics Circle award); editor: Best American Poetry, 2001. Bd. dirs. Internat. Rivers Network. Apptd. Poet Laureate of U.S., 1995-97; MacArthur "Genius" fellow; named Educator of the Yr., N.Am. Assn. on Environ. Edn., 1997, chancellor Acad. Am. Poets, 2000. Office: Steven Barclay Agy 321 Pleasant St Petaluma CA 94952-2648 E-mail: bobhass@uclink4.berkeley.edu.

HASSAN, FRED, pharmaceutical executive; b. Pakistan, Nov. 12, 1945; came to U.S., 1970; s. Syed Fida and Zeenat (Hussain) H.; m. Noreen Shah, Mar. 15, 1969. BS in Chem. Engring. with honors, Imperial Coll. of Sci. and Tech., 1967; MBA, Harvard U., 1972. Chem. engr., sales mgr. Dawood Corp., Lahore, Pakistan, 1967-70; sales rep. Richardson-Vicks, NYC, 1970; project mgr., corp. planning Sandoz Pharms. Corp., East Hanover, NJ, 1972-74; mgr. planning Dorsey Labs. div. Sandoz Pharms. Corp., Lincoln, Nebr., 1974-76, dir. mktg., 1975-80; CEO Sandoz Pakistan, Karachi, Pakistan, 1980-83; gen. mgr. Sandoz Pharms. Corp., East Hanover, NJ, 1984—86, COO, 1986—87, CEO, 1987-89; pres. Wyeth Ayerst Labs., St. David's, Pa., 1989-93; sr. v.p. global pharm. Am. Home Products, Madison, NJ, 1993—95, exec. v.p., bd. dirs., 1995-97; CEO Pharmacia Corp., Peapack, NJ, 1997—2003, chmn., 2001—03; chmn., dir., CEO Schering-Plough Corp., Kenilworth, NJ, 2003—. Bd. dirs. Avon Products Inc.; chmn. Health Care Inst. of NJ. Named CEO of Yr. in global pharmaceutical industry, Financial Times, 1999. Mem. Alliance for Aging Rsch. (past bd. dirs.), Pharm. Rsch. & Mfrs. Am. (past chmn.). Office: Schering-Plough Corp 2000 Galloping Hill Rd Kenilworth NJ 07033*

HASSAN, IBNE, lawyer, diplomat, political philosopher, international strategist; b. Najibabad, India, Jan. 2, 1938; s. Alhaj M. Abdul Aziz and Hasrat Jehan Begum. BA in Pub. Law and Govt., Purdue U., 1963; MA in Internat. Rels., Fordham U., 1964; PhD in Polit. Econ., Columbia U., 1966; PhD in Pub. Adminstrn., NYU, 1968; PhD in Internat. Rels., Oxford (Eng.) U., 1972; LLB, LLM, PhD in Internat. Law, Cambridge (Eng.) U., 1977. CEO Fgn. Devel. Corp., N.Y.C., London, Geneva, 1965-81; dir. gen. Kalos World Order Found., N.Y.C., 1971-81; prin. assessor Found. New World Edn., Geneva, 1972-77; sr. assoc. Fletcher Sch. Law and Diplomacy, Tufts U., Medford, 1978-79; permanent rep. to UN Ctr. Devel. Policy, Washington, 1981-85; spl. rep. Inst. Internat. Security Studies, Washington, 1981-85; chief commr. Commn. Mid. Ea. Affairs, Washington, 1981-85; disting. prof. Sch. Advanced Internat. Studies, Johns Hopkins U., Washington, 1981-83; regional pres. Internat. Law Chambers, Washington, Hague, Islamabad, 1986—. Sr. fellow UN, N.Y.C., 1970-71, spl. advisor, 1983-85, mission assessor, 1994-96, spl. rep., 1998—, chmn. culture peace commn., 2005—, coord. millennium devel. goals, N.Y., 2005—, spl. adv., goodwill amb. spirulina conv., Rome, 2005—; dir. Oxford Conf. Internat. Affairs, 1970, Philip Jessup Moot Internat. Law, Cambridge, Eng., 1975; mem. faculty bd. law, Cambridge (Eng.) U., 1974-77; vis. assoc. U. Inst. High Internat. Studies, Geneva U., 1971-72; mem. adv. bd. World Peace News, N.Y.C., 1977-81; sr. fellow, vis. scholar Harvard U., Cambridge, Mass., 1977-78, 86-87; vis. scholar Yale U., New Haven, 1978-79, Columbia U., N.Y.C., 1996-98; vis. fellow Princeton U., 1979-80; regional rep. World Fedn. UN Assns., 1970-71, Internat. Students Movement for the UN, 1970-71; legal assoc. Internat. Law Commn., 1971-72; jud. asst. Internat. Ct. Justice, 1973-74 Contbr. numerous treatises and articles to polit. and legal publs. Chmn. Culture of Peace Commn., N.Y.C., 2005—; coord. Millennium Devel. Goals, N.Y.C., 2005—; spl. advisor, goodwill amb. Spirulina Conv., Rome, 2005—. Recipient Hyder Meml. award of merit, Aligarh U., 1951, Lit. award of merit, Majlis-i-Ilmistan, 1958, Internat. award of merit, Purdue U., 1962, Purdue Calumet award, 1962, Coldrush Medallion award, 1963, Acad. Excellence award, Purdue Hassars, 1963, Student of Yr. award, Internat. Reporter, 1962, Quaid-i-Azan award of merit, Oxford U. Pakistan Soc., 1968, Meritorious Achievement award, New World Edn. Found., 1972, World Peace award, World Peace News, 1977, World Order award, Kalos World Order, 1978, Disting. Achievement award, WAFUNIF, 2001, Wall of Tolerance award, Campaign for Tolerance, 2004; fellow, UN, 1968, 1970, Hague Acad. Internat. Law, 1972, 1974—75, 1994, Internat. Inst. Human Rights, 1975—76, Inst. Internat. Law & Rels., 1976—77, 1979, 1981, 1986, 1994, 1996; scholar, Inst. World Affairs, 1964—65; Litigious fellow, European Ct. Human Rights, 1972—73. Fellow World Lit. Acad., Acad. of Polit. Sci.; mem. Am. Soc. Internat. Law, Global Policy Forum, Internat. Polit. Sci. Assn., Internat. Bar Assn., Internat. Peace Bur., Punjab Bar Coun., Internat. Soc. for Mil. Law, UN Assn. (UK, USA, Pakistan), Internat. Law Assn., Internat. Econ. Soc., Internat. Devel. Coun., Soc. for Internat. Devel., Royal Commonwealth Soc., Royal Inst. Internat. Affairs, Pakistan Inst. Internat. Affairs, Internat. Inst. Strategic Studies, Fedn. Internat. des Avocats, Carnegie Coun., Am. Polit. Sci. Assn., World Jurist Coun., Rhodes Scholars Assn., Oxford Soc., Oxford Union Soc., Cambridge Soc., Cambridge Union Soc., Harvard Coun. Internat. Rels., Harvard Grad. Soc., World Inst. Achievements, Oxford Mgmt. Soc., Pi Sigma Alpha. Avocations: gardening, painting, photography, music, riding. Office Phone: 212-963-3110. Personal E-mail: ibnehassan_un@yahoo.com. Business E-Mail: wafunif@wafunif.org.

HASSAN, SONIA SHAWKY, medical educator; BA, U. Mich., 1990; MD, Wayne State U., 1994. Bd. cert. ACOG, 2002, Am. Bd. Maternal Fetal Medicine, 2004. Intern, resident in ob-gyn. Wayne State U., Detroit, 1994—98, physician, asst. prof., 2001—. Fellow, ACOG, 2002; grantee, Children's Rsch. Ctr. of Mich., 2002—; Maternal-Fetal Medicine fellow, Wayne State U., 1998—2001, Women's Reproductive Health Rsch. scholar, NIH, 2002—. Assn. Profs. Ob-Gyn. Mem.: ACOG, Ctrl. Assn. Ob-Gyn. (Young Investigator's award 1999, Cert. of Merit 2000), Soc. Maternal-Fetal Medicine (assoc.). Office: WSU Hutzel Womens Hosp Dept OB GYN Divsn Maternal Fetal Med 3990 John R Box 163 Detroit MI 48201 Office Phone: 313-993-1368.

HASSE, JOHN EDWARD, music curator; b. Aberdeen, SD, Nov. 20, 1948; s. Merten Milton Hasse and Gladys Irene Elizabeth Johnson; 1 child, Leanne Alexandra. BA cum laude with distinction, Carleton Coll., 1971; MA, Ind. U., 1975, PhD, 1981; LHD (hon.), Walsh U., 2001. Cert. in Bus. Adminstrn. U. Pa., 1981. Founder, campaign mgr. Minnesotans for McGovern, Mpls., 1971—72; rsch. asst. Ind. U., Bloomington, 1973—74, assoc. instr., 1974—75, project coord., 1979—81; brand asst. Proctor & Gamble, Cin., 1982—83; dir. Sounds of Ind. Project, Cin., 1983—84; cur. Am. music Nat. Mus. Am. History, Smithsonian Instn., DC, 1984—. Chief advisor legends of Am. music stamp series US Postal Svc., 1989—99; founder Smithsonian Jazz Masterworks Orch., 1991, exec. dir., 1991—99; co-dir. Am.'s Jazz Heritage, 1992—96; pub. spkr. in field, 1993—; mem. Def. New Orleans Jazz Commn., 1996—; founder jazz appreciation month; interviewee in field. Co-prodr., co-annotator: Indiana Ragtime: A Documentary Album, 1981 (ASCAP Deems Taylor award, 1982); editor: Ragtime: Its History, Composers, and Music, 1985 (ASCAP Deems Taylor award, 1986), Jazz: The First Century, 2000; author, prodr.: book, Compact Disc set The Classic Hoagy Carmichael, 1988 (Grammy Award nominations for Best Hist. Album, Best Album Notes, 1989, Best Hist. Popular Album award by Music Retailers' Assn., 1989), curator: traveling exhbn. Beyond Category: The Musical Genius of Duke Ellington, 1993—2000; author: Beyond Category: The Life and Genius of Duke Ellington, 1993, (book) I Love You When, 2000; author, assoc. prodr.: booklet, Compact Disc set Beyond Category, 1995; co-curator Ella Fitzgerald: First Lady of Song, 1997—. Del. Dem. Nat. Conv., Miami Beach, 1972. Recipient Disting. Alumni Achievement award, Carlton Coll., 1996; vis. scholar fellow, Danforth Found., 1975—78. Mem.: Soc. Am. Music (mem. bd. trustees 1991—93), Nat. Acad. Recording Arts and Scis. (mem. hall of fame elections com. 1990—96), Internat. Assn. Jazz Edn. (sec. 2002—04), Am. Musicological Soc. (cultural diversity com. 1995—97), Soc. Ethnomusicology (life; editl. bd. mem. 1974—78).

HASSEL, RUDOLPH CHRISTOPHER, language educator; b. Richmond, Va., Nov. 16, 1939; s. Rudolph Christopher and Helen Elizabeth (Poehler) H.; m. Sedley Louise Hotchkiss, June 16, 1962; children: Bryan Christopher, Paul Sedley. BA, U. Richmond, 1961; MA, U. N.C., 1962; PhD, Emory U., 1968. English instr. Mercer U., Macon, Ga., 1962-65; asst. prof. Vanderbilt U., Nashville, 1968-73, assoc. prof., 1973-85, prof., 1985—. Dir. grad. studies English dept. Vanderbilt U., 1974-81, dir. undergrad. studies, 1991, 99-00; mem. exec. com. Folger Inst., Washington, 1986-95; cons. State of Tenn., Nashville, 1987-93; cons. for various univ. presses and profl. jours. Author: Renaissance Drama and the English Church Year, 1979, Faith and Folly in Shakespeare's Romantic Comedies, 1980, Songs of Death, 1987, Shakespeare's Religious Language: A Dictionary, 2005; contbr. articles to Shakespeare Quar., Shakespeare Jahrbuch, Comparative Drama, Studies in Philology, others, poems to Vanderbilt Rev., Arts and Letters. Mem. choir Christ Episcopal Ch., Nashville, 1974-95, outreach vol., 1974—, vestryman, 1980-83; vol. United Way, Vanderbilt U., 1980—, Habitat for Humanity. Woodrow Wilson Found. fellow, 1962; Emory U. fellow, 1965; Folger Libr. fellow, 1976; Am. Philol. Soc. fellow, 1986. Mem. MLA, Internat. Shakespeare Assn., Shakespeare Assn. Am., Malone Soc. New Variorum Editor (Richard 3 vol.), Omicron Delta Kappa. Avocations: biking, hiking, tennis, gardening, woodcrafting. Home: 107 Pembroke Ave Nashville TN 37205-3728 Office: PO Box 129B Nashville TN 37202-0129 Business E-Mail: r.chris.hassel@vanderbilt.edu.

HASSELBACH, KARLHEINZ, literature educator; b. Giessen, Germany; arrived in US, 1965; s. Adolf and Elisabeth Hasselbach; m. Ingrid Tiesler, June 10, 1972. PhD, Philipps U., Marburg, Germany, 1971. Asst. prof. Fla. State U., Tallahasse, 1965—72; assoc. prof. Tulane U., New Orleans, 1974—86, prof., 1986—, chmn. dept. Germanic and Slavic languages, 1978—82, dept. chair Germanic and Slavic languages, 1989—95, emeritus, 2005. Author: The Dialects of the Region of the Central Vogelsberg in Germany (vol. 76 of Deutsche Dialekt Geographie), 1971, Thomas Mann: Doktor Faustus, 1978, 1986, Thomas Mann: Doktor Faustus, vol. 24 of Oldenbourg-Interpretationen, 1988, 1996, Georg Büchner: Lenz, 1986, Georg Büchner: Lenz, vol. 5 of Oldenbourg-Interpretationen, 1988, Bertolt Brecht: Kalendergeschichten, vol. 32 of Odlenbourg-Interpretationen, 1990, 1997, Georg Büchner, Reclam, 1997, 2d rev. edit., 1999; contbr. articles to profl. jours. on Thomas Mann, Ernst Jünger, romanticism, and socio-linguistics. Mem.: AAUP. Home: 7325 Maple St New Orleans LA 70118 Office: Tulane Univ Dept Germanic/Slavic Studies New Orleans LA 70118 Business E-Mail: hasselk@tulane.edu.

HASSELBECK, MATT, professional football player; b. Westwood, Mass., Sept. 25, 1975; m. Sarah Hasselbeck, 2000; 2 children. Grad., Boston Coll. Player Green Bay Packers, 1999—2001; quarterback Seattle Seahawks, 2001—. Named to Pro Bowl, 2003. Achievements include became the Seahawks all-time, highest-rated passer (83.9) in 2003. Has 1,282 career attemps and 769 completions for 9,084 yards, 50 touchdowns, and 33 interceptions. Office: Seattle Seahawks Qwest Field 800 Occidental Ave S Seattle WA 98134*

HASSELHOFF, DAVID, actor; b. Balt., July 17, 1952; m. Catherine Hickland (div.); m. Pamela Bach; children: Taylor-Ann, Hayley Amber. TV appearances include: (series) The Young and the Restless, 1975-82, Semi-Tough, 1980, Knight Rider, 1982-86; exec. prodr., star Baywatch, 1989-2000, Baywatch Nights, 1995—97; (movies) Griffin and Phoenix: A Love Story, 1976, Pleasure Cove, 1979, The Cartier Affair, 1984, Bridge Across Time, 1985, Perry Mason: The Case of the Lady in the Lake, 1988, Knight Rider the Movie, 1988, Panic at Malibu Pier, 1989, Knight Rider 2000, 1990, Ring of the Muskateers, 1992, Avalanche, 1994, Gridlock, 1996, NightMan, 1997, Nick Fury: Agent of Shield, 1998, Shaka Zulu: The Citadel, 2001; films include: Starcrash, 1979, Starke Zeiten, 1988, W.B. Blue and the Bean, 1989 (also co-prodr.), The Final Alliance, 1989, Legacy, 1998, The Big Tease, 1999, The Target Shoots First, 2000, Layover, 2001, The Spongebob Squarepants Movie, 2004; albums include Looking for Freedom, 1989 (Platinum), Crazy for You, 1991 (Gold), David, 1991 (Gold), Everybody's Sunshine, 1992 (Gold), You Are Everything, 1993 (Gold), Du, 1994, Best of David Hasselhoff, 1995, David Hasselhoff, 1995, Hooked on a Feeling, 1997, Magic Collection, 2000; (video) Baywatch: Forbidden Paradise, 1995. Recipient Star, Hollywood Walk of Fame, 1996. Office: # 250-7 4720 Lincoln Blvd Marina Del Rey CA 90292-6972

HASSELL, CLINTON ALTON, chemist, educator; b. Seagraves, Tex., Oct. 26, 1945; s. Clinton Andrew (Brit) and Virginia Cotten Hassell; m. Patricia Darnell Berryhill, June 12, 1947; children: Clint Alan, Sharina Michelle. BS, Baylor U., 1969; PhD, Tex. A&M U., 1975. Lectr. Tex. A&M U., College Station, 1976—79, vis. asst. prof., 1979—82; lectr. Baylor U., Waco, 1982—2000, sr. lectr., 2000—. Tour spkr. Am. Chem. Soc., Washington, 1979—; lectr. Tex. Engring. Ext. Svc., College Station, 1981—82; area supr. Baylor in Israel Archaeol. Dig, Tel Malhata, Israel, 1990—2000. Author: Test Item File for General Chemistry, 1997, 2002, Solutions Manual for General Chemistry, an Integrated Approach, 1996, 2005, Selected Solutions Manual for General Chemistry, an Integrated Approach, 1996, 2005, Chemical Investigations for Changing Times, 1992, 2004, Solving Problems in Chemistry, 1977, 2d abridged edit., 1981, Advanced Problems in Applied Chemistry, 2000; contbr.: Test Item File for General Chemistry, 7th edit., 2002; author: (novel) Chemistry in Whispering Caves, 1998; contbr. articles to profl. jours. Team mem. Marriage Encounter, Waco, Tex., 1983—93; dir. sunday sch. Ctrl. Bapt. Ch., Bryan, Tex., 1980—82; asst. dir. sunday sch. Columbus Ave. Bapt. Ch., Waco, Tex., 1983—88. Mem.: Phi Lambda Upsilon (life; treas. 1974—75), Sigma Pi Sigma (life). Avocation: coin collecting/numismatics. Office: Baylor Univ One Bear Plaza # 97348 Waco TX 76798 Office Phone: 254-710-4414. Business E-Mail: alton_hassell@baylor.edu.

HASSELL, DARRIS ANTHONY, Spanish educator; b. Ft. Jackson, SC, Aug. 4, 1969; s. Ray Allen and Laura Betty Ann Hassell. BA in Spanish, Wofford Coll., 1991; MA in Spanish Lit., U. SC, 2001. Workflow clk. SC. Nat. Bank, Columbia, 1991—92; Spanish tchr. Sumter (SC) H.S., 1992—94; adj. instr. of Spanish U. SC, Columbia, 1996—97, Lancaster, 1997—2001, Spanish instr., 2002—; elem. sch. Spanish tchr. V.V. Reid Elem. Sch., Columbia, 1997—2000. Fgn. lang. cons. SC Dept. of Edn., Columbia, 1996; specialized instrn. in Spanish Springs Meml. Hosp., Lancaster, 2002. Musician church music department CD recording; team member Nat. Grass Champions BB Divsn. Ch. steward, musician, sec. Sons of Allen Brown Chapel A.M.E. Ch., Columbia, 1998—2003. Named Man of the Year, Brown Chapel A.M.E. Church, 2002—03. Mem.: Kappa Alpha Psi (assoc.; polemarch 1990—91). Democrat. Methodist. Avocations: volleyball, travel, food, Spanish, conversation. Home: 6410 Easter St Columbia SC 29203-5065 Office: U SC-Lancaster PO Box 889 Lancaster SC 29721 Personal E-mail: hassell@gwm.sc.edu.

HASSELL, LEROY ROUNTREE, SR., state supreme court chief justice; b. Norfolk, Va., Aug. 17, 1955; BA in Govt. and Fgn. Affairs, U. Va., 1977; JD, Harvard U., 1980. Bar: Va. Former ptnr. McGuire, Woods, Battle and Boothe; assoc. justice Va. Supreme Ct., Richmond, 1989—2003, chief justice, 2003—. Former mem. Va. gen. assembly task force to study violence on sch. property. Former mem. adv. bd. Massey Cancer Ctr.; mem. policy com., former chmn. Richmond Sch. Bd.,; former bd. dirs. Richmond Renaissance, Inc., Richmond chpt. ARC, Garfield childs Fund, Carpenter Ctr. for Performing Arts, St. John's Hosp., Legal Aid Ctrl. Va.; vol. Richmond Pub. Schs., Hospice vol.; elected sch. bd. chmn. 4 terms. Recipient Liberty Bell award 1985, 86, Black Achievers award, 1985-86, Outstanding Young Citizen award Richmond Jaycees, 1987, Outstanding Young Virginian award Va. Jaycees, 1987; one of youngest persons to both serve on the Richmond Sch. Bd. and to serve as bd. chmn. Mem. Va. Trial Lawyers Assn., Assn. Trial Lawyers Am., Va. Assn. Def. Attys., Old Dominion Bar Assn., Va. Bar Assn. Office: Supreme Ct of Virginia PO Box 1315 Richmond VA 23218-1315

HASSELL, STEPHEN C., information technology executive; BS, US Naval Acad., Annapolis, 1988; MBA, Kellogg Sch., Northwestern, Chgo., 1995. Mgr. Newport News Shipbuilding, 1995—98, dir., process innovation, CIO, 1998, v.p., 2000; pres. & CEO Naptheon Inc. (subs. Newport News); chief info. officer Invensys; v.p. & chief info. officer Emerson Elec. Co., St. Louis, 2004—. Decorated Navy Commendation medal; named one of top tech. innovators, Info. Week mag., 2004; recipient CIO 100 award, CIO Mag. Office: Emerson Elec Co 8000 W Florissant Ave PO Box 4100 Saint Louis MO 63136--850

HASSELMAN, RICHARD B., retired rail transportation executive; b. Jersey City, Nov. 28, 1926; s. Benjamin R. and Clara A. (Borchert) H.; m. Mildred E. Schaber, May 29, 1954; children: Richard Dwight, James Christopher. BME, Yale U., 1947; MBA, NYU, 1949. Student engr. N.Y. Ctrl. R.R., 1947-49, trainee, 1949-52, brakeman, 1952-53, signalman, freight agt., 1953; transp. insp. Ea. region Syracuse, NY, 1953-55; trainmaster Mohawk divsn. Albany, NY, 1955-57; divsn. trainmaster Syracuse divsn., 1957; divsn. supt. Boston & Albany divsn. Springfield, Mass., 1957-59; dist. transp. supt. Western region Cleve., 1959-60; gen. supt. yards and terminals N.Y. Ctrl. Sys., N.Y.C., 1960-63; gen. mgr. Ind. Harbor Belt and Chicago River & Ind. R.R., Hammond, Ind., 1963; gen. mgr. No. Region N.Y. Ctrl. R.R., Detroit, 1964, gen. mgr. So. Region Indpls., 1964-66, gen. mgr. Western Region Cleve., 1967; asst. v.p. transp. N.Y. Ctrl. Sys., N.Y.C., 1967-68; v.p. transp. Penn. Ctrl., Phila., 1968-76; pres. Ind. Harbor Belt R.R., 1968-87; sr. v.p. ops. Consol. Rail Corp., Phila., 1976-89; transp. cons., 1989—. Home and Office: 5289 Ladyfinger Lake Rd Sanibel FL 33957-2436

HASSELMEYER, EILEEN GRACE, medical researcher; b. Bklyn., May 23, 1924; d. Edwin Allen and Margaret Grace (Cody) H. RN, Bellevue Sch. Nursing, 1946; BS, NYU, 1954, MA, 1956, PhD, 1963. Mem. staff Pediatric Metabolic and Nutritional Rsch. Svc., NYU Children's Med. Svc., Bellevue Hosp., N.Y.C., 1946-56, study coord., 1951-56; rsch. nursing supr. Met. Hosp., N.Y.C., 1951; lectr. pediatric nutrition rsch. U. Tex. Sch. Nursing, 1952-53; nursing dir. nutritional rsch. studies Children's Hosp. of John Seely Hosp. (U. Tex. Med. Br.), Galveston, 1952-53; lectr. and nursing rsch. assoc. nutritional svc. pediat. dept. Hosp. Infantile, Mexico City, 1953; nursing dir. rsch. unit Willowbrook State Sch., S.I., 1953-54; commd. USPHS, 1956, advanced through grades to asst. surgeon gen.-rear adm., 1981; ret. 1989; nurse cons. Divsn. Nursing Resources, Bur. Med. Svcs., USPHS, Washington, 1956-59; prin. investigator Handling and Premature Infant Behavior project, NYU, N.Y.C., 1961-63; sr. nurse cons. Div. Nursing, Bur. State Svcs., USPHS, Washington, 1963; spl. asst. for prematurity Office of Dir., Nat. Inst. Child Health and Human Devel., Bethesda, Md., 1963-66, acting dir. perinatal biology and infant mortality program, extramural programs, 1967-68, dir., 1969-74, asst. to dir. for perinatology, 1974-80; chief pregnancy and infancy br. Ctr. for Rsch. for Mothers and Children, 1974-79, acting chief clin. nutrition and early devel. br., 1979-80; assoc. dir. for sci. rev. Office of Dir., 1979-89; spl. asst. to dir. N.C. for Nursing Rsch., 1986-89; exec. dir. Uniform Svcs. U. Health Sci., Fed. Coll. Nursing Feasability Study Task Force, 1989-92. Annie W. Goodrich vis. prof. Yale U. Sch. Nursing, New Haven, 1968-69; asst. surgeon gen. USPHS, Dept. Health and Human Svcs., 1981-89, chmn. interagy. panel on sudden infant death syndrome, 1974-82, others. Contbr. articles to profl. jours. Recipient NICHD Recognition of Outstanding Performance, 1973, plaque for 25 yrs. dedicated svc., 1987, Chief Nurse Officer's medal USPHS, 1989; USUHS Commendable Svc. medal, 1990; USPHS Surgeon Gen.'s Cert. of Appreciation, 1990; HEW-USPHS Commendation medal, 1975; recipient Perinatal Research Soc. award, 1979; NYU Sch. Edn., Health, Nursing and Arts Professions Creative Leadership award, 1980; Achievement award Nat. Sudden Infant Death Syndrome Found., 1987, Eileen G. Hasselmeyer Disting. Sci. Achievement award Sudden Infant Death Syndrome Alliance, 1990; Outstanding Performance award NCNR, 1987, Meritorious Svc. medal HHS-USPHS, 1989; cert. appreciation NIH-NCNR, 1989; Nat. League for Nursing Commonwealth fellow, 1959-62; NIH fellow, 1962-63; Am. Nurses Found. grantee, 1962-63; State of Conn. Maternal and Infant Program grantee, 1969; Sigma Theta Tau research grantee, 1969-71; Yale U. Sch. Nursing developmental grantee, 1969; disting. alumnae award Bellevue Alumnae Assn., 1997. Mem. Pub. Health Svc. Commd. Officers Assn., Bellevue Alumnae Assn.

HASSELMO, ANN HAYES DIE, executive recruiter, consultant, psychologist, educator, retired academic administrator; b. Baytown, Tex., Aug. 15, 1944; d. Robert L. and Dorothy Ann (Cooke) Hayes; 1 child, Meredith Anne. BS with highest honors, Lamar U., 1966; MEd, U. Houston, 1969; PhD, Tex. A&M U., 1977. Lic. psychologist. Asst. prof. dept. psychology Lamar U., Beaumont, Tex., 1977—82, assoc. prof., dir. Psychol. Clinic, 1982—86, Regents prof. psychology, 1986, dir. grad. programs in psychology, 1981—86, pres. faculty senate, 1985—86; pvt. practice clin. psychology Beaumont, 1979—87; prof. Tulane U., New Orleans, 1988—92, dean Newcomb Coll., 1988—92, assoc. provost, 1991—92; pres., prof. psychology Hendrix Coll., Conway, Ark., 1992—2001, pres. emerita, 2001—; v.p., ptnr. higher edn. practice A.T. Kearney, Inc., Alexandra, Va., 2001—02; mng. dir. Acad. Search Consultation Svc., Washington, 2002—. Adminstr. adolescent residential unit Mental Health/Mental Retardation S.E. Tex., 1979-80, mem. cmty. adv. com., 1981-87; cons. in field; coordinating bd. Tex. Coll. and Univ. Sys. Internship, 1986, chair, bd. dirs. Ednl. and Instl. Ins. Adminstrs., 2000-02; bd. dirs. Nat. Merit Scholarship Corp., Acxiom Corp., Found. for Ind. Higher Edn., Air U., USAF. Contbr. articles to profl. jours. Mem. cmty. adv. com. Beaumont State Ctr. Human Devel., 1981-88; chair So. Collegiate Athletic Conf., 1996-97; participant Nat. Identification Program for Women, Am. Coun. on Edn., 1985, mem. govt. rels. commn., 1993-96, chmn., 1994-96, chmn. coun. of fellows, 1995-96, bd. dirs., 1997-2000; bd. dirs. Beaumont Civic Opera, Lamar U. Wesley Found., Tulane U. Wesley Found.; bd. govs. Isidore Newman Sch., 1991-92; trustee Robert Morris Coll., 1990-98, chmn. edn. com., 1990-94, chmn. pers. com., 1994-98; mem. univ. senate United Meth. Ch., 1993-01, chair commn. on instnl. rev., 1997-01; 1st v.p. Nat. Assn. Schs. & Colls. United Meth. Ch., 1996, pres. 1997-98; bd. dirs. Ouachita coun. Girl Scouts U.S., 1996-2000; mem. bd. visitors Air U., 1999—; mem. Internat. Women's Forum, 1995—, Ark. Women's Leadership Forum, 1999-02, pres. 2000-01; mem. Ark. Commn. to Streamline State Govt., 1996-98; mem. pres. commn. NCAA, 1997-01, chmn. div. III, 1999-2001, mem. exec. com. 1999-2001; chair Assoc. Coll. of the South, 1997-99; bd. dirs. Ark. Repertory Theatre, 2000-01, United Way of Faulkner County, 2000-01. Am. Coun. Edn. fellow Coll. William and Mary, 1986-87; recipient Regents Merit award, 1979, Coll. Health and Behavioral Sci. Merit award, 1982, Lamar U.; named one of Top 100 Women in Ark., Ark. Bus., 1995-99. Mem. APA, Southwestern Psychol. Assn., Family Svcs. Assn. (bd. dirs. 1988-89), Tex. Psychol. Assn. (dir. divsn. acad. psychologists 1986), S.E. Tex. Psychol. Assn. (treas. 1978-80, pres. 1983), Mental Health Assn. Jefferson County, Nat. Register Health Svc. Providers in Psychology, Nat. Assn. Ind. Colls. and Univs. (bd. dirs., vice chmn. 1995, chair 1996). Office: Acad Search Consultation Svc Ste 705 1825 K St NW Washington DC 20006

HASSELMO, NILS, academic administrator, linguist, educator; b. Kola, Sweden, July 2, 1931; arrived in U.S., 1958; s. A. Wilner and Anna Helena (Backlund) Hasselmo; m. Patricia June Tillberg, Oct. 25, 1958 (dec. Dec. 30, 2000); children: Nils Peter, Michael Erik, Anna Patricia; m. Ann Hayes, Nov. 8, 2003. Fil. mag., Uppsala U., 1956, Fil. lic., 1962, PhD (hon.), 1979; BA, Augustana Coll., Ill., 1957, DHL (hon.), 1995; PhD, Harvard U., 1961; LHD (hon.), North Park Coll. Theol. Sem., 1992. Asst. prof. Swedish Augustana Coll., Rock Island, Ill., 1958—59, 1961—62; from assoc. prof. to prof. Scandinavian langs. and lit. U. Minn., Mpls., 1965—83, 1988—, chmn. Scandinavian langs. and lit., 1970—73; dir. U. Minn. Ctr. for N.W. European Langs. and Area Studies, Mpls., 1970—73; assoc. dean U. Minn. Coll. Liberal Arts, Mpls., 1973—78; v.p. for adminstrn. and planning U. Minn., Mpls., 1980—83, pres., 1988—97; sr. v.p. acad. affairs, provost U. Ariz., Tucson, 1983—88, prof. English and linguistics, 1983—88; pres. Assn. Am. Univs.,

Washington, 1998—. Vis. com. dept. Germanic langs. and lit. Harvard U., Cambridge, Mass., 1981—86; trustee Nat. Merit Scholarship Corp., 1992—97. Author: Amerikasvenska, 1974, Swedish America: An Introduction, 1976; editor: Perspectives on Swedish Immigration, 1978. Active Gov.'s Task Force on Technology and Improvement of Employment, Minn., 1982—83; trustee Am. Scandinavian Found., 1992—; bd. dirs. Swedish Coun. Am., 1978—, chmn. bd., 1999—2001; bd. dirs. Walker Art Ctr., 1989—95; bd. overseers Mpls. Coll. Art and Design, 1982—83; bd. dirs. Carnegie Found. for Advancement of Tchg., 2002—, Coun. Libr. and Info. Resources, 1999—. Sgt. Royal Signal Corps Swedish Army, 1951—54. Decorated Royal Order of North Star Sweden; named Swedish-Am. of Yr., Swedish Govt. and Vasa Order Am., 1991; recipient King Carl XVI Gustaf's Bicentennial medal in Gold, Sweden, 1976, Ellis Island medal of honor, 1993; Fulbright-Hays fellow, 1968—69. Mem.: MLA, Nat. Acad. Forum Info. Tech. and Rsch. U., Univ. Rsch. Assn. (trustee 1993—97), Nat. Assn. State Univs. and Land Grant Colls. (exec. com. acad. affairs coun. 1986—88, chmn. coun. pres. and chancellors 1992—93, chair bd. 1994—95), Swedish-Am. Hist. Soc. (chmn. bd. 1984—86), Royal Gustavus Adolphus Acad., Vetenskaps-Soc., Linguistic Soc. Am., Soc. for Advancement Scandinavian Study (pres. 1971—73). Office Phone: 202-408-7500. Business E-Mail: nils_hasselmo@aau.edu.*

HASSENFELD, ALAN GEOFFREY, consumer products company executive; b. Providence, Nov. 16, 1948; s. Merrill Lloyd and Sylvia (Kay) H.; married. BA, U. Pa., 1970. Asst. to pres. Hasbro, Inc., Pawtucket, RI, 1970—72, v.p. internat. ops., 1972-78, v.p. mktg. and sales, 1978-80, exec. v.p., 1980-84, pres., 1984-89, chmn., CEO, 1989—2003, chmn., 2003—. Dir. Hasbro, Inc., 1978; dir. exec. com. Internat. Tennis Hall Fame, 1998; dir. Salesforce.com, 2004. Dir. Hasbro Children's Found., Shoah Found., Milken Family Found., Jewish Fedn. RI, 1989, Refugees Internat., 1992; bd. gov. Miriam Hosp., 1984, Operation Smile, 2002; bd. overseers (dean's coun.) Sch. Arts and Sci., U. Pa., 1986, Kennedy Sch. Govt., Harvard, 1995, mem. exec. com., 2003; bd. overseers (dean's coun.) Harvard Sch. Pub. Health, 1997, Rosenberg Inst. Brandeis, 2002; trustee Deerfield Acad., 1996, U. Pa., 1999, US Coun. Internat. Bus., 2002, Save the Bay, 2003, Bryant Coll., 2004; trustee emeritus Brown U.; mem. adv. com. Big Brothers RI, Internat. Inst. RI; mem. exec. com. Brown U. Civic Leadership Coun., Commodores RI; chmn. Right Now! Coalition, 1991, World Scholar Athlete Games, 1996, RISOP, 2002, Jerusalem Found., 2004. Office: Hasbro Inc 1027 Newport Ave Pawtucket RI 02862

HASSENGER, JAMES MICHAEL, writer, retired small business owner; b. Sioux City, Iowa, Dec. 9, 1926; s. Ralph Joseph and Eva Sylvia Hassenger; m. Joann C. Bendixen, Nov. 14, 1951 (div. Oct. 14, 1983); children: Susan, Michael, Timothy, Juliana, Elizabeth, James, Daniel. BS, Creighton U., Omaha, 1948; MA, U. S.D., 1993. Sales exec. Hassenger Bros. Ins., Sioux City, Iowa, 1948—50; owner Quality Beverage, Sioux City, 1950—52, Hassenger Import Motors, Sioux City, 1952—63, Citizens Loan and Thrift, Sioux City, 1963—80, KBCM FM radio sta., Sioux City, 1973—83; author, pub. Marriage Enhancement Ctr., Sioux City, 1988—. Pres. Iowa Consumer Loan Assn., 1981—83. Author: (book) Marriage Enhancement Guide, 2001, Marriage #101, 2004. Divsn. mgr. Sioux City C of C., 1979; pres. Mariners Swim Club, Sioux City, 1980. Midshipman USN, 1944—46. Mem.: Am. Counseling Assn. Avocations: flying, golf. Home and Office: Marriage Enhancement Ctr 520 Buckwalter Dr Sioux City IA 51104 Office Phone: 712-239-2347. Office Fax: 712-239-2347. E-mail: jimhassenger@mindspring.com.

HASSETT, JAMES MANNING, small business owner, psychology educator; b. N.Y.C., June 22, 1947; s. John and Jean (Manning) H.; m. Patricia Ann Dugan, Nov. 26, 1977; 1 child, Eileen. BS in Psychology, Fordham U., 1969; MA in Psychology, Harvard U., 1971, PhD in Psychology, 1975. Asst. prof. Wellesley (Mass.) Coll., 1974-75, Boston U., 1974-84; assoc. editor Psychology Today, N.Y.C., 1977-80; cons. editor Addison-Wesley Pub., Reading, Mass., 1984; rsch. psychologist Sci. Systems, Inc., Cambridge, Mass., 1984-85; pres. Brattle Systems, Inc., Arlington, Mass., 1985—. Adj. assoc. prof. Boston U., 1985—93. Author: A Primer of Psychophysiology, 1978, Psychology in Perspective, 1984, (with others), 2d edit., 1989; contbr. articles to profl. jours. NSF fellow, 1969; recipient Sci. Writers award ADA, 1978; recipient Small Bus. Prime Contractor award of excellence SBA, 1997; named Prime Contractor of Yr. for New Eng. SBA, 1999. Office: Brattle Systems Inc 1100 Massachusetts Ave Arlington MA 02476-4332 E-mail: jhassett@brattlesystems.com.

HASSETT, JOSEPH MARK, lawyer; b. Buffalo, May 1, 1943; m. Carol A. Melton, June 23, 1984; children: Matthew, Meredith. BA summa cum laude, Canisius Coll., 1964; LL.B. cum laude, Harvard U., 1967; MA with 1st class honors, Univ. Coll. Dublin, 1981, PhD, 1985. Bar: N.Y. 1967, D.C. 1970, U.S. Supreme Ct. 1976. Assoc. Hogan & Hartson, Washington, 1970-74, ptnr., 1974—. Bd. trustees Canisius Coll. Author: Yeats and the Poetics of Hate, 1986; contbr. articles to profl. publs. Mem.: ABA, D.C. Bar Assn. Home: 6035 Crimson Ct Mc Lean VA 22101-1818 Office: 555 13th St NW Washington DC 20004-1109 Office Phone: 202-637-5600. Business E-Mail: jmhassett@hhlaw.com.

HASSETT, VALERIE JANE, interior designer, architect, educator; b. San Diego, Dec. 22, 1962; d. Roger John and Cecelia Virginia (Cibarich) H. Student, U. Tenn., 1982—86; BFA in Interior Design, Va. Commonwealth U., Richmond, 1988; MArch, Va. Poly. U., Alexandria, 1993. Registered profl. interior designer, Va., cert. constrn. documents technologist, registered profl. architect, Va., cert. Nat. Coun. of Archtl. Registration Bds., Nat. Coun. for Interior Design Qualification (NCIDQ). Interior arch. Washington Area Transit Authority, 1988-90, 91-92, Prince William County Va. Govt., 1993-96, RTKL, Balt., 1996-97; instr. Mt. Vernon Coll. at George Washington U., Washington, 1997-99; project mgr., head interior design dept. Sharadan, Behm, Eustice and Assocs. Ltd., Arlington, Va., 1997—; assoc. prof. No. Va. C.C., 2000—. Mem. professions fellowship rev. panel AAUW, 2003—. Exhibitions include Nat. Bldg. Mus., 1995, 1996. Chmn. women in architecture film festival Nat. Mus. Women in the Arts, 1998, 2000; Va. State Govt. & Industry Affairs Commn., 2003—. Mem. AIA (bd. dirs., 1998-, v.p. 2003, chair women in architecture com. No. Va. chpt. 1993—), Internat. Interior Design Assn. (past pres. Mid-Atlantic chpt., Herb Ginsburg Leadership award 2005), Neighborhood Design Ctr. Balt. Avocation: paper making. Office: Sheridan Behm Eustice & Assocs 3440 Fairfax Dr Arlington VA 22201-4431 Personal E-mail: vjhassett@aol.com.

HASSEVOORT, CHRISTINE, music educator, singer; b. Nebr. d. Bill and Sharon Beck; m. Darrin Hassevoort; 1 child, Sophia. MusM, Bob Jones U., 1997. Adj. instr. of music Bryan Coll., Dayton, Tenn., 1997—2000; instr. of music Chattanooga State Tech Comm Coll., 2000—; adj. instr. of music Lee U., Cleve., Tenn., 2000—03. Mem.: Music Educators Nat. Conf., Nat. Assn. of Teachers of Singing. Christian. Office: Chattanooga State Tech Comm College 4501 Amnicola Hwy Chattanooga TN 37404

HASSEY, L. PATRICK, metal products executive; married; 6 children. Degree, Calif. State U., Long Beach, Calif. From mgr. sales and mktg. to exec. v.p. Alcoa Inc., 1990—2000, exec. v.p., 2000—03, group pres. Alcoa Indsl. Components, 2000—03; cons. Allegheny Technologies Inc., Pitts., 2003, pres., CEO, 2003—, CEO, 2003—. Office: Allegheny Technologies Inc 1000 Six PPG Pl Pittsburgh PA 15222

HASSID, SAMI, architect, educator; b. Cairo, Apr. 19, 1912; came to U.S., 1957, naturalized, 1962; s. Joseph S. and Isabelle (Israel) H.; m. Juliette Mizrahi, June 29, 1941; children: Fred, Muriel. Diploma in architecture with distinction, Sch. Engring., Giza, Egypt, 1932; BA in Architecture with honors, U. London, Eng., 1935; M.Arch., U. Cairo, 1943; PhD in Architecture, Harvard U., 1956. Tchr. Alexandria (Egypt) Tech. Sch., 1932-34; successively tchr., lectr., asst. prof. U. Cairo, 1934-56; prof. architectural theory and design U. Ein-Shams, Cairo, 1957; mem. faculty U. Calif., Berkeley, 1957—, prof. architecture, 1964-79, prof. emeritus, 1979—; also assoc. dean U. Calif. (Coll. Environ. Design), 1977-83, faculty asst. to vice-chancellor for campus planning, 1980-85, dir. campus planning office, 1983-84; archtl. practice Cairo, 1932-57, Berkeley, 1957-85; from draftsman to sr. designer office Ali Labib Gabr (architect), Cairo, 1935-47; ptnr. Sami Hassid and Youssef Shafik, Cairo, 1947-57, Hassid and Kelemen, Berkeley, 1963-65. Author: The Sultan's Turrets, 1939, Architectural Construction Details, 1954, Development and Application of a System for Recording Critical Evaluations of Architectural Works, 1964, Architectural Education U.S.A, 1967, (with others) Innovations in Housing Design and Construction Techniques as Applied to Low-Cost Housing, 1969, Surface Materials in Architecture, 1970, Doctoral Studies in Architecture, 1971, Methods for the Development of Shipboard Habitability Design Criteria, 1974, Fire Safety in Buildings, A Course Offering Package, 1976, (with others) The Berkeley Campus Space Plan, 21 publs., 1981-83; Proc. Workshop on Seismic Upgrading of Existing Bldgs., NSF, 1982; prin. works include Hill House; student hostel, Am. U. Cairo, 1952. Commr. Calif. Bd. Archtl. Examiners, 1961-71. Fulbright grantee, 1954-56; recipient First prize Al-Chams Competition, Cairo, 1947, First prize San Francisco AIA Hdqrs. Competition, 1963 Fellow AIA; mem. Bldg. Research Inst., Assn. Collegiate Schs. Architecture. Democrat. Jewish (trustee temple; v.p. East Bay synagogue council 1970-71). Home: Sami Hassid FAIA 2851 Rockridge Dr Pleasant Hill CA 94523

HASSLER, DONALD MACKEY, II, English language educator, writer; b. Akron, Ohio, Jan. 3, 1937; s. Donald Mackey and Frances Elizabeth (Parsons) H.; m. Diana Cain, Oct. 8, 1960 (dec. Sept. 1976); children: Donald, David; m. Sue Smith, Sept. 13, 1977; children: Shelly, Heather. BA (Sloan fellow), Williams Coll., 1959; MA (Woodrow Wilson fellow), Columbia U., 1960, PhD, 1967. Instr. U. Montreal, 1961-65; instr. English Kent (Ohio) State U., 1965-67, asst. prof., 1967-71, assoc. prof., 1971-76, prof., 1977—, acting dean honors and exptl. coll., 1979-81, dir., 1973-83, coord. writing cert. program, 1986-91, chmn. undergrad. studies, 1987-91, dir. Wick Poetry Competition, 1987-91, coord. grad. studies, 1991-94; sec. faculty senate Kent (Ohio State U., 1996—, coord. maj. program, 1998—. Author: Erasmus Darwin, 1974, The Comedian as the Letter D: Erasmus Darwin's Comic Materialism, 1973, Asimov's Golden Age: The Ordering of an Art, 1977, Hal Clement, 1982, Comic Tones in Science Fiction, 1982, Patterns of the Fantastic, 1983, Patterns of the Fantastic II, 1984, Death and the Serpent, 1985, Isaac Asimov, 1991; mng. editor Jour. Extrapolation, 1986-87, co-editor, 1987-89, editor, 1990-2001, exec. editor, 2002—; co-editor (with Sue Hassler) Letters of Arthur Machen and Montgomery Evans, 1923-1947, 1993, (with Clyde Wilcox) Political Science Fiction, 1997; adv. editl. bd. Hellas, 1988—; editl. bd. Paradoxa, 1994—. Co-chmn. Kent Am. Revolution Bicentennial Commn., 1974-77; deacon Presbyn. Ch., 1971-74, elder, 1974-77; sec. Kent State Faculty Senate, 1996—, chancellor's faculty adv. com., 1996—, univ. priorities and budget adv. coun., 1998—; spkr. Smithsonian Yesterday's Tomorrow's exhibit, 2003; mem. Kent State U. Press Bd., 2004—; trustee Covington Hist. Soc., 2005—. Recipient J. Lloyd Eaton award, Eaton Libr. Collection U. Calif., Riverside, 1993. Mem. Sci. Fiction Rsch. Assn. (treas. 1983-84, 2005—, pres. 1985-86, Thomas D. Clareson award 2001), Kiwanis (bd. dirs. 1974-76), Phi Beta Kappa (pres. 1983-84). Home: 1226 Woodhill Dr Kent OH 44240-2832 Office Phone: 330-672-1706. Business E-Mail: extrap@kent.edu.

HASSLER, JON FRANCIS, novelist; b. Mpls., Mar. 30, 1933; s. Leo Blaise and Ellen Frances (Callinan) H.; children: Michael, Elizabeth, David. BA, St. John's U., 1955; MA, U. N.D., 1961; LLD (hon.), Assumption Coll., 1993, U. N.D., 1994, U. Notre Dame, 1996. Tchr. Melrose, Fosston, Park Rapids (Minn.) High Schs., 1955-65, Bemidji State U., Minn., 1965-68, Brainerd C.C., Minn., 1968-80; regents prof. St. John's U., Collegeville, Minn., 1981—97. Author: Staggerford, 1977 (Friends of Am. Writers Novel of Yr. award 1978), Four Miles to Pinecone, 1977, Simon's Night, 1979, Jemmy, 1980, The Love Hunter, 1981, A Green Journey, 1985, Grand Opening, 1987 (Soc. of Midland Authors Best Work of Fiction award 1988), North of Hope, 1990, Dear James, 1993, Rookery Blues, 1995, The Dean's List, 1997, The Staggerford Murders and The Life and Death of Nancy Clancy's Nephew, 2004, The Staggerford Flood, 2002, The New Woman, 2005. Guggenheim fellow, 1980, Minn. State Arts Bd. fellow, 1979, 85. Roman Catholic. Office: St John's Univ Collegeville MN 56321 E-mail: johassl@aol.com.

HASSON, JAMES KEITH, JR., lawyer, educator; b. Knoxville, Tenn., Mar. 3, 1946; s. James Keith and Elaine (Biggers) Hasson; m. Jayne Young, July 27, 1968; 1 child, Keith Samuel. BA, Duke U., 1967; JD, 1970. Bar: Ga. 1971, DC 1971. Assoc. Sutherland, Asbill & Brennan, Atlanta, 1970—76; ptnr., 1976; prof. law Emory U., Atlanta, 1976—94; chmn. bd. dir. House-Hasson Hardware Co., Knoxville, 2000—. Editor: Jour. Taxation; contbr. articles profl. jour. Mem. Atlanta Civilian Rev. Bd.; trustee Met. Atlanta Crime Commn., chmn., 1986—87; trustee Foxfire Fund, 1988—2001, chmn. bd. dirs.; chmn. bd. trustees Reinhardt Coll., 2001—. Recipient Pres. Disting. Svc. award, 1980. Mem.: ABA (com. chmn. 1983—85), Atlanta Bar Assn. (counsel 1977—80), Leadership Atlanta, Lawyers Club. Presbyterian. Home: 3185 Chatham Rd NW Atlanta GA 30305-1101 Office: Sutherland Asbill & Brennan 999 Peachtree St NE Ste 2300 Atlanta GA 30309-3996 Office Phone: 404-853-8083. Business E-Mail: jim.hasson@sablaw.com.

HASSON, KIRKE MICHAEL, lawyer; b. East St. Louis, Ill., Oct. 25, 1949; s. David S. and Audrey (Leber) Hasson. BA magna cum laude, Yale U., 1971; JD cum laude, Harvard U., 1974. Bar: Calif. 1974, U.S. Dist. Ct. (all dist. Calif.), US Ct. Appeals (2d, 5th, 9th cir.). Assoc. Pillsbury Winthrop Shaw Pittman LLP (formerly Pillsbury Winthrop LLP), San Francisco, 1974—81, ptnr., 1982—2005, ptnr., chmn. life sci. and tech. group, mem. mng. bd., 2004—. Office: Pillsbury Winthrop Shaw Pittman LLP 50 Fremont St San Francisco CA 94105 Office Phone: 415-983-1077. Office Fax: 415-983-1200. E-mail: kirke.hasson@pillsburylaw.com.

HAST, ADELE, editor, writer, historian; b. NYC, Dec. 6, 1931; d. Louis and Kate (Miller) Krongelb; m. Malcolm Howard Hast, Feb. 1, 1953; children: David Jay, Howard Arthur. BA magna cum laude, Bklyn. Coll., 1953; MA, U. Iowa, 1969, PhD, 1979. Rsch. assoc. Atlas Early Am. History Project, Newberry Library, Chgo., 1971-75; assoc. dir. Atlas Great Lakes Indian History Project, 1976-79, Hist. Boundary Data File Project, 1979-81; editor in chief Marquis Who's Who, Inc., Chgo., 1981-86; survey dir. Nat. Opinion Rsch. Ctr., U. Chgo., 1986-89; rsch. fellow Newberry Libr., Chgo., 1989-95, scholar in residence, 1995—; exec. editor St. James Press, Chgo., 1990-92; mng. editor Hist. Ency. of Chgo. Women U. Ill., Chgo., 1991-93, dir., editor Hist. Ency. of Chgo. Women project, 1993-2001, sr. rsch. assoc. Ctr. for Rsch. on Women and Gender, 1999—. Mem. faculty Newberry Libr. Summer Inst. Cartography, 1980. Author: Loyalism in Revolutionary Virginia, 1982, American Leaders Past and Present: The View from Who's Who in America, 1985; compiler: Iowa, Missouri, vol. 4 of Historical Atlas and Chronology of County Boundaries, 1788-1980, 1984; editor: International Directory of Company Histories, vols. 3-5, 1991-92, Women Building Chicago 1790-1990: A Biographical Dictionary, 2001; assoc. editor: Atlas of Great Lakes Indian History, 1987; curator exhibit on Chgo. history Spertus Inst. of Jewish Studies, 2002-03; contbr. articles to profl. jours. Mem. profl. adv. grad. program pub. history Loyola U., 1986—; treas., bd. dirs. Chgo. Map Soc., 1980-81, 93-95; mem. New Trier Twp. H.S. Bd. Caucus, 1972-74; mem. acad. coun. Am. Jewish Hist. Soc., 1985—; pres. Chgo. Jewish Hist. Soc., 1980-81, bd. dirs., 1977—. Recipient Alumna of Yr. award Bklyn. Coll., 1984, Colonial Williamsburg Found. grantee-in-aid, 1975, Brit. Acad. rsch. fellow, 1979; Am. Coun. Learned Socs. grantee-in-aid, 1980; NEH rsch. grantee, 1985, 87, 93-95, 97-98, fellow Jewish Women's Archive, 2003—. Fellow Royal Hist. Soc., Phi Beta Kappa, Kappa Delta Pi; mem. Am. Hist. Assn., Orgn. Am. Historians, Chgo. Area Women's History Coun. (sec., treas. 1994-2004, bd. dirs. 1990—), Caxton Club (coun. 1990-93, 2003—, v.p. 2005—). Office: Newberry Library 60 W Walton St Chicago IL 60610-3380

HAST, MALCOLM HOWARD, biomedical scientist, medical educator; b. NYC, May 28, 1931; s. Irving William and Rose Lillian (Berlin) H.; m. Adele Krongelb, Feb. 1, 1953; children: David Jay, Howard Arthur. BA, Bklyn. Coll., 1953; postgrad., U. So. Calif., 1955-57; MA, Ohio State U., 1958, PhD (NIH fellow), 1961; CBiol, FIBiol, Gt. Britain, 1991. Instr. U. Iowa, 1961-63; NIH spl. fellow U. Iowa (Coll. Medicine), 1963-65, asst. prof., 1965-69; assoc. prof. otolaryngology-head and neck surgery Northwestern U. Feinberg Sch. Medicine, Chgo., 1969—74, prof., 1974—; dir. research otolaryngology Northwestern U. Med. Sch., Chgo., 1969-93, prof. cell and molecular biology (anatomy), 1977—2001; prof. basic and behavioral scis. Northwestern U. Dental Sch., 1989-2001; assoc. med. staff Northwestern Meml. Hosp., 1969-90, health profl., 1990-93; rsch. assoc. zoology Field Mus. Natural History, 1995—; guest scientist Max Planck Inst. für Psychiatrie, 1976; vis. prof. Royal Coll. Surgeons Eng., 1980-86, U. Edinburgh, 1987; assoc. editor Clinical Anatomy, 1995—. Mem. task force on new materials Am. Bd. Otolaryngology, 1969-72; dir. Ill. Soc. Med. Rsch., 1973-77; mem. Internat. Anat. Nomenclature Com., 1983-91; guest scientist Zoologisches Forchungsinstitut und Mus. A. Koenig, 1988; mem. exec. com. of med. admissions com. Northwestern U. Feinberg Sch. Medicine, 1991-, chmn., 1998-2003; mem. exec. admissions com. MSTP, 2002-; Brodel meml. lectr. Assn. Med. Illustrators, 1995; mem. Chgo. Clin. Ethics Programs. Editor Annotated Translation of Vesalius' Fabrica, 1995-, elec. edit., 2003; contbr. articles to profl. jours., chpts. to books. Mem. adv. bd. Ctr. Deafness, 1977-80; bd. dirs. Cliff Dwellers Arts Found., 1979-82; trustee Wilmette Libr. Bd., 1982-83, Wilmette Bd. Health, 1999-. Served with U.S. Army, 1953-55. NATO sr. fellow in sci. Oxford U., Eng., 1978; NIH rsch. grantee, 1964-84, 95—2004, NSF rsch. grantee, 1975-77, NEH grantee, 1995-2002; recipient Gould Internat. award, 1971, Disting. Alumnus award of Honor, Bklyn. Coll., 1977, Alumnus of Yr. award, 1984; Arnott demonstrator Royal Coll. Surgeons Eng., 1985. Fellow AAAS, Linnean Soc. London, Inst. Biology, Am. Speech-Hearing Assn., Royal Soc. Medicine; mem. AMA, AAUP (chpt. pres. 1977-82), Am. Physiol. Soc. (animal care and experimentation com. 1976-82), Am. Assn. Clin. Anatomists, Chgo. Laryngol. and Otol. Soc. (coun. 1988-89), Am. Soc. Mammalogists, Anat. Soc. Gt. Britain and Ireland, Am. Assn. History Medicine, Soc. Med. History Chgo., Amnesty Internat. (coord. Chgo. Health profls. group 1986-87), Am. Assn. Anatomists, Nat. Eagle Scout Assn., Sigma Xi (chpt. pres. 1971-72), Sigma Alpha Eta. Achievements include research on neuromuscular physiology, embryology and comparative anatomy of the larynx, history of medicine. Office: 303 E Chicago Ave Chicago IL 60611-3008

HASTERT, DENNIS (JOHN DENNIS HASTERT), congressman; b. Aurora, Ill., Jan. 2, 1942; m. Thelma Jean Kahl, 1973; children: Joshua John, Ethan Allen. BA in Econ., Wheaton Coll., 1964; MS in Philosophy of Edn., No. Ill. U., 1967. Tchr., coach Yorkville (Ill.) High Sch., 1964—80; mem. Ill. House Reps., Springfield, 1980-86, U.S. Congress from 14th dist. Ill., 1987—, chief dep. majority whip, 1994-99, speaker of the house, 1999—, mem. commerce com., mem. govt. reform and oversight com. Permanent chair Rep. Nat. Conv., 2000; mem. bd. dirs. Aurora Family Support Ctr. Author: Speaker: Lessons from Forty Years of Coaching and Politics, 2004. Named Ill. Coach of the Year, 1976, Guardian of the Seniors Rights, 60 Plus Assn., 1999; named an Outstanding Am., Nat. Wrestling Hall of Fame, 2000; named one of The 20 Top Legislators, Chgo. Sun Times, 1985; recipient Build Life award, Nat. Coalition for Athletic Equity, 1999, Taxpayer Hero award, Americans for Tax Reform, 1999, Disting. Citizen award, Three Fires Coun. (St. Charles, Ill.) Boy Scouts of Am., 2000, Alumnus of the Year award for Disting. Svc. to Society, Wheaton Coll., 2002. Mem.: US Wrestling Assn., IL Wrestling Coaches Assn. (pres. 1977—78), US Olympic Com., US Olympic Movement, Farm Bureau, Lions (Yorkville). Republican. Protestant. Office: US Ho of Reps 235 Cannon House Office Bldg Washington DC 20515-1314

HASTINGS, ALCEE LAMAR, congressman, retired judge; b. Altomonte Springs, Fla., Sept. 5, 1936; s. Julius C. and Mildred L. H.; 3 children BA, Fisk U., 1958; postgrad., Howard U. Sch. Law, 1958-60; JD, Fla. A&M U., 1963. Bar: Fla. 1963. Mem. firm Allen and Hastings, Ft. Lauderdale, 1963-66; pvt. practice law Ft. Lauderdale, 1966-77; judge Cir. Ct. Broward County, Fla., 1977-79, U.S. Dist. Ct. (so. dist.) Fla., 1979-89; mem. U.S. Congress from 23d Fla dist., 1993—; mem. rules com., intelligence com. Adj. prof. criminal justice dept. Nova U.; lectr. So. Regional Council on Black Am. Affairs; lectr., cons. Internat. Juvenile Officers Assn., Peace Corps Vols. in Avon Park, Fla., 1966; legal counsel Community Action Migrant Program, Broward County Classroom Tchrs.; mem. Gov.'s Conf. on Criminal Justice, State of Fla.; lectr., cons. to elem. and secondary public and pvt. schs., chs., synagogues, social orgns., civic orgns., colls. and univs. in U.S.; co-propr. Tri-City News Host TV program: Pride, Sta. WPLG; columnist: West Side Gazette. Atty. various civic assns., Broward County and State of Fla.; mem. Bi-Racial Adv. Commn., Broward County Personnel Adv. Commn.; sec. Fla. Council on Aging; chmn. Broward Youth Services Task Force; mem. State of Fla. Edn. Commn., Task Force on Crime, Democratic Exec. Com; candidate for Fla. Ho. of Reps., Fla. Senate, U.S. Senate, Fla. Public Service Commn.; bd. dirs. Urban League of Broward County, Child Advocacy, Inc., The Starting Place, Broward County Sickle Cell Anemia Found., Fla. Voters League, Broward County Council on Human Relations; trustee Mt. Hermon A.M.E. Ch., Ft. Lauderdale, Broward Community Coll., Bethune Cookman Coll. Recipient numerous awards and honors including; Humanitarian award Broward County Young Democrats, 1978; Citizen of Year award Zeta Phi Beta, 1978; Sam Delevoe Human Rights award Community Relations Bd. of Broward County, 1978; Glades Festival of Afro Arts award Zeta Phi Beta, 1981; named Man of Year, Com. Italian Am. Affairs, 1979-80; Judge Alcee Hastings Day proclaimed for City of Daytona Beach in his honor on Dec. 14, 1980. Mem. ABA (standing com. profl. discipline), Nat. Bar Assn. (Chmn.'s award 1981), Am. Trial Lawyers Assn., Fla. Bar Assn., U.S. Dist. Judges Council., A.M.E. Ch. Clubs: Elks, KP. Democrat. Office: US Ho of Reps 2235 Rayburn Ho Office Bldg Washington DC 20515-0923 E-mail: alcee.pubhastings@mail.house.gov.

HASTINGS, DANIEL, aeronautical engineer, educator; b. Chardstock, Devon, Eng. BA in Math., Oxford U., 1967; SM in Aeronautics and Astronautics, MIT, 1978, PhD in Plasma Physics, 1980. Rsch. scientist Physical Sciences Inc., Andover, Mass., 1980—81, Oak Ridge Nat. Lab., Tenn., 1981—85; asst. prof. aeronautics and astronautics MIT, 1985—88, assoc. prof. aeronautics and astronautics, 1988—93, prof. aeronautics and astronautics, 1993—, dir. Space Grant Prog., 1990—93, assoc. dept. head of rsch., dept. aeronautics and astronautics, 1993—96, dir., Space Engring. Rsch. Ctr., 1996—97, prof. engring. systems, 2000—, dir. technol. and policy prog., 2000—03, assoc. dir. engring. sys. divsn., 2001—03, co-dir. engineering systems div., assoc. dean engring. systems, 2003—04, dir. engineering systems div., 2004—. Vis. scientist Phillips Lab., 1993—94; chief scientist US Air Force, Washington, 1997—99; mem. Applied Physics Lab Sci. and Technol. Advisory Bd.; bd. dir. Nat. Sci. Bd.; chair Air Force Scientific Advisory Bd.; mem. MIT Lincoln Lab. Advisory Com.; bd. trustees Aerospace Corp. Contbr. articles to profl. jours. Recipient Martin Marietta Superior Publ. award, 1988, Air Force Disting. Civilian award, 1997, 1999, Bur. Eagle award, Nat. Guard, 1999. Fellow: AIAA; mem.: Internat. Acad. Astronautics. Achievements include research in tethers, plasma conductors, and high voltage arching on solar arrays; research in new design paradigms for space systems, collaborating distributed satellite systems, changing the nature of the space economy and strategic space policy. Avocations: reading, walking. Office: MIT Engring Systems Divsn 77 Massachusetts Ave Bldg E40-251 Cambridge MA 02139-4307

HASTINGS, DEBORAH, bass guitarist; b. Evansville, Ind., May 11, 1959; d. Mortimer Winthrop Hastings and Margaret Hooper (Smith) Zimmerman. Student music, U. Wis. Bass guitarist, N.Y.C. and Madison, Wis., 1975—; freelance photographer Madison, 1976-81; band leader Bo Diddley, 1992—; founder A/Prompt Computer Telepromting Svcs., Inc., 1994—. Featured bassist with Duck Dunn for Bush inauguration, performing with Billy Preston, Dr. John, Koko Taylor, Willie Dixon, Carla Thomas, Eddie Floyd, Ron Wood, Steve Cropper, Bo Diddley, Jerry Lee Lewis, Chuck Berry, Joe Louis Walker; has also performed with Ben E. King, Little Anthony, Sam Moore, John Lee Hooker, Mick Fleetwood, Al Kooper, James Cotton; TV shows include Legends of Rock and Roll Live from Rome; appeared on David Letterman Show, 2003; subject of PBS Spl., 2003. Bass player TV shows Joan Rivers, 1987, Classics of Rock and Roll, 1988, Gunslingers tour Live from the Ritz with Ron Wood & Bo Diddley, 1988, Live from the Ritz, 1989, Legends of Rock and Roll (live from Australia), Legends of Guitar from Seville, Spain, 1991, Showtime at the Apollo, 1992, N.Y. at Night, 1992; performed Into The Night, 1991 (TV show) Nashville Now, 1991, American Musicshop, 1991, Johnny Carson Show, 1990, Pat Sajak Show, 1990, Carla Thomas, 1991, Arts & Entertainment Revue, 1990, (Madison Sq. Garden) Tribute to John Lee Hooker, 1990, Richard Nader's 25th Anniversary Show, 1994, Conan O'Brien Show, 1996; recordings include Bo Diddley's Grammy Nominated Album "A Man Amongst Men", 1996; performer in concert video "A Man Amongst Men", 1996; tours in Europe, Australia and Japan; performed at inaugurations of Pres. George Bush, 1989, Pres. Bill Clinton, 1997; performed with Bo Diddley opening of Seattle Music Experience Mus., 2000, Edgar Winter, 2003, Buffy Saint-Marie, 2003, Rock n'Roll Hall of Fame, 2005. Fundraiser, bassist polit. campaigns, Madison. Recipient numerous awards for pottery, award Arts Coun., Madison, Arts Coun., Ann Arbor, Mich.; played at Rock and Roll Hall of Fame Mus. Johnnie Johnson in Buenos Aires, Argentina, 2003. Mem. Musicians Union (local 802). Democrat. Avocations: computers, photography, graphics design, video. Office: Talent Cons Internat 1560 Broadway Ste 1308 New York NY 10036-1518

HASTINGS, DEREK K., history professor; b. Battle Creek, Mich., Aug. 11, 1968; s. Samuel and Judith Hastings; m. Kristine Chandler, Sept. 20, 1991; children: Erica, Sara. BA, Stony Brook U., 1995; PhD, U. Chgo., 2003. Asst. prof. history Oakland U., Rochester, Mich., 2003—. Contbr. articles to profl. jours. Fellow, German Acad. Exch. Svc., 1999—2000. Office: Oakland Univ 354 O'Dowd Hall Rochester MI 48309

HASTINGS, DOC (RICHARD NORMAN HASTINGS), congressman; b. Spokane, Wash., Feb. 7, 1941; m. Claire Hastings; 3 children. Student, Columbia Basin Coll., 1958—61, Ctrl. Wash. U., 1964. Mem. Wash. State Ho. of Reps., 1979-87; pres. Columbia Basin Paper & Supply, 1983-94; mem. U.S. Congress from 4th Wash. dist., 1995—; mem. rules com., budget com.; chmn. com. stds. ofcl. conduct com., 2005—. Bd. dirs. Yakima Fed. Savings & Loan; chmn. Franklin County Republican Com., 1974-78 USAR, 1962—68. Republican. Office: US House Reps 1323 Longworth Ho Office Bldg Washington DC 20515-0001*

HASTINGS, DONALD FRANCIS, actor, writer; b. Bklyn., Apr. 1, 1934; s. Charles Benedict and Hazel May (Kirk) H.; m. Noretta Kennedy, Dec. 29, 1956 (div. Feb. 1980); children: Jennifer, Julie Ann, Matthew; m. Leslie Denniston, June 7, 1980; 1 dau., Katharine Scott. Student pvt., pub. schs., N.Y. State. Appeared on network radio shows, 1940-53, including Cavalcade of Am; appeared in plays including Life With Father, 1941-43, I Remember Mama, 1944-45, On Whitman Avenue, 1946, Young Man's Fancy, 1947, Summer and Smoke, 1948; various TV shows, from 1947, including Captain Video, 1949-55, Studio One, 1955, Big Story, 1959, Chevrolet on Broadway, 1948, Edge of Night, 1956-60, As The World Turns, 1960—; author: scripts of As The World Turns, 1972-73, Guiding Light, 1974, 77, (films) Prisoner at Gilbert House, 1976, Decoys, 2003. Recipient Lifetime Achievement award, Nat. TV Acad., 2004. Mem. AFTRA (Amee award 2004), Screen Actors Guild, Actors Equity, Writers Guild-East. Roman Catholic. Office: 549 Tripp Rd Millerton NY 12546-4751

HASTINGS, DOUGLAS ALFRED, lawyer; b. Oak Park, Ill., July 28, 1949; s. Douglas A. and Elaine M. (Schramm) H.; m. Virginia Joslin, May 28, 1982; children: Corey, Douglas. BA, Duke U., 1971; JD, U. Va., 1981. Bar: D.C. 1981. Assoc. dir. Inst. for Govt. Studies, Memphis State U., 1976-77; adminstrv. intern Fed. Exec. Inst., Charlottesville, Va., 1977-78; project coord. Assn. Acad. Health Ctrs., Charlottesville, 1978-80; cons. Shenandoah PSRO, Charlottesville, 1980-81; ptnr. Epstein Becker & Green, Washington, 1981—. Vis. lectr. dept. health adminstrn. Duke U., Durham, N.C., 1985-90. Contbr. articles to profl. jours. Mem. ABA, Washington Coun. Lawyers, Am. Health Lawyers Assn. (bd. dirs. 1991—, pres. 2001-02), Inst. of Med. (bd. health svs. 2001—), Order of Coif, Phi Beta Kappa. Democrat. Unitarian Universalist. Avocations: baseball, tennis, basketball. Home: 5301 Burke Dr Alexandria VA 22309-3310 Office: Epstein Becker & Green 1227 25th St NW Fl 7 Washington DC 20037-1156 Office Phone: 202-861-1807. E-mail: dhastings@ebglaw.com.

HASTINGS, EDWARD WALTON, theater director; b. New Haven, Apr. 14, 1931; s. Edward Walton and Madeline (Cassidy) H. BA, Yale, 1952; postgrad., Royal Acad. Dramatic Art, London, 1953, Columbia U., 1955-56. Bd. dirs. Eugene O'Neill Found., 1993; guest instr. Shanghai Drama Inst., 1984. Dir. Australian premiere Hot L Baltimore, 1975, Shakespeare's People nat. tour, 1983, Nothing Sacred, Hong Kong, 1992, Come Back Little Sheba, Gogol Theater, Moscow, 1995, Dial M for Murder nat. tour, 1995, Beggars Opera, Santa Fe Opera, 2000, H.M.S. Pinafore, Santa Fe Opera, 2001, Italian Girl, Santa Fe Opera, 2002, Rock of Angels, Santa Fe Pro Musica, 2005, others; exec. dir. Am. Conservatory Theatre, San Francisco, 1965-80, artistic dir., 1986-92; freelance dir., 1980-86. Mem. Santa Fe Arts Commn. Served with U.S. Army, 1953-55. Mem. Coll. of Fellows of the Am. Theatre. Clubs: Elizabethan (New Haven). Office: Am Conservatory Theatre 30 Grant Ave San Francisco CA 94108-5800 Home: 945 Acequia Madre Santa Fe NM 87505

HASTINGS, GEORGE L., federal official; b. Detroit, July 24, 1953; m. Gail Hastings; children: Will, Helen, Emma. BA magna cum laude, U. Mich., 1974; JD cum laude, U. Mich. Law Sch., 1977. News editor Good Morning Michigan, 1975; atty., tax divsn., appellate sect. US Dept. Justice, 1978—85, asst. chief claims ct. sec., tax divsn., 1985—89; spl. master US Ct. Fed. Claims, 1989—. Recipient Tax Divsn. Outstanding Atty. award, 1981, 1984, Atty. Gen. Spl. Commendation, 1983. Mem.: US Supreme Ct. Bar, Mich. State Bar. Office: US Ct Fed Claims Office Spl Masters 717 Madison Pl NW Washington DC 20005 Office Phone: 202-219-9657.

HASTINGS, HAROLD MORRIS, science educator; b. Dayton, Ohio, Nov. 21, 1946; s. Julius M. and Celia A. (Morse) H.; m. Gretchen E. Saalbach, June 2, 1968; children: Curtis, Matthew. BS, Yale U., 1967; MA, Princeton U., 1969, PhD, 1972. From instr. to assoc. prof. math. Hofstra U., N.Y., 1968-81, prof., 1981—, dept. chmn., 1985-90, 93-96, assoc. dean, 1990-93, chair dept. physics, 1999—. Vis. assoc. prof. SUNY, Binghamton, 1974-75, U. Ga., Athens, 1978-79; prin. Hastings, Saalbach Assocs., Inc., Garden City, N.Y., 1983-96; prin. Prisma Med. Tech., 1999—; mem. working group on supercomputers NASA, Greenbelt, Md., 1985-90. Author: (with D. Edwards) Cech and Steenrod Homotopy Theory, 1974; editor: (with M. Kochen) Advances in Cognitive Sci., 1988, (with G. Sugihara) Fractals: A User's Guide for the Natural Scis., 1993, Fraktale: Ein Leitfaden für Anwender, 1996; contbr. articles to profl. jours. Patentee in field for computerized acoustic fetal monitor, ultrasonic tissue classification; research in non-linear dynamics, excitable media, bio-medicine. Pres., v.p. Garden City Lay Ecumenical Com., N.Y., 1983-93. Grantee NSF, Woodrow Wilson Found., NAS, NIH. Mem. Am. Phys. Soc., Soc. Math. Biology. Avocations: running, photography, music. Office: Hofstra Univ Dept of Physics CHPHB 102 151 Hofstra Univ Hempstead NY 11549-1510 Office Phone: 516-463-5586. Business E-Mail: harold.hastings@hofstra.edu.

HASTINGS, JOHN WOODLAND, biologist, educator; b. Salisbury, Md., Mar. 24, 1927; s. Vaughan Archelaus and Kathrine (Stevens) H.; m. Hanna Machlup, June 6, 1953; children: Jennifer, David, Laura, Karen. BA, Swarthmore Coll., 1947; MA, Princeton U., 1950, PhD, 1951; MA, Harvard U., 1966. AEC postdoctoral fellow Johns Hopkins, 1951-53; instr. to asst. prof. biol. scis. Northwestern U., 1953-57; from asst. prof. to prof. biochemistry U. Ill. at Urbana, 1957-66; prof. biology Harvard, 1966-87, Paul C. Mangelsdorf prof. natural scis., 1987—; master Pforzheimer House, 1976-96. Summer rsch. participant Oak Ridge Nat. Lab., 1958; vis. lectr. biochemistry Sheffield (Eng.) U., 1961-62; instr. physiology Marine Biol. Lab., Woods Hole, Mass., 1961-66, dir., 1962-66, dir. marine ecology, 1989-91, mem. corp., 1961, trustee, 1966-74, exec. com., 1968-74; guest prof. Rockefeller U., 1965-66, Inst. Biol. Phys. Chemistry Paris, 1972-73, U. Konstanz, Ger., 1979-80, Nat. Biology Inst., Okazaki, Japan, 1986, U. Munich, 1993; Disting. vis. scientist Calif. Inst. Tech., 2000, Jet Propulsion Lab., 2000--; mem. panel molecular biology NSF, 1963-66, mem. adv. com. biology and medicine, 1968-71; com. postdoctoral fellowships chemistry Nat. Acad. Scis., 1965-67, com. photobiology, 1965-71, com. on phototherapy, 1971-73, com. on low frequency radiation, 1975-77; mem. Commn. Undergrad. Edn. in Biol. Scis., 1965-66; space biology com. NASA, 1966-71; biochemistry tng. com. Nat. Inst. Gen. Med. Scis., 1968-72; mem. internat. adv. bd. Marine Biol. Lab., Eilat, Israel, 1968—; faculty assoc. Calif. Inst. Tech., 2000. Contbr. profl. jours. With USN, 1944—45. Guggenheim fellow, 1965-66, NIH fellow, 1972-73, Yamada Found. fellow, Osaka, Japan, 1986; recipient Alexander von Humboldt prize, 1979, Humboldt fellow, 1993. Fellow AAAS, Am. Soc. Biol. Chemists, Biophys. Soc., Soc. Am. Microbiologists, Am. Soc. Photobiology (pres. 1999-2001), Soc. Gen. Physiology (pres. 1963-65), Soc. Chemi- and Bio-luminescence (founding pres. 1994-98), Pierian Found. (pres. 1999—2001), Johns Hopkins Soc. Scholars, mem. Nat. Acad. Scis., Am. Acad. Arts and Scis. Home: 14 Concord Ave Cambridge MA 02138-2356 Office: 16 Divinity Ave Cambridge MA 02138-2020 Office Phone: 617-495-3714. Business E-Mail: hastings@fas.harvard.edu.

HASTINGS, L(OIS) JANE, architect, educator; b. Seattle, Mar. 3, 1928; d. Harry and Camille (Pugh) H.; m. Norman John Johnston, Nov. 22, 1969. B.Arch., U. Wash., Seattle, 1952, postgrad. in Urban Planning, 1958. Architect Boeing Airplane Co., Seattle, 1951-54; recreational dir. Germany, 1954-56; architect (various firms), Seattle, 1956-59, pvt. practice architecture, 1959-74; instr. archtl. drafting Seattle Community Coll., part-time 1969-80; owner/founder The Hastings Group Architects, Seattle, 1974—; lectr. design Coll. Architecture, U. Wash., 1975; incorporating mem. Architecta (P.S.), Seattle, 1980, pres., from 1980. Mem. adv. bd. U. Wash. YWCA, 1967—69; mem. Mayor's Com. on Archtl. Barriers for Handicapped, 1974—75; chmn. regional public adv. panel on archtl. and engring. services GSA, 1976; mem. citizens adv. com. Seattle Land Use Adminstrn. Task Force, 1979—; AWIU guest of Soviet Women's Con., 1983; spkr. Pacific Rim Forum, Hong Kong, 1987; guest China Internat. Conf. Ctr. for Sci. and Tech. of the China Assn. for Sci. and Tech., 1989; mem. adv. com. Coll. architecture and urban planning U. Wash., 1993; mem. accreditation team U. Oreg. Coll. Architecture, 1991, N.J. Inst. Tech. Sch. Architecture, 1992; juror Home of the Yr. ann. award AIA/Seattle Times, 1996; mem. architect selection com. Wash. State capital carillon project, Pratt Art Ctr. new bldg., 2001. Design juror for nat. and local competitions, including Red Cedar Shingle/AIA awards, 1977, Current Use Honor awards, AIA, 1980, Exhibit of Sch. Architecture award, 1981; Contbr. to: also spl. features newspapers, articles in profl. jours. Sunset mag. Mem. bd. Am. Women for Internat. Understanding, del. to, Egypt, Israel, USSR, 1971, Japan and Korea, 1979, USSR, 1983; mem. Landmarks Preservation Bd. City of Seattle, 1981-83; mem. Design Constrn. Rev. Bd. Seattle Sch. Dist., 1985-87; mem. mus. con. Mus. History and Industry, 1987—; leader People to People del. women architects to China, 1990. Recipient AIA/The Seattle Times Home of Month Ann. award, 1968; Exhbn. award Seattle chpt. AIA, 1970; Environ. award Seattle-King County Bd. Realtors, 1970, 77,; AIA/House and Home/The American Home Merit award, 1971, Sp. Honor award Wash. Aggregates and Concrete Assn., 1993, Prize bridge Am. Inst. Steel Contrn., 1993; Honor award Seattle chpt. AIA, 1977, 83; Women Achievement award Past Pres. Assembly, 1983, Washington Women and Trading Cards, 1983; Nat. Endowment for Arts grantee, 1977; others; named to West Seattle High Sch. Hall of Fame, 1989, Woman of Achievement Matrix Table, 1994; named Woman of Distinction, Columbia River Girl Scout Coun., 1994. Fellow AIA (pres. Seattle chpt. 1975, pres. sr. coun. 1980, state exec. bd. 1975, N.W. regional dir. 1982-87, Seattle chpt. found. bd. 1985-87, Bursar Coll. Fellows 1989-90, Coll. of Fellows historian 1994—, internat. rels. com. 1988-92, vice chancellor 1991, chancellor 1992, Seattle chpt. medal 1995, Northwest & Pacific region Medal of Honor 2002, Leslie N. Boney Spirit of Fellowship award 2003, Richard Upjohn Fellows medal), Internat. Union Women Architects (v.p. 1969-79, sec. gen. 1985-89, del. UIA Congress, Montreal 1990), Am. Arbitration Assn. (arbitrator 1981—), Coun. of Design Professions, Assn. Women Contrs., Suppliers and Design Cons., Allied Arts Seattle, Fashion Group, Tau Sigma Delta, Alpha Rho Chi (medal). *It is not the quantity but the quality of space that is important.*

HASTINGS, PAUL J., pharmaceutical executive; BS, U. R.I., 1984. With Hoffman LaRoche, 1984—94; v.p., mktg. and sales and European gen. mgr. Synergen, Inc., 1989—94; v.p. global mktg. Genzyme Corp., 1994—98; pres. Genzyme Therapeutics Europe, 1994—98, Genzyme Therapeutics Worldwide, 1994—98, Chiron BioPharms., 1999—2001; pres., CEO, dir. Axys Pharms.; pres., CEO QLT, Inc., Vancouver, Canada, 2002—. Bd. dirs. ViaCell, Inc., Leading Edge Endowment Fund, Arriva Pharms., Inc., Bio. Mem. leadership coun. Coll. Pharmacy, U. R.I. Recipient Entrepreneur award, U. R.I., 2004, Communicator of Yr. award, 2004, Contbn. to the Assn. award, BIOTECanada, 2004. Office: QLT Inc 887 Great Northern Way Vancouver BC Canada V5T 4T5

HASTINGS, PHILIP KAY, psychology educator; b. Worcester, Mass., Aug. 27, 1922; s. Rowland Eunice (Leach) H.; m. Elizabeth Frances Hann, Mar. 11, 1950; children: Pamela Dillenback, Elizabeth Leach (dec.), Ann Upton, Mary Florence. BA, Williams Coll., 1943; MA, Princeton U., 1949, PhD, 1950. Instr. psychology Williams Coll., 1946-48, lectr., asst. prof., asso. prof., 1951-61, prof. psychology and polit. sci., 1961—; instr. psychology Princeton U., 1950-51; chmn. Survey Research Consultants Internat., 1977—. Research asso. Psychol. Corp. N.Y.; cons. AT&T, 1944-58, Gen. Electric Co., 1975—. Contbr. articles to profl. jours.; editor: Index to International Public Opinion, 1979— . Served to lt. (j.g.) USNR, 1944-46. Fellow Am. Psychol. Assn., Am. Sociol. Assn.; mem. World Assn. Pub. Opinion Research (pres. 1971-72), Am. Assn. Pub. Opinion Research, Sigma Xi. Home: 156 Bulkley St Williamstown MA 01267-2021

HASTINGS, REED, film company executive, educational association administrator; Bachelors Degree, Bowdoin Coll.; M in Computer Sci., Stanford U. Founder Pure Software, 1990; co-founder, CEO Netflix, Inc., LosGatos, Calif., 1998—. Pres. Calif. State Bd. Edn., 2000—; founding mem. NewSchools.org, Aspire Pub. Schs., Pacific Collegiate Sch., EdVoice.net; CEO Technology Network; vol. Peace Corps, Swaziland, 1983—86. Named one of World's 100 Most Influential People, Time Mag., 2005. Office: NetFlix com Inc 970 University Ave Los Gatos CA 95032

HASTINGS, SUSAN C., lawyer; b. Mpls., 1959; BA, U. Iowa, 1980, JD with distinction, 1985. Bar: Ohio 1985, registered: US Dist. Ct. (No. Dist.) Ohio, US Ct. Appeals (6th cir.). Ptnr. Squire, Sanders & Dempsey LLP, Cleve., chmn., Labor & Employment Practice Group. Mem.: ABA (Labor & Employment Law Sect.), Ohio State Bar Assn. (Labor & Employment Law Sect.), Nat. Sch. Bd. Assn., Ohio Coun. of Sch. Bd. Attys. Office: Squire Sanders & Dempsey LLP 4900 Key Tower 127 Public Sq Cleveland OH 44114-1304 Office Phone: 216-479-8723. Office Fax: 216-479-8780. Business E-Mail: shastings@ssd.com.

HASTINGS, VIVIEN N., lawyer; b. Havana, Cuba, Dec. 22, 1951; BA, U. Conn., 1973; JD, Wash. U., 1977. Bar: Ill. 1977, Fla. 1990. Assoc. Winston & Strawn, 1977—82; v.p., co-gen. counsel Merrill Lynch Hubbard, Inc., 1982—89; various positions WCI Communities Ltd. Partnership, sr. v.p., gen. counsel; sr. v.p., gen. counsel, sec. WCI Communities, Inc., Bonita Springs, Fla. Office: WCI Communities Inc 24301 Walden Ctr Dr Bonita Springs FL 34134 Office Phone: 239-947-2600. Office Fax: 239-498-8277.

HASTINGS, WILLIAM CHARLES, retired state supreme court chief justice; b. Newman Grove, Nebr., Jan. 31, 1921; s. William C. and Margaret (Hansen) H.; m. Julie Ann Simonson, Dec. 29, 1946; children— Pamela, Charles, Steven. B.Sc., U. Nebr., 1942, JD, 1948; LHD (hon.), Hastings Coll., 1991. Bar: Nebr. 1948. With FBI, 1942-43; mem. firm Chambers, Holland, Dudgeon & Hastings, Lincoln, 1948-65; judge 3d jud. dist. Nebr., Lincoln, 1965-79, Supreme Ct. Nebr., Lincoln, 1979-88, chief justice, 1988-95; ret., 1995. Bd. dir. Nat. Conf. Chief Justices, 1989-91. Pres. Child Guidance Ctr., Lincoln, 1962, 63; v.p. Lincoln Community Coun., 1968, 69; vice chmn. Antelope Valley coun. Boy Scouts Am., 1968, 69; pres. 1st Presbyn. Ch. Found., 1968—; mem. Lincoln Parks and Recreation Adv. Bd., Govs. task force correctional dept. medical svcs., 2000; mem. Nebr. Pub. Employees Retirement Bd. Served with AUS, 1943-46. Named to Nebr. Jaycee Hall of Fame, 1998, U. Nebr. Lincoln-Greek Hall of Fame, 2005; recipient Merit award, Acacia Nat. Frat., 2004. Mem. ABA, Nebr. Bar Assn. (George H. Turner award 1991, Pioneer award 1992), Am. Jud. Soc., Lincoln Bar Assn., Nebr. Dist. Judges Assn. (past pres.), Nat. Conf. Chief Justices (past bd. dirs.), Am. Judicature Soc. (Herbert Harley award 1997), Phi Delta Phi. Republican. Presbyterian (deacon, elder, trustee). Club: East Hills Country (pres. 1959-60). Home: 1544 S 58th St Lincoln NE 68506-1407 Personal E-mail: hwchastings@aol.com.

HASTINGS, WILMOT REED, lawyer, writer; b. Salem, Mass., May 29, 1935; s. Abner Horace and Florence (Hylan) H.; m. Joan Amory Loomis, Aug. 30, 1958; children: W. Reed, Jr., Melissa H., Claire A. AB magna cum laude, Harvard U., 1957, LL.B. magna cum laude, 1961; postgrad., U. Paris, 1957-58. Bar: Mass. 1961. Law clk. Chief Justice Raymond S. Wilkins, Boston, 1961-62; assoc. firm Bingham, Dana & Gould, Boston, 1962-68; 1st asst. and dep. atty. gen. Mass., 1968-69; spl. asst. and exec. asst. to undersec. state, 1969-70; gen. counsel HEW, 1970-73; ptnr. Bingham, Dana & Gould (now Bingham McCutchen), Boston and London, 1973-90; writer, 1990—. Home and Office: 45 Ward Ave Northampton MA 01060 E-mail: hastings@crocker.com.

HASWELL, CARLETON RADLEY, banker; b. Milw., May 18, 1939; s. Clayton Lyman and Jane (Radley) H.; m. Almut Haberkamp, Dec. 10, 1966; children— Angela, Robin. BS, Northwestern U., 1961; MBA, NYU, 1967. Chief internat. credit officer Chem. Bank, N.Y.C., 1963-87; dir. Chem. Internat. Inc., N.Y.C., 1981-86, Chem. Internat. Fin., N.Y.C., 1981-84; pres. Carleton Haswell Assocs., 1987—. Treas. P.G. Islanders; counselor S.C.O.R.E. With U.S. Army, 1961—63. Republican. Home and Office: Villa 514 2645 W Marion Ave Punta Gorda FL 33950-5979

HATAMIYA, LON SHOSO, consultant, former state official; m. Nancy Hatamiya; 2 children. BS in Economics, Harvard U.; MBA in Internat. Bus. & Entrepreneurial Studies, UCLA; JD, UCLA Sch. of Law. Former atty. Procter & Gamble Co., Cincinnati, Ohio, Sony Corp., Tokyo; administrator Agricultural Mktg. Svc., USDA, 1993—97, Foreign Agricultural Svc., USDA, 1997—99; secy. Calif. Techn., Trade and Commerce Agy., 1999—2003; dir. LECG, 2004—. Mem. Calif. Rural Economic Develop. Infrastructure Panel; exec.-in-residence U. Calif. Grad. Sch. of Bus., Davis, 2004. Office: LECG 333 S Grand Ave Ste 3750 Los Angeles CA 90071*

HATCH, ANNIA, gymnast; b. Guantanamo, Cuba, June 14, 1978; arrived in U.S., 1997, naturalized, 2001; m. Alan Hatch, 1997. Gymnast Stars Academy/U.S. Natl. Team, 2002—; co-owner Stars Elite Gymnastics Academy; competed in World Championships, 1996, U.S. Gymnastics Championships, 2002; co-owner Stars Academy, West Haven, Conn. Achievements include Bronze medal, Women's Vault, World Championships, 1996; 1st, Women's Vault, U.S. Nat. Championships, Nashville, Tenn., 2003; Silver medal, Women's Vault, Athens Olympics, 2004; Silver medal, Women's Team Gymnastics, Athens Olympics, 2004. Office: 221 Bull Hill Ln West Haven CT 06516

HATCH, DENNY (ALDEN DENISON), publishing executive, writer; b. N.Y.C., Aug. 15, 1935; s. Alden R. Hatch and Ruth Brown Hatch Elwell; m. Margaret Cook, July 12, 1970. AB in English, Columbia U., 1958. Sales mgr. Franklin Watts, Inc., Pubs., N.Y.C., 1961—64; mem. staff advt. sales Libr. Jour. Mag., N.Y.C., 1965—66; copywriter, dir. new products Grolier Enterprises, N.Y.C., 1966—68; dir. book club Macmillan, N.Y.C., 1968—69; dir. book clubs Meredith Corp., Manhasset, N.Y., 1970—71; v.p., account exec. Walter Weintz & Co., Stamford, Conn., 1972—75; pres. Denison Hatch Assocs., Inc., 1976—. Editor, pub. Who's Mailing What! newsletter, 1984—95; editor Target Mktg. mag., 1992—97; contbg. editor Tarket Mktg., Catalog Success, Fundraising Success mags., 1997—. Author: Million Dollar Mailings, 1992, Method Marketing, 1999, Priceline.com: A Layman's Guide to Manipulating the Media, 2004, Cedarhurst Valley, 2005; co-author (with Don Jackson): 2,239 Tested Secrets for Direct Marketing Success, 1998; editor: www.businesscommonsense.com. Served with AUS, 1958—60. Mem.: Union League Club Phila., Delta Kappa Epsilon. Home and Office: 310 Gaskill St Philadelphia PA 19147-1503 Personal E-mail: dennyhatch@aol.com.

HATCH, FREDERICK TASKER, research scientist, consultant; b. Boston, Aug. 27, 1924; s. Frederick Southard and Beatrice (Tasker) H.; m. Virginia Weeks, Mar. 3, 1946; children: Daniel F., Daphne A., Deborah J., Douglas E. BA, Dartmouth Coll., 1944; MD, Harvard U., 1948; PhD, MIT, 1960. Diplomate Nat. Bd. Med. Examiners. Intern Roosevelt Hosp., N.Y.C., 1948-49; rsch. fellow Columbia U., N.Y.C., 1949-52; established investigator Am. Heart Assn./Mass. Gen. Hosp., Boston, 1960-65; sr. scientist, sect. leader Lawrence Livermore (Calif.) Nat. Lab., 1965-80, asst. assoc. dir., 1980-87, cons., 1987—. Mem. lipid metabolism adv. com. Nat. Heart, Lung and Blood Inst., Bethesda, Md., 1968-73. Assoc. editor Lipids Jour., 1964-73; author chpts. in books; contbr. numerous articles to profl. jours. Sec. Land Conservation Task Force, Meredith, N.H., 1989-90, chmn. Transp. Adv. Com., 1994—. Capt. USAR, 1952-55. Fellow Am. Inst. Chemists; mem. Am. Chem. Soc., Am. Soc. Biochemistry and Molecular Biology, Environ. Mutagen Soc., Arteriosclerosis, Thrombosis and Vascular Biology, Coun. of Am. Heart Assn. (exec. com. 1971-73). Avocations: tree farmer, skiing, hiking, biotechnology investing. Home and Office: 27 Pease Rd Meredith NH 03253-5506 Office Phone: 603-279-5142. Personal E-mail: fhatch@cyberportal.net.

HATCH, GEORGE CLINTON, television executive; b. Erie, Pa., Dec. 16, 1919; s. Charles Milton and Blanche (Beecher) Hatch; m. Wilda Gene Glasmann, Dec. 24, 1940; children: Michell Arnow, Diane Glasmann Orr, Jeffrey Beecher, Randall Clinton, Deepika Hatch Avanti. AB, Occidental Coll., 1940; MA in Econs., Claremont Coll., 1941; HHD (hon.), So. Utah U., 1988. Pres. Comms. Investment Corp., Salt Lake City, 1945-95; chmn. Double G Comm. Corp., Salt Lake City, 1956—; dir. Republic Pictures Corp., Los Angeles, 1971-94; pres. Sta. KVEL, Inc., 1978-94. Pres. Standard Corp., Ogden, 1993-98, Hatch Family LLC, 1998—; past mem. Salt Lake adv. bd. First Security Bank Utah; past chmn. Rocky Mountain Pub. Broadcasting Corp.; past chmn. bd. govs. Am. Info. Radio Network; past bd. govs. NBC-TV Affiliates. Past pres. Salt Lake Com. on Fgn. Relations; past mem. Utah Symphony Bd., Salt Lake City; past chmn. and mem. Utah State Bd. Regents, 1964-85. Recipient Svc. to Journalism award U. Utah, 1966, silver medal Salt Lake Advt. Club, 1969, Disting. Svc. award Utah Tech. U., 1984, Disting. Utahan Centennial Yr. award Margaret Thatcher U.K., Utah Festival, 1996. Mem. Nat. Assn. Broadcasters (past pres., radio bd. dirs., ambassador to Inter-Am. mtgs. in Latin Am. 1962), Utah Broadcasters Assn. (past pres., Mgmt. award 1964, Hall of Fame award 1981), Salt Lake City Advt. Club (silver medal 1969), Phi Beta Kappa, Phi Rho Pi (life). Democrat. Avocations: hiking, rock art. Office: Hatch Family LLC 1537 Chandler Dr Salt Lake City UT 84103-4220

HATCH, JOHN D., lawyer; b. Atlanta, Aug. 26, 1942; s. Ernest Healey and Charlotte Blanchard (Chazal) H.; m. Pamela Faye Carr, June 13, 1964; children: Wendy H. Duncan, A. Candice Hatch, Teresa H. Caraker. AA, Ctrl. Fla. Jr. Coll., Ocala, 1962; BS, Fla. State U., 1964; JD, Georgetown U., 1971. Bar: Fla. 1971, Conn. 1972, Tex. 1992, U.S. Dist. Ct. Conn. 1973, U.S. Dist. Ct. (no. dist.) Tex. 1992, U.S. Tax Ct. 1979, U.S. Supreme Ct. 1979; gen. securities lic., gen. prin. lic. Lt. USNR, 1964-71; atty. AEtna Life & Casualty, Hartford, Conn., 1971-74, counsel, 1974-83; v.p. and gen. counsel Continental Corp., N.Y.C., 1983-85; v.p. spl. ops. Comml. Life Ins. Co., Piscataway, N.J., 1985-87; v.p. and gen. counsel Associated Madison Cos., Inc., N.Y.C., 1987-88; sr. v.p. Resource Deployment, Inc., N.Y.C. and Ft. Worth, 1988-91;

pres. Ins. Horizons, Inc., Ocala, Fla., 1992—, John D. Hatch, P.C., Ocala, 1992—. Gen. counsel Am. Health & Life Ins. Co., Ft. Worth, 1995—; bd. dirs. Pub. Svc. Mut. Ins. Co., N.Y.C., London and Midland Gen. Ins. Co., London, Ont. Mem. ABA (chmn. TIPS employee benefits com. 1983-84, TIPS fin. svcs. com. 1992-93), Assn. Life Ins. Counsel, Fed. Bar Assn., Internat. Assn. Ins. Law. Republican. Roman Catholic. Avocations: reading, boating, tennis. Home and Office: 840 SE 5th St Ocala FL 34471-2306

HATCH, MICHAEL WARD, lawyer; b. Pittsfield, Mass., Nov. 19, 1949; s. Ward Sterling and Elizabeth (Hubbard) H.; m. Lisa Schilling, June 8, 1974; children: Stuart, Andrew, Gillian. AB in Econs., St. Lawrence U., 1971; JD, Yale U., 1974. Bar: Wis. 1974, N.Y. 1980. Ptnr. Foley & Lardner LLP, Milw., 1974—, chmn. real estate practice group. Mem. ABA, N.Y. State Bar Assn., Wis. Bar Assn., Milw. Bar Assn., Am. Coll. Real Estate Lawyers, Urban Land Inst., Nat. Multi Housing Coun., Mortgage Bankers Assn. Wis., Bldg. Owners and Mgrs. Assn., Local Initiatives Support Corp., Milw. Athletic Club, Town Club. Avocations: architecture, historic preservation. Office: Foley & Lardner LLP 777 E Wisconsin Ave Ste 3800 Milwaukee WI 53202-5367 Office Phone: 414-297-5706. Office Fax: 414-297-4900. Business E-Mail: mhatch@foley.com.*

HATCH, MIKE, state attorney general; m. Patti Hatch; 3 children. BS in Polit. Sci. with honors, U. Minn., Duluth, 1970; JD, U. Minn., 1973. Commr. of commerce State of. Minn., 1983—89; pvt. practice law; atty. gen. State of Minn., 1999—. Democrat. Office: Minn Atty Gen's Office 1400 Bremer Tower 445 Minnesota St Saint Paul MN 55101

HATCH, NATHAN ORR, academic administrator; b. May 17, 1946; m. Julia Gregg; 3 children. AB summa cum laude, Wheaton Coll., 1968; AM, Washington U., 1972, PhD, 1974. Postdoctoral fellow Johns Hopkins U., 1974-75; from asst. prof. to prof. history U. Notre Dame, South Bend, Ind., 1975-88, dir. grad. studies dept. history, 1980-83, assoc. dean Coll. Arts and Letters, dir. Inst. for Scholarship in the Liberal Arts, 1983-89, acting dean Coll. Arts and Letters, 1988-89, v.p. for grad. studies and rsch., 1989-96, prof., 1989, provost, 1996—2005, Andrew V. Tackes prof. history, 1999—2005; pres. Wake Forest U., Winston-Salem, NC, 2005—. Author: The Sacred Cause of Liberty: Republican Thought and the Millennium in Revolutionary New England, 1977, The Democratization of American Christianity, 1989 (Albert C. Outler prize Am. Soc. Ch. History 1989, 1989 Book prize Soc. for Historians of Early Am. Republic, co-winner John Hope Franklin Publ. prize Yale U. Press 1990); also articles; editor: The Professions in American History, 1988; co-editor: The Bible in America: Essays in Cultural History, 1982, Jonathan Edwards and the American Experience, 1988. Bd. dirs. United Way St. Joseph County, Ind., 1987-92; trustee St. Joseph's Med. Ctr., 1994, chair bd. trustees, 1997-99; mem. nat. adv. bd. Salvation Army, 1997-99; trustee Fuller Theol. Sem., 1998—; mem. Nat. Coun. Humanities, 2000—. Recipient Paul Fenlon Teaching award U. Notre Dame, 1981; Am. Coun. Learned Socs. fellow, 1976, Fred Harris Daniels fellow Am. Antiquarian Soc., 1977, Charles Warren fellow Harvard U., 1977-78; grantee Lilly Endowment, 1979, Ind. Com. for the Humanities, 1981-82, NEH, 1981-85. Mem. Johns Hopkins Soc. Scholars, Am. Soc. Ch. Hist. (pres. 1993), Phi Beta Kappa. Office: Wake Forest U 211 Reynolds Hall Box 7226 1834 Wake Forest Rd Winston Salem NC 27109*

HATCH, ORRIN GRANT, senator; b. Homestead Park, Pa., Mar. 22, 1934; s. Jesse and Helen (Kamm) H.; m. Elaine Hansen, Aug. 28, 1957; children: Brent, Marcia, Scott, Kimberly, Alysa, Jess. BS, Brigham Young U., 1959; JD, U. Pitts., 1962; LLD (hon.), U. Md., 1981; MS (hon.), Def. Intelligence Coll., 1982; LLD (hon.), Pepperdine U., 1990, So. Utah State U., 1990. Bar: Pa. 1962, Utah 1962. Ptnr. firm Thomson, Rhodes & Grigsby, Pitts., 1962-69, Hatch & Plumb, Salt Lake City, 1976; U.S. senator from Utah, 1977—; former chmn. labor and human resources com. U.S. Senate, mem., former chmn. Senate judiciary com., chmn. subcom. on internat. trade, mem. fin. com., senate Rep. policy com., com. on Indian affairs, aging com., mem. select com. on intelligence, 1997—. Author: The Equal Rights Amendmen: Myths and Realities, 1983, Understanding the Doctrines of Christ, 1995, Square Peg: Confessions of a Citizen Senator, 2003; contbr. articles to newspapers and profl. jours. Recipient Outstanding Legislator award Nat. Assn. Rehab. Facilities, Legislator of Yr. award Am. Assn. Univ. Affiliated Programs, Legis. Leadership award Health Profl. Assn., many others. Mem. Am., Nat., Utah, Pa. bar assns., Am. Judicature Soc. Republican. Mem. Lds Ch. Avocations: golf, poetry, piano playing, composer lyrics.*

HATCH, RONALD RAY, engineer; b. Freedom, Okla., Dec. 28, 1938; s. Richard Verni and Elma Lottie (Carberry) H.; m. Nancy Elene Bates, Dec. 30, 1960; children: Richard, Rebecca, Sondra, Wendy, Randall, Ronald, Jeffrey, Nathan, Abigail, Peter, Robert, Marcy, Melanie. BS in Physics and Math., Seattle Pacific Coll., 1962. Physicist Johns Hopkins Applied Physics Lab., Silver Spring, Md., 1963-65; engr. Boeing Co., Seattle, 1965-70, Magnavox, Torrance, Calif., 1970-93; cons. Wilmington, Calif., 1993—95; with NavCom Tech., Inc., 1995—. Author: Escape from Einstein, 1992; contbr. numerous articles to profl. jours. Mem. Inst. Navigation (marine rep. 1991-93, we. region v.p. 1992-93, chair Satellite Div. 1998-2000, pres. 2001-02, Johannes Kepler award 1994, Col. Thomas Thurlow award 2000). Republican. Baptist. Achievements include 13 patents most concerning Global Positioning System (GPS). Home and Office: 1142 Lakme Ave Wilmington CA 90744-3517

HATCH, WILDA GENE, broadcast company executive; b. Ogden, Utah, Nov. 28, 1917; d. Abraham Lincoln and Edris Alida (Toombs) Glasmann; m. George Clinton Hatch, Dec. 24, 1940; children: Michell Arnow, Diane G. Orr, Jeffrey B., Randall C., Deepika Avanti. BA, Stanford U., 1939; HHD (hon.), Weber State U., 1981. Pres. The Std. Corp., Ogden, 1955-93; v.p. Sta. KUTV, Salt Lake City, 1956-94. Pres. Women's State Legis. Coun., Salt Lake City, 1967-69; active LWV, Salt Lake City, 1965—. Democrat. Avocations: hiking, rock art, fishing. Home: 1537 Chandler Dr Salt Lake City UT 84103-4220

HATCHELL, STEVEN JAMES, collegiate sports association executive; b. Madison, Wis., Mar. 14, 1947; s. George Hatchell; m. Patricia Clarke, June 12, 1971; children: Matthew, Jonathan. BS in Journalism, U. Colo., 1970. Dir. equipment and grounds U. Colo., Boulder, 1970-71, asst. to athletic dir., 1971-74, asst. sports info. dir., 1973-74, co-sports info. dir., 1974-76; dir. external affairs/sports info. Colo. State U., Ft. Collins, 1976-77; dir. svc. bur. Big 8 Conf., Kansas City, Mo., 1977-78, assoc./asst. commr., 1978-85, acting commr., 1980; commr. Met. Collegiate Athletic Conf., Atlanta, 1983-87; exec. dir. Orange Bowl Com./Fed. Express Orange Bowl Game, Miami, Fla., 1987-93, commr. Southwest conf., 1993-95, commr. Big 12 conf., 1995—. Mem. team selection com. Peach Bowl, 1984, 85, 86; dir. basketball tournament NCAA, 1983-87; press liaison rep. U.S. Ski Team/U.S. Olympic Com., Lake Placid, N.Y., 1980, Calgary, Alta., Can., 1988, mem. adv. com., 1980-84; press liaison rep. U.S. Olympic Com., L.A., 1984, mem. pub. rels. com., 1981-85, mem. Kans. chpt. fund-raising com., 1982, mem. congress program com., 1991; mem. bd. govs. Doral Ryder Open, 1988, 89, 90, 91; Silver Knight judge The Miami Herald, 1988, 89, 90, 91. Coun. mem. Discovery of Am. Quincentennial Com.; mem. adv. bd. Dr. Martin Luther King Jr. Parade and Festival; bd. dirs. Dade County Pub. Edn. Fund; mem. adv. bd. St. Thomas U., 1990, 91. Named one of Outstanding Young Men Am., 1975, 80, Man of Yr. Coconut Grove (Fla.) Jaycees, 1988-89; recipient award Nat. Assn. Collegiate Dirs. Athletics, 1994. Mem. Nat. Assn. Collegiate Athletic Dirs. (at-large, mem. exec. com. 1990—), PO stseason Football Bowl Assn. (chmn. 1988-91), Football Writers' Assn. Am., Basketball Writers' Assn. Am., Greater Miami C. of C. (founding mem. exec. com. sports coun.). Democrat. Roman Catholic. Avocations: golf, tennis, skiing. Office: PO Box 569420 1300 W Mockingbird Ln Ste 444 Dallas TX 75247-4959

HATCHELL, SYLVIA, basketball coach; b. Gastonia, N.C., Feb. 28, 1952; m. Sammy Hatchell; 1 child, Van. B.Phys. Edn. cum laude, Carson-Newman Coll., 1974; MS, U. Tenn., 1975. Coach jr. varsity women's team U. Tenn.; head coach Francis Marion Coll.; head women's basketball coach U. N.C., Chapel Hill, 1986—. Asst. coach U.S. World Univ. Games team, 1983, 85; ct. coach U.S. Olympic basketball try-outs, 1984, 92; basketball events taff Olympic Games, L.A., 1984; asst. coach U.S. team 1988 Olympic Games, Goodwill Games and World Championships; coach USA team World Univ. Games, Fukuoka, Japan, 1995, R. william Jones Cup, 1994. Named Nat. Coach of the Yr., USA Today, 1994, Coll. Sports Mag., 1994, Converse NAIA Reg. Coach of the Yr., 1986, AMFVoit Championship Coach, 1986, Coll. Basketball Coach of the Yr., Athletes Internat. Ministries, 1995, Carson-Newman Disting. Alumnus of the Yr., 1994; inductee Francis Marion U. Athletic Hall of Fame, 1993. Mem. Women's Basketball Coaches Assn. (pres. 1996-97, past bd. dirs.), Amateur Basketball Assn. of U.S. (women's games com.).

HATCHER, CHARLES ROSS, JR., surgeon, health facility administrator; b. Bainbridge, Ga., June 28, 1930; s. Charles Ross and Vivian Elizabeth (Miller) Hatcher; m. Phyllis Gregory Slappey, July 9, 1988; children from previous marriage: Marian Barnett Thorpe, Charles Hatcher III. BS magna cum laude, U. Ga., 1950; MD cum laude, Med. Coll. Ga., 1954. Intern Johns Hopkins Hosp., Balt., 1954-55; resident surgery Peter Bent Brigham Hosp., Boston, 1955-56, Johns Hopkins Hosp., 1958-62; prof. surgery, chief cardiothoracic surgery Emory U. Sch. Medicine, Atlanta, 1971-90; dir., CEO Emory Clinic, Atlanta, 1976-84; v.p. health affairs, dir. Woodruff Health Scis. Ctr., Emory U., 1984-96, dir. emeritus; chmn., CEO Emory HealthCare, 1995-96. Bd. dirs. Life of the South Corp., Japan Am. Soc. Contbr. Capt. U.S. Army, 1956—58. Mem.: ACS, So. Thoracic Surg. Assn. (pres. 1984), So. Surg. Assn., Am. Cancer Soc., Soc. Thoracic Surgeons (pres. 1986—87), Am. Assn. Thoracic Surgery, Am. Surg. Assn., Am. Coll. Chest Physicians (bd. regents 1977—81, bd. govs. 1974—77), Am. Coll. Cardiology (bd. govs. 1976—80), Johns Hopkins Soc. Scholars, Gov.'s Club Tallahassee, Fla., Bainbridge Country Club, Piedmont Driving Club, Rotary Club (bd. dirs. Atlanta chpt. 1976—80), Capital City Club, Alpha Omega Alpha, Sigma Xi, Phi Beta Kappa. Methodist. Home: 1105 Lullwater Rd NE Atlanta GA 30307-1245 Office: Emory U Woodruff Health Scis Ctr 1365 A Clifton Rd NE Ste 5036 Atlanta GA 30322-1013 Office Phone: 404-778-5860. Business E-Mail: charles_hatcher@emoryhealthcare.org.

HATCHER, JAMES A., lawyer; b. Macon, Ga., Feb. 20, 1952; BA, Furman U., 1974; JD, SC Sch. Law, 1977. Assoc. Sell & Melton, Macon, Ga., 1977—79; corp. legal counsel, sec. Cox Communications Inc., Altanta, 1979—92; sec., gen. counsel Cox Enterprise (parent co. of Cox Communications), 1987—93; v.p., gen. counsel Cox Communications Inc., 1992, v.p. legal & regulatory affairs, 1995—99, sr. v.p. legal & regulatory affairs, 1999—. Mem.: Ga. Bar Assn., SC Bar Assn., Bd. Dir. Diversity Com. State Bar Assn. Ga. Office: Cox Communication Inc 1400 Lake Hearn Dr Atlanta GA 30319 Office Phone: 404-843-5000. Business E-Mail: jim.hatcher@cox.com.

HATCHER, JOE BRANCH, management consultant; b. Ft. Worth, July 28, 1936; s. W. Joe and Jessie Mae Hatcher; m. Irma Gail Collins, Apr. 18, 1957; children: Gregory Layne, Geoffrey Alan, Gailyn. BA, U. Wichita, 1960; MA, U. Kans., 1967, PhD, 1968. Mem. English lit. faculty Baker U., Baldwin City, Kans., 1966-74; asst. to pres. Park Coll., Kansas City, Mo., 1974-75; v.p. Albion (Mich.) Coll., 1976-81; pres. Hendrix Coll., Conway, Ark., 1981-91; vice chmn. 1st Comml. Bank, Little Rock, 1992-95, also bd. dirs., 1992-95; cons. Hatcher & Assocs., Conway, 1995—. Mem.: Conway C. of C. Methodist. Avocation: tennis. Office: 916 Heather Cir Conway AR 72034-9395 Office Phone: 501-269-3185. Personal E-mail: jhatcher@cyberback.com.

HATCHER, TERI, actress; b. Sunnyvale, Calif., Dec. 8, 1964; d. Owen and Esther Hatcher; m. Marcus Leithold, June 4, 1988 (div. 1989); m. Jon Tenney, May 27, 1994 (div. Mar. 2003); 1 child, Emerson Rose. Student, Deanza Jr. Coll., Am. Conservatory Theater. Spokeswoman Clairol Nice 'n Easy hair color. Actor: (films) Tango and Cash, 1989, The Big Picture, 1989, Soapdish, 1991, Straight Talk, 1992, Heaven's Prisoners, 1996, Two Days in the Valley, 1996, Dead Girl, 1996, Tomorrow Never Dies, 1997, Since You've Been Gone, 1998, Fever, 1999, Spy Kids, 2001, The Chester Story, 2003; (TV films) Dead in the Winter, 1991, The Brotherhood, 1991, Running Mates, 2000, Jane Doe, 2001, Say Uncle, 2001, Momentum, 2003; (TV series) The Love Boat, 1985-86, Capitol, 1986-87, Karen's Song, 1987, Lois and Clark: The New Adventures of Superman, 1993-97, Desperate Housewives (Golden Globe Award for best actress in a TV series - musical or comedy, 2005, Screen Actors Guild Award for outstanding performance by an ensemble in a comedy series, 2005), 2004-. Address: Desperate Housewives Touchtone Television 100 Universal City Plaza Bldg 2128 Ste G Universal City CA 91608*

HATCHETT, EDWARD BRYAN, JR., lawyer; b. Glasgow, Ky., Aug. 8, 1951; s. Edward Bryan and Leona Katherine (Azbill) H.; m. Judie Etta James, Aug. 3, 1973; children: Catherine Wade, Elizabeth Black, James Edward Bryan. BA, Centre Coll., Danville, Ky., 1973; JD, U. Louisville, 1976; diploma Nat. Grad. Trust Sch., Northwestern U., 1980; diploma Stonier Grad. Sch. Banking, U. Del., 1986; diploma Ky. Mgmt. Inst., Western Ky. U., 1988. Bar: Ky. 1976. Editorial asst. Dept. Agr., Washington, 1971; edn. rsch. asst. Ky. Legis. Rsch. Commn., Frankfort, 1972; law clk. Dept. Law, City of Louisville, 1973-76; pvt. practice Glasgow, 1978-88; v.p., trust officer New Farmers Nat. Bank, Glasgow, 1980-88, sec., 1986-88; asst. gen. counsel Ky. Dept. Fin. Instns., Frankfort, 1977, commr., 1988-94, dir. securities divsn., 1992-94; auditor pub. accts. Commonwealth of Ky., 1996—2004. Chmn. Ky. Fin. Instns. Bd., Frankfort, 1988-94; bd. dirs. Commonwealth Preservation Advs., Inc., Frankfort; pres. Barren County Bar Assn., Glasgow, 1988, Estate Planning Coun. So. Ky., Bowling Green, 1988. Gov.'s appointee Ky. Heritage Coun., Frankfort, 1985-88; pres. Mammoth Cave Area 4-H Found., Glasgow, 1981; lay reader Ch. of the Ascension, 1988—; elected Ky. Auditor of Public Accounts, 1995, re-elected, 1999. Named nat. pub. speaking champion, Future Farmers Am., 1970. Mem. N.Am. Securities Adminstrs. Assn., Nat. Assn. State Auditors, Controllers and Treasurers (bond com. 1997—2004), Frankfort Rotary Club. Democrat. Episcopalian. Avocations: historical research, golf. Home: 454 Chinook Trail Frankfort KY 40601-1602 E-mail: ebhatchett@aol.com.

HATELEY, J. MICHAEL, human resources executive; BA Psychology, U. Calif. Mgr. human resources Monogram Industries, ITT; v.p. pres. human resources Mil. Aircraft, Elec., Aircraft Northrop Grumman, Inc., L.A., 1976-99, corp. v.p. personnel, 1999; corp. v.p., chief human resourve Northrop Grumman Corp., L.A., 2000—. Mem. human resources adv. coun. conf. bd. USC Marshall Sch. Bus., mem. corp. adv. bd. Bd. dirs. Ind. Colls. So. Calif. Office: Northrop Grumman Corp 1840 Century Park E Los Angeles CA 90067-2101 Office Phone: 310-553-6262.*

HATFIELD, DONALD GENE, retired art educator; b. Detroit, May 23, 1932; s. Floyd Myrl Hatfield and Helen Regina Nehmer; m. Marilyn Ann Grindstuen, Sept. 10, 1960 (dec.); children: Suzanne Valadon, John Thomas-(dec.), Kathleen Marie. AA, Northwestern Mich. Coll., 1958; BA, Mich. State U., 1960, MA, 1961; MFA, U. Wis., 1962. Elem. art supr., art tchr. Auburndale Elem., Jr. HS, Wis., 1962—64; asst. prof. art Auburn U., Ala., 1964—71, assoc. prof. art, 1971—81, prof. art, 1981—94, prof. emeritus art, 1994—. Instr. history architecture and art Tuskegee Inst., Tuskegee, Ala., 1968—69; art accreditation team mem. So. Assn. Colls. and Schs., 1973—81; dep. art accreditation team mem. Nat. Assn. Schs. Art, 1975, mem. commn., Va., 76; spkr. in field. One-man shows include Home Savings & Loan, Madison, Wis., 1962, Parker Co., Madison, 1962, La Cross State Coll., Wis., 1963, Unitarian House, Auburn, Ala., 1966, Auburn U., Bradley Lounge, 1967, Columbus (Ga.) Mus. Arts and Crafts, 1968, Birmingham Mus. Art, 1968, Savannah Arts Assn. Gallery, 1969, Birmingham So. Coll., 1970, Montgomery Mus. Art., 1972, LaGrange (Ga.) Coll., 1972, Eufaula Bank and Trust Co., Mezzanine Gallery, 1972, Telfair Peet Theater, Auburn U., 1976, 1980, Chattahoochee Valley State Coll., Phenix City, Ala., 1983, others, exhibited in group shows at Greater River Fall Art Assn., Fall River, Mass., 1964—65, Birmingham Mus. Art, 1965—66, 1968—72, Callaway Gardens, Pine Mountain, Ga., 1968, Montgomery Mus. Art, 1969, 1973, 1979—81, Columbus Mus. Art, 1969, Greater Birmingham Arts Alliance Gallery, 1976—77, 1980, Auburn U., 1983, Marble Gallery, Charleston, SC, 1983, Del Mar Coll., Corpus Christi, Tex., 1983, Columbia (Mo.) Coll., 1983, numerous others, marble sculpture, Gov.'s Mansion, Montgomery, Ala., 1973. Art awards judge Chattanoochee Valley Fair, Columbus, Ga., 1966—90; v.p. Ala. Art League, Montgomery, 1969—70, pres., 1970—72; bd. trustees Opelika Arts Assn., Inc., Ala., 1971—73. Served with USN, 1952—56. Recipient Merit award and Kelly Fitzpatrick award, Centennial Painting Exhbn., Montgomery, 1972, Purchase award, Opelika Arts Festival, 1972, 5th Ann. Miniworks, Jackson State U., 1983, numerous other purchase and exhbn. awards; grantee, Auburn U., 1985, 1986; Faculty Improvement grantee, 1990—91. Mem.: Mil. Order of Cootie (Ala. grand comdr. 1994—95, 2005—), VFW (quartermaster post 5404 all state team 1991—92, 1996—97), Elks (vet. affairs vol. svc. rep. to Tuskegee Vets. Hosp. 1989—95). Avocations: genealogy, artifacts, gardening, reading. Home: 550 Forest Pk Cir Auburn AL 36830

HATFIELD, ELAINE CATHERINE, psychology professor; b. Detroit, Oct. 22, 1937; d. Charles E. and Eileen (Kalahar) H.; m. Richard L. Rapson, June 15, 1982. BA, U. Mich., 1959; PhD, Stanford U., 1963. Asst. prof. U. Minn., Mpls., 1963-64, assoc. prof., 1964-66; asso. prof. U. Rochester, 1966-68, U. Wis., Madison, 1968-69, prof., 1969-81; now prof. U. Hawaii, Honolulu, chmn. dept. psychology, 1981-83. Author: Equity: Theory and Research, 1978, Mirror, Mirror: The Importance of Looks in Everyday Life, 1986, Psychology of Emotions, 1991, Love, Sex and Intimacy, 1993, Emotional Contagion, 1994, Love and Sex: Cross-cultural Perspectives, 1996, Rosie, 2000; contbr. articles to profl. jours. Recipient Disting. Scientist award Soc. Exptl. Social Psychology, 1993. Fellow APA; mem. Soc. Sci. Study of Sex (pres., Disting. Scientist award 1996, Alfred Kinsey award 1998). Home: 3334 Anoai Pl Honolulu HI 96822-1418 Office: U Hawaii 2430 Campus Rd Honolulu HI 96822-2216 Office Phone: 808-956-6276. E-mail: elaineh1@aol.com.

HATFIELD, JACK KENTON, lawyer, accountant; b. Medford, Okla., Jan. 26, 1922; s. Loate L. and Cora (Walsh) H.; m. D. Ann Keltner, Dec. 5, 1943 (dec. Sept. 1988); children: Susan Kathryn Hatfield Bechtold, Sally Ann Hatfield Clark; m. K. Dean Walker, Aug. 7, 1997; m. Dores Hamaker, Aug. 9, 2000. BS in BA, Phillips U., Enid, Okla., 1947; BA, Phillips U., 1953; LLB, Oklahoma City U., 1954, JD, 1967. Bar: U.S. Dist. Ct. (we. dist.) Okla. 1954, U.S. Supreme Ct. 1961, U.S. Dist. Ct. (no. dist.) Okla. 1967, U.S. Ct. Appeals (10th cir.) 1968; CPA 1954. Pvt. practice, Enid, Okla., 1954-58; with Dept. Interior, Tulsa, 1958-77; pvt. practice, Tulsa, 1977—. Mem.: ABA, Okla. Bar Assn., Tulsa Bar Assn., Am. Inst. CPA's, Okla. Soc. CPA's, Petroleum Club. Avocations: photography, tennis. Home: 4013 E 86th St Tulsa OK 74137-2609 Office: 1302 S Florence Pl Tulsa OK 74104 Office Phone: 918-494-0545.

HATFIELD, JANE STAUFF, secondary school educator; b. Milw., Aug. 9, 1911; d. Grover Andrew and Marie Louise (Vogt) Stauff; m. Henry C. Hatfield, Mar. 15, 1937; children: Robert, Barbara Hatfield Bazyn. BA, Northwestern U., 1932. Instr. English Mass. Dept. Edn., Quincy, Mass., 1964-92. Sec. Cambridge Editorial Rsch., Inc, 1960-70. Author study guides for various English courses, 1964-92, including: The American Woman, 1974, Black History, 1972. Bd. dirs. Cambridge YWCA, 1972-78; active Cambridge Civic Assn.

HATFIELD, JERRY LEE, plant pathologist, meteorologist; b. Wamego, Kans., May 1, 1949; s. Virgil H. and Elsie L. (Fischer) H.; m. Patricia JoAnne Reigle, Sept. 1, 1968; children: Mark E., Andrew J. BS, Kans. State U., 1971; MS, U. Ky., 1972; PhD, Iowa State U., 1975. Biometeorologist U. Calif., Davis, 1975-83; plant physiologist USDA-Agrl. Rsch. Svc., Lubbock, Tex., 1983-89; lab. dir. Nat. Soil Tilth Lab., USDA-Agr. Rsch. Svc., Ames, Iowa, 1989—. Editor: Biometerology and Integrated Pest Management, 1982, Limitations to Plant Root Growth, vol. 19, Advances in Soil Science, 1992, Soil Biology: Impacts on Soil Quality, Advances in Soil Science, 1993, Crops Residue Management, Advances in Soil Science, 1994, Utilization of Manure as a Soil Resource, Advances in Soil Science, 1998, Innovative Weed and Soil Management, Advances in Soil Science, Nitrogen in the Environment, 2001; contbr. over 320 articles to profl. jours. Recipient Arthur S. Flemming award for outstanding svc. to fed. govt., 1997, Disting. Svc. award in agr., Kans. State U., 2002. Fellow Soil Sci. Soc. Am., Am. Soc. Agronomy (editor jour. 1989-95, editor-in-chief 1996-2002, Agronomic Svc. award 1999), Crop Sci. Soc. Am.; mem. Am. Geophys. Union, Am. Meteorol. Soc. (chair agrl./forest com. 1980-81, agrl. and forest meteorology com. 1999-2002), Indian Agrometeorol. Soc. (hon.), Soil and Water Conservation Soc. (program chair 1997-98, bd. dirs. 2005-2007, Pres. Leadership award 1998), Phi Kappa Phi, Gamma Sigma Delta (Disting. Alumni award 2005). Republican. Avocations: golf, reading, photography, landscaping. Office: USDA Agrl Rsch Svc Nat Soil Tilth Lab 2150 Pammel Dr Ames IA 50011-0001 Business E-Mail: hatfield@nstl.gov.

HATFIELD, JULIE STOCKWELL, journalist, editor-in-chief; b. Detroit, Mar. 22, 1940; d. William Hume and Ruth Reed (Palmer) Stockwell; m. Philip Mitchell Hatfield, Aug. 1, 1964 (div. 1979); children— Christian Andrew, Juliana, Jason David; m. Timothy Leland, Nov. 23, 1984; stepchildren— Christian Bourso, London Chamberlain BA, U. Mich, 1962. Staff reporter Women's Wear Daily, NYC, 1962-64; freelance feature writer Bath-Brunswick Times, Wis. State Jour., 1964-68, Quincy Patriot Ledger, Mass., 1968-77; freelance music critic, fashion editor Boston Herald, 1977-79; fashion editor Boston Globe, 1979-95, living/arts writer, 1995-96, soc. columnist, 1996-2001, travel writer, 2001, bus. columnist, 2005—; freelance travel writer, 2001—. Author: (with others) Guide to the Thrift Shops of New England, 1982, Felix, 2004; contbg. editor The Boston (Mass.) Courant. Recipient Lulu award, Men's Fashion Assn., 1985, Atrium award for Outstanding Writing on Fashion, U. Ga., 1987, 1992; Nat. Endowment Arts grantee, 1973. Mem.: Soc. of Am. travel writers. Episcopalian. Avocation: piano. Office Phone: 781-934-2624. E-mail: juliestockwell@peoplepc.com.

HATFIELD, KEVIN DEAN, history professor, researcher; b. Eugene, Oreg., Sept. 10, 1970; s. Kenneth Dean and Susan Gracia Hatfield. BA cum laude, U. Oreg., 1992; MA, Utah State U., 1994; PhD, U. Oreg., 2003. Editl. internship Western Hist. Quar., Logan, Utah, 1993—94; grad. tchg. fellowship dept. history U. Oreg., Eugene, 1994—98, instr. history, 1998—2003, adj. prof. history, 2003—, consulting historian Coll. Edn., Ctr. for Advanced Tech. in Edn., 2004—. Rsch. cons. KDH Rsch. & Consulting, Eugene, Oreg., 1998—2005. Tutor Gutenberg Coll., Eugene, Oreg., 2003—05; lectr., discussion leader Solvang Retirement Ctr., Eugene, Oreg., 2004—05; spkr./presenter Silver Sage Soc., U. Oreg., Bend, 2004—05. Scholar Cash Award, State of Oreg., 1988. Mem.: Deschutes County Hist. Soc., Oreg. Hist. Soc., Am. Hist. Assn., Western History Assn., Phi Kappa Phi, Golden Key Nat. Honor Soc., Pi Gamma Mu, Phi Alpha Theta, Phi Eta Sigma, Phi Beta Kappa. Avocation: numismatism. Home: 3170 Agate St Eugene OR 97405 Office: Univ Oreg 1288 Dept History Eugene OR 97403 Office Phone: 541-617-4660. Personal E-mail: kevhat@ispwest.com.

HATFIELD, MARK ODOM, former senator; b. Dallas, Oreg., July 12, 1922; s. Charles Dolen and Dovie (Odom) H.; m. Antoinette Kuzmanich, July 8, 1958; children: Mark, Elizabeth, Theresa, Charles. AB, Willamette U., 1943; AM, Stanford U., 1948. Instr. Willamette U., 1949, dean students, assoc. prof. polit. sci., 1950-56; mem. Oreg. Ho. of Reps., 1951-55, Oreg. Senate, 1955-57; sec. State of Oreg., 1957-59, gov., 1959-67; U.S. senator from Oreg., 1967-97. Chmn. appropriations com., energy and natural resources com., rules and adminstrn. com., joint printing com., joint libr. com., select com. Indian Affairs, Republican Policy Com.; chmn. Appropriations subcom. on transp. & related agencies. Author: Not Quite So Simple, 1967, Conflict and Conscience, 1971, Between A Rock and A Hard Place, 1976; co-author: Amnesty: The Unsettled Question of Vietnam, 1976, Freeze! How You Can Help Prevent Nuclear War, 1982, The Causes of World Hunger,

1982; co-author: What About the Russians, 1984, Vice Presidents of the United States 1789-1993, 1997. Lt. (j.g.) USN, 1943-45, PTO. Recipient over 100 hon. degrees Republican. Baptist. Office: PO Box 2 Marylhurst OR 97036

HATFIELD, ROBIN KATHERINE, chemist; b. Enid, Okla. d. Robert Dale and Krystyna Anne Hatfield. BA, U. Okla., 1990, MA, 1996, BS, 1998; MS, U. Wash., 2001. Analytical chemist FDA, Lenexa, Kans., 2002—. Fulbright scholar, 1994—95. Mem.: Am. Chem. Soc., Sierra Club, Mensa, Phi Lambda Upsilon, Phi Beta Kappa. Democrat. Avocations: reading, mathematics, knitting, swimming.

HATFULL, GRAHAM F., microbiologist, educator; BSc in biological sci., Westfield Coll., Univ. London; PhD in molecular biology, Edinburgh Univ., Scotland, 1981; postdoctoral studies, Yale Univ., Cambridge Univ., UK. Prof. to Eberly Family Prof. U. Pitts., 1988—, chmn. Dept. Biological Sci. Mem. editl. bd. Jour. of Bacteriology, jour. Molecular Microbiology, jour. Molecular Microbiology & Biotechnology. Grantee professorship, Howard Hughes Med. Inst., 2002—. Office: 376 Crawford Hall U Pitts 4249 5th Ave Pittsburgh PA 15260 Office Phone: 412-624-6975, 412-624-6976. Office Fax: 412-624-4870. E-mail: gfh+@pitt.edu.

HATGIL, PAUL PETER, artist, sculptor, educator; b. Manchester, N.H., Feb. 18, 1921; s. Peter and Katina (Karkadou) H.; m. Katherine Haritos. BS, Mass. Coll. of Art, 1950; MFA, Columbia U., 1951. Instr. art U. Tex., Austin, 1951-54, asst. prof., 1954-56, assoc. prof., 1956-67, prof., 1967-85, prof. emeritus, 1985—, design curator Archer M. Huntington Gallery Mus., 1965-68. Vis. instr. Columbia U. (summer) 1958; designed and installed Tex. Pavilion Exhbn., N.Y. World's Fair; coord. for Gov. John Connolly's Exhbn. of Art and Conf. on the Arts; aux. edn. officer Dist. 8 U.S. Coast Guard, 1965-74; bd. dirs. AHEPA Nat. Ednl. Found., 2003—. Author: Establishing Residency in Greece. 1988, (autobiography) Apostolos, The Immigrant's Son, 1990; (book) Contemporary Encaustic Painting, 1994; contbr. numerous articles and papers to profl. jours. One man shows include Baylor U. Gallery, Bass Concert Hall, U. Tex.; exhbns. include: 42 annual faculty exhbns. U. Tex., Austin, 2d, 3d, 4th Internat. Invitational Exhbn. of Ceramic Art Smithsonian Mus., Washington, 2d, 3d and 7th Nat. Decorative Arts Exhbns., Wichita, Kans., Internat. Invitational Exhbn. of Ceramic Art Iowa State U., Ceder Rapids, Flatbed Print Gallery, 1985-2003, St. Stephen's Emeriti Exhbn., Tex., Austin (Tex.) Mus. Fine Arts; pvt. collections including St. Paul's Luth. Ch., U. Tex. Bus. Administrn. Bldg., Huston Tillotson Coll., Seguin Luth. Coll., U. Tex. Faculty Club, U. Tex. Coll. Fine Arts, Woodlands Corp., Houston, Zapata Corp., Houston, Warren Cravens Corp., Houston, U.S. Mil. Ins. Corp., Harry Litwin Industries, Wichita, Kans., Coopers & Lybrand Corp., Houston, Cesar Design Inc., Cleve., Abilne (Tex.) 1st Nat. Bank, Tchr. Retirement Sys., Austin, FAA, Panama C.Z., Austin (Tex.) Mus. Art, Fox Collection, Austin, Tex., Voutsinas Collection, Elgin, Tex., Iatrou Collection, Austin, Tex.; videos collections include Ceramic History 1951-1976, Baylor U. Archives, Art in Texas - 1951-2000, Baylor U.; work featured in Encaustic Painting, 2000. With USAAF, 1943-45, PTO. Recipient Estelle Grey Meml. prize in art, Margaret Flowers prize in art, White Mus., San Antonio, Wolff and Marx prize in art, Dallas Mus. of Fine Arts; purchase prizes Dallas Mus. of Art, Laguan Gloria Mus. Austin; grantee U. Tex. Mem. Am. Hellenic Ednl. and Progressive Assn. (pres. Stephen F. Austin chpt. 312, dist. gov., 1999-2002, mem. nat. ednl. found. bd.). Home: 2203 Onion Creek Pky Unit 7 Austin TX 78747-1648

HATHAWAY, CARL EMIL, investment company executive; b. Boston, Aug. 12, 1933; s. Carl Barbour and Tekla (Neumaier) H.; m. Gail Humphries Oglee, Dec. 6, 1958 (div. Oct. 23, 1996); children: Brian Kent, Carl Nichols, Andrew Oglee; m. Martha Livingston, Jan. 1, 1999. BA, Harvard U., 1955; MBA, Cornell U., 1959. With Morgan Guaranty Trust Co. N.Y., 1959-81, sr. v.p. pension investments, vice chmn. trust and investments dept., 1969-81; pres. Hathaway & Assocs. Ltd. (instl. investment mgmt.), Rowayton, Conn., 1981—, Hathaway Ptnrs., Inc., Rowayton, Conn., 1994—. Served to lt. (j.g.) USNR, 1955-57. Mem.: Shorehaven Golf Club, Eastward Ho Country Club, Harvard Club, Blind Brook Club. Home: 526 Flax Hill Rd Norwalk CT 06854-2317 Office: Hathaway & Assocs Ltd Rowayton Ave Norwalk CT 06853

HATHAWAY, CHARLES E., academic administrator; BS in Physics, Tex. A&M U., 1958; PhD in Physics, U. Okla., 1965. Mem. faculty dept. physics Kans. State U., Little Rock, 1965-81, dept. head, 1971-81; dean Coll. Sci. and Engring. U. Tex., San Antonio, 1981-86; v.p. acad. affairs Wright State U., 1986-93; chancellor U. Ark., Little Rock, 1993—2002, Donaghey Disting. prof., chancellor emeritus, 2003—. Founder, sr. editor Met. Univs.: An Internat. Forum. Fellow Woodrow Wilson fellow, U. Okla. Mem.: Am. Assn. State Colls. and Univs. (bd. dirs.), Ark. Sci. and Tech. Authority. Office: U Ark Little Rock Office of Chancellor Emeritus 2801 S University Ave Little Rock AR 72204-1000 Office Phone: 501-569-3193. E-mail: cehathaway3@ualr.edu.

HATHAWAY, DEREK C., mining products executive; Founder, chmn. Dartmouth Investments (aquired by Harsco 1979), divsn. pres., 1979-84; group v.p. ops. Harsco Corp., 1984-86, sr. v.p. ops. for engineered products group, 1986-91, pres., COO, 1991-94, pres., CEO, chmn. bd. dirs., 1994—. Office: Harsco Corp PO Box 8888 350 Poplar Church Rd Camp Hill PA 17011

HATHAWAY, FRED WILLIAM, lawyer; b. Lewiston, Maine, Sept. 18, 1956; s. William Dodd and Mary Lee (Bird) H.; m. Lee Broadfoot, June 11, 1988; children: William Broadfoot, Benjamin Dodd. BA, Harvard U., 1979; JD, U. Maine, 1985. Bar: Maine 1985, D.C. 1986, U.S. Patent Office 1986, Virginia 1999. Assoc. Robbins & Laramie, Washington, 1985-90, Venable, Baetjer, Howard & Civiletti, LLP, Washington, 1990-95, Burns, Doane, Swecker & Mathis, LLP, Alexandria, Va., 1995—; ptnr., adj. prof. Georgetown U. Law Ctr., 1998—. Mem. ABA (chair various coms., sub.-coms). Episcopalian. Avocations: rowing, golf, carpentry. Office: Burns Doane Swecker & Mathis LLP 1737 King St Ste 500 Alexandria VA 22314-2727 E-mail: fredh@burnsdoane.com.

HATHAWAY, GERALD THOMAS, lawyer; b. Frankfurt, Fed. Republic of Germany, Aug. 5, 1954; came to U.S., 1955; s. Robert Ernest Hathaway and Jacqueline Anne (Hughes) Gouin; m. Kathleen Ann McCauley, Dec. 27, 1980; children: Michael, Anne, Thomas. BA, LaSalle U., 1976; JD, U. Pitts., 1979. Bar: Pa. 1979, N.J. 1980, N.Y. 1983, U.S. Dist. Ct. (ea. dist.) Pa. 1980, U.S. Dist. Ct. N.J. 1980, U.S. Ct. Appeals (3d cir) 1980, U.S. Dist. Ct. (cen. dist.) Ill. 1981, U.S. Dist. Ct. (so. and ea. dists.) N.Y. 1984, U.S. Supreme Ct., 1988, U.S. Ct. Appeals (2d cir.) 1988. Assoc. Cunniff, Bray & McAleese, Phila., 1979-82, Holtzmann, Wise & Shepard, NYC, 1982-86, ptnr., 1987-91, Marks & Murase, L.L.P., NYC, 1991-97, Bingham McCutchen LLP, NYC, 1997—2003; shareholder Littler Mendelson PC, NYC, 2003—. Author: (musical play) Ire, 1984; contbg. editor: The Developing Labor Law, 1987, 4th edit., 2005; contbr. articles to profl. jours. Vol. dir. NYU Grad. Sch. Bus., 1983-87; asst. sec. Riverside Opera Ensemble, NYC, 1984-91; pres. Barrow Group, NYC, 2000—. Mem. ABA, N.Y. State Bar Assn., Assn. Bar of City of N.Y. Episcopalian. Avocations: writing, theater, photography. Office: Littler Mendelson PC 885 Third Ave New York NY 10022-4614 Office Phone: 212-583-9600. Business E-Mail: ghathaway@littler.com.

HATHAWAY, JAMES C., law educator; JSD, LLM, Columbia U.; LLB with honors, York U. James E. and Sarah A. Degan Prof. Law U. Mich. Law Sch., Ann Arbor, dir. Refugee and Asylum Law Prog. Sr. vis. rsch. assoc. Refugee Studies Prog., Oxford U.; vis. prof. U. Tokyo, U. Calif., U. Cairo. Editor: Jour. Refugee Studies, Immigration and Nationality Law Reports. Office: U Mich Law Sch 970A Legal Research 625 S State St Ann Arbor MI 48109 Office Phone: 734-764-2359. Office Fax: 734-764-8309. E-mail: jch@umich.edu.*

HATHAWAY, LYNN MCDONALD, education advocate, administrator; b. N.Y.C., Mar. 28, 1939; d. William Douglas IV and Dorothy Edna (Homan) McDonald; m. Earl Burton Hathaway II, July 7, 1962; children: Earl Burton III, Amanda McDonald. BA, Bryn Mawr Coll., 1960. Editl. asst. Mademoiselle mag., N.Y.C., 1960-61; adminstrv. asst. Peace Corps office Nat. Coun. Chs., N.Y.C., 1961-62; vice chmn. cmty. rsch. N.Y. Jr. League, 1969-70; editor, chmn. N.Y. Entertains cookbook, 1973-74; edn. chair London Svc. League, 1979-80; pres., dir. London Svc. League, Jr. League, 1980-82; ind. writer, editor London, 1983. Bd. dirs. Friends of Ferguson Libr., Stamford, Conn., 1988, mem., rec. sec., v.p., pres., 1988-95, trustee, 1996-01, sec. bd. trustees, 2000—, citizen adv., 2001—, continuing chair student life com.; trustee, mem. exec. com., chair student life com. Conn. State U. Sys., 1991—, sec. bd. trustees, 1999—. Mem. Bryn Mawr Alumnae Assn. (pres. London 1983-86, internat. councillor 1988-90). Episcopalian. Home: 7 Oakmont Dr Falmouth ME 04105-1157 Fax: 203-359-2511. E-mail: lynnhath@aol.com.

HATHAWAY, PETER S, corporate financial executive; Auditor Arthur Anderson, LLP, 1979—91; contr. and fin. dir. BFI, 1991—95; chief acctg. officer Allied Waste Industries, 1995—2001, treas., 1996—97, v.p., 1996—2000, sr. v.p., fin., 2000—. Office: Allied Waste Industries Inc 15880 N Greenway Hayden Loop Scottsdale AZ 85260*

HATHAWAY, RICHARD DEAN, retired language educator; b. Chillicothe, Ohio, Aug. 8, 1927; s. Dale and Edith (Hart) H.; m. Viola Hale, Apr. 16, 1978; children by previous marriage: Linda Hathaway Ellis, Bruce. AB summa cum laude, Oberlin Coll., 1949; AM, Harvard U., 1952; PhD, Western Res. U., 1964. Instr. English Oberlin Jr. H.S., 1949-50; chief interviewer U.S. Bur. of Census, Boston, 1952-53; exec. sec. New Eng. Fellowship of Reconciliation, Boston, 1953-55; instr. in English, Rensselaer Poly. Inst., Troy, N.Y., 1957-62; from asst. prof. to assoc. prof. SUNY, New Paltz, 1962-69, prof., 1970—2001; ret., 2001. Assoc. prof. Millsaps Coll., Jackson, Miss., 1965-66. Author: Sylvester Judd's New England, 1981, The Henry James Scholar's Guide to Web Sites, 1997; (computer software) Text: A Program About Literature, 1990; contbr. articles to profl. jours. Chair legis. com. SCLC Poor People's Campaign, 1968. Served with USNR, 1945-46. Mem. MLA. Mem. Religious Soc. of Friends. Home: Apt 112 141 Fulton Ave Poughkeepsie NY 12603

HATHCOCK, BONITA CATHERINE (BONNIE HATHCOCK), managed health care company executive; b. Chambersburg, Pa., Oct. 30, 1948; d. John McGillis Gentry and Lola Vaneda (Showaker) Wood; m. Lindsay Levoy Hathcock, Apr. 14, 1984. BS in Bus., Shippensburg State U., 1971; MBA, Nova Southwestern U., 1989; grad. Exec. Human Resource Program, Stanford U. Instr. bus. Cen. Pa. Bus. Sch., Summerdale, 1972-75; with Xerox Corp., various locations, 1975-84, product planning mgr. Dallas, 1982-84; dir. mktg. edn. Datapoint Corp., San Antonio, 1984-85, sr. dir. corp. edn., 1985, sr. dir. worldwide edn., 1985-87; various positions including dir. corp. tng. and v.p. human resources Siemens-Rolm, Boca Raton, Fla.; v.p. human resources U.S. Airways; joined Humana Inc., Louisville, 1999, now sr. v.p., chief human resources officer. Prin. bcG Enterprises (profl. awareness tng. co.) Dallas, 1982-84. Avocations: cooking, swimming, reading, walking, writing. Office: Humana Inc The Humana Bldg 500 W Main St Louisville KY 40202*

HATHCOCK, JOHN EDWARD, vocalist; b. Memphis, Sept. 6, 1955; BA in Psychology, Memphis State U., (now U. Memphis), 1986; studied with Dr. David Williams, U. Memphis, 1992-97; studied with Ethel Maxwell, 1982-98; AAS in Graphic Art Tech. summa cum laude, S.W. Tenn. C.C., 2001; MA in Music summa cum laude, Am. World U., Iowa City, Iowa, 2001, PhD in music, 2004. Cert. Internet Webmaster 2003. Singer, performer, composer opera and sacred classical music; vocal coach, 1999—. Pres. Position Prodns., 1988-90; pres., founder Soaring Spirit Music, 1996—. Author: Seasons of Wonder, 1995; author poems; patentee in field; exec. prodr., vocal performer Grace: The Eternal Song. Mem. Bellevue Choir, 1991-92, Memphis Vocal Arts Ensemble, 1993, The Heritage Found. Recipient Mr. Wheelchair Am. award, 1990, Man of Yr. award, Happi Internat. Talent, 1990, Trailblazer award, City of Memphis, 1990. Mem.: Internat. Soc. Poets, Beethoven Club (dir. pub. rels. 1993), Phi Theta Kappa (Nat. Dean's List 1999—2000, 2000—01). Baptist. Fax: 901-683-6805. Office Phone: 901-761-5662.

HATHEWAY, JOHN HARRIS, advertising agency executive; b. Waterbury, Conn., Aug. 9, 1926; s. Fred Whipple and Louise (Wood) H.; m. Patricia Mary Flaherty, Sept. 24, 1955; children: John Harris, Geoffrey Mills, Sara Wood. AB, Dartmouth Coll., 1948; MBA, Amos Tuck, 1950. With Young and Rubicam Inc., N.Y.C., 1950-89, sr. v.p., mgmt. supr., 1968-74, sr. v.p., group dir., 1974-83, exec. v.p., group dir., 1983-87, exec. v.p., western regional dir., 1987-89, also dir. Bd. overseers Hanover Inn, N.H., 1968-78, 94—. Mem. editl. bd. Dartmouth Life, 1991—. Mem. Coun. of Alumni Dartmouth, 1968-90, mem. alumni awards com., 1982-86, chmn., 1986-90, chmn. pub affairs adv. com., 1990—; pres. Dartmouth Class 1948, 1994-98; assembly of overseers Dartmouth-Hitchcock Med. Ctr., 1996—; mem. Dean's Council, Dartmouth Med. Sch. 2001-; bd. dirs. Chappaqua Summer Sch. Program, Horace Greeley Ednl. Fund, 1978-85, Upper Valley Hostel, 1999—, Friends of Hopkins and Hood, 1990—; mem. Diocesan Mission Com.; mem. com. Parents' Fund, U. Vt., 1981-86. Served with AUS, 1945-46. Recipient Alumni award Dartmouth Coll., 1980 Mem. Dartmouth Coll. of N.Y. Alumni Assn. (pres. 1965-66, bd. dirs. 1958-64, 67-70, 72-87), Waccabuc Country Club, Manchester (Vt.) Country Club, Hanover Country Club, Dartmouth Club Upper Valley (dir. 1994—), Phi Beta Kappa. Episcopalian (vestryman, warden). Home: 10 Buell St Hanover NH 03755-2416 Office: Young and Rubicam Inc 285 Madison Ave New York NY 10017-6486

HATHORNE, GAYLE GENE, musician, family historian; b. Concordia, Kans., Sept. 3, 1953; d. Richard and R. Virginia (Huscher) Hathorne; 1 child, Amanda Kimberly. BMusic, Manhattan Sch. Music, N.Y.C., 1976; Artist's Diploma, Karajan Akademie, Berlin Philharm. Orch., 1980. Backstage hornplayer Bayreuth (Germany) Festival, 1977; 3d/1st solo hornist Stadt. Orch., Solingen, Germany, 1980-88; genealogy instr. Blue Ridge C.C., 1999—2002; dir. membership, office mgr. N.Y. Geneal. and Biog. Soc., 2002—. Substitute tchr. music and German, Henderson County Pub. Schs., 1988-98; pvt. horn tchr., Hendersonville, 1989— Sr. editor Tarheel Tattler, 1994-96, River Ramblings, 1994-96; editor Kuykendall Gazette, 1996-97; performer on CDs/cassettes; extra in film 28 Days, 1999. Nat. Fedn. Music Clubs nat. scholar, 1971. Mem. DAR (state pub. rels. N.C. Soc. 1997-99, organizing regent Abraham Kuykendall chpt. 1996), Children of Am. Revolution (organizing sr. pres. French Broad River Soc. 1992, state libr. 1996-98). Democrat. Avocations: genealogical research, photography, travel, writing, listening to opera. Personal E-mail: gaylegenehath@yahoo.com.

HATKOFF, CRAIG MITCHELL, real estate executive, educator; b. Albany, N.Y., Mar. 19, 1954; s. Leon and Doris (Wildove) H. BA magna cum laude, Colgate U., 1976; MBA, Columbia U., 1978. Mng. dir. Chem. Bank, N.Y.C., 1978-89; mng. ptnr. Victor Capital Group, N.Y.C., 1989—; cofounder Tribeca Film Festival, 2002—. Adj. prof. bus. Columbia U., N.Y.C., 1990—. Mem. Albany Academy (nat. adv. bd.), Columbia Bus. Sch. Alumni Assn. (bd. dirs.), Phi Beta Kappa. Avocations: collecting guitars, tennis, waterskiing.

HATLEN, BURTON NORVAL, language educator; b. Santa Barbara, Calif., Apr. 9, 1936; s. Julius Herbert and Lillie (Torvend) H.; m. Barbara Karlson, Sept. 20, 1961 (div. Nov. 1982); children: Julia, Inger; m. Virginia Nees, Nov. 10, 1983. BA, U. Calif., Berkeley, 1958; MA, Columbia U., 1959, Harvard U., 1961; PhD, U. Calif., Davis, 1972. Asst. prof. English King Coll., Bristol, Tenn., 1961-62; instr. U. Cin., 1962-65; asst. prof. U. Maine, Orono, 1967-72, assoc. prof., 1972-81, prof., 1981—, chmn. dept. English, 1985-88; interim dean Coll. Arts and Humanities, 1996-97. Dir. Nat. Poetry Found. Author: George Oppen: Man and Poet, 1981, (poems) I Wanted To Tell You, 1988. Mem.: MLA. Democrat. Office: U of Maine Dept Of English Orono ME 04469-0001

HATLEN, JOEL S., electronics manufacturing executive; b. 1958; With Ernst & Young LLP; sr. tax acct., tax mgr., corp. contr., chief acctg. officer Data I/O Corp., Redmond, Wash., 1991, v.p. fin., CFO, 1998—. Office: 10525 Willows Rd NE Redmond WA 98052-2545

HATLER, PATRICIA RUTH, lawyer; b. Las Vegas, Nev., Aug. 4, 1954; d. Houston Eugene and Laurie (Danforth) Hatler; m. Howard A. Coffin II; children: Sloan H. D. Coffin, Laurie H. M. Coffin. BS, Duke U., 1976; JD, U. Va., 1980. Bar: Pa. 1980, Ohio 2002. Assoc. Dechert, Price & Rhoads, Phila., 1980-83; assoc. counsel Independence Blue Cross, Phila., 1983-86, sr. v.p., gen. counsel, corp. sec., 1987-99; exec. v.p., chief legal, gov. officer Nationwide, Columbus, 1999—. Home: 17 N Parkview Ave Bexley OH 43209-1427 Office: Nationwide One Nationwide Plaza Columbus OH 43215 Office Phone: 614-677-8754. E-mail: hatlerp@nationwide.com.

HATT, CLIFFORD VAN, school system administrator, psychologist; b. Buffalo, Feb. 17, 1949; s. Clifford Milton and Mary Eileen Hatt; m. Cynthia Kay Ellis, July 21, 1979; children: Gregory Gerard Clifford, Catherine Marie. BA, Canisius Coll., Buffalo, 1969—71; MEd, Fla. Atlantic U., Boca Raton, 1973—75; EdD, U. No. Colo., Greeley, 1977—81. Diplomate in School Psychology Am. Bd. Profl. Psychology, 2004, Am. Bd. Med. Psychotherapists, 1998, cert. sch. psychologist Nat. Assn. Sch. Psychologists, 1989, lic. clin. psychologist Va. Bd. Psychology, 1987. Tchr. Cardinal Newman H.S., West Palm Beach, Fla., 1972—76; adj. assoc. prof., psychology Coll. William and Mary, Williamsburg, Va., 1988—; sch. psychologist Va. Beach City Pub. Schs., 1979—89, coord., psychol. svcs., 1989—, dir, doctoral psychology internship tng., 1997—; adj. prof., psychology Norfolk State U., Va., 1995—. Contbr. articles to profl. jours., chapters to books. Fellow: Am. Acad. Sch. Psychology; mem.: NASP, APA, Va. Acad. Clin. Psychologists, Va. Acad. Sch. Psychologists (pres. 1990—91), Va. Psychol. Assn. (pres. 1992—93). Roman Catholic. Avocations: music, travel, racquetball. Home: 1310 Plantation Lakes Cir Chesapeake VA 23320-8110 Office: Va Beach City Pub Schs 1413 Laskin Rd Virginia Beach VA 23451 Office Phone: 757-437-7589. Office Fax: 757-437-7596. Personal E-mail: chatt@vbschools.com.

HATTEBERG, LARRY MERLE, photojournalist; b. Winfield, Kans., June 30, 1944; s. Merle Lawrence and Mary Dorothy (Early) H.; m. Judy Beth Keller, June 6, 1965; children: Sherry Renee, Susan Michelle. Student, Kans. State Tchrs. Coll., 1962-63, Emporia-Wichita State U., 1963-66. Photographer Sta. KAKE-TV, Wichita, Kans., 1963, photojournalist, 1966-67, chief photographer, 1967-81, assoc. news dir., 1981-87, exec. news dir., 1987-88, co-anchor 5 p.m. newscast, 1988-92; co-anchor Evening News broadcasts KAKE-TV, Wichita, Kans., 1992—. Co-chmn. faculty Nat. Press Photographers TV Workshop, U. Okla., 1975—. Author: Larry Hatteberg's Kansas People,1991; developed Hatteberg's People series for TV, 1974. Served with USAR, 1966-72. Regional semi-finalist NASA Journalist-in-Spece Program; recipient Brotherhood award Kans. region NCCJ, 1995, regional lifetime Emmy award TV segment Hatteberg's People, Regional Emmy, 2000, 04. Life mem. Nat. Press Photographers Assn. (Nat. TV News Photographer of Yr. award 1975, 77, Joseph Sprague award 1983, Joseph Costa award 1991). Office: 1500 N West St Wichita KS 67203-1323

HATTEN, WILLIAM SEWARD, manufacturing executive; b. Chgo., Apr. 7, 1917; s. William Seward and Margaret (Ahearn) H.; m. Marjorie Popp, Dec. 29, 1939; 1 dau., Patricia Marie (Mrs. Dudley D. Pendleton III). BA, Lawrence Coll., 1939; MBA, Northwestern U., 1944; PhD, Kennedy-Western U., 2000. Indsl. engr. Sears, Roebuck & Co., 1940-43; mgr. control div. Chgo. Ordnance Dist., 1943-45; owner Eskimo Ice Cream Co., Tucson, 1945-50; gen. mgr. Utica Knitting Co., N.Y., 1950-54; cons. Worden & Risberg, Phila., 1954-64; pres., chief exec. officer, dir. Clayton Mark & Co., Evanston, Ill., 1964-67; chmn. bd. Ken-Ray Brass Products, Inc., Vermont, Ill., 1964-67; pres., chief exec. officer, dir. Harper-Wyman Co., Hinsdale, Ill., 1967-69; exec. v.p. Warner Electric Brake & Clutch Co., Beloit, Wis., 1969-72; group v.p. engines and generators, dir. Kohler Co., Wis., 1973-80; pres. Hatten & Assocs., Lakeland, Fla., 1980—. Mem. Am. Ordance Assn., Northwestern U. Grad. Bus. Alumni Assn., Lone Palm Golf Club (Lakeland, Fla.), Lakeland Yacht and Country Club (Lakeland, Fla.), Union League (Chgo.), Phi Delta Theta. Episcopalian. Office: Hatten & Assocs 4010 Cheverly Dr E Lakeland FL 33813-1207 Office Phone: 863-680-4117.

HATTERSLEY-SMITH, GEOFFREY FRANCIS, retired government agency administrator, retired government research scientist; b. London, Apr. 22, 1923; s. Wilfred Percy Ashby and Ethel Mary (Willcocks) H.-S.; m. Maria Kefallinou, May 12, 1955; children: Kara Mary, Fiona Anastasia Student, Winchester Coll., Eng., 1937-41; BA, Oxford U., Eng., 1948, MA, 1951, DPhil, 1956. Base leader Falkland Islands Dependencies Survey, 1948-50; def. sci. staff officer Def. Rsch. Bd., Ottawa, Ont., Can., 1951-73; prin. sci. officer Brit. Antarctic Survey, Cambridge, Eng., 1973-91. Sec. Antarctic place names com. Fgn. and Commonwealth Office, London, 1975-91. Author: North of Latitude Eighty, 1974, Present Arctic Ice Cover, 1974, The History of Place Names in the Falkland Islands Dependencies, 1980, The History of Place Names in the British Antarctic Territory, 1991, Geographical Names in the Ellesmere Island National Park Reserve, 1998; editor: The Norwegian with Scott, 1984. Sub-lt. Royal Navy, 1942-46. Fellow Royal Soc. Can. (Acad. Scis.), Royal Geog. Soc. (Founder's Gold medal 1966), Arctic Inst. N. Am. (gov. 1963-66), Arctic Circle Club (pres. 1967-69), Arctic Club (pres. 1976), Antarctic Club (London) (com. mem. 1983-85). Avocations: history, gardening. Home: The Crossways Kent Cranbrook TN17 2AG England Office Phone: 01580-712865.

HATTERY, ROBERT RALPH, radiologist, educator; b. Phoenix, Dec. 15, 1939; s. Robert Ralph and Goldie M. H.; m. D. Diane Sittler, June 18, 1961; children: Angela, Michael. BA, Ind. U., 1961, MD, 1964; cert. in diagnostic radiology, Mayo Grad. Sch. Medicine, 1971. Diplomate Am. Bd. Radiology. Intern Parkland Meml. Hosp.-Southwestern Med. Sch., Dallas, 1964-65; fellow Mayo Clinic, Rochester, Minn., 1967-70, cons., 1970-81, chmn. dept. diagnostic radiology, 1981-86; instr. radiology Mayo Med. Sch., 1973-75, asst. prof. radiology, 1975-78, assoc. prof. radiology, 1978-82, prof. radiology, 1982—. Chair Mayo Group Practice Bd., 1991-93; chmn. bd. govs Mayo Clinic, Rochester, 1994-98; trustee Mayo Found., 1992-2002; trustee Am. Bd. Radiology. Author numerous jour. articles and abstracts, book chpts. Capt. USAF, 1965-67, Willford Hall Hosp., San Antonio. Fellow Am. Coll. Radiology; mem. Radiol. Soc. N.Am. (bd. dirs. 1999—), Am. Roentgen Ray Soc., Soc. Computed Body Tomography (pres. 1982-83), Soc. Genitourinary Radiography (pres. 1986-88), Am. Bd. Radiology (exec. dir.). Office: American Bd Radiology 5441 E Williams Blvd Tucson AZ 85711 Office Phone: 520-790-2900. Business E-Mail: rhattery@theabr.org.

HATTIN, DONALD EDWARD, geologist, educator; b. Cohasset, Mass., Nov. 16, 1928; s. Edward Arthur and Una Vestella (Whipple) H.; m. Marjorie Elizabeth Macy, July 15, 1950; children: Sandra Jane, Ronald Scott, Donna Jean. BS, U. Mass., 1950; MS, U. Kans., 1952, PhD (Shell fellow), 1954. Asst. instr. geology U. Kans., 1950-52, instr., 1953-54; asst. prof. geology Ind. U., Bloomington, 1954-60, assoc. prof., 1960-67, prof., 1967-95, prof. emeritus, 1995—; asst. geologist Kans. Geol. Survey, 1952, research assoc., 1959-68, 70-74, 77-82, 86-87. Vis. prof. Ernst-Moritz-Arndt U., Greifswald, German Dem. Republic, 1985; geologist Ind. Geol. Survey, 1957-58; cons. in field; mem. N.Am. Commn. on Stratigraphic Nomenclature, 1987-94; vis. disting. prof. U. Kans., 1991. Author: Stratigraphy of the Wreford Limestone, 1957, Stratigraphy of the Carlile Shale, 1962, Stratigraphy of the Graneros Shale in Central Kansas, 1965, Stratigraphy and Depositional Environment of Greenhorn Limestone of Kansas, 1975, Upper Cretaceous Stratigraphy and Depositional Environments of Western Kansas, 1978, Stratigraphy and Depositional Environment of Smoky Hill Chalk, Niobrara Chalk, Western Kansas, 1982, W. Ferdinand Macy, 1852-1901: Painter of New England Landscapes, 2004. Capt. reserves USAF, 1950—59, lt. USAF, 1955—57. Recipient Erasmus Haworth Disting. Alumni honors in geology U. Kans., 1976, Alumni Disting. Tchg. award Coll. Arts and Scis. Ind. U., 1988, Disting. Tchg. and Mentoring award Grad. Sch. Ind. U., 1995; NSF grantee, 1975-77, 88-90, Am. Chem. Soc. grantee, 1978-80, 84-86; NSF fellow, 1969. Fellow:

Geol. Soc. Am. (grantee 1975); mem.: Paleontol. Soc., Soc. Econ. Paleontologists Mineralogists, Am. Assn. Petroleum Geologists (Outstanding Educator award Ea. sect. 1993). Office: Ind U Dept Geol Scis Bloomington IN 47405

HATTON, BARBARA R., academic administrator; b. La Grange, Ga., June 4, 1941; d. William H. and Katye (Tucker) H.; 1 child, Kera M. Washington. BS, Howard U., 1962; MA, The Atlanta U., 1966; MEA, Stanford U., 1971, PhD, 1976. Assoc. dir. Stanford (Calif.) U., 1970-72, asst. prof. edn. adminstrn. and policy studies, 1976-79; chair Dept. Adminstrn. & Supervision, acting assoc. dean The Atlanta U., 1979-80; dean, prof. Tuskegee U., Ala., 1984-88; dep. dir. The Ford Found., N.Y., 1988; scholar-in-residence So. Edn. Found., Atlanta, 1992—; pres. S.C. State U., Orangeburg, 1993—, Knoxville Coll., 1997—. Mem. adv. com. Tchr. Edn. Project Assn. Am. Colls.; mem. review panel Fifth Yr. Non-Trad. Edn. Programs Ala. Dept. Edn.; mem. futures task force Am. Assn. Colls. for Tchr. Edn.; noms. com. New Deans Orientation Com. Trainer New Dean's Inst. Am. Assn. of Colls. of Tchr. Edn.; commn. on edn1. quality So. Regional Edn. Bd.; mem. Math. Standardization Com. Atlanta Pub. Schs.; reader Jour. Ga. Ednl. Rsch. Assn.; chmn. subcommittee on provisional certification and reciprocity, exec. com. Bd. Regents and State Bd. of Edn., State of Ga. Mem. S.C. Humanities Coun., Orangeburg C. of C.; bd. dirs. Assn. Presbyn. Colls. and Univs., Tenn. Rsch. Valley, Knoxville Symphony; active Met. Drug Com., Coll. Bds. Equity 2000 Project. Fellow NDEA, EPDA; recipient The Rose award U. S.C., 1993, Drum Major for Justice awards, 1993. Mem. Am. Ednl. Rsch. Assn., Am. Assn. Sch. Adminstrs., Exec. Women's Assn., Rotary Knoxville, Alpha Kappa Alpha Sorority Inc., Phi Chi Hon. Soc., Phi Delta Kappa Hon. Soc. Office: Knoxville Coll 901 College St Knoxville TN 37921-4724 Office Phone: 865-524-6511. Business E-Mail: bhatton@knoxvillecollege.edu.

HATTON, RANDY C., pharmacist, educator; b. Peoria, Ill., July 20, 1954; s. Virginia Faye Hatton; m. Carla Ann Carmody, May 7, 1984; children: August Carl, Cara Agnes. BS in Pharmacy, St. Louis Coll. of Pharmacy, 1977; PharmD, U. of Fla., 1982. Cert. Bd. Pharm. Spltys. 1991, 1998, 2005. Pharmacist Meth. Med. Ctr., Peoria, Ill., 1977—80; postdoctoral fellow U. Fla., Gainesville, 1982—83, vis. instr., 1983—84; clin. pharmacist Pharmacokinetics, Travenol Labs., Longwood, Fla., 1984—85; clin. specialist, medicine, clin. asst. prof. pharmacy Shands Tchg. Hosp., U. Fla., Gainesville, 1985—86; co-dir. drug info., assoc. prof. pharmacy U. Fla., Gainesville, 1986—, clin. assoc. prof. pharmacy, 1988—95, clin. prof. pharmacy, 1995—. Fellow: Am. Coll. of Clin. Pharmacy (hon.); mem.: Fla. Soc. Hosp. Pharmacists (Glaxo Pharmacoecons. award 1995, Pres.'s award 1993, Outstanding regional soc. pres. award 1988, Upjohn Pharmacy Rsch. award 1998), North Ctrl. Fla. Soc. of Health-System Pharmacists, Fla. Soc. of Health-System Pharmacists, Am. Soc. of Health-System Pharmacists, Rho Chi, Phi Lambda Sigma. Home: 3924 SW 102nd Way Gainesville FL 32607 Office: Shands/U Fla PO Box 100316 Gainesville FL 32610-0316 E-mail: hatton@ufl.edu.

HATTON, VINCENT PAUL, lawyer; b. Hartford, Conn., June 2, 1950; s. Leo William and Rose J. (Delaura) H.; m. Anne Louise Sweet, Aug. 22, 1972; children: Sarah Anne, Matthew Thomas, Daniel Leo, Michael Robert. BA, U. Pa., 1972, JD, 1975. Bar: Pa. 1975, N.Y. 1982. Assoc. Ballard, Spahr, Andrews and Ingersoll, Phila., 1975-81; asst. corp. counsel, divsn. counsel, asst. gen. counsel Corning (N.Y.) Inc., 1981-95, asst. gen. counsel, dir. legal dept., 1995-97, v.p., 1998—2003, sr. v.p., 2003—. Mem. ABA (bus. law sect.), Am. Corp. Counsel Assn., Nature Conservancy, Atlantic Salmon Fedn., Trout Unltd., Rockwell Mus., Corning Glass Mus., Am. Chestnut Found. Republican. Roman Catholic. Avocation: fly fishing. Office: Corning Inc One Riverfront Plz Corning NY 14831 Office Phone: 607-974-8382. E-mail: hattonup@corning.com.

HAUBEGGER, CHRISTY, media consultant, publishing executive; b. Houston, Tex. d. David and Ann Haubegger. BA in philosophy, U. Tex., Austin, 1989; JD, Stanford U., 1992. Owner Alegre Enterprises, Inc.; founder, pub., CEO Latina Mag., N.Y.C., 1996—2001; bd. dirs. Latin Media Ventures, N.Y.C., 1996—; founder Latina Mag., N.Y.C., 2001—; cons. Hispanic-related initiatives Creative Artists Agy., 2003—. Assoc. prodr. (films) Chasing Papi, 2003. Bd. dirs. New Am. Alliance; mem. governing bd. Mgmt. Leadership for Tomorrow. Named to Am. Advt. Fedn. Advt. Hall of Achievement, 1999; David Rockefeller Fellow, N.Y.C. Partnership, 2002. Office: Latin Media Ventures 1500 Broadway Ste 700 New York NY 10036

HAUBER, DOROTHY MARIE, elementary school educator; b. Phila., Oct. 28, 1946; d. Frederick J. and Dorothy M. (Delaney) H. BS in Elem. Edn., Bloomsburg U., 1968; MEd in Elem. Edn., Lehigh U., 1971, student, 1986—; postgrad., Marywood Coll., 1978-79, Villanova U., 1979. Cert. elem. and secondary prin., Lehigh U., Pa. Tchr. reading and math. North Pa. Sch. Dist., Lansdale, 1968—2004, advisor CPR Core Group, 1980-85. Instr. CPR ARC, Lansdale, 1984-87; mem. North Pa. Sch. Dist. Found., Lansdale, 1988; co-chair United Way Campaign, Lansdale, 1983-88; judge St. Jude Sch. Sci. Fair, Chalfont, Pa., 1989-92. Named Honor for Devel. Core Group Concept for CPR ARC, 1983. Mem. NEA, ASCD, Pa. State Edn. Assn., Pa. Assn. for Supervision and Curriculum Devel., Nat. Coun. Tchrs. Math., Pa. Coun. Tchrs. Math., Northeastern Pa. Coun. Tchrs. Math. (v.p. 1979-82, pres. 1983-88), North Penn. Edn. Assn., Phi Delta Kappa. Democrat. Roman Catholic. Avocations: gardening, reading, cooking, crafts. Home: 391 Huckleberry Ln Harleysville PA 19438-2334

HAUBER, FREDERICK AUGUST, ophthalmologist; b. Pitts., July 3, 1948; s. Michael H. and Cecilia (Azinger) H.; m. Cathy Lu Rosellini, Aug. 3, 1981; children: Elizabeth Alexandra, Natalia Fredericka. BS in Microbiology cum laude, U. Pitts., 1970; MD, U. Tenn., 1974. Intern U. South Fla., Tampa, 1975, resident in ophthalmology, 1982; pvt. practice Pasco Eye Inst., New Port Richey, Fla., 1983—. Asst. clin. prof. U. South Fla., Tampa, 1984—; rechr., spkr. in field, 1990—; cons. Optimed, Inc. Contbr. articles to profl. jours. Advisor health care cost containment com., Tarpon Springs, Fla., 1988; founder Pasco County Diabetes Assn.; mem. bd. counsellors U. Tampa. Fellow ACS, Am. Acad. Ophthalmology; mem. Southeastern U.S. Debate Soc. Achievements include patent for achromatic intraocular lens; first to insert glaucoma pressure regulator; development of binary optical intraocular lens, color vision eye chart system. Office: Pasco Eye Inst 5347 Main St New Port Richey FL 34652-2506

HAUBIEL, CHARLES W., II, lawyer; b. July 1965; m. Michele R. Haubiel. B, Purdue U.; JD, Ohio State U. Bar: 1992. Atty. Vorys, Sater, Seymour & Pease; sr. staff counsel Big Lots Inc. (previously Consolidated Stores Corp.), Columbus, Ohio, 1997—99, dir., corp. counsel, asst sec., 1999—2000, v.p., gen. counsel, corp. sec., 2000—04, sr. v.p., gen. counsel, corp. sec., 2004—. Office: Big Lots Inc 300 Phillipi Rd Columbus OH 43228

HAUBOLD, SAMUEL ALLEN, lawyer; b. Watertown, S.D., July 29, 1938; s. Gustuv Herman and Leone Marjorie (York) H.; m. Caroline V. Thompson. Sept. 27, 1969; 1 child, Caroline A. BS in Engring., Northwestern U.; JD, Harvard U. Bar: Ill. 1966, N.Y. 1990, U.S. Dist. Ct. (no. dist.) Ill. 1966, U.S. Ct. Appeals (7th cir.) 1970, U.S. Ct. Appeals (9th cir.) 1979, U.S. Supreme Ct. 1974. Assoc. Kirkland & Ellis, Chgo., 1966, ptnr., 1972—; resident ptnr. Kirkland & Ellis Internat., London, 1994—. Served to lt. USN, 1960-63. Mem. ABA, Ill. Bar Assn., Internat. Bar Assn., Mid-Am. Club, Saddle and Cycle Club (Chgo.), The Hurlingham Club (London), City of London Club. Presbyterian. Home: 40 S Eaton Pl London SW1W 9JJ England Office: Kirkland & Ellis Internat Old Broad St London EC2N 1HQ England

HAUBRICH, ROBERT RICE, biology professor; b. Claremont, NH, May 4, 1923; s. Frederick William and Marion Norma (Rice) H. BS in Forestry, Mich. State U., 1949, MS in Zoology, 1952; PhD in Biology, U. Fla., 1957. Asst. prof. biology East Carolina U., Greenville, N.C., 1957-61, Oberlin (Ohio) Coll., 1961-62, Denison U., Granville, Ohio, 1962-64, assoc. prof. biology, 1964-67, prof. biology, 1968-88, chair dept. biology, 1968-69, alumni chair, 1983-89, prof. emeritus, 1988—. Assoc. dir. Earlham Coll. Biol. Sta., Syracuse, Ind., 1967-72; mem. marine sci. edn. consortium Duke Marine Lab., Beaufort, N.C., 1983-88; libr. reader Marine Biol. Lab., Woods Hole, Mass., 1965—. Contbr. articles to profl. publs. Sgt. USAF, 1943-46. Fellow AAAS, Ohio Acad. Sci.; mem. Internat. Soc. History, Philosophy and Social Studies. Avocations: swimming, hiking. Home and Office: PO Box M Denison U Granville OH 43023 Office Phone: 740-587-6538.

HAUCK, BARBARA JEAN, not-for-profit developer, writer, artist; b. Princeton, N.J., Mar. 11, 1948; d. Lester Winfield Hauck and Jean Catherine Dawson Rodda; stepdau. Paul Mott Rodda; m. Robert Francis Fogarty (div. Feb. 1984); children: Corey Michael, Matthew Robert; m. Richard David Claffey, Aug. 12, 1989; stepchildren: Kelly, Shannon Claffey Hughes; 1 adopted child, Martina Vidovic. BS in Art, Skidmore Coll., 1985; MA in Speech and Comm. Studies, Edinboro U., 1996. Graphic designer various cos., Lancaster and Erie, Pa., 1980-88, printing saleswoman Erie, 1988-93; publicist and dir. mktg. Bay City Promotions, Erie, 1992-95; freelance advt. and promotions, Erie, 1992-97; grad. asst. Edinboro (Pa.) U., 1994-96; exec. dir. Warner Theatre Preservation Trust, Erie, 1996—. Dir. devel. Arts Coun. Erie Endowment, 2000—; mem. adv. bd. Highland Festival, Edinboro, 2000-01. One-woman shows, 1983, 90, 91; exhibited in group shows, 1980—; contbr. articles and poems to various publs. Vol. tchr. Neighborhood Art House, Erie, 1996-2000; fundraiser Jane Earll for State Senate, Erie, 1996, Mike Dunlavey for Judge, Erie, 1999; coord. phone bank Tom Ridge for Gov., Erie, 1998; mem. exec. com. Erie Rep. Com., 1998-99. Recipient Golden Roosters award Erie Advt. Club, 1997; hon. Paul Harris fellow Rotary Club, Erie, 1997. Mem. Assn. Fund Raising Profls. (chmn. legis. and govt. affairs), Women's Roundtable. Roman Catholic. Avocations: painting, weaving, skiing, hiking, reading. Office: Warner Theatre Preservation Trust 811 State St PO Box 1645 Erie PA 16507-9645

HAUCK, FREDERICK HAMILTON, retired military officer, retired astronaut, retired aerospace executive; b. Long Beach, Calif., Apr. 11, 1941; s. Philip and Virginia (Hustvedt) H.; m. Dolly Bowman, Aug. 27, 1962 (div.); children: Whitney Irene, Stephen Christopher; m. Susan Cameron Bruce, June 27, 1993. BS in Physics, Tufts U., 1962; MS in Nuclear Engring., MIT, 1966. Commd. ensign USN, 1962, advanced through grades to capt., 1983; pilot Attack Squadron 35, USS Coral Sea, 1968-70; instr. pilot Attack Squadron 42, Oceana, Va., 1970-71; test pilot Naval Air Test Ctr., Patuxent River, Md., 1971-74; ops. officer Carrier Air Wing 14, Miramar, Calif., USS Enterprise, 1974-76; exec. officer Attack Squadron 145, Wash., 1976-78; astronaut NASA, Houston, 1978-89; space shuttle pilot shuttle transp. system mission 7, 1983; space shuttle comdr. STS-51A, 1984; assoc. adminstr. for external rels. NASA, 1986; space shuttle comdr. STS-26, 1988; dir. Navy Space Systems (OP-943), Washington, 1989-90, ret., 1990; pres., CEO AXA Space (formerly Internat. Tech. Underwriters), Bethesda, Md., 1990—2005. Comml. space transp. adv. com. Dept. Transp., 1990-98, chmn. COMSTAC task group on Soviet entry into world space markets; mem. comml. programs adv. com. NASA, 1991-92, mission rev. group on spacecraft salvage and repair, 1992; mem. panel on space launch industry U.S. Congress Office Tech. Assessment, 1994-95; chmn. NASA External Ind. Readiness rev. group for Second Hubble space Telescope Servicing Mission, 1995-97; mem. Nat. Rsch. Coun. Aeronautics & Space Engring. Bd., 1996-2002, internat. space sta. meteoroid/debris risk mgmt. com., 1995-97, chair space shuttle meteoroid/debris risk mgmt. com., 19976-97; chair bd. overseers Schs. Arts and Scis., Tufts U.; adv. coun. Inst. Nuc. Power Ops., 2005-. Contbg. author: The Greatest Adventure, 1995. Trustee Tufts U.; bd. govs. St. Albans Sch., 1989-95. Decorated Def. D.S.M. (2), Def. Superior Svc. medal, Legion of Merit, DFC, Air medal (9), Navy Commendation Medal with Gold Star and Combat V, NASA D.S.M, NASA medal for Outstanding Leadership, NASA Space Flight medal (3), Presdl. Cost Saving Commendation; named to U.S. Astronaut Hall of Fame, 2001; recipient AIAA Haley Space Flight award, Disting. Svc. award, Tufts U. Alumni Assn., 2000. Fellow: AIAA, Am. Astron. Soc. (bd. govs. 1997—2000), Soc. Exptl. Test Pilots; mem.: Astronaut Scholarship Found. (bd. govs.), Nat. Assoc. Nat. Academies, Early and Pioneer Naval Aviators Assn., Assn. Space Explorers (v.p. 1991—93, bd. govs. 2000), Winter Harbor Yacht Club (Maine).

HAUCK, JEFFREY PETER ARTORIUS MARTEL, lawyer, protective services official; b. Allentown, Pa., Sept. 9, 1968; s. William Lincoln Hauck, Jr. and Alberta Rita Dugan; m. Michelle Frances Wisser, Mar. 7, 1999; children: Jameson Romulus Maxwell children: Jeffrey Peter Artorius Martel Jr., Jacob Nathaniel Xavier, Jonathan Roland Magnus. BA, DeSales U., 1999; JD, Widener U., 2003; pvt. investigator cert., Global Sch. Investigation, 1991; paralegal/legal asst. cert., Blackstone Career Inst., 2004. Cert.: Widener U. Sch. Law (law and govt.) 2003; mcpl. police officer Allentown Police Acad./Pa. MPOTEC, 1991, police firearms instr. NRA, Allentown, Pa., 1992, police defensive tactics instr. Protective Safety Systems, LLC, Va., 1997, tactical sub-machine gun instr. HRT, Inc., Fla., 1998, defensive/control tactics instr. PPCT, Inc., Ill., 2000, spontaneous knife def. instr. PPCT, Inc., Ill., 2001, chem., distraction, spl. impact munitions and OC spray instr. Armor Holdings, The Tng. Acad., 2001, close quarter combat level I instr. Internat. Police Tactical Tng. Acad., 2002, martial arts asst. instr. Black Panther Martial Arts Acad., 2002, law enforcement trainer Am. Soc. for Law Enforcement Tng., 2002, law enforcement acad. instr. Pa. Mcpl. Police Officers' Tng. & Edn. Comm., 2003, self-def. specialist Black Panther Martial Arts Acad., Pa., 2004, specialist in martial arts conditioning Internat. Sports Scis. Assn., 2004, paralegal/legal asst. Blackstone Career Inst., 2004. Cpl. patrol supr. Bethlehem Twp. Police Dept., Pa., 1991—; pres. Hauck and Assocs. Corp., Allentown, Pa., 2002—; assoc. Law Offices of Karl J. Maehrer, Allentown, Pa., 2003—; sgt. Bethlehem Twp. Police Dept., 2004. Expert witness Hauck and Assocs. Corp., Allentown, Pa., 2002—. Author: (novel) Ports And Happy Havens, The Awful Grace Of God; actor: (independent film) The Test; contbr. periodical discussion. Notary pub. State of Pa., 2003—; mem. Allen Coun. No. 23 R.&S.M., Allen-Beauceant Commandery No. 20, Jordan Royal Arch chpt. No. 203, Lehigh Consistory S.P.R.S. 32 degrees, Bethlehem chpt. Rose Croix 18 degrees, Lafayette Coun. Princes of Jerusalem 16 degrees, Muhlenberg Lodge of Perfection 14 degrees, Rajah Shrine A.A.O.N.M.S., Ordo Templi Orientis Xanadu Camp. Staff sgt. U.S. Army, 1986—93. Named Knight Bachelor, Alliance of Karadjordjevic Knights, 2005; named to Instructor of Yr. for Police Control Tactics and Self Defense, World Karate Union Hall of Fame, 2004; recipient Legion of Honor award, Am. Police Hall of Fame, 1997, Honor award, 1998, John Edgar Hoover Meml. Gold medal, 1998, Knight Chevalier award, Venerable Order of The Knights of Michael The Archangel, 1998, President's Nat. Medal of Patriotism, Am. Police Hall of Fame, 1999, Profl. Devel. Spkr. Appreciation, 48th Ann. NECUSA Conf., 2001, Cert. of Achievement in Bus. Orgns., Widener U. Sch. Law, 2002, Student Yr., Black Panther Martial Arts Acad., 2002, Martial Arts Asst. Instr. Yr., Internat. Tae Kwon Do Union's World Wide Martial Arts Hall of Fame, 2002, Black-Belt Yr., Black Panther Martial Arts Acad., 2003, Knight Chevalier, Religious and Mil. Order Knights of the Holy Sepulchre of Jerusalem, 2005. Mem.: NRA (life), Internat. Tae Kwon Do Union (Asst. Instr. Yr. 2002), Nat. Tactical Officers Assn., Am. Soc. Criminology, Acad. Security Educators and Trainers, Police Exec. Rsch. Forum, Am. Soc. For Law Enforcement Tng., Lehigh County, Pa. Pro-Se/Pro-Bono Clinic (asst. counselor 2001—03), Fraternal Order of Police, Pa. Lodge 35, Gun Owners of Am. (life), Nat. Criminal Justice Assn., 82nd Airborne Divsn. Assn., Inc. (life), Rose Croix (Bethlehem chpt., 18°), Princes of Jerusalem (Lafayette coun.), Muhlenberg Lodge of Perfection (14th degree, Allentown, Pa.), H. Stanley Goodwin Lodge of Pa. Free and Accepted Masons, Chpt. 64, Spl. Forces Assn., Inc., Delta Theta Phi (pres. Fred Lick, Jr. senate 2002—03). Democrat. Lutheran. Achievements include research in Martial Science and the Law Enforcement Paradigm. Avocations: alchemy, writing, gourmet cooking, study and practice of European & Asian martial arts, Napoleanic era miniature wargaming. Home: 8312 Countryside Ln Fogelsville PA 18051-1505 Office: Hauck & Assocs Corp 1453 W Linden St Allentown PA 18102 Personal E-mail: thorenslk@cs.com. E-mail: haucktraining@cs.com.

HAUCK, STEVEN ARTHUR, III, planetary scientist, educator; b. Laurel, Md., Mar. 7, 1974; s. Steven and Barbara Hauck; m. Danette Jill Decker, Apr. 17, 1974; m. Danette Jill Decker, June 28, 1997. B in Aerospace Engring. and Mechanics, U. Minn., 1996; A.M. in Earth and Planetary Scis., Washington U., St. Louis, 1998, Ph.D. in Earth and Planetary Sci., 2001. Postdoctoral assoc. Carnegie Instn. Washington., 2001—03; asst. prof. Case Western Res. U., Cleve., 2003—. Assoc. editor Jour. Geophys. Rsch.-Planets, Am. Geophys. Union, 2003—. Contbr. articles to profl. jours. Mem.: Am. Geophys. Union. Office: Case Western Res Univ 10900 Euclid Ave Cleveland OH 44106-7216 Office Phone: 216-368-3675.

HAUER, ERWIN FRANZ, sculptor, educator; b. Vienna, Austria, Jan. 18, 1926; s. Johann and Margarete (Maehner) H.; m. Helen Takacs, Feb. 28, 1961; children— Nicholas James, Laura Leslie. M.F.A., Acad. Applied Arts, Vienna, 1954; M.F.A. (hon.), Yale U., 1983. Mem. faculty Yale U., New Haven, 1956-60, 63-90, prof. art, 1983-90, ret., 1990; artist in residence Dartmouth Coll., Hanover, N.H., 1976; vis. critic R.I. Sch. Design, 1963-64, U. Pa., 1979; vis. artist U. Mich., 1982, U. Maine, Orono, 1983; originator, sculpture Project Calif. Condor traveling exhbn. 1978-83. One-man shows Old Dominion Coll., Norfolk, Va., 1964, Am. Mexican Inst. Cultural Relations, Mexico City, 1963, Yale U., 1964, 65, Dartmouth Coll., Hanover, N.H., 1976, Sindin Galleries, N.Y.C., 1977, Mid Hudson Arts and Sci. Ctr., Poughkeepsie, N.Y., 1981, Smithsonian Instn., 1981, U. Conn., Storrs, 1981, Hartford Childrens Mus., 1982, 1708 E Main St., Richmond, Va., 1983, Nat. Soaring Mus., Elmira, N.Y., 1984; exhibited in group shows Vienna, Rome, Italy, Boston, Cleve., Ann Arbor, Hartford, Manchester, N.H., Yale U., Galerie Chalette, N.Y.C., 1961, 68, Sculptors Guild, N.Y.C., 1983, 84, Silvermine Collection, Westport, Conn., 1984, Silo Gallery, New Milford, Conn., 1984, Arrowwood, Purchase, N.Y.; sculpture commns. and indsl. designs in Austria, Can., Italy, Mexico, Netherlands, Antilles, U.S., Venezuela; represented in permanent collection Josef Albers Found., Am. Mexican Cultural Inst., Mexico City, Chase Manhattan Bank, N.Y.C., 1st Nat. Bank Chgo., Mus. Art, Basel, Switzerland, Wadsworth Atheneum, Hartford, Conn., Art Inst. Chgo., Nat. Soaring Mus.; prin. works include sculpture Conn. Superior Ct., New London. Recipient design award Indsl. Designers Inst. Chgo., 1959; Fulbright grantee, 1955; Morse fellow, 1968. Mem. AAUP, Sculptors Guild, Artists Equity Assn., Soaring Soc. Am. Avocations: soaring. Office: Yale U Sch Art 180 York St West Haven CT 06516-3549*

HAUER, JEROME M., city official; b. Manhattan, N.Y., Oct. 31, 1951; s. Milton and Rose Hauer; m. Glenda Hauer; 1 child, Michael. BA, NYU, 1976; MPH, Johns Hopkins U., 1978. Rsch. assoc. divsn. cardiac surgery Johns Hopkins Hosp., Balt., 1976-78; assoc. adminstr. Red Cross Blood Svcs., 1978-80; various positions IBM, 1983-87; dep. dir. Emergency Med. Scs., N.Y.C., 1987-88, spl. asst. to exec. dir., 1988-89; commr. State of Ind., Indpls., 1989-96; dir. N.Y.C. Office Emergence Mgmt., 1996—. Reachback cons. USMC, 1998; reviewer Heart and Lung Jour. Critical Care, 1987; lectr., presenter in field. Author: (with others) Auto-Transfusion, 1981, Current Problems in Surgery, 1982, Autotransfusion Units: Guideline Report, 1983, Advanced Emergency Care for Paramedic Practice, 1992; contbr. more than 30 articles to profl. jours. including Emergency Medicine, Resident and Staff Physician, Circulation, among others; mem. editl. bd. Natural Disaster Mgmt. Jour., 1998. Mem. exec. com. Interagy. Coun. Drugs, State Ind., 1989, vice chmn. state emergency response com., 1989-92; chmn., bd. dirs. Ind. Pub. Safety CInst., 1990-94; vice chmn., bd. dirs. Ctrl. U.S. Earthquake Consortium, 1990; chmn. The Leadership Coalition for Global Bus. Protection, 1997; mem. sci. adv. for hazardous materials response FBI, 1997; mem. Am. Heart Assn., Am. Lung Assn. Recipient bronze award Internat. Film and TV Festival, 1986, Legion of Hoosier Heros award Mil. Dept. Ind., 1994, Ind. Commendation medal for Exceptional Meritorious Svcs., Ind. Nat. Guard, 1994, Sagamore of the Wabash award, Gov. Evan Bayh, 1994, Outstanding Alumnus of Yr. Pub. Health Practice, Soc. Alumni Johns Hopkins U. Sch. Hygiene and Pub. Health, 1995, Disting. Alumni award NYU, 1997, Hon. Legion award N.Y.C. Police Dept., 1998; named Man of Yr. Fire Safety Dirs. N.Y., 1999. Fellow Internat. Soc. Hematology; mem. Nat. Emergency Mgmt. Assn. (regional v.p., treas. 1990), Nat. Assn. State EMS Dirs. (govt. affairs com. 1993-95), Nat. Fire Protection Assn. (tech. com. on disaster mgmt. 1993-95), Internal Security Assn., Assn. Contingency Planners, Am. Soc. for Indsl. Security, Ind. Arson and Crim Assn. (hon.), Internat. Assn. Fire Chiefs, Internat. Rescue and Emergency Care Assn., Acad. Surg. Rsch., Am. Soc. Hosp. Based Emergency Air Med. Svc., N.Y. Acad. Scis., Assn. Mil. Surgeons U.S., Internat. Soc. Blood Transfusion, Internat. Soc. Thrombosis and Haemostatis, Mass. Assn. Blood Banks.

HAUER, RUTGER, actor; b. Breukelen, The Netherlands, Jan. 23, 1944; s. Arend and Teunke Hauer; m. Inece Tencate, Nov. 22, 1985; 2 children. Film appearances include Turkish Delight, 1973, Pusteblume, 1974, Keetje Tippl'e, 1975, The Wilby Conspiracy, 1975, Max Havelaar, 1976, Mysteries, 1978, A Woman Between Dog and Wolf, 1979, Soldier of Orange, 1979, Spetters, 1980, Chanel Solitaire, 1981, Nighthawks, 1981, Blade Runner, 1982, Eureka, 1983, The Osterman Weekend, 1983, Outsider in Amsterdam, 1983, A Breed Apart, 1984, Flesh and Blood, 1985, Ladyhawke, 1985, The Hitcher, 1986, Wanted: Dead or Alive, 1986, Bloodhounds of Broadway, 1989, Blind Fury, 1989, The Blood of Heroes, 1990, Split Second, 1992, Buffy the Vampire Slayer, 1992, Beyond Justice, 1992, Past Midnight, 1992, Nostradamus, 1995, Surviving the Game, 1994, The Beans of Egypt, Maine, 1994, New World Disorder, 1999, Wilder, 2000, Lying in Wait, 2000, Partners in Crime, 2000, Wilder, 2000, The Room, 2001, Jungle Juice, 2001, The God Bankers, 2002, Scorcher, 2002, Confessions of a Dangerous Mind, 2002, In the Shadow of the Cobra, 2004, Tempesta, 2004, Sin City, 2005, Batman Begins, 2005, Dracula III: Legacy, 2005; co-prodr. film Mysteries, 1978; TV movie appearances include Inside the Third Reich, 1982, Escape from Sobibor, 1987 (Golden Glove award for best actor in a supporting role in a TV miniseries or motion picture), Deadlock, 1991, Blind Side, 1993, Voyage, 1993, Fatherland, 1994, Amelia Earhart: The Final Flight, 1994, Angel of Death, 1994, also in The Edge, 1989, Merlin, 1998, The 10th Kingdom, 2000, Salem's Lot, 2004. Founder Rutger Hauer Starfish Found. AIDS rsch.; with Dutch Army and Dutch Navy. Office: William Morris Agy 151 S El Camino Dr Beverly Hills CA 90212-2775*

HAUG, EDWARD JOSEPH, JR., engineering educator, director; b. Bonne Terre, Mo., Sept. 15, 1940; s. Edward Joseph and Thelma (Harrison) H.; m. Carol Jean Todd, July 1, 1979; 1 child, Kirk Anthony. BSME, U. Mo., Rolla, 1962; MS in Applied Mechanics, Kans. State U., 1964, PhD in Applied Mechanics, 1966. Rsch. engr. Army Armaments Command, Rock Island, Ill., 1969; chief sys. analysis Army Weapons Command, Rock Island, Ill., 1970, chief sys. rsch., 1971-72, chief concepts and tech., 1973-76; prof. U. Iowa, Iowa City, 1976—2003, Carver Disting. prof., 1990—2003, dir. Ctr. for Computer Aided Design, 1983-95; dir. Nat. Advanced Driving Simulator and Simulation Ctr., 1992-98. Author 9 books on computer aided design and dynamics; editor 5 books; contbr. numerous papers to profl. jours. Capt. U.S. Army, 1966-68. Recipient Innovative Info. Tech. award Computerworld/Smithsonian Instn., 1989, Colwell Merit award Soc. Automotive Engrs., 1989. Fellow ASME (Design Automation award 1991, Machine Design award 1992), Am. Acad. Mechanics. Achievements include patents for Constant Recoil Automatic Cannon, and for Real-Time Simulation System.

HAUGEN, CHRISTINE, plastic surgeon; d. Bjorn Hugo and Margit Haugen; m. Frederick Martin Haddad, Sept. 20, 2003; 1 child, Hunter Haugen Haddad. Student, U. So. Calif., 1986—87; AB in English Lit. cum laude, Bryn Mawr Coll., 1990; MD Med. Coll. Pa., 94. Diplomate Am. Bd. Plastic Surgery. Resident in gen. surgery Brown U., Providence, 1994—97; resident in plastic surgery U. Miami, Fla., 1998—2000; plastic surgeon Advanced Cosmetic Laser Ctr., Ft. Lauderdale, Fla., 2000—01; pvt. practice Ft. Lauderdale, 2001—. Med. dir. Med. Spa Ft. Lauderdale, 2003. Contbr. articles to profl. jours. Active Hospice Hundred, Ft. Lauderdale, 2002—,

Goodwill Amb., Ft. Lauderdale, 2004—. Hannah E. Longshore Meml. scholar, Bryn Mawr Coll., 1990. Mem.: Am. Soc. Plastic Surgeons. Avocations: skiing, surfing, travel. Office: 4604 N Federal Hwy Fort Lauderdale FL 33308

HAUGEN, JANE S., elementary school educator; b. Dubuque, Iowa, Feb. 18, 1950; d. Wilfrid L. and Frances E. Welter; m. Daryl A. Haugen, Aug. 9, 1974; 1 child, Alex M. BS, U. Wis., Platteville, 1972; MA, Clarke Coll., 1975. Cert. tchr. Iowa. Tchr. elem. sch. We. Dubuque (Iowa) Schs., Epworth, 1972—73, Dubuque (Iowa) Cmty. Schs., 1973—. Cons. Kendall Hunt co., Dubuque, Iowa, 2005. Recipient Tchg. award, Izaak Walton League, 1996, Excellence in Math. Sci. Tchg. award, Pres. U.S., 2000; vis. scholar, FINE Found. fellow, 2004—05. Mem.: NEA, Internat. Reading Assn., Nat. Sci. Tchrs. Assn., Iowa Acad. Sci. (facilitator projects 1999—, Excellence in Elem. Sci. Tchg. award 1999), Soc. Elem. Presdl. Awards, Nat. Coun. Tchrs. Math., Iowa Coun. Tchrs. Math., Iowa State Edn. Assn., Dubuque Edn. Assn., Phi Delta Kappa (pres. 2001—02, treas. 2002—03, v.p. membership 2000—04). Democrat. Roman Catholic. Avocations: reading, gardening. Home: 2989 Olde Country Ln Dubuque IA 52001 Office: Kennedy Elem 2135 Woodland Dr Dubuque IA 52002 Office Phone: 563-552-3900. Business E-Mail: jhaugen@dubuque.k12.ia.us.

HAUGEN, JANET B., corporate financial executive; B in Econ. magna cum laude, Rutgers U. Ptnr. Ernst & Young LLP; corp. v.p., contr. Unisys Corp., Blue Bell, Pa., 1996—2000, corp. sr. v.p., CFO, 2000—. Mem.: Conf. Bd. Coun. of CFOs, Fin. Exec. Inst., Forum Exec. Women. Office: Unisys Corp Unisys Way Blue Bell PA 19424

HAUGEN, MARGARET ELLEN, daycare administrator; b. Butte, Mont., June 14, 1948; d. W. Stewart and Margaret Anne (Murphy) Zeigler; children: Cherie Anne, Alek Hemmel Spach. Student, Scranton Coll., 1983—84. Dental asst. Dr.Stephen Jones, Butte, 1967—69; religious edn. tchr. St. Patrick's Ch., Butte, 1963—70; daycare provider, 1970—. Vol. tutor Lit. Program, Butte. Named to Wall of Tolerance, Nat. Campaign for Tolerance, 2002, 2005; recipient Cert. Appreciation, Wall of Tolerance, 2005. Home: 626 W Galena St Butte MT 59701-1508

HAUGEN, MARY MARGARET, state legislator; b. Camano Island, Wash., Jan. 14, 1941; d. Melvin Harry and Alma Cora (Huntington) Olsen; m. Basil Badley; children: Mary Beth Fisher, Katherine Heitt, Richard, James. Mem. Wash. Ho. Reps., Olympia, 1982-1992, past mem. natural resources com., transp. com., mem. joint legis. com. on criminal justice system; mem. Wash. Senate, Dist. 10, Olympia, 1993—, chair transp. com., mem. rules com. Mem. LWV, Stanwood Camano Soroptomists. Lodges: Order Ea. Star. Democrat. Methodist. Avocations: fishing, reading, collecting antique clothing. Office: Wash Senate Legis Bldg PO Box 40482 Olympia WA 98504-0482 E-mail: haugen_ma@leg.wa.gov.

HAUGER, JEFFREY BRUCE, educational consultant; BA, U. Calif., Irvine, Calif., 1998; MA, San Jose (Calif.) State U., 2001. Rsch. technician San Jose (Calif.) State U., 2001—02; grad. asst. U. Mass., Amherst, Mass., 2002—04; rsch. fellow Ctr. Ednl. Assessment, Amherst, 2004—. Cons. in field. Contbr. articles to profl. jours. Grantee, San Jose (Calif.) State U., 2000. Mem.: APA, N.E. Ednl. Rsch. Assn., Soc. Tchg. of Psychology, Am. Ednl. Rsch. Assn., Nat. Coun. Ednl. Measurement (chmn. grad. students issues com. 2004—05). Office: University of Massachusetts 152 Hills South Amherst MA 01003 Office Phone: 413-545-1947. Business E-Mail: jhauger@educ.umass.edu.

HAUGERUD, SUE ANN, elementary school educator; d. Russel C. and Norma J. Schneider; m. Donald N. Haugerud. BS in Chem. Engring., Iowa State U., 1978; MA in Tchg. and Learning, St. Mary's U., 2000. Cert. tchr. Nat. Bd. Edn., 2002. Tchr. St. Anthony/New Brighton (Minn.) Sch. Dist., 1993—. Finalist Tchr. of Yr., State of Minn., 2003; recipient Tchr. Excellence award, 2003. Mem.: Pi Lambda Theta, Phi Delta Kappa. Home: 3624 Rolling View Dr White Bear Lake MN 55110 Office: 3600 Highcrest Rd Saint Anthony MN 55418

HAUGHEY, JAMES MCCREA, lawyer, artist; b. Courtland, Kans., July 8, 1914; s. Leo Eugene and Elizabeth (Stephens) H.; m. Katherine Hurd, Sept. 8, 1938; children: Katherine (Mrs. Lester B. Loo), Bruce Stephens, John Caldwell. Student, Deep Springs Coll., 1930-31; LLB, U. Kans., 1939. Bar: Kans. 1939, Mont. 1943. Landman Carter Oil Co., 1939-43; practice in Billings, Mont., 1943-98; ptnr. Crowley, Haughey, Hanson, Toole & Dietrich, 1950-86, counsel, 1986-98; ret. dir. Mont.-Dakota Resources Group Inc., 1998. One-man shows include, U. Kans., U. Mont., Mont. State U., Concordia Coll., Nebr., C.M. Russell Mus., Great Falls, Mont., Boise Mus. Art, Mont. State Mus., Helena, Sandzen Gallery, Bethany Coll., Lindsborg, Kans., Yellowstone Art Mus., Billings, Mont., also numerous group shows. Pres. Rocky Mountain Mineral Law Found., 1957-58, trustee, 1955—; pres. Mont. Inst. Arts Found., 1965-67; pres. Yellowstone Art Center Found., 1969-71, trustee, 1964-81; mem. Mont. Ho. of Reps., 1960-64, Mont. Senate, 1966-70, senate minority leader, 1969-70. Recipient Gov.'s award Arts, 1981 Fellow Mont. Inst. Arts (Permanent Collection award 1960), Am. Artists Profl. League; mem. ABA, Am. Coll. Real Estate Lawyers, Yellowstone County Bar Assn. (pres. 1960-61), U. Kans. Law Soc. (bd. govs. 1989-92), Am. Watercolor Soc. (Midwest v.p. 1978-82), N.W. Watercolor Soc. (life), Midwest Watercolor Soc., Kans. Watercolor Soc. (hon.), Mont. Watercolor Soc. (hon.), Yellowstone Art Mus. (Pres.'s award svc. to Arts, 2005, Philanthropist of Yr.), Phi Delta Theta, Phi Delta Phi. Republican. Episcopalian. Office: Crowley Haughey Hanson Toole & Dietrich TransWestern Pla II 490 N 31st St Billings MT 59101-1256 Office Phone: 406-252-3441. Personal E-mail: jimhoy@bresnan.net. Business E-Mail: jhaughey@crowleylaw.com.

HAUGHT, JAMES ALBERT, JR., journalist, editor; b. Reader, W.Va., Feb. 20, 1932; s. James Albert and Beulah (Fish) H.; m. Nancy Carolyn Brady, Apr. 22, 1958; children: Joel, Jacob, Jeb, Cassie. Student, Morris Harvey Coll., 1950-52; part-time, W.Va. State Coll., 1960-63. Apprentice printer Charleston Daily Mail, 1951-53; reporter Charleston Gazette, 1953—, varied positions as night and weekend city editor, music and film critic, govt., schs., suburban, religion and investigative reporter, 1970-82, assoc. editor, 1983-92, editor, 1992—. Author: Holy Horrors, 1990, Science in a Nanosecond, 1990, The Art of Lovemaking, 1992, Holy Hatred, 1994, 2000 Years of Disbelief, 1996; sr. editor (part-time): Free Inquiry mag., 1996—. Recipient award Headliners Club, 1971, 1st Ann. Consumer Writing prize Nat. Press Club, 1973, Nat. Hwy. Safety Writing award Uniroyal Tire Co., 1975, First Amendment award Sigma Delta Chi, 1977, Merit award ABA, 1977, Consumer Writing prize Nat. Press Club, 1979, 83, Spl. award Religion Newswriters Assn., 1980, Health Journalism award Am. Chiropractic Assn., 1981, 83, First Amendment award People for Am. Way, 1986, Nat. award for edn. reporting Edn. Writers Assn., 1989, Hugh M. Hefner First Amendment award Playboy Found., 1989, Benjamin Fine award for edn. reporting Nat. Assn. Secondary Sch. Prins., 1990, Clarion award Women in Comms., 2000, 02, 03, Nat. Headliners award, 2001, Green Eyeshade award, 2003. Democrat. Unitarian Universalist. Home: 15 Killen Hollow Dr Cross Lanes WV 25313-3516 Office: Charleston Gazette 1001 Virginia St E Charleston WV 25301-2895 Office Phone: 304-348-5199. Personal E-mail: haught@wvinter.net. Business E-Mail: haught@wvgazette.com.

HAUGHT, WILLIAM DIXON, lawyer, writer; b. Kansas City, Kans., June 12, 1939; s. Walter Dixon and Florence Louise (Rhoads) H.; m. Julia Jane Hedstrom, July 22, 1967; 1 dau., Stephanie Jane. BS, U. Kans., 1961; LL.B., U Kans., 1964; LL.M., Georgetown U., 1968. Bar: Kans. 1964, Ark. 1971. Assoc. Stanley, Schroeder, Weeks, Thomas & Lysaught, Kansas City, Kans., 1968-70; ptnr. Wright, Lindsey & Jennings, Little Rock, 1970-91; pvt. practice Little Rock, 1991-95; ptnr. Haught & Wade, 1996—. Author: Arkansas Probate System, 1977, 6th ed. 1999, (with others) Probate and Estate Administration: The Law in Arkansas, 1983. Served to capt. USAR, 1964-68, Korea, Washington. Mem. ABA (coun. chmn. coms.), Am. Coll. Trust and Estate Counsel (regent, editor studies program, chmn. editl. bd., state chair), Internat. Acad. Estate and Trust Law, Am. Law Inst., Am. Counsel Assn., Ark. Bar Assn. (chmn. probate law sect., chmn. econs. of law practice com., chmn. agrl. law com., chmn. juris law reform com.), Ctrl. Ark. Estate Coun., Pulaski County Bar Assn., Ark. Bar Found., Country Club of Little Rock. Presbyterian. Office: Haught & Wade 111 Center St Ste 1320 Little Rock AR 72201-4405 Office Phone: 501-375-5257. Business E-Mail: wdh@haughtwade.com.

HAUGLAND, SUSAN WARRELL, education educator, consultant; b. Portland, Oreg., Aug. 29, 1950; d. George William and Commery Wallace (Coleman) Warrell; children from previous marriage: Charles, Michael. BS in Child Devel., Oreg. State U., 1972; PhD in Psychology, Saybrook Inst., 1976. Cert. family and consumer scis. Dir., head tchr. Lafayette Co-op Nursery Sch., Detroit, 1973-75; handicapped svcs. coord. OutWayne County Head Start, Wayne, Mich., 1975-76; asst. prof. child devel. Va. Poly. Inst. and State U., Blacksburg, 1976-79; prof. emeritus child devel. S.E. Mo. State U., Cape Girardeau, 1979-99, prof. emeritus, 1999—; pres. K.I.D.S. & Computers, Inc., Cape Girardeau, 1999—; prof. early childhood edn. The Met. State Coll. of Denver, 2000—. Dir. Ctr. for Child Studies, Cape Girardeau, 1979-99, Kids Interacting with Devel. Software, Cape Girardeau, 1985—; chair Human-Environ. Studies, Cape Girardeau, 1990-93; judge Developmental Software Awards, 1991—, Child Mag. Awards, 1992-99. Author: Helping Young Children Grow, 1980, Developmental Evaluations of Software for Young Children, 1990, Young Children and Technology: A World of Discovery, 1997, Haugland Developmental Software Scale, 1997, Haugland/Gertzog Developmental Scale for Web Sites, 1998; dept. editor Early Childhood Education Jour., 1992—; contbr. numerous articles to profl. jours. Grantee numerous orgns.; recipient Gov.'s award for Teaching Excellence, 1996. Mem. Assn. for Childhood Edn. Internat., Nat. Assn. for Edn. Young Children, Nat. Assn. for Early Childhood Tchr. Educators, Tech. and Young Children Caucus, Omicron Nu. Democrat. Methodist. Avocations: reading, travel, cooking, bicycling. E-mail: susanhaugland@hotmail.com.

HAUKE, KATHLEEN ARMSTRONG, writer, editor; b. Kalamazoo, Mich., Aug. 27, 1935; d. Robert J. and Katherine E. (Gall) Armstrong; m. Richard L. Hauke, Sept. 20, 1958; children: Katy DuGarm, Nellie Ohr, Andrew M., Henry J. BA Journalism, U. Mich., 1958; MA in English, U. R.I., 1962, PhD in English, 1981. Teaching asst. English U. R.I., Kingston, 1976-81; instr. Hopkinsville (Ky.) C.C., 1984; asst. prof. Morris Brown Coll., Atlanta, 1986-91. Vis. prof. Emory U., Atlanta, 1985; part-time instr. Ga. State U., Atlanta, 1986-88; vis. lectr. U. Nairobi, Kenya, 1988-89; lectr. Spelman Coll., Atlanta, 1994—. Author: Ted Poston: Pioneer American Journalist, 1998; editor: Dark Side of Hopkinsville, 1991; editor (newsletter) Citizens to Advance Negro Edn., 1969-71; contbr. articles to profl. jours. Grantee NEH, 1984. Mem. MLA, Coll. Lang. Assn., Langston Hughes Soc. Democrat. Roman Catholic. Home: 900 N Stafford St Apt 1103 Arlington VA 22203-1844

HAUN, CONSTANCE MORGAN, music educator; b. Pikeville, Tenn., Nov. 16, 1952; d. Rufus Samuel and Elizabeth Ann Morgan; m. David Welch Haun, Aug. 18, 1976; children: Andrew, Margaret. MusB cum laude, U. Tenn., 1974; MSc, George Peabody Coll., 1976. Pvt. piano tchr. Bledsoe County Schs., Pikeville, 1974—75, Street Piano Co., Goodlettesville, Tenn., 1976—81, Donelson, Tenn., 1977—85, Montessori Ctr. & Acad., Nashville and Brentwood, Tenn., 1982—88; activities leader Cumberland Sci. Mus., Nashville, 1986—91; pvt. piano tchr. Kingston Springs, Tenn., 1985—. Pianist South Cheatham Chorale Soc., Kingston Springs, 2003—, Cheatham County Cmty. Theatre, Kingston Springs, 2001—; adjudicator piano auditions, Tenn., 2003—; piano tchr. W.O. Smith Music Sch., Nashville, 1996—98. Vol. music tchr. ARC Charitable Orgn., Kingston Springs, 2004—05. Mem.: Music Tchrs. Nat. Assn., Nat. Guild Piano Tchrs., Tenn. Native Plant Soc., N.Am. Butterfly Assn. Avocations: hiking, butterflies, native plants. Home: 202 Harpeth Hills Dr Kingston Springs TN 37082

HAUN, GREGORY COSMO, artist; b. Atlanta, June 30, 1967; s. Cosmo L. and Lynn E. (Wilcox) H.; m. Jennifer Martin Davis, Aug. 20, 1995. BA, Reed Coll., Portland, Oreg., 1990; MS in Visual Studies, MIT, Cambridge, 1992. Instr. continuing edn. Pacific Northwest Coll. Art, Portland, 1994-98; instr. Mt. Hood C.C., Portland, 1996-97; sr. programmer analyst Mattel, Inc., 1998-99; arch. Cenquest, Inc., Portland, 1999—. Exhibited in group show at Portland Art Mus., 1995; author: Photoshop Collage Techniques, 1997, (CD) Personal Dictionaries, 1995; artist: (series of digital photos) Archaeological Collage I, 1993 (Purchase award City of Portland Visual Chronicle 1994, 2002). Land-use chmn. Creston-Kenilworth Neighborhood Assn., 1997. Project grantee Archaeological Collage II, Regional Arts & Culture Coun., Portland, 1996.

HAUN, JOHN DANIEL, petroleum geologist, educator; b. Old Hickory, Tenn., Mar. 7, 1921; s. Charles C. and Lydia (Rhodes) H.; m. Lois Culbertson, June 30, 1942. AB, Berea Coll., 1948; MA, U. Wyo., 1949, PhD, 1953. Registered profl. engr., Colo. Geologist Stanolind, Amoco, Vernal, Utah, 1951-52; v.p. Petroleum Research Corp., Denver, 1952-57; mem. faculty dept. geology Colo. Sch. Mines, Golden, 1955-80, prof., 1963-80, part time, 1980-85, emeritus prof., 1983—; cons. Barlow & Haun, Inc., Evergreen, Colo., 1957-90. Cons. Potential Gas Agy., 1966-78, mem. com., 1978—; mem. adv. com. Colo. Water Pollution Control Commn., 1969-70; mem. adv. council Kans. Geol. Survey, 1971-76; del. Internat. Geol. Congress, Sydney, Australia, 1976; U.S. rep. Internat. Com. on Petroleum Res. Classification UN, N.Y.C., 1976-77; mem. oil shale adv. com. Office of Tech. Assessment, Washington, 1976-79, mem. U.S. natural gas availability adv. panel, 1983; mem. Colo. Oil and Gas Conservation Commn., 1977-87, vice-chmn., 1983-85, chmn. 1985-87; mem. energy resources com. Interstate Oil and Gas Compact Commn., 1978—; mem. exec. adv. com. Nat. Petroleum Coun., 1968-70, 79-89, mem. com. on unconventional gas sources, 1978-80; com. on Arctic oil and gas resources, 1980-81; mem. U.S. Nat. Com. on Geology Dept. Interior and NAS, 1982-89, chmn., 1985-87; mem. com undiscovered oil and gas resources, 19881-91, com. status and rsch. objectives in solid-earth scis.: critical assessment, 1988-92, Nat. Rsch. Coun.; del. Internat. Geol. Congress, Paris, 1980, Moscow, 1984; mem. Colo. Oil and Gas legis. com., 1993-94. Editor: The Mountain Geologist, 1963-65, Future Energy Outlook, 1969, Methods of Estimating the Volume of Undiscovered Oil and Gas Resources, 1975; asst. editor: Geologic Atlas of the Rocky Mountain Region, 1972; co-editor: Subsurface Geology in Petroleum Exploration, 1958, Symposium on Cretaceous Rocks of Colorado and Adjacent Areas, 1959, Guide to the Geology of Colorado, 1960; contbr. articles to profl. jours. Served with USCG, 1942-46. Recipient Disting. Svc. award Am. Assn. Petroleum Geologists, 1973, Mines medal Colo. Sch. Mines, 1995. Fellow Geol. Soc. Am., AAAS; mem. Am. Assn. Petroleum Geologists (editor 1967-71, pres. 1979-80, hon. mem. 1984, Sidney Powers Meml. award 1995, Disting. Educator award 2000), Am. Inst. Profl. Geologists (hon. mem., v.p. 1974, pres. 1976, exec. com. 1981-82, Ben H. Parker Meml. award 1983), Am. Geol. Inst. (governing bd. 1976, 79-82, sec.-treas. 1977-78, v.p. 1980-81, pres. 1981-82, Ian Campbell medal 1988, William B. Heroy Jr. award 1996), Rocky Mountain Assn. Geologists (sec. 1961, 1st v.p. 1964, pres. 1968, hon. mem. 1974), Soc. Econ. Paleontologists and Mineralogists, Am. Petroleum Inst. (com. exploration 1971-73, 78-88), Nat. Assn. Geology Tchrs., Wyo. Geol. Assn. (hon. life), Colo. Sci. Soc. (hon. life), Sigma Xi, Sigma Gamma Epsilon, Phi Kappa Phi. Home: 1238 Kerr Gulch Rd Evergreen CO 80439-6397

HAUN, MARK WILLIAM, music educator; b. Phoenixville, Pa., Feb. 11, 1961; s. William D. and Joan F. Haun; m. Karla M. Cook, Sept. 26, 1987; children: Jacob Cook, Luke Cook. B, Southern Ill. U., 1983. Cert. music tchg. K-12, elem. classroom tchg. K-9. Band dir. Anna Jonesboro HS, Anna, Ill., 1983—84, Edwardsville Sch. Dist., Edwardsville, Ill., 1985—. Mem.: Madison County Band Dir. Assn., Music Educators Nat. Conf., Ill. Music Educators Assn. Luth. E-mail: mhaun@ecusd7.org.

HAUPT, ANDREA MOORE, psychologist, therapist; b. Princeton, N.J., Aug. 1, 1943; d. Frank Leslie and Lucille M. (Kipp) Moore; m. Raymond E. Haupt, Aug. 19, 1978. BA in Liberal Arts and Chemistry, SUNY, Binghamton, 1965; ABD in Biochemistry, U. Pa., 1967; MEd in Ednl. Psychology, Temple U., 1972, PhD in Counseling Psychology, 1990. Lic. psychologist. Caseworker Dept. Pub. Assistance, Phila., 1967-69; mental health worker Phila. State Hosp., 1969-72; counselor Horizon House, Phila., 1972-74; psychologist Jefferson Cmty. Mental Health Ctr., Phila., 1974-84; pvt. practice Phila., 1984—98. Consulting psychologist Grad. Hosp. Dept. Psychiatry, Phila., 1990—96; consulting psychol. examiner City of Phila., 1990—; bd. dirs. Women Therapist's Network, 1993—96. Juried mem. Phila. Watercolor Soc., 1982—. Recipient N.Y. Regents scholar, 1961-65; NIH fellow U. Pa., 1965-67, Univ. fellow Temple U., 1984-86. Fellow: Pa. Psychol. Assn.; mem.: APA. Avocations: gardening, pets, writing, travel, watercolor. Home and Office: 639 W Ellet St Philadelphia PA 19119-3428 Office Phone: 215-438-8175.

HAUPT, ROGER A., advertising executive; Joined Leo Burnett (became Leo Group), Chgo., 1984—2000; exec. v.p. Leo Group, 1989—97, 1999—2000, pres., CEO, 2000, COO, 1999; CAO Leo Group (became BCom3), 1997—99; chmn., CEO BCom3 (became Publicis Groupe SA), 2000—02; pres., COO Publicis Groupe SA, Chgo, 2002—04; chmn. Publicis Groupe Media. Office: Publicis Groupe SA c/o Leo Burnett Worldwide 35 W Wacker Dr Chicago IL 60601

HAUPTFUHRER, W. BARNES, bank executive; b. Apr. 29, 1954; BA in Polit. Economy, Princeton U.; JD/MBA, U. Va. Mng. ptnr., head First Union Capital Ptnrs., Inc.; with Kidder Peabody, NY, 1981—88; co-head investment banking Wachovia Corp., 1999, sr. exec. v.p., co-head corp. and investment banking Charlotte, NC, 1999—; sr. v.p. Wachovia Securities, Inc., 2000—02, co-head corp. and investment bank, 2000—02. Bd. mem. Wolverine Tube, Inc. Former co-chair Alexis de Tocqueville Soc. for Charlotte United Way Campaign.

HAUPTMAN, GREGORY B., lawyer; b. Washington, Apr. 5, 1951; AB, Washington U., 1973; JD with honors, George Washington U., 1976. Bar: Md. 1976, DC 1977. Ptnr., real estate group Venable LLP, Washington. Mem.: ABA (mem. real property section), Md. Bar Assn., DC Bar Assn. Office: Venable LLP 575 7th St NW Washington DC 20004 Office Phone: 202-344-8528. Office Fax: 202-344-8300. Business E-Mail: gbhauptman@venable.com.

HAUPTMAN, HERBERT AARON, mathematician, educator, researcher; b. NYC, Feb. 14, 1917; s. Israel and Leah (Rosenfeld) Hauptman; m. Edith Citrynell, Nov. 10, 1940; children: Barbara, Carol Hauptman Fullerton. BS in Math., CCNY, 1937; MA, Columbia U., 1939; PhD, U. Md., 1955, PhD (hon.), 1985, CCNY, 1986, U. Parma, Italy, 1989, D'Youville Coll., 1989, Bar-Ilan U., Israel, 1990, Columbia U., 1990, Tech. U., Lodz, Poland, 1992, Queen's U., Kingston, Ont., Can., 1994, Niagara U., 1996, U. Toledo, 1999, Medaille Coll., 2002. Statistician U.S. Census Bur., Washington, 1940—42; civilian instr. electronics and radar U.S. Army Air Force, Boca Raton, Fla., 1942—43; physicist, mathematician Naval Rsch. Lab., Washington, 1947—70; mathematician Hauptman-Woodward Med. Rsch. Inst., 1970—72, exec. v.p., rsch. dir., 1972—85, pres., rsch. dir., 1985—87, pres., 1988—, also bd. dirs.; prof. biophys. scis. SUNY, Buffalo, 1970—, prof. computer scis., 1992—, disting. prof. structural biology, 2001—. Chmn. N.Y. State Inst. on Superconductivity, 1988—98; mem. sci. adv. bd. Biocryst, 1989—; math. instr. U. Md., 1958—70; chmn. Intercongress Symposium Direct Methods in Crystallography, Buffalo, 1976; pres. Assn. Ind. Rsch. Insts., 1979—80; mem. U.S. Nat. Com. for Crystallography, 1979—81, 1982—85, 1988—89; mem. sci. adv. bd. Biophan, 2001—04. Author (with J. Karle): Solution of the Phase Problem, 1953; author: Crystal Structure Determination: The Role of the Cosine Seminvariants, 1972; editor: Direct Methods in Crystallography, Proceedings of the 1976 Intercongress Symposium, 1978; contbr. chapters to books, articles to profl. jours. Trustee Buffalo Gen. Hosp., 1990—96; chmn. comm. com. Philos. Soc. Washington, 1966—67, corr. sec., 1967—69. Lt. (j.g.) USNR, 1943—46. Named Western N.Y. Man of Yr., Buffalo C. of C., 1986, YMCA Dinner, 1986, 90th Nobel Ann. Dinner, 1991; named to Nobel Hall Mus. Sci. and Industry, 1986, Townsend Harris Hall of Fame, 1989, U. Md. Alumni Hall of Fame, guest of honor Roswell Park Meml. Inst., 1985, YMCA Luncheon, others, invited guest Am. Nobel Convocation, 1987, 1988, Weizmann Nat. Dinner, 1998, others; recipient Belden prize (Gold medal) in Math., 1935, RESA award in Pure Scis., 1959, Citizen of Yr. award, Buffalo Evenings News, 1986, Schoelkopf award, Am. Chem. Soc., 1986, Gold Plate award, Am. Acad. Achievement, 1986, Nat. Libr. Medicine medal, 1987, Law Sch. award, Maimonides Chabad House, 1986, others, (with J. Karle) Patterson award, 1984, Nobel Prize in Chemistry, 1985; grantee NSF, 1972—92, NIH, 1992—; sr. fellow for travel, lectures and rsch. in Italy, NATO, 1973. Fellow: Jewish Acad. Arts and Scis. (medal 1986), Washington Acad. Scis.; mem.: NAS, AAAS, Math. Assn. Am., Am. Crystallographic Assn. (mem. Fankuchen award com. 1988), Am. Phys. Soc., Am. Math. Soc., Saturn Club (guest of honor 1985), Cosmos Club, Sigma Xi (sec. Buffalo chpt. 1971—72), Phi Beta Kappa. Avocation: stained glass art, swimming, hiking . Office: Hauptman Woodward Med Rsch 700 Ellicott St Buffalo NY 14203 Office Phone: 716-898-8607. Business E-Mail: hauptman@hwi.buffalo.edu.

HAUPTMAN, MICHAEL, broadcasting company executive; b. Bklyn., Jan. 6, 1933; s. Hyman A. and Toba L. (Hershman) H.; m. Betty Holzman, Nov. 28, 1957; children: James, William. BA, U. Vt. 1954. Program dir. Sta. WSTC, Stamford, Conn., 1960-61; prodn. mgr. Sta. WABC, N.Y.C., 1961-62, advt., promotion mgr., 1962-63; with Sta. WINS, N.Y.C., 1963-67, Sta. KYW-TV, Phila., 1967-68; mgr. mktg. services Westinghouse Broadcasting Co., N.Y.C., 1968-69; dir. retail mktg. ABC owned radio stas., N.Y.C., 1969-72, dir. planning, 1972-73; v.p. ABC Radio, 1973-76, sr. v.p., 1976-81; v.p.-in-charge ABC Radio Enterprises, Inc., 1981-83; v.p. ABC Video Enterprises Inc., 1983-85; pres. Nat. Communications Corp., Cos Cob, Conn., 1985-89, 90—; pres. Physicians Radio Network div. Primark Corp., v.p. Health Info. Internat., 1989-90; pres. Group H Radio, Inc., 1992—. Address: 13 Carriage Rd Cos Cob CT 06807-1301 Personal E-mail: carriage13@optonline.net.

HAUPTMANN, RANDAL MARK, biotechnologist; b. Hot Springs, SD, July 6, 1956; s. Ivan Joy and Phyllis Maxine (Pierce) H.; m. Beverly Kay Suko, May 22, 1975; 1 child, Erich William. BS, S.D. State U., 1979; MS, U. Ill., 1982, PhD, 1984. Postdoctoral rschr. Monsanto Corp. Rsch., St. Louis, 1984-86; vis. rsch. scientist U. Fla., Gainesville, 1986-88; asst. prof. No. Ill. U., DeKalb, 1988-90, dir. plant molecular biology ctr., 1989-90; sr. rsch. scientist Amoco Life Sci. Techs., Naperville, Ill., 1990-94; dir. advanced tech. Seminis Vegetable Seeds, Woodland, Calif., 1994-98; gen. mgr. Ball Helix, West Chicago, Ill., 1998—2003; pres. Varro Inc., Chgo.; head raw product rsch. Fresh Express, Salinas, Calif. Author: (with others) Methods in Molecular Biology, 1990; contbr. articles to profl. jours. Mem. Internat. Assn. Plant Tissue Culture, Internat. Soc. Plant Molecular Biology, Am. Soc. Plant Physiologists, Tissue Culture Assn. (Virginia Evans award 1982), Sigma Xi, Gamma Sigma Delta. Democrat. Office Phone: 831-384-7388.

HAURI, PETER J., psychology professor, researcher; b. Sirnach, Switzerland, June 25, 1933; arrived in U.S., 1960; s. Rudolf and Verena Hauri; m. Cynthia A. Cleveland, Sept. 25, 1992; 1 child, Matthew R.; m. Debbie Jo Rea-Hauri (div.); children: Heidi J., David J., Katrin J. Sekundar lehr patent, SLS St. Gallen, Switzerland, 1958; PhD, U. Chgo., 1966. Bd. cert. sleep disorders medicine; lic. psychologist Minn. Bd. Profl. Psychology. Tchg. prin. Pestalozzi Jr. H.S., Trogen, Switzerland, 1956—59; asst. prof. psychology Sacramento State Coll., 1966—68; assoc. prof. psychology U. Va., Charlottesville, 1968—71; prof. psychology Dartmouth Coll., Hanover, NH, 1971—88, Mayo Med. Sch., Rochester, Minn., 1988—2000, prof. emeritus, 2000—. Adminstrv. dir. Mayo Sleep Disorders Ctr., Rochester, Minn., 1988—2000; chair Com. to Revise Internat. Classification Sleep Disorders, Chgo., 2002—04. Author: No More Sleepless Nights, 1990, The Sleep

Disorders (and revisions), 1977—98; contbr. articles to profl. jours. Scoutmaster Boy Scouts Am., Hanover, NH, 1980—88; vol. Habitat Humanity, Rochester, Minn., 2001—03; soccer coach Rochester Youth Hockey, 2002—03; bd. mem. The Sleep Found., Chgo., 1992—96. Lt. Swiss Army, 1952—59. Mem.: APA, Am. Acad. Sleep Medicine (bd. mem. 1988—92, Nathaniel Kleitman award 1989), Sleep Rsch. Soc. (pres. and exec. sec. 1974—75). Democrat. Mem. United Ch. Christ. Achievements include research in insomnia. Avocations: skiing, history, outdoor sports. Home: 422 Seventh Ave SW Rochester MN 55902 Office Phone: 507-266-7603.

HAUSDORFER, GARY LEE, management consultant; b. Indpls., Mar. 26, 1946; s. Walter Edward and Virginia Lee (Bender) Hausdorfer; children: Lisa Ann Turner, Janet Lee Fortner. AA, Glendale Coll., 1966; BS, Calif. State U.-L.A., 1968. Rsch. officer Security Pacific Bank, L.A., 1968-73; v.p., mgr. W. Ross Campbell Co., Irvine, Calif., 1973-81; sr. v.p. Weyerhaeuser Mortgage Co., Irvine, 1982-87; exec. v.p., ptnr. L.J. Melody & Co. of Calif., 1987-89; pres. Hausdorfer Co., 1989—, The Diamond Group, 1994—; chmn., CEO Cofiroute USA, 2003—. Councilman, City of San Juan Capistrano, 1978-94, mayor, 1980-81, 84-85, 88-90; chmn. Capistrano Valley Water Dist., 1980-81, San Juan Capistrano Redevel. Agy., 1983-84, 85-86, South Orange County Leadership Conf.; bd. dirs. Orange County Trans. Corridor Agy., Orange County Transit Dist.; chmn. Orange County Transp. Authority. Recipient cert. of commendation Orange County Bd. Suprs., 1981, congl. commendation, 1985, Theodore Roosevelt Conservation award Pres. Bush, 1990. Republican. E-mail: ghausdorfer@cofiroutusa.com.

HAUSER, BERNICE WORMAN, director; m. A. Daniel Hauser; children: Mitchell Alan, Lisa Ann. BA cum laude, Hunter Coll., 1953, MS, 1956; MS in Adminstrn. and Supervision, CUNY, 1978. Tchr. Yonkers Pub. Schs., N.Y.C., 1953-54, N.Y. Pub. Schs., N.Y.C., 1954-60; primary sci. tchr., cons. Pub./Parochial/Ind. Schs., N.Y.C., 1960-72; tchr., primary sci. chair Walden Sch., N.Y.C., 1972-80, coord. student tchrs., 1980-88, curriculum cons., prin. sci. chair, 1988-91; asst. to headministress Horace Mann Sch., N.Y.C., 1991-93, dir. inter-campus acitivities, 1993—. Cons. Scholastic Publs., N.Y.C., 1980—; bd. dirs. CUNY Pub.-Pvt. Schs. Partnership Coun. Author: How to Help Your Child at Home with Science, 1991, The Cat in the Hat Comes Back, 1997, You're the Apple of My Eye, 1998, (adoption issues) Am. Baby, 1984; primary corres. articles Tchr. Clearinghouse for Sci., 1987—; editor: Horace Mann Bull., 1993—; contbr. articles to Ind. Sch., Bull. of Sci. Tech & Soc., Parents League Bull., others. Mem. parks coun. Ctrl. Park Conservancy, 1970—; mem. Citizens Com. For Better N.Y., N.Y.C., 1980—; cons., spkr. and writer Adoptive Parents Com., N.Y.C., 1975—; trustee, v.p., nominating chair Louis Wise Svcs. for Children, N.Y.C., 1976—. Recipient Impact II award Exxon, 1987, Jeremy Rifkin award NASTS, 1991; honoree United Jewish Appeal for Disting. Vol. Svc. to Louise Wise Svcs., 1998; named to Hunter Coll. Hall Fame, 2003. Fellow Phi Delta Kappa; mem. AAUW, ASCD, NSTA (presenter 1985—), Nat. Assn. Ind. Schs., Nat. Assn. Sci. Tech. and Soc., Assn. Tchr. Ind. Schs. (program chairperson), N.Y. Assn. Ind. Schs. (liaison), Hunter Coll.H.S. Alumni Assn. (Hunter Coll. Hall of Fame 2003), Phi Beta Kappa, Epsilon Pi Tau, Cum Laude Soc. Avocations: indoor gardening, theater, opera, reading, writing. Office: Horace Mann Sch 231 W 246th St Bronx NY 10471-3430 E-mail: Bernice_Hauser@horacemann.org.

HAUSER, GEORGE, biochemist, educator; b. Vienna, Dec. 13, 1922; came to U.S., 1939. s. Hans Joseph and Juliane Therese (Gleissner) H.; m. Louise Jean Russo, July 2, 1955. BS, Ohio State U., 1949; PhD, Harvard U., 1955. Mem. faculty Harvard Med. Sch., Boston, 1952-55, from rsch. assoc. to prof., 1955-93, prof emeritus, 1993—; from asst. biochemist to biochemist McLean Hosp., Belmont, Mass., 1957-93, sr. biochemist, 1993—; rsch. affiliate Mass. Inst. Tech., 2000—. Mem. editl. bd. Neurochem. Rsch; adv. and editl. bd. Jour. Neurochemistry, 1977-86, dep. chief editor, 1986-92; interim dir. Ralph Lowell Labs., McLean Hosp., Belmont, 1983-93; reviewer many sci. jours.; cons. NIH, NSF, MIT. Co-editor: Inositol & Phosphoinositides: metabolism & metabolic regulation. Mem., treas. Dem. Ward Com., Newton, Mass., 1976—. With U.S. Army, 1943-48. Recipient Austrian Cross Honor Sci. and Art, 2000; grantee Nat. Insts. Health, 1965-92, Nat. Sci. Found., 1980-82; fellow Japan Soc. for the Promotion of Sci., 1988. Mem. Biochem. Soc., Am. Soc. Biochemistry and Molecular Biology, Internat. Soc. Neurochemistry, Am. Soc. Neurochemistry (coun. 1983-87), Soc. Neurosci. Democrat. Jewish. Home: 47 Windermere Rd Auburndale MA 02466-2521 Office: McLean Hosp 115 Mill St Belmont MA 02478-1048 Office Phone: 617-855-2408. Business E-Mail: george_hauser@hms.harvard.edu.

HAUSER, GUSTAVE M., cable television and electronic communications company executive; b. Cleve., Sept. 3, 1929; s. Abraham and Stella H.; m. Rita Abrams, June 10, 1956; children: Glenvil A., Patricia A. AB, Western Res. U., 1950; JD, Harvard U., 1953; LLM, NYU, 1957; diploma in law, U. Paris, 1958. Bar: Ohio 1953, N.Y. 1957. Instr. Harvard U. Law Sch., Cambridge, Mass., 1955-56; counsel internat. affairs Office Sec. Def., Washington, 1958-60; v.p. Gen. Telephone & Electronics Internat., N.Y.C., 1960-71; exec. v.p. Western Union Internat., N.Y.C., 1971-73; pres., CEO Warner Cable Corp., N.Y.C., 1973-75, chmn., chief exec. officer, 1975-79, Warner Amex Cable Communications, Inc., N.Y.C., 1979-83; chmn., CEO Hauser Comm., Inc., N.Y.C., 1983—. Chmn, bd. dirs. Orion Network Sys., Inc., Washington, 1996-98. Author: A Guide to Doing Business in the European Common Market, 1960. Chmn., bd. dirs. Hauser Found., Inc., 1989—; trustee Steep Rock Land Trust, 1992—; trustee, vice-chmn. The Mus. TV and Radio, 1992—; exec. com. Harvard U., com. on univ. resources, 1997—; bd. dirs. The Cable Ctr., 1997—. Served with AUS, 1953-55. Named to, Cable Hall of Fame, 2003. Mem. Nat. Cable TV Assn. (dir. 1976-84, exec. com. 1978-84, vice chmn. 1983-84). Office: Hauser Comm 712 5th Ave New York NY 10019-4108

HAUSER, JOHN REID, electrical engineering educator; b. Advance, N.C., Sept. 19, 1938; s. Reid R. and Lillian (Sheek) H.; m. Ann Covington, June 15, 1962; children: John R. Jr., James W., Daniel R. BS, N.C. State U., 1960; MS, Duke U., 1962, PhD, 1964. Mem. tech. staff Bell Telephone Labs., Winston-Salem, N.C., 1960-62; rsch. engr. Rsch. Triangle Inst., Rsch. Triangle Pk., N.C., 1963-66; asst. prof. N.C. State U., Raleigh, 1966-68, assoc. prof., 1968-73, Disting. prof., 1983—, prof., 1973—. Dir. Solid State Electronics Lab., N.C. State U., 1984—. Author: Fundamentals of Silicon Internal Devel. Tech., vol. II, 1968; contbr. over 150 articles to profl. jours. Recipient R.J. Reynolds Indsl. award for excellence N.C. State U., 1982, Univ. Rsch. award, Semiconductor Ind. Assn., 2002. Fellow IEEE (Outstanding Engr. in N.C. award, 1978); mem. Am. Phys. Soc., Am. Soc. for Engring. Edn. Home: 6800 Phillips Ct Raleigh NC 27607-4924

HAUSER, JOHN RICHARD, marketing and management science educator; b. Scranton, Pa., Apr. 19, 1949; s. Jesse Ransberry and Muriel Florence (Myers) H.; m. Marija Danūte Eiva Hauser, June 9, 1979; children: Marius John, Aleksas Jonas, Rolandas Aras. SB in Elec. Engring., SM in Elec. Engring. and Civil Engring., MIT, 1973, ScD in Ops. Rsch., 1975. Asst. prof. mktg. and transp. Northwestern U., Evanston, Ill., 1975-80; assoc. prof. mgmt. sci. MIT, Cambridge, Mass., 1980-84, prof. mgmt. sci., 1984-89, Kirin prof. mktg., 1989—, head mktg. group, 1988—2003, co-dir. Internat. Ctr. Rsch. on Mgmt. of Tech., 1993-2000, rsch. dir. Ctr. for Innovation in Product Devel., 1997-2000; Marvin Bower fellow Harvard U., Cambridge, Mass., 1987-88; prin. Applied Mktg. Sci., Waltham, Mass., 1989—. Vis. lectr. European Inst. Bus. Adminstrn., Fontainbleau, France, 1985; trustee Mktg. Sci. Inst., Cambridge, Mass., 2003—; spkr., lectr. in field; expert witness in field; cons. in field. Author: Applying Marketing Management: Four Simulations, 1986, (with others) Essentials of New Product Management, 1986, Design and Marketing of New Products, 2nd edit., 1993, Enterprise: An Integrating Management Exercise, 1989; editor-in-chief Mktg. Sci., 1989-94; contbr. articles to profl. jours. NSF fellow, 1971-74; grantee in field; recipient Parlin award, 2001. Mem. Am. Mktg. Assn. (1st Pl. Thesis Supervision award 1981, Paul D. Converse award 1996, MSI award 1996, Parlin award 2001), European Mktg. Acad., Inst. Mgmt. Sci. (1st Pl. Best Paper award 1982, 83, 93, 2003), Product Devel. and Mgmt. Assn., Tau Beta Pi, Eta Kappa Nu, Sigma Xi. Episcopalian. Avocations: sailing, skiing, basketball. Office: MIT E56-314 38 Memorial Dr Cambridge MA 02142-1347 Business E-Mail: jhauser@mit.edu.

HAUSER, JOYCE ROBERTA, marketing professional; b. NYC; d. Abraham and Helen (Lesser) Frankel; divorced; children: Mitchell, Mark, Ellen BA, SUNY, 1976; PhD, Union Inst. and U., 1987. Editor Art in Flowers, 1956-58; pres. Joyce Advt., 1958-65; ptnr. Hauser & Assocs., Pub. Rels., 1966-75; dir. broadcasting Bildersee Pub. Rels., 1973-75; pres. Hauser & Assocs., Inc., Pub. Rels., 1975-78; COO, pres. Hauser-Roberts, Inc., Pub. Rels./Mktg., N.Y.C., 1978—85; pres. Mktg. Concepts & Communications Inc., N.Y.C., 1985-92; moderator show Perceptions Sta. WEVD, 1975-77, Speaking of Health Sta. WNBC, 1977-89, 97 Health Line, Sta. WYNY, 1980-83, Conversations with Joyce Hauser, Sta. WNBC, 1975-86, What's on Your Mind, Sta. WYNY, 1983-84, Talk-Net, 1983-90; entertainment critic Sta. NBC, 1986-92. Instr. Baruch Coll., CCNY, 1980—85; assoc. prof. NYU, 1987—, prof. edn., 1992—. Sr. editor Art & Leisure News Svc., 1988—; editor-in-chief N.Y. State Comms. Annual, 1999—; contbg. editor Alive, 1976-77; author: Good Divorces, Bad Divorces: A Case for Divorce Mediation, 1995; contbr. 70 articles to profl. jours., chpts. to books. Mem. Citywide Health Adv. Coun. on Sch. Health, 1970-88, treas., 1980-92; mem. adv. bd. degree programs NYU Sch. Continuing Edn.; mediator/arbitrator Victim Svcs. Agy., 1986-87, Inst. Mediation and Conflict Resolution, 1985-86. Named one of 10 Top Successful Women, Cancer Soc., 1976, Tchr. of Yr., Zeta Beta Tau, 1989-90, one of 20 Top Women in Pub. Rels., 1981, Prof. of Yr. Sch. of Edn., 1999, Prof. of Yr., NYU Sch. Edn., 1999-2000; recipient Professionalism award Sta. WNBC, 1980; John E. Wilson fellow, 1996-97. Mem. AFTRA, Pub. Rels. Soc. Am., Nat. Assn. Communicators, Nat. Assn. Scholars, NY State Communicators (treas., v.p. 1996, pres. 1997), NY State Comms. Assn. (editor annual 1998), Acad. Family Mediators, Soc. Am. Travel Writers, Soc. Profl. Dispute Resolutions, Drama Desk (bd. mem. 2004), Outer Critics Cir., NY Press Club. Office Phone: 212-772-1625.

HAUSER, LA WAYNE, elementary school educator; b. Decatur, Tex., Nov. 6, 1943; d. Thomas and Tommie Ann Hodges; m. Karl-Heinz Hauser, Nov. 14, 1980; children: Aaron Cowan, Mican Cowan. BS in Elem. Edn. and English, U. North Tex., 1965; M in Edn. and Psychology, Tex. Women's U., 1977. Tchg. Cert. Tex. Tchr. Midland Ind. Sch. Dist., Tex., 1965—66, Irving Ind. Sch. Dist., Tex., 1966—67, Dept. Def., 1967—70, Child Study Ctr., Ft. Worth, 1971—72, Grapeville Ind. Sch. Dist., Tex., 1972—73, Birdville Ind. Sch. Dist., Ft. Worth, 1974—98; adj. prof. Tarrent County Coll. N.W., 1999; ret., 1999. Com. mem. Varied Ind. Sch. Dists. of Employment, 1965—98; proprietor Hauser Haus Rental Property, Hauser Haus Handmade. Author: (booklet) Students Expressing Fredom of Press, 1993. Arts and crafts leader East Ft. Worth 4-H, 2000—; editor newsletter Ea. Hills Homeowners Assn., 2002—; crime watch chair Easter Hills Homeowners Assn., 1997—. Mem.: DAR, Tex. Ret. Tchrs. Assn., Oak Crest Women's Club, Eastside Creative Arts Club. Achievements include patents in field.

HAUSER, MICHAEL GEORGE, astrophysicist; b. Chgo., Dec. 3, 1939; s. Julius and Sylvia Ann (Gross) Hauser; m. Miriam Freedman, Sept. 11, 1960 (div. May 1977); children: Karen Celia(dec.), Gerald Paul; m. Deanna Grove, May 8, 1981; stepchildren: Lisa Dawn Greening, Amy Lynne Canby, Elizabeth Ann Grove. B.Engring. Physics with distinction, Cornell U., 1962; PhD in Physics (NSF fellow), Calif. Inst. Tech., 1967. Instr. Princeton U., 1967-70, asst. prof. physics, 1970-72; sr. rsch. fellow in physics Calif. Inst. Tech., 1972-74; head infrared astronomy group lab. for high energy astrophysics Goddard Space Flight Center, Greenbelt, Md., 1974-77, head sect. infrared astrophysics Lab. for Extraterrestrial Physics, 1977-85, head infrared astrophysics br. Lab. Extraterrestrial Physics, 1985-87, head infrared astrophysics br. Lab. Astronomy and Solar Physics, 1987, chief Lab. Astronomy and Solar Physics, 1988-95; dep. dir. Space Telescope Sci. Inst., Balt., 1995—. Mem. joint sci. working group Infrared Astron. Satellite, 1977-84; prin. investigator Diffuse Infrared Background Experiment, Cosmic Background Explorer, 1977-97; mem. NASA Space Sci. Adv. Com., 1994-97; adj. prof. dept. physics and astronomy Johns Hopkins U., 1997—. Vice pres. PTA, Kensington (Md.) Jr. High, 1977-78, mem. exec. bd., 1978-79. Named Hon. Woodrow Wilson fellow, 1962; recipient Exceptional Sci. Achievement medal, NASA, 1984, 1991, John C. Lindsay award, Goddard Space Flight Ctr., 1986, Award of Merit, 1995, Meritorious Exec. award, Exec. Svc., 1994, AURA Sci. award, Assn. Univs. for Rsch. in Astronomy, 1998. Fellow Am. Phys. Soc., AAAS; mem. Am. Astron. Soc., Internat. Astron. Union (v.p. commn. 21, 1991-94), Sigma Xi Achievements include rsch. in elem. particle physics, astronomy, and cosmology. Office: Space Telescope Sci Inst 3700 San Martin Dr Baltimore MD 21218-2464 Office Phone: 410-338-4730. E-mail: hauser@stsci.edu.

HAUSER, RAY LOUIS, engineer, researcher, entrepreneur; b. Litchfield, Ill., Apr. 16, 1927; s. A. Vernon and Grace (Gregg) H.; m. Consuelo Wright Minnich, Sept. 2, 1951; children: Beth, Cynthia, Dewi, Chris. BS, U. Ill., 1950; M in Engring., Yale U., 1952; PhD, U. Colo., 1957. Registered profl. engr., Colo., safety engr., Calif. Sr. project engr. Conn. Hard Rubber Co., New Haven, 1950-52; rsch. staff U. Colo., Boulder, 1954-57; material tech. staff Martin Co., Denver, 1957-61; owner, mgr. Hauser Labs., Boulder, 1961-89; materials/process cons., expert witness Ray Hauser Expertise, Boulder, 2000—. Bd. dirs. Surface Solutions Inc.; vis. lectr. U. Colo., Boulder, 1957-63. Pres. Boulder Civic Opera, 1971-72. Sgt. U.S. Army, 1952-54. Recipient U. Colo. medal, 1995, Gold medal Colo. Engring. Coun., 1999. Fellow AAAS, Soc. Plastics Engrs. (bd. dirs. 1959-62, 2004—); mem. AIChE, Assn. Cons. Chemists and Chem. Engrs. (bd. dirs. 1986), Am. Assn. Lab. Accreditation (bd. dirs. 1986-91), Rotary (bd. dirs. 1975-77). Home and Office: 5758 Rustic Knolls Dr Boulder CO 80301-3029 Business E-Mail: ray@rayhauser.com.

HAUSER, RICHARD ALAN, lawyer, foundation administrator; b. Litchfield, Ill., Feb. 26, 1943; s. Melvin Henry and Helen Maxine (Roberts) H.; m. Carol E. Clampett, Jan. 2, 1965 (div. 1974); children: Jennifer Macey; Sarah Hampton; m. Karen Rollow Allen, July 26, 1977; children: Kristin Anne, Erica Christine, Alissa Marie. BS, U. Pa., 1965; JD cum laude, U. Miami, 1968. Bar: Fla., D.C. Law clk. US Dist. Ct. Fla., Miami, 1968-70; asst. U.S. atty. Dept. Justice, Miami, 1970-71, atty. adviser Dept. Atty. Gen.'s Office Washington, 1971-73, asst. dir. Office of Policy Planning, 1974-75; assoc. counsel White House, Washington, 1973-74, dep. counsel to pres., 1981-86; pvt. practice Washington, 1975-81; ptnr. Baker & Hostetler, Washington, 1986—2001; gen. counsel US Dept. HUD, Washington, 2001—04; pres. Nat. Legal Ctr. for Pub. Interest, Washington, 2004—. Chmn. Pennsylvania Ave. Devel. Corp., 1988-96; mem. Internat. Ctr. Settlement of Investment Disputes, 1986-94; chmn. bd. dirs. The Luther Inst., Washington; bd. dirs. Lutheran Brotherhood Mutual Funds. Bd. dirs. Washington Hosp. Ctr., 2000—. Recipient Spl. Asst. U.S. Atty. award for Superior Performance, Dept. Justice Mem. Fla. Bar Assn., D.C. Bar Assn., Va. Bar Assn., Chevy Chase Club, Met. Club (bd. govs.), Econ. Club. Office: Nat Legal Ctr for Pub Interest Ste 800 1600 K St NW Washington DC 20006 Office Phone: 202-466-9360. Office Fax: 202-466-9366.*

HAUSER, RITA ELEANORE ABRAMS, lawyer; b. N.Y.C., July 12, 1934; d. Nathan and Frieda (Litt) Abrams; m. Gustave M. Hauser, June 10, 1956; children: Glenvil Aubrey, Ana Patricia. AB magna cum laude, CUNY Hunter Coll., 1954; D in Polit. Economy with highest honors, U. Strasbourg, France, 1955; Licence en Droit, U. Paris, 1958; student, Harvard U., 1955-56; LLB with honors, NYU, 1959; LLD (hon.), Seton Hall U., 1969, Finch Coll., 1969, U. Miami, Fla., 1971, Colgate U., 1995. Bar: D.C. 1959, N.Y. 1961, U.S. Supreme Ct. 1967. Atty. U.S. Dept. Justice, 1959-61; pvt. practice N.Y.C., 1961-67; ptnr. Moldover, Hauser, Strauss & Volin, 1968-72; sr. ptnr. Stroock & Stroock & Lavan, N.Y.C., 1972-92, of counsel, 1992—; pres. The Hauser Found., N.Y.C., 1990—; presdl. apptd. mem. Pres.'s Fgn. Intelligence Bd. and Intelligence Oversight Bd., 2001—04. Handmaker lectr., Louis Brandeis Lecture Series, U. Ky. Law Sch.; lectr. internat. law Naval War Coll. and Army War Coll.; lectr. St. Anthony's Coll., Oxford (England) U., 2002; Mitchell lectr. in law SUNY, Buffalo; USIA lectr. constl. law Egypt, India, Australia, New Zealand; U.S. chmn. Internat. Ctr. for Peace in Middle East, 1984-92; bd. dirs. Internat. Peace Acad., chair 1993—; U.S. pub. del. to Vienna follow-up meeting of Conf. on Security and Cooperation in Europe, 1986-88; mem. adv. panel in internat. law U.S. Dept. State, 1986-92, Am. Soc. Internat. Law Award to honor Women in Internat. Law; mem. Pacific Coun. on Internat. Policy, 1998-2000; bd. dirs. The Rand Corp., Internat. Inst. Strategic Studies, London, The Lowy Inst. Internat. Policy, Sydney, The Ctr. Internat. Governance Innovation, Can.; chair internat. adv. bd. The Internat. Crisis Group, 2004—. Contbr. articles to profl. jours. U.S. rep. to UN commn. on Human Rights, 1969-72; mem. U.S. del. to Gen. Assembly UN, 1969; vice chmn. U.S. Adv. Com. on Internat. and Cultural Affairs, 1973-77; mem. N.Y.C. Bd. Higher Edn., 1974-76, Stanton Panel on internat. info., edn., cultural rels. to reorganize USIA and Voice of Am., 1974-75, Mid. East Study Group Brookings Inst., 1975, 87-88, U.S. del. World Conf. Internat. Women's Yr., Mexico City, 1975; co-chair Com. for Re-election Pres., 1972, Presdl. Debates project LVW, 1976, Coalition for Regan/Bush; adv. bd. Nat. News Coun., 1977-79; bd. dirs. Bd for Internat. Broadcasting, 1977-80, Internat. Peace Acad., The Aspen Inst., The RAND Corp.; chair internat. adv. bd. Internat. Crisis Group; trustee Lincoln Ctr. Performing Arts; adv. bd. Ctr. For Law and Nat. Security, U. Va. Law Sch., 1978-84; vis. com. Ctr. Internat. Affairs Harvard U., 1975-81, John F. Kennedy Sch. Govt., Harvard U., 1992—, chair adv. bd. Hauser Ctr. for Non-Profit Orgns. at Harvard U.; co-chair dean's bd. advisors Harvard Law Sch., 1996—, vice-chair, nat. co-chair univ. fund-raising campaign, 1997-2000, vice chmn. com. on univ. resources, 2002-; bd. advisors Mid. East Inst., Harvard U.; bd. visitors Georgetown Sch. Fgn. Svc., 1989-94; chmn. adv. panel Internat. Parlimentary Group for Human Rights in Soviet Union, 1984-86; mem. Lawyers Com. for Human Rights, 1995—; mem. spl. refugee adv. panel Dept. State, 1981; bd. fellows Claremont U. Ctr. and Grad. Sch., 1990-94; former trustee Internat. Legal Ctr., Legal Aid Soc. N.Y., Freedom House; mem. Lawyers Comm. Human Rights, 1996—. Fulbright grant U. Strasbourg, 1955; Intellectual Exch. fellow Japan Soc.; recipient Jane Addams Internat. Women's Leadership award, 1996, Women in Internat. Law award Am. Soc. Internat. Law, 1995, Fulbright award for Fulbright Alumni, 1997, Servant of Justice award, Legal Aid Soc. N.Y., 2000, Vanderbilt medal NYU Law Sch., 2004. Fellow ABA (life, mem. standing coms. on law and nat. security 1979-85, standing com. on world order under law 1969-78, standing com. on jud. selection, tenure, compensation 1977-79, coun. sect. on ind. rights and responsibilities 1970-73, advisor bd. jour. 1973-78); mem. Am. Soc. Internat. Law (v.p. 1988—, mem. exec. com. 1971-76), Am. Fgn. Law Assn. (bd. dirs.), Am. Arbitration Assn. (past bd. dirs.), Ams. Soc. (bd. dirs. 1988—), Coun. Fgn. Rels. (bd. dirs.), Internat. Inst. for Strategic Studies (London, bd. dirs. 1994—), Internat. Adv. Bd., Jaffee Ctr. for Strategic Studies, Tel Aviv Univ. (1999—), Am. Coun. on Germany, The Atlantic Coun. U.S., Friends of the Hauge Acad. Internat. Law (bd. dirs.), Assn. of Bar of City of N.Y., Catalyst (bd. dirs. 1989-96). Republican. Office: Stroock & Stroock & Lavan 180 Maiden Ln Fl 17 New York NY 10038-4937 also: The Hauser Found Office of Pres 712 5th Ave New York NY 10019-4108

HAUSER, ROBERT ALAN, neurologist, educator; b. Phila., Pa., Nov. 23, 1957; s. Norman and Judith Hauser; m. Susan Leslie Alden, Oct. 24, 1990; children: Allison Elizabeth, Evan Tyler. BA, Brandeis U., Waltham, Mass., 1978; MD, Temple U., Phila., 1982; MBA, U. South Fla., Tampa, 2000. Diplomate Am. Bd. Neurology and Psychiatry, 1989. Dir. Parkinson's disease and movement disorders ctr. U. South Fla., Tampa, Fla., 1994—. prof. neurology, pharmacology and exptl. therapeutics, 2001—. Author: (book) Parkinson's Disease: Questions and Answers, 2004; contbr. articles to profl. jours. Named one of Best Doctors in Am., 2002, 2003. Mem.: Am. Acad. Neurology (chair sect. interventional neurology 2003—). Achievements include research in med.and surg. treatments for Parkinson's disease and other movement disorders. Office: U S FL Ste 410 4 Columbia Dr Tampa FL 33606

HAUSER, SARAH B., artist; b. San Francisco, Calif., 1956; d. John Norman and Florence DeBonis Hauser; life ptnr. Jeffrey Warren Lerer. BFA, NYU, 1983; student, Art Students League, 1990—93, Cooper Union, 1996—, Manhattan Graphics, 1996—, Lower East Side Print Shop, 1996—, Koho Sch. Sumi-E, 2000—. Artist-tchr. Arts Connection, NYC, 1996—2001, Dieu Donne Papermill, NYC, 1996—2000; asst. instr. Japan Soc., N.Y.C., 2001. Exhibitions include Barrett Art Ctr., Poughkeepsie, NY, 1999, Woman Made Gallery, Chgo., 1999, 2000, 2001, Bedford Gallery, Dean Lesher Ctr. Arts, NYC, 1999, Feminist Expo, Balt., 2000, Purdue U. Galleries, 2000, 2001, Bklyn. Botanic Garden, 2000, 2001, 2002, Sumei Multidisciplinary Arts Ctr., NJ, 2000, Nommo Gallery, Kampala, Uganda, 2000, Open Space Gallery, Allentown, Pa., 2000, New Leaf Editions, Vancouver, Can., 2000, Hiram Blauvelt Mus., Oradell, NJ, 2000, Ga. Coll. and State U., 2000, Veliko Turnovo Mcpl. Art Gallery, Bulgaria, 2000, Beit Gavriel Cultural Ctr., Israel, 2000, Contemporary Mus. of Balt., 2000—02, Noho Gallery, 2000, Yad Lebanim Gallery, Israel, 2001, Fulton St. Gallery, NYC, 2001, La. State Univ., Baton Rouge, 2001, LSU Union Art Gallery, 2001, Canton Artists Guild, Conn., 2001, Conn. Graphic Arts Ctr., 2001, Fredericksburg Ctr. Creative Arts, Va., 2001, Woodward Gallery, NYC, 2001, 2002, 2003, Kirkland Arts Ctr., 2001 (Grand Prize for "Mona Is", 2001), Gallery of Que. Printmaking Coun., 2001—02, No. Nat., Rhinelander, Wis., 2002, 2003, Nat. Small Works Exhibit-Wash. Printmakers Gallery, 2002, 2003, AI&G 11 Ann. Nat. Exhbn., 2002, PrintAlliance Sept. 11 Meml. Portfolio, 2002, Perkins Ctr. Arts, NJ, 2002, Montreal Internat. Miniature Prints Biennial, 2002, Delta Nat. Small Prints Exhbn., 2002, Toy Theater Exhbn., NYC, 2003, Boston Printmakers, 2003, Internat. Print Ctr. of NY, 2003, Iowa State U., 2003, Holter Mus., 2003, Long Beach Arts, 2003, Hudson Opera House, 2003, Kirkland Arts Ctr., 2003, Printmaking Biennial, 2003, Target Gallery, 2003, Internat. Print Ctr. N.Y., 2004, La. State U. Sch. Vet. Medicine Libr., 2004, one-woman shows include Womanmade Gallery, 2001, John Jay Gallery, 2002, Woodward Gallery, 2004, 2005, Manhattan Graphics Ctr., 2004—05, Iowa Biennial Exhbn., 2005, Anchorage Mus. History and Arts, 2005—, Stone Metal Press, 2005, NYU Law Sch., 2005, Courthouse Gallery at Lake George Arts Project, 2005, Internat. Print Ctr. NY, 2005, Represented in permanent collections Woodward Gallery, NYC, RM Fine Arts, UK, Malloy Family Found., U. Oregon, Nat. Assn. Women Artists, Vivian and Gordon Gilkey Ctr. of Portland Art Mus., Spencer Mus. (U. Kans.), KIWA (Japan), Iowa U. Print Soc., The Australian Print Collections of Wagga Wagga Regional Art Gallery, NSW, Australia, NY Pub. Libr., NY Hist. Soc., Iowa Biennial Exhbn., prin. works include .Spiffy, 1998 (Esther K. Gayner Meml. award, 2001), Lady & 4 Dogs in Central Park, 1999, Chinese Crested with Red Sweater, 1999, 3 Dogs in a Truck, 1999, Mona Is, 2001 (Grand Prize Kirkland Arts Ctr. Printmaking Biennial, 2001), Little Jazz, 2001 (Medal of Honor, Elizabeth Morse Genius Found. printmaking award, 2003), La Vision du Bouledogue I, 2001 (Elizabeth Fenn Meml. award, Pen and Brush Galleries, Regional Juried Exhbn. for non-members, 2001), Panchito, 2002 (1st prize graphics, Pen and Brush Galleries, 2002, Hortense Ferne Meml. award Printmaking, Nat. Assn. Women Artists, 2002, 4th prize printmaking, 2003, Best Depiction of Chihuahua Art Show, Dog Show, 2003), Guadalupe Montaña I, 2003 (Silver award, Dialogue Magazine, 2003), Baby and a Seal, Target Gallery, 2003 (Hon. mention, 2003), Baby Monkey Playing, 2003, pub. art project, Art Unleashed, Lancaster, Pa., 2002, work included in books and periodicals, including Simple Printmaking, 2000, Japanese Woodblock Printmaking, 2001, studio Notes interview, 2001, CALYX: A Jour. of Art and Lit. by Women, 2003, Dialogue mag., 2003, website, www.sarahhauser.womanmade.net. Mem.: N.Y. Hist. Soc., Manhattan Graphics Ctr., Nat. Assn. Women Artists, New York Artist's Cir., Sumi-e Soc. Am., Lower East Side Printshop (keyholder). Office: Sarah Hauser PO Box 2234 New York NY 10009 E-mail: cucamongie@aol.com.

HAUSER, WILLIAM BARRY, historian, educator; b. Washington, May 2, 1939; s. Philip Morris and Zelda Barnett (Abrams) H.; children: Benjamin Lester, Aaron Davidson, Zachary Barnett. SB in Math., U. Chgo., 1960; MA in East Asian Studies, Yale U., 1962, PhD in History, 1969. Lectr., asst. prof. U. Mich., Ann Arbor, 1967-69, 70-74; asst. prof. history U. Rochester, N.Y., 1974-77, assoc. prof. history, 1977-83, prof. history, 1983—, chmn. dept.

history, 1979-85. Author: Economic Institutional Change in Tokugawa Japan, 1974, (with Jeffrey P. Mass) The Bakufu in Japanese History, 1985; contbr. articles and revs. to profl. publs. Fellow Fulbright-Hays fellow, U.S. Dept. State, Osaka, Japan, 1964—66, NEH fellow, 1972—73, 1982—83, Mellen Faculty fellow, U. Rochester, 1977, Japan Found. fellow, 1976, 1982. Mem. Assn. for Asian Studies (chmn. adv. com. Bibliography of Asian Studies 1984-96). Avocations: cooking, gardening. Home: 425 Westminster Rd Rochester NY 14607-3231 Office: U Rochester Dept History Rochester NY 14627-0070 Office Phone: 585-275-9359. Business E-Mail: wbha@mail.rochester.edu.

HAUSERMAN, JACQUITA KNIGHT, management consultant; b. Donalsonville, Ga., Apr. 23, 1942; d. Lendon Bernard and Ressie Mae (Robinson) Knight; m. Mark Kenny Hauserman, July 8, 1978 (div. Mar. 1998). BS in Math., U. Montevallo, Ala., 1964; MA in Tchg. Math., Emory U., 1973; MBA in Fin., Ga. State U., 1978. Fin. analyst Cleve. Electric Illuminating Co., 1982-83, gen. supr. employment svc., 1983-85, sr. corp. planning advisor, 1985-86, dir. customer svc., 1986-88, v.p. adminstrn., 1988-90; v.p. customer svc. & cmty. affairs Centerior Energy Corp., Independence, Ohio, 1990-93, v.p. customer support, 1993-95, v.p. bus. svcs., 1995-97; v.p., chief devel. officer Summa Health Sys., Akron, Ohio, 1999-2000; prin. Arcadia Consulting, Pepper Pike, Ohio, 2000—. Home and Office: 2901 Greenflower Ct Bonita Springs FL 34134-4387 E-mail: jhauserman@johnrwood.com.

HAUSFATHER, SAMUEL J., dean; s. Nathan Hausfather and Edythe Bienstock; m. Pamela Vinn; children: Ezekiel, Lisa. BA, Antioch Coll., 1972; MA, Calif. State U., Chico, Calif., 1988; PhD, U. Wis., Chico, Calif., 1994. Cert. tchr. Calif. Tchr. San Juan (Calif.) Ridge Sch. Dist., 1979—89; dir. field experiences Berry Coll., Mount Berry, Ga., 1992—97, asst. dean grad. studies, 1997—2001; dean profl. studies East Stroudsburg (Pa.) U., 2001—. Co-author: Reframing teacher education: Dimensions of a constructivist approach; contbr. articles to profl. jours. Grantee, BellSouth Found., 1997—2001, U. Sys. Ga. Title II Grants Program, 2000—03, U.S. Dept. Edn., 2001—, 2003—05, Nat. Writing Project, 2004—05. Mem.: Pa. Assn. Colls. and Tchr. Educators (founding mem. 2004), Am. Soc. Curriculum Devel., Am. Ednl. Rsch. Assn., Nat. Assn. Profl. Devel. Schs., Kappa Delta Pi. Office: East Stroudsburg University 200 Prospect St East Stroudsburg PA 18301 Office Phone: 570-422-3377. E-mail: shausfather@po-box.esu.edu.

HAUSFELD, JAMES FRANK, client services manager; b. Chgo., July 22, 1955; s. James J. and Geraldine M. (Nesladek) H.; m. Loretta Brown, Sept. 16, 2000; 1 child, Laura Beth. BA in Comm., Columbia Coll., 1976. Producer, cameraman Chgo. Bulls Basketball Team, 1976-77; media specialist Bell and Howell, Chgo., 1977-79; producer, dir. New Trier Technology Coop., Winnetka, Ill., 1979-94, exec. dir., 1994—2003, mem. adv. coun., 1995—2003; client svcs. mgr. Allied Vaughn, 2004—. Mem. State of Ill. Instnl. Tech. Adv. Coun., 1994-2003; mem. ind. video competition jury Chgo. Internat. Film Festival, 1979-86; freelance editor, cameraman On Location, Ltd., Chgo., 1983-90; freelance video editor, videographer Bougainville Prodns., 1991—. Producer, editor, dir.: (videotapes) North Suburban Spl. Edn. Dist.-One Child at a Time, 1984, The Pursuit of Excellence-Illinois Style, 1985, Social Service: A Committment to Caring, 1987, To Enrich Their Lives, 1989, Nazi Concentration Camps: an Eyewitness Account, 1990, Peer Helping: A Code of Friendship, 1992, Education and the Common Denominator: The Teacher, 1995, Abriendo Puertas: The Winnetka Schools Foreign Language Program, 1996, New Trier Technology Cooperative 1997 Institute Day: Thinking in the Future Tense, 1997, The Grade 3 Virtual Museum Project, 1999, Dancin' Through the Decades, 2001; editor (videotapes) Perspectives on China, 1987, The Other Side of Summer: The Wrecking of Old Comiskey Park, 1993, Wrigley Field: Beyond the Ivy, 2001. Mem. Internat. TV Assn. Clubs: Argyle-Magnolia Glenwood Block (capt. 1985-89), Montrose Elite (Chgo.); BMG Music Service (Indpls.). Roman Catholic. Avocations: softball, darts, music. Home: 1431 W Argyle St Chicago IL 60640-3502 Office: New Trier Tech Coop 385 Winnetka Ave Winnetka IL 60093-4238 E-mail: hausfelj@nttc.org.

HAUSFELD, MICHAEL D., lawyer; b. Bklyn., 1946; AB cum laude, Bklyn. Coll., 1966; JD with honors, George Washington U., 1969. Bar: Washington, DC 1969. Sr. ptnr. Cohen, Milstein, Hausfeld & Toll, P.L.L.C., Washington. Mem., bd. editors George Washington Law Rev., 1969—69; adj. prof. Georgetown U. Law Ctr., 1980—87, mem. adv. bd., Inst. Law and Econs., 1980—; bd. dirs. George Washington U. Law Sch., 1998—. Named one of 75 Best Lawyers in Washington, Washingtonian survey mag., Top 100 Influential Lawyers in Am., Nat. Law Jour., 2000; recipient Humanitarian of Yr. award, B'Nai Brith, 2002, Simon Wiesenthal Ctr. award for Disting. Svc., Human Spirit award, U.S. Dept. Energy. Mem.: Order of the Coif. Office: Cohen Milstein Hausfeld & Toll PLLC Ste 500 W 1100 New York Ave NW Washington DC 20005-3964

HAUSLER, RUDOLF HEINRICH, research chemist; b. Zurich, Switzerland, Apr. 9, 1934; came to U.S., 1963; s. Robert Ruppert and Elsa (Figi) H.; m. Joyce Ann Partridge, Sept. 19, 1998; 1 child, Natasha Louise. diploma chem. engring., Swiss Fed. Inst. Tech., Zurich, 1958, D.Tech.Scis., 1961. Research chemist, project leader Battelle Meml. Inst., Geneva, 1961-63; research chemist, research assoc. Universal Oil Products Co., Des Plaines, Ill., 1963-76; tech. dir. Gordon Lab., Inc., Great Bend, Kans., 1976-79; sr. research chemist corp. research and devel. Petolite Corp., St. Louis, 1979-81, prin. investigator, 1981-86, research fellow, 1986-91; sr. engring. advisor Mobil R&D Corp., Dallas, 1991-96; co-owner, v.p. tech. BJB Co., Post, Tex., 1996—; pres. Corro-Consulta; cons. in field of corrosion in nuc. energy generation, in oil and gas prodn.; investor in oil and gas prodn.; horse farmer, 2001; lectr. in field. Registered profl. engr., Calif. Author, co-author 3 books. Mem. Electrochem. Soc. (chmn. Chgo. sect. 1967-68, councilor 1972—), Nat. Assn. Corrosion Engrs. (chmn. Chgo. sect. 1974-75, Outstanding Achievement award 1990, fellow 2003), Chgo. Tech. Socs. Council (chmn. 1974-75), Am. Chem. Soc., Am. Soc. Metals. Unitarian-Universalist. Author, patentee in field. Office: 8081 Diane Dr Kaufman TX 75142-4607

HAUSLER, WILLIAM JOHN, JR., microbiologist, educator, public health service officer; b. Kansas City, Kans., Aug. 31, 1926; s. William John and Clifton (McCambridge) H.; m. Mary Lois Rice, Apr. 19, 1949 (dec. 1999); children: Cheryl Kaye Johnson, Kenneth Randall, Eric Rice, Mark Clifton; m. Jeanne Seeberger, May 26, 2001. AB in Microbiology, U. Kans., 1951, MA in Microbiology, 1953, PhD in Microbiology, Math., 1958. Diplomate Am. Bd. Med. Microbiology (chmn. 1979-82, Profl. Recognition award 1995). Asst. instr. U. Kans., Lawrence, 1951-56, rsch. asst., 1956-58; assoc. bacteriologist Iowa State Hygienic Lab., Iowa City, 1958-59, asst. dir., prin. bacteriologist, 1959-65, dir., 1965-95; dir. emeritus, 1995—; asst. prof. U. Iowa Coll. Medicine, Iowa City, 1959-66, assoc. prof., 1966-90, prof., 1990—; assoc. prof. U. Iowa Coll. Dentistry, 1966-90, prof., 1990—. Cons. to Iran WHO, 1969, U.S. EPA, 1970-72, CDC, 1965—, People's Republic China WHO, 1990, WHO Western Pacific Region, 1991, UNDP India, 1992; cons. to industry; mem. mil. infectious diseases rsch. program Am. Inst. Biol. Scis., 2002. Editor: Standard Methods for the Examination of Dairy Products, 1972, Manual Clinical Microbiology, 3d edit., 1980, 4th edit., 1985, 5th edit., 1991, Compendium of Methods for the Microbiological Examination of Foods, 1980, 2d edit., 1984, Diagnostic Procedures for Bacterial Mycotic and Parasitic Infections, 1981, Laboratory Diagnosis of Infections Diseases: Principles and Practice, 1988; co-editor: Topley & Wilson's Microbiology and Microbial Infections, 9th edit., 1997; mem. editl. bd. various profl. jours.; contbr. articles to profl. jours. Councilman City Govt., University Heights, Iowa, 1966-69; commr. Iowa Air Pollution Control Commn., 1967-74; mem. exec. com. Iowa Dept. Environ. Quality, 1974-80, Nat. Com. for Clin. Lab. Standards, bd. dirs., 1987-93. Lt. comdr. USNR, 1944-67. Recipient Henry Albert Meml. award Iowa Pub. Health Assn., 1974. Fellow APHA, Am. Acad. Microbiology (chmn. 1983-89, Profl. Recognition award 1995); mem. Am. Soc. Microbiology, Assn. State and Territorial Pub. Health Lab. Dirs. (pres. 1984-85, Lifetime Achievement award 1998), Sigma Phi Epsilon, Rotary (Paul Harris fellow). Avocations: photography, woodworking, wilderness backpacking. Home: 11 The Woods NE Iowa City IA 52240-7986 Office: U Iowa Hygienic Lab Oakdale Hall Iowa City IA 52242 E-mail: iahausler@yahoo.com.

HAUSMAN, ARTHUR HERBERT, electronics company executive; b. Chgo., Nov. 24, 1923; s. Samuel Louis and Sarah (Elin) H.; m. Helen Mandelowitz, May 19, 1946; children: Susan Lois, Kenneth Louis, Catherine Ellen. BSEE, U. Tex., 1944; MS, Harvard U., 1948. Electronics engr. Engring. Rsch. Assocs., St. Paul, 1946-47; supervisory electronics scientist U.S. Dept. Def., Washington, 1948-60; now advisor, v.p., dir. rsch. Ampex Corp., Redwood City, Calif., 1960-63, v.p. ops., 1963-65, group v.p., 1965-67, exec. v.p., 1967-71, exec. v.p., pres., CEO, 1971-83, chmn. bd., 1981-87, chmn. bd. emeritus, 1987—. Chmn. tech. adv. com. computer peripherals Dept. Commerce, 1973-75; mem. Pres.'s Export Coun.; chmn. Subcom. on Export Adminstrn., 1984-88; bd. dirs. Lasercard Inc., Vista Rsch. Inc., Calamp, Inc. Trustee United Bay Area Crusade.; mem. vis. com. dept. math. MIT; bd. dirs. Bay Area Coun. Served with USNR, 1944-54. Recipient Meritorious Civilian Svc. award Dept. Def. Mem. IEEE, Army Ordnance Assn. (dir. chpt. 1969-71), Am. Electronics Assn. (dir.), Commonwealth Club of Calif., Cosmos Club.

HAUSMAN, HARRIET SECELEY, administrator; b. Chgo., Apr. 8, 1924; d. Samuel and Lena Rubin; m. Martin C. Hausman, June 30, 1946 (dec. Apr. 1988); children: Daniel, Barbara. Student, U. Ill., 1941—42, Northwestern U., 1943—45; BS, Rosary Coll., 1972. Asst. tchr. Winfield (Ill.) Sch., 1945; psych testing Hines Vet. Hosp., Maywood, Ill., 1972-74; social worker Cook County Hosp., Chgo., 1973; pres. Power Parts Co., Chgo., 1947-87, CEO, 1987-92. Author: Reflections, A History of River Forest, 1975. Trustee River Forest (Ill.) Twp., 1978-90; bd. dirs. ACLU, 1988—, v.p.; bd. dirs. Jewish Childrens Bur., pres. 1970-92, v.p., 1992—; v.p., bd. dirs. Bldg. Better Futures (BBF), 1992-96, v.p. BBF Scholarship Bd., 1997-; vice chmn. scholarship com., 1998-; adv. bd. Bus. and Prolf. People for Pub. Interest, 1999—; plannig commn. Oak Pk. Temple, 2001—. Named Woman Entrepreneur of Yr., 1992, U.S. Transp. Cmty. Svc. award Oak Park and River Forest, 1980, 96, 90, 92, 96, 99, Carl Winter Svc. award, 1972, Lifetime Achievement award, 2005. Democrat. Jewish. Achievements include one of 4 who est. River Forest Cmty. Ctr. Avocations: symphony, opera, drama, gardening, travel.

HAUSMAN, HOWARD, electronics executive; b. N.Y.C., July 4, 1945; s. Edward A. and Bella H.; m. Gloria Lynn; children: Lawrence Stuart, Bradley Russel. BSEE, Poly. Inst. N.Y., 1967, MSEE, 1971. Computer programmer Harry Kahn Assocs., Great Neck, N.Y., 1965-67; engr. Airborne Instruments Lab., Deer Park, N.Y., 1967-72; dept. head Miteq Inc., Hauppauge, N.Y., 1972-81; pres. Syncom Industries Inc., Bohemia, N.Y., 1981—; chief scientist Microphase Systems Inc., Hauppage, N.Y., 1992—; v.p. engring. Miteq Inc., Hauppage, 1996—; pres. Syncom Industries, Bohemia, 1999—. Mem. tech. cons. com., v.p. local adv. counsel 1st supervisory dist. Bd. Coop. Ednl. Services, Suffolk County, N.Y., 1986—; cons. Arista Devices, Inc., Ronkonkoma, N.Y., 1974-81; prof. Hofstra U., Hempstead, N.Y., 1996; adj. prof. Polytech. U., Farmingdale, N.Y., 1978—. Contbr. articles to profl. jours. Mem. IEEE (sr.), AIAA (sr.), AAAS, Nat. Contracts Mgmt. Assn., N.Y. Acad. Scis., Am. Inst. Aeronautics and Astronautics (sr.). Home: 139 Hidden Ponds CIR Smithtown NY 11787-5233 Office: MITEQ Inc 100 Davids Dr Hauppauge NY 11788-4 E-mail: h.hausman@ieee.org, hhausman@miteq.com. *As we acquire more knowledge we realize how little we know. It is a very humbling experience that tends to limit our creativity. It is important that we realize the subliminal negative feedback effects inherent in our learning experience and consciously focus our energies on piercing the envelope of the psychologically comfortable known universe.*

HAUSMAN, JERRY ALLEN, economics professor, consultant; b. Weirton, W.Va., May 5, 1946; s. Harold H. and Rose (Hausman); m. Margaretta Stone, Dec. 21, 1968; children: Nicholas, Claire. AB, Brown U., 1968; B.Phil., Oxford U., 1972, D.Phil., 1973. Mem. faculty MIT, Cambridge, 1973—, prof. econs., 1979—. Contbr. articles to profl. jours. Marshall scholar, 1970-72; recipient Frisch medal Econometrics Soc., 1980; John Bates Clark award Am. Econs. Assn., 1985. Office: MIT Dept Econs 77 Massachusetts Ave Dept Econs Cambridge MA 02139-4307

HAUSMAN, JILL SUSAN, rabbi, cantor, vocalist, lyricist, poet, composer; d. Alan Louis Hausman and Roslyn Diamond Wolf; m. Harold John Hawkins, Apr. 4, 1975; children: Theodore Jeffrey Hawkins, Aaron David Hawkins. AB, Smith Coll., 1974. Ordination Rabbinical Seminary Internat., 2004. Environ. analyst U.S. Army Corps Engrs., N.Y.C., 1974; biologist Interstate Sanitation Commn., N.Y.C., 1975—78, Fred C. Hart Assocs., N.Y.C., 1978; cantor, asst. rabbi Progressive Temple Beth Ahavath Sholom, Bklyn., 1994—2004, asst. rabbi, cantor, 2004—. Actor: Ft. Salem Theater; singer: Amato Opera, N.Y. Choral Soc. Summer Sings; singer, lyricist (classical CD) Lieder in Our Language, 2001, poet (song cycle of 5 poems) Animals Like Me (Gerald Busby), 2002; composer: (music) Misheberach, Ahavat Olam, Ahava Raba, Ashreinu, Michamocha. Singer S.E.R.V.E. the Handicapped. Democrat. Avocations: cooking, biking, reading. Home: 12 W 96th St New York NY 10025 Office: Temple Beth Ahavath Sholom 1515 46th St Brooklyn NY 11219

HAUSMAN, KEITH LYNN, health facility administrator, physical therapist; b. Cleve., Nov. 20, 1949; s. Harold Herbert and Betty (Reed) H.; 1 child, Sierra Dawn. BS, Loma Linda U., 1972, MA in Pub. Health, 1975. Lic. real estate broker; cert. instrument multiengine flight instr., air transport pilot. Acting adminstr. Thomas Rehab. Hosp., Asheville, N.C., 1976-77; pres. Marion County Hosp., Jefferson, Tex., 1977-81, Jellico (Tenn.) Community Hosp., 1981-91; health care cons., 1991—; pres. Premier Rehab., Inc., 1994—, Premier Vending, Inc., 2000—, Premier Vending Wholesale, Inc., 2002—. Bd. dirs. Pvt. Indsl. Coun. SDA4, Tenn., 1989-2000. Fellow Am. Coll. Health Care Execs.; mem. Tenn. Hosp. Assn. (bd. dirs. 1991, pres. Mid-East dist. 1991), Campbell County C. of C. (bd. dirs. 1989-92). Republican. Seventh-Day Adventist. Home: PO Box 541 Jellico TN 37762-0541 Office Phone: 423-784-4704. E-mail: flyboy@2geton.net.

HAUSMAN, MARVIN S., research and development company executive; MD, NYU, 1967. Resident in urol. surgery UCLA Med. Ctr., L.A.; resident in gen. surgery Mt. Sinai Hosp., N.Y.C.; rsch. assoc. NIH, Bethesda, Md.; founder MedCo Rsch. Inc.; pres., CEO, dir. Axonyx Inc., N.Y.C., 1998—. Lectr., clin. instr., attending surgeon div. urology UCLA Med. Ctr., Cedars-Sinai Med. Ctr., L.A.; cons. clin./pharm. rsch. Bristol-Meyers Internat., Mead-Johnson Pharm. Co., MedCo Rsch. Inc., E.R. Squibb; pres. N.W. Med. Rsch. Ptnrs., Inc.; bd. dirs. Regent Assisted Living, Inc. Office: 500 Fashion Ave FL 10 New York NY 10018-0805

HAUSMAN, MICHAEL ROBERT, orthopedist, educator, surgeon; b. Bridgeport, Conn., Apr. 20, 1953; s. Sydney and Esther Hausman; m. Tracy Ellen Pogue, May 15, 1993; children: Sydney Claire, Laura Elise, Richard Allan. MS, Yale Coll., New Haven, Conn., 1971—75; MD, Yale Med. Sch., New Haven, Conn., 1975—79. Prof. Mt. Sinai Sch. Medicine, N.Y.C., 1988—2004. Dir. NDI Med., Cleve., 2004. Recipient Maimonides Award, Israel Bonds, 1998. Fellow: Am. Acad. Orthop. Surgeons. Achievements include patents for Bone Fixation, Wrist Sports Protection. Office: Mt Sinai Med Ctr 5 E 98th St 9th Fl New York NY 10029 Office Phone: 212-241-1658.

HAUSMAN, STEVEN JACK, health science association administrator; b. Phila., May 20, 1945; s. Leo and Bella Hausman. BA, U. Pa., 1967, MS, 1968, PhD, 1972. Postdoctoral fellow Inst. for Cancer Rsch., Phila., 1972-75; staff fellow Nat. Inst. on Aging, Balt., 1975-77; spl. asst. to assoc. dir. Nat. Inst. Arthritis, Metabolism and Digestive Diseases, Bethesda, Md., 1977-78, dir. ctrs. program, 1978-86; dep. dir. extramural program Nat. Inst. Arthritis and Musculosketal and Skin Diseases, Bethesda, 1986-90, dep. dir., 1990—, dir. extramural program, 1997—2002. Mem. AAAS, Am. Assn. Immunologists, Soc. In Vitro Biology, Am. Chem. Soc., Am. Soc. for Cell Biology. Office: NIAMS-NIH 31 Center Dr Msc2350 Bldg 31 Bethesda MD 20892-0001

HAUSMAN, WILLIAM RAY, fund raising and management consultant; b. Bradford, Pa., Apr. 22, 1941; s. Raymond Harvey and Eleanor Janet (Freeman) H.; m. Rosalyn Schmidt, Aug. 16, 1963; children: Valerie Noelle, Stephanie Carol. AB, Wheaton Coll., 1963; MA, Trinity Evang. Div. Sch., 1966, DD (hon.), 1981; postgrad., North Park Theol. Sem., 1968—69; EdM, Harvard U., 1977. Ordained to ministry Evang. Covenant Ch., 1971. Min. Christian edn. Glen Ellyn (Ill.) Covenant Ch., 1966-69; from registrar, dir. admissions to assoc. dean Trinity Evang. Div. Sch., Deerfield, Ill., 1969-80; pres. North Park Coll. and Theol. Sem., Chgo., 1980-86; from cons. to group mgr. Donald A. Campbell & Co., Inc., Chgo., 1986-94, v.p. ea. regional mgr., 1994—, sr. v.p., 1995—. Dir. Rockport Chamber Music Festival; trustee 1st Congl. Ch. of Rockport. Mem. Assn. Fundraising Profls. (cert.), Lehigh County Hist. Soc., Coun. Advancement and Support Edn., New Eng. Hist. Geneal. Soc. Office: Campbell & Co Eastern Regional Office 85 Eastern Ave Ste 305 Gloucester MA 01930-1869 Office Phone: 978-281-1235. E-mail: wrh@campbellcompany.com.

HAUSNER, JOHN HERMAN, retired judge; b. Detroit, Oct. 31, 1932; s. John E. and Anna (Mudrak) Hausner; m. Alice R. Kieltyka, Aug. 22, 1959. PhB cum laude, U. Detroit, 1954, MA, 1957, JD summa cum laude, 1966. Bar: Mich. 1967, U.S. Ct. Appeals (6th cir.) 1968, U.S. Supreme Ct. 1971, U.S. Tax Ct. 1976, U.S. Ct. Claims 1976, U.S. Ct. Mil. Appeals 1976. Tchr. Detroit Pub. Schs., 1954, 56-59; tchg. fellow U. Cin., 1959-61; instr. U. Detroit, 1961-74; pvt. practice Detroit, 1967-69; asst. U.S. atty., 1969-73; chief asst. U.S. atty. Ea. Dist. Mich., 1973-76; judge 3rd Jud. Cir. Mich., Wayne County, 1976-94; ret., 1994. Lectr. law sch.; faculty adviser Nat. Jud. Coll., 1978—79. Author: Sebastian, The Essence of My Soul, 1982; contbr. articles to profl. jours. Served with U.S. Army, 1954—56. Mem.: State Bar Mich., Fed. Bar Assn. (mem. exec. bd. Detroit chpt. 1976—82), Mich. Ret. Judges Assn., Blue Key, Alpha Sigma Mu. Republican. Home: 22433 Louise St Saint Clair Shores MI 48081-2034 also: 8420 E Desert Palm Tucson AZ 85730-4723

HAUSNER, MARTINA, microbiologist, educator; arrived in U.S., 2004; 1 child. BSc, U. Toronto, Ont., Can., 1987; MSc, U. Waterloo, Ont., Can., 1991; PhD, Ludwig Maximilian U., Munich, 1997. Postdoctoral rschr. Tech. U. Munich, 1997—2001, coord. microbiology, 2001—04; asst. prof. Northwestern U., Evanston, Ill., 2004—. Contbr. articles to profl. jours. Scholar, Tech. U. Munich, 2001—04. Mem.: Assn. Environ. Engring. and Sci. Profs., Internat. Water Assn., Am. Soc. Microbiology. Office: Northwestern Univ 2145 Sheridan Rd Evanston IL 60208 Office Phone: 847-467-7445. Business E-Mail: m-hausner@northwestern.edu.

HAUSRATH, DAVID L., lawyer; m. Debra Hausrath; 3 children. BSEE, Va. Tech. U., 1974; JD, U. Richmond, 1979. Law clk. Va. Supreme Ct.; project engr. DuPont, 1974—76; from lawyer to sr. v.p. Ashland, Inc., 1980—2004, sr. v.p., 2004—. gen. counsel, 2004—. sec., 2004—. Bd. vis. Salmon P. Chase Coll. Law, No. Ky. U.; mem. coun. chief legal officers The Conf. Bd.; mem. planning com. Met. Growth Alliance; mem. various coms. Ashland, Inc. Mem.: ABA, Va. Bar Assn., No. Ky. Bar Assn., Cin. Bar Assn., Ky. Bar Assn., Am. Soc. Corp. Secs., Am. Corp. Counsel Assn. Office: Ashland Inc Corp Hdqrs PO Box 391 Covington KY 41012-0391 Office Phone: 859-815-4711. Business E-Mail: dlhausrath@ashland.com.

HAUSSERMANN, OSCAR WILLIAM, JR., retired lawyer; b. Cambridge, Mass., Aug. 17, 1921; s. Oscar William and Eleanor (Drinker) H.; m. Mary Whitney, 1943 (div. 1951); children: William Burgess (dec.), Richard Hayward (dec.); m. Jean Saltonstall. BA, Harvard U., 1942, LL.B., 1948. Bar: Mass. Ptnr. Ropes & Gray, Boston, 1949-93, of counsel, 1994—. Mem. Country Club (Brookline, Mass.). Home: 28 Fresh Pond Ln Cambridge MA 02138-4602 Office: of counsel Ropes & Gray 1 International Pl Boston MA 02110-2602

HAUTMAN, PETE (PETER MURRAY), writer; b. Berkeley, Calif., 1952; V.p. mktg. Crowd Caps Inc., Minneapolis, 1981—88; owner Hautman Mktg. Svcs., 1988—91; writer, 1991—. Author: Drawing Dead, 1993 (selected NY Times Book Review Notable Books), Short Money, 1995, Mortal Nuts, 1996 (selected NY Times Book Review Notable Books), Mr. Was, 1996 (nominated Edgar Allan Poe Award, 1997), Ring Game, 1997, Stone Cold, 1998, Mrs. Million, 1999, Rag Man, 2001, Hole in the Sky, 2001 (Wis. Libr. Assn. Award, 2002), Doohickey, 2002, Sweetblood, 2003 (Best Young Adult Book of Yr., Mich. Libr. Assn., 2004), Godless, 2004 (Nat. Book Award for Young People's Lit., 2004). Office: c/o The Lazear Agency 800 Washington Ave N Ste 660 Minneapolis MN 55401-1111 E-mail: pete@petehautman.com.

HAUVER, CONSTANCE LONGSHORE, lawyer; b. Abington, Pa., Oct. 9, 1938; d. Malcolm Rettew and Margaret Evans (Lyon) L.; m. Arthur R. Hauver, 1962 (div. Mar. 1979); 1 child, Sian; m. Giles Toll, 1990. BA with high honors, Swarthmore Coll., 1960; MA, UCLA, 1962; JD magna cum laude, U. Denver, 1967. Bar: Colo. 1968, U.S. Dist. Ct. Colo. 1968, U.S. Tax Ct. 1970. Libr. Friends Com. on Nat. Legis., Washington, 1960-61; lectr. U. Hawaii, Honolulu, 1963-64; assoc. Sherman & Howard, Denver, 1968-73, ptnr., 1973-91; vol. naturalist Lookout Mountain Nature Ctr., 1998—. Mem. grievance com. Colo. Supreme Ct., 1981—86. Co-contbr. legal articles. Trustee Rocky Mountain Women's Inst., Denver, 1987-90, Swedish Med. Ctr. Found., Denver, 1978-85; bd. dirs. Women's Forum Colo. Inc., Denver, 1988-89, Girls Count, Denver, 1995-2000, pres., 1996-97. Named New Vol. Naturalist of Yr., Lookout Mountain Nature Ctr., 1998, Vol. Naturalist of Yr., 2001; recipient Athena award, Alliance Profl. Women, 1987. Fellow Am. Coll. Probate Counsel; mem. Colo. Bar Assn. (chair probate and trust law sect. 1982-83), Denver Bar Assn. (del. to ABA Ho. of Dels. 1986-88), Rocky Mountain Estate Planning Coun. (pres. 1980-81). Democrat. Mem. Soc. Of Friends. Avocations: mountain climbing, kayaking, skiing, reading, learning Spanish.

HAUX, HEATHER V., secondary school educator, consultant; d. George E. and Ann C. Haux. BA, SUNY, New Paltz, 1989, MA, 1992; MS, LI U., 2002. Permanent tchg. cert. N.Y. Cons. Very Spl. Arts, Washington, D.C., DC, 1989—90; tchr. Pine Bush (N.Y.) Ctrl. Schs., 1994—97, Southampton (N.Y.) Pub. Sch., 1997—. Writing instr. Summer Discovery Cambridge U., 1997. Recipient Departmental Honors, SUNY, New Paltz; fellow, 1991; Target scholar, Citizen's Scholarship Found. Am., 2001. Mem.: AAUW, Social Register (life). Avocations: travel, writing, piano. Office Phone: 631-591-4600. Personal E-mail: lotsofwanderlust@hotmail.com.

HAVEL, RICHARD JOSEPH, physician, educator; b. Seattle, Feb. 20, 1925; s. Joseph and Anna (Fritz) Havel; m. Virginia Johnson, June 25, 1947; children: Christopher, Timothy, Peter, Julianne. BA, Reed Coll., 1946; MS, MD, U. Oreg., 1949. Intern Cornell U. Med. Coll., NYC, 1949—50, resident in medicine, 1950—53; clin. assoc. Nat. Heart Inst., NIH, 1953—54, rsch. assoc., 1954—56; faculty Sch. Medicine, U. Calif., San Francisco, 1956—, prof. medicine, 1964—; assoc. dir. Cardiovasc. Rsch. Inst., 1961—73, dir., 1973—92. Chief metabolism sect., dept. medicine Sch. Medicine, U. Calif., San Francisco, 1967—97; dir. Arteriosclerosis Specialized Ctr. Rsch., 1971—96; mem. bd. sci. counselors Nat. Heart, Lung and Blood Inst., 1976—80; chmn. food and nutrition bd. NRC, 1987—90; pres. Lipid Rsch., Inc., 1999—. Editor: Jour. Lipid Rsch., 1972—75; assoc. editor: Am. Jour. Clin. Nutrition, 1997—, mem. editl. bd.: Jour. Biol. Chemistry, 1981—85, Jour. Arteriosclerosis, 1980—; contbr. chapters to books, articles to profl. jours. Established investigator Am. Heart Assn., 1956—61, chmn. coun. on arteriosclerosis, 1977—79. With USPHS, 1951—53. Recipient Disting. Achievement award, Am. Heart Assn., 1993, Bristol-Myers award for nutrition rsch., 1989, Gold medal, Charles U., Prague, Czech Republic, 1996. Fellow: AAAS (Theobald Smith award 1960), Am. Inst. Nutrition; mem.:

NAS, Western Soc. Clin. Investigation (Mayo Soley award 1997), Am. Soc. for Clin. Investigation, Assn. Am. Physicians, Am. Soc. Clin. Nutrition (McCollum award 1993), Am. Acad. Arts and Scis., Inst. Medicine of NAS, Alpha Omega Alpha, Phi Beta Kappa. Office: U Calif San Francisco Cardiovascular Rsch In San Francisco CA 94143-0130 Business E-Mail: richard.havel@ucsf.edu.

HAVEL, RICHARD W., lawyer; b. Fairmont, Minn., Sept. 20, 1946; s. Thomas Earl and Elizabeth (Shiltz) H.; m. Arlene Havel, July 6, 1968; children: Stephanie, Derek. BA, Notre Dame U., 1968; JD, UCLA, 1971. Bar: Calif., U.S. Dist. Ct. (no., ea., cen. and so. dists.) Calif., U.S. Ct. Appeals (9th cir.). Atty. Shutan & Trost, L.A., 1971—80, Sidley & Austin, L.A., 1980—2001, Sidley Austin Brown & Wood, L.A., 2001—. Trustee, instr. law U. Loyola, 1975-80; bd. govs. Fin. Lawyers Conf., 1991-94, 95-98, officer, 1998-2001; spkr., panelist Bankruptcy Litigation Inst., 1989-95, ALI-ABA, 1989, 90, 91; chmn. L.A. City Indsl. Devel. Authority, 1993-98, bd. dirs., 1998-2000. Contbr. articles to profl. jours. Trustee Jonsson/UCLA Cancer Ctr., 1998—; bd. dirs. Dollars for Scholars, So. Calif. region. Fellow Am. Coll. Bankruptcy, 1997; mem. ABA, Calif. Bar Assn., L.A. County Bar Assn. (comml. law and bankruptcy sect. bankruptcy subcom. 1986-89, exec. com. 1987-90, lawyer assistance com. 1985-90), UCLA Law Alumni Assn. (trustee 1996—2001). Office: Sidley Austin Brown & Wood 555 W 5th St 40th Fl Los Angeles CA 90013-1010 Office Phone: 213-896-6017. Business E-Mail: RHavel@Sidley.com.

HAVELKA, THOMAS EDWARD, retired secondary education educator; b. Wheeling, W.Va., July 10, 1947; s. Alfred and Marilyn Eleanor (Hays) H.; m. Susan Kay Wilson, June 16, 1973; children: Trevor Hays, Havaleh Ann. BFA, Ohio State U., 1969, MusM, 1975; postgrad., Akron U., Ashland U., Cleve. State U., Ohio State U. Cert. tchr., Ohio; national registered music tchr. M.E.N.C. Music instr., chmn. fine arts dept. Bellaire (Ohio) Bd. Edn., 1969-74; choir dir., chmn. music dept. Coshocton (Ohio) City Bd. Edn., 1975—. Founder Coshocton City Schs., Arts Festival, 1985—; state rep. All Am. Youth Honor Musicians, Miami, Fla., 1970-90; asst. condr. All Am. Youth Honor Choir, 1970, 77-78, condr., 1980-90; adjudicator Internat. Choir Fest., Mexico City, 1978, Dulcimer Festival, Roscoe Village, Ohio, 1986-88, Show Choir Festival, Portsmouth, Ohio, 1986, Lander Coll., S.C.; instr. Ohio U., 2002-; adj. faculty Ohio U., Zanesville, Ohio. Composer: Piece for String Quartet, 1974, (choral) Offertorium from Missae Requiem Brevis, 1974, Bless Ye the God of All, 1975, Joseph's Lullaby, 1997, Peter's Praise, 1999. Mem. Big Bros./Big Sisters Assn., Columbus, 1970—; dist. exec., chmn. bd. Boy Scouts Am., Coshocton, 1979-80; sect. leader, asst. accompanist, asst. conductor Coshocton Community Choir, 1984—; active various theater groups, Coshocton and Wheeling, 1974—; singer St. Matthew's Episcopal Ch., Wheeling, W.Va., 1973-75; asst. organist Grace United Meth. Ch., Coshocton, 1986—; pres., bd. dirs. Ohio U. Sch. of Music Soc. of Alumni and Friends. Recipient awards from Mayors of Malaga, Spain, 1981, Agnani and Fuiggi, Italy, 1984 and Paris, 1985, Istra, USSR, 1989, award of Merit Coshocton City Schs., 1984. Mem. NEA, Ohio Edn. Assn., Ohio Music Edn. Assn. (asst. contest chmn., approved adjudicator in piano, voice, and choir, chmn. county membership com. 1977-78), Internat. Soc. for Music Edn., Internat. Fedn. for Choral Music, Am. Guild Organists, Am. Choral Dirs. Assn., Ohio Choral Dirs. Assn. (chmn. county membership com. 1978-79), Coshocton City Edn. Assn. (sec. 1984-85, 88-89), Music Educators Nat. Conf., Soc. Music Tchr. Edn., Kappa Kappa Psi, Phi Mu Alpha, Pi Kappa Lambda. Republican. Methodist. Avocations: travel, camping, backpacking, coin collecting/numismatics. Home: 1628 Woodland Dr Coshocton OH 43812-3151 Personal E-mail: thavelka@adelphia.net.

HAVEMANN, JOEL, editor; b. N.Y.C., 1943; BA in Math., Harvard U., 1965. Gen. assignment reporter Portland Oregonian, 1965-67; edn. reporter Chicago Sun-Times, 1967-73; budget reporter National Journal, 1973-78, dep. ed., 1978-83; econ. reporter L.A. Times, 1983-84, projects editor, 1984-90, Brussels bur. chief, 1990-93, DC projects editor, news editor, 1993—. Author: (book) Congress and the Budget, 1978. Office: Los Angeles Times/Wash Bur 1875 Eye St NW Ste 1100 Washington DC 20006-5421

HAVEN, MILTON M., retired lawyer; b. Paterson, NJ, July 12, 1909; s. Harry and Minnie (Brown) H.; m. Phyllis Grossman, Dec. 23, 1938; children: Miles J., Constance A. AB, Syracuse U., 1931, LLB, 1933, JD, 1968. Bar: N.Y. Assoc. Hon. John E. Mack, Poughkeepsie, N.Y., 1933-46; rent examiner OPA, Poughkeepsie, 1946-50; acting sitting city judge, clk. of City Ct., Poughkeepsie, 1950-54; assoc. Edward J. Mack, Poughkeepsie, 1954-62, 66-70; judge City Ct., Poughkeepsie, 1962-66, 70-72; counsel to firm McCabe & Mack, Poughkeepsie, 1972-80, Corbally, Gartland & Rappleyea, Poughkeepsie, 1980—2003; jud. hearing officer 9th Jud. Dist., Poughkeepsie, 1978-81; ret., 2000. Mem. N.Y. State Mental Hygiene Coun. Pres. Poughkeepsie Jewish Ctr., 1942-43; pres. Temple Beth-El, Poughkeepsie, 1959-60, hon. trustee, 1985—; mem. adv. com. police sci. and correction adminstrn. CC, 1966-71; pres. Dutchess County Mental Health Assn., 1970-71, hon. trustee, 1990—; mem. adv. com. Pub. Welfare, Poughkeepsie, 1966-71; chmn. City Trial Com., Poughkeepsie, 1972-75; budget chair Dutchess County Area Chest and Coun., Poughkeepsie, 1952-54; mem. adv. bd. Marist Coll., Poughkeepsie, 1970-75; chmn. Dem. Com. City of Poughkeepsie, 1954-57; mem. bd. visitors Hudson River Psychiat. Ctr., 1977-88. Served with U.S. Army, 1942-43. Recipient Cert. of Appreciation Dutchess C.C., 1965, Dutchess Interfaith Coun., Poughkeepsie, 1990, Disting. Svc. award Mental Health Assn., Poughkeepsie, 1992, Van Bramer award, 1992. Mem. N.Y. State Bar Assn., Dutchess County Bar Assn. (pres. 1977-78), Masons, Harding Club (pres. 1937-38). Avocation: choir singing. Home: 3 Ivy Ter Poughkeepsie NY 12601-4804

HAVENS, CAROLYN CLARICE, librarian; b. Nashville, Sept. 11, 1953; d. Charles Buford and Iris Mae (Anderson) H.; m. Hilton Harris Huey, June 9, 1990; children: Heather Louise, Quentin Harris. AA, Sue Bennett Coll., 1973; BA in English, U. West Fla., 1974; MLS, U. Ky., 1981. Tchr. Escambia High Sch., Pensacola, Fla., 1974-75; salesperson Univ. Mall, Pensacola, 1975-77; libr. tech. U. Ky., Lexington, 1978-82; libr. Auburn (Ala.) U., 1982—. Contbr. articles to profl. jours. and newspapers; editorial bd.: A Dynamic Tradition, 1991. Bd. dirs. Nat. Kidney Found. Ala., Opelika, 1986-89; active Conscientious Alliance for Peace, Auburn, 1989—. Clergy and Laity Concerned, Atlanta, 1991—. Mem. ALA, Southeastern Libr. Assn., Ala. Libr. Assn., North Am. Serials Interest Group, Ala. Assn. Coll. and Rsch. Librs., Studio 218. Democrat. Methodist. Avocations: painting, writing, photography. Office: Auburn U Ralph Draughon Libr Auburn AL 36849-5606

HAVENS, CHARLES W., III, retired lawyer; b. Balt., Mar. 22, 1936; m. Lucille Bowman; children— Charles W. IV, Jessica Madaline AB, Franklin and Marshall Coll., 1958; LL.B., U. Va., 1961. Bar: D.C. 1961, Va. 1961, U.S. Supreme Ct. Assoc. Covington & Burling, Washington, 1961-66; spl. asst. to gen. counsel Dept. Def., Washington, 1966-67, spl. asst. to asst. sec. def., 1967-70; gen. counsel then pres. Reins. Assn. Am., Washington, 1970-81; ptnr. LeBoeuf, Lamb, Leiby & MacRae, Washington, 1981—2000; ret., 2000. Contbr. articles to profl. jours. Mem. AIDA Reins. and Ins. Arbitration Soc. (founding, bd. dirs.), Met. Club, John's Island Club. Clubs: Metropolitan (Washington). Avocation: golf. Home: # 396 1000 Beach Rd Vero Beach FL 32963 Home (Summer): 4045 Mansion Dr NW Washington DC 20007

HAVENS, HARRY STEWART, retired federal official, management consultant; b. Little Rock, Dec. 18, 1935; s. Ralph Murray and Catherine Clara (Clark) H.; m. Frances Jones, June 12, 1960. BA in Econs. magna cum laude, Duke U., 1957; BA in Philosophy, Politics, Econs., Oxford U., England, 1959, MA, 1963. Economist U.S. Budget Bur., Washington, 1964-66, budget examiner, 1966-70, chief housing br., 1970-72; chief income maintenance br. U.S. Office Mgmt. and Budget, Washington, 1972-74, dep. dir. human resources divsn., 1972—74; dir. program analysis divsn. U.S. GAO, Washington, 1974-80, asst. comptroller gen., 1980-93; pvt. practice cons. Washington, 1993—. Cons. Orgn. Econ. Coop. & Devel., Paris, 1993—, U.S. GAO, 1993-96, Supreme Soviet of Russian Fedn., 1992-93, State Duma of Russian Fedn., 1994. Contbr. articles to profl. jours.; contbr. book chpts. Rhodes scholar, 1957. Home and Office: 4515 Neptune Dr Alexandria VA 22309-3129 Personal E-mail: havensh@aol.com.

HAVENS, JASON EDWARD, lawyer; s. Edward A. and Mary Jane Havens; m. Daphne K. McDermit, June 1, 1996. BA magna cum laude, Lipscomb U., 1996; JD, U. Tenn., 1999; LLM in Estate Planning, U. Miami, 2000; LLM in Internat. Taxation, Regent U., 2003. Bar: Fla. 2000. Summer assoc. Henderson, Franklin, Ft. Myers, Fla., 1998—99, assoc. atty., 2000—01; shareholder atty. Hall & Runnels, P.A., Destin, Fla., 2002—03; pvt. practice Havens & Miller, PLLC, Destin, 2003—, Niceville, Fla., 2004—. Mem. legal adv. bd. Capital Trust Co., Wilmington, Del., 2004—; bd. dirs. Estate Plan Coun. Emerald Coast, Destin, pres., 2004—; spkr. in field; presenter in field. Contbr. articles to profl. jours. Chmn. Planned Giving com. Sacred Heart Hosp. Found., Destin, 2003—; ambassador The Able Trust, Tallahassee, 2004—; bd. dirs. Boys and Girls Club, Ft. Walton Beach, Fla., 2002—04. Mem.: ABA (editor Probate & Property mag., Best Article award 2004), Fla. Bar Assn., Christian Legal Soc. (v.p. gift, estate and trust sect. 2004—). Republican. Presbyterian. Office: Havens & Miller PLLC 4400 East Hwy 20 Ste 211 Niceville FL 32578 also: Ste 101 1223 Airport Rd Destin FL 32541 Office Phone: 850-897-6733. Business E-Mail: jasonhavens@havensmiller.com, jasonhavens@abanet.org.

HAVENS, JOHN P., investment company executive; Grad., Harvard U. Formerly with Kidder Peabody; principal in institutional equity Morgan Stanley, 1986, mng. dir., 1990—2000, head of worldwide instl. equity divsn., 2000—05. Bd. dirs. Nasdaq Stock Market Inc., 2003—.

HAVENS, LESTON LAYCOCK, psychiatrist, educator; b. Bklyn., July 31, 1924; s. Valentine Britton and Nellie Falk (Laycock) H.; m. Susan Elizabeth Miller, May 19, 1973; 1 child, Emily E.; children by previous marriage: Christopher W., Jeffry B. (dec.), Jennifer F., Sarah B. BA, Williams Coll., 1947; MD, Cornell U., 1952; MA (hon.), Harvard U., 1987; LHD, Mass. Sch. Profl. Psychology, 1993. Intern N.Y. Hosp., 1952-53, asst. resident internal medicine, 1953-54; resident, chief of svc. Mass. Mental Health Ctr., Boston Psychopathic Hosp., 1954-58, staff visit and asst. clin. dir., 1958-62, prin. investigator studies in visual word perception, 1960-66, program dir. psychiat. rehab. internship program, 1962-68, program dir. med. student teaching, 1964-81; asst. prof. psychiatry Harvard Med. Sch., Boston, 1963-64, assoc. clin. prof. psychiatry, 1965-71, psychoanalyst, 1967—, prof. psychiatry, 1971—. Cargnegie vis. prof. humanities MIT, 1968; H. B. Williams traveling prof. Australian and New Zealand Coll. of Psychiatrists, 1975; chief psychiat. cons. Mass. Rehab. Commn., 1959-65; mental health adminstr. Region VI, Mass. Dept. Mental Health, 1968-69; dir. residency tng. Cambridge Hosp., 1987-96, co-dir. edn., 1996—. Author: Approaches to the Mind, 1973, Participant Observation, 1977, Making Contact, 1986, A Safe Place: Laying the Groundwork of Psychotherapy, 1989, Coming to Life, 1993, Learning To Be Human, 1994, The Real Life Guide to Psychotherapy Practice, 2000; contbr. articles to profl. jours. Served to 2d lt. AUS, 1944-46. Recipient H.C. Solomon award, 1977, Benjamin Rush award, APA, 1995; Leston Havens award for excellence in tchg., Cambridge Hosp., 2003. Mem. Am. Psychiat. Assn., Soc. Biol. Psychiatry (A.E. Bennett award 1958), Mass. Soc. for Rsch. in Psychiatry (McCurdy prize 1962), Mass. Psychiat. Soc. (Lifetime Achievement award 2004), Phi Beta Kappa, Alpha Omega Alpha. Home: 151 Brattle St Cambridge MA 02138-2243 Office: Cambridge Hosp 1493 Cambridge St Cambridge MA 02139-1099

HAVENS, MURRAY CLARK, political scientist, educator; b. Council Grove, Kans., Aug. 21, 1932; s. Ralph Murray and Catherine Clara (Clark) H.; m. Agnes Marie Scharpf, July 5, 1958 (dec. 1969); children: Colin Scott, Theresa Agnes; m. Carolyn Trost, May 5, 1997. BA, U. Ala., 1953; MA, Johns Hopkins U., 1954, PhD, 1958. Postdoctoral fellow Brookings Instn., Washington, 1958-59; asst. prof. polit. sci. Duke U., 1959-61; from asst. prof. to prof. U. Tex., Austin, 1961-73; vis. lectr. U. Sydney (Australia), 1966; prof. polit. sci. Tex. Tech U., Lubbock, 1973-98, chmn. dept., 1975-83, prof. emeritus, 1999—. Author: City Versus Farm?, 1957, The Challenges to Democracy, 1965, The Politics of Assassination, 1970, Assassination and Terrorism, 1975, Texas Politics Today, 1995; book rev. editor Jour. Politics, 1971-83; contbr. numerous articles to profl. jours. Served with AUS, 1954—56. Mem.: AAUP, Am. Polit. Sci. Assn., So. Polit. Sci. Assn., Southwestern Polit. Sci. Assn. (pres. 1983—84), Phi Beta Kappa. Home: 8636 Sawyer Brown Rd Nashville TN 37221

HAVER-ALLEN, ANN, communications director; d. Vivian Faye Haver; m. William Allen, June 21, 1986; children: Jason Allen, Summer Allen. BA in Journalism, Thomas Edison State Coll., Trenton, N.J. Reporter Angleton Times, Tex., 1985—86; mng. editor Princeton Packet Group, NJ, 1986—90, Engel Pub. Ptnrs., West Trenton, NJ, 1990—92; dir. engring. comm. Princeton U., NJ, 1992—2004; dir. pub. rels. and mktg. Prescott (Ariz.) Coll., 2004—. Editor: EQuad News, Transitions, Payson (Ariz.) Roundup, 2005—. Commr. Red Heart Coastal Mvskoke Clan, Robertsdale, Ala., 2001—; bd. dirs. Cmtys. for Compassion and Justice, Prescott. Recipient APEX award for publ. excellence, 2002, 2003, 2004, Communicator award, 2002, Communicator award design/logo, 2004, Award of Merit, Internat. Assn. Bus. Communicators, 2002, 2004, Silver Quill award, Assn. Bus. Communicators, 2003, Crystal Award of Excellence, 2003, Clarion award, Assn. Women Comm., 2003, Clarion award for Strategic Planning Logo in the Nonprofit Logo category, 2004, Magnum Opus Gold award in Best Rewrite category, Mo. Sch. Journalism and industry comm. profls., 2004, Magnum Opus Hon. Mention in Best Series of Articles category, 2004, Dalton Pen Comms. Merit award for EQuad News in the Mags. category, 2004, Dalton Pen Comms. Merit award for Strategic Planning Logo in the Graphic Arts/Logos category, 2004. Mem.: NAFE, N.J. Press Assn. (hon. mention), Nat. Newspaper Assn. (Blue Ribbon Excellence 1988), Internat. Assn. Bus. Communicators (IRIS Award of Excellence 2002, IRIS award 2004), Women in Comm., Ednl. Press Assn. Am., Coun. for Advancement and Support of Edn. Personal E-mail: aha_prescottcollege@yahoo.com. Business E-Mail: ahaver-allen@prescott.edu.

HAVERBACK, CHESTER Z., plastic surgeon; b. Mass., Feb. 25, 1939; s. Morris M. and Tillie P. Haverback; m. Mary Carol Stanchfield; children: Brian Cheston, Craig Bradford, Gretchen Carol. BA cum laude, MS in Chemistry, Syracuse U.; studied, Cornell U.; MD, The Johns Hopkins U., Balt. Diplomate Am. Bd. Surgery, Am. Bd. Plastic Surgery. Asst. resident, gen. surgery N.Y. Hosp., Cornell Med. Ctr., U. Minn. Hosp., U. Wis. Hosps.; resident, plastic surgery St. Louis U. Hosps., chief resident, plastic surgery; plastic surgeon pvt. practice, Bethesda, Md. Asst. clin. prof., plastic surgery Georgetown U. Med. Sch. and Hosp., Washington. Sr. asst. USPHS, NIH, Bethesda, Md. Fellow: ACS; mem.: AMA, Am. Soc. for Aesthetic Plastic Surgery, Inc., Am. Assn. Hand Surgery, Assn. Military Surgeons U.S., Am. Cleft Palate Assn., Montgomery County Med. Soc., Am. Soc. Plastic Surgeons, Sigma Xi, Sigma Pi Sigma. Avocations: reading, music, poetry, writing, water sports. Home: 5104 Cammack Dr Bethesda MD 20816 Office: Chester Z Haverback MD 8218 Wisconsin Ave #320 Bethesda MD 20814

HAVERKAMPF, KATHLEEN LEA, economist; b. Elgin, Ill., Nov. 26, 1959; d. David Allen and Mary Louise (Warner) H; m. Thomas J. Schwartz; 1 daughter. BS, U. Wis., Stevens Point, 1982; Leadership Program cert., Johns Hopkins U., 1999. Cert. interior decorator 2003. Legis. asst. Wis. State Assembly, Madison, 1983-86; asst. personnel dir. Govs. Transition Team, Madison, 1986; dir. constituent rels. Govs. Exec. Office, Madison, 1987-88; econ. devel. cons. Wis. Dept. Devel., Madison, 1988-92; prin. KLH Comms., 1992-93; exec. dir. Wis. Rural Ptnrs., Inc., Madison, 1993—. Bd. dirs. Wis. Leadership Inst., 1994-2002, v.p., 1996-2000, bd. dirs. North Ctrl. Reg. Ctr. for Rural Devel., 2000-, pres. 2003. Recipient Pioneer Leader award Nat. Rural Devel. Partnership, 1996; named to Outstanding Young Women of Am., 1986. Mem. Wis. Soc. for Hist. Preservation. Home: 601 Bob White Ct Lodi WI 53555-1350 Office: Ste D 110 Baker St Waunakee WI 53597 E-mail: wirural@tds.net.

HAVERSTOCK, LYNDA M., lieutenant governor; m. Harley Olsen; 4 children. MEd, PhD in Clin. Psychology, U. Sask. Clin. psychologist; lt. gov. of Sask., 2000—. Past radio talk show host. Author: Fighting the Farm Crisis, Safety and Health in Agriculture, Saskatchewan Politics in the Twenty-First Century. Named hon. col., 2 Can. Forces Flying Tng. Sch.; recipient Triple E award, Gzowski award; Paul Harris fellow, Rotary Internat. Mem.: Army, Navy and Air Force Vets. Can. (hon. life). Office: Govt House 4607 Dewdney Ave Regina SK S4P 3V7 Canada

HAVIGHURST, CLARK CANFIELD, law educator; b. Evanston, Ill., May 25, 1933; s. Harold Canfield and Marion Clay (Perryman) H.; m. Karen Waldron, Aug. 28, 1965; children: Craig Perryman, Marjorie Clark. BA, Princeton U., 1955; JD, Northwestern U., 1958. Bar: Ill. 1958, N.Y. 1961. Assoc. Debevoise Plimpton Lyons & Gates, N.Y.C., 1958, 61-64; assoc. prof. law Duke U., Durham, NC, 1964-68, prof., 1968-86, William Neal Reynolds prof., 1986—2002, emeritus, 2005—; interim dean Duke U. Sch. Law, 1999. Dir. Program on Legal Issues in Health Care Duke U., 1969-88; adj. scholar Am Enterprise Inst. Pub. Policy Rsch., 1976—; resident cons. FTC, Washington, 1978, Epstein, Becker & Green, Washington, 1989-90; scholar in residence Inst. Medicine of NAS, Washington, 1972-73, RAND Corp., Santa Monica, 1999. Author: Deferred Compensation for Key Employees, 1964, Regulating Health Facilities Construction, 1974, Deregulating the Health Care Industry, 1982, Health Care Law and Policy, 1988, 2d edit., 1998, Health Care Choices: Private Contracts as Instruments of Health Reform, 1995; editor Law and Contemporary Problems jour., 1965-70. With U.S. Army, 1958-60. Mem. Inst. Medicine of Nat. Acad. Sci., Order of Coif Office: Duke U Sch Law PO Box 90360 Durham NC 27708-0360 Business E-Mail: hav@law.duke.edu.

HAVILAND, BANCROFT DAWLEY, lawyer; b. Yonkers, N.Y., May 13, 1925; s. Harold Bancroft and Dorothy (Dawley) H.; m. Dorothy MacFarland, Oct. 30, 1945; children: Lucy, William, Thomas, Amy. BA in Polit. Sci., U. Pa., 1947, LLB, 1949. Bar: N.Y. 1951, Pa. 1952. Gowen teaching fellow U. Pa. Law Sch., Phila., 1949-50; assoc. Donovan, Leisure, Newton & Irvine, N.Y.C., 1950-51, Schnader, Harrison, Segal & Lewis, N.Y.C., 1951-61, ptnr., 1961-90, ret., 1991. Trustee Westtown (Pa.) Friends' Sch., 1960-94, Media-Providence (Pa.) Friends' Sch., 1960-95; chmn. Westtown Sch. Com., 1988-93; commr. Rose Tree Soccer Club, Media, 1971-98, Aston Twp., Pa., 1954-61; justice of peace Middletown Twp., Pa., 1963-65. Lt. (j.g.) USN, 1943-45, PTO. Mem. ABA, Pa. Bar Assn., Phila. Bar Assn., Am. Judicature Soc., Order of Coif Lodges: Lions. Democrat. Mem. Soc. Of Friends. Avocations: woodworking, reading, gardening. Home: 21 Kendal Dr Kennett Square PA 19348 Office: Schnader Harrison Segal & Lewis 1600 Market St Ste 3600 Philadelphia PA 19103-7287 Office Phone: 215-751-2458.

HAVILAND, DAVID SANDS, architectural educator, researcher, administrator; b. Rome, N.Y., Apr. 26, 1942; s. William Erwin and Barbara Hannon (Huguenin) H.; m. Kathleen Anne Kelly, July 8, 1973; children: Kelly Sands, Wallace Sands. BS, Rensselaer Poly. Inst., 1964, BArch, 1965, MArch, 1967. Rsch. asst., instr. Rensselaer Poly. Inst., Troy, N.Y., 1965-67, asst. prof. architecture, 1967-70, assoc. prof., 1970-79, prof., 1979—, dean Sch. of Architecture, 1980-90, v.p., student life, 1994-2000, v.p. Inst. Advancement, 2000—. Vis. prof. constrn. mgmt. and engring. U. Reading, Eng., 1990-96. Editor: The Architect's Handbook fo Profl. Practice, 12th edit., 1994; contbr. articles to profl. jours. V.p. Rensselaer Newman Found.; pres. Howard and Bush Found. Recipient James L. Haecker award for disting. rsch. leadership, 1996, also numerous rsch. grants. Mem. AIA (Inst. award 1989), N.Y. State Assn. Architects. Home: 63 Pinewoods Ave Troy NY 12180-4701 Office: Rensselaer Polytech Inst Inst Advancement Troy Bldg 110 8th St Troy NY 12180-3590 Office Phone: 518-276-6247.

HAVILAND, PETER L., lawyer; BA, Harvard U., 1977; JD, Stanford Law Sch., 1989. Bar: Calif. 1989. Law clk. to Hon. Warren Ferguson, US Ct. Appeals 9th Circuit; litig. ptnr. Kaye, Scholer, Fierman, Hays & Handler LLP; ptnr., nat., internat. comml. disputes Akin Gump Strauss Hauer & Feld LLP, LA. Assoc. editor Stanford Law Review. Bd. dirs. Constl. Rights Found., So. Christian Leadership Conf. Named one of Am. Top Black Lawyers, Black Enterprise Mag., 2003. Mem.: Black Entertainment and Sports Lawyers Assn., State Bar Calif. Office: Akin Gump Strauss Hauer & Feld LLP 2029 Century Park E Ste 2400 Los Angeles CA 90067-3012 Office Phone: 310-229-1034. Business E-Mail: phaviland@akingump.com.

HAVIS, ALLAN STUART, playwright, theatre educator; b. N.Y.C., 1951; s. Mickey and Esther H. Havis; m. Julia Fulton; children: Simone Michelle, Julian Sage. BA, CCNY, 1973; MA, Hunter Coll., 1976; MFA, Yale U., 1980. Film animation tchr. Guggenheim Mus., N.Y.C., 1974-76; playwriting tchr. Dramatist Guild, N.Y.C., 1985-87, Ulster County C.C., Stoneridge, N.Y., 1985-88; prof. theatre, head playwriting program U. Calif.-San Diego, La Jolla, 1988—. Author: (novel) Albert the Astronomer, 1979, (plays) Morocco, 1986 (HBO award), Lilith, 1991, The Gift, 1998, (anthology) Plays by Allan Havis, 1989, A Daring Bridge, 1997, Ladies of Fisher Cove, 1997, Sainte Simone, 1997, (play) A Vow of Silence, 1996, (anthology) Plays by Allan Havis, 1997; editor, contbr.: American Political Plays of 1990's, 2000—. Dramaturg Young Playwrights Festival, N.Y.C., 1984, juror, 1993; juror N.J. Arts Coun., Trenton, 1987; panelist Theatre Communications Group, N.Y.C., 1987; juror McKnight Playwriting Fellowship, 1995. Playwriting fellow Nat. Endowment for the Arts, 1986, Rockefeller Found., 1987, Guggenheim Found., 1987-88; recipient New American Plays award Kennedy Ctr./Am. Express, Washington, 1988, Dramatists Guild/CBS award, 1995, HBO award, 1996; award San Diego Drama Critics, 2003. Democrat. Jewish. Avocations: tennis, motorcycles, Karate (black belt), swimming, horseback riding. Office: Dept of Theatre Univ Calif-San Diego La Jolla CA 92093 E-mail: ahavis@ucsd.edu.

HAVLICEK, FRANKLIN J., communications executive; b. N.Y.C., July 18, 1947; s. Raymond Joseph and Rosalia Maria (Zona) H.; m. Louise Sferrazza, Dec. 21, 1980. BA, Columbia U., 1968, JD, 1973, MA, 1977, MPhil, 1980; cert., Internat. Inst. Human Rights, Strasbourg, France, 1972. Bar: N.Y. 1974, U.S. Dist. Ct. (so. and ea. dists.) N.Y. 1974, U.S. Ct. Appeals (2d cir.) 1975, U.S. Supreme Ct. 1979, D.C. 1990. Atty. Battle & Fowler, N.Y.C., 1973-78; spl. advisor to Mayor of N.Y.C., 1978-82; ptnr. Seham, Klein, Zelman, N.Y.C., 1982-84; dir. labor rels. NBC, N.Y.C., 1984-88; v.p. personnel, indsl. rels. and environ. svcs. Washington Post, 1988-97; pres. stratagem adv. svcs. Washington, 1997-98; with Internat. Monetary Fund, Washington, 1998—. Adj. prof. internat. & pub. affairs Columbia U., N.Y.C., 1978-88, Sch. Pub. Affairs & Sch. Internat. Svc., Am. U., Washington, 1999—. Editor: Collective Bargaining, 1979, Presidential Selection, 1982, Election Communications, 1984; contbr. numerous articles on law, govt., communications to mags., newspapers. Exec. com. N.Y. Gov.'s Task Force in Schs. and Bus., 1986-88; counsel Vietnam Vets. Meml. Commn., 1982-85, State Commn. on Dioxin, 1983-85; candidate for U.S. Senate in N.Y., 1986; mem. U.S. U.S.S.R. Emerging Leaders Summit, 1988, 90; bd. dirs. World Affairs Coun., 1991-97, Washington Performing Arts Soc., 1995-97, Internat. Peace Acad., 1989-90, World Media Colloquium UNESCO, 1989; U.S. Tech. expert ILO, 1990; cons. to UN High Commr. for Human Rights in Bosnia, 1992; study grant on media and communications European Cmty., 1994; cons. Cath. Relief Svcs., Kosovo, 1999. With U.S. Army, 1968-70. Ford Found. fellow, 1977; study grantee on media and comms. European Cmty., 1994. Mem. ABA, Assn. of Bar of City of N.Y., Am. Polit. Sci. Assn., Am. Acad. Polit. Sci., N.Y. Acad. Scis. Clubs: City N.Y. (trustee 1985-87). Roman Catholic. Avocations: tennis, running, climbing, films, architectural restoration. Home: 6024 Western Ave Chevy Chase MD 20815-3344 Office: Internat Monetary Fund 700 19th St NW Washington DC 20431 Office Phone: 202-623-7732. Personal E-mail: fhavlicek@aol.com. Business E-Mail: fhavlicek@imf.org.

HAVLIN, JOHN LEROY, soil scientist, educator; b. Chgo., May 8, 1950; 1 child, Jonathon Cary. MS, Colo. State U., 1980, PhD, 1983. Asst. prof. U. Nebr., Scottbluff, 1983-85, Kans. State U., Manhattan, 1985-90, prof. dept. agronomy, 1990-96; prof. N.C. State U., Raleigh, 1996—. Author: Soil Fertility and Fertilizers; contbr. articles articles to profl. pubs., chapters to books. Named Researcher of Yr., Nat. Fertilizer Solutuions Assn., 1989; recipient Werner L. Nelson Rsch. award, 1991, R.E. Wagner award, 2003, Honors award, USDA, 2004; fellow Tchr. fellow, Nat. Assn. Coll. Tchrs. of Agr., 1994. Fellow: Soil Sci. Soc. Am. (pres. 2005, Edn. award 2002), Am. Soc. Agronomy; mem.: Soil and Water Conservation Soc., Phi Kappa Phi, Sigma Xi, Gamma Sigma Delta (Outstanding Tchr. award 1992). Republican. Presbyterian. Achievements include research in advancement of dryland soil and crop managment technologies to improve productivity and profitability; crop rotation and tillage effects on soil organic matter and productivity; dryland fertilizer managment and precision farming. Home: 8709 Bluff Pointe Ct Raleigh NC 27615-4195 Office: NC State U Dept Soil Sci Raleigh NC 27695-0001 Office Phone: 919-513-4411. E-mail: havlin@ncsu.edu.

HAWE, DAVID LEE, manufacturing consultant, venture capitalist; b. Columbus, Ohio, Feb. 19, 1938; s. William Doyle and Carolyn Mary (Hassig) H.; m. Margret J. Hoover, Apr. 15, 1962; children: Darrin Lee, Kelly Lynn. Lic. real estate broker, Calif. Project mgr. ground antenna systems W.D.L. Labs., Philco Corp., 1960-65; credit mgr. for Western U.S. Am. Hosp. Supply Corp., Burbank, Calif., 1965-74; owner, mgr. Hoover Profl. Equipment Co., Contract Health Equipment Co., Guasti, Calif., 1974-75; pres. Baslor Care Svcs.; owner convalescent homes Santa Ana, Calif., 1975-80; pres. Application Assocs., 1980-2000; CEO Xiron Inc., 1985—2004; owner Tripro Assocs.; chmn. bd. C-Squad, Anaheim, Calif., 1999—. Bd. dirs., chmn. bd. dirs. Xiron, Inc.; bd. dir. Medisco Co., Casa Pacifica, Broadway Assocs., C-Squard Inc., Xiron Corp., C and C Group, Application Assocs. Inc. Bd. dirs. Santa Ana Cmty. Convalescent Hosp., 1974-79, pres. 1975-79. With USN, 1954-56. Mem. Am. Vacuum Soc. Republican. Roman Catholic. Home: 18082 Hallsworth Cir Villa Park CA 92861-4503 Office Phone: 714-999-2791. Personal E-mail: triproassoc@att.net.

HAWES, BESS LOMAX, retired folklorist; m. Baldwin Hawes; children: Corey, Naomi, Nicholas. BA, Bryn Mawr U., 1941; MA, U. Calif., 1970; PhD (hon.), Kenyon Coll., 1994, U. N.C., 1995. With music divsn. N.Y. Pub. Libr.; prof. anthropology Calif. State U., Northridge, 1963—74, Smithsonian Instn., 1974—76; dir. Folk Arts Program Nat. Endowment for Arts, 1977—92; ret., 1992. Recipient Nat. Medal of Arts, Pres. Clinton, 1993. E-mail: bess.hawes@csun.edu.

HAWES, WILLIAM KENNETH, communication educator, author; b. Grand Rapids, Mich., Mar. 6, 1931; s. William Kenneth and Cora Elizabeth (Tibble) H.; m. Ella Margaret Plant, Aug. 13, 1961 (dec. 1998); children: William III, Robert Ernest. AB, Eastern Mich. U., 1955; AM, U. Mich., 1956, PhD, 1960. Tchg. asst. U. Mich., Ann Arbor, 1956-57; instr. English and speech Eastern Mich. U., Ypsilanti, 1956-60; asst. prof., mgr. KTCU Tex. Christian U., Ft. Worth, 1960-64; vis. assoc. prof., mgr. WUNC U. N.C., Chapel Hill, 1964-65; assoc. prof., mgr. KUHF U. Houston, 1965-76, prof., 1976—. Admissions bd. Biomed. Program, Sch. Allied Health Scis., U. Tex. Health Sci. Ctr., Houston, 1974-95; lectr. J. William Fulbright, Taiwan, 2001; resident Rockefeller Found., Bellagio, Italy, 2003. Author: The Performer in Mass Media, 1978, American Television Drama, 1986, Television Performing, 1991, Ante La Cámara, 1993, Chinese edit., 1999, Public Television: America's First Station, 1996, Live Television Drama, 1946-1951, 2001, Filmed Television Drama, 1952-1958, 2002; contbg. author: Understanding Radio, 1967, 85, La Radio: Une Carrière, 1970, Understanding Television, 1978, Television Station Management and Operations, 1989; editor: Pornography Cinema Community Standards, 1975, 3rd edit., 1993; prodr., creator TV series including Video Workshop, 1967—; film guest Fed. Republic of Germany, 1981. Active Houston Pub. TV, Fulbright Found. Recipient Avery Hopwood award U. Mich., 1957, Rockwell award, 1996, Gulf Coast Film and Video award, 2004; grantee U. Houston and/or NEH, 1981, 83, 86-87, 91, 2003; named to U. Houston London Program, 1984, 94 Mem.: ACLU, Mus. of Fine Arts Houston, Am. Film Inst., Nat. Trust for Historic Preservation. Home: Parc V-902 3600 Montrose Blvd Houston TX 77006-4658 Office: U Houston Sch of Comm Houston TX 77204-4072 Office Phone: 713-743-2863. Office Fax: 713-743-2604. Business E-Mail: whawes@mail.uh.edu.

HAWK, GEORGE WAYNE, retired electronics company executive; b. Warren, Ohio, Feb. 21, 1928; s. Oscar Wilmer and Morda Irene (Klingensmith) H.; m. Charline Hines Bond, Feb. 12, 1955; children: George Wayne, David James, John Robert. BS in Aero. Engring, Purdue U., 1951; MSME, U. So. Calif., 1955; postgrad., U. Tenn. Registered profl. engr., Ind. Asst. R & D officer gas dynamics facility Arnold Engring. Devel. Ctr., Tullahoma, Tenn., 1951-53; project engr. Hughes R & D Lab., Culver City, Calif., 1953-56; sr. rsch. engr. Goodyear Aircraft Corp., Akron, Ohio, 1956-57; with Moog Inc., East Aurora, N.Y., 1957-81, v.p. aerospace divsn., 1968-69, exec. v.p., dir., gen. mgr. controls divsn., 1969-76, exec. v.p., dir. pres. controls group, 1976-81; pres. G.W. Hawk Inc., 1981-86; pres., CEO Acme Electric Corp., 1986-91, chmn. bd. dirs., CEO, 1992-94; chmn. bd. dirs. Comptek Rsch. Inc., 1983-87, M.H.P. Machines, Inc., Buffalo, 1983-92. Chmn. bd. dirs. B.I.S. Ptnrs.; bd. dirs. Comptek Rsch., Inc., Western N.Y. Tech. Devel. Corp., past chmn. Contbr. articles profl. jours.; patentee in field. Past chair and vice chair bd. dirs. Buffalo Philharm. Orch., lifetime dir.; past pres. Greater Niagara Frontier coun. Boy Scouts Am.; past chmn. bd., pres. Greater Buffalo Devel. Found.; trustee, treas. Buffalo Gen. Hosp. Found.; pres. Niagara Aerospace Mus.; bd. dirs. Niagara Luth. Home Found.; past bd. dirs. Fluid Power Edn. Found.; bd. regents emeritus Canisius Coll. With U.S. Army, 1946—48, 1st lt. USAF, 1951—53. Inducted into Niagara Frontier Aviation Hall of Fame. Fellow AIAA (assoc.); mem. Air Force Assn. (pres. Larry D. Bell chpt. 1978), Navy League, Am. Def. Preparedness Assn., Nat. Fluid Power Assn. (past chmn. bd.), Nat. Conf. on Fluid Power (past conf. dir.) Buffalo C. of C. (past vice chmn.). Avocations: private pilot (twin engine-instrument), skiing, golf, fishing. Home: 1634 Hubbard Rd East Aurora NY 14052-3011 E-mail: hawkwabunk@msn.com.

HAWK, KATHLEEN PATRICIA, broadcast consultant; b. Butler, Pa., Feb. 12, 1945; d. Allen Clarence and Betty Ruth (Wilson) Pollock; m. Robert Ferdinand Hawk, Dec. 31, 1966; 1 child, Allen Robert. BSc, Parsons Coll., Fairfield, Iowa, 1966. Ind. internat. radiofrequency/microwave cons./personal wireless telecom./facilities siting cons., wireless facility siting cons., Butler, Pa., 1990—. Invited reviewer U.S. Congress, Office of Tech. Assessment, Wireless Technologies and the Nat. Info. Infrastructure, 1995; participant numerous seminars, confs., telecomms. adv. com.; mem. elec. sensitivity network. Author: Case Study in the Heartland, 1996; freelance writer Pitts. Post Gazette; contbr. articles to profl. jours. Worthy advisor Rainbow Girls, 1961; mem. Nat. Coalition of Citizens and Pub. Ofcls. for Local Control; founding mem., bd. dirs. Cellular Phone Task Force; bd. dirs. Delbert Parkinson Christian Cancer Coalition. Mem. Bioelectromagnetics Soc., Associated Bioelectromagnetics Technologists, Butler Natural Living Group, 1000 Club, Butler Country Club, 38 Year Card Club, Am. Legion Aux., Am. Golf Hall of Fame. Republican. Achievements include research on human and animal health in close proximity to telecomms. facilities. Home and Office: 122 Thornwood Dr Butler PA 16001-3442 E-mail: kathyhawk@webtv.net.

HAWK, PHILLIP MICHAEL, service corporation executive; b. Oklahoma City, June 14, 1939; s H. M. and Rosetta (Cross) H.; m. Nancy Batton, Aug. 13, 1966; children— Tabatha Lynn, Phillip Michael BBA, U. Okla., 1961. Pub. rels. exec. Coca Cola Co., Dallas, 1961-63; salesman svc. Reynolds Metals Co., Dallas, 1963-65; corp. dir. mktg. Cole Pubs. Co., Dallas, 1965-71; sr. v.p. Club Corp. of Am., Dallas, 1972-90; pres. Interclub Corp., Blackwell, Tex., 1990-93, CEO club acquisiton and devel., 1993—; CEO Clubnet, Kingwood, Tex., 1996—2001. Bd. dirs. Club Corp. Mex. Exec. v.p. United Golf Group, N.Y.C., 1998-2000; v.p. Acquisitions Renaissance Golf Group, LLC, 2001-. Republican. Avocation: golf. Office: 5362 Keswick Dr Frisco TX 75034 Office Phone: 281-853-7167. E-mail: phawk281@aol.com.

HAWK, TONY, professional skateboarder; b. Carlsbad, Calif., May 12, 1968; s. Frank Hawk and Judy; m. Cindy Hawk, 1990; 1 child, Riley; m. Erin Hawk, 1995; children: Spencer, Keegan. Profl. skateboarder, 1983—; founder Tony Hawk Found., Vista, Calif., 2002. Founder Tony Hawk's Demolition Radio, Sirus Satellite Radio. Actor: (films) Thrashin', 1986, Police Academy 4: Citizens on Patrol, 1987, Gleaming the Cube, 1989, xXx, 2002, Haggard: The Movie, 2003; (TV films) The Contest, 1989, Reunion X, 2004, (video) Destroying America, 2001, CKY 3, 2001, (guest appearances): (TV series) Arli$$, 1999; (TV series, voice) The Simpsons, 2003; prodr.: (soundtrack for Tony Hawk's Underground) T.H.U.G. (MTV Music award, 2004). Recipient 6 gold medals for skateboarding, ESPN X Games, 16 medals, No. 1 Vertical Skateboarder in the World, 1984—96, 3 time Favourite Male Athlete, Nickelodeon Kids Choice Awards, 3 time Male Athlete, Fox Teen Choice. Achievements include first skateboarder in history to do "The 900" skateboarding trick; Video Game Series is the top selling sports video game franchise in history. Office: Tony Hawk Found 1611-A Melrose Dr 360 Vista CA 92081 Office Phone: 760-477-2479.

HAWKE, BERNARD RAY, planetary scientist, researcher; b. Louisville, Oct. 22, 1946; s. Arvil Abner and Elizabeth Ellen (Brown) H. BS in Geology, U. Ky., 1970, MS, 1974, Brown U., 1977, PhD in Planetary Geology, 1978. Geologist U.S. Geol. Survey, 1967-68; researcher U. Ky., 1972-74, Brown U., 1974-78; planetary scientist Hawaii Inst. Geophysics, U. Hawaii, Honolulu, 1978—; dir. NASA Pacific Regional Planetary Data Ctr., 1981—; prin. investigator NASA grants. Assoc. dir. Hawaii Space Grant Coll. Author papers in field. Served with USAR, 1970-72. Decorated Bronze Star Mem. Geochem. Soc., Meteoritical Soc., Am. Geophys. Union, Am. Chem. Soc., Geol. Soc. Am., Sigma Xi, Sigma Gamma Epsilon, Alpha Tau Omega. Republican. Office: U Hawaii SOEST Hawaiian Inst Geophysics Honolulu HI 96822

HAWKE, ETHAN GREEN, actor; b. Austin, Tex., Nov. 6, 1970; m. Uma Thurman, May 1, 1998 (div.); children: Maya Ray Thurman-Hawke, Roan. Co-founder & artistic dir. Malaparte Theatre Co., NYC, 1992—. Actor: (plays) Casanova, 1991, A Joke, The Seagull, 1992, Sophistry, Henry IV, 2003—04, Hurlyburly, 2005; (TV series) Alias, 2003; (films) Explorers, 1985, Lion's Den, 1988, Dead Poet's Soc., 1989, Dad, 1989, White Fang, 1991, Mystery Date, 1991, A Midnight Clear, 1992, Waterland, 1992, Alive, 1993, Rich in Love, 1993, Floundering, 1994, Reality Bites, 1994, White Fang II, 1994, Quiz Show, 1994, Before Sunrise, 1995, Search & Destroy, 1995, Gattaca, 1997, Great Expectations, 1998, The Newton Boys, 1998, The Velocity of Gary, 1998, Joe the King, 1999, Snow Falling on Cedars, 1999, Tell Me, 2000, Hamlet, 2000, (voice) Waking Life, 2001, Tape, 2001, Training Day, 2001, The Jimmy Show, 2001, (dir., voice) Chelsea Walls, 2001, (& author) Before Sunset, 2004, Taking Lives, 2004, Assault on Precinct 13, 2005; dir.: Straight to One, 1994; author: (novels) The Hottest State, 1996, Ash Wednesday, 2002. Mailing: c/o Creative Arts Agency 9830 Wilshire Blvd Beverly Hills CA 90212*

HAWKE, JOHN DANIEL, JR., former federal official; b. N.Y.C., June 26, 1933; s. John Daniel and Olga (Buchbinder) H.; m. Marie Reddan, June 15, 1962 (dec. Mar. 1991); children: Daniel, Caitlin, Anne, Patrick BA, Yale U., 1954; LL.B., Columbia U., 1960. Bar: D.C. 1961, U.S. Supreme Ct. 1968. Law clk. to judge U.S. Ct. Appeals (D.C. cir.), Washington, 1960-61; counsel Select Subcom. on Edn., U.S. Ho. of Reps., Washington, 1961-62; assoc. Arnold & Porter, Washington, 1962-66, ptnr., 1967-75, 78-95; gen. counsel bd. govs. Fed. Res. System, Washington, 1975-78; under sec. for domestic fin. US Dept. Treasury, Washington, 1995-98, comptroller of the currency, 1998—2004; dir. Fed. Deposit Ins. Corp., Washington, 1998—2004. Adj. prof. law Georgetown U., Washington, 1971-87; lectr. law Columbia U., N.Y.C., 1979; bd. advisers Morin Ctr. for Banking Law Studies, Boston U. Sch. Law, 1982—, lectr., 1984-88; mem. Shadow Fin. Regulatory Com., 1986-95; lectr. in field. Author: Commentaries on Banking Regulation, 1985; chmn. editorial adv. bd. Banking Policy Report, 1982-95; contbr. numerous articles to profl. jours., chpt. to book. Mem. Fed. City Coun., 1990-95; trustee Found. for Nat. Capital Region, 1992-98; trustee Washington Opera, 1992-96; mem. Pres.'s Com. on the Arts and Humanities, 1996-2001. 2d lt. USAF, 1955-57. Mem. Fed. Bar Assn. (banking law com., chmn. 1976-78), Cosmos Club, Exchequer Club, Econ. Club, Yale Club, Vineyard Haven Yacht Club.

HAWKE, PAUL HENRY, historian; b. Canton, Ohio, Mar. 9, 1958; s. Richard Carl and Sara (Hemming) Hawke; m. Gaynel O. Allen, May 2, 1987; children: Cailean Stewart, Angela Jeanette, Tiffani Alahna. BA in History, Geography, Hist. Preservation, Mary Washington Coll., 1982; postgrad., Temple U., 1983, U. Ark., 1984-85; MA in History and Heritage Preservation, Ga. State U., 1993. Pk. tech. Petersburg (Va.) Nat. Battlefield, 1978-81; intern Fredericksburg (Va.) and Spotsylvania Nat. Mil. Pk., 1981-82; pk. ranger Independence Nat. Hist. Pk., Phila., 1982-83; pk. historian Pea Ridge (Ark.) Nat. Mil. Pk., 1983-85; historian S.E. Regional Office, Atlanta, 1985-95; S.E. coord. Am. Battlefield Protection Program, Atlanta, 1991—95, mem. Civil War sites adv. commn. staff, 1991—93, chief Washington, 2000—; chief interpretation and resources mgmt. Shiloh (Tenn.) Nat. Mil. Pk., 1995—2000. Coord. Nat. Hist. Landmarks Program, Atlanta, 1986—95. Co-author: Civil War Battlefield Guide, 1991; editor: The Parapet: Newsletter of the Civil War, 1992—2000; asst. editor, author: Jour. Civil War Fort Study Group, 1994. Water safety instr. Am. Nat. Red Cross, Benton County, Ark., 1975—80, water safety chmn., 1984—85; water safety instr. Am. Nat. Red Cross, Fredericksburg, Va., 1980—82; small craft safety instr. Canton, 1975—80, Benton County, Ark., 1984—85. Named Ky. Col., Gov. of Ky., 1992. Mem.: Soc. Mil. Historians, Civil War Trust, Nat. Trust Hist. Preservation, Assn. Preservation Civil War Sites, Assn. Nat. Pk. Rangers, Coast Def. Study Group, Civil War Fortification Study Group. Avocations: swimming, travel, movies, military history, sports. Home: 6314 Morning Dew Ct Clarksville MD 21029-1150 Office: Nat Park Svc 1849 C St NW 2255 Washington DC 20240 Office Phone: 202-354-2023. Business E-Mail: paul_hawke@nps.gov.

HAWKE, ROBERT DOUGLAS, retired state legislator; b. Gardner, Mass., July 20, 1932; s. Arthur Eugene Hawke and Gladys Emma (Waite) Sorton; m. Nancy Marie Moschetti, July 20, 1958; children: Linda, Cynthia, Heather, Dean, Mark. BA, Northeastern U., 1954; LLB, Boston U., 1956; MA, Fitchburg State U., 1970. Cert. tchr., Mass. Tchr. Murdock High Sch., Winchendon, Mass., 1956-66, Gardner (Mass.) High Sch., 1966-90; mem. Mass. Ho. of Reps., Boston, 1990-97. Trustee Heywood Hosp., Gardner, 1981-97, Gardner Mus., 1980-83, Baldwinville Nursing Home, templeton, Mass.; mem. So. Gardner Hist. Soc., 1984—; adv. bd. Mt. Wachusett C.C., Gardner, 1968-81; chmn. Gardner Rep. Com., Rep. City Com., 1966-76; area campaign coord. Reagan Com., North Ctrl. Mass., 1980-84; councillor at large to Gardner City Coun., 2001-04; pres. Consortium of New Eng. Cmty. Art Mus., 1999-2002. Named Citizen of Yr. Grange of Gardner, 1993, So. Gardner Hist. Soc., 1993, Legislator of Yr. award Worcester County League of Sportmen's Clubs, 1996. Mem. Nat. Rep. Legis. Assn., Nat. Conf. State Legislators, Polish Am. Citizens Club, Account Exec. for Greater Gardner C. of C., Eagles. Republican. Baptist. Avocations: reading, tennis, softball. Home: 162 Pearl St Gardner MA 01440-2357

HAWKE, ROBERT FRANCIS, dentist; b. Pasadena, Calif., Oct. 26, 1946; s. George Herbert and Mildred Estelle (Wood) H.; m. Emily Sue Wilkins, Aug. 17, 1973; 1 child, Kristen. BA, U. Ariz., 1969; DDS, Baylor U., Dallas, 1973. Assoc. B.J. Barber, Tucson, 1976-78; ptnr. Barber-Hawke, P.C., Tucson, 1978-87; pvt. practice Tucson, 1987—. Bd. dirs., pres. Delta Dental Ariz., Phoenix, 1985-91. Mem. Tucson Bus. Alliance, 1981—, pres., 1983, 94, Cmty. Auto Immune Deficiency Syndrome Adv. Coun., Tucson, 1987-90, Auto Immune Deficiency Syndrome Edn. Project, Tucson, 1988-90. Maj. U.S. Army. Fellow Am. Coll. Dentists, Internat. Coll. Dentists; mem. ADA (alt. del. 1988-92, del. 1994-2000, 14th dist. chmn. polit. action com. 1995-98), Ariz. State Dental Assn. (trustee 1988, v.p. 1991, pres.-elect 1992-93, pres. 1993-94, past pres. 1994-95, mem. legal liaison com. 1993-94, chmn. coun. on constitution and bylaws 1996-97, chmn. coun. on budget planning 1992-93, chmn. coun. on ins. 1998-2003, Svc. award 2002), So. Ariz. Dental Soc. (bd. dirs. 1983-89, pres. 1987-88), Pierre Fauchard Acad., Acad. Laser Dentistry, Acad. Gen. Dentistry, Tucson Advanced Cosmetic & Restorative Study Club, World Clin. Laser Inst., Give Kids a Smile Day (So. Ariz. chmn. 2003-04), Rotary (Paul Harris fellow), Beta Beta Beta. Republican. Evangelical. Avocations: golf, jogging, tennis, racquetball, reading. Home: 6745 E Tivani Dr Tucson AZ 85715-3348 Office: 1575 N Swan Rd Ste 200 Tucson AZ 85712-4068 E-mail: hawkerobertf@qwest.net, robertfhawke@comcast.net.

HAWKE, ROGER JEWETT, lawyer; b. NYC, July 2, 1935; s. John Daniel and Olga (Buchbinder) H.; m. Rose Marie Ferri, Aug. 15, 1964; children—Christopher, Allison, John BA cum laude, Amherst Coll., 1956; LL.B., Columbia U., 1959. Bar: NY 1960, U.S. Supreme Ct. 1976. Assoc. Donovan, Leisure, Newton & Irvine, NYC, 1960, 62-65; asst. U.S. atty. U.S. Atty.'s Office, So. Dist. N.Y., NYC, 1965-69; assoc. Brown, Wood, Ivey, Mitchell & Petty LLP, NYC, 1969-71, ptnr., 1971—2001, Sidley Austin Brown & Wood LLP, NYC, 2001—. Arbitrator Nat. Assn. Securities Dealers. Acting village justice Village of Lloyd Harbor, NY,1977-83, trustee, 1983-99; police commr., 1983-99, dep. mayor, 1983-99. With U.S. Army, 1961-62. Fellow: Am. Coll. Trial Lawyers; mem.: ABA, Am. Law Inst., NY Law Inst. (exec. com., treas.), Assn. of Bar of City of NY, Lloyd Neck Bath (pres. 1981). Office: Sidley Austin Brown & Wood LLP 787 Seventh Ave New York NY 10019

HAWKER, KENO, mayor, trucking company executive; BA, Wis. State U.; MBA, U. Wis. Owner & pres. Hawker Trucks & Materials, Inc.; mem. coun. City of Mesa, Ariz., 1986—94, 1998—2000, vice mayor, 1990—92, mayor, 2000—. Mem. U.S. Conf. Mayors, Ariz. League of Cities and Towns Bd., Williams Gateway Authority, Regional Public Transportation Authority, Regional Aviation System Policy Com., Ariz. Mcpl. Water Users Assn., Nat. League of Cities Transp. TEA 21 Reauthorization Task Force, Nat. League of Cities Transp. Infrastructure and Svcs. Steering Com., Nat. League of Cities, Maricopa Assn. Govt.'s, Mesa Chamber of Commerce, Valley Metro Rail Bd.; chair Maricopa Assn. Govt.'s Regional Coun., Regional Coun. Transp. Subcom.; pres. Ariz. Mcpl. Water Users Assn.; ex-officio mem. adv. bd. City of Mesa Econ. Develop. Mem.: Maricopa Assn. Govts. (treas.), Mesa HoHoKams, Mesa Baseline Rotary. Avocations: biking, hiking, climbing, rappelling, travel, rollerblading, owns his own palne and is a lic. pilot, dirt bike racing, river rafting, motorcycle riding. Office: Mesa City Plaza 20 E Main St Mesa AZ 85201 Address: Hawker Trucks and Materials Inc 315 S Morris Mesa AZ 85210 Office: Office of Mayor PO Box 1466 Mesa AZ 85211-1466 E-mail: mayor_hawker@ci.mesa.az.us.*

HAWKES, CAROL ANN, academic administrator; b. NYC; d. Howard N. and Lavinia M. (Lally) H. BA, Barnard Coll., 1943; MA, Columbia U., 1944, PhD, 1949. Dir. acad. English liberal arts div. Katharine Gibbs Sch., N.Y.C., 1950-57; prof. English, chmn. dept. English and comparative lit. Finch Coll., N.Y.C., 1957-75; v.p. for ednl. affairs, dean of coll. Hartwick Coll., Oneonta, NY, 1975-80; pres. Endicott Coll., Beverly, Mass., 1980-87; assoc. v.p. for acad. affairs Western Conn. State U., Danbury, 1987—. Trustee Norwich U., Hartwick Coll. Author: Master's Degree Programs and the Liberal Arts College, 1968. Harvard Sch. Dental Medicine fellow. Mem. MLA, LWV, Modern Humanities Rsch. Assn., Am. Assn. Higher Edn., Princeton Club (N.Y.C.), Columbia U. Club New Eng., Phi Beta Kappa. Office: Western Conn State U Academic Affairs Danbury CT 06810 Office Phone: 203-837-8851. Business E-Mail: hawkesc@wcsu.edu.

HAWKES, MARY NEWGEON, retired minister, educator; b. Thessaloniki, Greece, June 27, 1934; arrived in U.S., 1937; d. William Emory and Jessie Newgeon Hawkes. AB in Music, Doane Coll., 1956; MA in Religious Edn., Hartford Sem., 1958; EdD in Religious Edn., Columbia U. Tchrs. Coll./Union Theol. Sem., 1983. Ordained to ministry United Ch. of Christ, 1980. Dir. Christian edn. United Chs. of Christ, Middletown and Hartford, Conn., 1958—67; ecumenical ch. worker German Protestant Ch., Hamburg/Berlin, 1967—69; dir. Christian edn. United Chs. of Christ, Conn., N.Y., Mich., 1969—76, interim min. Conn., N.Y., Vt., 1986—88, 1994—98, pastor North Bennington, Vt., 1988—94; sec. edn. programs United Ch. Bd., Homeland Min., N.Y.C., 1981—85; pastor 1st Congl. Ch., Deer River United Cmty. Ch., Carthage, NY, 1998—2002. V.p., pres. Village Ecumenical Min, Carthage, NY, 1999—2002; resource person United Ch. of Christ N.Y. Women, 1999—2002. Mem. editl. bd.: hymnal Sing of Life and Faith, 1963—67, content editor: religious songbook Sing to God, 1981—84, co-author, editor: Festivals of Christmas, 1981—83. Mem. family life com. Bennington (Vt.) Pub. Schs.; bd. dirs. Adult Day Care Program, Bennington, 1990—93; editor newsletter, v.p. Adam Hawkes Family Assn., Saugus, Mass., 2002—; v.p. Greater Hartford Coun. Chs., 1963—66; mem., chair Task Force on the Homeless, Bennington, 1989—94; annuitant visitor UCC Pension Bds. for So. Vt., 2004—. Recipient Doane Builder award, Doane Coll., 1981. Mem.: AAUW (scholarship com. 2004), Alban Inst., Ptnrs. in Edn. United Ch. of Christ, Children's Def. Fund, Habitat for Humanity, Common Cause, So. Poverty Law Ctr., Amnesty Internat., N.H. Peace Found., Kappa Delta Pi. Democrat. United Ch. Of Christ. Avocations: music, travel. Home: 107 Morningside Commons Brattleboro VT 05301-3633 E-mail: mellyhaw@sover.net.

HAWKEY, G. MICHAEL, lawyer, real estate developer; b. Apr. 17, 1941; m. Frances Tripp, Feb. 27, 1971; children: Samuel, Eliza, MacKenzie. AB, Princeton U., 1963; postgrad., Columbia Bus. Sch., 1964; LLB, Cornell U., 1967. Bar: Mass. 1967. Atty. Sullivan & Worcester LLP, Boston. Founder Sun Valley Properties, Ketchum, Idaho, Mettowee Valley Properties, Pawlet, Vt.; lectr. Mass. Restaurant Assn. Bd. dirs. Pacific. Internat. Inst., Lewiston, Idaho, 1992—97, St. Lukes Cancer Rsch. Found., Cork, Ireland, 1994—97; N.Am. bd. Michael Smurfit Grad. Sch. Bus., Univ. Coll., Dublin, 1994—98; trustee Maruzen Hawthorne Coll., Antrim, NH, 1991—92; bd. govs. Wianno Club, Orteville, Mass., 1982—98; bd. dirs. Greyhawk Village Assn., Ketchum, 2001—. Mem. Internat. Coun. Shopping Ctrs., Mass. Real Estate Fin. Assn. (bd. dirs. 1989-92), Sr. Execs. Club of Mass. Real Estate Fin. Assn., The Country Club (Brookline, Mass.), Wianno Club (Osterville, Mass.). Home: 26 Arlington Rd Wellesley MA 02481-6129 Office: Sullivan & Worcester LLP 1 Post Office Sq Ste 2300 Boston MA 02109-2129

HAWKING, STEPHEN W., astrophysicist, mathematician; b. Oxford, England, Jan. 8, 1942; s. Frank and Isobel Hawking; m. Jane Wilde, 1965 (div. 1991); 3 children; m. Elaine Mason, 1995. BA, Oxford U., DSc (hon.), 1978; PhD, Cambridge U.; DSc (hon.), U. Chgo., 1981, Notre Dame U., 1982, NYU, 1982, Leicester U., 1982. Research asst. Inst. Astronomy, Cambridge, Eng., 1972-73, research asst. dept. applied maths. and theoretical physics, 1973-75, reader in gravitational physics, 1975-77, prof., 1977-79, Lucasian prof. math., 1979—. Author: The Large Scale Structure of Space-Time, 1973 (with G.F.R. Ellis), 300 Years of Gravity, 1987 (with W. Israel), A Brief History of Time: From the Big Bang to Black Holes, 1988, Black Holes and Baby Universes, 1993, Hawking on the Big Bang and Black Holes, 1993; The Universe in a Nutshell, 2001, The Theory of Everything: The Origin and Fate of the Universe, 2002; also author numerous jour. articles. Decorated comdr. Brit. Empire, 1981; recipient Eddington medal Royal Acad. Sci., 1975, Pius XI Gold medal Pontifical Acad. Sci., 1975, Danne Heinemann prize for math. and physics Am. Phys. Soc.-Am. Inst. Physics, 1976, William Hopkins prize Cambridge Philos. Soc., 1976, Maxwell medal Inst. Physics, 1976, Einstein award Strauss Found., 1978, Albert Einstein medal Albert Einstein Soc. of Berne, 1979, Wolf Prize in physics, 1988, Britannica award, 1989. Fgn. mem. Am. Philos. Soc., AAAS; fellow Royal Soc. (Hughes medal 1976). Address: DAMTP U Cambridge Silver St Cambridge England CB3 9EW

HAWKINS, ANITA LYNNE, primary school educator; b. Oklahoma City, May 5, 1959; d. Charles Richard and Juanita Lee Hilderbrand; m. Ephriam Albert Hawkins, Apr. 12, 1986 (div.); 1 child, Kyle Albert. BBA in Mktg., Cen. State U., Edmond, Okla., 1981; M of Early Childhood Edn. and Elem. Edn., lang. arts cert., U. Cen. Okla., Edmond, 1995. Cert. higher learning workshops. Preventive maintenance coord. Firestone, Oklahoma City, 1977—84; tchr. presch. Children's Lighthouse #1, Oklahoma City, 1997—2001; tchr. 1st grade Webster Elem., El Reno, 2001—; drummer Mustang (Okla.) Mkt. Ch., 2003—; com. mem. Curriculum Com., El Reno, 2004—05, Tech. Com., El Reno, 2004—05. Adviser, editor yearbook Webster

Elem., 2004—05. Bd. dirs. Parent Tchr. Orgn., El Reno, 2004—05; usher Yukon (Okla.) Philharm., 2004; parent mem. Project Graduation, Yukon, 2004—05. Named Terrific Tchr., Kiwanis Club, 2003. Mem.: Yukon Indian Edn. Orgn. (mem. tchr. com. 2001—), Chord - Ringers and Dirs. Democrat. Methodist. Avocations: gardening, tennis, country western dancing, singing, drums. Home: 800 Miller Dr Yukon OK 73099 Office: Tech Com 100 North L El Reno OK 73036-3130 Office Phone: 405-262-1943.

HAWKINS, BARBARA REED, mental health nurse; b. Burghettstown, Pa., July 20, 1945; d. John Francis Reed and Iona Eleanor Spring; m. Hal Kenneth Hawkins, Sept. 6, 1969; children: David, Heidi, Brian, Russell. BS in Nursing, Duke U., 1968; MSN, U. N.C., 1973; postgrad., Houston Montessori Ctr., 1992—93. RN N.C., 1968. Staff nurse pediatrics Duke U. Med. Ctr., 1968—69; psychiatric nurse, group co-therapist Durham County Mental Health Ctr., 1971—72; counselor Durham Crisis and Suicide Ctr., 1972—73; lectr. psychiat. nursing U. N.C., Sch. Nursing, Chapel Hill, 1972; lectr. U. N.C., 1972—73, instr., 1973—77; therapist Psychiat. Assocs. Chapel Hill, 1975—79; head nurse, nursing supr., acting unit dir. Ga. Mental Health Inst., 1979—80; coord. career devel. Emory U. Hosp., 1980—81. Avocations: shell collecting, gourmet cooking, gardening, interior decorating, needlecrafts. Home: 5500 N Braeswood Blvd Apt 198 Houston TX 77096

HAWKINS, BRANDON JAMES, podiatrist, surgeon; b. Murray, Utah, July 13, 1972; s. Lorin Robert and Evelyn Schoenfeld Hawkins; m. Jessica Ann Barron, Mar. 18, 1995; children: Nicholle, Emma, Micah. BS in BioChemistry, U. Utah, 1997; BS in Biol. Scis., Scholl Coll. Podiatric Medicine, 1998; D Podiatric Medicine, Finch U., 2001. Diplomate Am. Bd. Podiatric Medicine. Intern Lebanon DVAMC/Pa. State U., Lebanon, 2001—02; resident Hu Hu Kam Meml. Hosp., Sacaton, Ariz., 2002—03; chief resident South Western Podiatry Program, San Juan Capistrano, Calif., 2004—. Contbr. articles to profl. publs. Regional dir., scoutmaster Boy Scouts Am., Salt Lake City and Chgo., 1995—2001. Scholar, Scholl Coll. Podiat. Medicine, 1999. Mem.: Am. Podiatric Med. Assn., Am. Profl. Wound Care Assn. Office: Aestheticare Cosmetic Surgery Inst 30260 Rancho Viejo Rd San Juan Capistrano CA 92675 Home: 30001 Golden Lantern # 17 Laguna Niguel CA 92677

HAWKINS, BRETT WILLIAM, retired political science professor; b. Buffalo, Sept. 15, 1937; s. Ralph C. and Irma A. (Rowley) H.; m. Linda L. Knuth, Oct. 31, 1974; 1 child, Brett William. AB, U. Rochester, 1959; MA, Vanderbilt U., 1962, PhD, 1964. Instr. polit. sci. Vanderbilt U., 1963; instr. in polit. sci. Washington and Lee U., 1963-64, asst. prof., 1964-65, U. Ga., Athens, 1965-68, assoc. prof., 1968-70, U. Wis., Milw., 1970-71, prof., 1971-99, ret, 2000. Author: Nashville Metro, 1964, The Ethnic Factor in American Politics, 1970, Politics in the Metropolis, 2d edit, 1971, Politics and Urban Policies, 1971, The Politics of Raising State and Local Revenue, 1978, Professional Associations and Municipal Innovation, 1981; contbr. articles to profl. jours., chpts. in edited vols. Mem. Phi Beta Kappa, Iota of N.Y. Home: 5318 N Kent Ave Whitefish Bay WI 53217-5109 Personal E-mail: bretthwk@yahoo.com.

HAWKINS, BRIAN L., academic administrator, educator; b. Lafayette, Ind., Aug. 5, 1948; s. Robert H. and Marjorie Joan (Bradley) H.; m. Lisa Ellen Herrick, Dec. 30, 1970; children: Timothy, Steven. BA, Mich. State U., 1970, MA, 1972; PhD, Purdue U., 1975. Asst. prof. U. Tex., San Antonio, 1975-76, asst. dean of bus., 1976-81; assoc. v.p. acad. affairs Drexel U., Phila., 1981-86, assoc. v.p. computing and telecommunications, 1984-86; v.p. Brown U., Providence, 1986—, spl. asst. to pres., assoc. provost acad. planning, 1990-92, v.p. acad. planning and adminstrn., 1992-96, sr. v.p. acad. planning and adminstrv. affairs, 1997-98; pres., CEO EDUCAUSE, 1998—. Trustee EDUCOM, Washington, 1986-90, chmn. bd., 1989-90; trustee U. Richmond, 1999-2003; dir. Forum for Future of Higher Ed., 1999-, Am. Coun. Edn., 2005-. Author: Managerial Comm., 1981; editor: Managing & Organizing Info. Resources on Campus, 1990, The Mirage of Continuity: Reconfiguring Academic Info. Resources in the 21st Century, 1998; Tech. Everywhere, 2002. Bd. dir. CAUSE, 1992-96. Office: EDUCAUSE Ste 206 4772 Walnut Boulder CO 80301 Business E-Mail: hawkins@educause.edu.

HAWKINS, BRIDGETT BURNETT, elementary school educator; b. Jackson, Miss., Dec. 8, 1978; d. Tommy Bridges and June Lee Burnett; m. John Benton Hawkins, Sept. 4, 2004. B of Music Edn. cum laude, Miss. Coll., 2002. Tchr. music grades k-3 Tupelo Pub. Sch. Dist., 2002—. Mem.: Miss. Chpt. Orff-Schulwerk Assn., Am. Orff-Schulwerk Assn., Miss. Music Educators Assn., Music Educators Nat. Conf. Republican. Baptist. Office: Tupelo Pub Sch Dist Parkway Elem 628 Rutherford Rd Tupelo MS 38804 Business E-Mail: bbhawkins@tupelo.k12.ms.us.

HAWKINS, CAROLE ANN, elementary school educator; b. L.I., Dec. 25, 1944; d. Harold and Pauline Hawkins. BS, SUNY, Plattsborgh, 1967, MS, 1972. Tchr. elem. sch. James A. Dever Sch., Valley Stream, NY, 1967—, sci. coord., 1982—91. Trustee edn. Grace Luth. Ch., Malverne, NY, 2000—03, tchr. Sunday sch., 1993—2000; chair bd. edn. Grace Luth. Sch., 1989—91. Chair Ctrl. High Sch. Alumni Found., Valley Stream; life mem. James A. Dever PTA, 1978—. Mem.: ASCD, Valley Stream Tchrs. Assn. (unit leader 1987—), Kappa Delta Phi. Avocations: crafts, magic, camping, hiking, gardening. Office: James A Dever Sch 585 N Corona Ave Valley Stream NY 11580

HAWKINS, CLAUDIA L., social services executive; b. Mount Bayou, Miss., June 11, 1953; m. Vaughn Hawkins; children: Monica, Candace, Travis. BSBA in Acctg., Miss. Valley State U., 1975; postgrad., Greater Des Moines Leadership Inst., 1993; MPA, Drake U., 1995; M (hon.), The Grantsmanship Ctr. Tng. Program, 1998, Nat. YWCA Leadership Devel. Inst., 1998. Acctg. clk. Beacon Cmty. Fed. Credit Union, Chgo., 1975—77; jr acct. Marillac Cmty. Ctr., 1977—79; acct. Operation Rush Excellence Inc, 1979—82; adminstrv. exec. dir. Tiny Tot Family Outreach Ctr. Inc, Des Moines, 1983—92; acctg. supr. YWCA, 1993—95, assoc., devel. dir., 1995—98, exec. dir., 1998—2005. Achievements include development of Professional membership affiliates including the NAACP, Port of Entry, Food Bank of Iowa, Mt. Hebron Baptist Church, Greater Des Moines Leadership Institute, Des Moines Pastoral Counseling Center; The National Society Fund Raisers Executives, National Black Child Development Institute, and City of Des Moines Neighborhood Revitalization Board. Home: 1139 - 15th St West Des Moines IA 50265

HAWKINS, DAVID RAMON, psychiatrist, writer, researcher, spiritual studies educator; b. Milw., June 3, 1927; s. Ramon Nelson and Alice-Mary (McCutcheon) H.; m. Susan Humphrey; children: Sarah Humphrey. BS, Marquette U., 1950; MD, Med. Coll. Wis., Milw., 1953; PhD, Columbia Pacific U., 1995. Med. dir. North Nassau Mental Health Ctr., Manhasset, NY, 1956-80; dir. rsch. Brunswick Hosp., L.I., NY, 1968-79; pres. Acad. Orthomolecular Psychiatry, NYC, 1970-80; dir. Inst. Spiritual Rsch., Sedona, Ariz., 1979-88, The Rsch. Inst., Sedona, 1988—. Chmn. Inst. Advanced Theoretical Rsch., 1993—; guest on TV shows including McNeal-Lehrer, Barbara Walters, Today; chief of staff Mingus Mountain RTC, 1995; cons. USN, HEW, Congress; lectr. U. Notre Dame, U. Mich., Oxford U., others. Author (with Linus Pauling): Orthomolecular Psychiatry, 1973; author: Power vs. Force, 1995, The Eye of the I, 2001, I, 2002, Truth vs. Falsehood, 2005. With USN, 1945—46. Decorated knight Sovereign Order St. John of Jerusalem (Denmark); Tae Ryoung Sun Kak Tosun (Korea); recipient Mosby Book award, 1953. Mem. AMA, APA, Ariz. Med. Soc., Ariz. Psychiat. Soc., Alpha Omega Alpha. Avocations: inventing, designing, architecture. Office: Rsch Inst PO Box 3516 W Sedona Ave Sedona AZ 86340 E-mail: info@veritospub.com. *Our lives are created more by our vision of the future then they are by the details of our past.*

HAWKINS, DAVID ROLLO, SR., psychiatrist, educator; b. Springfield, Mass., Sept. 22, 1923; s. James Alexander and Janet (Rollo) H.; m. Elizabeth G. Wilson, June 8, 1946; children: David Rollo Jr., Robert Wilson, John Bruce, William Alexander. BA, Amherst Coll., 1945; MD, U. Rochester, N.Y., 1946. Intern Strong Meml. Hosp., Rochester, 1946-48; Commonwealth Fund fellow in psychiatry and medicine U. Rochester, 1950-52; instr. psychiatry U. N.C. Sch. Medicine, 1952-53, asst. prof., 1953-57, asso. prof. psychiatry, 1957-62, prof., 1962-67; prof., chmn. dept. psychiatry U. Va. Sch. Medicine, 1967-77, Alumni prof. psychiatry, 1967-79, asso. dean, 1969-70; psychiatrist-in-chief U. Va. Hosp., 1967-77; prof. psychiatry Pritzker Sch. Medicine, U. Chgo., 1979-90, U. Ill., 1990—; clin. prof. psychiatry U. N.C., Chapel Hill, 1992—. Dir. liaison and consultation svcs. dept. psychiatry Michael Reese Hosp., Chgo., 1979-87, chmn., 1987-92; assoc. attending physician N.C. Meml. Hosp., Chapel Hill, 1952-62, attending physician, 1962-67; cons. Watts Hosp., Durham, 1952-67, VA Hosp., Fayetteville, N.C., 1956-67, Eastern State Hosp., Williamsburg, Va., 1971—, VA Hosp., Salem. Va., 1969-79, mem. deans com., 1971-77; spl. rsch. fellow Inst. Psychiatry, U. London, 1963-64, Fogarty internat. rsch. fellow, 1976-77, U.S.-USSR and Romania health exch. fellow, 1978. Rev. editor Psychosomatic Medicine, 1958-70; assoc. editor Psychiatry, 1970-92. Mem. small grants com. NIMH, 1958-62; mem. nursing rsch. study sect. NIH, 1965-67; mem. Gov.'s Commn. Mental, Indigent and Geriatric Patients, 1968-72; mem. rsch. evaluation com. Va. Dept. Mental Hygiene and Hosps., 1970-73; mem. behavioral sci. test com. Nat. Bd. Med. Examiners, 1970-73. Served as capt. M.C., AUS, 1948-50. Fellow Am. Coll. Psychoanalysts (charter bd. regents 1979-81, treas. 1989-91, pres.-elect 1992, pres. 1994), Am. Psychiat. Assn.; mem. AAUP, Am. Psychosomatic Soc. (mem. coun. 1959), AMA, Group for Advancement Psychiatry (bd. dirs. 1987-89), Assn. Am. Med. Colls. (coun. acad. socs. 1973-78), Am. Psychoanalytic Assn., Am. Coll. Psychiatrists, AAAS, Va. Psychoanalytic Soc., Washington Psychoanalytic Soc., Chgo. Psychoanalytic Soc., N.C. Psychoanalytic Soc., Ill. Psychiat. Soc. (coun. 1981-82, pres.-elect 1987, pres. 1988-90), Soc. Neurosci., Am. Assn. Chmn. Depts. Psychiatry (sec.-treas. 1971-73, pres. 1974-75), Sleep Rsch. Soc., Nat. Bd. Med. Examiners (exam. com. 1983-87), Phi Beta Kappa, Sigma Xi, Alpha Omega Alpha. Home: 235 Cedar Club Cir Chapel Hill NC 27517

HAWKINS, EDWARD J., retired lawyer; b. Fall River, Mass., June 24, 1927; s. Edward Jackson and Harriet (Sherman) H.; m. Janet Schwerdt; children: Daniel, George, Robert, Harriet. Grad., Phillips Acad., Andover, Mass., 1945; AB summa cum laude, Princeton U., 1950; LLB magna cum laude, Harvard U., 1953. Bar: Ohio 1954, D.C. 1990. Assoc., ptnr. Squire, Sanders & Dempsey, Cleve., 1953-78, ptnr. Cleve. and Washington, 1982-96, counsel, 1997-99; ret., 2000. Chief tax counsel U.S. Senate Fin. Com., Washington, 1979-80, minority tax counsel, 1981; gen. chmn. Cleve. Tax Inst., 1969. Contbr. articles to profl. jours. With U.S. Army, 1945-46. Mem. ABA (vice chmn. govt. rels. tax sect. 1987-89), D.C. Bar Assn., Phillips Acad. Alumni Assn. (alumni coun. 1967-70), Quadrangle Club. Democrat. Home: 1843 Westerham St Keswick VA 22947 E-mail: ejhawkins2@earthlink.net.

HAWKINS, EMMA B., humanities educator; b. Ardmore, Okla., July 28, 1946; d. Bernard C. and Occie E. (Morris) H. BA, Okla. Bapt. U., 1968; MDiv, Southwestern Bapt. Theol. Sem., 1976; MA, U. North Tex., 1990, PhD in English (Medieval), 1995. Instr. U. North Tex., Denton, 1990-95; lectr. Lamar U., Beaumont, 1995-97, asst. prof., 1997—2002, assoc. prof., 2003—. Chair program and arrangements South Cen. Conf. on Christianity and Lit., 1999, mem. exec. bd., 1999-2004; presenter numerous papers at profl. confs. Contbr. chpt. to book, articles to profl. jours. Recipient Go the Extra Mile award, 1997. Mem. MLA (sec. Old and Mid. English sect. South Ctrl. chpt. 1997, chair Old and Mid Eng. sect. chpt. 1998), Tex. Medieval Assn., Conf. on Coll. Tchrs. English (CCTE award best paper Brit. Lit., 2004), South Ctrl. Conf. Christianity and Lit. (chair various sessions, James Sims award 2000), Phi Kappa Phi (pres. chpt. 95), Sigma Tau Delta. Office: Lamar U PO Box 10023 Beaumont TX 77710-0023

HAWKINS, FALCON BLACK, JR., federal judge; b. Charleston, S.C., Mar. 16, 1927; s. Falcon Black Sr. and Mae Elizabeth (Infinger) H.; m. Jean Elizabeth Timmerman, May 28, 1949; children: Richard Keith, Daryl Gene, Mary Elizabeth Hawkins Eddy, Steely Odell II. BS, The Citadel, 1958; LLB, U. S.C., 1963, JD, 1970. Bar: S.C. bar 1963. Leadingman electronics Charleston (S.C.) Naval Shipyard, 1948-60; salesman ACH Brokers, Columbia, S.C., 1960-63; from assoc. to sr. ptnr. firm Hollings & Hawkins and successor firms, Charleston, 1963-79; U.S. dist. judge Dist. of S.C., Charleston, 1979—, chief judge, 1990-93, sr. status, 1993—, inactive status, 2003—. Served with Mcht. Marines, 1944-45, with AUS, 1945-46. Mem. Jud. Conf. 4th Jud. Circuit, ABA, S.C. Bar Assn., Charleston County Bar Assn., Am. Trial Lawyers Assn., S.C. Trial Lawyers Assn., Fed. Judges Assn., Carolina Yacht Club, Hibernian Soc. Charleston, Masons. Democrat. Presbyterian. Fax: 843-579-1499.

HAWKINS, GERI SUE, interior designer, jewelry designer, realtor; b. Kansas City, Mo., Sept. 4, 1940; d. William S. McCune and Verla J. (Kempter) McCune Stoll; m. LeRay D. Long, Oct. 12, 1958 (div. Dec. 1961); 1 chld, Lori Diane Long Seidl; m. Ray Eldon Hawkins, Oct. 9, 1964; children: Lynn M., John Ted; stepchildren: Celeste, Steve. Student, Kansas City Bus. Coll., 1961-62, U. Mo., Kansas City, 1974-75; AA, Maple Woods Coll., 1974; student, Wm. Jewel Coll. Interior designer Carpenter Bros. Inc., Kansas City, 1975-77; pres., designer Gerry Hawkins Interiors, Kansas City, 1977-81; interior designer R.D. Mann Inc., Kansas City, 1981-83; owner, designer Designs By Geri, Kansas City, 1983-89, 95-96, Interior Designs by Geri Inc., Parkville, Mo., 1989—, Greenstreet Interiors, 1993-94; realtor assoc. ERA Martin House, Platte City, Mo., 1984-85; sales rep. Don Wood Real Estate, 1987-88; with J.D. Reece Realtors, 1988—. Owner Designs By Geri, Inc., 2003—. Leader, Winding River coun. Girl Scouts U.S., 1966-71; active Grace Notes Singing Ensemble, Kansas City, 1980; trustee Park Hill Bapt. Ch., Parkville, 1983-85; trustee First Bapt. Ch., North Kansas City, Mo., 1998—, choir, 1994—; extension coun. Platte City, Mo.; coord. Northland Master Gardener. Mem. Platte County Bus. and Profl. Assn. (bd. dirs. 1980-81), Am. Soc. Interior Designers, Nat. Assn. Women Bus. Owners, Greater Kansas City, Platte County Women's Exch., Women in Bus., Northland Genealogy Soc. (bd. dirs. 1997—), Platte County Ext. Coun., Gen. Fedn. Women's Clubs, Patricia Club, Lions (hon.), Habitat for Humanity, Master Gardeners of Greater Kans. City Mo., Women's Missionary Soc., First Bapt. NKC. Mo. (dir.), Internat. Soc. Glass Bead Designers. Democrat. Baptist. Avocations: jewelry designing, swimming, theater, gardening. Home: 9203 NW 76th Ter Weatherby Lake MO 64152-1723 E-mail: redhen@gbronline.com.

HAWKINS, H. RALPH, architectural firm executive; BArch, U. Tex., Arlington; MPH, U. Tex. Health Scis. Ctr.; MArch, Rice U. Registered Ala., Ariz., Calif., D.C., Fla., Ga., La., Mich., Miss., Nev., N.J., N.C., Ohio, Pa., Tex., Utah, Va. Pres., CEO HKS, Inc., Dallas. Adj. prof. U. Tex., Arlington, Tex. Fellow: AIA (pres. Acad. Arch. for Health 2003), Forum for Health Planning, Am. Coll. Healthcare Archs. Office: HKS Inc 1919 McKinney Ave Dallas TX 75201 Office Phone: 214-969-5599. E-mail: rhawkins@hksinc.com.

HAWKINS, HAROLD STANLEY, pastor, school director, police chaplain; b. Santa Ana, Calif., Oct. 16, 1927; s. Henry Jesse and Susan Brown (Young) H.; m. Paula Juanita Paeschke, Feb. 19, 1949 (dec. June 1999), m. JoAnn Faron, Feb. 12, 2005; children: Bert Stanley, Harold Paul, Kathleen Faith Meulstee. Grad., L.I.F.E. Bible Coll., 1950; cert., So. Bay Regional Police Acad., 1978; DD, Hawthorne Christian Sch./Coll., 1978. Pastor Internat. Ch. of the Foursquare Gospel, Redondo Beach, Calif., 1949-58, 69-97, Reseda, Calif., 1958-66; staff mem. Oral Roberts U., Tulsa, 1966-67; pastor Internat. Ch. of the Foursquare Gospel, Bell, Calif., 1967-69; chaplain Redondo Beach Police, 1978-98, res. police officer, 1978-88; master police chaplain L.A. Police Dept. Acad., 1988-92. Dir. Camp Cedar Crest, Running Springs, Calif., 1961-81, Wings of Mercy, Santa Ana, 1966-70, Hawthorne (Calif.) Christian Schs., 1973-96. Mem. Redondo Beach Round Table, 1974-2000, pres. 1991-92; commr. Harbor Commn., Redondo Beach, 1982-92, planning commn., 1996-2000. With USN, 1944-46, World War II. Mem.: Rotary (pres. 1982—83). Republican. Office Phone: 310-702-1695. E-mail: revhal@allvantage.com. *We live in exciting days! America needs a great revival to start the new millennium!.*

HAWKINS, IDA FAYE, elementary school educator; b. Ft. Worth, Dec. 28, 1928; d. Christopher Columbus and Nanie Idella (Hughes) Hall; m. Gene Hamilton Hawkins, Dec. 22, 1952; children: Gene Agner, Jane Hall. Student, Midwestern U., 1946-48; BS, North Tex. State U., 1951; postgrad., Lamar U., 1968-70; MS, McNeese State U., 1973. Tchr. DeQueen Elem. Sch., Port Arthur, Tex., 1950-54, Tyrrell Elem. Sch., Port Arthur, Tex., 1955-56, Roy Hatton Elem. Sch., Bridge City, Tex., 1967-68, Oak Forest Elem. sch., Vidor, Tex., 1968-91; ret., 1991. Elementary school educator; b. Ft. Worth, Dec. 28, 1928; d. Christopher Columbus and Nannie Idella (Hughes) Hall; m. Gene Hamilton Hawkins, Dec. 22, 1952; children: Gene Agner, Jane Hall. Student Midwestern U., 1946-48; BS, N. Tex. State U., 1951; student Lamar U., 1968-70; MS, McNeese State U., 1973. Tchr. DeQueen Elem. Sch., Port Arthur, Tex., 1950-54, Tyrrell Elem. Sch., Port Arthur, 1955-56, Roy Hatton Elem. Sch., Bridge City, Tex., 1967-68, Oak Forest Elem. Sch., Vidor, Tex., 1968-91, ret. 2d v.p. Travis Elem. PTA, 1965-66, 1st v.p., 1966-67; corr. sec. Port Arthur City coun. PTA, 1966-67; Sunday sch. tchr. Presbyn. Ch., 1951-53, 60-66. Named Tchr. of Yr., Oak Forest Elem., 1984-85. Mem. NEA, Tex. State Tchrs. Assn. 2d v.p. Travis Elem. PTA, 1965-66, 1st v.p., 1966-67; corr. sec. Port Arthur City Coun. PTA, 1966-67; Sunday sch. tchr. Presbyn. Ch., 1951-53, 60-66. Named Tchr. of Yr., Oak Forest Elem., 1984-85. Mem. NEA, Tex. State Tchrs. Assn. Home: 6315 Central City Blvd #611 Galveston TX 77551-3806 Personal E-mail: hawkinsshi@aol.com.

HAWKINS, JAMES ALEXANDER, II, mental health fund executive; b. N.Y.C., May 2, 1929; s. James Alexander and Janet Anand (Rollo) H.; m. Marian Slate Stoudemire, June 11, 1955; children: Anne Hawkins Ramsey, Elizabeth Hawkins Ende, James Alexander III. BA, Amherst Coll., 1950. Salesman Eastman Kodak Co., New Orleans and Richmond, Va., 1954-60, rep. Washington, 1961-65, mgr. govt. markets Rochester, 1966-71, mgr. Washington Office, 1972-84; mgr. pub. rels. Washington, 1987-89; vice-chmn. Am. Mental Health Fund, Washington, 1989-90, chmn., 1990, pres., 1991-92. Cons. to CEO, Nat. Mental Health Assn., 1992—1999, bd. dir. 1999—. Bd. dirs. Met. USO, Washington, 1986-92, Children's Hospice, Int., 1992—. 1st lt. U.S. Army, 1951-53. Mem. Nat. Security Indsl. Assn. (pres. Washington chpt. 1988), Washington Reps. Rsch. Group (pres. 1984), Navy League (v.p. D.C. coun. 1982-89), Circus Saints and Sinners (bd. dirs. Washington 1984—). Republican. Episcopalian. Home: 7010 Old Cabin Ln Rockville MD 20852-4532 Office Phone: 301-881-3846. E-mail: jhawkinssr@yahoo.com.

HAWKINS, JAMESETTA See JAMES, ETTA

HAWKINS, JASPER STILLWELL, JR., architect; b. Orange, N.J., Nov. 10, 1932; s. Jasper Stillwell and Bernice (Ake) H.; m. Patricia A. Mordigan, Mar. 22, 1980; children: William Raymond, John Stillwell, Karen Ann, Jasper Stillwell III. B.Arch., U. So. Calif., 1955. Registered architect, Calif., Ariz., N.Mex. Founder, prin. Hawkins & Lindsey & Assocs., L.A., 1958-90, Hawkins Lindsey Wilson Assocs., L.A. and Phoenix, 1978-85; pres. Fletcher-Thompson Assocs., 1981-84; prin. Jasper Stillwell Hawkins, F.A.I.A., architect, Phoenix, 1990—. Bd. visitors Nat. Fire Acad., 1978-80; bd. dirs. Nat. Inst. Bldg. Scis., 1976-85, chmn. bd. dirs., 1981-83, consultative council, 1978—; mem. com. protection of archives and records centers GSA, 1975-77; mem. archtl. adv. panel Calif. State Bldg. Standards Commn., 1964-70; mem. U.S. del. to UN Econ. Commn. for Europe Working Party on Bldg., 1978-84; mem. U.S. presdl. del. to Honduran Presdl. Elections, 1985; mem. com. standards and evaluation Nat. Conf. States on Bldg. Codes and Standards, 1971-74; mem. Am. Arbitration Assn., 1992-2002; trustee Underwriter's Labs., 1984-2002, mem. nat. coun. Archtl. Registration Bds., 1971—; participant and speaker numerous confs. Contbr. articles to profl. jours.; maj. works include Valley Music Theatre, L.A., Houston Music Theatre, Sundome Theatre and R.H. Johnson Ctr., Sun City West, Ariz., Bell Recreation Ctr., Sun City, U. Calif. at Irvine Student Housing, Oxnard (Calif.) Fin. Ctr., condominium develts., Lakes Club, Sun City. Mem. Nev. Gov.'s Commn. Fire Safety Codes, 1980-81, Pres. Reagan's Commn. on Housing, 1981-82, City of Phoenix ACDC Task Force, 1985-86, ACDC Aesthetics Commn., 1986-89, City of Phoenix Camelback East Village Planning Com., 1983-89; mem. fire rsch. panel Nat. Bur. Stds., 1978-81; chmn. NAS fire assessment rev. com., 1987-88, com. on analytical methods for designing bldgs. for fire safety, 1977-78; chmn. bldg. seismic safety coun. ind. rev. panel San Francisco War Meml. Opera House, 1995. Recipient design awards from Ariz. Rock Products Assn., Theater Assn. Am., Nat. Food Facilities, House and Home Mag., Practical Builders Mag., Am. Builders Mag., Nat. Inst. of Bldg. Sci. Inst. award, 1995, others. Fellow AIA (mem. codes and stds. com. 1970—, chmn. 1970-73, nat. liaison commn. with Assoc. Gen. Contractors 1969-70, chmn. nat. fire safety task force 1972-74, chmn. Calif. coun. AIA state code com. 1964-68, chmn. nat. conf. industrialized constrn. 1969-70, nat. com. bldg. industry coordination 1969-70, nat. rep. to Internat. Conf. Bldg. Ofcls. 1969, state Calif. AIA codes com. 1960-70, chmn. 1965-70, nat. AIA codes and stds. com. 1970-80, chmn. 1970-74, nat. crisis adv. com. 1988-89), 1976—; mem. ASCE (task force bldg. codes 1971-74), ASTM, Nat. Fire Protection Assn. (com. bldg. heights and areas 1965-72, chmn. 1968-72, fire prevention code com. 1974-76, bd. dirs. 1985-93, chmn. nat. model codes coordinating com. 1983-86, stds. coun. 1996—, bldg. code task force 2000—), Nat. Fire Acad. (bd. regents 1980-83), Nat. Bur. Stds. Fire (rsch. adv. com. 1979-82), Nat. Acad. Forensic Engrs., Ariz. C. of C. (policy com. 1983-84), Ariz. Biltmore Village Estates Homeowners Assn. (pres. 1981-83), Phoenix C. of C. (chmn. Water task force 1982-83). Office: 5332 N 24th Pl 220 Phoenix AZ 85016

HAWKINS, JEFF, information technology company executive; b. LI, NY, June 1, 1957; BSEE, Cornell U., 1979; student, U. Calif., 1986—88. Key tech. positions Intel Corp., 1982; with GRiD Sys. Corp., 1982—92, v.p. rsch.; founder Palm Computing (now palmOne Inc.), 1992, with, 1992—98; co-founder Handspring (merged with Palm Hardware Group to create new co. palmOne, Inc., 2003), 1998, chief product officer, bd. mem., 1998—2003; CTO palmOne, Inc., Milpitas, Calif., 2003—; and Exec dir, chmn Redwood Neuroscience Inst, Menlo Park, Calif. Founder Redwood Neuroscience Inst., 2002, exec. dir., chmn.; mem. sci. bd. dirs. Cold Spring Harbor Labs. Co-author (with Sandra Blakeslee): (non-fiction) On Intelligence, 2004 (Wired Mag RAVE award, 2005). Mem.: Nat. Acad. Engring. Achievements include invention of original PalmPilot, 1994; Treo smart phone; patents for nine various handheld devices and features; prin. architect and designer for GRiDPad (1989) and GRiD Convertible. Avocations: sailing, playing musical instruments. Office: palmOne Inc 400 N McCarthy Blvd Milpitas CA 95035 Office Phone: 408-503-7000. Fax: 408-503-2750.*

HAWKINS, JENNIFER REBEKAH, band director; d. Douglas Wayne and Kathleen Diane Needham; m. Kenneth Christopher Hawkins, June 24, 2004. BA in music edn., Lawrence U., 1996; MA in tchg., Grand Canyon U., 2002. Dir. of bands Parker Vista Mid. Sch., Parker, Colo., 1996—98, Pioneer Elem. Sch., Parker, 1996—, Sagewood Mid. Sch., Parker, 1998—. Pvt. music lessons tchr. Denver Metro Area, 1996—. Mem.: Colo. Music Educator's Assn., Music Educators Nat. Conf. Achievements include invited to perform at Colo. Music Educator's Assn. Convention, 2001. Office: Sagewood Mid Sch 4725 Fox Sparrow Rd Parker CO 80134 Office Phone: 303-387-4361. Office Fax: 303-387-4301.

HAWKINS, JOHN DONALD, JR., lawyer; b. Bronxville, N.Y., Dec. 30, 1956; s. John Donald and Lucille Phyllis (Sassano) H.; m. Alice Sherron Harward, May 17, 1980; children: Alison Lyn, Megan Leigh. BA cum laude in Govt. and Econ., Lehigh U., 1977; JD with honors, U. N.C., 1980. Bar: N.Y. 1981, U.S. Dist. Ct. (so. dist.) N.Y. 1983, U.S. Ct. Appeals (2d cir.) 1983, Conn. 1998. Ptnr. Mudge Rose Guthrie Alexander & Ferdon, N.Y.C., 1980—, Paul, Hastings, Janofsky & Walker LLP, chmn. global project practice. Mem. N.Y. State Bar Assn., Assn. of Bar of City of N.Y., Phi Beta Kappa. Roman Catholic. Office: Paul Hastings Janofsky & Walker LLP 1055 Washington Blvd Stamford CT 06901 Office Phone: 203-961-7486. Office Fax: 203-674-7686. Business E-Mail: johnhawkins@paulhastings.com.

HAWKINS, JOHN N., education educator; b. Sterling, Ill., May 18, 1944; m. Judith Ayami Takata, Aug. 12, 1967; children: Marisa Harumi, Larina Yasuko. BA with honors, U. Hawaii, 1967; MA, U. B.C., Vancouver, Can., 1969; PhD, Vanderbilt U., 1973. Dean internat. studies and overseas programs UCLA, chair dept. edn., dir. curriculum inquiry ctr., prof. comparative and internat. edn. Author: (with T. LaBelle) Education and Intergroup Relations: An Internat. Perspective, 1988, Education and Social Change in the People's Republic of China, 1983, (with B. Koppel) The Future Work in Rural Asia, 1993. Mem. internat. adv. com. Exxon Edn. Found. Fellow NDEA, Internat. Studies Ministry of Edn., Japan, U. B.C.; Mombusho Fgn. scholar; recipient numerous grants. Mem. AERA, Comparative and Internat. Edn. Soc. (bd. dirs., pres.), Am. Ednl. Studies Assn., Omicron Delta Kappa., Phi Delta Kappa. Home: 3847 Daguerre Ave Calabasas CA 91302-5816

HAWKINS, JOSEPH ELMER, JR., physiologist, educator; b. Waco, Tex., Mar. 4, 1914; s. Joseph Elmer and Maude Burke (Schlenker) H.; m. Jane Elizabeth Daddow, Aug. 24, 1939 (dec. Sept. 2002); children: Richard Spencer Daddow, Peter Douglas Huntington, James Marion Davis, William Alexander Parmley, Priscilla Ann (Mrs. Philip A. Leach). Student, Altes Realgymnasium, Munich, 1929-30; AB, Baylor U., 1933; postgrad., Brown U., 1933-34; BA in Physiology, U. Oxford, 1937, MA, 1966, DSc in Clin. Medicine, 1979; PhD in Med. Sci., Harvard U., 1941. Tchg. fellow in physiology Harvard Med. Sch., 1937-41, instr., 1941-45; asst. investigator Nat. Def. Rsch. Com.-Office Sci. Rsch. & Devel., Harvard U., 1941-43; spl. rsch. assoc. Harvard Psycho-Acoustic Lab., Cambridge, Mass., 1943-45; asst. prof. physiology Bowman Gray Sch. Medicine, Wake Forest Coll., Winston-Salem, N.C., 1945-46; rsch. assoc. neurophysiology Merck Inst. for Therapeutic Rsch., Rahway, N.J., 1946-56; assoc. prof. otolaryngology NYU Sch. Medicine, 1956-63; prof. physiol. acoustics U. Mich., Ann Arbor, 1963-84, prof. otolaryngology emeritus, 1984—, chmn. grad. program in physiol. acoustics, 1969-81. Disting. vis. prof. biology Baylor U., Waco, Tex., 1985-93; mem. NIH sensory diseases study sect., 1958-61, communicative disorders rsch. tng. com., 1965-69, communicative scis. study sect., 1975-79; mem. Nat. Libr. Medicine Communicative Disorders Task Force, 1977-79; lectr. Armed Forces Inst. Pathology, 1969-74; cons. various pharm. cos. Contbr. to: Ency. Brit., 1974, 86, 99, Ency. Neuroscience, 1987, 99, 2003; editor: (with M. Lawrence and W.P. Work) Otophysiology, 1973, (with S.A. Lerner and G.T. Matz) Aminoglycoside Ototoxicity, 1981; contbr. sci. articles to profl. jours. Mem. Bd. Edn., Cranford, NJ, 1958—61. Rhodes scholar Tex. and Worcester Coll., U. Oxford, 1934-37; USPHS spl. fellow Öronkliniken, Sahlgrenska Sjukhuset U. Göteborg, Sweden, 1961-63; NAS exch. lectr. to Yugoslavia and Bulgaria, 1977; Chercheur étranger de l'INSERM, Lab. d'Audiologie Expérimentale, U. Bordeaux II, 1978; recipient Disting. Achievement award Baylor U., 1982, City of Pleven, Bulgaria medal, 1982, U. Bordeaux medal, 1983, Humboldt Rsch. award for sr. U.S. scientists U. Würzburg, 1991, Hon. Citizen award, Bordeaux, 1991, Disting. Alumnus award Baylor U., 1996. Fellow AAAS, Acoustical Soc. Am.; mem. Am. Physiol. Soc., Assn. for Rsch. in Otolaryngology (award of merit 1985, Presdl. citation 2004), Collegium Oto-rhino-laryngologicum Amicitiae Sacrum, Bárány Soc., European Workshop for Inner Ear Biology, Am. Assn. for History of Medicine, Am. Otol. Soc. (assoc.), Prosper Menière Soc. (hon., Gold medal for basic sci. 1998), Pacific Coast Oto-ophthalmol. Soc. (hon.), Connétablie de Guyenne (Bordeaux, assoc.), Phi Beta Kappa, Sigma Xi. Anglican. Democrat. Achievements include research in ototoxic, noise-induced, and presbyacusic hearing loss; history of otolaryngology. Avocations: Germanic and Romance languages and literature, gardening. Home: Glacier Hills Apt 258 1200 Earhart Rd Ann Arbor MI 48105 Office: U Mich Med Sch Kresge Hearing Rsch Inst Ann Arbor MI 48109-0506 Office Phone: 734-764-0215. Business E-Mail: josehawk@umich.edu.

HAWKINS, KATHERINE ANN, hematologist, educator, lawyer; b. Teaneck, N.J., Oct. 25, 1947; d. Howard Robert and Helen Ann (Foley) Hawkins; m. Paul Jonathan Chrzanowski, June 29, 1974; children: Eric, Brian. AB, Manhattanville Coll., Purchase, N.Y., 1969; MD, Columbia U., 1973; JD, Fordham U., Sch. of Law, 2002. Intern Presbyn. Hosp., N.Y.C., 1973, Roosevelt Hosp., N.Y.C., 1974-75, resident, 1975-77; fellow NYU, 1977-79; attending hematologist Sickle Cell Ctr. St. Luke's Hosp., N.Y.C., 1985-87; assoc. attending physician St. Luke's - Roosevelt Hosp. Ctr., N.Y.C., 1989—; asst. clin. prof. medicine Columbia U., N.Y.C., 1987-94, assoc. clin. prof., 1994—96; assoc. dir. dept. medicine, dir. med. edn. St. Luke's Hosp., N.Y.C., 1991-96; assoc. residency program dir. Beth Israel Med. Ctr., N.Y.C., 1996—; assoc. prof. clin. medicine Albert Einstein Coll. Medicine Yeshiva U., N.Y.C., 1996—. Mem. attending staff Beth Israel Hosp., N.Y.C., St. Luke's-Roosevelt Hosp. Ctr., N.Y.C. Contbr. articles to profl. jours. Fellow ACP; mem. ABA, Am. Soc. Hematology, Am. Soc. Clin. Oncology, Am. Coll. Legal Medicine Roman Catholic. Office: Gair Gair Conason Steigman and Mackauf 80 Pine St New York NY 10005 Office Phone: 212-943-1090.

HAWKINS, KEVIN ANDREW, music educator; b. Springfield, Mo., June 2, 1962; s. Billy Wayne and Joyce Anne Hawkins; m. Judith Karol Miller, June 27, 1987; children: Klayton, Kyndal. BS in Music Edn., SW Mo. State U., 1985; MusM, Southwestern Bapt. Theol. Sem., 1988; student, S.W. Bapt. Theol. Sem., 1996—. Ordained to gospel ministry 1994. Min. of music and youth First Bapt. Ch., Clever, Mo., 1982—85; min. of music Travis Bapt. Ch., Corpus Christi, Tex., 1988—91, First Bapt. Ch., Picayune, Miss., 1991—96; dir. of choral activities Glendale H.S., Springfield, Mo., 1997—. Mem.: Music Educator's Nat. Conf., Am. Choral Dirs. Assn., Mo. Music Educators Assn., Mo. Choral Dirs. Assn. Republican. Baptist. Avocations: travel, woodworking. Home: 1052 E High Point St Springfield MO 65810 Office: Glendale HS 2727 Ingram Mill Rd Springfield MO 65804 Personal E-mail: k4hawkins1@juno.com. E-mail: khawkins@spsmail.org.

HAWKINS, LAWRENCE CHARLES, management consultant, educator; b. Greenville County, S.C., Mar. 20, 1919; s. Wayman and Etta (Brockman) H.; m. Earline Thompson, Apr. 29, 1943; children: Lawrence Charles Jr., Wendell Earl. BA, U. Cin., 1941, BEd, 1942, MEd, 1951, EdD, 1970; AA (hon.), Wilmington Coll., 1979; LittD (hon.), Cin. Tech. and C.C.; LHD (hon.), Mt. St. Joseph Coll. Cert. sch. supt. Ohio. Elem./secondary tchr. Cin. Pub. Schs., 1945-52, sch. prin./dir., 1952-67, asst. supt., 1967-69; dean U. Cin., 1969-75, v.p., 1975-77, sr. v.p., 1977-83; vis. asst. prof. Eastern Mich. U., Ypsilanti, summers 1955-60; mem. Cincinnatus Assn., 1971-87. Vice chair Student Loan Funding Corp., 1982-98; mem. cmty. rels. panel Cin. Mayors, 1979—, others; cons. U.S. Dept. Justice, Dept. Edn.; bd. dirs. We. and So. Fin. Group. Bd. dirs. exec. com. Ohio Citizens Coun. Health and Welfare, 1966-73; vice chair Ohio Valley Regional Med. Program, 1972-77, bd. trustees Cmty. Chest and Coun. Cin. Area Inc., 1970-72; bd. dirs. Wilmington (Ohio) Coll., 1980-90, Bethesda Hosp., Cin., 1980-90; trustee Children's Home of Cin., 1978-90, Coll. Mt. St. Joseph, 1989-93; pres., CEO Omni-Man, Inc., 1981-96; bd. dirs. emeritus Nat. Underground R.R. Freedom Ctr., 1994-98; owner The L.C.H. Resource; vice chmn. Greater Cin. TV Ednl. Found., WCET-TV, 1983; co-chmn. Cin. area NCCJ 1980-87; nat. bd. dirs. Inroads, 1982-87; bd. trustees Knowledge Works Found., 1999-2002. Served to lt. USAAF, 1943-45 (an original Tuskegee Airman). Recipient award of Merit, Cin. Area United Appeal, 1955, 73, cert. Pres.'s Coun. on Youth Opportunity, 1968, City Cin., 1968, Disting. Svc. citation Greater Cin. NCCJ, 1988; named Great Living Cincinnatian, Greater Cin. C. of C., 1989. Mem. NEA (life), ASCD, Am. Assn. Sch. Adminstrs. (conv., Golden Eagles Lifetime Achievement award 1998), Nat. Congress Parents and Tchrs. (hon. life; chmn. com.), Phi Delta Kappa, Kappa Delta Pi, Kappa Alpha Psi, Sigma Pi Phi. Home: 3544 Sherbrooke Dr Cincinnati OH 45241-3831 Office Phone: 513-563-8387.

HAWKINS, LINDA PARROTT, school system administrator; b. Florence, SC, June 23, 1947; d. Obie Lindberg Parrott and Mary Francis (Lee) Evans; m. Larry Eugene Hawkins, Jan. 5, 1946; 1 child, Heather Nichole. BS, U. S.C., 1969; MS, Francis Marion Coll., 1978; EdS in Adminstrn., U. S.C., 1994, PhD in Ednl. Adminstrn., 2002. Tchr. J.C. Lynch HS, Coward, SC, 1973—80; tchr., chair bus. dept. Lake City (SC) HS, 1980—89, assoc. prin., 1989—98; dir. Florence County Sch. Dist. 3, Lake City, 1998—2002, sr. dir. accountability, 2002—. Mem. Williamsburg Tech. Adv. Coun., Kingstree, S.C., 1985-90; adv. coun. Florence-Darlington (S.C.) Tech., 1981-87; co-chair Pee Dee Tech Prep consortia steering com.; co-chmn. allied health adv. com., 1990-93; spkr., presenter in field. Editor: Parliamentary Procedure Made Easy, 1983; contbr. articles to profl. jours. State advisor Future Bus. Leaders of Am., Columbia, S.C., 1978-86; treas. S.C. State Women's Aux., 1983-93; sec.-treas. J.C. Lynch Elem. Sch. PTO. Mary Eva Hite scholar, 2001; named Outstanding Advisor SC Future Bus. Leaders of Am., 1985, Tchr. of Yr., SC Bus. Edn. Assn., 1988-89, Secondary Tchr. of Yr., Nat. Bus. Edn. Assn., 1989-90, Educator of Yr. SC Trade & Indsl. Edn. Assn., 1993, SC Asst. Prin. of Yr., 1995, 2020 Vision Dist. Adminstr. award, 2000, Leadership award Nat. Assn. Fed. Program Adminstrs., 2005 Mem. Profl. Secs. Internat., Nat. Bus. Assn. (S.C. chpt. membership dir. 1986-89, so. region membership dir. 1989-92, secondary program dept. dir. 1991-92), SC Bus. Edn. Assn. (jour. editor 1985-86, v.p. for membership 1986-87, treas. 1987-88, pres. elect 1988-89, pres. 1989-90), Am. Vocat. Assn., SC Vocat. Assn. (parliamentarian 1985-86, v.p. 1989-90, treas. 1991-92), SC Assn. of Title I Admin. (pres. elect 2003-2004, pres. 2004-2005), Internat. Soc. Bus. Educators, Lake City C. of C., Kappa Kappa Iota, Delta Kappa Gamma. Democrat. Baptist. Avocations: cross-stitching, reading, softball. Office: Florence County Sch Dist 3 PO Box 1389 Lake City SC 29560-1389 Office Phone: 843-374-8652 115. Business E-Mail: lhawkins@florence3.k12.sc.us.

HAWKINS, LORETTA ANN, retired secondary school educator, playwright; b. Winston-Salem, N.C., Jan. 1, 1942; d. John Henry and Laurine (Hines) Sanders; m. Joseph Hawkins, Dec. 10, 1962; children: Robin, Dionne, Sherri. BS in Edn., Chgo. State U., 1965; MA in Lit., Governor's State U., 1977, MA in African Cultures, 1978; MLA in Humanities, U. Chgo., 1998. Cert. tchr., Ill. Tchr. Chgo. Bd. Edn., 1968—2002; lectr. Chgo. City Colls., 1987-89; tchr. English, Gage Park H.S., Chgo., 1988—2002; ret., 2002. Mem. steering com. Mellon Seminar U. Chgo., 1990; tchr. adv. com. Goodman Theatre, Chgo., 1992, mem. cmty. adv. coun., 1996—; spkr. in field; creator 5-4-3-2-1- Essay Writing Method, 1997. Author: (reading workbook) Contemporary Black Heroes, 1992, (plays) Of Quiet Birds, 1993 (James H. Wilson award 1993), Above the Line, 1994, Good Morning, Miss Alex; contbr. poetry, articles to profl. publs.; featured WYCC-TV-Educate, 1996. Mem. Chgo. Tchg. Connections Network, DePaul U. Ctr. Urban Edn., 2001; mem. Chgo. Pub. Schs. Mentoring and Induction of New Tchrs. Program. Fellow Santa Fe Pacific Found., 1988, Lloyd Fry Found. 1989, Andrew W. Mellon Found., 1991, Ill. Arts Coun., 1993; grantee Cmty. Arts Assistance Program Award, Chgo. Dept. Cultural Affairs; recipient Feminist Writers 3d pl. award NOW, 1993, Zora Neale Hurston-Bessie Head Fiction award Black Writer's Conf., 1993, Suave Tchr. Plus award, 2002; numerous others. Mem. AAUW, Nat. Coun. Tchrs. English (spkr. conv.), Am. Fedn. Tchrs., Women's Theatre Alliance, Dramatists Guild of Am., Internat. Women's Writing Guild. Achievements include invention of 5-4-3-2-1 essay writing method. Avocations: films, coins, reading, walking. Home: 8928 S Oglesby Ave Chicago IL 60617-3047

HAWKINS, MARGARET, art critic, writer, educator; Tchr. Sch. of the Art Inst. Chgo. Contbr. weekly column in the Chgo. Sun Times; Chgo. corr. ARTnews; contbr. articles to a number of other nat. and local art publs. Mem.: Chgo. Art Critics Assn. Mailing: 1835 Old Briar Rd Highland Park IL 60035 Fax: 847-831-0982. E-mail: Margahawk@aol.com.*

HAWKINS, MARY ELLEN HIGGINS (MARY ELLEN HIGGINS), retired state legislator, public relations executive; b. Birmingham, Ala., Apr. 18, 1923; m. James H. Hawkins, Feb. 13, 1960 (div. 1971); children: Andrew Higgins, Elizabeth, Peter Hixon. Student, U. Ala., Tuscaloosa, 1945-47. Congl. aide to several mems. U.S. Ho. Reps., 1950-60; instr. art Sumter County Schs., Americus, Ga., 1971-72; staff writer Naples (Fla.) Daily News, 1972-74; prin. Daniels-Hawkins, Naples, 1982-84; mem. Fla. Ho. Reps., Tallahassee, 1974-94; vice chmn. BancFlorida Fin. Corp., Naples, 1979-91, pres., CEO, 1991-92, chmn., 1991-93, also. bd. dirs. Columnist, contbr. articles to local newspapers. V.p. Naples Philharm., 1984-91; life mem., vice chair Big Cypress Basin bd. South Fla. Water Mgmt. Dist., 1999-2005; mem. adv. com. Lower Gulf Coast Water Supply Plan, 1999—; trustee CREW Land and Water Trust, 2002—, treas., 2004—; vice chair Fla. Children's Campaign, 1997—; various offices Rep. Party Ga., Americus, 1965-71. Mem. Zonta Internat. Avocation: painting. Office Phone: 239-262-4932. Personal E-mail: mhawk26249@aol.com.

HAWKINS, MICHAEL DALY, federal judge; b. Winslow, Ariz., Feb. 12, 1945; s. William Bert and Patricia Agnes (Daly) H.; m. Phyllis A. Lewis, June 4, 1966; children: Aaron, Adam. BA, Ariz. State U., 1967, JD cum laude, 1970; LLM, U. Va., 1998. Bar: Ariz. 1970, U.S. Ct. Mil. Appeals 1971, U.S. Supreme Ct. 1974. Pvt. practice law, 1973—77; U.S. atty. Dept. Justice, Phoenix, 1977—80; pvt. practice law, 1980—94; judge U.S. Ct. Appeals (9th cir.), Phoenix, 1994—. Mem. Appellate Cts. Jud. Nominating Commn., 1985—89. Staff editor: Ariz. State U. Law Jour., 1968—70. Mem. Ariz. Lottery Commn., 1980—83, Commn. on Uniform State Laws, 1988—93. Capt. USMC, 1970—73. Recipient Alumni Achievement award, Ariz. State U., 1995. Mem.: ABA, Nat. Assn. Former U.S. Attys. (pres. 1989—90), Adminstrv. Conf. U.S. (pub. mem. 1985—94), Phoenix Trial Lawyers Assn., Ariz. Trial Lawyers Assn. (bd. dirs. 1976—77, state sec. 1976—77), State Bar of Ariz. (James Walsh Outstanding Jurist Award 2003), Maricopa County Bar Assn. (bd. dirs. 1975—77, 1981—89, pres. 1987—88). Office Phone: 602-322-7310.

HAWKINS, PAMELA LEIGH HUFFMAN, biochemist; b. Washington, Oct. 7, 1950; d. Lauria Carl and Maryalice (Flinner) Huffman; m. James Lee Hawkins, Mar. 7, 1981 (div. Aug. 1993). BS in Biochemistry, Va. Polytech. Inst. & State U., Va., 1972; MS in Biochemistry, Pa. State U., Pa., 1975. Sci. info. specialist Inform., Inc., Rockville, Md., 1972; asst. rsch. scientist Union Carbide Corp., Tarrytown, NY, 1975; assoc. rsch. scientist Am. Hosp. Supply Corp., Gibbstown, NJ, 1976-78, rsch. scientist Miami, Fla., 1978-85; R & D scientist Baxter Healthcare Corp., Miami, Fla., 1985-95, sr. rsch. scientist, 1993-95; prin. scientist Sigma Diagnostics, St. Louis, 1995—2002; sr. scientist Biotech. Rsch. and Devel., Sigma-Aldrich, 2002—04; prin. scientist Internat. Lab., Orangeburg, NY, 2004—. Contbr. articles to profl. jour. Recipient Baxter Diagnostics Tech. award for Thromboplastin-IS, 1990, Baxter Internat. Tech. award, 1991. Mem. Mortar Bd., Phi Sigma, Gamma Sigma Delta, Phi Lambda Upsilon. Lutheran. Achievements include US and European patent for fresh blood (unfixed) hematology control, 3 US and 1 European patents for improved extraction methods for preparing thromboplastin reagents, patent for thromboplastins for recombinent tissue factor, US patent for thromboplastin reagents based on recombinent technology, production of thromboplastin IS, Innovin, Two US patents-US Pat. No. 6,528,273, 2003, Methods for Quality Control of Prothiombin Thromboplastin Time (PT) and Activated Partial Thromboplastin Time (APTT) Assays using coagulation controls-for coagulation controls for prothrombin time and activated partial thromboplastin time, various others. Office: Sigma Diagnostics 545 S Ewing Ave Saint Louis MO 63103-2991

HAWKINS, PHILIP LINTON, real estate executive; b. Phila., Dec. 27, 1955; s. Robert Bruce and Nancy (Perry) H.; m. Elizabeth Porter, June 28, 1980; children: Robert Bruce II, Jennifer Louise. BA, Hamilton Coll., 1978; MBA, U. Chgo., 1980. New products mgr. Avery Internat., Cleve., 1980-82; v.p., gen. mgr. LaSalle Ptnrs., Cin., 1982-85, v.p., regional mgr. Dallas, 1985—; COO CarrAmerica Realty, Wash., D.C. Dir. Dallas West End Assn.; mem. Cen. Dallas Assn. Mem. Dallas C. of C. Clubs: Canyon Creek Country, City Club of Dallas. Republican. Congregationalist. Avocations: tennis, golf, sailing, skiing. Home: 7713 Crossover Dr Mc Lean VA 22102-2507 Office: CarrAmerica Realty 1850 K St NW Ste 500 Washington DC 20006

HAWKINS, RICHARD ALBERT, medical educator, administrator; b. Greenwich, Conn., Mar. 27, 1940; s. Albert Rice and Florence Marie Elizabeth (Hansen) H.; m. Enriqueta Elias, May 9, 1964; children: Richard Alfred, Paul Andrés. BSc magna cum laude, San Diego State U., 1963; PhD, Harvard U., 1969; LHD (hon.), U. Phoenix, 1994. Rsch. fellow Metabolic Rsch. Lab. Radcliffe Infirmary, Oxford (Eng.) U., 1969-71; staff fellow in neurochemistry St. Elizabeth Hosp., Washington, 1971-72, NIMH/NIAAA sr. staff fellow in neurochemistry, 1972-74; chief phys. sci. br. FDA, Rockville, Md., 1974-76; assoc. prof. neurosurgery and physiology NYU Med. Ctr., N.Y.C., 1976-77; prof. anesthesia and physiology Pa. State U., Hershey (Pa.) Med. Ctr., 1977-88; prof., chmn. physiology and biophysics The Rosalind Franklin U. Medicine and Sci., North Chicago, Ill., 1988-93, prof., 1988—; exec. v.p. acad. affairs, chief academic officer Herman M. Finch U. Health Scis./Chgo. Med. Sch., North Chicago, Ill., 1993-98, provost, 1998, pres., CEO, 1999—2003. Hon. prof. U. Valencia, Spain, 1989—. Contbr. numerous articles to profl. jours. Recipient Meritorious Rsch. award Morris Parker Found., 1992. Fellow Am. Heart Assn.; mem. Am. Physiol. Soc., Am. Soc. Neurochemistry, Biochem. Soc., Soc. for Neurosci., Alpha Omega Alpha. Home: 950 N Michigan Ave Chicago IL 60611 Office: Finch U Health Scis Chgo Med Sch 3333 Green Bay Rd North Chicago IL 60064-3037 Office Phone: 847-578-3218. Business E-Mail: rah@post.harvard.edu.

HAWKINS, ROBERT B., think-tank executive; PhD, U Wash. Chmn. Adv. Commn. on Intergovt. Rels., Washington, 1982-93; dir. Am. pub. policy program Woodrow Wilson Internat. Ctr. for Scholars, Washington; pres., CEO Inst. for Contemporary Studies, Oakland, Calif. Tv co-host, That's Politics, 1987-91; radio California Political Review; Books American Federalism: A New Partnership for the Republic, Self-government by District: Myth and Reality. Office: Institute For Contemporary Studies 3100 Harrison St Oakland CA 94611-5526

HAWKINS, SHEILA J., purchasing agent; BS in Bus. Adminstrn., U. Maine; MBA in Internat. Supply Chain Mgmt., Atlantic Internat. U., Honolulu, 2004; post grad. in Advanced Comm. and Advanced Negotiations, Boston Coll.; post grad. in Constrn. Project Mgmt., U. Maine; grad., Dale Carnegie Course, Dynamic Comm. Course. Cert. internat. supply chain mgr., e-procurement profl., purchasing profl., purchasing mgr., prodn. and inventory mgmt. Mem.: Am. Purchasing Soc., S.W. Mich. Nat. Assn. Purchasing Mgrs., Inst. Supply Mgmt., Assn. Ops. Mgmt. (liaison Nat.Assn. Purchasing Mgrs., Mid-size Mfr. award 2004), S.W. Mich. Internat. Bus. Group (pres.). Address: 7844 N 26th St Kalamazoo MI 49004

HAWKINS, SIDNEY TAYLOR, mathematician, educator; s. Joe Dewitt and Odalie Elizabeth Hawkins; children: Sharon Celestine, Latafta Spivey. BS in Math., Grambling State U., 1973; MS in Math., La. Tech. U., 1975, Tulane U., 1995; PhD in Math., La. State U., 1999. Asst. chemist D.H.& J Industries, Monroe, La., 1976—78; instr. math. Grambling (La.) State U., 1979—81; asst. prof. math. Dillard U., New Orleans, 1981—88, Xavier U., New Orleans, 1988—95, La. State U., Baton Rouge, 1997—99; assoc. prof. math. Alcorn (Miss.) State U., 1999—. Asst. prof. of math. Dillard U., New Orleans, 1981—88, Xavier U. of New Orleans, New Orleans, 1988—95, La. State U., Baton rouge, La., Usa, 1997—99; assoc. prof. of math. Alcorn State U., Alcorn, Miss., Usa. Recipient Gov.'s Award, Gov. of La., 1988, Mayor's Award, Mayor of New Orleans, 1988. Mem.: Nat. Assn. Math. (life), Pi Mu Epsilon (life). Office: Alcorn State Univ 1000 ASU Dr #30 Alcorn State MS 39096 E-mail: shawkins@loman.alcorn.edu.

HAWKINS, TRIP, electronics company executive; Chmn. bd. dirs., CEO 3DO, Redwood City, Calif. Office: The 3DO Company 100 Cardinal Way Redwood City CA 94063-4755

HAWKINS, WILLIAM E. N., newspaper editor; b. N.Y.C., Dec. 4, 1943; s. Frank Nelson and Lottie (Norton) H.; m. Diane Taylor, Apr. 1, 1967; children: William E.N. Jr., Geoffrey W.T. BA, Cornell U., 1966. Reporter Patriot-News, Harrisburg, Pa., 1968-73, Balt. Evening Sun, 1973-78, city editor, 1978-83, asst. mng. editor, 1983-88; exec. editor The Herald-Sun, Durham, N.C., 1988—; v.p. The Durham Herald Co., 1994—. Vis. media fellow Duke U., 2002. Mem. bicentennial adv. com. U. N.C., 1992-93. 1st lt. U.S. Army, 1966-68, Vietnam. Decorated Bronze Star. Mem. Am. Soc. Newspaper Editors, AP Mng. Editors, N.C. Press Assn. (pres. 2001-2002, bd. dirs. 1992-96), N.C. Press Found., Soc. Profl. Journalists, Americal Divsn. Vets. Assn. Presbyterian. Avocation: skiing. Home: 7 Hartley Pl Durham NC 27707-2437 Office: The Herald-Sun 2828 Pickett Rd Durham NC 27705-5613 Office Phone: 919-419-6678.

HAWKINS, WILLIAM H., II, lawyer; b. Cin., July 18, 1948; BS, U. Cin., 1970, MEd, 1974; JD, No. Ky. U., 1978. Bar: Ohio 1978, Ky. 1979. Atty. then ptnr. Frost & Jacobs (now Frost Brown Todd); assoc. gen. counsel, sec. Convergys Corp., Cincinnati, Ohio, 1999—2001, gen. counsel, sec., 2001—03, sr. v.p., gen. counsel, sec., 2003—. Office: Convergys Corp PO Box 1638 Cincinnati OH 45201

HAWKINS DE GOLIER, DANIELLE, political activist; b. Valhalla, N.Y., Dec. 6, 1947; d. Daniel Livingston and Lucy Ann (Collesano) Wilson; m. David Frederick DeGolier, Apr. 8, 1967 (div. 1984); children: Jeffrey David De Golier, Amyjo MeLoon; m. Charles Edward LaGreca, Feb. 14, 1986 (div. May 1993); m. Steven Tracey Moore, July 7, 1996 (div. 1998); m. Robert Michael Hawkins, Oct. 16, 2004. AA in Liberal Arts Human and Social Scis., Niagara County C.C., 1991. Founder, pres. Citizens Against Pollution Niagara County, 1980—82; founder, facilitator Love Addicts Anonymous Niagara Falls, 1982—88; prof. dancer, 1998—2003. Author: (children's book) A Lap for Leonard, 1977; columnist The Niagara Gazette, 1975-76, Nat. Women's Polit. Caucus, 1978, Just Ask Danni, The Niagara Falls Reporter, 2000-2002. Lobbyist state/fed. upgrade adoption laws granting adopted adults access to med. info. via anonymous computer network, 1975; founder, pub. rels. dir. Peoples Animal Lovers Soc., 1975-76; pres. Niagara Area chpt., pub. rels. dir. Animal Birth Control Soc. Western N.Y., 1976; founder, pres. Citizens Against Pollution, Niagara County, 1980-82, Love Addicts Anonymous, Niagara Falls, 1982-89; lobbyist state/fed. stalkers act., Niagara Falls, 1991-93, fed. sponsorship to upgrade domestic violence laws, 1990-94. Statue erected in honor of her Citizens Against Pollution work, Lewiston, N.Y., 1982. Mem. NOW (pres. Niagara County chpt. 1993-94); People Animal Lovers Soc. (founder, pub. rels. dir. 1975-76), Animal Birth Control Soc. Western N.Y. (pres. Niagra County chpt., pub. rels. dir. 1975-77. Avocations: writing, animal, environmental and humanitarian work. Home: 550 Main St #2 Niagara Falls NY 14301

HAWKS, BARRETT KINGSBURY, lawyer; b. Barnesville, Ga., July 13, 1938; s. Paul K. and Nettie Glenn (Barrett) H.; m. S. Kathleen Pafford, Apr. 3, 1965 BBA, Emory U., 1960, LL.B., 1963; LL.M., Harvard U., 1964. Bar: Ga. Clk. Supreme Ct. Ga., 1963; Assoc. Gambrell, Russell, Moye & Richardson (now Smith, Gambrell & Russell), Atlanta, 1961-65; assoc. Sutherland, Asbill & Brennan, Atlanta, 1965-70, ptnr., 1970-82, 93—, Paul, Hastings, Janofsky & Walker, 1982-93. Served to lt. comdr. USNR. Mem. ABA (mem. coun. group pub. utility, transp. and comms. law sect.), State Bar Ga. (bd. govs. 1981-88), Atlanta Bar Assn., D.C. Bar Assn., Emory Law Sch. Alumni Assn. (pres. 1996-97), Emory Law Sch. Coun. (chmn., 1997-98), Capital City Club, Highlands Country Club. Presbyterian. Office: Sutherland Asbill & Brennan 999 Peachtree St NE Ste 2300 Atlanta GA 30309-3996 Office Phone: 404-853-8164. Business E-Mail: barrett.hawks@sablaw.com.

HAWKS, WESLEY HOWARD, retired director, music educator; b. San Diego, Calif., May 22, 1939; s. William Jewell Hawks; m. Katherine Marti, Sept. 11, 1965; children: Brian William, Kevin Marshall. AB, Oberlin Coll., Oberlin, Ohio, 1961; MA, Claremont Grad. Sch., Claremont, Calif., 1966. Cert. Special Secondary Credential in Music Edn. Calif., 1963. Instrumental music instr. Cucamonga Sch. Dist., Rancho Cucamonga, Calif., 1962—71, Alta Loma Sch. Dist., Rancho Cucamonga, Calif., 1963—2002. Clarinet and saxophone instr. Claremont Cmty. Sch. of Music, Claremont, Calif., 1968—95; prin. clarinetist West End Symphony Orch., Ontario, Calif., 1967—74; pres. San Bernardino County Music Educators Assn., San Bernardino, Calif., 1973—74; negotiations chmn. Alta Loma Educators Assn., Rancho Cucamonga, Calif., 1976—78, pres., 1978—80; manager-principal clarinetist Ea. Sierra Symphony Orch., Mammoth Lakes, Calif., 1983—. Musician: (songs) Clarinet Recital, 1988, 1993, 1999, 2004, (featured soloist)

Eastern Sierra Symphony Orch., 1985, Desert Cmty. Orch., 1985; conductor San Bernardino County Elem. Honor Band, Redlands, Calif., 1976, San Bernardino County Elem. Honor Band Ontario, Calif., 1991, San Bernardino County Honor Band Hesperia, 2005. Pres. Crystal Crag Water and Devel. Assn., Mammoth Lakes, Calif., 2003—05; fin. com. chmn. Claremont United Meth. Ch., Claremont, Calif., 1989—2002. Staff sgt. Air N.G., 1965—71, Ontario, Calif. Scholar Tuition, Oberlin Coll., 1957-1958. Mem.: Music Educators Nat. Conf., Internat. Clarinet Assn. (assoc.), Calif. Tchrs.Assn. (assoc.; regional coun. mem. 1978—80), Calif. Music Educators Assn. (assoc.). Democrat-Npl. United Meth. Avocations: backpacking, skiing. Home: 2068 N Palm Ave Upland CA 91784 Personal E-mail: whhawks@qnet.com.

HAWKS-JOHNSON, STEFANIE ANN, marine biologist, educator; b. Seattle, May 2, 1967; d. Harold Duffraine Sutherland (Stepfather), Gerald Wayne Hawks; m. Craig Alan Johnson, Mar. 21, 1997; children: Dylan Micheal Johnson, Danielle Katherine Johnson. BS in Biol. Oceanography, U. Wash., 1991, MS Animal Behavior with hons., 2003. Cert. trainer Am. Coun. Exercising, Calif., 2000. Intern Pacific Whale Found., Hervey Bay, Australia, 1991; naturalist Tandagusix Corp., St. Paul, Alaska, 1991; naturalist Beach Ranger Program City Edmonds, Wash., 1991—93; adminstr. marine programs King County Pks. and Recreation, Redmond, Wash., 1993—96; naturalist Mosquito Fleet Orca Whale Watch, Everett, Wash., 1994—97; programs adminstr. Adopt a Beach, Seattle, 1997—98; prin., owner Marine Mammal Connection Soc., North Bend, Wash., 1997—. Vol. Nat. Marine Fishery Svc., St. Paul, 1991, Marine Animal Resource Ctr., Seattle, 1992—93. Dir. N.W. Aquatic and Marine Educators, 1997—99. Grantee, Am. Cetacean Soc., 2001. Achievements include research in use of autonomous vessel for echosounder whale foraging research. Avocations: my children, yoga, exercise, scuba diving, snorkeling. Office Phone: 206-459-1398. Home Fax: 425-888-3174; Office Fax: 425-888-3174. Personal E-mail: sahawks@u.washington.edu.

HAWLEY, ANNE, museum director; b. Iowa City, Iowa, Nov. 3, 1943; d. Marshall Newton and Leone Ardith (Wilson) Hawley; m. Bruce Ivor McPherson, Sept. 4, 1977; 1 child, Katherine Black. BA, U. Iowa, 1966; MA, George Washington U., 1969; LHD (hon.), Lesley Coll, 1987; LHD (hon.), Williams Coll., 1989, Babson Coll., 1990, sr. exec. prog., Kennedy Sch. Govt, Harvard Univ., Intern in edn., Washington, 1967-69; research assoc. Nat. Urban League, Washington, 1969-71, Ford Found. Study Leadership in Pub. Edn., Washington, 1971-73; exec. dir. Cultural Edn. Collaborative, Boston, 1974-77, Mass. Council Arts/Humanities, Boston, 1977-89; mus. dir. Isabella Stewart Gardner Mus., Boston, 1989—; resident Nat. Hist. Soc. 1993—; adv. com. Nat. Trust of Historic Preservation, 1993—; vis. com. Fitchburg Art Mus., 1992-94. Bd. dirs. New Eng. Found. for Arts, 1978-89, Nat. Assembly/State Arts Agencies, Washington, 1981-83, Greater Boston Arts Fund, 1984-89, Boston Archtl. Found., 1986-89, Nat. Art Stabilization Fund, 1990-95, Boston Fenway Program, 1990-93. Trustee Inst. Contemporary Art, Boston, 1990—, Old Sturbridge Village, 1991-94; vis. comm. Sch. Mus. Fine Arts, Boston, 1989—, adv. bd. Mass. Coll. Art, 1979-81. Fulbright scholar, 1986; recipient Design Travel Grant, Women's Travel Club, Boston, Mass., 1982, Polaroid travel grant, 1987, Fund for Mutual Understanding travel grant to USSR, 1988, Art award Mass. Coll. Art, 1987, Lyman Ziegler award Commonwealth of Mass., 1988. Mem. Nat. Endowment for Arts (mus. panel 1978-81, task force on trng. and devel. of artists and art edu., 1978, dance panel 1982-84, design panel 1978-81, 88—, Pres. Clinton's transition team for arts and humanities, 1992-93), Boston Soc. Architecture (hon. mem. 1989); Radcliffe Alumnae Career Svcs. (adv. comm. 1974). Office: Isabella Stewart Gardner Mus 2 Palace Rd Boston MA 02115-5807*

HAWLEY, EDMUND S. (KIP HAWLEY), federal agency administrator; s. Edmund Blair and Greta (Crocker) H.; m. Janet Isak. AB, Brown U.; JD, U. Va., 1980; postgrad., Harvard U. Legis. asst. to Senator John Chafee U.S. Senate, Washington, 1977-78; assoc. Gaston, Snow and Ely Bartlett, Boston, 1980-81; dep. asst. sec. for govt. affairs US Dept. Transp., Washington, 1981-83; dep. asst. to the Pres. for intergovernmental affairs The White House, Washington; v.p. Union Pacific R.R.; asst. sec., Transp. Security Adminstrn. US Dept. Homeland Security, Washington, 2005—. Republican. Congregationalist. Office: US Dept Homeland Security E Bldg 601 S 12th St Arlington VA 22202*

HAWLEY, ELLIS WAYNE, historian, educator; b. Cambridge, Kans., June 2, 1929; s. Pearl Washington and Gladys Laura (Logsdon) H.; m. Sofia Koltun, Sept. 2, 1953; children— Arnold Jay, Agnes Fay. BA, U. Wichita, 1950; MA, U. Kans., 1951; PhD (research fellow), U. Wis., 1959. Instr. to prof. history North Tex. State U., 1957-68; prof. history Ohio State U., 1968-69, U. Iowa, 1969-94, prof. emeritus, 1994—, chmn. dept. history, 1986-89. Hist. cons. Pub. Papers of the Presidents: Hoover, 1974-78. Author: The New Deal and the Problem of Monopoly, 1966, The Great War and the Search for a Modern Order, 1979, (with others) Herbert Hoover and the Crisis of American Capitalism, 1973, Herbert Hoover as Secretary of Commerce, 1981, Federal Social Policy, 1988, Herbert Hoover and the Historians, 1989; contbr. articles to profl. jours., essays to books Investigator Project to Study Hist. in Iowa Pub. Schs., Iowa City, 1978-79; cons. Quad Cities hist. project Putnam Mus., Davenport, 1978-79. Served to 1st lt. inf. AUS, 1951-53 North Tex. State U. Faculty Devel. grantee, 1967-68, U. Iowa, 1975-76. Mem. Am. Hist. Assn., Orgn. Am. Historians, So. Hist. Assn., AAUP (mem. exec. coun. Iowa chapt. 1982-84), Iowa Hist. Soc. Democrat. Home: 2524 E Washington St Iowa City IA 52245-3724 Personal E-mail: e-hawley@worldnet.att.net.

HAWLEY, FRANK JORDAN, JR., venture capital executive; b. Roanoke Rapids, N.C., Oct. 3, 1927; s. Frank Jordan and Mary (Miller) H.; m. Alethea Wood, Sept. 12, 1959; children: Frank J. III, Mark R., Andrew D., Stuart W., Alethea S. BS in Physics, U. N.C., 1949; MBA, Harvard U., 1955. Rsch. analyst Eaton & Howard, Inc., Boston, 1955-59; banking assoc. Lazard Freres, N.Y.C., 1959-64; portfolio mgr. Stein, Roe & Farnham, N.Y.C., 1964-69; exec. v.p. Laidlaw Coggeshall, Inc., N.Y.C., 1969-74; gen. ptnr. Foster Mgmt. Co., N.Y.C., 1974-82; mng. ptnr. Saugatuck Capital Co., Stamford, Conn., 1982—. Chmn. bd. Floor & Decor. Inc., Atlanta; bd. dirs. Thorpe Corp., Statesville, NC. Chmn. bd. Waterloo Rest. Ventures, Inc., Vancouver, Oreg.; vice pres., treas. New Canaan (Conn.) YMCA, 1981-85; trustee Chocorua Chapel Assn., Squam Lake, N.H.; bd. visitors U. N.C., Chapel Hill, 1990-94; trustee Kenan Inst. Pvt. Enterprise of U. N.C. Lt. (j.g.) USN, 1950-53, Korea. Mem. Links Club, Harvard Club (N.Y.C.), New Canaan Country Club, Mill Reef Club (Antigua), Bald Peak Club (N.H.), Phi Beta Kappa. Republican. Episcopalian. Avocations: tennis, fly fishing, hunting. Office: Saugatuck Capital Co 1 Canterbury Grn Stamford CT 06901-2032

HAWLEY, HAROLD PATRICK, educational consultant; b. Paducah, Ky., Jan. 8, 1945; s. Mathew Mark and Mae (Herndon) H.; m. Ann Dunbar, 1971 (dec. 1982); Lucrecia Thomas, Aug. 27, 1983; children: Cherise, Charlotte. AA, Paducah Jr. Coll., 1965; BA, U. Ky., 1968; MS, Ind. U., New Albany, 1974; EdD, Ind. U., Bloomington, 1977; postgrad., Mary Baldwin Coll., 1988, Ala. A&M U., 1996. Liaison to adjutant gen. 5th army U.S. Army, Ft. Carson, 1970, Bien Hoa, Vietnam, 1969-70; diversity rschr. (with Christine Bennett) Indpls. Pub. Sch., 1977; English tchr. Southwestern Consol. Schs., Hanover, Ind., 1971-73; asst. prin. Whitewater Consol. Sch., Lyons, Ind., 1978-80; assoc. prof., dir. secondary edn. Birmingham (Ala.)-So. Coll., 1980-86, chmn. freshman seminar, 1984-86; 1988-95 Ga. Dept. Edn., Atlanta, 1988-95; evaluator So. Assn. Schs. and Colls., 1988—; ednl. cons. Ga. Dept. Edn., Atlanta, 1988-95; chmn. Effective Sch. Rsch. Program, 1991; asst. prof. elem. edn. program Ala. A&M U., 2000—01, asst. prof. secondary edn. and multicultural edn., 2001—, advisor svc. frat., 2003; dir. Harlem Renaissance Project, Lee H.S., 2003. Adj. prof. Ind. U., Bloomington, 1975-80, Samford U., 1980-84, Auburn U., 1987, U. Ala., Gadsen, 1984-85, Brenau U., Gainesville, Ga., 1988-96, Reinhardt Coll./Brenau Coll. Collaboration, 1995—; adj. prof. Ala. A&M U., 1999, univ. supr., 1996—; cons. Intervarsity Beach Project, 1982—, Ford Ednl. Found., Parker H.S., Birmingham, Ala., 1981-85, Christian Acad., Cornerstone, Baton Rouge, 1983-84, FCA, 1983, Happy Valley Elem., Fairview Elem. Schoolwide Project, 1995, Walker County Curriculum Specialist, 1995-96, Nicholas Soc., 1997—; tech. advisor Polk County Schoolwide Projects, 1995, Floyd County Schoolwide Project, 1995—, Dade County Schoolwide Project, 1996; ednl. cons. Ga. Dept. Edn., Atlanta, 1988-95, Attention Deficit Disorder/HD, 1995—, Effective Schs. Rsch./Authentic Ins.; coord. 9th Dist. Schs. of Excellence, Ga., 1988-92; team leader sch. improvement teams Ga. Dept. Edn., Calhoun, 1995; dir. 1st State Remedial Edn. Conf., Lafayette, Ga., 1994, 1st statewide instrnl. conf. ESEA, 1995-96, Title I Northwest Ga. Instrnl. Conf., 1996, Lone Oak Edn. Svcs. 1999—; 1983-86; student tchr. supr. Covenant Coll., Chattanooga, 1996—; rsch. asst. North Ala. Tchr. Exch., Normal, 2000—; frequent presenter in field. Author: (with Don Manlove) Classroom Climate Teacher-Student Relations, Expectancy Effects, 1976; rsch. asst. (with Floyd Coppedge) Binford Middle School Project, Bloomington, Ind., 1976, Individual Instrn. Project, 1975, Lebanon High Sch. Project, 1975-76, Katherine Hamilton Rsch. Project, New Albany, Ind., 1974 (with Carol Lewis). Bd. dirs. Boys Club Am., Paducah, 1963-65; tech. adv. Polk County Consol. Schs., 1995-96, Dade County Consol. Schs., 1995. Basketball scholar, 1965, attention deficit rsch. scholar univ. supr., Ala. A&M U., 1997—; Spenser grantee, 1981, Mellon grantee, 1985; grad fellow Okla. State Sch. Supt.,1975-77, Nat. Study Sch. Evaluation fellow Ind. U., 1977. Mem. Ga. Com. Leaders Assn., Internat. Platform Assn., Phi Delta Kappa. Achievements include music and brain research. Avocations: jogging, basketball, camping. Home: 117 Darlington Rd NE Huntsville AL 35801-1513 Office Phone: 256-539-1243, 256-539-1243. E-mail: phawley@aamu.edu.

HAWLEY, JOSEPH. B., property management executive, educator; b. Red Bank, N.J., May 1, 1963; s. Bart J. and Genevieve M. Hawley. BA, Kean Coll. N.J., 1986; MA, Rutgers U., 1989, PhD, 1998. V.p. Bay Haven Property Mgmt., Atlantic Highlands, NJ, 1985—. Founding mem. Kean U. Peace Edn. Resource Ctr., trustee, 1986—90; pres. Genevieve M. Hawley Meml. Found., 2002—; chmn. Atlantic Highlands Dem. Exec. Com., 1990—92, 1996—; mem. Atlantic Highlands Planning Bd., N.J. Dem. State Com., Trenton, 1994—, Henry Hudson Regional Bd. Edn., Highlands, NJ, 1986, Atlantic Highlands Bd. Edn.; pres. Kean U. Class of 1986, 1985—86, Kean U. Student Orgn., Inc., 1984—85. Mem. Kiwanis (pres. Phila. chpt. 1989-90), Phi Alpha Theta. Roman Catholic. Avocations: long distance running, weightlifting. Home: 25 Ocean Blvd Atlantic Highlands NJ 07716 Office: Bay Haven Property Mgmt 25 Ocean Blvd Atlantic Highlands NJ 07716 Office Phone: 732-291-2962.

HAWLEY, KIMRA, software company executive; BS in Psychology, Pitts. State U. Founding prin. MarketBound, Inc., Silicon Valley, Calif.; various mktg. mgmt. positions Amdahl Corp.; imaging mktg. dir. Action Point Software (formerly Cornerstone Imaging), 1992-96, gen. mgr. software divsn., pres., CEO, chmn. bd., 2001—04; interim CEO, pres. iUniverse, Inc., 2004, bd. dirs., 2005—. Office: iUniverse Inc 2021 Pine Lake Rd Ste 100 Lincoln NE 68512 Office Phone: 402-323-7800. Office Fax: 402-323-7824.*

HAWLEY, LUCRETIA MARLENE, retired accounting educator; b. Stillwater, Okla., Nov. 19, 1932; d. Owen Hartman Schneider and Maudee Dessie (Callicoat) Bearg; m. Robert Paul Hawley, Nov. 27, 1955; children: James Owen, Kathleen Francis Jeschke, John Robert. BS in Econs., BSBA in Acctg., Ctrl. Mo. State U., 1955, MA in Acctg., 1970. CPA, cert. mgmt. acct. Payroll clk. Westinghouse, Kansas City, Mo., 1951; internal auditor Spencer Chem., Kansas City, 1955-56; bus. skills and Am. history tchr. J.C. Penney H.S., Hamilton, Mo., 1965-67; bus. skills and speech tchr. Breckenridge (Mo.) H.S., 1967-70; bus. skills and acctg. tchr. various bus. schs., 1972-77; instr., asst. prof. acctg. Mo. Western State Coll., St. Joseph, Mo., 1970-71, 77-95; ret., 1995. Mem. acad. computing com. Mo. Western State Coll., St. Joseph, 1988-95. Co-pastor, treas. Cmty. of Christ Ch. Mem. Inst. Mgmt. Accts. (bd. dirs., CMA dir., student dir.), Sr. Citizens Found. (treas., bd. dirs. 1980-95), Gen. Fedn. Women's Clubs Monday Club (pres.), Phi Delta Kappa, Delta Kappa Gamma (v.p. 1994-96, pres. 1996-98). Republican. Avocations: reading, travel, sewing, crafts, church work. Home: 1004 S Hughes Hamilton MO 64644

HAWLEY, NANCI ELIZABETH, association administrator; b. Detroit, Mar. 18, 1942; d. Arthur Theodore and Elizabeth Agnes (Fylling) Smisek; m. Joseph Michael Hawley, Aug. 28, 1958; children: Michael, Ronald, Patrick (dec.), Julie Anne. Pres. Tempo 21 Nursing Svcs., Inc., Covina, Calif., 1973-75; v.p. Profl. Nurses Bur., Inc., L.A., 1975-83; owner, CEO Hawley & Assocs., Covina, 1983-87; exec. v.p. Glendora (Calif.) C. of C., 1984-85; dir. membership West Covina (Calif.) C. of C., 1985-87; exec. dir. San Dimas (Calif.) C. of C., 1987-88; mgr. pub. rels. Soc. for Advancement of Material and Process Engrs., Covina, 1988-92; small bus. rep. South Coast Air Quality Mgmt. Dist., 1992-94; bus. counselor Commerce and Trade Agy., Small Bus. Devel. Ctr., 1994; exec. v.p. Ontario (Calif.) C. of C., 1994-97; CEO, RMH Elec. Contractors, Colorado Springs, Colo., 1997-98; exec. v.p. Teen Resources, Inc., Colorado Springs, 1998; meetings mgr., registrar Am. Birding Assn., Colorado Springs, 1999—. V.p. Sangabriel valley chpt. Women in Mgmt. Recipient Youth Motivation award Foothill Edn. Com., Glendora, 1987. Mem. NAFE, Colo. Assn. Nonprofit Orgns., Pub. Rels. Soc. Am., Soc. Nat. Assn. Publs., Am. Soc. Assn. Execs., Nat. Assn. Membership Dirs., Profl. Communicators Assn. So. Calif., Profl. Conf. Mgrs. Assn., West End Bus. Assn. (pres. 1997-99), Western Assn. Chamber Execs. (Spl. merit award for mag. pub. 1995), Profl. Conv. Mgrs. Assn., Kiwanis (sec. 1989-90, pres. West Covina 1990-91, Kiwanian of Yr. 1989), Rotary. Avocations: reading, walking, painting, gardening, birdwatching. Office: PO Box 6599 Colorado Springs CO 80934-6599 Office Phone: 800-850-2473 233. Personal E-mail: nanmick58@aol.com. Business E-Mail: nhawley@aba.org.

HAWLEY, PHILIP METSCHAN, retired retail executive, management consultant; b. Portland, Oreg., July 29, 1925; s. Willard P. and Dorothy (Metschan) H.; m. Mary Catherine Follen, May 31, 1947; children: Diane (Mrs. Robert Bruce Johnson), Willard, Philip Metschan Jr., John, Victor, Edward, Erin (Mrs. Kevin Przybocki), George. BS, U. Calif., Berkeley, 1946; grad. advanced mgmt. program, Harvard U., 1967. With Carter Hawley Hale Stores, Inc., L.A., 1958-93, pres., 1972-83, chief exec. officer, 1977-93, chmn., 1983-93. Bd. dirs. Weyerhaeuser Co. Trustee Calif. Inst. Tech., U. Notre Dame; chmn. L.A. Energy Conservation Com., 1973-74. Decorated hon. comdr. Order Brit. Empire, knight comdr. Star Solidarity Republic Italy; recipient Award of Merit L.A. Jr. C. of C., 1974, Coro Pub. Affairs award, 1978, Medallion award Coll. William and Mary, 1983, Award of Excellence Sch. Bus. Adminstrn. U. So. Calif., 1987, Bus. Statesman of Yr. award Harvard Bus. Sch., 1989, 15th ann. Whitney M. Young Jr. award L.S. Urban League, 1988; named Calif. Industrialist of Yr. Calif. Mus. Sci. and Industry, 1975. Mem. Calif. Retailers Assn. (chmn. 1993-95, dir.), Beach Club, Calif. Club, L.A. Country Club, Bohemian Club, Pacific-Union Club, Newport Harbor Yacht Club, Multnomah Club, Links Club, Phi Beta Kappa, Beta Alpha Psi, Beta Gamma Sigma. Office: 800 W 6th St Ste 920 Los Angeles CA 90017

HAWLEY, PHILLIP EUGENE, investment banker; b. Tecumseh, Mich., Dec. 9, 1940; s. Paul P. and Vadah Arlene (Lawhead) H.; m. Linda Darlene Miller, Feb. 14, 1957; children: Pierre Lee, Paul Marvin, Danny Parke, David Eugene, Martin Edward. Student in mgmt., Yale U., 1959-63; BSBA, Northwestern Coll., Tulsa, 1980. With Credit Bur. Ft. Myers (Fla.), Inc., 1956—; chmn. bd. dirs., regional mgr. Credit Bur. Internat. Corp., Ft. Myers, 1993—; pvt. investigator Transworld Investigators, Inc., 1964, now v.p.; mgr., founder real estate co. Gold Coast Devel. Corp., 1965, pres., Phillip Hawley Investment Banking Co. Bd. dirs. Caribbean Industries Internat. Corp., Future Investment Corp. Author: Law and It's Alternative to Chaos, 1958, The Happiest Man in the World, 1970, The Best Buys in Fort Myers, 1982. Named Outstanding Individual, Fla. Fedn. Young Reps., 1971; recipient Presdl. Sports award, 1979. Mem. Am. Collectors Assn. (scholar degree Collection Bus. Acad. 1994, fellow degree 1996), Fla. Collectors Assn. (Outstanding Spkr. 1967), Assn. Credit Burs. Am., Med.-Dental Hosp. Burs. Am., Fla. Assn. Mortgage Brokers, Fla. Assn. Pvt. Investigators, Am. Numismatic Assn., Gideons Internat., Collier-Lee Wrestling Assn. (co-founder, bd. dirs. 1974—). Mem. Nazarene Ch. Home: 6535 Winkler Rd Fort Myers FL 33919-8167 Office: Internat Collection Svc Inc 255 Tamiami Trl S Nokomis FL 34275-3136 E-mail: philhawley@earthlink.net.

HAWLEY, RAYMOND GLEN, pathologist; b. Cambridge, Kans., Jan. 13, 1939; s. Pearl Washington and Gladys Laura (Logsdon) H.; m. Phyllis Ann Williams, Aug. 25, 1963; children: Bradford, Anthony, Douglas. BS, Kans. State U., 1961; MD, U. Kans., 1965. Intern Wesley Med. Ctr., Wichita, 1965-66; pathology resident Riverside Meth. Hosp., Columbus, Ohio, 1966-70; pathologist St. Joseph Hosp., Concordia, Kans., 1973-75, St. Joseph Med. Ctr., Wichita, 1975—82, Via Christi Regional Med. Ctr., Wichita, 1983—2000; with Coffeyville (Kans.) Regional Med. Ctr., 2000—, chief of staff, 2004. Maj. U.S. Army, 1970-73. Fellow Am. Coll. Pathologists; mem. AMA, Am. Soc. Clin. Pathologists, Kans. Soc. Pathology (sec.-treas. 1989-99, pres. 2004—). Home: 512 Spruce St Coffeyville KS 67337-4834 E-mail: rhawley@cox.net.

HAWLEY, RICHARD L., utilities executive; BBA, U. Wash. With PricewaterhouseCoopers LLP, 1973—98; CFO Puget Energy Inc., Bellevue, Wash., 1998—2002; exec. v.p. Nicor Inc., Naperville, Ill., 2003, CFO, 2003—; exec. v.p. Nicor Gas, Naperville, 2003—, CFO, 2003—. Office: Nicor Inc 1844 Ferry Rd Naperville IL 60563

HAWLEY, RODDICK, writer, editor; d. Harrison Arnold Roddick and Mary Elizabeth Henrici; 1 child, Luke Harrison Meade. BA, Wellesley Coll., 1958. Exec. dir. BoehmGroup, Inc., Santa Barbara, Calif., 2002—. Cons., trainer, editor, writer Hawley Roddick, Santa Barbara, 1968—. Author: (nonfiction) Young Filmmakers, 1967 (named one of 15 best books for young adults, N.Y. Pub. Libr., 1969), Business Writing Makeovers, 2002, (novels) Together, 1981, Holding Patterns, 1999. Founding mem. Seal Watch, Jenner, Calif., 1982—84, N.Mex. Green Party, Santa Fe. Mem.: Authors Guild, PEN Internat. (founding mem. N.Mex. chpt. 1996—97), Wellesley Club. Office: Hawley Roddick PO Box 3794 Santa Barbara CA 93130 Office Phone: 805-682-6366. Personal E-mail: hroddick@hawleyroddick.com.

HAWLEY, SANDRA SUE, electrical engineer; b. Spirit Lake, Iowa, May 7, 1948; d. Byrnard Leroy and Dorothy Virginia (Fischbeck) Smith; m. Michael John Hawley, June 7, 1970; 1 child, Alexander Tristin. BSEE, U. Dayton, 1981; BS in Math. and Stats., Iowa State U., 1970; MS in Stats., U. Del., 1975. Rsch. analyst State of Wis., Madison, 1970-71; rsch. asst. Del. State Coll., Dover, 1972-73; asst. prof. math. and statis. Wesley Coll., Dover, 1974-81, chmn. dept. math. and computer sci., 1978-80; elec. engr. Control Data Corp., Bloomington, Minn., 1982-85; sr. elec. engr. Custom integrated Circuits, 1985-89; sr. lead engr. Cardiac Pacemakers, Inc., 1989-90; mgr. Tech. Rosemount Inc., 1990-94; prin. cons. Tri-Ess, Mpls., 1994—. Contbr. articles to profl. jours. Elder Presbyn. Ch. U.S.A., 1975—, mem. session Oak Grove Presbyn. Ch., Bloomington, 1985-88; moderator Presbytery of Twin Cities Area, 1996, chair Presbytery Coun., 1994, chair Coun. United Action, 1989-92, adminstrv. comm., 1989-91, chair com. on ministry, 1998—, commr. to Synod of Lakes & Prairies, 1990, Gen. Assembly Coun., 1992-98, com. on coun., 1992, commr. Gen. Assembly, 1991, chair Nat. Ministries divsn. Gen. Assembly, 1992-98; bd. dirs. Presbyn. Investment and Loan Program, gen. assembly coun. ch. growth strategy team, 1997-99, mem. steering com. churchwide transformation, 2003—; coun. advisors Dubuque Theol. Sem., 1999—; bd. dirs. Presbyn. Homes of Minn., 2002-. NSF scholar U. Dayton, 1981. Mem. IEEE, Soc. Women Engrs. Office: Tri-Ess 7724 W 85th St Minneapolis MN 55438-1382

HAWN, GOLDIE, actress; b. Washington, Nov. 21, 1945; d. Edward Rutledge and Laura (Steinhoff) H.; m. Gus Trinkonis, May 16, 1969 (div. 1976); m. Bill Hudson 1976 (div. 1979); children: Oliver, Kate; 1 child (with Kurt Russell), Wyatt Russell. Student, Am. U.; D (hon.), Loyola Marymount Univ., 2004. Co-head (with Kurt Russell, Kate Hudson, Oliver Hudson) Cosmic Entertainment, 2003—. Profl. dancer, 1965; profl. acting debut in Good Morning, World, 1967-68; mem. company TV series Laugh-In, 1968-70; films include: The One and Only Genuine Original Family Band, 1968, Cactus Flower, 1969 (Acad. award best sup. actress, 1969, Golden Globe best sup. actress, 1969), There's A Girl In My Soup, 1970, $ (Dollars), 1971, Butterflies Are Free, 1971, The Sugarland Express, 1974, The Girl from Petrovka, 1974, Shampoo, 1975, The Duchess and the Dirtwater Fox, 1976, Travels with Anita, 1978, Foul Play, 1978, Seems Like Old Times, 1980, Lovers and Liars, 1981, Best Friends, 1982, Swingshift, 1984, Overboard, 1987, Bird on a Wire, 1989, Deceived, 1991, Housesitter, 1992, Death Becomes Her, 1992, Crisscross, 1992, The First Wives Club, 1996, Everyone Says I Love You, 1996, The Out of Towners, 1999, Town and Country, 1999, The Banger Sisters, 2002; exec. producer, actor Private Benjamin, 1980, Protocol, 1984, Wildcats, 1986; exec. prodr. My Blue Heaven, 1990, Something to Talk About, 1995 (TV films) When Billie Beat Bobby, 1991, The Matthew Shepard Story, 2002; exec. prodr., dir. (TV films) Hope, 1997; host TV spl. Pure Goldie, 1970, Goldie Hawn Special, 1978, Goldie and Liza Together, 1980, Goldie and Kids: Listen to Us!, 1982; author: (memoir) A Lotus Grows in the Mud, 2005 (NY Times Bestseller list, 2005). Named Woman of the Year, Hasty Pudding Theatricals, 1999; recipient Women in Film Crystal award, 1997. Office: Cosmic Entertainment 350 Park Ave New York NY 10022 also: Cosmic Entertainment 18th Fl 1888 Century Pk E Los Angeles CA 90067

HAWORTH, CHARLES RAY, lawyer; b. Little Rock, June 23, 1943; s. Clarence Frederick and Vinita Leona (Bowers) H.; m. Nancy Anne Patterson, Aug. 16, 1970; 1 child, Alan. BA, U. Tex., 1965, JD, 1967. Bar: Tex. 1967, U.S. Dist. Ct. (no. dist.) Tex. 1968, U.S. Dist. Ct. (we. and so. dists.) Tex. 1988, U.S. Dist. Ct. (ea. dist.) Tex. 1989, U.S. Ct. Appeals (5th cir.) 1968, U.S. Ct. Appeals (11th cir.) 1982, U.S. Supreme Ct. 1971; bd. cert. civil trial law Tex. Bd. Legal Specialization. Law clk. U.S. Ct. Appeals (5th cir.), Houston, 1967-68; assoc. Coke & Coke, Dallas, 1968-71; prof. law Washington U. Sch. Law, St. Louis, 1971-79; ptnr. Johnson & Gibbs, Dallas, 1979-85, Andrews & Kurth, Dallas, 1985-92; mng. ptnr. Scott, Douglass, Luton & McConnico, L.L.P., Dallas, 1992-95; ptnr. Owens, Clary & Aiken, L.L.P., Dallas, 1995—. Vis. prof. U. Va. Sch. Law, Charlottesville, 1975-76, U. Tex. Sch. Law, Austin, 1977; cons. Dept. Justice, Washington, 1978. Editor: Congress and the Courts, 1977; contbr. numerous articles to profl. jours. Bd. dirs. Dallas Opera, 1991—2000. Grantee Dept. of Justice, 1978; named Tex. Super Lawyer Tex. Monthly, 2003, 04, 05. Mem.: Dallas Bar Assn. (chair bus. litigation sect. 2002), Tex. Bar Assn. Republican. Avocation: fishing. Office: Owens Clary & Aiken LLP 700 N Pearl St Ste 1600 Dallas TX 75201 Office Phone: 214-698-2113. Personal E-mail: chaworth@flash.net.

HAWORTH, DANIEL THOMAS, chemistry professor; b. Fond du Lac, Wis., June 27, 1928; s. Arthur Valentine and Mary Lena (Wattawa) H.; m. Mary Hormuth, Dec. 27, 1952; children: Daniel G., M. Judith, Steven T. BS, U. Wis., Oshkosh, 1950; MS, Marquette U., 1952; PhD, St. Louis U., 1959. Nuclear chemist Bur. of Ships, Washington, 1952-53; rsch. chemist All-Chalmer Mfg. Co., Milw., 1958-60; instr. chemistry Marquette U., Milw., 1955, from asst. prof. to assoc. prof., 1960-68, prof., 1968—. Vis. prof. chemistry U. Wis.-Milw., 2001—02. Contbr. numerous articles to profl. jours.; patentee in field. Served as cpl. U.S. Army, 1953-55. Recipient Pere Marquette award for tchg. excellence Marquette U., 1971, Nicolos Salgo Outstanding Tchr. award, 1971. Mem. Am. Chem. Soc. (emeritus), N.Y. Acad. Scis., Wis. Acad. Arts/Scis./Letters, Sigma Xi (emeritus). Roman Catholic. Avocation: stamp collecting/philately. Home: 3483 N Frederick Ave Milwaukee WI 53211-2902 Office: Marquette Univ Dept Chemistry PO Box 1881 Milwaukee WI 53201-1881 Office Phone: 414-288-3534. Business E-Mail: daniel.haworth@marquette.edu.

HAWORTH, GERRARD WENDELL, office furniture manufacturing company executive; b. Alliance, Nebr., Oct. 9, 1911; s. Elmer R. and Lulu (Jones) H.; m. Dorcas A. Snyder, June 22, 1938 (dec.); children: Lois, Richard, Joan, Mary, Julie; m. 2d Edna Mae Van Tatenhove, Feb. 3, 1979. AB, Western

Mich. U., 1937; MA, U. Mich., 1940. Tchr. Holland High Sch., Mich., 1937-48; founding chmn. Haworth Inc., Holland, Mich., 1948—. Office: Haworth Inc 1 Haworth Ctr Holland MI 49423-9576

HAWORTH, JAMES CHILTON, pediatrics educator; b. Gosforth, Eng., May 29, 1923; emigrated to Can., 1957, naturalized, 1972; s. Walter Norman and Violet Chilton (Dobbie) H.; m. Eleanor Marian Bowser, Oct. 18, 1951; children— Elizabeth Marian, Peter Norman James, Margaret Jean, Anne Ruth. M.B., Ch.B, U. Birmingham, Eng., 1945, MD, 1960. House physician Birmingham Gen. and Children's Hosps., 1946-47; fellow Cin. Children's Hosp., 1949-50; house physician Hosp. for Sick Children, London, 1951; pediatric registrar Alder Hey Children's Hosp., Liverpool, Eng., 1951-52; sr. registrar Sheffield Children's Hosp., 1953-57; pediatrician Winnipeg (Man., Can.) Clinic, 1957-65; asst. prof. dept. pediat. U. Man., Winnipeg, 1965-67, assoc. prof., 1967-70, prof., 1970-94, head dept. pediat., 1979-85, senate mem., 1985-90, prof. human genetics, 1987-94, prof. emeritus, 1994—, sr. scholar dept. biochemistry and med. genetics, 1999—. Mem. active staff Health Scis. Centre-Children's, 1957-93; cons. staff St. Boniface Hosp., 1974-93; hon. staff Health Sci. Ctr., 1993—. Contbr. articles to profl. jours. Bd. dirs. Man. Med. Svc. found., 1988—, exec. dir., 1995-2004. Served with Royal Naval Vol. Res., 1947-49. Fellow Royal Coll. Physicians (Can., London), Can. Coll. Med. Geneticists (hon.); mem. Can. Soc. Clin. Investigation, Am. Pediatric Soc., Soc. Pediatric Rsch., Can. Pediatric Soc. Home: 301 Victoria Crescent Winnipeg MB Canada R2M 1X8 Office: Childrens Hosp Dept Pediatrics 678 William Ave Winnipeg MB Canada R3E 0W1

HAWORTH, JANICE L., music educator; b. Corpus Christi, Tex., Sept. 17, 1959; d. Alvin G. and Betty E. Haworth. MusB, Carson-Newman Coll., 1980; MusM, U. Tenn., 1981; PhD in Music Edn., U. Fla., 1995. Asst. prof. U. Ctrl. Ark., Conway, Ark., 1995—97, Ga. State U., Atlanta, 1997—2000, Bemidji State U., Minn., 2000—. Mem.: Am. Choral Directors Assn., Nat. Assn. for Year-Round Edn., Minn. Soc. of Music Tchr. Edn. (sec., treas. 2003—05), Minn. Music Educators Assn., Music Educators Nat. Conf. Office: Bemidji State Univ 1500 Birchmont Ave NE Bemidji MN 56601-2699 Office Phone: 218-755-3361. Office Fax: 218-755-4369. E-mail: jhaworth@bemidjistate.edu.

HAWORTH, LAWRENCE LINDLEY, philosophy educator; b. Chgo., Dec. 14, 1926; s. Lawrence Lindley and Ruth Ethyl (Johnson) H.; children: Lawrence Lindley III, Ruth Ellis. BA with highest distinction, Rollins Coll., 1949; MA, U. Ill., 1950, PhD (Univ. fellow), 1952. Asst. prof. U. Ala., 1952-54, asst. dean, 1953-54; asst. prof. Purdue U., 1954-59, assoc. prof., 1959-65; prof. philosophy U. Waterloo, Ont., Can., 1965-96, disting. prof. emeritus, 1996—, dir. Ctr. for Soc., Tech. and Values, 1984-86, chmn. dept. philosophy, asso. dean grad. studies, assoc. dean computing and rsch., 1967-70, 88-89. Author: The Good City, 1963, Decadence and Objectivity, 1977, Autonomy, 1986, Value Assumptions in Risk Assessment, 1991, A Textured Life: Empowerment and Adults with Developmental Disabilities, 1999; contbr. articles to profl. jours. Served with AUS, 1945-46. Purdue U. rsch. fellow, 1956, 59, 64; U. Waterloo rsch. fellow, 1967, 68, 69, 70; Can. Coun. leave fellow, 1971-72; Can. Coun. rsch. grantee, 1973-75, 81-83, 85-87, Social Sci. and Humanities Rsch. Coun. leave fellow, 1985-86, rsch. grantee 1981-84, 85-87, 91—. Fellow Royal Soc. Can.; mem. Canadian Philos. Assn., Phi Beta Kappa. Office: U Waterloo Dept Philosophy Waterloo ON Canada N2L 3G1 Office Phone: 519-888-1211. Personal E-mail: lhaworth@uwaterloo.ca.

HAWORTH, MICHAEL ELLIOTT, JR., aerospace company executive; b. Pitts., Dec. 18, 1928; s. Michael E. and Margarett (Thomas) H.; m. Elizabeth Jean Evans, Dec. 20, 1949; children: Michael Elliott III, Jean Evans. Student, U. Ala., 1946-50; BS, Samford U., 1958. Gen. mgr. Haworth Engring. & Mfg. Co., Birmingham, Ala., 1954-56; chief contract negotiator U.S. Army Ordnance, Birmingham, 1956-61; dir. procurement Kennedy Space Center NASA, 1961-67; v.p., sec. Hayes Internat. Corp., Birmingham, 1967-86, pres., chief exec. officer, 1986-88, also bd. dirs.; pvt. investor, 1989-99. Life mem. Bapt. Med. Ctr.-Montclair Aux. With Q.M. Corps, U.S. Army, 1952-54. Mem. Am. Def. Indsl. Assn. (life, chpt. pres. 1969-71, 82-85), Nat. Aerospace Svcs. Assn. (dir. 1971-74, chmn. 1972-73), Coun. Def. and Space Industry Assns. (vice chmn. 1973-74, chmn. 1974-75), Nat. Contract Mgmt. Assn. (bd. dirs. Birmingham area chpt. 1976-78, lifetime cert. profl. contracts mgr.), Birmingham Urban League (dir. 1971-75), Phi Gamma Delta, Country Club of Birmingham, The Club. Home: 4805 Mill Springs Cir Birmingham AL 35223-1682 Personal E-mail: melliotth@bellsouth.net.

HAWORTH, RANDAL DIGBY, plastic surgeon; b. L.A., Sept. 19, 1961; s. William and Annalise Haworth. BA in Biology, BA in Chemistry, U. Calif., Santa Cruz, 1982; MD, U. So. Calif., L.A., 1988. Diplomate bd. cert. Am. Bd. Plastic Surgeons. Resident gen. surgery Cornell N.Y. Hosp., 1988—93; fellow plastic surgery UCLA Med. Ctr., 1993—95; pvt. practice Beverly Hills, Calif., 1995—. Contbr. sci. articles to profl. jours.; contbg. editor: Fitness Mag., Swan Mag. Bd. dirs. Sheba Med. Ctr.; Mem. Pres.'s Cir. The Thalians, Cedars Sinai Med. Ctr., 1999—; Mem. L.A. Mus. Art, Mus. Contempory Art, L.A. Named one of Best Surgeons in Am., Rsch. Coun. Am. Mem.: Am. Soc. Plastic Surgeons, Alpha Omega Alpha. Avocations: art, music, skiing. Office: Ste 105 436 N Bedford Dr Beverly Hills CA 90210 Office Phone: 310-273-3000.

HAWPE, DAVID VAUGHN, newspaper editor, journalist; b. Pikeville, Ky., Feb. 4, 1943; s. Chester and Betty Frances (Fletcher) H.; m. Linda Shadoin, Aug. 13, 1966; children: Christopher Fidler, Jonathan Bragdon. AB in Journalism, U. Ky., 1965; postgrad. (Nieman fellow), Harvard U., 1974-75. Reporter, editor AP, Lexington and Louisville, 1965-67; editorial writer St. Petersburg Times, Fla., 1967-69; various positions Courier-Jour., Louisville, 1969-78, mng. editor, 1979-87, editor, 1987-96, edit. dir., 1996—; city editor Louisville Times, 1978-79; tchr. Appalachian studies Harvard U., spring 1975; tchr. Appalachian studies and journalism U. Louisville, U. Ky. Served with USAR, 1966-73. Named to Ky. Journalism Hall of Fame, 1994, U. Ky. Hall Disting. Alumni, 1995. Mem. Am. Soc. Newspaper Editors, AP Mng. Editors (pres. 1997-98), Ky. Press Assn. (pres. 1990, 96-97). Democrat. Presbyterian. Office: Courier-Jour Co 525 W Broadway St Louisville KY 40202-2206 Home: 507 Penwood Rd Louisville KY 40206-3031 Office Phone: 502-582-4613. Business E-Mail: dhawpe@courier-journal.com.

HAWRYLUK, RICHARD JANUSZ, physicist; b. Mansfield, Eng., June 7, 1950; came to U.S., 1952; s. Michal and Jozefa H.; m. Mary Katherine McMahon, Feb. 7, 1976; children: David, Kevin. BS, MS, MIT, 1972, PhD, 1974. Dep. dir. Princeton Plasma Physics Lab., 1974—. Cons. Lincoln Lab., Lexington, Mass., 1970-74, 79. Contbr. over 100 articles to profl. jours. and conf. proceedings. Recipient Disting. Assoc. award Dept. of Energy, 1995, Kaul Found. prize for excellence in plasma physics rsch. and technology, 1996. Fellow Am. Phys. Soc. (Excellence in Plasma Physics award 1988). Achievements include research on heating and confinement of Tokamak plasmas and electron beam lithography. Office: Princeton Plasma Physic Lab PO Box 451 Princeton NJ 08544-0451 E-mail: rhawryluk@pppl.gov.

HAWS, ELIZABETH ANNE, psychologist, director; b. Willingboro, N.J., Mar. 30, 1970; d. William Joseph and Mary Ruth (Datko) Haws. BA in Edn. of the Handicapped, Kean U., 1992; MA in Sch. Psychology, Rowan U., 1998, supr. curriculum and instrn., 2000, EdS, 2001, EdD in Ednl. Leadership, 2005. Spl. edn. tchr. Willingboro Bd. Edn., 1992—98, peer mediation supr., 1994—95, peer mediation coord., 1996—98, sch. psychologist, 1998—2000; supr. Union County ESC, Westfield, NJ, 2000—03; dir. special svcs. Eastampton (N.J.) Bd. Edn., 2003—. Mem. crisis response team Burlington County Sch.; mem. Burlington County Red Cross Disaster Relief Team. Mem.: NASP, N.J. Prin. and Supr. Assn., N.J. Assn. Sch. Psychologists, Coun. Exceptional Children (chpt. 461 programming com. 1988—89, pres. 1989—91, treas. 1991—92), Profl. Assn. Dive Instructors, Cara Irish Soc., Alpha Epsilon Lambda, Sigma Beta Chi. Republican. Roman Catholic. Avocations: writing, bicycling, walking, travel, collecting catchy quotations. Home: 202 E Union St Burlington NJ 08016 Personal E-mail: lizhaws@aol.com.

HAWS, HALE LOUIS, medical association administrator, consultant; b. Anaheim, Calif., June 15, 1923; s. Lloyd Albert and Nancy Jean (Hale) H.; m. JoAn Penn Haws; children: Kathleen Seghieri, Jay B., Jerald L. BA, Pepperdine Coll., 1947; MD, UCLA, 1958. Diplomate Med. Bd. Calif., Am. Bd. Preventive Medicine, Bd. Life Ins. Medicine. Intern Gorgas Hosp., Canal Zone, 1958-59; pvt. practice L.A., 1959-60; plant med. dir. Chrysler Corp., Commerce, Calif., 1960-71; physician, surgeon Narcotic Control, Dept. Corrections, L.A., 1961-75; v.p. med. svcs. Pacific Mut. Life Ins. Co., Newport Beach, Calif., 1962-81; consulting med. dir. Calif., 1981—. Dir. Best Life Assurance Co. of Calif., Irvine, 1981-97; med. adv. bd. Equifax Svcs., Inc., Atlanta, 1977-81; spkr. in field. Mem. Church of Christ. Recipient Cert. of Appreciation, Selective Svc. Sys., 1975; scholar Kaiser Family Found., 1957. Fellow Am. Coll. Preventive Medicine, Am. Coll. Angiology, Am. Coll. Occupl. and Environ. Medicine, Am. Geriatrics Soc.; mem. Am. Acad. Ins. Medicine, Am. Coun. Life Ins., Calif. Scholastic Soc. (life), Pepperdine Alumni Assn. (dir. 1968-70). Avocations: art collecting, classic/antique autos, continuing medical education, reading, gardening. Home: 5268 Royal Canyon Ln Paradise CA 95969-6683 E-mail: hale@dcsi.net.

HAWTHORNE, BRUCE N., lawyer, telecommunications industry executive; b. Dearborn, Mich., Sept. 21, 1949; BBA with distinction, U. Mich., 1971; MBA, U. Detroit, 1972; JD, Vanderbilt U., 1975. Bar: Ga. 1975. Atty., ptnr. King & Spalding LLP, Atlanta; lead outside counsel Sprint Corp., Overland, Kans., exec. v.p., chief staff officer, 2003—04; exec. v.p., gen. counsel, sec. EDS Corp., Plano, Tex., 2004—. Mng. editor Vanderbilt Law Rev., 1974-75. Mem. ABA (fed. regulation of securities com., corp., banking and bus. law sect. 1983—), State Bar Ga., Atlanta Bar Assn., Order of the Coif, Beta Gamma Sigma. Office: General Counsel EDS 5400 Legacy Dr Plano TX 75024

HAWTHORNE, DOUGLAS D., medical association administrator; b. N.J. two children. BBA, M in Health Care Adminstrn., Trinity U., San Antonio. Intern San Antonio Hosp.; with Presbyn. Health Care Sys., 1970—97, pres., CEO, 1983—97, Tex. Health Resources, Arlington, 1997—. Bd. dirs. United Way; mem. exec. com. Dallas Red Cross; active Circle Ten, Boy Scouts Am. Recipient Leonard A. Duce award for outstanding contbn. to the field of health care adminstrn., 1977; named Healthcare Leader of the 21st Century for State of Tex., Hosps. mag.; named to The Dallas Dozen Up-and-Comers to Watch, Dallas Times Herald, 1986.

HAWTHORNE, ENID RUTH, retired secondary school educator, social sciences educator; b. N.Y.C., Aug. 8, 1939; d. Irving Helfont and Lorraine (Kanarvogel) H; children: Erica, David. BA, CUNY, 1961, MS, 1965. Elem. tchr. N.Y.C. Bd. Edn., 1961-66, creative writing tchr., 1966-69; adult edn. tchr. Port Washington (N.Y.) UFSD, 1970-80, adult edn. counselor, 1979-82, alternative H.S. tchr., 1970-81, social studies tchr., 1981-82, Freeport (N.Y.) Union Free Sch. Dist., 1982—; human rels. tchr. Freeport (N.Y.) UFSD, 1989—, ret.; adj. prof. Oreonta Coll. Cons. Nassau County Commn. on Human Rights, Mineola, N.Y., 1989—; cons. H.S. mediation programs Nassau County Schs., Mineola, 1989—; adj. prof. edn. Oneonta Coll Recipient Exemplary Program in L.I. Schs. award Coun. Adminstrs. and Suprs., 1991, Sprit of Anne Frank Outstanding Educator award, 1998. Mem. ASCD, N.Y. State Coun. for Social Studies, Nat. Coun. for Social Studies. Democrat. Jewish. Avocations: reading, theater, music, bridge.

HAWTHORNE, LOU, genetic cloning research company executive, researcher; BA in English Lit., Princeton U., 1983. Founder Genetic Savings & Clone, Sausalito, Calif., 1999—, project coord. of "Missyplicity Project", 1997—, CEO, 1999—. Coord. large scale tech. and media projects both independently and for various Fortune 500 clients; media prodr. Involved with the "CC-Copy Cat" project resulting in the world's first cloned domestic cat and the Missyplicity Project, which hopes to genetically clone the first domestic dog; made first sale: a cloned male kitten, "Little Nicky", for $50,000 in December, 2004. Office: Genetic Savings & Clone Inc 80 Liberty Ship Way Ste 22 Sausalito CA 94965-3300 Office Phone: 415-289-2525. Office Fax: 415-289-2526.

HAWTHORNE, MARION FREDERICK, chemistry professor; b. Ft. Scott, Kans., Aug. 24, 1928; s. Fred Elmer and Colleen (Webb) Hawthorne; m. Beverly Dawn Rempe, Oct. 30, 1951 (div. 1976); m. Diana Baker Razzala, Aug. 14, 1977. BA, Pomona Coll., 1949; PhD (AEC fellow), UCLA, 1953; DSc (hon.), Pomona Coll., 1974; PhD (hon.), Uppsala U., 1992. Rsch. assoc. Iowa State Coll., 1953-54; rsch. chemist Rohm & Haas Co., Huntsville, Ala., 1954-56, group leader, 1956-60, lab. head Phila., 1961; prof. chemistry U. Calif., Riverside, 1962-68, UCLA, 1968—, U. Calif., 1998—. Vis. lectr. Harvard U., 1960, vis. prof., 68; vis. lectr. Queen Mary Coll., U. London, 1963; vis. prof. U. Tex., Austin, 1974; mem. sci. adv. bd. USAF, 1980—86, NRC Bd. Army Sci. and Tech., 1986—90; disting. vis. prof. Ohio State U., 1990; 1st Anton Burg lectr. U. So. Calif., 2004; mem. dir.'s external adv. bd. divsn. M Los Alamos Nat. Lab., N.Mex., 1991—94; lectr. in field. Editor-in-chief: Inorganic Chemistry, 1969—2000, assoc. editor:, 1966—69. Decorated Meritorious Svc. medal USAF; named Sr. Scientist Alexander von Humboldt Found., Inst. Inorganic Chemistry U. Munich, 1990—96, Centenary lectr., Royal Soc. Chemistry, London, 1998; recipient Chancellors Rsch. award, 1968, Herbert Newby McCoy award, 1972, Am. Chem. Soc. award Inorganic Chemistry, 1973, Glenn T. Seaborg medal, 1997, Tolman Medal award, 1986, Nebr. sect. Am. Chem. Soc. award, 1979, Disting. Svc. Advancement of Inorganic Chemistry award, Am. Chem. Soc., 1988, Disting. Achievements in Boron Sci. award, 1988, Bailar medal, 1991, Polyhedron medal and prize, 1993, Chem. Pioneer award, Am. Inst. Chemists, 1994, Willard Gibbs medal, Am. Chem. Soc., 1994, Internat. award in Polyhedral Borane Chemistry, Internat. Com. on Boron Chemistry, 1996, Basolo medal, Am. Chem. Soc., 2001, King Faisal Internat. Sci. prize, 2003; fellow Sloan Found., 1963—65, Japan Soc. Promotion Sci., 1986, Disting. Vis. scholar, Chinese U. Hong Kong, 2001. Fellow: AAAS; mem.: Nat. Acad. Sci. Bd. Army Sci. and Tech., Internat. Soc. Neutron Capture Therapy for Cancer (mem. exec. com. 1992—2000, pres. 1996—98), Am. Acad. Arts and Scis., U.S. Nat. Acad. Scis. (award in chem. scis. 1997), Göttingen Acad. Scis. (corr.), Aircraft Owners and Pilots Assn. (named Col. Confederate Air Force 1984), Cosmos Club, Sigma Nu, Alpha Chi Sigma, Sigma Xi (Monie A. Ferst award 2003). Home: 3415 Green Vista Dr Encino CA 91436-4011 Office Phone: 310-825-7378. Business E-Mail: mfh@chem.ucla.edu.

HAWTHORNE, MINNIE, elementary school educator; b. Jackson, Miss., Feb. 15, 1949; d. Tommie Lee and Rosetta (Tolbert) Harris; m. Cedric Hawthorne; 1 child, Cedric. BS, Jackson State U., 1970; MS, Ind. U., 1971. Tchr. Hinds C.C., Utica, Miss., 1974-80, Chgo. Bus. Coll., 1988-93; cadre tchr. Chgo. Pub. Schs., 1994-96; tchr. Yazoo County Schs., Yazoo City, Miss., 2000—. Co-sponsor, sponsor Phi Beta Lamba, Utica, 1974-80. Mem. Yazoo County Fair and Civic League, Yazoo City, 1996-97. Mem. Pi Omega Pi. Avocations: playing piano, community volunteering for americorps, vista. Home: 217 E 3d St Yazoo City MS 39194

HAWTHORNE, NAN LOUISE, Internet company executive, consultant, web site designer, writer; b. Hawthorne, Nev., Jan. 3, 1952; d. Louis Frederick Haas Jr. and Merle Forrest (Ohlhausen) Ritter; m. James Denver Tedford, Dec. 20, 1981. BS, No. Mich. U., 1981. Mng. dir. CyberVPM.com, Seattle, 1997—; content devel. eSight Careers Network, 1999—; mng. dir. nanhawthorne.com. Author: Loving the Goddess Within, 1990, Building Better Relationships with Volunteers, 1997, Managing Volunteers in Record Time, 1997, Recognizing Volunteers Right From the Start, 1998; contbr. articles to profl. jours. Mem. Assn. Vol. Adminstrs. (tech. com. 1998—), Soc. Profl. Journalists. Office: PO Box 1229 22833 Bothell-Everett Hwy 102 Bothell WA 98021-9366 E-mail: hawthorne@nanhawthorne.com.

HAWTHORNE, ROY JOHN, retired music educator; b. Cleve., Sept. 26, 1944; s. Clyde Schaefer and Helen Jean Hawthorne; m. Frances Carol Foote, Mar. 6, 1965; children: David Scot, Carol Jean. BS in Edn., Ohio State U., 1966; MA, Case Western Res. U., 1970. Permanent cert. Ohio Dept. of Edn. Music specialist South Euclid-Lyndhurst City Schs., Lyndhurst, Ohio, 1966—95. Choir dir. So. Euclid Hillcrest United Meth. Ch., 1968—86. Arranger (band) Four Scottish Songs, Happy Bros. (Vesili Bratri), Rapid Transit Rag; composer: (band compositions) Red Shirt waltz, Prelude, Waltz And Rondo, Karlin polka, Polka Sine Nomine, Bo and John polka, Brittany's Waltz, Ernie's Polka, DTJ polka, Freedom and Justice march, Ohio 200 march. Mem.: NEA (life), Ohio Edn. Association (life; ret. mem.), Phi Mu Alpha Sinfonia (life), Kappa Kappa Psi (life). Avocation: music performance.

HAWTHORNE, VICTOR MORRISON, epidemiologist, educator; b. Glasgow, Scotland, June 19, 1921; came to U.S., 1978; s. John Morrison and Isabel Stuart (Crowe) H.; m. Jean Christie Mackenzie, Aug. 19, 1948; children: Hilary June (dec.), Wendy Victoria, Joan Rosalind. MB ChB, U. Glasgow, 1951, MD, 1962, DSc (hon.), 1996; diploma, Scottish Coun. for Health Edn., 1976. Sr. lectr. dept. epidemiology U. Glasgow, 1967-78, sr. research fellow dept. community medicine, 1978-91; cons. physician Nat. Health Service, Glasgow Health Bd., 1966-78; coordinator Scottish MMR services Nat. Health Service Scotland, 1970-78; prof. epidemiology U. Mich., Ann Arbor, 1978-91, chmn. dept., 1978-86, prof. dept. family practice, 1982-91, prof. epidemiology emeritus, 1991—95. Chmn. epidemiology study sect. NIH, Bethesda, Md., 1979-83, active, 1979-93; chmn. kidney disease adv. com. Mich. Dept. Pub. Health, Lansing, 1979-95, mem. chronic disease adv. com., 1979; chmn. Continuing Med. Edn./Pub. Health Consortium Mich., 1987-2004; hon. dir. Bayer Rsch. unit Royal Coll. Physicians of Edinburgh, 1987-93, hon. cons. Royal Coll. Physicians of Edinburgh Diabetes Register, 1989-01, U. Mich. Complementary and Cardiovas. Rsch. Ctr., 1999-. Author: First Aid For Medical Students, 1978, Tuberculosis, Respiratory and Cardiovascular Risks of Dying in the West of Scotland, 1985; contbr. articles to profl. jours. Capt. Brit. Army, 1941—46. Recipient Bronze medal U. Helsinki, 1985; Victor Hawthorne: Young Investigator Rsch. Award Program established in his honor Mich. Dept. Pub. Health, 1986. Fellow Royal Coll. Physicians and Surgeons of Glasgow, Royal Coll. Physicians of Edinburgh, Faculty of Pub. Health Medicine, Am. Coll. Epidemiology, Gen. Med. Coun. UK Mem. Ch. of Scotland Avocations: sketching, gardening. Office: Univ Mich Sch Pub Health Dept Epidemiology 109 Observatory St Ann Arbor MI 48109-2029

HAWTHORNE, SIR WILLIAM (SIR WILLIAM REDE HAWTHORNE), aerospace and mechanical engineer, educator; b. May 22, 1913; s. William and Elizabeth H.; m. Barbara Runkle, 1939; 1 son, 2 daus. Ed., Trinity Coll., Cambridge, MIT. Devel. engr. Babcock & Wilcox Ltd., 1937-39; sci. officer Royal Aircraft Establishment, 1940-44; seconded to Power Jets, 1940-41; with Brit. Air Commn., Washington, 1944; dep. dir. engine rsch. Ministry of Supply, 1945; assoc. prof. mech. engring. MIT, 1946, George Westinghouse prof. mech. engring., 1948-51, Jerome C. Hunsaker prof. aero. engring., 1955-56; master Churchill Coll., Cambridge, 1968-83, now fellow; Hopkinson and ICI prof. applied thermodynamics U. Cambridge, 1951-80, head dept. engring., 1968-73. Chmn. Home Office Sci. Adv. Council, 1967-76, Adv. Council Energy Conservation, 1974-79; dir. Cummins Engine Co., Inc., 1974-86, dir. Dracone Devels. Ltd. Bd. govs. Westminster Sch., 1956-76. Recipient Royal medal Royal Society, 1982, R. Tom Sawyer award ASME, 1992. Fellow AIAA (hon.), ASME (hon.), Royal Soc., Royal Acad. Engring.; mem. NAE (fgn. assoc.), NAS (fgn. assoc.). Office: Churchill Coll Cambridge CB3 0DS England also: 19 Chauncy St Cambridge MA 02138-2549

HAWVER, DENNIS A., psychologist, consultant; s. Carl F. and Frances J. H.; m. Anne M. Augustyn, 1961 (div. Oct. 1974); children: Timothy, Laura, Derek; m. Judith M. Anderson, Jan. 28, 1977. BA, U. Akron, 1964, MA, 1965; PhD, Temple U., Phila., 1964-70. Dir. rsch. Temple U., Phila., 1964-70, instr. Grad. Sch., 1968-70, internal cons., 1964-70; mng. ptnr. Cardall Assocs., Princeton, N.J., 1970-72; nat. program dir. The RHR Inst., N.Y.C., 1972-80; pres. The Hawver Group, N.Y.C. and Princeton, 1980—. Pres. The Hawver Group, N.Y.C. and Princeton, 1980-; pres. Princeton chpt. Inst. Mgmt. Cons. Author: How to Improve Your Negotiating Skills, 1983; contbr. to bus. and profl. jours.; developer rsch. and tng. programs; internat. cons. in exec. identification and devel. and bus. negotiations. Chmn. Leadership Devel. Com. of Princeton C. of C. Mem. APA, Soc. Indsl. and Organizational Psychology, Internat. Assn. Applied Psychology, Inst. Mgmt. Cons. (CMC), Soc. Assessment Sys. Practitioners, Internat. Pers. Mgmt. Assn. Assessment Coun. Office: The Hawver Group 21 Park Place W Cranbury NJ 08512-3224 E-mail: hawvergrp@aol.com.

HAXO, FRANCIS THEODORE, marine biologist; b. Grand Forks, N.D., Mar. 9, 1921; s. Henry Emile and Florence (Shull) H.; m. Judith Morgan McLaughlin, Apr. 15, 1961; children: John Frederick, Barbara, Philip, Francis Theodore, Aileen. BA, U. N.D., 1941; PhD, Stanford U., 1947. Teaching, research asst. Stanford U., 1941-44, acting instr., 1943; research asst. Calif. Inst. Tech., 1946; research asso. Hopkins Marine Sta., Pacific Grove, Calif., 1946-47; from instr. to asst. prof. plant physiology Johns Hopkins U., 1947-52; mem. faculty U. Calif. Scripps Inst. Oceanography, La Jolla, 1952-88, prof. biology, 1963-88; prof. emeritus, 1988—; chmn. marine biology dept. U. Calif. Scripps Inst. Oceanography, 1960-65, chmn. marine biology research div., 1960-77; instr. marine botany Marine Biol. Lab., Woods Hole, Mass., 1949-52, 70. Vis. faculty botany U. Calif. at Berkeley, 1957, U. Wash. Marine Lab., Friday Harbor, 1963 Abraham Rosenberg fellow Stanford, 1945. Fellow AAAS, San Diego Zool. Soc.; mem. Am. Soc. Photobiology, Phycological Soc. Am., Western Soc. Naturalists, Internat. Phycological Soc., Phi Beta Kappa, Sigma Xi. Achievements include spl. rsch. photosynthesis, plant pigments, physiology of algae. Home: 6381 Castejon Dr La Jolla CA 92037-6933 Business E-Mail: fhaxo@ucsd.edu.

HAXTON, DAVID, filmmaker, photographer; b. Indpls., Jan. 6, 1943; s. John Laird and Dorothy Margaret (Peters) H.; m. Kay Elizabeth Keller, Feb. 8, 1969. BA, U. South Fla., 1965; MFA, U. Mich., 1967. Prof. computer graphics William Paterson Coll., Wayne, N.J., 1974-95, U. Ctrl. Fla., Orlando, 1995—. One-man shows include: Sonnabend Gallery, N.Y.C., 1979, 80, 81, 83, Paris, 1978, Mus. Modern Art, N.Y.C., 1978, Rosa Esman Gallery, N.Y.C., 1986, U. Ctrl. Fla., 1998, Ikon Galerie, 2001; group shows include: Whitney Mus. Am. Art, N.Y.C., 1979, 81, 83, Rosa Esman Gallery, N.Y.C., 1986, Anne Plumb Gallery, N.Y.C., 1987, Ringling Art Mus., Sarasota, Fla., 1987, Digital Film Exhbn., Ikon Galerie, Germany, 2001, True Fictions, Ludwig Forum, Aachen, Germany, 2002, Orlando Mus. Art, 2003; represented in permanent collections, Mus. Modern Art, N.Y.C., Whitney Mus. Am. Art, N.Y.C., Denver Art Mus., Australian Mus. Art. Recipient awards for computer animation direction Gold Plaque award Chgo. Internat. Film Festival, 1988, 89, Art Dream award Siggraph Film and Video Show, 1988, Nat. Computer Graphics Assn. 2d award, 1989, Siggraph Animation Screening award, 1990, NCGA Video Show 3rd award, 1991, 1st pl. award Alias Desing Competition, 1991, Siggraph Electronic Theater award, 1992, Pri Ars Electronica award, 1993, UN Cabinet D'Amateurs Cinematheque Francaise, Films, 1995, Siggraph Animation Screening Rm. award, 1997, Siggrapa Animation Theatre, 1999, 2000, Siggraph Art Show, 2001; N.Y. Coun. on Arts grantee, 1977-78, Nat. Endowment for Arts grantee, 1978-79; Individual Artist fellow, 1979-80; Nat. Computer Graphics Assn. faculty student, 1992, 2d prize award, 1991. Office: U Ctrl Fla Dept Art Orlando FL 32789 Business E-Mail: info@haxton.net.

HAY, ALEX, painter, sculptor; b. Fla., 1930; m. Deborah Hay. Retired from art world, 1969; began painting again, 2003. Exhibitions include Work From the 60's, Peter Freeman, NYC, 2002, Whitney Biennial, Whitney Mus. Am. Art, 2004. Mailing: c/o Whitney Museum American Art 945 Madison Ave New York NY 10021*

HAY, BRUCE L., law educator; b. Northampton, Mass., Jan. 9, 1963; BA in Polit. Sci., U. Wis., 1985; JD, Harvard U., 1988. Bar: Pa. 1991. Law clk. to Judge William A. Norris US Ct. Appeals 9th Cir., 1988—89; law clk. to Justice Antonin Scalia US Supreme Ct., 1989; assoc. Sidley Austin Brown & Wood, Washington; asst. prof. law Harvard Law Sch., Cambridge, Mass., 1992—98, prof., 1998—. Office: Harvard Law Sch 1563 Massachusetts Ave Cambridge MA 02138 Office Phone: 617-496-8277. Office Fax: 617-496-5156. Business E-Mail: hay@law.harvard.edu.

HAY, ELIZABETH DEXTER, embryologist, educator; b. St. Augustine, Fla., Apr. 2, 1927; d. Isaac Morris and Lucille Elizabeth (Lynn) H. AB, Smith Coll., 1948; MA (hon.), Harvard U., 1964; ScD (hon.), Smith Coll., 1973, Trinity Coll., 1989; MD, Johns Hopkins U., 1952, LHD (hon.), 1990. Intern in internal medicine Johns Hopkins Hosp., Balt., 1952-53; instr. anatomy Johns Hopkins U. Med. Sch., Balt., 1953-56, asst. prof., 1956-57, Cornell U. Med. Sch., N.Y.C., 1957-60, Harvard Med. Sch., Boston, 1960-64, Louise Foote Pfeiffer assoc. prof., 1964-69, Louise Foote Pfeiffer prof. embryology, 1969—, chmn. dept. anatomy and cellular biology, 1975-93; prof. dept. cell biology, 1993—. Cons. cell biology sect. NIH, 1965-69; mem. adv. coun. Nat. Inst. Gen. Med. Sci., NIH, 1978-81; mem. sci. adv. bd. Whitney Marine Lab., U. Fla., 1982-86; mem. adv. coun. Johns Hopkins Sch. Medicine, 1982-96; chairperson bd. sci. counselors Nat. Inst. Dental Rsch., NIH, 1984-86; mem. bd. sci. counselors Nat. Inst. Environ. Health Sci., NIH, 1990-93. Author: Regeneration, 1966; (with J.P. Revel) Fine Structure of the Developing Avian Cornea, 1969; editor: Cell Biology of Extracellular Matrix, 1981, 2d edit., 1991; editor-in-chief Developmental Biology Jour., 1971-75; contbr. articles to profl. jours. Mem. Scientists Task Force of Congressman Barney Frank, Massach, 1982-92. Recipient Disting. Achievement award N.Y. Hosp.-Cornell Med. Ctrl. Alumni Coun., 1985, award for vision rsch. Alcon, 1988, Excellence in Sci. award Fedn. Am. Socs. Exptl. Biology. Mem. Soc. Devel. Biology (pres. 1973-74, E.G. Conklin award 1997), Am. Soc. Cell Biology (pres. 1976-77, legis. alert com. 1982—, E.B. Wilson award 1989, chair 40th anniversary 2000), Am. Assn. Anatomists (pres. 1981-82, legis. alert com. 1982—, Centennial award 1987, Henry Gray award 1992), Am. Acad. Arts and Scis., Johns Hopkins Soc. Scholars, Nat. Acad. Sci., Inst. Medicine, Internat. Soc. Devel. Biologists (exec. bd. 1977, keynote spkr. 1st Australian EMT conf. 2003), Boston Mycol. Club. Home: 14 Aberdeen Rd Weston MA 02493-1733 Office: Harvard Med Sch Dept Cell Biology 220 Longwood Ave Boston MA 02115-5701 Office Phone: 617-432-1651. Business E-Mail: ehay@hms.harvard.edu.

HAY, FRED J., education educator, librarian, editor; b. Toccoa, Ga., Oct. 3, 1953; s. Samuel Hutson and Dorothy Churchill Hay; m. Valentina Maiewskij, Feb. 4, 1983; 1 child, Nikolai Mikhail. BA, Rhodes Coll., Memphis, Tenn., 1975; MA, U. Va., Charlottesville, Va., 1981; PhD, U. Fla., Gainesville, Fla., 1985; MLIS, Fla. State U., Tallahassee, Fla., 1987. Asst. prof. St. Cloud State U., Minn., 1985—86; libr. Fla. Hospitality Edn. Program (FSU), Tallahassee, 1987; ast. prof., social sciences libr. Kans. State U., Manhattan, 1988—89; reference libr. Harvard U., Cambridge, Mass., 1989—94; prof., libr. Appalachian State U., Boone, NC, 1994—. Adv. bd. mem. Appalachian Jour., Boone, NC, 2000—; editl. bd. mem. Coll. & Rsch. Libraries, Chgo., 1993—, book rev. editor, 1996—; grant reviewer Nat. Endowment for the Humanities, Washington, 2000—03. Author: (scholarly book) Goin' Back To Sweet Memphis: Conversations With The Blues, African-American Community Studies in North America; editor: When Night Falls, Kric Krac: Haitian Folktales, Documenting Cultural Diversity in the Resurgent American South; guest editor: Black Music Rsch. Jour., 3 issues. Mem. Bd. of Adjustments, Boone, NC, 1999—. Recipient Brenda McCallum Meml. Award, Am. Folklore Soc., 1997; grantee NEH Challenge Grant, Nat. Endowment for the Humanities, 2000-2003; Douglas W. Bryant Fellowship, Harvard U., 1992-93. Mem.: Ctr. Black Music Rsch., Assn. of Coll. and Rsch. Libraries, ALA, Am. Anthrop. Assocaition, Appalachian Studies Assn. Avocations: gardening, contemplation, music, social and environmental activism. Home: 261 East View Dr Boone NC 28607 Office: Appalachian State Univ WL Eury Appalachian Collection Boone NC 28608 Office Phone: 828-262-2887. Business E-Mail: hayfj@appstate.edu.

HAY, GEORGE ALAN, law and economics educator; b. N.Y.C., Feb. 4, 1942; s. George N. and Marjorie H. (Prote) H. BS, Le Moyne Coll., 1963; MA, Northwestern U., 1967, PhD, 1969. From asst. to assoc. prof. econs. Yale U., New Haven, 1967-74; dir. econs. antitrust div. U.S. Dept. Justice, Washington, 1973-79; prof. law and econs. Cornell U., Ithaca, N.Y., 1979-92, Edward Cornell prof. law, prof. econs., 1992—. Vis. prof. law U. Sydney, 1992, vis. fellow Balliol Coll., Oxford, 2001. Contbr. articles on antitrust to profl. jours. Fulbright scholar Oxford U., 1984-85. Mem. ABA, Am. Econ. Assn., Assn. Am. Law Schs. (chmn. antitrust sect. 1985-87). Office: Cornell Law Sch 214 Myron Taylor Hall Ithaca NY 14853-4901

HAY, GEORGE AUSTIN, actor, artist, musician, writer; b. Johnstown, Pa., Dec. 25, 1915; s. George and Mary Louise (Austin) H. BS, U. Pitts., 1938; postgrad., U. Rochester, 1939; MLitt, U. Pitts., 1948; MA, Columbia U., 1948. Dir. Jr. League hosp. shows, N.Y.C., 1948-53. *As a kind of legacy from his physician and surgeon father, Austin Hay has enjoyed a regimen of lifelong healthfulness. In his impressionable youth, he became markedly inspired by knowing two young local figures: an obscure endlessly exuberant, surprisingly skilled, astonishingly agile, indefatigable teacher in his own home town--by the name of Gene Kelly; and a lanky assistant to a prestidigitator in a neighboring small town--unknown Princeton student, James Stewart. To a youngster, all this exemplified magical adventureland. Manifestly from such extraordinary early influences, a career in theater and movies followed. Through ensuing halcyon times, friendships continued with notables in the field, among them, "the most trusted man in America," television's Walter Cronkite, in whose home and yacht, on Martha's Vineyard, Austin Hay has been welcomed. In a lively saga of effort to broaden horizons and enhance the quality of life, he performs in a variety of disciplines, is productive in different fields of creative endeavor. Being born on Christmas day, he helps nurture in a joyous way a continuing ethic of integrity, and healthful living.* Producer, dir. off-Broadway prodns., 1953-55; motion picture casting dir. for Dept. Def. films, Astoria Studios, N.Y., 1955-70, motion picture producer-dir., U.S. Dept. Transp., Washington, 1973—, Office Presdl. Personnel, The White House, 1993—; group exhbns. of paintings and sculpture include, Lincoln Ctr., N.Y.C., 1965, Parrish Art Mus., Southampton, N.Y., 1969, Carnegie Inst., 1972, Duncan Galleries, N.Y.C., 1973, Bicentennial Exhbn. Am. Painters, Paris, 1976, Chevy Chase Gallery, 1979, Watergate Gallery, 1981, Le Salon des Nations a Paris, 1983; rep. permanent collections, Met. Mus. Art, N.Y.C., Library Congress, also, pvt. collections; bibliog. reference to works pub. in History of Internat. Art, 1982; author, illustrator: Seven Hops to Australia, 1945, The Moving Image, A Career in Pictures, 1990; Dir.: Bicentennial documentary Highways of History, 1976; dir.: film World Painting in Museum of Modern Art, 1972; Composer: Rhapsody in E Flat for piano and strings, 1950; writer: TV program Nat. Council Chs., 1965; Broadway appearances include: What Every Woman Knows, 1954; original Broadway run of Inherit the Wind, 1955-57; created role of Prof. Fiveash in premiere of The Acrobats, White Barn Theater, Westport, Conn., 1961; feature films include: North by Northwest, 1959, Murder, Inc., 1960, Pretty Boy Floyd, 1960, The Landlord, 1970, Child's Play, 1971, Chekhov's The Bet, 1978, Being There, 1980, No Way Out, 1986, Her Alibi, 1988, Air Force One, 1997, Guarding Tess, 1994, Contact, 1997 The Contender, 2000, Head of State, 2003; TV appearances include Am. Heritage, 1961, Americans-A Portrait in Verses, 1962, Naked City, 1962, U.S. Steel Hour, 1963, Another World, 1965, Edge of Night, 1968, As the World Turns, 1969, Love Is a Many-Splendored Thing, 1972, The Adams Chronicles, 1976, A Woman Named Jackie, 1991; piano soloist in concerts and recitals, 1937; performer Cruise Ship, Europe, 1938; author, illustrator: The Arts Scene; contbr. articles to periodicals. App. time adv. panel, pres.'s coun. Col. William and Mary; mem. World Affairs Coun., Am. Archit. Found.; bd. govs. Home of Pres. James Monroe; trustee Home of Pres. James Monroe; mus. donor turn-of-century doctor's office from estate of surgeon father; With AUS, 1942—46; PTO; bd. dirs. Washington Film Coun. Recipient Loyal Svc. award Jr. League, 1953, St. Bartholomew's Silver Leadership award, 1966, Gold medal Accademia Italia, 1980, Smithsonian Instn. Pictorial award, 1982; Fed. Govt. Honor award in recognition 45 yrs. dedicated svc., 2000; subject of biog. work: Austin Hay, Adventures of a Christmas Child, 1970. Mem. NATAS, AFTRA, SAG, Am. Artists Profl. League, Allied Artists Am., Internat. Bach Soc., Rachmaninoff Soc., Beethoven Soc. (bd. dirs.), Nat. Soc. Arts and Letters (bd. dirs.), Music Libr. Assn., Nat. Symphony Orch. Assn., Actors Equity Assn., Nat. Trust Hist. Preservation, SAR, Nat. Parks and Conservation Assn., Shakespeare Oxford Soc., St. Andrew's Soc., Victorian Soc. (bd. dirs.), Cambria County Hist. Soc., Am. Philatelic Soc., Am. Mus. Moving Image, Jimmy Stewart Mus. (Indiana, Pa.), English Speaking Union (bd. dirs.), Nat. Arts Club (N.Y.C.), Players Club (N.Y.C.), Nat. Travel Club, Columbia U. Club, Nat. Press Club, Arts Club of Washington, Cosmos Club, Classic Car Club Am., Nat. Naval Med. Command, Sigma Chi, Phi Mu Alpha Office Phone: 202-366-9127.

HAY, HOWARD CLINTON, lawyer; b. Portland, Maine, Apr. 16, 1944; s. Willis and Ruth (Clark) H.; m. Carol Anne Newsome, Dec. 21, 1968; children: Mark, David, Scott. AB (with distinction), Duke U., 1966; JD magna cum laude, U. Mich., 1969. Bar: U.S. Supreme Ct. 1977, Calif. 1970. Law clerk U.S. Ct. Appeals, Boston, 1970; atty. NLRB; ptnr. Paul, Hastings, Janofsky & Walker, Costa Mesa, Calif., 1971—. Program chmn. Certificate in Employee Rels. Law; instr. U. S.C. Grad. Sch. Bus. Editor Mich. Law Review; contbr. articles to profl. jours. Mem. State Bar Calif. (exec. com. labor and employment sect.), Calif. Bar Assn. Office: Paul Hastings Janofsky & Walker 695 Town Center Dr Fl 17 Costa Mesa CA 92626-1924 Office Phone: 714-668-6266. E-mail: howardhay@paulhastings.com.

HAY, JESS THOMAS, retired finance company executive; b. Forney, Tex., Jan. 22, 1931; s. George and Myrtle Hay; m. Betty Jo Peacock, 1951; children: Deborah Hay Spradley, Patricia Hay Daibert. BBA, So. Meth. U., 1953, JD magna cum laude, 1955. Bar: Tex. Assoc. Locke, Purnell, Boren, Laney & Neely, 1955-61, partner, 1961-65; pres., chief exec. officer Lomas Fin. Corp., Dallas, 1965-69, chmn. bd., chief exec. officer, 1969-94; chmn. bd., chief exec. officer, trustee Lomas & Nettleton Mortgage Investors, 1969-92; chmn., CEO Capstead Mortgage Corp. (formerly Lomas Mortgage Corp.), 1985-91. Chmn. HCB Enterprises Inc; bd. dirs. Trinity Industries, Inc., Exxon Corp., Viad Corp., SBC Comm. Inc. Former mem. Dem. Nat. Com., also former nat. fin. chmn.; former chmn. bd. regents U. Tex. Sys.; former mem. Dallas Citizens Coun., Dallas Assembly; mem. Greater Dallas Planning Coun.; mem. WWII Meml. Adv. Bd.; bd. dirs. Tex. Rsch. League, North Tex. Food Bank, Child Care Partnership Dallas, Dallas County Hist. Found.; chmn. bd. Tex. Found. for Higher Edn.; trustee Southwestern Med. Found. Recipient Disting. Service award Assn. Governing Bds. of Univs. and Colls., 1987. Mem. ABA, Dallas Bar Assn., Tex. Bar Assn., Am. Judicature Soc., Newcomen Soc. N.Am., U.S. C. of C. Methodist. Home: 7236 Lupton Cir Dallas TX 75225-1737 Office: 5956 Sherry Ln Ste 1413 Dallas TX 75225 Office Phone: 214-969-9210.

HAY, JOEL W., health economist, educator; b. Boston, Nov. 22, 1952; BA, Amherst Coll., 1974; MPhil, Yale U., 1976, PhD, 1980. Asst. rsch. prof. U. So. Calif., 1978-80; asst. prof. U. Conn., Farmington, 1980-84, Storrs, 1981-84; sr. rsch. fellow Hoover Inst. Stanford U., Calif., 1985-92; assoc. prof. and chmn. U. So. Calif., 1992—. Sr. policy analyst, Project HOPE, Millwood, Va., 1983-85; vis. scholar, Chinese U., Hong Kong, 1990-91; health care advisor, Hungarian Parliament, Budapest, 1991-92; tech. cons., Health Care Financing Adminstrn., Balt., 1992; health care task force mem., Am. Heart Assn., Washington, 1992. Author: (book) Health Care in Hong Kong, 1992; contbr. numerous articles to profl. jours. Office: 1985 Zonal Ave Dept Pharm Los Angeles CA 90089-0105

HAY, LEWIS, III, utilities company executive; b. 1955; BS in Elec. Engring., Lehigh U., 1977; M in Indsl. Adminstrn., Carnegie-Mellon U., 1982. Gen. foreman U.S. Steel Corp., Pitts., 1977-80; v.p., mng. ptnr. strategy practice Strategic Planning Assocs., Washington, 1982-91; exec. v.p., CFO U.S. Foodsvc. Inc., Columbia, Md., 1991-99; CFO FPL Group, Inc., Juno Beach, Fla., 1999—2000; pres. FPL Energy, 2000—01. Office: FPL Group Inc PO Box 14000 North Palm Beach FL 33408

HAY, PETER HEINRICH, law educator; b. Berlin, Sept. 17, 1935; s. Edward and Margot (Tull) H.; 1 child, Cedric. BA, JD, U. Mich., 1958. Prof. law U. Ill., Champaign, 1963-91, dean Coll. Law, 1979—89; L.Q.C., Lamar prof. law Emory U., Atlanta, 1991—, interim dean, chief exec. and acad. officer, 2001—02. Hon. prof. U. Freiburg, Germany, 1976—; prof. U. Dresden, Germany, 1994-2000. Author: Law of the United States, 2002, 2d edit., 2005, Internationales Privatrecht, 2d edit., 2002; co-author: Conflict of Laws, 4d edit., 2004; contbr. over 70 articles to profl. jours. Recipient Rsch. prize von Humboldt Found., Germany, 1990; Fulbright rsch. prof., 1992; Jean-Monnet prof., Bonn, Germany, 1994. Mem. Am. Law Inst., Am. Acad. Fgn. Law, Internat. Acad. Comparative Law. Office: Emory U Sch Law G523 Gambrell Hall 1301 Clifton Rd Atlanta GA 30322-2770 Office Phone: 404-727-6896. Business E-Mail: phay@law.emory.edu.

HAY, RICHARD LE ROY, geology educator; b. Goshen, Ind., Apr. 29, 1926; s. Edward Le Roy and Angela H.; m. Barbara J. Herbert, Dec. 13, 1956; 1 child, Randall E.; m. Lynn Simonds, July 14, 1973. BS, Northwestern U., 1946, MS, 1948; PhD, Princeton U., 1952. Asst. prof. geology La. State U., Baton Rouge, 1955-57; asst. prof. to prof. geology and geophysics U. Calif., Berkeley, 1957-83; Ralph E. Grim prof. geology U. Ill., Urbana-Champaign, 1983-97. Geologist U.S. Geol. Survey, intermittently 1948-84; adj. prof. U. Ariz., 1999—. Author: Geology of the Olduvai Gorge, 1976. Recipient Arnold Guyot award, Nat. Geog. Soc., 1978, Leakey prize, L.S.B. Leakey Found., 2001. Fellow AAAS, Geol. Soc. Am. (Kirk Bryan award 1978, Rip Rapp award 2000), Mineral. Soc. Am., Calif. Acad. Sci. Home: 5121 N Soledad Primera Tucson AZ 85718-4822 Business E-Mail: rhay@geo.arizona.edu.

HAY, ROBERT DEAN, retired management educator; b. LaPorte, Ind., Nov. 17, 1921; s. Carl Roy and Almetta (Diedrich) H.; m. Margaret B. Appelman, 1944; children— Sue Ann, Carol Lynn, Taj Margaret. BS, U. Okla., 1949, MBA, 1950; PhD, Ohio State U., 1954. Mem. faculty U. Ark., Fayetteville, 1949-90, mem. emeritus, 1990—, prof. mgmt., 1959-86, Univ. prof., 1986-90. Author: (with F. Broyles) Athletic Administration, 1979, (with Ed Gray and Paul Smith) Business and Society, 1989, Strategic Management in Non-Profit Organizations, 1990; also 10 other books. Served with USAAF, 1942-47. Mem. Am. Bus. Communications Assn., Acad. Mgmt., Case Rsch. Assn., other profl. orgns. Office: U Ark Dept Mgmt Fayetteville AR 72701

HAY, SAMUEL ARTHUR, theater educator, playwright; b. Barnwell, S.C., Mar. 26, 1937; s. Thomas Jr. and Maebelle Glover H.; m. Delores Ricks Glover, June 1, 1986 (div. Aug. 1988). BA, Bethune-Cookman Coll., 1959; MA, Johns Hopkins U., 1967; PhD, Cornell U., 1971. Asst. prof. English and African Am. studies U. Md., Catonsville, 1971-74; dir. Africana studies and rsch. ctr. Purdue U., West Lafayette, Ind., 1974-78; prof. theatre arts and Afro-Am. studies Washington U., St. Louis, 1978-79, chair Afro-Am. studies, 1978-79; prof., chair dept. comm. and theatre arts Morgan State U., Balt., 1979-88; prof. theatre arts, exec. dir. theatre N.C. A&T State U., Greensboro, 1993—2002; vis. prof. Lafayette Coll., Easton, Pa., 2002—. Vis. prof. Afro Am. studies U. Calif., Berkeley, 1987-88; archivist The Ed Bullins Collection, Greensboro, N.C., 1988-2000; artistic dir. Cottage Theatre, Riviera Beach, Fla., 1988-93; mng. dir. The Bullins Meml. Theatre, Emeryville, Calif., 1987-88; instr. English and drama Roosevelt H.S., West Palm Beach, Fla., 1971-74; convener Nat. Symposium on Ed Bullins N.C. A&T State U., Greensboro, 1997, Nat. Symposium on Paul Robeson N.C. A&T State U., Greensboro, 1988, Nat. Symposium on Alice Childress N.C. A&T State U., Greensboro, 1996, Nat. Symposium on August Wilson N.C. A&T State U., Greensboro, 1995. Author: (books) Focus on Literature, 6 vols., 1978, African American Theatre: A Historical and Critical Analysis, 1994, Ed Bullins: A Literary Biography, 1997 (CHOICE award 1998), (plays) Cream and Brown Sugar, 1997 (Am. Coll. Theatre Festival Region IV winner 1997), David Richmond, 1999 (Best Play of 1999 Kennedy Ctr./Am. Coll. Theatre Festival 1999). Cons. N.C. Shakespeare Fest., High Point, 1994-99, Nat. Black Theatre Fest., Winston-Salem, N.C., 1998—, Simon & Schuster Lang. Arts, Nassau, Bahamas, 1992-94. Recipient Harvard U. Found. medallion Harvard U., 1995, Dist. scholar N.C. A&T State U., 1995, Achievement award Arena Players Balt., 1987, Best Play Nat. Theatre of Detroit, 1985. Fellow Nat. Conf. African Am. Theatre, Inc. (founder, pres 1980-90); mem. Nat. Asns. Schs. Theatre (bd. dirs. 2000—), Nat. Symposium on African Am. Theatre (founder, pres. 1993—), Assn. Theatre in Higher Edn., Black Theatre Network. Democrat. Episcopalian. Avocations: tennis, walking, travel. Home: PO Box 1183 Easton PA 18042-1183 Office: Lafayette Coll Dept Govt & Law Easton PA 18042 E-mail: samhay3@aol.com.

HAY, TERI B., artist, educator; b. York, Pa., Mar. 7, 1957; d. Richard MacDonald and Hazel Ring Bisker; m. Ike Hay, May 20, 1979; children: Mariah, Mistral. BS in Art Edn., Millersville (Pa.) U., 1979, MEd in Art, 1984. Tchr. Solanco Sch. Dist., Quarryville, Pa., 1980—82, Conestoga Valley Sch. Dist., Lancaster, Pa., 1979—80, New Sch. Lancaster, 1988—92, Penn Manor Sch. Dist., Millersville, 1993—. Adv. com. Lancaster (Pa.) Quilt Mus., 2004—. Avocations: bronze casting, felting, knitting, ceramics. Office: Penn Manor High Sch 100 E Cottage Ave Millersville PA 17551

HAYAKAWA, KAN-ICHI, retired food science educator; b. Shibukawa, Gumma, Japan, Aug. 12, 1931; arrived in U.S., 1961, naturalized, 1974; s. Chygoro and Kin (Hayakawa) H.; m. Setsuko Maekawa, Feb. 18, 1967. BS, Tokyo U. Fisheries, 1955; PhD, Rutgers U., 1964. Rsch. fellow Canners' Assn. Japan, 1955-60; asst. prof. food sci. Rutgers U., New Brunswick, NJ, 1964-70, assoc. prof. food sci., 1970-77, prof. food engring., 1977-82, Disting. prof. food engring., 1982-99, prof. emeritus, 1999—. Cons. to food processing cos.; organizer, chmn., participant NSF sponsored U.S.-Japan Coop. Conf., Tokyo, 1979; lectr. Industry R&D Inst. and Nat. Taiwan U., 1982, Wuxi Inst. Light Industry, China, 1986, Tokyo U. Fisheries, 1992. Co-editor: Heat Sterilization of Food, 1983; contbr. articles to books, profl. jours. and encys.; developer new math methods for predicting safety of food processes; found theoretical and exptl. theorems on heat and mass transfer in biol. material with or without strain--stress formation. Rsch. grantee USPHS, 1966-73, Nabisco Found., 1975-76, NSF, 1981-82, travel grantee NSF, 1972, Rutgers Rsch. Found., 1977, rsch. grantee Advanced Food Tech. Ctr., 1985-89, John von Neumann Nat. Supercomputer Ctr., 1989-90, Pitts. Nat. Supercomputer Ctrs., NSF, 1990-97, Cray Rsch. Inc., 1993-95, U.S. Army Natick R & D Ctr., 1992-94, USDA, 1994-98. Fellow Inst. Food Technologists; mem. ASHRAE (life, chmn. tech. com. on thermophys. property values of food 1981-85, mem. com. 1981-96).

HAYASHI, FUJIO, manufacturing executive; b. Tokyo, Jan. 12, 1954; came to U.S., 1964; s. Nisiki and Chikako H.; m. Susan Eleanor Haggard, Aug. 21, 1976; children: Stephen Tomio, Alan Kenji, Brian Makio. BSME, MSME, MIT, 1975; MBA, U. Rochester, 1978. Systems engr. Xerox Corp., Rochester, N.Y., 1975-78; sr. cons. Design and Devel. Group, Cleve., 1978-82; sr. assoc. Booz, Allen & Hamilton, Tokyo and N.Y.C., 1982-86; dir. market devel. Mead Imaging div. Mead Corp., Miamisburg, Ohio, 1986-91; mgr. bus. devel. Imaging Product div. Internat. Paper, Binghamton, N.Y., 1991-92; pres. Internat. Paper Co. (Japan) Inc., 1992-98; dir. stategic planning printing paper sector Internat. Paper Co., Memphis, 1998—. Patentee interlocking apparatus, 1978. Mem. IEEE, Beta Gamma Sigma, Pi Tau Sigma. Avocation: square dancing. Office: 6400 Poplar Ave Memphis TN 38197-0100

HAYASHI, FUMIKO, retail executive; Saleswoman Honda, 1977—87, BMW Japan, 1987—99, sales mgr., pres. BMW Tokyo, 2003—05; pres. Fahren Tokyo Volkswagen Group Japan, 1999—2003; adv. Daiei Inc., 2005, chairwoman & CEO, 2005—. Named one of world's 50 noteworthy female corp. mgr., Wall Street Jour., 2004, most powerful women, Forbes mag., 2005. Office: Daiei Inc 4-1-1 Minatojima Nakamachi Chuoku Kobe Hyogo 650 0046 Japan*

HAYASHI, KIM, music educator; b. Patterson, NJ, May 15, 1950; s. Mitsuru Hayashi and Mary Louise Hiyashi. MusB in Piano and Music Edn, U. Wash., 1978; MusM, U. Oreg., 1981, U. Ariz., 1987, D Mus Arts, 1995. Pvt. studio piano tchr. Seattle, Eugene, Oreg. and Tucson, 1972—; asst. undergrad. advisor Sch. Music U. Wash., Seattle, 1977—79; grad. tchg. asst. U. Oreg., Eugene, 1979—81, U. Ariz., Tucson, 1986—88; solo and chamber music performer, 1980—; dir. chamber music in pub. schs. Az. Friends of Chamber Music, Tucson, 1995—. Adj. faculty mem. Sch. Music U. Oreg., Eugene, 1982—86; adj. faculty dept. fine arts Pima Coll., Tucson, 1996—; preconcert lectr. Ariz. Friends of Chamber Music, 1999—; clinician Nev. State Music Tchrs. Assn., Las Vegas, 1997, Rosie's Music House, Phoenix, 2003. Chmn. Yamaha Corp. piano donation Berger Performing Arts Ctr., Ariz. State Schs. for Deaf and Blind, 1993—97. Named Theodore Presser Music Edn. scholar, U. Wash., 1971; Rotary fellow for study abroad, Staatliche Hochschule Musik, Freiburg, Germany, 1981—82, rsch. grantee, Grad. Coll. U. Ariz., 1988. Mem.: Phi Eta Sigma, Music Tchrs. Nat. Assn., Tucson Music Tchrs. Assn. (organizing chmn. command performances 1995, mem. command performancers com. 1995—2002), Ariz. State Music Tchrs. Assn. (adjudicator 1994—, chmn. James R. Anthony Honors Recital Auditions 1995—99, chmn. fundraising for James R. Anthony Honors Recital 1995—2002), Phi Beta Kappa. Office: 2925 E Adams St Tucson AZ 85716

HAYASHI, TETSUMARO, retired literature educator, writer, editor; b. Sakaide City, Japan, Mar. 22, 1929; arrived in U.S., 1954, naturalized, 1969; s. Tetsuro and Shieko (Honjyo) Hayashi; m. Akiko Sakuratani, Apr. 14, 1960; 1 child, Richard Hideki. BA, Okayama (Japan) U., 1953; MA, U. Fla., 1957; MALS, Kent State U., 1959, PhD, 1968; LHD (hon.), Wilmington Coll., Ohio, 2005. Assoc. and acting dir. Culver-Stockton Coll. Libr., Canton, Mo., 1959-63; instr. English Kent (Ohio) State U., 1965-68; from asst. prof. to assoc. prof. Ball State U., Muncie, Ind., 1968—77, prof., 1977-93; dir. Steinbeck Rsch. Inst., 1981-93; vis. grad. prof. Kwassui Women's Coll., Japan, 1993-96; v.p., grad. prof. English Yasuda Women's U., Hiroshima, Japan, 1996-2001, dir. grad. studies in English, 1997-99; ret., 2001. Sr. editl. cons. Steinbeck Yearbook, 2001—03; sr. cons. Steinbeck Soc. Japan, 1976—, New Steinbeck Soc. Am., 2004—; cons. Steinbeck Rev., 2004—. Author: (book) Sketches of American Culture, 1960, John Steinbeck: A Concise Bibliography, 1967, Arthur Miller Criticism, 1969, Robert Greene Criticism, 1971, Shakespeare's Sonnets: A Record of 20th Century Criticism, 1972, Index to Arthur Miller: Criticism, 1976; editor: A Looking Glass for London and England (Thomas Lodge, Robert Greene), An Elizabethan Text, 1970, Steinbeck's Literary Dimension, 1973, Steinbeck's Literary Dimension, Series II, 1991, A Study Guide to Steinbeck: A Handbook of His Major Works, 1974, 1979, 1993, 24 others; editor: (with Richard Astro) Steinbeck: The Man and His Work, 1971, John Steinbeck: A Dictionary of His Fictional Characters, 1976; founder, editor-in-chief: Steinbeck Quar., 1968—93, Steinbeck Monograph Series, 1971—91; contbr. articles to profl. jours. Executor Pruis Award Fund and Burkhardt Award Fund, Ball State U. Found., Muncie, 1978—. Named Disting. English Alumnus, Kent State U., 2002; grantee, Am. Philos. Soc., 1975, 1981, Am. Coun. Learned Socs., 1976, Bernard Boyd Meml. Found., 1986, Lyndon B. Johnson Found., 1987, others; Rotary Internat. Jr. fellow, U. Fla., 1957, Folger Sr. fellow, 1972. Mem.: MLA, Shakespeare Assn. Am., Am. Lit. Assn. Home: 4300 W Kings Row Muncie IN 47304-2436 Personal E-mail: rhaya16177@aol.com.

HAYCOCK, CHRISTINE ELIZABETH, retired medical educator, health educator; b. Mt. Vernon, NY, Jan. 7, 1924; d. John B. and Madeline (Sears) H.; m. Sam Moskowitz, July 6, 1958 (dec. Apr. 1997). SB, U. Chgo., 1948; MD, SUNY, Bklyn., 1952; MA in Polit. Sci., Rutgers U., 1981. RN, N.J.; diplomate Am. Bd. Surgery. Intern Walter Reed Army Med. Ctr., Washington,

1952-53; resident in surgery St. Barnabas Med. Ctr., Newark, 1954-58, St. John's Episcopal Hosp., Bklyn., 1958-59; pvt. practice Newark, 1959-68; asst. prof. surgery, N.J. Med. Sch. U. Med. and Dentistry N.J.-N.J. Med. Sch., Newark, 1968-75; assoc. prof. surgery, N.J. Med. Sch. UMDNJ, Newark, 1975-89, prof. clin. surgery, 1989-92; prof. emeritus, 1992—. Chief GYN Svc., VA Hosp., East Orange, NJ Trauma Soc.; pres. Med. Amature Radio Coun., 1981, bd. dirs. (Coun. award 1978); adv. com. NJ Phys. Conditioning of the Police Tng. Commn., 1984-96. Editor: Trauma and Pregnancy, 1985, Sports Medicine for the Athletic Female, 1980; mem. editl. bd. Jour. NJ Med. Soc., 1979-95, The Physician and Sports Medicine, 1975-98, The Main Event, 1987; contbr. articles to profl. jours. Chmn. bd. Essex County chpt. Am. Cancer Soc., West Orange, N.J., 1978-79, bd. mgrs., Livingston, N.J., 1962—, hon. life mem., 1992. With U.S. Army, 1947-86, col. Res. ret. Recipient Outstanding Alumnae award Bloomfield Coll., 1971, Res. Forces Achievement award, 1974, Distinguished Lecturer award Downstate Med. Ctr., 1976, Dr. Frank L. Babbott Meml. award SUNY Alumni Assn., 1982, Pres. Honor citation, N.J. Assn. Phys. Edn. and Health Tchrs., 1982, Commendation medal, 1982, Meritorious Svc. medal, 1986, Presdl. Citation, N.J. Assn. for Health, Phys. Edn. and Recreation, 1984, Med. Bd. Svc. award Newark City Hosp., 1986, Bertha Van Hoosen award Am. Med. Women's Assn., 1997, Alma Dea Morani MD Renaissance Women of Yr. award Found. for History of Women in Medicine, 2004; grantee Abbott Labs, 1981-82. Fellow ACS (hon., life, N.J. com. on trauma 1970-91), Am. Coll. Sports Medicine (trustee 1978-80), Photog. Soc. Am. (chmn. video/motion picture divsn. 1993-95; Silver medal jour. award 2000, 02); mem. AMA, Am. Med. Women's Assn. (bd. dirs. 1976-86, pres. 1980, hosp. assn. com. 1985—, Silver Medallion award 1980), Zonta Internat., Assn. Women Surgeons (treas. 1989-91, chair found. com. 1991-95, sec. 1995-99, Disting. Surgeon award 1990), N.J. Women's Assn. (pres. 1976, treas. 1989-92, Woman of Yr. 1987), Amateur Radio Relay League. Republican. Avocations: photography, dog training and showing, sports, collecting elephants, amateur radio. Home: 361 Roseville Ave Newark NJ 07107-1721 Personal E-mail: chrish2@juno.com.

HAYCOCK, KENNETH ROY, education educator, consultant; b. Hamilton, Ont., Can., Feb. 15, 1948; s. Bruce Frederick T. and Doris Marion P. (Downham) H.; m. Sheila Tripp, Jan. 28, 1990. BA, U. Western Ont., 1968, diploma in edn., 1969; specialist cert., U. Toronto, Can., 1971; MEd, U. Ottawa, Can., 1973; AMLS, U. Mich., 1974; EdD, Brigham Young U., 1991; MBA, Royal Roads, 2004. Tchr., dept. head Glebe Collegiate Inst., Ottawa, 1969-70, Col. By Secondary Sch., Ottawa, 1970-72; cons. Wellington County Bd. Edn., Guelph, Ont., 1972-76; coord. libr. svcs., supr. instrn. Vancouver (B.C.) Sch. Bd., Canada, 1976-84, acting mgr., elem./secondary edn. Canada, 1984-85, dir. instrn., head program svcs., 1985-89, 91-92; prin. Waverley Elem. Sch., 1989-91; prof. Sch. Libr., Archival and Info. Studies U. B.C., Vancouver, 1992—2005, dir., 1992—2002; prof. Sch. Libr. and Info. Sci., dir. San Jose State U., 2005—. Instr. univs. and colls.; pres. Ken Haycock and Assocs., Inc. Editor Tchr. Libr., 1978-2004; author various books; contbr. articles to profl. and scholarly jours. Trustee Guelph Pub. Libr., 1975-76; trustee West Vancouver Sch. Bd., 1993-99, chair, 1994-97, councilor Dist. of West Vancouver, 1999-2002; trustee West Vancouver Pub. Libr., 1999-2000. Recipient award Beta Phi Mu, 1976, Queen Elizabeth Silver Jubilee medal, 1977. Fellow: Can. Coll. Tchrs.; mem.: ASCD (urban curriculum leaders 1985—92, internat. panel 1990—94), ALA (exec. bd. 1999—2003, coun. 2004—, 1999—2003, Herbert and Virginia White Advocacy award 2001), Coun. for Can. Learning Resources (pres. 1995—98), Internat. Assn. Sch. Librarianship (dir. N.Am. 1993—95, exec. dir. 1995—2000, Ken Haycock Leadership Devel. award named in his honor 2001), B.C. Libr. Assn. (Ken Haycock Student Conf. award named in his honor 1999), Assn. for Libr. and Info. Sci. Edn. (sec. coun. dean and dirs. 1993—96, pres. 2005—), Ont. Libr. Assn., Can. Libr. Assn. (life; pres. 1977—78, Outstanding Svc. award 1991, Ken Haycock award for promoting librarianship named in his honor 2004), B.C. Tchr. Libr. Assn. (Ken Haycock Profl. Devel. award named in his honor 1984, Disting. Svc. award 1989, Helen Gordon Stewart Outstanding Contbns. award 2005), Can. Sch. Libr. Assn. (pres. 1974—75, Margaret B. Scott award of merit 1979, rsch. award 1984, Disting. Sch. Adminstr. award 1989, rsch. award 1995), Am. Assn. Sch. Librs. (pres. 1997—98, Baker and Taylor Disting. Svc. award 1996), Internat. Fedn. Libr. Assns. and Instns. (sect. on Edn. and Tng. 1997—2005, chair 1999—2001), Phi Delta Kappa (Young Leader in Edn. award). Home and Office: 5118 Meadfeild Rd West Vancouver BC Canada V7W 3G2 Office Phone: 604-925-0266. E-mail: ken@kenhaycock.com.

HAYDEN, CARLA DIANE, library director, educator; d. Bruce Kenard and Colleen (Dowling) Hayden. BA, Roosevelt U., 1973; MA in Libr. and Info. Sci., U. Chgo., 1977, PhD, 1987; LHD (hon.), U. Balt., 2000, Morgan State U., 2001. Children's and young adult libr. Chgo. Pub. Libr., 1973-81; asst. prof. Sch. Libr. and Info. Sci. U. Pitts.; libr. svcs. coord. Mus. Sci. and Industry, Chgo., 1982-87; mem. faculty Sch. Libr. and Info. Sci., Pitts., 1987-91; 1st dep. commr., chief libr. Chgo. Pub. Libr., 1991-93; exec. dir. Enoch Pratt Free Libr., Balt., 1993—. Adj. prof. U. Md., College Park, 1995—; faculty mem. L.I. U., NY, 1994, Columbia U., NYC, 1990, 91. Contbr. numerous articles to profl. jours. Bd. dirs. Md. African Am. Mus. Corp., Balt. City Hist. Soc., Balt. Reads, Goucher Coll., Md., Greater Balt. Cultural Alliance, Franklin and Eleanor Roosevelt Inst. and Libr., NYC, Balt., Md. Pub. Broadcasting Commn., Mercy Hosp., mem. adv. bd. Women's Ctr., Nat. Aquarium, mem. nat. adv. bd., Balt., PALINET, Sinai Hosp., U. Pitts. Sch. Info. Scis. Named Libr. of Yr. Libr. Jour., 1995, One of Md.'s Top 100 Women Warfield Bus. Record 1996, Daily Record, 2003, Woman of Yr. Ms. mag., 2003; recipient Legacy of Literacy award DuBois Cir., 1996, Torch Bearer award Coalition of 100 Black Women, 1996, Andrew White medal Loyola Coll., 1997, Pres.'s medal Johns Hopkins U., 1998, Pro Urbe award Coll. Notre Dame Md., 2004, Whitney M. Young Jr. award Greater Balt. Urban League, 2004, Leader award YWCA, Balt, 2004, Medal of Distinction Barnard Coll., 2005. Mem.: Md. Libr. Assn., Pub. Libr. Assn., ALA (pres.-elect 2002—03, pres. 2003—04, immediate past pres. 2004—05, chmn. com. on accreditation and spectrum initiative). Office: Enoch Pratt Free Library 400 Cathedral St Baltimore MD 21201-4401

HAYDEN, DONALD J., JR., pharmaceutical executive; Exec. v.p. health-care group Bristol-Myers Squibb Co., pres. Worldwide Medicines Group, corp. sr. v.p., 1998—2001, corp. exec. v.p., pres. N.Am. Medicines, 2002—. Office: Bristol-Myers Squibb Co 345 Park Ave New York NY 10154-0037

HAYDEN, HARROLD HARRISON, communications executive; b. Cin., Jan. 16, 1942; s. Harold Richard and Blanche Marie (Sargent) H. BA, Millikin U., Decatur, Ill., 1964; MA, DePaul U., Chgo., 1970. Dir. mktg. tng. Automatic Electric, Northlake, Ill., 1968-70; dir. Universal Tng. Co., Wilmette, Ill., 1970-80; pres. Performance Achievement Group, Chgo., 1980-85; v.p. Lead Mgmt. Service, Chgo., 1985-90, Qualified Lead Systems, Chicago Heights, Ill., 1990—; pres. Intramark, Chicago Heights, Ill., 1992-94, chmn., 1995-97, 2000—; pres. Pace Airline Svcs. USA, Chgo., 1994—97, 2000—01, v.p. Synergistic Networks, 2001—. Exec dir. Internat. Meetings Inst., 1997-2000. Author: (multimedia package) Successful Telephone Selling, 1979, Santa Fe Railroad Data, 1975, Best Ill. award, 1975; editor Secrets of Successful Telemarketing, 1985. Mem. Ohlmstead Hist. Soc., Riverside, Ill., 1985; bd. dirs. 44th Ward Bus. Com., Chgo., 1985-86; exec. mgr. British Consortium, 1989-91; bd. dirs. North Park Village, 1993-96; bd. dirs. Ill. Acad. Criminology, 1996-2000, pres., 2002-2003; vols. v.p. Am. Police Ctr. and Mus., 1996—. Recipient award Best Condo Bldg., Northside Real Estate Bd., Chgo., 1985. Mem. Am. Mgmt. Assn. (spkr. 1979-85), Pine Point Ski Club, Simply Singles (CEO). Avocations: sailing, skiing. Office: Intramark One World Trade Ctr 1540 Merchandise Mart Chicago IL 60654 Office Phone: 630-993-0460 41. Personal E-mail: hhh55@aol.com.

HAYDEN, JEFFREY LYNN, retired aerospace engineer; b. Hutchinson, Minn., Aug. 19, 1940; m. Brenda Bakken, 1970 (div. 1999); children: Eric, Nathan, Tyler. B Physics, U. Minn., 1969. Design engr. physics dept. U. Minn., 1964—76; design engr. Am. Med. Systems, Inc., 1976—78; sr. staff engr. Lockheed Martin, Waterton, Colo., 1978—99; prin., cons. PresciPoint Solutions, LLC, Littleton, Colo., 2000—. Contbr. articles to profl. jours. Staff sgt. USAF, 1963—69. Independent. Office: PresciPoint Solutions LLC Littleton CO Office Phone: 720-320-1568. Personal E-mail: jlhayden@earthlink.net.

HAYDEN, JOHN OLIN, English literature educator, writer; b. LA, Dec. 18, 1932; s. John Ellsworth and Norah Elizabeth (Bussens) H.; m. Mary Kathleen Garland, Dec. 18, 1965; children— Michael, John, Mark, Ann BA, U. Calif.-Santa Barbara, 1958; MA, Columbia U., 1959, PhD, 1965. Asst. prof. U. Colo., Boulder, 1964-66; assoc. prof. English lit. U. Calif.-Davis, 1966-75, prof. English lit., 1975-94, prof. emeritus, 1994—. Author: Romantic Reviewers, 1969, Polestar of the Ancients, 1979, William Wordsworth and the Mind of Man, 1993, Why the Great Books are Great, 1998; editor: Sir Walter Scott, 1970, Wordsworth: The Poems, 1977, Wordsworth: The Prose, 1988, Wordsworth: Selected Poetry, 1994. Served with USAF, 1951-55 E. J. Noble Found. fellow Columbia U., N.Y.C., 1959-61; fellow NEH, 1971, Am. Council Learned Socs., 1984 Republican. Roman Catholic. Avocation: coin collecting/numismatics. Home: 25199 Carlsbad Ave Davis CA 95616-9434 Office: U Calif English Dept Davis CA 95616 E-mail: johayden@ucdavis.edu.

HAYDEN, JOSEPH PAGE, JR., finance company executive; b. Cin., Oct. 8, 1929; s. Joseph Page and Amy Dorothy (Weber) H.; m. Lois Taylor, Dec. 29, 1951; children: Joseph Page III, William Taylor, John Weber, Thomas Richard. BS in Bus, Miami U., Oxford, Ohio, 1951; student, U. Cin. Law Sch., 1952; DL (hon.), Miami U., 1986. With mobile home div. Midland-Guardian Co., Cin., 1952-61, v.p., 1954-60; pres., chief exec. officer, dir. Midland Co., Cin., 1961-80, chmn. bd., CEO, dir., 1980-98, chmn. exec. com., bd. dirs., 1998—. Former bd. mem. Firstar Corp. (now U.S. Bank); former Cin. mem. bus. adv. com. Miami U., Oxford, Ohio; former mem. pres.'s council Xavier U., Cin.; former trustee Miami U. Found. Mem. Met. Club (Cin., Ohio), Comml. Club (Ohio), Boca Bay Pass Club (Fla.), Lemon Bay Golf (Fla.), Useppa Island Club (Fla.), Sigma Chi. Clubs: Queen City, Hyde Park Golf and Country, Cincinnati, Ohio. Office: 7000 Midland Blvd Amelia OH 45102-2608

HAYDEN, LINDA C., librarian, educator; b. Hazard, Ky. d. Walter H. and Nancy Catherine (Gott) Combs. BA, Coll. of William and Mary, 1966; MA in Teaching, Spalding U., 1976, postgrad., 1987; MSLS, U. Ky., 2002. Cert. elem. and early childhood edn. tchr., Ky., cert. public mgr., Governmental Svc. Ctr., Ky. Tchr. York County Pub. Schs., Poquoson, Va., 1966-67; asst. coord. children's svcs. Louisville Free Pub. Libr., 1969-74; tchr. Ursuline Spl. Edn. Ctr., Louisville, 1975-79; tchr., owner Multi-Handicapped Tutoring, Louisville, 1979-80; tchr. J-Town Presch., Inc., Jeffersontown, Ky., 1983-84; therapist Pine Tree Villa Nursing Home, Louisville, 1982-84; asst. prin., tchr. Brown's Lane Acad., Louisville, 1984-86; tchr. Jefferson County Pub. Schs., Louisville, 1986-94; access svcs. libr., reference and interlibr. loan libr., acad. libr., assoc. prof. Ky. State U., 1994—, faculty senate, 2005—. Part-time pub. rels. and outreach asst. Ky. Commn. on Cmty. Volunteerism and Svc., 1998-99; mem. faculty senate Ky. State U., 2005— Vol. tutor ESL with refugees, 1990—91. Mem.: ALA, Ky. Libr. Assn., Leadership Edn. Alumni Assn., Internat. Soc. for Tech. in Edn., Amnesty Internat., Pi Lambda Theta. Democrat. Avocations: music, sports, outdoors, cooking, computers.

HAYDEN, LISA C., interpreter, translator, language educator, writer; d. Thomas and Doris Hayden; m. Park Espenschade, July 1999. BA, U. Pa., 1985, MA, 1989. Comm. specialist Hannaford Bros. Co., Scarborough, Maine, 1990—92; resident dir. Am. Coun. Tchrs. of Russian, Moscow, 1992—93; program dir. United Way Internat., Moscow, 1993—94; dir., Moscow project office IREX, Internat. Partnerships Project, Moscow, 1995—96; dir. Inst. Internat. Edn., 1996—98; freelance writer Scarborough, Maine, 1998—; Russian interpreter and translator Maine Med. Ctr., Portland, 1999—2004; Russian tchr. and translator The Lang. Exch., Portland, 1999—; lectr. Russian lang. U. So. Maine, Portland, 2003—04. Cons. Eurasia Found., Christian Children's Fund, Moscow, 1994—95. Co-chair, treas. The Archangel Com., Portland, Maine, 1988—92; vol. Soup Kitchen, Children's Shelter, Moscow, 1993—94. Tchg. fellow, U. Pa., 1985—87. Avocations: gardening, cooking, travel, reading. Office: PO Box 6635 Scarborough ME 04070-6635 Personal E-mail: lisahesp@maine.rr.com.

HAYDEN, MICHAEL VINCENT, federal official, career military officer; b. Mar. 17, 1945; s. Harry V. Hayden Jr.; m. Jeanine Carrier; children: Margaret, Michael, Liam. BA in History, grad. Res. Officer Tng. Corps, Duquesne U., 1967, MA in Am. History, 1969; postgrad., Acad. Instr. Sch., Maxwell AFB, Ala., 1975, Squadron Officer Sch., 1976, Air Command and Staff Coll., 1978, Def. Intelligence Agy., Bolling AFB, D.C., 1980, Armed Forces Coll., Norfolk, Va., 1983, Air War Coll., Maxwell AFB, Ala., 1983. Commd. 2d lt. USAF, 1967, advanced through grades to gen., 2005, analyst, briefer Hdqrs. Strategic Air Command Offutt AFB, Nebr., 1970-72, chief intelligence divsn. Hdqrs. 8th Air Force Andersen AFB, Guam, 1972-75; acad. instr., cadet comdt. Res. Officer Tng. Corps St. Michael's Coll., Winooski, Vt., 1975-79; chief intelligence 51st Tactical Fighter Wing USAF, Osan Air Base, South Korea, 1980-82; air attache U.S. Embassy, Sofia, Bulgaria, 1984-86; politico-mil. affairs officer Strategy Divsn. USAF, Washington, 1986-89; dir. for def. policy and arms control NSC, Washington, 1989-91; chief Sec.'s Staff Group Office Sec. Air Force USAF, Washington, 1991-93, dir. intelligence directorate Hdqrs. U.S. European Command Stuttgart, Germany, 1993-95, spl. asst. to comdr. Hdqrs. Air Intelligence Agy. Kelly AFB, Tex., 1995, comdr. Air Intelligence Agy., dir. Joint Command Control, 1996-97; dep. chief of staff UN Command, U.S. Forces Korea, 1997—99; dir. Nat. Security Agy./Ctrl Security Svc., Ft. Meade, Md., 1999—2005; prin. dep. dir. Office Nat. Intelligence, Washington, 2005—. Decorated Air Force Achievement medal, Def. Disting. Svc. medal, Def. Superior Svc. medal with oak leaf cluster, Legion of Merit, Bronze Star, Meritorious Svc. medal with two oak leaf clusters, Air Force Commendation medal. Office: The White House 1600 Pennsylvania Ave NW Washington DC 20500

HAYDEN, PAUL ALLAN, speech pathology educator, consultant, researcher; b. Williston, N.D., Jan. 29, 1949; s. George L. Hayden and Ortense M. Bernier; m. Elaine Margret Stauder, Aug. 19, 1975; children: Dan, Jessica. BA in Speech Pathology summa cum laude, Moorhead (Minn.) State U., 1971, MS in Speech Pathology, 1972; PhD in Speech Pathology, Purdue U., 1975. Cert. speech pathologist. Prof. communicative disorders dept. U. Wis., River Falls, 1975—. Dept. chmn., 1988-2003; cons. area hosps., Wis., 1980—. Mem. Am. Speech Lang. and Hearing Assn. (presenter confs.), Wis. Speech Lang. and Hearing Assn., Phi Eta Sigma, Phi Kappa Phi. Office: Dept Communicative Disorders U Wis-River Falls River Falls WI 54022 Fax: (715) 425-3800. E-mail: paul.a.hayden@uwrf.edu.

HAYDEN, RAYMOND PAUL, lawyer; b. Rochester, N.Y., Jan. 15, 1939; s. John Joseph and Orpha (Lindsay) Hayden; children: Thomas Gerard, Christopher Matthew. BS in Marine Transit, SUNY Maritime Coll., 1960; LLB, Syracuse U., 1963. Bar: N.Y. 1963, U.S. Ct. Appeals (2d cir.) 1963, U.S. Dist. Ct. (ea. and so. dists.) N.Y. 1964, U.S. Supreme Ct. 1967. Assoc. Haight Gardner Poor & Havens, N.Y.C., 1963-70; asst. gen. counsel Commonwealth Oil Co., N.Y.C., 1970-71; ptnr. Hill Rivkins & Hayden LLP, N.Y.C., 1971—. Trustee Seamens Ch. Inst. of NY, 2004—; mem. coll. coun. SUNY Maritime Coll., 1977—98, chmn., 1983—98; mem. adv. coun. Tulane U. Admiralty Law Inst. Lt. (j.g.) USNR, 1960—70. Mem.: ABA (chmn. standing com. admiralty and maritime law 1982—86), Comité Maritime Internat., Maritime Law Assn. U.S. (chmn. com. admissions 1974—82, mem. exec. com. 1988—91, sec. 1996—98, 2d v.p. 1998—2000, 1st v.p. 2000—02, pres. 2002—04), Brookville Country Club, India House Club (bd. dirs. 2002—, v.p. 2005—). Office: Hill Rivkins & Hayden LLP 45 Broadway New York NY 10006-3739 Business E-Mail: rhayden@hillrivkins.com.

HAYDEN, RICHARD SETH, architectural firm executive; BArch, Syracuse U.; DFA (hon.), Hamilton Coll. Registered U.S. and U.K. Ptnr. Swanke, Hayden, Connell Archs., N.Y.C., 1972—, mng. prin., mem. exec. com. Chief restoration arch. Statue of Liberty; mem. archtl. leadership com. N.Y. Bldg. Congress. Co-author: Restoring the Statue of Liberty: Sculpture, Structure, Symbol, 1986. Trustee Syracuse U.; bd. dirs. N.Y. Hist. Soc. Fellow: AIA (past v.p. N.Y. chpt.); mem.: Royal Inst. Brit. Arch. Office: SHCA 295 Lafayette St New York NY 10012

HAYDEN, WILLIAM ROBERT, lawyer; b. Chgo., May 22, 1947; s. Robert George and Dorothy (Honan) H.; m. Carol Ann Brock, Aug. 12, 1978; 1 child, Nathaniel. BA, Kans. State U., 1969; JD with honors, George Washington U., 1972. Bar: D.C. 73, U.S. Dist. Ct. D.C. 75, U.S. Ct. Appeals (D.C. cir.) 75, Ariz. 78, U.S. Dist. Ct. Ariz. 78, U.S. Ct. Appeals (9th cir.) 79, U.S. Ct. Appeals (10th cir.) 97, U.S. Ct. Appeals (11th cir.) 01, Colo. (U.S. Dist. Ct.) 2002. Mem. gen. counsel's staff NLRB, Washington, 1973-75; assoc. O'Donoghue and O'Donoghue, Washington, 1975-78, Snell and Wilmer, Phoenix, 1978-82, ptnr., 1982—. Contbg. editor: Developing Labor Law, 1974, Employment Discrimination Law, 1989. Mem. ABA (labor and employment law sect.), Nat. Panel, Am. Arbitration Assn. (employment dispute resolution), Ariz. Bar Assn. (exec. com., past chmn. labor and employment law sect. 1984-89, employment civil jury instructions com.), Maricopa County Bar Assn., D.C. Bar Assn., Ariz. C. of C. (employee rels. subcom.). Avocations: tennis, softball, skiing. Office: Snell & Wilmer 1 Arizona Ctr Phoenix AZ 85004 E-mail: bhayden@swlaw.com.

HAYDOCK, WALTER JAMES, banker; b. Chgo., Dec. 14, 1947; s. Joseph Albert and Lillian V. (Adeszko) H.; m. Bonnie Jean Thompson, Aug. 22, 1970; children: Nicole Lynn, Matthew Michael. At, Harvard Bus. Coll., 1969—71, Daily Coll., 1971—73; BS in Acctg., DePaul U., 1976. Computer operator, jr. programmer Pepper Constrn. Co., Chgo., 1972—73; input analyst Continental Bank, Chgo., 1973—76, data control supr., 1976—79, corp. fixed asset adminstr., 1979—83, properties sys. analyst, 1983—87, props. sr. sys. supr., 1987—91; unit chief conversions Fed. Deposit Ins. Corp., Chgo., 1992—93, info. security specialist, 1993—96; info. security officer U. Ill., Chgo., 1996—2001, info. sys. adminstr., 2001—. Pres. Wal-Bon., Inc.; distbr. Lic. Disney Character Mdse. Dir. Dawnwood Homeowner Assn. Mem. Southwest Suburban Bd. Realtors. Home: 13525 Marissa Ct Homer Glen IL 60491 Office: 809 S Marshield Ave m/c 694 Chicago IL 60612-7209 Office Phone: 312-996-3768. Business E-Mail: whaydock@uic.edu.

HAYEK, SALIM MICHEL, pain medicine physician; b. Beirut, Dec. 12, 1967; s. Michel and Salwa Hayek; m. Addie Hayek. BS in Biology, Am. U. Beirut, 1982, MD, 1994; PhD, Case Western Res. U., 2001. Staff physician Cleve. Clinic Found., 2003—. Mem.: Internat. Assn. for Study of Pain, Am. Acad. Pain Medicine. Office: Cleve Clinic Found Dept Pain Mgmt 9500 Euclid Ave C25 Cleveland OH 44195

HAYEK, SALMA, actress; b. Coatzacoalcos, Veracruz, Mexico, Sept. 2, 1968; d. Sami Hayek Domingues and Diana H. Television work includes: Un Nuevo amanecer, 1988, Teresa, 1989, The Sinbad Show, 1993, Roadracers, 1994, El Vuelo del aguila, 1996, The Hunchback, 1997, In the Time of the Butterflies (also exec. prod.), 2001; Television appearances: Dream On, 1992, Nurses, 1992, Action, 1999. Films include Mi Vida Loca, 1993, Four Rooms, 1995, Desperado, 1995, Fair Game, 1995, From Dusk Til Dawn, 1996, Fled, 1996, Fools Rush In, 1997, Follow Me Home, 1997, Breaking Up, 1997, Sister Diastole, 1997, The Velocity of Gary, 1998, The Faculty, 1998, 54, 1998, Dogma, 1999, Wild Wild West, 1999, No One Writes to the Colonel, 1999, Shiny New Enemies, 2000, Frida, 2000, Timecode, 2000, Chain of Fools, 2000, Living It Up, 2000, Traffic, 2000, Hotel, 2001, Frida (also prod.), 2002, Spy Kids 3-D: Game Over, 2003, Once Upon a Time in Mexico, 2003, After the Sunset, 2004, Sian Ka'an, 2005, Ask the Dust, 2005; dir, exec. prod.: The Maldonado Miracle, 2003. Named one of 25 Most Influential Hispanics, Time Mag., 2005.*

HAYES, AILISH MAIRE, pediatrician; b. Limerick, Ireland, Feb. 1, 1951; arrived in U.S., 1984; d. Richard F. and Christina Beatrice (McDonald) H.; m. Haig Oghigian, Sept. 8, 1984 (div.). Grad., Univ. Coll., Dublin, Ireland, 1974, diploma in child health, 1976, diploma in obstetrics, 1978; MB, BCh, BAO, Nat. Univ. Ireland, Dublin, 1974. Bd. cert. in genetics. Intern in surgery Mater Miseriacordia Hosp., Dublin, Ireland, 1974-75; resident in pediatrics Children's Hosp., Crumlin, Dublin, 1975-77; fellow in neonatology Nat. Maternity Hosp., Dublin, Ireland, 1977-80; sr. resident in pediatrics Toronto Sick Children's Hosp., 1980-81; fellow in genetics Montreal Children's Hosp., 1981-84; instr. in pediatrics Med. Sch., Harvard U., Boston, 1984—; pediatrician Revere Pediatric Assocs., 1993—; asst. in pediatrics Mass. Gen. Hosp., Boston, 1990-93. Former attending physician Children's Hosp., Boston, Brigham and Women's Hosp., Boston, Beth Israel Hosp., Boston; cons. Nat. Birth Defects Ctr., Boston, 1986—; cons. in teratology Mass. Gen. Hosp., Boston, 1987-90; cons. pediatrics and genetics Retina Assocs., Boston, 1991-92; cons. Prenatal Diagnostic Ctr., Boston, 1994—; lectr. Harvard U. Med. Sch., Boston, 1989-91; presenter in field. Fellow Royal Coll. Physicians (fellow 1982), Royal Coll. Physicians. Home: 2 Stone Ter Marblehead MA 01945-1320 Office: Nat Birth Defects Ctr 40 2nd Ave Ste 460 Waltham MA 02451-1136

HAYES, ALICE BOURKE, academic administrator, biologist, researcher; b. Chgo., Dec. 31, 1937; d. William Joseph and Mary Alice (Cawley) Bourke; m. John J. Hayes, Sept. 2, 1961 (dec. July 1981). BS, Mundelein Coll., Chgo., 1959; MS, U. Ill., 1960; PhD, Northwestern U., 1972; DSc (hon.), Loyola U., Chgo., 1994; HHD (hon.), Fontbonne Coll., 1994; LHD (hon.), Mount St. Mary Coll., 1998; DSc (hon.), St. Louis U., 2002; EdD (hon.), Providence Coll., 2004. Rschr. Mcpl. Tb San., Chgo., 1960-62; faculty Loyola U., Chgo., 1962-87, chmn. dept., 1968-77, dean natural scis. divsn., 1977-80, assoc. acad. v.p., 1980-87, v.p. acad. affairs, 1987-89; provost, exec. v.p. St. Louis U., 1989-95; pres. U. San Diego, 1995—2003, pres. emerita, 2003—. Mem. space biology program NASA, 1980—86; mem. adv. panel NSF, 1977—81, Parmly Hearing Inst., 1986—89; del. Bot. Del. to South Africa, 1984, to People's Republic of China, 1988, to USSR, 1990; reviewer Coll. Bd. and Mellon Found. Nat. Hispanic Scholar Awards, 1985—86; bd. dirs. Loyola U. Chgo., Jack-in-the-Box, ConAgra; mem. Ill. Bd. Higher Edn., 2004. Co-author books; contbr. articles to profl. publs. Campaign mem. Mental Health Assn. Ill., Chgo., 1973-89; trustee Chgo.-No. Ill. divsn. Nat. Multiple Sclerosis Soc., 1981-89, bd. dirs., 1980-88, com. chmn., sec. to bd. dirs., vice chmn. bd. dirs.; trustee Regina Dominican Acad., 1984-89, Civitas Dei Found., 1987-92, Rockhurst Coll., Loyola U., Chgo., San Diego Found.; trustee St. Ignatius Coll. Prep. Sch., bd. dirs., 1984-89, sec., vice chmn.; bd. dirs. Urban League Met. St. Louis, St. Louis Sci. Ctr., 1991-95, Cath. Charities St. Louis, 1992-95, St. Louis County Hist. Soc., 1992-95, Cath. Charities San Diego, 1996—, San Diego Hist. Soc., 1996—; bd. dirs., trustee Old Globe Theater, 1996—. Named to Tchrs.' Hall of Fame Blue Key Soc.; fellow in botany U. Ill., 1959-60; fellow in botany NSF, 1969-71; grantee Am. Orchid Soc., 1967; grantee HEW, 1969, 76; grantee NSF, 1975; grantee NASA, 1980-85. Mem. AAAS, AAUP (corp. rep. 1980-85), Am. Assn. for Higher Edn., Am. Assn. Univ. Adminstrs. (mem. program com. nat. meeting 1988), Am. Soc. Gravitational and Space Biology, Assn. Midwest Coll. Biology Tchrs., Am. Soc. Plant Physiology, Bot. Soc. Am., Am. Inst. Biol. Scis. Acad., Chgo. Network, Soc. Ill. Microbiologists (edn. com. 1969-70, Pasteur award com. 1975, pub. rels. com. 1974, chair speakers' bur. 1974-79), Chgo. Assn. Tech. Socs. (acad. liaison 1982-85, awards com. 1984-89), Am. Coun. on Edn. (corp. rep. higher edn. panel), Ctr. Rsch. Librs. (nominating com. 1986), N.C. Assn. Colls. and Schs. (cons., evaluator Commn. on Higher Edn. 1984-95, commr.-at-large 1988-94), Mo. Women's Forum Club, Sigma Xi, Delta Sigma Rho, Sigma Delta Epsilon, Phi Beta Kappa, Alpha Sigma Nu. Roman Catholic. Home: 6801 N Loron Chicago IL 60646

HAYES, ANDREW WALLACE, II, consumer products company executive; b. Corning, Ark., Aug. 21, 1939; s. Andrew Wallace and Helen (Latimer) H.; m. Sandra Smith, Dec. 28, 1963; children: Andrew Wallace III, Helen Cathleen, Benjamin Bailey. AB, Emory U., 1961; MS, Auburn U., 1964, PhD, 1967. Diplomate Am. Bd. Toxicology, Am. Bd. Forensic Medicine, Am. Bd. Forensic Examiners; cert. nutrition specialist; Eurotox registered toxicologist. NIH postdoctoral fellow, rsch. assoc. div. toxicology Vanderbilt U. Sch. Med.,

Nashville, 1966-68; asst. prof. dept. microbiology U. Ala., Tuscaloosa, 1968-71, assoc. prof. dept. microbiology, 1971-75, prof. depts. microbiology and biochemistry, 1975; assoc. prof. dept. pharmacology and toxicology U. Miss. Med. Ctr., Jackson, 1975-76, prof. dept. pharmacology and toxicology, 1976-80, program dir. NIEHS tng. program in environ. toxicology, 1977-80; dir. toxicology rsch. Rohm and Haas Co., Spring House, Pa., 1980-84, dir. regulatory affairs, agrl. chems. (worldwide) Phila., 1984; corp. toxicologist RJR Nabisco Inc., Winston-Salem, N.C., 1984; corp. toxicologist, dir. biochem. and biobehavioral rsch., Bowman Gray Tech. Ctr. R.J. Reynolds Tobacco Co., Winston-Salem, N.C., 1984-86, corp. toxicologist, group dir. biochem. and biobehavioral rsch., 1986-87, corp. toxicologist, v.p. biochem. and biobehavioral rsch., 1987-92; prof. Bowman Gray Sch. Medicine Wake Forest U., Winston-Salem, 1992; v.p. corp. product integrity The Gillette Co., Boston, 1993—2002; IUTOX faculty risk assessment summer sch., 1990, 92, 94, 96, 98, 2000, 02, 2004; prin. Gradient Corp., Cambridge, Mass., 2002—03. Vis. sr. scientist biochemistry dept. Cen. Vet. Lab., New Haw, Weybridge, Surrey; Eng., 1977; disting. lectr. U. Calif., 1979; vis. prof. dept. vet. pub. health Tex. A&M U., 1979-91; rsch. prof. dept. physiology and biophysics Sch. Dentistry, Temple U., 1981-84, Phila. Coll. Pharmacy and Sci., 1982-84, dept. medicine and toxicology program Duke U., 1986-2001, dept. pharmacology and toxicology Med. Coll. Va., 1987—, Sch. Vet. Med., Va. Poly. Inst., 1988—, Sch. Pub. Health U. Mass, Armherst, 1994—, dept. pharmacology and toxicology Sch. Medicine, U. Louisville, 1997—; mem. faculty Wayne State U., 1987; vis. scientist Harvard U. Sch. Pub. Health, Boston, 2003—; collaborator Interlab. Collaborative Study for Aflatoxin B1, FDA, 1977, Aflatoxin Check Sample Survey, Internat. Agy. Rsch. on Cancer, 1978; mem. Target Organ Toxicity Conf. Steering Com., 1978-88, Panel on Equivalent Safety Concept of Maritime Hazardous Materials, Nat. Materials Adv. Bd., NAS, 1979-82, Safe Drinking Water Com., Bd. Toxicology and Environ. Health Hazards, NAS, 1979-81, Environ. Health Scis. Rev. Com. NIEHS, 1981-85, sci. program com. Internat. Congress Toxicology, 1982-83, Testing Task Group, CMA, 1981-84, Chem. Systems Lab. Toxin Def. Group Rev. Panel, U.S. Army, 1982, TDB/CIS User Assessment Panel Life Scis. Rsch. Office, FASEB, Bethesda, Md., 1982; alt. del. Internat. Union Toxicology, 1982-83; advisor U.S. Army Med. Command, 1982-84; del. Internat. Union Toxicology, 1984-86; cons. Walter Reed Army Inst. Rsch., 1984-86; mem. selection com. Immunotoxicology Found., 1986, Commn. on Comm., Internat. Union Toxicology, 1986-89, program com. Toxicology Forum, 1986-87, toxicology adv. bd. Raven Press, N.Y.C., 1982-96; mem. external adv. bd. La. Inst. Toxicology, 1996—; bd. dirs. Toxicology Edn. Found., 1997-2001, 2005—, pres., 1998-2000; mem. sci. adv. bd. Inst. In Vitro Scis., 1997-2002; commn. strategic devel. IUTOX, 1997, sec.-gen., 2004—; bd. dirs. Ctrs. for Alternatives to Animal Testing; sci. adv. com. on alternative toxicol. methods NIEHS, 2002-05; mem. sci. expert panel for environ. water monitors U.S. Army, 2004—; sci. adv. panel EPA FIFRA, 2004, 05; trustee Scientists Ctr. for Animal Welfare, 2004—. Author: Mycotoxin Teratogenicity, 1981; editor: Toxicology of the Eye, Ear and Other Special Senses, 1985, Extrapolation of Dosimetric Relationships for Inhaled Particles and Gases, 1989, Prinicples and Methods of Toxicology, 4th edit., 2001, Human and Experimental Toxicology, 1993—, Jour. Toxicology, Cutaneous and Ocular Toxicology, 2001—; co-author: Loomis's Essentials of Toxicology, 4th edit., 1996; co-editor: Target Organ Toxicity Series, 1989—; founding editor Comments of Toxicology, 1986—2003; assoc. editor Regulatory Toxicology and Pharmacology, 1986—, Toxicology and Applied Pharmacology, 1980, editor, 1981-86, mem. editl. bd., 1978-80; mem. editl. bd. Archives Environ. Contamination and Toxicology, 1987-2000, Environ. Toxin Series, 1987-95, Toxicology, 1978-83, Jour. Toxicology and Environ. Health, 1979—, Food and Chem. Toxicology, 1987—; mem. editl. coun. Toxicon, 1980-90; contbr. articles to profl. jours., chpts. to books. Mem. adv. coun. Auburn U., 1987—97; mem. dept. environ. health Harvard Sch. Pub. Health, 1997—; mem. nat. coun. Fla. Coll., 1980—97, bd. dirs., 1998—; trustee Scientists Ctr. for Animal Welfare, 2004—; bd. dirs. Join Hands--The Health and Safety Alliance, 1995—2001; trustee Am. Assn. for Accreditation of Lab. Animal Care, Chgo., 1984—89. Named Exec. of Yr., Winston-Salem chpt. Profl. Secs. Internat., 1989-90; recipient cert. of merit, EPA, 1981, Rsch. Career Devel. award NIH, 1973-78. Fellow Acad. Toxicological Scis. (bd. dirs. 1993-2001), Inst. Biology, Am. Coll. Forensic Examiners; mem. Inst. Toxicology (mem. external adv. bd. 1996—), Soc. Toxicology (co-chmn. tech. com. 1978, chmn. 1978-79, pres. Mid-Atlantic chpt. 1983-84, v.p. mech. sect., 1981-82, 82-83, animals in rsch. com. 1996-99, chmn. 1998-99, bd. dirs. toxicology edn. found. 1996-07, pres. 1998-2000), Am. Coll. Toxicology (edn. com. 1996-99, coun. 2003-05), The Cosmetic, Toiletry, and Fragrance Assn. (sci. adv. exec. com. 1999-2002), Am. Soc. Pharmacology and Exptl. Therapeutics (chmn. com. on environ. pharmacology 1981-82, coun. sect. toxicology), Am. Chem. Soc. (com. on chemistry and pub. affairs task force on TSCA Interagy. Testing Com.'s Preliminary List of Chem. Substances, 1977-80), Am. Soc. for Nutritional Scis., Am. Soc. for Microbiology (environ. microbiology com. 1975-76), Internat. Union Pharmacology (sect. on toxicology), Internat. Soc. Regulatory Toxicology and Pharmacology, Interant. Itamesis Soc. (chair exec. com. 2005—), Sigma Xi. Mem. Ch. of Christ. Avocation: fishing. Office: Harvard Sch Public Health Harvard Univ Boston MA 02142 Office Phone: 978-409-1153. E-mail: awallacehayes@comcast.net.

HAYES, ANN CARSON, computer services executive; b. Hamlin, Tex., Apr. 25, 1941; d. Fred Elbert and Nona Faye (Riddle) Carson; m. James Russell Brown, May 7, 1959 (div. July 1973); children: James Allen, Daniel Russell, Robert Anthony, Debra Faye Brown; m. Robert Lee Hayes, Nov. 15, 1975. AAS, Howard Coll., Tex., 1972; student, Regents Coll., N.Y.C., 1986. Lic. ins. agt., Nat. Assn. for Self-Employed. Freelance artist, Big Spring, Tex., 1956-76; real estate agt. Century 21, Littleton, Colo., 1976-78, Huntsville, Ala., 1978-79; art dir. Hayes and Co., Splendora, Tex., 1979—; CEO Hayes Enterprises, New Caney, Tex., 2000—. Executor Hayes Tax Svc., New Caney, 1992. Mem. NAFE. Democrat. Episcopalian. Avocations: sculpting, glass etching. Home and Office: 20152 Split Oak Dr New Caney TX 77357-3565

HAYES, BERNARD M., military officer, researcher; s. Robert and Hallie Hayes. BSc, NC Agrl. and Tech. State U., 1979—84. Officer US Army, Fayetteville, NC, 1984—88, maj., us army reserves Washington, 1984—, officer Little Rock, 1988—92, Korea (South), 1992—94, Warrenton, Va., 1994—96; rsch. analyst Northrop Grumman, Falls Ch., Va., 1996—. Co-founder The Greater Manassas Mentoring Network, Va., 1997—2000; mem. Christians Involved Together With Youth, Manassas, Va., 1995—2001; pres. Outreach Com. First AME Ch., Manassas, Va., 1999—2003; nominating com. chair Prince William County ARC, Manassas, Va., 1996—2000. Decorated Meritorious Svc. medal US Army, Master Parachutist Badge. Mem.: Women in Def. African Meth. Episcopal. Avocations: photography, running. Personal E-mail: bhayes5786@aol.com.

HAYES, BYRON JACKSON, JR., retired lawyer; b. L.A., July 9, 1934; s. Byron Jackson and Caroline Violet (Scott) H.; m. DeAnne Saliba, June 30, 1962; children: Kenneth Byron, Patricia DeAnne. Student, Pomona Coll., 1952-56; BA magna cum laude, Harvard U., LLB cum laude, 1959. Bar: Calif. 1960, U.S. Supreme Ct. 1963. Assoc. McCutchen, Black, Verleger & Shea, L.A., 1960-68, ptnr., 1968-89, Baker & Hostetler, 1990-97; ret., 1998. Gov. bd. Fashion Inst. Design & Mdse., 2003—. Trustee L.A. Urban Found., 1996—, CFO, 1998-2000, v.p., CFO, 2000—; trustee L.A. Ch. Ext. Soc. United Meth. Ch., 1967-77, pres., 1974-77, chancellor ann. conf. Pacific and S.W., 1979-86, dir. 1010 devel. corp., 1993—, v.p., 1995—; dir., pres. Pacific and S.W. United Meth. Found., 1978-84; dir., v.p. Padua Hills, Inc., 1999—. Named Layperson of yr. Pacific and S.W. Ann. Conf., United Meth. Ch., 1981; recipient Bishop's award, 1992, 2000. Mem. Am. Coll. Mortgage Attys. (regent 1984-93, pres. 1993-94), Calif. Bar Assn., Los Angeles County Bar Assn. (chmn. real property sect. 1982-83), Toluca Lake Property Owners Assn. (sec. 1990-94), Toluca Lake C. of C. (dir. 2001—), Pomona Coll. Alumni Assn. (pres. 1984-85), Pomona Coll. Torchbearers (pres. 2001-2003), Lakeside Golf Club. Office Phone: 818-752-4653. Personal E-mail: bhayes@earthlink.net.

HAYES, CHARLES, religious organization executive, clergyman; b. Chgo., Aug. 4, 1950; s. Charles and Doris Yvonne (Davis) H.; children: Tammy, Beverly, Christine, Crystal, Enda. Degree in Theology, Emmaus Bible Sch., 1977; AA in Data Processing, Kennedy King Coll., 1982, AS in Acctg., 1985; BA, Chgo. State U., 1986, MS in Libr. Sci., 1996, MA in Cmty. Coll. Adminstrn., 2000. Lic. minister. Instr. Kennedy King Coll., Chgo., 1980-82; asst. coll. libr. city colls. Chgo., 1985-86; agt. IRS, Chgo., 1986; assoc. pastor St. Mary's Missionary Bapt. Church, Chgo., 1980—; nat. pres. Christians Taking Action, Inc., Chgo., 1983—; libr., lectr. Olive-Harvey Coll., Chgo., 1997—. Contbr. articles to profl. jours. Recipient Recognition award Ch. Christ, 1977, Appreciation award U.S. Com. for UNICEF, 1985, Internat. World Leaders award. Democrat. Rep. Avocations: horticulture, aquariums. Office: 5942 S Michigan Ave Chicago IL 60637-2183 Office Phone: 773-324-5851. E-mail: charleshayesus@yahoo.com.

HAYES, CHARLES DEWAYNE, professional baseball player; b. Hattiesburg, Miss., May 29, 1965; Grad. high sch., Miss. With San Francisco Giants, 1988-89, 98-99; 3d baseman Phila. Phillies, 1989-91, 95; with N.Y. Yankees, 1992, 96-97, Colo. Rockies, 1993-94, Pitts. Pirates, 1996, Milwaukee Brewers, 2000—. Office: Milwaukee Briewers 1 Brewers Way Milwaukee WI 53214-3651

HAYES, CHARLES FRANKLIN, III, museum director, consultant; b. Boston, Mar. 6, 1932; m. Nannette J. Rhodes; children: Marna Brewster Dove, Tavia Frances. AB in Anthropology, Archaeology, and Ethnography, Harvard U., 1954; MA in Anthropology, U. Colo., 1958. Rsch. asst. Glen Canyon Archeol. Survey U. Utah., 1957; rsch. asst. Shoshone Indian Land Claims U. Colo., 1957; jr. anthropologist Rochester (N.Y.) Mus. and Sci. Ctr., 1959-61, assoc. curator anthropology, 1961-66, curator anthropology, 1966-79, coord. curator, mus. dir., 1970-79, dir. rsch., 1979-97, also instr. Sch. Sci. and Man; ret., 1997. Asst. lectr. U. Rochester, 1961-69, assoc. lectr., 1970-73; lectr. anthropology St. John Fisher Coll., 1986, 89, rsch. cons. 1997—; cons. Rochester Hosp. Soc., 2003 Contbr. 70 publs. on museology and archeology. Trustee Seneca Iroquois Nat. Mus., Salamanca, N.Y., 1977-2002; mem. restoration com. New City Hall, Rochester, 1977. 2nd lt. USAF, 1954-56, USAFR, 1956-67. Fellow N.Y. State Archeol. Assn. (sec. 2 yrs., v.p. 2 yrs., pres. 1967-69, chair publs. 1965-67, editor rschs. and transactions 1966-67, co-editor 1976-77, editor The Bull. 1983—, chmn. awards and fellowships com. 1975-77, sec. Lewis H. Morgan chpt. 2 yrs., pres. 4 yrs., exec. com. 20 yrs.).

HAYES, CLAUDE QUINTEN CHRISTOPHER, research scientist, inventor; b. N.Y.C., Nov. 15, 1945; s. Claude and Celestine (Stanley) H.; m. Solvi Wold, 2002. BA in Chemistry and Geol. Sci., Columbia U., 1971, postgrad., 1972-73, N.Y. Law Sch., 1973-75; JD, Thomas Jefferson Law Sch., 1978. Cert. community coll. tchr. earth scis., phys. sci., law, Calif. Tech. writer Burroughs Corp., San Diego, 1978-79; instr. phys. scis. Nat. U., San Diego, 1980-81; instr. bus. law, earth scis. Miramar Coll., 1978-82; sr. systems analyst Gen. Dynamics Convair, 1979-80, advanced mfg. technologist, sr. engr., 1980-81; pvt. practice sci. and tech. cons. Calif., 1979—; instr. phys. sci., phys. geography, bus. law San Diego Community Coll. Dist., 1976-82, 85-90; U.S. Dept. Def. contractor Def. Nuclear Agy., Strategic Def. Initiative Agy., USAF, Def. Advance Rsch. Projects Agy., 1986—, U.S. Army, 1991—, USN, 1995-2000. Adj. prof. phys. chemistry San Diego State U., 1986-87; bus. and computer sci. def. rsch. contractor to Maxwell Labs., Honeywell Inc., Naval Ocean Sys. Ctr.; tech. cons. Pizza Hut, Inc., Carts of Colo., Smiths Industries; guest lectr. in endothermics applied to protective devices and clothing; lectr. in field of invention and patent commercial litigation Contbr. articles to profl. jours.; patentee in field. Mem. Am. Chem. Soc., N.Y. Acad. Sci., Am. Inst. Aero. and Astronautics, Princeton Columbia Barnard Club. Avocations: travel, technical, ancient history, art, people. Home and Office: 3737 3rd Ave Apt 308 San Diego CA 92103-4133 Office Phone: 619-299-2267.

HAYES, COLLEEN BALLARD, journalist, photographer, writer; b. Kansas City, Mo. d. Charles Richard and Mary Frances (Ballard) Hayes. BA in English, U. Kans., 1972. Assoc. editor, reporter Johnson County (Kans.) Sun newspapers, 1967—68; editor, writer press releases and pub. rels. Met. Plan Agy., 1968-70; writer speeches, Freedom of Info. and other letters for Pres. U.S., U.S. Senators, U.S. Reps., midwest govs., EPA, 1972—82. Contbr. articles (with photography) Elle Mag., Travel-Holiday, Country Inns Mag., Archtl. Digest publs., Confederate Veteran Mag., The Boston Globe, The Phila. Inquirer, Chgo. Tribune, L.A. Times, The Balt. Sun, Odyssey, San Francisco Examiner, The Denver Post, Christian Science Monitor, The Detroit News, The Orlando Sentinel, St. Petersburg Times, St. Louis Post Dispatch, The Kansas City Star, San Jose Mercury News, N.Y. Daily News, The Plain Dealer, Chicago Sun-Times, Des Moines Register, Richmond (Va.) Times-Dispatch, Women's Sports and Fitness, The Calgary Herald, others; co-author: Anthology Am. Holidays; contbr. numerous nat. and regional poetry anthologies, Nat. Scholastic Mag. (recipient writing award), Mo. Hist. Rev., others; lead in drama prodns. at regional theaters and Topeka Civic Theater; commentator on WIBW-TV, performed role of Medea on KTWU Pub. TV, guest interview KCUR-FM, others. Named to, Honorable Order Ky. Cols.; recipient 1st Prize Bethany Coll. Creative Writing award, Key to City of St. Joseph, Mo., City and Regional Tennis awards, others. Mem. Jackson County Hist. Soc., Quantrill Hist. Soc., Pony Express Hist. Soc., St. Andrew Scottish Soc., Woodside Racquet Club. Avocations: history, international and adventure travel, lap swimming, tennis, golf. E-mail: bcolin77@hotmail.com, bballard7@yahoo.com.

HAYES, CYNTHIA ANN (C.A. HAYES), writer; b. L.A., Sept. 11, 1954; d. Lafayette and Verna (O'Gee) H.; 1 child, LaLaunie Charisse. Student, U. Calif., L.A., 1972-75. Author: The My Family Collection, 1985, That Lovely Piece of Art, 1997, The Death of Lillie Maroe, 1998, The Night Aunt Ives Went to Sleep, 1999. Donor The Brotherhood Crusade, The Donor's Welfare Plan. Mem. U. Calif. L.A., The Duvall Found. Democrat. Baptist. Avocations: sewing, creating graphic designs, sailing, bicycling, attending concerts and theater.

HAYES, DAVID C., actor, writer; b. Garden City, Mich., Nov. 24, 1971; s. David W. and Sally A. Hayes; m. Sandra R. Stankiewicz, Sept. 9, 2000. BA, Mich. State U., 1994; cert. in children's lit., Inst. Children's Lit., Conn., 2004. Singer: (feature films) Back Woods; author: Shower of Blood, Dark Places; actor: (feature films) Machined, Devil Girls, Deadly Scavengers, Silo Killer 2: The Wrath of Kyle. Recipient award, Internat. Telly Awards, 2003. Personal E-mail: davidchayes@hotmail.com.

HAYES, DAVID JOHN, lawyer; b. Rochester, NY, Oct. 7, 1953; s. John E. and Helen E. (Hendrick) H.; m. Elizabeth Haile, Oct. 2, 1982; children: Katherine, Stephen, Molly. AB summa cum laude, U. Notre Dame, 1975; JD, Stanford U., 1978. Bar: D.C. 1978. Law clk. to hon. William Jones U.S. Dist. Ct. D.C., Washington, 1978-79; assoc. Hogan & Hartson, Washington, 1979-86, ptnr., 1986-90, Latham & Watkins, Washington, 1990—97, ptnr., global chair, environmental land and resources dept., 2001—; dep. sec. US Dept. of Interior, Washington, 1997—2001. Chmn. bd. dirs. Environ. Law Inst., bd. dir. RESOLVE, Am. Rivers, Natural Heritage Inst., bd. of visitors, Stanford Law Sch. Mem. editorial adv. bd. RCRA and Superfund Quar.; contbr. articles to profl. jours. Mem. ABA, D.C. Bar (mem. steering com.), Phi Beta Kappa. Office: Latham & Watkins Ste 1000 555 11th St NW Washington DC 20004-1304

HAYES, DAVID JOHN ARTHUR, JR., legal association executive; b. Chgo., July 30, 1929; s. David J.A. and Lucille (Johnson) H.; m. Anne Huston, Feb. 20, 1963; children— David J.A. III, Cary AB, Harvard U., 1952, JD, 1961. Bar: Ill. Trust officer, asst. sec. First Nat. Bank of Evanston, Ill., 1961-63; gen. counsel Ill. State Bar Assn., Chgo., 1963-66; asst. dir. ABA, Chgo., 1966-68, div. dir., 1968-69, asst. exec. dir., 1969-87, v.p., 1987-88, assoc. exec. v.p., 1989-90, sr. assoc. exec. v.p., 1990, exec. dir., 1990-94, exec. dir. emeritus, 1994—; exec. dir. Naval Res. Lawyers Assn., 1971-75; asst. sec. gen. Internat. Bar Assn., 1978-80, 90—, Inter-ABA, 1984—. Contbr. articles to profl. jours. Capt. JAGC, USNR Fellow Am. Bar Found. (life); mem. Ill. State Bar Assn. (ho. of dels. 1972-76), Nat. Orgn. Bar Counsel (pres. 1967), Chgo. Bar Assn., Michigan Shores Club. Home: 908 Pontiac Rd Wilmette IL 60091-1349 Office: ABA 750 N Lake Shore Dr Chicago IL 60611-4403 E-mail: djahayes@aol.com.

HAYES, DAVID MICHAEL, lawyer; b. Syracuse, N.Y., Dec. 2, 1943; s. James P. and Lillie Anna (Wood) H.; m. Elizabeth S. Tracy, Aug. 26, 1972; children: Timothy T., AnnElizabeth S. AB, Syracuse U., 1965; LLB, U. Va., 1968. Bar: Va. 1968, N.Y. 1969. Assoc. Hiscock & Barclay, Syracuse, 1968-72; asst. gen. counsel Agway Inc., Syracuse, 1972-81, gen. counsel, sec., 1981-87, v.p., gen. counsel, sec., 1987-92, sr. v.p., gen. counsel, sec., 1992-2001; of counsel Bond, Schoeneck & King, Syracuse, 2001—. Adj. prof. law Syracuse U. Coll. Law, 1995—; former chmn. Nat. Coun. of Farmer Coops. Legal Tax and Acctg. Com. Bd. dirs., former pres. Boys and Girls Club of Syracuse. With Army N.G., 1968-74. Mem.: ABA, Va. State Bar, N.Y. State Bar Assn. (ho. of dels. 1995—99, 2002—, exec. com. of antitrust sect. 2001—), Onondaga County Bar Assn. (pres. 1998), N.Y. Bar Found., Skaneateles Country Club, Century Club. Democrat. Office: BS&K One Lincoln Ctr Syracuse NY 13202-1355 Office Phone: 315-218-8188. E-mail: dhayes@bsk.com.

HAYES, DAVID RYAN, mathematics professor; b. Raleigh, N.C., July 14, 1937; s. Woodrow Rufus and Eleanor Ruth (Crocker) H.; m. Carla Ann Bradshaw, Sept. 2, 1961 (div. 1980); children: Robert, Christopher, Jonathan; m. Irene P. Brown, Nov. 6, 2004. AB, Duke U., 1959, PhD, 1963. Asst. prof. U. Tenn., Knoxville, 1963-65, assoc. prof., 1965-67, U. Mass., Amherst, 1967-72, prof., 1972—2002, Emeritus prof., 2002—. Visiting prof. Oxford (Eng.) U., 1974-75, Harvard U., Cambridge, Mass., 1981, U. Calif., San Diego, 1983, Imperial Coll. of Sci. and Tech., London, 1989. Contbr. numerous articles to profl. jours. NSF postdoctoral fellow Harvard U., 1966-67. Mem. Am. Math. Soc., Math. Assn. Am. Democrat. E-mail: cftheorie@aol.com.

HAYES, DAVID VINCENT, sculptor; b. Hartford, Conn., Mar. 15, 1931; s. David Vincent and Adelaide (Brown) H.; m. Julia Moriarty, June 22, 1957; children: David Matthew, Brian James, Mary Judith, John Mark. AB, U. Notre Dame, 1953; MFA, Ind. U., 1955. Vis. lectr. visual and environ. studies Harvard U., 1972-73; regent U. Hartford, 1992-94. One man shows include Ind. U., 1955, Wesleyan U., Middletown, Conn., 1958, Mus. Modern Art, 1959, Willard Gallery, N.Y.C., 1961-64, 66, 69, 71, U. Notre Dame-Ind. U., 1963, Root Art Center, Clinton, N.Y., 1963, Galerie David Anderson, Paris, France, 1966, Columbus (Ohio) Mus., 1974, Martha Jackson Gallery, N.Y.C., 1974, Everson Mus., Syracuse, N.Y., 1975, DeCordova Mus., Lincoln, Mass., 1977, Springfield (Mass.) Mus., 1978, SUNY, Albany, 1978, Dartmouth Coll., 1979, Amherst Coll., 1979, Nassau County (N.Y.) Mus., 1979, Saratoga Performing Arts Center, Sarasota Springs, N.Y., 1980, Old State House, Hartford, 1981, Shippee Gallery, N.Y.C., 1984, 86, Elaine Benson Gallery, Bridgehampton, N.Y., 1993, Anderson Gallery, Buffalo, 1994, Prudential Ctr., Boston, 1996, U. New Haven, 1997, Orlando City Hall, Boca Raton Mus., 1998, Colgate U., Hamilton, N.Y., 1999, Sasaki Assocs., Watertown, Mass., 2000, Fordham U., New York, 2000, Denise Bibro Gallery, New York, 2000, Sculpture 2000, New London, Conn., Lyric Theatre, Stuart, Fla., 2001, U. Ctrl. Fla., Orlando, 2004, Fla. Internat. U., Miami, 2004, Michner Mus., Doylestown, Pa., 2004, City of Fort Pierce, Fla., 2004, Krasle Art Ctr., St. Joseph, Mich., 2005, Hartwick Coll., Oneonta, NY, Mobile Mus. Art, others; numerous group shows, 1959—; represented in permanent collections Mus. Modern Art, Guggenheim Mus., Carnegie Inst., Hirshhorn Mus., Washington, U. Notre Dame, Mus. Fine Arts, Houston, Wadsworth Atheneum, Hartford, Addison Gallery Am. Art, Andover, Mass., Currier Gallery Art, Manchester, N.H., Williams Coll., Dartmouth Coll., Harvard U., Colgate U., Hartwood Acres, Pitts., Hartford Pub. Library, Snite Mus., Notre Dame, Ind., Western Mich. U., Kalamazoo, U. Hartford, Hamilton Coll., Clinton, N.Y., others. Regent, U. Hartford, Conn., 1992-96. Recipient Logan medal Art Inst. Chgo., 1960; Fulbright research grantee, 1961; Guggenheim fellow, 1961; grantee Nat. Inst. Arts and Letters, 1965. Mem. Sculptors Guild N.Y. (bd. dirs. 1994-2000). Office Phone: 806-742-9687. E-mail: dvhayes@snet.net.

HAYES, DENNIS COURTLAND, civil rights association executive, lawyer; b. Jan. 29, 1951; BS in Am. History, Ind. U., Indpls., 1973; JD with high honors, Ind. U., 1977. Bar: Ind. 1977, U.S. Dist. Ct. (so. dist.) Ind. 1977. With Law Offices of Brooks and Schwartz, 1976-77; pvt. practice law Indpls., 1977—85; asst. gen. counsel NAACP, Balt., 1985—89, gen. counsel, 1989—, interim pres., CEO, 2005. Bd. dirs. Ind. Black Expo, Community Svcs. Addiction Agy.; asst. dir. Nat. Rsch. Inst., Washington; dir. Guide Right Program; trustee First Bapt. Ch., Indpls., mem. Mass Choir, Male Chorus. Mem. Marion County Bar Assn. (pres. 1980-81), Black Am. Law Student Assn. (pres.), Kappa Alpha Psi. Avocations: swimming, reading, guitar, backgammon. Office: NAACP 4805 Mount Hope Dr Baltimore MD 21215-3297

HAYES, DENNIS EDWARD, geophysicist, educator; b. St. Joseph, Mo., Oct. 3, 1938; s. William Franklin and Gertrude Margaret (Lorson) H.; m. Leslie Eve Price, May 17, 1978; children—Jennifer, Katharine, Elizabeth, Élan. BSE. summa cum laude, Kans. U., 1961; PhD, Columbia U., 1966. Research asso. Columbia U., 1966-71, sr. research asso., 1971-74, asso. prof., 1974-77, prof. geophysics, 1977—, chmn. dept. geol. scis., 1989—94, 1997—2002; chmn. exec. com. Arts and Scis. faculty, 1994-96; assoc. dir. Lamont-Doherty Geol. Obs., 1978—2002; deputy dir. edn. Lamont-Doherty Obs. Columbia U., 1998—2002. Mem. ocean scis. bd. and polar rsch. bd. NAS; mem. adv. panel to earth scis. divsn. NSF, polar programs divsn., ocean scis. divsn.; vis. prof. Stanford U., 1981, vis. prof., Ecole Normal Superior (ENS), Paris, 2002; mem. IOC Commn. on Non-living Resources, Joint Oceanographic Insts. for Deep Earth Sampling Planning Commn., 1977-87; mem. Univ. Nat. Oceanog. Lab. Sys. coun., 1991—. Editor books including Antarctic Oceanology II, 1972, Marine Geophysics of S.E. Asia, I and II, 1978, 83, Marine Geology/Geophysics of the Circum-Antarctic, 1991; contbr. numerous articles to profl. jours. Recipient Haworth Disting. Alumni Honors in Geology Kans. U., 1977; NSF fellow, 1961-65; John Simon Guggenheim fellow, 1980-81 Fellow Am. Geophys. Union, Geol. Soc. Am.; mem. Soc. Exploration Geophysicists, Am. Assn. Petroleum Geologists, Tau Beta Pi. Home: 6 Century Rd Palisades NY 10964-1503 Office: Lamont-Doherty Geol Obs Palisades NY 10964 Office Phone: 845-365-8470. Business E-Mail: deph@ldeo.columbia.edu. *I believe maintaining one's personal integrity may be the single most important ingredient in a successful and satisfying career.*

HAYES, DEWEY, lawyer; b. Ga., July 27, 1923; s. J.C. and Mary (Walsh) H.; m. Margaret Haley, June 16, 1951; children: Dewey Jr., Franklin, Candy. AB, Mercer U., JD, 1949. Bar: Ga. 1949, U.S. Supreme Ct. 1966. Mem. Ga. Ho. of Reps., 1953-56; dist. atty. Waycross Jud. Cir., Ga., 1957-80; sole practice Douglas, Ga., 1980—. Instr. law South Ga. Coll., 1973. Author: You and the Law, 1970, Georgia Warrants, 1972; Miranda, 1973; Search and Seizure, 1973. Mem. Ga. State Crime Commn., 1973-74. Served with U.S. Army, 1942-46, ETO, PTO. Mem. Nat. Dist. Atty.'s Assn., Dist. Attys. Assn. Ga. (pres. 1972), Am. Legion, V.F.W., Douglas Bar Assn. (pres. 1962—), Delta Theta Phi (pres. 1949), Kappa Sigma. Lodges: Elk, Lion, Woodman of World. Methodist. Office: 107 Madison Ave S Douglas GA 31533-5321

HAYES, DEWEY NORMAN, JR., lawyer; b. Douglas, Ga., May 7, 1955; s. Dewey N. and Margaret Harrell (Haley) H.; m. Clara June Carver, Mar. 10, 1984; child; Dewey N. Hayes, III. AB, U. Ga., 1976; JD, Mercer U., 1979. Bar: U.S. Dist. Ct. (so. and mid. dists.) Ga. 1979, U.S. Ct. Appeals (5th cir.) 1979. Sole practice, Douglas, 1979—; city atty. Ambrose, Ga., 1980—90; soliciter State Ct., Coffee County, Ga., 1985—89. V.p. Coffee County ARC, Douglas, 1980-85, Ga. Assn. Dem. County Chmn., 1985; mem. Dem. Exec. Com., Atlanta, 1985-90. Mem. Ga. Assn. Dems. (v.p. co-chmn. 1985-95), Nat. Coll. Advocacy (civil trial advocate 2002). Lodges: Lions (v.p. Douglas

1983-2004, pres. 1987, past pres. 1988, solicitor 1985-88). Democrat. Methodist. Home: 503 Dogwood Ave Douglas GA 31533-4714 Office: 105 S Madison Ave PO Box 37 Douglas GA 31534-0037 Office Phone: 912-384-9330. E-mail: dnhjrpc@alltel.net.

HAYES, DON, JR., physician, researcher; m. Keri A. Hayes. MD, U. of Ky. Coll. of Medicine, 1998. Pediatrics Am. Bd. of Pediat., 2002, Internal Medicine Am. Bd. of Internal Medicine, 2004. Adult and pediatric pulmonary fellow and sleep fellow U. of Wis. Hosp and Clinics, 2002. Recipient Clin. Fellowship award, Cystic Fibrosis Found., 2005, Nat. Ctr. on Minority Health and Health Disparities Scholar, US HHS, 2004, NIH Clin. Rsch. award, NIH, 2004—. Fellow: Am. Acad. Pediat.; mem.: ACP, Am. Acad. Sleep Medicine, Am. Coll. Chest Physicians, Am. Thoracic Soc. Achievements include research in investigating the acquisition of Pseudomonas aeruginosa in infants and younger children with cystic fibrosis. Office: Univ of Wis Hosp and Clinics 600 Highland Avenue Madison WI 53792 Office Phone: 608-263-8555. Personal E-mail: d.hayes@hosp.wisc.edu.

HAYES, EDWARD W., lawyer; b. 1947; married; 2 children. Attended, U. Va.; JD, Columbia Law Sch. Bar: 1973. Asst. dist. atty. homicide bureau Bronx Dist. Atty. Office; pvt. practice; co-anchor Both Sides, Court TV, 2000—. Office: Court TV 600 Third Ave 3rd Fl New York NY 10016

HAYES, EDWIN JUNIUS, JR., consumer products company executive; b. Brockton, Mass., July 20, 1932; s. Edwin Junius and Edith Franklin (Miller) H.; m. Brenda Storrs, Apr. 19, 1958; children: Bradford, Jonathan, Christopher. AB, Dartmouth Coll., 1954, MBA, 1955; cert., U. Manchester (Eng.) Inst. Sci. and Tech., 1972. Various mgmt. positions Gen. Mills, 1955-67; product group mgr. Quaker Oats Co., Chgo., 1967-69; dir. mktg. Quaker Oats Ltd. (U.K.), London, 1969-72, v.p. internat., mng. dir., 1972-76; v.p. internat. William Underwood Co., Boston, 1976-77, exec. v.p., 1977-79; pres., chief exec. officer M. Grumbacher, Inc., NYC, 1979-85; prin. and dir. Center for Concept Development Inc., NYC, 1985-88, 92-01; pres., chief executive officer Diethelm and Keller (USA) Ltd., 1988-92, Delta Tech. Coatings, Inc., 1988-92. Dir. Norfra Shipping Co. Advisor Nat. Art Edn. Assn. Mem. Nat. Maritime Mus. Greenwich (Eng.), Delta Upsilon.

HAYES, ELVIN ERNEST, retired basketball player; b. Rayville, La., Nov. 17, 1945; Grad., U. Houston, 1968. Basketball player San Diego Rockets, 1968-71, Houston Rockets, 1971-72, 81-83, Balt. Bullets, 1972-74, Capital Bullets, 1973-74, Washington Bullets, 1974-75. Named to Basketball Hall of Fame, 1989, All-NBA 1st Team, 1975, 77, 79, All-NBA 2d Team, 1973, 74, 76, NBA All-Defensive 2d Team, 1974, 75, NBA All-Rookie Team, 1969; record-holder single season most minutes played by rookie, 1969, NBa Finals single-game record most offensive rebounds, 1979; recipient Coll. Player of Yr. sporting News, 1968, All-Am. 1st Team, 1967, 68, All-Am. 2d Team, 1966. Home: 252 Piney Point Rd Houston TX 77024-7325

HAYES, ERNEST M., podiatrist; b. New Orleans, Jan. 21, 1946; s. Ernest M. and Emma Hayes; m. Bonnie Ruth Beigle, Oct. 16, 1970. BA, Calif. State U., Sacramento, 1969; BS, Calif. Coll. Podiat. Medicine, San Francisco, 1971, DPM, 1973. Diplomate Am. Coun. Cert. Podiatric Physicians and Surgeons. Resident in surg. podiatry Beach Cmty. Hosp., Buena Pk., Calif., 1973-74, dir. residency program, 1974-75; pvt. practice Anaheim, Calif., 1974-80, Yreka, Calif., 1980-95, Machias, Lubec and Calais, Maine, 1995—. Courtesy staff Down East Cmty. Hosp., 1997—2004; sr. clin. instr. So. Calif. Podiatric Med. Ctr., LA, 1975—78; vice chmn. podiatry dept. Good Samaritan Hosp., Anaheim, Calif., 1978—79; mem. med. staff Mercey Med. Ctr., Mt. Shasta, Calif.; CEO, Siskiyou Foot Group, Yreka, 1980—95, Nature's Pace, 1995, Underground Food and Seed, LLC, 1995; pres. Down East Podiatry, Machias, Maine, 1995—. Registrar POSM Horse Registry, 2000; bd. dir. Little Bogus Ranches Home Owners Assn., 1981—83, pres., 1983—84. Fellow: Nat. Coll. Foot Surgeons; mem.: Am. POSM Horse Assn. (trustee 1995), Am. Assn. Podiatric Physicians and Surgeons, 1989. Baptist. Home: PO Box 538 Lubec ME 04652-0538

HAYES, GERALD JOSEPH, lawyer; b. Bronx, NY, July 24, 1950; s. James Joseph and Gladys (Guest) H.; m. Diane Elizabeth Willoughby, July 21, 1984; children: Erin Jane, Thomas Joseph, Cara Elizabeth. BA, U. Mass., 1972; JD, U. Miami, 1978. Bar: NY 1979, U.S. Dist. Ct. (so. dist.) NY 1979. Assoc. Baker & McKenzie, NYC, 1978-85, ptnr., 1985—, mng. ptnr., 1995, 97, 99—, mem. policy com., 1997—, nominating com., 2002—. Mem. Bus. Coun. for UN, 1990-95. Nat. alumni adv. bd. U. Miami Sch. Law, 1992-1994. Mem. ABA (atomic energy com. pub. utility law sect. 1983, vice chair internat. tort and ins. law com., tort and ins. practice sect. 1997—), Assn. Bar City of NY (com. on nuc. tech. and law 1979-82, 85-88, com. on ins. law 1983-84), Nat. Assn. Ins. Commrs. (adv. com. on internat. law 1989-90), Nat. Risk Retention Assn. Office: Baker & McKenzie 805 3rd Ave New York NY 10022-7513 Office Phone: 212-751-5700. Business E-mail: gerald.j.hayes@bakernet.com.

HAYES, GORDON GLENN, civil engineer; b. Galveston, Tex., Jan. 2, 1936; s. Jack Lewis and Eunice Karen (Victery) H. BS in Physics, Tex. A&M U., 1969. Registered profl. engr., Alaska, Tex. Rsch. technician Shell Devel. Co., Houston, 1962-68; rsch. assoc. Tex. Trans. Inst., College Station, 1969-71, asst. rsch. physicist, 1971-74, assoc. rsch. physicist, 1974-80; traffic safety specialist Alaska Dept. Transp. & Pub. Facilities, Juneau, 1981-83, state traffic engr., 1983-85, traffic safety standards engr., 1985-90; owner Alaska Roadsafe Cons., Juneau, 1990-92, Hayes Highway Consulting, Carson City, Nev., 1992-93, Livingston, Tex., 1993—. Author of numerous pubs. in the hwy. safety field; producer of numerous documentary films in the hwy. safety field. Petty officer USN, 1953-57. Mem. ASCE, Nat. Com. on Uniform Traffic Control Devices (signs tech. com.) Inst. Transp. Engrs. Avocations: fishing, boating, camping. Home: 209 Crystal Creek Dr Livingston TX 77351-9730

HAYES, ISAAC, rhythm and blues singer, composer; b. Covington, Tenn., Aug. 20, 1942; 7 children. Formerly singer rhythm and blues recs., Stax Records; albums recorded included Hot Buttered Soul, 1969, Isaac Hayes Movement, 1970, Enterprise, 1970, Black Moses, 1971, Hotbed, 1978, Don't Let Go, 1979, U-Turn, 1986, Love Attack, 1988, Greatest Hit Singles, (with Dionne Warwick) A Man and A Woman, And Once Again, 1980, Lifetime Thing, 1981, Back to Back (with Barry White), Branded, 1995, Raw and Refined; (with Donald Dunn and Al Jackson Jr.), 1995; composer: musical score film Shaft (Grammy and Oscar awards); actor: voice of Jerome 'Chef' McElroy on TV series South Park, 1997-, (TV films) Betrayed by Innocence, 1986, Hammer, Slammer, & Slade, 1990, Acting On Impulse, 1993, Hallelujah, 1993, Soul Survivors, 1995, Book of Days, 2003, Anonymous Rex, 2004, (films) Truck Turner, 1974, Tough Guys, 1974, It Seemed Like a Good Idea at the Time, 1975, Escape from New York, 1981, Counterforce, 1987, Dead Aim, 1987, I'm Gonna Git You Sucka, 1988, Guilty as Charged, 1991, Prime Target, 1991, Final Judgement, 1992, Deadly Exposure, 1993, CB4, 1993, Posse, 1993, Robin Hood: Men in Tights, 1993, Oblivion, 1994, It Could Happen to You, 1994, Once Upon a Time...When We Were Colored, 1995, Oblivion 2: Backlash, 1996, Flipper, 1996, Illtown, 1996, Uncle Sam, 1997, Six Ways to Sunday, 1997, Blues Brothers 2000, 1998, Ninth Street, 1999, (voice) South Park: Bigger, Longer & Uncut, 1999, Reindeer Games, 2000, (voice) Dr. Dolittle 2, 2001, Dodge City: A Spaghetto Western, 2004, Dream Warrior, 2004, Return to Sleepaway Camp, 2005, Hustle & Flow, 2005. Named to Rock and Roll Hall of Fame, 2002, Songwriters Hall of Fame, 2005. Office: ILH Entertainment Inc 113 Pavonia Ave # 376 Jersey City NJ 07310*

HAYES, J. MICHAEL, lawyer; b. St. Louis, Dec. 10, 1946; s. Frank J. and Louise J. (Lough) H.; m. Vicky J. Verbocy, May 27, 1972; children: Thomas K., James M. BS summa cum laude, SUNY, Brockport, 1973; JD, SUNY, Buffalo, 1976. Bar: N.Y. 1977, U.S. Dist. Ct. (we. dist.) N.Y. 1977. Assoc. Smith, Murphy & Schoepperle, Buffalo, 1977-79, Tenney, Smith & Scott, Buffalo, 1979-82, Terry D. Smith, Buffalo, 1982-86; ptnr. Smith, Keller, Hayes & Miner, Buffalo, 1986-94; pvt. practice, Buffalo, 1994—. Office: 69 Delaware Ave Rm 1111 Buffalo NY 14202-3805 E-mail: jmh@jmichaelhayes.com.

HAYES, JACK IRBY, historian, educator; b. Danville, Va., Aug. 13, 1944; s. Jack Irby and Minnie Lee (Conner) H.; m. Bernadine Joy Arnn, June 5, 1966; children: Emily Wilson, Julia Arnn. BS in History, Hampden-Sydney Coll., 1966; MA in History, Va. Poly. Inst. and State U., 1968; PhD in History, U. S.C., 1972; BS in Bus., Averett Coll., 1987. Dir. continuing edn. U. S.C., Columbia, 1972-74; asst. prof. history Averett Coll., Danville, 1974-77, assoc. prof., 1977-82, prof., 1982-90, W.C. Daniel prof. history and polit. sci., 1990—, chmn. dept. history, 1976—. Adj. prof. grad. sch. Va. Poly. Inst. and State U., Blacksburg, 1977-79; archival cons. Dibrell Bros., Inc., Danville, 1990-91. Author:Dan Daniel and the Persistence of Conservatism in Virginia, 1997, South Carolina and the New Deal, 2001, The Lamp and The Cross: A History of Averett College, 1859-2001, 2004. Mem. jud. ethics adv. com. Commonwealth Va., 1999-; bd. dirs. The Womack Found., 1982-90, Danville Mus. of Fine Arts and History, 1992-98, 2004—; pres. Hughes Meml. Home, 1999-; mem. Danville Dem. Com., 1984-; elder, trustee First Presbyn. Ch., Danville; mem., past pres. Citizens Bd., Danville Corps., Salvation Army. Grantee Va. Found. for Humanities and Pub. Policy, Charlottesville, 1976-87, Commn. on Bicentennial of U.S. Constn., Washington, 1989, 90; Westmoreland Davis Meml. Found. fellow, 1967-68, Seminar for Hist. Adminstrs. fellow, Colonial Williamsburg, Va., 1967, Louis P. Jones fellow, U. S.C., 1998; named one of Outstanding Young Men of Am., 1977. Mem. So. Hist. Assn., Assn. for Preservation of Va. Antiquities (life), Kiwanis (lt. gov. div. 2 capital dist. 1991-92, pres. Danville club 1989, sec.,1998—), So. Assn. Colls. and Schs. (mem. re-accreditation com. 1986-99), German Club Danville, Danville Golf Club. Avocations: running, tennis, golf. Home: 245 Linden Dr Danville VA 24541-3523 Office: Averett Coll 420 W Main St Danville VA 24541-3612

HAYES, JANET GRAY, retired management consultant, retired mayor; b. Rushville, Ind., July 12, 1926; d. John Paul and Lucile (Gray) Frazee; m. Kenneth Hayes, Mar. 20, 1950; children: Lindy, John, Katherine, Megan. AB, Ind. U., 1948; MA magna cum laude, U. Chgo., 1950. Psychiat. caseworker Jewish Family Svc. Agy., Chgo., 1950-52; vol. Denver Crippled Children's Service, 1954-55, Adult and Child Guidance Clinic, San Jose, Calif., 1958-59; mem. San Jose City Coun., 1971-75, vice mayor, 1973-75; mayor San Jose, 1975—82; co-chmn. com. urban econs. U.S. Conf. Mayors, 1976-78, co-chmn. task force on aging, mem. sci. and teck task force, 1976-80, bd. trustees, 1977-82; bd. dirs. League Calif. Cities, 1976-82, mem. property tax reform task force, 1976-82; chmn. State of Calif. Urban Devel. Adv. Com., 1976-77; mem. Calif. Commn. Fair Jud. Practices, 1976-82; client-community relations dir. Q. Tech., Santa Clara, Calif., 1983-85; bus. mgr. Kenneth Hayes MD, Inc., 1985-88; CEO Hayes House, Book Distbr., 1998—. Mem. Dem. Nat. Campaign Com., 1976; mem. Calif. Dem. Commn. Nat. Platform and Policy, 1976; del. Dem. Nat. Conv., 1980; bd. dirs. South San Francisco Bay Dischargers Authority; chmn. Santa Clara County Sanitation Dist.; mem. San Jose/Santa Clara Treatment Plant Adv. Bd.; chmn. Santa Clara Valley Employment and Tng. Bd. (CETA), League to Save Lake Tahoe adv. bd., 2000—; past mem. EPA Aircraft/Airport Noise Task Group; bd. dirs. Calif. Center Rsch. and Edn. in Govt, Alexian Bros. Hosp., 1983-92; bd. dirs., chmn. adv. council Public Tech. Inc.; mem. bd. League to Save Lake Tahoe, 1984-2000; pres. bd. trustees San Jose Mus. Art, 1987-89; founder, adv. bd. Calif. Bus. Bank, 1982-85; polit. advisor Citizens Against Airport Pollution, 2003—. AAUW Edn. Found. grantee. Mem. Assn. Bay Area Govts. (exec. com. 1971-74, regional housing subcom. 1973-74), LWC (pres. San Francisco Bay Area chpt. 1968-70, pres. local chpt. 1966-67), Mortar Bd., Phi Beta Kappa, Kappa Alpha Theta. Personal E-mail: janetgrayhayes@sbcglobal.net.

HAYES, JOANNA, Olympic track and field athlete; b. Williamsport, PA, Dec. 23, 1976; Grad., UCLA, 1999. Mem. U.S Olympic Track Team, Athens, 2004. SMART Moves Coord. Jackie Joyner-Kersee Youth Center, East St. Louis, Ill., 2001—02. Achievements include NCAA Champion, 400m hurdles, 1999; Gold medal, 400m hurdles, Pan American games, 2003; Gold medal, 100m hurdles, Athens Olympic games, 2004. Office: c/o USOC 1 Olympic Plaza Colorado Springs CO 80909

HAYES, JOHN D., diversified financial services company executive; Grad. in Mktg. and Comm., Seton Hall U. Pres. Lowe & Ptnrs./SMS; various positions Geer DuBois, Saatchi & Saatchi Compton; exec. vp. global advt. and brand mgmt. Am. Express, N.Y.C., 1995—. Mem. planning and policy com. Am. Express; mem. Tiger Wood Found. Mem.: Assn. Nat. Advertisers (chmn. 2000—01, vice chmn. 2002—). Office: Am Express World Fin Ctr 200 Vesey St New York NY 10285

HAYES, JOHN FRANCIS, lawyer; b. Salina, Kans., Dec. 11, 1919; s. John Francis and Helen (Dye) H.; m. Elizabeth Ann Ireton, Aug. 10, 1950; children: Carl Ireton, Ann Chandler. AB, Washburn Coll., 1941, LLB, 1946. Bar: Kans. 1946, Mo. 1987. Pvt. practice, Hutchinson, Kans., 1946—; dir. Gilliland & Hayes, P.A. (and predecessors), 1946—. Mem. Commn. Uniform State Laws, 1975—; bd. dirs. Cen. Bank and Trust Co., Hutchinson, Cen. Fin. Corp., Waddell & Reed Funds. Mem. Kans. Ho. of Reps., 1953-55, 67-79, majority leader, 1975-77. Served as capt. AUS, 1942-46. Fellow Am. Bar Found., Am. Coll. Trial Lawyers; mem. Hutchinson C. of C. (pres. 1961), Kans. Assn. Def. Counsel (pres. 1972-73), Internat. Assn. Def. Counsel. Republican. Office: 20 W 2nd Ave Fl 2 Hutchinson KS 67501 also: 1211 Penntower Bldg 3100 Broadway St Kansas City MO 64111-2406 also: Epic Ctr 301 N Main Ste 1300 Wichita KS 67202 also: 900 Massachusetts Ste 400 Lawrence KS 66044-2868 Office Phone: 620-662-0537. E-mail: johnh@gh-hutch.com.

HAYES, JOHN FREEMAN, architect; b. Media, Pa., June 16, 1926; s. James Alfred and Katharine Stoddard (Williams) H.; m. Anne Gitt Fox, Apr. 5, 1952; children: John Fox, Thomas Freeman, Anne Clarke. Grad., Haverford Sch., 1944; BArch, U. Pa., 1950. With various cos., 1954-60; ptnr. Hayes & Hough Archs., Phila., 1960-95; sr. cons. Blackney Hayes Archs., Phila., 1995—. Pres. The Carpenters Co. of the City and County of Phila., 1993. Served with USNR, 1944-46; served with USAF, 1951-53. Fellow AIA (John Harbeson Svc. award 1995); mem. Martins Dam Club, Phila. Curling Club. Episcopalian. Office: Blackney Hayes Architects 105 S 12th St Philadelphia PA 19107-4809

HAYES, JOHN PATRICK, electrical engineering and computer science educator, consultant; b. Newbridge, Ireland, Mar. 3, 1944; s. Patrick Joseph and Christine (Duggan) H.; m. Joan Benson, June 7, 1969; children: Thomas, Michael. BE in Elec. Engring., Nat. U. Ireland, Dublin, 1965; MS in Elec. Engring., U. Ill., 1967, PhD in Elec. Engring., 1970. Systems engr. Royal Dutch Shell Co., The Hague, The Netherlands, 1970-72; asst. prof. elec. engring. and computer sci. U. So. Calif., L.A., 1972-77, assoc. prof., 1977-82; prof. U. Mich., Ann Arbor, 1982—2002, Shannon prof. engring. sci., 2002—. Cons. in field. Author: Computer Architecture and Organization, 1978, 3d edit., 1998, Digital System Design and Microprocessors, 1984, Hierarchical Modeling for VLSI Circuit Testing, 1990, Layout Minimization for CMOS Cells, 1992, Introduction to Digital Logic Design, 1993; contbr. articles to profl. jours. Fellow: IEEE (assoc. editor jour. 1989—94), Assn. Computing Machinery (assoc. editor jour. 1978—81); mem.: Sigma Xi. Office: U Mich Dept Elec Engring & Computer Sci Ann Arbor MI 48109 Office Phone: 734-763-0386. Business E-Mail: jhayes@eecs.umich.edu.

HAYES, JOHN PATRICK, retired manufacturing company executive; b. Manistee, Mich., May 9, 1921; s. John David and Daisy (Davis) H.; m. Margaret Barbara Butler, Apr. 12, 1947; children— John Patrick, Timothy Michael. BS, U. Detroit, 1947. With Nat. Gypsum Co., 1947-90, group v.p., 1970-75, pres., 1975-90, chmn. bd., chief exec. officer, 1983-90, also bd. dirs. Served to 1st lt. AUS, 1942-45.

HAYES, JOSEPH G., cardiologist, educator; b. Port Chester, N.Y., Jan. 13, 1938; s. Arthur Hill and Florence Gruber Hayes; m. Britt-Marianne Alfredsson, Dec. 10, 1968; children: Patricia, Diane, Joseph Jr., Kristin, Sean, Morgan. BA, Georgetown U., 1959, MD, 1963. Diplomate Am. Coll. Internal Medicine and Cardiology. Intern N.Y. (N.Y.) Hosp., 1963—65, resident, 1965—66, fellow cardiology, 1966—68; from asst. prof. to prof. Med. Coll. Cornell U., N.Y., 1970—86, prof., 1986—, N.Y. (N.Y.) Hosp., 1970—. Vice chmn. Dept. Medicine Cornell U., N.Y., 1987—96, assoc. dean Weill Med. Coll., 1998—; vis. prof. Georgetown U., Washington. Maj. USAF, 1968—70. Fellow: ACP, Am. Heart Assn. (bd. dir. N.Y. chpt. 1982—88, 1990—2004, vol., clin. coun. 1980—). Avocations: woodworking, landscaping, photography. Office: Weill Med Coll NYPH 525 E 68th St New York NY 10021 Business E-Mail: jghayes@med.cornell.edu.

HAYES, KATHARINEALICE, retired elementary school educator; b. San Francisco, Aug. 23, 1939; d. Herman Jesse and Lorraine Myrtle (Irwin) Hale; m. William Scott Hayes, Aug. 23, 1959; children: Jessica Alice, Jennifer Ann, Scott McKay, Johanna Alexandria. BA, San Francisco State U., 1962. Cert. elem. tchr. Kindergarten tchr. Old Adobe Sch. Dist., Petaluma, Calif.; tchr. lang., devel. specialist Petaluma (Calif.) City Schs.; kindergarten tchr. Novato (Calif.) City Schs.; ret. Site coun. chair Old Adobe Sch.; vice chair Kenilworth Jr. High Site Coun., Casa Grande High Site Coun. Active Camp Fire, Boy Scouts Am., 4-H and Girl Scouts Am.; vol. nature guide Terilliger Wild Care, San Rafael. Mem. AAUW (bd. dirs.), Mu Phi Epsilon (former pres. San Francisco alumni chpt.) Home: 1724 Tampico Ct Petaluma CA 94954-4547 E-mail: kandwhayes@earthlink.net.

HAYES, LYNDA MARGARET, elementary school educator; b. N.Y.C., NY, Oct. 15, 1951; d. Ernest Wyatt and Marie Eloise Hayes; 1 child, Christina Barretto. MusB, Mannes Coll. Music, 1972; MusM, SUNY at Stonybrook, 1974. Cert. elem. edn. William Paterson Coll., NJ, 1985, music edn. William Paterson Coll., NJ, 1992, supr. William Paterson Coll., NJ, 1997. Tchr. Orange BOE, Orange, NJ, 1980—85; instr., music methods William Paterson Coll., Wayne, NJ, 1984—85; tchr. Cornerstone Christian Acad., Edison, NJ, 1986—91; edn. coord. Hackensack Day Care, Hackensack, NJ, 1991—92; tchr. (summers) Teaneck BOE, Teaneck, NJ, 1996—2004; instr. Regional Tng. Ctr., Randolph, NJ, 2001—03; tchr. Little Ferry (N.J.) Bd. Edn., 1992—, tchr., presenter, intervention and referal svc. chair, 1995—2005, dir. summer sch., 1999—2000. Workshop presenter Bur. of Edn. and Rsch., Bellevue, Wash., 2003; classroom model for instructional video Pearson Learning Group, Parsippany, NJ, 2003, adv. bd. mem., 02; core curriculum arts framework com. mem. NJ Edn. Dept., NJ, 1997—98; affirmative action com. mem. Little Ferry Pub. Schs., Little Ferry, NJ, 2003—04; cast mem. Mama, I Want To Sing, NY Reach Ensemble Off Broadway Theatre Co., N.Y.C., NY, 1989—91; vocalist, flutist freelance performer. Author: My Special Friend, 1985; performer (solo recording artist): (albums) (gospel) Your Love Will Live On, 1999; song writer: CD's for Mother's Day Tribute to Mom, 1999—2005, Little Ferry, 1994; musician (solo flute debut): Carnegie Recital Hall, 1974. Donor Feed the Children, 1997—; mem., soloist NJ Conf. Choir, New Spirit Project, 1999—2005; dir. Faith Revival Ctr., Praise Warriors Young Adult Choir, Hackensack, NJ, 1988—; founder, dir. Life on Earth, 1990—93; min. Faith Revival Ctr. Ch., Hackensack, NJ, 1988—. Recipient Gov's. Tchr. Recognition award, State of NJ, 1998—99. Mem.: NEA, Assn. for Supr. and Curriculum Devel., Little Ferry Edn. Assn., Bergen County Edn. Assn., Gospel Music Workshop of Am., PTA, Kappa Delta Pi (Zeta Alpha chpt.). Avocations: dance, camping, health and fitness. Office: Wash Elem Sch 123 Liberty St Little Ferry NJ 07643 Office Phone: 201-641-6760. Office Fax: 201-265-1907. E-mail: lyndasing@msn.com, lhayes@littleferry.k12.nj.us.

HAYES, M. M.M., publishing executive; b. Chgo., Nov. 30, 1945; d. William C. and Minnie Marie (Prunty) Mitchell; m. James E. Hayes, July 12, 1969; children: James J., Will. BA, U. Ill., 1967; MFA in Writing, Vt. Coll., 1991. Promotion & continuity writer CBS, Chgo.; pub. rels. rep. J. Walter Thompson Advt. Agy., Chgo.; prof. Columbia Coll. Mo., Crystal Lake, Ill. Editor and pub.: StoryQuarterly, 1994—2005; contbr. New Stories from the South: Best of 1996, Best of the West, short stories to lit. jours. and anthologies (Katherine Anne Porter prize, 1995). Mem.: Heartland Literary Soc. (bd. dirs.), Poetry Ctr. Chgo. (bd. dirs.). Avocations: travel, photography, hiking, swimming, tango. Home and Office: 431 Sheridan Rd Kenilworth IL 60043 Personal E-mail: mmmhayes@gmail.com. E-mail: storyquarterly@yahoo.com.

HAYES, MARY DIANNE WIXTED, lawyer; b. Danbury, Conn., Jan. 4, 1942; d. Francis Joseph and Mary (Zwyner) Wixted; m. Paul P. Hayes, Jr., June 18, 1966. BA in Economics, Regis Coll., Weston, MA, 1961—64; JD, Suffolk U. Law Sch., Boston, 1968, LLM, 1968—70; MEd in Religious Edn., Boston Coll., Chestnut Hill, MA, 1989, MA in Theology, 1990—97; STL, Weston SJ Sch. of Theology, Cambridge, MA, 1997—2002. Bar: Mass. 1970, U.S. Dist. Ct. (Mass.) 1971, U. S. Supreme Ct. 1973, U.S. Ct. Appeals (1st cir.) 1979. Ptnr. Hayes and Hayes, Quincy, Mass., 1970—; vol. atty. Irish Pastoral Centre, 1998—, mem. adv. bd., 2004—. Town meeting mem. Town of Milton, Milton, Mass., 1977—93; mem. Secular Franciscan Order, Boston, 1985—. Mem.: Am. Immigration Lawyers Assn., Real Estate Bar Assn., Mass. Assn. Women Lawyers (pres. 1993—94), Mass. Bar Assn. (chair probate law sect. coun. 1995—97), S. Shore Regis Club, Weston, Mass. (pres. 1973—75). Roman Catholic. Office: Hayes and Hayes 31 Newcomb Street Quincy MA 02169-4507 Office Phone: 617-773-2800. Personal E-mail: Wixtedhaye@aol.com.

HAYES, MARY ESHBAUGH, editor, writer; b. Rochester, N.Y., Sept. 27, 1928; d. William Paul and Eleanor Maude (Sievert) Eshbaugh; m. James Leon Hayes, Apr. 18, 1953; children: Pauli, Eli, Lauri Le June, Clayton, Merri Jess Bates. BA in English and Journalism, Syracuse U., 1950. With Livingston County Republican, Geneseo, N.Y., summers, 1947-50, mng. editor, 1949-50; reporter Aurora Advocate, Colo., 1950—52; reporter-photographer Aspen Times, Colo., 1952-53, columnist, 1956—, reporter, 1972-77, assoc. editor, 1977-89, editor-in-chief, 1989-92, contbg. editor, 1992—. Instr. Colo. Mountain Coll., 1979; Aspen corr. Reuters, 1997—. Author, editor: The Story of Aspen, 1996 (1st prize, 1996); contbg. editor: Destinations Mag., 1994—97, Aspen Mag., 1996—; editor: Aspen Pot Pourri, 1968 (1st prize, 1990), rev. edit., 2002 (1st prize, 2002). Recipient Living Landmark award, Aspen Hist. Soc., 2002. Mem.: Colo. Press Women's Assn. (writing award 1974—75, 1978—85, sweepstakes award for writing 1977—78, 1984—85, 1991—2003, 2d pl. award 1976, 1979, 1982—83, 1994—95, Woman of Achievement 1986), Nat. Fedn. Press Women (1st prize in writing and editing 1976—80, 1st prize in adv. photography 1998). Home: PO Box 497 Aspen CO 81612-0497 Office: Box E Aspen CO 81612 Personal E-mail: meh@sopris.net.

HAYES, MAXINE DELORES, physician, pediatrician; b. Nov. 29, 1946; children: Leon Williams, Kevin Williams. AB in Biology, Spelman Coll., 1969; MD, SUNY Buffalo, 1973; MPH, Harvard U., 1977; DSc (hon.), Spelman Coll., 2000. Intern pediat. Vanderbilt Hosp., Nashville, 1973-75; resident Children's Hosp., Boston, 1975-76; dir. Divsn. Parent-Child Health Svcs., Olympia, Wash., 1988-90, asst. sec., 1990-93, Cmty. and Family Health, Olympia, 1993-2000, acting health officer, 1998-2000; state health officer Wash. State Dept. Health, 2000—. Pres. Assn. Maternal and Child Health Programs, Washington, 1995-97; nat. program dir. Robert Wood Johnson Child Health Initiative, 1994-97; chair, Comprehensive Health Edn. Found. Bd. Dir., Seattle Recipient Outstanding Contbns. in Field of Pub. Health award Wash. State Pub. Health Assn., 1994, Guardian of Women's Health award Aradia Women's Health Ctr., 1996, Stockton Kimball award for medicine SUNY, Buffalo, 2000, Dr. Nathan Davis award AMA, 2002, Richard P. Nelson Lecture Series award Iowa Pub. Health Assn., 2002, Lifetime Achievement award Wash. Health Found., 2003. Fellow Am. Acad. Pediatrics; mem. APHA. Avocations: opera, art, science. Office: Wash State Dept Health PO Box 47890 Olympia WA 98504-7890 Office Phone: 360-236-4018. Business E-Mail: maxine.hayes@doh.wa.gov.

HAYES, MICHAEL JOSEPH, investment banker, entrepreneur, retail executive; b. Altoona, Pa., June 8, 1941; s. Francis C. and Mary E. (Curren) H.; m. Christina L. Casselbury, Apr. 21, 1966; children— Barbara, Michelle, Michael Joseph BA in Econs., Lycoming Coll., 1963; postgrad., Gen. Motors Inst. Mgmt., 1965; cert., N.Y. Inst. Fin., 1969. Gen. ptnr. Oppenheimer and Co., N.Y.C., 1977-82, exec. v.p., mng. dir., 1982-85, co-mng. corp. fin. dept., 1983-85, dir., fin. services dept.; mortgage banker Advance Mortgage Co., Southfield, Mich., 1979-84; prin. Hayes Fin. Corp., N.Y.C.; dir. Petro Corp., Houston; CEO Fred's, Inc. Mem. fin. com. N.J. Republican Party, 1982. Served with USAR, 1963-68 Mem.: Ridgewood Country (N.J.). Roman Catholic. Avocations: golf; squash; bridge. Home and Office: 380 Mountain Ave Ridgewood NJ 07450-4021*

HAYES, MICHELLE CHRISTINE, artist, educator; d. Pablo Tyler Mendez and Ann Muriel Staffeld; m. James Francis Hayes, July 1, 1995; 1 child, William Maxwell. BFA, Boston U., 1983, MFA, 1990. Cert. Tchr. Visual Art (5-12) Commonwealth of Mass., 2003, Bridgewater State Coll., Mass., 2004. Mech. layout artist Harold Cabot & Co., Inc., Charlestown, Mass., 1985—87; adminstrv. asst. Mus. of Fine Arts, Boston, 1989—94; adminstrv. asst. to the pres. Nat. Textile Assn., 1995—2000; visual art tchr. Walpole HS, Mass., 2003—03, Canton HS, Canton, 2003—. Open studios arts coun. Ft. Point Artists Cmty., 1992—93; co-chair staff art exhbn. Mus. Fine Arts, 1993; art exhbn. coord. Boston Visionary Cell, 1993—94; sch. improvement coun. Tower Hill Sch., Randolph, 2003—04, Martin E. Young Sch., Randolph, 2004—. Exhibitions include Fuller Mus. Art, Nancy Lincoln Gallery, Ne Women Artist Exhibit, Faith Exhbn., U. Mass., Dartmouth, Episcopal Divinity Sch., Fed. Res. Bank Exhbn., Kahn Arts Festival Exhibit, Ticknor Gallery, Harvard U., Shelburne Farms, Vt., Bowery Gallery, NY, one-woman shows include, Iona, Scotland. Mural project artist Beechwood Cmty. Life Ctr., Quincy, 2001—02; issues and advocacy com. mem. Randolph Unity Network, 2002—03; warden of duncraig Iona Cornerstone Found., Isle of Iona, Scotland, 1994; clip art project coord. Episcopal Diocese of Mass., 1999—2000; artist-in-residence Trinity Ch. Youth Ministry, 2001—03, tchr., 2001—03; vestry Trinity Episcopal Ch., 1997—2005. Caumsett Landscape Painting Program scholarship, Queens Coll., 1981. Mem.: Mass. Tchrs. Assn., Nat. Art Edn. Assn., Mass. Art Educators Assn. Democrat. Episcopalian. Avocations: yoga, hiking. Office: Canton High School 960 Washington St Canton MA 02021 Office Phone: 781-821-5050. Personal E-mail: michellechayes@verizon.net.

HAYES, PAGE DURHAM, music specialist, harpist; b. Culpeper, Va., June 14, 1970; d. William Bryan and Annette Coker Durham; m. Shawn David Hayes, June 24, 1995; 1 child, Sydney Madison. MusB in edn., Shenandoah U., 1988—92; M in edn., Am. Intercontinental U., 2003—04. World Music Drumming Levels 1, 2, and 3 Univ. of Wis., 2005, Orff Level 1 James Madison U., 1997, Teaching Guitar Dusquene U., 2002. Gen. music specialist Culpeper County Pub. Schools- Farmington Elem., Va., 1997—; choral dir. Culpeper County Pub. Schools- Culpeper Mid. Sch., 1993—97; online music facilitator J. Sargeant Reynolds C.C., Richmond, Va., 2004—. Musician: Austrialian Ambassadors Residence, Canadian Embassy, Washington and Lee University. Mem. Orange Bapt. Ch., Va., 1999—2005. Mem.: Va. Music Educators Assn., Music Educators Nat. Conv. Office: Farmington Elementary School 500 Sunset Lane Culpeper VA 22701 Office Phone: 540-825-0713. Home Fax: 540-672-7188; Office Fax: 540-829-0865. Personal E-mail: pdhayes@ns.gemlink.com. E-mail: phayes@culpeperschools.org.

HAYES, PATRICIA ANN, health facility administrator; b. Binghamton, NY, Jan. 14, 1944; d. Robert L. and Gertrude (Congdon) H. BA in English, Coll. of St. Rose, 1968; PhD in Philosophy, Georgetown U., 1974. Tchr. Cardinal McCloskey H.S., Albany, NY, 1966-68; tchg. asst. Georgetown U., Washington, 1968-71; instr. philosophy Coll. of St. Rose, Albany, 1973-75, instr. bus., 1981, adminstrv. intern to acad. v.p., 1973-74, dir. admissions, 1974-78, dir. adminstrn. and planning, 1978-81, v.p. adminstrn. and fin., treas., 1981-84; pres. St. Edward's U., Austin, Tex., 1984-98; exec. v.p., COO Seton Healthcare Network, Austin, 1998—2001, 2003—, interim pres., CEO, 2001—02. Bd. dirs. Tex. Assn. Pub. and Nonprofit Hosps., Topfer Family Found. Roman Catholic. Office: Seton Med Ctr 1201 W 38th St Austin TX 78705-1006 Office Phone: 512-324-1102. Business E-Mail: phayes@seton.org.

HAYES, PAULA FREDA, federal agency administrator; b. Apr. 5, 1950; d. Ario Louis and Elena Marguerite (Gentile) Freda; m. Robert J. Hayes, Sept. 6, 1975; children: Brendan Michael, Lauren Ann. BA magna cum laude, R.I. Coll., 1972; MPA, Syracuse U., 1973. Criminal justice planner City of Syracuse, NY, 1973-75, asst. crime control coord., 1975-77; supervisory grants specialist Nat. Endowment Arts, Washington, 1977-78; criminal justice program analyst Dept. Justice, Washington, 1978-79, program mgr. arson discretionary grant program, 1979-80, sr. mgmt. analyst, 1980-81; dir. legis. and analysis divsn. Office of Insp. Gen., Dept. Agr., Washington, 1981—89, asst. insp. gen. for policy devel. and resources mgmt., 1989—2003, asst. insp. gen. for planning and spl. projects, 2003—04, asst. insp. gen. for mgmt. USAID, 2004—05, acting dep. insp. for gen. USAID, 2005—. Roman Catholic. Office: USAID Office Insp Gen 1300 Pennsylania Ave NW Washington DC 20253-2004 Office Phone: 202-912-0010. E-mail: phayes@usaid.gov.

HAYES, RANDY ALAN, family therapist; b. Johnston City, Ill., Jan. 12, 1950; s. Clarence Lee Jr. and Mable Marie (McClain) H.; m. Donna Faye Carriker, Oct. 9, 1971; 1 child, Colin. BA, So. Ill. U., 1972; postgrad., U. Dubuque Theol. Sem., 1973-74; MS, No. Ill. U., 1975; post grad., Columbia Pacific U., 1996. Cert. rational emotive therapy, family life educator; cert. substance abuse counselor; ordained as deacon United Meth. Ch., 1973; lic. local pastor United Meth. Ch.; lic. clin. profl. counselor; nat. cert. counselor; clin. cert. mental health counselor. Day sch. dir. Village of Progress, Oregon, Ill., 1974-76; team coord. Children's Devel. Ctr., Rockford, Ill., 1976-78; career counselor Highland C.C. CETA, Freeport, Ill., 1978-79; family therapist, clin. dir. Stephenson County Assn. for Prevention of Child Abuse, Freeport, 1979-92; dir. quality assurance Sinnissippi Ctrs., Inc., 1992—; pastor Zion United Meth. Ch., Mendota, Ill., 1996-98, Brookville-Elkhorn United Meth. Chs., Polo, Ill., 1996-98, 2004—. Pre-marriage cons. Rochelle (Ill.) United Meth. Ch., 1985—91; mem. adminstrv. bd. Polo United Meth. Ch., 1975—90; cons. quality assurance, 1998; guest faculty mem. Family Info. Svcs., 2001—; lectr. Joint Commn. Resources, 2000—. Pub.: Handbook of Quality Training and Implementation, 2001, Behavior Health Mgmt., 2000—, The Evidence Based Practice, 2004; contbr. JCAHO Advisor. Vol. Ogle County Hospice Assn., Oregon, 1990; campaign coord. Am. Cancer Assn., Polo, 1987-93; bd. dirs. Ogle County Mental Health Assn., Oregon, 1974-76; den leader Polo Cub Scouts, 1988-91; violinist Sauk Valley Coll. String Orch., 1992-96. Mem.: Ill. Counselors Assn., Ill. Coun. Family Rels. (bd. dirs. 1990—2000, pres. 1993, immediate past pres. 1994), Nat. Coun. Family Rels. Avocations: collecting asian art, crafting fiber and textile art, poetry. Home: 401 N Congress Ave Polo IL 61064-1306 Office: 325 IL Rt 2 Dixon IL 61021 Office Phone: 815-284-6611. E-mail: rahayes@essex1.com.

HAYES, RICHARD J., management consultant; BSBA, postgrad., William Jewell Coll. Contr., UNIX sys. adminstr. Webb Builders, Inc., Juno Beach, Fla., 1984—87; pvt. practice Tequesta, Fla., 1987—95, 2002—; dir. info. tech. and profl. svcs. ACI Worldwide Profl. Resources, Inc., Overland Park, Kans., 1995—2001; sr. project mgr. bus. transformation, tech. and ops. Bank of Am., Atlanta, 2001—02. Chmn. ComputerForHope; past bd. dirs. Kansas City Crime Commn. Home: 78 Fairview E Tequesta FL 33469

HAYES, RICHARD J., JR., engineering company executive; b. Evanston, Ill., Jan. 8, 1964; s. Richard J and Mary L Hayes; m. Danette G Kauffman, Aug. 25, 1990; children: David A Cansler, Makayla M Cansler, Kelly Ms. BA, U. Kans., 1982—86; grad. CGSOC, US Army Command and Gen. Staff Coll., 1998—2002; MBA in mil. mgmt., Touro U. Internat., 2002—03. Cert. hazardous materials manager, Inst. of Hazardous Materials Mgmt., 2000. Constrn. mgr. Hall Kimbrell, Lawrence, Kans., 1987—89; officer, US Army 1-127 FA Kans. Army N.G., Ottawa, Kans., 1987—89; project mgr. Fluor Daniel, Chgo., 1989—93; officer, US Army 2-122 FA Ill. Army N.G., Chgo., 1989—2002; v.p. RMS Inc., Mnpls., 1993—97, Profl. Svc. Industries, Inc., Hillside, Ill., 1997—; lt. col. -comdr. 2-122 F.A. Ill. Army N.G., Chgo., 2002—. Bd. mem. Ill. Assn. of Environ. Professionals, Chgo., 2002—. Co-author: Asbestos Control and Replacement Guidelines for the Electric Industry. Com. mem. Ill. Legislature Joint Task Force on mold in indoor environments. Home: 1140 Gail Dr Buffalo Grove IL 60089 Office: Patrick Engring Inc 4970 Varsity Dr Lislg IL 60532 Personal E-mail: rihayes@yahoo.com.

HAYES, ROBERT BRUCE, former college president, educator; b. Clarksburg, W.Va., Nov. 15, 1925; s. Bruce and Ruby (Hitt) H.; m. Ruth Harrison, July 19, 1947 (dec.); children: Steven, Ruthann, Mark; m. Kathleen Peters. Student, Fairmont (W.Va.) State Coll.; BA, Asbury Coll., Wilmore, Ky., 1950; MEd, U. Kans., 1956, EdD, 1960. Tchr., prin. elem. and secondary schs., Kans., 1951-57; chmn. dept. edn. and psychology Asbury Coll., Wilmore, Ky., 1957-59; dir. tchr. edn. Taylor U., Upland, Ind., 1959-65; dean Coll. Edn. Marshall U., Huntington, W.Va., 1965-74, pres., 1974-83; prof. ednl. adminstrn. Coll. Edn., Marshall U., 1983-90; exec. v.p. Warner So. Coll., Lake Wales, Fla., 1991-92; interim dean coll. bus. Marshall U., Huntington, W.Va., 1992-93, coord. accreditation, 1993-95, pres. emeritus, 1992-95, provost, 1996-97, 99; interim v.p. Cmty. & Tech. Coll., 1995-97. Mem. W.Va. Adv. Com. Tchr. Edn., 1965-74; dir. Twentieth St. Bank Editor, contbr.: 1966 Yearbook of Assn. Student Teaching. Bd. dirs. Cabell-Wayne United Way, 1981; chmn. bd. Green Acres, 1983; commr. Cabell County (W.Va.), 1983-88. Served with USMCR, 1944-46. Recipient Green Acres award for contbn. to mentally retarded, 1972, Golden Knight award Nat. Mgmt. Assn., 1981 Mem. Huntington Area C. of C. (dir. 1974-83), Phi Delta Kappa, Kiwanis. Methodist. Home: 347 Bradley Foster Dr Huntington WV 25701-9451 Office: Marshall U Sch of Medicine Huntington WV 25755-0001 Office Phone: 304-691-1558.

HAYES, ROBERT E., lawyer; b. Denver, Nov. 12, 1950; BA, U. S.D., 1973, JD with honors, 1976. Bar: S.D. 1976, U.S.Ct. Appeals (8th cir.), 1977, U.S. Supreme Ct. 1980, U.S. Ct. Claims 1988, U.S. Ct. Appeals (D.C. cir.) 1989. Law clk. to Hon. Fred J. Nichol U.S. Dist. Ct. S.D., 1976-77; assoc. Davenport, Evans, Hurwitz & Smith, Sioux Falls, SD, 1977—79, ptnr., 1980—. Editor-in-chief U. S.D. Law Rev., 1975-76. Mem. ABA, State Bar S.D. (chmn. debtor-creditor com. 1983-86, 1991-94, 1996-99, pres. 2002-03), Minnehaha County Bar Assn., Phi Beta Kappa. Address: Davenport Evans Hurwitz & Smith LLP 206 W 14th St PO Box 1030 Sioux Falls SD 57101-1030

HAYES, ROBERT EMMET, retired insurance company executive; b. Los Angeles, Nov. 21, 1920; s. Robert and Marion Verbeck (Weatherwax) H.; m. Alice McCarthy, June 26, 1943; children: Kathleen Byers, Joanne, Marianne Frank, Robert Emmet Jr., Janet Gheer, Philip. AB, Loyola U., Los Angeles, 1941. Group ins. rep. Aetna Life Ins. Co., N.Y., Conn., Calif., Oreg., 1941-46; co-pilot Matson Nav. Co., San Francisco, 1946-47; employee benefit cons. Cosgrove & Co., Los Angeles, 1947-57; v.p. Marsh & McLennan, Inc., Los Angeles, 1957-62, Equitable Life Assurance Soc., N.Y.C., 1962-67; sr. v.p., group nat. accounts Met. Life Ins. Co., N.Y.C., from 1967; now ret. Served with USN, 1941-45. Home: 18670 Polvera Dr San Diego CA 92128-1122

HAYES, ROBERT FRANCIS, lawyer; b. Boston, Jan. 1, 1941; s. Robert Francis and Miriam Frances (Comfrey) H.; m. Nancy Hite Roach, Apr. 26, 1969; children: Robert Francis III, Katherine M., Rebecca C. AB, Harvard U., 1962, JD, 1965. Bar: Mass. 1965. With Ropes & Gray, Boston, 1966—. Trustee Thayer Acad., Braintree, Mass., 1985-96; dir. Jordan Hosp., Inc., Plymouth, Mass., 1984-2004; trustee, dir. Duxbury (Mass.) Beach Reservation, Inc., 1986—. Office: Ropes & Gray One International Pl Boston MA 02110 Business E-Mail: RHayes@Ropesgray.com.

HAYES, ROBERT HERRICK, technology management educator; b. Wakeeney, Kans., July 17, 1936; s. Daniel Frank and Ruth Dee (Herrick) H.; m. Priscilla Jane Alden, Aug. 25, 1963; children: Melissa, Jonathan, Michelle. BA, Wesleyan U., 1958; MS, Stanford U., 1962, PhD, 1966; AM (hon.), Harvard U., 1973. Prof. Harvard U., Boston, 1966-91, Caldwell prof. bus. adminstrn., 1991-2000, sr. assoc. dean, 1992-98, emeritus, 2000—. Bd. dirs. Helix Tech. Corp., Mansfield, Mass., Applera Corp., Norwalk, Conn. Coauthor: Restoring our Competitive Edge, 1984 (Assn. Am. Pubs. award 1984), Dynamic Manufacturing, 1988, Manufacturing Renaissance, 1995, Strategic Operations, 1996, Operations, Strategy, and Technology: Pursuing the Competitive Edge, 2004. Trustee Wesleyan U., Middletown, Conn., 1985-88. Recipient McKinsey award 1980, 81, 82, Outstanding Alumnus award Wesleyan U., 1983. Avocations: sailing, reading, travel. Office: Harvard Bus Sch Soldiers Fld Boston MA 02163-1317 Office Phone: 617-495-6330. Business E-Mail: rhayes@hbs.edu.

HAYES, ROBERT MAYO, dean, library and information scientist, educator; b. N.Y.C., Dec. 3, 1926; s. Dudley Lyman and Myra Wilhelmina (Lane) H.; m. Alice Peters, Sept. 2, 1952; 1 son, Robert Dendrou. BA, UCLA, 1947, MA, 1949, PhD, 1952. Mathematician Nat. Bur. Standards, Washington and Los Angeles, 1949-52; mem. tech. staff Hughes Aircraft Co., 1952-54; head applications group Nat. Cash Register Co., 1954-55; head bus. systems group Magnavox Co., 1955- 60; pres. Advanced Information Systems, Inc., Los Angeles, 1960-64; v.p., sci. dir. Electrada Corp., Los Angeles, 1960-64; lectr. dept. math. UCLA, 1952-64, prof. library and info. sci., 1964-91, dean, 1974-89, dean emeritus, 1989—, dir. Inst. Libr. Rsch., 1965-70; prof. emeritus, 1991—. Vis. prof. U. NSW, 1979, 93, 2002, 03, Tskuba U., 1987, Nankai U., 1987, Loughborough U., 1989, Keio U., Japan, 1994, Khazar U., Azerbaijan, 1995; mem. adv. com. White House conf. Libr. and Info. Svcs., 1979; v.p. Becker & Hayes, Inc., 1969-73, 93-96; cons. On Line Computer Libr. Ctr., 1990-94; lectr. in field. Author: Strategic Management for Academic Libraries, 1993, Models for Library Management, Decision-Making and Planning, 2001; co-author: Introduction to Information Storage and Retrieval:Tools, Elements, Theory, 1963, Handbook of Data Processing for Libraries, 2d edit., 1974, Strategic Management for Public Libraries, 1996; U.S. regional editor: Problems in Info. Storage and Retrieval, 1959—63; editor: Info. Scis. Series, 1963—75; mem. editl. bd.: Libr. Info. Sci. Rsch., 1978—. Recipient Profl. Achievement award, UCLA Alumni Assn., Beta Phi Mu award, ALA, 1st Tezak award, U. Zagreb, 1990. Mem. ALA (pres. info. sci. and automation div. 1969), Am. Soc. Info. Sci. (pres. 1962-63, nat. lectr. 1968, Award of Merit 1993), Am. Math. Soc., Assn. for Computing Machinery (assoc. editor jour. 1959-69, nat. lectr. 1969), Cosmos Club, Phi Beta Kappa, Sigma Xi. Home: 3943 Woodfield Dr Sherman Oaks CA 91403-4239 Office: UCLA 405 Hilgard Ave Los Angeles CA 90095-9000 E-mail: rhayes@ucla.edu.

HAYES, ROBIN (ROBERT CANNON HAYES), congressman; b. Concord, N.C., Aug. 14, 1945; m. Barbara; children: Winslow, Bob. BA in History, Duke U., 1967. Businessman, Concord, 1967—; mem. NC Ho. Reps., 1992—96, U.S. Congress from 8th N.C. dist., 1999—; mem. agr. com., armes svcs. com., transp. and infrastructure com.; vice chair. Congress. Sportsmen's Caucus. Current owner, operator of Mt. Pleasant Hosiery Mill; other bus. ventures include Arctic So. Turbines, Mack Sales of Birmingham, Colville Environ. Svcs., Palmer Mt. Farms (hwy. contractor) and Central Motor Lines. Mem. Concord Bd. Aldermen, 1978-81; Wildlife Resources Commn., Coun. on Drug Abuse, Prison Fellowship in N.C., 1994-; chmn., Cabarrus County Drug Task Force, 1998-; Nominated 1996 as Rep. candidate for gov. of N.C.; Mem. 1st Presbyn. Ch. Concord. Recipient Charles Dick medal of Merit, Nat. Guard Assn. US, 2000, Guardian of Small Bus., Nat. Fedn. Ind. Bus., 2002, Legis. Achievement award, The Seniors Coalition, 2002, Spirit of Enterprise award, US C. of C., 2002; Chosen as Legislator of Yr. by Nat. Rep. Legislator's Assn., 1996. Republican. Office: 130 Cannon Ho Office Bldg Washington DC 20515-0001*

HAYES, SAMUEL LINTON, III, business educator; b. Phila., Feb. 23, 1935; s. Samuel L. and Ann Walsh (Barclay) H.; m. Barbara Frances Lloyd, Dec. 21, 1963; children: Elizabeth Ann, Susan Lloyd, Judith Linton. AB, Swarthmore Coll., 1957; MBA with distinction, Harvard U., 1961, DBA, 1966. Asst. prof. bus. adminstrn. Columbia U., N.Y.C., 1965-68, assoc. prof., 1968-70; vis. assoc. prof. Harvard U., Cambridge, Mass., 1970-72, prof., 1972-75, Jacob Schiff prof. investment banking, 1975—98, Jacob Schiff prof. emeritus, 1999—, chmn. faculty Research and Mgmt. Ctr. Vevey, Switzerland, 1979-81. Cons. in field; bd. dirs. Tiffany & Co., Eaton Vance Mut. Funds, Telect, Inc. Mem. editorial bd. Harvard Bus. Rev., 1976-84, Harvard Bus. Sch. Press, 1986-89; contbr. articles to profl. jours. Mem. Mass. Fin. Adv. Bd., 1976-87, chmn., 1978-87; trustee Swarthmore Coll., 1983-94, 96—, New Eng. Conservatory, 1989—; hon. dir. Nat. Scoliosis Found. With USN, 1957-59. Mem.: Am. Guild Organists, Fin. Mgmt. Assn., Dedham Country and Polo Club, Harvard Club (N.Y.C.). Office: Harvard U Sch Bus Cumnock Hall 300 Soldiers Field Rd Boston MA 02163 Office Phone: 617-495-6240. Business E-Mail: shayes@hbs.edu.

HAYES, SHIRLEY ANN, special education educator; b. Lindsay, Calif., June 15, 1955; d. Clarence Berwine and Betty Francis (Matthews) Fox; children: Norman Tony Whited Jr., Samuel Hayes, James Chodes. AA, Porterville Jr. Coll., Calif., 1982; BA, Calif. State U., Bakersfield, 1984; specialist credential, Fresno (Calif.) Pacific Coll., 1985. Resource specialist cert. Tchg. asst. Porterville (Calif.) Devel. Ctr., 1977-84, tchr. of severely handicapped, 1984—, chmn. employee adv. com., 2003. Sec. PTA, West Putnam Sch., Porterville, 1992. Mem. Ednl. Svc. Profl. Orgn. (chair 1990), Calif. State Employees Assn. (bargaining unit rep. 1990—), Ednl. Svc. Profl. Orgn. (chmn. 1990, 2004). Avocations: artist, cooking. Home: PO Box 8624 Porterville CA 93258-8624 Office: Porterville Devel Ctr CPS PO Box 2000 Porterville CA 93258-2000 E-mail: truefox4ever@yahoo.com.

HAYES, STEPHEN MATTHEW, librarian; b. Detroit, Sept. 30, 1950; s. Matthew Cleary and Evelyn Mary (Warren) H. BS in Psychology, Mich. State U., 1972; MLS, Western Mich. U., 1974; MS in Adminstrn., U. Notre Dame, 1979. Cons. Western Mich. U., Kalamazoo, 1974; libr. U. Notre Dame, Ind., 1974-76, ref. and pub. documents libr., 1976-94; libr. Bus. Svcs. Libr., 1994—. Adv. bd. Ebsco's Bus. Sch., 2003—. Author/contbr.: What is Written Remains: Historical Essays on the Libraries of Notre Dame, 1994; editor: Environmental Concerns, 1975; contbr.: Depository Library Use of Technology: A Practitioner's Perspective, 1993. Apptd. mem. Depository Libr. Coun. to Pub. Printer, 1994—97. Recipient Rev. Paul J. Foik award, 1998. Mem. AAUP, ALA (govt. documents roundtable 1978—, chair 1987-88, chair pubs. com. 1989-91, coord. com. on access to info. 1989-90, 93-95, exec. bd. dirs. 1988-91, awards com. 1991-93, chair Godort orgn. com. 1991-93, Godort legis. com., 1999-2002, bus. ref. and svc. sect. 1994—, bus. & adult ref. roundtable 1995—, edn. com. 1996-98, resolution com. 1997-99, task force or restrictions on access to govt. info. 2002-03), Assn. Pub. Data Users (census com., steering com. 1987-96), Indigo (fed. rec. commn. chair 1992-93). Roman Catholic. Avocations: horseback riding, quilting, gardening. Home: PO Box 6032 South Bend IN 46660-6032 Office: U Notre Dame L012 Mendoza Coll Of Business Notre Dame IN 46556-5646 Office Phone: 574-631-5268. Business E-Mail: shayes1@nd.edu.

HAYES, SYLVIA RICHMOND, music educator; b. Lawrenceburg, Tenn.; d. Edward David and Blanche Audrey (Sells) Richmond; m. Gene Edwin Hayes; B.S., George Peabody Coll. Tchrs., M.Mus. Edn., 1968; postgrad. Tenn. State U.; postgrad. in data processing Columbia State Community Coll. Band dir., tchr. English, high sch., Loretto, Tenn.; dir. band, tchr. music Coffman Sch., Lawrenceburg, 1972—89, Leoma (Tenn.) Sch., 1989-94; tech. coord. Lawrence County Sch. Sys., 1994— . Choir and music dir., sec. Immanuel Baptist Ch. Mem. Bus. and Profl. Women's Club (Career Woman of Yr. 1972), Lawrence County Edn. Assn. (treas. bd. dirs., sec. 1988-98, pres. 1998-99), Midele Edn. Assn. (Tenn.), Tenn. Edn. Assn., NEA, Middle Band and Orch. Assn., Music Educators Nat. Conf. Democrat. Club: Lioness (pres. 1977-78). Office: Lawrence County Bd Edn 700 Mahr Ave Lawrenceburg TN 38464

HAYES, TRENT ROBERT, music educator; b. Decatur, Ga., Apr. 17, 1976; s. Robert Franklin and Diane McKendrick Hayes; m. Paula Jean Maynard, July 11, 2003. Med, Valdosta State U., 1998—99, MusB, 1994—98. Florida Teaching Certificate State of Fla., 2003. Band dir. Tattnall CountyHigh Sch., Reidsville, Ga., 1999—2000, Baker County H.S., Glen St Mary, Fla., 2000—. V.p. Baker County Edn. Assn., Macclenny, Fla., 2004—05. Mem.: Fla. Bandmasters Assn., Phi Mu Alpha Sinfonia Frat. (life; pres., zeta gamma chpt. 1998—99). Independent. Avocations: writing, soccer. Home: 6073 Copper Dr Macclenny FL 32063 Personal E-mail: trhayes76@comcast.net.

HAYES, WILBUR FRANK, retired biology educator; b. Rhinelander, Wis., Nov. 10, 1936; s. Wilbur Mead and Evelyn (Stritesky) H.; m. Dawn Olivia Waldorf, July 21, 1979 (div. Feb. 1991); stepchildren: Lynn, Robert, Dana, Richard, Gary, Kevin. BA, Colby Coll., 1959; MS, Lehigh U., 1961, PhD, 1965. Postdoctoral fellow Yale U., New Haven, 1965-67; asst. prof. biology Wilkes Coll., Wilkes-Barre, Pa., 1967-71, assoc. prof., 1971-99, assoc. prof. emeritus, 2000—. Vis. prof. Northeastern U., Boston, 1987-88. Contbr. articles to profl. jours. Chmn. bd. dirs. N.E. Pa. chpt. Am. Heart Assn., Wilkes-Barre, 1986-87. Mem. Soc. for Integrative and Comparative Biology, Pa. Acad. Sci., Microscopy Soc. Am., Sigma Xi (pres. Wilkes Coll. chpt. 1976-77, sec.-treas. 1984-87, 88-91). Republican. Congregationalist. Avocations: downhill skiing, photography, travel, colonial american history. Home: 47 Stanley St Wilkes Barre PA 18702-2308 Office: Wilkes U Dept Biology Wilkes Barre PA 18766

HAYES, WILLIAM MEREDITH, pilot, retired military officer; b. San Antonio, Mar. 28, 1947; s. Oscar Junior and Mary Kathrn (Leuthart) Hayes; m. Beverly Jeanne Lowe, May 20, 1972; children: Loren Elaine, Colin Meredith. BA, Western Ky. U., 1971. Cert. naval aviator, airline transport pilot FAA. Commd. ensign USCG, 1973, advanced through grades to capt., 1994; asst. ops. officer USCG Base, Honolulu, 1973-74; pub. affairs officer USCG Air Sta., Mobile, Ala., 1975-78; tng. officer USCG Group/Air Sta., Corpus Christi, Tex., 1978-81; head Falcon jet tng. USCG Aviation Tng. Ctr., Mobile, 1981-87; air ops. officer USCG Air Sta., Miami, Fla., 1987-92, exec. officer Elizabeth City, N.C., 1992-94; commdg. officer USCG Activities, San Diego, 1994-97; chief office of ops. 8th C.G. Dist., New Orleans, 1997; pilot Humana, Inc., Louisville, Ky., 1997—. Bd. dirs. USO, San Diego, Armed Svcs. YMCA, San Diego; mem. mil. adv. coun. C. of C., San Diego, 1994—. Contbr. articles to profl. jours. Recipient Humanitarian Svc. medal USCG, Corpus Christi, 1978, Commendation medal USCG, Miami, 1992, Achievement medal USCG, Elizabeth City, 1994, Meritorious Svc. medal, 1997. Mem. SCV, Amateur Radio Relay League, Sons of the Am. Revolution, Delta Tau Delta (life, chpt. v.p. 1969-70). Avocations: fishing, amateur radio, golf. Home: 2420 Napoleon Blvd Louisville KY 40205-2011 Office: Humana 1180 Standiford Ct Louisville KY 40213-2019 Office Phone: 502-580-3395. Personal E-mail: wmhayes@humana.com.

HAYFLICK, LEONARD, microbiology educator, writer; b. Phila., May 20, 1928; s. Nathan Albert and Edna (Silbert) H.; m. Ruth Louise Heckler, Oct. 3, 1954; children: Joel, Deborah, Susan, Rachel, Anne. BA in Microbiology and Chemistry, U. Pa., 1951, MS in Med. Microbiology, 1953, PhD in Med. Microbiology and Chemistry, 1956. McLaughlin rsch. fellow in infection and immunity, dept. microbiology U. Tex. Med. Br., Galveston, Tex., 1956-58; assoc. mem. Wistar Inst. Anatomy and Biology, Phila., 1958-68; asst. prof. rshc. medicine U. Pa., Phila., 1966-68; prof. med. microbiology Stanford (Calif.) U. Sch. Medicine, 1968-76, senator-at-large, Basic Med. Scis., 1970-73, chmn. gen. rsch. support grant com., 1972-74; sr. research cell biologist Children's Hosp., Oakland, Calif., 1976-81; prof. zoology, prof. microbiology and immunology U. Fla., Gainesville, 1981-87, dir. Ctr. for Gerontol. Studies, Coll. Liberal Arts and Scis., 1981-87; prof. anatomy U. Calif. Sch. Medicine, San Francisco, 1988—. Mem. subcom. on mycoplasmataceae Internat. Com. Bacteriol. Nomenclature, 1965-78; mem. steering com. cell and devel. biology film program MIT, 1970-73; chmn. Calif. State

Com. Health White Ho. Conf. Aging, 1971-72, Calif. state rep., 1972; Nat. Cancer Planning Com. Nat. Cancer Inst., NIH, 1972; chmn., adult devel. and aging rsch. and tng. com. Nat. Inst. Child Health and Human Devel., NIH, 1972-73; non-resident fellow Inst. Higher Studies, Santa Barbara, Calif., 1973—; mem. Argonne Nat. Lab. rev. com. biol. and med. rsch. div. Argonne Nat. Lab., 1973-76; mem. rsch. adv. com. Tchrs. Ins. and Annuity Assn. Am.-Coll. Retirement Equities Funds, N.Y.C., 1974-80; founding mem. Nat. Adv. Coun. on Aging, Nat. Inst. on Aging, NIH, Bethesda, Md., 1975; cons. Office of Dir. Nat. Cancer Inst., Bethesda, 1963-74; vis. scientist Ctr. for Aging Weizmann Inst. Sci., Rehovoth, Israel, 1980, 86; mem. adv. bd. Internat. Exchange Ctr. Gerontology, Fla. Univ. System, Tampa, 1982-86; mem. jury for Sandoz prize in gerontology and geriatrics, 1985-89; bd. dirs. Ctr. for Climacteric Studies, Inc., Gainesville, 1985-88; expert cons. various coms. U.S. Congress, vis. prof. Oita Med. U., Japan, 1991-95, U. Parma, Italy, 1991, Kurume U. Med. Sch., Japan; lectr. in field. Author: How and Why We Age, 1996; editor: Biology of the Mycoplasmas, 1969, Handbook of the Biology of Aging, 1977; sr. editor Biol. Scis. Microfiche Collection Info. on Gerontology and Geriatric Medicine Univ. Microfilms Internat., Ann Arbor, Mich., 1984-98; editor-in-chief Exptl. Gerontology, 1984-98; asst. editor In Vitro jour. Tissue Culture Assn., 1969-75; editor biol. scis. sect. Jour. Gerontology, 1975-80; assoc. editor Cancer Rsch., 1972-80; mem. editorial bd. Jour. Bacteriology, 1964-72, Jour. Virology, 1967-70, Infection and Immunity jour., 1968-78, Exec. Health Report, 1970—, Mechanisms of Aging and Devel., 1972—, Gerontology and Geriatrics Edn., 1980—, A Revista Portuguesa de Medicina Geriatrica, 1987—; mem. adv. com. Bergey's Manual of Determinative Bacteriology, 1965-78; bd. dirs., mem. editorial bd. Bollettino Dell Instituto Sieroterapico Milanese, Archivo de Microbiologia ed Immunologia, Milan, Italy, 1968—; contbr. numerous articles in field to profl. jours. Staff sgt. U.S. Army, 1946-48. Recipient Samuel Roberts Noble Found. Rsch. Recognition award, 1984; co-recipient Sandoz prize Internat. Assn. Gerontology, 1991, Biomed. Scis. & Aging award U. So. Calif., 1974, Rsch. Recognition award Samuel Roberts Noble Found., 1984; Karl-Forster lectr. Acad. Sci. and Lit., Mainz, Germany, 1983, Hoffman-LaRoche lectr. Waksman Inst. Microbiology Rutgers U., 1984, Wadworth Meml. Fund lectr. Rush-Presbyn.-St. Luke's Med. Ctr., Chgo., 1984, hon. lectr. Rosenfield Program Pub. Affairs Grinnell Coll., 1989, invited speaker Sandoz lectrs. in Gerontology, Basle, Switzerland, 1986, 92, numerous other lectureships U.S.A., Can. and Europe, 1970—, Career Devel. award Nat. Cancer Inst., NIH, 1962-70, Lifetime Achievement award Soc. In Vitro Biology, 1996, Van Wezel prize Euro. Soc. Animal Cell Technology, 1999, Lord Cohen of Birkinhead medal Brit. Soc. Rsch. on Aging, 1999. Fellow AAAS, Gerontol Soc. Am. (program and awards com. 1972-77, chmn., exec. com. biol. scis. sect. 1972-74, com. on internat. rels. 1980-82, pub. policy com. 1980-82, pres. 1982-83, ann. Robert W. Kleemeier award 1972, Brookdale award 1980); mem. Am. Soc. for Microbiology, Tissue Culture Assn. (hon., trustee 1966-68, program com. 1970, mem. coun. 1972-74, v.p. 1974-76, pres. Calif. chpt. 1971-73), Soc. for Exptl. Biology and Medicine (councillor 1984-88), Assn. for Advancement of Aging Rsch. (adv. coun. 1970-71), Am. Aging Assn., Am. Cancer Soc. (virology and cell biology study sect. 1974-76), Internat. Assn. Microbiol. Standardization (sec. cell culture com. 1963-73, chmn. 1985—, mem. coun. 1987-89), Internat. Orgn. for Mycoplasmology (Presdl. award 1984), Am. Gerontol. Soc. (v.p., coun. 1972-74, 81-83, program com. 1977-79, bd. dirs. 1981-83), Am. Fedn. Aging Rsch. (bd. dirs., exec. com., rsch. adv. com. 1981—, chmn. study sect. 1987—, v.p. 1988—, Leadership award 1983), Fedn. Am. Socs. for Exptl. Biology, Aging Prevention Rsch. Found. (sci. adv. bd. dirs.), Am. Assn. for Cancer Rsch., Am. Soc. Pathologists, Calif. Found. for Biomed. Rsch., Am. Longevity Assn. (sci. adv. bd. dirs. 1981—), Western Gerontology Assn. (coun. 1972-74, bd. dirs. 81-83), Internat. Assn. Gerontology (mem. Am. exec. com. 1972-75, treas., exec. com. 1985-89, co-recipient Sandoz award gerontology 1991), Found. on Gerontology (sci. adv. bd. 1985—), Soc. Medicine and Natural Sci., Ukrainian Acad. Med. Scis. (fgn., academician 1991), French Biol. Soc. (fgn.), Euro. Soc. Animal Cell Tech. (Van Wezel prize), Brit. Soc. Rsch. on Aging (Lord Cohen of Burkinhead medal). Office: U Calif 36991 Greencroft Close PO Box 89 The Sea Ranch CA 95497-0089

HAYGOOD, ALMA JEAN, elementary school educator; d. John Thomas and Alma Perry Haygood. BS, Ala. A&M U., 1978; MA, George Mason U., 2001. Kindergarten tchr. Talladega (Ala.) County Pub. Schs., 1978—80; adult edn. tchr. Ft. Carson (Colo.) Mil. Base, 1980—82; day care ctr. tchr. KinderCare Learning Ctrs., Colorado Springs, Colo., 1982—84; child care ctr. dir. Open Hands Preschool, Colorado Springs, Colo., 1984—85; preschool tchr. Gum Springs Child Devel. Ctr., Alexandria, Va., 1985—87; tchr. Fairfax County Pub. Schs., Springfield, Va., 1987—. Cons., tutoring-mentoring program Lomax Ch., Arlington, Va., 1989—95. Sch. union rep. Fairfax Edn. Assn., Fairfax, Va., 2001—. Tchr. tng. grantee, Fairfax Edn. Assn., 2003. Mem.: Kappa Delta Pi (assoc.; mem. 2002—). Democrat. Baptist. Avocations: clarinet, aerobic exercise, piano, singing. Home: 5318 Harbor Court Dr Alexandria VA 22315-3934 Office: Mount Vernon Woods Elem Sch 4015 Fielding St Alexandria VA 22309 Personal E-mail: hhaggard86@aol.com. E-mail: Alma.Haygood@fcps.edu.

HAYGOOD, ROBERT COLLINS, industrial psychologist, educator, consultant; b. Jacksonville, Fla., Oct. 17, 1926; s. James Douglas and Margaret (Collins) H.; m. Danielle Hagerty Haygood, Aug. 23, 1963; children: Daniel Paul, Charles Douglas, Harold Bennett. BS, U. Ill., 1949; MS, U. Utah, 1959, PhD, 1963. Lic. psychologist, Ariz. Sr. rsch. engr. N.Am. Aviation-Autonetics, Anaheim, Calif., 1959-64; from asst. to assoc. prof. Kans. State U., Manhattan, 1964-69; prof. Ariz. State U., Tempe, 1970-97, prof. emeritus, 1997—. Vis. lectr. Calif. State Coll., Long Beach, 1969-70; cons. Advanced Risk Control Sys. Internat., Scottsdale, Ariz., 1994-97, VA, Kansas City, 1965-69; cons. various hosps., Phoenix, 1971-74. Mem. editl. staff, manuscript reviewer Jour. Exptl. Psychology, 1965-72; contbr. articles to profl. jours. Chmn. Ariz. State Bd. Psychol. Examiners, Phoenix, 1974-75; dist. leader Arizonans for McGovern, Phoenix, 1972. Staff sgr. USAF, 1953-57. Sr. rsch. assoc. Nat. Rsch. Coun., NASA, 1977-78; predoctoral rsch. fellow USPHS, U. Utah, 1958-59. Mem. Am. Psychol. Soc., Southwestern Psychol. Assn. (bd. dirs. 1973), Human Factors and Ergonomics Soc. (chpt. pres., sec.-treas. 1979—). Avocations: jazz, dance band arranging, international travel. Home: 6616 E Calle Redondo Scottsdale AZ 85251 Office: Ariz State U Dept Psychology Tempe AZ 85287 E-mail: danibobhaygood@cox.net.

HAYHURST, JAMES FREDERICK PALMER, career and business consultant, motivational speaker, writer; b. Toronto, Can., May 24, 1941; s. W. Palmer and Jean E. (Hunnisett) H.; children: Cindy, Jim, Barbara. H.BA, U. Western Ont., 1963. Brand man Procter & Gamble, Toronto, 1963-66, exec. v.p., 1975-82; pres. Hedwyn Communications Inc., Toronto, 1983-86; chmn. Saatchi & Saatchi Compton Hayhurst, Toronto, 1983-86; owner Wyldwyn Holdings Ltd., Toronto, 1986—; pres. The Hayhurst Career Ctr., Toronto, 1988—, The Right Mountain Crew, 1994—. Author: The Right Mountain, 1996, Where Have I Gone Right?, 2004. Chmn. Outward Bound Can., 1985-87; founding co-chmn. Trails Youth Initiatives. Mem. Toronto Golf Club, Olde Fla. Golf Club (Naples). Office: The Right Mountain Inc 378 Fairlawn Ave Toronto ON Canada M5M 1T8 E-mail: jim@therightmountain.com. *True success is the attainment of purpose without compromising your core values.*

HAYLON, MICHAEL E., insurance company executive; Degree, Bowdoin Coll.; MBA, U. Conn. Sr. v.p. The Phoenix Cos. Inc., Hartford, Conn., 1990—2002, exec. v.p., investment chief, 2002—03, exec. v.p., CFO, 2003—. Office: The Phoenix Cos Inc 1 American Row Hartford CT 06102-5056

HAYMAKER, DOUGLAS JAMES, psychologist, researcher; b. Evansville, Ind., Oct. 28, 1957; s. James Gallagher and Marjorie Louise (Uber) H.; m. Stephanie Elise Brody, Apr. 4, 1987. BA, Brown U., 1980; MS, U. Fla., 1984, PhD, 1988. Intern Bklyn. VA Med. Ctr., 1986-87; sr. clinician psychologist St. Clares-Riverside Med. Ctr., Denville, N.J., 1987-90; clin. psychologist Ctr. for Evaluation and Psychotherapy Morristown (N.J.) Meml. Hosp., 1989-98; clin. psychologist Princeton (N.J.) Psychiatric Recovery Network, 1990-92; field supr. Grad. Sch. of Applied and Profl. Psychology Rutgers U., Piscataway, N.J., 1990—. Clin. psychologist, CEO Oldwick (N.J.) Assocs. in Psychotherapy, 1991—. Contbr. articles to profl. jours. NSF fellow, 1978; recipient Recognition award Fla. Dept. Health and Rehab. Svcs., 1986. Mem. APA, N.J. Psychol. Assn. Republican. Avocations: sailing, photography. Office: Oldwick Assocs in Psychotherapy PO Box 242 Oldwick NJ 08858-0242

HAYMAN, HARRY, professional society administrator, electrical engineer; b. Lewistown, Pa., Mar. 20, 1917; s. Sidney and Nettie (Hirsch) H.; m. Edith Harriet Levitz, Mar. 18, 1946; children: Gail A., Beth (Mrs. Stanley Truman), Sidney F., Stuart A. BS, NYU, 1938; postgrad., George Washington U., 1947—50. Engr. FCC, Washington, 1940-54; pres., gen. mgr. radio sta. WPGC, Morningside, Md., 1954-55; project mgr. U.S. Navy and FAA, Washington, 1956-60; program mgr. NASA project Apollo, Washington, 1960-71; chmn. IEEE Computer Soc., Washington, 1965, exec. sec. N.Y.C., 1971-82, dir. confs. and tutorials Silver Spring, Md., 1982-89, coord. robotics and automation divsn., 1988—. Vice pres. Nat. Childrens Ctr., 1960; pres. Henryton State Hosp. Assn., 1970, 74; Bd. dirs. D.C. Assn. Retarded Children, 1956-70, pres. Washington chpt., 1953-55; pres. Gt. Oaks Aux., 1975-78. Served with USNR, 1944-46. Recipient Apollo Achievement award 1969. Mem. IEEE (treas. Computer Soc. Internat. Conf. 1970, treas. Internat. Conf. on Computer Comm. 1972, spl. asst. to chmn. Conf. on Computer Comm. 1974, coord., treas. Internat. Conf. on Robotics and Automation 1980-96). Home: 3037C Exeter Dr Boca Raton FL 33434 Office: 1201 Elm Grove Cir Silver Spring MD 20905-7020 Business E-Mail: h.hayman@ieee.org.

HAYMAN, MARTIN ARTHUR, psychiatrist, educator; b. NYC, Dec. 5, 1929; s. Louis and Cecelia (Klatzkin) H.; m. Traude E. Sighartner, June 9, 1957; children: Douglas, Kenneth. BA cum laude, NYU, 1951, MD, 1955. Diplomate Am. Bd. Psychiatry and Neurology, Nat. Bd. Med. Examiners. Intern Meadowbrook Hosp., East Meadow, NY, 1955-56; pvt. practice Nassau County, 1959-73; sr. physician VA Med. Ctr., Northport, 1973; resident in psychiatry SUNY Med. Ctr., Stony Brook, 1974-77, asst. prof. clin. psychiatry, 1977—. Dir. psychiatry South Brookhaven Health Ctr., Patchogue, NY, 1977—91; attending physician Brookhaven Meml. Hosp. Med. Ctr., 1977—91. Reviewer jour.; contbr. articles to profl. jours. Mem. ad hoc com. Helping Older People Emotionally, Suffolk County, 1981-82. Capt. M.C., USAF, 1956-58. Fellow Acad. Psychosomatic Medicine; mem. AMA (Physician's Recognition awards 1970—), Am. Psychiat. Assn., Med. Soc. N.Y., Suffolk County Med. Soc., Phi Beta Kappa, Beta Lambda Sigma (vice chancellor 1951). Home and Office: 20 Redwood Dr PO Box 626 Great River NY 11739-0626 E-mail: mhayman@pol.net.

HAYMAN, RANDY E., lawyer; b. St. Louis, Sept. 24, 1963; s. Robert B.E. and Roen Hayman. BA, U. Mich., 1985; JD, Georgetown U., 1989. Bar: Mo. 1995, Pa. 1990, D.C. 1990, U.S. Dist. Ct. (ea. dist. Mo.) 1999, U.S. Dist. Ct. (we. dist. Mo.) 1995, U.S. Supreme Ct. 1997. Intern ABC News, 1984; reporter KMOX Radio News CBS, St. Louis, 1985—86; law clk. Nat. Pub. Radio, Washington, 1987; assoc. Wilkes, Artis, Hedrick & Lane, Washington, 1989—92; counsel NAACP Legal Def. Fund, Inc., Washington, 1992—93; asst. atty. gen. Mo. Atty. Gen.'s Office, Jefferson City, Mo., 1994—96; assoc. Stinson, Mag & Fizzell PC, Kansas City, St. Louis, 1996—2000; gen. counsel Met. St. Louis Sewer Dist., 2000—, legal counsel Capital Improvement and Replacement program. Mem. Leadership St. Louis, 2002; bd. dirs. Crime Solvers, Washington, 1991—94, pres., 1993—94; bd. dirs. Build a Future Found., 1989—97, Trailnet, 2005—. Recipient 40 Under 40 award, St. Louis Bus. Jour., 2002, award, Leadership St. Louis, 2002. Mem.: ABA, Mo. Bar Young Lawyers' Coun. (bd. dirs. young lawyer's coun. 1998), Lawyers' Assn. Kansas City (bd. dirs. Young Lawyers divsn. 1997—98), Am. Met. Sewer Assn., Water Environment Fedn., Am. Corp. Counsel Assn., Bar Assn. Met. St. Louis (bd. dirs. Young Lawyers divsn. 1998—2001). Avocations: guitar, radio talk show host, public speaking. Office: Met St Louis Sewer Dist 2350 Market St Saint Louis MO 63103 Office Phone: 314-768-6209. E-mail: rhayman@stlmsd.com.

HAYMES, HARMON HAYDEN, retired economics professor; b. Lynchburg, Va., June 8, 1927; s. Joseph Albert and Reba (Hayden) Haymes; m. Beatrice Ann Mason, Nov. 26, 1952; children: Ann Elizabeth, William Hayden. BA magna cum laude, Lynchburg Coll., 1954; MA, U. Va., 1956, PhD, 1959. Acting asst. prof. Lynchburg Coll., 1956-57; instr. U. Va., 1957-59; asst. prof. Smith Coll., 1959-61, Washington and Lee U., 1961-64; asst. v.p. Fed. Res. Bank of Richmond, 1964-68; prof. econs. Va. Commonwealth U., 1968-77; chmn. dept. econs. Va. Commonwealth U., 1968-73, acting dir. Bur. Bus. and Econ. Rsch.; prof. econs. St. Mary's Coll. Md., 1977-91, provost, dean faculty, 1978-84, prof. econs. emeritus, 1991—. Mem. Gov.'s Adv. Com. Urban Incentive Fund, 1970—78, Gov.'s Revenue Resources and Econ. Study Commn., 1972—75. Editor: Va. Social Sci. Jour., 1970—73; assoc. editor: Atlantic Econ. Jour., 1973—80; contbr. articles to profl. jours. With U.S. Army, 1950—52. Recipient McKinsey award, Bus. Horizons, 1962; duPont fellow, 1954, John Y. Mason fellow, 1955, Virginia Mason Davidge fellow, 1955. Mem.: So. Econ. Assn., Am. Econ. Assn., Omicron Delta Epsilon. Home: 105 N Branch Rd Bedford VA 24523-1238

HAYMES, JERRY LYNN, entertainment industry executive; b. Verron, Tex., Aug. 30, 1940; s. Arthur L. and Georgia H.; m. Brenda Dee, Aug. 1, 1962 (div. June 1981); children: Tracy, Darren. BS, Abilene Christian Univ., 1975; AS, Kilgore Coll., 1988; MusD, London Conservatory of Music, London, 1963. Drummer/singer Norman Petty Studio, Clovis, N.Mex., 1955-57, Sun Records, Memphis, 1957; performer, 1960—; CEO, various radio stations., Longview, Tex., 1977, Umpire Entertainment, Longview, Tex., 1980—. Bd. dirs. Country Music Assn., Nashville, 1960's, Internat. Talent Buyer Assn., 1970's; adv. bd., bd. dirs. Texas County Music Assn., 1995—. Record promotor It's A Heart Ache, 1978 (Gold Record 1978); songwriter What Then?, 1956 (Gospel music award 1967), So Fine, 1959 (Triple Gold Record 1981); drummer Party Doll, 1957 (Gold Record 1957). Pres. S.W. Conf. Baseball Umpire Assn., Tex., 1993—98; adv. Vernon Reg. Jr. Coll. Fine Arts Dept., 1997—. With U.S. Army, 1960—62, with U.S. Army, 1967, Vietnam. Named to Tex. Music Hall of Fame; recipient Sun Legends Group Rock-a-Billy Artist award, Rock-n-Roll Hall of Fame, 1996, Top Ten Record Artist/Musician for Past 45 Years award, Billboard Mag., 1999. Mem. Sons of Confederate Vet., Am. Fed. of Musicians, Baseball Umpire Assn. (pres. 1992-98). Avocations: collecting music memorbilia, sports officiating. Office: Umpire Entertainment 1507 Scenic Dr Longview TX 75604-2319 Business E-Mail: umpire.shows@sbcglobal.net.

HAYMON, CHADRON ZONELLE, music educator, minister; b. Denver, June 28, 1974; s. Ronald Zonelle and Sheila Jo Haymon; m. Andrea Michelle Bunch, May 23, 1998; 1 child, Joya Isabelle. BA in Music Edn., Metro State Coll., Denver, 1997. Cert. music edn. K-12 vocal and instrumental Va. Bd. Edn., 2002. Music pastor Capital Cmty. Ch., Ashburn, Va., 1997—; orch. dir. Marsteller Mid. Sch., Bristow, Va., 1998—. Min. of music Capital Cmty. Ch., Ashburn, Va., 1997—. Clinician Heart Of Worship Ministries, Stockton, Calif., 2003—05. Mem.: Music Educators Nat. Conf. (licentiate). Republican. Pentecostal. Avocations: music, skiing. Home: 608 Nathan Pl Leesburg VA 20176 Office: Marsteller Mid Sch 14000 Sudley Manor Dr Bristow VA 20136 Office Phone: 703-393-7608. Personal E-mail: chaymon@capitalcommunity.org. E-mail: haymoncz@pwcs.edu.

HAYNALI, CAROLYN ANN, social services administrator; b. Clarksville, Pa., Oct. 22, 1934; d. George J. Nesto and Annie Kepan; m. Charles D. Haynali, Apr. 6, 1953; children: Denise Marie, Charles David Jr. Grad. high sch., Fredicktown, Pa., 1953. Founder, spokesperson Caregiver's Army Orgn., Berlin Center, Ohio, 1999—. Vol. Operation Blessing, Ohio, 1979—94; pub. spkr. Caregiver's Army Orgn., 1999—; spkr. Alzheimers Task Force Congress, Washington, 2000; pub. spkr. internet radio Thunderstar Showcase, Ohio, 2000—. Author, poet (book) Poetry from the Heart by An Alzheimer Care Giver, 2004;, author articles in short stories. Home: 14646 Ellsworth Rd PO Box 64 Berlin Center OH 44401 Office: Caregivers Army Orgn Box 64 Berlin Center OH 44401 Business E-Mail: carladydove1@juno.com.

HAYNES, CALEB VANCE, JR., geology and archaeology educator; b. Spokane, Wash., Feb. 29, 1928; m. Elizabeth Hamilton, Jan. 11, 1954 (div. 1991); 1 child, Elizabeth Anne. Student, Johns Hopkins U., 1947-49; degree in geol. engring., Colo. Sch. Mines, 1956; PhD, U. Ariz., 1965. Mining geology cons., 1958-60; sr. project engr. Am. Inst. Research, Golden, Colo., 1956-60; sr. engr. Martin Co., Denver, 1960-62; geologist Nev. State Mus. Tule Springs Expedition, 1962-63; research asst. U. Ariz., Tucson, 1963-64, asst. prof. geology, 1965-68, prof. geoscis., anthropology, 1974-99, Regents prof., 1991-99, Regents prof. emeritus, 1999; assoc. prof. So. Meth. U., Dallas, 1968-73, prof., 1973-74. Served with USAF, 1951—54. Guggenheim fellow 1980-81, Smithsonian sr. post doctoral fellow, 1987; grantee NSF, Nat. Geographic Soc., others. Fellow: AAAS, Geol. Soc. Am. (Archaeol. Geology award 1984, Kirk Bryan award 2003); mem.: Soc. Am. Archaeology (Fryxell award 1978), Am. Quaternary Assn. (pres. 1976—78, Disting. Career award 2002), Nat. Acad. Sci., Sigma Xi. Office: U Ariz Dept Anthropology Tucson AZ 85721-0001

HAYNES, CORNELL See NELLY

HAYNES, DOUGLAS MARTIN, obstetrician, gynecologist, educator; b. NYC, Jan. 25, 1922; s. Daniel Hagood and Courtenay (Collins) H.; m. Elizabeth B. Johnson, June 17, 1961; children: Douglas Marshall, Lewis Daniel. BA, BS, So. Meth. U., 1943; MD, Southwestern Med. Coll., 1946; MA, Louisville Presby. Theol. Sem., 1989, ThM, 1994. Diplomate Am. Bd. Obstetrics and Gynecology (assoc. examiner). Intern in pathology Parkland Meml. Hosp., Dallas, 1946-47, resident obstetrics and gynecology, 1949-52; asst. prof. obstetrics and gynecology U. Tex. Southwestern Med Sch., 1952-55; assoc. prof. obstetrics and gynecology U. Louisville Sch. Medicine, 1955-57, prof., 1957-87, prof. emeritus, 1987—, chmn. dept., 1957-69; interim dean U. Louisville Sch. Medicine (Sch. of Medicine), 1969-70, dean, 1970-72. Author: Medical Complications During Pregnancy, 1969; Contbr. articles to profl. jours. Served to capt., M. C. AUS, 1947-49. Fellow Am. Gynec. and Obstet. Soc.; mem. Am. Coll. Obstetricians and Gynecologists, A.C.S., Central Assn. Obstetricians and Gynecologists (v.p. 1977-78), So. Med. Assn., Phi Beta Kappa, Phi Chi, Delta Chi, Alpha Omega Alpha, Phi Kappa Phi. Democrat. Episcopalian. Home: 5204 Tomahawk Rd Louisville KY 40207-1643

HAYNES, GARY ALLEN, photojournalist, editor; b. Beloit, Kansas, Jan. 25, 1936; s. Blair W. and Evelyn H. (Allen) F.; children by previous marriage: Stephanie L., Philip A., Emily L.; m. Audrey M. (Edwards); stepchildren: Jane Kelly, Katie Kelly. BS in journalism, Kans. State U., 1957. Staff photographer Salina (Kans.) Jour., Salina, Kans., 1957; photographer UPI, Detroit, 1958, mgr. picture bur. Phila., 1959-62, Atlanta, 1962-63, spl. projects photographer N.Y.C., 1964, mgr. picture bur. L.A., 1964-68; photographer Internat. Olympic Photo Pool, Tokyo, 1964; mgr. divsn. news pictures UPI, Chgo., 1968-70, asst. to mng. editor newspictures N.Y.C., 1970-71; nat. picture editor N.Y. Times, N.Y.C., 1971-74; photo editor San Francisco Examiner, San Francisco, 1974; dir. graphic arts Phila. Inquirer, Phila., 1974-95, asst. mng. editor; with Photography weekly column, syndicated by Knight Newspapers (later Knight Ridder), 1976-87; cons. N.Y. Times, N.Y.C., 1996—. Photographer NASA Photo Pool, 1962-63; spkr., del., USA,USSR Photo Summit, Moscow, 1990, Washington, 1991. Contbg. photographer: (book) Four Days-The Historical Record of Death of President Kennedy, 1963, A Week at Kansas State, 1988; picture editor: Assignment Am.-N.Y. Times, 1972, A Day In the Life of Calif., 1989; judge, W.R. Hearst photojournalism competition, San Francisco, 1986-88; lectr., photography and photo editing, Am. Press Inst., Reston, Va., 1987-96, The New Sch., 1991, Internat. Ctr. Photography, NY, 1990, U. Arts, Phila., 1989-91, Kans. State U., Manhattan, 1989-99, 2000, 04, Kans. State U., photo workshop, Salina, 2002, 04, Temple U., Phila., 1992. Capt., Adj. Gen. Corps, U.S. Army, 1957-58. Recipient, first pl. award, Look mag., Sports Photo Contest, 1962, first and Best of Show award, The White House News Photographers Assn., 1962, Photo awards World Press Photo, first and third pl. gen. news, 1963, Sweepstakes award, Atlanta Press Assn., Sweepstakes first and third pl. awards Gen. News, 1964, Best Use of Pictures in a Newspaper award Nat. Press Photog. Assn., 1978, Judges Spl. award for newspaper picture editing, 1979, best use of photos in newspaper zoned edit NPPA/Pictures of Yr. Competition, Silver medal mag. photo editing, Soc. Newspaper Design, 1988, Pictures of Yr. eighteenth Ann. Competition first pl. spot news, first pl. feature, first pl. gen. news. Mem., Nat. Press Photographer's Assn., Sigma Delta Chi. Home: 1473 N Ill Rte 2 Oregon IL 61061 Personal E-mail: verity@rochelle.net.

HAYNES, GARY ANTHONY, archaeologist; b. Long Beach, Calif., Sept. 30, 1948; s. Ellsworth Wallace and Martha Louise (Ryan) H. BA, U. Md., 1970; MA, Cath. U. Am., 1978, PhD, 1981. Vis. asst. prof. anthropology Cath. U. Am., Washington, 1981; assoc. prof. lectr. George Washington U., Washington, 1982; research assoc. anthropology dept. Smithsonian Inst., Washington, 1981-85; asst. prof. anthropology U. Nev., Reno, 1985-88, assoc. prof. anthropology, 1988-95, prof. anthropology, 1995—, chair dept., 1998—2004. Founder, vice-chmn. bd. Hwange Rsch. Trust, 1987—. Author: Mammoths, Mastodonts and Elephants, 1991, The Early Settlement of North America, 2002; editor: Mammoths and the Mammoth Fauna, 2000; contbr. articles to profl. jours. Active Scientist Exchange Acad. Scis. U.S. Nat. Research Council, 1987. Smithsonian Inst. fellow, 1980; grantee Nat. Geog. Soc., 1981-88, 91, Leakey Found., 1990, 91, IREX, 1995, Wenner-Gren Found., 2000; Fulbright sr. scholar Subsaharan Africa Rsch. Program, 1993. Mem. Soc. Am. Archaeology (Fryxell com. chmn. 1986-89), Am. Quaternary Assn., Zimbabwe Sci. Assn., Inqua Commn. on Palaeoecology and Human Evolution (pres. 2003—). Office: U Nev Dept Anthropology Reno NV 89557-0001

HAYNES, JANICE JAQUES ELIZABETH, editor, elementary school educator; b. Casper, Wyo., May 31, 1924; d. George Havelock and Grace Mary (O'Keefe) Jaques; m. David Clark Haynes, Dev. 16, 1951; children: Judith J., David C. AB, Stanford Univ., 1945; MA, Claremont Grad. Sch., 1947. Tchr. Girls Collegiate Sch., Claremont, Calif., 1945-47, Fullerton (Calif.) Jr. Coll. H.S., 1947-48, Stanley Clark Sch., South Bend, Ind., 1963-69, Wis. Sch. for Deaf, Delavan, 1971-73; editor Gila Bend Herald, Gila Bend, Ariz., 1974-79; migrant coord. La. Paloma (Ariz.) Elem.; mid. sch. tchr. Humboldt (Ariz.) Jr. High., 1984-87. Coord. Yavapai Indian Reservation, Prescott, Ariz., 1988-92. Editor: Prescott Symphony Guild, 1997-98. Mem. Alpha Delta Kappa (pres. 1985-86), Philanthropic Edni. Orgn., Phi Beta Kappa. Avocation: short story writing. Home: 831 Bertrand Ave Prescott AZ 86303-4011

HAYNES, JOHN MABIN, retired utilities executive; b. Albany, N.Y., Apr. 22, 1928; s. John Mabin and Gladys Elizabeth (Phillips) H.; m. Marion Enola Hamilton, Apr. 7, 1956; children: John David, Douglas Hamilton, Robert Paul. BS, Utica Coll., Syracuse U., 1952. Accountant Price Waterhouse & Co., N.Y.C., Syracuse, N.Y., 1953-61; successively auditor, adminstrv. asst., asst. treas., treas., and v.p., sr. v.p. Niagara Mohawk Power Corp., Syracuse, 1961-88; past pres., chmn., dir. N.Y. Bus. Devel. Corp., Syracuse. Past dir., pres. N M Uranium, Inc.; past dir., treas. Canadian Niagara Power Co. Ltd.; past treas. Moreau Mfg. Co., St. Lawrence Power Co.; past treas. Empire State Power Resources, Inc.; past dir. and treas. Beebee Island Corp.; past bd. dirs. treas. Opinac Investments Ltd., Opinac Energy Ltd., Opinac Holdings Ltd.; past mng. dir. Niagara Mohawk Fin. N.V. Mem. Westhill Cen. Sch. Bd. Edn., 1968-73, pres., 1969-71; treas. Henderson County Humane Soc., 1989-90. With AUS, 1945-47. Mem. Nat. Assn. Accountants (past dir.), Am. Gas Assn. (fin. com.), Fin. Execs. Inst. Clubs: Bond of Syracuse (past dir.), Masons. Home: Apt 352 400 Wesley Dr Asheville NC 28803 Personal E-mail: jack_hay352@msn.com.

HAYNES, JOSEPH ALLEN, pharmacy operations coordinator, consultant pharmacist; b. St. Petersburg, Fla., Feb. 28, 1964; s. Sharon Ann Bates and Allen Elliott Haynes; m. Patricia Ann Dunphy, Jan. 15, 1993; children: Joseph Patrick, Brian Christopher. BS in Biology, Auburn U., Montgomery, AL, 1989; BS in Pharmacy, Northeastern U., Boston, 1994; MBA, St. Leo U., Fla., 2005. Registered pharmacist Fla., 1994, cert. cons. pharmacist Fla., 1994. Pharmacy mgr. NCS Healthcare, Pinellas Park, Fla., 1995—99; pharmacy ops. coord. All Children's Hosp., St. Petersburg, Fla., 1999—. Infusion pharmacist Bay Pharmacy, St. Petersburg, 1994—95. Membership com. Libertarian Party of Fla., Clearwater, 2004—05; affiliate organizer Rep. Liberty Caucus, Largo, Fla., 2005. Recipient Student Excellence Award, Mass. Soc. Hosp. Pharmacists, 1993. Fellow: Am. Soc. Pharmacy Law; mem.: Pinellas Pharmacists Assn., Am. Med. Informatics Assn., Fla. Soc. Health-Systems Pharmacists (legal and regulatory affairs coun. 2004—05), Fla. Pharmacy Assn. Libertarian. Evangelical Christian. Avocations: photography, bowling, reading, politics. Home: 10012 130th Ln N Seminole FL 33776-1709 Office: All Children's Hosp 8016th St S Box 7300 Saint Petersburg FL 33701 Office Phone: 727-767-8148. Personal E-mail: joehaynes@tampabay.rr.com. E-mail: haynesj@allkids.org.

HAYNES, KAREN SUE, academic administrator, educator; b. Jersey City, July 6, 1946; d. Edward J. and Adelaide M. (Hineson) Czarnecki; m. James S. Mickelson; children: Kingsley Eliot Mickelson, Kimberly Elizabeth Mickelson, David Mickelson. BA in Social Work, Goucher Coll., 1968; MSW, McGill U., 1970; PhD in Social Work, U. Tex., 1977. Dir., social work divsn., sociology dept. Mary Hardin-Baylor Coll., Tex.; faculty mem. S.W. Tex. State U., San Marcos, Tex.; cons. Inst. Nat. Planning, Cairo, 1977-78; asst. prof. Ind. U., Indpls., 1978-81, assoc. prof., 1981-85; prof. social work U. Houston, 1985-95, dean, 1985-95; pres. U. Houston-Victoria, Tex., 1995—2004, Calif. State, San Marcos, 2004—. Founding presdl. sponsor Tex. Network Women Higher Edn.; formula adv. com. Tex. Coord. Bd. Higher Edn. Author: (book) Sage Publications, 1984, Longman, 1986, 1996, Springer, 1989, Allyn and Bacon, 2000, 2003; contbr. articles to profl. jours. Mem.: NASW, Leadership Houston, Leadership Tex., Leadership Am., Nat. Alliance Info. and Referral (pres. 1983—87), Internat. Assn. Schs. Social Work, Coun. Social Work Edn., Am. Coun. Edn. Network (mem. exec. bd. dirs.), Am. Assn. State Colls. and Univs. (sec.-treas., mem. exec. bd. dirs. 2003—). Avocation: poetry. Office: Calif State U 333 S Twin Oaks Valley Rd San Marcos CA 92096-0001

HAYNES, LEONARD L., III, former government official, consultant, educator; b. Boston, Jan. 26, 1947; s. Leonard L. Haynes Jr. and Leila Louise (Davenport) H.; m. Mary Jane Sensley, Aug. 10, 1968; children: Leonard IV, Eboni Michelle, Jabari Kenyatta, Bakari Ali. BA, So. U., Baton Rouge, 1968; MA, Carnegie-Mellon U., 1969; PhD, Ohio State U., 1975, LLD (hon.), 1990, Ala. A&M U., 1990; DHL (hon.), Wiley Coll., 1990; LLD (hon.), Stockton (N.J.) State U., 1991. Instr. history So. U., 1969-70, exec. v.p., 1982-85, prof., 1985-88; edn. policy fellow Dept. Edn. State of Ill., Springfield, 1972-73; staff asst. to pres. Ohio State U., Columbus, 1974-75, asst. to provost, 1975-76; dir. desegregation policy Inst. Svcs. Edn., Washington, 1976-79; dir. Office Advancement Pub. Black Colls., Washington, 1979-82; asst. supt. acad program Dept Edn. State of La., Baton Rouge, 1988-89; asst. sec. U.S. Dept. Edn., Washington, 1989-91; pres. Haynes the Third and Assocs., Silver Spring, Md., 1993-94; sr. asst. to pres. The Am. V., 1994-95; spl. asst. to pres. Fine Host Corp., 1995—. Cons., HHS, Washington, 1991—; cons., dir. acad. programs USIA, Washington, 1991-93; vis. scholar edn. policy U. Md., 1994; sr. asst. to pres. Am. U., 1994—. Author: A Critical Examination-Adams Case, 1978; editor: An Analysis-Arkansas and Georgia Desegregation Plans, 1979; editorial bd. Jour. Negro Edn. Mem. fam. com. United Way, Baton Rouge, 1985-88; bd. dirs. NCCJ, Baton Rouge, 1988. Recipient Meritorious citation Pres.'s Bd. Advisors Black Colls., 1991, Nat. Svc. award S.C. State Coll., 1991, Disting. Alumni award So. U., 1991. Mem. Jack and Jill Inc., So. U. Nat. Lettermen's Club (pres. 1987-88), Ohio State U. Alumni Assn., So. U. Alumni Assn., Omega Psi Phi, Phi Delta Kappa. Methodist. Avocation: competitive sports. Home: 1346 Atwood Rd Silver Spring MD 20906-2087

HAYNES, LINDA ROSE, medical/surgical nurse; d. Floyd George Hilbers, Sr. and Mildred Ann Hilbers; children: Jinny Marie Millican, Thomas Baird. ADN, Vernon Regional Coll. Am. Nurses Credentialing Ctr., RN Tex. Dir. of patient care Outreach Health Svcs., Wichita Falls, 2002—. RN case mgr., 1994—2002. Mem.: Am. Diabetic Assn. (diabetic educator), Phi Theta Kappa (Omega Kappa). Roman Catholic. Avocations: crafts, reading. Office: Outreach Home Health Ste 3 1411 13th St Wichita Falls TX 76301

HAYNES, MOSES ALFRED, physician; b. Guyana, Nov. 17, 1921; came to U.S., 1947, naturalized, 1955; s. Milton Alphonso and Charlotte Mildred (Alleyne) Haynes; m. Hazel Louise Edgecombe, July 1, 1951; 1 child, Theresa Sue Aldrich. BS, Columbia U., 1951; MD, SUNY, 1954; MPH, Harvard U., 1963. Intern St. John's Episcopal Hosp., Bklyn., 1954-55; physician USPHS Indian Hosp., Cheyenne Agy., S.D., 1955-59; asst. prof. community medicine U. Vt., 1959-64; assoc. prof. Sch. Pub. Health, Johns Hopkins, 1966-69; prof. preventive and social medicine and pub. health UCLA, 1969-77; assoc. dean Drew Postgrad. Med. Sch., Los Angeles, 1969-77, chmn. dept. cmty. medicine, 1969-74, acting dean, 1975-76, dean, pres., 1979-86; dir. Drew/Meharry/Morehouse Consortium Cancer Ctr., 1986-90. Pres. SECON Inc., 1977-79; vis. prof. Med. Coll., Trivandrum, Kerala, India, 1964-66; mem. cancer support rev. com. Nat. Cancer Inst. Chmn. health task force Urban Coalition, 1968—69; mem. Pres.'s Com. Health Edn., 1972; exec. dir. Nat. Med. Assn. Found., 1968—69; mem. bd. sci. counselors, divsn. cancer prevention and control Nat. Cancer Inst., 1989—93, chmn., 1991—93; mem. adv. com. Nat. Ctr. Health Stats., 1974—76; bd. dirs. Ptnrs. for Prevention, 1991—92; chmn. bd. dirs. Charles Drew U. Medicine and Sci., 2001—03; mem. adv. bd. Fogarty Internat. Ctr., 1992—93; mem. U.S. Preventive Svcs. Task Force, 1985—86. With USPHS, 1955—59. Fellow Am. Coll. Preventive Medicine, (pres. 1983-85); fellow AAAS; mem. Inst. Medicine of Nat. Acad. Sci. (internat. health bd., com. human rights 1986-89), Inst. Medicine (council 1983-86), Hopkins Soc. Scholars, Alpha Omega Alpha. Home: 4161 Harbortown Ln Corona CA 92883 E-mail: mahaynes@comcast.net. ***Being is more important than doing.***

HAYNES, PETER LANCASTER, utilities executive; b. Ellsworth, Maine, July 8, 1939; s. Charles A. and Hazel G. (Giles) H.; m. Judith A. Bates, Aug. 26, 1961; children: Jeffrey, Timothy, Christopher. BS, U. Maine, 1961; MBA, Cornell U., 1963. Registered profl. engr., Vt. V.p. switched svcs. New Eng. Telephone, Boston, 1978-83, v.p. mktg., 1983-85; pres., CEO Nynex Enterprises, N.Y.C., 1985-90, Quality Logistics Mgmt., Inc., Bedford, N.Y., 1991-92, Consumers Water Co., Portland, Maine, 1992-99. Chmn. Boys and Girls Club Am., 1999—2001, bd. govs.; pres. Portland Symphony, 2002—04; chmn. Maine Med. Ctr., 2002—; vice chmn. MaineHealth, 2004—. Mem.: Cornell Club N.Y. Home: 98 Starboard Reach Yarmouth ME 04096-6158 Office Phone: 207-846-4561. Personal E-mail: plhaynes@aol.com.

HAYNES, R. MICHAEL, lawyer; b. Safford, Ariz., Oct. 3, 1940; s. Rodman and Angeline (Fragale) H.; m. Anne Marie de Almeida, Aug. 15, 1972; 1 child, Michelle Chloe. BA, Rutgers U., 1963, JD with honors, 1968. Bar: N.Y. 1969, N.J. 1977, D.C. 1992, U.S. Dist. Ct. (so. and ea. dists.) N.Y. 1973, U.S. Ct. Appeals (2d cir.) 1973, U.S. Supreme Ct. 1973, U.S. Dist. Ct. N.J. 1977, U.S. Dist. Ct. D.C. 1992. Assoc. Cooper, Ostrin, DeVargo & Ackerman, N.Y.C., 1968-69; asst. dist. atty., dep. chief rackets bur. N.Y. County Dist. Atty.'s Office, N.Y.C., 1969-74; exec. asst. dist. atty. spl. narcotics Prosecutor's Office, N.Y.C., 1974-76; asst. U.S. atty. Dist. N.J., Newark, 1976-79; minority counsel Com. on Small Bus., U.S. Senate, Washington, 1979-81, chief counsel, 1981-86; gen. counsel Nat. Assn. Small Bus. Investment Cos., Washington, 1986-90; founding ptnr. Law Offices R. Michael Haynes, Washington, 1990—2000; prin. Semmes, Bowen & Semmes, P.C., Washington, 2000—. Adj. prof. L.I. U., 1975-76; instr. N.Y. State Commn. Investigation, 1974-75, Atty. Gen.'s Adv. Inst., Dept. Justice, 1978-79; counsel White House Conf. on Small Bus., 1980 Advisor Washington Internat. Sch. Mock Trial Team, 1991-95. Recipient Atty. Gen.'s Spl. Achievement award, 1977 Mem. ABA (chmn. SBIC subcom. small bus. com. 1986-89), Fed. Bar Assn. (chmn. small bus. com. fin. insts. and economy sect. 1988-89), U.S. C. of C. (small bus. coun. 1987-89), SEC Govt. Bus. Forum on Capital Formation (exec. com. 1988-89). Republican. Office: 3509 Idaho Ave NW Washington DC 20016-3151 Office Phone: 202-966-5102. Business E-Mail: rmhaynes@lawyer.com. E-mail: mhaynes@semmes.com. *The law holds everyone equally accountable, but requires of a lawyer a higher duty to honor the principles that the law prescribes while at the same time serving the people whom it governs. To that end, a lawyer must insure that the law itself remains just and fair and that those who make and enforce the law do so with integrity.*

HAYNES, RAYMOND NEAL, JR., lawyer, state legislator; b. Merced, Calif., Aug. 26, 1954; s. Raymond Neal and Leona Faye (Ollar) H.; m. Diane Marie McDonald, Dec. 29, 1979 (div. May 1988); 1 child, Jennifer Marie; m. Pamela Davis, Sept. 9, 1989; children: Caitlin Joy, Sarah Elizabeth. BA, Calif. Luth. Coll., 1976; MPA, Ea. Ky. U., 1981; JD, U. So. Calif., 1980. Bar: Calif. 1980. Assoc. Best, Best and Krieger, Riverside, Calif., 1980-83; ptnr. Lawson and Hartnell, Redlands, Calif., 1983-88; pvt. practice Moreno Valley, Calif., 1988-92; assemblyman Calif. State Legis., Sacramento, 1992—; mem. CA State Senate, 1994—. Planning commr. City of Moreno Valley, 1985-86; dir. Youth Svc. Ctr., Riverside, 1984-86; treas. Citizens for Property Rights, Moreno Valley, 1986-90; chmn. Com. for No New Taxes, Moreno Valley, 1989-92. Republican. Office: CA State Senate Rm 2187 State Capitol Sacramento CA 95814

HAYNES, RICHARD, lawyer; b. Houston, Apr. 3, 1927; BBA, U. Houston, 1951, JD, 1956. Bar: Tex. 1956. Pvt. practice, 1956—. Adj. prof. law U. Houston, 1972—73; mem. permanent tchg. faculty Nat. Coll. for Criminal Def. Charter mem. Coll. Edn., Challenge Club, U. Houston; chmn. bd. regents Nat. Coll. for Criminal Def., 1980—81; mem. Nat. Neurofibromatosis Found.-Tex. Chpt.; bd. mem. Coll. Edn. Found. Bd., U. Houston. Paratrooper officer. Named one of Top Criminal Def. Lawyers, The Best Lawyers in Am., 5th edit. (book), 10 Best Trial Lawyers, The Trial Lawyers (book); recipient Tex. Lifetime Achievement award, Mexican Am. Bar Assn., 2004, Outstanding Alumni award, U. Houston, Law Alumni award, Golden Plate award, Am. Acad. Achievement. Fellow: Internat. Acad. Trial Lawyers, Tex. Bar Found.; mem.: ABA, Houston Law Found. (bd. dirs.), Houston Bar Assn. (bd. dirs.), Harris County Criminal Lawyers Assn. (bd. dirs., named Lawyer of Yr. 1999), Tex. Trial Lawyers Assn., Tex. Criminal Def. Lawyers Assn. (bd. dirs.), Tex. Bar Assn. (bd. dirs.), Nat. Assn. Criminal Def. Lawyers, Am. Judicature Soc., Am. Bd. Trial Advs., Internat. Soc. Barristers, Phi Alpha Delta (alumni advisor 1979—80). Office: Richard Haynes & Assocs PC 4300 Scotland Houston TX 77007-7394 Office Phone: 713-868-1111.

HAYNES, RICHARD TERRY, lawyer; b. Detroit, Dec. 10, 1946; s. Charles Hawley and Elizabeth (Powers) H.; m. Jan Michele Ouillette, Dec. 22, 1980. BBA, U. Mich., 1969; JD, Wayne U., 1972. Bar: Mich. 1973, U.S. Dist. Ct. (ea. dist.) Mich. 1973. Ptnr. Draugelis, Ashton, Scully and Haynes, Plymouth, Mich., 1973--. Capt. USAR, 1965-80. Mem. ABA, Mich. Bar Assn., Detroit Bar Assn., Washtenaw County Bar Assn., Def. Rsch. Inst. Office: Draugelis Ashton Scully & Haynes 843 Penniman Ave Plymouth MI 48170-1690 Office Phone: 734-453-4044. E-mail: janhaynes@msn.com.

HAYNES, ROBERT VAUGHN, retired academic administrator, historian; b. Nashville, Nov. 28, 1929; m. Martha Farr, Dec. 25, 1952; children: Catherine Anne, Carolyn Alice, Charles Allen. BA, Millsaps Coll., 1952; MA, Peabody Coll., 1953; PhD, Rice U., 1959. Mem. faculty U. Houston, 1956-84, prof. history, 1967-84, acting dir. Afro-Am. studies, 1969-71, interim dir. libraries, 1976-78; dir. libraries U. Houston central campus, 1978-80, assoc. provost, 1980-81, dep. provost, 1981-84; v.p. acad. affairs Western Ky. U., Bowling Green, 1984-96. Vis. prof., Black studies cons. U. Ala., 1970; dir. Inst. Cultural Understanding, 1971; mem. adv. planning com. Tex. Conf. on Library and Info. Services, 1978-79 Author: A Night of Violence: The Houston Riot of 1917, 1976, The Natchez District and the American Revolution, 1976; editor: The Houston Rev., 1981-84; Contbr. articles to profl. jours. Mem. Houston United Campus Christian Life com., 1973-81; chmn. ch. and soc. com. Synod of Tex., Presbyn. Ch. U.S.A., 1970-73; treas. Houston Com. on the Humanities, 1978-79. Served with USAF, 1950-51. Danforth assoc., 1969, Carnegie fellow, 1952—53, Nat. Endowment Humanities fellow, 1973. Mem. Am. Hist. Assn., Orgn. Am. Historians, So. Hist. Assn., Miss. Hist. Soc., Inst. Early Am. History and Culture, Tex. Assn. Coll. Tchrs. (past chpt. pres.), Phi Kappa Phi (past pres.). Democrat. Office: Dept History Western Ky U Bowling Green KY 42101

HAYNES, THOMAS MORRIS, philosophy educator; b. Waukesha, Wis., Oct. 24, 1918; s. George Albert and Lois (Morris) H.; m. Jane Louise Riggs, Sept. 12, 1942; children: Christopher Thomas, Jonathan Marshall, Carolyn Martha. AB, Butler U., 1941; PhD, U. Ill., 1949. Indsl. engr. RCA, Indpls., 1942-44; research and devel. engr. P.R. Mallory, Indpls., 1944-46; U. Ill. postdoctoral fellow Faculty Law U. Paris, 1949-50; instr. philosophy U. Ill., 1950-51; research asst. U. Ill. (Coll. of Law), 1950-51; instr. philosophy Lehigh U., 1952-54, asst. prof., 1954-61, asso. prof., 1961-69, prof., 1969-83, prof. emeritus, adj. prof., 1983-91. Founder, pres. World-Sense, Inc.; dir. World-Sense Dialogue. Mem. AAUP, Am. Philos. Assn., N.Y. Acad. Scis., Environ. Def. Fund, World Wildlife Fund, Natural Resources Def. Coun., The Wilderness Soc., Nat. Wildlife Fedn. (assoc.), The Nature Conservancy, Worldwatch Libr., Union Concerned Scientists (sponsor), Amnesty Internat., Woodrow Wilson Internat. Ctr. for Scholars (assoc.), Phi Beta Kappa, Phi Kappa Phi. Home: 175 W North St Apt 427A Nazareth PA 18064-1439

HAYNES, ULRIC ST. CLAIR, JR., retired dean; b. Bklyn., June 8, 1931; s. Ulric St. Clair and Ellaline (Gay) H.; m. Yolande Toussaint, Sept. 20, 1969; children: Alexandra, Gregory. BA, Amherst Coll., 1952; JD, Yale U., 1956; LLB (hon.), Ind. U., 1981, John Jay Coll., 1981, Fisk U., 1982, Ala. State Coll., 1982; JD, Butler U., 1988; LLB (hon.), Mercy Coll., 1994. Exec. asst. N.Y. State Dept. Commerce, Albany, 1956-57; adminstrv. officer UN European Office, Geneva, 1959-60; asst. to rep. Ford Found., Lagos, Nigeria, Tunis, Tunisia, 1960-63; asst. officer in charge Moroccan affairs Dept. State, Washington, 1963, officer in charge Southwest Africa and High Commn. Ters. Affairs, 1963-64; mem. NSC staff White House, 1965-66; pres. Mgmt. Formation Inc., N.Y.C., 1966-70; sr. v.p., ptnr. Spencer Stuart and Assocs. Mgmt. Consultants, N.Y.C., 1970-72; v.p. for mgmt. devel. Cummins Engine Co., Columbus, Ind., 1972-74, v.p. for Mid-East and Africa, 1974-77, v.p. internat. bus. planning, 1981-83; ambassador to Algeria Am. Embassy, Algiers, Algeria, 1977-81; acting pres. SUNY/Coll. at Old Westbury, 1985-86; pres. AFS Intercultural Programs, N.Y.C., 1986-88; cons. N.Y.C., 1989-91; exec. dean Hofstra U. Sch. Bus., Hempstead, NY, 1991-96; exec. dean internat. rels. Hofstra U., Hempstead, NY, 1996—2003; adj. prof. internat. rels Rollins Coll. and U. Ctrl. Fla., 2004—05. Bd. dirs. Pall Corp., ReliaStar Life Ins. Co. N.Y. Contbr. articles to profl. publs. Mem. selection com. Henry Luce Found. Asian Scholars Program; trustee Deep Springs Coll., 1999-2004. Root-Tilden scholar; John Hay Whitney scholar; Leopold Schepp Found. scholar. Mem. Coun. Fgn. Rels., Coun. Am. Ambs., Yale Club of N.Y.C., Am. Acad. Diplomacy, Atlantic Coun. U.S. Democrat. Episcopalian. Home: 2403 Timothy Ln Kissimmee FL 34743 Personal E-mail: uhaynesjr@yahoo.com.

HAYNES, VICTORIA F., science administrator; Chief tech. officer, v.p. Advanced Tech. Group, BFGoodrich Co., 1992—99; pres., CEO Rsch. Triangle Inst., Research Triangle Park, NC, 1999—. Bd. dir. Ziptronix Bd., Lubrizol Corp., Nucor Corp., MCNC, N.C. Biotech. Ctr., N.C. Bd. Sci. and Tech., PPG Ind.; appt. to Kans. Bioscience Authority, 2004—. Office: Rsch Triangle Inst Internat PO Box 12194 3040 Corwallis Rd Research Triangle Park NC 27709-2194

HAYNES, WILLIAM ERNEST, lawyer, financial consultant, educator; b. Peoria, Ill., Aug. 22, 1936; s. Clarence Ernest and Lucille Ann Haynes; m. Willette Lancia Rothschild, Dec. 2, 1972; children: Lancia Ann, Sharon Elizabeth. BA in Fin., Loras Coll., Dubuque, Iowa, 1959; JD, Marquette U., Milw., 1964; MBA in Bus. Econs., Loyola U., Chgo., 1969. Bar: Wis. 1964, Ill. 1965, Calif. 1970; cert. specialist taxation law, Calif. Corp. counsel Gen. Fin. Co., Evanston, Ill., 1964-69; asst. contr. internat. tax Wells Fargo Bank, San Francisco, 1969-76; tax counsel Kaiser Aluminum and Chem. Corp., Oakland, Calif., 1976-79; prin. Law Offices of William E. Haynes and Assocs., San Francisco, 1979—; chief fin. officer Pacific Rim Ptnrs. Ltd., San Francisco, 1989—; pres. Gryphon Group Ltd., econ. cons., 1981-86; prin. The Bus. Mart Bus. Brokers, San Francisco, 1987-94; prof. taxation, adj. faculty, McLaren Coll. of Bus., U. San Francisco; lectr. on law, taxation and fin. Mem. adv. com. on edn. State Bar of Calif.; bd. dirs. Meals on Wheels of San Francisco. With U.S. Army, 1959-61. Mem. ABA, Calif. Bar Assn., Am. Econs. Assn., San Francisco Internat. Tax Group, Internat. Assn. Fin. Planners, Calif. Hist. Soc., San Francisco Mus. Soc., World Affairs Council, Civil Air Patrol (capt.). Republican. Roman Catholic. Lodge: Rotary, Elks.

HAYNES, WILLIAM JAMES, II, lawyer; b. Waco, Tex., Mar. 30, 1958; s. William James and Caroline H.; m. Margaret Frances Campbell, 1982; 3 children. BA, Davidson Coll., 1980; JD, Harvard U., 1983; LLD (hon.), Stetson U., 1999. Bar: NC 1983, Ga. 1989, DC 1990. Law clk. to Hon. James B. McMillan US Dist. Ct. NC, Charlotte, 1983-84; assoc. Sutherland, Asbill & Brennan, Washington, 1989; spl. asst. to gen. counsel Dept. Def., Washington, 1989-90; gen. counsel Dept. Army, Washington, 1990-93; ptnr. Jenner & Block, Washington, 1993-96; v.p., assoc. gen. counsel Gen. Dynamics Corp., Falls Church, Va., 1996-98; gen. counsel Gen. Dynamics Marine Group, 1997-98; ptnr. Jenner & Block, Washington, 1999—2001; gen. counsel, def. legal svcs. agy. Dept. of Def., 2001—. Capt. US Army, 1984-88. Mem. ABA, NC Bar Assn., DC Bar Assn., Ga. Bar Assn. Presbyterian. Avocation: tennis. Office: General Counsel of Dept Def Rm 3E980 1600 Defense Pentagon Washington DC 20301 Office Phone: 703-695-3341. Office Fax: 202-693-7278.

HAYNIE, THOMAS POWELL, III, physician; b. Hearne, Tex., Aug. 9, 1932; s. Thomas Powell Jr and Sue Cummings Haynie; m. Bette Flossel, Mar. 10, 1956 (dec. Apr. 2002); children: David Powell, Amy Cummings, Sue Cummings, Garner Powell; m. Charlotte Peters, Dec. 18, 2004. Student, U. South, Sewanee, Tenn., 1949-51, U. Tex., Austin, 1951-52; MD, Baylor U., 1956. Diplomate Am Bd Internal Med, Am Bd Med Oncology, Am Bd Nuclear Med. Intern, then resident in internal medicine U. Mich. Med. Center, Ann Arbor, 1956-60, instr., 1960-62; asst. prof. medicine, dir. nuclear med. service U. Tex. Med. Br., Galveston, 1962-65; assoc. prof. medicine U. Tex.-M.D. Anderson Cancer Ctr., Houston, 1965-75; prof. U. Tex.-M.D. Anderson Hosp. and Tumor Inst., Houston, 1975-95, James E. Anderson prof. nuclear medicine, 1988-95, prof. emeritus of nuclear medicine, 1995—, chief sect. nuclear medicine, 1967-84, chmn. dept. nuclear medicine, 1984-93, head dept. internal medicine, 1977-84. Adj prof radiology Baylor Col Med, Houston, 1996—; pres Am Col Nuclear Med, 1993—94; consult in field. Contbr. articles in field, chapters to books; editor: Jour Nuclear Med, 1985—89. Mem.: AMA, ACP, AAAS, Am. Coll. Radiology, Tex. Assn. Physicians Nuclear Medicine, Tex. Med. Assn., Soc. Nuclear Medicine, Assn. Univ. Radiologists, Am. Thyroid Assn., Radiol. Soc. N.Am., Am. Coll. Nuclear Medicine, Am. Coll. Nuclear Physicians, Order St. Lazarus of Jerusalem, Sigma Xi, Phi Gamma Delta. Episcopalian. Home: 1222 Ripple Creek Dr Houston TX 77057 Office: U Tex-MD Anderson Hosp and Tumor Inst 1515 Holcombe Blvd Houston TX 77030-4009 Business E-Mail: thaynie@mdanderson.org.

HAYNOR, PATRICIA MANZI, nursing educator, consultant; children: Kelly Christine, Craig; m. Donald C. Maaswinkel. Diploma in nursing, Grasslands Hosp., Valhalla, N.Y.; BSN, Fairleigh Dickinsn U., 1967; MSN in Nursing Adminstrn., U. Pa., 1969; D Nursing Sci., Widener U., 1989. RN, Pa., N.J., N.Y., Del. Asst. dir. surg. nursing Thomas Jefferson U. Hosp., Phila., 1972-74; asst. dir. nursing care depts. Our Lady of Lourdes Hosp., Camden, N.J., 1974-76; assoc. dir. nursing West Jersey Hosp., Camden, 1976-79; dir. nursing West Jersey Health System, Camden, 1979-81, corp. dir. nursing, 1981-82; v.p. nursing Crozer-Chester (Pa.) Med. Ctr., 1982-85; coord. nursing adminstrn. program, asst. prof. Widener U., Chester, 1985-87; v.p. for nursing St. Francis Med. Ctr., Trenton, N.J., 1987-90; asst. prof. U. Del. Coll. Nursing, 1990-92; assoc. prof. Villanova (Pa.) U. Coll. Nursing, Phila., 1992—. Cons. Nurse Assocs., Haddon Heights, N.J., 1985—; spkr. in field. Contbr. articles to profl. publs. Mem. Am. Orgn. Nurse Execs., Am. Coll. Healthcare Execs., S.E. Pa. Orgn. Nurse Leaders. Home: 201 9th Ave Haddon Heights NJ 08035-1632 Office: Villanova U Coll Nursing Villanova PA 19085 Office Phone: 610-519-7751. E-mail: patriciahaynor@villanova.edu.

HAYNSWORTH, HARRY JAY, IV, law educator; b. Greensboro, N.C., Apr. 9, 1938; s. Harry J. Jr. and Ruth (Eberhardt) H. AB, Duke U., 1961, JD, 1964; postgrad., U. Denver Law Center, 1972; MAR, Luth. Theol. So. Sem., 1989; LLD (hon.), William Mitchell Coll. Law, 2004. Bar: SC 1965. Assoc. Haynsworth, Perry, Bryant, Marion & Johnstone, Greenville, S.C., 1964-69, ptnr., 69-71; assoc. prof. law U. S.C., 1971-74, prof., 1974-90, assoc. dean, 1975-76, 85-86, acting dean, 1976-77; of counsel Nexson, Pruet, Jacobs & Pollard, Columbia, S.C., 1986-90, Briggs & Morgan, Mpls., 2005—; dean, prof. law So. Ill. U., Carbondale, 1990-95; dean, pres. William Mitchell Coll. Law, St. Paul, 1995—2004; dean emeritus William Mitchell Coll. Law, 2004—. Vis. prof. U. Leeds, Eng., 1978-79; commr. Nat. Conf. Commrs. on Uniform State Laws, 1992—; mem. S.C. Legis. Consumer Law Com., 1975-80 Author: Comments, S.C. Consumer Protection Code, 1983, 2d edit. 1990, Organizing a Small Business Entity, 1986, Marketing and Legal Ethics: The Rules and Risks, 1990, others; contbr. articles to profl. jours.; mem. editorial bd.: Am. Bar Assn. Jour, 1977-83, chmn. editorial bd., 1982-83. Chmn. bd. S.C. Commn. for Blind, 1973-75; bd. dirs. Greenville County (S.C.) Housing Commn., 1970-71; v.p., dir. United Speech and Hearing Center, Greenville, 1970-71; trustee Heathwood Hall, 1976-86, Randolph-Macon Women's Coll., Lynchburg, Va., 1970-75. Mem. ABA (small bus. com., spl. cons. corp. laws com. 1978-82, coun. sect. bus. law 1988-92), S.C. Bar Assn. (vice chmn. consumer and comml. law com. 1975-78, sec., exec. com. 1972-75, exec. dir. 1971-72), Minn. State Bar Assn., Ramsey County Bar Assn., Hennepin County Bar Assn., Am. Law Inst., 4th Cir. Jud. Conf. Office: 2200 IDS Ctr Minneapolis MN 55402 Office Phone: 612-977-8298. Business E-Mail: hhaynsworth@briggs.com.

HAYNSWORTH, ROBERT FRANCIS, JR., anesthesiologist; b. El Paso, Tex., Aug. 11, 1954; MD, U. Tex., Houston, 1981. Cert. in anesthesiology, specialty in pain mgmt. Flex intern Tex. Tech. U. Health Sci. Ctr., Lubbock, 1981-82, resident in anesthesiology, 1982-84, chief resident in anesthesiology, 1983-84; fellow in pain mgmt. U. Tex. S.W. Med. Sch., Dallas, 1984—85; attending anesthesiologist Baylor U., Tex., 1992—2002, attending physician, 1992—2002; clin. dir. Baylor Pain Mgmt. Ctr., 1992—. Office: 530 Clara Barton Blvd Ste 215 Garland TX 75042-5740

HAYO, GEORGE EDWARD, management consultant; b. L.A., Nov. 2, 1934; s. George Edward Hayo Sr. and Esther Marie (Goodman) Arthur; m. Nixie Joanne Hunt, Aug. 4, 1956; children: Michael Edward, Kenneth Marvin, Michelle Virginia. BS in Applied Math., Calif. State U., 1960; MBA in Mgmt., U. Denver, 1968. Cert. mgmt. cons. Mathematician U.S. Naval Civil Engring. Lab., Port Hueneme, Calif., 1961-63; corp. systems planner No. Natural Gas Co., Omaha, 1963-66; asst. to pres. C.A. Norgren Co., Littleton, Colo., 1966-68; sr. staff cons. Emerson Electric, St. Louis, 1968-71; dir. adminstrn. Fisher Radio, N.Y.C., 1971-72; v.p., dir. The Emerson Cons., N.Y.C., 1973-87; pres. The Hayo Cons., Albuquerque, 1988—. Arbitrator Am. Arbitration Assn., N.Y., 1985—. Contbr. articles to profl. jours. Mem. Inst. Mgmt. Cons., Am. Inst. Plant Engrs., Am. Prodn. and Inventory Control Soc. Avocations: running, sailing, golf. Home and Office: The Hayo Cons 335 Pinon Creek Tr SE Albuquerque NM 87123-4123 Office Phone: 505-237-0313. Personal E-mail: hayocon@aol.com.

HAYON, ELIE M., chemist, educator; b. Cairo, May 15, 1932; came to U.S., 1965; s. Mayer E. and Regina (Cohen); m. Nina Mokady, 1982; 1 child, Rona B.Sc., U. Strathclyde, Glasgow, Scotland, 1954; PhD, Durham U., Newcastle-upon Tyne, Eng., 1957. Brit. Empire Cancer Research fellow Kings Coll., Newcastle-upon Tyne, 1957-58, Brookhaven Nat. Lab., Upton, N.Y., 1958-

60, Cambridge (Eng.) U., 1960-62, Centre Nuclear Studies, Saclay, France, 1963-65; head phys. chemistry Natick (Mass.) Labs., 1966-75, Gen. Foods Corp., Tarrytown, N.Y., 1976-78; dean grad. studies and research, prof. chemistry Queens Coll., City U.N.Y., 1978—. Contbr. articles to profl. jours. Mem. numerous profl. assns. in U.S. and U.K. Home: 240 E 82nd St New York NY 10028-2703 Office: 6 Einstein St Ra ananna Israel

HAY-ROE, MIRIAN MEDINA, education educator, researcher; d. Jose W. Medina and Yolanda Polanco; m. Keith A. Hay-Roe, Dec. 15, 1995; 1 child, Kyle G. B in Economics, U. San Martin de Porres, 1985; B in Biol. Sci., U. de San Marcos, 1991; MA, U. Tex., 1996; PhD, U. Fla., 2004. Tchr. asst. U. Tex., Austin, 1992—96; lectr. S.W. Tex. State U., San Marcos, 1996—97; tchr. asst. U. Fla., Gainseville, 1999—2003. Cons. Inst. Nacional de Planificacion, Lima, Peru, 1986—89, Junta del Acuerdo de Cartagena, Lima, 1987—88. Recipient Mulrenan Scholarship, U. Fla., 2000, Delores Azenne Scholarship, 2002—04. Mem.: Lepidopterological Soc., Entomological Soc. Am. Office: McGuire Ctr of Lepidoptch & Biodiversity U Fla PO Box 112710 Gainesville FL 32611-2710 Office Phone: 352-846-2000 478.

HAYS, DENNIS K., former ambassador; b. Calif., June 1, 1953; married; 4 children. B.Am. studies, U. Fla.; MPA, Harvard U.; grad., Nat. War Coll., 1993. Staff mem. Congressman Charles E. Bennett, Fla.; with U.S. Fgn. Svc., 1976—, dep. chief of mission Bujumbura, Burundi, 1985-88, dep. chief of mission, then charge d'affaires Georgetown, Guyana, 1988-93; coord. Cuban Affairs US Dept. State, 1993-95, dir. Office for Mex. Affairs, 1995-96, US amb. to Suriname Paramaribo, 1997—2000; pres. Fgn. svc. Assn., 1982-85; exec. v.p. Cuban Am. Nat. Found., 2000—. Advance man for presdl. and vice-presdl. visits overseas. Recipient Superior Honor award Dept. of State, 1981, 87, 91, 95, Meritorious Honor award, 1979. Office: Cuban Am Nat Found Embassy for a Free Cuba 1822 Jefferson Place NW Washington DC 20036

HAYS, DIANA JOYCE WATKINS, consumer products company executive; b. Riverside, Calif., Aug. 29, 1945; d. Donald Richard and Evelyn Christine (Kolvoord) Watkins; m. Gerald N. Hays, Jan 30, 1964 (div. Jan. 1970), 1 child, Tad Damon. BA, U. Minn., 1975, MBA, 1982; BS in Computer Sci. cum laude, Nat. U., 1997, MS in Software Engring. magna cum laude, 1998. Microsoft cert. sys. engr.; cert. in C and C++ programming, visual C++ and visual basic programming; NCR Teradata cert. profl. engr. Dir. environ./phys. sci. Sci. Mus. Minn., St. Paul, 1972-76; dir. mktg. rsch. No. Natural Gas Co., Omaha, 1977-78; mktg. asst., asst. product mgr. Gen. Mills, Inc., Mpls., 1978-81; product mgr. ortho pharms. Consumer Products div. Johnson & Johnson, Raritan, N.J., 1981-82, product dir. home diagnostics, 1982-86; mktg. dir. new market devel. Consumer Products div. Becton Dickinson & Co., Franklin Lakes, N.J., 1986-90; dir. home diagnostics worldwide program Becton Dickinson Advanced Diagnostics Div. Becton Dickinson & Co., Balt., 1990-93; founder, pres. Exec. Computing Solutions, Inc., Vista, Calif., 1991-99; product mktg. mgr. Jostens Learning Corp., San Diego, 1994-95; mgr. MIS Circus Distbn., Inc., Vista, Calif., 1995-96; product mktg. mgr. St. Bernard Software, San Diego, 1997; software engr. NCR Corp., San Diego, 1997—2004, sr. software engr., 2004—; founder, prin. CodeCare, Vista, 2001—. Chmn. energy exhibit com. Assn. Sci.-Tech. Ctrs., Washington, 1974-75. Producer Ecologenie, 1975. Recipient Tribute to Women and Industry award, YWCA, 1989. Mem. Am. Mktg. Assn., NAFE, Twin Mgmt. Forum, Am. Assn. of Health Svcs. Mktg., Capital PC User Group, Beta Gamma Sigma (life). Republican. Mem. Christian Ch. (Disciples Of Christ). Avocations: photography, travel. Office: NCR Corp 17095 Via del Campo San Diego CA 92127-1711

HAYS, E. EARL, retired youth organization administrator; b. Uniontown, Kans. s. Earl Loren and Avis Marie (Mccollum) H.; m. Betty Ann Frigo, Nov. 21, 1966. BA, Whittier Coll., 1962; MA, Ottawa U., 1993; PhD, Pacific Western U., 1993. Dir. pub. rels., fin., dist. exec. Boy Scouts Am. L.A. Area Coun., 1962-71; asst. dir. exploring Boy Scouts Am. Nat. Coun., North Brunswick, N.J., 1971-73; dir. fin. svcs. Boy Scouts Am. Golden Empire Coun., Sacramento, 1973-75; dir. field svc. Boy Scouts Am. Santa Clara County, San Jose, Calif., 1975-77; scout exec., CEO Boy Scouts Am. Clinton Valley Coun., Pontiac, Mich., 1977-82, Boy Scouts Am. Grand Canyon Coun., Phoenix, 1982—2004. Bd. dirs. Pontiac Oakland Symphony, 1980-82; pres. United Way Exec. Dirs. Assn., Phoenix, 1984-85. Fellowship honor Boy Scouts Am., 1991, James E. West fellow, 1994. Mem. Ottawa U. Alumni Assn. (bd. dirs. 1995-98), Nat. Eagle Scout Assn. (life, Disting. Eagle Scout 1998), Rotary (pres. Pontiac 1982, bd. dirs., sec.) Phoenix 100 Club (Paul H. Harris fellow). Democrat. Lutheran. Avocations: travel, music, reading, scuba, golf.

HAYS, HOWARD H. (TIM HAYS), editor, publisher; b. Chgo., June 2, 1917; s. Howard H. and Margaret (Mauger) H.; m. Helen Cunningham, May 27, 1947 (div. Dec. 1988); children: William, Thomas; m. Susie Gudermuth, Sept. 1992. BA, Stanford U., 1939; LLB, Harvard U., 1942. Bar: Calif. 1946. Spl. agt. FBI, 1942-45; reporter San Bernardino (Calif.) Sun, 1945-46; asst. editor Riverside (Calif.) Daily Press, 1946-49, editor, 1949-65, editor, co-pub., 1965-83, editor, pub., chief exec. officer, 1983-88, editor, chmn., chief exec. officer, 1989-92, chmn. bd., 1992-97, chmn. emeritus, 1997—. Mem. Pulitzer Prize Bd., 1976-86; mem. AP Bd., 1980-89, vice chmn. 1988-89. Mem. nat. com. Wash. U. Sch. of Art, 1992—2003; bd. visitors John S. Knight Fellowships for Profl. Journalists, Stanford U., 1983—98. Recipient Dist. award Calif. Jr. C. of C., 1951, William J. Brennan Def. of Freedom award, 2003; named Pub. of Year Calif. Press Assn., 1968 Mem.: New Directions for News (bd. dirs. 1982—86), Am. Press Inst. (bd. dirs. 1973—, chmn. 1978—83), Internat. Press. Inst. (chmn. Am. Com. 1971—72, mem. exec. bd. 1977—83), Am. Soc. Newspaper Editors (dir. 1969—76, pres. 1974—75), Calif. Bar Assn., Tower Grove Pk. (bd. dirs. 1999—, vice chmn. 2000—), Stanford Alumni Assn. (dir. 1970—74). Home: 3724 Utah Pl Saint Louis MO 63116-4831 Office Phone: 314-773-8082.

HAYS, JAMES FRED, geologist, educator; b. Little Rock, July 10, 1933; s. Orren Lee and Virginia (Russell) H.; m. Diane Lee Huntoon, Dec. 22, 1956; 1 dau., Lee Anne. AB, Columbia U., 1954; MS (NSF fellow), Calif. Inst. Tech., 1961; PhD, Harvard U., 1966. Geologist U.S. Geol. Survey, 1961; guest investigator Geophys. Lab., Carnegie Instn. of Washington, 1965; Soc. Fellows jr. fellow Harvard U., 1963-66, asst. prof. geology, 1966-69, assoc. prof., 1969-72, prof., 1972-84, chmn. dept. geol. scis., 1981-82; dir. div. earth scis. NSF, 1982-87, sr. sci. advisor, 1987-91, dir. earth scis. div., 1991-95. Cons. NASA Astronaut Tng. Program, 1969-73; mem. NASA Lunar Sample Analysis Planning Team, 1973-76, chmn. Lunar and Planetary Rev. Panel, 1978-81; prin. investigator Apollo Lunar Sample Program; vis. prof. chemistry and geology Ariz. State U., 1978-79; adminstrs. bd. Harvard and Radcliffe Colls., 1976-78; mem. Harvard Ctr. for Earth and Planetary Physics, 1970-84, sci. adv. bd. Mt. St. Helens Nat. Volcanic Monument, 1983-87, adv. com. on mining and minerals rsch. Dept. Interior, 1983-85, Working Group for U.S.-Peoples' Republic of China Agreement for Cooperation in Earth Scis., 1982-87, Space Grant Rev. Panel NASA, 1992-95; NRC com. on Rsch. Opportunities and Priorities for EPA, 1995-97; exec. sec. Pres.'s Com. on Nat. Medal Sci., 1987-91; vis. scholar U. Ariz., 1997—. Assoc. editor: Nature of the Solid Earth, 1970, Jour. Geophys. Research, 1978-80, 83-85. Served to capt. USNR, 1954-59. Recipient Presdl. Rank award U.S. Govt., 1994; NSF grantee, 1974-82, NASA grantee, 1971-82 Fellow AAAS (councilor 1989-92), Geol. Soc. Am. (councilor 1988-91), Mineral. Soc. Am.; mem. Am. Geophys. Union, Geol. Soc. Ariz. (councilor 2004—), Am. Ornithologists Union, Naval Res. Assn., Harvard Club, Cosmos Club, Phi Beta Kappa, Sigma Xi. Rsch. and publs. on exptl. petrology and geochemistry. Home: 3381 W Foxes Den Dr Tucson AZ 85745-5107 Personal E-mail: jhays@post.harvard.edu.

HAYS, KATHLEEN, news correspondent; B in Econs., M in Econs., Stanford U. Co-founder Market News Svc. Internat., served on NY bur., chief, mem. bd. dirs.; chief credit markets reporter Munifacts Fin. News; corr. Reuters' Money Desk, 1987—89; NY bur. chief, chief econs. corr. Investor's Bus. Daily, 1989—92; econs. editor, corr., commentator, segment host several CNBC programs, 1992—2001; joined CNN, 2001—; anchor CNN Money Morning and The Flipside; anchor, econs. corr. CNN Bus. News; contbr. Lou Dobbs' Moneyline; CNN Money contbg. columnist HaysWire. Office: CNN 5 Penn Plz Fl 20 New York NY 10001-1810

HAYS, KATHY ANN, elementary school educator; b. Council Bluffs, Iowa, Sept. 29, 1955; d. Leo P. and Monica G. (Schwery) Kenkel; m. Dan P. Hays, Aug. 20, 1988; children: Caitlin Leigh, Patrick Joseph. BS in Elem. Edn., Creighton U., 1977, MS in Elem. Edn., 1984. Cert. elem. tchr., Nebr. 6th grade tchr. Treynor (Iowa) Pub. Schs., 1977-79; from 6th grade tchr. to gifted cons. Ralston (Nebr.) Pub. Schs., 1979-86, 5th grade tchr., 1986-88, Blue Valley Pub. Schs., Overland Park, Kans., 1988-91, Elkhorn (Nebr.) Pub. Schs., 1991—. Lang. arts chair Elkhorn Pub. Schs., 1994—; leadership acad. Blue Valley Pub. Schs., Overland Park, 1991-92; presenter in field. Cantor St. Vincent De Paul Ch., Omaha, 1991—. Named Educator of Yr. Ralston Pub. Schs., 1988. Mem.: Internat. Reading Assn., Nat. Coun. Tchrs. English, Nebr. Assn. Gifted Children, Phi Delta Kappa. Democrat. Roman Catholic. Avocations: music, theater. Home: 519 S 215th St Elkhorn NE 68022-2058 Office: Elkhorn Pub Schs 400 S 210th St Elkhorn NE 68022-2166 E-mail: khays@epsne.org.

HAYS, MARGUERITE THOMPSON, nuclear medicine physician, educator; b. Bloomington, Ind., Apr. 15, 1930; d. Stith and Louise (Faust) Thompson; m. David G. Hays, Feb. 4, 1950 (div. 1975); children: Dorothy Adele, Warren Stith Thompson, Thomas Glenn. AB cum laude, Radcliffe Coll., 1951; postgrad., Harvard U. Med. Sch., 1954; MD, UCLA, 1957; ScD (hon.), Ind. U., 1979. Diplomate Am. Bd. Internal Medicine, Am. Bd. Nuc. Medicine. Intern UCLA Sch. Medicine, 1957-58, resident, 1958-59, 61-62, USPHS postdoctoral trainee, 1959-61, USPHS postdoctoral fellow, 1963-64, asst. prof. medicine, 1964-68, SUNY-Buffalo, 1968-70, asst. prof. biophys. sci., 1968-74, assoc. prof. medicine, 1970-76, clin. assoc. prof. nuc. medicine, 1973-77; asst. chief nuc. medicine VA Med. Ctr., Wadsworth, Calif., 1967-68; chief nuc. medicine Buffalo VA Med. Ctr., 1968-74, assoc. chief of staff for rsch., 1971-74; dir. med. rsch. svc. VA Ctrl. Office, Washington, 1974-79, asst. chief med. dir. for R & D, 1979-81; chief of staff Martinez VA Med. Ctr., Calif., 1981-83; prof. radiology Sch. Medicine U. Calif., Davis, 1981-93, prof. medicine and surgery, 1983-91, assoc. dean, 1981; clin. prof. radiology Stanford U. Sch. Medicine, 1990—; assoc. chief of staff for rsch. Palo Alto (Calif.) VA Med. Ctr., 1983-97, staff physician, 1997-99, cons., 1999—2001. Vis. rsch. scientist Euratom, Italy, 1962-63; chmn. radiopharm. adv. com. FDA, 1974-77; co-chmn. biomedicine com. Pres.'s Fed. Coun. on Sci., Engring. and Tech., 1979-81; mem. rsch. restructuring adv. com. Va. R & D Office, 1995-96, chair task group to restructure R & D Career Devel. Program, 1996-97; chmn. coop. studies evaluation com., Med. Rsch. Svc., VA, 1990-93; mem. sci. rev. and evaluation bd. Health Svcs. Rsch. and Devel. Svc., VA, 1988-91, chmn. career devel. com., 1991-99, chmn. career devel. com. Rehab. Rsch. and Devel. Svc., 1997-2003. Rsch. grantee VA, 1968-2003. NIH grantee, 1964-71; recipient Exceptional Svc. award Sec. Vets. Affairs, 2000. Fellow ACP; mem. Soc. Nuc. Medicine (chmn. publs. com., trustee, v.p. 1983-84), Am. Thyroid Assn. (bd. dirs. 1993-96), Endocrine Soc., Western Assn. Physicians. Home: 270 Campesino Ave Palo Alto CA 94306-2912 Office: 3801 Miranda Ave Palo Alto CA 94304-1207 E-mail: ritahays19@yahoo.com.

HAYS, PATRICK GREGORY, healthcare executive; b. Kansas City, Kans., Sept. 9, 1942; s. Vance Samuel and Mary Ellen (Crabbe) H.; m. Penelope Ann Hall, July 3, 1976; children: Julia L., Jennifer M., Emily J., Drew D. BS in Bus. Adminstrn, U. Tulsa, 1964; M.H.A., U. Minn., 1971; postgrad., U. Mich. Grad. Sch. Bus. Adminstrn., 1977. Mfg. analyst N.Am. Rockwell Corp., Tulsa, 1964-66; asst. adminstr., adminstr. for ops. Henry Ford Hosp., Detroit, 1971-75; exec. v.p. Meth. Med. Ctr. of Ill., Peoria, 1975-77; adminstr. Kaiser Found. Hosp., Los Angeles, 1977-80; pres. Sutter Community Hosps. and Sutter Health, Sacramento, 1980-95; pres., CEO Blue Cross Blue Shield Assn., Chgo., 1995—2000; faculty, School of Policy, Planning and Devel. U. So. Calif., Los Angeles. Trustee Cen. Area Teaching Hosps., Inc., L.A., 1977-79; mem. exec. com. St. Jude Children's Rsch. Hosp. Midwest Affilate, Peoria, 1975-77; past chmn. adv. bd. grad. program in health svcs. adminstrn. U. So. Calif., Sacramento; regent Am. Coll. Healthcare Execs., 1989-95, founding pres. Sacramento Regional Purchasing Coun.; mem. adv. bd. the Governance Inst.; mem. civil justice reform act com., U.S. Dist. Ct., Ea. Calif.; adj. faculty Ariz. State U.; bd. dirs. Trinity Health, Novi, Mich., chmn. HR and compensation com.; vice chmn. bd. dirs. Trinity Health, Novi, Mich., vice chmn. accrediting commn. for edn. in health adminstrn., adv. to mgmt. Contbr. articles on health services to publs. Mem. Pvt. Industry Coun., Sacramento Employment and Tng. Agy., 1984-85; bd. dirs. Consumer Credit Counselors Sacramento, 1984-87, Sacramento Area United Way, campaign chair, 1992-93; bd. dirs. Comstock Club, 1986-89; pres. Sacramento Camellia Festival Assn., 1987-88; chmn. Whitney M. Young Jr. Award, 1987; pres. Sacramento Regional Purchasing Coun., 1989-90. With U.S. Army, 1966-69. Decorated Army Commendation medal, cert. of appreciation Dept. Army; recipient Commendation resolution Calif. Senate, 1979, Whitney M. Young award Sacramento Urban League, 1983; named Chief Exec. Officer of Yr., Soc. for Healthcare Planning and Mktg. of Am. Hosp. Assn., 1991; USPHS fellow, 1969-71, Calif. Assn. Hosps. and Health Systems Walker fellow, 1989. Fellow Am. Coll. Healthcare Execs. (Calif. regent, Gold medal for career excellence 2003); mem. Calif. Assn. Hosps. and Health Systems (chmn. bd. dirs. 1991), Sacramento-Sierra Hosp. Assn. (exec. com., bd. dirs., pres. 1984), Royal Soc. Health (U.K.), Am. Mgmt. Assn. (Pres. Club), Hollywood C. of C. (revitalization com. 1979), Sacramento C. of C. (bd. dirs. 1982-85, 87-88), Vol. Hosps. Pacific (bd. dirs.), Rotary (bd. dirs. Sacramento 1987-89), Kappa Sigma (treas.). Presbyterian. *Personal philosophy: Most people want to excel at what they do. Management's job, at its essence, is to remove the barriers to their success.*

HAYS, RICHARD R, lawyer; b. Tulsa, Okla., Mar. 25, 1960; AB, Harvard Univ., 1982; MSc., Univ. Edinburgh, Scotland, 1984; JD, Vanderbilt Univ., 1986. Bar: Ga. 1986. Ptnr. Alston & Bird LLP, Atlanta, 1994, co-chair, litig., trial practice group, mngmt. com., 2005. Editor: Vanderbilt Law Rev.; co-author: Georgia Appellate Practice Handbook; contributing author Litigation Year 2000 Cases, 1999. Office: Alston & Bird LLP One Atlantic Ctr 1201 W Peachtree St NW Atlanta GA 30309-3424 Office Phone: 404-881-7360. Office Fax: 404-881-7777. Business E-mail: rhays@alston.com.

HAYS, ROBERT WILLIAM, communications consultant, educator, writer; b. Atlanta, Oct. 17, 1925; s. Calvin Samuel and Elizabeth (Green) H.; m. Rebecca Copeland, June 15, 1950; children: Michael, David, William. Student, Duke U., 1943-44; AB summa cum laude, Presbyn. Coll. S.C., 1947; MEd, Emory U., 1957. Comml. mgr. Sta. WSFT-AM, Thomaston, Ga., 1947-48, Sta. WLBG, Clinton, S.C., 1948; co-owner Clinton Plastic Co., 1948-49; instr. English So. Tech. Inst. (now So. Polytechnic State U.), Chamblee, Ga., 1950-51; supr. of tng. course devel. Lockheed Aircraft Corp., Marietta, Ga., 1951-52; asst. prof. So. Tech. Inst. (now So. Polytechnic State U.), Chamblee, Ga., 1952-57, head English dept. Marietta, 1953-73, assoc. prof., 1958-60, prof., 1960-85, prof. emeritus, 1985—. Cons. in comms., Marietta, 1965—, Mid. East, 1968—70; cons. Atlanta Exec. Svc. Corps, 1991—92; cons./lectr. Ga. Sch. Profl. Psychology, 1997—98. Author: Pacific Parodies, 1947, Principles of Technical Writing, 1965, Practically Speaking in Business, Industry and Government, 1969, Guide to Technical Writing, 1970, (with others) Getting Your Message Across, 1981; author poetry; contbr. numerous articles to profl. jours. Program dir. Marietta History Mus./Kiwanis Culture Capsule, 1999; active Cobb Arts Commn., 1988—99; mem. adv. bd. Salvation Army, Marietta, 1996—. Served to lt. (j.g.) USNR, 1943—46. Hixson fellow Kiwanis, 1996; recipient Arthur Williston award, 1967, Internat. Tech. Communications Conf. Honor, 1980, 83, Cmty. Svc. award King Ctr., 1994, 95. Fellow: Soc. for Tech. Comm. (life Disting. award 1993, Author one of 13 most significant articles 1954-2004); mem.: Ga. Poetry Soc., Kiwanis (program dir. 1991—). Home: 3360 Trickum Rd Marietta GA 30066-4683 Personal E-mail: haysR@aol.com.

HAYS, RONALD JACKSON, career officer; b. Urania, La., Aug. 19, 1928; s. George Henry and Fannie Elizabeth (McCartney) H.; m. Jane M. Hughes, Jan. 29, 1951; children: Dennis, Michael, Jacquelyn. Student, Northwestern U., 1945-46; BS, U.S. Naval Acad., 1950; HHD (hon.), Northwestern State U. Commd. ensign U.S. Navy, 1950, advanced through grades to adm., 1983; destroyer officer Atlantic Fleet, 1950-51; attack pilot Pacific Fleet, 1953-56; exptl. test pilot Patuxent River, Md., 1956-59; exec. officer Attack Squadron 106, 1961-63; tng. officer Carrier Air Wing 4, 1963-65; comdr. All Weather Attack Squadron, Atlantic Fleet, 1965-67; air warfare officer 7th Fleet Staff, 1967-68; tactical aircraft plans officer Office Chief Naval Ops., 1969-71; comdg. officer Naval Sta., Roosevelt Roads, P.R., 1971-72; dir. Navy Planning and Programming, 1973-74; comdr. Carrier Group 4, Norfolk, Va., 1974-75; dir. Office of Program Appraisal, Sec. of Navy, Washington, 1975-78; dep. and chief staff, comdr. in chief U.S. Atlantic Fleet, Norfolk, Va., 1978-80; comdr. in chief U.S. Naval Force Europe, London, 1980-83; vice chief naval ops. Dept. Navy, Washington, 1983-85; comdr. in chief U.S. Pacific Command, Camp H.M. Smith, Hawaii, 1985-88; pres., chief exec. officer Pacific Internat. Ctr. for High Tech. Rsch., Honolulu, Hawaii, 1988-92; tech. cons., 1992—. Chmn. Pacific Aviation Mus Pearl Harbor Bd. Decorated D.S.M. with 3 gold stars, Silver Star with 2 gold stars, D.F.C. with silver star and gold star, Legion of Merit, Bronze Star with combat V, Air Medal with numeral 14 and gold numeral 3, Navy Commendation medal with gold star and combat V; recipient Disting. Eagle Scout award, 1987. Republican. Baptist. Home and Office: 869 Kamoi Pl Honolulu HI 96825-1318 Office Phone: 808-739-7770. Personal E-mail: rjhayshawaii@msn.com.

HAYS, THOMAS S., medical educator, medical researcher; b. Winter Haven, Fla., Dec. 20, 1954; married. BS in Zoology, U. N.C., 1976, PhD in Cell Biology, 1985. Rsch. asst. dept. zoology U. N.C., Chapel Hill, 1975—76; rsch. asst. dept. biol. scis. Duke U., Durham, NC, 1976—79; asst. instr. quantitative and analytical microscopy Marine Biol. Lab., Woods Hole, Mass., 1981—83; asst. instr. optical microscopy U. Calif., Santa Cruz, 1982; postdoctoral fellow dept. molecular, cellular and devel. biology U. Colo., Boulder, 1985—89; asst. prof. dept. genetics and cell biology U. Minn., St. Paul, 1989—95, assoc. prof. dept. genetics and cell biology, 1995—. External reviewer NSF, 1989—. Reviewer: Jour. Cell Biology, Jour. Biol. Chemistry, Molecular Biology of the Cell, Molecular Cell Biology, Proceedings Nat. Acad. Sci. USA, Cell Motility and the Cytoskeleton, Jour. Cell Sci., Genetics; contbr. articles to profl. jours. Recipient Basil O'Connor Scholar award, March of Dimes, 1993, Establishe Investigator award, Am. Heart Found., 1996; fellow H.V. Wilson, U. N.C., 1983, R.J. Reynolds, 1983, Postdoctoral, NIH, 1985—88; grantee Tng., 1991—95, 1995—, Rsch. Tng., NSF, 1991—95, March of Dimes, 1995—; scholar Founders, Marine Biol. Lab., 1980. Mem.: Genetics Soc. Am., Am. Soc. Cell Biology. Office: U Minn Dept Genetics Cell Biology & Devel 6-160 Jackson Hall 321 Church St SE Minneapolis MN 55455

HAYS, TIMOTHY ODELL, musician, educator, writer; b. N.Y.C., May 6, 1954; s. Herman John and Ester Odell Hays; m. Karen Gordon Hays, June 19, 1983; children: Laurel, Eric, Ariana. BM, James Madison U., Harrisonburg, Va., 1981, MBA, 1984; PhD, Loyola U., Chgo., 1999. Performer Alliance, Washington, 1972—77; CEO, owner Ad Sound, Harrisonburg, Va., 1980—84; musician, band leader Moments Notice, Harrisonburg, Va., 1980—; assoc. editor Chgo. Musicate, 1984—89; prof., music dept. Elmhurst Coll., Ill., 1984—, chmn., music dept., 1991—; CEO, owner, prodr. Yodiah Prodns., Chgo., 1993—. Contbr. articles to profl. jours.; composer: (concerto) Laundromat Concerto, 1987. Grantee, Gretsch Inc., 1997, 1998. Mem.: Nat. Assn. of Music Bus. Instns., Nat. Acad. of Recording Arts and Scis., Music and Entertainment Industry Educators' Assn. (v.p., sec. 1990—98, pres. 1999—2003). Avocation: skiing. Office: Elmhurst Coll Music Dept 190 Prospect Ave Elmhurst IL 60126 Office Phone: 630-617-3515.

HAYSBERT, JOANN WRIGHT, academic administrator; b. Kingstree, S.C., Sept. 22, 1948; d. Norwood and Lillie Mae (Scott) Wright; m. Barral Stanley Hershel Haysbert, Mar. 7, 1981; children: Andre, Nineveh, Nazareth, Jordan. BA, Johnson C. Smith U., Charlotte, N.C., 1969; MEd, Auburn U., 1974, EdD, 1978. Coordinator rsch. and program planning Macon County Pub. Sch. System, Tuskegee, Ala., 1971-76; title IX coordinator Auburn (Ala.) U., 1976-78; instr. psychology Alexander City (Va.) State Jr. Coll., 1977-78; asst. prof. edn. Va. State U., Petersburg, 1978-80, prin. lab. sch., 1979-80; dir. women and minorities program Hampton (Va.) U., 1981-82, asst. v.p. acad. affairs, dir. summer session, various positions including asst. provost, provost, prof. and dean, acting pres., 2003—04; pres. Langston U., Langston, Okla., 2005—. Cons. in field. Author ednl. materials. Mem. Va. Nat. Identification Program for Advancement of Women in Higher Edn. Adminstrn. Ford Found. fellow, 1973. Mem. Nat. Assn. Women Deans, Adminstrs. and Counselors, Nat. Assn. Summer Sessions (chmn. com. 1986-88), Assn. Univ. Summer Sessions, AAUW, Phi Delta Kappa. Avocations: reading, music. Office: Langston Univ PO Box 907 Langston OK 73050 Office Phone: 405-466-3201. Office Fax: 405-466-3461. E-mail: jwhaysbert@lunet.edu.*

HAYSE, RICHARD FRANKLIN, lawyer; b. Kansas City, Mo., Sept. 6, 1943; s. Lewie Frank and Elizabeth Bronson (Humfreville) H.; m. Linda Rae Fairchild, Aug. 8, 1964; children: Adrienne Jennifer, Thomas Bronson. BA in Speech, Kansas State U., 1964; JD, Washburn Law Sch., 1969. Bar: Kans. 1969, U.S. Dist. Ct. Kans. 1969, U.S. Ct. Appeals (10th cir.) 1969, U.S. Supreme Ct. 1990. Broadcast journalist WIBW-TV-AM-FM, Topeka, 1964-68; asst. atty. gen. State of Kansas, Topeka, 1969-70; fgn. svc. info. officer U.S. Info. Agy., Washington, 1971-75; lawyer Eidson, Lewis, Porter & Haynes, Topeka, Kans., 1975-89, Hayse Law Offices, Topeka, 1989-90; ptnr. Morris, Laing, Evans, Brock & Kennedy, Chartered, Topeka, 1991—. Editor in chief Washburn Law Jour., author, 1969, co-author, 1970; contbr. chpts. to books. Pres. Topeka Lions Club, 1983-84, Topeka Youth Project, 1990-91, Topeka Symphony Soc., 1993-94, Cornerstone of Topeka, Inc., 1998-99. Mem. ABA, Kans. Bar Assn. (pres.-elect 2004, pres. 2005—), Topeka Bar Assn. (dir. 1986-91). Avocations: gardening, sailing. Home: 1724 SW Collins Ave Topeka KS 66604-3219 Office: Morris Laing Evans Brock & Kennedy Chartered 800 SW Jackson St Ste 1310 Topeka KS 66612-1216 Office Phone: 785-232-2662.

HAYT, THERESE D., newspaper executive; With Time-Life Books; deputy photo editor Sports Illustrated, NYC; photo editor San Diego Union-Tribune, Calif.; sports photo editor Newsday, NYC; photo editor Orlando Sentinel, Fla.; with mktg. and advt. divsn. The Walt Disney Co., Orlando; dir. photography Ariz. Daily Star, 2000—02, asst. mng. editor presentation, 2002—04, mng. editor, 2004—. Office: Ariz Daily Star 4850 S Park Ave Tucson AZ 85714

HAYTAYAN, ALITA **See GUILLEN, ALITA**

HAYTER, JOHN ELDON, retired music educator; b. Warsaw, Mo., Apr. 17, 1929; s. Clay Glen and Alta Grace (Gregory) Hayter. BS in Edn., Ctrl. Mo. State U., Warrensburg, 1952; MA, Sangamon State U., Springfield, Ill., 1974. Cert. tchr. Mo. Tchr. Logan Elem. Sch., Clinton, Mo., 1947—48; bandmaster USN Fleet Sonar Sch., Key West, Fla., 1954—56; tchr. Dept. Def. Dependent Sch., Ankara, Turkey, 1962—64, Wiesbaden, Germany, 1964—65; condr. Jacksonville Symphony Orch., Ill., 1968—70; tchr., orch. condr. Sch. Dist. 117, Jacksonville, Ill., 1965—90; ret., 1990. Orch. chmn. Ill. Music Educators Assn. Dist. IV, Jacksonville, Ill., 1965—89. Author: Sri Lanka-A Late 20th Century Adventure, 1996. Election judge Dem. Party, Jacksonville, Ill., 1990—. With USN, 1952—56. Mem.: Ansar Shrine Chanters (choral dir. 1984—), Ansar Masonic Shrine, Shawnee Lodge AF&AM. Democrat. Methodist. Avocations: travel, photography, cooking, gardening, sailing. Home: 3 Millwood Manor Jacksonville IL 62650

HAYTHE, WINSTON MCDONALD, lawyer, educator, real estate developer; b. Reidsville, N.C., Oct. 10, 1940; s. McDonald Swann and Henrietta Elizabeth (East) H.; m. Glennann Leigh Rogers, Aug. 17, 1963 (div. 1977);

children: Sheila Elaine, Kevin McDonald, Rhonda Leigh. BS, Mo. State U., 1963; JD, Coll. William and Mary, 1967; postgrad., U. Va., 1968—69; grad., Command and Gen. Staff Sch., Ft. Leavenworth, Kans., 1982, U.S. Def. U., 1984; LLM, U.S. Army JAG Sch., 1976. Bar: Va. 1967, D.C. 1969. Assoc. Rhyne & Rhyne, Washington, 1969-72; sr. trial atty. AEC, Washington, 1972-73; asst. gen counsel, sr. atty. Consumer Produce Safety Commn., Washington, 1973-82; staff dir. legal office EPA, Washington, 1982-83, sr. atty. for enforcement policy, 1985-91, sr. atty. Nat. Enforcement Tng. Inst., 1991-94, asst. dir., 1994-96, sr. legal counsel, 1996-2001; sr. counsel Office of Criminal Enforcement, Forensics and Tng., 2001—05; chief counsel Nat. Enforcement Tng. Inst., 2005—. Legis. fellow U.S. Senate, Washington, 1983-85; adv. com. paralegal studies U. Md., 1980-95, chmn., 1992-95; adj. prof. law, 1978-94; law faculty U.S. Army Judge Adv. Gen.'s Sch., Charlottesville, Va., 1969-94, Nat. Advocacy Ctr. U.S. Dept. Justice, Columbia, S.C., 1999—; cons. Barrister Ent., Washington, 1978—; elected mem. undergrad. programs adv. coun. U. Md., 1993-95; guest lectr. George Washington U. Sch. Law, 1999-2002, adj. prof. law, 2002-; mem. Strayer U. Bus. Admin. Program Adv. Coun., 2003-, Fed. Dispute Resolution Conf. Adv. Bd., 2004-. Trustee Georgetown Presbyn. Ch., 1995-98, v.p. trustees, 1996, pres. trustees, 1997-98, elder, mem. session, 2000-03, clk. of session, 2003—. Col. JAGC, USAR, 1967-94, ret. Fellow: Found. Fed. Bar Assn. (life); mem.: English Speaking Union, Found. of the Fed. Bar (sustaining life), Fed. Bar Assn. (fed. career svcs. divsn. 1974—90, nat. coun. 1998—, coun. mem. found. 2003—), DC Bar Assn., Va. State Bar Assn., Coll. William and Mary Law Sch. Assn. (bd. dirs. 1988—95), The English Speaking Union, Cosmos Club, Knights Templar, The Social List of Washington, Kappa Mu Epsilon. Presbyterian. Avocations: playing organ, piano, theater, concerts, reading. Home: 2141 P St NW Apt 402 Washington DC 20037-1031 Office: EPA (MC-2235A) 1200 Pennsylvania Ave NW Washington DC 20460-0001 Office Phone: 202-564-6057. Personal E-mail: winstonhaythe@verizon.net. Business E-Mail: haythe.winston@epa.gov.

HAYTHORNTHWAITE, ROBERT MORPHET, civil engineer, educator; b. Whitley Bay, Eng., May 5, 1922; came to U.S., 1953, naturalized, 1964; s. William and Doris (Morphet) H.; m. Beatrice Mary Swift, Mar. 29, 1952; children: Richard Swift, Jennifer Anne, Susan Mary, Sheila Margaret. BSc with honors, Durham U., 1942; BSc, London U., 1945, PhD, 1952; MS, Brown U., 1953, MA, 1957. Registered profl. civil engr., Pa. Sci. officer Bldg. Rsch. Sta., Watford, England, 1942-47; lectr. Sheffield U., 1947-53; instr. to assoc. prof. Brown U., 1953-59; prof. engring. sci. U. Mich., 1959-67; prof. engring. mechanics Pa. State U., 1967-79, head dept., 1967-74; dean Coll. Engring. Tech., Temple U., Phila., 1979-81, prof. engring. sci., 1979-96, prof. emeritus, 1996—. Vis. prof. Cambridge U., 1961, Manchester U., 1965-66, Lehigh U., 1974-75; cons. to Coun. Grad. Schs. U.S., Detroit Tank Arsenal, Engrs. Coun. for Profl. Devel., NASA, NSF; assoc. scientist Project Apollo Lunar Landing, 1962. Editor Proc. of the 3d U.S. Nat. Congress Applied Mechanics, 1958, Mechanics, 1972, 73, 88-97; contbr. articles to profl. jours. Pres. Robert M. and Mary Haythornwaite Found., 1985—. Commonwealth Fund fellow, 1950. Fellow ASCE (tech. editor jour. engring. mechanics divsn. 1967-70, chmn. engring. mechanics divsn. 1966-67, rsch. prize 1963), Am. Acad. Mechanics (pres. 1969-71, Disting. Svc. to Theoretical and Applied Mechanics medal 1996, pub. Mechanics jour. 1997—, conf. procs., 1999); mem. ASME, Am. Soc. Engring. Edn. (chmn. mechanics div. 1966-67), Sigma Xi, Tau Beta Pi (faculty adviser Pa. Beta chpt. 1968-79). Home: 313 Wellington Ter Jenkintown PA 19046-3831 E-mail: rmhay@astro.temple.edu.

HAYUTIN, DAVID LIONEL, lawyer; b. Phoenix, Apr. 19, 1930; s. Henry and Eva (Gaines) H.; m. Lee June Rodgers, June 15, 1951. AB, U. So. Calif., 1952, JD, 1958. Bar: Calif. 1958. Assoc. Pillsbury Winthrop Shaw Pittman LLP and predecessor firms, L.A., 1958-67, ptnr., 1967—. Author: Distributing Foreign Products in the United States, 1988, revised edit., 2000; assoc. editor So. Calif. Law Rev.; contbr. legal articles to profl. jours. Served to lt. (j.g.) USN, 1952-55. Mem. ABA, Internat. Bar Assn., Calif. Bar Assn., Maritime Law Assn. Republican. Avocations: opera, golf. Office: Pillsbury Winthrop Shaw Pittman LLP 725 S Figueroa St Los Angeles CA 90017-5524 Office Phone: 213-488-7351. Business E-Mail: dhayutin@pillsburylaw.com.

HAYWARD, EDWARD JOSEPH, lawyer; b. Springfield, Mo., Dec. 4, 1943; s. Joseph Hunter and Rosemary Hayward; m. Ellinor Duffey, Aug. 30, 1968; children: Jeffrey, Stephen, Susan. Student, U. d'Aix Marseille, Aix-en-Provence, France, 1963-64; AB, Stanford U., 1965; JD magna cum laude, Harvard U., 1971. Bar: N.Y. 1972, Minn. 1980. Assoc. Cleary, Gottlieb, Steen & Hamilton, N.Y.C. and Brussels, 1971-74, Oppenheimer Wolff & Donnelly, LLP, Brussels, 1975-79, ptnr. Mpls., 1978—. Pres. pres. Twin Cities Fgn. Trade Zone Inc., Mpls., 1983—84. Chmn. legis. com. Minn. World Trade Assn., Mpls., 1984—87. Served to capt. U.S. Army, 1965—68. Mem.: ABA, Minn. Bar Assn. (councillor internat. law sect. 1983—, sec. 1986—88, vice chmn. 1988—89, chmn. 1989—90), Dist. Export Coun. (chmn. 1996—), German-Am. C. of C. (bd. dirs. 1994—99, 2000—), French-Am. C. of C. (bd. dirs. 1983—, pres. 1985—87, 1996—2001, nat. sec. 1988—). Republican. Presbyterian. Avocations: languages, sports. Home: 6625 W Shore Dr Minneapolis MN 55435-1528 Office: Oppenheimer Wolff & Donnelly LLP 45 S 7th St Ste 3300 Minneapolis MN 55402-1609 Office Phone: 612-607-7280. Business E-Mail: ehayward@oppenheimer.com.

HAYWARD, JEAN, artist, musician, interior designer, performance artist; b. L.A., Calif., Apr. 4, 1917; d. Herbert Hastings Eastwood and Irma Isabel Arundell; m. William Hayward (dec.); m. George R. Collins (dec. Sept. 26, 1939); children: Julia Ann, Stephen, George, Mark. BA, U.C.L.A., L.A., 1938. Mime story telling with orchestras, all around the world; designer clothing line of denim for Bullock's Willshire; architecture and design houses, Santa Barbara. Contbr. articles to profl. jour.;, performer symphony soloist. Vol. Jr. League, Santa Barbara, Calif., 1946—70. Mem.: Birnam Wood Golf Club. Republican. Episc. Avocation: horseback riding. Home: 300 Hot Springs Rd Santa Barbara CA 93108

HAYWARD, OLGA LORETTA HINES (MRS. SAMUEL ELLSWORTH HAYWARD), retired librarian; b. Alexandria, La. d. Samuel James and Lillie (George) Hines; m. Samuel E. Hayward, July 12, 1945; children: Anne Elizabeth, Olga Patricia (Mrs. William Ryer). AB, Dillard U., 1941; BSLS, Atlanta U., 1944; MALS, U. Mich., 1959; MA in History, La. State U., 1977. Tchr. Marksville (La.) H.S., 1941-42; head libr. Grambling (La.) Coll., 1944-46; br. libr. br. nine New Orleans Pub. Libr. System, 1947-48; reference libr. So. U. Baton Rouge, 1948-73, libr. bus. and social scis. libr., 1973-84, libr. collection devel. consent decree program, 1984-86, chairwoman dept. reference, 1986-88, ret., 1988. Author: Graduate Theses of Southern University, 1959-71, A Bibliography of Literature By and About Whitney Moore Young Jr., 1929-71, 1972, The Influence of Humanism on Sixteenth Century English Courtesy Texts, 1977; also other bibliographies. Bd. dirs. La. Diocese Episcopal Cmty. Svcs., 1972-78; mem. banquet com. Baton Rouge chpt. Nat. Conf. Christians and Jews, 1981-2000, Nat. Conf. for cmty. and Justice, 2001-02. Recipient recognition, La. Llbr. Assn., 2003. Mem. life, La. Libr. Assn. (chair-elect subject specialists divsn. 1986-87, chairwoman subject specialists sect. 1987-88, Lucy B. Foote award subject specialists sect. 1990), Spl. Librs. Assn. (pres. La. chpt. 1978-79, Roll of Honor award 1995). Episcopalian. Home: 1632 Harding Blvd Baton Rouge LA 70807-5442 Office: 1632 Harding Bvd Baton Rouge LA 70807-5442

HAYWARD, ROBERT M., lawyer; s. Thomas Z. and Sally M. Hayward; m. Elizabeth R. Richards, June 15, 1971; children: Trevor R., Charlie N. BS, Northwestern U., 1994, JD, 1997. Bar: Ariz. 1997, U.S. Dist. Ct. Ariz. 1997, Ill. 1998, U.S. Dist. Ct. (no. dist.) Ill. 1998. Assoc. Snell & Wilmer LLP, Phoenix, 1997—2000, Kirkland & Ellis LLP, Chgo., 2000—03, ptnr., 2003—. Dir. Northwestern Gridiron Network, Evanston, Ill., 2003—; trustee Music Inst. Chgo., Winnetka, Ill., 2003—; mem. adv. bd. TheCorporateCounsel.net, Washington, 2003—; co-chair class gift Northwestern U. Alumni Assn., Evanston, 2003—. Contbr. articles to profl. jours. Mem.: ABA, Chgo. Bar Found. (dir. young profls. bd. 2004—), Ariz. Bar Assn., Chgo. Bar Assn., Econ. Club Chgo., Lawyers Club Chgo. Office: Kirkland & Ellis LLP 200 East Randolph Dr Chicago IL 60601 Office Phone: 312-861-2000. Office Fax: 312-861-2200.

HAYWARD, RONALD HAMILTON, surgeon; b. Wellington, N.Z., Nov. 7, 1927; s. Frederick Howard and Emma Mathilde (Hannibal) H.; m. Elizabeth Ruth Wells, Sept. 16, 1961; children— Maureen, John, Gregory, Jennifer. Ed., Wellington Coll., 1941-45; M.B., Ch.B., U. Otago, 1951; PhD in Surgery, U. Minn., 1961. Resident Mayo Clinic, Rochester, Minn., 1956-62; practice medicine specializing in thoracic and cardiovascular surgery Ft. Worth, 1962-65, Scott & White Clinic, Temple, Tex., 1965-93; prof., chmn. dept. surgery Tex. A&M Med. Sch., 1979-89. Recipient Alumni award Mayo Clinic, 1959 Mem. AMA, Tex. Med. Assn., Tex. Surg. Soc., So. Thoracic Surg. Assn., Soc. Thoracic Surgeons, Sigma Xi. Republican. Episcopalian. Patentee in field. Office: Scott & White Clinic Temple TX 76508-0001

HAYWARD, THOMAS ZANDER, JR., lawyer; b. Oct. 21, 1940; s. Thomas Z. and Wilhelmina (White) H.; m. Sally Madden, June 20, 1964; children: Thomas Z., Wallace M., Robert M. BA, Northwestern U., 1962, JD, 1965; MBA, U. Chgo., 1970. Bar: Ill. 1966, Ohio 1966, U.S. Dist. Ct. (no. dist.) Ill. 1966, U.S. Supreme Ct. 1970. Assoc. Defrees & Fiske, Chgo., 1965-69, ptnr., 1969-81, Boodell, Sears, Giambalvo & Crowley, Chgo., 1981-87, Bell, Boyd, Lloyd, Chgo., 1987—. Mem. mgmt. and exec. coms. Bell, Boyd, Lloyd. Trustee Northwestern U., 1980-84, 97—, vice-chmn., 2000—; bd. dirs. Ill. Continuing Legal Edn., 1987-92, Chgo. Area Found. for Legal Svcs., 1983—; bd. dirs. Nat. Cowboy and Western Heritage Mus., 2004—; pres. Sigma Alpha Epsilon Found., 2005—. Recipient Northwestern U. Alumni Svc. award, 1973. Mem. ABA (ho. of dels. 1984—, fed. jud. com. 1993-97, bd. govs., exec. com. 1998-2001, chmn. fin. com. 2000-01), ABA/Am. Law Inst. (pres. continuing profl. edn. 2005—), Fed. Judiciary Com. (chmn. 2003-05), Ill. State Bar Assn., Chgo. Bar Assn. (pres. 1983-84), Chgo. Bar Found. (bd. dirs., v.p. 2003—), Chgo. Club, Casino Club, Barrington Hills Country Club (pres. 1985-87). Republican. Presbyterian. Home: 8 W County Line Rd Barrington IL 60010-2613 Office: Bell Boyd & Lloyd 3 1st Nat Plz 70 W Madison St Ste 3100 Chicago IL 60602-4284 Office Phone: 312-807-4340. Business E-Mail: thayward@bellboyd.com.

HAYWOOD, B(ETTY) J(EAN), anesthesiologist; b. Boston, June 1, 1942; d. Oliver Garfield and Helen Elizabeth (Salisbury) H.; m Lynn Brandt Moon, Aug. 29, 1969 (div. Aug. 1986); children: Kaylin, Kristan, Kelly, Kasy R BSc, Tufts U., 1964; MD, U. Colo., 1968; MBA, Oklahoma City U., 1993; Grad., Air War Coll., 1997. Intern Wilford Hall AFB, San Antonio, 1968-69; resident in pediatrics U. Ariz., Tucson, 1971-72, resident in anesthesiology, 1972-74; dir. anesthesia dept. Pima County Hosp., Tucson, 1975-76; staff anesthesiologist South Community Hosp., Oklahoma City, 1977—, Moore (Okla.) Mcpl. Hosp., 1981-94, chief of anesthesia, 1990-94; staff anesthesiologist St. Anthony Hosp., Oklahoma City, 1982—; instr. dept. anesthesia U. Okla. Health Sci. Ctr., Oklahoma City, 1999—; col. USAF, active duty for Op. Enduring Freedom Wilford Hall Med. Ctr., Lackland AFB, Tex., 2001—02. Chief of ethics com. S.W. Med. Ctr., 1996. Bd. dirs. N.Am. South Devon Assn., Lynnville, Iowa, 1978—86; mem. med. com. Planned Parenthood Okla., 1992—; col. USAFR, 1968—. Mem. ASA, World South Devon Assn. (U.S. rep. 1985, 88), Tufts U. Alumni Assn. (rep.), Chi Omega (treas. 1963-64) Republican. Presbyterian. Avocations: skiing, sailing. Home: 705 NW 144th St Edmond OK 73013-1878 E-mail: Beej1942@sbcglobal.net.

HAYWOOD, BRUCE, retired academic administrator; b. York, Eng., Sept. 30, 1925; came to U.S., 1951, naturalized, 1957; s. Joseph Edgar and Eva (Street) H.; m. Isona Gretchen Shelley, June 21, 1947; children— Anne Margaret, Elizabeth Shelley. Student, U. Leeds, Eng., 1947-48; BA, McGill U., 1950, MA, 1951; PhD, Harvard, 1956. Mem. faculty Kenyon Coll., 1954, prof. German lit., 1960-63, dean coll., 1963-67, provost, 1967-80; pres. Monmouth (Ill.) Coll., 1980-94; ret., 1994. Author: The Veil of Imagery, 1959. Served with Brit. Army, 1943-47. Mem. Am. Assn. Tchrs. of German. Home: 311 E Simmons St Apt 706 Galesburg IL 61401

HAYWOOD, H(ERBERT) CARL(TON), psychologist, educator; b. Taylor County, Ga., July 2, 1931; s. Howard Chapman and Rosebud (Smith) H.; m. Nancy Patricia Roberts, Oct. 5, 1951 (div. Mar. 1971); children: Carlton, Terence, Elizabeth, Kristin; m. Dona June Wooldridge Tapp, Sept. 6, 1993 (div. Mar. 2000). AB, San Diego State Coll., 1956, MA, 1957; PhD, U. Ill., 1961. Lic. clin. psychologist Tenn. Mem. faculty George Peabody Coll. (merged with Vanderbilt U. 1979), Nashville, 1962-93, Alexander Heard disting. svc. prof., 1993-94, prof. psychology, 1969-93, prof. spl. edn., 1975-79, prof. emeritus, 1994—, dir. mental retardation research tng. program, 1968-70; dir. Inst. Mental Retardation and Intellectual Devel., 1970-73, Office Research Adminstrn., 1974-76, John F. Kennedy Center Research Edn. and Human Devel., 1971-83; prof. neurology Vanderbilt U. Sch. Medicine, 1971-93; prof. psychology and edn., dean grad. sch. edn. & psychology Touro Coll., N.Y.C., 1993-2000. Vis. prof. U. Toronto, 1965-66; sr. fellow Vanderbilt Inst. Pub. Policy Studies, 1983-88; chmn. Nat Mental Retardation Research Center Dirs., 1979-82; adv. bd. Ill. Inst. Developmental Disabilities, Chgo., 1970-78, Eunice Kennedy Shriver Center Mental Retardation, Waltham, Mass., 1973-80, Tenn. Dept. Mental Health, 1964-92; mem. nat. child health and human devel. council NIH, 1983-88; cons. President's Com. on Mental Retardation, 1968-73; mem. sci. rev. com., health research facilities br., div. edn. and research facilities NIH, 1967-71 Author (with Brooks and Burns): Bright Start: Cognitive Curriculum for Young Children, 1992; editor: Brain Damage in School Age Children, 1968, Social Cultural Aspects of Mental Retardation, 1970; editor: (with Begab and Garber) Prevention of Retarded Development in Psychosocially Disadvantaged Children; editor: (with J.R. Newbrough) Living Environments for Developmentally Retarded Persons, 1981; editor: (with D. Tzuriel) Interactive Assessment, 1992; editor: (with S. Friedman) Developmental Follow-Up: Domains, Concepts, and Methods, 1994; editor: Am. Jour. Mental Deficiency, 1969—79, Jour. Cognitive Edn. and Psychology, 1999—; mem. editl. bd.: Jour. Abnormal Child Psychology, 1973—89, Contemporary Psychology, 1982—85, Acta Paedologica, 1983—87, Jour. Mental Deficiency Rsch., 1984—2001, Internat. Rev. Rsch. in Mental Retardation, 1982—97; contbr. articles on child devel., motivation, cognitive edn., psycho assessment and mental retardation to profl. jours. Trustee Am. U. Rome, 2000—04. With USN, 1950-54. Recipient Myrtle Wreath Citation of Honor, So. Region Hadassah, 1979. Fellow Am. Assn. Mental Retardation (v.p. psychology 1975-77, 1st v.p. 1978-79, pres. 1980-81, Leadership award, 1985, Rsch. award, 1989), APA (pres. Div. 33 1978-79, mem. Coun. of Reps. 1980-82, Edgar A. Doll award, 1988), Am. Psychol. Soc.; mem. Internat. Assn. Cognitive Edn. (pres. 1988-92, Disting. Svc. award, 1995), Soc. Rsch. in Child Devel., Inst. Medicine. Democrat. Episcopalian. Avocations: piano, organist, choral conductor. Business E-Mail: carl.haywood@vanderbilt.edu. *Dominant values include enthusiasm for scholarship, equal parts of dedication to science for its own sake and concern for social progress, and the conviction that self-concern and self-seeking constitute the most dangerous threat to the collective goals of humanity. The future lies in education designed to stretch minds and develop processes of critical thought rather than to impart job-oriented skills.*

HAYWOOD, L. JULIAN, cardiologist, educator; b. Reidsville, N.C., Apr. 13, 1927; s. Thomas Woodly and Louise Viola (Hayley) H.; m. Virginia Elizabeth Paige, Dec. 3, 1953; 1 child, Julian Anthony. BS, Hampton Inst., 1948; MD, Howard U., 1952. Intern St. Mary's Hosp., Rochester, N.Y., 1952-53; resident L.A. County Hosp., 1956-58; fellow cardiology White Meml. Hosp., 1959-61; traveling fellow U. Oxford, Eng., 1963; instr. medicine Loma Linda (Calif.) U., 1960-61, asst. prof., 1961-73, assoc. clin. prof., 1973-82, clin. prof., 1982—; asst. prof. medicine U. So. Calif., 1963-67, assoc. prof., 1967-76, prof., 1976—; dir. EKG dept. L.A. County/U. Soc. Calif. Med. Ctr., 1996—. Past dir. coronary care unit, physicians tng. program Regional Med. Programs L.A. County/U. So. Calif. Med. Ctr, 1970-75; cons. Los Angeles County Coroner, Indsl. Accident Bd. Calif., Health Care Tech. Divsn., USPHS, Nat. Heart and Lung Inst.; past mem. cardiology adv. com. divsn. heart and vascular diseases; bd. dirs., pres. Sickle Cell Diseases Found.; mem. Armed Forces Epidemiol. Bd., 1996—; pres. U. So. Calif. Salerni Collegium, 1997-98; bd. dirs. Charles Drew U. Medicine and Scis., 1999—. Contbr. articles profl. jours.; Mem. editorial bds.: Jour. Nat. Med. Assn. Past pres., hon. mem., bd. dirs. Am. Heart Assn. Greater L.A., 1989—. With M.C. USNR, 1954-56. Recipient award of merit Los Angeles County Heart Assn., 1968, 69, 73, 75, Disting. Alumnus award Howard U. Sch. Medicine, 1982, Disting. Svc. award, 1996, Disting. Health Educator award, 2003; Louis B. Russel award Am. Heart Assn., 1988, Merit award, 1991, Heart of Gold award Am. Heart Assn./Greater L.A. Affiliate, 1989, Dedicated Svc. award, 1991, 93, award of Achievement in Rsch., 1994, 20th Anniversary Founder's award Assn. Black Cardiologists, 1994; J.B. Johnson Meml. lectr., 1975, 88; honoree Internal Medicine sect. Nat. Med. Assn., 1988; named Alumnus of Yr.-at-Large, Hampton U., 1993; nat. med. fellow Gala West 2004, 2004, Eagle Cert. Excellence award Nat. Med. Fellowships, N.Y.C., 2004. Fellow ACP, AAAS, L.A. Acad. Medicine, Am. Coll. Cardiology (Disting. Svc. award 2001, Cert. of Merit 2003, Cert. of Appreciation 2003), Am. Heart Assn. (coun. on clin. cardiology, coun. on atherosclerosis, exec. com. coun. on epidemiology, long range planning com., dir., past sec., v.p. Greater L.A. affiliate, pres.); mem. AMA, AAUP, Am. Fedn. Clin. Rsch., Western Soc. Clin. Investigation, Assn. Advancement Med. Instrumentation, Nat. Med. Assn. (Charles Drew Med. Soc.), N.Y. Acad. Scis., Hampton Inst. Alumni Assn. (past pres. L.A. chpt.), Med. Faculty Assn. U. So. Calif. Sch. Medicine (past pres.), Assn. Physicians L.A. County Hosp. (pres. 1991—), Western Assn. Physicians, Fedn. Am. Scientists, Assn. Black Cardiologists (Walter Booker Innovation award 1990), Assn. Acad. Minority Physicians (councilor, pres.-elect 1992-93, pres. 1993-94), Alpha Omega Alpha, Am. Coll. Physicians (Laureate award So. Calif. Region I 1997). Office: LACt USC Med Ctr 1200 N State St Box 305 Los Angeles CA 90033-1029 Office Phone: 323-226-7116. Business E-Mail: jhaywood@hsc.usc.edu.

HAYWOOD, THEODORE JOSEPH, physician, educator; b. Monroe, N.C., Feb. 13, 1929; s. Jesse Beman and Mary (McDonald) H.; m. Nancy Hume Ferguson, Dec. 21, 1959; children: Elizabeth Linscott, Keene McDonald, Mark Shepard. BS, The Citadel, 1948; MD, Vanderbilt U., 1952. Diplomate: Am. Bd. Pediatrics, Am. Bd. Allergy and Immunology. Pvt. practice allergy, Houston, 1958—; mem. staff Tex. Children's Hosp., 1958—, mem. active staff Pediatrics, 1963—; mem. faculty Baylor U. Coll. Medicine, 1958—, clin. assoc. prof. pediatrics and allergy, 1977—. Assoc. mem. U. Tex. McDonald Obs., 2000—. Served with M.C. AUS, 1955-57. Fellow Am. Coll. Allergists, Am. Acad. Allergy and Immunology, Am. Acad. Pediatrics; mem. Sigma Xi. Clubs: River Oaks Country (Houston). Republican. Episcopalian. Home: 2923 Ferndale Pl Houston TX 77098-1117 Office: McGovern Allergy & Asthma Clinic 4710 Bellaire Blvd Ste 200 Bellaire TX 77401-4505 Office Phone: 713-661-1444. Business E-Mail: mac@mcgovernallergy.com.

HAYWORTH, ANDREA ELIZABETH, lawyer; b. San Francisco, Nov. 5, 1966; d. Stephen Lee and Loureta Lamb Hayworth. BA, U. N.C., Chapel Hill, 1988; JD, Duke U., Durham, NC, 1994. Paralegal Branch, Pike, & Ganz, Atlanta, 1989—90, Chambliss & Bahner, Chattanooga, 1990—91; law clerk Hon. H. Ted. Milburn Ct. Appeals, Chattanooga, 1994—95; counsel Sutherland Asbill & Brennan, LLP, Atlanta, 1995—. Mem.: Ga. Assn. Women Lawyers (scholarship chair, sec., pub. chair 1995—2002). Avocations: tennis, dance, travel. Office: Sutherland Asbill & Brennan LLP 999 Peachtree St NE Atlanta GA 30309 Office Phone: 404-853-8354. Business E-Mail: andrea.hayworth@sablaw.com.

HAYWORTH, J(OHN) D(AVID), JR., congressman, former sportscaster; b. High Point, N.C., July 12, 1958; s. John David and Gladys Ethel (Hall) H.; m. Mary Denise Yancey, Feb. 25, 1989; children: Nicole Irene, Hannah Lynne, John Micah. BA in Speech and Polit. Sci., N.C. State U., 1980. Sports anchor, reporter Sta. WPTF-TV, Raleigh, N.C., 1980-81, Sta. WLWT-TV, Cin., 1986-87; sports anchor Sta. WYFF-TV (formerly Sta. WFBC-TV), Greenville, S.C., 1981-86, Sta. KTSP-TV, Phoenix, 1987-94; mem. U.S. Congress from 5th Ariz. dist., Washington, 1995—; mem. ways and means com., mem. resources com., asst. whip. Radio commentator; play-by-play broadcaster. Dist. committeeman Ariz. Rep. Com., Scottsdale, 1988-89; bd. dirs. Am. Humanics Found., Ariz. State U., Tempe, 1991-92; chmn. Scout-A-Rama, Theodore Roosevelt coun. Boy Scouts Am., 1991-92. Recipient honor roll award Atlantic Coast Conf., 1977, Young Am. award Unharrie coun. Boy Scouts Am., 1979, Friend of Edn. award Sch. Dist. Greenville County, 1985, Sch. Bell/Friend of Edn. award S.C. Dept. Edn., 1985. Mem. Rotary (bd. dirs. Phoenix 1989-90). Republican. Baptist. Avocations: reading, distance running, bible study, public speaking, television trivia. Office: US House Reps 2434 Rayburn Ho Office Bldg Washington DC 20515-0306*

HAYWORTH, SCOTT DAVID, physician; b. N.Y.C., Apr. 4, 1956; s. Henry Charles and Anne (Sinnreich) H.; m. Nan Alison Sutter, June 21, 1981; children: William, John. AB, Princeton U., 1978; MD, Cornell U., 1984. Diplomate Am. Bd. Ob/Gyn., Nat. Bd. Med. Examiners. Intern Mt. Sinai Hosp., N.Y.C., 1984-85, resident physician, 1985-87, chief resident, 1987-88; physician Mt. Kisco (N.Y.) Med. Group, 1988—, v.p., 1995-96, pres., 1996—, acting med. dir., 1996-98, CEO, 1998—. Co-chmn. laser com. No. Westchester Hosp., 1991-95, mem. pharmacy and therapeutics com., 1990-2004, mem. med. cabinet, 2002—, mem. found. bd., 2005—. Contbr. chpt. to book and articles to profl. jours. Bd. dirs. No. Westchester Hosp. Found., 2005—. Fellow NIH, 1981, David Barr, 1981; recipient award of merit Vis. Nurse Assn. Hudson Valley, 2005. Fellow Am. Coll. Ob-Gyn. (chmn. Hudson Valley sect. 2000-01, sec. Dist. II-NY 2002, treas. Dist. II-NY 2002-04, vice chair Dist. II-NY 2004—, Dist. Svc. award 2002); mem. Westchester Obstet. and Gynecol. Soc. (sec.-treas. 1995-96, co-pres. 1996-97, pres. 1997), Internat. Soc. Gynecol. Endoscopy, Gynecol. Laser Soc., Am. Med. Group Assn. (bd. dir. 2005—, chmn. membership com. 2005—). Office: Mt Kisco Med Group 90 S Bedford Rd Mount Kisco NY 10549-3412 Office Phone: 914-241-1050.

HAZAN, MARCELLA MADDALENA, writer, educator, consultant; b. Cesenatico, Italy, Apr. 15, 1924; d. Giuseppe and Maria (Leonelli) Polini; m. Victor Hazan, Feb. 24, 1955; 1 child, Giuliano. Dr. in Natural Scis., U. Ferrara, 1952, Dr. in Biology, 1954. Rschr. Guggenheim Inst., 1955-58; prof. math. and biology Italian State schs., 1963-66; founder Sch. of Italian Cooking, N.Y.C., 1969-94, Marcella Hazan Sch. of Classic Italian Cooking, Bologna, Italy, 1976-94, Master Classes in Classic Italian Cooking, Venice, Italy, 1986-98. Pres. Hazan Classic Enterprises, Inc., 1978-99. Author: The Classic Italian Cookbook, 1973, More Classic Italian Cooking, 1978, Marcella's Italian Kitchen, 1986, Essentials of Classic Italian Cooking, 1992, Marcella Cucina, 1997, Marcella Says, 2004. Decorated knight Presdl. Order Star of Italian Solidarity. Roman Catholic. Address: 1211 Gulf Of Mexico Dr # 109 Longboat Key FL 34228 Fax: (941) 387-0183.

HAZARD, CHRISTOPHER WEDVIK, international business executive; b. NYC, Aug. 9, 1943; s. Herbert Ray and Ellen Clausine (Wedvik) H.; m. Sally Grace Woodruff, Sept. 1, 1966; children: Mark Alexander, Julie Lynne. BA, Ohio State U., 1965; MPA, U. Colo., 1973; postgrad., U. Pa., The Wharton Sch. Lt. col. USAF, 1965-86; near east region dir. ops. Def. Security Assistance Agy., Washington, 1982-86; exec dir. internat. mktg. BAE Sys., Land and Armaments, Arlington, Va., 1986—2005, BAE Sys., Arlington, 2005—. Active Neighborhood Friends of Mt. Vernon Recipient Def. Superior Svc. award, Sec. of Def., 1986, Joint Svc. Achievement award, Dept. of Def., 1984; decorated Air Force Meritorious Svc. medal. Mem.: Mt. Vernon Citizens Assn. (pres. 1984—85), Soc. Am. Period Furniture Makers. Avocations: international affairs, historic preservation, gardening, woodworking. Office Phone: 703-312-6119.

HAZARD, GEOFFREY CORNELL, JR., law educator; b. Cleve., Sept. 18, 1929; s. Geoffrey Cornell and Virginia (Perry) H.; m. Elizabeth O'Hara; children: James G., Katherine W., Robin P., Geoffrey Cornell III. BA, Swarthmore Coll., 1953, LLD (hon.), 1988; LLB, Columbia U., 1954; LLD (hon.), Gonzaga U., 1985, U. San Diego, 1985, Ill. Inst. Tech., 1990, Republica Italiana, 1998. Bar: Oreg. 1954, Calif. 1960, Conn. 1982, Pa. 1994.

Assoc. Hart, Spencer, McCulloch, Rockwood & Davies, Portland, Oreg., 1954-57; exec. sec. Oreg. Legis. Interim Com. Jud. Adminstrn., 1957-58; assoc. prof. law, then prof. U. Calif., Berkeley, 1958-64; prof. law U. Chgo., 1964-71, Yale U., 1971-94, prof. mgmt., 1979-83, acting dean Sch. Orgn. and Mgmt., 1980-81, Sterling prof. law, 1986-94; trustee prof. U. Pa., Phila., 1994—; Thomas Miller prof. U. Calif. Law, Hastings, 2005—. Mem. Adminstrv. Conf. U.S., 1971-78; cons. jud. conf. U.S. com. on rules practice and procedure, 2004. Author: (Law text) Research in Civil Procedure, 1963, Ethics in the Practice of Law, 1978; author: (with D.W. Louisell, C. Tait, W. Fletcher) Pleading and Procedure, 1972; author: 8th rev. edit., 1999; author: (with M. Taruffo) (Law text) American Civil Procedure, 1994; author: (with S. Koniak and R. Cramton) Law and Ethics of Lawyering, 4th edit., 2004; author: (with W.W. Hodes) Law of Lawyering 3d edit., 2000; author: (with F. James and J. Leubsdorf) Civil Procedure 5th rev.edit., 2001; author: (with A. Dondi) Legal Ethics: A Comparative Study, 2004; editor: (Law text) Law in a Changing America, 1968; editor: (with D. Rhode) Legal Profession: Responsibility and Regulation, 1985; co-editor (with D. Rhode): Professional Responsibility and Regulation, 2002; contbr. articles to profl. jours. Served with USAF, 1948-49. Fellow Am. Bar Found. (exec. dir. 1964-70, rsch. award 1986); mem. ABA (cons. code jud. conduct 1970-72, reporter stds. jud. adminstrn. 1971-77, reporter model rules of profl. conduct 1978-83), Am. Law Inst. (reporter restatement of judgments 1973-81, dir. 1984-99, dir. emeritus, 1999-), Am. Acad. Arts and Scis., Am. Philos. Soc., Nat. Legal Aid and Defender Assn., Am. Judicature Soc., Selden Soc., Pa. Bar Assn., Calif. State Bar, Phi Beta Kappa. Episcopalian. Avocations: tennis, history, golf. Office Phone: 215-898-7494. Business E-Mail: ghazard@law.upenn.edu.

HAZARD, ROBERT CULVER, JR., hotel executive; b. Balt., Oct. 23, 1934; s. Robert Culver and Catherine B. H.; m. Mary Victoria Cranor, Jan. 2, 1981; children by previous marriage: Alicia W., Letitia A., Robert Culver, III, Thomas E.J., Anne. BA cum laude, Woodrow Wilson Sch., Princeton U., 1956; postgrad., Johns Hopkins U., U. Denver. Mktg. rep. IBM Corp., Denver, 1959-68; with Am. Express Co., 1968-74, v.p. exec. accounts, 1973-74; CEO Best Western Internat., 1974-80; CEO, retired chmn. Choice Hotels Internat., Silver Spring, Md., 1980-96; chmn. Creative Hotel Assocs., Phoenix, 1996—. Capt. USAF, 1956-59. Recipient Man of Yr. award Motel Brokers Assn. Am., 1976, Silver Plate award Hospitality mag., 1979, Albert E. Koehl award HSMA, 1992, Cecil B. Day Hospitality award AAHOA, 1993, Silver Plate award Lodging Hospitality Mag., 1995. Mem.: Am. Hotel and Lodging Assn. E-mail: roberthazard@msn.com.

HAZEL, MARIANNE ELIZABETH, elementary school educator; b. Bellefonte, Pa., Mar. 14, 1967; d. Joseph Edward and Patricia (Rumberger) H. BS, Pa. State U., 1990, MEd, 1995, MS, 1998, DEd, 2003. Cert. reading specialist; cert. adminstrn.; cert. curriculum and instrn. Tchr. 1st grade Carroll County Pub. Schs., Westminster, Md., 1991-97; elem. asst. prin. reading supr. Conewago Valley Sch. Dist., New Oxford, Pa., 1997—2000; asst. prof. Lock Haven U. of Pa., 2002—. Mem. ASCD, Pa. State U. Alumni Assn., Western Md. Coll. Alumni Assn., Pi Lambda Theta, Phi Delta Kappa Home: 223 W Curtin St Bellefonte PA 16823-1518 Office Phone: 570-893-6289. Business E-Mail: mhazel@lhup.edu.

HAZEL, MARY BELLE, university administrator; b. Orange, NJ, May 30, 1932; d. Morris M. Sr. and Robena (Brinkley) Thomas; m. James H. Hazel, Sept. 28, 1958 (div. Sept. 1976); children: Sharon Marie Hazel-Griggs, James Thomas. BSBA, Seton Hall U., South Orange, NJ, 1992, MA in Edn. cum laude, 1998. Publs. asst. advt. and pub. rels. dept. Foster Wheeler Corp., NYC, 1969-87; ind. contractor, 1987-92; adminstrv. coord. dean's office Univ. Medicine and Dentistry NJ Sch. Health Related Professions, Newark, 1992—. Elder Elmwood United Presbyn. Ch. Mem. AAUW, NAFE, Smithsonian Nat. Assn., Soc. Allied Health Professions NJ, YWCA, NJ Performing Arts Ctr., Jersey Ednl. Opportunity Fund Profl. Assn., Newark Mus. Assn., YWCA of Essex and West Hudson (NJ).

HAZELIP, HERBERT HAROLD, academic administrator; b. Bowling Green, Ky., Aug. 3, 1930; s. Herbert and Maggie Marie (Ferguson) H.; m. Helen Frances Royalty, Mar. 23, 1956; children: Patrick Harold, Jeffrey Alan. AA, Freed-Hardeman Coll., Henderson, Tenn., 1948; BA, David Lipscomb Coll., Nashville, 1950; MDiv, So. Bapt. Theol. Sem., 1958; PhD, U. Iowa, 1967. Ordained to ministry Ch. of Christ, 1947. Min. Cen. Ch. Christ, Owensboro, Ky., 1950-53, Taylor Blvd. Ch. Christ, Louisville, 1954-64, Cen. Ch. Christ, Cedar Rapids, Iowa, 1964-67, Highland St. Ch. Christ, Memphis, 1967-86; dean, prof. Harding U. Grad. Sch. Religion, Memphis, 1967-86; pres. Lipscomb U., Nashville, 1986-97, chancellor, 1997—. Author: Discipleship, 1977, A Devotional Guide to Bible Lands, 1979, Anchors in Troubled Waters, 1981, Lord, Help Me When I'm Hurting, 1984, Happiness in the Home, 1985, Questions People Ask Ministers Most, 1986, Jesus: Our Mentor and Model, 1987, Becoming Persons of Integrity, 1988, Anchors for the Asking, 1989. Mem. Rotary. Avocations: travel, reading. Office: David Lipscomb U 3901 Granny White Pike Nashville TN 37204-3903 Office Phone: 615-279-6064. E-mail: harold.hazelip@lipscomb.edu.

HAZELIP, LINDA ANN, musician, small business owner, executive assistant; b. El Campo, Tex., Oct. 20, 1952; d. Al Gareth and Annabelle (Black) Braswell; m. Richard Chris Hazelip, July 28, 1972 (div. Aug. 30, 1984). *It is only by God's grace I live a normal life, developing and using the talents given me. Born with a dislocated hip, I was chosen by a team of doctors from around the world to try to help. I learned to walk three times before age five. At age three, Jesus told me three times in a dream that I could walk. With childlike faith, I did walk while continuing my rehabilitation; a miracle in medical history. My continual prayer is for my life to be a living testimony of what is possible with God if we only believe.* Diploma in computer programming and data processing, Massey Bus. Coll., 1972. Cert. tchr. progressive series intermediate level piano St. Louis Conservatory Music, 1971. Tchr. basic music and piano, 1971—79; bookkeeper Millar Instruments, Houston, 1973—74; sec. St. Andrew's United Meth. Ch., Houston, 1975—79; various positions as exec. asst., mgmt. asst., exec. sec., adminstr., and other adminstrv. positions Houston, 1979—; bus. owner, organist/choirmaster, pianist, vocalist sacred occasions, select secular spl. occasions Met. Area, Houston, S.E. Tex., 1986—; dir., exec. sec. Exponet Trading Co., Houston, 1983—86; exec. sec. InterFirst Bank Post Oak, Houston, 1986; sec., adminstr., mgmt. asst. Halliburton Energy Svcs., Houston, 1991—96; tchr. voice, organ, piano, 2000—. Organist, vocalist, pianist, children's music dir. Faith United Methodist Ch., South Houston, 1972—77; organist, vocalist, children's music dir. Old River Ter. United Methodist Ch., Channelview, Tex., 1978—80; organist, vocalist, music dir. St. John's United Methodist Ch., Baytown, Tex., 1980—84; organist, vocalist St. Stephens United Methodist Ch., Houston, 1983—85; organist, choir dir., vocalist Parker Meml. United Methodist Ch., Houston, 1984—85; choir dir., vocalist Reid Meml. United Methodist Ch., Houston, 1985, Covenant United Methodist Ch., Houston, 1985—86. Vocalist, pianist Open Door Mission, Houston, 1997—; mem. First United Meth. Ch., Houston, 1986—. Mem.: NAFE, Chorister's Guild, Houston Area League PC Users, Am. Bus. Women's Assn. (Skyscraper chpt., Woman of Yr. 1993—94), Am. Guild Organists, Nat. Honor Soc., Nat. Math. Honor Soc. Republican. Methodist. Avocation: holy land study tours. Office: 2501 Westridge # 241 Houston TX 77054-1519 Office Phone: 713-668-2248. E-mail: lhazelip@hal-pc.org.

HAZELRIGG, GEORGE ARTHUR, JR., systems engineer, educator; b. Summit, NJ, Oct. 28, 1939; s. George Arthur Hazelrigg and Dorothy Hetty (Howell) Orr; m. Lauretta Blanche Powell, Aug. 31, 1968; children: George A. III, Geoffrey A. BS, N.J. Inst. Tech., 1961, MS, 1963; MA, Princeton U., 1966, MSE, 1968, PhD, 1969. Cert. glider flight instr. Engr. Curtiss-Wright, Wood Ridge, N.J., 1961-63, Jet Propulsion Lab, Pasadena, Calif., 1966-67; staff sci. Gen. Dynamics, San Diego, 1968-71; rsch. staff Princeton U., 1971-75; dir., systems engr. Econ, Inc, Princeton, 1976-82; sr. advisor for tech. integration NSF, Arlington, Va., 1982—; prof. of systems engring. (sabbatical) Inst. for Advanced Engring., Seoul, 1993. Dir. ECON, Inc., Princeton, 1974-84; cons. Princeton Synergetics, Inc., 1986—. Author: Systems Engineering: An Approach to Information-Based Design, 1996; editor: Opportunities for Academic Research in a Low Gravity Environment, 1986; assoc. editor Jour. Spacecraft and Rockets, 1977-82. Named Disting. Alumnus, N.J. Inst. Tech., Newark, 1989. Mem. AIAA, ASME, Am. Soc. for Engring. Edn., Tau Beta Pi. Avocation: commercial pilot. Home: 8427 Idylwood Rd Vienna VA 22182-5309 Office: NSF 4201 Wilson Blvd Arlington VA 22230-0001 E-mail: ghazelri@nsf.gov.

HAZELTINE, BARRETT, electrical engineer, educator; b. Paris, Nov. 7, 1931; came to U.S., 1932; s. L. Alan and Elizabeth (Barrett) H.; m. Mary Frances Fenn, Aug. 25, 1956; children: Michael B., Alice W., Patricia F. BSE, Princeton U., 1953, MSE, 1956; PhD, U. Mich., 1962; ScD (hon.), SUNY, Stony Brook, 1988. Registered profl. engr., R.I. Asst. prof. engring. Brown U., 1959—66, assoc. prof., 1966—72, prof., 1972—; asst. to dean Brown U. (The Coll.), 1962—63, asst. dean, 1968—74, assoc. dean, 1974—93; Robert Foster Cherry chair for disting. tchg. Baylor U., 1991—92; prof. U. Botswana, 1993. Lectr., vis. prof. U. Zambia, Lusaka, 1970-71, 76-77; vis. prof. U. Malawi-Poly., Blantyre, 1980-81, 83-84, 88-89, Africa U. Mutare, Zimbabwe, 1996-97, 2000; asst. to mgr. rsch. labs., space and info. sys. divsn. Raytheon Co., 1964-65, cons., 1965-67; cons. R.I. Utilities Commn., 1977-80, others. Author: Introduction to Electronic Circuits and Applications, 1980, Appropriate Technology: Tools, Choice and Implications, 1998, Field Guide to Appropriate Technology, 2003; editor: The Weaver, 1982—90. Trustee Stevens Inst. Tech. Recipient award for excellence in instrn. Western Electric, 1968; grantee NSF, Dept. Edn.; grantee Met. Life Ins. Ednl. Found.; Fulbright fellow 1988-89, 93. Mem. IEEE (sr., chmn. Providence sect. 1971-72), Providence Engring. Soc. (pres. 1977-78), Am. Soc. Engring. Edn., Sigma Xi, Tau Beta Pi. Congregationalist (deacon). Clubs: Providence Art, Providence Review. Achievements include patents for color recognition system. Home: 60 Barnes St Providence RI 02906-1502 Office: Brown U Divsn Engring Providence RI 02912-0001 Office Phone: 401-863-2673. Business E-Mail: Barrett_Hazeltine@brown.edu.

HAZELTINE, GERALD LESTER, food products executive; b. Beloit, Wis., Apr. 10, 1924; s. Frank Raymond and Ella (Bush) H.; m. Luella Agnes Heath, Aug. 15, 1953. Grad. high sch., Rockton, Ill., 1941. Farm hand, Wis., Ill., 1938-42; steelworker Carnegie Ill. Steel Corp., Gary, Ind., 1942-48; r.r. sect. hand Chgo. Northwestern R.R., Clarance, Iowa, 1948-49; machine operator Quaker Oats Co., Cedar Rapids, Iowa, 1950-81; owner, operator Hazeltine Honey Co., Toddville, Iowa, 1949—. Beekeeping cons., Linn County, Iowa, 1970—. With U.S. Army, 1942-45. Decorated Bronze stars, Victory medal. Jehovah'S Witness. Avocations: reading, writing, gardening. Home and Office: 8300 Tower Terrace Rd Toddville IA 52341-9617

HAZELTINE, JOYCE, former state official; b. Pierre, SD; m. Dave Hazeltine; children: Derek, Tara, Kirk (dec.). Student, Huron (S.D.) Coll., No. State Coll., Aberdeen, S.D., Black Hills State Coll., Spearfish, S.D. Former asst. chief clk. SD Ho. of Reps.; former sec. SD State Senate; sec. of state State of SD, Pierre, 1987—2003. Bd. dirs. SD Bankers Found., 2002—, chair, 2004—05; bd. dirs. Chiesman Found. Democracy, 2004—. Adminstrv. asst. Pres. Ford Campaign, S.D.; Rep. county chmn. Hughes County S.D.; state co-chair Phil Gramm for Pres., 1996; chair Custer Co. Rep. Women Mem. Nat. Assn. Secs. of State (exec. bd., pres.), Women Execs. in State Govts. (bd. dirs.). Republican.

HAZELTON, JUANITA LOUISE, librarian; b. Glendale, Calif., June 12, 1942; d. James Chester and Eddith Pearl (Henson) McCrain; m. Merrill Edward Hazelton, Apr. 27, 1968; children: Larry Scott, James Edward. BA in Arts and Letters, U. Oreg., 1964; MLS, U. Tex., 1970; tchg. cert., Tex. Woman's U., 1984. Cert. county libr., 1997. Librarian Dallas Pub. Libr., 1966-69; libr. asst. Austin Coll., Sherman, Tex., 1974-75; tchr., librarian Gunter (Tex.) Ind. Sch. Dist., 1984-94; librarian Plano (Tex.) Pub. Libr., 1994-95; libr. dir. Van Alstyne (Tex.) Pub. Libr., 1995—. Contbg. author: Telling Our Stories-Texas Family Secrets, 1997 (Gold Star award 1997); Bookshelf columnist Van Alstyne Leader, 1995—. Recipient Libr. of Yr., N.E. Tex. Libr. Sys., 1996; named Bus. Citizen of Yr. Van Alstyne C. of C., 1998, named to Tall Texans, 2003. Mem. Tex. Libr. Assn. (treas. dist. 5, 2000-01), TALL Tex., Toastmasters Internat., Van Alstyne Genealog. Assn., Tex. Storytelling Assn. Republican. Mem. Ch. of Christ. Avocations: collecting kachinas and folk tales, amateur storytelling, computers, genealogy, writing poetry and family history. Office: Van Alstyne Pub Libr PO Box 629 117 N Waco Van Alstyne TX 75495 Office Phone: 903-482-5991. Business E-Mail: jhazelton@vanalstynepl.lib.tx.us.

HAZELTON, PENNY ANN, law librarian, educator; b. Yakima, Wash., Sept. 24, 1947; d. Fred Robert and Margaret (McLeod) Pease; m. Norris J. Hazelton, Sept. 12, 1971; 1 child, Victoria MacLeod. BA cum laude, Linfield Coll., 1969; JD, Lewis and Clark Law Sch., 1975; M in Law Librarianship, U. Wash., 1976. Bar: Wash. 1976, U.S. Supreme Ct. 1982. Assoc. law libr., assoc. prof. U. Maine, 1976-78, law libr., assoc. prof., 1978-81; asst. libr. for rsch. svcs. U.S. Supreme Ct., Washington, 1981-85, law libr., 1985, U. Wash., Seattle, 1985—, prof. law, assoc. dean libr. and computing svcs., 1985—. Tchr. legal rsch., law librarianship, Indian law; cons. Maine Adv. Com. on County Law Librs., Lawyers Coop. Pub., 1993-94, Marquette U. Sch. Law, 2002, Georgetown U. Law Ctr., 2004. Author: Computer Assisted Legal Research: The Basics, 1993; author: (with others) Washington Legal Researcher's Deskbook, 3d edit., 2002; contbr. articles to legal jours.; gen. editor Specialized Legal Rsch. (Aspen). Recipient Disting. Alumni award U. Wash., 1992. Mem. ABA (sect. legal edn. and admissions to bar, chair com. on librs. 1993-94, vice chair 1992-93, 94-95, com. on law sch. facilities 1998—), Am. Assn. Law Schs. (com. law librs. 1991-94), Law Librs. New Eng. (sec. 1977-79, pres. 1979-81), Am. Assn. Law Librs. (program chmn. ann. meeting 1984, exec. bd. 1984-87, v.p. 1989-90, pres. 1990-91, program co-chair Insts. 1983, 95), Law Librs. Soc. Washington (exec. bd. 1983-84, v.p., pres. elect 1984-85), Law Librs. Puget Sound, Wash. State Bar Assn. (chair editl. adv. bd.), Wash. Adv. Coun. on Librs., Westpac. Office: U Wash Marian Gould Gallagher Law Libr William H Gates Hall Box 353025 Seattle WA 98195 Office Phone: 206-543-4089. Business E-Mail: pennyh@u.washington.edu.

HAZEN, PAUL MANDEVILLE, banker; b. Lansing, Mich., 1941; married. BA, U. Ariz., 1963; MBA, U. Calif., Berkeley, 1964. Asst. mgr Security Pacific Bank, 1964-66; v.p. Union Bank, 1966-70; chmn. Wells Fargo Realty Advisors, 1970-76, with San Francisco, 1979—2001, exec. v.p., mgr. Real Estate Industries Group, 1979-80, mem. exec. office Real Estate Industry Group, 1980, vice-chmn. Real Estate Industries Group, 1980-84, pres., chief oper. officer Real Estate Industries Group, 1984—, also dir. Real Estate Industries Group, 1984—; pres., treas. Wells Fargo Mortgage & Equity Trust, San Francisco, 1977-84; with Wells Fargo & Co., San Francisco, 1978—2001, from exec. v.p. to vice-chmn., pres., chief operating officer, 1981—95, chmn, CEO, 1995-2000, chmn. bd. dirs., Accel-Kohlbert, Kravis, Roberts and Co., Menlo Park, Calif., 2001—. Trustee Wells Fargo Mortgage & Equity Trust; bd. dirs. Pacific Telesis Group, Safeway Inc., Phelps Dodge Corp., Xstrata AG, E.piphany; dep. chmn. Vodafone. Office: Accel Kohlberg Kravis Roberts and Co 2500 Sand Hill Rd Ste 100 Menlo Park CA 94205

HAZEN, ROBERT MILLER, research scientist, writer; b. Rockville Centre, NY, Nov. 1, 1948; s. Dan Francis and Dorothy Ellen (Chapin) Hazen; m. Margaret Hindle, Aug. 9, 1969; children: Benjamin Hindle, Elizabeth Brooke. BS, SM, MIT, 1971; PhD, Harvard U., 1975. NATO fellow U. Cambridge, England, 1975—76; rsch. sci. Geophys. Lab., Carnegie Instn., Washington, 1976—; Robinson prof. earth sci. George Mason U., Washington, 1990—. Author: Comparative Crystal Chemistry, 1982, Music Men, 1987, The Breakthrough, 1988, Keepers of the Flame, 1991, Why Aren't Black Holes Black?, 1997, The Diamond Makers, 1999, The Sciences, 2000, Physics Matters, 2003, Genesis: The Scientific Quest for Life's Origins, 2005; co-author: Science Matters, 1990; contbr. articles to profl. jours.; musician (trumpeter): Nat. Gallery Orch., also recs. Recipient Deems Tayor award, ASCAP, 1989, Wood Sci. Writing prize, 1998. Fellow: AAAS, Mineral Soc. Am. (editor, coun. pres., Mineral Soc. Am. award 1982, Disting. Lectr.); mem.: Internat. Guild Trumpeters, History of Sci. Soc., Am. Chem. Soc. (Ipatief prize 1985), Am. Geophys. Union, Phi Lambda Upsilon, Sigma Xi. Avocations: volleyball, ballroom dancing, string quartets. Office: Geophys Lab 5251 Broad Branch Rd NW Washington DC 20015-1305 Business E-Mail: r.hazen@gl.ciw.edu.*

HAZEN, SAMUEL N, corporate financial executive; m. Glenna Hazen. B in fin., U. Ky., 1982; MBA, U. Nevada, 1988. Various positions HCA, 1983—; pres. Western group HCA Inc., 2002—. Office: HCA Inc 1 Park Pl Nashville TN 37203

HAZEN, WAYNE ESKETT, retired physicist; b. Three Rivers, Mich., Feb. 8, 1914; s. Wirt Mandeville and Elta (Brewer) Hazen; m. Jean Mary Shearer, Aug. 19, 1939; children: Priscilla, Gretchen, Virginia, Eric. BSc, MIT, 1936; PhD, U. Calif., Berkeley, 1941. Asst. prof. U. Calif., Berkeley, 1941—47; prof. physics U. Mich., Ann Arbor, 1948—84, ret., 1984, prof. emeritus, 1984—. Smith-Mundt prof. Am. U., Beirut, 1958—59; vis. prof. U. Leeds, England, 1972—84; cons. Agy. Internat. Devel., Siliguri, India, 1966. Author: Physics; contbr. articles to profl. jours. Fellow Guggenheim fellow, MIT, 1948; grantee, Imperial Coll., London, 1954; scholar Fulbright Com. scholar, Ecole Polytechnique, Paris, 1953. Fellow: Am. Phys. Soc. Achievements include development of of first measurement of the mass of a created elementary particle, the muoh, and later, its spin of 1/2; research in on cosmic rays and their interactions. Avocations: sailing, skiing, mountain backpacking, travel, home repair and construction. Office: Univ of Mich Dept Physics Ann Arbor MI 48109

HAZEN, WILLIAM A., secondary school educator; b. Grand Forks, N.D., Jan. 16, 1938; s. Gordon Bradford Hazen and Catherine Ellen Vassau; m. Frances Dee Pound, Dec. 21, 1964 (div. June 8, 1982); 1 child, Stephen James; m. Rachael A. Smith, Jan. 2, 1987. BA in History, U. Wash., 1960; MA in Edn., Chapman U., 1975; JD, San Joaquin Coll. Law, 1986. Bar: Calif. 1986; life diploma edn. Calif., 1971. Tchr. Hanford (Calif.) H.S., 1964—87; lawyer Law Offices of Steve Barnes, Hanford, 1987—89; tchr. Kings County Supt. Schs., Hanford, 1989—2002. Mem. state coun. edn. Calif. Tchrs. Assn., 1970—73, polit. edn. cons., 1972—74; chmn. resolutions com. Spkr. of Ho. Dels., Calif. Coun. for the Social Studies, 1971—72. Active State Dem. Ctrl. Com., 1975, 1977, 1979, Kings County Dem. Ctrl. Com., 1974—79, sec., 1974—75, vice chmn., 1975—76, chmn., 1977—78; pres. Ken Knudson Meml. Scholarship Fund, 1980—. Capt. U.S. Army, 1960—68. Mem.: Hanford Bonsai Soc., Taoist Temple Preservation Soc. Democrat. Avocations: travel, sailing, reading. Home: 235 W Amber Way Hanford CA 93230

HAZLEHURST, JOHN LIVINGSTON, surgeon; b. Wilmington, N.C., July 14, 1931; s. John Livingston Jr. and Elizabeth McLean (Graham) H.; m. Shirley Lord Coxe, Sept. 5, 1953 (dec. Apr. 8, 2000); children: Elizabeth Graham, John L. IV; m. Margaret S. Pennell, Nov. 4, 2000. AB, U. N.C., 1952, MD, 1956. Diplomate Am. Bd. Surgery. Commd. capt. USAF, 1958, advanced through grades to maj., 1964; pvt. practice surgery Asheville, NC, 1966—2000; surgeon VA Med. Ctr., Asheville, NC, 2004. Bd. dirs. Ashville Fed. Savs. & Loan; chief of staff St. Joseph Hosp., Ashville, 1974. Mem. dist. selection com. Morehead Scholarship, 1978-90. Morehead scholar Morehead Found., U. N.C., Chapel Hill, 1952-56. Fellow Am. coll. Surgeions, Southeastern Surgical Congress; mem. N.C. Surgical Assn., AMA, Civitan Club. Republican. Episcopal. Avocations: golf, travel, fishing, piano. Home: 11 Deerfield Rd Asheville NC 28803-3011

HAZLEHURST, ROBERT PURVIANCE, JR., lawyer; b. Spartanburg, S.C., Jan. 7, 1919; s. Robert Purviance and Lottie Lee (Nicholls) H.; m. Mary Kierulff, Feb. 20, 1947 (dec. July 1971); children: Ellen Hazlehurst Courtney, Charlotte Hazlehurst Leonesio, Anne Hazlehurst Goldberg; m. Dorothy Wilson Deemer, Jan. 7, 1972. AB, Princeton U., 1940; LL.B., Yale U., 1947. Bar: N.J. 1947. Since practiced in Newark and Morristown; ptnr. Pitney, Hardin, Kipp & Szuch, 1952-89. Bd. dirs. Princeton Fund, 1966-71, chmn. ann. giving campaign, 1967-68 Sec., trustee Greater Newark Hosp. Devel. Fund; trustee Kent Pl. Sch., Summit, N.J., 1960-70; trustee, v.p. Silver Hill Found., New Canaan, Conn., 1973-85; trustee United Hosps. Newark, 1958-73, pres., 1970-73. Served to capt. USAAF, 1942-45. Mem.: Short Hills (N.J.), Nassau (N.J.). Home and Office: 38 Sinclair Ter Short Hills NJ 07078-1714

HAZLETON, RICHARD A., chemicals executive; b. 1941; Pres., ceo Dow Corning Corp, Midland, Mich., 1965—, chmn., CEO. Former pres. Midland Jr. Achievement, Midland Co. United Way; dir. Chemical Bank and Trust Co.; pres., CEO Charles J. Strosacker Found. Office: Dow Corning Corp PO Box 994 Midland MI 48686-0994*

HAZLETT, COLLEEN MARIE, elementary school educator; d. Sheila Hazlett. AA, L.A. (Calif.) Valley Coll., 1983; BS, Calif. State U., Hayward, Calif., 1986, cert. in Tchg., 1994. Tchr. phys. edn. Calvin Simmons Jr. H.S., Oakland, Calif., 1992—94, Hayward (Calif.) Unified Sch. Dist., 1994—96, Richmond (Calif.) H.S., 1996—97, James Logan H.S., Union City, Calif., 1997—2000, Searles Elem. Sch., Union City, Calif., 2000—. Head coach water polo James Logan H.S., Union City, Calif., 1997—2000; head coach swimming Castro Valley (Calif.) H.S., 1987—89; head coach water polo Calif. H.S., San Ramon, Calif., 1990—90. Named Nat. Champion, U.S. Water Polo, 1982, U.S. Masters Swimming, 1999, 2001; recipient Outstanding Phys. Edn. Program award, CAPHERD-North Bay Area, 1992. Avocations: water polo, swimming, coaching. Office: Searles Elementary School 33629 15th ST Union City CA 94587 Office Phone: 510-471-2772. Office Fax: 510-471-8420. Personal E-mail: colleen_hazlett@nhusd.k12.ca.us.

HAZLETT, DAVID LAWRENCE, social studies educator; b. Rock Island, Ill., Nov. 20, 1956; s. Albert Dale and Orpha Ellen Hazlett; m. Theresa Ann Wright, June 21, 1997; children: Dahlton, Jennifer. BSc with distinction, U. So. Colo., Pueblo, 1978, BA with spl. distinction, 1980; MA, U. Colo., Colo. Springs, 1984. Cert. Colo. Profl. Tchrs. Lic. Social studies tchr. El Paso County Sch. Dist. 8, Fountain, Colo., 1980—. Mentor tchr. El Paso County Sch. Dist. 8, Fountain, Colo., 1997—; adj. prof. U.S. history Colo. State U., Pueblo, 1980—; in-svc. workshop presenter Fountain-Ft. Carson HS, Fountain, Colo., 2004. Vol. coach Colo. Springs Sch. Dist. 11, 1992—96, El Paso County Sch. Dist. 8, Fountain, Colo., 2002—. Named Disting. Tchr., El Paso County Sch. Dist. #8, 2005; recipient Tchr. Yr., Wal-Mart, 2002. Mem.: Orgn. History Tchrs., Am. Hist. Assn., Colo. HS Coaches Assn. (Svc. award 2000, 2004). Non-Denom. Christian. Avocations: travel, reading. Home: 11115 Peaceful Valley Rd Colorado Springs CO 80925 Office: Fountain Ft Carson HS 900 Jimmy Camp Rd Fountain CO 80817 Business E-Mail: dhazlett@ffc8.org.

HAZLETT, MARK A., lawyer; b. N.Y.C., Aug. 18, 1948; BA, Stanford U., 1970, JD, 1973. Bar: Hawaii 1973. Ptnr. Cades Schutte LLP, Honolulu. Mem. adv. com. to Commr. of Fin. Insts., 1984-86; adj. prof. law U. Hawaii Law Sch., 19952—2001. Co-editor: Hawaii Commercial Real Estate Manual, 1988; co-editor, co-author: Hawaii Real Estate Financing Manual, 1990, Hawaii Real Estate Law Manual, 1997. Mem. ABA, Hawaii State Bar Assn. (dir. fin. svcs. divsn. 1982-83, chmn. real property and fin. svcs. sect. 1984, bd. dirs. 1982-98). Office: Cades Schutte LLP PO Box 939 1000 Bishop St Honolulu HI 96808

HAZLETT, WILLIAM C., band director, trombonist; b. Pitts., Oct. 11, 1964; s. Charles G. and Patricia M. Hazlett. BA in Music Edn., Fla. State U., Tallahassee, 1989—2000; MA in Music Edn., U. NC, Jacksonville, 1996. Cert. tchr. 1989. Dir. bands Arlington Mid. Sch., Jacksonville, 1989—2000, Providence Sch., Jacksonville, 2000—. Trombonist St. John River City Band, Jacksonville, 1989—, Premiere Brass Quintet, Jacksonville, 1995—; orchestra dir. Arlington Baptist Ch., Jacksonville, 1994—96; bass ensemble dir. Arlington Meth. Ch., 2002—. Music arranger (wind ensemble) Sinfonia for Solo Trombone & WE, 2005. Mem.: Fla. Bandmasters Assn. Avocations: hiking, scuba diving, fishing, skiing, reading. E-mail: bhazlett@prov.org.

HAZUDA, HELEN PAULINE, sociologist, educator; b. San Francisco, Oct. 20, 1943; d. Alexander William and Dolores Underwood (Green) H.; children: Ann Elizabeth Richter, Sean. BA in Sociology and Philosophy, Incarnate Word Coll., 1965, MA in Edn. and History, 1968; PhD in Sociology, U. Tex., 1975. Asst. prin. Incarnate Word H.S., San Antonio, 1967-71; discipline head for curriculum, instrn., dir. bilingual edn. Our Lady the Lake U., San Antonio, 1976-79; asst. prof. clin. medicine in medicine and psychiatry U. Tex. Health Sci. Ctr., San Antonio, 1980-88, assoc. prof. medicine dept. medicine and psychiatry, 1988-96, prof. medicine dept. medicine and psychiatry, 1996—. Del. Gov's White House Conf. Children and Youth, Austin, 1970; admissions com. med. sch. U. Tex. Health Sci. Ctr., San Antonio, 1986-91, med. humanities curriculum planning com., 1989-91, tech. adv. panel for clin. and epidemiological rsch., 1991—; faculty mem. Ctr. Ethics and the Humanities in Health Care, 1992—, assoc. dir. Med. Humanities Course, 1997-98, Instnl. Rev. Bd., 1998—, dep. chair, 1999—; doctoral dissertation com. Sch. Nursing, 1992-93, adj. asst. prof. medicine and psychiatry, 1979-80; lectr. Incarnate Word Coll., San Antonio, 1971-72; cons. San Luis Valley Health and Aging Study/U. Colo. Health Sci. Ctr., Denver, 1992—; mem. nat. adv. panel RMC Rsch. Corp., 1977-81; mem. ad hoc study section NIH, 1988, mem. clin. applications and prevention adv. com. divsn. epidemiology and clin. applications Nat. Heart, Lung and Blood Inst., 1991-94, chair behavioral medicine working group, 1993-94, task force on rsch. in epidemiology and prevention cardiovascular disease, 1993-94; reviewer grants and proposals; mem. working group on epidemiology of hypertension in Hispanic-Ams., Native Ams., and Asian/Pacific Islanders-Ams., 1993-94; co-chair NHLBI Conf. socioeconomic status and cardiovascular health and disease, 1995, data and safety monitoring bd. multi-ethnic study atherosclerosis, 1999—, mem. external adv. group study of women's health issues, 1999—; cons. McDonnell-Douglas Automation Co., St. Louis, 1969-78, Devel. Assocs., 1975-77; spkr. and presenter in field. Contbr. articles to profl. jours. Panelist San Antonio Cmty. Symposium on the Changing Role Women in Personal and Profl. Life, 1976; resource person Leadership San Antonio, 1976; co-chair Working Women in Am.: Where Are They and Why are They There?, 1976-77; judge Hobby Middle Sch. Sci. Fair, San Antonio, 1984, John Jay H.S. Sci. Fair, San Antonio, 1987, Alamo Area Regional Sci. Fair, San Antonio, 1987; alumnae bd. dirs. Incarnate Word H.S., San Antonio, 1986-89; pledge vol. Womens Faculty Assn., San Antonio, 1991. U.S. Seminar on the Epidemiology and Prevention Cardiovascular Disease fellow, Lake Tahoe, Calif., 1983; instl. rsch. grantee U. Tex. Health Scis. Ctr./Hogg Found. for Mental Health, Austin, 1981-82; grantee Am. Heart Assn., 1983-84, Morrison Trust Found., 1986-87, NIH, 1979—, Nat. Cancer Inst., 1985-89. Mem. Sociol. Assn., Soc. for Behavioral Medicine, Am. Diabetes Assn., Soc. for Epidemiol. Rsch., Am. Heart Assn. (mem. coun. on cardiovasc. epidemiology), Am. Soc. Bioethics and Humanities, Gerontol. Soc. Am., Acad. Behavioral Medicine Rsch., Gerontol. Soc. Am., Phi Kappa Phi, Kappa Gamma Phi, Alpha Chi, Alpha Lambda Delta. Avocations: hiking, horseback riding, reading, travel, music. Office: U Tex Health Sci Ctr Dept Medicine/Epidemiology MC 7873 7703 Floyd Curl Dr San Antonio TX 78229-3900

HAZZARD, SHIRLEY, author; b. Sydney, Australia, Jan. 30, 1931; d. Reginald and Catherine (Stein) Hazzard.; m. Francis Steegmuller, Dec. 22, 1963 (dec. Oct. 1994). Ed., Queenwood Sch., Sydney, 1946. With Combined Services Intelligence, Hong Kong, 1947—48, U.K. High Commr. Office, Wellington, New Zealand, 1949—50, UN (gen. svc. category), N.Y.C., 1952—61. Boyer lectr., Australia, 1984, 88. Author: Cliffs of Fall and other stories, 1963; (novels) The Evening of the Holiday, 1966, People in Glass Houses, 1967, The Bay of Noon, 1970, The Transit of Venus, 1980, History Defeat of an Ideal: A Study of the Self Destruction of the UN, 1973, History Countenance of Truth, 1990; (novel) The Great Fire, 2003 (Nat. Book award, 2003); (memoir) Greene on Capri, 2000. Trustee N.Y. Soc. Libr. Named Hon. Citizen Capri, 2000; recipient Lit. Award, Nat. Inst. Arts and Letters, 1966, First prize, O. Henry Short Story Awards, 1976, Cir. Award for Fiction, Nat. Book Critics, 1981, Clifton Fadiman Medal for Lit., 2001, Nat. Book Award for Fiction, 2003, Medal of Honor, Nat. Arts Club Lit., 2004, Mary McCarthy award, Bard Coll., 2004, Miles Franklin award, Australia, 2004; Guggenheim Fellow, 1974. Fellow Royal Soc. Lit.; mem. AAAL (William Dean Howells medal, 2004), Nat. Arts and Sci., Century Club, N.Y.C. Address: 200 E 66th St Apt C1705 New York NY 10021-9187

HAZZARD, SUSAN PETERS, elementary school educator; b. Cleve., May 17, 1946; d. John Dennis and Dorothy Amanda (Tydeman) Peters; 1 child, Sheri Lynn. BA, Purdue U., 1968, MS, 1974. Grad. teaching asst. Purdue U., West Lafayette, Ind.; elem. tchr. Tippecanoe Sch. Corp., Lafayette, Ind., West Lafayette Community Sch. Corp. Presenter Ind. Tchrs. Writing Conf; co-author Education as Adventure Lessons from the Second Grade. Grantee. Mem. NEA, Nat. Coun. Tchrs. English, Nat. Reading Assn., Ind. Tchrs. Assn., West Lafayette Edn. Assn., Alpha Delta Kappa, Kappa Delta Pi, Delta Kappa Gamma.

HAZZARD, WILLIAM RUSSELL, geriatrician, educator; b. Ann Arbor, Mich., Sept. 5, 1936; s. Albert Sidney and Florence Bernice (Woolsey) Hazzard; m. Ellen Bennett Friedman, June 10, 1961; children: Susan Lovejoy Roque, Russell Holden, Rebecca Cornell Oliver, Daniel Bennett. AB, Cornell U., 1958, MD, 1962. Diplomate Am. Bd. Internal Medicine, Am. Bd. Geriatrics. Resident in internal medicine U. Wash. Sch. Med. and Affiliated Hosps., Seattle, 1966—67, fellow in endocrinology and metabolism, 1965—66, 1967—69; from instr. to prof. medicine U. Wash., Seattle, 1969—82, dir. Northwest Lipid Rsch. Clinic, 1972—78; investigator Howard Hughes Med. Inst., U. Wash., Seattle, 1972—80; chief divsn. gerontology and geriatric medicine, 1978—82; prof. medicine, assoc. dir. dept. medicine Johns Hopkins Med. Instns., Balt., 1982—86, dir. ctr. on aging, 1983—86; prof., chmn. dept. internal med. Bowman Gray Sch. Medicine of Wake Forest U., Winston-Salem, NC, 1986—98; dir. J. Paul Sticht Ctr. on Aging of Wake Forest U., Winston-Salem, NC, 1987—97; sr. adv. J. Paul Ctr. On Aging of Wake Forest U., 1998—; prof. medicine U. Wash., Seattle, 1999—; dir. geriatrics and extended care VA Puget Sound Health Care Sys., 1999—. Vis. lectr., hon. sr. registrar Oxford (Eng.) U., 1977—78, St. Thomas Sch. Medicine, London, 1977—78; dir. sect. gerontology and geriatric medicine VA Puget Sound Health Care Sys., Seattle, Tacoma, Wash., 1999—. Editor: Principles of Geriatric Medicine and Gerontology, 1984, 1989, 1993, 1999, 2003; contbr. over 200 articles to jours. in field. Lt. USNR, 1963—65. Fellow: ACP; mem.: Coun. on Aging (mem. nat. adv. coun. 1995—99), Nat. Inst. on Aging (aging rev. com. 1990—94, Geriatric Medicine Acad. award 1980), Am. Clin. and Climatol. Assn., Assn. Am. Physicians, Am. Soc. Clin. Investigation (mem. emeritus), Am. Fedn. Biomed. Rsch. (mem. emeritus), Am. Heart Assn. (Coun.on Arterosclerosis), Gerontol. Soc. Am. (chmn. clin. med. sect. 1984), Am. Geriatrics Soc. (bd. dirs. 1988—94, pres. 1993), Inst. Medicine of NAS. Avocations: gardening, conservation and nature study, music, athletics. Home: 3515 E Conover Ct Seattle WA 98122-6426 Office: VA Puget Sound Health Care Sys Geriatric Extended Care 1660 S Columbian Way Seattle WA 98108-1532 E-mail: william.hazzard@med.va.gov.

H'DOUBLER, FRANCIS TODD, JR., surgeon; b. Springfield, Mo., June 18, 1925; s. Francis Todd and Alice Louise (Bemis) H'D; m. Joan Louise Huber, Dec. 20, 1951 (dec. Dec. 1983); children: Julie H'Doubler Thomas and Sarah H'Doubler Muegge (twins), Kurt, Scott; m. Marie Ruth Duckworth, Jan. 18, 1986 Student, Washington U., St. Louis, 1943, Miami U., Oxford, Ohio, 1943-44; BS, U. Wis., 1946, MD, 1948. Intern Milw. Hosp., 1948-49; resident in surgery U.S. Naval Hosp., Oakland, Calif., 1950-51; practice medicine specializing in alternative medicine Springfield, Mo., 1952—; mem. courtesy staff St. John's Hosp., Springfield, L.E. Cox Hosp., Springfield. Bd. dirs. Union Planters Bank. Active Singing Doctors; chmn. fundraising drive YMCA, 1960-61, Sch. Bond and Tax Levy Com., 1958, Greene County Rep. Com., 1974-75; past bd. trustees Shriners Hosps., past chmn. spinal cord injury com., past chmn. rsch. com., past chmn. long range planning com., emeritus mem. rsch. com.; mem. Commn. to Reapportion Mo. Senate, 1971, Rep. State Fin. Com., 1972-75, steering com. Wilson's Creekl Battlefield Nat. Park, 1951-61, pres.'s adv. coun. Sch. Ozarks, Point Lookout, Mo., 1975-89; trustee Cottey Coll., Nevada, Mo., past bd. chmn.; bd. trustees Forest Inst. With USNR, 1943-46, 49-51. Decorated Bronze Star with V, Purple Heart with oak leaf cluster; recipient Disting. Service award Mo. Jaycees, 1959; Humanitarian award S.W. Mo. Drug Travelers Assn., 1971; named Young Man of Yr., City of Springfield, 1959 Fellow Am. Coll. Nuclear Medicine (founder's group); mem. AMA, Greene County Med. Assn., Mo. Med. Soc., Southwestern Surg. Congress, Mo. Surg. Assn., Soc. Nuclear Medicine, Am. Thyroid Assn., Springfield Jr. C. of C. (past pres.), Springfield C. of C., DAV, VFW, SAR, Am. Legion, Green Gang (co-founder), Sigma Nu (Outstanding Alumnus nat. award 1980), Nu Sigma Nu. Clubs: Hickory Hills Country. Lodges: Mason (33 deg.), Shriners (imperial potentate 1980-81), Red Cross of Constantine, Order DeMolay Legion Honor (hon.), Royal Order Scotland. Presbyterian.

HE, HUI, energy executive; arrived in U.S., 1992; m. Yumei Ning; children: Michael, Albert. BS, U. Sci. and Tech. of China, Hefei, 1992; MPhil, Yale U., 1994, PhD, 1998. Rsch. asst. Yale U., New Haven, 1992—98; rsch. assoc. U. Md. Balt. County, Balt., 1998—2000; sr. scientist Raytheon, Lanham, Md., 2000—01; sr. quantitative analyst BP, Houston, 2001—. Contbr. articles to profl. publs. Office: BP 501 Westlake Park Blvd Houston TX 77079 Office Phone: 281-366-4206. Office Fax: 281-366-7909. Personal E-mail: hui.he@aya.yale.edu. E-mail: hui.he@bp.com.

HE, JI XIANG, ecologist; b. Jilin, China, Jan. 6, 1961; arrived in U.S., 1993; s. Tong Xin He and Chun Lan Wang; m. Hong Liu, May 4, 1987; 1 child, Xiaomeng. BS, Shanghai U. Fisheries, 1982; MS, SUNY, Syracuse, 1996, PhD, 1999. Rsch. asst. Chinese Acad. Scis. Inst. Subtropical Agr., Changsha, China, 1982—85, rsch. assoc., 1986—94; sea grant fellow NY Sea Grant Inst., Syracuse, 1995—99; postdoctoral rsch. assoc. SUNY Coll. Environ. Sci. and Forestry, Syracuse, 2000—01; postdoctoral fellow zoology dept. Toronto (Can.) U., 2002; rsch. fishery biologist Mich. Dept. Natural Resources, Alpena, 2002—; adj. faculty mem. fish and wildlife dept. Mich. State U., East Lansing, 2003—. Leader fed. aid long-term rsch. project assessment of lake trout stocks in Lake Huron, Alpena, 2002—; peer reviewer jours. in field. Contbr. articles to profl. jours. Postdoctoral fellow, Nat. Sci. and Engring. Rsch. Coun., Toronto, 2002. Mem.: AAAS, Internat. Assn. Gt. Lakes Rsch., Am. Fisheries Soc., Am. Inst. Biol. Scis., Ecol. Soc. Am., Am. Soc. Limnology and Oceanography. Avocation: reading. Office: Mich Dept Natural Resources 160 E Fletcher St Alpena MI 49707

HE, LI-MING, environmental scientist; s. Zai-Sheng He and Yuf-Feng Weng; m. Min Lu, Mar. 8, 1985; children: Lucy, Ginny Ho. BS, Zhejiang Forestry U., China, 1982; MS, Zhejiang U., 1987; PhD, Va. Tech, 1995. Cert. profl. soil scientist. Rschr. Scripps Instn. Oceanography, San Diego, 1995—98, Los Alamos Nat. Lab., 1989—99; rsch. scientist San Diego State U. Found., 1999—2002; adj. prof. San Diego State U./Space and Naval Warfare Sys. Ctr., 1999—2003; environ. health specialist County of San Diego, 2002—. Author over 40 publications including journal articles, book chapters, and reports. County dry weather monitoring coord.; chair dry weather monitoring work group; mem. deacon bd. Chinese Bible Ch. of San Diego, 2002—04. Fellow, Va. Tech, 1994. Mem.: AAAS, Am. Geophys. Union, Internat. Neural Network Soc., Am. Chem. Soc., Phi Kappa Phi. Achievements include patents for advanced calibration algorism for oil content monitor; invention of advanced oil content monitor; advanced biological agent detector; discovery of uranium interaction with bacterial biopolymers; research in metal binding with spores; first to application of artificial neural networks to oil content monitors and water quality prediction; discovery of evidence of survival and growth of fecal indocators bacteria in southern Calif. Office: County of San Diego 9325 Hazard Way San Diego CA 92123 Office Fax: 858-495-5263. Business E-Mail: liming.he@sdcounty.ca.gov.

HE, LIN, chemistry professor; arrived in U.S., 1996; BSc in Chemistry, Peking U., 1996; PhD in Analytical Chemistry, Pa. State U., 2000. Scientist SurroMed, Inc., 2000—02; sr. scientist Nanoplex Technologies, Inc., 2002—03; asst. prof. NC State U., Raleigh, 2003—. Presenter in field. Contbr. articles to profl. jours. Mem.: AAAS, Am. Soc. Mass Spectrometry, Am. Chem. Soc., Sigma Xi. Achievements include patents in field. Office: NC State U Dept Chemistry 317 Partners III CB 8204 Raleigh NC 27695-8204

HE, MIN, mathematics professor; d. Baiwen He and Xueying Wu; m. Yidong Chen; 1 child, Kristy Xing Chen. BS (hon.), Northease Normal U., 1982, MS (hon.), 1984; PhD (hon.), So. Ill. U., 1994. Instr. Ne Normal U., Changchun, China, 1984—88; lectr. So. Ill. U., Carbondale, 1994—95; asst. prof. Kent State U. Trumbull, Warren, Ohio, 1995—2000, assoc. prof., 2001—. Author: Stability Theory In Ordinary Differential Equations; contbr. articles to profl. jours. Pres. Chinese Assn. Greater Youngstown Area, Ohio, 2001—03. Fellow, So. Ill. U., 1991—92; grantee, Assn. Women Math., 1997. Mem.: Assn. for Women Math., Math. Assn. Am., Am. Math. Soc. Avocations: reading, music, travel, cooking, gardening. Office: Kent State University Trumbull 4314 Mahoning Avenue Nw Warren OH 44483 Business E-Mail: mhe@kent.edu.

HEACOCK, DONALD DEE, social worker; b. Anthony, Kans., Feb. 21, 1934; s. C.W. and Thelma Olive (Hilton) H.; m. Margaret Newberry, Sept. 4, 1953; children: Teresa Ellen, Mark Dee. AB, Washburn U., 1956; BD cum laude, United Sem., 1959; MSW, Barry Coll., 1971; ThD, Slidell Bapt. Sem., 1999. Ordained priest Episcopal Ch., 1965; diplomate in clin. social work. Parish minister St. John's Ch., Clinton, Mich., 1961-66; chaplain Margarita, Canal Zone, 1966-69; tchr. Christ Ch. Acad. Secondary Sch., Colon, Panama, 1966-69; counselor South Fla. Neighborhood Youth Corp., Miami, 1969-70; chief social svc., instr. pediat. comprehensive health care U. Miami, 1971-72; asst. dir. Alpha House, Dade County, Fla., 1972-73; field supr. Barry Coll., 1972-73; marriage and family therapist Psychiat. Assocs., Shreveport, La., 1973-75; pvt. practice social work Shreveport, 1975—. Dir. Holy Cross Child Placement Agy., Inc., 1984; lectr. sociology Centenary Coll., 1981-88. With USAF, 1959-61. Mem. Am. Assn. Marriage and Family Therapy, Nat. Assn. Social Workers, Acad. Cert. Social Work, Masons, Phi Kappa Mu, Phi Gamma Mu. Home: 3820 Fairfield Ave # 113 Shreveport LA 71104 Office: Ste 357 910 Pierremont Rd Shreveport LA 71106-2063 Office Phone: 318-865-3199. Personal E-mail: domahea@aol.com.

HEAD, ALEXANDER HAMILTON, adult education educator; b. Chgo., Ill., Dec. 10, 1971; s. Henry Buchan and Suzanne Spletzer Head. MA, U. Colo., 2001, PhD in tchr. edn., 2005. Emt/ Wemt Colo., 2000; Teacher Certification Vt., 1995. Grad. instr. UCB Sch. Edn., Boulder, Colo., 2001—05; adj. instr. edn. U. Denver, 2002. Doctoral Fellowship in Edn., U. of Colo. at Boulder, 2001—04. Mem.: Phi Delta Kappa. Personal E-mail: a.head@colorado.edu.

HEAD, HAYDEN WILSON, JR., federal judge; Student, Washington and Lee U., 1962-64; BA, U. Tex., 1967, LLB, 1968. Bar: Tex. Assoc. Head & Kendrick, Corpus Christi, Tex., 1968-69, 1972-76, ptnr., 1976-81; judge US Dist. Ct. (So. Dist.) Tex., Corpus Christi, 1981—, chief judge. Chmn. 5th Cir. Com. on Criminal Pattern Jury Instr., 1986—; mem. jud. conf. U.S. Com. on Security and Facilities, 2002—. Lt. JAGC USNR, 1969—72. Fellow: Tex. Bar Found.; mem.: State Bar Tex., Am. Inn of Ct. (pres. 2001—). Office: US Dist Ct 1133 N Shoreline Blvd Corpus Christi TX 78401 Office Phone: 361-888-3142.

HEAD, JONATHAN FREDERICK, cell biologist; b. Syracuse, NY, Nov. 23, 1949; s. Arthur Everard and Lillian Myrtle (Hendra) H.; m. Priscilla Catherine Tambone, July 28, 1984; 1 child, Catherine Elizabeth. BS in Zoology, Syracuse U., 1971; MA in Biology, Bklyn. Coll., 1977; PhD in Biology, Fordham U., 1985. Rsch. asst. Naylor Dana Inst. Disease Prevention/Am. Health Found., Valhalla, NY, 1974-78, Cornell U. Med. Coll., NYC, 1978, Mt. Sinai Sch. Medicine, NYC, 1978-84, rsch. assoc., 1984-86, rsch. asst. prof., 1986-87; dir. tumor cell biology Ctr. Clin. Scis./Internat. Clin. Labs., Nashville, 1986-89; pres. Mastology Rsch. Inst., Baton Rouge, 1989—; dir. R & D Med. Thermal Diagnostics, Baton Rouge, 1995—2001, Innovative Drug Techs., Edmond, Okla., 1999—. High Complexity Clin. Lab. dir. Am. Bd. Bioanalysis, 1988—; med. lab. dir. Clin. Chemistry, State of Tenn., 1988—; clin. lab. scientist/specialist, State of La., 1995—; adj. assoc. prof. Tulane U. Sch. Medicine, New Orleans, 1989—, La. State U. Vet. Sch., BAton Rouge, 2005—; adj. prof. Delta State U., Cleveland, Miss., 1992—; rschr. and lectr. in field of cancer. Contbr. articles, abstracts and chpts. to sci. publs. Mem. State of La. Adoption Cmty. Adv. Bd., 1992-95. Mem. AAAS, Am. Assn. Cancer Rsch., Am. Soc. Clin. Oncology, Am. Acad. Thermology, Internat. Soc. Biol. Therapy Cancer, Am. Soc. Breast Disease, European Soc. Med. Oncology, NY Acad. Scis. Methodist. Home: 6144 Hagerstown Dr Baton Rouge LA 70817-3917 Office: Mastology Rsch Inst 17050 Med Ctr Dr 4th Fl Baton Rouge LA 70816 Office Phone: 225-755-3070. Business E-Mail: jhead@ehhbreastca.com.

HEAD, LOUIS ROLLIN, II, surgeon; b. Madison, Wis., Apr. 8, 1924; s. Jerome R. and Jean (Milne) H.; m. Emily Johnson, Sept. 15, 1951; children: Emily, Julia, Marjorie, Mary, Anne, Louis, Frederic. AB, Amherst Coll., 1945; MD, Johns Hopkins U., 1952. Diplomate Am. Bd. Surgery, Am. Bd. Thoracic Surgery. Intern Northwestern U. Hosp., Chgo., 1952-53; resident in gen. surgery U. Chgo., 1953-57; fellow in thoracic surgery Northwestern U., 1957-58; fellow in cardiac surgery St. Vincent's Charity Hosp., Cleve., 1958-60; assoc. in surgery Northwestern U. Med. Sch., Chgo., 1960-88; field rep. The Joint Commn. on Accreditation of Healthcare Orgns., Oakbrook Terrace, Ill., 1990-95, assoc. dir. standards interpretation, 1995-97; pvt. practice Evanston, Ill., 1997—. Author: Dancing in the Dark: Escape and Evasion During the Second World War, 2002. 2d lt. USAF, 1942—45, Italy. Rsch. grantee John Hartford Found., N.Y., 1963-71. Fellow Am. Assn. Cardiac and Thoracic Surgery, Ill. Thoracic Surg. Soc., Chgo. Surg. Soc.; mem. Air Force Escape and Evasion Soc. (life). Republican. Anglican. Achievements include development of implantable artificial lung. Avocations: tennis, fishing. Home: Apt 2-South 1107 Lake St Evanston IL 60201-4147 Office: 524 W Diversey Pkwy Chicago IL 60614-1610 Office Phone: 773-248-7246. E-mail: drlrhead@earthlink.net.

HEAD, MELVA ANN, artist; b. St. Louis, July 9, 1937; d. Melvin G. and Muriel J. (Hall) Irwin; m. Fred L. Head, Dec. 15, 1956; children: Allan L., Shawn M. Studied with, Thelma DeGoede Smith, 1973-83, Kwok Wai Lau, 1983—. V.p. gallery La Habra (Calif.) Art Assn., 1986-88, v.p. membership, 1988-89, v.p. programs, 1989-91, pres., 1991-92, dir., 1992-95. One person shows, including La Habra (Calif.) Art Assn., 1986, 90; exhibited in group shows at LA Art Assn., Chevron Oil and Field Rsch., La Habra, 1991, Long Beach (Calif.) Arts, 1994-2002, 05, Palm Springs (Calif.) Desert Mus., 1994, 97, 2000, 02-04, Gallery 825, LA, 1995-2004, Pasadena (Calif.) Presbyn. Ch., 1995-97, Guggenheim Gallery, Chapman U., Orange, Calif., 1997-98, Hollywood Los Feliz Jewish Cmty. Ctr., LA, 1997, San Bernardino County Mus., 2002, Women Painters West, 2001, 03-04, Orange County Ctr. for Contemporary Art, 2001, San Diego Watercolor Soc., 2003, 05, City of Brea (Calif.) Gallery, 2005 Mem. Artists Coun. Palm Springs, L.A. Arts, Long Beach Arts, La Habra Art Assn., Whittier Art Assn., Women Painters West. Avocations: sewing, reading. Personal E-mail: ma.head@spamex.com.

HEAD, WILLIAM CHRISTOPHER, military officer, health care administrator; b. Clarksville, Tenn., Apr. 24, 1944; s. Asbury Jefferson and Dorothy Lillian (Brown) H.; children: Sara Christine, William Christopher Jr.; m. Gwendolyn Marie More, Jan. 16, 1999. BSBA, U. Tenn., Knoxville, 1967; MHA, Duke U., 1969. Commd. 2nd lt. USAF, 1967, advanced through grades to col., 1990; asst. adminstr. USAF Hosp., Homestead AFB, Fla., 1969-72; adminstr. USAF Clinic, Greenham Common, U.K., 1972-74; asst. adminstr. USAF Regional Hosp., Lakenheath, U.K., 1974-77; instr. Sch. Health Care Scis., Sheppard AFB, Tex., 1977-79; health sys. planner Office of Surgeon Gen., Bolling AFB, 1979-80; health sys. analysis Air Firce Med. Svc. Ctr., Brooks AFB, Tex., 1980-82; chief med. sys. divsn. Sch. Health Care Scis., Sheppard AFB, 1982-86; adminstr. 325th Med. Group, Tyndall AFB, Fla., 1986-89, 1st Med. Group, Langley AFB, Va., 1989-91; dir. health care support Office of Command Surgeon, Langley AFB, 1991-92, 92-94; command surgeon Hdqrs. Air Combat Command (Provisional), Langley AFB, 1992; dep. command surgeon Hdqrs. Air Combat Command, Langley AFB, 1994-95; dep. comdr. 96th Med. Group, Eglin AFB, Fla., 1995—. Mem. cmty. adv. bd. Bay Med. Ctr. Panama City, Fla., 1986-89; mem. regional adv. bd. Am. Hosp. Assn., Chgo., 1982-85; bd. dirs. Young Execs. Healthcare Bus., Wichita Falls, Tex., 1982-86; bd. govs. Career Decision, Inc., 1993-94. Fellow Am. Coll. Healthcare Execs. (nominating com. 1995-98, chmn. bd. policy com. 1996-97, chmn. 1994-95, immediate past chmn. 1995-97, chmn.-elect 1993-94, chmn. credentialing task force 1993-94, fin. com. chmn. 1993-94, gov. dist. VIII 1989-93, strategic planning com. 1988-89, gov. dist VI 1985-86, regional adv. bd. Region 7 1982-85, regent-at-large 1982-85, many other coms., Fed. Excellence in Healthcare Leadership award 1996, Regent's Sr. Level Healthcare Exec. award 1997, 99); mem. Am. Hosp. Assn., Fla. Hosp. Assn., Tex. Hosp. Assn. Assn. Mil. Surgeons U.S. (Outstanding Fed. Svc. Adminstrs. award 1995, Ray E. Brown award 1986, Young Fed. Healthcare Adminstr. award 1984), Fla. Hosp. Assn., L.R. Jordan Healthcare Mgmt. Soc., Emerald Coast Healthcare Execs. Forum, Healthcare Adminstrs. of Tidewater, Royal Soc. Health, Air War Coll. Alumni Assn. (life), Interagy. Inst. for Fed. Health Care Execs., Duke U. Health and Hosp. Adminstrn. Alumni Assn., Profl. Soc. Svcs. Inc. (bd. govs., chmn. 1993-94), Northwest Fla. Track Club, Omicron Delta Kappa (pres. 1967), Kappa Alpha (pres. Pi chpt. 1965-67). Methodist. Avocations: scuba diving, travel, fine dining, classical music, running. Home: 2050 Kildare Cir Niceville FL 32578-7308 Office: 96 Medical Group 307 Boatner Rd Ste 114 Eglin Afb FL 32542-1391

HEAD, WILLIAM IVERSON, SR., retired chemical company executive; b. Tallapposa, Ga., Apr. 4, 1925; s. Iverson and Ruth Britain (Hubbard) H.; m. Mary Helen Ware, June 12, 1947; children: William Iverson, Connie Suzanne Head Toohey, Alan David. BS, Ga. Inst. Tech., 1949; D of Textile Engring. (hon.), World U., 1983; PhD in Indsl. Mgmt., Columbia Pacific U., 1988. Textile engr. Tenn. Eastman Co., Kingsport, 1949-56, quality control-mfg. sr. textile engr., 1957-67, dept. supt., 1968-74; supt. acetate yarn dept., bus. team, chem. divsn. Eastman Kodak Co., Kingsport, 1975-85. Info. officer U.S. Naval Acad., 1983-97; adv. bd., rsch. assoc. Point One Adv. Group, Inc., 1988-2005. Capt. USNR, 1943-83. Mem.: VFW, Internat. Soc. Philos. Enquiry (pers. cons. 1978—79, v.p. 1979—80, sr. rsch. fellow and internat. pres. 1980—85, diplomate, trustee 1986—, chmn. bd. trustees 1987—2002, Whiting Meml. award 1993), Wisdom Soc. (Award of Honor 2000), Mil. Officers Assn. Am., Sons of Confederate Vets., Sons of Revolution, Mil. Order World Wars, Naval Res. Assn., Prometheus Soc., Assn. Naval Aviation, Res. Officers Assn. (pres. Tenn. dept. 1981—82, nat. councilman 1991—98, nat. coun. steering com. 1993—97), Mensa (pres. Upper East Tenn. 1976—79). Unitarian Universalist. Achievements include patents for textured yarn technology in U.S., Great Britain, Federal Republic of Germany, Japan and France. Home: 4035 Lakewood Dr Kingsport TN 37663-3374

HEADDEN, SUSAN M., editor; Formerly reporter Indpls. Star, Indpls.; sr. editor to asst. mng. editor, spl. projects U.S. News & World Report, Washington, mng. editor, spl. projects, 2004—. Recipient Pulitzer prize for investigative reporting, 1991. Office: US News and World Report 1050 Thomas Jefferson St NW Washington DC 20007 Office Phone: 202-298-0485.

HEADLEE, RAYMOND, retired psychotherapist; b. Shelby County, Ind., July 27, 1917; s. Ortis Verl and Mary Mae (Wright) H.; m. Eleanor Case Benton, Aug. 24, 1941; children: Sue, Mark, Ann. AB in Psychology, Ind. U., 1939, A.M. in Exptl. Psychology, 1941, MD, 1944; grad., Chgo. Inst. Psychoanalysis, 1959. Diplomate: Am. Bd. Psychiatry and Neurology (examiner 1964—). Intern St. Elizabeth's Hosp., Washington, 1944-45, resident in psychiatry, 1945-46, Milw. Psychiat. Hosp., 1947-48, pres. staff, 1965-70; practice medicine specializing in psychiatry and psychoanalysis Elm Grove, Wis., 1949—; clin. asst. prof. psychiatry Med. Coll. Wis., 1958-59, clin. asso. prof., 1959-62, clin. prof., 1962-2000, chmn. dept. psychiatry, 1963-70; prof. psychology Marquette U., 1966-76; Bd. dirs. Elm Brook (Wis.) Meml. Hosp., 1969-71; ret., 2000. Author: (with Bonnie Corey) Psychiatry in Nursing, 1949, I Think, Therefore I Know, 1996; contbr. numerous articles to profl.

jours. 1st lt. Ft. Knox Armored Med. Rsch. Lab., AUS, 1945, to col. USPHS. Fellow Am. Psychiat. Assn. (life), Am. Coll. Psychiatry (emeritus); mem. State Med. Soc. Wis. (editorial dir. 1971-77), Wis. Psychiat. Assn. (pres. 1971-72), Milw. Club. *My life story represents a gradual and often difficult transition from the puritan ethic, which got me into this book, to a lighter style of living. This is what the Germans call Lebenskünstler.*

HEADLEY, CAROL ANN, elementary and secondary school educator; b. Butler, Mo., Oct. 4, 1937; d. William Harold and Fairy Anise (Hodges) Cain; m. Ralph Bruce Headley, Oct. 7, 1956; children: Kimberley Fritchie, Sandee McMillin. BS in Edn., Ctrl. Mo State Univ., Warrensburg, Mo., 1970, MS in Edn., 1975. Cert. Elem. Edn. K-8 1970, Remedial Reading K-12 1975, Learning Disabilities K-9 1975. Elem. tchr. Independence (Mo.) Sch. Dist., 1970—72, Lee's Summit (Mo.) Sch. Dist., 1972—95, substitute tchr., 1995—98, homebound tchr., 1995—97; reading tutor Laubach Literacy (K C Literacy), Kansas City, Mo., 1999—2000; adj. prof. Ctrl. Mo. State U., Warrensburg, 2000—01; substitute tchr. Lone Jack (Mo.) Sch. Dist., 2002—03, Pleasant Hill (Mo.) Sch. Dist. Mentor Mother's Refuge - Home for homeless pregnant teens, Independence, Mo., 1997—2002; presenter com. chmn. for Parents Univ. Lee's Summit Cares, Lee's Summit, Mo., 2003—, bd. mem., 2003—. Bd. mem. Hazel Dell Cmty. Ctr., Greenwood, Mo., 1993—95; mentor Lee's Summit Cmty. Ch., Lee's Summit, Mo., 1996—2000; bd. mem. Mother's Refuge (Shelter for homeless pregnant teens), Independence, Mo., 1999—2002; past. pres. Lee's Summit Internat. Reading Assn. Nominee Reading Tchr. of the Yr., Lee's Summit Internat. Reading Assn., 1989—90, 1992—93, 1995. Mem.: Lee' Summit Ret. Tchr. Assn., Mo. State Tchr. Assn., Mo. State Ret. Tchr. Assn. (life), Daughters of the Am. Revolution (regent, treas., vice regent 1990—2000, Past Chpt. Regent 1998), Daughter of the Am. Colonists (libr., treas., v.p., chaplain 1990—2003), CMSU Kappa Delta Pi Soc. (hon.). Conservative. Avocations: travel, reading, genealogy, writing. Personal E-mail: Carol55Bruce@aol.com.

HEADLEY, KATHRYN WILMA, secondary school educator; b. Grand Rapids, Mich., Mar. 10, 1940; d. William L. and Kathryn (Mekkes) H. BA, Hope Coll., 1967; MEd, Grand Valley Univ., 1981. Cert. tchr., Mich. Missionary Reformed Ch. in Am., N.Y.C., 1959—64; various ch. positions Ottawa Reformed Ch., West Olive, Mich., 1956—, Bible day camp dir., 1979—92; tchr. lang. arts/phys. edn. Jenison Pub. Schs., 1967—2002, head coach girls basketball, volleyball, 1967—78, head coach girls track, softball, 1967—73, head coach girls bowling, 1973—78, class advisor, 1983—90; numerous other sch. activities; coach girls soccer, basketball Borculo Christian Sch., Mich., 1981—88. Bd. dirs. Ottawa County Tchrs. Credit Union, Grand Haven, Mich., 1978-90, 94—, v.p., 1984-88. Mem. Mich. Edn. Assn. (rep.), NEA, Jenison Edn. Assn. (rep.), Mich. High Sch. Athletic Assn. (ofcl.), Hope Coll. Alumni Assn., Mich. Christian Endeavor Bd., Delta Kappa Gamma. Mem. Reformed Ch. in Am. Home: 9111 96th Ave Zeeland MI 49464 E-mail: kheadley@altelco.net. *Personal philosophy: After a life threatening experience following a 1982 surgery...I believe in the following quote, "I asked God for all things that I might enjoy life. He gave me life that I might enjoy all things." Each morning I wake up thanking God for another day and I try to make it a masterpiece.*

HEADLEY, MARK J., lawyer; s. Richard Jensen and Carol Ann Headley. BA in Philosophy magna cum laude, Yale U., 1981; JD, Columbia U., 1986. Bar: N.Y. 1987, U.S. Dist. Ct. (so. and ea. dists.) N.Y., U.S. Ct. Appeals (2d and DC cirs.), U.S. Supreme Ct. Law clk. to Hon. Pierre N. Leval, N.Y.C., 1986-87; assoc. Kramer, Levin, Naftalis & Frankel, N.Y.C., 1987-95; ptnr. Kramer Levin Naftalis & Frankel LLP, N.Y.C., 1996—. Editor-in-chief Columbia Law Rev., 1985-86; contbr. articles to profl. jours. James Kent scholar Columbia U. Mem. ABA, N.Y. State Bar Assn., Assn. of Bar of City of N.Y. Office: Kramer Levin Naftalis & Frankel LLP 1177 Ave of Americas New York NY 10036 Office Phone: 212-715-9119. Business E-Mail: mheadley@kramerlevin.com.

HEADRICK, DANIEL RICHARD, history and social sciences educator; b. Bay Shore, N.Y., Aug. 2, 1941; s. William Cecil and Edith (Finkelstein) H.; m. Rita Koplowitz, June 20, 1965 (dec. 1988); children: Isabelle, Juliet, Matthew; m. Kate Ezra, Aug. 23, 1992. B, Lycée de Garçons, Metz, France, 1959; BA, Swarthmore Coll., 1962; MA, Johns Hopkins U., 1964; PhD, Princeton U., 1971. Instr. history Tuskegee (Ala.) Inst., 1968-71, asst. prof., 1971-73, assoc. prof., 1973-75; assoc. prof. social scis. Roosevelt U., Chgo., 1975-82, prof., 1982—. Vis. NEH scholar Hawaii Pacific U., 2000. Author: Ejercito y Politica, 1981, The Tools of Empire, 1981, Tentacles of Progress, 1988, The Invisible Weapon, 1991, The Earth and Its Peoples, 1997, When Information Came of Age, 2000. Coll. Tchrs. fellow NEH, 1983-84, 88-89, Guggenheim fellow, 1994, Sloan fellow, 1998; recipient Faculty Achievement award Burlington No. Found., 1988, 92. Mem. Am. Hist. Assn., World History Assn. (exec. com. 1991—), Soc. for History Tech. (exec. com. 1992—). Home: 5483 S Hyde Park Blvd Chicago IL 60615-5827 Office: Roosevelt U Univ Coll 430 S Michigan Ave Chicago IL 60605-1394 E-mail: dan.headrick@att.net.

HEADRICK, THOMAS EDWARD, lawyer, educator; b. East Orange, NJ, June 28, 1933; s. Lewis Barnard and Marian Elizabeth Headrick; m. Mary Margaret Shontz, June 27, 1957; children— Trevor, Todd. BA, Franklin and Marshall Coll., 1955; LittB, Oxford (Eng.) U., 1958; LLB, Yale U., 1960; PhD, Stanford U., 1975. Bar: Conn. 1960, Calif. 1962. Asst. dir. Ansonia (Conn.) Redevel. Agy., 1959-60; law clk. to justice Wash. State Supreme Ct., Olympia, 1960-61; assoc. firm Pillsbury, Madison & Sutro, San Francisco, 1961-64; mgmt. cons. Emerson Cons., London, 1964-66, Baxter, McDonald & Co., Berkeley, Calif., 1966-67; asst. dean Stanford U. Law Sch., 1967-70; v.p. acad. affairs Lawrence U., 1970-76; dean law sch. U. at Buffalo, 1976-85, prof. law, 1976—, interim dean arts and letters faculty, 1990, disting. svc. prof., 1993—, provost, 1995-99, sr. counselor to pres., 1999, interim dean architecture and planning, 1999. Cons. NEH, NSF; legal commentator Sta. WKBW-TV, 1978-80. Author: The Town Clerk in English Local Government, 1962; co-editor Law and Policy, 1988-92. Named to, Franklin and Marshall Sports Hall of Fame, 2002. Mem. Phi Beta Kappa. Office: University at Buffalo 411 O'Brian Hall Buffalo NY 14260-1100 Business E-Mail: headrick@buffalo.edu.

HEAGARTY, MARGARET CAROLINE, retired pediatrician; b. Charleston, W.Va., Sept. 8, 1934; d. John Patrick and Margaret Caroline (Walsh) H. BA, Seton Hill Coll., 1957; BS, W.Va. Sch. Medicine, 1959; MD, U. Pa., 1961; DSc honoris causa, Iona Coll., 1989. Diplomate: Am. Bd. Pediatrics. Intern Phila. Gen. Hosp., 1961—62; resident in pediatrics St. Christopher's Hosp. for Children, Phila., 1962—64; dir. pediatric ambulatory care services N.Y. Hosp.-Cornell Med. Ctr., N.Y.C., 1969—78; dir. pediatrics Harlem Hosp. Ctr. Columbia U., N.Y.C., 1978—2000, prof. pediatrics coll. physicians & surgeons, 1987—2000, prof. emerita coll. physicians and surgeons, 2000—. Cons. Dept. HEW Promotion of Child Health, Washington; mem. Com. Community Oriented Primary Care Inst. Medicine, Washington; mem. Robert Wood Johnson Found. Program for Prepaid Managed Health Care, 1984; mem. governing council Inst. Medicine, Nat. Acad. Scis., 1986 Author: Changing the Medical Car System-Report of an Experiment, 1974, Medical Sociology: A Systems Approach, 1975, Child Health: Basics for Primary Care, 1980. Grantee Commonwealth Found., 1981, Robert Wood Johnson Found., 1983, Ctr. for Disease Control, 1985, Health Rsch. and Svc. Adminstrn., 1988, Nat. Inst. Allergy/Infectious Disease, 1988. Fellow Inst. Medicine (steering group for nat. forum on future of children and their families 1987—); mem. Ambulatory Pediatric Assn. (pres. 1976-77), Soc. Pediatric Research, Am. Pediatric Soc., Am. Acad. Pediatrics (com. on hosp. care 1988—), Assn. Pediatric Program Dirs., Nat. Bd. Med. Examiners. Home: 2520 Kingsland Ave Bronx NY 10469-6108 E-mail: mheagarty@aol.com.

HEAGGANS, RAPHAEL CHESARE, education educator; b. Kings Mountain, N.C. s. Joseph Theodore and Dorothy Seigle H. BA, Winston-Salem State U., 1994; MA, Winthrop U., 1997; EdD, W.Va. U., 2003. Cert. English tchr. Nat. Coun. Tchrs. English. Lang. arts tchr. Troutman (N.C.) Mid. Sch., 1997-98; instr. English Winston-Salem (N.C.) State U., 1998-2000; coll. instr. edn. W.Va. U., Morgantown, 2000—03. Grad. asst. W.Va. U., Morgantown, 2000-03; spkr. in field. Editor (newsletter) Bobcat Tales, 1997. DuBois fellow, 2001-2003, doctoral fellow Wash. State U. Mem. Alpha Phi Alpha. Democrat. Avocations: exercise, reading, writing, travel.

HEALD, BRUCE DAY, English and music educator, historian; b. Boston, June 5, 1935; s. Henry M. and Muriel D. (Day) H. m. Helen Peaslee, May 21, 1960; children: William Forristall III, Craig, Eric Bentley, Allyson Kaye. AA, Boston U., 1956; BS in Music Edn., Lowell State U., 1959; MA, Columbia Pacific U., 1984, PhD, 1985. Supr. music Ashland-Meredith Union 2, Meredith, N.H., 1959-64; dir. music, lectr. fine arts Belknap Coll., Center Harbor, N.H., 1963-65; dir. bands Plattsburgh (N.Y.) City Schs., 1969-70; supr. music Inter-Lakes Sch. Dist., Meredith, 1965-69, dir. music edn., 1970-77; dir. instrumental music Kennebunk (Maine) High Sch., 1977-79; prodn. mgr. Annalee Mobilitee Dolls, Meredith, 1979-81; lectr. English and journalism Moultonborough Acad., 1981-86; dir. music Congl. Ch., Laconia, N.H., 1985-86; chair English dept. Holy Trinity Sch., Laconia, 1987—2000; mentor Columbia Pacific U., 1986—; instr. music N.H. Coll., Manchester, 1988—95; historian Weirstimes Pub. Co., 1992—2001. Lectr. English lit. Plymouth State Coll., 1995-97, lectr. U.S. history Plymouth State U., 1998—. Author: Follow the Mount, 1968, 70, 93, 97, 2000, Postmaster of the Lake, 1971, Mail Service on the Lake, 1980, 2000, Steamboats in Motion, 1984, New Hampshire Learnin' Days, 1987, Boats 'n Ports I and II, 1989, Landmarks and Legacy, 1990, The Boston See Party, 1991, Reminisce the Valley, 1992, Shadows in the Window, 1995, Images of America: Meredith, 1996, Images of America: The Lakes Region of New Hampshire, 1996, vol. I and II, 1998, Images of America: The Upper Merrimack to Winnipesaukee by Rail, 1997, Images of America: Boats and Ports in Lake Winnipesaukee, vol. I and II, 1998, Images of America: The White Mountains Region by Rail, 1999, Image of America: Plymouth State College, 1999, Images of America: Stereoptic Memories of the White Mountains, 2000, Images of America: Lakes and Ponds of the Granite State, 2000, Images of Rail: The Boston and Maine in the 19th Century, 2001, Images of Rail: The Boston and Maine in the 20th Century, 2001, Images of the Civil War: N.H. in the Civil War, 2001, Images of America: Around Squam Lake, 2002, History & Guide: The Franconia Gateway, 2002, Images of Rail: Boston and Maine Locomotives, 2002, The Adventures to the Great American Railroads, 2003, Images of America: Main Streets in New Hampshire, 2003, Images of America: Meredith Then and Now, 2005, Images of Rail: Boston and Maine Trains and Services; composer: Kennebunk Concert March, The Hills of Old N.H., Moultonboro Concert March, Cascades, Trilogy. Commr. Parks and Playgrounds, Meredith, 1966-69; selectman Town of Meredith, 1971-76; mem. N.H. State Legislature, 2004—. Served with USMC, 1954-62. Mem. Masons. Republican. Home: PO Box 1052 Meredith NH 03253-1052 Office Phone: 603-279-8026. E-mail: bheald@metrocast.net.

HEALD, MORRELL, humanities educator; b. Oak Park, Ill., July 16, 1922; s. Howard Leslie and Helen (Morrell) H.; m. Barbara Legg, June 25, 1949; children: David M., Seth G., Sarah H. AB, Yale U., 1946, A.M., 1947, PhD, 1951. Instr. history Yale, 1950-53; mem. faculty Case Inst. Tech., 1953-68, assoc. prof. history, 1958-68, chmn. dept. humanities and social studies, 1959-62; prof. Am. studies Case Western Res. U., 1968-82, Samuel B. and Virginia C. Knight prof. humanities, 1982-88, prof. emeritus, 1988—, chmn. div. spl. interdisciplinary studies, 1971-78, 79-82. Vis. prof. Am. history Indian Inst. Tech., Kanpur, 1966-67; dir. Armington Research Program on Values in Children, 1978-80, chmn. adv. com., 1978-82 Author: The Social Responsibilities of Business: Company and Community, 1900-1960, 1970, Japanese edit., 1974, 2d edit., 1988, paperback edit., 2005, Transatlantic Vistas: American Journalists in Europe, 1900-1940, 1987; (with Lawrence S. Kaplan) Culture and Diplomacy: The American Experience, 1977; co-editor: The Aims and Organization of Liberal Studies, 1966; editor: Journalist At The Brink: Louis P. Lochner In Berlin, 1924-1942, 2005. Vice pres. Cleveland Heights Your Schools Com., 1962, pres., 1965; Pres. of the First Ward Democratic Club, Cleveland Heights, 1962; mem. Cleve. Heights Landmarks Commn., 1987-01. Served with AUS, 1943-45, ETO. Mem. Soc. for History of Am. Fgn. Rels., Western Res. Hist. Soc. (publs. com. 1981-89), Phi Beta Kappa. Episcopalian. Home: 10450 Lottsford Rd #4215 Mitchellville MD 20721 Office Phone: 301-925-7378.

HEALEY, DAVID LEE, investment company executive; b. Pomona, Calif., Dec. 13, 1950; s. Robert Lincoln Sr. and Bernice (Mayes) H.; children: Paul Marcus, Elaina Rose. BS, U. Tulsa, 1978, postgrad. in law, 1979-80; cert., N.Y. Inst. Fin., 1980. Sales mgr. Magnavox, Tulsa, 1978-80; dir. tng. First State Fin., Tulsa, 1980-81; asst. v.p. Prudential-Bache Securities, Tulsa, 1981-86, E.F. Hutton, Tulsa, 1986-91, UBS PaineWebber, Inc., Tulsa, 1991—. Sales cons., Tulsa, 1981—. Judge Miss Teen USA pageant, 1984; chair endowment fund adv. com. Tulsa YWCA. Sgt. USAF, 1974-78. Mem. Internat. Assn. Fin. Planners (bd. dirs. 1984), Toastmasters Internat. (speakers bur.). Republican. Baptist. Avocations: computers, auto restoration, public speaking. Home: RR 1 Box 120 Cleveland OK 74020-9729 Office: UBS 2431 E 61st St 8th Fl Tulsa OK 74136-1211

HEALEY, FRANK HENRY, retired chemicals executive; b. Worcester, Mass., Oct. 5, 1924; s. Frank H. and Elizabeth (MacGillivray) H.; m. Loretta Marguerite Finnigan, June 5, 1948; children: Steven Allan, Elaine Elizabeth, Frank Henry. AB, Clark U., 1947, PhD, 1949. Asst. prof. chemistry Lehigh U., Bethlehem, Pa., 1949-56; with Lever Bros. Co., Edgewater, N.J., 1956-88, v.p. research and devel., 1964-73, research v.p., 1973-78, v.p. research and engring., 1978-80, research v.p., dir., 1968-88; pres. Lever Research Inc., Edgewater, 1982-88. Served to lt. (j.g.) USN, 1943-46. Mem. Indsl. Rsch. Inst. (pres. 1977-78, bd. dirs. 1972-79), Assn. Rsch. Dirs., Am. Chem. Soc., Dirs. Indsl. Rsch., Am. Oil Chemists Soc., Soap and Detergent Assn. (steering com. tech. and materials divsn.), Ridgewood Country Club (sec. 1981-82, bd. dirs. 1990-94), Hobbyists Unlimited (v.p. 1994-95, pres. 1996). Home: 255 W Ridgewood Ave Ridgewood NJ 07450-3629

HEALEY, JUDITH KOLL, foundation executive; b. Alexandria, Minn., Mar. 26, 1939; d. Leo M. and Beatrice Loretta (Sanger) K.; m. Michael James Healey, Aug. 1, 1964; children: Sean, Paul, Michael Brian, Colin. BA cum laude, U. Minn., 1961, BS in Edn., 1968. Exec. dir. Joint Religion Legis. Com., Mpls., 1973-75, Minn. Council on Founds., Mpls., 1975-79; officer grants Gen. Mills Found., Mpls., 1979-81; v.p. Northwest Area Found., Mpls., 1981—. Bd. dirs. First Bank St. Paul. Author poems and fiction for various publs. Del. Dem. Nat. Conv., N.Y.C., 1976; mem. selection com. Rhodes Scholar Found., Mpls., 1984, 85, Task Force on Biomed. Ethics, Mpls., 1984-85; bd. dirs. Johnston Inst., Mpls., 1984-85; trustee Coll. St. Teresa, Winona, Minn., 1984—. Named one of Outstanding Young Women Am., 1973. Mem. Pub. Edn. Found. (trustee 1983—), Minn. Acad. Excellence Found. (trustee 1984—), Women and Founds. (bd. dirs. corp. philanthrophy 1979—, chmn. 1982-84), Women's Equity Action League (past bd. dirs.). Avocations: running, mountain climbing. Home: 4800 Fremont Ave S Minneapolis MN 55409-2209 Office: Northwest Area Found W-975 W First Bank Bldg Saint Paul MN 55101

HEALEY, KERRY MURPHY, lieutenant governor; b. Omaha, Apr. 30, 1960; d. Edward Morris and Shirley (Cumming) M.; m. Sean Michael Healey, Dec. 28, 1985; children: Alexander Edward, Averill Adair. AB in Govt., Harvard Coll., 1982; PhD in Law and Polit. Sci., Trinity Coll., Dublin, Ireland, 1991. Proctor freshman dean's office, vis. reseacher Law Sch. Harvard U., Cambridge, Mass., 1985—86; legal policy analyst ABT Assocs., Inc., Cambridge, 1986—87; pub. policy cons. Bklyn. and Boston, 1990—99; mem. Mass. Rep. State Com., 1999—; chmn. Mass. Republican Party, 2001—02; lt. gov. State of Mass., 2003—. Del. UN NGO assembly, 1994-95. Author: State and Local Experience with Drug Paraphernalia Laws, 1987, Victim and Witness Intimidation: New Developments and Emerging Responses, 1995; co-author: Compendium of Federal Justice Statistics, 1989, Handbook of Drug Control in the United States, 1990, Prosecutorial Response to Heavy Drug Case Loads, 1993. Bd. dirs., Mass. Women's Polit. Caucus, 1999-2001; bd. dirs., North Shore C.C. Found., Danvers, Mass., 1999-2002, Friends of Beverly (Mass.) Hosp., 1999-2001; co-chair North Shore United Way Campaign, Beverly, 2001, bd. dirs. YWCA, N.Y.C., 1992-95, mem. YWCA World Svc. Coun., 1992—. Grad. fellow Rotary Internat., 1983-84; rsch. grantee Mark DeWolfe Howe Fund of Harvard Law Sch., 1986. Mem. Coun. on Fgn. Rels., Harvard Club N.Y.C. (mem. schs. com. 1987-95), N.Y. Jr. League (rep. N.Y.C. ednl. priorities panel 1992-95), Cosmopolitan Club (N.Y.C.), Union Club (Boston). Republican. Office: State House Office of the Governor Room 360 Boston MA 02133 E-mail: khealey@romneyhealey.com.

HEALEY, LYNNE KOVER, editor, writer, broadcaster, educator; b. L.I., N.Y. d. R. Bascom and M Fuchs; div.; children: Christine Josepha, Lauren Teresa. BA in Comm., Rutgers U., 1983; MA in English, Drew U., 1987. Editor A.M. Best Co., Oldwick, N.J., 1985-91; communications cons. MetLife Ins. Co., 1992—2002; freelance writer, editor, 2002—. Adj. prof. English Middlesex County Coll., Edison, NJ, DeVry U., North Brunswick, NJ, Raritan Valley C. C., No. Branch, NJ, Rutgers U., New Brunswick, NJ. Bd. dirs. Women's Crisis Svcs. Mem. Meeting Planners Internat. (bd. dirs. N.J. chpt., co-chairperson com. for Give Kids the World project), Rutgers U. Alumni Assn. (exec. com.), Alpha Sigma Lambda (grad. sch. scholar 1986, bd. dirs. Rutgers chpt.). Avocations: photography, golf, dance, swimming, skiing.

HEALEY, THOMAS J., former government official, brokerage house executive; b. Balt., Sept. 14, 1942; m. Margaret Sachs Healey; children—Megan, Jeremiah AB, Georgetown U., 1964; MBA, Harvard U., 1966. Chartered fin. analyst, real estate counselor. Mgr. project fin. group Dean Witter, 1975-82; mng. dir., mgr. corp. fin. Dean Witter Reynolds Capital Markets, 1982-83; asst. sec. domestic fin. Dept. of Treasury, Washington, 1983-85; v.p. real estate Goldman Sachs & Co, N.Y.C., 1985-88, mng. dir. pension svcs. group, 1988-99, mng. dir. instl. sales and mktg., 1999-2000, adv. dir., 2001—; prin. Healey Devel. LLC, Morristown, NJ. Fellow, adj. lectr. John F. Kennedy Sch. Govt. Harvard U., 2001—. Home: Van Beuren Rd New Vernon NJ 07976 Office: Healey Devel LLC 310 South St Morristown NJ 07960 also: 85 Broad St New York NY 10004 Business E-Mail: tom.healey@healeydev.com.

HEALY, ALICE FENVESSY, psychology professor, researcher; b. Chgo., June 26, 1946; d. Stanley John and Doris (Goodman) Fenvessy; m. James Bruce Healy, May 9, 1970; 1 child, Charlotte Alexandra. AB summa cum laude, Vassar Coll., 1968; PhD, Rockefeller U., 1973. Asst. prof. psychology Yale U., New Haven, 1973-78, assoc. prof. psychology, 1978-81, U. Colo., Boulder, 1981-84, prof. psychology, 1984—. Rsch. assoc. Haskins Labs., New Haven, 1976—80; com. mem. NIMH, Washington, 1979—81; co-investigator rsch. contract USAF U. Colo., 1985—86, prin. investigator rsch. contract U.S. Army Rsch. Inst., 1986—; prin. investigator rsch. contract Naval Tng. Sys. Ctr., 1993—94; rsch. grant prin. investigator U.S. Army Rsch. Office U. Colo., 1995—2002, 2005—; rsch. grant prin. investigator NASA, 1999—. Co-author: Cognitive Processes, 2d edit., 1986; editor: Memory and Cognition, 1986—89, Experimental Cognitive Psychology and its Applications, 2005; co-editor (with S. M. Kosslyn and R. M. Shiffrin): (Essays in Honor of William K. Estes) From Learning Processes to Cognitive Processes Vol I, 1992; co-editor: (with S.M. Kosslyn and R.M. Shiffrin) From Learning Theory to Connectionist Theory: Essays in Honor of William K. Estes, Vol. II, 1992; co-editor: (with L.E. Bourne Jr.) Learning and Memory of Knowledge and Skills: Durability and Specificity, 1995, Foreign Language Learning: Psycholinguistic Studies on Training and Retention, 1998; co-editor: (with R. W. Proctor) Experimental Psychology, 2003; assoc. editor: Jour. Exptl. Psychology, 1982—84; contbr. articles to profl. jours. and chpts. to books. Recipient Sabbatical award, James McKeen Cattell Fund, 1987—88; grantee, NSF, 1977—86, 2003—, Spencer Found. Rsch., 1978—80. Fellow: AAAS (nominating com. 1988—91, chair nominating com. 1991, chair psychology sect. 1995—96), APA (chair membership com. 1992—93, exec. com. divsn. 3 2001—04, pres. 2004—05), Soc. Exptl. Psychologists; mem.: Soc. for Applied Rsch. in Memory and Cognition, Cognitive Sci. Soc., Rocky Mountain Psychology Assn. (pres. 1994—95), Soc. Math. Psychology, Psychonomic Soc. (governing bd. 1987—92, publs. com. 1989—93), Univ. Club, Sigma Xi, Phi Beta Kappa. Avocation: French pastries. Home: 840 Cypress Dr Boulder CO 80303-2820 Office: U Colo Dept Psychology 345 UCB Boulder CO 80309-0345 Office Phone: 303-492-5032. Business E-Mail: healy@colorado.edu.

HEALY, BERNADINE P., physician, educator, federal official; b. N.Y.C., Aug. 2, 1944; d. Michael J. and Violet (McGrath) Healy; m. Floyd Loop, Aug. 17, 1985; children: Bartlett Anne Bulkley, Marie McGrath Loop. AB summa cum laude, Vassar Coll., 1965; MD cum laude, Harvard Med. Sch., 1970. Diplomate Am. Bd. Med. Examiners, Am. Bd. Cardiology, Am. Bd. Internal Medicine, lic. physician Md., Ohio. Intern in medicine Johns Hopkins Hosp., Balt., 1970—71, asst. resident, 1971—72; staff fellow sect. pathology Nat. Heart, Blood & Lung Inst., NIH, Bethesda, Md., 1972—74; fellow cardiovascular div. dept. medicine Johns Hopkins U. Sch. Medicine, Balt., 1974—76, fellow dept. pathology, 1975—76, asst. prof. medicine and pathology, 1976—81, assoc. prof. medicine, 1977—82, asst. dean postdoctoral programs and faculty devel., 1979—84, assoc. prof. pathology, 1981—84, prof. medicine, 1982—84, dean Coll. Med. and Pub. Health, 1995—99, prof. internal medicine, physiology, 1995—99; active staff medicine and pathology Johns Hopkins Hosp., 1976—, dir. CCU, 1976—84; pres. ARC, 1999—2001; advisor on weapons of mass destruction & bioterrorism White House, DC, 2001—; med. & healthcare columnist, sr. writer U.S. News & World Report, 2002—. Dep. dir. Office Sci. and Tech. Policy Exec. Office of Pres., White House, Washington, 1984—85; chmn. Rsch. Inst. The Cleve. Clinic Found., 1985—91, sr. health and sci. policy advisor, 1994—95; dean Med. Sch. Ohio State U., 1995—97; dir. NIH, Bethesda, Md., 1991—93; vice-chmn. Pres.' Coun. Advisers on Sci. and Tech., 1990—91; mem. Spl. Med. Adv. Group, Dept. Vet.'s Affairs, 1990—91, chmn. adv. panel for Basic Rsch. for 1990s, Office Tech. Assessment, 1990—91, mem. NHLBI Task Force on Atherosclerosis, 1990; mem. Vis. Com. Bd. Overseers Harvard Med. Sch. and Sch. of Dental Medicine, Boston, 1986—91; councillor Harvard Med. Alumni Assn., 1987—90; mem. Nat. Adv. Bd. Johns Hopkins Ctr. for Hosp. Fin. and Mgmt., 1987—91, Bd. Overseers Harvard Coll., 1989—; chmn. Office of Tech. Assessment Panel New Devels. in Biotech., U.S. Congress, 1986—87; mem. U.S.-Brazil Panel on Sci. and Tech., 1987, White House Sci. Coun., 1988—89; cons. Nat. Heart, Lung and Blood Inst., NIH, 1976—91; mem. adv. com. to dir. NIH, 1986—91; chmn. steering com. Post-CABG Clin. Triai, 1987—91; bd. dirs. Medtronic, Inc., Mpls., Nat. City Corp., Cleve., Nova Pharms., Balt.; mem. adv. bd. Bayer Fund for Cardiovasc. Rsch., N.Y.C., 1987—89; trustee Edison BioTech. Ctr., Cleve., 1990—; chmn. Ohio Coun. on Rsch. and Econ. Devel., 1989—91; bd. dirs. Nat. City Corp., 1989—90, 1995—2001, 2003—. Editl. cons. numerous jours.:, abstract reviewer:, editl. bd.: Jour. Cardiovasc. Medicine, 1980—91, Am. Jour. Cardiology, 1981—82, Circulation, 1981—, Jour. Am. Coll. Cardiology, 1982—84, Am. Jour. Medicine, 1986—91; contbr. articles to profl. jours. Recipient Nat. Bd. Ann. award for Medicine, Med. Coll. Pa., 1983; fellow Eloise Ellery fellow, 1965—66, Stetler Rsch. fellow, 1976—77; scholar Matthew Vassar scholar, 1962—65, Harvard Nat. scholar, 1965—70. Mem.: ACP, Inst. Medicine NAS, Am. Bd. Internatl Medicine (bd. dirs. 1983—87, bd. govs. 1986—), Am. Soc. Clin. Investigation, Assn. for Women in Sci., Am. Med. Women's Assn., Internat. Acad. Pathology, Assn. Am. Med. Colls., Am. Coll. Cardiology (bd. govs. 1979—82), Am. Heart Assn. (fellow coun. on clin. cardiology, coun. on circulation, dir. 1983—84, pres. 1988—89, award 1983—84, 1990), Am. Fedn. Clin. Rsch. (pres. 1983—84), Johns Hopkins U. Soc. Scholars, Alpha Omega Alpha, Phi Beta Kappa.

HEALY, BRIDGET M., lawyer; b. Clinton, Iowa, Feb. 14, 1955; AB with honors, Brown U., 1976; JD magna cum laude, Georgetown U. Law Ctr., 1982. Assoc. Davis, Polk & Wardwell; ptnr. Strook & Strook & Lavan; atty. Becton, Dickinson & Co., Franklin Lakes, NJ, 1995—97, v.p., sec., 1997—, gen. counsel, 2000—. Mem.: Am. Soc. Corp. Sec. Inc., Am. Corp. Counsel Assn., ABA. Office: Becton Dickinson Co One Becton Dr Franklin Lakes NJ 07417-1880 Home: 601 Tenth St Brooklyn NY 11215 Office Phone: 201-847-6800. Office Fax: 201-847-6475.

HEALY, GEORGE WILLIAM, III, lawyer, mediator; b. New Orleans, Mar. 8, 1930; s. George William and Margaret Alford H.; m. Sharon Saunders, Oct. 26, 1974; children: George W. IV, John Carmichael, Floyd Alford, Hyde Dunbar, Mary Margaret. BA, Tulane U., 1950, JD, 1955. Bar: La. 1955, U.S. Supreme Ct. 1969. Assoc. Phelps, Dunbar, Marks, Claverie & Sims, New Orleans, 1955-58; ptnr. Phelps Dunbar LLP, 1958-95; of counsel Phelps Dunbar, 1996—. Mem. U.S. del. Comité Maritime Internat., Tokyo, 1969, Lisbon, 1985, Paris, 1990, Sydney, 1994, titulary mem. Mem. planning com. Tulane U. Admiralty Law Inst., dir. World Trade Ctr., 1993-2001; dir. New Orleans Pro Bono Project, 1995-97, La. Orgn. for Jud. Excellence, 1997—. Fellow Am. Bar Found., Am. Coll. Trial Lawyers, Maritime Law Assn. U.S. (mem. exec. com. 1984-87, 2d v.p. 1988-90, 1st v.p. 1990-92, pres. 1992-94), La. Bar Found.; mem. ABA (ho. dels. 1993-95, 97-2000), New Orleans Bar Assn. (pres. 1992), Def. Rsch. Inst., La. Assn. Def. Counsel, New Orleans Assn. Def. Counsel, Com. Maritime Internat. Am. Found. (dir. 1990—), New Orleans Bar Assn. Inn of Ct. (master), Boston Club., La. Club, Stratford Club, Plimsoll Club, Recess Club (pres. 1978), Pinfeathers Hunting Club, New Orleans Lawn Tennis Club, Propeller Club, Mariners Club. Republican. Episcopalian. Home: 6020 Camp St New Orleans LA 70118-5902 Office: Canal Place 365 Canal St Ste 2000 New Orleans LA 70130-6534 Office Phone: 504-584-9238. Office Fax: 504-568-9130. Business E-Mail: healyg@phelps.com.

HEALY, GERALD BURKE, otolaryngologist; b. Boston, Mar. 31, 1942; s. Gerald E. and Margaret C. (Burke) H.; m. Anne Herron, June 3, 1991; children: Elisabeth, Laurie. AB cum laude, Boston Coll., 1963; MD, Boston U., 1967; MBA (hon.), Harvard U., 1990. Diplomate Am. Bd. Otolaryngology, Am. Bd. Laser Surgery, Nat. Bd. Med. Examiners; lic. physician, Mass., Pa. Surg. intern Univ. Hosp., Boston, 1967-68, resident in surgery, 1968-69, resident in otolaryngology, 1969-72; instr. otolaryngology Boston U. Sch. Medicine, 1974-75, asst. prof., 1975-77, assoc. prof., 1977-83, prof., 1983—; assoc. dir. otolaryngology Boston VA Hosp., 1975-76; assoc. otolaryngologist-in-chief The Children's Hosp., Boston, 1976-79, otolaryngologist-in-chief, 1979—; exec. v.p. Am. Bd. of Otolaryngology, Houston. Instr. otolaryngology Tufts U. Sch. Medicine, 1975-88; assoc. prof. otolaryngology Harvard Med. Sch., 1979-88, prof. otology and laryngology, 1988—; chief otolaryngology Valley Forge Army Med. Ctr., Phoenixville, Pa., 1972-73, William Beaumont Army Med. Ctr., El Paso, 1973-74; assoc. dir. otolaryngology Boston City Hosp., 1975-76; bd. dirs. Am. Bd. Otolaryngology, 1986—; mem. com. on certification Am. Bd. Med. Specialists, 1988—. Reviewer Jour. Pediatrics, 1976—, Pediatrics, 1977—, New Eng. Jour. Medicine, 1979—, Annals of Otology, Rhinology and Laryngology, 1982-88, The Laryngoscope, 1986-88; mem. editorial bd. Internat. Jour. Pediatric Otolaryngology, 1979—, The Laryngoscope, 1988—, Annals of Otology, Rhinology and Laryngology, 1988—. Maj. U.S. Army, 1972-74. Fellow ACS, Am. Coll. Chest Physicians, Am. Acad. Pediatrics; mem. Am. Bd. Emergency Medicine (bd. dirs. 1988—), Am. Soc. Pediatric Otolaryn. (pres. 1987), Am. Laryngol. Assn. (exec. coun. 1985—), Am. Broncho-Esophagological Assn. (exec. coun. 1983—, pres. 1990-91), Am. Acad. Otolaryngology-Head and Neck Surgery (chmn. outcomes com. 1991), Am. Acad. Facial Plastic and Reconstructive Surgery, Soc. Univ. Otolargyngologists, Mass. Med. Soc., New Eng. Otolaryn. Soc., Pediatric Otolaryn. Study Group. Office: Childrens Hosp 300 Longwood Ave Boston MA 02115-5737

HEALY, HAROLD HARRIS, JR., lawyer; b. Denver, Aug. 27, 1921; s. Harold Harris and Lorena (Isom) H.; m. Elizabeth A. Debevoise, May 24, 1952; 1 son, Harold Harris III. AB, Yale U., 1943, LL.B., 1949. Bar: NY 1949, U.S. Supreme Ct. 1957. Exec. asst. to U.S. atty. gen., Washington, 1957-59; mem. Debevoise & Plimpton, NYC, 1959-89, resident ptnr. Paris, 1964-67, of counsel NYC, 1989-92. Mem. Am. adv. council Ditchley Found., 1972-99; bd. dirs. Legal Aid Soc., 1968-89, chmn., 1975-79, pres.'s coun., 1989—. Bd. dirs. Met. Opera Guild, 1975-2000, Acad. Am. Poets, 1993-94; nat. coun. Glimmerglass Opera, 1992-2004; adv. dir. Met. Opera Assn., 1986-95; trustee Vassar Coll., 1977-86. Capt. F.A., AUS, 1943-46, ETO. Decorated Bronze Star medal. Mem. ABA (mem. coun. sect. of internat. law and practice 1987-90), N.Y. State Bar Assn., Assn. Bar City of N.Y. (sec. 1959-61), Am. Law Inst., Order of Coif, Am. Soc. Internat. Law (mem. exec. coun. 1977-80), Internat. Law Assn., Internat. Bar Assn., Union Internationale des Avocats (pres. 1979-81), Am. Coll. Investment Counsel, Coun. Fgn. Rels., Pilgrims U.S., Yale Law Sch. Assn. (exec. com. 1974-82, v.p. 1980-82), Century Assn., Univ. Club, Met. Club, Phi Beta Kappa, Zeta Psi, Phi Delta Phi, Chevalier de la Legion d'Honneur. Republican. Episcopalian. Home: 1170 5th Ave New York NY 10029-3916 Office: Debevoise & Plimpton 919 3rd Ave New York NY 10022-6225 Office Phone: 212-909-6355. Business E-Mail: hhhealy@debevoise.com.

HEALY, J. KEVIN, lawyer; b. Bklyn., Feb. 1, 1949; s. Joseph John and Isabel Mark (O'Brien) H.; m. Carey Weiss; children: Christopher Robert, William Daniel. BS, St. Joseph Coll., Phila., 1970; JD, Forham U., N.Y.C., 1973. Bar: N.Y., U.S. Dist. Ct. (no., ea. and so. dists.) N.Y. Atty. enforcement div. EPA, NYC, 1973-78; gen. counsel Dept. Environ. Protection City of NY, 1978-82, NY Conv. Ctr. Devel. Corp., NYC, 1982-84; assoc. Stadtmauer, Bailkin, NYC, 1984-87, Teitelbaum, Hiller, NYC, 1987; ptnr., mem. exec. com. Bryan Cave LLP, NYC. Spl. master U.S. Dist. Ct. (so. dist.) N.Y. 1990. Vice chair citizens' adv. com. Delaware River Basin Commn. Capt. USAFR. Mem. N.Y. State Bar Assn. (co-chair global warming com.,air quality com.), N.Y.C. Bar Assn. (environ. law com.). Home: 235 Corlies Ave Pelham NY 10803-1903 Office: Bryan Cave LLP 1290 Ave of the Americas New York NY 10104 Office Phone: 212-541-1078. Business E-Mail: jkhealy@bryancave.com.

HEALY, JAMES CASEY, lawyer; b. Washington, Feb. 19, 1956; s. Joseph Francis Jr. and Patricia Ann (Casey) H.; m. Kelly Anne Quinn, Nov. 4, 1995; 1 child, Caitlin Quinn. BS, Spring Hill Coll., 1978; JD, Emory U., 1982. Bar: Ga. 1983, Conn. 1983, U.S. Dist. Ct. Conn. 1984, U.S. Tax Ct. 1984, U.S. Supreme Ct. 1987. Assoc. Gregory and Adams PC, Wilton, Conn., 1982-87, ptnr., 1988-89, mng. ptnr., 1990-94, v.p., 1995—. Spl. counsel Wilton Police Commn., 1986-98; mem. Wilton Parks and Recreation Commn., 1991-2002, sec., 1991-93, chmn., 1997-2002; corporator Ridgefield Bank, 1997—; mem. Wilton Fire Commn., 2002—, sec., 2002—. Bd. dirs. Mark Lavin Meml. Offshore Med. and Safety Found., Empire, Mich., 1987—97; bd. dirs. Village Market, Inc., 1988—90; chmn. leadership giving program United Way, 1991; bd. mgrs. Wilton Children's Ctr., 1996—98; athletic fields subcom.of building com. Wilton H.S., 1998—99; steering com. Wilton Family Recreation and Activity Ctr., 2000; bd. trustees Wilton Hist. Soc., 2001—; bd. dirs. Wilton Teen Ctr., 2001—. Mem. Internat. Mcpl. Lawyers Assn., State Bar Ga., State Bar Conn. (exec. com., planning and zoning sect. 1992-94), Am. Planning Assn., Fairfield County Bar Assn. (law office mgmt. com. 1994-96, co-chmn. land use com. 1996—, real estate broker's contract com. 1997-98), Real Estate Fin. Assn., Wilton C. of C. (bd. dirs. 1994-96). Republican. Roman Catholic. Office: Gregory and Adams 190 Old Ridgefield Rd Wilton CT 06897-4023 Office Phone: 203-762-9000. E-mail: jhealy@gregoryandadams.com.

HEALY, JANE ELIZABETH, newspaper editor; b. Washington, May 9, 1949; d. Paul Francis and Connie (Maas) H.; children: Randall, Kevin. BS, U. Md., 1971. Copy clk. N.Y. Daily News, Washington, 1971-73; met. reporter Orlando (Fla.) Sentinel, 1973-81, editorial writer, 1981-83, chief editorial writer, 1983-85, assoc. editor, 1985-92, mng. editor, 1993—2001, editl. page editor, 2001—. Recipient Pulitzer Prize, Columbia U., 1988, Sigma Delta Chi Disting. Service award, 1988. Mem. Am. Soc. Newspaper Editors. Office: Orlando Sentinel 633 N Orange Ave Orlando FL 32801-1349

HEALY, JOSEPH FRANCIS, JR., lawyer, retired air transportation executive; b. N.Y.C., Aug. 11, 1930; s. Joseph Francis and Agnes (Kett) H.; m. Patricia A. Casey, Apr. 23, 1955; children: James C., Timothy, Kevin, Cathleen M., Mary, Terence. BS, Fordham U., 1952; JD, Georgetown U., 1959. Bar: D.C. 1959. With gen. traffic dept. Eastman-Kodak Co., Rochester, N.Y., 1954-55; air transp. examiner CAB, Washington, 1955-59; practiced in Washington, 1959-70, 80-81; asst. gen. counsel Air Transport Assn. Am., 1966-70; v.p. legal Eastern Air Lines, Inc., N.Y.C. and Miami, Fla., 1970-80; ptnr. Ford, Farquhar, Kornblut & O'Neill, Washington, 1980-81; v.p. legal affairs Piedmont Aviation, Inc., Winston Salem, N.C., 1981-84, sr. v.p., gen counsel, 1984-89, ret., 1989; sr. v.p., gen. counsel Trans World Airlines Inc., Mt. Kisco, N.Y., 1993-94. Mem. bd. visitors Sch. Law Wake Forest U., 1988-96. 1st lt. USAF, 1952-54. Mem.: Nat. Aero. Assn., Phi Delta Phi, Beta Gamma Sigma. Home: 104 Overlink Ct Lynchburg VA 24503-3200

HEALY, JUDITH ANN, social worker; b. Nov. 4, 1942; d. Howard and Elenora (Hutchison) Crothers; children: Eric David (dec.), Mark Daniel. AAS, Moraine Valley Community Coll., Palos Hills, Ill., 1979; BS, Nat. Coll. Edn., 1980; postgrad., George Williams Coll., 1983-86; MSW, Loyola U., Chgo., 1987. Cert. sch. social worker, Ill.; lic. clin. social worker. Counselor Community Resources for Youth, Palos Park, Ill., 1977-79; case mgr., weekend coord. Proviso Assn. for Retarded Citizens, Hillside, Ill., 1979-87; sch. social worker Arbor Park Sch. Dist. 145, Oak Forest, Ill., 1987—; therapist Midwest Resources, 1994—99. Social worker cons. Village Inn, Intermediate Care Facility for Developmentally Disabled Adults, Dixon, Ill., 1987-89. Vol. Cmty. Response, Oak Park, Ill., 1991-96, ARC; case worker Armed Forces Svcs. Great Lakes Naval Base; maj. Civil Air Patrol, aerospace officer, dep. comdr. cadets; youth leader Morgan Park Bapt. Ch., Chgo., 1976-81, Christian edn. chair, 1995—; mem. cabinet Am. Bapt. Chs. Metro Chgo., 2000—. Named Sr. of Yr., Lewis Composite Squadron, 2001. Mem. NASW, Ill. Assn. Sch. Social Workers, Assn. Individual Devel. Home: 8148 W 111th St # 2A Palos Hills IL 60465-3234

HEALY, KAREN, automotive executive; B in Journalism, Mich. State U., 1976. With GM, 1976—95, staff pub. rels. fisher guide divsn., 1985—86, mgr. employee comm. Buick-Oldsmobile-Cadillac group, 1986, sr. adminstr. pub. affairs, dir. media comm. Delphi Corp. (formerly auto. components group worldwide), 1993—95; dir. comm. Delphi Corp., Troy, Mich., 1995—96, exec. dir. comm., 1997, v.p. corp. affairs, 1998—, v.p. mktg. comm. and facilities, 2000—. Trustee Music Hall Ctr. Performing Arts, Detroit; bd. visitors Oakland U. Bus. Sch.; bd. dirs. Forgotten Harvest, North Suburban Figure Skating Club. Named Businesswoman of Yr., Detroit News, 2000; named one of 100 Leading Women in Auto. Industry, Auto. News, 2000, Most Influential Women S.E. Mich., Crain's Detroit Bus., 2001. Mem.: Automotive Women's Alliance, Arthur Page Soc., Pub. Rels. Coun., Troy C. of C. (bd. dirs.). Office: 5725 Delphi Dr Troy MI 48098-2815

HEALY, MARTIN RUSSELL, lawyer; b. Yonkers, N.Y., Apr. 22, 1950; s. Thomas Joseph and Faith (DeBaun) H.; m. Joanne Ferrera, Aug. 5, 1972; children: Adam, Alexander, Craig, David. BA, Boston Coll., 1972, JD, 1975. Bar: Mass., U.S. Dist. Ct. Mass., U.S. Ct. Appeals (1st cir.). Law clk. Mass. Trial Ct., Boston, 1975-76; with Rackemann, Sawyer & Brewster, Boston, 1976—95; ptnr. Goodwin Procter LLP, Boston, 1995—. Editor, contbg. author: Massachusetts Zoning Manual, 1989. Mem. Needham (Mass.) Conservation Commn., 1983-86; trustee Capt. Robert Bennet Forbes House Charitable Trust, Milton, Mass., 1986-87. Fellow Mass. Bar Found.; mem. Mass. Bar Assn. (chmn. property law coun. 1986-88), Nat. Assn. Indsl. and Office Parks (chmn. pub. affairs com. Mass. chpt. 1990-91). Roman Catholic. Office: Goodwin Procter LLP Exchange Pl 53 State St Boston MA 02109 Office Phone: 617-570-1371. Office Fax: 617-523-1231. Business E-Mail: mhealy@goodwinprocter.com.

HEALY, NICHOLAS JOSEPH, retired lawyer; b. N.Y.C., Jan. 4, 1910; s. Nicholas Joseph and Frances Cecilia (McCarthy) H.; m. Margaret Marie Ferry, Mar. 29, 1937; children: Nicholas, Margaret Healy Parker, Rosemary Healy Bell, Mary Louise Healy White, Donall, Kathleen Healy Hamon. AB, Holy Cross Coll., 1931; JD, Harvard U., 1934. Bar: N.Y. 1935, U.S. Supreme Ct. 1949. Pvt. practice, N.Y.C., 1935—42; mem. Healy & Baillie (and predecessor firms), 1948—. Spl. asst. to atty. gen. U.S., 1945-48; tchr. admiralty law NYU Sch. Law, 1947-86, adj. prof., 1960-86; Niels F. Johnsen vis. prof. maritime law Tulane Maritime Law Ctr., 1986; vis. prof. maritime law Shanghai Maritime Inst. (now Shanghai Maritime U.), 1981, 86, 88. Contbr. chpts. to Ann. Survey Am. Law, 1948-87; author: (with Sprague) Cases on Admiralty, 1950; (with Currie) Cases and Materials on Admiralty, 1965; (with Sharpe) Cases and Materials on Admiralty, 1974, 3rd edit., 1998; (with Sweeney) The Law of Marine Collision, 1998; editor: Jour. Maritime Law and Commerce, 1980-90, mem. editl. bd., 1969-79, 91—; assoc. editor: American Maritime Cases; mem. scientific bd. Il Dirittimo Marittimo; contbr. to Ency. Brit. Chmn. USCG Adv. Panel on Rules of the Road, 1966-72; mem. permanent adv. bd. Tulane Admiralty Law Inst. Lt. (s.g.) USNR, 1942-45. Fellow Am. Coll. Trial Lawyers; mem. ABA (ho. of dels. 1964-66), N.Y. State Bar Assn., Assn. of Bar of City of N.Y., N.Y. County Lawyers Assn., Maritime Law Assn. U.S. (pres. 1964-66), Assn. Average Adjusters U.S. (chmn. 1959-60), Com. Maritime Internat. (exec. coun. 1972-79, v.p. 1985-91, hon. v.p. 1991—), Ibero-Am. Inst. Maritime Law (hon.). Home: The Hallmark 455 North End Ave Apt 203 New York NY 10282 Office: Healy & Baillie LLP 61 Broadway New York NY 10006-3201 Fax: 212-425-0131. E-mail: nhealy@healy.com.

HEALY, PATRICIA COLLEEN, social worker; b. Denver, Aug. 24, 1935; d. Cecil John and Gracia Maude (Walker) Schulte; m. John Patrick Healy III, Aug. 3, 1957 (div. Jan. 1972); 1 child, Sean Patrick. BA, Sacred Heart Coll., Wichita, 1957; MSW, U. Kans., 1983; postgrad., Wichita State U., 1974, 75, 89, Emporia (Kans.) State U., 1990, U. Kans., 1998. Lic. specialist clin. social worker, Kans.; cert. in spinal cord injury medicine. Proofreader Wichita Pub. Co., 1953; clk. typist Nat. Sales, Inc., Wichita, 1954-58, Dept. of Army, Ft. Leavenworth, Kans., 1958-60, Air Force, McConnell AFB, Kans., 1962-63; clk., typist VA Regional Office, Wichita, 1963-66; self-employed typist Wichita, 1966-70; ward clk., typist VA Regional Office and VA Med. Ctr., Wichita, 1970-73; vets. benefits counselor VARO, Wichita, 1973-83; social worker VA Med. Ctr., Wichita, 1983-2000; ret.; pvt. practice Wichita, 2000—. Author filmstrip, columns, book revs., feature stories and poetry. Former mem. Ctrl. Plains AAA Coun. on Aging; bd. dirs. Ind. Living Ctr. South Ctrl. Kans., 1990-96, Sedgwick Co. Dept. Aging Cmty. Svc. Adv. Bd.; mem. Clin. Social Work Fedn., 2003—; vol. Sr. Svcs. Mem.: Kans. Authors Club. Roman Catholic. Avocations: writing, reading, photography, music, knitting and sewing.

HEALY, SONDRA ANITA, consumer products company executive; b. 1939; married; 3 children. BFA, Goodman Sch. Drama, 1963; MA, Nat. Coll., 1964. Owner, chair Turtle Wax, Chgo., 1973—. Office: Turtle Wax 5655 S 73rd Ave Chicago IL 60638

HEALY, STEVEN MICHAEL, accountant, city official; b. Chgo., July 20, 1949; s. Daniel Francis and Angelina (Massino) H. BA, U. Ill., Chgo., 1971; MBA, Dominican U., 1984. Br. mgr. Assocs. Capital Co., Chgo., 1971-74; credit analyst Motorola, Inc., Schaumburg, Ill., 1974-76; office mgr. Triple "S" Steel Corp., Franklin Park, Ill., 1976-79; accounts payable supr. Zenith Electronics, Chgo., 1979-84; supr. acctg. Village of Oak Park, Ill., 1984-86; bus. analyst Cablevision of Chgo., Oak Park, 1986-87; dir. fin. Village of Maywood, Ill., 1988-91; dir. fin., treas. City of DeKalb, Ill., 1991-93; dir. fin. Village of Cahokia, Ill., 1993—. Mem. Friends of Oak Park Libr., Friends of the Conservatory, Oak Park Village Players Group, Cahokia Econ. Devel. Commn.; bd. dirs. Oak Park Employees Credit Union; treas. Cahokia Assn. for the Tricentennial; pres. sch. bd. Cahokia Unit Sch. Dist. 187; bd. dirs. Cahokia C. of C., 2000—. Mem.: Ill. Govt. Fin. Officers Assn., Nat. Govt. Fin. Officers Assn., Dominican U. MBA Alumni Assn. (founder, soc. com. 1984—), U. Ill. Alumni Assn., Village Oak Park Chess Club, Cath. Alumni Club, Kiwanis (Cahokia club), Kishwaukee Sunrise Rotary, Maywood Rotary, Rotary Club of St. Clair Valley (chair, sec.), Oak Park Area Jaycees. Avocations: participation sports, reading, travel, writing, chess. Home: 2013 Oak Tree Ln Cahokia IL 62206-1408 Office: 103 Main St Cahokia IL 62206-1019

HEALY, THERESA ANN, retired ambassador; b. Bklyn., July 14, 1932; d. Anthony and Mary Catherine (Kennedy) H. BA, St. John's U., 1954, LLD (hon.), 1985. Tchr. elem. and secondary schs., N.Y.C., 1951-55; with U.S. Fgn. Svc., 1955-94, amb. to Sierra Leone, 1980-83; with Ctr. for Internat. Affairs, U. South Fla., Tampa, 1983-84; faculty Nat. Def. U., Washington, 1984-86; with pers. and mgmt. policy bur. U.S. Dept. State, 1986-92; with Office of Freedom of Info., 1992-94; ret., 1994. Cons. Dept. State, 1996—, Office of Freedom Info., 1997—; arbitrator dispute resolution Nat. Assn. Security Dealers, 1999—. Mem. Am. Fgn. Svc. Assn., Diplomatic and Consular Officers Ret. Roman Catholic. Home: 6800 Fleetwood Rd Apt 1002 Mc Lean VA 22101-3610

HEANEY, GERALD WILLIAM, federal judge; b. Goodhue, Minn., Jan. 29, 1918; s. William J. and Johanna (Ryan) H.; m. Eleanor R. Schmitt, Dec. 1, 1945; children: William M., Carol J. Student, St. Thomas Coll., 1935—37; BSL, U. Minn., 1939, LLB, 1941, LLD for Pub. Svc., 2001. Bar: Minn. 1941. Lawyer securities div. Dept. of Commerce Minn., 1941—42; mem. firm Lewis. Hammer, Heaney, Weyl & Halverson, Duluth, 1946—66; judge U.S. Ct. Appeals (8th cir.), 1966—88, sr. judge, 1988—. Bd. regents U. Minn., 1964—65; Mem. Dem. Nat. Com. from Minn., 1955. Capt. AUS, 1942—46. Mem.: ABA, Am. Judicature Soc., Minn. Bar Assn. Roman Catholic. Office: US Ct Appeals 8th Cir US Courthouse & Federal Bldg 315 W 1st St Duluth MN 55802-1605 also: US Ct Appeals 8th Cir 111 S 10th St Rm 24-32 Saint Louis MO 63102*

HEANUE, ANNE ALLEN, retired librarian; b. Ft. Oglethorpe, Ga., Feb. 7, 1940; d. James Edward and Mary (Dennean) Allen; m. Kevin E. Heanue, July 20, 1963; children: Mary, Brian, Patricia. BA cum laude, Dunbarton Coll., 1962; MA, Georgetown U., 1966; MS in Libr. Sci., Cath. U. Am., 1976. Libr. Deloitte Haskins and Sells, Washington, 1977—79; asst. to dir. ALA, Washington, 1979—81, asst. dir., 1981—84, assoc. dir., 1984—98; ret., 1998. Bd. dirs. Alexandria (Va.) LWV, 1967-78; chmn. Alexandria Spl. Edn. adv. com., 1978-79; mem. Alexandria Gypsy Moth Control Commn., 1991-96; vol. White House, 1999—; trustee Freedom to Read Found., 2003—; mem. cancer care com. Inova Alexandria Hosp. Found., 2003—. Recipient Fed. Librs. Round Table Achievement award, 1988. Mem. ALA, Hist. Soc. Washington, D.C., Va. Hist. Soc., Rappahannock Hist. Soc., D.C. Libr. Assn. (bd. dirs. 1994-97), Beta Phi Mu, Pi Gamma Mu. Roman Catholic. Avocations: reading, travel, theater.

HEAPE, MARY WILLIS, music educator, soprano; b. Bartlesville, Okla., Jan. 12, 1957; d. Joseph Benjamin and Charlotte Velau Willis; m. Robert Loyd Heape, Feb. 6, 1988; children: Pedro Benjamin Willis-Barbosa, Cristie Elizabeth. MusB in Edn., Okla. Bapt. U., 1979; MusM, S.W. Bapt. Theol. Sem., 1990, MusD, 1995. Cert. tchr. music K-12 Okla. State Dept. Edn., 1979. Music instr. Seminario de Educadoras Cristas, Recife, Brazil, 1980—82, Instituto Biblico da Bahia, Feira de Santana, Brazil, 1982—85, Tarrant County C.C., Fort Worth, Tex., 1991—96; asst. prof. music, chmn. Dept. Music Bluefield (Va.) Coll., 1996—2000; assoc. prof. music McPherson (Kans.) Coll., 2000—02, MacMurray Coll., Jacksonville, Ill., 2002—. Dir. performing arts series Bluefield (Va.) Coll., 1997—2000; chmn. content area adv. com. Ill. State Dept. Edn., Springfield, Ill., 2003—03; adj. instr. Seminario Bapt. do Norte do Brasil, Recife, Brazil, 1981—82, S.W. Adventist Coll., Keene, Tex., 1994—96. S.W. Bapt. Theol. Sem., Fort Worth, Tex., 1995—96. Musician: Sacred Songs and Arias by Women Composers 1501 to the present; singer: A Night in Vienna: Songs and Arias by Viennese Composers, American as Apple Pie: Songs and Arias by American Composers, That's Amore: Love Songs and Arias Across the Centuries. Hist. interpreter Lincoln's New Salem, Petersburg, Ill., 2003—04. Mem.: Am. Choral Dirs. Assn., Nat. Assn. Tchrs. Singing (sec. Dallas-Fort Worth chpt. 1995—96), Music Educators Nat. Conf., Sorosis Lit. Soc. Avocations: reading, travel.

HEAPHY, JOHN MERRILL, lawyer; b. Escanaba, Mich., Apr. 27, 1927; s. John Merrill and Catherine R. (Feeney) H.; m. Martha Jean Knowles, Nov. 16, 1951; children— John Merrill III, Catherine Jean Heaphy DeThorne, Barbara H. Murphy. BA, U. Mich., 1950; JD, Wayne State U., 1953. Bar: Mich. 1954. Atty. office of gen. counsel HEW, Washington, 1954-57; ptnr. Vandeveer & Garzia, P.C. and predecessor firms, Detroit, 1958-86, pres. firm, 1986-92; ret. Served with USNR, 1945-46. Fellow Am. Coll. Trial Lawyers; mem. ABA, Internat. Assn. Def. Counsel, Mich. Bar Assn., Delta Theta Phi, Alpha Sigma Phi. Republican. Home: 14650 N Desert Rock Dr Tucson AZ 85737-7135 Personal E-mail: JMHeaphy@aol.com.

HEAPHY, LESLIE ANNE, history educator; b. Liberty, N.Y., Dec. 4, 1964; d. James Richard and Jean Isabel (Thomson) H. BA, Siena Coll., Loudonville, N.Y., 1987; MA, U. Toledo, 1989, PhD, 1995. Grad. asst. U. Toledo, 1987-93, instr., 1994-95; small group dir. Collingwood Presbyn. Ch., Toledo, 1993-95; asst. prof. Kent State U., Stark, 1995—2004, assoc. prof., 2005—. Speaker in field. Prodr.: The Negro Leagues, 1869-1960, 2003; contbr. articles and revs. Mem. Soc. for Am. Baseball Rsch. (chair com. women in baseball 1993—), Phi Alpha Theta. Presbyterian. Avocations: running, reading, collecting baseball cards. Home: 135 Hillcrest Ave North Canton OH 44720 Office Phone: 330-244-3304. Business E-Mail: lheaphy@kent.edu.

HEAPHY, MAUREEN S., management consultant; b. Detroit, Dec. 18, 1950; d. Edward A. and Lauretta H. MA, U. Mich., 1975; MS, Wayne State U., 1982, PhD, 1998. Cert. quality mgr., quality engr., reliability engr., Am. Soc. Quality. Computer counselor U. Mich., Dearborn, 1972-74; reliability engr. Detroit Diesel, Gen. Motors, 1974-77; sr. quality engr. Chevrolet Divsn., Gen. Motors, Warren, Mich., 1977-82; mgr. Corp. Quality, Gen. Motors, Detroit, 1982-84; dir. Gen. Motors, Ypsilanti, Mich., 1984-87; prin. cons. TTNI, Farmington Hills, Mich., 1987—. Adj. faculty various colls., 1976—2002; judge Mich. Quality Coun., Rochester, 1994—, Army Cmty. Excellence, Washington, 1996—. Co-author: MBNQA: A Yardsick for Quality Growth, 1995. Founding mem. Mich. Quality Coun., Rochester, 1991—. Recipient Koth award Milw. Automotive Divsn., 1996. Fellow Am. Soc. Quality; mem. Soc. Automotive Engrs., Automotive Divsn. Detriot Sect. (chmn. 1983-84, 95-96).

HEAPS, MARVIN DALE, retired food services company executive; b. Boone, Iowa, June 26, 1932; s. Donald and Mary Isabel (Robson) H.; m. Martha Coleman Davis, July 4, 1957; children— Mitchell, Matthew, Martha. BA in Econs, Whitworth Coll., 1953; postgrad., George Washington U., 1957; MBA (Achievement scholar), U. Pa., 1959. Asso. McKinsey & Co. (mgmt. cons.), Washington, Geneva and N.Y.C., 1960-66; dir. service systems engrng. Automatic Retailers of Am., Phila., 1967, v.p., 1968; sr. v.p. ARA Svcs., Inc., Phila., 1969-71; pres. ARA Food Svcs. Co., 1971-75; exec. v.p. ops. ARA Svcs., Inc., 1975-77, pres., chief operational officer, 1977-81; pres./chief exec. officer Marvin D. Heaps Assos., Inc., 1981—. Cons. to Office Edn., HEW; mem. food svc. industry adv. com. Exec. Office Pres., 1969—; chmn. bd. ACTS Retirement Life Communities, 1997-. Active Whitworth Coll.; chmn. Salvation Army. Lt. USN, 1955-59. Mem. Conf. Bd., Am. Mgmt. Assn., Assn. Internat. Devel., Nat. Automatic Mdse. Assn. (dir.), Wharton MBA Alumni Club. Republican. Presbyterian (elder). Home and Office: 1079 Kennett Way West Chester PA 19380

HEARD, EDWIN ANTHONY, banker; b. N.Y.C., Oct. 31, 1926; s. Edwin Anthony and Frances Weaver (Taylor) H.; m. Phyllis Marie Gregory, Dec. 18, 1948; children: Elizabeth Gregory, Edwin Anthony III. AB, Princeton U., 1948; grad., Advanced Mgmt. Program, Harvard U., 1966. V.p. Irving Trust Co., N.Y.C., 1960-71; treas. U.S. Trust Co., N.Y.C., 1971-73, exec. v.p., 1973-76, vice chmn., 1976-89; pres. Excelsior Income Shares, Inc., 1989-92, also bd. dirs., emeritus. Trustee Trinity Episcopal Sch. Corp. With USNR, 1944-46. Mem. Belle Meade Country Club (Nashville), Bond Club (N.Y.C.). Home: 3901 West End Ave Nashville TN 37205-1837

HEARD, JAMES HENRY, lawyer, educator, historian; b. Woburn, Mass., Sept. 28, 1940; s. James Henry Heard and Thelma Mae Bailey; m. Deloris Heard, Sept. 2, 1978; children: Patrick, Malcolm, Anthony. BS, Boston State Coll., 1963; MAT, U. Chgo., 1968; JD, DePaul U., 1974. Bar: Ill. 1975, U.S. Dist. Ct. (no. dist.) Ill. 1975, U.S. Supreme Ct. 1975. Chmn. social sci. Bloom Twp. H.S., Chgo. Heights, Ill., 1965-70; prof. of history Prarie State Coll., Chgo. Heights, 1970-71, Harold Washington Coll., Chgo., 1971—, chmn. social scis. dept., 1980-85, 90—, chmn. faculty coun., 1993—; dean applied scis. Kennedy-King Coll., Chgo., 1985-90; arbitrator Cook County Cir. Cts., Chgo., 1975—. Coord. common ground projects Harold Washington Coll., Chgo., 1995—. Contbr. to book and profl. jours.; chorister Kennedy King Coll. Cmty. Chorus, 1985—. Cantor St. Thomas the Apostle Ch., Chgo., 1985—; chmn. of adv. bd. Ill. Infant Mortality Project, 1980-85; chmn. bd. dirs. New City Health Ctr., Chgo., 1980-90. Named Educator of Yr., Comty. Coll. Assn. of Ill. and U. Mich. Consortium, 1995, Disting. Prof. Harold Washington Coll., 1995, Most Disting. Advisor, Phi Theta Kappa Internat. Honor Soc., Jackson Miss. chpt., 1995; recipient award Chgo. Urban League, 1985, Osterman Outstanding Svc. award City of Chgo., 1996. Mem. Comty. Colls. Humanities Assn. Avocations: music appreciation, running, reading.

HEARD, LARRY, real estate company executive; b. Houston; BBA in Fin., Baylor U. With devel. and leasing divsn. Joe A. McDermott, Inc., Houston, 1981—84; joined Transwestern Comml. Svcs., Inc., Houston, 1984, pres. S.W. region, 1996—2002, exec. v.p. Houston divsn., pres., CEO, 2002—, also bd. dirs. Bd. dirs. SEARCH. Mem.: Urban Land Inst. (mem. exec. com. Houston), Baylor Bear Found. (past pres. Houston chpt.), Young Pres. Orgn. Office: Transwestern Comml Svcs Ste 1300 1900 W Loop St Houston TX 77027

HEARD, WILLIAM ROBERT, retired insurance company executive; b. Inpls., Apr. 25, 1925; s. French and Estelle (Austin) Heard; m. Virginia Ann Patrick, Feb. 6, 1951; children: Cynthia Ann, William Robert II. Student, Ind. U., 1948—49. With Grain Dealers Mut. Ins. Co., 1948, exec. v.p. Indpls., 1978—79, pres., CEO, dir., 1979—90, also chmn. bd. dirs.; pres., CEO, dir. Companion Ins. Co., 1979—90, also chmn. bd. dirs.; ret., 1994. Past chmn. Alliance Am. Insurers; chmn., mem. exec. com. IRM. With USNR, 1942—46. Mem.: VFW, Sales and Mktg. Execs. Internat. (past bd. dirs.), Mill and Elevator Fire Prevention Bur. (bd. dirs.), Mill and Elevator Rating Bur. (bd. dirs.), Property Loss Rsch. Bur. (bd. dirs., chmn.), Ins. Claims Svc. (bd. dirs.), Ind. Mill and Elevator Rating Bur. (bd. dirs.), Hoosierland Rating Bur. (bd. dirs.), Ind. Insurors Assn. (bd. dirs.), Property and Casualty Ins. Coun., Sales and Mktg. Execs. Indpls. (past pres.), Excess Loss Assn. (vice chmn., bd. dirs.), Ind. BBB (bd. dirs., mem. exec. com., vice chmn.), Ins. Inst. Ind. (bd. dirs., mem. exec. com.), Assn. Mill and Elevator Ins. Cos. (chmn., bd. dirs.), Pearl Harbor Survivors Assn. (hon.), Indpls. Skyline Club, Econ. Club Indpls., Fla. 1752 Club (past pres.), Hon. Order Ky. Cols., Am. Legion, Pi Sigma Epsilon.

HEARLE, DOUGLAS GEOFFREY, public relations consultant; b. N.Y.C., Apr. 7, 1933; s. Douglas G. and Regina Irene (Booth) H.; m. Mary Elizabeth Hogan, July 13, 1957; children: Douglas, Christopher, Matthew. BA, Iona Coll., 1954, MBA, 1970. Reporter-editor N.Y. Jour.-Am., N.Y.C., 1954-63; pub. relations mgr. Borden Inc., N.Y.C., 1963-66; account exec. Hill & Knowlton, N.Y.C., 1966-70, v.p., 1970-73, sr. v.p., 1973-80, exec. v.p., 1980-86, vice chmn., 1989-90, also bd. dirs.; founder, pres. Douglas G. Hearle & Co., N.Y.C., 1993—. Pres. John W. Hill Found., N.Y.C., 1980-86; founder, pres. Douglas G. Hearle & Assoc., Inc., N.Y.C., 1986-89; pres., CEO Carl Byoir & Assocs., N.Y.C., 1990-92; adj. prof. Iona Coll., 1982-84, Coll. New Rochelle, 1996—, Fordham U., 1998-99; disting. lectr. Ball State U., 1981, U. Tex., 1984. V.p. Bd. Edn., Pelham, N.Y., 1972-78; v.p. N.Y. Newspaper Reporters Assn., 1961-63; mem. exec. coun. Boy Scouts Am., 1967-69; vice chmn. bd. trustees Coll. New Rochelle, 1989-95; bd. dirs. The Roper Ctr., U. Conn., 1990—2003; pres. Danny Fund, Pelham, N.Y., 2003-. Recipient Disting. Service award Asean P.R. Congress, Jakarta, Indonesia, 1981; recipient Citizen of Yr. award Pelham Men's Club, 1978, Five Most Respected award by PR Week, 1988, All Star award Inside PR Mag., 1992. Mem. Silurians, N.Y. Newspaper Reporters Assn., Asia Soc., Internat. C. of C., Grenock C. of C. Lee, Mass., Sky Club of N.Y. Republican. Roman Catholic. Home: 20 Maple Ave Pelham NY 10803-2220 Office: PO Box 480 Pelham NY 10803-0480

HEARN, BEVERLY JEAN, education educator; b. Lexington, Tenn., Sept. 10, 1953; d. James Lawrence and Marie (Sparks) Kee; m. Larry Joseph Hearn, June 15, 1973; children: Matthew Joseph, David Andrew. BA, Union U., 1974; MLS, George Peabody Coll. for Tchrs., 1975; EdD, Memphis State U., 1991. Acqusitions librarian Union U., Jackson, Tenn., 1975-80, reference librarian, 1980-86; tchr. Madison County Bd. Edn., 1986—2004; dir. reading ctr., asst. prof. reading U. Tenn., Martin, 2004—. Instr. Memphis State U., 1990-95, Jackson State C.C., 1992-97; freelance cataloger, 1978-86; multicultural edn. cons., 2004—. Grantee Fulbright Hayes Group Projects Abroad, US govt., 2000, 2002. Mem. TESOL, Tenn. TESOL (pres. 2004—), Internat. Reading Assn., Assn. for Curriculum Devel., TESCI (pres.). Democrat. Baptist. Home: 558 Wallace Rd Jackson TN 38305-2839 Office Phone: 731-881-7197. Business E-Mail: bhearn@utm.edu.

HEARN, FIL, architectural history professor, director; b. Lincoln, Ala., Aug. 18, 1938; s. Millard F. Hearn and Olivia Richey; m. Jana Srba Hearn, June 18, 1966; children: John V.R., Susannah M.O. Hearn Kerest. BA in History, Auburn U., 1960; MA in History, Ind. U., 1964, MA in Art History, 1966, PhD in Art History, 1969. From instr. to prof. U. Pitts., 1967—, chair art history dept., 1974—78, dean semester-at-sea, 1998, 2001. Vis. prof. Carnegie-Mellon U., Pitts., 1979; bd. mem. Internat. Ctr. Medieval Art, NYC, 1981—84. Author: (books) Romanesque Sculpture, 1981, Ripon Minster, 1983; editor: Arch. Theory of Viollet-Le-Duc, 1990, Ideas That Shaped Buildings, 2003. Bd. mem. Pitts. Chamber Music, 2001—. Lt. USNR, 1960—62. Vis. Sr. scholar, CASVA, DC, 1992. Mem.: Soc. Archtl. Historians. Avocation: writing. Office: Univ Pittsburgh 104 Frick Fine Arts Pittsburgh PA 15260

HEARN, GEORGE HENRY, lawyer, water transportation executive; b. Bklyn., July 4, 1927; s. Henry G. and Grace A. (Flaherty) H.; m. Cecelia Anne Philbin, June 28, 1952; children: Annemarie Jude, Margaret Mary, George Henry. BA, St. Francis Coll., 1950; student, Fordham U., 1948; LLB, St. John's U., 1954. Bar: N.Y. 1955, U.S. Supreme Ct. 1960, D.C. 1965. Jr. ptnr. Haight, Gardner, Poor and Havens, NYC, 1954—61; mem. CAB, 1961-64; commr. Fed. Maritime Commn., 1964-75; maritime adminstr. Govt. Sultanate of Oman, 1975-80; counsel to firm Hill, Rivkins, Carey, Loesberg & O'Brien (specializing in maritime and transp. law), N.Y.C., 1977-82; exec. v.p. Waterman Steamship Corp., N.Y.C., 1982—. Lectr. transp. Georgetown U., Am. U., Tulane U., St. Francis Coll. Contbr. articles to profl. jours. Pres. Fleet Week Found., 1990—; dist. commr. Boy Scouts Am., 1958—, mem. N.Y.C. coun., 1958—61; chmn. Kings County spkrs. com. 1960 presdl. election of John F. Kennedy; vice-chmn. com. nationalists and intergroup rels. N.Y. State Dem. Com., 1960—. Served USNR, WWII, PTO. Recipient Disting. Svc. award U.S. Jr. C. of C., 1958; named Man of Yr., N.Y. Freight Forwarders and Brokers Assn., 1968, Cathedral Club of Bklyn., 1974. Mem. D.C. Bar Assn., Fed. Bar Assn., Maritime Adminstrv. Bar Assn., Maritime Law Assn., Soc. Maritime Arbitrators, U.S. Maritime Assn. Port of N.Y. and N.J. (pres., Man of Yr. 2000), India House (bd. govs.), Adminstrv. Conv. U.S., St. Patrick's Soc. Bklyn. (past pres.), Am. Com. Italian Migration (rec. sec. Bklyn. divsn.), KC. Home: 250 Lido Blvd PO Box 143 Point Lookout NY 11569 Office: 1 Whitehall St New York NY 10004-2109 also: 1000 16th St NW Washington DC 20036-5705 Office Phone: 212-747-8550. Business E-Mail: hearngh@intship.com.

HEARN, INDIA L., sales executive; BA in Bus. and Adminstrn.-Mktg., Howard U., Washington, 1992. Account exec. Fairchild Publs., N.Y.C., 1995—96, EBONY Mag., 1996—97; ea. advt. sales mgr. W.G. Holdsworth & Assoc., Inc., 1997—2000; advt. sales cons. HealthQuest Mag., 2000—02; pvt. practice advt. sales cons., 2002—03; recruitment advt. sales rep. N.Y. Times, N.Y.C., 2003—, account mgr. Am. fashion and jewelry retail/bridal, 2003—. Recipient 8 sales awards, N.Y. Times, 2003. Address: 133 32 147th St South Ozone Park NY 11436

HEARN, JOYCE CAMP, retired state legislator, educator, consultant; b. Cedartown, Ga. d. J.C. and Carolyn (Carter) Camp; m. Thomas Harry Hearn; children: Theresa Hearn Potts Bailey, Kimberly Ann Johnson, Carolyn Lee Becker. Student, U. Ga.; BA, Ohio State U., 1957; postgrad., U. S.C. Former h.s. tchr.; dist. mgr. U.S. Census, 2d Congl. Dist., 1970; mem. S.C. Ho. of Reps., 1975-89. Asst. minority leader, 1976-78, 86-89; chmn., commn. alcohol beverage control, 1989-91; pres., cons. Hearn & Assocs., Columbia, S.C., 1995—. Mem. Richland County Planning Commn., 1974-76; bd. dirs. Meml. Youth Ctr. and Stage South; chmn. Sexual Assault Awareness Week; vice chmn. Dist. Rep. Com., 1968; Rep. chmn. 2d Congl. Dist., 1969; Rep. chmn. Richland County, 1972; del., platform com. Rep. Nat. Conv., 1980, 84; moderator Kathwood Bapt. Ch., 1979-80, former asst. Sunday Sch. tchr.; bd. dirs. Small Bus. Devel. Ctr., S.C., Columbia Coll. Bd. Vis., Columbia Urban League, Fedn. of Blind; trustee Columbia Mus. Art; apptd. to Alcohol Beverage Control Bd., 1989, apptd. chmn. commn., 1990-92, commr., 1991-94; bd. dirs. Lupus Found., 1990—; chair nat. adv. com. Occupl. Safety and Health, 1980-88. Recipient Outstanding Citizen award Columbia Rape Coalition, 1977, Disting. Svc. award Claims Mgmt. Assn., S.C., 1977, Nat. Fedn. Blind S.C., 1978, Columbia Urban League, 1983, MADD, 1985, Outstanding Legislator of Yr. award Alcohol and Drug Abuse Assn., 1980, Retarded Citizens Assn., 1982, S.C. Rehab. Assn., 1984, S.C. Assn. of Deaf, 1987, Legislator of Yr., Fedn. of Blind, 1988, Disting. Legislator, DAV, 1989; honoree Easter Seals, 1989; numerous other awards. Mem. Nat. Order of Women Legislators (v.p., pres.), Order of the Palmetto, S.C. Women's Club, Columbia Women's Club (bd. dirs.), Larkspur Garden Club, Spring Valley Country Club Golf Assn. (pres. 1973, 97), Spring Valley Country Club. Office Phone: 803-256-7255. E-mail: jchearn@bellsouth.net.

HEARN, PRISCILLA ROSE, music educator; b. Dodge City, Kans., July 9, 1952; d. Woodson Albert and Norma Allene Kingry; m. John Allen Hearn, Mar. 18, 1978. BMus in Piano performance, U. Kans., Lawrence, 1970—74; MMus in Piano performance, U. Tex., Austin, 1974—77. Piano instr. St. Mary of the Plains Coll., Dodge City, Kans., 1990—91; music instr. Hutchinson CC, Kans., 1990—. Staff accompanist High Plains Band Camp, Hays, Kans., 1995—. Mem.: Hutchinson Piano Tchrs. League. Home: 2122 W 17th Ave Hutchinson KS 67501 Office Phone: 620-665-3361.

HEARN, SHARON SKLAMBA, lawyer; b. New Orleans, Aug. 15, 1956; d. Carl John and Marjorie C. (Wimberly) Sklamba; m. Curtis R. Hearn. BA magna cum laude, Loyola U., New Orleans, 1977; JD cum laude, Tulane U., 1980. Bar: La. 1980, Tex. 1982, cert.: (tax specialist). Law clk. to presiding judge U.S. Ct. Appeals Fed. Cir., Washington, 1980—81; assoc. Johnson & Swanson, Dallas, 1981—84, The Kullman Firm, New Orleans, 1984—. Recipient Am. Legion award, 1970. Mem.: ABA, Dallas Women Lawyers Assn., Tex. State Bar Assn., La. State Bar Assn. Democrat. Roman Catholic. Home: 106 Bordeaux St Metairie LA 70005-4231 Office: The Kullman Firm 1600 Energy Ctr 1100 Poydras St New Orleans LA 70163-1101 Office Phone: 504-598-0088. E-mail: ssh@kullmanlaw.com.

HEARN, THOMAS K., JR., academic administrator; b. Opp, Ala., July 5, 1937; s. Thomas H. Hearn; m. Laura Walter; children: Thomas K., William Neely, Lindsay. BA summa cum laude, Birmingham-So. Coll., 1959; BD, Baptist Theol. Sem., 1963; PhD (NDEA fellow), Vanderbilt U., 1965. Instr. Birmingham-So. Coll., 1964—65; asst. prof. Coll. William and Mary, 1965—68, assoc. prof., 1968—74; prof. philosophy U. Ala., Birmingham, 1974—83, chmn. dept. philosophy, 1974—76; dean U. Ala. Sch. Humanities, Birmingham, 1976—78; v.p. U. Ala. Univ. Coll., Birmingham, 1978—83; pres. Wake Forest U., Winston-Salem, NC, 1983—2005, pres. emeritus, 2005—. Contbr. articles to profl. jours. Chmn. bd. govs. Ctr. for Creative Leadership; chair Knight Commn. on Intercoll. Athletics, 2005—. Recipient Thomas Jefferson Teaching award, 1970; fellow, Council Philos. Studies, 1968, Coop. Program in Humanities, 1969—70; grantee, Nat. Found. Humanities, 1967, Faculty Summer grant, Coll. William and Mary, 1970, 1972—73. Mem.: AAUP, Newcomen Soc. N.Am., David Hume Soc., Am. Philos. Assn., Soc. Philosophy Religion (pres. 1974—75), So. Soc. Philosophy, Psychology (exec. council 1974—77, Jr. award), Phi Kappa Phi, Omicron Delta Kappa, Phi Beta Kappa. Home: 2730 Chatham Farm Rd Winston Salem NC 27106-5824 Office: Wake Forest U Office of Pres Emeritus PO Box 7626 Winston Salem NC 27109 E-mail: tkh@wfu.edu.

HEARNSBERGER, KEITH ALAN, music educator; b. Warren, Ark., Dec. 17, 1981; s. Richard Alan and Patricia M. Hearnsberger. BA in Applied Music, BA in Music History, U. of Ark., Little Rock, 2005. Tchr. music edn. Luth. H.S., Little Rock, 2004—; children's choirmaster Trinity Episc. Cathedral, Little Rock, 2004—. Piano, voice instr. Hearnsberger Applied Music, Little Rock, 1997—. Mem.: Am. Choral Directors Assn. Republican. Protestant. Achievements include Development of Choral Programs. Avocations: cooking, reading, writing/research. Office: Lutheran High School 6711 West Markham Little Rock AR 72205-2897 Office Phone: 501-663-5117. Personal E-mail: keifus921@yahoo.com.

HEARON, SHELBY, writer, educator; b. Marion, Ky., Mar. 18, 1931; d. Charles Boogher and Evelyn Shelby (Roberts) Reed; m. William Halpern, Aug. 19, 1995; children from previous marriage: Anne Rambo, Reed. BA, U. Tex., 1953. Disting. vis. prof. U. Ill., Chgo., 1993, Colgate U., 1993, U. Miami, Fla., 1994, U. Mass., Amherst, 1994-96, Middlebury Coll., 1996-98. Author: Armadillo in the Grass, 1968, The Second Dune, 1973, Hannah's House, 1975, Now and Another Time, 1976, A Prince of a Fellow, 1978, Painted Dresses, 1981, Afternoon of a Faun, 1983, Group Therapy, 1984, A Small Town, 1985, Five Hundred Scorpions, 1987, Owing Jolene, 1989, Hug Dancing, 1991, Life Estates, 1994, Footprints, 1996, Ella in Bloom, 2001; contbr. articles, short fiction and book revs. to various publs. Pres. Tex. Inst. Letters, 1980; chair lit. panel Tex. Commn. on Arts, 1980; mem. lit. panel N.Y. Coun. on Arts, 1985. Named to, Tex. Lit. Hall of Fame, 2004; recipient Syndication prize, NEA/PEN, 1984—85, 1985, 1987, 1988, Lit. award, Am. Acad. Arts and Letters, 1990, Lifetime Achievement award, Tex. Book Festival, 2003; fellow, Guggenheim, 1982, Nat. Endowment Arts, 1983; grantee, Ingram Merrill, 1987. Mem.: PEN, Associated Writing Programs, Tex. Inst. Letters (Fiction award 1973, 1978), Poets and Writers Inc., Authors Guild. Democrat. Presbyterian. Home: 246 S Union St Burlington VT 05401-4514

HEARST, GEORGE RANDOLPH, JR., publishing executive, diversified ranching and real estate executive; b. San Francisco, July 13, 1927; s. George and Blanche (Wilbur) H.; m. Mary Thompson, Apr. 23, 1951 (dec. Dec. 1969); children: Mary, George Randolph III, Stephen T., Erin; m. Patricia Ann Bell, Nov. 30, 1969 (div. Nov. 1985) Pvt. bus., 1946-48; staff Los Angeles Examiner, 1948-50, San Francisco Examiner, 1954-56; with Los Angeles Evening Herald-Express, from 1956, bus. mgr., 1957, pub., from 1960, Los Angeles Herald-Examiner, from 1962; group head Hearst Real Estate; v.p. Hearst Corp., 1977—, chmn., 1996—. Pres. Hearst Found.; dir. Randolph William Hearst Found. Served with USNR, 1945-46; with AUS, 1950-54. Mem. V.F.W. Clubs: Burlingame Country, Jonathan, California, Riviera. Office: Chairman of Board Hearst Corp 1345 Sixth Avenue New York NY 10105*

HEARST, JOHN EUGENE, chemistry educator, researcher, consultant; b. Vienna, July 2, 1935; came to U.S., 1938; s. Alphonse Bernard and Lily (Roger) Hirsch; m. Jean Carolyn Bankson, Aug. 30, 1958; children: David Paul, Leslie Jean. B.E., Yale U., 1957; PhD, Calif. Inst. Tech., 1961; D.Sc. (hon.), Lehigh U., 1992. Postdoctoral rschr. Dartmouth Coll., Hanover, N.H., 1961-62; prof. chemistry U. Calif., Berkeley, 1962-95, prof. emeritus, 1996—, Miller rsch. prof., 1970-71; founder, dir. HRI Rsch. Inc., 1978—; sr. rsch. scientist Lawrence Berkeley Lab., 1980-99, faculty chemist, 2000—, dir. divsn. chem. biodynamics, 1986-89; founder, sr. cons. Advanced Genetics Rsch., Inc., Oakland, Calif., 1981-84; founder, dir. Steritech Inc., Concord, Calif., 1992-96; founder, dir., v.p. new sci. opportunities Cerus Corp., Concord, 1992—2004, cons., 2005—. Disting. lectr. Purdue U., 1986; Merck Centennial lectr. Lehigh U., 1992, Robert A. Welch Found. lectr., 1992-93; adv. bd. Pharm. and Chem. Scis. Graduate Program Univ. of the Pacific, 2000—; cons. Codon, Inc., 1993-97; scientific adv. bd. Thomas McNesney & Ptnrs., 2003—. Author: Contemporary Chemistry, 1976. editor: General Chemistry, 1974; exec. editor Nucleic Acids Rsch., 1990-93; inventor, patentee in field. Bd. dirs. U. No. Calif., 1993-95, dir. Disability Policy and Planning Inst., Berkeley, 2000-2002. Recipient Sci. Profl. Devel. award NSF, 1977-78, The Berkeley citation, 1999, Mortimer Bortin award for outstanding rsch. in bone marrow transplant, 2000; John Simon Guggenheim fellow, 1968-69, European Molecular Orgn. sr. fellow, 1973-74. Mem. AAAS, Am. Chem. Soc., Biophys. Soc., Am. Soc. Biol. Chemists, Am. Soc. for Photobiology (coun., pres. elect 1990-91, pres. 1991-92, Rsch. award 1994), Am. Phys. Soc. Home: 101 Southampton Ave Berkeley CA 94707-2036 Office: U Calif Dept Chemistry Berkeley CA 94720-1460 Office Phone: 510-407-4555.

HEARST, WILLIAM RANDOLPH, III, lawyer, former newspaper publisher; b. Washington, June 18, 1949; s. William Randolph and Austine (McDonnell) H.; m. Margaret Kerr Crawford, Sept. 23, 1990; children: William, Adelaide, Caroline. AB, Harvard U., 1972. Reporter, asst. city editor San Francisco Examiner, 1972-76, publisher, 1984-96; editor Outside Mag., 1976-78; asst. mng. editor Los Angeles Herald Examiner, 1978-80; mgr. devel. Hearst Corp., 1980-82, dir., 1992—; v.p. Hearst Cable Communications Div., 1982-84; dir. Hearst-Argyle TV; ptnr. Kleiner Perkins Caufield & Byers, Menlo Park, Calif., 1995—. Pres. William Randolph Hearst Found., 2003—; bd. dirs. Akimbo, Applied Minds, Juniper Networks, Oblix, OnFiber, RGB Networks. Bd. trustees Grace Cathedral, San Francisco, Carnegie Inst. of Washington, Math. Scis. Rsch. Inst. Fellow: AAAS; mem.: Calif. Acad. Scis. (bd. trustees). Office: Kleiner Perkins Caufield & Byers 2750 Sand Hill Rd Menlo Park CA 94025 Office Phone: 650-233-2750. Office Fax: 650-233-0300.*

HEARTH, BLAIR ANTHONY, fundraiser, clergyman; b. Fall River, Mass., Apr. 23, 1950; s. Theodore Frederick and Jacqueline (Blair) H.; m. Amy Hill. BA, Stetson U., DeLand, Fla., 1972; MDiv, Garrett Theol. Sem., Evanston, Ill., 1976; MEd, Rutgers U., 2001. Ordained elder United Meth. Ch. Assoc. pastor St. Paul's United Meth. Ch., Tallahassee, 1976-78, First United Meth. Ch., Ormond Beach, Fla., 1978-81; exec. dir. Halifax Urban Ministries, Daytona Beach, Fla., 1981-85; regional dir. N.Y.C. Easter Seal Soc., 1985-87; dir. devel./planned giving Mt. Sinai Med. Ctr., N.Y.C., 1987-90; nat. dir. planned giving Nat. March of Dimes Found., White Plains, N.Y., 1990-95; dir. gift planning Monmouth Health Care Found., Long Branch, NJ, 1995—99; min. visitation Red Bank United Meth. Ch., 2003—. Adj. prof. philosophy and religion Bethune Cookman Coll., Daytona Beach, 1981-85; v.p. N.Y. Conf. United Meth. Found., White Plains, 1988-98; reas. Planned Giving Group of Greater N.Y., N.Y.C., 1987-98, N.J. Dept. Aging, 1987-91. Founder, pres. Nova House, Daytona Beach., 1983-85. Recipient White House Citation for Pvt. Sector Initiatives, 1985. Mem. AAAS, N.Y. Acad. Scis., Assn. Health Philanthropy, Meth. Fedn. for Social Action. Avocation: archeoastronomy. Home: PO Box 314 Oceanport NJ 07757-0314 Office: Red Bank United Meth Ch 247 Broad St Red Bank NJ 07701 Office Phone: 732-747-0446.

HEARTNEY, ELEANOR, art critic; b. Des Moines, Aug. 5, 1954; d. Matthew Joseph and Marjorie Waite (Parker) H. BA in Humanities, U. Chgo., 1976, MA in Art History, 1980. Ind. art critic, N.Y.C., 1982—; contbg. editor New Art Examiner, N.Y.C., 1986—, Art in Am., N.Y.C., 1989—. Critic in residence Sculpture Mag., washington, 1989-90; vis. curator Inst. Contemporary Art, Boston, 1994; vis. lectr. U. N.Mex., Albuquerque, 1995-96; panelist, vis. critic, lectr. for various nat. and internat. orgns. Co-author: Angels of Language, 1988, Critical Condition: American Culture at the Crossroads, 1997, Out of the Ordinary, 2003; author: Parts: Work by Rita McBride, 1992, After Eden:Garden Varieties in Contemporary Art, 1998, Postmodernism (Movements in Modern Art), 2001, Postmodern Heretics: Catholic Imagination in Contemporary Art, 2004, A Capital Collection: Masterworks From the Corcoran Gallery of Art, 2004; contbr. articles to profl. publs. Recipient Creative Non-fiction award N.Y. Found. for Arts. Mem. Art Critics Assn., Coll. Art Assn. (Frank Jewett Mather award 1992), Etant Donnes (adv. bd. 1994-97); co-pres. Am. Chpt. Internat. Art Critics Assn. Home and Office: 313 E 6th St Apt 2 New York NY 10003-8447 Address: American Chpt Internat Art Critics Assn 105 Duane St Apt #40E New York NY 10007-3612 Office Phone: 212-566-6777.*

HEARTT, CHARLOTTE BEEBE, university official; b. N.Y.C., Nov. 12, 1933; d. Stacey Kile and Charlotte Beebe; m. William Hollis Peirce, 1954 (div. 1960); children: Daniel Converse, William Kile; m. Stephen Heartt, 1962 (div. 1968); children: Thomas Beebe, Sarah Lincoln. BA, Wellesley Coll., 1954. Intern Office of V.p. Richard Nixon, Washington, 1953; asst. Computing Numerical Analysis Lab. U. Wis., Madison, 1954-56; dir. fund raising Boston Arts Festival, 1961; asst. to dean coll. rels. Radcliffe Coll., Cambridge, Mass., 1961-62; sec. to chmn. dept. city planning Harvard U., Cambridge, 1962; Fulbright program adviser, study abroad adviser Brandeis U., 1966-71, dir. office internat. programs, 1971-76, dir. found. and corp. rels., 1976-79; dir. corp. rels., asst. dir. devel. Smith Coll., Northampton, Mass., 1979-81, dir. devel., 1981-95, dir. prin. gifts, 1995-98; ind. cons., 1999—. Mem. Commonwealth Task Force on the Open Univ., 1973; bd. dirs. Coun. on Internat. Ednl. Exch., 1973-77, mem. exec. com., 1975-77; bd. dirs. Boston Area Seminar for Internat. Students, 1973-76; mem. adv. com. New England Colls. Fund, 1981-95; trustee Berkshire Sch., 1989-98, trustee emerita, 1999—; bd. dirs. Hampshire Cmty. United Way, 1996-2000; mem. devel. com. Belmont Day Sch., Belmont, Mass., 2000-04, Boston (Mass.) Leadership Gift Com. Wellesley Coll., 2002—, chmn. spl. gifts 50th reunion, 2000-04. Mem. Sect. on U.S. Study Abroad (nat. sec., regional rep. 1972-74), Nat. Assn. Fgn. Student Affairs (nat. commr. liaison), Nat. Assn. Women Deans, Adminstrs. and Counselors (internat. students and programs com. 1974-76), Nat. Soc. Fund Raisers, Coun. for Advancement and Support Edn. Home: 11 Carver Rd Wellesley MA 02481-5351 E-mail: c.heartt@comcast.net.

HEASLEY, LAURA MICHELLE, elementary school educator; b. Clarion, Pa. d. Michael Keith and Judy Marie Hetrick; m. Alvin Lee Heasley, Oct. 7, 1989; children: Emily, Justin. BS in Edn., Clarion (Pa.) U., 1993, MS in Edn., 2002. Tchr. first grade Redbank Valley Sch. Dist., New Bethlehem, Pa., 1998—. Treas. family net Cmty. Group, New Bethlehem, 2003—. Mem.: PTO (pres. 1994—), 4-H Club (leader 1998—). Avocations: reading, swimming, time with children. Home: 1306 Heasley Rd New Bethlehem PA 16242 Office: New Bethlehem Elem School 600 Vine St New Bethlehem PA 16242-1163

HEASLEY, THOMAS ALLEN, composer, musician; b. Columbus, Ohio, July 26, 1956; s. Allen Sutcliffe and Bette Lorraine Heasley; m. Martina Gail Brown, Jan. 7, 2001; 1 stepchild, Erik Robert Klinger. Student, Dana Sch. Music, Youngstown State U., 1974—78. Guest lectr. Mills Coll., Oakland, Calif., 1997, Calif. Inst. Arts, Valencia, 2000, Timara/Oberlin Conservatory, 2001, CalArts, 2005. Freelance tubist, Youngstown, Ohio, 1974—79, L.A., 1981—84, NYC, 1985—86, San Francisco Bay, 1988—2002, tubist Charlie Haden's Liberation Orch., LA, 1983—85, Cabrillo Music Festival, Santa Cruz, Calif., 2000, composer, performer, San Francisco, 1999—2003, LA, 2003—, Meet the Composer Concerts, San Francisco, NYC, 2003, composer, performer, prodr. (CD) Where the Earth Meets the Sky, 2001; prodr.: (CD) On the Sensations Tone, 2002, Desert Triptych, 2005; featured (interview) BBC Radio 3, London, 2004. Grantee Am. Composers Forum, San Francisco, 2003, LA, 2005; Artists fellow musical composition, Arts Coun. Silicon

Valley, San Jose, 2002. Mem.: ASCAP (writer, pub. 2001—, award 2002, 2003, 2004), Nat. Assn. Rec. Arts and Scis., Musician's Union, Soc. Composers and Lyricists, Am. Composers Forum (Subito grant chpt. San Francisco Bay area 2003), Internat. Tuba Euphonium Assn. Democrat. Avocations: art, architecture, films. Office: Tom Heasley Full Bleed Music 9663 Santa Monica Blvd Ste 125 Beverly Hills CA 90210 Business E-Mail: tom@tomheasley.com.

HEATH, BERTHANN JONES, education administrator; b. Dallas, May 4, 1938; d. James Lafayette and Allie Mae (Hudson) Jones; m. John Willie Heath, Jr., July 14, 1963 (div. 1975); 1 child, John William, III. BS cum laude, Pepperdine U., 1959; MS, UCLA, 1960. Nat. cert. family and consumer scientist. Tchr., dept. chair L.A. Unified Sch. Dist., 1960—69, tchr. dist. resource, 1972—75; counselor L.A. H.S., 1968—72; regional supr., home econ. edn. Calif. State Dept. Edn., 1975—85; program mgr., sch.-to-career transition San Diego City Sch., 1985—2000; cons., 2000—; owner Berthann's Enterprises, 2000—. Trustee Consumer Credit Counselors of San Diego and Imperial Counties, Calif., 1986-2000; mem. adv. com. Calif. State Dept. Edn. Home Econs. and Health Careers, Sacramento, 1985-98; mem. articulation team SDUSD and San Diego C.C.s, 1987-2000. Author, contbr. to curriculum guides, pamphlets and leaflets. V.p. San Diego chpt. The Links, Inc., 1995-97; presenter TV-8 Looks at Learning and Inside San Diego, 1985-95. Recipient Appreciation/Commendation award Calif. Dept. Edn., 1987, Nat. Gourmet Cook award Nat. Assembly, Links, Inc., 1996, Fin. Literacy Program Svc. award Consumer Credit Counselors of San Diego and Imperial Counties, 1996, Am. Assn. Family and Consumer Scis. Nat. Leader of Yr. award, 1998; named Woman of Distinction, Women, Inc., 1999. Mem. Am. Vocat. Assn. (bylaws chair family and consumer scis. edn. divsn. 1993-97), Nat. Assn. Local Suprs. of Family and Consumer Scis. (pres. 1992-93), Am. Vocat. Assn. (policy and planning com. 1991-97), Calif. Assn. Family and Consumer Scis. (San Diego chpt., chair secondary edn. 1985-95, state chair edn. com. 1989-90, ex-officio mem. articulation com. 1989-96), So. Calif. Biotech. Consortium (charter 1994-96), Links, Inc., Alpha Rho Tau, Delta Sigma Theta, Kappa Omicron Nu, Phi Delta Kappa. Avocations: food design and recipe experimentation, writing, elder care research and development. Office: Berthann's Enterprises PO Box 10823 Marina Del Rey CA 90295

HEATH, DAVID CLAY, mathematics professor, consultant; b. Oak Park, Ill., Dec. 23, 1942; s. Wilbur Curtis and Margaret Helen (Wasson) H.; m. Judith Ellen Simonson, June 13, 1964; children: Kelley Dianne, Michael David, Susan Kathleen. AB, Kalamazoo (Mich.) Coll., 1964; MA, U. Ill., 1965, PhD, 1969. Asst. prof. Sch. Math. U. Minn., Mpls., 1969-75; asst. prof. Cornell U., Ithaca, N.Y., 1975-78, assoc. prof., 1978-88, prof., 1988-96, Merrill Lynch prof. fin. engrg., 1996—; prof. dept. math. scis. Carnegie Mellon U., Pitts., 1997-99, Hoch prof. math. scis., 1999—, head Ctr. for Computational Fin., 1998—. Vis. asst. prof. sch. stats. U. Calif., Berkeley, 1977-78; vis. assoc. prof. sch. math. and stats. U. Minn., 1983-84; vis. prof. U. Strasbourg, France, 1990, 92-93; cons. Galton-Gauss Ptnrs., Berkeley, 1978-81, IBM Corp., Endicott, N.Y., 1981-84, The Options Group, N.Y.C., 1984-87, U.S. Army C.E., 1987-88, Quaker Oats, 1990, Credit Suisse, 1993, Morgan Stanley, 1994, Falcon Asset Mgmt., 1997; bd. dirs. Lehman Bros. Fin. Products, Lehman Bros. Derivative Products. Mem. Am. Math. Soc., Inst. for Math. Statistics, Informs. Avocations: music, scuba, photography. Office: Carnegie Mellon Univ Dept Math Scis Pittsburgh PA 15213-3890 Office Phone: 412-268-2548. Business E-Mail: heath@andrew.cmu.edu. E-mail: dchcmu@comcast.net.

HEATH, DWIGHT BRALEY, anthropologist, educator; b. Hartford, Conn., Nov. 19, 1930; s. Percy Leonard and Luise (Hosp) H.; 1 child, David Braley (dec.). AB in Social Rels., Harvard U., 1952; PhD in Anthropology, Yale U., 1959. Mem. faculty Brown U., 1959—, prof. anthropology, 1970—. Dir. Ctr. for Latin Am. Studies, 1984-87, 88-89; vis. prof., U.S. and abroad, cons. in field. Author: A Journal of the Pilgrims at Plymouth, 1963, 86, Land Reform and Social Revolution in Bolivia, 1969, Historical Dictionary of Bolivia, 1972, Contemporary Cultures and Societies of Latin America, 1965, 74, 3d edit., 2002, Cross-Cultural Approaches to the Study of Alcohol, 1976, Alcohol Use and World Cultures, 1980, Cultural Factors in Alcohol Research and Treatment of Drinking Problems, 1981, International Handbook on Alcohol and Cultures, 1995, Drinking Occasions, 2000; contbr. articles to profl. jours. With AUS, 1952—54. Grantee Nat. Acad. Scis., 1974, Am. Philos. Soc., 1972, Social Sci. Research Council, 1958, Doherty Found., 1956-57, Nat. Inst. Alcohol Abuse and Alcoholism, 1976-81. Mem. AAAS, Am. Anthrop. Assn., Am. Ethnol. Soc., Am. Soc. Ethnohistory, Royal Anthrop. Inst., L.Am. Studies Assn. Office: Brown U Dept Anthropology PO Box 1921 Providence RI 02912-1921 Business E-Mail: Dwight_Heath@brown.edu.

HEATH, FRANK BRADFORD, retired dentist; b. Houston, Dec. 11, 1938; s. Robert Bradford and Maudie H. (Sweeney) H.; m. Heide J.M. Schmidt, Aug. 20, 1965; children: Dirk Alan, Shannon Erika, Kent Bradford. BA, Sam Houston State U., 1961; DDS, U. Tex., Houston, 1965. Pvt. practice, Houston, 1967-2000; ret., 2000. Capt. U.S. Army, 1965-67. Fellow Acad. Gen. Dentistry, Acad. Dentistry Internat.; mem. ADA, Tex. Dental Assn., Houston Dist. Dental Soc., Delta Tau Delta, Xi Psi Phi. Republican. Methodist. Home: 12904 W Shadow Lake Ln Cypress TX 77429-5907 E-mail: fbheath@houston.rr.com.

HEATH, FRED MILTON, library director, educator; b. Dothan, Ala., Aug. 26, 1944; s. Fred Milton and Mary Glenn Marsh Heath; m. Carol Jean Benton, Aug. 6, 1966; children: Laura Elizabeth Heath Case, Joseph Benton. BA in History, Tulane U., 1966; MA in History, U. Va., 1968; MLS, Fla. State U., 1973; EdD in Edn. Adminstrn., Va. Tech., 1980. Commd. 2d lt. USAF, 1968, rose through ranks to capt., 1972; reference libr. U. Richmond, Va., 1973—74; pub. svcs. libr. Radford (Va.) U., 1974—80; libr. dir. U. North Ala., Florence, 1980—87, Tex. Christian U., Ft. Worth, 1987—93; dean of librs. Tex. A&M U., College Station, 1993—2003; vice provost librs. U. Tex., Austin, 2003—. Interim dir. Network Ala. Acad. Librs., Montgomery, 1984—85; chair coun. libr. dirs. Assn. Higher Edn. North Tex., 1990—93; pres. Va. Libr. Assn., 1978—79; editor Libr. Adminstrn. and Mgmt. Assn. Jour. ALA, 1992—93; founding adv. bd. SPARC, 1999—2001. Co-editor: Libraries Act on Their Lilquid and Findings, 2004; mem. editl. bd. Tex. A&M U. Press., 1993—2003, mem. editl. adv. bd. Libr. Quar., 2003—. Grantee Fund for Improvement of Postsecondary Edn., 2000, NSF, 2001, Telecomm. and Informatics Task Force, Tex., 2002. Mem.: Tex. Coun. State Univ. Librs. (pres. 1998—2000), Greater Midwest Libr. Consortium (pres. 1998—99), Assn. Rsch. Librs. (pres. 2002—03). Avocations: golf, kayaking, running, photography. Home: 5909 Tom Wooten Dr Austin TX 78731 Office: U Tex at Austin Mail Stop 5400 Austin TX 78713

HEATH, GEORGE ROSS, oceanographer; b. Adelaide, Australia, Mar. 10, 1939; s. Frederick John and Eleanora (Blackmore) H.; m. Lorna Margaret Sommerville, Oct. 5, 1972; children: Amanda Jo, Alisa Jeanne. BSc, Adelaide U., 1960, BSc with honors, 1961; PhD, U. Calif., 1968. Geologist S. Australian Geol. Survey, Adelaide, 1961-63; asst. prof. oceanography Oreg. State U., Corvallis, 1969-72, assoc. prof., 1972-75, prof., dean, 1978-84; assoc. prof. oceanography U. R.I., Narragansett, 1974-77, prof., 1977-78; dean U. Wash., Seattle, 1984-96, prof., 1984—, dean emeritus, 1996—, chair, faculty, 2004—05; pres., exec. dir. Monterey Bay Aquarium Rsch. Inst., Moss Landing, Calif., 1996-97. Mem. bd. oceans and atmosphere Nat. Assn. State Univs. and Land Grant Colls., 1982-96, co-chmn. exec. com., 1992-93; chmn. legis. com. Commn. on Food, Environment and Renewable Resources, 1994-96; chmn. bd. ocean sci. and policy NRC, 1984-85, mem. bd. radioactive waste mgmt., 1982-90; bd. govs. Joint Oceanographic Instns., Inc., 1978-96, chmn., 1982-84; v.p. sci. com. on oceanic rsch. of Internat. Coun. of Sci. Unions, 1984-90; chmn. performance assessment peer rev. panel Waste Isolation Pilot Plant, 1987-98; bd. dirs. Monterey Bay Aquarium Rsch. Inst; found. com. Coll. Marine Sci. and Fisheries, Sultan Qaboos U., Muscat, Sultanate of Oman, 1994—; adv. panel Odyssey, 1990—, bd. govs., 1999-2000; environ. analyst Sta. KIRO-TV, Seattle, 1993; bd. govs. Consortium for Oceanographic Rsch. & Edn., 1994-98, chmn., 1996-98; bd. govs. Seattle Aquarium Soc., 1998—; mem. Nat. Sea Grant rev. panel, 2001—. Contbr. articles to profl. jours. Recipient Fulbright award, 1963. Fellow AAAS, Geol. Soc. Am., Am. Geophys. Union; mem. Oceanography Soc. Home: 12513 237th Way NE Redmond WA 98053 Office: U Wash Sch Oceanography PO Box 357940 Seattle WA 98195-7940 Office Phone: 206-543-3153. E-mail: rheath@u.washington.edu.

HEATH, JAN ELLEN, artist; b. New Brunswick, N.J., Oct. 1, 1949; d. Jack Howard and Angela Katherine Moran; m. Jonathan Alexander Heath, Oct. 2, 1970; 1 child, Damian. Student, U. Ky., 1967-69, U. Md., 1970, 74, Montgomery Coll., 1974-78. Exhibited in group shows Molloy Coll. Art Gallery, NY, Cultural Ctr., Charleston, WV, US Embassy, Copenhagen, Denmark, Eige Arts Festival, Carlow, Ireland, Arts and Letters Series, Governors Mansion, WV, Nat. Print Exhbn., Hunterdon Art Ctr, NJ, Internat. Print Exhbn., Silvermine Art Ctr., Ct. Mem. Morgan Arts Coun. Home: 250 Quail Run Ln Berkeley Springs WV 25411 Studio: 37 Depot St Berkeley Springs WV 25411

HEATH, JINGER L., cosmetics executive; b. 1952; Interior decorator, cons., Dallas, 1981; chmn. bd. Beauticontrol Cosmetics Inc., Carrollton, Tex., 1981—. Office: Beauticontrol Cosmetics Inc 2121 Midway Rd Carrollton TX 75006-5039

HEATH, JOSEPHINE WARD, foundation administrator; b. San Jose, Calif., Sept. 5, 1937; d. James Hugh and Adella Ward; m. Stratton Rollins Heath Jr.; children: Stratton, Kristin Heath-Colon, Joel. BS, Ea. Oreg. State U., 1959; MS, U. Wis., 1960. Commr. Boulder (Colo.) County, 1982-90; tchg. fellow John F. Kennedy Sch. of Govt., Harvard U., Cambridge, Mass., 1991; spl. asst. to the dir. White Ho. Office of Nat. Svc., Washington, 1993; pres. Jurismonitor, Boulder, 1993-95; tchr., project liberty John F. Kennedy Sch. Govt., Harvard U., Cambridge, 1994-98; pres. The Cmty. Found., Boulder, 1995—. Tchr. Bad Kreuznach, Germany, 1966-67, El Paso, Tex., 1963-64, Appleton, Wis., 1961-62; regional dir. ACTION, Denver, 1977-79. Editor: Alternative Work Patterns, 1977. Candidate U.S. Senate, Colo., 1992, 1990; commr. Met. Baseball Stadium Dist., Maj. League Colo. Rockies, 1991—; county commr. Boulder County, 1982-90; co-founder Women's Found. of Colo., 1987; trainer for elected offcls. in Ctrl. Europe, 1994-98. Named to Colo. Women's Hall of Fame, 2000; recipient William Funk award for Statewide Cmty. Leadership, Colo. Assn. Non Profits, 2004. Mem. Internat. Women's Forum (bd. dirs. 1986-89), Women's Forum of Colo. (pres. 1991). Democrat. Avocations: skiing, hiking, sports. Home: 2455 Vassar Dr Boulder CO 80305-5728 Office: The Cmty Found 1123 Spruce St Boulder CO 80302-4001 Office Phone: 303-442-0436. Personal E-mail: JosieHeath@aol.com.

HEATH, MARIWYN DWYER, writer, legislative issues consultant; b. Chgo., May 1, 1935; d. Thomas Leo and Winifred (Brennan) Dwyer; m. Eugene R. Heath, Sept. 3, 1956; chilren: Philip Clayton, Jeffrey Thomas. BJ, U. Mo., 1956. Mng. editor Chemung Valley Reporter, Horseheads, N.Y., 1956-57; freelance writer, platform spkr., editor Tech. Transls., Dayton, Ohio, 1966—. Cons. Internat. Women's Commn., 1975-76; ERA coord. Nat. Fedn. Bus. and Profl. Women's Clubs, 1974-82, 92—; polit. and mgmt. coms. ERAmerica, 1976-82, exec. dir., 1982-88; pres. Miami Valley Regional Transit Authority, 1986-88; chair Regional Transit Coalition, 1991-94. Author: 75 Years and Beyond-BPW/USA, 1994. Active Gov. Ohio Task Force Credit for Women, 1973, Ohio Womens Commn., 1990-98, vice-chair, 1993-96, chair, 1996-98; midwest regional adv. com. SBA, 1976-82; task force Women Ohio Bicentennial Commn., 1999—; pres. Dayton Pres. Club, 1973-74; chmn. Ohio Coalition ERA Implementation, 1974-75; appt. joint civilian orientation conf. U.S. Dept. Def., 1988. Recipient Legion of Honor award Dayton Pres. Club, 1987, Keeper of Flame award Ohio Sec. of State, 1990; named one of 10 Outstanding Women of World Soroptimist Internat., 1982; named to Ohio Womens Hall of Fame. Mem. AAUW (dir. Dayton 1965-72, Woman of Yr. award Dayton 1974), Nat. Fedn. Bus. and Profl. Womens Clubs (pres. Dayton 1967-69, Ohio 1976-77, nat. polit. action com. 1985-98, chmn. 1988-98), Miami Valley Mil. Affairs Assn. (bd. dirs.), Ohio Women (v.p. 1983-86, bd. dirs. 1977-89), Assn. Women Execs., Women in Comm. Republican. Roman Catholic. Address: Apt 128 100 Huffman Ave Dayton OH 45403-1960

HEATH, MARY ANN, elementary school educator; d. Charles Todd and Annie Lorene Reedy; m. Roy David Heath, Jan. 12, 1974; children: Todd David, Reed Douglas. BS in Edn. cum laude, U. North Tex., 1977; kindermusic cert., U. Dallas, 1991; reading recovery cert., Tex. Women's U., 2001. Slingerland lang. disability cert. Highland Park, Tex., 1977, remedial motor tng. cert. Scottish Rite Hosp., Dallas, 1991, cert. master reading tchr. Tex., ESL Tex., multisensory reading Tex., Dupont leadership cert. Region 10 Tex. Music/lang. arts educator Lubbock (Tex.) Ind. Sch. Dist., 1977—78, second grade educator, 1978—79; music specialist The Children's Workshop, Plano, Tex., 1985—93; fourth grade educator Plano Ind. Sch. Dist., 1993—98, ESL educator, 1998—99, team leader 4th grade, 1999—2000, literacy specialist, 2001—. Mem. Dyslexia edn. adv. bd. Plano Ind. Sch. Dist., 1987—90. Pres. Williams Band Boosters, Plano, 1995—96; 2nd v.p. Plano East Band Boosters, 1997—98; sr. v.p. Plano East Quarterback Club, 1999—2001; mem., bd. dirs., sect. leader, soloist Sweet Adelines, 1978—88. Named, Outstanding Young Women Am., 1982, KFYO (local radio sta.) Outstanding Tchr., 1977. Mem.: Reading Recovery Coun. N.Am., Tex. Staff Devel. Coun., Assn. Tex. Profl. Educators (bd. mem. 1993—95, bd. dirs. 1997—99, Local Educator of Yr. 2002—03, Regional Educator of Yr. 2002—03, State Finalist Educator of Yr. 2002—03), Alpha Delta Pi, Delta Kappa Gamma, Kappa Delta Pi (hon.). Methodist. Avocations: reading, gardening, singing, creative writing. Home: 2604 Winona Plano TX 75074 Office: Stinson Elem Sch 4201 Greenfield Richardson TX 75082

HEATH, MICHAEL R., physical education educator; b. Phila., Aug. 4, 1969; s. Robert and Alexandra Karctas Heath; m. Tara Diane Derstine, July 18, 1992; 1 child, Kylie. BS, Ursinus Coll., 1991. Health and phys. edn. tchr. Springfield (Pa.) Sch. Dist., 1992—, k-12 curriculum coord. health and phys. edn., 2002—. Office: Springfield High Sch 49 W Leamy Dr Springfield PA 19064

HEATH, RICHARD EDDY, lawyer; b. N.J., Nov. 15, 1930; s. W. Eddy and Dorothy (Brown) H.; m. Beth M., June 17, 1955; children: Ellen Louise, David Montgomery, Karen Elizabeth, Deborah Anne. BA cum laude, Swarthmore Coll., 1952; LLB cum laude, Harvard U., 1955. Bar: N.Y., Fla. Teaching fellowship Harvard Law Sch., Cambridge, Mass., 1955-56; assoc. Hodgson and Russ, Buffalo, N.Y., 1956-61, ptnr., 1961—. Bd. dirs. Cliffstar Corp., Dunkirk, N.Y. Trustee Children's Hosp., Buffalo, 1975-98; trustee U. at Buffalo Found., 1966-89, sec., 1976—. Recipient Walter P. Cooke award U. Buffalo, 1978. Office Phone: 561-394-0500.

HEATH, RICHARD RAYMOND, retired investment company executive; b. La Junta, Colo., June 22, 1929; s. Perry Stanford and Genevieve Anabelle (Whitney) H.; m. Arlene Newbrow, Nov. 3, 1961. BA in Econs., U. Colo., 1951, LLB, 1954. Bar: Colo. 1954, Calif. 1957, Ark. 1973. Mem. firm Neyhart & Grodin, San Francisco, 1957-66; dep. Peace Corps dir. Ivory Coast, 1966-68; dir., 1968-69; Peace Corps dir. Mali, 1969-72; dir. Ark. Dept. Fin. and Adminstrn.; also chief fiscal officer, commr. revenues State of Ark., mem. gov.'s cabinet, 1972-77; dir. San Francisco Internat. Airport, 1977-81; v.p., dir. mktg. AIS, Inc., 1981-84; exec. v.p., CFO United Bank, San Francisco, 1984-85; chmn., CEO Nat. Bus. Resources Inc., 1985-87; ptnr. Hakman & Co., Investment Bankers, 1987-2000; chmn., CEO Podarok Internat., Inc., 1993-96; chmn., pres. Heath Mgmt. Svcs., 1994-2000; chmn. Laser Design Internat., LLC, 1996—. Chmn., CEO 1st Calif. Bus. and Indsl. Devel. Corp., United Bus. Ventures; bd. dirs. V-Ray Imaging, Inc.; vice chmn. Multi-State Tax Commn., 1973-74, chmn., 1976-77, mem. exec. com., 1974-77; del. Conf. State Bar Dels. Bd. dirs., treas. San Francisco Midsummer Mozart Festival, 1986-92, chmn., 1999-2000; mem. nat. bd. dirs. Coalition for a Dem. Majority, 1973-76; chmn. bd. dirs. FORUM; mem. conservative caucus nat. Tax Limitation Com., 1980—; mem. rep. presdl. task force Rep. nat. Com., 1980-91. Mem. State Bar Calif., San Francisco Bar Assn. (past chmn. indsl. accident com.), San Francisco Lawyers Club, Am., Calif. trial lawyers assns., San Francisco Planning and Urban Renewal Assn., Nat. Parks Assn., Calif. Applicants Attys. Assn. (v.p.) Clubs: Little Rock Racquet, Little Rock Athletic, San Francisco Tennis (gov.), Rotary Internat., World Trade. Home: 1904 21st Ave E Seattle WA 98112-2906

HEATH, ROBERT F., lawyer; BA, Harvard U., 1969; JD, Georgetown U., 1975, MBA, 1982. Atty. Davison & Easton, Stowe, Vt.; various sr. legal positions U.S. Dept. Transp.; sr. counsel RCA Comm., 1981—84, GE Am. Com., 1984—88; assoc. gen. counsel GE Medical Systems, Milw., 1988—97; sr. v.p., gen. counsel Omnicare, 1997; gen. counsel Briggs & Stratton Corp., Milw., 1997—, asst. sec., 2001, v.p., 2001—, sec., 2002—. Office: Briggs & Stratton Corp 12301 W Wirth St PO Box 702 Wauwatosa WI 53222 Office Phone: 414-259-5333. Office Fax: 414-259-5773.

HEATH, ROSS BRADLEY, consulting company executive; b. Geneva, Ill., June 26, 1959; s. Donald Jeremiah Heath and Louise Zalithea H. BA in English, Augustana Coll., 1982; MS in Tech. Mgmt., U. Md., 1996. Program mgr. performance engrng. Getronics (formerly J.G. Van Dyke & Assocs.), Alexandria, Va., 1992-2000; cons. network architect EDS, Washington, 2001—04; network engr. Northrop Grumman, Washington, 2004—. Mem. City of Alexandria Commn. on Aging, 1989-92; master of ceremonies Annual Lighting of Nat. Christmas Tree, Ellipse, Washington, 1999. Grantee Andrew Mellon Found., 1979; recipient award of Merit City of Alexandria Commn. on Aging, 1993, Cert. of Recognition City of Alexandria, 1993, U.S. Dept. State, 2003, 2005. Mem. Toastmasters (pres. 1998-99, Schweitzer award 1998, Toastmaster of Yr. 1998-99). Avocation: composing music.

HEATHCOCK, CLAYTON HOWELL, chemistry educator, researcher; b. San Antonio, Tex., July 21, 1936; s. Clayton H. and Frances E. (Lay) H.; m. Mabel Ruth Sims, Sept. 6, 1957 (div. 1972); children: Cheryl Lynn, Barbara Sue, Steven Wayne, Rebecca Ann; m. Cheri R. Hadley, Nov. 28, 1980. BSc, Abilene Christian Coll., Tex., 1958; PhD, U. Colo., 1963. Supr. chem. analysis group Champion Paper and Fiber Co., Pasadena, Tex., 1958-60; asst. prof. chemistry U. Calif.-Berkeley, 1964-70, assoc. prof., 1970-75, prof., 1975—, Gilbert Newton Lewis prof., 2003—05, chmn., 1986-89, dean Coll. of Chemistry, 1999—2005; chief scientist Berkeley QB3 Calif. Inst. Quantitative Biomedical Rsch., 2005—. Chmn. Medicinal Chemistry Study Sect., NIH, Washington, 1981-83; mem. sci. adv. coun. Abbott Labs., 1986-97. Author: Introduction to Organic Chemistry, 1976; editor-in chief Organic Syntheses, 1985-86, Jour. Organic Chemistry, 1989-99; contbr. numerous articles to profl. jours. Recipient Alexander von Humboldt U.S. Scientist, 1978, Allan R. Day award, 1989, Prelog medal, 1991, Centenary medal Royal Soc. Chemistry, 1995. Mem. AAAS, Am. Acad. Arts and Scis., Am. Chem. Soc. (chmn. divsn. organic chemistry 1985, Ernest Guenther award 1986, award for creative work in synthetic organic chemistry 1990, A.C. Cope scholar 1990, H.C. Brown medal 2002, Paul Gassman award 2004), Nat. Acad. Scis., Royal Soc. Chemistry (Centenary medal 1995), Am. Soc. Pharmacology. Home: 5235 Alhambra Valley Rd Martinez CA 94553-9765 Office: U Calif Dept Chemistry Berkeley CA 94720-1460 Office Phone: 510-642-3360. Business E-Mail: heathcock@berkeley.edu.

HEATHCOCK, LEANN KAY, elementary school educator; b. Wichita, June 8, 1955; d. William Arthur and Marva Catherine Tarr; m. Steven Edwin Heathcock, Sept. 23, 1973. AA, Fullerton Jr. Coll., 1977; BS, Calif. State U., Fullerton, 1978. Tchr. elem. sch. Chino Unified Sch. Dist., Calif., 1982—. Recipient Hon. Svc. award, PTA, 1989; grantee, Rotary, 2001, 2002; Classroom Tchr. Instructional grantee, 1986. Republican. Avocations: miniatures, sewing, genealogy, travel. Office: Chino Unified Sch Dist 5130 Riverside Dr Chino CA 91710

HEATLEY, DANY, professional hockey player; b. Freibourg, Germany, Jan. 21, 1981; Right wing Atlanta Thrashers, 2001—; named WCHA's rookie of the yr., 1999—2000. Mem. Team Canada, World Cup of Hockey, 2004. Named to NHL All-Rookie Team, 2002, NHL All-Star game, 2003; recipient Calder Memorial Trophy, 2002, MVP, NHL All-Star game, 2003. Achievements include mem. World Cup Champion Team Can., 2004. Office: Atlanta Hockey Club Inc 1 CNN Ctr 13 S Atlanta GA 30303

HEATON, CHARLES LLOYD, dermatologist, educator; b. Bryan, Tex., May 8, 1935; BS, Tex. A&M U., 1957; MD, Baylor U., 1961; MA (hon.), U. Pa., 1973. Diplomate Am. Bd. Dermatology. Intern Jefferson Davis Hosp., Houston, 1961-62; resident Baylor U., 1962-65; sr. attending physician Phila. Gen. Hosp., 1965-69, chief of svc., 1970-77; mem. dept. dermatology U. Pa. Sch. Medicine, 1966-78; assoc. prof. dermatology U. Pa., 1973-78, U. Cin., 1978-85, prof., 1985—, interim dir. dept. dermatology, 1998. Author: Audiovisual Course in Venereal Disease, 1972, (with D.M. Pillsbury) Manual of Dermatology, 1980; contbr. 35 articles to profl. jours., 12 chpts. to books. Served to lt. comdr. USPHS, 1965-67. Named Ohio Dermatologist of Yr., 2000. Fellow ACP, AAD, Coll. Physicians of Phila.; mem. AMA, Soc. Investigative Dermatology, Am. Venereal Disease Assn., Am. Dermatol. Assn., Cin. Dermatol. Soc., Alpha Omega Alpha Home: 5534 E Galbraith Rd Apt 25 Cincinnati OH 45236-2840 Office: U Cin Coll Medicine Dept Dermatology 231 Albert Sabin Way Cincinnati OH 45229-2827 Business E-Mail: charles.heaton@uc.edu.

HEATON, LARRY CADWALDER, security firm executive; b. St. Louis, Aug. 19, 1934; s. John Raymond and Martha Elizabeth (Simpson) H.; m. Dorothy Mueller, Dec. 10, 1953; children: Tannice Jo, Larry C. II, Kent M., Eric S., Elmo D.J., David J. II. Student, So. Ill. U., 1959; BSBA, U. Tampa, 1962; postgrad., Chgo. Kent Coll. Law, 1962-65. Registered investment advisor. Adjuster N.Y. Ctrl. R.R., Chgo., 1962-65; salesman/sales mgr. SCM Inc., Chgo., 1965-68; agt., gen. agt. Thomas Jefferson Life Ins., Champaign, Ill., 1969-75; gen. agt. Ctrl. Nat. Life Ins., Jacksonville, Ill., 1975-80; pres., co-founder Nurses Guaranteed Retirement Life Ins., Jacksonville, Fla., 1980-85; gen. agt., mgr. Nat. Old Line Ins., Little Rock, 1985-95; pres., owner Larry C. Heaton & Assocs., Jacksonville, Fla., 1996—. Chmn. PFL Agts. Adv. Bd., Little Rock, 1992. Co-author state manual: Illinois Young Republicans, 1965 (Nat. Young Republican award). Adminstrv. asst., speech writer Ill. Young Republicans, 1962-68; precinct capt. Cook County Rep. Orgn., Oak Park, Ill., 1965-68; mem. Rep. Presdl. Task Force, Washington, 1982—; mem. House/Senate Adv. Bd., Washington, 1985—. Sgt. U.S. Army, 1953-56. Active vestry, jr. warden/vestry San Jose Episcopal Ch., 1999-2002, sr. warden/vestry, 2002-2003. Recipient Bronze plaque Nat. Assn. Life Underwriters, 1973, Nat. Performance award Nat. Assn. Life Underwriters, 1973, Nat. Quality award Nat. Assn. Life Underwriters, 1974, Million Dollar Round Table award Nat. Assn. Life Underwriters, 1970-85. Mem. Inst. CFPs, Internat. Assn. Fin. Planning, Certified Estate Planner, Certified Charitable Tax Deductible Adv., NCF, Masons (32d degree). Republican. Episcopalian. Avocations: family, golf, painting, sailing. Office Phone: 904-730-5130. E-mail: lcheaton@aol.com.

HEATON, PATRICIA, actress; b. Bay Village, Ohio, Mar. 4, 1958; d. Chuck and Pat Heaton; m. David Hunt Oct. 10, 1990; children: Sam, John Basil, Joseph Charles, Daniel Patrick. BA in Theater, Ohio State U., 1980. Spokesperson Albertsons, Inc. supermarkets. Actor (stage) The Johnstown Vindicator, 1987, Don't Get God Started, 1987-88, Miracle in the Woods, 1997, (TV series) Room for Two, 1992-93, Someone Like Me, 1994, Women of the House, 1995, Everybody Loves Raymond, 1996—2005 (Best Actress in Quality Comedy Viewers for Quality TV award 1998, Outstanding Lead Actress in Comedy Series Emmy award, 2000 and 2001); (TV movies) Shattered Dreams: The Charlotte Fedders Story, 1990, Miracle in the Woods, 1997, A Town Without Christmas, 2001, The Goodbye Girl, 2004, (films) Beethoven, 1992, Memoirs of an Invisible Man, 1992, The New Age, 1994, Space Jam, 1996; TV appearances include Alien Nation, 1989, Thirtysomething, 1989-91, Matlock, 1990, DEA, 1991, Party of Five, 1996, The King of

Queens, 1999, (voice) Danny Phantom, 2004; author (book): Motherhood and Hollywood, 2003. Hon. chairperson Feminists for Life. Mem.: Delta Gamma. Office: United Talent Agency 9560 Wilshire Blvd Ste 500 Beverly Hills CA 90212*

HEATON, STUART ALAN, lawyer; b. Orange, Calif., Mar. 28, 1956; m. Carolyn T. Heaton. BA, Calif. State U., Fullerton, 1979; JD, UCLA, 1982; MBA, Vanderbilt U., 1991. Bar: Fla. 1982, Tenn. 1989. Atty. Preddy, Kutner, Rubinoff, Brown & Thompson, Dixon, Dixon, Hurst & Nicklaus, Miami; v.p., gen. counsel Thomas Nelson Inc., 1989—96; asst. gen. counsel Lockheed Martin Corp., 1997—2002; v.p., gen. counsel, corp. sec. CarMax Inc., Glen Allen, Va., 2002—. Mem.: Assn. of Corp. Counsel, Richmond Bar Assn., Va. Bar Assn., Tenn. Bar Assn., Fla. Bar Assn., ABA. Office: CarMax Inc 4900 Cox Rd Glen Allen VA 23060

HEATWOLE, MARK M., lawyer; b. Pitts., Jan. 28, 1948; s. Marion Grove and Phyllis Adelle (Leiter) H.; m. Sarah Ann Collier, Dec. 30, 1970; children: Mary Phyllis, Elizabeth Collier, Anna Bell. BA, Washington and Lee U., 1969, JD, 1972. Bar: Ill. 1972, U.S. Dist. Ct. (no. dist.) Ill. 1972, U.S. Ct. Appeals (7th cir.) 1977, U.S. Supreme Ct. 1980, U.S. Tax Ct. 1987. Assoc. Chadwell & Kayser, Ltd., Chgo., 1972-79, ptnr., v.p., 1979-89; ptnr. Winston & Strawn LLP, Chgo., 1990—. Treas. Lyric Opera Chgo. Guild, 1980—81, v.p., 1980—81, chmn. fundraising, 1986; vice-chmn. Gorton Cmty. Ctr., 1986; chmn. bd. Gorton Cmty. Ctr. Found., 1986—89; trustee Barat Coll., 1982—85, The Admiral, Chgo., 1988—2001, Allendale Assn., 1991—2000; mem. Art Inst. of Chgo. Old Masters Soc., 1999—; Mem. 1st ward Rep. com. on candidates Lake Forest (Ill.) Caucus, 1985—88, chmn., 1987—88, vice-chmn., 1989—90, chmn., 1990—91; mem. session Lake Forest Presbyn. Ch., 1978—84, chmn. ch. and society com., 1980; bd. dirs. Lyric Opera Chgo. Guild, 1976—, Lake Forest Symphony, 1987—91, Rehab. Inst. Chgo. Enterprises, 1991—2001, Gorton Community Ctr., 1982—88. Mem.: ABA (continuing legal edn. com. 1978—79, mem. antitrust com. young lawyers sect. 1978—81, com. on civil practice and procedure antitrust sect. 1980, bus. law sect. 1986—, patent trademark and copyright sect. 1990—), Chgo. Bar Assn. (chmn. profl. responsibility com. young lawyers sect. 1977—78, mem. exec. com. 1978—79, bd. dirs.), Valley Club Montecito, Lawyers Club, Econ. Club Chgo., Shoreacres Club (bd. govs. 1996—, pres. 2002—04). Republican. Office: Winston & Strawn LLP 35 W Wacker Dr Ste 4200 Chicago IL 60601-1695 Office Phone: 312-558-5137. E-mail: mheatwole@winston.com.

HEAVEY, MIKE, judge; m. Connie Heavey; children: Michael James, Shana Marie, Christa Colleen. BA in Polit. Sci., U. Wash.; JD, U. Santa Clara. Pvt. practice; mem. Wash. Legislature, Olympia, 1995—2001, chair jud. com., mem. commerce, trade, housing and fin. instns. com., mem. transp. com.; judge Kings County Superior Ct., 2002—. Mem. 34th Dist. Dems.; mem. Fauntleroy Cmty. Assn.; fundraiser West Seattle chpt. YMCA. 1st lt. U.S. Army, Vietnam. Decorated Bronze Star. Mem. Wash. State Bar Assn., Am. Legion (Post 160), Tyee Club (U. Wash.), Pres.'s Club (U. Wash.), Kiwanis, Quad Club, Phi Alpha Delta. Democrat. Office: Kings County Superior Ct 516 3rd Ave Seattle WA 98104

HEAVICAN, MICHAEL G., prosecutor; b. 1947; BA, JD, U. Nebr. From dep. county atty. yo chief dep. county atty. Lancaster County, Nebr., 1975—81, county atty., 1981—91; chief of criminal div. U.S. Atty.'s Office Nebr. U.S. Dept. Justice, Nebr., 1991—2001, U.S. atty., 2001—. Office: 1620 Dodge St Ste 1400 Omaha NE 68102-1506

HEBARD, BARBARA ADAMS, conservator; b. Fort Dodge, Iowa, July 26, 1951; d. George D. and Bonnie J. Adams; m. Christopher G. Hebard, Jan. 10, 1981. B, U. Mass., 1975. Handbinder cert. North Bennet St. Sch., Mass., 1990. Book conservator Boston Athenaeum, 1990—. Chair alumni steering com. North Bennet St. Sch., Boston, 1998—2002, mem. corp., 2002—04, overseer, 2004—. Author: (catalogue) Boston Athenaeum Conservation Dept. Finishing Tools, 10 Years 10 Binders; exhibition, Roundup: Rocky Mountain chpt. Guild of Book Workers, 9th Wexford Artist Books Exhbn., Book Explorations, Arts Iowa City: Multiple Talents, 10 Years 10 Binders, Heaven on Earth: Lone Star Chapter of the Guild of Book Workers, Essence: The Art of Simplicity, Society of Arts and Crafts: Centennial Education Exhibition, Planet Dada Show, The Nurtured Spirit: Rocky Mountain Chapter of the Guild of Book Workers Exhibit, NE School of Art and Design exhibit, Bound Together: Ten Years of Bookbinding at North Bennet Street School, Boston Athenaeum Members Exhibition, New England Vignettes: NE Chapter of Guild of Book Workers, Leap of Faith, 1st International Collage Exhibition, North Bennet Street School Juried Show of Graduate Work; contbr. articles to Athenaeum Items, The Beacon, Pittock Papers. Mem. parish coun. St. Paul Ch., Cambridge, Mass., 2003—. Andrew Oliver Wellspring fellow. Fellow: Internat. Inst. Conservation Hist. and Artistic Works (profl. assoc.); mem.: New Eng. Conservation Assn., Assn. Coll. and Rsch. Librs., Am. Inst. Conservation Hist. and Artistic Works (assoc.), Guild Book Workers, Ticknor Soc. Achievements include design of design binding, Grace Raymond Hebard scrapbook purchased by the Marriott Rare Book Library at the University of Utah. Office: Boston Athenaeum 10 1/2 Beacon St Boston MA 02108 Office Phone: 617-720-7632. Business E-Mail: hebard@bostonathenaeum.org.

HEBB, MALCOLM HAYDEN, physicist; b. Marquette, Mich., July 21, 1910; s. Thomas Carlyle and Evelyn Shewell (Hayden) H.; m. Marion Elizabeth Evers, May 8, 1943. BA, U. B.C., 1931, D.Sc. (hon.), 1963; postgrad., U. Wis., 1931-34; PhD, Harvard, 1936. Instr. physics Harvard, 1936-37; Harvard Sheldon travelling fellow to U. Utrecht, 1937-38; instr. physics Duke, 1938-42; anti-submarine devices Harvard Underwater Sound Lab., Nat. Def. Research Com., 1942-45; physicist research lab. Sharples Corp., 1945-49; research asso. Gen. Electric Co., 1949-51, mgr. gen. physics research dept., 1951-68, physicist, 1968-75. Vis. com. physics Tufts U., 1967; mem. council Harvard Found., 1958-63; vis. com. elec. engring. Princeton, 1959-71 Recipient Gov. Gen. Medal B.C., 1931 Fellow Am. Phys. Soc.; mem. Netherlands Phys. Soc., Sigma Xi. Clubs: Mohawk, Mohawk Golf. Home: 1600 E Crooked Lake Dr Eustis FL 32726-5720 Office: Gen Electric Co Research Lab Schenectady NY 12345-0001

HEBBELER, REGIS J., lawyer; JD, George Mason U., 1977. Corp. counsel Diversifoods, Inc., Lafayette, La., The Pillsbury Co., Atlanta; asst. gen. counsel S&A Restaurant Corp.; assoc. legal counsel Real Estate Div. Goody's Family Clothing, Inc., Knoxville, Tenn., 1993—95, v.p., gen. counsel, asst. sec., 1995—. Mem.: ABA, Am. Corp. Counsel Assn., DC Bar Assn. Office: Goody's Family Clothing, Inc 400 Goodys Lane Knoxville TN 37922-1900 Office Phone: 865-966-2000.

HEBDA, LAWRENCE JOHN, data processing executive, consultant; b. East Chicago, Ind., Apr. 9, 1954; s. Walter Martin and Barbara (Matczynski) H.; m. Cynthia Ruta Aizkalns, June 17, 1978. BS, Purdue U., 1976; MBA, U. Iowa, 1983. Cert. data processor. Programmer Inland Steel Co., East Chicago, 1976-77; data analyst Deere & Co., Moline, Ill., 1977-82, systems analyst, 1982-83, project mgr., 1983-84, dealer systems cons., 1984-85, corp. planning analyst, 1985-87, systems edn. adminstr., 1987-88, telecommunications analyst, 1988; info. systems sr. cons. Hewitt Assocs., Lincolnshire, Ill., 1988-93, MIS bus. mgr., 1994-97, mgr. software distbn./oper. sys., 1997-2000, mgr. client/server application support, 2000—02, sr. application project mgr., 2002—. Instr. computer sci. dept. Coll. Lake County Ill., 1996—, mem. computer info. systems adv. bd., 1999—. Mem. Nat. Rep. Congl. Com., 1982-85; charter mem. Rep. Presdl. Task Force, 1980; chmn. pastoral coun. Roman Cath. Ch., 1994-95. Recipient Cert. Recognition, Nat. Rep. Congl. Com., 1982-85, Presdl. Achievement award Rep. Nat. Com., 1984. Mem. Data Processing Mgmt. Assn., Am. Legion, Internat. Platform Assn., DAV Comdr.'s Club, King's Men Religious Orgn. (v.p. 1985, pres. 1986-87), Toastmasters Internat. (assoc. area gov. 1983-84), K.C. (3d degree coun. 8022, 2001, Dep. Grand Knight 2002-03, fin. sec., 2003-). Roman Catholic. Home: 675 Sussex Cir Vernon Hills IL 60061-2123 Office: Hewitt Assocs 100 Half Day Rd Lincolnshire IL 60069-3242 Office Phone: 847-295-5000. E-mail: ljhebda@hewitt.com.

HEBEL, DORIS A., astronomer; b. Chgo., Jan. 1, 1935; d. Erich and Anna Dorothea (Hircy) H.; m. Leon L. Bram, Apr. 29, 1961 (div. Dec. 1973); 2 children. Libr. Campbell-Mithun, Chgo., 1958—61, Kenyon & Eckhardt, Chgo., 1961—64; pres. Astro-Technic Forecasting, Chgo., 1965—. Contbr. numerous articles in astrological jours. and mags.; author: Contemporary Lectures, 1975, Celestial Psychology, 1985. Mem. Am. Fedn. Astrologers (life), Nat. Coun. Geocosmic Rsch. (life, nat. bd. dirs. 1975-80), Nat. Astrol. Soc., Assn. for Astrol. Networking, Internat. Soc. for Astrol. Rsch. Avocations: reading, singing, walking, metaphysical subjects, arts. Home and Office: 150 W Maple St Apt 1518 Chicago IL 60610-5433 Office Phone: 312-751-9382. Business E-Mail: dorishebel@core.com.

HEBELER, HENRY KOESTER, retired electronics executive, aerospace engineer; b. St. Louis, Aug. 12, 1933; s. Henry and Viola O. (Koester) H.; m. Mirriam Robb, Aug. 12, 1978; children by previous marriage: Linda Ruth, Laura Ann. BS in Aero. Engring., MS, MIT, 1956, MBA, 1970. Gen. mgr. rsch./engring. Boeing Aerospace Co., Seattle, 1970-72, pres., 1980-85; v.p. bus. devel. The Boeing Co., Seattle, 1973-74, exec. coun. and corp. v.p. planning, 1988-89; pres. Boeing Engring. & Constrn. Co., Seattle, 1975-79, Boeing Electronics Co., Seattle, 1985-87. Bd. dirs. Microelectronics and Computer Tech. Corp.; mem. fusion panel Ho. of Reps., 1979-81, energy rsch. adv. bd. Dept. Energy, 1980-81, task force on internat. industry Def. Sci. Bd., 1982-84, adv. com. nat. strategic materials and minerals program U.S. Dept. Interior, 1986—. Author: Your Winning Retirement Plan, 2001. Bd. govs. Sloan Sch., MIT, 1980-84; bd. visitors Def. Systems Mgmt. Coll., Ft. Belvoir, Va. Recipient Mead prize for aero. engrs., 1956; Kuljian humanities award, 1954; Sperry Gyroscope fellow, 1956; Sloan fellow M.I.T., 1970 Mem. AIAA, Nat. Aeros. Assn., Assn. of U.S. Army, Armed Forces Comm. and Electronics Assn. (bd. dirs.), Aviation Hall of Fame, Ala. Space and Rocket Ctr. (sci. and adv. com. 1980-85), Nat. Space (bd. govs. 1980-85), Meridian Valley Country Club. Achievements include patents in field. Home and Office: 24600 140th Ave SE Kent WA 98042-5160

HEBENSTREIT, JAMES BRYANT, agricultural products executive, bank and venture capital executive; b. Long Beach, Calif., Mar. 8, 1946; s. William Joseph and Jean (Stark) H.; m. Marilyn Bartlett, Aug. 23, 1986. AB, Harvard U., 1968, MBA, 1973. Pres. Terra-Light div. Butler Mfg. Co., Boston, 1980-82, Capital for Bus., Inc. (SB/C, venture capital affiliate Commerce Bancshares), St. Louis and Kansas City, Mo., 1982-87; sr. v.p. fin., CFO Commerce Bancshares, Inc., Kansas City, 1985-87, bd. dirs., 1987—; pres. Bartlett and Co., Kansas City, 1992—. Lt. USNR, 1968-71. Home: 1016 W 58th St Kansas City MO 64113-1133 Office: Bartlett & Co 4800 Main St Kansas City MO 64112-2510

HEBENSTREIT, JEAN ESTILL STARK, religion educator, practitioner; d. Charles Dickey and Blanche (Hervey) Stark; m. William J. Hebenstreit, Sept. 4, 1942; children: James B., Mark W. Student Conservatory of Music, U. Mo. at Kansas City, 1933-34; AB, U. Kans., 1936. Authorized C.S. practitioner, Kansas City, 1955—; bd. dirs. 3d Ch., Kansas City, 1952-55, chmn. bd., 1955, reader, 1959-62; authorized C.S. tchr. C.S. Bd., 1964—, bd. dirs. Boston, 1977-83, chmn., 1981—82. Mem. Christian Sci. Bd. of Lectureship, Christian Sci. Bd. Edn.; bd. trustees The Christian Sci. Pub. Soc., bd. dirs. First Ch. Christ.Scientist, 1977-83, chmn., 1981-82. Contbr. articles to C.S. lit. Pres. Mother Ch., The First Ch. of Christ, Scientist, 1999. Mem. Art of Assembly Parliamentarians (charter, 1st pres.), Pi Epsilon Delta, Alpha Chi Omega (past pres.), Carriage Club. Home: 310 W 49th St Ste A-2 Kansas City MO 64112-2425 Office: 310 W 49th St Apt A-3 Kansas City MO 64112-2425

HEBERLING, TIMOTHY ALAN, information scientist; b. Portsmouth, Va., Sept. 3, 1955; s. Donald Anthony and Phyllis Elaine (McMillan) H.; m. Judith Ann Tohill, June 13, 1992; children: Ellen, Ben, Hanna. Student, James Madison U., 1973—74; BS in Computer Sci., Va. Tech., 1986. Commd. 2d lt. USAF, 1986, advanced through grades to capt., 1990, law enforcement specialist Hampton, Va., 1975—79, entry contr. Chievres, Belgium, 1979—82, security police flight chief Enid, Okla., 1982—83; comm.-computer officer Air Force Hdqts., Washington, 1987—91; info. sys. officer Def. Info. Sys., Reston, Va., 1991—94; sr. sys. adminstr. The White House, Washington, 1994—96; ret. USAF, 1995; sr. info. sys. engr. Mitretek Sys., McLean, Va., 1996—97; tech. mgr. AOL Internet Svcs., Sterling, Va., 1997—. Cons. WebVisor, Leesburg, Va., 1996—. Blood drive coord. Def. Info. System Agy., Reston, 1991-94, United Way vol. Decorated various Air Force medals. Mem. Air Force Security Police Assn. Home: 19553 Herndon Ct Leesburg VA 20175-6759 Office: Am Online Internet Svcs 22080 Pacific Blvd Sterling VA 20166-9304 Personal E-mail: wwwvisor@aol.com.

HEBERT, BLISS EDMUND, opera director; b. Faust, N.Y., Nov. 30, 1930; s. Wilfrid Joseph and Merle Addasah (Bliss) H. BA, Syracuse U., 1951, M.Mus., 1952; piano pupil of, Robert Goldsand, Simone Barrere, Lelia Gousseau. Gen. mgr. Washington Opera Soc., 1960-63; guest dir. Juilliard Sch., 1975-76; mem. faculty Boston U., 1952-53, U. Wash., 1969. Stage dir., Met. Opera, N.Y.C., 1973-75, N.Y. City Opera, 1963-75, Santa Fe Opera, 1957—; dir. opera companies of, San Francisco, 1963, Houston, 1964, Seattle Opera, 1967, Toronto, 1972, San Diego, 1970, Vancouver, B.C., 1969, Ft. Worth, 1966, Washington, 1959, Cin., 1968, Portland, Oreg., 1969, Caramoor Festival, Katonah, N.Y., 1966, La Gune Festival, 1968—, New Orleans, 1970, Balt., 1972, Tulsa, 1975, Miami, Fla., 1975, Charlotte, N.C., 1975, Dallas, 1977, Shreveport, La., 1977, Chgo., 1983, Montreal, 1984, Boston, 1984, Cleve., 1988, Opera Northern Ireland, 1988, Virginia Opera, 1991, Opera Mexico City, 1993, Austin Opera, 1993, Florentine Opera, Milw., 1994, Atlanta Opera, 2005; rec. artist, Columbia records; as stage dir. for Igor Stravinsky's major operas under his conducting. Served AUS, 1954-56. Mem. Lambda Chi Alpha, Phi Mu Alpha. Office: care John S Miller 2nd Fl 889 Ninth Ave New York NY 10019

HEBERT, JAY HOWELL, lawyer; b. Lake Charles, La., Jan. 31, 1961; s. John Roland and Cynthia Hope (Johnson) H.; m. Camille Renee Comeau, June 8, 1986; 1 child, Isabel Suzanne. BA summa cum laude, Rice U., 1983; JD magna cum laude, Harvard U., 1986. Bar: Tex. 1986, U.S. C. Appeals (5th cir.) 1987, U.S. Supreme Ct. 1990, D.C. 2001. Law clk. to presiding judge U.S. Ct. Appeals (5th cir.), Dallas, 1986-87; with Hughes & Luce LLP, Dallas, 1987—96, Vinson & Elkins LLP, Dallas, 1996—, ptnr. Bus. and Internat. Group Washington, DC, 1996—, chair Comm. Practice Group. Mem. Tex. Bar Assn., DC Bar Assn. Office: Vinson & Elkins LLP Ste 600 1455 Pennsylvania Ave NW Washington DC 20004 Office Phone: 202-639-6521. E-mail: jhebert@velaw.com.

HEBERT, PAUL B, insurance company executive; BS in acctg., Ctrl. Conn. State U. With Hartford Ins. Group; database adminstr. for corp. gen. ledger Aetna Inc., 1987—2001, v.p., dir. of internal audit, 2001—. Mem. accountancy adv. bd. Ctrl. Conn. State U. Mem.: Ctr. for Internal Audit of La. State U. (adv. bd.), Inst. of Internal Auditors (mem. So. New England chapt.). Office: Aetna Inc 151 Farmington Ave Hartford CT 06156

HEBERT, ROBERT D., academic administrator; b. Abbeville, La., Nov. 14, 1938; married. BA, U. Southwestern La., 1959; MA, Fla. State U., 1961, PhD, 1966. Asst. prof. history Miss. State U., 1962-69, assoc. prof. history, 1969-76; prof. McNeese State U., 1976—, v.p. acad. affairs, 1980-87, pres., 1987—. Office: McNeese State U Office Pres Lake Charles LA 70609-0001 E-mail: rhebert@mcneese.edu.

HEBERT, SCOTT F., assistant principal, consultant; b. Meadville, Pa., May 10, 1967; s. Clifford Harry and Beverly Ann Hebert; m. Sarah Lynn Haber, July 28, 1990; children: Teresa Nicole, Alexander Michael. BS in Edn., Slippery Rock (Pa.) U., 1988; MS in Ednl. Leadership, Nova Southeastern U., 1998; EDS in Sch. Guidance and Counseling, Argosy U. Cert. elem. educator Fla., ednl. leadership Fla., sch. guidance and counseling Fla. Tchr. grades K-6 Citrus County Schs, Inverness, Fla., 1989—94; tchr., guidance counselor, tech. specialist Citrus County Schs., Inverness, 1995—2004, asst. prin. Homosassa, Fla.; tchr. pre-k Wilmington (Del.) Friends Sch., 1994. Facilitator U.S. Dept. Edn., Washington, 2000—01. Edn. chair Fla. PTA, Orlando, 2001—03; mem. Fla. Edn. Stds. Commn., Fla. Dept. of Edn., Tallahassee, 1998—2000; mem. Commr.'s Cmty. Involvement Coun., Tallahassee, 1998—2001. Named Fla. Tchr. of the Yr., Fla. Dept. of Edn., 1999; named to Fla. Educators Hall of Fame, 1998; recipient Nat. Educator award, Milken Family Found., 1998. Mem.: ASCD (assoc.), Fla. League of Tchrs., Southea. Regional Vision for Edn. (assoc.). Republican. Avocations: reading, swimming, running, basketball. Home: 1388 E Bismark St Hernando FL 34442 Office: Homosassa Elem Sch PO Box 498 10935 W Yulee Dr Homosassa FL 34487 Office Phone: 352-628-2953. Home Fax: 352-628-5408; Office Fax: 352-628-5408. Personal E-mail: shebert@infionline.net. E-mail: heberts@citrus.k12.fl.us.

HEBERT, WILLIAM N., lawyer; b. Iowa City, Iowa, Oct. 19, 1960; AB with distinction, Stanford Univ., 1983; JD, Boalt Law Sch., Univ. Calif., Berkeley, 1988. Bar: Calif. 1988, US Dist. Ct. (no., ctrl. & ea. Calif., Colo.), US Ct. Appeals, 9th cir. Ptnr., Global Litigation practice Coudert Bros. LLP, San Francisco. Mediator US Dist. Ct., no. Calif. dist. Contbr. articles to profl. jours. Mem.: Fed. Bar Assn. (mem. steering com., no. dist. Calif.). Office: Coudert Bros LLP Suite 2100 1 Market Spear St Tower San Francisco CA 94105-1126 Office Phone: 415-267-6200. Office Fax: 415-977-6110. Business E-Mail: whebert@coudert.com.

HEBERTON, GEORGE H., lawyer; b. Phila., 1957; BA cum laude, Vanderbilt U., 1978; JD, U. Ga., 1981. Bar: Ga. 1981. Ptnr. Roberts, Isaf & Summers (acquired by McGuireWoods in 1999), McGuireWoods LLP, Atlanta, 1999—, mng. ptnr. Atlanta office, 2000—03, chair firm real estate & environ. dept. Office: McGuireWoods LLP Ste 2100 1170 Peachtree St NE Atlanta GA 30309-7649 Office Phone: 404-443-5710. Office Fax: 404-443-5767. Business E-Mail: gheberton@mcguirewoods.com.

HECETA, ESTHERBELLE AGUILAR, retired anesthesiologist; b. Cebu City, Philippines, Jan. 1, 1935; came to U.S., 1962, naturalized, 1981; d. Serafin Aquilar and Elsie (Nichols) Aguilar; m. Wilmer G. Heceta, Apr. 5, 1962; children: W. Cristina, W. Elgine, Wuela E. BS in Chemistry cum laude, Silliman U., Dumaguete City, Philippines, 1955, BS cum laude, 1956; MD cum laude, U. East Ramon Magsaysay, Quezon City, Philippines, 1961. Diplomate Am. Bd. Anesthesiology, Philippine Bd. Anesthesiology. Intern Youngstown (Ohio) Hosp. Assocs., 1962-63, resident in anesthesiology, 1963-66; anesthesiologist Salem (Ohio) City Hosp., 1967, St. Joseph's Hosp., Manapla, Philippines, 1967-72; instr. dept. anesthesiology U. Tenn., Memphis, 1972-74; staff anesthesiologist Ohio Valley Med. Ctr., Wheeling, W.Va., 1974—, Bellaire (Ohio) City Hosp., 1975—, East Ohio Regional Hosp., Martins Ferry, 1989—. Jt. conf. com. for profl. affairs, exec. com., sec.-treas. med. dental staff Ohio Valley Med. Ctr., 1992-96, pres.-elect, 1993-94, pres. med. dental staff, 1994-95; physician reviewer Anesthesiology W.Va. Med. Inst., 1992-96. Claims rev. panel W.Va. Med. Assn., 1990-95; vol. med.-surg. mission to Philippines, 1982-90. Fellow Am. Coll. Anesthesiology; mem. AMA, Am. Soc. Anesthesiologists, Ohio Valley Phillipine Med. Assn. (pres. 1988-90), Tri-State Phillipine-Am. Assn. (pres. 1991-92), Assn. Philippine Physicians in Am., Philippine Soc. Anesthesiologists in Am., W.Va. Soc. Anesthesiologists, Internat. Anesthesia Rsch. Soc., Am. Med. Womens Assn. (organizer, pres. 1983, regional gov. region IV 1987-89), W.Va. Med. Soc., Ohio County Med. Soc. Presbyterian. Home and Office: 15 Holly Rd Wheeling WV 26003-5656

HECHE, ANNE (ANNE CELESTE HECHE), actress; b. Aurora, Ohio, May 25, 1969; d. Donald Heche; m. Coley Laffoon, 2001; 1 child, Homer Heche Laffoon. Appearances include (film) An Ambush of Ghosts, 1993, The Adventures of Huck Finn, 1993, A Simple Twist of Fate, 1994, Milk Money, 1994, I'll Do Anything, 1994, The Wild Side, 1995, Pie in the Sky, 1995, Walking and Talking, 1996, The Juror, 1996, Volcano, 1997, Donnie Brasco, 1997, Wag the Dog, 1997, I Know What You Did Last Summer, 1997, Return to Paradise, 1998, Six Days Seven Nights, 1998, Psycho, 1998, The Third Miracle, 1999, Auggue Rose, 2000, Prozac Nation, 2001, John Q., 2002, Timepiece, 2003, Birth, 2004; (TV movies) O Pioneers!, 1992, Against the Wall, 1994, Girls in Prison, 1994, The Investigator, 1994, Kingfish: A Story of Huey P. Long, 1995, If These Walls Could Talk, 1996, Wild Side, 1996, SUBWAYStories: Tales from the Underground, 1997, One Kill, 2000, Gracie's Choice, 2004, The Dead Will Tell, 2004, Sexual Life, 2005,(TV series) Another World, 1987-91, Murphy Brown, 1991-92, Ally McBeal, 2001, Ellen, 1998, Everwood, 2004-05, (TV spls.) Soap Opera Digest, 1989, The 16th Ann. Daytime Emmy Awards, 1989, (stage) Getting Away with Murder, 1991-92, (Broadyway plays) Proof, 2002-03, Twentieth Century, 2004- (Tony nom. best actress in a play, 2004); prodr. (TV) The Dead Will Tell, 2004; writer Stripping for Jesus, 1998, If These Walls Could Talk 2, 2000 (also dir.), On the Edge, 2001 (also dir.); dir. (TV) Reaching Normal, 1999, Ellen De Generes: American Summer Documentary, 2001; author autobiography Call Me Crazy, 2001. Recipient Emmy award Another World; named one of the 50 Most Beautiful People in the World, People, 1998.*

HECHLER, KEN, former state official, former congressman, writer, political science professor; b. Roslyn, NY, Sept. 20, 1914; s. Charles Henry and Catherine Elizabeth (Hauhart) H. *Grandfather George Hechler emigrated from Germany in 1854, enlisted with Union infantry at Parkersburg, West Virginia, wounded at Antietam and discharged at Wheeling, West Virginia. Great Uncle John Hechler captured at Chickamauga, died in Andersonville Prison. Father University of Missouri graduate, managed Clarence H. Mackay's 600 acre farm estate on Long Island, elected to numerous Republican county offices and President of Board of Education, secretary-treasurer of New York Guernsey Breeders' Association, bank president. Mother was a school teacher in St. Louis County, elected to numerous Republican county offices on Long Island, noted raiser and exhibitor of Chrysanthemums.* BA, Swarthmore Coll., 1935, LLD (hon.), 2001; AM, Columbia U., 1936, PhD, 1940; HHD (hon.), W. Va. Inst. Tech., 1988. Lectr. govt. Barnard Coll., Columbia Coll., NYC, 1937-41; rsch. asst., Judge Samuel I. Rosenman, 1939-50; rsch. asst. Pres. Roosevelt's pub. papers, 1939-50; sect. chief Bur. Census, 1940; pers. technician Office Emergency Mgmt., 1941; adminstrv. analyst Bur. of Budget, 1941—42, 1946—47; spl. asst., Pres. Harry S. Truman, 1949-53; rsch. dir. Stevenson-Kefauver campaign, 1956; adminstrv. aide Senator Carroll of Colo., 1957; mem. 86th-94th Congresses from 4th W.Va. dist., 1959-77; sec. state State of W.Va., 1985-2001. Sci. and tech. com. 86th to 94th Congresses from 4th W.Va. Dist., chmn. Energy (Fossil Fuels) Subcom.; mem. Joint Com. on Orgn. of Congress, 1965-66, NASA Oversight Subcom. (US Congress); asst. prof. politics Princeton U., 1947-49; prof. polit. sci. Marshall U., Huntington, W.Va., 1957, 82-84, 2001-2003; sci. cons. US House Com. on Sci. and Tech., 1978-80; radio, TV commentator Sta. WHTN, Huntington, 1957-58, Sta. WWHY, 1978; adj. prof. polit. sci. U. Charleston (W.Va.), 1981; keynote spkr. Harry Truman lecture ser. USAF Acad., 1995; lectr. Harry S. Truman Libr., George C. Marshall Found., Washington & Lee U. Law Sch., 1996, Harry S. Truman Coll. of Chgo., 1997, So. Ill. U., 1998, Mid. Ga. Coll., Appalachian State U., Ill. Wesleyan, Ill. State U., 1999, U. Va., 2000, Ctrl. Mich. U. 2000, Yale U. Law Sch., 2001, Duquesne U. Sch. Law, 2002, U. No. Fla., 2003, U. Mich., Flint, 2003, Ea. Mich. U., 2003, others; disting. vis. scholar W.Va. State Coll., Institute, 2001, Bowling Green State U., 2003, Fla. Atlantic U., 2004-2005, Va. Military Inst., 2004. *Only Congressman to march with Martin Luther King in Selma, Alabama. First Congressman sponsoring legislation to limit coal dust and provide strict safety standards in Federal Coal Mine Health and Safety Act of 1969. Fought against corruption in coal union, risked life to campaign for Jock Yablonski, insurgent candidate later murdered. Crusaded against strip mining and mountain top removal of coal. Helped mobilize secretaries of state and attorneys general in 33 states to limit campaign spending. Led campaign to more fairly appraise and tax West Virginia natural resources owned by out-of-state corporations. Cracked down on West Virginia political corruption.* Author: Insurgency: Personalities and Politics of the Taft Era, 1940, The Bridge at Ramagan, 1957, rev. edit., tech. advisor of motion picture based on book, 1969, 1998, 2005, West Virginia Memories of President Kennedy, 1965, Toward the Endless Frontier, 1980,

The Endless Space Frontier, 1982, Working with Truman, 1982, 3d edit., 2001, Hero of the Rhine, 2004; weekly columnist Cabell Record, Hampshire Rev., Elk River and Little Kananha News, W.Va. Hillbilly, 1990—2000. Bd. dirs. W.Va. Humanities Coun., 1982-84; del. Dem. Nat. Conv., 1964, 68, 72, 80, 84; mem. W.Va. State Dem. Exec. Com., 1998-99. Served to maj. AUS, 1942—46, served to col. Res., 1947—74. Decorated Bronze Star; named W.Va. Son of Yr., W.Va. State Soc. of D.C., 1969, W.Va. Spkr. of Yr., W.Va. U., 1970, Grand Marshal, Annual Martin Luther King Parade, Huntington, 2003, Mountaineer of Yr., Graffiti Mag., 2003, Maverick Pub. Servant, 1987, Smithsonian Instn. lectr. on 50th Anniversary of Pres. Truman, 1985, Prof. of Yr., Marshall U. student senate, 2002; recipient Conservation award, Nat. Audubon Soc., 1973, Mother Jones award, W.Va. Environ. Coun., 1995, Civil and Human Rights award, Martin Luther King Commn. W.Va., 2001, Harry S. Truman award for pub. svc., 2002, Good Samaritan award for Svc., Martin Luther King Commn. W.Va.; subject of biography by Dr. Charles H. Moffat, Ken Hechler. Mem. Am. Polit. Sci. Assn. (assoc. dir. 1953-56), Civitan, Am. Legion, VFW, DAV, Judson Welliver Soc. of Presdl. Speech-Writers, Elks, Hon. mem. Golden Key Internat. hon. soc., 2002. Democrat. Episc. Walked 530 miles with Granny D on behalf of campaign reform. Home: 101B Greenbrier St Charleston WV 25311-2130 Office Phone: 304-395-4323.

HECHT, ALAN DANNENBERG, insurance executive; b. Balt., Aug. 31, 1918; s. Lee I. and Miriam (Dannenberg) H.; m. Margaret R. Moses, June 27, 1943 (dec. Nov. 1, 1984); children: Stephen Lee, Nancy H., Elizabeth Ann; m. Marcia Levin Oberfeld, Dec. 8, 1985. BS, Johns Hopkins U., 1940, M Liberal Arts, 1976. CLU, 1951. Solicitor Travelers Ins. Co., 1945-60; partner Hecht-Schoenfeld Ins. Agy., 1960-62; merged and formed Wolman-Hecht-Schoenfeld, Inc., 1962, v.p., 1962-64, Wolman-Hecht, Inc., 1964-91, pres., 1971-92, chmn., 1992; v.p. Tongne Brooks & Co., Inc. (merged with Wolman-Hecht, Inc.), 1992-95; founder, pres. Alan D. Hecht & Co., Inc., 1966—; gen. agt. Sunamerica Life Ins. Co. Am. and other cos., Balt., 1960—; assoc. Ins., Inc., Balt., 1995—. Pres. Balt. Estate Planning Coun., 1978-79; tchr. CLU econs. and fin. Johns Hopkins U., 1954-81; mem. faculty dept. econs. Mount St. Mary's Coll., Emmitsburg, Md., 1981-84; past bd. graders Am. Coll. Life Underwriters. Pres. Balt. Jewish Council, 1971-73; life and qualifying mem. Million Dollar Round Table, 1985, mem. resolutions com., 1976; bd. dirs. Balt. chpt. Am. Jewish Com., pres., 1958-60, former mem. nat. exec. com.; trustee Sinai Hosp. of Balt., 1959-68. Served to 1st lt. AUS, 1941-45. Recipient Nat. Quality award Nat. Assn. Life Underwriters; Nat. Sales Achievement award; Szold award Temple Oheb Shalom Brotherhood, 1980; George S. Robertson award Balt. Life Underwriters Assn., 1981 Mem. Soc. Fin. Svc. Profls. (CLU, ChFC, dir. 1957—, nat. sec. 1962-63, pres. 1964-65, Helen Hottenbacher award Balt. chpt. 1991), Omicron Delta Kappa, Pi Delta Epsilon. Jewish (pres. congregation 1968-70, past dir.). Home and Office: 111 Hamlet Hill Rd Apt 312 Baltimore MD 21210-1521 E-mail: heclev@aol.com. *With some background in economics, I believe that we can improve our life and environment only by greater productivity. Each person should accept responsibility for finishing assigned tasks at every level, no matter how menial or unimportant that task may seem. I would add that courtesy and respect for others should be a top priority for the successful growth and future of our great country.*

HECHT, DONALD D., lawyer; b. Newark, N.J., Sept. 30, 1957; BA, John Hopkins U., 1979; MBA, JD, U. Md., 1984. Bar: Md. 1985. Ptnr. Leslie L. Gladstone, P.A., Balt. Mem.: ABA, Md. Trial Lawyers Assn., Assn. Trial Lawyers of Am., Md. Bar Assn., Bar Assn. Baltimore City. Office: Leslie L Gladstone, PA 1040 N Calvert St Baltimore MD 21202-3856 Office Phone: 410-727-2322. E-mail: don@lesliegladstone.com.

HECHT, FREDERICK, pediatrician, educator, medical geneticist, researcher, consultant, writer, editor; b. Balt., July 11, 1930; s. Malcolm and Lucile Burger (Levy) H.; m. Irene Winchester Duckworth, Aug. 29, 1953 (div. 1977); children: Frederick Malcolm, Matthew Winchester, Maude Bancroft, Tobias Ochs; m. Barbara Kaiser McCaw, May 29, 1977; children: Kerrie Kristine, Brian Stuart. Student, U. Paris, 1950-51; BA with distinction, Dartmouth Coll., 1952; student, Boston U., 1955-56; MD with honors, U. Rochester, 1960. Lic. physician, Oreg., Ariz., Nev., Kans.; diplomate Am. Bd. Pediatrics, Am. Bd. Med. Genetics. Intern Strong Meml. Hosp., Rochester, NY, 1960-61, resident, 1961-62, U. Wash. Hosp., Seattle, 1962-64, asst. in pediat., med. genetics, 1962-64, instr. pediatrics, med. genetics, 1962-65; asst. in pediat. U. Rochester, 1960-62; prof. pediat. U. Oreg., Portland, 1965-78; founder, pres., dir. S.W. Biomed. Rsch. Inst., Scottsdale, Ariz., 1978-89; founder, pres. Hecht Assocs. Inc., Jacksonville, Fla., 1989—2004; prof. zoology Ariz. State U., Tempe, 1978-89; prof. ob-gyn. U. Nev., Reno and Las Vegas, 1983-89; dir. molecular medicine Children's Mercy Hosp., Kansas City, Mo., 1990-91; prof. medicine U. Mo., Kansas City, 1990-91; founder, dir. div. molecular medicine Children's Mercy Hosp., Kansas City, Mo., 1990-91. Vis. prof. cytogenetics and molecular genetics Adelaide Children's Hosp., North Adelaide, South Australia, 1992; prof. medicine Lab. de Génetique Moleculaire des Cancers Humains, l'Université de Nice, France, 1992-95; bd. dirs. Youth Law Ctr., San Francisco; prof. med. U. Mo., Kansas City, 1990-91. Author: Fragile Sites on Human Chromosomes, 1985; editor: Trends and Teaching in Medical Genetics, 1977; co-editor in chief: Webster's New World Medical Dictionary, 2000, 2003; mem. editl. bd. Am. Jour. Human Genetics, Cancer Genetics and Cytogenetics; chief editor MedTerms.com, 2000—04; assoc. chief editor MedicineNet.com, 1997—2004; contbr. over 600 articles to profl. jours. and over 200 articles to med. websites. Sgt. M.I. Corps, U.S. Army, 1952-55. NIH grantee, 1968-89, USPHS grantee, 1968-89; recipient Pediatric Rsch. award Ross Labs., 1970; Royal Soc. Medicine traveling fellow, London, 1971-73. Mem. Am. Pediatric Soc., Am. Soc. Human Genetics (bd. dirs.), Am. Acad. Pediatrics (charter mem. genetics sect. 1990), Soc. Pediatric Rsch., Western Soc. Pediatric Rsch. (bd. dirs.), Nat. Found. Jewish Genetic Diseases. Jewish. Avocations: gardening, writing, classical music, poetry. Office: 4134 McGirts Blvd Jacksonville FL 32210-4362 Fax: 904-384-5136. E-mail: TBHecht@AOL.com.

HECHT, HARVEY LEON, radiologist; b. Bklyn., Feb. 10, 1937; s. Samuel and Frieda Hecht; m. Gail Ellen Solomon, Oct. 28, 1962; children: Daniel, Jonathan, Elizabeth. BA, Amherst Coll., 1958; MD, Albert Einstein Coll. of Medicine, 1962. Cert. bd. Radiology and Nuclear Medicine. Intern Montefiore Hosp., Bronx, NY, 1962—63, resident in medicine, 1963—64; resident in radiology Columbia Presbyn., N.Y.C., NY, 1967—68, instr. radiology, 1968—70, clin. asst. prof., 1970—2005; radiologist Stanford Hosp., Stanford, Conn., 1970—2005. Contbr. articles various profl. jours. Cpt. U.S. Army, 1963—69. Mem.: AMA. Avocation: tennis. Office: Stamford Radiological Assoc 190 Shelburn Rd Stamford CT 06902 Office Phone: 203-276-7882.

HECHT, MARION B., mental health services professional; b. Bklyn., Nov. 21, 1966; d. Herman and Selma Sonnenblick; m. Ronald J. Hecht; 1 child, Henry. MA, Goddard Coll., Plainfield, Vt., 1991; postgrad., Goddard Coll., 1998, Hofstra U., U. Minn., U. Iowa, Montclair State U. Lic. profl. counselor, N.J., D.C.; registered art therapist Am. Art Therapy Assn.; cert. guidance counselor, tchr. of handicapped, N.J. Dept.Edn.; cert. cognitive behavioral therapist Nat. Assn. Cognitive Behavioral Therapists. Mental health specialist, gerontologist Bay Ridge Ctr. for Older Adults, Bklyn., 1989-90; art therapist, mental health therapist Rockaway Mental Health Svcs., Far Rockaway, N.Y., 1990-91, Coney Island Hosp., 1991—93; pvt. practice No. N.J. Counseling Svcs., 1996—; tchr. home instrn., spl. edn. Montclair & South Orange (N.J.) Pub. Schs., 1997-2000. Avocations: sports, reading, computer, drawing. Office: 15 Village Plaza South Orange NJ 07079 Office Phone: 973-762-1224. Office Fax: 973-597-1357. Personal E-mail: mbshinc@comcast.net.

HECHT, MARJORIE MAZEL, editor; b. Cambridge, Mass., Dec. 21, 1942; d. Mark and Theresa (Shuman) Mazel; m. Laurence Michael Hecht, July 2, 1972 BA cum laude, Smith Coll., 1964; postgrad., London Sch. Econs., 1964-65; MSW, Columbia U., 1967. Dir. Forest Neighborhood Service Ctr., N.Y.C., 1967-70, Wiltwyck Sch. for Boys, Bronx Center, N.Y., 1970-73; mng. editor Fusion Mag., Washington, 1977-87, 21st Century Sci. & Technol. Mag., Washington, 1987—; sci. editor Exec. Intelligence Rev., Washington, 1997—. Co-author: Beam Defense: An Alternative to Nuclear Destruction, 1983 (Aviation and Space Writers award 1983); editor: Colonize Space! Open the Age of Reason, 1985, The Holes in the Ozone Scare: The Scientific Evidence That the Sky Isn't Falling, 1992. Press rep. LaRouche Campaign, N.Y.C., 1984 Democrat. Jewish. Avocation: astronomy. Office: 21st Century Sci & Technol Mag PO Box 16285 Washington DC 20041-6285 E-mail: tcs@mediasoft.net.

HECHT, NATHAN LINCOLN, state supreme court justice; b. Clovis, N.Mex., Aug. 15, 1949; s. Harold Lee and Mary Loretta (Byerly) H. BA, Yale U., 1971; JD cum laude, So. Meth. U., 1974. Bar: Tex. 1974, D.C. 1975, U.S. Dist. Ct. D.C. 1975, U.S. Dist. Ct. (no. and we. dists.) Tex. 1976, U.S. Ct. Appeals (D.C. cir.) 1975, U.S. Ct. Appeals (5th cir.) 1976, U.S. Supreme Ct. 1979. Law clk. to judge U.S. Ct. Appeals (D.C. cir.), 1974-75; assoc. Locke, Purnell, Boren, Laney & Neely, Dallas, 1976-80, ptnr., 1981; dist. judge 95th Dist. Ct., Dallas, 1981-86; justice Tex. 5th Dist. Ct. Appeals, 1986-89, Tex. Supreme Ct., Austin, 1989—. Contbr. articles to profl. jours. Bd. visitors So. Meth. U., Dallas, 1984-87; trustee Children's Med. Found., Dallas, 1983-89; bd. dirs. Children's Med. Ctr. North, Dallas, 1985-89; elder Valley View Christian Ch., Dallas, 1981—. Lt. USNR, 1971—79. Named Outstanding Young Lawyer of Dallas, Dallas Assn. of Young Lawyers, 1984. Fellow Tex. Bar Found., Am. Bar Found.; mem. ABA, Dallas Bar Assn., D.C. Bar Assn., Am. Law Inst. Republican. Avocations: piano, organ, jogging, bicycling. Office: Tex Supreme Ct PO Box 12248 201 West 14th Room 104 Austin TX 78711

HECHT, ROBERT D., lawyer; b. Seneca, Kans., Oct. 17, 1934; s. Jesse J. and Flossie Isabel (Ridgeway) H.; children: Lisa Fay, Julia Paige. B.B.A., Washburn U., 1956, J.D., 1958. Bar: Kans. 1958, U.S. Dist. Ct. Kans. 1958, U.S. Ct. Appeals (10th cir.) 1969, U.S. Supreme Ct. 1969. Asst. county atty. Shawnee County, Kans., 1961-65, county atty., 1965-69, county counselor, 1969-75; ptnr. Gray, Freidberg & Davis, Topeka, 1965-69, Scott, Quinlan & Hecht, Topeka, 1969-2001, Dist Attorney Third Judicial Dist. Ks. 2002—; past adj. prof. Washburn U. Sch. Law, Topeka; dir. Benchmark Securities, Topeka; sch. atty. Unified Sch. Dist. 345, Topeka, 1979-; Contbr. articles to Kans. Trial Lawyers Jour. Co-chmn. Shawnee County March of Dimes, 1963; candidate for atty. gen. State of Kans., 1968. Served as capt. JAGC, USAF, 1958-61. Mem. ABA, Kans. Bar Assn., Assn. Trial Lawyers Am., Kans. Trial Lawyers Assn. (bd. govs. 1974-, v.p. 1981-82), Am. Judicature Soc. Republican. Office: Shawnee County Courthouse 200 E 7th Topeka KS 66603 Home: 3111 SW Sewll Topeka KS 66611

HECHT, RUDOLPH C., physician, educator; b. Hamburg, Germany, Apr. 16, 1927; arrived in U.S., 1954; s. Otto and Rose (Caro) Hecht; m. Ilse Hecht, May 22, 1958; children: David H., Martin O., Thomas C., Anita. BSc, Nat. U. Mex., 1947, MD, 1954. Diplomate Am. Bd. Family Medicine, lic. Tex., 1957, Wis., 1973, diplomate State Bd. Med. Examiners. Pvt. practice, LaFeria, Tex., 1957—73; prof. U. Wis., Madison, 1973—82, Med. Coll. Wis., Milw., 1985—88; pvt. practice Wis., 1988—99. Author: Autobiography: The Early Years, 2000. Hon. consul of Mexico, Madison County, 1974—, Dane County, 1974—. Internat. Travel fellow, Pan Am. Health Orgn., 1977. Home: 141 N Hancock St Madison WI 53703-2311 Office Phone: 608-283-6000. Business E-Mail: rchecht@facstaff.wisc.edu.

HECHT, SIDNEY MICHAEL, chemistry professor; b. N.Y.C., July 27, 1944; AB, U. Rochester, 1966; PhD, U. Ill., 1970. USPHS fellow U. Wis., 1970-71; from asst. prof. to assoc. prof. MIT, Cambridge, 1971-79; John W. Mallet prof. chemistry U. Va., Charlottesville, 1978—; v.p. preclin. research and devel. Smith Kline & French Labs., 1981-83, v.p. chem. research and devel., 1983-86. Mem. editl. adv. bd. Anti-Cancer Drug Design, 1986—,2002 Jour. Molecular Recognition, 1991-98, Bioconjugate Chemistry, 1992—, Molecules Online, 1997—99, Current Medicinal Chemistry, 2000—, Molecular Cancer Therapeutics, 2001—, Oncology Rsch./Anticancer Drug Design, 2002—; assoc. editor Medicinal Chemistry Rsch., 1990-91; assoc. editor Jour. Am. Chem. Soc., 1992—. Alfred P. Sloan research fellow, 1975-79, John Simon Guggenheim fellow, 1977-78, AAAS, 2004; NIH research career devel. grantee, 1975-80; recipient Arthur C. Cope Scholar award Am. Chem. Soc., 1996; recipient Rsch. Achievement award Am. Soc. of Pharmacognory, 1998; named Va.'s Outstanding Scientist, 1996. Mem. AAAS, Am. Chem. Soc., Royal Soc. Chemistry, Am. Soc. Biol. Chemists, Sigma Xi Office: U Va Dept Chemistry Charlottesville VA 22901

HECHT, WILLIAM DAVID, accountant; b. N.Y.C., Nov. 7, 1941; s. Adolph J. and Lillian (Shore) H.; m. Francine Rosen, Aug. 22, 1964; children: Peter, Dana, Allison. BS in Acctg., Queens Coll., 1962; JD, Bklyn. Law Sch., 1971; LLM in Taxation, NYU, 1974. Bar: N.Y. 1972. Ptnr., mem. mgmt. com. Weiser LLP, N.Y.C., 1964—. Mem. faculty Found. Acctg. Edn., N.Y.C.; lectr. in field. Contbr. articles to CPA Jour. Mem. ABA, AICPA, N.Y. State Soc. CPAs, N.J. State Soc. CPAs, N.Y. State Bar Assn. Republican. Jewish. Avocations: skiing, basketball. Home: 8 Tutor Pl East Brunswick NJ 08816-3658 Office: Weiser, LLP 399 Thornall St Edison NJ 08837-2236 Office Phone: 732-205-2001. Business E-Mail: whecht@mrweiser.com.

HECHT, WILLIAM F., electric power industry executive; b. 1943; BSEE, Lehigh U., 1964, MSEE, 1970. Engr. Pa. Power & Light Co., Allentown, 1964-68, project engr., 1968-72, sr. project engr., 1972-75, mgr. distbn. planning, 1975-76, exec. dir. corp. energy planning coun., 1976-78, mgr. systems planning, 1978-84, v.p. systems power, 1984-87, v.p. mktg., 1987-90, exec. v.p., 1990-93, CEO, chmn., pres., 1993—. Office: PP&L Utilities 2 N 9th St Allentown PA 18101-1139

HECHTER, MICHAEL NORMAN, sociologist; b. LA, Nov. 15, 1943; s. Oscar Milton and Gertrude (Horowitz) H.; children: Joshua, Eliana. AB, Columbia U., 1966, PhD, 1972. From asst. prof. to prof. U. Wash., Seattle, 1970-84; prof. sociology, dir. research group for instnl. analysis U. Ariz., Tucson, 1984—99; prof. sociology U. Wash., Seattle, 1999—2005; found. prof. global studies Ariz. State U., 2005—. Univ. lectr., fellow New Coll., Oxford (Eng.) U., 1994-96; vis. prof. U. Bergen, Norway, 1984. Author: Internal Colonialism, 1975, Principles of Group Solidarity, 1987, Containing Nationalism, 2000; editor: The Microfoundations of Macrosociology, 1983, Social Institutions, 1989, The Origin of Values, 1993, Social Norms, 2001, Theories of Social Order, 2003. Fellow Russell Sage Found., 1988-89, Ctr. Advanced Study Behavioral Scis., 1990-91, Udall Ctr. for Studies in Pub. Policy. Fellow: Am. Acad. of Arts and Sci.; mem.: Soc. for Comparative Rsch., Internat. Sociol. Assn., Sociol. Rsch. Assn., Am. Sociol. Assn. Office: School Global Studies Ariz State Univ Tempe AZ 85287 Office Phone: 206-543-4163. Business E-Mail: hechter@u.washington.edu.

HECHTMAN, HOWARD, financial analyst; b. N.Y.C., Sept. 1947; s. Charles and Pauline (Barmatz) H.; m. Marsha Louise Garwin, Dec. 19, 1976 (div. 1984). BS, Bklyn. Poly. U., 1968; MS in Physics, Adelphi U., 1970, MBA in Mgmt. with distinction, 1972; Cert. in Labor Rels., Cornell U., 1999, Advanced Cert. in Labor Rels., 2000. Grad. teaching asst. physics Computer Ctr. Adelphi U., Garden City, N.Y., 1970-72; from asst. to assoc. analyst N.Y.C. Transit Authority, 1973—. Capt. N.Y. State Guard. Named Patron of Arts Soc. for Theater Arts Resources, 1989-90; recipient Cert. of Merit Rep. Nat. Com., 1990. Mem. Soc. Am. Mil. Engrs., Civil Svc. Tech. Guild (del. 1994-2005), Poly U. Alumni Assn. (alumni bd. dirs. 1978—, life dir. 1996—). Office: NYC Transit Authority MOW Finance Rm 1261 370 Jay St Brooklyn NY 11201-3817 Office Phone: 718-243-4199. Personal E-mail: howardusaone@yahoo.com.

HECK, ALBERT FRANK, retired neurologist; b. Balt., Oct. 9, 1932; s. Albert Franklin and Dorothy Mary Heck; divorced; children: Albert William, Karl Andrew, Robert Conrad, Paul Christopher. AB, Johns Hopkins U., 1954; MD, U. Md., 1958. Diplomate: Am. Bd. Psychiatry and Neurology. Intern Mercy Hosp., 1958-59; NIH fellow in neurology U. Md., Balt., 1959-62, faculty, instr. to prof., 1964-77; prof., chmn. dept. neurology U. Tenn. Center for Health Scis., Memphis, 1977-82, dir. neurosci. program, 1978-82; prof. neurology W. Va. U., 1982-2000, ret., 2000—. Vis. prof. Medezinische Hochschule Hannover, W. Ger., 1973-74 Contbr. writings to profl. publs. Served with M.C. U.S. Army, 1962-64. Recipient jr. investigator award NIH, 1965, U.S. sr. scientist award, 1973; Humboldt Found. prize Fed. Republic Germany, 1973-74 Fellow Am. Acad. Neurology, ACP, Stroke Council Am. Heart Assn.; mem. Am. Neurol. Assn., Internat. Coll. Angiology, Alpha Omega Alpha. Achievements include research in field. Home: 10906 Baronet Rd Owings Mills MD 21117

HECK, DEBRA UPCHURCH, information technology, procurement professional; b. Valparaiso, Fla., Nov. 4, 1956; d. Robert P. and Sallaine S. (Sledge) Upchurch; m. Robert J. Heck, May 31, 1980; children: Andrew W., Jennifer A. BS in Math., Purdue U., 1978, MS in Mgmt., 1980. Analyst mgmt. sci. Monsanto Corp. Mgmt. Sci., St. Louis, 1980-81; sys. analyst Monsanto Agr. Group, St. Louis, 1981-82, sr. sys. analyst, 1982-84; sr. analyst mgmt. sci. Monsanto Polymer Products Group, St. Louis, 1984-86; total quality fundamentals instr. Monsanto Co., St. Louis, 1985-86; project mgr. Monsanto Chem. Co., St. Louis, 1986-88; group leader Monsanto Corp. MIS, St. Louis, 1988-92, sr. group leader, 1992-95; info. tech. dir. Monsanto Bus. Svcs. Fin. & Procurement, St. Louis, 1995—97, dir. strategic sourcing procurement strategic initiatives, 1997—2000; exec. dir. global procurement Pharmacia, St. Louis, 2000—03; exec. dir. global sourcing Pfizer, 2003—04; v.p. corp. procurement Express Scripts, St. Louis, 2005—. Trustee, chair fall gathering, doubles, social com. Ethical Soc., St. Louis, 1982—; mem. sci. adv. com., PTO bd. Parkway Sch. Dist., St. Louis, 1992—; vol. St. Louis Assn. for Retarded Citizens, 1978-85. Recipient Leader award, YWCA Monsanto Corp., 1999. Mem. Nat. Assn. Purchasing Mgmt., Human Resource Sys. Profls., Leadership Am. Alumni (award 1994), Winning Women. Avocations: travel, sports. Personal E-mail: debrauheck@aol.com.

HECK, HENRY D'ARCY, retired toxicologist, consultant; b. Bryn Mawr, Pa., Apr. 18, 1939; s. Harold Joseph and Lydia Suzanne (Holt) H.; m. Mercedes Casanova, Dec. 21, 1984; children: Katherine (Mrs. Daniel Troy), Julia, John Schmitz, Lara (Mrs. Daniel King). AB, Princeton U., 1962; PhD, Northwestern U., 1966. Asst. prof. chemistry U. Calif., Berkeley, 1968-72; chemist Stanford Rsch. Inst., Menlo Park, Calif., 1972-77; scientist Chem. Ind. Inst. Toxicology, Research Triangle Park, NC, 1977-85, sr. scientist, 1985-99; ret., 1999; prin. Casaheck Cons., 2004—. Adj. assoc. prof. U. NC, Chapel Hill, 1983-99, Duke U., Durham, NC, 1987-99 Assoc. editor: Fundamental and Applied Toxicology, 1986-1991, editor-in-chief, 1991-97. Fellow NSF, NIH, EMBO, 1963-68; mem. AAAS, Am. Chem. Soc., NC Soc. Toxicology (pres. 1995-96), Soc. Toxicology (Frank Blood award 1983, Inhalation Toxicol. Paper of Yr. award 1987, 93). Home: 4969 Adelia Dr Virginia Beach VA 23455 E-mail: casaheck@cox.net.

HECK, JAMES BAKER, retired education educator; b. Columbus, Ohio, Aug. 26, 1930; s. Arch O. and Frances (Agnew) H.; m. Jo Ann Gatton, Nov. 18, 1950; children: Janice M., Judith L., J. Jeffrey. BS in Edn., Ohio State U., 1953, MA, 1961, PhD, 1967. Comml. sales engr. Ohio Bell Tel. Co., Dayton, 1955-57; tchr. Ohio Pub. Schs., Dayton, 1957-59, sch. counselor, 1959-60; from instr. to assoc. dean Ohio State U., 1960—67, assoc. dean faculties Office Acad. Affairs, 1967-68, asst. prof. edn., 1967—68, prof., dean, dir. Mansfield campus, 1971-78; prof., dean Coll. Edn. U. Del., Newark, 1968-71; dean regional campus affairs U. South Fla., 1978-81, assoc. v.p. acad. affairs, 1981-84, prof., assoc. v.p. acad. affairs, dir. office of tech., 1984-86, prof., dean Sch. Extended Studies & Learning Techs., gen. mgr. pub. broadcasting Sta. WUSF-TV/FM, WSFP-TV/FM, spl. asst. to provost, dir. office tech., 1986-90; prof., gen. mgr. Sta. WSFP-TV/FM, 1990-96, Sta. WUSF-TV/FM, 1990—2002; exec. dir. WUSF advancement Sta. WUSF TV/FM, 2002—03; ret., 2003. Mem. bd. adminstrv. reps. U. South Fla. Pub. Broadcasting, 1999-2002; asst. state supr. for guidance svc. Ohio Dept. Edn., 1962-63; Am. Coun. on Edn. fellow in acad. adminstrn. U. Ill., 1965-66; evaluator Nat. Coun. for Accreditation Tchr. Edn., 1972-78; mem. planning com. Nat. Conf. Br. and Regional Campus Adminstrs., 1973-82, chmn., 1972, 80; chmn. planning com. Am. Coun. Edn. Acad. Fellows Working Reunion, 1972, 79, 85; vice chmn. Am. Coun. Edn. Coun. Fellows, 1980-81, chmn., 1981-82, exec. com., 1980-83, chmn. S.E. Region Conf., 1988, mem. alumni rels. com.; mem. U. South Fla. Interdisciplinary Ctr. on Digital and Computational Video, 1999-2002; co-chair Internat. Workshop on Digital and Computational Video, 1999, 2000; cons., lectr. in field. Co-author: Counseling; Selected Readings, 1962, Educational Administration: Selected Readings, 1965, 2d edit., 1971, Analysis of Educational Change in Ohio Public Schools, 1968; contbr. articles to profl. jours. Gen. chmn. Mansfield Area United Way campaign, 1975, bd. dir., 1976-78, v.p., 1977, 78; bd. dir. Mansfield Symphony Orch., 1972-78, pres., 1978; bd. dir. Rsch. for Better Schs., Inc., 1968-71, pres., 1970-71; mem. Kiwanis Club of Mansfield, 1971-78, bd. dir., 1974-78; mem. citizens adv. com. Richland County Regional Planning Commn., 1973-74, bd. dir., 1975-78, v.p.; mem. Manpower Adv. Coun. Richland and Morrow Counties, 1977-78; trustee Hillsbrough County Hosp. Authority, Tampa, Fla., 1980-84, Tampa Heart Ctr., 1982-84; sec.-treas., 1983-84; mem. Leadership Tampa, 1982-83, Leadership Tampa Alumni, 1983—2003, Leadership Tampa Bay, 1992—2003; mem. Tampa-Hillsborough Cable adv. com., 1984-92, vice chmn., 1987-88, chmn., 1988-92; instl. rep. PBS and Nat. Pub. Radio, Am. Pub. TV Stas. 1986-2001, Legis. adv., APTS, 1995-2001; market fund adv. com. CPB, 1996; steering com. Higher Edn. Telecomm. Consortium, 1995-2001; steering com., pub. broadcasting joint licensee Consortium, 1996-2001; bd. dir. Fla. Pub. Broadcasting Svc. Inc., 1986-2001, chair Long Range Planning Com., 1988-93, treas., 1991-93, vice chair, 1993-95, chair, 1995-97, chair programs and ops. com., 1993-95, exec. com. 1991-99; bd. dir. Program Resources Group, 1993-2001, exec. com., 1995-2001, vice-chair, sec., 1995-2001; mem. Palma Ceia United Meth. Ch., 1980—, chair coun. on ministries, 1985-86, chair pipe organ com., 1985-91, chair adminstrv. bd., coun., 1987-89, 93-98; mem. pastor parish com., 1990-92, 96-98, chair, 1992; mem. Master Chorale of Tampa Bay, 1983—; bd. dir. Chorale Masterworks Festival, Inc., 1987—, v.p., 1991-93, chair and pres., 1993-95, 97-99, 2000-01, exec. com., 2002—, sr. advisor, 2004-, co-chair longrange planning com., 2005-; bd. dir. So. Ednl. Comms. Assn., 1986-97, mem. budget and fin. com., 1989-91. bd. dir. Nat. Edn. Telecom. Assn., 1997-2002, long range planning coun. 1997-98; mem. Tampa Bay Area Com. Fgn. Rels., 2002—. With USAF, 1953-55; USAFR, ret. 1973. Nat. Def. Edn. Act fellow, Ohio State U., 1961. Mem. Assn. Higher Edn. (life), Ohio State U. Assn. (life), Nat. Univ. Continuing Edn. Assn. (instnl. rep., bd. dirs. region III, honors and awards com. 1986-90), Greater Tampa C. of C. (chmn. emergency preparedness task force 1991-94), Civitan (club founding pres. 1980-82), Rotary (Downtown Tampa), Phi Delta Kappa (life), Kappa Delta Pi, Phi Kappa Phi. E-mail: jheck1@tampabay.rr.com, jim@jbheck.com.

HECK, MELODY ANN, library director; b. Kewanee, Ill., July 8, 1957; d. Edwin and Helen M. Nelson; m. Michael Robert Heck, Feb. 25, 1984; children: David M., Holly Ann Elizabeth. Cert. libr. tech. asst., Black Hawk Coll., 1996. Cert. libr. tech. asst. Black Hawk Coll., 1996. Staff librarian Galva (Ill.) Pub. Libr., 1975-84, asst. dir., 1984-96, libr. dir., 1996—. Mem.: ALA, Ill. Libr. Assn. Avocations: reading, needlecrafts. Office: Galva Pub Libr Dist 120 NW 3rd Ave Galva IL 61434-1326 E-mail: galvanet@cin.net.

HECK, RICHARD T., tree farmer; b. Madison, Ind., Sept. 16, 1924; s. Richard Charles and Virginia (Tevis) H.; m. Ruth Irwin Heck, June 27, 1948; children: Richard Gregory, Rebecca Jeanne. Student, Admiral Farragut Naval Acad., Pine Beach, N.J., 1942-43, Hanover Coll. 1947-48. Tree farmer, Hanover, Ind., 1943—. Vol. firefighter, 1946—; mem. arson investigation team Jefferson County, Ind., 1983-90, Hanover Twp. Vol. Fire Co., 1956—; trustee Hanover Coll., 1991-2000. With USN, 1944-54, WWII, Korea. Named to Hon. Order of Ky. Cols., 1971, Sagamore of Wabash, 1973; named Ind. Outstanding Tree Farmer, Ind. Tree Farm Commn., 1983, Nat. Outstanding Tree Farmer Am. Forest Found., 1984, Good Steward award Nat. Arbor Day Found., 1984, North Ctrl. Region Outstanding Tree Farmer, 1984, Ind. Conservationist of Yr., Ind. Dept. Natural Resources, 1985, Forest Conservationist of the Yr. Ind. Wildlife Fedn., 1987. Mem. Soc. Am. Foresters (hon.), Nat. Forestry Assn. (life), Ind. Foresty and Woodland Owners Assn.

(bd. dirs. 1984-95, Ind. state tree farm com. 1984—), NRA (life), Ind. Vol. Firemans Assn. (life), Nat. Muzzle Loading Rifle Assn. (life), Internat. Assn. Arson Investigators, Inc., Nat. Eagle Scout Assn., Soc. Ind. Pioneers, Am. Legion, Wahpanipe Muzzle Loading Rifle Club, Connor Prairie Rifles Club, Masons, Elks. Republican. Presbyterian. Avocations: hunting, fishing, hiking, collecting indian artifacts, competitive muzzle loading shooting. Address: 110 Clemmons St Hanover IN 47243-9659

HECK, THOMAS F., librarian, performing arts educator; b. Washington, July 10, 1943; s. Harold Joseph and Suzanne Holt H.; m. Anne Elizabeth Goodrich, June 2, 1968; children: Larissa, John. French bac, 1 ere Partie, Paris, 1961; BA in Liberal Arts/Music History, U. Notre Dame, 1965; PhD, Yale U., 1970; MLS, U. So. Calif., 1977. Asst. prof., libr. Wis. Conservatory Music, Milw., 1977-78; head music and dance libr. Ohio State U., Columbus, 1978-2000; pres. Insights Cons., 2001—. Author: Commedia dell'arte: A Guide to the Primary and Secondary Literature, 1988, Mauro Giuliani: Virtuoso Guitarist and Composer, 1995, Picturing Performance: The Iconography of the Performing Arts in Concept and Practice, 1999; editor: The Music Information Explosion and its Implications, 1992; rev. editor Fontes Artis Musicae, 1988-92; gen. editor: Coll. Music Soc. Reports, 1992-95. 1st lt. U.S. Army, 1970-71. Fellow, Nederlands Inst. Advanced Study, Wassenaar, 1994—95, Fulbright fellow, 1968—69, 1995—96. Mem. Authors Guild, Am. Musicological Soc., Am. Soc. Theatre Rsch., Music Libr. Assn., Coll. Music Soc. (life), Internat. Assn. Music Librs., Internat. Fedn. Theatre Rsch., Guitar Found. Am. (founder, archivist 1978-94). Avocations: foreign languages and culture, foreign travel, photography, audiovisual media, bicycling. E-mail: insights@aya.yale.edu.

HECKATHORN, DARLENE, language educator; b. Kenton, Ohio; d. Paul and Emma Hensel; m. Dal Heckathorn, Apr. 16, 1966. BS, Bowling Green State U., 1966; MA, Wright State U., 1991. Tchr. Kenton city Schs., Ohio. Office: Kenton HS 200 Harding Ave Kenton OH 43326-1699

HECKATHORN, DOUGLAS D., sociologist, educator, epidemiologist; b. Wichita, Kans., May 15, 1948; s. Donald L. Heckathorn and Frances E. Haney; m. Susan N. LoBello, Oct. 4, 1949. PhD, U. Kans., 1974. Prof. sociology Cornell U. Sr. editor: Rationality and Society; contbr. articles to Harvard Jour. Law and Pub. Policy (Lon Fuller Prize in Jurisprudence, 1989). Office: Cornell Univ 344 Uris Hall Ithaca NY 14853 E-mail: douglas.heckathorn@cornell.edu.

HECKEL, JOHN LOUIS (JACK HECKEL), aerospace transportation executive; b. Columbus, Ohio, July 12, 1931; s. Russel Criblez and Ruth Selma (Heid) H.; m. Jacqueline Ann Alexander, Nov. 21, 1959 (div. 1993); children: Heidi, Holly, John; m. Linda Holleran, Aug. 1, 1994. BS, U. Ill., 1954; PhD with honors, Nat. U. San Diego, 1984. Divsn. mgr. Aerojet Divsn., Azusa, Calif., 1956-70, Seattle and Washington, 1956-70; pres. Aerojet-Space Gen. Co., El Monte, Calif., 1970-72, Aerojet Liquid Rocket Co., Sacramento, 1972-77; group v.p. Aerojet Sacramento Cos., 1977-81; pres. Aerojet Gen., La Jolla, Calif., 1981-85, chmn., CEO, 1985-87; pres., COO GenCorp., Akron, 1987-94, also bd. dirs. Bd. dirs. WD-40 Corp., Petritech, Corp. Bd. dirs. San Diego Econ. Devel. Corp., 1983-86, Akron Regional Devel. Bd., Akron Gen. Hosp., Summit County United Way; pres. Summit Edn. Partnership Found., Akron. Recipient Disting. Alumni award U. Ill. Ann. Alumni Conv., 1979 Fellow AIAA (assoc.); mem. Aerospace Industries Assn. Am. (gov. 1981), Navy League U.S., Am. Def. Preparedness Assn., San Diego C. of C. (bd. dirs.)

HECKEL, RICHARD WAYNE, metallurgical engineering educator; b. Pitts., Jan. 25, 1934; s. Ralph Clyde and Esther Vera (Zoerb) H.; m. Peggy Ann Simmons, Jan. 3, 1959 (dec. Apr. 1998); children: Scott Alan, Laura Ann Rowe. BS in Metall. Engring., Carnegie Mellon, 1955, MS, 1958, PhD, 1959. Sr. rsch. metallurgist E.I. duPont de Nemours & Co., Wilmington, Del., 1959—63; prof. metall. engring. Drexel U., Phila., 1963—71; head dept. materials sci. and engring. Carnegie Mellon, Pitts., 1971—76; prof. materials sci. and engring. Mich. Tech. U., Houghton, 1976—96, prof. emeritus, 1996—; tech. dir., owner Engring. Trends, Houghton, 2000—. Commr. at large Engring. Workforce Commn., 1997—, founder, tech. dir. Engring. Trends (e-commerce). Contbr. articles to profl. jours. Served as 1st lt. Ordnance Corps, U.S. Army, 1959-60. Recipient Lindback Teaching award Drexel U., 1968; Research award Mich. Tech. U., 1985 Fellow ASM Internat. (life; Bradley Stoughton Young Tchr. of Metallurgy award 1969, Phila. Ednl. Achievement award 1967); mem. The Metals, Minerals and Materials Soc., Am. Welding Soc. (Adams Meml. mem. 1966), Am. Soc. Engring. Edn., Sigma Xi, Omicron Delta Kappa, Tau Beta Pi, Phi Kappa Phi, Alpha Sigma Mu. Address: Engring Trends 1281 Hickory Ln Houghton MI 49931-1609 Office Phone: 906-482-1523. Personal E-mail: rheckel@chartermi.net. E-mail: engtrend@up.net.

HECKEN, HAROLD PHILIP, JR., management analyst, legislative analyst; b. Bklyn., Jan. 4, 1928; s. Harold P. and Dorothea Louise (Niclas) H.; m. Valerie Brown Hecken, Apr. 19, 1964; 1 child, H. Philip. BS, Cornell U., 1949; MPA, L.I. U., 1981. Mktg. mgr. Schrader Divsn. Scovill Mfg., Bklyn., 1949-66; gen. mgr. Auto Rsch. Corp. divsn. Bijur, Rochelle Park, N.Y., 1966-70; v.p. mktg. Allomatic Industries, New Hyde Park, N.Y., 1970-74; mktg. mgr. Soledyne, Inc., Bayshore, N.Y., 1974-77; dir. mgmt. analysis County of Nassau, Mineola, N.Y., 1977—; legis. analyst N.Y. State Senate, Albany, 1984—; mayor Inc. Village of Garden City, N.Y., 1999—. Trustee Inc. Village of Garden City, 1992-99; dir., treas., pres. Ea. Property Owners Assn., Garden City, 1976-91; committeeman Garden City of Rep. Com., 1976-99. Capt. U.S. Army Quartermaster Corp., 1951-53. Avocations: tennis, sailing. Home: 42 Huntington Rd Garden City NY 11530-3102 Office: Inc Village of Garden City 351 Stewart Ave Garden City NY 11530-4528

HECKER, MICHAEL HANNS LOUIS, retired electrical engineer, speech scientist; b. Hamburg, Germany, Mar. 30, 1936; came to U.S., 1948; s. Hanns Ewald Hecker and Wilhelmine (Corinth) H. Klopfer; m. Elizabeth Ann Bowen, Sept. 3, 1960 (div.); 1 child, Serena Suzanne; m. Dorothy Louise Dunlap, Mar. 12, 1971. BSEE with honors, Northeastern U., 1959; MSEE, MIT, 1961; PhD in Speech & Hearing Scis., Stanford U., 1974. Sr. rsch. engr. Bolt Beranek and Newman Inc., Cambridge, Mass., 1964-67, SRI Internat., Menlo Park, Calif., 1967-95. Cons. forensic acoustics, Los Altos, Calif., 1967-98; retained by White House during Watergate investigation to examine presdl. tapes; sci. cons. Nat. Commn. Rev. Fed. & State Laws Relating to Wiretapping & Electronic Surveillance, 1974-76. Author: Speaker Recognition, 1971; co-editor: Speech Evaluation in Psychiatry/Medicine, 1981; contbr. articles to profl. jours., chpts. to med. books. 1st lt. U.S. Army, 1962-64. Grantee, NIH, 1982—88. Mem. Eta Kappa Nu, Tau Beta Pi, Sigma Xi. Achievements include rsch. in speech changes related to emotional states, psychological stress, and neurologic disorders; developed methods of speech analysis to assess behavioral risk for coronary heart disease. E-mail: midohecker@earthlink.net.

HECKER, PETER S., lawyer; b. N.Y.C., Sept. 4, 1949; BA, Carleton Coll., 1970; JD, U. Calif., Berkeley, 1973. Bar: N.Y. 1974, Calif. 1975, Am. Bar. Assoc. Atty. Heller, Ehrman, White & McAuliffe, San Francisco, 1975—. Mem. ABA, Order of Coif, Phi Beta Kappa. Office: Heller Ehrman White & McAuliffe 333 Bush St San Francisco CA 94104-2806 Office Phone: 415-772-6080. E-mail: phecker@hewm.com.

HECKERT, PAUL CHARLES, sociologist, educator; b. May 30, 1929; s. Paul Kester and Clara Belle (Plessinger) H.; m. Sara Mae (Raezer), Sept. 6, 1952; children: Paul Andrew, Druann Maria, Daniel Alex, Nathanael Alan, Diane Manette. BA, Catawba Coll., 1951; BD, Lancaster Theol. Sem., 1954; MS, Cornell, 1959, PhD, 1964. Ordained min. United Ch. of Christ, 1954. Missionary United Ch. of Christ, Honduras, 1954—60; clergyman of various Meth. ch. NY, 1960—64; assoc. prof. sociology, also chmn. dept. Catawba Coll., NC, 1964—68; prof. Catawba Coll., NC, 1968—72; chmn. joint dept. sociology Livingstone Coll, Salisbury, NC; chmn. dept. sociology Frostburg State U., Md., 1972—87, prof., 1987—94. Support visitor, Prison, 1995—; del. Rowan Coop. Christian ministry, 1968-72; Spanish and sociology vol. tchr. fed. prison; mem. leadership devel. com. Pa. West Conf., United Ch. of Christ, 1973-78. Bd. dir. Salisbury Rowan Cmty. Svc. Coun., 1971-72. Served with AUS, 1948-50. Ford fellow, summer 1968, NASA, ASEE summer faculty fellow, 1969, 77, AEC summer faculty fellow, 1973. Contbg. book reviews. to profl. journals. Recipient Vol. of Yr. Award, Fed. Correctional Instn., 2001; grantee, NEH, 1975, 1979, 1983, 1986. Mem. AAAS, Am. Sociol. Assn., Rural Sociol. Soc., Allegany County Ret. Tchr. Assn. (mem. chmn. 1997, pres. elect 1998, 2003, pres. 1999, 2004), Phi Kappa Phi, Alpha Kappa Delta, Sigma Delta Pi, Delta Tau Kappa. Home: 13 N Woodlawn Ave Cumberland MD 21502-7254

HECKLER, FREDERICK ROGER, plastic surgeon; b. N.Y.C., Mar. 7, 1942; s. Frances George; children: Jeremy, Michael, Adrienne, Lauren. Student, Tufts U., 1959-62, MD, 1966. Diplomate Nat. Bd. Med. Examiners, Am. Bd. Surgery, Am. Bd. Plastic Surgery with qualification in surgery of the hand. Intern in surgery U. Chgo. Med. Ctr., 1966-67; resident in gen. surgery Tufts New Eng. Med. Ctr., Boston, 1967-69; fellow in surgery Malmo (Sweden) Gen. Hosp., 1969-70; resident in plastic surgery Wilford Hall USAF Med. Ctr., San Antonio, 1973-75; fellow in hand surgery Denver Gen. Hosp., 1976-77; chief surgery USAF Hosp., Taiwan, 1976-77; asst. prof. surgery U. Miss. Med. Ctr., Jackson, 1977-79, chief divsn. plastic surgery, 1979-82; dir. divsn. plastic surgery Allegheny Gen. Hosp., Pitts., 1982—; clin. assoc. prof. plastic surgery U. Pitts. Sch. Medicine, 1982—. Active med. staff Miss. Cripple Children's Treatment and Tng. Ctr., Miss., 1981-82; dir. cleft palate clinic Allegheny Gen. Hosp., Pitts., 1982-88; attending physician St. Margaret Meml. Hosp., Pitts., 1984-89, Montefiore Hosp., Pitts., 1986-89, Divine Providence Hosp., Pitts., 1991—, North Hills Passavant Hosp., Pitts., 1993; cons. med. staff Harmarville Rehab. Ctr., Inc., Pitts., 1985; cons. in plastic surgery VA Hosp., Pitts., 1993—, Miss. Meth. Rehab. Ctr., Jackson, 1977-82, VA Hosp., Jackson, 1977-82; dir. burn unit U. Miss. Med. Ctr., Jackson, 1979-82, co-dir. hand surgery svc., 1979-82; mem. med. staff Miss. Crippled Children's Treatment and Tng. Ctr., Jackson, 1981-82; presenter in field. Contbr. numerous articles to profl. publs., chpts. to books; assoc. editor Jour. Plastic and Reconstructive Surgery. Lt. col. USAF, 1972-76. Mem. AMA, ACS, Am. Soc. Plastic and Reconstructive Surgeons, Am. Assn. Plastic Surgeons, Assn. Mil. Plastic Surgeons, Soc. Air Force Clin. Surgeons, Am. Burn Assn., Internat. Soc. for Burn Injuries, Am. Cleft Palate Assn., Plastic Surgery Rsch. Coun., Am. Soc. for Surgery of Hand, Am. Assn. Hand Surgery, Royal Soc. Medicine, Assn. Acad. Chmn. of Plastic Surgery, Lipolysis Soc. N.Am., Allegheny County Med. Soc., Pa. Med. Soc., Ohio Valley Plastic Surg. Soc., Pitts. Surg. Soc. Office: Allegheny Gen Hosp 320 E North Ave Pittsburgh PA 15212-4756 Office Phone: 412-359-4352.

HECKLER, GERARD VINCENT, lawyer; b. Utica, N.Y., Feb. 18, 1941; s. Gerard Vincent and Mary Jane (Finocan) H. BA, Union Coll., 1962; JD, Syracuse U., 1970; MA in Clin. Psychology, Antioch U., 1994; postgrad., The Fielding Inst., 1995. Bar: Ill. 1971, Calif. 1980, Mass. 1986, N.Y. 1986, U.S. Supreme Ct. 1985. Assoc. Martin, Craig, Chester & Sonnenschein, Chgo., 1970—73, Goldstein, Goldberg & Fishman, Chgo., 1973—76; ptnr. Heckler & Enstrom, Chgo., 1976—80; pvt. practice law L.A., Irvine, 1980—85; sr. trial atty. Law Office of Harden Bennion, L.A., 1985—87, Rafferty & Polich, Cambridge, Mass., 1987—88; trial atty. Acret, Gropman & Turner, L.A., 1989—92; of counsel Lanak & Hanna PC, Santa Ana', Calif., 1992—. Instr. trial skills and evidence Calif. State Bar, 1987—; judge pro tem L.A. Mcpl. Ct., 1991—. Lt. USCG, 1964-67, Vietnam. Mem. Calif. State Bar (Bd. Govs. commendation 1986), L.A. County Bar Assn., Acad. Family Mediators, Ill. Bar Assn., Mass. Bar Assn., N.Y. Bar Assn. Avocations: sports, theater, public speaking. Office: 2070 Business Center Dr Ste 265 Irvine CA 92612 Office Phone: 714-550-0418. E-mail: hecklerlaw@sbcglobal.net.

HECKLINGER, RICHARD E., ambassador; b. Syracuse, N.Y. m. Carol Pratt. Grad., St. Lawrence U.; JD, Harvard U.; grad. in advanced internat. studies, Johns Hopkins U. Joined Fgn. Svc., Dept. State, Washington, 1967—, prin. dep. asst. sec. for econ. and bus. affairs, sr. advisor and exec. asst. to under sec. for econ. affairs; dep. chief mission U.S. Mission to OECD; dep. asst. sec. for European and Can. affairs Dept. State, sr. insp. Office Insp. Gen., advisor to under sec. for polit. affairs, dir. Internat. Energy Policy Office; acting dep. asst. sec. for internat. affairs Dept. Energy, Washington; amb. to Thailand, Am. Embassy, Bangkok.

HECKMAN, GARY WALTER, military career officer; b. Des Moines; m. Sally Mitchell; children: Wendy, Ryan, Benjamin. BA in Edn., U. No. Iowa, 1972; MPA, Troy State U., 1981; grad., Air Command and Staff Coll., 1981, Armed Forces Staff Coll., 1984, Air War Coll., 1989; M in Nat. Security and Strategic Studies, Naval War Coll., 1992. Commd. 2d lt. USAF, 1973, advanced through grades to brig. gen., 1997. C130 transport and AC-130 gunship aircrew and staff, 1974-79, with hdqs., 1979-80, 92-94, plans officer 1st spl. ops. wing, 1980-83, with hdqs. European Commandhdqrs., 1984-87, with hdqs. Air Force spl. ops., 1987-89, dep. dir. programming and policy Mil. Airlift Command Scott AFB, Ill., 1989-91, commdr. 16th Spl. Ops. Group Hurlburt Field, 1994-96; dir. resources (J8), chief of staff J7/J8 US Spec Ops Cmd., 1996—; co-dir. Air Force's base-closing analysis team, 2004—. Decorated Legion of Merit with one oak leaf cluster, Def. Meritorious Svc. medal, Meritorious Svc. medal with three oak leaf clusters, Air medal, Joint Svc. Commendation medal, Air Force Commendation medal, Air Force Achievement medal.*

HECKMAN, HENRY TREVENNEN SHICK, retired metal products executive; b. Mar. 27, 1918; s. H. Raymond and Charlotte E. (Shick) Heckman; m. Helen Clausen Wright, Nov. 28, 1946; children: Sharon Anita(dec.), Charlotte Marie. AB, Lehigh U., 1939. Advt. prodn. mgr. Republic Steel Corp., Cleve., 1940—42; editor Enduro Era, 1946—51, account exec., 1953—54, asst. dir. advt., 1957—65, dir. advt., 1965—82; ptnr. Applegate & Heckman, Washington, 1955—56; advt. mgr. Harris Corp., 1956—57; ret., 1982. Permanent chmn. Joint Com. Audit Comparability, 1968—93; chmn. Media Comparability Coun., 1969—83; chmn. indsl. advertisers com. Greater Cleve. Growth Assn., 1973—76; chmn. pubs. com. Lehigh U., 1971—76; pres.'s adv. coun. Ashland Coll., 1966—76; advt. adv. coun. Kent State U., 1976—81; exec. com. Cleve. chpt. ARC, 1968—74; mem. Rep. Fin. Exec. Com., 1966—87; coord. adv. coun. pub. svcs. campaign Employer Support Guard and Res., 1973—83, 1990—2003. Lt. USNR, 1942—46, comdr. USNR, 1951—53, Korea. Named Advt. Man of Yr., 1969; named to Advt. Effectiveness Hall of Fame, 1967, Cleve. Graphic Arts Coun. Hall of Distinction, 1981; recipient G.D. Crain, Jr. award, 1973, Disting. Alumnus award, Lehigh U., 1979. Mem.: SAR (pres. Western Res. Soc. 1979, Archibald Willard award 1996), New Eng. Soc., Steel Svc. Ctr. Inst. (advt. adv. com. 1965—77), Am. Iron and Steel Inst. (com. chmn. 1961—69), Assn. Nat. Advertisers (chmn. shows and exhibits com. 1966—74, dir. 1969—72), Bus. Mktg. Assn. (pres. 1968—69, Best Seller award 1966, Hall of Fame 1973), Indsl. Marketers Cleve. (past pres., Golden Mousetrap award 1968), Ctr. Mktg. Comm. (chmn. bd. 1965), Ohio Soc. SAR (Hub Scott award 1995), Mil. Order World Wars (comdr. 1980), Cleve. Grays (trustee 1980—82), Cheshire Cheese (pres. 1982), Cleve. Advt. Club (pres. 1961—62, Hall of Fame 1980), Early Settlers, Pi Delta Epsilon. Home: 6000 Nob Hill Dr Apt 401 Chagrin Falls OH 44022-3358

HECKMAN, JAMES JOSEPH, economist, educator; b. Chgo., Apr. 19, 1944; s. John Jacob and Bernice Irene (Medley) H.; m. Lynne Pettler, 1979; children: Jonathan Jacob, Alma Rachel. AB in Math. summa cum laude (Woodrow Wilson fellow), Colo. Coll., 1965, D (hon.), 2001; MA in Econ., Princeton U., 1968, PhD in Econ. (Harold Willis Dodds fellow), 1971; MA (hon.), Yale U., 1989; D (hon.), U. Chile, 2002, Universidad Autonoma del Estados de Mex., Toluca, 2003, U. Montreal, 2004; DHL (hon.), Bard Coll., 2004. From lectr. to assoc. prof. Columbia U., 1970-74; assoc. prof. econs. U. Chgo., 1973-76, prof., 1976—, Henry Schultz prof. of econ., 1985-95, Henry Schultz Disting. Svc. prof., 1995—, prof. econs. Harris Sch. Pub. Policy, 1990—, dir. Ctr. for Program Evaluation Harris Sch. Pub. Policy, 1991—, dir. Econs. Rsch. Ctr. dept. econs., 1997—; A. Whitney Griswold prof. econs. Yale U., New Haven, 1988-90, Sterling prof., 1990, prof., dept. stats., 1990; disting. prof. microeconometrics Univ. Coll., London, 2004—, disting. chair microeconomics, 2004—. Rsch. assoc. Nat. Bur. Econs. Rsch., 1970-77, sr. rsch. assoc., 1977-85, 87—; Irving Fisher prof. econs. Yale U., 1984; treas. Chgo. Econ. Rsch. Assocs.; rsch. assoc. Econs. Rsch. Ctr.-NORC, 1985—; cons. in field; cons. Chgo. Urban League, 1978-86; mem. status Black Ams. com. NRC; lectr. in field.; hon. prof. U. Tucuman, Argentina, 1998, Hangzhou U. Sci. and Tech., Wuhan, China, 2001, Wuhan U., 2003, Changjiang river scholar prof., 2004-. Co-author: (with Alan Krueger) Income Inequality in America: What Role for Human Capital Policy, 2004; editor Jour. Polit. Economy, 1981-87; assoc. editor Jour. Econometrics, 1977-83, Jour. Labor Econs., 1983—, Econs. Revs., 1987—, Rev. of Econs. and Statistics, 1994-2002, Jour. Econ. Perspectives, 1989-96, Labor Econs., 1992—; editor: (with B. Singer), Longitudinal Analysis of Labor Market Data, 1985; (with E. Leamer) Handbook of Econometrics, Vol. 5, 2001, vol. 6, 2005, (with Carmen Pages) Law and Employment Lessons from the Latin America and The Caribbean, 2004; Am. editor Rev. Econ. Studies, 1982-85; contbr. articles to profl. jours. Founding faculty and curriculum com. U. Chgo. Harris Sch. Pub. Policy. Recipient John Bates Clark prize, 1983, Louis Benezet Alumni prize Colo. Coll., 1985, Nobel Prize in Econs., 2000, Paul Harris award Internat. Rotary Assn., 2002, Jacob Mincer award, 2005; J.S. Guggenheim Found. fellow, 1978-79, Social Sci. Rsch. Coun. fellow, 1977-78, Ctr. for Advanced Study in Behavioral Scis. fellow, 1978-79. Fellow Am. Bar Found. (sr. rsch. affiliate 1989-91, sr. rsch. fellow 1991—), Econometric Soc. (mem. coun. 2001—), Am. Acad. Arts and Scis., Am. Statis. Assn., Soc. Labor Econs.; mem. NAS, Am. Econ. Assn. (exec. com. 2000-03), Midwest Econs. Assn. (pres.-elect 1996-97, pres. 1997-98), Western Econ. Assn. (pres.-elect 2005—), Indsl. Rels. Rsch. Assn., Econ. Sci. Assn. (founder), Phi Beta Kappa. Office: U Chgo Dept Econs 1126 E 59th St Chicago IL 60637-1580 Office Phone: 773-702-0634. Business E-Mail: jjh@uchicago.edu.

HECKMAN, JEROME HAROLD, lawyer; b. Washington, June 7, 1927; s. Morris and Pauline (German) H.; m. Margot Resh, June 16, 1948 (div. Oct. 1977); children: Eric Stephen, Carey Eugene; m. Ilona Ely Grenadier, Jan. 2, 1986. BSS, Georgetown U., 1948, LLB, 1953, JD, 1967. Bar: D.C. 1953, U.S. Supreme Ct. 1965. Assoc. Dow, Lohnes & Albertson, Washington, 1954-59, ptnr., 1959-62; sr. ptnr. Keller and Heckman, Washington, 1962—. Gen. counsel Soc. of Plastics Industry Inc., N.Y.C., Washington, 1954—, Broadcasting Publs. Inc. Mag., Washington (co. sold to L.A. Times), 1968-87, Disposables Assn. Inc. (now named Internat. Nonwovens and Disposables Assn.), 1958-67. Contbr. articles to profl. jours. Chmn. regional Rep. com., Md., 1966-72; pres. Plastics Acad., 1995-97. Named to Hall of Fame of Plastics Industry, 1987; recipient Spes Hominum award, Nat. Sanitation Found., 1987, William Bradbury award, Soc. Plastics, 2000, Paul R. Dean Disting. Alumni award Georgetown U. Law Ctr., 2001; Dirs. Citation, Ctr. Food Safety and Applied Nutrition, 2000, FDA. Mem. ABA, Bar Assn. D.C., George Town Club, Woodmont Country Club, Phi Delta Phi. Avocations: golf, tennis. Office: Keller & Heckman 1001 G St NW Ste 500 Washington DC 20001-4545 Office Phone: 202-434-4110. Business E-Mail: heckman@khlaw.com.

HECKMAN, JYOTSNA (JO) L., bank executive; married; 2 children. With Denali State Bank, Fairbanks, Alaska, 1986—, pres., CEO, 2003—. Named One of 25 Women to Watch, U.S. Banker Mag., 2003. Office: Denali State Bank 119 N Cushman PO Box 74568 Fairbanks AK 99707-4568

HECKMAN, LUCY T., librarian; b. Queens, N.Y., June 9, 1954; d. Charles and Ruth Heckman. BA in English, St. John's U., Jamaica, N.Y., 1976, MLS in Libr. Info. Sci., 1977; MBA, Adelphi U., 1981. Catalog libr. St. John's U. Libr., Jamaica, 1977—82, reference libr., 1982—2001, head reference, 2002—. Author: Franchising in Business, 1989, The New York Stock Exchange, 1992, Nasdaq, 2001, Damascus, 2004. Mem.: ALA (sec. bus. ref. and svcs. sect. 1998—), Beta Phi Mu. Avocations: photography, antiques. Home: 100-50 223 St Queens Village NY 11429

HECKMANN, RICHARD J., sporting goods company executive; m. Mary Heckmann; 6 children. Attended, Univ. Hawaii, Small Co. Mgmt. Prog., Harvard Bus. Sch. Founder & chmn. Tower Scientific Corp., 1971—77; assoc. adminstr. SBA, Washington, 1978—79; founding shareholder Callaway Golf Inc.; owner & dir. Smith Goggles, Sun Valley, Idaho; founder & chmn. USFilter Inc., 1990—99; chmn. Vivendi Water, 1999—2001; dir. K2 Inc., Carlsbad, Calif., 1997—, chmn., 2000—, CEO, 2002—. Trustee Eisenhower Med. Ctr., Univ. Calif., Riverside; mem. Bus. Council Univ. Notre Dame Bus. Sch. Office: K2 Inc 2051 Palomar Airport Rd Carlsbad CA 92009*

HECKT, MELVIN DEAN, lawyer; b. Dysart, Iowa, Apr. 21, 1924; s. Wesley T. and Ada Merle(Lawyer) H.; m. Dorothy M. Simons, Sept. 4, 1948; children— Janice, Paul, Mary, Barbara, William, Thomas. B.A. in Econs., State U. Iowa, 1948, J.D., 1950. Bar: Minn., 1950, Iowa 1950, U.S. Dist. Ct. (Minn.), U.S. Supreme Ct. Assoc. Snyder, Gale, Hoke, Richards, Janes (name changed to Bassford, Heckt, Lockhart & Mullin), Mpls., 1950-55, ptnr., 1955—94, prtnr. Luther, Heckt & Cameron, 1994-. Served with USMC, 1943-45. Decorated Bronze Star. Mem. Iowa Bar Assn., Minn. Bar Assn., Am. Legion, VFW, past dir. Marine Corps Heritage Found., U.S. Marine Raider Assn. (past pres.). Republican. Lutheran. Contbr. articles to profl. jours. Address: 601 Carlson Pkwy Ste 750 Minnetonka MN 55305-5241 Office Phone: 952-449-4145. E-mail: melheckt@aol.com.

HECOX, WALTER EDWIN, economics educator; b. Denver, Sept. 23, 1942; s. Morris Brown and Elizabeth (Rogers) H.; m. Ann Elizabeth Gourlay, Dec. 26, 1970; children: Sarah, Eric. BA in Econs., Colo. Coll., 1964; MA in Econs., Syracuse U., 1967, PhD in Econs., 1969. Research economist US Aid/Pakistan, Lahore, 1968, U.S. Mil. Acad., West Point, N.Y., 1969-70; project supr. Nat. Resources Dept. State of Colo., Denver, 1979-81; adv. trade and tariffs Ministry of Fin., Nairobi, Kenya, 1982-84; from asst. prof. to assoc. prof. econs. Colo. Coll., Colorado Springs, 1970-85, prof., 1985—. Sr. lect. Fulbright program, Islamabad, Pakistan, 1976-77; vis. scientist Internat. Inst. for Applied Systems Analysis, Vienna, 1981; cons. Ford Found., Islamabad, 1976-77, Kenyan Minister of Fin., Nairobi, 1982, U.S. Aid/Kenya, Nairobi, 1984, U.S. Aid/Sudan, Khartoum, 1985-86. Contbr. articles to profl. jours. Served to capt. U.S. Army, 1969-70. Fulbright scholar, 1964-65, Nat. Def. Edn. Act fellow, 1965-69, Sr. fellow Grand Canyon Trust, 1994—. Mem. Am. Econ. Assn., Western Social Sci. Assn., assn. Environ. and Resource Economists, Soc. Internat. Devel., African Studies Assn. Office: Colo Coll Econs Dept Colorado Springs CO 80903 Business E-Mail: whecox@coloradocollege.edu.

HECTOR, LOUIS JULIUS, lawyer; b. Fort Lauderdale, Fla., Dec. 11, 1915; s. Harry Howard and Grace Elizabeth (Kellerstrass) H.; m. Dorothy Anne Dooley, Aug. 12, 1950 (dec. 1973); children: Denis Howard, Dorothy Anne, William Frederic, Louis Julius; m. Nancy Bean Hilles, Dec. 11, 1976. BA, Williams Coll., 1938; postgrad., Christ Church Oxford (Eng.) U., 1939; LLB, Yale U., 1942. Atty. Dept. Justice, Washington, 1942-43; asst. to under sec. Dept. State, 1944; pvt. practice Miami, 1946-47; pres. Hector Supply Co., Miami, 1948-56; mem. CAB, 1957-59; sr. ptnr. Steel, Hector & Davis, Miami, 1959—. Trustee emeritus U. Miami, Rockefeller U., Nat. Humanities Ctr., 1985-91; dir. emeritus Chamber Music Soc. Lincoln Ctr., 1987—; chmn. Lucille P. Markey Charitable Trust, 1983-97 . Served with OSS. Mem. Am. Acad. Arts and Scis. Home: One Grove Isle Dr # 809 Miami FL 33133-6530

HEDAHL, GORDEN ORLIN, theatre educator, university dean; b. Minot, N.D., Jan. 2, 1946; s. Chester Owen and Delores May (Johnson) H.; m. Kathleen Josephine Sawin, Sept. 2, 1967 (div.); children: Marc Oscar, Melissa Ann; m. Jean Louise Loudon, Dec. 31, 1983. BS, U. N.D., 1968, MA, 1972; PhD, U. Minn., 1980. Postdoctoral fellow Purdue U., West Lafayette, Ind., 1981-82; prof. theater U. Wis., Whitewater, 1970-92, chair dept. theatre and dance, 1986-89, assoc. dean Coll. Arts, 1989-90, acting assoc. vice chancellor, 1991-92, dean Coll. Arts. and Scis. River Falls, 1998—; dean Coll. Liberal

Arts U. Alaska, Fairbanks, 1993-98; acad. planner U. Wis. System, 1990-91. Author: (plays) Tall Tales and True, 1976, The Brothers Grimm, 1977, Land of the Rising Sun, 1979, Trolls and Other Fjord Folk, 1983, Andersen's Storybook, 1986, The Magic of Oz, 1987, African Folk Tales, 1989, Tell Me a Story, 1992; assoc. editor: Guide to Curriculum Planning in Classroom Drama and Theatre, 1989. Recipient Roseman Excellence in Teaching award U. Wis., Whitewater, U. Wis. Mem. Am. Coun. of Colls. of Arts and Scis., Am. Alliance for Theatre and Edn., Internat. Coun. of Fine Arts Deans, Theatre in Higher Edn., Rotary. Lutheran. Office: U Wis Coll Arts and Scis 410 S 3d St River Falls WI 54022-5001 Office Phone: 715-425-3777. E-mail: gorden.o.hedahl@uwrf.edu.

HEDBERG, PAUL CLIFFORD, broadcast executive; b. Cokato, Minn., May 28, 1939; s. Clifford L. and Florence (Erenberg) Hedberg; m. Juliet Ann Schubert, Dec. 30, 1962; children: Mark, Ann. Student, Hamline U., 1959-60, U. Minn., 1960-62. Program dir. Sta. KRIB, Mason City, Iowa, 1957-58, Sta. WMIN, Mpls., 1959; staff announcer Time-Life broadcast Sta. WTCN-AM-TV, Mpls., 1959-61, Crowell Collier Sta. KDWB, St. Paul, 1961-62; founder, pres. Sta. KBEW, Minn., 1963-81; founder, owner Sta. KQAD and KLQL-FM, Luverne, Minn., 1971-88; co-founder Sta. KMRS-AM, KKOK-FM, Morris, Minn., 1956-94, pres., 1974-94; founder, pres. Courtney Clifford Inc., Mpls., 1977-79; founder, owner Market Quoters Inc., Blue Earth, Iowa, 1974-96; pres. Complete Commodity Options Inc., Blue Earth, 1977-91; pres., owner Sta. KEEZ-FM, Mankato, Minn., 1977-92; founder, pres. Sta. KUOO-FM, Spirit Lake, Iowa, 1984-99; owner Sta. KRIB and KLSS-FM, Mason City, 1984-97; owner, pres. Sta. KAYL-AM-FM, Storm Lake, Iowa, 1990-99; pres. KLGA AM-FM, Algona, Iowa, 1993-99; CEO Hedberg Broadcasting Group, Blue Earth, 1976-99; pres. KSOU AM-FM, Sioux Center, Iowa, 1996-99. Pres. Blue Earth Indsl. Svcs. Corp., 1970—76, bd. dirs., Minn. Good Rds., v.p., 1976—79, pres., 1979—81; bd. dirs. Spirit Lake Industries; mem. affiliates bd. NBC Radio Network, 1990—95, chmn., 1991—95; pres., CEO Arnolds Park (Iowa) Amusement Pk., 1990—95; founder Sta. KUQQ-FM, Spirit Lake-Milford, 1996—99, Sta. KIHK-FM, Rock Valley, Iowa, 1997—99; founder, developer Bridgewater Devel., Spirit Lake, 1999. Mem. Iowa Gt. Lakes Airport Commn., 1986—92; bd. dirs. Pavek Mus. Wonderful Wireless, St. Louis Park, Minn., 1987—. Named to, Mus. Broadcasting Hall of Fame, 2002; recipient Disting. Svc. award, Blue Earth Jaycees, 1971. Mem.: Iowa Broadcasters Assn. (Broadcaster of the Yr. 1998), Minn. AP Broadcasters (pres. 1966, bd. dirs. 1976—78), Minn. Assn. Broadcasters (radio bd. dirs. 1975—86, v.p. 1980—81, pres. 1983—84), Nat. Assn. Broadcasters (bd. dirs. 1985—89, 1993—95), Blue Earth C. of C. (pres. 1967, Leadership Recognition award 1967), Iowa Lakes C. of C. (bd. dirs. 1985—86), Shriners, Masons, Gredeh L. C. (founder 1995—). Lutheran. Office: Bridgewater Devel Office PO Box 157 Spirit Lake IA 51360-0157 Office Phone: 239-434-8261. E-mail: Grebdeh@aol.com.

HEDBERG, STEVEN MICHAEL, lawyer; b. Coeur d'Alene, Idaho, Dec. 30, 1958; s. Robert J. and Helenmarie (Nielsen) H.; m. Mary P. Dever, July 10, 1982. BBA, cert. in fin. law, Portland State U., 1981; JD, Lewis and Clark Coll., 1984. Bar: Oreg. 1984, Wash., US Dist. Ct. Oreg. 1984, US Dist. Ct. (We. Dist.) Wash. 1985, US Dist. Ct. (Ea. Dist.) Wash. 1987. Assoc. Weaver & Layne, Portland, 1984-85, Miller, Nash, Wiener, Hager & Carlsen, Portland, 1985-88, ptnr., 1988-92, Perkins Coie LLP, Portland, Seattle, 1992—, mng. ptnr. Portland office. Bd. dir. Spl. Deliveries, 2000—, Am. Red Cross, 1994—2000; pres. adv. coun. U. Portland, 2000—. Mem.: Wash. State Bar Assn., Oreg. Bar Assn., ABA. Office: Perkins Coie 1211 SW 5th Ave Ste 1500 Portland OR 97204-3715

HEDBRING, CHARLES, computer consultant, writer; b. Wadsworth, Ohio, July 26, 1945; s. Olle S. and Margaret (Dickers) H. BA, Northwestern U., Evanston, Ill., 1969; MS, SUNY, Geneseo, 1974; EdS, Vanderbilt U., 1975; EdD, Columbia U., 1982. Nat. and internat. cons. Rsch. grantee N.Y.C. Bd. Edn., 1983-87; award Assn. of Gifted and Talented, 1979, Computer Software award Nat. Assn. Schs., 1990. Avocations: computers, sports, piano, guitar, motorcycles. Home and Office: 310 Riverside Dr Apt 1712 New York NY 10025-4127 E-mail: steppec@aol.com.

HEDDELL, GORDON S., federal agency administrator; b. St. Louis, Aug. 13, 1943; BA in Polit. Sci., U. Mo., 1971; MA, U. Ill. (formerly Sangamon State U.), 1975. Asst. spl. agt. in charge U.S. Secret Svc., Phila., deputy asst. dir. office tng., spl. agt. in charge v.p. protective divsn., 1995—98, asst. dir. office inspection, 1998—2000; inspector gen. U.S. Dept. Labor, Washington, 2000—. Aviator, chief warrant officer U.S. Army, 1966—69. Former Woodrow Wilson Pub. Svc. fellow. Office: US Dept Labor 200 Constitution Ave NW Washington DC 20210 Office Phone: 202-693-5100. Business E-Mail: gheddell@oig.dol.gov.

HEDDEN, ANDREW S., lawyer; b. Hempstead, NY, June 3, 1941; BA, Hamilton Coll., 1963; LLB, Duke Univ., 1966. Bar: NJ 1966, NY 1970. Atty. Coudert Bros. LLP, NYC, 1968—, ptnr., Global Securities, Mergers & Acquisitions practices, former mem. exec. bd. Mem.: ABA, NY State Bar Assn. Office: Coudert Bros LLP 1114 Ave of the Americas New York NY 10036 Office Phone: 212-626-4422. Office Fax: 212-626-4120. Business E-Mail: heddena@coudert.com.

HEDENBERG, BETTY BARSHA, secondary education educator, writer, artist; b. Bklyn., Dec. 3, 1932; d. John Barsha and Daisy (Lack) Ferrari; m. Arthur Nathaniel Schwartz, Jan. 13, 1968 (div. Feb. 1980); 1 child, Jonathan Matthew (dec.); m. John W. Hedenberg, Aug. 24, 1997. BA, Syracuse U., 1954; MPA, Calif. State U., Northridge, 1994. Ind. researcher, writer, LA, 1980-85; acct. exec. AT&T, LA, 1985-92; policy analyst LA County Met. Transp. Authority, 1993; mem. tchg. staff William S. Hart HS Dist., Santa Clarita, Calif., 1994—. Project cons., guest lectr. Pasadena City Coll. Author: Tracking Transit Art, 1994, Art on Track, 1994, From the Dark Side, 2004; one-woman shows include Paideia Gallery, L.A., 1964, 1966, Orange County Art Assn., Fullerton, Calif., 1964; exhibited in group shows at Paideia Gallery, L.A., 1963, 64, 65, L.A. Art Assn., 1964, 65, Calif. State Coll., Long Beach, 1965, Bakersfield (Calif.) Coll., 1966, Long Beach Mus. Art, 1967, Fine Arts Fedn., Burbank, Calif., 1982, Orange County Art Assn., Brea, Calif., 1983, 86, Riverside (Calif.) Art Mus., 1987, Long Beach (Calif.) Arts Gallery, Second City Coun., Long Beach, Irvine (Calif.) Fine Arts Ctr., City of Brea (Calif.) Gallery; represented in pvt. collections. Recipient Second award modern oil All Calif. Art Exhibit, Riverside, 1966, Honorable Mention award Joslyn Ctr. of Arts, Torrance, Calif., 1984. Mem.: Nat. Assn. Women Artists, Inc., Women Painters West. Home: 21927 Parvin Dr Santa Clarita CA 91350-3008 Office Phone: 661-254-8258.

HEDGE, ARTHUR JOSEPH, JR., manufacturing executive; b. Hudson County, N.J., Sept. 19, 1936; s. Arthur Joseph and Mary Cecelia (Kieran) H.; m. Julie Norton Dahm, Apr. 15, 1961; children: Arthur Joseph III, Peter Michael, Gregory Carlton. BS, St. Peter's Coll., Jersey City, 1960; MS, MIT, 1973. Several mktg. postions Data Processing divsn. IBM, N.Y.C., 1960-68, sr. mktg. mgr. Data Processing divsn. Chgo., 1968-70, br. mgr. Data Processing divsn. N.Y.C., 1970-73, dir. mktg. practices Data Processing divsn. White Plains, N.Y., 1973-74, regional mgr. Data Processing divsn. Chgo., 1974-77, v.p. mgmt. svcs. Data Processing divsn. White Plains, 1977-80, v.p. Real Estate and Constrn. divsn., 1980-85, pres. Real Estate and Constrn. divsn., 1985-87, IBM v.p. and pres. Real Estate and Constrn. divsn., 1987-88, IBM v.p. Corp. Real Estate and Constrn. divsn. Stamford, Conn., 1988-90, v.p. environ. affairs, 1990-93; pres., CEO, bd. dirs. Kroll Environ. Enterprises Inc. subs. Kroll Assocs., Stamford, 1993-97; chmn. Jannon Holdings, LLC, Stamford, 1997-2001, ABR Group, LLC, Westport, Conn., 2003—. Mem. adv. bd. Wharton Real Estate Ctr., Phila., 1988-94. Mem. vis. com. Harvard U. Grad. Sch. Design, Cambridge, 1985-91, Chgo. Crime Commn., 1974-77, Urban Gateways Exec. Com., Chgo., 1974-77, Conn. Bus. and Industry Assn. Exec. Com., Hartford, 1989-92, trustee, 1988-92; chmn. Bd. Regents Fairfield (Conn.) Coll. Prep. Sch., 1978-84; chmn. bd. dirs. White Plains Hosp. Ctr., 1985-92, trustee, bd. dirs., 1978—; chmn. bd. trustees Am. Festival Theatre, Stratford, Conn., 1988-93; trustee Coun. for Arts, White Plains, 1982-89, The Presbyn. Hosp. N.Y.C., 1993—; bd. dirs. N.Y. and Presbyn. Hosps., Inc., 1996—; vice chmn. HealthStar Network, 1996-97, 99, chmn., 1998. Alfred P.Sloan fellow MIT, 1972-73. Mem. Westchester County Assn. (vice-chmn. 1989-92, trustee bd. dirs. 1986-96), Southwestern Area Commerce and Industry Assn. of Conn. (bd. dirs. 1992-2001), Conn. Golf Club (bd. dirs. 1980-85). Roman Catholic. Avocations: golf, reading, the arts. Office: ABR Group LLC 320 Post Rd West Westport CT 06880 Office Phone: 203-221-3117.

HEDGES, DONALD WALTON, lawyer; b. Kansas City, Mo., May 24, 1921; s. Byron C. and Irma (McCleary) H.; m. Mary Elizabeth Mancill, Jan. 29, 1944 (div.); children: Judith Elizabeth, Donna Louise, Byron C. II, Steven M.; m. Diane Scheid, Jan. 15, 1965; children: Scott Andrew, Hillary Carson. Student, Principia Coll., 1939-40; BS, U. Pa., 1943, LLB, 1947; D. Bus. Sci. (hon.), Webber Coll., 1947. Bar: Pa. 1949, U.S. Ct. Appeals (3d cir.) 1979, U.S. Dist. Ct. (ea. dist.) Pa. 1949. Law clk. to Chief Justice Horace Stern Pa. Supreme Ct., 1948-49; mem. firm Mancill, Cooney, Semans & Hedges, 1949-64; ptnr. Wolf, Block, Schorr & Solis Cohen, Phila., 1965-82, Obermayer, Rebmann, Maxwell & Hippel, Wayne, Pa., 1986-88; pvt. practice law, Wayne, Pa., 1948—. Dir. Servotronics, Inc. Former trustee Atwater Kent Mus. Lt. (j.g.) Air Force USNR, 1943—46. Decorated Distinguished Flying Cross, Air medal. Mem. ABA, Pa. Bar Assn., Phila. Bar Assn., Juristic Soc. Phila., Beta Theta Pi. Clubs: Union League (Phila.); Sharswood Law (U. Pa.), Merion Cricket. Episcopalian. Home: 538 Whitford Hills Rd Exton PA 19341-2050

HEDGES, HARRY GEORGE, retired computer scientist; b. Lansing, Mich., Oct. 7, 1923; s. Charles William and Elsie (Frost) H.; m. Mary J. Corbishley, June 14, 1944 (dec.); children: Susan, Martha; m. Kamla J. King, July 24, 1988. BS, Mich. State U., 1949, PhD, 1960; MS, U. Mich., 1954. Electronics engr. USAF Wright Air Devel. Center, Dayton, Ohio, 1949-51; research asso. U. Mich., 1951-54; instr. Mich. State U., East Lansing, 1954-60, asst. prof., 1960-63, asso. prof., 1963-69, prof., chmn. dept. computer sci., 1969-84, prof. emeritus, 1988—; sr. staff assoc. NSF, 1984-88, head Office Cross-Disciplinary Activities, 1988-92, program dir. undergrad. edn., 1992, program dir. exptl. and integrative activities, 1993—2003. Dir. Nat. Electronics Conf., Inc., 1968-75 Tech. editor: Analysis of Discrete Physical Systems, 1967; mem. Computer Sci. Bd, 1973-84; chmn., 1974-75. Chmn. Selective Service Bd. 264, Lansing, 1970-76. Served with AUS, 1943-46, PTO. NSF sci. faculty fellow, 1960 Mem. Am. Soc. Engring. Edn. (chmn. N.Central sect. 1968-69), IEEE (dir. 1967-69, treas. 1969, vice chmn. 1973, chmn. 1974, Southeastern Mich. sect.). Home: 4331 Embassy Park Dr NW Washington DC 20016-3607 E-mail: hedgeshk@comcast.net.

HEDGES, INEZ KATHLEEN, comparative literature educator; b. Washington, Jan. 20, 1947; d. Irwin Randolph and Janice H.; m. Victor E. Wallis, July 2, 1988. BA, Harvard U., 1968; PhD, U. Wis., 1976. Asst. prof. Duke U., Durham, N.C., 1976-82, Northeastern U., Boston, 1983-88, assoc. prof., 1988-90, prof., 1990—. Author: Languages of Revolt, 1983, Breaking the Frame, 1991, Framing Faust: Twentieth Century Cultural Struggles, 2005. Office: Northeastern U 360 Huntington Ave Boston MA 02115-5000 Office Phone: 617-373-3654. E-mail: i.hedges@neu.edu.

HEDGES, JERRIS, medical educator, health services researcher; MS, MD. Chmn. dept. emergency medicine Oreg. Health & Scis. U., 1997—2005, vice-dean Sch. Medicine, 2005—. Editor: (med. jour.) Acad. Emergency Medicine, 1993—97; co-editor: (med. text) Clinical Procedures in Emergency Medicine, 4th edit. Mem.: Nat. Acad. Scis. Inst. of Medicine, Soc for Acad. Emergency Medicine. Achievements include research in the evaluation of Trauma System impact and effectiveness. Office: Oreg Health Scis U 3181 SW Sam Jackson Pk Rd Portland OR 97201-3098 Business E-Mail: hedgesj@ohsu.edu.

HEDGES, KAMLA KING, library director; b. Covington, Va. d. John Wilton and Rhoda Alice (Loughrie) K.; m. Harry George Hedges, July 24, 1988. AB, Coll. of William and Mary, 1968; MLS, Vanderbilt U., 1969. Law and legis. reference libr. Conn. State Libr., Hartford, 1969-74; dep. law libr. Steptoe and Johnson, Washington, 1974-78; law libr. Wilkinson, Cragun and Barker, Washington, 1978-83; corp. libr. The Bur. of Nat. Affairs, Inc., Washington, 1983-94, dir. libr. rels., 1995—. Compiler: (directories) BNA's Directory of State and Federal Courts, Judges, Clerks, 1995, BNA's State Administrative Codes and Registers, 1995; contbr. chpt. to law manual. Bd. dirs. Friends of the Law Libr. of Congress, 2000—05. Mem. Am. Assn. Law Librs. (exec. bd. dirs. 1984-87), Spl. Libr. Assn. Episcopalian. Home: 4331 Embassy Park Dr NW Washington DC 20016-3607 Office: Bur Nat Affairs Inc 1231 25th St NW Washington DC 20037-1197

HEDGES, MARK STEPHEN, clinical psychologist; b. Chgo., Feb. 15, 1950; s. Norman T. and Doris Mae (Walters) H.; m. Janice Finnie, Aug. 16, 1975; children: Anna, Miriam. BS, Purdue U., 1972; MA, U. S.D., 1974, PhD, 1977. Psychology intern Western Mo. Mental Health Ctr., Kansas City, 1975-76; psychologist, dir. psychol. svcs. Northeastern Mental Health Ctr., Aberdeen, SD, 1977—2003; psychologist Luth. Social Svcs., Aberdeen, SD, 2003—; sch. psychologist Aberdeen Pub. Schs., 2003—. Mem. citizens rev. panel S.D. Dept. Social Svcs. Mem. APA, S.D. Assn. Sch. Psychologists, Phi Beta Kappa, Psi Chi, Phi Kappa Phi. Methodist. Office: Aberdeen Pub Sch 314 S Main St Aberdeen SD 57401 Business E-Mail: mhedges@lsssd.org.

HEDGES, MOLLIE ELLEN, elementary school educator; b. Columbus, Ohio, Oct. 14, 1952; d. Tracy Wheat and Maxine (Christy) Peters; m. Robert William Frampton, Sept. 15, 1973 (div. Feb. 1980); m. Charles Richard Hedges, Dec. 20, 1981; 1 child, Colin Harrison. BS in Elem. Edn., Kent State U., 1974; MA in Guidance and Counseling, Ohio State U., 1979; postgrad., Ashland U., Ohio U. Cert. tchr., Ohio. Substitute thcr. Columbus Pub.Schs., 1974-76; tchr. 5th grade Circleville (Ohio) City Schs., 1976-77, tchr. 4th grade, 1977-91; tchr. 3rd grade Circleville (Ohio) City Sch., 1991—; coop. tchr. edn. field experience students Ohio U. & Circleville Bible Coll., 1999—; coop. tchr. student teaching program Ashland U., 2000—. Deacon Presbyn. Ch. Circleville, 1990-92, moderator of deacons, 1992—, elder, 1993-95, 2001-03, chmn. Christian edn. commn., 2001-03; bd. dirs. Parents' Assn. Culver Mil. Acad., 1991-94; coord. shepherding program Presbyn. Ch. Circleville, 1995—. Named Circleville Elem. Tchr. of Yr., VFW, 1999, Educator of Yr., Jr. Achievement Ohio Inc., 2003—04. Mem.: CEA, OEA, NEA, AAUW. Republican. Avocations: cooking, reading, travel.

HEDGES, PATRICK ARMAND, security firm executive; b. Ft. Bragg, N.C., June 2, 1948; adopted s. Harold and Marcelle Marie Julienne (Zeyen) H.; m. Penelope Ann Huff, Aug. 20, 1968 (div. Feb. 1981); children: John Patrick, Sean Armand, Cristina Marie. *Patrick Hedges father was in the United States Army of the 562nd Ambulance Company, 425th Battalion, during WWII, when he and his wife were introduced in Belgium. His mother was born in Houffalize, Belgium. During the war she worked in the Hospital Baviere as a registered nurse, in Liege, and fought as a member of the Belgium underground army as an information courier. She was also an adjutant of a resistance group to the occupying Germans during the war and she saw 40 of her group lost during her five years in the Belgian resistance. She has six medals and a number of citations that she received for her allegiance during WWII, including the Cross of War. She received her US citizenship on June 27, 1957.* AA, St. Leo Coll., Ft. Monroe, Va., 1985, Air Command and Staff Coll., Langley AFB, Va., 1990, Air War Coll., Kelly AFB, Tex., 1993. Computer programmer Applied Tech. Lab., Ft. Eustis, Va., 1978-81, computer sys. analyst, 1983—84; dep. dir. intelligence support Hdqrs. Tactical Air Command, Langley AFB, 1984—85, tech. advisor intelligence support, 1985—86; chief sys. application, computer sys. analyst 1912 Computer Sys. Group, Langley AFB, 1986—91; chief air force computer security Air Force Info. Warfare Ctr., San Antonio, 1991-94; chief info. protection tech. support Air Force Comm. Agy., Scott AFB, Ill., 1994—2001, chief comm. Air Force security program, 2001—. Contbr. articles to profl. jours. With U.S. Army, 1968-77, Vietnam. Decorated Bronze Star, Vietnam Cross of Gallantry Unit, Meritorious Svc. medal, Army Commendation medal with oak leaf, Vietnam Svc. medal with three campaign stars. Mem.: Vet. Foreign Wars. Avocations: collecting books, coins and stamps, woodworking. Home: 2412 Antiquity Ln Belleville IL 62221

HEDGES-GOETTL, LEONARD, minister, psychologist; b. Jefferson, Wis., Dec. 5, 1956; s. Leonard Conrad and Gladys Mary Goettl; m. Barbara Hedges, Aug. 13, 1958; children: Kathryn Lynn, Robert James, Elizabeth Joy, Nathaniel Len. BA in Math., U. Wis., Madison, 1979; BA in Computer Sci., U.in Wis., Madison, 1979; MDiv, Princeton Theol. Sem., 1989; MA in Psychology, Widener U., 1997, PhD in Psychology, 1999. Ordained min. Presbyn. Ch., 1989; lic. psychologist Ga., Pa., cert. sch. psychologist Pa. Computer sys. engr. Bethlehem Steel, Pa., 1983—84; pastor various Presbyn. Chs., 1989—2004; pvt. practice Roswell, Ga., 1999—; forensic and clin. psychologist West Ctrl. Ga. Regional Hosp., Columbus, Ga., 2004—. Keynote spkr. NCCJ, NJ, 1991—91; clergy witness U.S. Adv. Bd. on Child Abuse and Neglect, Washington, 1993; mem. Gov.'s Taskforce on Abuse and Neglect, NJ, 1996—98; presenter Soc. for Personality Assessment, 2002; seminar leader Am. Assn. Mental Retardation, 2004. Author: Sexual Abuse: Pastoral Responses, 2004. Lt. USN, 1979—83. Recipient Humanitarian Svc. award, U.S. Navy, 1983; scholar, 1975—79; Zigmunt Piatrowski scholar, Widener U., 1998. Mem.: APA, Internat. Rorschach Soc., Soc. for Personality Assessment, Big Top Theatre (pres. bd. dirs.). Avocations: sewing, acting, singing. Office: 425 E Crossville Rd Ste C-105 Roswell GA 30075 Office Phone: 678-641-9757. Personal E-mail: the2revs@aol.com.

HEDGPETH, KIM ROBERTS, trade association administrator; m. Gilbert W. Hedgpeth. BA, Harvard U.; JD, Georgetown U. Bar: Calif., NY. Contract adminstr., asst. exec. dir./house counsel, co-exec. dir. AFTRA, NYC, 1981—86, exec. dir. San Francisco, 1987—92, asst. nat. exec. dir. news and broadcast, 1992—97, assoc. nat. exec. dir., 1997—2005, nat. exec. dir., 2005—. Dir. labor and employee rels. Harvard U.; v.p. human resources Safe Horizon. Mem.: Associated Actors and Artists Am. (exec. sec.). Office: AFTRA 260 Madison Ave New York NY 10016-2401 Office Phone: 212-532-4219.*

HEDIN, EDNA JENKS, musician, educator; b. Ft. Worth, Nov. 15, 1924; d. Edward Lee and Tressie (Jackson) Jenks; m. Alvin Morris Hedin, Apr. 1, 1947; children: John Alvin, Edward Morris, James Lee. AA, Ctrl. Coll. Women, Conway, Ark., 1945; BMus, Okla. Baptist U., 1948; MEd, Tex. Tech. U., 1972. Grad. asst. Ctrl. Coll. Women, Conway, Ark., 1946—47; pvt. tchr., piano, mus. dir., kindegarten Shawnee, Okla., 1948—49; dir. jr. high choir Crooked Oak Sch., Oklahoma City, 1950—51; music tchr. Norfolk Consol. Sch., Cushing, Okla., 1951—55, Artesia Pub. Schs., N.Mex., 1955—87; adj. instr. N.Mex. State U., Carlsbad. Organist First Bapt. Ch., Artesia, N.Mex., 1955—87. Mem.: Music Tchrs. Nat. Assn. (nat. cert. mem.), Nat. Guild Piano Tchrs., Delta Kappa Gamma, Kappa Delta Pi, Sigma Alpha Iota, Phi Kappa Phi. Republican. Baptist. Home: 1 Cajun Ct Roswell NM 88201-3408 Office: Chapel at New Mex Mil Inst Roswell NM 88201 Office Phone: 505-623-8054. E-mail: studio1@cableone.net.

HEDIN, ROBERT ALEXANDER, writer; b. Red Wing, Mont. s. Raymond F. and Lydia E. Hedin; m. Carolyn Hedin, Sept. 3, 1971; children: Alexander, Benjamin. BA in English and religion, Luther Coll., 1971; MFA in creative writing, U. Alaska, 1973. Grad. asst., English U. Alaska, Fairbanks, 1972—73; English instr. Sheldon Jackson Coll., 1973—76; vis. instr. creative writing U. Alaska, Fairbanks, Alaska, 1976—77, vis. asst. prof. English, 1979—80; poet in residence Wake Forest U., 1980—92; instr. Loft Literary Ctr., Mpls., 1993—94; lectr. U. Minn., 1995—96; vist. poet in residence English Wake Forest U., 1995—96; vis. writer in residence Assoc. Coll. of the Twin Cities, 1995—96; instr. Loft Literary Ctr., Mpls., 1996—97; exec. dir. Anderson Ctr. for Interdisciplinary Studies, 1997—; vis. poet in residence St. Olaf Coll., 2000—01; Edelstein-Keller Minn. writer of distinction U. Minn., 2001—02. Contbr. articles numerous profl. jours. Founder, bd. dirs. Anderson Ctr. for Interdisciplinary Studies, 1995—; bd. dirs. Loft Literary Ctr., 2000—04, Hedin-Hartnagel Edn. Fund, 2000—; judge John Haines Poetry Award, 2004, Wick Poetry Award, 2003; poetry panelist Mid-Atlantic Arts Found, Pa. Artist Fellowships, 2001; various positions numerous others. Named to Wall of Honor, Red Wing HS, 2004; recipient William Stafford award in poetry, Wash. State Poetry Assn., 1973, Poetry of Distinction award, The Loft Literary Ctr., 2000, Minn. Arts Leadership award, 1998; Alaska State Humanities grant, Alaska State Humanities Comm., 1983, fellowship in poetry, Minn. State Arts Bd., 1994, Bush Found. fellow, 1997, McKnight Found. fellow, 2000. Address: PO Box 59 Frontenac MN 55026 Office Phone: 651-388-2009.

HEDLEY-WHYTE, ELIZABETH TESSA, neuropathologist; b. London, Jan. 17, 1937; came to U.S., 1960; d. George Stanley and Elizabeth Margery (Hacking) Waller; m. John Hedley-Whyte, Sept. 19, 1959. MB, BS, Durham (U.K.) U., 1960, MD, U. Newcastle Upon Tyne (U.K.), 1976; AM (hon.), Harvard U., 1992. Diplomate Am. Bd. Pathology, Examiner neuropathology. Resident in pathology Children's, New Eng. Deaconess and Peter Bent Brigham Hosps., Boston, 1960-65; fellow Cerebral Palsy Found., 1965-66; asst. neuropathologist Children's Hosp., 1966-68, neuropathologist, 1968-77; pathologist New Eng. Deaconess Hosp., 1977-81; asst. prof., assoc. prof., prof. pathology Harvard Med. Sch., Boston, 1968—; assoc. neuropathologist Mass. Gen. Hosp., Boston, 1981-83, neuropathologist, 1983—, dir. neuropathology tng., 1983—, dir. pathology residency tng., 1985-96; cons. neuropathologist Children's Hosp., Boston, 1997—2000, Beth Israel Deaconess Hosp., Boston, 1977—. Cons. NIH, 1976-81; mem. residency rev. com. for pathology Accreditation Coun. on Grad. Med. Edn., 1996-2001. Mem. editl. bd. Jour. Neuropathology and Exptl. Neurology, 2000-2004, Human Pathology, 2000—; N.Am. editor Neurobiology and Applied Neurobiology, 1991-99; contbr. articles to profl. jours. Wellcome Trust fellow, 1984-85; recipient Meritorious award for contbns. to neuropathology Am. Assn. Neuropathologists, 2005. Mem. Nat. Insts. for Nervous and Communicative Disorders and Stroke (chair program project com. 1979-81), Am. Assn. Neuropathologists (pres. elect 1994-95, pres. 1995-96, v.p., chair coms. 1976-90, Meritorious Contbns. to Neuropathology award, 2005), Diagnostic Slide Session (moderator 1995—), New Eng. Soc. Pathologists (sec., treas., pres. 1980-86), Boston Soc. Neurology and Psychiatry (pres. 1994-95). Avocations: gardening, skiing, needlecrafts. Office: Mass Gen Hosp 14 Fruit St Boston MA 02114-2620

HEDLEY-WHYTE, JOHN, anesthesiologist, educator; b. Newcastle-upon-Tyne, Eng., Nov. 25, 1933; arrived in U.S., 1960, naturalized, 1965; s. Angus and Nancy (Nettleton) H.-W.; m. Elizabeth Tessa Waller, Sept. 19, 1959. Student, Harrow Sch., 1947-52; BA (Rothschild scholar Clare Coll.), Cambridge U., 1955, MB, 1958, MA, 1959, MD, 1972; AM (hon.), Harvard U., 1967. House surgeon St. Bartholomew's Hosp., London, 1958-59; resident in anesthesia Mass. Gen. Hosp., 1960-62, hon. anesthetist, 1977—; clin. asst. anesthesia Harvard U., 1961-63, instr., 1963-65, clin. assoc., 1965-67, assoc. prof., 1967-69, prof., 1969-76, 1st David S. Sheridan prof. anaesthesia and respiratory therapy, 1976—; prof. dept. health policy and mgmt. Harvard U. Sch. Pub. Health, 1988-2000, mem. leadership coun., 2003—; chmn. faculty seminar in health and medicine Harvard U., 1975—76, 2003—; anesthetist-in-chief Beth Israel Hosp., Boston, 1967-88, chmn. com. on rsch., 1976-82. Cons. in field; mem. tech. adv. bd. on med. devices tech. Am. Nat. Stds. Inst., 1973-83; U.S. del. Internat. Electrotech. Commn., 1989-91, 92—; leader U.S. del. Internat. Orgn. Standardization, Geneva, 1973-89, chmn. com. TC 121, SC 3 on anaesthetic and respiratory equipment, 1978—. Author: Respiratory Care, 1965, Applied Physiology of Respiratory Care, 1976, Continuous Anesthesia Vapor Monitoring, 1990, Operating room and Intensive Care Alarms and Information Transfer, 1992; contbr. articles to profl. jours. Recipient Hichens prize St. Bartholomew's Hosp., London, 1957. Fellow ACP (life), German Soc. Anaesthesia and Intensive Care Medicine (hon., life), ASTM (hon., chmn. com. F29 1983-89, Merit award 1994, user vice chmn. 2000-05, sec. 2005-), Royal Coll. Anaesthetists (hon., life); mem. Am. Physiol. Soc., Abernethian Soc. (past pres.), Am. Soc. Anesthesiologists (chmn. com. mech. equipment 1977-82, chmn. com. on equipment and standards 1982-84), Mass. Soc. Anesthesiologists (pres. 1973-74), Am. Soc.

Pharmacology and Exptl. Therapeutics, Roxbury Soc. Med. Improvement (libr. 1970-88, sec.-treas. 1988—), Mass. Med. Soc. (coun. 1975-78), Fairhaven Preservation Assn. (pres. 1990—), Boodle's Club, Carlton Club (hon., life), The Country Club, Somerset Club, Harvard Club of Boston, Harvard Travellers' Club, Vicarage Club Democrat. Episcopalian. Achievements include discovery that human blood has a constant relative solubility for oxygen. Office: VA Med Ctr 1400 VFW Pkwy Boston MA 02132-4927

HEDLUND, ELLEN LOUISE, state agency administrator, educator; b. Omaha, Feb. 17, 1943; d. Edwin Hugo and Olga Josephine Parrish; m. Ronald David Hedlund, Aug. 22, 1964; children: Karen Marie, David Peter. BA, Augustana Coll., 1965; MA, U. Iowa, 1966; PhD, U. Wis. Milw., 1989. Cert. life cert. in guidance and counseling Wis. Dept. Pub. Instr., 1977. Counselor Clear Creek Cmty. Schs., Oxford, Iowa, 1966—67; counselor, tchr. Nicolet H.S., Glendale, Wis., 1967—72, 1979; tchr. asst., project mgr. U. Wis., Milw., 1982—89, proposal writer, 1989; cons. R.I. Coll., Providence, 1990; adj. prof. U. R.I., Kingston, 1991; assessment coord. R.I. Dept. Edn., Providence, 1991—. Ptnr., cons. Wis. Pub. Opinion Mktg. Rsch., Milw., 1976—89. Adv. bd. U. Wis., Milw. Coll. for Kids, 1980—89; Sunday sch. supr. Bay Shore Luth., Whitefish Bay, Wis., 1987—89; congl. pres. Luth. Ch. of the Good Shepherd, Kingston, RI, 1996. Named Viking of Distinction, North HS, Omaha, Nebr., 2003. Mem.: Am. Edn. Rsch. Assoc., Assoc. for Supervision and Curriculum Devel., R.I. Assoc. Supervision and Curriculum Devel. Lutheran. Avocations: reading, gardening, home decor, stained glass. Office: RI Dept Elem Secondary Edn 255 Westminster St Providence RI 02903 Office Phone: 401-222-4600.

HEDLUND, RONALD, baritone; b. Mpls., May 12, 1934; s. Cyril and Mildred H.; m. Barbara Smith, Nov. 12, 1974; children: Eric, Alexander. BA, Hamline U.; MusM, Ind. U. Mem. faculty dept. music U. Ill., 1970-74, 83—; bass soloist, instr. classical music seminar Eisenstadt and Vienna, Austria. Singing voice cons. Carle Clinic Speech Ctr., Urbana, 1994—. Appeared throughout U.S. including opera cos. of San Francisco, Chgo., Houston, Miami, Seattle, Dallas, Ft. Worth, Phila., Washington, Omaha, Santa Fe, Lake George, Boston, N.Y.C. Opera, Met. Opera Nat. Co., New Orleans, Spoleto Festival, Edinburgh Festival, Vancouver Opera, Conn. Opera, Aspen Festival, R.I. Opera, Chgo. Opera Theater, Opera Theatre St. Louis, Utah Opera, Peoria Civic Opera, Ill. Opera Theatre; soloist with numerous orchs., recitals throughout U.S. Served with USNR, 1958-63. Office: 1st Choice Music Svcs 505 Eliot Dr Urbana IL 61801-6727 Business E-Mail: rhedlund@uiuc.edu.

HEDLUND, RONALD DAVID, academic administrator, researcher, educator; b. Joliet, Ill., June 16, 1941; s. Henry Gustav and Betty Marie (Nelson) H.; m. Ellen Louise Parrish, Aug. 22, 1964; children: Karen Marie, David Peter. BA, Augustana Coll., 1963; MA, U. Iowa, 1964, PhD, 1967. Asst. prof. U. Wis., Milw., 1967-73, assoc. prof., 1973-77, dir. social sci. rsch. facility, 1978-80, prof., 1977-89, assoc. dean of rsch. Grad. Sch., 1980-89; vice provost of rsch., prof. U. R.I., Kingston, 1989-96, acting dean grad. sch., 1995-96; prof. Northeastern U., Boston, 1996—, vice provost, 1996—2004. Co-chair rsch. network R.I. Partnership Sci. & Tech., Providence, 1990-93; bd. dirs. Econ. Innovation Ctr., Newport, R.I.; mem. R.I. legis. commn. on creating high-tech jobs and Univ. Contbr. numerous articles to profl. jours. Mem. Kingston Fire Dist. Study Com., 1990. NSF grantee, 1967, 77, 84, 95, Ford Found. grantee, 1985. Mem. Am. Polit. Sci. Assn., Internat. Polit. Sci. Assn., Nat. Coun. Univ. Rsch. Adminstrs., Midwest Polit. Sci. Assn. (exec. coun. 1987-90), Soc. of Rsch. Adminstrs., Southern Polit. Sci. Assn., Western Polit. Sci. Assn. Lutheran. Avocation: gardening. Office: Northeastern U 313 Meserve Hall Huntington Ave Boston MA 02115 Business E-Mail: r.hedlund@neu.edu.

HEDREN, PAUL LESLIE, parks director, historian; b. New Ulm, Minn., Nov. 12, 1949; s. Thomas Harry and Muriel Mary (Kunz) H.; m. Janeen Margaret Wolcott, June 19, 1974 (div. 1997); children: Ethne Olivia, Whitney Elizabeth. BA, St. Cloud State Coll., 1972. Park ranger, historian Ft. Laramie (Wyo.) Nat. Hist. Site, 1971-76; historian Big Hole Nat. Battlefield, Wisdom, Mont., 1976-78; chief ranger, historian Golden Spike Nat. Hist. Site, Brigham City, Utah, 1978-84; supt. Fort Union Trading Post Nat. Hist. Site, Williston, N.D., 1984-97, Niobrara Nat. Scenic River/Mo. Nat. Recreational River, O'Neill, Nebr., 1997—. Author: First Scalp for Custer, 1980, With Crook in the Black Hills, 1985, Fort Laramie in 1876, 1988 (Best Book of 1988 Wyo. State Hist. Soc.); editor: Campaigning with King, 1991 (Merit award State Hist. Soc. Wis. 1991), The Great Sioux War 1876-77, 1991, Traveler's Guide to the Great Sioux War, 1996, We Trailed the Sioux, 2003; contbr. articles to profl. jours. Bd. dirs. Conv. and Vis. Bur., Williston, 1984-96, pres., 1994-96. Named Supt. of Yr. for Nat. Resources Mgmt., NPS, 2004. Mem. Co. Mil. Historians, Western History Assn. (mem. coun. 1990-93). Avocations: writing, lecturing. Office: Nat Park Svc PO Box 591 Oneill NE 68763-0591 Office Phone: 402-336-3970. Business E-Mail: paul_hedren@nps.gov.

HEDRICH, CLEDA POLLARD, real estate broker, writer; b. Richmond, Va., July 3, 1940; d. Herschel Newton and Frances Morton Pollard; m. Norman Hedrich, Mar. 27, 1967; children: Norman Lee, Bradley Charles. BA, U. of N.C., 1960—62. Real Estate Broker State of Fla., 1974. Exec. asst. to the pres. London & Cheshire Ins. Co., London, 1962—63; exec. asst. Eurofinance, Paris, 1963—64; psychiat. asst. Emory U. (Grady Hosp.), Atlanta, Ga., 1965—66; elem. tchr. City of Chgo. Sch. Sys., Chgo., 1967—67; book editor MacMillan Pub. Co., N.Y.C., 1967—69; editor Internat. Jour. of Psychiatry, Internat. Jour. of Child Psychotherapy, Internat. Jour. of Psychoanalytical Psychotherapy, N.Y.C., 1970—72; real estate broker/owner Pollard & Hedrich Realty Inc., Bonita Springs, Fla., 1976—; vice pres./owner Hickory Homes, Inc., Bonita Springs, 1976—. Author: (novels) A Pl. to Go Someday, (mystery novel) Threat of a Stranger, (novels) Where Paths Meet, (screenplays) Threat of a Stranger. Personal E-mail: cleda@hedrichgroup.com.

HEDRICH, OLAF, medical educator, researcher; b. Johannesburg, Mar. 14, 1973; s. Falk and Helga Hedrich. MBBCh, U. Witwatersrand, 1996. Cert. Am. Bd. Internal Medicine, 2003. Intern physician U. Witwatersrand Med. Sch., Johannesburg Hosp., 1997—97, sr. med. officer, 1998—98; residing med. officer BMI The Pk. Hosp., Nottingham, England, 1999—99; resident St. Louis U. Health Scis. Ctr., 1999—2002, chief med. housestaff, 2002—03, instr. medicine, 2002—03; tchg. attending John Cochran VA Med. Ctr., 2002—03; instr. medicine Tufts U. Sch. Medicine, Boston, 2003—; clin. fellow cardiovasc. disease Tufts-New Eng. Med. Ctr., 2003—. Co-author: (textbook chapter) The Pharmacologic Management of Chronic Heart Failure, Syncope: Mechanisms and Management, 2nd Ed. Recipient 34th Ann. Ralph A. Kinsella, Sr. Meml. Tribute award, St. Louis U., 2002, Best Intern award, Johannesburg Hosp., Johannesburg, South Africa, 1997; scholar, U. Witwatersrand, Johannesburg, South Africa, 1991. Mem.: ACP, AMA, St. Louis U. Residents Assn. (pres. 2001—02), Heart Failure Soc. Am., Am. Coll. Cardiology. Achievements include research in Investigated Progression of Coronary Artery Disease in Non-ischemic Cardiomyopathy. Office: Tufts-New England Med Ctr 750 Washington St Box # 315 Boston MA 02111 Office Phone: 617-636-5114 2089.

HEDRICK, WILLIAM DAVID, secondary school educator, musician; b. Greenfield, Tenn., Aug. 30, 1944; s. John Charles and Christine Lenore Hedrick. BS, Campbellsville (Ky.) U., 1966; M in Music Edn., Ea. Ky. U., 1969; EdD, U. Sarasota, Fla., 1981. Cert. Ky. Tchr. Internship Program Ky. Dept. Edn., 1995, tchr. music K-12 Ky. Dept. of Edn. Assoc. musical dir./cast mem. Stephen Foster - The Musical, Bardstown, Ky., 1972—; chmn., dir. vocal music Shelby County H.S., Shelbyville, 1976—82, 1989—; instr. voice and keyboard St. Catherine Coll., Springfield, Ky., 1985—89. Singer: Lexington Singers, Inc., Shelby County Cmty. Theater; music arranger, composer Ky. Opera Assn. Amb. of goodwill Commonwealth of Ky., 1986; min. of music/organist First Bapt. Ch., Shelbyville, 1992—98; choirmaster, organist First Presbyn. Ch., Ashland, Ky., 1983—86. Named one of Outstanding Young Men of Am., 1979. Mem.: NEA (assoc.), Music Tchrs. Nat. Assn., Ky. Music Educators Assn. (dist. choral chmn. 1990—93), Shelby County Edn. Assn. (assoc.), Am. Choral Dirs. Assn. (assoc.), Ky. Choral Dirs. Assn. (assoc.), Music Educators Nat. Conf. (assoc.), Ky. Cols., Commonwealth of Ky. (hon.). Republican. Baptist. Achievements include patents for digital automated piano tuner. Avocation: computer music/digital technology. Office: Shelby County HS 1701 Frankfort Rd Shelbyville KY 40066-0069 Personal E-mail: dochedrick@aol.com. E-mail: dhedrick@shelby.k12.ky.us.

HEDRICK, WYATT SMITH, pharmacist; b. Roswell, N.Mex., Sept. 28, 1951; s. Wyatt Smith and Roberta Walker (Triser) H. BS in Pharmacy, U. N.Mex., 1974; MS in Hosp. Pharmacy, U. Houston, 1978. Registered pharmacist, N.Mex., Tex. Pharmacy intern St. Mary's Hosp., Roswell, N.Mex., 1973, Ea. N.Mex. Med. Ctr., 1973-74, U-SAVE Drug, 1974-75; pharmacy resident U. Tex. Med. Br. Hosps., Galveston, 1977-78; staff pharmacist Meml. Gen. Hosp., Las Cruces, N.Mex., 1978, Las Palmas Med Ctr., El Paso, Tex., 1978—. Mem. Am. Soc. Health-Sys. Pharmacists, Tex. Soc. Health-Sys. Pharmacists, El Paso Area Soc. Health-Sys. Pharmacists. Avocations: reading, travel, physical fitness. Home: 1028 Quinault Dr El Paso TX 79912-1223 Personal E-mail: whedr34182@aol.com.

HEEB, MARY JO, research biologist; b. Louisville, Sept. 20, 1942; d. John J. and Mary R. (Bohn) Holzknecht; m. Michael A. Heeb, Nov. 10, 1962 (div. Sept. 1987); children: Angela L., Randall V., Derek M., Cynthia A. BS in Chemistry, U. Fla., 1966, MS in Microbiology, 1968; PhD, Georgetown U., 1983. Technician U. Fla., Gainesville, 1963-65; rsch. asst. U. Miami (Fla.), 1969-71; algebra tchr. Hoggard High Sch., Wilmington, N.C., 1971-72; instr. chemistry U. N.C., Wilmington, 1973-75; rsch. group leader Hazelton Labs., Vienna, Va., 1975-78, 81-82; postdoctoral fellow Scripps Rsch. Inst., La Jolla, Calif., 1983-88, sci. assoc., 1988-92, asst. mem., 1993—. Cons. Office of Saline Water, Dept. of the Interior, Wrightsville Beach, N.C., 1972-73. Contbr. articles to Jour. Biol. Chemistry, Blood, Biochim. Biophys. Acta, Archives Mikrobiol., Infection and Immunity, Thrombosis Rsch., Biochemistry, Fedn. Am. Socs. Exptl. Biology Jour., and others. Fellow Am. Heart Assn., 1986; recipient Wilhelm Turk prize Austrian Soc. for Hematology and Oncology, 1986. Mem. AAAS, Thrombosis Coun. of Am. Heart Assn., Scripps Soc. of Fellows (officer 1986). Democrat. Roman Catholic. Achievements include discovery of several Plasma Protease Inhibitors of Protein C., that Protein C Inhibitor is identical to Plasminogen Activator Inhibitor-3; demonstration that Protein C is activated during Intravascular Coagulation; that protein S inhibits factors Xa and Va. Home: 801 Summerhill Ct Encinitas CA 92024-5450 Office: Scripps Rsch Inst 10550 N Torrey Pines Rd La Jolla CA 92037-1000

HEEBNER, ALBERT GILBERT, retired economist, retired educator, retired bank executive; b. Phila., Mar. 7, 1927; s. Albert and Julia (Zwada) Heebner; m. Dorothy Mae Kiler, Aug. 16, 1952. AB, U. Denver, 1948; AM, U. Pa., 1950, PhD, 1967. Instr. econs. Coll. Wooster, Ohio, 1950-52; with Phila. Nat. Bank subs. CoreStates Fin. Corp, 1952-87, economist, 1960-87, asst. v.p., 1961-64, v.p., 1964-70, sr. v.p., 1970-73, exec. v.p., 1973-83; exec. v.p., chief economist CoreStates Fin. Corp., Phila., 1983-87; Disting. prof. econs. Eastern Coll., St. Davids, Pa., 1987-97, disting. prof. econs. emeritus, 2000—. Lectr. fin. Wharton Sch., U. Pa., 1968—69; spl. asst. to chmn. Coun. Econ. Advisers, Washington, 1971—72; vis. prof. econs. Swarthmore (Pa.) Coll., 1976; chmn. Econ. Adv. Com., Am. Bankers Assn., 1978—80; adj. prof. Ea. Coll., St. Davids, 1982; mem. Inflation Policy Task Force adv. com. to Pres.-elect Reagan, 1980; mem. investment adv. bd. to City of Phila. Bd. Pensions, 1980—85; bd. dirs. Nat. Bur. Econ. Rsch., 1983—85, Market St. Fund, 1989—2003; bd. dirs., vice-chmn. Global Interdependence Ctr., 1992—. Author: (book) Negotiable Certificates of Deposit: The Development of a Money Market Instrument, 1969; contbr. articles to profl. jours. Mem. Internat. Visitors Coun. Phila.; trustee Eastern U., 2001—. With USNR, 1945—46. Named to Wall of Fame, N.E. HS, Phila., 1996; recipient Alumni Cmty. Svc. award, 1995. Fellow: Nat. Assn. Bus. Econs. (contbr. Econ. Policy Survey, pres. 1975—76); mem.: Phila. Coun. Bus. Economists, Fgn. Policy Rsch. Inst., World Affairs Coun. Phila., Union League Phila., Conf. Bus. Econs. (chmn. 1987—88), Am. Econ. Assn., Sunday Breakfast Club. Baptist. Home: 1515 The Fairway 471 Rydal PA 19046-1491 Personal E-mail: agheebner@aol.com. *I have always striven for excellence in everything that I undertake-reaching for the highest standards of which I am capable, not just meeting requirements. While I like to think that I have earned my way, I am deeply indebted to key people who encouraged me, mentored me, and steered me to opportunities. Thus, I do not see my career as a solo venture.*

HEED, PETER W., former state attorney general; b. West Chester, Pa., Apr. 2, 1950; s. Walter R. and Elizabeth Allen Heed; m. Patricia Longo, Oct. 3, 1983; children: Travis, Ethan. BA, Dartmouth Coll., 1972; JD, Cornell U., 1975. Bar: N.H. 1975, U.S. Dist. Ct. N.H. 1975, U.S. Ct. Appeals (1st cir.) 1976. Asst. atty. gen. State of NH, Concord, 1975-80; assoc. Cristiano and Krumphold, Keene, NH, 1980-82; sr. ptnr. Green, McMahon & Heed, Keene, NH, 1982—2001; county atty. Cheshire County, NH, 2001—03; atty. gen. State of NH, 2003—04. Instr., paralegal studies, Keene State Coll., 1980-84; bd. govs. N.H. Health & Welfare Coun., Keene, 1985-90. Co-author: Canoe Racing: The Competitor's Guide, 1992; dir./prodr. (video) The General Clinton Regatta, 1989. Moderator, Town of Westmoreland, N.H., 1998—; mem. zoning bd. adjustment, Town of Roxbury, N.H., 1989-90; bd. govs., v.p. Norris Cotton Cancer Ctr., Dartmouth-Hitchand Hosp., Lebanon, N.H., 1993—; mem. U.S. Marathon Canoe and Kayak Team, 1982-83. Mem. ATLA (sustaining mem. 1987-2000), N.H. Trial Lawyers Assn. (bd. dirs. 1987-93). Republican. Avocations: canoe and kayak racing (7 times National Marathon and Downriver Canoe Champion, World Masters Marathon Canoe Champion, Nike World Masters Games, 1998), nordic ski racing, marathon running, history.

HEEG, PEGGY A., lawyer, former gas industry executive; b. Louisville, June 25, 1959; BA with honors, U. Louisville, 1983, JD, 1986. Bar: Ky. 1986, DC 1987, Tex. 1987. Various Tenneco Energy, El Paso Corp., Houston, 1996—97, v.p., assoc. gen. counsel regulated pipelines, 1997—2001, sr. v.p., dep. gen. counsel, 2001, exec. v.p., gen. counsel, 2002—04; ptnr. Fulbright & Jaworski L.L.P., 2004—. Legal advisor to commr. Charles Stalon Fed. Energy Regulatory Commn., 1988; bd. dirs. El Paso Tenn. Pipeline Co. Mem.: ABA, Interstate Natural Gas Assn. Am., DC Bar, State Bar Tex., Ky. Bar Assn., Energy Bar Assn. Office: Fulbright & Jaworksi LLP 1301 McKinney Ste 5100 Houston TX 77010-3095 Office Phone: 713-651-5151.

HEEGER, ALAN JAY, physicist, educator; b. Sioux City, Iowa, Jan. 22, 1936; s. Peter J. and Alice (Minkin) Heeger; m. Ruthann Chudacoff, Aug. 11, 1957; children: Peter S., David J. BA, U. Nebr., 1957; PhD, U. Calif., Berkeley, 1961; degree (hon.), U. Mons, Belgium, 1993; DTech (hon.), Linköping (Sweden) U., 1996; PhD (hon.), Abo Akademie, Turku, Finland, 1998; DHL (hon.), U. Mass., 1999; DSc (hon.), U. Nebr., 1999, So. China U. Tech., Japan Adv. Inst. Sci. & Tech., Bar Ilan U., Israel. Asst. prof. U. Pa., Phila., 1962—64, assoc. prof., 1964—66, prof. physics, 1966—82, U. Calif., Santa Barbara, 1982—, dir. Inst. for Polymers and Organic Solids, 1983—2000; pres. UNIAX Corp., Santa Barbara, 1990—94, chief tech. officer, 1999—2002; chmn. Digital Solutions, Inc., 2005—. Dir. Lab. for Rsch. on Structure of Matter, U. Pa., 1974—81; acting vice provost for rsch. U. Pa., 1981—82; Morris Loeb lectr. Harvard U., 1973. Editor-in-chief Synthetic Metals jour., 1983—2000, contbr. sci. articles to profl. jours. Recipient John Scott medal, City of Phila., 1989, Oliver P. Buckley prize, 1983, Pres. medal for disting. achievement, U. Pa., 2000, Balzan prize for sci. of new materials, Balzan Found., Italy and Switzerland, 1995, Nobel prize in Chemistry, 2000; fellow, Alfred P. Sloan, Guggenheim; grantee, Govt. Fellow: Am. Physics Soc. (Buckley prize for solid state physics 1983); mem.: NAE, NAS, Korean Acad. Scis. (fgn.). Achievements include patents in field. Office: U Calif Dept Physics Santa Barbara CA 93106 Business E-Mail: ajhe@physics.ucsb.edu.

HEEGER, DAVID J., psychology educator; b. Berkeley, Calif., Oct. 3, 1961; s. Alan J. and Ruth (Chadacoff) H.; m. Anne Gelman, Oct. 21, 1990; 2 children. BA, U. Pa., 1983, MS in Engring., 1985, PhD, 1987. Rsch. assoc. Stanford (Calif.) U., 1990-91; rsch. scientist NASA-Ames Rsch. Ctr., Moffett Field, Calif., 1991; assoc. prof. Stanford U., 1991—. Contbr. articles to profl. jours.; patentee in field. Rsch. fellow U. Pa., Phila., 1983-87, Vis. fellow SRI Internat., Menlo Park, Calif., 1984-85, Postdoctoral Rsch. fellow MIT Media Lab., Cambridge, Mass., 1987-90, Fairchild Found. Postdoctoral fellow, 1987, Sloan Rsch. Found. fellow, 1994; NIH Rsch. grantee, 1993; recipient David Marr prize Internat. Conf. Computer Vision, London, 1987. Office: Stanford U Dept Psychology Stanford CA 94305

HEEGER, GERALD ARTHUR, university president; b. Akron, Iowa, Jan. 15, 1943; s. Peter J. and Alice (Minkin) H.; m. Geraldine Ruth Gyarfas, June 16, 1968; children— Brian, Robin. BA, U. Calif.-Berkeley, 1965; MA, U. Chgo., 1968, PhD, 1971. Dir. South Asia Studies program U. Va., Charlottesville, 1971-72; chmn. dept. polit. studies Adelphi U., Garden City, N.Y., 1976-79, dean, univ. coll., 1980-83, provost, 1983-87, exec. v.p., 1985-87; dean The New Sch., 1987-90; dean Sch. Continuing Edn. NYU, N.Y.C., 1991-99; pres. U. of Maryland University Coll., College Park, Md., 1999—. Recipient Cert. of Appreciation Assn. for Vol. Adminstrn. 1981, Sesquicentennial Associateship Inst. for Advanced Studies, 1973; Fulbright-Hayes grantee, 1973 Mem. Am. Polit. Sci. Assn., Assn. for Asian Studies Office: U MD U Coll 3501 Univ Blvd E Adelphi MD 20783 Office Phone: 301-985-7077. Business E-Mail: president-office@umuc.edu.

HEEKIN, JAMES ROBSON, III, advertising executive; b. Cin., Aug. 12, 1949; s. James Robson and Jane (Jessup) H.; children: Katie, James. BA, Williams Coll., 1971; cert., N. Adams State Tchrs. Coll., 1974. V.p. account supr. J. Walter Thompson, NYC, 1975-78, exec. v.p., gen. mgr., 1986; sr. product mgr. Gen. Foods, White Plains, NY, 1978-80; exec. v.p., mgmt. dir. Bozelle Jacobs Kenton-Echardt, NYC, Detroit, 1980-85; pres. McCann-Erickson North Am., 1994-97; regional dir. for Europe McCann-Erickson, 1997—2000; chmn., CEO McCann-Erickson WorldGroup, 2000—03; pres., COO Euro RSCG Worldwide, NYC, 2003—04, chmn, CEO, 2004—. Office: Euro RSCG Worldwide 350 Hudson St New York NY 10014*

HEEKIN-CANEDY, SCOTT H., publishing executive; m. Anne Heekin-Canedy; 1 child, Siobhan. BA in Polit. Sci., Williams Coll., 1974; LLD, Northeastern U., 1979; MBA in Mktg. and Fin., Columbia U., 1985. Positions with Dow Jones, Doubleday; circulation market planning analyst NY Times, NYC, 1987—89, circulation systems support mgr., 1989, asst. mgr. fin. planning dept., 1992—93; project mgr. to project dir. strategic planning NY Times, NYC, 1993—94; group dir. strategic planning NY Times, NYC, 1994—97, v.p. strategic planning, 1994—97, sr. v.p. circulation, 1999—2004, pres., 2004—, gen. mgr., 2004—; circulation acctg. mgr., fin. planning mgr. LA Times, 1989—92. Office: NY Times 229 W 43rd St New York NY 10036*

HEELAN, PATRICK AIDAN, philosophy educator; b. Dublin, Mar. 17, 1926; s. Matthew Henry and Pauline (Beirens) H. Student, Belvedere Coll., 1938-42; BA, Univ. Coll., Dublin, 1947, MA, 1948; PhD, St. Louis U., 1952; STL, Jesuit Theol. Faculty, Dublin, 1959; student, Princeton U., 1960-62; PhD, U. Louvain, 1964. Ordained priest Soc. Jesus, Roman Catholic Ch., 1958; lectr. math. physics Univ. Coll., Dublin, 1964-65; research asso. Dublin Inst. Advanced Studies, 1952-54, 64-65; asst. prof. philosophy Fordham U., 1965-67, asso. prof., 1967-70; prof. philosophy, chmn. dept. SUNY at Stony Brook, 1970-74, acting v.p. liberal studies, 1975-77, v.p. liberal studies, 1977-79, prof. philosophy, 1979-92, dean humanities and fine arts, 1990-92; exec. v.p. Georgetown U., Washington, 1992-95, William Gaston prof. philosophy, 1995—; external appraiser philosophy and arts and scis. programs U. Western Ont., Lowell U., John Carroll U., San Diego State U. Acad. adv. coun. Inst. for Advanced Cath. Studies. Author: Quantum Mechanics and Objectivity, 1965, Space-Perception and Philosophy of Science, 1983; festschrift: Hermeneutic Philosophy of Science, Van Gogh's Eyes and God: Essays in Honor of Patrick A Heelan, S.J., 2002. Fulbright fellow, 1960-62; NSF sr. fellow, 1983 Mem. AAAS, Am. Cath. Philos. Assn. (coun. 1973-75), Ctr. for Integrative Edn. (coun. 1972-74), Am. Philos. Assn. (program com. Ea. sect. 1975, nominating com. 1988), Philosophy Sci. Assn., Brit. Soc. Philosophy Sci., Soc. Phenomenology and Existential Philosophy, N.Y. Acad. Scis., Internat. Orgn. for Hermeneutics and Sci., Phi Beta Kappa, Sigma Xi. Address: 3612 O St NW Washington DC 20007-2615 Office: Georgetown Univ Philosophy Dept 234 New N Washington DC 20057-0001 Office Phone: 202-687-5222. E-mail: heelanp@georgetown.edu.

HEENAN, MICHAEL TERENCE, lawyer; b. Pitts., Jan. 28, 1942; s. Paul Joseph and Helen (Chemas) Heenan; m. Maryte Victoria Narkevicius, Feb. 12, 1970 (dec. Dec. 1999); children: Garrett, Leslie, Suzanne. BS, Mount St. Mary's Coll., Emmitsburg, Md., 1964; JD, U. Pitts., 1967. Bar: Pa. 1967, D.C. 1972, U.S. Supreme Ct. 1974, U.S. Ct. Appeals (D.C. cir.), U.S. Ct. Appeals for Armed Forces 1974, U.S. Ct. Fed. Claims 1975, U.S. Customs Ct. 1975, U.S. Ct. Appeals (3d cir.) 1979, U.S. Ct. Appeals (Fed. cir.) 1982, U.S. Ct. Appeals (4th cir.) 1987. Atty. advisor Bd. Vets. Appeals, Washington, 1971—73; trial atty., divsn. mine safety and health Office of Solicitor, Dept. of the Interior, 1973—74; assoc. Webster, Kilcullen & Chamberlain, 1974—75; ptnr. Kilcullen, Smith & Heenan, 1975—80, Heenan, Althen & Roles, Washington, 1980—2003; shareholder Ogletree Deakins, 2003—. Instr., internat. law U.S. Navy Reserve Officers Sch., 1971—72; adj. instr. New Century Coll., George Mason U., 2004—, adj. prof., 2004—. Author: Understanding MSHA, 1981, Enforcement, Administrative and Judicial Review, Coal Law and Regulation, 1983, Inspections and Investigations, Workplace Safety and Health, 1995, Employer Liability Related to Workplace Safety and Health Obligations at Cement Operations, 1996, Safety and Health at Mines: A Manual for Operators and Contractors, 1999, Federal Regulation of Mine Safety and Health, Mine Health and Safety Management, 2001, MSHA - The Mine Operator and the Law, 2003; co-author (with Ronald E. Meisburg): Federal Regulation of Mine Safety and Health, Administration, Practice and Procedure, 1986; co-author: (with C. Gregory Ruffennach) National Institute of Occupational Safety and Health: Limits of Authority in Rulemaking Under the Federal Mine Safety and Health Act of 1977, 1992; co-author: (with Lynn M. Rausch) Vicarious Liability for Contract Mine Operations: Expanding Liability for Mineral Owners and Lessees, 1994; co-author: (with William K. Doran) Employee Protections, 1995; legal editor Pit & Quarry, 1996—; with Margaret S. Lopez: Self Audits, Occupational Safety and Health Handbook, 2001. Trustee Energy & Mineral Law Found., 1996—. Lt. USN, 1968—71. Mem.: ABA (mem., labor and employment sect.), D.C. Bar Assn., Pa. Bar Assn., Nat. Stone and Gravel Assn. (coun. of counsel). Office: Ogletree Deakins Nash Smoak & Stewart PC 2400 N St NW 5th Fl Washington DC 20037 Business E-Mail: michael.heenan@odnss.com.

HEER, DAVID MACALPINE, sociology educator; b. Chapel Hill, N.C., Apr. 15, 1930; s. Clarence and Jean Douglas (MacAlpine) H.; m. Nancy Whittier, June 29, 1957 (div. 1980); m. Kaye S. Heymann, Dec. 11, 1980 (dec. Apr. 2000); children: Douglas (dec.), Laura, Catherine. AB magna cum laude, Harvard U., 1950, MA, 1954, PhD, 1958. Statistician population div. U.S. Bur. Census, Washington, 1957-61; lectr., asst. research sociologist U. Calif., Berkeley, 1961-64; asst. prof. demography Harvard U. Sch. Public Health, Boston, 1964-68, assoc. prof., 1968-72; dir. Population Rsch. Lab., U. So. Calif., L.A., 1995—2000, prof. sociology, 1972—2000, prof. sociology emeritus, 2000—; sr. fellow Ctr. Comparative Immigration Studies, U. Calif. San Diego, 2000—. Mem. population research study sect. NIH, 1971-73 Author: After Nuc. Attack: A Demographic Inquiry, 1965, Soc. and Population, 1968; author: (with Pini Herman) A Human Mosaic: An Atlas of Ethnicity in Los Angeles County, 1980—86, 1990, Undocumented Mexicans in the United States, 1990, Immigration in America's Future: Social Sci. Findings and the Policy Debate, 1996, Kingsley Davis: A Biography and Selections from his Writings, 2005; editor: Readings on Population, 1968, Social Stats. and the City, 1968. Mem. Population Assn. Am. (dir. 1970-73), Internat. Union Sci. Study Population. Home: 3890 Nobel Dr Unit 1002 San Diego CA 92122-5782 Business E-Mail: dheer@ucsd.edu.

HEER, EWALD, engineer; b. Friedensfeld, Germany, July 28, 1930; came to U.S., 1956; s. Johannes and Lilli Friedericke (Jauch) S.; m. Hannelore M. Oehlers, Jan. 26, 1952; children: Thomas Ewald, Eric Martin. Diploma Archtl. Engring., Sch. Hamburg, 1953; BS, CUNY, 1959; MS, Columbia U., 1960, CE, 1962; Dr Engring. Sci. magna cum laude, Tech. U. Hannover, Fed.

Republic Germany, 1964. Engr. Hinz Architects, Hamburg, Fed. Republic Germany, 1952-55; design engr. Hewitt Robins Co., N.Y.C., 1956-59; rsch. engr. Weidlinger Cons., N.Y.C., 1959-62, McDonnell Douglas, St. Louis, 1964-65; rsch. mgr. GE, Phila., 1965-66, Jet Propulsion Lab., Pasadena, Calif., 1966-70, program mgr. advanced studies, 1971-76, dir. rsch. program autonomous systems and space mechanics, 1976-84; pres. Heer Assocs., Inc., 1984—. Program mgr. Lunar exploration office NASA, Washington, 1970-71; adj. prof. U. So. Calif., 1973-84, dir. Inst. Technoecon. Studies, 1978-84. Author: Operation Systems-Humans-Intelligence-Machines, 1998; editor: Remotely Manned systems, 1973, Robots and Manipulator Systems I and II, 1977, Machine Intelligence and Autonomy for Aerospace Systems, 1988; contbr. articles to profl. jours. Fellow ASME; assoc. fellow AIAA; mem. ASCE, IEEE, Am. Mgmt. Assn., Internat. Fedn. Theory Machines and Mechanisms, Sigma Xi. Home: 5329 Crown Ave La Canada Flintridge CA 91011-2807 Office: 4800 Oak Grove Dr Pasadena CA 91109-8001 Office Phone: 818-790-3799. Personal E-mail: ewheer@yahoo.com, ewaldheer@aol.com.

HEER, NICHOLAS LAWSON, language educator; b. Chapel Hill, N.C., Feb. 8, 1928; s. Clarence and Jean Douglas (MacAlpine) H. BA, Yale U., 1949; PhD, Princeton U., 1955. Transl. analyst Arabian Am. Oil Co., Saudi Arabia, 1955-57; asst. prof. Stanford U., Calif., 1959-62; vis. lectr. Yale U., New Haven, 1962-63; asst. prof. Harvard U., Cambridge, Mass., 1963-65; assoc. prof. U. Wash., Seattle, 1965-76, prof. Near Eastern langs. and civilization, 1976-90, prof. emeritus, 1990—; chmn. dept. Near Eastern langs. and civilization U. Wash, 1982-87. Middle East curator Hoover Instn., Stanford, Calif., 1958-62 Editor: Tirmidhi: Bayan al-Farq, 1958, Jami: Al-Durrah al-Fakhirah, 1981, Islamic Law and Jurisprudence: Studies in Honor of Farhat J. Ziadeh, 1990; translator: Jami: The Precious Pearl, 1979, (with Kenneth Honerkamp) Three Early Sufi Texts, 2003. Mem. Am. Oriental Soc., Middle East Studies Assn., Am. Assn. Tchrs. of Arabic (treas. 1964-76, pres. 1981, dir. 1982-84) Home: 1821 10th Ave E Seattle WA 98102-4214 Office: U Wash Dept Near Ea Langs & Civ PO Box 353120 Seattle WA 98195-3120 Personal E-mail: heer@eskimo.com. Business E-Mail: heer@u.washington.edu.

HEERE, KAREN R., astrophysicist; b. Teaneck, NJ, Apr. 9, 1944; d. Peter N. and Alice E. (Hall) H. BA, U. Pa., 1965; MA, U. Calif., Berkeley, 1968; PhD, U. Calif., Santa Cruz, 1976. Rsch. assoc. NRC NASA Ames Rsch. Ctr., Moffett Field, Calif., 1977—79; rsch. astronomer NASA Ames Rsch. Ctr., U. Calif., Santa Cruz, 1979—86, sr. analyst, 2004—; assoc. prof. San Francisco State U., 1986-87; scientist Sci. Applications Internat. Corp., Los Altos, Calif., 1974-76, 87-93; rsch. specialist Sterling Software, Redwood City, Calif., 1993-98; sr. scientist Raytheon, Moffett Field, 1998—2003, mgr. space and earth sci., 2001—03. Vis. scientist TATA Inst. for Fundamental Rsch., Bombay, 1984. Contbr. articles to profl. jours. Mem.: Am. Astron. Soc. Avocations: hiking, birding, adventure travel. Home: PO Box 2427 El Granada CA 94018-2427 Office Phone: 650-604-6524.

HEERENS, ROBERT EDWARD, physician; b. Evanston, Ill., July 2, 1915; s. Joseph and Karen (Larsen) H.; m. Martha Virginia Lysne, Aug. 21, 1943; children: Kisti Lyn, Martha Jill, Nancy Ann, Robin Jan, Sara Bryce. AB, Kalamazoo Coll., 1938; postgrad., U. Ala. Med. Sch., 1939, 41; MD, Northwestern U., 1944. Diplomate Am. Bd. Family Practice. Intern U.S. Naval Hosp., Great Lakes, Ill., 1943-44, resident, 1946-47; gen. practice medicine Rockford, Ill., 1947—; pres. med. staff Swedish-Am. Hosp.; mem. staffs St. Anthony, Rockford hosps.; clin. assoc. prof. family medicine Rockford Sch. Medicine, also dir. ind. studies, mem. exec. com.; mem. admissions com. U. Ill. Coll. Medicine, 1970—, promotions com., 1973-75, mem. Senate Med. Ctr., 1975-77, also mem. acad. council, mem. adv. com. on family practice. Bd. dirs. Rockford Community Chest, 1954-60, Vis. Nurse Assn.; pres. Winnebago Tb Assn., 1960-61, Winnebago County Bd. Health, 1961-69; mem. Rockford Community Devel. Com.; mem. Community Action Com., 1969-71; pres. Northwestern Area Agy. on Aging, 1991-93. Served with M.C., USN, 1942-47. Recipient Disting. Svc. award Pub. Health Winnebago County Health Dept., 1997, Unique Achievement award Gov. of Ill., 1992, Betty Henry award for Cmty. Svc., 2000, Sr. of Yr. award Lifescape Cmty. Svcs., 2000. Mem. AMA, Am. Acad. Family Physicians (Ill. del. to congress of dels. 1959-71, mem. pub. relations com. 1967-74, chmn. pub. relations com. 1971-74, bd. dirs. 1970-73, exec. com. 1972-73, v.p. 1974), Ill. Acad. Gen. Practice (pres. 1958), Ill. Acad. Family Physicians (Pres.'s award 2000), Ill. Med. Soc. (chmn. pub. relations com. 1961-62, Pub. Svc. award 1994), Winnebago County Med. Soc. (v.p. 1965, pres. 1966), Rockford C. of C. (pres. 1962, chmn. edn. com.), Phi Beta Phi Home: 5664 Spring Brook Rd Rockford IL 61114-5553

HEESCHEN, DAVID SUTPHIN, astronomer, educator; b. Davenport, Iowa, Mar. 12, 1926; s. Richard George and Emily (Sutphin) H.; m. Eloise St. Clair, June 11, 1950; children: Lisa Clair, David William, Richard Mark. BS, U. Ill., 1949, MS, 1951; PhD, Harvard U., 1954; ScD (hon.), W.Va. Inst. Tech., 1974, New Mex. Inst. Tech., 1989. Instr. Wesleyan U., Middletown, Conn., 1954-55; lectr., rsch. assoc. Harvard U., 1955-56; scientist Nat. Radio Astronomy Obs., 1956-77, sr. scientist, 1977-92; emeritus, 1992—; dir. Nat. Radio Astronomy Obs., 1962-78; rsch. prof. astronomy U. Va., 1980-92; Karl Jansky lectr., 1993. Cons. NASA, 1960-61, 68-72, Univs. Space Rsch. Assn., 1996-99, Nat. Radio Astronomy Obs., 1997-99. Contbr. sci. jours. Bd. dirs. Fla. Keys Land and Sea Trust, 2000—. With Army Air Corp., 1944—45. G.R. Agassiz fellow Harvard Obs., 1953-54; Recipient Disting. Public Svc. award NSF, 1980, Alexander von Humboldt Sr. Scientist award 1985 Fellow AAAS; mem. NAS, Am. Acad. Arts and Sci., Am. Philos. Soc., Am. Astron. Soc. (v.p. 1969-71, pres. 1980-82), Internat. Astron. Union (v.p. 1976-82), Internat Sci. Radio Union. Personal E-mail: dheeschen@earthlink.net.

HEESE, WILLIAM JOHN, retired music publishing company executive; b. N.Y.C., June 4, 1936; s. William Theodore and Anna Marie (Bissinger) H.; m. Charlotte Anne Schlosser, Feb. 11, 1961; children: William, Philip, Peter. Student, Bronx C.C., 1971, Sch. for Visual Arts, 1972. Clk. Music Dealers Svc., Inc., N.Y.C., 1953-60; salesman Hansen Publs., N.Y.C., Miami Beach, Fla., 1960-61; mgr. sales Shapiro, Bernstein & Co., Inc., N.Y.C., 1961-69, M.C.A. Music (divsn. Music Corp. Am.), N.Y.C., 1970—71; gen. mgr. Sam Fox Music, N.Y.C., 1971—74; v.p. sales Carl Fischer, Inc., N.Y.C., 1974—2003, v.p. spl. projects, 2003—05; ret., 2005. Dir. Scott Tower Housing Co., Inc., 1970-80, pres., v.p., sec.; dir. Our Lady of Angels Ch., 1978-82, mem. parish coun., Our Lady of Fatima Parish, 1983-; dir. Vets. Little League, mgr., coach, 1976-88, Fountain 1&Cad Corp., East Coast Conf. Baseball League, 1989-91, mgr., coach sr. divsn., 1989-90; mgr., coach Unltd. Age Baseball Team, Westchester Baseball Assn., 1991-93. With Army N.G., 1959-65. Mem.: Retail Print Music Dealers Assn. (bd. dirs.), Music Pubs. Assn. (dir. 1980—84, sec. 1982—84, dir. 1984—92, treas. 1985—87, dir. 1996—2000), KC. Republican. Home: 1 Fountain Ln Scarsdale NY 10583-4654 E-mail: billh@carlfischer.com.

HEETER, JAMES A., lawyer; b. Monett, Mo., Oct. 28, 1948; AB with honors, U. Mo., Columbia, 1970; JD cum laude, Harvard U., 1973. Bar: Mo. 1973. Mem. Stinson, Mag & Fizzell PC, Kansas City, Mo., 1973—95; ptnr. Sonnenschein Nath & Rosenthal LLP, Kansas City, Mo., 1995—, mng. ptnr. Kansas City office, 2001—, mem. exec. com. Mem. City Coun., Kansas City, Mo., 1983—87. Mem. Civic Coun. of Greater Kansas City. Mem. ABA, Mo. Bar, Kansas City Met. Bar Assn. Office: Sonnenschein Nath & Rosenthal LLP Ste 1100 4520 Main St Kansas City MO 64111 Office Phone: 816-460-2452. Office Fax: 816-531-7545. Business E-Mail: jheeter@sonnenschein.com.

HEFFELFINGER, THOMAS BACKER, prosecutor, lawyer; b. Mpls., Feb. 13, 1948; BA in History, Stanford U., 1970; JD, U. Minn., 1975. Bar: Minn. 1976, U.S. Dist. Ct. Minn. 1977, U.S. Ct. Appeals (8th cir.) 1983. Law clk. Office of the Hennepin County Atty., 1974-76, asst. atty. juvenile divsn., 1976, asst. atty. criminal divsn. trial sect., 1977-82, asst. atty. major offender unit, 1978-81, supr. burglary unit, 1981-82; asst. U.S. atty. criminal divsn. U.S. Dept. Justice, Minn., 1982-88, atty. white collar crime sect., 1982-85, supr. narcotics and firemans sect., 1985-86, U.S. atty., 1991-93, 2001—; ptnr. Opperman Heins & Paquin, 1988-91, Bowman and Brooke, 1993—2000, Best & Flanagan, 2000—01. Contbr. articles to profl. jours. Candidate Hennepin County Atty., 1986; bd. dirs. Mpls. Chpt. ARC, 1987—; mem. Hennepin County Task Force on Youth and Drugs, 1987-88, Minn. Ho. of Reps. Rep. Caucus Drug Task Force, 1989-90, Minn. Commn. on Violent Crime, 1991; chmn. Minn. Commn. on Jud. Selection, 1990-91; lectr. in field. Mem. Fed. Bar Assn., Minn. Bar Assn., Hennepin County Bar Assn. Office: 600 US Courthouse 300 S 4th St Minneapolis MN 55415

HEFFERAN, COLIEN JOAN, economist; b. Mpls., May 13, 1949; d. Bernard and Rosemary Arnsdorf; m. Hollis Spurgeon Summers, Oct. 14, 1987; 1 child, Margaret Vimont Summers. BS, U. Ariz., 1971; MS, U. Ill., 1974, PhD, 1976. Asst. prof. Pa. State U., University Park, 1975-79; econ., rsch. leader Agrl. Rsch. Svc., USDA, Hyattsville, Md., 1979-88; adminstr. Coop. State Rsch., Edn. and Ext. Svc., 1988—. Adj. prof. U. Md., University Park, 1982-88; chmn. Ctr. for Family, Washington, 1985-87; vis. fellow Australian Nat. U., Canberra, NSW, 1989-91. Mem. editl. bd. Jours.-Family Econ. Issues, 1987—. Recipient Outstanding Citizen award U. Ariz., 1985, Outstanding Alumni award U. Ill., 1986, Presdl. Rank award as Disting. Fed. Exec., 2000. Mem. Am. Econ. Assn., Am. Coun. on Consumer Interests. Democrat. Roman Catholic. Office Phone: 202-720-4423. Business E-Mail: chefferan@csrees.usda.gov.

HEFFERNAN, JAMES ANTHONY WALSH, language and literature educator; b. Boston, Apr. 22, 1939; s. Roy Joseph and Kathleen (Walsh) H.; m. Nancy Coffey, June 27, 1964; children: Virginia, Andrew. AB cum laude, Georgetown U., 1960; PhD, Princeton U., 1964. Instr. English U. Va., 1963-65; asst. prof. English Dartmouth Coll., Hanover, N.H., 1965-70, assoc. prof., 1970-76, prof., 1976—2004, chmn. dept. English, 1978-81, Frederick Sessions Beebe prof. in art of writing, 1997—2004, prof. emeritus, 2004—. Cons. Mt. Holyoke, 1986, PMLA, 1986-87, Johns Hopkins U., 1987, NYU, 1987, 89, U. Press New Eng., 1987, U. Press Chgo., 1988, NEH, 1988, 90, Rutgers U., 1988, U. Md., 1988, Vanderbilt U., 1989, Barnard Coll., 1992; dir. summer seminar English romantic lit. and visual arts NEH/Dartmouth Coll., Hanover, 1987, 89; spkr. various seminars; lectr. in field. Author: Wordsworth's Theory of Poetry: The Transforming Imagination, 1969, The Re-Creation of Landscape: A Study of Wordsworth, Coleridge, Constable and Turner, 1985, Museum of Words: The Poetics of Ekphrasis from Homer to Ashbery, 1993; co-author: Writing: A College Handbook, 5th edit., 2000, Writing: A Concise College Handbook, 1st edit., 1996; editor: Space, Time, Image, Sign: Essays on Literature and the Visual Arts, 1987, Representing the French Revolution: Literature, Historiography and Art, 1992; contbr. articles to profl. jours. Trustee Vermont Acad., 1992-01. Woodrow Wilson fellow, 1960-61, Franklin Murphy, Jr. fellow, 1961-62, R.K. Root fellow, 1962-63, Dartmouth Coll., 1968-69, NEH fellow, 1991; grantee Dartmouth Coll., 1971, 74, 87, NEH, 1984, 87, 89. Mem. MLA (evaluator essays, presenter, del. various convs.), Assn. Literary Scholars and Critics (coun. 1996-99). Office: English Dept Dartmouth College Hanover NH 03755 E-mail: jamesheff@dartmouth.edu.

HEFFERNAN, JAMES VINCENT, lawyer; b. Washington, Oct. 6, 1926; s. Vincent Jerome and Hazel Belle (Wiltfong) Heffernan; m. Virginia May Adams, June 26, 1954; children: David V., Douglas J., Alan P., Margaret L., Thomas A. AB, Cornell U., 1949, JD with distinction, 1952. Bar: D.C. 1953, Md. 1959, U.S. Ct. Claims 1955, U.S. Tax Ct. 1953, U.S. Supreme Ct. 1958. Assoc. Sutherland, Asbill & Brennan, Washington, 1952-59, ptnr., 1959—. Adj. prof. Georgetown U., Washington, 1978—79. Contbr. articles to profl. jours. With USN, 1945—46. Mem.: ABA, Bar Assn. D.C., Fed. Bar Assn., Kenwood Golf and Country Club, Met. Club (Washington), KC, Order Coif, Phi Alpha Delta. Democrat. Roman Catholic. Home: 5216 Falmouth Rd Bethesda MD 20816-2913 Office: Sutherland Asbill & Brennan LLP 1275 Pennsylvania Ave NW Washington DC 20004-2415 Personal E-mail: jvh3@cornell.edu. Business E-Mail: james.heffernan@sablaw.com.

HEFFERNAN, JOHN WILLIAM, retired journalist; b. Stockbridge, Eng., Oct. 21, 1910; came to U.S., 1946; s. John and Alice Ann (Edwards) H.; m. Edith Curry, Dec. 10, 1948 (dec. Aug. 1990); 1 stepchild, Anthony Edward; m. Martha Powell Hensley, Apr. 25, 1992 (dec. June 2003); m. Ewa Joanna Janowski, Aug. 17, 2004. Student, Clarks Coll., Eng., 1924-26. Sub-editor Central News, London, 1929-34, Press Assn., London, 1934-36, sports reporter, 1936-39; fgn. corr. Reuters, N.Y.C., 1946; fgn. corr. at UN, N.Y.C., 1946-57; chief corr. Reuters, Washington, 1957-76; ret., 1976. Bd. dirs. Gasparilla Island Bridge Auth., 1995—97. Co-author: Frontlines, 2001. Pres. Gasparilla Island Conservation and Improvement Assn., Boca Grande, Fla., 1994; bd. dirs. Gasparilla Island Bridge Com., 1996-97. With Brit. Army, 1941-46, promoted maj. 1945. Decorated Comdr. Order of Brit. Empire. Mem. Nat. Press Club (pres. 1969), UN Corr. Assn. (pres. 1956), Overseas Press Club. Avocations: golf, swimming. Home: 7622 Desert Inn Way Bradenton FL 34202 Personal E-mail: johnwheffernon@verizon.net.

HEFFERNAN, NATHAN STEWART, retired state supreme court chief justice; b. Frederic, Wis., Aug. 6, 1920; s. Jesse Eugene and Pearl Eva (Kaump) H.; m. Dorothy Hillemann, Apr. 27, 1946; children: Katie (Mrs. Howard Thomas), Michael, Thomas. BA, U. Wis., 1942, LLB, 1948, LLD, 1999; postgrad., Harvard U. Sch. Bus. Adminstrn., 1943-44; LLD, Lakeland Coll., 1995. Bar: Wis. 1948, U.S. Dist. Ct. (we. dist.) Wis. 1948, U.S. Dist. Ct. (ea. dist.) Wis. 1950, U.S. Ct. Appeals (7th cir.) 1960, U.S. Supreme Ct. 1960. Assoc. firm Schubring, Ryan, Peterson & Sutherland, Madison, Wis., 1948-49; practice in Sheboygan, Wis., 1949-59; partner firm Buchen & Heffernan, 1951-59; counsel Wis. League Municipalities, 1949; research asst. to gov. Wis., 1949; asst. dist. atty. Sheboygan County, 1951-53; city atty. City of Sheboygan, 1953-59; dep. atty. gen. State of Wis., 1959-62; U.S. atty. Western Dist. Wis., 1962-64; justice Wis. Supreme Ct., 1964—, chief justice, 1983-95. Lectr. mcpl. corps., 1961-64, appellate procedure and practice U. Wis. Law Sch., 1971-83; faculty Appellate Judges Seminar, Inst. Jud. Adminstrn., NYU, 1972-87; former mem. Nat. Council State Ct. Reps., chmn., 1976-77; ex-officio dir. Nat. Ctr. State Cts., 1976-77, mem. adv. bd. appellate justice project; former mem. Wis. Jud. Planning Com.; chmn. Wis. Appellate Practice and Procedure Com., 1975-76; mem. exec. com. Wis. Jud. Conf., 1978-95, chmn., 1983; pres. City Attys. Assn., 1958-59; chair Citizens Panel on Election Reform; co-chair Equal Justice Coalition. Wis. chmn. NCCJ, 1966-67; past exec. bd. Four Lakes Coun., Boy Scouts Am.; gen. chmn. Wis. Dem. Conv., 1960, 61; mem. Wis. Found.; bd. dirs. Inst. Jud. Adminstrn.; visitors U. Wis. Law Sch., 1970-83, chmn., 1973-76; past mem. corp. bd. Meth. Hosp.; former curator Wis. Hist. Soc., curator emeritus, 1990; trustee Wis. Meml. Union, Wis. State Libr., William Freeman Vilas Trust Estate; v.p. U. Wis. Meml. Union Bldg. Assn.; former deacon Conglist. Ch. Lt. (s.g.) USNR, 1942-46, ETO, PTO. Recipient Disting. Svc. award NCCJ, 1968, Ann. Disting. Svc. award Wis. Mediation Assn., 1995, Lifetime Achievement award Milw. Bar Assn., 1995, Disting. Svc. award Dem. Party Sheboygan County, 1995; Disting. Jud. fellow Marquette U. Law Sch., 1996. Fellow Am. Bar Found. (life), Inst. for Jud. Adminstrn. (hon., bd. dirs., mem. faculty seminar), Wis. Bar Assn. (chmn. Wis. bar com. study on legal edn. 1995-96, hon. chmn. Equal Justice Coalition 1997—, Goldberg award for disting. svc.), Wis. Bar Found.; mem. ABA (past mem. spl. com. on adminstrn. criminal justice, mem. com. fed.-state delineation of jurisdiction, jud. adminstrn. com. on appellate ct., com. appellate time standards), Am. Law Inst. (life, adv. com. on complex litigation), Dane County Bar Assn., Sheboygan County Bar Assn., Am. Judicature Soc. (dir. 1977-80, chmn. program com. 1979-81), Wis. Law Alumni Assn. (bd. dirs., Disting. Alumni Svc. award 1989), Nat. Conf. Chief Justices (bd. dirs.), Nat. Assn. Ct. Mgmt., Wis. Rivers Alliance (bd. dirs.), Order of Coif, Iron Cross, U. Club (Madison, Wis.), Phi Kappa Phi, Phi Delta Phi. Clubs: Madison Lit. (pres. 1979-80); Harvard (Milw.); Harvard Bus. Sch. (Wis.). Home: 17 Thorstein Veblen Pl Madison WI 53705 Office Phone: 608-233-0736.

HEFFERNAN, PETER JOHN, state official; b. Hartford, Conn., Feb. 19, 1945; s. Kenneth F. and Vivian (Lacourse) H. m. Rosemary Margaret Eagan, May 29, 1971; children: Peter John, Matthew Paul. BA, Providence Coll., 1967; MBA, George Washington U., 1971. Adminstrv. resident Waltham (Mass.) Hosp., 1970-71, asst. dir., 1971-74, v.p. adminstrn. and gen. svcs., 1974-78, exec. v.p., 1978-86; pres., chief exec. officer Cardinal Cushing Gen. Hosp., Brockton, Mass., 1986-87; regional v.p. Weatherby Health Care, Norwell, Mass., 1987-90; regional adminstr. health svcs. divsn. Mass. Dept. Correction, Jamaica Plain, 1990—2003, dep. dir., 2004—; sr. surveyor Nat. Commn. on Correctional Health Care, 1999—. Co-preceptor health care adminstrn. George Washington U., 1977; mem. faculty evening div. Stonehill Coll., 1990—. Mem. instructional conf. coun. New Eng. Hosp. Assembly Inc., 1976; bd. dirs. Waltham Boys Club, 1977, Hosp. Svcs. of New Eng., 1980-83. USPHS trainee, 1967-70. Fellow Am. Coll. Hosp. Adminstrs.; mem. Health Care Mgmt. Assn. Mass., ACHE Regents Adv. Council, 1994—, Lions. Roman Catholic. Home: 352 Mayflower Cir Hanover MA 02339-2119 Office: Dept of Correction PO Box 426 Bridgewater MA 02324-0426

HEFFERNON, SHEILA LOUISE, music educator; b. Fort Benning, Ga., Feb. 15, 1954; d. Elmer Wesley and Ann Catherine (Daly) H.; m. Thomas P. Sullivan, Aug. 5, 1978 (div. Dec. 1986); children: Wesley, Kelsey; m. Wilbur Stauch Hattendorf, July 9, 1988; 1 child, Spencer. BA with honors, Smith Coll., 1976; MusM, New Eng. Conservatory, 1978. Asst. condr. New Eng. Conservatory, Boston, 1976-78; assoc. condr. Princeton (N.J.) U., 1978-80; music tchr. Miss Mason's Sch., Princeton, 1979-80; dir. choral music Northfield (Mass.) Mount Hermon, 1980—, chmn. performing arts dept., 2003—; lectr. music edn. U. Mass., 2001—. Dir. Summer Choral Conf., Mass., 1992-94; mgr. Mass. Music Educators, 1992; Plug fellowship tchr. Northfield Mount Hermon; music dir. The Country Players. Composer choral works; soloist for Alice Parker. Organist St. Andrews, Turnels Falls Mass., 1997- Mem. Am. Choral Dirs. Assn. (sec. 1982—, exec. bd. 1990-95, 2005-), Mass. Am. Choral Dirs. Assn. (exec. bd. 1990—), Nat. Music Educators Assn., Nat. Assn. Tchrs. of Singing, Pi Kappa Lambda. Avocations: theater, travel, working with small children, sports. Office: Northfield Mount Hermon Sch 206 Main St Northfield MA 01360-1089 Office Phone: 413-498-3341. Business E-Mail: sheffernon@nhschool.org.

HEFFERON, THOMAS MICHAEL, lawyer; b. Mt. Vernon, N.Y., Sept. 20, 1960; s. George Joseph and Julia Theresa Hefferon; m. Elizabeth Ann Rosnagle, May 27, 1990; children: David, Margaret, Robert. BA, Trinity Coll., 1982; JD, U. Chgo., 1986. Bar: Mass. 1986, Va. 2001, U.S. Dist. Ct. Mass. 1987, U.S. Ct. Appeals (1st cir.) 1987, U.S. Dist. Ct. (we. dist.) Mich. 1997, U.S. Dist. Ct. D.C. 1998, U.S. Dist. Ct. Va., Md., No. Ill., 2002, U.S. Ct. Appeals (D.C., 6th and 11th cirs.) 1998, U.S. Ct. Appeals (2d, 4th, 9th cir.) 2002, U.S. Supreme Ct. 1998, D.C. 1999. Asst. prof. Boston Coll. Law Sch., Newton, Mass., 1989-90; assoc. Goodwin, Procter & Hoar, Boston, 1986-89, 90-95; ptnr., co-chair, litig. dept., ptnr.-in-charge Goodwin Procter LLP (formerly Goodwin, Procter & Hoar), Washington, 1995—; chair, consumer fin. svcs. litig. practice group Goodwin Procter LLP, Washington. Mem. ABA, Boston Bar Assn., Order of Coif. Office: Goodwin Procter LLP 901 New York Ave NW Washington DC 20001 Office Phone: 202-346-4029. Office Fax: 202-346-4444. Business E-Mail: thefferon@goodwinprocter.com.

HEFFNER, DANIEL JASON, film producer; b. N.Y.C., Mar. 30, 1956; s. Richard Douglas and Elaine Peggy (Segal) H.; m. Beth Klein, May 26, 1991; children: Jeremy Aaron, Zachary David. BS in Comm., Ithaca Coll., 1978. Prodn. exec. Columbia Pictures, L.A., 1982-85; prodn. exec., prodr. Walt Disney Pictures, L.A., 1985-88; v.p. prodn. Buena Vista Pictures Distbn. divsn. Walt Disney Co., L.A., 1988-91; prodr. Serendipity Prodns., Inc., 1991—. Asst. dir. (film) The Big Chill, 1982; co-prodr. (film) Cocktail, 1988; exec. prodr. (film) The Good Mother, 1988; co-exec. prodr. (film) Holy Matrimony, 1993; asst. dir., 2d unit dir. (film) The Seventh Veil, 1999; line prodr., 1st asst. dir. (films) Highway 395, 1999, Sheer Bliss, 2000, Flying Virus, 2001; co-prodr. (films) George of the Jungle 2, 2002, Saw, 2003 Checking Out, 2004, Saw II, 2005; prodr. (film) Anonymous Rex, 2004. Mem.: Prodrs. Guild Am., Dirs. Guild Am. Democrat. Jewish. Home: 4119 Woodman Ave Sherman Oaks CA 91423-4331 Fax: 818-789-0213. Office Phone: 818-789-3035. E-mail: danheffner@earthlink.net.

HEFFNER, LINDA J., obstetrician-gynecologist, educator; d. Carl B. and Thelma W. Heffner; children: Jennifer M Richardson, Craig T Richardson, Timothy C Richardson. BS, Bucknell U., 1970; PhD, Cornell U., 1975; MD, Johns Hopkins U., 1977. Diplomate Am. Bd. Ob-Gyn., Am. Bd. Maternal-Fetal Medicine. Asst. prof. of ob-gyn. U. Pa. Sch. Medicine, Phila., 1983—85; asst. prof. of ob-gyn. and reproductive biology Harvard Med. Sch., Boston, 1987—93, assoc. prof. of ob-gyn. and reproductive biology, 1993—2003, prof. of ob-gyn. and reproductive biology, 2003; prof. and chair ob-gyn. Boston U. Sch. of Medicine, Boston, 2003—. Dir. of maternal-fetal medicine Brigham and Women's Hosp., Boston, 1994—2003; chief ob-gyn. Boston Med. Ctr., 2003—. Author: (textbook) Human Reproduction at a Glance, 2001. Recipient Excellence in Tchg. award, Coun. on Resident Edn. in Ob-Gyn., 2003. Fellow: ACOG; mem.: Assn. of Professors of Gynecology and Obstetrics (Excellence in Tchg. award 1995, 2004), Perinatal Rsch. Soc., Boston Obstet. Soc., Endocrine Soc., Soc. for Maternal-Fetal Medicine, Soc. for Gynecologic Investigation. Office: Boston U Med Ctr 85 E Concord St 6th floor Boston MA 02118 Office Phone: 617-414-5175.

HEFFNER, RICHARD DOUGLAS, historian, educator, communications consultant, television producer; b. NYC, Aug. 5, 1925; s. Albert Simon and Cely (Bender) H.; m. Anne de la Vergne, Dec. 14, 1946; m. Elaine Segal, July 30, 1950; children: Daniel Jason, Charles Andrew. AB, Columbia U., 1946, MA (Mitchell fellow), 1947. Tchg. asst. history U. Calif., Berkeley, 1947-48; instr. Am. history Rutgers U., 1948-50, univ. prof. comm., pub. policy, 1964—; lectr. history Columbia, 1950-52; prof. history Sarah Lawrence Coll., 1952-53; dir. pub. affairs WNBC-TV, NYC, 1955-57; dir. programs Met. Ednl. TV Assn., NYC, 1957-59; editl.l cons. CBS, Inc.; mem. editl. bd., dir. spl. projects CBS-TV Network, 1959-61; v.p., gen. mgr. ednl. TV Channel 13 WNET, NYC, 1961-63; pres. Richard Heffner Assocs., Inc., NYC, 1964—. Mem. program adv. bd. Teleprompter Corp.; dir. commn. campaign costs 20th Century Fund, 1968-69; dir. study TV's environ. messages Ford Found., 1970-72; chmn. bd. classification rating adminstrn. Motion Picture Assn. Am., 1974-94. Producer-moderator The Open Mind, NBC-TV, 1956—59, Channel 13, NYC, 1973—, moderator-host National Educational TV series People and Politics, 1964, exec. editor-host WPIX-TV From the Editor's Desk, 1981—86; author: A Documentary History of the United States, 1952, 7th 50th Anniversary edition, 2002, Conversations with Elie Wiesel, 2001, A Conversational History of Modern America, 2003; editor: Alexis de Tocqueville's Democracy in America, 1956. Mem. exec. com., vice chmn. bd. NYC Police Found.; chmn. judiciary com. cameras cts. NY State, 1987-89. Sr. fellow Freedom Forum Media Studies Ctr., NYC, 1994-95. Mem. AAAS, Acad. Motion Picture Arts Scis., Am. Hist. Assn., Nat. Assn. Ednl. Broadcasters, Phi Beta Kappa. Clubs: Century. Home: 90 Riverside Dr New York NY 10024-5306 Office: 320 Park Ave New York NY 10022-6815 Office Phone: 212-224-1368. E-mail: richarddheffner@aol.com, openmindtv@aol.com.

HEFFNER, WILLIAM RUDOLPH, engineer, consultant; b. Lancaster, Pa., Oct. 20, 1950; s. Scott Hamilton and Marian Anna Heffner; m. Susan F. Heffner, Feb. 22, 1949; children: Daniel D., Sarah D. BA in chemistry, Millersville U., 1971; MS in chemistry, Ind. U., 1977; PhD in physics, Stevens Inst. Tech., 1985. Rsch. scientist Upjohn Co., North Haven, Conn., 1975—77; staff mem. Bell Lab., Murray Hill, NJ, 1978—88; disting. staff mem. Agere Sys., Reading, Pa., 1988—2002; sr. engr. Scitonics Con., Sinking Springs, Pa., 2002—04; assoc. dir. Internat. Materials Inst., Lehigh U., Bethlehem, Pa., 2005—. Sci. adv. bd. Pa. State U. Berks, Reading, 2000—; advisor to Optoelectronics Initiative Lehigh U., Bethlehem, Pa., 2002—03; assoc. dir. Internat. Materials Inst., Bethlem, Pa., 2004—. Contbr. scientific papers. Founder N. Jersey Regional Sci. Fair, Murray Hill, 1985; fedn. chief YMCA Indian Guides, 1990; mem. Berks Sci. and Engrng. Fair, Reading, 1998—2004. Recipient Red Triangle Leadership award, YMCA, 1992. Mem.: Inst. Microelectronics Packaging Soc., Am. Assn. Physics Tchrs., Optical Soc. Am., Tristates Chpt. Optical Soc. (pres. 2002—04). Achievements include invention of 6 US patents; first in-wafer laser testing; bistable liquid crystal display, used in most laptop PCs. Avocation: science education. Home: 478 Rebers Bridge Rd Sinking Spring PA 19608 Office: Scitonics 478 Rebers Bridge Rd Sinking Spring PA 19608 Business E-Mail: wheffner@comcast.net.

HEFFRON, HOWARD A., lawyer; b. N.Y.C., Oct. 3, 1927; s. Jack and Sophie (Malkin) H.; m. Stella Meller, July 4, 1946; children: James, Robert, Nancy. AB, Columbia U., 1948; LL.B., Harvard U., 1951. Bar: N.Y. State 1953, D.C. 1953. Practiced in, N.Y.C. and Washington, 1953-58, 61-66, 69-77, 79—; asst. U.S. atty. So. Dist. N.Y., 1953-57; 1st asst. tax div. and asst. dep. atty. gen. Dept. Justice, Washington, 1958-61; chief counsel Fed. Hwy. Adminstrn., Dept. Transp., Washington, 1967-69; apptd. by Pres. and confirmed by Senate as dir. Office Rail Pub. Counsel, Washington, 1977-79; prof. law U. Wash., Seattle, 1965-67. Cons. Pres.'s Commn. on Law Enforcement and Adminstrn. of Justice, Washington, 1965-66, Nat. Commn. on Product Safety, Washington, 1969-70 Author: Federal Consumer Safety Legislation, 1970. With U.S. Army, 1946-47.

HEFFRON, WARREN A., physician, educator; b. St. Louis, Nov. 7, 1936; s. Willard Page H. and Alma Alberta Revington; m. Rosalee Bowdish, June 10, 1961; children: Kimberly, Wanda, Kara, Arthur. AB, U. Mo., 1958, MD, 1962. Diplomate Am. Bd. Family Practice (pres. 1998—). Rotating intern U. Calif., Orange, 1962-63; physician Hosp. Castaner (P.R.), 1966-68; resident internal medicine U. N. Mex., Albuquerque, 1968-71, asst. prof., chief divsn., 1971-76; assoc. prof., asst. chair Family Cmty. and Emergency Medicine, Albuquerque, 1976-82; prof., chmn. Family Committee and Emergency Medicine, Albuquerque, 1982-93; chief med. staff U. N. Mex. Hosp., Albuquerque, 1993—. Bd. dirs. Am. Acad. Family Physicians, Am. Bd. Family Practice; dir. family Med. Residency Program, Albuquerque, 1971-82; vis. prof., cons. Dept. Cmty. Health, Punjab, India, Christian Med. Coll., Punjab U., Ludihiana; prof. Dept. Family and Cmty. Medicine, Albuquerque, 1993—; various internat. vis. professorships; internat. cons. family medicine residences in missionary settings. Contbr. numerous articles to profl. jours. Mem. free clinic Albuquerque Rescue Mission. Lt. comdr. USPHS, 1964-66. Recipient Recognition award Am. Med. Assn. Physicians, 1971, 74, 77, 80, 83, 86, 89, 92, 95, 98, N. Mex. Family Physician of the Yr. award, 1990. Mem. N. Mex. Am. Acad. Family Physicians (pres. 1985, N. Mex. Family Dr. of Yr. award, chpt. svc. award 1988), Am. Bd. Family Practice (pres. 1998-99), N. Mex. Med. Soc. (pres. 1996-97, Robbins award Cmty. Svc. 1981), Soc. Tchrs. of Family Medicine (bd. dirs., treas. 1997, Smilkstein award for internat. family medicine edn. 1998), Christian Med. and Dental Soc. (bd. dirs. 1998-05, pres. 2003-05, residence rev. com. for family practice 1999-05), World Orgn. Family Drs. (pres. for the Ams. 2000-05). Methodist. Home: 2406 Ada Pl NE Albuquerque NM 87106-2550 Business E-Mail: wheffron@salud.unm.edu.

HEFLEY, JOEL MAURICE, congressman; b. Ardmore, Okla., Apr. 18, 1935; s. J. Maurice and Etta A. (Anderson) H.; m. Lynn Christian, Aug. 25, 1961; children: Jana, Lori, Juli. BA, Okla. Baptist U., 1957; MS, Okla. State U., 1962. Exec. dir. Community Planning and Research, Colorado Springs, Colo., 1966-86; mem. Colo. State Ho. of Reps., 1977-78, Colo. State Senate, 1979-86, U.S. Congress from 5th Colo. dist., 1987—; mem. armed svcs. com.; mem. natural resources com.; mem. small bus.-SBA com.; mem. nat. security com.; chmn. stds. ofcl. conduct com., 2001—05. Mem.: Rotary, Colorado Springs Country. Republican. Presbyterian. Office: Ho of Reps 2372 Rayburn Ho Office Bldg Washington DC 20515-0605

HEFLIN, MARTIN GANIER, diplomat, political scientist; b. Oklahoma City, July 5, 1932; s. Martin Henry and Eugenia Marie (Gabel) H.; m. Sydney Daffin Lewis, Nov. 24, 1954; children— Martin Hays, Stephanie Anne Heflin Pace BA, U. Okla., 1954, MA, 1957; postgrad., U. Redlands, 1955, U. Tex., 1958-59. Vice consul U.S. Consulate, Ponta Delgada, Portugal, 1960-62, U.S. Consulate Gen., São Paulo, Brazil, 1962-64; 2d sec. U.S. Embassy, Tokyo, Japan, 1964-68; prin. officer U.S. Consulate, Sapporo, Japan, 1968-71; fgn. affairs officer U.S. Dept State, Washington, 1971-74; consul, econ. and commerce U.S. Consulate Gen., São Paulo, 1974-76; dir. U.S. Trade Ctr. U.S. Dept. Commerce, São Paulo, 1976-78; counselor econ. and comml. affairs U.S. Embassy, New Delhi, India, 1979-83; minister-counselor, sr. Fgn. Service; prin. officer U.S. Consultate Gen., Monterrey, Mexico, 1983-87; sr. fellow Ctr. for Study of Fgn. Affairs, Fgn. Service Inst., Dept. State, 1987-89; mng. dir. The Naiad Corp., 1990—. Served to 1st lt. USAF, 1954-56. Mem. Am. Fgn. Service Assn., Am. Legion, Phi Delta Theta Roman Catholic. Avocations: golf, photography. Home: 4411 NW 12th Pl Gainesville FL 32605-5500 Personal E-mail: nikkihef@cox.net.

HEFNER, CHRISTIE ANN, publishing executive; b. Chgo., Nov. 8, 1952; d. Hugh Marston and Mildred Marie (Williams) H. BA in English and Am. Lit., summa cum laude, Brandeis U., 1974. Freelance journalist, Boston, 1974-75; spl. asst. to chmn. Playboy Enterprises, Inc., Chgo., 1975-78, v.p., 1978-82, bd. dirs., 1979—, vice chmn., 1986-88, pres., 1982-88, COO, 1984-88, chmn., CEO, 1988—. Bd. dirs. Playboy Found., Mag. Pubs. Assn. Bd. dirs. Creative Coalition, Rush Med. Ctr., Canyon Ranch, Bus. Com. for the Arts, NCTA Diversity Com. Named Advocate of Yr., AIDS Legal Coun., 1998, Friend for Life, Howard Brown Med. Ctr., 1998; named one of 100 Most Powerful Women in World, Forbes mag., 2005; named to Today's Chgo. (Ill.) Woman Hall Fame, 2002; recipient Agness Underwood award, L.A. chpt. Women in Comm., 1984, Founders award, Midwest Women's Ctr., 1986, Human Rights award, Am. Jewish Com., 1986, Harry Kalven Freedom of Expression award, ACLU, Ill., 1987, Spirit of Life award, City of Hope, 1988, Eleanor Roosevelt award, Internat. Platform Assn., 1990, Will Rogers Meml. award, Beverly Hills C. of C. and Civic Assn., 1993, Humanitarian award, Rainbow/PUSH Coalition, 1998, Corp. Leadership award, AIDS Pastoral Care Network, 1998, Exec. Leadership award, Nat. Soc. Fundraising Execs., 1998, Champion of Freedom award, ADL, 2000, Spirit of Hope award, John Wayne Cancer Ctr., 2001, Bettie B. Port Humanitarian award, Mt. Sinai, 2001, Christopher Reeve 1st Amendment award, Creative Coalition, 2001, Bette B. Port Humanitarian award, Sianai Health Sys., 2001, Vanguard award, Nat. Cable & Telecommunications Assn., 2002, Philanthropic Innovator Luminary award, Com. of 200, 2002, Family Bus. Coun. Leadership award, U. Ill., Chgo., 2003, Friends of Cmty. award, Diversity Healthcare, Inc., 2005, Lifetime Achievement award, 25-Yr. Club, 2005. Mem. Nat. Cable and Telecomm. Assn. (Vanguard award 2002, Interlochen's Path of Inspiration award 2003), Mus. of TV and Radio Media Ctr., Brandeis Nat. Women's Com. (life), Com. of 200, World Pres. Orgn., Chgo. Network, Sierra Club, Emilys List, Phi Beta Kappa. Democrat. Office: Playboy Enterprises Inc 680 N Lake Shore Dr Chicago IL 60611-4455

HEFNER, HARRY SIMON, retired art educator; b. Kalamazoo, Nov. 20, 1911; s. Charles Roscoe Hefner and Clara Belle Heiney; m. Leona Dorothea Adolf, Sept. 1946; children: Holly Hefner Stephenson, Lynne Hefner Serafin. BA, Western Mich. U., 1936; MA, Columbia U., 1939; postgrad., Ohio State U., 1952. Tchr. Muskegon (Mich.) Pub. Schs., 1937—38, Skidmore Coll., Saratoga Springs, NY, 1939, Western Mich. U., Kalamazoo, 1940—88. Served with U.S. Army, 1942—46, PTO. Named one of 100 Art Alumni Reaching Excellence and Leadership, Western Mich. U., 2004, Excellence in Art award established in his name, 2003. Mem.: Medici Soc. Republican. Presbyterian. Avocations: collecting ancient Oriental antiques, teaching adult education art classes, travel, museums. Home: 1700 Bronson Way Apt 147 Kalamazoo MI 49009

HEFNER, HUGH MARSTON, editor-in-chief; b. Chgo., Apr. 9, 1926; s. Glenn L. and Grace (Swanson) H.; m. Mildred M. Williams, June 25, 1949 (div.); children: Christie A., David P.; m. Kimberley Conrad, July 1, 1989 (div.); children: Marston G., Cooper B. BS, U. Ill., 1949. Subscription promotion writer Esquire mag., 1951; promotion mgr. Pubs. Devel. Corp., 1952; circulation mgr. Children's Activities mag., 1953; chmn. bd. HMH Pub. Co. Inc. (now Playboy Enterprises, Inc.), 1953-88; editor-in-chief Playboy mag., 1953—; pres. Playboy Clubs Internat., Inc., 1959-86; editor, pub. VIP mag., 1963-75, Oui mag., 1972-81. Occasional film appearances include History of the World, Part I, 1981, The Comeback Trail, 1982, Beverly Hills Cop II, 1987. Served with AUS, 1944-46. Recipient 1st Amendment Freedom award B'nai B'rith Anti-Defamation League, L.A., 1980, Internat. Pub. award Internat. Press Directory in London, 1997; named Man of Yr. Mag. Industry Newlsetter, 1967; named to Pub. Hall of Fame, 1989; honored with Hugh M. Hefner chair in study of Am. film U. So. Calif. Sch. Cinema/TV, 1996, Henry Johnson Fisher award, 2002. Mem.: N.Y. Friars Club (hon.). Office: Playboy Enterprises Inc 2706 Media Ctr Dr Los Angeles CA 90065-1733

HEFNER, JAMES A., academic administrator; b. Brevard, N.C. BBA, N.C. A&T U., 1961; MA in Econs., Atlanta U., 1962; PhD in Econs., U. Colo., 1971. Tchr. econs. Atlanta U., Clark Coll., Fla. A&M U.; prof. econs., chmn. dept. econs. and bus. adminstrn. Morehouse Coll., also holder Charles E. Merrill chair; provost Tuskegee (Ala.) U.; pres. Jackson State U.; now pres. Tenn. State U., Nashville, 1991—. Vis. rsch. assoc. Harvard U., Princeton U., U. Wis.; econ. and bus. cons. to numerous pvt. and pub. orgns. Co-author and/or co-editor: Black Employment in Atlanta, Public Policy for the Black Community: Strategies and Perspectives; contbr. articles to profl. jours. Bd. dirs. Am. Coun. on Edn., Am Assn. State Colls. and Univs.; trustee ACT. Recipient NAFEO Achievement award in rsch. Mem. Mensa, Phi Beta Kappa, Phi Kappa Phi. Office: Tenn State U 3500 John A Merritt Blvd Nashville TN 37209-1500

HEFNER, THOMAS L., real estate company executive; BA, Purdue U. With Continental Bank, Ind. Nat. Bank, Ind. Mortgage Corp.; mng. gen. ptnr. Duke Assocs., 1981-93; pres., CEO Duke Realty Investments (merged with Weeks Corp.), 1993-99; chmn., CEO Duke-Weeks Realty Corp., Indpls., 1999—. Bd. dirs. Project e. Mem. dean's adv. coun. Krannert Sch. Bus., Purdue U. Mem. Nat. Assn. Real Estate Investments Trusts (bg. govs.), Ctrl. Ind. Corp. Partnership (bd. dirs.), Nature Conservancy Ind. (bd. dirs.).

HEFNER, WILLIAM JOHNSON, JR., (W. JOHN HEFNER JR.), oil and gas industry executive; b. Oklahoma City, July 29, 1952; s. William Johnson and Eloise (Wallace) H.; m. Deborah Seyan Raulston, Nov. 23, 1979; children: Margaret Leigh, Virginia Lynn. BA in Journalism, U. Okla., 1980; MBA, Oklahoma City U., 1983. Reporter city desk The Daily Oklahoman, Oklahoma City, 1978-79; field landman Gerald D. Whitfield, Oklahoma City, 1980, W.W. Blair, Oklahoma City, 1980-81; field landman, in-house landman T.S. Dudley Land Co., Oklahoma City, 1981-82; landman, part owner Arbuckle Enterprises, Inc., Oklahoma City, 1984-88; mng. ptnr. Hefner Co., Oklahoma City, 1986-93, Hefner Prodn. Co., Oklahoma City, 1986-93; leasing agt. First Resource Realty, Inc., Oklahoma City, 1987; leasing agt., property mgr. Alquest Property Corp., Oklahoma City, 1987-88; pres. Hefner Corp., Oklahoma City, 1988-93, Hefner Co., Inc., Oklahoma City, 1994—. Bd. dirs. Hist. Preservation, Inc., 1982—, pres. 2000-03, mem. trees, parks and beautification com., 1983-85, 88-89, 95, chmn. trees, parks and beautification com., 1986, mem. projects com., 1986, 89, 91, 94-99, chmn., 2002, mem. enforcement com., 1984-85, 88, mem. long range planning com., 1988-89, 2004, mem. oil and gas com., 1988-89, 2004, mem. fin. and budget com., 1989, 1st v.p., 1988, 2d v.p., 1989, mem. assoc. bd., 1992, chmn. pub. rels. com., 1992, mem. real estate com., 1998-99; reporter, editor The Heritage Hills Herald, 1987-89, vice-chmn., 1993-97; participant Heritage Hills Housetour, 1982, 87, 93; pres. Midtown Redevel. Corp., 2000-02; bd. dirs. Uptown 23 Devel. Assn., 2001-; assoc. bd. dirs. Okla. Med. Rsch. Found., 1988-92, mem. fin. and investment com., 1991, exec. com., 1991-2001, bd. dirs., 1992-2001; bd. dirs. Lyric Theatre, 1990-92, adv. bd. dirs., 1992-95; bd. dirs. Deaconess Hosp., 1991—, mem. exec. com., 1993-95, 2d v.p., 1994-95; bd. dirs. Deaconess Health Care Corp., 1994-2003; mem. leadership circle com. Casady Sch., 1994-99, co-chair leadership circle, 1994, 2001-02; active Leadership Oklahoma City Class XI, 1993; vestry mem. St. Paul's Cathedral, 1990-92, mem. Usher's Guild, 1988-97, 99—2003; bd. dirs. Children's Med. Rsch., 1992-94; bd. dirs. Okla. Heritage Assn., 1994-99; active Downtown Now, 1989-2000, Oklahoma City Art Mus., 1985—, U. Okla. Found., Norman, 1990—, YMCA, 1988-94, Com. of 100, 1993-99—, bd. dirs. 1996-97; bd. dirs. St. Anthony Hosp. Found., 2004—; mem. com. Leadership Cir. Casady Sch., 1999; bd. visitors U. Okla. Coll. Fine Arts, 2004—, U. Okla. Pres. Associates, 2004—. Mem. Ind. Petroleum Assn. Am., Okla. Ind. Petroleum Assn., Chafing Dish Soc., Okla. Hist. Soc., Oklahoma City/County Hist. Soc. (life), Beacon Club, Oklahoma City Golf and Country Club, Magna Charta Barons, Lotus Club. Republican. Episcopalian. Avocation: historical preservation. Office: Hefner Co Inc PO Box 2177 Oklahoma City OK 73101-2177

HEFTER, LAURENCE ROY, lawyer; b. N.Y.C., Oct. 13, 1935; s. Charles S. and Rose (Postal) H.; m. Jacqulyn Maureen Miller, June 13, 1957; children: Jeffrey Scott, Sue-Anne. B.M.E., Rensselaer Poly. Inst., 1957, MS in Mech. Engring., 1960; JD with honors, George Washington U., 1964. Bar: Va. 1964, N.Y. 1967, D.C. 1973. Instr. Rensselaer Poly. Inst., Troy, N.Y., 1957-59; patent engr. Gen. Electric Co., Washington, 1959-63; sr. patent atty. Atlantic Research Corp., Alexandria, Va., 1963-66; assoc. firm Davis, Hoxie, Faithfull & Hapgood, N.Y.C., 1966-69; mem. firm Ryder, McAulay & Hefter, N.Y.C., 1970-73, Finnegan, Henderson, Farabow, Garrett & Dunner, LLP, Washington, 1973—. Professorial lectr. trademark law George Washington U., 1981-90; mem. adv. com. U.S. Patent and Trademark Office, 1988-92, Trademark Rev. Commn., 1986-89. Bd. govs. Brand Names Edn1. Found., 2001-05. Named one of best lawyers in intellectual property law, Best Lawyers in Am., 2005—06. Mem. ABA (chmn. patent office affairs com. patent, trademark and copyright sect. 1976-80, unfair competition com. 1980-81, governing com. franchise forum 1994-97), N.Y. State Bar Assn., D.C. Bar Assn., Va. Bar Assn. (dir. patent, trademark and copyright sect. 1976-78), Internat. Bar Assn. (chmn. trademark com. 1986-90), Am. Patent Law Assn. (chmn. trademark com. 1979-81, dir. 1981-84), U.S. Trademark Assn. (dir. 1982-84), Order of Coif, Alpha Epsilon Pi. Office: Finnegan Henderson Farabow Garrett & Dunner LLP 901 New York Ave NW Washington DC 20001-4413 Office Phone: 202-408-4053. Office Fax: 202-408-4400. Business E-Mail: larry.hefter@finnegan.com.

HEFTER, MICHAEL C, lawyer; b. Brooklyn, New York, Apr. 22, 1966; BA, U. of Mich., 1988; JD, Emory U. School of Law, 1991. Bar: New York 1992, U.S. District Ct., Am. Bar Assoc. Ptnr. Dewey Ballantine LLP. Named one of Top 40 Lawyers Under 40, The National Law Journal, 2002. Mem.: U. of Mich., Dept. of Organizational Studies (Mem., Faculty Advisory Comm. 2002—), Volunteer Lawyers for the Arts (Bd. Dir. 2002—). Office: Dewey Ballantine LLP 1301 Avenue of the Americas New York NY 10019

HEFTLER, THOMAS E., lawyer; b. Jersey City, 1943; AB, Princeton U., 1965; JD cum laude, NYU, 1968. Bar: NY 1968. Mng. ptnr., mem. operating exec. com. Stroock & Stroock & Lavan LLP, N.Y.C. Office: Stroock & Stroock & Lavan LLP 180 Maiden Ln New York NY 10038-4925 Office Phone: 212-806-6052. Office Fax: 212-806-6006. Business E-Mail: theftler@stroock.com.

HEFTMANN, ERICH, biochemist; b. Vienna, Mar. 9, 1918; came to U.S., 1939; s. Salomon and Rosa (Seifert) H.; m. Lily Rubin (div. 1966); children: Rex, Lisa, Erica; m. Brigitte Hedwig Sander, Mar. 14, 1968; children: Karen, David. BS, NYU, 1942; PhD, U. Rochester, 1947. Cert. clin. chemist. Biochemist USPHS, Boston, 1947-48, NIH, Bethesda, Md., 1948-63, USDA, Pasadena, Calif., 1963-70, Berkeley, Calif., 19790-83; editor Jour. of Chromatography, Amsterdam, The Netherlands, 1983—. Author: Biochemistry Steroids, 1960, Steroid Biochemistry, 1970, Chromatography of Steroids, 1976; editor: Chromatography, 1961, 67, 75, 83, 92, 2004, Modern Methods of Steroid Analysis, 1973. Recipient Humboldt prize German Govt., 1975. Fellow AAAS; mem. Am. Chem. Soc., Am. Soc. of Biol. Chemists. Home: 2482 Saklan Indian Dr Walnut Creek CA 94595 Personal E-mail: chromatography@comcast.net.

HEGARTY, CHRISTOPHER JOSEPH, management and financial consultant; b. Jersey City; s. Michael John and Catherine Mary (Morrissey) H.; children: Mahren, Cahlil, Michael. PhD in Mgmt. Edn., Creative Devel. Inst. Internat., 1977; DD, Am. Inst. Theology, 1998. Investors exec., zone mgr. Investors Diversified Svcs., Mpls., 1960-65; pres. Hegarty & Co., N.Y.C., 1965-67; founder, sr. v.p. Competitive Capital Corp., San Francisco, 1967-69; founder, pres. Charter St. Corp., San Francisco, 1969-71; pres. C.J. Hegarty & Co., Payson, Ariz., 1971—. Chmn. bd. dirs. Advanced Resources Mgmt.; faculty for continuing edn. U. So. Calif.; cons. SRI Internat.; founder, regent Coll. Fin. Planning; prin. Inst. Exceptional Performance, 1989; chmn. emeritus bd. govs. Nat. Ctr. for Fin. Edn.; spl. adv. Alternative Medicine.com., 1991—. Author: How To Manage Your Boss, 1980, Financial Planning for Chief Executives, 1983, Consistently Exceptional Leadership, 1989, Fiscal Fitness for Organizations, 1992, 7 Secrets of Exceptional Leadership, 1997, The Future Belongs to the Omnicompetent, 1997; co-author: Peak Performance for Executives and Professionals, 1983, Out of Harm's Way, 2001, Tyranny of the Familiar, 2002; contbg. editor Fin. Planning mag., 1973-77; mem. editl. bd. Health Consciousness mag., 1989, Alternative Medicine Mag., 1995; spl. advisor Future Medicine Pub., 1992—. Adv. bd. Small Bus. Coun. Am., 1982—; advisor Calif. Gov.'s Task Force for Emergencies, 1981-83; advisor Nat. Foun. Alternative Medicine, 2002; maj. Nat. Chaplains Corps, 1999; bishop Original Ch. of Apostles of Christ, 2002; chmn., bd. govs. Digest Fin. Planning, 1983—; pres., CEO Internat. Ctr. Life Improvement, 1987. Recipient Judge U.S. C. of C. Blue Chip Enterprise award, 1991, Top Preview Spkr. of Yr. award Internat. Platform Assn., 1972, Spl. award Sci. Found., 1977, Leadership and Comm. award Toastmasters Internat., 1978-79, Innovative Mktg. award Sales and Mktg. Assn., 1979, Outstanding Spkr. award Am. Soc. Tng. and Devel., 1980, Spkr. of Decade award Internat. Comm. Congress, 1980, Legion of Honor award Nat. Chaplains Assn., 1981, Leadership award UN, 1981, Excellence award Am. Film Guild; named Spkr. of Yr., Young Pres.'s Orgn., 1982. Mem. Nat. Spkrs. Assn. (founding dir., Continuare Professos Articulatus Excellence award 1977, named to Spkrs. Hall of Fame 1998), Am. Inst. Mgmt. (pres. coun. 1981—), Sales and Mktg. Execs. Internat., Internat. Assn. Fin. Planners (founder, nat. adv. bd., Spokesman of Yr. 1974), Commonwealth Club. Office: CJ Hegarty & Co 1116 S Elk Ridge Dr Ste A Payson AZ 85541 Home: 1116 S Elk Ridge Dr Payson AZ 85541 Office Phone: 800-247-4738. E-mail: hegarty@cutting-edge.com.

HEGARTY, GEORGE JOHN, academic administrator, literature educator; b. Cape May, N.J., July 20, 1948; s. John Joseph and Gloria Anna (Bonelli) H.; m. Joy Elizabeth Schiller, June 9, 1979. Student, U. Fribourg, Switzerland, 1968-69; BA in English, LaSalle U., Phila., 1970; Cert., Coll. de la Pocatiere, Que., Can., 1970; postgrad., U. Dakar, Senegal, 1970, Case Western Res. U., 1973-74, U. N.H., 1976; MA in English, Drake U., 1977; cert., U. Iowa, 1977; DA, Drake U., 1978; Cert., UCLA, 1979, U. Pa., 1981. Tchr. English, Peace Corps vol. College d'Enseignment General de Sedhiou, Senegal, 1970-71; tchr. English Belmore Boys' and Westfields High Schs., Sydney, Australia, 1972-73; teaching fellow in English Drake U., Des Moines, 1974-76; mem. faculty English Des Moines Area Community Coll., 1976-80; assoc. prof. Am. lit. U. Yaounde, Cameroon, 1980-83; prof. Am. lit. and civilization Nat. U. Cote D'Ivoire, Abidjan, 1986-88; dir. ctr. for internat. programs and svcs. Drake U., Des Moines, 1983-91; prof. grad. program intercultural mgmt. Sch. for Internat. Tng., The Experiment in Internat. Living, Brattleboro, Vt., 1991-93; provost, prof. English Teikyo Loretto Heights U., Denver, 1992-94; pres., prof. English, Teikyo Westmar U., Le Mars, Iowa, 1994-95; program dir. Am. degree program Taylor's Coll., Malaysia, 1996-97; v.p. academic affairs, prof. English Teikyo Loretto Heights U., Denver, 1997—2001; rector Webster U., Thailand, 2002—03; prof. Am. lit. & civilization U. Antananarivo, Madagascar, 2003—. Acad. specialist USIA, 1983-84; workshop organizer/speaker Am. Field Svcs., 1986; cons. Coun. Internat. Ednl. Exch., 1986; evaluator Assn. des Univ. Partiellment Entierément de Langue Francais, 1987, Iowa Humanities Bd., 1990-91, USAID's Ctr. for Univ. Coop. and Devel., 1991; Fulbright lectr., rschr. Am. Lit U., 2003—; cons. in field. Book reviewer African Book Pub. Record, Oxford, Eng., 1981—, African Studies Rev., 1990—; host, creator TV show Global Perspectives, 1989-91; exhibitor of African art, 1989—; contbr. articles to profl. jours. Commr. Des Moines Sister City Commn., 1984-87, 91; bd. dirs. Iowa Sister State Com., 1988-91; pres. Chautauqua Park Nat. Hist. Dist. Neighborhood Assn., 1991; bd. dirs. Melton Found., 1994-95. Drake U. fellow, 1971-72, 74-76; Nat. Endowment for Humanities grantee, 1981; Fulbright grantee, USIA, 1980-83, 86-88. Mem.: NAFSA: Assn. Internat. Educators (sectional chmn. region VI 1986—87, Vt. rep. 1992). Avocations: collecting tribal art, travel, swimming, writing. Office: 2040 Antananarivo Pl Dulles VA 20189-2040 E-mail: georgehegarty@aol.com.

HEGARTY, MARY FRANCES, lawyer; b. Chgo., Dec. 19, 1950; d. James E. and Frances M. (King) H. BA, DePaul U., 1972, JD, 1975. Bar: Ill. 1975, U.S. Dist. Ct. (no. dist.) Ill. 1976, U.S. Supreme Ct. 1980. Ptnr. Lannon & Hegarty, Park Ridge, Ill., 1975-80; pvt. practice Park Ridge, 1980—. Dir. Legal Assistance Found. Chgo., 1983—. Mem. revenue study com. Chgo. City Coun. Fin. Com., 1983; mem. Sole Source Rev. Panel, City of Chgo., 1984; pres. Hist. Pullman Found., Inc., 1984-85; apptd. Park Ridge Zoning Bd., 1993-94. Mem. Ill. State Bar Assn. (real estate coun. 1980-84), Chgo. Bar Assn., Women's Bar Assn. Ill. (pres. 1983-84), N.W .Suburban Bar Assn., Women's Bar Found. (v.p. 2003), Park Ridge Women Entrepreneurs, Chgo. Athletic Assn. (pres. 1992-93), Park Ridge C. of C. (pres. 2002-). Democrat. Roman Catholic. Office: 301 W Touhy Ave Park Ridge IL 60068-4204 Personal E-mail: mfhegarty@sbcglobal.net.

HEGARTY, THOMAS JOSEPH, academic administrator, history educator; b. Boston, Dec. 6, 1935; s. Thomas John and Abigail Barbara (Dunlap) H.; m. Louisa Ivanova, May, 1959; children: Alton Dunlap, Allison McAndrew. AB, Harvard U., 1957, AM, 1958, PhD, 1965; cert., Inst. Ednl. Mgmt. Harvard U., 1973. Asst. prof. history and history of ideas Brandeis U., Waltham, Mass., 1962-67; assoc. prof. history, chmn. Soviet and East European studies program Boston U., 1967-71; assoc. prof. history, dean grad. studies Boston State Coll., 1971-78; prof. history, v.p. provost SUNY-Potsdam, 1978-82; v.p. acad. affairs Butler U., Indpls., 1982-88, prof. history, 1982-89; sr. cons. Am. Assn. State Colls. and Univs., 1988-89; provost, prof. history U. Tampa, Fla., 1989—. Assoc. Russian Research Ctr., Harvard U., 1968—72; summer 2000 fellow U.S. Holocaust Meml. Mus., 2000. Mem. Tampa Bay Coun. on Fgn. Rels., 1989—; bd. dirs. Internat. Ctr., Indpls., 1983-85, Park-Tudor Sch., 1983-88; mem. 100 Friends of Fla., 1990—. Fellow Ford Found., 1957-61, Holocaust Ednl. Found., 1999,Inst. for Study of Conflict, Ideology and Policy U. Boston. Mem. Indpls. Coun. World Affairs (bd. dirs. 1988), Indpls. Com. on Fgn. Rels., Am. Assn. State Colls. and Univs., Resource Ctr. for Planned Change, Greater Tampa C. of C., Greater Tampa World Affairs Coun. (pres. 1992—), Japan-Am. Soc. Cen. Fla. Inc. (bd. dirs. 1990, chair edn. coun. 1993), Greater Tampa Internat. Trade Coun., Rotary, Harvard Club of West Cen. Fla., Lit. Club of Indpls., Tampa Club (mem. com. 1990—), Fla. Humanities Coun. (bd. dirs. 1986—), Phi Beta Kappa (Alpha of Harvard U. 1956), Phi Kappa Phi, Phi Alpha Theta. Office: U Tampa Box B Tampa FL 33606-1490 Office Phone: 813-253-3333. Business E-Mail: thegarty@ut.edu.

HEGDE, VENKATESH L., immunologist, researcher; s. Laxminarayan V. and Sharada L. Hegde; m. Shweta Hegde, June 25, 2004. PhD, Mysore U., 2003. Rsch. scholar Va. Commonwealth U., Richmond, 2003—. Fellow, Coun. Sci. and Indsl. Rsch., New Delhi, 1998—2000, 2000—03. Achievements include patents pending for An anti-carbohydrate antibody to mannitol. Home: 300 W Franklin St Apt 1402E Richmond VA 23220 Office: Virginia Commonwealth U 1217 E Marshall St Richmond VA 23298 Office Phone: 804-828-2603. Personal E-mail: vlhegde@gmail.com.

HEGEDUS, L. LOUIS, chemical engineer, research and development company executive; arrived in U.S., 1968; s. Lajos and Anna Hegedus; m. Eva Judith Brem, Mar. 28, 1968; children: Caroline Nora, Monica Michelle. MSChemE, Tech. U., Budapest, 1964, D honoris causa, 1991; PhD, U. Calif., Berkeley, 1972. Rsch. engr. Rsch. Inst. Organic Chem. Industry, Budapest, 1964-65; group leader Daimler-Benz AG, Manheim, Germany, 1965-68; supr. catalysis rsch. Gen. Motors Rsch. Labs., Warren, Mich., 1972-80; dir. inorganic rsch. W.R. Grace Co., Columbia, Md., 1980-84, v.p. rsch. dept., 1984-94, v.p. corp. tech. divsn., 1994-96; v.p. R&D Arkema Inc., King of

Prussia, Pa., 1996—2001, sr. v.p. R&D, 2001—. Allan P. Colburn lectr. U. Del., 1976; Union Carbide lectr. SUNY, Buffalo, 1983; B.F. Dodge lectr. Yale U., 1988; J.A. Gerster lectr. U. Del., 1988, Regents lectr. UCLA, 1991, Mason lectr. Stanford U., 1991, disting. faculty lectr. U. Tex., Austin, 1992, Ashton Cary lectr. Ga. Inst. Tech., 1993, Hugh Hulburt Meml. lectr. Northwestern U., 1993, Warren K. Lewis lectr. MIT, 1994; Disting. Landegger lectr. Sch. of Fgn. Svc. Georgetown U., 1995; R.L. Pigford Meml. lectr. U. Del., 1998; mem. adv. bd. chem. thermal bioengring. divsn. NSF, 1985; mem. adv. bd. dept. chem. engring. Princeton U., 1980-92, U. Calif., Berkeley, 1988-95, U. Wis., Madison, 1987-95, Lawrence Berkeley Lab. Ctr. for Advanced Materials Surface Sci. Program, 1989-93; mem. governing bd. Coun. Chem. Rsch., 1987-90, 92-95, chmn., 1993-94; mem. bd. on chem. sci. and tech., NRC, 1991-95, chmn. com. critical techs., 1992; mem. Commn. on Phys. Scis., Math. and Applications, 1995-98; catalysis and reaction engring. award lectr. AIChE, L.A., 2000. Author: Catalyst Poisoning, 1984; editor 3 books on catalysis; mem. editl. bd. Inds. and Engring. Chem. Rsch., 1992-95, Hungarian Jour. Chemistry, 1992—, Catalysis Letters, 1993-2002, Topics in Catalysis, 1994—; contbr. articles to profl. jours. Fellow Am. Inst. Chem. Engrs. (editl. bd. jour. 1978-83, 85-88, R.H. Wilhelm award 1988, Profl. Progress award 1980, Chem. Engr. of Yr. award Detroit 1978, Catalysis and Reaction Engring. Divsn. award 2000)); mem. NAE (chmn. chem. engring. sect. 2000), Am. Chem. Soc. (Chemtech Leo Friend award 1981, editl. bd. Indsl. and Engring. Chemistry Rsch., 1992-95, adv. bd. Chem. and Engring. News 2004—), Md. Acad. Scis. (sci. coun. 1987-91), Hungarian Nat. Acad. Engring. (hon.). Avocation: flying. Home: 1104 Beech Rd Bryn Mawr PA 19010 Office: Arkema Inc 900 First Ave King Of Prussia PA 19406 Business E-Mail: louis.hegedus@arkemagroup.com.

HEGENDERFER, JONITA SUSAN, public relations executive; b. Chgo., Mar. 18, 1944; d. Clifford Lincoln and Cornelia Anna (Larson) Hazzard; m. Gary William Hegenderfer, Mar. 12, 1971 (dec. 1978). BA, Purdue U., 1965; postgrad., Calif. State U., Long Beach, 1966-67, Northwestern U., 1969-70. Tchr. English, Long Beach (Calif.) Schs., 1965-68; editl. asst. Playboy Mag., Chgo., 1968-70; comms. specialist AMA, Chgo., 1970-72; v.p. Home Data, Hinsdale, Ill., 1972-75; mktg. mgr. Olympic Savs. & Loan, Berwyn, Ill., 1975-79; sr. v.p. Golin/Harris Comms., Chgo., 1979-89; pres. JSH & A, Chgo., 1989—. Bd. dirs. Chgo. Internat. Film Festival, 1989, 90. Author: Slim Guide to Spas, 1984, (video) PR Guide for Chicago LSCs, 1991; editor: Financial Information National Directory, 1972; contbr. articles to profl. jours. Co-chmn. pub. rels. com. Am. Cancer Soc., Chgo., 1984; mem. com. March of Dimes, Chgo., 1986; mem. pub. rels. com. Girl Scouts Chgo., 1989-90, bd. dirs., 1994-95; bd. dirs. Greater DuPage Women's Bus. Coun., 1992-93, Girl Scouts U.S. DuPage County, 1994—; vol. ctr. adv. com. United Way, Chgo., 1990-93; mem. cmty. svc. com. Publicity Club Chgo., 1990—. Recipient 5 Golden Trumpet awards Publicity Club Chgo., 1983, 96, 94, Silver Trumpet awards, 1984, 86, 88, Spectra awards Internat. Assn. Bus. Communicators, 1984, 85, 87, Gold Quill aard, 1985, Bronze Anvil award Pub. Rels. Soc. Am., 1985, award Nat. Creativity in Pub. Rels. award, 1995; named Influential Woman in Bus., 1998. Mem. Am. Mktg. Assn., Publicity Club Chgo., Pub. Rels. Soc. Am., Chgo. Women in Pub., Nat. Assn. Women Bus. Owners, DuPage Area Assn. Bus. Tech. (bd. dirs. 1997), Coun. on Fgn. Rels., Met. Women's Forum, Cinema Chgo. (bd. dirs. 1988-89, 2005-). Avocations: travel, photography. Office: JSH & A Ltd 2 Transam Plaza Dr Ste 450 Oakbrook Terrace IL 60181-4290 Office Phone: 630-932-4242. Business E-Mail: jonni@jsha.com.

HEGER, HERBERT KRUEGER, education educator; b. Cin., June 15, 1937; s. J. Herbert and Leona (Krueger) H.; m. Thyra Cleek. AS, Ohio Mechanics Inst., 1956; BS, Miami U., 1962, MEd, 1965; PhD, Ohio State U., 1969. Tchr. Marshall Jr. High Sch., Pomona, Calif., 1962—63; tchr. math. Mt. Healthy High Sch., Ohio, 1963—66; grad. asst., grad. assoc. Miami U.-Ohio State U., 1966—69; asst. prof. U. Ky., 1969—75; assoc. dir. Louisville Urban Edn. Ctr., 1971—75; vis. prof. Sch. Profl. Studies, Pepperdine U., 1975—78; dir. student teaching U. Tex., San Antonio, 1975—77, coord. curriculum and instrn., 1977—78; assoc. prof. edn. Whitworth Coll., Spokane, Wash., 1978—82, chmn. dept., 1978—79, dean Grad. Sch., 1979—82; prof. edn. U. Tex., El Paso, 1982—99, prof. emeritus, 1999—. Cons. in field Contbr. articles to profl. jours. Mem. Am. Ednl. Rsch. Assn., Nat. Soc. Study Edn., Phi Delta Kappa. Republican. Mem. Church Of Christ. Home: 2495 Tiffany Dr Las Cruces NM 88011-2008

HEGGEN, ARTHUR WILLIAM, insurance company executive; b. Eureka, Calif., Aug. 9, 1945; s. Arlo Murray and Edna Marie (Nelson) H.; m. Betty Louise Roddy, Nov. 21, 1970; children: Cherilyn, Christopher. BS in Indsl. Adminstrn., Acctg., Iowa State U., 1967. CPA, Iowa, Fla.; CPCU, FLMI, AIAF. Audit staff mgr. Ernst & Whinney, Des Moines, 1971-84; sr. v.p., treas. Am. Bankers Ins. Group, Inc., Miami, Fla., 1984-96; exec. v.p. Am. Bankers Ins. Co., Miami, 1996-99, Assurant Solutions (formerly Assurant Group), Miami, 1999—. Bd. dirs. YMCA of Greater Miami; pres. Iowa Ptnrs. of the Yucatan, Des Moines, 1984; pres., treas. Des Moines Hearing Speech Ctr., 1976-82. Capt. USMC, 1967-70, Vietnam. Fellow Life Mgmt. Inst.; mem. AICPA, Soc. CPCU, Fla. Inst. CPAs, Ins. Acct. & Sys. Assn. Office: Assurant Solutions 11222 Quail Roost Dr Miami FL 33157-6543 also: Assurant Solutions 260 Interstate North Cir NW Atlanta GA 30339-2210

HEGGEN, IVAR NELSON, lawyer; b. Tulsa, Sept. 22, 1954; s. Ivar George Lewis and Marley L. (Whitson) H.; m. Caroline Ann Driscoll, Dec. 20, 1976 (div. 1980); children: Kristin Dominique. BS, Charter Oaks Coll., 1979; JD cum laude, U. Houston, 1983. Bar: Tex. 1983, U.S. Ct. Appeals (5th cir.) 1987, U.S. Ct. Appeals (11th cir.) 1994; cert. in personal injury and civil trial law Tex. Bd. Legal Specialization and Nat. Bd. Trial Advocates. Assoc. Dibrell & Greer, Galveston, Tex., 1983-86, Schmidt & Matthews, Houston, 1986-87, Hornbuckle & Windham, Houston, 1987-89; pvt. practice, Houston, 1989—. Mem. ABA, ATLA (lectr., writer), Tex. Bar Assn., Coll. of State Bar Tex., Houston Bar Assn., Tex. Trial Lawyers Assn. (lectr.), Order of the Barons. Avocations: theater, music. Office: 7910 Kendalia Houston TX 77036-8701 Home: 7822 Kendalia Dr Houston TX 77036-8701 Office Phone: 713-995-9988. E-mail: inh@nelsonheggen.com.

HEGI, FREDERICK B., JR., mobile home manufacturing executive; b. 1943; Grad., So. Meth. U., 1966; MBA, Harvard U., 1968; PhD, U. Tex., 1970. With First Chgo. Co., 1970-73; v.p. Cooper Industries, Dallas, 1973-82; pres. Valley View Capital, Dallas, 1982-87; founding ptnr. to prin. Wingate Ptnrs., Dallas, 1987—; dir. United Stationers Inc., 1995—, chmn., interim pres. & CEO, 1996—97, chmn., 1997—; chmn., pres., CEO Kevco Inc., 1999—2002. Bd. dir. Lone Star Tech Inc., Drew Industries Inc., Tex. Capital Bancshares Inc. Office: Wingate Partners 750 N Siant Paul St Ste 1200 Dallas TX 75201 also: United Stationers Inc 2200 E Golf Rd Des Plaines IL 60016*

HEGSTROM, WILLIAM JEAN, retired mathematics professor; b. Macomb, Ill., Oct. 21, 1923; s. Carl William and Thelma (Canavit) Hegstrom; m. Grace Ann Paladino, May 3, 1944; children: Elizabeth Louise, William Jean II, Jean Kilbourne. Studied, Western Ill. U., 1941—42; BSc, Rutgers U., 1949, EdM, 1952; postgrad., U. Fla., 1961; MA in Tchg., Purdue U., 1964; postgrad., Fla. Atlantic U., 1965—68; EdD, U. Miami, 1971. Tchr. S. Plainfield Jr. H.S., NJ, 1949—52, Bernardsville H.S., NJ, 1952—54, Oak St. Sch., Bernardsville, NJ, 1954—55, Summit H.S., NJ, 1955—58, Delray Beach Jr. H.S., Fla., 1958—65; chmn., math. dept. John I. Leonard H.S., Lake Worth, Fla., 1965—68; dir. Palm Beach County Rsch. Project, 1966—68; adj. prof. Fla. Atlantic U., 1965—69, assoc. prof., 1969—70; counselor coord. John Leonard Adult Ctr., Lake Worth, Fla., 1965—68; supr. rsch. and evaluation Palm Beach County Sch. Bd., West Palm Beach, Fla., 1970—74; adj. prof. Palm Beach Jr. Coll., 1981—88, Palm Beach Atlantic Coll., 1984—86, asst. prof., 1986—87; cons. math. prof. Palm Beach County Sch. Bd., 1985—87; ret., 1987. Contbr. articles to profl. jours. With USAAF, 1942—46. Mem.: NEA, Am. Assn. Individual Investors, Phi Delta Kappa. Home: 225 NE 22nd St Delray Beach FL 33444-4221

HEHENBERGER, MICHAEL, chemist, researcher; b. Gmunden, Austria, Aug. 22, 1945; arrived in U.S., 1993; s. Ernst and Gretchen L. Hehenberger; m. Ulla Margareta Larsson, Mar. 24, 1971; children: Karin Margareta, Lisa Katarina, Anna Maria. Dipl.Ing. in Physics, Tech. U., Vienna, Austria, 1969; PhD in Quantum Chemistry, U. Uppsala, Sweden, 1975; Docent in Quantum Chemistry, U. Uppsala, 1979. Vis. assoc. prof. U. Fla., Gainesville, 1975—77; rsch. asst. U. Uppsala, 1977—79; rsch. mgr. Sandvik Hard Materials, Stockholm, 1979—85; acad. info. systems mgr. IBM Sweden, Stockholm, 1985—89; chem. info. tech. dir. IBM Europe, Paris, 1989—93; sci. and tech. chem./pharm. R&D mgr. IBM Rsch./IBM US, Almaden/San Jose, Calif., 1993—96; solutions exec. IBM Bus. Cons., Somers, NY, 1996—2003, IBM Info.-Based Medicine, Somers, 2004—. Bd. dirs. Infotech Pharma Sci. Adv. Bd., London. Contbr. articles to profl. jours. Mem.: AAAS, Math. Assn. Am., Am. Chem. Soc. Achievements include research in rigorous numerical treatment of Stark effect in H atom; first finite element treatment of power compaction in dies; application of text mining to genetic polymorphism literature. Office: IBM Healthcare and Life Sciences Rt 100 Somers NY 10589 Office Phone: 914-766-3408. Business E-Mail: hehenbem@us.ibm.com.

HEHIR, J. BRYAN, priest, educator, social services administrator; BA, MA, St. John's Sem., Boston; ThD in Applied Theology, Harvard Div. Sch. Ordained priest Archdiocese of Boston, 1966; served St. Elizabeth of Hungary Parish, Acton, Mass.; pastor St. Paul Parish, Cambridge, Mass.; positions with US Cath. Conf. Bishops, Washington, 1973—92, sec. dept. social devel. & world peace, dir. office internat. affairs, counselor social policy; mem. faculty Georgetown U., 1984—92; Joseph P. Kennedy Prof. Christian Ethics Kennedy Ctr. Ethics; rsch. prof. ethics & internat. politics Sch. Fgn. Svc.; mem. faculty Harvard Div. Sch., 1992—2001, chair exec. com., 1998—2001; counselor Cath. Relief Services, 1996—2001; pres. & CEO Cath. Charities USA, 2001—03; Parker Gilbert Montgomery Prof. of the Practice of Religion and Pub. Life Hauser Ctr. Nonprofit Organizations, John F. Kennedy Sch. Govt., Harvard U., 2004—; sec. social services Archdiocese of Boston, 2004—; pres. Cath. Charities Archdiocese of Boston, 2004—. Bd. dirs. Ind. Sector. Recipient 2004 Vision Award, Cath. Charities USA; MacArthur Fellow, 1984. Mem.: Arms Control Assn. (bd. dirs.), Coun. Fgn. Rels., Am. Philos. Soc., Am. Acad. Arts & Sciences. Roman Catholic. Office: Archdiocese of Boston 49 Franklin St Boston MA 02110-1304 Office Phone: 617-451-7955. Office Fax: 617-451-0337.*

HEIBERG, ROBERT ALAN, lawyer; b. St. Cloud, Minn., June 29, 1943; s. Rasmus Adolph and Irene (Shaffer) H.; m. Sharon Ann Olson, Aug. 2, 1969; children— Eric Robert, Mark Alan, Maren Ann BA summa cum laude, U. Minn., 1965, JD summa cum laude, 1968. Bar: Minn. 1968. Law clk. to assoc. justice Minn. Supreme Ct., 1968-69; assoc. Dorsey & Whitney, Mpls., 1969-73, ptnr., 1974—2003, of counsel, 2004—; instr. Law Sch., U. Minn., 1968-72, instr. legal assts. program, 1972-77. Articles editor Minn. Law Rev., 1967-68 Mem. adv. com. U. Minn. Legal Assts. Program, 1977-84, bd. visitors Law Sch., 1991-96. Mem. ABA (sect. real property, probate and trust law), Minn. Bar Assn. (chmn. com. on legal assts. 1979), Hennepin County Bar Assn., Am. Rose Soc. (accredited judge 1996), Order of Coif, Phi Beta Kappa Republican. Lutheran. Home: 4510 Wooddale Ave Minneapolis MN 55424-1137 Office: Dorsey & Whitney 50 S 6th St Ste 1500 Minneapolis MN 55402-1498 Office Phone: 612-340-2751. Business E-Mail: heiberg.robert@dorseylaw.com.

HEICHEL, GARY HAROLD, agronomist, educator; b. Park Falls, Wis., Nov. 9, 1940; s. Harold H. and Bernice I. (Comp) Heichel; m. Iris Fehl Martin, Apr. 24, 1988. BS, Iowa State U., 1962; MS, Cornell U., 1964, PhD, 1968; D in Natural Scis. (hon.), Swiss Fed. Inst. Tech., Zurich, 1998. Asst. plant physiologist Conn. Agrl. Expt. Stats., New Haven, 1968-73, assoc. plant physiologist, 1973-76, plant physiologist, 1976, USDA Agrl. Rsch. Svc., St. Paul, 1976-90, acting rsch. leader, 1988-90; head agronomy dept. U. Ill., Urbana, 1990-95, interim head plant pathology dept., 1994-95, head crop scis. dept., 1995—2004, prof. emeritus, 2004—. Adj. prof. agronomy U. Minn., 1976—90; program mgr. USDA Competitive Rsch. Grants Office, 1981; bd. dirs. Coun. Agrl. Sci. and Tech. Contbr. chapters to books, articles to profl. jours. Pres., mem. adminstrv. bd. Cheshire (Conn.) United Meth. Ch., 1973—76, v.p. Cheshire Land Trust, 1975—76. Named Civil Servant of the Yr., Twin Cities Fed. Exec. Bd., St. Paul, 1984; Paul Harris fellow, Rotary Internat., 2002. Fellow: AAAS (chair sect. 0 1997—98); mem.: Coun. Agrl. Sci. & Tech., Am. Soc. Plant Physiologists (trustee 1988—90), Am. Soc. Agronomy (pres. North Ctrl. sect. 1991—93, pres. 1997—98, Svc. award 2001), Crop Sci. Soc. Am. (pres. 1991—92, bd. dirs. 2004—), Urbana Rotary (bd. dirs. 1997—99). Avocations: classical music, reading, hiking, gardening. Office: U Ill Dept Crop Scis 1102 S Goodwin Ave AW-101 Urbana IL 61801-4730 Business E-Mail: gheichel@uiuc.edu.

HEID, MICHAEL PATRICK, surgeon; b. Miami, Fla. s. Patrick Joseph and Yvonne (Gregory) H. BS in Biology, BA in Psychology, U. South Fla., 1987; D of Osteo. Medicine, Nova Southeastern Coll. Osteopathic Medicine, 1993. Resident in gen. surgery Sun Coast Hosp., Largo, Fla., 1994-98; fellow in surg. critical care Ryder Trauma Ctr., U. Miami, 1998-99; gen. surgeon Surg. Assocs., Clearwater, Fla., 1999—. With USCG, 1979-91. Mem. AMA, Am. Osteo. Assn., Am. Coll. Osteo. Surgeons, Soc. Critical Care Medicine. Democrat. Roman Catholic. Avocations: running, bicycling. Fax: 727-443-6604.

HEIDBRINK, MARSHA LEA, artist, art association administrator; b. Memphis, Tenn., Dec. 16, 1946; d. Byron L. and Mary A. Mauck; m. Robert J. Heidbrink, June 15, 1968; children: Jenny, Chris. BS, Auburn U., 1968; BFA, Western Ky. U., 1984, MA in Edn., 1988. Owner, dir. Memphis Marsha's Art Gallery and Classes, Bowling Green, Ky., 2002—. Lectr. in art appreciation Western Ky. U., 1988—91; gallery dir. Capitol Art Ctr., Bowling Green, 1996—98; discussion facilitator Michaele Ann Harper Painting Workshop, London, 1998; visual arts tchr. Very Spl. Arts Festival, Bowling Green, 1997, Bowling Green, 99, Bowling Green, 2002; juror Capitol Art Ctr., Scholastic H.S., 1990—92, 2002, Very Spl. Arts Ky., 1998, Austin Peay State U., 1999, The Living Arts and Sci. Ctr., Lexington, 1999; spkr. Visual Arts, Kiwanis Club, Bowling Green, 1990—92; vis. artist Rich Pond Elem. Sch., Bowling Green, 1998; event coord. World's Greatest Studio Tour and Sale, 1996—2000, Memphis Marsha's gallery, Bowling Green, 2002. One-woman shows include Bowling Green (Ky.) Pub. Libr., 1987, Horse Cave (Ky.) Theatre, 1988, Campbellsville (Ky.) Coll., 1989, B. Deemer Gallery, Louisville, 1990, Acklen Gallery, Nashville, 1992, Rivendell Children and Youth Ctr., Bowling Green, 1992, Yellow House Gallery, Ft. Worth, 1997, Phoenix Theatre, Bowling Green, 1998, Bowling Green C. of C., 1999, Lindsey Wilson Coll., Columbia, Ky., 2000, exhibitions include Capital Arts Ctr., Bowling Green, 1985, 1987, 1989, Ky. State Capitol Art Lobby, Frankfort, 1984, Western Ky. U., Bowling Green, 1986, 1997, Kingman Found. Gallery, Quito, Ecuador, 1989, B. Deemer Gallery, Louisville, 1991, Yellow House Gallery, Ft. Worth, 1999, Ky. Wesleyan Coll., Owensboro, 2000, Represented in permanent collections Western Ky. U., U. Louisville, First Nat. Bank, Louisville, TVA, Springfield, Trans Fin. Bank, Ky., one-woman shows include Mammoth Cave Nat. Pk., 2001, exhibitions include Owenboro Mus. Art, 2001. Recipient Best of Show award, Western Ky. U. Gallery, 1984, Bowling Green/Warren County Arts Commn. Merit award, 1987, Terry Tichenor Merit award, Capitol Arts Ctr., 1988, Best of Category award, Trans Fin. Bank, 1991, Terry Tichenor Merit award, Capitol Arts Ctr., 1988, Drawing award, Karstlands Juried Art Exhbn., 2000, Profl. Works on Paper award, 15th Ann. Firstar Celebration of the Arts, Bowling Green, 2000, Woman of Achievement award for Arts, Bowling Green Human Rights Commn., 2000; grantee Individual Artist Profl. Devel. grantee, Ky. Arts Coun., 2001; scholar Russel M. and Mary Z. Yeager grad. scholar, Western Ky. U., 1988. Office: Memphis Marsha's Art Gallery 524 E 12th Ave Bowling Green KY 42101 E-mail: marsha@marsha-arts.com.

HEIDE, JOHN WESLEY, engineering executive; b. Chgo., Sept. 14, 1946; s. Frederick Bernard Heiner-Heide and Eleanor Francis (Tuttle) Heide; m. Patricia Ann Lynn, Aug. 5, 1967 (div. Jan. 1973); m. Carol G. Gutierrez, Sept. 27, 1999; children: John Wesley, Joseph Edward, Adela B., Monica, Nicholas B., Johanna M. AA, Phoenix Jr. Coll., 1972; BS, Ariz. State U., 1975. Quality assurance engr. Tex. Instruments, Dallas, 1969-70, ITT Courier, Tempe, Ariz., 1975-79; sr. project engr. GTE Comms., El Paso, 1979-83, Telxon Corp., Houston, 1983-87; engring. mgr. United Techs., Niles, Mich., 1987-91, Automotive Industries, Midland, Tex., 1991-94; divsn. quality assurance mgr. Pec Golden Triangle Plastics, El Paso, Tex., 1994-95; indsl. engring. mgr. Elcom, Inc., El Paso, Tex., 1995-97; quality assurance mgr. United for Excellence Inc., El Paso, 1997-99; TQM mgr. Dayco Inc., El Paso, 1999—. Instr. engring. Houston C.C., 1984—85; instr. plastic technology El Paso Cmty. Coll., 2003—04; superior woodwork auditor, 2004—05. Author: Reflections, 1990, Scan-It, 1991, A Step Beyond the Fog, 1992, How Cheap Is Cheap, 1993, None but the Brave Walk Alone, 1994, Beyond the Scope, 2001, Tootsie Roll Man, 2002, Saga, 2003, Behind the Scene: U.S. Economics, 2004. Candidate for mayor, El Paso, 1980, 82, 84; candidate for State Rep., Berrien Springs, Mich., 1990. With USMC, 1965-69, Vietnam. Mem. NSPE, Soc. Plastics Engrs. (pres.), Inst. Indsl. Engring. (v.p. 1982-83), Soc. Mfg. Engrs. (v.p.), Am. Soc. Quality Control (v.p.). Republican. Lutheran. Avocations: European travel, genealogy, stamp and coin collecting. Home: 9920 Minuteman El Paso TX 79924-1647

HEIDELBERG, MICHAEL, paintings conservator; s. Shlomo and Florence Eidelberg; m. Hillary Lynn Morris, Oct. 7, 1969; 1 child, Julian Raphael; 1 child, Luca Orion. BA, Columbia U., 1980. Certificate in Conservation NYU/Inst. of Fine Arts Conservation Ctr., 1986. Owner Heidelberg Congregation, LLC, NYC, 1988—. Fellow: Am. Inst. Conservation Hist. Works Art (assoc.). Achievements include Restoration of important 17th century Italian paintings. Office Phone: 212-420-0255. Personal E-mail: mhcons@yahoo.com.

HEIDELBERG, PAUL, writer; b. Austin, Tex., Dec. 23, 1948; s. James Martin and Alice Huebinger Heidelberg. BFA, San Francisco Art Inst., 1975. Author: (novels) Oceans Apart, 1988, Cook's Return, 1991, (Internet publ.) Paris, Prague and Salzburg: A Remembrance, 1999, poems; contbr. to jours. and mags. With USAF, 1966—70. Mem. Poetry Soc. Am., Hemingway Collection, J.F. Kennedy Libr. Avocations: hiking, bicycling. Home and Office: c/o Jeanette Heidelberg 245 Seford Dr San Antonio TX 78209 E-mail: info@paulheidelberg.com.

HEIDELBERGER, KATHLEEN PATRICIA, physician; b. Bklyn., Apr. 13, 1939; d. William Cyprian and Margaret Bernadette (Hughes) H.; m. Charles William Davenport, Oct. 8, 1977. BS cum laude, Coll. Misericordia, 1961; MD cum laude, Woman's Med. Coll. Pa., 1965. Intern Mary Hitchcock Hosp., Hanover, N.H., 1965-66, resident in pathology, 1966-70; mem. faculty U. Mich., Ann Arbor, 1970—, assoc. prof. pathology, 1976-79, prof., 1979—2002; ret., 2002. Mem. Am. Soc. Clin. Pathologists, U.S.-Can. Acad. Pathology, Soc. for Pediatric Pathology, Coll. Am. Pathologists.

HEIDEMAN, LYLE, retail executive; B, No. Ill. U., 1967. Asst. mgr. Sears Roebuck and Co., 1967—71, mdse. mgr., 1971—74, staff asst., 1974—76, mdse. mgr. III, 1976—79, gen. mdse. mgr. II, 1979—80, gen. mdse. mgr. IV, 1980—83, ter. gen. mdse. mgr., 1983—85; nat. mgr. mdse. sys., 1985—89; spl. assignment logistics mgmt. Sears Roebuck and Co., 1989—90, nat. logistics mgr., 1990—91, nat. mdse. mgr., 1991—92, divsn. v.p., gen. mgr. lawn and sporting goods, 1992—96, v.p., gen. mgr. home appliances, 1996—97, v.p. appliances and electronics, 1997—98, sr. v.p., appliances and electronics, 1998—99, exec. v.p., gen. mgr. hardlines, 1999—2003, exec. v.p., gen. mgr. home and off-mall stores, 2003—.

HEIDEMAN, RICHARD D., lawyer; b. Detroit, Apr. 4, 1947; s. Theodore Samuel and Marion (Yura) H.; m. Phyllis Greenberg, June 23, 1968; children: Stefanie Jo, Elana Rene, Ariana Michele. BA, U. Mich., 1969; student, Am. U./Hebrew U., Jerusalem, 1970-72; JD, George Washington U., 1972; grad., Nat. Coll. of Criminal Def. Lawyers and Pub. Defenders, 1974. Bar: Md. 1972, Ky. 1972, U.S. Dist. Ct. (we. dist.) Ky. 1972, U.S. Ct. Appeals (6th cir.) 1974, Wyo. 1979, Ind. 1979, U.S. Dist. Ct. Wyo. 1981, U.S. Dist. Ct. (ea. dist.) Ky. 1982, U.S. Dist. Ct. (so. dist.) Ind. 1982, U.S. Ct. Mil. Appeals 1982, U.S. Supreme Ct. 1983, U.S. Ct. Appeals (D.C. cir.) 1984, U.S. Dist. Ct. Md. 1989, U.S. Dist. Ct. D.C. 1989, U.S. Ct. Internat. Trade 1990, U.S. Ct. Claims 1992, U.S. Ct. Appeals (4th cir.) 1993. Sr. counsel The Heideman Law Group, P.C., Washington, 1973—. Markham's negligence counsel, 1989; vice-chmn. legislative com. Nat. Assn. Criminal Def. Lawyers. Past chmn. bd. dirs. Am. Indoor Soccer Assn.; past mayor Spring Valley, Ky.; past gen. co-chmn. State of Israel Bonds, Louisville; past mem. Ky. Crime Commn. Juvenile Delinquency Task Force; Non-Govtl. Orgn. del. U.S. Conf. on Women, Nairobi, Kenya, 1985; del.-prime minister Israel Solidarity Conf., 1989; past bd. dirs. Health Care for Am., Inc., No. Va. Family Svcs., Inc. Recipient Heritage award State of Israel Bonds, 1988; designated People to Watch, Louisville Mag., 1986. Mem. ABA, D.C. Bar Assn. (mem. criminal law steering com.), 1997-2000, Ind. Bar Assn., Ky. Bar Assn., Md. Bar Assn., Wyo. Bar Assn. (past v.p. Teton county chpt.), Am. Trial Lawyers Assn., Am. Inst. of Parliamentarians, Main St. Assn. (past v.p.), U. Mich. Club (past pres.), Nat. Coll. of Criminal Def. Lawyers (past resident faculty), Am. Soc. of Criminology (past chmn. criminal def. com.), B'nai Brit. (internat. v.p. 1988-92, sr. internat v.p. 1992-96, past chmn. pub. affairs and polit. action network, past co-chmn. internat. coun., past chmn. dist. 2 pres.'s coun., past dist. 2 pres., past chmn. internat. young leadership com., assoc. nat. commr. Anti-Defamation League, past internat. pres. youth orgns., internat. chmn. Ctr. for Pub. Policy, del. 50th World Jewish Congress 1986, pres. 1998—, Internat. Young Leadership award 1983), Internat. Assn. Jewish Lawyers and Jurists (past bd. dirs.), Am.-Israel C. of C. Inc. (pres.). Home: 7229 Armat Dr Bethesda MD 20817-2107 also: The Heideman Law Group PC 1714 N St NW Washington DC 20036-2907 Office: B'nai B'rith Perlman Intl 2020 K St NW #7700 Washington DC 20006-1806 Fax: 202-462-8995. E-mail: rdheideman@heidemanlaw.com.

HEIDEN, CHARLES KENNETH, metal products executive, consultant, retired military officer; b. Detroit, July 7, 1925; s. Carl William and Elsie Mae (Langley) H.; m. Nancy Earle Gray, June 7, 1949; 1 son, Charles Gray. BS, U.S. Mil. Acad., 1949; MS in Mech. Engring, U. Mich., 1957; grad. mgmt. execs. program, U. Pitts., 1971. Registered profl. engr., Ky. Enlisted U.S. Army, 1943, commd. 2d lt., 1949, advanced through grades to maj. gen., 1977; services in Panama, France, Korea and Vietnam; dep. dir. ops. Nat. Mil. Command Center, Joint Chiefs of Staff, 1973-74; dir. enlisted personnel U.S. Mil. Personnel Center, Washington, 1974-76; comdr. U.S. Army Mil. Personnel Center, 1977-80; comdg. gen. U.S. Army Tng. Ctr., Ft. Dix, N.J., 1980-81; pres., dir. Montel Metals Inc., 1981-83, Cedar Lake Lodge Inc., La Grange, Ky., 1985-86, chmn. bd. dirs., 1982—98, dir. emeritus, 1998—; cons. Computer Simulation, 1987-98. Bd. dirs. Park Glen Heights Assn., Annandale, Va., 1974-76; bd. dirs. Seven Counties Svcs., 2000—, treas., 2004—; pres. Our Saviour Luth. Ch., Arlington, Va., 1974-76; mem. code enforcement bd. City Jeffersontown, Ky., 1998-2000. Decorated D.S.M., D.F.C., Legion of Merit with 3 oak leaf clusters, Air medal with 10 oak leaf clusters, Joint Services Commendation medal, Army Commendation medal with 2 oak leaf clusters, Meritorious Service medal with oak leaf cluster; Cross of Gallantry with silver star Vietnam; recipient Pace award Office Sec. Army, 1963 Mem. Armed Forces Relief and Benefit Assn. (dir. 1977-81), West Point Alumni Assn., Forest Garden Assn. (chmn. and pres. 2001—04), Am. Legion, U.S. Army War Coll. Alumni Assn. Home: 10500 Forest Garden Ln Louisville KY 40223-6166 E-mail: heiden@juno.com.

HEIDENFELDER, KATHRYN M., educational administrator; b. Chgo., May 26, 1939; d. Roland John and Florence Anna (Cooke) Heidenfelder; children: Erick Joseph, Charles George. Student, Milw. Downer Coll., Lawrence U. Distbr., county mgr. Vanda Beauty Counselors, Orlando, Fla., 1965-80; sales assoc., adminstrv. asst. Resource Data Systems, Northbrook, Ill., 1981-87; dept. asst. Northwestern U., Evanston, Ill., 1987—; internat. conf. editl. asst. IEEE, 1994-97. Conf. planner, 1997—; pvt. piano tchr.

Leadership trainer, dist. commr. Boy Scouts Am.; mem. exec. coun. bd. N.W. Suburban Coun., Mt. Prospect, Ill., 1993—. Recipient Silver Beaver award Boy Scouts Am. Mem.: Historic Mt. Vernon Found., Nat. Trust, Colonial Williamsburg.

HEIDENREICH, DONALD EDWARD, JR., historian, educator; b. Sacramento, Aug. 30, 1958; s. Donald Edward Heidenreich and Faye Irene Corella; m. Lynn Marie King, Jan. 5, 1985; 1 child, Ana Katrina. BA, San Francisco State U., 1982; MA, U. Ariz., 1987; PhD, U. Mo., 1999. Instr. history Kemper Mil. Sch. and Coll., 1989—93, 1994—98, 1999—2000; assoc. prof. history Lindenwood U., St. Charles, 2000—. Historian 135th Mil. History Detachment, Mo. Army N.G, 1996—2002. 2d Lt. USAR, 1982—85, 1st Lt. USAR, 1985—89, cpt. USAR, 1989, cpt. Mo. Army Res. N.G., 1989—97, maj. Mo. Army Res. N.G., 1997—2002. Decorated Meritorious Svc. medal with Oak Leaf Cluster, Army Commendation medal, Mo. Army N.G. Meritorious Svc. medal, Army Achievement medal,; recipient Govs. award Tchg. Excellence, 1995. Mem.: US F.A. Assn., Am. Hist. Assn., Pi Gamma Mu, Phi Alpha Theta. Office: Lindenwood University 209 S Kingshighway Saint Charles MO 63301 Personal E-mail: donald.heidenreich@att.net. E-mail: dheidenreich@lindenwood.edu.

HEIDENRY, JOHN M., editor; b. St. Louis, May 15, 1939; s. John Joseph Heidenry and Margaret Adele Morrison; m. Patricia Ann Reynolds, May 30, 1964; children: Mary, John Shakespeare, James Joyce, Margaret. BA, St. Louis U., 1961; Dr. Arts, Inst. for Advanced Study of Human Sexuality, San Francisco, 1999. Reporter St. Louis Rev., 1961—63; mng. editor Herder and Herder, N.Y.C., 1963—73; editor, founder St. Louis Lit. Supplement, 1976—77; editor-in-chief St. Louis Mag., 1977—82; editor Forum Mag., N.Y.C., 1982—89; exec. editor The Week Mag., N.Y.C., 2000—. Author: Theirs Was the Kingdom, 1993, What Wild Ecstasy, 1997. Democrat. Episcopalian. Home: 33-51 80th St Jackson Heights NY 11372 Office: The Week 1040 Sixth Ave New York NY 10018 E-mail: jmheidenry@aol.com.

HEIDER, ANNE HARRINGTON, music educator; BA, Wellesley Coll., 1963; MA, NYU, 1965; DMA, Stanford U., 1981. Assoc. prof., resident choral condr. Roosevelt U.; artistic dir. Bella Voce Profl. Chamber Choir. Recipient Tempo All-Prof. Team, Humanities award, 1993. Office: Roosevelt U Coll Performing Arts 430 S Michigan Ave Chicago IL 60605

HEIDER, JON VINTON, retired lawyer; b. Moline, Ill., Mar. 1, 1934; s. Raymond and Doris (Hinch) H.; m. Barbara L. Bond, Dec. 27, 1960 (div.); children: Loren P., John C., Lindsay L.; m. Mary R. Murray, Jan. 27, 1984. AB, U. Wis., 1956; JD, Harvard U., 1961; grad., Advanced Mgmt. Program, 1974; LLD (hon.), U. Akron, 2005. Bar: Pa. 1962, U.S. Dist. Ct. (ea. dist.) Pa. 1962, U.S. Ct. Appeals (3d cir.) 1962, U.S. Supreme Ct. 1991. Assoc. Morgan Lewis & Bockius, Phila., 1961-66; counsel Catalytic, Inc., Phila., 1966-68, Houdry Process & Chem. Co., Phila., 1968-70; counsel chems. group Air Products & Chems., Inc., Valley Forge, Pa., 1970-75, asst. gen. counsel, 1975-76, assoc. gen. counsel, 1976-78, gen. counsel Allentown, Pa., 1978-80; v.p. corp. affairs, sr. adminstrv. officer-Europe, Air Products Europe, Inc., London, 1980-83; v.p. corp. devel. Air Products & Chems., Inc., 1983-84; v.p., gen. counsel BF Goodrich Co., Akron, Ohio, 1984-88, sr. v.p., gen. counsel, 1988-94, exec. v.p., gen. counsel, 1994-98; ret., 1998. Trustee U. Akron, 2001-04; dir. Bluecoats, Inc.; mem. distbn. com. Charles E. and Mabel M. Ritchie Meml. Found.; mem. bd. overseers Blossom Music Cytr.; chmn. distbn. com. Sisler McFawn Found. Lt. USNR, 1956-58. Mem. Portage Country Club, Rolling Rock Club, Key Biscayne Yacht Club. E-mail: JHeider-Fl@msn.com.

HEIDKAMP, MARY LOUISE, leadership management consultant; b. Chgo., Feb. 5, 1949; d. Herbert John and Mary Anne (Dunsheath) Heidkamp; m. James R. Lund, Aug. 19, 1978; children: Maura, Matthew. BA in Sociology, Clarke Coll., 1971; D in Ministry, McCormick Theol. Sem., 1993. Tchr., Kyoto and Tokyo, Japan, 1971, 74-75; coord. Social Ministry Diocese Providence, 1977-80; dir. Office Peace and Justice Diocese Rochester, N.Y., 1980-86; cons. Louisville, 1986-1989; co-dir. Office Peace and Justice Archdiocese Chgo., 1989-1999; cons. Oak Park, Ill., 1999—. Vis. asst. prof. U. Ill., Chgo., 2000—. Author: (with Jim Lund) Moving Faith into Action, 1990; columnist New World Newspaper, 1997—. Mem. adv. bd. Chgo. Project Violence Prevention, 1996—. Recipient Disting. Alumnae award for humanitarian svc. Clarke Coll., Dubuque, Iowa, 1996, Cardinal Bernardin award Assn. Chgo. Priests, 1997. Mem. Assn. Cons. Non-Profits, Nat. Assn. Social Action Dirs. of The ROUNDTABLE (founding mem., bd. dirs. 1982-86, 93-99, co-recipient with J. Lund Harry A. Fagan ROUNDTABLE award 1996), Nat. Interfaith Com. Worker Justice (bd. dirs. 1996—), Internat. Grail. Roman Catholic. Avocations: running marathons, travel. Fax: 708-386-8375. E-mail: mary@dynamic-insights.com.

HEIDLBERGER, FRANK, music educator; b. Bad Orb, Germany, May 22, 1962; MA, U. Wuerzburg, Germany, 1988, PhD in Musicology, Philosophy and German Lit., 1993, D of Musicology, 1999. Rsch. asst. U. Wuerzburg, 1988—93, asst. prof. musicology, 1993—99; adj. prof. music history Musikhochschule Wuerzburg, 1999; assoc. prof. music theory U. North Tex., Denton, 2001—. Author: Weber und Berlioz. Studien zur französischen Weber-Rezeption, 1994, Canzon da sonar. Studien zur Terminologie, Gattungsgeschichte und Stilwandel in der Instrumentalmusik Oberitaliens um 1600, 2000; editor: Von Isaac bis Bach. Studien zur älteren deutschen Musikgeschichte, 1991, Hector Berlioz: Les Troyens. Dossier de presse parisienne, 1995, Carl Maria von Webers Klaviermusik im Kontext des 19. Jahrhunderts, 2001, Berlioz-Schriften: Selected Writings, 2002, (music edition) Carl Maria von Weber: Concertino for Clarinet and Orchestra, 2001; supervising editor: Jour. Theoria, Aspects of History in Music Theory, 2001—. Recipient Jubilee award for rsch., Wuerzburg, 1996, Rsch. Work Printing award, German Rsch. Coun., 2000; grantee Cultural Exch., German Acad. Exch. Svc., 1989, Heisenberg-Stipendium, Deutsche Forschungsgemeinschaft (German Research Council), 2000—01. Fellow: Internat. Carl Maria von Weber Soc. (v.p. 1999—); mem.: Am. Musicol. Soc., Deutscher Hochschulverband, Coll. Music Soc., Internat. Musicol. Soc., Gesellschaft fuer Musikforschung. Home: 1416 Weatchee Dr Krum TX 76249 Office: U North Tex Denton TX 76203 Personal E-mail: fheidlbe@music.unt.edu.

HEIDORN, ROBERT E., lawyer; b. 1963; married; 2 children. BA, Miami U.; JD, U. Wis.-Madison. Bar: 1988. Pvt. practice Barnes and Thornburg, Indpls.; with Indiana Gas, 1995—2002; v.p., gen. counsel Vectren Corp., Evansville, Ind., 2002—. Bd. dirs. Evansville Coalition for the Homeless, Inc. Office: Vectren Corp 20 NW Fourth St PO Box 209 Evansville IN 47702-0209 Office Phone: 812-491-4000.

HEIDRICH, ROBERT WESLEY, lawyer; b. Chgo., Aug. 1, 1927; s. Carl G. and Harriet B. (Butzlaff) H.; m. Lennice L. Hubenbecker, June 19, 1948; children: John G., Robert G., Kimberly L. Student, U. Wis., 1944-45, 47-48; JD, DePaul U., 1951. Bar: Ill. 1951, Calif. 1974, Tenn. 1980. Atty. Brunswick Corp., Chgo., 1953-60, 65-69; v.p. Brunswick AG (Switzerland), 1960-61; dir. Brunswick Internat. Fin. AG (Switzerland), 1962-65; sec., corp. counsel Nat. Can Corp., Chgo., 1969-73; v.p., sec., gen. counsel, dir. Rohr Industries, Inc., Chula Vista, Calif., 1973-79; corp. v.p., gen. counsel Holiday Inn Hotels, Memphis, 1979-85; counsel Kaiser Steel Corp., LaVerne, Calif., 1985-87, San Diego Real Estate Devel., 1987—. Chmn. Riverside-Brookfield CMty. Caucus, 1972; bd. dirs., Am. Internat. Sch. Zurich, 1964-65; chmn. Jr. Achievement, Chgo., 1970-75. Served with U.S. Army, 1945-47. Mem. Frederick Law Olmstead Soc. (founding pres. 1967-69). Home: 5157 Long Branch Ave Apt 4 San Diego CA 92107-2032 Office: San Diego Devel PO Box 70075 San Diego CA 92167 E-mail: derobdude@aol.com.

HEIKAL, AHMED A., biophysicist, researcher; PhD, Calif. Inst. Tech., 1995. Rsch. fellow chemistry Calif. Inst. Tech., Jet Propulsion Lab., Pasadena, 1995—97; rsch. assoc. Cornell U., Ithaca, NY, 1997—2003; assoc. prof. bioengring. Pa. State U., University Park, 2003—. Contbr. articles to numerous profl. jours. Mem.: SPIE, Optical Soc. Am., Am. Phys. Soc., Am. Chem. Soc., Am. Soc. Cell Biology, Biophysical Soc. (assoc.). Achievements include research in biophysical research using a combination of fluorescence microscopy and ultrafast laser-induced fluorescence spectroscopy. Office: Pa State Univ 231 Hallowell Bldg University Park PA 16802 Office Phone: 814-865-8093. Office Fax: 814-863-0490. E-mail: aah12@psu.edu.

HEIKEN, JAY PAUL, physician; b. NYC, Aug. 31, 1952; s. Martin and Sylvia (Fisher) H.; m. Barbara Ellen Rayburn, Dec. 11, 1976 (div. 1982); m. Francine J. Rosen, Apr. 29, 1990; 1 child, Lauren M. BA, Williams Coll., 1974; MD, Columbia U., 1978. Intern Emory U. Hosp., Atlanta, 1978-79; resident in radiology Columbia-Presbyn. Med. Ctr., N.Y.C., 1979-82; fellow abdominal radiology Mallinckrodt Inst. Radiology, St. Louis, 1982-83; asst. prof. Washington U. Sch. Medicine, St. Louis, 1983-87, assoc. prof., 1988-93, prof., 1993—. Dir. abdominal imaging Mallinckrodt Inst. Radiology, St. Louis; mem. Washington U. Cancer Ctr. Author, editor: Manual of Clinical Magnetic Resonance Imaging, 1986, 2d edit., 1991, Computed Body Tomography with MRI Correlation, 2005; contbr. articles to profl. jours. Mem. AMA, Radiol. Soc. N.Am., Am. Roentgen Ray Soc., Am. Coll. Radiology, Greater St. Louis Soc. Radiologists, Soc. Computed Body Tomography and Magnetic Resonance (pres. 2003-04), Internat. Soc. Magnetic Resonance in Medicine, Soc. Gastrointestinal Radiologists, Assn. Univ. Radiologists, Internat. Cancer Imaging Soc. Avocations: skiing, tennis, softball, wine tasting. Home: 157 Gay Ave Saint Louis MO 63105-3665 Office: Mallinckrodt Inst Radiology 510 S Kingshighway Blvd Saint Louis MO 63110-1076 Office Phone: 314-362-1053. E-mail: heikenj@mir.wustl.edu.

HEIKES, KEITH, science administrator; b. 1957; With Ralston Purina, Chilicothe, Mo., 1978—81, Kabsu, Inc., Manhattan, Kans., 1981—90, Noba Inc., Tiffin, Ohio, 1990—, now COO; v.p. internat. programs 21st Century Genetics; with Coop. Resources Internat., Shawano, Wis. Office: Coop Resources Internat 100 Mbc Dr Shawano WI 54166-6095

HEIKS, JAMES ROBERT, education educator; b. Columbus, June 22, 1949; s. Ramond Emerson and Elizabeth Ann (Bixel) Heiks; m. Gail Lorraine Mitchell, Mar. 4, 1970; children: Samuel, Claire, Elizabeth. BA, Bluffton Coll., 1972; MusM, Nothwestern U., Evanston, Ill., 1973. Music tchr. Appleton (Wis.) Area Sch. Dist., 1973—84; dir. choral studies Appleton East HS, 1984—95, Appleton North HS, 1995—2003; assoc. prof. music Goshen (Ind.) Coll., 2004—. Adv. bd. Melodious Accord, NYC, 2001—. Editor: Alice Parker's Hand-Me-Down-Songs, 2004. Founder, bd. dirs. Appleton Boychoir, 1979—, adv. bd., 2004—. Named Outstanding Tchr. in Wis., Lawrence U., 1998; Kohl Tchr. fellow, US Senator Herb Kohl, 1997. Mem.: Voice Care Network, Music Educators Nat. Conf., Am. Choral Dirs. Assn. Mennonite. Avocations: fly fishing, prarie restoration. Home: N 9445 Pleasant Hill Rd Iola WI 54945 Office: Goshen Coll 1700 S Main St Goshen IN 46526 Office Phone: 574-535-7929.

HEIL, ALAN LEWIS, JR., retired radio broadcast executive, writer; b. Louisville, Oct. 21, 1935; s. Alan Lewis and Edna Mae Welch Heil; m. Dorothy Finnegan Heil, Aug. 23, 1959; children: Wendy Heil Packer, Susan Heil Cheatham, Nancy Heil Knor. BA in English, Duke U., 1957. Reporter Newark Evening News, 1957-58, 60-62; corr. Voice of Am., Beirut, Cairo, Athens, 1965—71, chief N.Y. bur., 1972-73, chief news and current affairs Washington, 1973-81; dir. broadcast ops. Washington, 1983-87, dep. dir. programs, 1987-95, dep. dir., 1996-98. Author: Voice of America: A History, 2003; contbr. chpts. to books, articles to mags. Mem. Presbyn. peacemaking study missions Bosnia, 1998, Palestine/Israel, 1999; OSCE election monitor Bosnia-Herzegovina, 1998, 2000, Kosovo, 2000. Recipient Meritorious Honor award USIA, Washington, 1972, Disting. Honor award, 1987; Disting. Honor award Voice of Am., 1998. Mem. Sr. Execs. Assn., USIA Alumni Assn., Pub. Diplomacy Coun. Presbyterian. Home: 8401 Porter Ln Alexandria VA 22308-2140

HEIL, KATHLEEN ANN, librarian; b. Easton, Pa., Sept. 22, 1949; d. Peter J. and Emily Elizabeth (Miller) H.; m. John Edward Zampier, Aug. 21, 1971; children: Kirsten Lynn, Heather Ann. BS, Millersville State U., 1971; MLS, U. Md., 1987. Librarian Caroline County Sch. System, Denton, Md., 1971-73; library asst. Meml. Hosp., Easton, Md., 1973-76; grants adminstr. Talbot County Public Library, Easton, 1976-80; cons. U. Md. Ctr. on Aging, College Park, 1979-84; grant adminstr. Somerset County Pub. Library, Princess Anne, Md., 1980-82; librarian U. Md., Solomons, Md., 1983—. Sec. Talbot County Interagency Council, Easton, Md., 1977-79, sec. U. Md. Sys. Library Dirs., 1996-97. Contbr. articles to profl. jours. Pres. Calvert H.S. Band Boosters, Prince Frederick, Md., 1990-91; sec. South Middle Sch. Music Supporters, Lusby, Md., 1988-89, 92-93; lay leader Olivet United Methodist Ch., Lusby, 1984-91, 98—; leader-disciple Olivet-Solomons Charge, Lusby, 1996—. Recipient Curve Bar Girl Scouts, Easton, Penn., 1967. Mem. Internat. Assn. of Aquatic and Marine Sci. Librs. and Info. Ctrs. (treas. 1996-98). Avocations: gardening, costume design, choir. Home: 12963 Ottawa Dr Lusby MD 20657-3255 Office: U Md Ctr for Environ Sci Chesapeake Biol Lab 1 William St Solomons MD 20688 Office Phone: 410-326-7287. Business E-Mail: heil@cbl.umces.edu.

HEIL, MARY RUTH, retired counselor; b. Westerville, Ohio, June 8, 1921; d. George Walter and Bertha Ellen (Shrodes) H. BS in Edn., Ohio State U., 1944; MEd, Wayne State U., 1956; cert. advanced study, Western Carolina U., 1987; cert. theol. edn., U. South, 1987. Cert. counselor, tchr. Ohio, Ky., Mich., Fla., NC. Tchr. 7th grade Cheshire (Ohio) Sch., 1942-43; tchr. biology, English Ohio Soldiers' and Sailors' Orphans' Home, Xenia, 1943-47; tchr. 7th grade Lakeview High Schs., Winter Garden, Fla., 1947-48; tchr. English, journalism Pine Mountain (Ky.) Settlement Sch., 1948-49; field and established camp dir. Columbus (Ohio) and Franklin County Girl Scouts, 1949-50; tchr. Mary Lyon Jr. High Sch., Royal Oak, Mich., 1950-56, 57-62, Coston Secondary Modern Girls' Sch., Greenford, Middlesex, Eng., 1956-57; tchr. English West Henderson High Sch., Hendersonville, N.C., 1962-65, guidance counselor, 1965-86. Chmn. Mayor's Com. Employment of Handicapped, Hendersonville, 1972-74; v.p. Mountain Ramparts Health Planning Bd., Asheville, N.C., 1972-76, Western Carolina Health Systems Agy. Bd., Morganton, N.C., 1976-82; bd. dirs., sec., com. chmn., Henderson County Dispute Settlement Bd., 1989-95; exec. com., bd. dirs. Western Carolina Presbyn. Retirement Com., 1987-94; active Henderson County Coun. Women, Hendersonville, 1994-96, treas.; mem.-at-large Pisgah coun. Girl Scouts U.S., 1994-98, chair fund devel. com., 1995-98, exec. com., 1997-98; bd. dirs. Henderson County Coun. on Aging, 1998-2001, chair nominating com., 1999. Named Woman of Achievement, Hendersonville Bus. and Profl. Women's Club, 1978, Civitan Citizen of Yr., Civitan Club, Hendersonville, 1986; named to Order Ky. Cols., 1988; recipient award, Galludent U., Washington, 1986, Thanks Badge, Pisgah Coun., Girl Scouts U.S., 1998, state degree of Style, Dignity, Title and Honor of Dame, Baron of Shalford, Eng., 2000, cert., Rt. Hon. Thomas de Shalford, 2000. Mem. NEA, ACA, Royal Oak Edn. Assn. (pres. 1954-56), N.C. Assn. Educators (pres. dist. 1970-72), Henderson County Mental Health Assn. (bd. dirs. 1965-74), Alpha Delta Kappa (N.C. 1st v.p. 1978-80, state pres. 1980-82, S.E. region grand v.p. 1987-89), Kappa Delta Pi. Democrat. Episcopalian. Avocations: golf, bowling, raising irish setters, classical music. Home: 726 Academy Rd Hendersonville NC 28792-9428

HEIL, MICHAEL LLOYD, military officer, academic administrator; BS in Engring. Scis., USAF Acad., Colo., 1975; MS in Flight Structures, Columbia U., 1976; PhD in Solid Mechanics, Air Force Inst. Tech., 1986; MS in Nat. Resource Strategy, Indsl. Coll. of Armed Forces, 1994. Registered profl. engr., Colo. Commd. 2d lt. USAF, 1975, advanced through grades to col., 1995; structural engr. F-15 Sys. Program Office, Wright-Patterson AFB, 1976—79; asst. prof., exec. officer dept. engring. mechanics USAF Acad., 1979—83; chief C-17 Structures Divsn., C-17 Sys. Program Office, Wright-Patterson AFB, Ohio, 1986—88; advanced cruise missile variant program mgr. Advanced Cruise Missile Sys. Program Office, Wright-Patterson AFB, Ohio, 1988—89; dep. dir. Astronautical Scis. Divsn., Astronautics Lab., Edwards AFB, Calif., 1989—90, Propulsion Directorate, Phillips Lab., Edwards AFB, Calif., 1990—93; asst. dir. countermeasures Ballistic Missile Def. Orgn., The Pentagon, Washington, 1994—95; comdr. Air Force Phillips Lab., Kirtland AFB, N.Mex., 1995—97; insp. gen. Hqrs. Air Force Material Command, Wright-Patterson AFB, 1997—98; comdr. Arnold Engring. Devel. Ctr., Arnold AFB, Tenn., 1998—2001; comdt. Air Force Inst. Tech., Wright-Patterson AFB, 2001—03; dir. propulsion directorate Air Force Rsch. Lab., Wright-Patterson AFB, 2003—. Decorated Legion of Merit with two oak leaf clusters, Air Force Commendation medal. Office: Air Force Rsch Lab Office of Pub Affairs Dayton OH 45433-7765 Home: 2247 Princess Dr Beavercreek OH 45434 Office Phone: 937-255-2520. E-mail: mlheil@aol.com.

HEIL, PAUL SAMUEL, radio producer; b. Reading, Pa., June 8, 1947; s. David Paul and Virginia May (Gaul) H.; m. Shelia Kay Troyer, Dec. 19, 1982; children: Jason David, Andrew Troy. BA in English, Elizabethtown Coll., 1969. News dir. Sta. WGAL Radio, Lancaster, Pa., 1969—77; news anchor Sta. WSBA Radio, York, Pa., 1977; news dir. Sta. WGAL-TV, Lancaster, 1977—79; owner, exec. prodr. The Gospel Greats, Lancaster, 1979—; owner Springside Mktg., Lancaster, 1986—. Prodr., host weekly 2 hour nationally syndicated Gospel Greats program, 1980—. Monthly columnist Christian Music News, 1986-87, Singing News Mag., 1987-94. Recipient Fan award Singing News, 1986-98, Marvin Norcross award, 1991; named Favorite Gospel Disk Jockey So. Gospel Music News, 1984, People's Choice Favorite Disk Jockey Gospel Music News, 1985, 86, 87; inducted into Pa. So. Gospel Music Hall of Fame, 2003. Mem. So. Gospel Music Guild (founder 1986, pres. 1990-99), Gospel Music Assn. (v.p. 1991-92), So. Gospel Music Assn. (adv. bd. 1995—, Silver Mike award 1983-84). Republican. Mennonite. Office: Heil Enterprises 921 Nissley Rd Lancaster PA 17601-1456 Office Phone: 717-898-9100. E-mail: paul@heilenterprises.com.

HEILBORN, GEORGE HEINZ, investor; b. Cologne, Germany, Feb. 27, 1935; arrived in U.S., 1941; s. Walter and Christine (Spiegel) H.; m. Phyllis Dorothy Ehrhardt, Sept. 30, 1972; children: Stephanie, Allison. BA, Northwestern U., 1956; AM, Harvard U., 1958. With Thompson Ramo Wooldridge Products Co., El Segundo, Calif., 1958—60; project mgr. Electronics divsn. Gen. Mills, Mpls., 1960—61; project mgr. Philco Corp., Willow Grove, Pa., 1961—63; pres., chmn. Info. Processing Sys., Inc., Hackensack, NJ, 1963—92; pres. G.H. Heilborn & Co., Inc., 1992—. Bd. vis. Coll. Arts and Scis., Northwestern U., 1992—, alumni regent, 1997—; grad. sch. alumni coun. Harvard U., 1993—, chmn., 1996-98; trustee Family Counseling Svc., Ridgewood, N.J., 1992-95; fin. and investment com. Children's Aid and Family Counseling, N.J., 1996—. Mem. Computer Dealers and Lessors Assn. (founding mem., pres. 1980-82, chmn. 1982-84), Equipment Leasing Assn. Am., US-USSR Trade and Econ. Coun., N.Y. Acad. Scis., Harvard Club N.Y. Home: 385 Knollwood Rd Ridgewood NJ 07450-4814 Office: G H Heilborn & Co Inc One University Plz Hackensack NJ 07601

HEILBRON, DAVID MICHAEL, lawyer; b. San Francisco, Nov. 25, 1936; s. Louis H. and Delphine A. (Rosenblatt) H.; m. Nancy Ann Olsen, June 21, 1960; children: Lauren Ada, Sarah Ann, Ellen Selma. BS summa cum laude, U. Calif., Berkeley, 1958; AB first class, Oxford U., Eng., 1960; LL.B. magna cum laude, Harvard U., 1962. Bar: Calif. 1962, U.S. Dist. Ct. (no. dist.) Calif. 1963, U.S Ct. Appeals (9th cir.) 1963, U.S. Ct. Appeals (D.C. cir.) 1972, U.S. Ct. Appeals (8th cir.), 1985, U.S. Ct. Appeals (1st cir.) 1987, U.S. Ct. Appeals (10th cir.) 1988, U.S. Ct. Appeals (7th cir.) 1988, U.S. Ct. appeals (11th cir.) 1988, U.S. Dist. Ct. Nev. 1982, U.S. Dist. Ct. (cen. dist.) Calif. 1983, U.S. Supreme Ct. 1988, U.S. Ct. Appeals (3rd cir.) 1992, (6th cir.), 1995, U.S. Ct. Appeals (2d cir.) 1998, U.S. Ct. Appeals (5th cir.) 1998. Assoc. McCutchen, Doyle, Brown & Enersen, San Francisco, 1962-69, ptnr., 1969—, mng. ptnr., 1985-88. Vis. lectr. appellate advocacy U. Calif., Berkeley, 1981-82, 82-83. Bd. trustees Golden Gate U., 1993-97, vice chair, 1995-97; bd. dirs. San Francisco Jewish Cmty. Ctr., 1974—, Legal Aid Soc., 1974-78, Legal Assistance to Elderly, San Francisco, 1980, San Francisco Renaissance, 1982—; pres. San Francisco Sr. Ctr., 1972-75; co-chmn. San Francisco Lawyers' Com. for Urban Affairs, 1976. Rhodes scholar. Fellow Am. Bar Found.; mem. ABA, Am. Coll. Trial Lawyers, Am. Arbitration Assn. (bd. dirs. 1986-98, 2002--, adv. coun. No. Calif. chpt. 1982—, chmn. 1987, jud. coun. 1986-88, exec. bd. 1994-98, instr. and panelist arbitrator tng. programs), Am. Acad. Appellate Lawyers, State Bar Calif. (chmn. com. cts. 1982-83. bd. govs. 1983-85, mem. commn. on discovery 1984-86, pres. 1985-86), Calif. Acad. Appellate Lawyers, Coll. Comml. Arbitrators, Bar Assn. San Francisco (chmn. conf. dels. 1975-76, pres. 1980). Clubs: Calif. Tennis. Democrat. Office: Bingham McCutchen LLP 3 Embarcadero Ctr San Francisco CA 94111-4003 Office Phone: 415-393-2177. Business E-Mail: david.heilbron@bingham.com.

HEILBRUN, JAMES, economist, educator; b. N.Y.C., Dec. 13, 1924; s. Maurice L. and Hortense (Unger) H.; m. Carolyn Gold, Feb. 20, 1945 (dec. Oct. 2003); children: Emily, Margaret, Robert. BS, Harvard Coll., 1945; MA, Harvard U., 1947; PhD, Columbia U., 1964. Asst. economist Prentice Hall Inc., N.Y.C., 1947-50; econ. analyst Chase Manhattan Bank, N.Y.C., 1951-55; instr. Columbia U., N.Y.C., 1961-65, asst, prof. econs., 1965-70; assoc prof. econs. Fordham U., Bronx, 1970-74, prof., 1974-97, prof. emeritus, 1997—. Research dir. Harlem Devel. Project, Columbia U., 1967-68 Author: Real Estate Taxes and Urban Housing, 1966, Urban Economics and Public Policy, 1973, 3d edit., 1987, (with Charles M. Gray) Economics of Art and Culture, 1993, 2d edit., 2001. Served with USN, 1944-46. Fellow Com. on Urban Econs., 1960-61; fellow Ford Found., 1969-70; UCLA resident scholar, 1978. Mem. Am. Econ. Assn. Home: 151 Central Park W New York NY 10023-1514 E-mail: jheilbrun@wordnet.att.net.

HEILENDAY, FRANK TOD, science educator; b. Jersey City, Dec. 31, 1927; s. Frank Walter and Helma Heilenday; m. Joan Heilenday. BS, MIT, 1948, M, 1949, postgrad., 1965—66. Chief office of ops. analysis Hdqs. 8th Air Force, Westover Air Force Base, Mass., 1959—65; chief applied rsch. SAC, Offutt Air Force Base, 1966—84; adj. prof. George Wash. U., Washington, 1986—93; cons. RAND Corp., Santa Monica, Calif., 1992—95; ret., 2003. Cons. Sandia Nat. Lab., Albuquerque, 1988—93, Toyon Rsch., Santa Barbara, 1984—88. Author: (textbook) Principles of Air Defense and Air Vehicle Penetration. Mem.: Rotary. Home: 720 Sherman St NW Olympia WA 98502 Personal E-mail: todjoan@yahoo.com.

HEILICSER, BERNARD JAY, emergency physician; b. Bklyn., Jan. 19, 1947; s. Murray and Esther (Dubrow) H.; m. Marcia Cherry, June 2, 1976; children: Micah, Seth, Jacob. BA, SUNY, Binghamton, 1968; MS, Hahnemann Med. Coll., Phila., 1971; DO, Coll. Osteo. Medicine/Surgery, Des Moines, 1976. Diplomate Am. Bd. Emergency Medicine. Instr. anatomy and physiology U. Pa. and Hahnemann Med. Coll., Phila., 1971-73; staff physician Va. Inst. Tech., Blacksburg, 1977-78; asst. prof. emergency medicine Chgo. Coll. Osteo. Medicine, 1979; emergency physician St. Margaret Hosp., Hammond, Ind., 1979-83, Michael Reese Med. Ctr., Chgo., 1989-91, Ingalls Hosp., Harvey, Ill., 1983—; project med. dir. South Cook County Emergency Med. Svc., Harvey, 1984—. Faculty Chgo. Osteo. Med. Ctr., 1987-99; faculty trauma nurse specialist St. James Hosp., Chicago Heights, Ill., 1980—; preceptor nurse practitioners Purdue U., Hammond, 1981-90; fellow MacLean Ctr. Clin. Med. Ethics, U. Chgo., 1993-94; chmn. ethics com., hosp. med. ethicist Ingalls Hosp., Harvey, Ill., 1994—; cons. Nat. Bd. Osteo. Med. Examiners, Harvey, 1994-95, ethics com. Am. Coll. Osteo. Emergency Physicians, 1997—; chmn. disaster com. Ill. Region 7 Emergency Med. Svcs./Trauma, 1997—; chair Ill. Region VII EMS Adv. Coun., 2001-04; adj. faculty Coll. Health Professions, Govs. State U., 1999—; exec. coun. Ill. Med. Emergency Response Team, 1999—; med. advisor Combined Agy. Response Team, 1999—. Vol. fireman Flossmoor (Ill.) Fire Dept., 1985—, Matteson (Ill.) Fire Dept., 1980-90; mgr. med. team Ill. Task Force One Urban Search and Rescue, 2004—. Fellow Am. Coll. Emergency Physicians, Am. Coll. Osteo. Emergency Physicians; mem. Am. Osteo. Assn., Nat. Assn. Emergency Med. Svcs. Physicians, Nat. Assn. Emergency Med. Technicians, Sigma Sigma Phi. Jewish. Avocations: running, basketball. Office: Ingalls Hosp One Ingalls Dr Harvey IL 60426 Office Phone: 708-915-6900. E-mail: bernardh47@yahoo.com.

HEILIGENSTEIN, CHRISTIAN ENRIC, lawyer; b. St. Louis, Dec. 7, 1929; s. Christian A. and Louisa M. (Dixon) H.; children: Christie; m. Liselotte Warbanoff, Feb. 6, 1981. BS in Law, U.Ill., 1953, JD, 1955. Bar: Ill. 1956, U.S. Dist. Ct. (so. dist.) Ill. 1956, U.S. Ct. Appeals (7th cir.) 1956, U.S. Dist. Ct. (cen. dist.) Ill. 1960, U.S. Supreme Ct. 1978. Assoc. Listeman & Bandy, East St. Louis, Ill., 1955-61; sole practice Belleville, Ill., 1962-84; ptnr., pres. Heiligenstein & Badgley, Belleville, 1984-98; pres. C.E. Heiligenstein, P.C., Belleville, 1998—. Bd. dirs. Union Planters Corp., Union Planters Bank NA, 1998-2000, audit com. 1999-2000, Magna Bank and Magna Group, Inc., 1984-98; chair audit com. Magna Group, Inc., 1994-98. Bd. visitors U. Ill. Coll. of Law, 2000. Recipient Alumni of Month award U. Ill. Law Sch., 1982; C.E. Heiligenstein Chair in Law named in his honor U. Ill., 1999. Mem. Ill. State Bar Assn., Internat. Acad. Trial Lawyers (bd. dirs. 1991-97), St. Clair County Bar Assn., St. Louis Bar Assn., Inner Circle Advs., Am. Bd. Trial Advs. (nat. bd. dirs. 1992, pres. St. Louis, So. Ill. region 1993), Am. Acad. Profl. Liabilities Attys. (Nat. bd. dirs., 1990-99), ATLA (bd. govs. 1985-87), Ill. Trial Lawyers Assn. (bd. mgrs. 1975-88, pres. 1989), Beach Club (bd. dirs. 1996, v.p. 1998), Old Guard Soc. of Palm Beach (bd. dirs. 2005). Democrat. Office Phone: 618-476-1112. Personal E-mail: l.warbanoj@aol.com.

HEILMAN, ELIZABETH, education educator, researcher; b. Phila., Nov. 8, 1962; d. Daniel Hugh Heilman and Mary Ann Loughrey; m. Yang Wang (div.); 1 child, Alexander Wang; children: Maryrose Stattelman, Anneliese Stattelman, Kathleen Stattelman. BS, Coll. William and Mary, 1985; MS, Ind. U., 1993, PhD, 1998. Assoc. instr. dept. ednl. leadership and policy studies Ind. U., Bloomington, 1993—98, assoc. instr. dept. curriculum and instrn., 1994—98, assoc. instr. Coll. Arts and Scis., 1996; asst. prof. dept. curriculum and instrn. Purdue U., West Lafayette, 1998—2002; asst. prof. Coll. Edn. Mich. State U., East Lansing, 1998—. Adj. instr. dept. ednl. leadership and policy studies Ind. U., Indpls., 1996—97. Editor: (book) Social Studies: The Next Generation Re-searching Social Studies in the Postmodern, Harry Potter's World: Multidisciplinary Critical Perspectives; contbr. articles to profl. jours., chpts. to books. Grantee, Carnegie Corp. NY, 2002—. Mem.: Nat. Coun. Social Studies (exec. bd. mem. 2004—05), Am. Ednl. Rsch. Assn. (divsn. b program chair 2005—). Home: 401 Highland Ave East Lansing MI 48823 Office: Mich State U 360 Erickson Hall East Lansing MI 48824-1034 Office Phone: 517-432-4860. E-mail: eheilman@msu.edu.

HEILMAN, KENNETH MARTIN, neurologist, educator; b. N.Y.C., June 2, 1938; m. Patricia C. Phillips; children: David N., Nicole B., Eden B. MD, U. Va., 1963. Diplomate Am. Bd. Psychiatry and Neurology. Intern 2d Cornell divsn. Belleview Hosp., N.Y.C., 1963-64, asst. resident, 1964-65; asst. resident neurology Harvard neurologic unit Boston City Hosp., 1967-68, resident to chief resident neurology, 1968-70; asst. prof. to assoc. prof. U. Fla. Coll. Medicine, Gainesville, 1970-77, prof. dept. neurology, 1975—; prof. dept. clin. psychology U. Fla., Gainesville, 1977—; staff physician VA Med. Ctr., Gainesville, 1977—; dir. Ctr. Neuropsychological Studies U. Fla. Coll. Medicine, Gainesville, 1984—, disting. prof., 1998—. Review group NIH, 1979, 81-84. Author: Clinical Neuropsychology, 1979, 4th edit., 2003, The Differential Diagnosis of Neurological Diseases, 1977, Neuropsychology of Human Emotion, 1983, Apraxia, 1997, Matter of Mind, 2002, Clinical Neuropsychology, 2003, Creativity and the Brain, 2005; author numerous book chpts.; contbr. over 300 articles to profl. jours. Recipient numerous NIH grants; Med. Rsch. Svc. grant, VA; various fellowships. Fellow Am. Acad. Neurology; mem. Am. Acad. Aphasia (governing bd. 1987-90), Am. Neurol. Assn., Fla. Med. Soc., Fla. Soc. Neurology, Internat. Neuropsychology Soc. (exec. com. 1974-77, pres. 1982-83), Aphasia Rsch. Group of World Fedn. Neurology, Behavioral Neurology Soc. (pres. 1982-83), Sigma Xi, Alpha Omega Alpha, Phi Kappa Phi. Achievements include research in attentional and emotional disorders and diseases of the nervous system. Office: U Fla Coll Medicine Dept Neurology Gainesville FL 32610-2102

HEILMAN, MARLIN STEPHEN, medical products executive; b. Tarentum, Pa., Dec. 25, 1933; s. Glenn Harold and Hilda Barnes; m. Drusilla Carswell, Aug. 18, 1956; children: Philip, Glenda, Carl Barnes, Stephen James, Karen. BA, U. Pa., 1955, MD, 1959. Pvt. practice, Pitts., 1963—65; cons. Westinghouse R & D, Pitts., 1965—67; pres. Medrad, Inc., Pitts., 1968—80, Intec Systems, Inc., Pitts., 1980—84; chmn., CEO Medrad/Intec, Inc., Pitts., 1984—86; chmn. bd. dirs., CEO Vascor, Inc., Pitts., 1986—, Lifecor, Inc., Pitts., 1986—. Founder Medrad, Intec, Medrad/Intec, Vascor & Lifecor; chmn. Alle-iski Med. Ctr. Contbr. articles to profl. jours. Capt. USAF, 1961—63. Named Entrepreneur of Yr., Arthur Young/Venture Mag., 1987; named to Nat. Inventors Hall of Fame, 2002; recipient Michel Mirowski Excellence in Cardiology award, 1992. Office: Vascor Inc 566 Alpha Dr Pittsburgh PA 15238-2912

HEILMAN, PAMELA DAVIS, lawyer; b. Buffalo, July 2, 1948; d. George Henry and Natalie (Maier) Davis; m. Robert D. Heilman, June 27, 1970. AB, Vassar Coll., 1970; JD, SUNY, Buffalo, 1975. Bar: N.Y. 1976, Fla. 1980. Assoc. Hodgson, Russ, Andrews, Woods & Goodyear, Buffalo, 1975-84, ptnr., 1984—. Bd. dirs. United Way Buffalo, 1985-97, vice chmn., 1989-92, chair, 1993-97, gen. campaign chair, 1992; bd. dirs. D'Youville Coll., Buffalo, 2001—, WNY Internat. Trade Coun., Inc., Buffalo, 2001—, Fin. Instns., Inc., Warsaw, 2002—. Mem. ABA, N.Y. State Bar Assn. (vice chmn., exec. com., sect. on internat. law and practice 1988-90), Fla. Bar Assn., Erie County Bar Assn. Office: Hodgson Russ Andrews Woods & Goodyear LLP One M&T Plz Buffalo NY 14211-1638 E-mail: pheilman@hodgsonruss.com.

HEILMANN, CHRISTIAN FLEMMING, manufacturing executive; b. Apr. 26, 1936; s. Poul Bent and Hedvig Buchwald (Moller) Heilmann; m. Marilyn Mildred Harter, July 9, 1959 (div. 1973); children: Christian Philip, Nicholas John, Claire Marie; m. Judith Lucy Tucker, Sept. 15, 1973; children: Per Flemming, Niels Henrik. MA, Cambridge (Eng.) U., 1957. Mng. dir., CEO Metal Box South Africa Ltd., Johannesburg, 1970-77; trustee Nat. Devel. and Mgmt. Found., South Africa, 1970-75; v.p. Continental Can Co., Stamford, Conn., 1977-78; pres. Continental Group Europe, Brussels, 1978-80, Continental Diversified Industries, Stamford, Conn., 1980-81; exec. v.p., chief administrative officer Continental Group, Inc., Stamford, Conn., 1982-84; dir., pres, CEO Am. Can Canada, Inc. (name changed to Onex Packaging Inc. 1986), Rexdale, 1984-89; N.Y. rep. Danes Worldwide, 1996; chmn., CEO Brockway Standard, Inc., Atlanta, 1989-94; dir., bd. dirs. Whitlock Packaging Co., Okla., 1998—2004. Mem. adv. coun. U. Toronto Bus. Sch., 1985—92; bd. dirs. Porter Chadburn, Inc., Porter Chadburn PLC, O'Shaughnessy Funds, Inc. U.S. rep. Nat. Olympic Com. Denmark, 1994—96; attache Paralympic Games Danish Sports Orgn. for Disabled, Atlanta, 1996; trustee Am. Scandinavian Found., 1998—, Paul Smith's Coll., St. Regis, NY, 1999—; mem. coun. Cornell U., 1996—2000, 2002—; bd. dirs. Cambridge in Am., 1996—2002, Jacob Riis Settlement House, N.Y.C., 1996—, v.p., 1999; elected Wilkins fellow Downing Coll., Cambridge U., 2000. Decorated knight Order of Dannebrog (Denmark); recipient Ellis Island medal of honor, 2002. Mem.: Danish Am. C. of C., Greenwich Country Club, Danish-Am. Soc. (bd. dirs. 1990—2003, pres. 1996—2001). Office Phone: 203-831-0367. E-mail: cfheilmann@aol.com.

HEILMEIER, GEORGE HARRY, electrical engineer, researcher; b. Phila., May 22, 1936; s. George C. and Anna I. (Heineman) Heilmeier; m. Janet S. Faunce, June 24, 1961; 1 child, Elizabeth. BEE, U. Pa., 1958; MS in Engring., Princeton U., 1960, MA, 1961, PhD in Solid-State Electronics, 1962; DEngring (hon.), Stevens Inst. Tech., 1995, Technion, Israel Inst. Tech., 1997. With RCA Labs., Princeton, NJ, 1958—66, dir. solid state device rsch., 1966—69, dir. device concepts, 1969—70; White House fellow, spl. asst. to sec. def. Washington, 1970—71; asst. dir. def. rsch. and engring. Office Sec. Def., 1971—74; dir. Def. Advanced Projects Agy., 1974—77; v.p. corp. rsch., devel., engring. and strategic planning Tex. Instruments Inc., 1977—83, sr. v.p., chief tech. officer, 1983—91; pres., CEO Bell Comm. Rsch., Inc., Livingston, NJ, 1991—96, chmn., CEO, 1996—97; chmn. emeritus Bell Comm. Rsch., Inc. "Bellcore" (now Telecordia Technologies, Inc.), 1997—. Vis. com. MIT, 1988—; mem. Princeton U. Sch. Engring. and Applied Sci. Leadership Coun.; bd. overseers. Sch. Engring. and Applied Sci. of U. Pa., 1989—; adv. group on electron devices Office Undersec. of Def., 1989—; bd. dirs. TRW, Compaq Computer Corp., Automatic Data Processing, MITRE Corp., 1993—, INET Technologies, Inc., Teletech Holdings; mem. Pres.'s Com. on Nat. Medal of Sci., 1992—94, U.S. Adv.Coun. on Nat. Info. Infrastructure, 1994—; mem., Def. Sci. Bd. Pres.'s Nat. Security Telecommunications Adv. Com., 1979—; mem. Alamos Nat. Security Adv. Bd., 1988—; sci. adv. bd. Nat. Security Agy., 1992—; chmn. adv. bd. GM Technology. Named Tech. Leader of Yr., Industry Week, 1994; recipient IR-100 New Product award, Indsl. Rsch. Assn., 1968—69, Disting. Civilian Svc. award, U.S. Sec. Def., 1975, 1977, Arthur Fleming award, U.S. Jaycees, 1974, Nat. medal of Sci., NSF, 1991, Indsl. Rsch. Inst. medal, 1993, John Fritz award, Am. Assn. Engring. Soc., 1999, Kyoto prize (Advanced Technology award), Inamori Found., 2005. Fellow: IEEE (David Sarnoff award 1976, Outstanding Achievement award Dallas chpt. 1984, Philips award 1985, Founder's award 1986, Japan Computers and Comm. prize 1990, Pres. Nat. Medal of Sci. 1991, Medal of Honor 1997), Am. Acad. Arts and Scis. (John Scott award for sci. achievement 1996); mem.: NAE (Founders award 1992), Princeton U. Grad. Alumni Assn., U. Pa. Alumni Assn., Eta Kappa Nu (Outstanding Young Engr. in U.S. 1969, Vladimir Karapetoff Eminent Mem. award 1993), Tau Beta Pi, Sigma Xi. Achievements include discovery of several new electro-optic effects in liquid crystals leading to the development of the first liquid crystal displays for watches, calculators, and instrumentation; Holds 15 Patents. Avocations: reading, sports.*

HEIM, CHERI D., mathematics educator; b. Emporia, Kans., Nov. 28, 1962; d. Roy Lee and Leona Ruth Sparks (Stepmother), Nancy Dean Crane; m. John Randall Heim, Apr. 13, 1961; children: Bart Randall, Brandon Eric, John Bradley. BS in Edn., Emporia State U., Kansas, 1985; post grad., Baker U., Baldwin, Kans., 2004—. Math. educator Unified Sch. Dist. 469, Lansing, Kans., 1986—88; sci. educator Unified Sch. Dist. 449, Easton, Kans., 1995—2000, math. educator, 2000—. Mem.: NEA (bldg. rep. 2003—). Personal E-mail: cheim@easton449.org.

HEIM, CHRISTINE MARCELLE, psychiatrist, educator; arrived in US, 2001; Psychology diploma, U. Trier, 1993; MA summa cum laude, PhD summa cum laude, U. Trier, Germany, 1993. Rsch. assoc. U. Trier, Dept. Clin. and Physicological Psychology, Germany, 1993—94, U. Trier, Dept. Ctr. for Psychobiological and Psychosomatic Rsch., Germany, 1994—96; post doctoral fellow Emory U. Sch. Medicine, Dept. Psychiatry and Behavioral Scis., Atlanta, 1996—99; scientific asst. U. Trier, Dept. Clin. and Physiological Psychology, Germany, 1999—2001; asst. prof. Emory U. Sch. Medicine, Dept. Psychiatry and Behavioral Scis., 2001—, Emory U. Sch. Medicine, Atlanta, 2001—. Affiliated scientist Centers for Disease Control & Prevention, Atlanta, 2001—. Contbr. chapters to books, articles to profl. jours. Recipient Young Investigator award, Nat. Alliance for Rsch. in Depression and Schiophrenia, 2002—04; scholar, German Govt., 1994—96, Soc. for Biol. Psychiatry, 2003; postdoctoral fellow, German Sci. Found., 1997—98, Rsch. grantee, 2000—02. Mem.: Internat. Soc. for Traumatic Stress Studies (Chaim Danieli Young Profl. award 2004), Am. Psychosomatic Soc., Psychoneuroimmunology Rsch. Soc., Internat. Soc. for Psychoneuroendocrinology, Soc. for Neuroscience. Achievements include research in first evidence in humans that adverse experience in childhood is associated with increased biological responses to subsequent stress, which in turn is related to mental disorders. Office: Emory University School of Medicine Ste 4000 101 Woodruff Circle WMB Atlanta GA 30322 Office Phone: 404-727-5835.

HEIM, VICTORIA LYNNE, writer; b. Denver; d. Kenneth Carlton and Fleta Jean (Gwyn) Fagan. BA in History, U. Ariz., 1981. Poetry writer, lectr. internat. topics; lectr. U. Ariz., Ariz. Dept. Corrections, pub. schs., Ariz. Freelance writer; creator Elko (Nev.) Internat. Forum. Mem. Toastmasters (area gov. 1990-91, DTM 1992).

HEIMAN, DAVID GILBERT, lawyer; b. Cin., Apr. 12, 1945; s. Marcus G. and Ardith S. H.; m. Lynn Greentree, July 12, 1969; children: Stacy, Alisa. BBA, U. Cin., 1967, JD, 1970. Bar: Ohio 1971, U.S. Dist. Ct. (no. dist.) Ohio 1971, U.S. Ct. Appeals (5th and 6th cirs.)., U.S. Dist. Ct. (no. dist.) Tex. Ptnr. Hahn, Loeser, Freidheim, Dean & Wellman, Cleve., 1970-84, Jones, Day, Reavis & Pogue, Cleve., 1984-95, corp. group coord., 1995; now ptnr., coord. firm-wide bus. practice group Jones Day, Cleve., and practice area leader, bus. restructuring and reorganization practice area. Editor Lender Liability Law Reporter. Vice chmn. Am. Jewish Com., Cleve., 1978-88. With U.S. Army, 1969-75. Recipient Young Leadership award Am. Jewish Com., Cleve., 1978. Mem. ABA (past chmn. comml. fin. svcs.), Ohio State Bar Assn. (chmn. com. 1979-82), Cleve. Bar Assn. (chmn. com. 1975-76). Office: Jones Day North Point 901 Lakeside Ave E Cleveland OH 44114-1190

HEIMAN, GROVER GEORGE, JR., editor, writer; b. Galveston, Tex., July 26, 1920; s. Grover George and Rose Mary (Ulch) H.; m. Virginia D. Williamson, Feb. 14, 1942 (dec.); children: Virginia, Grover, Deborah, Richard. Student, Lee Coll., 1937-40, U. Tex., 1940-41; BS in Commerce cum laude, U. So. Calif., 1959. With USAAF, 1941-45; News reporter Corsicana (Tex.) Daily Sun, 1945-47; commd. 2d lt. USAAC, 1942; advanced through grades to col. USAF, 1963; spl. asst. to USAF Chief of Staff, Pentagon, Washington, 1959-63; chief of info. Allied Air Forces So. Europe, Naples, Italy, 1963-66; chief mags. and books divsn. Dept. Def., Pentagon, 1966-68; ret., 1968; mng. editor Armed Forces Mgmt. mag., Washington, 1968-70; assoc. editor Nation's Business mag., Washington, 1970-76, industry editor, 1976-78, mng. editor, 1978-80, editor, 1980-82, editor emeritus, 1982-99. Chmn. Naples Dependent Schs. bd., 1964-65. Author: (with Rutherford Montgomery) Jet Navigator, 1959, Jet Tanker, 1961, Jet Pioneers, 1963, (with Virginia Myers) Careers For Women In Uniform, 1971, Aerial Photography, 1973. Decorated DFC, Legion of Merit. Mem. Nat. Press Club, Beta Gamma Sigma. Roman Catholic.

HEIMAN, MARVIN STEWART, finance company executive; b. Chgo., Sept. 16, 1945; s. Samuel J. and Mildred (Miller) H.; m. Adrienne Joy Nathan, Aug. 7, 1966; children: Scott, Michelle, Adam. Student, Roosevelt U., 1963-67. Pres. Curtom Record Co., Chgo., 1969-80, Gold Coast Entertainment, Chgo., 1980-82; ptnr. Profl. Real Estate Securities Co., Lincolnwood, Ill., 1982-86; pres., chmn. bd. Sussex Fin. Group, Inc., Skokie, Ill., 1986—; ptnr. Spago Restaurant, Chgo., 1997—. Bd. dirs. Skokie Bank, Drovers Bank, Chgo., Met. Health Care; ptnr. Cole Taylor Banks, Chgo., 1984—, bank examining com., 1986—, ptnr. Chgo. White Sox Am. League Baseball Club, 1981—, Gore/Bronson Bancorp, 1988, Sun Life of Can., 1993. Mem. Rep. Nat. Com., 1980—, Simon Wiesenthal Ctr., 1988. Recipient Men of Achievement award Cambridge, Eng., Nat. Quality award Nat. Assn. Life Underwriters, 1992. Mem. Internat. Assn. Fin. Planners, Chgo. Assn. Life Underwriters, Real Estate Securities Syndication Assn. Am., Nat. Assn. Securities Dealers (registered rep.), Am. Jewish Com. (Humanitarian award 1978), Internat. Platform Assn., Million Dollar Round Table, Pres.'s Club (Am. funds com. 1992). Avocations: baseball, tennis, music. Office: Sussex Fin Group Inc 707 Lake Cook Rd Deerfield IL 60015-5613

HEIMANN, JOHN GAINES, investment banker; b. N.Y.C., Apr. 1, 1929; s. Sidney M. and Dorothy V.B. (Gainesburg) H.; m. Margaret E. Fechheimer, Dec. 2, 1956 (div.); children: Joshua Gaines, Eliza Faith; m. Maria Cristina Anzola, Oct. 17, 1989. BA in Econs., Syracuse (N.Y.) U., 1950; LLD (hon.), St. Michael's Coll., 1979. V.p. Smith, Barney & Co., N.Y.C., 1955-66; sr. v.p., dir. E.M. Warburg, Pincus & Co., Inc., N.Y.C., 1967-75; N.Y. State supt. banks, 1975-76; N.Y. State commr. housing and community renewal, 1976-77; compt. of the currency Washington, 1977-81; co-chmn. exec. com. Warburg, Paribas, Becker, N.Y.C., 1981-82; dep. chmn. A.G. Becker Paribas Inc., Paribas Internat., 1982-84; vice chmn. Merrill Lynch Capital Markets, N.Y.C., 1984-91; chmn. Europe/Middle East Merrill Lynch, London, 1988-90; chmn. global fin. instns. group office of chmn. Merrill Lynch & Co. Inc., N.Y.C., 1991-99; chmn. Fin. Stability Inst. of the Bank for Internat. Settlements, N.Y.C., 1999-2001; sr. advisor Fin. Stability Inst. Bank for Internat. Settlements, 2001—; sr. advisor Merrill Lynch & Co., Inc., 2001—03. Chmn. Merrill Lynch Internat. Bank; chmn. Fin. Svcs. Coun.; mem. exec. com. Inst. Internat. Fin.; chmn. Fed. Fin. Instns. Exam. Coun., 1979-81, Comml. Reinvestment Task Force, 1978-81, 20th Century Task Force on Internat. Debt Crisis; lectr. Harvard U., Yale U., Columbia U., U. Calif., NYU; chmn. Brit.-N.Am. com.; trustee Nat. Policy Assn.; vice chmn., chmn. securities subcom. Am. Banking and Securities Assn. of London; chmn. N.Y. State Supt.'s Adv. Com. on Transnat. Banking Instns., 1981; co-chmn. Derivatives Policy Group; mem. Fed. Res. Bank of N.Y.'s Internat. Capital Markets Adv. Com.; mem. adv. com. on fin. svcs. Dept. U.S. Treasury; mem. governing coun. Ctr. for Study of Fin. Instns.; trustee French-Am. Found.; bd. dirs. NewSmith Hedge Fund LP, Interaudi Bank, Assured Guaranty ltd., NewSmith UK Hedge Fund Ltd. Bd. dirs., mem. Group of Thirty, Am. Ditchley Found.; trustee Hampshire Coll.; mem. strategic com. France Tresor; mem. Citizens Com. for N.Y. C., bd. dirs. Inst. Internat. Fin.; mem. adv. coun. Ctr. for Econ. Policy Rsch.; mem. Coun. Fgn. Rels. Named Housing Man of Yr. Nat. Housing Conf., 1976; recipient Bank Adminstrn. Key for Disting. Svc., 1980, Alexander Hamilton award Treasury Dept., 1981, Brotherhood award NCCJ, 1986, Pacesetter award Nat. Assn. Bank Women, Inc., 1986. Mem. Nat. Policy Assn. (vice chmn.), Fgn. Rels. Coun. Democrat. Office: Warburg Pincus 466 Lexington Ave Fl 11 New York NY 10017 Office Phone: 212-878-6118. E-mail: heimannjo@aol.com.

HEIMANN, M.L. (DICK HEIMANN), auto dealership executive; BS biology and languages, Univ. Colo. Dist. mgr. Chrysler Corp., 1967—70; pres., COO Lithia Motors Inc., Medford, Oreg. Mem.: Medford New Car Dealers Assn., Jeep Dealer Coun., Oregon Auto Dealers Assn. Office: Lithia Motors Inc 360 E Jackson St Medford OR 97501

HEIMANN-HAST, SYBIL DOROTHEA, literature and language professor; b. Shanghai, May 8, 1924; arrived in U.S., 1941; d. Paul Heinrich and Elisabeth (Halle) Heimann; m. David G. Hast, Jan. 11, 1948 (div. 1959); children: Thomas David Hast, Thomas David Hast, Dorothea Elizabeth Hast-Scott. BA in French, Smith Coll., 1946; MA in French Lang. and Lit., U. Pitts., 1963; MA in German Lang. and Lit., UCLA, 1966; diploma in Spanish, U. Barcelona, Spain, 1972. Cert. German, French and Spanish tchr. Calif. Assoc. in German lang. UCLA, 1966-70; asst. prof. German Calif. State U., L.A., 1970-71; lectr. German Mt. St. Mary's Coll., Brentwood, Calif., 1974-75; instr. French and German, diction coach Calif. Inst. of Arts, Valencia, 1977-78; coach lang. and diction UCLA Opera Theater, 1973-93, ret., 1993, lectr. dept. music, 1973-93; interviewer, researcher oral history program UCLA, 1986-93; dir., founder ISTMO, Santa Monica, Calif., 1975—. Cons. interpreter/translator LA Music Ctr., U.S. Supreme Ct., LA, J. Paul Getty Mus., Malibu, Calif., Warner New Media, Panorama Internat. Prodn., Sony Records, 1986—; voice-over artist; founder, artistic dir. Westside Opera Workshop, 1986—94. Author: numerous poems. Mem. KCET Founder Soc. Grantee, UCLA, 1990—91. Mem.: AFTRA, SAG, MLA, AAUP, German Am. C. of C., Sunset Succulent Soc. (v.p., bd. dirs., reporter, annual show chmn.). Avocations: performing arts, literature, history, plants, designing and knitting sweaters. Home and Office: River's Edge 111 Dekoven Dr Apt 606 Middletown CT 06457-3463

HEIMBERG, MURRAY, pharmacologist, biochemist, physician; b. Bklyn., Jan. 5, 1925; s. Gustav and Fannie (Geller) H.; children by previous marriage: Richard G., Steven A.; m. Anna Frances Langlois Knox, July 12, 1964; stepchildren: Larry M. Knox, David S. Knox. BS, Cornell U., Ithaca, N.Y., 1948, MNS, 1949; PhD in Biochemistry (NIH fellow), Duke, 1952. NIH Postdoctoral fellow in biochemistry Med. Sch. Washington U., St. Louis, 1952-54; research asso. physiology Med. Sch. Vanderbilt U., 1954-59, asst. prof. to prof. pharmacology, and asst. prof. medicine, 1959-74; prof., chmn. dept. pharmacology, prof. medicine U. Mo., 1974-81; prof. and chmn. dept. pharmacology, prof. medicine, endocrinology and metabolism U. Tenn., Health Sci. Ctr., Memphis, 1981-96; Van Vleet prof. pharmacology U. Tenn., Memphis, 1986-96, Disting. prof. pharmacology and medicine, 1996-99, disting. prof. pharmacology and medicine emeritus, 2000—. Cons. NSF, NIH; cons., established investigator Am. Heart Assn.; attending physician U. Tenn. Hosps. and Memphis VA Hosp.; dir. lipid metabolism clinic U. Tenn. Med. Group. Contbr. articles to profl. jours. Served with inf., AUS, 1943-45, ETO. Decorated Purple Heart, Bronze Star; recipient Lederle Med. Faculty award; research grantee. Fellow AAAS, Am. Coll. Clin. Pharmacology, Am. Heart Assn.; mem. Am. Soc. Biol. Chemistry and Molecular Biology, Am. Soc. Pharmacology and Exptl. Therapeutics, Endocrine Soc., Am. Diabetes Assn., So. Soc. Clin. Investigation. Home: 105 Devon Way Memphis TN 38111-7711 Office Phone: 901-448-4748. Business E-Mail: mheimberg@utmem.edu. E-mail: mheimberg@midsouth.rr.com.

HEIMBERG, SCOTT M., lawyer; b. Glen Ridge, NJ; BA, Franklin and Marshall Coll, 1981; JD with honors, George Washington Univ., 1984. Bar: Md. 1985, DC 1987, US Ct. of Appeals (fed. cir.), US Ct. of Fed. Claims. Atty.-adv. Hon. E.P. Snyder, chief adminstrv. judge Bd. of Contract Appeals, US Dept. Transporation, 1985—87; assoc. Akin Gump Strauss Hauer & Feld LLP, 1987—93, ptnr., govt. contracts, litig. and tech. practice groups Washington, 1993—. Mem. George Washington Jour. of Internat. Law and Econ. Mem.: ABA (sect. on public contract law), Bd. of Contract Appeals Bar Assn., DC Bar Assn., Nat. Contracts Mgmt. Assn. Office: Akin Gump Strauss Hauer & Feld LLP Robert S Strauss Bldg 1333 New Hampshire Ave NW Washington DC 20036-1564 Office Phone: 202-887-4085. Office Fax: 202-955-7623. Business E-Mail: sheimberg@akingump.com.

HEIMBINDER, ISAAC, lawyer; b. Bklyn., May 15, 1943; s. David and Evelyn (Brown) H.; m. Sheila Marie Mooney, Aug. 3, 1970; children: Susan, Daniel, Erin, Michael. BS in Bus., Am. U., 1965; JD, NYU, 1968. Atty. Debevoise and Plimpton, N.Y.C., 1969-72; corp. counsel U.S. Home Corp., Clearwater, Fla., 1973-77, v.p. legal affairs Houston, 1977-79, CFO, 1979-86, pres. COO, 1986-95, co-CEO, pres. COO, 1995-99; chmn., CEO HomeWrite Inc., Houston, 2000—01; vice chmn., pres., COO Kimball Hill Homes, 2001—. Policy adv. bd. Harvard U. Joint Ctr. for Housing Studies. Named one of 100 Most Influential People in Homebuilding Industry in 20th Century, Builder Mag., 1999; co-recipient Homebuilder of Yr. award Profl. Builder, 1994. Mem. N.Y. Bar Assn., Fla. Bar Assn., Tex. Bar Assn., Nat. Assn. Home Builders (mem. high prodn. home builders coun.), Order of Coif, Omicron Delta Kappa. Office Phone: 713-647-4159. Personal E-mail: heimbinder@aol.com.

HEIMBOLD, CHARLES ANDREAS, JR., former ambassador; b. Newark, May 27, 1933; s. Charles Andreas and Mary Joseph (Corrigan) Heimbold; m. Monka Astrid Barkvall, Sept. 22, 1962; children: Joanna, Eric, Leif, Peter. BA cum Laude, Villanova U., 1954; LLB cum laude, U. Pa., 1960; LLM, NYU, 1966; postgrad., Hague Acad. Internat. Law, 1959. Bar: N.Y. 1962. Assoc. Milbank, Tweed, Hadley & Mc Cloy, 1960-63; staff atty. Bristol-Myers Squibb Co., N.Y.C., 1963-70, dir. corp. devel., 1970-73, v.p. planning and devel., 1981-84, sr. planning and devel., 1981-84, pres., health care group, 1984-88, pres., health care group and sr. v.p. planning and devel., 1988-89, dir., 1989, exec. v.p., 1989-92, pres., 1992-94, pres., CEO, 1994-95, chmn., CEO, 1995-2001, chmn. bd. dirs., 2001; U.S. amb. to Sweden, 2001—04. Trustee U. Pa., mem. bd. overseers Law Sch. With USN, 1954—57. Mem.: Assn. Bar City of N.Y., Causeway Club, Riverside Yacht Club.

HEIMBOLD, MARGARET BYRNE, publisher, educator, consultant; came to U.S., 1966, naturalized, 1973; d. John Christopher and Anne (Troy) Byrne; m. Arthur Heimbold, Feb. 26, 1984; children: Eric Thomas Gordon, Victoria Byrne Heimbold. BA, Queens Coll.; MA in Libr. studies, Georgetown U., 2003; cert., Dale Carnegie, 1977, Psychol. Corp. Am., 1981, Wharton Sch., 1983, Stanford U., 1989. Group advt. mgr. N.Y. Times, N.Y.C., 1978-85; pub. Am. Film, Washington, 1985-86; v.p., pub. Nat. Trust for Hist. Preservation, Washington, 1986-90; pres. Summerville Press, Inc., Washington, 1990—; realtor Long and Foster, Washington. Pub. Metro Golf, 1992—; advisor Mag. Pubs.; mentor Women's Ctr. Va.; judge various publ. competitions; judge various mags. awards programs. Trustee Nat. Mus. Women in Arts, Choral Arts Soc. Washington, Kidsave Internat. Office Phone: 202-944-8400. E-mail: summervillemedia@erols.com.

HEIMBUCH, BABETTE E., bank executive; b. 1948; BS in Math Summa Cum Laude, U. Calif., Santa Barbara, 1972. Sr. v.p., CFO FirstFed. Bank Calif., Santa Monica, 1982—85, exec. v.p., CFO, 1985—87, dir., 1986—, FirstFed. Fin. Corp., 1987—; sr. exec. v.p., CFO FirstFed. Fin. Corp. & FirstFed Bank Calif, 1987—88, pres., COO, 1989—97, pres., CEO, 1997—2002, chmn., pres., CEO, 2002—. Bd. dirs. Water Pik Technologies Inc., 2002—, Scape Industries. Chair bd. advisors Santa Monica-UCLA Med. Ctr.; fin. oversight com. Santa Monica/Malibu Unified Sch. Dist. Named one of 25 Women to Watch, US Banker Mag., 2003. Office: First Fed Bank Calif 401 Wilshire Blvd Santa Monica CA 90401-1416

HEIMER, ROBERT, medical educator, researcher; b. Brooklyn, Ny, Feb. 22, 1952; s. Ralph and Caryl P. Heimer; m. Noel S. Heimer, June 18, 1983; children: Alison Caryl, Madeleine Irene. PhD, Yale U., 1988. Asst. prof. to assoc. prof. Yale Sch. of Medicine, New Haven, 1992—. Contbr. articles various profl. jours. Editl. bd. mem. Internat. Jour. of Drug Policy, United Kingdom, 2003—. Achievements include first to efficacy of syringe exchange programs; durability of HIV in syringes. Home: 56 Cold Spring St New Haven CT 06511 Office: Yale Sch Medicine 60 College St New Haven CT 06520-8034 Office Phone: 203-785-6732. Personal E-mail: robert.heimer@yale.edu.

HEIMERDINGER, JOHN FREDERICK, association executive; b. N.Y.C., June 3, 1932; s. Frederick M. and Jane R. (Rosenthal) H.; AB magna cum laude, Princeton U., 1954; MSSW, Columbia U., 1956; m. Suzanne Schrier, June 20, 1954 (dec. Aug. 1987); m. Marilyn Zurow Wilkes, Apr. 2, 1989; children: Charles F., Daniel J., Linda R. With Ladenburg, Thalmann & Co., N.Y.C., 1956-73, adminstrv. mgr., 1958-64, gen. ptnr., 1964-72, sr. exec. v.p., vice chmn. bd., 1972-73; assoc. exec. dir. Jewish Guild for Blind, N.Y.C., 1973-77, pres., chief exec. officer, 1977-97; dir. On-Line Systems Inc., 1968-73, Cooperstown Corp. Md.; adj. assoc. prof. Columbia U. Sch. Social Work, ret. 2005; mem. panel arbitrators Nat. Assn. Security Dealers, Ret., 2004; The N.Y. Stock Exchg. Mem. Byram Hills Sch. Bd., 1965-70, v.p., 1969, 70; active Armonk Ind. Fire Co., 1958—, chief dept., 1979-81; dist. fire commr., Town of North Castle, 1981-1984; mem. adv. coun. Sch. Social Work, Columbia U., 1975-88, vice chmn., 1979-83, chmn., 1983-88; trustee No. Westchester Hosp., 1982-94; dir. Westchester Medical Ctr., 1998—; dir. chmn. bd. Vis. Nurse Svc. Hudson Valley; mem. nat. com. A Campaign for Columbia; mem. spl. gifts com. A Campaign for Princeton, N.Y.C. Recipient medal Alumni Fedn. of Columbia U., 1980. Mem. NASW, Nat. Assn. Emergency Med. Technicians, Internat. Assn. Fire Chiefs, Am. Arbitration Assn., Phi Beta Kappa. Democrat. Jewish. Clubs: Sunningdale Country. E-mail: joheim@aol.com. Home: 13 Thornewood Rd Armonk NY 10504-2807 Office: Cooperstown Corp 707 Westchester Ave White Plains NY 10604 E-mail: johheim@aol.com.

HEIMFELD, SHELLY, hematologist, immunologist, researcher; b. May 11, 1955; PhD, U. Calif., 1983. Rsch. scientist, co-principal investigator SyStemix, Palo Alto, Calif., 1988—90; vis. scientist dept. of immunology DNAX Rsch. Inst., 1990—91; rsch. scientist, dir. biol. rsch. CellPro, Bothell, Wash., 1991—95, dir. discovery and intellectual property, 1995—98; staff scientist, dir. facility cellular therapy Fred Hutchinson Cancer Rsch. Ctr., Seattle, 1998—2001, assoc. mem., dir. facility cellular therapy, 2001—; dir., facility cellular therapy Seattle Cancer Care Alliance, 2001—; dir., c-gmp cell processing facility Fred Hutchinson Cancer Rsch. Ctr., 2001—. Mem.: AAAS, Internat. Cytokine Soc., European Hematology Assn., Am. Soc. Blood and Bone Marrow Transplantation, Am. Soc. Gene Therapy, NY Acad. Scis. Achievements include patents for 1992 Patent # 5, 087, 570; Homogeneous Mammalian Hematopoietic Stem Cell Composition; Methods and Devices for Culturing Human Hematopoietic Cells and Their Precursors; Apparatus and Method for Particle Separation in a Closed Field. Office: Fred Hutchinson Cancer Rsch Ctr 1100 Fairview Ave N D5-390 PO 19024 Seattle WA 98109 Business E-Mail: sheimfel@fhcrc.org.

HEIMLICH, HENRY J., physician, surgeon, educator; b. Wilmington, Del., Feb. 3, 1920; s. Philip and Mary (Epstein) Heimlich; m. Jane Murray, June 3, 1951; children: Philip, Janet, Elisabeth. BA, Cornell U., 1941, MD, 1943; DSc (hon.), Wilmington Coll., 1981, Adelphi U., 1982, Rider Coll., 1983, Alfred U., 1993. Diplomate Am. Bd. Surgery, Am. Bd. Thoracic Surgery. Intern Boston City Hosp., 1944; resident VA Hosp., Bronx, 1946—47, Mt. Sinai Hosp., N.Y.C., 1947—48, Bellevue Hosp., N.Y.C., 1948—49, Triboro Hosp., Jamaica, NY, 1949—50; attending surgeon divsn. surgery Montefiore Hosp., N.Y.C., 1950—69; dir. surgery Jewish Hosp., Cin., 1969—77; prof. advanced clin. scis. Xavier U., Cin., 1977—89; assoc. clin. prof. surgery U. Cin. Coll. Medicine, 1969—78. Pres. Heimlich Inst.; mem. Pres.'s Commn. on Heart Disease, Cancer and Stroke, 1965; pres. Nat. Cancer Found., 1963—68, bd. dirs., 1960—70; founder Heimlich Inst. Found. Author: Postoperative Care in Thoracic Surgery, 1962; author: (with M.O. Cantor, C.H. Lupton) Surgery of the Stomach, Duodenum and Diaphragm, Questions and Answers, 1965; contbr. chapters to books, articles to profl. jours.; prodr.(film): Esophageal Replacement with a Reversed Gastric Tube (Medaglione Di Bronzo Minerva, 1961), Reversed Gastric Tube Esophagoplasty Using Stapling Technique, How to Save a Choking Victim: The Heimlich Maneuver, 1976, 1982, How to Save a Drowning Victim: The Heimlich Maneuver, 1981, Stress Relief: The Heimlich Method, 1983, (video): Dr. Heimlich's Home First Aid Video, 1989 (Vira award, 1989); editl. bd. films Reporte's Medicos, 1962. Cmty. Devel. Foünd., 1967—70; Save the Chidlren FEdn., 1967—68; United Cancer Coun., 1967—70. Served to lt. (s.g.) USNR, 1944—46. Recipient Lasker award for Pub. Svc., Lasker Found., 1984, China-Burma-India Vets. Assn. Americanism award, 1988, 1st Heimlich Humanitarian award, Spirit of Am. Festival, 1994, Heimlich Inst. established in perpetuity by Deaconness Assns., Inc. Fellow: ACS (chpt. pres. 1964), Am. Coll. Gastroenterology, Am. Coll. Chest Physicians; mem.: AMA (cons. to jour.), Ctrl. Surg. Assn., Collegium INternat. Chirurgiae Digestive, Pan Am. Med. Assn., Am. Gastroent. Assn., Soc. Surgery Alimentary Tract, N.Y. Soc. Thoracic Surgery, Cin. Soc. Thoracic Surgery, Soc. Thoracic Surgeons (founding mem.). Achievements include development of Heimlich Operation (reversed gastric tube esophagoplasty) for replacement of esophagus; invention of Heimlich chest drain valve, Heimlich Micro-Trach (HMT) for COPD, emphysema and cystic fibrosis; development of Heimlich Maneuver to save lives of victims of food choking and drowning and prevents and overcomes asthma attacks (listed in Random House, Oxford Am. and Webster dictionaries); Computers for Peace, a program to maintain peace throughout world and A Caring World. Office: Heimlich Inst Found Inc 311 Straight St Cincinnati OH 45219 Office Phone: 513-559-2391. Personal E-mail: heimlich@iglou.com. *I have never been satisfied with existing methods and seek to simplify and improve them. After devising an operation for replacement of the esophagus, I became aware that with one such discovery I could help more people in a few weeks than in my entire lifetime as a surgeon in the operating room. The Heimlich Maneuver, which saves thousands of choking and drowning victims as well as asthmatics annually, confirmed this realization. My ultimate goal is to avoid needless death and promote well-being for the largest number of people by establishing a philosophy that will eliminate war and promote a caring world. Seeking to find a cure for cancer, AIDS, and Lyme disease through immunotherapy.*

HEIN, JANET EILEEN FICKEN, secondary school educator; b. Eustis, Nebr., Mar. 13, 1939; d. Herman Henry William and Edna Eileen (Buell) Ficken; m. Robert Lyle Hein, June 17, 1960; children: Laura E. Hein Preston, Randall Lyle. AA, McCook Coll., 1974; BA, Kearney Coll., 1975, MA, 1982. Cert. Tchr. Nebr. Elem. tchr. dist. 5 Frontier County Pub. Schs., Stockville, Nebr., 1958-60; dist. 23 Red Willow County Pub. Schs., McCook, Nebr., 1960-61, North Platte (Nebr.) Schs., 1961-62, St. Patrick's Sch., McCook, 1972—74; secondary tchr. Ft. Campbell (Ky.) Dependent Schs., 1964—65; clk. Burlington No. R.R., McCook, 1974—75; elem. tchr. McCook City Schs., 1975—2001. Instr. psychology McCook Coll., 1984-88; cert. instr. Project T.E.A.C.H.; coord./facilitator Artrain USA, McCook, 2002. Recipient Excellence in Teaching award McCook Schs., 1984, Cooper Found. award, 1986, 87. Mem. NEA (life), Nebr. Edn. Assn., McCook Edn. Assn. (com. mem. 1975-2001), Delta Kappa Gamma (com. mem. 1981—). Lutheran. Home: 1108 W 1st St McCook NE 69001-2503

HEIN, KAREN KRAMER, pediatrician, epidemiologist; b. NYC, Feb. 2, 1944; d. Irving W. and Ruth (Eisenberg) Kramer: m. Ralph Dell, Aug. 28, 1983; children: Ethan, Molly. BA, U. Wis., 1966; B of Med. Sci., Dartmouth Med. Sch., 1968; MD, Columbia U., 1970. Intern Bronx Mcpl. Hosp., Bronx Mcpl. Hosp. Ctr., 1970, resident, 1971-73; dir. adolescent AIDS program Montefiore Med. Ctr., NYC, 1987-94; prof. pediat. Albert Einstein Coll. Medicine, NYC, 1991—, prof. epidemiology and social medicine, 1993—, clin. prof. pediat., epidemiology and social medicine, 1995—; exec. officer Inst. Medicine NRC, Washington, 1995—98; pres. William T. Grant Found., NYC, 1998—2003. Cons. NYC Dept. Health, 1980-85, NYC Bd. Edn., 1987-93; bd. dirs. Dartmouth Med. Sch., Hanover, NH. Author: AIDS: Trading Fears for Facts Consumer Reports Books, 1989; contbr. articles to profl. jours. Named Outstanding Physician, Dept. Health and Human Svcs., 1989, Adminstrs. Citation award, 1993. Fellow Am. Bd. Pediat.; mem. Am. Pediatric Soc., Soc. for Pediatric Rsch., Am. Acad. Pediat., Soc. for Adolescent Medicine (pres. 1992-93). Address: Box 607 Jacksonville VT 05342

HEIN, LAURIE SNOW, artist, educator; b. Lakewood, NJ, Feb. 23, 1949; d. Lawrence Parlin and Jeanne Marion Opdyke Snow; m. William L. Casey (div.); 1 child, Shannon; m. Robert Carl Hein, Dec. 13, 1976; children: Karl, Caryn, Kristin, Lauren. Student, Columbus Coll. Art & Design, 1967-68, Austin Peabody U., 1969-70, Palm Beach Jr. Coll., 1970-71. Instr. art Delray (Fla.) Elem. Sch., 1974; owner, ptnr. Casey & Jolly Gallery, Palm Beach, Fla., 1974-76, instr., portrait artist, 1974-88; instr. workshops Duluth (Ga.) Art Club, 1991, 95, DeKalb County (Ga.) Art, 1993; illustrator, fine artist ARTS Unique, Cooksville, Tenn., 1993—. Instr. Everglades Club, Palm Beach, 1990—, Lost Tree Village, North Palm Beach, Fla., 1991—, Hope Sound Art Club, Jupiter, Fla., 1995, Symbionic Gallery, Stuart, Fla., 1995—; lectr. workshops Portrait Soc. Atlanta, 1997; commd. artist Reminiscence Gallery, Lake Worth, Fla., 1972-74; featured artist Artigras, Palm Beach, 2003; instr. oil painting Graham Ingels Studio, 1973-79; presenter workshops Gwinnet County (Ga.) Coun. of Art, 1993, pvt. classes, Atlanta, 1995; instr. workshops Lucca Italy, 1996, Indiantown (Fla.) Art League, others; lectr. in field. Exhibited in group shows at Ann Arbor State Street, Winter Park Art Fetival, Gasparilla Art Festival, Naples Nat. Art Festival, Fla., Gateway Gallery, Palm Beach, 1985—86, 1994—95, Renee Rand Gallery, Delray Beach, 1994—95, Mossy Creek Art Festival, Ga., 1995—96, Fernandina Shrimp Festival Art Shop, 1995—97, Los Olas Mus., 1997, Miami Mus. Sci. Invitational, 1997—99, Creative Inspirations Gallery, Fla., 1997—98, Mainsail, St. Petersburg, 1999, Dan Goad Gallery, St. Simons, St. Simons Island Gallery, Ga., 1999, Moot Mus., Brandon, Fla., 1998, Represented in permanent collections City Hall of Plantation, Fla.; illustrator Once Upon A Christmas, 2001, Love Like No Other, 2002, Mommy Don't Cry, 2003. Recipient People's Choice award South Fla. Fair, 1985, 1st place in oil painting exhibit award Delray Affair, 1995, Best of Show award Wellington Art Festival, Palm Beach, 2002; Columbus Coll. Art and Design scholar, 1967-68; Catherine Tuttle scholar, 1968-69. Mem. Am. Soc. Portrait Artists, Washington Soc. Portrait Artists, Atlanta Portrait Soc., Palm Beach Watercolor Soc. (v.p. 1995), Soc. Classical Realism, Nat. Portrait Soc. Baptist. Avocations: raising haflinger horses, art festivals, gardening. Home: 14494 Peace River Way Palm Beach Gardens FL 33418 Office Phone: 561-324-0100. Personal E-mail: artistlsh@aol.com.

HEIN, LEONARD WILLIAM, accounting educator; b. Forest Park, Ill., Feb. 17, 1916; s. Harry Christian and Clara Antoinette (Klein) H.; m. Akemi Kishi, Feb. 28, 1981. BSC., Loyola U., Chgo., 1952; MBA, U. Chgo., 1954; PhD (U. Calif. at Los Angeles Bus. Sch. Alumni Assn. fellow, Univ. fellow, Ford Found. fellow), U. Calif. at Los Angeles, 1962. C.P.A., Ill. With San. Dist. Chgo., 1941-56; asst. prof. accounting Calif. State U. at Los Angeles, 1956-59, asso. prof. accounting, 1959-65, prof. accounting, 1965—, coordinator program bus. info. systems, 1956-73, asst. dean grad. studies, 1963-72. Mem. nat. panel arbitrators Am. Arbitration Assn., 1972— Author: Introduction to Electronic Data Processing for Business, 1961, Quantitative Approach to Managerial Decisions, 1967, Contemporary Accounting and the Computer, 1969, The British Companies Acts and the Practice of Accountancy, 1844-1962, 1978; Contbr. articles to profl. jours. Served with USNR, 1942-45. Mem. Am. Inst. C.P.A.'s, Am. Accounting Assn., Calif. Soc. C.P.A.'s, Beta Gamma Sigma, Beta Alpha Psi, Alpha Kappa Psi, Phi Kappa Phi. Office: Calif State U 5151 State University Dr Los Angeles CA 90032-4226

HEINDEL, NED DUANE, chemistry professor; b. Red Lion, Pa., Sept. 4, 1937; s. Penrose Horace and Dorothy May (Strayer) H.; m. Linda Clarella Heefner, Aug. 26, 1959. BS, Lebanon Valley Coll., Annville, Pa., 1959; D.Sc. (hon.), Lebanon Valley Coll., 1985; MS, U. Del., 1961, PhD, 1963; postdoctoral studies, Princeton U., 1964; DSc (hon.), Albright Coll., 1993. Instr. chemistry U. Del., 1962-63; asst. prof. chemistry Ohio U., Ironton, 1964-65, Marshall U., Huntington, W. Va., 1964-66; asst. prof. to assoc. prof. chemistry Lehigh U., Bethlehem, Pa., 1966-73, H.S. Bunn prof., 1973—, dir. Ctr. Health Scis., 1980-88; prof. nuclear medicine Hahnemann Med. U., Phila., 1971—. Cons. Pa. State Police Crime Lab., Bethlehem, 1975-88; cons. safety program J.T. Baker Chem. Co., Phillipsburg, N.J., 1978-83; regional lectr. Mid. Atlantic region Sigma Xi. Author: Iron, Armor and Adolescents, 1982; editor: Chemistry of Radiopharmaceuticals, 1978; contbr. numerous articles to profl. jours. Trustee Keystone Jr. Coll., LaPlume, Pa., 1975-90, Ctr. for History of Chemistry, Phila., 1982—, Nat. Found. for History of Chemistry, Phila., 1988—. Recipient Alumni Assn. award Lebanon Valley Coll., 1971; fellow NSF, 1963-64; recipient numerous rsch. grants. Mem. Am. Chem. Soc. (councilor, bd. dirs., pres. 1994, Harry and Carol Mosher award 1995), Royal Soc., Soc. Nuclear Medicine, Am. Assn. Pharm. Scientists, Sigma Xi. Republican. Methodist. Home: 200 Hexenkopf Rd Easton PA 18042-9570 Office: Dept Chem Lehigh U Bethlehem PA 18015 Business E-Mail: ndh0@lehigh.edu.

HEINDL, CLIFFORD JOSEPH, physicist, researcher; b. Chgo., Feb. 4, 1926; s. Anton Thomas and Louise (Fiala) H. BS, Northwestern U., 1947, MS, 1948; AM, Columbia U., 1950, PhD, 1959. Sr. physicist Bendix Aviation Corp., Detroit, 1953-54; student rschr. Oak Ridge Nat. Lab., 1954-55; asst. sect. chief Babcock & Wilcox Co., Lynchburg, Va., 1956-58; rsch. group supr. Jet Propulsion Lab., Pasadena, Calif., 1959-65, mgr. rsch. and space sci., 1965—2005. Served with AUS, 1944-46. Mem. AIAA, Am. Nuclear Soc., Health Physics Soc., Planetary Soc., Am. Phys. Soc. Home: 179 Mockingbird Ln South Pasadena CA 91030-2047 Office: 4800 Oak Grove Dr Pasadena CA 91109-8001

HEINDL, PHARES MATTHEWS, lawyer; b. Meridian, Miss., Dec. 14, 1949; s. Paul A. and Leila (Matthews) H.; m. Linda Ann Williamson, Sept. 21, 1985; children: Lori Elizabeth, Jesse Phares, Jared Matthews. BSChemE, Miss. State U., 1972; JD, U. Fla., 1981. Bar: Fla. 1981, Calif. 1982, U.S. Dist. Ct. (cen. dist.) Calif. 1983, U.S. Dist. Ct. (mid. dist.) Fla. 1983; cert. civil trial lawyer Fla. Bar. Assoc. Lafollette, Johnson et al, L.A., 1982-83, Sam E. Murrell & Sons, Orlando, Fla., 1983-84; pvt. practice Orlando, Fla., 1984-93, Altamonte Springs, Fla., 1993—. Program com. Volie Williams Jr. Inns of Ct., 2003—. Precinct coord. Freedom Coun., Orlando, 1986; pres. Friends of the Wekiva River, 1999—2001. Mem. Fla. Bar Assn., Calif. Bar Assn., Seminole County Bar Assn. (pres. civil trial sect. 1998), ATLA, Christian Legal Soc. (past pres. Ctrl. Fla.), Fla. Acad. Trial Lawyers, Workers Compensation Rules Com. Republican. Avocation: kayak racing. Home: 2415 River Tree Cir Sanford FL 32771-8334 Office: 222 S Westmonte Dr Ste 208 Altamonte Springs FL 32714-4269 Office Phone: 407-865-5700. Business E-Mail: phares@heindllaw.com.

HEINEKEN, FREDERICK GEORGE, biochemical engineer; b. Chgo., Oct. 22, 1939; s. Frederick W.G. Heineken and Marie Helene Faber Heineken; divorced; 1 child, Christopher P. BS, Northwestern U., 1962; PhD, U. Minn., 1966. Sr. biochem. engr. Monsanto, St. Louis, 1966-71; postdoctoral fellow U. Colo., Denver, 1972-74, rsch. assoc., instr., 1974-76; sr. project engr. Cobe Labs., Lakewood, Colo., 1977-79, dept. head, 1979-81, therapy scientist, 1981-84; cons. Heineken & Assocs., Potomac, Md., 1985—; program dir. NSF, Washington, 1985—. Trustee 1st Universalist Ch., Denver, 1980-83, vice-moderator, 1984. Recipient Young Investigator award, NIH, 1974. Mem. AIChE, AAAS, Am. Chem. Soc. (councilor 1990—), Assn. for Advancement of Med. Instrumentation, Am. Soc. for Artificial Organs, St. Louis Ski Club (pres. 1971). Home: 7908 Turncrest Dr Potomac MD 20854-2772 Office: NSF Engring 4201 Wilson Blvd Arlington VA 22230-0001 Office Phone: 703-292-7944. Business E-Mail: fheineke@nsf.gov.

HEINEMAN, ANDREW DAVID, retired lawyer; b. N.Y.C., Nov. 5, 1928; s. Bernard and Lucy (Morgenthau) H. BA, Williams Coll., 1950; LLB, Yale U., 1953. Bar: N.Y. 1953. Assoc. Proskauer Rose Goetz & Mendelsohn, N.Y.C., 1953—63; ptnr. Proskauer Rose LLP, N.Y.C., 1963—2002; ret., 2002. Pres., chmn. bd. dirs. Ernest and Mary Hayward Weir Found., N.Y.C., 1969-87, trustee Mt. Sinai Hosp. Med. Sch. and Med. Ctr., 1976—, Williams Coll., 1980-95, Abelard Found., 1976-96; Asphalt Green, 1992-96; bd. dirs. Jewish Home and Hosp. for Aged, 1967—, vice chmn. bd. dirs., 1992, chmn. bd. dirs. 1993-97; exec. asst. Citizens for Kennedy and Johnson, N.Y.C., 1960; mem. N.Y. Gov.'s Commn. on Minorities in Med. Schs., 1982. Mem. Yale Law Sch. Assn. N.Y. (pres. 1970-73), Yale Law Sch. Alumni Assn. (v.p. 1973-76, exec. com.), Audubon Soc., North Country Bird Club, Linnaean Soc. (life), Fedn. N.Y. State Bird Clubs, Brit. Naval Photog. Club.

HEINEMAN, BEN WALTER, corporation executive; b. Wausau, Wis., Feb. 10, 1914; s. Walter Ben and Elsie Brunswick (Deutsch) H.; m. Natalie Goldstein, Apr. 17, 1935; children: Martha Heineman Pieper, Ben Walter. Student, U. Mich., 1930-33; LLB, Northwestern U., 1936; LLD (hon.), Lawrence Coll., 1959; LL.D. (hon.), Lake Forest Coll., 1966, Northwestern U., 1967; LHD, DePaul U., 1986. Bar: Ill. 1936. Pvt. practice law and govt. svc., Chgo., Washington, Algiers, 1936-56; chmn. bd. dirs. Four Wheel Drive Auto Co., 1954-57; chmn. C. & N.W. Ry. Co., 1956-72; founder, former chmn., CEO Northwest Industries, Inc., 1968-85. Dir., chmn. exec. com., bd. dirs. 1st Nat. Bank, Chgo.; chmn. orgn. com. First Chgo. Corp., 1965-86; Chmn. White House Conf. to Fulfill These Rights, 1966, Pres.'s Task Force on Govt. Orgn., 1966-67, Pres.'s Commn. Income Maintenance Programs, 1967-69 Life trustee U. Chgo.; chmn. Ill. Bd. Higher Edn., 1962-69; trustee, mem. investment com. Savs. and Profit Sharing Fund Sears Roebuck Employees, 1966-71; trustee, mem. exec. com., chmn. audit com. Rockefeller Found., 1972-78; life dir. Lyric Opera, Chgo.; life trustee Orchestral Assn.; sustaining fellow Art Inst. Chgo., 20th century acquisition com.; dir. emeritus The Corning (N.Y.) Glass Mus. Fellow ABA, AAAS, Am. Bar Found. (life); mem. Am. Law Inst. (life), Ill. Bar Assn., Chgo. Bar Assn., Ephraim Club (Wis.), Yacht Club, Mid-Am. Club, Chgo. Club, Wayfarers Club, Std. Club (life), Quadrangle Club, Comml. Club (life), Carlton Club, Order of Coif, Phi Delta Phi (hon.). Office: 180 E Pearson St Apt 4304 Chicago IL 60611-2171 E-mail: BWH@hmansr.net.

HEINEMAN, BENJAMIN WALTER, JR., lawyer; b. Chgo., Jan. 25, 1944; s. Benjamin Walter and Natalie (Goldstein) H.; m. Jeanne Cristine Russell, June 7, 1975; children: Zachary R., Matthew R. BA magna cum laude, Harvard U., 1965; B.Letters, Balliol Coll., Oxford U., Eng., 1967; JD, Yale U., 1971. Bar: DC. 1973, U.S. Supreme Ct. 1973. Reporter Chgo. Sun Times, 1968; law clk. to Assoc. Justice Potter Stewart U.S. Supreme Ct., 1971-72; staff atty. Center for Law and Social Policy, 1973-75; with Williams Connolly and Califano, Washington, 1975-76; exec. asst. to sec. HEW, Washington, 1977-78, asst. sec. for planning and evaluation, 1978-79; partner Califano, Ross & Heineman, Washington, 1979-82, Sidley & Austin, Washington, 1982-87; sr. v.p., gen. counsel, sec. Gen. Electric Co., Fairfield, Conn., 1987—2004, sr. v.p., law & pub. affairs, 2004—. Author: The Politics of the Powerless: A Study of the Campaign Against Racial Discrimination, 1972, Memorandum for the President: A Strategic Approach to Domestic Affairs in the 1980's, 1981; editor-in-chief: Yale Law Jour., 1970-71. Rhodes scholar, 1965-67; Lifetime Achievement award, Am. Law mag., 2005 Mem. Phi Beta Kappa. Office: General Electric Co 3135 Easton Tpke Fairfield CT 06431-0001

HEINEMAN, DAVID EUGENE, governor; b. Falls City, Nebr., May 12, 1948; s. Jean Trevers and Irene Larkin H.; m. Sally Ganem, 1977; 1 child, Sam. BS, U.S. Mil. Acad., 1970. Sales rep. Procter & Gamble, 1976-77; campaign mgr. Hal Daub for Congress, 1977-78; dep. dir. Policy Rsch. Office, Nebr., 1979; dir. Nebr. State Rep. Exec. Com., 1979-81; chief of staff to Congressman Hal Daub, 1983-88; office mgr. for Congressman Doug Bereuter, 1990-94; city councilman City of Fremont, Nebr., 1990-94; state treas. State of Nebr., 1994—2000, lt. gov., 2001—05, gov., 2005—. Served in U.S. Army, 1970—75. Decorated Army Commendation medal; recipient Outstanding Rep. Vol. award Douglas County Rep. Party, 1976, Outstanding Young Am. award Jaycees, 1980. Mem. Nat. Assn. State Treas. (pres. 1999-2000), Nat. Electronic Commerce Coordinating Coun. (exec. com. 1998-2000). Republican. Office: Office Gov PO Box 94848 Lincoln NE 68509 E-mail: dave.heineman@email.state.ne.us.

HEINEMAN, NATALIE (MRS. BEN W. HEINEMAN), civic worker; Formerly med. social worker, Chgo.; bd. dirs. Child Welfare League Am., 1960-86, pres., 1971-74, now hon. life mem.; chmn. citizens com. Ill. Adoption Svc., 1959-71; bd. dirs. Chgo. Child Care Soc., 1959-97, pres., 1967-71, now hon. life mem.; mem. citizens' com. Juvenile Ct. of Cook County, 1984-95. Bd. dirs. Children and Family Justice Ctr., Northwestern U. Sch. Law, 1991-96; mem. women's bd. Field Mus. Natural History, U. Chgo., Northwestern U.; vis. com. U. Chgo. Sch. Social Svc., 1956-91. Bd. dirs. United Way Met. Chgo., 1975-86, United Way Am., 1974-80, Erikson Inst. for Advanced Study Child Devel., 1966-88. Address: 180 E Pearson St Chicago IL 60611-2143

HEINEMANN, HEINZ, chemist, educator, researcher, consultant; b. Berlin, Aug. 21, 1913; came to U.S., 1938; s. Felix and Edith (Boehm) H.; m. Elaine Patricia Silverman, Feb. 12, 1948 (dec. Dec. 1993); children: Susan Carol, Peter Michael; m. Barbara A. Tenenbaum, Apr. 23, 1995. Diploma, U. Berlin, 1935; PhD, U. Basel, Switzerland, 1937. Rsch. chemist Danciger Oil & Refineries, Pampa, Tex., 1940-41, Attapulgus Clay Co., Phila., 1941-48; sect. chief Houdry Process Corp., Marcus Hook, Pa., 1948-57; dir. chem. & engring. rsch. M.W. Kellogg Co., N.Y.C., 1957-69; mgr. catalysis rsch. Mobil R & D Corp., Princeton, N.J., 1969-78; disting. scientist Lawrence Berkeley Lab., U. Calif., 1978—; lectr. in chem. engring. U. Calif., Berkeley, 1979-90. Pres. Internat. Congress on Catalysis, 1956-60; cons. numerous chem. and petroleum cos., 1978—. Editor Catalysis Revs. jour., 1966-86; author 130 publs. on catalysis and fuel chemistry; contbr. 6 chpts. to books, numerous articles to publs. Mem. Flood Control Commn. Princeton Twp., 1970-75, Gov's. Adv. Coun. Rsch., Trenton, N.J., 1976-78; dir. Princeton Art Assn. Recipient Phila. Catalysis Soc. award, 1976, Disting. Scientist award U.S. Dept. Energy, 1978, Homer H. Lowry award U.S. Dept Energy, 1994; Advances in Catalysis Chemistry II symposium held in his honor, Salt Lake City, 1982. Fellow AAAS; mem. Am. Chem. Soc. (Indsl. and Engring. Chem. award 1972, numerous offices), Catalysis Soc. N.Am. (Applied Catalysis award 1975), Nat. Acad. Engring., Internat. Congress Catalysis (pres. 1956-60), Ret. Chemists Group (pres. 2001). Achievements include over 50 patents in field; invention of and participation in commercialization of 16 industrial processes. Home: 4600 Connecticut Ave NW Apt 206 Washington DC 20008-5702 Office: Lawrence Berkeley Lab 905 D St SW Washington DC 20024-2115 Office Phone: 202-646-7862. Business E-Mail: hheinemann@lbl.gov.

HEINEMANN, LARRY C., writer; b. Chgo., Jan. 18, 1944; s. John Hubert and Dorothy Heinemann; m. Edith Jane, Apr. 27, 1968; children: Sarah Catherine, Preston John. BA, Columbia Coll., 1971; AA, Kendall Coll., 1966. Tchr. Columbia Coll., Chgo., 1971—86; writer-in-residence U. Mass., Boston, 1991—2002, DePaul U., Chgo., 2000—02. Writer-in-residence Northwestern U., Evanston, Ill., spring 1996, U. So. Calif., L.A., fall 1996. Author: Close Quarters, 1977, Paco's Story, 1986 (Nat. Book award, 1987), Cooler by the Lake, 1992, Black Virgin Mountain: A Return to Vietnam, 2005; contbr. articles to numerous mags. Bd. dirs. City Chgo. Adv. Com. Vets. Affairs, 1988-90, Nat. Vets. Legal Svcs. Project, 1990, My Lai Peace Park Project, Madison, Wis., 1995—. Sgt. U.S. Army, 1966-68, Vietnam. Recipient Nat. Book award Nat. Book Found., 1987, Carl Sandburg award Chgo. Pub. Libr. Assn., 1987, Fiction award Soc. Midland Authors, 1987; fellow NEA, 1982, 86, Guggenheim, N.Y.C., 1988-89, Steinberg/Pen U. Pa., 1989; Regent's scholar U. Calif., Davis, spring 1995. Buddhist. Office: c/o Doubleday Random House 1745 Broadway New York NY 10019 Office Phone: .*

HEINEMANN, PETER, artist, educator; b. Denver, Apr. 22, 1931; s. Arthur Mason Heinemann and Stella Irene Diana (Peckham) Cohen; m. Gisella Gross (div. Aug. 1970); children: Mark Elliot, Johanna Ellen; m. Marie Savettieier. Student, Black Mt. Coll., 1948-49. Tchr. Sch. Visual Arts, N.Y.C., 1960—. One-person shows at Roko Gallery, 1954, 56, 59, Hacker Gallery, 1963, Gallery 120, 1983, Gallery Schlesinger, 1985, 87, 89, 92; group exhbns. at Ctr. Figurative Painting, 55 Mercer St. Gallery, NY Studio Sch. Gallery, 1984, Prince St. Gallery, 1986, Lake Placid Ctr. for Arts, 1986, Visual Arts Mus. Recipient Creative Artists Program grant, 1972, 74, 77, NEA grantee, 1983, N.Y. Found. for Arts grantee, 1986; recipient Nat. Inst. Arts and Letters Childhassam Purchase award, 1972. Office: Sch Visual Arts 209 E 23rd St New York NY 10010-3994*

HEINEN, JAMES ALBIN, electrical engineering educator; b. Milw., June 23, 1943; s. Albin Jacob and Viola (DeBuhr) H. BEE, Marquette U., 1964, MS, 1967, PhD, 1969. Registered profl. engr., Wis. Data analyst Med. Sch. Marquette U., Milw., 1963, teaching asst. elec. engring. dept., 1964-65, 65-66, research asst., 1966, NASA trainee, 1966-69, asst. prof., 1969—71, research assoc. Provost's Office, 1970, asst. prof. and grad. adminstr., 1971-73, assoc. prof., chmn. elec. engring. dept., 1973-76, assoc. prof., 1976-80, prof. elec. engring. and computer sci., 1980-87, prof., dir. grad. studies elec. and computer engring., 1987-95, prof. elec. and computer engring., 1995—99, rsch. prof., 1999—2000, prof. emeritus, 2000—, dir. signal processing rsch. ctr., 1990-99, co-dir. ctr. intelligent syss., controls, and signal processing, 1999—. Cons. in field. Contbr. numerous articles and revs. on elec. engring. and computer sci. to profl. jours. Recipient Outstanding Engring. Tchr. award Marquette U., 1979, Teaching Excellence award Marquette U., 1985. Mem. IEEE (various coms., tech. reviewer Trans. Automatic Control 1969—, Trans. Circuits and Systems Soc. 1980—, Signal Processing Soc. 1980—, sr. mem., Meml. award Milw. sect. 1981, assoc. editor Trans. Circuits and Systems 1983-85, assoc. editor Trans. Indsl. Electronics 1996-2000), Am. Soc. Engring. Edn., Sigma Xi, Tau Beta Pi, Eta Kappa Nu (Most Oustanding Elec. Engring. Tchr. in U.S. award 1974), Pi Mu Epsilon, Alpha Sigma Nu. Home: 8200 W Menomonee River Pky Wauwatosa WI 53213-2537 Office: Marquette U Haggerty Hall Rm 211 PO Box 1881 Milwaukee WI 53201-1881 Office Phone: 414-288-3500. Business E-Mail: james.heinen@marquette.edu.

HEINEN, JOHN TIMOTHY, environmental engineer; b. Oshkosh, Wis., Sept. 30, 1966; s. Larry John and Marie Jane Heinen, John Paul Fink and Judith Loretta Bloedow; m. Leslie Dawn Gahagan (div. Jan. 2, 1997); children: Timothy J., Zoë N. BS in Indsl. Tech. summa cum laude, U. Wis., Platteville, 1989. Cert. hazardous waste mgmt. Lion Tech., Inc. R & D engr. Intermet Foundries, Inc., Lynchburg, Va., 1990—93; indsl. engr. Richland Ctr. Foundry Co., Richland Center, Wis., 1993—95, indsl. systems engr., 1995—2000, environ. dir., 2000—. Chmn. Richland County Local Emergency Planning Com., Richland Center, 1999—. Contbr. articles to profl. jours. Mem.: AAAS, Ocean Arks, Internat., Am. Foundry Soc. (sec. 1996—99, environ. com.), Gt. Lakes Pollution Prevention Roundtable, Fedn. of Environ. Techs. (cert.), Am. Chem. Soc., Nature Conservancy, Smithsonian Instn., Nat. Geog. Soc., Am. Black Holocaust Mus., Sierra Club, Epsilon Pi Tau, Phi Kappa Phi. Avocation: studies in: cosmology, philosophy, cultural anthropology, complex systems, natural & artificial intelligence and ecology. Home: 215 South Park St Richland Center WI 53581 Office: Richland Ctr Foundry Co 1000 Foundry Dr Richland Center WI 53581 Office Phone: 608-647-1420. Personal E-mail: atla201@yahoo.com. Business E-Mail: jheinen@rcfoundry.com.

HEINEY, JOHN WEITZEL, former utilities executive; b. Lancaster, Pa., Nov. 9, 1913; s. George and Gertrude G. (Weitzel) H.; m. Betty M. Horn, Apr. 12, 1941. BS in Bus. Adminstrn, Lehigh U., 1935. With various subsidiaries Am. Water Works Co., 1935-41, 46-60; pres., chief exec. officer, dir. Indiana Gas Co., Inc., Indpls., 1960-73, chmn. bd., chief exec. officer, 1973-78, chmn. bd., 1978-84; pres., dir. Ohio River Pipe Line Corp., 1964-73, chmn. bd., 1973-78; pres., chmn. Gen. Assurance Services, Ltd., 1975-84. Bd. dirs. United Fund Greater Indpls., 1960-77; bd. dirs. Community Hosp. Indpls., 1968-73, 75-81, chmn., 1972-73; bd. dirs., chmn. Community Hosps. Found., 1983-89. Served to lt. col., inf. AUS, 1941-46. Decorated Bronze Star medal; named Sagamore of Wabash, Gov. of Ind., 1997. Mem. Am. Gas Assn. (past chmn. spl. com. on consumer affairs, 1st vice chmn. 1968, chmn. 1969, dir. Disting. Svcs. award com. 1975), Ind. Gas Assn. (past pres. and dir.), Inst. Gas Tech. (trustee 1965, chmn. bd. trustees 1968), Internat. Gas Union (mem. council and bur. 1973-75), Ind. C. of C. (dir. 1973-80), Newcomen Soc. N.Am., Beta Theta Pi, Am. Legion. Clubs: Meridian Hills Country.

HEINICKE, RALPH MARTIN, science administrator, consultant; b. Hickory, N.C., Sept. 3, 1914; s. Martin John and Lydia Sophia (Kurth) H.; m. Sarah Anne Hall, July 31, 1944; 1 child, Mark. BS, Cornell U., 1936; PhD, U. Minn., St. Paul, 1950. Agr. chemist Shell Oil Co., N.Y.C., 1939-43; tech. advisor Jintan-Dolph, Osaka, Japan, 1962-86; assoc. faculty U. Hawaii, Honolulu, 1950-86; chemist Pineapple Rsch. Inst., Honolulu, 1950-55; dir. rsch. Dole Co., Honolulu, 1955-72; v.p. Biol. Control Systems, Honolulu, 1981-86; pres. Biotech. Resources Inc., Clarksville, Ind., 1990-94; cons. Morinda, Inc. Cons. various drug cos., 1972—; cons. on the xeronine-sys. Inventor, patentee on xeronine; inventor, patentee on nerve toxin insecticide. Master sgt. U.S. Army, 1942-45, CBI. Democrat. Avocations: music, writing, philosophy. Personal E-mail: rhein1@msn.com.

HEINKE, REX S., lawyer; b. Harrisburg, Ill., 1950; s. William Richard and Versa Lee Heinke; m. Margaret Ann Nagle, 1978; children: William Rex, Meghan Bradley. BA, U. Witwatersrand, Johannesburg, Republic of South Africa, 1971; JD, U. Columbia, 1975. Bar: Calif. 1975. Ptnr. Gibson, Dunn & Crutcher, LA, 1983-99, Greines, Martin, Stein & Richland, 1999—2001, Akin, Gump, Strauss, Hauer & Feld, 2001—. Office: 2029 Century Park E Ste 2400 Los Angeles CA 90067 Office Phone: 310-229-1000. Business E-Mail: rheinke@akingump.com.

HEINLE, BEVERLY DIANE, publishing executive; d. Charles William Hoffman and Beryl Dorothy Hoffman-Ferree; m. Charles A.S. Heinle, Dec. 25, 1973; children: Beverly Elisabeth, Katherine Margaretta. MA, W.Va. U., Morgantown, W. Va., 1966. Editl. sec. Ginn & Co., Boston, 1966—66; asst. to editor-in-chief Blaisdell Pub., Waltham, Mass., 1967—67; dir. distbn. Ctr. for Curriculum Devel. in Audio-Visual Lang. Tchg., Phila., 1967—72; editor-in-chief/dir. of advt. and promotion F.W. Faxon Co., Dedham, Mass., 1973—82; pres. H & H Advt., Concord, Mass., 1983—91; editor-in-chief Pimsleur Internat., Concord, Mass., 1992—97; exec. editor Pimsleur Lang. Programs/Simon & Schuster Audio, Concord, Mass., 1997—. Editor (foreign-lang. courses) 30 different Lang.:, author created model for future pimsleur program. Avocations: ice skating, classical music, science fiction. Home: 29 Lexington Rd Concord MA 01742 Office: Pimsleur Lang Programs 30 Monument Sq Concord MA 01742 Office Phone: 978-369-7525 202. Business E-Mail: beverly.heinle@simonandschuster.com.

HEINLE, RICHARD ALAN, lawyer; b. New Kensington, Pa., May 13, 1959; s. Robert Alan and Barbara Jane (Klimeck) H.; m. Sharon Eileen Farrell, Oct. 20, 1990; children: Kelly, Kyra, Casey. AB with highest honors, U. Chgo., 1981; JD cum laude, Georgetown U., 1984. Bar: Ill. 1984, Fla. 1994. Assoc. Arnstein & Lehr, Chgo., 1984-89, Foley & Lardner, Chgo., 1989-93, ptnr. Orlando, Fla., 1994—2003; with Pohl & Short, P.A., Winter Park, Fla., 2003—. Counsel Better Bus. Bur. Ctrl. Fla., Orlando, 1996-2003, bd. dirs., 2003-. Bd. dirs. Better Bus. Bur. Ctrl. Fla., 2003—. Mem.: Fla. C. of C. (bd. dirs. 1999—2000), Mfrs. Assn. Ctrl. Fla. (bd. dirs. 1995—), Phi Beta Kappa. Roman Catholic. Avocations: golf, running. Home: 8100 Vineland Oaks Blvd Orlando FL 32835-8215 Office: Pohl & Short PA 280 W Canton Ste 410 Winter Park FL 32789 Business E-Mail: rheinle@alumni.uchicago.edu.

HEINLEN, DANIEL LEE, alumni organization administrator; b. Columbus, Ohio, Nov. 16, 1937; s. Calvin Xenophon and Charlotte Elizabeth (Lanman) H.; m. Roberta Bishop, Mar. 20, 1966 (div. 1975); m. Gelene Vogel Kozlowski, June 17, 1978; children: Stephanie Heinlen, Kate Kozlowski Isler, Amy Heinlen. BS in Social Work, Ohio State U., 1960. Youth program dir., ext. dir. YMCA, Pitts., 1960-65; field dir. Alumni Assn., Ohio State U., Columbus, 1965-67, assoc. dir., 1967-73, dir. alumni affairs, 1973-92; pres., CEO Ohio State U. Alumni Assn., Inc., Columbus, 1992—2003, pres., CEO emeritus, 2004—; sec. Alumni Assn. Bd., Columbus, 1973—2003; pub. mag. Alumni Assn., Ohio State U., 1973—2003; pres. DLH. LLC, Lewis Center, Ohio, 2004—; sr. consulting v.p. Grenzebach Glier and Assoc., Inc., Chgo., 2004—. Ex-officio trustee Ohio State U. Found.; presdl. search com. Ohio State U., 1990, 97, 2002; trustee Coun. for Advancement and Support of Higher Edn., Washington, 1986-88, 90-94, chmn., 1992-93; chmn. 75th anniversary Colloquium, Columbus, 1988, chmn. ann. assembly alumni track, 1988, chmn. ann. assembly, 1990; chmn. Mgmt. Inst. for Alumni Assn. Execs., Chgo., 1996, pres., 1994-96, bd. dirs., 1988-96; founding bd. Coun. Alumni Assn. Execs. 1989-96, pres. 1992-93; chmn. Univ. ProNet, Inc., Palo Alto, Calif., 1996-99, chmn. alumni dirs. Big Ten, 1973, 84, 93; mem. Ohio State U. Pres.'s Coun., 1991-98; bd. dirs. River Road Hotel Corp.; founding chmn. Self-Governing Alumni Forum, 2000-2003; chmn. task force on alumni advocacy Inter Univ. Coun., 2002. Author chpts. in books. Mem. exec. com. N.W. Ordinance U.S. Constn. Bicentennial Commn., Ohio, 1986-88; bd. dirs. Non-profit Mailers Fedn., Wash., 1985-88; mem. OSU Com. on Student Fin. Aids, Columbus, 1973-99, exec. com. Acad. Disting. Tchg., 1995-2003, Newcomen Soc. N.Am., 1975-90, 93-2003. Recipient Ohio State U. Coll. of Social Work Disting. Svc. award, 1996, Disting. Svc. award CASE, 2003, Disting. Svc. award Dist. 5, 2003, Everett Reese medal Svc. in Philanthropy Ohio State U., 2003, Frank Ashmore award CASE Internat., 2004, Ohio State U. Disting. Svc. award, 2005; named Hon. Trustee Easter Seal Rehab. Ctr. of Ctrl. Ohio, Columbus, 1988-92; D.L. Heinlen award for univ. advocacy named in his honor Ohio Sate U. Alumni Assn., Inc., 1995. Mem. Rotary (bd. dirs. Columbus Club 1986, v.p. 1987-89, pres. 1989-90), Univ. Club (bd. dirs., 2nd v.p. 1985-88, 94-95, 1st v.p. 1996), Faculty Club (mem. bd. control 1978-80, pres.-elect 1999, pres. 2000-01), Kit Kat (exec. com. 1999-2002, sec. 2001—), Golden Key Nat. Honor Soc. (hon.), Sphinx Coun. (convener, 1983-2003). Avocations: tennis, sporting clays. Home and Office: 2981 E Powell Rd Lewis Center OH 43035-9517 Office Phone: 614-885-1713. E-mail: heinlen.4@osu.edu.

HEINLEN, RONALD EUGENE, lawyer; b. Delaware, Ohio, May 28, 1937; s. Carl Elwood and Evelyn Lucille (Scott) H.; m. Mary Pauline Turney, Dec. 28, 1955; children: James Michael, Deborah Lynn, Robert Christopher. AB, Harvard U., 1959, JD, 1962. Bar: Ohio 1962. Assoc. Frost & Jacobs, Cin., 1962-69, ptnr., 1969—. Lectr. Tax Inst. NYU. Contbr. articles to profl. jour. Trustee Cin. Nature Ctr., 1986-95. Fellow Am. Soc. Hosp. Attys.; mem. ABA, Ohio State Bar Assn., Cin. Bar Assn. (chmn. tax sect.), Cin. Country Club, University Club. Office: Frost & Jacobs 2500 PNC Ct 201 E 5th St Ste 2500 Cincinnati OH 45202-4182

HEINLY, MARK DAVID, music educator; b. Boyertown, Pa., June 23, 1960; s. Robert Harvey and Hilda Ruth Heinly; m. Sharalyn Roberts Heinly; children: Matthew Paul, Joshua Daniel, Kaitlyn Alison. MusB, West Chester U., 1978—82; MusM, Towson State U., 1983—90. Orch. dir. Aberdeen H.S., Md., 1983—86, North Harford Elem., Mid. and H.S., Pylesville, Md., 1986—. Home: 5110 Buttermilk Rd Pylesville MD 21132 Office: North Harford HS 211 Pylesville Rd Pylesville MD 21132 Office Phone: 410-638-3650.

HEINRICH, BERND, biologist, educator; b. Bad Polzin, Germany, Apr. 19, 1940; came to U.S., 1950, naturalized, 1958; s. Gerd Hermann and Hildegard Maria (Bury) H. BA in Zoology, U. Maine, 1964, MS in Zoology, 1966; PhD in Zoology, UCLA, 1970; PhD (hon.), U. Maine, 1999, Unity Coll., Maine, 1986, PhD (hon.), 2000. Teaching and research asst. UCLA, 1966-70; asst. prof. entomology U. Calif., Berkeley, 1971-75, assoc. prof., 1975-78, prof., 1978-80; prof. biology U. Vt., Burlington, 1981—2003, prof. emeritus, 2004—. Author: Bumblebee Economics, 1979, Insect Thermoregulation, 1981, In a Patch of Firewood, 1984, One Man's Owl, 1987, Ravens in Winter, 1989, The Hot-Blooded Insects, 1993, A Year in the Maine Woods, 1994, The Thermal Warriors, 1996, The Trees in My Forest, 1998, Mind of the Raven, 1999, Racing the Antelope, 2001, The Winter World, 2003, The Geese of a Beaver Bog, 2003; co-author: Biology, 1979; contbr. numerous articles to sci. jours. Recipient Burroughs, Winship and Rutstrums Author's awards, 1984, 95; Guggenheim fellow, 1976-77, von Humboldt fellow, 1988-89. Mem. Am. Ornithological Union, NAS, Sigma Xi; Fellow Am. Acad. Arts & Sciences. Office: U Vermont Dept Biology Marsh Life Science Bui Burlington VT 05405-0001*

HEINRICH, DANIEL J., chemicals executive; b. Gridley, Calif. BBA, U. Calif., Berkeley, Calif.; MBA, Saint Mary's Coll. CPA. With Ford Fin. Svcs. Group; acct. Ernst and Young; sr. v.p., treas. Transamerica Fin. Corp., San Francisco; controller The Clorox Co., Oakland, Calif., 2001—03, CFO, 2003—. Office: Clorox Co 1221 Broadway Oakland CA 94612-1888

HEINRICH, RANDALL WAYNE, lawyer; b. Houston, Nov. 29, 1958; s. Albert Joseph Sr. and Beverly June Earles; m. Linda Carol Cheek, June 6, 1993; children: Angela Leigh, Conrad Randall. BA, Baylor U., 1980, postgrad., 1981, Rice U., 1981-82; JD, U. Tex., 1985. Bar: Tex. 1985. Assoc. Baker & Botts, Houston, 1985-87, Chamberlain, Hrdlicka, White, Williams & Martin, Houston, 1987-91, Norton & Blair, Houston, 1991-92; mem. Gillis Paris & Heinrich, Houston, 1992—; mng. dir. Baytree Investors, Houston, 1993-97. Mem. dirs.' circle Houston Grand Opera, 1991, The Arts Symposium, 1991, Center Stage, Alley Theater, Houston, 1992-93, Houston Entrepreneurs' Forum, 1990-91; bd. dirs. The Cadre, 1991-92; pres. Exchange Club of Bayou City, 1992-93. Mem. ABA (YLD securities law com. 1993-95, vice chmn. 1994-95), NASD Pool Securities Arbitrators, Am. Arbitration Assn. (mem. nat. panel neutrals), Houston Bar Assn., Forum Club Houston, Phi Delta Theta. Baptist. Home: 4318 Saint Michaels Ct Sugar Land TX 77479-2986 Office: Gillis Paris & Heinrich 8 Greenway Plz Ste 818 Houston TX 77046 Office Phone: 713-951-9100. E-mail: heinrich@pdq.net.

HEINRICHS, APRIL, soccer coach; b. Charlottesville, Va., Feb. 27, 1964; BA in Radio, TV and Motion Pictures, U. N.C., 1986. Lic. U.S. Soccer Federation "A" coaching license. Player U.S. Nat. Team, 1986—91; profl. soccer player Prato, Italy, 1987—92; head coach Princeton U., 1990, U. Md., 1991—95, U. Va., 1996—99; full time asst. U.S. Women's Nat. Team, 1995—97; mem. coaching staff 1995 Women's World Cup, 1995, 1996 Olympic Women's Soccer Team, 1996; head coach U.S. U-16 Nat. Team, 1997—2000; head coach, tech. dir. U.S. Women's Nat. Team, 2000—. Mem. NCAA Championship Team, 1983, 84, 86. Recipient U.S. Soccer Female Athlete of Yr. award, 1986, 89; voted female player of the 1980s Soccer America Magazine; first female inducted into Nat. Soccer Hall of Fame, 1998; named First Team All-American U. N.C. (3 times); inaugural recipient NSCAA Women's Com. award of Excellence, 2000. Achievements include coached U.S. Women's Soccer Team to Silver Medal, Sydney Olympic Games, 2000. Office: US Soccer House 1801-1811 S Prairie Ave Chicago IL 60616

HEINS, ESTHER, artist, illustrator; b. Bklyn, Nov. 10, 1908; d. Israel and Margaret (Brown) Berow; m. Harold Heins; Sept. 8, 1929 (dec. 1987); children: Marilyn Heins, Judith Leet. BS in Edn., Mass. Coll. Art, 1929. Freelance artist, Boston, 1930-60; bot. artist, illustrator plant introductions Arnold Arboretum, Boston, 1960—. Contbr. bot. illustrations to profl. jour.; one-woman shows include Graham Arader Gallery, NYC, Harvard Radcliffe Hilles Libr., Arnold Arboretum, Boston Pub. Libr., Schlesinger Libr., Cambridge, Mass.; group shows include Hunt Inst. for Bot. Documentation, Pitts., Arnold Arboretum, Munich, Germany, Smithsonian, Washington, Oakland, Calif., others; represented in permanent collections at Mus. Fine Arts, Boston, Hunt Inst. for Bot. Documentation, Schlesinger Libr., Radcliffe Coll., Arnold Arboretum, Boston Pub. Libr., Fogg Mus., Cambridge, and numerous others in pvt. collections; illustrator, contbr. essay: (book) Flowering Trees and Shrubs: The Botanical Paintings of Esther Heins, 1987; illustrator many covers Jour. AMA., the most recent 2002. Mem. Guild of Natural Sci. Illustrators. Avocations: attending concerts of Boston Symphony, gardening. Home: 8 Mitchell Rd Marblehead MA 01945-1130

HEINS, JOHN, Internet company executive, former publishing executive; Staff writer Forbes Mag., N.Y.C. and L.A.; asst. to CEO Gruner and Jahr Internat., Paris; pres., CEO Parents Mag., N.Y.C., 1994-2000, Gruner and Jahr USA Pub., N.Y.C., 1994-2000; v.p. sales and internat. ops. Netscape Comm., 2000—01; sr. v.p., gen. mgr., fin. svc. Am. Online, 2001—.

HEINS, SAMUEL DAVID, lawyer; b. Providence, May 31, 1947; s. Maurice Haskell and Hadassah (Wagman) H.; children: Madeleine Sarah, Nora Anne. BA, U. Minn., 1968, JD, 1972. Bar: Minn. 1973, U.S. Dist. Ct. Minn., U.S. Ct. Appeals (8th cir.). Law clk. U.S. Dist. Ct. Minn., Mpls., 1972-73; assoc. Firestone Law Firm, St. Paul, 1973-76; ptnr. Tanick & Heins, Mpls., 1976-89, Opperman & Heins, Mpls., 1989-94, Heins, Mills & Olson, Mpls., 1994—. Vis. asst. prof. Sch. Architecture, U. Minn.-Mpls., 1974-89. Mem. Mpls. Charter Commn., 1983-84; pres. Minn. Lawyers Internat. Human Rights Com., Mpls., 1983-85, Minn. Ctr. for Torture Victims, Mpls., 1985-87, chmn., pres. Mem. ABA, Minn. State Bar Assn. (bd. govs. 1978-84). Office Phone: 612-338-4605. E-mail: sheins@heinmills.com.

HEINSEN, LINDSAY, newspaper editor; b. Berwyn, Ill., May 6, 1950; d. Henry Arthur and Mabel Scott (Witt) H. BA in French Lit., U. Ill., 1972, postgrad., 1972-76. Features editor D Mag., 1977-80; home and design editor Dallas Morning News, 1980-81, arts editor, 1981-89; freelance writer and editor Dallas, 1989-92; fine arts editor Houston Chronicle, 1992—2002, arts & entertainment editor, 2002—. Recipient Matrix award for Best Mag. Feature in Dallas, 1978; James scholar. Mem. Kappa Tau Alpha, Phi Kappa Phi. Office: Houston Chronicle 801 Texas Ave Houston TX 77002-2996

HEINTZ, CAROLINEA CABANISS, retired home economics educator; b. Roanoke, Va., Jan. 19, 1920; d. Luther Bertie and Emblyn Bird (Jennings) Cabaniss; m. Howard Elmer Smith, Dec. 19, 1942 (div. Aug. 1975); children: Emblyn Davis, Cynthia Shannon, Cheryl Peterson, Melyssa Sexton; m. Raymond Walter Heintz, May 21, 1977; 1 stepchild, James. BS in Home Econ. Edn., U. Ala., Tuscaloosa, 1941; vocat. home econ. degree, Montevallo Coll., 1941. Cert. vocat. home econs. tchr. Swimming instr. Camp Mudjekeewis, Centerlovel, Maine, summer 1940; home econs. tchr. Roanoke Pub. Schs., 1941-43; dietitian U. Va., Charlottesville, 1943; nutrition edn. specialist Liberty Health Ctr. Svcs., Liberty Center, Ohio, 1974-80; home economist Dayton Hudson Dept. Store, Toledo, 1980-84; splty . food instr., continuing edn. U. Toledo, 1984-85. Pres., mem. Greater Toledo Nutrition Coun., 1966-98; pres. Sunset House Aux., 1999-2001, bd. dirs. 2001-2005. Co-editor ch. cookbook Loaves and Fishes and Other Dishes, 2000. Spkr. United Way, Toledo, 1965-90; founder, pres. Mobile Meals Toledo, Inc., 1968-71, mem. adv. bd., 1988-95, 2001-05, bd. dirs., 2005, chmn. pub. rels., 1997-99, nominating com., 2000-04, Spirit of Mobile Meals award, 1998; affiliate mem. Arts Commn., Toledo, 1976-77; chmn. Saphire Ball, Toledo Symphony Orch., Toledo Opera, 1978; adminstrv. coord. Feed Your Neighbor program Met. Chs. United, Toledo, 1979-86; deacon Collingwood Presbyn. Ch., 1969-71, elder, 1972-74, 77-79, 97-99, 2001-05, trustee, 1984-86, elder, clk. of session, 1991-94, stewardship chmn., 1996-97, del. to Maumee Valley Presbytery, 1991-99; mem. steering com. Interfiath Hospitality Network, 1992-94, bd. dirs., 1993-94; alt. del. Gen. Assembly Presbyn. Ch. U.S.A., 1993, del.-commr., 1994. Recipient Woman of Toledo award St. Vincent Hosp. and Med. Ctr. Guild, 1967, 80, Outstanding Community Svc. award United Way, 1987, Henry Morse vol. award, Greater Toledo award United Way, 1998, runner-up Nat. Vol. of the Year award Project Meal Found., Reynolds Metal Co., 1998. Mem. AAUW (bd. dirs. 1974-76, 94-96, 97-98, chmn. mem. gourmet group 1966-99, 2001, 03, edn. found. chmn. 1994-96, book sale chmn. 1998, chair nominating com. 2005), Ohio Med. Aux. (1st v.p. 1973-74), Aux. Acad. Medicine (pres. 1967-68, chmn. edn. gourmet group 1966-99, 2001-03, Health Care award 1974), Indian Trails Garden Club (pres. 1997-98), Sigma Kappa (various alumni offices). Republican. Avocations: volunteering, gourmet cooking, travel, entertaining, bridge. Home: # 108 4030 Indian Rd Toledo OH 43606-2225

HEINTZ, FLORENT M., art appraiser; ThM, Harvard Univ., 1993, PhD in Classical Archaeology, 1999. Keeper of coins Harvard Univ. Art Mus.; curatorial asst. Worcester Art Mus, Mass.; antiquities specialist to asst. v.p. Sotheby's, NYC, 2001—. Author: Agnostic Magic in the Late Antique Circus, 1999. Named a Dumbarton Oaks Jr. Fellow, Harvard Univ., 1998—99. Office: Sotheby's NY 1334 York Ave New York NY 10021 Office Phone: 212-606-7266. Office Fax: 212-894-1371. Business E-Mail: florent.heintz@sothebys.com.

HEINTZ, JOHN EDWARD, lawyer; b. Bronxville, N.Y., Dec. 12, 1948; s. Howard Theodore and Ruth Janet (Brodhead) Heintz; m. Lynn Ann Ohman, June 21, 1980; children: Eric John, Jennifer Ann. BA, Cornell U., 1970; MPA, Princeton U., 1974; JD, NYU, 1977. Assoc. Covington & Burling, Washington, 1977-86; shareholder Popham, Haik, Schnobrich & Kaufman, Ltd., Washington, 1986-91; ptnr. Howrey, Simon, Arnold & White, LLP, Washington, 1991-2000, Gilbert Heintz & Randolph LLP, Washington, 2000—. Contbr. articles to profl. jours. Democrat. Avocations: sailing, swimming. Office: Gilbert Heintz & Randolph LLP Ste 700 1100 New York Ave NW Washington DC 20005-3987 E-mail: heintzj@ghrdc.com.

HEINTZLEMAN, RACHEL S., psychologist; b. Harrisburg, Pa. d. Jeffrey Heintzleman and Cynthia Minnich. BS in Psychology, Pa. State U., Middletown, 1999; post grad., Millersville U., Pa., 0199—. Cert. sch. psychologist Pa. Sch. psychologist Harrisburg City Sch. Dist., Pa., 2002—. Mobile therapist and behavior specialist Edgewater Psychiatric Svcs., Harrisburg, Pa., 2003—. Mem.: Nat. Assn. Sch. Psychologists. Independent. Roman Catholic. Avocation: travel.

HEINZ, E(DWARD) RALPH, neuroradiologist, educator; b. Cleve., Sept. 8, 1929; s. Edwin George and Gail (Reeve) H.; m. Ann McCardle, June 19, 1976; children: Tad, Christopher, Dana, Lindsey. AB, W.Va. U., 1951; MD, U. Pa., Phila., 1955. Diplomate Am. Bd. Radiology, 1963. Intern Phila. Gen. Hosp., 1955-56; resident in internal medicine U. Calif., San Francisco, 1958-59; NIH fellow in neuroradiology Neurol. Inst. Columbia U., N.Y.C., 1962-67; asst. prof. radiology Emory U., Atlanta, 1964-66, assoc. prof. radiology, 1967, Yale U., New Haven, 1967-69; prof., chmn. radiology U. Pitts., 1969-77, prof. radiology, 1977-78; chief divsn. neuroradiology Duke U. Hosp., Durham, N.C., 1978—; prof. radiology Duke U., Durham, N.C., 1978—. Mem Com. A, Neurol. Scis. Rsch. & Tng. Com., Nat. Inst. Neurol. Diseases and Stroke NIH, Bethesda, Md., 1966-79, mem. Neurol. Disorders Program Project Com., 1975-79. Editor: Clinical Neurosciences Part 4 Neuroradiology, 1984; assoc. editor Archives of Neurology, 1975-80; contbr. over 150 articles to profl. publs. concerning angiography, myelography, computed tomography, and magnetic resonance applications to diagnostic neuroradiology. Sr. asst. surgeon USPHS, 1956-58. Fellow Am. Coll. Radiology; mem. Am. Soc. Neuroradiology (v.p. 1975-76, Gold medal 2004), Am. Soc. Pediat. Neuroradiology (founding), Durham-Chapel Hill Torch Club. Republican. Achievements include development of C1-2 spinal fluid puncture used in neuroradiology. Office: Duke Univ Hosp Box 3808 Erwin Rd Durham NC 27710 E-mail: Heinz003@mc.duke.edu.

HEINZ, JOHN PETER, lawyer, educator; b. Carlinville, Ill., Aug. 6, 1936; s. William Henry and Margaret Louise (Denby) H.; m. Anne Murray, Jan. 14, 1967; children: Katherine Reynolds, Peter Lindley Murray. AB, Washington U., St. Louis, 1958; LLB, Yale U., 1962. Bar: D.C. 1962, Ill. 1966, U.S. Supreme Ct. 1967. Teaching asst. polit. sci. Washington U., St. Louis, 1958-59, instr., 1960; asst. prof. Northwestern U. Sch. Law, Chgo., 1965-68, assoc. prof., 1968-71, prof., 1971-88, Owen L. Coon prof., 1988—, dir. program law and social scis., 1968-70, dir. rsch., 1973-74, prof. sociology, 1987—. Affiliated scholar Am. Bar Found., Chgo., 1974—, vis. scholar, 1974-76, exec. dir., 1982-86, disting. research fellow, 1987—. Author: (with A. Gordon) Public Access to Information, 1979, (with E. Laumann) Chicago Lawyers, 1982, rev. edit., 1994, (with E. Laumann, R. Nelson, R. Salisbury) The Hollow Core, 1993, (with R. Nelson, R. Sandefur and E. Laumann) Urban Lawyers, 2005; contbr. articles to profl. jours. Served to capt. USAF, 1962-65 Grantee NIMH, 1970-72, NSF, 1970, 78-81, 84-86, 94-97, CNA Found., 1972, Am. Bar Found., 1974—, Russell Sage Found., 1978-80. Fellow: Am. Bar Found.; mem.: ABA, Chgo. Coun. Lawyers, Law and Soc. Assn. (Harry Kalven prize for disting. rsch. 1987). Home: 525 Judson Ave Evanston IL 60202-3083 Office: Northwestern U Sch Law 357 E Chicago Ave Chicago IL 60611-3059 Office Phone: 312-503-8473. Business E-Mail: j-heinz@law.northwestern.edu.

HEINZ, WILLIAM DENBY, lawyer; b. Carlinville, Ill., Nov. 26, 1947; s. William Henry and Margaret (Denby) H.; children: Kimberly, Rebecca, Elizabeth; m. Catherine Lamb Heinz. BS, Millikin U., 1969; JD, U. Ill., 1973. Bar: Ill. 1973, U.S. Dist. Ct. (no. dist.) Ill. 1974, U.S. Ct. Appeals (3d cir.) 1982, U.S. Ct. Appeals (5th cir.) 1973, U.S. Ct. Appeals (7th cir.) 1976, U.S. Supreme Ct. 1979. Law clk. to judge U.S. Ct. Appeals (5th cir.), Tuscaloosa, Ala., 1973-74; assoc. Jenner & Block, Chgo., 1974-80, ptnr., 1980—; mem. faculty NITA, 1981—. Adj. prof. Northwestern U. Sch. Law, 1995—; mem. bd. dir. The North Am. Co. for Life and Health Ins., 2002—; bd. visitors U. Ill. Coll. Law, 1990-93, pres.'s coun. U. Ill.; bd. dirs., chair Legal Aid Bur., Chgo.; bd. dirs. exec. com. Met. Family Svcs. Chgo; mem, bd. dirs. Ptnrs Fin. Holdings, Inc., 2003—. Recipient Disting. Grad. award U. Ill. Coll. Law, 1995. Fellow Am. Coll. Trial Lawyers; mem. ABA, Ill. Bar Assn. (civil practice and procedure sect. coun., com. on liaison with Ill. ARDC, task force on multi-disciplinary practice), Chgo. Bar Assn. (jud. evaluation com. 1990-93), ARDC Ill. Profl. Responsibility Inst., Cribbett Soc., U. Ill. Coll. Law, Legal Club (bd. dirs. 1998-2000), Westmoreland Country Club. Home: 437 Sheridan Rd Kenilworth IL 60043-1220 Office: Jenner & Block 1 E Ibm Plz Fl 46 Chicago IL 60611-3586 Office Phone: 312-923-2763. E-mail: wheinz@jenner.com.

HEINZELMAN, KRIS F., lawyer; b. Monroe, Wis., Jan. 9, 1951; AB, MA magna cum laude, Brown U., 1973; JD, Yale U., 1976. Bar: N.Y. 1977. Assoc. Cravath, Swain & Moore, N.Y.C., 1976—83, ptnr., corp. dept, 1983—. Named one of 12 Dealmakers of the Yr., The Am. Lawyer, 2004. Mem.: ABA, Am. Coll. Investment Counsel, Assn. of the Bar of the City of N.Y., N.Y. State Bar Assn. Office: Cravath Swain & Moore Worldwide Plz 825 8th Ave Fl 38 New York NY 10019-7475 also: 1 Chase Manhattan Plz New York NY 10005-1401 Office Phone: 212-474-1336. Office Fax: 212-474-3700. Business E-Mail: kheinzelman@cravath.com.

HEINZEN, BERNARD GEORGE, lawyer; b. Hendricks, Minn., Sept. 18, 1930; s. Bernard Martin and Thelma Harrington (Bowers) H.; m. Maryann Mullen, Aug. 25, 1978; children from previous marraige: John Masters, Robert Kenneth (dec.), James Warren, William Martin. BA, Carleton Coll., 1953; LLB, NYU, 1956. Bar: Minn. 1956, U.S. Supreme Ct. 1969, Pa. 1978. Atty., legal adviser U.S. Dept. State, Washington, 1956-58; assoc. Dorsey & Whitney, Mpls., 1960-65, ptnr., 1966-76; spl. asst. atty. gen. State of Minn., St. Paul, 1967-70; gen. counsel Consol. Rail Corp., Phila., 1976-77; counsel Harvey, Pennington, Herting & Renneisen, Ltd., Phila., 1977-83; pres. Bernard G. Heinzen, Ltd., Phila., 1978—2004; ptnr. Stassen, Kostos & Mason, Phila., 1983-85; pres., bd. dirs. Rittenhouse Town Watch, Inc., Phila., 1993—; gen. counsel Logan Capital Mgmt., Inc., Ardmore, 1995—. Dir. Chamber Orch. of Phila., 1995—; adviser U.S. del. to Geneva Conf. on Law of Sea, 1958. Contbr. Stanford Law Rev., 1959; assoc. editor NYU Law Rev., 1955-56. Mem. Citizens Com. on Pub. Edn., Mpls., 1964-76; exec. com. state cen. com. Minn. Rep. Party, 1967-71; vestryman The Ch. of the Holy Trinity, Phila., 1998—. 1st lt. U.S. Army, 1957-60. Mem. ABA, Phila. Bar Assn., Minn. Bar Assn. (chmn. com. on ins. 1970-73), Am. Judicature Soc. (life), Racquet Club Phila., Union League Phila., Phi Beta Kappa. Republican. Episcopalian. Home: 1901 Walnut St Philadelphia PA 19103-4640 Office: 6 Coulter Ave Suburban Sw Ardmore PA 19003-2308

HEINZERLING, LARRY EDWARD, communications executive; b. Elyria, Ohio, Aug. 28, 1945; s. Lynn Louis and Agnes Corinne (Dengate) H.; m. Sharyn Lee Jorgensen, Jan. 11, 1969 (div. 1985); children: Jesse, Kristen, Benjamin; m. Sieglinde Wolf, Aug. 1, 1985 (dec. Mar. 1998); stepchildren: Andreas Klohnen, Eva Klohnen; m. Ann Kathleen Cooper, May 12, 2001; 1 stepchild: Tom Keller. BA in Polit. Sci., Journalism, Ohio Wesleyan U., 1967; MA in Internat. Journalism, Ohio State U., 1969. Reporter AP, Columbus, Ohio, 1969-71, corr. Lagos, Nigeria, 1971-74, bur. chief Johannesburg, South Africa, 1974-78, mng. dir. Frankfurt, Germany, 1978-83, dir. world services N.Y.C., 1983-87; dep. dir. AP World Svc., N.Y.C., 1987-2000, also spl. asst. to AP pres., dep. internat. editor, 2000—. News coverage includes: coverage West Africa including Sahel drought, 1971-74, coverage Soweto riots, Mozambique independence, Angola, Rhodesia (now Zimbabwe); co-editor: Fundamental Analysis Worldwide: Investing and Managing Money in International Capital Markets, 1996. Trustee Ohio Wesleyan U., 1993-96, Bancroft, Inc., 1993-97, Bancroft Schs. and Cmtys., 1997-2002. Recipient Headliners award Headliners Club, Atlantic City, 1977, AP reportorial Performance award Mng. Editors, N.Y.C., 1977; nominated for Pulitzer Prize, 1976. Mem. Phi Delta Theta. Roman Catholic. Avocations: foreign affairs, history, philosophy, science. Office: AP 50 Rockefeller Plz New York NY 10020-1605 Business E-Mail: lheinzerling@ap.org.

HEINZ KERRY, TERESA F., foundation administrator; b. Mozambique, Oct. 5, 1938; d. Jose Simoes Ferreira and Irene Thierstein; m. John Heinz, 1966 (dec. 1991); children: John, Andre, Christopher; m. John Kerry, 1995; stepchildren: Alex, Vanessa. BA in Romance Langs., Lit., U. Witwatersrand, Johannesburg, South Africa, 1960; grad., U. Geneva, 1963; PhD (hon.), Beloit Coll., Wis., Bank ST. Coll. Edn., N.Y., Drexel U., Pa., Med. Coll. Pa. Cons. UN Trusteeship, NYC; chmn. Heinz Family Found., Pitts., Howard Heinz Endowment; trustee Vira I. Heinz Endowment; founder Women's Inst. for Secure retirement, 1996—. Endowed creation of professorship environ. mgmt. Harvard Bus. Sch., chair environ. policy John F. Kennedy Sch. Govt.; vice chair Environ. Def.; past mem. external adv. bd. Inst. Biospheric Studies, Yale U.; mem. adv. bd. Earth Comm. Office; founder Second Nature; co-founder, bd. dirs. Alliance to End Childhood Lead Poisoning; bd. dirs. Carnegie Corp., Family Comm.; trustee Brookings Inst.; former bd. dirs., trustee Phillips Exeter Acad., St. Paul's Sch., Georgetown U.; co-founder Nat. Coun. Families TV; featured speaker Dem. Nat. Convention, Boston, 2004. Founding mem., co-chair Congl. Wives Soviet Jewry; trustee governing bd. Yale Art Gallery; mem. trustees coun. Nat. Gallery Art; bd. dirs. Carnegie Inst., Pitts. Women's Leadership award, Save the Children Found., 2003, World Ecology award, Internat. Ctr. for Tropical Ecology, U. Mo., 2003, Albert Schweitzer Gold medal for Humanitarianism, John Hopkins U., 2003. Fellow: Am. Acad. Arts and Sciences. Avocation: art collecting. Office: Heinz Family Offices Ste 619 1201 Pennsylvania Ave NW Washington DC 20004-2401

HEIPLE, JAMES DEE, state supreme court justice; b. Peoria, Ill., Sept. 13, 1933; s. Rae Crane and Harriet (Birkett) H.; B.S., Bradley U., 1955; J.D., U. Louisville, 1957; Certificate in Internat. Law, City of London Coll., 1967; grad. Nat. Jud. Coll., 1971; LLM U. Va., 1988; m. Virginia Kerswill, July 28, 1956 (dec. Apr. 16, 1995); children: Jeremy Hans, Jonathan James, Rachel Duffield. Bar: Ill. 1957, Ky. 1958, U.S. Supreme Ct. 1962; partner Heiple and Heiple, Pekin, Ill., 1957-70; circuit judge Ill., 10th Circuit 1970-80; justice Ill. Appellate Ct., 1980-90; justice Ill. Supreme Ct., 1990—, ret., 2000. V.p., dir. Washington State Bank (Ill.), 1959-66; dir. Gridley State Bank (Ill.), 1958-59; village atty., Tremont, Ill., 1961-66, Mackinaw, Ill., 1961-66; asst. pub. defender Tazewell County, 1967-70., jud. clerk Ill. Appellate Ct., 1968-70. Chmn. Tazewell County Heart Fund, 1960. Pub. Adminstr. Tazewell County, Ill., 1959-61; sec. Tazewell County Republican Central Com. 1966-70; mem. Pekin Sch. Bd., 1970; mem. Ill. Supreme Ct. Com. on Profl. Responsibility, 1978-86. Recipient certificate Freedoms Found., 1975, George Washington honor medal, 1976, Bradley Centurion award Bradley U., 1995; named Disting. Alumnus, U. Louisville, 1992. Fellow ABA (life), Ill. Bar Found. (life), Ky. Bar Found. (life); mem. Ky., Ill. (chmn. legal edn. com. 1972-74, chmn. jud. sect. 1976-77, chmn. Bench and Bar Council 1984-85), Tazewell County Bar Assn. (pres. 1967-68), Ill. Judges Assn. (pres. 1978-79), Ky., Ill., Pa. hist. socs., S.A.R., War of 1812, Sons of Union Vets., Delta Theta Phi, Sigma Nu, Pi Kappa Delta. Methodist. Clubs: Filson; Union League (Chgo.), Country (Peoria). Lodge: Masons (33 degree). Office: PO Box 10495 Peoria IL 61612-0495 Office Phone: 309-689-0592. Business E-Mail: jamesdheiple@insightbb.com.

HEIRMAN, DONALD NESTOR, training engineering company executive, consultant; b. Mishawaka, Ind., Aug. 16, 1940; s. Chester J. and Agnes M. Heirman; m. Lois M. Heirman. BSEE, Purdue U., 1962, MSEE, 1963. Mem. tech. staff, then disting. mem. tech. staff AT&T Bell Labs., Holmdel, N.J., 1963-83; mem. tech. staff Am. Bell, Holmdel, 1983-84; supr. AT&T Info. Systems, Holmdel, 1984-88; mgr. global product compliance lab. AT&T Bell Labs., Holmdel, 1989-1996, Lucent Technologies Inc., 1996-97; adj. prof., sr. rsch. scientist, assoc. dir. wireless EMC Ctr. for Study of Wireless EMC, U. Okla., 1997—. Cons. in field, 1998—; course dir. Ctr. for Profl. Advancment, East Brunswick, N.J., 1988—; mem. exec. and tech. mgmt. coms. U.S. Nat. Com. IEC, 1995—; U.S. tech. expert subcoms. (SC) A and I, Internat. Spl. Com. on Radio Interference (CISPR), 1986—; sec. SC A, 1998-2000, chair, 2000--; chmn. SC A, WG1, 1998-2002; chmn. Am. Nat. Stds. Inst. Accredited Stds. Com. C63, vice chair, 2002—, chair Subcom. 1, 1986—; pres. Nat. Coop. for Lab. Accreditation, 1999-2001. Contbr. articles to profl. jours. Cmdr. USNR, 1963—85, ret, . Named Disting. Mem. Tech. Staff, AT&T Bell Labs., 1982. Fellow IEEE (stds. bd. 1990-2003, vice chmn. 1998-99, chmn. 2000-2001, bd. govs. 2001—, pres.-elect 2004, Centennial medal 1984, Disting. Svc. award 1993, Charles Proteus Steinmetz award 1996-97, Millennium medal 2000); mem. IEEE Electromagnetic Compatibility Soc. (bd. 1981-93, 97-99, pres. 1980-81, chmn. stds. com. 1982-2000, v.p. for stds. 1997—, Laurence G. Cumming award 1986, Stoddart award 1995), Am. Nat. Stds. Inst (Finegan medal, 2003). Office: Don Heirman Consultants 143 Jumping Brook Rd Lincroft NJ 07738-1442

HEIRTZLER, JAMES RANSOM, geophysicist; b. Baton Rouge, Sept. 16, 1925; s. William Ransom and Jimmie Lemon (Clark) H.; m. Phyllis Virginia Trossen, Feb. 7, 1951 (div. July 1986); children: Fenton Ransom, Jason Dean; m. Katherine Alexandrovna Nazarova, Apr. 5, 1991; 1 stepchild, Ilya Nazarov. BS, La. State U., 1947, MS, 1948; PhD, NYU, 1953. Asst. prof. Am. U. Beirut, 1953-56; sr. physicist Gen. Dynamics Corp., Rochester, NY, 1956-59; sr. rsch. assoc. Lamont-Doherty Geol. Obs., Palisades, NY, 1959-67; dir. Hudson Labs. Columbia U., Dobbs Ferry, NY, 1967-69; chmn. dept. geology and geophysics Woods Hole (Mass.) Oceanog. Inst., 1969-76, sr. scientist, 1976-86; head geology and geomagnatism br. NASA Goddard Space Flight Ctr., Greenbelt, Md., 1986-91, staff scientist geophysics, 1991—2004, emeritus scientist, 2004—. Co-organizer workshop on geomagnetism in the study of earth's interior, Pune, India, 1994; chief scientist various oceanog. cruises, 1959-76. Editor: Understanding the Mid-Atlantic Ridge-A Comprehensive Program, Indian Ocean Geology and Biostratigraphy, Initial Reports of the Deep Sea Drilling Project Vol. 46, Initial Reports of the Deep Sea Drilling Project Vol. 27; dir. (movie) Where the Earth Turns Inside Out; contbr. over 165 sci. papers, reports atlases to profl. publs. With USN, 1942-44, PTO. Recipient citation classic award Inst. Sci. Found., Inc., 1980, Otto Schmidt medal Inst. Physics Earth, Moscow, 1994. Fellow AAAS, Geol. Soc. Am., Am. Geophys. Union (various editl. positions 1984-89); mem. Am. Inst. Physics (bd. govs. 1990-93). Achievements include research in microfossil Pithonella heirtzleri, Antarctic topographic feature Heirtzler Ice Piedmont, and Heirtzler Fracture Zone in South Pacific Ocean. Home: 1607 Hugo Cir Silver Spring MD 20906-5921 Office: NASA Goddard Space Flight Ctr Code 920 Greenbelt MD 20771-0001

HEISE, JOHN IRVIN, JR., lawyer; b. Balt., Dec. 13, 1924; s. John Irvin and Ruby Belle (Carpenter) H.; m. Jacqueline Mosey Morley, Sept. 3, 1949; children: John Irvin III, Liane Des Roches, Jeff Howard, Suzanne Wolfrom. AB, U. Md., 1947; JD, U. Va., 1950. Bar: Md. 1950, D.C. 1953, U.S. Supreme Ct. 1962. Trial atty. civil divsn. Dept. Justice, Washington, 1950-52; assoc. Shea Greenman Gardner & McConnaughey, Washington, 1952-57; ptnr. Heise Jorgensen & Stefanelli, P.A., Silver Spring, Md., Gaithersburg, Md., 1957, 1968—. Committeeman, merit badge counselor, dist. chmn. sustaining mem. dr. Boy Scouts Am.; chmn. Md. Ednl. Found., Inc., 1972-92. Maj. USAF, 1942-45. Recipient Gottwals award U. Md., 1978. Mem. ABA, Fed. Bar Assn., Md. Bar Assn., D.C. Bar Assn., Montgomery County Bar Assn., Md. Alumni Assn. (pres. 1966-67), Terrapin (pres. 1961-62), Omicron Delta Kappa, Phi Kappa Phi. Republican. Episcopalian. Office Phone: 301-258-0400. E-mail: heisejacks@aol.com.

HEISE, STEVEN ANTHONY, surveyor, consultant; b. Arnprior, Ontario, Can., Apr. 21, 1964; s. Gerald William and Barbara Marie Heise; m. Marcia Christine Hanes, Oct. 10, 1987; children: Alix Ashley, Connor William Anthony. Civil engring., Loyalist; geomatics, Brit. Columbia Inst. ASCT. Pres. Heise Cons., Ottawa, Canada, 1987—97; surveyor Eagle Mapping, Vancouver, 1997—99, Naismith Engring., Inc., Corpus Christi, Tex., 1999—2001, Cmty. Land Surveying, Lincoln, Nebr., 2001—03, Algert Engring., Inc., Chula Vista, Calif., 2003—. Profl. spkr. Robbins Rsch., Los Angeles, 1993—96. Recipient Cert. of Achievement, ASTT, 1999. Christian. Achievements include use of global positioning system for land surveying and telecommunications. Avocations: golf, kayaking, hiking, bicycling, surfing. Office: Algert Engring, Inc 428 Broadway Chula Vista CA 91910 Personal E-mail: sheisecls@aol.com.

HEISER, ARNOLD MELVIN, astronomer; b. Bklyn., Feb. 9, 1933; s. Hyman Samuel and Sadie (Kretchmer) H.; m. Vivian Carol Jacobs, June 6, 1964; children: Naomi Elizabeth, David Alan. AB, Ind. U., 1954, MA, 1956; PhD, U. Chgo., 1961. Rsch. asst. Ind. U., 1954-56; rsch. fellow U. Chgo., 1956-61; asst. prof. physics and astronomy Vanderbilt U., Nashville, 1961-66, assoc. prof., 1966-99, prof. emeritus, 1999—. Dir. A.J. Dyer Obs., 1972-86; H. Shapley vis. prof. Am. Astron. Soc., 1969—. Subscriptions editor Comms. of the Internat. Amateur-Profl. Photoelectric Photometry, 1993-99; contbr. articles to profl. jours. Mem. Am. Astron. Soc., Internat. Astron. Union, Tenn. Acad. Sci., Sigma Xi. Home: 6132 Gardendale Dr Nashville TN 37215-5602 Office: Vanderbilt Univ Dyer Obser 1000 Oman Dr Brentwood TN 37027-4143 Office Phone: 615-373-4897. E-mail: a.heiser@vanderbilt.edu.

HEISER, CHARLES BIXLER, JR., botany educator; b. Cynthiana, Ind., Oct. 5, 1920; s. Charles Bixler and Inez (Metcalf) H.; m. Dorothy Gaebler, Aug. 19, 1944; children— Lynn Marie, Cynthia Ann, Charles Bixler III, Leslie Nosier Dakins. AB, Washington U., St. Louis, 1943, MA, 1944; PhD, U. Calif. at Berkeley, 1947. Instr. Washington U., St. Louis, 1944-45; assoc. botany U. Calif. at Davis, 1946-47; mem. faculty Ind. U., Bloomington, 1947—, prof. botany, 1957—, Disting. prof., 1979-86, disting. prof. emeritus, 1986—. Author: Nightshades, The Paradoxical Plants, 1969, Seed to Civilization, The Story of Man's Food, 1973, The Sunflower, 1976, The Gourd Book, 1979, Of Plants and People, 1985, Weeds in my Garden, 2003. Guggenheim fellow, 1953; NSF Sr. Postdoctoral fellow, 1962; recipient Pustovoit award Internat. Sunflower Assn., 1985. Mem. Am. Soc. Plant Taxonomists (pres. 1967, Asa Gray award 1988, Raven Outreach award 2002), Bot. Soc. Am. (Merit award 1972, pres. 1980), Soc. Study Evolution (pres. 1974), Soc. Econ. Botany (pres. 1978, Disting. Econ. Botanist 1984), Nat. Acad. Scis., Phi Beta Kappa, Sigma Xi. Achievements include research and numerous publications on systematics flowering plants, natural and artificial hybridization, origin cultivated plants. Home: 605 Bell Trace Ct Bloomington IN 47408-4410 E-mail: cbheiser@bio.indiana.edu.

HEISER, DEBORAH SUE, geriatrics services professional, researcher; d. Larry Joe and Mildred Mary Heiser; m. Joel Lee Weinberger, June 27, 2002; 1 child, Liam Heiser Weinberger. BA, Purchase Coll. SUNY, 1996; PhD, Fordham U., 2003. Rsch. asst. N.Y. Hosp./Cornell-Weill, White Plains, NY, 1996—97, asst. mgr. clin. core, 1997—98; rschr. Isabella Geriatric Ctr., N.Y., 2002—. Co-editor: Spiritual Assessment and Intervention with Older Adults: Current Directions and Applications, 2005. Recipient Nat. Excellence in Student Rsch. award, Psychologists in Long Term Care, 2003. Mem.: APA, Ea. Psychol. Assn., Psychologists in Long Term Care, State Soc. Aging N.Y. (conf. chmn. 2003, mem. exec. bd. 2003—05), Sigma Xi. Office Phone: 212-342-9392. Office Fax: 212-342-9876. E-mail: dheiser@isabella.org.

HEISER, JAMES S., manufacturing executive; b. 1956; BA in Econs., U. Va.; JD, Stanford U. Asst. gen. counsel, v.p. Ducommun Inc., Long Beach, Calif., 1985—96, gen. counsel, treas., CFO, 1996—. Office: Ducommun Inc 23301 Wilmington Ave Carson CA 90745 Office Phone: 310-513-7280. E-mail: jheiser@ducommun.com.

HEISER, ROLLAND VALENTINE, former army officer, foundation administrator; b. Columbus, Ohio, Apr. 25, 1925; s. Rudolph and Helen Cecile H.; m. Gwenne Kathleen Duquemin, Feb. 26, 1949; children: Helen Heiser Sanford, Charlene Heiser Wolff. BS, U.S. Mil. Acad., 1947; MS in Internat. Affairs, George Washington U., 1965. Commd. 2nd lt. U.S. Army, 1947; advanced through grades to lt. gen., 1976; army planner Washington, 1973-74; comdr. 1st Armored divsn. Germany, 1974-75; chief of staff U.S. Army, Europe, 1975-76, U.S. European Command, 1976—78; ret., 1978; pres. New Coll. Found., Sarasota, Fla., 1979—2003. Trustee New Coll. Fla., New Coll. Found. Decorated D.S.M. with oak leaf cluster, Def. Superior Svc. medal, Legion of Merit (3), Bronze Star, others. Mem.: Mil. Officers Assn., Greater Sarasota C. of C., Sarasota Devel. Com. 100, Ret. Officers Sarasota (past pres., dir.), Masons. Republican. Episcopalian. Home: 4104 Las Palmas Way Sarasota FL 34238-4532 E-mail: rrh2@comcast.net.

HEISER, WALTER CHARLES, librarian, priest, educator; b. Milw., Mar. 16, 1922; s. Walter Matthew and Lauretta Katherine (Kopmeier) H. AB, St. Louis U., 1945, AM, 1947, STL, 1955; MSLS, Cath. U. Am., 1959. Ordained priest Roman Cath. Ch., 1953. Latin tchr. St. Louis U. HS, 1947-50; div. libr. St. Louis U., 1955—; mem. faculty dogmatic systematic theology St. Louis U. Div. Sch., 1966-92; ret. Cons. catalog Cath. supplement Wilson Sr. HS Libr., 1968—77. Editor (Rev.): (digest) Theology Digest, 1963. Mem.: Mem. Cath. Libr. Assn. Home: 3601 Lindell Blvd Saint Louis MO 63108-3301 Office: 3650 Lindell Blvd Saint Louis MO 63108-3302 Business E-Mail: heiserwc@slu.edu.

HEISERMAN, ROBERT GIFFORD, lawyer; b. El Paso, July 5, 1946; s. Robert Gifford and Nancy Mildred (Wardlow) H.; m. Nancy Fay Price, Oct. 20, 1973; 1 child, Laura. BA, U. Oreg., 1968; JD, U. Denver, 1971. Bar: Ct. Colo. 1972, US Dist. Ct. Colo. 1972, US Dist. Ct. N.Mex. 1972, US Dist. Ct. DC 1972, US Dist. Ct. (so. dist.) Ala. 1974, US Ct. Appeals (10th cir.) 1975, US Supreme Ct. 1976. Legis. draftsman N.Mex. Legislature, Santa Fe, 1972-73; pvt. practice Santa Fe, 1973, Denver, 1974—. Adj. prof. immigration and nationality law and profl. responsibility courses U. Denver, 1981—. Active Emergency Med. Svc. Coun., Denver, 1981—84. Mem. ABA, Am. Immigration Lawyers Assn. (nat. bd. gov., chmn. profl. ethics and grievances com. 1982-89, 98-2000, founder Colo. chpt., treas. Colo. chpt. 1978-81), Colo. Bar Assn., Denver Bar Assn., DC Bar Assn. Democrat. Methodist. Office: 1675 Broadway Ste 2280 Denver CO 80202-4675 Home: Ste 2280 1675 Broadway Denver CO 80202-4675 E-mail: info@heiserman.com.

HEISKELL, MARIAN SULZBERGER (MRS. ANDREW HEISKELL), newspaper executive, civic worker; b. N.Y.C., Dec. 31, 1918; d. Arthur Hays and Iphigene (Ochs) Sulzberger; m. Orvil Eugene Dryfoos, July 8, 1941 (dec. May 1963); children: Jacqueline Hays, Robert Ochs, Susan Warms; m. Andrew Heiskell, Jan. 30, 1965. Grad., Frobeleague Kindergarten Tng. Sch., N.Y.C., 1941; LL.D. (hon.), Poly. Inst. N.Y., 1974, Dartmouth Coll., 1975. Dir. N.Y. Times Co., 1963—; Bd. dirs. N.Y.C. Partnership; chmn. Council on Environment N.Y.C.; bd. dirs. Regional Plan Assn., Inc.; bd. mgrs., exec. com. N.Y. Bot. Garden; mem. State Park and Recreation Commn. for City N.Y.; bd. dirs. Nat. Audubon Soc.; trustee Parks Council, Consol. Edison Co. N.Y., Inc.; co-chmn. We Care About N.Y., Inc. Dir. Ford Motor Co., Merck & Co., Inc. Recipient Mrs. Lyndon B. Johnson ann. award Keep Am. Beautiful, 1974; with husband) Disting. Service award Citizens Union, 1975 Home: 870 Un Plz New York NY 10017: 237 Long Neck Point Rd Darien CT 06820-5817 Office: Room 1031 NY Times 229 W 43rd St New York NY 10036-3913

HEISLER, ELWOOD DOUGLAS, hotel executive; b. Wilmington, Del., June 29, 1935; s. Elwood Dean and Laura Matilda (Hutchison) H. BA, Mich. State U., 1957; postgrad., Johns Hopkins U., 1979—. Asst. mgr. Kents Restaurants, Atlantic City, 1957; innkeeper Treadway Inns Corp., NY and Mass., 1960—68, Holiday Inns, Inc., Lansing and Troy, Mich., 1969—77; gen. mgr. Quality Inns, Inc., Towson, Md., 1977—89, Quality Suites Hotel, Mt. Laurel, NJ, 1989—94, Accor Hotels, Windsor Locks, Conn., 1994—98, Best Western Inn on River, Niagara Falls, NY, 1999, Milner Hotel, Boston, 1999—2001, Wellesley (Mass.) Travel Inn, 2001—02, Wellesley Inn On-the-Square, 2002—. Author manual for resort ops., 1965, The Rising Sun of the Japanese Hotel Industry, 1980. Sec. Md. adv. coun. Future Bus. Leaders Am.; bd. dirs. Gunpowder Youth Camps, Inc.; mem. Balt. Coun. on Fgn. Affairs; v.p. Ea. Shore Soc. Balt. 1st lt. U.S. Army, 1957-59. Named Top Ten Innkeeper, Holiday Inns Internat., 1975, Md. Bus. Person of Yr., Future Bus. Leaders Am., 1981, Bus. Person of Yr. nat. chpt. 1981; recipient award of merit Baltimore County C. of C., 1982, Outstanding Svc. award Md. Future Bus. Leaders Am., 1984, Balt. Mayor's citation, 1984; Paul Harris fellow Rotary Found., 1983. Mem. Am. Hotel and Motel Assn., Mass. Lodging Assn., Hotel Sales Mgmt. Assn., Baltimore County C. of C. (v.p.), St. George Soc. N.Y., Advt. Club. Balt. (bd. govs.), SAR, Soc. Sons of St. George Phila., German Soc. Md., German Soc. Pa., Amicale Soc. Francaise Balt., Welsh Soc. Phila., St. David's Soc. N.Y., St. Andrew's Soc. Conn., St. Davids Soc. Conn., Mass. Lodging Assn., German Soc. N.Y.C., Rittenhouse Family Assn., Supreme Ct. Hist. Soc., Hist. Soc. Del., Md. Hist. Soc., Nantucket Hist. Assn., Burlington County Hist. Soc., Md. Ret. Officers Assn., Balt. Yacht Club, Liedeerkranz Club, Williams Club (N.Y.C.). Republican. Congregationalist. Home and Office: PO Box 812662 Wellesley MA 02482-0023 Office Phone: 617-653-8894. Personal E-mail: edouglasheisler@yahoo.com.

HEISLER, NORMA BOODMAN, psychotherapist; b. N.Y.C., Nov. 11, 1933; d. David Louis and Belle (Hochstein) Boodman; m. Arthur Heisler, Aug. 9, 1952 (dec. 1997); children: Miriam, Daniel. Cert. art, Pratt Inst., 1956; BA in Psychology, Bklyn. Coll., 1972; MSW, NYU, 1977; postgrad., N.Y. Sch. for Study Psychoanalytic Psychotherapy, 1979—83, Karen Horney Inst. Study Psychoanalysis, 1984—86, Erickson Inst., 1992—93; PhD, Nat. Inst. Expressive Therapy, 1996. Cert. clin. social worker, art therapist, Am. Acad. Bereavement. Pers. asst. R.H. Miller, N.Y.C., 1952—56; freelance comml. artist Wolf Studios and Lowenstein Studios, 1957—69; tchr. Yeshivab Onel Moshe, N.Y.C., 1971—72; family counselor, art therapist Lillian Sklar Filler Day Care Ctr., N.Y.C., 1973—76; therapy intern L.I. Coll. Hosp., N.Y.C., 1976—77; tchr. adult edn. Kingsborough C.C., N.Y.C., 1978—79; psychotherapist N.Y. Psychotherapy and Counseling Ctr., N.Y.C., 1978—89; field instr., supr. social work C.I.H., 1989—92; pvt. practice Bklyn., 1993—. Instr. hypnotherapy for Dental Practice, 2001; gallery artist World Fine Art Gallery, N.Y.C., Monterrat, N.Y.C. One-woman shows include Jewish Cmty. House, NYC, 1960, Montserrat Gallery, 1998—, 2004—05, Javits Art Expo, 2002—03, Monserrat-Salon, 2003—04, 584 Broadway, 2004, Gora Gallery, Montreal, Can., 2005, exhibited in group shows at Stephen Gang Gallery, Art Expo Javits Ctr., 2002—03, Gora Gallery, Montreal, 2004, World Fine Art,

2005, Monserrat and World Fine Art Gallery, N.Y.C., 2005. Recipient Latham award for Brotherhood, 1954, 1955, 1956, 1957, 1959, Grumbacher award of Merit, 1960, Art awards. Fellow: Soc. Clin. Social Workers; mem.: NASW, N.Y. Artists Equity Assn., Am. Orthopsychiat. Assn., Soc. Advancement of Psychoanalytic Devel. Psychology, Nat. Expressive Therapy Assn. Jewish. Home: 2373 E 7th St Brooklyn NY 11223-5434 Office Phone: 718-934-9125. Personal E-mail: drnorma@aol.com.

HEISLER, QUENTIN GEORGE, JR., lawyer; b. Jefferson City, Mo., June 30, 1943; s. Quentin George and Helen R. Heisler; m. Susan D., Jan. 24, 1970; children: Sarah, Thomas, Margaret. AB magna cum laude, Harvard U., 1965, JD, 1968. Bar: Ill. 1968, U.S. Dist. Ct. (no. dist.) Ill. 1969, Fla. 1977. Assoc. McDermott, Will & Emery, Chgo., 1968-69, 70-75, ptnr., chmn. firm pvt. client dept., 1975—; legal counsel Office Minority Bus. Enterprise, Dept. Commerce, Washington, 1969-70. Co-author: Working With Family Businesses, 1995; gen. editor: Trust Administration in Illinois, 1979. Chmn. Winnetka Caucus, Ill., 1983; mem. Winnetka Bd. Edn., 1985-89; trustee Shedd Aquarium, 2002-, Hadley Sch. for the Blind, 1998-2002; bd govs. Winnetka Cmty. House, 1998-99. Fellow Am. Coll. Trust and Estates Counsel; mem. Chgo. Coun. Estate Planning, Univ. Club (Chgo.), Harvard Club (bd. dirs. Chgo. chpt. 1984-95, pres. bd. 1989-91), Skokie Country Club (Glencoe, Ill.), Racquet Club (Chgo.). Office: McDermott Will & Emery 227 W Monroe St Ste 3100 Chicago IL 60606-5096 Office Phone: 312-984-7606. Business E-Mail: qheisler@mwe.com.

HEISLER, STANLEY DEAN, lawyer; b. The Dalles, Oreg., Jan. 11, 1946; s. Donald Eugene and Roberta (Van Valkenburgh) Heisler. BA, Willamette U., 1968, JD, 1972. Bar: Oreg. 1972, U.S. Ct. Claims 1972, U.S. Tax Ct. 1972, U.S. Ct. Appeals (9th cir.) 1972, D.C. 1973, U.S. Ct. Appeals (fed. cir.) 1973, U.S. Ct. Mil. Appeals 1973, N.Y. 1985, U.S. Supreme Ct. 1985. Assoc. Heisler & Van Valkenburgh, The Dalles, 1973-74; ptnr. Heisler, Van Valkenburgh & Coats, The Dalles, 1975-81, Heisler & Heisler, The Dalles, 1982-84, Cohen & Shalleck, N.Y.C., 1985-88, Phillips, Nizer, Benjamin, Krim & Ballon, N.Y.C., 1988-91, Squadron, Ellenoff, Plesent, Sheinfeld & Sorkin, N.Y.C., 1991-94; mng. ptnr. Shays & Kemper, LLP, N.Y.C., 1994-98, Shays, Rothman, & Heisler, LLP, N.Y.C., 1999-2000, Shays, Heisler & Rosenthal, LLP, N.Y.C., 2000-01; pvt. practice Stanley D. Heisler, PC, N.Y.C., 2001—. Speechwriter Sec. of State Tom McCall, Salem, 1965, Gov. Tom McCall, Salem, 1966—68; speechwriter, legis. asst. U.S. Senator Bob Packwood, Washington, 1969—73; vice chmn. Pres.'s Air Quality Adv. Bd., Washington, 1973—76. Recipient Most Venerable Order of the Hosp. of St. John of Jerusalem, HRH Queen Elizabeth II, Knight of the Order of Saints Maurice and Lazarus, HRH Victor Emmanuel, the Prince of Naples and Duke of Savoy. Mem.: SAR, ABA, Assn. of Bar of City of N.Y., N.Y. State Bar Assn., The Pilgrims of the U.S., Colonial Soc. of Pa., St. George's Soc. NY, Sons of the Revolution, Edmund Rice (1638) Assn., Soc. Mayflower Descs. (bd. dirs. N.Y. chpt. 2001—, capt. N.Y. chpt. 2005—), Soc. of the Descs. Washington's Army at Valley Forge, Soc. for the Promotion of Hellenic Studies, New Eng. Soc. in City of N.Y., Soc. Colonial Wars (mem. coun. N.Y. State chpt. 2003—), St. Andrews Soc. of State of N.Y., Nassau Club, Princeton Club, Univ. Club (N.Y.C. and Portland, Oreg.), Arlington Club. Republican. Episcopalian. Home: 400 E 77th St Apt 8J New York NY 10021-2342 Office: Stanley D Heisler PC 276 5th Ave New York NY 10001-4509 E-mail: s.heisler@worldnet.att.net.

HEISLEY, MICHAEL E., SR., manufacturing executive, professional sports team executive; b. Washington; m. Agnes Heisley; 5 children. BA, Georgetown U., 1960. Formerly with Robertson-Ceco Corp., Toms Foods, Inc., WorldPort Comm. Inc., Pettibone Corp.; chmn., CEO Heico Cos. LLC, St. Charles, Ill., 1979—; owner Memphis Grizzlies (formerly Vancouver Grizzlies), 2000—. Chmn. Davis Wire Corp., Toms Foods, Inc. Mem. St. Patrick's Cath. Ch. Mem. Turnaround Mgmt. Assn., Union League Club, Chgo. Club. Office: Heico Cos LLC 70 W Madison St Ste 5600 Chicago IL 60602*

HEISS, DAVID JAMES, editor; b. Siagon, Vietnam, Oct. 1972; BA in English, U. Redlands, 1995. Writer Redlands (Calif) Daily Facts, 1999—. Contbg. author: Coming of Dawn, 1993. Instr., coach volleyball Redlands YMCA, 1998—. Mem. Redlands Hort. and Improvement Soc. (newsletter editor 2000—), Town and Gown, Sigma Kappa Alpha (alumni assn. officer 2001-04), Internat. Knights of Round Table. Office: Redlands Daily Facts 700 Brookside Redlands CA 92373 Office Phone: 909-793-3221. E-mail: dheiss@redlandsdailyfacts.com.

HEISS, HARRY GLEN, archivist; b. Fort Smith, Ark., Jan. 3, 1953; s. Fred William and Mary Kathryn (Hall) H. BA, U. Ark., 1975, MA, 1984; archives cert., Western Wash. U., 1979. Archives intern Oreg. State Archives, Salem, 1979; asst. archivist Smithsonian Instn. Archives, Washington, 1980-85; archivist Nat. Air and Space Mus., Washington, 1985-87, Jefferson Nat. Expansion Meml., Nat. Pk. Svc., St. Louis, 1988-91, Libr. Congress, Washington, 1991-2000, Shenandoah Nat. Park, Nat. Pk. Svc., Luray, Va., 2000—02, Bur. Pub. Debt, U.S. Dept. Treasury, Washington, 2002—. Democrat. Avocations: family history, bicycle touring, camping. Home: PO Box 50061 Arlington VA 20091-0061 Office: Bur Pub Debt US Treasury Washington DC 20239 Office Phone: 202-504-3516. E-mail: Harry.Heiss@bpd.treas.gov.

HEITING, JAMES OTTO, lawyer; b. Chicago, Apr. 21, 1949; m. Cindy Heiting; 3 children. BS, Riverside Univ., 1971; JD, Western State Univ., 1975. Bar: Calif. 1976, U.S. Supreme Court and U.S. District Ct. 1977, Central Dist. of Calif., U.S. Dist. Ct., So. Dist. of Calif. 1982. Founder, partner Heiting & Irwin, 1976—. Mem. bd. dirs The Other Bar, 1998—2003, pres., chmn., 1991—93. Mem.: Calif. State Bar Assn. (v.p., treas. 2004—05, pres. elect 2005—), Am. Soc. Law and Medicine, Am. Bar Assoc. Office: Heiting & Irwin 5885 Brocton Avenue Riverside CA 92506*

HEITKAMP, SANDY M., elementary school educator; b. Coldwater, Ohio, June 3, 1969; BA, Bluffton Coll., 1991; Cert. in Elem. Edn., Wright State U., 2002; MA in Tchg., Marygrove Coll., 2003. 5th grade tchr. Immaculate Conception Sch., Celina, Ohio, 1997—99; health, phys. edn. and sci. tchr. Houston Jr. and Sr. H.S., Ohio, 1999—. Named Tchr. of Yr., Hardin-Houston Schs., 2000, 2004; recipient Educator award, McDonald's, 2001. Mem.: Ohio Edn. Assn. (treas. 2003—05). Avocation: softball. Home: 446 E Third St Minster OH 45865 Office: Houston Jr and Sr HS 5300 Houston Rd Houston OH 45333

HEITLAND, JASON ERIC, voice educator; b. Clear Lake, Iowa, May 12, 1971; s. Gerald L. and Laura A. Heitland; m. Stacie Elizabeth Whitchelo, July 31, 1993; children: Jasie Elizabeth, Jillian Jo, Eric Edward. AA, North Iowa Area C.C., 1991; BME, U. No. Iowa, 1993, MM, 2000. Cert. master tchr. State of Iowa, 1993, athletic coach State of Iowa, 1993. Vocal music instr. grades pre-k through 12 Greene Cmty. Schs., Iowa, 1994—96; vocal music instr. grades 7-12 Garner-Hayfield Schs., Garner, 1996—. Pvt. voice instr. Pvt. Studio, Clear Lake, Iowa, 1993—. Dir.: 7-8 Grade Boys Opus Honor Choir, 2002. Vocalist Zion Luth. Ch., Clear Lake, 1986—2005. Mem.: Music Educators Nat. Conf. (assoc.), Iowa Choral Dirs. Assn. (assoc.). Lutheran. Achievements include Director for many vocal festivals and honor choirs; Private voice students have earned top places as state, regional, and national competitions. Avocations: golf, old car restoration, fishing, hunting, skiing. Office: Garner-Hayfield Schs 605 Lyons Garner IA 50438 Office Phone: 641-923-2632.

HEITLER, GEORGE, lawyer; b. N.Y.C., Sept. 3, 1915; s. John J. and Celia (Zeichner) H.; m. Florence A. Posner, Apr. 21, 1940; children: James B., Richard S. BS, Columbia U., 1936, JD, 1938. Bar: NY 1938, Ill. 1962. Asso. firm Cutler, Wilson & McMahon, N.Y.C., 1938-40; spl. asst. to David L. Podell; counsel to Hays, Podell & Schulman, N.Y.C., 1940; asso. atty. firm Coughlan & Russell; also mng. agt. and asst. sec. Central Manhattan Properties, Inc., N.Y.C., 1940-43; chief clk., legal adviser rents and claims bd. 4th Service Command, U.S. Army, 1943-45; engaged as bus. exec., also house counsel various comml. orgns., 1946-57; asst. sec., staff counsel Blue Cross Assn., N.Y.C., 1957-60, corporate sec., staff counsel, 1960-61; v.p., sec. Chgo., 1961-71; sr. v.p., corporate sec., gen. counsel, 1971-81; sr. v.p., legal counsel Nat. Blue Shield Assn., 1978-81; counsel to Kaye, Scholer, Fierman, Hays & Handler, N.Y.C., 1981-85. Spl. adviser Dept. Labor, also speaker and panelist. Author articles. Mem. Am., Chgo. bar assns., Assn. Bar City N.Y. Home: 700 John Ringling Blvd Apt 1408 Sarasota FL 34236-1555 Personal E-mail: fgheitfl@aol.com.

HEITMANN, GEORGE JOSEPH, business educator, consultant; b. N.Y.C., Nov. 27, 1933; s. Frederick Charles and Henrietta (Boesl) H.; m. Marian Kingsley, Sept. 3, 1960; children: James, Noel, Peter. AB, Syracuse U., 1956; MA, Princeton U., 1960, PhD, 1963. Prof. mgmt. sci. Pa. State U., University Park, 1958—94, chmn. dept., 1978—87, dir. internat. programs Coll. Bus. Adminstrn., 1989—94, prof. emeritus, 1994—; prof. econs. Muhlenberg Coll., Allentown, Pa., 1994—, chmn. dept. acctg., bus. and econs., 1994—2003, dean internat. program, 1994—2004. Econ. advisor Ministry of Planning and Devel., Govt. of Libya, Tripoli, 1964-66; cons. energy policy staff Exec. Office of Pres., Washington, 1968-70; vis. prof. Universität zu Köln, Cologne, Fed. Republic of Germany, 1974; vis. prof. Ruhr Universität, Bochum, Fed. Republic of Germany, 1970, 74, 77, W.Va. U., Morgantown, 1975, Shanghai Inst. Mech. Engring., Peoples Republic of China, 1985, U. Maastricht, 2002; cons. Helsinki Inst. Bus. Econs., Finland, 1980; Pa. State U. resident advisor U. West Indies, Kingston, Jamaica, 1987-89. Contbr. articles to profl. jours. Served as 1st lt. U.S. Army, 1957. Mem. Am. Econ. Assn., Decision Scis. Inst., Phi Beta Kappa. Home: 930 S 24th St Allentown PA 18103-3706 Office: Muhlenberg Coll Ettinger Bldg Allentown PA 18104-5586 Office Phone: 484-664-3283. E-mail: heitmann@muhlenberg.edu.

HEITNER, JOHN A. (JACK HEITNER), literature and language professor, writer; b. Bklyn., May 7, 1931; s. Samuel and Constance (Stannage) H.; m. Susanne James, 1956 (div. 1985); children: Randall, Steven, Wendi. BA cum laude, Hofstra U., 1959; MA, Cornell U., 1960; PhD, U. Rochester, 1968. Instr. SUNY, Albany, 1962-65; assoc. prof. Ctrl. Conn. State U., New Britain, 1965—. Lectr. Am. lit. N.W. U., Lanzhou, China, summer 1990, Chingdao (China) U., summer 1990; presenter in field; reader Borders Bookstore, 2004, 05. Author: The Search for the Real Self, 1978, At the Edge of Consciousness, 1987, rev. edit., 1996, Songs of the Spirit, 2004; contbr. articles and poems to profl. jours. Chmn. Caucus of Local Party Presdl. Nominations, New Britain, 1976; del. Dem. Congl. Caucus, New Britain, 1976, Dem. State Caucus, Southington, Conn., 1972; founder, coord. Ctrl. Literary Soc., 1983—, Humanistic Edn. Support Group, 1973. 1st lt. USMC, 1951-54. N.Y. State Coll. tchg. fellow N.Y. State Regents, 1959-61. Mem. AAUP, Melville Soc., Hawthorne Soc., Mark Twain Circle, John Gardner Soc. (paper presenter 2000), Kappa Delta Pi. Mem. Eckankar Ch. Avocations: world travel, rock climbing, hiking, mountain climbing. Office: Ctrl Conn State U Stanley St New Britain CT 06053 Office Phone: 860-832-2763. E-mail: jheitner@snet.net.

HEITNER, KENNETH HOWARD, lawyer; b. Jersey City, Apr. 1, 1948; s. Charles Fred and Molly (Vogelman) H.; m. Anne Barbara Siegel, June 14, 1970; children: Douglas, Andrew, Elizabeth. BA, Rutgers U., 1969; JD, NYU, 1973, LLM in Taxation, 1977. Bar: NY 1974, US Dist. Ct. (So. and Ea. dists.) NY 1975, US Tax Ct. 1976. Assoc. Weil, Gotshal & Manges, NYC, 1973-81, ptnr., co-head tax dept., 1981—. Gen. counsel, mem. bd. trustee Central Park Conservancy. Author: (articles) Tax Lawyer and Jour. of Partnership Taxation. With US Army, 1969-75. Mem. ABA tax sect., NY State Bar Assn., (exec. com. and former chmn. of committees on bankruptcy, corps., practices and procedure and net oper. losses, reorgns.) tax sect., Assn. Bar City NY, Fairview Country Club (Greenwich, Conn., bd. govs. 1983-90), Tax Club (past pres.), Phi Beta Kappa. Office: Weil Gotshal & Manges LLP 767 5th Ave Fl Concl New York NY 10153-0119 Office Phone: 212-310-8288. Office Fax: 212-310-8007. Business E-Mail: kenneth.heitner@weil.com.

HEITSCH, DOROTHEA BEATE, literature educator; b. Regensburg, Germany, Jan. 11, 1968; came to U.S., 1992; d. Ernst and Paula H. MA, U. Tübingen, Germany, 1992, U. Wash., Seattle, 1994, PhD, 1997. Instr. So. Ill. U., Edwardsville, 1998-99; asst. prof. of French Shippensburg (Pa.) U., 1999—. Author: Practising Reform in Montaigne's Essais, 2000; co-editor: Printed Voices: The Renaissance Culture of Dialogue, 2004. Mem. Modern Lang. Assn., Renaissance Soc. Am. Office: Shippensburg U 1871 Old Main Dr Shippensburg PA 17257 E-mail: dbheit@ship.edu.

HEITSCH, LEONA MASON, artist, writer; b. Pontiac, Mich., Jan. 6, 1931; d. Russell Leonard and Margaret M. (Arnold) Mason; m. Charles Weyand Heitsch, July 5, 1952; children: Russell, Carrie, Grace, Charles, Irene. BA in chemistry, U. Mich., 1952. Ednl. asst. Spl. Sch. Dist., St. Louis County, Mo., 1969-81. Commentator Sta. KUMR, Rolla, Mo., 1996—. Author: (pvt. printing) Echoes of the Ridge, 1985, Get Him to St. Louis, 1983; contbg. author: (poem anthology) Seasons of the Ozarks, 1998, Missourians Write About Reading, 2002, Apples, Apples Everywhere; contbr. poetry, articles to various publs. Sec., activist Mo. Assn. Children with Learning Disabilities, St. Louis, 1973-75; fundraising, writing Friends of Foster-Dolbeer Farm, Walled Lake, Mich., 1996—; contbg. poet Wis. Breastfeeding Coalition, Lac du Flambeau, 1996—; activist Poets Against the War, 2003. Recipient honorable mention Mo. Writers Week award for poetry, 1992, 94, grand prize Artists Embassy Internat., San Francisco, 1997, Editors Challenge award Internat. Soc. Authors and Artists, Abilene, Tex., 1997, included in Memories and Memoirs, Anthology of Mo. authors, 2000; featured in Grandmother Earth IX, 2003, Grist, Mo. State Poetry Soc., 2003. Mem. St. Louis Poetry Soc., Rolla Area Writers Guild. Home and Office: Ridge Orchards 13321 Hwy N Bourbon MO 65441-9305 E-mail: clheitsc@fidnet.com.

HEITZ, EDWARD FRED, freight traffic consultant; b. Chgo., May 18, 1930; s. Fredo and Hildur (Olson) H.; m. Gaymae Woodrow Heitz, Apr. 28, 1960 (dec. Jan. 2005); children: Merry, Ted. Student, Northwestern U., Chgo., 1950-55. Registered I.C.C. practitioner. Supr. transp. rsch. Internat. Minerals and Chem. Corp., Chgo., 1946-58; asst. freight traffic mgr.-rate rsch. C.&N.W.Ry., Chgo., 1958-64; traffic mgr. U.S. Dept. Agriculture, Washington, 1964-78; agriculture transp. analyst Fed. R.R. Adminstrn., Washington, 1978-82; freight traffic cons. Falls Church, Va., 1982-96; ret., 1996. Participant with Am. Arbitration Assn. in program applying arbitration techniques to settlement of class action insur. claims for first time, 1998-2000. Commr. Boy Scouts Am., Fairfax County, Va., 1974-77; chmn. Community Action Agy. County of Fairfax, 1975-77; v.p. Coun. of Fairfax PTAs, 1975; deacon Arlington Ch. of Christ, Falls Ch. Ch. of Christ; mem. Fairfax Com. of 100. *In my techinical work, I found that a problem properly defined is a problem solved, or on the way to a rational solution. The same approach to social and civic problems has brought good benefits with one addition: Define what's important.*

HEITZENRODER, WENDY ROBERTA, elementary school educator; b. Erie, Pa., Nov. 14, 1948; d. Robert Walfred and Ruth Wilhelmena (Sandberg) Gustavson; m. Frederick Charles Heitzenroder, June 20, 1970; 1 child, Matthew Frederick. BA, Thiel Coll., Greenville, Pa., 1970; MA, W.Va. U., 1980, EdD, 1988. Caseworker Philadelphia County, Phila., 1970-71; spl. edn. tchr. John E. Davis Sch., East. Pa. Psychiat. Inst., Phila., 1971-77, Marion County Schs., Fairmont, W.Va., 1977-90, Fox Chapel Area Schs., Pitts., 1990—. Instr. spl. edn. W.Va. U., Morgantown, 1989-90; cons. Marion County Bd. Edn., Fairmont, 1989-90. Mem. Jr. League of Fairmont, 1980s; mem. choir Salem Luth. Ch., 1990—, mem. bell choir, 1990—. Jr. League of Fairmont grantee, 1989; Excellence for Edn. grantee, Pitts., 1991, 92; Thanks to Tchrs. finalist Giant Eagle award, 1994-95; recipient, Silver award Tchr. Excellence Found., 2001, 2002. Mem. Phi Delta Kappa. Avocations: reading, swimming, tennis, needlecrafts. Home: RR 9 Box 543 Greensburg PA 15601-9255 Office: Fox Chapel Area Sch Dist 611 Field Club Rd Pittsburgh PA 15238-2406

HEITZMAN, FRANK EDWARD, architect; b. Litchfield, Ill., Aug. 24, 1946; s. Carroll Kramer and Mary Patricia (Hanafin) H.; m. Sandra Frensko, June 14, 1969; children: Christopher, Nicholas, Alexandra. BArch, U. Ill., 1970, MArch, 1975. Assoc. Skidmore, Owings & Merrill, Chgo., 1971—83; owner Heitzman Architects, Oak Park, Ill., 1983—85, 1987—; ptnr. Heitzman & Thorpe Architects, Oak Park, 1986—87; pres. Urban Resource Group Inc., Oak Park, 1989—. Instr. Triton Coll., River Grove, Ill., 1983—, head dept. architecture and interior design, 1999—; adj. faculty interior design So. Ill. U., 1987—, mem. interior design program adv. com., 1987—; adj. faculty mem. U. Ill. Sch. Architecture, 1989—; chmn. Oak Park (Ill.) Hist. Preservation Commn., 1990-96; juror NCIDQ nat. interiors qualification exam, 1991; chair Oak Park Universal Access Commn., 1997—; ADA for Ill. steering com., 1997—; bd. dirs. chair restoration com. Pleasant Home Found., 1999—. Mem. Oak Park Landmarks Commn., 1979-86; mem. Mayor's Adv. Commn. Bldg. Code Amendments, Chgo., 1983-86; chmn. accessibility code task force State Ill., Chgo., 1986, intern devel. coord., 1994—; mem. Oak Park Accessibility Policy Task Force, 1994; bd. dirs. Historic Pleasant Home Found., 1998—, chair restoration com., 1999—. Recipient Disting. Service award Landmarks Preservation Coun., 1986, Faculty of Yr. award Ill. C.C. Trustees Assn., 2000; Tnamed Vol. of Yr., Village of Oak Park, 2003; Triton Coll. grantee, 1985. Mem. AIA (bd. dirs. Chgo. chpt. 1984—, bd. dirs. Ill. Coun. 1984-88, pres. Chgo. chpt. 1988-89, Excellence in Edn. award 2002), AIA Found. (sec. Chgo. chpt. 1989—, pres. Chgo. chpt. 1990-91), Nat. Coun. Archtl. Registration Bds. (juror 1979, 86), Am. Soc. Interior Designers, Met. Planning Coun., Landmarks Preservation Coun. Ill. (easement monitor 1983—, mem. adv. bd. Ill. statewide program com. 1987—), Chgo. Archtl. Assistance Ctr. (bd. dirs. 1989—), Bright New City Bd., Oak Park-River Forest C. of C. Democrat. Roman Catholic. Home: 213 S Euclid Ave Oak Park IL 60302-3205 Office: Heitzman Architects 111 N Marion St Oak Park IL 60301-1004 Office Phone: 708-848-8844. E-mail: heitzman@comcast.net.

HEITZMANN, WM. RAY, education educator, athletic coach; b. Hoboken, NJ, Feb. 12, 1948; s. William Henry and Mary B. (Tolland) H.; m. Kathleen Heitzmann (div.); children: Richard, Mary. BS, Villanova U.; MAT, U. Chgo.; PhD, U. Del. Cert. tchr., N.Y., Ill. Pvt. practice cons. various pub. and pvt. schs. and bus.; prof. Villanova (Pa.) U. Dir. grad. tchr. edn., dir. Writing for Pub. workshops Villanova U.; basketball, baseball, men and women's football coach, NJ, Ill., Pa., NY. Author 50 Political Cartoons for Teaching U.S. History, 1975, American Jewish Political Behavior: History and Analysis, 1975, The Newspaper in the Classroom, 1979, 84, Educational Games and Simulations, 1987, Opportunities in Marine and Maritime Careers, 1988, 4th edit., 2006, Opportunities in Sports and Athletics, 1992, Opportunities in Sports Medicine, 1993, Careers for Sports Nuts and Other Athletic Types, 1997, 3d edit., 2004, Super Study Skills for Success, 1997, 2d edit., 1998, Opportunities in Sports and Fitness Careers, 2003; contbr. articles to profl. jours. Recipient Outstanding Alumnus award, Sch. Edn., U. Del., 1986, plaque, Weehawken (N.J.) Bd. Edn. Mem.: Pa. Coun. for Social Studies, N.J. Marine Educators, Nat. Social Sci. Assn. (Recognition award 2004), Nat. Marine Educators Assn., Nat. Maritime Hist. Soc., Nat. Coun. for History Edn., Mid. States Coun. for the Social Studies (Outstanding Rsch. award 1989, Carman award 2000), Nat. Coun. Social Studies (Outstanding Svc. award 1980), U.S. Naval Inst., Nat. Assn. Basketball Coaches, Phi Delta Kappa. Office: Villanova U Dept Edn Human Svcs Villanova PA 19085 Business E-Mail: ray.heitzmann@villanova.edu.

HEIVILIN, DONNA MAE, retired government executive; b. Clear Lake, Iowa, May 12, 1937; d. Nels Oliver Ouverson and Nellie Bernice (Humphrey) Ouverson-Loats; m. Thomas Stuart Heivilin, Dec. 26, 1961 (div. Dec. 1971); children: Vincent Stuart, James Edward. Student, Iowa State U., 1956-57; BA, U. Minn., 1959; MPA, George Washington U., 1974, DPA, 1988. Assoc. dir. Navy issues, nat. security and internat. affairs U.S. Gen. Acctg. Office, Washington, 1985-88, dir. logistics issues, nat. security and internat. affairs, 1988-93, dir. def. mgmt., NASA issues, 1993-95, vice chair job process reengring. team, 1995-96, dir. planning & reporting, nat. security & internat. affairs, 1996-99, dir. quality and risk mgmt., 1999-2000, dir. applied rsch. and methods, 2000—04; ret., 2004. Pres. Nat. Coun. Assn.'s Policy Scis., Washington, 1980-83. Profiler editor Pub. Budget and Fin. Jour, 1985-98. Mem. Exec. Women in Govt. (pres. 1996-97), Am. Assn. Budget and Programming Analysts (bd. dirs. 1980-83, 98-99), Coun. Logistics Mgrs., Soc. Logistics Engrs., World Future Soc., Profl. Futurists Assn., The Internat. Alliance for Women (bd. dirs. 1997—, treas. 1998, 1st v.p. 1999, pres. 2000-01, amb. at large 2004—), Phi Kappa Phi. Avocations: recreational walking, plays, shakespeare, country music. Home: 5330 36th St N Arlington VA 22207-1816 Office Phone: 703-532-0610. Personal E-mail: donna.heivilin@verizon.net.

HEIZER, EDGAR FRANCIS, JR., venture capitalist; b. Detroit, Sept. 23, 1929; s. Edgar Francis and Grace Adelia (Smith) H.; m. Molly Bradley Hunt, June 17, 1952; children: Linda Heizer Seaman, Molly Hunt, Edgar Francis III. BS, Northwestern U., 1951; JD, Yale U., 1954. Bar: Ill. 1954; CPA, Ill. Mem. audit and tax staff Arthur Andersen & Co., Chgo., 1954-56; fin. analyst Kidder, Peabody & Co., Chgo., 1956-58; mgmt. cons. Booz, Allen & Hamilton, Chgo., 1958-62; asst. treas., mgr. venture capital divsn. Allstate Ins. Co., Northbrook, Ill., 1962-69; chmn., founder, CEO Heizer Corp., a venture capital & bus. devel. co., Chgo., 1969-85; venture capitalist Tucker's Town, Bermuda, 1985—. Bd. dirs. Needham & Co., N.Y., Material Sci. Corp., Elk Grove Village, Ill., Manus Health Systems Inc., Lake Forest, Ill., Chesapeake Energy Corp., Oklahoma City, Okla.; mem. adv. bd. Kellogg Sch. Mgmt., Northwestern U.; chmn. Heizer Ctr. for Entrepreneurship at Kellogg Sch. Mgmt. Chmn. task force on capital formation for White House Conf. on Small Bus., 1978-80. Mem. Nat. Venture Capital Assn. (founder, 1st pres., chmn.), Nat. Assn. Small Bus. Investment Cos., Delta Upsilon (chmn. bd. dirs. 1985-88, chmn. ednl. found. 1990-98). Clubs: Chgo. Curling, Shoreacres, Econ. of Chgo., Coral Beach and Tennis, Mid-Ocean; Riddells Bay Golf (Bermuda). Republican. Presbyterian. Home: 28 S Shore Rd Tuckers Town HS 02 Bermuda also: 261 Bluffs Edge Dr Lake Forest IL 60045-3301

HELAIRE, LUMAS JOSEPH, foundation administrator; b. Lafayette, La., Mar. 16, 1978; s. Joseph Helaire Jr. and Shirley Mae Helaire. BS, Morehouse Coll., 2000; postgrad., U. Mich., 2000—. Program coord. Office Acad. Multicultural Initiatives, Ann Arbor, Mich., 2001—; instr. U. Mich., Ann Arbor, 2003—04. Cons. Office Acad. Multicultural Initiatives, 2002—; presenter in field. Mem.: Phi Beta Kappa, Golden Key Nat. Honor Soc. Achievements include development of Co-Founder, Co-Developer, & Co-Director THREADS Mentoring Program est. 2002. E-mail: lhelaire@umich.edu.

HELANDER, ROBERT CHARLES, lawyer; b. Chgo., Oct. 30, 1932; s. William Eugene and Grace Pauline H.; m. Betty Jane Vinson, Apr. 8, 1961; children: Diana Chaffin, Alexander Christian, Nicholas Charles. BA, Amherst Coll., 1953; JD, Harvard U., 1956, PMD, 1971. Bar: D.C. 1956, Ill. 1956, N.Y. 1979, U.S. Supreme Ct. 1960. Practice law, Chgo., 1956-62; Amherst fellow in Mid. East, 1960-61; mem. firm Helander, Farmanfarmaian & Ghany, Tehran, Iran, 1962-65; assoc. gen. counsel Internat. Basic Economy Corp., Lima, Peru, 1965-68, v.p., 1968-71, v.p. devel. and adminstrn., gen. counsel N.Y.C., 1971-73, group v.p. and pres., 1973-76; ptnr. firm Jones, Day, Reavis & Pogue (Surrey & Morse), N.Y.C., 1976-93; ptnr. Kaye, Scholer, Fierman, Hays & Handler, LLP, N.Y.C., 1993—2001; mng. ptnr. InterConsult., LLP, 2002—. Pres. Accion Internat., 1978-88; chmn. Pan Am. Soc., 1979-88, Am. Fund for Ind. Univs., 1987—, Fund for Multinat. Mgmt. Edn., 1981-91; bd. dirs. Internat. Law Inst., 1975, Ams. Soc., 1982—, Univ. Andes Found., 1983—, Near East Found., 1977—, Bolivarian Soc., 1980—, IESA Found., 1991—, chmn. Internat. Coun. Escuela Superior Adminstrn. de Negocios, 1999—; dir. The Americas Endowment (Orgn. Am. States), 2003-. Named Comendador, Orden del Sol (Peru). Fellow Am. Bar Found. (life); mem. ABA (chmn. inter-Am. law com. sect. internat. law and practice 1978-83, editor-in-chief Inter-Am. Legal Materials 1983-91, del. to Inter-Am. Bar Assn.), Assn. of Bar of City of N.Y. (inter-Am. affairs com.), Inter-Am. Bar Assn. (pres.), Am. Fgn. Law Assn. (pres. 2001-04), Coun. Fgn. Rels.,

Carnegie Coun., Century Club. Republican. Episcopalian. Home: 3 Mountainview Dr Mountainside NJ 07092-2510 Office: PO Box 1337 Mountainside NJ 07092 Office Phone: 917-345-8250. E-mail: rch@interconsultllp.com.

HELD, DAVID W., science educator, researcher; s. Robert C. and Nancy L. Held; m. Michelle L. Scharber, Sept. 9, 1970; children: Mary E., Michael E. R. Doctorate, U. Ky., 2003. Rsch. assoc. U. Ky., Lexington, 1995—2003; asst. prof. Miss. State U., Starkville, 2003—. Assoc. subject editor: jour. Applied Turfgrass Mgmt.; co-editor: ESA Handbook of Turfgrass Insect Pests (rev.). Recipient William White Spl. Project award, Miss. State U., 2004; grant, USDA, Plant Rsch. Initiative. Mem.: Miss. Entomol. Soc., La. Miss. Golf Course Superintendents Assn., South Miss. Lawn and Landscape Assn., Fla. Entomogical Soc., Entomol. Soc. of Am. (John Henry Comstock award 2003), Gamma Sigma Delta. Republican. Methodist. Avocations: fishing, music. Office: Mississippi State University 1815 Popps Ferry Rd Biloxi MS 39532 Office Fax: 228-388-1375. Personal E-mail: david.held@msstate.edu. Business E-Mail: david.held@msstate.edu.

HELD, GILBERT, computer communications consultant; b. N.Y.C., July 19, 1973; s. Milton and Selma Held. BSEE, Pa. Mil. Coll., 1965; MSEE, NYU, 1966; MSTM, Am. Univ., 1971, MBA, 1976. Commd. 2d lt. U.S. Army, 1965, advanced through grades to col., 1987, ret., 1995; dir. 4 Degree Consulting, Macon, Ga., 1977—. Author over 100 books. Recipient Karp award, Inerface, 1982, 1984; Endowed scolarship in sci., Wesleyan Coll., 2000. Republican. Jewish. Avocation: Corvette restoration. Home: 4736 Oxford Rd Macon GA 31210

HELD, IVAN, publishing executive; b. Pa. BA, Georgetown Univ. Various positions in publicity to v.p., dir. publicity Random House, 1989—97, founding pub., trade paperbacks group, assoc. pub. hardcover divsn., 2000—04; mktg. dir., co-assoc. pub. Viking Penguin, 1997—2004; v.p., assoc. pub. Warner Books, 2004—05; pres. G.P. Putnam's Sons (a divsn. of Penguin Group), 2005—. Office: Penguin Putnam Frnt 2 375 Hudson St New York NY 10014*

HELD, JOE ROGER, retired veterinarian; b. L.A., June 23, 1931; s. Edward Samuel and Carmen Antoinette (Planas) H.; m. Carolyn Ann Friderich, May 26, 1956; children: Lisa Held Doseff, Robert Joseph Held, Leslie Held Barnett, Teresa Held Johnson. AA, Pasadena City Coll., 1950; BS, U. Calif., Davis, 1953, DVM, 1955; MPH, Tulane U., 1959. Lic. veterinarian, Calif. Pvt. practice, Pasadena, Calif., 1957-58; various positions USPHS, 1959-72; dir. div. rsch. svcs. NIH, Bethesda, Md., 1972-84; asst. surgeon gen. USPHS, Bethesda, 1975-84; dir. Pan Am. Zoonoses Ctr., Buenos Aires, 1984-87; coord. vet. pub. health Pan Am./WHO, Washington, 1987-89; v.p. primate ops. Charles River Labs., Arlington, Va., 1989-91, dir. Washington office, 1991; dir. Lab. Animal Health Svcs. of Microbiol. Assocs., Rockville, Md., 1992-96, ret., 1996. Cons., Arlington, 1991—; chmn. AID Rinderpest Biosafety Commn., Washington, 1991; mem. USDA, APHIS panel on sci. and tech., Washington, 1987-91; mem. Pew Health Profl. Com. adv. panel on vet. medicine, Durham, N.C., 1991. Contbr. over 70 publs. to scientific jours. Rear adm. USPHS, 1955-84. Recipient Outstanding Svc. medal Uniformed Svcs., Univ. Health Sci., Bethesda, 1985. Mem. AAAS, Am. Vet. Med. Assn. (alt. del. 1981-84, Charles River prize 1984, XII Internat. Vet. Congress prize 1989), Am. Vet. Epidemiology Soc. (pres. 1990-93, K.F. Meyer award 1982), Assn. Mil. Surgeons of U.S. (chmn. vet. med. sect. 1977, McCallam award 1990), Am. Assn. for Lab. Animal Sci., Am. Assn. for World Health, NIH Alumni Assn. (pres. 1991-93), Am. Coll. Lab. Animal Medicine (hon.). Home: 1300 Crystal Dr Apt 505 Arlington VA 22202-3234 Personal E-mail: joe.held@att.net.

HELD, PETER ALLEN, academic administrator; b. Dallas, July 1, 1949; s. Lawrence Charles and Mary (Talmadge) H.; m. Robin Greiner, June 30, 1973; children: Rachel, Amanda. BS, John Brown U., 1971; ThM, Dallas Theol. Sem., 1975; MAE., U. Ala., Birmingham, 1988, EdD, 1994. Adminstr. North Hills Christian Schs., Salisbury, N.C., 1975-79; chmn. dept. Christian edn. Southeastern Bible Coll., Birmingham, 1979-83, dean students, 1983-94; v.p. for student life Bryan Coll., Dayton, Tenn., 1994—. Dir. edn. Faith Chapel, Birmingham, 1987-91. Chaplain, Birmingham Stallions Football Team, 1983-86; bd. dirs. Greater Birmingham Youth for Christ, 1980-83; adv. bd. Rowan County, Boy Scouts Am., Salisbury, N.C., 1976-79; mem. Kiwanis, Salisbury, 1975-79. Mem. Evang. Theol. Soc., Assn. for Christians in Student Devel., Am. Assn. for Counseling and Devel., Chi Sigma Iota. Office: Bryan Coll PO Box 7000 Dayton TN 37321-7000

HELD, SHEILA ANNE, artist; b. Niles, Mich., July 20, 1946; d. Charles Jacob anb Olive Helen (Jena) Dillman; m. HArvey Held, Sept. 13, 1968; 1 child, Maya Anjori. BA in COmparative Religions, Western Mich. U., 1968. Exhibited in group shows at The Arts Ctr., Iowa CIty, Iowa, 1984, Mussavi Gallery, N.Y.C., 1985, Adams Meml. Gallery, Dunkirk, N.Y., 1987, Chautauqua (N.Y.) Art Assn. Galleries, 1988, West Bend (Wis.) Gallery, 1990, Milw. Art Mus., 1992, John Michael Kohler Arts Ctr., Sheboygan, Wis., 1993, Pitts. Ctr. Arts, 1993, State of the Art Gallery, Ithaca, N.Y., 1993, Art Ctr. Gallery, Warrensburg, Mo., 1994; represented in Mindscape Gallery, Evanston, Ill., Tustin (Calif.) Renaissance. Wis. Arts Bd. Individual Artist's fellow, 1994; recipient Chautauqua Nat. Exhbn. of Am. Art award, 1995. Avocations: writing, reading, art, literature. Home: 2762 Mayfair Ct Wauwatosa WI 53222-4105

HELDER, JAN PLEASANT, JR., lawyer; b. Marysville, Calif., Jan. 18, 1963; s. Jan Pleasant Sr. and Roleane Phylis (Harrison) H.; m. Barbara Irene Loring, July 14, 1990; children: Russell Wright, Zachary Allen, David Grant. BA in Econs., Calif. State U., Sacramento, 1986; JD, Georgetown U., 1989. Bar: Mo. 1989, U.S. Dist. Ct. (we. dist.) Mo. 1989, Kans. 1990, U.S. Dist. Ct. Kans. 1990, U.S. Ct. Appeals (10th cir.) 1994, U.S. Tax Ct. 1994. Exec. asst. to pres. Sacramento Trade Exch., 1983-84; legis. asst. Calif. Postsecondary Edn. Commn., Sacramento, 1985-86; assoc. Spencer, Fane, Britt & Browne, Kansas City, Mo., 1989-94, Sonnenschein Nath & Rosenthal, Kansas City, Mo., 1994-96, ptnr., 1996-2000, Stueve Helder Siegel LLP, 2001—04; mng. ptnr. Helder Law Firm, 2004—. Judge pro tem City of Prairie Village (Kans.) Mcpl. Ct.; bd. dirs. Edn., Inc., bd. sec., 1994-95; bd. dirs. Young Audiences, vice pres., 1997-98, vice chmn., 1999-2001, sec., 2001-02. Bd. editor Bus. Torts Reporter, 1996—. Chair Calif. State Student Assn., Sacramento and Long Beach, 1984-85; mem. Leadership Mo., Jefferson City, 1992; mem. Centurions Leadership Program, 1993-95, mem. steering com., 1994-95; bd. dirs. Ivanhoe Neighborhood Coun., 2003—. Pursuit of Worthwhile Endeavors scholar Calif. State U., Sacramento, 1982. Mem. ABA (vice-chair bus. torts subcom., bus. and corp. litigation com., bus. sect. 1993-95, task force on Litigation Reform, chair bus. torts subcom. 1995—, co-chair, Task Force on Year 2000 Legislation, 1999—), co-chair, Task Force on Litigation Reform and Rule Revision, 1999—, ATLA, Nat. Inst. Trial Advocacy (western regional 1993), Am. Law Inst., 2003—, Kans. Assn. Trial Lawyers, Mo. Bar Assn., Kans. Bar Assn., Kansas City Met. Bar Assn., Johnson County Bar Assn., Greater Kansas City C. of C. (chair subcom. on labor and jud. 1990-91, fed. affairs com. 1989—), Ross T. Roberts Inn Ct. (barrister 1991-92), Am. Law Inst. Republican. Presbyterian. Avocations: jazz and classical and choral music, golf, tennis, running, politics. Home: 2216 W 63rd St Shawnee Mission KS 66208-1903 Office Phone: 816-561-5000. Business E-Mail: jan@helderlaw.com.

HELDING, KAREN A, science educator; b. Arlington Hieghts, Ill., Nov. 19, 1969; d. Philip G and Julia D Helding; m. Paul D Robertson, Feb. 26, 2000; 1 child, Christian P Robertson. BA, Marquette U., 1991; MS in edn., Fla. State U., 2000. National Board of Professional Teaching Standards Fla., 2001. Sci. educator Miami Dade County Pub. Schools, 1994—. Mem.: Am. Edn. Rsch. Assn. Personal E-mail: khelding@hotmail.com.

HELDMAN, BETTY LOU FAULKNER, retired health facility administrator; b. Washington, NC, June 3, 1937; d. Basil Frank Faulkner and Willie Mae Rose; m. Arthur Charles Heldman Jr., Aug. 23, 1959; children: Ruth Victoria, Andrew Basil. BS in Biology, Davis and Elkins Coll., Elkins, W.Va., 1959; MS in Med. Biology, C.W. Post Coll., 1978. Cert. eye bank technician Eye Bank Assn. Am. Lab. asst. Portsmouth (Va.) Gen. Hosp., 1954—58; lab. technician Johnson & Johnson Rsch., New Brunswick, NJ, 1959—62; med. assoc. Brookhaven Nat. Lab., Upton, NY, 1973—86; adminstrv. dir. Lions Eye Bank for L.I., Great Neck, NY, 1986—97; ret. Presenter in field; pres., v.p. exec. bd. Brookhaven Women in Sci., 1979—86; chairperson United Fund Brookhaven Nat. Lab., 1983—84; elected mem. lectr. com. Brookhaven Lab., 1978—84. Author, pub.: Faulkner, Cannon, Rose, Brickell-Families of Eastern North Carolina, 2003; contbr. rsch. papers to profl. jours. Recipient Outstanding Svc. in Sci. award, Town of Islip, 1985, Plaque of Appreciation, Lions and Lioness Clubs, 1991, Disting. Recognition award, Knights of the Blind, 2004. Mem.: Assn. for Women in Sci. Home: 2146 Seaton Springs Rd Sevierville TN 37862 E-mail: bheldman@bellsouth.net.

HELDMAN, JAMES GARDNER, lawyer; b. Cin., Mar. 7, 1949; s. James Norvin and Jane Marie (Gardner) H.; m. Wendy Maureen Saunders, Sept. 3, 1978; children: Dustin A., Courtney B. AB cum laude, Harvard U., 1971; JD with honors, George Washington U., 1974. Bar: D.C. 1975, U.S. Dist. Ct. (D.C. dist.) 1975, U.S. Ct. Appeals (D.C. cir.) 1975, U.S. Supreme Ct. 1980, Ohio 1981. Assoc. Perazich & Kolker, Washington, 1974-79, Wyman, Bautzer, Kuchel & Silbert, Washington, 1979-81, Strauss & Troy, Cin., 1981-83, ptnr., 1984—. Mem. ABA, Ohio State Bar Assn., Cin. Bar Assn. Avocations: tennis, platform tennis, biking. Office: Strauss & Troy The Fed Res Bldg 150 E Fourth St Cincinnati OH 45202-4018 Office Phone: 513-621-2120. Business E-Mail: jgheldman@strausstroy.com.

HELDMAN, PAUL W., lawyer, food service executive; BS, Boston U., 1973; JD, U. Cin., 1977. Bar: Ohio 1977. Assoc. Beckman, Lavercombe & Well, 1977-82; atty. The Kroger Co., Cin., 1982-86; sr. atty. Kroger Co., Cin., 1986-87, sr. counsel, 1987-89, v.p., gen. counsel, 1989-92; v.p., sec., gen. counsel The Kroger Co., Cin., 1992-97, sr. v.p., sec., gen. counsel, 1997—. Office: The Kroger Co 1014 Vine St Ste 1000 Cincinnati OH 45202-1100

HELDT, CARL RANDALL, design educator, painter; b. Stanford, Ill., Sept. 8, 1925; s. Carl Rudolf and Charlotte Amenda (Prayther) Heldt; m. Shirley Ann Cunningham (dec.); children: Pamela, Aaron, Tim; m. Doralee Jane Wilkins, Dec. 23, 1989. Degree, Witteneurg Coll., 1944; BFA, U. Ill., 1950. Med. illustrator U. Ill., Urbana, 1949—53, instr. graphic design, 1956—60; art dir. Our Wonderful World, Champaign, Ill., 1953—56; prof. graphic design U. Ariz., Tucson, 1961—90. Artist in residence Hallmark Cards, Kansas City, Kans., 1968; bd. dirs. Waste Mgmt. SYMP, Tucson, 1993. Achievements include patents for structural toy clip sticks; brace extension locking pliers. Home: 4560 N Via Sinuosa Tucson AZ 85745-9764

HELENIAK, DAVID WILLIAM, diversified financial services company executive, lawyer; b. St. Paul, June 27, 1945; s. George L. and Elizabeth (Child) H.; m. Kathryn Moore, Jan. 14, 1967; children: Claire Elizabeth Moore, Charlotte Margaret Moore. AB, U. Mich., 1967; MSc in Econ., London Sch. of Econ., 1969; JD, Columbia U., 1974. Bar: NY 1975. Exec. asst. to dep. sec. US Dept. Treasury, Washington, 1977-78, asst. gen. counsel, domestic fin., 1978-79; head Shearman & Sterling LLP, Hong Kong, 1981—84, co-head mergers & acquisitions group NYC, 1987—95, ptnr. mergers & acquisitions, 1995—2005, from assoc. to sr. ptnr., 1974—2001, sr. ptnr., 2001—05; vice chmn. Morgan Stanley, 2005—. Instr. in econs. U. Wis., Eau Claire, 1969-71; dir. NYC Partnership, 2001-, NYC Ballet, 2001-; mem. Coun. Fgn. Rels.; corp. ptnr. In Motion. Contbr. articles to profl. publs. Pres. The MacDowell Colony Inc., Peterborough, NH 1987-93, also bd. dir.; bd. visitors Coulmbia U. Law Sch.; dir. London Sch. Economics Centennial Fund. Mem. ABA, Bar Assn. City NY (mem. com. on securities regulation, com. to enhance diversity in the profession), Lawrence Beach Club, Century Assn. Office: Morgan Stanley 1585 Broadway New York NY 10036

HELENTJARIS, DIANE, physician, medical association administrator; bachelor degree, MD, Mich. State U. Rep. for Loudoun County Va. Dept. Health, 1993—2000; interim dir. Lord Fairfax Health Dist., 1999—2000, dir., 2000—; pres. Am. Med. Women's Assn., 2004—. Grad. Leadership Loudoun, 1995. Avocation: photography. Office: Lord Fairfax Health Dist 107 N Kent St Ste 201 Winchester VA 22601 Office Phone: 540-722-3480. Office Fax: 540-722-3479.

HELEY, GARY LEE, social studies educator; b. Butler, Pa., May 19, 1968; s. James and Mary Sue Woolcock; m. Lisa Ann Bogart, Aug. 1, 1992; children: Justin Christopher Haley, Joshua Andrew Haley. Bachelor, Bloomsburg U., 1991. Tchr. social studies Wyalusing Sch. Dist., Pa., 1992—. Home: RR 2 132-B Wyalusing PA 18853

HELFAER, MARK ALLEN, anesthesiologist; b. Niagara Falls, N.Y., Mar. 9, 1957; s. Betram Meyer and Sally Ann (Bernstein) H.; m. Michele Wilson, Sept. 1, 1984; children: Samuel Joshua, Jonathan Meyer. BA magna cum laude, Colgate U., 1978; MD, Albert Einstein Coll. Medicine, 1982. Diplomate Am. Bd. Pediatrics, Am. bd. Anesthesiology, Am. Bd. Pediatric Critical Care; lic. physician, Md., D.C. Resident in pediatrics Children's Hosp. Nat. Med. Ctr., Washington, 1982-85; resident in anesthesiology Johns Hopkins Hosp., Balt., 1985-87, chief resident in anesthesiology and critical care medicine, 1987-88, fellow in pediatric intensive care/pediatric anesthesia, 1987-89, instr. anesthesiology, div. pediatric anesthesia, 1988-89, asst. prof. anesthesiology, 1989-93, asst. prof. pediatrics, div. pediatric critical care, 1990—, assoc. prof. anesthesiology, 1993—. Lectr. in field. Co-editor: Casebook of Pediatric Intensive Care Unit, 1993; contbg. editor: Yearbook of Critical Care Medicine, 1992-93, Handbook of Pediatric Intensive Care; contbr. articles to profl. jours., chpts. to books. Children's Hosp. grantee, 1984-85, NIH, CRC grantee. Fellow Soc. of Critical Care Medicine; mem. AMA, Am. Soc. Anesthesiologists, Internat. Anesthesia Rsch. Soc., Soc. of Pediatric Anesthesia, Phi Beta Kappa. Home: 453 Clothier Rd Wynnewood PA 19096-2310 Office: Johns Hopkins Hosp Blalock 1508 A 600 N Wolfe St Baltimore MD 21287-0005

HELFAND, ARTHUR E., podiatrist; b. Phila., Jan. 12, 1935; s. Nathan H. and Esther H.; m. Myra Werner, May 23, 1976; children— Jennifer Bess, Lewis Aaron. D.Podiatric Medicine, Temple U., 1957. Diplomate Am. Bd. Podiatric Orthopedics, Am. Bd. Podiatric Pub. Health, Am. Bd.Podiatrics and Primary Podiatric Medicine (bd. dirs. 1992-95). Pvt. practice, Phila., 1957—2002; active staff James B. Giuffre Med. Ctr., Phila., 1958-89, coord. dept. podiatry, 1959-68, co-chief, 1968-78, chief, 1978-89, dir. podiatric edn., 1968-89; dir. clin. rsch. Pa. Coll. Podiatric Medicine, Phila., 1963-64, prof. podiatry, coord. clinics, 1964-70, prof. podiatry, chmn. dept. community health and aging, 1970—2002, prof. podiatric medicine, podiatric orthopedics, 1998—2002; prof. Sch. Podiatric Medicine Temple U., Phila., 1998—2002, prof. emeritus, 2002—. Mem. staff Thomas Jefferson U. Hosp., Phila., 1973-2002, now hon. staff; hon. staff Temple U. and Temple U. Children's Hosp., 2002—; cons. podiatry dept. surgery Phila. VA Hosp., 1973-82, 89-93; adj. prof. depts. orthopedic surgery and medicine Jefferson Med. Coll., Phila., 1976-2002, adj. prof. orthopedic surgery, podiatry, vis. assoc. prof. cmty. health and preventive medicine, 1977-79; cons. staff Wills Eye Hosp., 1980-2002; affiliate staff Joslin Ctr. for Diabetes, Boston, 1993-96, Joslin Ctr. for Diabetes at Wills and Jefferson, 1993-96; hon. staff Temple U. Hosp.; cons. staff Temple U. Children's Hosp.; cons. Dept. Vets. Affairs, Podiatric Svc., Washington; cons. in field. Mem. editl bd. Rehab. Today, 1990-93; contbr. chpts. to books and over 332 articles to profl. jours.; editor six textbooks. Bd. dirs. Pa. Diabetes Acad., 1988-2002, treas., 1991-93, 95-97, chmn. 1993-95; bd. dirs. Phila. Corp. for Aging. Recipient Lifetime Achievement award Podiatry Mgmt., 1991. Fellow ACP, Pa. Pub. Health Assn.; fellow emeritus Am. Geriatrics Soc., Am. Pub. Health Assn. (task force on aging), Royal Soc. Health; mem. AMA, Am. Coll. Foot Orthopedists, Am. Soc. Podiatric Medicine (pres. 1994-95), Am. Podiatry Assn. (pres. 1982-83), Pa. Podiatry Assn., Phila. County Podiatry Soc., Am. Soc. Podiatric Dermatology, Am. Assn. Hosp. Podiatrists, Del. Valley Geriatrics Soc. (bd. dirs. 1989-2004, pres. 1999-2000), Gerontol. Soc., Temple U. Alumni Assn., Internat. Acad. Preventive Medicine, Am. Assn. Colls. Podiatric Medicine. Personal E-mail: hehelfand@aol.com.

HELFAND, EUGENE, chemist; b. Bklyn., Jan. 8, 1934; s. Saul and Helen Helfand; m. Sondra Ruth Yoskowitz, Nov. 17, 1957; children: Robin Hope, Dawn Alisa, Russ Daniel. BS summa cum laude, Poly. Inst. Bklyn., 1955; MS, Yale U., 1957, PhD, 1958. Mem. tech. staff AT&T Bell Labs., Murray Hill, N.J., 1958-60, supr. chem. computations group, 1960-83, disting. mem. tech. staff, 1983-96; cons. Lucent Techs., Bell Labs., Murray Hill, 1996-98. Adj. prof. Yeshiva U., N.Y.C., 1960-62, Poly. Inst. Bklyn., 1963-64; mem. panel on polymer sci. and engring. NRC, 1979-81. Contbr. articles to profl. jours. Guggenheim Meml. Found. fellow Stanford U., 1969-70. Fellow Am. Phys. Soc. (chmn. divsn. high polymer physics 1987-88, prize 1989); mem. Am. Chem. Soc., Soc. of Rheology, Soc. Info. Display, Sigma Xi, Phi Lambda Upsilon. Achievements include research in theory of polymers, colloids and liquid crystal displays. Office: Lucent Techs Bell Labs PO Box 636 New Providence NJ 07974-0636

HELFENBEIN, ERIC D., electrical engineer, researcher; s. Abraham and Muriel Helfenbein; m. Cheryl Anton; children: L., A. BS in Math. and Computer Sci., UCLA, 1977; MS in Elec. Engring. and Computer Sci., MIT, 1980. Programmer/analyst Tech. Svc. Corp., Santa Monica, Calif., 1974—77; rsch. asst. UCLA Brain/Computer Interface Lab., 1976—77, MIT Lab. for Info. and Decision Systems, Cambridge, Mass., 1978—80; cons. Cardio-Dynamics Labs., Santa Monica, Calif., 1978; clin. engr. Mass. Gen. Hosp., Boston, 1979—80; engr. / project leader Hewlett-Packard Patient Monitoring Divsn., Waltham, Mass., 1980—93; rsch. engr. Hewlett-Packard Rsch. Labs, Palo Alto, Calif., 1993—2000; engr. / rsch. scientist Agilent Technologies Rsch. Labs, Palo Alto, Calif., 2000—01; engr. /scientist Philips Med. Systems - Advanced Algorithm Rsch. Ctr. - Cardiology, Milpitas, Calif., 2001—. Contbr. articles to profl. jours., conf. procs. Scholar, UCLA scholar, 1977. Mem.: IEEE, Drug Info. Assn., Internat. Soc. of Computerized Electrocardiology. Achievements include patents for Intramyocardial Wenckebach activity detection in high-resolution ECGs; determination of respiratory effort from muscle tremor in ECG signals; time-diversity filter for removal of electromagnetic interference from ECGs; real-time physiologic artifact removal from respiratory waveforms. Office: Philips Med Systems 540 Alder Dr Bldg 4 Milpitas CA 95035 E-mail: eric.helfenbein@philips.com.

HELFENSTEIN, JOSEF, museum director; b. Lucerne, Switzerland, 1958; m. Dorothee Sauter; 2 children. MA, U. Geneva; PhD, U. Bern, Switzerland. Dir. Kunstmuseum, Bern, 1983—2000, assoc. dir., 1995—2000, chief curator prints and drawings dept. Paul Klee Found., 1988—2000, project head nine-volume catalogue raisonné of the artist's work Paul Klee Found., 1990—; dir. Krannert Art Mus. U. Ill., Urbana-Champaign, 2000—04, prof. Sch. of Art and Design, 2000—04; dir. The Menil Collection, Houston, 2004—. Guest curator various museums, United States, Czech Republic, Japan, Republic of Korea, Brazil. Author: Louise Bourgeois, 2002; co-author: Maria Lassnig. Zeichnungen und Aquarelle 1946-1995, 1995, Deep Blues: Bill Traylor 1854-1949, 1999, Lipchitz and the Avant-Garde, 2002, Drawings of Choice from a New York Collection, 2003; editor, co-editor and contbr.: numerous internat. exhbn. catalogues and scholarly jours. Achievements include scholar on nineteenth- and twentieth-century and contemporary art. Office: The Menil Collection 1511 Branard Houston TX 77006

HELFER, MICHAEL STEVENS, lawyer, corporate financial executive; b. NYC, Aug. 2, 1945; s. Robert Stevens and Teresa (Kahan) H.; m. Ricki Tigert Helfer; children: Lisa, David, Matthew. BA summa cum laude, Claremont Men's Coll., 1967; JD magna cum laude, Harvard U., 1970. Bar: D.C. 1971, N.Y. 2004. Law clk. to chief judge U.S. Ct. Appeals D.C., 1970-71; asst. counsel subcom. on constl. amendments Senate Judiciary Com., 1971-73; assoc. Wilmer, Cutler & Pickering, Washington, 1973-78, ptnr., 1978-2000, mgmt. com., 1990-98, chmn., 1995-98; exec. v.p. for corp. strategy Nationwide Ins./Fin. Svcs., Columbus, Ohio, 2000—03; pres. Nationwide Strategic Investments, 2002—03; gen. counsel Citigroup Inc., NYC, 2003—. Bd. dirs. Lawyers for Children Am., 1997-, Legal Aid Soc. NY, 2005-, Lincoln Ctr. Theater, 2005-. Mem. Am. Law Inst. Democrat. Office Phone: 212-559-5152.

HELFER, RICKI TIGERT, banking consultant; b. N.C., Feb. 4, 1945; m. Michael S. Helfer; 1 child, Matthew. BA with honors, Vanderbilt U.; MA, U. N.C.; JD with honors, U. Chgo. Law. clk. to hon. John Minor Wisdom U.S. Ct. Appeals; counsel to Jud. Com. U.S. Senate, Washington, 1978-79; assoc., ptnr. Leva, Hawes, Symington, Martin and Oppenheimer, 1979-83; sr. counsel internat. fin. Treasury Dept., Washington; chief internat. lawyer Fed. Reserve Bd., 1985-92; ptnr. Gibson, Dunn & Crutcher, Washington, 1992-94; chmn. FDIC, Washington, 1994-97; nonresident sr. fellow The Brookings Inst., Washington, 1998-99; prof. law, dir. fin. instns. program Washington Coll. Law, Am. U., Washington, 2000—; cons. Am. Cmty. Bankers, Washington, 2000—. Bd. govs., chmn. audit com. Phila. Stock Exch., 1997-99; cons. internat. banking and fin. regulation. Bd. dirs. Girl Scouts U.S., 1995-99, Life Pt. Hosps., Inc., 1999—; mem. vis. com. U. Chgo. Law Sch., 1989-92, 94-97. Mem. ABA (former chair internat. banking and fin. com.), Am. Law Inst., Coun. Fgn. Rels., Washington Fgn. Law Soc. (past pres.), Basle Com. Banking Supervision.*

HELFERT, ERICH ANTON, management consultant, writer, educator; b. Aussig/Elbe, Sudetenland, May 29, 1931; came to U.S., 1950; s. Julius and Anna Maria (Wilde) H.; m. Anne Langley, Jan. 1, 1983; children: Claire L., Amanda L. BS, U. Nev., 1954; MBA with distinction, Harvard U., 1956, DBA, 1958. Newspaper reporter, corr., Neuburg, Germany, 1948—52; rsch. asst. Harvard U., 1956-57; asst. prof. bus. policy San Francisco State U., 1958-59; asst. prof. fin. and control Grad. Sch. Bus. Adminstrn. Harvard U., 1959-65; internal cons., then asst. to pres., dir. corp. planning Crown Zellerbach Corp., San Francisco, 1965-78, asst. to chmn., dir. corp. planning, 1978-82, v.p. corp. planning, 1982-85; mgmt. cons. San Francisco, 1985—. Co-founding dir., chmn. Modernsoft, Inc.; mem. Dean's adv. coun. San Francisco State Bus. Sch., sch. fin. Golden Gate U.; bd. dirs., past chmn. and pres. Harvard U. Bus. Sch. No. Calif.; trustee Saybrook Inst. Author: Techniques of Financial Analysis, 1963, 11th edit., 2003, Valuation, 1966, Valley of the Shadow, 1997, (with others) Case Book on Finance, 1963, Controllership, 1965; contbr. articles to profl. jours. Exch. student fellow U.S. Inst. Internat. Edn., 1950, Ford Found. doctoral fellow, 1956. Mem. Assn. Corp. Growth (past pres., bd. dirs. San Francisco chpt.), Inst. Mgmt. Cons., Commonwealth Club, Forensic Expert Witness Assn., Phi Kappa Phi. Roman Catholic. Home: 111 St Matthews Ave No 307 San Mateo CA 94401-4519 Office Phone: 650-377-0540. E-mail: heleassoc@rcn.com.

HELFGOTT, GLORIA VIDA, artist; b. NYC, May 25, 1928; d. Charles and Anna (Cohen) Wolff; m. Roy B. Helfgott; 1 child, Daniel Andrew. Grad. in fine arts, Cooper Union, 1948. Faculty mem. Ctr. for Book Arts, N.Y.C., 1989-98, San Francisco Ctr. for the Book, 1998-, Brookfield (Conn.) Craft Ctr., 1988—, Art New Eng. at Bennington (Vt.) Coll., 1992, Womens Studio Workshop, Rosendale, N.Y., 1992, Long Beach Art Mus., 1997-98. Solo and group exhbns. include P.S.I., L.I., N.Y., 1979, Handin Hand Gallery, N.Y.C., 1985, Grad. Ctr. for the Arts, W.Va. U., Morgantown, 1988, Berkshire Mus., Pittsfield, Mass., 1988, Ctr. for the Arts, Avado, Colo., 1989, Hoffman Gallery, Portland, Oreg., 1990, Granary Books, N.Y.C., 1990, Ted Cronin Gallery, N.Y.C., 1990, Boca Raton (Fla.) Mus., 1991, Sazama Gallery, Chgo., 1992, Harper-Collins Exhbn. Space, N.Y.C., 1993, 1998, 2000, Istvan Kiraly Mus., Hungary, 1994,1996, 1998, Meml. Art Mus., Ormond Beach, Fla., 1994, Brown U., 1995, Nexus Gallery, Phila., 1995, Ctr. for Book Arts, 1996, 2002, 2005, UCLA Art Libr., 1997; traveling exhbn. U.S. State Dept., 1996-98, San Francisco Libr., 1999, 2001, U. Judaism, L.A., 2004; represented in permanent collections Ruth and Marvin Sackner Archive of Concrete and Visual Poetry, Miami Beach, Fla., Nat. Mus. Women in the Arts, Washington, Victoria and Albert Mus., London, Bklyn. Mus., Stanford U., UCLA, Swarthmore Coll., Oberlin Coll, U. of Alberta, LIU; curator, So

Called Books, 1995-2002, San Francisco, NYC, Salt Lake City, Los Angeles; Beyond the Page, 1995, NYC; Metafiction, 1992, Kent, Conn. Mem. Guild of Book Workers. Home: 1784 Palisades Dr Pacific Palisades CA 90272-2117

HELFGOTT, ROY B., economist, educator; b. Bklyn., Oct. 27, 1925; s. Moses N. and Dorothy A. (Levine) H.; m. Gloria Wolff, July 4, 1948; 1 son, Daniel Andrew. BS in Social Sci, City Coll., N.Y., 1948; MA, Columbia U., 1949; PhD, New Sch., 1957. Rsch. dir. N.Y. coat bd. Internat. Ladies Garment Workers Union, N.Y.C., 1949—57; indsl. rels. analyst Wage Stblzn. Bd., N.Y.C., 1952; economist N.Y. Met. Regional Study, 1957—58; asst. prof. econs. Pa. State U., University Park, 1958—60; rsch. dir. Indsl. Rels. Counselors, N.Y.C., 1960-66, 67-68; adj. assoc. prof. Baruch Coll., 1961—68; indsl. devel. officer UN, N.Y.C., 1966—67; head UN mission, Lower Mekong Basin, 1967; disting. prof. econs. N.J. Inst. Tech., Newark, 1968—93, disting. prof. econs. emeritus, 1993—. Cons. Orgn. Resources Counselors, Inc., N.Y.C., 1968-2005; pres. Indsl. Rels. Counselors, Inc., N.Y.C., 1996-2005. Author: Computerized Manufacturing and Human Resources, 1988, Labor Economics, 1974, 2d edit., 1980; co-author: Industrial Planning, 1969, Management, Automation and People, 1964, Made in New York, 1959; co-editor: Industrial Relations to Human Resources and Beyond, 2003; editor IR Concepts, 1993-2005. Served with AUS, 1944-46, ETO. Decorated Bronze Star with oak leaf cluster, Combat Inf. badge; fellow Inter-Univ. Inst. Social Gerontology, Berkeley, Calif., 1959; sr. Fulbright rsch. scholar U.K., 1955-56. Mem. Am. Econ. Assn., Indsl. Rels. Rsch. Assn., Met. Econ. Assn. (pres. 1978-79), Phi Beta Kappa.

HELFGOTT, SAMSON, lawyer; b. N.Y.C., May 10, 1939; s. Benjamin Wolf and Hannah (Stern) H.; m. Joyce Ann Miller, Feb. 21, 1965; children—Yaffa, Eliezer, Batsheva, David. B.E.E. cum laude, CCNY, 1961; M.E.E., NYU, 1963; J.D. cum laude, Fordham U., 1972; M.H.L., Yeshiva U., 1962, D.H.L., 1974. Bar: N.Y. 1973, U.S. Patent Office 1973, U.S. Supreme Ct. 1978, Patent agt. Eugene S. Lovette, N.Y.C., 1961-65, Leonard H. King, N.Y.C., 1965-67; patent engr. IBM Corp., Rockville, Md., 1967-69; patent atty. Western Electric Co., N.Y.C., 1971-74; patent counsel Gen. Electric Co., N.Y.C., 1969-71, 1974-86; ptnr. Helfgott & Karas, P.C., 1986; ptnr. Katten Muchin Zavis Rosenman . Editor: Foreign Patent Litigation 1983. Contbr. articles to profl. jours. Patentee in communications systems. Vice pres. Jewish Community Council, West Lawrence, N.Y., 1980-84, Congregation Kneseth Israel, West Lawrence, 1982-83. Mem. ABA, Am. Patent Law Assn. (chmn. fgn. patent com., Japanese sub-com., harmonization com.), N.Y. Patent Law Soc. (bd. dirs., chmn. fgn. com.), Internat. Patent Club (bd. dirs.), Eta Kappa Nu. Jewish. Home: 611 Caffrey Ave Far Rockaway NY 11691-5322 Office: 575 Madison Ave New York NY 10022-2511 Office Phone: 212-940-8683. Office Fax: 212-940-8987. E-mail: samson.helfgott@kmzr.com.

HELFMAN, CAROLYN RAE, middle school educator; b. Dallas, July 15, 1941; d. Alfred Sallinger and Hermine Rita Morgenstern; m. Kenneth Harvey Helfman, Aug. 10, 1963 (div. June 1980); children: Theresa, Daniel, Kory. BA, Washington U., St. Louis, 1963; MEd in Counseling, U. North Tex., 1992. Tchr. Richardson (Tex.) Ind. Sch. Dist., 1963-64; homebound tchr. Garland (Tex.) Ind. Sch. Dist., 1970-71; tchr. Hockaday Sch., Dallas, 1971-84, 88-99, asst. head mid. sch., 1993-96, head mid. sch., 1996-99, assoc. head of sch., 1999—; mktg. mgr. Omniplan Architects, Dallas, 1984-88; assoc. head sch. Bryn Mawr Sch., Balt., 1999—. Mem. bd. dirs. devel. com. Temple Emanu-El, Dallas, 1998-99; bd. dirs. Anti Defamation League, Dallas, 1996-98. Mem. AAUW, ASCD, Nat. Mid. Sch. Assn., Ind. Schs. Assn. of S.W. (mem. adv. planning com. 1995—, mem. evaluation team 1998), Assn. Ind. Schs. MD, Phi Delta Kappa. Jewish. Home: 4100 N Charles St Apt 714 Baltimore MD 21218-1030 Office: Apt 714 4100 N Charles St Baltimore MD 21218-1030 E-mail: helfmanc@brynmawrschool.org.

HELFRICH, CORNELIUS DAVID, lawyer; b. 1939; BS, Univ. Pa.; LLB, Univ. Md.; LLM, George Washington Univ. Nat. Law Ctr. Pvt. law practice. Recipient Pro Bono award for outstanding svc., Md. Volunteer Lawyers Svc., 1989, David Hjortsberg award. Mem.: ABA, Harford County Bar Found. (bd. dir.), Harford County Bar Assn. (pres.), Maryland State Bar Assn. (pres.-elect 2003, pres. 2004, sec., bd. gov.). Office: 31 E Lee St Bel Air MD 21014

HELGASON, SIGURDUR, mathematician, educator; b. Akureyri, Iceland, Sept. 30, 1927; arrived in US, 1952; s. Helgi and Kara (Briem) Skulason; m. Artie Gianopulos, June 9, 1957; children: Thor Helgi, Anna Loa. Student, U. Iceland, 1946, D honoris causa, 1986; MS, U. Copenhagen, 1952, D honoris causa, 1988; PhD, Princeton U., 1954; D honoris causa, Uppsala U., 1996. C.L.E. Moore instr. MIT, Cambridge, 1954-56, asst. prof. math., 1960-61, assoc. prof. math., 1961-65, prof. math., 1965—; lectr. Princeton (N.J.) U., 1956-57; Louis Block asst. prof. math. U. Chgo., 1957-59; asst. prof. Columbia U., 1959-60. Vis. mem. Inst. Advanced Study, Princeton, 1964-66, 74-75, 83-84, 98, Mittag-Leffler Inst., 1970-71, 95. Author: Differential Geometry and Symmetric Spaces, 1962, Differential Geometry, Lie Groups and Symmetric Spaces, 1978, Groups and Geometric Analysis, 1984, Geometric Analysis on Symmetric Spaces, 1994, Radon Transform, 1999; editor Progress in Math., 1980-86, Perspectives in Math. Academic Press, Cambridge, 1985—; contbr. articles to profl. jours. Decorated Major Knight's Cross of Icelandic Falcon; recipient Jessen diploma, Danish Math. Soc., 1982, Gold medal, U. Copenhagen, 1951; Guggenheim fellow, 1964—65. Mem. Am. Acad. Arts and Scis., Royal Danish Acad. Scis. and Letters, Icelandic Acad. Scis., Am. Math. Soc. (Steele prize 1988). Avocations: music, photography. Office: MIT 77 Massachusetts Ave Dept Math Cambridge MA 02139-4307 Business E-Mail: helgason@mit.edu.

HELGENBERGER, MARG, actress; b. Fremont, Nebr., Nov. 16, 1958; m. Alan Roseberg Sept. 9, 1989; 1 child, Hugh. BS, Northwestern U., 1982. Appeared in TV series Ryan's Hope, 1984-86, The Shell Game, 1987, China Beach, 1988-91 (Emmy award; named Primetime Programming Individual Outstanding Supporting Actress in Drama Series, 1990, 91), CSI:Crime Scene Investigation, 2000-; co-host of New Year's Rockin' Eve, 1988, Home, 1989, (TV movies) Blind Vengence, 1990, Death Dreams, 1991, In Sickness and In Health, 1992, Through the Eyes of a Killer, 1992, When Love Kills: The Seduction of John Hearn, 1993, Stephen King's The Tommyknockers, 1993, Where Are My Children?, 1994, Lie Down with Lions, 1994, Partners, 1994, Perfect Murder, Perfect Town: Jon Benet and the City of Boulder, 2000; appeared in films Always, 1989, After Midnight, 1989, Crooked Hearts, 1991, Desperate Motive, 1993, The Cowboy Way, 1994, Bad Boys, 1995, Species, 1995, Erin Brockovich, 2000, In Good Company, 2004; TV appearances include Spenser: For Hire, 1986, Matlock, 1987, Thirtysomething, 1987, Tales from the Crypt, 1991, The Larry Sanders Show, 1995, ER, 1996, Frasier, 2000, (voice) King of the Hill, 2004.*

HELGERSON, JOHN LEONARD, federal agency administrator; b. Madison, S.D., Feb. 8, 1944; B, St. Olaf Coll., 1966; M, Duke U., 1968, PhD, 1970. With CIA, 1971—, deputy dir. intelligence, 1989—93, chmn. nat. intelligence coun. Washington, 2001—02; dep. dir. Nat. Imaging and Mapping Agy., 2000—01; inspector gen. CIA, 2002—. Office: CIA Office of Inspector General Washington DC 20505

HELGERSON, KAY, writer, publishing executive; d. Lyle M. and Jennette A. Crandall; m. Lyle V. Helgerson, 1969; children: Lance, Krista. BS in Bus., U. Minn., 1963. Staff, rsch. adminstr. Apache Corp., Mpls., 1964—69; tchr., spkr. Patricia Stevens Sch., Mpls., 1970—72; freelance writer, 1972—; owner L'Kayle, Stone Mountain, Ga., 1998—. Author: Crinkles the Cricket, 2001; contbr. columns in newspapers. Mem.: Nat. League Am. Pen Women (pres. Atlanta br. 2000—04), U. Minn. Alumni Assn., Kappa Kappa Gamma. Avocations: golf, tennis, photography. Office Phone: 770-469-1264. Office Fax: 770-469-6163. Personal E-mail: lkayle@juno.com.

HELGERSON, RICHARD, English literature educator; b. Pasadena, Calif., Aug. 22, 1940; s. Donald Theodore and Viola Dolores (Huss) H.; m. Marie-Christine David, June 8, 1967; 1 child, Jessica. BA, U. Calif., Riverside, 1963; MA, Johns Hopkins U., 1964, PhD, 1970. Prof. English Coll. Notre-Dame d'Afrique, Atakpamé, Togo, 1964-66; asst. prof. English U. Calif., Santa Barbara, 1970-76, assoc. prof., 1976-82, chair dept. English, 1989-93, prof. English, acting. chmn., 1982—. Vis. prof. Calif. Inst. Tech., Pasadena, 1987-88; chair Huntington (Calif.) Libr. Rsch. Rev., 1986-87; faculty rsch. lectr. U. Calif., Santa Barbara, 1998. Author: The Elizabethan Prodigals, 1976, Self-Crowned Laureates, 1983, Forms of Nationhood, 1992 (James Russell Lowell prize MLA, Brit. Coun. prize in humanities), Adulterous Alliances, 2000; contbr. numerous articles to profl. jours. Fellow Woodrow Wilson Found., 1963-64, NEH, 1979-80, Huntington Libr., 1984-85, Guggenheim Found., 1985-86, Folger-NEH, 1993-94, NEH, 1998-99, U. Calif. Pres.'s fellow, 1998-99, Borchard Found. fellow, 2003. Mem. MLA (exec. com. English renaissance div. 1988-92), N.Am. Conf. on Brit. Studies, Renaissance Soc. Am., Spenser Soc. Am. (pres. 1988), Shakespeare Assn. Am., Western Humanities Conf. (exec. com. 1988-91). Democrat. Home: 334 E Arrellaga St Santa Barbara CA 93101-1106 Office: U Calif Dept English Santa Barbara CA 93106

HELGERT, MARK JAMES, music educator; b. Waukesha, Wis., Feb. 10, 1955; s. Edward Joseph and Elsie Josephine (Olsen) H.; m. Gwenda Lynn Noah, July 1, 1978. BA, Carroll Coll., 1977. Dir. of bands Butler Mid. Sch., Waukesha, Wis., 1977—; lectr. saxophone Carroll Coll., Waukesha, Wis., 1977-96. Conductor, music dir. Waukesha Area Jazz Ensemble, 1978—. Composer Portals of Xanth, 1991, Nightingales Wept in Tiananmen Square, 1992, Cornerstone of Liberty, 1993. Avocations: chess, cinema, stamp collecting/philately. Home: 705 S Grandview Blvd Waukesha WI 53188-4749 Office: Butler Mid Sch 310 N Hine Ave Waukesha WI 53188-4320

HELGESON, DUANE MARCELLUS, retired librarian; b. Rothsay, Minn., July 2, 1930; s. Oscar Herbert and Selma Olivia (Sateren) H. BS, U. Minn., 1952. Libr. Chance-Vought Co., Dallas, 1956-59, Sys. Devel. Corp., Santa Monica, Calif., 1959-62, Lockheed Aircraft, Burbank, Calif., 1962-63, C.F. Braun Co., Alhambra, Calif., 1963-74; chief libr. Ralph M. Parsons Co., Pasadena, Calif., 1974-79; pres. Mark-Allen/Brokers-in-Info., L.A., 1976-80; phys. sci. libr. Calif. Inst. Tech., Pasadena, 1980-84; corp. libr. Montgomery Watson, Pasadena, 1985-94; ret., 1994. Mem. adv. bd. L.A. Trade Tech. Coll., 1974-79, U. So. Calif. Libr. Sch., 1974-79. Editor: (with Joe Ann Clifton) Computers in Library and Information Ctrs., 1973. With USAF, 1952-54. Mem. Spl. Librs. Assn. (chmn. nominating com. 1974). Home: Fergus Falls, Minn. Died Jan. 20, 2005.

HELGESON, JOHN PAUL, plant physiologist, researcher; b. Barberton, Ohio, July 25, 1935; s. Earl Adrian and Marguerite (Dutcher) H.; m. Sarah Frances Slater, June 10, 1957; children: Daniel, Susan, James. AB, Oberlin Coll., 1957; PhD, U. Wis., 1964. NSF postdoctoral fellow dept. chemistry U. Ill., Urbana, 1964-66; from asst. to prof. botany and plant pathology U. Wis., Madison, 1996—2002, prof. emeritus, 2003—. Plant physiologist USDA Argl. Rsch. Svc. plant disease resistance unit, Madison, 1966-90, rsch. leader, 1990-2003; program dir. USDA, Washington, 1982-83; vis. scientist Lab. of Cell Biology, Versailles, France, 1985-86. Lt. USAF, 1957-60. Mem. Bot. Soc. Am., Am. Phytopathol. Soc., Internat. Soc. Plant Molecular Biologists, Am. Soc. Plant Physiologists. Achievements include development of tissue culture procedures for studying interactions of plants and fungi, of somatic hybridizations to obtain new disease resistances in plants. E-mail: jph@plantpath.wisc.edu.

HELINSKI, DONALD RAYMOND, biologist, educator; b. Balt., July 7, 1933; s. George L. and Marie M. (Naparstek) H.; m. Patricia G. Doherty, Mar. 4, 1962; children: Matthew T., Maureen G. BS, U. Md., 1954; PhD in Biochemistry, Western Res. U., 1960; postdoctoral fellow, Stanford U., 1960-62. Asst. prof. Princeton (N.J.) U., 1962-65; mem. faculty U. Calif., San Diego, 1965—, prof. biology, 1970—, chmn. dept., 1979-81, dir. Ctr. for Molecular Genetics, 1984-95, assoc. dean Natural Scis., 1994-97. Mem. com. guidelines for recombinant DNA research NIH, 1975-78 Author papers in field. Mem. Am. Soc. Biol. Chemists, Am. Soc. Microbiology, AAAS, Am. Acad. of Arts and Scis., Am. Acad. Microbiology, Nat. Acad. Scis., European Molecular Biology Orgn. (assoc.). Office: Bonner Hall 9500 Gilman Dr La Jolla CA 92093-0322

HELLAND, CAROL JEAN, literature educator, dean; d. Earl C. Anthony and Helen Lorraine Shallbetter-Anthony; m. Barry M. Helland, June 26, 1971; children: Melissa, Heather, Gregg. BS cum laude, Winona (Minn.) State U., 1972; MS, Coll. of St. Scholastica, Duluth, Minn., 2000. Writer The Filmmakers, Mpls., 1973—75; tchr. Duluth Christian Acad., 1975—76, McKinley (Minn.) Christian Acad., 1976—87; tchr. speech Mesabi East H.S., Aurora, Minn., 1991—92; instr. English Mesabi Range Cmty. and Tech. Coll., Virginia, Minn., 1992—, interim dean acad. affairs strategic planning leader. Mem. leadership team for Higher Learning Commn. Mesabi Range Coll., 1996—; spkr. in field. Author: A Plan and Handbook for the Assessment of Student Academic Achievement and Institutional Effectiveness, 2000. Advisor Aurora Libr. Bd., 1997—99; pres. Boys' Swimming Boosters Club, Aurora, 2003—. Mem.: NEA, Nat. Coun. Tchrs. of English. Avocations: travel, piano, directing choir, writing, reading. Home: PO Box 384 101 W 2d Ave N Aurora MN 55705 Office: Mesabi Range Cmty and Tech Coll 1001 Chestnut St W Virginia MN 55792 Office Phone: 218-749-7710. Business E-Mail: c.helland@mr.mnscu.edu.

HELLAND, GEORGE ARCHIBALD, JR., manufacturing executive, federal official; b. San Antonio, Nov. 28, 1937; s. George Archibald and Ruth (Gorman) H.; m. Josephine Howell, June 9, 1962 (div. 1989); children: Jane Elizabeth, Thomas Gorman; m. Antonia Scott Day, Nov. 24, 1990. BS in Mech. Engring., U. Tex., 1959; MBA with distinction, Harvard U., 1961. Registered profl. engr., Tex. With Cameron Iron Works, Inc., Houston, 1961-77, asst. sales mgr., 1963, dist. sales mgr., 1964, dist. sales mgr., U.K., Africa, 1965, product mgr., 1966, plant mgr., Leeds, Eng., 1967, mgr. oil tool products, 1968, v.p., 1969-75, exec. v.p., 1975-77; with Weatherford Internat., Inc., Houston, 1977-79, v.p., 1977, pres., CEO, dir., 1978-79; pres. McEvoy Oilfield Equipment Co. (name changed to Sii McEvoy div. Smith Internat., Inc. 1980), Houston, 1979-85, McCall Industries, Inc., Houston, 1986-87, bd. dirs.; gen. mgmt. cons., 1987-90; dep. asst. sec. of energy for export assistance U.S. Dept. Energy, Washington, 1990-93; v.p. Dresser Industries, Inc., Houston, 1993-97. Sr. assoc. Cambridge Energy Rsch. Assocs., 1997—; pres. Lockwood Corp., Gering, Nebr., 1986—87; chmn. bd. dirs. SIE Internat., Inc., Ft. Worth, Gas Turbine Efficiency Holdings Corp., 2002—04; prin. Innova Ptnrs., 1988—90; bd. dirs. NSGroup, Newport, Ky., Hunting PLC, London, High Voltage Engring. Corp.; chmn. bd. dirs. Tokheim Corp., Ft. Wayne, Ind., 2001—03, High Voltage Engrs. Corp., 2004—05. Bd. dirs. Jr. Achievement Internat., Briarwood Sch., Houston; trustee S.W. Rsch. Inst., Eurasia Found., Washington; mem. exec. com. Jr. Achievement of S.E. Tex. Recipient Five Outstanding Young Texans award Tex. Jr. C. of C., 1972; named Outstanding Young Houstonian Houston Jr. C. of C., 1972; Disting. Grad. Sch. Engring. U. Tex., 1977. Mem. ASME, Am. Inst. Mining, Metall. and Petroleum Engrs., Am. Petroleum Inst. (bd. dirs.), Inst. Gas Engrs. (U.K.), Tex. Soc. Profl. Engrs., Am. Wellhead Equipment Assn. (pres. 1967), Petroleum Equipment Suppliers Assn. (pres. 1976-77), Houston C. of C., Tau Beta Pi, Phi Eta Sigma, Pi Tau Sigma, Sigma Nu, Friars Soc. Presbyterian. Home and Office: 3635 Overbrook Ln Houston TX 77027-4127 Office Phone: 713-961-4475. Personal E-mail: ghelland@worldnet.att.net.

HELLAND, MARK DUANE, small business owner; b. Eldora, Iowa, May 19, 1949; s. Duane J. and Mary Carolyn (Bloomberg) H.; m. Lois Ann Lebakken, Aug. 15, 1970; children: Alissa, Jonathan. BA, Luther Coll., 1971; JD, U. Minn., 1974; postgrad., Harvard U., 1985, 88. Bar: Minn. 1974, Wis. 1980. Assoc. Berg Law Offices, Stewartville, Minn., 1974-77; v.p. Legal Systems, Inc., Eau Claire, Wis., 1977-78; sr. editor Lawyers Coop. Pub. Co., Rochester, N.Y., 1978-80; exec. dir. Profl. Edn. Systems, Inc., Eau Claire, 1980-81, chief exec. officer, 1981-88, pub., 1988-91, Wiley Law Publs., Colorado Springs, Colo., 1991-93; pres. PESI, Eau Claire, 1993—, PESI Law Publ., LLC, Eau Claire, 2001—. Author: Minnesota Probate System, 1980, Wisconsin Rules of the Road, 1985. Mem. Greater Eau Claire C. of C. Office: PESI 200 Spring St Eau Claire WI 54703-3225 Office Phone: 715-833-5205. Business E-Mail: mark@pesi.com.

HELLAND, SHERMAN M., writer; b. Racine, Wis., Nov. 16, 1913; s. Severin and Marie Kutinka (Fyhrie) H.; m. Rose Martha Steuck, Aug. 12, 1939; children: Mary, Sandra, Karen, Harold. Mgr. retail meats C&W Haummersen, Racine, Wis., 1933-35; sales area developer George A. Hormel Co., Austin, Minn., 1936-51; mgr. bus. analysis U.S. Govt., Richmond, Va., 1951-53; sales mgr., beef grader Donner Packing Co., Milw., 1953-54; supr. chain store meat Godfrey Co., Waukesha, Wis., 1954-55, purchaser, merchandiser select beef and lamb, 1956-57, with, 1958-76. Cons. agr., livestock, breeding feeding, merchandising retail meat, 1991—. Author: Hoofs, Amen, 1978, E. Coli Kills--Wake Up or Die, 1997. Pres. Old Jr. Club of Milw. County, 1980. With USN, 1945. Mem. Am. Legion (chpt. pres. 1981-82). Republican. Lutheran. Avocations: flying, hunting, golf, fishing, philosophy. Home: 236 Oakland Ave Waukesha WI 53186-5548

HELLE, STEVEN JAMES, journalism educator, lawyer; b. Manchester, Iowa, Nov. 9, 1954; s. Roger John and Mary Anna Helle; m. Susan Hanes. BS, U. Iowa, 1976, MA, JD, U. Iowa, 1979. Bar: Iowa 1979, Ill. 1980. Prof. journalism and advt. U. Ill., Urbana, 1979—, head dept. journalism, 1988-97, interim head dept. advt., 2004—05. Contbr. articles to legal jours. Recipient Freedom Forum Journalism Tchr. of the Yr. award, 1998, IPA James C. Craven Freedom of the Press award, 2001; U. Ill. at Urbana tchr./scholar, 2002-. Mem. Assn. for Edn. in Journalism and Mass Comm. (head law divsn. 1984-85). Office: Univ Ill 810 S Wright St Ste 119 Urbana IL 61801-3645

HELLEBOID, OLIVIER, information technology executive; Degree in engring., Ecole Nationale Superieure des Telecom. de Paris; MS, MIT. Participant in design and launch of data network for indsl. automation Telemecanique Electrique, Valbonne, France; with Hewlett-Packard, 1982—2002, mktg. mgmt. positions, gen. mgr. comml. svc. bus., v.p., gen. mgr. HP OpenView Software Bus. Unit; CEO, pres. Rainfinity; exec. v.p. corp. devel. BEA Systems, Inc., San Jose, Calif., 2002—. Office: BEA Systems Inc 2315 N First St San Jose CA 95131

HELLEINER, GERALD KARL, economics professor; b. St. Pölten, Austria, Oct. 9, 1936; s. Karl Ferdinand and Grethe (Deutsch) H.; m. Georgia Stirrett, Aug. 16, 1958; children— Jane Leslie, Eric Noel, Peter David. BA, U. Toronto, 1958; PhD, Yale U., 1962; LLD (hon.), Dalhousie U., 1988; DLitt (hon.), U. W.I.; LLD (hon.), U. London, 2005. Asst. prof. Yale U., 1961—65; assoc., then prof. U. Toronto, 1965—98, prof. emeritus, disting. rsch. fellow Munk Ctr. Internat. Studies, 1998—. Dir. Econ. Rsch. Bur., Dar es Salaam, Tanzania, 1966-68; vis. fellow Inst. Devel. Studies, 1971-72, 75, Queen Elizabeth House, Oxford, 1979. Dir. Econ. Rsch. Bur., Dar es Salaam, Tanzania, 1966-68; vis. fellow Inst. Devel. Studies, Sussex, 1971-72, 75, Queen Elizabeth House, Oxford, 1979. Rsch. coord. Group of 24, 1990-98; bd. dirs., chmn. bd. trustees Internat. Food Policy Rsch. Inst., 1988-94; bd. dirs. North-South Inst., 1976-92, chmn., 1990-92; bd. dirs. Internat. Devel. Rsch. Ctr., 1985-91, Econ. and Social Rsch. Found., 1995-2000, African Capacity Bldg. Found., 1997-2003; chmn. Internat. Lawyers and Economists Against Poverty, 2003—. Guggenheim fellow, 1971-72 Fellow Royal Soc. Can.; mem. Can. Econs. Assn., Can. Assn. Study Internat. Devel., Am. Econs. Assn., Can. African Studies Assn., Order of Can. (officer). Office: 150 Saint George St Toronto ON Canada M5S 3G7 E-mail: ghellein@chass.utoronto.ca.

HELLEMOSE, AAGE, minister; b. Aarhus, Denmark, July 7, 1940; s. Harry and Sylvia (Nielsen) Hellemose Hansen; m. Janie Katzmar. Degree in indsl. engring., Holly Royde Coll.and Odense Indsl. Coll., Manchester, Eng. and Odense, Denmark, 1964; diploma, Rhema Bible Sch., Tulsa, 1992. Min. Worldwide Evangelical Chs., 1986. Mgr. Gen. Bearings Co., Nyack, NY, 1967—68, Electrolux, Old Greenwich, Conn., 1968—69; owner, cons. Hellemose, Inc., New Rochelle, NY, 1970—83; pres., dir. Praise Jesus Ministries, Inc., Washington, 1984—. Author: (book) A Strong Tower -- Building Character Through Fasting and Prayer, 2002; editor: (newsletter) Praise Jesus. Mem.: Worldwide Evangelical Chs. (dir. 1986—88). Avocation: writing. Home: 2468 Springbrook Rd Medford OR 97504 Office: Praise Jesus Ministries PO Box 1447 Medford OR 97501 Business E-Mail: praise4@earthlink.net.

HELLENBRAND, SAMUEL HENRY, lawyer; b. NYC, Nov. 11, 1916; s. Louis H. and Fannie (Cohen) H.; children: Kathy Noreen, Linda Caryn. LL.B., Bklyn. Law Sch. St. Lawrence U., 1941, LL.M., 1942. Bar: NY 1942. With NY Ctrl. R.R., NY, 1942-68, atty., asst. to gen. atty., tax atty., 1947-52, gen. tax atty., 1952-56, dir. taxes fin. dept., 1956-63, v.p. planning and devel., 1963-64, v.p. real estate, 1964-68; v.p. indsl. devel. and real estate Penn Ctrl. Co., 1968-70, v.p. real estate and taxes, 1970-71; pres. Pa. Co., Pa., 1970-71; v.p. exec. asst. to pres., dir. real estate affairs ITT, 1971-81; chmn. fin. com., vice-chmn. AMTRAK, 1982-90. Mem. ABA, Assn. Bar City NY Home: 177 E 75th St New York NY 10021-3230

HELLER, ABRAHAM, psychiatrist, educator; b. Claremont, N.H., Mar. 17, 1917; s. David and Rose Heller; m. Lora S. Levy, June 16, 1957; 1 child, Judith Rose. BA, Brandeis U., 1953; MD, Boston U., 1957. Diplomate Am. Bd. Med. Examiners, Am. Bd. Psychiatry and Neurology. Resident in psychiatry U. Colo., Denver, 1958-61; chief in-patient psychiatry Denver Gen. Hosp., 1961-65, asst. dir. psychiat. services, 1965-70, assoc. dir. psychiat. services, 1970-73, dir., community mental health services, 1970-72; chief psychiatry, dir. community mental health ctr. Newport (R.I.) Hosp., 1973-77; clin. assoc. prof. psychiatry Brown U., Providence, 1973-77; prof. psychiatry, community health Wright State U., Dayton, Ohio, 1977-91, vice chmn. dept., 1980-91, prof. emeritus, 1991—. Fellow Am. Psychiat. Assn. (disting. sr.), Am. Orthopsychiat. Assn., Am. Assn. for Social Psychiatry. Jewish. Home: 1400 Runnymede Rd Dayton OH 45419-2924 Office: Wright State U Sch Medicine Dept Psychiatry PO Box 927 Dayton OH 45401-0927 Office Phone: 937-223-8840. E-mail: abraham.heller@wright.edu.

HELLER, ADAM, chemist, researcher; b. Cluj, Romania, June 25, 1933; came to U.S., 1962; s. Ephraim and Blanche (Nissel) H.; m. Ilana Grossbard, July 26, 1956; children: Ephraim, Jonathan. MSc, Hebrew U., 1957, PhD, 1961; D honoris causa, Uppsala U., Sweden, 1991. Postdoctoral rsch. assoc. U. Calif., Berkeley, 1962-63; mem. tech. staff Bell Labs., Murray Hill, N.J., 1963-64, 75-77, GTE Labs., Bayside, N.Y., 1964-70, mgr. exploratory rsch. Waltham, Mass., 1970-75; head electronic materials rsch. dept. AT&T Bell Labs., Murray Hill, 1977-88; prof. chem. engring. U. Tex., Austin, 1988—. Lectr. in field; adv. bd. Nat. Renewable Energy Lab., Golden, Colo., 1987-93, Basic Energy Scis. Dept. Energy, 1993-96; adj. prof. Brandeis U., Waltham, 1972-75, CUNY, 1968-88; lectr. UCLA, 1984, Weizmann Inst., Israel, U. Guelph, Ont., Can., 1984, Tel-Aviv U., 1987; guest prof. Coll. de France; co-founder, chief sci. advisor TheraSense Inc., 1996—2003. Editor: Semiconductor Liquid Junction Solar Cells, 1977, Inorganic Resists, 1982; contbr. articles to profl. jours.; patentee in field. Recipient Faraday medal Royal Chem. Soc. (London), 1996, Spiers medal, 2000. Fellow AAAS, Electrochem. Soc. (Battery Divsn. award 1978, Grahame award Phys. Electrochemistry divsn. 1987, Vittorio De Nora-Diamond Shamrock medal 1988, De Nora Gold medal 1988); mem. Am. Chem. Soc. (Chemistry of Materials award 1994), Electroanalytical Soc. (Charles N. Reilley award 2004), U.S. Nat. Acad. Engring., Am. Inst. Chem. Engrs., Soc. German Chemists (prize 2005). Jewish. Achievements include glucose microsensors for the management of diabetes; electrochemical biosensors; lithium batteries; liquid lasers; electrochemical solar cells; miniature biofuel cells. E-mail: heller@che.utexas.edu.

HELLER, ARTHUR, advertising agency executive; b. Bklyn., Mar. 14, 1930; s. Max and Tecla (Jacobs) H.; m. Phyllis Olarsch, Dec. 25, 1954; children: Todd, Tracy. BA, Bklyn. Coll., 1951, MA, 1952. Speech and speech correction tchr. N.Y.C. Bd. Edn., 1951-55; v.p., assoc. media dir., media analysis and planning Benton & Bowles, Inc., 1955-66; with Ted Bates & Co., N.Y.C., 1966—, v.p., media dir., 1966-69, v.p., assoc. dir. media-program dept., 1969-71, sr. v.p., 1971—, also account dir., 1974-78; sr. v.p., dir. media-programming-mktg. services Griffin Bacal Inc., N.Y.C., 1978-82, exec. v.p., 1982-97, also bd. dirs.; pres. Heller Mktg. & Comms. Former dir. media programming worldwide, former gen. mgr. Griffin Bacal Can. Served with AUS, 1952-54. Mem. Actors Equity Assn.

HELLER, AUSTIN NORMAN, chemical and environmental engineer; b. Elizabeth, N.J., Aug. 18, 1914; s. Samuel Sidney and Bessie (Rosenfield) H.; m. Frances Sandler, Mar. 21, 1943; children: Richard David, Susan Starr. AB in Chemistry, Johns Hopkins U., Balt., 1938; MS, Iowa State U., 1941. Diplomate Am. Acad. Environ. Engrs. Emeritus. Rsch. asst. environ. sci. Rutgers U., New Brunswick, N.J., 1935-38, 39; chemist, bacteriologist Wallace and Tiernan Co., Belleville, N.J., 1942; rsch. assoc. dept. civil engring. N.Y.U. Coll. Engring., N.Y.C., 1946-48; supr. indsl. waste devel. sect., coord. long range planning Allied Chem. Corp., N.Y.C., 1948-61; dep. chief tech. assistance br. Air Pollution div. USPHS, Cin., 1961-66. Cons. E.F. Drew and Co., Boonton, N.J., 1946-48; U.S. del. OECD, Sci. Div., Air Pollution Rsch. Survey Techniques Group, Paris, 1962-66, Surgeon Gen., Belgian Govt., 1965, Royal Commn. for Air Purification, Govt. Sweden, 1965; pres. Austin N. Heller, Inc., Annapolis, Md., 1977-88, cons. 1991-92; environ. adv. com. Fed. Energy Adminstrn., Washington, 1973-75; adj. prof. engring. Cooper Union Coll., 1966-67; mem. adv. coun. dept. chem. engring. Princeton (N.J.) U., 1967-70; adj. assoc. prof. environ. Columbia U., Contbr. articles to profl. jours. Trustee Engirng. Index, Inc., N.Y.C., 1969-72; expert testimony Pres. Nixon's Adv. Bd. on Water Pollution and Ocean Dumping, Washington, 1974; commr. Dept. Air Resources, N.Y.C., 1966-70; sec. Dept. Natural Resources and Environ. Control, Dover, Del., 1970-73; exec. dir. N.Y. State Coun. Environ. Advisers, N.Y.C., 1973-75; asst. adminstr. conservation U.S. Energy R&D Adminstrn., Washington, 1975-76. Lt. USN, 1942-46, PTO; lt. comdr. USN Rsch. Res., 1948-61. Recipient Cert. of award corp. planning seminar Am. Mgmt. Assn., N.Y.C., 1960, Engring. award ASME, N.Y.C., 1967, 15th Ann. Honor award N.Y. State Soc. Profl. Engrs., N.Y.C., 1968, Humanitarian award Children's Asthma Rsch. Inst. N.Y.C., 1969; Wallace and Tiernan rsch. fellow Iowa State U., Ames, 1940-41. Fellow APHA, Am. Chem. Soc., Am. Inst. Chemists; mem. Am. Inst. Chem. Engrs., Am. Water Works Assn. (life), Air and Waste Mgmt. Assn. (bd. dirs. 1960-63, 67-70), Fedn. Water Pollution Control Assn. (life), N.Y. Acad. Sci., Masons. Republican. Jewish. Achievements include patents for Cyclic Method for Removal of Impurities from Coke Over Tar by Water Washing, Recovery of Phenolics from Industrial Wastes, Process for Production of High Grade Naphthalene and Preparation of B-Naphthol from Acidic Waters Therefrom, Solvent Dephenolization of Aqueous Solutions; development of the use of process research and development as a primary method to solve industrial waste problems in chemical and allied industries at a profit; first use of a telemetry/computer system to measure, on a continuous basis, the air quality of urban atmospheres. Home and Office: c/o Susan Zakem 22043 E Peakview Pl Aurora CO 80016 Address: 5465 Cedar Village Dr Apt #138 Mason OH 45040

HELLER, BARBARA R., former dean, nursing educator; BS, Boston U., 1962; MS, Adelphi U., 1966; EdM, Columbia U., 1971, EdD, 1973; postgrad., U. Md., 1986-90. RN Md., Mass., N.Y., Pa., Va. Chmn. dept. nursing SUNY, Farmingdale; asst. dean acad. programs, Coll. Nursing Villanova U.; prof. and chair dept. edn., adminstrn. and health policy, Sch. Nursing U. Md., Balt., dean Sch. Nursing, 1990—2002, prof., 2002—. Dir. rsch. and edn. nursing dept., Clin. Ctr., NIH, 1983-84; congl. fellow in health policy and edn. Hon. Constance A. Morella, U.S. House of Reps., 1989-90; vice chair, mem. bd. dirs. Computer Based Patient Record Inst., 1992-94, So. Coun. on Collegiate Edn. for Nurses, So. Regional Edn. Bd., chmn. task force on telecomms., numerous others; cons. in field. Co-editor: (book) Information Management in Nursing and Health Care, 1995; contbr. chpts. to books, articles to profl. jours. Mem. bd. dirs. Paul's Place, Open Gates; chair adv. bd. Gov's. Wellmobile. Recipient Innovative Health Program award Md. Found. for Nursing, 1995, Outstanding Educator of Am. award, Alumni award for Nursing Excellence Boston U., Alumni award for Nursing Practice Tchr's Coll. Columbia U.; numerous grants. Fellow Am. Acad. Nursing; mem. ANA, Am. Assn. Colls. Nursing, Am. Soc. Med. Informatics Assn., Am. Assn. Higher Edn., Nat. League Nursing, Md. Nurses Assn., Md. Assn. Higher Edn., Gerontological Soc., Nurses in Washington Roundtable, Women's Pol. Caucus Md., Exec. Women's Network Balt., Sigma Theta Tau, Phi Kappa Phi. Office: Univ MD Sch Nursing 655 W Lombard St Rm 725 Baltimore MD 21201-1506

HELLER, DAVID S., lawyer; BA, Northwestern U., 1974; JD, Georgetown U., 1978. Bar: Ill. 1978. Ptnr. fin. and real estate dept., co-chmn. insolvency and restructuring group Latham & Watkins LLP, Chgo. Spkr. in field. Named one of Top 10 Bankruptcy Attorneys in Country, Turnarounds & Workouts, 1997, Top 12 Outstandingy Bankruptcy Lawyers of Yr., 2000. Office: Latham & Watkins LLP Sears Tower Ste 5800 233 S Wacker Dr Chicago IL 60606 Office Phone: 312-876-7670. Office Fax: 312-993-9767. E-mail: david.heller@lw.com.

HELLER, DEAN, state official; b. Castro Valley, Calif., May 10, 1960; m. Lynne Brombach, children: Hilary, Harrison, Andrew, Emmy. BS with honors, USC. Former mem. Ways & Means & Carson City Rep. Cent. Committee; former Rep. Assembly Caucus; former Nev. St. Assembly; former sr. cons. Bank of Amer.; former stockbroker, broker, trader Pac Stock Exchange; chief dep. Office of State Treas.; sec. state State of Nev., Carson City, 1995—. Bd. dirs. Western Nev. Cmty. Coll. Found. Mem.: N.Am. Securities Adminstrs. Assn., Natl. Assn. Sec. of State. Republican. Achievements include being the first secretary of state in the nation to demand a voter-verifiable paper audit trail printer on touchscreen voting machines. Home: 110 Plantation Dr Carson City NV 89703-5410 Office: Sec State 101 N Carson St Ste 3 Carson City NV 89701-4786 Office Phone: 775-684-5709. Business E-Mail: sosexec@sos.nv.gov.

HELLER, DONALD HERBERT, lawyer; b. N.Y.C., June 1, 1943; s. Nathan and Sylvia Heller; m. Lesley Siskin, July 24, 1976; children: Michael, Joshua, Alexandra. BA in Econs., Queens Coll., 1966; JD, Bklyn. Law Sch., 1969. Bar: N.Y. 1969, Calif. 1973, U.S. Dist. Ct. (cen., no., so. and ea. dists.) Calif. 1974, U.S. Ct. Appeals (9th cir.) 1974. Asst. dist. atty. N.Y. County, N.Y.C., 1969-73; asst. U.S. atty. Calif. Dist. Ct. (ea. dist.), Sacramento, 1973-77; sole practice Sacramento, 1977—; judge pro tempore Sacramento County Superior Ct., 1986—. Mem. ABA, Sacramento County Bar Assn. Republican. Avocation: golf. Home: 205 Dunbarton Cir Sacramento CA 95825-6808 Office: 3638 American River Dr Ste 100 Sacramento CA 95864 E-mail: dheller@donaldhallerlaw.com.

HELLER, ERIC JOHNSON, physicist, educator, digital abstract artist; b. Washington, Jan. 10, 1946; PhD, Harvard U., 1973. Camile and Henry Dreyfus tchr.-scholar, 1977—82; Alexander von Humboldt Sr. Fellow, 1985; prof. physics Harvard U., Cambridge, Mass. Digital abstract artist. Author of 130 scientific papers. John Simon Guggenheim Fellowship, 1992. Fellow: Am. Physical Soc., AAAS, Am. Acad. of Arts and Scis.; mem.: Am. Chem. Soc. (Award in Theoretical Chemistry 2005). Research involves theoretical investigation of wave behavior, chaos and quantum mechanics, and collision theory. Office: Harvard U Jefferson 352 17 Oxford St Cambridge MA 02138 Office Phone: 617-496-7537. Business E-Mail: heller@physics.harvard.edu.

HELLER, ESTHER A., writer, educator; b. Malden, Mass., Nov. 14, 1947; d. Eugene Gregory and Goldie (Stern) Heller; m. Nicholas A. Corsano, Sept. 4, 1971. BA with honors, Brandeis U., 1969; MS, Stanford U., 1971; postgrad., U. Calif., Davis, 1979. Cert. diversity trainer Equity Inst., 1995. Engr. DCA Reliability, Sunnyvale, Calif.; firmware engr. ISS/Sperry-Univac, Cupertino, Calif., 1979-81; hardware engr. Hewlett-Packard, Cupertino, 1981-86, software engr., 1986-95; ind. cons., trainer and diversity coach self employed, Menlo Park, Calif., 1995—. Author diversity columns, 1996—; staff writer Voices of New Bridges-Connections in Judaism, 1999-2003. Bd. dirs. San Francisco Bay coun. Girl Scouts U.S.A., 1988—95, troop leader, 1972—2003; trainer San Francisco Bay coun. Girls Scouts U.S.A., 1982—, subchair capital campaign, 1997—98; founding mem. Silicon Valley Partnership, 1999, co-chair, 2001—02, 2005—; mem.-at-large Jewish Cmty. Rels. Coun., San Francisco area, 2000—; bd. dirs. Keddem Congregation, 2002—. Recipient Thanks badge San Francisco Bay coun. Girl Scouts U.S.A., Ora award Nat. Jewish Girl Scout Com., 1997, Maude Whalen award, 2003. Mem.: Profl. and Tech. Diversity Network of Bay Area (founding mem.), Soc. Women Engrs. (chair Santa Clara Valley sect. diversity com. 1996—, mem. multicultural com. 2000—, chair nat. Girl Scout com. 2000—, leadership coach 2003—). Jewish. Avocations: needlecrafts, orienteering, photography. Office: Ind Cons and Trainer 665 Gilbert Ave Menlo Park CA 94025-2731 E-mail: esther@galarc.com.

HELLER, FRANCIS HOWARD, retired political science professor, retired law educator; b. Vienna, Aug. 24, 1917; came to U.S., 1938, naturalized, 1943; s. Charles A. and Lily (Grunwald) H.; m. Donna Munn, Sept. 3, 1949 (dec. Dec. 1990); 1 child, Denis Wayne. Student in Law, U. Vienna, 1935—37; JD, MA, U. Va., 1941, PhD, 1948; DHL (hon.), Benedictine Coll., 1988. Asst. prof. govt. Coll. William and Mary, 1947; asst. prof. polit. sci. U. Kans., Lawrence, 1948-51, assoc. prof., 1951-56, prof., 1956-72, Roy A. Roberts prof. law and polit. sci., 1972-88, prof. emeritus Lawrence, 1988—, assoc. dean Coll. Liberal Arts and Scis., 1957-66, assoc. dean of faculties, 1966-67, dean, 1967-70, vice chancellor for acad. affairs, 1970-72. Vis. prof. Inst. Advanced Studies, Vienna, 1965, U. Vienna Law Sch., 1985, 97, Trinity U., Tex., 1992. Author: Introduction to American Constitutional Law, 1952, The Presidency: A Modern Perspective, 1960, The Korean War: A 25-Year Perspective, 1977, The Truman White House, 1980, Economics and the Truman Administration, 1982, USA: Verfassung und Politik, 1987, NATO: The Founding of the Alliance and the Integration of Europe, 1992, The Kansas State Constitution: A Reference Guide, 1992, The United States and the Integration of Europe, 1996. Mem. Kans. Commn. on Constl. Revision, 1957-61, Lawrence City Planning Commn., 1957-63, ednl. adv. commn. U.S. Army Command and Gen. Staff Coll., 1969-72; bd. dirs. Harry S. Truman Libr. Inst., 1958-96, v.p., 1962-96; bd. dirs. Benedictine Coll., chmn., 1971-79; mem. nat. adv. coun. Ctr. for Study of Presidency, 1991-97. Pvt. to 1st lt. arty. AUS, 1942-47, capt. 1951-52, maj. USAR, ret. Decorated Silver Star, Bronze Star with cluster; recipient Career Teaching award Chancellor's Club, 1986, Silver Angel award Kans. Cath. Conf., 1987, Disting. Svc. citation U. Kans., 1998; Cross Hon. for Sci. and Art First Class award Austria, 2004, Austrian Cross of Honor fo Sci. and Arts, 2004. Mem. Am. Polit. Sci. Assn. (exec. council 1958-60), Order of Coif, Phi Beta Kappa, Pi Sigma Alpha (mem. nat. council 1958-60) Home: 1510 St Andrews Dr Lawrence KS 66047-1634 Business E-Mail: fheller@ku.edu.

HELLER, FREDERICK, retired mining executive; b. Detroit, May 6, 1932; s. Robert and Lois Heller; m. Catherine C. Flynn, Mar. 26, 1955; m. Rosamund Clifford, July 10, 1964; children: Thomas M., John G., Cynthia R. BA, Harvard U., 1954. With Hanna Mining Co., Cleve., 1957-87, v.p. sales, 1973-76, sr. v.p. sales and transp. Cleve., 1976-81, sr. v.p. mktg., 1981-84; sr. v.p. sales and mktg. M.A. Hanna Co., Cleve., 1984-87; dir. exec. com. Tucson Bot. Gardens, 2002—04. Trustee, exec. com. Cleve. Inst. Art, 1977-82; trustee, fin. com. McGregor Home, 1978-86. 1st lt. U.S. Army, 1954-56. Mem. Tucson Country Club. Home: 4825 N Camino Sumo Tucson AZ 85718-7403

HELLER, JACK ISAAC, lawyer; b. Passaic, N.J., July 12, 1932; m. Naomi Heller AB, U. Chgo., 1952; LLB, Columbia U., 1958. Teaching fellow, research asst. internat. program in taxation Harvard Law Sch., 1958-61; tax economist Latin Am. Bur., U.S. AID, 1962-65; with Office Gen. Counsel, AID, 1965-66; legal adviser AID, Brazil, 1966-67, asst. dir., 1967-68; dir. Office of Devel. Programs, Latin Am. Bur., AID, 1969-72; atty., mgr. spl. projects Office Gen. Counsel, Gen. Electric Co., 1972-74; pvt. practice Washington, 1974—; ptnr. Heller & Rosenblatt, Washington, 1991—. Co-dir. programs in Latin Am. U. Ill. Coll. Law, 1975-80, spl. programs in China, 1982-86; pres. 1998-2000, dir. Pan Am. Devel. Found. Author: Tax Incentives for Industry in Less Developed Countries, 1963. Served with AUS, 1953-55. Home: 3431 Porter St NW Washington DC 20016-3125 Office: Heller & Rosenblatt 1101 15th St NW Washington DC 20005-5002 Office Phone: 202-466-4700. Personal E-mail: hellerji@erols.com.

HELLER, JOHN RODERICK, III, lawyer, corporate financial executive; b. Harrisburg, Pa., Aug. 14, 1937; s. John Roderick and Susie May (Ayres) H.; children: Elizabeth, Carolynn, John. AB summa cum laude, Princeton U., 1959; AM in History, Harvard U., 1960, JD magna cum laude, 1963. Bar: D.C. 1964. Assoc. Wilmer, Cutler & Pickering, Washington, 1963-65, 68-71, ptnr., 1971-82, of counsel, 1982-85; spl. asst. to dir. for India, AID, New Delhi, 1966-67, regional legal adviser for Pakistan, 1967-68; pres. Bristol Compressors, Inc., Va., 1982-85; pres., dir. NHP, Inc., 1985-97, also bd. dirs.; chmn. Carnton Capital Assocs., Washington, 1997—. Bd. dirs. CCC Info. Svcs. Inc., First Potomac Realty Trust, York Internat. Corp., The Phillips Collection; former chmn. Civil War Trust, WETA, Nat. Capital Revitalization Corp.; prof. law George Washington U., 1976—81. Author: The Confederacy Is On Her Way Up the Spout: Letters to South Carolina 1861-64, 1992, An Upcountry Chronicle, 1998. Recipient Meritorious Honor award U.S. Dept. State, 1967. Mem. ABA, Soc. of Cincinnati, Cosmos Club, Met. Club (Washington). Presbyterian. Office: Carnton Capital Assocs 2445 M St NW Ste 460 Washington DC 20037-1435

HELLER, JULES, artist, educator, writer; b. N.Y.C., Nov. 16, 1919; s. Jacob Kenneth and Goldie (Lassar) H.; m. Gloria Spiegel, June 11, 1947; children: Nancy Gale, Jill Kay. AB, Ariz. State Coll., 1939; AM, Columbia U., 1940; PhD, U. So. Calif., 1948; DLitt, York U., 1985. Spl. art instr. 8th St. Sch., Tempe, Ariz., 1938-39; dir. art and music Union Neighborhood House, Auburn, N.Y., 1940-41; prof. fine arts, head dept. U. So. Calif., 1946-61; vis. asso. prof. fine arts Pa. State U., summers 1955, 57; dir. Pa. State U. (Sch. Arts), 1961-63; founding dean Pa. State U. (Coll. Arts and Architecture), 1963-68; founding dean Faculty Fine Arts York U., Toronto, 1968-73; prof. fine arts Faculty of Fine Arts, York U., 1973-76; dean Coll. Fine Arts, Ariz. State U., Tempe, 1976-85, prof. art, 1985-90; prof. emeritus, dean emeritus, 1990—. Vis. prof. Silpakorn U., Bangkok, Thailand, 1974, Coll. Fine Arts, Colombo, Sri Lanka, 1974, U. Nacional de Tucumán, Argentina, 1990, U. Nacional de Cuyo, Mendoza, Argentina, 1990; lectr., art juror; Cons. Open Studio, 1975-76; mem. vis. com. on fine arts Fisk U., Nashville, 1974; co-curator Leopoldo Méndez exhbn. Ariz. State U., Tempe, 1999. Printmaker; exhibited one man shows, Gallery Pascal, Toronto, U. Alaska, Fairbanks, Alaskaland Bear Gallery, Visual Arts Center, Anchorage, Ariz. State U., Tempe, Lisa Sette Gallery, 1990, Centro Cultural de Tucumán, San Miguel de Tucumán, 1990; retrospective exhbn. Ariz. State U., Tempe, 1999, Town Hall, Paradise Valley, Ariz., 1999-2000; exhibited numerous group shows including Canadian Printmaker's Showcase, Pollack Gallery, Toronto, Mazelow Gallery, Toronto, Santa Monica Art Gallery, L.A. County Mus., Phila. Print Club, Seattle Art Mus., Landau Gallery, Kennedy & Co. Gallery, Bklyn. Mus., Cin. Art Mus., Dallas Mus. Fine Arts, Butler Art Inst., Oakland Art Mus., Pa. Acad. Fine Arts, Santa Barbara Mus. Art, San Diego Gallery Fine Arts, Martha Jackson Gallery, N.Y.C., Yuma Fine Arts Assn., Ariz., Toronto Dominion Centre, Amerika Haus, Hannover, Fed. Rep. Germany, U. Md., Smith-Andersen Galleries, Palo Alto, Calif., Grunewald Ctr. Graphic Arts, L.A., Steel Pavilion, Phoenix, 2003, Univ. So. Fla., Tampa, Sheldon Meml. Gallery, Lincoln, Nebr., Santa Cruz (Calif.) Mus., Drake U., Iowa, Bradley U., Ill., Del Bello Gallery, Toronto, Honolulu Acad. Fine Arts, New Orleans Mus. Art, Steel Pavilion, Phoenix, 2003, Robert Roman Gallery, Scottsdale, Ariz., 2004, Raper Politics, Ariz. State U, 2005; represented in permanent collections, Nat. Mus. Am. Art Smithsonian Instn., Washington, Long Beach Mus. Art, Library of Congress, York U., Allan R. Hite Inst. of U. Louisville, Ariz. State U., Tamarind Inst., U. N.Mex., Zimmerli Mus. Rutgers U., N.J., Can. Council Visual Arts Bank, also pvt. collections; author: Problems in Art Judgment, 1946, Printmaking Today, 1958, revised, 1972, Papermaking, 1978, 79; co-editor: North American Women Artists of the Twentieth Century, 1995, Codex Méndez, 1999; contbg. artist: Prints by California Artists, 1954, Estampas de la Revolución Mexicana, 1948; illustrator: Canciónes de Mexico, 1948; author numerous articles. Adv. bd. Continental affairs com. Americas Soc., 1983-86. With USAAF, 1941-45. Can. Coun. grantee; Landsdowne scholar U. Victoria; Fulbright scholar, Argentina, 1990. Mem. Coll. Art Assn. (Disting. Teaching of Art award 1995), Authors Guild, Internat. Assn. Hand Papermakers (steering com. 1986—), Nat. Found. Advancement in the Arts (visual arts panelist 1986-90, panel chmn. 1989, 90), Internat. Assn. Paper Historians, Internat. Coun. Fine Arts Deans (pres. 1968-69), So. Graphics Coun. (printmaker emeritus award 1999). Business E-Mail: jules.heller@asu.edu.

HELLER, KENNETH JEFFREY, physicist; b. Port of Spain, Trinidad, Nov. 7, 1943; s. George M. and Florence (Gelb) H.; m. Patricia Margaret Autry, Sept. 29, 1972. BA, U. Calif., Berkeley, 1965; PhD, U. Wash., 1973. Physicist Naval Rsch. Lab., Corona, Calif., 1965; tchr. U.S. Peace Corps, Nigeria and Kenya, 1966-68; rsch. asst., teaching asst. U. Wash., Seattle, 1968-73; rsch. assoc., lectr. U. Mich., Ann Arbor, 1973-78; asst. prof. U. Minn., Mpls., 1978-82, assoc. prof., 1982-86, prof., 1987—, chair senate edn. policy com., 1993-95, mem. consultative com., 1993-95, dir. undergrad. studies Sch. of Physics and Astronomy, 1992-98, assoc. head Sch. Physics and Astronomy, 1998—, chair pres.'s com. on tchg. and learning, 1993-95, Morse alumni prof., 1997—. Mem. users exec. com. Fermilab, Batavia, Ill., 1984-86, 98—, bd. overseers, 1988-92; trustee Univs. Rsch. Assn., 1985-88, 94. Editor: High Energy Spin Physics, 1988, 94; contbr. articles to profl. jours.; editor procs. Fellow Am. Phys. Soc. (chair forum on edn. 1999—), Am. Assn. Phys. Tchrs. (chair grad. edn. com.), Symposium of High Energy Spin Physics (internat. adv. com. 1988-96), Acad. Disting. Tchrs. Achievements include discovery of large polarization in high energy particle production technique for the precise measurement of hyperon magnetic moments; application of the quark model to understand the mechanism for polarized particle production technique of spin transfer to high energy hyperons; first observation of tau neutrino interactions. Office: U Minn Sch Physics & Astronomy Minneapolis MN 55455

HELLER, MARK A., lawyer; b. 1947; BA with honors, Univ. Wis., Madison, 1970, JD, 1973. Bar: Wis. 1973, DC 1981. Sr. trial atty. FTC, Washington, 1973—81; assoc. chief counsel, enforcement FDA, Washington, 1981—84, assoc. chief counsel, med. devices, 1984—91; ptnr., chmn. FDA dept. Wilmer Cutler Pickering Hale & Dorr, Washington, 1997—. Author: Guide to Medical Device Regulation; contbr. chapters to books, articles to profl. jours. Named a Top Lawyer in Washington, Washingtonian mag., 2004. Office: Wilmer Cutler Pickering Hale & Dorr 1899 Pennsylvania Ave NW Washington DC 20006 Mailing: Wilmer Cutler Pickering Hale & Dorr Willard Office Bldg 1455 Pennsylvania Ave NW Washington DC 20004 Office Phone: 202-663-6005. Office Fax: 202-663-6363. Business E-Mail: mark.heller@wilmerhale.com.

HELLER, MARY BERNITA, psychotherapist; b. Roland, Iowa, Feb. 11, 1934; d. Casper and Blanche (Hanson) Stenberg; m. John R. Heller, June 7, 1958; children: Kristen, Jonathan, Kathryn. BA, St. Olaf Coll., 1956; MSW, Fordham U., 1970. Lic. Social Worker NY, Bd. Cert. Diplomate in Social Work. Psychiat. social worker Beloit Children's Home, Ames, Iowa, 1957—58; caseworker Luth. Cmty. Svcs., N.Y.C., 1958—59, Soc. Seamen's Children, S.I., NY, 1971—75; psychiatric social worker S.I. Mental Health, 1971—75; psychotherapist Mid-Hudson Cons. Ctr., Wappinger Falls, NY, 1976—84; pvt. practice Poughkeepsie, NY, 1977—; psychotherapist Windsor Counseling Group, New Windsor, NY, 1989—2003. Supr. Luth. Cmty. Svcs., NYC, 1987-96. Bd. dirs. Children's Home of Poughkeepsie, 1983-88; resident, bd. dirs. Seafarers and Internat. House, N.Y.C., 1990-96, v.p., 2002-2005, pres., 2005—; mem. candidacy com. Met. N.Y. Synod, N.Y.C., 1986-94, v.p., 1992-2002; mem. coun. Hudson Valley Philharm., Poughkeepsie, 1983-88. Fellow Am. Orthopsychiat. Assn.; mem. NASW, Acad. Cert. Social Workers. Democrat. Lutheran. Avocations: alpine skiing, plants. Home: 24 Thornwood Dr Poughkeepsie NY 12603-4633 Office: 55 Wilbur Blvd Poughkeepsie NY 12603-3424 Office Phone: 845-473-5451. Personal E-mail: maryheller211@hotmail.com.

HELLER, MARY WHEELER, photographer; b. Sterling, Ill., Mar. 4, 1928; d. LeRoy Coe and Gladys (Lawrence) Wheeler; m. Peter Seton Heller, June 30, 1956; 1 child, Kate Heller O'Reilly. B in Philosophy, U. Chgo., 1947; BA, U. Ariz., 1950; student, Internat. Ctr. Photography, N.Y.C., 1979-81, Maine Photographic Workshop, 1980. Editl. asst. The New Yorker, N.Y.C., 1951-56, reporter, 1957-60; art photographer N.Y.C., 1970—. Stock photographer Swanstock, Getty Images, 1985—; com. mem. Internat. Ctr. Photography, 1990—. One-woman shows include James Hunt Barker Gallery, Nantucket, Mass., 1979, Siasconset Bookstore, Nantucket, 1984, Studio Gallery, Siasconset, 1982, 1986—88, 1990, Ledel Gallery, N.Y.C., 1990, X Gallery, Nantucket, 1992—95, Lisa Steinmetz Gallery, Clayton, Mo., 1997, U.S. Embassy, Yemen, 1998, Old Spouter Gallery, Nantucket, 1998, New Gallery, 1999, Artists Assn. Nantucket, 2000, 2002, Century Assn., 2000, exhibited in group shows at Vision Gallery, San Francisco, 1987—88, Ledel Gallery, N.Y.C., 1987—88, Main St. Gallery, Nantucket, 1987—91, 1996—98, U.S. Embassy, Oman, 1997, One Pleasant St. Art Ctr., Nantucket, 1996—97, Artists' Assn. Nantucket, 1998—2005, Gallery N., Setauket, N.Y., 1999, Photo Dist. Gallery, N.Y.C., 2003, Phillips Mill Gallery, New Hope, Pa., 2005, others. Trustee N.Y.C. Sch. Vol. Program (now named Learning Leaders), 1961—, classroom tutor, 1961—62, chmn. bd. trustees, 1967—72, chmn. search com. for new exec. dir., 1976; bd. dirs. Pub. Edn. Assn., N.Y.C., 1966—74, pres. bd. dirs., 1972—74; co-chmn. edn. com. N.Y. Philharm, N.Y.C., 1970—80; bd. dirs. Chamber Music Soc. Lincoln Ctr., N.Y.C., 1975—91, chmn. exec. com., 1979—82, pres. bd. dirs., 1988—91; bd. dirs. Nantucket Land Coun., 1986—; v.p. bd. dirs. MacDowell Colony, Peterborough, NH, 1975—79, chmn. search com. for new dir., 1977. Mem.: Profl. Women Photographers, Am. Soc. Media Photographers. Episcopalian. Avocations: reading, visual and performing arts, travel, golf, tennis. E-mail: photocomp@earthlink.net.

HELLER, MICHAEL A., law educator; AB, Harvard U., 1985; JD, Stanford U., 1989. Bar: Calif. 1989, US Ct. Appeals (9th cir.) 1989. Rsch. asst. Urban Inst., Washington, 1985-86; law clk. to Hon. James R. Browning US Ct. Appeals (9th cir.), San Francisco, 1989-90; legal policy cons. World Bank, Washington, 1990-94; asst. prof. law U. Mich. Law Sch., Ann Arbor, 1994—99, prof. law, 1999—2002; WDI rsch. dir. for corp. governance U. Mich. Bus. Sch., 1998—; Lawrence A. Wien prof. of real estate law Columbia Law Sch., NYC, 2002—, vice dean for rsch., 2005—. Vis. lectr. Yale Law Sch., 1991; vis. prof. NYU Law Sch., 2001. Contbr. articles to law jours. Fellow Ctr. for Advanced Study in Behavioral Scis., 2004—05. Office: Columbia U Law Sch 435 W 116th St New York NY 10027 Office Phone: 212-854-9763. E-mail: mhelle@law.columbia.edu.*

HELLER, PAUL MICHAEL, film company executive, producer; b. N.Y.C., Sept. 25, 1927; s. Alex Gordon and Anna (Rappaport) H.; children: Michael Peter, Charles Paul. Student, Drexel Inst. Tech., 1944-45; BA, Hunter Coll., 1950. Freelance scenic designer, N.Y.C., 1952-61; film producer, 1961—; instr. NYU, N.Y.C., 1964-66; prodn. exec. Warner Bros., 1970-71; pres. Paul Heller Prodns. Inc., Beverly Hills, Calif., 1973—. Producer over 30 films including David and Lisa, 1962, Enter the Dragon, 1973, First Monday in October, 1981, Withnail and I, 1987, My Left Foot, 1989, The Lunatic, 1990, The Annihilation of Fish, 1999; mus. multi-media prodr. The Skirball Cultural Center Museum, 1997, The Hong Kong Museum of History, 2000. Founding mem. Com. 100, Am. Film Inst. Served with U.S. Army. Recipient spl. award Nat. Assn. Mental Health. Mem. Dirs. Guild Am., Screen Actors Guild, Actors Equity Assn., Acad. Motion Picture Arts and Scis., Brit. Acad. Film and TV Arts (bd. dirs.), Hearst Castle Preservation San Simeon (bd. dirs.), Lotos Club (N.Y.C.). Home and Office: 1666 N Beverly Dr Beverly Hills CA 90210-2316 E-mail: pheller@earthlink.net.

HELLER, PETER SETON, composer; b. N.Y.C., Aug. 4, 1926; s. M.J. and Rose Backer H.; m. Mary Wellington Wheeler, June 30, 1956; 1 child: Kate Lawrence Heller O'Reilly. AB, Harvard U., 1949, LLB, 1952. Bar: N.Y.

Assoc. Webster & Sheffield, N.Y.C., 1952-60, ptnr., 1960-86, mng. ptnr., 1986-90, retired, 1990—; composer. Overseer Harvard Coll., 1983—90; trustee The Brearley Sch., 1965—80, Radcliffe Coll., 1977—83, William Matheus Sullivan Musical Found. Staff sgt. U.S. Army, 1944—46. Mem. Cambridge Boat Club, Century Assn., Harvard Club N.Y.C., Nantucket Yacht Club, Shimmo Rowing Club, Siasconset Casino Assn., Sankaty Head Golf Club. Avocations: rowing, archaeology, painting, golf, tennis.

HELLER, PHILIP, lawyer; b. N.Y.C., Aug. 12, 1952; s. Irving and Dolores (Soloff) Heller; married; children: Howard Philip, John Philip, Madison Irene Sarah. Attended, Harvard Coll.; BA summa cum laude, Boston U., 1976, JD, 1979. Bar: Mass 1979, NY 1980, US Ct Appeals (1st, 2d & 9th cirs) 1980, US Supreme Ct 1983, Calif 1984, US Dist Ct (all dists) Calif, US Dist Ct (ea & so dists) NY, US Dist Ct Mass. Law clk. to Judge Cooper U.S. Dist. Ct. N.Y., N.Y.C., 1979; ptnr. Fagelbaum & Heller LLP, L.A. Mem.: ABA (litigation sect), Los Angeles County Bar Asn, Calif Bar Asn. Office: Fagelbaum & Heller LLP 2049 Century Park E Ste 2050 Los Angeles CA 90067-3168 Office Phone: 310-286-7666. Office Fax: 310-286-7086. Business E-Mail: ph@philipheller.com.

HELLER, RICHARD H., editor, writer, retired publishing executive; b. Yonkers, N.Y., Oct. 16, 1924; s. Otto and Mary (Cohen) H.; m. Sonja Mentikov; 1 son, Matthew. AB cum laude, Syracuse U., 1948. Editor, also editorial dir. Sterling Group, N.Y.C., 1954-62; editor Dell Pub. Co.; also editorial dir. Dell Mags., N.Y.C., 1962-68; v.p., editor-in-chief Pyramid Books, N.Y.C., 1968-72; pres., editor, pub. Heller & Son, Inc., New Rochelle, N.Y., 1972-82; book critic Gannett Westchester Newspapers, 1976-81; dir. mktg. Macmillan Pub. Co., 1979-80. Author: Who's Who in TV, 1967, The Adventure Book, 1976; Editor: The President Speaks, 1964, The Life and Death of Robert F. Kennedy, 1968. Served in USMC, 1941-43. Mem. Am. Soc. Mag. Editors, Nat. Book Critics Circle, Sigma Delta Chi, Sigma Alpha Mu. Clubs: Dutch Treat.

HELLER, RICHARD MARTIN, lawyer, educator; b. Phila., Sept. 15, 1944; s. Leonard and Helen Heller. BS, West Chester U., 1966; postgrad., U. Nev., Las Vegas, 1968, U. Md., 1970-71; JD, Villanova U., 1974. Bar: Pa. 1974, U.S. Dist. Ct. (ea. dist.) Pa. 1975, N.J. 1977, U.S. Dist. Ct. N.J. 1979, U.S. Ct. Appeals (3d cir.) 1979, U.S. Supreme Ct. 1979. Sole practice, Norwood, Pa., 1975-77, Media, Pa., 1977, 1980—; ptnr. Serini, Heller & Dilullo, Broomall, Pa., 1980. Instr. Pa. State U., Media, 1978—, Suburban West Assn. Realtors Malvern, Pa., 1985—; curriculum and course planner, instr. Pa. Bar Inst., Adv. to Joint State Govt. Commn. (Real Estate Task Force) of Pa. Gen. Assembly; adj. prof. Grad. Bus. Sch. Phila. (Pa.) U., 2005—. Recipient George Washington Honor medal Freedoms Found., Valley Forge, Pa., 1968. Mem. Pa. Bar Assn. (vice-chmn. real estate divsn., real property, trust and probate sect. 1995-97, chmn. 1997-98), Am. Coll. Real Estate Lawyers. Republican. Roman Catholic. Office: 11 S Olive St Ste 200 Media PA 19063-3301 Office Phone: 610-565-9260. Personal E-mail: rei1031@erols.com.

HELLER, ROBERT, financial executive, economist; b. Cologne, Germany, Jan. 8, 1940; m. Emily Mitchell, Dec. 5, 1970; children: Kimberly, Christopher. MA in Econs., U. Minn., 1962; PhD, U. Calif., Berkeley, 1965. Instr. U. Calif., Berkeley, 1965; assoc. prof. econs. UCLA, 1965-71; prof. U. Hawaii, Honolulu, 1971-74; chief fin. studies divsn. Internat. Monetary Fund, Washington, 1974-78; sr. v.p., dir. internat. econ. rsch. Bank of Am., San Francisco, 1978-86; mem., bd. govs. Fed. Res. System, Washington, 1986-89; exec. v.p. VISA Internat., San Francisco, 1989-91; pres., CEO VISA, U.S.A., San Francisco, 1991-93; exec. v.p. Fair, Isaac and Co., San Rafael, Calif., 1994-2001; chmn. Govs. Group, 2001—. Bd. dirs. Fair, Isaac and Co., Plus Sys. Inc., Interlink, Mcht. Bank Svcs. Corp., Bay Area Coun., San Francisco, Sonic Automotive; bd. dirs., mem. adv. bd. BMW of N.Am., Inc.; vice-chmn. Fed. Fin. Instns. Exam. Coun., 1988-89; mem. Nat. Adv. Coun. Internat. Monetary and Fin. Policies, 1987-89, U.S. Coun. Internat. Bus., N.Y.C., 1979—; trustee World Affairs Coun., 1990-96; mem. adv. bd. Nat. Ctr. Fin. Svcs., U. Calif., Berkeley, 1984-90, Ctr. Fin. Sys. Rsch., Ariz. State U., Tempe, 1989, Inst. Internat. Edn., San Francisco, 1989; mem. Bay Area Internat. Forum, 1989, Bay Area Coun., 1992; dir. Am. Inst. Contemporary German Studies, Johns Hopkins U., Washington, 1989; dir. Wharton Fin. Instns. Ctr., U. Pa., 1989—2004. Author: International Trade, 1968, rev. edit. 1973, International Monetary Economics, 1974, The Economic System, 1972, Japanese Investment in the U.S., 1974; mem. editorial bd. Jour. Money, Credit and Banking, 1975-83, Internat. Trade Jour., 1985-88. Bd. dirs. Marin Gen. Hosp., 2001— Mem. Bankers Club of San Francisco, Royal Econ. Soc., Am. Econ. Assn., Western Econo. Assn. (exec. bd. 1977-81), San Francisco Yacht Club, Tiburon Peninsula Club. Avocations: sailing, skiing.

HELLER, ROBERT MARTIN, lawyer; b. N.Y.C., Feb. 12, 1942; s. Philip B. and Mildred S. (Friedman) H.; m. Amy S. Wexler, July 11, 1965; children: David B., Pamela L. BA, Columbia U., 1963, LLB, 1966. Bar: N.Y. 1967, D.C. 1992, U.S. Dist. Ct. (so. and ea. dists.) N.Y. 1970, U.S. Ct. Appeals (2d cir.) 1967, U.S. Supreme Ct. 1976. Law clk. to judge U.S. Ct. Appeals (2d cir.), N.Y.C., 1966-67; atty. adviser to commr. FTC, Washington, 1967-69; asst. to mayor for housing, city planning, transp. and model cities, sec. to cabinet City of N.Y., 1971-73; ptnr. Kramer Levin Naftalis & Frankel LLP, N.Y.C., 1974—, mng. ptnr., 1991-94. Adj. prof. architecture Columbia U., 1975—77; bd. visitors Columbia Law Sch., 1992—2000. Chair Union for Reform Judaism, 2003—; bd. govs. Hebrew Union Coll./Jewish Inst. Religion, 1996—; pres. bd. dirs. 1056 Fifth Ave. Corp., 1994-96; trustee Rabbi Marc H. Tanenbaum Found. James Kent scholar; Harlan Fiske Stone scholar. Mem. ABA, N.Y. State Bar Assn., Assn. of Bar of City of N.Y. (com. on antitrust and trade regulation 1996-99), Phi Beta Kappa. Avocations: aerobic walking, photography. Home: 1056 5th Ave New York NY 10028-0112 Office: Kramer Levin Naftalis & Frankel LLP 1177 Ave of the Americas New York NY 10036 Office Phone: 212-715-9100.

HELLER, RONALD IAN, lawyer; b. Cleve., Sept. 4, 1956; s. Grant L. and Audrey P. (Lecht) Heller; m. Shirley Ann Stringer, Mar. 23, 1986 (dec. 2001); 1 child, David Grant. AB with high honors, U. Mich., 1976, MBA, 1979, JD, 1980. Bar: Hawaii 1980, U.S. Ct. Claims 1982, U.S. Tax Ct. 1981, U.S. Ct. Appeals (9th cir.) 1981, U.S. Supreme Ct. 1992; Trust Ter. Pacific Islands 1982, Rep. Marshall Islands 1982; CPA, Hawaii. Assoc. Hoddick, Reinwald, O'Connor & Marrack, Honolulu, 1980-84; ptnr. Reinwald, O'Connor & Marrack, Honolulu, 1984-87; stockholder, bd. dirs. Torkildson, Katz, Fonseca, Moore & Hetherington, Honolulu, 1988—. Adj. prof. U. Hawaii Sch. Law, 1981; arbitrator ct.-annexed arbitration program First Ct., State of Hawaii; author, instr. Hawaii Taxes. Bd. dirs. Hawaii Women Lawyers Found., Honolulu, 1984-86, Hawaii Performing Arts Co., Honolulu, 1984-93; panel of arbitrators Am. Arbitration Assn., 1987-99; actor, stage mgr. Honolulu Cmty. Theatre, 1983-87, Hawaii Performing Arts Co., Honolulu, 1982-87. Named Hawaii Outstanding Small Bus. Vol., NFIB, 1998, Small Bus. Champion for State of Hawaii and S.W. U.S., 2004. Fellow Am. Coll. Tax Counsel; mem. AICPA (coun. 1994-96, 2002-04), ABA, Hawaii State Bar Assn. (chair tax sect. 1997-98, chair state and local tax com. 1994-95), Hawaii Soc. CPAs (chmn. tax com. 1985-86, legis. com. 1987-88, bd. dirs. 1988-2003, pres. 1994-95), Hawaii Women Lawyers. Office: Torkildson Katz Fonseca Moore & Hetherington 700 Bishop St Ste 1500 Honolulu HI 96813-4187 Office Phone: 808-523-6000. E-mail: rheller@torkildson.com.

HELLER, SANDERS D., lawyer; b. Montpelier, Vt., Apr. 19, 1923; s. Hymon and Annie Dorothy Heller; m. Helen Heller, Jan. 22, 1948; children: Howard, Jeffrey, David, Stephen. BA, Ohio State U., 1948, JD, 1950. Bar: Ohio 1950, N.Y. 1952. Sole practitioner, Columbus, Ohio, 1950-51, Gouverneur, N.Y., 1952—. Asst., acting dist. atty. St. Lawrence County, Canton, N.Y., 1961-64, spel. prosecutor, 1983-84, adminstr. assigned counsel plan, 1965-81. N.Y. state chmn. March of Dimes, 1970-73; v.p. Congregation Anshe Zophen, 1985—. Recipient Disting. Vol. Svc. award Nat. Found. March of Dimes. Mem. Fedn. Bar Assns. Fourth Judicial Dist. (past pres.), St. Lawrence County Bar Assn. (past pres.), Gouverneur Lions Club (past dist. gov., Melvin Jones fellow 1993-94), Tau Epsilon Phi (past pres., C.C. Lilienfield award 1981). Office: 23 E Main St Gouverneur NY 13642

HELLER, THOMAS CHARLES, law educator; b. Phila., Feb. 17, 1944, married; 2 children. AB, Princeton U., 1965; LLB, Yale U., 1968. Bar: Wis. 1975. Atty. Cleary, Gottlieb, Steen & Hamilton, Brussels, Belgium, 1968; fellow Internat. Legal Ctr., Bogota, Colombia, 1968-70; fellow law and modernization Yale Law Sch., 1970-71; asst. to assoc. prof. U. Wis., Madison, 1971-79; co-dir. Ctr. Pub. Representation, Madison, 1976-77; assoc. Yale Inst. Social Policy Studies, 1978-79; vis. assoc. prof. Stanford Law Sch., 1978-79, prof. law, 1979—96, Lewis Talbot and Nadine Hearn Shelton prof. internat. legal studies, 1996-, assoc. dean, 1997-2001; dir. Overseas Studies Program Stanford U. 1985-92, dep. dir. Internat. Studies Inst., 1989-92, sr. fellow, 1993- . Vis. prof. Ctr. for Law and Economics U. Miami, 1977-78, Catholic U., Louvian, 1998; Jean Monnet vis. prof. European U. Inst., 1992-93, 96-99. Fellow, Humanities Rsch. Inst., U. Calif., Irvine, 1989. Office: Stanford Law Sch 559 Nathan Abbott Way Stanford CA 94305-8610 Office Phone: 650-723-7650. Business E-Mail: theller@stanford.edu.*

HELLERER, MARK R., lawyer; b. 1949; BA, Fordham Univ., 1971; JD, Univ. Buffalo, 1976. Bar: NY 1977, US Dist. Ct. (ea., so., we. dist. NY), US Ct. Appeals (2d cir.) DC. Law clk. Judge John T. Curtin, US Dist. Ct., We. Dist. NY, 1976—78; asst. U.S. atty. So. Dist. NY, U.S. Dept. Justice, NYC, 1983—89, chief Major Crimes unit, 1989—92; ptnr., co-chmn. Corp. Investigations & White Collar Def. practice, head NY Litigation practice Pillsbury Winthrop Shaw Pittman, NYC. Chmn. N.Y.C. Water Bd., 1995—2004. Recipient Dir. award, US Dept. Justice, 1988, John Marshall award, 1990. Mem.: ABA, Assn. Bar City of NY, Fed. Bar Coun., NY Coun. Criminal Def. Lawyers. Office: Pillsbury Winthrop Shaw Pittman 1540 Broadway New York NY 10036 Office Phone: 212-858-1787. Office Fax: 212-858-1500. Business E-Mail: mark.hellerer@pillsburylaw.com.

HELLERICH, MAHLON HOWARD, academic administrator; b. Allentown, Pa., Jan. 20, 1919; s. Raymond John Hellerich and Mabel Mary Conrad; m. Frieda Cecilia Steiff, Dec. 26, 1942; children: Constance Marie, Conrad Mahlon. PhB, Mahlenberg Coll., 1940; MA, Columbia U., 1947; PhD, U. Pa., 1957. Tchd. social studies Upper Moreland Jr./Sr. H. S., Willow Grove, Pa., 1942—44; asst. prof. history, polit. sci. Elizabethtown (Pa.) Coll., 1946—51; instr. social scis. Towson State Tchrs. Coll., Md., 1951—59; dean, prof. history Albright Coll., Reading, Pa., 1959—66; vice pres. acad. affairs Wartburg Coll., Waverly, Iowa, 1966—70; coord. Lehigh Valley Assn. Ind. Colls., Bethlehem, Pa., 1970—74; mus. dir. Lehigh County, Allentown, 1974—84. Vice chmn. City of Reading, Charter Study Commn., 1961—62; bd. trustees Luth. Theol. Sem., Phila., 1990—96. Author: Lehigh Heritage, 1979; co-author: Allentown: 1762-1987, 1987, Richard Peter Hoffman, 1990. Pres. Pa. German Soc., Kutztown, 1972—78; pres. bd. Bethlehem Housing Authority, 1995—96; committeeman Lehigh County Rep. Com., Allentown, 1978—2001. Sgt. U.S. Army, 1944—46. Fellow higher edn. adminstrn., U. Mich., Ann Arbor, 1958—59. Mem.: Pa. Hist. Assn., Am. Hist. Assn. Republican. Lutheran. Avocations: reading, teaching church and community service. Home: 1940 Turner St Flat 304 Allentown PA 18104

HELLERSTEIN, ALVIN KENNETH, federal judge; b. NYC, Dec. 28, 1933; s. Max and Rose (Lichtenstein) H.; m. Mildred Markow; children—Dina, Judith, Joseph AB, Columbia U., 1954, LL.B., 1956. Bar: N.Y. 1956, U.S. Ct. Appeals (2d cir.) 1960, U.S. Supreme Ct. 1964, U.S. Ct. Appeals (D.C. cir.) 1978, U.S. Ct. Appeals (3d and 9th cirs.) 1980, U.S. Ct. Appeals (10th cir.) 1981, U.S. Ct. Appeals (1st cir.) 1985, U.S. Ct. Appeals (8th cir.) 1996. Ptnr. Stroock & Stroock & Lavan, N.Y.C., 1969-98, retired, 1998—; judge U.S. Ct. Dist. Ct. (So. Dist. NY), 1998—. Lectr. Am. Law Inst., Practicing Law Inst. Contbr. articles to profl. jours. Past chmn. Bd. Jewish Edn. Served to capt. JAGC, U.S. Army, 1957-60 Fellow Am. Bar Found. (life); mem. ABA, Assn. Bar City N.Y. (past chmn. com. on judiciary 1992-95, past exec. com., past chmn. com. on fed. cts., v.p. 2004—), Fed. Bar Coun., Internat. Assn. Jewish Lawyers and Jurists, N.Y. State Bar Assn. Democrat. Office Phone: 212-805-0152.

HELLERSTEIN, DAVID JOEL, psychiatrist, researcher, writer; b. Cleve., Dec. 30, 1953; s. Herman Kopel and Mary Leah (Feil) H.; m. Lisa Perry, Oct. 16, 1983; children: Sarah Nicole, Benjamin, Jason Samuel. AB, Harvard U., 1976; MD, Stanford U., 1980. Intern, then resident psychiatry N.Y. Hosp. Cornell Med. Ctr., 1980-84; fellow pub. psychiatry Columbia Presbyn. Med. Ctr.-N.Y. State Psychiat. Inst., N.Y.C., 1984-85; attending psychiatrist Beth Israel Med. Ctr., N.Y.C., 1985-2000; instr. psychiatry Mt. Sinai Med. Ctr., N.Y.C., 1985-88, asst. prof. psychiatry, 1988-93; physician in charge psychiat. outpatient svcs. Beth Israel Med. Ctr., N.Y.C., 1989-96, chief outpatient psychiatry divsn., 1996-2000; asst. prof. psychiatry Albert Einstein Coll. Medicine, N.Y.C., 1993-96, assoc. prof. psychiatry, 1996-2000, dir. mood disorders rsch. unit, 1994-2000; clin. dir. N.Y. State Psychiatric Inst., 2000—05; assoc. prof. clin. psychiatry Columbia U. Coll. of Physicians and Surgeons, NYC, 2000—; dir. mood disorders rsch. unit St. Luke's Roosevelt Hosp. Ctr., 2001—; med. dir. Columbia Psychiatry Clin. Trials Program, 2005—. Author: (novel) Loving Touches, 1987, (essay collection) Battles of Life and Death, 1986, (non-fiction) A Family of Doctors, 1994, A Guide for the Journey, 2005; (novel) Stone Babies, 2000; contbr. articles to profl. jours.; contbg. editor N.Am. Rev., 1981—, Sci. Digest, 1986-87, 7 Days mag., 1988-90, M.D. Mag., 1990-95. MacDowell Colony fellow, 1984, 86, 88. Fellow APA (disting.); mem. PEN, Am. Psychiat. Assn. (editor N.Y. County Dist. newsletter, 1989-2001; chmn. publs. com. N.Y. County chpt. 1989-2001, pres.-elect 1997-98, pres. 1998-99), Author's Guild. Democrat. Jewish. E-mail: djh102@columbia.edu.

HELLERSTEIN, WALTER, lawyer; b. NYC, June 21, 1946; s. Jerome Robert and Pauline Alice H.; m. Nina Laurie Salant, Aug. 31, 1970; children; Michael, Margaret. AB, Harvard U., 1967; JD, U. Chgo., 1970. Bar: D.C. 1970, Ill. 1976, N.Y. 1989. Law clk. U.S. Ct. Appeals (2d cir.), N.Y.C., 1967-71; atty. Air Force Gen. Counsel's Office, Washington, 1971-73; assoc. Covington & Burling, Washington, 1973-75; asst. prof. law U. Chgo., 1976—78; assoc. prof. law U. Ga., Athens, 1978-84, prof. law, 1984-98, Francis Shackelford prof. taxation, 1999—; of counsel Morrison & Foerster, N.Y.C., 1986-96; ptnr. Sutherland, Asbill & Brennan, Atlanta, 1996-98, of counsel Washington, 2004—. KPMG, 1999—2004. Cons. Orgn. Econ. Coop. and Devel., 1999—, UN, 2000—; sci. com. Centro Europeo di Studi Tributarie sall'Electronic Commerce, 1999—. Co-author: State and Local Taxation of Natural Resources, 1986, State Taxation, vols. 1 & 2, 3d edit., 1998, Electronic Commerce and Multijurisdictional Taxation, 2001, Streamlined Sales and Use Tax, 2nd edit., 2005, State and Local Taxation, 8th edit., 2005; mem. edtl. bd. Nat. Tax Jour., 1983-2004, Multistate Tax Analyst, 1986—; chmn. editl. adv. bd. State Tax Notes, 1991—, Jour. Taxation, 1993—; contbr. articles to profl. jours. Recipient Multistate Tax Commn. 25th Ann. award for outstanding contbn. 1992. Fellow Am. Coll. Tax Counsel; mem. ABA, Nat. Tax Assn. (dir. 1981-83), Ill. State Bar Assn., D.C. Bar Assn., N.Y. State Bar Assn., Am. Law Inst., Order of Coif, Phi Beta Kappa. Home: 239 Westview Dr Athens GA 30606-4731 Office: U Ga Law Sch Athens GA 30602-6012 Office Phone: 706-542-5175. Business E-Mail: wallyh@uga.edu.

HELLIE, RICHARD, historian, educator; b. Waterloo, Iowa, May 8, 1937; s. Ole Ingeman and Mary Elizabeth (Larsen) H.; children: Benjamin, Michael; m. Shujie Yu, Feb. 26, 1998. BA, U. Chgo., 1958, MA, 1960, PhD, 1965; postgrad., U. Moscow, 1963-64. Vis. asst. prof. Rutgers U., 1965-66; asst. prof. Russian history U. Chgo., 1966-71, assoc. prof., 1971-80, prof., 1980-2001, dir. Ctr. for East European, Russian and Eurasian Studies, 1997—2004, Thomas E. Donnelley prof., 2001—. Presenter in field; chmn. Coll. Russian Civilization course U. Chgo., 1967—, chmn. undergrad. studies in Russian Civilization, 1970—, chmn. Ea. European NDEA Title VI Area Com., 1974—78, coord. Coll. History, 1971—73, mem. Coun. U. Senate, 1976—79, mem. coll. com. academic standing, 1984—87, co-coord. Moscow exchange program, 1990—96, co-coord. Russian and Soviet studies workshop, sole coord. Russian and Soviet studies workshop, 1993—94, dir. Nat. Resource Ctr. Slavic, East European/Russian and Eurasian studies, 1997—2004, mem. faculty oversight com. on computing, 1999—2002. Author: Muscovite Society, 1967, Enserfment and Military Change in Muscovy, 1971 (Am. Hist. Assn. Adams prize 1972), Slavery in Russia 1450-1725, 1982 (Laing prize U. Chgo. Press 1985, Russian translation with new post-Soviet foreword Kholopstvo v Rossii, 1450-1725, 1998), 1982, The Russian Law Code (Ulozhenie) of 1649, 1988, The Economy and Material Culture of Russia 1600-1725, 1999; editor: The Plow, the Hammer and the Knout: An Economic History of Eighteenth Century Russia, 1985, Ivan the Terrible: A Quarcentenary Celebration of His Death, 1987, The Frontier in Russian History, 1993, The Soviet Global Impact 1945-1991, 2003; editor quar. jour. Russian History;, 1988 contbr. numerous articles to profl. jours. Fgn. area tng. fellow Ford Found., 1962-65, Inter-Univ. Com. on Travel Grants award, 1963-64, Quantrell grant for the Improvement of Tchg., 1969, Social Sci. Divsional Rsch. grants U. Chgo., 1970-88, 1991-94, 1996-97, 1998-99, Guggenheim fellow, 1973-74, fellow NEH, 1978-79; grantee NEH, 1982-83, summer, 1988, NSF, 1988-90, Bradley Found., 1988-91. Mem. PEN, Nat. Hist. Soc., Am. Soc. Legal History (program com. for ann. meetings 1976), Am. Assn. Advancement Slavic Studies (editorial bd. Slavic Rev. 1979-81), Econ. History Assn., Assn. for Comparative Econ. Studies, Nat. Assn. Scholars, Jean Bodin Soc. for Comparative Instl. History, Chgo. Consortium Slavic and East European Studies (pres. 1990-92), Nat. Hist. Soc. (founding, bd. govs. 1999-2002). Office: U Chgo Dept History 1126 E 59th St Box 78 Chicago IL 60637-1580 Home: 5811 S Dorchester Ave Apt 2G Chicago IL 60637-1775 Office Phone: 773-702-8377. Business E-Mail: hell@midway.uchicago.edu.

HELLIKER, KEVIN, journalist; BA in English lit., U. Kans. With Wall St. Jour., Houston, 1982—83, London, 1993—94, reporter Dallas, 1990—92, special writer New York, 1992—93, Dallas bureau chief, 1994—96, Chgo. bureau chief, 1996—; reporter Kans. City Times, 1983—85; asst. editor Corp. Report Kansas City Mag., 1985—86; writer to mng. editor Ariz. Trend mag., 1986—89. Recipient Pulitzer Prize for explanatory reporting, 2004; grantee writing fellowship, Duke U., 1989. Office: Wall St Jour 200 Liberty St New York NY 10281

HELLINGA, HOMME WYTZES, biochemist, educator, researcher; PhD, Cambridge U., 1986. Prof. biochemistry Duke U. Med. Ctr. Contbr. articles to profl. jour. Recipient Feynman prize, Foresight Inst., 2004, Pioneer award, NIH, 2004, Emil Thomas Kaiser award, Protein Soc., 2004; grantee, Whitaker Found. Achievements include research in combined theoretical and experimental approaches to protein and drug design, molecular simulation, and protein engring. Office: Duke U Med Ctr Dept Biochemistry Nanaline H Duke Box 3711 DUMC Durham NC 27710 Office Phone: 919-681-5885. Office Fax: 919-684-8885. Business E-Mail: hwh@biochem.duke.edu.

HELLIWELL, THOMAS MCCAFFREE, physicist, researcher; b. Mpls., June 8, 1936; s. George Plummer and Eleanor (McCaffree) H.; m. Bernadette Egan Busenberg, Aug. 9, 1997. BA, Pomona Coll., 1958; PhD, Calif. Inst. Tech., 1963. Asst. prof. physics Harvey Mudd Coll., Claremont, Calif., 1962-67, assoc. prof., 1967-73, prof., 1973—, chmn. dept. physics, 1981-89, chair of faculty, 1990-93, Burton Bettingen prof. physics, 1990—2004, interim dean of faculty, 2004—05. Author: Introduction to Special Relativity, 1966; author papers in field of cosmology, gen. relativity and quantum theory. Sci. faculty fellow NSF, 1968. Mem.: AAAS, Am. Phys. Soc., Am. Assn. Physics Tchrs. Avocations: music, hiking. Office: Harvey Mudd Coll Dept Physics 301 E 12th St Claremont CA 91711-5901

HELLMAN, ARTHUR DAVID, law educator, consultant; b. N.Y.C., Dec. 9, 1942; s. Charles and Florence (Cohen) H. BA magna cum laude, Harvard U., 1963; JD, Yale U., 1966. Bar: Minn. 1967, U.S. Ct. Appeals (3d cir.) 1976, U.S. Ct. Appeals (9th cir.) 1979, U.S. Supreme Ct. 1980, Pa., 1985. Law clk. to assoc. justice Minn. Supreme Ct., 1966-67; asst. prof. William Mitchell Coll. Law, St. Paul, 1967-70, U. Conn. Sch. Law, West Hartford, 1970-72; vis. asst. prof. U. Ill. Coll. Law, Champaign, 1972-73; dep. exec. dir. Commn. on Revision Fed. Ct. Appellate System, Washington, 1973-75; assoc. prof. U. Pitts. Sch. Law, 1975-80, prof., 1980—, Sally Ann Semenko endowed chair, 2005—. Supervising staff atty. U.S. Ct. Appeals 9th cir., San Francisco, 1977-79, evaluation com., 1999-2001; vis. assoc. prof. U. Pa. Sch. Law, Phila., 1979; faculty Practicing Law Inst. Program on Fed. Appellate Practice, N.Y.C., 1984, Fed. Jud. Ctr. Nat. Workshop for Judges of U.S. Cts. of Appeals, 1993; planner Nat. Conf. Empirical Rsch. in Judicial Adminstrn., Tempe, Ariz., 1988; gen. editor U.S. Ct. Appeals 9th Cir. Project Improvements in Judicial Adminstrn., 1987-91; prin. investigator intercir. conflicts study Fed. Jud. Ctr., 1990; lectr., cons. and expert witness in field. Author: Laws Against Marijuana-The Price We Pay, 1975, Restructuring Justice-The Innovations of the Ninth Circuit and the Future of the Federal Courts, 1990, (with Russell Weaver) The First Amendment: Cases, Materials and Problems, 2002, The Federal Judiciary: Is There a Ned for Judges?, 2003, Ninth Circuit Court of Appeals Judgeship and Reorganization Act of 2004, 2004, (with Lauren K. Robel) Federal Courts: Cases and Materials on Judicial Federalism and the Lawyering Process, 2005, Holmes Group, The Federal Circuit, and the State of Patent Appeals, 2005; editor: Major Cases in First Amendment Law: Freedom of Speech, the Press, and Assembly, 1984; bus. editor: Yale U. Law Jour. Mem. liaison task panel on psychoactive drug use/misuse Pres.'s Commn. on Mental Health, 1977-78; conferee Pound Conf., 1976, The Future and the Courts Conf., 1990; conferee Nat. Conf. on State-Fed. Jud. Relationships, 1992; adv. bd. Western Legal History, 2001—. Recipient Chancellor's Disting. Rsch. award, U. Pitts., 2002; U. Pitts. Sch. Law disting. faculty scholar, 2001—. Fellow Am. Bar Found.; mem. ABA (subcom. on stds. of com. appellate staff attys., jud. adminstrn. divsn., future of cts. com. 1992—, conferee Nat. Conf. on State-Fed. Jud. Rels. 1992, conferee summit on civil justice improvements 1990), Pa. Bar Assn. (discovery rules com. 1995—), Am. Law Inst., Supreme Ct. Hist. Soc., Am. Judicature Soc. (drafting com. project on jud. election campaigns, bd. dirs. 1985-89, justice reform com. 1992-95, chair civil justice reform subcom. 1993-95, chair civil justice reform com. 1995-97, invited witness, hearings of the Subcommittee on Cts., the Internet and Intellectual Property of the US House Judiciary Com. on: Final Report of the Commn. on Structural Alternatives for Fed. Cts. Appeals, 1999, Fed. Jud. Discipline, 2001, unpublished jud. opinions, 2002). Office: U Pitts Law Sch Pittsburgh PA 15260 Office Phone: 412-648-1340. Business E-Mail: hellman@law.pitt.edu.

HELLMAN, F(REDERICK) WARREN, investor; b. NYC, July 25, 1934; s. Marco F. and Ruth (Koshl) H.; m. Patricia Christina Sander, Oct. 5, 1955; children: Frances, Patricia, Marco Warren, Judith. BA, U. Calif., Berkeley, 1955; MBA, Harvard U., 1959. With Lehman Bros., N.Y.C., 1959-84, ptnr., 1963-84; exec. mng. dir. Lehman Bros., Inc., N.Y.C., 1970-73, pres., 1973-75; ptnr. Hellman Ferri Investment Assocs., 1981-89, Matrix Ptnrs., 1981—; chmn. Hellman & Friedman LLC, San Francisco. Bd. dirs. DN & E Walter, Levi Strauss & Co., Offit Hall Capital Mgmt., LLC, Sugar Bowl Corp.; hon. trustee emeritus The Brookings Inst.; chmn. Voice of Dance. Former chmn. The San Francisco Found., trustee; trustee emeritus The Brookings Instn.; co-chair Calif. Commn. for Jobs and Econ. Growth; mem. Governor's Coun. Econ. Advisors, Com. on JOBS; mem. adv. bd. Walter A. Haas Sch. Bus., UC Berkeley; chmn. Voice of Dance; bd. dirs. Bay Area Coun., San Francisco C. of C. Mem. Bond Club, Piping Rock Club, Century Country Club, Pacific Union Club. Office: Hellman & Friedman LLC 1 Maritime Plz Fl 12 San Francisco CA 94111-3404

HELLMAN, RICHARD, endocrinologist; b. N.Y.C., Jan. 19, 1943; s. Gabriel Michael and Rose Hellman; m. Julie Lynn Hellman, Aug. 17, 1997; children: Leslie Gayle. BA in Math., NYU, 1962; MD, Chgo. Med. Sch., 1966. Diplomate Am. Bd. Internal Medicine, Am. Bd. Endocrinology and Metabolism, Nat. Bd. Med. Examiners. Intern in straight medicine U. Kans., Kansas City, 1966-67, resident in internal medicine, 1967-68, 71-72, fellow in endocrinology and metabolism, 1972-73; asst. prof. medicine U. Mo., Kansas City Sch. Medicine, 1973-75, assoc. prof. medicine, 1975-81, clin. assoc. prof. medicine, 1981-95, clin. prof. medicine, 1998—; pvt. practice physician

North Kansas City, Mo., 1981—. Chmn. adv. bd. Mo. Diabetes Control program CDC, ATlanta, 1981-86; med. dir. Midwest Diabetes Care Ctr., Kansas City, 1981-86, Diabetes Treatment Ctr., Trinity Luth. Hosp., Kansas City, Mo., 1986-94; med. dir., founder, Heart of Am. Diabetes Rsch. Found., North Kansas City, 1991—; mem. Physicians Consortium for Performance Improvement, 2000—, co-chmn. work group depression, 2001—, work group implementation, 2002—, mem. exec. com., 2005—; cons. in field. Contbr. articles to profl. jours. Active Mo. Inst. Quality Health Care Mo. Patient Care Rev. Found., 1999—; mem. Mayor's Health Commn., Kansas City, Mo., 2001—, mem. minority health com., 2001—, mem. improvement com., 2001—; chair patient safety com. Health Commn., 2005—. Mem. AMA (accreditation program 1998-99, work group, cons. on applications of med. informatics and performance measures 2001), Am. Assn. Clin. Endocrinologists (bd. dir. 1999—, chair continuing med. edn. 2000-01, chair legis. and regulatory com. 2001-03, strategic planning com. 2000-01, sec. 2003-04, chmn. task force on patient safety 2003—, treas. 2004-05, bd. liaison legis. and regulatory com. 2001-04, Kansas City, chair patient and safety com. 2005—, v.p. 2005-), Am. Coll. Endocrinology (bd. dir. 2001-02, task force on cert. 2002-03), Met. Med. Soc. Greater Kansas City (sec. 1999, bd. dir. 1999-2000, pres. 2000-01, Meritorious Svc. award 2002), Physicians Coalition (exec. com.), Nat. Diabetes Alliance (tech. expert panel), Alpha Omega Alpha. Office: Ste 210 2750 Clay Edwards Dr North Kansas City MO 64116 Office Phone: 816-421-3700. Office Fax: 816-421-1654.

HELLMAN, SAMUEL, radiologist, educator; b. N.Y.C., July 23, 1934; s. Henry Sidney and Anna (Egar) Hellman; m. Marcia Sherman, June 30, 1957; children: Jeffrey, Richard, Deborah Susan. BS magna cum laude, Allegheny Coll., 1955, DSc (hon.), 1984; MD cum laude, SUNY, Syracuse, 1959, DSc (hon.), 1993; MS (hon.), Harvard U., 1968. Med. intern Beth Israel Hosp., Boston, 1959—60; asst. resident radiology Yale Sch. Medicine and Grace-New Haven Hosp., 1960—62, postdoctoral fellow radiotherapy and cancer research, 1962—64; postdoctoral fellow Inst. Cancer Research and Royal Marsden Hosp., London, 1965—66; asst. prof. radiology Yale Sch. Medicine, 1966—68; assoc. prof. radiology Harvard Med. Sch., 1968—70; dir. Joint Center for Radiation Therapy, 1968—83, assoc. prof., chmn. dept. radiation therapy, 1971, prof., chmn. dept., 1971—83, also Alvan T. and Viola D. Fuller-Am. Cancer Soc. prof.; physician-in-chief Meml. Sloan Kettering Cancer Ctr., 1983—88, Benno Schmidt chair in clin. oncology, 1983—88; dean div. biol. sci. and Pritzker Sch. Medicine, v.p. for Med. Ctr. U. Chgo., 1988—93, Pritzker Prof., 1988—93, Pritzker Disting. Svc. Prof., 1993—. Chmn. bd. sci. counselors divsn. cancer treatment Nat. Cancer Inst., 1980—84; bd. govs. Argonne Nat. Lab., 1990—93; trustee Brookings Inst., 1992—; bd. dirs. Varian Med. Systems Inc., Insightec; mem. sci. adv. bd. Ludwig Inst. for Cancer Rsch. Contbr. numerous articles to med. jours. Trustee Allegheny Coll., 1979—98, chmn. bd. trustees, 1987—93. Recipient Rosenthal award for cancer rsch., 1980, medal, City of Paris, 1986, award for Outstanding Contbns. to Cancer Care, Assn. Cmty. Cancer Ctrs., 1993. Fellow: AAAS; mem.: N.Y. Acad. Scis., Soc. Chmn. Acad. Radiology Depts., Inst. Medicine NAS, Assn. Am. Physicians, Am. Cancer Soc., Am. Soc. Hematology, Am. Assn. Cancer Rsch., Am. Soc. Clin. Oncology (pres. 1986, David A. Karnovsky lectr. 1994), Assn. Univ. Radiologists, Am. Coll. Radiology (gold medal 2003), Am. Soc. Therapeutic Radiologists (pres. 1983, Gold medal 1991), Am. Radium Soc., Alpha Omega Alpha, Sigma Xi, Phi Beta Kappa. Home: 1122 N Dearborn St Apt 25H Chicago IL 60610 Office: U Chgo Divsn Biol Scis 5841 S Maryland Ave Chicago IL 60637-1463 Office Phone: 773-702-4346. Business E-Mail: s-hellman@uchicago.edu.

HELLMAN, THEODORE ALBERT, JR., lawyer; b. Orange, N.J., June 4, 1946; s. Theodore A. Sr. and Jean Florence (Chrystie) H.; m. Janice Anne Reed, July 12, 1969; children: Theodore A. III, Anne, Karen, Julia. BA, Yale U., 1968; MA in Govt., Georgetown U., 1971; JD, U. Va., 1974. Bar: Calif. 1974. Assoc. Pettit & Martin, San Francisco, 1974-78; ptnr. Hanson, Bridgett, Marcus, Vlahos & Rudy, San Francisco, 1978—. Dir. Pacific Presbyn. Med. Found., San Francisco. Author: (supplement) Drafting California Irrev. Intervivos Trusts 1985, 1984; co-author: (chpt.) California Will Drafting, 1982; mem. editorial bd. U. Va. Law Rev. Lt. (j.g.) USNR, 1968-71. Mem. Bar Assn. of San Francisco (chmn. estate planning and probate sect. 1991—). Avocation: running. Home: 445 Lovell Ave Mill Valley CA 94941-1053 Office: Hanson Bridgett Marcus Vlahos & Rudy 333 Market St Fl 23D San Francisco CA 94105-2102

HELLMANN, DAVID BRUCE, medical educator; b. Louisville, Mar. 2, 1951; BA magna cum laude, Yale U., 1973; MD, Johns Hopkins U., 1977. Diplomate Am. Bd. Internal Medicine, Am. Bd. Rheumatology, lic. physician Md. Intern, resident Johns Hopkins Hosp., Balt., 1977-80; fellow in rheumatology/clin. immunology U. Calif., San Francisco, 1980-82, asst. clin. prof. medicine, 1982-86; chief Moffitt Arthritis Clinics, San Francisco, 1984-86; acting chief divsn. rheumatology/clin. immunology U. Calif., San Francisco, 1985—86; dep. dir. dept. medicine Johns Hopkins U., Balt., 1986-94, exec. vice chmn. dept. medicine, 1995-2000, med. dir. Faculty Practice Ctr., 1991-93, dir. Osler Med. Housestaff Tng. Program, 1992-2000, Mary Betty Stevens Prof. Medicine, 1996—; chmn. dept. medicine Johns Hopkins Bayview Med. Ctr., 2000—; acting dir. dept. medicine Johns Hopkins Hosp., Balt., 1994-95. Assoc. physician-in-chief Johns Hopkins Hosp., Balt., 1986-94, acting physician-in-chief, 1994-95; lectr. in field. Assoc. editor Medicine, 1993—; co-author: Rheumatology Committee, MKSAP II, 1995—; reviewer Jour. Rheumatology, Arthritis and Rheumatism, Western Jour. Medicine, Medicine, Jour. Clin. Investigation, Jour. of AMA; contbr. articles to profl. jours. Chmn. profl. edn. com. Md. chpt. Arthritis Found., 1991, 92, 93, 94. Recipient Kaiser Award for excellence in teaching U. Calif.-San Francisco, 1986, Cert. of Distinction in Teaching, 2d Yr. Med. Sch. Class, 1986, Profl. Edn. award Md. chpt. Arthritis Found., 1991, Disting. Svc. award for profl. edn., 1993, Faculty Teaching award Osler Med. Housestaff, 1992, Johns Hopkins Minority Faculty Assn. award, 1993; Henry Strong Denison scholar, 1975. Master ACP (gov. 1998-2002), Am. Coll. Rheumatology; mem. Am. Bd. Internal Medicine (dir. 2000—), Assn. Program Dirs. Internal Medicine, Internat. Network for Study of the Systemic Vasculitides, Alpha Omega Alpha. Office: Johns Hopkins Bayview Med Ctr A-I-W 4940 Eastern Ave Baltimore MD 21224

HELLMERS, NORMAN DONALD, retired historic site director; b. New Orleans, Feb. 3, 1944; s. Leonard H. and Meta J.C. (Wegener) H.; m. Patricia I. O'Brien, May 29, 1966; children: Jennifer L, Jeffrey N. BA, Concordia U., River Forest, Ill., 1966; postgrad., U. Iowa, 1966-67, La. State U., 1968. Writer, photographer Nebr. Game and Pks. Commn., Lincoln, 1969-71; ranger nat. pks. various locations, 1972-73; dist. naturalist Shenandoah Nat. Pk., Luray, Va., 1973-76; chief interpretation Grand Portage (Minn.) Nat. Monument, 1976-81; supt. Lincoln Boyhood Nat. Meml., Lincoln City, Ind., 1981-90, Lincoln Home Nat. Hist. Site, Springfield, Ill., 1990—2003; ret., 2003. Lutheran. Avocations: photography, genealogy.

HELLMUTH, GEORGE WILLIAM, architect; b. Detroit, Nov. 21, 1942; s. George Francis and Mildred Lee (Henning) H.; m. Camille Byrns Carmody, Feb. 20, 1965 (div. 2003); children: George, Holly, Julie, Emily. BA in Architecture, Yale U., 1964; MBA, Eastern N.Mex. U., 1969; BArch, CCNY, 1979. Sr. prin. Hellmuth, Obata & Kassabaum, Washington, 1971—. Capt. USAF, 1965-69. Mem. AIA, Sky Club (N.Y.C.). Roman Catholic. Office: Hellmuth Obata & Kassabaum PC 3223 Grace St NW Washington DC 20007-3614 Home: 2721 N Ohio St Arlington VA 22207 E-mail: george.hellmuth@hok.com.

HELLMUTH, THEODORE HENNING, lawyer; b. Detroit, Mar. 28, 1949; s. George F. and Mildred Hellmuth; m. Laurie Hellmuth, May 29, 1970; children: Elizabeth Ann, Theodore Henning, Sara Marie. BA, U. Pa., 1970; JD cum laude, U. Mo.-Columbia, 1974. Bar: Mo. 1974, U.S. Dist. Ct. (ea. dist.) Mo. 1974, U.S. Ct. Appeals (8th cir.) 1978. Assoc., then ptnr. Armstrong Teasdale LLP, St. Louis, 1974—2002. Author: Missouri Real Estate, 1985, 2d edit., 1998, Lease Audits: The Essential Guide, 1994; editor Distressed Real Estate Law Alert, 1987-88, Litigated Commercial Real Estate Document Reports, 1987-95. Mem.: ABA, Am. Coll. Real Estate Lawyers, Order of Coif. Office: Armstrong Teasdale LLP 1 Metropolitan Sq Ste 2600 Saint Louis MO 63102-2740 E-mail: thellmuth@armstrongteasdale.com.

HELLMUTH, WILLIAM FREDERICK, economics professor; b. Washington, Jan. 8, 1920; s. William Frederick and Sybel (Grant) H.; m. Jean A. Dieffenbach, Feb. 14, 1943; children: James (dec.), Suzanne, William L., Peter G. BA, Yale U., 1940, PhD, 1948. Instr. econs. Yale U., 1945-48; mem. faculty Oberlin Coll., 1948-68, prof. econs., 1958-68; dean Oberlin Coll. (Coll. Arts and Scis.), 1960-67; dep. asst. sec. treasury for tax policy, 1968-69; v.p. arts, prof. econs. McMaster U., Hamilton, Ont., Can., 1969-73, also bd. govs., 1969-73; prof. econs. Va. Commonwealth U., 1973-87, chmn. dept. econs., 1973-82; emeritus prof., 1987—. Economist Fed. Res. Bd., 1954-56; prof. U. Wis., 1959, Univ. Coll., Dar es Salaam, Tanzania, 1965, 66 Mem. Nat. Com. Taxation with Representation; mem. Oberlin City Coun., 1957-63, 67-68; pres. 1st Unitarian Ch., Richmond, 1976-78; mem. welfare adv. bd. City of Richmond, 1976-83; staff dir. Capital City Govt. Commn., 1980-81; treas. adv. bd. Richmond Cmty. H.S., 1986-92; bd. dirs. Common Cause Va., 1988-96, Shepherd's Ctr. of Richmond, 1985-91, 94-96, Va. Interfaith Ctr. for Pub. Policy, 1987-96, Va. State Dem. Com., 1994-96; fin. comm., Eskaton, 2001— Maj. aus U.S. Army, WWII. Decorated Air medal, Bronze Star. Mem. SAR, Nat. Tax Assn., Beta Gamma Sigma, Phi Beta Kappa. Democrat. Home: 3939 Walnut Ave # 187 Carmichael CA 95608-7309 Personal E-mail: bjhcool@sbcglobal.net.

HELLON, MICHAEL THOMAS, financial analyst, political organization worker; b. Camden, NJ, June 24, 1942; s. James Bernard and Dena Louise (Blackburn) H.; m. (div.); 2 children. BS, Ariz. State U., 1972. Ins. investigator Equifax, Phoenix, 1968-69; exec. v.p. Phoenix Met. C. of C., 1969-76; exec. Londen Ins. Group, 1976-78; pres. Hellon and Assocs., Inc., 1978—. Small claims hearing officer Pima County Justice Ct., 1990—; mem. Pima County Bd. Adjustments, 1993-00, Pima County Merit Commn., 2000—, Ariz. Jud. Performance Rev. Commn., 2004-; nat. def. exec. res. U.S. Dept. of Commerce, 1986-97; bd. dirs. Equity Benefit Life Ins. Co., Modern Income Life Ins. Co. of Mo., First Equity Security Life Ins. Co., Tucson Classics; mem. commn. jud. performance rev., Ariz., 2004—. Mem. Ariz. Occupl. Safety and Health Adv. Coun., 1972-76, mem. Speaker's Select Com. Auto Emissions, 1976; Phoenix Urban League, 1972-73, Area Manpower Planning coun., 1971-72, Phoenix Civic Plaza Dedication Com., 1972, Phoenix Air Quality Maintenance Taks Force, 1976; pres. Vis. Nurse Svc., 1978-79; Rep. precinct capt., 1973—; state campaign dir. Arizonans for Reagan Com., 1980; alt. del. Rep. Nat. Conv., 1980, 84, 88; mem. staff Reagan-Bush Nat. Conv., 1984; campaign mgr. for various candidates, 1972-82; mem. exec. com. Ariz. Rep. Party, 1989-90, chmn., 1997-99; mem. Rep. Nat. Com., 1992-04, mem. exec. com., 1997-04; bd. dirs. ATMA Tng. Found., 1981-84. Served with USAF, 1964-68. Decorated Bronze Star medal, Purple Heart; Recipient George Washington Honor medal Freedom's Found., 1964; commendation Fed. Bar Assn., 1973. Mem. U.S. C. of C. (pub. affairs com. western divsn. 1974-76), Inst. of Property Taxation, Internat. Assn. Assessing Officers, U.S. Dept. Commerce Exec. Res., Ariz. C. of C. Mgrs. Assn. (bd. m em. 1974-76), Tucson C. of C., Trunk 'N Tusk Club, Catalina Soccer Club (bd. dirs. 1984-88). Home: 1261 W Hopbush Way Tucson AZ 85704-2647 Address: 6700 N Oracle Rd #110 Tucson AZ 85704

HELLRUNG, STEPHEN ANDREW, lawyer; b. St. Louis, July 7, 1947; s. J. W. and Alice T. Hellrung; m. Margaret M. Frailey; children: Margaret, Carolyn, Joseph, Leigh. AB, U. Notre Dame, 1969, JD, 1972. Bar: Mo. 1972, U.S. Dist. Ct. (ea. dist.) Mo. 1972, Ill. 1978, N.Y. 1983, Minn. 1998, N.C. 2000. Assoc. Rassieur, Long, Yawitz & Schneider, 1972—78; asst. gen. counsel A.E. Staley, Decatur, Ill., 1978—82; sr. v.p., sec., gen. counsel Bausch & Lomb, Inc., Rochester, NY, 1983—97; sr. v.p., gen. counsel, sec. Pillsbury Co., Mpls., 1997—98, Lowe's Cos., Inc., 1999—2003, Graphic Packaging Corp., Marietta, Ga., 2003—. Mem.: Am. Corp. Counsel Assn., Mo. Bar Assn., NC State Bar Assn., Ill. State Bar Assn., NY State Bar Assn., Minn. State Bar Assn. Office: Graphic Packaging Corp 814 Livingston Ct Marietta GA 30067

HELLSTRÖM, INGEGERD, medical researcher; b. Stockholm; permanent resident, US, 1966, US citizen, 1996; m. Karl Erik Hellström; children: Katarina Elisabet, Per Erik. MD of Medicine, Karolinska Inst. Med. Sch., Stockholm, 1964, PhD of Medicine (Tumor Biology), 1966. Rsch. assoc. (docent), dept. Tumor Biology Karolinska Inst. Med. Sch., Stockholm, 1959-66, asst. prof. dept. tumor biology, 1966; asst. prof. microbiology U. Wash., Seattle, 1966—, rsch. assoc. prof. microbiology, 1969-72, prof. microbiology/immunology, 1972—85, adj. prof. pathology, 1972—85, affiliate prof. pathology, 1985—; mem. and program head, divsn. tumor immunology Fred Hutchinson Cancer Rsch. Ctr., Seattle, 1975—83; sr. scientist Oncogen, Seattle, 1983—85, lab. dir., 1985—86; v.p. Oncogen/Bristol-Myers Squibb, Seattle, 1986-90; v.p. immunological diseases Bristol-Myers Squibb Pharm. Rsch. Inst., Seattle, 1990—97; pron. investigator Pacific Northwest Rsch. Inst., Seattle, 1997—. Patents in the field: 17 US patents and 1 UK Patent; mem. editl. adv. bd., Jour. of Nat. Cancer Inst.; assoc. editor, Cancer Research, 1980-87, 1988-93, 1995-; mem. editl. bd., Anticancer Research; mem. gen. assembly, GM Cancer Rsch. Found.; mem. external adv. com, Specialized Ctr. for Cancer Rsch., U. Ill. at Chgo., Coll. Medicine, 1991-; contbr. to 400 sci. publs. Recipient Lucy Wortham James award, Ewing Soc., 1971, Matrix Table award, 1972, Pap award Outstanding Contbn. Cancer Rsch., Papanicolaou Cancer Rsch. Inst., 1973, Am. Cancer Soc. Nat. award 1974, RNO (Knight of Northern Star, First Class Swedish Order of Merit), 1976, Humboldt award to Sr. US Sci., Humbolt Stiftung Bonn, W. Germany, 1980. Mem. AMA, Am. Assn. Immunologists, Am. Fedn. Clin. Rsch., Am. Assn. Cancer Rsch., Soc. Biol. Therapy. Office: Harborview Med Ctr Box 359939 325 Ninth Ave Seattle WA 98104-2499 Office Phone: 206-341-5908. Business E-Mail: ihellstr@u.washington.edu.

HELLSTRÖM, KARL ERIK, science educator, researcher; b. Stockholm; permanent resident, US, 1966, US Citizen, 1996; m. Ingegerd Hellström; children: Katarina Elisabet, Per Erik. Candidate of medicine, Karolinska Inst. Med. Sch., Stockholm, 1955, MD, PhD, Karolinska Inst. Med. Sch., Stockholm, 1964. Rsch. fellow, dept. histology Karolinska Inst. Med. Sch., Stockholm, 1953—57, rsch. assoc., dept. histology, 1957, docent in tumor biology, 1958—62, asst. prof., dept. tumor biology, 1962—66; investigator in cell biology funded by Swedish Medical Rsch. Coun, 1964—66; assoc. prof. pathology U. Wash. Sch. Medicine, Seattle, 1966—69, prof. pathology, 1969—83, adj. prof. microbiology and immunology, affiliate prof. pathology, 1984—; prin. investigator Pacific Northwest Rsch. Inst., Seattle, 1997—2004; mem. and head, program of tumor immunology Fred Hutchinson Cancer Rsch Ctr., Seattle, 1975—83; sr. scientist Oncogen, Seattle, 1983—85, lab. dir., 1985—86; v.p. Oncogen/Bristol-Myers, 1986—90; v.p. oncology drug discovery Bristol-Myers Squibb Pharm. Rsch. Inst., 1990—95, v.p. immunotherapeutics drug discovery, 1995—97. Bd. dirs. Seattle Genetics, Inc.; sci. adv. coun. Cancer Rsch. Inst. Inc. Editl. bd.: Cancer Immunology and Immunology; contbr. to 460 sci. publs. Assessor Anti-Cancer Coun., Victoria, Canada; Can. reviewer Netherlands Cancer Found. Recipient Lucy Wortham James award, Ewing Soc., 1971, Parke Davis award in Exptl. Pathology, 1972, Pap award for Outstanding Contbn. in Cancer Rsch., Papanicolaou Cancer Rsch. Inst., Miami, Fla., 1973, Nat. award for Cancer Rsch., Am. Cancer Soc., 1974, RNO (Knight of the Northern Star, 1st Class, Swedish Order of Merit), 1976, Humboldt award to Sr. US Sci., Humboldt Stiftung, Bonn, Germany, 1980. Mem.: Clin. immunology Soc., Am. Assn. for Clin. Rsch., AAAS, Am. Assn. of Immunologists, Am. Assn. Exptl. Pathology, Am. Assn. for Cancer Rsch., NY Acad. Sciences, Sigma XI, The Sci. Rsch. Soc., Alpha Omega Alpha, U. Wash. Chap. Achievements include patents in field. Office: Harborview Med Ctr Box 359939 325 Ninth Ave Seattle WA 98104-2499 Office Phone: 206-341-5907. Business E-Mail: hellsk@u.washington.edu.

HELLWEGE, NANCY CAROL, special education educator; b. Bridgeport, Conn., Dec. 28, 1933; d. Emil and Dorothy Alma (Sell) Rosenoch; children: Michael, Christie, Patricia. BS with distinction, Ind. U., Ft. Wayne, 1972, MS, 1977; EdS, Ball State U., 1984. Tchr. 1st grade Luth. Schs., Ft. Wayne, Ind., 1962—66; coord. Head Start, Ft. Wayne, 1967—68; tchr. kindergarten Luth. Schs., Ft. Wayne, 1968—78; tchr. resource rm. East Allen County Schs., New Haven, Ind., 1978—81; cons. N.E. Colo. BOCES, Haxtun, 1982—84; strategist South Ctrl. BOCES, Pueblo, Colo., 1984—86; supr. Mt. BOCES, Leadville, Colo., 1986—87; coord. Broward Cunty Schs., Ft. Lauderdale, Fla., 1987—88; pres. Learning Power, Inc., 1988—; prin., owner Sch. for Learning Disabled Christi Acad., 2000—. Author handbooks: Helping Children Reach Their Potential, 1991, Different Strokes/Different Folks, 1990. Mem.: NAFE, Phi Delta Kappa. Avocations: swimming, reading, camping. Office Phone: 954-597-0645. E-mail: nhellwege@christiacademy.com.

HELLY, WALTER SIGMUND, engineering educator; b. Vienna, Aug. 22, 1930; came to U.S., 1938, naturalized, 1944; s. Edward and Elizabeth (Bloch) H.; m. Dorothy Oxman, Mar. 4, 1956; 1 dau., Miranda. BA, Cornell U., 1950; MS, U. Ill., 1954; PhD, Mass. Inst. Tech., 1959. With Sylvania Electric Co., Waltham, Mass., 1954-56; sr. engr. Melpar Co., Boston, 1956-59; mem. tech. staff Bell Telephone Labs., N.Y.C., 1959-62; sr. engr. Port of N.Y. Authority, 1962-65; prof. ops. rsch. Poly. Inst. N.Y., 1966—96. Cons. on traffic flow. Author: Urban Systems Models, 1975; Book rev. editor: Jour. Ops. Research, 1970—; Contbr. articles to profl. jours. Mem. Ops. Research Soc. Am. (past chmn. transp. sci. sect.) Home: 91 Central Park W New York NY 10023-4600 Office: 333 Jay St Brooklyn NY 11201-2907 Personal E-mail: whelly@nyc.rr.com.

HELLYER, CHRISTINE FRANCES, secondary school educator, art educator; d. Norman Earle and Frances Marie Hellyer. BFA, BA, U. Minn., 1981; MA, U. Tex., 1987. Tchr. T.K. Gorman, Tyler, Tex., 1981—88; instr. scuba Virgin Islands Dive Sch., St. Thomas, 1988—90; co-mgr. Lane Bryant, Morrow, Ga., 1990—91; coord. summer programs Fulton County Arts Coun., Atlanta, 1992—98; instr. scuba Divers Supply, Doraville, Ga., 1995—97; tchr. Henry County Bd. Edn., McDonough, Ga., 1991—2003, Gwinnet County, Norcross, Ga., 2003—. Recipient Goldfine Purchase award, Tweed Mus. Art, 1980. Mem.: Nat. Art Edn. Assn., Ga. Assn. Educators. Home: 612 Sweet Stream Way Lawrenceville GA 30044 Office: Meadowcreek High School 4455 Steve Reynolds Blvd Norcross GA 30093-3323

HELLYER, CONSTANCE ANNE (CONNIE ANNE CONWAY), writer, musician; b. Puyallup, Wash., Apr. 22, 1937; d. David Tirrell and Constance (Hopkins) H.; m. Peter A. Corning, Dec. 30, 1963 (div. 1977); children: Anne Arundel, Stephanie Deak Cunningham; m. Don W. Conway, Oct. 12, 1980 (dec. 2005) BA with honors, Mills Coll., 1959. Grader, rschr. Harvard U., Cambridge, Mass., 1959-60; rschr. Newsweek mag., N.Y.C., 1960-63; author's asst. Theodore H. White and others, N.Y.C., 1964-69; freelance writer, editor Colo., Calif., 1970-75; writer, editor Stanford (Calif.) U. Med. Ctr., 1975-79; comm. dir. No. Calif. Cancer Program, Palo Alto, 1979-82, Stanford Law Sch., Palo Alto, 1982-97; mgr., vocalist, pianist String of Pearls Band, 1991—, co-leader China tours, 1999, 2001, 2002. Founding editor (newsletters) Insight, 1978-80, Synergy, 1980-82, Stanford Law Alum, 1992-95; editor (mag.) Stanford Lawyer, 1982-98; contbr. articles to profl. jours. and mags. Recipient silver medal Coun. for Advancement and Support Edn., 1985, 89, award of distinction dist. VII, 1994. Mem. Nat. Assn. Sci. Writers, Phi Beta Kappa. Democrat. Home: PO Box 828 Cannon Beach OR 97110 Personal E-mail: conniepearl@yahoo.com.

HELLYER, TIMOTHY MICHAEL, protective services officer; b. Chgo., Nov. 30, 1954; s. William Al and Dotha Helen (Bucknum) H.; m. Nancy Ruth O'Donnell, Nov. 29, 1986; children: Jennifer Lynn, Allyson Jean. Student, So. Ill. U., 1985-86; BA, Nat. Louis U., 2002; MA, Aurora U., 2003. Cert. firefighter III; cert. paramedic. Firefighter, paramedic Palatine (Ill.) Fire Dept., 1980—2000; ret., 2000; program chair paramedic scis. Ivy Tech. State Coll., South Bend, Ind., 2005—. Instr. CPR, Chgo. Heart Assn., 1976—; pres. N.W. Assn. Provider Emergency Med. Svcs. Sys., 1989-92; mem. No. Ill. Critical Stress Debriefing Team. Deacon Palatine Presbyn. Ch., 1989-92; mem. comm. coun. Sch. Dist. 300, 1993-2003, mem. Year Round Sch. com., 1998-99; mem. improvement team Westfield Cmty. Sch., 1993-2004. Named Firefighter of the Yr., Jaycees of Palatine, 1987. Mem. Prehosp. Care Providers Ill. (bd. dirs. 1990), St. Francis Hook and Ladder Soc., Ill. Profl. Firefighters Assn., Smithsonian Instn., Nat. Trust Historic Preservation, Nat. Geographic Soc., U.S. Naval Inst., Nat. Space Soc. Republican. Presbyterian. Avocations: collecting disney memorabilia, gardening, model railroading. Office: Ivy Tech State College 220 Dean Johnson Blvd South Bend IN 46601 Home: 51288 Harbor Ridge Dr Granger IN 46530-4840 Office Phone: 574-289-7001 6344. Personal E-mail: hellyer4@aol.com. E-mail: thellyer@ivytech.edu.

HELM, DEWITT FREDERICK, JR., professional society administrator, consultant; b. Charlotte, NC, Apr. 24, 1933; s. DeWitt Frederick Sr. and Blanche Buchanan (DeBusk) H.; divorced; children: DeWitt Frederick III, Mary McNair Helm Bishop; m. Anne M. Valle, Mar. 1, 2002. BS in History, Davidson (N.C.) Coll., 1956. Mgr. advt. Vick Chem. Co., N.Y.C., 1956-63; mgr. consumer products Pfizer, Inc., N.Y.C., 1963-66; mgr. consumer product acquisition and devel. A.H. Robins Co., Richmond, Va., 1966-69; exec. v.p. Miller Morton Co., Richmond, 1969-72, pres., 1972-81, Miller Morton of Can. Ltd., 1969-81; sr. v.p. Jack Morton Prodns. Inc., Washington, 1981-84; exec. v.p. Assn. Nat. Advertisers, Inc., N.Y.C., 1984, pres., 1984-93, also bd. dirs.; mng. ptnr. DH Assocs., Palm City, Fla., 1994-97, The Advt. Partnership LLC, Bearfort, SC, 1996—. Deacon, elder Presbyn. Ch., United Meth. Ch., 1990-2003; trustee Christ Ch., NYC, 2000-03; bd. dirs. Nat. Tobacco Festival, Richmond, 1977-81, Traffic Audit Bur., NYC, 1984-93. With U.S. Army, 1956-58. Mem. Consumer Healthcare Products Assn. (bd. dirs., exec. com. 1972-80, chmn. 1973-75), Coun. Better Bus. Burs. (bd. dirs. 1989-93), Am. Advt. Mus. (founding dir., nat. bd. 1987—), Smithsonian Instn.'s Ctr. for Advt. History (adv. bd. 1989—), Advt. Coun. (bd. dirs., treas. 1984-93, life bd. dirs. 2002—), Advt. Rsch. Found. (bd. dirs. 1984-93), World Fedn. Advertisers (bd. dirs., mgmt. com. 1984-93), Media-Advt. Partnership for Drug-Free Am. (mgmt. bd.), Wintergreen (Va.) Club, Sky Club, Met. Club (N.Y.C.), Harbour Ridge Club (Fla.). Office Phone: 843-322-0302. Personal E-mail: taphelm@charter.net.

HELM, DONALD CAIRNEY, geologist, engineer, educator; b. Yokohama, Japan, Mar. 26, 1937; s. Nathan Teal and Rebecca Forsyth (Cairney) H.; m. Usha Monica Sundari Muliyil, Dec. 1961 (div. 1982); m. Karen Emily Reed, Sept. 3, 1982; 1 child, Rebecca Bernice Vera. *Grandparents Verling Winchell Helm (1875-1907) and Martha Teal Helm (1873-1952) moved from Indiana to Japan as newlyweds in the late 19th century to help establish the Japanese YMCA. Father Nathan, uncle Winchell, and aunt Kathryn Helm Turner were born in Japan, whereas aunt Margaret Helm Starn was born in the U.S. The Rev. Dr. Nathan Helm (1904-84) returned to Japan in 1927 with Rebecca (1904-95) his Scottish-American bride whom he met at Wooster College. He taught Latin and Greek at Meiji Gakuin in Tokyo. Siblings Charles William Helm (1931-) of Perth, Australia and Martha Christina Helm Miller (1928-89) of Dallas and Jakarta were also born in Japan.* AB in Math. cum laude, Amherst Coll., 1959; MDiv in Theology, Hartford Sem. Found., 1962; postgrad., Colo. Sch. Mines, 1962-63, 64-65; MS in Geol. Engring., U. Calif.-Berkeley, 1970, PhD in Civil Engring., 1974. Registered profl. engr., Australia. Vol. in rural devel. Mitraniketan Project, Kerala State, India, 1963-64; hydraulic engr. U.S. Geol. Survey, Portland, Oregon, 1965-68, Berkeley, Calif., 1968-69, research hydrologist Sacramento, 1969-78, Las Vegas, Nev., 1991-93, Carson City, Nev., 1993-96; ret., 1999; research physicist Lawrence Livermore Nat. Lab., U. Calif., 1978-84, ret. 1990, group leader, geohydrology and environ. studies group, 1981-84; prin. research scientist Geomechanics Div. Commonwealth Sci. and Indsl. Research Orgn. (CSIRO), Melbourne, Australia, 1984-92, ret. 1992, hydraulics group leader, 1984-86, chmn. selection com. for hiring research scientists, 1986, rep. to Research Officers Assn., 1986-87, mem. ex-officio divisional staff cons. com., 1986-87; rsch. hydrogeologist Nev. Bur. Mines and Geology U. Nev., Reno, Las Vegas, 1989-98, vis. rsch. scientist Nev. Bur. Mines and Geology Reno, 1989-92; chief Las Vegas Office, 1989-93; prof. geology U. Nev., Reno, 1992-98, adj. prof., 1998—; Samuel P. Massie prof. civil engring. Morgan

State U., Balt., 1996—. Instr. U.S. Geol. Survey Advanced Groundwater Sch., Denver, 1972-78, UNESCO Internat. Workshop on Land Subsidence, Mexico City, 1979, Pacific Sch. Religion, Berkeley, Calif., 1982, courses on subsidence for various mining cos., Western Australia, 1985, for U.S. Geol. Survey rsch. hydrologists, Tucson, 1987; advisor, nat. steering com. Geothermal Subsidence Rsch. Program, U.S. Dept. Energy, 1976-84; vis. sr. rsch. scientist State Elec. Commn. Victoria, Australia, 1982-83, U.S. Bur. Reclamation, Phoenix, 1984; subcom. on math. modeling of subsidence NSW Dept. Mineral Resources, 1984-86; internat. exch. scientist from Australia to Inst. Soil and Rock Mechanics, Acad. Sinica (Chinese Acad. Sci.), Wuhan, 1988, to dept. civil engring. U. Colo., Boulder, 1990; grad. faculty joint CSIRO-James Cook U. program in rock engring., 1989-90, dept. geol. scis. U. Nev., Reno, 1990-98, hydrology/hydrogeology program, 1991-95, hydrol. scis. program, 1995-98, dept. civil engring., 1994-98, dept. geosci. U. Nev., Las Vegas, 1992-93; coord. multi-agy. rsch. project on subsidence of the Las Vegas Valley, 1989-91; nat. liaison com. between ASCE, Geol. Soc. Am. and Assn. Engring. Geologists, 1997-2000; adj. prof. Royal Melbourne Inst. Tech., 1997—, U. Nev., Reno, 1998—, Va. Poly. Inst. and State U., 1999—. Contbr. articles to sci. jours., chpts. to books. Co-chmn. New Eng. Student Christian Movement, 1958-59; high sch. com. Am. Friends Service Com., Salem Oreg., 1966-68; bd. dirs. Ctr. Theology and Natural Scis., Grad. Theol. Union, Berkeley, Calif., 1981-84, Montessori Sch. Council, Melbourne, 1986-87; mem. Md. Tributary Team for Protecting the Chesapeake Bay, 1997-2000, Balt. Mayor's Transition Team (water and waste-water com.), 2000. Recipient Bennett-Tyler award in systematic theology, 1962, Award for Best Paper of Yr. Disciplines of Environ. and Engring. Geology from Assn. Engring. Geologists, 1994, Cert. of Appreciation Chinese (Taiwanese) Inst. of Civil and Hydraulic Engring. Com. of Geotech. Engring., 1992, U. Jos, Nigeria, 1998, Fed. U. Tech., Minna, Nigeria, Ahmadu Bello U., Nigeria, 1998; Innaugural occupant of U.S. Dept. Energy's Samuel P. Massie Chair of Excellence in Environ. Disciplines, Morgan State U., 1996—. Fellow Geol. Soc. Am., Inst. Engrs. Australia (Coll. Civil Engrs.); mem. NSPE, ASTM (com. solid waste disposal), AAUP, AAAS, ASCE, ASME, Am. Geophys. Union, Am. Water Resources Assn., Assn. Engring. Geologists, Assn. Geoscientists for Internat. Devel., Nat. Water Well Assn., N.Y. Acad. Scis., Internat. Soil Mechanics and Found. Engring., Internat. Assn. Engring. Geology, Internat. Soc. Rock Mechanics, Nev. Water Resources Assn., Md. Soc. Profl. Engrs. (pres. Balt. chpt., Md. bd. dirs., state v.p.), SAR (mem. bd. mgrs. John Eager Howard chpt.), Berkeley City Club, Outlook Club, Balt. Engrs. Club (bd. dirs.). Home: 1413 Bolton St Baltimore MD 21217-4202 Business E-Mail: helm@eng.morgan.edu.

HELM, JUDITH, retired clergywoman; b. Washington, Nov. 1, 1939; d. Walter Scott and Marian Florence (Pyles) Beck; m. Neil Richard Helm, June 2, 1962 (div. July 1981); 1 child, Karl Andrew. BA, Dickinson Coll., 1960; MDiv, Luth. Theol. Sem., Gettysburg, Pa., 1985. Ordained to ministry Luth. Ch., 1985. Editor William R. Hamilton & Staff, polls, market surveys, Washington, 1968-79; pastor Zion Lehigh Luth. Ch., Alburtis, Pa., 1985-90, Nativity Luth. Ch., Allentown, Pa., 1991—2003; ret., 2003. Author: Tenleytown, DC, 1981, 2d edit., 2000. Democrat.

HELM, LENORA ZENZALAI, musician, music educator; b. Chgo., Ill., Aug. 15, 1961; d. Reginald and Vera H Helm. Studied privately at, Am. Consveratory of Music, 1974—75; BA, Berklee Coll. of Music, 1979—82. Voice and piano instr. Palomba Music, Portchester, NY, 1991—93; voice and drama instr. Dance Cavise, Mammaroneck, NY, 1992—93; vocal and piano instr. Pvt. Instrn., 1991—94; music. dir., theatre arts program Ctr. Sch., NYC, 1992—94; music coord., piano instr. Jacob Riis Settlement, Long Is. City, NY, 1994—97, sr. citizens choir accompanist, 1995—96; tchg. artist and performance artist Young Audiences, NYC, 1999—; LinkUP! tchg. artist Carnegie Hall, NYC, 1999—2003; vocal jazz instr. Nassau BOCES Cultural Arts Ctr., 2000—; jazz educator, 2000—. Co-founder and artistic dir. HARMONY, 2002—; pres., owner, writer, pub. Holly's Hits Music Pub., 1997—; artist mgr. Self Mgr. to Lenora Zenzalai Helm and the Zenzalai Project, 1981—; pres. Internat. Women in Jazz, 1998—2001; dir. of youth services Jacob Riis Settlement, Long Is. City, 1995—97. Musician: (albums) Voice Paintings, 2003, Precipice, 2002 (top 100 jazz CDs in the U.S. by JazzWeek, 2002), Awakenings, 1997, Spirit Child, 1999; mem. vocal quartet Sepia, 1990—, featured guest vocalist Jazzpar 2003 tour in Europe (Chamber Music Am. New Works Creation and Presentation Jazz Composers Commn. award, 2004). Recipient U.S. Jazz Amb., 1998—99, Best New Jazz Artist, Jazz From the City (Internat. Radio Show), 1994, Maj. Young Artist award, Universal Jazz Coalition, 1998, The Dakota award, Dakota Station, 1999, Young Entrepreneur award, Universal Jazz Coalition, 2001, Artist-in-the-Sch. Cmty. award, NY Found. Arts, 2002, New Works Creation and Presentation Jazz Composers Commn. Award, Chamber Music Am., 2004—05, Manhattan Cmty. Arts Fund award, Lower Manhattan Cultural Coun., NYC Dept. Cultural Affairs, 2005. Mem.: SAG, ASCAP, AFTRA, NYC Arts in Edn. Roundtable (bd. dirs.), Grammy in Schs. Com., SESAC, Composer and Publisher, Nat. Acad. of Recording Arts and Sciences, Local 802 Musicians Union, Japan Ctrl. Music Pub. Composer, Internat. Women in Jazz (past pres. 1998—2001, bd. mem.), Internat. Assn. of Jazz Educators, Chamber Music Am. Office: PO Box 20085 New York NY 10014 Office Phone: 212-969-8756. Office Fax: 212-645-1260. E-mail: baoule.music@verizon.net.

HELM, LEWIS MARSHALL, communications executive; b. Riverdale, Md., Sept. 9, 1931; s. William P. and Selma S. (Snyder) Helm; m. Alice L. Kupferman, Sept. 12, 1953 (dec.). AA in Comms., Am. U., 1957, MS in Pub. Rels., 1979; grad., U.S. Army War Coll., 1977. Newspaper reporter Wichita (Kans.) Eagle, 1950-51, Washington Times-Herald, 1951-54; press asst. Republican Nat. Com., 1954-55; dir. pub. rels. Plumbing Fixture Mfrs. Assn., Washington, 1956-59, Home Mfrs. Assn., 1961-63; pub. rels. cons., 1959-60, 64-68; info. dir. Citizens for Nixon, 1968; asst. to sec. U.S. Dept. Interior, Washington, 1969, dep. asst. sec. mineral resources, 1969-72; asst. sec. for pub. affairs HEW, Washington, 1973-76; pres. Capital Counselors, Inc., Washington, 1976-86; govt. rels. and mktg. cons., 1987—; commr. Washington Suburban Sanitary Commn., 1991-95, vice-chair, 1992-93, chair, 1993-94. Instr. econs. Cath. U. Am., 1974; assoc. lecturing prof. polit,. sci. George Washington U., 1980; commentator Sta. WAMU-FM, Washington, 1995—2002; adj. prof. Montgomery Coll., 1996—97; adj. instr. Coll. Journalism U. Md., 1998—2002; adj. instr. MBA program and and pub. safety leadership divsn. Johns Hopkins U., 1999—. Co-author: Informing the People: A Public Affairs Handbook, 1981; author: Black Horse Cavalry Defend Our Beloved Country, 2004. Exec. dir. Sr. Army Res. Comdrs. Assn., 1985—2004; mem. Soc. of the Cin. in the State of Va.; mem. adv. bd. Vietnam Vets. Inst., 1993—96; bd. dirs. Mid-Atlantic region Audubon Naturalist Soc., 1995—97. Brig. gen. USAR, 1984—88. Decorated Legion of Merit with oak leaf cluster; named to Hall of Fame, Sr. Army Res. Comdrs. Assn.; recipient Meritorious Svc. medal, Dept. Interior, USPHS, Dept. Army, Spl. Citation for Disting. Svc., Sec. HEW, Meritoreous Svc. medal with two Oak Leaf Clusters.

HELM, PEYTON RANDOLPH, academic administrator, educator; b. Louisville; s. Thomas Kennedy and Nell Hunt (Hoge) H.; m. Patricia Burtow, July, 1980; children: Randolph Burton, Alexander Veasey. BA, Yale U.; PhD, U. Pa.; MA, Colby Coll., 1988. Sr. adminstrv. fellow U. Pa., Phila., 1979-81, corod. coll. house programs, 1981-84, asst. dean advising, 1979-84, assoc. dir. devel., 1984-86, dir. devel., 1986-88; v.p. devel., prof. Colby Coll., Waterville, Maine, 1988—. Adj. asst. prof. U. Pa., 1979-88. Contbr. articles to profl. jours. Mem. Am. Philological Assn., Am. Oriental Soc., CASE.

HELM, ROBERT WILBUR, federal official; b. LaCrosse, Wis., Aug. 19, 1951; s. Wilbur and Avis (Smale) H.; m. Sandra K. Howard, May 31, 1975 BA, U. Wis., LaCrosse, 1973; MA, Fletcher Sch. Diplomacy, Tufts U., 1975. Profl. staff mem. Los Alamos Lab., 1975-79; profl. staff mem. Senate Budget Com., Washington, 1979-82, Nat. Security Council, Washington, 1982-84; asst. sec. def., comptroller Dept. Def., Washington, 1984-88; v.p., business development Honeywell Inc., 1989; corp. v.p., legislative affairs Northrop Grumman Corp., 1989—93, corp. v.p., government relations, 1993—. Office: Northrop Grumman Corp 1840 Century Park East Los Angeles CA 90067

HELM, SHANNON MARIE, special education educator; b. Kingston, N.Y., Sept. 10, 1976; d. Ronald Edward and Nancy Joan Swart; m. Steven Helm, May 29, 1999; 1 child, Julia Caitlin. BSc, SUNY, 1999, MA, 2003. Cert. spl. edn. educator N.Y. Spl. edn. tchr. Children's Home Kingston, NY, 2000—02, Highland (N.Y.) Sch. Dist., 2003—. Exec. dir. scholarship program Miss Apple Valley Scholarship Program, Kingston, 2004—. Named Miss Ulster County, 1996; recipient Pride of Ulster County award, Ulster County Legis., 1996. Mem.: Assn. Supervision and Curriculum Devel.

HELM, STEVEN M, lawyer; b. Monmouth, Ill., Mar. 1, 1948; BA with honors, MacMurray College, U. Ill., 1970; JD, U. Ill., 1973. Corp. counsel, Allied Waste Industries, Scottsdale, Ariz., 1995—2003, corp. sec., v.p.-legal, 1996—, gen. counsel, 2003—. Mem.: Civil Justice Reform Act Adv. Com. and Rules Com., US Dist. Court, Ctrl. Dist. Ill.; Ill. State Bar Assn. Office: Allied Waste Industries Inc 15880 N Greenway-Hayden Loop Scottsdale AZ 85260 Home: 850 E Wetmore Rd Apt 1831 Tucson AZ 85719 Office Phone: 480-627-2700. Office Fax: 480-627-2728. Business E-Mail: shelm@awin.com.

HELMAN, ALFRED BLAIR, retired academic administrator, educational consultant; b. Windber, Pa., Dec. 25, 1920; s. Henry E. and Luie (Pritt) H.; m. Patricia Ann Kennedy, June 22, 1947; children: Harriet Ann Helman Hill, Patricia Dawn Helman Magaro. AB magna cum laude, McPherson Coll., 1946, DD, 1956; MA, U. Kans., 1947, postgrad., 1948-51; LLD, Juniata Coll., 1976; LHD, Bridgewater Coll., 1977, Ind. U., 1981, Manchester Coll., 1986. Ordained to ministry Ch. of Brethren, 1942; pastor Newton, Kans., 1944-46, Ottawa, Kans., 1946-54, First Ch. of Brethren, Wichita, Kans., 1954-56; faculty Ottawa U., 1947- 48, 51-54, chmn. div. social scis., 1952-54; faculty U. Kans., 1951-54, Friends U., 1955-56; pres. Manchester (Ind.) Coll., 1956-86, pres. emeritus, 1986—. Chmn. com. on higher edn. Ch. of Brethren, 1965-67, 76-78, nat. moderator, 1975-76, mem. rev. and evaluation com., 1983-85, mem. denominational structure rev. com., 1989-91, mem. pension bd. restructure com., 1986-87; trustee McPherson Coll., 1951-56, chmn., 1955-56; trustee Kans. Found. Pvt. Colls. and Univs., 1955-56; pres. Ind. Conf. Higher Edn., 1960-61; mem. policy bd. dept. higher edn. Nat. Coun. Chs. of Christ Am., 1960-71; mem. pres.'s adv. com. Nat. Assn. Intercollegiate Athletics, 1966-70; mem. exec. com. Ind. Coun. Chs., 1960-62, bd. dirs., 1992-94; bd. dirs. Independent Colls. and Univs. of Ind., 1977-83, 84-86, chmn., 1978-79, 85-86; chmn., interim pres. Coun. Protestant Colls. and Univs., 1967, bd. dirs., 1961-69; bd. dirs. Ctrl. States Coll. Assn., 1965-77, chmn., 1968; pres. Assoc. Colls. of Ind., 1970-72, bd. dirs., 1956-86; mem. commn. on religion in higher edn. Assn. Am. Colls., 1968-71; bd. dirs. CTB, Inc., 1977-92. Author articles on religion and higher edn. Mem. IAUP-UN Commn. on Arms Control Edn., 1991—2002. Named Sagamore of Wabash, Gov. of Ind., 1980, Ky. Col., Gov. of Ky., 1964; recipient Outstanding Local Citizen award, 1972, Sparks-Jones award Associated Colls. Ind., 1977, Legion of Honor award Kiwanis Club North Manchester, 1976, Alumni Honor award, Manchester Coll., 1981, Citation of Merit, McPherson Coll., 2001, Citation for Responsible Philanthropy, Manchester Coll., 2003; elected to Ind. Acad., 1987. Mem. Soc. Historians of Am. Fgn. Rels., Internat. Assn. Univ. Presidents (mem. steering com. N.Am. coun. 1982-84), Ind. Assn. Ch.-Related and Ind. Colls. (pres. 1966-67), Am. Assn. Higher Edn., Am. Acad. Polit. and Social Sci., Nat. Assn. Ind. Colls. and Univs. (bd. dirs. 1983-84), Ind. Acad. Social Scis., Ind. Hist. Assn., Ft. Wayne Rotary (Paul Harris fellow), Quest Club (mem. bd. govs. 1988-90, 92-94, 97-99), Phi Beta Kappa, Phi Alpha Theta, Pi Sigma Alpha, Pi Kappa Delta, Tau Kappa Alpha (hon.).

HELMAN, GERALD BERNARD, diplomat; b. Detroit, Nov. 4, 1932; s. Leo and Ann (Glassman) H.; m. Dolores Hammel, May, 1953; children: Ruth Leea, Deborah Gayle, David Robert. AB, U. Mich., 1953, LLB, 1956. Bar: Mich. 1956. Rsch. asst. U. Mich., 1955; intelligence rsch. specialist Dept. State, 1957, econ. consular officer Milan, Italy, 1958, polit. officer Vienna, Austria, 1960-62, econ. officer Barbados, 1962-63, fgn. affairs officer Washington, 1963-68; polit. mil. affairs officer, counselor U.S. Mission to NATO, Brussels, Belgium, 1968-73, dep. dir. NATO-Atlantic polit. mil. affairs Washington, 1974-76, dir. UN polit. affairs, 1976-77; dep. asst. sec. Bur. Internat. Orgn. Affairs, 1977-79; U.S. ambassador to UN Orgns. in Europe, 1979-81; dep. and sr. advisor to undersec. for polit. affairs Dept. State, Washington, 1982-91, cons. on Internat. and Telecomm. matters, 1991-92; v.p. Ellipso, Inc., 1992—. Woodrow Wilson fellow Princeton U., 1973 Jewish. Home: 2900 Maplewood Pl Alexandria VA 22302-2424 Business E-Mail: ghelman@ellipso.com.

HELMAN, ROBERT ALAN, lawyer; b. Chgo., Jan. 27, 1934; s. Nathan W. and Esther (Weiss) H.; m. Janet R. Williams, Sept. 13, 1958; children: Marcus E., Adam J., Sarah E. Student, U. Ill., 1951-53; BSL, Northwestern U., 1954, LLB, 1956. Bar: Ill. 1956. Asso. firm Isham, Lincoln & Beale, Chgo., 1956-64, ptnr., 1965-66; ptnr. firm Mayer, Brown, Rowe & Maw, Chgo., 1967—. Bd. dirs. No. Trust Corp., No. Trust Co. Co-author: Commentaries on 1970 Illinois Constitution, 1971; assoc. editor Northwestern U. Law Rev., 1955-56; contbr. articles to profl. jours. Chmn. Citizens' Com. on Juvenile Ct., Cook County, 1969-81; pres. Legal Assistance Found., Chgo., 1973-76; chmn. vis. com. Northwestern U. Law Sch., 1989-92; bd. dirs. United Charities Chgo., 1967-73; hon. trustee Brookings Instn., Aspen Inst., 1986-92, Mus. of Contemporary Art. Mem. ABA, Chgo. Bar Assn., Am. Law Inst., Chgo. Coun. Lawyers, Legal Club Chgo., Law Club Chgo., Comml. Club, Chgo. Club, Mid-Day Club, Econ. Club, Order of Coif. Home: 4950 S Chicago Beach Dr Chicago IL 60615-3207 Office: Mayer Brown Rowe & Maw 71 S Wacker Dr Chicago IL 60606 Office Phone: 312-701-7020. Business E-Mail: rhelman@mayerbrown.com.

HELMAN, STEPHEN JODY, lawyer; b. Houston, Dec. 14, 1949; m. Gail Stevenson, 1974; children: Kimberley Brooke, Courtney Elizabeth, Caitlin Rebecca. BA in Spanish and Religion, So. Meth. U., 1971; postgrad., Perkins Sch. Theology, 1971—73; JD with honors, U. Tex., 1978. Bar: Tex., 1978; cert. estate planning and probate law, 1987. Assoc. Graves, Dougherty, Hearon & Moody, Austin, Tex., 1978-85, ptnr., shareholder, 1985-93; ptnr. Osborne, Lowe, Helman & Smith, L.L.P., Austin, 1993-2000, Osborne & Helman, L.L.P., Austin, 2001—. Exam commr. in estate planning and probate law, Tex. Bd. Legal Specialization, 1990-94. Contbr. articles to profl. jours. Fellow Am. Coll. Trust and Estate Counsel (mem. profl. standards com. 1990-93); mem. ABA (mem. real property, probate, and trust law sects.), Coll. of the State Bar of Tex., State Bar Tex. (mem. real property, probate and trust law sects.), Travis County Bar Assn. (mem. probate and estate planning sect., pres. 1991-92, dir. 1989-92, ex-officio dir. 1992-93), Order of Coif. Avocations: nature photography, hiking. Office: Osborne & Helman LLP 301 Congress Ave Ste 1910 Austin TX 78701-4041 Office Phone: 512-542-2000. E-mail: sjhelman@osbornehelman.com.

HELMER, DAVID ALAN, lawyer; b. Colorado Springs, May 19, 1946; s. Horton James and Alice Ruth (Cooley) H.; m. Jean Marie Lamping, May 23, 1987 (div.). BA, U. Colo., 1968, JD, 1973. Bar: Colo. 1973, U.S. Dist. Ct. Colo. 1973, U.S. Ct. Appeals (10th cir.) 1993, U.S. Ct. Claims 1990, U.S. Supreme Ct. 1991. Assoc. Neil C. King, Boulder, Colo., 1973-76; mgr. labor rels., mine regulations Climax Molybdenum Co., Inc. divsn. AMAX, Inc., Climax, Colo., 1976-83; prin. Law Offices David A. Helmer, Frisco, Colo., 1983—. Sec., bd. dirs. Z Comm. Corp., Frisco, 1983-90; cmty. bd. dirs. Wells Fargo Bank, N.A., Frisco, 1996—. Editor U. Colo. Law Rev., 1972-73; contbr. articles to legal jours. Bd. dirs. Summit County Coun. Arts and Humanities, Dillon, Colo., 1980-85; advisor Advocates for Victims of Assault, Frisco, 1984—; legal counsel Summit County United Way, 1983-95, v.p., bd. dirs., 1983-88; bd. dirs., legal counsel Summit County Alcohol and Drug Task Force, Inc., Summit Prevention Alliance, 1984—, Pumpkin Bowl Inc./Chldren's Hosp. Burn Ctr., 1989—; chmn. Summit County Reps., 1982-89; chmn. 5th Jud. Dist. (Colo.) Rep. Com., 1982-89; chmn. resolutions com. Colo. Rep. Conv., 1984, del. Rep. Nat. Com., 1984; chmn. reaccreditation com. Colo. Mountain Coll., Breckenridge, 1983, mem. steering com., 1997-99; founder, bd. dirs. Dillon Bus. Assn., 1983-87, Frisco Arts Coun., 1989—; atty. N.W. Colo. Legal Svcs. Project, Summit County, 1983—; mcpl. judge Town of Dillon, 1982—, Town of Silverthorne, Colo., 1982—; bd. dirs. Snake River Water Dist., 1998—, chmn., 2002—. Master Sgt. USAR, 1968-74. Mem. ABA, Colo. Bar Assn., (bd. govs. 1991-93, mem. exec. com. 1995-97), Continental Divide Bar Assn. (prs. 1991-95, v.p. 1995-97), Summit County Bar Assn. (pres. 1990-99), Dillon Corinthian Yacht Club (commodore local club 1987-88, 95-97, vice commodore 1994, club champion 1989-91, 94, 95, 97, 98, 2002, winner Colo. Cup, Colo. State Sailing Championships 1991, Dist. Champion 2000, 02, Champion Dillon Open Regatta 2001), Phi Gamma Delta. Lutheran. Home: PO Box 300 352 Snake River Dr Dillon CO 80435-0300 Office: PO Box 868 611 Main St Frisco CO 80443-0868 Business E-Mail: dave@helmerlaw.com.

HELMER, M(ARTHA) CHRISTIE, lawyer; b. Portland, Oreg., Oct. 8, 1949; d. Marvin Curtis and Inez Bahl (Corwin) H.; m. Joe D. Bailey, June 23, 1979; children: Tim Bailey, Bill Bailey. BA in English magna cum laude, Wash. State U., 1970; JD cum laude, Lewis & Clark Coll., 1974; LLM in Internat. Law, Columbia U., 1998. Bar: Oreg. 1974. Assoc. Miller Nash, Portland, 1974-81, ptnr., 1981—. Adj. prof. Lewis & Clark Law Sch., 1999—; guest lectr. Xiamen U. Law, China, 1995; mem. Oreg. Bd. Bar Examiners, Portland, 1978-81; del. 9th Cir. Jud. Conf., 1984-87, mem. exec. com., 1987-90. Author: Arrest of Ships, 1985, Has China Adopted the UCC?, 1999. Mem.: ABA (internat. and litig. sections), Internat. Bar Assn., Maritime Law Assn., Oreg. Bar Assn. (bd. govs. 1981—84, treas. 1983—84, ho. of dels. 2003—), World Affairs Coun. (chair bd. dirs.), Multnomah Athletic Club, Phi Beta Kappa. Avocations: antiques, travel, fashion. Office: Miller Nash 111 SW 5th Ave Ste 3500 Portland OR 97204-3699 Office Phone: 503-205-2464. Business E-Mail: chris.helmer@millernash.com.

HELMER, ROBERT C., academic administrator; b. Jan. 30, 1960; m. Linda Helmer; 2 children. BA, U. Notre Dame, 1982; MA, Cath. U., Louvain, Belgium, 1986; PhD, Marquette U., 1988. Various tchg. positions Ind. U., Ancilla Domini Coll., 1986—90; tchg. fellow, lectr. Marquette U., 1991—96; retention developer, asst. prof. history and religion Lourdes Coll., Sylvania, Ohio, 1996, v.p. acad. affairs, interim pres., 2003, pres., 2003—. Mem.: Sylvania C. of C. (bd. dirs.), Cath. Bibl. Assn. Am. Office: Lourdes Coll 6832 Convent Blvd Sylvania OH 43560

HELMERS, SCOTT, orthopedic oncologist, military officer; s. Ralph and Mary Helmers; m. Robin Wood, Sept. 7, 1993; 1 child, Claire. MD, Uniformed Svcs. U., Bethesda, Md., 1990. Cert. Am. Bd. of Orthop. Surgery, 1998. Advanced through grades to comdr. U.S. Navy, 1982—; orthop. surgeon US Naval Hosp., Yokosuka, Japan, 1996—98, U.S. Naval Hosp., Bremerton, Wash., 1998—2000; orthop. oncologist Naval Med. Ctr., Portsmouth, Va., 2001—. E-mail: swhelmers@mar.med.navy.mil.

HELMERS, STEVEN J., lawyer, energy executive; m. Wanda Helmers; 4 children. BA magna cum laude, SD State U., 1978; JD cum laude, U. SD, 1981. Law clerk We. Div., U.S. Dist. Ct., 1981—83; atty. Lynn, Jackson, Shultz & Lebrun, P.C, 1983—87, Truhe, Beardsley, Jensen, Helmers & VonWald; gen. counsel, corp. sec. Black Hills Corp., Rapid City, SD, 2001—. Mem. Black Hills Area Boy Scout Coun., Rapid City Arts Coun., Black Hills Red Cross, Calvary Luth. Ch. Coun. Mem.: ABA, Rocky Mountain Mineral Law Found., Pennington County Bar Assn (pres. 1999), State Bar SD (Bar Commr. 1995—98). Office: Black Hills Corp 625 9th St Rapid City SD 57701 Office Phone: 605-721-2300. E-mail: shelmers@blackhillscorp.com.

HELMETAG, CHARLES HUGH, foreign language educator; b. Camden, NJ, Apr. 7, 1935; s. Charles Henry and Agnes Beatrice (Gibb) H.; m. Ruth Judith Crispin, Aug. 22, 1959; children: Steven, Diana. BA, U. Pa., 1957; MA, U. Ky., 1959; PhD, Princeton U., 1968. Instr. German Purdue U., West Lafayette, Ind., 1960-62; asst. prof. German Villanova U., Pa., 1964-75, assoc. prof., 1975-80, prof., 1980—, chmn. dept. modern lang. and lit., 1973-88. Contbg. editor Lit./Film Quar., 2000—; contbr. articles to book chpt., revs., profl. jour. Pres. Rosemont Elem. Sch. PTA, 1973—74, bd. dirs., 1974—75. Fulbright scholar U. Goettingen (Ger.), 1959-60; Germanistic Soc. Am. grantee, 1968; German Acad. Exchange Svc. grantee, 1978 Mem. Am. Assn. Tchr. German, MLA, N.E. MLA (exec. coun. 1991-92), Soc. Exile Studies, AAUP (pres. local chpt. 1972-73), Internat. Brecht Soc., Lit./Film Assn., Internationale Vereinigung für Germanistik, Internat. Soc. for the Study of European Ideas, Phi Kappa Phi (pres. Villanova chpt. 1984). Office: Villanova U Dept Classical &Modern Lang & Lit Villanova PA 19085-1699 Office Phone: 610-519-7794. Business E-Mail: charles.helmetag@villanova.edu.

HELMETAG, DIANA, music educator; b. Bryn Mawr, Pa., 1965; d. Charles and Ruth Helmetag; m. Steven Glanzmann, 1993. BS in Music Edn. cum laude, Duquesne U., 1987; MusM, Pa. State U., 1990. Instr. Sch. Music Pa. State U., University Park, 1988, 90, lectr. Delaware County campus Media, 1991-95; music tchr. Radnor (Pa.) Twp. Sch. Dist., 1993-94, 95, 96; piano accompanist Villanova (Pa.) Voices Villanova U., 1995-99; instr. Delaware County C.C., Media, 1996; orch. dir. Upper Merion Area Sch. Dist., King of Prussia, Pa., 1996—, subject area leader, 1997—2001, pit orch. dir., 1997, 1998, 2001—; choir dir., chamber music coach and children's orch. dir. Strings Internat. Music Festival Bryn Mawr (Pa.) Coll., 2001—. Pianist, violinist Mu Phi Epsilon recitals, Phila., 1991, 92, 94; orch. dir. Schuylkill Valley Area Orch. Festival, Wayne, Pa., 1996—; founding mem. Montgomery County Honors String Orch. Festival, Plymouth Meeting, Pa., 1999—; music dir. King of Prussia Players, 2000; guest condr. Bucks County String Day, 2003, 04. Orch. dir., pianist, violinist Narberth (Pa.) Cmty. Theatre, 1997—. Recipient grad. assistantship Pa. State U., 1987-90. Mem. Am. String Tchrs. Assn. with Nat. Sch. Orch. Assn., Music Educators Nat. Conf., Music Tchrs. Nat. Assn., Coll. Music Soc., Pa. Music Educators Assn. (host. dist. 11 orch. festival 1998, orch. dir. and presiding chair in-svc. conf. 2001, host all-state orch. festival 2002, chamber group selected to perform for All-State Conf., 2005), Phi Kappa Phi, Pi Kappa Lambda. Office: Upper Merion Area Sch Dist 435 Crossfield Rd King Of Prussia PA 19406 Business E-Mail: dhelmetag@umasd.org.

HELMHOLZ, R(ICHARD) H(ENRY), law educator; b. Pasadena, Calif., July 1, 1940; s. Lindsay and Alice (Bean) H.; m. Marilyn P. Helmholz. AB, Princeton U., 1962; JD, Harvard U., 1965; PhD, U. Calif., Berkeley, 1970; LLD, Trinity Coll., Dublin, 1992. Bar: Mo. 1965. Asst. prof. history to prof. law & history Washington U., St. Louis, 1970-81; prof. law U. Chgo. Law Sch., 1981—84, Ruth Wyatt Rosenson prof. law, 1984—99, Ruth Wyatt Rosenson disting. svc. prof. law, 2000—. Maitland lectr. Cambridge U., 1987; Goodhart prof. Cambridge U., 2000-01. Author: Marriage Litigation, 1975, Select Cases on Defamation, 1985, Canon Law and the Law of England, 1987, Roman Canon Law in Reformation England, 1990, Spirit of Classical Canon Law, 1996, The Ius Commune in England: Four Studies, 2001, Oxford History of the Laws of England, Vol. 1, 2004. Guggenheim fellow, 1986; recipient Von Humboldt rsch. prize, 1992. Fellow Brit. Acad. (corr.), Am. Acad. Arts and Scis., Am. Law Inst., Medieval Acad. Am.; mem. ABA, Am. Soc. Legal History (pres. 1992-94), Selden Soc. (v.p. 1984-87), Univ. Club, Reform Club. Home: 5757 S Kimbark Ave Chicago IL 60637-1614 Office: U Chgo Law Sch 1111 E 60th St Chicago IL 60637-2776 Office Phone: 773-702-9580. Business E-Mail: dick_helmholz@law.uchicago.edu.

HELMICK, RAYMOND GLEN, priest, educator; b. Arlington, Mass., Sept. 7, 1931; s. Raymond Glen and Alice Cecilia (Clancy) H. BA, Boston Coll., 1956, MA in philosphy, 1957; lic. philosphy, Weston Coll., 1957; lic. theol., Hochschule St. Georgen, Frankfurt, 1964. Joined Jesuit Order, 1949, ordained priest Roman Cath. Ch., 1963. Assoc. dir. Ctr. for Human Rights and Responsibilities, London, 1973-79, Inst. Soc. Rsch., London, 1973-79; found., co-dir. Ctr. of Concern for Human Dignity, London, 1979-81; sr. assoc. Conflict Analysis Ctr., Washington, 1982—; prof. of conflict resolution Boston Coll., 1984—; sr. assoc. Ctr. Strategic and Internat. Studies, Washington, 2000—04. Exec. comm. U.S. Interreligious Comm. for Peace in the Middle East, Seattle, 1987—, adv. bd. Orgn. for Human Rights in Iraq, Boston, 1992—; bd. dirs. Refugee Immigrant Ministry, Boston. Author: (with

Richard Hauser) A Social Option, 1975, La Question Libanaise Selon Raymond Edde, 1990; editor: (with Rodney Petersen) Forgiveness and Reconciliation: Religion, Public Policy and Conflict Transformation, 2001, Negotiating Outside the Law: Why Camp David Failed, 2004; video documentaries (with John Michalczyk) Out of the Ashes Northern Ireland's Fragile Peace, 1998, Prelude to Kosovo: War and Peace in Bosnia and Croatia, 1999, South Africa: Beyond a Miracle, 2000, Unexpected Openings: Northern Ireland's Prisoners, 2001, Different Drummers: Daring to Make Peace in the Middle East, 2003, Killing Silence: Taking on the Mafia in Sicily, 2004; exec. prodr. video documentaries. Mediation No. Irish conflict, 1972-81, 92—, Kurdish conflict, 1973-81, 87—, Lebanese conflict, 1982—, Israeli-Palestinian conflict, 1986—, Balkan conflict, 1995—. Democrat. Roman Catholic. Office: Boston Coll Chestnut Hill MA 02467 Business E-Mail: helmick@bc.edu.

HELMKE, PAUL (WALTER PAUL HELMKE JR.), mayor, lawyer; b. Bloomington, Ind., Nov. 24, 1948; s. Walter P. and Rowene Mary (Crabill) H.; m. Deborah Jane Andrews, Aug. 23, 1969; children: Laura Andrews, Kathryn Elizabeth. BA with highest honors, Ind. U., 1970; JD, Yale U., 1973. Bar: Ind. 1973, Fla. 1982. Lawyer Helmke Beams Boyer Wagner, Ft. Wayne, Ind., 1973-87, 2003—; mayor City Ft. Wayne, 1988-2000; atty. Barnes & Thornburg, Ft. Wayne, 2000—02. Asst. county atty. Allen County, Ft. Wayne, 1974-87; pres. Nat. Rep. Mayors and Local Ofcls. Orgn., 1993; pres. U.S. Conf. of Mayors, 1997-98. Chmn. Allen-Wells chpt. ARC, Ft. Wayne, 1985-87; candidate for Rep. nomination 4th U.S. Congl. Dist.-Ind., 1980; Rep. nominee for U.S. Senate, Ind., 1998; bd. dirs. Nat. League of Cities, 1995-97, chair pub. safety and crime prevention com., 1995; candidate for Rep. nomination 3d U.S. Congl. Dist. Ind., 2002. Recipient J.C. Gallagher prize Law Sch. Yale U., New Haven, Conn., 1972 Mem. Ind. Assn. Cities and Towns (pres. 1996-97). Republican. Lutheran. Home: 1215 Korte Ln Fort Wayne IN 46807-2920 Office: Helmke Beams Boyer & Wagner 202 W Berry St Ste 300 Fort Wayne IN 46802-2216 Office Phone: 260-422-7422. Personal E-mail: paulhelmke@aol.com. Business E-Mail: paulhelmke@hbbwlaw.com.

HELMLY, JAMES R., career military officer; b. Savannah, Ga. married; two children: Lisa, Melanie. BS, SUNY; grad., Army Command Gen. Staff Coll., Armed Forces Staff Coll., Army War Coll. Enlisted U.S. Army, commd. 2d lt., advanced through grades to lt. gen., 2002; early commd. svc. includes platoon leader 101st airborne divsn., U.S. Army, Ft. Campbell, Ky., and Vietnam; co. comdr. Ft. Benning, Ga.; res. assignments include regimental ops. officer Panama; logistics supply and maintenance officer assignments; comdr. 352d maintenance bn. Macon, Ga.; dep. chief of staff for tn., dep. chief of staff personnel 449th area support group, Forest Park, Ga.; dep. chief U.S. Army Res., Office to Chief Army Res., Washingtin, 1995—99; comdr. join task force conducting Oper. Provide Refuge, Fort Dix, NJ, 1999—99; military asst., manpower and reserve affairs Office of the Asst., Sec. of the Army, Washington, 1999—2001; commdg. gen. U.S. Army Res.,78th Div., Edison, NJ, 2001—02; comdr. U.S. Army Res. Command, Ft. McPherson, Ga., 2002—; chief U.S. Army Res., 2002—. Office: Office of Chief Army Res 2400 Army Pentagon Washington DC 20310-2400

HELMS, BENJAMIN PRESTON, music educator; b. Albany, Ga., Jan. 15, 1978; s. Danny Preston and Bette Bonnett Helms; m. Kimberly Dawn Smith, Dec. 27, 2003. MusB, Valdosta State U., 2000; MEd, Troy State U., 2005. Band dir. Tattnall County Bd. of Edn., Reidsville, Ga., 2001—. Marching band dir. Tattnall County H.S., Reidsville, 2001—; head baseball coach Collins (Ga.) Mid. Sch., 2001—. Mem.: PA of Ga. Educators, Collegiate Music Educators Nat. Congress, Ga. Music Educators. Mem. Nazarene Ch. Avocations: baseball, hunting, fishing, golf. Office: Reidsville Mid Sch 148 W Brazell St Reidsville GA 30453 Office Phone: 912-557-3993.

HELMS, BOBBY GILLESPIE, music educator, consultant; b. Cordele, Ga., Feb. 4, 1972; s. Marvin Eugene and Dorothy Ruth Helms. BS in Music Edn., Ga. Southwestern State U., Americus, 1994. Choral, band and drama dir. Seminole County Mid. Sch., Donalsonvile, Ga., 1995—97; choral and drama dir. Crisp County Mid. Sch., Cordele, Ga., 1997—. Youth dir. First Presbyn. Ch., Donalsonville, Ga., 1994—96; music dir. Swamp Garvy, Colquitt, Ga., 1995—96; performer Kennedy Ctr. Performing Arts, Washington, 1996, Olympics, Atlanta, 1996; min. of music Springfield Bapt. Ch., Jakin, Ga., 1996—98, Warwick (Ga.) United Meth. Ch., 2001—; dir. Crisp Area Theatrical Stars, Cordele, Ga., 2000—; exec. dir. Miss Cordele/Miss Heart of Ga. Scholarship Pageant; mem. Colquitt/Miller County Arts Coun., 1995—96. Actor: (musical) Dames at Sea, 1993, Pippin, 1992. Recipient Outstanding Graduating Music Maj., Ga. Southwestern State U., 1995, Scholarship, 1990-1994, Directors Award, 1994. Mem.: Nat. Music Educators Conf., Ga. Music Educators. Home: 1393 Musselwhite Rd Cordele GA 31015 Office: Crisp County Middle Sch 1116 24th Ave E Cordele GA 31015 Personal E-mail: bgillhelms@musician.org.

HELMS, CINDY S., elementary school educator; b. Alliance, Ohio, July 24, 1953; d. Arthur Louis and Emma L. Beach; m. Greg R. Helms, July 26, 1975; children: Erin L., Stephanie L. BA in Edn., Mt. Union Coll., 1975; MS in Reading, Youngstown State U., 2002. Cert. tchr. Ohio. Ad account exec., teletype setter Alliance Review, Ohio, 1971—74; 4th grade tchr. Manpower/Marlington Leed, Alliance, Ohio, 1975—76; 2d grade tchr. Youngstown Diocese, Alliance, Ohio, 1976—78; 1st grade tchr. Alliance City, Ohio, 1979—80; kindergarten tchr. Youngstown Diocese, Louisville, Ohio, 1983—85; 1st grade tchr. West Br. Local, Beloit, Ohio, 1985—. Named Tchr. of Month, Alliance C. of C., 2000. Mem.: Internat. Reading Assn. (Mahoning Valley Coun. 1st v.p. 2003—04, v.p. 2004—05, pres. 2005—), Phi Delta Kappa (10 Yr. award 2004). Republican. Roman Catholic. Avocations: reading, spectator sports, movies, shopping, vacationing.

HELMS, DORIS R., academic administrator; BA, Bucknell Univ.; PhD, Univ. Ga. Joined Clemson (S.C.) U., 1973—, provost, 2002—, also vice-pres. academic affairs. Office: Clemson Univ Office VP and Provost 206 Sikes Hall Clemson SC 29634

HELMS, ED, comedian, actor; b. Atlanta, Jan. 24, 1974; BA, Oberlin Coll., 1996. With The Upright Citizens Brigade, N.Y.C. Actor: (films) Blackbird: The Bobby Dukes Story, 2004; (TV series) Premium Blend, 2002, The Daily Show with Jon Stewart, 2002—. Office: c/o Agy for the Performing Arts 9200 Sunset Blvd #900 Los Angeles CA 90069

HELMS, J. LYNN, retired federal agency administrator; b. DeQueen, Ark., Mar. 1, 1925; s. Frank and Mamie (Johnson) H.; m. Lorraine Bisgard, Mar. 16, 1947; children: Loralyn, Jon, Carole, Zack. Dir. mktg. and sales N. Am. Aviation Co., Columbus, Ohio, 1956-62; group v.p. Bendix Corp., Ann Arbor, Mich., 1962-70; pres. Norden div. United Technologies Corp., Norwalk, Conn., 1970-74, Piper Aircraft Corp., Lock Haven, Pa., 1974-81, chmn. bd., 1978-81; adminstr. FAA, Washington, 1981-83. Dir. Birchminster Industries. Served to lt. col. USMC, 1944-55. Decorated Air medal with oak leaf cluster. Fellow AIAA; mem. Soc. Exptl. Test Pilots.

HELMS, JESSE, retired senator; b. Monroe, NC, Oct. 18, 1921; s. Jesse Alexander and Ethel Mae (Helms) H.; m. Dorothy Jane Coble, Oct. 31, 1942; children: Jane (Mrs. Charles R. Knox), Nancy (Mrs. John C. Stuart), Charles. Student, Wingate (N.C.) Jr. Coll., Wake Forest Coll. City editor Raleigh (N.C.) Times, 1941-42; news and program dir. Sta. WRAL, Raleigh, 1948-51; adminstrv. asst. to U.S. senators Willis Smith and Alton Lennon, 1951-53; exec. dir. N.C. Bankers Assn., 1953-60; exec. v.p., vice chmn. Capitol Broadcasting Co., Raleigh, 1960-72; U.S. senator from N.C., 1973—2002; sr. mem. Com. on Fgn. Relations; mem. Rules & Adminstrn. Com., Republican Policy Com. Chmn. bd. Specialized Agrl. Publs., Inc., Raleigh, 1964-72; mem. Raleigh City Council, 1957-61. Author: Here's Where I Stand, 2005. Bd. dirs. N.C. Cerebral Palsy Hosp., Durham, United Cerebral Palsy N.C., Wake County Cerebral Palsy and Rehab. Center, Raleigh, Camp Willow Run, Littleton, N.C.; former trustee Campbell Coll., Wingate Coll., Meredith Coll., John F. Kennedy Coll. Served with USNR, 1942-45, World War II. Recipient Freedoms Found. award for best TV editorial, 1962, for newspaper article, 1973, So. Bapt. Nat. award for Service to mankind, 1972; Gold medal VFW; Conservative Congressional award, 1976; Liberty award Am. Econ. Council, 1978; Disting. Public Service award Public Service Research Council, 1978; Watchdog of Treasury award; Guardian of Small Bus. award; named Man of Yr. Women for Constl. Govt., 1978; Legislator of Yr. award Nat. Rifle Assn., 1978, Taxpayer's Best Friend award Nat. Taxpayer's Union, 1993; other awards. Mem.: Masons (33d degree), Raleigh Execs. Club (past pres.), Rotary (past pres. Raleigh). Republican. Baptist (Deacon).

HELMS, MICKY, engineering executive; b. Oklahoma City, July 25, 1934; d. John Talbert and Lora V. (Lyons) Kelly; m. Jimmie A. Helms, July 14, 1953; children: Kelly Janine, James Michael, Jennifer Ann. AS, Midland (Tex.) Coll., 1975. Engring. technician TU Electric, Midland, 1958-92; corp. sec., treas. Helms and May Engring, Inc., Midland, 1992—2002; pres. Helms and May Aggregation, Inc., Midland, 2002—04; pres., CEO MH & KP, Inc., 2004—. Mem. Dachshund Club of Am., Basset Hound Club of Am. Avocations: breeding and showing wirehaired dachshunds and basset hounds, painting, photography. Home: 1909 W County Road 140 Midland TX 79706-6975 Office: MH & KP Inc 701-B W Indiana Ave Midland TX 79701-5007 Office Phone: 432-683-8016. Business E-Mail: micky@mhkpinc.com.

HELMS, ROBERT BRAKE, economist, science administrator; b. Mobile, Ala., Jan. 12, 1940; s. Osburn Charles and Julia May (Moore) H.; m. Sharon Gay Schliebe, Aug. 8, 1964; children— Elissa Lynelle, Julianne Nanette BS in Agrl. Adminstrn., Auburn U., 1962; MA in Econs., UCLA, 1966, PhD in Econs., 1973. Asst. prof. Loyola Coll., Balt., 1971-74; dir. health policy studies Am. Enterprise Inst., Washington, 1974-81, resident scholar, dir. health policy studies, 1990; dep. asst. sec. planning and evaluation/health HHS, Washington, 1981-84, acting asst. sec. planning and evaluation, 1984-86, asst. sec. for planning and evaluation, 1986-89; exec. dir. Am. Pharm. Inst., 1989-90. Chmn. Sec.'s Task Force on Hosp. Deregulation, Washington, 1981-83, Sec.'s Task Force on Drug Reimbursement, Washington, 1983-85; mem. White House Working Group on Health Policy and Econs., Washington, 1984-85; mem. steering com. Health Policy Agenda Am. People, Chgo., 1984-88; mem. working party on social policy OECD, Paris, 1984-89; mem. nat. adv. coun. Agy. Health Care Rsch. and Quality, 2005—, mem. HHS Med. Commn., 2005—. Author: Natural Gas Regulation, 1974; editor: Drug Development and Marketing, 1975, The International Supply of Medicines, 1980, Drugs and Health, 1981, American Health Policy: Critical Issues for Reform, 1993, Health Care Policy and Politics: Lessons From Four Countries, 1993, Health Care Reform: Competition and Controls, 1993, Competitive Strategies in the Pharmaceutical Industry, 1996, Medicare in the Twenty-first Century: Seeking Fair and Efficient Reform, 1999. Served to capt. U.S. Army, 1962-64 Republican. Lutheran. Avocations: tennis, travel, internet. Home: 1404 Foggy Glen Ct Silver Spring MD 20906-2092 Office: Am Enterprise Inst 1150 17th St NW Washington DC 20036-4603 Office Phone: 202-862-5877. Personal E-mail: RBHelms@sprintmail.com. Business E-Mail: rhelms@asi.org.

HELMSING, FREDERICK GEORGE, lawyer; b. Mobile, Ala., Dec. 30, 1940; s. Joseph Herman and Mary Gertrude (Zimlich) H.; m. Margaret Sue Oswalt, Mar. 22, 1969; children: Frederick George, Joseph Guy, Margaret Sue. BS in Acctg., Spring Hill Coll., 1963; JD, U. Ala., 1965; LLM in Taxation, NYU, 1967. Bar: Ala. 1965, Fla. 1989. Assoc. Gallalee, Denniston & Edington, Mobile, 1966-76; ptnr. Helmsing, Leach, Herlong, Newman & Rouse, Mobile, 1976—. Instr. U. South Ala., Mobile, 1969-78; instr. law U. Ala., Mobile, 1982 Dem. chmn. 1st Congl. Dist. Campaign, 1976. Fellow: Am. Coll. Trial Lawyers; mem.: ABA (mem. civil and criminal tax penalties com.), Mobile Area C. of C. (mem. taxation and world trade coms.), Mobile Bar Assn., Mobile County Bar Assn. (treas. 1969), Ala. State Bar Assn. (chmn. tax sect. 1979—80), Athelstan Country Club, Mobile County Club. Roman Catholic. Home: 240 Ridgelawn Dr E Mobile AL 36608-2417 Office: Helmsing Leach Herlong Newman & Rouse 200 LaClede Bldg 150 Government St Mobile AL 36602-3114 Office Phone: 251-432-5521. Personal E-mail: FGH@helmsinglaw.com.

HELMSLEY, LEONA MINDY, hotel executive; b. N.Y.C. m. Harry B. Helmsley, Apr. 8, 1972 (dec. Jan., 1997). Vice pres. Pease & Elliman, N.Y.C., 1962-69; pres. Sutton & Towne Residential, N.Y.C., 1967-70; sr. v.p. Helmsley Spear, N.Y.C., 1970-72, Brown, Harris, Stevens, N.Y.C., 1970-72; pres., CEO, chmn. bd. Helmsley Hotels, Inc., N.Y.C., 1980—. Named Woman of Yr. N.Y. Council Civic Affairs, 1970; named Woman of Yr. Town & Country Condos & Coops., 1981; recipient Service award Ort Sch. Engring., 1981, Profl. Excellence award Les Dames d'Escoffier, 1981, Spl. Achievement award Sales Execs. Club N.Y., 1981, Woman of Yr. award Internat. Hotel Industry, 1982 Home: 36 Central Park S New York NY 10019-1600 Office: Helmsley Hotels Inc 230 Park Ave New York NY 10169-0005

HELMSTETTER, CHARLES EDWARD, microbiologist; b. Newark, Oct. 18, 1933; s. Charles Edward and Elsa Simpson (Taylorson) H.; m. Wendy Lee; children— Charles Edward, Michael Frederick, Lee Grisetti. BA, Johns Hopkins U., 1955; MS, U. Mich., 1956, U. Chgo., 1957, PhD, 1961. Scientist NIH, Bethesda, Md., 1961-63; USPHS fellow U. Copenhagen, 1963-64; scientist Roswell Park Meml. Inst., Buffalo, 1964-89, dir. dept. exptl. biology, 1974-89; prof. biol. scis. Fla. Inst. Tech., Melbourne, 1989—. Contbr. articles to sci. jours.; mem. editorial bd.: Jour. Bacteriology, 1970-76, 80-86. Recipient Selman A Waksman award Theobald Smith Soc., 1970; yearly NIH grantee, 1965— Mem. AAAS, Am. Soc. Microbiology, Am. Soc. Biol. Chemists, Sigma Xi. Home: 854 Hawksbill Island Dr Melbourne FL 32937-3850 Office: Fla Inst Tech Dept of Biol Scis Melbourne FL 32901 E-mail: chelmste@fit.edu.

HELMSTETTER, WENDY LEE, librarian; b. Port Arthur, Ont., Can., Aug. 31, 1947; came to U.S., 1960; d. Estyn Lloyd and Vera Gertrude (Derwa) Edwards; m. Glenn Charles Grisetti, June 17, 1967 (div.); 1 child, Lee Glenn Grisetti; m. Charles Edward Helmstetter, July 1, 1988. BA in Psychology summa cum laude, SUNY, Buffalo, 1985; MLS, U. South Fla., 1994. Adminstrv. asst. to libr. dir. Roswell Pk. Cancer Inst., Buffalo, 1973-89; reference libr. Fla. Inst. Tech., Melbourne, 1994—96, academic info. svcs. libr., 1996—2002, asst. libr. dir., 2002—, dir. resources and svcs., 2005—. Bd. dirs. Friends of Evans Libr., Melbourne, 1996-98. Recipient Excellence Scholarly Achievement award SUNY/Buffalo, 1986. Mem. ALA, Assn. Coll. and Rsch. Librs. (instrn. sect., policy com. 1996-98, sci. and tech. sect., univ. librs. sect., membership com. 1996-98), Libr. Adminstrn. and Mgmt. Assn., Reference and User Svcs. Assn., Fla. Inst. Tech. Faculty Senate (enhancing tchg. excellence com. chair 2003-), Fla. Libr. Assn., Libr. Assn. Brevard (continuing edn. com. 1994-95), Ctrl. Fla. Libr. Cooperative (del.), Phi Kappa Phi, Beta Phi Mu, Alpha Sigma Lambda. Home: 854 Hawksbill Island Dr Satellite Beach FL 32937-3850 Office: Fla Inst Tech 150 W University Blvd Melbourne FL 32901-6975 E-mail: whelmste@fit.edu.

HELMS-VANSTONE, MARY WALLACE, anthropology educator; b. Allentown, Pa., Apr. 15, 1938; d. Samuel Leidich and Mary (Wallace) Helms; divorced. BA, Pa. State U., State College, 1960; MA, U. Mich., 1962, PhD, 1967. Instr. Wayne State U., Detroit, 1965-67; asst. prof. Syracuse (N.Y.) U., 1967-68; lectr. Northwestern U., Evanston and Chgo., Ill., 1969-79; prof. U. N.C., Greensboro, 1979—2004, prof. emerita, 2004—, head dept. anthropology Greensboro, 1979-85. Author: Asang: A Miskito Community, 1971, Middle America, 1975, Ancient Panama, 1979, Ulysses' Sail, 1988, Craft and the Kingly Ideal, 1993, Creations of the Rainbow Serpent, 1995, Access to Origins, 1998, The Curassow's Crest, 2000; contbr. articles to profl. jours. Fellow: Am. Anthrop. Assn.; mem.: Medieval Acad. Am., So. Anthrop. Soc. (pres. 1980—81, procs. editor 1982—94), Am. Ethnological Soc., Am. Soc. Ethnohistory (pres. 1976). Avocations: travel, painting, musical activities, crafts. Office: Univ NC Dept Anthropology PO Box 26170 Greensboro NC 27402-6170

HELMUTH, NED D., financial planner; b. Kokomo, Ind., Mar. 24, 1928; s. Dewey J. and Mildred C. (Norton) H.; m. Arlene J. Schwartz, Oct. 5, 1952 (div. 1971); children: Pamela M. Jones, Michael J., Gretchen L.; m. S. Patricia Broadhurst Tautfest, Jan. 4, 1973; 1 child, Carol E. Green. BS in Mktg., Ind. U., 1952; MS in Fin. Services, Am. Coll., 1981. Cert. fin. planner; chartered fin. cons.; chartered life underwriter. Agt. Equitable Life Assurance Soc., Houston, 1952-53, Lafayette, Ind., 1953-58, Nat. Life Ins. Co., Lafayette, 1958—; prin. Ned D Helmuth Fin. Svcs., Lafayette. Nat. trustee Life Underwriters Tng. Council, Washington, 1975-78. Author: The Client Approach-A Quality Method of Selling, 1963, There's No Fun Like Work, 1989. Bd. dirs. South Side Cmty. Ctr., Lafayette, 1955-57, Lafayette Urban MInistry, 1975-78, Big Bros./Big Sisters, Lafayette, 1981-83, Million Dollar Round Table Internat. Found., 1990-93; life mem. Million Dollar Round Table; mem. adv. bd. Salvation Army, Lafayette, 1985-88; trustee Family Svcs., Inc., Lafayette, 1991-93; vol. Network Ind. U. Found. Cpl. U.S. Army, 1946-48, Korea. Named Underwriter of Yr., Lafayette Ind. Assn. Life Underwriters, 1972, Hoosier Underwriter of Yr., Ind. State Assn. Life Underwriters, 1972. Mem.: Fin. Planning Assn., Am. Soc. CLUs (bd. dirs., v.p. 1965—68), Nat. Assn. Ins. and Fin. Advisors, Rotary Club, Phi Gamma Delta. Avocation: old Porsches. Office: Ned D Helmuth Fin Svcs 14 N 2d St Ste 200B Lafayette IN 47901-1204 Home (Winter): 7037 S Tamiami Trl Ste A Sarasota FL 34231-5552 Home: 4325 E 3rd St Bloomington IN 47401-5551

HELOISE, columnist, writer; b. Waco, Tex., Apr. 15, 1951; d. Marshal H. and Heloise K. (Bowles) Cruse; m. David L. Evans, Feb. 13, 1981. BS in Math. and Bus, S.W. Tex. State U., 1974. Owner, pres. Heloise, Inc. Asst. to columnist mother, Heloise, 1974-77, upon her death took over internationally syndicated column, 1977; author: Hints from Heloise, 1980, Help from Heloise, 1981, Heloise's Beauty Book, 1985, All-New Hints from Heloise, 1989, Heloise: Hints for a Healthy Planet, 1990, Heloise from A to Z, 1992, Household Hints for Singles, 1993, Hints for All Occasions, 1995, In The Kitchen With Heloise, 2000, Heloise Conquers Stinks & Stains, 2002, Get Organized with Heloise, 2004; featured on radio show Ask Heloise, Liberty Broadcasting; contbg. editor Good Housekeeping mag., 1983, Speaker for the House; co-founder, 1st co-pilot Mile Pie in the Sky Balloon Club. Mem. Good Neighbor Coun. Tex.-Mex.; sponsor Nat. Smile Week. Recipient Mental Health Mission award Nat. Mental Health Assn., 1990, The Carnegians Good Human Rels. award, 1994. Mem. AFTRA, SAG, Women in Comm. (Headliner 1994), Tex. Press Women, Internat. Women's Forum, Women in Radio and TV, Confrerie de la Chaine des Rotisseurs (bailli San Antonio chpt.), Ordre Mondial des Gourmets De'Gustateurd de U.S.A., Death Valley Yacht and Racket Club, Zonta. Home: PO Box 795000 San Antonio TX 78279-5000

HELPHAND, BEN J., actuary, consultant; b. Columbus, Nebr., Feb. 2, 1915; s. David and Bess (Krupinsky) H.; m. Bessie H. Stine, Sept. 16, 1937; 1 child, Cathy Dee. Student, U. Nebr., 1932-35; BA, U. Iowa, 1936, MA, 1937. Actuarial asst. Pacific Mut. Life Ins. Co., Newport Beach, Calif., 1937-42, v.p., actuary, 1947-80; corp. actuary Best Life Assurance Co., Irvine, Calif., 1980-87. Actuary Dept. Ins. State S.C., Columbia, 1946-47 Served to maj. USAAF, 1942-46. Fellow Soc. Actuaries (bd. govs.); mem. actuarial clubs Pacific States (past pres.), Los Angeles (past pres.), Am. Acad. Actuaries, Sigma Xi. Home: 1321 Keel Dr Corona Del Mar CA 92625-1238

HELPINGSTINE, DANIEL WALLACE, cultural organization administrator, writer; b. Hammond, Ind., Apr. 16, 1953; s. Wallace William and Jean (Janerski) H.; m. Delia Lynn Szendrey, Sept. 10, 1977; 1 child, Leah Jo. BA in Polit. Sci., Ind. U., Gary, 1977, B Gen. Studies in Labor Studies, 1982. Gen. laborer Inland Steel Co., East Chicago, Ind., 1978-82; bus. and labor corr., stringer The Times, Hammond, 1982-84; employee specialist Ind. Employment Security Divsn., Hammond, 1984-89; area supr. Lake County Assn. for Retarded, Gary, 1989-90; program mgr. job readiness and placement Chgo. Lighthouse, 1990—. Contbr. articles to newspaper, short stories to lit. publs. Recipient 1st place awards and cert. for novel and short stories Mississippi Valley Writers Conf., 1981, 92, 85, 86, 96, 98, 99. Office: Chgo Lighthouse 1850 W Roosevelt Rd Chicago IL 60608 E-mail: wallynn@aol.com.

HELPPIE, CHARLES EVERETT, III, financial consultant; b. Highland Park, Mich., Feb. 1, 1952; s. Charles Everett and Patricia Elizabeth (Cote) H.; m. Vali Renée Terhune, July 29, 1972. Student, Ea. Mich. U., 1970-73. Sales rep., sales mgr. Mich. Autosonics, Inc., Ann Arbor, 1972-74; mgr. World Wide Movers, Inc., Ypsilanti, Mich., 1973; sales rep. Godfrey Moving & Storage Co., Ann Arbor, 1974-78; account exec. Merrill Lynch Pierce Fenner & Smith, Detroit, 1978-83, E. F. Hutton, Ann Arbor, 1983-87; asst. br. mgr. Shearson Lehman Hutton, Ann Arbor, 1987-90; fin. cons. Shearson Lehman Bros., Detroit, 1991-92; investment exec. Paine Webber, Inc., Farmington Hills, Mich., 1992-99, br. office ins. coord., 1993—, accounts v.p., 1999-2000, v.p. investments, divisional life ins. cons. Birmingham, Mich., 2000—. Artist and engr. auto. models including MPC World Champion, 1977 (1st Pl. 1977). Campaign worker Dem. Com., Ypsilanti, 1965-71; organizer Anti-War Workshops, Ypsilanti, 1968-70; pres., organizer Fin. Svcs. Softball League, Detroit, 1979-83; mem. Colonial Leadership Coun., Boston. Mem. Am. Funds Group (All-Am. Team), Nameless Nat. Luminaries (founder, chartered), Detroit Tigers Fantasy Camp (chartered), Key and Kite Club, Aim Summit Club (chmns. coun. 1992—), Franklin Group of Funds, Paine Webber Premium Producers Guild, Paine Webber Preservation Planning Inst. (cons. forum "Top 75" mem. managed and retirement accounts svcs.), Paine Webber Pacesetter Club. Avocations: model car building and collecting, automobile and auto racing photography, baseball. Office: Paine Webber Inc 210 S Old Woodward Ave Ste 250 Birmingham MI 48009-6114

HELPRIN, MARK, author; b. N.Y.C., June 28, 1947; s. Morris A. and Eleanor (Lynn) H.; m. Lisa Kennedy, June 28, 1980; children: Alexandra Morris, Olivia Kennedy. AB, Harvard U., 1969, AM, 1972; postgrad., Magdalen Coll., Oxford (Eng.) U., 1976-77. Sr. fellow Claremont Inst. Study of Statesmanship and Polit. Philosophy. Aaron and Helen L. De Roy disting. vis. fellow Hillsdale Coll. Author: A Dove of the East and Other Stories, 1975, Refiner's Fire, 1977, Ellis Island and Other Stories, 1981, Winter's Tale, 1983, Swan Lake, 1989, A Soldier of the Great War, 1991, Memoir from Antproof Case, 1995, A City in Winter, 1996, The Veil of Snows, 1997, The Pacific and Other Stories, 2004, Freddy and Fredericka, 2005; contbg. editor The Wall Street Jour. Mem. Coun. on Fgn. Rels.; adviser in def. and fgn. rels. Rep. presdl. nominee Robert Dole. Served with Israeli Army and Air Force, 1972-73. Recipient Prix de Rome, Am. Acad. and Inst. Arts and Letters, 1982, Nat. Jewish Book award, 1982. Fellow Am. Acad. in Rome.

HELRICH, AMY LOUISE, nurse; b. Teaneck, N.J., Feb. 11, 1958; d. Henry William and Helen Irene Oehlrich; m. Steven Mark Helrich, June 26, 1983. Lic. LPN, N.Y., Pa., Fla., 1976. Pvt. duty oncology, geriatric nurse, Cornwall, NY, 1976—78; charge nurse, supr. Doane's Nursing Home, Campbell Hall, NY, 1978; charge nurse Oneonta (N.Y.) Nursing Home, 1979—81, United Health Svcs., Johnson City, NY, 1981—83; pharmacy owner, corp. officer, v.p. and treas. corp. Terry's Rexall Drug Store, Mansfield, Pa., 1983—90; charge nurse Fred and Harriet Taylor Health Ctr., Bath, NY, 1990—97; sr. charge nurse, supr. Homestead Nursing Home, Penn Yan, NY, 1997—. Editor: (yearbook) The Dragon, 1976; illustrator Easy Guide to Understanding Football, 1990; author: (cookbook) Aunt Amy's Country Cookbook, 2002, (craftbook) Aunt Amy's Country Crafts, 2002. Mem.: Nat. Psoriasis Found. Avocations: crafts, music, writing, poetry.

HELSBY, KEITH R., stock exchange executive; BA in bus. adminstrn., Gettysburg Coll., 1966. Audit divsn. Deloitte Haskins and Sells; dir. internal audits N.Y. Stock Exch., mem. mgmt. com., v.p. fin., 1989—95, sr. v.p. and CFO, 1995—. Office: NY Stock Exch Attn: Ray Pellecchia 11 Wall St New York NY 10005

HELSEL, ELSIE DRESSLER, retired special education educator; b. Butler, Pa., July 10, 1915; d. Adolph and Nelle Simpson Dressler; m. Robert Griffith Helsel, Sept. 2, 1939; children: William Griffith Waring, Robert Griffith Helsel, Jr., Marjorie Lynn. AB in Biology and Pre-Medicine magna cum laude, Chatham Coll., 1937; MS in Genetics, U. Pitts., 1939, PhD in Genetics, 1942; MA in Spl. Edn., Ohio State U., 1962. Biology tchr. Wilkinsburg (Pa.) H.S., 1937—41; instr. human genetics dept. zoology Ohio State U., Cole, 1951—53; cons. med. and sci. dept. United Cerebral Palsy Assn., N.Y.C., 1955, dir. Washington, 1968—74; coord. spl. edn. Ohio U. Coll. Edn., Athens, 1974—77, prof. emeritus, 1981—; dir. Ohio U. Affiliated Ctr. for Human Devel., 1975—81. Asst. dir. divsn. spl. studies Am. Assn. Mental Deficiency, 1964—68; project coord. Protective Svcs. Project Ohio Dept. Mental Health and Mental Retardation, 1967—69; chairperson Ohio Devel. Disabilities Planning Coun., 1993—98; mem. govs. vision com. Dept. Mental Retardation and Devel. Disabilities, 1997—99. Contbr. articles to profl. jours. Mem. govtl. activities com. United Cerebral Palsy Assn., 1965—97, bd. dirs., 1976—94, mem. cmty. svcs. com., 1995—97; Ohio coun. rep. Nat. Assn. Devel. Disabilities Couns., 1985—87, mem. policy com., 1995—97; bd. dirs. United Cerebral Palsy Ohio, 1955—76, 1990—96, v.p., 1977—83, vol. exec. dir., 1991—97; chairperson cmty. svcs. programs Ohio U. Coll. Medicine, 1995—98. Home: 8900 Lavelle Rd Athens OH 45701 Office Phone: 740-593-8775.

HELSLEY, ALEXIA JONES, archivist; b. Louisville, Ky., Sept. 9, 1945; d. George Alexander and Evelyn (Masden) J.; m. Terry Lynn Helsley, Oct. 11, 1969; children: Cassandra Keiser Paschal, Jacob Henry. BA in History, Furman U., 1967; MA in History, U. S.C., 1974; cert., Modern Archives Inst., Washington, 1978, S.C. Exec. Inst., Columbia, 1995. Archival asst. S.C. Dept. Archives and History, Columbia, 1968-69, archivist I, 1969-72, asst. reference archivist, 1972-76, supr. reference and rsch., 1976-88, dir. pub. programs divsn., 1988-96, dir. edn., 1996-99; dir. spl. projects, editor Biograph. Directory S.C. House of Reps., 1999—. Historian Am. Lodging Resources, Inc.; rsch. fellow Inst. So. Studies, U. S.C., 2001-02; adj. faculty Midlands Tech. Coll., 2001-02, U. S.C., Aiken, 2002— Author: Harbison: an Historical Sketch, 1986, First Baptist Church of Irmo: Historical Overview, 1992, Researching Family History: A Workbook, 1992, 96, The 1840 Revolutionary Pensioners of Henderson County, North Carolina, 1996, Unsung Heroines of the Carolina Frontier, 1997, Silent Cities: Cemeteries and Classrooms, 1997, South Carolina's African American Confederate Pensioners, 1923-1925, 1998, South Carolinians in the War for American Independence, 2000, The Map of South Carolina this historical Annontation, 2003, Beaufort, South Carolina a History, 2005, South Carolina: One State, Two Flags, 2006, (TV series) Branches, 2005; co-author: The Many Faces of Slavery, 1999, S.C. Court Records, 1993, The Changing Face of S.C. Politics, 1993, African American Genealogical Research, 1997; contbr. articles to profl. jours. Chair social and recreation com. Harbison Cmty. Assn., Columbia, S.C., 1984-89; trustee S.C. Hall of Fame, Myrtle Beach, 1988-96; vice-chair Columbia Quincentennial Commn. S.C., 1989-93; pres. Richland Sertoma, Columbia, 1998-99; bd. vis. Presbyn. Coll., 2001-2003. Recipient Willie Parker Peace History Book award, 1997, Lifetime Achievement award, SC Archival Assn., 2002; named to Hon. Order of Ky. Cols., Richland Sertoman of Yr., 2000. Mem.: S.C. Coun. for Social Studies, S.C. Hist. Assn., Soc. Am. Archivists (chair reference, access, outreach sect. 1981—83), Joseph McDowell Nat. Soc. DAR, Pace Soc. Am. (trustee), Henderson County Geneal. and Hist. Soc. (v.p. 1998—2005, charter), S.C. Archival Assn. (pres. 2005). Baptist. Home: 1 Northpine Ct Columbia SC 29212-2911 Office: SC Dept Archives History 8301 Parklane Rd Columbia SC 29223-4905 E-mail: helsley@scdah.state.sc.us, alexiahelsley@yahoo.com.

HELSON, HENRY BERGE, publisher, educator, retired mathematician; b. Lawrence, Kan., June 2, 1927; s. Harry and Lida G. (Anderson) H.; m. Ravenna W. Mathews, June 12, 1954; children— David M., Ravenna A., Harold E. AB, Harvard U., 1947, PhD, 1950. Lectr. U. Uppsala, Sweden, 1950-51; instr., then asst. prof. math. Yale, 1951-55; mem. faculty U. Calif. at Berkeley, 1955—, prof. math.; retired, 1993. Vis. prof. Swedish univs., spring 1962, U. Paris, Orsay, France, 1966-67, U. Sci. and Tech., Kumasi, Ghana, spring 1969, U. du Languedoc, Montpellier, France, 1971-72, Marseille, France, fall 1976; vis. prof. Indian Statis. Inst., Calcutta, spring 1980; lectr. St. Mary's Coll. of Calif., 2001-02. Author: Invariant Subspaces, 1964, Harmonic Analysis, 1983, The Spectral Theorem, 1986, Linear Algebra, 1990, Honors Calculus, 1992, Calculus and Probability, 1998, Dirichlet Series, 2005. Mem. Soc. Friends; treas. Friends Com. on Legis. Calif., 1989-95. Sheldon Traveling fellow, Warsaw and Wroclaw, Poland, 1947—48. Home: 15 The Crescent Berkeley CA 94708-1701 E-mail: hhelson@aol.com.

HELSTAD, ORRIN L., lawyer, educator; b. Ettrick, Wis., Feb. 9, 1922; s. Albert J. and Martha H. (Gimse) H.; m. Charlotte Dart Ankeney, June 26, 1954. Student, U. Wis., La Crosse, 1940-42; BS, U. Wis., Madison, 1948, LL.B., 1950. Bar: Wis. 1950. Research assoc. Wis. Legis. Council, 1950-61; assoc. prof. law U. Wis., Madison, 1961-65, prof., 1965-85; assoc. dean U. Wis. (Sch. Law), 1972-75, acting dean, 1975-76, dean, 1976-83, dean emeritus, 1985—, prof. emeritus, 1985—. Mem. consumer advisory council Wis. Dept. Agr., 1970-72; vice chmn. Wis. Supreme Ct. com. on the State bar, 1977; mem. Fed. Jud. Nominating Commn. Western Dist. Wis., 1979-83 Contbr. articles to law revs.; co-author, editor: Wisconsin Uniform Comml. Code Handbook, 1965, 1971. Recipient Disting. Svc. award Wis. Law Alumni Assn., 1991. Fellow Am. Bar Found.; mem. State Bar Wis., ABA (council sect. on local govt. law 1975-79), Wis. Bar Assn., Dane County Bar Assn., Am. Judicature Soc. Unitarian Universalist. Home: 8 Sebring Ct Madison WI 53719-3521

HELTNE, PAUL GREGORY, researcher, museum director; b. Lake Mills, Iowa, July 4, 1941; s. Palmer Tilford and Grace Katherine (Hanson) H.; children— Lisa, Christian. BA, Luther Coll., Decorah, Iowa, 1962; PhD, U. Chgo., 1970. Asst. prof. Johns Hopkins U. Sch. Medicine, Balt., 1970-82; dir. Chgo. Acad. Scis., 1982-91, pres., 1991—99, pres. emeritus, 1999—; co-dir. Nature Polis and Ethics Project, 1994—2002; co-dir., sr. rsch. scholar Ctr. for Humans and Nature, 2003—. Cons. WHO, Am. Petroleum Inst. Author, editor: Neotropical Primates: Status and Conservation, 1976, Lion-Tailed Macaque, 1985, Science Learning in the Informal Setting, 1988, Understanding Chimpanzees, 1989, Chimpanzee Cultures, 1994. Trustee Balt. Zool. Soc., 1972-82. Mem. Am. Assn. Mus. (edn. task force, accreditation site visitor), Assn. Sci. Mus. Dirs. (sec.-treas. 1986-96), Internat. Primatology Soc., Soc. Integrative and Comparative Biology, Soc. for Study Evolution, Systematic Zoology Soc. Office: Ctr for Humans and Nature 2430 N Cannon Dr Chicago IL 60614 E-mail: paulheltne@humansandnature.org.

HELTON, KATHLEEN JACOBSON, neuroradiologist; d. Gerald Jacobson and Mary Margaret Fitzgerald; m. Stephen Lane Helton, June 7, 1981. MSN, U. of Tenn. Coll. of Nursing, 1979—80; MD, U. of Tenn. Coll. of Medicine, 1986—91. Radiologist Am. Bd. of Radiology, 1996. Neuroradiology fellow Vanderbilt U. Med. Ctr., Nashville, 1996—98, clin. instr., neuroradiology, 1998; neuroradiologist St Jude Children's Rsch. Hosp., Memphis, 1999—. Interim dir. mri St. Jude Children's Rsch. Hosp., 2003—. Recipient Achievement Citation for Scholastic Achievement, Janet M. Glasgow Meml. Fund, 1991; Josephine Cir. scholarship, U. of Tenn. Sch. of Nursing, 1975—77. Mem.: Am. Soc. of Neuroradiology, Am. Soc. of Pediatric Neuroradiology (assoc.), Southeastern Neuroradiological Soc. (assoc.), Am. Coll. of Radiology (assoc.), Alpha Omega Alpha Soc. (assoc.). Avocations: swimming, travel, music. Office: St Jude Children's Rsch Hosp 332 N Lauderdale St Memphis TN 38105 Office Phone: 901-495-2412. E-mail: kathleen.helton@stjude.org.

HELTON, SANDRA LYNN, telecommunications industry executive; b. Paintsville, Ky., Dec. 9, 1949; d. Paul Edward and Ella Rae (Van Hoose) H.; m. Norman M. Edelson, Apr. 15, 1978. BS, U. Ky., 1971; MBA, MIT, 1977. Capital budget adminstr. Corning (N.Y.) Glass Works, 1978-79, fixed assets mgr., 1979-80, contr. electronics divsn., 1980-82, mgr. customer fin. svcs., 1982-84, dir. fin. svcs., 1984-86, asst. treas., 1986-91, v.p., treas., 1991-94, sr. v.p., treas., 1994—97; exec. v.p. fin., CFO TDS Telecom, Chgo., 1998—2000, exec. v.p., CFO, 2001—. Bd. dirs. U.S. Cellular Corp., The Prin. Fin. Group. Vol. Mass. Gen. Hosp., Boston, 1976; treas. Corning Mus. of Glass; treas pres. bd. dirs. Chemung Valley Arts Coun., Corning, 1981-87; bd. dirs. Corning Summer Theatre, 1987-91, Arnot Hosp. Found., 1988—; mem. fin. com. Clemens Performing Arts Ctr., Elmira, N.Y., 1985-92; mem. adv. bd. Chase Lincoln, 1988-91; mem. bus. com. Met. Mus. Art, 1992—; pres. bd. dirs. Rockwell Mus., 1992—; mem. Regional Cultural Adv. Com., 1992—; mem. FEI com. on Corp. Fin., 1995—; bd. dirs. Arnot Ogden Meml. Med. Ctr., Arts of the So. Finger Lakes. Mem. Nat. Assn. Corp. Treass., Fin. Women's Assn., Soc. Internat. Treas., Fin. Execs. Inst. Avocations: music, tennis.

HELTON, TODD, professional baseball player; b. Knoxville, Tenn., Aug. 20, 1973; m. Kristi Helton, Jan. 29. Student, U. Tenn. Player Colorado Rockies, 1997—. Named to Nat. League All-Star Team, 2000—04; recipient Nat. League Gold Glove Award, 2001, 2002, 2004. Achievements include led Nat. League in Hits (216), RBI's (147), and Batting Avg. (.372), 2000. Office: Colo Rockies 2001 Blake St Denver CO 80205-2008

HELVEY, WILLIAM CHARLES, JR., communications specialist; b. Springfield, Mo., Sept. 4, 1942; s. William C. Sr. and Alice (Essary) H.; m. Julia Faye Howard, June 16, 1962; children: Howard, Harold. BS in Art Edn., S.W. Mo. State U., 1965; MA in Art, U. Mo., 1970. Tchr. art Marshfield (Mo.) H.S., 1965-67; med. illustrator, program emphasis mgr. Mo. Regional Med. Program, Columbia, 1968-80; dir. instrl. media Ctrl. Meth. Coll., Fayette, Mo.; comm. cons., Columbia, 1981-83; state comm. sys. specialist Univ. Ext., Lincoln U., Jefferson City, Mo., 1983—2005; ret. Profl. artist, photographer, presenter in field; juror for art and photography. One-man shows (83), in art and photography, group shows (over 100) in arts, including, Arts Ctr. of the Ozarks, Boone County Hist. Mus., Columbia, Mo., Arrow Rock State Hist. Site, Rozier Gallery, Jefferson City, Mo., Columbia Art League, U.S. Social Security Adminstrn., Nat. 4-H Ctr., Silver Springs, Md.; contbr. numerous articles to profl. jours. Project leader Boone County 4-H Clubs, Columbia, 1977-2002. Recipient Unsung Hero award U.S. Dept. Agr., 1988, Mo. Specialist award Mo. State Extension, 1990, 93, numerous awards in art, photography, film and video prodn. Mem.: Columbia Art League (chmn. Boone County art show 1975—, Lifetime Achievement award in art), Aircraft Owners and Pilots Assn. Avocations: nature, aviation, screenplay writing, fine art photography. Home: 908 Shepard Ct Columbia MO 65201-6135 E-mail: bhelvey@aol.com.

HELWEG, OTTO JENNINGS, civil engineer, educator; b. Kalamazoo, Mich., Feb. 1, 1936; s. Otto John and Laura Virginia (Jennings) H.; m. Virginia Mae Caldwell, June 28, 1964; children: Otto John II, Mark Web, Steven Jennings. MDiv, Fuller Theol. Sem., Pasadena, Calif., 1966; MS, UCLA, 1967; PhD, Colo. State U., 1975; MS, Memphis State U., 1992; MBA, U. Memphis, 1994. Registered profl. engr., Calif., Colo., Tenn., Tex. Assoc. prof. civil engring. U. Calif., Davis, 1975-83; vis. prof. Tex. A&M U., College Station, 1983-88; prof., dept. chairperson Memphis State U., 1988-92; prof., 1992—96; dean Coll. Engring. and Arch. ND State U., Fargo, 1996—. Cons. U.N.D.P., Ludiana, India, 1980. Author: Improving Well and Pump Efficiency, 1983, Water Resources Planning and Management, 1983, Microcomputer Applications, 1991; contbr. over 100 articles to profl. publs. Capt. USNR, 1958-62. Recipient Nat. Sci. award Nat. Water Well Assn., Worthington, Ohio, 1983. Fellow: ASCE (editor jour. Irrigation and Drainage Engineering 1989-92, Hoover medal 1997); mem. many profl. socs. Home: 14656 Beaufort Cir Naples FL 34119 Office: ND State U Coll Engring and Arch Fargo ND 58105 Personal E-mail: ottoj@helweg.com. Business E-Mail: otto.helweg@nosu.edu.

HELWICK, CHRISTINE, lawyer; b. Orange, Calif., Jan. 6, 1947; d. Edward Everett and Ruth Evelyn (Seymour) Hailwood; children: Ted C., Dana J. BA, Stanford U., 1968; MA, Northwestern U., 1969; JD, U. Calif., San Francisco, 1973. Bar: Calif., U.S. Supreme Ct. U. S. Ct. Appeals (9th cir.), U.S. Dist. Ct. (no., ctrl., so. and ea. dist.) Calif. Tchr. history New Trier Twp. High Sch., Winnetka, Ill., 1968-69; sec. to the producer Flip Wilson Show, Burbank, Calif., 1970; assoc. Crosby, Heafey, Roach & May, Oakland, Calif., 1973-78; asst. counsel litigation U. Calif., Oakland, 1978-84, mng. univ. counsel, 1984-94, counsel Berkeley campus, 1989-94; gen. counsel Calif. State U. Sys., 1994—. Lectr. in field. Mem. instnl. rev. bd. Devel. Studies Ctr., Oakland, 1990—; mem. Alameda County Fee Arbitration Panel. Mem. Nat. Assn. Coll. and Univ. Attys. (bd. dirs. 1995-98, 2000-2004, pres. 2002-03), Nat. Assn. Coll. and Univ. Bus. Officers (bd. dirs. 2002—), State Bar Calif. (exec. com. 1980-83, Leadership Calif. 1998), dirs. 1977), Alameda County Bar Found. (adv. trustee 1988-90, bd. dirs. 1991), Order of Coif. Episcopalian. Office: Calif State U 401 Golden Shore 4th Fl Long Beach CA 90802-4275

HELWIG, ARTHUR WOODS, retired chemical company executive; b. St. Louis, Feb. 1, 1929; s. Gunther Albert and Emma (Schumacher) H.; m. Evelyn Morgan, July 10, 1954; children: Paul, Katherine, Elizabeth, Mary. BSChemE, U. Mo.-Rolla, 1950, ChemE (hon.), 1966; MSChemE, U. Ill., 1952. Process engr. Ethyl Corp., Baton Rouge, 1952-53, econs. engr., 1953-56, supr., 1956-59, gen. supt., 1959-64, dir. planning Baton Rouge and Richmond, Va., 1964-74, v.p. planning Richmond, 1974—94; ret., 1994. Bd. dirs. Solite Corp., Richmond, Albemarle Corp. Trustee Sci. Mus. Va., Richmond, 1987-99, chmn., 1992, pres. Found., 1984-87. Mem. Va. Inst. Marine Sci. (marine scis. devel. coun. 1994-99), Met. Richmond C. of C. (bd. dirs. 1986), Engrs. Club Richmond (v.p. 1987—, pres. 1988-89). Methodist. Home: 8911 Highfield Rd Richmond VA 23229-7756 Personal E-mail: helwig1@comcast.net.

HELZ, GEORGE RUDOLPH, chemistry professor; b. Silver Spring, Md., Mar. 4, 1942; married, 1970; 1 child. AB, Princeton U., 1964; PhD in Geochemistry, Pa. State U., 1971. From asst. prof. to assoc. prof. U. Md., College Park, 1970-84, prof. chemistry, 1984—; dir. Md. Water Resources Rsch. Ctr., 1990—2001. Mem. disinfectants chem. subcom. NAS-NRC, 1978; vis. prof. Stanford U., 1983-84, Cox vis. prof., 1998-99; sr. vis. fellow Manchester (Eng.) U., 1989-90. AAAS Environ. fellow, 1988. Mem. Am. Chem. Soc. (chmn. geochem. divsn. 1985), Am. Geophys. Union, Geochem. Soc. (treas. 1975-78), Geol. Soc. Am., Geol. Soc. Washington (pres. 1996). Achievements include research in aqueous geochemistry; geochemistry of mineral deposits; environmental chemistry; fate of pollutants in estuaries. Office: 3101 Chemistry Bldg 091 College Park MD 20742-0001

HELZER, JAMES DENNIS, retired health facility administrator; b. Fresno, Calif., Apr. 27, 1938; s. Alexander and Katherine (Scheidt) H.; m. Joan Elaine Alinder, Feb. 25, 1967; children: Amy, Rebecca. BS, Fresno State Coll., 1960; M.Hosp. Adminstrn., U. Iowa, 1965. Adminstrv. asst. Twilight Haven, Fresno, Calif., 1960-61, adminstr. resident, 1964-65; asst. adminstr. U. Calif. Hosps. and Clinics, San Francisco, 1965-68, Fresno Community Hosp., 1968-71, exec. adminstr., 1971-82, pres., chief exec. officer, 1982-91, Community Hosps. Cen. Calif., 1982-91, cons., 1991-95; adminstr. Veterans Home of Calif., Yountville, Calif., 1995-99; ret., 1999. Served with U.S. Army, 1961-63. Fellow Am. Coll. Hosp. Adminstrs.; mem. Am., Calif. hosp. assns. Clubs: Rotary. Presbyterian. Home: 1164 Secret Lake Loop Lincoln CA 95648-8404

HEMANN, RAYMOND GLENN, research company executive; b. Cleve., Jan. 24, 1933; s. Walter Harold and Marsha Mae (Colbert) H.; m. Lucile Tinnin Turnage, Feb. 1, 1958; children: James Edward, Carolyn Frances; m. Pamela Schaap Lehr, Dec. 18, 1987. BS, Fla. State U., 1957; postgrad., U.S. Naval Postgrad. Sch., 1963-64, U. Calif., Los Angeles, 1960-62; MS in Systems Engring., Calif. State U., Fullerton, 1970; MA in Econs., Calif. State U., 1972; cert. in tech. mgmt., Calif. Inst. Tech., 1990. Comml., glider and pvt. pilot. Aero. engring. aide U.S. Navy, David Taylor Model Basin, Carderock, Md., 1956; analyst Fairchild Aerial Surveys, Tallahassee, 1957; research analyst Fla. Rd. Dept., Tallahassee, 1957-59; chief Autonetics divsn. N.Am. Aviation, Inc., Anaheim, Calif., 1959-69; v.p., dir. R.E. Manns Co., Wilmington, Calif., 1969-70; mgr. Avionics Design and Analysis Dept. Lockheed-Calif. Co., Burbank, 1970-72, mgr. Advanced Concepts divsn., 1976-82; gen. mgr. Western divsn. Arinc Research Corp., Santa Ana, 1972-76; dir. Future Requirements Rockwell Internat., 1982-85, dir. Threat Analysis, Corp. Offices, 1985-89; pres., CEO Advanced Systems Rsch., Inc., 1989—. Adj. sr. fellow Ctr. Strategic and Internat. Studies, Washington, 1987—; bd. dirs., mem. exec. com. Fla. State U. Rsch. Found., 1995-2003; bd. dirs. Assn. Mgmt. Svc. Inc., Numedeon, Inc., Am. Heart Assn., Pasadena Civic Auditorium Found. Inc., 2000-02; chmn. adv. coun. Coll. Engring. Fla. State U./Fla. A&M U., 1995—; cons. to dir. Ctrl. Intelligence, Nat. Intelligence Coun., Nat. Air Intelligence Ctr., Inst. Def. Analyses, Battelle Meml. Inst., Ctr. Strategic and Internat. Studies; sec., bd. dirs. Calif State U., Fullerton, Econs. Found.; mem. naval studies bd. panels, 1985—, chmn. indsl. panel Nat. Labs. Infrastructure Study, Office Sec. Def., 1995; chmn. indsl. panel Future Dirs. Mil. Aeronautics Study, 1996; asst. prof. ops. analysis dept. U.S. Naval Postgrad. Sch., Monterey, Calif., 1963-64, Monterey Peninsula Coll., 1963; instr. ops. analysis Calif. State U., Fullerton, 1964-67, instr. quantitative methods, 1969-72; program developer, instr. systems engring. indsl. rels. ctr. Calif. Inst. Tech., 1992-96; lectr. Brazilian Navy, 1980, U. Calif., Santa Barbara, 1980, Yale U., 1985, Princeton U., 1986, U.S. Naval Postgrad. Sch., 1986, Ministry of Def., Taiwan, Republic of China, 1990; Calif. Inst. Tech. Assocs., 1992—; mem. exec. forum Calif. Inst. Tech., 1991—. Contbr articles to profl. jours. and new media. Chmn. comdr.'s adv. bd. CAP, Calif. Wing; reader Recording for the Blind, 1989—; bd. dirs. Pasadena Civic Auditorium Found., 2000-02, Boy Scouts Am., 2971-79; bd. dirs., sec.-treas. Jr. All-Am. Football; trustee Art Ctr. Coll. Design, Pasadena, Calif., 2003—. Syde P. Deeb scholar, 1956; recipient honor awards Nat. Assn. Remotely Piloted Vehicles, 1975, 76; named to Hon. Order Ky. Cols., 1985. Fellow AAAS, AIAA (assoc.); mem. IEEE (life), Ops. Rsch. Soc. Am., Air Force Assn., US Marines Meml. Club (life), N.Y. Acad. Scis., Assn. Old Crows., L.A. World Affairs Coun., Phi Kappa Tau (past pres.). Episcopalian. Office: Advanced Sys Rsch Inc 33 S Catalina Ave Ste 202 Pasadena CA 91106-2426

HEMBREE, JAMES D., retired chemical company executive; b. Morris, Okla., Feb. 27, 1929; s. James D. and Mary Eleanor H.; m. Joyce Pickrell, Aug. 25, 1951; children: Victoria Lee Krivacs, Alex James, Kent Douglas. BSCh.E., Okla. State U., 1951; MSCh.E., U. Mich., 1952. Dir. mktg. inorganic chems. Dow Chem U.S.A., Midland, Mich., 1968-78, gen. mgr. designed products dept., 1976-78, v.p., 1978-80, group v.p., 1980-83; pres., chief exec. officer Dow Chem. Can., Sarnia, Ont., 1983-86; ret., 1986. Home and Office: 4620 Jupiter Dr Salt Lake City UT 84124-3900 Personal E-mail: jandj_84124@yahoo.com.

HEMBREY, SHEA, artist; b. Newport, Ark., Aug. 21, 1974; s. Jackson and Sandy Hembrey. BA in art and English, Lyon Coll., 1996; COP, U. Canterbury, New Zealand, 1998; MA, Ark. State U., 1999. Cultural and profl. exchange to Chile Rotary Internat., 2003. Exhibitions include Helen Day Art Ctr., 2005, Georgetown Internat. Fraser Gallery, 2004, US Artists Am. Fine Art Show, Pa., exhibitions include Still Life Today Davidson Galleries, 2003, exhibitions include J. Cacciola Gallery, N.Y.C., 2003. Recipient Ambassador scholarship, Rotary Internat., 1998; Individual Artist grant, Ark. Arts Coun., 2003. Home: 610 Jackson 63 Newport AR 72112 E-mail: sheahembrey@yahoo.com.

HEMBROOK, ANOLA MARY, English language educator; b. Auburndale, Wis., May 3, 1950; d. Walter Andrew and Barbara Jeanne Willfahrt; m. William Lee Hembrook, Sept. 18, 1976; 1 child, Dani Jeanne. BS, U. Wis., Green Bay, 1972; MS, U. Wis., Stevens Point, 1983. Cert. tchr. Tchr. Auburndale Sch. Dist., 1972. Adviser Nat. Honor Soc. Home: 623 N Anton Ave Marshfield WI 54449

HEMBY, JAMES BENJAMIN, JR., college president; b. Ayden, N.C., Mar. 1, 1934; m. Joan Edwards Hemby; children: James B. III, Scott Edwards, Thomas Simmen. BA, Barton Coll., 1955; BD, Vanderbilt U., 1958; MA, Tex. Christian U., 1964, PhD, 1965. Grad. teaching fellow Tex. Christian U., Ft. Worth, 1962-64; instr. Memphis State U., 1964-65; dir. admissions Barton Coll., Wilson, NC, 1959-62, assoc. prof. English, 1965-68, prof., 1968-73, chmn. English dept., 1973-79, Am. Coun. Edn. fellow in acad. adminstrn., 1979-80, provost, 1980-83, pres., 1983—2003, pres. emeritus, 2003. Dir. N.C. Writing Project, 1980-85; pres. N.C. Lit. and Hist. Assn., 1983-84; chmn. N.C. Writer's Conf., 1982-83; pres. Carolinas Intercollegiate Athletic Conf., 1989-91, N.C. Assn. Colls. and Univs., 1993-94, pres. N.C. Assn. Ind. Colls. and Univs., 1995-99; ptnr. Administrv. Cons., 2005-. Editor: Crucible, 1973-83. Bd. dirs. Wilson County chpt. ARC, 1985-96, Flynn Home, 1998-02, Budget & Comm. United Way, 1997-02, Novopharm, 1998-00; mem. Wilson County Bd. Edn., 1974-86, N.C. Humanities Coun., 1988-91; exec. com. Triangle East, 1985-91; bd. dirs. The Lost Colony, 1998-00. Lilly Found. vis. scholar, Duke U., 1977; Fulbright grantee, 1990; recipient Disting. Svc. award N.C. High Sch. Athletic Assn., 1993. Mem. MLA, Am. Coun. Edn., Nat. Assn. Ind. Colls. and Univs. (bd. dirs. 2000-02, pres. NC chpt. 1995-99), NC Assn. Colls. and Univs. (pres. 1993-94), Internat. Assn. Univ. Pres., Coun. Ind. Colls., Am. Assn. Higher Edn., Nat. Assn. Intercollegiate Athletics (coun. pres. 1991-93), Rotary Club (Harris fellow), Wilson C. of C. (bd. dirs.). Democrat. Avocations: tennis, bicycling, chess, creative writing. Personal E-mail: jhembyjr@nc.rr.com.

HEMENWAY, ROBERT E., academic administrator, language educator; b. Sioux City, Iowa, Aug. 10, 1941; s. Myrle Emery and Katharine Leone (Cook) H.; m. Marilyn Wickstrom, June 16, 1962 (div. 1970); children: Gina, Jeremy; m. Mattie Fenter, May 12, 1972 (div. 1980); children: Robin, Karintha, Matthew, Langston; m. Leah Renee Hattemer, Dec. 19, 1981; children: Zachary, Arna. BA, U. Nebr., Omaha, 1963; PhD, Kent (Ohio) State U., 1966. Asst. prof. English U. Ky., Lexington, 1966-68; assoc. prof. Am. studies U. Wyo., Laramie, 1968-73; prof. U. Ky., Lexington, 1973-86; dean arts and scis. U. Okla., Norman, 1986-89; chancellor U. Ky., Lexington, 1989-95, U. Kans., Lawrence, 1995—. Dean Gov.'s Scholar's Program, Ky., 1984-86; bd. dir., Am. Coun. on Edn. Author: Zora Neale Hurston, 1977 (Best Biography of 1977 award Soc. Midland Authors 1978, Rembert Patrick prize Fla. Hist. Soc. 1978). Mem. Gov.'s Task Force on Literacy, Okla., 1987-89; bd. dirs. Okla. HS Sci. and Math., Oklahoma City, 1985-86, Coun. Colls. Arts and Scis., 1987-89. NEH fellow, 1974-75. Mem. MLA, Am. Studies Assn. (nat. coun.), South Atlantic Assn. Depts. English (pres. 1984-85). Lutheran. Avocation: duplicate bridge. Office: Univ Kansas Office of the Chancellor 230 Strong Hall Lawrence KS 66045-7501

HEMINGWAY, RICHARD WILLIAM, law educator; b. Detroit, Nov. 24, 1927; s. William Oswald and Iva Catherine (Wildfang) H.; m. Vera Cecilia Eck, Sept. 12, 1947; children: Margaret Catherine, Carol Elizabeth, Richard Albert. BS in Bus, U. Colo., 1950; JD magna cum laude (J. Woodall Rogers Sr. Gold medal 1955), So. Meth. U., 1955; LL.M. (William S. Cook fellow 1968), U. Mich., 1969. Bar: Tex. 1955, Okla. 1981. Assoc. Fulbright, Crooker, Freeman, Bates & Jaworski, Houston, 1955-60; lectr. Bates Sch. Law, U. Houston, 1960; assoc. prof. law Baylor U. Law Sch., Waco, Tex., 1960-65; vis. assoc. prof. So. Meth. U. Law Sch., 1965-68; prof. law Tex. Tech U. Law Sch., Lubbock, 1968-71, Paul W. Horn prof., 1972-81, acting dean, 1974-75, dean ad interim, 1980-81; prof. law U. Okla., Norman, 1981-83, Eugene Kuntz prof. oil, gas and natural resources law, 1983-92, Eugne Kuntz prof. emeritus oil, gas & natural resources law, 1992—. Author: The Law of Oil and Gas, 1971, 2d edit., 1983, lawyer's edit., 1983, 3d edit., 1991, West's Texas Forms (Mines and Minerals), 1977, 2d edit., 1991; contbg. editor various law reports, cases and materials. Served with USAAF, 1945-47. Mem. Tex. Bar Assn., Scribes, Order of Coif (faculty), Beta Gamma Sigma. Lutheran. Avocation: amateur radio. Home: Apt 1024 5000 Old Shepard Pl Plano TX 75093-4404 E-mail: rheming1@sbcglobal.net.

HEMINGWAY, THOMAS L., career military officer, lawyer; b. Evanston, Ill., Feb. 7, 1940; m. Judith Casey. BA in Sociology, Willamette U., 1962, JD, 1965. Bar: Oreg., U.S. Ct. Fed. Claims, U.S. Ct. Appeals Fed. cir. Commd. 2d lt. USAF, 1965, advanced through grades to brig. gen., 1992, chief civil law Davis-Monthan AFB, Ariz., 1965-69, chief mil. justice, provincial liaison

Udorn Royal Thai AFB, Thailand, 1969-70, chief mil. justice 15th Air Force March AFB, Calif., 1970-71; assoc. prof. law USAF Acad., Colorado Springs, Colo., 1971-75; staff judge adv. USAF, McChord AFB, Wash., 1975-79, Rhein-Main Air Base, West Germany, 1979-82, sr. judge ct. mil. rev. hdqs. Washington, 1982-83, chief mil. justice divsn. office of judge adv. gen., 1983-85, staff judge adv. 17th Air Force Sembach Air Base, West Germany, 1985-88, staff judge adv. Europe Ramstein Air Base, Germany, 1988-90, dir. judiciary, vice comdr. Air Force legal svcs. ctr. Washington, 1990-91, chief counsel U.S. transp. command, staff judge adv. hdqs. mil. airlift command Scott AFB, Ill., 1991-92, chief counsel U.S. transp. command, staff judge adv. air mobility command, 1992—96; legal adv. U.S. Office Mil. Commn. for mil. tribunals at Guantanamo Bay, Cuba, Washington, 2003—. Chmn. Joint Svc. Com. Mil. Justice; chmn. Mil. Justice Act of 1983 adv. commn. Dept. Def. Decorated Legion of Merit with oak leaf cluster, Bronze Star medal, Air Force Commendation medal, Mil. Achievement medal (Fed. Republic of Germany); recipient Justice Tom C. Clark award D.C. chpt. Fed. Bar Assn., 1985; recipient Disting. Alumni citation, Willamette Univ. 2002. Mem.: Judge Adv. Assn. (pres. 2005). Office: Office of Military Commissions The Pentagon Washington DC 20301

HEMKE, FREDERICK L., academic administrator; b. July 11, 1935; s. Fred L. and May H. (Rowell) H.; m. Junita Borg, Dec. 26, 1959; children: Elizabeth Hemke Shapiro, Frederic John Borg. Premiere prix, Cons. Nat. de Musique, Paris, 1956; BS in Music Edn., U. Wis., Milw., 1958; MusM in Music Edn., Eastman Sch. of Music, Rochester, N.Y., 1962; DMA in Musical Arts, U. Wis., 1975. Chmn. dept. preparatory wind and percussion Sch. of Music Northwestern U., Evanston, Ill., 1962-75, chmn. dept. music performance and studies, 1962-94, prof. of music (saxophone), 1963—, sr. assoc. dean, 1994—2003, acting dean, 2002, Louis and Elsie Snydacker Eckstein prof. music, 2003—, Charles Deering McCormick prof. tchg. exellence, 2004—. Faculty athletics rep. Northwestern U., Big 10 Conf., NCAA 1982-2003; cons. La Voz Corp., Sun Valley, Calif., Frederick Hemke Saxophone Reeds, So. Music Co., San Antonio, Hemke Saxophone Series, The Selmer Co., Elkhart, Ind. Instrumental soloist (recordings) The American Saxophone, Music for Tenor Saxophone, Allan Pettersson, Symphony No. 15 (with Stockholm Philharmonic); Quintet for String Quartet & Saxo-Warren Benson, Concerto-Ross Lee Finney, Simple Gifts for saxophone and organ; author: The Early History of the Saxophone, Hemke Saxophone Series, So. Music Co. Recipient Excellence in Teaching award Northwestern U. Alumni Assn., Music Alumni Achievement award, U. Wis., Milw.; grantee: Nat. Endowment for the Arts. Mem. Ill. Music Educators Assn., Pi Kappa Lambda, Kappa Kappa Psi, Phi Mu Alpha Sinfonia (past province gov.) Office: Northwestern U Sch of Music 1965 S Campus Dr Evanston IL 60208-0874

HEMMENDINGER, NOEL, retired lawyer; b. Bernardsville, N.J., Dec. 25, 1913; s. Max and Jeannette (Harris) H.; m. Marjorie Knebelman, Aug. 28, 1948; children: Eric, Lucy, John. AB, Princeton U., 1934; JD, Harvard U., 1937. Bar: D.C. 1937, N.Y. 1938, U.S. Dist. Ct. (so. dist.) N.Y. 1938, U.S. Supreme Ct. 1956. Law clk. U.S. Ct. Appeals (2d cir.), N.Y.C., 1937-38; asst. U.S. atty. So. Dist., N.Y.C., 1938-40; spl. asst. to U.S. atty. gen. U.S. Dept. Justice, N.Y.C., 1940-42; staff official U.S. Dept. State, Washington, 1946-56; ptnr. Stitt & Hemmendinger and successor firms, Washington, 1957-77, Arter, Hadden & Hemmendinger, Washington, 1977-83, Wald, Harkrader & Ross, Washington, 1983-85; of counsel Willkie, Farr & Gallagher, Washington, 1985—; now ret. Dep. dir. U.S. Japan Trade Council, Washington, 1957-77, bd. dirs. Trustee, counsel Japan Am. Soc. Washington, 1957—. Served to capt. U.S. Army, 1942-46, ETO. Decorated Bronze Star, 1945; named to Japanese Order of the Sacred Treasure 2d class, 1981. Mem. ABA, D.C. Bar Assn. Clubs: Cosmos. Democrat. Avocation: tennis. Home: 2007 Marthas Rd Alexandria VA 22307-1954 Office: Willkie Farr & Gallagher 1155 21st St NW Fl 6 Washington DC 20036-3384

HEMMER, J. MICHAEL, lawyer; b. Stillwater, Okla., May 28, 1949; BA with honors, Stanford U., 1971; JD with honors, U. Calif., Berkeley, 1976. Atty. Covington & Burling, Washington, 1976—2002, ptnr., 1984—2002; v.p. law Union Pacific Corp., Omaha, 2002—04, sr. v.p. law, gen. counsel, 2004—. Office: Union Pacific Corp 1400 Douglas St Omaha NE 68179

HEMMER, JAMES PAUL, lawyer; b. Oshkosh, Wis., Mar. 28, 1942; s. Joseph John and Margaret Louise (Nuernberg) H.; m. Francine M. Chamallas, June 4, 1967; children— James, Christopher, Sarah. A.B. summa cum laude, Marquette U., 1964; LL.B., Harvard U., 1967. Bar: Ill. 1967. Assoc. Bell, Boyd & Lloyd, Chgo., 1967-74, ptnr., 1975—, mng. ptnr., 1990-93; adj. prof. law Marquette U., 1985-86, Chgo. Kent Coll. Law, 1991-93; lectr. Ill. Inst. Continuing Legal Edn.; bd. dirs. Sanford Corp., Constrn. Projects Mgmt. Inc., Holco Corp. Mem. Kenilworth (Ill.) Sch. Dist. 38 Bd. Edn., v.p. 1985-87, pres. 1987-89, Kenilworth Citizens Adv. Caucus; bd. dirs. Joseph Sears Sch. Devel. Fund. Wickersham fellow; Fulbright scholar. Mem. ABA, Ill. Bar Assn. (editor banking and comml. law newsletter), Alpha Sigma Nu, Phi Theta Psi, Phi Sigma Tau, Sigma Tau Delta. Clubs: University, Law, Legal (Chgo.); Kenilworth. Contbr. articles to legal jours.

HEMMER, PAUL EDWARD, musician, communications executive, composer; b. Dubuque, Iowa, Oct. 12, 1944; s. Andrew Charles and Elizabeth Marie (Goerdt) H.; m. Janet T. Demmer, Feb. 7, 1970; children: Michelle, Steven. BS in Music Edn., U. Wis., Platteville, 1966. Program dir. Sta. WDBQ-AM, Dubuque, Iowa, 1967-93; leader Paul Hemmer Orch., Dubuque, 1967-96; pres. Hemmer Broadcasting, Dubuque, Iowa, 1994—2000; v.p. Radio DBQ, Inc., Dubuque, 2000—. Composer: (musical comedies) Get the Lead Out, 1976, Joe Sent Me!, 1978, Key City Komedy Company, 1981, Steamboat Comin', 1991, Here's to Dubuque, 1998, Sketches from a Drawing Room, 1996; appeared in film Field of Dreams, 1989. Named Citizen of Yr., Dubuque Telegraph-Herald, 1976, Disting. alumni, U. Wis, Platteville, 1999. Mem. Internat. Radio Broadcasters Idea Bank, Rotary. Roman Catholic. Home: 2375 Simpson St Dubuque IA 52003-7720 Office: Radio DBQ 8th Bluff Dubuque IA 52001 Office Phone: 563-690-0830. Personal E-mail: dbqpaul@mchsi.com.

HEMMERDINGER, H. DALE, real estate executive; b. Washington, Oct. 31, 1944; s. Monroe Elliott Hemmerdinger and Carol Phyllis (Weil) Haussamen; m. Elizabeth Gould, June 25, 1969; children: Damon John, Katherine Molly. BA, NYU, 1967, postgrad., 1967-68. Cert. real estate broker, N.Y. Pres., chief exec. officer The Hemmerdinger Corp., N.Y.C., 1968—, Atco Properties & Mgmt., Inc., N.Y.C., 1968—. Bd. dirs. Realty Found. of N.Y., N.Y.C.; trustee mem. ex-com. fin. com. NYU, 1994—; chmn. citizens budget commn., N.Y.C., 1995—; spkr., author articles on real estate and economy Bank Credit Analyst and Grant's Interest Rate Observer publs. Commr. conciliation and appeals bd. City of N.Y., 1978-84; mem. Dem. County Com., N.Y.C., 1978—, N.Y. State Senate Adv. Com., 1980-93, N.Y. State Fin. Control Bd., 1990—; mem. N.Y. State Senate Adv. Coun. on State Productivity, 1990-94; gov. Citizens Housing and Planning Coun., N.Y.C., 1982—; mem. exec. com. Assn. for Better N.Y., N.Y.C., 1984—; trustee, mem. exec. com. Nightingale Bamford Sch., N.Y.C., 1985-93; trustee, vice chmn., mem. exec. com. Police Found., 1986—; trustee NYU, 1993—. Mem. Real Estate Bd. N.Y., Manhattan C. of C., Queens C. of C., Harmonie Club (pres. 1985-86), Sky Club, Univ. Club, Commanderie de Bordeaux, N.Y. Yacht Club, Century Club, Princeton Club. Avocations: sailing, sculling. Office: Atco Properties & Mgmt Inc 555 5th Ave Fl 16L New York NY 10017-2416

HEMMERDINGER, WILLIAM JOHN, artist; b. Burbank, Calif., July 7, 1951; s. William John Jr. and Eileen Patricia (Fitzmaurice) H.; m. Catherine Lee Cooper, Aug. 8, 1981. Student, Art Ctr. Coll. Design, 1967-69, Nat. Palace Mus., Taiwan, 1973; AA, Coll. of Desert, 1971; BA, U. Calif., Riverside, 1973; MFA, Claremont Grad. Sch., 1975, PhD, 1979; postgrad., Harvard U., 1977. Curator Calif. Mus. Photography, 1973-74; instr. Coll. of Desert, 1974-79, 80-84, Calif. State U., Long Beach, 1979-80, Otis Art Inst. Parsons Sch. Design, 1979-80, U. Calif., Riverside, 1981-82; co-owner Hemmerdinger Fine Art and Appraisal, Palm Desert, Calif. Vis. artist, lectr. sculpture and environ. design Calif. State Summer Sch. for Arts, Calif. Inst. for Arts, Valencia, 1989; vis. prof. of art Pomona Coll., Claremont, Calif., 1990-92. One-man shows include Cirrus Editions, Ltd., 1982, 84, Brand Libr. and Art Ctr., Glendale, Calif., 1991, Old Selectmen's Bldg. Gallery, West Barnstable, Mass., 1995, 96, 97, 98; group shows include NAD, N.Y.C., L.A. County Mus. Art, Boyusan Citizens Hall, Internat. Contemporary Art Fair, Olympic Arts Festival, L.A., 1984, Seoul Korea, 1988; works in permanent collections Mus. Contemporary Art, L.A., Tate Gallery, London, Smithsonian Instn., Washington, Mobil Oil Co., N.Y.C., Fed. Reserve Bank, San Francisco, Cape Internet, Osterville, Mass.; contbr. articles to profl. jours. REcipient Calif. Nat. Watercolor Soc. award, 1974, 79, Lifetime Achievement award La Quinta Arts Found., 1991; Ford Found. grnatee, 1979; NEA grantee, 1979, NEH grantee, 1980. Mem. Nat. Watercolor Soc. (v.p. 1981-82, 83). Home: 44489 Town Ctr Way Ste D Palm Desert CA 92260-2789

HEMMING, NANCY LOUISE, elementary school educator; d. Robert Miles and Mary Cecile Grass; m. Richard Wale Hemming, Aug. 7, 1976; children: Ryan Richard, Matthew Louis. BS, U. SD, 1972; MEd, U. Utah, 1976. Teaching credential Calif., 1989. Elem. tchr. Jordan Sch. Dist., Salt Lake City, 1972—77; elem. educator Ogden Sch. Dist., Ogden, Utah, 1977—79, Napa Valley Unified Sch. Dist., Napa, Calif., 1989—. Bd. mem. Napa Valley Reading Assn., Napa, Calif., 1995—99; mentor tchr. Napa Valley Unified Sch. Dist., Napa, Calif., 1996—2000. Mem. Jr. League, Ogden, Utah, 1978—80, Chi Omega Sorority, Vermillion, SD, 1968—71; sec. of women's orgn. Relief Soc., Napa, Calif. Grantee Money to provide a sch. garden, Napa Valley Edn. Found., 1998, Money for a sound and lighting sys. for the multi-use Rm. at Mt. George. Mem.: NEA, Napa Valley Edn. Assn., Napa Valley Reading Assn. Office: Mt George Sch 1019 Second Ave Napa CA 94558 Office Phone: 707-253-3766.

HEMMING, VAL G., retired dean, educator; b. Rexburg, Idaho, July 9, 1937; m. Alice Bell Hemming; children: Heidi, Julie, Jill, Patrick. BA in Entomology, U. Utah, 1962; MD, U. Utah Coll. Medicine, 1966. Diplomate Am. Bd. Pediatrics, Nat. Bd. Med. Examiners. Commd. 2d lt. USAF, 1965, advanced through grades to col.; pediatric intern U. Utah Affiliated Hosps., 1966—67; resident physician in pediatrics Wilford Hall USAF Med. Ctr., Lackland AFB, Tex., 1968—70; staff pediatrician USAF Hosp., Wiesbaden, Germany, 1970—74; chmn., dir. pediatric residency tng. David Grant USAF Med. ctr., Travis AFB, Calif., 1976—80; assoc. prof. dept. pediatrics Uniformed Svcs. U. Health Scis., Bethesda, Md., 1980—84, prof. dept. pediatrics, 1984—87, prof., chmn. dept. pediatrics, 1987—95, from interim dean to dean F. Edward Hebert Sch. Medicine, 1995—2002, prof. emeritus in pediats., 2002—; splty. cons. in pediatrics to Air Force Surgeon Gen., 1983—90; ret., 1990. Cons. in pediatrics to the asst. sec. for health affairs Dept. of Def., 1988-91; adv. coun. Nat. Inst. of Child Health and Human Devel. Contbr. numerous articles to profl. jours. Mem. Am. Acad. Pediatrics, Am. Pediatric Soc., Infectious Disease Soc. of Am., Western Soc. for Pediatric Rsch., Pediatric Infectious Disease Soc., Lancefield Soc., Internat. AIDS Soc., Am. Soc. for Microbiology. Office: Uniformed Svcs U Health Scis 4301 Jones Bridge Rd Bethesda MD 20814-4712 Office Phone: 301-275-3742. Business E-Mail: vhemming@usuhs.mil.

HEMMING, WALTER WILLIAM, financial planner, consultant; b. Vineland, NJ, Oct. 2, 1939; s. Percy A. and Marguerite E. (Smith) H.; m. Shirley L. Derocher, June 10, 1961; children: Cynthia, Catherine, Walter Jr. BS, Syracuse U., 1961. CPA, NY, NH. Prin. Arthur Young & Co., Stamford, Conn., 1961-72; contr. Coca-Cola Bottling Co. NY, Hackensack, NJ, 1972-78; exec. v.p., chief oper. officer KW Inc., Manchester, NH, 1978-81; exec. v.p. fin. and adminstrn., chief fin. officer Coca-Cola Bottling Co. NY, Greenwich, Conn., 1981-86, Coca-Cola Bottling Plants of Maine, South Portland, 1987-88; gen. ptnr. Pleasant Ave. Assoc., 1988—2001, H&H Assoc., 1989-99; v.p. bus devel. Coca-Cola Bottling Co. No. New Eng., Bedford, NH, 1989; prin. Hemming Assoc., 1989—; treas. Island Approaches, Sunset, Maine, 1991—; also bd. dir., Island Approaches, Sunset, Maine. Mem. fin. rev. com. Coca-Cola Bottlers Assn., Atlanta, 1985-89; treas. NH Soft Drink Assn., Manchester, 1979-81; bd. dirs. Centerpoint Bank, 1990-96, mem. exec. com., chmn. audit com., chmn. exec. com., 1995-96; bd. dir. Cmty. Bankshares, Inc., mem. audit com., 1996-97; bd. dir. Centrix Bank & Trust, mem. exec. com., audit com., loan com., chmn. audit com., 1999-2000, chmn. exec. com., 2001-2003, 2005- Treas. Clinton (Conn.) United Meth. Ch., 1969-72, Jesse Lee Meth. Ch., Ridgefield, Conn., 1974-77; treas. Hollis (NH) Congl. Ch., 1981, 92-95, asst. treas., 1982-92, deacon, 1988-92, 04-, trustee, 1997-02. Mem. AICPA, NH Soc. CPAs, NY Soc. CPAs. Republican. Avocations: fishing, gardening, woodworking. Home: PO Box 610 Brookline NH 03033-0610 Office: Hemming Assocs 74 Northeastern Blvd Unit 11 Nashua NH 03062-3192

HEMMINGER, PAMELA LYNN, lawyer; b. Chgo., June 29, 1949; d. Paul Willis and Lenore Adelaide (Hennig) H.; m. Robert Alan Miller, May 14, 1979; children: Kimberly Anne, Jeffrey Ryan, Eric Douglas. BA, Pomona Coll., 1971; JD, Pepperdine U., 1976. Tchr. Etiwanda (Calif.) Sch. dist., 1971-74; law clerk Gibson Dunn & Crutcher, Newport Beach, Calif., 1974-76, assoc. L.A., 1976-84, ptnr., 1985—. Contbg. author Sexual Harassment, 1992, Employment Discrimination Law, 3d edit. and supplements, 1996, Employment Litigation, Calif. Practice Guide; contbr. articles to profl. jours. Mem. Comparable Worth Task Force Calif., Sacramento, 1984, Pepperdine U. Sch. of Law Bd. Visitors, 1990—, Calif. Law Revision Commn., 1998-99, 2005-; mem., bd. dirs. Dispute Resolution Svcs., 1998—. Named alumnus of yr. Pepperdine Sch. Law, 1996; listed in Best Lawyers in Am., 1998--. Mem. L.A. County Bar Assn. (chair, labor and employment sect. 1996-97), Calif. C. of C. (employment rels. com. 1984—). Republican. Lutheran. Office: Gibson Dunn & Crutcher Ste 4921 333 S Grand Ave Los Angeles CA 90071-3197

HEMMINGHAUS, ROGER ROY, energy company executive, chemical engineer; b. St. Louis, Aug. 27, 1936; s. Roy George and Henrietta E.M. (Knacht) H.; children: Sheryl Ann, Susan Lynn, Sally Ann; m. Dorotyh O'Kelly, Aug. 18, 1979; children: R. Patrick, Kelley Elizabeth, Roger Christian. Student, Purdue U., 1954-56; BS in Chem. Engring., Auburn U., 1958; grad. cert., Bettis Reactor Engring., Pitts., 1959; postgrad., La. State U., 1963-66. Various tech. and mgmt. positions Exxon Co. U.S.A., Baton Rouge, 1962-66, Benicia, Calif., 1967-70, Houston, 1970-76; refinery gen. mgr. C.F. Industries, East Chicago, Ind., 1976-77; pres. Petro United Inc., Houston, 1977-80; v.p. planning United Gas Pipe Line, Houston, 1980-82, United Energy Resources, Houston, 1982-84; v.p. corp. planning and devel. Diamond Shamrock Corp. (name changed to Maxus Energy Corp., 1987), Dallas, 1984-85, past exec. v.p.; pres. Diamond Shamrock Refining & Mktg., San Antonio, 1985-99; chmn., dir., former CEO UltraMar Diamond Shamrock, Inc., San Antonio, until 1999; chmn., fed. res. agt. Fed. Res. Bank of Dallas, 1999-2000; dir. Luby's Inc., San Antonio, 2001—04. Dir. InterFirst Bank, San Antonio Adviser Jr. Achievement, Baton Rouge, 1956-66; pres. congregation Lutheran Ch., Baton Rouge, 1965, Moraga, Calif., 1969; chmn. indsl. div. United Crusade, Solano County, Calif., 1970; assoc. gen. chmn. United Way, Tex. Gulf Coast, 1983-84. Served to lt. USN, 1958-62. Mem. Am. Chem. Soc., Am. Inst. Chem. Engrs., Naval Architects and Marine Engrs., Am. Petroleum Inst., San Antonio C. of C. (dir.), Tau Beta Pi, Phi Lambda Upsilon, Phi Kappa Phi, Kappa Alpha Clubs: Fair Oaks Country; Plaza, Petroleum (San Antonio). Office: 2211 NE Loop 410 San Antonio TX 78217-4673*

HEMMINGS, MADELEINE BLANCHET, management consultant, not-for-profit administrator, media consultant; b. Bryn Mawr, Pa., Aug. 14, 1942; d. Wilfred Loyola and Feroline (Sissenere) Blanchet; m. Richard B. Hemmings, Mar. 14, 1970; 1 child, Laurie Cornwall Hemmings Stull. Cert. in lang. and linguistics, U. Fribourg, Switzerland, 1961; BS in Indsl. and Labor Rels., Cornell U., 1976. Owner Hallmark Pers. of Pa., Harrisburg, Pa., 1964-70; assoc. dir. human resources Cornell U., Ithaca, NY, 1972-77; policy dir. employee benefits NAM, Washington, 1977-79; policy dir. edn., employment and tng. C. of C. U.S., Washington, 1979-83; v.p. policy Nat. Alliance Bus., Washington, 1983-85; pres. W.Va. Roundtable, Charleston, 1985—96; exec. dir. Nat. Assn. State Dirs. Vocat. Tech. Edn., Washington, 1987-96; mng. dir. Nat. Telelearning Network, Inc., Washington, 1996-98; pres. Hemmings Assocs., Inc., 1998—2002; grants coord. Wayne-Finger Lakes Bd. of Coop. Edn. Svcs., Newark, NY, 2002—. Select adv. com. to asst. sec. edn., 1989—93; pres. adv. com. Fed. Office Vocat. Edn. Performance Stds., 1992—95; ant. adv. bd. Ctr. Edn. and Work, U. Wis., 1992—96, Nat. Ctr. Rsch. Vocat. Edn., Berkeley, Calif., 1993—96. Author: (book) The New Job Training Partnership Act, 1982, Economic Development Plan, State of West Virginia, 1987, Education for a Working America, 1994, (newsletter) The Techocrat, 1988—95. Exec. dir. Nat. Vocat. Tech. Edn. Found., 1987—96; campaign mgr. Connie Cook for Congress, Ithaca, 1984; sponsor U.S. Pony Club, Olney, Md., 1987—96. Mem.: Greater Washington Soc. Assn. Execs. (chief exec. coun. 1989—98), U.S. C. of C. (edn. com. 1987—96), Cornell Pres.' Club. Avocations: thoroughbred breeding and racing, combined training, painting. Home: 111 Lea Dr Newark NY 14513 Office: Wayne-FInger Lakes BOCES 131 Drumlin Ct Newark NY 14513 Fax: 301-570-9104. Office Phone: 315-332-7379. E-mail: mhemming@rochester.rr.com, mhemmings@wflbecks.org.

HEMMINGSEN, BARBARA BRUFF, retired microbiologist; b. Whittier, Calif., Mar. 25, 1941; d. Stephen Cartland and Susanna Jane Bruff; m. Edvard Alfred Hemmingsen, Aug. 5, 1967; 1 child, Grete. BA, U. Calif., Berkeley, 1962, MA, 1964; PhD, U. Calif., San Diego, 1971. Lectr. San Diego State U., 1973-77, asst. prof., 1977-81, assoc. prof., 1981-88, prof., 1988—2004; ret., 2004. Vis. asst. prof. Aarhus U., Denmark, 1971—72; cons. AMBIS, Inc., San Diego, 1984—85, Woodward-Clyde Cons., 1985, 1987—91, Novatron, Inc., 2000—04. Author (with others): (book) Microbial Ecology, 1972; contbr. articles to profl. jours. Mem. Planned Parenthood, San Diego. Mem.: AAAS, San Diego Assn. Rational Inquiry (sec. 1998—2001, treas. 2002—), Am. Women Sci., Am. Soc. Microbiology, Phi Beta Kappa (corr. sec. Nu chpt. Calif. 1994—2002, past pres., historian 2003—), Sigma Xi. Democrat.

HEMON, ALEKSANDER, writer; b. Sarajevo, Bosnia, 1964; arrived in U.S., 1992; BA, U. Sarajevo, 1990; MA, Northwestern U., 1995. Former journalist. Part-time tchr. Northwestern U. Author: (novels) The Question of Bruno, 2000 (named Best Book LA Times, NY Times Notable), Nowhere Man, 2002, numerous short stories in various publications including Esquire and The New Yorker. Named MacArthur Fellow, John D. and Catherine T. MacArthur Found., 2004.*

HEMPE, A. HENRY, labor relations specialist, lawyer; b. Milw., Mar. 16, 1938; s. Arnold Herman and Marcia Fleer Hempe; m. Cornelia Macy Gordon, June 26, 1965; children: Andrew, Amy. BS, U. Wis., 1962, JD, 1965. Bar: Wis. 1965, U.S. Dist. Ct. (we. dist.) Wis. 1966. Asst. dist. atty. Rock County, Janesville, Wis., 1965-67, county corp. counsel, 1967-72; ptnr. Hempe & Daniel, Janesville, 1972-76; shareholder, pres. Hempe, Hunsader & Schulz, S.C., Janesville, 1975-86; dep. sec. Wis. Dept. Employment Rels., Madison, 1987-88; commr. Wis. Employment Rels. Commn., Madison, 1987—2003, chair, commr., 1989-97; pres. Midwest Employment Rels. Cons., LLC, Madison, 2003—. Author: Labor-Management Relations in the Public Sector, 2000, Labor-Management Cooperation: A New Way to Do Business. Mem., pres., v.p. Beloit (Wis.) Sch. Bd., 1980-86. bd. dirs. Sinnissipi Coun. Boy Scouts Am., Janesville, 1985-90, Rock County Humane Soc., Janesville, 1978-83, Assn. Labor Rels Agys. USA and Can., Washington, 1991-94; chair Human Rels. Commn., Beloit, 1972-76, Bd. Rev., Beloit. With USMCR, 1960—66, also res. Mem.: Wis. Bar Assn. Avocations: fishing, hunting, softball, jogging, dog training. Home: 5413 Trempealeau Trail Madison WI 53705 Office: MER Consultants PO Box 5344 Madison WI 53705-0344

HEMPEL, JOHN P., mathematics professor; b. Salt Lake City, Oct. 14, 1935; s. Edgar W. and Emma B. (Johnson) H.; m. Edith Froese-Gertzen, Sept. 1, 1965; 1 child, Kristian J. BS, U. Utah, 1957; MS, U. Wis., 1959, PhD, 1962. Asst. prof. Fla. State U., 1962-63, Rice U., Houston, 1964-69, assoc. prof., 1969-76, prof., 1976—. With Inst. Advanced Study, 1971-72; vis. assoc. prof. U. Utah, 1976; vis. prof. U. Mich. 1980-81, U. B.C., 1987-88. Postdoctoral fellow Inst. Advance Study, 1963-64. Mem. Math. Sci. Rsch. Inst. Office: Rice University Dept Math PO Box 1982 6100 South Main Houston TX 77251 Office Phone: 713-348-5126. E-mail: hempel@math.rice.edu.

HEMPFLING, CHRISTOPHER GEORGE, director; b. Miamisburg, Ohio, Apr. 22, 1981; s. Richard and Melissa Hempfling. BA, Ohio State U., 2004. Asst. dir. Addams Ctr. Civic Engagement Rockford (Ill.) Coll., 2004—. Mem. Project Welcome Home adv. bd. Youth Build, Rockford, 2004—; vol. fire fighter Loves Park (Ill.) Fired Dept., 2004—; asst. scoutmaster Boy Scouts Am. Democrat. Avocations: softball, hiking, skiing. Office: Rockford Coll 5050 E State St Rockford IL 61108

HEMPFLING, LINDA LEE, nurse; b. Indpls., July 28, 1947; d. Paul Roy and Myrtle Pearl (Ward) H. Diploma, Meth. Hosp. Ind. Sch. Nursing, 1968; postgrad., St. Joseph's Coll. Cert. med. audit specialist, 2000. Charge nurse Meth. Hosp., Indpls., 1968; staff nurse operating rm. Silver Cross Hosp., Joliet, Ill., 1969; charge nurse oper. rm. Huntington (NY) Hosp., 1969-73; night supr. oper. rm., post anesthesia care unit Hermann Hosp., Houston, 1973-76, unit mgr., purchasing coord. oper. rms., 1976-83; RN med. auditor, quality improvement and tng. coord. Nat. Healthcare Rev., Inc., Houston, 1984—98; RN med. auditor Integra Solutions, 1999—. Future Nurses Am. scholar, 1965, Nat. Merit scholar, 1965. Mem.: Am. Assn. Med. Auditor Specialists, Tex. Med. Auditors Assn., Assn. PeriOperative Registered Nurses. Office: 9401 SW Freeway # 631B Houston TX 77074

HEMPHILL, JAMES S., investment management executive, financial advisor; b. Richmond, Va., Sept. 13, 1956; s. John Mickle and Marie Jeanne (de Kiewiet) H.; m. Amy Guise, Oct. 16, 1993; children: John Reagan, Katharine Guise, Alexander Dallett. BA with high honors, Swarthmore Coll., 1978. CFP, CLU, ChFC, CIMA. Legal asst. Schnader, Harrison, Phila., 1978; stockbroker, 2d v.p. Shearson/Am. Express, Media, Pa., 1978-84; asst. v.p. Merrill Lynch, Media, 1984-90; pres. TGS Fin. Advisors, Media, 1990—. Bd. dirs. Suburban Music Sch., Media, 1993-2000, chmn. capital campaign, 1995-96, v.p., 1996-97, pres., 1997-99; founder Third Thursday Wine Club, Media, 1993—; commr. Media Sports League, 1985-86; mem. vestry Holy Trinity Episc. Ch., 2001—. Mem. Fin. Planning Assn., Investment Mgmt. Cons. Assn. Republican. Avocations: travel, wine appreciation. Office: TGS Financial Advisors 103 Chesley Dr Media PA 19063-1757 Office Phone: 610-892-9900. Business E-Mail: jim.hemphill@tgsfinancial.com.

HEMPHILL, JOHN LINDSAY, III, administrative assistant; b. Phila., Nov. 13, 1971; s. John L. and Elsie Hemphill. Student, C.C. Phila., 2004. Cook Phila. Naval Yard, 1994; with Health Dept., Phila., 1995, Phila. Libr., 1996; with revenue and acctg. dept. City of Phila., 2004—. Author: Genesis, Human History in the Eyes of God, 2003, Abraham, Man With Uncommon Faith, 2004, (songs) Private Show for Two, 2003. Missionary Immigration Mission, Sharon Bapt. Ch., Phila. & Arab World Ministries, London, 2003—04. 1st airman USAF, 1990—93, Gulf War. Avocations: calligraphy, art, rollerblading, walking, exercise. Office: City of Phila 1401 John F Kennedy Blvd Philadelphia PA 19102-1663 Personal E-mail: hemphilljl@yahoo.com.

HEMPHILL, LINDA CASHIN, medical educator; b. Lowell, Mass., Oct. 13, 1948; d. Kenneth D. Cashin; m. Thomas Scott Hemphill, July 21, 1984. BS, Beirut Coll. for Women, 1970; MD, Boston U., 1975. Diplomate Am. Bd. Internal Medicine, Am. Bd. Cardiology. Asst. prof. clin. medicine U. So. Calif., L.A., 1980-94; lectr. Harvard/MIT, Cambridge, Mass., 1994—. Contbr. articles to profl. jours. Fellow Am. Heart Assn. (arteriosclerosis coun.), Am. Coll. Cardiology. Office: Mass. Gen. Hosp. Yawkey Ctr Ste 5800 55 Fruit Boston MA 02114

HEMPHILL, PAUL JAMES, writer; b. Birmingham, Ala., Feb. 18, 1936; s. Paul James Hemphill and Velma Rebecca Nelson; m. Susan Olive, Sept. 1961 (div. Oct. 1975); children: Lisa, David, Molly; m. Susan Farran Percy, Nov. 6, 1976; 1 child, Martha. BA, Auburn U., 1959. Sports writer News, Birmingham, Ala., 1959-61; sports info. dir. Fla. State U., Tallahassee, 1962;

sports editor Chronicle, Augusta, Ga., 1963, Times, Tampa, Fla., 1964; gen. columnist Atlanta Journal, 1965-69; editor Atlanta Magazine, 1981; writer-in-residence Brenau Coll., Gainesville, Ga., 1986-92; faculty Emory U., Atlanta, 2000—. Author: The Nashville Sound, 1970, Mayor: Notes on the Sixties, 1972, (with Ivan Allen Jr.), The Good Old Boys, 1974, Long Gone, 1979, Too Old to Cry, 1981, T he Sixkiller Chronicles, 1985, Me and the Boy, 1986, King of the Road, 1989, Leaving Birmingham, 1993, The Heart of the Game, 1996, Wheels, 1997, The Ballad of Little River, 2000, Nobody's Hero, 2002, Lovesick Blues: The Life of Hank Williams, 2005. With USAF, 1959-62. Nieman fellow Harvard U., 1969. Avocations: camping, hiking, fishing.*

HEMPHILL, SHARON JEVERT, lawyer; b. Chgo., Nov. 22, 1946; d. Axel William and Helen Jevert; children: Sean James, Stephen Glenn. BS, U. Ill., 1968; JD, U. Houston, 1988, LLM in Taxation, M in Tax Law, 1992. Bar: Tex. 1988, D.C. 1989, U.S. Dist. Ct. (so. dist.) Tex. 1989. Model Berry Burke, Richmond, Va., 1975-78; tchr. Burlington (Iowa) High Sch., 1970-72; briefing atty. Supreme Ct. of Tex., Austin, 1990-91; com. mem. on penal code Tex. Legis., Austin, 1992; lawyer sole practice Houston, 1991—; exec. dir. A.A. White Dispute Resolution Inst., Houston, 1991-92; mediator, arbitrator A.D.R. Svcs. Internat., Inc., Houston, 1993—. Arbitrator Nat. Assn. Securities Dealers, Chgo. Bd. Options Exch., pvt. arbitrator and mediator, Houston, 1988—. Exec. editor South Tex. Law Jour., 1985-86. Recipient Am. Jurisprudence award Bankcroft & Whitney, 1986. Mem. ABA, Houston Bar Assn. Baptist. Home: 16419 Graven Hill Dr Spring TX 77379-7146 Office: The Lyric Ctr Ste 2120 440 Louisiana Houston TX 77002 also: ADR Svcs Internat Inc 6420 Richmond Ave Ste 675 Houston TX 77057-5925

HEMPLEMAN, BARBARA FLORENCE, archivist; b. Bellevue, Pa., Mar. 3, 1925; d. Warren Wilson and Florence Permelia (Firth) Hampe; m. David William Hempleman, Aug. 4, 1956; children: Warwick, Terence. BA, Coll. of Wooster, 1947; MA, NYU, 1953; MLS, Atlanta U., 1973. Dir. Christian edn. Calvary Reformed Ch., Reading, Pa., 1951-52; libr. asst. Duke U., Durham, N.C., 1957-59; asst. prof. history Warren Wilson Coll., Asheville, N.C., 1948-51, 54-56, 66-69, libr. dir., 1978-86, archivist, 1986-98, adj. prof. women's history, 1983-96; vis. prof. libr. sci. Emory U., Atlanta, 1973-74; adj. prof. libr. sci. Atlanta U., 1973, 78, reference libr., 1974-78. Contbr. numerous articles to Owl and Spade mag. Bd. dirs. YWCA, Asheville, 1978-79; libr. developer, adminstr. Black Mountain (N.C.) Correctional Ctr. for Women, 1997—. Nat. Assn. Fgn. Student Affairs grantee, 1975. Mem. Women's History Club Asheville (historian 1996—). Democrat. Presbyterian. Avocations: travel, reading. Personal E-mail: firthhampe@aol.com.

HEMPSTONE, SMITH, JR., diplomat, journalist; b. Washington, Feb. 1, 1929; s. Smith and Elizabeth (Noyes) H.; m. Kathaleen Fishback, Jan. 30, 1954; 1 dau. Student, George Washington U., 1946-47; BA with honors, U. of South, 1950, LittD (hon.), 1969; Nieman fellow, Harvard U., 1964-65. Rewrite man AP, Charlotte, N.C., 1952; with Nat. Geog. mag., Washington, 1954; reporter Louisville Times, 1953, Evening Star, Washington, 1955-56; fgn. corr. Africa, Asia, Europe and Latin Am. for Chgo. Daily News, 1960-66, Washington Evening Star, 1966-69, assoc. editor, 1970-75; exec. editor Washington Times, 1982-84, editor-in-chief, 1984-85; nationally syndicated newspaper columnist, 1970-89; ambassador to Kenya, 1989-93; diplomat in residence U. of the South, Sewanee, Tenn., 1993, Va. Mil. Inst., Lexington, 1994. Fellow Inst. Current World Affairs, 1956-60 Author: Africa, Angry Young Giant, 1961, Rebels, Mercenaries and Dividends-The Katanga Story, 1962, Rogue Ambassador, 1997; (novel) A Tract of Time, 1966, In the Midst of Lions, 1968; mem. editl. bd. Nieman Reports, 1965-73. Alumni trustee U. South, 1974-78; bd. govs. Inst. Current World Affairs, 1974-78. Recipient Fgn. Corr. award Sigma Delta Chi and Overseas Press Club. Mem. Chevy Chase Club (Md.), Met. Club (Washington). Episcopalian. Home and Office: 7611 Fairfax Rd Bethesda MD 20814-1313 Office Phone: 301-657-2918.

HEMRY, JEROME ELDON, lawyer; b. Kirksville, Mo., July 22, 1905; s. U.S.G. and Rose M. (Plumb) H.; m. Martha L. Langston, Aug. 1, 1934; children: Jerome Louis, Kenneth Marshall. AB, Oklahoma City U., 1926; JD, U. Okla., 1928; LL.M., Harvard U., 1929. Bar: Okla. 1928. Partner Hemry & Hemry, Oklahoma City, 1931-82, of counsel, 1983—; prof. law Central Okla. Sch. Law, 1931-41; dean, prof. law Langston U., 1948-49; dir., counsel Am. Gen. Life Ins. Co. Okla., 1959-79. Pres., gen. counsel Gen. Constrn. Corp., 1941-45; legislative counsel Okla. Chain Store Assn., 1941-44; Mem. Bd. Conf. Claimant's Okla. Ann. Conf.; treas. Oklahoma City S. Dist. Contbr. articles legal jours. Bd. dirs. Family and Children's Service, 1939-56. Mem. Okla. Assn. Mcpl. Attys. (pres. 1956-57), Am., Okla. bar assns., Order of Coif, Phi Delta Phi, Lambda Chi Alpha. Methodist (pres., counsel trustees). Clubs: Lions (Oklahoma City), Men's Dinner (Oklahoma City). Home: 2255 NW 55th St Oklahoma City OK 73112-7716 Office: 531 Couch Dr Oklahoma City OK 73102-2251

HEMRY, LARRY HAROLD, former federal agency official, writer, inventor; b. Seattle, Jan. 4, 1941; s. Harold Bernard and Florence Usborne (Achilles) H.; m. Nancy Kay Ballantyne, July 10, 1964 (div. Apr. 1976); children: Rachel Dalayne, Aaron Harold, Andrew LeRoy. BA, Seattle Pacific Coll., 1963; postgrad., Western Evang. Sem., Portland, Oreg., 1969, 70. Ordained to ministry Free Meth. Ch., 1968. Clergyman Free Meth. Ch., Vancouver, B.C., Can., 1963-64, Mt. Vernon, Wash., 1968-69, Colton (Oreg.) Community Ch., 1969-71; edit clk. Moody Bible Inst., Chgo., 1964-66; pres., founder Bethel Enterprises, Colton, 1969-71; immigration insp. U.S. Immigration and Naturalization Svc., Sumas, Wash., 1972-96. Author, historian: Some Northwest Pioneer Families, 1969, The Hemry Family History Book, 1985; author: An Earnest Plea to Earnest Christians, 1969; contbr. articles to profl. publs.; patentee mech. nut cracker. Chmn. com. to establish and endow the James A. Hemry meml. scholarship fund Seattle Pacific U., 1975. Fellow Seattle Pacific U. (Centurians Club); mem. The Nature Conservancy, The Sierra Club, The Audubon Soc. Avocations: camping, nature study, woodcarving. Home: PO Box 532 Sumas WA 98295-0532

HEMSLEY, STEPHEN J., healthcare company executive; Mng. ptnr. strategy and planning Arthur Andersen and Co.; sr. exec. v.p. UnitedHealth Group, 1997-99; pres., CEO United Am. Health Group, Detroit, 1999—. Office: United Healthgroup Ct 9900 Bren Rd E Minnetonka Mills MN 55343

HENCE, JANE KNIGHT, designer; b. Pitts., June 27, 1937; d. Luther and Doris (Ayers) Knight; m. Carleton Campbell Hence, May 12, 1962 (div. 1975); children: Kyle Fitz-Randolph Hence, Maxson Bentley Hence, Juliellen Hence Casey. Grad., Emma Willard Sch., Troy, N.Y., 1955; student, Skidmore Coll., Saratoga Springs, N.Y., 1955—58; Grad., Traphagen Sch. of Design, N.Y.C., 1960; student, Yale U., 1986—90, R.I. Sch. of Design, 1988—90. Owner various bus. ventures including Bed and Breakfast, catering bus., free-lance interior design, 1982—; owner, prin. JKH Design, 1989—; consulting assoc. and designer Michael McKinley & Assocs., Stonington, Conn., 1993—2001. Mem. Westerly Sch. Facilities Com., Westerly, R.I., 1993-96, Westerly Sch. Bldg. Com., 1992-93; mem. Bd. S.E. Mus., Brewster, N.Y., 1970-74; photographer, interviewer Green Light, Newport Designer over 50 bldgs., renovations and additions in New Eng.; co-designer overn 40 bldgs. in R.I. and Conn.; interior designer, 1998—; painter various media in collections in Midwest, South, N.Y. and New Eng.; photographer, interviewer Green Light Quar. bulletin, Newport. Alt. Westerly Zoning Bd., RI, 2000—02. Avocations: travel, reading, opera, theater. Home and Office: 73 Washington St Newport RI 02840-1533 Office Phone: 401-847-3767. Personal E-mail: rockbound@earthlink.net.

HENCK, ANITA FITZGERALD, academic administrator, educator; b. Norfolk, Va., June 27, 1957; d. Owen Ray and Jean Eyre Fitzgerald; m. William Edward Henck, Jr., July 21, 1978; children: Alayna Henck Effinger, Andrew Fitzgerald. BA, Ind. U., 1978; MA, Am. U., Washington, 1993; PhD, Am. U., 1996. Asst. to the provost Am. U., Washington, 1979—90, exec. asst. to the interim pres. and provost, 1990—91, exec. asst. to the provost, 1991—93, adj. faculty, 1995—98; v.p. for student devel. and retention, prof. Ea. Nazarene Coll., Quincy, Mass., 1998—. Higher edn. cons., Quincy, Mass., 1996—. Fellow Greenberg scholar, Am. U., 1993—96, Doctoral fellow, 1993—96. Home: 109 Grand View Ave Quincy MA 02170 Office: Eastern Nazarene College 23 East Elm Ave Quincy MA 02170 Office Phone: 617-745-3717. Business E-Mail: anita.f.henck@enc.edu.

HENDEE, JOHN CLARE, academic administrator, forester, educator; b. Duluth, Minn., Nov. 12, 1938; s. Clare Worden and Mary Myrtle H.; m. Marilyn R. Riley; children: John Jr., James, Landon, Joy, Joni, Jared. BS in Forestry, Mich. State U., 1960; MF in Forestry Mgmt., Oreg. State U., 1962; PhD in Forestry, Econs. and Sociology, U. Wash., 1967. With USDA Forest Svc., 1961-85; with timber mgmt. dept. Waldport and Corvallis, Oreg., 1961-64; fire rsch. forester Pacific S.W. Forest Experiment Sta., Berkeley, Calif., 1964; recreation rsch. unit leader Pacific N.W. Forest Expt. Sta., Seattle, 1967-76; legis. affairs staff Washington, 1977-78; asst. sta. dir. Southeastern Forest Experiment Sta., Asheville, N.C., 1978-85; dean Coll. Forestry, Wildlife, and Range Sci. U. Idaho, Moscow, 1985-94, prof. forest resources and resource recreation and tourism, 1985, dir. wilderness rsch. ctr., 1994—; dir. Idaho Forest, Wildlife and Range Experiment Sta., 1985-94. Mem. affiliate faculty in forestry U. Wash., Seattle, 1968-76; vice chmn. for sci. 4th World Wilderness Congress, 1987. Co-author: Wildlife Management in Wilderness, 1978, Introduction to Forests and Renewable Resources, 6th edit., 1994, 7th edit., 2002; sr. co-author: Wilderness Management, 1978, 2d edit., 1990, 3d edit., 2002; founding mng. editor Internat. Jour. of Wilderness, 1995-2000, editor-in-chief, 1995—; contbr. numerous articles to profl. jours. Bd. dirs. WILD Found., 1984—; co-leader Wilderness Transitions. Recipient Spl. Merit award Keep Am. Beautiful, 1972, Nat. Conservation Achievement award Am. Motors, 1974, Spl. award for Wilderness Rsch. and Edn. Nat. Outdoor Leadership Sch., 1985, Merit award USDA-Forest Service, 1979, 80, 85, Lifetime Achievement award Am. Soc. Pub. Adminstrn., 1988; Fed. Congl. fellow, Washington, 1976-77. Fellow Leisure Sci. Assn.; mem. Nat. Assn. Profl. Forestry Schs. and Colls. (chmn. western div. 1987-89), Soc. Am. Foresters (edn. and communication working group chmn. 1986-89). Avocations: hiking, camping, gardening.

HENDEE, WILLIAM RICHARD, medical physics educator, academic administrator, radiologist; b. Owosso, Mich., Jan. 1, 1938; s. C.L. and Alvina M. H.; m. Jeannie Wesley, June 16, 1960; children: Mikal, Shonn, Eric, Gareth and Gregory (twins), Lara and Karel (twins). BS, Millsaps Coll., Jackson, Miss., 1959; PhD, U. Tex., 1962; DSc (hon.), Millsaps Coll., Jackson, Miss., 1988. Diplomate Am. Bd. Radiology, Am. Bd. Health Physics. AEC fellow Nat. Reactor Testing Sta., Idaho Falls, Idaho, 1960; asst. prof., then assoc. prof. physics Millsaps Coll., 1962-65, chmn. dept., 1964-65; instr. Miss. State U. (extension), 1963; asst. prof., then assoc. prof. radiology (med. physics) U. Colo. Med. Center, 1965-73, prof., 1974-85, chmn. dept., 1978-85; mem. staff VA Hosp., Denver, 1970-85, Mercy Hosp., 1971-85, Denver Gen. Hosp., 1971-85, Beth Israel Hosp., 1974-85; v.p. sci. and tech. AMA, Chgo., 1985-1991; prof. radiology, biophysics, radiation oncology, bioethics Med. Coll. Wis., Milw., 1991—, clin. prof. radiology and biophysics, 1985-91, sr. assoc. dean, v.p., 1991—2005, dean grad. sch., 1995—, pres. rsch. found., 2005—. Prof. bioengring. Marquette U., 1993—; vis. lectr. Oak Ridge Assoc. Univs., 1964; adj. prof. radiology Northwestern U. Sch. Medicine, 1986-91. Editor Med. Phys., 2005—; contbr. articles to profl. jours. Served with USMC, 1957-62. Recipient Disting. Alumnus award Millsaps Coll., 1967, Disting. Svc. award Nat. Wildlife Fedn., 1990, Wright Langham Meml. award U. Ky., 1991, Gold medal Am. Roentgen Ray Soc., 2005, Med. Coll. Sic. Disting. Svc. award, 2005; Gilbert X-ray fellow, 1960-62, summer fellow NSF, AEC; campus assoc. Danforth Found. Fellow Am. Coll. Radiology, Am. Inst. Med. and Biol. Engring. (pres. 1998-99); mem. AAAS, Health Physics Soc. (chmn. coms., Elda E. Anderson award 1972), Am. Assn. Physicists in Medicine (pres. 1976-77, Robert S. Landauer Meml. award 1977, William D. Coolidge award 1989), Nat. Wildlife Fedn. (Disting. Svc. award 1990), Soc. Biomed. Engring., (sr. mem.), Soc. Nuclear Medicine (pres. 1980-81, Benedict Cassen Meml. award 1984), Am. Acad. Home Care Physicians (Disting. Svc. award 1991), Am. Bd. Radiology (trustee 1995-05, pres. 2002-04), Omicron Delta Kappa, Theta Nu Sigma. Office: Med Coll Wis 8701 W Watertown Plank Rd Milwaukee WI 53226-3548

HENDERSHOT, CAROL MILLER, physical therapist; b. Lancaster, Pa., July 24, 1959; d. Richard Horace and Joan Marie (Nonnenmocher) Miller; m. Richard A. Hendershot, Dec. 29, 1989; 1 child, Scott Michael. BS in Phys. Therapy, Quinnipiac U., 1981. Staff phys. therapist Easter Seal Rehab. Ctr., Lancaster, 1981-85, phys. therapy dept. head, 1986-89; staff phys. therapist Cmty. Hosp. of Lancaster, 1985—86, Guilds' Sch. & Neuromuscular Ctr., 1990—. Dir. publicity and pub. rels. Lancaster Dist. United Meth. Women, 1988—89; chmn. ch. and soc. com. Covenant United Meth. Ch., 1987, 1988, mem. chancel choir, 1981—89, mem. adminstrv. bd., 1975—88; trustee Audubon Pk. United Meth. Ch., 1990—93, mem. chancel choir, 1990—92, mem. staff parish rels. com., 1993—94, mem. Jubilee Bell Choir, 1990—, mem. worship com., 1996—, chair worship com., 2003—, dir. Bethlehem and Joy Bells Handbell Choirs, 1994—96, dir. Jubilee Handbell Choir, 1996—. Mem.: Lancaster County Vis. Nurse Assn. (prof. adv. com. 1987—89), Neuro-Devel. Treatment Assn., Beta Beta Beta. Democrat. Methodist. Avocations: sewing, music, cooking, needlecrafts, gardening, stamping. Home: 6007 W Hopi Ct Spokane WA 99208-9046

HENDERSON, ALBERT KOSSACK, publishing executive, consultant, food products executive; b. Phila., July 9, 1938; s. Harry Brinton, Jr. and Beatrice (Conford) H.; m. Tamara Ann McCormick, Feb. 14, 1968; children: Christopher Findley, Theodore Leon. Mus.B., Ithaca Coll., 1960; postgrad., N.Y. U. Editorial asst. Hearst Headline, 1960-62; asst. sales mgr. Royal McBee, 1960-64; editor Johnson Reprint Corp., 1964-69; gen. mgr., v.p., treas. Brit. Book Centre, Inc., N.Y.C., 1969-77; dir. Pergamon Press, Inc., v.p., treas., 1971-77; exec. v.p., dir. Newman Grove Creamery Co., Nebr., 1977-81; dir. publs. Am. Solar Energy Soc., N.Y.C., 1981-83; pres. Henderson Assoc. Cons., Bridgeport, Conn., 1980—, Chess Combination, Inc., Bridgeport, 1984—; editor Pub. Rsch. Quar., 1994-2000. Exec. sec. Com. for Preservation Academic and Sci. Info. Resources. Co-chairperson adv. panel for sci. publs. Found. for Internat. Sci. Coop., 1990-92. Mem. Am. Soc. Info. Sci. and Tech., Soc. Scholarly Publs., Coun. Sci. Editors. Home: 655 West Ave Milford CT 06460-3003 E-mail: 70244.1532@compuserve.com.

HENDERSON, ALICIA YVETTE TERRY, psychotherapist; b. Milw., Wis., Aug. 16, 1966; d. Robert Earl and Theresa Maye Terry; m. Leon Henderson Jr., Sept. 4, 1993; children: Raina, Ragan. BA, Howard U., 1988; MSW, U. Md., 1992; PhD, NYU, 2001. LCSW NY. Counselor Regional Inst. for Children and Adolescents, Rockville, Md., 1988—92; clin. social worker Boston, 1992—93; psychotherapist August Archborn Ctr., N.Y.C., NY, 1993—98; author, pub. Royal Regal Books, Englewood, NJ, 2002—; lecturer NYU, N.Y.C., NY, 2001—. Author: Call Me Block Call Me Beautiful, 2002. Recipient Golden Key Nat. Honor Soc. Honoree, Miracle Makers, 2003, Outstanding Citizen award, Englewood Charter Sch., 2004. Mem.: The Links, Inc. (co-chair of membership 2002—), Jack and Jill of Am., Alpha Kappa Alpha Sorority. Avocations: writing, bowling, kickboxing, crafts, outdoor activities. Home: 18 Old Quarry Rd Englewood NJ 07631 E-mail: ath@royalregalbooks.com, athenderson@earthlink.net.

HENDERSON, ARNOLD GLENN, architect, educator; b. Shawnee, Okla., Nov. 10, 1934; s. Henry Glenn and Pearlalee H.; m. Beatriz Eugenia Chavez Escandon; children: Eric Neal, Alex Jon. B.Arch., BS in Archtl. Engring, U. Okla., 1961; MS in Architecture, Columbia U., 1964. Asst. prof. architecture U. Ill., Urbana, 1964-68; assoc. prof. U. Okla., 1968-73, prof., 1973—2002, prof. emeritus, 2002—, disting. lectr. Norman, 1984, 88; pvt. practice architecture Norman, Okla., 1975—. Author: Document for an Anonymous Indian, 1974, The Surgeon General's Collection, 1976, (with others) Architecture in Oklahoma, 1978, (with others) The Point Riders Great Plains Poetry Anthology, 1982; co-editor: (with others) Point Riders Press, 1974-; painting exhbns. in Ind., Ill., Okla., La., Wyo., Ark., Kans., Ala., Colo., Tex. and London; author of poetry. Chmn. Norman Housing Authority, 1972-77; mem. Hist. Preservation and Landmark Commn., Guthrie, Okla., 1979-81; chmn. Okla. Hist. Preservation Rev. Com., 2004—. Served with U.S. Army, 1953-55. Grantee NSF, Nat. Endowment Arts, AIA, Okla. Arts Coun., Okla. Humanities Com., Graham Found. for Advanced Studies in the Fine Arts. Fellow AIA (award of excellence 1976); mem. Vernacular Architecture Forum, Nat. Trust Hist. Preservation, Okla. Hist. Soc. (Shirk Meml. award 1991), Soc. Archl. Historians, Sigma Tau. Democrat. Roman Catholic. Home: 1208 Barkley Ave Norman OK 73071-4812 Office: U Okla Coll Arch Norman OK 73019-0001 Business E-Mail: ahenderson@ou.edu.

HENDERSON, ARVIS BURL, data processing executive, biochemist; b. Abilene, Tex., Oct. 24, 1943; s. Arvis Vernon and Aubra Lee (Patton) H.; m. Mary Ann Pickett, Mar. 17, 1966 (div. Sept. 1983); 1 child, Michelle Rene; m. Jo Nell Hartsell, July 2, 1985 (dec. May 1996); m. Sally Wolfson, May 25, 2001. AA, San Angelo Coll., 1964; BA, U. Tex., 1966; MAS, So. Meth. U., 1969; PhD, U. Tex. Health Sci. Ctr., 1976. Postdoctoral fellow U. Tex., Austin, 1976-80; dir. rsch. lab. Instrumentation Specialities Co., Lincoln, Nebr., 1980-81; asst. prof. pediatrics U. Tex. Health Sci. Ctr., Houston, 1981-84; dir. sci. computing S.W. Found. for Biomed. Rsch., San Antonio, 1984-91; assoc. v.p. info. tech. U. Tex., San Antonio, 1991-96, vice provost for computing and info. tech. Arlington, 1996-2000; chief info. officer Howard U., 2000—02, Dept. Health and Family Svcs., State of Wis., Madison, 2002—03; dir. continuing edn. U. Tex. at Arlington, 2003—. Mem. strategic leadership coun. U. Tex., 1997-2000; co-prin. investigator Students' Work Consortium, 1997-99; mem. State Wis. Tech. Leadership Coun., 2002—. Contbr. articles on biomed. research to profl. jours., chpts. to books. Chmn. Alamo Area Quality Workforce Planning Com., 1990-92; active Class XII Gov. Exec. Devel. Program, 1993; reader North Tex. Taping and Radio for the Blind, 1999-2000, bd. dirs., 1999-2003. Recipient Research Service award NIH, 1976-79; fellow U. Tex., 1976-80, Clayton Found. Biochemistry Inst., 1980. Mem. NIH spl. study sect. 9, Data Processing Mgmt. Assn., Assn. Systems Mgmt., Assn. for Computing Machinery. Republican. Episcopalian. Avocation: photography. Office: Dept Health and Family Svcs 1 W Wilson St Madison WI 53707 E-mail: abhender@uta.edu, abhphd@comcast.net.

HENDERSON, BRIAN EDMOND, dean, physician, educator; b. San Francisco, June 27, 1937; s. Edward O'Brien and Antoinette (Amstutz) H.; m. Judith Anne McDermott, Sept. 3, 1960; children: Sean, Maire, Sarah, Brian John, Michael. BA, U. Calif.-Berkeley, 1958; MD, U. Chgo., 1962. Resident Mass. Gen. Hosp., Boston, 1962-64; chief arbovirology Ctr. Disease Control, Atlanta, 1969-70; assoc. prof. pathology U. So. Calif., LA, 1970-74, prof. pathology, 1974-78, prof. preventive medicine, dept. chmn., 1978-88, dir. Kenneth Norris Jr. Comprehensive Cancer Ctr., 1983—93, rschr., 1994—96, prof. dept. preventative medicine, Kenneth T. Norris Chair in Cancer Prevention, 1996—, dir. Zilkha Neurogenetic Inst., 2002—, dean Keck Sch. Medicine, 2004—; pres. Salk Inst. Biol. Studies, La Jolla, Calif., 1993—94. Established LA Cancer Surveillance Program, U. So. Calif., 1972, Hawaii-LA Multiethnic Cohort, 1993; cons. WHO, South Pacific Commn., U.S.-Japan-Hawaii Cancer Program; mem. Charles S. Mott selection com. Gen. Motors Cancer Research Found., 1982-88; bd. councillors Nat. Cancer Inst., 1979-82; mem. sci. council Internat. Agy. for Rsch. on Cancer, 1982-86 Contbr. articles to profl. jours., chpts. to books; mem. editorial bd. Jour. Clin. Oncology; assoc. editor: Cancer Research. Served to lt. col. USPHS, 1964-69 Nat. Acad. Sci. disting. scholar to China, 1982; recipient Richard & Hinda Rosenthal Found. award, Am. Assn. Cancer Research, 1987, Rsch. Excellence in Cancer Epidemiology and Prevention Award, Am. Acad. Cancer Rsch., U. Chgo. Disting. Svc. Award, Presdl. Medallion., U. So. Calif., 1999. Fellow Los Angeles Acad. Medicine; mem. AAAS, NAS, Inst. Medicine, Infectious Disease Soc. Am., Am. Epidemiol. Soc., Alpha Omega Alpha. Democrat. Roman Catholic. Office: Comprehensive Cancer Ctr 1441 Eastlake Ave # 44 Los Angeles CA 90089-0112

HENDERSON, CATHERINE LYNN, retired secondary school educator; b. Charleston, W.Va., Oct. 19, 1946; d. Raymond Anis Frame and Alma Madalene Green; m. W. Elliott Henderson, Apr. 12, 1978 (dec. 1985). BA in English, Morris Harvey Coll., 1968; MA in Journalism, Marshall U., 1976. Tchr. Kanawha County Bd. Edn., Charleston, W.Va., 1968—2001; ret., 2001. Stringer Offcl. Detective Group. Author: Fairs, Festivals & Funnin' in West Virginia, 1996; co-author: Essential Strategies for School Security, 2001; contbr. to Wonderful W.Va. Mag., Charleston City Mag. Mem.: Nat. Writers Assn., Mystery Writers of Am., Am. Crime Writers League, Sisters in Crime, Soc. of Profl. Journalists. E-mail: murdermostfoul@charter.net.

HENDERSON, CHARLES BROOKE, research and development company executive; b. Washington, Mar. 13, 1929; s. Robert Neel and Dorothy (Brooke) H.; m. Elizabeth Ann Carter, June 6, 1954; children: Katherine, Roger, Sally. BS, Purdue U., 1950; SM in Chem. Engring, MIT, 1952. With Atlantic Research Corp., Alexandria, Va., 1954-88, dir. research and tech., 1971-76, v.p., 1976-80, sr. v.p., 1980-88, also dir. Chmn. bd. dirs. Arctech Inc., 1988-92. Patentee in field. Active Boy Scouts Am., 1965-69, Girl Scouts U.S.A., 1969-71; treas. Loudoun Symphony, 1993-97, bd. dirs., 1993-2001; bd. dirs. Loudoun Arts Coun., 1997-99. Named Nat. Capital Outstanding Young Engr., 1961, One of Maj. Innovators, Tech. Mag., 1981. Fellow: AIAA (assoc.); mem.: Sigma Xi.

HENDERSON, CONNIE CHORLTON, city planner, artist, writer; b. Cedar Rapids, Iowa, July 16, 1944; d. Robert Brown and Lorraine Madeline (Marquardt) Chorlton; m. Dwight Franklin Henderson, Dec. 24, 1966; 1 child, Patricia. BA, Anderson U., 1966; MA in Edn., St. Francis Coll., Ft. Wayne, Ind., 1972; MPA, U. Tex. San Antonio, 1987. Art coord. Ft. Wayne Cmty. Schs., 1966-67; art tchr. East Allen County Schs., New Haven, Ind., 1968-71, 74-79; instr. Manchester Coll., N. Manchester, Ind., 1971-72; rsch. assoc. Tremar Real Estate Rsch., San Antonio, 1983-84; planning asst. (vol.) City of San Antonio, Tex., 1985-88, planner I, 1988-89, project mgmt. specialist, 1990, conservation edn. coord., 1990-91; planner II San Antonio Water Sys., 1991-96, 2003—, water edn. coord., 1996-97, spl. events. coord., 1998—2002; youth edn. specialist, 2003—. Docent (vol.) San Antonio Mus. Assn.; rsch. mgr. N. San Antonio C. of C., 1988. Artist: numerous paintings and fiber sculptures in juried and invitational shows, 1966-80; poetess: (2d prize Iowa Poetry Day Assn., 1961). Bd. dirs. Tex. Soc. to Prevent Blindness, San Antonio, 1981-83; v.p. U. Tex. at San Antonio Women's Club, 1981-82, pres. 1983-84; mem. San Antonio Conservation Soc., 1985—, mem. Assistance League of San Antonio, 1988—, liason Thrift House, San Antonio, 1995-96; co-pres. River Gardens Family and Friends, 1993-94, sec., 1995-96. Mem. Am. Planning Assn. (cert. planner, asst. dir. San Antonio sect. 1990, dir., 1991-93, Am. Water Works Assn., Univ. of Tex. at San Antonio Alumni Assn. Avocations: travel, reading, landscape design, swimming, music. Home: 18222 Redriver Sky San Antonio TX 78259 Office: San Antonio Water System PO Box 2449 San Antonio TX 78298-2449 Office Phone: 210-704-7254. Business E-Mail: chenderson@saws.org.

HENDERSON, CYNTHIA, medical librarian; d. Donald and Frances Henderson. BS in Ednl. Psychology cum laude, Alcorn State U., 1985; MS in Info. and Libr. Sci., U. Mich., 1991. Asst. prof. Iowa State U., Ames, 1991—92; asst. dir. libr. svcs. Charles R. Drew U. Medicine and Sci., L.A., 1992—95; asst. prof. U. Ill., Chgo., 1995—97; dir. John A. Graziano Meml. Libr. Samuel Merritt Coll., Oakland, Calif., 1997—2000; asst. prof. health and human sciences program Samuel Merritt Coll., 1997—2000; dep. dir. multi-media ctr. academic med. libr. Morehouse Sch. Medicine, Atlanta, 2000—04, dir. multi-media ctr. academic med. libr., 2004—. Spl. collections and collections devel. libr. Iowa State U., Ames, 1991—92; health sciences libr. U. Ill., Urbana, 1995—97; reviewer Jour. AMA. Contbr. articles to Bull. Med. Libr. Assn. Mem.: Med. Libr. Assn. Mem. Ame Ch. Avocations: reading, writing, cooking, dancing, sewing. Office: Morehouse Sch Medicine 720 Westview Dr Atlanta GA 30310 Office Phone: 404-752-1531. Office Fax: 404-752-1049. E-mail: chenderson@msm.edu.

HENDERSON, CYNTHIA ANNE, theater educator, actress; b. Mobile, Ala., May 11, 1966; d. Geraldine D. P. Henderson and Bobbie R. Henderson, Sr.; 1 child, Justin C. Baldessare. BS, Troy State U., 1994; MFA, Pa. State U., 1997. Asst. prof. Ithaca (N.Y.) Coll., 1999—. Actor: stage, film and TV (Best

Supporting Actress in Musical, European Tournament of Plays, 1991). Demonstrator, Washington, 2003. Fulbright Scholar, CIES - Fulbright, 2003—. Mem.: Actor's Equity Assn. Avocations: hiking, camping, poetry, pastels, travel. Office: Ithaca Coll Dept Theatre 201 Dillingham Ctr Ithaca NY 14850 Personal E-mail: chenderson@ithaca.edu.

HENDERSON, DAN W., psychiatric educator; b. Huntington, W.Va., Oct. 18, 1948; s. VanBuren and Laura Treavel (Mounts) H. BA in Elem. Edn., Marshall U., 1981, MA in Spl. Edn., 1982, MA in Counseling, 1985; PhD in Spiritual Psychology, Christian Bible Coll./Seminary, 2000. Cert. tchr., Calif., Ky., W.Va. cert. counselor, Calif., Ky., W.Va.; lic. profl. counselor nationally cert. counselor and psychologist. Grad. asst. Marshall U., Huntington, 1981-85; tchr. Cabell County Schs., Huntington, 1981-85; program dir. N.E.W. Inc., Hamlin, W.Va., 1986-89; psychiat. therapist Appalachian Regional Hosp., South Williamson, Ky., 1995—; mem. faculty depts. psychology and sociology W.Va. C.C., 1995—; pvt. practice, N.Y.C. Wrestling coach Cammack Jr. High Sch., Huntington, 1983-85; track coach West Jr. High Sch., Huntington, 1983-85; radio announcer, 1987-89; guest spkr. TV and radio, 1996—; condr. seminars and workshops, 1996—; conv. spkr. state conf., 1998—; facilitator, therapist Coalition Against Domestic Violence, 1998—; therapist pediatric weight mgmt. program, 2001—; facilitator anti-smoking cmty. program, 2001— Author: I the Antichrist, 2001. Facilitator Men's Batterers Group, 1998—. Sgt. USAF, 1967-71, Vietnam. Recipient cert. of appreciation ARC, 1993; grad. fellow Marshall U., 1981. Mem. ACA, N.Am. Masters in Psychology, Am. Mental Health Counselors Assn., Lic. Profl. Counelors Assn. (bd. dirs. 2000—), W.Va. Coling Assn. (bd. dirs. 1998—), Rotary. Democrat. Avocations: writing, photography, travel. Home and Office: 420 8th Ave W Huntington WV 25701-2516

HENDERSON, DELANEY, artist; b. Nice, France, Aug. 13, 1952; came to U.S., 1953; d. James Leal and Eva Jo Henderson. BS, San Francisco State U., 1983; BFA, Acad. Art, San Francisco, 1998. Artist, Oakland, 1998—. Cons. videos on local women artists Gayble TV, Oakland, 1999; represented by Sticks Gallery, Berkeley, Calif., 1999—. Exhibited in group shows at Bolinas Mus., 2000, San Diego Mus. Art, 1995, Ctr. for Visual Arts, 1996, San Bernardino (Calif.) County Mus., 1998 (Barr Art Svc. award), Pro Arts No. Calif. Competitions, 1998, 99, 2000, Somar Gallery, San Francisco, 2000, Oakland Artship, 2000; artist-in residence Mill Gallery, 2001. Co-leader painting group Wilderness Women, 1998-99. Recipient City of Oakland Honorarium, 1997. Mem. Pro Arts, Lesbians in Visual Arts.

HENDERSON, DONALD AINSLIE, public health service officer; b. Lakewood, Ohio, Sept. 7, 1928; s. David Alexander and Grace Eleanor (McMillan) Henderson; m. Nana Irene Bragg, Sept. 1, 1951; children: Leigh Ainslie, David Alexander, Douglas Bruce. BA, Oberlin (Ohio) Coll., 1950; MD, U. Rochester, 1954; MPH, Johns Hopkins U., 1960; DS (hon.), U. Rochester, 1977, Oberlin (Ohio) Coll., 1978; LLD (hon.), Marietta (Ohio) Coll., 1978; DS (hon.), U. Ill., 1979, U. Md., 1980; MD (hon.), U. Geneva, 1977; LHD (hon.), SUNY, 1981, Johns Hopkins U., 1994, Towson State U., 1994; DS (hon.), Yale U., 1986, Albany Med. Coll., 1989, Lafayette Coll., 1991, U. Mo., 1992; LLD (hon.), U. Minn., 2003, U. S.C., 2004, U. Medicine and Dentistry N.J., 2004. Diplomate Am. Bd. Preventive Medicine. Intern, then resident Mary Imogene Bassett Hosp., Cooperstown, N.Y., 1954-55, 57-59; chief epidemic intelligence service Center Disease Control, USPHS, Atlanta, 1955-57, chief surveillance sect., 1960-66; chief med. officer smallpox eradication WHO, Geneva, 1966-77; dean Johns Hopkins U. Sch. Hygiene and Pub. Health, 1977-90; assoc. dir. Office Sci. and Tech. Policy, Exec. Office Pres. of U.S., Washington, 1991-93; dep. asst. sec., sr. sci. advisor HHS, Washington, 1993—95; prof. Johns Hopkins U. Sch. Pub. Health, Balt., 1977—; dir. Hopkins Ctr. Civilian Biodefense Strategies, 1998—2001; dir., prin. advisor Office of Pub. Health Emergency Preparedness Dept. Health and Human Svcs., 2001—03; resident scholar Ctr. for Biosecurity U. Pitts. Med. Ctr., 2003—; prof. medicine and pub. health U. Pitts. Sch. Medicine, 2003—. Contbr. articles to profl. jours. Named Burroughs Wellcome Vis. Prof., Royal Soc. Medicine, 1996; recipient Ernest Jung Found. prize, 1976, Govt. India-Indian Soc. Malaria and Other Communicable Diseases award, 1975, Rosenhaus Internat. award for excellence, 1975, George MacDonald medal, London Sch. Hygiene and Tropical Medicine, Royal Soc. Tropical Medicine and Hygiene, 1976, Health medal, Govt. Afghanistan, 1976, Spl. Albert Lasker Pub. Health Svc. award, WHO, 1976, Health for All medal, 1990, Joseph C. Wilson award in internat. affairs, 1978, James D. Bruce Meml. award, 1978, Outstanding Alumnus award, Delta Omega, 1980, Disting. Alumnus award, Johns Hopkins U., 1982, Dean's medal, 2002, Internat. Merit award, Gairdner Found., 1983, Albert Schweitzer Internat. prize for medicine, 1985, Nat. Medal Sci., 1986, Richard T. Hewitt award, Royal Soc. Medicine, 1986, Edward Jenner medal, 1996, Charles Dana Found. award for pioneering achievement in health, 1986, Japan prize in preventative medicine, 1988, Health medal 1st Grade, People's Republic China, 1988, Medal of Abnegation Uruguay, 1988, Honor award, Pan Am. Health Orgn., 1990, Abraham Lilienfeld award, Am. Coll, Epidemology, 1991, Award of Excellence, Ronald McDonald Children's Charities, 1992, Surgeon Gen.'s medallion, USPHS, 1992, City of Medicine award, 1993, Walter Reed medal, Am. Soc. Tropical Medicine and Hygiene, 1993, Merit award, Nat. Coun. Internat. Health, 1993, Gold medal, Albert B. Sabin Found., 1994, Oswaldo Cruz Gold medal of merit, Govt. of Brazil, 1995, Soc. citation, Infectious Diseases Soc. Am., 1996, L. Frank Calderone prize, Columbia U. Sch. Public Health, 1999, Takeru Higuchi Meml. award, U. Kans., 1999, Presdl. Medal Freedom, 2002, Joseph Smadel Medal, Infectious Diseases Soc. Am., 2002, Arthur Kornberg Rsch. award, U. Rochester, 2002, Disting. Alumnus award, 2003, Silver medal, Govt. Italy Ministero Della Salute, 2004, Hutchinson Medal for Disting. Pub. Svc., U. Rochester, 2005; fellow Paul Harris fellow, Rotary Internat., 1993. Fellow: Nat. Acad. Arts and Scis., Nat. Acad. Medcine Mex. (hon.), N.Y. Acad. Medicine (hon. John Stearns award 1995, Annapolis Ctr. Sci. award 2000, Silvia and Hebert Berger award 2001), London Sch. Tropical Medicine and Hygiene (hon.), Am. Acad. Pediat. (hon.), Royal Coll. Physicians (hon.); mem.: APHA, Indian Soc. Malaria and Other Communicable Diseases, Royal Soc. Tropical Medicine and Hygiene, Royal Coll. Physicians Edinburgh (Eng.), Internat. Epidemiol. Assn., Inst. Medicine NAS (Pub. Welfare medal 1978). Home: 3802 Greenway Baltimore MD 21218-1825 Office: U Pitts Med Ctr for Biosecurity The Pier IV Bldg Ste 210 Baltimore MD 21202 Office Phone: 443-573-3323. E-mail: dahzero@aol.com.

HENDERSON, DONALD BERNARD, JR., lawyer; b. Birmingham, Ala., June 27, 1949; s. Donald B. and Pauline V. (Szulinski) H.; m. Ruth Ann Jeffers, Sept. 12, 1981. BS, U. Ala., 1971, JD, 1974; LLM in Taxation, NYU, 1976. Bar: Ala. 1974, N.Y. 1983. Ptnr. Sirote & Permutt, Birmingham, 1976—83, Kroll & Tract, NYC, 1985-88, LeBoeuf, Lamb, Greene & MacRae, L.L.P., NYC, 1988—; sr. assoc. Mound, Cotton, Wollan and Greengrass, NYC, 1983—85. Lectr. Birmingham chpt. Am. Coll., Bryn Mawr, Pa., 1977-82; bd. dirs. Jackson Nat. Life Ins. Co. NY, SunLife Assurance Co. NY; counsel Bronxville Planning Bd., 1994-2001. Contbr. articles to profl. jours. Pres. Lenox Hill Dem. Club, N.Y.C., 1989-90; mem. Ala. State Dem. Com., 1978-83, N.Y.C. Cmty. Bd. Number 8, 1987-88, Republican Club of Bronxville; mem., chair Bronxville Planning Bd., 2001—. Mem. ABA, N.Y. Bar Assn., Ala. Bar Assn. (sec. tax sect. 1982-83). Home: 108 Midland Ave Bronxville NY 10708-3206 Office: LeBouf Lamb Greene & MacRae LLP 125 E 55th St New York NY 10022-3502 Office Phone: 212-424-8694. Business E-Mail: dhenderson@llgm.com.

HENDERSON, DOUGLAS BOYD, lawyer; b. Pitts., Sept. 21, 1935; s. Arthur G. and Mildred E. (Rickenbach) H.; m. Olivia Lauer, July 6, 1957; children: Scotland Weaver, Keith Arthur, Heather Alice Atkinson. BS in Indsl. Engring., Pa. State U., 1957; JD with honors, George Washington U., 1963. Bar: Va. 1962, D.C. 1963. Mfrs. agt. firm Arthur G. Henderson & Assocs., Pitts., 1957-59; patent agt. Swift & Co., Washington, 1959-62; law clk. to Hon. Donald E. Lane US Ct. Claims, Washington, 1962-63; assoc. Irons, Birch, Swindler & McKie, 1963—65; founding ptnr. Finnegan, Henderson, Farabow, Garrett and Dunner LLP, 1965—. Adv. coun. U.S. Ct. Fed. Claims, 1982—; legal adv. bd. Martindale-Hubbell/LEXIS NEXIS, 1996—; mem. Nat. Patent Adv. Coun. Author: Third Party Practice in the United States Court of Claims or Two's Company, Three's A Crowd, 1976; contbr. articles to profl. jours. Bd. advisors George Washington U. Law Sch., 1991-97. Fellow: Am. Bar Found. (life); mem.: ABA (ho. of dels. 1999—), CPR Inst. for Dispute Resolution, Assn. Conflict Resolution, Nat. Patent Adv. Coun., Am. Arbitration Assn. (panel of neutrals), U.S. Ct. Fed. Claims Bar Assn. (bd. dirs. 1987—90, founder), Supreme Ct. Hist. Soc., Intellectual Property Owners Assn., Internat. Trademark Assn., Am. Intellectual Property Law Assn., US C. of C. (chmn. patent, trademark and copyright coun. 1980—82), ITC Trial Lawyers Assn. (founder), Bar Assn. D.C. (chmn. Ct. Claims com. 1973—74, chmn. patent, trademark and copyright law sect. 1974—75, bd. dirs. 1975—76, trustee rsch. found. 1980—81, chmn. Ct. Appeals for Fed. Cir. Com. 1982—83), Fed. Cir. Bar Assn. (founder 1985, bd. dirs. 1985—86, mem. jud. selection com. 1990—, bd. dirs. 1996—99), D.C. Bar Assn., Va. State Bar, Va. Bar Assn., Internat. Bar Assn., Capital Soc. of Clubs, Tournament Players Club at Avenel, Congl. Country Club, Univ. Club, Burning Tree Club, City Club of Washington (bd. govs. 1990—95), Delta Theta Phi, Phi Gamma Delta. Office: Finnegan Henderson Farabow Garrett & Dunner LLP 901 New York Ave NW Washington DC 20001-4413 Office Phone: 202-408-4001. Office Fax: 202-408-4400.

HENDERSON, DOUGLAS JAMES, physicist, chemist, researcher; b. Calgary, Alta., July 28, 1934; arrived in U.S., 1956; s. Donald Ross and Evelyn Louise (Scott) Henderson; m. Rose-Marie Steen-Nielssen, Jan. 21, 1960; children: Barbara, Dianne, Sharon. BA in Math., U. B.C., Vancouver, 1956; PhD in Physics, U. Utah, 1961. Instr. dept. math. U. Utah, Salt Lake City, 1960-61; asst. prof. physics U. Idaho, Moscow, 1961-62, Ariz. State U., Tempe, 1962-64, assoc. prof., 1964-67, prof. physics, 1967-69; assoc. prof. physics U. Waterloo, Can., 1964-67, prof. applied math. and physics, 1967-69; rsch. sci. IBM Almaden Rsch. Ctr., San Jose, Calif., 1969-90, IBM Corp., Salt Lake City, 1990-92, Utah Supercomputing Inst., U. Utah, Salt Lake City, 1990-95; Manuel Sandoval Vallarta prof. physics U. Autonoma Metropolitana, Mexico, 1985—86, Juan de Oyarzabal prof. physics, 1993—95; prof. chemistry Brigham Young U., Provo, Utah, 1995—. Vis. sci. CSIRO Chem. Rsch. Labs., Melbourne, Australia, 1966—67, Inst. Phys. Chemistry, Polish Acad. Scis., 1973, Korea Advanced Inst. Sci., Seoul, 1974, Inst. Theoretical Physics, Ukranian Acad. Scis., 1989; vis. prof. physics Nat. U. La Plata, Argentina, 1973; sabbatical visitor IBM Watson Rsch. Ctr., Yorktown Heights, NY, 1973—74; mem. evaluation panel Commn. Human Resources, NRC, 1976; vis. prof. chemistry U. Utah, 1976, adj. prof. chemistry and math, 1990—, Henry Eyring lectr., 1994; Manuel Sandoval Vallarta Disting. vis. prof. physics U. Autonoma Met., Mexico, 1985, 88, Juan de Oyarzabal prof. physics, Mexico, 1993—95; vis. prof. chem. physics U. Pisa, Italy, 1989; vis. prof. Scoula Normale Superiore, Pisa, Italy, 1989; adj. prof. applied math. and physics U. Waterloo, 1969—85; mem. adv. bd. Chem. Abstracts Svc., 1981—83; vis. prof. chemistry, math, and physics U. Guelph, Canada, 1991; adj. prof. physics Utah State U., 1990—93; hon. prof. chemistry and math. U. Hong Kong, 1992—. Author: (book) Statistical Mechanics and Dynamics, 1964, Statistical Mechanics and Dynamics, 2d rev. edit., 1982; editor: Physical Chemistry - An Advanced Treatise, Vols. 1-15, 1966—75, Theoretical Chemistry-Advances and Perspectives, Vols. 1-5, 1975—81, Fundamentals of Inhomogeneous Fluids, 1992; editor: (assoc. editor) Jour. Chem. Physics, 1974—76; mem. editl. bd.:, 1990—92, bd. editors: Ultitas Mathematica, 1971—87, Jour. Phys. Chemistry, 1984—89, Jour. Chem. Phys., 1990—92; editor (assoc. editor): Electrochimica Acta, 1991—, Condensed Matter Physics, 2005—; contbr. articles to profl. jours. Vol. Loma Prieta Vol. Fire Dept., Los Gatos, Calif., 1983—89; missionary Ch. Jesus Christ Latter Day Saints, 1957—59. Recipient Johnathan Rodgers award, 1954, Bursary award, NRC of Can., 1956, Outstanding Rsch. Contbn. award, IBM, 1973, Outstanding Innovation award, 1987, Catedra Patrimoniales de Excelencia, Mex., 1993—95; fellow, Corning Glass Found., 1959, Alfred P. Sloan Found., 1964, 1966, Ian Potter Found., 1966, CSIRO Rsch., 1966, Guggenheim Found., 1997; scholar Univ. Great War, 1953, Daniel Buchanan, 1955, Burbridge, 1955. Fellow: Am. Inst. Chemists, Am. Phys. Soc., Inst. Physics; mem.: N.Y. Acad. Scis., Mex. Nat. Acad. Sci. (corr.), Math. Assn. Am., Am. Chem. Soc. (Joel Henry Hildebrand award 1999, Utah award 2005), Can. Assn. Physicists, Sigma Pi Sigma, Sigma Xi, Phi Kappa Phi. Democrat. Member Lds Church. Achievements include statistical mechanics of liquids; co-developer first successful perturbation theory of liquids; statis. mechanics of surfaces and solid-fluid and liquid-vapor interfaces; structure and electronic properties of amorphous solids; theory of electric double layer; theory of selectivity and transport of ions in biological membranes. Office: Brigham Young U Dept Chemistry Provo UT 84602 Office Phone: 801-422-5934. Business E-Mail: doug@chem.byu.edu.

HENDERSON, DWIGHT FRANKLIN, dean, educator; b. Austin, Tex., Aug. 14, 1937; s. Ottis Franklin and Leona (Bady) H.; m. Connie Chorlton, Dec. 24, 1966; 1 dau., Patricia Ross. BA, U. Tex., 1959, MA, 1961, PhD, 1966. Assoc. prof. Ind. U., Ft. Wayne, 1966-68, chmn. dept. history, 1968-71, assoc. prof. history, 1971-80, chmn. arts and scis., 1971-76, dean arts and letters, 1976-80, acting chancellor, 1978-79; prof. history, dean Coll. Social and Behavioral Scis. U. Tex., San Antonio, 1980-2000, acting v.p. acad. affairs, 1986-87, interim dean Coll. Engring., 2000-2001; dir. Learning Cmtys. Jour., 2003—; Fulbright lectr. East China Normal U., Shanghai, 2002; dir. Freshman Initiative, 2003—. Author: Private Journals of Georgiana Gholson Walker, 1963, Courts for a New Nation, 1971, Congress, Courts, and Criminals, 1985. Bd. dirs. Ft. Wayne Philharm. Orch., 1973-74, Pub. Transp. Corp., Ft. Wayne, 1975-77, Vis. Nurse Assn., San Antonio, 1989-94, 95-96, Vis. Nurse Assn. Hospice South Tex., 1996-2002, Employment Network, 1990-96, Mitchell Lake Wetlands Soc., 2003—; docent Mitchell Lake Audubon Ctr., 2004—. With AUS, 1962-64. Tex. Soc. Colonial Dames fellow, 1964-65, 65-66; Ind. U. fellow, 1968, 70, 72, Fulbright U.S.-German Internat. Edn. Adminstrs. Program, 1993. Mem.: Tex. Assn. Deans of Liberal Arts and Scis. (bd. dirs. 1992—98, v.p. 1994, pres. 1995—97), So. Hist. Assn., Assn. Am. Historians, Phi Alpha Theta, Delta Sigma Rho. Home: 18222 Redriver Sky San Antonio TX 78259 Office: U Tex Dept History 6900 N Loop 1604 W San Antonio TX 78249 Office Phone: 210-458-7488. E-mail: dwight.henderson@utsa.edu.

HENDERSON, E. SUZANNE, elementary school educator; b. Champaign, Ill., Nov. 18, 1947; d. Donald Albert Fackler and Fiana B. Warfel Hardig; m. William Arthur Henderson, Aug. 17, 1968; children: Holly Janel, Rachel Eileen. BS, So. Ill. U., 1968; MEd, U. Ill., 1976. Tchr. grade 4 Pulaski County Spl. Sch. Dist., Jacksonville, Ark., 1968-70; tchr. grade 5 Tuscola Cmty. Unit Sch. Dist., Tuscola, Ill., 1970—. Recipient Presdl. Award for Excellence in Teaching of Math. and Sci., 1994. Mem. NEA, Ill. Edn. Assn., Tuscola Edn. Assn. (v.p. 1994-95), Nat. Coun. Tchrs. Math., Ill. Coun. Tchrs. Math. Avocations: flower gardening, golf. Home: 105 E Scott St Tuscola IL 61953-1834 Office: Tuscola Sch Dist 409 S Prairie St Tuscola IL 61953-1770 Business E-Mail: shenderson@net66.com.

HENDERSON, ERNEST, III, healthcare executive; b. Boston, Oct. 25, 1924; s. Ernest and Mary G. (Stephens) H.; m. Mary Louise Campbell, Dec. 31, 1953; children: Ernest Flagg IV, Roberta Campbell. S.B., Harvard, 1944, MBA, 1949; L.H.D. (hon.), Bard Coll., 1976; DPS, Northeastern U., 1992. With Sheraton Corp. Am., 1946-69, dir., 1953-69, treas., 1956-63, pres., 1963-69, chief exec. officer, 1967-69; pres. Henderson Houses Am., Inc. (and affiliates), 1969-89, chmn., 1989—; pres. Fidelity Products Corp., 1985-89. Bd. dirs. Boston Biotech. Corp. Mem. permanent com. Harvard Class, 1946; permanent sec. Harvard U. Bus. Sch. Class, 1952-2002; Mass. Republican jr. nat. committeeman, 1956-57; mem. Wellesley Town Meeting, 1970-89; grand marshal Wellesley Vets. Day Parade, 1978; vice chmn. emeritus bd. trustees Northeastern U.; trustee Henderson Found., George B. Henderson Found., Cape Cod Symphony, Bard Coll.; trustee Boston Biomed. Rsch. Inst.; bd. dirs. Wellesley Cmty. Ctr. Inc., Robin Moore Entertainment, Inc.; vice chmn. Nat. Ctr. for Family Homelessness. Lt. (j.g.) USNR, World War II. Named hon. Big Chief Many Tepees and blood brother Creek Indian Nation. Mem. Chief Exec.'s Orgn. Marlowe-Shakespeare Soc. (dir.), Mensa. Clubs: Harvard Business School Assn. (Boston) (past pres.), Travelers Century Club; Circumnavigators. Home: 171 Edmunds Rd Wellesley Hills MA 02481-1331 Office: Henderson Houses Am Inc PO Box 420 Sudbury MA 01776-0420

HENDERSON, FLORENCE, actress, singer; b. Dale, Ind., Feb. 14, 1934; d. Joseph and Elizabeth Elder H.; m. Ira Bernstein, Jan. 9, 1956 (div.); children: Barbara, Joey, Robert Norman, Elizabeth; m. John Kappas, Aug. 4, 1987. Attended, St. Francis Acad., Owensboro, Ky; studied at, Am. Acad. Dramatic Arts. Broadway and stage debut in Wish You Were Here, 1952; on tour in Oklahoma!, 1952-53, at N.Y.C. Ctr., 1953, Fanny, 1954, The Sound of Music, 1961, in revival of Annie Get Your Gun, 1974; appeared in The Great Waltz, Los Angeles Civic Light Opera Assn., 1953, on Broadway in The Girl Who Came to Supper, 1963, in revival of South Pacific, 1967, in revival The Sound of Music, Los Angeles Civic Light Opera Assn., 1978, Bells are Ringing, Los Angeles Civic Light Opera Assn., 1979; appeared in Oldsmobile indsl. shows, 1958-61; actress: (movies) Song of Norway, 1970, Shakes The Clown, 1991, Naked Gun 33 1/2: The Final Insult, 1994, The Brady Bunch Movie, 1995, Holy Man, 1998, Get Bruce, 1999; appeared on TV in Sing Along, 1958, The Today Show, 1959-60, The Brady Bunch, 1969-74, The Brady Bunch Hour, 1977, The Brady Girls Get Married, 1981, A Very Brady Christmas, 1988, The Bradys, 1990, Fudge-A-Mania, 1995, (host) Bradymania, 1993; numerous other TV appearances include The Love Boat, 1976, 83, The Brady Brides, 1981, Hart to Hart, 1981, Fantasy Island, 1981, 83, Alice, 1983, Murder She Wrote, Dean Martin TV Series; hostess Country Kitchen; appeared in TV spl. Just a Regular Kid; guest appearances It's Garry Shandling's Show, Wil Shriner Show, Jay Leno Family Spl.; first female host of The Tonight Show; co-host: Later Today, 1999-2000; writings, A Little Cooking, A Little Talking, and A Whole Lotta Fun; films include: Speaking of Women's Health, Lifetime. Recipient Sarah Siddons award Office: Don Buchwald and Assoc 6500 Wilshire Blvd Ste 2200 Los Angeles CA 90048 Office Phone: 310-479-0612. E-mail: askflo@flohome.com.*

HENDERSON, FRANCES J., lawyer; b. Glasgow, Scotland, Feb. 17, 1957; LLB with honors, U. Glasgow, Scotland, 1978; LLM, U. Va., 1979; JD, U. Minn., 1984. Bar: DC 1985. Of counsel Graham & James, Washington; ptnr. Sonnenschein Nath & Rosenthal, Washington, 1998—. Office: Sonnenschein Nath & Rosenthal LLP Ste 600, E Tower 1301 K St NW Washington DC 20005 Office Phone: 202-408-6357. Office Fax: 202-408-6399. Business E-Mail: fhenderson@sonnenschein.com.

HENDERSON, FREDA LAVERNE, elementary school educator; b. Parker County, Tex., June 18, 1939; d. Johnnie C. and Golda Arlene (Porter) Holbrooks; m. Ronald S. Henderson, Apr. 12, 1958; children: Ronald Kevin, Kelly Doyle, Chetley Brian, Terry Dean. AA, Am. Inst. Art, 1960; BEd, U. Colo., 1991; MEd, Lesley Coll., 1997. Pvt. tchr. art, Calhan, Colo., 1981-86; elem. tchr. art Ellicott Schs., Colo., 1986—90, tchr. chpt. I, 1991-96, classroom tchr., 1996—2005, Title I reading tchr., 2005—. Sec. Ellicott Sch. PTA; chmn. High Sch. Booster Club, 1979-80; active vol. activities, 1964-79. Named Walmart Tchr. of Yr., 2002. Home: 1975 Buck Rd Calhan CO 80808-8515 Office: Ellicott Schs # 22 399 S Ellicott Hwy Calhan CO 80808-8963 Personal E-mail: fredahenderson@hotmail.com.

HENDERSON, FREDERICK A. (FRITZ HENDERSON), automotive executive; b. Nov. 29, 1958; m. Karen Henderson; 2 children. BBA with high distinction, U. Mich., 1980; MBA with high distinction, Harvard U., 1984. From sr. analyst to dir. GM Corp., NY, 1984—87; from dir. to v.p. mortgage banking GMAC, 1987—90, from v.p. fin. to group v.p. fin. Detroit, 1991—92; exec. in charge of ops. automotive compontents group GM Corp., Pontiac, Mich., 1993, v.p., gen. mgr. Delphi Saginaw steering sys. Saginaw, Mich., 1996, v.p., mng. dir. Brazil Sao Paulo, Brazil, 1997—2000, group v.p., 2000—; pres. Latin Am., Africa and Middle East region GM Corp, 2000—02; pres. GM Asia Pacific GM Corp., 2002—04, chmn. GM Europe, 2004—. Mem. GM Automotive Strategy Bd. GM Corp.; chmn. bd. dirs. Shanghai GM Co., Ltd., 2002; vice-chmn., bd. dirs. Pan Asia Tech. Automotive Ctr.; bd. dirs. Fuji Heavy Industries Ltd.; chmn. bd. dirs. GM Daewoo Auto & Tech. Co. George F. Baker scholar, 1984. Mem.: Conf. Bd. Fin. Execs. Internat., Japan Automobile Mfrs. Assn. (bd. dirs. 2002). Office: GM Corp PO Box 300 300 Renaissance Ctr Detroit MI 48265-3000

HENDERSON, GENE M., marketing professional; BA, Coe Coll.; MBA, U. Chgo. Former sr. cons. Stuart Weiner and Assocs., Chgo.; former exec. v.p. strategic devel., pres. fund raising and membership svcs., COO Epsilon, Boston; pres., CEO, bd. dirs. DIMAC Mktg. Corp., 1997-98, Transmedia Network, Miami, 1998—. Mem. Direct Mktg. Assn. (ethical bus. practices com., operating com. non profit coun., spkr. ann. conf.). Office: Transmedia Network 11900 Biscayne Blvd Miami FL 33181-2743

HENDERSON, GEORGE, educational sociologist, educator; b. Hurtsboro, Ala., June 18, 1932; s. Kidd Large and Lula Mae (Crawford) H.; m. Barbara Ann Beard, Aug. 9, 1952; children: George, Michele, Faith, Lea, Joy, Lisa, Dawn. Student, Mich. State U., 1950-52; BA, Wayne State U., 1957, MA, 1959, PhD in Ednl. Sociology, 1965. Caseworker Ch. Youth Service, Detroit, 1957-59; social economist Detroit Housing Commn., 1960-61; dir. cmty. svcs. Detroit Urban League, 1961-63; program dir. Mayor's Com. for Detroit Youth, 1963-64; asst. dir. delinquency control tng. center Wayne State U., 1964-65; asst. dir. intercultural rels. Detroit Pub. Schs., 1965-66, asst. to supt., 1966-67; assoc. prof. sociology and edn. U. Okla., 1967-69, Sylvan N. Goldman prof. human rels., 1969—, prof. edn., assoc. prof. sociology, 1969—, David Ross Boyd prof. human rels., 1985—, Regents' prof. human rels., 1989—, Kerr-McGee Presdl. prof., 2001—05; dean U. Okla. Coll. Liberal Studies, 1996-2000; dir. human rels. U. Okla., 2000—. Chmn. dept. human rels. U. Okla., 1969-95; vis. prof. sociology Langston U., 1969-70; disting. vis. prof. U.S. Air Force Acad., 1980-81; cons. in field. Author: Foundations of American Education, 1970, Teachers Should Care, 1970, America's Other Children, 1971, To Live in Freedom, 1972, Education for Peace, 1973, Human Relations, 1974, Human Relations in the Military, 1975, A Religious Foundation of Human Relations, 1977, Introduction to American Education, 1978, Understanding and Counseling Ethnic Minorities, 1979, Police Human Relations, 1981, Transcultural Health Care, 1981, Physician-Patient Communication, 1981, The Human Rights of Professional Helpers, 1983, The State of Black Oklahoma, 1984, Psychosocial Aspects of Disability, 1984, Mending Broken Children, 1984, College Survival for Student Athletes, 1985, International Business and Cultures, 1987, Understanding Indigeneous and Foreign Cultures, 1989, Values in Health Care, 1991, Social Work Interventions, 1994, Cultural Diversity in the Workplace, 1994, Migrants, Immigrants and Slaves, 1995, Human Relations Issues in Management, 1996, Our Souls to Keep, 1999, Rethinking Ethnicity and Health Care, 1999, Ethnicity and Substance Abuse, 2002. Recipient Outstanding Achievement award Human Rels. Assn., 1975, Human Rels. award Met. Human Rels. Commn. Nashville, 1979, Okla. Dept. of Mental Health award, 1996, Okla. Found. for Excellence medal for outstanding coll./univ. tchr., 2000; named to Okla. Higher Edn. Hall Fame, 2003, Okla. Hall Fame, 2003. Mem. AAUP, ACD, Am. Sociol. Assn., Nat. Assn. Human Rights Works, Assn. Black Sociologists, Inter-Univ. Seminar on Armed Forces and Soc., Internat. Soc. Law Enforcement and Criminal Justice Instrs., Am. Assn. High Edn. (Black Caucus award for Ednl. Svc. 1993), Golden Key, Omicron Delta Kappa, Delta Tau Kappa, Phi Kappa Phi, Kappa Alpha Psi. Democrat. Home: 2616 Osborne Dr Norman OK 73069-5031 Office: 601 Elm Ave Norman OK 73019-3100 Office Phone: 405-325-1756. Business E-Mail: clsdean@ou.edu.

HENDERSON, GEORGE ERVIN, lawyer; b. Pampa, Tex., June 7, 1947; s. Ervin L. and Elizabeth (Yoe) Henderson; m. Linda L. Dalrymple, Aug. 22, 1970; children: Andrew, Elizabeth. BA, Tex. Christian U., 1969; JD, Yale U., 1972. Bar: Tex. 1972, U.S. Dist. Ct. (so. dist.) Tex. 1974, U.S. Dist. Ct. (we. dist.) Tex. 1978. Assoc. Fulbright & Jaworski, Houston, Austin, Tex., 1972-79, ptnr. Austin, 1983—, Sneed & Vine, Austin, 1979-82. Adj. instr. law U. Tex., Austin, 1983—85. Contbr. articles to profl. jours. Mem. rules com. S. Tex. Youth Soccer Assn., 1993—; mem. Greater Austin Soccer Coalition, Austin, 1995—98; elder Univ. Presbyn. Ch., Austin, 2001—04. Capt. USAR, 1972—78. Mem.: ABA, Am. Bankruptcy Inst., Turnaround Mgmt. Assn., San

Antonio Bankruptcy Bar Assn., Tex. Law Found., Travis County Bar Assn. (chmn. 1988—89, vice-chmn. 1997—98, mem. bankruptcy law sect.), Tex. Assn. Bank Counsel (pres. 1985—86), State Bar Tex. (chmn. corp. banking and bus. law sect. 1983, mem. coun. corp. banking and bus. law sect. 1985—88, mem. articles Z and ZA revision subcomittee 0205—), Capital Soccer Club (pres. 1993—95), Austin Yacht Club. Office: Fulbright and Jaworski 600 Congress Ave Ste 2400 Austin TX 78701-3271

HENDERSON, GEORGE MILLER, foundation executive, former banker; b. Indpls., Aug. 19, 1915; s. Ben Wymond and Verlinda (Miller) H.; m. Janice Himmelwright, Sept. 2, 1952; children: Donna, Bonnie, Heather, Randall, Darcy. Student, Harvard U., 1960. With S.H. Kress & Co., 1933-36; fire control supr. U.S. Forest Svc., Zig Zag, Oreg., 1936-42; asst. mgr. fgn. trade dept. Portland C. of C., 1946-47; with 1st Nat. Bank Oreg., Portland, 1947-80, v.p., 1953-62, sr. v.p., 1962-71, exec. v.p., 1971-80; pres. Oreg. Ind. Coll. Found., 1980-94. Chmn. Portland Aviation Commn., 1950-51, Oreg. Pks. Commn., 1956-86, Columbia Basin Export-Import Conf., 1961-62; pres. Rose Festival Assn., 1953-54, Family Counseling Svc., 1959-60, Pacific Internat. Livestock Exposition, 1965-67; chmn. woorld brotherhood banquet NCCJ, 1963; bd. dirs. Ind. Coll. Funds Am., 1980-94, Nature Conservancy, 1987-90. Mem. Oreg. Bankers Assn. (pres. 1962), Assn. Res. City Bankers, Pacific Northwestern Ski Assn. (pres. 1947-48), Pacific N.W. Trade Assn. (pres. 1964-65), Arlington Club, Multnomah Club, Cascade Club. Home: 7255 SW Benz Park Dr Portland OR 97225-3207

HENDERSON, HAROLD L., retired lawyer; b. IA, Nov. 11, 1935; married. BA, U. Chgo., 1962, JD, 1964; postgrad., Harvard U., 1984. Bar: Ill. 1966. With Cravath Swaine & Moore, 1964-66, Isham Lincoln & Beal, 1966-67, Brown & Platt, 1967-68; counsel resources group Gen. Dynamics Corp., 1968-70; sr. v.p., gen. counsel Firestone Tire & Rubber Co., 1970-85; v.p., gen. counsel RJR Nabisco Inc., Atlanta, 1985-2001, then sr. v.p., gen. counsel, 1985-89, exec. v.p., gen. counsel; ret., 2001; sr. vice-pres. and gen. counsel Eastman Chem. Co., Kingsport, TN. With USAF, 1954-58. Office: Eastman Chem Co PO Box 511 Kingsport TN 37662-5000

HENDERSON, HARRIET, librarian; b. Pampa, Tex., Nov. 19, 1949; d. Ervin Leon and Hannah Elizabeth (Yoe) H. AB, Baker U., 1971; MLS, U. Tex., 1973. Sch. libr. Pub. Sch. Sys., Pampa, 1971-72; city libr. City of Tyler, Tex., 1973-80, City of Newport News, Va., 1980-84, dir. librs. and info. svcs., 1984-90; dir. Louisville Free Pub. Libr., 1990-97, Montgomery County (Md.) Pub. Librs., 1997—. Del. White House Conf. Librs. and Info. Svcs., 1991; mem. Leadership Louisville, 1991—97, Alliant Health Sys. Adult Oper. Bd., 1991—97; mem. adv. com. dept. edn. Spalding U., 1991—95; mem. Md. Adv. Coun. on Librs., 2001—; diaconate Hiddenwood Presbyn. Ch., Newport News, 1983—85; bd. dirs. Tex. Libr. Sys. Act adv. bd., 1979—80, Peninsula Women's Network, Newport News, 1983—85. Recipient Tribute to Women in Bus. and Industry, Peninsula YWCA, Newport News, 1984. Mem.: ALA (councillor 2001—05), Pub. Libr. Assn. (v.p. 1998, pres. 1999), Va. Libr. Assn. (chmn. legis. com. 1981—84, v.p. 1985, pres. 1986), Ky. Libr. Assn. (chair pub. libr. sect. 1995, Outstanding Pub. Libr. Svc. award 1997). Office: Montgomery County Pub Librs Office of Dir 99 Maryland Ave Rockville MD 20850-2330

HENDERSON, HAZEL, economist, writer; b. Bristol, Somerset, U.K., Mar. 27, 1933; came to U.S., 1957, naturalized, 1962; d. Kenneth and Dorothy May (Jesseman) Mustard; m. Carter Henderson (div. 1981); 1 child, Alexandra Leslie Camille Henderson Cassidy; m. Alan F. Kay, 1996 Baccalaureate, Clifton Sch., Bristol, U.K., 1950; ScD (hon.), Worcester (Mass.) Poly. Inst., 1975; ScD (hon.), Soka U., 2000, U. San Francisco, 2001. Freelance writer, various locations, 1967—. Vis. regent's lectr. U. Calif., Santa Barbara, 1979, Horace Albright chair dept. forestry, Berkeley, 82; advisor Calvert Social Investment Funds, 1982—2005, others; ptnr. Calvert-Henderson Quality of Life Indicators; internat. adv. bd. Inst. Ethos, São Paulo, Brazil; dir. Worldwatch Inst., 1975—2001; guest Today Show, AM Am., Bill Moyers's Jour.; prodr. Sunrise Semester series, CBS, 1977, 78, informative series, PBS, 1984; founder Ethical Markets Media LLC; commn. on globalization; cons., lectr., presenter in field. Author: Creating Alternative Futures: The End of Economics, 1978, 2d edit., 1996, The Politics of the Solar Age: Alternatives to Economics, 1981, 2d edit., 1988, Paradigms in Progress, 1991, 2d edit., 1995, Building a Win-Win World, 1996, Beyond Globalization, 1999; co-author: Planetary Citizenship, 2004; editor: The United Nations: Policy and Financing Alternatives, 1996; syndicated columnist InterPress Svc., L.A. Times-Mirros Syndicate; contbr. articles to Christian Sci. Monitor, U.S. News and World Report, Time, N.Y. Times, InterPress Svc., to anthologies; mem. editl. bd. Futures U.K., Foresight U.K., Futures Rsch. Quar., Future Survey, Resurgence; prodr.: Sunrise Semester series, CBS, 1977, 1978, informative series, PBS, 1984, co-exec. prodr.: PBS series Ethical Markets, 2005. Adv. coun. U.S. Congress Office Tech. Assessment, Washington, 1974-80; adv. Com. on Future Fla. State Legislature, Tallahassee, 1984-86; mem. Commn. on Globalization; internat. adv. bd. Forum 2000, Prague. Named Citizen of Yr. N.Y. Med. Soc., 1967; awardee UN Environ. Program; co-winner Global Citizen award, 1996. Fellow: Findhorn Found., World Futures Study Fedn., World Bus. Acad., World Wisdom Coun., Club of Budapest (hon.). Avocations: bicycling, gardening, swimming. Office: PO Box 5190 Saint Augustine FL 32085-5190

HENDERSON, HORACE EDWARD, World War II historian, peace advocate; b. Henderson, NC, July 30, 1917; s. T. Brantley and Maude (Duke) H.; m. Vera S. Schubert; children by previous marriage: Terri Kelley, Elizabeth Smith. Student, Coll. William and Mary, 1934-37, Yale U., 1941-42. Owner Henderson Real Estate & Ins., Williamsburg, Va., 1947-52; coordinator Nat. Automobile Dealers Assn., Washington, 1954-56; dir. gen. World Peace Through Law Center, Geneva, 1964-69; chmn. bd. Henderson Real Estate, McLean, Va., 1964-66; exec. dir. World Assn. Judges, 1968-69; pres. Community Methods, Inc., 1969-76; chmn. Congress Reform Com., Washington, 1976; exec. v.p. Am. Lawmakers Assn., Washington, 1977; pres. Williamsburg Vacations, Inc., 1983-84. Chmn., pres. Nat. Assn. for Free Trade, San Francisco, 1986-87; mem. adv. bd. Mut. Security Agy., 1952-53; mem. Pres.'s Conf. on Indsl. Safety, 1952-53; exec. com. U.S. Com. for UN, 1954; dir. Nat. Citizens Com. for Hoover Report, 1954; indsl. adv. com. Fed. Civil Def. Adminstrn., 1952-53; cons. to dir. ICA, 1956; dir. spl. liaison, spl. asst. to dep. under sec. state, Washington, 1958, dep. asst. sec. state internat. orgn. affairs, Washington, 1959-60; dir. Exile Orgns. Free Europe Com., 1962; U.S. del. to ILO, UNESCO, FAO, WHO, ECOSOC, UN. Author: The Greatest Blunders of World War II, 2002, The Scots of Virginia--America's Greatest Patriots, 2001, The Final Word on War and Peace, 2004. Chmn. Va. Rep. party, 1962-64, Americans for Asian Security and Freedom, 1961; campaign dir. Am. Nationalities for Nixon-Lodge, 1960, Rep. candidate for Congress, 1956, for lt. gov. Va., 1957; permanent chmn. Va. Rep. Conv., 1957; asst. nat. dir. Rockefeller for Pres. campaign, 1964, Scranton for Pres. Campaign, 1964; ind. Candidate for U.S. Senator, 1972; mem. Williamsburg (Va.) City Coun., 1948-50; chmn. Com. Against Recognition Red Hungary, 1963; World vice chmn. Operation Brotherhood. 1954-55; owner Powhatan Hist. Corp., Williamsburg, Va., 1957; chmn. World Campaign Conv. for Peaceful Settlement Internat. Disputes, 1975-95, Assn. for Devel. Edn., Washington, 1978-80, World Peace Treaty Campaign, 1997-; pres. Internat. Domestic Devel. Corp., 1975; trustee Valley Forge Found., 1952-55, Jr. C. of C. War Meml. Hdqrs.; elder, deacon Presbyn. Ch. Capt., C.E. AUS, 1942-46. Recipient spl. citizenship award Am. Heritage Found., 1953; named Outstanding Jaycee of World, 1954 Mem. Jaycees (internat. v.p. 1951), Jr. C. of C. (nat. pres. 1952-53), U.S. C. of C. (dir. 1954), Yale Club, St. Andrew's Soc., Sigma Alpha Epsilon. Visited 47 countries organizing young men's civic groups, 1953-54. Home: Apt 822 1925 Burnt Bridge Rd Lynchburg VA 24503-2246 Personal E-mail: hDukeHen@aol.com. *As my father always told me, "Life is not getting what you want, but making the best of what you get.".*

HENDERSON, ISAAC CRAIG, oncologist, researcher; b. Paullina, Iowa, Aug. 10, 1941; s. Isaac C. and Ora E. (Tjossem) H.; m. Mary Turner Henderson, June 11, 1966; children: Isaac Craig, Amy Hudson. AB, Grinnell (Iowa) Coll., 1963; MD, Columbia U., 1970. Cert. internal medicine, 1977, med. oncology, 1979. Intern Presbyn. Hosp., N.Y.C., 1970-71; resident, 1971-72; rsch. assoc. NIH, 1972-74; instr. medicine Harvard U. Med. Sch., Boston, 1975-76; asst. prof., 1976-84; assoc. prof., 1984-92; dir. Breast Evaln. Ctr. Dana Farber Cancer Inst., 1980-92; dir. clin. cancer program U. Calif., San Francisco, 1992-95; chmn., CEO Sequus Pharm., Inc., Menlo Park, Calif., 1995—99; sr. med. advisor and mem. bd. of dir. Alza Corp., Mountain View, Calif., 1999—2002; CEO Access Oncology, NY, 2001—04; pres. Keryx Biopharmaceuticals, Inc., San Francisco, 2004—. Adj. prof., U. Calif., San Francisco, 1995—. Contbr. articles to profl. jours. Served with USPHS, 1972-74. Fulbright Rsch. scholar, 1964-65; Merck, Sharp & Dohme Internat. fellow, 1966; recipient Columbia Presbyn. Med. soc. rsch. prize, 1970. Fellow ACP; mem. Am. Soc. Clin. Oncology, Am. Assn. Cancer Rsch., Soc. Friends. Achievements include research on clin. protocols evaluating new treatment of breast cancer. Office: Keryx Biopharmaceuticals Inc 1373 Bay St San Francisco CA 94123-2201 Office Phone: 415-674-5148. E-mail: ichenderson@hotmail.com.

HENDERSON, JANET E. E., lawyer; b. 1956; BA, U. Okla., 1978; JD, Columbia U., 1982. Bar: Okla. 1982, U.S. Dist. Ct. (no. dist.) Okla. 1982, Ill. 1986, U.S. Dist. Ct. (no. dist.) Ill. 1986. With Sidley & Austin, Chgo., 1985—, ptnr., 1990—. Lectr. on lender liability issues and bankruptcy to legal orgns., including Midwest Assn. Secured Lenders. Harlan Fiske Stone scholar Columbia U., 1982. Mem. ABA, Chgo. Bar Assn., Am. Bankruptcy Inst., Phi Beta Kappa. Office: Sidley & Austin Bank One Plz 10 S Dearborn St Chicago IL 60603 Fax: 312-853-7036.

HENDERSON, JANET LYNN, small business owner; b. Chgo., Sept. 14, 1943; d. Howard Charles and Lucille Laura (Lambrecht) Harris; m. Todd Dierks Nelson, Jan. 30, 1965 (div. May 1997); children: Erik Nelson, Brooks Nelson, Jessica Nelson, Jillian Nelson; m. Phil M. Henderson, Dec. 26, 1997. BS in Bus. Adminstrn., Elmhurst Coll., 1966. Lic. real estate broker. Career counselor Employee Svcs., Inc., Chgo., 1966-67; acctg. mgr. Ins. Mgmt., Inc., Milw., 1967-70, Hosp. Coun. Greater Milw., 1970-84; broker assoc. Klein & Heuchan, Inc., Clearwater, Fla., 1994-99; pres., owner Weddings On Water, Clearwater, Fla., 2003—. Mem. leadership tng. coun. Nat. League Cities, Washington, 1999—2002; mem. internat. com. Fla. League Cities, Tallahassee, 1999—2002. Pres. Dunedin Youth Guild, 1993—; chair Relay for Life, 2003, Pinellas County Heart Ball, 2000, Tour of Kitchens, 2005—, Krewe of Venus Debutante Ball, 2005; co-chair Tour of Kitchens, 2005; v.p. Arms of Venus, 2005—; city commr. City of Dunedin, Fla., 1997—2002, vice mayor, 1999, 2002; bd. dir. Childrens Svc. Soc., 1983—86, Ruth Eckerd Hall Found., Clearwater, Fla., 1998—2004, Pinellas Planning Coun., Clearwater, Fla., 1998—2002, Watson Ctr., 1999—2005, Pinellas County Cmty. Found., Bowman Meml. Scholarship Fund Com., 2003—05, Leading Ladies, 2001—05; v.p. Dunedin Hist. Soc., 2004—05; bd. dir. Dunedin C. of C., 2003—, vice-chair membership, 2005—; chmn. steering com. Women in Philanthropy, 2004; active Leadership Pinellas, 1993—. Ill. State scholar, 1962. Mem.: Dunedin Hist. Soc., Friends Libr., Rotary. Republican. Office: Weddings on Water Inc 200 Seminole St Clearwater FL 33755 Office Phone: 727-466-0969. Business E-Mail: janet@weddingsonwater.com.

HENDERSON, JANICE ELIZABETH, law librarian; b. N.Y.C., Dec. 22, 1952; d. James and Adeline M. (Fitzgerald) H. BA in Psychology, Hunter Coll., 1974; MS in Spl. Edn., CUNY, 1979; MLS in Library Sci., Pratt Inst., 1980; JD, Bklyn. Law Sch., 1986. Law librarian Morgan, Lewis & Bockius, N.Y.C., 1977-83; reference librarian Weil, Gotshal & Manges, N.Y.C., 1983-85; law librarian Tenzer, Greenblatt et al, N.Y.C., 1985-86, Robinson, Silverman et al, N.Y.C., 1986-88; assoc. law libr. prof. CUNY Law Sch., N.Y.C., 1989-91; law librarian Kirkland & Ellis, N.Y.C., 1991-93; dir. libr. svcs. Epstein, Becker & Green, PC, 1993-98; dir. profl. devel. and libr. svcs. Baker & McKenzie, N.Y.C., 1998—2002; cons. law librarianship N.Y.C., 2003; reference and rsch. libr. Covington & Burling, 2004—05; rsch. libr. Lovells, 2005—. Assoc. adj. prof. Sch. Libr. and Info. Sci., St. John's U., N.Y.C., 1990-93; spkr. in field. Book reviewer Legal Info. Alert newsletter, 1984-86. Mem. Am. Assn. Law Librs. (mem. centennial celebration com. 2003—), Law Libr. Assn. Greater N.Y. (advt. mgr. 1986-89, bd. dirs. 1989-90, mem. continuing legal edn. com. 1990-92, co-chair 1992-94, v.p. 1995-96, pres. 1996-97, past pres. 1997-98, chair 65th anniversary com., 2003-2004), Practicing Law Inst. (mng. the law libr. 1997-98, program chair 1999-2000, program co-chair 2001—). Democrat. Roman Catholic. Home: PO Box 23060 Brooklyn NY 11202-3060 Office Phone: 212-841-1172. E-mail: jhenderson@cov.net.

HENDERSON, JEFFREY J., dean, educator; b. Montclair, N.J., June 21, 1946; s. Frank I. and Amy J. Henderson; m. Patricia J. Johnson, June 21, 1996. PhD, Harvard U., 1972; BA, Kenyon Coll., 1968, LHD (hon.), 1994. Asst. prof. Yale U., New Haven, 1972—78; assoc. prof. U. of Mich., Ann Arbor, 1978—82; prof. U. of So. Calif., L.A., 1982—91, Boston U., 1991—, dean of arts and scis., 2002—. Editor Loeb Classical Libr., Cambridge, Mass., 1998—. Author: (book) The Maculate Muse, 1975; translator: Aristophanes: Plays, 4 vols., 1998—2002 (Goodwin Award of Merit, Am. Philol Assn., 2001); editor: (collection of essays) Aristophanes: Essays in Interpretation, 1981. Recipient sr. faculty fellowship, NEH, 1991—92; fellow, John Simon Guggenheim Found., 1997—98, Danforth Found., 1968—72, Woodrow Wilson Found., 1968—72. Mem.: Am. Philol Assn., Harvard Club of Boston. Democrat. Avocations: softball, tennis, chess. Office: Boston U 725 Commonwealth Ave Boston MA 02215 E-mail: jhenders@bu.edu.

HENDERSON, JOAN BLUST, lawyer, educator, writer, mediator; b. Paterson, N.J., July 7, 1936; d. Vincent M. and Ellen Kennedy (Adams) Blust; m. J. Eber henderson, June 26, 1959 (div. 1976); children: Ian Scott, Heather Jo. BA, Cedar Crest Coll., 1958; MA, U. Louisville, 1967; JD, 1978. Bar: Ind. 1979, U.S. Dist. Ct. (so. dist.) Ind. 1979, U.S. Supreme Ct. 1988. Tchr. New Providence (N.J.) Sch., 1960-61, Army Sch., Ft. Campbell, Ky., 1961-62; tchr. chronically ill Louisville Pub. Schs., 1962-65; exec. dir. Rauch Ctr. Handicapped, New Albany, Ind., 1965-72; instr. Webster U. Jeffersonville Campus, St. Louis, 1983; dept. chmn. health svcs. mgmt., 1988—; sole practice Jeffersonville, Ind., 1979—. Lectr. various orgns. Author: A Good Worker, 1971, A Good Citizen, 1973, A Good Neighbor, 1976. Mem. adv. com. on child abuse Clark County Welfare, Jeffesonville, 1980-84; edn. com. ARC, Louisville, 1982—. Recipient Jeffersonville United to Make Progress Bus. aard, 1985. Mem. Am. Bus. Women's Assn. (Jeffersonville chpt.), Ind. Bar Assn., Clark County Bar Assn., Assn. Trial Lawyers Am., Kappa Delta Pi, Phi Alpha Delta. Home: 400 E Terrace Hts Jeffersonville IN 47130-4720 Office: 521 E 7th St Jeffersonville IN 47130-4031

HENDERSON, JOHN DREWS, architect; b. St. Louis, July 30, 1933; s. Russell Dewey and Hazel Agnes (Drews) H.; m. Barbara Lee Beckman, June 25, 1955; children: Susan Lee, John Beckman. BArch, U. Ill., 1956. Registered architect, Calif. With Delawie, Macy & Henderson, San Diego, Calif., 1966-77, Macy, Henderson & Cole, AIA, San Diego, 1977-86; pres. John D. Henderson, FAIA, 1986—. Mem. San Diego Hist. Sites Bd., 1972-78, Gaslamp Quarter Task Force, 1976-78, Gaslamp Quarter Coun., 1984-86; mem. City Mgr.'s Com. for Seismic Retrofit for Older Bldgs., 1986-92; bd. dirs. Hist. Am. Bldgs. Survey Found., 1984-86; Calif. Hist. Bldgs. Code Safety Bd., 1976-96; apptd. by Gov. of Calif. to State Hist. Resources Commn., 1990-02, reapptd., 1994-98, 98-02, chmn. 1992-93, 2000-01, chmn. Calif. Heritage Fund com. 1993—2001; Calif. advisor Nat. Trust Hist. Preservation, 1975-78; bd. dirs. Gaslamp Quarter Found., 1984-86. Lt. USNR, 1956-59. With USN, 1956—59, with USNR, 1959—64. Recipient Hist. Preservation awards from City San Diego, San Diego Hist. Soc., San Diego chpt. and Calif. Coun. AIA, La Jolla Women's Club, Am. Assn. State and Local History, Am. Inst. Planners, Save Our Heritage Orgn., Rancho Santa Fe Assn., Calif. Preservation Found., Ctrl. City Assn., Gaslmp Quarter Assn. Fellow AIA (officer, dir. local chpt. 1969-73, chpt. pres. 1972, editor guidebooks 1970, 76, state bd. dirs. 1971-73, nat. hist. resources com. 1974-76, 78—, emeritus 2002, regional rep. 1976-78, mem. guidebook com., 2002); mem. San Diego Archtl. Found. (bd. dirs. 1984-86, 89-91), San Diego Hist. Soc. (officer, bd. dirs. 1975, pres. 1975), San Diego Geneal. Soc., San Diego History Campaign (exec. com. 1981-86), San Diego Host Golf Club, Clan Henderson Soc. Republican. Presbyterian. E-mail: jhende@tns.net.

HENDERSON, JOHNNY, mathematician, educator; b. Santa Monica, Calif., Mar. 26, 1951; s. Ernest Elijah and Madora Allene Henderson; m. Darlene Baxter; 1 child, Kathryn Strunk. BS, U. Ark., 1973, MS, 1975; PhD, U. Nebr., 1981. Asst. prof. math. U. Mo., Rolla, 1981—84; alumni prof. math. Auburn U., Auburn, 1984—2000, Scharnagel prof. math., 2000—02; disting. prof. math. Baylor U., Waco, Tex., 2002—; adv. bd., math. dept. Abilene Christian U., Tex., 2004—. Author: Boundary Value Problems for Functional Differential Equations, 1995; contbr. articles to profl. jours.; mem. editl. bd. Jour. Math. Analysis and Applications, Comms. on Applied Nonlinear Analysis, Internat. Jour. Applied Math., Math. Scis. Rsch. Jour., others. Vol. Wesley Terr. Retirement Ctr., Auburn, 1984—2002, Meadowlands Terr. Retirement Ctr., Waco, 2002—. Recipient Outstanding Achievement award, Ark. Coll., 1993, Ark. Trio Achievement award, Ark. Assn. Student Assistance Programs, 1994, Alumni Achievement award, U. Nebr., 1995, Outstanding Tchg. award, Lamdba Sigma Soc., 2002; fellow, Tamkang U, Taiwan, 1999; Raybould fellow, U. Queensland, Australia, 1997, U. New South Wales fellow, 2003. Mem.: Internat. Soc. Difference Equations (adv. bd. 2001—03), Internat. Fedn. Nonlinear Analysts, Math. Assn. Am. (Disting Tchg. award 2001), Am. Math. Soc., Sigma Xi. Office: Baylor University Dept Math One Bear Pl #97328 Waco TX 76798

HENDERSON, KAREN LECRAFT, federal judge; b. Oberlin, Ohio, 1944; BA, Duke U., 1966; JD, U. N.C., 1969. Ptnr. Wright & Henderson, Chapel Hill, NC, 1969—70, Sinkler, Gibbs & Simons, P.A., Columbia, SC, 1983—86; asst. atty. gen. Columbia, 1973—78; sr. asst. atty. gen., dir. of spl. litigation sect., 1978—82; deputy atty. gen., dir. of criminal div., 1982; judge U.S. Dist. Ct. S.C., Columbia, 1986—90, U.S. Ct. Appeals (D.C. cir.), Washington, 1990—. Apptd. Dist. Ct. Adv. Com. Mem.: ABA (litigation sect. and urban, state and local government law sect.), Am. Law Inst., Supreme Ct. Hist. Soc., Fed. Judges Assn., Fed. Am. Inn of Ct., Am. Judicature Soc., SC Bar Assn. (government law sect., trial and appellate practice sect., fed. judges assn.), NC Bar Assn. Office: US Ct Appeals 333 Constitution Ave NW Washington DC 20001-2802*

HENDERSON, KENNETH LEE, lawyer; b. Atlanta, Nov. 2, 1954; s. Hugh T. and Norma (Zollars) H.; m. Kathryn Graves, Aug. 14, 1976; children: Christine Mary, Jack Kenneth. BA with high honors, Auburn U., 1976; JD cum laude, NYU, 1979. Bar: N.Y. 1980, U.S. Dist. Ct. (so. and ea. dists.) N.Y. 1980. Assoc. Webster & Sheffield, NYC, 1979-84, Finley, Kumble, Wagner, Heine, Underberg, Manley, Myerson, & Casey, NYC, 1984-87; ptnr. Robinson Silverman Pearce Aronsohn & Berman, NYC, 1987—2003, Bryan Cave LLP, NYC, 2003—; mem. exec. com. Editor (with others): State Ltd. Partnership Law, 1987; articles editor Annual Survey Am. Law, 1978-79. Elder, trustee Fifth Ave. Presbyterian Ch., N.Y.C., 1987—; bd. dirs. Population Communications Internat., Inc., 1985-2002, chmn., 1999-; bd. dirs. Activisiion, Inc., 2001-; Coral World Internat., 2004-. Root-Tilden scholar, 1976-79. Mem. ABA, N.Y. State Bar Assn., Assn. of Bar of City of N.Y., Order of Coif, Omicron Delta Kappa (leadership hon.), Phi Kappa Phi (scholastic hon.), Phi Gamma Delta. Democrat. Office: Bryan Cave LLP 1290 Avenue Of The Americas Fl 33 New York NY 10104-3300 Business E-Mail: klhenderson@bryancave.com.

HENDERSON, LENNEAL JOSEPH, JR., political science educator; b. New Orleans, Oct. 27, 1946; s. Lenneal Joseph and Marcelle (Heno) H. AB, U. Calif. at Berkeley, 1968, MA, 1969, PhD, 1976; postgrad. in Sci., tech. and pub. policy, George Washington U. Asst. dean students, asst. prof. govt. St. Mary's Coll., Calif., 1969-71; dir. ethnic studies, asst. prof. govt. U. San Francisco, 1971-75; prof. Morgan State U., Balt., 1975—; asst. dean Sch. of Mgmt. John F. Kennedy U., Martinez, 1974-75; also lectr. polit. sci. Morgan State U., Balt.; asso. dir. research Joint Center Polit. Studies, Washington, 1977-78; pub. adminstrn. fellow U.S. Dept. Energy, 1978-79; lectr. urban studies Inst. Urban Studies U. Md., College Park; for U.S. State Dept. in, Somalia, Tanzania and Nigeria, South Africa; prof. Sch. Bus. and Public Adminstrn., Howard U., 1979-87; v.p. sci. and tech. Ronson Mgmt. Corp., Alexandria, Va., 1986-88; prof., head dept. polit. sci., dir. Bur. Pub. Adminstrn. U. Tenn., Knoxville, 1988-89; Disting. prof. govt. and pub. adminstrn., sr. fellow, Henry C. Welcome fellow William Donald Schaefer Ctr. for Pub. Policy, U. Balt., 1989—. Vis. prof. polit. sci. Xavier U., New Orleans, 1970, Howard U., Washington, 1971, 75-76; instr. Ottawa U. of Kans., Ipoh, Penang, Malaysia and Hong Kong, 1997; vis. faculty city and regional planning dept. U. Calif., Berkeley, 1974-75; cons. Booz-Allen Pub. Adminstrn. Services, Inc., 1973-74, Shepard Assos., 1973-74, Morrison & Rowe, Inc., 1974, Dukes, Dukes & Assos., 1974-75; mem. U.S. del. Energy and Human Habitat Conf., EEC, Ottawa, Can., 1977; part-time faculty Fielding Inst., Santa Barbara, Calif., 1991—; lectr. USIA Tour, Namibia, Kenya, Ehiopia, Australia; spkr. internat. consulting seminar, Fielding Inst., Czech Republic, 1994. Editor: Black Political Life in the U.S, 1972; mem. editorial bd. Bureaucrat; contbr. articles to profl. jours. Pres., bd. dirs. Children and Youth Service Agy. of San Francisco, 1974-75; chmn. local reviewing com. San Francisco County Campaign for Human Devel., 1973-74; pres. San Francisco Youth Assn., 1964-65; mem. regional task force on open space Assn. of Bay Area Govt., 1973-75; pres., bd. dirs. African Am. Hist. and Cultural Soc., Inc., 1975-76; chmn. Mayor's Citizen Adv. Com. for Washington, 1981, Mayor's Budget Adv. Com., Washington, 1983; bd. dirs. Youth Svcs. Internat., Inc., 1998; apptd. Md. Commn. on African Am. History and Culture; bd. trustees Cath. Charities of the Archdiocese of Balt. Recipient Disting. Faculty award Howard U., 1984, Outstanding Faculty award, 1986; Calif. State fellow, 1969-71; Urban Affairs fellow, 1969-70; fellow Moton Center Ind. Studies, summer 1978; Nat. Assn. Schs. Public Affairs and Public Adminstrn. fellow U.S. Dept. Energy, 1978-79; research fellow Rockefeller Found.; research asso. Harvard U.; NRC postdoctoral fellow Johns Hopkins U. Sch. Advanced Internat. Studies, 1983-84; Kellogg nat. fellow, 1986 Mem. Am. Polit. Sci. Assn., Am. Soc. Pub. Adminstrn., AAAS, Western Govtl. Research Assn., Internat. Personnel Mgmt. Assn., Am. Social and Behavioral Sci. Assn. Independent. Roman Catholic. Home: 4530 Mustering Drum Ellicott City MD 21042-5949 Office: U Balt William D Schaefer Ctr Pub Policy 1304 Saint Paul St Baltimore MD 21202-2713 *Service is the heart of my life. Its demands hold me to the highest humanitarian ideals. Its standards teach me the value of mistakes made right. Without service, humanity falls below the lowest of life forms; for all animals serve God's purpose. So service will continue to lead me to others; to their needs, hopes, desires. And, as I fulfill these needs, hopes, desires, I fulfill my own.*

HENDERSON, MADELINE MARY (BERRY HENDERSON), chemist, researcher, consultant; b. Merrimac, Mass., Sept. 3, 1922; d. Burton B. and Irene R. (Murphy) Berry; m. Richard S. Henderson, Nov. 5, 1957; children: Anne M., Matthew R., Katherine M., Laura J. AB in Chemistry, Emmanuel Coll., Boston, 1944; MPA, Am. U., Washington, 1977. Chemist E.I. DuPont, Gibbstown, NJ, 1944—45, MIT, Cambridge, Mass., 1946—52; info. specialist Battelle Meml. Inst., Columbus, Ohio, 1953—55; rsch. assoc. NSF, Washington, 1956—62; computer specialist Nat. Bur. Standards, Washington, 1964—79; cons. Bethesda, 1980—. Chmn. Gordon Rsch. Conf. on Sci. Info. Problems, 1972. Author, co-author, editor books on info. sci.; co-author, author papers, articles on info. sci., standards, and libr. automation. Dept. of Commerce Sci.-Tech. fellow, 1971-72; Am. U. Key Exec. scholar, 1975-77. Fellow AAAS (sec. sect. info. scis. 1978-85); mem. Am. Chem. Soc., Am. Soc. Info. Sci. & Tech. (mem. publs. com. 1983-87, chmn. pub. affairs com. 1987-89, Watson Davis award 1989), Pi Alpha Alpha (nat. honor soc. pub. adminstr.). Office: 7401 Willow Rd #425 Frederick MD 21702-2500

HENDERSON, MARY STANLEY, museum director, writer; b. Norfolk, Va., Nov. 30, 1953; d. Stanley Wadsworth and Mary Scaffe Henderson; m. Donald Francis Valdivia, Sept. 27, 1980 (div. Aug. 1, 1986); 1 child, Mary Francis Valdivia. BA, Goucher Coll., Towson, Md., 1974; MA, George Wash. U., Washington, 1983; MPA, Am. U., Washington, 1994. Program asst. Nat. Found. for the Arts and Humanities, Washington, 1974—76; curator Smithsonian Instn., Washington, 1976—97; pres. Magic Wand Mus. Svcs., Inc., McLean, Va., 1997—99; chief curator of collections Am. Mus. of the Moving Image, New York, 1999—2001; dir. Lafayette Natural History Mus., La., 2001—. Panelist N.Y. State Coun. on the Arts, N.Y., 2000—01. Author: Star Wars: The Magic of Myth; curator (exhibitions) Star Wars: The Magic of Myth, Star Trek: An American Odyssey (Parade Mag. Best Exhbn. of 1992, 1993). Chmn. Lafayette Cultural Tourism Com., Lafayette, La., 2003—04. Fellow William Wilson Corcoran Fellowship, Corcoran Sch. of Art, 1971. Mem.: Am. Assn. of Mus. Episcopal. Office: Lafayette Natural History Mus 433 Jefferson St Lafayette LA 70501 Office Phone: 337-291-5544. Business E-Mail: mhenderson@lafayettegov.net.

HENDERSON, MAUREEN MCGRATH, medical educator; b. Tynemouth, Eng., May 11, 1926; arrived in U.S., 1960; d. Leo E. and Helen McGrath Henderson. MB BS, U. Durham, Eng., 1949, DPH, 1956. Prof. preventive medicine U. Md. Med. Sch., 1968—75, chmn. dept. social and preventive medicine, 1971—75; assoc. epidemiology Johns Hopkins U. Sch. Hygiene and Pub. Health, 1960—75; prof. epidemiology and medicine U. Wash. Med. Sch., 1975—96, prof. emeritus epidemiology and medicine, 1996—, asst. v.p. and assoc. v.p. health scis., 1975—81, head cancer prevention rsch. program Fred Hutchinson Cancer Rsch. Ctr., 1983—94; mem. Nat. Inst. Environ. Health Scis. Adv. Coun., 1994—97. Chmn. epidemiology and disease control study sect. Nih, 1969—82; chmn. clin. trial rev. com. Nat. Heart Lung and Blood Inst., 1975—79; mem. Nat. Cancer Adv. Bd., 1979—84; mem. bd. Robert Wood Johnson Health Policy Fellowship, 1989—93; bd. radiation effects rsch. NRC, 1991—97. Decorated Order of Brit. Empire; recipient John Snow award, Am. Pub. Health Assn., 1990; scholar Luke-Armstrong, 1956—57, John and Mary Markle, Acad. Medicine, 1963—68. Mem.: Nat. Rsch. Coun. (mem. report rev. com. 1996—2002, mem. com. rsch. priorities for airborne particulate matters 1998—2000), Am. Epidemiol. Soc. (pres. 1990—91), Internat. Coun. Cancer Rsch. (sci. adv. bd. 1989—92), Soc. Epidemiol. Rsch. (chmn. 1969—70), Assn. Tchrs. Preventive Medicine (pres. 1972—73), Am. Coll. Epidemiology, Inst. Medicine N.A.S. Home: 5309 NE 85th St Seattle WA 98115-3915 E-mail: mhenders@w-link.net.

HENDERSON, MAXINE, writer; b. Rusk, Tex., May 30, 1926; d. A.J. and Johnnie I. (Lewis) Ralson; widowed; children: Kenneth, Gerald, Richard, Nancy, Sally. BS, U. Denver. Registered med. technologist. Med. technologist, Denver and Ypsilanti, Mich., 1947-85. Author: Country Cuisine from Maxine, 1989, Snax from Max, 1996. Gourmet cook AAUW Study Group, Ypsilanti, 1979—. Mem. AAUW, Am. Soc. Clin. Pathology. Methodist. Home: A 105 1740 S Grove St Ypsilanti MI 48198-6658

HENDERSON, MELFORD J., epidemiologist, molecular biologist, chemist; b. Birmingham, Ala., Dec. 28, 1950; s. Robert Burton and Rena Henderson; 1 child, Erica. BS, Bishop Coll., Dallas, 1972; MA, Johns Hopkins U., 1976; student, NYU Dental Sch., 1977—79; MPH, Yale U., 1984. Ordained min. Rsch. assoc. Bishop Coll., 1972-73; rsch. assoc. Sch. of Pharmacy U. Md., Balt., 1976-77; microbiologist Torigian Labs., Queens, NY, 1979-81; pub. health analyst internat. program cardiovasc. diseases NIH, Bethesda, Md., 1984; epidemiologist, analyst Task Force on Black and Minority Health, Bethesda, 1985—. Epidemiologist DC Govt., DC Health Dept., 1985-88, U.S. Govt., Agy. for Health Care Policy and Rsch., 1990; epidemiologist, sr. rsch. assoc. Prospect Assocs., 1989; epidemiologist, program ofcl. U.S. Dept. HHS; program ofcl. Mayor's Health Policy Coun. DC Govt. Author 7 scholarly sci. publs. Recipient numerous awards in chemistry and pub. health; NIH fellow, 1973-76, USPHS fellow, 1982-84, rsch. fellow Assn. Black Cardiologists, 1984-85. Mem. APHA, Md. Pub. Health Assn., Blacks in Govt., Soc. for Epidemiol. Rsch., Assn. Black Cardiologists, Beta Kappa Chi. E-mail: mhenders@ahrq.gov.

HENDERSON, MICHAEL HOWARD, artist, educator; b. Dallas, Aug. 30, 1958; s. Ralph Howard and Barbara Ruth Henderson. BFA, U. North Tex., 1983, MFA, 1986; postgrad., Whitney Ind. Study Program, N.Y.C., 1986-87. Vis. lectr. Princeton (N.J.) U., 1994; adj. faculty mem. Tex. Christian U., Ft. Worth, 1995; vis. asst. prof. U. Tex., Arlington, 1996; adj. instr. Navarro Coll., Corsicana, Tex., 1997-98, Tarrant County Jr. Coll., Ft. Worth, 1998-99, Brookhaven Coll., Dallas, 1998-99; lectr. in painting U. Tex., Dallas, 1999—2001; asst. prof. art Sam Houston State U., Huntsville, Tex., 2001—. Co-dir. Gray Matters, Dallas, 1996-97; adj. asst. prof. U. Tex., Arlington, 1999—2001. One-man shows at alternate Gallery, Dallas, 1985, Artists Space, N.Y.C., 1990, Gray Matters, 1995, 97, John Michael Kohler Art Ctr., Sheboygan, Wis., 1997; exhibited in group shows at Chatauqua (N.Y.) Inst., 1984, D-Art Visual Ctr., Dallas, 1984, Theater Gallery, Dallas, 1984, Ark. Art Ctr., Little Rock, 1985, Arts Warehouse, Austin, Tex., 1986, Brown-Lupton Gallery, Tex. Christian U., Ft. Worth, 1986, 500X Gallery, Dallas, 1986, Soho Ctr. for Visual Arts, N.Y.C., 1987, Laguna Gloria Art Mus., Austin, 1989, Visual Arts Ctr. of Alaska, Anchorage, 1990, B4A Gallery, N.Y.C., 1990, Clocktower Gallery, N.Y.C., 1990, MMC Gallery Marymount Manhattan Coll., N.Y.C., 1991, Gray Matters, 1992, Lynn Goode Gallery, Houston, 1992, TZ'Art and Co. Gallery, N.Y.C., 1994, Islip Art Mus., East Islip, N.Y., 1995, Galeria de Arte Plastica Contemporania, Guatemala City, Guatemala, 1996, Diverse Works, Houston, 1996, Ft. Worth Contemporary Art Ctr., 1998, Webb Gallery, Waxahachie, Tex., 1998, McKinney Ave. Contemporary, Dallas, 1999, Hallwalls, Buffalo, N.Y., 1999, Arlington Mus. of Art, 1999, Barry Whistler Gallery, Dallas, 1999, SF Camerawork, San Francisco, 2000, Art League Houston, 2000, Pixxelpoint, Nova Gorica, Slovenia, 2002, Dallas Video Festival, 2002, Ky. State U., 2002, Tex. Tech. U., 2003; prodr. video Videokronografy, 1996. Grantee Artists Space, 1987, Pollock Krasner Found., 1989; tchg. fellow U. North Tex., 1984-88. Mem. Coll. Art Assn. Home: 1319 Avenue N Huntsville TX 77340-4435 E-mail: mhenderson@shsu.edu.

HENDERSON, MILTON ARNOLD, professional society administrator; b. Chattanooga, June 22, 1922; s. Milton Arnold and Margaret (Rawlings) H.; m. Joyce Crowder (dec. Nov. 13, 1977); children: George, Linda, Philip.; m. Betty Ann Harnage, Aug. 20, 1982. BS, Northwestern U., 1948. Asst. sales mgr. Coca-Cola Bottling Co., Savannah and Macon, Ga., 1948—54; with Gideons Internat., Chgo., 1954-63, field rep., 1954-55, promotion mgr., 1955-56, with Nashville, 1964—, exec. dir., 1956-87, exec. dir. emeritus, 1987—. Editor The Gideon Mag., Gideon Info. Bull., Gideon News Brief, 1956-87; author: Sowers of the Word, a 95-Year History of The Gideons International, 1899-1994, 1995; attended Gideon convs. and meetings in 74 countries, 1956—. 1st lt. USAAF, 1942-46; capt. USAF, 1951-52. Recipient Community Leader of Am. award, 1969, Personalities of the South award, 1975, Disting. Alumnus award Howe Mil. Sch., Ind., 1985. Mem. Am. Mgmt. Assn., Nashville City Club. Republican. Presbyterian. Home: 2524 Stones River Ct Nashville TN 37214-1425

HENDERSON, RALPH HALE, physician; b. N.Y.C., Mar. 5, 1937; s. Ralph Ernest and Clifford West (Sellers) H.; m. Ilze Sarma, May 21, 1966. AB, Harvard U., 1959, MD, 1963, MPH, 1970, M.Pub. Policy, 1972. Intern, then resident in internal medicine Boston City Hosp., 1963-65; joined USPHS, 1965, capt., 1973-81, asst. surgeon gen., 1981-90, svc. in, 1965-69. Asst. chief venereal disease br., state and cmty. svcs. divsn. Ctrs. Disease Control, Atlanta, 1972-73; dir. venereal disease control divsn. Bur. State Svcs., 1973-76; program mgr. expanded program on immunization WHO, Geneva, 1977-78, dir. expanded program immunization, 1979-89, asst. dir. gen., 1990-98, spl. advisor to dir. gen., 1998-99; Lilly lectr. Royal Coll. Physicians, 1989; lectr. disting. lecture series Baylor Coll. Medicine, 1995. Contbr. to med. publs. Trustee Dermatology Found., 1975-77. Recipient Commendation medal USPHS, 1969, Meritorius Svc. medal, 1984, Disting. Svc. medal, 1990, Donald MacKay Meml. medal Royal Soc. Tropical Medicine and Hygiene, 1990, Internat. Child Survival award U.S. Com. UNICEF and the Task Force for Child Survival and Devel., 1992, Ann. Pub. Health Forum award London Sch. of Hygiene and Tropical Medicine, 1994. Mem. Am. Coll. Preventive Medicine. Home: 1098 Mcconnell Dr Decatur GA 30033-3402

HENDERSON, RITA ELIZABETH, literary agent, journalist; b. Bitburg, German, Mar. 7, 1964; came to U.S., 1964; d. Walter Wanzley and Lola Bell (Boles) H.; adopted children: Christopher Allan Jackson, Kayla Elizabeth Octavia Davis. AAS, Camden County Coll., Blackwood, N.J., 1984; BS, Glassboro (N.J.) State Coll., 1987. Owner Henderson Lit. Representation, Sicklerville, N.J., 1994—; real estate agt. Weichert Realtors, Medford, N.J., 1998—. Author: The Boyz II Men Success Story: Defying the Odds, 1995; entertainment writer The N.Y. Amsterdam News, 1991-95, The Phila. Tribune, 1993-95. Democrat. Roman Catholic. Avocations: music, archery, antique collecting, baseball, computers. Office: Weichert Realtors 107 Taunton Blvd Medford NJ 08055-3400

HENDERSON, ROBB ALAN, minister; b. Wilkes Barre, Pa., Mar. 21, 1956; s. Robert Alan and Mary (Gallup) H.; m. Norma Jean Davis, Nov. 26, 1994; children: Jason Allyn, Gareth Kent. BA in Theology, King's Coll., Wilkes Barre, 1981; MDiv, Lancaster Theol. Sem., 1985; D Ministry, Bethany Theol. Sem., 1990. Ordained to ministry United Meth. Ch. as deacon, 1986, as elder, 1988; ordained into So. Episc. Ch., 1997. Pastor Luzerne (Pa.) United Meth. Ch., 1985-88, Carverton United Meth. Ch., Wyoming, Pa., 1988—93, St. Paul's United Meth. Ch., Scranton, Pa., 1993-94, So. Episcopal Ch. of Wyoming Valley, 2000—. Owner R&R Bus Line, Luzerne, 1990—; chmn. interreligious and ecumenical affairs com. Coun. of Chs., 1989—; bd. dirs. Wyoming Valley Coun. of Chs.; safety dir., dispatcher First Class Coach Co., St. Petersburg, Fla. Chaplain Mt. Zion Vol. Fire Dept., Mt. Zion, Harding, Pa. Mem. Masons (chaplain Kingston lodge 1989), Irem Temple. Home and Office: 230 Harland St Exeter PA 18643 E-mail: marauder-robb@juno.com.

HENDERSON, ROBERTA MARIE, librarian, educator; b. Mosinee, Wis., July 27, 1929; d. Roy H. and Marie Helena (Dittman) H. BS, Ctrl. State Tchrs. Coll., Stevens Point, Wis., 1951; MS, U. Wis., 1958; MA, No. Mich. U., 1975; Cert. of Adv. Studies, U. Denver, 1980. Librarian Wiesbaden (Ger.) Am. High Sch., 1954-55, Ashland (Wis.) High Sch., 1955-56; tchr./librarian Clark AFB, Philippines, 1956-57; librarian Prescott (Ariz.) Jr. High Sch., 1958-59, Frankfurt (Ger.) Am. High Sch., 1959-63; tchr./librarian Zama Am. High Sch., Camp Zama, Japan, 1963-66; librarian Ankara (Turkey) Am. High Sch., 1966-68; tutor Nkozi Tchr. Tng. Coll., Mpigi, Uganda, 1968-70; ref. librarian/prof. No. Mich. U., Marquette, 1971-93; retired, 1993; cons. No. Mich. U. and Pub. Librs., 1993—. Coord. faculty workshops No. Mich. U., 1986-88; cons. Escanaba (Mich.) Pub. Libr., 1987, 90, 92. Author slide/tape: Locating Materials in Periodicals and Documents, 1977, Library Materials for Literature Students, 1979. Mem. libr. com. Marquette County Hist. Soc., 1981—; mem. Upper Peninsula Environ. Coalition, Houghton, 1985—; host Marquette-Japan Sister Coalition City Program, 1988, mem. Marquette Sister City adv. bd., 2005—, No. Ctr.Lifelon Learning bd., 2003— Title II-B fellow, U. Denver, 1979-80; Human Resources Dept., No. Mich. U. grantee, 1986, 87; recipient Disting Faculty award No. Mich. U., 1988. Mem. ALA, AAUP, Libr. Instrn. Roundtable, Phi Kappa Phi (chpt. treas. 1987-91), Marquette Century Club, No. Mich. U. Women Avocations: interior decoration, gardening, hiking, cats. Home: 515 E Ridge St Marquette MI 49855-4216

HENDERSON, ROGENE FAULKNER, toxicologist, researcher; b. Breckenridge, Tex., July 13, 1933; d. Philander Molden and Lenoma (Rogers) F.; m. Thomas Richard Henderson II, May 30, 1957; children: Thomas Richard III, Edith Jeanette, Laura Lee. BSBA, Tex. Christian U., 1955; PhD, U. Tex., 1960. Diplomate Am. Bd. Toxicology. Research assoc. U. Ark. Sch. Med., Little Rock, 1960-67; from scientist to sr. scientist and group supr. chemistry and toxicology Lovelace Inhalation Toxicology Research Inst., Albuquerque, 1967—; deputy dir. Nat. Environ. Respiratory Ctr. Lovelace Respiratory Rsch. Inst., Albuquerque, 1998—. Mem. adv. com. Burroughs Wellcome Toxicology Scholar award, 1987-89, NIH toxicology study sect., 1982-86, Nat. Inst. Environ. Health Scis. adv. coun., 1992-95, EPA scientific adv. bd. environ. health commn., 1991-95; mem. bd. sci. counselors EPA, 2002—; mem. Com to Assess the Sci. Base for Tobacco Harm Reduction, adv. group Am. Cancer Soc.on Cancer and the Environment, 1999—, Health Effects Inst. Rsch. Com., 1997—; vice chmn. US Environ. protection Agy. Bd. of Sci. Counselors, 2001—; chair Clean Air Science Adv. Com., 2004—; chmn. clean air sci. adv. com. U.S. Environl. Protection Agy., 2004— Assoc. editor Toxicology Applied Pharmacology, 1989-95, Jour. Exposure Analysis and Environ. Epidemiology, 1991-95; contbr. articles to profl. jours. Named Woman on the Move YWCA, Albuquerque, 1985; grantee NIH, 1958-60, 1960-62, 1986—. Mem. AAAS, NAS (bd. on environ. studies and toxicology 1998—), Am. Chem. Soc. (chmn. ctrl. N.Mex. sect. 1981), Soc. Toxicology (pres. Mountain-West Regional chpt. 1985-86, pres. inhalation specialty sect. 1989—), N.Y. Acad. Scis., Nat. Acad. Scis. (com. toxicology 1985-98, chair 1992-98, com. epidemiology of air pollution 1983-85, com. biol. markers 1986—, com. on risk assessment methodology 1989-92, bd. environ. studies and toxicology 1998—), Nat. Acad. (nat. assoc.) Presbyterian. Home: 5609 Don Felipe Ct SW Albuquerque NM 87105-6765 Office: Lovelace Respiratory Rsch Inst 2425 Ridgecrest Ave SE Albuquerque NM 87108 Office Phone: 505-348-9464. Business E-Mail: rhenders@lrri.org.

HENDERSON, SALATHIEL JAMES, I, minister, clergy; b. Key West, Fla., June 15, 1944; s. James Joseph and Merlice Yvone (McIntosh) H.; m. Mary Louise Henderson, June 28, 1969; children: Salathiel James II, Shane Jamal. Diploma, LaSalle Extension U., 1977; AA, St. Leo U., 1987, BA, 1988, degree in Clin. Pastoral Edn., 2003. Ordained to ministry Bapt. Ch. 1989. Deacon Antioch Bapt. Ch., Hampton, Va., 1980—87, assoc. min., 1987—; vol. chaplain Hospice unit VA Med. Ctr., Hampton, 1987—. Substitute tchr. Hampton City Schs., 1991-95, adminstrv. asst., 1995—; sr. fed. supply cataloger Mason & Hanger Svcs., Inc., NASA/Langley AFB, Va., 1988-91; dir. Christian Edn., Antioch Bapt. Ch., Hampton, 1986-2001, mem. fin. com., 1984-94, spiritual advisor Youth Usher Bd., 1984-90, sec. Ministerial Staff, 1991-94; dir. Bereavement Ministry, Antioch Bapt. Ch., Hampton, 1988; cubmaster Cub Scouts Am., Antioch Bapt.-Hampton, 1990-95; chartered scouting rep. Antioch Bapt., 1995-97; sec. Ministers' Coalition for Hampton and Vicinity, 1992-94, coord. ministerial staff., 2003—; v.p. Ministers' Coalition for Hampton & Vicinity, 1994-98, pres., 1998—; co-founder Jericho Walls Ministry, 2000—. Mem. Hampton U. Min.'s Conf., 1990—; co-chmn. publicity com. Peninsula United Clergy Coun., 1994-96; vol. Am. Heart Assn., 1992—. With USAF, 1962-85. Mem. NAACP (life, cmty. coordination com. Hampton br. 1997-98, chmn. religious affairs 1999—, grad. Hampton Neighborhood Coll. 1999), DAV (life), Am. Assn. Christian Counselors, Masons. Democrat. Home and Office: 607 Allendale Dr Hampton VA 23669-1621 Office Phone: 757-508-3511. E-mail: salathielh@aol.com. *As one views society in its present state, and before an attempt is made to criticize the actions and values of the current generation (our future leaders) it is essential and imperative to carefully scrutinize today's grotesque situations as we focus upon the home and society. I believe our future leaders have many goals, with every hope of attaining them (when afforded the opportunity), but it is necessary that they receive proper mentoring from competent role models. Not just any role model, but one who institutes integrity and ethics, while propelling a greater force toward pride, trustworthiness and a genuine love for God, justice and all of mankind.*

HENDERSON, STANLEY DALE, lawyer, educator; b. Monona, Iowa, June 17, 1935; s. Leon Gilbert and Iva Elizabeth H.; m. DeArliss Garretson, June 15, 1957; children: Lesli Kara, Heidi Elizabeth, Holly Ann. AB, Coe Coll., 1957; postgrad. (Woodrow Wilson fellow), Cornell U., 1957-58; postgrad., U. Chgo. Law Sch., 1958-59; JD, U. Colo., 1961. Bar: Colo. 1961, Va. 1973. Law clk. U.S. Dist. Ct., Denver, 1961-62; mem. firm Williams and Zook, Boulder, Colo., 1962-64; mem. faculty U. Wyo. Coll. Law, 1964-69; prof. law U. Va. Law Sch., Charlottesville, 1970—2004, F.D.G. Ribble prof. law, 1976—2004. Vis. prof. law Ind. U., 1974, Harvard Law Sch., 1978-79, Pepperdine U., 1992-93. Author: Labor Law; author: (with Dawson and Harvey) Contracts; author: (with Meltzer) Labor Law; contbr. articles to profl. jours. Mem. Va. State Bar, Am. Law Inst., Am. Arbitration Assn., Order of Coif, Phi Beta Kappa, Phi Kappa Phi. Democrat. Presbyterian. Home: 1615 King Mountain Rd Charlottesville VA 22901-3003 Office: U Va Sch Law Charlottesville VA 22901 Office Phone: 434-924-3522. Business E-Mail: sdh6k@virginia.edu.

HENDERSON, STANLEY ELWOOD, academic administrator, consultant; b. Peoria, Ill., Jan. 13, 1947; s. Francis Wilford and Evelyn Mae Henderson; m. Diane Denise Matthews, Apr. 4, 1970; children: Derek Eaton, Duncan Timothy, Daniel Reining. BA with High Honor, Mich. State U., 1969; MA, Cornell U., 1971. Admissions counselor Mich. State U., East Lansing, 1970—71; dir. admissions Wichita State U., Kans., 1971—84; dir. enrollment mgmt. and admissions Western Mich. U., Kalamazoo, 1984—95; assoc. v.p. enrollment mgmt. U. Cin., 1995—2003; assoc. provost enrollment mgmt. U. Ill., Urbana, 2003—. Enrollment mgmt. cons. Bell-Trice Enterprises, Washington, 2003—; admissions cons. Michael Dolence Assocs., Claremont, Calif., 1993—95; enrollment mgmt. cons. pvt. practice, Champaign, 1990—. Co-author: ACT/APP and Other Admissions Uses of the ACT Assessment Program, Good Users of ACT Data and Services; editor: The Admissions Profession: A Guide to Staff Development and Program Management; co-editor: Handbook for the College Admissions Profession; contbr. articles to profl. jours., chapters to books. Vice chair Minorities Math., Sci., and Engring., Cin., 2001—03; academic resource coord. Gates Millenium Scholarship Program, Washington, 2000—03; developer and presenter of college-planning seminars for students and parents Personal Profl. Activity (gratis), 1995—2003, developer and presenter of coll. planning seminars for students and parents Kalamazoo, developer and presenter of coll. planning seminars for parents and students Wichita, Kans., 1974—84. Recipient Leadership Kans., Kans. C. of C., 1985; fellow, U. Ill., Urbana-Champaign, 1976—77; grantee, Cornell U., 1969—70; scholar, Nat. Merit Scholarship Corp., 1965. Mem.: Coll. Bd. (instl. rep. 1984—2003), Nat. Assn. Coll. Admission Counseling, Am. Assn. Collegiate Registrars and Admissions Officers (v.p. enrollment mgmt., admissions, and fin. 1990—93, pres. elect 1994—95, pres. 1995—96, past pres. 1996—97), Phi Beta Kappa, Omicron Delta Kappa, Kappa Delta Pi, Phi Delta Kappa, Phi Kappa Phi. Achievements include development of Co-creator of national enrollment management conference now in its 14th year; Keynote address at national Enrollment Planners Conference, 1995; Closing Plenary at SEM XI Enrollment Management Conference, 2001; Plenary Speaker National Enrollment Management Institute, 2003; Co-principal Presenter, Symposium on US Universities, Taipei, Taiwan; Principal Workshop Participant, Association of University Administrators, United Kingdom. Avocations: american presidents, travel, food. Office: University of Illinois at Urbana-Champai 901 West Illinois Street Urbana IL 61801 Office Phone: 217-333-2034.

HENDERSON, STEPHEN PAUL, lawyer; b. Oakland, Calif., July 14, 1949; s. Carl Edward and Esther Minnie (Miller) Henderson; m. Josephine Ann Bartlett; children: Catherine Anne, Lauren Elizabeth. BA, Wash. State U., 1971; JD, U. Oreg., 1974. Bar: Oreg. 1974, Ohio 1979, U.S. Ct. Mil. Appeals 1978, U.S. Tax Ct. 1979, U.S. Ct. Appeals (9th cir.) 1979, U.S. Ct. Appeals (6th cir.) 1990, U.S. Supreme Ct. 1979. Atty. GE Credit Corp., Providence, 1979-81; dept. counsel GE, Schenectady, N.Y., 1981-83, operation counsel Atlanta, 1983-86, divsn. counsel, 1987-89, GE Aircraft Engines, Cin., 1990-97; gen. counsel GE Engine Svcs., Inc., Cin., 1998—. Editor U. Oreg. Law Rev., 1972-73. 2d lt. inf. U.S. Army, 1971, capt. JAGC U.S. Army, 1974—79. Nat. Merit scholar, 1967. Mem.: ABA, Phi Eta Sigma, Fed. Bar Assn., Corp. Counsel Assn. of Atlanta Bar Assn., Cin. Bar Assn., Ohio Bar Assn., Oreg. Bar Assn., Phi Kappa Phi, Phi Beta Kappa. Democrat. Roman Catholic. Office: GE 1 Neumann Way F125 Cincinnati OH 45215-1915 Office Phone: 513-243-8251. Business E-Mail: stephen.p.henderson@ae.ge.com.

HENDERSON, TERRY DEAN, secondary school educator; b. Plainview, Tex., Nov. 22, 1963; s. Ronald S. and Freda L. Henderson; m. Gail M. Henderson; children: C.J., Cody. BA in Exercise Physiology & Leisure Sci., Adams State Coll., 1990; MA in Tchg. Integrated Natural Scis., Colo. Coll., 2000. Cert. secondary tchr., Colo., 1990. Biology and chemistry tchr., head sci. dept. Ellicott Sch. Dist. #22, Calhan, Colo., 1990—2005, head varsity boys track and field coach, 1991—2001, 2004, head football coach, 2000—03; athletic dir., bus. mgr. Wasson H.S., Colorado Springs, Colo., 2005—. Mem. Colo. H.S. Coaches Assn. (10 yr. svc. cert. football coaching 2000, track 2001). Republican. Avocations: outdoor activities, sporting events. Office: Wasson HS 2115 Afton Way Colorado Springs CO 80909 E-mail: torghenderson@hotmail.com.

HENDERSON, THELTON EUGENE, federal judge; b. Shreveport, La., Nov. 28, 1933; s. Eugene M. and Wanzie (Roberts) H.; 1 son, Geoffrey A. BA, U. Calif.-, Berkeley, 1956, JD, 1962. Bar: Calif. 1962. Social case worker County of Los Angeles, 1958; jr. rsch. scientist Sys. Devel. Corp., Santa Monica, Calif., 1958—59; atty. U.S. Dept. Justice, 1962-63; assoc. firm FitzSimmons & Petris, 1964, assoc., 1964-66; directing atty. San Mateo County (Calif.) Legal Aid Soc., 1966-69; asst. dean Stanford (Calif.) U. Law Sch., 1968-76; ptnr. firm Rosen, Remcho & Henderson, San Francisco, 1977-80; judge U.S. Dist. Ct. (no. dist.) Calif., San Francisco, 1980-90, 98—, chief judge, 1990-97. Asso. prof. Sch. Law, Golden Gate U., San Francisco, 1978-80 Bd. mem. Rosenberg Found. Served with U.S. Army, 1956-58. Recipient Bernard Witkin Medal, State Bar of Calif., 2004, Pearlstein Civil Rights award, Anti-Defamation League. Bd. mem. Am. Inns of Ct. (Professionalism award, 9th cir., mem. exec. com. Edward J. McFetridge Inn of Ct.); mem. ABA, Am. Law Inst., Fed. Judges Assn., Nat. Bar Assn. (Disting. Svc. award), Charles Houston Law Assn. Office: US Dist Ct US Courthouse PO Box 36060 San Francisco CA 94102

HENDERSON, THOMAS EMMETT, retired educator, antiquarian bookseller and publisher; b. Middletown, N.Y., Aug. 17, 1934; s. Thomas O'Connor and Elsie Eleanor Henderson; m. Barbara Lynn Meade; stepchildren: Ralph Courtney, Donald Courtney, Guy Courtney, Robert Lynn; m. Florence Cosgrove Tomlins (div. May 6, 1981); children: Lisa, Bruce, Samuel 1 stepchild, Mark Boujikian. BS, SUNY, 1958; MS (magna cum laude), U. Albany, 1979. Permanent tchg. cert. N.Y., 1958, lic. real estate salesperson N.Y., 1989, life and health insurance N.Y., 1992. Owner Quality Book Svc., Middletown, NY, 1954—2004; English tchr. N.Y. Dept. of Correctional Svcs., Fishkill, NY, 1962—89; owner T. Emmett Henderson, Publ. House, Middletown, NY, 1969—79; instr. Dutchess Cmty. Coll., Poughkeepsie, NY, 1979—81, Mercy Coll., Dobbs Ferry, NY, 1983—95; assoc. prof. English Sullivan County Cmty. Coll., Loch Sheldrake, NY, 1990—2003. Founder, dir Middletown Exptl. Coll. Assn., Middletown, 1975—79. Pres. Vanburenville Sch. Preservation Soc., Pine Bush, 1970—75; bd. dirs. Middletown and Waalkill Precinct Hist. Soc., 1963—78; chairperson Employee Assistance Program, Fishkill, 1984—89. With Res. Officers Tng. Corp. USAF, 1952—54. Recipient One Idea Ahead of its Time, Atlantic Richfield Corp., 1974, Cert. Appreciation, Port Jervis Antique Study Club. Home: 130 W Main St Middletown NY 10940 Office: Quality Book Svc 130 W Main St Middletown NY 10940 Office Phone: 845-343-1038. Office Fax: 845-344-4866. Business E-Mail: booker@frontiernet.net.

HENDERSON, THOMAS HENRY, JR., lawyer, former legal association executive; b. Birmingham, Ala., Feb. 4, 1939; s. Thomas Henry and Edna (Green) H.; m. Elaine Dauphin (div. 1983); children: Ashley, Michelle; m. Paulette Maehara, June 1988. BSBA, Auburn U., 1961; JD, U. Ala., 1966; LLM, Nat. Law Ctr., George Washington U., 1987. Bar: D.C. 1970, Ala. 1966. Trial atty. organized crime and racketeering sect. U.S. Dept. Justice, Washington, 1966-70, dep. sect. chief mgmt. labor sect., 1970-73; dep. chief counsel, subcom. on adminstrn. practice and procedure U.S. Senate, Washington, 1973-74; dep. sect. chief mgmt. and labor sect. Dept. Justice, Washington, 1974-76, chief pub. integrity sect., 1976-80, sr. counsel criminal divsn., 1980-83; bar counsel D.C. Ct. Appeals, Washington, 1983-87; CEO ATLA, Washington, 1988—2005, ret., 2005—. Columnist Bar Counsels Page, Washington Lawyer mag., bi-monthly, 1983-87. Pres. Christmas in April, Washington, 1986-87. Named Disting. Practitioner of Law, U. Ala.

Law Sch., 2004; recipient Justic Howell Heflin award, ATLA, 2004. Mem. Am. Soc. Assn. Execs. (bd. dirs. 1994-97, vice chair 1997-98, Key award 2003), Omicron Delta Kappa. Avocations: golf, skiing, exercise, outdoor adventure.

HENDERSON, VICTOR WARREN, behavioral and geriatric neurologist, epidemiologist, researcher, educator; s. Philip S. and N. Jean (Edsel) H.; m. Barbara Ann Curtiss; children: Gregory, Geoffrey, Stephanie, Nicole. BS, U. Ga., 1972; MD, Johns Hopkins U., 1976; MS, U. Wash., 1996. Diplomate Am. Bd. Psychiatry and Neurology. Intern Duke U., Durham, NC, 1976—77; resident Washington U., St. Louis, 1977—80; fellow Boston U., 1980—81; asst. prof. neurology U. So. Calif., LA, 1981—86, assoc. prof. neurology, gerontology & psychology, 1986—93, prof. neurology, gerontology & psychology, 1993—2001, chief divsn. cognitive neurosci. & neurogerontology, 1989—2001, Kenneth and Bette Volk prof. neurology, 1999—2001; prof. geriat., neurology, pharmacology and epidemiology U. Ark. Med. Scis., Little Rock, 2001—04, vice chair dept. geriat., 2001—04; prof. health rsch. and policy and neurology and neurological scis. Stanford (Calif.) U., 2004—, dir. grad. program in epidemiology, 2004—. Dir. NIH Alzheimer's Disease Rsch. Ctr. Clin. Core, 1985—2001; dir. neurobehavior Clinic/Bowles Ctr. for Alzheimer's and Related Diseases, 1988—2001; chair neurology svc. LA County, U. So. Calif. Med. Ctr., 1992—97; vis. scientist MIT, 1988—89; vis. prof. U. Melbourne, 2002; co-dir. State of Calif. Alzheimer's Disease Rsch. Ctr. U. So. Calif., 1999—2001, NIH Alzheimer's Disease Ctr., 2001—03; Kearney vis. prof. Mental Health Rsch. Inst. Victoria, Australia, 2002; dir. Rural Aging and Memory Study, 2001—; prof. fellow dept. psychiatry U. Melbourne, 2003—; assoc. chief of staff geriat. and extended care Ctrl. Ark. Vets. Healthcare Sys., 2003—04; lectr. and spkr. in field. Author: (with others) Principles of Neurologic Diagnosis, 1985, Hormone Therapy and the Brain, 2000; mem. editl. bd. profl. jours.; contbr. articles to profl. jours. Recipient Simons Lecture, Alzheimer's Assn. (Boston chpt.), 1995, Solvay Lecture, British Menopause Soc., 1997, Rsch. award, Alzheimer's Assn. (LA chpt.), 1998, Faculty Recognition award, Phi Kappa Phi, 2001, Vis. Rsch. Scholars award, U. Melbourne Collaborative Research Program, 2002; grantee, Alzheimer's Assn., Calif. Dept. Health Svcs., Adminstrn. on Aging, NIH, French Found., 1984—. Fellow: Am. Acad. Neurology; mem.: N.Am. Menopause Soc. (trustee 2002—), French Found. Alzheimer Rsch., Nat. Aphasia Assn., World Fedn. Neurology, Internat. Menopause Soc., Internat. Neuropsychol. Soc., Soc. for Behavioral and Cogntive Neurology, Gerontol. Soc. Am., Acad. Aphasia, Am. Neurol. Assn. Office: Stanford U Sch Medicine 259 Campus Dr HRP Redwood Bldg Stanford CA 94305-5405

HENDERSON, WADE J., civil rights advocate, law educator; b. 1948; BA, Howard Univ.; JD, Rutgers Univ., Newark. Bar: DC, NJ, US Supreme Ct. Asst. dean & dir. minority affairs Rutgers Univ. Sch. Law; exec. dir. Council on Legal Edn. Opportunity; assoc. dir. nat. office ACLU, Washington; dir. Washington Bureau NAACP; exec. dir. & counsel to Edn. Fund Leadership Conf. on Civil Rights, Washington; Joseph L. Rauh Jr. Prof. Pub. Interest Law David A. Clarke Sch. Law, Univ. of DC, 1999—. Recipient Civil Rights Leadership award, Israeli Embassy & Religious Action Ctr Reform Judaism, 1999, Everett C. Parker award, United Church of Christ, William J. Brennan award, DC Bar, 2002, Cong. Black Caucus Chair award, 2003. Office: Leadership Conference on Civil Rights 10th Fl 1629 K St NW Washington DC 20006 Office Phone: 202-466-3311.*

HENDERSON, WILLIAM CHARLES, editor; b. Phila., Apr. 5, 1941; s. Francis Louis and Dorothy Price (Galloway) H. BA, Hamilton Coll., 1963; postgrad., Harvard U., 1963, U. Pa., 1965-66. Assoc. editor Doubleday & Co., N.Y.C., 1972-73; pub. Pushcart Press, Wainscott, N.Y., 1972—; sr. editor Coward, McCann & Geohagan, Inc., N.Y.C., 1973-75; cons. editor Harper & Row Inc., 1976—. Guest lectr. Harvard U., summer 1974, Sarah Lawrence Coll., U. Rochester, summers 1978, 87; lectr. Columbia U., 1978-80, Princeton U., 1984, 86, 87, Johns Hopkins U., 1989, Radcliffe Pub. Course, 1989; mem. nat. adv. bd. Ctr. for the Book Library of Congress, 1979; pres. Pushcart Found.; fiction judge Nat. Book Award, 2001. Author: His Son: A Child of the Fifties, 1981, The Kid That Could, 1990, Her Father, 1995, Tower, 2000; editor, pub.: The Publish It Yourself Handbook, 1973, The Pushcart Prize: Best of the Small Presses, 1976—, The Pushcart Book of Short Stories, 2002; editor: Rotten Reviews, 1986, Minutes of the Lead Pencil Club, 1996. Recipient Author award N.J. English Tchrs. Assn., 1972; Newsboy award Horatio Alger Soc., 1973, Carey-Thomas award, 1978, Poor Richard award, 2001. Mem. P.E.N., The Lead Pencil Club (founder). Home and Office: Pushcart Press PO Box 380 Wainscott NY 11975-0380

HENDERSON HALL, BRENDA FORD, computer company executive; d. Frances Long and Johnny Dell Ford, William Alfred Randall; m. Joseph Aubrey N/A, Jan. 1, 2001. BSc, U. of NC, 1974—81, MBA, 1982—85. Six Sigma Green Belt 2003. Bookkeeper, transit operator Wachovia Bank, Wilmington, NC, 1968—73; cost acctg. technician, staff reliever E I du Pont de Nemours and Co., Inc., Wilmington, NC, 1973—86; acctg. instr. Shaw U., Wilmington, NC, 1985—86; systems engr. Electronic Data Systems, Dallas, 1986—87; edp mgr. Potomac Savs. Bank, Silver Spring, Md., 1987—88; v.p. Fin. Comm. Sys. Services Inc., Clinton, Md., 1987—89; sr. systems analyst The Maxima Corp., Lanham, Md., 1988—94; adj. acctg. instr. Prince George CC, Largo, Md., 1990—93; pres. Your Efficient Tax Service, Oxon Hill, Md., 1992—93; sr. mem. of the tech. staff Computer Sciences Corp., Falls Church, Va., 1994—95; account mgr., developer, analyst The Maxim Group, Reston, Va., 1995—97; prin. cons. Computer Sciences Corp., Falls Church, Va., 1997—2002; team leader, developer, analyst The Maxim Group, Reston, Va., 1997; sr. mem. of the exec. staff Computer Sciences Corp., Lanham, Md., 2002—04, acct. exec. - fed. sector, 2003—04, sr. cons. engr. Annapolis Junction, Md., 2004—. Charter mem. Williston Alumni Assn., Wilmington, NC, 1974—78; pres. -master of bus. adminstrn. assn. U. of NC, 1983—85; bd. mem. DuPont's Cape Fear Employees' Credit Union, Wilmington, NC, 1979—80; charter mem. nat. assn. of accountants U. of NC, 1980—81. D-Liberal. Baptist. Achievements include facilitated the effort that resulted in the achievement of the first software acquisition capability maturity model level 3 rating. Avocations: travel, swimming, reading, philanthropic activities, writing. Office: Computer Scis Corp 2711 Technology Dr Annapolis Junction MD 20701 Personal E-mail: bhall540@comcast.net. E-mail: bhall25@csc.com.

HENDIN, BARRY ALLEN, physician; b. St. Louis, Apr. 23, 1942; s. Gus and Lillian (Shanker) H.; m. Rita Ellen Scissors, Aug. 2, 1964; children: Julie ann Hendin Thikoll, Lori Beth Hendin Travis, Holly Hendin. AB, Washington U., St. Louis, 1964, MD, 1968. Intern Jewish Hosp., St. Louis, 1968-69; resident in neurology Washington U., 1969-72, instr., 1972; clin. lectr. U. Ariz., 1988-95, clin. prof. of neurology, 1995—. Chief neurology svc. Good Samaritan Med. Ctr., Phoenix, 1979—, chmn. Divsn. Neuroscis., 1991-92, vice chief of staff, 1993-95; bd. dirs. Samaritan Health Systems, 1995-2000, Banner Health, 2000—. Contbr. articles to profl. jours. Mem. Gov.'s Coun. on Head and Spinal Cord Injuries, Ariz. State Govt., Phoenix, 1994, 95; Maj. USAF, 1972-74. Fellow Am. Acad. Neurology; mem. Maricopa County Med. Soc., Royal Soc. of Medicine. Office: Phoenix Neurol Assocs 1331 N 7th St # 350 Phoenix AZ 85006

HENDIN, DAVID BRUCE, literary agent, writer, numismatist, educator; b. St. Louis, Dec. 16, 1945; s. Aaron and Lillian (Karsh) H.; m. Jeannie Luciano, Oct. 4, 1985; children: Sarah Tsvia, Benjamin Judah, Alexander Jacob. BS in Biology Edn, U. Mo., 1967, MA in Journalism, 1970. Sr. v.p., editorial dir., pub. United Media Inc., N.Y.C., 1970-93; clin. prof. off campus U. Mo. Sch. Journalism, 1971-86; pres. Pharos Books, 1992-3, DH Literary, Inc., Nyack, N.Y., 1993—. Adj. lectr. Columbia U. Sch. Journalism, 1974-76; numismatist Joint Sepphoris Excavation, 1985-88. Author: Everything You Need to Know About Abortion, 1971, The Doctor's Save-Your-Heart Diet, 1972, Death As a Fact of Life, 1973, 1984, Save Your Child's Life, 1973, 86, The Life Givers, 1975, Guide to Ancient Jewish Coins, 1975, The World Almanac Whole Health Guide, 1977, The Genetic Connection, 1978, Collecting Coins, 1979, Guide to Biblical Coins, 1987, 96, 2000, Not Kosher: Forgeries of Ancient Jewish and Biblical Coins, 2004; mem. editl. bd. Israel Numismatic Jour., 1992-96, Publs. Bd. Union of Am. Hebrew Congregations, 1993. Bd. dirs. Holyland Conservation Fund, 1973-83; v.p. Council Advancement Sci. Writing, 1975-84; trustee Scripps-Howard Found., 1978-87, Kinsey Inst., 1985-92, Mus. Cartoon Art, 1986-92; chmn. numis. com. The Jewish Mus., 1980-85; mem. adv. com. Sch. Journalims, U. Fla., 1991-97. Recipient award merit Am. Assn. Blood Banks, 1972, Claude Bernard Sci. Journalism award, 1972, cert. commendation Am. Acad. Family Physicians, 1973, Med. Journalism award AMA, 1973, Blakeslee award Am. Heart Assn., 1973, Book of Yr. award Am. Med. Writers Assn., 1977, Best Column award Numismatic Literary Guild, 1993, 2000, Ben Odesser Judaic Literary award 1997, Disting. Alumni award Ladue H.S., 2002, Pres. award Am. Numismatic Assn., 2003. Fellow Am. Numismatic Soc.; mem. Coun. for Advancement Sci. Writing, Am.-Israel Numismatic Assn. (v.p. 1979-85), Kappa Tau Alpha, Sigma Alpha Mu. Office: PO Box 805 Nyack NY 10960-0990 E-mail: dhendin@aol.com.

HENDIN, HERBERT, psychiatrist, researcher; b. NYC, Oct. 10, 1926; s. Louis and Pauline Hendin; m. Josephine Gattuso, June 7, 1968; children: Neil, Erik. BA, Columbia U., 1945; MD, NYU, 1949; degree in psychoanalytic medicine, Columbia U., 1959. Cert. N.Y., lic. psychiatry Am. Bd. of Neurology and Psychiatry. From asst. to assoc. prof. of psychiatry Columbia U., N.Y.C., 1960—78; dir. Posttraumatic Stress Disorder (PTSD) rsch. and treatment program VA Hosp., Montrose, NY, 1978—83; dir. Ctr. for Psychosocial Studies N.Y. Med. Coll., Valhalla, NY, 1983—87. Chair search com. for chief of psychiatry VA Hosp., Montrose, NY, 1981—82; mem. editl. bd. Suicide and Life-Threatening Behavior, N.Y.C., 1996—. Author: (book) Suicide and Scandinavia: A Psychoanalytic Study of Culture and Character, 1964; co-author: Psychoanalysis and Social Rsch.: The Psychoanalytic Study of the Non-Patient, 1966; author: Black Suicide, 1966, The Age of Sensation, 1975; co-author: (monograph) Adolescent Marijuana Abusers and their Families, 1981, (book) Wounds of War: The Psycho-logical Aftermath of Combat in Vietnam, 1984, Living High: Daily Marijuana Use in Adults, 1987; author: Suicide in Am., 1995, Seduced by Death: Doctors, Patients, and Assisted-Suicide, 1998; co-author (book) The Clin. Sci. of Suicide Prevention, 2001, The Case Against Assisted Suicide: For the Right to End of Life Care, 2002. Pres. 1045 Pk. Ave Coop., N.Y.C., 1988—96, Columbia U. Tennis Ctr., N.Y.C., 1970—97. Lt. USPH, 1949—50. Recipient Disting. Rschr. award, Gralnick Found., 1962, Original Rsch. award, Assn. for Psychoanalytic Medicine, 1963, Yearly Lectureship award, Chgo. Inst. for Psychoanalysis, 1966, Louis Dublin award, Am. Assn. of Suicidology, 1982, Langer award, Psychohistory Rev., 1984, Scholar in Residence award, Rockefeller Found., 1994. Fellow: Am.-Scandinavian Found. (hon.); mem.: Intern. Assoc. Suicide Prevent., Intern. Acad. for Suicide Rsch., Am. Found. for Suicide Prevention (pres. 1987—88, dir. nat. suicide data bank project 1988, exec. dir. 1988—97, med. dir. 1998—), Am. Assn. of Suicidology (Louis Dublin award 1982), Assn. for Psychoanalytic Medicine (dir. 1978—81, Original Rsch. award 1963), Am. Psychoanalytic Assn., Am. Psychiat. Assn., US Pub. Health Svc. (Lt. 1949—50), Coop. (pres., 1045 Pk. Ave., NYC 1988—96), Columbia U. Tennis Ctr. (pres., NYC 1970—97). Avocations: tennis, American and Greek civilization history, painting and art history, opera, Shakespeare's plays. Office: AFSP 22d Fl 120 Wall St New York NY 10005 also: Ste 3C 1045 Pk Ave New York NY 10028 E-mail: hhendin@afsp.org.

HENDIN, JOSEPHINE GATTUSO, language educator, writer; m. Herbert Hendin, June 7, 1968; children: Neil, Erik. BA, CCNY, 1960—64; MA, Columbia U., 1964—65, PhD, 1964—68. Asst. prof. Yale U., New Haven, 1968—69; adj. prof. New Sch. Social Rsch., New York, 1969—79; prof. NYU, 1979—, tiro a segno prof. italian am. studies, 2001—. Author: The Right Thing to Do (Am. Book award, 1989), Vulnerable People: A View of American Fiction Since 1945, 1978 (Notable Book Yr., 1978), Heartbreakers: Women and Violence in Contemporary Culture and Literature, 2004, The World of Flannery O'Connor, 1970; contbr. The Bostonians, articles to profl. jours.; editor: Concise Companion to Postwar American Literature and Culture, 2004. Dir., expository writing program NYU, 1983, chair, English dept., 1995—99. Recipient Elena Lucrezia Cornaro Award, Nat. Order Sons and Daughters Columbus, 1983-1984, Am. Book Award, Before Columbus Found., 1989; fellow Woodrow Wilson Fellowship, Woodrow Wilson Found., 1964-1966, Vera B. David Fellowship, Columbia U., 1965-1966, President's Fellowship, 1967-1968, John Simon Guggenheim Fellowship, John Simon Guggenheim Found., 1975-1976. Mem.: MLA, Nat. Book Critics Cir., Am. Italian Hist. Assn. (mem. exec. bd. 2001), Nat. Italian Am. Found. Avocations: speedwalking, travel, reading. Office: NYU English Dept 19 University Pl New York NY 10003 Personal E-mail: josephine.hendin@nyu.edu.

HENDL, WALTER, conductor, composer, musician; b. West New York, N.J., Jan. 12, 1917; s. William and Ella (Wittig) H.; m. Barbara Heisley; 1 dau by previous marriage, Susan. Pvt. study piano with, David Saperton; with, Clarence Adler, 1934-37; pvt. study conducting with, Fritz Reiner; faculty, Sarah Lawrence Coll., 1939-41, Curtis Inst. Music, 1937-41; MusD (hon.), Cin. Coll. Music, 1954; LHD (hon.), Edinboro U. Pa., 1990. Dir. Eastman Sch. Music, Rochester, N.Y., 1964-72; prof. conducting D'Angelo Sch. Music Mercy Hurst Coll., Erie, Pa., 1990-94. Active as condr. and pianist, Berkshire Music Center, 1941-42, asst. condr., pianist, N.Y. Philharmonic 1945-49, mus. dir., Dallas Symphony, 1949-58, Chautauqua (N.Y.) Symphony Orch., 1953-74, asso. condr., Chgo. Symphony Orch., 1958-64, mus. dir., Ravinia (Ill.) Festival, 1959-63; orchestral dir., Erie (Pa.) Philharm., 1976-89, condr. emeritus, 1989—; guest condr. in Europe, USSR, S. Am., Japan, Asia; also recs.; composer: Broadway prodn. Dark of the Moon, 1945, A Village Where They Ring No Bells, Loneliness (recipient Alice M. Ditson award, Columbia 1953).

HENDLER, JAMES ALEXANDER, computer science educator, consultant; b. NYC, Apr. 2, 1957; s. Samuel I. and Marjorie J. (Rosenblum) H.; m. Terry Spring Horowit, June 16, 1985; 1 child, Sharon Horowit-Hendler. BS in Computer Sci., Yale U., 1978; MS in Psychology, So. Meth. U., 1982; ScM in Computer Sci., Brown U., 1983, PhD in Computer Sci., 1986. Instr. dept. computer sci. Wellesley (Mass.) Coll., 1983, 84; lectr. dept. psychology Brown U., Providence, R.I., 1984; asst. prof. computer sci. U. Md., College Park, 1986-92, with Inst. Sys. Rsch., 1988—, with Inst. Advanced Computer Studies, 1988—, head Parallel Understanding Sys. Lab., 1989—, assoc. prof. computer sci., 1992—99, prof. computer sci., 1999—, head, founder Autonomous Mobile Robotics Lab., 1993—2002; dir. semantic web tech. Md. Info. and Network Dynamics Lab., 2001—, dir., 2004—. Vis. scientist Internat. Computer Sci. Inst., Berkeley, Calif., 1989, Australian AI Inst., Melbourne, 1991; vis. rschr. NEC Corp., Miyazaki-dia, Japan, 1992; vis. prof. Bar-Ilan U., Ramat Gan, Israel, 1994, Hebrew U., Jerusalem, 1995-96; cons. Pfizer Pharmaceuticals, Sandwich, Eng., 1984—, Gould Corp., 1984-85, Symbolics, Inc., 1984, Dept. Energy, 1988, Traisys Inc., 1989—, others; program mgr. Def. Advanced Rsch. Project Agy., 1999-2001, chief sci., 2000-01; chief scientist Info. Sys. office Def. Advanced Rsch. Project Agy., 2000—; guest lectr. IBM, 1991. Author: Integrating Marker-passing and Problem Solving: A spreading activation approach to improved choice in planning, 1987; editor: Expert Systems: The User Interface, 1987, Artificial Intelligence Planning Systems: Procs, of First International Conference, 1992, Massively Parallel Artificial Intelligence, 1994, Robots for Kids, 2000, Spinning the Semantic Web, 2003; editor-in-chief IEEE Intelligent Systems, 2004—; bd. rev. Ed. Sci., 2005-; co-editor: Readings in Planning, 1990, Semantic Web Technology, 2001; contbr. numerous articles to profl. jours., chpts. to books. Bd. dirs. Beth Tikva Synagogue, Rockville, Md., 1990, v.p. 1998—; v.p. Tikvat Israel Congregation, 1999—; mem. Inst. for Def. Analysis Def. Sci. Study Group, 1996-97; mem. sci. adv. bd. USAF, 1999. Fulbright fellow Ctr. Internat. Exch. Scholars, 1995, founding Rsch. fellow Kiss Inst. Practical Robotics, 1994; Exceptional Civilian Svc. Medal, U.S.A.F., 2002. Fellow Am. Assn. Artificial Intelligence (chair symposium com. 1993-94, workshop program 1992, conf. com. 2001-05). Democrat. Jewish. Avocations: scuba diving, travel. Office: Univ Md Dept Computer Sci College Park MD 20742-0001 Office Phone: 301-405-2696. Business E-Mail: jah2@cs.umd.edu.

HENDLER, NELSON HOWARD, physician, health facility administrator, director; b. N.Y.C., Aug. 15, 1944; s. Albert and Winifred (Lee) H.; m. Lee Meyerhoff, Oct. 20, 1974; children: Samuel, Alexander, Lindsay, Josepha. BA, Princeton U., 1966; MD, U. Md., 1972, MS, 1974. Diplomate Am. Bd. Psychiatry and Neurology. Resident in psychiatry Johns Hopkins Hosp., Balt., 1975; asst. prof. neurosurgery sch. medicine Johns Hopkins U., 1975—; owner, clin. dir. Mensana Clinic, Stevenson, Md., 1978—; assoc. prof. physiology sch. dental surgery U. Md., 1986—. Pres. Reflex Sympathetic Dystrophy Syndrome of Am., 1995-97; bd. dirs. Lightning Strike Elec. Injury Survivors. Author: Diagnosis and Non-Surgical Management of Chronic Pain, 1981; (with others) Coping with Chronic Pain, 1979; editor Diagnosis and Treatment of Chronic Pain, 1982; contbr. 51 articles and 31 chpts. to books and profl. jours.; co-patentee direct current motor protector, 1972. Bd. dirs. Md. Mental Health Assn., Balt., 1976-78, Balt. Zool. Soc., 1978-85; bd. dirs. Am. Orgn. Rehab. through Tng., 1983—, pres. Balt. chpt.; bd. dirs. Am. Technion Soc., 1980-92, pres. Balt. chpt. Recipient Janet Travell award for outstanding contbr. to pain medicine Am. Acad. Pain Mgmt.; Falk fellow Am. Psychiat. Assn., 1975. Fellow Acad. Psychosomatic Medicine, Am. Psychiatric Assn.; mem. Am. Inst. Stress (v.p. 1978-89), Internat. Soc. for Study of Pain, Am. Acad. Pain Mgmt. (bd. dirs. 2002—, pres.), Am. Pain Found. (bd. dirs. 1997-2001), Israeli Pain Soc. (hon.), Princeton U. Alumni Assn. Md. (bd. dirs., pres.), Princeton Club N.Y.C., Safari Internat. Club, Loch Raven Skeet and Trap Club. Republican. Jewish. Avocations: bird hunting, skeet and trap shooting, fishing, record big game hunter. Office: Mensana Clinic 1718 Greenspring Valley Rd Stevenson MD 21153-0642 Office Phone: 410-653-2403. Personal E-mail: docmelse@aol.com.

HENDLEY, DAN LUNSFORD, retired finance company executive; b. Nashville, Apr. 26, 1938; s. Frank E. and Mattie (Lunsford) H.; m. Patricia Fariss, June 18, 1960; children: Dan Lunsford, Laura Kathleen. BA, Vanderbilt U., 1960; grad., Stonier Grad. Sch. Banking, Rutgers U., 1969; postgrad., Program Mgmt. Devel., Harvard, 1972. With Fed. Res. Bank Atlanta, 1962-73, v.p., officer in charge Birmingham br., 1969-73; v.p., exec. v.p. AmSouth Bancorp, 1973-77; exec. v.p. First Nat. Bank Birmingham, 1976-77, pres., 1977-79, chmn. bd., chief exec. officer, 1979-83; pres., chief operating officer, bd. dirs. Am South Bank, N.A., 1983-90; v.p. bus. affairs Samford U., Birmingham, Ala., 1991-94; ret., 1994. Trustee Children's Hosp., Samford U. With Tenn. Air N.G., 1961-67. Mem. Kiwanis, Mountain Brook Club, Shoal Creek Club, The Club. Baptist. Home: 3258 Dell Rd Birmingham AL 35223-1318 Personal E-mail: dlhendleys@aol.com.

HENDRA, TONY, writer, comedian, actor; b. England; m. Carla Hendra; 3 children. Attended, Cambridge U. Founding editor Nat. Lampoon Mag.; editor Spy Mag., 1993—94. Actor: (films) This Is Spinal Tap, 1984, Jumpin' Jack Flash, 1986, Life with Mikey, 1993, Real Blonde, 1997, Suits, 1999; author: (TV series) That Was the Week That Was, 1962, (screenplays) National Lampoon's Lemmings, 1973, Le Big-Bang, 1984, The Great White Hype, 1996, Not the Bible, 1983, The 90's: A Look Back (with Peter Elbling), 1989, Born to Run Things: An Utterly Unauthorized Biography of George Bush, 1992, The Book of Bad Virtues: A Treasury of Immorality: A Parody, 1994, The GIGAWIT Dictionary of the E-nglish Language, 2000, Father Joe: The Man Who Saved My Soul, 2004.

HENDREN, JIMM LARRY, federal judge; b. 1940; BA, U. Ark., 1964, LLB, 1965. With Little & Enfield, 1968-69; pvt. practice Bentonville, Ark., 1970-77, 79-92; chancellor, probate judge Ark. 16th Chancery Dist., 1977-78; judge US Dist. Ct. (we. dist.) Ark., 1992-96, chief judge, 1997—. Served to lt. comdr. JAGC, USN, 1965-70, USNR, 1970-83. Mem. ABA, Ark. Bar Assn. Office: US Dist Ct PO Box 3487 Fayetteville AR 72702-3487*

HENDREN, ROBERT LEE, JR., academic administrator; b. Reno, Oct. 10, 1925; s. Robert Lee and Aleen (Hill) H.; m. Merlyn Churchill, June 14, 1947; children: Robert Lee IV, Anne Aleen. BA magna cum laude, LLD (hon.), Coll. Idaho; postgrad., Army Univ. Ctr., Oahu, Hawaii. Owner, pres. Hendren's Inc., 1947—; pres. Albertson Coll. Idaho, Caldwell, 1987—. Bd. dirs. 1st Interstate Bank Idaho. Trustee Boise (Idaho) Ind. Sch. Dist., chmn. bd. trustees, 1966; chmn. bd. trustees Coll. Idaho, 1980-84; bd. dirs. Mountain View coun. Boy Scouts Am., Boise Retail Merchants, Boise Valley Indsl. Found., Boise Redevel. Agy., Ada County Marriage Counseling, Ada County Planning and Zoning Com.; chmn. bd. Blue Cross Idaho. Recipient Silver and Gold award U. Idaho, Nat. award Sigma Chi. Mem. Boise C. of C. (pres., bd. dirs.), Idaho Sch. Trustees Assn., Masons, KT, Shriners, Rotary (Paul Harris fellow). Home: 3504 Hillcrest Dr Boise ID 83705-4503 Office: Albertson Coll Idaho 2112 Cleveland Blvd Caldwell ID 83605-4432

HENDRICK, GEORGE, retired English language educator; b. Stephenville, Tex., Mar. 30, 1929; s. Hoyt and Bessie Lea (Sears) H.; m. Willene Lowery, Jan. 21, 1955; 1 dau., Sarah. BA, Tex. Christian U., 1948, MA, 1950; PhD, U. Tex., 1954. Mem. English faculty S.W. Tex. State U., 1954-56, U. Colo., 1956-60; prof. Am. studies J.W. Goethe U., Frankfurt, Germany, 1960-65; prof. U. Ill., Chgo., 1965-67, Urbana, 1967-99, spl. curator Univ. Libr., 1994-97. Author: Katherine Anne Porter, 1965, Henry Salt: Humanitarian Reformer and Man of Letters, 1977, Remembrances of Concord and the Thoreaus, 1977, (with Fritz Oehlschlaeger) Toward the Making of Thoreau's Modern Reputation, 1980, (with Willene Hendrick) On the Frontier: Dr. Hiram Rutherford, 1981, Thoreau Amongst Friends and Philistines, 1982, (with Margaret Sandburg) Ever the Winds of Chance, 1983, the Selected Letters of Mark Van Doren, 1987; (with Willene Hendrick) Katherine Anne Porter, rev. edit., 1988, Fables, Foibles, and Foobles, 1988, (with Willene Hendrick) The Savour of Salt: A Henry Salt Anthology, 1989, To Reach Eternity: The Letters of James Jones, 1989, (with Willene Hendrick) Ham Jones, Antebellum Southern Humorist: An Anthology, 1990, (with Willene Hendrick and Fritz Oehlschlaeger) Salt's Life of Thoreau, 1993, More Rootabagas, 1993, (with Willene Hendrick) Billy Sunday and Other Poems, 1993 (with Nancy Romero) Literary Treasures of the University Library, 1995, (with Willene Hendrick) Selected Poems of Carl Sandburg, 1996, (with Nancy Romero and Maarten van de Guchte) Alvin Langdon Coburn and H.G. Wells: The Photographer and the Novelist, 1997, (with Willene Hendrick) Incidents in the Life of A Slave Girl and A True Tale of Slavery, 1999, (with Barbara Jones and Jean Geil) Learning About Lincoln at the University of Illinois at Urbana-Champaign, 1999, (with Willene Hendrick) Two Slave Rebellions at Sea: The Heroic Slave by Frederick Douglass and Benito Cereno by Herman Melville, 2000, (with Howe and Sackrider) James Jones and the Handy Writers' Colony, 2001, (with Howe and Sackrider) Writings from the Handy Colony, 2001, (with Willene Hendrick) The Creole Mutiny: A Tale of Revolt Aboard A Slave Ship, 2003, (with Willene Hendrick) Fleeing for Freedom: Stories of the Underground Railroad, 2004, (with Willene Hendrick) Why Not Every Man? African Americans and Civil Disobedience and the Quest for the Dream, 2005. Grantee Am. Coun. Learned Socs., Ford Found., NEH. Mem. MLA, James Jones Soc. (pres. 1991-92). Home: 502 W Main St Apt 122 Urbana IL 61801-2537

HENDRICK, HAL WILMANS, human factors educator; b. Dallas, Mar. 11, 1933; s. Harold Eugene and Audrey Sarah (Wilmans) H.; m. Mary Francis Boyle; children: Hal L., David A., John A. (dec.), Jennifer G. BA, Ohio Wesleyan U., 1955; MS, Purdue U., 1961, PhD, 1966. Cert. profl. ergonomist; bd. cert. forensic examiner. Asst. prof. U. So. Calif., L.A., assoc. prof., 1979-86; exec. dir. Inst. of Safety and Systems Mgmt., U. So. Calif., L.A., 1986-87; prof., dean Coll. of System Sci., U. Denver, 1987-90; prof. U. So. Calif., 1986-95, prof. emeritus L.A., 1995—; prin. Hendrick and Assocs., 1996—. Pres. Bd. Cert. in Profl. Ergonomics, 1992-94. Author: Behavioral Research and Analysis, 1980, 2d edit., 1989, 3rd edit., 1990, Macroergonomics: An Introduction to Work System Design, 2001, Good Ergomomics is Good Economics, 1996; editor 10 books; contbr. articles to profl. jours. Lt. col. USAF, 1956-76. Fellow APA, Am. Psychol. Soc., Human Factors Ergonomics Soc. (pres. L.A. chpt. 1986-87, 95-96, pres. Rocky Mountain chpt. 1989-90, pres. 1995-96), Internat. Ergonomics Assn. (pres. Geneva 1990-94, sec. gen. 1987-89, exec. com. 1984—2000, U.S. rep. 1981-87); mem. Ergonomics Soc. (U.K.), Soc. for Indsl. and Orgnl. Psychology.

Democrat. Avocations: travel, camping, hiking, reading, fishing. Home and Office: 7100 E Crestline Ave Greenwood Village CO 80111-1600 Office Phone: 303-843-6365. Personal E-mail: hhendrick@aol.com.

HENDRICK, JAMES T., lawyer; b. Fostoria, Ohio, Mar. 21, 1942; BA with honors and distinction in econs., U. Ill., 1963; JD, Harvard U., 1967. Bar: Ill. 1967, Calif. 1970. Ptnr. Thelen, Reid & Priest (formerly known as Thelen, Marrin, Johnson & Bridges), San Francisco, 1978—. Lt. USN JAG, 1968-71. Mem. ABA. Office: Thelen Reid & Priest 101 2nd St Ste 1800 San Francisco CA 94105-3659 Office Phone: 415-371-1200.

HENDRICKS, DONALD DUANE, retired school librarian; b. Flint, Mich., Nov. 3, 1931; s. Edgar F. and Marion (Scoble) Hendricks; m. Mary Jean Elrich, Feb. 17, 1951; children: Phillip, Scott, Randall. AB, U. Mich., AMLS, 1955; PhD, U. Ill., 1966. With Detroit Pub. Libr., 1955-57; head libr. Owosso Pub. Libr., Mich., 1957-60, Millikin U., 1960-63; dir. librs. Sam Houston State Univ., 1966-70; dir. S. Ctrl. Regional Med. Libr. Program, Dallas, 1970-78, U. Tex. Health Sci. Ctr. Libr., 1971-78, Earl K. Long Libr., U. New Orleans, 1978, dean libr. svcs., 1981-89, reference libr., 1989-92; mgr. St. Tammany Parish Libr. Sys., Mandeville, 1993-96; libr. Delgado C.C., Slidell, La., 1996—2003. Cons. in field. Co-author: (book) Resources of Texas Libraries, 1968, Centralizaed Processing and Regional Library Development - The Midwestern Regional Library System, 1970, The Louisiana State Library Processing Center: An Evaluation, 1971, Medical Libraries, Needs and Services, 1972; author: Centralized Processing and Regional Library Development, 1970; contbr. articles to profl. jours. Grantee, U.S. Office of Edn., 1965. Mem.: ALA, Bibliog. Soc. Am., Bibliog. Soc. (London), Grolier Club (N.Y.C.). Home: 61324 Brittany Dr Lacombe LA 70445-2818

HENDRICKS, J(AMES) EDWIN, historian, educator, consultant, author; b. Pickens, S.C., Oct. 19, 1935; s. J.E. and Cassie (Looper) H.; m. Sue James, June 28, 1958; children— James, Christopher, Lee BA, Furman U., 1957; MA, U. Va., 1959, PhD, 1961. Vis. prof. history U. Va., Charlottesville, summer 1961; asst. prof. history Wake Forest U., Winston-Salem, N.C., 1961-66, assoc. prof., 1966-75, prof., 1975—, chmn. dept. history, 1995-99, dir. Hist. Preservation Program, 1973—. Vis. prof. history U. Tex.-El Paso, summer 1965; preservation cons.; vis. dir. Mus. Albermarle, Elizabeth City, N.C., summer 1975; dir. Preservation Field Sch., summers 1983-86, 88-90, 92-95. Author: (with others) Liquor and Anti-Liquor in Virginia, 1619-1919, 1967; Charles Thomson and the Making of a Nation, 1729-1824, 1979; editor, contbg. author: Forsyth, The History of a County on the March, 1976; author: Wake Forest University School of Law; One Hundred Years of Legal Education, 1994, Seeking Liberty and Justice: A History of the North Carolina Bar Association, 1999. Pres. Hist. Winston, 1979—; chmn. Winston-Salem/Forsyth County Hist. Dists. Commn., 1978-79; pres. Wachovia Hist. Soc., 1983-87. Served with U.S. Army, 1958-59. Recipient R.J. Reynolds rsch. leave, 1973, 87, 01; Am. Philos. Soc. rsch. grantee, 1969, 70. Mem. N.C. Lit. and Hist. Assn. (pres. 1980-81), Hist. Soc. N.C., So. Hist. Assn., Nat. Trust Hist. Preservation, others Lodges: Kiwanis (pres. 1987-88), Torch (pres. Winston-Salem 1987-88). Democrat. Baptist. Office: Wake Forest U Dept History PO Box 7806 Winston Salem NC 27109-7806 E-mail: hendrije@wfu.edu.

HENDRICKS, JAMES POWELL, retired artist; b. Little Rock, Aug. 7, 1938; s. Leland Fuller and Christia Beatrice (Powell) H.; m. Betty Jean Fleming, Nov. 6, 1960 (div. 1977); children: Elizabeth Jane, Valerie Lee; m. Marcia Reed-Hendricks, 1978 (div.); m. Leslie Jill Cernak, 1999. BA, U. Ark., 1962; M.F.A., U. Iowa, 1964. Instr. art State U. Iowa, 1962-64, Mt. Holyoke Coll., 1964-65; mem. faculty U. Mass., Amherst, 1965—, prof. art, 1977—, dir. undergrad. programs in art, 1968-71, dir. grad. programs art, 1974-77; ret., 2004. Vis. artist Seoul Inst. of the Arts, Korea, 1986, Portland Sch. Arts, Maine, 1985, San Diego State U., 1986, Internat. Artist Colony, Ctr. Contemporary Visual Arts, Prilep, Macedonia, 1994. One-man exhbn., Nat. Air and Space Mus., Smithsonian Instn., fall 1969, Hudson River Mus., Yonkers, N.Y., 1970, U. Mass., Amherst, 1971-78, French and Co. Gallery, N.Y.C., 1972, Warren Benedek Gallery, N.Y.C., 1974, Helen Shlien Gallery, Boston, 1980, 82, 84, Smith Coll., Northampton, Mass., 1983, 84, SUNY-Oswego, 1983, Deerfield Acad., Mass., 1984, Portland Sch. Art, 1985, Space Art Gallery, Seoul, 1986, Mus. Fine Arts, Springfield, Mass., 1986, Slater-Price Fine Arts Gallery, N.Y.C., 1989, 90, Ark. Arts Ctr., Little Rock, 1993, Anderson Gallery, 1993, Art Gallery at Macedonia, Skopje, 1994, Westwood Gallery, Inc., N.Y.C., 1996, 2001, 2002, Hart Gallery, Northampton, Mass., 1996; group exhbns. include, Nat. Gallery Art, 1970, Nat. Air and Space Mus., 1976, 4th Internat. Biennial, Medellín, Colombia, 1981, Assemblage/Collage Exhbn. Seoul Inst. of Arts, Korea, in conjunction with World Olympics Arts Festival, 1988, Joy Moos Gallery, Miami, Fla., 1991, Ark. Arts Ctr., Little Rock, 1993, Vesti-dane Gallery, Scottsdale, Ariz., 1997; comms. include: Nat. Gallery Art, NASA, cover for Time mag., 1971, 2 album covers for Neuma Records, Fall 1991; cover commn. for The Mass. Rev., Vol. XXXVII, No. 4, Winter, 1997. Named Ark. Traveler, 1971

HENDRICKS, JOHN STANLEY, computational physicist; b. Hollywood, Calif., June 9, 1949; s. Richard and Grayce Ann (Houseman) H.; m. Margaret Hendricks; children: Dianne, Suzanne, James, David, Lisa. BS, MS, UCLA, 1972; PhD, MIT, 1975. Mem. staff Los Alamos (N.Mex.) Nat. Lab., 1975-84, assoc. group leader, 1984-87, congl. liaison, 1987-89, Monte Carlo team leader, 1989-97, mcnpx principal developer, 2001—. Cons. TRW, L.A., 1985-87, Martin Marietta, Denver, 1987, Gearhart, Austin, Tex., 1985. Organist IHM Ch., Los Alamos; 3d trombone Los Alamos Big Band. NSF fellow MIT, 1972-75. Mem. Am. Nuclear Soc. (chmn. Trinity chpt. 1980), Toastmasters (area gov. 1978). Roman Catholic. Achievements include co-development of Monte Carlo N-particle extended radiation transport computer code. Home: 102 Loma Del Escolar Rd Los Alamos NM 87544-2525 Office: Los Alamos Nat Lab D 5 K575 Los Alamos NM 87545-0001 Office Phone: 505-667-6997. E-mail: jxh@lanl.gov.

HENDRICKS, KENNETH, wholesale distribution executive; b. Sept. 8, 1941; m. Dianne Hendricks. Founder, CEO, chmn. ABC Supply, Beloit, Wis., 1982—. Owner AmCraft Bldg. Products, Mulehide Products, Hendricks Devel., Corporate Contractors, Inc., Cay Home Furnishing, Fed. Heath Sign Co., Pur Pac, Stratford Simmons. Named one of Richest People in Am., Forbes mag., 2004. Office: ABC Supply One ABC Pkwy Beloit WI 53511-4466 Office Phone: 608-362-7777. Office Fax: 608-362-2717.*

HENDRICKS, MINNIE MARIE, secondary school educator; b. St. Charles, Va., Dec. 30, 1933; d. James and Mary Minnie (Robbins) Poe; m. George Hendricks, Nov. 19, 1955; children: Phyllis, Elizabeth. BA and BS in Edn., Union Coll., 1955; MS in Biology, Marshall U., 1970. Tchr. jr. high sci. Big Walnut Local, Sunbury, Ohio, 1955; tchr. third grade Beaver (Ohio) Bd. Edn., 1958-59; tchr. biology, chemistry and earth sci. Ea. Local Sch. Bd., Beaver, 1964—2001. Mem. choir Beaver Emmanuel United Meth. Ch., mem. sec., lay delegate, Sunday Sch. tchr. Recipient tuition/stipend NSF, Capital U., 1966, Marshall U., 1967, Ohio U., 1969, Ohio Bd. Regents, Miami U., 1992. Mem.: Ea. Local Classroom Tchrs. Assn. (pres. 1981—98), S.E. Ohio Edn. Assn. (mem. exec. com. 1976—2001), Ohio Edn. Assn., NEA, Nat. Sci. Tchrs. Assn. Avocations: sewing, walking, travel, gardening. Home: PO Box 166 Beaver OH 45613-0166 Office: Ea High Sch 1170 Tile Mill Rd Beaver OH 45613-9435

HENDRICKS, RANDAL ARLAN, lawyer; b. Nov. 18, 1945; s. Clinton H. and Edith T. (Anderson) H.; m. Suann Rose, June 1, 1965 (div. 1976); children: Kristin Lee, Daehne Lynn; m. Jill Edith Duke, Mar. 22, 1982; 1 child, Bret Larson-Hendricks. Student, U. Mo., Kansas City, 1963-65; BS with honors, U. Houston, 1968, JD with honors, 1970. Bar: Tex. 1970, U.S. Dist. Ct. (so. dist.) Tex. 1970, U.S. Tax Ct. 1985. Assoc. Baker & Botts, Houston, 1970-71; pvt. practice Houston, 1971—; sr. v.p., mng. dir. Baseball, SFX Sports Group, Inc., 1999-2001; chmn., pres., CEO SFX Baseball Group LLC, 2001—03; pres. Hendricks Sports Mgmt. LLC, 2003—; mng. mem. Hendricks Interests LLC, 1999—. Ptnr. Hendricks Sports Mgmt., Houston, 1977-81; pres. Hendricks Mgmt. Co., Inc., Houston, 1981-99; expert witness U.S. Senate Subcom. on Antitrust and Monopoly, 1972; mem. pub. adv. com. Houston/Harris County Sports Facility, 1995-96. Author: Inside the Strike Zone, 1994. Dir. profl. div. Excellence Campaign, U. Houston, 1971; bd. dirs. Cypress Creek Christian Ch., Spring, Tex., 1979-85. Mem. Houston Bar Assn., Assn. Reps. Profl. Athletes (bd. dirs. 1978-88, mem. at large 1978-79, treas. 1979-80, v.p. 1980-81, pres. 1981-82, chmn. ethics com. 1978-80, chmn. baseball com. 1981-88), Sports Lawyers Assn. (bd. dirs. 1992-2000), Order of Barons (chancellor 1969-70), Phi Kappa Phi, Phi Delta Phi. Office: 400 Randal Way Ste 106 Spring TX 77388-8908 Home: 5 Winston Woods DR Houston TX 77024-7049 E-mail: randy.hendricks@hendricks-sports.com.

HENDRICKSON, ANITA ELIZABETH, biology professor; b. LaCross, Wis., Feb. 20, 1936; d. Walter V. and Alno (Larkin) Schnell; m. Morris N. Hendrickson, June 8, 1957; children: Lisa, Karin, Gordon. BA, Pacific Luth. Coll., 1957; PhD, U. Wash., Seattle, 1964. Instr. anatomy Northwestern Med. Sch., Chgo., 1964-65; rsch. assoc. Children's Meml. Hosp., Chgo., 1964-65; rsch. instr. dept. biol. structure U. Wash., Seattle, 1965-67, instr. dept. ophthalmology, 1967-69, asst. prof. dept. ophthalmology, 1969-73; affiliate/assoc. prof. dept. ophthalmology Reg. Primate Ctr./U. Wash., 1972—, 1973-81; affiliate Child Devel. & Mental Retardation Ctr., U. Wash., 1975; prof. dept. opthalmology U. Wash., 1981-97, prof. dept. biol. structure, 1984—, chair dept. biol. structure, 1994—, adj. prof. ophthalmology, 1997—. Vis. assoc. prof. neuropathology Harvard Med. Sch., Boston, 1975-76; adj. assoc. prof. dept. psychology U. Wash., 1975-78; mem. NIH VisB study section, 1976-80. Editorial bd. Jour. of Neurosci., 1982-88, Investigative Ophthalmology, 1977-82, Vision Research, 1990-95; contbr. articles to profl. jours. Dolly Green rsch. grantee, 1981; named Alumnus of the Yr., Pacific Luth. U., 1982. Mem. AAAS, Am. Assn. Anatomists, Soc. for Neurosci. (mem. nat. coun. 1982-86), Internat. Soc. for Eye Rsch., Assn. for Rsch. in Vision and Ophthalmology (prog. chmn. 1983-84, trustee 1993—), Cajal Club. Home: 1029C NE 120th St Seattle WA 98125-5003 Office: U Washington Dept Biol Structure Box 357420 Seattle WA 98195-7420

HENDRICKSON, BRUCE CARL, life insurance company executive; b. Holdrege, Nebr., Apr. 4, 1930; s. Carl R. and Ruth E. (Bosserman) H.; m. Carol Schepman, June 12, 1952; children: Julie, Mark Bruce. BA, U. Nebr., 1952. C.L.U., chartered fin. cons. Sr. agt. Prin. Life Ins. Co., Holdrege, 1950—. Bd. govs. Central Nebr. Tech. Community Coll.; mem. Nebr. Edn. Commn. of States, Nat. Hwy. Safety Advisors Com.; elder First Presbyterian Ch., Holdrege; pres. Holdrege City Council, 1979-86; pres. Phelps County Community Found.; trustee U. Nebr. Found.; moderator Cen. Nebr. Presbytery, Presbyn. Ch. USA, 1986-88, Gen. Assembly Coun., 1998-2004; dir. Nebr. Art Collection Found., 1996-2002; mem. pres. club U. Nebr., mem. chancellors club. Served with USNR, 1953-56. Bruce Hendrickson Week declared by Gov. of Nebr., 1975; recipient Distinguished Alumni Achievement award U. Nebr., 1977, Disting. Svc. award Nebr. State Assn. Life Underwriters, 1998. Mem. Nat. Assn. Life Underwriters (pres. 1975-76), Assn. Advanced Life Underwriting, Am. Soc. C.L.U.s., Life Underwriters Polit. Action Com. (chmn. 1989), Life Underwriters Tng. Coun. (trustee 1979-82), Million Dollar Round Table, Phi Kappa Psi. Clubs: Rotary (pres. 1960-61), Holdrege Country (Holdrege); Am. Legion, Elks. Republican. Office: Prin Fin Group PO Box 765 Holdrege NE 68949-0765

HENDRICKSON, CHRIS THOMPSON, civil and environmental engineering educator, researcher; b. Oakland, Calif., Mar. 31, 1950; s. Harold Thompson and E. Jean (Loomis) H.; m. Kathleen Devine, May 28, 1977; children: Andrew, Thomas, Peter. BS, MS, Stanford U., 1973; PhB, Oxford U., 1975; PhD, MIT, 1978. Asst. prof. Carnegie-Mellon U., Pitts., 1978-83, assoc. prof., 1983-87, prof., 1987—; assoc. dean Carnegie Inst. Tech., 1991-96, Duquesne Light Co. prof. engring., 1996—, head dept., 1996—. Author: (with others) Transportation Investment and Pricing Principles, 1984, Project Management for Construction, 1989, Knowledge-based Process Planning for Construction and Manufacturing, 1989, Computer Integrated Building Design, 1993; editor Jour. Transp. Engring.; contbr. articles to profl. publs. Bd. mem. St. Edmund's Acad., Pitts. Recipient C.E. Ladd Rsch. award Carnegie Inst. Tech., 1979; Rhodes scholar, 1973. Mem.: ASCE (com. chmn. 1983—, chmn. urban transp. divsn. 1989—90, dept. heads exec. com. 2000—02, Huber Rsch. award 1989, Masters Transp. Engring. award 1994, Fenves Systems award 2002, Turner Lecture award 2002), Transp. Rsch. Bd. (com. chmn. 1989—96), Am. Econ. Assn., Tau Beta Pi, Phi Beta Kappa. Home: 6933 Rosewood St Pittsburgh PA 15208-2638 Office: Carnegie Mellon U Pittsburgh PA 15213-3890 Office Phone: 412-268-2941.

HENDRICKSON, D. JOHN, lawyer; b. Berkeley, Calif., July 16, 1955; BA with distinction, Stanford U., 1977; JD cum laude, Pepperdine U., 1981. Bar: Calif. 1981, Tenn. 1996, US Ct. Appeals, 9th Cir., US Dist. Ct., Ctrl. Dist Calif., US Supreme Ct. Ptnr. Katten Muchin Zavis Rosenman, LA. Instr. Inst. of Advanced Advertising Studies; adj. assoc. prof. Southwestern U. Sch. Law. Mem.: State Bar Tenn., State Bar Calif. (mem. Bus. Law Sect.), LA County Bar Assn. Office: Katten Muchin Zavis Rosenman Ste 2600 2029 Century Park E Los Angeles CA 90067 Office Phone: 310-788-4400. Office Fax: 310-788-4471. E-mail: john.hendrickson@kmzr.com.

HENDRICKSON, DAVID NORMAN, chemistry educator; b. Mpls., Jan. 1, 1943; s. Henry N. and Lorraine M. Hendrickson; m. Sherry J. Hendrickson, June 19, 1966; children: Shelley A. Radziminski, Susanne M. McCarthy. BS, UCLA, 1966; PhD, U. Calif., Berkeley, 1969; postgrad., Calif. Tech. U., 1970. From asst. prof. to assoc. prof. U. Ill., Urbana, 1970-78, prof., 1979-88, U. Calif., San Diego, 1989—. Fgn. expert Nanjing U. as part of World Bank Program for Refurbishing Univs. of China, 1984; vis. prof. Tokyo Met. U., 1986, U. Colo., Boulder, 1988, U. Sydney, Australia, 1990, Osaka (Japan) U., 1991; assoc. Ctr. Advanced Study, U. Ill., 1988. Contbr. numerous articles to rsch. jours. Councilor Am. Chem. Soc., Washington, 1986-88. Recipient Humboldt Found. Rsch. prize for sr. U.S. scientists, 1993; DuPont Young Faculty fellow, 1973, U. Ill. Ctr. for Advanced Study fellow, 1975, Camille and Henry Dreyfuss Tchr.-Scholar fellow, 1972-77, A. P. Sloan Found. fellow, 1976-78, Japan Soc. for Promotion of Sci. Sr. Faculty fellow, 1986; Brown & Williamson vis. scholar U. Louisville, 1992. Achievements include research on electron transfer in mixed-valence compounds and properties of single-molecule magnets. Office: U Calif Dept Chemistry and Biochem 9500 Gilman Dr Dept 358 La Jolla CA 92093-0358

HENDRICKSON, JAMES BRIGGS, chemistry professor; b. Toledo, Jan. 3, 1928; s. Philip and Dorothy (Briggs) H.; m. Sybil Pardee, May 30, 1953; children— Jared Jeffrey Raymond, Sonia Catherine Angell. BS, Calif. Inst. Tech., 1950; MA, Harvard, 1951, PhD, 1955. NRC postdoctoral fellow U. London, Eng., 1954-55; asst. prof. UCLA, 1957-63; assoc. prof. chemistry Brandeis U., Waltham, Mass., 1963-66, prof., 1966—. Author: Biosynthesis of Steroids, Terpenes and Acetogenins, 1963, The Molecules of Nature, 1965, (with others) Organic Chemistry, 1970; also research papers. Served with AUS, 1946-48, Korea. Sloan fellow, 1962-66; Guggenheim fellow, 1964; Fulbright prof. U. Cape Coast, Ghana, 1974-76 Mem. Am. Chem. Soc., Chem. Soc. (London). Home: 9 Acacia St Cambridge MA 02138-4818 Office: Brandeis U Dept Chemistry Waltham MA 02454-9110 Office Phone: 781-736-2520. E-mail: hendrickson@brandeis.edu.

HENDRICKSON, JEROME ORLAND, trade association administrator, lawyer; b. Eau Claire, Wis., July 25, 1918; s. Harold and Clara (Halvorson) H.; m. Helen Phoebe Harty, Dec. 27, 1948 (dec. Oct. 1988); children: Jaime Ann, Jerome Orland. Student, Wis. State Coll., 1936-39; JD, U. Wis., 1942. Bar: Wis. 1942, U.S. Supreme Ct. 1955. Sole practice, Eau Claire, Wis., 1946; sales & advt. mgr. Eau Claire Coca-Cola Bottling Co., Inc., 1947-48; exec. sec. Eau Claire Cmty. Chest, 1948-49; in charge dist. Office Am. PEtroleum Inst., Kansas City, Mo., 1950-53, Chgo., 1953-55; exec. dir. Nat. Assn. Plumbing-Heating-Cooling Contractors, 1955-64; sec. Joint Apprentice Text, Inc., 1955-64; exec. v.p. Cast Iron Soil Pipe Inst., Washington, 1964-74; pres. Valve Mfrs. Assn., McLean, Va., 1975-80; exec. v.p. Plumbing and Pipe Industry Coun., Inc., 1981-90. Ret. treas. Wis. Cmty. Chest, 1948-49; treas. All-Industry Plumbing & Heating Modernization Com., 1956-57; co-sec. Joint Industry Program Com., 1958-64. Lt. USNR, 1943-46. Mem. ABA, Wis. Bar Assn., Am. Soc. Assn. Execs., Washington Soc. Assn. Execs., Wis. State Soc. Washington (pres. 1966-68), Nat. Conf. Plumbing-Heating-Cooling Industry (chmn. 1967-69), NAM, U. Wis. Alumni Assn., U. Wis. Law Sch. Alumni Assn. Washington (pres. 1970-74), C. of C. of U.S., Mason (32 degree, Shriner), Washington Golf and Country Club, Internat. Club (Washington), Gamma Eta Gamma (pres. Upsilon chpt. 1941-42). Episcopalian. Home and Office: 1200 Partridge Ln Charlottesville VA 22901-1787

HENDRICKSON, JOHN P., lawyer; b. Oct. 7, 1955; m. Lisa A. Hendrickson. BS, S.D. State U., 1977; JD, U. Notre Dame, 1980. Ptnr., chmn. firm employee benefits dept. McDermott Will & Emery LLP, Chgo. Named one of top employee benefits lawyers in U.S., Nat. Law Jour. Office: McDermott Will & Emery LLP 227 W Monroe St Chicago IL 60606-5055 Home: 721 Taft Rd Hinsdale IL 60521-4934 Office Phone: 312-984-7645. Office Fax: 312-984-7700. Business E-Mail: jhendrickson@mwe.com.

HENDRICKSON, PAUL JOSEPH, journalist, writer, educator; b. Fresno, Calif., Apr. 29, 1944; s. Joseph Paul and Rita Bernice Hendrickson; m. Sunday Hendrickson, Sept. 10, 1969 (div. Feb. 1974); m. Cecilia Regina Hendrickson, Mar. 10, 1979; children: Matthew, John. Classical AB in English, St. Louis U., 1967; MA, Pa. State U., 1968. Writer, prodr., publicist WPSX-TV, University Park, Pa., 1969-71; writer Holiday Mag., Indpls., 1971-72; reporter Detroit Free Press, 1972-74, The Nat. Observer, Washington, 1974-77, The Washington Post, 1977-2001; lectr. in creative writing U. Pa., Phila., 1998—. Author: Seminary: A Search, 1983, Looking for the Light, 1992, The Living and the Dead, 1996, Sons of Mississippi, 2003 (Nat. Book Critics Circle award for nonfiction, 2004). Fellow, Alicia Patterson Found., 1980, Lyndhurst fellow, 1985—87, Guggenheim fellow, 1999; grantee, Nat. Endowment for the Arts, 2002. Rman Catholic. Avocation: fly fishing. Home: 30 Colfax Rd Havertown PA 19083 Office Phone: 215-898-7341. E-mail: phendric@english.upenn.edu.

HENDRICKSON, WAYNE A(RTHUR), biochemist, educator; b. Spring Valley, Wis., Apr. 25, 1941; s. Olaf and Margaret (Oare) H.; children: Helen Margaret, Inga Marie. BA, U. Wis., River Falls, 1963; PhD in Biophysics, Johns Hopkins U., 1968; PhD (hon.), Uppsala U., 1995. Rsch. assoc. Johns Hopkins U., Balt., 1968-69; postdoctoral rsch. assoc. Naval Rsch. Lab., 1969-71, rsch. biophysicist, 1971-84; prof. biochemistry and molecular biophysics Columbia U. Coll. Physicians and Surgeons, N.Y.C., 1984—; investigator Howard Hughes Med. Inst., 1986—. Sci. adv. bd. mem. Progenics Pharms., 1987—; sci. adv. bd. mem., Kinetix Pharms., 1997—; sci. policy com. Stanford Linear Accelerator Ctr., 1992-94; program evaluation bd. Advanced Photon Source, 1988—; biomed. adv. com. for Pitts. Supercomputing Ctr., 1987-92; DOE Synchrotron Rev. Com., 1987-88; proposal rev. panel Cornell High Energy Synchrotron Source, 1987—; mem. NSF Molecular Adv. Panel, 1980-83, NIH Biophys. Chemistry Study Sct., 1986-89; mem. sci. adv. bd. Burnham Inst., 1995—; mem. nat. adv. Gdn. Med. Scis. Coun., 1997—; mem. sci. adv. vom. European Synchrotam Radiation Facility, 1997—, Rutgers Ctr. Advanced Biotech. & Medicine, 1998—; investigator, Howard Hughes Med. Inst. Mem. editl. bd. Jour. Biomolecular Structure and Dynamics, 1986-91; assoc. editor Jour. Molecular Biology, 1987-93; editor Current Opinion in Structural Biology, 1989—, Macromolecular Structures, 1990—, Structure, 1993—; contbr. numerous articles to profl. jours. Recipient Biol. Scis. award Washington Acad. Scis., 1976, Meritorious Civilian Svc. award U.S. Navy, 1978, Arthur S. Flemming award Outstanding Young Fed. Employees, 1979, Aminoff prize Royal Swedish Acad. Scis., 1997, Anfinsen award Protein Soc., 1997, Gairdner award, 2003. Fellow AAAS, Am. Acad. Arts and Scis; mem. NAS (Alexander Hollaender award 1998), Am. Crystallographic Assn. (chmn. biol. macromolecules group 1980, A.L. Patterson award 1981, Fankuchen award com. 1982), Am. Soc. Biochemistry and Molecular Biology (mem. pubs. com. 1997—, Fritz Lipmann award 1991), Biophys. Soc. (coun. mem. 1987-90, mem. publs. com. 1989—), Internat. Union Crystallography (commn. on biol. macromolecules 1981-87, commn. on crystallographic computing 1984-87, commn. on synchrotron radiation, 1990-93). Achievements include rsch. in macromolecular structure and function, in principles of protein structure, dynamics and assembly, in properties of specific proteins, in diffraction methods, in crystallographic computing, and in synchrotron radiation. Office: Columbia U Dept Biochem & Molecular Biophys 630 W 168th St New York NY 10032-3795

HENDRICKX, IRENE S., elementary school educator; b. Moline, Ill., Sept. 15, 1954; d. Walter F. and Adela F. Kacprzyk; m. Daniel P. Hendrickx, Mar. 9, 1954; children: Christopher Robert, Michael Walter, Amy Marie. AA, Black Hawk Coll., 1974; BA in Elem. Edn., St. Ambrose U., 1976; MA in Edn. Adminstrn., Western Ill. U., 1996. Libr. D.B. Hoffman, East Moline, Ill., 1979—80, tchr. 6th grade math., 1980—81; tchr. 5th grade math. Jordan Cath. Schs., Rock Island, 1981—82; tchr. math., sci. Audubon, 1991—98; tchr. intermediate lang. arts Longfellow Sch., 1998—2001, tchr. 2d grade, 2001—04, tchr. math., 2004—. Tech. coach Rock Island Sch. Dist., 1991—. Tech. support Heritage Wesleyan, Rock Island, 2003—, mem. leadership team, 2004—. Mem.: Rock Island Coun. Educators (treas. 2004—05), Delta Kappa Gamma (v.p. 1994—96, pres. 1996—98). Avocations: jet skiing, scrapbooks, reading, travel. Home: 2433 23 Ave Rock Island IL 61201

HENDRIE, JOSEPH MALLAM, physicist, nuclear engineer; b. Janesville, Wis., Mar. 18, 1925; s. Joseph Munier and Margaret Prudence (Hocking) H.; m. Elaine Kostell, July 9, 1949; children: Susan Debra, Barbara Ellen. BS, Case Inst. Tech., 1950; PhD, Columbia U., 1957. Registered profl. engr., NY, Calif. Asst. physicist Brookhaven Nat. Lab., Upton, NY, 1955-57, assoc. physicist, 1957-60, physicist, 1960-71, sr. physicist, 1971-97, chmn. steering com., project chief engr. high flux beam reactor design and constrn., 1958-65, acting head exptl. reactor physics divsn., 1965-66, project mgr. pulsed fast reactor project, 1967-70, assoc. head engring. divsn., dept. applied sci., 1967-71, head, 1971-72, chmn. dept. applied sci., 1975-77, spl. asst. to dir., 1981-96; dir. Entergy Ops., Inc., 1987-95; ret. Dir. Houston Industries, Inc., Houston Lighting & Power Co., 1985-96; dep. dir. licensing for tech. rev. U.S. AEC, 1972-74; chmn. U.S. Nuc. Regulatory Commn., Washington, 1977-79, 81, commr., 1980, mem. adv. com. on enforcement policy, 1984-85; lectr. nuc. power plant safety MIT, Ga. Inst. Tech., Northwestern U., summers 1970-77; cons. radiation safety com. Columbia U., 1964-72; mem. adv. com. reactor safeguards AEC, 1966-72, chmn., 1970; U.S. mem. sr. adv. group on reactor safety stds. IAEA, 1974-78; mem. nat. rsch. coun. com. Internat. Cooperation in Magnetic Fusion, 1983-85; cons. AEC, Nuc. Regulatory Commn., 1974-75, GAO, 1975-77, Electric Power Rsch. Inst., 1982, various nuc. utilities, 1981—. Mem. editl. adv. bd. Nuc. Tech., 1967-77. Served with AUS, 1943-45. Recipient E.O. Lawrence award, 1970, George C. Laurence Pioneering award Am. Nuc. Soc., 1998, Henry DeWolf Smyth Nuc. Statesman award, 2004; decorated comdr. Order of Leopold II (Belgium), 1982. Fellow Am. Nuc. Soc. (dir. 1976-77, v.p. 1983-84, pres. 1984-85), ASME; mem. IEEE, NAE, Am. Phys. Soc., ASTM (com. on rsch. and tech. planning 1985-90), Am. Concrete Inst., Inst. Nuc. Power Operation (adv. coun. 1984-90), NSPE, Sigma Xi, Tau Beta Pi. Achievements include research and publications on physics nuclear reactors, nuclear power plant safety, engineering design reactors, electrical power transmission, chem. physics nitrogen dissociation process, structure oxygen molecule. Office: Brookhaven Nat Lab Upton NY 11973 Office Phone: 631-286-8664.

HENDRIE, LAURA GIBSON, writer; b. Colorado Springs, Colo., May 8, 1954; d. John Gibson and Nipppy Elmes Hendrie. Student, Hampshire Coll., 1972—74, Metro State Coll., 1978; BA, U. Iowa, 1981; postgrad., U. Ala., 1985—87. Author: (short stories) Stygo, 1994 (Rosenthal award, 94), (novels) Remember Me, 1999. Vol. fireman Ojo Sarco (N.Mex.) Fire Dept., 1990—98; vol. Hospice, Hancock County, Maine, 2001. Recipient Richard and Hinda Rosenthal award, Am. Acad. Arts and Letters, 1999, Mountains and Plans Booksellers award, Booksellers of the West, 1999. Avocation: walking. Home and Office: 301 Wood Ave Salida CO 81201-3433

HENDRIKSEN, NEIL EVAN, music educator; b. Salt Lake City, Sept. 27, 1955; s. Oscar James and Dorothy Hendriksen; m. Marie Updegraff, Oct. 20, 1977; children: Jacob Thomas, Daren Bradford, Nathan Edward, Douglas Neil, Lauren Clarice. MusB, U. Utah, 1985. Cert. Secondary Tchr. State of Utah, 1985. Dir. choral activities Woods Cross H.S., Woods Cross, Utah, 1986—; adj. faculty mem. U. Utah, Salt Lake City, 1989—. Clinician, adjudicator Heritage Festivals, Salt Lake City, 1990—, Utah H.S. Activities Assn., Midvale, 1987—; trombonist, bass trombonist Ballet West/Utah Chamber Orch., Salt Lake City, 1989—; aux. trombonist Utah Symphony Orch., Salt Lake City, 1982—89; trombonist, bass trombonist Pioneer Theatre Co. Orch., Salt Lake City, 1983—89. Musician: numerous symphonic studio performances; singer: numerous soundtracks and studio recordings; musician: numerous studio, movies, advertising and tv appearances; singer: numerous live vocal solo and ensemble performances. Zone commr. Boy Scouts Am., Salt Lake City, 1990—97. Recipient Golden Apple Award, Utah PTA, 1996, Secondary Tchr. of Yr., Davis Sch. Dist., 1996, Tchr. of Yr., Woods Cross H.S., 1996. Mem.: Davis Educators Assn. (assoc.), Utah Educators Assn. (assoc.), NEA (assoc.), Utah Music Educators Assn. (assoc.; vice president.choral 2000—02), Am. Choral Dirs. Assn. (life; Utah repertoire/standards chair h.s. 1987—96, dir. choir at nat. conv. 2004—05). Avocations: hiking, target shooting, knife collecting, sight-seeing/travel, camping. Office: Woods Cross High School 600 West 2200 South Woods Cross UT 84087

HENDRIX, ALBERT RANDEL, social services administrator; b. Batesville, Miss., Aug. 17; s. Howard Roy Sr. and Marjorie Corine (Oliphant) H.; m. Sandra June Reynolds, July 15, 1973; children: Jo Ellen, Sarah Elizabeth, Albert Randel Jr., Sandra Louise. BA, U. Miss., 1968, MEd, 1971; PhD, U. So. Miss., 1979. Grants coord. Ellisville (Miss.) State Sch., 1971-75; dir. North Miss. Retardation Ctr., Oxford, 1975-86; exec. dir. Miss. Dept. Mental Health, Jackson, 1986—. Adj. instr. health care adminstrn. U. Miss. Pharmacy Sch., 1977—, acting asst. prof. spl. edn., dept. of curriculum and instrn. Sch. Edn., 1979-87; instr. human svcs. technician program Itawamba Jr. Coll., Fulton, 1981-83; dir. div. of mental retardation, dept. mental health, Jackson, Miss., 1981-82; adv. bd. Congress of Advocates for the Retarded, 1978—. Exec. dir. Miss. Arts Fair for the Handicapped, 1980—; adv. bd. U. Miss. Sch. Edn. (bd. dirs. 1989—), Jackson State U. Sch. Liberal Arts, 1986—; bd. dirs., adv. bd. Jackson State U. Sch. Social Work, 1990—; social work adv. bd. U. So. Miss., 1987-90; v.p. U. Miss. Health Coun., 1986-89; adv. coun. Foster Grandparent Program, Oxford, Miss., 1975-89; mem. Govs. Coun. on Aging, 1976-80. With U.S. Army, 1968-70. Mem. Phi Theta Kappa, Phi Kappa Phi, Phi Delta Kappa. Office: Miss Dept Mental Health Robert E Lee Bldg 239 N Lamar St Ste 1101 Jackson MS 39201-1325

HENDRIX, CHRISTINE JANET, retired government agency administrator, retired small business owner, volunteer; b. Corry, Pa., Dec. 3, 1939; d. Merle Alvin and Janet May Besson; m. Alfred E. Hendrix, Mar. 27, 1965; 1 child, Lee Andrew. BS in Edn., Clarion (Pa.) State Teacher's Coll., 1961. Tchr. Montour Schs., McKees Rocks, Pa., 1961—62, Newcomerstown (Ohio) Exempted Schs., 1962—65; welcome wagon hostess Welcome Wagon Internat., Newcomerstown, 1965—71; mgr. Amos Placement Bur., New Phila., Ohio, 1972—75; paralegal Pros. Atty.'s Office, New Phila., 1976—79; small bus. coowner Child Care Alternatives, New Phila., 1980—85; dir. Tuscarawas County Sr. Ctr., Dover, Ohio, 1985—89; relocation agt. Ohio Dept. of Transp., Fairlawn, Ohio, 1989—98; assignment commr. Mcpl. Ct., New Phila., 1998—2000, ret., 2000. Editor: Child Care Alternatives Newsletter, 1980—85. Vol. Cats N Us, Dover, Ohio, 2002, Ret. Sr. and Vol. Program, New Phila., 2003; ctr. and exec. com. Tuscarawas County Dem. Party, New Phila., 1980; various offices New Phila. (Ohio) Dem. Club, 1994—2001; mem. Bd. of Zoning Appeals, New Phila., 1979—89; rep. sr. citizens United Way, New Phila., 1983—85; mem. Domestic Violence Orgn., New Phila., 1987—89; various offices NOW, New Phila., 1974—79; vol. COMPASS Inc., New Phila., 2000. Democrat. Protestant. Avocations: genealogy, antiques. Home: 183 Wabash Avenue NW New Philadelphia OH 44663 Personal E-mail: cjhendrix@wilkshire.net.

HENDRIX, JOHN SHANNON, architecture educator; b. Ithaca, N.Y., Apr. 27, 1959; s. John David and Margaret Shannon Hendrix. BFA, Art Inst., 1983; MA, R.I. Sch. Design, 1984; MArch., U. Ill., 1993; PhD in Architecture, Cornell U., 2001. Adj. prof. art and archtl. history Roger Williams U./RI. Sch. Design, Bristol, RI, 2000—. Author: The Relation Between Architectural Forms and Philosophical Structures in the Work of Francesco Borromini in Seventeenth-Century Rome, 2002, Architectural Forms and Philosophical Structures, 2003, History and Culture in Italy, 2003, Platonic Architectonics: Platonic Philosophies and the Visual Arts, 2004, Aesthetics and the Philosophy of Spirit, 2005. Home: 212 Hope St Bristol RI 02809 Office: Roger Williams Univ One Old Ferry Rd Bristol RI 02809 Business E-Mail: jhendrix@rwu.edu.

HENDRIX, JON RICHARD, biology professor; b. Passaic, N.J., May 4, 1938; s. William Louis and Velma Lucile (Coleman) H.; m. Janis Ruth Rouhselange, Nov. 24, 1962; children— Margaret Susan, Joann Ruth, Amy Therese BS, Ind. State U., 1960, MS, 1963; Ed.D., Ball State U., 1974. Sci. supr. Sch. Town of Highland, Ind., 1960-71; instr. Ind. U., Gary, 1968-69; assoc. prof. biology Ball State U., Muncie, 1972-80, prof., 1980-98, prof. emeritus, 1998—. Cons. Ind. Dept. Pub. Instrn., 1967-71, Ctr. for Values and Meaning, 1971—; mem. Ind. Sci. Edn. Adv. Bd., Dept. Pub. Instrn., 1967-71 Author: The Wonder of Somehow, 1974, The Wonder of Someplace, 1974, The Wonder of Sometime, 1974, Becomings: A Parent Guidebook for In-Home Experiences with Nine to Eleven Year Olds, 1974, Becomings: A Clergy Guidebook for Experiences with Nine to Eleven Year Olds and Their Parents, 1974; contbr. articles to profl. jours. Recipient Outstanding Young Educator award Highland Jr. C. of C., 1968, Outstanding Faculty award in edn. Ind. U. N.W. Campus, 1970, Outstanding Teaching Faculty award Ball State U., 1982, Ball State U. fellowship, 1971-73, Hon. Mem. award Nat. Assn. Biology Tchrs., 1992, Outstanding Undergrad. Sci. Tchr. in Nation, Soc. of Coll. Sci. Tchrs./Kendall Mgmt., 1997; named Ind. Prof. of Yr., Coun. for Advancement and Support of Edn./Carneige, 1997. Fellow Ind. Acad. Sci.; mem. Nat. Sci. Suprs. Assn. (dir. 1969-71), Ind. Sci. Suprs. Assn. (pres. 1968-69), AAUP, Assn. Suprs. and Curriculum Devel., Nat. Biology Tchrs. Assn. (bd. dirs. 1986, 91—), Nat. Sci. Tchrs. Assn. (life), Nat. Soc. Coll. Sci. Tchrs. (undergrad. tchg. award 1997), Central Assn. Coll. Biology Tchrs., Hoosier Assn. Sci. Tchrs. Inc. (bd. dirs. 1968-71, Disting. Svc. award 1997), Ind. Assn. Tchr. Educators, Ind. Assn. Suprs. and Curriculum Devel., Ind. Biology Tchrs. Assn., Kappa Delta Pi, Phi Delta Kappa, Sigma Xi. Home: 8800 W Eucalyptus Ave Muncie IN 47304-9365 Personal E-mail: jonh49@comcast.net.

HENDRIX, LYNN PARKER, lawyer; b. McCook, Nebr., Apr. 24, 1951; s. Jack Hall and Betty Lee (Parker) H.; m. Theresa Louise Zabawa, June 19, 1976; children: Paige Ashley, Parker Jerome, Pierce Reid. BSEE, U. Nebr., 1973, JD with distinction, 1978. Bar: Nebr. 1978, U.S. Dist. Ct. Nebr. 1978, Colo. 1979, U.S. Dist. Ct. Colo. 1979, U.S. Ct. Appeals (10th cir.) 1993, Wyo. 1993, Mont. 1995, N.Y., 2000, U.S. Patent Office, 1994, U.S. Supreme Ct. 2004. Surveyor Nebr. Dept. Roads, McCook, 1973; constrn. adminstr. Commonwealth Electric Co., Lincoln, Nebr., 1974, cons. engr., 1975; instr. U. Nebr., Lincoln, 1974-75; law clk. Nebr. Atty.-Gen., Lincoln, 1976-77; assoc. Holme Robert & Owen, LLP, Denver, 1978-83; ptnr. Holme Robert & Owen, Denver, 1984—. Editor-in-chief Nebr. Law Rev., 1977-78, exec. editor, 1976-77; contbr. articles to profl. jours. Sec., bd. dirs. Girls Club Denver, 1984-90, Girls Inc. of Metro Denver, 1992-94; trustee, sec. Rocky Mountain Minn. Law Found. Named Adm., Nebr. Navy. Mem. ABA, Colo. Bar Assn., Mont. Bar Assn., Nebr. Bar Assn., Wyo. Bar Assn., N.Y. Bar Assn., S.E. Law Club (pres. 1990-91), Meridian Golf Club, Sigma Alpha Epsilon, Tau Beta Pi, Sigma Tau (pres.), Eta Kappa Nu. Home: 8125 S Glencoe Ct Centennial CO 80122-3876 Office: Holme Roberts & Owen LLP 1700 Lincoln St Ste 4100 Denver CO 80203-4541

HENDRIX, MARY ELIZABETH, language educator, researcher; b. Tuscaloosa, Ala., Mar. 17, 1973; d. Lawrence Thomson and Evelyn Jacobs Hendrix. BA in English & Dance cum laude, U. Ala., 1998, MA in Secondary Edn., 2000, postgrad., 2005—. Coord. Am. reads program U. Ala., Tuscaloosa, 1999—2000; tchr. English Meadow Creek High Sch., Lawrenceville, Ga., 2000—01, The Capitol Sch., Tuscaloosa, 2001—02, Shelton State C.C., 2001—04; rsch. asst. U. Ala., 2003—; English tchr. Mem. adv. bd. cmty. svc. & vol. U. Ala., 1999—2000. Mem. Ala. Citizens Constl. Reform, Tuscaloosa, 2004—, Ala. Arise, Birmingham, 2005—; grad. sen. U. Ala., 2004—; ctrl. region coord. Constl. Reform Edn. Campaign Greater Birmingham Ministries, coord. ctrl. region constnl. reform edn. campaign, 2005—. Recipient Eddy Fulks award, The Elliott Soc., U. Ala., 1997; scholar, U. Ala., 2005. Mem.: The Blackburn Inst., Sigma Tau Delta, Kappa Delta Pi, Phi Delta Kappa. Democrat. Achievements include patent on game for stimulating reading. Avocations: writing, dance, exercise, reading, theater. Home: 2706 31st Ave Way Northport AL 35476-3610 Office: U Ala Coll Edn 210 Wilson Hall Box 870302 Tuscaloosa AL 35487 Office Phone: 205-826-5549. Personal E-mail: ehendrix@cobra.simplecom.net. Business E-Mail: elizabeth@gbm.org.

HENDRIX, SHERMAN SAMUEL, biology professor, researcher; b. Bridgeport, Conn., June 1, 1939; m. Carol Ann Seibel, June 10, 1961; children: Marc, Robin. BA in Biology, Gettysburg Coll., 1961; MS in Zoology, Fla. State U., 1964; PhD in Zoology, U. Md., 1972. Instr. biology Gettysburg (Pa.) Coll., 1964-70, asst. prof., 1970-77, assoc. prof., 1977-90, prof., 1990—, chmn. dept., 1985—90, 1997—2001, coll. marshal, 2000—. Contbr. articles to Jour. Parasitology, Zeitschrift für Parasitenkunde, Comparative Parasitology, Proc. Helminthological Soc. Washington, Jour. Helminthological Soc. Washington, Fisheries Bull., Internat. Jour. for Parasitology, Folia Parasitologica. Bd. dirs. United Way Adams County, Gettysburg, 1983-86. Interam. fellow in tropical medicine NIH, 1973. Mem. Am. Soc. Parasitologists (mentor com. 2003—, chair 2004—), Helminthological Soc. Washington (pres. 1984, v.p. 2002-04, corr. sec.-treas. 2005—, editl. bd. 1985-2002, editor jours. 1993-98, Anniversary award 1998), Pa. Acad. Sci. (pres. 1990-92, Lifetime Achievement award 1998), Wildlife Diseases Assn., Am. Malacological Union. Lutheran. Achievements include research on aquatic animal parasites. Office: Gettysburg Coll Dept Biology Gettysburg PA 17325

HENDRIX, STEPHEN C., financial executive; b. Phila., Feb. 24, 1941; s. Houston W. and Helen Hendrix; children: Kimberly, Jeffrey, Julie. BA, Tex. Christian U., 1964; M in Internat. Svc., Am. U., 1966; MBA, Ohio State U., 1972. Jr. officer U.S. Dept. State, AID, Washington, 1967-68; mgr. mktg. adminstrn. Amecom divsn. Litton Industries, College Park, Md., 1968-70; mgr. fin. and planning internat. divsn. Anchor Hocking Corp., Lancaster, Ohio, 1970-73; bank rels. mgr. E.I. Dupont de Nemours & Co., Wilmington, Del., 1973-78; corp. treas. mgr. SmithKline Beckman Corp., Phila., 1978-79, asst. treas. domestic, 1979-82, asst. treas. internat., 1982-87, v.p., asst. treas. internat., 1987-89; v.p., treas. SmithKline Beecham Corp. (formerly SmithKline Beckman Corp.), Phila., 1989-91; treas. Armstrong World Industries, Lancaster, Pa., 1993-96; cons. AstraZeneca, Wayne, Pa., 1997-99, LifeSensors Inc., Wayne, 2000—. Contbr. articles to profl. jours. Mem. CFA Inst., Fin. Execs. Inst., Nat. Assn. Corp. Treas. Home and Office: 2403 Woodview Way Malvern PA 19355-3231 E-mail: stevehendrix@yahoo.com.

HENDRIX-MITCHELL, PANCHITA LAVONNE, retired voice educator, retired music educator; b. Jacksonville, Fla., May 31, 1947; d. Henry and Viola Williams (Little) Johnson; m. Daniel Wilbert Hendrix (dec.); children: Gia Michelle Hendrix-Lawe, Piagét Hendrix, Danielle Hendrix; m. Ronnie Tyrone Mitchell, July 5, 1993. AA, Palm Beach CC, 1969; BFA, Fla. Atlantic U., 1972, MA in Edn., 1979. Music instr. Palm Beach County Sch. Bd., West Palm Beach, Fla., 1972—2003; ret., 2003. CEO, pres. Agapé Music, West Palm Beach, 1995—. Asst. coord. cmty. outreach Ephesus Seventh Day Adventist Ch., West Palm Beach, 2005—; vol. music tchr. Ephesus Jr. Acad., West Palm Beach, 2005—; musician Ephesus Seventh Day Adventist Ch., West Palm Beach. Named Tchr. of Excellence, Palm Beach County Schs., 1998—99. Mem.: Fla. Music Educators Assn. (25 Yr. Svc. award 1997). Adventist. Avocation: music. Home: 1549 6th St West Palm Beach FL 33401

HENDRIXSON, PETER S., lawyer; b. Wilmington, Del., Apr. 9, 1947; s. Philip Roe and Betty Jane (Schillo) H.; m. Carolyn Hodge Ford, June 14, 1969; children: Julie Elise, Bradley Scott. BA, Northwestern U., 1969; JD magna cum laude, Harvard U., 1972. Bar: Minn. 1973, U.S. Dist. Ct. Minn. 1973, U.S. Supreme Ct. 1978. Law clerk U.S. Ct. Appeals, Boston, 1972-73; assoc., ptnr. trial dept. Dorsey & Whitney, Mpls., 1973—, chair trial dept., 1989-93, chair trial and adminstrv. group, 1994—, mng. ptnr., 2000—. Editor, officer Harvard Law Review, 1970-72. Treas. Fraser for Mayor Com., Mpls., 1983-95; bd. govs. Children's Theatre, Mpls., 1987-92; various positions Mayflower Congl. Ch.; bd. dirs. La Creche Early Childhood Ctrs., Mpls., 1990-98, Children's Home Soc., St. Paul, 1990—, Guthrie Theater, 1995-00. Mem. Minn State Bar (chair anti-trust law sect. 1992-93), Phi Beta Kappa. Democrat. Congregationalist. Office: Dorsey & Whitney LLP 50 S 6th St Ste 1500 Minneapolis MN 55402 Office Phone: 612-340-2917. Office Fax: 612-340-2868. Business E-Mail: hendrixson.peter@dorsey.com.*

HENDRON, MICHAEL G., management consultant; children: Kaden, Bronte, Corbett. BA in polit. sci., Brigham Young U., 1995; MBA, U. Va., 2000; postgrad., U. Tex., 2002—. Devel. intern U.S. C. of C., Wash., 1995; bus. devel. coord. Kanematsu USA, Sunnyvale, Calif., 1995—98; supply chain analyst United Technologies Corp., Hartford, Conn., 1999; sr. strategy cons. Alliance Consulting Group, San Jose, Calif., 2000—01; founder Arcwise Consulting, Walnut Creek, Calif., 2001—02. Program co-director ACCESS Big Sibling Program, Provo, Utah, 1993—94; missionary svc. LDS Ch., Japan, 1990—92. Mem.: Strategic Mgmt. Soc., Acad. Mgmt., Pi Sigma Alpha, Golden Key, Phi Kappa Phi.

HENDRY, ANDREW DELANEY, lawyer, consumer products company executive; b. N.Y.C., Aug. 9, 1947; s. Andrew Joseph and Virginia (Delaney) H.; 1 child, Robert. AB in Econs., Georgetown U., 1969; JD, NYU, 1972. Bar: N.Y. 1973. Va. 1981, Mich. 1984, Pa. 1987. Assoc. Battle and Fowler, N.Y.C., 1972-79; sr. corp. and fin. atty. Reynolds Metals Co., Richmond, Va., 1979-82; sr. staff counsel Burroughs Corp., Detroit, 1982-83, assoc. gen. coun., 1983-86, dep. gen. counsel, 1986-87; v.p. legal affairs Unisys Corp, Blue Bell, Pa., 1987-88, v.p., gen. counsel, 1988-91; sr. v.p., gen. counsel, sec. Colgate-Palmolive Co., N.Y.C., 1991—. Mem. adv. bd. Georgetown U. Law Ctr. Corp. Counsel Inst., 1999—; bd. editors The M&A Lawyer, 1996—, The Met. Corp. Counsel, 1993—. Trustee The O'Neal Sch., 2001—; mem. Georgetown Coll. Adv. Bd., 2002—; bd. dirs., chmn., corp. adv. bd. Nat. Legal Aid and Def., Washington, 1992—99; bd. dirs. Lawyers Alliance for N.Y., 2000—, Lawyers Com. for Civil Rights Under Law, 2004—. With JAGC USAF, 1973. Fellow: Am. Bar Found.; mem.: ABA (com. on corp. laws, standing com. on substance abuse), Ctrl. European and Eurasian Law Inst. (bd. dirs. 2002—04), N.Y. State Bar Assn. (steering com. on commerce and industry 1997—), Am. Corp. Counsel Assn. (pres. Mich. chpt. 1985, chmn. nat. pro bono com. 1985—88, bd. dirs. emeritus N.Y. chpt.), Am. Law Inst., N.Y. Athletic Club. Office: Colgate-Palmolive Co 300 Park Ave New York NY 10022-7499 E-mail: andrew_hendry@colpal.com.

HENDRY, JOHN V., state supreme court justice; b. Omaha, Aug. 23, 1948; BS, U. Nebr., 1970, JD, 1974. Pvt. practice, Licoln, 1974-1995; county ct. judge 3d Jud. Dist., 1995-98; chief justice Nebr. Supreme Ct., 1998—. Fellow: Nebr. State Bar Found.; mem.: Nebr. State Bar Assn. Office: Nebr Supreme Ct Rm 2214 State Capitol Lincoln NE 68509

HENEGAN, JOHN C(LARK), lawyer; b. Mobile, Ala., Oct. 14, 1950; s. Virgil Baker and Marie (Fife) Gunter; m. Morella Lloyd Kuykendall, Aug. 5, 1972; children: Clark, Jim. BA in English and Philosophy, U. Miss., 1972, JD with honors, 1976. Bar: Miss. 1976, U.S. Dist. Ct. (no. dist.) Miss. 1976, N.Y. 1978, U.S. Dist. Ct. (so. dist.) N.Y. 1979, U.S. Ct. Appeals (5th and 11th cirs.) 1982, U.S. Ct. Appeals (2nd cir.) 1984, U.S. Dist. Ct. (so. dist.) Miss. 1984, U.S. Ct. Appeals (fed. cir.) 1995, U.S. Supreme Ct. 1995. Law clk. to judge U.S. Ct. Appeals (5th cir.), 1976-77; atty. Dewey, Ballantine, Bushby, Palmer & Wood, N.Y.C. and Washington, 1977-81; exec. asst., chief of staff to Gov. William Winter Jackson, Miss., 1981-84; mem. Butler, Snow, O'Mara, Stevens & Cannada, PLLC, Jackson, 1984—. Lectr. U. Miss. Ctr. for Continuing Legal Edn., 1985, 87, Miss. Jud. Coll., Oxford, 1982; mem. lawyers adv. com. U.S. Ct. Appeals for 5th Cir. Jud. Conf., 1991-93. Editor-in-chief Miss. Law Jour., 1976; editor Miss. Lawyer, 1985; contbr. articles to legal jours. Bd. dirs. Mississippians for Ednl. Broadcasting, Jackson, 1983-90, North Jackson Youth Baseball, Inc., 1991-97, Ctr. and Ctrl. S.W. Miss. Legal Svcs., 1997-2004; co-pres. Chastain Mid. Sch. Parent Tchrs. Students Assn., 1995-96; mem. Miss. Ethics Commn., Jackson, 1984-87; mem. resources bd. William Winter Inst. Racial Raconciliation, 2004—; del. Hinds County Dem. Conv., 1988; mem. Miss. Dem. Fin. Coun., 1988, Hinds County Dem. Exec. Com., 1989-92; Sunday sch. supt. Covenant Presbyn. Ch., 1989-90, deacon, 1991-96, moderator of diaconate, 1993-94, elder, 1996-2002, 04—. Recipient Cmty. Svc. award Hinds County Bar Assn., 1998. Mem. ABA, FBA, Miss. Bar Assn. (chmn. Law Day U.S.A. 1983), Miss. Def. Lawyers Assn., Miss. Law Jour. Alumni Assn. (bd. dirs. 1985—), 5th Cir. Bar Assn., Hinds County Bar Assn. (bd. dir. 2002-04, sec., treas. 2004—), Jackson C. of C., Am. Inns of Ct. (barrister Charles Clark chpt. 1991-93, assoc. 2004—), Phi Kappa Phi, Phi Delta Phi, Omicron Delta Kappa. Avocation: reading. Home: 2441 Eastover Dr Jackson MS 39211-6727 Office: 210 E Capitol St Fl 17 Jackson MS 39201-2306 Office Phone: 601-985-4530. E-mail: john.henegan@butlersnow.com.

HENEGHAN, THOMAS P., real estate company executive; From v.p., CFO, treas. to pres., CEO Manufactured Home Cmtys. Inc., Chgo., 1995—2004, pres., 2004—, CEO, 2004—. Office: Manufactured Home Communities Inc 2 North Riverside Plaza Chicago IL 60606

HENES, DONNA, artist, writer; b. Cleve., Sept. 19, 1945; d. Nathan and Adelaide (Ross) Trugman. Student, Ohio State U., 1963-66; BS, CCNY, 1971, MS in Art Edn., 1972. Prodr. series pub. participatory celebratory events in parks, museums and univs., 100 cities in 9 countries, 1970—. Designer Olympic Medalist Tickertape Parade, N.Y.C., 1984; ednl. cons. New Wilderness Foundation, N.Y.C., 1985; judge Jane Addams Peace Assn. Children's Book Award, N.Y.C., 1983-89; ritual cons. Mama Donna's Tea Garden. Author, designer Dressing Our Wounds in Warm Clothes, 1982, Noting the Process of Noting the Process, 1977, Celestially Auspicious Occasions, 1996, The Moon Watcher's Companion, 2004, The Queen of My Self, 2005, author, performer (CD) Reverence to Her: Part I Mythology, the Matriarchy & Me, 1998, pub., editor quar. Always in Season: Living in Sync with the Cycles; author (with others): Peace: Piece by Piece; editor: Celebration News, 1986—92; internationally syndicated columnist; contbr. numerous articles to profl.jours. Co-founder, pres. STAND (Stand Together Affirmative Neighborhood Devel.), N.Y.C.; composer Chants for Peace/Chance for Peace, Sta. WNYC, first peace message in space, 1982. Fellow Nat. Endowment for Arts, 1982, interarts, 1983, N.Y. Found. for Arts, 1986, 90; grantee N.Y. State Coun. on Arts, N.Y.C. State Bicentennial Commn., Com. for Visual Arts, Money for Women, Beard's Fund, Jerome Found., Ctr. for the Media Arts; recipient Citation award Mayor of N.Y.C. David Dinkins. Mem. Internat. Ctr. for Celebration (bd. dirs., co-founder). Avocations: dance, travel, reading, walking, swimming. Office Phone: 718-857-1343. Personal E-mail: cityshaman@aol.com.

HENES, SAMUEL ERNST, lawyer; b. Oberlin, Ohio, Jan. 28, 1937; s. Ernst Louis and Martha Hannah (Artz) H. AB with honors, Cornell U., 1959; LL.B., Harvard U., 1962. Bar: Ohio, 1962. Assoc. Arter & Hadden, Cleve., 1962-70, ptnr., 1971-89. Trustee Musart Soc., Cleve., 1980—, pres. 1985-94; trustee Young Audiences Greater Cleve., Inc., 1982-85, George P. Bickford Found., 1981-90; hon. trustee So. Lorain County Hist. Soc., Wellington, Ohio, 1988—. Served to 1st lt. U.S. Army, 1963-65 Mem. ABA, Cleve. Bar Assn., Ohio State Bar Assn. Clubs: Rowfant (Cleve.) (sec. 1985-89). Republican. Methodist. Avocations: book collecting, amateur harpsichordist, swimming, travel. Home: 13605 Shaker Blvd Apt 2B Cleveland OH 44120-1503 Office Phone: 216-991-3574. Personal E-mail: shenes@msn.com.

HENEVELD-STORY, CHRISTY JEAN, educational researcher; b. San Jose, Calif., June 30, 1967; d. Sally Jean Dudley and Robert Michael Heneveld, Charles Gustav Sieloff (Stepfather) and Barbara Leech Heneveld (Stepmother); m. Robert David Duis, July 22, 1992; children: James Michael Story, Charles David Story, Christopher Robert Story. PhD, U. Calif., 1998. Lectr. U. Calif., Santa Cruz, 1999—2000; rschr. Ctr. for Study of Law and Soc. - UC Berkeley, 2000—02; tchr. Castilleja Sch., Palo Alto, Calif., 2002—. Internship coord. Castilleja Sch., Palo Alto, Calif., 2002—04. Sec. Ladera Cmty. Assn., unincorporated San Mateo County, Calif., 1999—2002; tutor Los Lomitas Sch. Dist., Atherton, Calif., 2001—04. Fellow, UC Regents, 1991-1992; Post Doctoral fellow, Ctr. for Study of Law and Soc., 2001-2002, Rsch. fellow, Ctr. for Study of Russia and Soviet Union, Moscow, Russia, 1996. Mem.: Western Assn. Women Historians, Am. Assn. Women in Slavic Studies, Am. Hist. Assn. D-Liberal. Avocations: scuba diving, travel, cooking. Home: 170 Pecora Way Portola Valley CA 94028 Office: Castilleja Sch 1310 Bryant St Palo Alto CA 94301 Office Phone: 650-328-3160. Personal E-mail: story@alum.vassar.edu.

HENG, DONALD JAMES, JR., lawyer; b. Mpls., July 12, 1944; s. Donald James and Catharine Amelia (Strom) H.; m. Kathleen Ann Bailey, Sept. 2, 1967; 1 child, Francesca Remy BA cum laude, Yale U., 1967; JD magna cum laude, Minn., 1971. Bar: Calif. 1971, U.S. Dist. Ct. (no. dist.) Calif. 1971, U.S. Ct. Appeals (9th cir.) 1971. Assoc. Brobeck, Phleger & Harrison, San Francisco, 1971-73, ptnr., 1978-90; atty.-adviser Office Internat. Tax Counsel, Dept. Treasury, Washington, 1973-75; pvt. practice law San Francisco, 1990—. Lectr., writer on tax-related subjects Note and comment editor Minn. Law Rev., 1970-71 Co-recipient award for outstanding performance Am. Lawyer Mag., 1981; Fulbright scholar, Italy, 1967-68 Mem. ABA, Calif. Bar Assn., Oakland Mus. Assn. (pres. 1985-87, bd. dirs. 1983-89), Mus. Soc. San Francisco, Fine Arts Mus. (bd. dirs. 1989-90), Order Coif. Republican. Congregationalist. Office: 388 Market St Ste 500 San Francisco CA 94111-5313

HENGST, HERBERT RANDALL, retired educator; b. Grand Rapids, Mich., May 22, 1924; s. Marion Cecil and L. Elnora H.; m. Georgina Jane, Apr. 1, 1950; children H. Randall II, Julie Ann. AB, Albion Coll., 1948; MS in Edn., Bowling Green State U., 1949; PhD, Mich. State U., 1960. Tchr. Lake Orion (Mich.) H.S., 1949-51; prin. Ortonville (Mich.) H.S., 1951-53, Barnum Jr. H.S., Birmingham, Mich., 1953-58; instr., asst. prof. Mich. State U., East Lansing, 1958-61; dir. higher edn. Mich. Edn. Assn., Lansing, 1961-64; from assoc. prof. to prof. emeritus U. Okla., Norman, 1964—88, asst. dean edn., 1968—71, dir. ctr. studies higher edn., 1971-88, interim dean edn., 1973-74, prof. emeritus, 1988—. Cons. Ministry Edn. Riyadh, Saudi Arabia, 1972-79, Arab Bur. Edn. Gulf States, Riyadh, 1979-87; vis. prof. King Saud U., Riyadh, 1974-75; lectr. in field. Co-author: Contemporary Educational Administration, 1982; co-author, editor: The Geo Lynn Cross Chrestomathy, 1998; editor: Planning & Utilization of Instructional Space, 1960, An Institutional Profile, 1972. Pastor Emanuel, Meth. Charge Gunnisonville, Lansing, 1958-60; co-founder Okla. Inst. Viable Future, Norman, 1975—; bd. dirs., tchr., conf. del. McFarlin Meth. Ch., 1998-99. Recipient Disting. Flying Cross, USAF, 1945; vis. scholar, Harvard U., 1986. Mem. Canterbury Choral Soc. (life), Omicron Delta Kappa, Alpha Tau Omega. Democrat. Avocations: reading, gardening, poetry, singing. Home: 2643 S Pickard Norman OK 73072

HENGSTLER, GARY ARDELL, publisher, editor, lawyer; b. Wapakoneta, Ohio, Mar. 23, 1947; s. Luther C. and N. Delphine (Sims) H.; m. Linda K. Spreen, Mar. 8, 1969 (div. Aug. 1986); children: Dylan A., Joel S.; m. Laura M. Williams, Dec. 15, 1986. BS, Ball State U., 1969; JD, Cleve. State U., 1983. Bar: Ohio 1984, U.S. Dist. Ct. (no. dist.) Ohio 1984, Nev. 2005. Assoc. Blaszak, Schilling, Coey & Bennett, Elyria, Ohio, 1984-85; editor: The Tex.

Lawyer, Austin, 1985-86; news editor ABA Jour., Chgo., 1986-89, editor, pub., 1989-2000; dir. Donald W. Reynolds Nat. Ctr. Cts. & Media, Reno, 2000—. Home: 5055 Carnoustie Dr Reno NV 89502-9724 Office: Donald W Reynolds Nat Ctr Cts & Media U Nev Jud Coll Bldg 358 Reno NV 89557-0001 Office Phone: 775-327-8270. Office Fax: 775-327-2160. Business E-Mail: hengstler@judges.org.

HENICAN, ELLIS, columnist, political correspondent; m. Stephanie Carvlin. Bachelor's Degree in Polit. Sci., Hampshire Coll.; Master's Degree, Columbia U. Sch. Journalism. Reporter Kentucky Post, Knickerbocker News, Albany, NY; joined Newsday, 1985—, gen. assignment reporter, 1985, staff columnist; polit. contbr. FOX News Channel, 1999—. Daily commentator, host Bloomberg Radio Network; host nationally syndicated weekend show on the Talk Radio Network. Contbr. articles to New Republic and Cosmopolitan; voice Sealab 2021, 2001—. Co-recipient Pulitzer Prizes for Spot News (two); recipient Meyer Berger award for disting. writing about NYC, Nat. Clarion award for column writing. Office: FOX News Channel 1211 Avenue of the Americas New York NY 10036*

HENIG, SUZANNE, retired academic administrator, editor, writer; b. N.Y.C., Jan. 12, 1936; d. Samuel G. and Gicia (Gottesdiener) Henig. BA, NYU, 1957, MA, 1961, PhD, 1968. V.p. Am. Heritage Soc., Washington, 1975-80; editor Va. Woolf Quar., San Diego, 1976-79; pres. India Expo, San Diego, 1976-81; mng. dir. Aeolian Press, San Diego, 1976—. Pres. Genesis Prodns. of Hollywood, San Diego, 1990-96. Editor Internat. Jour. Medicine, 1996; contbr. articles to profl. jours. V.p. N.Y. Young Reps., N.Y.C., 1953-54. Recipient Thomas Wolfe award for poetry NYU, 1957; grantee ACLS, Leopold Schepp Found., Am. Philos. Soc. Address: 5303 La Jolla Hermosa La Jolla CA 92037

HENIKOFF, LEO M., JR., academic administrator, educator, medical educator; b. Chgo., May 9, 1939; m. Carole E. Andersen; children from previous marriage: Leo M. III, Jamie Sue. MD with highest honors, U. Ill., Chgo., 1963. Diplomate Am. Bd. Pediat., Am. Bd. Pediat. Cardiology. Intern Presbyn.-St. Luke's Hosp., Chgo., 1963-64, resident, 1964-66, fellow in pediatric cardiology, 1968-69; clin. instr. U. Ill. Coll. Medicine, Chgo., 1964-66; clin. instr. pediatrics Georgetown U. Med. Sch., Washington, 1966-68, clin. asst. prof., 1968; asst. prof. U. Ill. Coll. Medicine, Chgo., 1968-71; asst. prof. pediat. Rush Med. Coll., Chgo., 1971-74, assoc. prof., 1974-79, asst. dean admissions, 1971-74, assoc. dean student affairs, 1974-76, assoc. dean med. scis. and svcs., 1976-79, acting dean v.p. med. affairs, 1976-78, prof. pediatrics, prof. medicine, 1984—; v.p. inter-instl. affairs Rush-Presbyn.-St. Luke's Med. Ctr., Chgo., 1978-79, pres., 1984—; pres., CEO; trustee Rush-Presbyn.-St. Luke's Med. Ctr., Chgo., 1984—; dean and v.p. med. affairs Temple U. Sch. Medicine, Phila., 1979-84, prof. pediat. and medicine, 1979-84; pres. Rush U., Chgo., 1984—. Adj. attending Presbyn.-St. Luke's Hosp., 1969, asst., 1970-72, assoc., 1973-76, sr. attending, 1977-79, 84—; staff Temple U. Hosp., 1979-84; assoc. staff St. Christopher's Hosp. for Children, 1979-84; mem. Ill. Coun. of Deans, 1977-79; vice chmn. Chgo. Tech. Pk., 1984-85, 86-87, chmn., 1985-86, 87-88; chmn. bd. dirs. Mid-Am. Health Programs, Inc., 1985—; bd. dirs. Harris Trust and Savs. Bank, Harris Bankcorp. Inc.; chmn. bd. dirs. Rush North Shore Health Svcs., 1988—, Rush/Copley Health Care Sys. Inc., 1988—. Contbr. chpts. to books, articles to profl. jours. Bd. dirs. Fishbein Found., 1975-79, Chgo. Regional Blood Program, 1977-79, Sch. Dist. 69, 1974-75, Johnston R. Bowman Health Ctr. for Elderly, 1984—; mem. bd. mgrs. St. Christopher's Hosp. for Children, 1979-84; mem. bd. govs. Temple U. Hosp., 1979-84, Heart Assn. S.E. Pa., 1979-84; trustee Episc. Hosp., 1983-84, Otho S.A. Sprague Meml. Inst., 1984—; mem. adv. bd. Univ. Village Assn., 1984—; mem. exec. com. Gov.'s Build Ill. Com., 1985—. Lt. comdr. USPHS, 1964-68, Res. 1968—. Recipient Roche Med. award, 1962, Mosby award, 1963, Raymond B. Allen Instructorship award U. Ill. Coll. Medicine, 1966, also Med. Alumni award, 1988, Phoenix award Rush Med. Coll., 1977. Fellow Am. Acad. Pediat., Inst. Medicine Chgo., Coll. Physicians Phila., Am. Coll. Physicians Execs.; mem. Assn. Am. Med. Colls. (chmn. nominating com. 1980, mem. coun. deans 1977-84, mem. audit com. 1984), Coun. Tchg. Hosps. (adminstrv. bd. 1987-90), Pa. Med. Sch. Deans Com., AMA (mem. coun. on ethical and jud. affairs 1984-88), Pa. Med. Soc., Philadelphia County Med. Soc., Assn. Acad. Health Ctrs. (bd. dirs. 1988-94, chmn.-elect 1991-92, chmn. 1992-93), Alpha Omega Alpha (chmn. nat. nominating com. 1981-90, nat. dir. 1979-90, pres. 1989-90), Omega Beta Pi, Phi Eta Sigma, Phi Kappa Phi. Office: Rush-Presbyn-St Luke's Med Ctr 1653 W Congress Pkwy Chicago IL 60612-3833

HENINGER, GEORGE ROBERT, psychology professor, researcher; b. L.A., Nov. 15, 1934; s. Owen P. and Rachel (Cannon) H.; m. Julie Hawkes, June 27, 1957; children: Steven, Catharine, Karen, Brian. BS, U. Utah, 1957, MD, 1960. Diplomate Am. Bd. Psychiatry and Neurology. Intern Boston City Hosp., 1960-61; resident in psychiatry Mass. Mental Health Ctr., 1961-63, chief resident, 1963-64; clin. assoc., clin. neuropharmacology rsch. ctr. St. Elizabeth's Hosp. NIMH, Washington, 1964-65, program specialist, office of dir. Bethesda, Md., 1965-66; asst. prof. psychiatry, assoc. chief rsch. ward Yale U., New Haven, 1966-71, assoc. prof., 1971-76, chief rsch. ward, 1971-78, prof. clin. psychiatry, 1976-78, prof. psychiatry, dir. Abraham Ribicoff Rsch. Facilities, 1978-93, assoc. chmn. rsch. dept. psychiatry, 1988-93, dir. lab. clin. and molecular neurobiology, 1993—. Cons. NIMH, 1975-86, 88-94, NIH, 1987, McGill U., 1989, VA, 1990-94, Nat. Rsch. Coun. Can., 1991-93, Nat. Inst. Aging, 1992-93, Wellcome Trust, 1992-94, Pfizer Inc., Merck, Sharp & Dohme, Inc., The Upjohn Co., Hoffman La Roche, Inc., Burroughs Wellcome Co., Bristol-Meyers Co., Squibb Corp., Kali DuPhar, Inc.; bd. sci. advisors, Neurogen Corp. REviewer manuscripts Archives Gen. Psychiatry, Am. Jour. Psychiatry, Psychiatry Rsch., Biol. Psychiatry, Jour. Affective Disorders, Jour. Clin. Psychopharmacology, Life Scis., Neurochemistry Internat., Psychiatry, Schizophrenia Bull., Psychoneuroendocrinology, Jour. AMA. Sr. asst. surgeon USPHS, 1964-66. Recipient Rsch. Sci. Devel. award Type II, NIMH, 1971, 1st prize Anna Monika Found., 1995; grantee NIMH, 1971, 74, 77, 82, 85, 89, 91. Fellow Am. Coll. Neuropsychopharmacology, Am. Psychiat. Assn.; mem. AAAS, Am. Psychopath. Assn., Soc. Neurosci., Soc. Biol. Psychiatry, Psychiat. Rsch. Soc., N.Y. Acad. Scis., Conn. Psychiat. Soc., Sigma Xi, Phi Kappa Phi, Alpha Omega Alpha. Avocation: running. Office: Yale U 34 Park St New Haven CT 06511

HENINGER, SIMEON KAHN, JR., language educator; b. Monroe, La., Oct. 27, 1922; s. Simeon Kahn and Elsye (Lieber) H.; m. Irene Callen, July 16, 1957; children— Dale Callen, Kathryn Leigh, Philip Ward, Polly Elizabeth, Simeon Kahn III; m. Dorothy Cooper Langston, May 30, 1971 BS, Tulane U., 1944, BA, 1947, MA, 1949; B.Litt. (Fulbright scholar), Oxford (Eng.) U., 1952; PhD, Johns Hopkins U., 1955. Instr. Duke U., Durham, N.C., 1955-57, asst. prof., 1957-62, assoc. prof., 1962-65, prof., 1965-67; prof. English U. Wis.-Madison, 1967-71; chmn. dept. U. Wis., Madison, 1968-70; prof. English U. B.C., Vancouver, Can., 1971-82; disting. prof. English and comparative lit. U. N.C., Chapel Hill, 1982—. Author: A Handbook of Renaissance Meteorology, 1960, Touches of Sweet Harmony, 1974, The Cosmographical Glass, 1977, Sidney and Spenser: The Poet as Maker, 1989, Proportion Poetical: The Subtext of form in the English Renaissance, 1994; editor: Thomas Watson, The Hekatompathia, 1964, Edmund Spenser, Poetry, 1970, Edmund Spenser, Shepheardes Calender, 1979, Kalendar of Sheepehards, 1979, Framing Fact and Fiction: Perspective in Early Modern England, 1992; asst. editor Modern Language Notes, 1953-55; mem. editorial bd. Duquesne Studies in Lang. and Lit., 1976-93, Renaissance and Reformation, 1976-93, Spenser Studies, 1977-93, Studies in English Lit., 1978-93, John Donne Jour., 1982-93, Huntington Libr. Quar., 1982-86, Spenser Newsletter, 1986-92, Studies in Philology, 1987-93, ANQ: A Quarterly Jour., 1988-93; contbr. articles to profl. jours. Exec. sec.-treas. Southeastern Renaissance Conf., 1958-67; mem. Nat. Shakespeare Anniversary Com., 1963-64; mem. ctrl. exec. com. Folger Inst. Renaissance and 18th Century Studies, 1982-92. Capt. USAAF, 1943-46. Folger Library fellow, 1961, Guggenheim fellow, 1962-63, Southeastern Inst. Medieval and Renaissance Studies fellow, 1967, Huntington Library fellow, 1970-71, 81, Killam Sr. fellow, 1975-76, Folger Inst. fellow, 1984, Ariz. Ctr. for Medieval and Renaissance Studies fellow, 1990. Mem. MLA, ACLU, Renaissance Soc. Am. (adv. coun. 1958-68, 75-80), Spenser Soc. (adv. coun. 1977-80, 86-90, pres. 1988-89), Milton Soc. (adv. coun. 1980-83), Medieval Acad. Am., Phi Beta Kappa Home: 750 Weaver Dairy Rd #247 Chapel Hill NC 27514-1493 E-mail: timdothening@mindspring.com.

HENINGTON, CARLEN, psychologist, educator; d. Carl Frank and Betty Jean Votapka; m. William Leonard Henington, 1978; children: Blake Leonard, Robin Leonard, Brianne Marie. PhD, Tex. A&M U., Coll. Sta., Tex., 1991—96. Cert. Sch. Psychol. NASP, 1996. Asst. prof. Miss. State U., 1996—2000, assoc. prof., 2000—. Cons. Miss. Early Intervention Program, Jackson, Miss., 1997—2003. Children's adv. Statewide Sch. Districts, Miss., 1994—2003. Mem.: APA, Behavior Spl. Interest Group - NASP (sec. 1999—2001), Nat. Assn. Sch. Psychol. (Miss. state del. 2005—, Miss. com. chmn.). Office: Mississippi State University 508 Allen Hall Box 9727 Mississippi State MS 39762 Office Phone: 662-325-7099. E-mail: cdh@colled.msstate.edu.

HENINGTON, DAVID MEAD, retired library director; b. El Dorado, Ark., Aug. 16, 1929; s. Bud Henry and Lucile Check (Scranton) H.; m. Barbara Jean Gibson, June 2, 1956; children— Mark David, Gibson Mead, Paul Billins. BA, U. Houston, 1951; MS in L.S., Columbia U., 1956. Young adult libr. Bklyn. Pub. Libr., 1956-58; head lit. and history dept. Dallas Pub. Libr., 1958, asst. dir., 1962-67; dir. Waco (Tex.) Pub. Libr., 1958-62, Houston Pub. Libr., 1967-95; ret., 1995. Served with USAF, 1951-55. Council on Library Resources fellow, 1970-71; recipient Liberty Bell award Houston Bar Assn., 1976 Mem. ALA, AIA (hon. mem. Tex. chpt.), Am. Mgmt. Assn., Tex. Libr. Assn. (Libr. of Yr. 1976, Disting. Svc. award 1993), Philos. Soc. Methodist. Home: 6225 San Felipe St Houston TX 77057-2809 Office Phone: 713-780-3798. Personal E-mail: dmhenington@ev1.net.

HENKE, MARCIA ANN, secondary school educator; b. Buffalo Center, Iowa, Sept. 4, 1957; d. Dean Kermit and Ruby Pauline (Durby) Farland; m. Duane Anthony Henke, July 19, 1980; children: Kayla, Brandon. BA, U. No. Iowa, 1979; MA, U. S.D., 1985. Cert. permanent tchr., Iowa. Tchr. bus. edn., coach Ctrl. Webster Cmty. Sch., Burnside, Iowa, 1979—80, South Clay Cmty. Sch., Gillett Grove, Iowa, 1980—81, Cherokee Cmty. Sch. Dist., Iowa, 1981—. Mem. NEA, Nat. Bus. Edn. Assn., Iowa Edn. Assn., Iowa Bus. Edn. Assn., Iowa Assn. Career and Tech. Educators Office: Washington HS PO Box 801 Cherokee IA 51012-1364

HENKE, MICHAEL JOHN, lawyer, educator; b. Evansville, Ind., Aug. 3, 1940; s. Emerson Overbeck and Beatrice (Arney) H.; m. Leni Edith Anderson, Mar. 20, 1966; children: Blake, Paige, Britt. BA summa cum laude, Baylor U., 1962, LLB, 1965; LLM, NYU, 1966. Bar: Tex. 1965, D.C. 1967, Va. 2005. Assoc. Covington & Burling, Washington, 1966-73, Vinson & Elkins, Washington, 1974—75, ptnr., 1976—2004; sec., gen. counsel, sec. Space Adventures, Ltd., 2005—. Adj. prof. U. Va. Law Sch., 1988-94, 96—; chmn. pro bono adv. com. Legal Aid Soc., D.C., 1990-96, trustee, 1992—, chmn. ways & means com., 1997-2000, v.p., 2000—02, pres., 2002-04; Washington adv. coun. Baylor Washington Program, 1989-92; sesquicentennial coun. of 150 Baylor U., 1993-95. Author: (with others) Petroleum Regulation Handbook, 1980, Natural Gas Yearbook, 1995; mem. editl. bd. Nat. Gas Mag., 1992-97, Best Lawyers in America, 1989—, Best Lawyers in Washington, 1997, Worlds Leading Competition and Antitrust Lawyers, 1997—, World's Leading Litigation Lawyers, 1997—; contbr. articles to profl. jours. Founder, chmn. Old Presbyn. Meeting House Day Care Ctr., Alexandria, Va., 1970-74; trustee Alexandria Country Day Sch., 2000-03. Recipient Gladys award La. State U. Sch. Law, 2003; Kenneson fellow. Mem. ABA (chmn. energy antitrust subcom. litigation sect. 1987-88, vice chmn. energy litigation com. 1988-89, chmn. 1989-92, chmn. ann. fall meeting 1993, divsn. dir. 1993-95, co-chmn. audiotaping and videotaping com. 1995-96, co-chmn. ins. coverage litigation com. 1996-98, coun. 1998-2001, co-chair task force on judiciary 2001-03, Pres.'s Commn. on 21st Century Judiciary 2002-03), D.C. Bar Assn., Tex. Bar Assn., Va. State Bar (corp. counsel), Coll. State Bar Tex., Baylor U. Alumni Assn. (bd. dirs. 1994-98), Am. Civil Trial Bar Roundtable, Met. Club, Belle Haven Country Club, Farmington Country Club (Charlottesville). Democrat. Avocations: skiing, flyfishing, tennis, backpacking. Home: 310 Charles Alexander Ct Alexandria VA 22301-1500 Office: Vinson & Elkins 1455 Pennsylvania Ave NW Ste 600 Washington DC 20004-1013 Business E-Mail: mhenke@velaw.com.

HENKEL, CATHY, newspaper sports editor; News reporter Wichita Beacon, 1966—76; sports reporter Eugene Register-Guard, 1976—87; asst. sports editor Seattle Times, 1987—90, sports editor, 1990—. Recipient AWSM Pioneer award, 2005. Office: The Seattle Times 1120 John St Seattle WA 98109-5321*

HENKEL, HERBERT LUDWIG, manufacturing executive; b. Reid, Austria, Apr. 22, 1948; m. Gloria Henkel; 2 children. BS in Aerospace Engring. and Applied, MS in Mech. Engring., Poly. U.; MBA, Pace U. Mem. tech. staff Bell Labs.; design engr. Grumman Aerospace; v.p. sales and mktg. Chgo. Pneumatic Tool Co., Hilti, Inc.; pres., COO Southern Fastening Sys. and Unifast Industries, Inc.; pres. Greenlee Textron, Rockford, Ill., 1987-93; pres. indsl. products segments Textron, Inc., 1993-98, exec. v.p., 1998-99, COO, 1998-2000, pres., 1999-2000; also chmn.; CEO Ingersoll-Rand, Montvale, NJ, 2000—; chmn., pres., 2000—. Bd. dirs. C.R. Bard Corp., AT&T Corp. Avocations: woodworking, golf, tennis. Office: Ingersoll-Rand 155 Chestnut Ridge Rd Montvale NJ 07645

HENKEL, KATHRYN GUNDY, lawyer; b. West Columbia, Tex., Oct. 16, 1952; d. Louis Ory Jr. and Patricia Dolores (Fields) Gundy. BA cum laude, Rice U., 1973; JD cum laude, Harvard U., 1976. Bar: Tex. 1976, U.S. Dist. Ct. (no. dist.) Tex. 1982, U.S. Ct. Appeals (5th cir.) 1994, U.S. Tax Ct. 1981, U.S. Supreme Ct. 1983; bd. cert. estate planning and probate law, Tex. Bd. Legal Specialization. Ptnr. Hughes & Luce, L.L.P., Dallas, 1982—. Author: Estate Planning and Wealth Preservation: Strategies and Solutions, 1997. Mem. adv. coun. Cmtys. Found. Tex. Inc., 1982—; mem. planned giving adv. com. Children's Med. Ctr., Dallas; trustee, chmn. bd. advisors to found. com. Dallas Opera. Named one of Best Lawyers in Dallas, D Mag., 2003, 2005. Fellow Am. Coll. Trust and Estate Counsel; mem. ABA (vice chair sect. real property, probate and trusts com. on generation-skipping transfers 1992-95, chair sect. of taxation com. on estate and gift taxes 1993-95, coun. dir. sect. taxation 1996-99, co-chair sect. real property, probate and trust law estate planning study com. on law reform), State Bar Tex. (chair sect. taxation 1992-93), Dallas Bar Assn. (past chair sect. taxation), Tex. Bar Found. Roman Catholic. Avocations: reading, travel. Office: Hughes & Luce LLP 1717 Main St Ste 2800 Dallas TX 75201-4685 E-mail: henkelk@hughesluce.com.

HENKEL, KATHY, composer; b. Los Angeles, Nov. 20, 1942; d. Norman Nicholas and Lila Rhea (Lee) Henkel; m. Michael Eric Manes (div.). BA in hist., UCLA, 1965; BM in music, Calif. State U., Northridge, 1976, MA in music, 1982. Music rschr. Paramount Pictures, L.A., 1978—81; music reviewer L.A. Times, 1979; scriptwriter, prod. KUSC-FM, L.A., 1984—89; program annotation, edn. cons. Chamber Music/LA, 1987—95; program annotation L.A. Chamber Orch., 1988—98, edn. cons., 1998—; liner note writer Pro Piano Records, N.Y.C., 1994—2003; composer, owner Sign of the Silver Birch Music, L.A., 2004—. Adv. bd. Los Angeles City Coll. Music Dept., 1994—. Composer various chamber music, song cycles. Recipient Commn. for Music award, State of Alaska, 1994. Mem.: Nat. Acad. Rec. Arts and Scis., Profl. Musicians Local 47, Phi Beta Kappa Alumni, Phi Beta Women's Profl. Fraternity. Avocation: hiking Cornwall coastal path. Home: 2367 Creston Dr Los Angeles CA 90068

HENKES, KEVIN, illustrator, writer; married; 2 children. Author illustrator: (children's picture books) All Alone, 1981, Bailey Goes Camping, 1985, A Weekend with Wendell, 1986, Jessica, 1989, Julius, the Baby of the World, 1990, Chrysanthemum, 1991, Owen, 1993 (Caldecott Honor Book, 1994), Lilly's Purple Plastic Purse, 1996, Wemberly Worried, 2000, Wemberly's Ice-Cream Star, 2003, Lilly's Chocolate Heart, 2003, Olive's Ocean, 2003 (Newbery Honor Book), A Box of Treats: Five Little Picture Books about Lilly and Her Friends, 2004, Kitten's First Full Moon, 2004 (NY Times Best Illustrated Books award, Randolph Caldecott medal, 2005), others. Office: c/o Greenwillow HarperCollins 1350 Ave Of The Americas New York NY 10019*

HENKIN, ROBERT ELLIOTT, nuclear medicine physician; b. Pitts., June 7, 1942; s. Hyman and Nettie (Jaffee) H.; m. Denise Dulberg, June 26, 1966 (dec. 1985); children: Gregory, Joshua, Steven; m. Renae Marley, Nov. 27, 1988. Student, Cornell U., 1960-62; BA, NYU, 1965, MD, 1969. Diplomate Am. Bd. Nuclear Medicine, Nat. Bd. Med. Examiners. Internship gen. surgery Bellevue Med. Ctr., NYU, NYC, 1969—70; resident in diagnostic radiology Northwestern U., Chgo., 1970—72, resident in nuc. medicine, 1972—74, asst. prof. radiology, 1974—76; from asst. prof. to assoc. prof. radiology Loyola U., Maywood, Ill., 1976—80, prof. radiology, 1980—, dir. nuc. medicine, 1976—98, 2002—, acting chair dept. radiology, 2000—02, vice chair dept. radiology, 2002—. Fellow Am. Coll. Radiology, Am. Coll. Nuc. Physicians (pres. 1990); mem. AMA, Am. Coll. Physician Execs., Soc. Nuc. Medicine (bd. dirs., trustee 1983-89, 2000-04, v.p. 1995-96, ho. dels. 1998-2004). Home: 875 E 22d St #202 Lombard IL 60148-5013 E-mail: unm@mindspring.com.

HENLE, PETER, retired economist, arbitrator; b. N.Y.C., Feb. 12, 1919; s. James and Marjorie (Jacobson) H.; m. Theda W. Ostrander, Aug. 25, 1941; children: Michael G., James M., Paul J. BA, Swarthmore Coll., 1940; MA, Am. U., 1947. Mem. rsch. staff, asst. dir. rsch. Am. Fed. Labor, Washington, 1946-55; asst. dir. rsch. AFL-CIO, Washington, 1955-61; chief economist Bur. Labor Stats., U.S. Dept. Labor, Washington, 1961-71; dep. asst. sec. U.S. Dept. Labor planning, evaluation research, 1977-79; sr. specialist Labor Congl. Research Service, Library of Congress, Washington, 1972-77; vis. economist Brookings Instn.; econ. cons., arbitrator Arlington, Va., 1979-92. Contbr. articles to profl. jours. Chmn. Arlington County (Va.) Manpower Planning Council, 1975-77; trustee Arlington County Employees Retirement System, 1985-89. With AUS, 1941-42; with USAAF, 1942-45. Recipient Disting. Achievement award U.S. Dept. Labor, 1968; Brookings Instn. fed. exec. fellow, 1971-72 Mem. Nat. Acad. Arbitrators, Indsl. Rels. Rsch. Assn. Address: Collington Retirement 10450 Lottsford Rd Mitchellville MD 20721

HENLEY, ARTHUR, writer, editor; b. Rockaway Beach, N.Y., Sept. 9, 1921; s. Nathan Siegel and Theresa (Hohauser) H.; m. Janet Radskin, June 3, 1950; children: Eric, Kenneth. Engr. Assoc., Pratt Inst., 1944; BA, CCNY, 1969. Tech. writer Fairchild Camera Co., 1944-45; TV program cons., 1960—; mem. faculty NYU, 1969-70. Mental health cons., Nat. Assn. Mental Health Keynoter, coll. lectr. Radio writer, producer shows Bob & Ray, Make Up Your Mind, 13 by Henley; others; also writer advt. jingles; TV producer Kate Smith Show, Make Up Your Mind, Broadway Open House; TV writer, producer, also indsl. films, others; mag. contbr. Ladies Home Jour., McCalls, Family Health, Public Affairs Com., N.Y. Times, Sat. Eve Post, others, 1961—; author: The Mathematics of Humor, 1948, Demon In My View, 1966, Make Up Your Mind, 1967, Yes Power, 1969, The Right to Lie, 1970, Schizophrenia, 1971, revised edit. 1987, What Other Child-Care Books Don't Tell You, 1972, The Complete Alibi Handbook, 1972, The Difficult Child, 1973, How to Be a Perfect Liar, 1978, Don't Be Afraid of Cataracts, 1978, Don't be Afraid of Cataracts, rev. edit., 1983, Phobias The Crippling Fears, 1987, paperback edit., 1988, Lily & Joel: A Novel of Life, Love and Audio Tapes, 1992, Talking Book and Braille edit., 1994; contbr. to anthologies How to Write for Pleasure and Profit, You and Your Mind, Treasury of Tips for Writers, How to Write Television Comedy, Tools of the Writer's Trade; editor: Interdisciplinary Communications Program, Smithsonian Inst., 1975. Cons. med. editor: Globe Communications, 1976-79; columnist Brides Mag, 1970. Recipient Russell Sage Found. award., TV-Radio Mirror Gold medals (2).; work included in U. Wyo. Am. Heritage Ctr. Mem. Am. Soc. Journalists and Authors, Nat. Assn. Sci. Writers, PEN, AFTRA. Clubs: Nat. Press. Home and Office: 73-37 Austin St Forest Hills NY 11375-6219 E-mail: ah55@webtv.net. *If I have learned anything from living it is that a static life is no life at all while a life of change without direction is only half a life.*

HENLEY, DARL HEATHCOTT, librarian, educator; b. Dyersburg, Tenn., Dec. 23, 1944; d. Hobert Valentine and Martha Erle (McClearn) Heathcott; m Paul N. Herron III, June 6, 1964 (div. Sept. 1987); m. James Robert Henley, Feb. 20, 1988; children: Dawn Michele Herron, Mark Heathcott Herron. BS in Elem. Edn. and Libr. Sci., Murray (Ky.) State U., 1966; postgrad., U. Ky., 1970-71. 6th grade tchr. Weaverton Elem. Sch., Henderson, Ky., 1966-68; substitute tchr. Henderson City Schs., 1970; libr., remedial tchr. Henderson City High, 1971-73; 6th grade tchr. Marion (Ky.) Elem., 1980-81, Crittanden County Elem. Sch., Marion, 1980-84, elem. libr., 1984—2001; ret., 2001. Past state pres. Kappa Kappa Iota Nat. Tchrs. Sorority. Mem. Cumberland Presbyn. Women Fellowship. Democrat. Avocations: reading, walking, fishing, travel, cooking. Home: 6208 Us Highway 60 W Marion KY 42064-7015

HENLEY, DEBORAH S., newspaper editor; City editor New York Newsday, N.Y.C.; exec. editor The News Journal, New Castle, Del.; asst. mng. editor, Long Island Newsday, mng. editor, 2005—. Office: Newsday 235 Pinelawn Rd Melville NY 11747

HENLEY, DON, singer, drummer, songwriter; b. Linden, Tex., July 22, 1947; m. Sharon Summerall, May 20, 1995. Drummer with band Eagles, L.A.; performer: (albums) The Eagle, 1972, Desperado, 1973, On the Border, 1974, One These Nights, 1975, Hotel California, 1976, The Long Run, 1979, Hell Freezes Over, 1994; performer: (solo, singer, composer) I Can't Stand Still, 1982, Building the Perfect Beast, 1985 (Grammy award for song The Boys of Summer), The End of Innocence, 1989, Actual Miles: Henley's Greatest Hits, 1995, Inside Job, 2000, (songs) Dirty Laundry, 1982, Long Way Home, I Will Not Go Quietly, New York Minute, If Dirt Were Dollars, Little Tin God, The Heart of the Matter. Mem. Active So. Poverty Law Ctr., Walden Woods Project. Named to Songwriters' Hall of Fame, 2000. Office: c/o Warner Bros Records Inc 3300 Warner Blvd Burbank CA 91505

HENLEY, DOUGLAS E., medical association administrator; b. Hope Mills, NC, Jan. 1, 1951; m. Mary Henley. MD, U. NC Sch. Medicine, Chapel Hill, 1977. Diplomate Am. Bd. Family Practice. Resident NC Memorial Hospital, Chapel Hill, NC, 1977—80; pvt. practice Hope Mills, NC; exec. v.p. Am. Acad. Family Physicians; assoc. clinical instructor U. NC Sch. of Medicine. Mem. editl. bd. Family Practice News, Jour. Family Practice. Mem. N.C. Cervical Cancer Task Force, U.S. Congress' Office of Tech. Assessment Adv. Panel; bd. dirs. Am. Acad. Family Physicians Found. Office: Heritage Family Phys 4092 Prof Dr Hope Mills NC 28348

HENLEY, ERNEST JUSTUS, chemical engineering professor; b. Sept. 30, 1926; BS, U. Del., 1950; D Engring. Sci., Columbia U., 1953. Asst. prof. nuc. and chem. engring. Columbia U., NYC, 1953-59; prof. chemistry and chem. engring. Stevens Inst. Tech., Hoboken, NJ, 1959-64; chief of party AID Mission, Rio de Janeiro, 1964-66; prof. chem. engring. U. Houston, 1964—. Founder, bd. dirs. Maxxim Med., St. Petersburg, Fla.; bd. dirs. Circon Corp., St. Petersburg, Fla., Serve Houston, Main St. Theater, Houston, Procedyne Corp., New Brunswick, NJ; tech. cons.; founding dir. RAI Rsch., 1953-82, Henley Healthcare, 1984-2000. Pres. The Henley Found. Office: U Houston Dept Chemical Engineering Houston TX 77204-0001 Office Phone: 713-743-4326. Personal E-mail: henleyej@aol.com.

HENLEY, ERNEST MARK, physics professor, retired dean; b. Frankfurt, Germany, June 10, 1924; came to U.S., 1939, naturalized, 1944; s. Fred S. and Josy (Dreyfuss) H.; m. Elaine Dimitman, Aug. 21, 1948; children: M. Bradford, Karen M. BEE, CCNY, 1944; PhD, U. Calif., Berkeley, 1952; DSc (hon.), Ohio State U., 2004, Justus Liebig U., Germany, 2005. Physicist Lawrence Radiation Lab., 1950-51; research assoc. physics dept. Stanford U., 1951-52; lectr. physics Columbia U., 1952-54; mem. faculty U. Wash., Seattle, 1954—, prof. physics, 1961-95; prof. emeritus, 1995—; chmn. dept. U. Wash., 1973-76, dean Coll. Arts and Scis., 1979-87, dir. Inst. for Nuclear

Theory, 1990-91; assoc. dir. Inst. for Nuclear Theory U. Wash., 1991—. Chmn. Nuclear Sci. Adv. Com., 1986-89. Author: (with W. Thirring) Elementary Quantum Field Theory, 1962, (with H. Frauenfelder) Subatomic Physics, 1974, 2nd edit. 1991, Nuclear and Particle Physics, 1975; mng. editor Internat. Jour. Modern Physics, 1992-; contbr. articles to profl. jours. Bd. dirs. Pacific Sci. Ctr., 1984-87, Wash. Tech. Ctr., 1983-87; trustee Associated Univs., Inc., 1989—, chmn. bd., 1993-96. Recipient Sr. Alexander von Humboldt award, 1984, T.W. Bonner prize Am. Physics Soc., 1989, Townsend Harris medal CCNY, 1989; F.B. Jewett fellow, 1952-53, Sr. fellow NSF, 1958-59, Guggenheim fellow, 1967-68, Sr. fellow NATO, 1976-77. Fellow AAAS (chmn. physics sect. 1989-90), Am. Phys. Soc. (chmn. divsn. nuclear physics 1979-80, pres. 1992, sec. treas. N.W. sect. 1999-2005, Disting. Svc. award 2004), Am. Acad. Arts and Scis.; mem. NAS (chmn. physics sect. 1998-2001), Sigma Xi. Achievements include research in symmetries, nuclear reactions, weak interactions and high energy particle interactions. Office: Univ Wash Physics Dept PO Box 351560 Seattle WA 98195-1560 Office Phone: 206-543-2896. Business E-Mail: henley@phys.washington.edu.

HENLEY, JEFFREY O., computer software company executive; b. Phoenix, Nov. 6, 1948; s. Justin Oniel and Jane Ellen (Rice) H.; children: Amy, Julie, Todd BA in Econ., U. Calif.-Santa Barbara, 1966; MBA in Fin., UCLA, 1967. Cost acctg. supr. Hughes Aircraft Co., Culver City, CA, 1967-70; div. controller Tridair Industries, Redondo Beach, Calif., 1970-72; div. controller internat. ops. Fairchild Camera & Instrument, Mountain View, Calif., 1972-75; dir. fin. Memorex Corp., Santa Clara, Calif., 1975-79; v.p., controller Saga Corp, Menlo Park, Calif., 1979-86, exec. v.p., CFO, 1986-91, Pacific Holding Co., Menlo Park, Calif., 1986—91, Oracle Corp., Redwood City, Calif., 1991—2004, chmn., 2004—, bd. dir., 1995—, serves on exec. mgmt. com. Bd. dir. CallWave, Inc. Bd. dirs. Herbert Hoover Boys' & Girls' Club, Menlo Park, Calif., 1983, pres., 1984—; chmn. Mid-Pacific Region Trustees for Boys & Girls Club of Am. Mem. Fin. Exec. Inst., Sigma Phi Epsilon Republican. Presbyterian. Avocations: golf, running. Office: Oracle Corp 500 Oracle Pkwy Redwood City CA 94065-1675

HENLEY, JOSEPH OLIVER, manufacturing executive; b. Sikeston, Mo., June 25, 1949; s. Fred Louis and Bernice (Chilton) H. m. Jane Ann Rhodes, Aug. 21, 1971 BSBA, U. Mo., 1972; MBA, Mich. State U., 1973. Ops. analyst Midland-Ross, Inc., Cleve., 1974, prodn. control mgr., 1974—75; engrng. sys. mgr. Cameron-Waldron divsn., Somerset, NJ, 1989—95, prodn. control mgr., 1976—77; prodn. planning and mfg. sys. mgr. ICM divsn. Massey Ferguson, Inc., Akron, Ohio, 1977—78; sr. audit specialist mfg. United Techs. Corp., Hartford, 1978—82, mfg. control sys. mgr. Diesel Sys. divsn., 1983—84, materials mgr. Diesel Sys. divsn., 1983—84, internal cons. Diesel Sys. divsn., 1984—86; inventory mgr. Aircraft divsn. Pratt & Whitney, Hartford, 1986—89, mgr. synchronous mfg. Aircraft divsn., 1989—95; dir. mfg. Case Corp., Racine, Wis., 1996—2000; mfg. exec. cons., 2000—. With Army N.G., 1970-72 Mem. Nat. Assn. Purchasing Mgmt., Am. Prodn. and Inventory Control Soc., Assn. for Mfg. Excellence (N.E. region bd. dirs.), Beta Gamma Sigma, Sigma Iota Epsilon, Omicron Delta Epsilon. Presbyterian. Home: 2400 SW Winterfield Ct Lees Summit MO 64081 Office: 2400 SW Winterfield Ct Lees Summit MO 64081

HENLEY, PATRICIA JOAN, principal; b. Harrison, Ark., Dec. 30, 1944; d. Durward Milford and Nola V. (Foresee) Ellis; m. Robert Lee Henley; children: Robert, Kevin, Laura. BA, Wichita State U., 1968; MS, Pittsburg (Kans.) State U., 1973, EdS, 1976; PhD, Kans. State U., 1980. Tchr. Wichita (Kans.) Pub. Schs., 1968-70; tchr. Oswego (Kans.) Pub. Schs., 1970-73; elem. prin. Aurora (Mo.) Schs., 1973-77; grad. teaching asst. Kans. State U., Manhattan, 1977-78; asst. supt. Turner Unified Sch. Dist. #202, Kansas City, Kans., 1978-82; supt. Platte County Schs., Platte City, Mo., 1982-89; dep. supt. Kansas City (Mo.) Schs., 1989-91; elem. prin. Ft. Osage Schs., Independence, Mo., 1991—. Instr. grad. courses U. Mo. Kansas City; assessor, supt. mem. Mo. Dept. Elem. and Secondary Edn. Spl. Edn. Panel; founding dir. Mo. Ctr. Safe Schs., 1995-2000; prin., CEO U. Acad., 2000—. Recipient Outstanding Leadership award Jackson County Inter-Agy. Coun., 1995, Heroes in Edn. award Reader's Digest, 1995; named Bus. Woman Yr. Townsend Publs., 1989. Mem. Nat. Assn. Elem. Sch. Prins. (Nat. Disting. prin. 1994), Mo. Assn. Elem. Sch. Prins., Kansas City Suburban Assn. Elem. Sch. Prins., Rotary. Office Phone: 816-412-5900. E-mail: henleyp@sbcglobal.net.

HENLEY, PAUL THOMAS, music educator, researcher; b. Aberdeen, SD, Dec. 2, 1966; s. Gerald Dennis and Nadene Audrey Henley; m. DeAnn Francis Lybeck, Aug. 4, 1990; children: Victoria Ann, Micah Gerald, Katrina Louise. MusB, U. of SD, 1985—89; MA in edn., fine arts and humanities, Chadron State Coll., 1990—95; PhD in music edn., La. State U. and A&M Coll., 1996—99. Dir. of bands Belle Fourche Ind. Sch. Dist., SD, 1989—91, Chadron City Schools, Nebr., 1991—94, Wahlert H.S., Dubuque, Iowa, 1994—96; asst. prof. music U. of Montana-Western, 1999—2000; asst. prof. of music SW Mo. State U., 2000—03; tchg. and learning specialist Tex. State Tchrs. Assn. NEA, 2003—. Chair Mo. Soc. of Music Tchr. Edn., 2000—; membership coord. MayDay Group, 2001—; advisor Student Mo. NEA, 2002—03. Author: (book reviews) Choral Journal; mem. editl. com. Missouri Journal of Research in Music Education, 2002—; contbr. articles to profl. jours. Mem. PTA; mem. youth com. Immanuel Lutheran Ch., Pilvergville, Tex. U. fellowship, La. State U. and A&M Coll., 1996—99, Funding for Results award, SW Mo. State U., 2001, Music Educators Scholarship Found., 1990, scholar, Blue Cross/Blue Shield of Nebr., 1992. Mem.: MayDay Group (membership coord. 2001—02), NEA, Am. Choral Directors Assn., Music Educators Nat. Conf., Pi Kappa Lambda. Evangelical Lutheran Church Of America. Office: Tex State Tchrs Assn 316 W 12th St Austin TX 78701 Office Phone: 512-476-5355. E-mail: paulh@tsta.org.

HENLEY, RICHARD JAMES, health facility administrator; b. Wroclaw, Poland, May 31, 1956; came to US, 1959; s. Henry and Lidia (Alper) Horczak. BA and MA summa cum laude, CCNY, 1978. Asst. v.p. fin. Mt. Sinai Med. Ctr., NYC, 1978-80, dir. fin. planning, 1980-81, assoc. dir. fin., 1982-84, dir. fin. profl. svcs., 1984-85; v.p. fin., treas. Vassar Bros. Med. Ctr., Poughkeepsie, NY, 1985-92, sr. v.p. for adminstrn., treas., 1992-97, exec. v.p., treas., 1997—; exec. v.p., COO, CFO Health Quest, Poughkeepsie, 1999—. Treas. VBH Corp., Poughkeepsie, 1986-99, Found. for Vassar Bros. Med. Ctr., 1986-2003, VBH Ins. Co., Ltd., 1988-, pres., 1991—, Riverside Diversified Svc., Inc., 1986-92, pres., 1992—, Riverside Mgmt. Svc., Inc., 1986-92, pres., 1992—, Alamo Amulance Svc., 1986-92, pres., 1992-; pres. Hudson Valley Home Care, Inc.; pres. HealthServe, LLC; bus. adv. coun. SUNY, New Paltz, 1999—; bd. dirs. Dutchess County Econ. Devel. Corp., chmn., 2003-05. Contbr. articles to profl. jours. Treas. Bardavon 1869 Opera House, Poughkeepsie, 1986-91, Family Svcs. Dutchess County, Poughkeepsie, 1987-88, Samuel F. B. Morse Hist. Site, 1998-99; pres. Hudson Terr. Owners' Corp., Poughkeepsie, 1987-88. Fellow Healthcare Fin. Mgmt. Assn. (nat. dir. 1994-96, nat. sec. 1996-97, nat. treas. 1997-98, nat. chmn. elect 1998-99, nat. chmn. 1999-2000, cost effectiveness award 1979-80, William G. Follmer Merit award 1986, Robert H. Reeves Merit award 1989, Fredric T. Muncie Mert award 1991, Medal of Honor award 1994, Stephen A. Ryan Meml. award 2003), Am. Heart Assn. (bd. dirs.), Am. Coll. Health Exec. (regent Hudson Valley Adirondack 2002—). Office: Health Quest 45 Reade Pl Poughkeepsie NY 12601-3947 Office Phone: 845-431-5607. Business E-Mail: rhenley@health-quest.org.

HENLEY, ROBERT LEE, school system administrator; b. Aug. 7, 1934; m. Patricia J. Ellis; 3 children. BA, Washington U., St. Louis, 1957, MEd, 1958; EdD, U. Mo., 1967. Tchr., counselor, pers. office, bus. mgr., asst. supt. Mehlville Sch. Dist., St. Louis, 1958-75; supt. schs. Independence (Mo.) Pub. Schs., 1975-93; asst. prof. U. Mo., Kansas City, 1991—. Cons. in field; instr. various colls. & univs., St. Louis and Columbia, 1975—. Trustee Andrew Drumm Inst., Independence, 1980—; bd. dirs. Am. Cancer Soc., Independence, 1978—; adv. com. Kansas City Arts Ptnrs. Program, 1990—. Recipient Community Leader award Comprehensive Mental health Svcs., Jackson County, Mo., 1983, Disting. Svc. award Mo. chpt. Am. Assn. on Mental Deficiency, 1983, Outstanding Educator award State of Mo., 1985, Innovation in Edn. award Nat. Ctr. for Ednl. Computing, 1985-86, Exec. Educator 100 award Exec. Educator Mag., 1987, Sch. Adminstr. award Kennedy Ctr./Alliance for Arts Edn., Washington, 1988, Disting. Svc. award Am. Assn. Sch. Adminstrs., 1993; named Mo. Supt. of Yr., 1992. Mem. Am. Assn. Sch. Adminstrs., Mo. Assn. Sch. Adminstrs. (exec. com. 1988—, Robert L. Pearce award 1991, Disting. Svc. award 1993), Jackson County Sch. Adminstrs. Assn. (pres. 1981), Mid-Am. Assn. Sch. Supts., Met. Sch. Study Group (pres. 1985-86), Independence C. of C.

HENMAN, TIM, professional tennis player; b. Oxford, England, Sept. 6, 1974; m. Ivy Henman (div.); m. Lucy Henman, Dec. 11, 1999; 1 child, Rose Elizabeth. Profl. tennis player, 1993—; mem. Davis Cup squad, 1994. Mem. player coun. ATP, 1997—98, charities chmn., 2000. Recipient Silver medal at Olympics with Neil Broad, 1996; winner Syndney Task Kent, 1997; winner Under 18 singles and doubles Nat. Titles, 1992; winner doubles title Guardian Direct Cup, 1999; winner 11 singles titles, 4 doubles titles. 430-219 career singles record. Office: Internat Mgmt Group 1 Erieview Plz Ste 1300 Cleveland OH 44114-1715

HENN, BARBARA JEANNE, academic librarian; b. Indpls., Aug. 2, 1936; d. George Louis and Kathryn Frances (Stewart) H. BS in Edn., Concordia Tchrs. Coll., 1958; MLS, Ind. U., 1967. Reference librarian Purdue U., W. Lafayette, Ind., 1967-68; with Ind. U., Bloomington, 1968—, asst. acquisitions librarian, 1980-85, head acquisitions sect., 1986—2000; ret. Author: chpt. Advances in Library Administration and Organization, 1989. Mem. ALA (chair com. 1986-87, 90-92, speaker San Francisco conf. 1987), Ind. Libr. Assn. (div. chair 1984-85), Ohio Valley Group of Tech. Svc. Librs., Ind. Consortium for Internat. Progress (speaker Indpls. chpt. 1986), Beta Phi Mu (pres. Chi chpt. 1973-74). Democrat. Methodist. Avocations: raising schnauzers, gardening, college basketball. Home: 4407 E Kinser Dr Bloomington IN 47408-2827 Office: Ind U Librs Main Libr E350 Bloomington IN 47405

HENN, FRITZ ALBERT, psychiatrist; b. Alden, Pa., Mar. 26, 1941; s. Fredrich and Luise (Kimm) H.; m. Suella Weiland, Aug. 1, 1964; children: Sarah, Stephen. BA, Wesleyan U., Middleton, Conn., 1963; PhD, Johns Hopkins U., 1967; MD, U. Va., 1971. Dir. rsch. tng. U. Iowa Hosps. and Clinics, Iowa City, 1975; asst. prof. U. Iowa, Coll. of Medicine, Iowa City, 1974-78, assoc. prof., 1978-81, prof. dept. psychiat., 1981; prof., chmn. SUNY, Stony Brook, 1982-94; dir. L.I. Rsch. Inst., Stony Brook, 1982-83, Inst. of Mental Health Rsch., Stony Brook, 1983—; prof. psychiatry U. Heidelberg, Germany, 1994; dir. Ctrl. Inst. for Mental Health, Germany, 1994. Pres. Winter Conf. on Brain Rsch., 1990-92. Mem. editorial bd. Jour. Neurochemistry, 1980-90, Archives Gen. Psychiatry, 1983—. Cons. Project Dawn Justice Dept., 1973-74. Fellow Life Ins. Medicine Rsch. Fund, 1968-71, Falk fellow Am. Psychiat. Assn., 1972-74. Mem. AMA, Am. Coll. Psychiatrists, Am. Coll. Neuropsychopharmacology, Soc. for Neurol. Sci., Psychiat. Rsch. Soc. (pres. 1992), Am. Soc. Neurochemistry, Sigma Xi, Alpha Omega Alpha. Office: Mental Health Inst PO 12 21 20 68072 Mannheim Germany Fax: 49-621-1703760. Office Phone: 49 621 1703739. E-mail: henn@zi-mannheim.de.

HENNAH, VIVIAN LISA, school system administrator; b. New Haven, Conn. d. George Albert and Bernaddette Keen; m. Allen Harold Stanley, Nov. 20, 1996; children: Harold Beid, Stanley Rudloph; 1 child, Allen Jr. Pub. sch., New Haven. Writer Gifted and Talented, New Haven, 1975—78. Contbr. poet: poetry book Young Words and Vision, Whisper, Giggles Laugh, Patterns of Life, 2003, Best Poets and Poems of 2003. Home: 151 Cedar St New Haven CT 06519

HENNE, JAMES PATRICK, marine biologist; s. James L. and Rhea E. Henne; m. Joy Seymour, June 21, 2000; 1 child, Jude. AA in Gen. Studies magna cum laude, Anne Arundel C.C., Arnold, Md., 1996; BS in Marine Biology, U. of N.C., Wilmington, 1995; MS in Marine Biology, U. of N.C., 2001. Fisheries technician N.C. Wildlife Resources Commn., Watha State Fish Hatchery, Watha, NC, 1997—98; rsch. and tchg. asst. U. of N.C. at Wilmington, Wilmington, NC, 1998—2000; hatchery supr. Southland Fisheries Corp., Yonges Island, SC, 2000—01; fisheries biologist US Fish and Wildlife Svc., Mora Nat. Fish Hatchery and Tech. Ctr., Mora, N.Mex., 2001—03; fisheries biologist, asst. sta. mgr. US Fish and Wildlife Svc., Bears Bluff Nat. Fish Hatchery, Wadmalaw Island, SC, 2003—. Contbr. articles to profl. jours. Mem.: Am. Fisheries Soc., World Aquaculture Soc. Avocation: outdoors activities. Office: United States Fish and Wildlife Service PO Box 69 Wadmalaw Island SC 29487 Office Phone: 843-559-2315.

HENNEKENS, CHARLES HENRY, physician, epidemiologist; b. N.Y.C., June 12, 1942; s. Charles Henry and Pauline (Garciello) H.; m. Deborah Cole; children: charles, Jennifer, Alissa. BS, Queens Coll., 1963; MD, Cornell U., 1967; MPH, Harvard U., 1972, MS, 1973, DPH, 1975. Diplomate Am. Bd. Preventive Medicine, Nat. Bd. Med. Examiners. Intern in medicine Cornell U. Hosps., N.Y.C., 1967-68, resident in internal medicine, 1968-69; epidemic intelligence officer USPHS, Dade County Dept. Pub. Health, Miami, Fla., 1969-71; asst. prof. epidemiology, pub. health chief chronic disease U. Miami Sch. of Medicine, 1972-74; asst. prof. medicine Channing Lab. Harvard U., Boston, 1975-81, assoc. prof. medicine and clin. epidemiology, 1981-88, prof. medicine and preventive medicine, 1990—, acting chair dept. preventive medicine, 1990—; physician Brigham and Women's Hosp., Boston, 1982-92, sr. physician, 1992-93, prof. medicine, ambulatory care and prevention chief divsn. preventive medicine, 1993—; acting chair dept. preventive medicine Med. Sch. Harvard U., Boston, 1990-92. Asst. vis. physician Boston City Hosp., 1975—; vis. epidemiologist with Sir Richard Doll, FRS, Regius Prof. of Medicine at the Radcliffe Infirmary, Oxford (Eng.) U., 1978-79; vis. prof. dept. epidemiology and pub. health U. Miami Sch. of Meidcine, 1980—; vis. prof. medicine N.Y. Hosp. Cornell U. Med. Ctr., 1990; Kroc. vis. prof. medicine U. N.Mex., 1990; adj. assoc. prof. div. biostatistics and epidemiology, Boston U. Sch. of Pub. Health, 1990—; rsch. dir. East Boston Neighborhood Health Ctr., 1988—; cons. Pan Am. Health Orgn., Caracas, Venezuela, 1975-77, Nat. Cancer Inst., Bethesda, Md., 1979.; sr. fellow Francis Weld Peabody Soc. Harvard Med. Sch., 1989—, rev. com. for ednl. programs, 1986-87; mem. admissions com. Sch. Pub. Health Boston U., 1984—, preventative medicine adv. com., 1985—; cons. Brockton (Mass.) VA Hosp., 1982—, U. Miami (Fla.) Sch. Medicine, 1983—, West Roxbury (Mass.) VA Hosp., 1984—, many others; mem. numerous other coms. and orgns.; lectr., speaker in field; instr., course dir. numerous instns. Author: Epidemiology in Medicine, 1987; editor in chief: Am. Jour. Preventive Medicine, Prevention of Myocardial Infarction, 1995; founding editor in chief: Annals of Epidemiology, 1989—; bd. overseers Am. Jour. Epidemiology, 1991—; mem. editorial bd. Statistics in Medicine, 1981—, Am. Jour. Preventive Medicine, 1987—, Exec. Health Report, 1988—, Circulation, 1988-91, Harvard Heart Letter, 1990—; epidemiology reviewer Jour. AMA, 1983-86; contbr. numerous articles to profl. jours. including Jour. Gen. Internal Medicine, Clin. Cardiology, Current Opinion in Cardiology. Mem. pediatric hypertension subgroup Nat. Heart, Lung and Blood Inst., 1977-78, task force on rsch. in epidemiology and prevention of cardiovascular diseases, 1992—, numerous others; mem. external adv. com. U. Ill. Comprehensive Cancer Ctr., 1980-82; mem. arteriosclerosis and hypertension in childhood com. Am. Heart Assn., 1981-83, mem. epidemiology and lipoprotein metabolism rev. com., 1986-90, others; mem. adv. com. for studies of chemoprevention of cancer in Beijing Nat. Cancer Inst., 1982-83; mem. profl. adv. com. Am. Coun. on Alcoholism, 1986-87; mem. Vietnam vets. studies adv. panel Office of Tech. Assessment, 1988-90; mem. expert panel cancer prevention advances Nat. Cancer Inst. 1993, chmn. data safety and monitoring bd. for TIMI-7 trial, 1991-94, mem. numerous others. Recipient Butcher scholarship U. Pa., 1959-60, N.Y. State Regents scholarship, 1960-63, Teagle scholarship Cornell U., 1963-67, Postdoctoral Rsch. Paper prize Soc. for Epidemiologic Rsch., 1975, Rsch. Ctr. Devel. award NIH, 1977-82, Esquire Mag. Disting. Achievement award 1988, James D Bruce Meml. award Am. Coll. Physicians, 1992, VERIS Outstanding Contribution to Antioxidant Vitaman Rsch. award, 1995. Fellow Am. Coll. Epidemiology (bd. dirs. 1984-88), Am. Coll. Cardiology (hon.); mem. APHA, AAAS, Am. Epidemol. Soc., Am. Fedn. for Clin. Rsch., Am. Soc. for Clin. Pharmacology and Therapeutics, Am. Soc. for Preventive Oncology, Argentine Soc. of Cardiology (hon.), Assn. Tchrs. Preventive Medicine, Internat. Assn. for Vitamin and Nutritional Oncology, Internat. Epidemiol. Assn., Soc. for Epidemiologic Rsch. (pres. 1991-92), Mass. Heart Assn., Mass. Pub. Health Assn., Mass. Med. Soc., N.Y. Acad. Sci., Norfolk Dist. Med. Soc., Sci. Coun. on Epidemiology and Prevention, Internat. Soc. and Fedn. for Cardiology Soc., Soc. for Clin. Trials, Soc. for Epidemiologic Rsch., Phi Beta Kappa. Achievements include research in epidemiology of cardiovascular disease and cancer, teaching and training in clinical epidemiology, and epidemiology of infectious diseases and methodology. Office: Apt 11J 2800 S Ocean Blvd Boca Raton FL 33432-8374

HENNELL, ROBERT WILLIAM, III, secondary school educator; b. Mount Vernon, Ohio, Sept. 9, 1952; s. Robert William Hennell, Jr. and Emily Gloria (Catrino) Hennell; m. Elizabeth Ellen Jameson, July 7, 1984; children: Joseph Robert, Jaclyn Grace. MusB magna cum laude in music edn., Bowling Green (Ohio) State U., 1974, MusM in Conducting, 1977. Cert. tchr. Ohio, 1974, music educator Music Educator's Nat. Conf., 1991. Dir. of bands Antwerp (Ohio) Local Schs., 1974—75; grad. asst. Bowling Green (Ohio) State U., 1975—77; dir. of bands Antwerp (Ohio) Local Schs., 1977—80; project coord. - LPGA pro-am golf tournament The J.M. Smucker Co., Orrville, Ohio, 1991—92; asst. golf coach Orrville (Ohio) HS, 2001—; dir. of bands Orrville (Ohio) City Schs., 1980—. Cons. Capital U. Complete Band Dir. Workshop, Columbus, Ohio, 1990; guest condr. Firelands Conf. Honor Band, Greenwich, Ohio, 2000. Condr. Orrville (Ohio) Cmty. Band, 1981—90; mem. Orrville Exch. Club, Ohio, 1982—, chmn. youth of month project, 1989—90; civilian participant US Army War Coll., Carlisle Barracks, Pa., 1991; coach Orrville (Ohio) Youth Baseball League, 1993—96. Recipient Golden Apple Achiever award, Ashland Oil Co., 1995. Mem.: Am. Sch. Band Dirs. Assn. (state chair 1986—88, state band clinic chair 1987, all-state band chair 1987), Ohio Music Edn. Assn. (adjudicated event chair 1984—86, band affairs chair 1989—91, dist. pres. 1991—93, adjudicator 1980—99), Music Educator's Nat. Conf. (profl. certification steering com. 1993—94), Ohio HS Golf Coach's Assn., Phi Kappa Phi, Phi Beta Mu. Avocations: reading, book collecting, travel, golf, baseball. Home: 1331 Independence Drive Orrville OH 44667 Office: Orrville City Schools 841 North Ella Street Orrville OH 44667 Office Phone: 330-682-4448. E-mail: orvl_hennell@tcom.net.

HENNEMAN, STEPHEN CHARLES, psychotherapist; b. Chgo., June 17, 1949; s. Charles Philip Jr. and Marion Louise (Eichberger) Henneman; m. Patricia Anne York, Feb. 14, 1975 (div. Sept. 1980); 1 child, Charles Philip III; m. Marion Jean McDermand, Oct. 4, 1980; stepchildren: Ervin F. Jr. Schrock, Lisa Ann Schrock, Thomas M. Schrock. BA in Journalism, Colo. State U., 1971; MA in Counseling, U. N.D., 1987. Cert. profl. counselor, Am. Counseling Assn. Commd. 2d lt. USAF, 1971, advanced through grades to maj., 1984; missile launch officer 570th Strategic Missile Squadron, Davis Monthan AFB, Ariz., 1972-76; info. officer 321st Strategic Missile Wing, Grand Forks AFB, N.D., 1976-79; missile combat crew flight comdr. 446th Strategic Missile Squadron, Grand Forks AFB, 1980-82; missile combat crew comdr. evaluator 321st Strategic Missile Wing, Grand Forks AFB, 1982, wing nuclear surety officer, 1982-83, chief weapon safety branch, 1983-85; asst. ops. officer 320th Strategic Missile Squadron, F E Warren AFB, Wyo., 1985-86; dep. wing inspector 90th Strategic Missile Wing, F E Warren AFB, 1986-88; ops. officer 319th Strategic Missile Squadron, F E Warren AFB, 1988-89; dep. chief war res. materiel div. Hdqrs. U.S. Air Forces in Europe, Ramstein Air Base, Fed. Republic Germany, 1989-92; vol. and outreach coord. Safe House/Sexual Assault Svcs., Inc., Cheyenne, Wyo., 1992-93; quality control investigator Dept. Employment State of Wyoming, Cheyenne, 1993-95; counselor Wyo. State Penitentiary, Rawlins, 1995-96, counseling team leader, 1996-97; residential counselor Aurora (Colo.) Cmty. Mental Health Ctr., 1997-99, mental health clinician, 1999-2001, profl. counselor, 2001—. Advocate, counselor Safehouse/Sexual Assault Svcs., Inc., Cheyenne, 1985-89; sec., bd. dirs. Carbon County Citizens Organized to See Violence Ended, 1996-97. Mem. ACA, Am. Mental Health Counselors Assn., Colo. Counselors Assn., Nat. Cert. Counselors. Avocations: photography, popular music recordings collecting, reading. Office Phone: 303-617-2723. Business E-Mail: schenneman@comcast.net.

HENNEMEYER, ROBERT THOMAS, diplomat; b. Chgo., Dec. 1, 1925; s. Rudolph Johannes and Mary Matilda (Petersen) H.; m. Joan Therese Renaud, Dec. 28, 1954; children— Christian, Paul, Robin Ph.B., U. Chgo., 1947, MA, 1950; student, Chgo. Tchrs. Coll., African area studies Oxford U., Eng., 1960-61, U. Md., 1965-67. Tchr. high schs., Chgo., 1948-50; instr. Woodrow Wilson Jr. Coll., Chgo., 1951; commd. fgn. service officer U.S. Dept. State, 1952; cultural officer Bremen, Fed. Republic Germany, 1952-53; officer-in-charge Bremerhaven, Fed. Republic Germany, 1953-54; asst. U.S. sec. Allied Gen. Secretariat, Bonn, Fed. Republic Germany, 1954-56, spl. asst. to ambassador, 1954-56; econ. officer Consulate Gen., Munich, 1956-58; internat. relations officer Dept. State, 1958-60; consul, dep. chief mission Dar es Salaam Tanganyika, 1961-64; faculty adviser U.S. Naval Acad., Annapolis, 1964-66; personnel officer Dept. State, Washington, 1966-68; chief polit. sec. Am. embassy Oslo, Norway, 1968-71; consul gen. Dusseldorf, Fed. Republic Germany, 1971-75; dep. asst. sec. Bur. of Security and Consular Affairs Dept. State, 1976-78; consul gen. Munich, 1978-80; sr. insp. and exec. dir. Dept. State, 1980-83, exec. asst. to Under Sec., 1983-84; U.S. ambassador Banjul, The Gambia, 1984-86; fgn. affairs advisor U.S. Cath. Conf., Washington, 1986-88, dir. office internat. justice and peace, 1988-90; pvt. cons., 1990—. Served with AUS, 1943-46 Mem. DACOR, Fgn. Service Assn., Alpha Delta Phi

HENNES, ROBERT TAFT, former management consultant, investment executive; b. Jamestown, N.Y., Mar. 8, 1930; s. Theodore Preston and Lucille (Kane) H.; m. Frances Walker Pratt, May 9, 1953 (div. 1962); children: Robert Taft, Duncan Pratt, Margaret Nickerson, Theodore Preston II; m. Grace Margaret Bruton, Oct. 9, 1971. AB, Harvard U., 1951; MBA, U. Pa., 1952. With Lummus Co., N.Y.C., 1952-62; exec. v.p., dir. Conahay & Lyon, Inc. (advt.), N.Y.C., 1962-70; sr. v.p. Cole & Assos., Boston, 1970-72; chmn., dir. Hennes & Cox Inc., N.Y.C., 1972-77; sr. dir. Spencer Stuart & Assos., N.Y.C., 1977-88. Dir. Oldwyck Industries, Inc., N.Y.C. Mem. Kennett Square Golf and Country Club, Harvard Club of N.Y. Home: PO Box 728 Kennett Square PA 19348-0728

HENNESSEY, AUDREY KATHLEEN, computer researcher, educator; b. Fairbanks, Apr. 4, 1936; d. Lawrence Christopher and Olga Virginia (Strandberg) Doheny; m. Gerard Hennessey, Mar. 10, 1963; children: Brian, Kate. BA, Stanford U., 1957; HSA, U. Toronto, Ont., Can., 1968; PhD, U. Lancaster, Eng., 1982. Asst. dir. European sales Univ. Soc., Heidelberg, Germany, 1959—61; landman's asst. Union Oil Co. Calif., Anchorage, 1962; sys. analyst No. Telephones, New Liskeard, Canada, 1962—63; adminstr. group pension Mfgs. Life Ins., Toronto, 1963—65; instr. office systems Adult Edn. Ctr., Toronto, 1965—68; lectr. office sys. Salford Coll. Tech., Lancashire, England, 1968—70; sr. lectr. data processing Manchester (Eng.) Met. U., 1970—79; lectr. computation U. Manchester Inst. Sci. and Tech., 1979—82; assoc. prof. computer sci. Tex. Tech. U., Lubbock, 1982—86, assoc. prof. info. sys., 1987—94, prof. info. sys., 1994—2001; pres., CEO ISOA Inc., 1994—2002; dir. Internat. Ctr. Informatics Rsch., 1996—2000; v.p., gen. mgr. YMG/Rudolph Tech. Inc., 2002—03; pres., CEO, ICIR Inc., Richardson, Tex., 2002—; mng. dir. Konsult Europe Ltd., Stourport, England, 2002—. Dir. Inst. for Studies of Orgn. Automation/Tex. Tech. U., Lubbock, 1987-95; vis. instr. Fed. Law Enforcement Tng. Ctr., Glynco, Ga., 1984-88; adj. prof. West Tex. A&M U., Canyon, 1994-95, U. Alaska, Anchorage, 1995, U. Tex., Dallas, 1995-98; mem. NATO panel of experts on visualization of massive data sets, 1996-98. Author: Computer Applications Project, 1982; contbg. author: Semiconductor International, 1998, 2002; editor (procs.) Office Document Architecture Internat. Symposium, English version, 1991; contbr. articles to profl. jours.; 14 patents in field. Organizer Explorer Scouts Computer Applications, Lubbock, 1983-85. Recipient various awards, Tex. Instruments, 1982—86, 1994, Xerox Corp., 1985, Halliburton, 1986, Sys. Exploration, 1987, State of Tex., 1988—93, 1996—99, Knowledge-based Image Analysis award, USN Tencap, 1991—96, Immunization Tracking Sys.

award, Robert Wood Johnson Found., 1993, Sematech S77 award, 1994, award, Leica GmbH, 1994—2001. Mem.: IEEE (contbg. author Systems Man Cybernetics 1984), Assn. Info. Tech. Profls. (chpt. pres. 1989, Disting. Info Sci. award 1992), Assn. Computing Machinery, Soc. Mfg. Engrs., Spl. Interest Group for Artificial Intelligence (JEDEC working group ISO semiconductor defect data stds. 1999—2002), Sigma Xi Rsch. Soc. (chpt. pres. 1996—97). Office: Konsult Europe/ICIR Ste 141 1221 W Campbell Rd Richardson TX 75080 Office Phone: 972-690-3398. E-mail: icirinc@aol.com.

HENNESSEY, JOHN WILLIAM, JR., academic administrator, educator; b. Danville, Pa., Mar. 25, 1925; s. John William and Martha Scott (Braun) H.; m. Jean Marie Lande, June 26, 1948; children: John William III, Martha Scott. AB, Princeton U., 1948; MBA, Harvard U., 1950; PhD, U. Wash., 1956; MA (hon.), Dartmouth Coll., 1959; LHD (hon.), York Coll. of Pa., 1978, U. N.H., 1981. From instr. to assoc. prof. orgn. and adminstrn. Coll. Bus. Adminstrn., U. Wash., 1950-57; prof. Amos Tuck Sch. Bus. Adminstrn., Dartmouth Coll., 1957-87, assoc. dean, 1962-68, dean, 1968-76, Charles H. Jones 3d Century prof. mgmt., 1976-87, now emeritus; provost U. Vt., Burlington, 1987-89, interim pres., 1990. Prof. Inst. pour l'Etude des Methodes de Direction de l'Enterprise, Lausanne, Switzerland, 1959; trustee NH Cmty. Loan Fund, 2005—. Author: (with Austin Grimshaw) Organizational Behavior, 1960, (with others) Hospital Policy Decisions, 1966. Trustee Mary Hitchcock Meml. Hosp., Hanover, 1963-86, chmn. bd. 1977-83; trustee Ednl. Testing Svc. 1975-80, 81-85, chmn. bd. 1978-80, 84-85; chmn. governing coun. Dartmouth Hitchcock Med. Ctr., 1977-83, trustee, 1983-86, 91—, chmn. bd. trustees, 1992-95; bd. visitors Grad. Sch. Bus., U. Pitts., 1970-76, 79-88; mem. Pres.'s Coun. on Bus. Sch., U. Vt., 1982-87; dir. Milbank Meml. Fund, 1982-87; trustee U. Vt., 1985-87, Med. Ctr. Hosp. Vt., 1988-90, Vt. Law Sch., 1999—; bd. dirs. Kendal at Hanover, 1995-01, chmn., 1998-2001; bd. dirs. Ams. for Campaign Reform, 2003—, New Hampshire Cmty. Loan Fund, 2005-; mem. Citizens' Commn. NH Ct. Sys., 2005-. 1st lt. U.S. Army, 1943-46. Mem. Am. Assembly Collegiate Schs. Bus. (dir. 1970-77, pres. 1975-76), Phi Beta Kappa. Home: 80 Lyme Rd Apt 1038 Hanover NH 03755 Business E-Mail: john.hennessey@dartmouth.edu.

HENNESSEY, KEITH, federal official; BAS, Stanford U.; M in Pub. Policy, Harvard U. Program designer Symantec Corp., Cupertino, Calif., 1990—92; rsch. asst. Bipartisan Commn. Entitlement and Tax Reform, 1994—95; health economist budget com. U.S. Senate, 1995—97, policy dir. for senate majority and Senator Trent Lott, 1997—2002; dep. asst. to Pres. for econ. policy and devel. The White House, 2002—; dep. dir. Nat. Econ. Coun., 2002—. Office: The White House 1600 Pennsylvania Ave Washington DC 20500*

HENNESSEY, PATRICK DANIEL, musician, educator, musicologist; b. New Orleans, La., Sept. 30, 1952; m. Heidi Rebecca Burgo, June 27, 1981. MusB (performance), Calif. State U., Long Beach, 1979; MA in Music Edn., U.Hawaii, Honolulu, 1995. Prin. trombone Royal Hawaiian Band, Honolulu, 1983—; dir. jazz ensembles U. of Hawaii, Honolulu, 1983—. Adj. faculty Chaminade U., Honolulu, 2000—. Musician: (freelance musician) Live and Recorded Performances with numerous nationally recognized artists.; contbr. articles on Royal Hawiian Band to popular publs. Clinician; guest performer Numerous Schools throughout the state of Hawaii, Hawaii, 1983—2003. Petty officer second class USN, 1970—74, Vietnam; Long Beach. Recipient Outstanding Achievement award Musicology, U. Hawaii Dept. Music, 1996, 1997, 1999, Donald Matsumori Rsch. award, 1992, Humanities in the Arts Founder's Award, 2002; grantee, Grad. Student Orgn., 1999. Mem.: Musicians Assn. of Hawaii, Internat. Assn. for Jazz Edn., Hawaiian Hist. Soc., Coll. Music Soc., Soc. for Am. Music, Internat. Trombone Assn., Mortar Board.

HENNESSEY, ROBERT JOHN, pharmaceutical company executive; b. Danbury, Conn., Dec. 5, 1941; s. James P. and Helen H.; m. Carol Stankwitz, Feb. 8, 1964; children: Jil, Christopher, Michele, Matthew. AB, U. Conn., 1963, MA in Internat. Affairs, 1967. Mgmt. intern Sec. of Commerce, Washington, 1967-69; assoc. dir. market planning MSD Internat., Rahway, N.J., 1969-71, dir. strategic planning, 1971-74; dir. corp. strategy devel. SmithKline, Rixensart, Belgium, 1974-76, regional dir. biols. Europe, 1976-79; dir. internat. bus. devel. Abbott Labs., North Chgo., Ill., 1979-82; dir. corp. planning Sterling Drug Inc., N.Y.C., 1980-82, v.p. corp. planning, 1982-86, v.p. corp. devel., 1986-90; pres. Hennessey & Assoc., Ltd., pharm. cons., Westport, Conn., 1990-93; chmn., pres., CEO, Genome Therapeutics Corp. (former Collaborative Rsch., Inc.), Waltham, Mass., 1993—. Bd. dirs. Maggioni-Winthrop, Milan, Steinberg & Lyman Health Care Ventures, N.Y.C. Mem. Fayerweather Yacht Club (Black Rock, Conn.). Office: Genome Therapeutics Corp 100 Beaver St Waltham MA 02453-8425

HENNESSY, DANIEL KRAFT, lawyer; b. Summit, NJ, Jan. 4, 1941; s. Robert Emmett and Agnes Lyons (Lindle) H.; m. Susan Elizabeth (Bettina) Ware, June 17, 1972; children— Mary Elise, Daniel Joseph, Michael Ware, Catherine Anne. BS with highest honors, U.S. Naval Acad., 1963; JD cum laude, Harvard U., 1970. Bar: Tex. 1970. Commd. ensign U.S. Navy, 1963, advanced through grades to lt., 1966; service in Vietnam; resigned, 1967; ptnr. Hughes & Luce (formerly Hughes & Hill), 1973—. Bd. regents Ave Maria U., 2005—. Editor: Harvard Law Rev, 1969-70. Mem. bd. advisers Jesuit Coll. Prep. Sch., Dallas, 1975-88; bd. dirs. Dallas-North Tex. region NCCJ, 1976-83, Catholics United for Faith, Inc., 1982-99, Greater Dallas Right to Life Ednl. Found., 1974-86, The Highlands Sch., 1986—, Cath. Pro-life Com. of North Tex., 2001—, Legatus Internat. (Dallas chpt.), 2003—. Decorated knight grand cross Equestrian Order of Holy Sepulchre of Jerusalem, Knight of Malta. Mem. Dallas Bar Assn., State Bar of Tex., Legatus Internat. Roman Catholic. Home: 4405 Beverly Dr Dallas TX 75205-3001 Office Phone: 214-939-5506. E-mail: hennesd@hughesluce.com.

HENNESSY, DEAN MCDONALD, lawyer, director, municipal official; b. McPherson, Kans., June 13, 1923; s. Ernest Weston and Beulah A. (Dunn) H.; m. Marguerite Sundheim, Sept. 6, 1946 (div. Sept. 1979); children: Joan Hennessy Wright, John D., Robert D. (dec.), Scott D. (dec.); m. Darlene MacLean, Apr. 4, 1981. AB cum laude, Harvard U., 1947, LLB, 1950; MBA, U. Chgo., 1959. Bar: Ill. 1951. Assoc. Carney, Crowell & Leibman, Chgo., 1950-53; atty. Borg-Warner Corp., Chgo., 1953-62; with Emhart Corp., Farmington, Conn., 1962-88, asst. sec., 1964-67, sec., gen. counsel, 1967-74, v.p., sec., gen. counsel, 1974-76, v.p., gen. counsel, 1976-86, sr. v.p., gen. counsel, 1986-88, ret., 1988. Incorporator Ill. Citizens for Eisenhower, 1952; chmn. Citizens Activities, Ill. Citizens for Eisenhower, 1952, 56; Justice of the peace, mem. bd. suprs. Proviso Twp., Ill., 1952-56; vice chmn. Jr. Achievement Chgo., 1959; program chmn. trade and industries divsn. United Rep. Fund Ill., 1961; trustee West Hartford Bicentennial Trust, Inc., 1976-77, Friends and Trustees of Bushnell Meml., Hartford, 1978-84; bd. dirs. Royal Homestead Condominium Assn., Juno Beach, Fla., 1990-93. Served to lt. (j.g.) USNR, 1943-46. Sheldon fellow Harvard U., 1947. Mem. ABA, Mfrs. Alliance for Productivity and Innovation (vice chmn. law coun. 1984-87, chmn. 1987, 88), John Harvard Soc., Oliver Wendell Holmes Soc. Republican. Presbyterian.

HENNESSY, ELLEN ANNE, lawyer, financial analyst, educator; b. Auburn, N.Y., Mar. 3, 1949; d. Charles Francis and Mary Anne (Roan) H.; m. Frank Daspit, Aug. 27, 1974. BA, Mich. State U., 1971; JD, Cath. U., 1978; LLM in Taxation, Georgetown U., 1984. Bar: D.C. 1978, U.S. Ct. Appeals (D.C. cir.) 1978, U.S. Supreme Ct. 1984. Various positions NEH, Washington, 1971-74; atty. office chief counsel IRS, Washington, 1978-80; atty.-advisor Pension Benefit Guaranty Corp., Washington, 1980-82; assoc. Stroock & Stroock & Lavan, Washington, 1982-85, Willkie Farr & Gallager, 1985-86, ptnr. Washington, 1987-93; dep. exec. dir. and chief negotiator Pension Benefit Guaranty Corp., Washington, 1993—98; sr. v.p. and dir. Actuarial Sci. Assoc. Holdings Inc., 1998—2000; sr. v.p. Aon Cons. Inc., Washington, 2000—03; pres. Fiduciary Counselors, Inc., 1999—. Adj. prof. law Georgetown U., Washington, 1985—; mem. com. on continuing profl. edn. Am. Law Inst./ABA, 1994—97. Mem. ABA (supervising editor taxation sect. newsletter 1984-87, mem. standing com. on continuing edn. 1990-94, chair joint com. on employee benefits 1991-92, mem. standing com. on tech. and info. sys. 2002—, mem. task force on corp. responsiblity, 2002-03), Worldwide Employee Benefits Network (pres. 1987-88), D.C. Bar Assn. (mem. steering com. tax sect. 1988-93, chair continuing legal edn. com. 1993-95), Am. Coll. Employee Benefits Counsel (bd. govs. 2000-03). Democrat. Avocation: whitewater canoeing. Home: 1926 Lawrence St NE Washington DC 20018-2734 Office: Ste 700 700 12th St NW Washington DC 20005-3949 Office Phone: 202-558-5141. Business E-Mail: nell.hennessy@fiduciarycounselors.com.

HENNESSY, JOHN FRANCIS, III, engineering executive, mechanical engineer; b. N.Y.C, Nov. 27, 1955; s. John Francis Jr. and Barbara (McDonnell) H. AB, Kenyon Coll., 1977; BSME, Rensselaer Poly Inst., 1978; MS, MIT, 1988. Registered profl. engr., N.Y., N.J., Mass., Va., Del., Calif. Project engr. Syska & Hennessy, N.Y.C., 1978-83, project mgr. San Francisco, 1983-86, v.p. L.A., 1986-87, Cambridge, Mass., 1987-88, sr. v.p., 1988-89, CEO N.Y.C., 1989—, chmn., 1989—. Chmn., bd. dirs. N.Y. Bldg. Congress, N.Y.C., 1992-96; chmn. Times Square Subway Sta. Improvement Corp., N.Y.C., 1989—. Mem. USO of Met. N.Y.; chmn. Salvation Army of N.Y., 2001—; mem. Bldg. Futures Coun.; bd. dirs. Internat. Alliance for Interoperability, 1998—; trustee Nat. Bldg. Mus., 2000—. Sloan fellowship, 1987. Mem. ASHRAE, NSPE, ASME, Coun. on Tall Bldgs. and Urban Habitat, Univ. Club, Olympic Club, Union League Club, Met. Club (Washington), Lyford Cay Club (Nassau), Winged Foot Golf Club (Mamaroneck, N.Y.), Nat. Golf Links of Am., Princeton Club, The Links. Roman Catholic. Avocations: golf, tennis, skiing, squash. Office: Syska Hennessy Group 11 W 42nd St New York NY 10036-8002

HENNESSY, JOHN L., academic administrator; b. New York, NY, Sept. 22, 1952; m. Andrea Hennessy; children: Thomas, Christopher. B in Engring. in Elec. Engring., Villanova U., 1973; MS in Computer Sci., SUNY, Stony Brook, 1975, PhD in Computer Sci., 1977, DSc (hon.), 2001; DHL (hon.), Villanova U., 2001; Doctor honoris causa, Universitat Politecnica de Catalunya, 2002; Docteur honoris causa, Ecole Polytechnique Federale de Lausanne, 2003. Asst. prof. elec. engring. Stanford U., Calif., 1977—83, assoc. prof. elec. engring., 1983—86, dir., computer rsch. lab., 1983—93, prof. elec. engring. and computer sci., 1986—, Willard and Inez Kerr Bell Endowed Prof. Elec. Engring. and Computer Sci., 1987—2001, chmn. dept. computer sci., 1994—96, dean Sch. Engring., 1996—99, provost, 1999—2000, pres., 2000—. Founder, chief scientist MIPS Computer Sys., 1984—92; chief arch. Silicon Graphics Computer Sys., 1992—98; founder MIPS Techs. (formerly MIPS Computer Sys.), 1998—; chmn. bd. dirs. T-span; mem. com. study internat. devels. in computer sci. and tech. NRC, 1988, mem. computer sci. and tech. bd., 1989—94, mem. com. study acad. careers for exptl. computer scientists, 1992—93, mem. status and direction of high performance computing and comm. initiative, 1995, mem. commn. phys. scis., math. and applications, 1998—99; mem. adv. com. computer and info. sci. and engring. NSF, 1992—96, chair oversight rev. of computer and info. sci. and engring. instnl. infrastructure program, 1992, mem. task force on future supercomputer ctrs. program, 95; tech. adv. bd. Microsoft Corp., 1992—96, Virtual Machine Works, 1995—96, Tensilica, 1998—99; strategic adv. bd. NetPower, 1992—95; mem. fellowship sel. com. Sloan Found., 1993—96; chmn. info. sci. and tech. Def. Advances Rsch. Projects Found., 1993—96, chair, 1994—95; mem. com. study investment strategy DARPA Def. Sci. Bd., 1998—99; mem. various conf. coms.; spkr. in field; bd. dirs. Alantec Corp., 1995—96, Cisco Systems, 2002—; chmn., bd. dirs. Atheros, 1998—. Co-author (with D.A. Patterson): Computer Organization and Design: The Hardware/Software Interface, 1993, Computer Organization and Design: The Hardware/Software Interface, 2d edit., 1998; co-author: Computer Architecture: A Quantitative Approach, 1990; contbr. articles to profl. jours. Named Profl. Young Investigator, NSF, 1984; recipient Disting. Alumnus award, SUNY, Stony Brook, 1991, John J. Gallen Memorial award, Villanova U., 1983, J. Stanley Morehouse Meml. award, 1997, Benjamin Garver Lamme medal, Am. Soc. Engring. Edn., 2000, Eckert-Mauchly award, ACM and IEEE Computer Soc., 2001, Seymour Cray Award, 2001. Fellow: IEEE (Emmanuel R. Piore award 1994, John Von Neumann medal 2000), Am. Acad. Arts and Scis., Assn. Computing Machinery; mem.: NAS, Royal Acad. Engring. Spain (corr.), Nat. Acad. Engring. (peer selection com. computer sci. and engring. 1996—99, chair 2000), Pi Mu Epsilon, Eta Kappa Nu, Tau Beta Pi. Office: Stanford U Office of the Provost Bldg 10 Stanford CA 94305-2061 Fax: 650-724-4062. E-mail: hennessy@stanford.edu.*

HENNESSY, PAMELA JOAN, elementary and secondary education educator; b. Danvers, Mass., May 30, 1961; d. Allan G. and Constance M. (Morgan) Hopkinson; m. Peter Hennessy, Oct. 12, 1985. BS, Framingham (Mass.) State Coll., 1983; MA, Worcester (Mass.) State Coll., 1990. Dir. Kinder Care Learning Ctrs., Framingham, 1983-84; tchr. Holliston (Mass.) pub. schs., 1984-86, Milford (Mass.) pub. schs., 1986—. Mem. Nat. Assn. for Edn. of Young Children, Am. Assn. Family and Consumer Sci., Cert. Family and Consumer Scis., Phi Upsilon Omicron, Kappa Delta Pi.

HENNESSY, SEAN P., retail executive; From mem. staff to sr. v.p. fin., CFO Sherwin-Williams, Cleve., 1984—2001, sr. v.p. fin., 2001—, CFO, 2001—. Office: Sherwin Williams 101 Prospect Ave NW Cleveland OH 44115-1075

HENNESSY, THOMAS CHRISTOPHER, priest, educator, retired dean; b. NYC, Nov. 3, 1916; s. Thomas C. and Anna E. (Regan) H. AB, Georgetown Coll., 1940; MA in Latin and Greek Classics, Fordham U., 1947, MS in Edn., 1957, PhD, 1962. Joined S.J., 1934, ordained priest Roman Cath. Ch., 1947. Tchr. Fordham Prep. Sch., NYC, 1941-44, 49-52, high sch. counselor, 1952-61; counselor educator Fordham U. at Lincoln Ctr., NYC, 1961-81; dean, prof. counselor edn. Sch. Edn. Marquette U., Milw., 1981-85. Editor: The Inner Crusade: The Closed Retreat in the US, 1965, The High School Counselor Today, 1966, The Interdisciplinary Roots of Guidance, 1966, Values and Moral Development, 1976, Value-Moral Education: The Schools and the Teachers, 1979, Fordham: The Early Years, 1998; How the Jesuits Settled in NY, A Documentary Account, 2003; cons. editor: Pers. and Guidance Jour., 1978-81; contbr. numerous articles to profl. jour. Mem. APA. Office: Fordham U Loyola Hall Bronx NY 10458

HENNESSY, WILLIAM JOSEPH, prosecutor; b. St. Paul, May 18, 1942; s. William E. and Julia R. (Luger) H.; m. Sandra Hennessy, July 3, 1965 (div. Jan. 7, 1977); m. Sally Ann Kroiss, Dec. 31, 1996; 1 child, Patricia Lee. BA, St. Thomas U., 1964; LLB, JD, William Mitchell U., 1968. Bar: Minn. 1968, U.S. Supreme Ct. 1975. Sr. ptnr. Hennessy & Richardson, St. Paul, 1970—93; chief prosecutor Cook County, Grand Marais, Minn., 1995—. Mem. adv. com. on the Criminal Rules, Minn. Supreme Ct., 1997-99. Mem. Minn. County Attys. Assn. (bd. dirs. 1996-2001). Avocation: commercial and instrument airplane pilot. Office: Cook County 411 W 2nd St Grand Marais MN 55604-2307 Office Phone: 218-387-1105.

HENNESY, GERALD CRAFT, artist; b. Washington, June 11, 1921; s. Gerald Craft and Frances Lee (Moore) H.; m. Elizabeth Ann Lovering, Mar. 4, 1950; children: Kathleen, Paul, Brian, Shawn, Hugh, Craig. Student, Corcoran Sch. Art, 1939, George Washington U., 1940; BS, U. Md., 1948. Enlisted U.S. Navy, 1942, advanced through grades to comdr., 1956; mgmt. analyst U.S. Air Force Hdqrs., Pentagon, Washington, 1948-52, 53-56; asst dir. for orgn. and mgmt. AEC, 1956-72; artist, dir. Studio of Hennesy, Clifton, Va., 1972—. One man shows include PLA Gallery, McLean, Va., 1967, Tolley Galleries, Washington, 1983, Venable Neslage Galleries, Washington, 1993, Marin-Price Galleries, Chevy Chase Md., 1995-96, 98, 2000, 02, 04 Prince Royal Gallery, Alexandria, Va., 1999, 2003, 2005; exhibited works at Corcoran Gallery Art, Washington, 1957, 59, 67, Smithsonian Inst., Washington, 1962, 64, Allied Artists of Am., N.Y.C., 1974, 75; represented in permanent collections at U.S. Ho. of Reps., Washington, Md. State Exec. Mansion, Annapolis, Nat. Hdqrs. Am. Legion, Washington, Nat. Hdqrs. DAR, Washington, Hdqrs. FDIC, Washington, others. Decorated Air medal with one star. Republican. Home and Office: 6811 White Rock Rd Clifton VA 20124-1434

HENNEY, CHRISTOPHER SCOT, immunologist; b. Sutton-Coldfield, Eng., Feb. 4, 1941; s. William Scot and Rhoda Agnes (Bateman) Henney; m. Janet Barnsley, June 20, 1964; children: James Scot, Samantha Jane. BS with honors, U. Birmingham, Eng., 1962, PhD in Exptl. Pathology, 1965, DSc. in Research Immunology (hon.), 1973. Immunologist WHO, Lausanne, Switzerland; assoc. prof. medicine and microbiology med. sch. Johns Hopkins U., Balt., 1978; prof. microbiology and immunology U. Wash., Seattle, 1978-81; head. basic immunology Fred Hutchinson Cancer Research Ctr., Seattle, 1978-81; co-founder, sci. dir., vice chmn. Immunex Corp., Seattle, 1981-89; co-founder, sci. dir., exec. v.p. ICOS Corp., Seattle, 1989—2000; CEO Dendreon Corp., Seattle, 1995—2003, chmn., 1995—2004, Structural Genomix Inc., Xcyte Therapier, Inc. Mem. Am. Assn. Immunology (sect. editor 1972-73), Reticuloendothelial Soc. (sect. editor 1978-79), Am. Cancer Soc. (chmn. immunology rev. com. 1982-83), NIH (mem. pathology study sect. 1978-82). Personal E-mail: chenney@comcast.net.

HENNEY, JANE ELLEN, health facility administrator, educator, oncologist; b. Kendallville, Ind., Mar. 26, 1947; d. Harry H. and Jeanette (Park) H.; m. J. Robert Graham, June 6, 1975. BS, Manchester Coll., North Manchester, Ind., 1969; MD, Ind. U.-Indpls., 1973. Intern St. Vincent's Hosp., Indpls., 1973-74; with Nat. Cancer Inst., Bethesda, Md., 1976—85, dep. dir., 1980—85; assoc. prof. medicine U. Kans. Med. Ctr., Kansas City, Kans., 1985—92, assoc. vice chancellor, acting dir. Mid Am. Cancer Ctr., 1985—92; prof. medicine, v.p. for health svcs. U. N.Mex., 1994—98; dep. commr. for ops. FDA, Rockville, Md., 1992—94, commr., 1998—2001; sr. v.p, provost for health affairs U. Cin., 2003—. Scholar in residence Assoc. Acad. Health Ctrs., 2001—03. Served with USPHS, 1976-86. Recipient commendation USPHS, 1979, 81, Sec.' Recognition award HHS, 1985. Mem.: Inst. Medicine.

HENNIG, ALFRED WALTER, lawyer; b. Istanbul, Turkey, July 15, 1952; came to the U.S., 1958; s. Rolf Alfred Hennig and Clara Del Favero. Student, Western Res. Acad., Hudson, Ohio, 1970, Albert-Ludwigs U., Freiburg, Germany, 1973; BA, U. Redlands, Calif., 1974; postgrad. in internat./comparative law, Sorbonne, Paris, 1977; JD, Santa Barbara Coll. Law, 1979; postgrad. in internat. bus. mgmt., UCLA, 1993. Bar: Calif. 1982. Lab. asst. Dr. Paul Lohmann Chem. Firm GmbH, Emmerthal, Germany, 1973; exec. ast. Sadolin & Stimman Co., Lima, Peru, 1974; legal asst. Santa Barbara (Calif.) County Pub. Defender, 1977; enumerator U.S. Dept. Commerce, Bur. of the Census, San Diego, 1980; atty. intern internat. law Barrera, Siqueiros & Torres Landa, Mexico City, 1981; atty. Cardenas & Fifield, El Centro, Calif., 1983-85, Read, Miguelez & Dib, L.A., 1985-90, Oliver Law Offices, L.A., 1990-92; pvt. practice L.A., 1993—. Pres. Internat. Club, Redlands, Calif., 1973-74. Mem. Internat. Law Soc., Country Club Woods (bd. mem. 1997-99), Turner Club, Alpha Mu Gamma, Pi Gamma Mu. Avocations: photography, equitation, bicycling, travel, foreign languages. Office: 3440 Torrance Blvd Ste 104 Torrance CA 90503-5805 Office Phone: 310-543-9185. E-mail: derfla715@hotmail.com.

HENNIGAR, DAVID JOHN, portfolio manager, director; b. Windsor, N.S., Can., July 5, 1939; s. Dean S. and Jean B. (Jodrey) H.; m. Carolyn Hiltz, June 8, 1964; children: Brian, Jan. B of Commerce, Mt. Allison U., 1960; MBA, Queen's U., 1962. Investment analyst Burns Fry Ltd. and predecessor co., Toronto, Ont., Can., 1963-66, br. mgr. Halifax, N.S., Can., 1966-71, Atlantic regional dir., 1971-93. Chmn. bd. dirs. Annapolis Group Inc., Extendicare Inc., Acadian Securities Inc., Aquarius Coatings Inc., High Liner Foods, Inc., VR Interactive Inc.; bd. dirs. Crown Life Ins. Co., Minas Basin Pulp & Power Co. Ltd., Scotia Investment Ltd., Crombie Properties, Ltd., Maritime Paper Products Ltd., Sentex Systems Ltd., CentrSource Corp., KLJ Field Svcs., Inc., Salumatics Inc., Solutioninc Ltd.; chmn. bd. dirs., CEO Landmark Global Fin. Inc. Bd. dirs., treas. Izaak Walton Killam Hosp. for Children, Halifax, 1976-82; bd. dirs. Inst. for Rsch. on Pub. Policy, 1983-89; active Trilateral Commn., 1988-94; bd. govs. Dalhousie U., 1983-90, Internat. Oceans Inst. Can., 2000-04; dir. Hope Air Inc. Mem. Investment Dealers Assn. Can. (nat. bd. dirs. 1985-87), Halifax Club. Home: 51 Forest Ln Bedford NS Canada B4A 1H8 Office: 3 Bedford Hills Rd Bedford NS Canada B4A 1J5 also: Extendicare 3000 Steeles Ave E Ottawa ON Canada L3R 9W2

HENNIGAR, WILLIAM GRANT, JR., dentist; b. Buffalo, Dec. 25, 1947; s. William Grant and Donnette (Glaeser) H.; m. Jennie Carcaud, Mar. 22, 1975 (div.); children: William Grant III, Charlotte Carcaud, Travis Welshofer(dec.), Brittany Lines. AB, Colgate U., 1970; DMD, U. Pa., 1973; cert., U. Rochester, 1975; JD, Cleve. State U., 1992. Bar: Mass., N.Y. 1993. With Harvard U. Health Inc., Cambridge, Mass., 1974; ptnr. Am. Family Dental Group, P.C., Cheektowaga, N.Y., 1982-97; pres. Grand Island, Cheektowaga, N.Y., 1988—. Bd. dirs. West River Homeowners Assn., Grand Island, 1985-88, Alumni Bd. Nichols Sch., Buffalo, 1988-89. Lic. capt. U.S. Coast Guard, 1989—. Fellow Acad. of Gen. Dentistry, ADA, Town of Grand Isl. Long Range Planning Com., 1998; mem. ABA, N.Y.State Bar Assn., Internat. Assn. for Orthodontics, Am. Acad. Dental Group Practice, U.S. Dental Inst. (cert. 1985), Erie County Bar Assn.,Buffalo Launch Club (Grand Island), Phi Kappa Psi, Psi Omega, U.S. Power Squadron. Libertarian. Episcopalian. Avocations: volleyball, boating, softball, geneology, running. Home: PO Box 691 Grand Island NY 14072-0691 Office: Am Family Dental Group 2025 Whitehaven Rd Grand Island NY 14072-2024

HENNING, GEORGE THOMAS, JR., steel company executive; b. West Reading, Pa., Sept. 26, 1941; s. George Thomas and Helen Virginia (Spangler) H.; m. Susan Young, July 21, 1962; children: George Thomas III, Michael Kevin. BA, Pa. State U., 1963; MBA, Harvard, 1965. Mgr. econ. analysis Eastern Gas & Fuel, Boston, 1967; mgr. gen. acctg. Ohio River Co., Cin., 1968; asst. to contr. Eastern Gas & Fuel Assos., Boston, 1969; dir. corp. planning Boston Gas Co., 1970; contr. Eastern Assoc. Coal Corp., Pitts., 1971-74; v.p., contr. Lykes Resources, Inc., 1974-78; asst. contr. Jones & Laughlin Steel Corp., 1979-85; gen. mgr. coal mine ops. and raw materials sales LTV Steel Co., Cleve., 1986, gen. mgr. asset mgmt., 1986-89; v.p., chief fin. officer Pioneer Chlor Alkali Co., Inc., Houston, 1988-95; v.p., CFO Pioneer Cos., Inc., 1995; v.p., contr. The LTV Corp., Cleve., 1995-99, v.p., CFO, 1999—2001, ret., 2001; bus. cons., 2002—. Mem. planning commn. Ferguson Twp., Pa.; trustee Mt. Nittany Conservancy; pres. Ctr. County Fedn. Librs.; bd. dirs. Schlow Ctr. Region Libr.; mem. bd. trustees Pa. State Univ., Univ. Pk. Mem. Pa. State Alumni Assn. (bd. dirs. Centre County chpt.), Lion's Paw Alumni Assn. (bd. dirs.), Omicron Delta Kappa. Methodist. Business E-Mail: ghenning63@psualum.com.

HENNING, JOEL FRANK, lawyer, writer; b. Chgo., Sept. 15, 1939; s. Alexander M. and Henrietta (Frank) H.; m. Grace Weiner, May 24, 1964 (div. July 1987); children: Justine, Sarah-Anne, Dara; m. Rosemary Nadolsky, June 21, 1992; 1 child, Alexandra. AB, Harvard U., 1961, JD, 1964. Bar: Ill. 1965. Assoc. Sonnenschein, Levinson, Carlin, Nath & Rosenthal, Chgo., 1965-70; fellow, dir. program Adlai Stevenson Inst. Internat. Affairs, Chgo., 1970-73; nat. dir. Youth Edn. for Citizenship, 1972-75; dir. profl. edn. Am. Bar Assn., Chgo., 1975-78; asst. exec. dir. comm. and edn. ABA, 1978-80; ptnr. Joel Henning & Assocs., 1980-87; sr. v.p., gen. counsel, mem. exec. com. Hildebrandt, Internat., Inc., 1987—; pres., pub. LawLetters, Inc., 1980-89; pub. Lawyer Hiring and Tng. Report, 1980-89; Chgo. theater critic Wall St. Jour., 1989—; pub. Almanac of Fed. Judiciary, 1984-89; editor Bus. Lawyer Update, 1980-87. Mem. faculty Inst. on Law and Ethics, Council Philos. Studies; chmn. Fund for Justice, Chgo., 1979-85 Author: Law-Related Education in America: Guidelines for the Future, 1975, Holistic Running: Beyond the Threshhold of Fitness, 1978, Mandate for Change: The Impact of Law on Educational Innovation, 1979, Improving Lawyer Productivity: How to Train, Manage and Supervise Your Lawyers, 1985, Law Practice and Management Desk Book, 1987, Lawyers Guide to Managing and Training Lawyers, 1988, Maximizing Law Firm Profitability: Hiring, Training and Developing Productive Lawyers, 1991-98, also articles. Chmn. Gov.'s Commn. on Financing Arts in Ill., 1970-71; bd. dirs. Ill. Arts Council, 1971-81, Columbia Coll., Chgo.; bd. dirs., v.p., pub. edn. exec. com. ACLU of Ill.; trustee S.E. Chgo. Commn.; mem. Joseph Jefferson Theatrical Awards Com. Fellow Am. Bar Found. (life); mem. Am. Law Inst., ABA (ho. of dels.),

Chgo. Bar Assn., Chgo. Council Lawyers (co-founder), Social Sci. Edn. Consortium. Office: 150 N Michigan Ave Ste 3600 Chicago IL 60601-7572 Office Phone: 312-578-0663. E-mail: jfhenning@rcn.com. *The hardest question for me to answer is, "What do you do?" I do a lot. Some of it returns money and satisfaction. Some returns more of one than the other. And, I do some things that make me feel fit. The best of what I do helps integrate my various selves and improves my relations with the world. But I have no facile way to say all of this at cocktail parties when, invariably, that question is popped.*

HENNING, LLOYD CRAIG, retired inventory executive; b. Lyons, Ill. s. Laverne Ellsworth Fredericke and Lillian Celeste (Krieg) Henning; married, Aug. 15, 1955; children: Cheryl Cox, Richard. Degree in materials mgmt. concepts (hon.), U. Ill., Northlake, 1982. Clk. Chgo. and Ill. Western R.R., Chgo., 1947—56; inventory records clk. Internat. Harvester, Melrose Park, Ill., 1956—57; inventory analyst Automatic Electric Co. GT&E, Northlake, Ill., 1957—74; supr., mgr. Sys. and Procedures (AECO), Northlake, 1974—84; co-owner Westchester Jewelers, Lombard, Ill., 1995—97; inventory analyst, master scheduler Reliable Electric/McClain Rogg, Bensenville, Ill., 1985—92; ret.; mem. Automatic Electric Jr. Staff, Northlake, 1972—73. Participant 23 mission projects at Presbyn. colls. and campgrounds. Comms. officer Nat. Presbyn. Mariners, Lombard, 1984—86, ext. officer, 1987—88; grade sch. mentor Kiwanis Club Hot Springs Village, Ark., 1998—2004. Mem.: Village Writers Club (v.p. 2004—05, pres. 2001—03). Republican. Methodist. Avocations: writing children's stories, writing monthly column for church newsletter. Home: 13 Halago Pl Hot Springs Village AR 71909

HENNINGS, DOROTHY GRANT (MRS. GEORGE HENNINGS), education educator; b. Paterson, N.J., Mar. 15, 1935; d. William Albert and Ethel Barbara (Moll) Grant; m. George Hennings, June 15, 1968. AB, Barnard Coll., 1956; EdM, U. Va., 1959; EdD, Columbia U., 1965. Tchr. Pierrepont Elem. Sch., Rutherford, NJ, 1956-58, Thomas Jefferson Jr. H.S., Fair Lawn, NJ, 1959-64; prof. edn. Kean U. of N.J., Union, 1965-99, disting. prof. edn., 1999—2002, disting. prof. emeritus, 2002—. Author citation N.J. Inst. Tech., Divsn. Continuing Edn., 1982; author: (with B. Grant) Teacher Moves, 1971; Content and Craft: Written Expression in the Elementary School, 1973; Smiles, Nods and Pauses: Activities to Enrich Children's Communication Skills, 1974; Mastering Classroom Communication: What Interaction Analysis Tells the Teacher, 1975; (with G. Hennings) Keep Earth Clean, Blue and Green: Environmental Activities for Young People, 1976; Words, Sounds, and Thoughts: More Activities to Enrich Children's Communication Skills, 1977; Communication in Action: Teaching the Language Arts, 1978, 8th edit. 2002 (with D. Russell) Listening Aids Through the Grades, 1979; (with G. Hennings) Today's Elementary Social Studies, 1980, 2d edit., 1989; Written Expression in the Language Arts, 1981; Teaching Communication and Reading Skills in the Content Areas, 1982; (with L. Fay) Star Show, 1989, Grand Tour, 1989, Previews, 1989, Reading with Meaning: Strategies for College Reading, 1990, 6th rev. edit., 2004, Poets Journal, 1991, Beyond the Read Aloud: Learning to Read Through Listening to and Reflecting on Literature, 1992, Vocabulary Growth: Strategies for College Word Study, 2001, Words Are Wonderful: An Interactive Approach to Vocabulary, books 1 and 2, 2003, book 3, 2004, book 4, 2005; contbr. articles to Edn., The Record, Lang. Arts, Sci. Tchr., The Reading Tchr., Jour. of Adolescent & Adult Lit., Jour. of Reading, Tchr. to Tchrs., Sci. and Children, Early Years, Reading Rsch. and Instrn., New Eng. Jour. of History, Jour. Reading Edn., others. Mem. Unitarian Ch., Summit, NJ. Recipient Edn. Press award, 1974, Outstanding Article award, 1999; NSF Acad. Yr. Inst. grantee, 1959, Field Enterprise grantee, Columbia U., 1965. Mem. Nat. Coun. Tchrs. English, N.J. Reading Assn. (Disting. Svc. to Reading award 1993), Internat. Reading Assn. (Outstanding Tchr. Educator in Reading award 1992), Suburban Reading Coun., Phi Beta Kappa, Phi Delta Kappa, Phi Kappa Phi, Kappa Delta Pi. Achievements include building named in her honor at Kean University in 2005. Home: 21 Flintlock Dr Warren NJ 07059-5014 Personal E-mail: hennings@verizon.net.

HENNINGSEN, PETER, JR., manufacturing executive; b. Mpls., Oct. 6, 1926; s. Peter and Anna O. (Kjelstrup) H.; m. Donna J. Buresh, June 19, 1948; children— Deborah, Pamela, James. BBA, U. Minn., 1950. Packaging engr. govt. and aero. products div. Honeywell, Inc., Mpls., 1950-72; mgr. packaging Internat. Tel. & Tel., N.Y.C., 1972-80; v.p. Raymond Eisenhardt & Son, Inc., 1980-90; ind. packaging and material handling cons., 1990—. Mem. Inst. Packaging Profls. (formerly Soc. Packaging and Handling Engrs.), 1951—, fellow, 1970, pres., 1970-71, chmn. bd., 1972-73, named Man of Yr., 1968. Editl. cons. mags. in field. With USNR, 1944-46. Elected to Packaging Hall of Fame, Packaging Edn. Forum, 1995. Mem. ASTM, Aerospace Industries Assn. (chmn. packaging com. 1967), Masons, Shriners. Methodist. Home and Office: 7610 Smetana Ln # 211 Eden Prairie MN 55344 E-mail: phenningsen@mn.rr.com.

HENNION, REEVE LAWRENCE, communications executive; b. Ventura, Calif., Dec. 7, 1941; s. Tom Reeve and Evelyn Edna (Henry) H.; m. Carolyn Laird, Sept. 12, 1964; children: Jeffrey Reeve, Douglas Laird. BA, Stanford U., 1963, MA, 1965. Reporter Tulare (Calif.) Advance-Register, 1960-62; reporter UPI, San Francisco, 1963-66, mgr. Fresno, Calif., 1966-68, regional exec. Los Angeles, 1968-69, mgr. Honolulu, 1969-72, San Francisco, 1972-75, Calif. editor, 1975-77, gen. news editor, 1977-81, bus. mgr., 1981-83, v.p., gen. mgr. Pacific div., 1983-85; v.p., gen. mgr. Calif.-Oreg. Broadcasting, Inc., 1985-86; pres. Viatech Inc., 1986-92; propr. Buncom Ranch; pres. Keypoint Svcs. Internat., Inc., Medford, Oreg., 1992—2002; interim exec. dir. Rogue Valley Coun. of Govts., 1998. Editor: The Modoc Country, 1971, Buncom: Crossroads Station, 1995. Chmn. Calif. Freedom of Info. Com., 1983-84; chair Jackson County Planning Commn., Jackson County Roads Com.; mayor of Buncom, Oreg.; pres. Buncom Hist. Soc.; active Rogue C.C. Found. Bd. Mem. Am. Planning Assn. (exec. bd. Oreg. chpt.), Delta Kappa Epsilon. Home: 3232 Little Applegate Rd Jacksonville OR 97530-9303

HENRETTA, DEBORAH A., consumer products company executive; m. Sean Murray; 3 children. Grad., St. Bonaventure U., 1983; MA, Syracuse U. Brand asst. Procter & Gamble, Cin., 1985, v.p., 1999—; gen. mgr. global baby care Proctor & Gamble, Cin., 1999—2001; pres. global baby care Procter & Gamble, Cin., 2001—. Bd. dirs. Sprint Corp., 2004—. Mem. adv. com. Newhouse Sch. Pub. Comm., Syracuse U. Named one of 50 Most Powerful Women in Bus., Fortune, 2002. Office: Procter & Gamble Procter & Gamble Plaza Cincinnati OH 45202

HENRICH, WILLIAM JOSEPH, JR., lawyer; b. Phila., Jan. 13, 1929; s. William J. and Helen (Moylan) H.; m. Dorothy Kolsun; children: William III, Michael, David, Richard. BA in Econs., LaSalle U., 1950; JD, Temple U., 1956. Bar: Pa. 1957, Ct. Common Pleas 1957, U.S. Dist. Ct. (ea. dist.) Pa. 1957. Assoc. Dilworth, Paxson, Kalish & Kauffman, Phila., 1957-65, ptnr., 1965-84, sr. ptnr., 1988—; pres., gen. counsel Triangle Pub. Inc., Radnor, Pa., 1985-88. Bd. mgrs. Beneficial Bank, Phila. Bd. dirs. LaSalle U., Phila., Pa., 1985—; trustee The Annenburg Sch. Comm., U. Pa., 1985—, The Annenburg Sch. Comm., U. So. Calif., L.A., 1985—. Mem. ABA. Office: Dilworth Paxson LLP 1735 Market St Fl 32 Philadelphia PA 19103-7595

HENRICHS, ALBERT MAXIMINUS, classicist, educator; b. Cologne, Germany, Dec. 29, 1942; came to U.S., 1971; s. Johannes and Berti H.; m. Ingrid Ursula Schaadt, June 4, 1965 (div. Mar. 1990); children: Markus, Helen Felicitas; m. Maura Giles, June 19, 1997 (div. Apr. 2001). Student, U. Cologne, 1962-66, U. Bonn, 1962-63; Dr.phil., U. Cologne, 1966, habilitation, 1969; A.M. (hon.), Harvard U., 1972. Vis. lectr. U. Mich., Ann Arbor, 1967-69; prof. U. Cologne, 1970-71; asso. prof. classics U. Calif., Berkeley, 1971-73; prof. Greek and Latin. Harvard U., Cambridge, Mass., 1973-84, Eliot prof. Greek lit., 1984—, chmn. dept. classics, 1982-88, mem. affiliated faculty Div. Sch., 1982—90; Sather prof. classical lit. U. Calif., Berkeley, 1990. Sr. fellow Ctr. for Hellenic Studies, Washington, 1992—97. Author: Didymos der Blinde Kommentar zu Hiob (Tura-Papyrus), 2 vols., 1968, Die Phoinikika des Lollianos, 1972, Die Götter Griechenlands, 1987, Warum soll ich denn tanzen? Dionysisches im Chor der griechischen Tragödie, 1996; editor: Harvard Studies in Classical Philology, 1975-79, 2001-05; adv. bd. Harvard Libr. Bull., 1981-95, Greek, Roman and Byzantine Studies, 1984—; contbr. articles on ancient Greek lit., papyrology, mythology and religion to scholarly jours. Fellow Am. Acad. Arts and Scis.; mem. Am. Philos. Soc., Am. Philol. Assn., Assn. Internationale de Papyrologues., Egypt Exploration Soc. Home: 272 Concord Ave Cambridge MA 02138-1338 Office: Harvard U Dept Classics 212 Boylston Hall Cambridge MA 02138 E-mail: henrichs@fas.harvard.edu.

HENRICHS, W(ALTER) DEAN, dermatologist; b. Smith Center, Kans., Oct. 26, 1939; s. Walter George and Mildred (Kubias) H.; m. Barbara Ann Bremer, Apr. 7, 1967; children: Matthew, Mark, Jonathan. BA, U. Kans., 1961, MD, 1965. Diplomate Am. Bd. Dermatology, Am. Bd. Dermatopathology. Commd. ensign USN, 1964, advanced through grades to capt.; chmn. dept. dermatology Winston-Salem (N.C.) Health Care Plan, 1984—. Methodist. Avocations: golf, reading. Office: Winston Salem Health Care 250 Charlois Blvd Winston Salem NC 27103-1579 Office Phone: 336-718-1006. Office Fax: 336-718-1296. Business E-Mail: wdhenrichs@novanthealth.org.

HENRICK, MICHAEL FRANCIS, lawyer; b. Chgo., Feb. 29, 1948; s. John L. and A. Madeline (Hafner) H.; m. Cissi F. Henrick, Aug. 9, 1980; children: Michael Francis Jr., Derry Patricia. BA, Loyola U., 1971; JD with honors, John Marshall Law Sch., 1974. Bar: Ill. 1974, U.S. Dist. Ct. (no. dist.) Ill. 1974, U.S. Supreme Ct. 1979, Wis. 1985, U.S. Dist. Ct. (ea. dist.) Wis. 1985. Ptnr. Hinshaw & Culbertson, Chgo., Waukegan, Ill., 1974—. Named Ill. Super Lawyer Chgo. Mag.; recipient Corpus Juris Secundum award West Publ. Co., 1974. Fellow Am. Coll. Trial Lawyrers; mem. ABA, Def. Rsch. Inst., Ill. Bar Assn., Lake County Bar Assn., Ill. Hosp. Attys. Assn., Internat. Assn. of Def. Counsel, Ill. Def. Attys. Assn., Soc. Trial Lawyers Def. Rsch. Inst., Am. Inns of Ct. Office: Hinshaw & Culbertson 110 N West St Waukegan IL 60085-4330 Business E-Mail: mhenrick@hinshawlaw.com.

HENRICKSON, LESLIE ANN, educational consultant, researcher; b. Sioux Falls, S.D., May 20; d. Reynolds Keith Henrickson and A. Jeanne Burkhalter; m. Joseph Dairmuid Deely, Jan. 2, 1983 (div. 1993); m. Donald Grurg, 2005; children: Brenda Kathleen Deely, Brian Seamus Deely. B in Chem. Engring., U. Ill., 1982; M in Physics, San Jose State U., 1990; MPhil, U. Calif., Riverside, 1997; PhD in Edn., UCLA, 2003. Rsch. engr. in advanced tech. Lockheed Missiles and Space Co., Sunnyvale, Calif., 1983—89; rsch./process engr. Censtor Corp., San Jose, Calif., 1989—90; physics and chemistry instr. San Jose City Coll., 1992—94; philosophy and physics instr. San Jose State U., 1993—94; physics instr. Foothill C.C., Menlo Park, Calif., 1993—94; CEO, pres. Tech. Edn. Consulting and Rsch., L.A., 1999—; edn. rschr. Ctr. for Governance, L.A., 2001—03, Ctr. for Assessment and Evaluation Student Learning, L.A., 2001—03; prof. Touro U. Internat., Cypress, Calif., 2003—. Contbr. articles to profl. jours. Fellow Nat. Sci. Found. for Assn. for Instl. Rsch., NSF, 2000, Nat. Sci. Found. for Ctr. for Assessment and Evaluation of Student Learning Project, 2002; grantee Doctoral Incentive Program, Calif. State U., 1995; Resident fellow at the Ctr. for Ideas and Soc., U. Calif., Riverside, 1995, Kneller scholar, UCLA, 1999. Mem.: Comparative and Internat. Edn. Soc. (assoc.), Computer Using Educators (assoc.), Assn. Instl. Rsch. (assoc.), Inst. of Strategic Thinking and Tech. Develop.l (exec. bd. mem. 2004), Sigma Pi Sigma (life). Methodist. Achievements include copyright on Student Technology Assessment Tool (Qwik-STAT) survey; copyright on computer program, Higher Education Enrollment Flow Predictor. Avocations: reading, running, needlecrafts. Home and Office: TECR PO Box 15264 Irvine CA 92623 Office: Touro U Internat 5665 Plaza Dr 3d Fl Cypress CA 90630 Office Phone: 949-400-4316. Personal E-mail: henrickson@techedcr.com.

HENRICSON, BETH ELLEN, microbiologist; b. Johnson City, N.Y., Apr. 22, 1947; d. Clifford Lyle and Margaret Addison (Moore) Hevenor; m. Lawrence Karl Henricson, Aug. 9, 1969; children: Erik Karl, Karen Jeanette. BS in Microbiology, Pa. State U., 1969; postgrad., U. Rochester, 1969-70; MEd, Boston U., Sechenheim, Germany, 1987; PhD in Biomed. Sci., Uniformed Svcs. U. Hlth. Scis., 1992. Registered clin. pub. health microbiologist Am. Acad. Microbiologists. Med. technologist Dept. of Army, Ft. Hood, Tex., 1981-84; microbiologist, med. technician Dept. of Army 5th Gen. Hosp., Stuttgart, Germany, 1986-87; predoctoral rsch. fellow USUHS, Bethesda, Md., 1987-92; NRC fellow FDA Ctr. Biol. Evaluation & Rsch., NIH, Bethesda, Md., 1992-93; postdoctoral rsch. fellow Henry M. Jackson Found., Bethesda, Md., 1993-95; microbiologist supr., quality assurance coord. Va. Dept. Agr. and Consumer Svcs., Warrenton, 1995—2002; adminstrv. officer Vet. Med. Assistance Team-2, Nat. Disaster Med. Sys., 2000—. Contbg. author: Endotoxin Research, 1990, Bacterial Endotoxins, 1995, Bioterrorism Agents: Implications for Animals, 2001, author, editor: VDACS Office of Animal Industry Lab. Svcs. Quality Assurance Guidance Manual; contbr. articles to profl. jours. Leader Boy Scouts Am., Germany, 1978—85, Girls Scouts Am., Germany, 1982—87, Boy Scouts Am., Hawaii, 1978—85, Boy Scouts Am., Tex., 1982—87, Girls Scouts Am., Tex., 1982—87; vol. Washington AIDS Ride, 1996. Scholar N.Y. State Regents, 1965. Mem.: AAUW, ACLU, LWV, AAAS, Am. Acad. Vet. Disaster Medicine, Am. Chem. Soc., Nat. Environ. Health Assn., Internat. Endotoxin Soc., Am. Soc. Microbiology, U.S. Animal Health Assn., Assn. Vet. Microbiologists (v.p. Colonial States chpt. 1996—98, pres. 1999—2001), N.Y. Acad. Scis., Am. Assn. Vet. Lab. Diagnosticians (life; Bacteriology, Mycoplasmology, Mycology steering com. 1998—, subcom. for antimicrobial susceptibility testing 1998—, co-chair lab. biosafety com. 2002), Phi Kappa Phi, Phi Beta Kappa, Phi Sigma, Iota Sigma Pi. Achievements include research in in cellular and molecular mechanism of endotoxic shock and early endotoxin tolerance; systemic inflammatory response to endotoxin analogs; in LPS (lipopolysaccharide)-inducible gene expression; in systemic inflammatory response syndrome; in acyloxyacyl hydrolase contribution to LPS detoxification; in LPS and Taxol or paclitaxel activation of Lyn Kinase autophosphorylation and LPS-induced cytokine production; contribution of C. diphtheriae to wound infection in an equine; contribution in agents of bioterrorism: consequences in animals; contribution in NCCLS antimicrobial QC for aqua culture. Office: VMAT 2 Inc c/o Office Emer Response/NDMS Office 12300 Twinbrook Pky Ste 520 Rockville MD 20852 E-mail: bhenricson@aol.com.

HENRIKSEN, EVA H., retired anesthesiology educator; b. Petaluma, Calif., Jan. 1, 1929; d. Peder Henrik Boas and Karen (Nielsen) Henriksen; m. Daniel Edward MacLean, Aug. 25, 1957 (dec. Dec. 1981); children: Elizabeth, Mary Ann. AA, U. Calif., Berkeley, 1948, BA, 1950; MD, Yale U., 1954. Diplomate Am. Bd. Anesthesiology. Intern, resident Los Angeles County Hosp., L.A., 1954-57; from instr. to asst. prof. anesthesia Loma Linda U. (formerly Coll. Med. Evangelists), L.A., 1957-68; from instr. to assoc. prof. surgery anesthesiology Sch. Medicine U. So. Calif., L.A., 1957-94, assoc. prof. anesthesiology emeritus, 1994—. Anesthesia cons. L.A. Coroner's Office, 1992—2005. Mem. governing coun. Angelica Luth. Ch., 1992—2000, 2002—05. Democrat. Avocation: patchwork quilt making. Home: 957 Arapahoe St Los Angeles CA 90006-5703

HENRIKSEN, MELVIN, mathematician, educator; b. NYC, Feb. 23, 1927; s. Kaj and Helen (Kahn) Henriksen; m. Lillian Viola Hill, July 23, 1946 (div. 1964); children: Susan, Richard, Thomas; m. Louise Levitas, June 12, 1964 (dec. Oct. 1997). BS, Coll. City N.Y., 1948; MS, U. Wis., 1949, PhD in Math, 1951. Asst. math., then instr. extension div. U. Wis., 1948-51; asst. prof. U. Ala., 1951-52; from instr. to prof. math. Purdue U., 1952-65; prof. math., head dept. Case Inst. Tech., 1965-68; research assoc. U. Calif. at Berkeley, 1968-69; prof., chmn. math. dept. Harvey Mudd Coll., 1969-72, prof., 1972-97, prof. emeritus, 1997—. Mem. Inst. Advanced Study, Princeton, 1956-57, 63-64; vis. prof. Wayne State U., 1960-61; rsch. assoc. U. Man., Winnipeg, Can., 1975-76; vis. prof. Wesleyan U., Middletown, Conn., 1978-79, 82-83, 86-87, 93-94. Author: (with Milton Lees) Single Variable Calculus, 1970; assoc. editor: Algebra Universalis, 1993—, Topology Atlas, 1996-2002, Topological Commentary, 1996-2002; mem. editl. bd. Functiones et Approximatio Commentario Mathematici, 2001–; author articles on algebra, rings of functions, gen. topology. Sloan fellow, 1956—58. Mem. Am. Math. Soc., Math. Assn. Am. (assoc. editor Am. Math. monthly 1988-91, assoc. editor Algebra Universalis 1993—). Office: Harvey Mudd Coll Math Dept Claremont CA 91711 Office Phone: 909-626-3676. Business E-Mail: henriksen@hmc.edu.

HENRIKSEN, THOMAS HOLLINGER, academic administrator; b. Detroit, Nov. 16, 1939; s. Paul and Irene (Hollinger) H.; m. Margaret Mary Mueller, Sept. 9, 1968; children— Heather Anne, Damien Paul Hollinger BA, Va. Mil. Inst., 1962; MA, Mich. State U., 1966, PhD, 1969. Asst. prof. SUNY, Plattsburgh, 1969-73, assoc. prof., 1973-79, prof., 1979-80; Peace fellow Hoover Instn. on War, Revolution and Peace Stanford (Calif.) U., 1979-80, research fellow, 1980-82, sr. research fellow, 1982-86, sr. fellow, 1986—, assoc. dir., 1983—2003, exec. sec. nat. fellows program, 1984—, mem. Pres.'s Commn. on White House fellows, 1987-93. Mem. U.S. Army Sci. Bd., 1984-90. Author: Mozambique: A History, 1978, Revolution and Counter-revolution: Mozambique's War of Independence, 1964-74, 1983, The New World Order: War, Peace and Military Preparedness, 1992, Clinton's Foreign Policy in Somalia, Bosnia, Haiti, and North Korea, 1996, Using Power and Diplomacy to Deal With Rogue States, 1999; co-author: The Struggle for Zimbabwe: Battle in the Bush, 1981; contbg. author, editor: Soviet and Chinese Aid to African Nations, 1980; Communist Powers in Sub-Saharan Africa, 1981; assoc. editor Yearbook on Internat. Communist Affairs, 1982-91; contbg. author, editor: One Korea? Challenges and Prospects for Reunification, 1994. Trustee George C. Marshall Found., 1993—. Served to lt. U.S. Army, 1963-65 Home: 177 Lundy Ln Palo Alto CA 94306-4563 Office: Stanford U Hoover Instn Stanford CA 94305 Office Phone: 650-723-4255.

HENRIKSON, ARTHUR ALLEN, political cartoonist, educator; b. Oak Park, Ill., June 1, 1921; s. Allen Bernhardt and Florence Ella (Dixon) H.; m. Lois Elizabeth Wessling, July 3, 1943; children: Diane Elizabeth Russell, Janet Christine, Michele Charlene Smetana. Student, Austin Acad. Fine Arts, Chgo., Chgo. Acad. Fine Arts, 1936-37; BS, Northwestern U., 1946, postgrad., 1946-51. With advt. dept. Snips Mag., Chgo., 1947-56; advt. and layout Des Plaines (Ill.) Jour., 1956; with Wessling Svcs., Des Moines. Illustrator: Living the Good Life Microwave Recipebook, 1990, PMS-Solving the Puzzle, 1995; editl. polit. cartoonist for The Daily Herald, Paddock Pubs., Arlington Heights, Ill., 1955-2001, Des Plaines Jour., 1956-69, Rockford Newspapers, Inc., 1959-73, Reporter/Progress, Downers Grove, Ill., 1959-2001, The Doings, Hinsdale, Ill., 1960-73, Ill. Cartoon Svc., 1961-81, Ind. Register, Libertyville, Ill., 1961-75, Suburban Life, Berwyn, Ill., Harvey (Ill.) Tribune, 1962-73, St. Petersburg Times/Brandon Times, Fla., 2003—, others; contbr. cartoons to Modern Medicine, Esquire, Nat. Enquirer, AMA, Christian Sci. Monitor; cartoons reprinted in Today's Cartoon, 1962, Best Gag Cartoons of the Year, 1964, Best Editorial Cartoons of the Year, 1972-2002, also in Chgo. Sun Times, Chgo. Daily News, Chgo. Tribune, L.A. Times, Sacramento Bee, San Diego Union, U.S. News and World Report, numerous others; cartoons exhibited at Columbia U., 1960, Art Inst. Chgo., 1962, White House, Washington, 1963, LWV, Washington, 1963, others; promotional cartoons for NBC-TV, for Motorola; cartoons in permanent collections at Libr. of Congress, Lyndon Baines Johnson Libr., Mus. of Cartoon Art, State Hist. Soc. Mo., others. Mem. bd. deacons First Congl. Ch., United Ch. of Christ, Des Plaines, 1970-74, chmn., 1972, 74, moderator, 1976, also mem. mission bd. and music bd.; bd. dirs. Northwest Cmty. coun. Girls Scouts U.S., 1972-79; mem. Sch. Bd. Caucus, Des Plaines, 1968-72, pres., 1970. Lt. USAF, 1942—46, capt. Med. Adminstrv. Corps USAF, 1946. Recipient numerous awards for cartoons including Sigma Delta Chi Peter Lisagor award, George Washington Honor medal Freedoms Found., 1962, 63, 64, 65, 66, 69. Mem. Assn. Am. Editl. Cartoonists, Ret. Officers Assn. Avocations: music, theater, art, travel. Home and Office: 27 N Meyer Ct Des Plaines IL 60016-2243 Office Phone: 847-296-1309. E-mail: lahenrkson@aol.com.

HENRIKSON, C. ROBERT, insurance company executive; BA, U. Pa.; JD, Emory U.; grad., Wharton U. Pension sales rep. Metlife, 1972—79, nat. dir. N.Y.C., 1979—81, asst. v.p., 1981—83, v.p. group pensions, 1983—91, sr. v.p. pensions dept., 1983—95, exec. v.p., 1995—96, instl. bus., 1996—97, sr. exec. v.p., 1997—99, pres. instl. bus., 1999—2002; pres. U.S. instl. and fin. svcs. Metlife Inc., N.Y.C., 2002—, pres., COO, 2004—. Bd. dirs. Met. Property and Casualty Ins. Co., MetLife Bank, MetLife Found., MetLife Auto & Home; bd. mem. emeritus Am. Benefits Coun.; bd. mem. Wharton Sch. S.S. Huebner Found. Ins. Edn., 1998—, chmn. bd.; mem. commn. on global aging CSIS; bd. mem. Ron Brown Award for Corp. Leadership. Bd. dirs. Wharton Sch.'s S.S. Huebner Found. Inst. Edn., 1998, chmn. Mem.: Health Inst. Assn. Am. (bd. dirs.). Office: Metlife Inc 27-01 Queens Plaza N Long Island City NY 11101 Business E-Mail: rhenrickson@metlife.com.

HENRIKSON, DONALD MERLE, forensic pathologist; b. Walla Walla, Wash., May 2, 1947; s. James Christan and Carol Jean (DuBois) H.; m. Eileen Ruth Mikita, Oct. 12, 1980. BA, Harvard U., 1969; MD, U. Calif., Davis, 1981. Diplomate Am. Bd. Pathology. Assoc. pathologist Lab. Medicine Cons., Inc., Auburn, Calif., 1986-87, FPMG, Inc., 1987-88; owner, pathologist FFPMG, 1989-94; assoc. pathologist NCFP, Inc., Sacramento, 1994—2002; pathologist Placer County Coroner's Office, Auburn, 2002—. Mem. med. staff Sierra Valley Dist. Hosp., Loyalton, Calif., 1992-95, Oroville Hosp. and Med. Ctr., 1986-95, Sierra Nev. Meml. Hosp., Grass Valley, Calif., 1986—, Sutter Auburn Faith Hosp., 1986—; asst. clin. prof. U. Calif. Sch. of Medicine, Davis, 1994—. Mem. Placer County Child Death Rev. Team, Auburn, 1990—; mem., former chair Sacramento County Child Death Rev. Team, Sacramento, 1994-2001; mem. Nevada County Child Death Rev. Team, Nevada City, 1996—. Sgt. U.S. Army, 1969-71. Fellow Coll. of Am. Pathologists; mem. AMA, AAAS, Am. Acad. Forensic Scis., Am. Soc. for Clin. Pathology. Avocations: hiking, golf, playing piano. Office: Placer County Coroner DeWitt Ctr 11500 A Ave Auburn CA 95603

HENRIQUES, DIANA BLACKMON, journalist; b. Bryan, Tex., Dec. 17, 1948; d. Lawrence Ernest and Pauline (Webb) Blackmon; m. Laurence Barlow Henriques, Jr., June 7, 1969. BA with distinction, George Washington U., 1969. Editor Lawrence Ledger, Lawrenceville, N.J., 1969-71; reporter Asbury Park (N.J.) Press, 1971-74; copy editor Palo Alto (Calif.) Times, 1974-76; investigative reporter Trenton (N.J.) Times, 1976-82; bus. writer The Phila. Inquirer, 1982-86; writer Barron's Fin. Weekly, N.Y.C., 1986-89, The New York Times, 1989—. Vis. fellow, cons. Woodrow Wilson Sch., Princeton U., N.J., 1981-82, Guggenheim Found., N.Y., N.J., 1981-82. Author: (books) The Machinery of Greed, 1986, Fidelity's World, 1995, The White Sharks of Wall Street, 2000; contbr. articles to profl. jours. Mem. internat. coun. Elliott Sch. Internat. Affairs George Washington U. Recipient Bell Prize N.J. Press Assn., 1977, Investigative Reporting prize Deadline Club, 1997, George B. Polk award for military reporting, 2005; co-recipient Loeb award Deadline Reporting, 1999. Mem. N.Y. Fin. Writers Assn., Phi Beta Kappa, Lectr. Am. Press Inst. Avocations: walking, reading. Office: The New York Times 229 W 43rd St New York NY 10036-3959*

HENRIQUES, GREGG ROS, psychology professor; b. Fairfax, Va., Aug. 30, 1970; s. Peter and Marlene Henriques; m. Andrea Somoroff, Apr. 21, 1970; children: Sydney Ros, Jonathan Matthew, Melana Somor. PhD, U. Vt., 1999. Lic. psychologist Va. Asst. prof. psychology James Madison U., Harrisonburg, Va., 2003—; rsch. asst. prof. U. Pa. Contbr. articles to profl. jours. Grantee, NIMH. Mem.: APA. Democrat. Achievements include discovery of new theoretical framework that unifies the sciences. Home: 22 Ashley Rd Stuarts Draft VA 24477 Office: James Madison U MSC 7401 216 Johnston Hall Harrisonburg VA 22807 Office Phone: 540-568-7857. Personal E-mail: henriqgx@jmu.edu.

HENRIQUEZ, ALLEN, artist, concierge; b. NYC, June 4, 1953; s. Charles Leo and Rosetta (Martin) Henriquez; m. Regina Millicent Thomas; children: Shad Alan Bert, Sean Allen. Radiology, Cmty. Coll. Air Force, 1978; Fire Safety, John Jay Coll., 1989. Artist, writer The 7th Renaissance, NYC, 2004, 3 on a Rock, 1995—2004. Writer: numerous screenplays, manuscripts, novels, plays. Sgt. USAF, 1974—78. Recipient Drawing award, The Sch. Art

League, 1972, NAACP (Jamaica Branch), 1972. Mem.: Ward Nasse Gallery, Long Island Black Artist Assn. Avocations: bongo, trumpet. Home: 120 Beach 19th St Apt 21L Far Rockaway NY 11691 Office: The 7th Renaissance PO Box 53 Lawrence NY 11559

HENRY, BARBARA A. ANN, publishing executive; b. Oshkosh, Wis., July 23, 1952; d. Robert Edward and Barbara Frances (Aylesworth) Henry BJ, U. Nev., 1974. With Gannett Co., 1974—; reporter Reno Gazette-Jour., 1974—78, city editor, 1978-80, mng. editor, 1980-82; asst. nat. editor USA Today, Washington, 1982-83; exec. editor Reno Gazette-Jour., 1981-86; editor, dir. Rochester (N.Y.) Dem. and Chronicle and Times-Union, 1986—91; pub. Great Falls (Mont.) Tribune, 1992-96; pres., pub. Des Moines Register, 1996—2000, The Indianapolis Star, 2000—; pres. Ind. Newspaper Group, 2002—. Recipient Publisher of the Year, Gannett Newspaper Group, 2001. Mem. Soc. Profl. Journalists, Associated Press Mng. Editors, Am. Soc. Newspaper Editors Avocation: skiing. Mailing: Indianapolis Star PO Box 145 Indianapolis IN 46206-0145

HENRY, C. BRAD (BRAD HENRY), governor; b. Shawnee, Okla., June 10, 1963; m. Kimberley Blain; children: Leah, Laynie. BA, Okla. U., 1985, JD, 1988. Bar: Okla. 1988, U.S. Ct. Appeals (10th cir.), U.S. Dist. Ct. (we. dist.) Okla. Staff researcher Okla. State Senate, Oklahoma City, summer 1984, senator; econs. tchg. asst. U. Okla., Norman, 1983-85; legal asst. Henry Henry & Henry, Shawnee, summer 1985; law clk. Andrews Davis Legg Bixler Milsten & Murrah, Oklahoma City, summer 1987; pres. Brad Henry Oil Co., Inc., Shawnee, 1987-89; legal intern Cleveland County Legal Aid Office, Norman, 1987-88; assoc. atty. Andrews Davis Legg Bixler Milsten & Price, Oklahoma City, 1988-89; atty. City of Shawnee, 1989—2002, state senator, 1989—2002; assoc. Charles T. Henry, Inc. & Assocs., Shawnee, 1989—; gov. State of Okla., Oklahoma City, 2003—. Mng. editor Okla. Law Rev., 1988. Trustee St. Gregory's Coll.; bd. dirs. Gateway to Prevention and Recovery, Inc.; mem. Okla. Acad. for State Goals, First Bapt. Ch., Shawnee; active Muscular Dystrophy Assn.; commr. U. Okla. Election Commn., 1987-88; bd. govs. U. Okla., 1982-84; Okla. and Cleveland County coord. Robert Henry for Atty. Gen. Campaign, 1986. Mem. ABA, ATLA, Okla. Bar Assn., Am. Inn of Ct., Pottawatomie County Bar Assn. (pres. 1991), Shawnee C. of C. (amb.), Lions, Jaycees, Delta Tau Delta (pres. 1984), Phi Delta Phi. Democrat. Baptist. Office: Gov Office State Capitol Bldg Ste 212 Oklahoma City OK 73105

HENRY, CANDY A., education educator, writer; b. Indiana, Pa., Apr. 21, 1966; d. John William and Katherine Barbara (Greczek) Henry. BA, St. Vincent Coll., 1998; MA, Indiana U. of Pa., 1991; PhD, Indiana U. Pa., 1995. Writing ctr. coord. Seton Hill U., Greensburg, Pa., 1995—2000, ESL instr., 1995—2000; adj. eng. prof. Cmty. Coll. of Allegheny County, Monroeville, Pa., 1999—2002, Penn State U., New Kensington, Pa., 1999—2002, Westmoreland County Cmty. Coll., Youngwood, Pa., 1991—2002, bus. and tech asst. eng. prof., 2002—. Mem.: Pa. State Edn. Assn. Roman Catholic. Avocations: golf, painting, spanish language, animal charities. Home: 1243 West Fir Dr Latrobe PA 15650 Office: Founders Westmoreland County Cmty Coll Armbrust Rd Rm 405 Youngwood PA 15697 Office Phone: 724-925-4044.

HENRY, CARL NOLAN, lawyer; b. Washington, Sept. 30, 1965; s. Robert Benjamin Covington III and Inola Francis Henry. BA in Polit. Sci., U. Calif., Berkeley, 1987, JD, 1993. Bar: Calif. 1993, U.S. Supreme Ct. 1997, U.S. Ct. Appeal (9th cir.) 1993, U.S. Dist. Ct. (no., ctrl. dists.) Calif. 1993. Dep. atty. gen. Calif. Dept. Justice, L.A., 1994-99, 99—; staff atty. to Hon. Janice Rogers Brown Calif. Supreme Ct., San Francisco, 1999. Career Awareness Acad. scholar Home Savings Am., 1983; Liberal Arts award Bank Am., 1983. Mem. L.A. Angel City Links Assn. (O. J. Simpson Acad. scholar 1983), L.A. Ephebian Honor Soc. Democrat. Methodist. Avocations: sports, politics, music, history, education. Office: Calif Dept Justice 300 S Spring St Ste 5000 Los Angeles CA 90013-1230

HENRY, CHARLES HOWARD, non-commissioned officer; b. Aurora, Ill., Oct. 14, 1966; s. Howard Hufford and Barbara Jeanne (Keller) H.; m. Trisha Barnhisel, May 8, 1999. Personnelman 3d class, USS Guardfish USN, San Diego, 1986-89, yeoman 2d class, comdr. submarine group 5, 1989-92, yeoman 2d class, USS Alabama Silverdale, Wash., 1993-96, pers. officer, cmdr. submarine squadron 22 La Maddalena, Sardinia, Italy, 1996-98, yeoman divsn. leading petty officer USS Jefferson City San Diego, 1998-2000; comdr. submarine force U.S. Pacific Fleet, shipyard representative Puget Sound Naval Shipyard, 2000—. Mem. U.S. Naval Inst., 1991-98. Named Sr. Sailor of Yr., Cmdr. Submarine Squadron 22, USN, 1997. Mem.: Non-Commissioned Officers Assn., F&Am. Warren G Harding Lodge, Lodge No. 260 Free and Accepted Masons of Wash. Republican. Lutheran. Avocations: reading, music, motorcycling, personal finance. Personal E-mail: billiebighead@aol.com.

HENRY, CHARLES JAY, library director; b. Washington, June 17, 1950; s. Charles J. and June (Statz) H.; m. Nancy C. Todd, Oct. 4, 1986. BA, Northwest Mo., 1972; MA, Columbia U., 1977, MPhil, 1980, PhD, 1987. Instr. Columbia U., N.Y.C., 1981-82; asst. to dean Columbia Coll., N.Y.C., 1982-85; asst. dir., divsn. humanities, hist. Columbia Libr., N.Y.C., 1985-91; dir. libr. Vassar Coll., Poughkeepsie, N.Y., 1991-96; dir. Am. Arts and Letters Network, 1995-96; vice-provost Rice U., Houston, 1996—, univ. libr., 1996—; exec. dir. Two Ravens Inst., 1998—. Internat. rsch. fellow London Guildhall U., 1995—; chair nat. steering com. for computer scis. and humanities, 1998—; sr. advisor Internat. U., Bremen, Germany. Co-author: Computing and Humanities: New Dir., 1990; contbr. articles to profl. jours; panel mem., speaker in field. Lectrs., symposia peace edn. UN, Peace Edn. Columbia U.; pres. Nat. Initiative for a Networked Cultural Heritage, 2002-03. Fulbright scholar Vienna, 1980-81; Lilian Becker scholar Middlebury Coll., 1977; MacArthur Found. grantee, 1984-87; Presidents fellow Columbia U. 1978-79, 79-80; recipient Best Paper award humanities architecture divsn. Conf. Cybernetics and Systems Rsch., Vienna, 1992, All Conf. award, 1996; Fulbright fellow New Zealand, 2003. Mem. AAAS, ALA, Assn. Computers and Humanities (exec. coun. 1994-96), Am. Soc. for Info. Sci., N.Y. Acad. Sci., Coalition for Networked Info. (project leader 1991—), Bd. of Governors, TX Digital Libr. Alliance. Democrat. Achievements include rsch. in cybernetics and systems rsch. Office: Foundren Libr MS44 Rice U PO Box 1892 Houston TX 77251 Office Phone: 713-348-4022. Office Fax: 713-348-5258. E-mail: chhenry@rice.edu.

HENRY, CHRISTOPHER JOEL, software consultant; b. Santa Maria, Calif., Dec. 18, 1958; s. Stacey Chumard Henry and Elvera Pauline (Ruggerio) Talley; m. Trudy Hawkes-Henry, Dec. 27, 1999. Student, City Coll. San Francisco, 1977-80, Dale Carnegie Sch., 1980; AS in Computer Sci., Andover Coll., Portland, Maine, 1994. Ops. mgr. MACCO, 1985-90; sr. lab technician IDEXX Labs., Portland, Maine, 1991-92; cons., subcontractor Douglass/400, Boston, 1993-94, EMC Corp., Hopkington, Mass., 1994; programmer G.H. Bass Inc., Portland, 1994; cons. QCC, Inc., Westwood, Mass., 1995-96, Douglas Cons. Inc., info. mgmt., contract cons. svcs., Boston, 1997—2001; with Next Step Enterprises, Inc., Orlando, Fla., 2001—. CEO, Next Step Enterprises, Inc. Inventor anti-nail biting product. Mem. New Eng. Sys. Group. Republican. Roman Catholic. Avocations: road racing, camping, reading. Office: Next Step Enterprises Inc 2212 S Chickasaw # 202 Orlando FL 32825 Office Phone: 888-850-8216. E-mail: chrishenry@stopbitingnails.com.

HENRY, DALE, artist; b. Anniston, Ala., Feb. 8, 1931; s. Elbert Postell and Vivian Penn (Dunlap) Henry. Grad. h.s. Various positions as civil servant; tchr. Sch. of Visual Arts, N.Y.C., 1970—86; ret. One-man shows include Gallery Nine, Berkeley, Calif., 1961, Calif. Palace of Legion of Honor, San Francisco, 1961, Esther Robles Gallery, L.A., 1965, Mills Coll. Art Gallery, Oakland, Calif., 1968, Fischbach Gallery, 1971, Galleria Toselli, Milan, 1972, John Weber Gallery, N.Y.C., 1972, 1973, 1976, 1977, 1979, The Clocktower, 1975, Hal Bromm Gallery, 1978, William Paterson Coll., Ben Shahn Gallery, Wayne, N.J., 1980, Sarah Lawrence Coll., Yonkers, N.Y., 1985, exhibitions include Witte Meml. Mus. Ann., San Antonio, 1952, Dallas Mus. for Contemporary Art, 1960, Legion of Honor Mus., 1960—65, Poindexter Gallery, N.Y.C., 1962, Va. Mus. Fine Arts, Richmond, 1962, John Weber Gallery, 1971—80, Gallery of Loretta Hilton Ctr., Webster Coll., St. Louis, 1976, Inst. for Art and Urban Resources, Long Island City, 1976, G.M. Vieville and S.P. Najar Gallery, Paris, 1977, Moore Coll of Art, Pa., 1977, USIA World Traveling Exhbn., 1977—80, Munson-Williams-Proctor Gallery, Utica, N.Y., 1981, Bard Coll., 1981; works featured in publs. including: San Francisco Chronicle, Art in Am., N.Y. Times, Village Voice; collections, Estate of Marconi, Milan, Hamburg & Family, Tang, L.I., Estate of John Reeves White, N.Y., Mills Coll., Oakland, Calif., Adirondack Planning Commission, Bickford, Nathaniel & Family, Legion of Honor; contbr. articles in field. Recipient Creative Pub. Svc. award, State of N.Y., 1981, Bd. Trustees' Calif. Legion of Honor, 1962; grantee, NEA, 1982.

HENRY, DAVID B., real estate company executive; With GE, 1978—2003, chmn. GE Capital Investment, chief investment officer, sr. v.p. GE Capital Real Estate; chief investment officer Kimco Realty, New Hyde Park, NY, 2001—, vice chmn. bd. dirs. Mem. Real Estate Credit Com., 1991—, chmn. investment com., 1997—; bd. mem. Health Care Property Investors, Inc. Office: Kimco Realty Corp 3333 New Hyde Park Rd New Hyde Park NY 11042

HENRY, DAVID HOWE, II, retired diplomat; b. Geneva, N.Y., May 19, 1918; s. David Max and Dorothy (Buley) H.; m. Margaret Beard, Nov. 16, 1946; children: David Beard, Peter York, Michael Max, Susan. Student, Hobart Coll., 1935-37, Sorbonne, 1937-38; AB, Columbia U., 1939; student, Russian Inst., 1948-49, Harvard U., 1944-45, Nat. War Coll., 1957-58. Ins. agt., 1939—41; mem. fgn. svc. Dept. State, 1941—71, assigned Montreal, 1941—42, assigned Beirut, 1942—44, Washington, 1944—45, 1948—52, 1957—66, 1970, Moscow, 1945—48, Vladivostok, 1945—46, Berlin, 1955—57; acting dir. Office Rsch. and Intelligence Sino-Soviet bloc, 1958—59; dir. dept. polit. affairs Nat. War Coll., 1958—61; dep. dir. Office Soviet Affairs, 1961—64, dir., 1964—65; mem. Policy Planning Coun., 1965—66; dep. chief of mission Am. Embassy, Reykjavik, Iceland, 1966—69; info. sys. specialist, 1970; specialist polit. and security coun. affairs UN, N.Y.C., 1971—79. Mem.: Rotary, Kappa Alpha. Presbyterian. Home: 2551 SW Brookwood Ln Palm City FL 34990-4752

HENRY, DAVID PATRICK, lawyer; b. Terre Haute, Ind., June 2, 1960; s. Joseph C. and Sara F. Henry; children: Hannah Lane, Blake Ryan. BS, U. Mo., 1982; JD, Oklahoma City U., 1985. Bar: Okla., U.S. Dist. Ct. (we., no. and ea. dists.) Okla., U.S. Ct. Appeals (10th cir.). Assoc. Hughes & Nelson, Oklahoma City, Okla., 1985-88; ptnr. Coyle & Henry, P.C., Oklahoma City, 1988-91, Henry Law Office, Oklahoma City, 1991—. Mem. ATLA, Okla. Criminal Def. Bar Assn., Okla. County Bar Assn. Democrat. Baptist. Avocations: golf, poker. Office: Henry Davidson & Hill 3315 NW 63rd St Oklahoma City OK 73116-3787

HENRY, DEWITT PAWLING, II, literature educator, art association administrator, writer; b. Wayne, Pa., June 30, 1941; s. John and Kathryn (Thralls) Henry; m. Constance Joy Sherbill, Aug. 25, 1973; children— Ruth Kathryn, David Jung Min. AB, Amherst Coll., 1963; A.M., Harvard U., 1965, PhD, 1971; postgrad., U. Iowa-Iowa City, 1964-66. Editor Ploughshares, dir. Ploughshares, Inc., Watertown, Mass., 1971-89, exec. dir., 1989-95; dir. Book Affairs, Inc., Watertown, 1975-85. Adj. prof. Emerson Coll., Boston, 1982-83, asst. prof. creative writing and lit., 1983-89, assoc. prof., 1989—, acting chair div. writing, pub. and lit., 1987-88, chair, 1989-93; mem. adv. panel Mass. Coun. on the Arts, Boston, 1981-83; literature panelist Nat. Endowment for the Arts, Washington, 1982-85, 92-93; mem. adv. bd. New England Found. for Arts, 1983-85; mem. Watertown Arts Lottery coun., 1987-92; bd. dirs., treas. Associated Writing Programs, 1988-90, pres., 1990-91. Author: The Ploughshares Reader, New Fiction for the 80s, 1985, Other Sides of Silence, New Fiction from Ploughshares, 1993, Fathering Daughters, 1998, Breaking Into Print, 2000, Sorrow's Company: Writers on Loss and Grief, 2001, The Marriage of Anne Maye Potts, 2001; columnist Wilson Libr. Bull., 1979-81; staff editor The Pushcart Prize, 1978—. Fellow Woodrow Wilson found., 1963; fellow Coordinating Council of Literary Mags., 1979, Nat. Endowment for Arts, 1979 Mem. Associated Writing Programs, Phi Beta Kappa Presbyterian. Home: 33 Buick St Watertown MA 02472-2176 Office: Emerson Coll Writing Lit Pub Divsn 120 Boylston St Boston MA 02116-4624 Office Phone: 617-824-8241. Personal E-mail: bakofpak@aol.com.

HENRY, EDWARD FRANK, data processing executive; b. East Cleveland, Ohio, Mar. 18, 1923; s. Edward Emerson and Mildred Adelia (Kulow) H.; m. Nicole Annette Peth, June 18, 1977. BBA, Dyke Coll., 1948; postgrad., Case Western Reserve U., 1949, Cleve. Inst. Music, 1972. Internal auditor E.F. Hauserman Co., 1948-51; sales and radio announcer Sta. WSRS, 1951; office mgr. Frank C. Grismer Co., 1951-52, Broadway Buick Co., 1952-55; sec., treas. Commerce Ford Sales Co., 1955-65; nat. mgr. Auto Acctg. divsn. United Data Processing Co., Cin., 1966-68; v.p. Auto Data Sys. Co., Cleve., 1968-70; pres. Profl. Mgmt. Computer Sys., Inc., Cleve., 1970—2003, Profl. Mgmt. Computer Sys. Became Internat., 1999—2003, ComputerEASE, Small Bus. Computer Ctrs. divsn. Profl. Mgmt. Computer Sys., Inc., 1985—2003, VideoEASE CompuAIDE Computerized Video Rental Sys. divsn. Profl. Mgmt. Computer Systems, Inc., 1987-89; pres. CompuPRINT divsn. Profl. Mgmt. Computer Sys., Inc., 1995—, pres. TravelEASE divsn., 1996—. Drum maj., musician Wurlitzer Marching Band, Cleve., 1939—42, The Ed Henry Dance Band, 1939—42; with USAF Marching Band, Kearns, Utah, 1943; dramatic dir., actor Euclid Little Theatres, Jewish Cmty. Ctr.; actor Cleve. Playhouse, 1961—63; dramatic dir., actor various other theatres; exec. artistic dir. NorthCoast Cultural Ctr., 1989—. Contbr. photography, Travel Agents Internat. mag., 1990 (hon. mention, 1990); prodr., dir. (Jesters) (plays) National Book of the Play Acapulco, Mexico, 1985, nat. prodr., dir. (Jesters) Nat. Book of the Play Reno, 1988—, Bally's Celebrity Rm., Las Vegas, 1989—96, Hyatt Regency O'Hare, 1998, Millennium, 2000, Nat. Book of the Play Bally's Las Vegas. Charter pres. No. Ohio Coun. Little Theatre, 1954—56; founder, artistic and mng. dir. Exptl. Theatre, Cleve., 1959—63; bd. dirs. Cleve. Philharm. Orch., 1972—74, Cleve. Jazz Orch., 1991—, Cleve. Opera League, Back on Board, 2002. 1st lt. USAF, 1943—46, PTO, capt. USAF, 1946—58, capt. USAFR, 1995. Decorated Bronze Star with 3 oak leaf clusters; named and featured in Showtime in Cleveland: The Rise of A Regional Theater Center (John Vacha). Mem.: APA, Res. Officers Assn., Internat. Soc. Photographers, Associated Photographers Internat., Internat. Platform Assn., Am. Soc. Profl. Cons., Nat. Assn. Profl. Cons., Data Processing Mgmt. Assn., Mil. Order World Wars (comdr. Cleve. chpt. 1994—95, dept. comdr. State of Ohio 2001—, adjutant 2001—, nat. staff mem. 2003—), Inst. Mgmt. Accts., Am. Mgmt. Assn., Air Force Assn. (life), Art Inst. Chgo., Cleve. Mus. Art, Nat. Assn. Met. Mus. Art of N.Y., Mayfield Area C. of C., Ky. Cols., Rotary, Univ. Club, Acacia Country Club, Hermit Club, Cleve. Grays Club, Deep Springs Trout Club, Jesters (dramatic dir. 1971—, dir. 1981, impresario 1984—99, impresario emertus 2000, Cleve. Ct. # 14, SOBIB, Kachina), Grotto, Scottish Rite (dramatic dir. 1967—, thrice potent master 1982—84, class named in his hon. 1994), DeMolay (master Cleve. chpt. 1942, Legion of Honor 1970), Sojourners (Nat. President's cert. 1977—78, pres. Cleve. chpt. #23 1978), Masons (60 yr. honor 2004, hon. 33d degree), Am. Legion, VFW, KT, Heroes of '76 (comdr. Cleve. 1977), Cuyahoga County Meml. Lodge (worshipful master 1993—94), Shriners (dramatic dir. 1968—88), Phi Kappa Gamma (charter pres., past nat. pres.). Republican. Presbyterian. Home: 666 Echo Dr Gates Mills OH 44040-9606 Office: Profl Mgmt Computer Systems Inc 19701 S Miles Rd Cleveland OH 44128-4257 Office Phone: 216-581-5337. Office Fax: 216-663-9822. E-mail: efhenry@aol.com.

HENRY, FRANCES ANN, journalist, educator; b. Denver, July 23, 1939; d. Lewis Byford and Betsy Mae (Lancaster) Patten; m. Charles Larry, June 28, 1963 (div. May 1981); children: Charles Kevin, Tracy Diane. BA in English, Carleton Coll., 1960; MA in Social Sci., U. Colo., Denver, 1988; MA in Journalism, Memphis State U., 1989. Cert. tchr. Lang. arts tchr. Rolla (Mo.) Pub. Schs., 1963-66; journalism/English tchr. Douglas County Pub. Schs., Castle Rock, Colo., 1976-99, retired, 1999, chmn. English dept., 1992-98; asst. prof. Memphis State U., 1991-92; mng. editor Douglas County News-Press, Castle Rock, 1986-87; editor Fourth World Bulletin, 1988; exec. editor Daily Helmsman Memphis State U., 1988-89, gen. mgr. Daily Helmsman, 1991-92; sole proprietor The Editor's Desk, 1997—. Contbr. articles to profl. jours. Recipient Gov.'s award for excellence in edn. Colo. Endowment for Humanities, 1997. Mem. ACLU, Colo. H.S. Press Assn. (sec. 1981-83, pres. 1983-91, bd. dirs., named Colo. Journalism Tchr. of Yr. 1985), Mensa, Kappa Tau Alpha. Democrat. Episcopalian. E-mail: fhenry1@comcast.net.

HENRY, FREDERICK B., foundation administrator; Pres. Bohen Found., 1984—. Bd. mem. Am. Ctr., Paris, 1991; chmn. Am. Ctr. Found.; bd. dir. Georges Pompidou Art & Culture Found., Paris & Houston, Aspen Valley Cmty. Found., Aspen, Colo., Bklyn. Acad. Music, Des Moines Art Ctr., Iowa, Dia Ctr. for Arts, NYC, Public Agenda Found., NYC, Whitney Mus. Am. Art, NYC; bd. trustee Solomon R. Guggenheim Mus., NYC, 2002—. Office: Bohen Foundation 415 W 13th St New York NY 10014 Office Phone: 212-414-4575.*

HENRY, FREDERICK EDWARD, lawyer; b. St. Louis, Aug. 28, 1947; s. Frederick E. and Dorothy Jean (McCulley) H.; m. Vallie Catherine Jones, June 7, 1969; children: Christine Roberta, Charles Frederick. AB, Duke U., 1969, JD with honors, 1972. Bar: Ill. 1972, U.S. Dist. Ct. (no. dist.) Ill. 1972, Calif. 1982. Assoc. Baker & McKenzie, Chgo., 1972-79, ptnr., 1979—. Elder, session mem. Fourth Presbyn. Ch., Chgo., 2000—02; bd. dirs. Lincoln Park Conservation Assn., 1983—85, Old Town Triangle Assn., Chgo., 1980—83, pres., 1984. Recipient Willis Smith award, Duke U. Law Sch., 1972. Mem.: ABA, Calif. State Bar, Chgo. Bar Assn., Order of Coif. Office: Baker & McKenzie 1 Prudential Plz 130 E Randolph St Ste 3700 Chicago IL 60601-6342 Home: 230 W Division Apt 1508 Chicago IL 60610 E-mail: frederick.e.henry@bakernet.com.

HENRY, GLORIA JEAN MULLINS, secondary school educator; b. Davenport, Iowa, Nov. 26, 1952; d. Luther Mannon and Eva Mae (Smith) Mullins; m. Jerry L. Henry, Aug. 19, 1972; children: Carie Suzanne Henry, Austin Luke Henry. BA, Okla. Bapt. U., 1975; MA, Baker U., 1992. Cert. secondary speech tchr. Tchr., coach Valley Center (Kans.) High Sch., 1976-78; speech tchr., debate coach Ruskin High Sch., Kansas City, Mo., 1979—. Chair Consol. Sch. Dist. #1, Kansas City, 1989—, profl. devel. and comm./ theatre cirriculm, Mo. staff devel. coun. steering com., consortium steering com., presenter for conf. Mem. NEA, Nat. Forensic League (double-diamond coach 1990, steering com. for the nat. debate, 1983, com. for nat. debate, 1993, judges chair for dist. debate 1980—), Speech Comm. Assn., Speech-Theatre Assn. of Mo., Nat. Fedn. of High Sch. Activities, Mo. NEA, United Tchrs. of Hickman Mills, Nat. Activities Fedr., Mo. Staff Devel. Coun., Nat. Staff Devel. Coun. Avocations: reading, gardening, quilting. Home: 24214 South Hunter Peculiar MO 64078 Office: Ruskin High Sch 7000 E 111th St Kansas City MO 64134-3399

HENRY, J. MYRLE, pharmacist; b. Jacksonville, Fla., Aug. 30, 1938; s. Joseph Mason and Ovieda Ida (Dossey) H.; m. Tommie Claire Williams, Aug. 28, 1959; children: Cheri Kim, Kathy Lynn. BSP, U. Fla., 1961. Registered pharmacist Fla. Pharmacist Barwick Drugs, Plant City, Fla., 1961, Magnolia Pharmacy, Plant City, 1962-66, pharmacist, co-owner, 1966-80; co-owner H&R Drug Ctr., Plant City, 1973-85, owner, 1985-93, Herring Drug, Plant City, 1977-86; pharmacist, owner Magnolia Pharmacy, 1980-2000; pharmacist Kash n Karry Pharmacy, Plant City, 2000—. Past mem. Hillsborough County Citizens Adv. Com.; pres. The Fla. Opry; past pres. East Hillsboro Hist. Soc.; Plant City Down Town Bus. and Merchants Assn.; founder, pres. Bapt. Towers Plant City, Inc.; deacon 1st Bapt. Ch.; pres. Christian Living Ctr., Inc.; trustee So. Fla. Bapt. Hosp.; past bd. dirs. Hillsborough County unit Am. Cancer Soc., past chmn. Plant City br.; founder, past chmn. Strawberry Classic Car Show. Named Plant City's Citizen Yr., group of 10 clubs Kiwanis, Civitan, Rotary, C. of C., Pilot, Optimist, Lions, Womans, Jr. Womans and Rotary Daybreak, 2001. Mem.: East Hillsborough C. of C. (past bd. dirs., past treas.), Fla. State Pharm. Assn., Am. Pharm. Assn., Hillsborough County Pharmacy Assn. (past pres.), Plant City Lions Club, Kappa Psi. Avocations: swimming, tennis, gardening. Office: Kash n Karry Pharmacy Wheeler St Plant City FL 33566

HENRY, JOHN BAILEY, art director; s. John Bailey and Maxine Henry; m. Janice Moore, Nov. 4, 2000; children: Megan Lee Rolf, Jack. BFA in Sculpture, U. S.C., 1971; MFA in History, U. Miss., 1982. Gen. curator fine arts Columbus (Ga.) Mus. Arts and Crafts, 1973—77; dir. collections and exhibitions Miss. Mus. Art, Jackson, Miss., 1977—85; exec. dir. Ctr. for Arts, Inc., Vero Beach, Fla., 1985—96, Flint (Mich.) Inst. Arts, 1996—. Adv. bd. Ctr. Grad. Studies Baker Coll., Flint, 1997—99; dirs. adv. coun. Nat. Trustee Assn., Flint, 1999—2002; v.p. Southeastern Sculptors Assn., Columbus, Ga., 1973—78. Author (editor): American Art At The Flint Institute Of Arts, 2003; author: (board game) Artist: The Game, (art catalogue) New New Painters. Trustee Flint (Mich.) Classroom Support Fund, 2000—05. Named Man of Yr., Am. Arab Assn., 2002; recipient Pres. award, Flint C. of C., 2005. Mem.: Am. Assn. Mus., Assn. Art Mus. Dirs. (assoc.), Rotary. Avocations: tennis, golf, skiing. Office: Flint Institute Of Arts 1120 East Kearsley Street Flint MI 48503 Office Phone: 810-234-1695. Office Fax: 810-234-1692. E-mail: jhenry@flintarts.org.

HENRY, JOHN BERNARD, pathologist, educator, academic administrator; b. Elmira, NY, Apr. 26, 1928; m. Georgette Boughton, June 10, 1953; children: Maureen Anne, Julie Patricia, William Bernard, Paul Bernard, John Bernard, Thomas David. AB, Cornell U., 1951; MD, U. Rochester, 1955. Diplomate: Am. Bd. Pathology (v.p. 1974-75, 76-79, pres. 1976-78, trustee). Intern ward med. service Barnes Hosp., St. Louis, 1955-56; resident pathology Presbyn. Hosp., N.Y.C., 1956-58, New Eng. Deaconess Hosp., Boston, 1958-60; trainee Nat. Cancer Inst., NIH, 1958-60; clin. pathologist, chmn. clin. lab. com., dir. Blood Bank and Clin. Labs. Teaching Hosp. and Clinic, U. Fla., 1960-64; asst. medicine Washington U. Sch. Medicine, St. Louis, 1955-56; asst. pathology, then instr. pathology Columbia Coll. Phys. and Surg., 1956-58; teaching fellow pathology Harvard U. Med. Sch., 1959-60; asst. prof., then asso. prof. pathology U. Fla. Coll. Medicine, 1960-64; prof. pathology Coll. Medicine; dir. clin. pathology SUNY, Upstate, Syracuse, 1964-79; dean Coll. Health Related Professions SUNY Upstate Med Ctr., 1971-77; dean, prof. pathology Georgetown U. Sch. Medicine, Washington, 1979-84; pres. SUNY Upstate Med. U., Syracuse, 1985-92, prof. pathology, past pres., 1992—. Author numerous articles on chemistry, med. edn. and immunopathology field. Bd. dirs. FACT, 1985-90. With USN, 1946-48, capt. USNR, 1967-95. Recipient S.C. Dyke Founder award Assn. Clin. Pathologists, 1979. Fellow Coll. Am. Pathologist, Am. Soc. Clin. Pathologists (bd. dirs. 1974-82, pres. 1980-81, Distinguished Serv. Clin. Pathology award 1993), Am. Coll. Physician Execs.; mem. AMA, AAAS, Am. Blood Commn. (pres. 1978-80), Am. Assn. Blood Banks (pres.), Am. Assn. Clin. Chemists, Assn. Am. Med. Colls., Am. Assn. Pathologists, Am. Soc. Histocompatibility and Immunogenetics, Internat. Soc. Blood Transfusion, Soc. Med. Consultants to Armed Forces, Med. Soc. D.C. (exec. bd. 1982-84), CAP (chmn. future tech. com. 1985-92, bd. dirs. council on edn. and pubs. 1986-92), Onondaga Med. Soc. (bd. dirs.), Alpha Omega Alpha. Office: SUNY Upstate Med Univ Dept Pathology 750 E Adams St Syracuse NY 13210-1834 Business E-Mail: henryjb@upstate.edu.

HENRY, JOHN DUNKLIN, SR., hospital executive; b. Atlanta, Dec. 23, 1937; married. B, Emory U., 1957. Cert. in hosp. adminstrn. Georgia State Univ., 1964, in hosp. methods improvement Georgia Inst. of Tech., 1966. Adminstrv. asst. Emory Crawford Long Hosp., Atlanta, 1963, adminstrv. resident, 1963-64, asst. dir., 1964-73, asst. adminstr., 1973-77, assoc. adminstr., 1977-84, sr. adminstrv. officer, 1984—95, adminstr., CEO, 1995—2003, Emory Hosp., Atlanta, 1995—2003; CEO Wesly Woods Ctr., Atlanta, 1995—2003; exec. v.p., COO Grady Health System, 2003—. Chmn. Georgia Hosp. Assn. Med. svc. corps officer U.S. Army, 1959—63. Recipient Lifetime Achievement award, Atlanta Bus. Chronicle, 2003; fellow, Am. Coll. of

Healthcare Executives, 1978, 1988, 1998. Mem.: Univ. Health System Consortium, Nat. Fire Protection, Am. Hosp. Assn., Am. Coll. of Healthcare Exec. Home: 2054 Imperial Dr NE Atlanta GA 30345-3436

HENRY, JOHN RAYMOND, sculptor; b. Lexington, Ky., Aug. 11, 1943; s. Arthur Raymond and Catherine (Campbell) H.; m. Pamela Kathryn, May 12, 1984; 1 child from previous marriage, Katherine Leigh Henry-Barrett. Student, U. Ky., 1961-65, U. Wash., 1962, Ill. Inst. Tech., 1967, U. Chgo., 1968-69; BFA, Sch. of Art Inst., 1969; PhD of Art (hon.), U. Ky., 1996. Pres., CEO ConStruct Corp., 1979-81. Vis. prof. sculpture U. Iowa, 1969, U. Wis. Green Bay, 1970, U. Chgo., 1971, Sch. of Art Inst. Chgo., 1979-80; coord., advisor Art Inst. Chgo., City of Chgo., 1974; advisor Art Coun., New Orleans, 1976; mem. adv bd. Lawyers for Creative Arts, Chgo.; spkr. in field. Solo exhbns. include retrospective Art Mus. South Tex., Corpus Christi, Mus. Art, Ft. Lauderdale, Fla., Mus. Fine Arts, St. Petersburg, Fla., Hunter Mus. Art, Chattanooga, 1988-89, Richard Gray Gallery, Chgo., 1969, 71, Ill. State Mus., 1973, Gallery 10, Aspen, Colo., 1980, Nina Owen Ltd., Chgo., 1990, Jaffee, Baker Gallery, Boca Raton, Fla., 1991, Ann Norton Sculpture Garden, Palm Beach, Fla., 1991, Ctr. for Arts, Vero Beach, Fla., 1991, Seo Hwa Gallery, Seoul, Korea, 1993, Springfield (Mo.) Art Mus., 1995, many others; exhbns. include U. South Fla. Art Mus., Tampa, 1988, traveling Marseille, France, Geneva, Hasselet, Belgium, Barcelona, Spain, 1988, Thomas Ctr. Gallery, Gainesville, Fla., 1989, North Miami (Fla.) Ctr. Contemporary Art, 1989-90, Internat. Art Expo, Tokyo, 1991, European Fine Art Fair, Maastricht, The Netherlands, 1992, Polk Mus. Art, Lakeland, Fla., 1992, Internat. Art Expo, Chgo., 1992, 93, Art Chgo., 1992, New Pier Show, Chgo., 1993, FIAC, Paris, 1993, Lineart, Ghent, Belgium, 1993, Manif 95, Manif 96, Seoul, Art Chgo. 96, Pier Walk 96, Chgo., Art in Chgo., Mus. Contemporary Art, 1996, numerous others; represented in permanent collections Mint Mus. Art, Charlotte, N.C., Springfield (Mo.) Art Mus., Ft. Worth Art Mus., Bradley Sculpture Garden, Milw. Art Mus., Oklahoma City Art Ctr., Brit. Mus., Miami Dade C.C., others, numerous pvt. collections. NEA Individual Artist fellow/grantee, 1975, State of Fla. Individual Artist fellow, 1989, Edward L. Reyerson fellow Art Inst. Chgo., 1969, Ford Found. grantee Sch. Art Inst. Chgo. Mem. Nat. Found. Advancement in Arts (trustee 1991—, chair programs 1993—), Internat. Sculpture Ctr. (bd. dirs., vice chmn. bd. dirs.), SE Sculptors Assn. (hon., life).

HENRY, JOHN W., professional sports team executive; b. Quincy, Ill. m. Peggy Henry; 1 child. Founder, chmn. John W. Henry & Co., Inc., Boca Raton, Fla., 1981—, Westport, Conn., 1981—; chmn., majority owner Class AAA Tucson Toros, Pacific Coast League, 1989-97; co-owner W. Palm Beach Tropics, Sr. Baseball League, 1989—; limited ptnr. N.Y. Yankees, 1992—; chmn. Fla. Marlins Baseball Club, Miami, 1999—2002; majority owner Boston Red Sox, 2002—. Mem. Nat. Assn. Futures Trading Advisors (bd. dirs.), Managed Futures Trade Assn. (bd. dirs.), Nat. Futures Assn. (mem. nominating com.), Futures Industry Assn. (bd. dirs.). Office: Boston Red Sox 4 Yawkey Way Boston MA 02215-3496

HENRY, JOSEPH PATRICK, chemical company executive; b. Mansfield, Ohio, Mar. 3, 1925; s. Harold H. and Louise A. (Droxler) Henry; m. Jeanette E. Russell, Oct. 26, 1957; 1 child, Jeanette Louise. Attended, Bowling Green State U., 1943—44; BS, Ohio State U., 1949. Ohio sales mgr. NaChurs Plant Food Co., Marion, 1949—55; organizer, pres. Growers Chem. Corp., Milan, 1955—, Sandusky Imported Motors, Inc., Ohio, 1958—78; pres. Homestead Motors, Inc., 1978—83. Co-owner Homestead Inn Restaurant, Homestead Farms; v.p. South Avery Corp. Motels, 1961, Homestead Inn, Inc. Motels, 1963—; dir. Erie County Bank, Vermilion, Ohio, Soc. Bank of Firelands. Mem. Milan C. of C. Served with USMCR, 1943—46, PTO. Named to Lakewood (Ohio) HS Athletic Hall of Fame, 1997; recipient Bus. Adv. Coun. Gold Medal, Rep. Congressional Com., 2003, Businessman of Yr., Rep. Congl. Com., 1999. Mem. Nat. Fedn. Ind. Bus. (nat. adv. coun.), AAAS, Ohio Farm Bur. Fedn., Aircraft Owners and Pilots Assn., Internat. Flying Farmers, Ohio Restaurant Assn., Ohio Motel-Hotel Assn., Ohio Licensed Beverage Assn., Am. Horse Show Assn., Nat. Trust for Hist. Preservation, N.A.M., Internat. Platform Assn., Huron County Hist. Soc., Ohio Farm Bur. (pres.), Ohio, Internat. (dir. 1978-84), Arabian Horse Assns., Antique Auto. Club Am., Sports Car Am., N. Am. Yacht Racing Union, Sandusky Yacht Club, Sandusky Sailing Club, Catawba Island Club. Achievements include developing (with V.A. Tiedjens) foliage fertilization and direct to seed fertilization of commercial field crops. Home: 128 Center St Milan OH 44846-9757 Office: Growers Chem Corp PO Box 1750 Milan OH 44846-1750 also: Homestead Farms RR 1 Milan OH 44846-1700 Office Phone: 419-499-2508.

HENRY, KATHLEEN MARIE, marketing executive; b. Stillwater, Okla., Sept. 24, 1950; d. Irl Wayne and Hulda Mary Henry. BS, U. Cen. Okla., Edmond, 1972. Community relations dir./account exec. Lowe Runkle Advt., Oklahoma City, 1972-74, account coordinator, 1975; sales promotion cons. McDonald's Corp., Houston, 1974, regional advt. supr. Southfield, Mich., 1975, regional advt. mgr., 1976-78, local store mktg. mgr. Oak Brook, Ill., 1978-80, staff dir., store mktg./sales promotion, 1980-82, home office dir. store mktg./sales promotion, 1982-83, dir. nat. sales promotion, 1983-84, internat. mktg. dir., 1984-85; mktg. dir. McDonald's System France, 1985-86, McDonald's System Europe, 1985-88, v.p. mktg., 1988-97; pres. Henry Jamieson Assocs., Tulsa, Okla., 1997—, Zepper Entertainment, Tulsa, 2004—. Publicity chmn. Keep Okla. Beautiful, 1973-74; publicity chmn. Muscular Dystrophy Assn. Am., Okla. chpt., 1973-74; bd. dirs. Southfield Arts Coun., Mich., 1976-78; commr. Lake Keystone Planning and Zoning Commn., 1999—; bd. dirs. Perry High Sch. Alumni Assn., 1999-; bd. dirs. sec. Keystone Peninsula Property Owners Assn., 1998—; commr. State of Okla. Film and Music Commn. Recipient Chgo. YWCA Leadership award, 1978, Disting. Former Student award U. Ctrl. Okla., 1979, Bronco award U. Ctrl. Okla. Centennial, 1991; named Outstanding Sr. Woman U. Ctrl. Okla., 1972, Outstanding Greek Woman, 1972. Mem. U. Ctrl. Okla. Alumni Assn. (dir. 1974, 1998-2002, found. bd. dirs. 1999—), U. Ctrl. Okla. Centennial Commn., Sigma Kappa. Office: Henry Jamieson Assocs Rte 3 Box 150A Cleveland OK 74020

HENRY, KEVIN GUDGEL, lawyer; b. Lexington, Ky., June 23, 1953; s. Edward Joseph and Sue H.; m. Ann M., Apr. 23, 1983. BA in History, Ctr. Coll., 1975; JD, U. Ky., 1978. Bar: Ky. 1978, U.S. Supreme Ct. 1992. Law clerk Chief Justice, Supreme Ct. Ky., Frankfort, 1978-79; assoc. atty. Trimble, Stapleton, Reaves, Slone & Driesler, Lexington, Ky., 1979-80; mem. Trimble & Henry, Lexington, 1980-91, Sturgill, Turner, Barker & Moloney, Lexington, 1991—. Editor It's A New Age For You, 1990-91 (Ky. Bar Found. award 1990). Mem. Leadership Lexington, 1983-84; bd. mgrs. Beaumont Family YMCA, Lexington, 2000-2001. Mem. Ky. Acad. Trial Lawyers (bd. govs. 1987-90), Ky. Def. Counsel, Def. Rsch. Inst., Fayette County Bar Assn. (pres. 1991-92), Employment Law Alliance. Episcopalian. Avocations: golf, women's basketball. Office: Sturgill Turner Barker Moloney PLLC 155 E Main St # 400 Lexington KY 40507

HENRY, LAURIN LUTHER, public affairs educator; b. Kankakee, Ill., May 23, 1921; s. Laurimer Luther and Jeanette Belle (Wagner) H.; m. Kathleen Jane Stephan, May 18, 1946; children— Stephanie Jane, Robin Leigh. BA, DePauw U., 1942; MA, U. Chgo., 1948, PhD, 1960. Staff asst. Public Adminstrn. Clearing House, Chgo. and Washington, 1950-55; research asso., sr. staff mem. Brookings Instn., Washington, 1955-64; prof. govt. and fgn. affairs U. Va., 1964-78; dean Sch. Community and Public Affairs, Va. Commonwealth U., Richmond, 1978-86, prof., 1986-87, prof. emeritus, 1987—. Guest scholar U. Va., 1988-95; vis. prof. Johns Hopkins U.; cons. to govt. Author: Presidential Transitions, 1960, The NASA-University Memorandum of Understanding, 1967; co-author: Presidential Election and Transition of 1960-61, 1961; contbr. articles profl. publns. Served with USNR, 1942-46. Recipient L.D. White prize Am. Polit. Sci. Assn., 1961. Fellow Nat. Acad. Pub. Adminstrn. (sr.); mem. Nat. Assn. Schs. Public Affairs and Adminstrn. (pres. 1971-72), Am. Soc. Pub. Adminstrn., Phi Beta Kappa, Phi Kappa Phi. Home: 500 Crestwood Dr Apt 1204 Charlottesville VA 22903-4853

HENRY, MARTIN DANIEL, university president; b. Pitts., Dec. 13, 1940; s. Martin A. and Margaret (Fisher) H.; m. Aimee Monteverde, Nov. 21, 1973; children: Donna, Nicholas, Bryan. BA, St. Vincent Coll., 1962; MEd, Duquesne U., 1965; MBA, Barry U., 1973; PhD, U. Pitts., 1979; JD, U. Dayton, 1984. Bar: Ohio, 1984. Tchr. South Hills Cath. High Sch., Pitts., 1963-65; adminstr. U. Pitts., 1966-71; dean LaRoche Coll., Pitts., 1971-74; v.p. acad. affairs Barry U., Miami, Fla., 1974-79; v.p. adminstrn. U. Dayton, Ohio, 1979-85; pres. St. Leo (Fla.) Coll., 1985-87, Gannon U., Erie, Pa., 1987-91. Speaker numerous univs., seminars, confs. Author: The Practice of Management, 1980; author invited and juried papers. Recipient Disting. Alumnus award St. Vincent Coll., Latrobe, Pa., 1985, Bicentennial Medallion of Distinction U. Pitts, 1987. Mem. Ohio State Bar Assn. Roman Catholic. Avocations: racquet sports, spectator sports, movies, travel. Home: 10163 Woodbury Dr Wexford PA 15090 Office: Gannon U Office of Pres University Sq Erie PA 16507 Office Phone: 412-919-1042. E-mail: dan.henry@cancer.org.

HENRY, MATTHEW CREIGHTON, lawyer; b. Taylor, Tex., July 13, 1969; s. William J. and Martha Kay Henry; m. Alicia Jo McCarter, Aug. 3, 1991; children: Victoria Shae, William Reed, Matthew Ryan. BS cum laude, Howard Payne U., 1991; JD cum laude, SMU, 1994. Atty., Counselor at Law: Tex. Supreme Ct. 1994. Assoc. Worsham, Forsythe, Wooldridge, LLP, Dallas, 1994—2002; ptnr. Hunton & Williams, LLP, 2002—. Adv. bd. Love for Children, Inc., Dallas, 2004—05; bd. dirs. Douglas MacArthur Acad. Freedom, Brownwood, 2000—05. Recipient Tex. Monthly Rising Star, Tex. Monthly Mag., 2004. Fellow: Dallas Bar Found. Avocations: travel, reading, baseball, football. Office: Hunton & Williams LLP 1601 Bryan 30th Fl Dallas TX 75201 Office Fax: 214-880-0011. Business E-Mail: mhenry@hunton.com.

HENRY, MYRON, academic administrator; Provost Kent State U., 1992—98, U. So. Miss., Hattiesburg, Miss., 1998—2001, faculty senate pres., 2003—04, faculty senate pres.-elect, 2005—. Office: The Univ Southern Mississippi 2701 Hardy Street Hattiesburg MS 39406 Office Phone: 601-266-4739. Business E-Mail: myron.henry@usm.edu.

HENRY, NANCY LOUISE, hospitality executive, mayor; b. Somerville, N.J., July 18, 1940; d. Robert Lewis and Mary Louise (Skinner) Twyman; student Rutgers U., 1973-75, Trenton State Coll., 1976-77; children: Lionel N., Robert Lewis. With Johnson & Johnson, New Brunswick, N.J., 1959-77, v.p., 1965-77; conv. coordinator Nat. Conf. Center, East Windsor, N.J., 1977-78; sales mgr. Scanticon-Princeton (N.J.) Conf. Center-Hotel, 1982—; dep. mayor City of Somerset (N.J.), 1982—; mayor Franklin Twp. (N.J.), 1982—; pres. Henry's Constrn. Clean Up Service; spl. asst. to gov. State of N.J., Trenton, 1978-79, dir. resources and community participation Office of Ombudsman for Instnl. Elderly, Trenton, 1979— . Councilwoman Franklin Twp. (N.J.), 1977—; committeewoman 4th Ward, Franklin Twp., 1977-79, ward chmn., 1978-79; mem. adv. council Somerset County Employment and Tng. Agy., 1977-81, chmn. youth adv. council, 1978-80; del. Democratic Nat. Conv., 1980; v.p. N.J. Fedn. Dem. Women. Methodist. Mailing: PO Box 1204 La Quinta CA 92247

HENRY, NICHOLAS LLEWELLYN, public administration educator; b. Seattle, May 22, 1943; s. Samuel Houston and Ann (Connor) H.; m. Muriel Bunney; children: Adrienne Richardson, Miles Houston. BA, Centre Coll. Ky., 1965; MA, Pa. State U., 1967; MPA, Ind. U., 1970, PhD, 1971. Asst. to dean Coll. Arts and Scis.; instr. Ind. State U., 1967-69; vis. asst. prof. U. N.Mex., 1971-72; asst. prof. polit. sci. U. Ga., 1972-75, assoc. prof., 1975-78, prof., 1978-87, dir. Ctr. Pub. Affairs, 1975-80, dean Coll. Pub. Programs, 1980-87; prof., pres. Ga. So. U., Statesboro, 1987-98, prof. polit. sci., 1998—. Author or editor 12 books; contbr. numerous articles to profl. jours. Recipient Author of Yr. award Assn. Sci. Jours., Laverne Burchfield award ASPA, 2002; named One of 100 Most Influential People in Ga., Ga. Trend, 1994. Fellow Nat. Acad. Pub. Adminstrn.; mem. Cosmos Club (Washington). Office: Ga So U PO Box 8009 Statesboro GA 30460-1000 Office Phone: 912-644-7953. Business E-Mail: nic_henry@georgiasouthern.edu.

HENRY, PETER YORK, lawyer, mediator; b. Washington, Apr. 28, 1951; s. David Howe III and Margaret (Beard) Henry; m. Deidra B. Hagdorn, May 1995; 1 child, Chance Hagdorn stepchildren: Nathan Hebert, Christpher Hebert;children from previous marriage: Ryan York, Zachary Price. BBA, Ohio U., 1973; JD, St. Mary's U., San Antonio, 1976. Bar: Tex. 1976. Sole practice, San Antonio, 1976—. Mem.: ATLA, San Antonio Bar Assn., San Antonio Trial Lawyers Assn. (bd. dirs. 1989—90), Tex. Trial Lawyers Assn., Tex. Bar Assn., Phi Delta Phi. Home: 7642 Bluesage Cove San Antonio TX 78249-2541 Office Phone: 210-223-9244. Personal E-mail: lawofpyh@aol.com.

HENRY, PHILIP LAWRENCE, marketing professional; b. LA, Dec. 1, 1940; s. Lawrence Langworthy and Ella Hanna (Martens) H.; m. Claudia Antonia Huff, Aug. 9, 1965 (div. 1980); children: Carolyn Marie, Susan Michelle; m. Carrie Katherine Hoover, Aug. 23, 1985. BS in Marine Engring., Calif. Maritime Acad., 1961. Design engr. Pacific Telephone Co., San Diego, 1963-73; svc. engr. Worthington Svc. Corp., San Diego, 1973-78; pres. Realmart Corp., San Diego, 1978-81; dir. mktg. Orbit Inn Hotel and Casino, Las Vegas, 1981-84; pres. Comml. Consultants, Las Vegas, 1984—2002, Gray Electronics Co., Las Vegas, 1986—. Chmn. bd. dirs. Las Vegas Accomodations Unltd., 1997-2000; mng. mem. G/Tracker Techs., LLC, 1998, Strobe Detector Techs., LLC, 1998; bd. dirs. Silver State Classic Challenge, Inc. Inventor electronic detection devices, 1986—. Served to lt. (j.g.) USNR, 1961-67. Republican. Avocations: amateur radio, open road auto racing, storm chasing. Office Phone: 775-289-6254. Personal E-mail: mak@philhenry.com.

HENRY, RENE ARTHUR, writer, consultant; b. Charleston, W.Va., June 13, 1933; s. Rene A. and Lillian E. (Reveal) H.; children: Deborah Marie, Bruce Rexford. AB, Coll. William and Mary, 1954; postgrad., W.Va. U., 1954-56. Account exec. Flournoy & Gibbs, Toledo, 1956-59; publicity dir. Lennen & Newell, Inc., San Francisco, 1959-67; sr. v.p., dir. Daniel J. Edelman, Inc., Los Angeles, 1967-70; pres. Rene A. Henry, Jr., Inc., L.A., 1970-74; ptnr. Allen, Ingersoll, Segal & Henry, Inc., L.A., 1974-75; prin. ICPR, L.A., 1975-81; pvt. practice mgmt. and sports mktg. cons., 1981-86, 90-91; pres., chief exec. officer Nat. Inst. Bldg. Scis., Washington, 1986-88; confidential asst. to adminstr. Farmers Home Adminstrn. USDA, 1989; cons., designate asst. adminstr. AID, Dept. State, 1989-90; spl. asst. to dir. Office of Fed. Contract Compliance Programs, U.S. Dept. Labor, Washington, 1991; exec. dir. univ. rels. Tex. A&M U., College Station, 1991-96; dir. Office of Comm. and Govt. Rels. U.S. EPA, Phila., 1996—2001; v.p. pub. rels. Innovative Comm. Corp., West Palm Beach, Fla., 2003—. Exec. sec. to bd. dirs. Coun. Housing Producers, 1968-78; spl. advisor The Pres.'s Coun. on Phys. Fitness and Sports, 1981-89; spl. cons. Nat. Fitness Found., 1981-89. Author: How to Profitably Buy and Sell Land, 1977, Marketing Public Relations, 1995, You'd Better Have a Hose If You Want to Put Out the Fire: The Complete Guide to Crisis and Risk Communications, 1999, Offsides!; Fred Wyant's Provocative Look Inside the National Football League, 2001; co-author: MIUS and You--The Developer Takes a Look at a New Utility Concept, 1980, Bears Handbook, 1996. Adv. bd. Arthur R. Marshall Found.; mem. adv. bd. Internat. Children's Mus.; asst. to. pres., media coms. internat. rels., pub. rels., long range strategic planning task force U.S. Olympic Com., 1984—89; campaign dir. for athletes and entertainers Bush for Pres. and Bush/Quayle '88 presdl. election campaigns; mem. adv. bd. Ctr. Crisis Pub. Rels. and Litigation Lehigh U. With U.S. Army, 1956—58. Decorated Knight of Honor, The Sovereign Order of St. John Jerusalem, Knights Hospitaller; named San Francisco Bay Area Pub. Relations Man of Year, 1963; recipient Clarion award for human rights Women in Communication, 1980, Alumni Svc. award Coll. William and Mary, 2003; inductee Granby HS Hall of Fame, Norfolk, Va., 2001. Mem.: Acad. Motion Picture Arts and Scis., Pub. Rels. Soc. Am. (chmn. Coll. Fellows 2001, Disting. Citizen award L.A. chpt. 1979, 3 Silver Anvils), Acad. TV Arts and Scis. (past chair bld. com.), Sigma Nu. Episcopalian. Office: Innovative Comm Corp Phillips Point East Tower 777 S Flagler Dr # 1201-E West Palm Beach FL 33401 Home: 255 Evernia St Apt 1306 West Palm Beach FL 33401-5688 also: 1305 E Republican St #1 Seattle WA 98102 Office Phone: 561-514-0600. Business E-Mail: rene_henry@iccvi.com. E-mail: sail2gold@yahoo.com.

HENRY, RICKEY ROY, electrical engineer, educator; b. Muskogee, Okla., Sept. 19, 1953; s. Roy E. and Avis Lee Henry; m. Suzanne Jordan Henry, Jan. 28, 1976; children: Nicole, Brandi Singleton. AS, Connor State Coll., 1978; BS, Northeastern State U., 1996. Electrical contractor H & H Electric, Gore, Okla., 1996—2000; tchr. Indian Capital Career Tech., Muskogee, Okla., 2000—. Adv. VICA, Muskogee, Okla., 2000—05; electrical contractor, Gore, Okla., 1996—2005. Vol. Habitat for Humanities, Muskogee, Okla., 2005—. E-4 USN, 1972—75. Bapt. Home: Rt 3 Box 440 Gore OK 74435 Office: Indian Capital Career Tech 2403 N 41st St E Muskogee OK 74403 Office Phone: 918-687-6383. E-mail: rhenry@mus.icatstech.ok.us.

HENRY, ROBERT E., dean, educator; s. Hiram H. and Wanda J. Henry; m. Anna M. Whitlock, May 0, 1989; 1 child, Scott A. PhD, U. North Tex., 1987; MEd.-Music, U. Mo. Columbia, 1978; BME, Okla. State U., 1972. Cert. tchr. Am. Orff-Schulwerk Assn., 1990, Orgn. Am. Kodaly Educators, 1990. Assoc. dean Coll. Visual and Performing Arts Tex. Tech U., Lubbock, Tex., 2002—, assoc. dir. Sch. Music, 1987—2002, prof. music edn., 1985—. Pres. Tex. Music Educators Assn., Austin, Tex., 1999—2001. Musician: (profl.) Symphony, Jazz.

HENRY, ROBERT HARLAN, federal judge, former attorney general; b. Shawnee, Okla., Apr. 3, 1953; BA, U. Okla., 1974, JD, 1976. Bar: Okla. 1976. Atty. Henry, West, Still & Combs, Shawnee, Okla., 1977—83, Henry, Henry & Henry, Shawnee, 1983—87; mem. Okla. Ho. of Reps., 1976—86; atty. gen. State of Okla., Oklahoma City, 1987—91; dean, prof. Okla. City U. Law Sch., 1993—94; judge U.S. Ct. Appeals (10th cir.), Oklahoma City, 1994—. Mem. Nat. Conf. Commrs. on Uniform State Law. Fellow: Am. Bar Found.; mem.: William J. Holloway, Jr. Am. Inn of Ct., ABA, Okla. City Bar Assn., Nat. Assn. Attys. Gen. (chmn. state constl. law adv. com., vice-chmn. civil rights com.), Am. Coun. Young Polit. Leaders, Okla. Bar Assn. Office: US Ct Appeals 10th Cir 200 NW 4th St Rm 2021 Oklahoma City OK 73102-3026 also: Byron White US Cthse 1823 Stout St Denver CO 80257*

HENRY, ROBERT JOHN, lawyer; b. Chgo., Aug. 1, 1950; s. John P. and Margaret P. (Froelich) Henry; m. Sara Mikuta; children: Cherylyn, Deanna, Laurin, Joseph Mikuta, Nicholas Mikuta. BA cum laude, Loyola U., Chgo., 1973, JD cum laude, 1975. Bar: Ill 1975, U.S. Dist. Ct. (no. dist.) Ill. 1975. Atty. Continental Ill. Nat. Bank, Chgo., 1975-77, Allied Van Lines, Inc., Chgo., 1977-81, assoc. gen. counsel, 1981-88, gen. counsel, 1988-90, v.p. adminstrn., gen. counsel, 1990-93, v.p. gen. counsel, 1993-99; v.p., assoc. gen. counsel SIRVA, Inc., Chgo., 1999—. Gen. counsel NFC N.Am., 1996-99. Alt. scholar Weymouth Kirkland Found., 1971. Mem. Chgo. Bar Assn., Am. Corp. Counsel Assn. Office: SIRVA Inc PO Box 4403 Chicago IL 60680-4403 Office Phone: 630-570-3573. E-mail: robert.henry@sirva.com.

HENRY, ROBERT S., art educator; b. Bklyn., Aug. 3, 1933; s. Charles and Dorothy Henry; m. Selina Hanna Trieff, Nov. 25, 1955; children: Sarah, Jane. Student, Hofmann Sch. Art, 1952—53; BA, Bklyn. Coll., 1955. Prof. Bklyn. Coll., 1960—90, prof. emeritus, 1990—. Pres. bd. dirs. Provincetown Art Assn. & Mus., Mass., 2001—05; mem. adv. bd. Truro Ctr. Arts, 2000—05; mem. faculty Fine Arts Work Ctr., Provincetown, 2001—04, Truro Ctr. Arts, 1997—2005; guest critic Vt. Studio Ctr., 1990—. Author: Selina in Hospital, 2001. Mem.: N.Y. Artists Equity Assn., Cape Cod Mus. Art. Democrat. Avocation: music. Home: 801 Greenwich St #6 New York NY 10014 E-mail: selrobert@earthlink.net.

HENRY, RONALD JAMES WHYTE, academic administrator, physicist, educator; b. Belfast, No. Ireland, Feb. 5, 1940; came to U.S., 1965; s. William James Louis and Mary Ann (Whyte) H.; children: Norah Lynn, Andrea Marie. BSc, Queen's U., Belfast, 1961, PhD, 1964. Asst. lectr. Queen's U., 1964-65; rsch. assoc. Goddard Space Flight Ctr., Greenbelt, Md., 1965-66; asst. physicist Kitt Peak Nat. Obs., Tucson, 1966-69; assoc. prof. La. State U., Baton Rouge, 1969-73, prof., 1973-89, chmn. dept. physics and astronomy, 1976-82, dean basic scis., 1982-89; v.p. acad. affairs Auburn (Ala.) U., 1989-91; provost, exec. v.p. for acad. affairs Miami U., Oxford, Ohio, 1991-94; provost, v.p. acad. affairs Ga. State U., Atlanta, 1994—. Com. on undergrad. sci. edn. Nat. Rsch. Coun., 1998-2004; bd. trustees CAEL, 2005-. Fellow Am. Physics Soc. Republican. Avocation: golf. Office: Ga State U Atlanta GA 30303 Office Phone: 404-651-2574. E-mail: rhenry@gsu.edu.

HENRY, RONALD KENNETH, lawyer; b. Detroit, Jan. 12, 1951; s. Charles G. and Barbara J. (Retz) H.; m. Constance B. Henry, Apr. 23, 1983; children: Laura, Rebecca. BA, U. Mich., 1973, JD, 1976. Bar: DC 1976; US Supreme Ct. 1982. Ptnr. Dickstein, Shapiro & Morin, Washington, DC; ptnr. litig., chair Govt. Contracts Dept. Kaye Scholer LLP, Washington, DC. Lectr. govt. contracts law, 1978—. Counsel Nat. Council for Children's Rights, Washington, 1987—. Mem. ABA, DC Bar Assn. Avocations: tennis, racquetball, chess. Office: Kaye Scholer LLP McPherson Bldg 901 Fifteenth Street, NW, Ste 1000 Washington DC 20005 Office Phone: 202-682-3590. E-mail: rhenry@kayescholer.com.

HENRY, ROY MONROE, financial planner; b. Oct. 27, 1939; s. Roy Monroe and Nancy Lowe (Morse) H.; m. Meredith Elaine Hjelmstad, Aug. 20, 1961; children: Robin E., Roy M. III. BBA, Kennedy-Western, 1990. Registered prin., rep.-NASD; LUTCF. Airman 1st class USAF, Turkey, 1957-61; estimator Con P. Curran Printing Co., St. Louis, 1961-64; sales mgr. Prudential Ins. Co., St. Louis, 1964-72; pres. Roy M. Henry & Assocs., Chesterfield, Mo., 1972-76, St. Louis Fin. Planners, Chesterfield, Mo., 1976-83, First Fin. Planners, Chesterfield, Mo., 1983—. Guest spkr. Purdue U., Yale U., Stanford U. Appeared on (TV show) 20/20, 1991; contbr. articles to profl. jours. Named Fin. Planner of Yr., 1987; commd. mem. Hon. Order of Ky. Cols. Fellow Life Underwriting Tng. Counsel; mem. Internat. Assn. Fin. Planners (bd. dirs. 1984-86), Mo. Athletic Club, Internat. Assn. of Registered Fin. Cons. (emeritus). Republican. Lutheran. Avocations: travel, model trains, cars, video and career. Home: 2031 Kehrsboro Dr Chesterfield MO 63005-6512

HENRY, SARAH M., museum director, historian; b. N.Y.C., May 30, 1961; d. Robert Henry and Selina Trieff; m. Michael Gorin, July 23, 1958; children: Emma May Gorin, Molly Rose Gorin. BA, Yale U., 1983; PhD, Columbia U., 1995. Asst. prof. Union Coll., Schenectady, NY, 1996—2001; dep. dir. Mus. of City of N.Y., 2001—. Office: Mus of City of NY 1220 Fifth Ave New York NY 10029 Office Phone: 212-534-1672.

HENRY, SHERRYE P., political advisor, radio personality; b. Memphis, July 13, 1935; Grad. magna cum laude, Vanderbilt U.; MBA, Fordham U. Asst. adminstr. Office Women's Bus. Ownership SBA; sr. advisor to Congresswoman Louise M. Slaughter, 2000—. Vice-chair interagy. com. on women's bus. enterprise. Author of 2 books including The Deep Divide: Why American Women Resist Equality; contbr. numerous articles to nat. mags.; creator, host Woman! program on Sta. WCBS-TV, N.Y.C.; ind. prodr., broadcaster Sherrye Henry Program WOR Radio, N.Y.C. Active Group for the South Fork, eastern end of L.I., N.Y., Fedn. Protestant Welfare Agys. N.Y., The Retreat, East Hampton, N.Y. Mem. Women's Forum N.Y. (founding mem.).*

HENRY, STEPHEN LEWIS, former lieutenant governor, orthopedic surgeon, educator; b. Owensboro, Ky., Oct. 8, 1953; s. Virgil Lewis and Wanda (Harper) Henry; m. Heather Reneé French, Oct. 27, 2000. BS, We. Ky. U., 1976; MD, U. Louisville, 1981. Diplomate Am. Bd. Orthopaedic Surgery. Intern gen. surgery U. Louisville Med. Ctr., 1981-82, resident, 1982-86, instr. orthopedic surgery, 1986—; lt. gov. Commonwealth of Ky., 1995—2003. Clin. investigator Richards Med. Co., Memphis, 1986—; athletic physician football teams U. Louisville, 1987—, Seneca High Sch., 1987—, Ky. State

Football Championships, 1986—; commr. "A" dist. Jefferson County, 1992-95. Editor: Sports Medicine; contbr. abstracts and articles to profl. jours., chpts. to books. Treas. Louisville Tyler Park Neighborhood Assn., 1983-88, pres., 1988-89 Recipient best paper award So. Med. Assn., 1985, best clin. rsch. award U. Cin., 1986, outstanding resident rsch. award U. Louisville, 1988, Edwin G. Bovill rsch. award Orthopaedic Trauma Assn., 1989, Bell award for outstanding vol., Louisville, 1989, Presdl. recognition Nat. Vol. Week, The White House, 1989; named Outstanding Young Leader in Ky., 1988, One of 10 Outstanding Young Ams., U.S. Jaycees, 1989, Bell award, 1989, Jefferson award, 1989, Owensboro award for excellence, 1990, Lawrence-Grever award, 1990; grantee Richards Med. Co., 1986, Dept. Navy, 1989. Mem. Jefferson County Med. Soc., So. Orthopedic Assn., Ky. Med. Assn., U. Louisville House Staff Assn. (com. on health, phys. edn. and med. aspects of sports 1987—). Democrat. Office Phone: 502-464-0955.

HENRY, SUE, social worker, educator; b. Marion, Ind., Aug. 25, 1934; d. William Floyd and Mildred Ethel (Schwark) H. AB, Earlham Coll., 1956; MSc in Social Adminstrn., Western Res. U., 1964; DSW, U. Denver, 1972. Teenage program dir. YWCA, Lima, Ohio, 1956-62; br. exec. YWCA Met. Cleve., 1964-67; spl. svcs. dir. YWCA Met. Denver, 1967-70; asst. prof. U. Pa., Phila., 1972-76; assoc. prof. U. Denver, 1976-82; faculty fellow Colo. Divsn. Mental Health, Denver, 1984-85; adj. faculty Met. State Coll., Denver, 1985-89; prof. U. Denver, 1982-99, prof. emerita, 2000—. Cons. Denver Internat. Program, 1977—; rsch. assoc. Applied Social Sci. Cons., Denver, 1982-87. Author: Group Skills in Social Work, 1981, revised edit., 1992; sr. editor: Social Work with Groups Mining the Gold, 2002; mem. editl. bd. Social Work with Groups, 1981—; contbr. articles to profl. jours. Com. chair Am. Friends Svc. Com., Phila., 1972-76; mem. Planning Commn., Gilpin County, Colo., 1985-88, chair Citizen Adv. Bd. Health and Human Svcs., 1997-2002; bd. pres. Columbine Family Health Ctr., 1988-92. W.T. Grant fellow YWCA of U.S.A., N.Y.C., 1962-64, doctoral tng. grantee Children's Bur., U.S. Govt., 1970-72; recipient Contbn. to Profl. Lit. award Assn. Social Group Workers, 1986, Contbn. to Profl. Lifetime Achievement award Assn. Social Group Workers, 2001. Mem. AARP (mem. nat. legis. coun. 2002-04), Coun. Social Work Edn. (ho. of dels. 1981-83), Assn. for Advancement Social Work with Groups. Democrat. Avocations: international cuisine cooking, travel, skiing, weaving. E-mail: shenry@du.edu.

HENRY, SUSAN ARMSTRONG, biology professor, dean; b. Alexandria, Va., June 27, 1946; d. Frederic Sylvester and Frederica Ann (Thompson) A.; m. Peter Edward Henry, July 20, 1968; children: Rebecca Alice, Joshua Armstrong. BS in Zoology, U. Md., 1968; PhD in Genetics, U. Calif., Berkeley, 1971. Postdoctoral fellow Brandeis U., Waltham, Mass., 1971-72; asst. prof. genetics, molecular biology Albert Einstein Coll. Medicine, Bronx, N.Y., 1972-77, assoc. prof. genetics and molecular biology, 1972-82, prof., 1972-87, dir. Sue Golding grad. div., 1983-87; prof. biol. scis. Carnegie Mellon U., Pitts., 1987-2000, head dept. biol. scis., 1987-91, program dir. undergrad. biol. scis. edn. initiative, Howard Hughes Med. Inst., 1989-2000, dean Mellon Coll. Sci., 1991-2000; dean Coll. of Agrl. and Life Sci. Cornell U., Ithaca, NY, 2000—. Mem. nat. adv. gen. med. scis. coun. NIH, 1995-98, adv. com. rsch. on minority health, 1998-00, chmn., 1999-00; co-dir. W.M. Keck Ctr. Advanced Tng. Computational Biology, 1992-97; bd. dirs. Agrium, Inc. Contbr. over 100 articles to profl. jours. Mem. N.Y. Farm Bur. Recipient Merit award NIH, 1991, 95, Career Devel. award, 1975-80, Irma T. Hirschl Faculty award Hirschl Found., 1980-85; rsch. grantee NIH, 1972—. Fellow AAAS (mem. com. coun. affairs 2004—, sect. biol. scis. coun. del. 2004—); mem. Genetics Soc. Am., Am. Soc. Biol. Chemists, Am. Soc. Microbiologists (grad. microbiology tchg. award nominating com. 2003-), Nat. Acads. (nat. rsch. coun. com. sci. and tech. to support health care, sustainability, and other aspects of devel. assistance 2004-05). Office: Office of the Dean CALS Cornell U 260 Roberts Hall Ithaca NY 14853-5905 Office Phone: 607-255-2241. E-mail: sah42@cornell.edu.

HENRY, VIC HOUSTON, lawyer; b. Big Spring, Tex., Apr. 23, 1958; s. Don Vernor and Patricia Jean (Ezell) H.; m. Candace Lee McComb, Dec. 27, 1980; children: Taylor McComb, Lee Houston. BA with highest honors, U. Tex., 1980; JD cum laude, Georgetown U., Washington, 1983. Bar: Tex. 1983, U.S. Ct. Appeals (5th, 8th, 10th and D.C. cirs.) 1985, U.S. Ct. Appeals (fed. cir.) 1987, U.S. Dist. Ct. (no. dist.) Tex. 1983, U.S. Dist. Ct. (ea. and we. dists.) Tex. 1985, U.S. Dist. Ct. (ea. and we. dists.) Okla. 1985, U.S. Dist. Ct. (ea. and we. dists.) Ark. 1985, U.S. Dist. Ct. (no. dist.) Ala. 1985, U.S. Claims Ct. 1986, U.S. Supreme Ct. 1985. Law clk. to presiding justice U.S. Dist. Ct., Dallas, 1983—84; assoc. Storey Armstrong Steger & Martin, Dallas, 1984—88, ptnr., 1989—97, Henry Oddo Austin & Fletcher, P.C., Dallas, 1997—. Mem. faculty U. Tex. Arlington Asbestos Abatement, 1987; mem. adv. group Civil Justice Reform, U.S. Dist. Ct. (no. dist.) Tex., 1990; speaker seminars including Am. Corp. Counsel Assn., 1987, Notre Dame U. Sch. of Law, 2000-02, Georgetown U. Law Ctr., 2001. Adminstrv. asst. Tex. senate, Austin, 1976-78, Tex. Ho. of Reps., Austin, 1979-80, U.S. Ho. of Reps., Washington, 1980-82; chmn. deacons Gaston Ave. Baptist Ch., Dallas, 1988, 2002-04. Mem. ABA (chmn. litig. subcom. firms 5-15 lawyers), Tex. State Bar, Conf. Freight Counsel, Transp. Lawyers Assn., Dallas Inn Ct. (barrister 1988-91). Avocations: basketball, travel, fly fishing. Home: 4903 Heritage Cir Sachse TX 75048-4560 Office: Henry Oddo Austin & Fletcher PC 1700 Pacific AVe Ste 2700 Dallas TX 75201-7353 Office Phone: 214-658-1900. E-mail: vhhenry@hoaf.com.

HENRY, WILLIAM RAY, business administration educator; b. Russellville, Ark., Dec. 30, 1925; s. Mace Leon and Violet May (Shinn) H.; m. Norma Talmadge Wright, Nov. 27, 1954; children— William Ray, Lisa Carolyn, Linda Carol, Lara Carlene. BS, U. Ark., 1948, MS, 1953; PhD, N.C. State U., 1957. Asst. prof., then assoc. prof., prof. N.C. State U., Raleigh, 1956-70; prof. bus. adminstrn. Ga. State U., Atlanta, 1970—, prof. emeritus fin., 1993—. Author: (with others) Managerial Economics, 1978; contbr. (with others) articles to profl. jours. Served with USAAF, 1944-45. Recipient award of merit Am. Agrl. Econs. Assn., 1957, 61

HENRYSON, HERBERT, II, lawyer; b. N.Y.C., Mar. 9, 1940; s. Herbert and Adeline (Grey) H.; m. Maxine Mosher, Sept. 4, 1965; children: Dylan Melville, Stefan Friend. BSE, Princeton U., 1962; PhD, U. Calif., Berkeley, 1968; JD, U. Chgo., 1984. Bar: N.Y., Pa., Minn. Vis. scientist U.K. Atomic Energy Authority, Winfrith, Eng., 1967; sr. scientist, mgr. LMFBR physics design Argonne (Ill.) Nat. Lab., 1968-84; assoc., vis. prof. Northwestern U., Evanston, Ill., 1982-84; assoc. Skadden Arps Slate Meagher & Flom, N.Y.C., 1984-92; dep. gen. counsel Honeywell Inc., Mpls., 1992-96; ptnr., co-chair corp. dept. Wolf, Block, Schorr & Solis-Cohen LLP, Phila., 1996—. Vis. assoc. prof. U. Pa., Phila., 1998-99. Contbr. articles to profl. jours. Bd. dirs. Hyde Park Neighborhood Club, Chgo., 1980-84, Honeywell Found. Arts Com., Mpls., 1994-96, Theatre de la Jeune Lune, Mpls., 1994-96, Venture Theatre, Phila., 1997-99. U.S. AEC spl. fellow in sci. and engring., 1962-65, U. Calif. sci. fellow, 1965-66, Fulbright Hays fellow, London, 1966-67. Mem. Phi Beta Kappa. Achievements include participation in many of the most significant negotiated and unsolicited merger and acquisitions of 1980s and 90s. Home: 478 W Broadway New York NY 10012-3168 Office: Wolf Black et al 250 Park Ave New York NY 10177-0001

HENSARLING, JEB, congressman; b. Stephenville, Tex., May 29, 1957; m. Melisa Fore; 1 child, Claire; m. Melissa Fore. BA in Econs. magna cum laude, Tex. A&M, 1979; JD, U. Tex., 1982. Atty. Oppenheimer, Harrison, Blend and Tate, San Antonio; v.p. Maverick Capital, Dallas; prin.-owner F-H and Assocs., Dallas; congressman 5th Dist. Tex. U.S. Ho. Reps., 2003—. Bd. dirs. IMCO Recycling Inc. Co-founder Family Support Assurance Corp.; mem. adv. bd. Children's Edn. Fund; exec. dir. Nat. Rep. Senatorial Com., 1991—93; Tex. dir. U.S. Senator Phil Gramm, 1985—89, chair re-election campaign, 1990; bd. dirs. Am. Cancer Soc.-Dallas Metro Area, Tex. Pub. Policy Found. Republican. Episcopalian. Office: 423 Cannon House Office Bldg Washington DC 20515*

HENSCHEL, JOHN JAMES, lawyer; b. Mineola, NY, Aug. 11, 1954; s. John Jr. and Lilyan Marie (Dodge) H.; m. Yasmin Islami, May 26, 1980; children: John Christopher, Theodore Martin, Jessamyn Susanna. BA in Psychology, Fairfield U., 1976; JD, Seton Hall U., 1984. Bar: N.J. 1984, U.S. Dist. Ct. N.J. 1984, U.S. Dist. Ct. (so. and ea. dists.) N.Y. 1985, U.S. Ct. Appeals (3d cir.) 1996. Law sec. Hon. Marshall Selikoff, J.S.C., Freehold, NJ, 1984-85; assoc. McElroy, Deutsch & Mulvaney, Morristown, NY, 1985-88, Bumgardner, Hardin & Ellis, Springfield, NJ, 1988-90; ptnr. Tompkins McGuire & Wachenfeld, Newark, 1990-97; trial counsel Caron McCormick Constants & Wilson, Rutherford, NJ, 1997—2003; mediator Superior Ct. N.J., 1999—; corp. counsel Atlas Copco North Am. Inc., 2003—. Trustee Abdol H. Islami M.D. Found. for Med. Edn. Mem. ABA, N.J. Bar Assn., N.J. Bar Found. (trustee 1995-99, treas. 1999-2001, second v.p. 2001-2003, 1st v.p. 2003-05, pres. 2005—), Am. Inns of Ct. (Justice William Brennan Jr. chpt.; master Seton Hall Law Alumni chpt., Marie L. Garibaldi chpt.), Essex County Bar Assn. Avocations: reading, sports. Home: 12 Christy Dr Warren NJ 07059-6804 Office: 34 Maple Ave Pine Brook NJ 07058

HENSCHEL, SANDI, English, speech and drama educator, actor, writer; b. Bklyn., Dec. 27, 1938; d. Sydney Henschel and Helen Sara (Kellner) Mione; div.; children: Lisa Richele Piccione, Rachel Astarte Piccione, Sarah Rebecca Piccione. BS in Edn., English, SUNY, Potsdam, 1960, MS in English, Edn., 1966; MA in Creative Writing, SUNY, Brockport, 1984. Cert. K-12 tchr., secondary English tchr., N.Y. Tchr. English Potsdam Jr. Sr. H.S., 1960-61, Norwood (N.Y.)-Norfolk H.S., 1961-63, Scotia (N.Y.)-Glenville Jr. H.S., 1964-67; supr. student tchrs. No. Ill. U., DeKalb, 1968-69; instr. writing SUNY, Brockport, 1973-74; tchr. English Kendall (N.Y.) H.S., 1974—. Supr. student tchrs. SUNY, Brockport, 1997; dir. prodns., curriculum cons. Kendall H.S., 1997—. Auhor poetry (calendar) The Sound of a Few Leaves, (pamphlet) In March, Longing for Bees, (chapbook) After a Long Time Waiting, Polar Sun, (anthology) On Turtle's Back; actor numerous prodns. Mem. pub. rels. Steve Ireland for N.Y. State Senate, Brockport, 1996. Recipient Outstanding Tchr. award U. Rochester Excellence in Tchg., 1990, Educator of Excellence award N.Y. State English Coun., 1995. Mem. NEA, Kendall Faculty Assn. Home: 37 Chappell St Brockport NY 14420-2224

HENSCHKE, CLAUDIA INGRID, physician, radiologist; b. Berlin, Mar. 3, 1941; d. Ulrich Konrad and Gisela Franziska H. BA in French, So. Meth. U., 1962, MS in Math. Stats., 1966; PhD in Stats., U. Ga., 1969; MD, Howard U., 1977; Radiologist, Harvard U., 1981. Diplomate Am. Bd. Radiology. Internship, residency dept. radiology Harvard Med. Sch./Brigham and Women's Hosp., 1977-81, clin. fellow in radiology, 1977-81; rsch. fellow in radiology Brigham and Women's Hosp., 1981-82, Harvard Med. Sch., Boston, 1981-82; rsch. fellow in epidemiology Harvard Sch. of Pub. Health, 1981-82; assoc. radiologist Brigham and Women's Hosp., 1982-83, co-dir. Thoracic Divsn., 1983; asst. attending radiology to assoc. radiologist The N.Y. Hosp. - Cornell Med. Ctr., 1983-87, 87-92, sect. chief, chest imaging to chief of divsn., 1988-92, 92-95, attending radiologist, 1992—, chief, Divsn. of Health Care Policy and Tech. Assessment, 1995—, chief, Divsn. of Chest Imaging, 1995—. Various acad. positions to prof. radiology, Cornell U. Med. Coll., 1992—; cons. Rockefeller U., 1986—, Med. Billing Program Devel. and Med. Computer Systems Planning, 1986—; lectr. in field; mem. numerous coms. in field; vis. prof. numerous unvis., including Columbia U., 1999, Roy Castle Internat. Ctr. for Lung Cancer Rsch., Liverpool, Eng., 1999, Washington U., 1999, Clinica U., Pamplona, Spain, 1999, U. Rochester, N.Y., 1999, others. Mem. editl. bd. Complications in Surgery, 1995—, Investigative Radiology, 1990-94, Clin. Imaging, 1988—, Acad. Radiology, 1994—, others; reviewer Am. Jour. Cardiology, 1982—, Chest, 1992—, Radiology, 1993—, Jour. of Computed Assisted Tomography, 1995—, Am. Jour. of Radiology, 1995—, others; contbr. numerous books, including: Women's Complete Handbook, 1994, Introduction to Statistics and Computer Programming, 1975, Instructions for General Purpose Program Package, 1971, First and Second Biomedical Computing Symposium 1965 and 1966, 1967; contbr. numerous articles to profl. jours. and publs. Named Ky. Col. by Gov. of Ky., 1963; grantee in field. Mem. Am. Statis. Soc., Am. Assn. Women Radiologists (Marie Curie award/2d place 1994), Radiol. Soc. N.Am., Am. Coll. Radiology, Soc. Thoracic Radiology, Sigma Xi, Phi Kappa Phi. Office: New York Hosp/Dept Radiol Cornell Med Ctr New York NY 10021 Business E-Mail: chensch@med.cornell.edu.

HENSE, DONALD LANGFORD, educational association administrator; b. St. Louis, July 4, 1942; s. Fred Hense and Lillie Ivy H.; 1 child, Dana. AB, Morehouse Coll., 1970; postgrad., Stanford U., 1973. Dir. govtl. rels. Howard U., Washington, 1973-79, Boston U., 1979-81, Dartmouth Coll., Hanover, N.H., 1984-86; v.p. for devel. and univ. rels. Prairie View (Tex.) A&M U., 1986-88; v.p. for devel. Nat. Urban League, N.Y.C., 1988-90. Dir. Nat. Fedn. of Interfaith Vol. Caregivers, Kansas City, Mo., 21st Century Found., N.Y. Pres., CEO Friendship House Assn.; chmn., founder Edison Friendship Pub. Charter Sch. Merrill scholar Charles E. Merrill Trust, U. Ghana, 1969, Rockefeller Intern in Econs., Rockefeller Found., Cornell U., 1968, Ford Found. Dissertation fellow, Stanford U., 1973, NDEA fellow, 1970-72. Mem. Nat. Soc. Fundraising Exec. (DC chpt. bd. dirs. 1993-96, Fundraising Exec. of Yr. 1999), Kappa Alpha Psi. Baptist. E-mail: dhense@friendshiphouse.net.

HENSEL, KATHERINE RUTH, portfolio manager, investment strategist, securities analyst; b. Summit, N.J., Nov. 24, 1959; d. John Charles and Carolyn (Bahle) Hensel; m. Jean-Paul Fouillade, Sept. 24, 1994 (div. Dec. 2001); . AB, Harvard U., 1981, MBA, 1985. Securities analyst Donaldson Lufkin & Jenrette, N.Y.C., 1981-83; investment banker Paine Webber, N.Y.C., 1985, Shearson Lehman Bros., N.Y.C., 1986, sr. v.p., securities analyst, 1987-91; mng. dir. Lehman Bros., N.Y.C., 1992, chief investment strategist, 1993-95; sr. equity rsch. analyst Chancellor Capital Mgmt., N.Y.C., 1996—97; mng. dir., dir. rsch. Chancellor LGT, N.Y.C., 1997—98; mng. ptnr. Sage Asset Mgmt., N.Y.C., 1999—. Contbr. articles to profl. jours. Named Instl. Investor All Am. Rsch. Team, 1989-93. Office: Ste 930 500 Fifth Ave New York NY 10110 E-mail: Khensel@sageasset.com.

HENSEL, NANCY H., academic administrator; 1 child. BA, MA, Calif. State U., San Francisco; EdD, U. Ga., 1973. Prof. early childhood edn., Calif.; dean coll. of edn., health and rehab. U. Maine, Farmington, 1992—95, provost and v.p. academic affairs, 1995—99; pres. U. Maine at Presque Isle, 1999—. Named to Fourteenth Maine Women's Hall of Fame, 2003. Office: U Maine at Presque Isle 181 Main St Presque Isle ME 04769-2888

HENSEL, PAUL H., lawyer; b. Hinsdale, Ill., Apr. 11, 1948; BS in Fin. with high honors, U. Ill., 1969; JD cum laude, U. Mich., 1972. Bar: Ill. 1972. Assoc. to ptnr., chief administrative ptnr. Winston & Strawn, Chgo., 1972—, chmn. assoc. programs, chmn. bldg. com. Bd. dirs. B.F. Shaw Printing Co. Bd. trustees NALP Found. Rsch. and Edn.; mem. auxiliary bd. Art Inst. Chgo. Mem. ABA, Chgo. Bar Assn., Ill. State Bar Assn. Office: Winston & Strawn LLP 35 W Wacker Dr Ste 4200 Chicago IL 60601-9703 Office Phone: 312-558-5750. Office Fax: 312-558-5700. E-mail: phensel@winston.com.

HENSELER, CHRISTINE, language educator; b. London, Mar. 31, 1969; d. Klaus Henseler and Trin-Madlen Winden. BA with honors, BSJ in Advt., U. Kans., 1993, MA, 1995; PhD, Cornell U., 1999. Asst. prof. SUNY, Fredonia, 1999—2001, Union Coll., Schenectady, NY, 2001—. Editor: Escritoras Españolas ante el Mercado Literario, 2003; author: Contemporary Spanish Women's Narrative and the Publishing Industry. Named John T. and Catherine MacArthur jr. prof., Union Coll., 2002; grantee, NEH, 2000, NEH summer seminar, 2002. Mem.: MLA, Am. Assn. Tchrs. Spanish and Portuguese, Am. Coun. Tchg. Fgn. Lang., Soc. for History Authorship, Reading and Pub., Twentieth Century Spanish Assn. Am., Sigma Delta Pi, Phi Beta Kappa.

HENSELMANN, CASPAR GUSTAV FIDELIS, sculptor; b. Mannheim, Germany, Mar. 13, 1933; came to U.S., 1950; s. Albert Edward and Lore Elfriede (Feist) Henselmann; m. Evangeline Karantzaki, Dec. 30, 1961; children: Xavier, Samuel. Student, Northwestern U., 1950-52; diploma in med. art, U. Ill. Coll. Medicine, 1955; BFA, Art Inst., Chgo., 1956; postgrad. studies, Wayne State U., Columbia U., 1958-61. Fellow W. B. Saunders Pub. Co., Phila., 1956; med. illustrator pvt. practice, N.Y.C., 1968—; art dir. Aron & Falcone Advtg., Chatham, N.J., 1972-73; assoc. prof. sculpture CW Post Ctr. Long Island (N.Y.) Univ., 1976-77, Hofstra Univ., Hempstead, N.Y., 1987-88; assoc. prof. Long Island U., Brooklyn, 1996—. Vis. artist St. Cloud (Minn.) State Coll., 1975, Ox-Bow Sch. of Painting, Sugatuck, Mich., 1976, Memphis Acad. Fine Arts, 1982, Md. Art Inst., 1982, Univ. N.C., Chapel Hill, 1983; lectr. and critic Grad. Sch. of Architecture, U. Pa., Phila., 1993, Grad. Sch. Architecture, Columbia U., N.Y.C., 1994; mem. Berlin-Spandau Internat. City Planning Project Team, Columbia U., 1993. One-man shows include Rice Gallery, N.Y.C., 1961, 63, Kern County Mus., Bakersfield, Calif., 1965, Stable Gallery, 1968, 55 Mercer Gallery, 1972, 74, 75, 76, 77, Sculpture Now, NYC, 1979, Fredericsburg (Va.) Ctr. for Creative Arts, 1979, Walter Bischoff Gallery, Chgo., 1986, Drothea Van Der Koelen, Mainz, Germany, 1989, Walter Bischoff, Stuttgart, Berlin, Germany, 1990, 94, 97, Kunstverein Bielefeld Mus. in Waldhof, Germany, 1991, Bill Bace Gallery, N.Y.C., 1992, 95, Stadt Gallery, Lahr, Germany, 1993, Offenberg Mus., Germany, 1994, View Pardo Gallery, N.Y.C., 1996, Kingsborough C.C., Bklyn., 1997, Lindenau Mus., Altenburg, Germany, 1991, Rosenberg & Kaufman Gall., NYC, 1995, Villa Haiss Mus., Altenburg, Neuberger Mus., Purchase, N.Y., 1999, Robert Pardo Gallery, 1999, Forum Munich, 2003, Artefact, Zurich, Wooster Artspace, NY, 2004; exhibited in group shows Am. Painting and Sculpture Annual, Phila., 1964, Nat. Design Ctr., Chgo., 1964, New Eng. Artists Annual, Silvermine, Conn., 1964, Arts Coun. of Great Britain, Whitechapel Gallery, London, 1970, Marika Malacorda Gallery, Geneva, 1976, Memphis (Tenn.) Acad. Fine Arts, 1982, Nina Owen Gallery, Chgo., 1987, U. Mass., Amherst, 1989, Bischoff Gallery, 1998, U. L.I., 1998, Pardo Gallery, 1999-2002, Chelsea Studio Gallery, N.Y.C., 2002, Berlin, 2002, Wooster Artspace, 2003, Robert Pardo, 2003, Milano Artefact, 2005; represented in collections in Marshall-Isley Bank Lobby, Milw., 1971, Mannesmann Internat. Hdqrs., Dusseldorf, Germany, 1985, Deutsche Bank, N.Y.C., 1990, Julius Baer Bank, N.Y.C., 1992, Kunsthalle, Bremen Germany, 1993, Collection Hurrle, Durbach, Germany, 1994, Lindenau Mus., Villa Haiss Mus., Neuberger Mus., Swiss Paraplegic Ctr., Nottwil. Commr. City of Denver, 2004—05. Home: 21 Bond St New York NY 10012-2451 E-mail: chenselmann@earthlink.net.

HENSELMEIER, SANDRA NADINE, retired training services executive; b. Indpls., Nov. 20, 1937; d. Frederick Rost Henselmeier and Beatrice Nadine (Barnes) Henselmeier Enright; m. David Albert Funk, Oct. 2, 1976; children: William H. Stolz Jr., Harry Phillip Stolz II, Sandra Ann Stolz. AB, Purdue U., 1971; MAT, Ind. U., 1975. Exec. sec. to dean Ind. U. Sch. Law, Indpls., 1977—78; adminstrv. asst. Ind. U.-Purdue U., Indpls., 1978—80, assoc. archivist, 1980—81; program and comm. coord. Midwest Alliance in Nursing, Indpls., 1981—82; tng. coord. Coll./Univ. Cos., Indpls., 1982—83; pres. Better Bus. Comms., Indpls., 1983—96; ret., 1996. Adj. lectr./lectr. U. Indpls. Ctr. Continuing Mgmt. Devel. and Edn., Indpls., 1984—94. Author: Successful Customer Service Writing, Winning with Effective Business Grammar, Successful Telephone Communication and Etiquette, Management Writing; contbr. articles to profl. jours. Mem.: Econ. Club of Indpls. Republican. Presbyterian. Avocations: travel, walking, reading, learning new ideas. Personal E-mail: shenselmeier@iquest.net.

HENSEN, STEPHEN JEROME, lawyer; b. Durango, Colo., Nov. 8, 1961; s. Ronald Jerome and Sandra Lucille (Monroe) H.; m. Janice Lynn Lamunyon; children: Amanda, Stephanie, Cory. BS in Econs., Colo. State U., 1984; JD, Gonzaga U., 1987. Bar: Colo. 1987, U.S. Dist. Ct. Colo. 1987, U.S. Ct. Appeals (10th cir.) 1988, U.S. Supreme Ct. 1994. Atty. Cortez Friedman, P.C., Denver, 1987-93; atty. McKenna & Cuneo, Denver, 1993-95; ptnr. Richman & Hensen, P.C., Denver, 1995-99, Hensen & Drake, Denver, 1999—. Mem. Colo. Bar Assn., Denver Bar Assn., Colo. Supreme Ct. Bar Com. Republican. Office: Tiemeier and Hensen PC #1300 1515 Arapahoe St Denver CO 80202-2113

HENSGEN, HERBERT THOMAS, medical technologist; b. Cin., May 28, 1947; s. Herbert and Carolyn Elizabeth (Stites) H. BS, U. Cin., 1973, MS, 1978; AAS, Cin. State Tech. and C.C., 1981. Reg. med. technologist. Grad. tchg. asst. U. Cin., 1976-77; lectr. Xavier U. (formerly Edgecliff Coll.), Cin., 1977-78; tech. Our Lady of Mercy Hosp. (now Mercy Hosp. Anderson), Cin., 1979-81, med. lab. tech., 1981—84, med. technologist, 1984—86; rsch. asst. Cin. Children's Hosp. Med. Ctr., 1986—. Instr. Cin. State Tech. and C.C., 1984-85. Contbr. article to Gen. and Comparative Endocrinology; co-author abstracts for Soc. for Pediat. Rsch., Endocrine Soc. Deacon Madisonville Bapt. Ch., 1977. Mem. Am. Soc. Clin. Pathologists, Triple Nine Soc., Am. Mensa Ltd. Achievements include production of data suggesting lack of insulin-like growth factor-1 (IGF-I) may mediate growth retardation in the neonatal rat; discovery of evidence that IGF-I may be one of several growth factors regulating differentiation of the fetal brain; demonstration that the antigonadal effect of prolactin in the lizard Anolis carolinensis is directed toward the smaller ovarian follicles; research on effects of IGF-I and its binding proteins on fetal and neonatal development. Home: 7420 Drake Rd Cincinnati OH 45243-1422 Office: Cin Children's Hosp Med Ctr Dept Endocrinology 3333 Burnet Ave Cincinnati OH 45229-3026

HENSHAW, GUY RUNALS, management consultant; b. Moscow, Idaho, Sept. 27, 1946; s. Paul C. and Helen E. Henshaw; m. Susan S. Seigel, Dec. 29, 1968; children: Christine, Victoria. BA, Ripon Coll., 1968; MBA, U. Pa., 1970. V.p. Security Nat. Bank, Walnut Creek, Calif., 1970-80, Bank Am., San Francisco, 1980-84; pres., dir. CivicBan Corp., Oakland, Calif., 1984-93; chmn. Payday, Payroll Co., San Francisco, 1993-96; mng. dir. Henshaw/Vierra, LLC, San Francisco, 1996—. Dir. Calif. Banker's Ins. Svcs., Inc., San Francisco, 1989-92, Fair Isaac & Co., San Rafael, Calif., 1994—, R&D Diagnostic Antibodies, Benicia, Calif., 1997, Sleepy Cat Software, Boston, 2001; v.p., Eubel Brady & Suttman Asset Mgmt., Dayton, 2000—; bd. dirs. I Sys. LLC, Burlington, Vt., IKEN Tissue Therapeutics, Inc. Chmn. bd. trustees Head Royce Sch., Oakland, 1982-90; trustee Ripon (Wis.) Coll., 1994—; dir. John Muir Health Sys., Walnut Creek, 1999—. Lt. col. U.S. Army, 1968-96. Mem.: Penn Club NY, Skyline Country Club, Diablo Country Club, Pacific Union Club. Episcopalian. Avocations: tennis, travel. Office: Henshaw/Vierra LLC 1460 Maria Ln Ste 290 Walnut Creek CA 94596 E-mail: guy@henshawvierra.com.

HENSHAW, JONATHAN COOK, retired manufacturing executive; b. Dobbs Ferry, NY, Jan. 29, 1922; s. Elmer Ellsworth and Leonora Agnes (Scott) H.; m. Martha Emily Stock, July 14, 1948; children: William (dec.), Jane, Mary, Thomas, Daniel, Anne. BS, Fordham U., 1950; MBA, NYU, 1952; AA in Real Estate, Bucks County C.C., 1988. CPA NY. Staff acct. Coopers & Lybrand, NYC, 1951-55, 68-69; v.p., treas. J.A. Ewing & McDonald, Inc., NYC, 1955-62; asst. treas. Block Drug Co., Jersey City, 1962-64; contr., asst. treas. Turner Jones Co., Inc., NYC, 1964-68; treas. Visual Electronics, NYC, 1969—, Crane Co., NYC, 1970-80; assoc. broker Fox & Lazo Realtors, 1980-83, John T. Henderson, Inc., 1983-87, Richard A. Weidel Corp., Newtown, Pa., 1987—2002; ret., 2002. Served as sgt. AUS, 1943-46. Decorated Purple Heart. Roman Catholic. Home: 48 Falcon Rd Levittown PA 19056-1906

HENSHEL, HARRY BULOVA, watch manufacturer; b. NYC, Feb. 5, 1919; s. Harry D. and Emily (Bulova) H.; m. Joy Altman, Nov. 4, 1948; children—Dale, Patti, Diane, Judith. AB, Brown U., 1940; grad., U.S. Army Command and Gen. Staff Sch., 1945; MBA, Harvard U., 1951. With Bulova Watch Co., Inc., Flushing, N.Y., 1938—, asst. sec., 1950, sec., 1951, v.p. finance, 1957, exec. v.p., 1958, pres., 1959-74, chmn., 1973-96, vice-chmn., 1996—. Bd. dirs. Ampal Corp., mem. audit com., Universal Holdings Corp., mem. audit com.; chmn. bd. dirs. Bulova Internat., Ltd., 11961-81; chmn. Atlantic Time Products Corp., 1991—; chmn. chief execs. coun. The Omega Group, 1991; chmn. Bulova Watch Co., 1973-96, vice chmn., 1991—. Vice chmn., trustee Adelphi U., 1955-88, emeritus trustee, 1989—; bd. overseers parsons Sch. Design; bd. dirs. U.S. Com. for UNICEF, 1979-87, Fedn. Employment and Guidance Svcs., Westchester Philharm. Orch., 1990; mem. bus. coun. UN Bus. Adv. Com., policy study com. Heller Inst., 1979-85; mem. adv. bd.

N.Y.C. chpt. Am. Cancer Soc., N.Y. State Bus. Venture Partnership. Mem. Amateur Athletic Union U.S. (timing com.), N.Y. C. of C. (dir.), Am. Ordnance Assn (life), Newcomen Soc. N.Am., UN Assn. U.S. (dir.), Thoroughbred Owners and Breeders Assn., Sigma Chi (Significant Sig medal) Clubs: Harvard Business School, Sales Executives, New York (dir.), Brown Univ, Harmonie, Economic; Army and Navy (Washington); Old Oaks Country (Purchase, N.Y.); Turf and Field; Town (Scarsdale). Republican. Home: 24 Murray Hill Rd Scarsdale NY 10583-2828 Office: Bulova Corp 1 Bulova Ave Flushing NY 11377-7826

HENSLER, DAVID J., lawyer; b. Alexandria, Va., June 9, 1943; AB cum laude, St. Louis U., 1965, JD cum laude, 1967. Bar: Mo. 1967, D.C. 1969; U.S. Supreme Ct. 1971. Atty., gen. counsel's office Securities and Exchange Commn., 1967-68; ptnr. Hogan & Hartson, Washington, dir. litig. practice group. Adj. prof. Georgetown U. Law Ctr., 1978-86; mem. exec. com. Council for Ct. Excellence, 1986-90. Notes and Comments Editor: St. Louis U. Law Jour., 1966-67. Mem. ABA (litigation sect.), D.C. Bar Assn., Mo. Bar Assn., Fed. Bar Assn., Defense Rsch. Inst. Office: Hogan & Hartson LLP Columbia Square 555 13th St NW Ste 800E Washington DC 20004-1161 Office Phone: 202-637-5600. Office Fax: 202-637-5910. Business E-Mail: djhensler@hhlaw.com.

HENSLER, DEBORAH ROSENFIELD, law educator; b. Syracuse, NY, May 23, 1942; d. Nathan and Vivian (Feller) Rosenfield; m. Carl Peter Hensler, May 23, 1965; children: Benjamin, Rebecca. AB in Polit. Sci. summa cum laude, CUNY, 1963; PhD in Polit. Sci., MIT, 1973. Asst. to dir., mgr. tech. ops. Survey Rsch. Ctr. UCLA, 1969-73; social scientist RAND Corp., Santa Monica, Calif., 1973—80, sr. social scientist, 1980—98, dir. survey rsch. group, 1975—85, assoc. head social sci. dept., 1975-80, rsch. dir. Inst. Civil Justice, 1986—90, dir. Inst. Civil Jusice, 1993—98, mem. faculty grad. sch., 1980—93, sr. fellow, 1998—2001; prof. law and social sci. U. So. Calif. Law Ctr., 1993—98; Judge John W. Ford. prof. dispute resolution Stanford Law Sch., 1998—; dir. Stanford Ctr. on Conflict & Negotiation, 2000—. George E. Allen Chair U. Richmond Law Sch., spring 1990; scholar-in-residence U. So. Calif. Law Sch., LA, fall 1990, vis. prof. social sci. in law, 1991-93; vis. prof. U. Chgo. Law Sch., spring 1991; presenter in field, 1970—; mem. law and social sci. adv. panel NSF, 1991-94; mem. study com. of Fed. Employers' Liability Act, Nat. Transp. Bd., 1992-93; mem. steering com. Nat. Conf. Lawyers and Scientists AAAS-ABA, 1994; mem. editl. bd. Pub. Opinion Quarterly, 1988-91, Law & Soc. Rev., 2000-03; cons. editor Psychology, Pub. Policy, and Law. Bd. dirs. Calif. Supreme Ct. Hist. Soc., 1998-. Recipient Achievement Award Soroptomist Club, LA, 1977, Woman of Yr. Award YWCA, Santa Monica, 1980; named to Hunter Coll. Hall of Fame, CUNY, 1985; Woodrow Wilson Fellow, 1963-64, Woodrow Wilson Dissertation Fellowship, 1965, NSF Fellowship, 1966-67, Stouffer Fellowship Harvard-MIT Joint Ctr. for Urban Studies, 1966-67, NSF Dissertation Rsch. Fellowship, 1967-68. Fellow Am. Acad. Polit. and Social Sci.; mem. Am. Judicature Soc. (bd. dirs. 1993-99), Law and Soc. Assn. (bd. trustees 1993-96, chmn. nominating com. 1993-94), Am. Arbitration Assn. (bd. dirs. 1990-95), Soc. for Profls. in Dispute Resolution (pub. policy com. 1990-94), Am. Assn. for Pub. Opinion Rsch. (chmn. stds. com. 1982-84), Am. Inns of Ct. (leadership coun., 1997-2001), Phi Beta Kappa, Pi Sigma Alpha. Office: Stanford Law Sch Crown Quadrangle 559 Nathan Abbott Way Stanford CA 94305-8610 Office Phone: 650-723-0146. E-mail: dhensler@stanford.edu.*

HENSLEY, ELIZABETH CATHERINE, nutritionist, educator; b. Mpls., Feb. 27, 1921; d. Erich Christian and Lulu Mabel (Elliott) Selke; m. Eugene B. Hensley, June 10, 1954 (dec. 1992). BS in Edn., U. N.D., 1942; MS, Cornell U., 1944, postgrad., 1950-51. Instr. food and nutrition U. Del., 1944-47; asst. prof. Okla. A&M U., 1947-50; mem. faculty U. Mo., Columbia, 1951—, prof. food and nutrition, 1954-84, prof. emeritus, 1984—, chmn. dept. home econs., 1954-55, head dept. food and nutrition, 1955-65, co-chmn. dept. human nutrition, 1973-76. Author: Basic Concepts of World Nutrition, 1981. Mem. Am. Home Econs. Assn., Nutrition Today Soc., Mo. Home Econs. Assn., Boone County Hist. Soc., PEO, Pi Lambda Theta, Omicron Nu, Phi Upsilon Omicron, Gamma Sigma Delta, Kappa Alpha Theta Mem. Christian Ch. (Disciples Of Christ). Home: 802 Greenwood Ct Columbia MO 65203-2841

HENSLEY, JOHN CLARK, religious organization administrator, minister; b. Sullivan County, June 16, 1912; s. Truman and Ivan (Moddrell) H.; m. Margaret Sipes, Nov. 24, 1946; children: Gary, Clark, Dana. Ordained to ministry So. Bapt. Conv., 1930. Pastor, Moberly and Kansas City, Mo., 1935-46, Nashville and Pulaski, Tenn., 1947-58; supt. missions Hinds County Bapt. Assn., Jackson, Miss., 1958-66; exec. dir. Christian Action Commn. Miss. Bapt. Conv., Jackson, 1966-82, exec. dir. emeritus, 1982—, cons. family life, 1982-90, rec. sec., 1982-90. Assoc. prof. Cen. Bapt. Theol. Sem., 1943-46. Author: The Pastor as Educational Director, rev. edit., 1950, My Father is Rich, 1956, In the Heart of the Young, 1952, Behaving at Home, 1972, 99, Help for the Single Parents and Those Who Love Them, 1973, Coping With Being Single Again, 1978, Preacher Behave! Pointers on Ministerial Ethics, 1978, 99, rev., 2001, Good News for Todays Single, 1985, The Autumn Years, 1987, The Pastor in Family Ministry, 1990. Pres. bd. CONTACT, 1973—; trustee Radio and TV Commn. So. Bapt. Conv., 1980-88; mem. Gov. Miss. Com. Alcohol Abuse and Alcoholism, 1972—; mem. bd. Am. Coun. Alcohol Problems, 1972—; trustee Hannibal, Mo. LaGrange Coll., 1939-45. Recipient Disting. Svc. award for leadership in Christian ethics Christian Life Commn., 1975, Disting. Svc. award Family Ministry Bapt. Sunday Sch. Bd., 1988, Brooks Hays Christian Citizenship award, 1992, Ctrl. Bapt. Theol. Sem. Alumnus of the Yr. award, 1996. Mem. Nat. Coun. Family Problems, Southeastern Coun. Family Problems, Miss. Couns. Family Problems, Am. Judicature Soc., Am. Acad. Polit. Assn., Am. Assn. Sex Educators and Counselors. Home: 130 Caribbean Cv Clinton MS 39056-6101 E-mail: j.clarkhen@aol.com. *God must have intended that we have enough of Heaven in our homes here to get us a little bit prepared for what Heaven is like. The spiritual temperature of our churches is controlled by thermostats in the homes of the members.*

HENSLEY, MARBLE JOHN, SR., civil engineer, consultant; b. Ball Ground, Ga., Nov. 6, 1922; s. C. Paul and Ober Odel (Penland) H.; m. Ruth Ann Collins, Sept. 11, 1948; children: Carol Hensley Hastey, Sandra Hensley Wise, Kathy Hensley McFarlane, Marble John Jr. BS in Civil Engring., Ga. Inst. Tech., 1950. Registered profl. engr., Ala., Ga., Ind., Ky., La., Miss., NC, SC, Tenn., Va., W.Va., NJ, Pa.; registered land surveyor, Ga., Ky., Tenn., La. Aviation loftsman Bell Aircraft, Marietta, Ga., 1942-44; jr. engr. Ga. Hwy. Dept., 1949-50; asst. traffic engr. City of Atlanta, Ga., 1950-54; traffic engr. City of Chattanooga, Tenn., 1954-58, city coord., 1958-63; pres. Hensley & Assocs., Marietta, Ga., 1957-63, Hensley-Schmidt, Inc., Chattanooga, 1963-81, chmn. of bd., 1981-91; dir. Piedmont Olsen Hensley, Chattanooga, 1991—95; sr. v.p. Arcadis, Chattanooga, 1995—. Del. President's Hwy. Conf., Miami, Fla., 1957; col., aide de camp Govs. Staff State of Tenn., Nashville, 1989—,dir. Interfed Saving and Loan, (later First Fed. Savings and Loan, then Am. South Bank of TN), 1981-1995. Trustee Bryan Coll. Dayton, Tenn., 1983—, Memphis Theol. Sem., 1981-89; elder First Cumberland Presbyn. Ch., Chatanooga, 1961-89, Brainerd Presbyn. Ch., Chatanooga, 1989—; bd. dir. Chatanooga Automobile Club, 1955-59, Chatanooga Kiwanis Club, 1962-63. With US Navy, 1944-46. Marble J. Hensley award created in his honor by So. Dist. Inst. Transp. Engrs.; named Engr. of Yr. Chattanooga Engr. Club, 1961. Fellow ASCE, Inst. Transp. Engr. (mem. tech. coun. 1959-64, chm. tech. program annual meeting 1964, pres. 1969), Consulting Engr. Coun. (pres. consulting engr. Tenn., del. nat. coun. 1970). Office: Arcadis G&M Inc 1210 Premier Dr Chattanooga TN 37421 Office Phone: 423-756-7193.

HENSLEY, NOEL M. B., lawyer; b. LA, Dec. 25, 1944; BS magna cum laude, North Tex. State U., 1975; JD cum laude, So. Meth. U., 1978. Bar: Tex. 1978. Law clk. to Hon. Robert W. Porter US Dist. Ct. (No. Dist.) Tex., 1978-80; mem. Haynes & Boone LLP, Dallas, 1980—, ptnr., Bus. Litig. Arbitrator Nat. Assn. Securities Dealer, 1986—; instr. Nat. Inst. Trial Advocacy, 1989—, So. Meth. U. Sch. Law, 1990—92. Editor: Southwestern Law Jour., 1977—78. Rsch. fellow, Southwestern Legal Found. Fellow: Tex. Bar Found., Dallas Bar Found.; mem.: Am. Law Inst., State Bar Tex. (Litig. Sect.), ABA (Litig. Sect.), Order of Coif. Office: Haynes & Boone LLP 3100 NationsBank Plz 901 Main St Ste 3100 Dallas TX 75202-3789 Office Phone: 214-651-5631. Office Fax: 214-200-0470. Business E-Mail: noel.hensley@haynesboone.com.

HENSLEY, PATRICIA DRAKE, principal; BLS in Liberal studies, MA in Edn., PhD in Edn. Adminstrn., St. Louis U., Mo. Cert. use of tech. in sch. setting Tech. Leadership Acad. Tchr. grades 7 and 8 math. and sci., 1976—82; prin. St. Mary Magdalen, St. Louis, 1982—86; vice-prin. St. Elizabeth Acad., St. Louis, 1986—91; prin. St. Francis of Assisi, St. Louis, 1991—95; acad. adviser grad. programs Webster U., St. Louis, 1990—2002; prin. Ursuline Acad., St. Louis, 1995—. Adj. instr. math. and computer sci. Webster U., St. Louis, 1986—; nat. media cons. FM radio stas.; fellow St. Louis Prin. Acad., 1994; state prin. assessor NASSP, 1994; grant reviewer U.S. Dept. Edn., 2002. Mem. Archdiocesan Com. for Rev. of H.S. Admissions, 1997—99; bd. dirs., co-chair ednl. policies com. DeSmet Jesuit H.S., 1998—; bd. dirs. Vianney H.S., 1999—. Office Phone: 314-966-4556 ext. 212. Personal E-mail: pdrakehensley@hotmail.com.

HENSLEY, RALPH HENRY, III, public information officer; b. Balt., June 8, 1967; s. Charles Junior (Stepfather) and Donna Rae Turner. Assoc. in Gen. Studies, Piedmont Va. C.C., Charlottesville, 1996; diploma in internat. hotel and restaurant mgmt., ATI Career Inst., Falls Church, Va., 1996. Edn. analyst Chief of Naval Ops., Washington, 1993—95; mgmt. analyst, family svcs. Bur. of Naval Pers., Washington, 1996; lead, manpower analyst Field Support Activity, Washington, 1996—99; sr. program analyst EER Systems Inc., Chantilly, Va., 1999—2002; exec. asst. to dep. for resource mgmt. Missile Def. Agy., Washington, 2002—04, chief staff officer, resource mgmt., 2004—05, asst. chief infrastructure planning & policy, 2005—. Sr. chief petty officer USNR, 1985—. Decorated Meritorious Svc. Medal Comdt., Naval Dist. Wash., Joint Svc. Achievement Medal Joint Task Force Armed Forces Inaugural Commitee, Navy Commendation Medal (Gold Star in lieu of Second Award) Chief of Naval Ops., Joint Svc. Commendation Medal (2nd Award) U.S. European Command, Navy Achievement Medal Commdg. Officer, Naval Air Facility Wash. DC, Navy Commendation Medal Chief of Naval Ops.; recipient DSM, Piedmont Va. C.C., 1991-1993. Mem.: VFW, Am. Legion (life). Democrat. Methodist. Avocations: cycling, reading, volunteering. Office Phone: 703-486-6841. Personal E-mail: ralphhensley2003@yahoo.com.

HENSLEY, STEPHEN M., music educator; b. Whittier, Calif., Feb. 18, 1955; s. Maxwell Clement and Berenice Ester Hensley. Mu B in Performance, U. So. Calif., 1977, MusM, 1990. Elem. tchr. gen. music Beverly Hills (Calif.) Unified Sch. Dist., 1978—79; elem. tchr. gen., instrumental and choral music Irvine (Calif.) Unified Sch. Dist., 1979—90; tchr. choral music and theatre La Quinta H.S., Westminster, Calif., 1990—. Named Disney Creative Challange Tchr. of Yr., Westminster Tchr. of Yr., Irene Schoepfle Outstanding Music Tchr. of Orange County. Mem.: Music Educators Nat. Conf., Am. Choral Dir. Assn., Calif. Music Educators Assn. (sec. 1992—93, pres. so. sect. 1991—92). Office: La Quinta High Sch 10372 McFadden Ave Westminster CA 92683

HENSON, C. WARD, mathematician, educator; b. Worcester, Mass., Sept. 25, 1940; s. Charles W. and Daryl May (Hoyt) H.; m. Faith deMena Travis, August 31, 1963; children: Julia Rebecca, Suzanne Amy, Claire Victoria. AB, Harvard U., 1962; PhD, MIT, 1967. Asst. prof. Duke U., Durham, N.C., 1967-74, N.Mex. State U., Las Cruces, 1974-75, U. Ill., Urbana, 1975-77, assoc. prof., 1977-81, prof., 1981—, chmn. dept. math., 1988-92. Vis. assoc. prof. U. Wis., Madison, 1979-80; vis. prof. RWTH Aachen, Fed. Republic Germany, 1985-86, Univ. Tübingen, Fed. Republic Germany, 1992-93. Mem. Assn. for Symbolic Logic (sec.-treas. 1982-2000, pub. 1999—), Am. Math. Soc., London Math. Soc., European Assn. Theoretical Computer Sci. Office: U Ill Dept Math 1409 W Green St Urbana IL 61801-2943 Office Phone: 217-333-2768. E-mail: henson@math.uiuc.edu.

HENSON, DELORES NADINE, music educator; b. Orange, Tex., Mar. 15, 1963; d. Carl K. and Lois I. Howerter; m. James Ronald Henson, July 6, 1991; 1 child, Alexis Miah-Valentina. BA, Calif. State U.-Hayward, 1990. Tchg. credential Calif., 1990. Music tchr. Wash. Unified Sch. Dist., West Sacramento, 1990—. Musician (music arranger): (performance with saxophone trio) Le Trio A Mule. Evangelism chairperson First Christian Ch., Sacramento, 2003. Mem.: Calif. Music Educators Assn.

HENSON, GLENDA MARIA, newspaper writer; b. Marion, N.C., June 17, 1960; d. Douglas Bradley and Glenda June (Crouch) H. BA in English cum laude, Wake Forest U., 1982. Reporter Ark. Dem., Little Rock, 1982-84; bur. reporter Tampa Tribune, Crystal River, Fla., 1984; statehouse reporter Ark. Gazette, Little Rock, 1984-87, bur. chief Washington, 1987-89; editl. writer Lexington (Ky.) Herald-Leader, 1989-94; editl. writer, columnist The Charlotte (N.C.) Observer, 1994-98; dep. editl. page editor Austin (Tex.) American-Statesman, 1998-2001, asst. mng. editor enterprise, 2001—. Lectr. journalism, Indonesia, 2001; juror Nat. Headliner Awards, 2002—04, ASNE Writing Awards, 2001—03; mem. Nieman Selection Com., 2004. Mem. Wake Forest Presdl. Scholarship Com., Ky., 1992, Wake Forest Bd. Visitors, 1995-99; Pulitzer Prize juror, 1994, 95, 99, 2000. Recipient Pulitzer prize, 1992, Walker Stone award Scripps Howard Found., 1992, award Ky. Press Assn., 1992, N.C. Press Assn., 1995, 96, Leadership award Duke U., 1995, Nat. Headliner award, 1996; named Wake Forest Woman of Yr., 1992; Nieman fellow Harvard U., 1993-94; Found. Am. Comm. Econs. fellow, 1997. Mem. Soc. Profl. Journalists (Sigma Delta Chi award 1991, Green Eyeshade award Atlanta chpt. 1992), Nat. Conf. Editorial Writers, Investigative Reporters & Editors Assn., Am. Soc. Newspaper Editors, Omicron Delta Kappa. Avocations: skiing, bicycling, swimming, travel, rafting. Home: 6506 Santolina Cove Austin TX 78731-2806 Office: Austin Am-Statesman 305 S Congress Ave Austin TX 78704-1200 Office Phone: 512-445-3965.

HENSON, HOWARD KIRK, lawyer; b. Chgo., Apr. 28, 1956; s. Howard I. and Constance M. (Evanhoff) H.; m. Annette Whorton, May 3, 1991. BA, Ga. State U., 1979; JD, U. Ga., 1982; postgrad., Harvard U., 1996. Bar: Ga. 1982, U.S. Dist. Ct. (no. dist.) Ga. 1983, U.S. Dist. Ct. (mid. dist.) Ga. 1986. Pvt. practice, Atlanta, 1982-86; of counsel Corlew, Smith & Wright, Atlanta, 1984-86; house counsel Am. States Ins. Co., Atlanta, 1986-88; atty. Amoco Corp., Atlanta, 1988-95; pvt. practice Atlanta, 1995—. Mem. ABA, State Bar Ga., Atlanta Bar Assn., Ga. Trial Lawyers Assn., Am. Trial Lawyers Assn. State & Fed. Litigation. Office: 4615 Lake Forrest Dr NE Atlanta GA 30342-2537 Home: 3713 Concord Way Atlanta GA 30340-2814

HENSON, LOLETIA SOULÉ, retired language educator, translator, consultant; b. Meridian, Miss., Dec. 31, 1940; d. Robert Gara and Loletia Cooper Soulé; widowed; children: John W., Connie A.; m. Robert Lee Walker, Aug. 25, 1989; 1 child, Chelsea Ann Walker. BA, Tulane U., 1963; MA, U. Wis., 1964; postgrad., U. Mich., Ann Arbor, 1973—74. Instr. Spanish Oakland CC, Highland Lakes, Mich., 1965—76; tchr. Spanish, English and French Forrest County Agrl. HS, Bklyn., Miss., 1980—86; fgn. lang. instr. Chipola Coll., Marianna, Fla., 1986—2004. Bd. dirs. So. Conf. on Lang. Tchg. Mem.: Am. Assn. Tchrs. Spanish and Portuguese. Southern Baptist. Avocations: skiing, travel, reading. Home: 5162 Woodgate Way Marianna FL 32446

HENSON, O'DELL WILLIAMS, JR., retired anatomy educator; b. Kansas City, Mo., Jan. 11, 1934; s. O'Dell Williams and Natalie (Smith) H.; m. Miriam Morgan, Aug. 1, 1964; 1 child, Phillip William. BA, U. Kans., 1957, MA, 1960; PhD, Yale U., 1964. From instr. to assoc. prof. dept anatomy Yale U., New Haven, 1964-74; prof. dept cell biology and anatomy U. N.C., Chapel Hill, NC, 1974—2004, ret., 2004. Chmn. Commn. Anatomy, N.C., 1982-2003. Recipient Phi Sigma award 1960, Alexander Von Humbolt award 1982, Cen. Carolina Bank Excellence in Teaching award 1982, NIH-Nat. Inst. Deafness and Other Communicative Disorders Claude Pepper award, 1989. Fellow AAAS. Home: 317 Reade Rd Chapel Hill NC 27516-1509 E-mail: owh@med.unc.edu.

HENSON, PAMELA TAYLOR, secondary education educator; b. Mobile, Ala., Aug. 31, 1958; d. Richard Dowdy and Martha Jo (Hanson) Taylor; m. Thomas Baird Henson III, Mar. 7, 1987; 1 child, Joshua Taylor. BS in Secondary Edn./Biology, U. South Ala., 1983; MS in Secondary Edn./Biology, U. Mobile, 1989, Adminstrv. Cert., 1990; Edn. Specialist Adminstrn., Ala. State U., 1995; postgrad., U. West Fla. Cert. secondary edn. educator. Sci. tchr. Fairhope (Ala.) Middle Sch., 1984-91, Foley (Ala.) H.S., 1991-97; sci. supr., grant writer Baldwin County Schs., 1994—. Christa McAuliffe fellow State Dept. of Edn., 1994, Outstanding Biology tchr. Nat. Assn. Biology Tchrs., 1994, Outstanding Instr. in Environ. Edn., Legacy Found., 1995, Outstanding Sci. Supr. award, 2002, Mobile Bay NEP award, 2002, YWCA Woman of Profl. Achievement award, 2002; recipient Presdl. award NSTA, 1994, Melvin Paul Jones award Tuskegee U., Outstanding Svc. to Edn. award. Mem. NSTA, Nat. Assn. Biology Tchrs., Ala. Sci. Tchrs. Assn., Nat. Marine Educators Assn., Baldwin County Assn. Profl. Educators (pres. 1994—), Alpha Delta Kappa (treas. 1994-96). Republican. Baptist. Avocations: travel, walking, outdoor summer sports. Home: PO Box 1676 810 Juniper Ct Daphne AL 36526-4358

HENSON, PEGGY A., literary agent, consultant; d. Robert and Alice Natalee Anderson; m. Donn Henson, Jan. 27, 1969; children: Daron, Julie Werner. MS, Drake U. Cert. curriculum, instruction, andreading Iowa, 1988. Classroom tchr. Lamoni (Iowa) Cmty. Sch., 1971—99; literacy cons. Green Valley AEA 14, Osceola, Iowa. Founding mem. SAFE Coalition, Lamoni, Iowa; common ground facilitator Independence, Mo. Recipient Tchr. of Yr., Sam's Club, Iowa Tchr. of Yr., NASA Internat. Space Camp, Right Stuff award. Mem.: ASCD (assoc.), Internat. Reading Assn. (assoc.). Office: Green Valley AEA 14 1003 N Main Osceola IA 50213 Office Phone: 1.641.342.2398.

HENSON, RAY DAVID, law educator, consultant; b. Johnston City, Ill., July 24, 1924; s. Ray David and Lucile (Bell) Henson. BS, U. Ill., 1947, JD, 1949. Bar: Ill. 1950, U.S. Supreme Ct. 1960. Assoc. CNA Fin. Corp., Chgo., 1952-70; prof. law Wayne State U., 1970-75, Hastings Sch. Law, U. Calif., San Francisco, 1975—95, prof. emeritus, 1995—. Author: Landmarks of Law, 1960, Secured Transactions, 1973, 2d edit., 1979, Documents of Title, 1983, 2d edit., 1990, The Law of Sales, 1985; editor: The Business Lawyer, 1967-68; contbr. rev. to profl. jours Mem. legal adv. com. N.Y. Stock Exch., 1971-75. Served with USAAC, 1943-46. Mem. Am. Law Inst. (life), ABA (chmn. bus. law sect. 1969-70, adv. bd. jour. 1974-80, chmn. uniform comml. code com.), Ill. Bar Assn. (chmn. corp. banking and bankruptcy law sect. 1963-65, chmn. uniform comml. code com.), Chgo. Bar Assn. (chmn. uniform comml. code com.), Univ. Club (San Francisco). Home: 1400 Geary Blvd San Francisco CA 94109-6561 Office: U Calif Hastings Sch Law 200 Mcallister St San Francisco CA 94102-4707 Office Phone: 415-563-0435.

HENSON, RICHARD NELSON, dean, biologist, educator; b. Asheville, N.C.; s. Nelson Hilliard and Edith Mason Henson; m. Betty Jo Henson, Sept. 3, 1966; children: Angela Lee, Mark Nelson. BSc, Lamar State U., 1963; MSc, Tex. A&M U., 1966, PhD, 1970. Instr. biology Tex. A&M U., Coll. Station, Tex., 1969—70; from asst. prof. biology to prof. Appalachian State U., Boone, NC, 1970—80, prof. biology, 1980—, acting chmn. biology, 1998—99, asst. dean Arts and Scis., 1999—2001, assoc. dean Arts and Scis., 2002—. Advisor grad. students major Appalachian State U., 1970—. Contbr. articles to profl. jours. Mem.: Am. Assn. Higher Edn., Am. Entomological Soc., Am. Arachnological Soc. Democrat. Methodist. Avocation: outdoor activities. Office: College Arts and Sciences ASU 201 IG Greer Hall Boone NC 28608 Office Phone: 828-262-2413.

HENSON, ROBERT FRANK, lawyer; b. Jenny Lind, Ark., Apr. 10, 1925; s. Newton and Nell Edith (Kessinger) H.; m. Jean Peterson Henson, Sept. 14, 1946; children: Robert F., Sandra Henson Curfman, Laura, Thomas, David, Steven. BS, U. Minn., 1948, JD, 1950. Bar: Minn. 1950, U.S. Supreme Ct. 1972. Atty. Soo Line R.R., 1950-52; ptnr. Cant, Haverstock, Beardsley, Gray & Plant, Mpls., 1952-66; sr. ptnr. Henson & Efron, Mpls., 1966-94, of counsel, 1995—; !. Chmn. Minn. Lawyers Profl. Responsibility Bd., 1981-86; co-chmn. Supreme Ct. Study Com. on Lawyer Discipline, 1992-94. Trustee Mpls. Found., 1974-85, Emma Howe Found, 1986-90; chmn. Hennepin County Mental Health and Mental Retardation Bd., 1968-70. Served with USN, 1943-46. Fellow Am. Bar Found.; mem. ABA, Hennepin County Bar Assn. (pres. 1968-69), Minn. Bar Assn., Order of Coif. Unitarian Universalist. Office: 220 S Sixth St Ste 1800 Minneapolis MN 55402-4503 Office Phone: 612-339-2500. Personal E-mail: rhenson@mn.rr.com. Business E-Mail: rhenson@hensonefron.com.

HENTGES, DAVID JOHN, microbiology educator; b. LeMars, Iowa, Sept. 18, 1928; s. Romaine Francis and Geneva Mae (Kruger) H.; m. Kathleen Edwina Mullan, Dec. 28, 1957; children: Stephen Edward, Kathleen Marie, Margaret Ann. BS, U. Notre Dame, 1953; MS, Loyola U., Chgo., 1958, PhD, 1961. Asst. prof. Creighton U. Sch. Medicine, Omaha, 1964-67, assoc. prof., 1967-68, U. of Mo. Sch. of Medicine, Columbia, 1968-72, prof., 1972-81, interim chmn., 1976-79; prof., chmn. Tex. Tech. U. Sch. Medicine, Lubbock, 1981-96, vice provost for rsch., dean grad. sch. biomed. scis., 1996-98, assoc. dean basic scis., 1996-98, dean emeritus, 1998—. Editor: Human Intestinal Microflora, 1983, Medical Microbiology, 1986, Microbiology and Immunology, 2d edit., 1995; regional editor Microbial Ecology in Health and Disease, 1987-96; mem. editl. bd. Infection and Immunity, 1983-92, Anaerobe, 1998-2004; contbr. chpts. to books and articles to profl. jours. Lay gen. chmn. Diocesan Cath. Appeal, Lubbock, 1989, 1997; co-exec. dir. Cath. Found. Diocese of Lubbock, 1998—2002. Decorated knight grand cross Order of the Holy Sepulchre, knight of merit with star Constantinian Order of St. George. Fellow Am. Acad. Microbiology (emeritus); mem. Cath. Acad. Scis., Soc. for Microbial Ecology and Disease (pres. 1987-89), Rotary Club, Sigma Xi. Roman Catholic. Avocations: gardening, fly fishing. Home: 4601 88th St Lubbock TX 79424-4107

HENTIC, YVES FRANK MAO, investment banker, industrial engineer; b. Paris, Dec. 7, 1946; came to U.S., 1947; s. Pierre Yves and Alberta Dorothy (Smith) H.; m. Donna May Woods, Aug. 3, 1981 (div. Dec. 1990); 1 child, Frank Hilton Wadsworth Hentic; m. Pandora Duke Biddle, Jan. 19, 1991; 1 child, Katherine Yvette Biddle Hentic. AB in Econs., Georgetown U., 1970; AS in Engring., Fashion Inst. Tech., N.Y.C., 1972; MBA, Harvard U., 1975. Plant engr. Lynn Lee Fabrics, N.Y.C., 1972-73; cons. Emanuel Weintraub Assocs., N.Y.C., 1974; securities analyst Wertheim & Co., N.Y.C., 1975-77; arbitrage analyst Colin Hochstin & Co., N.Y.C., 1977-78; rsch. ptnr. Bodkin, DePaolis, Hentic, Satloff & Co., N.Y.C., 1978-80; mng. ptnr. Y.H. Assocs., N.Y.C., 1980-95; pres. Yves Hentic & Co., Jersey City, 1983-86, Merger, Inc., Reno, 1987-95, Send It In, Mex., 1993-95, Archimedes Mgmt. Inc., 1995-97, OX Pasture Devel., Inc., Southampton, 1997—. Pres. 18 pub. cos. for Merger Inc., Reno, 1987-92; mem. N.Y. Stock Exch., 1983-86. Mem. Southampton (N.Y.) Assn., 1992—. Mem. St. Nicholas Soc. (treas. 1990-95), Soc. Colonial Wars N.Y. (3d v.p. 1992-94), U.S. Croquet Assn., Kane Lodge, Colonial Order of the Acorn, Sons of the Revolution N.Y. Avocations: fishing, croquet, scuba diving, cave exploring. E-mail: yves@hamptons.com.

HENZE, WILLIAM F., II, lawyer; b. Cleve., Apr. 20, 1949; m. Nancy A. Harmel, Oct. 3, 1980. BA, Ohio Wesleyan U., 1971; JD, U. Ariz., 1974; LLM, NYU, 1976. Bar: Ariz. 1974, N.Y. 1977, Tex. 1984. Ptnr. Jones Day, N.Y.C. Instr. in law NYU, 1974-76. Trustee Phoenix Country Day Sch., 1997—. Mem. Phi Beta Kappa. Office: Jones Day 222 E 41st St New York NY 10017-6702

HENZLIK, RAYMOND EUGENE, zoophysiologist, educator; b. Casper, Wyo., Dec. 26, 1926; s. William H. Henzlik and Adeline Adele (Brown) Wolff; m. Wilma Louise Bartels, Oct. 1, 1950; children: Randall Eugene, Nancy Jo. BS, U. Nebr., 1948, MS, 1952, PhD, 1960; postgrad., Cornell U., 1961-62. Tchr. biology and chemistry York (Nebr.) High Sch., 1948-50; sci. edn. supr. Tchrs. Coll., U. Nebr., Lincoln, 1951-53; tchr. biology Omaha North High Sch., 1953-56; instr. biology Nebr. Wesleyan U., Lincoln, 1957-59; asst. prof. zoology and biology U. Nebr., Lincoln, 1959-61; asst. prof. biology Ball State U., Muncie, Ind., 1962-67, assoc. prof. physiology, 1967-69, prof. physiology, 1970—. Adj. vis. prof. vet. physiology Tex. A&M U., College Station, 1984-85; anatomy cons. Nat. Prescription Footwear Applicators Assn., Muncie, 1962—; lectr. Pedorthics Tech. Program, Muncie, 1977—; cons. ednl. affairs Argonne (Ill.) Nat. Lab., 1970-76; dir. ednl. program Am. Diabetes Assn., Muncie, 1979-83; vis. prof. health sci. USAF European Ctr., Ramstein and Rhein Main, Germany, 1977-78; lectr. Ind. Health Care Assn., 1985-91. Author: Human Physiology Lab Manual, 1976-92; contbr. articles to profl. jours. Pres. Muncie Tech. Soc., 1975—80; mem. bd. Am. Diabetes Assn. Delaware County, Muncie, 1979—85. Radiation biology fellow NSF/AEC, U. Mich., 1960, Radiobiology fellow AEC/NSF, Cornell U., 1961-62, Radiation Biology Rsch. fellow U.S. Radiobiology Lab N.C. State U., 1965, P.R. Nuclear Ctr., 1967. Mem. AAAS, Nutrition Today Soc., Ind. Acad. Sci., Muncie Tech. Soc., Mensa, Sigma Xi, Phi Delta Kappa. Avocations: renting houses, reading, book collecting. Home: 5009 N Somerset Dr Muncie IN 47304-6501 Office Phone: 765-285-5961.

HEO, YOUNG-WOO, research scientist, educator; b. Taegu, Korea, July 18, 1968; s. IL-Rang Heo and Jeong-Ja Lee; m. Sookyung Lee; children: Donghyun, Hannah. BE in Inorganic Materials Engring., Kyungpook Nat. U., Taegu, 1994, ME in Inorganic Materials Engring., 1996; PhD in Materials Sci. Engring., U. Fla., 2003, post doctorate, 2004. Rschr. LG Chem. Ltd./Rsch. Pk., Daejon, Republic of Korea, 1996—2000. Author more than 50 articles to profl. jours. such as Applied Physics Letters. Mem. of voluntary svc. club for rehab. facility Doldari, Taegu, Korea (South), 1987—95. Mem.: Am. Ceramic Soc., Am. Vacuum Soc., Electrochem. Soc., Alpha Sigma Mu. Achievements include development of Phosphors for PDP display. Home: Jisan-dong 436 Daegu 706-839 Republic of Korea Office: Kyungpook Nat U Dept Inorganic Materials Engring Daegu 702-701 Republic of Korea Office Phone: 82-53-950-7587. Personal E-mail: ywheo@hanmail.net. Business E-Mail: ywheo@knu.ac.kr.

HEPFORD, JOHN P., music educator; b. Topeka, Kans., Mar. 14, 1974; s. Charles and Marie Hepford; m. Stefani Hepford, Dec. 18, 1999. B Music Edn., U. Kans., 1998. Band and choir dir. Pleasant Ridge H.S. and Jr. High, Easton, Kans., 1998—2002; band dir. Chisholm Trail Jr. High, Olathe, Kans., 2002—. Music min. Lawrence (Kans.) Life Fellowship, 2000—; percussionist Kansas City (Kans.) Wind Symphony, 2003—, Johnson County Wind Symphony, Overland Park, Kans., 2003—; performer Am. Musical Salutes, 2005. Mem.: N.E. Kans. Music Educator's Assn. (assoc.; asst. jr. high band chmn. 2004). Avocations: road cycling, tennis. Office: 16700 W 159th St Olathe KS 66062 Office Phone: 913-780-7240. Personal E-mail: jhepfordcst@olatheschools.com.

HEPLER, LOWELL EUGENE, music educator, musician; b. Sligo, Pa., Dec. 23, 1950; s. John Lynn and Carla Jane Hepler; m. Julie Elizabeth Morton, July 27, 2003; children from previous marriage: David Loren, Laura Leigh. BMusEd, Clarion U. Pa., 1972; MFA, Carnegie Mellon U., Pitts., 1974; PhD, Case Western Reserve U., Cleve., 1986. Cert. tchr. Commonwealth of Pa. Prof. music and dir. bands Allegheny Coll., Meadville, Pa., 1974—; prin. tuba Erie Philharmonic Orch., 1982—, Sulkowski & Savelli Concert Band, 1983—, Lake Erie Ballet Orch., 1985—. Guest condr. music festivals Pa. Music Educators Assn., 1982—, guest adjudicator festivals, 1985—, condr. all state band, 1998; mem. orch. com. Erie Philharmonic Orch., 2004—; adjudicator and clinician Festivals at Sea, Fla., 2005; orchestral and solo tuba Erie Chamber Orch.; piano soloist Allegheny Summer Music Festival, Allegheny Coll. Band Camp Adult Musicians; leader European study tours Allegheny Coll. Ctr. Experiential Learning. Recipient Pub. Partners in Edn. award, Crawford Ctrl. Sch. Dist., 1988, citation of Excellence, Pa. Music Educators Assn., 1995. Mem.: Coll. Band Dir. Nat. Assn. (Pa. state chair 1988—93), Rotary (pres. Meadville chpt. 2005—), Phi Beta Mu (pres. 2005—). Avocations: reading, travel, chamber music. Home: 944 Limber Rd Meadville PA 16335 Office: Allegheny Coll Dept Music Box 31 Meadville PA 16335

HEPLER, MERLIN JUDSON, JR., real estate broker; b. Hot Springs, Va., May 13, 1929; s. Merlin Judson and Margaret Belle (Vines) H.; m. Lanova Helen Roberts, July 25, 1952; children: Nancy Andora, Douglas Stanley. BS in Bus., U. Idaho, 1977; grad., Realtors Inst., 1979. Cert. residential specialist. Enlisted USAF, 1947, advanced through grades to sgt., 1960, ret., 1967; service mgr. Lanier Bus. Products, Gulfport, Miss., 1967-74; sales assoc. Century 21 Singler and Assn., Troy, Idaho, 1977-79; broker B&M Realty, Troy, 1979—. Mem. Nat. Assn. Realtors, Am. Legion, U. Idaho Alumni Assn., Air Force Sgts. Assn. Lodges: Lions. Republican. Avocations: hunting, fishing. Home: 1081 Driscoll Ridge Rd Troy ID 83871-9605 Office: B&M Realty W 102 A St PO Box 187 Troy ID 83871-0187 E-mail: mhepler@idaho.tds.net.

HEPNER, JON R., investment company executive; b. Freeport, Ill., June 10, 1942; s. John and Sara Jane Hepner; m. Gail K. Hepner; children: Lisa L., E. Elizabeth. BBS in Bus. Adminstrn., Northwestern U., 1964. V.p. La Salle Nat. Bank, Chgo., 1965—75, Hibernia Bank, New Orleans, 1975—77, Corpus Christi (Tex.) Bank and Trust, 1977—81; investment cons. Merrill Lynch, 1981—86; sr. v.p. investment A.G. Edwards & Sons, Corpus Christi, 1986—. Dir. Karen Henry Found., 1996—2000, Padre Isles Property Owners Assn., Corpus Christi, 1998—; trustee Corpus Christi Fire Fighters Pension Fund, 2001—. Mem.: Corpus Christi Execs. Assn. (pres. 1991), Corpus Christi Rotary Club (treas. 1987). Office: A G Edwards and Sons 409 S Carancahua Corpus Christi TX 78401 Office Phone: 361-882-1600.

HEPP, DAVID WORTHINGTON, draftsman; b. Thousand Oaks, Calif., Sept. 29, 1973; s. William and Nancy Hepp; 1 child, Brandon. A, Fresno City Coll., 1995. Cert. archtl., mech design, MTI Coll., Calif., 2001. Computer aided drafter BFL Owen and Assocs., Irvine, Calif., 2001—03, Vulcraft Inc., Santa Ana, 2003—04, Wright Engineers, Irvine, 2004—. Author: (poetry) The Bard's Tale of Darkness (Editor's choice award, 2001), Valor Of Battle (Editor's choice award, 2002), Tell About The Time (One of 2003's Best Poets award, 2003), Whisper in the Wind (Editor's Choice award, 2004). Home: 350 St Vincent Irvine CA 92618 Personal E-mail: fantasywriterdh@hotmail.com.

HEPP, JOHN HENRY, IV, historian, lawyer; b. West Chester, Pa., Oct. 21, 1959; s. John Henry Hepp, III and Rose Hunt Hepp; m. Julie Kay Benigni, Dec. 29, 1984; 1 child, John Henry V. BA, Temple U., 1982; JD, U. of Pa., 1986; PhD in History, U. of NC, 1997. Bar: Pa. 1986. Atty. Dechert Price and Rhoads, Phila., 1986—91; lectr. U. of NC, Chapel Hill, NC, 1998—99; asst. prof. Wilkes U., Wilkes-Barre, Pa., 1999—2005, assoc. prof., 2005—. Author: The Middle-Class City: Transforming Space and Time in Philadelphia, 1876-1926, 2003. Mem.: Soc. for Historians of the Gilded Age and Prog. Era (mem. H-SHGAPE editl. bd. 1997—2000), Orgn. of Am. Historians, Am. Studies Assn., Am. Hist. Assn., Athenaeum of Phila., Order of the Coif. Home: 437 Rutter Avenue Kingston PA 18704 Office: Wilkes U Dept History Wilkes Barre PA 18766 Office Phone: 570-408-4225. E-mail: heppj@wilkes.edu.

HEPPA, DOUGLAS VAN, computer specialist; b. Bklyn., May 26, 1945; s. Joseph Charles and Antoinette Palmer (Vanasco) H.; m. Barbara Zanlunghi. BS in Social Sci., Poly. Inst. N.Y., 1968, BS in Math., 1971, MS Insl. & Applied Math., 1973, postgrad., 1983—. Assoc. engr. Raytheon Co., Portsmouth, R.I., 1968-70; systems engr. PRD Electronics, Syosset, N.Y., 1970-71; mathematician USN, New London, Conn., 1971; asst. computer engr. George Sharp, N.Y.C., 1972-73; programmer N.Y.C. Dept. Social Svcs., 1975; quantitative analyst N.Y.C. Fire Dept., 1976-80, assoc. staff analyst, 1980-81, computer specialist, 1991—99; with Algorithm Devel. Co., Maspeth, NY, 1999—. Pres. Algorithim Devel. Co., Queens, NY, 1985—. Mem. Math. Assn. Am., Am. Mgmt. Assn., Soc. for Indsl. & Applied Math., Assn. for Computing Machinery, IEEE, Am. Math. Soc. Avocations: fishing, swimming, boating, amateur radio, astronomy. Home: 64-08 60 th Rd Maspeth NY 11378 Office: Algorithm Devel Co 64-08 60th Rd Maspeth NY 11378-3433

HEPPER, CAROL, artist, educator; b. McLaughlin, SD, Oct. 23, 1953; d. Adolph and Lavern Hepper. BS, S.D. State U., 1975. Instr. drawing Standing Rock C.C., Ft. Yates, N.D., 1980-82, Sch. Visual Arts, N.Y.C., 1984. Vis. lectr. RISD, Providence, 1986-88, Md. Art Inst., Balt., 1988, SUNY, Purchase, 1989, U. Mass., Amherst, 1989, Princeton (NJ), 1989, 2005, U., Williams Coll., Williamstown, Mass., 1992, U. Colo. Boulder, 1990, Brandeis U., Waltham, Mass., 1992, Cranbrookl Acad. Art, Birmingham, Ala., 1992, Worcester Art Mus., Mass., 1992, Portland (Oreg.) State U., 1993, Harvard U., 1999. One-woman shows include Inst. for Art and Urban Resources, Queens, NY, 1982, Hill Gallery, Birmingham, Mich., 1988, 92-93, 96, Rosa Esman Gallery, NYC, 1988-89, 91, Worcester (Mass.) Art Mus., 1992, Miss. Mus. Art, Jackson, 1995, Orlando (Fla.) Art Mus., 1995, Portland Inst. for Contemporary Art, 1996, Hopkins Ctr. Dartmouth Coll., Hanover, NH, 2000, Md. Inst. Coll. Art, Balt., 2002, Burapha U., Chonburi, Thailand, 2003, others; exhibited in group shows at Contemporary Art Ctr., Cin., 1987, Sculpture Ctr., NYC, 1987, Art Gallery Western Australia, 1986, Art Gallery New South Wales, Sidney, 1986, Guggenheim Mus., 1987, Aldrich Mus. Art, 1988, Walker Art Ctr., Mpls., 1989, Phillips Collection, Washington, 1992, Portland Art Mus., 1993, Decordova Mus., and Sculpture Park, Lincoln, Mass., 1993-94, Laumeier Sculpture Park, St. Louis, 1995—, White House Sculpture Garden, Washington, 1995, Neuberger Mus. Art, Purchase, NY, 1997; represented in permanent collections Walker Art Ctr., Minn., Guggenheim Mus., NYC, Mus. Contemporary Art, Chgo., SD Meml. Art Ctr., New Sch. Social Rsch., NYC, Met. Mus., NYC, NY Pub. Libr., Hood Mus., Hanover, N.H., Detroit Inst. Arts, New Sch. for Social Rsch., NYC, ND Mus. Art, Grand Forks, Newark Mus., Portland Art Mus., Detroit Inst. Arts, Orlando (Fla.) Art Mus., NY Pub. Libr., Am. Telephone and Telegraph, NY, Phoenix Art Mus., NYC, Champion Paper, Stanford Conn., Aterrana Found., Vaduz, Leichtenstein, Mus. Modern Art, NY Betty Brazil meml. sculpture grantee, 1981, Louis Comfort Tiffany Found. sculpture grantee, 1984, Pollock-Krasner Found. sculpture grantee, 1986, N.Y. Found. for Arts sculpture grantee, 1989, Nat. Endowment for Arts grantee, 1990. Office Phone: 212-619-8108. E-mail: carolhepper@yahoo.com.

HEPPNER, DONALD GRAY, JR., immunology research physician, army officer; b. Lynchburg, Va., Jan. 17, 1956; s. Donald Gray Sr. and Nathalie (Ward) H.; m. Mary Virginia Leach, June 12, 1983; children: Charlotte Nathalie, Virginia Dearing, William Lynch. BA in Biochemistry/German Lit., U. Va., 1978, MD, 1983. Diplomate Am. Bd. Internal Medicine, Am. Bd. Infectious Diseases. Commd. capt. U.S. Army, 1987, advanced through grades to col., 2002; intern in internal medicine U. Minn. Hosps. and Clinics, Mpls., 1983-84, resident in internal medicine, 1984-86; rsch. assoc. Dight Lab., U. Minn., Mpls., 1987; with emergency medicine dept. Abbot North Western Hosp., Mpls., 1986-88; fellow infectious diseases U. Md., Balt., 1988-90; infectious disease officer Dept. Immunology, Walter Reed Army Inst. of Rsch., Washington, 1990-93; asst. chief dept. immunology Armed Forces Rsch. Inst. Med. Scis., 1993-94, chief dept. immunology and medicine Bangkok, 1994-97; overseas malaria vaccine trial coord. dept. immunology Walter Reed Army Inst. Rsch., Forest Glen, Md., 1997-99, chief dept. immunology, 1999—; dir. U.S. Army Malaria Vaccine Program, 2001—. Attending physician Walter Reed Army Med. Ctr., Washington, 1991-93, 2003—; advisor NRC, 1995-97; mem. Fed. Malaria Vaccine Steering Com. Contbr. more than 50 articles to profl. jours. Mem. Com. on Fgn. Rels., Charlottesville, Va., 1983—. Fellow ACP; mem. Am. Soc. Tropical Medicine and Hygiene, Multilateral Initiative n Malaria, Armed Forces Infectious Disease Soc. Achievements include development and testing of human malaria vaccines for military and public health indications. Office: Walter Reed Army Inst Rsch Dept Immunology 503 Robert Grant Ave Silver Spring MD 20910 Office Phone: 301-319-9414. E-mail: donald.heppner@na.amedd.army.mil.

HEPTINSTALL, ROBERT HODGSON, physician; b. Keswick, Eng., July 22, 1920; s. James A. and Mabel (Sanders) H.; m. Ann Enraght Porter, Jan. 25, 1950; children: Bridget, Gillian, Jonathan, James, Caroline, Christopher. MB, BS, London U., 1944, MD, 1948. Intern, house surgeon Charing Cross Hosp., London, 1944; jr. lectr. pathology St. Mary's Hosp., London, 1947-50, sr. lectr. pathology, 1950-60; vis. prof. pathology Washington U., St. Louis, 1960-62; assoc. prof. pathology Johns Hopkins Med. Sch., Balt., 1962-67, prof. pathology, 1967-69, 88—, Baxley prof. pathology, dir. dept., 1969-88; pathologist in chief Johns Hopkins Hosp., 1969-88; disting. svc. prof. pathology, 1992—. Pathology study sect. NIH, 1963-67, pathology tng. com., 1967-71; sci. adv. bd. Nat. Kidney Found., 1969-73. Author: Pathology of the Kidney, 1966, 5th edit., 1998; editor Lab. Invest, 1976-81; mem. editl. bd. Kidney Internat., Lab Investigation. With M.C., Royal Army, 1944-47. Recipient gold medal Danish Surg. Soc., 1984, David M. Hume Meml. award Nat. Kidney Found., 1986. Mem.: Renal Pathology Soc. (pres. 1980—83), Internat. Soc. Nephrology (v.p. 1981—84, Jean Hamburger award 1999), Am. Soc. Nephrology (pres. 1972—73, John P. Peters award 1993), Internat. Acad. Pathology (Maude Abbott lectr. 1983, Disting. Pathologist award 2002), Danish Soc. Nephrology (hon.), Alpha Omega Alpha.

HEPWORTH, JOHN LEONARD, chemist, researcher; b. Salt Lake City, Nov. 2, 1927; s. Peter Leonard and Flora Victoria (Burningham) H.; m. Caryl Peterson, Mar. 19, 1951; children: Dale, Diana, Vicki, Joseph, James, John T. BS, U. Utah, 1952; MS, U. Idaho, 1958. Chemist GE Co., Richland, Wash., 1953-57, Am. Potash and Chem. Corp., Henderson, Nev., 1957-58; sr. chemist Thiokol Corp., Brigham City, Utah, 1958-90, supr. propellant devel. sect., 1960, sr. scientist, 1967, dept. mgr. asst., 1970. Instr. propellant chemistry Utah State U., Logan, 1962; cons. Battelle Inst., Hanford, Wash., 1965-68, McGraw-Hill, Inc., 1968-90; vol. substitute tchr. math., chemistry, physics, religion Box Elder H.S., Brigham City, Utah, 1998—; vol. tchr. for young adults with spl. needs, 1999—. Author: A Review of Hydrazinium Diperchlorate, 1967; contbr. articles to profl. publs. Missionary LDS Ch., 1948-50, 90-93; instr. Early Morning Seminary, 1954-57; officer PTA, 1960-62; coach Little League Sports, 1964-75; H.S. athletic official, 1972-92. With USN, 1946-48. Republican. Achievements include patents for development of separation process of Uranium and Plutonium from fission products, separation of radioactive Cesium from fission products, development of first stage propellant for Minuteman, C-4 and C-5 Trident, and Peacekeeper missiles, supervision of space shuttle development, development of delayed quick-cure catalyst employed in all three stages of Trident missiles; effect of di-n-butyl phosphate on the partition of zirconum between aqueous solutions and 2.2.4. trimethylpentane. Home: 560 Holiday Dr Brigham City UT 84302-2387 Personal E-mail: jhepworth@besstek.net.

HERA, sculptor; b. New Orleans, Sept. 28, 1940; d. Maury Mason Calvert and Mary Eleanor Rodenhauser; m. Richard John Voelker, Jr., Aug. 27, 1960 (div. Aug. 21, 1972); children: Richard John Voelker III, Jordan Calvert Voelker, Kurt Manfred Voelker. BA, U. Dallas, 1970; MFA, So. Meth. U., Dallas, 1973. Procession designer First Night, Boston, 1978; vis. lectr. Harvard U., Cambridge, Mass., 1983; vis. artist Gerrit Rietveld Acad., Amsterdam, 1985; instr. Cooper Union, N.Y.C., 1991—92; guest lectr. SUNY, New Paltz, 1996; pub. and environ. sculptor Georgetown, Mass., 1973—79, N.Y.C., 1979—96. Artist in residence Bear Mountain (N.Y.) State Pk., 1981; guest critic Parsons Sch. Design, N.Y.C., 1982; cons. Townscape Inst., Cambridge, Mass., 1982—83, Wonder Woman Cons., Bearsville, NY, 1998—. Represented in permanent collections Niagara-Knossos-Carranza Connector, Vaulted Arbor, Spirit House, Singing Rock Sitting Place, Orbital Connector (Unity Day citation Borough Pres. Manhattan, 87), Tower as Inland Lighthouse. Vol. Guildette Woodstock (NY) Guild, 1997—; firefighter Woodstock Fire Co. #2, 1999—; active Woodstock Commn. Civic Design, 1999—. Recipient Unity Day Citation for Orbital Connector award, Borough Pres. of Manhattan, David Dinkins, 1987; grantee, NEA, 1975—76, Fla. Fine Arts Coun., 1975—76, Mass. Coun. on Arts and Humanities, 1979, NEA and Contemporary Arts Ctr. New Orleans, 1980, Glickenhaus Found., Money for Women Fund, Com. for Visual Arts, 1981, Com. for Visual Arts, 1983, N.Y.C. Dept. Cultural Affairs, 1983, N.Y. State Coun. on Arts, 1983, N.Y.C. Dept. Culural Affairs, 1987, Thanks Be To Grandmother Winifred Found., 1995, Artist in Residence at Bear Mountain State Pk., Am. the Beautiful Fund. Mem.: Woodstock Guild of Craftsmen (Guildette 1986—), Kingston Sailing Club (com. chair 2000—), Mohonk Singles Hiking Club (hike leader 1996—). Democrat-Npl. Mem. Soc. Of Friends. Avocations: sailing, hiking, cross country skiing. Home: 145 Coldbrook Rd Bearsville NY 12409 Office: 145 Coldbrook Rd Bearsville NY 12409 Office Phone: 845-679-4439. Home Fax: 845-679-4441. Personal E-mail: hera@netstep.net.

HERALD, CHERRY LOU, medical researcher, educator; b. Beeville, Tex., 1940; m. Delbert Leon Herald, Jr., July 31, 1964; children: Heather Amanda, Delbert Leon, III. BS, Ariz. State U., 1962, MS, 1965, PhD, 1968. Faculty rsch. assoc. Cancer Rsch. Inst. Ariz. State U., Tempe, 1973-74, sr. rsch. chemist, 1974-77, asst. to dir. and sr. rsch. chemist, 1977-83, asst. dir., assoc. rsch. prof., 1984-88, assoc. dir., rsch. prof., 1988—. Co-author: Biosynthetic Products for Cancer Chemotherapy, vols. 4, 5, & 6, 1984, 85, 87, Anticancer Drugs from Animals, Plants & Microorganisms, 1994; contbr. articles to sci. jours. Mem. Am. Soc. Pharmacognosy, Am. Chem. Soc. Office: Ariz State U Cancer Rsch Inst Tempe AZ 85287-2404 Business E-Mail: cherald@asu.edu.

HERALD, GEORGE WILLIAM, news correspondent; b. Berlin, Jan. 3, 1911; arrived in U.S., 1941; s. Bruno H. and Paula J. (Levy) Herald; m. Martha A. Dubois, Mar. 24, 1948; children: Steve Andrew, Patricia Claudia. LLD cum laude, Basle (Switzerland) U., 1934; postgrad., Columbia U., 1950-52. Staff corr. INS, N.Y.C., London, Paris, 1945-46, bur. chief Berlin and Vienna, 1946—49; spl. writer United Features, N.Y.C., 1949-52; assoc. editor UN World mag., N.Y.C. and Europe, 1952-55; head bur. Vision, Inc., Paris, 1955—. Author: My Favorite Assassin, 1943, The Big Wheel, 1963; author: (with others) Off the Record, 1952, Tatiana, 1955; author: (with Soraya Esfandiary) My Life as an Empress, 1962; contbg. editor: Am. Peoples Ency., 1952—62; contbr. articles to mags. including Reader's Digest, Harper's, McCall's. Capt. U.S. Army, 1942—45. Recipient Best Spl. Reporting from Abroad award, Mex. Press, 1989. Mem.: Anglo-Am. Press Club, Overseas Press Club Am., Internat. Arts Coun., Authors League Am. Office: Vision Inc Vision Bldg 310 Madison Ave Rm 1412 New York NY 10017-6006 E-mail: geoherald@noos.fr.

HERALD, J. PATRICK, lawyer; b. Latrobe, Pa., Sept. 27, 1947; s. John P. and Doris Faye (Galvin) H.; m. Bridget Grace Tobin, Aug. 17, 1973; children: Brian Michael, Matthew Patrick, Molly Bridget, John Francis. AB in History, John Carroll U., 1969; JD, U. Notre Dame, 1972. Bar: Ill. 1972, U.S. Dist. Ct. (no. dist.) Ill. 1972, U.S. Ct. Appeals (7th cir.) 1975, U.S. Supreme Ct. 1978. Assoc. Baker & McKenzie, Chgo., 1972-79, ptnr., 1979—. Fellow Am. Coll. Trial Lawyers, Internat. Acad. Trial Lawyers; mem. ABA, Ill. Bar Assn., Chgo. Bar Assn., 7th Cir. Bar Assn., Soc. Trial Lawyers (bd. dirs. 1987-89), Internat. Assn. Def. Counsel, Chgo. Trial Lawyers Club (pres. 1982-83). Roman Catholic. Home: 1721 N Normandy Ave Chicago IL 60707-3925 Office: Baker & McKenzie 1 Prudential Plz 130 E Randolph St Fl 3500 Chicago IL 60601-6213 Office Phone: 312-861-2830. Business E-Mail: j.patrick.herald@bakernet.com.

HERBEL, LEROY ALEC, JR., telecommunications engineer; b. Ft. Carson, Colo., July 24, 1954; s. LeRoy Alec and Mabel Bertha (Huffman) H. BS, S.W. Mo. State U., 1976; MEd, Ga. So. U., 1978; MS in Telecom., Golden Gate U., 1987, MBA, 1990. Asst. mgr. toy dept. Dillard's Dept. Store, Springfield, Mo., 1971-76; material contr. GTE of the South, Durham, NC, 1979-80; asst. prof. mil. sci. Army ROTC, U. NH, Durham, 1982-85; tech. instr., course developer No. Telecom Inc., Raleigh, NC, 1988-91, sr. engr., 1991-93; field engr. mgr. We. Wireless Corp., Bellevue, Wash., 1994-95; switch supr. Palmer Wireless (CellularOne), Ft. Myers, Fla., 1995-96; sr. network analyst Sprint PCS, Lenexa, Kans., 1996-97; instrl. sys. specialist Dept. Def., Fort Gordon, Ga., 1997—2004, Army Tng. Support Ctr., For Eustis, Va., 2004—. Adj. prof. DeKalb (Ga.) C.C., 1978—79, NC Wesleyan Coll., Rocky Mount, 1991. Dist. commr. Kiokee dist Ga. Carolina Coun., Augusta, Ga., 2000—, asst. coun. commr., 2004—; scoutmaster troop 213 Boy Scouts Am., Cary, NC, 1990—93, asst. dist. commr. Dan Beard dist., 1992—96, mem. merit badge staff Nat. Jamboree, 1993, 2001, mem. troop 213 com., 1993—. Capt. U.S. Army, 1980—88, maj. USAR, 1988—. Recipient Scoutmaster award of merit Boy Scouts Am., 1991, Disting. Leadership citation Boy Scouts Am., 1991, Scoutmaster Key award Boy Scouts Am., 1992, Dist. Order of Merit Boy Scouts Am., 1994, Boy Scout Commr. Key award, 1995, Disting. Commr. Svc. award, 2002. Mem. Tel. Pioneers Am., Phi Delta Kappa. Avocations: golf, running, trains, camping, music.

HERBER, STEVEN CARLTON, physician; b. LA, Aug. 25, 1960; s. Raymond and Marilyn Joyce (Dart) H.; m. Katherine Carol Jones, Apr. 23, 1989. BS, Pacific Union Coll., 1982; Dr.med., Loma Linda U., 1986. Diplomate Nat. Bd. Med. Examiners, Am. Bd. Plastic Surgery. Resident surgeon Med. Ctr. Loma Linda (Calif.) U., 1986-90; resident plastic surgery Yale U., New Haven, Conn., 1990-92; asst. prof. surgery Loma Linda (Calif.) U., 1993-98; med. dir. Ctr. for Plastic Surgery at St. Helena Hosp., 1998—. Bd. dirs. St. Helena Hosp., Adventist Health. Contbr. articles to profl. jours. NIH grantee, 1988, MacPherson Soc. Clin. Sci. fellow, 1992; recipient Leadership award, AMA, 1991, 98. Fellow ACS; mem. Am. Soc. Plastic Surgeons (bd. dirs.), Am. Cleft Palate, Craniofacial Assn., Calif. Med. Assn., Napa County Med. Soc., Yale Plastic Surgery Soc. Republican. Adventist. Avocations: travel, collections of watches, books. Office: 1030 Main St Ste 206 Saint Helena CA 94574-2056 Office Phone: 707-968-0800. E-mail: sch@napanet.net.

HERBERGER, DOUGLAS J., automotive executive; B in Fin., St. Bonaventure U.; MBA, Mich. State. U. With GM Corp., Lockport, NY, 1973—, various analyst pos. Detroit, 1976, fin. analyst, 1980—83, dir. cost analysis, 1983, dir. treasurer's office, 1984, asst. div. comptroller, 1985, dir. bus. ops., 1986; exec. asst. to group exec.-in-charge component ops. GM Automotive Component Group, 1988; gen. dir. costing measuring systems GM Corp., 1988; div. comptroller GM Ctrl. Foundry Div., 1990; gen. dir. fin. GM Svc. Parts. Ops., 1992; gen dir. GM ACDelco Aftermarket, 1996; pres. GM Japan, Japan, 1997; reg. gen. mgr. GM North Am., 1998—.

HERBERMAN, RONALD BRUCE, medical association administrator, immunologist; b. Bklyn., Feb. 26, 1940; married, 1963; children: Steve, Holly. BA, NYU, 1960, MD, 1964; MD (hon.), U. Rome, 1986. Intern, asst. resident medicine Mass. Gen. Hosp., 1964-66; clin. assoc. immunologist USPHS, 1966-68; sr. investigator immunology br. Nat. Cancer Inst. NIH, Bethesda, Md., 1968-71, head cellular and tumor immunology sect. Lab. Cell Biology, 1971-74, chief Lab. Immunodiag., 1975-81, chief biol. therapeutic br., 1981-85; dir. U. Pitts. Cancer Inst., 1985—; prof. medicine and pathology Sch. Medicine U. Pitts., 1985—. Acting assoc. dir. biol. response program Nat. Cancer Inst., NIH, 1981-85, dir. immunodiag. contract program, 1972-76; mem. FDA rev. panel diagnostic tests, 1979-83; mem. AIDS clin. drug devel. com. Nat. Inst. Allergy and Infectious Disease, 1986—. Sect. editor: Jour. Immunology, 1974-77; assoc. editor Cancer Rsch., 1975-80, Clin. Immunology and Immunopathology, 1978-85, Jour. Immunol. Methods and Clin. Immunol. Therapy, 1980-90, Jour. Clin. Immunology, 1981—, Jour. Nat. Cancer Inst., 1972-80. Fellow Am. Acad. Microbiology, Clin. Immunol. Soc., Soc. Biol. Therapy (pres. 1996-98), Am. Soc. Clin. Oncology; mem. Soc. Leukocyte Biology (pres. 1984), Am. Soc. Clin. Investigation, Am. Assn. Immunologists, Am. Assn. Cancer Rsch., Internat. Soc. Interferon Rsch. Achievements include research in cancer immunology and immunotherapy; immunodiagnstic tests for cancer; natural killer cells characterization and in vivo role in resistance to cancer and AIDS. Office: Univ Pitt Cancer Inst 5150 Centre Ave Ste 500 Pittsburgh PA 15232 Office Phone: 412-623-3205. Business E-Mail: herbermanrb@upmc.edu.

HERBERS, TOD ARTHUR, publisher; b. Cin., Sept. 11, 1948; s. Walter Fred and Jeanette Ruth (Dalton) H.; m. Suzanne Jeannine Daly, Sept. 7, 1974. BA, Catholic U. Am., 1970. With Nation's Bus. mag., Washington, 1972-75, promotion dir., 1974-75, Washingtonian mag., Washington, 1975-76, circulation and promotion dir., assoc. pub., 1976-77; pub. Am. Film mag., Washington, 1977-82; mng. pub. Science 86 Mag., Washington, 1982-86; pub. Sci. Illustrated Mag., Washington, 1987-89; pres. Jour. NIH Rsch., Washington, 1989-94; pub. On Target Media, Inc., Washington, 1994—2003; pub., pres. Home & Design Mag., Homestyles Media Inc., Silver Spring, Md., 2002—. Home: 8428 Holly Leaf Dr Mc Lean VA 22102-2224 Office: Homestyles Media Inc Ste 150 12501 Prosperity Dr Silver Spring MD 20904 Office Phone: 301-622-0040. Business E-Mail: therbers@homeanddesign.com.

HERBERT, ADAM WILLIAM, JR., academic administrator, educator; b. Muskogee, Okla., Dec. 1, 1943; s. Addie Herbert; m. Karen Y. Lofty, Apr. 1980. BA, U. So. Calif., 1966, MPA, 1967; PhD, U. Pitts., 1971. Instr., asst. prof., coord. acad. programs Ctr. Urban Affairs Sch. Pub. Adminstrn., U. So. Calif., L.A., 1969-72; assoc. prof., chmn. urban affairs program div. environ. and urban systems Va. Poly. Inst. State U., Blacksburg, 1972-75, prof., dir. North Va. programs, Ctr. for Pub. Adminstrn. and Policy, 1978-79; White House fellow, spl. asst. sec. HEW, Washington, 1974-75; spl. asst. to under sec. HUD, Washington, 1975-77; prof., dean Fla. Internat. U., Miami, 1979-87, assoc. v.p. for acad. affairs, chief acad. officer North Miami campus, 1985-88, v.p., chief adminstrv. officer, 1987-88; pres. U. North Fla., Jacksonville, 1989—98; chancellor State Univ. Sys. of Fla., 1998—2001; Regents prof., exec. dir. Fla. Ctr. for Pub. Policy and Leadership U. North Fla., Jacksonville, Fla.; pres. Ind. Univ. System, Bloomington, 2003—. Office: Indiana Univ System Bloomington IN 47405

HERBERT, ALBERT EDWARD, JR., interior and industrial designer; b. Detroit, June 12, 1928; s. Albert Edward and Gladys Mae (Speechley) H. Student, Pratt Inst., 1947-50. Owner, operator Albert Herbert Designs, 1957—; designer for V'Soske, Inc. Baker Furniture. Author: (with Roger P. Myers) The Last Survivor, 1976, Killer Pack, 1976, The Skytower Disaster, 2000, The Quest, 2001; contbr. articles to mags. Served with USAF, 1952-56. Fellow Am. Soc. Interior Designers (life). Home: Fords Colony 104 Baltusrol Williamsburg VA 23188 Business E-Mail: mrdesign8240@verizon.net.

HERBERT, BOB, columnist; b. Mar. 7, 1945; m. Suzanne. BS, Empire State Coll., SUNY, 1989. Reporter, night city editor Star-Ledger, Newark, 1970-76; reporter Daily News, N.Y., 1976-81, city hall bur. chief, 1981-83, city editor, 1983-85, columnist, 1985-93; panelist Sunday Edition talk show WCBS-TV, N.Y., 1990-91; host Hotlines issues show WNYC-TV, N.Y., 1990-91; nat corr NBC News, 1991—93; op-ed columnist N.Y. Times, N.Y., 1993—. Taught journalism Bklyn Coll, Columbia Univ. Author: Promises Betrayed: Waking Up from the American Dream, 2005. Avocations: reading, tennis, rotisserie baseball. Office: New York Times 229 W 43rd St New York NY 10036-3959*

HERBERT, EUGENIA WARREN, history educator; b. Summit, N.J., Sept. 8, 1929; s. Robert Beach and Mildred (Fisk) Warren; m. Robert Louis Herbert, June 6, 1953; children— Timothy D., Rosemary, Catherine. B.A., Wellesley Coll., 1951; M.A., Yale U., 1953, Ph.D., 1957. Asst. prof. history Quinnipiac Coll., Hamden, Conn., 1970; lectr. history Yale U., New Haven, 1972-73, 76, collaborator with R.S. Lopez, 1971, research affiliate, 1976-79; asst. prof. history Mt. Holyoke Coll., South Hadley, Mass., 1978-82, assoc. prof., 1982-85, E. Nevius Rodman prof., 1985—, prof. emeritus, 1997—; sr. assoc. mem. St. Anthony's Coll., Oxford U. (Eng.), 1978. Author: The Artist and Social Reform, 1961; (with Claude-Anne Lopez) The Private Franklin (Boston Globe award 1976), 1975; Red Gold of Africa, 1984; Red Gold: Copper Arts of Africa; film (with Candice Goucher and Carlyn Saltman) the Blooms of Banjeli, 1986; Iron, Gender, and Power, 1993; Twilight on the Zambezi, 2002; review editor African Studies REview, 1997—; contbr. articles to profl. jours. Mem. Bethany Democratic Com., 1970-77; mem. Bethany Sch. Bd., 1964-68; pres. Ctr. for Ind. Study, New Haven, 1977. Fulbright fellow, Vienna, Austria, 1951-52; Mellon faculty fellow Mt. Holyoke Coll., 1982; Donner Found. fellow, 1982-85; NEH mus. grantee, 1984; Social Sci. Rsch. Coun. grantee, 1989. Fellow Royal Geog. Soc.; mem. African Studies Assn., Am. Hist. Assn., Hist. Metallurgy Soc., Assn. Concerned African Scholars. Office: Mt Holyoke Coll Dept History South Hadley MA 01075 Business E-Mail: eherbert@mtholyoke.edu.

HERBERT, GARY RICHARD, lieutenant governor; b. American Fork, Utah, May 7, 1947; s. Duane and Carol Herbert; m. Jeanette Snelson; children: Nathan, Daniel, Bradley, Kimberli Cahoon, Shannon Child, Heather. Lic. real estate broker 1969. Pres. Herbert & Associates Inc., Orem, Utah; county commr. State of UT, 1990—2004, lt. gov. Salt Lake City, 2005—. Pres. Utah State Assn. County Commrs. and Couns., 2000; chmn. Mountainland Assn. Govts., Utah County Coun. Govts., Utah Adv. Coun. on Intergovernmental Relations. Bd. dirs. Provo/Orem C. of C. Mem.: Utah Assn. Counties (v.p. 2002, pres. 2003), Utah Assn. Counties Insurance Mutal (past pres.), Utah Assn. Realtors (past pres.), Nat. Assn. Realtors (chmn. Local Fiscal Affairs Com. 1999). Republican. Avocations: golf, tennis. Office: Utah State Capitol Complex East Office Bldg, Ste E220 PO Box 142220 Salt Lake City UT 84114-2220 Office Phone: 801-538-1000. Office Fax: 801-538-1528.*

HERBERT, GAVIN SHEARER, health care products company executive; b. L.A., Mar. 26, 1932; s. Gavin and Josephine (D'Vitha) H.; children by previous marriage Cynthia, Lauri, Gavin, Pam; 2d. m. Ninetta Flanagan, Sept. 6, 1986. BS, U. So. Calif., 1954. With Allergan, Inc., Irvine, Calif., 1950—, v.p., 1956-61, exec. v.p., pres., 1961-77, chmn. bd., CEO, 1977-91, chmn. bd., 1992-95, chmn. emeritus; pres. Eye and Skin Care Products Group Smith Kline Beckman Corp., 1981-89. Exec. v.p. Smith Kline Beckman Corp., 1986-89; bd. dirs. Beckman Instruments, Inc., Calif. Healthcare Inst. Mem. Rsch. to Prevent Blindness (bd. dirs.), Big Canyon Country Club, Newport Harbor Yacht Club, Pacific Club, Beta Theta Pi. Republican.

HERBERT, JAMES ARTHUR, artist, filmmaker; b. Boston, Feb. 13, 1938; s. James Arthur and Bernice Frances (Burns) H. AB magna cum laude, Dartmouth Coll., 1960; M.F.A., U. Colo., 1962. Instr. U. Colo., 1962; artist-in-residence Yale Summer Sch. Art and Music, 1965; mem. faculty dept. art U. Ga., Athens, 1962—, prof., 1973—, rsch. prof., 1992—, disting. rsch. prof. art, 1999—. One-man shows include Babcock Galleries, N.Y.C., 1967, U. Colo., Boulder, 1972, Poindexter Gallery, N.Y.C., 1972, 1973, 1974, 1976, Mus. Modern Art, 1970, 1972, 1974, 1977, 1981, 1988, 1994, 1998, 1999, 2005, Walker Art Ctr., Mpls., 1973, 1982, Harvard U., 1973, High Mus. Art, Atlanta, 1979, Kennedy Ctr., Washington, 1981, Libr. of Congress, 1983—, Museu Tropical, Lisbon, Lisbon, Portugal, 1993, Art Gallery Toronto Can., 1994, Oberhausen Internat. Film Festival, Germany, 1999, Brit. Coun., Cologne, Germany, 1999, Film Mus. Munich, 1999, Atl. Contemporary Art Ctr., 2000, Mus. Modern Art, N.Y.C., 2005, exhibited in group shows at Krannert Art Mus., Urbana, Ill., 1974, New Orleans Mus. Art, 1975, 1980, 1989, Whitney Mus. Am. Art, 1969, 1973, 1974, 1983, Westdeutsche Kurzfilmtage, Oberhausen, W. Ger., 1970, 1972, 1989, 1992, 2001, La Cinémathèque Royale de Belgique, Knokke-Heist, Belgium, 1974—75, Mus. Modern Art, 1979, P.S. 1, N.Y.C., 1979, Stedelijk Mus., Amsterdam, 1982, Kennedy Ctr., Washington, 1983, Monique Knowlton Gallery, N.Y.C., 1983, IRCAM, Pompidou Ctr., Beaubourg, France, 1984, Cinémateque Française, Beaubourg, 1985, Bibliotheque Nat., Avignon, France, 1985, Mus. Modern Art, N.Y.C., 1986, 1991, L.A. County Mus. Art, 1988, Carnegie-Mellon U. Art Gallery, Pitts., 1988, Va. Mus. Fine Art, Richmond, Va., 1988, Southeastern Ctr. for Contemporary Art, Winston-Salem, N.C., 1988, Corcoran Gallery of Art, Washington, 1989, Kuznetsky Most Exhbn. Hall, Moscow, 1989, Art Gallery of Ont., 1989, Long Beach Mus. Art, Calif., 1989, 1991, Norton Galley Art, Palm Beach, 1989, Sheridan Opera House, Telluride, Colo., 1989, 1991, 1993, Mus. Fine Arts, Boston, 1990, Art Inst., Chgo., 1990, Pacific Film Archive, Berkeley, Calif., 1991, Walker Art Ctr., Mpls., 1991, Sundance Theatre, Park City, Utah, 1992, Melbourne Internat. Film Theatre, Australia, 1992, European Media Art Theatre, Osnabrück, Germany, 1992, Toronto (Can.) Film Festival Theatre, 1992, N.Y. Film Festival at Lincoln Ctr., 1992, Inst. de Estadios Norteamericanos, Barcelona, Spain, 1992, Melbourne (Australia) Internat. Film Mus., 1992, Eldorado Theatre, Royal Palace, Antwerp, Belgium, 1993, Odense (Denmark) Internat. Film Theater, 1993, Fifth Media Festival Theatre, Hertogenbosch, The Netherlands, 1993, Vienna Shortfilm Mus., Antwerp (Belgium) Sinema festival Theatre, 1993, Rio Internat. Festival Hall, Rio de Janiero, Brazil, 1993, Sydney (Australia) Internat. Film Mus., 1994, Vherskě Hradiště, Czech Republic, 1994, Kunstencentrum, Leuveen, Netherlands, Gaumont Marignan Theater, Paris, 1995, Toronto Internat. Film Festival, 1997, 1999, Sundance Film Festival Theater, Park City, Utah, 1998, 1999, Rotterdam Internat. Film Festival, The Netherlands, 1998, 1999, 2000, Edinburgh (Scotland) Internat. Film Festival, 1999, Rio Internat. Film Festival, Brazil, 1999, Sao Paulo (Brazil) Internat. Film Festival, 1999, Film Theatre Brit. Coun., Cologne, Germany, 1999, Staatliche Galerie Moritzburg, Halle, Germany, 1999, Mus. Nat. Ctr. de Arte Reina Sofia, Madrid, Spain, Regensburger Kurzfilmwoche, Germany, 2003, Metropolis Kino Hamburg, 2003, Oberhausen Internat. Film Festival, 2004, Represented in permanent collections NYU, Am. Fedn. Arts, Royal Film Archives Belgium, Centre Beaubourg, Paris, Mus. Modern Art, Whitney Mus. Am. Art, Cornell U., Am. Film Inst., Chase Manhattan Bank, Coca Cola USA, Herbert F. Johnson Mus. Art at Cornell U., Walker Art Ctr., Mpls., Anthology Film Archives, N.Y.C.; author: Stills: Photographs by James Herbert, 1992. Recipient Awards in the Visual Arts, Rockefeller Found., 1987; Woodrow Wilson fellow, 1960-62, Guggenheim Found. fellow, 1971-72, 89-90; grantee Am. Film Inst., 1969, Nat. Endowment Arts, 1975, 78, 81, 82, Louis Comfort Tiffany Found., 1980, Rockefeller Found., 1993; commn. Libr. of Congress, 1983, Adolph and Esther Gottlieb Found., 1991. Office: U Ga Sch Art Athens GA 30602

HERBERT, JAMES CHARLES, academic administrator; b. Dayton, Ohio, Nov. 22, 1941; s. Charles August and Helen Louise (Korte) H.; m. Sandra Lynn Swanson, June 4, 1966; children: Kristen, Sonja. BA, U. Dayton, 1963; MA, Brandeis U., 1965, PhD in History of Ideas, 1970. Instr. history Cath. U. Am., Washington, 1967-69; asst. prof. history and philosophy U. D.C., Washington, 1971-73; asst. prof. gen. honors program U. Md., College Park, 1973-79; Am. Coun. on Edn. fellow U.S. Dept. Edn., Washington, 1979-80; dir. governance study Carnegie Found. for Advancement Teaching, Washington, 1980-82; dir. acad. rels. Coll. Bd., N.Y.C., 1982-84, exec. dir. acad. affairs, 1984-89; dir. edn. programs NEH, Washington, 1989-95, dir. rsch. and edn. programs, 1995-99, dir. rsch. programs, 1999—2004. Mem. Nat. Performance Review, Office of V.P. of U.S., 1993; vis. rsch. scholar Inst. for Philosophy and Pub. Policy, U. Md., 1998-99; acting chmn. NEH, 2001; sr. adv. NSF/NEH, 2003—. Gen. editor Academic Preparation Series, 6 vols., 1985-86; editor, writer: Academic Preparation for College, 1983; writer: Control of the Campus, 1982. GM scholar, 1959-63, NDEA fellow, 1963-66, Folger Shakespeare Libr. fellow, 1971, Am. Coun. on Edn. fellow, 1979-80. Mem. Am. Philos. Assn., AAUP, Nat. Collegiate Honors Coun. (exec. com. 1978-80, 81-84, pres. N.E. region 1978-79), D.C. Edn. Licensure Commn. Avocations: writing, swimming, travel, gardening. Office: NEH 1100 Pennsylvania Ave NW Washington DC 20506

HERBERT, KATHY J., retail executive; MBA, Lake Forest Grad. Sch. Mgmt., 1985. Dir. personnel tng. Jewel-Osco divsn. Am. Stores Co., 1996—98, v.p. human resources, 1998—2001; exec. v.p. human resources Albertson's, Inc., Boise, 2001—. Chair Jewel-Osco United Way Campaign; bd. dirs. Chgo. Sinfonietta, Kohl's Childrens Mus. Office: Albertsons Inc 250 Parkcenter Blvd PO Box 20 Boise ID 83706 Office Phone: 208-395-6200. Office Fax: 208-395-6349.*

HERBERT, KEVIN BARRY JOHN, classics educator; b. Chgo., Nov. 18, 1921; s. William Patrick and Margaret (Lomasney) H.; m. Margaret Frances Lambin, Dec. 28, 1946; children: John Barry (dec.), Catherine Ann (Mrs. John Reilly). BA, Loyola U., Chgo., 1946; MA, Harvard U., 1949, PhD, 1954. Instr. classics Marquette U., Milw., 1948—52; instr. Ind. U., Bloomington, 1952—54; master St. Paul's Sch., Concord, NH, 1954—55; asst. prof. Bowdoin Coll., Brunswick, Maine, 1955—62; asso. prof., prof. Washington U., St. Louis, 1962—92, chmn. dept., 1982—92, prof. emeritus, 1992—, curator emeritus, 1994—; reader Advanced Placement Latin, 1962—68, chief reader, 1969—73; mem. Latin test com. Coll. Entrance Exam. Bd., 1968—73; dir. tours to Europe and Mid. East, 1973—96; referee Am. Coun. Learned Socs., 1990—94; mem. editorial and adv. bd. Internat. Jour. Classical Tradition, 1993—. Curator John Max Wulfing Coin Collection, 1966—94. Author: Hugh of St. Victor: Soliloquy on the Earnest Money of the Soul, 1956, Ancient Art in Bowdoin College, 1964, Greek and Latin Inscriptions in the Brooklyn Museum, 1972; co-editor: Ancient Collections in Washington University, 1973; contbr. to: Great Events from History, 2 vols., 1972, Greek Coins in the Wulfing Collection of Washington University, 1979, Maximum Effort The B-29s Against Japan, 1983, Roman Republican Coins in the Wulfing Collection of Washington University, 1987, Roman Imperial Coins in the Wulfing Collection of Washington U.: 31BC-AD180, 1996; prodr. exhbns. and descriptive catalogs Washington U. Gallery of Art: Greek Coins, Fall term, 1989, Roman Republican Coins, Fall term, 1990, Goddesses, Queens and Women of Achievement: 550 B.C.-A.D. 1979, Spring Term, 1993; guest editor Classical Bull., 1998, 99; translator (Greek and Latin commentaries) St. Paul Epistle to the Romans, 1999-2000; contbr. articles and revs. to profl. jours. With USAAF, 1942-45. Decorated DFC, Air medal with two silver oak leaf clusters; Wilbour fellow Bklyn. Mus., 1967. Fellow Am. Numis. Soc.; mem. Am. Philol. Assn., Classical Assn. Middle West and South. Home: 1124 Basswood Ln Saint Louis MO 63132-3008 Office Phone: 314-935-5123. Personal E-mail: kherbert@artsci.wustl.edu.

HERBERT, LEROY JAMES, retired accounting firm executive; b. Long Branch, N.J., Aug. 3, 1923; s. LeRoy J. and Edna Hazel (Keller) H. BS, U. Md., 1950. CPA, N.J., N.Y., Ohio, Tenn., La., N.C., Va.; chartered acct. South Africa. Profl. staff mem. Ernst & Ernst, Balt., 1950-58, asst. mgr., 1958-60, mgr. internat. ops. N.Y.C., 1960-63, ptnr., 1963-67; sr. U.S. ptnr. Whinney Murray Ernst & Ernst, London and Paris, 1967-70; ptnr. in charge internat. ops. N.Y.C., 1970-78; internat. exec. ptnr. Ernst & Whinney Internat., N.Y.C., 1979-83. Bd. dirs. U. Md. Found., St. Barnabas Health Care Sys., Ronald McDonald House, Long Branch, N.J., Monmouth Med. Ctr. Found.; past chmn. Monmouth Med. Ctr., Long Branch. With U.S. Army, 1942-46. Recipient Disting. Alumnus award U. Md. Coll. Bus. and Mgmt., 1980, Disting. Acctg. Alumnus award, 1991; named to Long Branch H.S. Disting. Alumni Hall of Fame, 1996. Mem. AICPA, N.Y. Assn. CPAs, Ohio Assn. CPAs, Md. Assn. CPAs, Transvaal Soc. Accts. (South Africa), Deal Country Club, Harpoon and Needle Club, Pres.'s Club (U. Md.), Beta Alpha Psi Episcopalian. Home: 1 Channel Drive Apt 1111 Monmouth Beach NJ 07750

HERBERT, MARILYNNE, public relations executive, freelance photographer; b. Columbus, Ga., Aug. 12, 1944; d. Herbert Paul and Victoria (Raskin) Gruber; m. Victor Daniel Herbert, June 23, 1968 (div. 1990), remarried Oct. 6, 2002; children: Alissa, Laura. BA, Colo. Woman's Coll., 1966. Adminstrv. asst. pub. rels. dept. Mt. Sinai Med. Ctr., NYC, 1966-68; freelance photographer NYC, 1977—; sr. account exec. Ruder-Finn, Inc., NYC, 1986-93; dir. pub. rels. Iona Coll., New Rochelle, NY, 1993-94; sr. account exec. Coll. Connections Inc., NYC, 1994-96; sr. mgr. media rels. Halstead Comm., NYC, 1997—2002, exec. v.p., 2002—; cmty. rels. coord. Osborn Retirement Cmty., 1995—2003. Bd. dirs. Women of Westchester, White Plains, NY, 1977-79, Byrdcliffe Performing Arts Orgn., New Rochelle, 1987-91, Nat. Women's Polit. Caucus, Westchester County, 1988-90, Sr. Pers. Placement Bur., Inc., 1989-92; bd. dirs., sec. New Rochelle Cmty. Fund, 1986-91. Recipient Spl. Recognition award Nat. Women's Polit. Caucus, 1989, Clarion award Assn. Women in Comm., 2001. Mem. Am. Soc. Mag. Photographers, Assn. for Women in Comm., Lake Katonah Club (bd. govs. 1995-98). Jewish. Home: 77 Upper Lake Shore Dr Katonah NY 10536-2646 Office: Halstead Comm 329 E 82d St New York NY 10028 E-mail: halstead@halsteadpr.com.

HERBERT, PAUL, paper company executive; Sr. v.p., pulp and paper divsn. Rust Internat. Corp.; bd. chmn. Zanders, Bergish-Gladbach, Germany; staff v.p., engring. Internat. Paper Co., Memphis, 1992—2002, sr. v.p. printing and comm. paper, 2003—. Office: Internat Paper Co 6400 Poplar Ave Memphis TN 38197

HERBERT, WILLIAM CARLISLE, lawyer; b. Gainesville, Fla., Aug. 25, 1947; s. Thomas Walter and Jean Elizabeth (Linton) H.; m. Mary Lee Dedinsky. AB, Princeton U., 1969; MSJ, Northwestern U., 1970, JD cum laude, 1976. Bar: Ill. 1976, US Ct. Appeals (7th cir.) 1977, Fla. 1978, US Dist. Ct. (no. dist.) Ill. 1978, US Supreme Ct. 1980, US Tax Ct. 1982. Law clk. to Hon. Latham Castle US Ct. Appeals (7th cir.), 1976-77; ptnr. Foley & Lardner, Chgo. Exec. editor Northwestern U. Law Rev., 1976. Mem. ABA, Ill. State Bar Assn., Fla. Bar, Chgo. Bar Assn., Legal Club Chgo., U. Club Chgo. Presbyterian. Office: Foley and Lardner 321 N Clark St 270o Chicago IL 60610 Office Phone: 312-832-4551. E-mail: wcherbert@aol.com.

HERBICH, GREGORY J., dermatologist, plastic surgeon; b. Mpls., July 5, 1956; s. John B. and Margaret P. Herbich; m. Sue L. Vo, Jan. 5, 1993 (div. Oct. 2002). BSEE, Rice U., 1978; MD, U. Tex., Galveston, 1981. Diplomate Am. Bd. Dermatology, Am. Bd. Cosmetic Surgery. Intern in internal medicine U. Conn., Farmington, 1982; resident in dermatology Coll. Medicine Baylor U., Houston, 1982—85, resident in plastic surgery Coll. Medicine, 1985; pvt. practice Honolulu, 1986—. Contbr. articles to profl. jours., chapters to books. Brown and Root scholar, Rice U., 1977—78. Fellow: Am. Acad. Cosmetic Surgery, Am. Acad. Dermatology; mem.: Hawaii Dermatol. Soc. (sec./treas. 2002—03, v.p. 2003—04, pres. 2004—). Republican. Roman Catholic. Avocation: travel. Office: 1001 Bishop St # 390 Pauahi Twr Honolulu HI 96813 Office Phone: 808-538-0123. E-mail: herbich2000@yahoo.com.

HERBIG, GÜNTHER, conductor; b. Aussig, Germany, Nov. 30, 1931; s. Emil and Gisela (Hieke) H.; m. Jutta Czapski, Oct. 30, 1958; children: Beate, Thomas. Diploma, Franz Liszt Hochschule, Weimar, Germany, 1956. Mus. asst. Erfurt Theatre, 1956-57; condr. German Nt. Theatre, Weimar, 1957-62; prin. condr. Potsdam (Germany) Theatre, 1962-66; condr. Berlin Symphone Orch., 1966-72, chief condr., artistic dir., 1977-83, Dresden (Germany) Philharm. Orch., 1972-77; prin. guest condr. Dallas Symphony Orch., 1979-81, BBC Philharm., 1982-85; music dir. Detroit Symphony Orch., 1984-90; artistic advisor Toronto (Ont., Can.) Symphony Orch., 1988, music dir., 1988-94; chief condr. Saarbrücken (Germany) Radio Symphony Orch., 2001—. Recipient Theodor Fontane Arts prize, 1975; arts prize Govt. of German Dem. Republic, 1970, nat. prize, 1977. Roman Catholic. Personal E-mail: gherbig@comcast.net.

HERBISON, PRISCILLA JOAN, social services administrator, law educator; b. Mpls., Sept. 13, 1943; d. Charles W. and Vonda C. (Rogers) H. BA, Coll. St. Catherine, St. Paul, 1965; MSW, U. Ill., Urbana, 1969; JD, U. Minn., 1982. Social worker Cath. Social Svc., St. Paul, 1965-67, Cath. Welfare Svc., Mpls., 1969-71; prof. social work U. W.V., 1971-74; prof., dir. social work program St. Cloud (Minn.) State U., 1974—, chmn. dept. sociology, anthropology and social work, 1987—. Prof., dir. human devel. and psychology St. Mary's U. Minn., 1987—; cons., researcher in law; staff aide to speaker of Ill. Ho. of Reps., 1968-69; founder, dir. early childhood ctrs. in rural Appalachia, 1971-72. Author: God Knows We Get Angry, 2002, God Knows Grandparents Make a Difference: Sharing Grandparent's Wisdom, 2003. Recipient Grad. Advisor of Yr. award, 1996, George R. Christenson award for Excellence in Edn., 1998; Fairchild fellow, 1980. Mem. NASW, Acad. Cert. Social Workers (cert.), Conf. Social Work End., Delta Theta Phi. Roman Catholic. Home: 5905 Columbus Ave Minneapolis MN 55417-3107 Office: St Mary's U 2500 Park Ave Minneapolis MN 55404-4403 E-mail: pherbiso@smumn.edu.

HERBOLD, ROBERT J., former software company executive; b. July 1942; m. Patricia L. Kruse, June, 1966; 3 children. BS, U. Cin., 1964; MS in Math., Case Western Reserve U., 1966, PhD in Computer Sci., 1968. Info. tech. and mktg. positions Procter & Gamble Co., 1968—88, sr. v.p. advtsg. and info. svcs., 1988—94; exec. v.p., COO Microsoft Corp., Redmond, Wash., 1994—2001, exec. v.p., 2001—03; mng. dir. Herbold Group, LLC, Bellevue, Wash., 2001—. Bd. dirs. Weyerhaeuser Corp., Agilent Corp., Cintas Corp., ICOS Corp., First Mut. Bank. Trustee Case We. Res. U., Seattle Found., Overlake Hosp., Heritage Found., Hoover Instn. Avocations: hiking, fishing.

HERBST, ARTHUR LEE, obstetrician, gynecologist; b. NYC, Sept. 14, 1931; s. Jerome Richard and Blanche (Vatz) H.; m. Lee Ginsburg, Aug. 10, 1958. AB magna cum laude, Harvard Coll., 1953, MD cum laude, 1959; DSc (hon.), N.E. Ohio U., 2001. Diplomate Am. Bd. Ob-gyn. (bd. dirs. 1985-93, dir. div. gynecol. oncology 1989-91). Intern Mass. Gen. Hosp., Boston, 1959—60, resident, 1960—62; resident in ob-gyn. Boston Hosp. for Women, 1962—65; instr., assoc. prof. ob-gyn. Mass. Gen. Hosp. and Harvard U. Med. Sch., Boston, 1965—76; Joseph B. DeLee prof. ob-gyn. U. Chgo., 1976—84, Joseph B. DeLee Disting. Service prof., 1984—2005, disting. prof. emeritus, 2005—; chmn. dept. ob-gyn. Chgo. Lying In Hosp., 1976—2001; chmn. exec. com. U. Chgo. Hosps. and Clinics, 1980. Contbr. articles to profl. jours. Fellow Royal Coll. Obstetricians and Gynecologists (hon.), Inst. Med., Nat. Acad. Scis.; mem. AMA, ACS, ACOG, Am. Gynecol. and Obstet. Soc. (pres. 1997-98), Am. Assn. Profs. Ob-Gyn., Ctrl. Assn. Obstetricians and Gynecologists, Chgo. Gynecologic Soc., Soc. Pelvic Surgeons, Endocrine Soc., Infertility Soc., Soc. Gynecologic Oncologists. Home: 1234 N State Pkwy Chicago IL 60610-2219 Office: U Chgo Med Ctr 5841 S Maryland Ave MC2050 Chicago IL 60637-1463 Office Phone: 773-702-6671.

HERBST, ERIC, physicist, astronomer, chemist; b. NYC, Jan. 15, 1946; s. Stuart Karl and Dorothy (Polakoff) H.; m. Judith Strassman, Oct. 15, 1972; children: Elisabeth, Andrea, Seth. AB, U. Rochester, 1966; MA, Harvard U., 1969, PhD, 1972. Asst. prof. chemistry Coll. of William and Mary, Williamsburg, Va., 1974-79, assoc. prof.chemistry, 1979-80; assoc. prof. physics Duke U., Durham, N.C., 1980-86, prof. physics, 1986-91. Univ. zu Köln, Cologne, Germany, 1988-89, Ohio State U., Columbus, 1991—, prof. astronomy, 1992—, prof. chemistry, 2003—. Cons. NASA, Washington, 1985-90, NSF, Washington, 1989-92. Contbr. over 270 articles and 25 revs. to profl. jours. Recipient Humboldt award Humboldt Found., 1988, Max Planck prize Max Planck Soc., 1993. Fellow Am. Phys. Soc., Royal Soc. Chem. (Centenary medal 2004); mem. Am. Astron. Soc., Am. Chem. Soc., Inst. Physics Achievements include theory of how organic molecules are formed in space; theory of floppy molecules. Office: Ohio State U Dept Physics 191 W Woodruf Ave Columbus OH 43210-1106 E-mail: herbst@mps.ohio-state.edu.

HERBST, JAN FRANCIS, physicist, researcher; b. Tucson, May 1, 1947; s. Alva and Frances Theresa (Feler) H.; m. Margaret Mae Priest, July 24, 1982; children: Helen, John, Mary. BA in Physics, MS, U. Pa., 1968; PhD, Cornell U., 1974. Postdoctoral rsch. assoc. Nat. Bur. Standards, Gaithersburg, Md., 1974-76; asst. physicist Brookhaven Nat. Lab., Upton, N.Y., 1976-77; assoc. sr. rsch. physicist GM Rsch. Labs., Warren, Mich., 1977-81, staff rsch. scientist, 1981-85, mgr. magnetic materials sect., 1984—2002, sr. staff rsch. scientist, 1985-93, prin. rsch. scientist, 1993—, mgr. solid state materials for energy storage and conversion group, 2002—. Mem. basic energy scis. adv. com. Dept. Energy, 1996-2000, panel chair workshop on devel. of secure energy future, 2002; mem. panel for physics Nat. Rsch. Coun. bd. assessment NIST Programs, 2000—03. Contbr. articles over 100 to profl. jours. Recipient Campbell award GM Rsch. Labs., 1983, McCuen award GM Rsch. Labs., 1987, Kettering award GM Corp., 1987. Fellow Am. Phys. Soc. (sec.-treas. div. condensed matter physics 1985-90, nominating com. 1996-98, Internat. prize for new materials 1986). Achievements include patents for in field. Avocations: reading, numismatics. Office: GM R&D Ctr MC 480-106-224 30500 Mound Rd Warren MI 48090-9055 Business E-Mail: jan.f.herbst@gm.com.

HERBST, JOHN EDWARD, ambassador; b. Rockville Center, N.Y., Aug. 12, 1952; s. Christopher and Mary Rose (Vaccheli) H.; m. Nadezda Christoff, May 22, 1977; children: Maria, Ksenia, Aleksandra. BSFS, Georgetown U., 1974; MA, Tufts U., 1978; MALD, Fletcher Sch., Medford, Mass., 1979. Staff asst. Am. Embassy, Jidda, Saudia Arabia, 1980-82, polit. officer Moscow, 1985-87, Office of Israel, Arab-Israeli Affairs, 1982-84; dir. policy devel. NSC, Washington, 1977-88; dep. dir. econs. Office Soviet Affairs, U.S. State Dept., Washington, 1988-97; consul gen. Am. Consulate, Jerusalem, 1997-2000; amb. to Republic of Uzbekistan U.S. Fgn. Svc., 2000—03; amb. to Ukraine U.S. Dept. State, Washington, 2003—. Contbr. articles to profl. publs. Mem. Phi Beta Kappa, Phi Alpha Theta. Avocations: reading, sports. Office: Dept of State 5850 Kiev Pl Washington DC 20521-5850*

HERBST, JURGEN, historian, educator; b. Braunschweig, Germany, Feb. 22, 1928; came to U.S., 1954, naturalized, 1957; s. Hermann and Annemarie Herbst; m. Susan Lou Allen, Sept. 16, 1951; children: Christian, Annemarie, Stephanie. Student, U. Gottingen, 1947-48; BA, U. Nebr., 1950; MA, U. Minn., 1952; PhD, Harvard U., 1958. Instr. edn. and history Wesleyan U., Middletown, Conn., 1958-59, asst. prof., 1959-65, asso. prof., 1965-66; assoc. prof. ednl. policy studies and history U. Wis., 1966-69, prof., 1969-94, prof. emeritus, 1994—; profl. assoc. Ft. Lewis Coll., Durango, Colo., 1999—. Author: The German Historical School in American Scholarship, 1965, The History of American Education, 1973, From Crisis to Crisis: American College Government, 1636-1819, 1982, And Sadly Teach: Teacher Education and Professionalization in American Culture, 1989, The Once and Future School: 350 Years of American Secondary Education, 1996, Requiem for a German Past: A Boyhood among the Nazis, 1999; editor: Our Country, 1963, History of Elementary School Teaching Curriculum, 1990, Aspects of Antiquity in the History of Education, 1992, German Influences on Education in the United States to 1917, 1995, Mutual Influences on Education: Germany and the United States in the Twentieth Century, 1997. Am. Coun. Learned Socs. grantee, 1960; Fulbright Commn. grantee, 1963, 81; Nat. Endowment for Humanities grantee, 1972-73; Nat. Inst. Edn. grantee, 1973-76; Internat. Research and Exchanges Bd. grantee, 1977; Guggenheim Found. grantee, 1978-79; Wis. Inst. Research in Humanities grantee, 1978-79; Spencer Found. grantee, 1986, 99. Mem. Nat. Acad. Edn., Am. Hist. Assn., Orgn. Am. Historians, History of Edn. Soc. (pres. 1978-79), Historische Kommission der Deutschen Gesellschaft für Erziehungswissenschaft, Internat. Standing Conf. for the History of Edn. (mem. exec. com., pres. 1988-91). Democrat. E-mail: jurgenherbst@cs.com.

HERBST, ROBERT LEROY, organization executive; b. Mpls., Oct. 5, 1935; s. Walter Peter and Bernice Mickey (Mikkelson) H.; m. Evelyn Clarice Elford, Sept. 22, 1956; children— Eric Elford, Peter Robert, Amy Jo. BS in Forest Mgmt, U. Minn., St. Paul, 1957. Dep. commnr. Minn. Conservation Dept., 1966-69; nat. exec. dir. Izaak Walton League Am., 1969-70; commr. natural resources State of Minn., 1971-77; asst. sec. fish, wildlife and parks Dept. Interior, Washington, 1977-81, sec., Jan. 20-26, 1981; exec. dir. Trout Unltd., 1981-90; pres. Lake Superior Ctr., Washington, 1990-92, A-S5 Energy Co., Reno, Nev., 1997-98; Washington rep. TVA, Washington, 1992-96; CEO, chmn. bd. dirs. Global Environment & Tech. Found., Annandale, Va., 1996—. Instr. U. Minn., 1954; mem. adv. faculty N. Am. Sch. Conservation, 1969-77; chmn. Gt. Lakes Fisheries Commn., 1978-80, steering com. Nat. Fishing Week, 1991; mem. U.S. Commn. UNESCO, 1978-79, Pres. Carter's Interagency Coun., 1978-80; co-chmn. Nat. Adv. Coun. Environ. Edn., 1989, chmn., 1990-92; mem. U.S. bd. Environ. Ctr. for Ctrl. and Ea. Europe, 1997—, chmn. bd. dirs.; chmn. bd. dirs. Nat. Wildlife Refuge Assocs., 1998-2001. Author: Careers in Environment, 1973; contbr. articles to profl. jours. Mem. nat. bd. Boy Scouts Am., 1969—77; exec. bd. Viking Coun., 1975—76; bd. govs. African Inst. Econs. Edn. and Devel., 1980; pres. Nat. Watershed Protection Ctr., 1994; U.S. rep. Regional Environ. Ctr. for Ctrl. and Ea. Europe, chair bd. dirs.; chmn. bd. Nat. Reach Coun.; mem. Annandale United Meth. Ch., 1969—77. Recipient Nat. Svc. award Izaak Walton League Am., 1971; Silver Beaver award Boy Scouts Am., 1977; Disting. Svc. award U. Minn., 1969, 2003, Washington Acad. Sci. award, 2001, Outstanding Achievement award U. Minn., 2003; named Pub. Adminstr. of Yr. in Minn. Am. Soc. Pub. Adminstrn., 1976; elected Nat. Fresh Water Fishing Hall Fame, 2003. Mem. Natural Resource Coun. Am. (chmn. 1989-91, Honor award 1994), Land Between Lakes Assn.(chmn. 1982-91, trustee 1981-91). Democrat. Office: Global Environment & Tech Found Ste 460 7010 Little River Tpke Annandale VA 22003-3241 Office Phone: 703-379-2713. Business E-Mail: bherbst@getf.org.

HERBST, TODD L., lawyer; b. N.Y.C., July 15, 1952; s. Seymour and Charlotte (Wolper) H.; m. Robyn Beth Kellman, June 3, 1979; children: Scott Marshall, Carly Nicole. BA, CUNY, 1974; JD, John Marshall Law Sch., 1977. Bar: NY 1978. Assoc. Max E. Greenberg, Cantor & Reiss, N.Y.C., 1977-83, mng. ptnr., 1984-87; sr. ptnr. Greenberg, Trager & Herbst LLP, N.Y.C., 1988—. Bus. cons. Gottlieb Skanska, Inc., N.Y.C., 1980—, Shimizu Corp., U.S., 1983—, Dillingham Constrn. Holdings, Inc., San Francisco, 1987—2001, Jolly Hotels, Italy, 1993—, NTT Internat. Corp., Japan and U.S., 1996—, Legal Commentary UPN News, N.Y., Apollo Real Estate Advisors, LP, Rose Assocs., Inc., Kreisler Borg Florman Gen. Constrn. Co., Inc., Madison Equities, LLC; lectr. Nat. Assn. Corp. Real Estate Execs. Exec. editor: John Marshall Law Rev. Mem. ABA (A/V rated), Am. Inst. Archs., N.Y. State Bar Assn., Am. Corp. Counsel Assn., N.Y. County Lawyers Assn. Avocations: poetry, automobiles. Home: 7 Brookwood Ln New City NY 10956-2203 Office: Greenberg Trager & Herbst LLP 12th Fl 767 Third Ave New York NY 10017-2023 Office Phone: 212-688-1900. Business E-Mail: therbst@gthny.com.

HERCEG, TREVOR JOHN, artist, educator; b. Binghamton, N.Y., Dec. 15, 1970; s. Ernest and Nadine Herceg. BS in Art Edn., Mansfield (Pa.) U., 1993; MA in Art, Edinboro (Pa.) U., 1996; MFA in Ceramics, Wolverhampton (Eng.) U., 1997. Cert. tchr. N.Y. State Dept. Edn., 1994. Asst. lectr. Wolverhampton (Eng.) U., 1996—97; tchr. art Union Endicott (N.Y.) H.S., 1997—. Adj. instr. art Keystone Coll., La Plume, Pa., 1998—. Exhibitions include Keystone Fine Arts Faculty Exhibit. Co-chmn. Ducks Unlimited, Binghamton, NY, 2002. Mem.: Nat. Coun. Edn. for Ceramic Arts. Home: 11 Aitchison Rd Binghamton NY 13905 Office: Union Endicott High School 1200 E Main Street Endicott NY 13760 Office Phone: 607-757-2170. Personal E-mail: therceg@uegw.stier.org.

HERCULES, DAVID MICHAEL, chemistry professor, consultant; b. Somerset, Pa., Aug. 10, 1932; s. Michael George and Kathryn (Saylor) H.; m. Nancy Catherine Miller, Sept. 23, 1957 (div. 1968); 1 dau., Kimberly Ann; m. Shirley Ann Hoover, Dec. 14, 1970; children: Sherri Kathryn, Kevin Michael. BS, Juniata Coll., 1954; PhD, MIT, 1957. Asst. prof. Lehigh U., 1957-60; assoc. prof. Juniata Coll., Huntington, Pa., 1960-63; asst. prof. MIT, 1963-68, assoc. prof., 1968-69, U. Ga., Athens, 1969-74, prof., 1974-76; prof. dept. chemistry U. Pitts., 1976-94, chmn., 1980-89, Miles prof., 1990-94; Centennial prof. Vanderbilt U., Nashville, 1995—, chmn. dept., 1995—2003. Mem. vis. com. for chemistry Lehigh U., 1980-84; vis. prof. Mich. State U., 1972; chmn. Gordon Research Conf. on Electron Spectroscopy, 1974, Gordon Research Conf. on Analytical Chemistry, 1966; co-chmn. Internat. Conf. Chemiluminescence, 1972; univ. rep. Council on Chem. Research, 1980-88; mem. program com. Pitts. Conf. on Analytical Chemistry and Applied Spectroscopy, 1977-94; mem. vis. scientist program NSF, 1964-76 Mem. editorial bds.: Applied Spectroscopy, 1963-65, Analytical Chemistry, 1964-67, Jour. Electron Spectroscopy, 1971-77, Environ. Analytical Chemistry, 1973—, Spectrochimica Acta, 1973-83, Talanta, 1974-80, Spectroscopy Letters, 1975—, The Scis., 1979-84, Trends in Analytical Chemistry, 1980-88, Jour. Trace and Microprobe Techniques, 1980-93, Fresenius Zeitschrift für Analytische Chemie, 1987-; patentee (in field). Recipient Benedetti-Pichler award Am. Microchem. Soc., 1987, Achievement in Analytical Chemistry award Ea. Analytical Symposium, 1988, prize Alexander von Humboldt Found., 1984, Disting. Alumnus award Juniata Coll., 1989, Pres.'s Disting. Rsch. award U. Pitts., 1990; John Simon Guggenheim Meml. fellow, 1973. Mem. Am. Chem. Soc. (Petroleum Research Fund adv. bd. 1978-80, chmn. div. analytical chemistry 1977-78, analytical chemistry award 1986, Arthur W. Adamson award disting. svc. in advancement of surface chemistry 1993, Pitts. sect. award 1997), Soc. Applied Spectroscopy (Lester W. Strock medal New Eng. sect. 1981, Pitts. Spectroscopy award 1996), Am. Vacuum Soc., Photoelectric Spectrometry Group, Pa. Acad. Scis., Spectroscopy Soc. Pitts. (award 1996), Soc. Analytical Chemists Pitts., Sigma Xi Home: 200 Olive Branch Rd Nashville TN 37205-3220 Office: Vanderbilt U Dept Chemistry Box 1822, Sta B Nashville TN 37235

HERDEG, HOWARD BRIAN, retired physician; b. Buffalo, Oct. 14, 1929; s. Howard Bryan and Martha Jean (Williams) H.; m. Beryl Ann Fredricks, July 21, 1955; children: Howard Brian II, Erin Ann Kociela. Student, Paul Smith's Coll., 1947-48, U. Buffalo, 1948-50, Canisius Coll., 1949; DO, Phila. Coll. Osteo. Medicine, 1954; MD, U. Calif., Irvine, 1962. Diplomate Am. Acad. Pain Mgmt. Intern Burbank (Calif.) Hosp., 1954-55; practice medicine specializing in gen. medicine, surgery and pain mgmt., Woodland Hills, Calif., 1956—; ret., 2004. Chief med. staff West Park Hosp., Canoga Park, Calif., 1971-72, trustee, 1971-73; chief family practice dept. West Hills Hosp. and Med. Center (formerly Humana Hosp. West Hills, 1982-85, 88-89), exec. com., 1984-85, 88-89. Mem. Hidden Hills (Calif.) Pub. Safety Commn., 1978-82; bd. dirs. Hidden Hills Cmty. Assn., 1971-73, pres. 1972; bd. dirs. Hidden Hills Homeowners Assn., 1973-75, pres. 1976-77; bd. dirs. Woodland Hills Freedom Season, 1961-67, pres. 1962; mem. Hidden Hills City coun., 1984-2001, mayor pro tem, 1987-90, mayor, 1990-92. Recipient Disting. Svc. award Woodland Hills Jr. C. of C., 1966. Mem. Woodland Hills C. of C. (dir. 1959-68, pres. 1967), Calabasas C. of C., Rotary, Theta Chi, Gamma Pi. Republican. Home: 13368 Savanna Tustin CA 92782-9143 Personal E-mail: docherdeg@cox.net.

HERDEG, JOHN ANDREW, lawyer; b. Buffalo, Sept. 15, 1937; s. Franklin Leland and Susannah Estelle (Clark) H.; m. Judith Coolidge Carpenter, June 24, 1961; children: Judith Leland Herdeg Wilson, Andrew Carpenter Herdeg, Fell Coolidge Herdeg. BA, Princeton U., 1959; LLB, U. Pa., 1962. Bar: Conn. 1963, Del. 1964. Atty. Wilmington (Del.) Trust Co., 1963-75, sr. v.p. in charge of trust dept., 1975-85, bd. dirs., chmn. trust com., corp. sec., 1977-85; pres. Herdeg & Assocs., Wilmington, 1986-98; ptnr. Herdeg, duPont & Dalle Pazze, LLP, Wilmington, 1999—. Co-founder, chmn. bd. dirs. Christiana Bank & Trust Co., Greenville, Del., 1992—. Co-author: Delaware Total Return Unitrust Statute, 2001. Bd. trustees Henry Francis duPont Winterthur (Del.) Mus., 1970—, chmn., 1977—86; bd. trustees Historic Deerfield, Inc., 2004—; supr. Pennsbury Twp., Chester County, Pa., 1968—74. Mem.: Soc. Colonial Wars, Walpole Soc., Conferie des Chevalier du Tastevin, Soc. Colonial Wars (gov. 2005—, Del., gov. 2005—), Walpole Soc., West Chop Club, Mill Reef Club, Vicmead Hunt Club (bd. govs. 1977—84), Wilmington Club (bd. govs. 1997—, prs. 2005—). Avocations: tennis, photography, decorative arts. Home: PO Box 614 Mendenhall PA 19357-0614 Office: Herdeg DuPont & Dalle Pazze LLP 12th & Orange St Ste 500 Wilmington DE 19801-1140 Office Phone: 302-655-6500. E-mail: jherdeg@dellaw.com.

HERDLE, WILLIAM BRUCE, chemist; b. Rochester, N.Y., Dec. 2, 1947; s. Lloyd and Rebecca Herdle. BA in Chemistry with honors, Swarthmore Coll., 1969; PhD, U. Wis., 1975. Chemist Union Carbide Corp., Tarrytown, N.Y., 1975-81, project scientist, 1981-84, rsch. scientist, 1984-85, group leader, 1985-88, tech. mgr., 1988-94; R&D mgr. Europe OSiSpecialties S.A., Geneva, 1995-96; tech. dir. Witco Corp., South Charleston, W.Va., 1996-99; dir. R & D Crompton Corp., Tarrytown, NY, 2000—03; rsch. fellow GE Advanced Materials, Tarrytown, 2003—. Game system designer Trans Fiction Systems, N.Y.C., 1984-90. Contbr. articles to profl. jours.; patentee in field. NIH fellow, 1970-75. Mem. AAAS, Am. Chem. Soc., Soc. Plastics Engrs., Sigma Xi, Phi Lambda Upsilon. Democrat. Avocations: microcomputer, programming, role-playing games. Home: 104 Hungerford Rd N Briarcliff Manor NY 10510-1362 Office: GE Advanced Materials 771 Old Saw Mill River Rd Tarrytown NY 10591

HEREK, STEPHEN, film director, film producer; b. San Antonio, Nov. 10, 1958; Dir. films Bill & Ted's Excellent Adventure, 1989, Don't Tell Mom the Babysitter's Dead, 1991, The Mighty Ducks, 1992, The 3 Musketeers, 1993, Mr. Holland's Opus, 1995, 101 Dalmations, 1996, Rock Star, 2001, Life or Something Like It, 2002, Man of the House, 2005, (TV series) Young MacGyver, 2003; dir., prodr. Holy Man, 1998; dir., writer Critters, 1986. Office: Endeavor care Steve Rabineau 9701 Wilshire Blvd Fl 10 Beverly Hills CA 90212-2010*

HEREMANS, JOSEPH PIERRE, physicist; b. Leuven, Belgium, Jan. 8, 1953; came to U.S., 1984; s. Joseph Felix Heremans and Marie Therese Bracke; m. Claire Pierre Mali, July 1, 1978; children: Hilde Anne, Joseph Paul. Elec. Engr., U. Louvain, Belgium, 1975, PhD in Applied Physics, 1978. Aspirant Belgium Nat. Sci. Found., Louvain, 1978-80, charge de recherche, 1980-83; rsch. scientist GM Rsch. and Devel. Ctr., Warren, Mich., 1984-85; group leader GM Rsch., Warren, Mich., 1985-87, sect. mgr., 1987-99; rsch. fellow Delphi Rsch. Labs., Shelby Township, 1999—. Invited prof. U. Louvain, 1989; vis. scientist U. Tokyo, 1982, MIT, Cambridge, 1980-81. Editor: Growth, Characterization and Properties of Ultrathin Magnetic Films and Multilayers, 1989, Survey of Semiconductor Physics, 2002; contbr. articles to profl. jours. Fellow Am. Phys. Soc.; mem. AAAS, Materials Rsch. Soc. Achievements include patents in field. Office: Delphi Rsch Labs 51786 Shelby Pkwy Shelby Township MI 48315 Business E-Mail: joseph.p.heremans@delphi.com.

HERENTON, WILLIE W., mayor; b. Memphis, Apr. 23, 1943; divorced; children: Errol, Rodney, Andrea. BS, LeMoyne-Owen Coll., 1963; MA, Memphis State U., 1966; PhD, So. Ill. U., 1971; PhD (hon.), Rhodes Coll., Christian Brother's Coll. Elem. sch. tchr. Memphis City Sch. System, 1963-67, elem. sch. prin., 1967-73; dept. supt. Memphis City Schs., 1974-78, supt. of schs., 1979-91; mayor Memphis, 1991—. Bd. dirs. Nat. Urban League Edn. Adv. Coun., 1978, Nat. Jr. Achievement, Jr. Achievement of Memphis 1979—, United Way Greater Memphis, 1979-, Promous Cos., Inc., First Tenn. Nat. Corp.; mem. Nat. Alliance of Black Educators, 1974—, Am. Assn. Sch. Adminstrs., Am. Mgmt. Assn.; mem. exec. bd. Nat. Conf. Christians and Jews.; served March of Dimes, United Way, Rotary Club, Boy Scouts of Am., Econ. Club Memphis. Named one of Top 100 Sch. Adminstrs. in U.S. and Can., Exec. Educator Jour., 1980, 84, Municipal Leader of Yr., American City & County Mag., 2002; Fellow Rockefeller Found., 1973; recipient Horatio Alger award, 1988. Mem.: Am. Mgmt. Assn., Am. Assn. of Sch. Adminstrn. Baptist. Office: Office of the Mayor 125 N Main St Ste 700 Memphis TN 38103-2017 Office Phone: 901-576-6007. Office Fax: 901-576-6023. Business E-Mail: mayor@cityofmemphis.org.

HERGE, DONNA CAROL, secondary school educator; b. Rockford, Ill., Nov. 11, 1948; d. William Carl and Grace Wilma Kling; m. John Arthur Herge, June 9, 1973; 1 child, Thomas William. BA in Math. and Philosophy, Rockford Coll., 1970; MS in Math., Wright State Univ., 1973; PhD and MS in Stats., Fla. State Univ., 1992. Commd. 2d lt. USAF, 1971, advanced through grades to lt. col., 1989, comdr. Detachment 1, 6th Weather Squadron Kelly AFB, Tex., 1974—75, contract monitor 16th Surveillance Squadron Shemya AFB, Alaska, 1975—76, asst. prof. math USAF Acad. Colorado Springs, Colo., 1976—80, comm.-electronics br. chief Offutt AFB, Nebr., 1980—83, stats. br. chief Air Force Inst. Tech. Wright Patterson AFB, Ohio, 1986—91; dir. rsch. and analysis AF Quality Inst., Maxwell AFB, Ala., 1991—95; ret. USAF, 1995; math tchr. Cath. H.S., Montgomery, Ala., 1996—. Adj. prof. stats. Troy State U., Montgomery, 1995—96, Auburn U., Montgomery, 1995—96. Editor: (book) Process Improvement Guide: Tools for Today's Air Force, 1992. Alto St. Bede Ch. Adult Choir, Montgomery, 1995—. Decorated Commendation medal USAF, Meritorious Svc. medal; recipient Comm. Electronics Profl. Achievement award, Aerospace Def. Command, 1976. Mem.: Am. Soc. for Quality, Am. Statis. Assn., Phi Beta Kappa (hon.). Business E-Mail: d.herge@knights.pvt.k12.al.us.

HERGE, HENRY CURTIS, JR., information technology executive, consultant; b. Hartford, Conn., Sept. 13, 1950; s. Henry Curtis and Josephine (Breen) Herge; m. Donna Gay Takeda, Dec. 20, 1974 (div. Dec. 1982); m. Madge Lynn Henley, Feb. 19, 1983; children: H. Curtis III, Erika Ainsley, Alyssa Taylor, Whitney Meghan. BSME, Rutgers U., 1972, BA, 1972. Prodn. splst. GE, Columbia, Md., 1972-73, engring. foreman med. sys. divsn. Milw., 1973-74, buyer internat. sales divsn. N.Y.C., NY, 1974-76; sr. sys. analyst Arthur Andersen & Co. (now Accenture), N.Y.C., 1976-78, cons. mgr. Stamford, Conn., 1978-85, ptnr., 1985—, practice dir. cons. divsn. Rochester (N.Y.) office, 1987-92. Sr. v.p. Tech. Solutions Co., 1992—94; ptnr. Diamond Tech. Ptnrs., Chgo., 1994—95; prin. A. T. Kearney divsn. Electronic Data Sy., Plano, Tex., 1995—, global contracts mgr., 1997—, svc. delivery quality, 1998—; cons. strategic devel. mgr. Electronic Data Sys., 2002—, strategic devel. mgr. solutions cons. N.E. USA; dir. Value-2-Xerox Corp., 2000—, Xerox Client Industry Exec., 2004—. Mem.: Am. Prodn. and Inventory Soc. (v.p. 1985). Presbyterian. Avocations: skiing, travel, canoeing, kites. Home: 16 Lancashire Way Pittsford NY 14534-9786 Office Phone: 585-231-4475. E-mail: curt.herge@eds.com.

HERGE, J. CURTIS, lawyer; b. Flushing, N.Y., June 14, 1938; s. Henry Curtis and Josephine E. (Breen) H.; m. Joyce Dorean Humbert, Aug. 20, 1960 (div. 1988); children: Cynthia Lynda, Christopher Curtis; m. Shirley Brooks Labonte, Dec. 22, 1989. Student, Cornell U., 1956-58; BA, Rutgers U., 1961, JD, 1963. Bar: N.Y. 1964, U.S. Supreme Ct. 1970, U.S. Ct. Claims 1974, D.C. 1974, Va. 1976. Assoc. Mudge Rose Guthrie & Alexander, N.Y.C., 1963-71; spl. asst. to atty. gen. U.S. Dept. Justice, Washington, 1973; assoc. solicitor conservation and wildlife U.S. Dept. Interior, Washington, 1973-74, asst. to sec. and chief staff, 1974-76; ptnr. Sedam & Herge, McLean, Va., 1976-85, Herge, Sparks & Christopher LLP, McLean, Va., 1985—. Bd. dirs. Diversified Labs., Inc., Ann E.W. Stone & Assocs., Inc., Palmer Tech. Svcs., Inc., Eaton Design Group, Inc., George Washington Banking Corp., Eaton Purchase Mgmt., Inc., George Washington Nat. Bank, Congl. Inst. Inc., Citizens United for Am., Am. Def. Lobby, Coun. Nat. Def., Renascence Found., The Am. Lobby Econ. Recovery Taskforce, Nat. Bank No. Va., Am. Freedom Found., Creative Response Concepts Inc., Congl. Inst., Inc.; spkr. in field. Adv. bd. Washington Legal Found., Nat. Taxpayers Legal Fund; Va. Commonwealth escheator Loudoun County and City of Fairfax, 1979-83; co-dir. spokesmen resources Com. for Re-election of Pres., 1971-72; mem. No. Va. Estate Planning Council; mem. natural resources coun. Rep. Nat. Com.; mem. Fairfax County Rep. Com., Conservative Rep. Com.; mem. Office Pres.-Elect Fed. Election Commn. Transition Team, 1980; co-chmn. N.Y. Honor Am. Day, 1970; expert witness, charitable fund-raising, U.S. Tax Ct. Sebastian Gaeta scholar Rutgers U., 1963. Mem. ABA, N.Y. State Bar Assn., Va. Bar Assn., D.C. Bar Assn., Capital Hill Club, Phi Kappa Sigma. Clubs: Capitol Hill. Home: 35 Rutherford Cir Potomac Falls VA 20165-6221 Office: Herge Sparks & Christopher LLP 6862 Elm St Ste 360 Mc Lean VA 22101-3867

HERGENHAN, KENNETH WILLIAM, lawyer; b. N.Y.C., Apr. 21, 1931; w. William Otto and Neva H.; m. Jane Steinruck Stahl, Aug. 24, 1959; children: Lisa Fevery, Susan Mitchell, William, John. BS, Lehigh U., 1953; LLB, Harvard U., 1958. Bar: Oreg. 1958, U.S. Dist. Ct. Oreg. 1958. Assoc., then ptnr. Miller Nash and predecessors, Portland, Oreg., 1958-96; dir. Willamette Industries, Inc., Portland, 1997-2001. Contbr. articles to legal publs. 1st lt. U.S. Army, 1953-55. Mem. Oreg. Bar Assn., Multnomah Athletic Club. Democrat. Episcopalian. Avocations: aviation, gardening.

HERGER, WALLY W., congressman; b. Yuba City, Calif., May 20, 1945; m. Pamela Sargent; 8 children. Mem. Calif. State Assembly, 1980—86, U.S. Congress from 2nd Calif. dist., 1987—; mem. ways and means com.; mem. human srvc. subcom.; owner Herger Gas, Inc. Republican. Mem. Lds Ch. Office: US Ho of Reps 2268 Rayburn Bldg Washington DC 20515-0502

HERGERT, HERBERT LAWRENCE, consultant; b. Portland, Oreg., Feb. 20, 1927; s. John Edward and Elizabeth (Blahm) H.; m. Lois Marion Lilly, Dec. 20, 1949; children: Lawrence A., Gregory K., David E., Daniel W. BA, Reed Coll., 1948; MS, Oreg. State U., 1951, PhD, 1954. Asst. prof. Oreg. State U., Corvallis, 1952-54; rsch. chemist Rayonier Inc., Shelton, Wash., 1954-70; asst. dir. R&D ITT Rayonier Inc., N.Y.C., 1970-72, v.p., dir. R&D, 1972-80, dir. quality, 1971-79, v.p., dir. tech. mktg., 1980-87; sr. scientist Repap Techs. Inc., Valley Forge, Pa., 1987-97. Trustee Textile Rsch. Inst., Princeton, N.J., 1976-82, Tech. Assn. Pulp & Paper Industries, Atlanta, 1980-83; forest products con., Pottstown, Pa., 1987-97; adj. prof. N.C. State U., 1998—. Contbr. over 90 papers to profl. jours. and 7 chpts. to books. Chmn., bd. dirs. Shelton (Wash.) Gen. Hosp., 1962-66, Shelton Sch. Dirs., 1966-70; adv. bd. Cons. Bapt. Theol. Seminary, Denver, 1968-79. Corp. USAAF, 1945-46. Fellow Internat. Acad. Wood Sci.; mem. Am. Botanical Soc., Internat. Paleobotanical Soc., Soc. Wood Sci. and Tech., Am. Chem. Soc., Tech. Assn. Pulp and Paper Industry. Republican. Baptist. Achievements include 6 U.S. patents and 36 foreign patents. Home: 901 Burdan Dr Pottstown PA 19464-4475 Office Phone: 610-970-1882.

HERGO, JANE ANTOINETTE, music educator, composer; b. Dayton, Ohio, Apr. 16, 1946; d. Frank Gustav and Antoinette Rosalyn (Jean) Hergo. BMus, U. Dayton, 1968, BS in Music Edn., 1975; MMus, Wright State U., 1980. Cert. music tchr., Ohio. Kindergarten tchr., Englewood, Ohio, 1971; elem. tchr. Dayton, Ohio, 1976—77, 1978—81; class piano instr. Sinclair C.C., Dayton, Ohio, 1981, piano accompanist for ballet and modern dance, 1983—84; ind. piano tchr. Dayton, Ohio, 1984—. Composer (book) Five Finger Frolics, 1988, Keyboard Confections, 1992 (sheet music) Gems on the Lake, 1991 (Ohio Music Tchrs. Assn. award 1990), Skeleton Skedaddle, 1993 (hon. mention award composition contest), Forest in the Rain (hon. mention award composition contest), Jazz Spooks (hon. mention award composition contest), Ghostly Gathering, 1991, Chilipeppers, 1998, Snowswirls, 2002 (hon. mention award composition contest). Piano soloist Dayton Philharm. Designer Show House, 1985, 87; adjudicator Jr. Music Club Festivals, Dayton, 1989—. Recipient Jr. Composer award Ohio Fedn. Music Club, 1998, Piano Compositions awards Key Piano Mag., 1990, 93, Merit award Nat. Fedn. Music Clubs, 1990. Mem. ASCAP, Music Tchrs. Nat. Assn. (nat. cert.), Ohio Music Tchrs. Assn. (officer student composition sect. Western dist. 1988-90, composition panel 1989, state conv. 1992), Jr. Music Club, Dayton Music Club (composer), Sigma Alpha Iota. Avocations: emboidery, drawing, sewing, reading, flower gardening.

HERGUTH, ROBERT JOHN, retired columnist; b. Chgo., Apr. 4, 1926; s. Harry Conrad Herguth and Loretta (Oberreither) Herguth-Slimmer; m. Margaret Ann Silsbee, Apr. 16, 1966; children: Amy Rene, Robert Charles, Mary Jennifer BA in Journalism, U. Mo., 1948. Copy editor, reporter Peoria Star, Ill., 1948-54; reporter, feature writer, columnist Chgo. Daily News, 1954-78; columnist Chgo. Sun Times, 1978-97, freelance weekly columnist, 1997-2001. Mem. editl. bd. Chgo. Sun Times., 1985-86. With U.S. Army, 1950-52. Inducted into Chgo. Journalism Hall of Fame, 1996. Mem. Chgo. Newspaper Guild (Page One award 1973), Chgo. Press Club (v.p. 1984-87, pres. 1987). Democrat. Roman Catholic.

HERING, DORIS MINNIE, dance critic; b. N.Y.C., Apr. 11, 1920; d. Harry and Anna Elizabeth (Schwenk) H. BA cum laude, Hunter Coll., 1941; MA, Fordham U., 1985. Freelance dance writer, 1946-52; assoc. editor, prin. critic Dance mag., N.Y.C., 1952-72; exec. dir. Nat. Assn. for Regional Ballet, N.Y.C., 1972-87; adj. assoc. prof. dance history NYU, 1968-78; freelance dance writer, lectr., cons., 1987—. Mem. dance panel NEA, 1972-75, cons., 1991—; mem. dance panel N.Y. State Coun. Arts, 1992-96, program auditor, 1997—; bd. dirs. Walnut Hill Sch., 1975—, Internat. Ballet Competition, 1981—; hon. bd. dirs. Phila. Dance Alliance, 1980—; cons. Regional Dance Am.; adj. assoc. prof. dance history NYU Grad. Sch. Edn. Author: 25 Years of American Dance, 1950, Dance in America, 1951, Wild Grass, 1965, Giselle and Albrecht, 1981; sr. editor Dance mag., 1989—. Howard D. Rothschild Rsch. fellow Harvard U., 1991-93; recipient 33d ann. Capezio Dance Found. award for lifetime svc., 1985, Award of Distinction Dance mag., 1987, Sage Cowles Land Grant chair in dance U. Minn., 1993, Sr. Critics tribute Dance

Critics Assn., 2002, Annual award, Martha Hill Dance Fund, 2002; named to Hunter Coll. Alumni Hall of Fame, 1986. Mem. Dance Critics Assn., Assn. Dance History Scholars, Phi Beta Kappa, Chi Tau Epsilon (hon.). Office Phone: 212-787-3834.

HERING, WILLIAM MARSHALL, medical organization executive; b. Indpls., Dec. 26, 1940; s. William Marshall and Mary Agnes (Clark) H.; m. Suzanne Wolfe, Aug. 10, 1963. BS, Ind. U., 1961, MS, 1962; PhD, U. Ill., Urbana, 1973. Asst. dir. sociol. resources project Am. Sociol. Assn., 1966-70; dir. social sci. curriculum Biomed. Interdisciplinary Project, Berkeley, Calif., 1973-76; staff assoc. Tchrs. Ctrs. Exch., San Francisco, 1976-82; dir. rsch. Far West Lab. Ednl. R&D, San Francisco, 1979-85; mgr. human resource devel. Bank Am., San Francisco, 1985-94. Mem. Nat. Adv. Bd. Educ. Resource Info. Ctr.; cons. U.S. Dept. Edn.; pres. Social Sci. Educ. Consortium, 1981-82, bd. dirs., 1979-81. Contbr. over 100 articles, book chpts. Bd. dirs. San Francisco Chamber Orch., 1986-94. Nat. Inst. Edn. grantee, 1979-82. Mem. ASTD (v.p. 1986), Alliance Continuing Med. Edn., Alpha Tau Omega, Phi Delta Kappa. Republican. Episcopalian. Home: 731 Duboce Ave San Francisco CA 94117-3214 Office: 655 Beach St San Francisco CA 94109-1336 E-mail: williamhering@comcast.net.

HERKERT, CRAIG R., retail executive; BS in Mktg., St. Francis Coll.; Master's, No. Ill. U. With Albertson's, Inc., Boise, Idaho; sr. v.p. fresh food mktg. Acme Supermarkets, 1998—99, pres. ea. region Malvern, Pa., 1999—2000; exec. v.p. and COO internat. div. Wal-Mart Stores, Inc., 2000—04, exec. v.p., pres., CEO Americas, 2004—. Office: Wal-Mart Stores Inc 702 SW Eighth St Bentonville AR 72716*

HERKSTROETER, KRISTIN BRIGITTE, music educator; b. Rochester, N.Y., Jan. 26, 1969; d. William George and Ingeborg Dorothea Herkstroeter; m. Babar Ali, July 29, 2001; 1 child, Sekander Nikolai Herkstroeter Ali. BM.E, Baldwin-Wallace Coll., 1987—91; MM in violin, U. of Cin., 1991—93; PhD in music edn., Fla. State U., 1998—2001. Music tchr. Penfield Ctrl. Schools, Penfield, NY, 1993—98; music dept. chair/dir. of strings Viewpoint Sch., Calabasas, Calif., 2001—. Pvt. music tchr., Valley Village, Calif., 1988—. Contbr. articles to profl. jours. Grad. Rsch. grant, Fla. State U., 2001. Mem.: Coll. Music Soc., Southern Calif. Sch. Band and Orch. Assn., Suzuki Assn. of the Americas, Music Educators Nat. Conf., Am. String Teachers Assn. Achievements include research in an investigation of the college decision making process among undergraduate string majors, and comparison of music education and performance majors; the comparison of the background of music education and music performance undergraduate majors. Home: 12706 Tiara St Valley Village CA 91607 Office: Viewpoint Sch 23620 Mulholland Hwy Calabasas CA 91302 Office Phone: 818-591-6517. Personal E-mail: kherkstroeter@hotmail.com.

HERLIHY, EDWARD D., lawyer; BA, Hobart Coll., 1969; JD, George Washington U., 1972. Bar: N.Y. 1973, D.C. 1973. Ptnr. Wachtell, Lipton, Rosen & Katz, N.Y.C. Contbr. articles to profl. jours. Office: Wachtell Lipton Rosen & Katz 51 W 52nd St Fl 29 New York NY 10019-6150 Office Phone: 212-403-1207. E-mail: edherlihy@wlrk.com.

HERLIHY, SCOTT C., lawyer; BBA, Coll. of William & Mary, 1985; JD, Univ. Notre Dame, 1991. CPA; bar: Va. 1991, DC 1992. Litig. cons. Peterson & Co., 1985—88; mng. ptnr., No. Va. office Latham & Watkins LLP, Reston, Va., now ptnr., corp. dept. Washington. Mem.: ABA. Office: Latham & Watkins LLP Ste1000 555 Eleventh St NW Washington DC 20004-1304 Business E-Mail: scott.herlihy@lw.com.

HERLONG, HENRY MICHAEL, JR., federal judge; b. Washington, June 1, 1944; s. Henry Michael Sr. and Josie Payne (Blocker) H.; m. Frances Elizabeth Thompson, Dec. 30, 1983; children: Faris Elizabeth, Henry Michael III. BA, Clemson U., 1967; JD, U. S.C., 1970. Bar: S.C. 1970, U.S. Ct. Appeals (4th cir.) 1972, U.S. Dist. Ct. S.C. 1972. Legis. asst. U.S. Senator Strom Thurmond, Washington, 1970-72; asst. U.S. atty. Dept. Justice, Greenville, S.C., 1972-76, Columbia, S.C., 1983-86; U.S. Magistrate judge U.S. Dist. Ct., Columbia, S.C., 1986-91, U.S. Dist. judge Greenville, S.C., 1991—; prin. Coleman & Herlong, Edgefield, S.C., 1976-83. Dir. Edgefield (S.C.) Devel. Bd., 1978-83, S.C. Assn. of Counties, 1980-83; active S.C. Rural Devel. Bd., 1980-83, Edgefield County Coun., 1979-83. Capt. USAR, 1970-75. Mem. S.C. Bar, Edgefield County Bar, Lions Club, Sertoma Club. Republican. United Methodist. Avocations: hunting, fishing, gardening. Office: US Dist Courts PO Box 10469 300 E Washington St Greenville SC 29603-1000

HERMAN, ALEXIS M., former secretary of labor; b. Mobile, Ala., July 16, 1947; Student, Edgewood Coll. Sacred Heart, 1966—67; BA, Xavier U., New Orleans, 1969; Ph.D (hon.), Lesley Coll. Community worker Interfaith, Inc., Mobile, Ala., 1969; social worker Catholic Social Svc., Mobile, Ala., 1969—72; consult., supr. Recruitment & Training Program Inc., NYC, 1973—74; nat. dir. Minority Women's Employment Program, Washington, 1974—77; dir., founder, Women's Bur. US Dept. Labor, Washington, 1977-81; v.p., co-founder Green, Herman & Associates, 1981—85; founder, pres., CEO A.M. Herman & Assocs., Washington, 1985—93; chief staff, then dep. chair Dem. Nat. Conv. Com., Washington, 1989—91, CEO, 1991-92; dep. dir. Clinton-Gore Presdl. Transition Office, Washington, 1992-93; asst. to Pres., pub. liaison dir. The White House, Washington, 1993-96; sec. U.S. Dept. Labor, Washington, 1997-2001; chmn., CEO New Ventures, Inc., Washington, 2001—; chairperson Coca-Cola Human Resources Diversity Task Force, Ga., 2001—; chmn. Toyota N Am. Diversity Bd., 2002—. Mem. bd. dirs. Entergy Corp., 2003—, Cummins Inc., President Life Insurance Co., MGM Mirage. Recipient Outstanding Young Person in Atlanta award, 1974, Atlanta's First Woman award, 1976, Dorothy I. Height Leadership award, Ctrl State U., Sara Lee Front Runner award, 1999. Mem. Atlanta Black Woman's Coalition, Am. Soc. Bus. & Profl. Women, Diocesan Commn. Social Justice, Internat. Personnel Mgmt. Assn., Nat. Coun. Negro Women, Delta Sigma Theta. Democrat.*

HERMAN, ANDREA MAXINE, newspaper editor; b. Chgo., Oct. 22, 1938; d. Maurice H. and Mae (Baron) H.; m. Joseph Schmidt, Oct. 28, 1962. BJ, U. Mo., 1960. Feature writer Chgo.'s Am., 1960-63; daily columnist News Am., Balt., 1963-67; feature writer Mainichi Daily News, Tokyo, 1967-69; columnist Iowa City Press-Citizen, 1969-76; music and dance critic San Diego Tribune, 1976-84; asst. mng. editor features UPI, Washington, 1984-86, asst. mng. editor news devel., 1986-87; mng. editor features L.A. Herald Examiner, 1987-91; editor/culture We/Mbl Newspaper, Washington, 1991—. Recipient 1st and 2d prizes for features in arts James S. Copley Ring of Truth Awards, 1982, 1st prize for journalism Press Club San Diego, 1983. Mem. Soc. Profl. Journalists, Am. Soc. Newspaper Editors, AP Mng. Editors, Women in Communications. Avocations: music, art. Office: We Mbl Newspaper 1350 Connecticut Ave NW Washington DC 20036-1722 Office Phone: 858-459-3625. Business E-Mail: jdschmidt@ucsd.edu.

HERMAN, CHARLES KENNETH, plastic surgeon, researcher; s. Marvin Jules and Janice Deborah Herman. BS summa cum laude, Rensselaer Poly. Inst., 1996; MD summa cum laude, Albany Med. Coll., 2000. Lic. physician N.Y., 2001, Pa., Conn., 2005. Rsch. asst. Roswell Pk. Cancer Inst., Buffalo, 1997—98; resident in plastic surgery Albert Einstein Coll. of Medicine and Montefiore Med. Ctr., N.Y.C., 2003—04, chief resident in plastic surgery, 2004—05, attending surgeon, 2005—; med. dir. of plastic and reconstructive surgery Pocono Health Systems, East Stroudsburg, Pa., 2005—. Student dir. Young Scientist Rsch. Program, Canisius Coll., Buffalo, 1994—94; med. student editor Albany Med. Rev., NY, 1998—99; guest reviewer Jour. of Reconstructive Microsurgery, Bronx, NY, 2000—00; mem. curriculum com. dept. plastic surgery Albert Einstein Coll. of Medicine, N.Y.C., 2004—05; med. dir. of plastic and reconstructive surgery Pocono Health Systems, East Stroudsburg, Pa., 2005. Author: (research) Synthesis and Evaluation of Cationic Photosensitizers for Photodynamic Therapy (Nat. Winner of the ACP' Med. Student Rsch. Competition, 1998), (case presentation) Churg-Strauss Vasculitis Presenting with Cardiac Tamponade in Association with Zafirlukast (Nat. Winner of the ACP' Med. Student Clin. Competition, 1999), (textbook chpt.) Nerve Conduits in Peripheral Nerve Repair, Nutrition and the Geriatric Surgery Patient; contbr. articles to profl. jours. Recipient Hon. Sci. award, Bausch and Lomb Corp., 1993, 1994, Rensselaer medal, Rensselaer Poly. Inst., 1994, 1995, 1996, 1997, 1998, Commendation in Med. Ethics, Ctr. for Med. Ethics, Albany Med. Coll., 1997, Rsch. Competition award, ACP, 1998, Dean's Rsch. award, Albany Med. Coll., 1998, 1999, 2000, Trustees' Prize in pharmacology, 1999, Clin. Competition award, ACP, 1999, W. Brandon Macomber Prize in plastic surgery, Albany Med. Coll., 2000, Charles Eckert Prize in Surgery, 2000, Kevin Barron Hon. Award in the neuroscis., 2000; fellowship, NSF, 1993, Richard T. Beebe, M.D. fellowship in medicine, Albany Med. Coll., 1999. Mem.: Alpha Omega Alpha. Achievements include research in Research in Photodynamic Cancer Therapy; discovery of Churg-Strauss Vasculitis Presenting with Cardiac Tamponade in Association with Zafirlukast. Avocations: drummer and trumpeter, tennis, racquetball, travel. Personal E-mail: charleshermanmd@hotmail.com.

HERMAN, CLAUDIA BERNICE, elementary school educator; b. Manchester, Iowa, Nov. 6, 1952; d. Vernon Claude and Vivian Rita Northrop; m. Jean-Claude Rene Herman, Aug. 9, 1975; children: Sean, Mark. BA in Elem. Edn., History/Secondary Edn., Upper Iowa U., 1975. 1st grade tchr. New Hampton Schs., Iowa, 1975—. Mem.: NEA, New Hampton Edn. Assn., Iowa State Edn. Assn., Chickasaw Co. Hist. Soc. Avocations: gardening, travel. Home: 507 N Hartwell Ave New Hampton IA 50659 Office: New Hampton Schs 206 W Main St New Hampton IA 50659 E-mail: c_herman@new-hampton.k12.ia.us.

HERMAN, DAVID J., infectious diseases physician; b. St. Louis, Nov. 19, 1958; MD, U. Mo., 1985. Diplomate Am. Bd. Internal Medicine, Am. Bd. Infectious Disease. Resident in internal medicine Northwestern U., Chgo., 1985—88; fellow in infectious disease U. Minn., Mpls., 1988—91; physician Somerset Med. Ctr., 1991—, Med. Ctr. Princeton, NJ, 1991—, R.W. Johnson Univ. Hosp., 1991—, St. Peter's Univ. Hosp., 1996—. Named one of Top Drs. in N.Y. Metro Area, Castle Connolly, Top Drs. 2003, N.J. Monthly Mag. Office: 411 Courtyard Dr Hillsborough NJ 08844 also: 11 State Rd Ste 200 Princeton NJ 08540-1318 also: 81 Veronica Ave Somerset NJ 08873 Office Phone: 732-725-2522.

HERMAN, DAVID JAY, orthodontist; b. Rome, N.Y., Oct. 4, 1954; s. Maurice Joseph and Bettina S. (Stiener) H.; m. Mary Beth Appleberry, Apr. 11, 1976; children: Jeremiah D., Kellin A. BA in Biology, San Jose State U., 1976; DDS, Emory U., 1981; MS in Orthodontics, MPH, U. N.C., 1992. Comdr. USPHS, 1981-97; advanced gen. practice resident Gallup (N. Mex.) Indian Med. Ctr., 1983-84; Navajo area dental br. chief Window Rock, Ariz., 1986-89; mem. grad. residency com. U. N.C., Chapel Hill, 1990-91; Navajo area orthodontic specialist Shiprock, N. Mex., 1992-97; clin. dir. Nizhoni Smiles Inc., 1997-99; pvt. practice Farmington, N.Mex., 1998—; pres. Four Corners Orthodontics, Inc., 1998—. Mem. health adv. bd. Navajo Reservation Headstart, 1986—89; health promotion/disease prevention cons. USPHS/Indian Health Svc. Navajo Area, Window Rock, 1986—89; cons. Ariz. IHS Periodontal Health Task Force, 1986—90. Asst. wrestling coach Winslow (Ariz.) H.S., 1984-86, Gallup High Sch., 1987-89, Chapel Hill H.S., 1991-92, Farmington H.S., 1992—, Aztec H.S., 1998-2000; mem. H.S. Youth Wrestling Program, 1992-2000; mem. corp. bd. San Juan Reg. Med. Ctr., 1996—. Recipient Healthy Mothers/Healthy Babies Disease Prevention award, 1988, USPHS Achievement medal, 1985, Headstart Achievement award, 1989, Ariz. Pub. Health Assn. Hon. award, 1989; Nat. Health Svc. Corp. scholar Emory U., 1977-81. Mem. ADA, Am. Assn. Orthodontists, Rocky Mountain Soc. Orthodontists, N.Mex. Soc. Orthodontists (pres. 1998-99), Northwestern N.Mex. Sco. Orthodontists (pres. 1999-00), Navajo Area Dental Soc. (pres. 1985), Am. Assn. Mil. Orthodontists (sec.reas. 1992, v.p. 1993-94, pres. 1995-97). Avocations: wrestling, weightlifting, jogging, skiing, backpacking. Office Phone: 505-564-9000.

HERMAN, EDITH CAROL, journalist; b. Edgewood, Md., July 1, 1944; d. Herbert R. and Thirza E. (Simmons) H.; m. Leonard Wiener. BA, Purdue U., 1966. Reporter Hollister Newspaper Chain, Wilmette, Ill., 1966-68, Chgo. Tribune Newspaper, 1968-79, edn. editor, 1971-74, feature writer, 1976-79; sr. editor TV Digest Inc., 1980-83; pub. rels. mgr. AT&T, 1983-90; pub. rels. cons. Bethesda, 1990—93, Warren Comm., 1994—, assoc. mng. editor, 2001—. Bd. dirs. Sigma Delta Chi Found. of Washington, 1990—92. Recipient Journalism award Ill. Edn. Assn., 1969-70; Editorial award Ill. Automatic Merchandising Council, 1977 Mem.: Soc. Profl. Journalists. Home: 5501 Burling Ct Bethesda MD 20817-6309 E-mail: eherman@warren-news.com.

HERMAN, ELLEN ROMBS, literature and language educator; d. Vincent Joseph and Ruth (Burns) Rombs; m. James Paul Herman, June 24, 1967; children: Laura Brooks, Julia. BA, Marquette U., Milw., 1966, MEd, 1995. Cert. reading specialist pre-k-12, elem. tchr. Tchr. grades 3 and 5 Holy Family Sch., St. Louis Park, Minn., 1967—70; tchr. grade 2 Greendale (Wis.) Sch. Dist., 1970—71; tchr. grade 5 art St. Mary Parish Sch., Hales Corners, 1982—83, tchr. and reading tutor, 1990—94; tchr. reading and lang. arts grade 8 Holy Angels Sch., West Bend, 1994—98; tchr. art grades 6-8 St. Mary Parish Sch., Hales Corners, 1998—99, tchr. reading and lang. arts grades 6 and 7, 1999—. Sec. Friends of Hales Corners Libr., 1990—92, pres., 1992—95. Mem.: Wis. State Reading Assn., Nat. Coun. Tchrs. English, Pi Lambda Theta. Avocations: painting, reading, boating, skiing, hiking. Office: St Mary Parish Sch 9553 W Edgerton Ave Hales Corners WI 53130

HERMAN, ELVIN E., retired consulting electronic engineer; b. Mar. 17, 1921; s. John Lawrence and Martha Elizabeth (Conner) H.; m. Grace Winifred Eklund, Sept. 29, 1945; 1 child, Jane Ann Herman Fischer. BSEE, State U. Iowa, 1942. Engr., sect. head Naval Rsch. Lab., Washington, 1942-51; sect. head Corona (Calif.) Labs., Nat. Bur. Stds., 1951-53; sect. head, lab. mgr., tech. dir. radar sys. group Hughes Aircraft Co., El Segundo, Calif., 1953-83; cons. electronic engr., Pacific Palisades, Calif., 1983-88; ret., 1988. Recipient Meritorious Civilian Svc. award Naval Rsch. Lab., 1946. Fellow IEEE. Achievements include 24 patents in field. Home: 1200 Lachman Ln Pacific Palisades CA 90272-2228 Personal E-mail: alherm@earthlink.net.

HERMAN, FRED L., lawyer; b. New Orleans, Mar. 25, 1950; s. Harry and Reba (Hoffman) H.; m. Amanda Luria, Mar. 4, 1975. BA, Tulane U., 1972; JD, Loyola U.-New Orleans, 1975. Bar: La. 1975, U.S. Dist Ct. (ea. dist.) La. 1975, U.S. Ct. Appeals (5th cir.) 1978, U.S. Dist. Ct. (we. and mid. dists.) La. 1981, U.S. Ct. Appeals (11th cir.) 1981. Assoc. Herman & Herman, New Orleans, 1975-80; ptnr. Herman, Hermán, Katz & Cotlar, New Orleans, 1980-87; pvt. practice New Orleans, 1987—. Ltd. ptnr. New Orleans Saints, 1985, legis. counsel, chief negotiator for mng. ptnr., 1987; adj. faculty Tulane U.; lectr. Loyola Sch. Law, New Orleans, La.; spl. master Civil Dist. Ct. Parish of Orleans. Trial Lawyers Assn. Commr. New Orleans Pub. Belt R.R. Commn., 1983-93; mem. Jefferson Parish Child Abuse Advocacy Program, 1980-81; spl. counsel litigation, State of La.; spl. counsel City of New Orleans; judge pro tem., First City Ct., New Orleans, 1998; mem. adv. coun. Adult Rehab. Ctr. Salvation Army, 1991—. Mem. ATLA, Am. Arbitration Assn. (mediator, arbitrator), Nat. Health Lawyer Assn. (panel of mediators and arbitrators), La. Bankers' Assn. (bank counsel sect.), La. State Bar Assn. Office: 1010 Common St Ste 3000 New Orleans LA 70112-2421 Office Phone: 504-581-7070. Business E-Mail: fherman@acadiacom.net.

HERMAN, GEORGE ADAM, writer, literature educator; b. Norfolk, Va., Apr. 12, 1928; s. George Adam and Minerva Nevada (Thompson) H.; m. Patricia Lee Glazer, May 26, 1955 (div. 1989); children: Kurt, Erik, Karl, Lisa, Katherine, Christopher, Jena, Amanda; m. Patricia Jane Piper Dubay, Aug. 25, 1989; children: Lizette, Paul, Kirk, Victoria. PhB, Loyola Coll., 1950; MFA, Cath. U., 1954; cert. of fine arts, Boston Coll., 1953. Asst. prof. Clarke Coll., Dubuque, Iowa, 1955-60, Villanova (Pa.) U., 1960-63; asst. prof., playwright in residence Coll. St. Benedict, St. Joseph, Minn., 1963-65; chmn. theatre dept. Coll. Great Falls, Mont., 1965-67; media specialist Hawaii State Dept. Edn., Honolulu, 1967-75, staff specialist, 1975-83; sr. drama critic Honolulu Advertiser, 1975-80; artistic dir. Commedia Repertory Theatre, Honolulu, 1978-80; freelance writer, lectr., composer Portland, Oreg., 1983—. Author: (plays) Company of Wayward Saints, 1963 (McKnight Humanities award 1964), Mr. Highpockets, 1968, A Stone for Either Hand, 1969, Tenebrae, 1984, (novels) Carnival of Saints, 1994 (finalist Oreg. Book Awards 1994), A Comedy of Murders, 1994, Tears of the Madonna, 1995, The Florentine Mourners, 1999, The Toys of War, 2002, Little Rome, Iowa, 2003, Nine Dragons, 2003, Necromancer, 2003; composer (ballets) The Dancing Princesses, Fraidy Cat. Pres. local chpt. Nat. Sch. Pub. Rels. Assn., Honolulu, 1981-83; bd. dirs. Honolulu Community Theatre, 1981-82, Hawaii State Theatre Coun., Honolulu, 1981. With U.S. Army, 1950-52. Recipient Hartke Playwrighting award Cath. U., 1954, Humanities award McKnight Found., 1963, Excellence award Am. Security Coun., 1967. Avocations: directing theatre, lecturing. Personal E-mail: gadamo@aol.com.

HERMAN, HANK, writer; b. N.Y.C., Nov. 13, 1949; s. Philip and Stella (Rubenfeld) H.; m. Carol K. Korngut, Dec. 30, 1972; children: Matt, Greg, Robby. BA, U. Pa., 1971. Advt. copywriter Prentice-Hall, Englewood Cliffs, N.J., 1972-73; assoc. editor Travel Mgmt. Daily, N.Y.C., 1973-74; mng. editor TravelScene, N.Y.C., 1975-77, Health Mag., N.Y.C., 1978-79, editor in chief, 1980-88; freelance writer, 1989—. Health reporter Sta. WINS-Radio, N.Y.C., 1987-90. Award-winning columnist Westport News, 1993—; author numerous mag. articles and youth sports fiction books, 1973—. Avocations: running, tennis, skiing, coaching youth sports.

HERMAN, JAMES EDWARD, lawyer; b. Kansas City, July 14, 1945; s. Everton Paul and Virginia May (Hutchinson) Herman; m. Denise deBellefeuille. BA, U. Calif., Santa Barbara, 1971; JD, Calif. Western Law Sch., San Diego, 1975; LLM, NYU, 1976. Bar: Calif. 1976. Sr. fellow Criminal Law Edn. Rsch. Ctr. NYU, 1975—76; atty. Pub. Defender's Office, Riverside County, Calif., 1976—80, Defenders Inc., San Diego, 1979—80, Santa Barbara County Pub. Defenders Office, 1980—84; assoc. Cappello and Foley, Santa Barbara, 1984—; ptnr. Reicker, Prau, Pyle, McRoy & Herman LLP, Santa Barbara. Trustee Calif. Western Sch. Law; lectr. voir dire and dramatic arts techniques applied to trials various profl. orgns. Author: articles to profl. jours. Bd. dirs. Ensemble Theatre Project. Recipient Bernard E. Witkin Disting. Svc. Amicus Curiae award, Judicial Coun., State of Calif., 2003. Mem.: Calif. Attys. Criminal Justice, Assn. Trial Lawyers Am., State Bar Calif. (pres., bd. govs. 1999, pres. 2002—03), Santa Barbara County Bar Assn. (pres., past chair, bench/bar com.). Office: Reicker Pfau Pyle McRoy & Herman LLP 1421 State St Ste B PO Box 1470 Santa Barbara CA 93102-1470

HERMAN, JOAN ELIZABETH, insurance company executive; b. N.Y.C., June 2, 1953; d. Roland Barry and Grace Gales (Goldstein) Herman; m. Richard M. Rasiej, July 16, 1977. AB, Barnard Coll., 1975; MS, Yale U., 1977. Actuarial student Met. Life Ins. Co., N.Y.C., 1978-82; asst. actuary Phoenix Mut. Life Ins. Co. (name now Phoenix Life Ins.), Hartford, Conn., 1982-83, assoc. actuary, dir. underwriting rsch., 1983-84, 2d v.p., 1984-85, v.p., 1985-89, sr. v.p., 1989-98; pres. splty. bus. WellPoint Health Networks, Woodland Hills, Calif., 1998, group pres., 1999—2001, pres., sr., splty. and state sponsored programs divsn., 2002—04; pres., CEO, sr., splty. and state sponsored programs divsn WellPoint, Inc., Indpls., 2004—. Bd. dirs. PM Holdings, Inc., Phoenix Group Holdings, Inc., Phoenix Am. Life Ins. Co., Emprendimiento Compartido, S.A.; v.p. BC Life & Health Co., Profl. Cliams Svcs. Inc., Proserv., MEDIX. Contbr. articles to profl. jours. Bd. dirs. Health Ins. Assn. Am., 2002—03; capt. fundraising team Greater Hartford Arts Coun., Hartford, 1986; bd. dirs. Children's Fund Conn., 1992—98, My Sister's Pl. Shelter, Hartford, 1989—94, Western Mass. Regional Nat. Conf. Conn., 1995—98, Greater Hartford Arts Coun., 1997—98, Hartford Ballet, 1989—95, corporator, 1995—98; bd. dirs. Leadership Greater Hartford, 1989—94, chmn. bd. dirs., 1993—94; bd. dirs. So. Calif. Leadership Network, 2003—; mem. bd. founders Am. Leadership Forum Hartford, 1991—98; corporator Hartford Sem., 1994—98; bd. dirs. Hadassah, Glastonbury, Conn., Temple Beth Hillel, South Windsor, Conn., 1983—84. Fellow: Soc. Actuaries (chairperson health sect. coun. 1994—95); mem.: Am. Leadership Forum, Am. Acad. Actuaries (bd. dirs. 1994—97). Jewish. Avocations: reading, swimming, bicycling, jogging, aerobic dancing, hiking. Office: WellPoint Inc 1 Wellpoint Way Thousand Oaks CA 91362-3893 Office Phone: 805-557-6333. Business E-Mail: joan.herman@wellpoint.com.

HERMAN, KENNETH BEAUMONT, lawyer; b. Medford, Mass., Jan. 23, 1944; s. Beaumont Alexander and Winifred (Small) H.; m. Agnes Anne Burch, Sept. 18, 1976; children: Alexander Beaumont, Juliana Burch. AB, Harvard U., 1966; JD, Harvard Law Sch., 1969. Bar: N.Y. 1971. Tchr. St. Dominic Savio High Sch., East Boston, Mass., 1969-70; assoc., then ptnr. Fish & Neave, N.Y.C., 1970—2004; ptnr. Ropes & Gray LLP, N.Y.C., 2005—. Mem. Larchmont (N.Y.) Recreation Com., 1983-94, trustee Larchmont Hist. Soc., 1987-88. Mem. ABA, N.Y. State Bar Assn., N.Y. Intellectual Property Law Assn. (chmn. com. on incentives for innovation 1987-88), Licensing Execs. Soc., Internat. Trade Commn. Trial Lawyers Assn., Fed. Cir. Bar Assn., Am. Intellectual Property Law Assn., Assn. Bar of City of N.Y., Am. Arbitration Assn. (panel arbitrators). Avocations: sailing, skiing, kayaking, reading. Home: 810 Pirates Cv Mamaroneck NY 10543-4717 Office: Fish & Neave IP Group Ropes & Gray LLP 1251 Sixth Ave Avenue of the Americas New York NY 10020-1105 Office Phone: 212-596-9020.

HERMAN, LETA GWEN, columnist; b. Sommerville, N.J., Apr. 26, 1967; d. Stephen Jay and Gail (Neary) H.; m. Neal Stuart Parks. BA, Smith Coll., 1989. Vol. U.S. Peace Corps, Kiffa, Mauritania, 1990; corp. cons. Hybridon, Worcester, Mass., 1991; dir. comm. Complete Bus. Solutions, Inc., Farmington Hills, Mich., 1991—93; dir. mktg. Software Alliance Corp., Berkeley, Calif., 1993—94; nat. syndicated columnist, 1995—. Sys. engr. Avaya Inc., 1998—2005. Sara Williston scholar Mt. Holyoke Coll., 1987. Mem. NOW, NAFE, Nat. Orgn. Returned Peace Corps Vols., Phi Beta Kappa. Democrat. Avocations: creative writing, photography, travel, languages. Home and Office: 122 Old Bay Rd Belchertown MA 01007-9348

HERMAN, LYNN BRIGGS, state legislator; b. Philipsburg, Pa., Oct. 30, 1956; s. Frederick Jr. and Barbara Ann (Briggs) H. BA, U. Pitts., Johnstown, 1978; MPA, U. Pitts., 1980. Adminstrv. asst. Pa. Dept. Edn., Harrisburg, 1980-81; adminstrv. analyst Pa. Dept. Transp., Harrisburg, 1981-82; mem. Pa. Ho. of Reps., Harrisburg, 1982—. Chmn. local govt. com. Pa. Ho. of Reps., 1997—, chmn. legis. data processing com., 1994—, co-chmn. house history caucus; founder, co-chmn. Pa. State Forum Capitol, Centennial Commn., 2004—. Elected pres. Centre County's 148th Pa. Vol. Inf. Regiment Civil War reenactment group, 1998-2003. Named Outstanding Legislator, Pa. Rifle and Pistol Assn., 1987, State Ofcl. of Yr., Nat. Assn. Home Builders, 2004; named to Outstanding Young Men of Am.; recipient Presdl. Recognition award Moshannon Valley Econ. Devel. Partnership, 1990, Champion of Good Govt. award Common Cause of Pa., 1999, Disting. Svc. award Pa. Mcpl. Authorities Assn., 2002. Mem. Pa. Assn. State Retirees (Legislator award 2003), Frat. Order Police, Pa. State Alumni Assn., Ctrl. Pa. Civil War Round Table (pres. 2004—), Centre County Hist. Soc., Centre County Geneaol. Soc., Pa. SAR, Philipsburg Hist. Found. (hon. trustee), Sons Union Vets. Civil War, Pa. State Quarterback Club, Grange, Elks, Kiwanis, Masons. Republican. Office: Pa Ho of Reps State Capitol Rm 45 East Wing Harrisburg PA 17120 Office Phone: 717-787-8594. E-mail: lherman@pahousegop.com.

HERMAN, MARTIN NEAL, neurologist, educator; b. Washington, July 19, 1939; m. Sydney Beryl Epstein, July 1, 1962; children: Kenneth Dayan, Heidi Felice. AA, George Washington U., 1960; BS, Northwestern U., 1961, MD, 1964. Diplomate Am. Bd. Electroencephalography, Am. Bd. Psychiatry and Neurology, Nat. Bd. Med. Examiners; lic. N.J. Intern Georgetown U./D.C. Gen. Hosp., Washington, 1964; resident psychiatry U. Rochester (N.Y.)/Strong Meml. Hosp., 1964; resident neurology U. Va., Charlottesville, 1967-70; rsch. fellow clin. neurophysiology NIH, Bethesda, Md., 1970-71;

asst. prof., dir. electroencephalography N.J. Coll. Medicine and Dentistry, Newark, 1971-74; dir. neurology Monmouth Med. Ctr., Long Branch, N.J., 1974—. Asst. clin. prof. Hahnemann Med. Coll. and Hosp., 1974-91; clin. assoc. prof. Pa. U., Drexel U. Coll. Medicine, 1991—; attending physician Martland Hosp., Newark, 1971-74, East Orange (N.J.) VA Hosp., 1971-74, Riverview Med. Ctr., Red Bank, N.J., 1983—. Contbr. chpts. to books and articles to profl. jours. Mem. AMA, Am. Acad. Neurology, Am. Med. Electroencephalographic Soc., Am. Clin. Neurophysiology Soc., N.J. Med. Soc., N.J. Acad. Medicine, Ea. Assn. Electroencephalographers, Phi Eta Sigma. Office Phone: 732-935-1850. Personal E-mail: mnhermes1@comcast.net.

HERMAN, MARY MARGARET, neuropathologist; b. Plymouth, Wis., July 26, 1935; d. Elmer Fredolein and Esther Lydia (Bross) H.; m. Lucien Jules Rubinstein, Jan. 31, 1969. BS in Med. Sci., U. Wis., 1957, MD, 1960. Diplomate Nat. Bd. Med. Examiners, Am. Bd. Anatomic Pathology, Am. Bd. Neuropathology. Intern Mary Hitchcock Meml. Hosp., Hanover, NH, 1960-61; resident in neurology U. Wis. Hosps., 1961-62; intern in pathology Yale U., New Haven, 1962-63, asst. resident in pathology, 1963-64, fellow in neuropathology, 1964-65, rsch. assoc. pathology, 1967-68; fellow in neuropathology Stanford U., Palo Alto, Calif., 1965-66, fellow, acting instr. neuropathology, 1966-67, asst. prof. pathology, 1967-74, assoc. prof., 1974-81; prof., co-dir. divsn. neuropathology U. Va. Sch. Medicine, Charlottesville, 1981-91, prof. clin. pathology, 1991-92; spl. expert neuropathology in clin. brain disorders br. NIMH, Washington, 1991-96, sr. staff scientist, 1996—; neuropathologist NIMH Brain Collection, 1992—, Stanley Fund Brain Collection, 1992—2002. Vis. asst. prof. Albert Einstein Coll. Medicine, Bronx, NY, 1971—72; mem. program project rev. com. Nat. Inst. Neurol. and Communicative Diseases NIH, 1973—77; cons. lab. svc. VA Hosp., Salem, Va., Ctrl. Va. Tng. Ctr., Lynchburg, 1982—92, ad hoc mem. pathology A study sect., 1986—91; cons. neuropathologist DC Med. Examiner's Office, Washington, 1992—, Med. Examiner's Office, No. Va. Dist., Fairfax, 2000—, DC Gen. Hosp., 1992—2002; mentor scientist NIH Intramural Rsch. Tng. award, Fogarty Fellows, Howard Hughes Med. Inst./MCPS/NIH student and tchr. internships program, Stanley Found. scholar's program. Mem. editl. bd.: Jour. Neuropathology and Exptl. Neurology, 1989—93, 2001—; contbr. over 200 articles to profl. jours. Recipient Rsch. Career Devel. award, NIH, 1967—72, Staff Recognition award, 2000—05, Faculty Devel. award, Merck Found., 1969. Mem.: AAAS, AMA, Am. Assn. Anatomists, Soc. Biol. Psychiatry, Am. Assn. Neuropathologists (Weil award 1974), Am. Soc. for Investigative Pathology, Soc. for Devel. Biology, Internat. Soc. Neuropathology, Am. Soc. Cell Biology (rsch. fellowship program, mentor scientist summer tchr. 1994), Internat. Acad. Pathology, Soc. In Vitro Biology, Soc. Neurosci. Achievements include research in neuropathology of serious mental disorders, neurodegeneration and aluminum neurotoxicity, and embryonal tumors of the CNS. Avocations: tennis, gardening, music. Home: 10008 Stedwick Rd Apt 304 Montgomery Village MD 20886-3718 Office: Clin Brain Disorders Br NIMH NIH Msc 9402 5625 Fisher Ln Rm 4N03 Bethesda MD 20892-9402 Office Phone: 301-480-0042. Business E-Mail: mh230t@nih.gov.

HERMAN, MICHELLE RAE, writer; b. Bklyn., Mar. 9, 1955; d. Morton and Sheila Marcia (Weiss) Herman. BS, Bklyn. Coll., 1976; MFA in English, U. Iowa, 1986. Manuscript editor Van Nostrand Reinhold Co., N.Y.C., 1976; reporter Assoc. Press, City Desk, N.Y.C., 1977; freelance editor various pubs., N.Y.C., 1977-84; instr. U. of Iowa, Iowa City, 1984-86; assoc. prof., English Ohio State U., Columbus, 1988—. Author: (novel) Missing, 1990 (Harold U. Ribdow award Hadassah 1990), Dog, 2005 (memoir) The Middle of Everything: Memoirs of Motherhood, 2005; short stories; playwright: Tyler and Althea, 1980; editor (lit. mag.) The Journal. NEA fellow, 1986; recipient Tchg.-Writing award U. Iowa, 1985, 86, James Michener award 1987, Ohio Arts Coun. award 1989. Democrat. Jewish.*

HERMAN, MINDY, broadcast executive; d. Leonard and Flora Herman. BS in Economics, Wharton Sch. Bus., U. Penn, 1982; JD, MBA, UCLA; student, London Sch. Economics. With News Corp., 1990—98; v.p. bus. affairs Twentieth Century Fox, 1990—93; sr. v.p. bus. affairs FX Networks, 1993—95; exec. v.p. bus. ops. Tele-TV, 1995—97; exec. v.p. Fox Television Studios, 1997—99; pres., CEO Viewer's Choice (renamed In Demand, 2000), 1999—2000, E! Networks, N.Y.C., 2000—04. Recipient Women of Vision in Cable award, 2002, Larry Stewart Leadership and Inspiration award, Prism Awards, The Entertainment Industries Coun., 2004. Office: E! Networks 11 W 42d St Fl 19 New York NY 10036

HERMAN, PETER WINDLEY, lawyer; b. N.Y.C., 1944; AB, Columbia U., 1965, JD cum laude, 1970. Bar: N.Y. 1971. Ptnr. & head, Real Estate Dept. Milbank, Tweed, Hadley & McCloy, N.Y.C. Contbr. columns in newspapers. Chmn. Regional Plan Assn., NY; sec. Downtown Lower Manhattan Assn. Mem. ABA, N.Y. State Bar Assn. (mem. environ. law com.), Assn. Bar City N.Y. (chmn. transp. com. 1979-82), Urban Land Inst. Office: Milbank Tweed Hadley & McCloy 1 Chase Manhattan Plz Fl 47 New York NY 10005-1413 Office Phone: 212-530-5742. Office Fax: 212-530-5219. Business E-Mail: pherman@milbank.com.

HERMAN, RAYNA S., pharmaceutical consultant; BA in Chemistry, Ind. U., 1991; MBA, Washington U., 1996. Sales/mktg. staff Merck & Co., Inc., West Point, Pa., 1991-99; prin., owner Health Strategies Group, Lambertville, N.J., 1999—. Bd. dirs. Big Bros. Big Sisters, Montgomery County, 1999-2001; collegiate advisor Sigma Sigma Sigma, 2002-03; active Jr. League, 2002—. Mem.: Healthcare Bus. Women's Assn. Office Phone: 609-397-5282.

HERMAN, RICHARD GERALD, research chemist, consultant, educator; b. Springville, NY, Mar. 11, 1944; s. Richard Arthur and Mary Ann (Hoffman) H.; m. Helen Lynn Ramer; children: Richard David, Sarah Louise, Jonathan Garett. BS, SUNY, Fredonia, 1966; PhD, Ohio U., 1972. Cert. secondary edn. tchr., N.Y. Postdoctoral fellow Lund (Sweden) U., 1972-73, Tex. A&M U., College Station, 1973-75; rsch. scientist I Lehigh U., Bethlehem, Pa., 1975-82, rsch. scientist II, 1982-89, prin. rsch. scientist, 1989—, interim dir. Zettlemoyer Ctr. for Surface Studies, 1989; exec. dir. Zettlemoyer Ctr. for Surface Studies, Bethlehem, Pa., 1995-2001. Adj. assoc. prof. dept. chemistry Lehigh U., 1980—81, adj. prof. dept. chem. engring., 2002—. Editor: Catalytic Conversions of Synthesis Gas and Alcohols to Chemicals, 1984, Advances in Clean Fuel Technology and Control of Atmospheric Emissions, 2000, Catalytic Surface Centers and Mechanisms, 2002; contbg. author: New Trends in CO Activation, 1991, also others; contbr. over 110 articles to Catalysis, Chem. Engring. Sci., Inorganic Chemistry, Chem. Comm., also others. Tchr. Bible class Christ Evang. Luth. Ch., Schoenersville, Pa., 1981—, youth retreat asst., 1987-90; asst. coach Tri-Boro Youth Soccer, Whitehall, Pa., 1987-92, Lehigh Valley United Sr. Soccer Team, 1998—. Recipient Outstanding Achievement award SUNY, Fredonia, 1991, Disting. Svc. award Tri-Boro Youth Soccer, 1995. Mem.: Catalysis Soc. N.Am., Am. Chem. Soc. (chmn. Lehigh Valley chpt. 1989), Sigma Xi. Republican. Achievements include 5 patents for methanol synthesis, amine synthesis and water gas shift; development of new process for obtaining high cetane liquid fuels from alcohols; development of new catalytic process for low temperature abatement of NOx emissions. Office: Lehigh U Dept of Chemistry 6 E Packer Ave Bethlehem PA 18015-3102 Office Phone: 610-758-3486. E-mail: rgh1@lehigh.edu.

HERMAN, RICHARD H., academic administrator; m. Susan Herman. BA cum laude, Stevens Inst. Tech., 1963; PhD in Math., U. Md. Various positions UCLA, 1968—72, Pa. State U., 1972—90; dean Coll. Computer, Math. and Phys. Scis. U. Md., College Park, 1990—98; provost, vice chancellor acad. affairs U. Ill., Urbana-Champaign, 1998—, interim chancellor, 2004—05, chancellor, 2005—. Chmn. adv. com. for directorate math. and phys. sci. NSF; chair Joint Policy Bd. for Math.; mem. adv. bd. Mellon Coll. Sci. Contbr. articles to profl. jours. Bd. dirs. United Way, Champaign County C. of C. Fellow, Alexander von Humboldt Found. Mem.: Assn. Univs. for Rsch. in Astronomy, Inc. (mem. obs. coun.), Sigma Xi, Tau Beta Pi. Office: 204 Swanlund Adminstrn Bldg 601 E John St Champaign IL 61820*

HERMAN, ROBERT LEWIS, cork company executive; b. N.Y.C., July 16, 1927; s. Nat W. and Ruth (Stockton) H.; m. Susan Marie Volper, Dec. 10, 1966; children: Candia Ruth, William Neal. AB, Columbia U., 1948, BS, 1949. V.p. Joseph Samuels & Sons, Inc., Whippany, N.J, 1953-62; pres. Dependable Cork Co., Inc., Morristown, N.J, 1962—. Sr. chmn. Amorim Indsl. Solutions, Inc., Trevor, Wis., 1999—; bd. dirs. Concorco LDA, Lisbon, Portugal, Oporto, Portugal, Amorim Indsl. Solutions, LDA, Oporto, Portugal. Inventor Corticiera natural cork wallcovering. Comdr. C.E. Corps, USNR, 1949-53. Mem. N.J. Mfrs. Assn., Naval Res. Assn., U.S. C. of C., Navy League Club, Columbia U. Club, Princeton Club (N.Y.C.). Home: PO Box 1023 Morristown NJ 07962-1023 Office: PO Box 1102 Morristown NJ 07962-1102

HERMAN, RONALD ALTON, pharmacokineticist, educator; b. Waukon, Iowa, Nov. 5, 1953; s. Alton Earl and Margaret Elaine (Christianson) H.; m. Beverly Ann Leistikow, May 17, 1975; children: Andrea Faith, Alicia Joy, Joshua Benjamin, Rebecca Grace. BS in Pharmacy, U. Iowa, 1976, MS in Clin. Pharmacy, 1978, PhD in Pharmacokinetics, 1992. Registered pharmacist, Iowa. Tng. pharmacists Bophuthatswana Dept. of Health, Mmabatho, So. Africa, 1979-84; teaching asst. U. Iowa, Iowa City, 1985-92; clin. pharmacist U. Iowa Hosp. and Clinics, Iowa City, 1992-94; asst. prof. U. Iowa, Iowa City, 1994—. Contbr. articles to Jour. Rheumatology, Jour. Burn Care and Rehab., Jour. Pharm. Scis., Biopharmaceutics and Drug Disposition. Host Family Friends of Interant. Students, Iowa City, 1985—; host Coun. Internat. Visitors, Iowa City, 1988—. Abbott Labs. fellow, 1986-87. Mem. Am. Assn. Pharm. Scientists, Am. Soc. Clin. Pharmacology and Therapeutics, Am. Burn Assn., Am. Assn. Colls. Pharmacy, Christian Pharmacists Fellowship Internat. (bd. dirs. 1995—), Rho Chi. Soc. Republican. Evangelical. Home: 1939 Calvin Ave Iowa City IA 52246-3101 Office: U Iowa S525 Coll Pharmacy Iowa City IA 52242

HERMAN, SARAH ANDREWS, lawyer; b. Fargo, N.D., June 20, 1952; d. Mark and Mary Ann (Willming) Andrews; m. Douglas Ray Herman, July 7, 1976; children: Matthew, Samuel, Joseph. BA magna cum laude, U. N.D., 1974; JD, U. Mich., 1977. Bar: N.D. 1977, U.S. Dist. Ct. N.D. 1978. With Nilles, Hansen & Davies, Ltd., Fargo, ND, 1977, bd. dirs.; ptnr., trial and labor and employment practice groups Dorsey & Whitney LLP, Mpls., and group head, regulatory. Mem. Fed. Practice Com., 8th Cir. Gender Task Force. Co-chair N.D. Gender Fairness, 1993-94. Mem. ND State Bar Assn. (pres.), Cass County Bar Assn., Alpha Lambda Delta, Phi Beta Kappa. Republican. Episcopalian. Office: Dorsey & Whitney LLP Ste 402 Dakota Ctr 51 N Broadway Fargo ND 58107-4933 Office Phone: 701-235-6000. Office Fax: 701-235-9969. Business E-Mail: herman.sarah@dorsey.com.

HERMAN, SIDNEY N., lawyer; b. Chgo., May 14, 1953; s. Leonard M. and Suzanne (Nierman) H.; m. Meg Dobies. BA, Haverford Coll., 1975; JD, Northwestern U., 1978. Bar: Ill. 1978, U.S. Dist. Ct. (no. dist.) Ill. 1978, U.S. Ct. Appeals (7th cir.) 1982, U.S. Supreme Ct. 1983. Assoc. Kirkland & Ellis, Chgo., 1978-84, equity ptnr., 1984-93; founding ptnr. Bartlit Beck Herman Palenchar & Scott, Chgo., 1993—. Bd. dirs. Todd Shipyards Corp., Sigmatron, Inc., Chgo., Global Material Techs., Chgo. Lawyers' Com. for Civil Rights Under Law, Inc.; mem. law bd. Northwestern U. Sch. Law. Articles editor Northwestern U. Law Rev. Trustee Francis W. Parker Sch.; bd. mem. Chgo. Lawyers' com. for Civil Rights Under Law. Mem. ABA, Ill. Bar Assn. Jewish. Office: Bartlit Beck Et Al Courthouse Pl 54 W Hubbard St Ste 300 Chicago IL 60610-4668 Office Phone: 312-494-4400. Business E-Mail: skip.herman@bartlit-beck.com.

HERMAN, STEPHEN CHARLES, lawyer; b. Johnson City, N.Y., Apr. 28, 1951; s. William Herman and Myrtle Stella (Clark) Keithline; m. Jeanne Ellen Nelson, Sept. 9, 1972; children: Neelie Kristine, Stefanie Anne, Christopher William. Student, Cedarville Coll., 1969-72; BA, Wright State U., 1973; JD, Ohio No. U., 1976. Bar: Mo. 1977, Ill. 1977, Tex. 2004; U.S. Dist. Ct. (ea. dist.) Mo. 1978, U.S. Dist. Ct. (no. dist.) Ill. 1979, U.S. Dist. Ct. (ea. dist) Mich. 1988, U.S. Dist. Ct. (so. dist.) Tex. 1997; U.S. Ct. Appeals (D.C. cir.) 1979, U.S. Ct. Appeals (7th cir.) 1979, U.S. Ct. Appeals (5th cir.) 1980, U.S. Ct. Appeals (10th cir.) 1992; U.S. Supreme Ct. 1986, U.S. Ct. Internat. Trade, 1998. Atty. Mo. Pacific Railroad Co., St. Louis, 1977-78; assoc. Belnap, McCarthy, Spencer, Sweeney & Harkaway, Chgo., 1978-82; ptnr. Belnap, Spencer & McFarland, Chgo., 1982-83, Belnap, Spencer, McFarland & Emrich, Chgo., 1983-84, Belnap, Spencer, McFarland, Emrich & Herman, Chgo., 1984-89, Belnap, Spencer, McFarland, Herman, 1990-96, McFarland & Herman, 1996-01; atty. Stephen C. Herman, P.C., Chgo., 2001—03, Waco, Tex., 2003—. Mem. Mo. Bar Assn., Met. Bar Assn. St. Louis, Ill. State Bar Assn., Chgo. Bar Assn., Tex. Bar Assn., Assn. Transp. Law Profls., Transp. Lawyers Assn. Office: 3426 Austin Ave Waco TX 76710-7338 Home: 3426 Austin Ave Waco TX 76710-7338 Office Phone: 254-753-4472. Personal E-mail: schrmn@aol.com.

HERMAN, WILLIAM ARTHUR, engineering and physics laboratory director; b. Washington, Mar. 9, 1947; s. William Jackson and Alma Rebecca (Wattwood) H. BSEE, George Washington U., 1968. Chief microwave sect. Southeastern Radiol. Health Lab., Montgomery, Ala., 1968-70; chief microwave measurements unit FDA, Rockville, Md., 1970-73, dep. chief. electromagnetics br., 1973-74, sr. engr. electromagnetics br., 1974-79, assoc. dir. divsn. electronic products, 1979-83, dir. divsn. phys. scis., 1983—2004; dep. dir. Office Sci. and Engring. Labs. CDRH/FDA, 2004—. Mem. Interagy. Group on Sci. Performance Measures, Rockville, 1994—96; staff mem. blue ribbon panel FDA, Washington, 1990; FDA coord. scholar-in-residence program NSF/FDA, 2003—; expert panelist NAS Symposium on Video Display Terminals and Vision, 1981, NIH Bioengring. Symposium: Bldg. the Future of Biology and Medicine, Instruments and Devices Panel, 1998; expert bioengring. panelist NSF, 1999—; mem. planning com. White Houe Conf. on emerging tech. for Am. with Disabilities, 2004. Contbr. articles to profl. jours.; patentee in field. With USPHS, 1968-74. Mem. IEEE (sr.), World Future soc., Mensa, Tau Beta Pi, Amnesty Internat., Sigma Tau, Omicron Delta Kappa, Phi Eta Sigma, Alpha Theta Nu.

HERMAN, WILLIAM GEORGE, municipal official; b. West Chester, Pa., Sept. 2, 1956; s. Albert William Jr. and Beverly Lou (Marshall) H.; m. Mary Jo Batchelder, July 7, 1983; children: Brian William, Andrew Albert. Grad. H.S., Weare, N.H., 1974. Cert. pub. mgr. Reporter, photographer Union Leader Corp., Manchester, NH, 1973—80; prin., owner Herman Assocs. P.R., Manchester, 1980—82; press sec. Gov. John H. Sununu, Concord, NH, 1982—83; programs info. officer N.H. Divsn. Human Svcs., Concord, 1984—86, Divsn. Econ. Devel., Concord, 1986—92; pub. info. officer Fed. Emergency Mgmt., Boston, 1992—; town adminstr. Town of Milton, NH, 1993—95, Town of New Durham, NH, 1995—. Affiliate, cons. Mcpl. Resources, Inc., Meredith, 1995—; bd. dirs. N.H. Sch. Health Care Coalition, treas., 2002-2003, chmn. 2003-, NH Pub. Works Mut. Aid Program, 1999—, sec., treas. 2003—, N.H. Pub. Works Stds. and Tng. Coun., 2000—, vice-chmn., 2000-03, chmn., 2003—; mem. U.S. Selective Svc. #4, Merrimack County, 1999-2004. Vice chmn. U.S. Selective Svc. #10, Hillsborough County, 1982-98; chmn. Bd. Selectmen, Weare, N.H., 1984-96; commr., officer So. N.H. Planning Commn., Manchester, 1984-96; chmn. Concord Regional SW/RRC, Corcord, 1987—; dir. Greater Manchester ARC, 1988-94; trustee YMCA Camp Coniston, Grantham, N.H., 1989-93; dir. ARC Blood Svc., Dedham, Mass., 1989-98. Recipient George Washington honor medal Freedom Found., Valley Forge, Pa., 1973, Svc. award Town of Weare, 1996, Grassroots govt. leadership award Nat. Assn. Towns & Twps., Washington, 1991. Mem. Am. Acad. Cert. Pub. Mgrs. (ho. of dels. 2000—, chmn. integrated mktg. com. 2001-04, bylaws com. 2001-02, bd. dirs. mem.-at-large 2002-04, pres-elect 2005), Internat. City/County Mgmt. Assn. (small cmtys. task force 1999-2001), N.H. Assn. Cert. Pub. Mgrs. (officer, sec. 1999-2001, treas. 2001-04), N.H. Mcpl. Mgmt. Assn. Republican. Avocations: reading, travel, computers. Home: 203 Loudon Rd Unit 721 Concord NH 03301 Office: Town of New Durham PO Box 207 New Durham NH 03855-0207

HERMAN, archbishop, head of Orthodox Church in America; b. Briarford, Pa., Feb. 1, 1932; Degree in bus. admin. and secretarial sci. with honors, Robert Morris Coll., Pitts.; grad., Saint Tikhon Seminary, South Canaan, Pa., 1963. Rector Saint John the Baptist Ch., Dundaff, Pa., Saints Peter and Paul Church, Uniondale, Pa.; tonsured to monastic rank Orthodox Ch. in Am., 1970, dep. abbot Saint Tikhon Monastery, 1971, ordained Holy Diaconate and Holy Priesthood, 1964, bishop of Wilkes-Barre, 1973—81, rector Saint Tikhon Monastery, 1981—, bishop of Phila., 1981—2002; elevated to archbishop, 1994—; archbishop of Washington, metropolitan of Am., Canada Orthodox Ch. in Am., 2002—. Adjutant Gen. Corps U.S. Army, Labrador. Office: Orthodox Church in Am Saint Tikhon's Monastery South Canaan PA 18459*

HERMANCE, MYRON E., JR., conductor, educator; b. Hudson, Ny, May 7, 1928; s. Myron Erastus and Thelma Evelyn Hermance; m. Alicia Van Zoeren Hermance, June 21, 1952; children: Susan Adella, Dirk Edward, Melanie Jo, Peter Alan, Gay Marie, Rhonda Kay, Philip Jon. MusM, Ind. U., 1956; BA, Hope Coll., 1950. Cert. Secondary Teaching Mich., 1950, Music Education NY State, 1961. Profl. vocalist chs., colls. and theater, Western Mich. and Ea. NY, 1952—; pvt. voice educator NY, 1952—; vocal and instrumental educator Fremont (Mich.) H.S., 1952—57; music supr. Holton (Mich.) Pub. Schs., 1957—60; condr., pvt. educator chs., sr. citizen homes and cmty. theatre, Albany, NY, 1960—; vocal music educator Schenectady (NY) City Schools, 1960—87. Orchestral condr. Albany and Schenectady Sr. Ctrs., 1994—; ch. music ministry Ref. Chs., Schenectady and Albany, NY, Congl. Ch., Fremont, Mich., 1952—60. Recipient Teacher's Performance Inst., Rockefeller Found., Oberlin Coll., 1968. Mem.: NY State Sch. Music Assn. (all-state voice judge 1997—), Music Educators Nat. Conf., NY State Fedn. Tchrs., Nat. Assn. Tchrs. of Singing. Democrat-Npl. Reformed Church In America. Avocations: lay preacher, civil war historian, geneologist, theology, artist. Home: 25 Alvey Street Schenectady NY 12304

HERMAN-GIDDENS, GREGORY, lawyer; b. Birmingham, Ala., Aug. 8, 1961; BA, U. N.C., 1984; JD, Tulane U., 1988; LLM in Estate Planning, U. Miami, 1993. Bar: N.C. 1988, U.S. Dist. Ct. (mid. dist.) N.C. 1988, Fla. 1992, U.S. Tax Ct. 2001, U.S. Supreme Ct. 1998, U.S. Tax Ct. 2001, Tenn. 2004; cert. specialist in estate planning and probate law, N.C. State Bar Bd. Legal Specialization; grad. leadership triangle program 1996. Assoc. N. Joanne Foil, Atty. at Law, Durham, N.C., 1988-92, Catalano, Fisher, Gregory & Crown, Chartered, Naples, Fla., 1993, Northen, Blue, Rooks, Thibaut, Anderson & Woods, L.L.P., Chapel Hill, N.C., 1994-96; pvt. practice Chapel Hill, 1996—. Profl. adv. com. Triangle Cmty. Found., 1999—. Mem. Chapel Hill Bd. Adjustment, 1989—92; bd. dirs. Friends of Chapel Hill Sr.Ctr., 1994—97; mem. Orange County Adv. Bd. on Aging, 1994—97, vice chair, 1996—97; treas., bd. dirs. Orange County Literacy Coun., Carrboro, NC, 1994—98. Mem.: ABA (probate and trust sect. 1996—, coms. on stds. of tax practice and tax practice mgmt. of tax sect., coms. on lifetime and testamentary charitable gift planning, com. on planning for execs. and profls. of real property), Durham/Orange Estate Planning Coun., Nat. Acad. Elder Law Attys., NC Bar Assn. (career devel. com. young lawyers divsn. 1990—91, law and aging com. young lawyers divsn. 1994—98, dir. young lawyers divsn. 1997—98, endowment com. 1997—, elder law sect. coun. 1998—2001, newsletter editor 2001—03), Psi Chi, Phi Beta Kappa. Office: 205 Providence Rd Chapel Hill NC 27514 Office Phone: 919-493-6351. E-mail: ghgiddens@trustcounselpa.com.

HERMANIES, JOHN HANS, retired lawyer; b. Aug. 19, 1922; s. John and Lucia (Eckstein) H.; m. Dorothy Jean Steinbrecher, Jan. 3, 1953 AB, Pa. State U., 1944; JD, U. Cin., 1948, D of Law (hon.), 1992. Bar: Ohio 1948. Atty. Indsl. Commn. Ohio, 1948-50; asst. atty. gen. State of Ohio, 1951-57, asst. to gov., 1957-59; ptnr. Hermanies & Major (formerly Beall, Hermanies, Bortz & Major), Cin., 1958-99; mem. bd. grievances and discipline Supreme Ct. Ohio, 1976-82; ret., 1999. Mem. Ohio Bd. Bar Examiners, 1963-68. Mem. Southwest Ohio Regional Transit Authority, 1973-76; trustee U. Cin, 1977-92, Found. Bd., 1992-99, trustee emeritus, 1999—; mem. bd. elections Hamilton County, Ohio, 1984-88; chmn. exec. com. Hamilton County Rep. Party, 1974-88. With USMC, WWII. Mem. ABA, Ohio Bar Assn., Cin. Bar Assn., Queen City Club, Highland Country Club, Hyde Park Golf and Country Club. Home: 1201 Edgecliff Pl Cincinnati OH 45206-2847

HERMANN, ALLEN MAX, physics professor; b. New Orleans, July 17, 1938; s. Edward Frederick and Miriam (Davidson) H.; m. Leonora Christopher, May 19, 1979; children: Miriam, Mary, Neil, Scott. BS with honors in Physics, Loyola U., New Orleans, 1960; MS in Physics, U. Notre Dame, 1962; PhD in Physics, Tex. A&M U., 1965. Sr. research scientist Jet Propulsion Lab, Pasadena, Calif., 1965-67, tech. mgr., 1985-86; asst. prof. physics Tulane U., New Orleans, 1967-70, assoc. prof. physics, 1970-75, prof. physics, 1975-81; task mgr. Solar Energy Research Inst., Golden, Colo., 1980-85; prof., chmn. dept. physics U. Ark., Fayetteville, 1986-89, Disting. prof., 1989; prof. dept. physics U. Colo., Boulder, 1990—2005; vis. prof. dept. elec. and computer engring. U. Ky., Lexington, 2005—; dir. Ctr. Nanoscale Sci. and Engring. U Ky., 2005—. Cons. Jet Propulsion Lab., 1978-81, 86-87, NASA-Lewis Rsch. Ctr., Cleve., 1978-80, Cardiac Pacemakers Inc., Mpls., 1976-79, Radiation Monitoring Devices, Newton, Mass., 1990-93, Superconducting Core Techs., Denver, 1989-95, Sumitomo Electric Industries, Osaka, Japan, 1991-98, MV Sys., Inc., Golden, 1999—. Founding co-editor Applied Physics Communication; editor: Applied Physics Book Series; contbr. numerous articles to profl. jours. Bd. dirs. Colo. Assn. Retarded Citizens, Denver, 1983-85. Recipient NASA Outstanding Achievement award 1970, 72, Disting. Scientist award Am. Assn. Physics Tchrs., 1987; named Hero, State of Ark., Ark. Times mag.; named Person of the Yr., Superconductivity Week, 1989; elected to Acad. Disting. Grads., Coll. Sci., Tex. A&M U., 1999. Fellow Am. Phys. Soc.; mem. IEEE (sr.), Materials Rsch. Soc. Home: 2704 Lookout View Dr Golden CO 80401-2520 Office: U Colo PO Box 390 Boulder CO 80309-0390 Business E-Mail: allen.hermann@colorado.edu.

HERMANN, DONALD HAROLD JAMES, law educator; b. Southgate, Ky., Apr. 6, 1943; s. Albert Joseph and Helen Marie (Snow) H. AB (George E. Gamble Honors scholar), Stanford U., 1965; JD, Columbia U., 1968; LLM, Harvard U., 1974; MA, Northwestern U., 1979, PhD, 1981; MA in Art History, Sch. Art Inst. Chgo., 1993; MLA, U. Chgo., 2001. Bar: Ariz. 1968, Wash. 1969, Ky. 1971, Ill. 1972, U.S. Supreme Ct. 1974. Mem. staff, directorate devel. plans U.S. Dept. Def., 1964-65; With Legis. Drafting Research Fund, Columbia U., 1966-68; asst. dean Columbia Coll., 1967-68; mem. faculty U. Wash., Seattle, 1968-71, U. Ky., Lexington, 1971-72, DePaul U., 1972—, prof. law and philosophy, 1978—, dir. acad. programs and interdisciplinary study, 1975-76, assoc. dean, 1975-78, dir. Health Law Inst., 1985—2000; lectr. dept. philosophy Northwestern U., 1979-81; counsel DeWolfe, Poynton & Stevens, 1984-89. Vis. prof. Washington U., St. Louis, 1974, U. Brazilia, 1976, U. P.R. Sch. Law, 1993; lectr. law Am. Soc. Found., 1975-78, Sch. Edn. Northwestern U., 1974-76, Christ Coll. Cambridge (Eng.) U., 1977, U. Athens, 1980; vis. scholar U. N.D., 1983; mem. NEH seminar on property and rights Stanford U., 1981; participant law and econs. program U. Rochester, 1974; mem. faculty summer seminar in law and humanities UCLA, 1978; Bicentennial Fellow of U.S. Constitution Claremont Coll., 1986; Law and Medicine fellow Cleve. Clinic., 1990; bd. dirs. Coun. Legal Edn. Opportunity, Ohio Valley Consortium, 1972, Ill. Bar Automated Rsch. Corp., 1975-81, Criminal Law Consortium Cook County, Ill., 1977-80; cons. Adminstrv. Office Ill. Cts., 1975-90; reporter cons. Ill. Jud. Conf., 1972-90; mem. Ctr. for Law Focused Edn., Chgo., 1977-81; faculty Instituto Superiore Internazionale Di Science Criminali, Siracusa, Italy, 1978-82; cons. Commerce Fedn., State of São Paulo, Brazil, 1975; residential scholar Christ Ch., Oxford, 1999. Editor: Jour. of Health and Hosp. Law, 1986-96, DePaul Jour. Healthcare Law, 1996—, AIDS Monograph Series, 1987—. Mem. Cook County States Atty. Task Force on Gay and Lesbian Issues, 1990—, Contemporary Arts Coun. Chgo., 1999—; bd. dirs. Ctr. Ch.-State Studies, 1982—, Horizons Cmty. Svcs., 1985—88, Chgo. Area AIDS Task Force, 1987—90, Howard Brown Health Ctr., 1994—; v.p. Inst. Genetics, Law and Ethics, Ill. Masonic Hosp., 1993—2000; trustee 860 N. Lakeshore Trust,

Chgo., 1993—95; bd. visitors Oriental Inst. U. Chgo., 1995—; co-chair parity and inclusion com. Ill. HIV Prevention Cmty. Group Ill. Dept. Pub. Health; dir. Inst. Genetics, Law and Ethics, Ill. Masonic Hosp., 1993—2000; bd. dirs. Gerber-Hart Libr. and Archives, Mostly Music of Chgo., 1998—2001; mem. scholars' group ethics and med. rsch. NIH/U. Ill. Med. Sch. John Noble fellow Columbia U., 1968, Internat. fellow, NEH fellow, Law and Humanities fellow U. Chgo, 1975-76, Law and Humanities fellow Harvard U., 1973-74, Northwestern U., 1978-82, Criticism and Theory fellow Stanford U. 1981, NEH fellow Cornell U., 1982, Judicial fellow U.S. Supreme Ct., 1983-84, U. Ill. fellow med. ethids rsch. group; Dean's scholar Columbia U., 1968, Univ. scholar Northwestern U., 1979. Mem.: ABA, Am. Inn of Ct. (Abraham Lincolm Marowitz chpt.), Chgo. Coun. Fgn. Rels., Ill. Assn. Hosp. Attys., Am. Acad. Healthcare Attys., Am. Assn. Law Schs. (del., sect. chmn., chmn. sect. on jurisprudence), Soc. Am. Law Tchrs., Internat. Penal Law Soc., Soc. Writers on Legal Subjects, Soc. Phenomenology and Existential Philosophy, Soc. Bus. Ethics, Am. Philos. Assn., Am. Judicature Soc., Nat. Health Lawyers Assn., Internat. Assn. Philosophy of Law and Soc., Am. Soc. Polit. and Legal Philosophy, Am. Soc. Law, Medicine and Ethics, Am. Law Inst., Am. Acad. Polit. and Social Sic., Chgo. Bar Assn., Ill. Bar Assn., Soc. Contemporary Art Art Inst. Chgo., Evanston Hist. Soc., Northwestern U. Alumni Assn., Chgo. Literary Soc., Quadrangle Players, Renaissance Soc. (bd. dirs. 1995—), Lawyers Club Chgo., Arts Club Chgo., Cliff Dwellers Club, Tavern Club, Quadrangle Club, University Club, Hasty Pudding Club, Signet Club Harvard. Episcopalian.

HERMANN, PHILIP J., lawyer; b. Cleve., Sept. 17, 1916; s. Isadore and Gazella (Gross) H.; m. Cecilia Alexander, Dec. 28, 1945; children: Gary, Ann. Student, Hiram Coll., 1935-37; BA, Ohio State U., 1939; JD, Western Res. U., 1942. Bar: Ohio 1942. With Hermann Cahn & Schneider and predecessors, Cleve., 1946-86. Founder, former chmn. bd. Jury Verdict Rsch., Cleve.; pres. Legal Info. Pubs. Author: 1956, Better Settlements Through Leverage, 1965, Do You Need a Lawyer?, 1980, Better, Earlier Settlements through Economic Leverage, 1989, Injured? How to Get All the Money You Deserve, 1990, The 96 Billion Dollar Game: You are Losing, 1993, How to Select Competent Cost-effective Legal Counsel, 1993, Profit With the Right Lawyer, I Was Raised by a St. Bernard, 2003; contbr. articles to profl. jours. Served to lt. comdr. USNR, 1942-46, PTO. Mem. ABA (past vice chmn. casualty law com., past chmn. use of modern tech. com.), Ohio Bar Assn. (past chmn. ins. com., past chmn. fed. ct. com., past mem. ho. of dels.), Cleve. Bar Assn. (past chmn. membership com.), Am. Law Firm Assn. (past chmn. bd.), Fedn. Ins. Counsel. Home: 23287 Blue Water Cir Apt A104 Boca Raton FL 33433-7016 *Being what some people label "a perfectionist" is not easy and certainly not popular. It takes time and effort to collect information, to analyze it, to apply these to decisions and to insist upon careful work, but in the long run it is rewarding.*

HERMANN, ROBERT BELL, physical chemist, consultant; b. Bellevue, Pa., Dec. 12, 1930; s. Gustave Adolph and Alida Hermann; m. Phyllis Ann Halley, Aug. 7, 1958 (div. Feb. 1982); children: Deborah, David, Stephen; m. Carol Sue Lester, June 12, 1985. BS in Chemistry, U. Mich., 1953; MS, Wayne State U., 1960, PhD, 1962. Organic chemist Parke-Davis & Co., Detroit, 1953-58; NSF postdoctoral fellow U. Wis., Madison, 1962-63; postdoctoral fellow Ill. Inst. Tech., Chgo., 1963-64; computational chemist Eli Lilly & Co., Indpls., 1964-93. Vis. prof. Ind. U.-Purdue U. Ind., Indpls., 1994—; cons. Eli Lilly & Co., 1994—. Contbr. articles to profl. jours. Presbyterian. Achievements include research of relationship between molecular surface area and solubility especially with regard to hyrdophobic interactions; patent for inhibitors of phospholipase A2. Office Phone: 317-277-8608. Personal E-mail: robeherma@aol.com.

HERMANN, ROBERT EWALD, retired surgeon; b. Highland, Ill., Jan. 28, 1929; s. Ewald E. and Erna (Pabst) H.; m. Barbara Bower, Aug. 23, 1952 (dec. Aug. 1980); m. Polly Dreher, Mar. 8, 1986; childrn: Robert Jr., Barry, Monty. AB cum laude, Harvard U., 1950; MD, Washington U., St. Louis, 1954. Diplomate Am. Bd. Surgery. Intern, resident Univ. Hosps., Cleve., 1954-61; chmn. gen. surgery Cleve. Clinic, 1969-94, emeritus cons. dept. gen. surgery, 1994—; clin. prof. surgery Case Western Res. Sch. Medicine, Cleve., 1970—. Dir. Am. Bd. Surgery, Phila., 1975-81; mem. Residency Rev. Com., Chgo., 1975-81. Author: Surgery of Gallbladder, Bile Ducts, Pancreas, 1979, Surgical Practice of Cleveland Clinic, 1985; contbr. over 180 articles to med. jours., 53 chpts. to books. Trustee Cleve. Clinic Found., 1976-77. Capt. M.C. U.S. Army, 1956-57. Recipient Roswell Park Gold medal Buffalo Surg. Soc., 1993. Mem. ACS (gov. 1981-87, v.p. 1996-97, Disting. Svc. award 1994), Am. Surg. Soc., German Surg. Soc. (hon.), Internat. Surg. Soc., Internat. Coll. Surgeons (hon.), Soc. Surg. Oncology, Soc. Surgery Alimenatary Tract (pres. 1988-89), Assn. Program Dirs. Surgery (pres. 1979-81), Ea. Surg. Soc. (pres. 1985-86), Pan-Pacific Surg. Assn. (v.p. 1991-93), Joint Commn. on Accreditation of Healthcare Orgns. (bd. commrs. 1997-2002). Republican. Avocations: tennis, golf, sailing, music. Home: 1 Bratenahl Pl Apt 1403 Bratenahl OH 44108-1156 Office: Cleve Clinic A-80 9500 Euclid Ave Cleveland OH 44195-0001 Personal E-mail: rhermannmd@aol.com.

HERMANN, ROBERT JAY, former manufacturing executive, consultant; b. Sheldahl, Iowa, Apr. 6, 1933; s. John and Ellen Melinda (Ericson) H.; m. Darlene Velda Lowman, Mar. 20, 1954; children: Scott Alan, Sherie Lynn. BSEE, Iowa State U., 1954, MSEE, 1959, PhD, 1963. Dep. dir. research and engring. Nat. Security Agy., Ft. Meade, Md., 1973-75; spl. asst. to supreme allied comr. Europe SHAPE, Casteau, Belgium, 1975-77; dep. under sec. of def. for research and engring. Dept. Def., Washington, 1977-79, asst. sec. of Air Force for research, devel. and logistics, 1979-81; dir. Nat. Reconnaissance, 1979-81; spl. asst. for intelligence to under sec. of def. for research engring. Dept. Def., Washington, 1981-82; v.p. systems tech. and analysis United Techs., Hartford, Conn., 1982-84, v.p. advanced systems def. and space group, 1984-87, v.p. sci. and tech., 1987-92, sr. v.p. sci. and tech., 1992-98; sr. ptnr. Global Tech. Partners, LLC, 1998—. Cons. Def. Sci. Bd., 1985-; mem. vis. com. advanced tech. Nat. Inst. Stds. and Tech., 1992-97; mem. Pres. Fgn. Intelligence Adv. Bd., 1993-01; mem. commn. on phys. scis., math. and applications NRC, 1993-98; bd. dirs. Draper Labs., 1992-01, Am. Nat. Stds. Inst., 1994-02. 1st lt. USAF, 1955-57. Recipient Arthur Fleming Washington Jaycees, 1972; recipient Nat. Capital Nat. Capital Area Architects and Engrs., Washington, 1967, Air Force Disting. Service medal USAF, Washington, 1980, Disting. Grad. award Iowa State U., 1995. Mem. NAE, AIAA, Armed Forces Comms. and Electronics Assn. (bd. dirs. 1979-83), Security Affairs Support Assn. (pres. 1983-86, award 1994), Navy League (chmn. indsl. exec. bd. 1989, Dept. Def. Fubini award 2004). Home: 5 Stonepost Simsbury CT 06070-2511 Office: Global Tech Ptnrs LLC 14th Fl 100 Pearl St Hartford CT 06103 Office Phone: 860-249-7242. Personal E-mail: rjhinct@aol.com.

HERMANN, ROBERT JOHN, lawyer; b. Chgo., Apr. 17, 1944; s. Jacob L. and Rose E. (McCrudden) H.; m. Lyn D. Johnson; children by a previous marriage: Kelly, Brenna, Richard, Edana. Student, U. Ill., 1962-65; BS, No. Ill. U., 1967; JD, DePaul U., 1970. Bar: Ill. 1970, U.S. Supreme Ct. 1988; CPA, Ill., Tex. Tax staff Deloitte Haskins & Sells, Chgo., 1968-81; dir. corp. tax Houston Natural Gas, 1981-82, v.p. corp. tax, 1982-85, Enron Corp., Houston, 1985-99, mng. dir., gen. tax counsel, 2000—. Mem. ABA, Nat. Assn. Mfrs. (taxation com.), Tax. Execs. Inst., Sweetwater Country Club. Home: 4002 S Oak Cir Sugar Land TX 77479-2426

HERMANSEN, JOHN CHRISTIAN, application developer, linguist, consultant; b. Athens, Greece, Oct. 21, 1949; s. John Theodore and Lois Ann Hermansen; m. Sharyl Lynn Miner (div. 1994); children: John Theodore, Janet Lois. BA in Speech, Linguistics, Pa. State U., 1975; PhD in Computational Linguistics, Georgetown U., 1985. Cert. knowledge engr., 1992. Propr. CompAssociates, Inc., Washington, 1974-78; lectr., univ. fellow computational linguistics Georgetown U., Washington, 1980-83, dir. Lang. Processing Ctr., Sch. Langs. and Linguistics, 1982-85; artificial intelligence rsch. scientist Planning Rsch. Corp., McLean, Va., 1985-88, computational linguistics cons., 1988-90; cons. knowledge engring. Sterling Software, Inc., McLean, 1991-95; lead scientist linguistics analysis team State Dept. CLASS Project, Lang. Analysis Systems, Inc., Herndon, Va., 1986—; computational linguistics cons. Ctr. for Applied Linguistics, Washington, 1985-94; CEO Lang. Analysis Systems, Inc., Herndon, 1991—. Instr. effects of Asian organized crime on U.S., Fla. NG, 2000; spkr. in field Co-author: Southeast Asia Refugee Testing Report, Vols. I and II, 1985, Report on the Evaluation of Kenya Radio Language Arts Project, 1985, PAKTUS Version 1 User's Guide, 1986, Building NLU Systems in the PAKTUS Environment: Developer's Introduction, 1987, Message Processing Systems: Evaluation Factors, 1987, Meronomy, Word Experts and Prepositional Phrase Attachment in PAKTUS, 1989, Techniques in Multilingual Name Searching, 1989, The Automated Templating System for Database Update from Unformatted Message Traffic, 1995, The On-Line Name Reference Library Project, 1999, Combatting Asian Organized Crime, 2001, Advanced Name Matching for Enhanced Airline Security, 2002, Predictive Technology and Border Security, 2002, Name Recognition Tech., 2003, Names Have Currency, Technology for Finance, 2003, Asian Name Tracing, Interpol, 2005, Tracking Terrorists, 2005, Metadata about Names, 2005, Global Security: The Asian Perspective, Singapore, 2005; contbr. articles to profl. jours.; patentee in field. Recipient Fast 50 Champion CEO, Fast Co. mag., 2003, Fed. Computer Week "Fed. 100" award, 2004. Mem. IEEE, Assn. for Computational Linguistics, Internat. Assn. Knowledge Engrs., Data Adminstrn. Mgmt. Assn. Home: 12012 Robin Dr Catharpin VA 20143-1307 Office: Lang Analysis Systems Ctr for Innovative Tech 2214 Rock Hill Rd Herndon VA 20170-4214 Office Phone: 703-834-6200 ext. 222.

HERMES, CLINTON DANIEL, lawyer; s. Terry and Lisa Hermes; m. Susan Fieselman, Aug. 11, 2001. BA, Yale U., New Haven, Conn., 1994—98; JD, Harvard Law Sch., Cambridge, Mass., 1998—2001. Atty. Ropes & Gray LLP, N.Y.C., 2001—. Panelist, spkr. in field., 2001—. Co-author: (book) HIPAA and Human Subjects Research, 2003; editor: (journal) Harvard Journal of Law and Technology, 2000—01; contbr. articles to profl. jours. Dir., pres. Tutoring in Elem. Schools, New Haven, 1995—97; dir. Battered Women's Advocacy Project Legal Rsch. Bur., Cambridge, Mass., 1999—2001; vice chmn., instl. rev. bd. Judge Baker Children's Ctr., Boston, 2003—04; pro-bono counsel Psychoanalytic Couple and Family Inst. of New Eng., Boston, 2004—; mem. adv. bd. Am. Law Found. Named New Haven Youth of the Yr., Mayor of the City of New Haven, 1997; named one of the 15 Outstanding Young Healthcare Lawyers (under 40) nationally, Nightingale's Healthcare News, 2004; recipient Deb Levi Pro Bono award, 2005; scholar, Ala. Law Found., 2000; Nat. Merit Scholar, 1994. Mem.: ABA, Am. Health Lawyers Assn., Mass. Bar Assn., Boston Bar Assn., Nat. Polit. Sci. Honor Soc. Avocations: hiking, travel. Office: Ropes & Gray LLP 45 Rockefeller Plaza New York NY 10111 Office Phone: 212-841-0694. Office Fax: 212-841-5725. E-mail: chermes@ropesgray.com.

HERMINGHOUSE, PATRICIA ANNE, foreign language educator; b. Melrose Park, Ill., Mar. 13, 1940; m. 1964; 2 children. BA, Knox Coll., 1962; MA, Washington U., 1965, PhD in German, 1968. Asst. prof. German U. Mo.-St. Louis, 1966-67, vis. lectr., 1968-69; asst. prof. Washington U., St. Louis, 1967-78, assoc. prof. German, 1978-83; Fuchs prof. German studies U. Rochester, NY, 1983—, chmn. dept. fgn. langs., lits. and linguistics, 1983—89. Lectr. German, Fontbonne Coll., 1965-66. Internat. Research & Exchanges Bd. ad hoc grantee, 1976. Editor or co-editor: Literatur der DDR in den siebziger Jahren, 1983, Literatur und Literaturtheorie in der DDR, 1976, Frauen im Mittelpunkt, 1987, Gender and Germaness, 1997, Ingeborg Bachmann and Christa Wolf, 1998, German Feminist Writings, 2000; editor GDR Bull., Newsletter Lit. and Culture in German Dem. Republic, 1975-83; co-editor: Women in German Yearbook, 1994-2002. Recipient Susan B. Anthony Lifetime Achievement award, 2003; grantee Fulbright German Studies Summer Seminar, 2005; sr. fellow, NEH, 1991. Mem. MLA, Am. Assn. Tchrs. German (exec. coun. 1979-81), German Studies Assn. (exec. com., v.p./pres. 2001-02, pres. 2003-04), Coalition Women German (coord. 1974-75, nat. steering. com. 1976-79, 94-2002), Assn. Depts. Fgn. Langs. (exec. com.). Address: U Rochester Dept Modern Lang and Cultures Rochester NY 14627 Business E-Mail: pahe@troi.cc.rochester.edu.

HERMINIO, PLANAS MANUEL (TITO), mathematician, consultant; s. Herminio Planas Vazquez and Ana Luisa Lisboa Valentin; m. Diana Crespo, June 24, 2000; 1 child, Manuel Planas. BS in Computer Sci., U. Of Bridgeport, Conn., 1994; MS in Elem. Edn., U. Of Bridgeport, 1995; Sixth Yr. Degree Bilingual/TESOL, Fairfield U., Conn., 2001. Lic. tchr. math. 7-12 Conn., 1996, cert. tchr. bilingual edn.K-12 Conn., 1996, TESOL edn. Conn., 2001. Tchr.'s aide / talented and gifted program Elias Howe Sch., Bridgeport, Conn., 1990—93; student tchr. Bassick H.S., Bridgeport, Conn., 1994; sch. intern Maplewood Sch., Bridgeport, 1994—95; 5th grade bilingual tchr. Columbus Sch., Bridgeport, 1995—2000; numeracy coach Elias Howe Sch., Bridgeport, Conn., 2000—. Co-founder/co-director St. Peter's Ch. Music Acad., Bridgeport, Conn., 2000—02; bd. mem. Bridgeport Pub. Edn. Fund, Bridgeport, Conn., 1996—98; profl. trombonist; profl. caddy, 1986—. Author: (musical/Latin jazz composition) Fuego A La Lata, (musical/intrumental composition) Dreams Of Love. Mem. St. Peter's Ch. Brass Ensemble, Bridgeport, Conn., 1985—2005. Named Outstanding Puerto Rican Tchr., Puerto Rican Parade of Fairfield County, 2005; recipient Tchr. of the Yr. award, Bridgeport Pub. Sch., 2004, Theodore and Margaret Beard Award of Excellence in Tchg., Bridgeport Area Found., 2004, Title I Nat. Disting. Grad. Honoree, State of Conn., Title I / Nat., 2001, Coll. of Edn. and Human Resources Dean's award, U. of Bridgeport, 1995; grantee, Bridgeport Pub. Edn. Fund grantee, 1998, 2000, 2004; scholar G.E. Scholar's Program, U. of Bridgeport, 1990—94. Mem.: ASCD (assoc.), Assn. of Tchrs. of Math. in Conn. (assoc.), Nat. Coun. Of Tchrs. of Math. (assoc.), NEA (assoc.), Conn. Edn. Assn. (assoc.), Bridgeport Edn. Assn. (assoc.; treas. 2004—05, cmty. action com. chair 2000—). Roman Catholic. Avocation: arranger/composer. Office: Elias Howe School 287 Clinton Ave Bridgeport CT 06606 Office Phone: 203-576-8044. Office Fax: 203-576-8398. E-mail: hplanas@bridgeportedu.net.

HERMSEN, JAMES R., lawyer; b. Orange, Calif., Oct. 2, 1945; BA, U. Wash., 1967, JD, 1970. Bar: Wash. 1971, Oreg. 2004. Mem. Bogle & Gates, PLLC, Seattle, Dorsey & Whitney, Seattle, 2000—, ptnr., trial, regulatory, tech. group. Mem. Bur. of Competition Fed. Trade Commn., 1971-73. Mem. Seattle-King County Bar Assn., Wash. State Bar Assn., Phi Beta Kappa, Omicron Delta Epsilon, Phi Delta Phi. Office: Dorsey & Whitney 1420 5th Ave Ste 3400 Seattle WA 98101-4010 Office Phone: 206-903-8852. Office Fax: 206-903-8820. E-mail: hermsen.james@dorsey.com.

HERNANDEZ, ALBERTO H., librarian, researcher; b. Santurce, P.R., Jan. 21, 1952; s. Humberto F. Hernández and Carmen Ligia Banuchi; m. Mildred B. Bou, Apr. 19, 1984; children: Ana Sofía, Cecilia Maria, Maria Mercedes. BA, U. P.R., Rio Piedras, 1974; MLS, SUNY, Geneseo, 1976; MA, Columbia U., 1983, EdD, 1990. Humanities rsch. libr. rsch. divsn. N.Y. Pub. Libr., N.Y.C., 1979—82; head libr. Conservatorio de Musica de PR, Hato Rey, PR, 1983—85; libr. dir. Am. U., Bayamon, PR, 1985—91; art and music libr. U. No. Iowa, Cedar Falls, 1991; reference mgr., bibliographer Boston Coll., Newton, Mass., 1994—2000; univ. libr. U. West Fla., Pensacola, 2000—. Guest lectr. Simmons Coll., Boston, 1995—99. Contbr., articles to profl. jours. Mem. N.W. Fla. Ballet, Fort Walton, 2002—04; jury mem. Sanromá Piano Competitions, San Juan, PR, 1988—90; libr. evaluator Coun. of Higher Edn., San Juan; exec. dir. Con Brio, Inc., Bayamon, 1988—91, Pensacola Chamber Music Soc., 2003—04. Grantee Plan Renovacion Cultural, Puerto Rican Inst. Culture, 1988; Faculty Rsch. grant, Alumni Assn. U. West Fla., 2001. Mem.: MLA (assoc.), Coll. Music Soc. (assoc.). Achievements include research in Jesús María Sanromá Project. Avocations: music, travel, writing, research. Office: Univ West Florida 11000 University Parkway Pensala FL 32514 Office Phone: 850-474-2168. Office Fax: 850-474-3338. E-mail: webmaster@albertohernandez.com, ahernandez@uwf.edu.

HERNANDEZ, ANDRIANA, artist, poet, performer; b. Bello, Antioquia, Colombia, Oct. 17, 1968; d. Luis E. Hernandez and Amparo Muñoz; m. Guillermo Uribe, Aug. 22, 1991; children: Ariadna, Waira, Emmanuel, Santiago. Attended, Medellin U., Colombia, 1992; studied poetry and lit., U. Antioquia, 1993; studied social comm., Colombian Coop. U., 2001. Performing arts cert. Ministry of Edn. Colombia, 1990. Cultural panelist Caja Compensación Familiar, Medellin, Colombia, 1986—90; journalist El Colombiano Newspaper, 1990—91; artist/performer HITN-Edn. TV Channel, NYC, 2003—. Author, interpreter (CDs and tapes) Ensueño, Una Voz para decir la belleza, 1986—98; author: (poems) Esperando Abril (Awaiting April), 2000; participated in Fiesta de Gala de la Parada Cubana, Waldorf Astoria Hotel, NYC, Semana Cultiral, Independencia de Colombia, Anniversary of September 11th, Fiesta de la Vida, Colombian Center, UN Mission, Jazz Concerts, Natives Theater, Queens, Kennedy Ctr. for Performing Arts, Washington, DC, La Poesía Tiene la Palabra, Venezuelan Ctr., NYC, Saludo a las Américas. Avocations: music, dance, photography. Home: 8811 3rd Ave 3rd Flr North Bergen NJ 07047

HERNANDEZ, ANN MARGARET, education educator; b. Williamsport, Pa., Feb. 19, 1939; d. Adam E. and Helen A. Sieminski; m. Jorge E. Hernandez, June 20, 1970; children: James, Natalia, David. BS in Edn., Ohio U., 1961; MEd in Adminstrn., Pa. State U., 1969; EdD in Instrnl. Leadership, U. Ala., 1984. Tchr. Greenwich (Conn.) Sch. Sys., 1961-65, L.A. (Calif.) City Schs., 1965-66, Colegio Bolivar, Cali, Colombia, 1966-68, elem. prin., 1968-88; dir. early childhood and lower sch. Canterbury Sch., Ft. Wayne, Ind., 1988-95; prof. edn. U. St. Francis, Ft. Wayne, Ind., 1995—. Adj. prof. Ind. Vocat. Tech. Coll., Ft. Wayne, 1989-95, Ind. U.-Purdue U., Ft. Wayne, 1993-95; bd. dirs. WFWA-TV Pub. Broadcasting, Ft. Wayne, 1995-97; presenter and cons. in field. Bd. dirs. Found. Art and Music in Elem. Schs., 1997—, Stop Child Abuse and Neglect, Sci. Ctrl., 2005—. Named Nat. Disting. Prin., U.S. Dept. Edn., 1987. Mem. So. Assn. Colls. and Schs. (evaluator for overseas schs.), Phi Delta Kappa, Kappa Delta Pi. Home: 7012 Blake Dr Fort Wayne IN 46804-1016 Office: Univ of St Francis 2701 Spring St Fort Wayne IN 46808-3939 Office Phone: 260-434-3254. E-mail: ahernandez@sf.edu.

HERNANDEZ, CARLOS I., historian, educator; b. Mayaguez, P.R., Aug. 2, 1965; s. Americo and Armida Hernandez; m. Xenia I. Medina, July 4, 1993; children: Diego, Rocio I. BA, U. P.R., Mayaguez, 1990; PhD in History, U. P.R., Rio Piedras, 2005; MA in History, Ctr. Advanced Studies P.R.and the Caribbean, San Juan, P.R., 1996. Instr. U. P.R., Aguadilla, 1997—99, Ponce, 1999—2002, Utuado, 2002—02, Río Piedras. Coord. com. for the autonomy U. P.R., Aguadilla, 1997—99. Contbr. articles to profl. jours. Rschr. Atlantea Project U. P.R., Rio Piedras, 1997—2005. Decanato de Estudios Graduados e Investigacion grantee, U. P.R., 2003—04. Mem.: Ramey AFB Hist. Assn. (assoc.), Internat. Assn. Oral History (assoc.), Puerto Rican Assn. Historians (assoc.). Avocations: surfing, chess. Home: Urb Constancia LafayetteSt #3264 Ponce PR 00717 Home Fax: 787-848-6539. Personal E-mail: caivhernandez@yahoo.com.

HERNANDEZ, DANIEL MARIO, lawyer; b. Tampa, Fla., Sept. 26, 1951; s. Mario and Margaret (Alvarez) H.; m. Debra Sue Coleman, Dec. 6, 1980. BA, U. South Fla., 1972; JD, U. Fla., 1976. Bar: Fla. 1977, U.S. Dist. Ct. (mid. dist.) Fla. 1977, U.S. Supreme Ct. 1977. Asst. state atty. State Atty.'s Office, Tampa, 1977-82; assoc. Wilson and Sawyer P.A., Tampa, 1983; sole practice Tampa, 1983—. Mem. NCDFL, FBA, Hillsborough County Bar Assn. Democrat. Baptist. Avocations: tennis, jogging. Office: 902 N Armenia Ave Tampa FL 33609-1707

HERNANDEZ, DAVID N(ICHOLAS), lawyer; b. Albuquerque, Nov. 5, 1954; s. B.C. and Evangeline (C De Baca) H.; m. Alice A. McLish, June 7, 1975. BA, U. N.Mex., 1975, MBA, 1978, JD, 1979. Bar: N.Mex. 1979, U.S. Dist. Ct. N.Mex. 1979. Law clk. to presiding justice N.Mex. Supreme Ct., Santa Fe, 1979-80; assoc. Knight, Custer & Duncan, Albuquerque, 1980-82; sole practice David N. Hernandez & Assoc., Albuquerque, 1982—; of counsel Western Glass & Panels, Albuquerque. Mem. com. rules appellate ct. procedure N.Mex. Supreme Ct., 1984—; bd. dirs. Delta Dental N.Mex., Albuquerque. Mem. Environ. Planning Commn., Albuquerque, 1984-86, PHS assocs. Presbyn. Healthcare Found., 1985—. Named one of Outstanding Young Men Am., 1980. Mem. ABA, N.Mex. Bar Assn. (pres. 2000-01), Albuquerque Bar Assn., Am. Judicatur Soc., Greater Albuquerque C. of C. (bd. dirs. 1982-86, polit. action com. 1983-85). Avocations: tennis, golf, reading, fishing, politics.

HERNANDEZ, ENRIQUE, gynecologist, educator; b. Vega Baja, P.R., Oct. 25, 1951; s. Nathaniel and Ana Luisa (Lopez) H.; children: David Enrique, Daniel Antonio. BS, U. P.R., Rio Piedras, 1973, MD, 1977. Diplomate Am. Bd. Med. Examiners, Am. Bd. Ob-Gyn, Am. Bd. Gynecol. Oncology. Resident in ob-gyn Johns Hopkins Hosp., Balt., 1977-81, fellow in gynecol. oncology, 1981-83; instr. ob-gyn Johns Hopkins U., Balt., 1981-82, asst. prof., 1982-83; chief gynecol. oncology service Tripler Army Med. Ctr., Honolulu, 1983-87, asst. dir. intern tng., 1984-87; assoc. prof. Med. Coll. of Pa., Phila., 1987-89, prof., 1989-98; dir. divsn. gynecologic oncology Med. Coll. Pa./Hahneman Univ., Phila., 1987-98; vice chair dept. ob-gyn. Med. Coll. Pa./Hahneman U., Phila., 1995-98. Pres. med. and dental staff Med. Coll. Pa. Hosp., 1992—93; chief ob-gyn. svc. Allegheny U. Hosp. for Women, 1997—98, Allegheny U. Hosps./Med. Coll. Pa., 1997—98; prof. ob-gyn. Temple U. Sch. Medicine, 1998—, prof. pathology and lab. med., 1998—, chmn., dept. obstetrics and gynecology, 2002—, dir. divsn. gynecol. oncology, 1998—, Abraham Roth prof., 2002—; dir. ob/gyn. residency program Temple U. Hosp., 1998—; corp. mem. Himark (Blue Shield Western Pa., 2005—. Author: Manual of Gynecologic Oncology, 1989; editor: Clinical Gynecologic Pathology, 1995; mem. editl. bd. Revista de Ginecologia; contbr. articles to profl. jours. Pres. Pfhaler Found. of Philadelphia County Med. Soc., 2005—; bd. dirs. Allegheny Health, Edn. and Rsch. Found., 1992—93, Found. Obstet. Soc. Phila., 1998—; bd. dirs. Pa. divsn. Am. Cancer Soc., 2002—. Maj. U.S. Army, 1983—87. Recipient Bristol award P.R. Med. Assn., 1977. Fellow: ACOG, ACS (treas. met. Phila. chpt. 1995—99, pres.-elect 2000—01, pres. Phila. chpt. 2001—02); mem.: Phila. County Med. Soc. (bd. dirs. 1999, treas. 2001—03, pres.-elect 2003—, pres. 2004—05), Pa. Med. Soc. (ho. of dels. 1998—, chmn. pub. health and edn. com. 2003, pres. 2004—05), Soc. Ibero Latin Am. Med. Profls. (pres.-elect 1999—2001, pres. 2001—03), Colposcopy Soc. of Phila. (pres. 1999—2001), Am. Cancer Soc. (mem. adv. bd. Southeastern Pa. chpt. 1998—), Mid-Atlantic Gynecologic Oncology Soc. (pres. 1996—97), Obstet. Soc. Phila. (sec. 1994—96, pres.-elect 1996—97, pres. 1997—98), Soc. Gynecologic Oncologists (co-chair bylaws com. 2003—), Am. Soc. Clin. Oncology. Roman Catholic. Avocation: long distance running. Office: Temple Univ Hosp 3401 N Broad St Philadelphia PA 19140-5189

HERNANDEZ, FERNANDO VARGAS, lawyer; b. Irapuato, Mex., Sept. 8, 1939; came to U.S., 1942, naturalized, 1957; s. José Espinosa and Ana Maria (Vargas) H.; m. Bonnie Corrie, Jan. 8, 1966 (div. Feb. 1991); children: Michael David, Alexandra Rae, Marcel Paul. BS, U. Santa Clara, 1961; MBA, 1962; JD, U. Calif., Berkeley, 1966. Bar: Calif. 1967, U.S. Dist. Ct. (no. dist.) Calif. 1967. Sole practice law, San Jose, Calif., 1967—. Lectr. law Lincoln U.; lectr. bus. U. Santa Clara. Mem. San Jose Housing Bd., 1970-73; arbitrator Santa Clara County Superior Cts., 1979-2005, judge pro tem, 1979—. Contbg. editor to legal pleadings books. Active San Jose Civic Light Opera, 1981-83. With AUS, 1962-63. Mem. Calif. State Bar Assn., Santa Clara County Bar Assn. (chmn. torts sect. 1977-78, features editor In Brief mag. 1990-93), Calif. Trial Lawyers Assn. (bd. govs. 1979-82), Santa Clara County Trial Lawyers Assn., La Raza Lawyers Assn., Tapestry in Talent (bd. dirs. 2000—), Greater San Jose Hispanic C. of C. (founder, corp. counsel, bd. dirs. 2003-04), Silicon Valley Capital Club Democrat. Roman Catholic. Office: 46 S 1st St San Jose CA 95113-2406 Office Phone: 408-280-5800. E-mail: fvhlaw@pacbell.net.

HERNANDEZ, FRANK PATRICK, lawyer, judge; b. Galveston, Tex., June 18, 1939; s. Herculano and Elida (Vidaurri) H.; m. Jeanine Dishman, Dec. 27, 1960 (div. Dec. 1978); children: Elida Maria de Luna, Jeanine Bartolo, J. Frank. BA in Econs., Tex. A&M U., 1961; LLB, So. Meth. U., 1964, LLM,

1965. Bar: Tex. 1964, U.S. Dist. Ct. (no. dist.) Tex. 1965, U.S. Ct. Appeals (5th cir.) 1970, U.S. Supreme Ct. 1968. Judge County Ct. at Law No. 3, Dallas, 1976-78. Democrat. Avocation: filmmaking. Home and Office: 716 Wayne St Dallas TX 75223-1645

HERNANDEZ, GARY A., lawyer; b. Merced, Calif., Feb. 15, 1959; s. Rosendo and Margaret (Salazar) Hernandez; m. Teri L. Bond, Sept. 9, 1989. AB, U. Calif., Berkeley, 1981; JD, U. Calif., Davis, 1984. Bar: Calif. 1985. Dep. city atty. City and County of San Francisco, 1988-90; dep. ins. commr. Calif. Dept. Ins., San Francisco, 1991—95; ptnr. Long & Levit, San Francisco, 1995-97, Sonnenschein Nath & Rosenthal, San Francisco, 1997—. Bd. dirs. Iteris Inc., 1999—. Co-author eBusiness and Insurance: A Legal Guide To Transacting Insurance and Other Business on the Internet, 2001; editor (newspaper) Perspectiva, 1984-88; mem. editl. bd. Calif. Ins. Law & Regulation Reporter, 1998—. Bd. dirs. Calif. Coastal Conservancy, Oakland, 1998—, Ins. Regulators Examiners' Soc. Found.; trustee Latino Cmty. Found., U. Calif. Merced Found. Mem. Internat. Assn. Ins. Receivers, City Club of San Francisco, Club Mercedes. Democrat. Roman Catholic. Office: Sonnenschein Nath & Rosenthal LLP 685 Market St, 6th Fl San Francisco CA 94105 Office Phone: 415-882-2466. Fax: 415-543-5472. Business E-Mail: ghernandez@sonnenschein.com.

HERNANDEZ, GILBERTO JUAN, accountant, auditor, management consultant; b. Havana, Cuba, July 12, 1943; came to U.S., 1960; s. Gilberto E. and Zoila M. (Mendez) H.; m. Maria-Elena Diaz Lugo, Jan. 19, 1968 (div. 1971); 1 child, A. Patrick; m. Maria-Carmen Marcet, Dec. 23, 1972; children: Martin J., David J., Thomas J. BBA, Pace U., 1968. CPA, N.Y., Fla. Auditor sr. Arthur Andersen LLP, N.Y.C., Tampa, 1968—73; v.p., treas. Coaxial Comms., Inc., Sarasota, Fla., 1973—81; tax mgr. Laventhol & Horwath, Tampa, Fla., 1981—83; mem. firm ValienteHernandez P.A., CPAs, Auditors and Consultants, Mems. Polaris Internat., Tampa, 1983—. Chmn. N.Am. region Polaris Internat., 2002-04 Commr. City of Tampa Housing Authority, 1981-93; treas., bd. dirs. Ybor City Devel. Corp., Tampa, 1988—; past chmn. Tampa Bay Econ. Devel. Corp. Mem. AICPA, N.Y. State Soc. CPA, Fla. Inst. CPA (bd. dirs., pres. West Coast chpt., past chmn. com. on unauthorized practice of pub. accountancy 1993-94, Outstanding Chmn. of Yr. 1994), Nat. Assn. Housing and Redevel. Ofcls. (bd. govs. 1988-94), Govt. Fin. Officers Assn., Fla. Assn. Govt. Fin. Officers, Ybor City C. of C. (chmn. 1997-98, chmn. 1998-99), Ybor City Rotary Club (pres. 1990-91). Avocations: geography, travel, hiking. Office: ValienteHernandez PA 1715 N Westshore Blvd Ste 950 Tampa FL 33607-3920 Office Phone: 813-933-3943. Business E-Mail: ghernandez@vhcpa.com.

HERNANDEZ, GONZALO CRIS, literature and language educator, photographer; b. Mexico City, Jan. 27, 1966; s. Hernandez Joaquin and Suarez Roberta; m. Anna A. Arellano-Hernandez, Jan. 9, 1997; 1 child, Sydney. Grad., Nat. U. Mex., 1992, Purdue U., 2005. Tchr. Spanish Gary Cmty. Sch. Corp., Ind., 2000—. Mem.: Am. Fedn. Tchrs. (assoc.). Personal E-mail: sydneyproductions@sbcglobal.net.

HERNANDEZ, JO FARB, museum director, consultant; b. Chgo., Nov. 20, 1952; BA in Polit. Sci. & French with honors, U. Wis., 1974; MA in Folklore and mythology, UCLA, 1975; postgrad., U. Calif., Davis, 1978, U. Calif., Berkeley, 1978-79, 81. Registration Mus. Cultural History UCLA, 1974-75; Rockefeller fellow Dallas Mus. Fine Arts, 1976-77; asst. to dir. Triton Mus. Art, Santa Clara, Calif., 1977-78, dir., 1978-85; adj. prof. mus. studies John F. Kennedy U., San Francisco, 1978; grad. advisor arts adminstrn. San Jose (Calif.) State U., 1979-80; dir. Monterey (Calif.) Peninsula Mus. Art, 1985-93, cons. curator, 1994—2000; prin. Curatorial and Mus. Mgmt. Svcs., Watsonville, Calif., 1993—. Cons.SPACES (Saving and Preserving Art and Cultural Environ.), 2000—; panelist Creative Works Fund, 2001; adj. prof. gallery mgmt. art dept. U. Calif., Santa Cruz, 1999—; cons. Archives Am. Art., 1998—2000; dir. Thompson Gallery, San Jose State U., 2000—; lectr., panelist, juror, panelist in field USIA, Calif. Arts Coun., Calif. Confedn. for Arts, Am. Assn. Mus., Western Mus. Assn., Am. Folklore Soc., Calif. Folklore Soc., Internat. Coun. on Mus., others; vis. lectr. U. Wis., 1980, U. Chgo., 1981, Northwestern U., 1981, San Jose State U., 1985, UCLA, 1986, Am. Cultural Ctr., Jerusalem, 1989, Tel Aviv, 89, Binational Ctr., Lima, Peru, 1988, Daytona Beach Mus. Art, 1983, UCLA, 1986, Israel Mus., 1989, Mont. State U., 1991, Oakland Mus., 1996, High Mus. Art, Atlanta, 1997, Mus. Am. Folk Art, NY, 1998, San Francisco Mus. Modern Art, 1998, U. Calif., 1998, Grinnell Coll., Iowa, 1999, Arts Coun. Silicon Valley, 2000, U. Calif., Santa Cruz, 2000, ICOM, Barcelona, 2001, Intuit Gallery, Chgo., 2004, Chgo., 04; guest curator San Diego Mus. Art, 1995—98; guest on various TV and radio programs. Author: (mus. catalogs) The Day of the Dead: Tradition and Change in Contemporary Mexico, 1979, Three from the Northern Island: Contemporary Sculpture from Hokkaido, 1984, Crime and Punishment: Reflections of Violence in Contemporary Art, 1984, The Quiet Eye: Pottery of Shoji Hamada and Bernard Leach, 1990, Alan Shepp: The Language of Stone, 1991, Wonderful Colors: The Paintings of August Francois Gay, 1993, Jeannette Maxfield Lewis: A Centennial Celebration, 1994, Armin Hansen, 1994, Jeremy Anderson: The Critical Link/A Quiet Revolution, 1995, A.G. Rizzoli: Architect of Magnificent Visions, 1997 (one of 10 Best Books in field Amazon.com), Misch Kohn: Beyond the Tradition, 1998, Fire and Flux: An Undaunted Vision/The Art of Charles Strong, 1998, Mel Ramos: The Galatea Series, 2000, Holly Lane: Small Miracles, 2001, Irvin Tepper: When Cups Speak/Life with the Cup, 2002; co-author: Sam Richardson: Color in Space, 2002, Marc D'Estout: Domestic Objects, 2003, Peter Shire: Go Beyond the Ordinary, 2004, Forms of Tradition in Contemporary Spain, 2005; mem. internat. editl. bd. Raw Vision Mag., 2001-; contbr. articles to profl. publs. Bd. dirs. Bobbie Wynn and Co. of San Jose, 1981-85, Santa Clara Arts and Hist. Consortium, 1985, Non-Profit Gallery Assn., 1979-83, v.p., 1979-80; mem. nat. adv. bd. The Fund for Folk Culture, Santa Fe, 1995-98; mem. founding and exec. bd. Alliance for Calif. Traditional Arts, 2002—; mem. founding internat. adv. bd. Friends of Fred Smith, 2002—. Recipient Golden Eagle award, Coun. Internat. Non-theatrical Events, 1992, Leader of Decade award, Arts Leadership Monterey Peninsula, 1992, merit award, N.Y. Book Show, 1997; Rsch. grantee, Calif. State U., 2001, 2002, 2003, Dean's grantee, 2001, Lottery Fund grantee, 2000, 2004. Mem.: Nat. Coun. for Edn. in Ceramic Arts, Western Mus. Conf. (bd. dir., exec. com. 1989—91, program chair 1990), Am. Folklore Soc., Art Table, Calif. Assn. Mus. (bd. dirs. 1985—94, v.p. 1987—91, chair nominating com. 1988, chair ann. meeting 1990, chair nominating com. 1990, pres. 1991—92, chair nominating com. 1993), Am. Assn. Mus. (lectr. 1986, mus. assessment program surveyor 1990, nat. program com. 1992—93, mus. assessment program surveyor 1994), Phi Beta Kappa. Office: Curatorial Mus Mgmt Svcs 345 White Rd Watsonville CA 95076-0429 Office Phone: 408-924-4328. E-mail: jfh@cruzio.com.

HERNANDEZ, JOHN E., musician, music educator; arrived in U.S., 2001; s. Gerardo E. Hernandez and Dolores Ludena de Hernandez. Bachelor's Degree, Conservatory Salvador Bustamante Celi, Loja, 1992; Bachelor's Degree with honors and excellence, Conservatory Rimsky-Korsakov, Ecuador, 1999; MusM, U. Louisville, 2003. Tchr. Conservatory Salvador Bustamante Celi, Loja, 1990—94, Conservatory Rimsky-Korsakov, Guayaquil, Ecuador, 1997—2001, Ctr. for the Arts, Guayaquil, 1998—99; pianist Home of Culture Chamber Ensemble, Loja, 1992—94; pianist, soloist, accompanist Symphony Orch. Guayaquil, 1990—2001; grad. asst. U. Louisville, 2002—. Arranger, pianist: recording Te Voy a Dejar Vivir, 1991, Que Bonita Es La Vida, 1992, Un Lugar en La Musica, 2000. Recipient Cultural Merit award, City Hall Loja, 1990, first prize nat. contest, German-Ecuadorian Cultural Ctr., 1993. Mem.: Casa de la Cultura, Music Tchrs. Nat. Assn. Avocations: reading, soccer, movies, theater, gardening. Office: Univ Louisville Belnak Campus Louisville KY 40292

HERNANDEZ, JOSE, professional baseball player; b. Vega Alta, Puerto Rico, July 14, 1969; m. Melanie Hernandez; children: Jolanie, Jose Orlando. Student, Interamerica University, Bayamon, Puerto Rico. Player Tex. Rangers, 1991, Cleve. Indians, 1992, 2005—, Chgo. Cubs, 1994—99, 2003, Atlanta Braves, 1999, Milw. Brewers, 2000—02, Colo. Rockies, 2003, Pitts. Pirates, 2003, LA Dodgers, 2004. Named to Nat. League All-Star Team, 2002. Office: c/o Cleveland Indians 2401 Ontario St Cleveland OH 44115

HERNANDEZ, JOSE YOLANDO BALAGTAS, surgeon; b. Manila, Philippines, Dec. 30, 1938; came to U.S., 1964; s. Pablo Manio and Leoncia (Balagtas) Hernandez; m. Minerva Cuadrante, Dec. 17, 1966; children: Jay, Myra, Maureen. U. St. Thomas, Manila, Philippines, 1962. Diplomate Am. Bd. Surgery, Am. Bd. Colon-Rectal Surgery, Internat. Bd. Proctology. Fellow: Soc. Philippine Surgeons in Am., Southeastern Surgical Congress, Internat. Acad. Proctology, InterAm. Coll. Physicians and Surgeons, Internat. Coll. Surgeons, Am. Soc. Colon Rectal Surgeons, Am. Soc. Abdominal Surgeons; mem.: AMA, Coll. Internat. Chirurgiae Digestiva, Endoscopic Surgeons, Am. Gastroent. Roman Catholic. Avocations: ballroom dancing, golf, music. Home and Office: 3053 Carlow Cir Tallahassee FL 32309-3302

HERNANDEZ, KATHY-ANN C., education educator; d. Peter Hernandez and Jean Calliste. Ph.D., Temple U., 2004. Lectr. H. L. Stoutt C.C., Tortola, British Virgin Islands, 1997—2000; rsch. asst. Temple U., Phila., 2000—02, rsch. assoc. CRHDE, 2002—04; asst. prof. Ea. U., St. Davids, Pa., 2004—. Contbr. chapters to books. Mentor Achieving Independence Ctr., Phila., 2004—05; cons. First African Cmty. Devel. Corp. Cmty. Arts Initiative, Phila., 2004—05. Recipient award, Temple U., Coll. of Edn., 2002—03, Marlene S. Korn Humanitarian award, Temple U., 2004; scholar, Temple U., Coll. of Edn., 2000—04. Mem.: Am. Ednl. Rsch. Assn. Seventh-Day Adventist. Office Phone: 610-225-5686.

HERNANDEZ, LUIS SERGIO, JR., editor, researcher; s. Luis Sergio and Rita Teresa Hernandez. B.A., U. of Miami, 1998; M.S., Boston Coll., 2000; MTS, Harvard U., 2002; postgrad., Columbia U., 2002—. Editor in chief Harvard Jour. of Hispanic Policy, Cambridge, Mass., 2000—01, chair, editl. adv. bd., 2001—. Co-chair Harvard Latino and Latin Am. Studies Initiative, Cambridge, Mass., 2001—02. Editor, author (scholarly journal) Harvard Journal of Hispanic Policy. Fellow, David Rockefeller Ctr. for Latin Am. Studies, 2001-02. Mem.: Am. Ednl. Rsch. Assn., Am. Polit. Sci. Assn. Roman Catholic. Achievements include research in African American and Latino political coalitions. Avocation: collecting fine art. Home: 8335 Menteith Terrace Miami Lakes FL 33016 Office: Teachers College Columbia University 525 West 121st Street Box 67 New York NY 10027 Personal E-mail: luis_hernandez@post.harvard.edu.

HERNANDEZ, MARIE, nurse; b. Edgefield, SC, Mar. 15, 1945; d. Mary Lue (Hill) Curry; m. Noel Manuel Hernandez, Apr. 2, 1965; children: Nadine Marisa, Nolan Maurice. BSN, Long Island U., 1978. Registered nurse, legal nurse cons. RN Hariem Hosp., N.Y.C., NY, 1971—73, Elmir Richmond Hosp., N.Y.C., NY, 1976—79; domestic nurse Home, Venezuela, 1980—89; RN Lenox Hill Hosp., N.Y.C., NY, 1989—96, Baptist Health Sys., Miami, Fla., 1999—. Named Nurse of Yr. Emergency Room, Baptist Health Sys., 2005. Mem.: Nurse Cons., Fla. Nurses Assn. Democrat. Cath. Avocations: cooking, baking, crocheting, reading. Office: Bapt Health Sys 8900 No Kendall Dr Miami FL 33173 E-mail: marie@baptisthealthsystem.net.

HERNANDEZ, MICHELLE A., lawyer; d. Stella V. Martinez; m. Jon J Hernandez, Aug. 4, 2000; 1 child, Mia Estella. BA magna cum laude in Polit. Sci., U. N.Mex, 1990—93; JD, UCLA, 1994—97. Bar: (U.S. Ct. Appeals, 10th cir.) 1999, N.Mex (U.S. Dist. Ct.) 2000, N.Mex 1997. Jud. law clk. N.Mex Supreme Ct., Sr. Justice Joseph F. Baca, Santa Fe, 1997—99; atty. Modrall Sperling Law Firm, Albuquerque, 1999—. Co-author: (insurance article) Def. Lawyers Assn. Mem. Verne Payne Inns of Ct., Albuquerque, 1999—2002, Leardership Albuquerque, 2004—; local advance team Clinton/Gore, Albuquerque; bd. mem., exec. comittee mem., treas. U. N.Mex Alumni Assn., 1999—2003; founding mem. U. N.M. Young Alumni Assn., 1999—2000. Lubric Pioneering Women in Law Scholarship, 1997. Mem.: Hispanic Bar Assn., N.Mex Bar Assn., UCLA La Raza Law Students Assn., Phi Beta Kappa. Office: Modrall Sperling Law Firm 500 4th St NW Albuquerque NM 87102 Office Phone: 505-848-1800. Office Fax: 505-848-1889.

HERNANDEZ, MINERVA CUADRANTE, physician, consultant; d. Arsenio Francisco Cuadrante and Mercedes Rontas Relunia; m. Jose Yolando Balagtas Hernandez, Dec. 17, 1966; children: Jay, Myra, Maureen. *Daughter, Myra, received a BS in Manufacturing Engineering from Boston University and a Doctor of Dental Medicine degree from Boston University, Goldman School of Dental Medicine. Son, Jay, is a 1989 graduate from Florida State University with a BA in Humanities. He currently resides in Beverly Hills, California and works in the movie film production industry as an associate producer. Daughter, Maureen, is a 1996 graduate from Florida State University, College of Law, cum laude. She is practicing in Atlanta, Georgia. She has a BA in Diplomatic History from the University of Pennsylvania and a BS in Economics from the Wharton School of Business.* MD, U. St. Tomas, Manila, 1962. Intern St. Clare's Hosp., Schenectady, NY, 1964—65; jr. resident Springfield Hosp., Mass., 1965—66; pediatric resident Trumbull Meml. Hosp., Warren, Ohio, 1966—69; resident, gen. pathology Allentown Hosp., Pa., 1969—70; staff physician Fla. State Hosp., Chattahoochee, 1974—78, Southwestern State Hosp., Thomasville, Ga., 1980—85; physician advisor Profl. Found. for Health Care, Tampa, Fla., 1985—89; staff physician Tricare Clinic, Atlantic Beach, Fla., 1993—97; med. dir. Spectrum Health Care Partnership, Cecil Field, Fla., 1995—96; physician Fla. State U., Thagard Student Clinic, Tallahassee, 1997—2004. Mem. Springtime Tallahassee, 1983. Fellow: Am. Bd. Disability (analyst), Am. Coll. Utilization Rev. Physicians; mem.: Panhandle Med. Soc., Assn. Am. Philippine Physicians, Am. Acad. Family Physicians. Avocations: ballroom dancing, creative writing, reading. Home: 3053 Carlow Cir Tallahassee FL 32309 Office: Fla State Univ Thagard Student Health Ctr Tallahassee FL 32309

HERNANDEZ, RAMON ROBERT, retired minister, school librarian; b. Chgo., Feb. 23, 1936; s. Eleazar Dario and Marie Helen Hernandez; m. Fern Ellen Muschinske, Aug. 11, 1962; children: Robert Frank, Maria Marta. BA, Elmhurst (Ill.) Coll., 1957; BD, Eden Theol. Sem., St. Louis, 1962; MA, U. Wis., 1970. Co-pastor St. Stephen United Ch. Christ, Merrill, Wis., 1960-64; dir. youth work Wis. Conf. United Ch. Christ, Madison, 1964-70; dir. T.B. Scott Free Library, Merrill, 1970-75, McMillan Meml. Library, Wisconsin Rapids, Wis., 1975-83, Ann Arbor (Mich.) Pub. Library, 1983-94; pastor Comty. Congl. Ch., Pinckney, Mich., 1994-98. Seminar leader on pub. libr. long-range planning, budgeting and handling problem patrons. Editl. com. mem. Songs of Many Nations Songbook, 1970; contbr. articles to profl. jours. Treas. Ann Arbor Homeless Coalition, 1985-88; bd. dirs., sec., v.p. Riverview Hosp. Assn., Wisconsin Rapids, 1977-83; bd. dirs. Hist. Soc. Mich., 1988-90, Ind. Living, Inc., Dame County, Wis., 2001-03; trustee Madison Pub. Libr, Wis., 2000—. Mem. ALA, Wis. Libr. Assn. (Leadership award 1980, pres. 1980), Rotary (pres. Merrill chpt. 1974-75, Community Svc. award 1975, pres. Ann Arbor chpt. 1990-91, Paul Harris fellow 1994).

HERNANDEZ, ROBERTO REYES, secondary school educator; b. Juarez, Chihuahua, Mex., Apr. 30, 1950; came to U.S., 1953; s. Felipe de Jesus and Juanita (Reyes) H.; m. Joanne Dora Richard; adopted children: Rosellor, Ledores, Joetta, Harriett, Barbara, Richard, Ray. AA in Edn., El Paso C.C., 1976; BS in Psychology, U. Tex., El Paso, 1978, BE in Secondary Edn., 1981, BS in Biology, 1982, MS in Biology, 1986; grad. sci. fellow, Baylor Coll. Medicine, 1984-85. Cert. secondary edn. teacher, Tex. Pharmacy technician Southwestern Gen. Hosp., El Paso, 1974—79, William Beaumont Army Med. Ctr. U.S. Civil Svc., Ft. Bliss, Tex., 1979—81; tchr. phys. sci., anatomy, physiology, biology Socorro Ind. Sch. Dist., El Paso, 1981—84; tchr. life and earth sci. Houston Ind. Sch. Dist., 1984—85; tchr. phys. sci., biology, astronomy, chemistry, computer sci., psychology, sociology and GED Ysleta Ind. Sch. Dist., El Paso, 1985—. Instr. English El Paso C. C., spring, 1986; grad. asst. interdisciplinary edn. Tex. A & M U., summer, 1989, 90; mem. evaluation team So. Assn. of Accreditation, El Paso, 1984; mem. textbook adoption team Tex. Biology Textbook Adoption Com., El Paso, 1983-84. Pres. Tex. Student Edn. Assn., El Paso, 1980-81; vol. instr. ESL The Westin Paso Del Norte Hotel, El Paso, 1990; den leader Wolf and Bear Cub Scout Pack 201, 1994-95. Recipient Hidalgo award Heftel Broadcasting Corp., 1997. Mem.: NEA, Ysleta Tchrs. Assn. (area rep. 1994—97), Tex. State Tchrs. Assn., Blue Jackets Cmty. Svc. Orgn. (faculty sponsor 2001—), Eastwood Stargazers Club (faculty sponsor 2001—05), Bow and Arrow Sci. Club (faculty sponsor 1985—96), Vista Hills Lions Club (lion tamer 1992—94, LEO Advisor 1992—2001, editor newsletter 1993—95, 2d v.p. 1994—95, dir. 1995—96, chair dist 2--T3 Leo Clubs 1997—2001, exec. v.p. 1998—99, sec. 2001, Lion of Yr. 1992—93, 1996—97, 1999—2000). Home: 10310 Kellogg St El Paso TX 79924-2902 Office: Eastwood HS 2430 Mc Rae Blvd El Paso TX 79925-6097 Office Phone: 915-434-4000. Personal E-mail: RobertHernandez@hotmail.com. E-mail: roberthernandex67@yahoo.com.

HERNANDEZ, ROLAND, broadcast executive; Pres., CEO Telemundo Group, Inc., Hialeah, Fla., chmn. bd., CEO. Office: Telemundo Group Inc 2290 W 8th Ave Hialeah FL 33010-2017 also: Telemundo 3000 W Alameda Ave Burbank CA 91523-0001

HERNANDEZ, VICTOR RENÉ CHRISTIAN, medical researcher, consultant; b. San Francisco, Mar. 22, 1960; s. Victor Gonzales and Maria Christina (Martinez) H. B in psychology and biology, U. San Francisco, 1981; postgrad., U. Calif., 1989; MEd, Harvard U., 1990, D in pub. health, 1993. Cert. tchr., Calif., cert. HIV/AIDS counseling and testing, N.Y. Cons. Boston Mus. Sci., Boston, 1990; researcher, AIDS educator, cons. Mass. Dept. Correction Health Svcs. div., Boston, 1990; rsch. devel. cons. dept. epidemiology & social medicine Montefiore Medical Ctr., N.Y.C., 1990-91; dir. substance abuse prevention project Streetwork Project, N.Y.C., 1991; rsch. devel. cons. Columbia Sch. Social Work, N.Y.C., 1991; resource devel. cons. NENA Health Clinic, N.Y.C., 1992; project devel. cons. Am. Indian Community House, 1992—; cons. Cicatelli Assocs., Inc., N.Y., 1992-93, Hispanic AIDS Forum, N.Y.C., 1993, NDA Internat., N.Y.C., 1992—. Rsch. assoc. Found. Integrated Rsch., Bernard Behari, N.Y.C., 1993—, Rsch. Focus Narcolepsy and Benign Epilepsy Pastuer Inst., Paris, 1985-87, Children's Hosp., San Francisco, 1984-85, rsch. assoc., cons. Centre Hospitalier et Universitaire de Montpellier, France, 1983-84, rsch. assoc., technician Stanford Disorders Clinic, Stanford U. Medical Ctr., 1981-83; tchr. in field. Contbr. articles to profl. jours. Bd. dirs. Direct AIDS Alternative Info. Resource, Illusion Prodns., ACT UP; adv. bd. Mt. Sinai Medical Ctr.; bd. dirs. Three Corners Adolescent Persons with AIDS Housing. AIDS and Adolescent Network N.Y., substance abuse com., Nat. Pediatric AIDS Com. Mem. Internat. AIDS Soc., Internat. Neuropsyhcological Soc., N.Y. Acad. Scis., Am. Fedn. Tchrs., Harvard AIDS Inst. Home: 4998 Sterling Dr Fremont CA 94536-7125

HERNANDEZ-DENTON, FEDERICO, state supreme court justice; b. Santurce, PR, Apr. 12, 1944; s. Federico and Teresa (Denton) Hernandez-Morales; m. Isabel Pico, 1966. BA, Harvard U., 1966, JD, 1969. Bar: PR 1971. Dir. Consumer Rsch. Ctr. and Bus. Adminstrn. Rsch. Ctr. U. PR, 1970-72; dir. PR Consumer Svc. Adminstrn., 1973; sec. PR Dept. Consumer Affairs, 1973-76; asst. prof. Law Sch. Interam. U., PR, 1977-84, dean, 1984-85; justice Supreme Ct. PR, San Juan, 1985—2004; pres. PR Bd. of Bar Examiners, 1987—2004; chief justice PR Supreme Ct., San Juan, 2004—. Pres. PR Bd. Bar Examiners, 1987—2004; chairperson Jud. Code Comm., 2003—05. Mem. ABA, Am. Law Inst., PR Bar Assn. Office: Supreme Ct of PR PO Box 9022392 San Juan PR 00902-2392 Office Phone: 787-724-3535. E-mail: federicoH@tribunales.gobierno.pr.

HERNDON, ALICE PATTERSON LATHAM, public health nurse; b. Macon, Ga., Dec. 18, 1916; d. Frank Waters and Ruby (Dews) Patterson; m. William Joseph Latham, July 21, 1940 (dec. Apr. 1981); children: Jo Alice Latham Miller, Marynette Latham Herndon, Lauruby Latham Herndon; 1 adopted child, Courtney Marie Herndon; m. Sidney Dumas Herndon, Apr. 26, 1985. Diploma, Charity Hosp. Sch. Nursing, New Orleans, 1937; student, George Peabody Tchrs. Coll., 1938-39; BS in Pub. Health Nursing, U. N.C., 1954; MPH, Johns Hopkins U., 1966. Staff pub. health nurse assigned spl. venereal disease study USPHS, Darien, Ga., 1939—40; county pub. health nurse Bacon County, Alma, Ga., 1940—41; USPHS spl. venereal disease project Glynn County, Brunswick, 1943—47, county pub. health nurse, 1949—51, Ware County, Waycross, 1951—52; pub. health nurse surp. Wayne-Long-Brantley-Liberty Counties, Jesup, 1954—56; dist. dir. pub. health nursing Wayne-Long-Appling-Bacon-Pierce Counties, Jesup, 1956—70; dist. chief nursing S.E. Ga. Health Dist., 1970—79, organizer mobile health svcs., 1973—. Founder, exec. dir. Wayne County Home Health Agy., 1968—80; exec. dir. Ware County Home Health Agy., 1970—79, mem. exec. com., 1978—85; mem. governing bd. S.E. Ga. Health Sys. Agy., 1975—82; organized and mem. governing bd. Health Dept. Home Health Agy., 1978—, also author numerous grant proposals; governing bd. Brunswick Civic Orch., 1993—97. Contbr. to state nursing manuals. Mem. adv. coun. Ware Meml. Hosp. Sch. Practical Nursing, Waycross, Ga., 1958; mem. Altar Guild St. Paul's Episc. Ch., 1979—86, vestrywoman, 1981—82; mem. Altar Guild St. Marks Episcopal Ch., Brunswick, Ga., 1994—2001; bd. dirs. Wayne County Mental Health Assn., 1959—61, 1981—82, Wayne County Tb Assn., 1958—62, a non-alcoholic organizer Jesup group Alcoholics Anonymous, 1962—63. Recipient recognition Gen. Svc. Bd., Alcoholics Anonymous, Inc. Fellow APHA; mem. ANA, 8th Dist. (pres. 1954-58, sec. 1958-60, dir. 1960-62, 1st v.p. 1962), Ga. Nurses Assn. (exec. bd. 1954-58, program rev. continuing edn. com. 1980-86, Dist. 21 Excellence in Nursing award 1994), Ga. Pub. Health Assn. (chmn. nursing sect. 1956-57), Ga. Assn. Dist. Chiefs Nursing (pres. 1976). Home: 192 Bluff Dr Brunswick GA 31523-6225

HERNDON, JAMES FRANCIS, retired political science educator; b. Indpls., Aug. 11, 1929; s. Francis Earl and Agnes (Demmer) H.; m. Doris Arlene Beall, Dec. 24, 1952; 1 son, David Lyle. Student, John Herron Sch. Fine Arts, 1949; BA, Ind. U., 1952; MA, Wayne State U., 1956; PhD, U. Mich., 1963. Instr. Drake U., Des Moines, 1959-60; asst. prof. U. N.D., 1960-63, asso. prof., 1963-67; coordinator U. N.D. (Honors Program), 1965-66, asso. dean arts and scis., 1967; asso. prof. Va. Poly. Inst., Blacksburg, 1967-70, prof., chmn. dept. polit. sci., 1970-74, also dir. summer course math. models in polit. sci., 1973, prof. emeritus, 1994. Dir. Summer Inst. in Math. Applications in Polit. Sci., 1969-73 Co-editor: Selected Bibliography of Materials in State and Local Government, 1963, Mathematical Applications in Political Science, Vols. V-VII, 1971-74; editorial bd.: Jour. Politics, 1973-75. Mem. adv. bd. Americans for Religious Liberty. With CIC, U.S. Army, 1952-54. Recipient Faculty-Student Teaching award U. N.D., 1965; Faculty lectr., 1966 Mem. Va. Social Sci. Assn. (v.p. 1979-80, pres. 1980-81, Disting. Svc. award 1989, scholar award 1984), Ams. for Democratic Action, ACLU, Omicron Delta Kappa, Pi Sigma Alpha. Unitarian Universalist. Home: 1110 Roanoke St E Blacksburg VA 24060-5050

HERNDON, JAMES HENRY, orthopedic surgeon, educator; b. L.A., Oct. 31, 1938; s. James Greene and Kathleen Theresa (Murphy) H.; m. Geraldine Grace Armiger, Feb. 26, 1971; chidlren: Jennifer, Jonathan. BS, Loyola U., L.A., 1961; MD, UCLA, 1965; MA, Brown U., 1979; MBA, Boston U., 1990; MA (hon.), Harvard U., 1999; DHL (hon.), Loyola-Marymount U., 2004. Diplomate Am. Bd. Orthopaedic Surgery (bd. dirs., pres. 1991-92). Intern Hosp. of U. Pa., Phila., 1965-66, resident in surgery, 1966-67; resident in orthopaedics Mass. Gen. Hosp., Boston, 1970, chief resident in orthopaedics, 1967-70; asst. clin. prof. orthopaedic surgery Mich. State U., Grand Rapids, 1974-77, assoc. clin. prof., 1977-78; prof., chmn. dept. orthopaedics Brown U., Providence, 1979-88; surgeon-in-chief dept. orthopaedic surgery R.I. Hosp., Providence, 1979-88; Silver prof., chmn. dept. orthopaedic surgery U. Pitts., Pitts., chief orthopaedics, 1988-98; chief dept. orthopeadics and rehab. Presbyn. U. Hosp., Pitts., 1988-98; assoc. sr. vice chancellor Health Svcs. U. Pitts. Med. Ctr., 1995-98, v.p. med. svcs., 1995-98; chmn. ptnrs. dept. orthopaedic surgery Mass. Gen. Hosp., 1998—2004, Brigham and Women's Hosp., 1998—2004. Examiner Am. Bd. Orthopaedic Surgery, Chgo., 1977—2004, pres., 1990-91; William H. and Johanna A. Harris prof. Harvard Med. Sch., 1998—. Reviewer Jour. Bone and Joint Surgery, 1975—, bd. trustees, 2005-; contbr. articles to profl. jours., chpts. to books; author books in field. Trustee Meeting St. Sch., Providence, 1984-88, Harmarville Rehab. Hosp., Pitts., 1989-95; mem. bd. govs. Arthritis Found., Providence, 1984-88, Pitts., 1989—98, Boston, 1998-2004; bd. dirs. Make A Wish Found., chmn., 1998-99. Recipient Edith and Carl Lasky Meml. award UCLA Med. Sch., 1965, Bronze award Am. Congress Rehab. Medicine, 1972, Clin. Rsch. award N.Y. Med. Soc., 1974. Fellow ACS, Am. Acad. Orthopaedic Surgeons (treas. 1994-97, pres. 2003—04); mem. Am. Orthopaedic Assn. (pres. 1999-00), Orthop. Rsch. Soc., Residence Rev. Com. Orthopaedic Surgery (past chmn.), Am. Soc. Surgery of Hand, Internat. Soc. for Quality in Health Care. Office: Massachusetts Gen Hosp Gray 624 55 Fruit St Boston MA 02114-2696

HERNDON, JOHN LAIRD, accounting firm executive; b. Shreveport, La., 1958; s. Jack and Irene Herndon. BS Econs., Millsaps Coll., Jackson, Miss., 1981; MBA, U. Miss., Oxford, 1997. Cons., Jackson, Miss., 1981-84; fin. analyst Coldwell Banker, L.A., 1984-86; sr. fin. analyst Kenneth Leventhal & Co., L.A., 1986-87; asst. contr. E&Y Real Estate Group, L.A., 1987-89, contr., 1989-95; dir. Ernst & Young LLP, N.Y., 1996—. Developer multiple e-bus. applications; author numerous articles; speaker in field. John Palmer scholar U. Miss., Oxford, 1996-97. Mem. Mensa Internat., Urban Land Inst. Episcopalian. Avocations: tennis, golf. Office: Ernst & Young LLP 125 Chubb Ave Lyndhurst NJ 07071-3504 E-mail: jlherndon@yahoo.com.

HERNDON, MERLE PUCKETTE, principal; b. Lynchburg, Va., Jan. 5, 1954; d. Walter William and Marion (Layne) Puckette; m. William Robertson Herndon III, June 19, 1976; children: William Robertson IV, Stuart Thomas, Caroline Whitney. BS in Elem. Edn., Averett Coll., 1974; MEd in Reading, Lynchburg Coll., 1977, EdS, 1986; EdD in Ednl. Leadership, U. Va., 1993. Cert. elem. tchr., prin., supt., reading specialist, devel. reading tchr., Va. Remedial math. and reading tchr. T. C. Miller Elem. Sch., 1974-75; remedial math. and reading tchr., reading specialist Dearington Elem. Sch.; reading specialist Linkhorne Elem. Sch., Lynchburg, Va., 1975-86, unit leader, 1984-86, staff devel. specialist, 1986-87, prin., 1987—; staff devel. specialist Lynchburg City Schs., 1986-87. Coord. partnership programs with bus. and Linkhorne Elem. Sch.; presenter in field. Mem. Madeline Hunter Inst., Williamsburg, Va., 1987; active Brookneal Elem. PTA, William Campbell Mid. Sch. PTA, Staunton River Hist. Soc.; past pres. Red Hill Garden Club; mem. adminstrv. coun. Brookneal Meth. Ch.; den leader Cub scouts Boy Scouts Am., Brookneal, 1986-89. Mem. ASCD, Piedmont Area Reading Coun., Va. Assn. Elem. Prins. (chmn. grand session 1992, mem. conf.), Nat. Assn. Elem. Prins. (Va. state del. to conv. 1992, session presider), Lynchburg Assn. Elem. Sch. Prins. (chair supt. and legislators forum 1989), Lynchburg Coll. Alumni Assn., Averett Coll. Alumni Assn., Optimist Club (chmn. youth essay contest 1988-90, project designer youth recognition program 1989—, children at risk ct. project 1988), Phi Delta Kappa, Kappa Delta Pi, Delta Kappa Gamma. Office: Linkhorne Elem Sch 2501 Linkhorne Dr Lynchburg VA 24503-3398 Home: 2286 Swinging Bridge Rd Brookneal VA 24528-2598

HERNDON, ROBERT MCCULLOCH, neurologist, researcher; b. Richmond, Va., May 29, 1935; s. Lee Roy and Lois Ruth (McCulloch) H.; m. Kathryn Lucille Stearns, June 11, 1955; children: Robert McCulloch, William, Cynthia. BA, U. Chgo., 1955; MD, U. Tenn., 1958. Diplomate Am. Bd. Psychiatry and Neurology. Intern, then resident in neurology Wayne State U. Hosp., Detroit, 1959-61; fellow in neuropathology Montreal (Que., Can.) Neurol. Inst., 1962-63; fellow in anatomy Harvard U. Med. Sch., 1965-66; asst. prof. neurology Stanford U. Med. Sch., 1966-69; neurologist, then chief neurology Palo Alto (Calif.) VA Hosp., 1966-69; assoc. prof. Johns Hopkins U. Med. Sch., 1969-77; prof. neurology Ctr. Brain Rsch., U. Rochester (N.Y.) Med. Ctr., 1977-88, chmn., 1977-87; chief neurology Good Samaritan Hosp., Portland, Oreg., 1988-94; prof. neurology Oreg. Health Scis. U., Portland, 1988-96; chief, chairperson neurol. svcs. dept. Legacy Portland Hosps., 1993-94; prof. U. Miss., Jackson, 1996—; staff neurologist VA Med. Ctr., Jackson, Miss., 1996—2000, U. Miss. Med. Ctr., 2000—. Dir. Multiple Sclerosis Soc. Clinic, Rochester, 1978-88; mem. med. adv. bd. Multiple Sclerosis Soc. U.S., Internat. Fedn. Multiple Sclerosis Socs.; editor Internat. Jour. MS Care, 1999—. Pres. Consortium of Multiple Sclerosis Ctrs., 1993-94. With USAF, 1963-65. Fellow Am. Acad. Neurology; mem. Am. Neurol. Assn., Am. Acad. Sci., Am. Assn. Neuropathologists (Arthur Weil award 1969, 72, Moore award 1983), Soc. Exptl. Neuropathology (pres. 1988-91), Alpha Omega Alpha. Office: Jackson VAMC 1500 E Woodrow Wilson Ave # 127 Jackson MS 39216-5116

HERNDON, ROY CLIFFORD, physicist; b. Washington, Sept. 25, 1934; BS, Washington and Lee U., 1955; PhD, Fla. State U., 1962. Staff physicist Lawrence Livermore (Calif.) Lab., 1962—67; prof. Nova U., Ft. Lauderdale, 1967—75; dir. CBTR Ctr. for Biomed. & Toxicol. Rsch., Fla. State U., Tallahassee, 1983—. Dir. Inst. Internat. Coop. Environ. Rsch.; exec. dir. Fla. Hazardous Waste Adv. Coun., Tallahassee, 1980-82; mem. adv. bd. Fla. State U. System, Tallahassee, 1988—; hon. prof. Tech. U. Budapest, 1992. Author: (with others) Methods of Computational Physics, 1966, Land Use: A Spatial Approach, 1980, Theories of Electrons in Disordered Systems, 1982; contbr. over 100 articles to profl. jours. Mem. AAAS, Am. Phys. Soc., Phi Beta Kappa, Sigma Xi. Office: CBTR Fla State U 226 Morgan Bldg 2035 E Paul Dirac Dr Tallahassee FL 32310-3713

HERNON, PETER, library science educator; b. Kansas City, Mo., Aug. 31, 1944; s. Robert M. and Ethel S. (Grazier) H.; m. Elinor Hernon, Dec. 30, 1972; children: Alison K., Linsay C. BA, U. Colo., 1966, MA, 1968, U. Denver, 1971; PhD, Ind. U., 1978. From asst. prof. to assoc. prof. Simmons Coll., Boston, 1978-83; from assoc. prof. to prof. U. Ariz., Tucson, 1983-85; prof. Simmons Coll., 1986—. Vis. prof. Victoria U., Wellington, New Zealand, 1995-96. Author: Federal Information Policies, 1987 (Best Book award 1988), Service Quality in Academic Libraries, 1996, Assessng Service Quality (Best Book award ALA), U.S. Government on the Web, 1999, 3d edit., 2003, also others; editor Govt. Info. Quar., 1984-2000, Jour. Acad. Librarianship, 1993-2002; co-editor Libr. & Info. Sci. Rsch., 1992—. Recipient Best Article award Coll. & Rsch. Libraries, 1993. Avocation: jogging. Home: 23 Westgate Rd Framingham MA 01701-8843 Office: Simmons Coll 300 Fenway Boston MA 02115-5820 Office Phone: 617-521-2794. E-mail: peter.hernon@simmons.edu.

HERNSTADT, JUDITH FILENBAUM, city planner, real estate executive, broadcast executive; b. NYC, Nov. 18, 1942; d. Alex and Ruth Selena (Silberman) Filenbaum. BA, NYU, 1964, M Urban and Regional Planning, 1966; cert. smaller co. mgmt. program, Harvard Bus. Sch., 1977. With Office Planning Coordination, State of N.Y., 1966-68; ptnr. Devel. Planning Assocs., N.Y.C., 1967-68; with engring. scis. dept. Svc. Bur. Corp., N.Y.C., 1968-69; planning cons. Llewelyn-Davies Assocs., N.Y.C., 1969-71, Arlen Realty & Devel. Corp., N.Y.C., 1971-73; ptnr. Planning & Devel. Team, N.Y.C. and Las Vegas, 1974—; v.p. Sta. KVVU-TV Nev. Ind. Broadcasting Corp., Las Vegas, 1974-75, pres., 1976-77, Hernstadt Broadcasting Corp., 1978-81. Chmn. adv. bd. Internat. Film and TV Exch., Inc., 1996—2000; mem. coun. Rockefeller U., 1998—. Condr. TV interview programs. Bd. dirs. Nat. Com. on Am. Fgn. Plicy, Decorative Arts Trust, 1980—98, Eastside Internat. Cmty. Ctr., 1988—96; bd. advisors ACORN Found.; mem. fine arts com. U.S. Dept. State, 1976—; del. Fine Arts Fedn. N.Y., 1970—90; mem. Hudson Inst., 1980—92. Mem.: Nat. Inst. Social Scis., Women's Fgn. Policy Group, Hadji Baba Soc., Harvard Club (N.Y.C.), Lotos Club, Explorers Club. Home: 927 5th Ave New York NY 10021-2650

HERO, RODNEY E., political science professor; b. Tampa, Fla., Feb. 15, 1953; s. Henry Hero and Josie HeroRaynor; m. Kathryn S. Sween, May 22, 1982; children: Lindsay M, Christopher R Eden. PhD, Purdue U., 1980. Prof., polit. sci. U. Colo., Boulder, 1989—2000; Packey J. Dee prof., Am. democracy, polit. sci. U. Notre Dame, Ind., 2000—. Polit. sci. prof. Ariz. State U., Tempe, Ariz., 1988—89. Author: Faces of Inequality: Social Diversity in American Politics (Woodrow Wilson award, Am. Polit. Sci. Assn., 1999). Recipient Ralph Bunche award, Am. Polit. Sci. Assn. Office: U Notre Dame 217 O'Shaughnessy Hall Notre Dame IN 46556 Office Phone: 517-631-5189. Personal E-mail: rhero@nd.edu.

HEROD, CHARLES CARTERET, Afro-American studies educator; b. Florence County, S.C., Nov. 18, 1924; s. George William and Essie Lee (Johnson) H.; m. Agustina Benedicto; children: Charles-Francis, Ilona-Nora, Olivia Maria. A.B. in History and English magna cum laude, Rutgers U., 1964, A.M. in History, 1968, Ph.D. in History, 1973. Lic. tchr. N.J. Tchr. dept. social studies East Orange High Sch., N.J., 1964-66; instr. dept. history Rutgers U., New Brunswick, N.J., 1966-73; prof. Afro-Am. studies, SUNY-Plattsburgh, 1974—; lectr. in field. Author: The Nation in the History of Marxian Thought, 1976; Afro-American Nationalism, 1986. Mem. editorial bd. Can. Rev. Studies in Nationalism, P.E.I. U., Can. Contbr. revs., articles to profl. jours. Names Hon. Squadron Comdr. 380th Bomb Wing, Plattsburgh AFB, 1978; grantee NDEA, 1966, U. Vienna, 1970-73, Ctr. for East Asian Studies, 1975; recipient Special Diplome, French Guerelme. Mem. Am. Assn. for Advancement of Slavic Studies, N.Y. State Assn. European Historians, Royal Archaeol. Inst. Great Britain and Ireland, N.Y. African Studies Assn., Univ. Coll. Honor Soc. of Rutgers U., Habsburg Discussion Group, Pi Sigma Alpha.

HEROLD, JEFFREY ROY MARTIN, retired library director; b. Chgo., Aug. 9, 1941; s. Roy George and Anne (Polacek) H.; m. Carol Ann Courtial, June 20, 1964; children: Kristin Ann, Timothy Scott. MEd, SUNY, Buffalo, 1966; PhD, Ohio State U., 1969; MLS, Kent State U., 1986. Teaching assoc. Ohio State U., Columbus, 1965-69; asst. prof. edn. SUNY, Cortland, 1969-74, Ind. U. Pa., 1974-75; lectr. in edn. Kelvin Grove Coll., Brisbane, Australia, 1976-78; assoc. dir. office continuing edn. Ohio State U., Columbus, 1979-84; extension libr. Columbus Pub. Libr., 1985-87; dir. Bucyrus (Ohio) Pub. Libr., 1987-2000, Bucyrus Libr. Consortium, 1989-2000; mem. adv. coun. Nat. Multiple Sclerosis Soc., Idaho, 2002—. Book reviewer: Libr. Jour., 1988-97. Chair McGovern for Pres. Com., Cortland County, N.Y., 1972; founder and pres. SUNY Founds. of Edn. Assn., 1971-72. Grantee Timken Found., 1989, 1996, Ohio Humanities Coun., 1994, 1995, 1997, Libr. Svcs. and Tech. Act, 1998, Leidy Found., 2002, 2003, Kissler Family Found., 2003, Morrison Found., 2003, Idaho Cmty. Found., 2004. Avocations: reading, walking.

HERON, DAVID WINSTON, librarian; b. Los Angeles, Mar. 29, 1920; s. Charles Morton and Elizabeth (Atsatt) H.; m. Winifred Ann Wright, Aug. 24, 1946; children— Holly Winston, James, Charles. AB, Pomona Coll., 1942; B.L.S., U. Calif. at Berkeley, 1948; MA, U. Calif. at Los Angeles, 1951. Reference asst. U. Calif. at Los Angeles Library, 1948-52; librarian Am. embassy, Tokyo, Japan, 1952-53; staff asst. to librarian Grad. Reading Room U. Calif. at Los Angeles, 1953-55; asst. to dir. Stanford Libraries, 1955-57, asst. dir., 1959-61; asst. librarian Hoover Instn., Stanford, 1957-59; dir. libraries U. Nev., Reno, 1961-68, U. Kans., Lawrence, 1968-74; univ. librarian U. Calif. at Santa Cruz, 1974-78, emeritus librarian, 1979—; sr. lectr. Sch. Library and Info. Studies, 1978-79; head reader services Hoover Instn., 1980-86. Library adviser U. Ryukyus, Naha, Okinawa, 1960-61; mem. Kans. Library Adv. Commn., 1973-74 Author: Forever Facing South, 1991, Night Landing, 1999; editor: A Unifying Influence, 1981; mem. editorial bd. Coll. and Rsch. Librs.; contbr. articles to gen. and profl. jours. Served as 1st lt. AUS, 1942-46, ETO. Mem. ALA (exec. bd.), Kans. Library Assn., Nev. Library Assn. (pres. 1963-65), Assn. Research Libraries (bd. dirs. 1974), ACLU, Assn. Coll. and Research Libraries (editor monographs; chmn. U. libraries sect. 1970-71). Democrat. Home: 120 Las Lomas Dr Aptos CA 95003-3221

HEROS, ROBERTO COSME, neurosurgeon; b. Havana, Cuba, Sept. 27, 1942; m. Deborah O.; children: Elsa, Rob, Carlos. MD, U. Tenn., Memphis, 1968. Diplomate Am. Bd. Neurol. Surgery. Intern in surgery Mass. Gen. Hosp., Boston, 1968-69; asst. resident gen. surgery, 1969-70; resident in neurosurgery, 1972-77; asst. in neurosurgery, 1976-77; attending neurosurgeon Presbyn. U. Hosp., Pitts., 1977-79; assoc. chief neurosurgery, 1979-80; asst. prof. neurosurgery U. Pitts., 1977-80, dir. neurosurgery residents ednl. program, 1979-80; asst. prof. surgery Harvard Med. Sch., Boston, 1980-83; assoc. prof. surgery, 1983-89; prof. surgery, 1989-90; Lyle A. French prof., chmn. dept. neurosurgery U. Minn., 1990-95; prof., chair dept. neurol. surgery U. Miami, 1995—. Dir. U. Miami Internat. Health Ctr. Chmn. editl. bd. Neurosurgery, 1988; contbr. articles to profl. jours. Chmn. Brain Attack Nat. Coalition, neurovasc. com. World Fedn. Neurosurg. Soc. Recipient Medal of Surgery U. Tenn., 1968, Dean's medal, 1968. Fellow: ACS; mem.: Congress Nuerol. Surgeons (v.p. 1986—87), Neurosurg. Soc. Am., Am. Acad. Neurol. Surgeons (pres. 2001), Am. Assn. Neurol. Surgeons (pres. 2002), Alpha Omega Alpha. Office: U Miami Med Sch 1095 NW 14th Terr Miami FL 33136-1407 Office Phone: 305-243-4572. E-mail: rheros@med.miami.edu.

HERPST, ROBERT DIX, lawyer, research and development company executive; b. Teaneck, N.J., Jan. 23, 1947; s. Harold Dix and Anita Augusta (Adams) H.; children: Katherine Elizabeth, Lauren Gabrielle, Sarah Elizabeth; m. Theresa M. Jacobini, Oct. 24, 1987. BS, NYU, 1969; JD, Rutgers U., 1972. Bar: NJ 1972, US Supreme Ct. 1979. Assoc. Pitney, Hardin & Kipp, Morristown, N.J., 1972-77, BOC Group, Inc., Montvale, N.J., 1977-89, div. counsel, 1978-82, corp. counsel, asst. sec., 1982-88. Pres. Internat. Crystal Labs., Garfield, NJ, 1982—88, mng. dir., chmn. bd. dirs., 1988—; bd. suprs. Solaris Optics, S.A., Warsaw, 2003—04. Achievements include patents in field. Avocations: golf, politics, stock market, graphic arts. Office: Internat Crystal Labs 11 Erie St Garfield NJ 07026-2307 Personal E-mail: rherpst@internationalcrystal.net.

HERR, DAVID FULTON, lawyer, educator; b. St. Paul, July 13, 1950; s. Robert and Janet (Fleischbein) H.; m. Mary Kay Strand, Oct. 25, 1986; children: Ehrland A. Truitt, Alec F. BA, U. Colo., 1972, MBA, 1977; JD cum laude, William Mitchell Coll. Law, 1978. Bar: Minn. 1978, U.S. Dist. Ct. Minn. 1978, U.S. Ct. Appeals (8th cir.) 1978, U.S. Ct. Appeals (3rd cir.) 1983, U.S. Claims Ct. 1986, U.S. Supreme Ct., 1989. Assoc. Robins, Davis & Lyons, Mpls., 1978-81; from assoc. to ptnr., applleate litig. Maslon Edelman Borman & Brand, Mpls., 1981—. Adj. prof. William Mitchell Coll. Law, St. Paul, 1978—. Author: Multidistrict Litigation, 1986, (with others) Motion Practice, 1986, 3d edit., 1998, Discovery Practice, 1982, 3d edit., 1996, Minnesota Practice, 1986, 3d edit., 1995, Annotated Manual for Complex Litig., 2005, and other works. Fellow Am. Acad. Appellate Lawyers (pres. 2004-05); mem. ABA, Am. Law Inst., Minn. State Bar (chmn. litigation sect. 1985-86, task force on complex litigation 1990—, Advocate's award 1999), Hennepin County Bar Assn., Ramsey County Bar Assn., Lawyers-Pilots Bar Assn. Office: Maslon Edelman Borman & Brand LLP 3300 Wells Fargo Ctr 90 S 7th St Minneapolis MN 55402 Office Phone: 612-672-8350. Office Fax: 612-642-8350. Business E-Mail: david.herr@maslon.com.

HERR, HARRY WALLACE, medical researcher, educator, surgeon, urologist; b. Saint Louis, Mo., Oct. 1, 1943; s. Harry M. and Harriet Wallace Herr; m. Sheri Machele Herr, Oct. 23, 1999; children: Julie Christine Rozell, Nicole Alison, Annek Lynn Smith, John William. BA, U. Calif., Davis, 1965; MD, U. Calif., Irvine, 1969; student, Columbia U., 2004—. Diplomate Am. Bd. Urology, 1976. Intern U. So. Calif. Med. Ctr., LA, 1969—70; urology resident U. Calif., Irvine, 1970—74; immunology, urologic oncology fellow Cornell Grad. Sch. Med. Scis./Meml. Sloan-Kettering Cancer Ctr., NYC, 1974—76; attending surgeon Meml. Sloan-Kettering Cancer Ctr., NYC, 1979—. Prof. urology Meml. Sloan-Kettering/Cornell U. Med. Coll., NYC, 1997—. Contbr. papers, book chpts., revs. in field. Recipient FC Valentine award, NY Acad. Medicine, 1976, Jane Ewing award, Soc. Surg. Oncology, 1980; fellow, ACS, 1978. Fellow: Am. Assn. Genito-Urinary Surgeons; mem.: Am. Assn. Cancer Rsch., Am. Soc. Clin. Oncology, Am. Urologic Assn. Office: Memorial Sloan Kettering Cancer Ctr 1275 York Ave New York NY 10021

HERR, PETER HELMUT FRIEDERICH, sales executive; b. Hamburg, Germany, Apr. 23, 1951; came to U.S., 1978; s. Helmut and Ellen (Schmidt) H.; m. Kim Lovett, Sept. 29, 1984 (div. Nov. 1991); 1 child, Andrew; m. Monika Berns, Nov. 19, 1991; children, Jan, Maximilian. BS in Mech. Engring., U. Braunschweig, 1974, MS in Aero. Engring., 1978. Aero. engr. R & D Beech Aircraft Corp., Wichita, Kans., 1978-81, regional mgr., 1981-86, sr. regional mgr., 1987-92, dir. internat. market devel., 1992-93, regional dir. western Europe and Africa, 1993-94; v.p. internat. sales for Europe, Africa Mid. East Raytheon Aircraft, Wichita, Kans., 1994—. Sec., treas. Euroflight, Inc., Wichita, 1985—. Cpl. German Air Force, 1970-72. Lutheran. Avocations: flying, golf, boating. Home: 15229 E Zimmerly Ct Wichita KS 67230-9244 Office: Raytheon Aircraft Co 10511 E Central Ave Wichita KS 67206-2557 also: Raytheon Internat Inc Am Fronhof 1 D-53177 Bonn Germany E-mail: n1721@aol.com.

HERR, PHILIP MICHAEL, lawyer, accountant; b. NYC, June 22, 1955; s. Norman and Grace (Sporn) H.; m. Lorrie Wiener, Nov. 23, 1978; children: Gabrielle, Nicole, Adam. BS, BA magna cum laude, L.I. U., 1977; JD, Ohio No. U., 1980. CPA NY, 1995; bar: NY 1981, US Tax Ct. 1982; registered rep. Nat. Assn. Securities Dealers, 1999. Tax staff Ernst & Young, N.Y.C., 1980-83; tax supr. Wiss & Co., Livingston, N.J., 1983-88; tax mgr. Goldstein Golub Kessler & Co., N.Y.C., 1988-93; cons. N.Y.C., 1992-95; cons. estate bus. and fin. planning Guardian Life Ins. Co. of Am., N.Y.C., 1995-98; dir. advanced underwriting Kingsbridge Fin. Group, Inc., Pt. Pleasant Beach, NJ, 1998—; registered rep. AXA Advisors, LLC, 1998—. Adj. prof. bus. Ohio No. U., Ada, 1978-80, Fairleigh Dickinson U., Teaneck, N.J., 1983—, NYU Sch. Continuing Edn., N.Y.C., 1992-95. Contbr. articles to profl. jours., chpt. to book. Mem.: N.Y. State Soc. CPAs, N.Y. State Bar Assn., Assn. Advanced Life Underwriting. Jewish. Avocations: racquetball, tennis, power walking. Office: Kingsbridge Financial Group Inc 501 Broadway Point Pleasant Beach NJ 08742 Office Phone: 732-899-1000 ext. 109. Business E-Mail: philh@kingsbridge.com.

HERR, RICHARD, history professor; b. Guanajuato, Mexico, Apr. 7, 1922; s. Irving and Luella (Winship) H.; m. Elena Fernandez Mel, Mar. 2, 1946 (div. 1967); children: Charles Fernandez, Winship Richard; m. Valerie J. Jackson, Aug. 29, 1968; children: Sarah, Jane. AB, Harvard U., 1943; PhD, U. Chgo., 1954; Doctorate (hon.), U. Alcalá de Henares, Spain, 2001. Instr. Yale U., 1952-57, asst. prof., 1957-59; assoc. prof. U. Calif., Berkeley, 1960-63, prof. history, 1963-91, prof. emeritus, 1991—, chancellor's fellow, 1987-90. Directeur d'études associé, sixième sect. Ecole Pratique des Hautes Etudes, Paris, 1973; dir. Madrid Study Ctr., U. Calif., 1975-77; chair Portuguese Studies Program, U. Calif., Berkeley, 1994-98, chair Spanish Studies Program, U. Calif. Berkeley, 2002-04; vis. life mem. Clare Hall, Cambridge, Eng., 1985—; vis. prof. U. Alcalá. Henares, Spain, 1991; bd. dirs. Internat. Inst. Found. in Spain, Boston, 1997-2000; fellow Ctr. for History of Freedom, Washington U., St. Louis, 1994. Author: The Eighteenth Century Revolution in Spain, 1958, Tocqueville and the Old Regime, 1962, An Historical Essay on Modern Spain, 1974, Rural Change and Royal Finances in Spain at the End of the Old Regime, 1989 (Leo Gershoy award Am. Hist. Assn. 1990); co-author: An American Family in the Mexican Revolution, 1999; editor: Memorias del cura liberal don Juan Antonio Posse, 1984; co-editor, contbr.: Ideas in History, 1965, Iberian Identity, 1989; editor, contbr.: The New Portugal: Democracy and Europe, 1993, Themes in Rural History of the Western World, 1993; asst. editor: Jour. Modern History, 1949-50; mem. editl. bd. French Historical Studies, 1966-69, Revista de Historia Economica, 1983-91. With AUS, 1943-45. Decorated Comendador of the Orden de Isabel la Católica (Spain); recipient Bronze medal Collège de France, Paris, The Berkeley citation U. Calif., 1991; Social Sci. Rsch. Coun. grantee, 1963-64; Guggenheim fellow, 1959-60, 84-85; NEH sr. fellow, 1968-69. Fellow Am. Acad. Arts and Scis.; mem. Am. Philos. Soc., Real Academia de la Historia Madrid (corr.), Soc. for Spanish and Portuguese Hist. Studies. Office: U Calif Dept History Berkeley CA 94720-2550

HERR, SHARON MARIE, retired librarian; b. St. Cloud, Minn., June 23, 1950; d. Lawrence James and Avis Christina (Klein) Blenkush; m. Dennis Wilfred Herr, June 8, 1985. BA cum laude, Coll. St. Benedict, 1972; MA in LS, U. Mich., 1974. Scheduling asst. South Jr. H.S., St. Cloud, 1968; asst. to libr. Coll. of St. Benedict, St. Joseph, Minn., 1972-73; sci. libr. Ohio No. U., Ada, 1974-78, cataloging libr., 1978—2005; ret., 2005. Mem. univ. coun. Ohio No. U., Ada, 1989-91, 97-2001, mem. pers. com., 1979-80. Author essay. Judge elections Hardin County Bd. Elections, Kenton, Ohio, 1995-2001. Recipient Betty Crocker Homemaker award Gen. Mills, 1968. Mem.: Stearns History Mus., Smithsonian Instn. Democrat. Avocations: antiques, gardening, christmas tree ornament collecting, investing. Home: 822 S Johnson St Ada OH 45810-1521

HERRANEN, KATHY, artist; b. Zelienople, Pa., Dec. 22, 1943; d. John and Helen Elizabeth (Sayti) D'Biagio; m. John Warma Herranen, Dec. 31, 1974 (div. Feb. 1994); 1 child, Michael John. Student, Scottsdale (Ariz.) C.C., 1990—. Cert. tchr. art, State Bd. Dirs. for Cmty. Coll. Ariz. Horseback riding instr. Black Saddle Riding Acad., Lancaster, Calif., 1960—65; tel. co. supr. Bell Tel., Bishop, Calif., 1965; reporter, part-time photographer Ellwood City (Pa.) Ledger, 1967—70; back-country guide and cook Mammoth Lakes (Calif.) Pack Outfit, 1970; motel mgr. Mountain Property Mgmt., Mammoth Lakes, 1970—72; reporter, bookkeeper Hungry Horse (Mont.) News, 1973—74; pig farmer Columbia Falls, Mont., 1973—75; fine artist, illustrator, graphic designer Mont., Calif., and Ariz., 1980—; fine arts cons. Collector's Gallery, Galleri II, Yuma, Ariz., 1983—84; wind chime designer, creator Phoenix, 1995—; represented by Backstreet Furniture and Art, Phoenix, 1995—2001, Marcella's Ariz. Collection, Phoenix, 1995—2003, Hohn Gallery Fine Arts, Ltd., Scottsdale, 1997—, Magickal Paths, Tempe, Ariz., 2003—04, Coomers Mall, Phoenix, 2003—04, Wilson's Antiques, Coraopolis, Pa., 2003—. Guest lectr. Paradise Valley Tchrs Acad., Phoenix, 1993, Sr. Adult Edn. Program, Scottsdale (Ariz.) C.C., 1994, pastel painting instr., 1996—; guest demonstrator Binder's Art Ctr., Scottsdale, 1995, Backstreet Furniture and Art, Phoenix, 1995-96; guest lectr., demonstrator Summer Edn. Program Paradise Valley Sch. Dist., 1996, 99, 2000; guest demonstrator Phoenix Artists Guild, 2000, Paradise Valley Artists, 2000. Solo shows include Pinnacle, Phoenix, 1993, Villas of Sedona, Ariz., 1995. Sec. Young Dems., Ellwood City, Pa., late 1960's, Vistas Home Owners Assn., Phoenix, 1995—; troubleshooter Maricopa County Elections Dept., Phoenix, 1994-96, 2000-05. Recipient 1st pl. award, Potpourri Artists, Yuma, 1981, Subscriber award, Butte (Mont.) Arts Coun., 1981, 2d pl. award, Desert Artists, Yuma, 1982, hon. mention, Yuma County Fair, 1983, Wildlife Painting Exhibit, Scottsdale, 1993, Fountain Festival Juried Competitive exhbn. Fine Arts, 1993, Scottsdale Studio 13, 1991, 1992, Spl. award, 1993, Merit award, 1993, 2 Merit awards, 1994, 1st pl. award, Phoenix Ctr. for the Arts, 2003. Mem. Nat. Assn. Sr. Friends Fine Artists (chair 1995-2003, hon. mention 1993, People's Choice award 1996, 1st pl. award, hon. mention, 2001), Women's Caucus for Art, Phoenix Artists Guild (hon. mention 2003), Ariz. Pastel Artists Assn. (charter mem., juried mem., membership chair 1995-96, 2002—, 2d v.p., show chair 1996, guest demonstrator 1995, guest lectr. 1998, Merit award 1995), Ariz. Art Alliance (juried mem., publicity chmn. 2000—), Artists and Craftsmen of Flathead Valley Mont. (founder, charter mem., pres. 1981-82), Desert Sage Artists (charter mem., juried mem., v.p. 2003-04), Phi Theta Kappa. Republican. Lutheran. Avocations: public speaking and acting, dance, stamp collecting/philately, photography, interior decorating. Office Phone: 602-569-6209. Personal E-mail: kathyherranen@aol.com.

HERREGAT, GUY-GEORGES JACQUES, banker; b. Oostende, West Flanders, Belgium, July 22, 1939; came to U.S., 1966; s. Georges-Albert Maurice and Marie-Gerard S. (Elleboudt) H. Licence en philosophie, U. Louvain, 1961, licence en philosophie et lettres, 1964; postgrad., Yale U., 1966-67, PhD in Econs., 1972. Rsch. asst. U. Louvain (Belgium), 1964-66; rsch. assoc. Nat. Bur. Econ. Rsch., N.Y.C., 1967-72; internat. economist Brown Bros. Harriman & Co., N.Y.C., 1973-74; asst. v.p. Chem. Bank, N.Y.C., 1974-76; dep. chief economist European Am. Bank, N.Y.C., 1977-80; sr. advisor, sr. v.p. Societe Generale de Banque, N.Y.C., 1980-85; mgr. Banque Worms, N.Y.C., 1985-86; sr. v.p., dep. gen. mgr. Credit du Nord, N.Y.C., 1986-93; sr. v.p. Banque Paribas, N.Y.C., 1993-2000; mgr. dir. risk mgmt. BNP-Paribas, N.Y.C., 2000—04; ret. Cons. Am. Bankers Assn., N.Y.C., 1971, SEIDEIS-Futuribles, Paris, 1967-80, Ford Found., N.Y.C., 1972-73. Author: Managerial Profiles and Investment Patterns, 1972, (with others) The Diffusion of New Industrial Processes, 1974, The Finances of the Performing Arts, 1974; contbr. articles to profl. jours. Yale U. fellow, 1966-67,

Nat. Bur. Econ. Rsch. fellow, 1971-72; named Aspirant de Recherches Fonds National Belge de la Recherche Scientifique, 1967-72. Mem. Am. Econ. Assn., Acad. Polit. Sci., Yale Alumni Assn., Japan Soc., Inst. Internat. Bankers, Belgian-Am. C. of C. (bd. dirs. 1986—). Home: 30 E 81st St New York NY 10028-0222 also: 253 Atlantic Fire Island Pines NY 11782 also: 800 West Ave Miami Beach FL 33139-5542 Office Phone: 212-841-2942.

HERREN, MICHAEL WAYNE, classical studies educator; b. Santa Ana, Calif. s. Cecil Ray Herren and Carol Jean McCollum; m. Dana Tenny, Aug. 28, 1962 (div. Feb. 1975); m. Shirley Ann Brown, Apr. 12, 1975; children: Sarah, Michael Aidan. BA, Claremont McKenna Coll., 1962; MSL, Pontif. Inst. Mediaeval Studies, 1967; PhD, U. Toronto, 1969. Asst. prof. classics York U., Toronto, 1969—74, assoc. prof. classics, 1974—78, prof. classics, 1978—98, disting. rsch. prof. classics, 1998—. Adj. prof. medieval studies U. Toronto, 1990—; cons. Royal Irish Acad. Latin Texts, Dublin, 1995—. Author: Chirst in Celtic Christianity, 2002; editor, translator: The Hisperica Famina, 2 vols., 1974, 87, Social Sciences and Humanities Research Coun., 1974, 87, Aldhelm the Prose Works, 1979, Iohannis Scotti Eriugenae Carmina, 1993, Latin Letters in Early Christian Ireland, 1996, Latin Culture in the Eleventh Century, 2002; editor Jour. Medieval Latin, 1991-2001, gen. editor, pub., 1996—; mem. adv. bd. Filologia Mediolatina Spoleto It jour., 1994—. Bd. dirs. Mozart Soc., Toronto, 1990—. Sr. Rsch. fellow Kings Coll., London, 1987-88, Alexander von Humboldt fellow, 1981-82, 88-89, Killam Rsch. Can. Coun. fellow, 1995-97, Guggenheim Rsch., 1998-99; recipient Konrad Adenauer prize, AvH Stiftung, 2003. Fellow Royal Soc. Can.; mem. Medieval Acad. Am., Classical Assn. Can., Soc. for Promotion of Eriuenian Studies, Hon. mem. Royal Irish Acad. Avocations: classical music vocalist, opera and lieder. Office: Atkinson Coll York U 2300 Toronto ON Canada M3J 1P3 E-mail: aethicus@yorku.ca.

HERRERA, CAROLINA, fashion designer; b. Caracas, Venezuela, Jan. 8, 1939; d. Guillermo and Maria Cristina Pacanina; m. Reinaldo Herrera, 1968; children: Mercedes, Ana Luisa, Carolina Adriana, Patricia. Founder, head designer Carolina Herrera, 1981—, launched bridal collection, 1987; opened Carolina Herrera / New York boutique, NYC, 2000. Released fragrance Carolina Herrera, 1988, Carolina Herrera for Men, 1991, Aqua Flore, 1995, 212 Carolina Herrera, 2003, 212 Men, 2004. Recipient Red Cross, 1979, Best Design Hall of Fame, 1980, Latin Am. Designer "Fashion award", 1987, Pratt Inst., 1990, Mary Ann Magnin awards, 1994, Special Distinction to a Career in the World of Design, Internat. Fashion Ctr. de New York, 1995, Reward to an enterprising spirit, Women's Div., Albert Einstein Coll. of Med. of Yeshiva U., 1996, Women with Heart award, Am. Aevet Assn., 2001. Office: 501 7th Ave Fl 17 New York NY 10018-5903 Office Phone: 212-944-5757. Office Fax: 212-944-7996.

HERRERA, DENNIS J., lawyer; b. Bay Shore, NY, Nov. 6, 1962; m. Anne Herrera; 1 child, Declan. BA, Villanova U.; JD, George Washington U. Bar: Calif. 1989. Dep. city. atty. City of San Francisco, city atty., 2002—; ptnr. Kelly, Gill, Sherburne & Herrera, San Francisco; chief staff U.S. Maritime Adminstrn., Washington; pres. San Francisco Police Commn.; with San Francisco Pub. Transp. Commn. Office: City Hall Rm 234 1 Doctor Carlton B Goodlett Pl San Francisco CA 94102 Business E-Mail: cityattorney@ci.sf.ca.us.*

HERRERA, GILBERT VICTOR, engineering executive; b. Albuquerque, Mar. 23, 1959; s. Carlos Placido and Martha Trujillo Herrera; m. Cynthia Villareal, Sept. 1, 1984; children: Aubrey Victoria, Brian Edward. Cadet, U.S. Mil. Acad., 1977—79; BS in Computer Engring., U. N.Mex, 1981; MS in Elec. and Computer Engring., U. Calif., Berkeley, 1982. Mem. tech. staff Sandia Nat. Labs., Albuquerque, 1982—88, supr. radiation-hardened semiconductors divsn., 1988—91, mgr. govt. rels., 1992—93, program mgr. electronic packaging, 1993—97, mgr. electronic and optical materials rsch., 1999—2000, dep. dir. corp. bus. devel. and partnerships, 2000—03, dir., mfg. S&T, 2003—; AAAS/Sloan White House sci. fellow White Ho. Office Sci. and Tech. Policy, Washington, 1991—92; COO SEMI/SEMATECH, Austin, Tex., 1997—99. Adj. asst. prof. U. N.Mex., Albuquerque, 1983—84, mem. external adv. bd. elec. and computer engring. dept., 1989—96, mem. faculty search com. elec. and computer engring., 1996—96; mem. AAAS Nat. Sci. Journalism Award Tech. Rev. Com., Washington, 1991—; mem., chair SEMATECH Tech. Adv. Bd., Electronic Packaging, Austin, Tex., 1993—97; mem. Semiconductor Industry Assn./Nat. Tech. Roadmap for Semiconductors Packaging Working Group, San Jose, 1994—97, Nat. Electronic Mfg. Initiative Packaging Tech. Working Group, Washington, 1995—96, Hispanic Engr. Nat. Achievement Award Selection Com., L.A., 1995—95, Army Sci. Bd., Washington, 1999—, co-chair summer study on force protection, 2002—; mem. AAAS DoD Fellowship Selection Com., Washington; presenter in field. Contbr. articles to profl. jours. Pres. Thomas Village Neighborhood Assn., Albuquerque, 1990—91; mentor Stay in Sch. Program Albuquerque Hispano C. of C., 1987—89; precinct chmn. Rep. Party, Albuquerque, 1980—81; mem., players rep. Altamont Little League, Albuquerque, 1999—99. Recipient Ann. Rising Star in Engring. award, Albuquerque Tribune, 1989; fellow, Am. Ctr. for Internat. Leadership, 1992; scholar, grantee, Minority Access for Rsch. Careers, 1980—81, White Ho. Sci. fellow, AAAS/Sloan Found., 1991—92. Mem.: AAAS, IEEE, Mexican Am. Engring. Soc., Assn. of the U.S. Army, Materials Rsch. Soc., Kappa Mu Epsilon, Etta Kappa Nu, Tau Beta Pi. Republican. Roman Catholic. Achievements include patents pending for Fringing Field Effect Transistor with Integrated Memory Function. Avocations: military history, basketball, science history, science and public policy, singing. Home: 10522 City Lights Dr NE Albuquerque NM 87111 Office: Sandia Nat Labs PO Box 5800 Albuquerque NM 87185-0157 E-mail: herrergv@sandia.gov.

HERRERA, JOHN, professional football team executive; married; 9 children. BA in History, U. Calif., Davis. Tng. camp asst. Oakland Raiders, 1963-68, pub. rels. asst., 1968, dir. pub. rels., 1978-80, sr. exec., 1985—; dir. player pers. B.C. Lions, 1981-82; gen. mgr. Sask. Roughriders, 1983-84; with scouting depts. Tampa Bay Buccaneers, 1975-76, Washington Redskins, 1977. Office: Oakland Raiders 1220 Harbor Bay Pkwy Alameda CA 94502-6570 Office Phone: 510-864-5000. E-mail: jherrera@raiders.com.

HERRERA, PALOMA, dancer; b. Buenos Aires, Dec. 21, 1975; d. Alberto Oscar and Diana Lia (Rube) H. Attended, Olga Ferri Studio, 1982, Ballet Sch. of Minsk, 1987, English Nat. Ballet, London, 1990, Sch. Am. Ballet, N.Y.C., 1991; diploma, Inst. Superior Art at The Colon Theatre, Buenos Aires, 1991. Soloist Am. Ballet Theatre, N.Y.C., 1992-95, prin. dancer, 1995—. Dancer (ballets) Don Quixote, 1987, 88, soloist La Bayadere, The Sleeping Beauty, Don Quixote, Met. Opera, N.Y.C., 1992, Etudes, The Sleeping Beauty, Swan Lake, Symphonie Concertante, Voluntaries, 1993, prin. Symphonie Concertatne, Symphonic Variations, 1993; prin. Peasant Pas de Deux in Giselle, Colon Theatre, Buenos Aires, 1992, La Bayadere, 1993; prin. Don Quixote, soloist Etudes, Voluntaries, Theme and Variations, Kennedy Ctr., Washington, 1993; prin. The Nutcracker, Dorothy Chandler Pavilion, L.A., 1993, Palace Theatre, Stamford, Conn., 1993; repertoire Met. Opera House Symphonic Variations, Theme and Variations, The Nutcracker, Cruel World, Symphonie Concertante, Gala Performance, 1994, La Bayadera, Don Quixote, Paquite, How Near Heaven, Les Sylphides, Cruel World, Tchaikovsky Pas de Deux, Romeo and Juliet, 1995; guest artist Ballet Gala, Toronto, 1993, Colon Theatre, Buenos Aires, 1993, Gala Ballet of Aix-En-Provence, France, 1993, New Generation Ballet, Moscow, Gala Tribute to Nureyev, Toronto, Le Gala des Etoiles, Montreal, Internat. Evenings of Dance, Vail, Colo., Don Quixote, Kremlin Palace, Moscow, 1995. Recipient First prize Latino Am. Ballet Contest, Lima, Peru, 1985, Coca-Cola Contest of Arts and Scis., 1986, Finalist diploma XIV Varna (Bulgaria) Internat. Competition of Ballet, 1990; scholar Colon Theatre Found., 1989; Dance scholar Antorchas Found., 1991. Home: One Lincoln Plz 20 W 64th St Apt F New York NY 10023-7129 also: Billinghurst 2553 10 Piso Dto CP 1425 Buenos Aires Argentina Office: American Ballet Theatre 890 Broadway Fl 3 New York NY 10003-1278

HERRERA, PAUL FREDRICK, accountant; b. Manilla, Philippines, Aug. 31, 1948; came to U.S., 1949 (parents Am. citizens); s. Raymond Mix and Emily Irene (Smith) H.; m. Valerie Ann Derryberry, June 24, 1982; 1 child, Charles. BA, Washington U., 1970; M in Acctg., U. Ariz., 1977. CPA, Tex., N.Y. Capt. U.S. Army, 1970-75; sr. mgr. Price Waterhouse, Houston, 1976-86; ptnr. Deloitte Tax, N.Y.C., 1986—. Frequent speaker on internat. tax issues. Contbr. articles to profl. publs. Mem. Am. Inst. CPA's. Office: Deloitte & Touche LLP Two World Fin Ctr New York NY 10281

HERRERO, LOWELL, artist, painter; BA, Calif. Coll. Arts and Crafts, 1949. Part-time illustrator San Francisco Chronicle, 1946—49; studio illustrator Standford and Sanvick, San Francisco, 1950—53; ptnr. Butte, Herrero and Hyde Studio, 1953—66. Ann. calendars for Shell Oil Co., 1963-70, whale painting series, 1979-81, cat calendar series, 1981-, cow calendar series, 1988-; one-man shows include Bill Dodge Gallery, Carmel, Calif., 1983-93, Sailor's Valentine Gallery, Nantucket, Mass., 1986-, New Masters Gallery, Carmel, Calif., 1993-, Franklin Mint, 1995, I. Wolk Gallery, St. Helena, Calif., 1996, 1998, 2000; Represented in permanent collections Spago Restaurant, Beverly Hills, Calif.; ltd. edition collectibles, Franklin Mint (Best in Show, Best in Class, 1994), 1993-. Office: PO Box 192305 San Francisco CA 94119

HERRERO RODRIGUEZ DE MIÑON, MIGUEL, lawyer, consultant, legislator; b. Madrid, June 18, 1940; s. Miguel Herrero and Carmen Rodriguez de Miñon; m. Cristina de Jauregui Segurola, Nov. 6, 1975; children: Miguel, Cristina, Amaya. Student, U. Oxford, England, 1958, U. Luxembourg, 1962, U. Geneva, 1964; LLD, U. Madrid, 1965; BA, Licentiate Philosphy, U. Louvain, Belgium, 1966, 68; Licentiate Literature, U. Madrid, 1969. Sr. legal advisor Spanish Adminstrn. (Conejo de Estado), Madrid, 1966—; gen. sec. Ministry of Justice, Madrid, 1976-77; mem. parliament, 1977—93; leader parliamentary majority, 1980-81; leader opposition parliamentary group, 1982-87; spokesman fgn. affairs opposition parliamentary group, 1987—91. Drafter Spanish Constitution, 1977—78; mem. Trilateral Commn., 1982—2004, Real Acad. Ciencias Morales y Politicas, 1991—, Constitutional Ct., Andorra, Spain, 2001—. Author: numerous books on constitutional law; contbr. articles to profl. jours. Decorated Gran Collar Merito Civil, Gran Cruz San Raimundo de Peñafort, Gran Cruz Isabel La Catolica, Orden del Merito Constitucional (Spain); Order of Merit (Italy). Mem. Bar Assn. Madrid, Nuevo Club, Gran Peña, Madrid Club de Campo. Roman Catholic. Avocations: hunting, collecting antique books. Office: Mayor 70, bajo izq 28013 Madrid Spain Office Phone: 3491-5166262.

HERRETT, RICHARD ALLISON, agricultural research institute administrator; b. Buffalo, Aug. 4, 1932; s. Wilbert Atherton and Loys (Richards) H.; m. Virginia Walker, July 28, 1958 (div. July 1978); children: Steven Jay, Jeffrey James, William Allan; m. Joan Hanhauser Maurer, Aug. 26, 1978; 1 child, Maxwell. BS in Agrl. Rsch., Rutgers U., 1954; MS in Agronomy/Organic Chemistry, U. Minn., 1956, PhD in Plant Biochemistry/Organic Chemistry, 1959; postgrad., George Washington U., U. Calif., Berkeley. Leader rsch. team Boyce Thompson Inst., Yonkers, N.Y., 1959-61, Union Carbide Corp., Clayton, N.C., 1961-70; tech. mgr. ICI Ams. Inc., Wilmington, Del., 1970-75, dir. rsch. and devel., 1975-87, mem. govt. rels., sci. liaison, 1987-92; pres., cons. EnvirAg Assocs., Bethesda, Md., 1992-94; exec. dir. Agrl. Rsch. Inst., Bethesda, 1995—2002; ind. contractor, 2002—. Bd. dirs., treas., trustee N.C. Biotech Ctr., Research Triangle Park; bd. dirs. Agrl. Rsch. Inst./Bio, Washington; treas. C.V. Riley Found., Washington, 1988-92; vice chmn. exec. bd. Bus. Coun. on Indoor Air; appointee N.C. Bd. Sci. and Tech.; presenter in field. Contbr. chpts. to books, articles to profl. jours.; patentee in field. Upton Meml. scholar Rutgers U. Mem. AAAS, Internat. Union of Pure and Applied Chemists (fin. chmn.), Nat. Agrl. Chems. Assn. (chmn., mem. rsch. dirs. com.), Am. Chem. Soc., Weed Sci. Soc. Am., Sigma Xi, Inst. Food Technologists. Avocations: racquetball, skiing. Home: 23 Sonneborn Ln Severna Park MD 21146-4803 Office: Nat Assn State Depts Agr 1156 15th St NW Ste1020 Washington DC 20005 Office Phone: 202-296-9680. Personal E-mail: ariherrett@aol.com.

HERRICK, ELBERT CHARLES, chemist, consultant; b. Joliet, Mont., Oct. 16, 1919; s. Charles Albert and Marie (Johnson) H.; m. Doris Christine Brock, June 1, 1962; children: David, Dennis, Douglas, Donna. BSChemE, Mont. State U., 1941; degree of ChemE, Princeton U., 1942; PhD in Organic Chemistry, MIT, 1949. Rsch. chemist Cen. Rsch. Dept. E.I. duPont de Nemours, 1949-54; assoc. rsch. chemist Houdry Process Corp., 1955-58; supr. chem. rsch. Climax Molybdenum Co., Mich., 1958-59; sr. rsch. chemist R&D div. Sun Oil Co., 1959-61; sr. rsch. chemist Textile Fibers div. Dow Chem. Co., 1962-64; pvt. practice cons. chemist and chem. engr., 1964-65; organic sect. head Great Lakes Rsch. Corp., 1965-67; dir. chem. rsch. Escambia Chem. Corp., 1967-69; sr. rsch. chemist Air Products and Chems., Inc., 1969-77; sr. chem. engr., scientist Tracor Jitco, Inc., 1977; environ. systems scientist The MITRE Corp., 1977-88; sr. staff specialist Dynamac Corp., 1988-89; pvt. practice Woodbine, Md., 1989—. Patentee in field; contbr. articles to profl. jours. Lt. USAF, 1942-45, ETO. Fellow Am. Inst. Chemists; mem. Am. Inst. Chem. Engrs., Am. Chem. Soc., N.Y. Acad. Scis., Sigma Xi, Tau Beta Pi, Phi Kappa Phi. Democrat. Adventist. Avocations: gardening, reading. Home and Office: Sunset Summit 2403 Vine Cir Rocklin CA 95765-4716

HERRICK, GREGORY EVANS, computer company executive; b. Ottumwa, Iowa, Nov. 23, 1951; s. Walter Edward and Doris Ann (Evans) H. BS, U. Iowa, 1974. Gen. mgr. retail stores Amana (Iowa) Soc., 1975-77; mktg. mgr. Meredith Corp., Des Moines, 1977-80; mktg. devel. mgr. Fingerhut Corp., Minnetonka, Minn., 1980-82; founder, pres., chief exec. officer, chmn. Zeos Internat., Mpls., 1982-95; CEO Yellowstone Aviation, Inc., Jackson, Wyo., 1996—; founder, mgr. Golden Wings Flying Mus., Mpls., 1998—; pres. Sky Media Historic Aviation and Flying Books, 1999—; founder, chmn. Aviation Found. Am., 2002—. Organizer Nat. Air Tour, 2003; founder Aircraft Owner mag., 2004. Editor: Complete Desk Reference, 1973; patentee and inventor electronics equipment. Mem.: Inst. Am. Entrepreneurs (Minn. Entrepreneur of Yr. 1991). Republican. Roman Catholic. Avocations: flying, skiing, sailing. Address: PO Box 6291 Jackson WY 83002-6291

HERRICK, JOHN DENNIS, financial planner, consultant, retired food products executive; b. St. Paul, Oct. 8, 1932; s. Willard R. and Gertrude (O'Connor) H. BA, U. St. Thomas, 1954; MBA (hon.), U. Laval, 1969. Field auditor Gen. Mills, Inc., Mpls., 1954-59, acctg. supr. Kankakee, Ill., 1959-61, adminstrv. mgr. Chgo., 1961-62, mgr. auditing Mpls., 1962-65, mgr. new bus. devel., 1965-66, dir. adminstrn. and controller Smiths Food Group (subs.) London, 1966-68; pres. Gen. Mills Cereals Ltd., Toronto, Ont., Can., 1969-71; chmn. bd., pres., chief exec. officer Gen. Mills Canada, Inc., Toronto, Ont., Can., 1971-86; chief operating officer Borden & Elliot, Toronto, 1986-89; cons. Palm Beach Gardens, Fla., 1989—; pres. J.D. Herrick Found. Past chmn. Grocery Products Mfrs. of Can., Toronto; dir. CP Express & Transport, Toronto. Past pres. Jr. Achievement Can., Toronto, 1970-71; past chmn. Toronto Area Inds. Devel. Bd.; past pres., mem. coun. Bd. Trade Met. Toronto; past chmn. Emmanuel Convalescent Found., Toronto; past pres. Am. Club; past vice-chmn. Nat. Theater Sch. Can., Montreal; past chmn. Toronto Harbour Commn.; bd. dirs., past pres. Cath. Charities Palm Beach; bd. dirs. Pub. Voice for Food and Health Policy, Washington; mem. pres.'s coun. U. St. Thomas; chmn.'s adv. bd. Rep. Nat. Com., pres. Roundtable NRSC; mem., treas. Rep Exec. Com., Palm Beach County; bd. dirs., pres. DePorres P.L.A.C.E.; bd. dirs., chmn. Liberty Ednl. Forum; bd. govs. U. St. Thomas Law Sch. Capt. USAF, 1954-57 Decorated knight grand cross Knights of Holy Sepulchre, Order of St. John, knight comdr. Order of Polonia Restituta; recipient Queen's Silver Jubilee medal, 1978, Queen's Golden Jubilee medal, 2003, Bishop Cretin award, 2004; named Disting. Alumnus, U. St. Thomas, 1984. Mem.: Can. C. of C. (past chmn., gov.), Palm Beach Yacht Club, Capital Hill Club (Washington), KC, Accademia Italiana Della Cucuna Club, Hot Stove Club, NY Athletic Club, Gov. Club, Lambton Golf and Country Club, Royal Can. Yacht Club, Empire Club, Beefeater Club. Roman Catholic. Home: 529 S Flagler Dr 2 H West Palm Beach FL 33401-5933

HERRICK, KATHLEEN MAGARA, retired social worker; b. Mpls., Oct. 18, 1943; d. William Frank and Mary Genevieve (Gill) Magara; m. John M. Herrick, Feb. 5, 1966; children: Elizabeth Jane, Herrick-Chapman, Kathryn Mary. BA in Social Work and French, Coll. St. Benedict, St. Joseph, Minn., 1965; MSW, Mich. State U., 1976. Cert. diplomate Am. Psychotherapy Assn., 1998; cert. Acad. Cert. Social Workers. Social worker II Carver County Social Svcs., Chaska, Minn., 1965—70; therapist St. Lawrence Cmty. Mental Health Ctr., Lansing, Mich., 1974—75; sch. social worker Ingham Intermediate Sch. Dist., Mason, Mich., 1975—76; home/sch. coord. Eaton Intermediate Sch. Dist., Charlotte, Mich., 1976—81; sch. social worker, 1994—2005; ret., 2004. Caseworker St. Vincent Home for Children, Lansing, 1979-80; tchr. cons. for severely emotionally impaired, 1981-83; behavior disorder cons., 1983-85; sch. social work cons., 1985-87, prevention specialist profl. and program svcs. region XIII SAPE, 1987-94. Chmn. bd. dirs. Eaton County Child Abuse and Neglect Prevention Coun., 1986—; Dem. precinct del.; bd. dirs. Cath. Social Svcs., Lansing. Recipient Eaton County Svc. to children award Eaton County Child Abuse and Neglect Prevention Coun., 1997; named Region E Sch. Social Worker of Yr., 2004; Mildred B. Erickson fellow Mich. State U., 1976. Mem.: NOW, NEA, NASW, Am. Psychotherapy Assn., Am. Orthopsychiat. Assn., Mich. Assn. Emotionally Disturbed Children, Mich. Assn. Sch. Social Workers, Mich. Edn. Assn., Nat. Women's Health Network, Amnesty Internat., Glasser Inst. Reality Therapy & Choice Theory, Mich. Assn. Suicidology, Phi Alpha, Phi Kappa Phi. Democrat. Home: 2113 Long Leaf Trl Okemos MI 48864-3210 E-mail: kherrick@eaton.k12.mi.us.

HERRICK, MARK ANTHONY, entrepreneur; b. Princeton, Ill., Oct. 23, 1960; s. Clifford Leon and Judith Meldene Herrick. Student, Northern Ill. U., 1978—79. Registered agt. Dept Of Ins., Ind., 1993; stockbroker SEC, Fla., 1989. Agt. Am. Income Life, Waco, Tex., 1990—98; owner S.L.I. Industries, Fort Wayne, Ind., 1998—. Libertarian. Achievements include patents for Pipe with improved cutting edge; invention of Eight different designs for tobacco smoking systems; Two designs for portable cigarette snuffing devices; Point of sale candy dispenser. Avocations: vending, golf, fishing, inventing. Home and Office: SLI industries 820 Lillian Ave Fort Wayne IN 46808 Office Phone: 260-745-7499. Personal E-mail: onehitwunder1@yahoo.com. Business E-Mail: onehitwunder1@earthlink.net.

HERRICK, NITA MARIE, music educator; b. Lebanon, Mo., June 1, 1943; d. Clarence Ellsworth and Esther Edna Clark; m. Lloyd F. Herrick Jr., Nov. 27, 1963; 1 child, Alisa Herrick Jeffrey. B Music Edn., Ctrl. Mo. State U., 1966; MEd, U. Mo., 1969. Vocal music tchr. Sweet Springs (Mo.) Sch. Dist., 1966, Odessa (Mo.) Sch. Dist., 1966—73; adminstrv. asst. Gov.'s Office Traffic Safety, Austin, Tex., 1973—75; assoc. prof. Ark. Tech. U., Russellville, Ark., 1976—. Choir dir. 1st Presbyn. Ch., Morrilton, Ark., 1989—. Mem.: Nat. Assn. Tchrs. Singing (chmn. nat. conv. 2004, gov. so. region 1997—2000). Home: 86 Sturgeon Cir Russellville AR 72802 Office: Ark Tech U 407 W Q St Russellville AR 72801 Office Phone: 479-968-0469. Business E-Mail: nita.herrick@mail.atu.edu.

HERRICK, TODD W., manufacturing executive; b. Tecumseh, Mich., 1942; Grad., U. Notre Dame, 1967. Dir. Tecumseh (Mich.) Products Co., 1973—, pres., COO, 1984—, CEO, 1987—, chmn. bd., 2003—. Bd. dirs. Comerica, Inc.; bd. trustees Howe Military Sch.; mem. adv. bd. sch. engring. U. Mich.; mem. adv. bd. sch. bus. U. Notre Dame. Bd. mem. US C. of C. Capt. U.S. Army. Office: Tecumseh Products Co 100 E Patterson St Tecumseh MI 49286-2087 Office Fax: 517-423-8760.

HERRICK, TRACY GRANT, fiduciary; b. Cleve., Dec. 30, 1933; s. Stanford Avery and Elizabeth Grant (Smith) Herrick; m. Maie Kaarsoo, Oct. 12, 1963; children: Sylvi Anne, Alan Kalev. BA, Columbia U., 1956, MA, 1958; postgrad., Yale U., 195-57; MA, Oxford U., England, 1960. Economist Fed. Res. Bank, Cleve., 1960-70; sr. economist Stanford Rsch. Inst., Menlo Park, Calif., 1970-73; v.p., sr. analyst Shuman, Agnew & Co., Inc., San Francisco, 1973-75; v.p. Bank of Am., San Francisco, 1975-81; pres. Tracy G. Herrick, Inc., 1981—. Lectr. Stonier Grad. Sch. Banking Am. Bankers Assn., 1967—76; commencement spkr. Memphis Banking Sch., 1974; bd. dirs. Jefferies Group, Inc., chmn. bd. audit com., 1989—96, chmn. bd. compensation com., 1991—96, dir., 1983—99; bd. dirs. Jefferies & Co., Inc.; dir. Com. Monetary Rsch. and Edn., Inc.; chief economist Pvt. Bank of the Peninsula, Palo Alto, Calif., 2003—. Author: Bank Analyst's Handbook, 1978, Timing, 1981, Power and Wealth, 1988; contbr. Mem. adv. bd. Kara Found., Palo Alto, Calif. Fellow: Fin. Analysts Fedn.; mem.: San Francisco Soc. Security Analysts, Assn. Investment Mgmt. Rsch. Republican. Congregationalist. Home: 1150 University Ave Palo Alto CA 94301-2238 Office Phone: 650-321-4540.

HERRIDGE, CATHERINE, political correspondent; Bachelor's Degree, Harvard Coll.; Master's Degree in Journalism, Columbia U. Graduate Sch. Journalism. Corr. ABC News, London; polit corr. FOX News Channel, 1996—, Homeland Defense corr., 2001—. Corr. Fox Files, 1998; gen. field reporter The Pulse. Recipient Bronze World Medal, NY Festivals. Office: FOX News Channel 400 N Capitol St NW Ste 550 Washington DC 20001*

HERRIDGE, ELIZABETH, museum director; Mng. dir. Guggenheim Hermitage Mus., Las Vegas, 2003—. Office: Guggenheim Hermitage Mus 3355 Las Vegas Blvd S Las Vegas NV 89109 Office Phone: 702-414-2002. E-mail: eherridge@guggenheim.org.

HERRIFORD, ROBERT LEVI, SR., army officer; b. Lewistown, Ill., May 4, 1931; s. John and Lola (Braden) H.; m. Muriel Jean Davis, July 10, 1949; children: Robert Levi, Thomas Merle, David William, Deborah S., Traci Ann. BS, U. Ariz., 1966, MBA, 1968. Enlisted in U.S. Army, 1948, commd. 2d lt., 1952, advanced through grades to maj. gen., 1979; service in Vietnam, 1966-67; comdr. 269th Ordnance Group Ft. Bragg, N.C., 1969-71; chief spl. items mgmt. Tank Automotive Command Detroit, 1971-72; comdr. Korean Procurement Agy. Seoul, 1973-74; dir. procurement Armaments Command Rock Island, Ill., 1974-76; comdr. Def. Contracts Region N.Y., 1976-78; asst. dep. chief of staff logistics Pentagon, 1978-80; dir. procurement and prodn. Devel. and Readiness Command Alexandria, Va., 1980-83; assoc. chief ops. officer, dir. support services Argonne Nat. Lab., 1983-95. Chmn. Minority Bus. Opportunity Council, N.Y.C., 1976-78. Decorated Legion of Merit, D.S.M., Def. Superior Service medal, Bronze Star, Airmedal, numerous others. Mem. Am. Def. Preparedness Assn., Assn. U.S. Army, Am. Legion, Nat. Contracts Mgmt. Assn. (chpt. pres. 1975-76) Personal E-mail: RobLHerr@insightbb.com. *There is no substitute in any career, but particularly in an Army officer's career, for hard work, dedication and absolute integrity. Subordinates, peers, and superiors can sense it in training, in garrison, and in battle. Many people, in all pursuits and professions, are created equal in talent. Only a very few are willing to give to that talent all the care and dedication that is required to bring it to the top of their chosen field. It is often easier to explain why you didn't make it than to devote all that is required to develop this talent.*

HERRIN, BARRY SCOTT, lawyer, writer; b. Columbia, SC, Sept. 29, 1965; s. Glen Willis and Cora Jean (Scott) Herrin; m. Deborah June Fry, Aug. 29, 1987; children: Scott Fergusson, Abigail Margaret. BA, Ga. State Univ., Atlanta, 1987, JD, 1990. Bar: Ga. 1990, NC 2005. Assoc. atty. Booth, Wade & Campbell, Atlanta, 1990—91, Brock, Clay, Calhoun, Wilson & Rogers, P.C., Marietta, Ga., 1991—96, Kilpatrick Stockton LLP, Atlanta, 1996—98; assoc. atty., spl. healthcare coun. Nelson Mullins Riley & Scarborough LLP, Atlanta, 1998—2000; ptnr. Smith Moore LLP, Atlanta, 2000—. Chmn. So. Clams Conf., Atlanta, 2002—03. Co-author ins. law vol., Law Manual; contbr. articles pub. to profl. jour. Asst. scoutmaster Boy Scout Troop 69, Alpharetta, Ga.; lt. col. U.S. A. F. Aux.; pres. United Meth. Men Christ UMC, Roswell, Ga.; ch. lay spkr. United Meth Ch. Recipient Silver Beaver, Atlanta Area Coun. Boy Scouts of Am., 1996. Mem.: Ga. Assn. of Healthcare Exec., Am. Coll. of Healthcare Exec. (diplomate), Ga. Acad. of Healthcare Attys., Am. Health Lawyers Assn., Nat. Eagle Scout Assn. (life), Lawyers Club of

Atlanta. Republican. Meth. Home: 700 Barrington Way Roswell GA 30076 Office: Smith Moore LLP One Atlantic Ctr Ste 3700 1201 W Peachtree St NE Atlanta GA 30309 Office Phone: 404-962-1000. Business E-Mail: barry.herrin@smithmoorelaw.com.

HERRING, BERNARD DUANE, physician; b. Massillon, Ohio, Jan. 27, 1929; s. James and Eva (Lancaster) H.; m. Odessa Mae Appling, Sept. 6, 1950; children: Kevin, Duane, Terez, Sean. BS magna cum laude, Kent State U., 1952; MD, U. Cin., 1956; LLB, LaSalle Extension U., 1964. Real estate broker, Calif.; diplomate Am. Coll. Forensic Examiners, Am. Bd. Forensic Medicine; bd. cert. in family practice, geriatrics. Intern San Francisco Gen. Hosp., 1956-57; resident internal medicine VA Hosp., Bklyn., 1957-58, Cleve., 1958-59; asst. clin prof. medicine U. Calif. Med. Sch., San Francisco, 1982—. Legal document asst., 2003. Fellow Am. Coll. Legal Medicine; mem. AMA, Am. Soc. Internal Medicine, ASCAP, Am. Geriat. Soc. Home: 712 Longridge Rd Oakland CA 94610-2325 Office: PO Box 10286 Oakland CA 94610-0286

HERRING, CHARLES DAVID, lawyer, educator; b. Muncie, Ind., Mar. 18, 1943; s. Morris and Margaret Helen Herring; children: David, Margaret, Christopher. BA, Ind. U., 1965, JD cum laude, 1968. Bar: Ind. 1968, U.S. Dist. Ct. (so. dist.) Ind. 1971, Calif. 1971, U.S. Dist. Ct. (so. dist.) Calif. 1971. Rsch. assoc. Ind. U., 1965-68; intern Office of Pros. Atty., Monroe County, Ind., 1967-68; ptnr. Herring, Stubel & Lehr and predecessor Herring and Stabel, San Diego, 1972—92; pvt. practice San Diego, 1972—. Prof. law Western State U., 1972—91. Author: (with Jim Wade) California Cases on Professional Responsibility, 1976. Vice chmn. Valle de Oro Planning Com., Spring Valley, Calif., 1972-75; chmn. Valle de Oro Citizens Exec. Com. for Community Planning, Spring Valley, 1975-78. Served with JAGC, U.S. Army, 1968-72. Mem.: ABA (Best Brief award 1968), Calif. Trial Lawyers Assn., Conf. Spl. Ct. Judges, San Diego County Bar Assn., Calif. Bar Assn., Ind. Bar Assn., San Diego Lions Club (dir., bd. trustees, past pres.), Order of Coif. Republican. Avocations: computers, gardening, swimming, golf. Home: 284 Sunnybrook Ln El Cajon CA 92021-7801 Office: Herring & Herring 755 Broadway Cir 2d Fl San Diego CA 92101-6160 Office Phone: 619-231-0877. Business E-Mail: dherring@cox.net.

HERRING, DAVID JOHN, dean, law educator; b. Detroit, July 9, 1958; s. John Edward and Hermia Rowena (Schellenberg) H.; m. Lu-in Wang, May 17, 1986; children: An-Li Wang Herring, Maia Tao Herring. BBA, U. Mich., 1980, JD, 1985. Bar: Mich. 1985, Ill. 1987, Pa. 1991. Jud. law clk. Mich. Ct. Appeals, Southfield, 1985-86; Bigelow fellow, instr. law U. Chgo. Sch. Law, 1986-87; asst. clin. prof. law U. Mich. Law Sch., Ann Arbor, 1987-90; dir. Legal Clinics U. Pitts. Sch. Law, 1990—98, assoc. dean for academic affairs, 1990—98, interim dean, 1998, dean, 1998—. Mem. Pa. Legal/Med. Adv. Bd. Child Abuse, Harrisburg, 1990—; mem., cons. Child Devel. Office, U. Pitts., 1990—. Author: (atty. tng. manual) Agency Attorney in Child Abuse Cases, 1990; contbr. articles to profl. jours. Grantee HHS, 1988, Legal Svcs. Corp., Pitts., 1990—. Mem. ABA, Mich. Bar Assn., Pa. Bar Assn. Avocation: running. Office: U Pitts Sch of Law 3900 Forbes Ave Pittsburgh PA 15213

HERRING, JERONE CARSON, retired lawyer, bank executive; b. Kinston, N.C., Sept. 27, 1938; s. James and Isabel (Knight) H.; m. Patricia Ann Hardy, Aug. 6, 1961; children— Bradley Jerone, Ansley Carole. AB, Davidson Coll., 1960; LL.B., Duke U., 1963. Bar: N.C. 1963. Assoc. McElwee & Hall, North Wilkesboro, N.C., 1965-69; ptnr. McElwee, Hall & Herring, North Wilkesboro, 1969-71; exec. v.p., sec., gen. counsel Br. Banking & Trust Co., Winston-Salem, NC, 1971—2003, BB&T Corp., Winston-Salem, 1995—2003. Mem. bd. adv. U. N.C. Ctr. Banking and Fin.; mem. bd. visitors Davidson Coll. Served to capt. U.S. Army, 1963-65. Mem. ABA, N.C. Bar Assn., Am. Soc. Corp. Secs. Presbyterian. Personal E-mail: jherring123@charter.net.

HERRING, KEVIN WARD, lawyer; BBA with distinction, U. Hawaii at Manoa, Honolulu, 1989—93; JD cum laude, Case Western Res. U., Cleveland, Ohio, 1993—96. Bar: Hawaii 1996. Assoc. atty. Tam O'Connor, Hederson Taira & Yamauchi, Honolulu, 1997—2000, Ashford & Wriston, LLP, Honolulu, 2000—04; ptnr. Ashford & Wriston, LLLP, Honolulu, 2004—. Mem.: ABA, Hawaii State Bar Assn. Avocation: soccer. Office: Ashford & Wriston LLLP 1099 Alakea St Ste 1400 Honolulu HI 96813

HERRING, LYNNE D., secondary school educator; b. Orange, Calif., June 20, 1962; BA in Comms., Azusa Pacific U., 1984. Tchr. L.A. Unified Sch. Dist., 1987—89, Edison Mid. Sch., L.A., 1992—94, Armijo H.S., 1996—. Office: Armijo Hs 824 Washington St Fairfield CA 94533 Office Phone: 707-438-3451.

HERRING, MARK YOUNGBLOOD, librarian, university dean; b. Dothan, Ala., Oct. 10, 1952; s. Reuben and Dorothy Lavina (McCorvey) H.; m. Brenda Carol Lane, Aug. 11, 1972; children: Adriel, Areli Allene. BA, George Peabody Coll. Tchrs., 1974; MLS, Vanderbilt U., 1978; EdD, East Tenn. State U., 1990. Libr. dir. King Coll., Bristol, Tenn., 1979-87; instr. East Tenn. State U., Johnson City, 1990; dean libr. svcs. Okla. Bapt. U., Shawnee, 1992-99; dean Winthrop U., Rock Hill, S.C., 1999—. Exec. dir. Am. 21, Bristol, Tenn., 1990-92; founder, pres. Electronic Conservative Clearinghouse Libr., Shawnee, 1998—. Author: (monographs) Controversial Issues in Librarianship, 1986, Ethics and the Professor, 1988, Organizing Friends Group, 1993, Historic Guide to the Pro-Life Pro-Choice Debate, 2003, At the Core of the Problem-Reforming Teacher Education in Oklahoma, 2001, Raising Funds with Friends Groups, 2004. Fellow East Tenn. State U., 1987-90; grantee Noble Found., Okla., 1999, S.C. Humanities Found. Mem. Nat. Assn. Scholars, Assn. Libr. and Learning Ctr. Dirs. (pres. 1996-97), Okla. Libr. Assn. (exec. bd. 1993-95), Okla. Assn. Scholars (pres. 1997-99). Republican. Presbyterian. Avocations: reading, running, hiking. Office: Winthrop U Dacus Libr Rock Hill SC 29733-0001 Office Phone: 803-323-2131. Office Fax: 803-323-2215. Business E-Mail: herringm@winthrop.edu.

HERRING, TERRY MICHAEL, medical educator; b. Lumberton, N.C., Aug. 15, 1965; s. Roland Mitchell and Shirley Ann Herring. Diploma in surgl. tech., Fayetteville Tech. C.C., 1986, AS with honors in Mktg., 1990; MS in Psychology, Fayetteville State U., 1993; MS in Health Adminstrn., Coll. Health Sci., 2000. Cert. surgl. technologist, surgl. asst. Surgl. technologist S.E. Regional Med. Ctr., Lumberton, NC; rep. Midwest Surgl., Bloomington, Minn.; dept. chair Fayetteville Tech. C.C., NC, 2003—. Dir. Surgl. Tech. Adv. Bd., Fayetteville. Instr. Am. Heart Assn., NC, 1998—2003, Am. Red. Cross, NC, 1998—2003. Mem.: Assn. Surgl. Assts., Assn. Surgl. Technologists, Delta Epsilon Tau. Republican. Baptist. Avocations: bicycling, running. Home: 2140 Wisteria Ln #103 Fayetteville NC 28314 Office: Fayetteville Tech Cmty Coll 2201 Hall Rd Fayetteville NC 28303

HERRING, WILLIAM CONYERS, retired physicist, educator; b. Scotia, N.Y., Nov. 15, 1914; s. William Conyers and Mary (Joy) H.; m. Louise C. Preusch, Nov. 30, 1946; children— Lois Mary, Alan John, Brian Charles, Gordon Robert. AB, U. Kans., 1933; PhD, Princeton, 1937. NRC fellow Mass. Inst. Tech., 1937-39; instr. Princeton, 1939-40, U. Mo., 1940-41; mem. sci. staff Div. War Research, Columbia, 1941-45; prof. applied math. U. Tex., 1946; research physicist Bell Telephone Labs., Murray Hill, N.J., 1946-78; prof. applied physics Stanford (Calif.) U., 1978-81, prof. emeritus, 1981—. Mem. Inst. Advanced Study, 1952-53 Recipient Army-Navy Cert. of Appreciation, 1947; Distinguished Service citation U. Kans., 1973; J. Murray Luck award for excellence in sci. reviewing Nat. Acad. Scis., 1980; von Hippel award Materials Rsch. Soc., 1980, Wolf prize in Physics, 1985. Fellow Am. Phys. Soc. (Oliver E. Buckley solid state physics prize 1959), Am. Acad. Arts and Scis.; mem. AAAS, NAS, Am. Soc. Info. Scis. Home: 3945 Nelson Dr Palo Alto CA 94306-4524 Office: Stanford U Lab for Advanced Materials MS 4045 Stanford CA 94305-4045 Office Phone: 650-723-0686.

HERRINGER, FRANK CASPER, diversified financial services company executive; b. NYC, Nov. 12, 1942; s. Casper Frank and Alice Virginia (McMullen) H.; m. Maryellen B. Cattani; children: William, Sarah, Julia. AB magna cum laude, Dartmouth, 1964, MBA with highest distinction, 1965. Prin. Cresap, McCormick & Paget, Inc., NYC, 1965-71; staff asst. to Pres. of U.S., Washington, 1971-73; adminstr. U.S. Urban Mass Transp. Adminstrn., Washington, 1973-75; gen. mgr. San Francisco Bay Area Rapid Transit Dist., 1975-78; exec. v.p. Transam. Corp., San Francisco, 1979-86, pres., dir., 1986-99, CEO, 1991-99, chmn., 1996—; mem. exec. bd. AEGON N.V., 1999-2000; chmn. AEGON USA, 1999-2000. Bd. dirs. AT&T Corp., Amgen Corp., Charles Schwab & Co., Mirapoint, Inc., Aegon USA, Calif. Pacific Med. Ctr Mem. Cypress Point Club, San Francisco Golf Club, Nanea Golf Club, Olympic Club, Claremont Country Club, Pacific Union Club, Stock Farm Club, Phi Beta Kappa. Office: Transam Corp 600 Montgomery St San Francisco CA 94111-2702

HERRINGER, MARYELLEN CATTANI, lawyer; b. Bakersfield, Calif., Dec. 1, 1943; d. Arnold Theodore and Corinne Marilyn (Kovacevich) C.; m. Frank C. Herringer; children: Sarah, Julia. AB, Vassar Coll., Poughkeepsie, N.Y., 1965; JD, U. Calif. (Boalt Hall), 1968; Exec. Program, Stanford Grad. Sch. Bus., 1994. Assoc. Davis Polk & Wardwell, N.Y.C., 1968-69, Orrick, Herrington & Sutcliffe, San Francisco, 1970-74, ptnr., 1975-81; v.p., gen. counsel Transamerica Corp., San Francisco, 1981-83, sr. v.p., gen. counsel, 1983-89; ptnr. Morrison & Foerster, San Francisco, 1989-91; sr. v.p. gen. counsel APL Ltd., Oakland, Calif., 1991-95, exec. v.p., gen. counsel, 1995-97; gen. counsel allied bus. Littler & Mendelson, San Francisco, 2000. Bd. dirs. Golden West Fin. Corp., World Savs. Bank, ABM Industries Inc. Author: Calif. Corp. Practice Guide, 1977, Corp. Counselors, 1982. Regent St. Mary's Coll., Moraga, Calif., 1986—, pres., 1990-92, trustee, 1990-99, chmn., 1993-95; trustee Vassar Coll., 1985-93, The Head-Royce Sch., 1993-2002, Mills Coll., 1999—, The Benilde Religious & Charitable Trust, 1999—, Alameda County Med. Ctr. Hosp. Authority, 1998-2002, Univ. Calif. Berkeley Art Mus., 2001—; bd. dirs. The Exploratorium, 1988-93. Mem. ABA, State Bar Calif. (chmn. bus. law sect. 1980-81), Bar Assn. San Francisco (co-chair com. on women 1989-91), Calif. Women Lawyers, San Francisco C. of C. (bd. dirs. 1987-91, gen. counsel 1990-91), Am. Corp. Counsel Assn. (bd. dirs. 1982-87), Women's Forum West (bd. dirs. 1984-87). Democrat. Roman Catholic. E-mail: mherringer@aol.com.

HERRINGTON, JAMES BENJAMIN, JR., job recruiting executive; b. New Orleans, Jan. 17, 1953; s. James Benjamin Sr. and Ruby Mae (Collins) H. BS in Edn., La. Tech U., 1975; MEd, Tarleton State U., 1982. Tchr., coach Briarfield Acad., Lake Providence, La., 1975-76; material expeditor Brown & Root Constrn. Corp., Luling, La., 1976-77, Mid-Tex Constrn., Ft. Worth, 1977; tchr., coach Glen Rose (Tex.) High Sch., 1977-78; tchr., head coach Smith Middle Sch., Killeen, Tex., 1978-82, Manor Middle Sch., Killeen, 1982-84; tchr., coach Channelview (Tex.) High Sch., 1984-85; sci. tchr. Miller Intermediate Sch., Pasadena, Tex., 1985-88; counselor San Jacinto Intermediate Sch., Pasadena, 1988-93; orgnl. specialist Tex. Faculty Assn., 1993-97; owner DataTrain Inc., Houston, 1996—. Mem. NEA (rec. sec. Rep. Educators Caucus 1991-93), Tex. Tchrs. Assn. (pub. rels. chmn. Dist. IV 1989-92, polit. activist team 1986-93, instrnl. and profl. devel. com. 1986-91, media rels. chmn. Dist. IV 1990-92, bd. dirs. 1990-92), Pasadena Educators Assn. (bd. dirs. 1986-87, pres. 1988-90, v.p. 1990-91, sec.-treas. 1991-92, editor 1986-87), Optimists. Presbyterian. Avocations: sports, baseball card collector. Office: DataTrain Inc 14115 Lost Meadow Ln Houston TX 77079-3111

HERRINGTON, JOHN B., astronaut, military officer; b. Wetumka, Okla., Sept. 14, 1958; s. James E. and Mrs. Harrington; m. Debra Ann Farmer; 2 children. BS in Applied Math., U. Colo., Colo. Springs, 1976; MS in Aeronautical Engrng., USN Postgrad. Sch., 1995. Commd. ensign USN, 1984, student pilot, 1984—85; from student pilot to patrol plane commdr., instr. pilot USN Pacific Theater, 1985—89; student USN Test Pilot Sch., Patuxent River, Md., 1990; test pilot USN Force Warfare Aircraft Test Directorate, 1991—93; student USN Postgrad Sch., Monterey, Calif., 1993—95; astronaut NASA Johnson Flight Ctr., Houston, 1996—. Fellow: Am. Indian Sci. and Engrng. Soc.; mem.: Sequoyah, Assn. Naval Aviation (life), U. Colo. at Colo. Springs Alumni Assn. Avocations: bicycling, rock climbing, skiing, running. Office: Astronaut Office/CB Johnson Space Ctr Houston TX 77058*

HERRINGTON, JOHN DAVID, III, retired lawyer, director; b. Warren, Ohio, Nov. 19, 1934; s. John David Jr and Gertrude Francis (Herlinger) Herrington; m. Phoebe Jane Henderson, Mar. 16, 1957; children: Gay Annette, Joy Ann, Jennifer John. BSBA, Ohio State U., 1956. CPA Pa. With Price Waterhouse & Co., Pitts., 1956-63; asst. to sec.-treas. Fisher Sci. Co., Pitts., 1963-65, controller, 1965-71, v.p. fin., treas., 1971-78, sr. v.p. fin., treas., 1979-82; exec. dir. Reed Smith Shaw & McClay, Pitts., 1982-86; ret., 1986. Bd. dirs. Hi Pure, Inc, Rochester Sci., Pfeiffer Glass, E & A Bldg. Corp., F. S. de Mex., Conco Inc. Bd. dirs. Family and Children Svcs. Pitts. With AUS, 1957—58. Mem.: AICPA, Assn. Legal Adminstrs., Pa. Soc. CPAs, Planning Execs. Inst., Tax Execs. Inst., Fin. Execs. Inst. Home: 9402 Babcock Blvd Allison Park PA 15101-2011 also: 9721 S Old Oregon Inlet Rd Nags Head NC 27959-9376

HERRINGTON, JOHN SCOTT, conductor, music educator; b. Odessa, Tex., Nov. 24, 1953; s. Ollie Jack and Edna Herrington; m. Sarah Kathryn Greenwood, Dec. 16, 2000. MusB, West Tex. State U., 1972—76; M of ch. music, Southwestern Bapt. Theol. Sem., 1978—80; MusM, West Tex. State U., 1981—83; MusD, U. of Mo., 1986—92. Assoc. dir. of choral studies West Tex. State U., Canyon, Tex., 1984—86, Baylor U., Waco, Tex., 1984—86; dir. of choral studies Wayland U., Plainview, Tex., 1992—. Conductor Lubbock Chorale Fall Concert, Tex. Bapt. All-State choir, High School Choral Clinician, clinician Amarillo Independent School District Choral Music Guest Clinician, conductor Region XVI All-Region High School Choir, Region XX All-Region High School Choir, Region XVI All-Region High School Choir. Interime music min. First Bapt. Ch., Hereford, Tex., 1994—95, interim music min., 1999—2000, 2000—01. Mem.: Am. Choral Directors Assn., Tex. Music Educators Assn., Tex. Choral Directors Assn. (r & s chair of youth and activities 2002—04). Office: Wayland Univ 1900 W 7th St CMB 399 Plainview TX 79072 Office Phone: 806-291-1062.

HERRLING, CHRISTOPHER J., lawyer; BA, Univ. Rochester, 1976; JD, Catholic Univ., Washington, 1980. Bar: DC 1981, NY 1981. Staff atty. Legal Aid Soc., DC, 1984—94, exec. dir., 1994—97; pro bono counsel Wilmer Cutler Pickering Hale & Dorr, Washington, 1997—. Mem. ABA AIDS Coord. Com., 2003—03. Recipient Pub. Svc. award, Bar Assn. DC, 1997. Office: Wilmer Cutler Pickering Hale & Dorr 2445 M St NW Washington DC 20037 Office Phone: 202-663-6780. Office Fax: 202-663-6363. Business E-Mail: christopher.herrling@wilmerhale.com.

HERRMAN, MARCIA KUTZ, child development specialist; b. Boston, June 16, 1927; d. Cecil and Sonia (Schneider) Kutz; m. Bayard F. Berman, July 23, 1949 (div. 1960); m. William H. Herrman, June 23, 1961; 1 child, Fred. BA, Smith Coll., 1949; MA, Pacific Oaks Coll., 1974. Credentialed tchr., Calif. NIMH intern Cedars-Sinai Med. Ctr., L.A., 1966-67; ednl. therpist L.A. Child Guidance Clinic, 1967-69, Child and Family Study Ctr., Cedars-Sinai Med. Ctr., 1969-71; dir. tng., asst. project dir. handicapped early edn. program Dubnoff Ctr., North Hollywood, Calif., 1972-76; child devel. cons. schs., agys. and families L.A. Co., Calif., 1969—. Cons. L.A. Child Guidance Clinic, Head Start, Child Care and Devel. Svcs., 1969-73; cons. child and parenting program St. Joseph's Ctr., Venice, Calif., 1992-98; profl. expert L.A. Unified Sch. Dist., 1976-80; vis. faculty Pacific Oaks Coll., Pasadena, Calif., 1970-76. Vol. Alliance for Children's Rights, 1992-94, Child Advocate's Office, Superior Ct., L.A., 1983—; mem. Dependency Ct. Com., 1988-92, Task Force on Rep. of Children in Dependency Ct., Superior Ct., L.A. County, 1994; mem. oversight and resource coms. Placement Project, joint com. of program policy adv. com. Dept. Children and Family Svcs., 1995-98; steering com. Cmty. Based Placement Project, Joint Effort of Youth Law Ctr., L.A. Dept. Children. & Family Svcs. and Calif. Dept. Social Svcs., 1995; mem. L.A. Foster Care Network, 1987-94, L.A. County MacLaren Children's Ctr. Task Force, 1990-95, cmty. mem., 1996—; cmty. adv. com. St. Joseph's Ctr., 1992-96; policy and implementation coms. Cmty. of Care Integration Project, 1998—, L.A. County bd. suprs., policy and implementation coms.; bd. chair Keeping Families Together, L.A., 1987-88; trustee Ruth Pearce Fund for Therapeutic Companions, 1994—. Recipient Vol. of Yr. award L.A. County Bd. Supr., 1986, Commendation for Dedicated Svc. to Cmty., 1991, Recognition award for Outstanding Svc. to Children L.A. County Inter-Agy. Coun. on Child Abuse, 1991; Sophia Smith scholar, 1949. Fellow Am. Orthopsychiat. Assn. (life); mem. N.Y. Acad. Scis., Assn. Child Devel. Specialists, Nat. Ct. Appointed Spl. Advocate Assn. Democrat. Jewish. Avocations: music, theater, hiking, travel. Home and Office: 3919 Ethel Ave Studio City CA 91604-2204

HERRMANN, BENJAMIN EDWARD, former insurance executive; b. Bensonhurst, N.Y., May 9, 1919; s. Benjamin Edward and Ethel (Cuff) H.; m. Jean Clare Yancey, Oct. 19, 1946 (dec. Mar. 1, 1994); children: Benjamin E., Elizabeth M.; m. Mary Anne O'Connor, Oct. 20, 1995. BS, Columbia, 1941. C.L.U. With Home Life Ins. Co. N.Y., N.Y.C., 1941-68; regional v.p. Northeastern U.S., P.R., 1960-68; agy. v.p. Acacia Mut. Life Ins. Co., Washington, 1968-75; exec. com., dir. Acacia Nat. Life Ins. Co.; Acacia Equity Sales Corp. regional v.p. Met. N.Y., Home Life Ins. Co., N.Y.C., 1975-78, v.p. sales adminstrn., 1978-80, v.p. mktg., 1980-84; pres. Nat. Benefit Plans Inc., Norfolk, Va., 1986-93. Mem. Planning Bd., Madison, N.J., 1963-68, chmn., 1967-68; mem. Zoning Bd. Adjustment, 1964-68, chmn., 1966. Served to 1st lt. USAAF, 1943-46, PTO. Fellow Life Mgmt. Inst.; mem. Life Ins. Mgmt. and Rsch. Assn. (exec. devel. com., chmn. agy. officers roundtable com. 1968-76, chmn. 1976, chmn. tng. dirs. subcom. 1974-76, grad. sch. agy. mgmt., agy. officer sch., sr. mktg. officers' seminar), Soc. CLUs, Golden Key Soc., U.S. Squash Racquets Assn. (bd. dirs. 1986-95), Va. Squash Racquets Assn. Inc. (pres. 1986-91, chmn. 1991-95), Intertel, Mensa, Kingsmill Golf Club, The Jesters Club, Nat. Eagle Scout Assn. Republican. Presbyterian. Home: 105 Elizabeth Page Williamsburg VA 23185-5108

HERRMANN, DEBRA MCGUIRE, chemist, educator; b. Ft. Benning, Ga., Dec. 28, 1955; d. Delbert Wayne and Twyla Pauline (Moran) McGuire; m. David Read Hermann, Aug. 2, 1980; children: Adam James Hermann, Jesse Read Hermann, Aaron Matthew Hermann. BS in chemistry, U. Tex., 1979, U. Ark., 1989. Rsch. chemist Dow Chem., Oyster Creek, Freeport, Tex., 1980-84; chemist Aluminum Co. Am., Bauxite, Ark., 1984-87; tchr. Little Rock Sch. Dist., 1987-90; tchr. chemistry and integrated physics and chemistry Carroll Ind. Sch. Dist., Southlake, Tex., 2002—04; tchr. chemistry Keller (Tex.) Ind. Sch. Dist., 2004—. Pres., bd. dirs. Little Peoples Acad. Sch. Montessori, Ottumwa, Iowa, 1990—93; den leader Cub Scouts. Mem.: PEO, Phi Beta Kappa. Democrat. Presbyterian. Avocations: walking, watercolor, dogs, sailing, gardening. Home: 1100 Harbor Haven St Southlake TX 76092-2811

HERRMANN, FRANK (HENRY), painter, educator; b. Westmont, N.J., Mar. 1, 1945; s. Francis H. and Carolyn (Vance) C.; m. Stephanie Karanzalis, Feb. 2, 1969; children: Jason Thomas, Zachary Francis. BA, Western Ky. U., 1969; MFA, U. Cin., 1972. Instr. Western Mich. U., Kalamazoo, 1972-73; prof. fine art U. Cin., 1973—. One-man shows include Western Ky. U., 1968, U. Cin., 1971, 72, 82, 83, 92, U. Akron, 1974, Colo. State U., 1979, Ga. Southwestern State U., Americus, 1980, First Inst. Art and Design, Hong Kong, 1980, Toni Birckhead Gallery, Cin., 1983, 89, Centre Coll., Danville, Ky., 1983, U. Ky., 1985, Ohio U., Athens, 1990, Henri Gallery, Washington, 1984, 86, 91, Taylor's Contemtoraea, Hot Springs, Ark., 1993, Linda Schwartz Gallery, Cin, 2002; exhibited in group shows at Miami U., Oxford, Ohio, 1970, 71, Findlay Coll., 1978, Dayton Art Inst., 1979, Murray State U., Ky., 1980, Toni Birckhead Gallery, Cin., 1981, 83, 90, 91, Nornberg Gallery Contemporary Art, St. Louis, 1983, Henri Gallery, Washington, 1983, 84, 85, 87, 89, Contemporary Arts Ctr., Cin., 1991, Ruschman Gallery, Indpls, 1998, Closson's Art Gallery, Cin., 1996, 98, Frank Herrmann Aronoff Ctr. Gallery, Cin., 1998, 99, Weber State U., UT, 2002, Contemporary Arts Fedn., 2002, Invitational Siatama Mus. of Modern Art, 2002, Found. and Ctr. for Contemporary Art, Prague, many others; represented in numerous pub. and pvt. collections. Bd. dirs. Contemporary Arts Ctr., CIn., 1990-91. Fellow Ohio Arts Coun., 1983, Arts Midwest Nat. Endowment Arts, Mpls., 1990; grantee Ohio Arts Coun., Columbus, 1983, 86, 2001, Summer Fair Inc., Cin., 1990, 2000, U. Cin. Rsch. Coun., 1982, 91, 99; artist-in-residence Cinelice Castle, Czech Republic, 2001. Office: U Cin Sch Art Daap Ml0016 Cincinnati OH 45221-0016 E-mail: fherrman@fuse.net.

HERRMANN, HERBET GEORGE, IV, music educator; s. Herbert George Herrmann III and Marilyn Jean Herrmann; m. Denise Nichole Wyant, Mar. 20, 2004; children: Helene Ruth, Herbert George. BA in Music Edn., Va. Tech., Blacksburg, 1998; MS in Sch. Adminstrn., Shenandoah U., Winchester, Va., 2002. Lic. tchg. K-12 1999. Choral dir. Patrick County HS, Stuart, Va., 1998—2000; band dir. Sterling HS, Va., 2000—02, Heritage HS, Leesburg, Va., 2002—. Mem.: Va. Music Educators Assn., Va. Band and Orchestra Dirs. Assn. (Superior Ensemble Ranking 2003), Music Educators Nat. Conf. Avocations: reading, model trains, furniture construction. Office: Heritage HS 520 Evergreen Mill Rd Leesburg VA 20175

HERRMANN, LACY BUNNELL, investment company executive, entrepreneur, venture capitalist; b. New Haven, May 12, 1929; s. James Joseph and Helen Georgia (Bunnell) H.; m. Elizabeth Ocumpaugh Beadle, May 23, 1953; children: Diana Parsons, Conrad Beadle. AB, Brown U., 1950; postgrad., London Sch. Econs., 1953-54; MBA, Harvard U., 1956. Asst. to purchasing mgr. and buyer Westinghouse Elec. Corp., Metuchen, N.J., 1956-60; asst. v.p. Douglas T. Johnston & Co., Inc., N.Y.C., 1960-66; v.p. Johnston Mut. Fund, Inc., N.Y.C., 1964-66; gen. ptnr. Tamarack Assocs., N.Y.C., 1966-84; chmn. bd., pres. Family Home Products, Inc., N.Y.C., 1972-84, Buxton's Country Shops, Jamesburg, N.J., 1973-86. Founder, pres. STCM Corp., moneymarket fund, N.Y.C., 1974-76; vice chmn. bd. trustees, v.p. Centennial Capital Cash Mgmt. Trust, N.Y.C. successor to STCM Corp., 1976-81; chmn. bd. trustees, pres. successor fund Capital Cash Mgmt. Trust, 1981—; founder, chmn. bd. trustees, pres. Trinity Liquid Assets Trust, 1982-85, Oxford Cash Mgmt. Fund, 1982-88, Prime Cash Fund, 1982—; chmn., CEO, Aquila Mgmt. Corp., 1983—; founder, sponsor, mgr. Pacific Capital Cash Assets Trusts, 1984—, Hawaiian Tax-Free Trust, 1985—, Churchill Cash Reserves Trust, 1985—, Tax-Free Trust Ariz., 1986—, Tax-Free Trust Oreg., 1986—, Tax-Free Fund Colo., 1987—, Churchill Tax-Free Fund of Ky., 1987—, Pacific Capital Tax-Free Cash Assets Trusts, 1988—, Pacific Capital U.S. Govt. Securities Cash Assets Trust, 1988—, Narragansett Insured Tax-Free Income Fund, 1992—, Tax-Free Fund for Utah, 1992—, Aquila Rocky Mountain Equity Fund, 1994—, Aquila Cascadia Equity Fund, 1996—, VP Aquila Distributors, Inc.; bd. dirs. Quest for Value Fund Investment Trust, Quest for Value Accumulation Trust, Quest Cash Res., Inc.; trustee Oppenheimer/Quest group funds global Value Fund, 1994—, Oppenneimer Rochester Funds; organizer, bd. dirs. and/or cons. to numerous sml. to medium sized-corps. and orgns.; founding dir. mgmt. cons. firm merged with Towers, Perrin, Forster & Crosby; instr. Rutgers U., 1958-59; chmn., pres. bd. dirs. In-Cap Mgmt. Corp, 1984-98; speaker various profl. investment orgns. Contbr. articles to profl. jours. Organizer, trustee endowed award Internat. div. Grad. Sch. Journalism, Columbia U., 1962—; trustee Meml. and Endowment Trust of St. Paul's Ch., Westfield, N.J., 1968-96; mem. capital devel. com. St. Luke's Ch., Darien, Conn., 1978-85, mem. coll. scholarship fund com., 1976-85; trustee Brown U., 1990-96, trustee emeritus, 1996—, Hopkins Sch., New Haven, 1993-2003. Lt. (j.g.) USN, 1951-54, Korea; lt. USNR ret. Mem. N.Y. Soc. Security Analysts, Harvard Bus. Sch. Club N.Y. (bd. dirs., officer, 1958-71), Assoc. Alumni Brown U. (bd. dirs. 1978-87, exec. com. 1980-85, pres. 1983-85), Harvard Club, N.Y. Athletic Club, Brown U. Club, Brown U. of Fairfield Country Club (pres. 1977-82, bd. dirs. 1977—), Univ. Club (R.I.), Faculty Club Brown U., Stratton Mountain Country Club, Orleans Yacht Club, Ariz. club, Outrigger Canoe Club (Honolulu), Lahaina Yacht Club (Maui). Republican. Episcopalian. Office: 380 Madison Ave New York NY 10017-2513 Home: 3310 Kendal Way Sleepy Hollow NY 10591 Office Phone: 202-697-6666. E-mail: lherrmann@aquilafunds.com.

HERRMANN, ROBERT LAWRENCE, biochemist, educator; b. NYC, July 17, 1928; s. Philip Charles and Florence Gertrude (Benn) Herrmann; m. Elizabeth Ann Cook, Aug. 12, 1950; children: Stephen, Karen, Holly, Anders. BS in Chemistry, Purdue U., 1951; PhD in Biochemistry, Mich. State U., 1956. Postdoctoral fellow MIT, 1956-59; from asst. prof. to assoc. prof. biochemistry Boston U. Sch. Medicine, 1959-76; prof., chmn. dept. biochemistry Oral Roberts U. Sch. Medicine and Dentistry, Tulsa, 1976-81, assoc. dean biomed. sci., 1978-79; lectr. chemistry Gordon Coll., Wenham, Mass., 1981, adj. prof., 1982-97; exec. dir. Am. Sci. Affiliation, 1981-93; program dir. John Templeton Found., 1992—2002. Judge Templeton Prize Progress in Religion, 1999—2001. Editor: Prog. in Theology newsletter of John Templeton Found., 1992—2000; contbr. chapters to books, articles to profl. jours. Mem. Bd. Health, Bedford, Mass., 1975—76; trustee Christian Med. Soc., 1976—79, Barrington Coll., 1975—78, Templeton Found., 1987—95, 1996—2002, Southeastern Mass. U., 1988—91. With USN, 1946—48, with USN, 1951—52. Fellow: AAAS, Gerontol. Soc.; mem.: Am. Sci. Affiliation, European Soc. Study Sci. and Theology, Sci. and Religion Forum, Am. Soc. Biochem. and Molecular Biology. Evangelical Christian. Home and Office: 12 Spillers Ln Ipswich MA 01938-2430 Personal E-mail: r.herrmann@comcast.net.

HERRMANN, THOMAS FRANCIS, systems administrator; b. Kenosha, Wis., Sept. 28, 1951; s. Matthias Bernard and Sebastiana J. (Placente) H.; m. Gail Ann Sipsma, Oct. 25, 1975; children: Aaron Matthew, Joel Michael, Andrew Jacob, Justin Thomas. Student, Gateway Tech. Inst., 1969, U. Wis., Kenosha, 1973, Kennedy-We. U., 1995—97; BA magna cum laude, Shefferton U., 2001. Programmer Snap-On Tools Corp., Kenosha, 1975—79; project leader Jacobsen Mfg. Co., Racine, Wis., 1979—80; database analyst Jupiter Transp. Co., Kenosha, 1980—82; sys. programmer Citibank S.D., Sioux Falls, 1982—85; database adminstr. Sandoz Crop Protection, Chgo., 1985—86; cons. data processing Applied Info. Devel., Inc., Oak Brook, Ill., 1986—89, Trilogy Cons. Corp., Waukegan, Ill., 1989; database adminstr. Waste Mgmt., Inc., 1989—93; mgr. database Newark Electronics, Inc., 1993—97, ADP/Adminstrv. Solutions Group, 1997—2000; mgr. change control, customer svc. delivery team Washington Mut., 2000—. Pres. Software AG User Group, Chgo., 1991-95, v.p. midwest region; pres. CD Cleavers, 1995-99 Editor newsletter Open Channel, 1985-92 Candidate Common Coun., Kenosha; dir./sec. Vernon Hills Youth Baseball/Softball Assn.; youth and young adult sports coach, 1970—. Mem. Data Processing Mgmt. Assn. (reporter newsletter 1981-82), Nat. Youth Sports Coach Assn. (life, cert.), Chgo. Indsl. Chess League, USS Halsey Club (Sioux Falls), USS Voyager Club (Vernon Hills, Ill.) Roman Catholic. Avocations: sports, music, books. E-mail: tfhermann@yahoo.com, thomas_f_herrmann@hotmail.com.

HERRNSTADT, RICHARD LAWRENCE, American literature educator; b. N.Y.C., Nov. 4, 1926; s. Oscar Edward and Helen (Lidz) H.; m. Helen Lea Appel, June 18, 1950; children— Steven, Ellen Sara, Owen BS, U. Wis., 1948, MS, 1950; PhD, U. Md., 1960. Instr. English Iowa State U., Ames, 1954-58, asst. prof., 1958-61, assoc. prof., 1961-65, prof., 1965-92, prof. emeritus, 1992—. Editor: The Letters of A. Bronson Alcott, 1969; contbr. articles to profl. jours. Bd. dirs. Ames Cmty. Sch. Dist., 1967-74, Iowa Humanities Programs, 1973-79, v.p., 1978-79; bd. dirs. Area Edn. Agy. 11, Johnston, Iowa, 1977-91, v.p., 1980-84, pres., 1984-87; bd. dirs. Youth and Shelter Svcs., Ames, 1980-91, v.p., 1984-85, pres., 1985-87; bd. dirs. Joint Action in Cmty. Svc., 1994—. Served with USN, 1945-46. Recipient faculty citation Iowa State U. Alumni Assn., 1983 Mem. MLA, Am. Studies Assn. (exec. council 1969-76), Thoreau Soc., Mid-Am. Am. Studies Assn. (v.p. 1961-62, pres. 1962-63), AAUP. Democrat. Jewish. Home: 5320 N Via Sempreverde Tucson AZ 85750-5970

HERROD, HENRY GRADY, III, dean, allergist, immunologist; b. Oakland, Calif., Apr. 30, 1945; MD, U. Ala., 1972. Cert. allergy and immunology; cert. pediats. Intern U. Wash., Seattle, 1972-73, resident in pediats., 1973-74; resident rsch. assoc. in allergy and immunology NIH, Bethesda, Md., 1974-76; fellow in allergy and immunology Duke U., Durham, 1976-78; physician Le Bonheur Childrens Med. Ctr., Memphis; prof. U. Tenn., Memphis, dean, 1998—. Mem. AAAI, AAI, AAP, APS. Office: Dean Coll Medicine U Tenn 62 S Dunlap St Ste 400 Memphis TN 38163-0001 E-mail: hherrod@utmem.edu.

HERRON, CINDY, actress, vocalist; b. San Francisco, Sept. 26, 1965; m. Glenn Braggs; 1 child, Donovan Andrew. Vocalist En Vogue, Atco/Eastwest Records, N.Y.C. Albums include Born to Sing (Platinum 1990), Funky Divas, Remix to Sing, Runaway Love, The Best of En Vogue, 1999; actress (motion picture) Juice, 1992. Recipient Soul Train Music award, 1991; nominated Grammy award, 1990. Office: care En Vogue Atco Eastwest Records 75 Rockefeller Plz New York NY 10019-6908

HERRON, DAVID A., stock exchange executive; Floor reporter Pacific Stock Exch., mem. and specialist, Boston Stock Exch., 1982—84; various positions Fidelity Investments, 1984—98; v.p. listed equities Charles Schwab & Co., Inc., 1998—; CEO Chgo. Stock Exch., 2002—. Gov. Boston Stock Exch., 1991—; trustee Cin. Stock Exch., 1996—2001; ofcl. Am. Stock Exch. Office: Chgo Stock Exch One Financial Pl 440 S LaSalle St Chicago IL 60605*

HERRON, EDWIN HUNTER, JR., energy consultant; b. Shreveport, La., June 7, 1938; s. Edwin Hunter and Helen Virginia (Russell) H.; m. Frances Irvine Hunter, June 27, 1959; children: Edwin, David, Ashley. BS in Chem. Engring., Tulane U., 1959, MS, 1963, PhD (NSF fellow 1963-64), 1964. Rsch. engr. Exxon Rsch. & Engring. Co., Linden, N.J., 1959-61; sr. rsch. egnr. Exxon Prodn. Rsch. Co., Houston, 1964-66; corp. planning advisor Esso Europe, London, Eng., 1966-74; fin. analyst Exxon Corp., N.Y.C., 1974-78; v.p. Gruy Petroleum Tech., Inc., McLean, Va., 1978-84; pres. Petro-Analysis, Inc. (named changed to Hunter Trading Co. Inc.), 1984—, Petroleum Equities, Inc., 1987—; dir. petroleum projects CORE Internat., Inc., 1989—; pres. Petroleum Holdings, Inc., 1993—; dir. World Energy Sys. Inc., 1999—2005. Contbr. articles to profl. publs. Recipient Levey award Tulane U., 1970. Mem. Soc. Petroleum Engrs., Am. Inst. Chem. Engrs., Sci. Rsch. Soc., Soc. Tulane Engrs., Tau Beta Pi. Office Phone: 703-734-0253. Business E-Mail: hunter.herron@petroleumequities.com.

HERRON, FLORINE PERNELL, retired music educator; b. Pitts., Mar. 14, 1951; d. Samuel Melvin and Sadie Leah Herron. BA in Music Edn., Duquesne U., Pitts., 1973; MA in Music Edn. and Performance, Ill. State U., 1975. Cert. tchr. Pa., Fla., Miss., La., Kans., Ill. Prof. music, chmn. dept. Donnelly Coll., Kansas City, Kans., 1983—84; min. music, clinician AME Ch., La., 1973—, chaplain Eighth Episcopal Dist. various locations, La., 2004—. Cons./clinician AME Ch., La., 1973—2003. Author: (piano/organ book) Harmonic Praise, (songbook - sacred and polit. music) In Thee O Lord Do I Put My Trust, (guitar method book) ProgressiveGuitar Melodies. Mem. La. Women's Legis. Caucus, La., 2003. Mem.: Am. Fedn. Of Tchrs., Nat. Coun. Of Negro Women, Connectional Music Com. (assoc. dir., keyboards 2000—03), Music Educators Nat. Conf., Women's Missionary Soc., Mu Phi Epsilon. African Methodist Episcopalian. Avocations: raising birds, composing and arranging music. Office: Florimusic Studios PO Box 1420 Slidell LA 70459 Personal E-mail: florineflorimusic@juno.com.

HERRON, GAYLE ANN, forensic specialist, health facility administrator, psychotherapist, mental health services professional, consultant; b. L.A., Sept. 21, 1953; d. Robert Owen Sr. and Rachel Rebecca (Lemley) Colvin; m. Curtis William Sr. Herron, Feb. 14, 1997; children: Freddie, Brian, Ian, Abbi. AA in Psychology, Okla. City C.C., Oklahoma City, 1986; BS in Sociology, Okla. State U., 1989, BS in Psychology, 1990, MS in Counseling, 1992; postgrad., U. Okla., 1994—95, U. Nev., Las Vegas, 1995—96. Lic. profl. counselor N.C., Mo., Nebr., cert. nat. bd. master psychologist, forensic clin. counselor Nat. Bd. Cert. Forensic Counselors. Adminstr., fin. cons. Security Fin. Cons., Oklahoma City, 1980-88; case worker Big Bros./Big Sisters, Stillwater, Okla., 1988-89; counselor Payne County Family Practices, Stillwater, 1989; social worker Dept. Human Svcs. Child Welfare, Stillwater, 1990-91; asst. to v.p. bus. and fin. Okla. State U., Stillwater, 1990-91; adj. instr. Langston (Okla.) U., 1992; counselor Christian Counseling Assocs., Stillwater, 1993-95; social worker U. Nev. Las Vegas Health Ctr., 1995, Clark County, Las Vegas, Nev., 1995—96; counselor Payne County Health Dept. Child Guidance Clinics, Stillwater and Cushing, Okla., 1992—95; clin. dir., clin. psychotherapist New Beginnings Clin. Svcs. Corp., Las Vegas, 1995—2003; clin. dir., masters psychologist/psychotherapist New Beginnings Diagnostic and Clin. Svcs., Brunswick City, NC, 1997—2003, clin. dir., psychotherapist Branson, Mo., 1999-2001; forensic masters psychologist, clin. dir. Crisis Intervention Svcs., Branson, Mo., 2001—02; cons. masters psychologist Tri-Lakes Primary Care, Hollister, Mo., 2001—02; dir., forensic clin. counselor, masters psychologist Ozark Child, Adolescent and Adult Counseling, Branson, 2002—04; clin. dir., psychotherapist New Beginnings Family Counseling, Hollister, Mo., 2004—. Vol. mental health clinician Crisis Incident Response Team, S.W. Mo., 2001-03. Columnist Brunswick County News, 1997-98. Disaster vol. ARC, Oklahoma City, 1987-88; vol. disaster inquiry team, Oklahoma City, Las Vegas, 1995; vita site coord. IRS, Oklahoma City, 1982-84; emergency room EMT Hillcrest Hosp., Oklahoma City, 1994; EMT/intermediate paramedic Amcare Ambulance Svcs., 1994. Mem. ACA, APA, NASW, Am. Assn. for Christian Counselors, Nat. Assn. Social Workers, Okla. Psychol. Assn., Okla. Assn. Counseling and Devel., Assn. for Humanist Psychology, N.C. Assn. Lic. Counselors and Therapists, Am. Coll. Forensic Counselors, Golden Key Soc., Phi Theta Kappa, Psi Chi. Democrat. Mem. LDS Ch., Roman Catholic. Avocations: travel, drafting, hiking, flying, sports. Address: PO Box 557 Hollister MO 65673-0557 Office: 2257 State Bus Hwy 65 Ste 9 Hollister MO 65672 Office Phone: 417-239-3434. Personal E-mail: gayleannherron@earthlink.net. E-mail: newbeginningscounseling@earthlink.net.

HERRON, J. JAY, lawyer; b. Lake City, MN, 1954; Attended, Calif. State U., Fullerton; BS, U. Calif., Berkeley, 1977; JD, Stanford U., 1980. Passed CPA examination, 1981; bar: Calif. 1980, US Dist. Ct. (Ctrl. Dist. Calif.) 1980. Ptnr. O'Melveny & Myers LLP, Irvine, Calif., co-chair bus. practice group. Lectr. Calif. Continuing Edn. of the Bar-Financing Bus. & other programs, 1990, 1992—93, 1995—96, Advanced Course of Study: Mergers & Acquisitions, 1990, 1992—93, 1995—96, 2000, 2000—04, US Securities and Exchange Commn., 2004. Mem.: Order of the Coif, Beta Alpha Psi, Phi Beta Kappa. Office: O'Melveny & Myers LLP 114 Pacifica Ste 100 Irvine CA 92618-3318 Office Phone: 949-737-2902. Office Fax: 949-737-2300. Business E-Mail: jherron@omm.com.

HERRON, ORLEY R., college president; b. Olive Hill, Ky., Nov. 16, 1933; s. Orley R. and Hyllie W. (Weaver) H.; m. Donna Jean Morgan, Aug. 24, 1956; children: Jill Donette, Morgan Niles, Mark Weaver. BA, Wheaton Coll., 1955; MA, Mich. State U., 1959, PhD, 1965; LittD (hon.), Houghton Coll., 1972; LHD (hon.), Lesley Coll., 1983. Dean of students Westmont Coll., Santa Barbara, Calif., 1961-67; dir. doctoral program/student pers. U. Miss., 1967-68; asst. to pres. Ind. State U., 1968-70; pres. Greenville (Ill.) Coll., 1970-77, Nat Louis U. (formerly Nat. Coll. Edn.), Evanston, Ill., 1977-97; chmn., pres. ORH group eBooks Interactive, 1998—; founder AutoeDirect-.com, Inc., 2000—; chmn., CEO Herron Multimedia, 2001—, BOT-Best of Thrift Travel, 2003—; chmn. Significant Living, 2003—. Mem. Ill. Commn. for Improvement Elem. and Secondary Edn., 1983-1985; chmn. bd. Harris Bank, Wilmette, Ill., 1991—, also bd. dirs.; bd. dirs. Corp. Cmty. Schs. Am., 1989—. Author: Role of the Trustee, 1969, Input-Output, 1970, New Dimensions in Stude Personnel Administration, 1970, A Christian Executive in a Secular World, 1979, Who Controls Your Child?, 1980, Words to Live By, 1997, Notes for the New Millennium, 2000, Song of Blessing, 2004; (cassette) Governing Higher Education in the 70's, 1970; exec. prodr., composer, songwriter (CD) I Love You My Dearest Darling, 2001. Rep. of Pres. U.S. 25th Anniversary UNESCO, 1971; adv. bd. Expt. on Internat. Living, Santa Barbara, 1961-67; mem. Gov.'s Task Force on Encouraging Citizen Involvement in Edn., 1986-87; nat. dir. educators for reelection of Pres., 1972; bd. dirs. Ch. Centered Evangelism; mem. Chgo. Sun. Evening Club, 1987-97; founder Santa Barbara Industries. Lt. comdr. U.S. Naval Res., 1973-77. Recipient Crusader Christian Contbn. award Wheaton Coll., 1955, 74, Outstanding Citizen award Greenville Jaycees, 1971, Outstanding Educator award Religious Heritage of Am., 1987, Disting. Alumnus award Wheaton Coll., Outstanding Alumnus award New Philadelphia H.S., Amicus Polonae award, 1996. Mem. SAG, AAUP, Am. Assn. Higher Edn., Coun. on Inter-Instnl. Cooperation (pres.), Council Advancement Small Colls. (sec.), Christian Coll. Consortium (exec. com.), Fedn. Ind. Ill. Colls. (exec. bd. 1971-97), Assn. Free Meth. Ednl. Instns. (pres. 1973-75), Rotary, Kiwanis. Office: One Westminster Pl Ste 101 Lake Forest IL 60045 Office Phone: 847-295-4221.

HERRON, SHERRY SHELTON, biology professor; b. Hattiesburg, Miss., Sept. 4, 1954; d. John Joseph III and Alice English Shelton; m. John Larkin Herron, June 1, 1974; children: Alicia Hope, John Lark, Forrest Boyd, Lauren Guess. BS, U. South Ala., 1975, MEd, 1988; PhD, U. So. Miss., 1999. Sci. tchr. Baldwin County Sch. Sys., Fairhope, Ala., 1975-80, Bayside Acad., Daphne, Ala., 1981-83, Baldwin County Sch. Sys., Bay Minette, Ala., 1983-93; freshman biology program coord. U. So. Miss., Hattiesburg, 1993-2000, dir. Biol. Scis. Freshman Ctr., 1995-2000; staff biologist Biol. Scis. Curriculum Study, Colorado Springs, Colo., 2001—. Author: General Biology Laboratories: Investigations Into the Unity and Diversity of Life, 1998, 2nd edit., 2000, Investigations Into the Issues of Human Biology, 1998, Inquiries into Introductory Biology, 1999. Officer Alpha Delta Gamma, Bay Minette, Ala., 1984-95. Recipient award USM Coll. Discovery, Inst. Higher Learning, 1993-95, award Using Constructivist-Based Investigations and Cooperative Learning in Introductory Coll. Biology, NSF, 1999-2001. Mem. AAAS, Nat. Assn. for Rsch. in Sci. Tchg., Miss. Acad. Sci. (corp. coord. 2000), Sigma Xi, Gamma Beta Phi. Methodist. Avocations: piano, organ. Office: Biol Scis Curriculum Study 5415 Mark Dabling Blvd Colorado Springs CO 80918-3842 Office Fax: 719-531-9104. E-mail: sherron@bscs.org.

HERRON, VINCENT H., lawyer; b. Santa Monica, Calif., June 1, 1967; s. Thomas Litchfield and Bonnie (Quinn) H. BA in Econs., UCLA, 1990; JD, U. So. Calif., 1994. Bar: Calif., U.S. Tax Ct. Assoc. Latham and Watkins, L.A., 1994-98, ptnr., 1998—2005; prin. Abelson/Herron LLP, L.A., 2005—. Office: Abelson Herron LLP 333 South Grand Ave ste 650 Los Angeles CA 90071 Office Phone: 213-402-1900. Business E-Mail: vherron@abelsonherron.com.

HERSCH, DENNIS STEVEN, lawyer; b. Bklyn., Mar. 20, 1947; s. Alfred and Florence (Flom) H.; m. Huguette Marcelle Lefebvre, June 20, 1976; children: Gregory Alain, Jeremy Lawrence. AB cum laude, Bklyn. Coll., 1967; JD cum laude, NYU, 1970. Bar: N.Y. 1971, U.S. Dist. Ct. (so. dist.) N.Y. 1972, U.S. Ct. Appeals (2nd cir.) 1975. Assoc. Davis Polk & Wardwell, N.Y.C., 1970-78, ptnr., 1978—, co-head mergers & acquisitions practice group. Contbr. articles to profl. jours. Recipient Judge Learned Hand Award, Am. Jewish Com., 2003. Mem. ABA, N.Y. State Bar Assn, Lawyer's Com N.Y. Pub. Library, Horiticultural Soc. N.Y. (chmn. & dir.). Jewish. Office: Davis Polk & Wardwell 450 Lexington Ave Fl 23 New York NY 10017-3982 Office Phone: 212-450-4545. Office Fax: 212-450-3545. Business E-Mail: dennis.hersch@dpw.com.

HERSCH, JONI, economist, educator; b. Chicago, Ill., 1956; d. Lawrence Hersch; m. W. Kip Viscusi. PhD, Northwestern U., Evanston IL, 1977—81. Assoc. prof. of economics U. of Wyo., Laramie, Wyo., 1989—95; vis. assoc. prof. of economics Calif. Inst. of Tech., Pasadena, Calif., 1992—93; prof. of economics U. of Wyo., Laramie, Wyo., 1995—99; vis. prof. of economics Duke U., Durham, NC, 1995—96, Harvard U., Cambridge, Mass., 1998—98; lectr. on law Harvard Law Sch., Cambridge, Mass., 1999—2004; adj. prof., co-dir. Harvard Law Sch., Empirical Legal Studies Program, 2004—. Author: (journal articles) Am. Econ. Rev., Rev. of Economics and Stats., Jour. of Human Resources, Jour. of Risk and Uncertainty, Indsl. and Labor Rels. Rev., Econ. Inquiry, Managerial and Decision Economics. Fellow Vis. Professorship for Women, NSF, 1992-93. Mem.: Am. Econ. Assn. (bd., com. on the status of women in the economics profession 1994—96). Office: Harvard Law School Lewis 425 Cambridge MA 02138

HERSCHBACH, DUDLEY ROBERT, chemistry professor; b. San Jose, Calif., June 18, 1932; s. Robert Dudley and Dorothy Edith (Beer) Herschbach; m. Georgene Lee Botyos, Dec. 26, 1964; children: Lisa Marie, Brenda Michele. BS in Math., Stanford U., 1954, MS in Chemistry, 1955; AM in Physics, Harvard U., 1956, PhD in Chem. Physics, 1958; DSc (hon.), U. Toronto, 1977, Cornell Coll., 1988, Framingham State Coll., 1989, Adelphi U., 1990, Dartmouth Coll., 1992, Charles U., Prague, 1993, U. Ill., Chgo., 1994, Wheaton Coll., 1995, Franklin & Marshall Coll., 1998. Asst. prof. U. Calif., Berkeley, 1959—62, assoc. prof., 1961—63; jr. fellow Harvard U., Cambridge, Mass., 1957—59, prof. chemistry, 1963—76, Frank B. Baird prof. sci., 1976—2002, mem. faculty coun., 1980—83, master Currier House, 1981—86, rsch. prof., 2002—. Cons. editor W.H. Freeman lectr. Haverford Coll., 1962; Falk-Plaut lectr. Columbia U., 1963; vis. prof. Göttingen (Germany) U., 1963, U. Calif., Santa Cruz, 1972; Harvard lectr. Yale U., 1964; Debye lectr. Cornell U., 1966; Rollefson lectr. U. Calif., Berkeley, 1969; Reilly lectr. U. Notre Dame, 1979; Phillips lectr. U. Pitts., 1971; disting. vis. prof. U. Ariz., 1971, U. Tex., 1977, U. Utah, 1978; Gordon lectr. U. Toronto, 1971; Clark lectr. San Jose State U., 1979; Hill lectr. Duke U., 1988; Priestly lectr. Pa. State U., 1990; Kaufman lectr. U. Pa., 1990; Polanyi lectr. U. N.C., 1991; Dreyfus lectr. Dartmouth Coll., 1992; Pauling lectr. Calif. Inst. Tech., 1993; Bernstein lectr. UCLA, 1994; Brown lectr. Rutgers U., 1995; chair bd. trustees Sci. Service. Assoc. editor Jour. Phys. Chemistry, 1980—88, pub. over 400 rsch. papers. Named to Calif. Pub. Edn. Hall of Fame, 1987; recipient pure chemistry award, Am. Chem. Soc., 1965, Centenary medal, 1977, Pauling medal, 1978, Spiers medal, Faraday Soc., 1976, Polanyi medal, 1981, Langmuir prize, 1983, Nobel Prize in chemistry, 1986, Nat. Medal of Sci., NSF, 1991, Heyrovsky medal, 1992, Sierra Nevada Disting. Chemist award, 1993, Kosolapoff medal, 1994, William Walker prize, 1994, Council of Scientific Society President's award for support of science, 1999; fellow Guggenheim fellow, U. Freiburg, Germany, 1968, vis. fellow, Joint Inst. for Lab. Astrophysics, U. Colo., 1969, Sloan fellow, 1959—63, Exxon Faculty fellow, 1980—96, Miller fellow, U. Calif. Berkeley, 1997; scholar Fairchild Disting. scholar, Calif. Inst. Tech., 1976. Fellow: Am. Acad. Arts and Scis., Am. Phys. Soc. (chmn. chem. physics divsn. 1971—72), N.Y. Acad. Sci. (hon.; life); mem.: Am. Philos. Soc., NAS, Royal Soc. Chemistry (fgn.) (hon.), Am. Chem. Soc., AAAS, Sigma Xi, Phi Beta Kappa (orator Harvard U. 1992). Office: Harvard U Dept Chemistry Mallickrodt Lab 035 12 Oxford St Cambridge MA 02138-2902*

HERSCHLEIN, JAMES D., lawyer; AB magna cum laude, Boston Coll., 1982; JD, St. John's U., 1985. Bar: NY 1986, DC. Ptnr. litig. dept., mem exec. com. Kaye Scholer LLP, NYC. Named one of Fifteen Lawyers 40 and Under Shaping the Law for the 21st Century, NY Lawyer, 2001; recipient Thurgood Marshall award, 1988, Legal Aid Pro Bono Publico award for affirmative litigation, 2001. Mem.: ABA (mem. poduct lability ltigation com., mem. pharma. & med. devices subcom.), Fed. Bar Coun., Assn. Bar of City NY (chair young lawyers com. 1991—93, sec. 2000—03). Office: Kaye Scholer LLP 425 Park Ave New York NY 10022 Office Phone: 212-836-8655. E-mail: jherschlein@kayescholer.com.

HERSETH, STEPHANIE, congresswoman, lawyer; b. Aberdeen, SD, Dec. 3, 1970; BA in Govt., Georgetown U., 1993, MA in Govt., 1996; JD, Georgetown U. Law Sch., 1996. Law clerk to US Dist. Judge Charles Kornmann, Pierre, 1998—99, to Judge Diana Gribbon, US Ct. Appeals (4th cir.), Balt., 1999—2000; atty. Skadden, Arps, Slate, Meagher & Flom LLP, Washington, 2001; exec. dir. SD Farmers Union Found., 2003—04; mem. US Ho. Reps., SD, 2004—, mem. agriculture and resources com., veterans affairs com. Prof. Augustana Coll., 2003, SD State U., 2003; teacher Fund for Am. Studies; prof. Georgetown U.; counsel SD Public Utilities Commn. Mem.: SD Bar Assn. Democrat. Office: US Ho of Reps 331 Cannon Ho Office Bldg Washington DC 20515-4101*

HERSEY, GEORGE LEONARD, retired art historian; b. Cambridge, Mass., Aug. 30, 1927; s. Milton Leonard and Katharine (Page) H.; m. Jane Maddox Lancefield, Sept. 2, 1953; children: Donald, James. BA, Harvard U., 1951; MFA, Yale U., 1954, MA, 1961, PhD, 1964. Instr. art Bucknell U., Lewisburg, Pa., 1954-55, asst. prof., 1955-59, acting chmn., 1958-59; instr. Yale U., New Haven, 1963-65, asst. prof., 1965-68, assoc. prof., 1968-74, prof., 1974-98, ret., 1998. Mem. adv. bd. Conn. Preservation Trust, 1977-79; mem. Conn. State Commn. Capitol Restoration, 1977-79; lectr. Princeton U., Columbia U., other univs., orgns. Author (some books have been translated into German, Italian, Japanes, Turkish, and Russian): Alfonso II and the Artistic Renewal of Naples, 1969, The Aragonese Arch at Naples, 1443-1475, 1973; High Victorian Gothic: A Study in Associationism, 1972, Pythagorean Palaces: Magic and Architecture in the Italian Renaissance, 1976, Architecture, Poetry and Number in the Royal Palace at Caserta, 1983, The Lost Meaning of Classical Architecture, 1988, (with R. Freedman) Possible Palladian Villas, 1992, High Renaissance Art in St. Peter's and the Vatican, 1993, The Evolution of Allure, Sexual Selection from the Medici Venus to the Incredible Hulk, 1996, The Monumental Impulse: Architecture's Biological Roots, 1999, Architecture and Geometry in the Age of the Baroque, 2001; also numerous articles and revs.; co-editor: Architectura, 1971—; editor: Yale Publ. in History of Art, 1974-90; art exhbn. co-organizer The Taste of Angels: Neapolitan Paintings in North America, 1650-1750, Yale Univ. Art Gallery and other museums, 1987-88. With U.S. Mcht. Marine, 1945-46, U.S. Army, 1946-47. Recipient Monticello prize, 1961; Fulbright scholar, Italy, 1962; Morse fellow, London, 1966, Schepp fellow, Florence, Italy, 1972; resident Am. Acad. Rome, 1994. Mem.: Soc. Archtl. Historians (bd. dirs. 1971—73), Dunky Club (hon.). Democrat. Home: 167 Linden St New Haven CT 06511-2407 E-mail: g.hersey@comcast.net.

HERSH, IRA PAUL, tax specialist, financial consultant; b. Bklyn., July 14, 1948; s. Saul and Mildred (Leibowitz) Hershkowitz; m. Jan Bennett; children: Marcy Fay, Gregory Alexander, Carrie Elizabeth. Tax mgr. Wiss and Co., NYC, 1970—77; contr. Assets Adminstrn. and Mgmt., Stamford, Conn., 1978—79; tax mgr. Exec. Monetary Mgmt., Inc., NYC, 1980—84; pvt. practice Wilton, Conn., 1985—. Pres. MacArthur Equities Ltd., 1985—. Mem. Rolling Hills Country Club. Home and Office: 20 Branch Brook Rd Wilton CT 06897-1520 E-mail: taxplan@optonline.net.

HERSH, RICHARD H., academic administrator; b. N.Y.C. m. Judith C. Meyers. BA in Polit. Sci. and History, Syracuse U., 1964, MA in Social Sci. Edn., 1965; EdD, Boston U., 1969. Prof., chmn. secondary edn. Coll. Edn. U. Toledo, Ohio, 1968-75; assoc. dean tchr. edn., prof. edn. Coll. Edn. U. Oreg., 1976-80, dean grad. sch., assoc. provost rsch., 1980-83, v.p. rsch. Eugene, 1983-85; v.p. acad. affairs U. N.H., Durham, 1985-89; v.p. acad. affairs, provost Drake U., Des Moines, 1989-91; pres. Hobart and William Smith Coll., Geneva, N.Y., 1991-99; dir. grants program Christian A. Johnson Endeavor Found., 1999—2000; sr. advisor C.A. Johnson Endeavor Found., New York, NY, 2000—02; sr. fellow Council for Aid to Education, 2000—02; pres. Trinity College, Hartford, Conn., 2002—03. Vis. prof., dir. moral edn. project Ont. Inst. Studies Edn. U. Toronto, 1975-76, Ctr. Moral Devel., Harvard U., Cambridge, Mass., 1975-76; vis. prof. Western Australia Inst. Tech., Perth, 1978; speaker in field. Co-author: No G.O.D.'s in the Classroom: Inquiry into Inquiry, 1972, Inquiry and Elementary Social Studies, 1972, Inquiry and Secondary Social Studies, 1972, Perspectives in Moral and Values Education, 1976, Promoting Moral Growth: From Piaget to Kohlberg, 1979, 83, Models of Values and Moral Education, 1980, The Structure of School Improvement, 1983. Stanford U. fellow, 1979, Congl. fellow, 1982-83, Ger. Acad. Exch. Svc. fellow, 1983. Avocations: skiing, tennis, rowing (mem. U.S. rowing team competed World Championships, Bled, Yugoslavia, 1966).

HERSH, ROBERT MICHAEL, retired lawyer, retired insurance company executive; b. N.Y.C., Feb. 12, 1940; s. Isaac and Esther (Cohen) H.; m. Louise Sobin, Sept. 23, 1984; 1 child, Lauren. BA, Columbia U., 1960; JD, Harvard

U., 1963. Bar: N.Y. 1964. Assoc. Malcolm A. Hoffmann, N.Y.C., 1964-66, Valicenti, Leighton, Reid & Pine, N.Y.C., 1966-68; atty. Kraftco Corp., N.Y.C., 1968-74; assoc. counsel Equitable Life Assurance Soc. U.S., N.Y.C., 1974-76, asst. gen. counsel, 1976-78, v.p., counsel, 1978-83, v.p., assoc. gen. counsel, 1983-88; v.p., gen. counsel Integrity Life Ins. Co., N.Y.C., 1988-93; assoc. gen. counsel Met. Life ins. Co., N.Y.C., 1994—2004, ret., 2005. Dir. Ideal Mut. Ins. Co., 1972-74; chief announcer Madison Sq. Garden Track Meets, 1974—; chief Eng. lang. athletics announcer Olympic Games, 1984, 88, 92, 96, 04, World Championships, 1991, 93, 95, 97, 99, 2001, 03, 05, World Indoor Championships, 1987, 99, World Jr. Championships, 1994, 98. Columnist: Track and Field News, 1973-84, sr. editor, 1974—; contbg. editor Runner Mag., 1980-87; contbr. articles to profl. jours. With USAR, 1963—69. Mem. Assn. Life Ins. Counsel, Assn. Bar City N.Y. (com. profl. and jud. ethics 1978-81, consumer affairs com. 1984-85, ins. com. 1985-88), USA Track & Field (dir. 1979—, chmn. records com. 1979-88, chmn. rules com. 1989-02, gen. counsel 1989-98, chmn. grand prix 1982-96, Robert Giegengack award for outstanding svc. 1997), Internat. Assn. Athletics Fedns. (tech. com. 1984-99, coun. 1999-, competition commn. 1999-, mktg. commn. 1999—, juridical commn. 2000-, doping review bd. 2001-), Assn. Track and Field Statisticians, Fedn. Am. Statisticians of Track. Home: 92 Club Dr Roslyn Heights NY 11577-2732 Personal E-mail: bobhersh@compuserve.com.

HERSH, SEYMOUR MYRON, journalist, writer; b. Chgo., Apr. 8, 1937; s. Isadore and Dorothy (Margolis) H.; m. Elizabeth Sarah Klein, May 30, 1964; children: Matthew, Melissa, Joshua. BA in History, U. Chgo., 1958. Police reporter City News Bur., 1959-60; UPI Corr. Pierre, SD, 1962-63; AP corr. Chgo. and Washington, 1963-67; with staff NY Times, Washington, DC, 1972-75, 1979, NYC, 1975-78; nat. corr. Atlantic Monthly, 1983-86; corr. New Yorker Mag., 1992—. Press sec. Senator Eugene J. McCarthy of Minn. (in NH primary), 1968 Offered stories on the My Lai Massacre through Dispatch News Service., reports on US military actions in Afghanistan, 2001, breaking stories on Iraqi prisoner abuse in Abu Ghraib prison, May 2004; author: Chemical and Biological Warfare: America's Hidden Arsenal, 1968, My Lai 4: A Report on the Massacre and Its Aftermath, 1970, Cover-Up: The Army's Secret Investigation of the Massacre of My Lai 4, 1972, The Price of Power: Kissinger in the Nixon White House, 1983 (Los Angeles Times Book prize, 1983, Nat. Book Critics Circle award, 1983, Investigative Reporters amd Editors prize, 1983), The Target Is Destroyed, What Really Happened to Flight 007 and What America Knew About It, 1986, The Samson Option: Israel's Nuclear Arsenal and America's Foreign Policy, 1991 (Investigative Reporters and Editors prize, 1992), The Dark Side of Camelot, 1997, Chain of Command: The Road From 9/11 to Abu Ghraib, 2004; contbr. articles to magazines. Recipient Worth Bingham prize, Sigma Delta Chi Disting. Service award, Pulitzer prize for internat. reporting, 1970; George Polk award, 1970; Scripps-Howard Pub. Service award and 2nd Polk award for stories on B-52 bombing in Cambodia, 1973; Sidney Hillman and 3rd Polk awards for stories on domestic CIA spying, 1974; John Peter Zenger Freedom of The Press award, 1975; Drew Pearson prize for stories on CIA involvement in Chile.; 2nd Sigma Delta Chi Disting. Service award, 1981 and 4th Polk award, 1981, for articles on CIA involvement in Libya, 5th Polk award, 2004, for reports on torture of Iraqis at Abu Ghraib prison; Nat. Mag. Award for pub. interest for 3 articles on US intelligence used to justify the war in Iraq, 2004. Office: The New Yorker 4 Times Sq New York NY 10036*

HERSH, STEVEN LANCE, hypnotherapist, writer; BA in English, Upsala Coll., 1976. Cert. advanced clin. hypnotherapist, master hypnocounselor Inst. of Hypnotherapy. Dir. mktg. Monmouth County Arts Coun.-Count Basie Theatre, Red Bank, NJ, 1990—91; entertainment columnist The Two River Times, 1991-93; founder, exec. dir. Silent Running Soc., 1985—; with Meridian Healthcare Sys./Jersey Shore Med. Ctr., Neptune, NJ. Host Names in the News, WHTG (FM), Eatontown, N.J., 1993-96. Author: Written Out of Television: The Encyclopedia of Cast Changes and Character Replacements, 1945-94, 1996, Written Out of Television: A TV Lover's Guide to Cast Changes 1945-94, 1996; rsch. asst. (Vincent Terrace) Television Character and Story Facts, 1993, Television Specials, 1995; (James Robert Parish) Rosie: Rosie O'Donnell's Biography, 1997, others; actor Star Trek: The Motion Picture, 1980, Stardust Memories, 1981. Office: Inst Integrated Health and Wellness 1820 Corlies Ave Ste 1B Neptune NJ 07753 E-mail: stevenlance@netscape.net.

HERSHAFT, ELINOR, space planner, interior designer; b. N.Y.C., Aug. 12, 1940; d. Solomon and Rose (Cohen) Klausner; m. Arthur Hershaft, June 21, 1959 (div. 1983); children: Karin, Peter; m. Alan J. Hoffman, Sept. 2, 1990. Student, Skidmore Coll., 1956-58; BA, N.Y.U., 1960; postgrad., N.Y. Sch. Interior Design, 1977-78. Lic. home improvement contractor, Conn. Interior designer Elinor Hershaft Interiors, Greewich, Conn., 1979—. Major projects house constrn. with interior design, 1985-87, additions, 1982—; projects pub. in House Beautiful, 1988, Tile News, 1988, Kitchen and Bath Concepts, 1989; numerous comml. and residential interior design projects in Fairfield, Conn. and Westchester, N.Y. Counties, Mass., So. Fla., Boulder, Colo., Wilmington, N.C.; also custom furniture design and fabrication. Creative dir. Greenwich Jewish Fedn., 1983—86; creator logo Bobbie Silverman Inst. for Jewish Culture, Greenwich, Conn., 2001; developer design format, logo and calligraphy spl. fund raising campaign Temple Sholom, Greenwich, 1994—95; pro bono office design and space planning Jewish Cmty. Svcs. Recipient Svc. award Jewish Community Svcs. of Greenwich, 1985, Greenwich Jewish Fedn., 1983, 84, 85. Mem. ASID (allied mem.), Allied Bd. Trade, AIA (allied individual), AAF (allied individual). Jewish. Avocations: calligraphy, reading, swimming, piano. Studio: 115 Old Mill Rd Greenwich CT 06831-3015

HERSHATTER, RICHARD LAWRENCE, lawyer, writer; b. New Haven, Sept. 20, 1923; s. Alexander Charles and Belle (Blenner) Hershatter; m. Mary Jane McNulty, Aug. 16, 1980; 1 stepchild, Kimberly Ann Matlock Kleiman-;children from previous marriage: Gail Brook, Nancy Jill, Bruce Warren. BA, Yale U., 1948; JD, U. Mich., 1951. Bar: Conn 1951, Mich 1951, US Supreme Ct 1959. Pvt. practice, New Haven, 1951—85, Clinton, Conn., 1985—99; state trial referee, 1984—. Author: The Spy Who Hated Licorice, 1966, The Spy Who Hated Caramel, 1968, The Spy Who Hated Fudge, 1970;; 2d edit., 2001, Hung Jury, 2001, The Spy Who Hated Taffy, 2001; columnist Longboat Key News. Mem. Branford Bd. Edn., Conn., 1963—71; bd. dirs. Longboat Key Fedn. of Condominium Assns.; mem. Clinton Rep. Town Com., Conn., 1982—2000, chmn., 1984—88. With Air Corps U.S. Army, 1942—44, With U.S. Inf., 1944—46. Mem.: Mystery Writers Am, Middlesex County Bar Asn, Conn. Sch. Attys. Coun. (pres. 1977), Longboat Key Fedn. of Condominium Assns. (bd. dirs.), Banyan Bay Club (v.p., bd dirs 1988—), Masons. Personal E-mail: hershatter@aol.com.

HERSHBERGER, ROBERT GLEN, architect, educator; b. Pocatello, Idaho, Apr. 4, 1936; s. Vernon Elver and Edna Syvilla (Kinsley) H.; m. Deanna Marlene Van Dyke, Mar. 25, 1961; children: Vernon, Andrew. AB, Stanford U., 1958; BArch, U. Utah, 1959; MArch, U. Pa., 1961, PhD, 1969. Registered architect, Idaho, Ariz. Project architect Spencer & Lee, Architects, San Francisco, 1961-63; project designer GBQC Architects, Phila., 1967-69; asst. prof. Idaho State U., Pocatello, 1963-65; adj. asst. prof. Drexel U., Phila., 1967-69; practicing architect Archtl. & Planning Cons., Tempe, Ariz., 1969-87; prof. Sch. of Architecture Ariz. State U., Tempe, 1969-87, acting dir. Sch. Architecture, 1986-87, assoc. dean. Coll. of Architecture and Environ. Design, 1987; prof. U. Ariz. Coll. Arch., Tucson, 1988—2001, dean, 1988-96; ptnr. Hershberger and Nickels Archs./Planners, 1998—. Chmn. Environ. Design Rsch. Assoc., Washington, 1976-79, chair Archs. in Edn. Com. AIA, Washington, 1983-85; v.p. Arch. Rsch. Ctrs. Consortium, 1994-96; prin. Hershberger, Arch. and Planner, Payson, Ariz., 2002—. Prin. works include Covenant Bapt. Ch. (AIA Excellence award), Urban Renewal Plan Downtown Tempe (AIA Citation), Hershberger residence (AIA honor 1990); author: Architectural Programming and Predesign Manager, 1999; Archtl. Programming in Architect's Handbook of Professional Practice, 2001, Handbook of Environmental Psychology, 2002. Bd. dirs. Rio Salado Found.; mem. Tempe Design Rev. Com., 1985-87, Tempe Elec. Adv. Com., 1982-85, Pocatello Planning Commn., 1962-65; mem. Tucson Planning Commn., 2000-02; mem. pub. arts com. U. Ariz., 1988-96, chmn., 1994-96, mem. campus design rev. adv. com., 1990-96, chmn., 1990-93; chair staff parish com. Catalina United Meth. Ch., 1995; bd. dirs. Catalina Day Care Ctr., 1990-93, So. Ariz. chpt. Make-A-Wish Found., 1995-96; mem. fin. com. Christ Ch. United Meth., 2000-01; conservation comm. Payson Hist. Preservation, 2003—; archtl. rev. com. Portal 4, Pine, Ariz., 2003—; chair Payson Design Rev., 2003—. Recipient Crescordia Environ. Excellence award Valley Forward Assn., 1986, Hon. Mention award Ariz. Hist. Mus. competition, 1985. Fellow AIA (pres. Rio Salado chpt. 1981, 74-88, bd. dirs. So. Ariz. chpt. 1988-96, pres., 1993, Gold medal adv. bd. 1992-95). Democrat. Methodist. Avocations: fly fishing, skiing, hunting, tennis, golf, photography. Office: PO Box 2266 Payson AZ 85547 Home: 204 N Forest Park Dr Payson AZ 85541 Office Phone: 928-970-9280. E-mail: hershberger@npgcable.com.

HERSHBERGER, SCOTT LAURENCE, psychologist, educator, statistician, researcher; b. N.Y.C., July 27, 1963; PhD, Fordham U., Bronx, N.Y., 1990. Prof. U. Minn., 1994—95, Calif. State, Long Beach, 1995—97; pres. Statistical and Measurement Cons. Grp. Author: Multivariate Statis. Methods. Fellow: Royal Statis. Soc.; mem.: Internat. Acad. Sex Rsch., Internat. Statis. Inst., Soc. Multivariate Exptl. Psychology. Achievements include author of over 80 published articles; contributed to the fields of behavior genetics, multivariate analysis, and sexual behavior. Home: 319 Bonito Ave #8 Long Beach CA 90802 Office: Calif State U Long Beach Psychology 1250 Bellflower Blvd Long Beach CA 90840 Office Phone: 562-985-5012. Personal E-mail: scotth@csulb.edu.

HERSHCOPF, GERALD THEA, lawyer; b. Feb. 8, 1922; s. Paul and Rose (Thea) Hershcopf; m. Elaine Yeckes, June 10, 1950; 1 child, Jane. AB, Columbia U., 1943; cert. in French Civilization, U. Paris, 1945; JD, Harvard U., 1949. Bar: N.Y. 1949, U.S. Dist. Ct. (so. dist.) N.Y. 1960, U.S. Supreme Ct. 1981. Assoc. Marshall, Bratter, Greene, Allison & Tucker, N.Y.C., NY, 1949—54; ptnr. Starr & Hershcopf, N.Y.C., 1954—56, Hershcopf, Stevenson, Tannenbaum, San Filippo, Donovan & Korn, 1956—91, Eisen, Hershcopf & Schulman, 1991—. Gen. ptnr. Norfolk Realty Corp., N.Y.C., 1961—86; chmn. bd. N.Am. Planning Corp., N.Y.C., 1968—71; pres. Consortium Met. Law Schs., N.Y.C., 1983—. B. dirs. N.Y. divsn. Am. Cancer Soc., 1997—98. Served with U.S. Army, 1943—46, ETO. Mem.: Real Estate Bd. N.Y., Judge Advs. Assn., N.Y. State Bar Assn. (gen. practice sect.), Assn. Bar City N.Y., Doubles Club (N.Y.C.), French-Am. C. of C., Harvard Club, N.Y. Athletic Club, Columbia U. Tennis Club, Beta Sigma Rho. Home: 737 Park Ave New York NY 10021-4256 Office: 609 5th Ave Fl 6 New York NY 10017-1021 Office Phone: 212-832-4000.

HERSHENHORN, ROBERT GENE, bank executive; b. St. Louis, Nov. 2, 1943; s. Isadore and Dorothy Hershenhorn; m. Dittany R. Felker, June 11, 1963 (div. Feb. 1975); children: Lindsay, Alexis; m. Judith Marie Holmberg, Aug. 5, 1995; 1 child, Sarah. BA, Washington U., 1965; JD, Chgo.-Kent Coll. of Law, 1968. Chmn. of the bd. First Bank of Ill., 1976—. Owner Hershenhorn Bancorp. holding co.; past chmn. bd. dirs. Chgo. Econometrics & Forecasting Assocs.; past chmn. bd., prin. Petroco, Sierra Hotel, Concoco. Bd. dirs. Joffrey Ballet, Chgo., 1996-97, Lincoln Park Zoo, Chgo., 1998-2003; founding mem. fin. com. Peter Fitzgerald for U.S. Senate, 1998; past trustee Barat Coll., Lake Forest, Ill., Chgo. Acad. of Sci. and Mus.; past bd. dirs. Little City, Devel. Office of Chgo. Province of the Soc. of Jesus, Chgo. Hearing Soc., Chgo. Internat. Film Festival, U. Chgo. Cancer Rsch. Found., Lake Forest Symphony, United Way, Northlight Theater, Touchstone Theater, Drexel Hom for the Aged, others; mem. vis. com. U. Chgo. Divsn. Biol. Scis., 2001-, Pritzker Sch. Medicine, 2001-. Mem. ABA, Ill. Bar Assn., Chgo. Bar Assn., Ind. Bankers of Am., Am. Bankers Assn., Banker's Club of Chgo. Jewish. Avocations: travel, tennis, biking. Home: 808 E Deerpath Rd Lake Forest IL 60045-2273 Office: First Bank & Trust Co of Ill 300 E Northwest Hwy Palatine IL 60067-8133

HERSHENOV, BERNARD ZION, research and development company executive; b. N.Y.C., Sept. 22, 1927; s. Joseph and Rebecca (Landes) H.; m. Miriam Leah Gold, Oct. 27, 1950; 1 dau., Ruth Lois. BS, U. Mich., 1950, MS, 1952, PhD, 1959. Asso. research engr. U. Mich., Ann Arbor, 1951-59; devel. engr. Gen. Electric Co., Schenectady, 1959-60; mem. tech. staff, head microwave integrated circuits RCA Research Labs., Princeton, N.J., 1960-72; dir. Research Labs., Tokyo, 1972-75, head energy systems Princeton, 1976-79, dir. Solid State Devices Lab., 1979-83, dir. Optical Systems and Display Materials Lab., 1983-84, dir. Optoelectronics Research Lab., 1984-87; dir. mktg. coordination David Sarnoff Research Ctr. (subs. of SRI Internat.), Princeton, 1987-88; dir. internat. bus. devel., 1989-93; sr. advisor Sarnoff Research Ctr. (subs. of SRI Internat.), Princeton, 1994-95; cons., 1993-95. Contbr. articles in field. V.p. Jewish Community Center, Princeton, 1970-71, pres., 1971-72, trustee, 1977-79; mem. physics adv. com. U. Mich., 1988—. Served with USN, 1946-47. Recipient RCA Outstanding Achievement awards, 1963, 66, Microwave Application award Microwave Theory and Techniques Soc. of IEEE, 1992. Fellow IEEE; mem. Sigma Xi, Phi Kappa Phi. Jewish. Home: 22 Raleigh Rd Kendall Park NJ 08824-1007

HERSHENSON, MARTHA BRADFORD, history educator; b. Chgo., June 20, 1944; d. William Stephen Bradford and Barbara Hearn Kennedy; m. Loren Victor Hershenson, Sept. 4, 1988; 1 child, Holly Ann Boes. BA in History, Lake Forest Coll., 1966; M in Edn., Nat. Lewis U., 1971. Cert. K-8 edn. Ill., 6-12 edn. Ill. 6th grade educator Deerfield (Ill.) Grammar Sch., 1966—68, Woodland Intermediate Sch., Gages Lake, Ill., 1968—70; 4th-6th grade educator North Shore Sch. Dist., Highland Park, Ill., 1970—. Suicide phone worker Reed Zone Ctr., Chgo., 1973; supr. for student tchrs. North Shore Sch. Dist. 112, Highland Park, Ill., 1978—2002; mentor Lake Forest Coll.; 6th grade team leader Edgewood Mid. Sch., Highland Park, 2003—04. Bd. dirs. Highland Park Cmty. Orgn., 1995—97; mem. alumni bd. Lake Forest Coll., 1996—2000; mem. Youth, Edn. and Arts, Highland Park, 1998; sponsor trip to Ireland with h.s. students Rotary Internat. Project- Towards a Better Understanding (TABU), Highland Park, 1997; coll. scholarship sponsor Highland Park C. of C., 1992—2005. Named Best Tchr. on North Shore, Pioneer Press Survey of 17 Counties, 1994. Mem.: DAR (life), Ill. Fedn. Tchrs. (various edn. orgns. 1974—75), Maine Hist. Soc. (life), Descendants of Mayflower Soc. (life; bd. assts. for Ill. 2002—05), John Butler Civil War Soc. for Ill. (life), Highland Pk. Rotary Internat. (life). Avocation: genealogy. Home: 600 Beverly Pl Lake Forest IL 60045 Office: Edgewood Mid Sch 929 Edgewood Rd Highland Park IL 60035

HERSHENSON, MIRIAM HANNAH RATNER, librarian; b. Springfield, Mass., July 23, 1944; d. David and Thelma (Wasserman) Ratner; children: Trent M., Scott D. AB, Syracuse U., 1966; MS, Simmons Coll., 1967; postgrad., Nova U., 1987-89. Cert. tchr./librarian, Mass. Media specialist Quincy (Mass.) Pub. Schs., 1967-71, Virginia Beach (Va.) Pub. Schs., 1982-84, Portsmouth (Va.) Pub. Schs., 1984; regional children's coord. Broward County Libr., Ft. Lauderdale, Fla., 1985-88, br. liaison, 1988-89, br. librarian, 1989-93, regional br. supr., 1993-2001; head pub. svc. Nova Southeastern U./ Broward County Libr., 2001—03; pub. svc. adminstr. Broward County Libr., 2003—. Mem. ALA, Pub. Libr. Assn., Fla. Libr. Assn. (caucus chair 1990-91), Broward County Libr. Assn. (pres. 1994-95), Hadassah (life, chpt. pres. 1983-84), Nat. Coun. Jewish Women (life), Jewish Women Internat. (life), Brandeis Univ. Women (life). Office: Broward County Libr 100 South Andrews Ave Fort Lauderdale FL 33301 Office Phone: 954-357-7335. Business E-Mail: mhershen@browardlibrary.org.

HERSHEY, APRIL M., music educator, school system administrator; b. Ephrata, Pa., Apr. 16, 1969; d. Ronald A. and Linda M. Horning; m. Richard C. Hershey, Oct. 1, 1994. BS in Music Edn., Lebanon Valley Coll., Annville, Pa., 1991; MEd in Tchg. and Curriculum, Pa. State U., 2001. Cert. instrnl. II Pa., elem./secondary prin. Pa. Substitute tchr. Cornwall-Lebanon Sch. Dist., Lebanon, Pa., 1991—97; elem. music educator Annville-Cleona Sch. Dist., 1997—2002, dean of elem. students, 2000—02; prin. Reamstown Elem. Sch., Cocalico Sch. Dist., 2002. Dir. adult and youth choirs Annville United Meth. Ch., 1991—2000. Mem.: ASCD, Lancaster-Lebanon Elem. Prins. Assn., Phi Delta Kappa. Democrat. Brethren. Avocations: reading, singing at weddings, travel. Office: Reamstown Elem School Cocalico School Dist 44 S Reamstown Rd Reamstown PA 17567

HERSHEY, BARBARA (BARBARA HERZSTEIN), actress; b. Hollywood, Calif., Feb. 5, 1948; d. William H. Herzstein; 1 child, Tom; m. Stephen Douglas, Aug. 8, 1992 (div. 1995). Student public schs., Hollywood. Appearences include (TV series) The Monroes, 1966-67, From Here to Eternity, 1979, (mini-series) A Man Called Intrepid, 1979, Return to Lonesome Dove, 1993, Abraham, 1994; other TV appearances include Gidget, 1965, The Invaders, 1967, Daniel Boone, 1967, Love Story, 1973, Bob Hope Chrysler Theatre, 1967, High Chaparral, 1967, Kung Fu, 1973, CBS Playhouse, 1967, (TV movies) Flood, 1976, In the Glitter Palace, 1977, Just a Little Inconvenience, 1977, Sunshine Christmas, 1977, Angel on My Shoulder, 1980, The Nightingale, 1985, My Wicked, Wicked Ways... The Legend of Errol Flynn, 1985, Passion Flower, 1986, Killing in a Small Town, 1990 (Emmy award 1990, Golden Globe award 1991), Paris Trout, 1991 (Emmy award nomination), Stay the Night, 1992, Abraham, 1994, (films) With Six You Get Egg Roll, 1968, Last Summer, 1969, Heaven with a Gun, 1969, The Liberation of L.B. Jones, 1970, The Baby Maker, 1970, The Pursuit of Happiness, 1971, Dealing, 1971, Boxcar Bertha, 1972, Angela (Love Comes Quietly), 1974, The Crazy World of Julius Vrooder, 1974, Diamonds, 1975, You and Me, 1975, Dirty Night's Work, 1975, The Stunt Man, 1980, Take This Job and Shove It, 1981, The Entity, 1982, The Right Stuff, 1983, Americana, 1983, The Natural, 1984, Hoosiers, 1986, Hannah and Her Sisters, 1986, Tin Men, 1987, Shy People, 1987 (Best Actress Cannes Film Festival, 1987), A World Apart, 1988 (Best Actress Cannes Film Festival, 1988), The Last Temptation of Christ, 1988, Beaches, 1988, Tune in Tomorrow, 1989, Defenseless, 1991, The Public Eye, 1992, Falling Down, 1993, Swing Kids, 1993, Splitting Heirs, 1993, A Dangerous Woman, 1993, Last of the Dogmen, 1995, Portrait of a Lady, 1996 (nominated Golden Globe Best Supporting Actress, nominated Academy award Best Supporting Actress), The Pallbearer, 1996, A Soldier's Daughter Never Cries, 1998, Frogs for Snakes, 1998, The Staircase, 1998, Breakfast of Champions, 1999, Passion, 1999, Lantana, 2001, 11:14, 2003, Riding the Bullet, 2004; (theatre, Broadway) Einstein and the Polar Bear, 1981. Recipient Golden Palm award for best actress Cannes Film Festival, 1987, 1988. Office: CAA care Jenny Rawlings 9830 Wilshire Blvd Beverly Hills CA 90212-1804 also: Bymel O'Neill Mgmt care Suzan Bymel N Vista Los Angeles CA 90046

HERSHEY, DALE, lawyer, educator; b. Pitts., Mar. 24, 1941; s. Henry E. and Elizabeth (Loeffler) H.; m. Susanne Jarrett Wilson, July 8, 1967; children: Lauren Dixon, Justin Alexander. BA, Yale U., 1963; LLB, Harvard U., 1966. Bar: Pa. 1966, U.S. Dist. Ct. (we. dist.) Pa. 1966, U.S. Ct. Appeals (3d cir.) 1971, U.S. Tax Ct. 1978, U.S. Supreme Ct. 1979, Ct. Internat. Trade 1999. Assoc. Eckert Seamans Cherin & Mellott, LLC, Pitts., 1966-75, mem., 1975—. Sr. lectr. law Tepper Sch. of Bus. Carnegie Mellon U., 2001—, lectr. Acad. for Lifelong Learning; pres. Charleston Trust/U.S.A.; vis. prof. E.M. Lyon, Ecully, France, 2003, 05. Bd. dirs. Legal Aid Soc. Pitts., pres., 1983-89; hon. pres. Gateway to the Arts, Inc.; bd. dirs. Friends of Carnegie Libr., Kids Voice, Inc., Pitts. Chamber Music Soc., pres., 1992-94; active Leadership Pitts., 1989-90. Mem. ABA, Internat. Bar Assn., Pa. Bar Assn. (Pro Bono award 1988), Allegheny County Bar Assn. (bd. dirs. Bar Found., 2001-04, mem. judiciary com. 1997-2000), Am. Law Inst., Harvard Law Sch. Assn. Western Pa. (pres. 1985-86), Harvard-Yale-Princeton Club, Yale Club (Pitts.) (pres. 1987-89). Unitarian Universalist. Home: 311 Dorseyville Rd Pittsburgh PA 15215-1022 Office: Eckert Seamans Cherin & Mellott LLC 600 Grant St Ste 4400 Pittsburgh PA 15219-2702 Office Phone: 412-566-6058. Business E-Mail: dhershey@eckertseamans.com.

HERSHEY, NATHAN, lawyer, educator; b. N.Y.C., Apr. 28, 1930; s. Harry and Hannah (Horwitz) Hershey; m. Carol Fine, July 13, 1958; children: Suzanne, Madeleine. AB, NYU, 1950; LLB, Harvard U., 1953. Bar: D.C. 1953, Pa. 1977. Individual practice law, N.Y.C., 1955—56; rsch. assoc. in health law U. Pitts., 1956—58, asst. prof., 1958—63, assoc. prof., 1963—68, prof., 1968—; mem. Pa. Bd. Med. Edn., 1974—80; of counsel Markel, Schafer, and Goldman P.C., Pitts., 1977—, Post & Schell, Phila., 1984—94. Cons. Pa. State Com. on Pub. Health and Welfare, 1973—80; v.p. U. Pitts. Senate, 1995—98, pres., 1998—2001. Author (with others): Hospital Law Manual, 1959; author: (with Robert D. Miller) Human Experimentation and the Law, 1976; author: Hospital-Physician Relations, 1982; editor: Hosp. Law Newsletter; contbr. articles to profl. jours. Bd. dirs. Women's Health Svcs., 1976—91, bd. v.p., 1982—91; bd. dirs. Hill House Assn., Pitts., 1964—71. Served with U.S. Army, 1953—55. Mem.: Am. Pub. Health Assn., Soc. Hosp. Attys. Western Pa. (dir. 1974—85, past pres.), Am. Soc. Hosp. Attys. (past pres.), Inst. Medicine of NAS. Democrat. Jewish. Home: 5423 Northumberland St Pittsburgh PA 15217-1128 Office: 2200 Lawyers Bldg Pittsburgh PA 15219

HERSHEY, NONA, artist, printmaker, educator; b. N.Y.C., Oct. 31, 1946; d. Don and Rita (Meyrson) H.; m. Richard Akre Trythall, Jan. 19, 1972; (div. 1992). BFA, Temple U., 1967; MFA, Temple U., Rome, 1969; studied lithography, Istituto Statale d'Arte, Urbino, Italy, 1979, 80; studied woodcut and printing, Yoshida Hanga Acad., Tokyo, 1990-91. Asst. prof. drawing and printmaking Daeman Coll., Buffalo, 1972-73; mem. faculty studio art St. Stephen's Sch., Rome, 1973-79; lectr. studio art John Cabot Coll., Rome, 1979; asst. prof. printmaking Temple Abroad, Tyler Sch. of Art, Rome, 1979-90; vis. assoc. prof. drawing and printmaking Study Abroad Program, Temple U., Tokyo, 1990-91; vis. assoc. prof. printmaking Wesleyan U., Middletown, Conn., 1991-92; vis. assoc. prof. drawing and painting U. Iowa, Iowa City, 1992; assoc. prof. printmaking Mass. Coll. Art, Boston, 1993—. Vis. artist-critic Calcografica Nazionale, Rome, 1986, Istituto per la Grafica, Latina, Italy, 1987, R.I. Sch. Design, Rome, 1987, 89, 90, 93, U. Conn, Storrs, 1992, SUNY, Albany, 1993, Syracuse (N.Y.) U., 1993, N.Y. Grad. Sch. Figurative Art, N.Y.C., 1993; artist-in-residence The MacDowell Colony, Peterborough, N.H., 1989, 93, Ucross Found., Clearmont, Wyo., 1992. One-woman shows include Jane Haslem Gallery, Washington, 1976, Laboratorio Artvisive, Foggia, Italy, 1979, 86, Villa Schifanoia Gallery, Florence, Italy, 1980, Il Patio Gallery, Ravenna, Italy, 1982, Galleria Il Ponte, Rome, 1985, 90, Mary Ryan Gallery, N.Y.C., 1983, 87, Dolan/Maxwell Gallery, Phila., 1987, Palazzo Sormani, Milan, 1993, RI Sch. Design, 1994, Miller/Block Gallery, Boston, 1995, 99, 02, Robert Lehman Art Ctr., AIA, 2001, Soprafina Gallery, Mass., 2002; group exhbns. include Smithsonian Inst., Washington, 1973, Honolulu Acad. Arts, 1973, USIS, Rome, 1973, Jane Haslem Gallery, 1974, 75, Mus. Fine Arts, Boston, 1975, Garden Gallery Modern Art, Raleigh, N.C., 1975, Met. Mus., Fla., 1977, USIS, Bucharest, Hungary, 1978, Am. Acad., Rome, 1978, Laboratorio Artivisive, 1981, 92, Rassegna di Grafica Contemporanea, Casalpusterlungo, Italy, 1982, Clark Gallery, Lincoln, Mass., 1983, Mary Ryan Gallery, 1983, 84, 85, 86, 88, 91, 92, Noyes Mus., N.J., 1984, Galleria Il Ponte, 1984, Dolan/Maxwell Gallery, 1985, Calcografia Nazionale, Rome, 1986, Palazzo Ducale, Pesaro, Italy, 1986, Bklyn. Mus., 1986, Walker Art Ctr., Mpls., 1986, Garton & Cooke Gallery, London, 1987, Istituto per la Grafica, Latina, Italy, 1987, Premio Sassoferrato, Italy, 1987, Premio Internazionale Biella per l'Incisione, Italy, 1987, Pa. Acad. Fine Arts, Phila., 1987, Premio Internazionale d'Arte Contemporanea, Campobello di Mazara, Italy, 1988, Greenville Mus. Fine Arts, N.C., Taipei Fine Art Mus., 1988, Dedalos Gallery, San Severo, Italy, 1990, Gallery Kabutoya, Tokyo, 1991, Art Multiple, Dusseldorf, Germany, 1992, G.W. Einstein Gallery, N.Y.C., 1993, Meml. Hall Ctr. for Arts, Vt., 1999, Atrium Mus., St. Louis, 1999, Rose Art Mus., Mass., 2000, ARTcetera, BCA, Boston, 2000, Hess Gallery, Mass., 2000, Corcoran Gallery of Art, Washington, DC, 2001, John Elder Gallery, N.Y.C., Plum Gallery, Mass, 2002, Parchman Stremmel Gallery, San Antonio, 2002, Andersen Fine Art, Mass., 2003, Newton Art Ctr., Boston, 2003; public collections include Met. Mus. Art, N.Y.C., Minn. Mus. Art, St. Paul, Pa. Acad. Fine Arts, Mint Mus., N.C., Nat. Print Cabinet, Rome, Civic Mus., Piacenza, Italy, Mcpl. Mus. Graphic Art, Caracas, Venezuela, Crakow Nat. Mus., Poland, Skopje Mus. Contemporary Art, Yugoslavia, Yale U. Art Gallery, S-E Banken, Stockholm, Mus. Fine Arts, Boston, Boston Pub. Library, Corcoran Mus. Art, Washington

DC, Davidson Coll., N.C., Fogg Art Mus., Mass., Free Library of Phila., Georgetown U., Washington DC, Haper Coll., Ill., Harvard U. Law Sch., Hunterdon Art Ctr., N.J., Library of Congress, Washington DC. Mem. Printmaking Coun. N.J. Democrat. Office: Mass Coll Art 621 Huntington Ave Boston MA 02115-5801*

HERSHEY, ROBERT LEWIS, mechanical engineer, management consultant; b. Chgo., Dec. 18, 1941; s. Maurice and Rose Beverly (Barrish) H. BSME summa cum laude, Tufts U., 1963; MSME, MIT, 1964; PhD in Engring., Cath. U. Am., 1973. Registered profl. engr., D.C., N.Y.; cert. mfg. engr. Engr. Bell Telephone Labs., Whippany, N.J., 1963-67; acoustics mgr. Weston Instruments, Inc., Poughkeepsie, N.Y., 1967-68; sr. scientist Bolt Beranek & Newman, Washington, 1968-71; acoustics program mgr. Booz Allen & Hamilton, Bethesda, Md., 1971-79; program v.p. Sci. Mgmt. Corp., Washington, 1979-80, divsn. v.p., 1980-88; exec. engr. O'Donnell Cons. Engrs., Inc., Washington, 1988—. Sec. Engring. Registration Bd., D.C., 1987-98, D.C. Profl. Coun., Washington, 1974; mem. coordinating com. on productivity Am. Assn. Engring. Socs., Washington, 1984-88. Author: How to Think With Numbers, 1982, All the Math You Need to Get Rich, 2001. Sci. policy analyst George H.W. Bush Presdl. Campaign, Washington, 1988, 92, Bob Dole Presdl. Campaign, Washington, 1996, George W. Bush Presdl. Campaign, Washington, 2000, 04; pres. Hamilton House Assn. Resident Tenants, Washington, 1987-88, 90—; mem. Joint Bd. on Sci. Engring. Edn., Washington, 1972-78 Recipient Design award Machinery Mag., 1963. Fellow ASME (chmn. Washington chpt. 1978-79, Dedicated Svc. award 2001), NSPE (sec. profl. engrs. in industry 1973-75); mem. AAAS, DC Sci. Writers Assn., Philos. Soc. Washington (pres.), Capital PC User Group, Acoustical Soc. Am. (chmn. Washington chpt. 1982-83), D.C. Soc. Profl. Engrs. (pres. 1975-76, 2002-03, nat. dir. 1980-86, pres.-elect 2005—, Young Engr. of Yr. 1974), D.C. Coun. Engring. and Archtl. Socs. (del. 1969—, pres. 1978-79, Pres.'s award 1989, Nat. Capital award 1974), Soc. Mfg. Engrs. (chmn. Washington Robotics Internat. chpt. 1986-87), Mensa, Washington Coal Club, MIT Club of Washington (pres. 1979-80), Cosmos Club, Washington Tufts Alliance (v.p. 1970-71, steering com. 1999—), Tau Beta Pi (pres. Tufts student chpt. 1962-63, v.p. Washington alumni chpt. 1988-89), Sigma Xi. Republican. Avocations: chess, tennis, sports cars, golf. Home: Apt 1033 1255 New Hampshire Ave NW Washington DC 20036-2328 E-mail: hershey@cpcug.org.

HERSHISER, OREL LEONARD, IV, professional baseball player; b. Buffalo, Sept. 16, 1958; s. Orel Leonard H. III and Millie H. Hershiser; m. Jamie Byars, Feb. 7, 1981; children: Orel Leonard V, Jordan Douglass. Student, Bowling Green State U. Pitcher minor league teams, Clinton, Iowa, 1979, San Antonio, 1980—81, Albuquerque, 1982—83; with LA Dodgers, 1983—94, Cleve. Indians, 1995—97; pitcher San Francisco Giants, 1997—98, NY Mets, 1998—99; with LA Dodgers, 1999—2000; analyst ESPN, 2001; pitching coach Texas Rangers, Arlington, Tex., 2002—. Named Most Valuable Player, World Series, 1988, Major League Player of Yr., Sporting News, 1988, Pitcher of Yr., 1988; named to All-Star Team, Nat. League, 1987, 1988, Sporting News Nat. League, 1988, Silver Slugger Team, Sporting News, 1993, All-Star Games, 1987—89; recipient Cy Young award, Nat. League, 1988, Gold Glove award, 1988. Achievements include playing in the World Series, 1988. Office: Los Angeles Dodgers 1000 Elysian Park Ave Los Angeles CA 90012-1199*

HERSHKOFF, HELEN, law educator; b. 1953; AB, Radcliffe-Harvard Coll., 1973; BA, Oxford U., 1975, MA, 1979; JD, Harvard Law Sch., 1978. Bar: NY 1979. Assoc. Paul, Weiss, Rifkind, Wharton & Garrison, NYC, 1978—83; staff atty. The Legal Aid Soc. of NY, NYC, 1983—87; assoc. legal dir. ACLU, NYC, 1987—95; asst. prof. law NYU Sch. Law, 1995—98, assoc. prof., 1998—2000, prof., 2000—, co-dir. Arthur Garfield Hays civil liberties program. Cons. World Bank. Bd. dirs. Urban Justice Ctr., NYC. Office: NYU Sch Law Vanderbilt Hall Rm 334 40 Washington Sq S New York NY 10012-1099 Office Phone: 212-998-6285. E-mail: helen.hershkoff@nyu.edu.

HERSHNER, ROBERT FRANKLIN, JR., judge; b. Sumter, S.C., Jan. 21, 1944; s. Robert Franklin and Druie (Goodman) H.; m. Sally Sinclair, May 19, 1990; children: Bryan, Andrew. AB, Mercer U., 1966, JD, 1969. Bar: Ga. 1971, U.S. Dist. Ct. (mid. dist.) Ga. 1971, U.S. Dist. Ct. (so. dist.) Ga. 1979, U.S. Ct. Appeals (11th cir.) 1981, U.S. Supreme Ct. 1978. Atty. Ga. Legal Svcs. Corp., Macon, 1972; assoc. Adams, O'Neal, Hemingway & Kaplan, Macon, 1972-76; ptnr. Kaplan & Hershner, P.A., Macon, 1976-80; judge U.S. Bankruptcy Ct. for Mid. Dist. Ga., Macon, 1980—, chief bankruptcy judge, 1986—. Active Fed. Jud. Ctr. Com. on Bankruptcy Edn., 1990—99, chmn., 1994—99; elected mem. bd. Fed. Jud. Ctr., 2001—. Contbr. Georgia Lawyers Basic Practice Handbook, 2d edit., Post-Judgment Procedures, 1979; cons. Norton Bankruptcy Law and Practice. V.p. Macon Heritage Found., 1977-78. Capt. U.S. Army, 1970-75. Mem. Ga. Bar Assn., Macon Bar Assn., Nat. Conf. Bankruptcy Judges (gov., v.p. 1996-97, pres. 1997-98), Blue Key, Phi Eta Sigma. Methodist. Office: US Bankruptcy Ct PO Box 86 Macon GA 31202-0086

HERSHONIK, SHERYL ANN, secondary school educator; b. New Haven, Dec. 8, 1955; m. Stanley Paul Hershonik, Jr., Sept. 22, 1984; children: Stanley Paul III, Julia Elizabeth. BS, U. Conn., 1977; MS, So. Conn. State U., 1984. Tchr. math. New Haven Bd. Edn., 1977—. Panelist Conn. Mastery Test Standards Com. Fellow Yale-New Haven Tchrs. Inst. Mem. ASCD, Nat. Coun. Tchrs. Math., Assn. Tchrs. Math. in New Eng., Assn. Tchrs. Math. in Conn., New Haven Fedn. Tchrs. (exec. bd.). Office: 175 Water St New Haven CT 06511

HERSI, DOROTHY TALBERT, education educator; b. Pine Bluff, Ark., Nov. 13, 1953; d. Ernest and Dorothy Georgie (Burkett) Talbert; m. Hersi M. Hersi, May 29, 1977; 1 child, Sidin. BA cum laude, Howard U., 1975, MEd, 1976, postgrad., 1983-84, PhD, 1991. Counselor Alexandria (Va.) City Schs.; tchr. English, Charles County Pub. Schs., La Plata, Md.; instr. Upward Bound, Howard U., Washington, instr. devel. skills, adj. asst. prof., coord./dept. chair Ctr. for Academic Reinforcement, 1991-94; assoc. prof., asst. v.p. Student and Acadademic Support Svcs. Del. State U., Dover, Del., 1997—. Presenter Coll. Bd. Forum, 1984. Author: How To Develop a Better Memory: The ICARE System of Memorization. Mem. APGA, ACPA, Internat. Reading Assn. (past mem. U.S. legis. com.), D.C. Reading Coun. (past bd. dirs.), Phi Delta Kappa, Kappa Delta Pi (past sec.). Home: 35 Deer Cir Bear DE 19701-2718

HERSON, MICHAEL HARRY, lobbyist, consultant; b. N.Y.C., Apr. 30, 1965; s. Milton and Arlene Rita Herson; m. Vicki Siegel Herson, Nov. 20, 1999; children: Molly, Kyle. BA in Am. Govt., Georgetown U., 1987, MA in Nat. Security Studies, 1993; JD, Rutgers U., 1990. Bar: Pa. 1991, N.J. 1992, D.C. 1992, U.S. Dist. Ct. N.J. 1992. White House intern Exec. Office Pres. Reagan, Washington, 1986; spl. asst. Office Sec. Def. Cheney, Washington, 1990—93; base closure cons. Great Lakes (Ill.) Naval Tng. Ctr., 1993; asst. v.p. Healthcare Imaging Svcs., Red Bank, NJ, 1993—94; Rep. nominee for Congress N.J. 6th Congl. Dist., 1994; pres., CEO Am. Def. Internat., Inc., Washington, 1995—. Office: Am Def Internat Inc 1100 N Y Ave NW Ste 630 Washington DC 20005

HERSON, VICTOR CHARLES, pediatrician; b. NYC, June 30, 1948; s. Irving and Shirley Herson; m. Gail Williams Herson, June 19, 1970; children: Heather, Andrew, David. AB, Colgate U., 1969; MD, U. Vt., 1973. Diplomate Am. Bd. Pediat., 1981. Intern, resident in pediat. U. Colo., Denver, 1973—76; prof. pediat. U. Conn., Farmington, 2002—; med. dir. neonatal ICU Conn. Children's Med. Ctr., Hartford, 1981—. Fellow: Am. Acad. Pediat. Achievements include research in over 40 original articles in peer reviewed journals of neonatal medicine. Office: Conn Childrens Med Ctr 282 Washington St Hartford CT 06106 E-mail: vherson@ccmckids.org.

HERSPRING, DALE ROY, political science educator, consultant; b. Oakland, Calif., Sept. 28, 1940; s. Frank E. and Ruby F. Herspring; m. Maureen C. Phillip, June 11, 1965; children: Larissa, Kurt, Kyle. AB, Stanford U., 1965; MA, Georgetown U., 1967; PhD, U. So. Calif., 1972. Fgn. svc. officer Dept. State, Washington, 1971-91; ret., 1991; prof. Nat. War Coll., Washington, 1991-93; prof. polit. sci., head dept. Kans. State U., Manhattan, 1993-2000. Weekly contbr. Manhattan Mercury, 1993—. Author: East German Civil-Military Relations, 1973, Civil-Military Relations in Communist Systems, 1978, (with Robbin Laird) The Soviet Union and Strategic Arms, 1984, The Soviet High Command, 1964-1987, 1990, Russian Civil-Military Relations, 1996, Requiem for an Army: The Demise of the East German Military, 1998, Soldiers, Commissions and Chaplains: From Cromwell to the Present, 2001; guest editor: Studies in Comparative Communism, 1978; mem. editl. bd. Communist and Post Communist Studies, 1995—; contbr. over 60 articles to profl. jours. Capt. USNR, 1967-2000. Fulbright fellow, 1969-71, Woodrow Wilson fellow, 1985-92, Inst. of Peace fellow, 1991-92. Republican. Roman Catholic. Home: 3912 Barbara Ln Manhattan KS 66503-7573 Office: Kans State U Dept Polit Sci Waters Hall Manhattan KS 66506 E-mail: falka@ksu.edu.

HERSTAM, CHRIS, academic administrator; B, M, Ariz. State U. Mem., majority whip Ariz. Ho. Reps., Phoenix, 1983—90; head govtl. rels. practice Lewis and Roca, Phoenix; mem. Ariz. Bd. Regents, 1998—, treas. Active Phoenix C. of C., Ariz. Town Hall, Ctrl. Ariz. Shelter Svcs. Mem.: Ariz. State U. Alumni Assn. Office: Ariz Bd Regents Ste 230 2020 N Central Ave Phoenix AZ 85004

HERSTAND, JO ELLEN, librarian; b. Iowa City, Sept. 14, 1937; d. Arnold Simpson and Josephine (Jay) Gillette; m. Theodore Herstand, Aug. 23, 1957; children: Sarah Ellen, Michael Simpson. BA, U. Minn., 1970; MLS, Case Western Res. U., 1975; MSE in counseling, Okla. City U., 1994. Reference libr. Shaker Heights (Ohio) Pub. Libr., 1973-75, head reference libr., 1975-77; libr. U. Okla., Norman, 1978-80; pub. svc. libr. Met. Libr. System, Oklahoma City, 1977-78, chief materials selection, 1980—94. Bd. dirs. Temple B'Nai Israel, 2003—. Mem. ALA, Okla. Library Assn., Beta Phi Mu., Norman Area Quilters' Guild and Art Quilt Guild. Avocations: reading, gardening, weightlifting, jazz music, quilting. Home: 4418 Manchester Ct Norman OK 73072-3915 Personal E-mail: joherstand@hotmail.com.

HERSTAND, THEODORE, retired theatre artist, retired educator; b. N.Y.C., May 14, 1930; s. Max Arthur and Rose (Shyatt) H.; m. Jo Ellen Gillette, Aug. 23, 1957; children: Sarah Ellen, Michael Simpson. Cert. Advanced Studies, U. Birmingham (Eng.), 1951; BA, U. Iowa, 1953, MA, 1957; PhD, U. Ill., 1963. Instr. theatre Parsons Coll., Fairfield, Iowa, 1953-54, Eastern Ill. U., Charleston, 1957-59; asst. prof. SUNY, Plattsburgh, 1960-64, asso. prof., 1963-64; asst. prof. U. Ill., 1964-66; asso. prof. U. Minn., Mpls., 1966-70; prof., chmn. dept. theatre, drama and dance Case Western Res. U., Cleve., 1970-77, chmn. faculty senate, 1975-76; dir. Sch. Drama, U. Okla., Norman, 1977-79, prof., 1979-92; prof. emeritus U. Okla., Norman, 1992—; artistic dir., actor Okla. Profl. Theatre, 1978; ret., 1992. Vis. prof. Mpls. Coll. Art and Design, 1969; vis. dir. Colo. Shakespeare Festival, Boulder, 1968, 82; theatre bldg. cons. Eastern Ill. U., Charleston, Ill. State U., Bloomington, Jewish Community Center Theater, Mpls.; ednl. cons. in arts; spl. contbr. Silver Burdett Music Series. Profl. actor, dir. over 70 plays; author: (plays) Sugar and Lemon, 1968; new version Oedipus, 1978, Dov, 1982, The Emigration of Adam Kurtzik, 1985, 89, It Should Be So, 1989, The Minor Matter of Cynthia Smith, 1990, Bittersweet, 1996, It Should Be, 2003; assoc. editor: Drama Survey, 1967-70; contbr. revs., articles to profl. jours.; founder Klein Nat. Playwriting award, 1974, Bliss Nat. Playwriting award, 1980. Bd. dirs. Theater-in-the-Round, Mpls., 1968, v.p., 1969; bd. dirs. Gt. Lakes Shakespeare Festival, 1970-71, Okla. Arts Inst., mem. theatre panel, 1991-2003, chair 1994-2003; chmn. bd. dirs. Okla. Hillel Found., 1981-82; trustee Karamu House, 1975-77, Temple B'nai Israel, Oklahoma City, 1989-92, 1999-2002; chmn. new plays program S.W. Theatre Assn., 1985-89; bd. dirs. Okla. Israel Exch., 2003—, v.p., 2004—. Fellow, Coll. Fellows of Am. Theatre, 2004—. Mem.: Jewish Theatre Assn., Nat. Theatre Conf., Dramatists Guild, Omicron Delta Kappa. Home: 4418 Manchester Ct Norman OK 73072-3915 Personal E-mail: herstand@att.net.

HERSTEIN, CARL WILLIAM, lawyer; b. Plainfield, N.J., Jan. 8, 1953; s. Robert L. and Marie (Burke) H.; m. Charlene Ruth Mosher, Aug. 16, 1975; children: Janette, Matthew, Diana, Jennifer. BA in Polit. Sci. with high distinction, highest honors, U. Mich., 1973; JD, Yale U., 1976. Bar: Mich. 1976. Congl. intern to Congressman Clarence Long Washington, 1972; acting divsnl. paymaster Parts Divsn. GM, Flint, Mich., 1973; law clk. Benton Hicks Beltz Behm & Nikola, Flint, 1974; ptnr. Honigman Miller Schwartz and Cohn LLP, Detroit, 1976—. Mem. fin. instns. adv. bd. U. Detroit-Mercy, 1985-95. Editor Yale Law Jour., 1975-76. Trustee John and Marnee Divine Found., Detroit, 1985—90; active in Detroit Zool. Soc., Ann Arbor Hands-on Mus., Detroit Art Inst., Nat. Trust Hist. Preservation; treas. Cath. Soc. Svcs. of Washtenaw County, Mich., 1990—92, chair, 1992—93; bd. dirs. St. Francis Parish, Ann Arbor, 1985—91, edn, commn, rep, 1990—91. Recipient William Jennings Bryan prize, 1973; James B. Angell scholar, 1973. Fellow Mich. State Bar Found.; mem. ABA (real property and trust law sect.), State Bar Mich., Cath. Lawyers Guild, Shehyan Superior Ct. Hist. Soc., U. Mich. Pres. Club, U. Mich. Victors Club, U. Mich. Alumni Assn., Yale U. Alumni Assn., KC, Otsego Ski Club, Ann Arbor Golf & Outing Country Club, Huron Valley Swim Club, Phi Beta Kappa. Republican. Roman Catholic. Avocations: reading, skiing, golf, travel, drawing. Office: Honigman Miller Schwartz & Cohn LLP 2290 1st National Bldg 660 Woodward Detroit MI 48226

HERTEL, SUZANNE MARIE, musician, retired training and development specialist; b. Hastings, Neb., Aug. 8, 1937; d. Louis C. Hertel and W. Lenore (Cross) Budd. BA, Doane Coll., Crete, Nebr., 1959; MSM, Union Theol. Sem., 1961; postgrad., U. Hartford, 1966, U. Conn., 1975; MA, Merrill Palmer Inst., 1977; EdD, Boston U., 1982. Tchr. music Pub. Sch., Wethersfield, Conn., 1962—63; libr. serials Hartford Sem. Found., 1963—64; tchr. elem. Pub. Sch., Glastonbury, Conn., 1965—79; asst. prof. U. No. Iowa, Cedar Falls, 1979—81; tng. mgr. Focus Rsch. Sys. Inc., W. Hartford, Conn., 1982—89; pers. adminstr. City of Hartford, 1989—99; cons., 1999—2002. Mem. leadership educators program John F. Kennedy Sch. Govt., Harvard U., 1999; mem. Human Resource Mgmt. Del., Russia and Estonia, 1992, Initiative Edn., Sci. and Tech., South Africa, 1995. Recipient Maria Miller Stewart award, 1992. Mem.: Am. Guild Organists. Democrat. Personal E-mail: smher82@aol.com.

HERTEL, WILLIAM JOHN, music educator; b. Chgo., Jan. 31, 1946; s. John Joseph and Caroline Theresa (Schmidt) Hertel; m. Janet Sue Hudson, June 14, 1969; 1 child, John William. B in Music Edn., Ill. Wesleyan U., 1968; M in Music Edn., Ill. State U., 1974; M in Edn. Adminstrn., No. Ill. U., 1985. Cert. music tchr. grades K-12 Ill., adminstrn. grades K-12 Ill. Band dir., fine arts chair El Paso (Ill.) Cmty. Unit Dist. #375, 1968—73; band dir., music coord. Sterling (Ill.) Cmty. Unit Dist. #5, 1973—96; band dir. Mattoon (Ill.) Cmty. Unit Dist. #2, 1996—2001; instr., cons. Kidder Music Svc., Inc., Sterling, 2001—. Founder, chmn. Sterling Festival of the Arts, 1974—96; cons. Ill. State Bd. Edn., 1975—80; state chmn. Am. Guild English Handbell Ringers, Ill., 1980—83; guest lectr. in field; guest condr., adjudicator, Ill. Named Educator of the Month, WAND-TV, Decatur, Ill., 2000; recipient Those Who Excel award, Ill. State Bd. Edn., 1994. Mem.: Ill. Music Educators Assn., Music Educators Nat. Conf. Lutheran. Avocations: church musician, bicycling, photography. Home: 1666 Hill Dr Dixon IL 61021

HERTELENDY, PAUL, critic, writer, poet; b. Budapest, Hungary, June 10, 1932; arrived in U.S., 1940; s. Andor and Elizabeth (Hitt) Hertelendy; children: Glen, Ann, Ralph. BSE, Princeton (N.J.) U., 1953; MSE, Stanford (Calif.) U., 1957; PhD, U.Calif., Berkeley, 1965. Rsch. engr. Nat. Bur. of Standards, Washington, 1958—64; music and dance critic Oakland (Calif.) Tribune, 1964—79, San Jose (Calif.) Mercury News, 1979—99; webmaster, CEO artssf.com, Berkeley, Calif., 1999—; poet laureate Smithsonian Instn. Nat. Bd., Washington, 2000—. Nat. bd. mem. Smithsonian Instn., Washington, 1995—2001; chair of adv. coun. Lawrence Hall of Sci., Berkeley, Calif., 1999—2003; mem., bd. dirs. SAM Tech., San Francisco, 1997—; bd. mem.; bd. chair Chinese Culture Ctr., San Francisco, 1980—93. Author: (books of poetry) The Very Slender Volume, 1999, Vietnam, Venice, Varied Vales, 2000, Poetrose in the 'Oughties, 2001, Glaciers and Butterflies, 2002, Too good to Last, 2004; contbr. articles to Performing Arts, Dance Mags, Contra Costa Times, others. Trustee Coll. Prep. Sch., Oakland, 2001—03. Ensign US Coast and Geod. Survey, 1953—56, Washington, DC. Mem.: U. of Calif. (Berkeley) Alumni Assn. (life). Roman Catholic. Avocations: hiking, tennis, travel, language study, soccer refereeing. Office: artssf.com Box 1290 Berkeley CA 94701 Office Phone: 510-652-9482.

HERTNEKY, RANDY LEE, optometrist; b. Burlington, Colo., Jan. 9, 1955; s. Harry Francis and Darleen Mae (Walters) H.; m. Laura Ann Ciaccio, Nov. 28, 1981; children: Lisa Kay, Erin Elizabeth. BA, U. Colo., 1977; OD, So. Calif. Coll. Optometry, Fullerton, 1981. Pvt. practice optometry, Yuma and Wray, Colo., 1982—. Precinct committeeman Yuma County Rep. Com., 1986—; mem. bd. rev. Boy Scouts Am., Yuma, 1982—; chmn. bldg. com. Yuma H.S., 1987-89; bd. dirs. Yuma Hosp. Found., 1990-97, vice chmn., 1994-97; chmn. Yuma Sch. Curricculum Com., 1993. Mem. APHA, KC (sec. 1990-95, dep. grand knight 1995-96, grand knight 1996-98), Am. Optometric Assn. (coord. Colo. Polit. Action Com. 1995—, nominee Keyperson of Yr. 1999, 2000), Colo. Optometric Assn. (trustee 1989-90, vice chmn. legis. com. 1994—, nominee Optometrist of Yr. 1996, 2000, 01, named Optometrist of Yr., 2003), Coll. Optometrists in Vision Devel. (assoc.), Yuma C. of C. (Bus. of Yr. 1996), Wray C. of C., Lions (treas. 1987-88, pres. 1991-92, Lion of Yr. award 1992). Roman Catholic. Avocations: golf, coin collecting/numismatics, skiing. Office: 105 S Main St Yuma CO 80759-1913

HERTOG, ROGER, investment company executive; Grad., City Coll. of NY. Securities analyst Oppenheimer & Co.; exec. v.p. Sanford C. Bernstein & Co., Inc., 1973—93, pres., CEO, 1993—2000; vice chmn. Alliance Capital Mgmt. Corp. (merged with Bernstein), 2000—. Chmn. Manhattan Inst.; trustee Am. Enterprise Inst. Public Policy Rsch., Washington; mem. NY Society Security Analysts. Office: Alliance Capital 1345 Avenue of the Americas New York NY 10105

HERTWECK, ALMA LOUISE, sociology and child development educator; b. Moline, Ill., Feb. 6, 1937; d. Jacob Ray and Sylvia Ethel (Whitt) Street; m. E. Romayne Hertweck, Dec. 16, 1955; 1 child, William Scott. AA, Mira Costa Coll., 1969; BA in Sociology summa cum laude, U. Calif., San Diego, 1975, MA, 1977, PhD, 1982. Cert. sociology instr., multiple subjects tchg. credential grades k-12, Calif. Staff rsch. assoc. U. Calif., San Diego, 1978-81; instr. sociology Chapman Coll., Orange, Calif., 1982-87; instr. child devel. Mira Costa Coll., Oceanside, Calif., 1983-87, 88-89; instr. sociology U.S. Internat. U., San Diego, 1985-88; exec. dir., v.p. El Camino Preschools, Inc., Oceanside, 1985—2005. Author: Constructing the Truth and Consequences: Educators' Attributions of Perceived Failure in School, 1982; co-author: Handicapping the Handicapped, 1985. Mem. Am. Sociol. Assn., Am. Ednl. Rsch. Assn., Nat. Coun. Family Rels., Nat. ASsn. Edn. Young Children, Alpha Gamma Sigma. Avocations: foreign travel, sailing, bicycling. Home: 2024 Oceanview Rd Oceanside CA 92056-3104 Personal E-mail: ahertweck@cox.net.

HERTWECK, E. ROMAYNE, psychology professor; b. July 24, 1928; s. Garnett Perry and Nova Gladys (Chowning) H.; m. Alma Louise Street, Dec. 16, 1955; 1 child, William Scott. BA, Augustana Coll., 1962; MA, Pepperdine U., 1963; EdD, Ariz. State U., 1966; PhD, U.S. Internat. U., 1978. Cert. sch. psychologist, Calif. Night editor Rock Island (Ill.) Argus Newspaper, 1961; grad. asst. psychology dept. Pepperdine Coll., L.A., 1962; counselor VA Ariz. State U., Tempe, 1963; assoc. dir. Conciliation Ct., Phoenix, 1964; prof. Phoenix Coll., Phoenix, 1965, Mira Costa Coll., Oceanside, Calif., 1966—2003, ret., 2003. Mem. senate coun. Mira Costa Coll., 1968-70, 85-87, 89-91, chmn. psychology-counseling dept., 1973-75, chmn. dept. behavioral sci., 1976-82, 87-88, 90-91; part-time lectr. dept. bus. adminstrn. San Diego State U., 1980-84, Sch. Human Behavior U.S. Internat. U., 1984-89; prof. psychology Chapman Coll. Mem. World Campus Afloat, 1970; pres. El Camino Preschs., Inc., Oceanside, Calif., 1985—; CEO Nutri-Cal, Inc., Oceanside, Calif., 1996-2003. Bd. dirs. Lifeline, 1969, Christian Counseling Center, Oceanside, 1970-82; mem. City of Oceanside Childcare Task Force, 1991—1992; mem. City of Oceanside Community Rels. Commn., 1991-96, vice chair, 1994; mem. steering com. Healthy Cities Project City of Oceanside, Calif., 1993-95. Mem. Am. Western, North San Diego County (v.p. 1974-75) psychol. assns., Am. Assn. for Counseling and Devel., Nat. Educators Fellowship (v.p. El Camino chpt. 1976-77), Am. Coll. Personnel Assn., Phi Delta Kappa, Kappa Delta Pi, Psi Chi, Kiwanis (charter mem. Carlsbad club, dir. 1975-77). Home: 2024 Oceanview Rd Oceanside CA 92056-3104 Personal E-mail: rhertweck@cox.net.

HERTZ, ADAM ELLIOTT, director; b. Morristown, N.J., June 22, 1962; m. Laura Lennon Lennon, Nov. 2, 1991; children: Jacob, Rachel. BA, U. Redlands, 1985; MEd, Temple U. Head coach soccer and golf Arcadia U., Glenside, Pa., 1991—96; dir. athletics, men's soccer coach Alvernia Coll., Reading, Pa., 1996—2001; assoc. v.p., dir. phy. edn. and athletics Swarthmore (Pa.) Coll., Pa., 2001—. Chai, nat. soccer com. NCAA, Divsn. III. Mem.: NACDA (corr.). Home: 500 College Ave Swarthmore PA 19081 Office Phone: 610-328-8325. Personal E-mail: ahertz1@swarthmore.edu.

HERTZ, ARTHUR HERMAN, communications executive; b. Bklyn., Sept. 10, 1933; s. Edwin Carl and Blanche H.; Stephen R., Andrew P. BBA, U. Miami, Fla., 1955, postgrad., 1955-56. Acct. Aetna Mortgage Co., Miami, Fla., 1955, Wometco Enterprises, Inc., Miami, 1955-60, contr., v.p., 1960-64, sr. v.p., 1964-71, exec. v.p., treas., CFO, 1971-81, COO, 1981-84, chmn., CEO, 1985—; exec. v.p., COO WEI Enterprises Corp., Miami, 1984-85; exec. v.p. Wometco Broadcasting Co., Inc., Miami, 1984-85. Past pres. Orange Bowl Com.; past chair City of Miami Off St. Parking Authority; past chair Pub. Health Trust, Miami Dade County; chmn. audit com. bd. trustees U. Miami. Mem. AICPA, Fla. Inst. CPAs, Greater Miami C. of C. (gov. 1975-78), Iron Arrow, Phi Kappa Phi, Omicron Delta Kappa, Phi Eta Sigma. Home: 610 Fluvia Ave Coral Gables FL 33134-7016 Office: Wometco Enterprises Inc PO Box 141609 Coral Gables FL 33114-1609 Office Phone: 305-529-1403. Business E-Mail: Arth@wometcoent.com.

HERTZ, DANIEL LEROY, JR., entrepreneur; b. Montclair, N.J., Feb. 27, 1930; s. Daniel Leroy and Elizabeth Nielsen (Beet) H.; m. Valerie A. Smith, Mar. 15, 1956 (div. 1962); m. Isabel Waud Hurd, Apr. 18, 1970; children: Valerie H. Boyle, Suzanne E., Daniel L. III, Seana L. Burdge. Degree in mech. engring., Stevens Inst. Tech., 1952, MSME (hon.), 1982. Sales engr. C.E. Conover & Co., Fairfield, N.J., 1953-58; founder, pres. Seals Eastern, Red Bank, N.J., 1958—. Ex-officio. adv. bd. polymer tech. cons. Tex. A&M U., College Station, 1990-94, CHEMTECH, Washington, 1983-91, Elastomerics, Atlanta, 1984-92. Contbr. chpts. to Intermediate Rubber Technology, 1983, Handbook of Elastomers, 1988, 2d edit., 2000, Vanderbilt Handbook, 1990, 14th edit., 2000, Engineering with Rubber, 1992, 2d edit., 2000, Rubber Products Manufacturing Technology, 1993, Rubber Technology, 2001, Elastomer Technology- Special Topics, 2003; contbr. articles to profl. jours. Vis. com. mech. engring. dept. Stevens Inst. Tech., 1992-96; sec. Riverside Dr. Assn., Red Bank, 1980-85; mem. vestry, treas. All Saints Meml. Ch. Cpl. U.S. Army, 1950-51, Korea Mem. Am. Chem. Soc. (treas. rubber divsn. 1988-90, chmn. 1996, Disting. Svc. award 2000), N.Y. Rubber Group (chmn. 1983), Rumson Country Club, Nassau Club, Seabright Tennis Club. Republican. Episcopalian. Achievements include 5 U.S. patents. Home: 8 Hasler Ln Little Silver NJ 07739-1650 Office: 134 Pearl St Red Bank NJ 07701-1525 Office Phone: 732-747-9200. Business E-Mail: dhertz@sealseastern.com.

HERTZ, HARRY STEVEN, government official; b. N.Y.C., Feb. 25, 1947; s. Marcus and Alice (Oppenheimer) H.; m. Francine Turkowitz, June 21, 1969; children: Matthew Adam, Joshua Lee BS in Chemistry, Poly. Inst. Bklyn., 1967; PhD in Organic Chemistry, MIT, 1971. Alexander von Humboldt fellow U. Munich, Fed. Republic Germany, 1971-73; research chemist Nat. Bur. Standards (now Nat. Inst. Standards and Tech.), Gaithersburg, Md., 1973-78, chief organic analytical rsch. div., 1978-83; dir. Ctr. for

Analytical Chemistry Nat. Bur. Standards, Gaithersburg, Md., 1983-91, acting dir. Nat. Measurement Lab., 1989, dir Chem. Sci. and Tech. Lab., 1991-92, dep. dir. Office Quality Programs and Malcolm Baldrige Nat. Quality Award, 1992-96; dir. Baldrige Nat. Quality Program and Malcolm Baldrige Nat. Quality award, 1996—. Mem. health environ. research adv. com. Dept. Energy, Washington, 1984-89, good mfg. practices adv. com. FDA, 1988-90; mem. steering com. conf. bd. Global Ctr. Performance Excellence, 1996—2000; mem. nat. quality com. United Way Am., 1997—2000; mem. operating com. Juran Ctr. for Leadership in Quality. Co-editor: Trace Organic Analysis, 1979; mem. editorial adv. bd. Analytical Chemistry, 1984-86, Chem. and Engring. News, 1990-92; contbr. numerous articles to profl. jours. Recipient Bronze medal Dept. Commerce, 1981, Arthur S. Flemming award for Outstanding Fed. Service, 1985, Silver medal Dept. Commerce, 1986, Gold medal Dept. Commerce, 1998. Fellow AAAS, mem. Am. Soc. for Mass Spectroscopy (sec. 1983-85), Am. Chem. Soc., Nat. Com. for Clin. Lab. Standards (pres. 1986-88), Sigma Xi. Avocations: racquetball, hiking. Office: Nat Inst Standard & Tech A600 Adminstrn Bldg Gaithersburg MD 20899-1020 Business E-Mail: harry.hertz@nist.gov.

HERTZ, KENNETH THEODORE, healthcare executive; b. Jackson Heights, NY, Aug. 19, 1951; s. Irwin R. and Dorothy S. H.; m. Debra Pitre, July 12, 1997. BA in Spl. Studies, SUNY, Fredonia, 1974; cert. med. and dental practice mgmt., Loyola U., 1992. Cert. med. practice exec. Gen. mgr. Cape Cod Symphony, West Barnstable, Mass., 1974-75; mng. dir. Tulsa Philharm., 1975-78; pres., gen. mgr. Atlanta Ballet, 1979-89; instr. continuing edn. Oglethorpe U.; dir. Atlanta Great Artists Series, 1989-90, Atlanta Arts Devel. Svcs., 1989-90; exec. dir. New Orleans Symphony, 1990-91; adminstr. M.D. Care, Inc., New Orleans, 1991-95; dir. acquisitions and network devel. Tenet Healthcare, New Orleans, 1995-96, area mgr. practice ops., 1996-97; adminstr. MacArthur Surg. Clinic, Alexandria, La., 1977—2002, KTH Cons. LLC, 2003—, MGMA Health Care Cons. Group, 2005—. Mem. dance panel City of Atlanta, 1983-89, Ga. Coun. for Arts, 1984-88, NEA, 1985-87; dir. Dance/USA, 1985-89; mem. adv. bd. cert. program in med./dental practice mgmt. Loyola U., 1993—; mem. Pres.'s Adv. Coun., De La Salle H.S., 1993-2000. Chmn. Atlanta C. of C. Cultural Programming Task Force, 1987—89, Atlanta C. of C. "Arts Alive", art celebration, 1986, Ga. Profl. Arts Caucus, 1983—85; bd. dirs. Big Bros./Big Sisters, 1988—89, Arts Festival Atlanta, BVA, 1986—90, Bus. Vols. for Arts, New Orleans Ballet Assn., 1996—98, Rapides Symphony Orch., 1998—2000, Ballet Alexandria, 2000—, Am. Jewish Com., Atlanta, 1967. Mem. Midtown Bus. Assn. (dir. 1984-89), Ga. Citizens for Arts, Am. Symphony Orch. League, La. Med. Group Mgmt. Assn. (bd. dirs. 2001—, sec. 2003—, v.p., 2004-05), Ctrl. La. Med. Group Mgmt. Assn. (v.p. 2001-02, pres. 2002—), Alpha Phi Omega

HERTZ, LEON, publishing executive; b. Perth, Australia, Aug. 1, 1938; came to US, 1975; s. A. and Rose (Traub) H.; m. Linda Paula Cooper, June 1, 1980; 1 child, Monique. Student, U. Western Australia, Perth. Dir. Mirror Newspapers News Ltd., Sydney, Australia, 1967-75; gen. mgr., dir. Australian Nationwide News, Sydney, Australia, 1969-75; v.p., gen. mgr. Express News Corp. Am., San Antonio, 1975-80; v.p., assoc. pub., gen. mgr. NY Post Am., NYC, 1980-86; gen. mgr., dir. News Internat., London, 1986-87; exec. v.p. charge global mktg. News Corp. Ltd., NYC, 1987; exec. v.p. News Am., NYC, 1987—. Bd. dirs. Media Council of Australia, Sydney, 1970-75; chmn. Australian Newspaper Council, Sydney, 1973-75. Mem. Am.-Scandinavian Found., Am. Australian Assn. (dir.). Clubs: Cruising Yacht (Sydney); Friars (NYC), Metro. Club (NYC). Avocation: sailing. Home: 4 E 88th St New York NY 10128-0509 Office: News America Inc Ste 303 1211 Avenue Of The Americas New York NY 10036-8701 Office Phone: 212-852-7009. E-mail: lhertz@newscorp.com.

HERTZ, MICHAEL K., lawyer; b. Indpls. BS, Georgetown U., 1982; MA, U. Chgo., 1984; JD, Columbia U., 1988. Bar: NY 1989. Ptnr. (currently on indefinite leave of absence) Latham & Watkins LLP, NY, 1988—98; co-founder, exec. dir. and pres. Probono.net, 1998—. Bd. dir. NPower. Office: Pro Bono Net 151 West 30th St 10th Floor New York NY 10001 Office Phone: 212-760-2554 x479. Business E-Mail: mhertz@probono.net.

HERTZBERG, ARTHUR, rabbi, educator; b. Lubaczow, Poland, June 9, 1921; s. Zvi Elimelech and Nehamah (Alstadt) H.; m. Phyllis Cannon, Mar. 19, 1950; children: Linda, Susan. AB, Johns Hopkins U., 1940; MHL, Jewish Theol. Sem., 1943; PhD, Columbia U., 1966; DD, Lafayette Coll., 1970; DHL (hon.), Balt. Hebrew Coll., 1974, Jewish Theol. Sem., 1987, Balt. Hebrew U., 1997, Boston Hebrew Coll., 1999, Hebrew Union Coll., Cin., 2000, CUNY Grad. Ctr., 2001, Johns Hopkins U., 2005. Rabbi, 1943; Hillel dir. Mass. State and Smith Coll., 1943-44; rabbi Congregation Ahavath Israel of Oak Lane, Phila., 1944-47, West End Synagogue, Nashville, 1947-56, Temple Emanu El, Englewood, N.J., 1956-85, rabbi emeritus, 1985—; prof. religion Dartmouth Coll., 1985-91, prof. emeritus, 1991—. Lectr. Columbia U., 1961-68, adj. prof. history, 1968-90; vis. scholar Mideast Inst., 1991—; vis. assoc. prof. Jewish studies Rutgers U., 1966-68; lectr. religion Princeton U., 1968-69; vis. prof. history Hebrew U., Jerusalem, 1970-71; vis. prof. Ecole des Hautes Etudes, Paris, 1989; vis. scholar St. Antony's Coll., Oxford, 1989; pres. Conf. Jewish Social Studies, 1967-72; mem. exec. com. World Zionist Orgn., 1969-78, Jewish Agy. for Israel, 1969-71, bd. govs., 1971-78; pres. Am. Jewish Congress, 1972-78, Am. Jewish Policy Found., 1978—; v.p. World Jewish Congress, 1975-91, co-chmn. adv. coun., 1991—; vis. prof. humanities NYU, 1991—. Author: The Zionist Idea, 1959; (with Martin Marty and Joseph Moody) The Outbursts that Await Us, 1963, The French Enlightenment and the Jews, 1968, Being Jewish in America, 1979, The Jews in America: Four Centuries of an Uneasy Encounter, 1989, Jewish Polemics, 1992; (with Aron Hirt-Manheimer) Jews: The Essence and Character of a People, 1998, A Jew in America, 2002, The Fate of Zionism, 2003; editor: Judaism, 1961, 2d rev. edit., 1991; introduction author At Home Only With God, 1992; sr. editor: Ency. Judaica, 1972; contbr.: Ency. Britannica, 1975. Vice pres. bd. dirs. Meml. Found. for Jewish Culture, 1965-98. Served 1st lt., chaplain USAF, 1951-53. Recipient Amram award, 1967, award for Lifetime Achievement Present Tense, 1989, Jewish Cultural Achievement award Nat. Found., 2001, Book award N.J. Coun. for Humanities, 2003, Book award Jewish Book Coun., 2003; Inst. Advanced Studies fellow, Jerusalem, 1982 Jewish. Home: 83 Glenwood Rd Englewood NJ 07631-1909 Office: NYU 269 Mercer St Rm 203/203AA New York NY 10003-6687 *I cannot even imagine improving on Hillel's dictum, nearly 20 centuries ago; what is hateful to you, don't do to your fellow man.*

HERTZBERG, DAVID GORDON, retired lawyer; b. Detroit, Feb. 21, 1918; s. Harry Aaron and Sarah Silk Hertzberg; m. Millicent Brower, Aug. 28, 1942 (dec. Oct. 2000); children: Richard York, Jane Elyse Litin. BBA, U. Mich., 1939; LB, Harvard Law Sch., 1942, JD (hon.), 1969. Bar: Mich. 1946, U.S. Supreme Ct. 1958. Estate tax agt. U.S. IRS, Detroit, 1946; tax atty. Hertzberg & Noveck, Detroit, 1947—88; ret., 1989. Trustee, v.p. Sigmund and Sophie Rohlik Found., Southfield, Mich., 1990—2005. Sr. lt. USN, 1942—46. Mem.: Masons (32 degree), Phi Beta Kappa. Avocations: sailing, skiing, running. Home: 22855 Shagbark Beverly Hills MI 48025-4771

HERTZBERG, HENRY, retired radiologist; b. Bklyn., Oct. 21, 1933; s. Louis and Bessie (Eisman) H.; m. Dori Balter, June 10, 1962; children: Richard, Lisa. BS, CCNY, 1955; MD, SUNY, Bklyn., 1959. Diplomate Am. Bd. Radiology. Intern Kings County Med. Ctr., Bklyn., 1959-60; resident Roosevelt Hosp., N.Y.C., 1960-63; dir. radiology Fort Gordon (Ga.) Army Hosp., 1963-65; pvt. practice Green Brook, N.J.; assoc. dir. dept. radiology Somerset Med. Ctr., Somerville, N.J., 1975-85; dir. dept. radiology Muhlenberg Med. Ctr., Plainfield, NJ, 1985-92, attending radiologist, 1992—2002. Clin. asst. prof. radiology Rutgers U. Med. Ctr., 1985—. Capt. M.C., U.S. Army, 1963-65. Mem. AMA. Avocation: travel. Home: 182 Deer Run Watchung NJ 07069-6222 Office: Assoc Radiologists PA 239 Us Highway 22 Green Brook NJ 08812-1916

HERTZEL, DOROTHY, librarian; b. Cleve., Aug. 5, 1915; d. Walter and Helen (Metz) Hoffstetter; m. Franklin William Hertzel, July 22, 1944 (dec. May 1987); children: Franklin Dale, Brian James. BS, Baldwin-Wallace Coll., 1938; MLS, Case Western Res. U., 1965, DPhil, 1985. Tchr. math. Garfield Heights High Sch., 1939-49; asst. children's libr. Cuyahoga County Pub. Libr., Parma, Ohio, 1960-64, children's libr., 1964-65, Brooklyn, Ohio, 1965-66, libr. mgr., 1966-79. Founder Friends of Bklyn. Br. Cuyahoga County Pub. Libr., 1973—, trustee; vol. Brooklyn Sr. Ctr., 1979—; mem. Bklyn. City Sch. Vol. Tutor com., 1980-88; mem. Bklyn. City Sch. Bd. Edn., 1990-93, v.p., 1992, pres., 1993; mem. Brooklyn City Sch. Fin. com., 1993-97, Cmty. Edn. Adv. Com., 1987-90. Mem. Ohio Libr. Coun., Brooklyn Hist. Soc. (co-founder 1970, v.p. 1970-73, corr. sec. 1973-78), Soc. Ohio Archivists, Mid-Atlantic Regional Archives Conf., Greater Cleve. Genealogical Soc., Ohio Hist. Soc., Cleve. Archival Roundtable, Brooklyn Genealogical Soc. (founder 1996, pres.1996-2001, program chair 2003).

HERTZIG, MARGARET E., psychiatrist; b. N.Y.C., Feb. 9, 1935; d. Morris and Grace Koenig Hertzig; m. Herbert George Birch, Dec. 11, 1961 (dec. Feb. 5, 1973); children: Sarah Ellen Birch, Martin Lawrence Birch. AB, Vassar Coll., 1956; MD, NYU, 1960. Diplomate psychiatry Am. Bd. Psychiatry and Neurology, 1968, child psychiatry Am. Bd. Psychiatry and Neurology, 1977. Rotating intern Jewish Hosp. Bklyn., 1960—61, pediat. resident, 1961—62; psychiatric resident Bellevue Psychiat. Hosp., 1962—64; rsch. fellow NYU Sch. Medicine, 1964—66; assoc. prof. psychiatry Cornell U. Med. Coll., N.Y.C., 1977—95; assoc. attending psychiatrist N.Y. Hosp.-Cornell Med. Ctr., N.Y.C., 1977—95; dir. child and adolescent outpatient dept. Payne Whitney Clinic-N.Y. Presbyn. Hosp., N.Y.C., 1977—; prof. psychiatry Weill Med. Coll. Cornell U., N.Y.C., 1995—, interim vice-chair child and adolescent psychiatry, 2002—; attending psychiatrist N.Y. Presbyn. Hosp., Weill Cornell Med. Ctr., N.Y.C., 1995—. Cons. Spl. Citizens Inc., N.Y.C., 1980—. Fellow, NYU Sch. Medicine, 1964—66. Fellow: Am. Acad. Child and Adolescent Psychiatry. Office: Weill Med Coll Cornell Univ 525 East 68th St New York NY 10021 Office Phone: 212-746-5712. Business E-Mail: mehertzi@med.cornell.edu.

HERWITZ, DAVID RICHARD, law educator; b. Lynn, Mass., Dec. 8, 1925; s. Harry M. and Sarah (Shapiro) Herwitz; m. Carla B. Cowett, Jan. 22, 1960; children: Andrew B., Juliet F. Student U. Wis., 1942-43; SB, MIT, 1946; LLB magna cum laude, Harvard U., 1949. Bar: Mass 1949. Atty US Tax Ct., 1949-50; pvt. practice, Boston, 1951-54; teaching fellow Harvard Law Sch., 1950-51, asst. prof. law, 1954-57, prof. law, 1957—, Austin Wakeman Scott prof. law, 1980-2003, Royall prof. law, 2003-, dir. program of instrn. for lawyers, 1984-; faculty supr. Harvard-Brandeis coop. research for Israel's legal devel., 1957-59; lectr. Northeastern Sch. Law, 1951-54. Cons., US Treasury Dept., 1961-64. Author: Business Planning: Materials on the Planning of Corporate Transactions, 1984; co-author: Accounting for Lawyers, 1997, Materials on Accounting for Lawyers, 2001. Office: Harvard Law Sch 1563 Massachusetts Ave Cambridge MA 02138 Office Phone: 617-495-3121. Office Fax: 617-495-1082. Business E-Mail: herwitz@law.harvard.edu.*

HERZ, ANDREW LEE, lawyer; b. NYC, Nov. 12, 1946; s. John W. and Elise J. H.; children: Adam, Matthew, Daniel, Michael. BA, Columbia U., 1968, JD, 1971. Bar: N.Y. 1972. Assoc. Milbank, Tweed, Hadley & McCloy, N.Y.C., 1971-75, Nickerson, Kramer, Lowenstein, Nessen, Kamin & Soll, N.Y.C., 1975-76, Marshall, Bratter, Greene, Allison & Tucker, N.Y.C., 1977-80; gen. counsel N.Y. State Mortgage Loan Enforcement and Adminstrn. Corp., N.Y.C., 1980—81; ptnr. Richards & O'Neil, LLP, N.Y.C., 1981-2001, Bingham McCutchen LLP, N.Y.C., 2001—04, Patterson, Belknap, Webb & Tyler LLP, N.Y.C., 2004—. Lectr. Real Estate Inst., NYU, 1988-93; cons. N.Y. Real Property Svcs., 1987. Author: Office Lease Operating Expense Clauses-Definitional Problems, 1986, Renegotiating Commercial Leases, 1993, Liability Risks for Ducking Loan Commitments, 1995; co-author: Japanese Yen Financing of U.S. Real Estate, 1989, Real Estate Management Agreements, 1990, Subleases: The Same Thing as Leases, Only Different, 2000; contbr. articles to profl. jours. Chmn. zoning bd. appeals Village of Ossining, N.Y., 1980-88; bd. dirs. Planned Parenthood N.Y.C., 1987-94, AIDS Resource Ctr., 1991-94, Commercial Real Estate Law Advisor, Realcomm, 2001-02. Harlan Fiske Stone Scholar, 1971. Mem.: ABA (vice chmn. 1988—90, chair real estate mgmt. com. 1990—91, co-chair real estate asset mgmt. com. 1992—94, chair real estate asset mgmt. com. 1994—95, lending and financing subcom. 1997—99, comml. office leasing com. 1999—2001, co-chair comml. leasing com. 1999—2001, real property divsn.), Urban Land Inst. (dir.), Real Estate Bd. N.Y., Assn. Bar City N.Y., N.Y. State Bar Assn. (co-chmn. comml. leasing com. 1991—96, exec. com. 1991—96, editor N.Y. Real Property Jour. 1996—97, real property sect.), Am. Coll. Real Estate Lawyers (vice chair office leasing com. 1997—98, chair office leasing com. 1999—2001), Columbia Law Sch. Alumni Assn. (dir. 1999—2003). Democrat. Home: 6 Park Ave Larchmont NY 10538-3807 Office: Patterson Belknap Webb & Tyler LLP 1133 Ave of the Americas New York NY 10036 Office Phone: 212-336-2910. Business E-Mail: alherz@pbwt.com.

HERZ, ARNOLD D., lawyer; b. LI, Mar. 8, 1962; BA in Polit. Sci., U. Mich., 1984; JD, Fordham U., 1991. Bar: NY 1992, US Dist. Ct. (ea. and so. dists.) NY 1992. Assoc. Weil, Gotshal & Manges, LLP, N.Y.C., 1991—94, Leader & Berkon, LLP, N.Y.C., 1994—95, Kupfer, Rosen, N.Y.C., 1995; ptnr. Kupfer, Rosen & Herz, LLP, N.Y.C., 1996—2000; pvt. practice Port Washington, NY, 2000—. Mem. legal/bus. adv. bd. Prasad Project, N.Y.C., 2002—; mem. panel mediators U.S. Dist. Ct. (ea. dist.) and comml. divsn. Supreme Ctr State of N.Y., 2000—. Mem.: ABA, Fed. Bar Assn., N.Y. State Bar Assn. Office: 14 Vandervanter Ave Ste 255 Port Washington NY 11050 also: 40 Wall St 32d Fl New York NY 10005 Office Phone: 516-767-0800. Business E-Mail: arnie@arnieherz.com.

HERZ, MARVIN IRA, psychiatrist, researcher; b. N.Y.C., Dec. 24, 1927; s. Jules Edward and Vivian M. (Becker) Herz; m. Beatrice Leslie Mittelman, Sept. 13, 1952; 3 children. BA, U. Mich., 1949; MS in Psychology, Yale U., 1950; MD, Chgo. Med. Sch., 1955; cert. in Psychoanalysis, Columbia U., 1968. Diplomate Am. Bd. Psychiatry and Neurology (sr. examiner). Intern U. Ill. Rsch. and Ednl. Hosps., 1955-56; resident in psychiatry Michael Reese Hosp., Chgo., 1956-59; dir. inpatient svc. divsn. psychiatry Montefiore Hosp., N.Y.C., 1961-63; dir. Westchester Sq. Day Hosps., N.Y.C., 1963-65; asst. prof. psychiatry Albert Einstein Coll. Medicine, N.Y.C., 1963-65; assoc. in psychiatry Columbia U., 1965-68, asst. prof., 1968-72, assoc. prof., 1972-77; ward adminstr. Washington Heights Cmty. Svc., N.Y. State Psychiat. Inst., 1965-68, dir., 1968-72; asst. attending psychiatrist Vanderbilt Clinic, Presbyn. Hosp., N.Y.C., 1965-68; dir. cmty. svcs. N.Y. State Psychiat. Inst., 1972-77, acting clin. dir., 1975-76; med. dir. Ga. Mental Health Inst., Atlanta, 1977-78, dir. ops. rsch., 1977-78; prof. Emory U., 1977-78; prof., chmn. dept. psychiatry SUNY Sch. Medicine, Buffalo, 1978-91; dir. psychiatry Erie County Med. Ctr., Buffalo, 1978-91; head dept. psychiatry Buffalo Gen. Hosp., 1978-91; prof., dir. Mental Health Svcs. Rsch. U. Rochester, NY, 1991—2002, prof. emeritus, 2002; vol. prof. U. Miami, Fla., 2003; attending psychiatrist Jackson Meml. Hosp. Cons. Task Panel Pres.'s Commn. Rsch. Mental Illness, 1977, Robert Wood Johnson Found., 1992, Nat. Heart and Lung Inst.; cons. psychiatry VA Hosp., Buffalo, 1978—91; sr. sci. advisor to dir. NIMH, 1989—91; cons. psychiatry edn. br., 1978; chmn. psychiat. adv. com. N.Y. State Office Mental Health, 1980—87. Contbr. articles to med. jours. Served to lt. comdr. USNR, 1959—61. Recipient award for outcomes rsch., World Assn. Psychosocial Rehab., U.S. Br., 1994, Heinz Lehmann Rsch. award, N.Y. State Office Mental Health, 1994, award for svcs. rsch., 2002. Fellow: Am. Coll. Psychoanalysts (treas. 1991—95, v.p. 1996—97, pres. elect 1997—98, pres. 1998—99), Am. Coll. Psychiatrists (bd. regents 1990—93, 2d v.p. 1994—95, v.p. 1995—96, pres. elect 1996—97, pres. 1997—98, Dean award for Rsch. in Schizophrenia 1993), Am. Psychiat. Assn. (chmn. com. to develop practice guidelines schizophrenia 1992—97, chair rsch. prize com. 1996—2000, disting. life, prize in hosp. psychiatry rsch. 1988, Alexander Gralnick award for Rsch. in Schizophrenia 2003); mem.: Am. Psychoanalytic Assn., Assn. Psychoanalytic Medicine (chmn. com. comm. psychiatry 1975—76), Assn. Clin. Psychosocial Rsch. (pres. 1993—95), Alpha Omega Alpha. Address: 10175 Collins Ave Apt 402 Bal Harbour FL 33154 Office: Dominion Towers 1400 NW 10th Ave Ste 704M Miami FL 33136 Office Phone: 305-243-2000. Personal E-mail: marvles@aol.com. Business E-Mail: mherz@med.miami.edu.

HERZ, WERNER, chemist, educator; b. Stuttgart, Germany, Feb. 12, 1921; came to U.S., 1937, naturalized, 1944; s. Alfred and Hedwig (Loewenstein) H.; m. Marcia Lucile King, Feb. 22, 1945; children— Michael John, Patrick Werner, Monica Lucile, Andrea Lauren. BA, U. Colo., 1943, MA, 1945, PhD, 1947. Instr. math. U. Colo., 1946-47; Am. Cyanamid fellow U. Ill., 1947-49; with Fla. State U., Tallahassee, 1949—, prof. chemistry, 1959—, Robert O. Lawton disting. prof., 1987—; mem. chemistry panel Cancer Chemotherapy Nat. Service Center, 1959-62, NSF, 1961-64; cons. Nat. Cancer Inst., 1962-65; mem. cancer chemotherapy study sect. NIH, 1962-66, mem. medicinal chemistry study sect., 1970-74. Author: The Shape of Molecules, 1963; editorial bd.: Jour. Organic Chemistry, 1962-63, sr. editor, 1963-89; editor: Fortschritte der Chemie Organischer Naturstoffe, 1969—; bd. editors: Planta Medica, 1978—, Phytochemistry, 1981—. Mem. Am. Chem. Soc. (councilor Fla. sect. 1960-79, adv. bd. Petroleum Research Fund 1970-72), Chem. Soc. London, Phi Beta Kappa, Sigma Xi, Sigma Pi Sigma, Alpha Chi Sigma, Pi Mu Epsilon, Phi Lambda Upsilon. Research and numerous publs. on isolation and structure determination of plant products with emphasis on possible applications to chemotaxonomy and cancer chemotherapy, structure synthesis and transformations of terpenoid substances; studies of molecular rearrangements in chemistry. Home: 314 Saratoga Dr Tallahassee FL 32312-2041 Office: Fla State U Dept Chemistry Tallahassee FL 32306-4390 Office Phone: 850-644-2774. E-mail: herz@chem.fsu.edu.

HERZBERG, PETER JAY, lawyer; b. Newark, Feb. 3, 1950; s. Arno and Annelle (Baruch) Herzberg; m. Lisa F. Chrystal, Mar. 13, 1982. BA, Haverford Coll., 1972; JD, U. Pa., 1975. Dep. atty. gen. N.J. Dept. Law and Pub. Safety, Trenton, 1975-78, 80, 82-83; staff atty. Sierra Club Legal Def. Fund, Washington, 1978-80; acting asst. counsel to gov. of N.J. Trenton, 1981; John F. Baker scholar, 1971; atty. Pitney Hardin, Morristown, NJ. Mem. Phi Beta Kappa. Office: Pitney Hardin PO Box 1945 Morristown NJ 07962-1945 Office Phone: 973-966-8058. Business E-Mail: pherzberg@pitneyhardin.com.

HERZBERG, THOMAS, artist, educator, illustrator; b. Chgo., Feb. 3, 1954; s. Carroll Alexander and Victoria Herzberg; m. Rosemary Ann Morrissey, Aug. 11, 1979; 1 child, Kyli Rose. BA, Northeastern U., 1975; MFA, No. Ill. U., 1979. Instr. Am. Acad. Art, Chgo., 2000—, chair dept. fine art, 2005—. Illustrations appeared in Chgo. mag., Advertising Age, Playboy mag., World Book, Chgo. Tribune, Washington Post, Art Inst. Chgo., Goodman Theatre, Chg. Exhibited Art Inst. Chgo., 1978, 84, De Cordova Mus., Lincoln., Mass., 1978, 79, 83, Silvermine Guild Artists, New Canaan, Conn., 1980, Met. Mus. and Art Ctr., Coral Gables, Fla., 1980, 82, Hunterdon Art Ctr., Clinton, N.J., 1982, U. Dallas, 1983, 10th, 12th and 13th Ann. Soc. Newpaper Design, Am. Soc. Illustrators 28th, 39th and 41st Ann. Exhbns.; represented in permanent collections USAF, De Cordova Mus., Terrance Gallery, Palenville, N.Y., Met. Mus. and Art Ctr., Silvermine Guild Artists, Carnegie Inst., Art Inst. Chgo., Lincoln Park Zoo, Chgo. Symphony Orch.; over 1900 illustrations in newspapers, mags., books, mus. graphics, 1981—. Mem. Air Force Art Program, 1998—. Named Best of Show 3 Ann. Ill. Regional Print Show, 1980; recipient Award of Excellence New Horizons in Art North Shore Art League, 1980-82, Weston Press and Gallery award 8th Internat. Miniature Print Exhbn. Pratt Graphic Ctr., 1981, Cert. of Design Excellence Print's Regional Design Ann., 1994-96, 97, also numerous awards Art Direction mag. creativity show, 1992-93, Soc. Newspaper Design, Cert. of Merit Soc. Illustrators. Office Phone: 312-461-0600.

HERZBERGER, EUGENE E., retired neurosurgeon; b. Sotchi, USSR, June 7, 1920; came to U.S., 1957, naturalized, 1964; s. Eugene S. and Mary P. H.; married; children— Henry, Monica MD, U. King Ferdinand I, Cluj, Rumania, 1947. Diplomate Am. Bd. Neurol. Surgery. Intern Univ. Hosp., Cluj, Rumania, 1946-47, resident in surgery, 1947-48; resident in neurosurgery Beilinson Hosp., Tel Aviv, 1949-53; chief neurosurgeon Tel Hashomer Govt. Hosp., Tel Aviv, 1953-57; research asst. Yale U., 1958-59; instr. neurosurgery Med. Coll. Ga., 1959-60; attending neurosurgeon St. Clare Hosp., Monroe, Wis., 1960-76, Mercy Hosp. and Finley Hosp., Dubuque, Iowa, 1976-94. Contbr. articles to med. jours. Mem. Am. Assn. Neurol. Surgeons, Iowa Midwest Neurosurg. Soc., Congress Neurol. Surgeons, Am. Acad. Neurology, Iowa State Med. Soc.

HERZECA, LOIS FRIEDMAN, lawyer; b. July 7, 1954; d. Martin and Elaine Shirley (Rapoport) Friedman; m. Christian S. Herzeca, Aug. 15, 1980; children: Jane Leslie, Nicholas Cameron. BA with honors, SUNY-Binghamton, 1976; JD cum laude, Boston U., 1979. Bar: NY 1980, US Dist. Ct. (so. dist.) NY 1980, US Dist. Ct. (ea. dist.) NY 1980. Atty. antitrust div. U.S. Dept. Justice, Washington, 1979-80; assoc. Fried, Frank, Harris, Shriver & Jacobson LLP, NY, 1980-86, ptnr., 1986—. Editor Am. Jour. Law & Medicine, 1978—79. Dir. Volunteers of Legal Svc., Children for Children Found. Mem.: Legal Aid Soc. (Cmty. Devel. Adv. Com.), Assn. Bar City NY, ABA. Office: Fried Frank Harris Shriver & Jacobson LLP 1 New York Plz Fl 22 New York NY 10004-1980 Office Phone: 212-859-8076. Office Fax: 212-859-4000. Business E-Mail: lois.herzeca@friedfrank.com.

HERZENBERG, ARVID, physicist, researcher; b. Vienna, Apr. 16, 1925; m. Marjorie Swift, Nov. 30, 1949; children: Catherine, Anne, Stephen. BS, U. Manchester, Eng., 1949, DSc, 1964. Mem. faculty U. Manchester, 1952-69; prof. applied physics Yale U., 1969—, emeritus prof. physics & applied physics, 1995—. Contbr. articles to profl. jours. Fellow Brit. Physics Soc., Am. Physics Soc. Achievements include research in geomagnetism, electron-molecule collisions, x-ray analysis of macromolecules. Home: 6 Legrand Rd North Haven CT 06473-1013 Business E-Mail: arvid.herzenberg@yale.edu.

HERZENBERG, CAROLINE STUART LITTLEJOHN, physicist; b. East Orange, N.J., Mar. 25, 1932; d. Charles Frederick and Caroline Dorothea (Schulze) Littlejohn; m. Leonardo Herzenberg, July 29, 1961; children: Karen Ann, Catherine Stuart. SB, MIT, 1953; SM, U. Chgo., 1955, PhD, 1958; DSc (hon.), SUNY, Plattsburgh, 1991. Asst. prof. Ill. Inst. Tech., Chgo., 1961-66, research physicist ITT Research Inst., 1967-70, sr. physicist, 1970-71; lectr. Calif. State U., Fresno, 1975-76; physicist Argonne (Ill.) Nat. Lab., Ill., 1977-2001. Prin. investigator NASA Apollo Returned Lunar Sample Analysis Program, 1967—71; disting. vis. prof. SUNY, Plattsburgh, 1991; mem. final selection com. Bower award and prize for Achievement in Sci., 1993—94, bd. adv.; mem. nat. panel advisors PBS TV Bill Nye the Sci. Guy, 1991—95; mem. steering com. Midwest Consortium Internat. Security Studies, 1994—95. Prodr., host (TV series) Camera on Science; author: Women Scientists from Antiquity to the Present: An Index, 1986; author: (with R. H. Howes) Their Day in the Sun: Women of the Manhattan Project, 1999; contbr. articles to profl. jours. Past chmn. NOW chpt., Freeport, Ill.; candidate for alderman Freeport, 1975. Finalist Am. Phys. Soc. Congl. Scientist Fellowship, 1976—77; recipient award in sci., Chgo. Women's Hall of Fame, 1989. Fellow: AAAS, Assnq. Women in Sci. (nat. sec. 1982—84, pres. 1988—90), Am. Phys. Soc. (past chmn. com., past sec.-treas. Forum Physics and Soc., chair elect, past exec. bd. Forum History Physics, mem. panel pub. affairs); mem.: Sigma Xi. Home and Office: 1700 E 56th St Apt 2707 Chicago IL 60637-5092 E-mail: carol@herzenberg.net.

HERZER, MARIAN DAY, not-for-profit developer, educator; b. Williston, N.D., July 1, 1933; d. Joseph Rollin and Catherine Elizabeth (Bissett) Day; m. Kaye H. Herzer, June 12, 1954; children: Scott Kaye, Kent Day, Brett Herbert. BS in Music, Drama, Business, U. N.D., 1955; AA in real estate, Whatcom Cmty. Coll., 1979. Cert. mgmt. tng. Spokane (Wash.) Leadership Inst., 1975, lic. real estate Wash., 1976, real estate instr. Wash., 1977. Program dir. YWCA, Grand Forks, ND, 1954—56; tchr. secondary edn. Montgomery, Ala., Schertz, Tex., Redondo Beach, Calif., 1957—67; exec. dir. Sinto Ctr., Project JOY, Spokane, Wash., 1969—75; realtor Arnasons & Century 21, Seattle and Bellingham, Wash., 1976—85; corp. sales mgr. Fairwood Village,

Spokane, 1985—87; devel. dir., vol. mgr. Hospice of North Idaho, Coeur d'Alene, Idaho, 1987—89; vol. mgr. Wash. County, Hillsboro, Oreg., 1989—95; retired, 1995. Pres. Prevention, Edn. and Devel., Spokane, 2000—03; sec. N.W. Regional Mental Health Bd., Bellingham, Wash., 1978—82, Whatcom County Bd. of Realtors, Bellingham, 1976—82; generalist com. Health Improvement Partnership, Spokane, 1997—99. Editor: Living, Loving, Letting Go, 2002; author: Six Scripts for Seniors, 1988. Sec. No. Va. Action Com., Washington, 1967; mem. So. Poverty Law Ctr., Montgomery, 1993—2002, Poor People's Campaign; bd. dirs. Citizens League, Spokane, 1997—2001. Recipient Disting. Svc. award, ACTION - Region X, 1993, Marian Herzer award, Spokane Parks & Recreation, 1985, Outstanding Vol. Mgr. award, Retirement and Sr. Vol. Program, 1998, Ethel Percy Andrus Award for Cmty. Svc., Wash. State, 2002, Spokane Woman of Achievement award for Cmty. Svc., 2002, Outstanding Vol. award, Retirement and Sr. Vol. Program, 2002, Outstanding Cmty. Svc. award, DAR, 2003, Outstanding Vol. award, 2003. Mem.: AARP, Sr. Svc. of Wash. Achievements include founder numerous civc orgns. Avocations: music, reading, travel, art collecting, writing. Home: 8230 No Pamela St Spokane WA 99208 Office: Prevention Education and Devel Inc 315 W Mission Ste 22 Spokane WA 99201 Office Phone: 509-326-1971. E-mail: dayher@msn.com.

HERZFELD, CHARLES MARIA, physicist, educator; b. Vienna, June 29, 1925; came to U.S., 1942, naturalized, 1949; s. August Alfred and Frieda Auguste (Poehlman) H.; children: Charles Christopher, Thomas Augustine, Paul Vincent; m. Shannon Stock Shuman, June 9, 1990. BS in Chem. Engring. cum laude, Cath. U. Am., 1945; PhD (Carnegie Found. fellow), U. Chgo., 1951. Lectr. chemistry Cath. U. Am., 1946; lectr. gen. sci. Coll. U. Chgo., 1946-47; lectr. physics DePaul U., Chgo., 1948-50; physicist Ballistic Research Lab., Aberdeen, Md., 1951-53, Naval Research Lab., Washington, 1953-55; lectr. physics U. Md., 1953-57, prof. physics, 1957-61; cons. chief heat and power div. Nat. Bur. Standards, 1955-56, acting asst. chief, 1956-57, chief heat div., 1957-61, asso. dir. bur., 1961; asst. dir. Advanced Research Project Agy., Dept. Def., 1961-63, dir. ballistic missile def., 1963; dep. dir. Advanced Research Projects Agy., 1963-65, dir., 1965-67; tech. dir. def. space group ITT, Nutley, N.J., 1967-74, tech. dir. aerospace-electronics-components-energy group, 1974-76, tech. dir. telecommunications and electronics group N.Am., 1978-79; v.p., dir. research ITT Corp., 1979-83, v.p., dir. research and tech., 1983-85; vice chmn. Aetna, Jacobs and Ramo, N.Y.C., 1985-90; dir. def. rsch. and engring. Dept. Def., Washington, 1990-91; cons. to Office Sci. and Tech. Policy, Exec. Office Pres. of U.S., Washington, 1991. Chmn. bd. Westronix Co., Midvale, Utah, 1985-88; mem. Def. Sci. bd., 1968-83, Def. Policy Bd., 1985-90, Nat. Commn. on Space, 1985-86; cons. in field; fellow Hudson Inst., 1970-90; mem. Brookings Inst. 5th Conf. for Career Execs. in Fed. Govt., 1958, mem. chief of Naval Ops. exec. panel, 1970-2000; mem. Tech. Review Bd. Hong Kong, 1993-94, Nat. Security Advisory Bd., Los Alamos Nat. Lab.; adj. fellow Ctr. Strategic and Internat. Studies, Washington, 1995—; mem. bd. regents, sr. fellow Potomac Inst. for Policy Studies. Editor: Temperature, Its Control in Science and Industry, vol. III, 1962; contbr. articles to profl. jours. Recipient Flemming award, 1963; Meritorious Civilian Service medal Dept. Def., 1967 Fellow AAAS, Am. Phys. Soc., Conf. on Sci., Philosophy and Religion, Coun. Fgn. Rels., Ctr. for Strategic and Internat. Studies (Washington); mem. Explorers Club, Inst. for Strategic Studies (London), Cath. Assn. Internat. Peace (pres. 1959-61), Cosmos Club (Washington).

HERZFELD, SIEGFRIED, manufacturing executive, consultant; arrived in U.S., 1938, naturalized, 1946; s. William and Irma (Rapp) Herzfeld; m. Bruna Leoni, June 16, 1960; children: William, Oliver, Doris. B in Engring., City U., N.Y., 1945; M in Engring., Polytech. Inst., 1948; postgrad., Columbia U., 1948—53. Design engr. Farrand Optical Co., N.Y.C., 1945—46; quality evaluation engr. Macy's Bur. Stds., N.Y.C., 1946—47; founder, pres. Internat. Machine Co., N.Y.C., 1947—89; dir. purchasing Stark Carpet Inc., N.Y.C., 1989—. Founder, pres. Internat. Rug Co., N.Y.C., 1947—89, Internat. Rare Book Co., N.Y.C., 1960—95; cons. Tech. Adv. Svc. for Attys., Blue Bell, Pa., 1990—. Editor: (book) The Setting Sun, 1985; author: Orden de Oraciones de Mes Arreo, 2002, How Even A Bungler Can Make A Million, 2004. Treas. West Side Block Assn., N.Y.C., 1997—. Mem.: Oriental Rug Inst., Verein der Diplom-Ingenieure, Soc. Bibliophiles. Avocations: calligraphy, Ju Jitsu, studies in philology, Italian and Hebrew incunabula.

HERZIG, DAVID JACOB, retired pharmaceutical company executive, consultant; b. Cleve., Dec. 13, 1936; s. Marvin Laurence and Lillian Gertrude (Blaine) H.; m. Phyllis Glicksberg, Sept. 2, 1962; children: Michael, Pamela, Roberta, Karen. BA, Oberlin Coll., 1958; PhD in Chemistry, U. Cin., 1963. Vis. scientist NIH, Bethesda, Md., 1963-65, staff fellow, 1965-67; sr. rsch. assoc. NYU Sch. Medicine, N.Y.C., 1967-68, Warner Lambert, Parke-Davis Co., Ann Arbor, Mich., 1968-77, dir. immunopharmacology, 1977-81, dir. sci. devel., 1981—91; v.p. drug devel. and sci. devel. Mich. Biotechnology Inst., 1991—99, acting v.p. bus. devel. genetics, 2005—, also bd. dirs. Bd. dirs. Metabasis, Inc. Contbr. articles to profl. jours. Bd. dirs. Mich. Ctr. High Tech., 1992-95. Fellow Damon Runyon Meml. Fund. Mem. Licensing Exec. Soc., Mich. Biotech. Assn. (bd. dirs. 1993-96, pres. 1994-96), N.Y. Acad. Scis., N.Y. Fencers Club (bd. dirs. 1970-77), Sigma Xi. Avocations: squash, fencing, furniture building. Home and Office: 3540 Windemere Dr Ann Arbor MI 48105-2842 Office Phone: 734-662-3411. E-mail: davidjhherzig@world.oberlin.edu.

HERZLICH, HAROLD J., chemical engineer; b. Bklyn. m. Carol Ast; children: Amy, Adam. BSChemE, NYU, 1956; student, So. Conn. Coll., Quinnipiac Coll. Mem. prodn. squadron Goodyear Tire & Rubber Co., Akron, Ohio, 1956-57, mem. process devel., 1957-58; prodn. compounder Armstrong Rubber Co., New Haven, 1958-61, sr. compounder, 1961-62, divsn. compounder, 1962-65, mgr. pass tire comp. devel., 1965-66, mgr. auto tire comp. devel., 1966-68, mgr. pass car tire comp. devel., 1968-70, sr. rsch. chemist, 1970-73, mgr. compound rsch., 1973-75, mgr. compound devel., 1975-85, dir. tire engring., legal matters and product reliability, 1985-88, Pirelli Armstrong Tire Co., New Haven, 1988-90; consulting tire engr. Tire Engring., Chemistry and Safety, Las Vegas, 1990—. Pres. Elasphalt Corp.; chmn. Internat. Tire Conf.; speaker in field. Tech. editor Rubber and Plastics News. With USCG. Mem. ASTM (mem. E-40), Am. Chem. Soc. (chmn. rubber divsn. 1982—, chmn.-elect 1981, mem. membership com., mem. edn. com., mem. budget and fin. com., treas. rubber divsn. 1978-81, bus. mgr. rubber chemistry and tech., mem. divsn. chemistry and law, hon. life), Soc. Automotive Engrs., Acad. Forensics Sci. (engring. divsn.), Tire Soc., Conn. Rubber Group (edn. chmn., vice chmn., chmn. 1966, hon. life). Avocations: sports, community service, travel. Home and Office: Tire Engring Chemistry & Safety 8908 Desert Mound Dr Las Vegas NV 89134-8801

HERZLINGER, REGINA, economist, educator, writer; d. Alexander and Ella Elbinger; m. George Herzlinger. BS, MIT; Doctorate, Harvard Bus. Sch. Economist, Washington; v.p. Various Cons. Firms, Cambridge; asst. sec. Gov. Commonwealth Mass.; prof. Harvard Bus. Sch., Boston, 1971—. Bd. dirs. 13 cos. Author: (books) Market-Driven Health Care, 2000, Consumer-Driven Health Care, 2004, 4 other books. Avocations: art, gardening, aerobics. Office: Harvard Bus Sch Soldier's Field Boston MA 02163 Business E-Mail: rherzlinger@hbs.edu.

HERZOG, ARTHUR, III, author; b. N.Y.C., Apr. 6, 1927; s. Arthur Jr. and Elizabeth Lindsay (Dayton) H.; 1 son by previous marriage, Matthew Lennox. Student, U. Ariz., 1945-46; BA, Stanford U., 1950; MA, Columbia U., 1956. Editor Fawcett Publs., 1957-59. Cons. Peace Corps, 1967-68; polit. cons., 1969-71; bd. dirs. Leslie Mandel Enterprises, Mandel Airplane Funding and Leasing Co. Author: (with others) Smoking and the Public Interest, 1963, The War-Peace Establishment, 1965, The Church Trap, 1968, McCarthy for President, 1969, The B.S. Factor, 1973, The Swarm, 1974, Earthsound, 1975, Orca, 1977, Heat, 1977, rev. edit., 1989, IQ 83, 1978, Make Us Happy, 1978, Glad to be Here, 1979, Aries Rising, 1981, The Craving, 1982, L.S.I.T.T., 1983, Vesco-From Wall Street to Castro's Cuba, The Rise, Fall and Exile of the King of White Collar Crime, 1987, Takeover, 1987 (formerly L.S.I.T.T.), The Woodchipper Murder, 1989, Seventeen Days: The Katie Beers Story, 1993, How to Write Almost Anything Better and Faster, 1995, Body Parts, 2001, Imortalon, 2003, The Village Buyers, 2003, Icetopia, 2004, The Town That Moved to Mexico, 2004, Murder in Our Town, 2005 (almost all works transl. and published in Hungary); contbr. articles profl. jours. Campaign mgr. Oreg., nat. pub. rels. dir. Eugene McCarthy Presdl. Campaign, 1968; founder New Democratic Coalition, N.Y. and nationally, 1968-69, Lexington Dem. Club, 1974. With USNR, 1944-45. Mem.: PEN, Authors League, Authors Guild, Pigeon Point Club Tobago. Address: PO Box 294 Wainscott NY 11975-0294 Office Phone: 212-879-3089. E-mail: artherzog@aol.com. *I do not believe that money and success should figure as strongly as it does in our estimate of what is a good life. Since it often does, though, I would point to perseverance as a major element of success. Another, mostly overlooked, is a lack of dogmatism and a belief in skepticism and personal happiness as ends in themselves.*

HERZOG, DAVID BRANDEIS, psychiatrist; b. Newark, Oct. 18, 1946; s. Harry William H.; m. Jennifer Mary Rathbun; children: Jonathan Rathbun, Matthew Alden. BA, Rutgers U., 1966; MD with highest honors, U. Mex., 1973. Intern in pediatrics U. Wis. hosp., Madison, 1973-74, resident in pediatrics, 1974-75; sr. resident in pediatrics Boston City Hosp., 1975-76; resident in child psychiatry Children's Hosp. Med. Ctr. & Judge Baker Guidance Ctr., Boston, 1976-78; chief resident psychosomatic unit Children's Hosp. Med. Ctr., 1977-78; resident in adult psychiatry Mass. Gen. Hosp., Boston, 1978-80, dir. psychosomatic outpatient clinic, 1980-81, chief consultation and liaison svc., 1980—2000, dir. eating disorders unit, 1981—. Pres. and founder Harvard Eating Disorders Ctr., 1994-, pres. Eating Disorders Coalition for Rsch. Policy and Action; prof. psychiatry, Harvard U., Boston, 1998—. Author 185 refereed articles, revs., chpts. and two books. Grantee, NIMH, 1987, 93. Fellow Am. Acad. Pediatrics, Am. Acad. Child and Adolescent Psychiatry, mem. AMA (Joseph B. Goldberger award 1994), Am. Psychiat. Assn. (Blanche F. Ittleson award 1992), New Eng. Coun. Child and Adolescent Psychiatry (bd. dirs. 1983-87). Office: Mass Gen Hosp 15 Parkman St Boston MA 02114-3117

HERZOG, DON, law educator, political science professor; AB, Cornell U.; AM, PhD, Harvard U. Prof. law and polit. sci. U. Mich., Ann Arbor, 1983—, Edson R. Sunderland Prof. Law. Author: Without Foundations: Justification in Political Theory; contbr. articles to law jours. Office: U Mich 410 Hutchins Hall 625 S State St Ann Arbor MI 48109-1215 Office Phone: 734-647-4047. Office Fax: 734-763-9375. E-mail: dherzog@umich.edu.

HERZOG, DOUG, broadcast executive; BS, Emerson Coll. Assoc. prodr. Turner Broadcasting Sys.; segment prodr. Entertainment Tonight; with MTV, 1984—98, news dir. music news, 1984, v.p. news and spl. programming, sr. v.p. programs and devel., exec. v.p. programming, pres. productions; with Comedy Central, 1995—98; pres. entertainment Fox Broadcasting, LA, 1998—2000; pres. USA Network, 2001—04, Comedy Central, LA, 2004—. Bd. dirs. Emerson Coll., Boston, Teach Am. LA Chpt. Exec. prodr.: (TV series) Remote Control, 1987. Office: Comedy Central 2049 Century Park E Ste 4170 Los Angeles CA 90067*

HERZOG, FRED F., law educator; b. Prague, Czech Republic, Sept. 21, 1907; s. David and Anna (Reich) H.; m. Betty Ruth Cohen, Mar. 27, 1947 (dec. Sept. 1984); children: Stephen E., David R. Dr. Juris, U. Graz (Austria), 1931; JD with high distinction U. Iowa, 1942; LLD (hon.), John Marshall Law Sch., 1983. Bar: Iowa 1942, Ill. 1946, U.S. Supreme Ct. 1965. Judge, Vienna, Austria, 1937-38; prof., dean Chgo.-Kent Coll. Law, 1947-73; spl. atty. Met. San. Dist. Greater Chgo., 1962-70; 1st asst. atty. gen. Ill., 1973-76; dean John Marshall Law Sch., Chgo., 1976-83, prof., 1976—. Recipient Americanism award DAR, 1978; Golden Doctor diploma U. Graz, 1981; award of Excellence, John Marshall Law Sch. Alumni Assn., 1981; cert. of appreciation Ill. Dept. Registration and Edn., 1978; Ill. Atty. Gen.'s award for Outstanding Pub. Service, 1976; Torch of Learning award Am. Friends of the Hebrew U., 1986; named to Sr. Citizens Hall of Fame, City of Chgo., 1983. Mem. ABA, Ill. Bar Assn., Chgo. Bar Assn., Ill. Appellate Lawyers Assn., Decalogue Soc. Lawyers, Mid-Am. Club, Internat. Club (Chgo.), Union League Club (Chgo.). Contbr. articles to profl. jours. Office: John Marshall Law Sch 315 S Plymouth Ct Chicago IL 60604-3969 Office Phone: 312-427-2437.

HERZOG, GODOFREDO MAX, physician; b. Chemnitz, Germany, Jan. 12, 1931; came to U.S., 1950; s. Heinrich and Louise (Gittler) H.; m. Eva r. Muller, Sept. 2, 1956; children: Jacques A., Patricia M., Elsa M. BS, La. State U., 1953; MD, Washington U., St. Louis, 1957. Diplomate Nat. Bd. Med. Examiners, Am. Bd. Ob-Gyn. Intern Jewish Hosp., St. Louis, 1957-58, Sch. Aerospace Medicine, San Antonio, 1960; resident in surgery Jewish Hosp., Cin., 1958-59, resident in ob-gyn. St. Louis, 1964-67; assoc. prof. ob-gyn. Washington U., St. Louis, 1967—; practice medicine specializing in ob-gyn. St. Louis, 1967—. Chmn. dept. ob-gyn. Christian Hosps. NE/NW, St. Louis; sr. med. cons. Premenstrual Program Ctr., St. Louis; gynecol. cons. med. laser program DePaul Hosp., St. Louis; cons. med. sys. optimization and clin. effectiveness, Sarasota, Fla., 2002—. Contbr. articles to profl. jours. Med. advisor, bd. dirs. Life Seekers, Planned Parenthood, Abortion Rights Alliance; mem. Hispanic Leadership Conf., St. Louis. Capt. USAF, 1959-64. Fellow Am. Coll. Ob-Gyn.; mem. AMA, St. Louis Met. Med. Soc., Pan Am. Med. Assn., Israel Med. Assn., Mo. Med. Assn., Mo. Gynecol. Soc., St. Louis Gynecol. Soc., Am. Soc. Gynecol. Laparascopists, Am. Soc. Reproductive Medicine, Am. Coll. Medicine Execs., Gynecol. Laser Soc., N.Y. Acad. Scis. Jewish. Home: 2425 Gulf Of Mexico Dr Unit 1E Longboat Key FL 34228-3211 E-mail: godoherzog@msn.com.

HERZOG, JOHN E., numismatist; b. N.Y.C., Mar. 18, 1936; s. Robert I. and Norma (Englander) H.; m. Diana E. Rigby; children: Mary, Sarah. BA, Cornell U., 1957; postgrad., N.Y. Inst. Fin., 1958; MBA, NYU, 1970. With Eastman Dillon (Paine Weber), Phila., 1957-59; chmn. Herzog, Heine, Geduld, N.Y.C., 1959—2002, R.M. Smythe & Co. Inc., 1996—. Charter mem. regulatory policy adv. com. N.Y. Stock Exch., 1981—, mem. regional firms adv. com. Bd. dirs. Resources for Children with Spl. Needs, N.Y.C.; trustee The Knox Sch., 1986-91, Randolph Macon Woman's Coll., Securities Industry Inst.; bd. regents L.I. Coll. Hosp., Bklyn.; founder, chair Mus. Am. Fin.; mem. adv. coun. Cornell Libr.; mem. bd. overseers NYU Stern Sch. Bus. Mem.: Smithsonian Instn. (nat. bd. dirs.), Securities Industry Assn. (chmn. N.Y. Area firms com., econ. edn. com. N.Y.dist.). Office: R M Smthye & Co Inc 2 Rector St New York NY 10006-1844 Office Phone: 212-312-6333.

HERZOG, PETER EMILIUS, retired legal educator; b. Vienna, Dec. 25, 1925; came to U.S., 1950, naturalized, 1955; s. Paul and Leopodine (Mannhart) H.; m. Brigitte Ecolivet, June 29, 1970; children: Paul, Elizabeth Ann. Student, U. Vienna, 1949-50; BA, Hobart Coll., 1952; LLB summa cum laude, Syracuse U., 1955; LLM, Columbia U., 1956. Bar: N.Y. 1957. Dep. asst. atty. gen. N.Y. State Dept. Law, Albany, 1955-57, asst. atty. gen., 1957-58; asst. prof. law Syracuse U. Coll. Law, 1958-62, assoc. prof., 1962-66, prof., 1966-83, Crandall Melvin prof., 1983-94, Crandall Melvin prof. emeritus, 1995—, law librarian, 1960-68; staff mem. Columbia U. Project on Inter Procedure, 1960-63; assoc. dir. Project on European Legal Instns., 1968-73; ret. Staff mem. UN Commn. on Internat. Trade Law, 1968-69; rsch. fellow Procedural Aspects Internat. Law Inst., 1968-71; lectr. Hague (Netherlands) Acad. Internat. Law, 1992; cons. N.Y. State Eminent Domain Commn., 1971; vis. prof. U. Paris, 1976-77, U. Dijon, France, 1987, U. Fribourg, Switzerland, 1987. Author: (with Martha Weser) Civil Procedure in France, 1967, (with Ivan Head and Frank Dawson) International Law, National Tribunals and the Rights of Aliens, 1971, (with Hans Smit) The Law of the European Economic Community, A Commentary, 1976, (with Schlesinger, Baade and Wise) Comparative Law, 6th edit., 1998; contbr. articles to legal publs. Jervey fellow Columbia U., 1956. Mem. Am. Soc. Internat. Law, Soc. de Législation Comparée, Internat. Law Assn., Internat. Acad. Comparative Law (assoc.), Order of Coif, Phi Beta Kappa. Roman Catholic. Home: 112 Erregger Rd Syracuse NY 13224-2220 Personal E-mail: 72560.1122@compuserve.com.

HERZSTEIN, BARBARA See HERSHEY, BARBARA

HERZSTEIN, ROBERT EDWIN, history educator, author; b. N.Y.C., Sept. 26, 1940; BA, NYU, 1961, MA, 1963, PhD, 1964. Asst. prof. Carnegie-Mellon U., Pitts., 1964-65, MIT, Cambridge, Mass., 1966-72; assoc. to prof. U. S.C., Columbia, 1972—, Carolina disting. prof., 1990—. Spl. aide to gov. Conn., Hartford. Author: Waldheim: The Missing Years, 1988, Roosevelt & Hitler: Prelude to War, 1980, Henry R. Luce: A Political Portrait, 1994, The War that Hitler Won, 1978, Henry R. Luce, Time, and the American Crusade in Asia, 2005. Advisor, witness Govt. Reform subcom. U.S. Ho. of Reps., 1994-98; co-organizer Conf. on the legacy of Nuremberg trials, Columbia, 1997. Recipient Founders Day award NYU, 1965, Russell award U. S.C., 1978, Signing pen by Pres. Clinton upon signing Nazi War Crimes Disclosure Act, 1998. Mem. German Studies Assn., WWII Studies Assn., Soc. for Historians of Am. Fgn. Rels. Jewish.

HERZSTEIN, ROBERT ERWIN, lawyer; b. Denver, Feb. 26, 1931; s. Sigmund Edwards and Estelle Ruth (Borwick) H.; m. Priscilla Holmes, July 11, 1956; children: Jessica Anne, Emily Holmes, Robert Holmes. AB, Harvard U., 1952, LLB, 1955. Bar: Colo. 1956, D.C. 1959, U.S. Supreme Ct. 1962. Sr. ptnr., other positions Arnold & Porter, Washington, 1958-80, sr. ptnr., 1981-89; undersec. for Internat. Trade U.S. Dept. Commerce, Washington, 1980-81; ptnr. Shearman & Sterling, Washington, 1989-95, counsel, 1995-99; mem. Miller & Chevalier, Washington, 1999—2004, of counsel, 2004—. Contbr. articles to profl. jours. Trustee Internat. Law Inst., Washington, 1974—; bd. dirs. Ptnrs. for Dem. Change, Appleseed Found., Washington, Coun. of Ams., NY, 1990—2004; bd. dirs., mem. faculty Salzburg Seminar in Am. Studies, 1986—93. Mem. ABA, Am. Soc. Internat. Law, Coun. on Fgn. Rels. Home: 4710 Woodway Ln NW Washington DC 20016-3241 Office: 655 15th St NW Ste 900 Washington DC 20005-5701 Office Phone: 202-626-5983. Business E-Mail: rherzstein@milchev.com.

HESCHEL, MICHAEL SHANE, retail food products executive; b. June 18, 1941; m. Judi Heschel; 2 children. BS in Indsl. Engring., Ohio State U., 1964, MBA, 1965, MS in Indsl. Engring., 1967; PhD in Indsl. Engring., Ariz. State U., 1970. Former sr. mgmt. systems analyst Boeing Aircraft Co.; former corp. mgr. ops. rsch. FMC Corp.; former corp. v.p. info. svcs. Am. Hosp. Supply Corp.; former corp. v.p. info. resources Baxter Internat. Inc.; former chmn., CEO Security Pacific Automation Co.; group v.p. info. systems The Kroger Co., Cin., 1991-94, sr. v.p., 1994-95, exec. v.p., chief info. officer, 1995—. Office: The Kroger Co 1014 Vine St Cincinnati OH 45202-1100 Office Phone: 513-762-4374.

HESER, CHERYL J., library director; b. Iowa City, Mar. 14, 1948; d. Eugene W. and Myrtle A. Elliott; m. Douglas C. Heser, June 8, 1974; children: Clinton D., Anne J. Heser Robinson, Joshua R. BA, Ea. Mont. Coll., 1970, tchg. cert., 1972; postgrad., Western Mont. Coll., 1995. Tchr. Rosebud (Mont.) Schs., 1986—91, tchr., sch. libr., 1993—98; advt. mgr. Ind. Enterprise, Forsyth, Mont., 1991—93; dir. Rosebud County Libr., Forsyth, 1997—. Author: Lewis & Clark Activity Book, 2003, Look to the Mountains: A Lewis & Clark Cantata with Narration, 2004, Living History Presenter: Tea with Dolly Madison, 2005. Judge speech and drama meets, Forsyth, 1997—; mem. Immaculate Conception Ch., Forsyth, 1986—. Mem.: Mountain Plains Libr. Assn., Mont. Libr. Assn. (dir. at large 1997—99, chair Lewis & Clark task force 1999—2003, Mountain Plains Libr. Assn. rep. 2000—03, Media award 2002). Roman Catholic. Avocations: writing, music, backpacking. Office: Rosebud County Libr 201 N Ninth Ave Forsyth MT 59327 Office Phone: 406-346-7561. Personal E-mail: relib@rangeweb.net.

HESHMAT, HOOSHANG, manufacturing executive; b. Tabriz, Iran, Aug. 20, 1950; BS, Pa. State U., 1977; MS, Rensselaer Poly. Inst., 1979, PhD in Mech. Engring., 1988. With Reliance Electric Co.; co-founder, pres., CEO, tech. dir. Mohawk Innovative Tech., Inc. Co-author: (chpt.) Compressor Handbook; contbr. over 146 articles to profl. jours.; Patentee in field. Recipient Tech. Creativity award Mech. Tech. Inc., 1990; Thomas A. Edison Patent award, 2002. Fellow Soc. Tribologists and Lubrication Engrs./ASME (chmn. internat. joint conf. 1994, vice chmn. rsch. com. tribology, tribology divsn. exec. com., Wilbur Deutsch Meml. award 1983, Burt L. Newkirk award 1985, Capt. Alfred E. Hunt award 1993, Creative Rsch. award 1995, Al Sonntag award 1996, Thomas A. Edison Patent award 2002, Frank P. Bussick award 2003). Office: Mohawk Innovative Tech Inc 1037 Watervliet Shaker Rd Albany NY 12205-2033

HESKETH, THOMAS A.E., lawyer, arbitrator, educator; b. Toronto, July 22, 1951; s. Thomas William Hesketh and Mary Patricia Bell Kindermann. BA, Claremont Men's Coll., 1975; JD, U. Calif., San Franciso, 1979. Bar: Calif. 1980, U.S. Supreme Ct. 1989. Tchr. Peace Corps, Morocco, 1973-76; atty. Law Offices of Daryl R. Hawkins, San Francisco, 1980-87, Dinkelspiel & Dinkelspiel, San Francisco, 1987-90; instr. legal rsch. and writing Hastings Coll. of the Law, U. Calif., San Francisco, 1985-88; atty., arbitrator Chickering & Gregory, San Francisco, 1990-94, Law Offices of Thomas A.E. Hesketh, San Francisco, 1995—; judge pro tem, arbitrator San Francisco Mcpl. Ct., 1988-99; settlement judge pro tem, arbitrator San Francisco Superior Ct., 1992—; arbitrator settlement judge pro tem Marin Superior Ct., Calif., 1996—; tchr. San Francisco Unified Sch. Dist., 1996—. Arbitrator Nat. Assn. Securities Dealers, 1988—, Pacific Stock Exch., 1992—. Sr. articles editor Hastings Constnl. Law Quar., 1978-79. Mem. Civil Grand Jury, San Francisco, 1991-92. Calif. State scholar, 1969-73. Mem. Bar Assn. San Francisco (vol. legal svcs. program). Democrat. Avocations: chess, baseball, international affairs. Office: Law Offices Thomas AE Hesketh PO Box 420587 San Francisco CA 94142-0587

HESS, ADAM R., lawyer; b. Reading, Pa., Apr. 22, 1965; BS Chem. Engring., Lehigh Univ., 1987; JD, George Washington Univ., 1992. Bar: Pa. 1992, DC 1994, Va. 2002, US Dist. Ct. (DC, ea., we. dist. Mich., ea. dist. Va.), US Ct. Appeals (Fed. cir.) 1994, US Ct. Appeals (DC cir.) 1997, US Supreme Ct. 2001. Ptnr., leader No. Va. IP Litigation group Pillsbury Winthrop Shaw Pittman, McLean, Va. Mem.: ABA, Bar Assn. DC, Fed. Cir. Bar Assn., Am. Intellectual Property Law Assn., Am. Inst. Chem. Engineers, Giles Sutherland Rich Am. Inns of Ct. Office: Pillsbury Winthrop Shaw Pittman 1600 Tysons Blvd Mc Lean VA 22102 Office Phone: 703-905-2089. Office Fax: 703-905-2500. Business E-Mail: adam.hess@pillsburylaw.com.

HESS, CHARLES EDWARD, environmental horticulture educator; b. Paterson, NJ, Dec. 20, 1931; s. Cornelius W. M. and Alice (Debruyn) H.; children: Mary, Carol, Nancy, John, Peter; m. Eva G. Carroad, Feb. 14, 1981. BS, Rutgers U., 1953; MS, Cornell U., 1954, PhD, 1957; DAgr (hon.), Purdue U., 1983; DSc (hon.), Delaware Valley Coll., Doylestown, Pa., 1992. From asst. prof. to prof. Purdue U., West Lafayette, Ind., 1958-65; rsch. prof., dept. chmn. Rutgers U., New Brunswick, NJ, 1966, assoc. dean, dir. NJ Agrl. Exptl. Sta., 1970, acting dean Coll. Agrl. and Environ. Sci., 1971, dean Cook Coll., 1972-75; assoc. dir. Calif. Agrl. Exptl. Sta., 1975-89; asst. sec. sci. and edn. USDA, Washington, 1989-91; dean Coll. Agrl. and Environ. Scis. U. Calif., Davis, 1975-89, prof. dept. environ. horticulture, 1975-94, prof. emeritus, 1994—, dir. internat. programs Coll. Agrl. and Environ. Scis., 1992-98, spl. asst. to provost, 1994—2003, spl. asst. to chancellor, 2003—04. Cons. U.S. AID, 1965, Office Tech. Assessment, U.S. Congress, 1976-77; chmn. study team world food and nutrition study NAS, 1976; mem. Calif. State Bd. Food and Agr., 1984-89; mem. Nat. Sci. Bd., 1982-88, 92-98, vice-chmn., 1984-88; co-chmn. Joint Coun. USDA, 1987-91; mem. external adv. com. Western Ctr. for Agrl. Health and Safety, 2005—. Mem. West Lafayette Sch. Bd., 1963-65, sec., 1963, pres., 1964; mem. Gov.'s Commn. Blueprint for Agr., 1971-73; bd. dirs. Davis Sci. Ctr., 1992-94; trustee Internat. Svc. for Nat. Agrl. Rsch., The Hague, Netherlands, 1992-98, bd. chmn., 1995-96. Mem. U.S. EPA (mem. biotech. sci. adv. com. 1992-96), AAAS (chmn. agriculture sect. 1989-90), Am. Soc. Hort. Sci. (pres. 1973), Internat. Plant Propagators Soc. (pres. 1973), Agrl. Rsch. Inst., U. Calif. Davis Emerti Assn. (pres. 2004—), Phi Beta Kappa, Sigma Xi, Alpha Zeta, Phi Kappa Phi, Gamma Sigma Delta (Disting.

Achievement in Agr. award 2004). Office: U Calif Coll Agrl Environ Scis Dept Environ Horticulture Davis CA 95616 Office Phone: 530-752-8117. Business E-Mail: cehess@ucdavis.edu.

HESS, DARLA BAKERSMITH, cardiologist, educator; b. Valparaiso, Fla., June 4, 1953; d. James Barry and Irma Marie (Baker) Bakersmith; m. Leonard Wayne Hess, July 20, 1988; 1 child, Ever Marie. BS, Birmingham So. Coll., 1975; MD, Tulane U., 1979. Diplomate Am. Bd. Internal Medicine, Am. Bd. Cardiovascular Disease. Resident in internal medicine Portsmouth (Va.) Naval Hosp., 1979-82, cardiologist, head non-invasive cardiology, 1986-88; fellow in cardiology San Diego Naval Hosp., 1982-84; cardiologist, head med. officer in charge ICU Camp Lejeune (N.C.) Naval Hosp., 1984-85; dir. noninvasive sect. cardiology, dir. fetal echocardiography U. Mo., Columbia, 1991—99; asst. prof. medicine U. Miss. Med. Ctr., Jackson, 1988-91, asst. prof. ob/gyn., 1990-91; co-dir. fetal echocardiogaphy U. Mo., Columbia, 1991—99, co-dir. Adult Congenital Heart Disease Clinic, 1991—99, assoc. prof. medicine, assoc. prof. ob/gyn., 1998—2001; commd. ensign USNR, 1979, advanced through grades to lt. comdr., 1988. Author: (with others) Obstetrics and Gynecology Clinics, 1992, Clinical Problems in Obstetrics & Gynecology, 1993, General Medical Disorders During, 1991; co-editor: Fetal Echocardiography, 1999; contbr. articles to So. Med. Jour., Ob/Gyn. Clinics N.Am., Soc. Perinatal Obs., Jour. Reproductive Medicine, others. Fellow Am. Coll. Cardiology, Fellow Am. Heart Assn. (fellow stroke coun.), Fellow Am. Soc. Echocardiography; mem. Am. Assn. Nuclear Cardiology, Phi Beta Kappa, Alpha Omega Alpha. Republican. Episcopalian. Home: 7945 Springhouse Rd New Tripoli PA 18066 Office Phone: 610-217-5753. E-mail: darlahess@aol.com.

HESS, DENNIS JOHN, investment banker; b. Manila, July 7, 1940; s. Carl and Anna (Harris) H.; m. Marilyn Golchert, July 7, 1977; children: Whitney, Christine, Craig. BS, U. Calif., Berkeley, 1962. With Merrill Lynch & Co., 1969—, v.p., 1977-80; chmn. bd., chief exec. officer Merrill Lynch, Hubbard, Inc., N.Y.C., 1980—; dir. diversified fin. svcs. Merrill Lynch, Pierce, Fenner & Smith, 1985-2000; pres., chief oper. officer ML Realty, 1983-2000; chmn., CEO, ML Equity Mgmt. Corp., 1984-2000, Paine Webber Life Ins. Co.; chm. bd. Tandem Fin. Corp.; CEO, Merrill Lynch Ins. Group, 1986-2000; pres. DJH, Inc., Greenwich, Conn.; ret. Bd. dirs. United First Mortgage Corp., M.L. Huntoon Paige, Inc., MLH Puerto, SA, Family Life Ins. Co., DJH, Inc.; exec. v.p. Payne Webber Inc.; chmn., CEO Paine Webber Life Ins. Co. Served to 1st lt. USAF, 1962-66. Mem. Greenwich Country Club. Republican. Roman Catholic.

HESS, DONALD MARC, diversified financial services company executive; b. Bern, Switzerland, Aug. 3, 1936; s. Hector Albert and Louise (McNeir) H.; divorced; 1 child, Alexandra. Ecole Superieure De Commerce, Neuchatel U.; brewmaster, Doemens, Munich, 1957. Pres. Steinholzli Brewery, Bern, 1957-68; chmn. Hess Holding, Bern, 1968—. Chmn. Valser Mineral Water, Ltd., Vals, CH, Hess Ltd., Bern, Blue Lake, Ltd., Blausee, CH, Hess Internat., V.V., Rotterdam, The Netherlands; CEO The Hess Collection Winery, Napa, Calif.; bd. dirs. Kambly Bisquits, Ltd., Trubschachen, CH, 1988—, Hess Art Collection Ltd., Bern, CH, 1998—; founder Hess Collection Contemporary Art Mus., Napa, Calif., 1989—, Hess Collection Art Exbhn. Space at Vinopolis-City of Wine, 1 Bank End, London, 1999—. Editor: Hess Collection, 1989 (named one of best books in Switzerland 1989), Hess Collection New Works, 1998, Franz Gertsch, Hess Collection, 1999. Co-founder Kunst Heute Found., Bern, 1982; pres., mem exec. com. International Green Cross Switzerland, 1994-96. Named one of Top 200 Collectors, ARTnews Mag., 2004. Avocation: Collector Contemporary Art. Office: Hess Holding Steinholzli CH-3097 Bern Switzerland

HESS, EVELYN VICTORINE, medical educator; b. Dublin, Nov. 8, 1926; arrived in U.S., 1960, naturalized, 1965; d. Ernest Joseph and Mary (Hawkins) H.; m. Michael Howett, Apr. 27, 1954. MB, B.Ch, BAO, U. Coll., Dublin, 1949; MD, Univ. Coll., Dublin, 1980. Intern West Middlesex Hosp., London, Eng., 1950; resident Clare Hall Hosp., London, 1951-53, Royal Free Hosp. and Med. Sch., London, 1954-57; rsch. fellow in epidemiology of Tb Royal Free Med. Sch., London, 1955; fellow U. Tex. Southwestern Med. Sch., Dallas, 1958—59, asst. prof. internal medicine, 1960-64; assoc. prof. dept. medicine U. Cin. Coll. Medicine, 1964-69, McDonald prof. medicine, 1969—, dir. div. immunology, 1964-95. Sr. investigator Arthritis and Rheumatism Found., 1963-68; attending physician Univ. Hosp., VA Hosp.; cons. Children's Hosp., Cin., 1967—, Jewish Hosp., Cin., 1968—; mem. various coms., mem. nat. adv. coun. NIH; mem. various coms. FDA, Cin. Bd. Health. Contbr. articles on immunology, rheumatic diseases to jours., chpts. to books. Active Nat. Pks. Assn., Smithsonian Instn., others. Recipient Arthritis Found. award, 1973, 78, 83, Am. Lupus Soc. award, 1979, Am. Acad. Family Practice award, 1980, award for AIDS work State of Ohio, 1989, Spirit of Am. Women award, 1989, Daniel Drake medal U. Cin., 2001; travel fellow Royal Free Med. Sch., Scandinavia, 1956, Empire Rheumatism Coun., 1958-59. Master ACP (gov. Ohio chpt. 1999-2003, Master Tchr. award 1995); fellow AAAS, Am. Acad. Allergy, Royal Soc. Medicine, ACR (master, Disting. Rheumatologist award 1996); mem. Heberden Soc., Am. Coll. Rheumatology, Pan-Am. League Assns. for Rheumatology (Gold medal 2003), Ctrl. Soc. Clin. Rsch., Am. Fedn. Clin. Rsch., Am. Assn. Immunologists, Am. Soc. Nephrology, Am. Med. Womens Assn. (Local Hero award 2004), Am. Soc. Clin. Pharmacology and Therapeutics, N.Y. Acad. Scis., Soc. Exptl. Biology and Medicine, Rheumatological Soc. Colombia (hon.), Rheumatological Soc. Peru (hon.), Rheumatological Soc. Italy (hon.), Clin. Immunol. Soc. Japan (hon.), Cuban Soc. Rheumatology (hon.), Alpha Omega Alpha. Home: 2916 Grandin Rd Cincinnati OH 45208-3418 Office: U Cin Med Ctr ML 563 ML 563 MSB Cincinnati OH 45267-0001 Office Phone: 513-558-4701. Business E-Mail: hessev@email.uc.edu.

HESS, FRANCES ELIZABETH, retired secondary school educator, retired director; b. Trenton, N.J. d. George Alfred and Frances Randall Hess. BS in Edn., Temple U., 1956, MS in Edn., 1964. Tchr. Bd. Edn., Trenton, 1956—60, Fallsington, Pa., 1960—93, aquatics dir., 1981—97; ret., 1997. Instr., trainer ARC, Levittown, Pa., 1983—2005, mem. health & safety, 1981—2005; tech. v.p. U.S. Synchronized Swimming, Indpls., 1999—2005, ofcls. v.p., 2004—. Named to Hall of Fame, Temple U., 1983, Pennsbury Sch. Dist. Hall of Fame, 2004; recipient Lillian Mac Kellar Disting. Svc. award, U.S. Synchronized Swimming, 2003. Avocations: swimming, jigsaw puzzles, gardening. Home: 718 S Olds Blvd Fairless Hills PA 19030 Personal E-mail: bettyhess@verizon.net.

HESS, FREDERICK J., lawyer; b. Highland, Ill., Sept. 22, 1941; s. Fred and Matilda (Maiden) H.; m. Mary V. Menkhus, Nov. 13, 1976; children: Frederick, M. Elizabeth. BS in Polit. Sci. and History, St. Louis U., 1963; JD, Washburn Sch. Law, Topeka, 1971. Bar: Kans. 1971, Ill. 1975, U.S. Supreme Ct. 1975, D.C. 1977, U.S. Tax Ct. 1977. Asst. U.S. atty. Dept. Justice, East St. Louis, Ill., 1971-73, 1st asst. U.S. atty., 1973-76; ct. appt. U.S. Atty. E. Dist. of Ill., 1977; ptnr. Stiehl & Hess, Belleville, Ill., 1977-82; U.S. atty. U.S. Dist. Ct. (so. dist.) Ill., East St. Louis, 1982-93; pvt. practice Lewis Rice & Fingersh, Belleville, 1993—. Bd. dirs., past pres. Nat. Assn. Former U.S. Attys., 1996; judge Ill. Ct. of Claims, 1997-2003; commr. Ill. Exec. Ethics Commn., 2004—. Served to capt. USAF, 1964-68. Fellow ABA Found., ISBA Found., Ill. Bar Assn.; mem. Kans. Bar Assn., D.C. Bar Assn., Tamarack Golf Club, Stone Wolf Golf Club. Republican. Office: Lewis Rice & Fingersh 325 S High St Belleville IL 62220-2116 Office Phone: 618-234-8636.

HESS, FREDERICK SCOTT, artist; b. Balt., July 12, 1955; s. Charles Stevens and Katherine Ruth Hess; m. Gita Tabatabai, Dec. 28, 1989; children: Ava Katarina, Atiyeh Mehri. BS, U. Wis., 1977; postgrad., Vienna Acad. Fine Art, 1979-84. Artist in residence Bahman Cultural House, Tehran, Iran, 1992, Cité Internat. des Arts, Paris, 1993. Solo exhibitions include Gallery Herzog, Vienna, Austria, 1979, Galerie im Tabak Museum, Vienna, Austria, 1982, Ovsey Gallery, L.A., Calif., 1985, 86, 88, 89, 90, 92, 94, U. So. Calif. Fisher Art Gallery, 1987-88, Santa Clara U. de Saisset Mus., Santa Clara, Calif., 1987-88, Mt. San Jacinto Coll., San Jacinto, Calif., 1989, Fresno (Calif.) Art Mus., Calif., 1991, Underground Exhibition, Tehran, Iran, 1993, Art Inst. So. Calif., Laguna Beach, 1996, Mt. S. Antonio Coll. Walnut, Calif., 1997, Hackett-Freedman Gallery, San Francisco, 1999, Orange County Mus. Art, Newport Beach, 2001, Loyola-Marymunt U., L.A., 2002; exhibited in group shows at Taipei (Taiwan) Fine Arts Mus., 1987, U. So. Calif., L.A., 1987-88, Laguna Art Mus., Laguna Beach, Calif., 1988, Henry Art Gallery, U. Washington, Seattle, 1988, Fresno (Calif.) Art Mus., 1988-89, Flint (Mich.) Inst. Art, 1991, San Diego Mus. Art, 1991, Triton Mus., Santa Clara, Calif., 1992, Oakland (Calif.) Mus., 1992, Flint (Mich.) Inst. Art, 1992, Nev. Inst. Contemporary Art, Las Vegas, 1995, L.A. County Mus. Art, 1997, Armory Ctr. for Arts, Pasadena, 1997, Laband Art Gallery, L.A., 1998, Frye Art Mus., Seattle, 2000. Recipient Theodor Koerner award Austrian Min. Culture, Vienna, 1981, WESTAF award Nat. Endowment for the Arts, 1990; fellow J. Paul Getty Trust, 1991, Nat. Endowment for the Arts, 1991. Mem. The Drawing Group. Avocations: writing, polo, sailing. Address: 1830 Lake Shore Ave Los Angeles CA 90026-1716 E-mail: shess@artcenter.edu.

HESS, GEORGE FRANKLIN, II, lawyer; b. Oak Park, Ill., May 13, 1939; s. Franklin Edward and Carol (Hackman) H.; m. Diane Ricci, Aug. 9, 1974; 1 child, Franklin Edward. BS in Bus., Colo. State U., 1962; JD, Suffolk U., 1970; LLM, Boston U., 1973. Bar: Pa. 1971, Fla. 1973, U.S. Tax Ct. 1974, U.S. Dist. Ct. (so. dist.) Fla. 1975. Assoc. Hart, Childs, Hepburn, Ross & Putnam, Phila., 1970-72; instr. Suffolk U. Law Sch., Boston, 1973-74; ptnr. Henry, Hess & Hoines, Ft. Lauderdale, Fla., 1974-79, Mousaw, Vigdor, Reeves & Hess, Ft. Lauderdale, Fla., 1979-94; pvt. practice Ft. Lauderdale, Fla., 1995—. Bd. dirs. Childrens Home Soc., Ft. Lauderdale, 1985-89, Nadeau Charitable Found., 1985-2000; trustee endowment fund All Sts. Ch., 1995—. Lt. USNR, 1963-66. Mem. ABA, SAR, Fla. Bar Assn., Broward County Bar Assn., Lauderdale Yacht Club, USN League, Phi Alpha Delta. Episcopalian. Home: 2524 Castilla Is Fort Lauderdale FL 33301-1505 Office: 333 N New River Dr E Fort Lauderdale FL 33301-2241 Office Phone: 954-764-2068. E-mail: gfhess2@aol.com.

HESS, GEORGE PAUL, biochemist, educator; b. Vienna; came to U.S., 1938; s. Henry Steven Hess and Edith Muller; children: Alvis, Peter, Richard, Paul, David. AB, U. Calif., Berkeley, 1951, PhD, 1953. Postdoctoral fellow MIT, 1953—55, Nat. Infantile Paralysis, 1953-55; instr. Cornell Med. Sch., 1955; asst. prof. biochemistry Cornell U., Ithaca, N.Y., 1956-60, assoc. prof., 1960-64, prof., 1964—. Vis. fellow chemistry Yale U., 1960, U.S. Dept. State Cultural Exchange prof. to Europe, 1963, 70; vis. prof. biophysics U. Pa., Phila., 1964-65, biochemistry U. Hawaii, Honolulu, Jan. 1966, chemistry U. Ariz., Tucson, Feb. 1968, biology MIT, 1990; lectr. Naito Found., Japan, 1988. Mem. Biochemistry Editl. Adv. Bd.; adv. bd. Ctr. Molecular and Behavioral Neuroscis., Universidad del Caribe Ctr., P.R. With U.S. Army, 1945—47. Recipient Alexander von Humboldt Sr. Scientist award U. Konstanz, 1982, Outstanding Educator Recognition award Cornell Merrill Presdl. scholar, 1994, 97, Wellcome vis. professorship, 1998; Guggenheim fellow, sr. Fulbright grantee Max-Planck-Inst. fur physikalische Chemie, 1962-63; spl. NIH fellow Med. Rsch. Coun. Lab Molecular Biology, 1969-70; Churchill Coll. U. Cambridge vis. fellow 1969-70; NIH Nat. Inst. of Neurol. Diseases and Stroke Fogarty scholar, 1999-2000. Fellow AAAs, Am. Acad. Microbiology; elected mem. NAS, mem. Am. Soc. Cell Biol.; Am. Chem. Soc., Biophys. Soc., Fedn. Am. Soc. of Exptl. Biologists, N.Y. Acad. Scis., Soc. Neurosci., Protein Soc. Home: 123 Heights Ct Ithaca NY 14850-2450 Office: Cornell Univ 216 Biotechnology Bldg Ithaca NY 14853-2703 Office Phone: 607-255-4809. Business E-Mail: gph2@cornell.edu.

HESS, GLEN E., lawyer; b. Evergreen Park, Ill., Feb. 4, 1942; m. Victoria G. Hess. AB summa cum laude, Cornell U., 1964; LLB magna cum laude, Harvard U., 1967. Bar: Ill. 1987, N.Y. 1990. Ptnr., mem. mgmt. N.Y.C. Office Kirkland & Ellis LLP. Lecturer U. Chgo. Law Sch., 1977—89. Office: Kirkland & Ellis LLP Citigroup Ctr 55 E 52nd St New York NY 10022-5907 Office Phone: 212-446-4808. Office Fax: 212-446-4900. Business E-Mail: ghess@kirkland.com.

HESS, JOHN B., oil industry executive; s. Leon Hess. BA, Harvard Univ., 1975, MBA, 1977. With Amerada Hess Corp., 1980—; chmn., CEO Amerada Hess Corp., N.Y.C., 1995—. Office: Amerada Hess Corp 1185 Avenue Of The Americas New York NY 10036-2601*

HESS, JOHN WARREN, professional society administrator; b. Lancaster, Pa., May 6, 1947; s. John Warren and Barbara Kathryn (Spencer) H.; m. Letitia Jean Schrantz, Mar. 20, 1971; children: Nathan James, Joshua Kyle. BS in Geol. Scis., Pa. State U., 1969, PhD in Geology, 1974. Asst. rsch. prof. water resources ctr. Desert Rsch. Inst., Las Vegas, Nev., 1974-78, assoc. rsch. prof., 1978-86, rsch. prof., 1985—2001, dir. environ. isotope lab., 1981-87, dep. dir., 1987-89, exec. dir., 1989-2000, interim v.p. rsch., 1994-95, v.p. acad. affairs, 1995—2001, congrl. fellow, 2000—01; exec. dir. Geol. Soc. Am., Boulder, Colo., 2001—04. Chmn. bd. dirs. Karst Waters Inst., Charlestown, W.Va. Contbr. over 85 articles to profl. jours. Adult leader Boy Scouts Am., Las Vegas, 1978—2001, Boulder, Colo., 2002—. Recipient Alumni Achievewment award Coll. Earth and Mineral Scis., Pa. State U., 2004; Hon. Rsch. fellow U. Glasgow, Scotland, 1980-81; Centennial fellow Coll. Earth and Mineral Scis., Pa. State U. Fellow Geol. Soc. Am. (chair hydrogeology divsn., 1995-96), Nat. Speleological Soc.; mem. AAAS, Am. Geophys. Union, Internat. Assn. Hydrogeologists, Geochem. Soc. Office: Geol Soc Am 3300 Penrose Pl Boulder CO 80301 Office Phone: 303-357-1039. Business E-Mail: jhess@geosociety.org.

HESS, JUDITH A., secondary school educator; b. Port Jervis, N.Y., May 2, 1952; d. Harold N and Caroline I (Schields) Hess. B in English cum laude, Marywood Coll., 1975; MA in English lit., Wroxton Coll., 1978. English tchr. Delaware Valley H.S., Milford, Pa., 1975—. Exec. com. Delaware Valley Edn. Assn., Milford, Pa., 1985—99, editor, union newsletter, 1989—90, 1998—99; principal's adv. coun. Delware Vally Sch. Dist., 1992—98, superintendent's com., 1986—89. Mem.: Delaware Valley Edn. Assn., Pa. State Edn. Assn., Nat. Edn. Assn., Lambda Iote Tau. Avocations: travel, reading. Home: 416 Twin Lakes Rd Shohola PA 18458

HESS, KARL, electrical and computer engineering educator; b. Trumau, Austria, June 20, 1945; came to U.S. 1977; naturalized 1988; s. Karl Joseph and Gertrude (Resch) H.; m. Sylvia Horvath, Sept. 1967; children: Ursula, Karl. PhD, U. Vienna, Austria, 1970; DSc (hon.), ETH, Zurich, Switzerland, 2003. Rsch. asst. U. Vienna, 1969-71, asst. prof., 1971-77, univ. lectr., 1977; vis. assoc. prof. U. Ill., Urbana, 1977-80, prof. elec. and computer enging., 1988—, adj. prof. supercomputing applications, 1990—, Swanlund Endowed chair, 1996—, prof. physics. Contbr. articles to profl. jours.; patentee in field Univ. scholar U. Ill., 1982-83; Fulbright scholar, 1973-74. Fellow AAAS, IEEE (J.J. Ebers award 1994, David Sarnoff field award 1995, H. Welker Meml. medal 2001), NAS, NAE, Am. Phys. Soc., Am. Acad. Arts and Scis. Avocations: classical music, chess. Home: 1805 Bentbrook Dr Champaign IL 61822-9220 Office: U Ill Beckman Inst 405 N Mathews Ave Urbana IL 61801-2325 Office Phone: 217-333-6362. Business E-Mail: k-hess@uiuc.edu.

HESS, KERI A., music educator; d. Donald E. and Virginia K. Smith; 1 child, William E. BS in Composite Music, Dickinson State U., 1994. Choral dir. Simle Mid. Sch., Bismarck, ND, 1994—95, Mandan H.S., 1995—. Musical dir. Mandan H.S., 1995—. Recipient Golden Apple award, Kxmb 12, 2002. Mem.: Am. Choral Dirs. Assn., N.D. Music Educators Assn. Home: 1307 Monte Dr Mandan ND 58554 Office: Mandan High Sch 905 8th Ave NW Mandan ND 58554-2400 Office Phone: 701-663-9532. Personal E-mail: presto39@bis.midco.net.

HESS, LEONARD WAYNE, obstetrician gynecologist, perinatologist; b. Richlands, Va., Nov. 23, 1949; s. Ralph Eugene and Lucille Cindy (Kennedy) H.; m. Sarah Mahala Leedy, Nov. 27, 1969 (div. July 1988); children: Gregory Scott, Lauren Ashley; m. Darla Irma Bakersmith, July 20, 1988; 1 child, Ever Marie. BSChemE, Va. Poly. Inst., 1973; MD, Va. Commonwealth U., 1977. Diplomate Nat. Bd. Med. Examiners, Am. Bd. Ob-Gyn., also sub.-bd. Maternal-Fetal Medicine. Intern U.S. Naval Hosp., Portsmouth, Va., 1977-78, resident in ob-gyn., 1978-81; fellow in maternal-fetal medicine Naval Med. Command, Walter Reed Army Med. Ctr., Washington and Bethesda, 1981-83; staff dept. ob-gyn. U. Health Scis., Bethesda, 1981-85; dept. ob-gyn. U.S. Naval Hosp., Portsmouth, 1985-87; comdr. USNR, 1987-88; asst. prof. dept. ob-gyn. U. Miss. Med. Ctr., Jackson, 1987-91; assoc. prof. ob-gyn. U. Mo. Med. Ctr., Columbia, 1991-96, head obstetrics and maternal-fetal medicine, 1991-96, prof., chmn. ob-gyn., 1996—2001; chmn. ob-gyn. Lehigh Valley Hosp. and Health Network, 2001—; prof. ob/gyn. Pa. State U. Sch. Medicine. Mem. Med. Ethics Com., U.S. Naval Hosp., Portsmouth, 1985-87; mem. Patient Care Com., U. Miss. Med. Ctr., Jackson, 1988-91, Infection Control Com., 1988-91; bd. examiner Am. Bd. Ob-Gyn., 1996—. Author: Fetal Echocardiography, 1999; cons. editor Obstetrics and Gynecology, 1988—, Am. Jour. Obstetrics and Gynecology, 1988—, Am. Jour. Med. Genetics, 1989—; contbr. numerous articles to profl. jours. Mem. AMA, USP (ob-gyn. adv. panel 1995-2001), Am. Coll. Obstetricians and Gynecologists, Soc. Perinatal Obstetricians, Am. Inst. Ultrasound in Medicine, Assn. Profs. Gynecology and Obstetrics, Cen. Assn. Obstetricians and Gynecologists, Am. Soc. Human Genetics, So. Med. Assn., Winifred L. Wiser Soc., Miss. State Obstet. and Gynecol. Soc., Cen. Med. Soc., Gynecol. Soc., Med. Soc. Va., Portsmouth Acad. Medicine, Med. and Surgical Soc. of Md., Miss. State Med. Assn., Assn. Mil. Surgeons, Miss. Perinatal Assn., So. Perinatal Assn. Republican. Episcopalian. Office: Lehigh Valley Hosp 17th and Chew Sts Allentown PA 18105 Office Phone: 610-402-9504. Business E-Mail: l_wayne.hess@lvh.com.

HESS, MARK DAVID, lawyer; b. Huntsville, Ala., Feb. 12, 1962; s. James Henry and Dorothy Brown Hess; m. Margaret Wilborn Hess, May 12, 1990; children: Thomas Jackson, Aaron Daniel, Jonathan David. BA, U. Ala., Huntsville, 1984; JD, U. Ala., Tuscaloosa, 1987. Law clk. U.S. Dist. Ct. Ala., Montgomery, 1987-88; legal advisor to the gov. Office of the Gov., Montgomery, 1989-92; assoc. Spain & Gillon, LLC, Birmingham, 1993-95; mem. London & Yancey, LLC, Birmingham, 1995—. Mem. Ala. State Bar Assn., Ala. Def. Lawyers Assn. (amicus curiae com. 1999), Bar of Supreme Ct. of U.S. Republican. Presbyterian. Avocations: reading, wood working, hunting, team sports. Home: 4033 Marthas Cir Birmingham AL 35243-4961 Office: London & Yancey LLC 2001 Park Pl Ste 400 Birmingham AL 35203-2787

HESS, MICHAEL DAVID, lawyer; b. NYC, Nov. 8, 1940; s. Jacques J. and Lee B. (Berman) H.; m. Lynn Carol Levine, June 16, 1963; children: Laurie R., Geoffrey N. AB, Yale Coll., 1962; JD, Harvard U., 1965. Bar: N.Y. Chief civil divsn. Office of U.S. Atty., N.Y.C., 1966-73; ptnr. Weil Gotshal, N.Y.C., 1973-83; sr. ptnr. Gelberg & Abrams, N.Y.C., 1983-86, White & Case, N.Y.C., 1986-93, Chadbourne & Parke, N.Y.C., 1993-98; corp. counsel, law dept. head City of N.Y., 1998—2001; ptnr., sr. mng. dir. Giuliani Partners LLC, N.Y.C., 2002—. Chmn., bd. trustees Horace Mann Sch., Bronx, N.Y., 1994-2001. Mem. ABA, N.Y. State Bar Assn., N.Y.C. Bar Assn., Phi Beta Kappa. Office: Giuliani Partners LLC 5 Times Sq New York NY 10036 Office Phone: 212-931-7396. Business E-Mail: michael.hess@giulianipartners.com.

HESS, MICHAEL E., federal agency administrator; m. Teresa Crawford; children: Ken, James. B in Engring., U.S. Military Acad.; M in European History, Columbia U.; MBA, NYU; grad. Nat. Strategic Studies Program, Army War Coll. Liaison office chief, Kosovo Forces Hdqs. Dept. U.S. Army, spl. asst. to chief of staff, Office of High Rep., dep. chief of staff, Coalition Provisional Authority, humanitarian coord. Office Reconstrn. and Humanitarian Assistance; v.p. banking Citigroup, Inc., v.p. audit and risk review; asst. adminstr. Bur. Democracy Conflict and Humanitarian Assistance U.S. Agency Internat. Devel., Washington, 2005—. Office: US Agency Internat Devel Ronald Reagan Bldg 1300 Pennsylvania Ave NW Rm 806-084 Washington DC 20523-6100 Office Phone: 202-712-0100.*

HESS, PATRICK HENRY, chemist, researcher; b. Albia, Iowa, Aug. 6, 1931; s. John Henry and Mary Ellen (Judge) H.; m. Ann Marie Malone, June 6, 1959; children: Michelle, Maria, Margaret, Catherine, John. BS in Chemistry, U. Iowa, 1953; MS in Organic Chemistry, U. Nebr., 1958, PhD in Organic Chemistry, 1960. Chemist Iowa State Hygienic Labs., 1953-54; teaching asst. U. Nebr., 1956-57, rsch. asst., 1957-58, rsch. fellow, 1958-60; rsch. chemist Chevron Research Co., Richmond, Calif., 1960-64, Chevron Oil Field Rsch. Co., La Habra, Calif., 1964-65; sr. rsch. chemist Chevron Oil Field Research Co., La Habra, Calif., 1965-69, sr. rsch. assoc., 1969-92; ret., 1992. Rsch. group supr. Chevron Corp. Contbr. articles to profl. jours.; patentee crude oil recovery. Active youth sports PTA. Served with USAF, 1954-55. Rsch. fellow 3-M, 1958-59, Monsanto, 1959-60. Mem. Am. Chem. Soc., Soc. Petroleum Engrs., Sigma Xi, Alpha Chi Sigma, Alpha Tau Omega Republican. Roman Catholic. Home: 12463 Jeremiah Dr Auburn CA 95603-9051 *Retirement is great - so long as one doesn't become too retired.*

HESS, PETER ANDREAS, German language educator; b. Sept. 20, 1955; BA, U. Zurich, 1977; MA, U. Mich., 1980, PhD, 1984. Assoc. prof. German, U. Tex., Austin, 1987—, grad. advisor, 1994—. Vis. asst. prof. U. Ky., 1984-85, U. Ariz., 1985-86; dir. Austria-Ill. Exch. program, Vienna, 1986-87. Pres. Barton Hills Neighborhood Assn., Austin, 1998-99. Home: 2502 Rock Terrace Dr Austin TX 78704-3840 Office: U Tex Dept German 3 102 Ep Schoch Bldg Austin TX 78712-1190 E-mail: phess@mail.utexas.edu.

HESS, RICHARD CHRISTIAN, JR., obstetrician/gynecologist, educator; b. Bethlehem, Pa., June 21, 1943; MD, Johns Hopkins U., 1967. Diplomate Am. Bd. Ob-Gyn. Intern Cleve. Metro Gen. Hosp., 1967-68; resident ob-gyn U. Wash. Hosp., Seattle, 1968-72; ob-gyn USN, Keflavik, Iceland, 1972-74, Fairbanks (Alaska) Meml. Hosp., 1974—. Clin. instr. U. Wash., 1978—. Fellow Am. Coll. Ob-Gyn; mem. AMA, Alaska Med. Assn. Office: Tanana Valley Med-Surg Group 1001 Noble St Fairbanks AK 99701-4978 Office Phone: 907-459-3540. Personal E-mail: alaska_rich43@yahoo.com.

HESS, SIDNEY J., JR., lawyer; b. Chgo., June 26, 1910; s. Sidney J. and Alma (Katz) Hess; m. Jacqueline Engelhardt, Aug. 28, 1948; children: Karen E. Hess Freeman, Lori Hess Pleiss. PhB, U. Chgo., 1930, JD, 1932. Bar: Ill. 1932. Practiced in, Chgo., 1932—; mem. firm Aaron, Aaron, Schimberg & Hess, 1933—84, D'Ancona & Pflaum, 1985—2003, Seyarth Shaw L.L.P., 2003—. Bd. dirs., legal counsel Jewish Fedn. of Met. Chgo., 1968-75, v.p., 1972-74, pres., 1974-76; dir., legal counsel Jewish United Fund Met. Chgo., 1971-75, pres., 1974-76; legal counsel Jewish Welfare Fund Met. Chgo., 1969-73; bd. dirs. S. Silberman & Sons, Chgo. Metallic Products, Inc., Vienna Sausage Mfg. Co. Mem. exec. com. Anti-Defamation League, 1954-57, HIAS, 1974-90; mem. nat. devel. coun., aims com., citizens bd. U. Chgo.; bd. dirs. Schwab Rehab. Hosp., 1957-65, pres., 1959-64; trustee Michael Reese Health Trust, 1991—. Recipient Judge Learned Hand Human Rels. award Am. Jewish Com., 1979, Julius Rosenwald Meml. award Jewish Fedn. Met. Chgo., 1994, Army Commendation Medal (USAF); elected to Jewish Cmty. Ctrs. Hall of Fame, 1985, City of Chgo. Sr. Citizens Hall of Fame, 1987. Fellow Ill. Bar Found. (charter mem.); mem. ABA, Ill. State Bar Assn., Chgo. Bar Assn., Am. Judicature Soc., U. Chgo. Law Sch. Assn. (dir.), Standard Club (past pres., dir.), Mid-Day Club (Chgo.), Northmoor Country Club (Highland Park, Ill.), Tamarisk Country Club (Rancho Mirage, Calif.), Phi Beta Kappa, Pi Lambda Phi. Home: 1040 N Lake Shore Dr Chicago IL 60611-1165 Office: Ste 4200 55 E Monroe St Chicago IL 60603-3713 Office Phone: 312-781-8624. Office Fax: 312-269-8869. Business E-Mail: shess@seyfarth.com. *In my judgment the principles and standard of conduct which one must observe in daily life include a clear recognition of the rights and privileges of others, coupled with a desire to provide assistance to those who are less fortunate and unable to provide for themselves. No conduct of one's affairs can be adequate and fulfilling without recognition and observance of relationships with family. In all dealings, one must act with the highest degree of integrity and conscientious application.*

HESS, SIDNEY WAYNE, management consultant, educator; b. Ames, Iowa, Oct. 21, 1932; s. Edwin M. and Mina Hess; m. Grayce Ann Medici, Oct. 9, 1954; children: Debra, Peter, Diana. BS, M.I.T., 1953; postgrad., Delft Technische Hogeschool, 1953-54; PhD, Case Inst. Tech., 1960; MA (hon.), U. Pa., 1971. Mgr. ops. research Atlas Chem. Industries, Inc., Wilmington, Del., 1959-66; assoc. prof., dir. Mgmt. and Behavioral Sci. Center, U. Pa., 1966-75; dir. pharm. program devel. ICI Americas, 1974-76, v.p. planning and rsch., 1976-80, v.p., gen. mgr. aerospace div., 1980-86; v.p. mfg. Synthes Ltd. (USA), 1986; sr. v.p. Chase Enterprises, 1987-89; prof. mgmt. Drexel U., Phila., 1989-94; pres. Hess Assoc., 1986—. Bd. dirs. Ketron, Inc.; prin. Becknell, Frank, Gross & Hess, Inc., 1986-71 Contbr. articles to profl. jours. Bd. dirs. Girls Inc. of Del., 1980-96, 98—, also treas., former sec.; trustee Concord Presbyn. Ch., 1978-80; mem. Adv. Com. on Indsl. Innovation, Dept. Commerce, 1978-79. Served to 1st lt. U.S. Army, 1954—56. Fulbright fellow, 1953 Mem. Inst. Mgmt. Sci. (past internat. sec. and pres., Disting. Svc. medal 1992), Ops. Rsch. Soc. Am. (past pres. Delaware Valley sect.), Am. Def. Preparedness Assn. (past bd. dirs. Phila. sect.), Chem. Mktg. Rsch. Assn. (Meml. award), Inst. for Ops. Rsch. and Mgmt. Sci. (pub. info. com.), Coun. of Ringfield Pvt. Resdl. Devel. (past pres.), Greenville Country Club, MIT Club of Delaware Valley (bd. dirs., pres.), Tau Beta Pi, Theta Chi.

HESS, STANLEY O., retired art educator; b. Weatherford, Okla., July 8, 1923; s. Otto Mathias Hess and Julia Telford Claunch; m. Mildred Ann Elmenhorst, Jan. 26, 1948 (dec. Apr. 1991); children: Patricia, Catherine, Thomas, Rebecca, Mary, Michael; m. Joanne Lenore Gravelin, June 6, 1992. BFA in Art, U. Okla., 1948, MFA in Art, 1950. Spl. instr. art U. Okla., 1948—50; instr. art William Woods Coll., 1951; prof. art Drake U., 1951—85. Supt. Iowa State Fair Art Salon, 1952—70. One-man shows include U. Okla., 1950, 1956, Sioux City Art Ctr., 1958, Des Moines Art Ctr., 1958, Mabee-Gerrer Mus. Art, St. Gregory's U., Shawnee, Okla., 1994, exhibited in group shows at Renwick Gallery, Washington, 1978, Okla. Arts Workshop, Tulsa, 1993—95, Tulsa Mayfest Gallery, 1994—2000, Leslie Powell Found., Lawton, Okla., 1995, Holliman Gallery, Tulsa, 1996, Mabee-Gerrer Mus. Art, 1997, Anderson Gallery, DesMoines, 1997, Okla. Artists Painting Biennial, 1997, Okla. Forestry Mus., Idabel, 1998, Okla. City Art Ctr., 1999, Drake U. Beinnial Faculty Exhbn., Butler Inst. Am. Art, others; contbr. articles to profl. jours. 1st lt. U.S. Army, 1942—45, PTO. Avocations: reading, bridge. Home: 5412 S 76th East Ave Tulsa OK 74145-7819 E-mail: stanleyohess@mailstation.com.

HESS, STEPHEN, political scientist, author; b. NYC, Apr. 20, 1933; s. Charles and Florence (Morse) Hess; m. Elena Shayne, Aug. 23, 1959 (div. 1979); children: Charles P., James R.; m. Beth Amster, Aug. 22, 1982. Student, U. Chgo., Ill., 1950-52; BA, Johns Hopkins U., 1953. Jr. instr. polit. sci. Johns Hopkins U., 1953-55; staff asst. to US Pres., 1959-61; asst. to minority whip US Senate, 1961; assoc. fellow Inst. for Policy Studies, 1964-65; fellow Inst. Politics J.F. Kennedy Sch. Govt., Harvard, 1967-68; dep. asst. to US Pres. for urban affairs, 1969; nat. chmn. White House Conf. on Children and Youth, 1969-71; sr. fellow Brookings Inst., Washington, 1972—2004, sr. fellow emeritus, 2004—. Mem. Washington regional selection panel Pres.'s Commn. White Ho. Fellows, 1973; cons. Ford Found., 1974—76; mem. DC Bd. Higher Edn., 1973—76; chmn. DC Coun. Home Rule Transition Commn., 1974; U.S. alt. rep. UNESCO Gen. Conf., 1974; mem. Alumni fellows adv. com. Inst. Politics, J. F. Kennedy Sch. Govt., Harvard U., 1974—; mem. 20th Century Fund Task Forces, 1975, 78, US Nat. Commn. UNESCO, 1975—77; editor-in-chief Nat. Rep. Platform, 1976; mem. adv. coun. gen. govt. Rep. Nat. Com., 1978—81; U.S. alt. rep. UN Gen. Assembly, 1976; cons. USIA, 1976, US Office Mgmt. and Budget, 1977; mem. vis. com. Gerald R. Ford Inst. Pub. Svc., Albion Coll., 1979—82; fellow faculty govt. Harvard U., 1979—82; mem. adv. com. Fund Investigative Journalism, 1981—; mem. sr. adv. bd. ctr. for press, politics and pub. policy John F. Kennedy Sch. Govt., Harvard U., 1987—; vis. prof. Johns Hopkins U., 1990, UCLA, Washington Program, 1990; disting. rsch. prof. media and pub. affairs The George Washington U., Washington, 2004—. Author (with Malcolm Moos): Hats in the Ring: The Making of Pres. Candidates, 1960, America's Polit. Dynasties, 1966; author: (with David S. Broder) The Rep. Establishment, 1967; author: (with Milton Kaplan) The Ungentlemanly Art: A History of Am. Polit. Cartoons, 1968; author: (with Earl Mazo) Nixon: A Polit. Portrait, 1968, Nixon: A Polit. Portrait, rev. edit., 1969, The Presdl. Campaign, 1974; author: (with Milton Kaplan) The Ungentlemanly Art: A History of American Political Cartoons, rev. edit., 1975; author: Organizing the Presidency, 1976, The Washington Reporters, 1981, The Government/Press Connection: Press Officers and Their Offices, 1984, The Ultimate Insiders: U.S. Senators in the National Media, 1986, The Presdl. Campaign, rev. edit., 1987, Live from Capitol Hill! Studies on Congress and the Media, 1991, Internat. News & Fgn. Correspondents, 1995, Presidents & The Presidency, 1995, News & Newsmaking, 1995; author: (with Sandy Northrop) Drawn & Quartered, 1996; author: America's Polit. Dynasties, rev. edit., 1996, International News & Foreign Correspondents, rev. edit., 1997, The Little Book of Campaign Etiquette, 1998, The Little Book of Campaign Etiquette, rev. edit., 2000, Organizing the Presidency, rev. edit., 2002, Through Their Eyes: Foreign Correspondents in the United States, 2005; editor (with Marvin Kalb): The Media and the War on Terrorism, 2003. With AUS, 1956—58. Fellow: Nat. Acad. Pub. Adminstrn. Home: 2801 New Mexico Ave NW Apt 1417 Washington DC 20007 Office: Brookings Instn 1775 Massachusetts Ave NW Washington DC 20036-2103 Office Phone: 202-797-6078. E-mail: shess@Brookings.edu.

HESS, SUZANNE HARRIET, newspaper publisher, photographer; b. Steubenville, Ohio, Nov. 8, 1941; d. Roswell J. and Ruth R. (Feuer) Caulk; m. Richard Robert Hess, Aug. 28, 1960 (div. Oct. 1989); children: Richard, Rebecca. Student, Lane C.C., 1961. Cert. radiologist, Oreg.; cert. ofcl. nat. level USA Track and Field, 1992-2002. Med. asst. Dr. John Burket, Medford, Oreg., 1970-72; sec. receptionist Dr. Paul Saarinen, Eugene, Oreg., 1982-84; office mgr. Europcar Internat., Sicily, Italy, 1989-91; visitor svcs. mgr. Conv. and Visitors Assn. Lane County, Eugene, Oreg., 1991-94; office mgr. Nat. Masters News, Eugene, Oreg., 1994-97, adminstrv. editor, 1998—2001; pub. Nat. Masters News, 2002—. Bd. dirs. U.S. Amateur Track and Field, Oreg., Photographer Nat. Masters News; nat. sec. USA Track and Field-Masters Com., 1997-98, 99-2004, 2005—, vice-chair master's com. Sec. Oreg. Track Club, Eugene, 1993-96, com. person for preservation of Prefontaine Rock, 1995; protester Preservation of Old Growth Timber, Eugene, 1994; elected nat. sec. USA Track and Field Masters Com., 1996, elected vice chair, 2000-. Recipient Appreciation award Oreg. Track Club, 1995, 2 Nat. Championship awards U.S. Amateur Track and Field, 1995, Silver medal 16# and 25# weight throw U.S. Amateur Track and Field Nat. Masters Indoor Championship, 1995, Bronze medal discus and hammer U.S. Amateur Track and Field Nat. Masters Outdoor Championships, 1995, Gold medal 16# weight throw and 25# superweight throw U.S. Amateur Track and Field Nat. Masters Weight and Superweight Championships, 1995, Gold medal U.S. Amateur Track and Field Nat. Masters Weight Pentathlon, 1995, Bronze medal 16# weight throw, Silver medal 25# super weight throw U.S. Amateur Track & Field Indoor Nat. Championships, Boston, 1997, Gold medals 16# and 25# superweight U.S. Amateur Track and Field Indoor Nat. Championships, Boston, 1998; named All Am. U.S. Amateur Track and Field, 1995, 97-99, 2000, 2001, 2002, 2003, Adminstr. Yr., U.S. Amateur Masters Track and Field, 1999, Silver medals 16# weight, 25# superweight Indoor Nat. Championships, Boston, 2000, Bronze medal, Seattle. Democrat. Avocations: track and field, bicycling, golf, travel. Office: Nat Masters News Ste 5 2791 Oak Alley Eugene OR 97405 Office Phone: 541-343-7716. Personal E-mail: natmanews@aol.com.

HESS, TERRY LEE, writer, educator, logistician; b. Balt., July 22, 1954; d. Lee Hess Ray and Ruth Carol Smith, Iva Estelle Teague (Stepmother). MA in English Creative Writing Nonfiction, U. Ctrl. Fla., 2002, postgrad. Program mgr., logistic engr. TRW Aerospace, Redondo Beach, Calif., 1982—89; sr. logistics engr. Boeing/McDonnell Douglas, Kennedy Space Ctr., Cape Canaveral, Fla., 1990—97; mng. editor Fla. Rev., Orlando, 1999—2002, non-fiction editor, 2001—02; sr. proposal specialist Johnson Controls, Inc., Cape Canaveral, 2003, proposal mgr., 2003—. Instr. U. Ctrl. Fla., 2001—03. Author: (Memoir) Bellingham Review, 2002 (AWP Intro Award for Creative Nonfiction, 2001), Cypress Dome, 2000, 4th edit., 2003. Fin. advisor 53rd Assembly Dist., 27th Congl. Dist., Rep. Party, L.A., 1985—87. With USAF, 1972—76, with USMC, 1978—82. Recipient United Arts Emerging Writers award, First Place Nonfiction and Second Place Fiction, United Arts, Orlando, Fla., 1999. Home: 3242 Angelica St Cocoa FL 32926 Office: Johnson Controls Inc 7315 N Atlantic Ave Cape Canaveral FL 32926 Office Phone: 321-784-7136. Personal E-mail: hes1of6@bellsouth.net.

HESSE, BILL L., music educator, conductor; b. Waterloo, Iowa, Sept. 2, 1952; s. LaVerne W. and Marietta M. Hesse; m. Patricia A. Erion, Oct. 1, 1988. BA, U. No. Iowa, 1974, MA, 1978. Cert. tchr. Iowa Dept. Edn., 1974. Music educator Dubuque Cmty. Sch. Dist., Iowa, 1974—; children's choir condr. Dubuque Symphony Orch., 1993—2001; adj. instr. Loras Coll., 1998—2002; children's choir condr. Colts Youth Orgns., 2001—, Dubuque Colts Youth Orgns., 2001—; music coord. Westminster Presbyn. Ch., 2002—. Clinician Ill. Music Educators Assn., Ill., 1987—. Bd. mem., pres. ARC, 1982—88; bd. mem., vol. coord. Kids for Dubuque, 1985—88. Mem.: Iowa Choral Dirs. Assn., Dubuque Edn. Assn. Presbyterian. Avocations: singing, theater, ballet, bicycling. Office Phone: 563-588-8370.

HESSE, JERRY EDWARD, music educator; s. William G. Wessling and Merlyn E. Hesse; m. Pamela Jane Hesse, Aug. 11, 1967; 1 child, Suzanne Michelle Vinson. BS, Cinn. Bible Sem., 1968; EdM, U. Cinn., 1989. Music tchr. Cinn. Pub. Sch., 1969—99; substitute organist Am. Guild Organists, Cinn., 1999—2003; dir. music, organist Trinity United Meth. Ch., Arcadia, Fla., 2003—05. Organist Madiera C.C., Ohio, 1996—99. Choir dir., organist Westwood Ch. of Christ, Cinn., 1973—92, elder, 1982—92, edn. supr., 1974—89. Mem.: Am. Guild Organist, Rotary, Phi Delta Kappa. Republican. Mem. Church Of Christ. Home: 8183 SW Aviary Lake Suzy FL 34269 Office: Trinity UMC 304 W Oak St Arcadia FL 34266

HESSE, KAREN (KAREN SUE HESSE), writer, educator; b. Balt., Aug. 29, 1952; d. Alvin Donald and Frances Broth Levin; m. Randy Hesse; children: Kate, Rachel. BA, U. Md., 1975. Reference libr. U. Md., 1973-75, leave benefit coord., 1975-76; advt. sec. Country Journal mag., 1976-77, typesetter, proofreader, 1978-88; mental health care provider, 1989-91; children's lit. reviewer, 1993-94. Author: (children's books) Wish on a Unicorn, 1991 (Hungry Mind Rev. Children's Book of Distinction 1992), Letters From Rifka, 1992 (Nat. Jewish Book award 1993, IRA Children's Book award 1993, Christopher award 1992, Sydney Taylor Book award 1992, ALA Notable Book 1992, ALA Best Book for Young Adults 1992, Sch. Libr. Jour. Best Book of Yr. 1992, Horn Book Outstanding Book of Yr. 1992, Booklist Editors' Choice 1992, NY Pub. Libr. 100 Titles for Reading and Sharing 1992), Poppy's Chair, 1993 (Am. Booksellers Assn. Pick of List 1993), Lester's Dog, 1993 (Best Book of Yr. Sch. Libr. Jour. 1993, Notable Children's Trade Book in Field of Social Studies 1993), Lavender, 1993, Sable, 1994 (Sch. Libr. Jour. Best Book of Yr. 1994, NY Pub. Libr. 100 Titles for Reading and Sharing 1994, Boston Globe 10 Best Trade Books 1994, Parenting Mag. 40 Outstanding Children's Books 1994), Phoenix Rising, 1994 (Sch. Libr. Jour. Best Book of Yr. 1994, IRA Tchr.'s Choice 1995, NY Pub. Libr. Books for the Teenage 1995, Best Book for Young Adults ALA 1995, Notable Book, 1995, Wilson Libr. Bull. 33 Favorite Reads 1994 (S.C. Jr. Book award, 1996, 97, others), A Time of Angels, 1995 (IRA Tchr's Choice 1996, IRA Young Adults' Choice, 1997, NY Pub. Libr. Books for the Teenager 1995), The Music of Dolphins, 1996 (Pub.'s Weekly Best Book of Yr. 1996, Best Book of Yr. Sch. Libr. Jour. 1996, Book Links, 100 Titles for Reading and Sharing NY Pub. Libr. Children's Book 1996, Best Books for Young Adults ALA, 1997, Golden Kite Honor Book, 1997), Out of the Dust, 1997 (Newbery medal 1998, Scott O'Dell award 1998), Just Juice, 1998 (100 Titles for Reading and Sharing NY Pub. Libr. 1998, Notable Children's Trade Book in the Field of Social Studies 1998), Come On, Rain!, 1999 (BCCB Blue Ribbon Book, NYPL 100 Books for Reading & Sharing, Jr. Library Guild selection, Book of the Month Club selection, Hon. Mention award, Columbus Internat. Film Fest., ALA Notable Video, 2004); contbr. When I Was Your Age, Vol. II, 1999 (2000 Books for the Teen Age), A Light in the Storm, 1999 (Notable Children's Trade Book in the Field of Social Studies 1999, Kennedy Ctr. Stage Adaptation, 2001), Stowaway, 2000 (SLJ Book of Yr., 2001, Capitol Choice Noteworthy Books for Children (10-14), 100 Titles for Reading and Sharing NY Pub. Libr., 2000, Jr. Libr. Guild Selection), Witness, 2001 (NY Pub. Libr. 100 Books for Reading and Sharing, ALA Notable Children's book, LA 100 Best Books 2001, 2002 IRA Notable 2002, CBC Choice 2002, Myers Award 2002, NCTE Notable 2002, Christopher award 2002, Parents Guide to Children's Media award); Aleutian Sparrow, 2003 (Jr. Libr. Guild selection 100 Titles for Reading and Sharing), The Stone Lamp, 2003 (NY Pub. Libr. 100 Titles, Assn. Jewish Librs. Notable), The Cats in Krasinski Square, 2004 (PW Best Book award 2004, Kirkus Editor's Choice 2004, N.Y. Pub. Libr. 100 Titles for Reading and Sharing, Parent Choice Gold award, Book Sense Children's Picks List for Winter 2004-2005, ALA Notable, Koret Jewish Book award); contbr. articles to profl. jours. Chmn. Sch. Bd., 1989; sec. bd. dirs. Moore Free Libr., 1989-91; active Hospice, 1988—. MacArthur fellow, 2003—. Mem. Soc. Children's Book Writers and Illustrators, So. Vt. Soc. Children's Book Writers (leader 1985-92), Ctr. for Children's Environ. Lit., Author's Guild. Avocations: reading, hiking, cultivating friendships, music. Office: Scholastic 557 Broadway New York NY 10012-3919

HESSE, MARTHA O., gas industry executive; b. Hattiesburg, Miss., Aug. 14, 1942; d. John William and Geraldine Elaine (Ossian) H. BS, U. Iowa, 1964; postgrad., Northwestern U., 1972-76; MBA, U. Chgo., 1979. Research analyst Blue Shield, 1964-66; dir. div. data mgmt. Am. Hosp. Assn., 1966-69; dir., chief operating officer SEI Info. Tech., Chgo., 1969-80; assoc. dep. sec. Dept. of Commerce, Washington, 1981-82; exec. dir. Pres.' Task Force on Mgmt. Reform, 1982; asst. sec. mgmt. and adminstrn. Dept. of Energy, Washington, 1982-86; chmn. FERC, Washington, 1986-89; sr. v.p. 1st Chgo. Corp., 1990; CEO Hesse Gas Co., Houston, 1990—2003. Bd. dirs. Pinnacle West Capital Corp., Ariz. Pub. Svc. Co., Mut. Trust Life, AMEC plc, Terra Industries, Enbridge Energy Prnrs. Home: 4171 Autumn Hills Dr Winnemucca NV 89445

HESSE, MICHAEL, physicist; s. Josef and Margret Hesse; m. Therese Moretto-Jorgensen; children: Benjamin Moretto-Krog, Sebastian Moretto-Krog, Sabrina. Dr.rer.nat. in Theoretical Physics, Ruhr U., 1988. Sr. scientist Hughes Sys. Corp., Lanham, Md., 1991—93; sr. staff scientist NASA Goddard Space Flight Ctr., Greenbelt, 1993—. Dir. cmty. coord. modeling ctr. NASA Goddard Space Flight Ctr., 1999—; alt. mem. US Com. Space Weather, Silver Spring, 2000—; cons. DoD Nat. Security Space Arch., Alexandria, Va., 1999—2000; mem., steering com. NSF Geospace Environment Modeling Program, Arlington, 1993—98, campaign co-coord.; guest lectr. Niels Bohr Inst., U. Copenhagen, 2000—00; mem. NASA Sun-Earth Connection Roadmap, Washington, 2002—03. Recipient Grad. "mit Auszeichnung", Ruhr U., Bochum, 1985, Space Sci. Achievement award, NASA Goddard Space Flight Ctr., 2002, Group Achievement award, for Cmty. Cooordinated Modeling Ctr., 2004, Air Force Directorate of Weather medal, USAF Dir. Weather, BGen. Johnson, 2003; Dir. postdoctral fellow, Los Alamos Nat. Lab., N.Mex., 1988—91. Achievements include research in Produced complete theoretical description of the dissipation region in collisionless magnetic reconnection; first to Founding director of the Community Coordinated Modeling Center, a multi-agency partnership that aims at the development of advanced space science models for space weather applications. Avocations: sailing, skiing, hiking. Office: NASA Goddard Space Flight Center Code 612.3 Greenbelt MD 20771 Office Phone: 301-286-8224. E-mail: michael.hesse@nasa.gov.

HESSELBEIN, FRANCES RICHARDS, foundation administrator, consultant, editor; b. South Fork, Pa. d. Burgess Harmon and Anne Luke (Wicks) Richards; widowed, 1978; 1 child, John Richards. DHL (hon.), Buena Vista Coll., 1987, Juniata Coll., 1990, Hood Coll., 1991; D Mgmt. (hon.), GM Inst., 1990; LLD (hon.), Wilson Coll., 1991; LHD (hon.), Marymount-Tarrytown Coll., 1993; DHL (hon.), Boston Coll., 1994, U. Nebr., Kearney, 1994, Lafayette Coll., 1995, Carroll Coll., 1996, Fairleigh Dickinson U., 1996, Muhlenburg Coll., 1996; LLD (hon.), Moravian Coll., 2000; D in Pub. and Internat. Affairs, U. Pitts., 2001; DHL (hon.), Mt. Mary Coll., 2002, Union Inst. and Univ., 2003, U. Cin., 2003. CEO Talus Rock Girl Scout Coun., Johnstown, 1970-74, Penn Laurel Girl Scout Coun., York, Pa., 1974-76, Girl Scouts U.S., N.Y.C., 1976-90; pres., CEO Peter F. Drucker Found. Nonprofit Mgmt., N.Y.C., 1990-99, chmn., 1999—2003, Leader To Leader Inst., N.Y.C., 2003—. Chmn. Nat. Bd. Vols. Am.; bd. dirs. Mut. of Am. Ins. Co., N.Y.C.; nat. bd. visitors Peter F. Drucker Grad. Mgmt. Sch. Claremont (Calif.) Grad. Sch., 1987—; chmn. bd. govs. Josephson Ethics Inst., 1989-99; adv. com. to bd. dirs. N.Y. Stock Exch., 1988-91; bd. govs. Ctr. for Creative Leadership, Greensboro, N.C., 1992-98; adv. bd. Harvard Bus. Sch.'s Initiative on Social Enterprise, Harvard's Kennedy Sch. Hauser Ctr. Nonprofit Policy and Leadership Program; chmn. Vols. Am., 2002-, Leader to Leader Inst., 2003—. Editor-in-chief Leader to Leader; co-editor The Leader of the Future, The Organization of the Future, The Community of the Future, Drucker Found. Future Series, Leader to Leader Book, 1999, Leading Beyond the Walls, 1999; author: Hesselbein on Leadership, 2002. Trustee Juniata Coll., Huntingdon, Pa., 1988—, Allentown (Pa.) Coll., 1988-97; mem. Pres.'s Adv. Com. on Points of Light Initiative Found., 1989; bd. dirs. Nat. Exec. Svc. Corps., N.Y., Commn. on Nat. and Cmty. Svc., 1991-94; adv. bd. The Leadership Inst., U. So. Calif., 1991, Harvard U.'s John F. Kennedy Sch. Govt. Nonprofit Policy and Leadership Program. Recipient Outstanding Achievement award Inter-Svc. Club Coun., Johnstown, 1976, Entrepreneurial Woman award Women Bus. Owners of N.Y., 1984, Nat. Leadership award United Way of Am., Washington, 1985, Disting. Cmty. Svc. award Mut. of Am. Ins. Co., 1985, Dir.'s Choice-award Nat. Women's Econ. Alliance, 1989, Pa. Soc. Disting. Citizen award, 1991, Wilbur M. McFeeley award Internat. Mgmt. Coun. YMCA, 1993, U. Pitts. Legacy Laureate award, 2000, Internat. Leadership award Athena Found., 2001, Henry Russo award Ind. U. Ctr., 2001, Dwight D. Eisenhower Series Nat. Security award, 2002, Leadership Devel. award, Boston U., 2003, Juliette award Women of Distincton Girl Scouts USA, 2004, Visionary award Am Soc. Assn. Execs., 2004; named to Bus. Hall of Fame, Johnstown, 1995; named Outstanding Exec., Savvy Mag., 1985, Disting. Alumni Fellow U. Pitts., 1999, Disting. Dau. of Pa., Gov. Ridge, 1999, Woman of Yr., Boy Scouts of Greater N.Y., Legacy Laureate, U. Pitts., 2000; on cover BusinessWeek, 1990, Presdl. Medal of Freedom, 1998; featured in Chief Exec. mag., 1995, Fortune, 1995-96, Chapel of Four Chaplains Gold Legion of Hon. medal, 1999, Athena Found.-Internat. Leadership award, 2001, Henry Rosso award for lifetime ethical fundraising Ind. U. Ctr., 2001-02, Marion Gisalon award Boston U., 2003, Juliette award Girl Scouts U.S., 2004, Visionary award A.S.A.E., 2004; Frances Hesselbein How To Be Leadership award for Ethical Leadership established at Jur. Achievement, 2003. Mem. Sky Club, Pa. Soc., Cosmos Club (Washington). Office: Leader to Leader Inst 320 Park Ave 3d Fl New York NY 10022-6815 Office Phone: 212-224-1154. Office Fax: 212-224-2508. Business E-Mail: frances@leadertoleader.org.

HESSELINK, LAMBERTUS, electrical engineering and physics educator; b. Enschede, The Netherlands, Dec. 4, 1948; came to U.S., 1971; s. Lambertus and Wilhelmina (ten Tye) H. BSME, Twente Inst. Tech., Enschede, 1970, BS in Applied Physics, 1971, postgrad., 1974; MSME, Calif. Inst. Tech., 1972, PhD in Applied Mechs., Physics, 1977. Rsch. fellow Calif. Inst. Tech., Pasadena, 1977-78, instr. applied physics, 1978-80, sr. rsch. fellow fluid mechs., 1979-80; asst. prof. aeros. and astronautics Stanford (Calif.) U., 1980-85, asst. prof., 1985—, assoc. prof. elec. engring., 1980-85, asst. prof., 1985-90, prof. electrical engring. and aeronautics/astonautics, 1990—. Cons. Hughes Aircraft Corp., Culver City, Calif., 1978-79, MCC Corp., 1986-92; invited scientist mem. image processing work group for Hubble Space Telescope, 1990; assoc. editor Jour. Applied Sci. and Applied Optics, 1990; founder Siros Technologies, Inc.; cons. to industry and govt.; mem. scientific adv. bd. USAF, 1995—; founder Senvid, Inc. Patentee in field. Recipient Stheeman prize Twente Inst. Tech., 1970; Fulbright fellow 1971-74; Josephine de Karman fellow, 1974-75. Fellow SPIE, Optical Soc. Am.; mem. AIAA (Engr. of Yr. 1982), Soc. Photo-Optical Instrumentation Engrs. Optical Soc. Am., Am. Phys. Soc., Royal Dutch Acad. Arts and Scis. (corr.), Sigma Xi. Office: Stanford U Mail Code 4075 CISX Bldg Rm 325 Stanford CA 94305-4075 E-mail: bert@kaos.stanford.edu.

HESSER, CHRISTA E., secondary school educator; b. Springfield, Ill., Feb. 2, 1949; d. James Lowell and Christa Gisela (Grabski) Lawhorn; m. Francis Edward Hesser, July 27, 1974; children: Karen Ann, Heidi Noel. BA, Ill. State U., 1972, MA, 1973. Cert. secondary tchr. Ill. Tchr. English, Lincoln-Way HS, New Lenox, Ill., 1973—. Mem. ASCD, NEA, Nat. Coun. Tchrs. English, Kappa Delta Epsilon, Kappa Tau Delta, Pi Omega Pi. Office: Lincoln-Way HS English Dept Rt 30 New Lenox IL 60451

HESSERT, WILFRED, retired military officer; BS in Acctg. magna cum laude, Husson Coll., 1969; M in Bus. Adminstrn., Auburn U., 1974; grad., Air Command and Staff Coll., 1974, Air War Coll., 1982, CAPSTONE, 1997. Commd. 2d lt. USAF, 1968, advanced through grades to maj. gen., 1997; pilot 132d Fighter Inceptor Squadron, Maine Air N.G., Dow AFB, Maine, 1967-72; aircraft maintenance and flight test officer Maine Air N.G., Bangor Internat. Airport, 1972-76, chief of maintenance, 1976-79; comdr. 101st Consol. Aircraft Maintenance Squadron Maine Air N.G., Bangor Air N.G. Base, 1979-84, dep. comdr. for maintenance 101st Consol. Aircraft Main. Sq., 1984-87, dep. comdr. for ops. Hdqs., 1987-91, vice wing comdr. 101st Air Refueling Wing, 1991, wing comdr. 101st Air Refueling Wing, 1991-96; Air N.G. asst. to comdr. US Air Forces in Europe, Ramstein Air Base, Germany, 1996-97; dep. inspector gen. Hdqs. USAF, Washington, 1997—99; mil. exec. (ret.) Res. Forces Bd. Policy, Arlington, Va., 1999—2000. Decorated Legion of Merit, Meritorious Svc. medal with oak leaf cluster.

HESSINGER, GREG, entertainment company executive; Grad., Lebanon Valley Coll.; JD, St. John's U., 1990. Atty. Skadden, Arps, Slate, Meagher & Flom, NY, 1990—94, Westinghouse Broadcasting Co., 1994—98; nat. asst. exec. dir. news/broadcast AFTRA, N.Y.C., 1998—2000, exec. dir., 2000—05; CEO, nat. exec. dir. Screen Actors Guild, 2005—. Office: SAG 5757 Wilshire Blvd Los Angeles CA 90036-3600 Office Phone: 323-954-1600.*

HESSLER, DAVID WILLIAM, information and multimedia systems educator; b. Oak Park, Ill., May 9, 1932; s. William Wigney and Gwendolyn Eileen (Butler) H.; m. Helen Montgomery, Aug. 27, 1955; children: Leslie Susan, Laura Lynne. BA, U. Mich., 1955, MA, 1961; PhD, Mich. State U., 1972. Comml. photographer Oscar & Assocs., Chgo., 1950; equipment engr. Western Electric Co., Chgo., 1958-59; dir. librs. and media Ann Arbor (Mich.) Pub. Schs., 1966-67; asst. prof. edn. Western Mich. U., 1967-72, assoc. prof., 1974-77; dir. instrnl. svcs., dir. broadcasting, prof. edn. U. S.C., 1973-74; cons., asst. dir. Audio-Visual Edn. Ctr. U. Mich., Ann Arbor, 1960-66, prof. Sch. Info., 1977-98, prof. emeritus, 1998—, dir. instrnl. strategy svcs. for schs. of edn., libr. sci., 1979-81, pres. Ann Arbor sys. and tech., 1987—, exec. dir. for info. svcs. Info-Span, 1991-92; exec. v.p. Infotronix, Ann Arbor, 1993-97. Cons. Presdl. Commn. on World Hunger; cons. media and tech.; instrnl. designer and evaluator; bd. dirs. Kirsch Techs.; vis. prof., cons. dept. biblioteconomia U. Brazil, 1981. Author: (with J. Smith) Student Production Guide, 1975, Technology for Communication and Instruction, 1983; producer/dir. numerous films, filmstrips, TV programs and sound/slide programs for various ednl. levels. Lt. USAF, 1955-58; capt. Res. ret. Decorated Air Force Commendation medal; named Mich. Most Valuable Tchr. Chrysler Corp., 1965; Ednl. Profl. Devel. Act fellow, 1968-69. Mem. ALA, ASTD, Assn. Image and Info. Mgmt., M Club, Phi Kappa Phi. Home: 24 Southwick Ct Ann Arbor MI 48105-1410 Office: Univ Mich Sch Info W Hall 550 E University Ave Ann Arbor MI 48109-1092 Business E-Mail: dwh@umich.edu.

HESSLER, WILLIAM GERHARD, tax specialist, consultant; b. Chgo., May 20, 1926; s. William Gerhard and Rosemary (Kalb) Hessler; m. Kazuko Yonetsu, June 2, 1956 (dec. Mar. 1995); children: Martha, George, Kay, Emmy. BSEE, Purdue U., 1946; MBA, Northwestern U., 1956. Cert. data processor, individual tax profl. Tech. intelligence investigator U.S. Army, Tokyo, 1947-50, electronics engr. signal corps. Yokohama, Japan, 1952-54;

mfg., devel. engr. Western Electric, Chgo., 1955-61; engring. specialist Goodyear Aerospace Corp., Akron, Ohio, 1961-65; computer applications programmer analyst Goodyear Tire & Rubber Co., Akron, 1965-83, computer operating systems programmer, 1983-87; cons. Cutler-Williams, Independence, Ohio, 1987; systems engineer Profl. Support, Inc., Brecksville, Ohio, 1989. Tax cons. and return preparer H & R Block, Greater Akron, 1969—80, Akron Nat. Tax & Notary, 1981, Tax Ctr. and Fin. Solutions, Inc. (formerly Hammer Tax Ctr.), Akron, 1982—2001; cons. in field; agt. enrolled to practice U.S. Dept . Treasury IRS, 1984—2002. Scoutmaster Boy Scouts Am., Silver Lake, Ohio, 1972—77. With U.S. Army, 1950—52, Japan. Mem.: AARP (pres. chpt. 3515 2003). Roman Catholic. Avocation: amateur radio (w8dxt). Home: 3046 Lake Rd Stow OH 44224-3814 E-mail: J2QBI@aol.com.

HESTER, BRUCE EDWARD, library media specialist, lay worker; b. Clarksville, Tenn., June 26, 1956; s. Edward Vaughan and Mabel Sarah (Chandley) H. BS, Middle Tenn State U., 1978; MEd, Trevecca Nazarene Coll., 1987. Cert. elem. tchr., cert. secondary tchr. and libr., Tenn. Tchr. Met.-Davidson County Schs., Nashville, 1993-98; libr. Clarksville/Montgomery County Schs., Clarksville, Tenn., 1998—. Adj. faculty-vol. State C.C., Gallatin, Tenn., 1993-2001; choir dir. First Christian Ch., Dover, Tenn., 1983-95, Sunday sch. tchr., deacon, 1988-93, chmn. bd. dirs., 1989-95; dir. Stewart County Cmty. Choir, 1987-89. Co-chmn. Stewart County Rep. Party, 1986-89. Recipient Vol. Svc. award Cystic Fibrosis Found., 1984, Mayor's Acts of Excellence award, 1994; named E. Middle Sch. Tchr. of Yr., 1996. Mem. ALA, NEA, Tenn. Edn. Assn., Tenn. Assn. Sch. Librs. (conf. coord.), Tenn. Assn. Mid. Schs., Clks. Montgomery County Edn. Assn. (editor The Collective Voice, mem. CMCEA negotiations team 2002-03, East Mid. Sch. Tchr. of Yr. 1995, N.E. Mid. Sch. Tchr. of Yr. 2000). Mem. Christian Ch. (Disciples Of Christ). Home: 1724 Valley Rd Clarksville TN 37043-4537 Office: Northeast Middle Sch 3703 Trenton Rd Clarksville TN 37040-5622 Personal E-mail: hesterb@charter.net. *Our heritage is the foundation of our future. As children, our parents help to build us to be able to meet the challenge of life and embrace the future. The option is ours; to add to that foundation or remain unfinished.*

HESTER, D. MICAH, education educator; b. Pomona, Calif., July 16, 1966; s. James D. and Darylin J. Hester; m. Kelly Nugent Sherman, Oct. 1, 1993; children: Emily Sherman, Joshua Davis. BA, Pomona Coll., Calif., 1988; MA, Vanderbilt U., Nashville, 1995, PhD, 1998. Adj. asst. prof. philosophy Tenn. State U., Nashville, 1993—99; asst. prof. biomedical ethics and humanities Mercer Univ. Sch. of Medicine, Macon, Ga., 1999—2004; asst. prof. med. humanities U. Ark. for Med. Sci., Little Rock, 2004—. Sec. treas. William James Soc., 2001—. Author: (scholarly monograph) Community As Healing, 2001, On James, 2004; editor: (textbook anthology) Computers and Ethics in the Cyberage, 2001, (scholarly anthology) Dewey's Logical Theory, 2002, A William Ernest Hocking Reader, 2004. Office: UAMS 4301 W Markham St #646 Little Rock AR 72205 Office Phone: 501-661-7970. Personal E-mail: hesterdm@alum.pomona.edu. E-mail: hesterdm@uams.edu.

HESTER, DOUGLAS BENJAMIN, lawyer; b. McKenzie, Ala., Sept. 18, 1927; s. Mack Ellis and Carrie Lottie (Taylor) H.; m. Melissa Hood Fuller, Apr. 16, 1960; children: Carlotta Marie, Benjamin Alexander. BS, U. Ala., 1950, LL.B., 1952. Bar: Ala. 1952, D.C. 1960, U.S. Supreme Ct. Law asst. Office Legis. Counsel-U.S. Senate, Washington, 1952-54, asst. counsel, 1954-69, sr. counsel, 1969-80; legis. counsel U.S. Senate, 1980-91; mem., liaison between Ala. and U.S. Congress Svc. Corps. of Retired Execs., 1992-93. Trustee Centro Anglo-Espanol, Washington, 1990. Served with AUS, 1945-47. Mem. ABA, D.C. Bar Assn., Ala. Bar Assn., Farah Order of Jurisprudence, Pi Alpha Delta, Omicron Delta Kappa, Sigma Delta Pi, Pi Kappa Phi. Home: 2171 Vaughn Ln Montgomery AL 36106-3252

HESTER, JAMES MCNAUGHTON, retired foundation administrator, artist; b. Chester, Pa., Apr. 19, 1924; s. James Montgomery and Margaret (McNaughton) H.; m. Janet Rodes, May 23, 1953; children: Janet McN., Margaret, Martha. BA, Princeton U., 1945, LL.D. (honoris causa), 1962; BA (Rhodes scholar 1947-50), Oxford (Eng.) U., 1950, D.Phil., 1955; LL.D., Lafayette Coll., 1964, Morehouse Coll., 1967; L.H.D., Hartwick Coll., 1964; LHD (hon.), Pace U., 1971, U. Pitts., 1971, Colgate U., 1974; L.H.D., N.Y. U., 1977; DCL, Alfred U., 1965; LLD (hon.), Hofstra U., 1967, Hahnemann Med. Coll., 1967, Fordham U., 1971, Amherst Coll., 1975, New Sch. for Social Rsch., 1975, Union Coll., 1983. Civil information officer Fukuoka Mil. Govt. Team, Japan, 1946-47; asst. to Am. sec. to Rhodes Trustees, 1950; asst. to pres. Handy Assocs., Inc. (mgmt. cons.), N.Y.C., 1953-54; account supr. Gallup and Robinson, Inc., Princeton, N.J., 1954-57; provost Bklyn. center L.I. U., 1957-60, v.p., 1958-60; prof. history, exec. dean arts and sci., dean Grad. Sch. Arts and Sci. N.Y.U., 1960-61, pres., 1962-75; rector UN U., Tokyo, 1975-80; pres. N.Y. Bot. Garden, 1980-89, The Harry Frank Guggenheim Found., N.Y.C., 1989—2004, also bd. dirs.; ret., 2004. Bd. dirs. various Alliance Funds. Trustee Lehman Found. Served with USMCR, 1943-46, 51-52. Mem. Assn. Am. Rhodes Scholars Clubs: Century Assn., University, Pretty Brook Tennis.

HESTER, JULIA A., lawyer; b. L.A., Nov. 14, 1953; d. Robert William and Bertie Ella (Gilbert) Hester; children: Allison Hester-Haddad, Nancy Hester-Haddad. BA, Fla. Atlantic U., 1984; JD, Nova U., 1990. Bar: Fla. 1990, U.S. Dist. Ct. (mid. dist.) Fla. 1993. Asst. pub. defender Broward Pub. Defender, Ft. Lauderdale, Fla., 1990-93; atty., ptnr. Haddad & Hester, Ft. Lauderdale, 1993-95, 97—. Bd. dirs. St. Anthony Found., Ft. Lauderdale, Ft. Lauderdale Billfish Tournament, 1992—96; bd. dirs., mem. exec. bd. St. Thomas Aquinas Found.; mem. Sunrise Intercoastal Bd., Ft. Lauderdale, 1995; bd. dirs., officer Kids Inn Distress Aux., Ft. Lauderdale, 1984—87. Office: 1 Financial Plz Ste 2612 Fort Lauderdale FL 33394-0061

HESTER, KARLTON EDWARD, composer, musician, educator; b. El Paso, Tex., Feb. 11, 1949; s. Webb and Clara (Briggs) Hester; m. Bette Jean Hered (dec.); 1 child, Karlton William; m. Alissa J. Roedig; 1 child, Nanaiya Fabaynima. MusB, U. Tex., El Paso, 1971; MusM, San Francisco State U., 1978; PhD in Composition, CUNY, 1990. Music dir. Eisenhower HS, Rialto, Calif., 1971-74, San Francisco and Oakland (Calif.) Pub. Schs., 1977-82, Contempory Jazz Art Movement, San Francisco, N.Y.C., 1977-82; pres. Hesteria Records & Pub. Co., San Francisco, N.Y.C., 1981—; asst. prof. Coll. S.I., NY, 1990-91, 1990-91; artist in residence N.Y. Found. Arts, N.Y.C., 1984-88, 1984-91; composer in residence Western Edition Cultural Ctr., San Francisco, 1980-81; Herbert Gussman dir. jazz studies Cornell U., Ithaca, N.Y., 1991-2000; dir. jazz studies U. Calif., Santa Cruz, 2000—; pres. Interdisciplinary Artists Aggregation, Inc., Ithaca, NY. Adj. prof. Bronx (N.Y.) CC, 1985—88, Coll. S.I., 1988—91; composer in residence, music dir. Cazadero Music Camp, Berkeley, Calif., 1982; dir. Hesterian Musicism, 1990—; founding dir. Global African Music Festival/Symposium, UC Santa Cruz, 2002—03, Fillmore Jazz Preservation Big Band, San Francisco, 2003—. Author: The Melodic and Polyrhythonic Development of John Coltrane's Spontaneous Composition in a Racist Society, 1997, Bigotry and the Afrocentric Jazz Evolution, 2004, From Africa to Afrocentric Innovations Some Call Jazz, 2000; editor: Juba Jour.; editor-in-chief: Living Encyclopedia of Global African Music, 2000—, prodr., composer: record albums. Recipient S.I. Cmty. TV NOVA Video award for a children's jazz video, Merit award in Composition, Howard Found., 1996; fellow, Mellon Found., 1991—92; grantee, NEA, 1985, 1989, New Eng. Coun. Arts, 1986, S.I. Coun. Arts, 1987, 1990, 1991, Fund U.S. Artists Internat. Festival & Exhbns., 1994—95. Mem.: ASCAP (Popular and Std. awards), Am. Fedn. Musicians, Nat. Flute Assn. Rosicrucian Order. Avocation: sports. Office: U Calif Santa Cruz Music Dept Santa Cruz CA 95064 Office Phone: 831-459-2575.

HESTER, LINDA HUNT, retired dean, counseling administrator, sociology educator, health and physical education educator; b. Winston-Salem, NC, June 16, 1938; d. Hanselle Lindsay and Jennie Sarepta (Hunt) H. BS with honors, U. Wis., 1960, MS, 1964; PhD, Mich. State U., 1971. Lic. ednl. counselor, Wis. Instr. health and phys. edn. for women U. Tex., Austin, 1960—62; asst. dean women U. Ill., Urbana, 1964—66; dean of women, asst. prof. sociology and phys. edn. Tex. Woman's U., Denton, 1971—73; ret., 1973. Rsch. assoc. bur. higher edn. Mich. Dept. Edn., Lansing, 1969-70; vol. counselor Dallas Challenge and Dallas Ind. Sch. Dist., 1989-90 Bd. dirs. Dallas Opera, Dallas, 1986—; Stradivarious mem. Dallas Symphony, 1991—; assoc. mem. Dallas Mus. Art, 1991—; friend of Kimbell Art Mus., com. of 1000 Philharmonic Ctr. for Arts, Naples, Fla.; mem., donor Naples Mus. Art; founder Women's Mus., Dallas; founding mem. Dallas Ctr. Performing Arts; mem. governing bd. TACA; mem. Friends Art Dist., Dallas. Fellow coll. edn. Mich. State U., 1968 Mem. ACA, Am. Coll. Pers. Assn., Nat. Assn. Women in Edn., Brookhaven Country Club, Wyndemere Country Club, Delta Kappa Gamma, Alpha Lambda Delta. Republican. Presbyterian. Avocations: golf, music, sailing, cooking, travel. Home: 7606 Wellcrest Dr Dallas TX 75230-4857

HESTER, MARTIN LUTHER, publishing executive; b. Greensboro, N.C., Aug. 18, 1947; s. Martin Luther Hester Sr. and Avis E. Hester; m. Marsha Ann Hutchins, 1966 (div. 1978); 1 child, Leigh Ann Hester Hutchens. Student, Western Carolina Coll., 1965—66, Gulford Coll., 1966—67, U. N.C. Greensboro, 1968—71, student, 1975—77. Editor Tudor Pubs., Inc., Greensboro, NC, 1985—89, v.p., sr. editor, 1990—94; v.p., editor Morgan Reynolds, Inc., 1993—95; pres., pub. Avisson Press, Inc., 1995—. Bd. advisors Simmer Pot Press, Boone, NC, 1990. Author: Looking At You, 1984, Country Girl - The Life of Sissy Spacek, 1988, Another Jackie Robinson, 1996. Recipient Poetry prize, St. Andrews Rev., 1976. Mem.: Soc. Children's Book Writers and Illustrators, Nat. Writers Union, U. N.C. Greensboro Alumni Assn. Avocations: reading, guitar. Office: Avisson Press Inc PO Box 38816 Greensboro NC 27438

HESTER, NANCY ELIZABETH, county government official; b. Miami, Fla., Jan. 20, 1950; d. George Temple and Lorraine Patricia (Cluney) Hester. BA, Bucknell U., 1972; MIA, Columbia U., 1974; MBA, Fla. Internat. U., 1979; postgrad, Fla. Atlantic U., 2000—. Treasury rep. Westinghouse Electric Co., N.Y.C., 1974—76; adminstrv. officer serving in bldg. and zoning, gen. svcs. and corrections and rehab. depts. Metro Dade County, Fla., 1979—2000, bur. comdr. corrections and rehab. dept., 1990—2000. Adj. prof. Fla. Internat. U., Miami, 1980-83. Bd. dirs. YWCA Greater Miami, 1988-92, LWV Dade County, 1993-98; pres. bd. dirs., pres. bd. trustees edn. fund, 1994-96; mem. adv. bd. SafeSpace, 1995-2001, v.p. adv. bd., 2000.

HESTER, NORMAN ERIC, chemical company technical executive, chemist; b. Niangua, Mo., Dec. 16, 1946; s Eric Ira and Norma Josephine (Wright) H.; m. Sylvie Jean Hunt, June 16, 1973; children: Jenay Aimee, Yvette Joy, Trinity Marie. AA, El Camino Coll., 1966; BS, Calif. State U., Long Beach, 1968; MS, U. Calif., Riverside, 1971, PhD, 1972. Postdoctoral rsch. chemist U. Calif. Air Pollution Ctr., Riverside, 1972-74; air quality chemist EPA, Las Vegas, Nev., 1974-77; program mgr. Rockwell Internat., Newbury Park, Calif., 1977-80; group head Occidental Petroleum Rsch. Ctr., Irvine, Calif., 1980-83; tech. dir. Truesdail Labs. Inc., Tustin, Calif., 1983—. Pvt. environ. cons., Mission Viejo, Calif., 1983. Contbr. articles to profl. jours. Mem. Am. Chem. Soc., Assn. Ofcl. Racing Chemists. Republican. Avocations: growing hybrid roses, hiking, travel. Office: Truesdail Labs Inc 14201 Franklin Ave Tustin CA 92780-7008 Office Phone: 714-730-6239. E-mail: norman@truesdail.com, normanhester@netscape.net.

HESTER, PERRIETTA BURKE, artist, educator; b. El Centro, Calif., Mar. 8, 1925; d. Perry Alexander and Agnes M. (Pedersen) Burke; m. Henry Hartwell Hester, Aug. 23, 1947 (div. May 1967); children: Henry Hester Jr., Loraine Hester Dyson, Heather Hester Duckett. BA in Fine Art, San Diego State U., 1947, MA in Fine Art, 1967. Cert. tchr., Calif. Art educator L.A. Unified Schs., 1948-51, La Jolla (Calif.) Mus. Art, 1967-68, U. Calif., San Diego, 1968-70, San Diego Cmty. Coll., 1969—, U. Calif., Irvine, 1985, San Diego (Calif.) Zoological Inst., 1970-95. Lectr. in field. One- woman shows include The Atheneum, La Jolla, 1979, The Art Garden, Del Mar, Calif., 1980, San Vicente, Ramona, Calif., 1982, Knowles Gallery, La Jolla, 1989. Vol., counselor San Diego Artists, 1985—. Mem. San Diego Portrait Soc. (co-founder, chmn.), Calif. Art Club, San Diego Art Guild, Helga Gallery. Republican. Presby. Avocations: travel, painting, walking, golf. Home: 2600 All Torrey Pines Rd La Jolla CA 92037-0052

HESTER, THOMAS PATRICK, lawyer; b. Tulsa, Okla., Nov. 20, 1937; s. E.P. and Mary J. (Layton) H; m. Nancy B. Scofield, Aug. 20, 1960; children: Thomas P. Jr., Ann S., John L. BA, Okla. U., 1961, LLB, 1963. Bar: Okla. 1963, Mo. 1967, N.Y. 1970, D.C. 1973, Ill. 1975. Atty. McAfee & Taft, Okla. City, 1963-66, Southwestern Bell Telephone Co., Okla. City, St. Louis, 1966-72, AT&T, N.Y.C., Washington, 1972-75; gen. atty. Ill. Bell Telephone Co., Springfield, 1975-77, gen. solicitor Chgo., 1977-83, v.p., gen. counsel, 1983-87; sr. v.p., gen. counsel Ameritech, Chgo., 1987-91, exec. v.p., gen. counsel, 1991-97; ptnr. Mayer, Brown & Platt, Chgo., 1997—; sr. v.p., gen. counsel, sec. Sears, Roebuck and Co., 1998-99, FMC Corp., 2000. Corp. counsel ctr. adv. bd. Northwestern U., 1987-97. Mem. Taxpayers Fedn. Ill., Springfield, 1987-97, chmn. bd. trustees 1987-88; mem. adv. bd. Ill. Dept. Natural Resources, 1991-2000—, chmn., 1993-98; trustee Art Inst. Chgo., 1995-2000. Fellow Am. Bar Found.; mem. Am. Law Inst.

HESTER, THOMAS ROY, anthropologist, educator; b. Crystal City, Tex., Apr. 28, 1946; s. Jim Tom and Mattie Laura (Umphres) H.; m. Lynda Sue Broadway, July 2, 1966; children: Lesley Elise, Amy Lynne. BA with honors, U. Tex., Austin, 1969; PhD, U. Calif., Berkeley, 1972. Acting asst. prof. anthropology U. Calif., Berkeley, 1972-73; asst. prof. anthropology U. Tex., San Antonio, 1973-75, assoc. prof., 1975-77, prof., 1977-87, prof. anthropology Austin, 1987—2003, prof. emeritus, 2003—; dir. Ctr. for Archaeol. Research, 1974-87, Tex. Archeol. Rsch. Lab., 1987—2000. Vis. assoc. prof. U. Calif., Berkeley, 1976. Author: (with R. Heizer and J. Graham) Field Methods in Archaeology, 1975, Digging into South Texas Prehistory, 1980, (with R. Heizer and C. Graves) Archaeology: A Bibliographical Guide to the Basic Literature, 1980, (with G. Ligabue, S. Salvatori, M. Sartor) Colha e I Maya Dei Bassipiani, 1983, (with E.S. Turner) A Field Guide to the Stone Artifacts of Texas Indians, 1985, 2d edit., 1993, (with G. Ligabue) Robert F. Heizer's Age of Giants, 1990, (with H.J. Shafer) Maya Stone Tools, 1991; Ethnology of Texas Indians, 1991, (with H.J. Shafer and K.F. Feder) Field Methods in Archaeology, 7th edit., 1997; editl. bd. numerous jours.; contbr. articles to profl. jours. Woodrow Wilson fellow, 1969-70 Fellow Tex. Archeol. Soc. (pres. 1993); mem. Soc. Am. Archaeology (exec. com. 1984-86, award 2000), Assn. Field Archaeology (exec. com. 1979-82), Soc. Archaeol. Sci., Accademia Nazionale dei Lincei (fgn.), Sigma Xi (pres. Alamo chpt. 1979). Democrat. Methodist. Office: U Tex Archeol Rsch Lab Austin TX 78712-1100 Home: PO Box 625 Utopia TX 78884-0625

HESTHOLM, STIG, author; BS in Applied Math. & Numerical Analysis, U. Bergen, 1985, MS in Applied Math., 1987; PhD in Geophys., Rice U., 1999; DS in Seismology, U. Bergen, 1999. Rsch. scientist Norst Hydro, Bergen, 1985; teaching asst. dept. math. U. Bergen, 1986-87; teaching asst. Bergen AOF, 1989-91; rsch. scientist IBM, Bergen, 1987-94; with seismic rsch. project U. Bergen, 1995. Contbr. articles to profl. publs. Rsch. fellow MIT, 1993, 2001—, postdoctoral fellow U. Bergen, 2000-01. Office: MIT Earth Resources Lab 42 Carleton St Cambridge MA 02142

HESTON, CHARLTON (JOHN CHARLTON CARTER), actor; b. Evanston, Ill., Oct. 4, 1924; s. Russell Whitford and Lilla (Charlton) Carter; m. Lydia Marie Clarke, Mar. 17, 1944; children— Fraser Clarke, Holly Ann. Student, Northwestern U., 1941-43. Mem. Nat. Council on the Arts, 1967-72 Author: The Actor's Life, 1979, In the Arena, 1995; performances include: (stage) Antony and Cleopatra, 1947, Leaf and Bough, 1948, Design for a Stained Glass Window, 1949, The Tumbler, 1960; (TV appearances) Wuthering Heights, Macbeth, Taming of the Shrew, Of Human Bondage, Jane Eyre, The Nairobi Affair, 1984, The Proud Men, 1987, TNT, 1988, 90, 91, A Man For All Seasons (also dir.), 1988, Original Sin, 1989, Treasure Island, 1990, The Little Kidnappers, 1990, The Crucifer of Blood, Crash Landing: The Rescue of Flight 232, 1992, The Avenging Angel, 1995; (TV series) The Colbys, 1985-87, Chiefs (miniseries), 1983, (also writer) Charleton Heston Presents the Bible, 1993; (films) Dark City, Greatest Show on Earth, 1952, The Savage, 1952, Ruby Gentry, 1952, The President's Lady, 1952, Pony Express, 1983, Arrowhead, 1953, Bad for Each Other, 1954, Naked Jungle, 1954, The Secret of the Incas, 1954, The Far Horizons, 1955, Lucy Gallant, 1955, Private War of Major Benson, 1955, The Ten Commandments, 1956, Three Violent People, 1956, Touch of Evil, 1958, The Big Country, 1958, Ben Hur, 1959 (Acad. award for best actor), The Wreck of Mary Deare, 1959, El Cid, 1961, The Pigeon That Took Rome, 1962, 55 Days of Peking, 1963, Diamond Head, 1963, The Agony and The Ecstasy, 1963, The War Lord, 1965, The Greatest Story Ever Told, 1965, Khartoum, 1966, Planet of the Apes, 1967, Will Penny, 1968, Number One, 1969, Beneath The Planet of the Apes, 1969, Julius Caesar, 1970, The Hawaiians, 1970, The Omega Man, 1971, Antony and Cleopatra (also dir.), 1971, Skyjacked, 1972, Call of the Wild, 1972, Soylent Green, 1973, The Three Musketeers, 1973, Airport, 1974, The Four Musketeers, 1974, Earthquake, 1974, Midway, 1976, Two-Minute Warning, 1976, The Last Hard Men, 1976, The Prince and the Pauper, 1977, Gray Lady Down, 1977, Mountain Men, 1980, The Awakening, 1980, Mother Lode (also dir.), 1982, Solar Crisis, 1989, Almost An Angel, 1990 (cameo), Wayne's World 2 (cameo), Tombstone, 1993, True Lies, 1994, In the Mouth of Madness, 1995, Hamlet, 1996, Alaska, 1996, Ben Johnson: Third Cowboy On The Right, 1996, Hercules (voice), 1997, Illusion Infinity, 1998, Gideon's Webb, 1998, Armageddon (voice), 1998, Toscano, 1999, Any Given Sunday, 1999, Town & Country, 1999; TV movie Avenging Angel, 1995, I Am Your Child, 1997; dir. The Caine Mutiny Court-Martial (Beijing), 1988. Trustee Los Angeles Center Theatre Group, Am. Film Inst., 1971—, chmn., 1973; head President's Task Force on Arts and Humanities, 1981—; led the Pledge of Allegiance at the Republican Conv., New Orleans, 1988. Served in USAAF, World War II. Recipient Jean Hersholt award as Humanitarian of Yr. Am. Acad. Motion Picture Arts and Scis., 1978, Citizenship medal VFW, 1982, Golden medal City of Vianna, 1995. Mem. Screen Actors Guild (pres. 1966-71), NRA (pres. 1998-2003) Office: care Jack Gilardi ICM 8942 Wilshire Blvd Beverly Hills CA 90211-1934*

HESTON, JOAN, artist, art educator; b. Hartford, Conn., Sept. 20; m. Charles Heston; children: Lynne, Rand. Grad., Pratt Inst.; student, Art Students League N.Y.C., Studio II, Westport, Conn., Silvermine Guild, New Canaan, Conn. Tchr., critic, Stamford, Conn.; juror various art shows, 1979—. Exhibited in group shows at Nat. Acad., N.Y.C., Conn. Acad. Fine Arts, Stamford Mus., Am. Acad. and Inst. Arts and Letters; contbr. chapters to books on painting, articles to profl. jours. Recipient Philip Isenberg award, Knickerbocker Artists, 1988, Silver medal, 1987. Mem.: Nat. League Am. Penwomen (v.p. Pioneer br. 1980—84, Achievement award Conn. chpt. 1985—86), Conn. Watercolor Soc., Silvermine Guild Artists (trustee 1989—), Conn. Acad. Fine Arts (Best Portrait 1975), Audubon Artists (Emily Lowe award 1981), Nat Arts Club (Silver medal 1981, B. Stevensen Portrait award 1985, Salzman award 1990), Allied Artists Am. (bd. dirs., pres. 1984—85, Salmagundi award 1976, S. Anthony D'Orai award 1984, Silver medal 1985), Pen and Brush Club (Solo Show award 1979, 1983), Catharine Lorillard Wolfe Art Club (Gold medal 1981, 1983). Home: 29 Hemlock Dr Stamford CT 06902-1808 Personal E-mail: joanheston@aol.com.

HESTON, THOMAS J., historian, educator; b. Bethesda, Md., Nov. 2, 1945; s. Walter Enoch and Vivian Janney Heston; m. Susan Luella De Vore, Oct. 1969; 1 child, Timothy Michael. AB, Gettysburg Coll., 1967; MA, Case Western Res., 1972, PhD, 1975. Grad. fellow Case Western Res., 1970—74; veterans benefits counselor VA, Cleve., 1974—75; asst. prof. West Chester State Coll., Pa., 1975—81; assoc. prof. West Chester U., Pa., 1981—86, prof., 1986—. Acting asst. dean Coll. of Arts & Sci., West Chester U., 1986—87, dept. chair, 1990—92; cons. Delaware County Vets. Mus., 2003—04, Sta. WPHL-TV, 1995, Phila. Inquirer. Author: (book) Sweet Subsidy, 1987; contbr. articles to profl. jours. and encys. With U.S. Army, 1968—70. Grantee Bernadette E. Schmitt fellowship, Case Western Res. U., 1973. Mem.: Soc. of Mil. History, US Naval Inst., Soc. of Historians of Am. Fgn. Rels., Orgn. of Am. Historians. Office: Dept of History West Chester U West Chester PA 19383 Office Phone: 610-436-2972. Business E-Mail: theston@wcupa.edu.

HETFIELD, JAMES, singer; b. Los Angeles, Calif., Aug. 3, 1963; Former co-founder, singer Phantom Lord; former co-founder, lead singer, songwriter & rhythm guitarist Leather Charm; co-founder, lead singer, songwriter & rhythm guitarist Metallica, 1981—. Albums include Kill 'em All, 1983, Ride the Lightning, 1984, Master of Puppets, 1986, ...And Justice for All, 1988, Metallica, 1991, Live Sh*t: Binge and Purge, 1993, Kill 'Em All, 1995, Load, 1996, Reload, 1997, Garage Inc., 1998 (Grammy award), S & M, 1999, St. Anger, 2003 (Grammy award best metal performance, 2003); played on compilation albums including Metal Massacre, 1982, The Good, The Bad and The Live, 1990, Rubaiyant: Elektra's 30th Anniversary, 1990, For Those About To Rock: Moscow, 1992, Woodstock '94, 1994, Spawn: The Album, 1997, Woodstock '99, 2000, WCW: Mayhem The Music, 1999, M:I-2, 2000, NASCAR: Full Throttle, 2001, Swizz Beatz Presents G.H.E.T.T.O. Stories, 2002, Biker Boyz Soundtrack, 2003, We're A Happy Family: Tribute to the Ramones, 2003, I've Always Been Crazy: Tribute to Waylon Jennings, 2003. Recipient Grammy award, 1990, 91. Office: c/o Metallica Elektra Records 75 Rockefeller Plz New York NY 10019-6908*

HETH, DIANA SUE, psychotherapist; b. Robinson, Ill., Sept. 25, 1948; d. Quentin Wilson and Marguerite (Bird) Abraham; m. Kenneth Lewis Greider, Aug. 16, 1970 (div. Mar. 1985); children: Kathryn Elizabeth Greider, Susan Nicole Greider, Jonathan Abraham Greider; m. Harold Eugene Heth; children: Joseph Brockwell, Kiley Joy, Mark Quentin. BSE, Ea. Ill. U., 1970; MSW, U. Ill., 1992. Cert.: (criminal justice specialist); LCSW. Exec. dir. Nat. Assn. Downs Syndrome, Chgo., 1977—78, Heartland Hospice, Effingham, Ill., 1983—88; office adminstr. Am. Family Life Assurance, Effingham, 1988—90; sec. design engring. dept. Fedders N.Am., Effingham, 1990; co-owner H&S Vending, 1990—98; therapist sexual abuse Heartland Human Svcs., Effingham, 1992—94; advanced specialist child protection Ill. Dept. Children and Family Svcs., Effingham, 1994. Mem. profl. adv. com. Hospice Lincolnland; social work cons. Effingham County Health Dept., 1995—, Clay County Health Dept., 2004—. Author: One Gift to the Next, 1983, Sundance Lady, 1990. Vol. Belleville (Ill.) Hospice, 1981—83; co-chmn. svc. and rehab. com. Am. Cancer Soc.; mem. steering com. Coun. Domestic Violence, 1998; mem. Interfaith Com. on Domestic Violence Coun.; mem. parent adv. bd. Ill. State U., 1996—99. Mem.: NASW, Nat. Assn. Forensic Counselors, County Orgn. Svc. Providers, Ill. Pub. Health Assn., Assn. Christian Counselors, Ill. State Hospice Orgn. (bd. dirs. 1985—86), Topnotcher's 4-H Club (leader), Compassionate Friends Club (bd. dirs. 1985—86), Newcomers Club (pres. 1984—85). Republican. Methodist. Avocations: bridge, bowling, needlecrafts, gardening, cooking. Home: 9973 E 1735th Ave Shumway IL 62461-2229 Office: Effingham Field Office Ill Dept Child/Family Svcs 401 Industrial Ave Ste 2 Effingham IL 62401-2835 Office Fax: 217-868-5082. Personal E-mail: heheth@frontiernet.net.

HETHERINGTON, EILEEN MAVIS, psychologist, educator; b. Nov. 27, 1926; BA, U. B.C., 1947, MA, 1948; PhD in Psychology, U. Calif.-Berkeley, 1958. Clin. psychologist B.C. Child Guidance Clinic, 1948-51, sr. psychologist, 1951-52; clin. internship Langley Porter Clinic, 1956-57; instr. psychology San Jose State Coll., 1957-58; asst. prof. Rutgers U., 1958-60; from asst. prof. to prof. U. Wis., 1960-70; prof. psychology U. Va., Charlottesville, 1970-99, James Page prof. psychology, 1976-99, prof. emeritus, 1999—, dept. chmn., 1980-84. Editor Child Devel., 1971-77; rschr. in personality devel. and childhood psychopathology, the role of family process and parent characteristics on normal and deviant behavior in children, the effects of divorce and remarriage on families, parents and children. Bd. dirs. Found. for Child Devel. Recipient Disting. Scientist award Am. Assn. for Marriage and Family Therapy, 1988, Am. Family Therapy Assn., 1992, Burgess award Nat. Coun. on Family Rels., 2000. Mem. APA (pres. divsn. 7, 1978-79, Stanley Hall Disting. Scientist award 1987, Disting. Scientist award 1993), Soc. Rsch. in Child Devel. (pres. 1985-87, Disting. Scientist award 1995), Soc. Rsch. in

Adolescents (pres. 1986-88, Disting. Scientist award 1988, William James Disting. Scientist award 1994), Am. Psychol. Soc. (Disting. Scientist award 2004). Address: 2533 Midway Farm Charlottesville VA 22901

HETHERINGTON, JOHN WARNER, lawyer; b. N.Y.C., Aug. 15, 1938; s. John Kells and Susanna Louisa (Warner) H.; m. Hope Luke, Nov. 6, 1976; children: Kells, Jane. BA, Yale U., 1960, JD, 1963. Bar: N.Y. 1964, U.S. Dist. Ct. (ea. and so. dists.) N.Y. 1965, U.S. Ct. Mil. Appeals 1974, Conn. 1987. Atty. Fed. Res. Bank, N.Y.C., 1964-65; assoc. Dickerson & Reilly (formerly Brown, Hyde & Dickerson), N.Y.C., 1965-67; atty. MeadWestvaco Corp., N.Y.C., 1967-77, asst. sec., asst. gen. counsel, 1977-78, sec., asst. gen. counsel, 1978—, v.p., 1987—. Apptd. to adv. com. on shareholder comm. SEC, 1981-82. Mem. New Canaan (Conn.) Planning and Zoning C., 1986-89; mem. New Canaan Town Coun., 1989-97; chmn. New Canaan Bd. Assessment Appeals, 2000—. Capt. JAGC, USNR ret. Mem. SR, Am. Soc. Corp. Secs. (chmn. tender offers com. 1986-89, dir. 1990-93), Assn. Bar City N.Y., Country Club New Canaan. Republican. Congregationalist. Avocation: sailing. Office: Westvaco Corp One High Ridge Park Stamford CT 06905

HETHERWICK, GILBERT LEWIS, lawyer; b. Winnsboro, La., Oct. 30, 1920; s. Septimus and Addie Louise (Gilbert) H.; m. Joan Friend Gibbons, May 31, 1946 (dec. Aug. 1964); children: Janet Hetherwick Pumphrey, Ann Hetherwick Lyons Winegeart, Gilbert, Carol Hetherwick Sutton, Katherine Hetherwick Hummell; m. Mertis Elizabeth Cook, June 7, 1967 (dec. May 2003). BA summa cum laude, Centenary Coll., 1942; JD, Tulane U., 1949. Bar: La. 1949. With legal dept. NorAm Energy Corp., Shreveport, La., 1949-53; dir. Blanchard, Walker, O'Quin and Roberts, PLC, Shreveport, 1953-99, of counsel, 2000—. Mem. Shreveport City Charter Revision Com., 1955; mem. Shreveport Mcpl. Fire and Police Civil Svc. Bd., 1956-92, vice chmn., 1957-78, chmn., 1978-88. Served with AUS, 1942-46. Recipient Tulane U. Law Faculty medal, 1949. Mem. ABA, La. Bar Assn., Shreveport Bar Assn. (pres. 1987), Energy Bar Assn., Order of Coif, Phi Delta Phi, Omicron Delta Kappa. Episcopalian. Home: 4604 Fairfield Ave Shreveport LA 71106-1432 Office: Bank One Tower Shreveport LA 71101

HETLAGE, ROBERT OWEN, lawyer; b. St. Louis, Jan. 9, 1931; s. George C. and Doris M. (Talbot) H.; m. Anne R. Willis, Sept. 24, 1960; children: Mary T., James C., Thomas K. AB, Washington U., St. Louis, 1952, LLB, 1954; LLM, George Washington U., 1957. Bar: Mo. 1954, U.S. Dist. Ct. (ea. dist.) Mo. 1954, U.S. Supreme Ct. 1957. Ptnr. Hetlage & Hetlage, 1958-65, Peper, Martin, Jensen, Maichel & Hetlage, St. Louis, 1966-97, chmn., 1994-97; of counsel Blackwell Sanders Peper Martin LLP, St. Louis, 1998—. 1st lt. U.S. Army, 1954-58. Fellow Am. Bar Found. (life, v.p. 2002-04, pres. 2004—); mem. ABA (chmn. real property, probate and trust law sect. 1981-82), Bar Assn. Met. St. Louis (pres. 1967-68), Mo. Bar (pres. 1976-77), Am. Coll. Real Estate Lawyers (pres. 1985-86), Anglo-Am. Real Property Inst. (chmn. 1991). Office: Blackwell Sanders Peper Martin LLP 720 Olive St 24th Fl Saint Louis MO 63101-2338 Office Phone: 314-345-6421. Business E-Mail: rohetlage@blackwellsanders.com.

HETLAND, JAMES LYMAN, JR., banker, lawyer, educator; b. Mpls., June 9, 1925; s. James L. and Evelyn E. (Lundgren) H.; m. Barbara Anne Taylor, Sept. 10, 1949; children: Janice E., James E., Nancy L., Steven T. BSL., U. Minn., 1948, JD, 1950. Bar: Minn. 1950. Law clk. Minn. Supreme Ct., 1949—50; asso. firm Mackall, Crounse, Moore, Helmey & Palmer, Mpls., 1950-56; prof. U. Minn. Coll. Law, 1956-71; v.p. urban devel. First Nat. Bank Mpls., 1971-75, sr. v.p. law and urban devel., 1975-82, sr. v.p., gen. counsel, sec., 1982-88; sr. v.p. First Bank System, 1987-88; counsel to bd. and sec. First Bank, N.A., 1988-90; of counsel Rasmussen & Assocs., Ltd., 1990-99, Leighton, Hetland & Stein, PLLP, Mpls., 2002—. Adj. prof. Hubert Humphrey Inst., U. Minn., 1976—90, regents adv. com., 1982—90; adj. prof. Bus. Coll. ext., 1975—81, Coll. Law, 1980—90; labor arbitrator, 1967—; chmn. Minn. Citizens Coun. Crime and Delinquency, 1978—83; chmn. adv. coms. Minn. Supreme Ct., 1958—90; chmn. Telecommuters, Inc., 1992—96. Co-author: Minnesota Jury Instruction Guides, 1963, 2d edit., 1974, Minnesota Practice, 3 vols., 1970. Chmn. Met. Coun. Twin Cities, St. Paul, 1967-71, Mpls. Charter Commn., 1963-70; chmn. Mpls. Citizens League, 1963-64, bd. dirs., 1953-67; bd. dirs. Mpls. Downtown Coun., 1971—, vice chmn., 1978-82, chmn., 1982-83; chmn. bd. Minn. Zool. Garden, 1978-83; nat. v.p., mem. exec. com. Nat. Mcpl. League, 1979-82, pres., 1982-85, chmn. bd., 1985-87; vice chmn. Minn. Press Coun., 1973-81; vice chmn. bd. Minn. Health Care Cost Coalition, 1980; bd. dirs. Interstudy, 1972-79, chmn., 1974; mem. Bus. Urban Issues Coun., Conf. Bd., 1980-89; bd. dirs. Freshwater Biol. Rsch. Found., 1971-85, adv. bd., 1985—; bd. dirs. Mpls. Community Coll. Found., 1978-83, Minn. Exptl. City, 1972-75, Minn. Campfire Girls, 1974-79, Mpls. YMCA, 1957-76; bd. dirs. Health Central, Inc., 1973-87, exec. com., 1977-87; bd. dirs. Citizen Coun. on Crime and Justice, 1977—, chmn., 1979-82; bd. dirs. Ctr. for Policy Studies, 1983—, Twin Cities Habitat for Humanity, 1988-95; mem. exec. com. Partnership Dataline U.S.A., 1983; bd. dirs., exec. com. Health One, 1987-93; trustee Metro State U., 1989-98, Mpls. United Way, 1988-99; chmn. Mpls. Urban Tennis, 1987-94. With AUS, 1943-46. Mem.: ABA, Hennepin County Bar Assn., Minn. Bar Assn., Rotary. Republican. Lutheran. E-mail: JBH@mninter.net. *Seeking to improve services for urban citizens through new public and private service delivery systems has been a keystone for setting involvement priorities. Effective service delivery systems are essential if an urban society is to preserve a free public-private economic democracy. Involvement and change in the private sector is as important as in the public sector.*

HETLAND, JOHN ROBERT, law educator; b. Mpls., Mar. 12, 1930; s. James L. and Evelyn (Lundgren) H.; m. Mildred Woodruff, Dec. 1951 (div.); children: Lynda Lee Catlin, Robert John, Debra Ann Allen; m. Anne Kneeland, Dec. 1972; children: Robin T. Willcox, Elizabeth J. Pickett. BSL., U. Minn., 1952, JD, 1956. Bar: Minn. 1956, Calif. 1962, U.S. Supreme Ct, 1981. Practice law, Mpls., 1956-59; prof. law U. Calif., Berkeley, 1959-91; prof. emeritus, 1991—; prin. Hetland & Kneeland, PC, Berkeley, 1959—. Vis. prof. law Stanford U., 1971, 80, U. Singapore, 1972, U. Cologne, Fed. Republic Germany, 1988. Author: California Real Property Secured Transactions, 1970, Commercial Real Estate Transactions, 1972, Secured Real Estate Transactions, 1974, 1977; co-author: California Cases on Security Transactions in Land, 2d edit., 1975, 3d edit., 1984, 4th edit., 1992; contbr. articles to legal, real estate and fin. jours. Served to lt. comdr. USNR, 1953-55. Fellow Am. Coll. Real Estate Lawyers, Am. Coll. Mortgage Attys., Am. Bar Found.; mem. ABA, State Bar Calif., State Bar Minn., Order of Coif, Phi Delta Phi. Home and Office: 20 Red Coach Ln Orinda CA 94563-1112 Office Phone: 510-548-5900. E-mail: johnhetland@comcast.net.

HETRICK, CHARLES BRADY, retired county official; b. Linton, Ind., Jan. 16, 1932; s. Norman Charles and Emma (Klinger) H.; divorced; children: Keith Charles, David Kent, Steven John. BA, Ind. U., 1953; MPA, U. Mich., 1957. Adminstrv. asst., asst. to city mgr., asst. city mgr. City of Park Ridge, Ill., 1956—68; exec. dir. Miami Valley Coun. Govts., Dayton, Ohio, 1968—69; cons. to pres., divsn. mgr., dir. corp. planning Dayton Progress Corp., 1969—71, 1973—74; exec. v.p., gen. mgr. Ft. Worth Area C. of C., 1971—73; sr. assoc. Louis A. Allen Assocs., Inc., Palo Alto, Calif., 1974—75; coord. econ. devel. State of Wis., Madison, 1975—76; asst. county mgr. Volusia County, Daytona Beach and Deland, Fla., 1975—80; county adminstr. Rock County, Janesville and Beloit, Wis., 1980—84, Charleston County, SC, 1984—85, Hernando County, Brooksville, Fla., 1985—97; coord. cmty. devel. Fla. Dept. Cmty. Affairs, Tallahassee, 1997—2000; ret., 2000. Adj. instr. bus. and pub. svc. program Tallahassee C.C. Contbr. articles on mcpl. problems and urban affairs to various publs. 1st lt. U.S. Army, 1953-55. Recipient resolution S.C. Ho. of Reps. and Senate, 1985; U. Mich. Met. Community fellow, 1955-56. Mem. Internat. City Mgmt. Assn., Am. Soc. for Pub. Adminstrn. Home: PMB 251 400 Capital Cir SE Ste 18 Tallahassee FL 32301-3802 Personal E-mail: chetrick9@comcast.net.

HETRICK, ESTHER, music educator; b. Lafayette, Ind., Feb. 23, 1960; d. Loren J. and Patricia A. Hetrick. BA in Sacred Music, Lincoln Christian Coll., 1982; M of Ch. Music, So. Bapt. Theol. Sem., 1989; D of Worship Studies, Inst. Worship Studies, 2004. Dir. youth music Union Christian Ch., Terre Haute, Ind., 1982—87; music min. Clifton Christian Ch., Louisville, 1987—89; prof. music Great Lakes Christian Coll., Lansing, Mich., 1989—; min. worship Meridian Christian Ch., Okemos, 1992—. Mem. exec. com. Nat. Ch. Music Conf., Plainfield, Ind., 2002—05. Mem.: Assn. Chs. Coll. Music Educators. Office: Great Lakes Christian Coll 6211 W Willow Hwy Lansing MI 48917

HETRICK, JOAN WILLETTE, critical care nurse, nursing administrator; b. Oct. 14, 1959; d. Wilbert D. Sproul and Lois Diane (Wilson) Pinette Anderson; m. Charles Vance Frum, May 4, 2002. B in Health Scis., Fla. Atlantic U., 1996; ASN, Miami-Dade Med. Ctr., 1998. RN, Fla., Ga. Adminstrv. asst., cons. Holiday Prime Foods, 5 Star Mktg. Group, Davie, Fla., 1996—2002; RN critical care Aventura (Fla.) Hosp., 1999; RN Meml. Reg. Hosp., Hollywood, Fla., 1999, Hollywood Med. Ctr. Telemetry and Prog. Care, 1998-99; charge nurse Hallandale Rehab. Ctr., 2000—02; ER nurse Plantation Gen. Hosp., 2001—02; RN specialist Agy. for Health Care Adminstrn., Fla., 2001—02; RN Agy., 2002—03; oncology nurse Kennestone Hosp., Ga., 2003—04; gynecol. oncology nurse Northside Hosp., 2004—; oncology nurse Atlanta Med. Ctr., 2004—, oncology, 2004—. Health instr. Miami Book Fair Internat., Miami-Dade C.C., 1997; health care rschr. for 104th Congress, 1995. Mem. Oncology Nurses Soc., Internat. Thespian Soc., Fla. Nurses Assn., Oncology Nursing Soc., Kappa Delta Pi, Alpha Phi Omega. Republican. Avocations: critical care nursing studies, business studies, real estate studies, pets, surfing the internet. Home: 282 Hood Pkwy Kennesaw GA 30152-

HETSKO, JEFFREY FRANCIS, lawyer; b. Glen Ridge, N.J., Apr. 25, 1950; s. Cyril Francis and Josephine (Stein) Hetsko; m. Nicolletta D. White, Nov. 17, 2001; stepchildren: Joshua Taylor White, Noah Carson White. BA, Williams Coll., 1972; JD, U. Fla., 1978. Bar; Fla. 1978, Ga. 1978. Assoc. Troutman, Sanders, Lockerman & Ashmore, Atlanta, 1978-86, ptnr., 1987; v.p., gen. counsel Grove Properties, Inc., Atlanta, 1987-89; ptnr. Troutman Sanders LLP, Atlanta, 1989—. Mem. State Bar Assn. Ga., Fla. State Bar Assn. Office: Troutman Sanders LLP 600 Peachtree St NE Ste 5200 Atlanta GA 30308-2231

HETTCHE, L. RAYMOND, engineering educator, retired research scientist; b. Balt., Mar. 24, 1938; s. Leroy and Dorothy (Curtain) H.; m. Patricia Durkan, July 1965; children: Lisa, Kathleen, Matthew, Craig. BSCE, AB in Math., Bucknell U., 1961; MSCE, Carnegie-Mellon U., 1961, PhD in CE, 1965. Asst. prof. Rutgers U., New Brunswick, N.J., 1964-66; resident rsch. assoc. Nat. Bur. Standards, Washington, 1966-68; structural engr. metallurgy div. Naval Rsch. Lab., Washington, 1968-71, head thermomech. effect sect., 1971-73, head mech. br. metallurgy div., 1973-75, supt. materials sci. div., 1975-81; now, dir. Applied Rsch. Lab. Pa. State U., State College, 1981—2002, prof. engring. rsch., 2002—, prof. engring. rsch. emeritus. Navy rep. Tech. Working Group Export Control, Washington, 1979-81; navy rep. subgroup P materials panel for metals Tech. Cooperation Program, Washington, 1977-81; session chmn. Submarine Tech. Symposium, Columbia, Md., 1990. Contbr. numerous articles to profl. jours. Tau Beta Pi Nat. fellow, 1961-63; NSF fellow, 1963; recipient Outstanding Achievement award Am. Def. Preparedness Assn., 1986. Office: Pa State U Applied Rsch Lab PO Box 30 State College PA 16804-0030 Business E-Mail: lrh3@psu.edu.

HETTMANSPERGER, SUE, artist; b. Akron, Ohio, Nov. 20, 1948; d. Hilton E. Hettmansperger and Dorothy E. Stone. Student, Yale U., summer 1971; BFA in Lithography and Drawing cum laude, U. N.Mex., 1972, MA in Lithography and Drawing, 1974. Grad. tchg. asst. U. N.Mex., 1972—74; instr. lithography, intaglio and drawing Pa. State U., State College, 1974—75; prof. painting and drawing U. Iowa, Iowa City, 1977—. Vis. lectr. U. N.Mex., Albuquerque, 1985; invited artist in residence in painting and drawing Roswell Art Mus., N.Mex., 1990; artist in residence in drawing U Cross Found., Wyo., 1992; curator of prints Tyler Graphics, Bedford Village, N.Y., 1976; nat. affiliate A.I.R. Gallery, N.Y.C., 1989—; lectr. in field. One-woman shows include, Frumkin & Struve Gallery Chgo., 1981, A.I.R. Gallery, NYC, 1990, 1994, 1999, 2003, CSPS Alternative Space, Cedar Rapids, Iowa, 1992, U. No. Iowa Gallery, Cedar Falls, 1994, Artemisia Gallery, Chgo., 1995, S.D. Sch. Mines and Tech., 2004, exhibited in group shows at Artemisia Gallery, Chgo., 1996, Arts Iowa City Gallery, 1998, Galeria Article 26, Carer de Ferlandina, Barcelona, Spain, 1999, U. Tex. San Antonio Gallery, 2002, Faulconer Gallery, Grinnell Coll., 2003, others, Represented in permanent collections; contbr. artwork to New Am. Paintings Midwest. MacDowel Colony Drawing fellow, 1977; NEA fellow in drawing, 1983; recipient Faculty Scholar award U. Iowa, 1997-99; arts and humanities interdisciplinary grantee U. Iowa, 2001. Office: U Iowa E 100 AB Riverside Dr Iowa City IA 52242

HETTRICK, GEORGE HARRISON, lawyer; b. Piney River, Va., Aug. 15, 1940; s. Ames Bartlett and Frances Caryl (O'Brian) H.; m. Lee Ann Hettrick; children: Heather White Hettrick Brugh, Edward Lord. BA, Cornell U., 1962; JD, Harvard U., 1965. Bar: Va. 1965. Assoc. Hunton & Williams LLP, Richmond, Va., 1965-73; spl. counsel Gov. of Va., 1970—71; ptnr., bus. practice group Hunton & Williams LLP, Richmond, Va., 1973—, and chmn., cmty. svc. com. Ptnr. in charge Church Hill Neighborhood Law Office Hunton & Williams, 1990—, chmn. Community Svc. com.; dir. Richmond Community Hosp., 1992—. Contbr. articles to profl. jours. Pres. bd. trustees Va. Episcopal Sch., Lynchburg, 1978—81; spl. counsel Gov. of Va., Richmond, 1971—72; vice-chmn. bd. dirs. Va. Port Authority, Norfolk, 1970—75, former commr., vice-chmn.; Va. State adv. com. Neighborhood Assistance Program; past dir., chmn. Peter Paul Devel. Ctr., Inc.; bd. dirs. Lawyers Helping Lawyers, St. Mary's Hosp., St. Francis Hosp., Regional Meml. Med. Ctr; bd. dirs., pres. Greater Richmond Bar Found., 2003—; mem. Henrico County (Va.) Cmty. Svcs. Bd., 1997—, chmn., 2002—; bd. dirs. Chesterfield/Colonial Heights Drug Ct. Found., 2002—; bd. dirs., vice chair Va. Network Nonprofit Orgns. Capt. U.S. Army, 1966—68. Fellow Va. Law Found.; mem. ABA, Va. Bar Assn. (chmn. substance abuse com. 1995-96), Va. State Bar, Richmond Bar Assn. (chmn. pro bono com. 1998-2001). Republican. Episcopalian. Office: Hunton & Williams LLP Riverfront Plz East Tower 951 E Byrd St Richmond VA 23219-4074 Office Phone: 804-788-8324. Office Fax: 804-788-8218. E-mail: ghettrick@hunton.com.

HETZ, MATTHEW, composer, educator; b. L.A., Mar. 26; s. William and Frances Hetz. BA cum laude, Calif. State Dominguez Hills, 1985. Pres. Westchester Symphony Soc., L.A., 2004—05; active Friends for EXPO, L.A., 2004—05, Friends of the Greenline, L.A., 2002—05; mem. Transit Coalition, L.A., 2002—05; sec. Ind. Composers Assn., L.A., 1991—99; pres. Culver City Symphony Orch., 2004—05. Recipient hon. mention, Mu Phi Epsilon, 1985. Mem.: Nat. Assn. Composers U.S.A. (contbr. newsletter 1985—2004), Am. Music Ctr. Democrat. Roman Catholic.

HETZEL, ALICE M., statistician, researcher; b. Guthrie, Okla., Feb. 9, 1922; d. Eugene Tilden and Ina (Pence) H. BS, Okla. State U., 1942; postgrad., Georgetown U., 1945. Economist Navy Dept., Washington, 1943-46; statistician USPHS, Washington, 1946-50, U.S. Navy Dept., Washington, 1950-61; spl. asst. to chief Nat. Office Vital Stats., Washington, 1961-68, chief marriage and divorce stats., 1968-74; dep. dir. divsn. vital stats. NCHS, Washington, 1974-83; rschr. self employed, Silver Spring, Md., 1983—. Author: U.S. Vital Statistics System 1950-1995, 1997, Marriage and Divorce Statistics and the Health Department, 1971, Health Survey of the Trust Territory of the Pacific Islands, 1959; co-author: Vital Statistics Rates in the U.S. 1940-1960, 1968. Recipient Exemplary Svc. award Nat. Vital Statistics Program, 1983. Mem. Argyle Country Club. Home: Unit 615 19385 Cypress Ridge Ter Leesburg VA 20176-5167

HETZLER, MARK MICHELET, music educator; b. Sarasota, Fla., June 2, 1968; s. Kemper Michelet Hetzler and Diana Lynn Horton; m. Svetha Seshadri, May 24, 1992; children: Monika Louise, Marisa Louise. MusB, Boston U., 1990; MusM, New Eng. Conservatory, Boston, 1992. Trombone player Empire Brass Quintet, West Stockbridge, Mass., 1996; asst. prof. music trombone U. Wis., Madison, 2004—, trombone player Wis. Brass Quintet, 2004—. Musician: (albums) American Voices, Serious Songs, Sad Faces, 20th Century Architects. Office: U Wis Madison 455 N Park St #5442 Madison WI 53706 Office Phone: 608-263-1932.

HETZNER, DONALD RAYMUND, social studies educator, forensic social scientist; b. Ottawa, Ill., Jan. 1, 1938; s. James Hyatt and Thelma Margaret (Sheedy) H.; m. Coralia Josefina Lora, July 9, 1966; children: Sean, Matthew. AA, LPO Jr. Coll., 1957; BA in Social Sci., Shimer Coll., 1961; MA in Polit. Sci., No. Ill. U., 1965; EdD in Social Studies, SUNY, Buffalo, 1972. Cert. tchr. social studies, N.Y. Tchr. English, social studies Medina (N.Y.) Pub. Sch. System, 1966-68; tchr. Kenmore-Tonawanda (N.Y.) Union Free Sch. Dist. 1, 1968-69; prof. SUC, Buffalo, 1970—. Scholar in residence Am. Assn. Cmty. and Jr. Colls., Washington, 1986-87; cons. restructuring post-secondary edn. in The Acad. Namibia, Southwest Africa, 1989; founder Applecore Consulting. Co-author: Practical Methods for the Social Studies, 1977, Working in America, 1976, Historian: Building a New Nation in 1789; editor: The Social Science Record, 1975-78; contbr. articles to ednl. jours. Mem. World Assn. for Case Rsch. and Application, Nat. Coun. for Social Studies, N.Y. State Coun. for Social Studies (exec. bd. dirs. 1975-78, jour. editor), Rsch. and Planning for the Future (founder), Internat. Coun. for Innovation in Higher Edn. Democrat. Avocations: travel, historical research. Home: 67 Lancaster Ave Buffalo NY 14222-1403 Office: SUC Dept History & Social Studies 1300 Elmwood Ave Buffalo NY 14222-1004 Office Phone: 716-883-0455. Personal E-mail: hetznerd@aol.com.

HEUBEL, WILLIAM BERNARD, lawyer, consultant; b. Sharon, Pa., Mar. 7, 1928; s. Herman J. and Margaret (Becker) H. Student, Gannon U., 1948-49; BS, Purdue U., 1954; JD, Ind. U., 1954. Bar: Ind. 1955, U.S. Dist. Ct. (so. dist.) Ind. 1955. Mem. project mgmt. staff AT&T Long Lines, 1955—61; contract adminstr. nuclear and def. Westinghouse Electric Corp., Pitts., 1961-68, mgr. mktg. adminstrn. nuclear, 1968-73, contract mgmt. cons. corp. mktg., 1973-81, contract cons. internat. sales contracts-law dept., 1981-87; pvt. practice, 1988—. Served with AUS, 1946-48. Roman Catholic. Office: 123 Franklin Dr Greensburg PA 15601-1304

HEUBI, JAMES EDWARD, pediatrician, educator; b. Indpls., Nov. 13, 1948; s. John Edward and Elizabeth Ruth Heubi; m. Margo A. Hungerford; children: Elizabeth C., Christine H. BS, Ind. U., 1970; MD, Ind. U., Indpls., 1973. Asst. prof. pediat. U. Cin. Coll. Medicine, 1979—83, assoc. prof. pediat., 1983—89, prof. pediat., 1989—, assoc. dean clin. rsch., 2003—; program dir., Gen. Clin. Rsch. Cin. Children's Hosp. Med. Ctr., 1988—. Contbr. articles to med. rsch. jours. Mem.: Am. Gastroenterol. Assn., Am. Assn. Study Liver Disease, Am. Pediat. Soc., Alpha Omega Alpha, Phi Beta Kappa. Achievements include research in finding new defects of bile acid synthesis which could be treated medically with liver transplantation; instrumental in increasing understanding of importance of early recognition of Reyes Symdrome and its effect on prognosis. Avocations: indoor soccer, reading, water sports. Office: Cincinnati Childrens Hosp Med Ctr 3333 Burnet Ave Cincinnati OH 45229

HEUER, GERALD ARTHUR, mathematician, educator; b. Bertha, Minn., Aug. 31, 1930; s. William C. F. and Selma C. (Rosenberg) Heuer; m. Jeanette Mary Knedel, Sept. 5, 1954; children: Paul, Karl, Ruth, Otto. BA, Concordia Coll., 1951; MA, U. Nebr., 1953; PhD, U. Minn., 1958. Math. instr. Hamline U., 1955-56, Concordia Coll., Moorhead, Minn., 1956-57, asst. prof., 1957-58, assoc. prof., 1958-62, prof., 1962-95, Sigurd and Pauline Prestegaard Mundhjeld prof., 1988-95, chmn. dept., 1963-70, research prof., 1970-71, prof. emeritus, mathematician-in-residence, 1995—; mathematician Remington Rand Univac, summer 1958. Vis. prof. U. Nebr., Lincoln, 1960—61, Wash. State U., Pullman, 1980—81; mathematician Control Data Corp., 1960—62, cons., 1960—63; vis. lectr. Math. Assn. Am., 1964—66; cons. NSF-AID, India, 1968—69; guest spkr. Minn. sect. Math. Assn. Am., 1956, Nebr. sect. Math. Assn. Am., 1961, No. Ctrl. sect. Math. Assn. Am., 1974; vis. prof., scholar Math. Inst. Cologne (Germany) U., 1973—74; vis. prof., scholar Inst. Stats., Econs. and Ops. Rsch. Graz U., Austria, 1987—88, rsch. prof., Austria, 1990, vis. prof., Austria, 94, Austria, 97; dir. U.S. Math. Olympiad Tng. Session; leader U.S. team Internat. Math. Olympiad, 1988—90; invited plenary spkr. Internat. Symposium Ops. Rsch., Passau, Germany, 1995. Author (with Ulrike Leopold-Wildburger): (book) Balanced Silverman Games on General Discrete Sets, 1991, Silverman's Game, 1995; contbr. articles to profl. jours.; reviewer: Zentralblatt für Mathematik, 1967—, Math. Revs., 1978—. Grantee Rsch., NSF, 1963, 1964, 1966; scholar Bush Rsch., Concordia Coll., 1983—84, Centennial Rsch., 1992, 1993, 1994, 1995; Faculty fellow, NSF, Univ. Calif. Berkeley, 1966—67. Mem.: Österreichische Math. Gesellschaft (Vienna), Deutsche Math.-Vereinigung e.v. (Berlin), Nat. Geographic Soc., Am. Math. Soc., Math. Assn. Am. (pres. Minn. sect. 1959—60, nat. bd. govs. 1971—73, com. Putnam prize 1987—90, com. Am. math. competitions 1988—, problem books editl. bd. 1999—, cert. meritorious svc. 1994), Sigma Xi. Lutheran. Home: 1216 Elm St S Moorhead MN 56560-4049 Office: Concordia Coll Dept Math Moorhead MN 56562-0001 Office Phone: 218-299-3348. Business E-Mail: heuer@cord.edu.

HEUER, MARTIN, retired human resources specialist; b. Algoma, Wis., Oct. 16, 1934; s. Orland Fred and Gertrude Mayme (Zimmerman) Heuer; m. Rita Mae Prokash, Oct. 27, 1954; children: Martin Joseph, Ronald James. AA, SUNY, 1973, AS, 1975. Commd. 2d lt. C.E. U.S. Army, 1954, advanced through grades to lt. col., 1968; flight comdr., adminstrv. and maintenance officer 1st Aviation Co., Ft. Riley, 1958-61; with 937th Engr. Aviation Co. Panama and Lima, Peru, 1961-65; maintenance officer 174th Aviation Co., Vietnam, 1966; adj. 14th Combat Aviation Bn., 1966-67; dir. sys., curriculum and spl. projects divsn. Army Primary Helicopter Sch., Ft. Wolters, Tex., 1967-69; aviation advisor Wis. Army N.G., West Bend, 1969-70; airfield comdr. Cu Chi Army Airfield, Vietnam, 1970-71; airfield comdr., adj. 165th Combat Aviation Group, Vietnam; engr. advisor Wis. N.G., Eau Claire, 1971-73; mgr., area mgr. Manpower Temp. Svcs., 1973-76; exec. v.p. Aide Svcs. Inc. and KARI Svcs. Inc., Tampa, Fla., 1976-80, pres., chmn., 1980—2002; ret., 2002. Pres. Seminole HS Band Boosters, 1974—79; v.p. Pinellas County Band Boosters, 1977—78; v.p. and bd. dir. Vietnam Helicopter Air Crew Mus., Tampa, 1999—2002; bd. dir. Seminole HS Booster Assn., 1975—79, pres., 1978—79. Decorated Legion of Merit with 1 oak leaf cluster, Bronze Star with 3 oak leaf clusters, Air medal with 3 oak leaf clusters; recipient First Band Booster Pres. award, Seminole HS, 1979, Svc. to Mankind award, Sertoma, 1980. Mem.: Nat. Assn. Temp. Svcs. (treas./sec. Fla. chpt. 1991—94), Soc. Am. Mil. Engrs., Assn. Manpower Franchise Owners (dir. 1980—82, treas. 1981—82, dir. 1983—86, chmn. 1984—86), Vietnam Helicopter Pilots Assn. (bd. dir. Fla. chpt. 1993—2002, v.p. 1996—98, pres. 1998—2000, chmn. bd. dir. 2000—02), Future Farmers Am. Alumni Assn., Ret. Officers Assn., Res. Officers Assn., Air Force Assn., Army Aviation Assn. Am., Assn. U.S. Army (chmn. bd. govs. 1981—82, asst. state v.p. Suncoast chpt. and Fla. 1981—82, state v.p. 1982—84, chmn. chpt. comms. nat. adv. bd. 1982—86, mem. corp. adv. coun. 1985—90, FLA exec. coun. 1985—90, bd. dir. Sun Coast chpt. 1994—2002). Republican. E-mail: martyheuer@aol.com.

HEUER, ROBERT MAYNARD, II, opera company executive; b. Detroit, Nov. 27, 1944; s. Robert Maynard and May Elizabeth (Quinn) H. Student, Capital U., 1963-64; BA, Wayne State U., 1976. Youth dir. Grace Luth. Ch., Detroit, 1964-66; costume designer, prodn. mgr. U. Windsor, Ont., Can., 1967-69; program coord. Detroit Youtheatre, Detroit Inst. Arts, 1970-71; mng. dir. Mich. Opera Theatre, Detroit, 1971-79; prodn. dir. Fla. Grand Opera (formerly Greater Miami Opera), 1979-83; asst. gen. mgr. Greater Miami Opera, 1984-85, gen. mgr., CEO, 1986-97, gen. dir., CEO, 1997—. Mem. Performing Arts Ctr. Found. Greater Miami. Recipient Narot Humanitarian award, 2001. Mem.: Opera Am., Greater Miami C. of C. Home: 547 Navarre Ave Coral Gables FL 33134-4231 Office: Fla Grand Opera 1200 Coral Way Miami FL 33145-2927 E-mail: rmheuer@fgo.org.

HEUERMANN-NOWIK, PATRICIA CALHOUN, theater director; d. William Royal Calhoun and Nancy Lee Griffitts; m. Eric Heuermann (div.); children: Beryl Lee, William Whitney, Lana Amanda, Linda Dilwara; m. Vete Nowik, Mar. 29, 1985. Grad., Curtis Inst. Music, 1951—55. Dir. opera theatre Emory U., Atlanta, 1968—75, Clark Coll., 1972—75; founder, artistic music dir. Atlanta Opera, 1975—80; mng. dir., touring ednl. program N.C. Opera, Charlotte, 1980—82; founder, artistic dir. Singers Theatre N.Y., N.Y.C., 1983—92; instr. stage artistry Am. Inst. Musical Studies, Graz, Austria, 1994—2001; dir. opera theatre Hofstra U., Hempstead, NY, 2000—05. Chair internat. opera singers competition Ctr. Contemporary Opera, 1990—94, chair artistic adv. bd., 1990—96. Mem.: Opera for Youth (bd. dirs. 2000—02, program chair nat. conf. 1995), N.Y. Singing Tchrs. Assn. (bd. dirs. 1998—99), Opera Am., Nat. Opera Assn. (N.E. regional gov. 1991—94, bd. dirs. 1991—95, v.p. resources 1995—98, v.p. programs 1998—2000, pres. 2000—02). Democrat. Avocations: cooking, reading, travel. Home: 20-49 48th St Astoria NY 11105 Office: Hofstra U Music Dept 112 Hofstra Univ Hempstead NY 11549-1120 Personal E-mail: patruschhka@mindspring.com.

HEUKELS, RUDY, sales executive, consultant; BA in internat. econ., U. Amsterdam; at, Sch. Retail Sales and Mktg., Sch. Textile, Tilburg, Netherlands. Dir. sales Dollfus Mieg & Cie (DMC) USA, South Kearney, N.J. and Paris, 1983—87, Zetag AG., Hauptwil, Switzerland, 1987—98, Zweigart, Inc., Piscataway, N.J. and Sindelfingen, Germany, 1987—98; sales and mktg. cons. RH Internat., USA, Long Valley, NJ, 1998—. Named Internat. Sales Mgr. of Yr., Dollfus Mieg & Cie (DMC) USA, 1987, Internat. Mgr. of Yr., Zetag AG., 1997. Address: 2 Eagle Nest Ln Long Valley NJ 07853 E-mail: rh99int@aol.com.

HEUSCH, CLEMENS AUGUST, physicist, researcher; b. Aachen, Germany, Apr. 19, 1932; s. Hermann and Elisabeth (Pauli) H.; m. Karin von Gilgenheimb, July 6, 1968; children: Marina, Bettina. Student, Bowdoin Coll., 1951-52; Dipl. Phys., U. Aachen, 1955; postgrad., U. Paris, 1956; Dr. rer. nat., Tech. U. Munich, 1959. Rsch. asst. Dipl. Phys. Tech. U., Munich, 1956-59; project leader rsch. div. AEG, Frankfurt, Germany, 1960-61; rsch. scientist DESY Accelerator Lab., Hamburg, Germany, 1961-63; from rsch. fellow to assoc. prof. Calif. Inst. Tech., Pasadena, Calif., 1963-69; prof., co-prin. investigator U. Calif., Santa Cruz, Calif., 1969—. Cons., referee Am. Inst. Physics, N.Y.C., European Orgn. for Nuclear Rsch., Geneva; cons. Nat. Acad. Scis.; mem. various internat. adv. coms., 1965—; founding dir. Santa Cruz Inst. for Particle Physics; lectr. musical criticism Porter Coll., U. Calif., vis. prof., RWTH Aachen, Germany, 1995—, U. Rome (Italy), La Sapienza, 1999. Free-lance music critic. Recipient Humboldt prize, 1990; Fulbright scholar, 1951; grantee Dept. Energy, NSF, 1963—. Roman Catholic. Office: U Calif Inst Particle Physics Dept Physics 1156 High St Santa Cruz CA 95064-1077

HEVEL, GARY FRANCIS, public information officer, consultant; b. Salida, Colo., Nov. 30, 1941; s. Francis Marion and Doris Hevel; m. Julie Ann Fortin, July 18, 1980; 1 child, Amanda Simone; m. Susan Platkin, June 30, 1970 (div. 1980). BS, Pittsburg State U., 1969. Mus. specialist Dept. Entomology, Washington, 1969—73, collections mgr., 1973—95, pub. info. officer, 1995—. Cons. Dorling Kindersley, N.Y.C., 2000—01, USA Weekend Mag., Arlington, Va., 2003—03, Fish & Wildlife Dept., Cabin John, Md., 2000—02. Editor: (production of united states stamps) Insects and Spiders; co-creator (species biodiversity inventory) First National Bio-Blitz; author: (educational website) BugInfo website, Smithsonian Entomology; co-developer (exhibition) BugFest; contbr. articles to profl. jours. Mem.: Coleopterists Soc., N.Y. Entomol. Soc., Entomol. Soc. Wash., Entomol. Soc. Am., Kans. Entomol. Soc. Achievements include discovery of some 200 new insect species; World record for kinds of insects collected at residence; Published photo in book, Magnificent Foragers; Tarantula wrangler for National Geographic Explorer; Collected insects in 24 countries and territories; Featured in Washington Post, USA Today and other newspapers; Interviewed by BBC, CBS, CNN, Nat. Pub. Radio, Spanish television, Chinese television, Wisconsin Public Radio. Avocations: collecting postcards & stamps, bird watching, photography. Home: 15410 Johnson Rd Silver Spring MD 20905 Office: Smithsonian Institution PO Box 37012 10th Street & Constitution Avenue NW Washington DC 20013-7012 Office Phone: 202-633-1016. Personal E-mail: hevels@comcast.net. E-mail: hevel.g@si.edu.

HEVENER, FILLMER, JR., English language educator, writer, portrait artist; b. Churchville, Va., May 14, 1933; s. Fillmer Sr. and Estie (Harper) H.; m. Celia Achenbach, Aug. 27, 1954; children: Dennis Lyle, Yolanda Mae. BA, Columbia Union Coll., 1954; MA, James Madison U., 1957; EdD, U. Va., 1973. Cert. tchr., Va.; ordained pastor, 2001. Secondary English tchr. State of Va., 1954-55, Shenandoah Valley Acad., New Market, Va., 1955-57; tchr. ESL Bugema Missionary Coll., Kampala, Uganda, 1957-58; secondary English tchr. State of Mich., 1958-60; asst. prof. English Frostburg (Md.) State Coll., 1960-64, LaSierra Coll., Riverside, Calif., 1965-66; assoc. prof. English edn. Longwood Coll., Farmville, Va., 1966-92; owner Fillmer Hevener Studio-Gallery, Farmville, Va., 1995—; owner, pres. health food divsn. Fillmer Hevener Studio, Inc., 1997—; owner Green Meadows Farm and Village, 1997—; owner, mgr. Blue Ridge Boys, 1999—; pres., owner Hevener Homes. Cons. student tchrs. Longwood Coll., Farmville, Va.; pres., owner Fillmer Hevener Studio, Inc., Farmville, 1992—; presenter seminar on home schooling, Farmville, 1997; interim pastor Farmville S.D.A. Ch., 1999-00; lectr. on vegetarianism Southside Cmty. Hosp. Farmville, 2000-04; founder Good Samaritan Soc., 2003. Author: Successful Student Teaching: A Handbook for Elementary and Secondary Student Teachers, 1981, Hot Tips for Student Teachers, 1985, Technical Writing: A Theoretical Basis, 1991, Tithing: Not Required After the Cross, 1993; contbr. articles to profl. publs.; one-man shows include Eisenhower Sch., Ft. Leavenworth, Kans., Richmond (Va.) Pub. Libr., Appomattox (Va.) Pub. Libr., Jefferson Hotel Gallery, Richmond; portraits exhibited at Mayflower Hotel Gallery, Washington, New England Fine Arts Inst., Boston Trade Ctr., Chateau Elan Gallery, Braselton, Ga.; commd. portraits include H. Ross Perot, Gen. Douglass MacArthur, Gen. Robert E. Lee, Pres. George Bush, Pres. Bill Clinton, Pres. J.F. Kennedy, Will Rogers, Pres. Thomas Jefferson, Sir Winston Churchill, Pres. Abraham Lincoln, Pres. Dwight D. Eisenhower, Pres. Woodrow Wilson, Stone Mountain (Ga.) carving; portrait of Mayor Rudolph Giuliani, 2002. Mem. bd. regents Gen. Conf. Seventh Day Adventists, 1977-80; supr. Buckingham County (Va.). 1984-87; pres. Lower Francisco Fire Assn., Buckingham County, 1981—; vice chair Crossroads Mental Health Svcs., Va., 1985-87; elected sec. Ctrl. Va. Fine Arts Assn., 1993-94, 94—; chair Farmville Post Office Adv. Com., 1997—; bd. dirs. Va. Arts., 1996-97, 2001—, pres. 2000-01; pres. Ctrl. Va. Arts, Inc., 2000-01; bd. dirs. Longwood Ctr. Visual Arts, 2000-01; founder Hevenerites, 2001, Good Samaritan Soc., 2002; pastor Guthrie Meml. Adventist Chapel, Cumberland, Va., 2001—, delivered series of sermons The Christian Answers the Atheist. Mem. ASCD, Va. Conf. English Educators (chmn. 1988-90), Nat. Coun. Tchrs. English, Va. Assn. Tchrs. English, Univ. Profs. for Acad. Order, Internat. Platford Assn., Am. Culture/Popular Culture Assn. (presenter 1990), Good Samaritan Soc. (founder 2002), Lions Club Internat. Avocations: playing mandolin and violin, travel. Home and Office: RR 2 Box 1425 Farmville VA 23901-9502 Office Phone: 434-392-6255. E-mail: fhevener@oilart.com.

HEWES, LAURENCE ILSLEY, III, lawyer, management consultant; b. Palo Alto, Calif., Sept. 18, 1933; s. Laurence Ilsley, Jr. and Patricia Esther (Jackson) H.; m. Mary Clarke Darling, Oct. 1, 1960; children: Laurence Ilsley IV, Henry Patrick Darling, Mary Clarke Danforth. AB, Yale U., 1956, LLB, 1959. Bar: D.C. 1961, U.S. Dist. Ct. D.C., 1961, U.S. Ct. Appeals (D.C. cir.) 1961, U.S. Supreme Ct. 1966. Assoc. counsel U.S. Senate Comm. Labor and Human Resources, Washington, 1961; assoc. counsel Econ. Devel. Adminstrn. U.S. Dept. Commerce, Washington, 1961-62; staff dir., counsel Pres.'s Com. on Equal Opportunity in Armed Forces, Washington, 1962-63; assoc. then ptnr. Hydeman & Mason and successor firms, Washington, 1963-72; ptnr. Boasberg & Hewes (and successor firms), Washington, 1972-80, Wald Harkader & Ross, Washington, 1980-85; exec. dir., gen. counsel The Support Ctr., 1985-88; pres., chief exec. officer, gen. counsel Corp. Against Drug Abuse, 1989-93; legal, devel. and mgmt. cons. Washington, 1994—. Bd. dirs., Officer Taft Corp., Washington and N.Y.C., 1967-72; bd. dirs., mgr. Grants Mgmt. Adv. Svc., Inc., 1975-80; lectr. non-profit orgn. field. Contbr. articles to profl. jours., chpts. to books. Bd. trustees, Wooster Sch., Danbury Conn., 1981-89, Friends of Superior Ct. of D.C., 1973-87. Served with USAFR, 1959-66. Mem. ABA, D.C. Bar Assn., Cosmos Club, Yale Club (N.Y.C.), Mountain View Country Club. Democrat. Avocations: music, reading, walking, fly fishing, tennis. Home: Lawrence I & Mary D Hewes III 4944 Western Ave Bethesda MD 20816-1714 Office Phone: 301-320-4944. Personal E-mail: lhewes@starpower.net.

HEWES, THOMAS FRANCIS, physician; b. Boston, Mar. 5, 1929; s. Walter Raymond and Margaret Frances (Fallon) Hewes; m. Catherine Rene Lemaitre, June 29, 1958; children: Christine, Philip, Gerald, Nancy. AB, Coll. of the Holy Cross, 1950; MD, Tufts U., 1954. Diplomate Am. Bd. Internal Medicine. Intern U. Rochester (N.Y.) Strong Meml. Hosp., 1954-55, resident, 1955-56; sr. med. resident VA Hosp., Boston, 1958-59; clin. and rsch. fellow in gastroenterology Mass. Gen. Hosp., Boston, 1959-60; physician Am. Hosp. Paris, Neuilly-sur-Seine, France, 1961-98, dir. ICU, 1968-87, v.p. med. staff, 1978-80, 82-85, pres. med. staff, 1980-82, 85-87, chmn. dept. medicine, 1978-92. Adj. clin. prof. medicine Tufts U. Sch. Medicine, Boston, 1993—2001; bd. govs. Am. Hosp. Paris, 1976—87; trustee Am. Sch. Paris, Garches, France, 1971—80. Pres. bd. regents Marymount Internat. Sch., Neuilly-sur-Seine, 1997—2000, v.p., trustee, 2000—01. Capt. U.S. Army, 1956—58. Recipient Profl. Svc. citation, FAA, 1994. Mem.: AMA, Mass. Med. Soc. Democrat. Roman Catholic. Avocations: sailing, gardening, travel. Home: 23 High Meadow Rd 92200 Little Compton France Personal E-mail: tomfhewes@yahoo.com.

HEWITSON, WILLIAM CRAIG, physician, career officer; b. Park City, Utah, July 4, 1961; s. William Glenn and Darlene Marie Hewitson; m. children: William Brent, Staci Anne, Andrew Craig. BA with honors, U. Utah, 1986; MD, USUHS, 1991; MPH, Johns Hopkins U., 1995. Diplomate Am. Bd. Preventive Medicine. Officer U.S. Army, advanced through grades to lt. col., 1986; transitional intern Fitzsimons Army Med. Ctr., Aurora, Colo., 1991-92; 2d brigade surgeon 7th Inf. Divsn., Ft. Ord, Calif., 1992-93, divsn. surgeon Ft. Lewis, Wash., 1993-94; resident in general preventive medicine Walter Reed Army Inst. Rsch., Washington, 1994-96; chief injuries and occupation illnesses U.S. Army Ctr. for Health Promotion and Preventive Medicine, Aberdeen Proving Grounds, Md., 1996-98; chief preventive medicine divsn. Gen. Leonard Wood Army Cmty. Hosp., Ft. Leonard Wood, Mo., 1998-2000; healthcare adminstrv. fellow Baylor U., Ft. Sam Houston, Tex., 2000—02; chief epidemiology and disease surveillance Brooke Army Med. Ctr., Ft. Sam Houston, Tex., 2002—03; chief cmty. health practices br. Army Med. Dept. Ctr. & Sch., Ft. Sam Houston, Tex., 2003—. Dir. The Preventive Health Care Mgmt. Group, Salt Lake City, 1996-97; cons. Med. Adv. Sys., Owings, Md., 1995-98. Contbr. articles to profl. jours. Advancement chmn. Big Piney dist., Boy Scouts Am., Waynesville, Mo., 1999, Four Rivers dist. health and safety com., 1998, Pack com. chmn., Ft. George G. Meade, 1995-97, health and safety com. Eagle dist., 2001-02; missionary, Argentina, 1980-82. Fellow Am. Coll. Preventive Medicine; mem. AMA (Physician Recognition award 1997, 2000, 03), Assn. Mil. Surgeons U.S., Masons. Avocations: running, exercise, flying, golf, tennis. Office: 2250 Stanley Rd # 574 Fort Sam Houston TX 78234-2641 Business E-Mail: pmdoc@satx.rr.com.

HEWITT, BENJAMIN ATTMORE, psychologist, consultant; b. Westerly, R.I., Dec. 20, 1921; s. Benjamin Henry and Anne Mildred (Wangelin) H. BA, Yale U., 1943, MA, 1950, PhD, 1952. Lic. psychol., Conn. Dean Mitchell Coll., New London, Conn., 1948-51; dir. counseling Wesleyan U., Middletown, Conn., 1952-53; pres. Psychol. Svcs., Inc., New Haven, Conn., 1958-70; rsch. assoc. Yale U., New Haven, 1960-68; cons. psychologist New Haven, 1969-92; furniture cons. Wakefield, R.I. Guest curator Work of Many Hands; Card Tables in Fed. Am. Yale U. Art Gallery, New Haven, 1981-82; furniture researcher, 1965—. Author: The Work of Many Hands: Card Tables in Federal America, 1982. With U.S. Army, 1943-46, PTO. Mem. APA, Conn. State Psychol. Assn. (coun. 1960-64, ethics com. 1983-84), Friends of Am. Arts at Yale (sec. 1969-83, exec. com. 1969-92). Avocations: gardening, furniture collecting, boating. Office Phone: 401-789-8571.

HEWITT, DENNIS EDWIN, financial executive; b. Los Angeles, Apr. 9, 1944; s. Robert Sherwood and Anna Marie (Linge) H.; m. Kathryn Dale Lefler, June 11, 1966; children— Denise, Dawn BS, UCLA, 1966; MBA, U. So. Calif., 1968. Fin. analyst Rockwell Internat., L.A., 1967-72; div. contr. Arcata Co., N.Y.C., 1972-76; v.p., contr. Weeden Co., N.Y.C., 1976-78; sr. v.p., treas. Young & Rubicam Inc., N.Y.C., 1979-88; treas. Omnicom Group Inc., N.Y.C., 1988—; pres., CEO Omnicom Capital Inc., N.Y.C., 2000—. Republican. Avocations: golf, tennis. Home: 1 Richmond Dr Old Greenwich CT 06870-1413 also: 3794 Bayside Walk San Diego CA 92109 Office: Omnicom Capital Inc 1 E Weaver St Greenwich CT 06831-5146 Office Phone: 203-625-3010. E-mail: parents@mindspring.com.

HEWITT, DON S., television news producer; b. N.Y.C., Dec. 14, 1922; s. Ely S. and Frieda (Pike) H.; children: Jeffrey, Steven, Jill, Lisa; m. Marilyn Berger, Apr. 14, 1979. Student, NYU, 1941; hon. degree, Brandeis U., 1990; DFA (hon.), Am. Film Inst., 1993. War corr., World War II; prodr. 1st Kennedy-Nixon TV debate, 1960; exec. prodr. CBS Evening News with Walter Cronkite, 1960-65, 60 Minutes, 1968—2004, CBS News, 2004—. Delivered 1st ann. William S. Paley lectr. Mus. of TV and Radio, 1993. Recipient Paul White award Radio and TV News Dirs. Assn., 1987; Gold medal Internat. Radio and TV Soc., 1987, Broadcaster of Yr. award, 1980; Gold Baton award Columbia DuPont, 1988, Peabody award, 1989, Lowell Thomas Centennial award, 1992, 1st ann. Goldsmith award for Investigative Reporting, John F. Kennedy Sch. Govt. Harvard U., 1992, Lifetime award Prodrs. Guild Am., 1993, Founders award Internat. Coun. of TV Acad. Arts and Scis., 1995, Com. to Protect Journalists 9th Ann. Burton Benjamin Meml. award Internat. Press Freedom, 1999; named to Hall of Fame, NATAS, 1990. Office: CBS News 524 W 57th St New York NY 10019-2924 *Sometimes I think I am not sure of what I absolutely know is so.*

HEWITT, EMILY CLARK, federal judge, minister; b. Balt., May 26, 1944; d. John Frank and Margaret Genevieve (Gray) H. AB, Cornell U., 1966; MPhil, Union Theol. Sem., 1975; JD, Harvard U., 1978. Bar: Mass. 1978, U.S. Dist. Ct. Mass. 1979, U.S. Ct. Appeals (1st cir.) 1984, U.S. Ct. Appeals (fed. cir.) 1999, U.S. Supreme Ct. 2003; ordained priest Protestant Episcopal Ch. 1974. Adminstr. Upward Bound Programs Cornell and Hofstra U., NYC, 1967-69; asst. min. St. Mary's Episcopal Ch., Manhattanville, NY, 1972-73; lectr. Union Theol. Sem., NYC, 1972-73, 74-75; asst. prof. Andover Newton Theol. Sch., Newton Centre, Mass., 1973-75; assoc. Hill & Barlow, Boston, 1978-85, ptnr., 1985-93; gen. counsel GSA, 1993-98; judge US Ct. of Fed. Claims, Washington, 1998—. Co-author: Women Priests: Yes or No?, 1973; contbr. works in field. Bd. dirs. Mass. Found. for Humanities and Pub. Policy, South Hadley, 1983-89. Mem.: Mass. Conveyancers Assn. (exec. com. 1990—93), New Eng. Women in Real Estate (dir. 1985—89), ABA (vice chair Bid Protest com. sect. pub. contract law 2000—02). Office: US Ct Fed Claims 717 Madison Pl NW Washington DC 20005

HEWITT, HOLLY E., workforce development professional, reporter; b. Geneva, N.Y., Aug. 3, 1951; d. Richard Elliott and Elise Harriet (DeMeritt) Hewitt. BA in English Lit., SUNY Fredonia, 1973. Cert. workforce devel. profl. News reporter/bur. chief Observer, Dunkirk, N.Y., 1973—79; pub. info. coord. Chautauqua County Govt., Maryville, NY, 1979—80; mgr. corp. comm. Sunmaster Corp., Corning, NY, 1980—82; TV and radio news dir. WENY TV/Radio, Elmira, 1982—83; dir. tourism devel. and promotion Cheming County C. of C., Elmira, 1983—86; pub. rels. dir. Elmira City Schs., 1986—88; owner/cons. Hewitt Assocs. Mktg., N.Y. and Va., 1988—98; employment svcs. case mgr. Winchester Dept. Social Svcs., Va., 1995—96; mgr. career devel. svcs. Chautauqua Opportunities, Inc., Dunkirk, 1996—2002; workforce devel. specialist Jamestown C.C., N.Y., 2002—. Mem. cmty. coun. Cassadaga Job Corps, NY, 2001—03; mem. Diversity Coun., Jamestown; mktg. cons. various cos., N.Y. and Va. Freelance reporter: Buffalo News. Mem. Lily Dale Assembly, 1989—; mem. coun. on women's issues Chautauqua County, 2001—03; bd. dirs. Ch. Living Spirit, Lily Dale, N.Y., 1989—2002. Recipient Tourism award, N.Y.S. Gov. Mario Cuomo, 1985, Pub. Rels. award, Nat. Sch. Pub. Rels. Assn., 1987. Spiritualist. Avocations: travel, reading, cats. Home: 40 Summer St Fredonia NY 14063 Personal E-mail: hehewitt@yahoo.com.

HEWITT, JACQUELINE N., astronomy educator; AB in Econs., Bryn Mawr Coll., 1980; PhD in Physics, MIT, 1986. Prof. physics MIT, 1989—; dir. MIT Kavli Inst. for Astrophysics and Space Rsch., 2002—. Recipient Annie Jump Cannon award in Astronomy, 1989; David and Lucille Packard fellow, 1990; Henry G. Booker prize award, 1993; Maria Goeppart-Mayer award Am. Phys. Soc., 1995; Alfred P. Sloan rsch. fellow, 1990. Fellow: Am. Phys. Soc. Office: MIT Dept Physics Room 37-241 Cambridge MA 02139 Business E-Mail: jhewitt@mit.edu.

HEWITT, JAMES WATT, retired lawyer; b. Hastings, Nebr., Dec. 25, 1932; s. Roscoe Stanley and Willa Manners (Watt) H.; m. Marjorie Ruth Barrett, Aug. 8, 1954; children: Mary Janet, William Edward, John Charles, Martha Ann. Student, Hastings Coll., 1950-52; BS, U. Nebr., 1954, JD, 1956, MA, 1994, PhD, 2003. Bar: Nebr. 1956. Practice, Hastings, 1956—57, Lincoln, Nebr., 1960—2003; v.p., gen. counsel Nebco, Inc., Lincoln, 1961—2003. Vis. lectr. U. Nebr. Coll. Law, 1970—71; adj. prof. Am. history Nebr. Wesleyan U., 2001—. Mem. state exec. com. Rep. Party, 1967-70, mem. state ctrl. com., 1967-70, legis chmn., 1968-70; bd. dirs. Lincoln Child Guidance Ctr., 1969-72, pres., 1972; bd. dirs. Lincoln Cmty. Playhouse, 1967-73, pres., 1972-73; trustee Bryan Meml. Hosp., Lincoln, 1968-74, 76-82, chmn., 1972-74; bd. dirs. Lincoln Libr., 1990-97; trustee U. Nebr. Found., 1979—; dir. Bryan Meml. Hosp. Found., Lincoln, 1994—; pres, dir. Nebr. State Hist. Soc. Found., Lincoln, 1994—; dir. Nebr. state chpt. The Nature Conservancy, 1993-97. Capt. USAF, 1957-60. Fellow: Am. Bar Found. (Nebr. state chmn. 1988—92, 1999—2003, chmn. 1994—95); mem.: ABA (Nebr. state del. 1972—80, bd. govs. 1981—83), Lincoln Bar Assn., Fed. Bar Assn., Nebr. State Bar (chmn. ins. com. 1972—76, chmn. pub. rels. com. 1982—84, pres. 1985—86), Newcomen Soc. (Nebr. chair 1995—2003), Lincoln Rose Soc., Am. Rose Soc., Nebr. Rose Soc., Round Table, Country Club of Lincoln, Phi Alpha Theta, Phi Delta Phi, Beta Theta Pi. Congregationalist. Home: 2990 Sheridan Blvd Lincoln NE 68502-4241 Office Phone: 402-465-2554. Business E-Mail: jhewitt@nebrwesleyan.edu.

HEWITT, JENNIFER LOVE, actress, singer; b. Waco, Tex., Feb. 21, 1979; d. Danny and Pat. Actress: (films) Munchie, 1992, Little Miss Millions, 1993, Sister Act 2: Back in the Habit, 1993, Little Miss Millions, 1993, House Arrest, 1996, Trojan War, 1997, I Know What You Did Last Summer, 1997, Can't Hardly Wait, 1998, Telling You, 1998, Zoomates (voice), 1998, I Still Know What You Did Last Summer, 1998, The Suburbans, 1999, Heartbreakers, 2001, The Devil and Daniel Webster, 2001, The Tuxedo, 2002, Garfield: The Movie, 2004; (TV series) Kids Inc., 1989-91, Shaky Ground, 1992, The Byrds of Paradise, 1994, McKenna, 1994-95, Party of Five, 1995-99. Actress, prodr.: (films) If Only, 2004; (TV series) Time of Your Life, 1999, Ghost Whisperer, 2005. Actor, co-exec. prodr.: (TV movies) The Audrey Hepburn Story, 2000. Prodr. (films) One Night, 2002. Singer: (albums) Let's Go Bang, 1995, Jennifer Love Hewitt, 1996, Love Songs, 1998, BareNaked, 2002. Office: William Morris Agy 151 S El Camino Dr Beverly Hills CA 90212-2775

HEWITT, LESTER L., lawyer; b. Houston, Mar. 11, 1942; BSME, U. Houston, 1965, LLB cum laude, 1968. Bar: Tex. 1968. Examiner U.S. Patent Office, 1968-69; atty. Pravel, Hewitt, Kimball & Krieger, Houston, 1971-98; ptnr., co-head intellectual property practice nationally Akin Gump, Strauss, Hauer & Feld LLP, Houston. Assoc. prof. engring. law U. Houston, 1973-80. Mem. Am. Intellectual Property Law Assn. (treas. 1985-88), Houston Intellectual Property Law Assn. (pres. 1991-92), Order of the Barons, Phi Delta Phi, Pi Tau Sigma, Tau Beta Pi, Omicron Delta Kappa. Office: Akin Gump Strauss Hauer & Feld LLP 44th fl 1111 Louisiana St Houston TX 77002 Office Phone: 713-220-5851. Business E-Mail: lhewitt@akingump.com.

HEWITT, LISA CAROL (LISA CAROL VER HOEF), elementary school educator; b. Rock Rapids, Iowa, Oct. 7, 1963; d. Floyd Raymond and Carol Ann (Hollander) Ver Hoef; m. Douglas Ray Hewitt, July 22, 1995; 1 child, Mackenzie Ann Hewitt. BA summa cum laude, Buena Vista Coll., Storm Lake, Iowa, 1986. Cert. in elem. edn. and Spanish. Bilingual tchr. 2d grade Twombly Elem. Sch., Ft. Lupton, Colo., 1986—; elem. tchr., technology trainer Rolling Green Elem. Sch., Urbandale, Iowa, 1988—. Jr. webmaster supr. Rolling Green Elem. Sch., 1988—, mem. bldg. assistance team, 1988—2004; new tchr. mentor, 2004—; math com. mem., 2002—. Mem. NEA, Iowa Edn. Assn., Urbandale Edn. Assn., Iowa Jaycees (state dir. 1989-90, mgmt. v.p. 1990-91, pres. 1991-92, dist. dir. 1992-93), Iowa Jaycee (adminstrv. v.p. 1993-94, region 7 regional dir. 1994-95). Methodist. Avocations: golf, travel, reading, swimming. Home: 5143 69th St Des Moines IA 50322-6907 Office: Rolling Green Elem Sch 8100 Airline Ave Urbandale IA 50322-2446 E-mail: hewittl@urbandale.k12.ia.us.

HEWITT, LLEYTON, professional tennis player; b. Adelaide, Australia, Feb. 24, 1981; s. Glynn and Cherilyn. Profl. tennis player Assoc. of Tennis Profl. (ATP), 1998—. Mem. Australian Davis Cup Team, 1999—. Named Male Athlete of the Yr., Australian Sports Awards, 2002, Sportsman of the Yr., GQ (Australia), 2003. Achievements include winner U.S. Open, 2001, Wimbledon, 2002; doubles champion (with Max Mirnyi), U.S. Open, 2000; winner 24 career singles titles, 2 doubles titles, ATP Tour; mem. Australian Davis Cup Championship Team, 1999. Office: Octagon 1751 Pinnacle Dr Ste 1500 Mc Lean VA 22102

HEWITT, PAUL BUCK, lawyer; b. St. Louis, July 27, 1949; s. John York and Kathryn Louise (Buck) H.; m. Marla Ivy Zimmers, Feb. 17, 1985; children: Anna Ruth, Rachel Elizabeth. BA in Econs., Northwestern U., 1971; JD cum laude, U. Wis., 1974. Bar: D.C. 1979, Wis. 1974. Law clk. to chief justice Wis. Supreme Ct., Madison, 1974-75; atty. Bureau of Competition FTC, Washington, 1975-78; assoc. Akin Gump Strauss Hauer and Feld, Washington, 1978-82, ptnr., 1983—. Articles editor Wis. Law Rev., 1973—74. Mem. ABA, D.C. Bar, Wis. Bar Assn. Office: Akin Gump Strauss Hauer and Feld LLP 1333 New Hampshire Ave NW Washington DC 20036-1564 Office Phone: 202-887-4120. Business E-Mail: phewitt@akingump.com.

HEWITT, PAUL HARRINGTON, basketball coach; b. Jamaica, May 4, 1963; m. Dawnette Hewitt; 3 children. BA in Journalism and Econs., St. John Fisher Coll., 1985. Jr. varsity head coach Westbury H.S., L.I., NY, 1985—88; asst. coach C.W. Post U., 1988—89, So. Calif. U., 1989—90, Fordham U., 1990—92, Villanova, 1992—97; head coach Siena Coll., 1997—2000, Georgia Tech Men's Basketball Team, 2000—. Achievements include coached Georgia Tech to NCAA Final Four appearance, 2004. Office: 150 Bobby Dodd Way NW Atlanta GA 30332-0455

HEWITT, THOMAS F., hotel executive; Grad., Bryant Coll., 1967; hon. doctorate, Johnson and Wales U. With Sheraton Corp., pres. N.Am. divsn., 1983-85; pres., COO Carnival Resorts and Casinos, Miami, Fla., 1997-99; chmn. Interstate Hotels Corp., Pitts., 1999—. Chmn. Am. Hotel Found., Greater Miami Conv. and Visitors Bur.; dean Pres. Acad.; bd. dirs. Fla. Internat. Univs. Sch. of Hospitality; bd. trustees Bryant Coll., Smithfield. Mem. Am. Hotel and Motel Assn. Ednl. Inst. (bd. dirs.), Am. Hotel and Motel Assn. (officer's adv. coun.), Dade County's Beacon Coun., Coconut Grove C. of C. Office: Interstate Hotels and Resorts 4501 Fairfax Dr Arlington VA 22203-1656

HEWITT, VIVIAN ANN DAVIDSON (MRS. JOHN HAMILTON HEWITT JR.), retired librarian; b. New Castle, Pa., Feb. 17, 1920; d. Arthur Robert and Lela Luvada (Mauney) Davidson; m. John Hamilton Hewitt, Jr.,

Dec. 26, 1949; 1 son, John Hamilton III. AB with honors, Geneva Coll., 1943, LHD, 1978; BSLS, Carnegie Mellon U., 1944; postgrad., U. Pitts., 1947-48. Sr. asst. libr. Carnegie Libr., Pitts., 1944-49; instr., libr. Sch. Libr. Sci. Atlanta U., Atlanta U., 1949-52; with Readers Reference Svc., Crowell-Collier Pub. Co., N.Y.C., 1953-55; libr. Rockefeller Found., N.Y.C., 1955-63; librarian Carnegie Endowment Internat. Peace, N.Y.C., 1963-83; librarian Mexican Agrl. Program, Rockefeller Found., summer 1958; dir. libr. and info. svcs. Katherine Gibbs Sch., N.Y.C., 1984-86; reference asst. Coun. on Fgn. Rels., 1986-89. Lectr. spl. librarianship at grad. schs. of L.S. and info. throughout U.S. and Can., 1968-88; condr. profl. seminars Am. Mgmt. Assn., 1968-69, UN Inst. Tng. and Rsch., 1973, 74, Grad. Sci. Libr. and Info. Sci., Rutgers U., 1986; mem. faculty Grad. Sch. Libr. and Info. Sci., U. Tex., Austin, summer 1985; SLA rep. to Internat. Fedn. Libr. Assns., 1970-73, 73-75, 75-77; mem. nat. adv. com. Ctr. for the Book, Libr. of Congress, 1979-84; mem. adv. bd. Who's Who Among African Ams., 1975—. Contbr. chpt. to: The Black Librarian in America, 1970, What Black Librarians Are Saying, 1972, New Dimensions for Academic Library Service, 1975, A Century of Service, 1976, Handbook of Black Librarianship, 1977, 2d edit., 2000, The Black Librarian in America Revisited, 1994, Notable Black American Men, 1999. Bd. dirs. Graham-Windham, 1967, sec., 1980—87; bd. dirs. Laymen's Club, Cathedral Ch. of St.John the Divine, 1975—82, sec., 1986—93. Recipient Outstanding Cmty. Svc. awards, United Fund N.Y., 1965—77, Disting. Alumna award, U. Pitts.-Carnegie Mellon U. Alumni Assn., 1978, Merit award, Carnegie Mellon U. Alumni Assn., 1979, Leadership award, Carnegie Mellon U. Black Alumni, 2001. Mem.: ALA (Disting. Svc. to Librarianship award Black Caucus 1978, Leadership in Profession award Black Caucus 1992), Jack and Jill Am., Inc. (ea. regional dir. 1967—69), Spl. Librs. Assn. (rep. to Pacem in Terris Convocation 1965, rep. to White House Conf. Internat. Coop. Yr. 1965, pres. N.Y. chpt. 1970—71, nat. pres. 1978—79, Hall of Fame 1984, Leadership award 2001), Am. Soc. Order of St. John, Pierians, Inc. (hon.), Alpha Kappa Alpha, Tower Soc. Geneva Coll. Democrat. Episcopalian. Home: 862 West End Ave New York NY 10025-4959 E-mail: jhh2nyc@aol.com.

HEWLETT, GLORIA LOUISE, rancher, retired educator, civic volunteer; b. Clifton, Tex., Nov. 28, 1930; d. Dock Simpson and Leona Martha (Fricke) Martin; m. Robert Eckhart Hewlett, Jr., Sept. 3, 1950; children: Robert Eckhart, III, Jeffrey Martin Hewlett. BS, Tex. A&M, Corpus Christi, 1962; MEd, Northwestern State U., Natchitoches, La., 1974; DEd, East Tex. State U., 1988. Tchr. Terrebonne Parish Sch. Dist., Houma, La., 1962-69, Natchitoches (La.) Parish Sch. Dist., 1970-76, Mesquite (Tex.) Sch. Dist., 1977-91; ret., 1991. Author: A Descriptive Study of Textbook Preparation Programs and State Level Textbook Adoption in Texas, 1988, Bosque County Armed Forces, Vol. 1, 2004. Mem. sr. affairs commn. Dallas City Coun., 1995-97; pres. Eta Zeta chpt. Delta Kappa Gamma, Dallas, 1992-94. Named Gift to the Ednl. Found. of AAUW, 1992-93, 94-95. Mem. AAUW (pres. Dallas br. 1991-93, v.p. Tex. 1994-96), Dallas Ret. Tchrs. Assn. (pres. 1997-99), Am. Legion Aux., DAR, Dallas County Hist. Soc., Dallas Geneology Soc. Avocations: reading, genealogy, gardening. Home and Office: 9402 Mill Hollow Dr Dallas TX 75243-6338 E-mail: gloriamh28@earthlink.net.

HEWLETT, RICHARD GREENING, historian; b. Toledo, Feb. 12, 1923; s. Timothy Younglove and Gertrude Josephine (Greening) H.; m. Marilyn Eloise Nesper, Sept. 6, 1946. Student, Dartmouth, 1941-43, Bowdoin Coll., 1943-44; MA, U. Chgo., 1948, PhD, 1952. Intelligence specialist USAF Hdqrs., Washington, 1951-52; reports analyst AEC, Washington, 1952-57, chief historian, 1957-75, ERDA, Washington, 1975-77, U.S. Dept. Energy, 1977-80; sr. assoc., sr. v.p., chmn. bd. History Assoc., Inc., Rockville, Md., 1980—. Regents' lectr. U. Calif., 1982; historiographer Episcopal Diocese of Washington, also Washington Cathedral, 1978—, honorary canon, 2003-; chmn. fed. govt. resource group Nat. Coordinating Com. for Promotion of History, 1977-81; mem. U.S. Del. 2d UN Internat. Conf. on Peaceful Uses Atomic Energy, 1958. Author: Jessie Ball du Pont, 1992; co-author: The New World, 1939-46, 1962, Atomic Shield, 1947-52, 1969, Nuclear Navy, 1946-52, 1974, Atoms for Peace and War, 1953-61, 1989. Served with USAAF, 1943-46. Recipient David D. Lloyd prize Harry S. Truman Libr. Found., 1970; Distinguished Service award AEC, 1973. Mem. Am. Hist. Assn., Orgn. Am. Historians (Richard W. Leopold prize 1970), Soc. History Tech., Hist. Soc. Episc. Ch., Nat. Coun. Pub. History, Soc. for History in Fed. Govt. (v.p. 1983-85, Henry Adams prize 1990, Franklin D. Roosevelt award 1994), Cosmos Club. Episcopalian. Home: 7909 Deepwell Dr Bethesda MD 20817-1927 Office: History Assocs Inc 300 N Stonestreet Ave Rockville MD 20850 E-mail: rhewlett6@cs.com.

HEWLETT, SANDRA MARIE, clinical consultant; b. Chgo., Jan. 28, 1959; d. Stanley Vincent and Angeline Sajkiewicz. BS, Rush U., 1988, MS, 1989; postgrad., U. Ill., Chgo., 1992-95, Tex. Woman's U., 1997—. RN, Ill.; cert. BLS instr. Am. Heart Assn.; cert. breast health awareness instr.; cert. advanced oncology nurse; cert. rehab. RN and advanced cardiac life support certification. Acct., comptr. McKinsey Steel Co., Inc., Forest Park, Ill., 1976-79; exec. dir. Adolescent Youth Svcs., Village of Stone Park, Ill., 1979-81; coord. Midwest Therapeutic Assocs., Morton Grove, Ill., 1981-83, adminstr., 1983-86; in-outpatient oncology nurse Rush North Shore Med. Ctr., Skokie, Ill., 1988-89; oncology resource nurse West Suburban Hosp. Med. Ctr., Oak Park, Ill., 1989-90; oncology clin. nurse specialist Holy Family Hosp., Des Plaines, Ill., 1990-92; oncology clin. specialist, dir. autologous transplant program N.W. Oncology, Hematology S. C., Elk Grove Village, Ill., 1992-95; dir. Breast Ctr. The Dr.'s Hosp., Dallas, 1996-97; cons. Schering Plough Pharms., Mansfield, Tex., 1997—2002; dir. patient care svcs. Healthsouth Rehab. Hosp., 2002—. Asst. prof. Wright Coll., Chgo., 1990-95; profl. adv. bd. Rainbow Hospice, Park Ridge, Ill., 1990-93; profl. educator Ill. Cancer Pain Initiative, N.W. Suburban Cook County, Ill., 1991—. Author: AIDS-Facts & Myth, 1988, (cassettes) Chemo-Induced Sequelae, 1989, Lymphoscintigraphy and Sentinel Lymph Node Biopsy, 1999. Rush U. scholar, 1987-88; recipient Luther Christman award and scholarship Rush U./Rush Presbyn. St. Lukes Med. Ctr., 1988, Excellence in Gerontol Nursing award, 1988, Spl. Project award, 1988. Mem. Oncology Nursing Soc. (pres. elect local chpt., chmn. com., continuing edn. approval panel bd. dirs. 1999—), Am. Cancer Soc. (nurses ednl. com. 1990—, profl. educator 1990—, grad. scholar 1988-89, bd. dirs. unit 113 1992—), Soc. Otolaryngology and Head-Neck Nurses (treas. 1990-93, legis com. 1991, editor newsletter 1991), Gamma Phi chpt. Sigma Theta Tau. Republican. Roman Catholic. Avocations: reading, writing, travel, classical and jazz music. Home and Office: 9745 Corral Dr Keller TX 76248-5522 Personal E-mail: shewlett11@aol.com. Business E-Mail: sandra.hewlett@healthsouth.com.

HEWSON, PAUL See BONO

HEXBERG, KARIN, language arts educator, writer; b. Hayes, Kans., May 17, 1945; d. Caspar Jul and Patricia Marcelle (Phillips) H.; m. Gary Edward Brandt, Sept. 5, 1965 (div. 1977); 1 child, Christopher Gary (dec.); 1 child, Kirsten Annamarie. BA, U. S.D., 1966; postgrad., U. Md., 1972-73, U. Tex., Houston, 1975, U. Houston, 1977-81. Tchr. Wilson Jr. High Sch., Cedar Rapids, Iowa, 1966-68; mng. editor Union Express, Houston, 1975, Am. Jour. Med. Tech., Houston, 1975-77; copywriter Boone Advt., Houston, 1977-79; coord. advt./tng. FMC Corp., Houston, 1979-80; v.p. LeFevre Assocs., Houston, 1981-83; assoc. creative dir. Pinne Garvin Herbers & Hock, San Francisco, 1983-87; v.p., group creative dir. Foote Cone & Belding, San Francisco, 1987-90; sr. copywriter Young and Rubicam, San Francisco, 1990—93; tchr. Ione Jr. H.S., Calif., 1998—. Author short stories, poetry. Founder, dir. Volcano Writers Retreat, 1998—. Mem. Phi Beta Kappa, Kappa Alpha Theta. Democrat. Lutheran.

HEXT, KATHLEEN FLORENCE, college adminstrator; b. Bellingham, Wash., Oct. 7, 1941; d. Benjamin Byron and Sarah Debell (Youngquist) Gross.; m. George Ronald Hext, June 13, 1964 (div. 1972); m. William H. Lewis, Nov. 14, 1992. BA magna cum laude, Lewis & Clark Coll., Portland, Oreg., 1963; MA, Stanford U., 1964; MBA, UCLA, 1979. CPA; chartered bank auditor; cert. info. systems auditor. Chief exec. officer Internat. Lang. Ctr., Rome, 1970-77; sr. auditor Peat, Marwick, Mitchell & Co., L.A., 1979-81; mgr. fin. audit Lloyds Bank, L.A., 1981-83, mgr. EDP audit, 1983-85; dir. corp. audit First Interstate Bancorp, L.A., 1985-89, sr. v.p., gen. auditor, 1989-91, sr. v.p., chief compliance officer, 1991-94; compliance cons. Proactive, Inc., 1993—; dir. internal audit Calif. State U., Long Beach, 1996—; treas., Arcadia H.O. Assoc., El Monte, Calif., 1982-84, 86-88, pres., 1985. Recipient Edward W. Carter award UCLA, 1979. Mem. AICPA, Calif. Soc. CPA. Republican. Avocations: photography, microcomputers, reading. *I sincerely believe that the key to a happy, successful life is to do all that you do in truth and love.*

HEY, NANCY HENSON, educational administrator; b. Cleve., Apr. 1, 1935; d. Henry Brumback Henson and Isabelle (Smock) Selverstone; m. Robert Pierpont Hey, July 4, 1959; 1 child, Julie Dean. AB, Bates Coll., 1957; MS in Edn., Bank Street Coll. Edn., 1961. Cert. advanced profl. in early childhood nursery thru grade 3 Md. Primary tchr. Concord Pub. Sch., Mass., 1958-59; tchr. The Potomac Sch., McLean, Va., 1959-60, Galloway Sch., Atlanta, 1968-69; head tchr. Beauvoir Sch. Nursery Dept., Washington, 1969-70; supr. student tchr. U. Md. Coll. Edn., Coll. Pk., Md., 1973-76, Tufts U., Medford, Mass., 1978-79; head tchr. Newton Ctr. Day Care Ctr., 1980-81, Cmty. Child Devel. Ctr., Peabody, Mass., 1981-82; dir. Greater Lawrence YWCA Children's Ctr., Mass., 1982-86; tchr. Prince George's County Pub. Sch., Md., 1986-88; dir. Child Devel. Ctr., FTC, Washington, 1988-92; dir. Chevy Chase Plz. Children's Ctr., Washington, 1992-93; assoc. dir. Ctr. for Young Children, U. Md., Md., 1994—. Supr. student tchrs. Simmons Coll., Boston, 1965-67; teaching asst. to head of lower sch.Shady Hill Sch., Cambridge, Mass., 1960-61; mem. task force com. Region III Dept. of Social Svcs., Middleton, Mass., 1984-86; bd. dirs. Greater Lawrence Coun. for Children, 1984-86. Mem.: Nat. Coalition for Campus Children's Ctrs. (D.C. area chpt. pres. 2004—05), Dirs. Exch., Congressional and Fed. Child Care Dir. Assn. (sec. 1990—92), Nat. Assn. Edn. of Young Children. Home: 10908 Candlelight Ln Potomac MD 20854-2756 Office: U Md Ctr for Young Children Valley Dr College Park MD 20742-0001

HEY, ROBERT PIERPONT, retired editor; b. East Providence, R.I., Jan. 24, 1935; s. Daniel Chase and Grace (Pierpont) H.; m. Nancy Henson, July 4, 1959; 1 dau., Julie. AB, Harvard U., 1955. Gen. assignment reporter, local edn. reporter Christian Sci. Monitor, Boston, 1960-64, asst. to Am. news editor, then asst. Am. news editor, 1964-67, S.E. U.S. corr., then Washington corr., 1967-76, asst. mng. editor, 1976-79, mng. editor features Boston, 1979-83, editorial writer, 1983-86, Washington Corr., 1986-91; mng. editor AARP Bull., 1991-2000; purchasing agt. Arkell Safety Bag Co., N.Y.C., 1956-58; with public relations dept. U. Pitts., 1964. Served with AUS, 1958-60.

HEYBURN, JOHN GILPIN, II, federal judge; b. Boston, 1948; m. Martha Keeney, 1976. BA, Harvard U., 1970; JD, U. Ky., 1976. Ptnr. Brown, Todd & Heyburn, Louisville, 1976-92; judge US Dist. Ct. (we. dist.), Louisville, 1992—, chief judge, 2001—. Mem. Budget Com. Jud. Conf.of US, 1994-04, chmn. 1997-04; chair Jefferson County Crime Commn.; mem. vis. com. U. Ky., 1980; active Leadership Louisville Found. With USAR, 1970-76. Mem. ABA, Ky. Bar Assn., Louisville Bar Assn., U. Ky. Coll. Law Alumni Assn. Office: US Dist Ct Gene Snyder US Courthouse 601 W Broadway Ste 239 Louisville KY 40202-2227

HEYCK, THEODORE DALY, lawyer; b. Houston, Apr. 17, 1941; s. Theodore and Richard and Gertrude Paine (Daly) H. BA, Brown U., 1963; postgrad., Georgetown U., 1963-65, 71-72; JD, N.Y. Law Sch., 1979. Bar: N.Y. 1980, Calif. 1984, U.S. Ct. Appeals (2d cir.) 1984, U.S. Supreme Ct. 1984, U.S. Dist. Ct. (so. and ea. dists.) N.Y. 1980, U.S. Dist. Ct. (we. and no. dists.) N.Y. 1984, U.S. Dist. Ct. (cen. and so. dists.) Calif. 1984, U.S. Ct. Appeals (9th cir.) 1986. Paralegal dist. atty., Bklyn., 1975-79; asst. dist. atty. Bklyn. dist., Kings County, N.Y., 1979-85; dep. city atty. L.A., 1985—. Bd. dirs. Screen Actors Guild, N.Y.C., 1977-78. Mem. ABA, ATLA, AFTRA, NATAS, SAG, Bklyn. Bar Assn., N.Y. Trial Lawyers Assn., N.Y. State Bar Assn., Calif. Bar Assn., Fed. Bar Coun., L.A. Coun. Bar Assn., Actors Equity Assn. Home: 2106 E Live Oak Dr Los Angeles CA 90068-3639 Office: Office City Atty City Hall E 200 N Main St Los Angeles CA 90012-4110

HEYDARI, EZAT, geologist, physics professor; b. Village of Laibid, Esfahan, Iran, Apr. 22, 1954; s. Alamdar Heydari and Kokab Izadi; m. Shahrzad Aseel, Sept. 6, 1971. PhD, La. State U., 1990. Tchg. asst. dept. geology & geophysics La. State U., Baton Rouge, 1981—86, rsch. asst. dept. geology & geophysics, 1986—90, rschr., 1990—99; adminstr. Miss. Dept. Environ. Quality, Jackson, 1999—2001; asst. prof. dept. physics Jackson State U., Miss., 2001—. Assoc. editor Jour. of Sedimentary Rsch., Tulsa, Okla., 1997—2004. Author: about 30 jour. articles in sci. publs. Recipient Best Paper award, 2d pl., Gulf Coast Assn. Geol. Socs., 2001. Fellow: Geol. Soc. Am. (life). Achievements include research in the study of the cause of the mass extinction of animals and plants at the Permian - Triassic boundary, about 251 million years ago. Office: Jackson State University Dept of Physi 1400 Lynch St PO Box 17660 Jackson MS 39217 Office Phone: 601-979-7012. Office Fax: 601-979-3630. E-mail: ezat.heydari@jsums.edu.

HEYDARI, PAYAM, engineering educator; m. Negah Arman, Dec. 13, 1974. PhD, U. So. Calif., 2001. Author (prin. investigator): (rsch.) Analysis and Design of Silicon-Based Performance-Optimized Integrated Circuits for High-Frequency Wideband Wireless Communication Systems. Tech. program com. Internat. Symposium on Low-Power Electronics and Design, Calif., 2004—. Recipient Best Paper award, IEEE Internat. Conf. in Computer Design, 2000, Tech. Excellence award, Assn. of Profs. and Scholars of Iranian Heritage, 2001, IEEE Darlington Best Jour. award, IEEE Circuits and Systems Soc., 2005, Career award, NSF, 2005-2009. Mem.: IEEE (Orange County chpt. faculty advisor 2003—). Achievements include patents pending for A Novel Silicon-Based Differential Non-Uniform Downsized Distributed Amplifier; A Novel Delay-Locked Loop Based Clock and Data Recovery Circuit; Design and Analysis of a Novel Ultra-Wideband CMOS Mixer. Office: Univ Calif Engring Tower 644C Irvine CA 92697-2625

HEYDE, MARTHA BENNETT (MRS. ERNEST R. HEYDE), psychologist; b. New Bern, N.C., Jan. 31, 1920; d. George Spotswood and Katherine (McIntosh) Bennett; m. Ernest R. Heyde, Aug. 17, 1946. AB, Columbia U., 1941, MA, 1949, PhD, 1959. Instr. psychol. founds and svcs. Tchrs. Coll., Columbia U., N.Y.C., 1957-59, rsch. assoc., 1960-70, cons., 1970-73. Contbg. author: (rsch. monograph) The Vocational Maturity of Ningh Grade Boys, 1960, Floundering and Trial After High Sch., 1967; co-author: Vocational Maturity During the High School Years, 1979. Mem. Barnard Coll. alumnae coun. Columbia U., 1956-61, 69—, pres. class, 1956-61, trustee, 1974-79, hon. vice chmn. Barnard Coll. Centennial, 1987-89. Mem. APA, Sigma Xi, Kappa Delta Pi, Pi Lambda Theta. Home: 530 E 23rd St Apt 8E New York NY 10010-5030

HEYDERMAN, ARTHUR JEROME, engineer, civilian military employee; b. Bklyn., Jan. 1, 1946; s. Herbert Robert and Sally (Baron) H.; m. Renee Linda Pearlman, July 4, 1967; children: Brian Douglas, Deborah Ann, Cathy Ruth. BS in Applied Math., Poly. Inst. Bklyn., 1966, MS in Applied Math., 1973; postgrad., Stevens Inst. Tech., 1982, Brookings Inst., 1992, Wharton Sch. Bus., U. Pa., 1993. Nuclear weapons engr. U.S. Army Armaments R&D Ctr., Picatinny Arsenal, N.J., 1971-83, asst. tech. dir., 1983-84, chief prodn. program planning, 1984, assoc. tech. dir., 1984-86; armaments rsch. and devel. prog. mgr. U.S. Army Armaments Munitions and Chem. Command, Rock Island, Ill., 1986-93, chief of rsch. devel., test and evaluation integration, 1993-94; chief improved armor engring. U.S. Army Armaments Rsch., Devel. and Engring. Ctr., Rock Island, Ill., 1994-96; chief armor engring. U.S. Armaments Rsch. Devel. & Engring. Ctr., Rock Island, Ill., 1996-98, chief arty. sys. & armor divsn., 1998—99; chief prodn. and logistics engring. support U.S. Armaments Rsch. Devel. and Engring. Ctr., Rock Island, Ill., 1999—2003; enterprise mgr. U.S. Army Armaments Rsch., Devel. and Engring. Ctr., Rock Island, 2003—. Bd. dirs., sec./treas., pres. Iowa-Ill. chpt. Am. Def. Preparedness Assn., Rock Island; lt. col. nuclear weapons officer USAR, Ft. Sheridan, Ill., 1989-93; pres. OPICON, Bettendorf, Iowa, 1989—; nat. coun. Am. Def. Preparedness Assn.; coun. mem. Quad-Cities Engring. and Sci. Coun.; adj. faculty U.S. Army Command and Gen. Staff Coll., Ft. Leavenworth, Kans., 1981-89, Scott C.C., 1997. Contbr. column to Rock Island Argus/Moline Dispatch; guest editor Quad Cities Times; contbr. tech. papers on weapons and weaponry assessment to profl. meetings. Pres., bd. dirs. Sussex County Jewish Ctr., Newton, N.J., 1979-86; fundraiser United Jewish Fedn., Davenport, Iowa, 1986-99; mem. Rock Island Arsenal Com. for Disabled, 1987-93, Quad Cities Coalition for Choice; dir. intake Quad City chpt. ACLU; mem. platform com. Scott County Dem. Ctrl. Com., 1994—; mem. 1st dist. Iowa Dem. Ctrl. Com., 1994—; mem. platform com. Iowa State Dem. Party; chmn. Quad Cities WWII Commemoration Com., 1995, Quad Cities Vietnam Wall Com., 1997, Quad Cities Korean War Commemoration Com., 2003; mem. Iowa Sesquecentennial Commemoration Com., 1995, Rock Island County, Ill. C. of C. Spkrs. Bur., 1996; bd. dirs. Jewish Fedn. of Quad Cities, 1996-99; funds distbn. panelist United Way of Quad Cities, 1999-2000; bd. dirs. Iowa Civil Liberties Union, 1997—, sec.-treas., 2004—; bd. dirs. Iowa Civil Liberties Found., 1997—; mem. Scott County Foster Care Citizens Rev. Bd., 2000-2001. Capt. U.S. Army, 1968-71, Vietnam; maj./lt. col. USAR, 1971-93. Decorated Bronze Star; Cross of Gallantry (Vietnam); named to Hon. Order St. Barbara, U.S. Army Field Arty. Assn.; recipient Civilian of Yr. award Fifth Region Assn. of the U.S. Army, 1998; recipient Nat. President's award, Women in Def., 2003. Mem. VFW, ACLU (nat. bd. dirs. 1998—), NAACP (bd. dirs. Quad Cities chpt. 1996-2001), U.S. Army Acquisitions Corps, U.S. Army Engr. Assn., Assn. U.S. Army (v.p. Ft. Armstrong chpt. 1993—, acting pres. chpt. 1996-97), Soc. Am. Mil. Engrs. (scholar 1966), Soc. Am. Mil. Comptrs., Federally Employed Women, Planned Parenthood (mem. cmty. coun.), Nat. Soc. Scabbard and Blade (chpt. v.p. 1965-66), Nat. Def. Indsl. Assn. (pres. Iowa Ill. chpt.), Res. Officers Assn., Women in Defense, Poly. Alumni Assn. (pres. Quad City chpt. 1989—), Mensa, Intertel, Vietnam Vets. Jewish. Avocations: horticulture, art, bonsai, cooking, photography. Home: 1430 Grappler Ct Bettendorf IA 52722-1847

HEYDON, PETER NORTHRUP, farmer, educator, philanthropist; b. Hackensack, NJ, Nov. 25, 1940; s. Clark A. and Elizabeth VanFleet (Northrup) H.; m. Henrietta M. Heydon, Aug. 24, 1968. BA, Princeton U., N.J., 1962; MA, U. Mich., Ann Arbor, 1963, PhD, 1970. Lectr. in humanities & English U. Mich., Ann Arbor, 1963-80, adj. prof., 1980-86. Chmn. Clements Library Assocs., Ann Arbor, 1970-2004; trustee Folger Shakespeare Libr., Washington D.C., 1986-99, Nat. Pub. Radio Found., 1994—; dir. Farrar, Straus & Giroux, NYC, 1970-94; pres. Browning Inst., NYC, 1971-85, Firenze, 1971-85; pres. Beacon Theatre Assocs., NYC, 1990—. Founder, bd. dirs. The Mosaic Found., 1989—. Mem. The Lotos Club, The Grolier Club, The Century Assn., Maitre, Commanderie de Bordeaux á Detroit, Commandeur Chevaliers du Tastevin. Avocations: restoration of classic and special interest automobiles, historic preservation of national register buildings, wine, food, horse breeding. Office: Heydon Washington St Prop 324 E Washington St PO Box 7801 Ann Arbor MI 48107-7801

HEYDRICK, LINDA CAROL, consulting company executive, editor; b. Pomona, Calif., July 25, 1947; d. Robert Bruce and Wanda Georgine (Wellman) Middough; m. Stephen R. Bova, Jan. 20, 1968 (div. May 1981); children: Karen E., Lori L.; m. Allen L. Heydrick, Mar. 15, 1995. Student, El Camino Coll., Gardena, Calif., 1965-66. Sec. TRW, Inc., Manhattan Beach, Calif., 1967-68, USAF NCO Clubs, Mildenhall, England, 1968-70; adminstrv. asst. Prudential-Bache Securities, N.Y.C., 1970-73, Tex. Instruments, Inc., Dallas, 1980-83; asst. to pres. Acclivus Corp., Dallas, 1983-85, mgr. design and prodn., 1985-88, mgr. ops., 1988-89, v.p. ops., 1989—. Cons. Digital Equipment Corp., Boston, 1984-89, coord. internat. translations of books, audiotapes and videotapes, 1993—. Editor: (books and videotapes) BASE for Sales Performance, 1984, Acclivus Sales Negotiation, 1985, The New BASE for Sales Excellence, 1989, Major Account Planning and Strategy, 1993, rev., 1996, Building on the BASE (award for best new tng. products Human Resource Exec.), 1993, R3 Service, (award for best new tng. product Human Resource Exec. 1998), 1997, Creating R3 Value, 2002; editor, pub. Denton Bible Ch., The Titus 2 Woman, More of Christ, 1993-. Mem.: ASTD, Instrnl. Sys. Assn. Republican. Avocations: christian studies, fine arts, design, performing arts. Office: Acclivus Corp 14500 Midway Rd Dallas TX 75244-3109

HEYDRON, JO ANN, writer; b. Sacramento, Sept. 2, 1953; d. Herman Heydron and Mary Faye Hill; m. Herbert Pluemer, Apr. 19, 1979 (div. Nov. 1984); 1 child, Alexander William Pluemer; m. Warren Kenneth Miller, Dec. 21, 1984; children: Victor Kenneth, Mary Lauren. BA in English, U. Calif., Berkeley, 1977; MA in English, San Jose State U., 1993. Tech. editor geophys. dept. Stanford (Calif.) U., 1978-95; pub. rels. profl. Advanced Micro Devices, Sunnyvale, Calif., 1983-85; prof. English Santa Clara (Calif.) U., West Valley Coll. and Foothill Coll., San Jose area, 1993-96; freelance writer, 1994—. Contbr. short stories, poems and book revs. to profl. publs. Vol. St. Anthony's Dining Rm., Redwood City, Calif., 1999—. Mem. Green Party. Presbyterian.

HEYER, CAROL ANN, illustrator; b. Cuero, Tex., Feb. 2, 1950; d. William Jerome and Merlyn Mary (Hutson) H. BA, Calif. Luth. U., 1974. Freelance artist various cos., Thousand Oaks, Calif., 1974-79; computer artist Image Resource, Westlake Village, Calif., 1979-81; staff writer, artist Lynn-Davis Prodns., Westlake Village, Calif., 1981-87; art dir. Northwind Studios Internat., Camarillo, Calif., 1988-89; illustrator Touchmark, Thousand Oaks, 1989—. Cons. art dir., writer Lynn-Wenger Prodns., 1987-89; guest spkr. Ariz. Kidney Found. Children's Art and Lit. luncheon 2000, Thousand Oaks Libr., Author's Faire, Calif. Luth. U., Soc. Children's Book Writers and Illustrators, Illustrators Day, Ventura County Reading Assn.'s Author's Faire; guest artist/spkr. Oxnard Libr.; booksignings/appearances Anaheim Conv. Ctr., L.A. Conv. Ctr., Am. Booksellers Assn.; guest 1996 Readout, grand opening Barnes and Noble, Thousand Oaks; represented by Art Works, N.Y.C.; SCBWI workshop leader Trading Spaces; invited artist Ann. Art Show, Chemers Gallery; spkr. and presenter in field. Illustrator Once Upon A Cool Motorcycle Dude, 2005, (children's books) Down the Grand Canyon Harcourt, A Star in the Pasture, 1988, The Dream Stealer, 1989, The Golden Easter Egg, 1989, All Things Bright and Beautiful, 1992, Rapunzel, 1992, The Christmas Carol, 1995, Prancer, Gift of the Magi, Black Beauty, Dinosaurs Strange and Wonderful, Down the Great Unknown, 1999, Abraham Lincoln, 2002, Teacher of the Year, Two Fridas, Down the Grand Canyon, The First Easter, 2003, The First Christmas, 2003, Flame and Clay (teachers' big book) 1998, 3 Repeat Jobs for Hampton/Brown (teacher's big book), (illustrator) Night Journey, 1999, Here Come the Brides, (adult book) The Artist's Market, also L.A. Times, Daily News, The Artist's Mag., News Chronicle; also cover art for Troll Assoc., Top Secret, The Loveless Cafe (cookbook), Ellery Queen's Mystery Mag., Frontispiece Collectors Leather Bound Edition, Crippen and Landru Mystery Covers, Dragon mag., Dungeon mag., Aboriginal Sci. Fiction mag., Wizards of the Coast, (game covers) F.X. Schmid - Puzzle Wizards of the Coast (fantasy collector cards, Dune and Hobbit), 4 covers, frontspieces and chpt. headings for Henry Winkler's Hank Zipzer series, Georgw W. Bush Scholastic, 2003, also various novels, books and games; illustrator Bugs Bunny Coloring Book, Candyland Work Book, The Dragon Sleeps Step Ahead Workbook, City of Sorcers, CD-ROM cover for Memorex/Roaring Mouse Prodns., George W. Bush Scholastic; interior art for various publs. including (mags.) Amazing Stories two covers, Interzone, Aboriginal Sci. Fiction Mag., Alfred Hitchcocks Mystery Mag., Ideals mag., Ellery Queen's Mystery mag. two covers, Realms of Fantasy mag., Sci. Fiction Age mag., Tomorrow mag., (book) Tome of Magic, Spider Magazine, (book) Top Secret, (book, interiors) Star Trek Next Generation, (also art for game cards), (repeat covers) Crippen and Landru, (game book cover) Wizards of the Coast; writer (screenplay) Thunder Run, 1986; illustrator, writer (children's books) Black Beauty, Beauty and the Beast, 1989, The Easter Story, 1989, Excalibur, Robin Hood, 1993, Sleeping Beauty in the Wood, 1996, The Christmas Story, 1996, Down the Great Unknown, 1999, Flame and Clay, 1998, Black Beauty, The First Easter, 2003, The First Christmas, 2003; paintings for line of Fantasy Art Prints, Scafa/Tornabene, religious art prints; rep. by Every Picture Tells a Story Gallery, Worlds of Wonder; cover art/bookmark for Antioch Pub.; new cover for Baen Books; art for Maruri USA Corp.; 2 covers for young adults Hyperion/Disney Press; one-woman show Adventures for Kids Gallery; illustrator poster for motion picture and TV fund; writer Disney ednl. prodns., others; freelance artist Disney Interactive. Guest spkr. Ariz. Kidney Found. Recipient Lit. award City of Oxnard Cultural Arts Commn. and Carnegie Art Inst., 1992, Best Cover Art Boomerang award, 1989, Cert. of Merit, Career Achievement award Calif. Luth. U., 1993, Cert. of Excellence Alumni Career Achievement award, 1993, Print's Regional Design Ann. award, 1992, Best Paper Backs award Internat. Reading Assn. Children's Book Coun. Joint Com., 1994, Spectrum Internat. Competition for Best in Contemporary Fantastic Art, Spectrum 7 award, Spectrum 9 Art Competition award, award Ventura Soc. of Children's Bookwriters and Illustrators, 2002. Mem. Soc. Children's Book Writers (judge 1990, Mag. Merit award 1988, Keynote spkr.), Assn. Sci. Fiction and Fantasy Artists (nominated for Chelsey award), Soc. Illustrators (Cert. of Merit 1990-92, winner Ann. Illustration West show, award L.A. chpt. 1998). Achievements include being featured in articles. Home and Office: Touchmark 925 Ave Arboles Thousand Oaks CA 91360

HEYER, ERICA RITTENHOUSE, marketing professional; d. Stanley V. Heyer, Jr. and Daryl B. Heyer. BA magna cum laude, Muhlenberg Coll., 2000; MA, Ind. U., 2002. Mktg. intern Phila. Orch., 2000; program assoc. Phila. Classical Symphony, Merian, 2001—02; mktg. & devel. asst. Haddonfield Symphony, NJ, 2002—. Arts Adminstrn. Fellowship, Ind. U., 2002. Mem.: Am. Guild Organists (publicity chair 2005—), Phi Mu. Avocations: music, ice skating, photography, hiking.

HEYER, STEVEN J., hotel executive, former beverage company executive; Former sr. v.p., mng. ptnr. Booz Allen & Hamilton, N.Y.C.; former pres., COO Young & Rubicam Advt. Worldwide; former pres., COO Turner Broadcasting Sys., Inc. subs. AOL Time Warner; former pres., COO Coca-Cola Ventures; pres., COO The Coca-Cola Co., Atlanta, 2002—04; CEO Starwood Hotels & Resorts Worldwide, Inc., White Plains, NY, 2004—. Bd. dirs. Equifax Inc., Coca-Cola Enterprises, Inc., Coca-Cola FEMSA, Internet Security Systems Inc., 2004—. Bd. advisors Amos Tuck Sch., Dartmouth Coll.; bd. dirs. Piedmont Hosp., Atlanta, Trinity Sch., Atlanta; bd. visitors Emory U., Atlanta; ret. chmn. bd. dirs. Cable Advt. Bur.; bd. dirs. Ad Coun. Office: Starwood Hotels & Resorts Worldwide Inc 1111 Westchester Ave White Plains NY 10604

HEYERDAHL, JENS P., investment company executive; b. Oslo, Feb. 17, 1943; s. Jens and Sessan (Lyche) H.; widowed; 2 children. Student, Cavalry Officers Sch., 1961-63; degree in law, Oslo U., 1968; MBA, European Inst. Adminstrn. Affairs, Fontainebleau, France, 1970. Atty. Thommessen, Karlsrud, Heyerdahl & Brunsvig, Oslo, 1969; staff Directorate for Legal Harmonization, EEC, Brussels, 1969; legal cons. Insp. of Taxes, Oslo, 1970-71; dep. judge of Lier Røyken and Hurum Magistrate, 1971-72; co. sec. Dyno Industrier A.S., Oslo, 1972-75; v.p. indsl. devel. and investments Orkla Industrier A/S, 1975-79, CEO, 1979—2001. Bd. dirs. BASF Norge, Hafslund ASA, Oslo, subs. cos. Orkla ASA. Avocation: riding (Grand Prix). Office: Orkla ASA PO Box 423 Skøyen N-0213 Oslo Norway E-mail: jens.p.heyerdahl@orkla.no.

HEYL, ALLEN VAN, JR., geologist; b. Allentown, Pa., Apr. 10, 1918; s. Allen Van and Emma (Kleppinger) H.; m. Maxine LaVon Hawke, July 12, 1945; children: Nancy Caroline, Allen David Van. BS in Geology, Pa. State U., 1941; PhD in Geology, Princeton U., 1950. Field asst. major regional exploration, govt. geologist Nfld. Geol. Survey, summers 1937-40, 42; jr. geologist U.S. Geol. Survey, Wis., 1943-45, asst. geologist, 1945-47, assoc. geologist, 1947-50, geologist Washington and Beltsville, Md., 1950-67, staff geologist Denver, 1968-90; cons. geologist, 1990—. Disting. lectr. grad. coll. Beijing, China and Nat. Acad. Sci., 1988; disting. invited lectr. Internat. Assn. Genesis Ore Deposits 9th Symposium, Beijing, 1994; chmn. Internat. Commn. Tectonics of Ore Deposits. Contbr. numerous articles to profl. jours., chpts. to books. Fellow Instn. Minin and Metallurgy (Gt. Britain), Geol. Soc. Am., Am. Mineral Soc., Soc. Econ. Geologists, Inst. Genesis of Ore Deposits (hon., life), Geol. Soc. Wash., Colo. Sci. Soc., Rocky Mountain geol. Soc., Friends of Mineralogy (hon., life), Evergreen Naturalist Audubon Soc., Sigma Xi, Alpha Chi Sigma. Lutheran. Home: PO Box 1052 Evergreen CO 80437-1052

HEYL, JAMES TAYLOR, retired physician; b. Chgo., Feb. 21, 1912; s. Ernst Oscar and Charlotte Taylor Heyl. AB, Hamilton Coll., Clinton, NY, 1933; MD, Harvard U., Boston, 1937. Intern in medicine Mass. Gen. Hosp., Bsoston, 1937—38; instr. in pharmacology Phila., 1938—39; lab. dir. Am. Hosp., England, 1939—40; fellow in medicine Harvard Medicine, Boston, 1941—43; med. dir. Exeter Acad.; intern Exeter Hosp. Clinic. Country staff Exeter Hosp. Lt. MC USNR, South Pacific, Boston, Nebr. Independent. Avocations: fishing, skiing. Home: River Woods 7 Riverwoods Dr Apt F114 Exeter NH 03833-4394

HEYLER, GROVER ROSS, retired lawyer; b. Manila, June 24, 1926; s. Grover Edwin and Esther Viola (Ross) H.; m. Caroline Yarbrough, Aug. 10, 1949; children: Richard Ross, Sue Louise, Randall Arthur BA, UCLA, 1949; LLB, U. Calif., Berkeley, 1952. Bar: Calif. 1953. Atty. Latham & Watkins, L.A., 1952—93, chmn., corp. securities dept., 1967-89. Chmn. Nat. Alliance for Rsch. into Schizophrenia and Depression, NYC, 2002—04. Mem. Calif. Bar Assn. (com. on drafting Calif. corps. code 1971-75), Order of Coif, UCLA ALumni Assn. (bd. dirs. 1966-70, 1988-90), L.A. Country Club. Home: 491 Homewood Rd Los Angeles CA 90049-2713

HEYMACH, GEORGE JOHN, III, physician, educator, health facility administrator, consultant; b. N.Y.C., Nov. 17, 1942; s. George John and Bertha Vina (Floerke) H.; m. Barbara Lynne Lerew, Oct. 26, 1968; children: Brooke Lerew, G. John IV, Bria Lerew. BSCE, CCNY, 1964; MS, U. Pa., 1966, PhD, 1969; MD, Jefferson Med. Coll., 1976; MBA, U. Pitts., 1997. Diplomate in internal medicine, pulmonary medicine, critical care medicine, geriatrics Am. Bd. Internal Medicine. Asst. prof. chem. engring. Kans. State U., Manhattan, 1969—72; resident in medicine Thomas Jefferson U. Hosp., Phila., 1976—79; fellow in medicine Washington U., St. Louis, 1979—81; physician Pitts. Pulmonary Assn. Ltd., 1981—96; v.p. med. affairs Bapt. Med. Ctr., Kansas City, Mo., 1997—98; med. dir. Health Midwest, Kansas City, Mo., 1998—2000; sr. v.p. healthcare Fleishman-Hillard, 2000—01; pres. Physicians' Health Care Cons., 2001—. Clin. asst. prof. medicine U. Pitts., 1982-2003; adj. prof. biomed. engring. Carnegie-Mellon U., Pitts., 1982—96. Contbr. articles to profl. jours. Fire surgeon Fox Chapel (Pa.) Vol. Fire Dept., 1984-92; Tb physician Allegheny County Health Dept., Pitts., 1986-90. Served to capt. U.S. Army, 1970-72. Grantee in field. Fellow ACP, Am. Coll. Chest Physicians. Avocations: boating, travel, racketball, music. Home: 801 W 57th Ter Kansas City MO 64113-1166 Office: 801 W 57th Terr Kansas City MO 64113 Office Phone: 816-333-0224. E-mail: Breathdoc@aol.com.

HEYMAN, IRA MICHAEL, federal agency administrator, law educator, museum executive; b. NYC, May 30, 1930; s. Harold Albert and Judith (Sobel) H.; m. Therese Helene Thau, Dec. 17, 1950 (dec.); children: Stephen Thomas (dec.), James Nathaniel. AB in Govt., Dartmouth Coll., 1951; JD, Yale U., 1956; LLD (hon.), U. Pacific, 1981, Hebrew Union Coll., 1984, U. Md., 1986, SUNY, Buffalo, 1990, Dartmouth Coll., 2001. Bar: NY 1956, Calif. 1961. Legis. asst. to U.S. Senator Ives, 1950-51; assoc. Carter, Ledyard & Milburn, N.Y.C., 1956-57; law clk. to presiding justice U.S. Ct. Appeals (2d cir.), New Haven, 1957-58; chief law clk. to Supreme Ct. Justice Earl Warren, 1958-59; acting assoc. prof. law U. Calif., Berkeley, 1959-61, prof. law, 1961—93, prof. city and regional planning, 1966-93, prof. emeritus, 1993—, vice chancellor, 1974-80, chancellor, 1980-90, chancellor emeritus, 1990—; counselor to Sec. of Interior Dept. Interior, Washington, 1993-94; sec. Smithsonian Inst., Washington, 1994-99, sec. emeritus, 2000—; mem. Citizens' Stamp Adv. Com., 2000—. Vis. prof. Yale Law Sch., 1963—64, Stanford Law Sch., 1971—72; bd. dirs. Presidio Trust. Editor Yale Law Jour.; contbr. articles to profl. jours. Sec. Calif. adv. com. U.S. Commn. Civil Rights, 1962-67; trustee Dartmouth Coll., 1982-93, chmn., 1991-93, Smith Coll., 2004—; mem. Lawyers' Com. for Civil Rights under Law, 1977-95, Citizens Stamp Advisory Com., USPS, 2000-; chmn. exec. com. Nat. Assn. State Univs. and Land Grant Colls., 1986; bd. regents Smithsonian Instn., 1990-94; bd. dirs. Presidio Trust, 2000-04. 1st lt. USMC, 1951-53, capt. Res. ret. Decorated chevalier Legion of Honor (France). Mem. Am. Acad. Arts and Sci. Office Phone: 510-642-1731. Business E-Mail: mheyman@law.berkeley.edu.

HEYMAN, JOHN H., energy executive; BBA acctg., Univ. Ga.; MBA, Harvard Bus. Sch. With Arthur Andersen, LLP, 1983—87; vice-pres. acquisitions Forsch Corp., 1989—91; vice-pres., CFO Phoenix Comm., Inc., 1991—95; CFO Radiant Systems Inc., Atlanta, pres., 1999—, CEO, 2002—. Office: Radient Systems Inc 3925 Brookside Pkwy Alpharetta GA 30022*

HEYMAN, JOSEPH MARTIN, obstetrician, gynecologist; b. Bklyn., May 21, 1942; s. Ezekiel and Elaine Olga (Adelman) H.; m. Laurel Ann Taylor, June 10, 1967; children: Eve Renata, Todd Sanford. BS, CCNY, 1963; MD, SUNY, Bklyn., 1967. Diplomate, Am. Bd. Ob.-Gyn. Intern USPHS Marine Hosp., Staten Island, N.Y., 1967-68; chief outpatient dept., venereal disease control officer USPHS Northern Navajo Indian Hosp., Shiprock, N.Mex., 1968-70; resident in ob.-gyn. Sinai Hosp., Balt., 1970-73; staff ob.-gyn. Women's Health Care, West Newbury, Mass., 1973—, former pres.; pres. med. staff Anna Jaques Hosp., Newburyport, Mass., 1990-92; ob.-gyn. private practice. Bd. dirs. Tufts Associated HMO, Waltham, Mass., 1986-96; exec. com. bd. trustees Anna Jaques Hosp., 1995-99; pres. Healthy Women & Babies, L.L.C.; mem. Health and Human Svcs. Practicing Physics Adv. Coun., 1999-2003; mem. steering com. Connecting for Health, 2003—; mem. bd. commrs. Joint Commn. on Accreditation Health Care Orgns., 2003—. Contbr. articles to profl. publs. Pres., West Newbury PTA, 1978; mem. adv. com. Physician Edn. Ctr. Found., 1996—. Fellow ACOG; mem. AMA (coun. on med. scis. 1996-2002, chair 2000-01, ho. dels. 1986—, accreditation program governing body 1997-2000, bd. trustees 2002-, sec. 2005—), Mass. Med. Soc. (exec. bd. 1983—2004, spkr. ho. dels. 1992-94, v.p. 1994-95, pres.-elect 1995-96, pres. 1996-97), Whittier Ind. Practice Assn. (pres. 1985-95, exec. bd. 1985—). Democrat. Avocations: computers, reading, music, medical politics. Office: 24 Morrill Pl Amesbury MA 01913 Office Phone: 978-388-1259.

HEYMAN, LAWRENCE MURRAY, printmaker, painter; b. Washington, June 30, 1932; s. Philip I. and Gertrude B. H. BFA, Tyler Sch. Fine Arts, Temple U., 1954, BS in Edn., 1955; MFA, Am. U., 1972. Instr. fine arts in printmaking R.I. Sch. Design, 1967-69, asst. prof. fine arts and printmaking, 1972-79, dir. printmaking program, 1976-79; lectr. Am. U., 1971-72. Exhibited in one-man shows, Mickelson Gallery, Washington, 1966, 77, R.I. Sch. Design, 1969, 79, St. John's U., St. Paul, 1980, Mus. City of N.Y., 1984, Starr Gallery, Newton, Mass., 1985, Plum Gallery, Kensington, Md., 1986, 88, NIH, Bethesda, Md., 1990, Vets.' Meml. Auditorium, Providence, 1991; group shows including, Providence Art Club, (prize 1974, 76), Bibliotheque Nationale, Paris, 1977 (purchase honor 79), San Francisco Art Mus., 1977, Plum Gallery, Kensington, Md., 1985, 86, 89, Starr Gallery, Newton, Mass., 1991, Galerie Foret-Verte, Paris, 2004; represented in permanent collections Bibliotheque Nationale, Paris, Bklyn. Mus., Brooks Meml. Mus., Tenn., Mus. City of N.Y., Portland (Oreg.) Art Mus.; U.S. rep. Art in Embassies program exhbn., Istanbul, Turkey, 1976; Commd.: print edits. for Associated Am. Artists, N.Y.C., 1964, 68, 69, Antares Editions d'Art, Paris, 1970, 71, 72, Judith Selkowitz Fine Arts, N.Y.C., 1978; featured in book Painting the Town, 2000. Served with U.S. Army, 1955-57. Nominee and finalist for Nat. Arts medal Nat. Endowment for Arts, 1987; finalist 1989 Portrait Painting Competition Artist's Mag. Mem. Whitegate Features Syndicate Fine Arts. Office: 71 Faunce Dr Providence RI 02906-4805

HEYMAN, RALPH EDMOND, lawyer; b. Cin., Mar. 14, 1931; s. Ralph and Florence (Kahn) H.; m. Sylvia Lee Schottenstein, Jan. 2, 1984; children: Michael Cary, Cynthia Ann Heyman Eeg, Ginger Florence. AB magna cum laude (Rufus Choat scholar), Dartmouth Coll., 1953; LLB cum laude, Harvard U., 1956; LLM, U. Cin., 1957. Bar: Ohio 1956, Ill. 1957. Pvt. practice, Cin., 1956-58, Dayton, 1958—; assoc. Freiden & Wolf, 1956-58; from assoc. to ptnr. Smith & Schnacke, 1958-88; ptnr. Chernesky, Heyman & Kress, Dayton, Ohio, 1988—. Lectr. estate planning U. Cin., 1958-61; lectr. participant Southwestern Ohio Tax Inst., 1957-65; lectr., moderator Dayton Bar Assn. Tax Insts., 1975-79, 94; lectr. continuing edn. program U. Dayton, 1989; lectr. estate planning Dayton Area Tax Profls., 1993; lectr. on venture capital Miami Valley Venture Assn., 1998; dir., gen. counsel Towne Properties, Ltd., Hills Developers LLC, Aristocrat Products, Inc., K.K. Motorcycle Supply, Inc., The Sportsman's Guide. Mem. Bd. Rural Zoning Commn. Montgomery County, 1969-71; bd. dirs., pres. Jewish Fedn. Dayton, 1993-97; nat. trustee NCCJ; past pres. Temple Israel; pres. Temple Israel Found., 1999-2001; bd. dirs. United Way Greater Dayton Area, 1999. Recipient Humanitarian award NCCJ, 1997, Robert A. Shapiro Vol. award Jewish Fedn., 1998; named Ohio Super Lawyer, Law and Politics Mag., Cin. (Ohio) Mag Mem. ABA, Ohio Bar Assn., Dayton Bar Assn. (past chmn. tax com.), Cin. Bar Assn., Lawyers Club, Bicycle Club, Meadowbrook Country Club, Dayton City Club (past pres.), B'nai Brith, Phi Beta Kappa Office: Chernesky Heyman & Kress PLL PO Box 3808 1100 Courthouse Plz SW Dayton OH 45401-3808 Office Phone: 937-449-2820. E-mail: reh@chklaw.com.

HEYMAN, RONNIE FEUERSTEIN, lawyer; b. NYC, 1948; m. Samuel J. Heyman, Nov. 1970; children: Lazarus, Eleanor, Jennifer, Elizabeth. BA, Harvard U., 1969; JD, Yale U., 1973. Bar: Conn. 1973. Atty. & prin. Heyman Properties, Westport, Conn. Established The Heyman Chair in Legal Ethics Yale Law Sch.; The Samuel and Ronnie Heyman Ctr. for Ethics, Pub. Policy and the Professions Duke U.; The Samuel & Ronnie Heyman Ctr. on Corp. Governance Yeshiva U., bd. trustees, bd. dirs. Benjamin N. Cardozo Sch. Law; trustee Barnard Coll.; exec. com. internat. directors' coun. Guggenheim Mus.; collectors' com. Nat. Gallery, Washington. Named one of Top 200 Collectors, ARTnews mag., 2004. Avocation: Collector modern and contemporary art, especially Miró, Léger, Gorky, Giacometti, and Dubuffet. Office: Heyman Properties 333 Post Rd W Westport CT 06880*

HEYMAN, SAMUEL J., chemical manufacturing company executive; b. NYC, Mar. 1, 1939; s. Lazarus S. and Annette (Silverman) Heyman; m. Ronnie Feuerstein, Nov. 1970; children: Lazarus, Eleanor, Jennifer, Elizabeth BS magna cum laude, Yale Coll., 1960; LLB, Harvard U., 1963. Bar: Conn. 1963. Atty. US Dept. Justice, Washington, 1963-64; asst. US atty. Dist. Conn., New Haven, 1964-67, chief asst. US atty., 1967-68; CEO Heyman Properties, Westport, Conn., 1968—; chmn. G-I Holdings Inc. (formerly GAF Corp.), Wayne, NJ, 1983—, Internat. Specialty Products Inc., Wayne, NJ, 1991—, CEO, 1991—99. Hon. dir. Benjamin N. Cardozo Sch. Law Yeshiva U., established The Samuel & Ronnie Heyman Ctr. on Corp. Governanance; bd. visitors Terry Sanford Inst. Pub. Policy Duke U., established The Samuel and Ronnie Heyman Ctr. for Ethics, Pub. Policy and the Professions; dean's adv. bd. Harvard Law; established The Heyman Chair in Legal Ethics Yale Law Sch.; founder & chmn. Partnership for Pub. Svc., Washington, 2001—. Named one of Top 200 Collectors, ARTnews mag., 2004. Avocation: Collector modern and contemporary art, especially Miró, Léger, Gorky, Giacometti, and Dubuffet. Office: Internat Specialty Products Inc 1361 Alps Rd Wayne NJ 07470*

HEYMAN, WILLIAM HERBERT, financial services executive; b. NYC, Apr. 20, 1948; s. George Harrison and Edythe Jane (Forman) H., Jr. AB magna cum laude, Princeton U., 1970; JD cum laude, Harvard U., 1973. Bar: NY 1974, DC 1991. Assoc. Cravath, Swaine & Moore, NYC, 1975-78, White & Case, NYC, 1973-75, Stroock & Stroock & Lavan, NYC, 1978-79; gen. ptnr., COO Mercury Securities, NYC, 1979-88; mng. dir. Smith Barney, Harris Upham & Co., Inc., NYC, 1989-91; dir. divsn. market regulation SEC, Washington, 1991-93; mng. dir. Salomon Bros. Inc., Washington, 1993-95; exec. v.p. Citigroup Investments, Inc., NYC, 1995—2000, chmn., 2001—02; CEO Tribecca Investments LLC, NYC, 1996—2002; vice chmn., chief investment officer St. Paul Travelers Cos., 2002—. Bd. dirs. Max Re Capital Holdings Ltd., Max Re Ltd., Nuveen Investments Inc.; bd. govs. Nat. Assn. Securities Dealers. Trustee Mt. Sinai-NYU Med. Ctr., 1994-99, Hosp. for Joint Diseases, 1994-98; mem. NY area firms adv. com. NY Stock Exch., 1996-2002; mem. adv. bd. fin. math. Courant Inst. Math. Scis. NYU; bd. dirs. Student/Sponsor Partnership of NY, 1989-91, 93-2003, mem. adv. bd., 2004-; bd. dirs. 92d St. YM&YWHA, NYC, 1979-90, hon. bd. dirs., 1991-; coun. overseers United Jewish Appeal-Fedn. NY, 1986-88; mem. fin. com. NY State Reps., 1986-90, v.p. NY County Reps. Com., 1987-90; mem. nat. fin. com. George Bush for Pres., 1987-88; hon. chmn. Bicentennial Presdl. Inaugural, 1989; pub. mem. Adminstrv. Conf. of the U.S., 1989-90; mem. NY regional panel for selection of White House Fellows, 1989, 2002-05; mem. fin. products adv. com. Commodity Futures Trading Commn., 1992-93. Mem. Securities Industry Assn. (chmn. adv. coun.), Coun. on Fgn. Rels., Harvard Law Sch. Assn. (nat. coun. 1986-90), Econ. Club NY, Century Country Club (Purchase, NY), Army and Navy Club (Washington), Univ. Club (NY), Nassau Club (Princeton, NJ), Mid Ocean Club (Bermuda), Doonbeg Golf Club (County Clare, Ireland), Phi Beta Kappa. Jewish. Office: St Paul Travelers Cos 385 Washington St Saint Paul MN 55102-1396 Office Phone: 651-310-7289. Personal E-mail: wheyman103@aol.com. Business E-Mail: william.h.heyman@stpaultravelers.com.

HEYMANN, C(LEMENS) DAVID, author; b. N.Y.C., Jan. 14, 1945; s. Ernest Frederick and Renee K. (Vago) H.; m. Jeanne Ann Lunin, Nov. 10, 1974 (div. 1995); children: Chloe Colette, Paris Kent Fineberg-Heymann; m. Rebecca Ellen Coughlan, 1995 (div. 1996). BS, Cornell U., 1966; MFA, U. Mass., 1969. Lectr. English lit. SUNY-Stony Brook, 1969-74, Antioch Coll., N.Y.C. campus, 1975. Mem. judges panel Am. Book Awards, 1979-80, Nat. Book Critics Circle, 1978-79 Author: (poetry) The Quiet Hours, 1969; Ezra Pound: The Last Rower, 1976, American Aristocracy: The Lives and Time of James Russell, Amy and Robert Lowell, 1980, Poor Little Rich Girl: The Life and Legend of Barbara Hutton, 1983, A Woman Named Jackie: An Intimate Biography of Jacqueline Bouvier Kennedy Onassis, 1989, Liz: An Intimate Biography of Elizabeth Taylor, 1995, RFK: A Candid Biography of Robert F. Kennedy, 1998, The Georgetown Ladies' Social Club: Power, Passion, and Politics in the Nation's Capital, 2003; also book revs. and articles for nat. mags. and newspapers. Israeli govt. writer's grantee, 1984-85 Address: William Morris Agy 1325 Avenue Of The Americas New York NY 10019-6026

HEYMANN, PHILIP BENJAMIN, law educator; b. Pitts., Oct. 30, 1932; m. Ann Ross Heymann; 2 children. AB in Philosophy, Yale U., 1954; grad. studies, U. Sorbonne, Paris, 1954—55; JD, Harvard U., 1960. Bar: DC 1960, Mass. 1970. Law clk. to Justice John Harlan US Supreme Ct., Washington, 1960—61; asst. to Solicitor Gen. US Dept. Justice, Washington, 1961-65; acting adminstr. bur. security & consular affairs US Dept. State, Washington, 1966—67, dep. asst. sec. state for bur. internat organizations, 1967, exec. asst. to Under Sec. of State, 1967-69; asst. atty. gen. criminal divsn US Dept. Justice, Washington, 1978-81, dep. atty. gen., 1993-94; lectr. law Harvard Law Sch., Cambridge, Mass., 1969—71, prof. law, 1971—, James Barr Ames prof. law, 1989—, named dir. Ctr. Criminal Justice, 1981, assoc. dean, 1985—87. Assoc. prosecutor and cons. to Watergate Spl. Prosecution Force, summers 1973-75 Author: The Politics of Public Management, 1987, Towards Peaceful Protest in South Africa, 1992, Terrorism and America: A Commonsense Strategy for a Democratic Society, 2000, Terrorism, Freedom, and Security, 2003; co-author (with William N. Brownsberger): Drug Addiction and Drug Policy: The Struggle to Control Dependence, 2001; editor: South Africa: Policing the Conflict, 1993. Served with USAF, 1955-57. Office Phone: 617-495-3137. Office Fax: 617-496-4913. Business E-Mail: heymann@law.harvard.edu.

HEYMANN, S. RICHARD, lawyer; b. Chgo., Sept. 18, 1944; s. Samuel R. and Ann (Menning) H.; m. Jane Ann Gebhart, June 14, 1980; children: Elizabeth Jane, Catherine Claire. BS, U. Wis., 1966; JD, U. Mich., 1969. Bar: Mo. 1969, Wis. 1988. Law clk. Minn. Supreme Ct., St. Paul, 1970-72; assoc. Bryan, Cave, McPheeters & McRoberts, St. Louis, 1972-79, ptnr., 1980-87, Foley & Lardner, Madison, Wis., 1987-99; dir. Inst. for Environ. Studies U. Wis., Madison, 1996—. Adj. prof. U. Wis. Law Sch.; fellow U. Wis. Bus. Ctr.Urban Land Econs. Rsch. Fellow, Ctr. for Urban Land Econs. Mem. U. Wis. Found., Wis. Alumni Assn. (bd. dirs. 1985-87), Madison Club, Maple Bluff Country Club. Office: U Wis Law Sch 801 Magdeline Rd Madison WI 53704 E-mail: srheymann@wisc.edu.

HEYNEMAN, DONALD, parasitology and tropical medicine educator; b. San Francisco, Feb. 18, 1925; s. Paul and Amy Josephine (KLauber) H.; m. Louise Davidson Ross, June 18, 1971; children: Amy J., Lucy A., Andrew P., Jennifer K., Claudia G. AB magna cum laude, Harvard U., 1950; MA, Rice U., 1952, PhD, 1954. Instr. zoology UCLA, 1954-56, asst. prof., 1956-60; head dept. parasitology U.S. Navy Med. Research unit, Cairo, also co-dir. Malakal, Sudan, 1960-62; assoc. research parasitologist Hooper Found. U. Calif., San Francisco, 1962-64, assoc. prof., 1966-68, prof., 1968-91, prof. emeritus, 1991—, asst. dir. Hooper found., 1970-74, acting chmn. dept. internat. health, 1976-78, assoc. dean Sch. Pub. Health Berkeley and San Francisco, 1987-91, assoc. dean emeritus, 1991—, chmn. joint med. program, 1987-91, chmn. emeritus, 1991—. Research coordinator U. Calif. Internat. Ctr. Med. Research and Tng., Kuala Lumpur, Malaysia, 1964-66; cons. physiol. processes sect. NSF, 1966-91; environ. biology div. NIH, 1968-91; mem. tropical medicine and parasitology study sect. NIAID-NIH, 1973-76; mem. adv. sci. bd. Gorgas Meml. Inst., 1967-90; cons. WHO, 1967, mem. sci. tech. rev. com. on Leishmaniases, 1984; cons. UN Devel. Program, 1978-91, US-AID, others; panel reviewer Internat. Nomenclature of Diseases, 1984—; Am. cons. and U.S. prin. investigator U. Linkage Project, Egypt-U.S., 1984—; mem. Calif. Health Adv. Com., 1983—. Author: (with R. Boolootian) An Illustrated Laboratory Text in Zoology, 1962, An Illustrated Laboratory Text in Zoology, A Brief Version, 1977, International Dictionary Medicine and Biology, (with R. Goldsmith) Textbook of Tropical Medicine and Parasitology, 1989;co-author, contbg. editor Phytolacca dodecandra: Endod, 1984, Endod II, 1987; contbr. articles to jours., chpts. to books.; editorial cons. Am. Jour. Tropical Medicine and Hygiene, Jour. Parasitology, Jour. Exptl. Parasitology, Sci., 1968—, other jours. Served with AUS, 1943-46. NIH grantee, 1966-85. Mem. Am. Soc. Parasitologists (council 1970-74, pres. 1982-83), Am. Micros. Soc. (exec. com. 1971-75), Am. Soc. Tropical Medicine and Hygiene (councilor 1981-84), So. Calif. Parasitol. Soc. (pres. 1957-58), No. Calif. Parasitologists (sec.- treas. 1969-72, pres. 1977-78), Phi Beta Kappa. Home: 1400 Lake St San Francisco CA 94118-1036 Office: U Calif Dept Epidemiology Biostat PO Box 0560 San Francisco CA 94143-0001 Personal E-mail: dheyneman@attglobal.net.

HEYNES, AEDHMAR, public relations executive; b. Galway, Ireland; married; 4 children Econs. degree, Univ. Coll., Galway, Ireland; postgrad. diploma in mktg. With London office Text 100, account mgr., 1990—96, regional dir. N.Am. ops. San Francisco, 1997—2000; CEO Text 100 NA, San Francisco, 2000—. Bd. dir., in charge of client svc. Text 100, 1996.

HEYWARD, ANDREW JOHN, television producer; b. Roslyn, N.Y., Oct. 29, 1950; s. E.J.R. and Elisabeth Heyward; m. Jody Gaylin Heyward, May 23, 1976; children: David, Emily, Sarah. BA, Harvard U., 1972. Producer Sta. WNEW-TV News, N.Y.C., 1974-76, Sta. WCBS-TV News, N.Y.C., 1976-78, exec. producer, 1978-81; producer CBS Evening News CBS News, N.Y.C., 1981-84, sr. producer, 1984-87; exec. producer 48 Hours, N.Y.C., 1987-93, Eye to Eye, 1993-94; v.p. CBS News, 1994-96; exec. producer CBS Evening News, 1994-96; pres. CBS News, 1996—. Mem. NATAS (Emmy award 1977-78, 84, 88-93, 95). Office: CBS News 524 W 57th St New York NY 10019-2924

HEYWARD, PETER E., lawyer; b. NYC, June 23, 1953; BA, Wesleyan U., 1974; JD, Columbia U., 1979. Bar: NY 1980, DC 1991. Law clerk to Judge John R. Bartels US Dist. Ct., NY, 1979—81; sr. atty. Federal Reserve Bd., 1986—89; of counsel Jones Day Reavis & Pogue, Washington; ptnr., banking and fin. svcs. Venable LLP, Washington, 2001—. Mem.: ABA (mem. banking law com. 1990—, vice chair internat. banking subcom. 1998—2000, chair fin. holding co. subcom. 2000—), Federal Bar Assn. (mem. banking law com. 2003—, mem. exec. council), NYC Bar Assn. (mem. banking law com. 1999—2001, mem. insurance law com. 2001—03, mem. banking law com. 2003—). Office: Venable LLP 575 7th St NW Washington DC 20004 Office Phone: 202-344-4616. Office Fax: 202-344-8300. Business E-Mail: peheyward@venable.com.

HEYWOOD, ANNE, artist, educator, author; b. Newport, RI, Sept. 15, 1951; d. Albert Paul and Eileen Frances (Laforest) Boretti; m. Ciro DiGiovanni, May 24, 1969 (div. 1980); 1 child, Carlo; m. Henry Robert Heywood, Nov. 9, 1985. BA in Art summa cum laude, Bridgewater (Mass.) State Coll. Tchr. drawing and pastels Silver Lake Reg. H.S. Adult Edn., Kingston, Mass., 1991—95; art educator pastels, drawing South Shore Art Ctr., Cohasset, Mass., 1996—; art educator pastels Fuller Mus. Art, Brockton, Mass., 1996—2003, Pastel Painters Soc. Cape Cod, Barnstable, Mass., 1997; art educator drawing Swinburne Sch., Newport, RI, 1995, Round Top Ctr. for Arts, Damariscotta, Maine, 1996, 2004; workshop instr. Northwest Pastel Soc., Gig Harbor, Wash., 2002. Pastel demonstrator, spkr. in field; artist residency Carillon Beach Inst., Panama City, Fla., 2002; juror Renaissance in Pastel, 1999; juror N.W. Pastel Soc., 2002, workshop instr., Wash., 02. Author: Pastels Made Easy, 2003; contbg. artist: Best of Pastel, 1996, Landscape Inspirations, 1997, Best of Sketching and Drawing 1999; one-woman shows include East Bridgewater (Mass.) Pub. Libr., 1992, 95, Mass. Audubon Soc., Marshfield, 1992, South Shore Natural Sci. Ctr., Norwell, Mass., 1993, Marion (Mass.) Art Ctr., 1994, Fuller Art Mus., Brockton, Mass., 1995, 2000, Passage Gallery, South Shore Art Ctr., Cohasset, Mass., 1996, 98, Sparrow House, Plymouth, Mass., 1997, 2000, 04, Landmark Bldg., Boston, 1999; exhibited in group shows at Duxbury Art Assn., Mass., 1993, Trenton (N.J.) State Coll., 1994, Bridgewater State Coll., 1994, Zullo Gallery, Medfield, Mass., 1995, 99, 2001, Maine Art Gallery, Wiscasset, 1995, Pastel Soc. Am., N.Y.C., 1995, 97, Internat. Assn. Pastel Socs., 1997, 99 (Convention Image award), Left Bank Gallery, Wellfleet, Mass., 1997, Gallery at C3TV, South Yarmouth, Mass., 1997, Salmagundi Club, N.Y. 1999 (George Inness Jr. Meml. award for pastel), Degas Soc., La. (La. Watercolor Soc. award of merit), Colo. History Mus., Fla. Pastel Soc., Soc. Western Artists, Mass., 1999, Pastel Soc. of the West Coast, 2001, Audubon Artists, 2001, Newington-Cropsey Found., N.Y., 2001, Attleboro Mus. Ctr. for Arts, 2003; pvt. collections; contbr. articles to profl. jours.; editor Pastel Painter's Soc. Cape Cod newsletter, 1998-99, bd. dirs. Sec. East Bridgewater Arts Coun., 1992-97, Artists Cir. at Fuller Mus., Brockton, Mass., 1995-97; juror Renaissance in Pastel, 1999, Northwest Pastel Soc., Harbor, Wash., 2002. Recipient 1st pl. drawing East Bridgewater Art Festival, 1991, 1st pl. awards Wickford (R.I.) Art Assn., 1992, Taunton (Mass.) Art Assn., 1993, South Shore Art Ctr. Blue Ribbon Members Show, Cohasset, 1994, Fuller Art Mus., Brockton, 1994, 1st pl. pastels Plymouth Guild May Members Show, 1994, award Providence Art Club, 1996, award of distinction All New Eng. Color Show, Cohasset, 1996; Vt. Studio Ctr. Residency fellow, 1999. Mem.: Copley Soc. (artist mem.), Nat. Assn. Women Artists (D.Wu and Elsie Jeck-Key Meml. award 2000), Oil Pastel Assn./United Pastellists Am. (signature mem.), Pastel Soc. Am. (signature mem., Holbein award 1995), Conn. Pastel Soc. (signature mem.), Pastel Painters Soc. Cape Cod (founding mem., signature mem., bd. dirs. 2000—, Canson-Talens award 1997), Allied Artists of Am., Associated Pastelists on Web (signature mem.), Am. Artists Profl. League, Internat. Assn. of Pastel Socs. (Masters Cir. award 2005), Salmagundi Club. Roman Catholic. Avocations: reading, walking, biking, choir. Address: PO Box 651 East Bridgewater MA 02333 E-mail: aheywood@anne-heywood.com.

HEYWOOD, GAIL ANNE, music educator, musician; b. Hartford, Conn., July 25, 1958; d. Laurier Joseph and Shirley Lucille Alix; m. Neil Chaplain Heywood, June 29, 1991; m. Steven James Barber, Sept. 5, 1981 (div. Nov. 29, 1990); children: Katelyn Rose, Kimberly Anne Barber, Daniel Steven Barber. AA in Liberal Studies, Bay Path Jr. Coll., 1976—78; BA in Music, Ctrl. Conn. State Coll., 1981. Cert. in religious edn. Diocese of LaCrosse, Wis., 1995. Nurses aid Prospect Hill Rehab. Ctr., East Windsor, Conn., 1976—78; music instr. Inst. of Living, Hartford, Conn., 1980—86; music min./cantor St. Philip the Apostle Ch., Rudolph, Wis., 1992—; gen. music tchr., k-8 St. Philip Sch., Rudolph, Wis., 1994—97; music instr./sole operator Heywood Music Studios, Rudolph, Wis., 1986—; webmaster Wis. Music Tchrs. Assn., Racine, Wis.; accompanist/musician St. Vincent de Paul Parish, Wisconsin Rapids, Wis., 2002—. Clinician, adjudicator Wis. Music Tchrs. Assn., Racine, Wis., 1998—2004; childrens choir dir. St. Stanislaus Parish, Stevens Point, Wis., 1991; substitute accompanist St. Stanislaus Ch., Stevens Point, Wis., 2003—; chair, north ctrl. divsn. badger keyboard competition Wis. Music Teachers Assn., Stevens Point, Wis., 1997—97, North Ctrl. divsn. badger keyboard competition chair, 2001—01; employee adv. group Inst. of Living, Hartford, Conn., 1984—86. Musician: (featured soloist) Womens Composer Concert, (solo performance) Charity Auction, Sam Kimble Band, 1980—84; actor: Guys & Dolls, 1979. Mem. St. Francis Group, PCCW, Rudolph, Wis., 1991—2004; litury comm. St. Philip the Apostle Parish, Rudolph, Wis., 1991—; mem. Greater Hartford Youth Chorale, 1974—75; treas. St. Philip Home and Sch. Assn., Rudolph, Wis., 1994—97; com. mem. Boy Scout Troop 114, Rudolph, Wis., 1995—2004. Recipient Outstanding Music Dept. Mem., Granby Meml. H.S., 1973—75, Excellence in Tchg. award, 2004; grantee MTNA Local Assn. grantee, Music Teachers Nat. Assn., 1999. Mem.: Wis. Music Teachers Assn. (assoc.; pres. 2003—, membership sec. 1998—2003, Excellence in Tchg. award 1995, 1997, Member of the Yr. for Stevens Point ares 1999, Outstanding Svc. award 2000, Excellence in Tchg. award 2001, 2004). Avocations: travel, gardening, crafts. Home: 1531 Main St Rudolph WI 54475 Office: Heywood Music Studios 1531 Main St Rudolph WI 54475 Office Phone: 715-459-8180. E-mail: heywood@tznet.com.

HEYWOOD, JOHN BENJAMIN, mechanical engineering educator; b. Sidcup, Kent, Eng., Jan. 11, 1938; s. Harold and Frances Dora (Weaver) H.; m. Marguerite Gilkerson, Dec. 28, 1961; children: James, Stephen, Benjamin. BA, Cambridge U., 1960, DSc, 1984; MS, MIT, 1962, PhD, 1965; DTech (hon.), Chalmers U. Tech., 1999; DSc (hon.), City U., London. Lectr. Northeastern U., Boston, 1963-65; rsch. officer Cen. Electricity Generating Bd., Leatherhead, 1965-67, group leader, 1967-68; rsch. assoc. mech. engring. dept. MIT, Cambridge, 1964-65, asst. prof. mech. enginrg., 1968-70, assoc. prof., 1970-76, prof., 1976-92, dir. Sloan Automotive Lab., 1972—, co-dir. leaders for mfg. program, 1991-93; Sun Jae prof. mech. engring., 1992—; dir. Ctr. for 21st Century Energy, 2002—; co-dir. Ford-MIT Alliance, 2003—. Author, editor: (with others) Open-Cycle MHD Power Generation, 1969; author: (with others) The Automobile and the Regulation of its Impact on the Environment, 1975, Internal Engine Combustion Fundamentals, 1988, (with E. Sher) The Two-Stroke Engine, 1999; contbr. Ency. Britannica, chpts. to books, numerous articles, papers to profl. jours., confs., symposia U.S.A, Eng., Europe. Recipient Ayerton Premium Inst. Elec. Engrs., U.K., 1969; Fulbright travel scholar, 1960; Richard C. Mellon Overseas fellow Churchill Coll., Cambridge, Eng., 1976-77; recipient Nat. award for Advancement of Motor Vehicle R&D, US DOT, 1996. Fellow U.K. Instn. Mech. Engrs. (George Stephenson Internat. Lectr. 1997); mem. Soc. Automotive Engrs. (Ralph R. Teeter Outstanding Young Engr. award 1971, Arch T. Colwell Merit award 1973, 81, 89, Outstanding Oral Presentation award 1980, 2001, Horning Meml. Best Paper award 1984, Rsch. on Automotive Lubricants award 2001), ASME (Freeman scholar 1986, Honda lectr. 1990, Honda medal 1999), Nat. Acad. Engring., Am. Acad. Arts and Scis. Achievements include rsch. interests in thermodynamics, combustion, energy, power and propulsion, performance, efficiency and emissions of spark-ignition and diesel engines, control of air pollution, engine design and manufacture. Office: MIT Dept Mech Engring 77 Mass Ave # 3-340 Cambridge MA 02139-4307 Office Phone: 617-253-2243.

HEYWOOD, ROBERT GILMOUR, lawyer; b. Berkeley, Calif., May 18, 1949; m. Carolyn Cox, June 10, 1972. AB with distinction, Stanford U., 1971; MA, U. Calif., Berkeley, 1972; JD cum laude, Santa Clara U., 1975. Bar: Calif. 1975, U.S. Dist. Ct. (no. and ea. dists.) Calif. 1975, U.S. Ct. Appeals (9th cir.) 1976, U.S. Supreme Ct. 1979; cert. specialist workers' compensation law Calif. Bd. Legal Specialization, State Bar Calif. Of counsel Hanna, Brophy, MacLean, McAleer & Jensen, Oakland, Calif., 1976—. Instr. Santa Clara U., 1975-77, advocacy skills workshop Stanford U. Law Sch., 1994—; faculty ctr. for trial and appellate adv. Hasting Coll. of Law, San Francisco; mem. faculty Calif. Ctr. for Jud. Edn. and Rsch., 1998; mem. intensive advocacy program faculty U. San Francisco Sch. Law, 1995—; adj. prof. law U. Calif., Hastings, 1982-86; arbitrator Alameda County Superior Ct. Mem. bd. editl. cons. Calif. Compensation Cases. Bd. dirs. Alameda County Legal Aid Soc., Oakland, 1978-87, Cazadero Performing Arts Camp, 1994—; bd. govs. Oakland East Bay Symphony, pres., 1991-93. Mem. ABA, Calif. Bar Assn., Calif. Continuing Edn. of Bar (editor, lect., author), Alameda County Bar Assn., Calif. Compensaton Def. Attys. Assn. Office: Hanna Brophy MacLean Et Al 155 Grand Ave Ste 600 Oakland CA 94612-3747

HEYZER, NOELEEN, international organization official; BS, U. Singapore; PhD in social scis., Cambridge U. Exec. dir. UN Devel. Fund for Women, 1994—. Sociology tutor U. Singapore; keynote spkr. for numerous univs. and orgns. Author: Gender, Economic Growth and Poverty, The Trade in Domestic Workers, Working Women in South-East Asia. Named Woman of Distinction, NGO Com. on the UN Commn. on the Status of Women, 2003; recipient Global Tolerance award for humanitarian svc., Friends of the UN, 2000, Lifetime Achievement award, Inst. for Leadership Devel., 2000, Leadership award, Ending Violence Against Women, Mt. Sinai Hosp., N.Y.C., 2004, UN Assn. Greater Boston-Harvard U. Kennedy Sch., 2004; fellow, Inst. Devel. Studies U. Sussex. Mem.: Isis Internat., Asia Pacific Women in Law and Devel., Devel. Alternatives with Women for a New Era. Office: UNIFEM 304 E 45th St 15th fl New York NY 10017

HEZIR, JOSEPH S., energy and environmental executive; b. Pitts., Pa., Aug. 27, 1950; s. Joseph F. and Elizabeth G. F.; m. Joyce Ann Martincic, May 12, 1979; children: Alexandra M., Damjan S. BS, Carnegie-Mellon U., 1972, MS, 1974. Rsch. engr. St. Joe Minerals Corp., Monaca, Pa., 1971, Carnegie-Mellon U., Pitts., 1972; planning analyst City of N.Y., 1973; budget examiner U.S. Office Mgmt. and Budget, Washington, 1974-82, dep. assoc. dir., 1986-92; sr. corp. analyst Exxon Rsch. and Engring. Corp., Florham Park, N.J., 1982; mng. ptnr. The EOP Group, Inc., Washington, 1992—. Mem. adv. bd. Competitiveness Policy Coun., Washington, 1992-94, NASA Adv. Coun., Washington, 1992-93. Dir. nat. capital chpt. ARC, Washington, 1987-90. Fellow Coun. Excellence in Govt.; mem. NAS (mem. study bds.), Croatian Fraternal Union Am. Roman Catholic. Home: 1509 Pennycress Ln Vienna VA 22182-1473 Office: EOP Group Inc 819 7th St NW Washington DC 20001-3762 Office Phone: 202-833-8940. E-mail: jshezir@819eagle.com.

HIAASEN, CARL, writer, reporter; b. 1953; Attended, Emory U.; BA in Journalism, U. Florida, 1974. Gen. assignment reporter then investigative reporter The Miami Herald, Miami, Fla., 1976. Co-author: (novels) (with Bill Montalbano) Powder Burn, 1981, Trap Line, 1982, A Death in China, 1984; author Tourist Season, 1986, Double Whammy, 1987, Skin Tight, 1989, Native Tongue, 1991, Strip Tease, 1993, Stormy Weather, 1993, Lucky You, 1997, Team Rodent, 1998, Sick Puppy, 2000, Basket Case, 2002, Hoot, 2002, Skinny Dip, 2004 (Publishers Weekly Bestseller, 2005), (collection of columns) Kick Ass, 1999, Paradise Screwed, 2001. Office: c/o Esther Newberg Internat Creative Mgmt 40 W 57th St New York NY 10019

HIATT, ARNOLD, apparel executive, retail executive; b. May 26, 1927; s. Alexander and Dorothy H.; m. Anne Wechsler. BA, Harvard U., 1948. Pres., founder Blue Star Shoe Co., Lawrence, Mass., 1952-69; pres., chief exec. officer Stride Rite Corp., Boston, 1969-89, chmn. bd., 1982-92; chmn. Stride Rite Found., Boston, 1982—. Bd. dirs. Dreyfus Fund. Former mem. bd. regents of higher edn. Commonwealth of Mass.; mem. bd. trustees Isabela Stewart Gardner Mus., The John Merck Found.; former mem. vis. com. Boston U. Sch. Medicine; bd. overseers Harvard U., 1984-90; former chair Bus. for Social Responsibility. Mem. Am. Footwear Industries Assn. (dir., chmn. 1980).

HIATT, FRED, journalist; b. Washington, Apr. 30, 1955; m. Margaret Shapiro; 3 children. BA in History, Harvard U., 1977. City Hall reporter Atlanta Jour.-Constitution, 1979—80; reporter The Washington Star, 1981; Va. reporter The Washington Post, 1981—83, Pentagon reporter, 1983—86, Northeast Asia co-bur. chief, 1987—90, Moscow co-bur. chief, 1991—95, editl. page editor & editl. writer, 1996—. Author: (novels) The Secret Sun, 1992, (children's book) If I Were Queen of the World, 1997, Baby Talk, 1999. Office: The Washington Post 1150 15th St NW Washington DC 20071-0001*

HIATT, HOWARD H., internist, educator; b. Patchogue, N.Y., July 22, 1925; s. Alexander and Dorothy (Askinas) Hiatt; m. Doris Bieringer, Nov. 29, 1947; children: Jonathan, Deborah, Frederick. MD, Harvard U., 1948. Intern, then resident medicine Beth Israel Hosp., Boston, 1948—50; research fellow Cornell U. Med. Coll., 1950—53; clin. investigator USPHS, 1953—55; mem. faculty Med. Sch., Harvard U., 1955—, H.L. Blumgart prof. medicine, 1963—72, prof. medicine, 1972—, prof. medicine Sch. Pub. Health, 1984—92, dean Sch. Pub. Health, 1972—84; physician-in-chief Beth Israel Hosp., 1963—72; sr. physician Brigham Women's Hosp., Boston, 1984—, co-chief Divsn Social Medicine and Health Inequalities, 2003—. Mem.: NAS Inst. Medicine, Partners in Health, Bd. Physicians for Human Rights (bd. dirs. 1996—2002), Am. Acad. Arts and Scis. (sec. 1992—97, dir. Initiatives for Children 1992—2002), Assn. Am. Physicians, Am. Soc. Clin. Investigation, Alpha Omega Alpha. Home: 130 Mt Auburn St Cambridge MA 02138-5757 Office: Brigham and Women's Hosp Boston MA 02115 Office Phone: 617-732-5155.

HIATT, JONATHAN PAUL, lawyer, labor union administrator; b. 1949; married; 3 children. BA, Harvard U.; JD, U. Calif., Berkeley, 1974. Bar: Calif. 1975. Ptnr. Angoff Goldman Manning Pyle Wagner & Hiatt, Boston, 1974—95; gen. counsel Svc. Employees Internat. Union, 1988—95, AFL-CIO, Washington, 1995—. Exec. dir. lawyers coordinating com. AFL-CIO, Washington; practitioner-in-residence Ctr. for Social Justice Boalt Hall Sch. Law., U. Calif., Berkeley. Bd. dirs. Nat. Employment Law Project, NYC, Appleseed Found., Washington; adv. bd. Peggy Browning Fund, Phila.; bd. advisors DC Employment Justice Ctr.; adv. bd. ex-officio NYU Ctr. for Labor and Employment Law. Mem.: Am. Arbitration Assn. (bd. dirs. 2002—). Office: Gen Counsel AFL CIO 815 16th St NW Washington DC 20006

HIATT, PETER, retired library and information scientist; b. N.Y.C., Oct. 19, 1930; s. Amos and Elizabeth Hope (Derry) H.; m. Linda Rae Smith, Aug. 16, 1968; 1 child, Holly Virginia. BA, Colgate U., 1952; MLS, Rutgers U., 1957, PhD, 1963. Libr. intern Elizabeth (N.J.) Pub. Libr., 1955-57; head Elmora Br. Libr., Elizabeth, 1957-59; instr. Grad. Sch. Libr. Svc., Rutgers U., 1960-62; libr. cons. Ind. State Libr., Indpls., 1963-70; asst. prof. Grad. Libr. Sch., Ind. U., 1963-66, assoc. prof., 1966-70; dir. Ind. Libr. Studies, Bloomington, 1967-70; dir. continuing edn. program for libr. pers. Western Interstate Commn. for Higher Edn., Boulder, Colo., 1970-74; dir. Grad. Sch. Libr. and Info. Sci., U. Wash., Seattle, 1974-81, prof., 1974-98; dir. libr. insts. at various colls. and univs.; adv. projects U.S. Office Edn.-ALA, 1977-80; prof. emeritus U. Wash., 1998—. Bd. dir. King County Libr. Sys., 1989-97, pres., 1991, 95, sec., 1993, 94; prin. investigator Career Devel. and Assessment Ctrs. for Librs.: Phase I, 1979-83, Phase II, 1990-93. Author: (with Donald Thompson) Monroe County IN Public Library: Planning for the Future, 1966, The Public Library Needs of Delaware County, 1967, (with Henry Drennan) Public Library Services for the functionally Illiterate, 1967 (with Robert E. Lee and Lawrence A. Allen) A Plan for Developing a Regional Program of Continuing Education for Library Personnel, 1969, Public Library Branch Services for Adults of Low Education, 1964; dir., gen. editor: The Indiana Library Studies, 1970-74; author: Assessment Centers for Professional Library Leadership, 1993; mem. editl. bd. Coll. and Rsch. Librs., 1969-73; co-editor Leads: A Continuing Education Newsletter for Library Trustees, 1973-75, Octavio Noda; author chpts., articles on libr. continuing edn., staff devel. and libr. adult svcs. Mem. selection com. Jefferson County Pub. Libr., Washington, 2000—01; bd. dir., sec., pres. Port Townsend Pub. Libr. Found., 2002—; mem. bd. dirs. Turtle Bluff Chamber Orch., Jefferson County, Wash., 2000—03, mem. soloist competition jury, 2000—03, mem. scholarship com., 2000—04, chair spl. fundraising com., 2002—03, mem. new music group, 2002—; founder, bd. dir. Camerata Olympica, North Olympic Peninsula, 2004—05. Mem. ALA (life mem., officer), Pacific N.W. Libr. Assn., Assn. Libr. and Info. Sci. Educators (officer, Outstanding Svc. award 1979), ACLU. Home: 20 Sequim Pl Port Townsend WA 98368-9414 Personal E-mail: phiatt@cablespeed.com. *I know of no other profession which helps so many people and organizations change and grow--from pre-school years through retirement, as does librarianship. It is a joy to be part of that.*

HIBBARD, JUDITH USHER, obstetrician; b. Chgo. m. Mark C. Hibbard. Studied, Edgewood Coll., Madison, Wis., 1966—68; BS in Secondary Edn., Gen. sci. & History, MS in sci. Edn., U. Wis., Madison, 1968—72; studied, Coll. of DuPage, Glen Ellen, Ill., 1977—78, Ill. Benedictine Coll., Lisle, 1978—79; MD, Loyola U., Maywood, Ill., 1979—82. Diplomate Nat. Bd. Med. Examiners, 1983, Am. Bd. Ob-Gyn., 1990, in Maternal-Fetal Medicine 1991. Sci. tchr. Verona Mid. Sch., Wis., 1970—72, Toledo Jr. H.S., Oreg., 1972—74; sci. and math. tchr. Mesquite H.S., Ridgecrest, Calif., 1975—77; resident, ob-gyn. U. Chgo., 1982—86, fellow, instr., maternal-fetal medicine, 1986—89, asst. prof., maternal-fetal medicine, 1989—96, acting dir., ob-gyn. ultrasound, 1999—2000, assoc. prof., clin. ob-gyn., 1996—2001, fellowship dir., maternal-fetal medicine, 2001—, prof., maternal-fetal medicine, 2001—, sect. chief, maternal-fetal medicine, 2003—. Reviewer for various jours. Recipient Hon. Sci. award, Bausch and Lomb, 1968, Scholastic Achievement award, Am. Med. Women's Assn., 1982, Young Investigator's award, Am. Diabetes Assn., 1988, Faculty Devel. Tng. award, Berlex Found., 1991, Young Investigator's Travel award, NIH, 1994. Mem.: Chgo. Soc. Perinatal Obstetricians, Chgo. Gyn. Soc., Ill. Perinatal Assn., Ctrl. Assn. of Ob-Gyn., Internat. Soc. of Ultrasound in Ob-Gyn., Internat. Soc. for Study of Hypertension in Pregnancy, Nat. Perinatal Assn., Soc. Obstetric Medicine, Soc. Maternal Fetal Medicine, Am. Coll. Ob-Gyn., Pi Lambda Theta, Alpha Omega Alpha. Office: Dept Ob-Gyn U Ill 820 S Wood St MC808 Chicago IL 60612

HIBBARD, RICHARD PAUL, industrial ventilation consultant, educator; b. Defiance, Ohio, Nov. 1, 1923; s. Richard T. and Doris E. (Walkup) H.; m. Phyllis Ann Kirchoffer, Sept. 7, 1948; children: Barbara Rae, Marcia Kae, Rebecca Ann, Patricia Jan, John Ross. BS in Mech. Indsl. Engring., U. Toledo, 1949. Mech. engr. Oldsmobile divsn. GM, Lansing, Mich., 1950-56; design and sales engr. McConnell Sheet Metal, Inc., Lansing, 1956-60; chief heat and ventilation engr. Fansteel Metall. Corp., North Chicago, Ill., 1960-62; sr. facilities and ventilation engr. The Boeing Co., Seattle, 1962-63; ventilation engr. environ. health divsn. dept. preventive medicine U. Wash., Seattle, 1964-70, lectr. dept. environ. health, 1970-82, lectr. emeritus, 1983—; prin. Indsl. Ventilation Cons. Svcs., Bellevue, Wash., 1983—. Chmn. Western Indsl. Ventilation Conf., 1962; com. indsl. ventilation Am. Conf. Govtl. Indsl. Hygienists, 1966—; staff Indsl. Ventilation Conf., Mich. State U., 1955—. Contbr. articles on indsl. hygiene and ventilation to profl. jours. With USAAF, 1943-45; maj. C.E., USAR ret. Recipient Disting. Svc. award Indsl. Ventilation Conf., Mich. State U., 1975, 93. Mem.: VFW, ASHRAE, Am. Foundrymen's Soc., Am. Indsl. Hygiene Assn. (J.M. Dallevalle award 1977), Am. Inst. Plant Engrs., Am. Soc. Safety Engrs. (R.M. Gillmore Meml. award Puget Sound chpt.), Elks, Masons. Home: 41 165th Ave SE Bellevue WA 98008-4721

HIBBERT, DAVID WILSON, lawyer; b. Atlanta, Nov. 21, 1950; s. George Wilfred and Dorothy Marie H.; m. Mary Frances Disco, June 21, 1975; children: Jaxon, Taj. BA, Mercer U., 1972; JD, Emory U., 1972. Bar: Ga. 1975, U.S. Dist. Ct. (no. dist.) Ga. 1975. Sole practice, Atlanta, Tucker, Ga., 1975-89. Mem. ATLA, Ga. Bar Assn., Atlanta Bar Assn. (chmn. referral com. 1981-89). Clubs: Lawyers of Atlanta, Atlanta Radio, Atlanta Bonsai (treas. 1982). Democrat. Baptist. Avocations: bonsai, amateur radio.

HIBBETT, DANIEL LEE, music educator, director; b. McPherson, Kans., Dec. 27, 1952; s. William Pierce and Dorothy Marie Hibbett; m. Becky Lynn Spangler, Aug. 21, 1976; children: Cherie Lynn, Kevin Daniel. BA magna cum laude in Music Edn., Seattle Pacific U., 1976; MA in Music, Ctrl. Wash. U., 1981; D magna cum laude in Musical Arts, U. Wash., 1998. Music tchr. Orchard Jr. H.S., Wenatchee, Wash., 1978—80; prof. music Ctrl. Coll., McPherson, Kans., 1981—88; dir. music Edmonds (Wash.) United Meth. Ch., 1988—97; prof. music N.W. Nazarene U., Nampa, Idaho, 1997—2000; dir. music St. Luke Luth. Ch., Portland, Oreg., 2000—05. Dir. music Wenatchee Free Meth. Ch., 1979—81; adj. music prof. Seattle Pacific U., 1994—95; music dir., conductor McPherson Chorale, 1986—87; conductor South Sorohomish County Assn. Combined Ch. Choir, Edmonds, 1995—97. Singer: Portland Symphonic Choir, 2005. Bd. dirs. McPhearson Arts Coun., 1985—87. Mem.: Chorister's Guild, Am. Choral Dir. Assn., Am. Guild Eng. Handbell Ringers (presenter 1990—96). Avocations: jogging, golf, hiking, backpacking, gardening. Office: St Luke Luth Ch 6835 SW 46th Ave Portland OR 97219 Personal E-mail: dlhibbett@comcast.net.

HIBBS, CLAIR M., retired pathologist; b. Lucerne, Mo., Oct. 10, 1923; s. Grover Clarence and Bertha Cassiday H.; m. Ann Elisabeth Robinson, Dec. 26, 1946; children: Drew Robinson, Gerald Wayne. BS in Agr., U. Mo., Columbia, 1949, DVM, 1953; MS in Pathology, Kans. State U., Manhattan, 1962, PhD in Pathology, 1965. Gen. vet. practice Philips Magilton & Hibbs, David City, Nebr., 1953—60; instr. Kans. State U., Manhattan, 1960—65, 1965—68, assoc. prof., 1968—69, U. Nebr., North Platte, 1969—73, prof., 1973—79; dir. N.Mex. Diagnostic Lab N.Mex. State U., Albuquerque, 1979—90. Advisor Norden Labs. (divsn. SmithKline), Lincoln, Nebr., 1988—89; cons. Triple J Zahnis Lab., Bellingham, Wash., 2000—; bd. dirs. Nebr. Med. Rsch. Com., 1977; pres. Western Vet. Conf., 1997—98. Contbr. more than 60 articles to profl. publs. Mm3/c USN, 1943—46. Recipient Disting. Svc. award, Nebr. Vet. Med. Assn., 1978—79, N.Mex. Vet. Assn., 1986, N.Mex. Dept. Agr., 1986; fellow kidney rsch. fellow, Mark Morris Found., 1962. Mem.: Western Vet. Med. Assn. (past pres. 1998), Rotary (past pres. 1977, pres. Mt. Baker club 2005—), Am. Legion (comdr. 1958). Home: 1172 Edgewater Ln Lynden WA 98264-1079

HIBBS, JOHN DAVID, computer company executive, electrical engineer, small business owner; b. Del Norte, Colo., Jan. 26, 1948; s. Alva Bernard and Frances Ava (Cathcart) Hibbs; m. Ruthanne Johnson, Feb. 28, 1976. BSEE, Denver U., 1970. Elec. engr. Merrick and Co., Denver, 1972-73; lighting engr. Holophane div. Johns Manville, Denver, 1973-79; lighting products mgr. Computer Sharing Svcs., Inc., Denver, 1979-83; pres., owner Computer Aided Lighting Analysis, Boulder, Colo., 1983-86, Hibbs Sci. Software, Boulder, Colo., 1986—; chmn. bd. Sport Sail Inc., 1996-97. Co-founder Sport Sail, Inc. Author: CALA, CALA/Pro, PreCALA. With USNR, 1970—72. Recipient 1st prize, San Luise Valley Sci. Fair, 1963. Mem.: IEEE, Computer Soc. of IEEE (chmn. computer problem set com. 1991—95), Illuminating Engring. Soc. N.Am. (chmn. computer com. 1988—91). Achievements include patents in field. Avocations: woodworking, bicycling, sailing, skiing. Home and Office: PO Box 1920 Boulder CO 80306-1920 E-mail: jdhibbs@ieee.org.

HIBBS, LOYAL ROBERT, lawyer; b. Des Moines, Dec. 24, 1925; s. Loyal B. and Catharine (McClymond) H.; children: Timothy, Theodore, Howard, Dean. BA, U. Iowa, 1950, LLB, JD, 1952. Bar: Iowa 1952, Nev. 1958, U.S. Supreme Ct. 1971. Ptnr. Hibbs Law Offices, Reno, 1972—. Moderator radio, TV Town Hall Coffee Breaks, 1970-72; mem. Nev. State Bicycle Adv. Bd., 1996-2000, Reno Bicycle Coun., 1995-99; mem. Reno Parks, Recreation and Cmty. Svc. Commn., 1998—, chmn., 2001—. Fellow Am. Bar Found. (Nev. chmn. 1989-94); mem. ABA (standing com. Lawyer Referral Svc. 1978-79, steering com. state dels. 1979-82, consortium on legal svcs. and the pub. 1979-82, Nev. State Bar del. to Ho. of Dels. 1978-82, 89-90, bd. govs. 1982-85, mem. legal tech. adv. coun. 1985-86, standing com. on nat. conf. groups 1985-91, chmn. sr. lawyers divsn. Nev. 1988—), Nat. Conf. Bar Pres.'s Iowa Bar Assn., Nev. Bar Assn. (bd. govs. 1968-78, pres. 1977-78),

Washoe County Bar Assn. (pres. 1966-67), Nat. Jud. Coll. (bd. dirs. 1986-92, sec. 1988-92), Assn. Def. Counsel No. Calif., Assn. Def. Counsel Nev., Assn. Ski Def. Attys., Aircraft Owners and Pilots Assn. (legal svcs. plan 1991—), Washoe County Legal Aid Soc. (co-founder), Lawyer-Pilots Bar Assn. (chmn. Nev.), Greater Reno C. of C. (bd. dirs. 1968-72), Washoe County Golf Task Force, Phi Alpha Delta. Home: 3600 Salerno Dr Reno NV 89509 Office: 421 Court St Ste 100 Reno NV 89501-1793 Office Phone: 775-786-3737. Personal E-mail: loyalhibbs@aol.com.

HIBBS, ROBERT ANDREWS, analytical chemistry professor; b. Cocoa, Fla., Sept. 9, 1923; s. Charles Harold and Virginia Hibbs; m. Pauline Johnson (div. 1950); 1 child, Sally; m. Lois Elaine Boberg, May 10, 1952; children: Bruce, Laura, Ellen, Dale, Martha, James. BSA, U. Fla., 1947, MS in Agr., 1948; PhD, Wash. State U., 1951. With quality control Darigold Farms, Spokane, Wash., 1951-54; asst. prof. dairy mfg. U. Idaho, Moscow, 1954-61; dir. Hibbs Labs., Boise, Idaho, 1961-90; from asst. prof. to assoc. prof. chemistry Boise State Coll., 1965, 67; prof. analytical chemistry Boise State U., 1971-90, prof. emeritus, 1990—; tech. dir. Hibbs Analytical Labs. Inc., Boise, 1991-95; pres. Refrigerated Foods Tech. Inc., Boise, 1991—99. Adv. bd. Ctr. for Entrepreneurial and Econ. Devel., 1997—99. Contbr. articles to profl. jours. Served as sgt. Infantry, 1942-45, ETO. Decorated Bronze Star. Mem. Inst. Food Technologists (profl. emeritus 1994—, councilor 1977-89). Lodges: Masons, Shriner. Republican. Episcopalian. Avocation: hiking.

HIBNER, MICHAEL, obstetrician, educator; b. Otwock, Poland, Apr. 29, 1968; s. Barbara and Cezary Antoni Hibner; m. Greta Olson; children: Jack Michael, Annika Susan. MD, PhD, Med. U. Warsaw, Poland, 1986—92. Cert. Am. Bd. Ob-Gyn., 2004. Resident, ob-gyn. Cook County Hosp., Chgo., 1995—2000; fellow gynecol. surgery Mayo Clinic Scottsdale, Ariz., 2000—03; gynecol. surgeon St. Joseph's Med. Ctr., Phoenix, 2003—, Maricopa Med. Ctr., Phoenix, 2003—; asst. prof., clin. ob-gyn. U. Ariz. Coll. Medicine, Tuscon, 2004—. Dir. gynecol. surgery Maricopa Med. Ctr., Phoenix, 2003—; dir., med. student edn. in ob-gyn. Maricopa Med. Ctr., U. Ariz. Coll. Medicine, Phoenix, 2004—. Contbr. chapters to books. Grantee, Hektoen Rsch. Inst., 1995, Mayo Found., 2001, 2002. Fellow: Am. Coll. Ob-Gyn.; mem.: Am. Acad. Pain Mgmt., Am. Acad. Gynecol. Laparoscopists. Liberal. Roman Catholic. Achievements include patents pending for the transilluminating rod used at laparoscopic hysterectomy; the needle guide for transurethral bulking agent injection in women; research in the effects of Raloxifene Hydrochloride on endometrial cancer; the three-dimensional reconstruction of the MRI images of the anal sphincter, and correlation between sphincter volume and pressure; a new method for the detection and localization of apoptosis in mouse blastoc; Urinary Incontinence and Sexual Function in Morbidly Obese Female Patients Before and After Surgically Induced Weight Loss; how dilution plays a significant role in the assessment of blood loss during vaginal hysterectomy; the postoperative restrictions in patients after antiincontinence/antiprolapse surgery. Avocations: skiing, sailing, photography. Office: St Joseph's Hosp and Med Ctr 500 W Thomas Ste 700 Phoenix AZ 85013 Office Phone: 602-909-5509.

HICK, KENNETH WILLIAM, marketing company executive; b. New Westminster, B.C., Can, Oct. 17, 1946; s. Les Walter and Mary Isabelle (Warner) H. BA in Bus., Ea. Wash. State coll., 1971; MBA, U. Wash., 1973, PhD, 1975. Regional sales mgr. Hilti, Inc., San Leandro, Calif., 1976-79; gen. sales mgr. Moore Internat., Inc., Portland, 1979-80; v.p. sales and mktg. Phillips Corp., Anaheim, Calif., 1980-81; owner, pres., CEO K.C. Metals, San Jose, Calif., 1981-87, Losli Internat., Inc., Portland, 1987-89; pres. Resources N.W., Inc., Portland, 1989—. Comms. cons. Asso. Pub. Safety Comm. Officers, Inc., State of Oreg., 1975-93; numerous cons. assignments, also seminars, 1976-2004. Contbr. articles to numerous publs. Mem. Oreg. Gov.'s Tax Bd., 1975-76; pres. Portland chpt. Oreg. Jaycees, 1976; bd. fellows U. Santa Clara, 1983-90. With USAF, 1966-69. Decorated Commendation medal; U. Wash. fellow, 1973. Mem. Am. Mgmt. Assn., Am. Mktg. Assn., Assn. MBA Execs., Assn. Gen. Contractors, Soc. Advancement Mgmt., Home Builders Assn. Roman Catholic. Home: 21462 SW St James Pl West Linn OR 97068 Office: Resources Northwest Inc 8415 SW Seneca # 210 Tualatin OR 97062 Office Phone: 503-612-6628. Personal E-mail: rnwi@aol.com.

HICKAM, KENT LEWELL, lawyer; b. Albany, Oreg., July 10, 1950; s. Howard R. and Jeanette L. (Salzman) H.; m. Judith A. Petreny, July 9, 1983; children: Christopher, Brennan. BA, Stanford U., 1974; JD, MA, Willamette U., 1980. Bar: Oreg. 1980, U.S. Dist. Ct. Oreg. 1982. Atty. Minor Yeck & Beeson, Newport, Oreg., 1980-81; sole practitioner Albany, Oreg., 1982—. Office: 250 Broadalbin St SW Ste 210 Albany OR 97321-2290 E-mail: hicklaw@hotmail.com.

HICKCOX, LESLIE KAY, health educator, consultant, trainer; b. Berkeley, Calif., May 12, 1951; d. Ralph Thomas and Marilyn Irene (Stump) H. BA, U. Redlands, 1973; MA in Exercise Physiology, U. of the Pacific, 1975; MEd in Continuing Teaching, Columbia U., 1979; MEd in Health Edn., Oreg. State U., 1987, MEd in Guidance & Counseling, 1988, EdD in Edn., 1991. Cert. Calif. State C.C. instr. (life). Phys. edn. instr., dir. intramurals SUNY, Stony Brook, 1981-83; instr. health edn. Linn-Benton C.C., Oreg., 1985-94; instr. human studies and comm. studies Marylhurst U., Portland, 1987-96, 2002—; edn. supr., instr. Oreg. State U., Corvallis, 1988-90; health and phys. edn. instr. Portland C.C., 1994-95, 2003—; instr. health edn. U. Auckland, New Zealand, 1991; instr., coord. dept. health, phys. edn. and recreation Rogue C.C., Grants Pass, Oreg., 1995-97; assoc. prof., coord. health and phys. edn. Western Mont. Coll., Dillon, Mont., 1997-99; asst. prof. health edn. Northeastern Ill. U., Chgo., 1999—2002; health edn. instr. Portland C.C., 2003—05; assoc. prof. health edn. West Liberty (W.Va.) State Coll., 2005—. Founder Experiential Learning Inst., 1992—, found., Lilly N.W. High Edn. Tchg. Conf., 1996; founding v.p. Home Health Diagnostics, Portland, Oreg., 1996, dir. health info., 1996-2003. Contbr. articles to profl. jours. Mem. ASCD, Am. Pub. Health Assn., Am. Sch. Health Assn., Am. Assn. Health Edn., Higher Edn. R&D Soc. Australasia, Coun. for Adult and Experiential Learning, Adult Higher Edn. Alliance, Kappa Delta Phi, Phi Delta Kappa. Office: 2635 N Baldwin St Portland OR 97217 Office Phone: 503-244-6111 ext. 3266. E-mail: lesliekayh@msn.com.

HICKEL, WALTER JOSEPH, investment firm executive, forum administrator; b. nr. Claflin, Kans., Aug. 18, 1919; s. Robert A. and Emma (Zecha) H.; m. Janice Cannon, Sept. 22, 1941 (dec. Aug. 1943); 1 child, Theodore; m. Ermalee Strutz, Nov. 22, 1945; children: Robert, Walter Jr., Jack, Joseph, Karl. DEng (hon.), Stevens Inst. Tech., 1970, Mich. Tech. U., 1973; LLD (hon.), St. Mary of Plains Coll., 1970, St. Martin's Coll., 1971, U. Md., Adelphi U., 1971, U. San Diego, 1972, Rensselaer Poly. Inst., 1973, U. Alaska, 1976, Alaska Pacific U., 1991, Benedictine Coll., Kans., 2003; D in Pub. Adminstrn. (hon.), Willamette U., 1971. Founder Hickel Investment Co., Anchorage, 1947—; gov. State of Alaska, 1966-69, 90-94; sec. U.S. Dept. Interior, 1969-70; sec. gen. 24 arctic & sub-arctic regional govts. The Northern Forum, 1994—. Nominated for pres. at Rep. Nat. Convention, 1968; founder Commonwealth North, 1979—; co-founder Yukon Pacific Corp. Author: Who Own's America?, 1971, Crisis in the Commons--The Alaska Solution, 2002; contbr. articles to newspapers. Mem. Rep. Nat. Com., 1954-64; bd. regents Gonzaga U.; bd. dirs. Salk Inst., 1972-79, NASA Adv. Coun. Exploration Task Force, 1989-91; USAR amb. representing Alaska. Named Alaskan of Year, 1969, Man of Yr. Ripon Soc., 1970; recipient DeSmet medal Gonzaga U., 1969, Horatio Alger award, 1972, Grand Cordon of the Order of Sacred Treasure award His Imperial Majesty the Emperor of Japan, 1988. Mem. Pioneers of Alaska, Equestrian Order Holy Sepulchre, KC. Home: 1905 Loussac Dr Anchorage AK 99517-1225 Office: PO Box 101700 Anchorage AK 99510-1700 Personal E-mail: wjhickel@gci.net. *We shall never understand peace, justice and the living of life until we recognize that all people are human and that humans are the most precious things on earth.*

HICKENBOTHAM, ALVIN LYLE, contractor; b. Aberdeen, S.D., June 30, 1925; s. Charles Edwin and Emma Christian Hickenbotham; m. Clarice Dawn Hickenbotham (div.); children: Michael Warne, Lawrence A., Daniel Allen; m. Gabrielle T.M. Hickenbotham, Dec. 3, 1976. BS in Bus. and Econs., Northern State U., Aberdeen,. S.D., 1948. Radar prodn. release mgr. Hughes Aircraft Co., Culver City, Calif., market analyst, sr. contracts adminstr., supr., misc. elec. sales, asst. to dir. of materials, supr., product purchasing, sr. subcontract adminstr.; mgr., subsidiary contracts McDonnel Douglas Aircraft Co., Long Beach, Calif., sr. subcontracts adminstr., asst. product mgr.; ret. V.p., mgr. Garden Grove N.W. Lit. League, Calif., 1957—72; Sunday Sch. supt. LDS Ch., South Bay, Calif., 1954—57, fin. chmn., 1955—57. Cadet USN, 1943—45. Mem.: VFW, Elks. Republican. Mem. Lds Ch. Avocations: coin collecting/numismatics, stamp collecting/philately, writing. Home: 5110 Ruby St Torrance CA 90503

HICKENLOOPER, JOHN W., mayor; m. Helen Thorpe; 1 child, Teddy. BA in English, Wesleyan U., 1974, MS in Geology, 1980. Exploration geologist Buckhorn Petroleum, Denver, 1981—86; founder The Wynkoop Brewing Co., 1988—98; mayor City and County of Denver, 2003—. Co-founder CultureHaus, Chinook Fund; bd. dirs. Colo. Bus. Com. for the Arts, Denver Metro Conv. and Visitors Bur., Denver Art Mus., Denver Civic Ventures, Volunteers for Outdoor Colo. Office: Denver City and County Bldg 1437 Bannock St Ste 350 Denver CO 80202 Office Phone: 720-865-9000. Office Fax: 720-865-8787. Business E-Mail: MileHighMayor@ci.denver.co.us.

HICKERSON, GLENN LINDSEY, leasing company executive; b. Burbank, Calif., Aug. 22, 1937; s. Ralph M. and Sarah Lawson (Lindsey) H.; m. Jane Fortune Arthur, Feb. 24, 1973. BA in Bus. Adminstrn., Claremont McKenna Coll., 1959; MBA, NYU, 1960. Exec. asst. Douglas Aircraft Co., Santa Monica, Calif., 1963; sec., treas. Douglas Fin. Corp., Long Beach, Calif., 1964-67, regional mgr. customer financing, 1967; exec. asst. to pres. Universal Airlines, Inc., Detroit, 1967-68, v.p., treas., asst. sec., 1968-69, pres., 1969-72; v.p., treas., asst. sec. Universal Aircraft Service, Inc., Detroit, 1968-69, chmn. bd., 1969-72; v.p., treas. Universal Airlines Co., Detroit, 1968-69, pres., 1969-72; group v.p. Marriott Hotels, Inc., Washington, 1972-76; dir. sales Far East and Australia Lockheed Calif. Co., 1976-78, dir. mktg. Americas, 1978-79, dir. mktg. Internat., 1979-81, v.p., internat. sales, 1981-83; v.p. comml. mktg. internat. Douglas Aircraft Co., McDonnell Douglas Corp., 1983-89; mng. dir. GPA Asia Pacific, El Segundo, Calif., 1989-90; exec. v.p. GATX Air Group, San Francisco, 1990-95, pres., 1995-98, chmn. adv. bd., 1998—, GATX Fin. Corp., San Francisco, 1998—; pres. Hickerson Assocs., 1998—. Bd. dirs. Willis Lease Fin. Corp. Lt. (j.g.) USCGR, 1960—62. H.B. Earhart Found. fellow, 1962 Mem.: St. Francis Yacht Club, Pacific Union Club. Office Phone: 415-955-3413. Business E-Mail: glenn.hickerson@gatx.com.

HICKEY, BOBBY RAY, underwriting assistant; b. Louisville, Apr. 13, 1960; s. Virgle Ray and Doris Jean (Adams) H. Student, U. Louisville, 1990. Various positions Kroger, Louisville, 1980-87; student asst. U. Louisville, 1987-91, libr. asst. I, 1991-95; mail courier Ky. Farm Bur. Ins., Louisville, 1995, underwriting asst., 1995—2001, Adecco, 2001—02, Today's Staffing, 2003—04; dep. clk. Jefferson County Cir. Ct., Clk.'s Office, 2004—. Auto underwriting dept. rep. to safety com. Ky. Farm Bur., 1996. Neighborhood rep. West Jefferson County Cmty. Task Force, Inc., Louisville, 1996—, v.p. 2002-03, pres. 2003—; neighborhood rep. Family Health Ctrs., Louisville, 1986—, vice chmn., 1991-2003, chmn., 2003—, chairperson nominating com., 1994-2003, mem. mktg. com., 1997. Recipient Barney H. Kroger Cert. Merit Cmty. Svc., 1982, William O. Cowger award Jefferson County Rep. Com., Louisville, 1986, Mayor's citation City of Louisville, 1990, 96, cert. of recognition Jefferson County Commr., 1996. Mem. Toastmasters (v.p. pub. rels. Ky. Farm Bur. chpt. 1996). Roman Catholic. Avocations: theater, reading, community service, theater, travel, music. Office: 700 W Jefferson St Louisville KY 40202 Personal E-mail: brh6078@juno.com.

HICKEY, BRUCE WILLIAM, lawyer; b. Washington, Mar. 2, 1973; s. Lien Huong H. AB, Princeton U., 1995; BA, MSt, Oxford U., England, 1998; JD, Harvard U. Bar: N.Y. 2001, D.C., 2002. Editor Harvard Law Review, Cambridge, Mass., 1999-2001; atty. Sullivan & Cromwell LLP, Washington, 2001—. Dir. Washington-Lee H.S. Edn. Found., Inc., Arlington, Va., 1999—. Scholar Brit. Marshall scholar, 1995—98. Mem. ABA, Phi Beta Kappa. Home: 1302 N Utah St Arlington VA 22201-4822 Office: Sullivan & Cromwell LLP 1701 Pennsylvania Ave NW Washington DC 20006 Fax: 202-293-6330. Office Phone: 202-956-7500. E-mail: bwhickey@alumni.princeton.edu, hickeyb@sullcrom.com.

HICKEY, DAMON DOUGLAS, library director; b. Houston, Oct. 30, 1942; s. Thomas Earl and Ethel Elizabeth (Place) Hickey; m. Mary Lyons Temple, May 27, 1967; 1 child, Doralyn Temple Hickey Rossmann. BA, Rice U., 1965; MDiv, Princeton (N.J.) Theol. Sem., 1968; cert. in clin. pastoral care, Inst. of Religion, Houston, 1969; MSLS, U. N.C., 1975; MA, U. N.C., Greensboro, 1982; PhD, U. S.C., 1989. Assoc. pastor First Presbyn. Ch., Irving, Tex., 1969-71, Southminster Presbyn. Ch., Oklahoma City, 1971-72; pastor First Presbyn. Ch., Moore, Okla., 1971—72; catalog libr. U. N.C., Chapel Hill, 1972-73; acting curator rare books Duke U., Durham, NC, 1973-74; assoc. libr. dir. Guilford Coll., Greensboro, 1975-91, curator Friends Hist. Collection, 1980-91; dir. libr. Coll. Wooster, Ohio, 1991—. Adj. asst. prof. history Guilford Coll., 1990—91. Author: Sojourners No More: The Quakers in the New South, 1865-1920, 1997, When Chage is Set in Store: An Analysis of Seven Academic Libraries, 2001, Learn Library Management, 2003; editor: (jour.) The Southern Friend, 1983—91; contbr. chapters to books, articles and book revs. to profl. jours. Recipient Twiford Religious History Book award N.C. Soc. of Historians, Inc., 1998. Mem.: ALA, Assn. Coll. and Rsch. Librs. (chair coll. librs. sect. 2004—), Hist. Soc. N.C. (elect), Friends Hist. Assn., So. Hist. Assn., Orgn. Am. Historians, N.C. Friends Hist. Soc. (bd. dirs. 1977—91), Beta Phi Mu, Phi Alpha Theta. Democrat. Episcopalian. Avocations: church work, baseball. Office: Coll of Wooster Libraries Wooster OH 44691-2364 Office Phone: 330-263-2483. E-mail: dhickey@wooster.edu.

HICKEY, FRANCIS ROGER, physicist, researcher; b. Troy, N.Y., June 8, 1942; s. Frank R. and Ann M. (O'Malley) H.; m. Paula Williamson, Aug. 29, 1964; children: Sharon Ann, Kevin Derus (dec.). BS, Siena Coll., 1964; MS, Clarkson U., 1967, PhD, 1970. From asst. to assoc. prof. Physics Hartwick Coll., Oneonta, N.Y., 1969-83, prof. Physics, 1983—. Adv. bd. Sci. Discovery Ctr. of Oneonta, 1989—, Oneonta Newman Found, 1988—; nat. councillor Soc. Physics Students, 1974-75. Contbr. articles to profl. jours. Founding mem. Oneonta region chpt. The Compassionate Friends. Mem. Am. Phys. Soc., Am. Assn. Physics Tchrs. Roman Catholic. Achievements include development of Physics Educational Computer Programs. Home: 117 Glen Dr Oneonta NY 13820-3553 Office: Hartwick Coll Physics Dept Oneonta NY 13820 Office Phone: 607-431-4739. Business E-Mail: hickeyr@hartwick.edu.

HICKEY, JEROME EDWARD, investment company executive; b. Chgo., June 25, 1937; s. Matthew Joseph and Naomi (Pope) H.; m. Denise Coakley, May 20, 1967; children: J. Graham, Matthew, Elizabeth, George, Peter. BS in Econs., Coll. of the Holy Cross, 1959; MA in Philosophy, Boston Coll., 1964. Instr. Cranwell Sch., Lenox, Mass., 1964-66; acct. exec. Paine Webber, N.Y.C., 1966-68; v.p. Hickey & Co., Chgo., 1968-72, Ralph W. Davis, Chgo., 1972-75, Weeden & Co., Chgo., 1975-78; founder, pres. Jerome Hickey Assocs., Chgo., 1979-84; pres. No. Trust Brokerage, Chgo., 1984-87; sr. v.p. Stein Roe & Farnham, Chgo., 1988-93; sr. v.p., mng. dir. SEI Corp., Chgo., 1993-96; founder, mng. dir. Dearborn Ptnrs., Chgo., 1997—. Dir. Western Golf Assn., Golf, Ill., 1979—, chmn. exec. com., 1991-96; trustee St. Ignatius Coll. Prep., Chgo., 1988-93, chmn., 1990-93; dir. USO of Ill., Inc., 2002—. Named Outstanding Young Man in Am., 1971. Mem. Knollwood Club (Lake Forest, Ill., dir. 1976-79), Bond Club Chgo. (dir. 1974-75), Econ. Club Chgo., Desert Forest Golf Club, The Boulders, Burning Tree Club. Roman Catholic. Home: 245 Leeds Ct Lake Bluff IL 60044 Office: Dearborn Ptnrs 200 W Madison St Chicago IL 60606-3414 E-mail: jhickey@dearpart.com.

HICKEY, JOHN THOMAS, retired electronics company executive; b. Chgo., Oct. 28, 1925; s. Matthew J., Jr. and Naomi (Pope) H.; m. Joanne R. Keating, Sept. 17, 1949; children: Kathleen Coakley Barrie, John, Michael, James, Roger. BS in Commerce, Loyola U., Chgo., 1948; MBA, U. Chgo., 1952. With Motorola Inc. (and subs.), 1943—55, gen. mgr. semicondr. div., 1955-58, asst. to pres., 1958-62, dir. long range planning, 1962-65, v.p. planning, 1965-70, v.p. finance, sec., 1970-74, sr. v.p., chief fin. officer, dir., 1974-84, exec. v.p., chief fin. officer, dir., 1984-86, chmn. fin. com., dir., 1986-96; ret., 1996. Served with AUS, 1944-46. Mem. Skokie Country Club (Glencoe, Ill.), Ocean Forest Golf Club, Sea Island (Ga.) Club. Home (Summer): 2320 Indigo Ln Glenview IL 60026 Home (Winter): PO Box 31065 Sea Island GA 31561-1065

HICKEY, JOHN THOMAS, JR., lawyer; b. Evanston, Ill., July 9, 1952; s. John Thomas and Joanne (Keating) H.; m. Candis Bailey, July 7, 1979; children: Alison, Jack, Patrick, Claire, Matthew. AB magna cum laude, phi beta kappa, Georgetown U., 1974; JD, U. Chgo., 1977. Bar: Ill. 1977, U.S. Dist. Ct. (no. dist.) Ill. 1977, U.S. Ct. Appeals (7th cir.) 1977, U.S. Ct. Appeals (10th cir.) 1987. Assoc. Kirkland & Ellis, Chgo., 1977-83, ptnr., mem. firm mgmt. com., 1983—. Mem. adv. bd. Leading Lawyers Network. Fellow Am. Coll. Trial Lawyers. Office: Kirkland & Ellis 200 E Randolph St Fl 59 Chicago IL 60601-6609 Office Phone: 312-861-2348. Office Fax: 312-861-2200. Business E-Mail: jhickey@kirkland.com.

HICKEY, JOSEPH MICHAEL, investment banker; b. Greenburgh, Pa., June 6, 1940; s. Joseph Michael and Margaret (Nelson) H.; m. Suzanne Klempay, July 2, 1970. BS, Ind. U. Pa., 1963. Sales rep. 3M Co., St. Paul, 1967-69; acct. exec. Hornblower & Weeks, Helphill, Noyes, Cleve., 1970-75; pres. Prescott, Ball & Turben, Cleve., 1976-88; dist. chmn. Nat. Assn. Security Dealers, Cleve., 1979-81; mem. mktg. com. SIA, N.Y.C., 1982-86, mem. regional firms com., 1989; chmn. bd. Canregie Capital Mgmt. Co., Cleve., 1983-86; pres. J.W. Charles Group, Cleve., 1988-90; chmn. Pierman Golf Co., North Palm Beach, Fla., 1991-92; pres. Greyfriar Capital Corp., North Palm Beach, Fla. Bd. dirs. No. Trust Corp. Fla. Capt. U.S. Army, 1963-67. Mem. Kirtland Country Club (Willoughby, Ohio), Loxahatchee club (Fla.), Castle Pines Golf Club (Castle Rock, Colo.), Lost Tree Club (Fla.), The Bear's Club (Jupiter, Fla.).

HICKEY, KEVIN FRANCIS, insurance company executive; b. Bridgeport, Conn., June 20, 1951; s. Herbert Augustine and Anne Therese (Pisani) H.; m. Christine Marie Hackett, June 10, 1973 (div. 1978); m. Eileen Michael O'Gara, July 4, 1981; children: Frances, Augustine. AB, Harvard U., 1973; MHSA, U. Mich., 1976; JD, Loyola U., Chgo., 1984. Bar: Ill. 1984. Dir. Am. Hosp. Assn., Chgo., 1978-83; exec. v.p. First Health Assocs., Chgo., 1983-85; v.p., gen. counsel Metlife Healthcare Mgmt. Corp., St. Louis, 1985-88; sr. v.p. Lincoln Nat. Life Ins. Co., Ft. Wayne, Ind., 1988-92; regional v.p. Aetna Health Plans, Chgo., 1992-94, sr. v.p. ops. Hartford, Conn., 1994-96; pres. Health Plans of Am., Farmington, Conn., 1996-97; exec. v.p. Oxford Health Plans, Norwalk, Conn., 1997-98; chmn., CEO IntelliClaim, Inc., Norwalk, Conn., 1998—2005. Chmn. NEIC, Secaucus, N.J., 1994-95. Contbr. articles to profl. publs. Office Phone: 203-847-8553, 860-614-7037. Personal E-mail: khickey@mail.com.

HICKEY, LADY JANE, librarian, minister; d. William Edgar and Betty Jane (Black) Hickey. BS in edn., U. Tulsa, 1969—71; MLS, Drexel U., Phila., Pa., 1981—85; MBA, St. Mary's U., San Antonio, Tex., 1995—98. Cert. Ordination Light Ho. Gospel Fellowship, 1969, Agape, Internat., 2001. Cataloging technician Messiah Coll., Grantham, Pa., 1979—86; catalog libr. St. Mary's U. Law Libr., San Antonio, 1986—2001; head cataloging unit Sam Houston State U., Huntsville, Tex., 2001—. Author: (reviews) Am. Reference Books Ann.; author: (reviewer) books and online jours.; co-author: (guides) Layperson's Guide to Legal Rsch.; author: (book chapter) E-Serials Collection Mgmt.: Transitions, Trends, and Technicalities/David C. Flowler, ed. Haworth Press. Chpt. 3: Collection Devel. and Cataloging of Online Materials: What Libraries Are Doing Now., 2004; reviewer: Choice. Mem.: ALA, AAUW, AAUP, Assn. of Christian Librians, Tex. Libr. Assn., Southwestern Assn. Law Librs., Assn. Libr. Collections and Tech. Svcs., North Am. Serials Interest Group, Am. Assn. Law Librs. Christian. Avocations: water aerobics, reading, dog obedience. Office: Sam Houston State U PO Box 2281 Huntsville TX 77341

HICKEY, LEO J(OSEPH), museum curator, educator; b. Phila., Apr. 26, 1940; s. James J(oseph) and Helen Marie (Schwarz) H.; m. Judith McKendry, June 29, 1968; children: Geoffrey Alan, Damian Michael, Jason Alexander. BS, Villanova U., 1962; MA, Princeton U., 1964; postgrad., Rutgers U., 1963-65; PhD, Princeton U., 1967; MA (privatim), Yale U., 1983. Postdoctoral fellow NRC-Smithsonian Inst., Washington, 1966-69, assoc. curator, 1969-80; chmn. exhibits com. Natural History Mus., Smithsonian, 1973-75, curator, 1980-82; prof. geology Yale U., New Haven, 1982—; dir. Peabody Mus., Yale U., 1982-87; prof. biology Yale U., 1982-97, chair dept. geology and geophysics, 2003—; curator of paleobotany Peabody Mus. Nat. History, 1982—. Adj. prof. botany U. Md., College Park, 1981-85; adj. prof. geology U. Pa., Phila., 1982-, chmn. dept. geology and geophysics, 2003-; past pres., pres., v.p. Yellowstone-Bighorn Rsch. Assn., Red Lodge, Mont., 1979-86; dir. Mus. of Am. Theatre, New Haven, 1983-87; mem. Mars Lander Sci. Team, 1999—. Author: Stratigraphy and Paleobotany of Golden Valley Formation, 1977, On Wood and the Forest Primeval: The Geological History of Wood, 2003; co-author: The Great Dinosaur Mural, 1990; editor: (with D.W. Taylor) Origin, Early Evolution, and Phylogeny of the Flowering Plants, 1996. Recipient H.A. Gleason award NY Bot. Gardens, 1977, Best Paper award Geol. Soc. Washington, 1981, Disting. Alumnus award Villanova U., 1982, Ann. Book award Dinosaur Soc., 1992; grantee Smithsonian Rsch. Found., 1972-76, Nat. Geog. Soc., 1979, 84-85, NSF, 1984, 90, 92, 2000, 03, Bay Found., 1995-96, 2000, Nason Found., 2002. Fellow Geol. Soc. Am.; mem. AAAS, Bot. Soc. Am., Paleontol. Soc. Democrat. Roman Catholic. Office: Peabody Mus Natural History PO Box 208118 170 Whitney Ave New Haven CT 06520-8118 Office Phone: 203-432-5006. Business E-Mail: leo.hickey@yale.edu.

HICKEY, PAUL ROBERT, anesthesiologist, educator; b. Corinth, N.Y. s. William Joseph Hickey; m. Ann Marie Murphy, Oct. 9, 1956; children: Julia, Brendan, Claire, Connor, Meghan. BA cum laude, Yale U., 1966; MD, Columbia U., 1970. Diplomate Am. Bd. Anesthesiology, Nat. Bd. Med. Examiners; lic. physician, N.Y., Mass., Ohio. Surg. intern Columbia Presbyn. Med. Ctr., N.Y.C., 1970-71, asst. resident, 1971-72; resident anesthesia Mass. Gen. Hosp., Boston, 1978-80, fellow cardiac anesthesia svc., 1980-81; clin. and rsch. assoc. in surgery Nat. Heart and Lung Inst., NIH, Bethesda, Md., 1972-74; clin. fellow anesthesia Harvard Med. Sch., 1978-80, rsch. fellow anesthesia, 1980-81, instr. anesthesia, 1981-83, asst. prof., 1983-86, assoc. prof., 1986-96, prof. anaesthesia, 1996—, chair exec. com. dept. anesthesia, 1997—. Staff physician emergency rm. St. Anne's Hosp., Fall River, Mass., 1974-78, Falmouth (Mass.) Hosp., 1974-78; asst. in anesthesia Children's Hosp. Med. Ctr., Boston, 1981-83; clin. assoc. in anesthesia, Mass. Gen. Hosp., 1981—; cons. in anesthesia Brigham and Women's Hosp., Boston, 1982—; assoc. in anesthesia The Children's Hosp., 1984-86, sr. assoc. in anesthesia, 1986-92, anesthesiologist-in-chief, 1992—, chmn. physican orgn., 1998—; cons. cardiac anesthesia Project Hosp., Washington, 1984—; vis. prof. various univs., 1983—; chmn. anesthesia/intensive care subcom. Project Hope steering com. for Sino-Am. Children's Med. Ctr., 1990-93; assoc. examiner Am. Bd. Anesthesiology, 1988—, assoc. oral examiner, 1991—; lectr. various orgns., univs., hosps. Cons., editl. bd. Anesthesiology, 1981-91, Jour. Thoracic and Cardiovascular Surgery, 1984—, New Eng. Jour. Medicine, 1992—, Pediatric Rsch., 1994—; editl. bd. Jour. Cardiothoracic Anesthesia, 1986-92, Anesthesia and Analgesia, 1987-97; contbr. articles to profl. jours., chpts. to books. Grantee Janssen Pharmaceutica, Inc., 1982-83, 85-88, NIH, 1985—, Mass. Humane Soc., 1982-83, Medasonics, 1990-91. Fellow Am. Acad. Pediatrics; mem. AAAS, Andrew G. Morrow Surg. Soc., Am. Soc. Anesthesiologists (com. on circulation 1983-85, com. on pediatric anesthesia 1992-94), Internat. Anesthesia Rsch. Soc., Soc. Cardiovascular Anesthesiologists (internat. affairs com. 1987—), Assn. Univ. Anesthetists, Soc. Pediatric Anesthesia, Soc. Acad. Anesthesia Chmn., Mass. Med. Soc. Office: Children's Hosp Anesthesia Dept 300 Longwood Ave Boston MA 02115-5724

HICKEY, REBECCA GENE, healthcare educator, mental health nurse; b. Cin., Ohio, Jan. 13, 1965; d. Frederick Eugene and Barbara Gene Wallace; m. Gerard Edwin Hickey, May 20, 1989; children: Ryan, Shawn, Kevin, Benjamin. RN, Miami Valley Sch. of Nursing, Dayton, Ohio, 1986; BA Health Psychology, Graceland U., Lamoni, Iowa, 2003. RN Ohio Bd. Nursing. Med. group nurse Wright Health Assocs., Dayton, 1990—99; critical care nurse Nurse Finders, Cin., 1999—2003, Inteli Staff, Cin./Dayton, Ohio, 1998—2003, Mercy Health Ptnrs., Batavia, Ohio, 2001—02; health consultative coord. Butler Technology & Career, Hamilton, Ohio, 2002—. Adjunct faculty Warren County Career Sch., Lebanon, Ohio, 2001—, U. Cin., 2004—; health cons. Emergency Tng. and Consulting, Hamilton, Ohio, 2001—; adv. bd. Warren County Career Ctr/, Lenanon, Ohio, 2004—05; reviewer textbooks Elsevier Publs., Lippincott Williams & Wilkins Publs., Delmac Publs., 2004—. Instr. ARC, Hamilton, Ohio, 1999—, Am. Heart Assn., Cin., 1999—; merit badge counselor Boy Scouts Am., Hamilton, 2001—; active parent Cub Scouts, Hamilton, 2000—; active in Butler County Spl. Olympics. Scholar Alumni scholarship award, Miami Valley Sch. of Nursing, 2001—03. Mem.: Miami Valley Sch. of Nursing Alumni Assn. (Cheer Com. 2000—), Am. Med. Techs. (cert.). Avocations: gardening, reading, travel, history. Office Phone: 513-868-6300 ext.4408. Fax: 513-844-8916. E-mail: HickeyRN@aol.com.

HICKEY, ROBERT CORNELIUS, surgeon, educator; b. Hallstead, Pa., Dec. 9, 1917; s. Cornelius E. and Jennie (Murphy) H.; m. Rose Van Vranken, June 11, 1942; children: Kathryn Ann (Mrs. Geoffrey White), Robert C., Stephen P., Dennis V., Sarah E. (Mrs. Rodney Laird). BS, Cornell U., 1938, MD, 1942; postgrad., State U. Iowa, U.S. Naval Hosp., San Diego, Meml. Hosp. Cancer and Allied Diseases, N.Y.C. Diplomate Am. Bd. Surgery. Staff U. Hosp. and State U. Iowa, 1951-62, successively assoc. surgery, clin. asst. prof., assoc. prof., 1951-57, prof. surgery, 1957-62, assoc. dean research in medicine, 1955-62; assoc. dir. research U. Tex. M.D. Anderson Hosp. and Tumor Inst., 1962-63, dir., 1969—, exec. v.p., 1976-84; prof. surgery U. Tex., 1962-63, 68—; prof., chmn. dept. surgery U. Wis. Med. Sch., Madison, 1963-68. Cons. surgeon gen. USPHS, 1959-68 Dir. Iowa div. Am. Cancer Soc., 1954-62; pres. Iowa div., 1959-60; dir.-at-large Tex. div., 1968-84; mem. U.S. nat. com. Internat., Union Against Cancer, 1977-87, chmn., 1984-87, Internat. Colloborative Activity UICC, 1988—; mem. nat. cancer adv. bd. USPHS, 1980-86. Served to lt. M.C. USNR, 1943-46. Fellow ACS (gov. 1968-71, vice chmn. bd. govs. 1971-73, chmn. bd. 1973-74, pres. So. Tex. chpt.); mem. AMA, AAAS, AAUP, Am. Assn. Endocrine Surgeons (pres. elect 1991), Houston Surg. Soc. (v.p. 1987-88), Am. Soc. Clin. Oncology, Am. Radium Soc. (v.p. 1964-65), Central Surg. Assn., N.Y. Acad. Scis., Soc. Surg. Oncology, Western Surg. Assn. (v.p. 1973-74), Iowa Acad. Surgery (pres. 1962), Am. Surg. Assn., Soc. Surgery Alimentary Tract (v.p. 1977-78), Tex. Surg. Soc., Sigma Xi. Home: 3964 Plymouth Cir Madison WI 53705-5212

HICKEY, WILLIAM V., manufacturing executive; b. 1945; BS U.S. Naval Acad, MBA Harvard U. With W.R. Grace & Co.; joined Sealed Air Corp., Saddle Brook, NJ, 1980, exec. v.p., 1994—96, pres., COO, 1996—2000, pres., CEO, 2000—. Bd. dirs. Universal Foods Corp. Office: Sealed Air Park 80 East Saddle Brook NJ 07663*

HICKEY, WIN E(SPY), former state legislator, social worker; b. Rawlins, Wyo. d. David P. and Eugenia (Blake) Espy; children: John David, Paul Joseph. BA, Loretto Heights Coll., 1933; postgrad., U. Utah, 1934, Sch. Social Svc., U. Chgo., 1936; LLD (hon.), U. Wyo., 1991. Dir. Carbon County Welfare Dept., 1935—36; field rep. Wyo. Dept. Welfare, 1937—38; dir. Red Cross Club, Europe, 1942—45; commr. Laramie County, Wyo., 1973—80; mem. Wyo. Senate, 1980—90; dir. United Savs. & Loan, Cheyenne; active Joint Powers Bd. Laramie County and City of Cheyenne. Pub. Where the Deer and the Antelope Play, 1967; pres. Meml. Hosp. of Laramie County, 1986—88, Wyo. Transp. Mus., 1990—92; pres. county and state mental health assn., 1959—63; trustee U. Wyo., 1967—71; active Gov. Residence Found., 1991—93, Wyo. Transp. Mus., 1993—; trustee St. Mary's Cathedral, 1986—; active Nat. Coun. Cath. Women; pres., bd. dirs. U. Wyo. Found., 1986—87; chmn. adv. coun. div. cmty. programs Wyo. Dept. Health and Social Svcs.; chair Am. Heritage Assocs. of U. Wyo., 1992—96. Named Outstanding Alumna, Loretto Heights Coll., 1959, Woman of Yr., Commn. for Women, 1988, United Med. Ctr., Cheyenne, 1998, Legislator of Yr., Wyo. Psychologists Assn., 1988, Family of the Yr., U. Wyo., 1995, Person of Yr., United Med. Ctr., Cheyenne, Wyo., 1998. Mem.: Altrusa Club (Cheyenne).

HICKINGBOTHAM, FRANK D., food product executive; b. 1936; With Nat. Investors Life Ins., 1959; prin. McGehee High School, 1958-61; pres., CEO FDH Entprs. Inc., 1970; founder TCBY Entprs. Inc., 1981-87, 97—, chmn., CEO, 1981-97. Office: Tcby % Riverport Equipment Co 2855 E Cottonwood Pkwy Ste 400 Salt Lake City UT 84121-7050

HICKMAN, BERT GEORGE, JR., economist, educator; b. LA, Oct. 6, 1924; s. Bert George and Caroline E. (Douglas) H.; m. Edythe Anne Warshauer, Feb. 9, 1947; children: Wendy Elizabeth, Paul Lawrence, Alison Diane. BS, U. Calif.-Berkeley, 1947, PhD, 1951. Instr. Stanford U., 1949-51; research asso. Nat. Bur. Econ. Research, 1951-52; asst. prof. Northwestern, 1952-54; mem. sr. staff Council Econ. Advisers, 1954-56; research assoc. Brookings Instn., 1956-58, mem. sr. staff, 1958-66; prof. Stanford U., 1966-95, prof. emeritus, 1996—. Vis. prof. U. Calif. at Berkeley, 1960, London Grad. Sch. Bus Studies, 1972-73, Inst. Advanced Studies, Vienna, Austria, 1974, 1975, Kyoto U., 1977; NSF fellow Netherlands Econometric Inst., Rotterdam, 1964-65; Ford Found. Faculty research fellow, 1968-69; mem. com. econ. stability Social Sci. Research Council, 1959-61, chmn., 1962-95; chmn. exec. com. Project Link, 1969—; chmn. Energy Modeling Forum working group on macroecon. impacts of energy shocks Stanford U., 1982-83; Am. coord. US-USSR program on econ.-math. macromodeling Am. Coun. Learned Socs., 1988-90. Author: Growth and Stability of the Postwar Economy, 1960, Investment Demand and U.S. Economic Growth, 1965, (with Robert M. Coen) An Annual Growth Model of the U.S. Economy, 1976; Editor: Quantitative Planning of Economic Policy, 1965, Econometric Models of Cyclical Behavior, 1972, Global International Economic Models, 1983, International Monetary Stabilization and the Foreign Debt Problem, 1984, International Productivity and Competitiveness, 1992; co-editor: Global Econometrics, 1983, Macroeconomic Impacts of Energy Shocks, 1987, Link Proceedings, 1991, 92, Studies in Applied Economics, Vol. 1, 1997; contbr. articles to profl. jours. Served with USNR, 1943-46. Vis. fellow Internat. Inst. Applied Systems Analysis, 1979, 80; resident fellow Rockefeller Found., 1989; named Hon. Prof. U. Vienna, Austria, 1985. Fellow Econometric Soc.; mem. Am. Econ. Assn. (chmn. census adv. com. 1968-71, tech. subcom. to rev. bus. cycle devels. 1962-68, nominating com. 1978-79, chmn. seminar on global modeling, conf. on econometrics and math. econs. 1975-83), Phi Beta Kappa, Phi Eta Sigma. Home: 904 Lathrop Pl Stanford CA 94305-1060 Office: Stanford U Dept Econs Stanford CA 94305 Business E-Mail: bhickman@stanford.edu.

HICKMAN, CHARLES WALLACE, Internet executive; b. Des Moines, Sept. 19, 1952; s. James Charles and Margaret Wallace (McKee) H.; m. Rebecca Ann Nyman, July 31, 1993; children: Matthew, Heidi. BBA, U. Iowa, 1974, MA, 1975. Economist U.S. Dept. Labor, Washington, 1976; project coord. Ind. U., Bloomington, 1977; dir. mem. rels. Am. Assembly Collegiate Schs. Bus./Internat. Assn. Mgmt. Ed., St. Louis, 1978-99; v.p. for acad. affairs Quisic, L.A., 1999—2000; exec. dir. Ohio Coun. on Higher Edn., Fairlawn, Ohio, 2001—. E-mail: chickman@noche.org.

HICKMAN, FREDERIC W., retired lawyer; b. Sioux City, Iowa, June 30, 1927; s. Simeon M. and Esther (Nixon) Hickman; m. Katherine Heald, July 15, 1964; children: Mary Sanders, Sara Ridder. AB, Harvard U., 1948, LLB magna cum laude, 1951. Bar: Ill. 1951. Assoc. Sidley & Austin, Chgo., 1951-55; ptnr. Hopkins & Sutter, Chgo., 1956-71, 75-92, sr. counsel, 1993-2001. Asst. sec. tax policy Dept. Treasury, Washington, 1972—75; draftsman Ill. Income Tax, 1969; author, lectr. taxation. Pres. Nat. Tax Assn., 1989—90; mem. Ill. Humanities Coun., 1977—82, Citizens Commn. Pub. Sch. Fin., 1977—78; chmn. bd. trustees Am. Conservatory Music, 1980—90. With USN, 1945—46. Mem.: ABA, Am. Coll. Tax Counsel (regent 1989—92), Internat. Fiscal Assn. (dir. 1973—77), Chikaming Country Club (Lakeside, Mich.), Legal Club (pres. Chgo. 1980—81), Mid-Day Club (Chgo.), Union League Club (Chgo.), Comm. Club (Chgo.). Republican. Methodist. Home: 360 Green Bay Rd # 4E Winnetka IL 60093-4032 Office: Foley & Lardner 321 N Clark St Chicago IL 60610 E-mail: fwhickman@comcast.net.

HICKMAN, HUGH V., science educator, researcher; b. Washington, June 3, 1947; s. Jack Wallis Hickman and Mary Cecelia (Regar) McCoy; m. Kayoko K. Hickman, Dec. 30, 1997; 1 child, Hugh Yamato. BSEE, U. South Fla., 1984, PhD, 1989. Entrepreneur, 1969-80; vis. prof. elec. engring. U. South Fla., Tampa, 1989-90; vis. prof. computer sci. Eckerd Coll., St. Petersburg, Fla., 1990-91; prof. physics Hillsborough CC, Tampa, Fla., 1991—2001. Contbr. articles to profl. jours. Mem. AAAS, IEEE, Am. Assn. Physics Tchrs., Am. Phys. Soc., Ye Mystic Krewe of Gasparilla, Phi Kappa Phi. Republican. Roman Catholic. Achievements include research into temporal dynamics. Home: 5010 W Dante Ave Tampa FL 33629-7513 E-mail: kayoko@tampabay.rr.com.

HICKMAN, J. KENNETH, finance company executive; b. Bklyn., July 8, 1928; s. Walter E. and Mildren C. (Ehrhardt) Hickman; m. Irene A. Davis, May 12, 1956; children: Patricia, Carolyn, Beth. BS cum laude, Fordham U., 1951. With Arthur Andersen & Co. CPAs, 1953-91, mng. ptnr. N.J. office, 1963-72, ptnr. N.Y. office, 1972-91; sr. mng. dir. Grubb & Ellis Real Estate, 1992—2000. Mem. US Coun. for Internat. Bus., Nat. Com. Am. Fgn. Policy, Inc., Carnegie Coun. Ethics and Internat. Affairs; mem. Bus. Coun. UN, mem. Am. Coun. on Germany, mem. Nat. Com. for US-China Rels.; mem. Ireland-US Coun. for Commerce and Industry, 1978—, v.p., 1979—93. Trustee Fordham U., 1983—. 1st lt. AUS, 1951—53. Mem.: AICPA, NJ Soc. CPAs (trustee 1971—73), Inst. Mgmt. Accts., Beacon Hill Club, Econ. Club NY, Fordham U. Alumni Fedn. (nat. chmn. 1973—75), Am.-Irish Hist. Soc. (exec. coun. 1981—), Beta Gamma Sigma, Alpha Kappa Psi. Home: 45 Templar Way Summit NJ 07901-3730 Office: JKH Assocs 45 Templar Way Summit NJ 07901-3730 Office Phone: 908-277-1699. *Never fold. Play every hand as it is dealt to you.*

HICKMAN, JAMES CHARLES, finance educator, dean; b. Indianola, Iowa, Aug. 27, 1927; s. James C. and Mabel L. (Fisher) Hickman; m. Margaret W. McKee, June 12, 1950; children: Charles Wallace, Donald Robert, Barbara Jean. BA, Simpson Coll., 1950; MS, U. Iowa, 1952, PhD, 1961. Actuarial asst. Bankers Life Co., Des Moines, 1952-57; from asst. prof. to assoc. prof. dept. stats. U. Iowa, 1961—67, prof., 1967-72; prof. bus. and stats. U. Wis., Madison, 1972-93, dean Sch. Bus., 1985-90, emeritus prof. and dean, 1993—; Warren prof. U. Man., 1990; Bowles prof. George State U., 1996. Mem. panel cons. social security fin. Senate Fin. Com., Ho. Ways and Means Com., 1975—76; mem. adv. com. Joint Bd. Enrollment Actuaries, 1976—78; mem. Actuarial Stds. Bd., 1985—92; dir. Mems. Capital Advisors; vis. prof. Nankai U., Tianjin, China, 1993, 96. Mem. editl. bd. N.Am. Actuarial Jour., 1997—. Mem. bd. pensions Presbyn. Ch. U.S., 1989—2003. With USAAF, 1945—47. Recipient Alumni Achievement award, Simpson Coll., 1979, David Halmstad award for actuarial rsch., Actuarial Ednl. Rsch. Fund, 1979, 1981, Disting. Alumni award, U. Iowa, 1993; Coll. Liberal Arts Alumni fellow, 1999. Fellow: Soc. Actuaries (bd. govs. 1971—74, v.p. 1975—77, bd. govs. 1991—94, J. E. O'Connor Disting. Svc. award 2000); mem.: Nat. Acad. Social Ins., Am. Statis. Assn., Swiss Assn. Actuaries (corr.), Casualty Actuarial Soc. (assoc.), Am. Acad. Actuaries (Jarvis Farley award for svc.), Actuarial Found. (trustee 1994—2000), Beta Gamma Sigma (bd. govs. 1988—92). Presbyterian. Home: 2822 Marshall Ct #3 Madison WI 53705-2271 Office: U Wis Sch Bus 975 University Ave Madison WI 53706-1324 Personal E-mail: jandmhickman@aol.com.

HICKMAN, LUCILLE, physical therapist; b. Chgo., July 21, 1949; d. Louis Melvin and Edna (Edwards) H. BA in Sociology, Lake Forest Coll., 1972; BS in Physical Therapy, Chgo. Med. Sch., 1975; MS in Health Sci., Gov.'s State U., 1985. Staff phys. therapist Michael Reese Hosp., Chgo., 1975-79; dir. phys. therapy Provident Med. Ctr., Chgo., 1979-83; instr. phys. therapy Chgo. State U., 1983-87; pres. adminstrv. dir. R.O.C. Phys. Therapy Svcs., Chgo., 1985—93; founder, pres. PhysioCare Ltd., Chgo., 1988—93. Pvt. practice therapy cons., Chgo., 1983—93. Mem. Am. Phys. Therapy Assn., Nat. Soc. Allied Health. Democrat. Episcopalian. Achievements include patents for exercise machine, 1998. Avocations: piano, composing, cooking, writing.

HICKMAN, R(OBERT) HARRISON, political pollster, strategist; b. Whiteville, N.C., Feb. 10, 1953; s. Robert Raymond and Marietta (Harrison) H.; m. Caroline Isabelle Mesrobian, Aug. 15, 1981; 1 child, Ralfe Harrison. AB, Guilford Coll., 1975; MA, U. Nebr., 1977; postgrad., Tulane U., 1980, U. Mich., 1979. V.p. Hamilton & Staff, Inc., Chevy Chase, Md., 1980-84; ptnr. Hickman-Brown Rsch., Inc., Washington, 1984—; adj. prof. George Washington U., Washington, 1993—. Election cons. CBS News, N.Y.C., 1982—. Disting. Alumni lectr. Guildford Coll., Greensboro, N.C., 1987; named most valuable pollster 1986 elections, U.S. News & Report, 1986; recipient Good Guy award Nat. Women's Polit. Caucus, 1987, Alumni Excellence award Guilford Coll., 1991; named Best in the Bus., Cable News Network Inside Politics, 1988. Mem. Am. Assn. Polit. Cons., Am. Assn. Pub. Opinion Rsch., Am. Polit. Sci. Assn., Kenwood Country Club (Bethesda, Md.). Democrat. Methodist. Avocations: golf, reading. Home: 3828 Gramercy St NW Washington DC 20016-4226 Office: 4445 Willard Ave STE 1040 Chevy Chase MD 20815-3694

HICKMAN, RONALD LEE, media broker, broadcast executive; b. Belmar, N.J., Sept. 23, 1932; s. Charles Alfred and Thelma Hefter Hickman; m. Barbara Alice Sanders; children: Ronald Hickman, II, David, Todd. Student, Pikeville Coll., 1953—55. Announcer, sportscaster, salesman WPKE-AM, Pikeville, Ky., 1952—55; salesman, news dir., gen. mgr. WNNJ-AM & FM, Newton, NJ, 1955—63; gen. mgr., part-owner WKER-AM, Pompton Lakes, NJ, 1963—69; pres., gen. mgr. WKFD-AM, Wickford, RI, 1969—78; founder, gen. mgr., pres. WOTB-FM, Middletown/Newport, RI, 1978—83; media broker Hickman Assocs. Author: Touching the Stars, 1986, The Media Brokers, 2000. Pres. Newton Country Club, 1995—97; founder Newton (N.J.) Jaycee Chpt., 1959—60; pres. N.J. Broadcasters Assn., 1964; bd. dirs. People's Credit Union, Middletown, RI, 1982—86. Pvt. USAF, 1951—51. Recipient Best News Story, AP to WOTB-FM, 1982. Mem.: Men's Golf Assn. (pres. 1998—2000), Tiger Point Golf and Country Club. Episcopalian. Avocations: golf, music, photography. Home: 48 Timberton Dr Hattiesburg MS 39401 Office Phone: 601-544-4466. Personal E-mail: ronhickman@bellsouth.net.

HICKMAN, RUTH VIRGINIA, Bible educator; b. Sac City, Iowa, Oct. 15, 1931; d. Ronald Minor and Ida E. (Willcutt) Wilson; m. Charles Ray Hickman, Aug. 25, 1962; children: Ronald Everett, Lisa Michelle. BS in Home Econs., Morningside Coll., 1953. Ordained to ministry Christian Ch., 1985. Instr. Nat. Ednl. TV, 1964-76; staff coord., tchr. Life for Layman, Denver, 1974-77; founder, tchr. Abundant Word Ministries, Lakewood, Colo., 1980—; tchr. Bible Calvary Temple, Denver, 1980—; sales/trainer Hillestad Internat., Woodruff, Wis., 1978—. Women's com. Billy Graham Assn., Denver, 1986-87. Author: (book) Hope for Hurting People, 1987; spkr., instr. audio and video tape series, 1980—. Leader pilgrimages to Israel, 1984, 87, 94, 96, 98, 2001. Republican. Home: 3043 S Holly Pl Denver CO 80222-7010 Office: Abundant Word Ministries 2109 S Wadsworth Lakewood CO 80227 Personal E-mail: ruthabundant@cs.com, abundant_word@hotmail.com.

HICKMAN, SHERRY LYNNE, biology professor; d. Guy Herbert and Esther Lillian Hickman; children: Christian, Marten. BS in Agr., U. Fla., 1979; MA in sci. Edn., U. South Fla., 1993. Prof. biology Hillsborough C.C., Plant City, Fla., 1984—2000, mem. adj. faculty Tampa, Fla., 2000—, Indian River C.C., Vero Beach, Fla., 2000—. Author: Wow I Don't Want to Get That! A Guide to STDs, 2002. Grantee Coalition for Sci. Literacy. Home: 914 Jasmine Ln Vero Beach FL 32963 Office: Indian River CC College Ln Vero Beach FL 32966

HICKMAN, TRAPHENE PARRAMORE, retired library director, consultant; b. Dallas, Jan. 31, 1933; d. Redden Travis and Stella (Moore) P.; m. John Robert Hickman, June 9, 1950; children: Lynn Kleifgen, Laurie Ward AA, Mountain View C.C.; BA, U. Tex-Arlington; MLS, U. North Tex. Cert. libr., Tex. Libr. Cedar Hill (Tex.) Pub. Libr., 1959-77; dir. Dallas County Libr. Sys., Dallas, 1977-93; libr. cons. Dallas County, 1993-95; libr. High Pointe Elem. Sch. Cedar Hill Ind. Sch. Dist., 2003—. Chair leadership coun. and family ministries FUMC of Cedar Hill. Editor: History and Directory of Cedar Hill, 1976; editor News and Views newsletter Dallas county Employees, 1986-92. Chmn. Bicentennial Com., Cedar Hill, 1976; del. Dem. Nat. Conv. 9th Senate Dist., Tex., 1976; chmn. Sesquicentennial Com., Cedar Hill, 1984-86; Dallas County Dem. Forum; mem. Electoral Coll., 1988; chairperson Women's Bd. Northwood Inst., Cedar Hill; active Dallas County Sesquicentennial Com., 1996-; lay speaker United Methodist Ch., 2004. Recipient Newsmaker of Yr. award Cedar Hill Chronicle, 1976; named Amb. of Goodwill, State of Tex., 1976 Mem. ALA, Tex. Libr. Assn. (legis. com. 1984-95, councillor 1982-83, trustee com. 1987-95, pub. info. com. 1987-95), Pub. Libr. Adminstrs. of North Tex. (sec., v.p., pres. 1980, 87), Dallas County Libr. Assn., N.E. Tex. Libr. Sys. (legis. commn. 1978-95, Libr. of Yr. 1987), U. North Tex. Sch. Libr. and Info. Scis. Alumni Assn. (pres. 1987-88), Cedar Hill C. of C., Cedar Summit Book Club (officer), Dallas Area Storytelling Guild (pres. 1995-99) Democrat. Methodist. Avocations: writing, reading, storytelling, gardening, bridge, travel, square dancing. Home and Office: 421 Lee St Cedar Hill TX 75104-2697

HICKMAN, VIVIAN T., elementary school educator; b. McComb, Miss., Jan. 6, 1956; d. Jerry Jim and Elena Arnold Tillotson; m. Terry W. Hickman, Dec. 17, 1976; children: Jeremy W., Jeffry C., J. J. BA, Sul Ross State U., 1984. Cert. tchr. Tex. Substitute tchr. Ft. Stockton (Tex.) Sch. Dist., 1982—84, 1984—. Pres. Am. Cancer Soc., Ft. Stockton, Tex., 1983. Mem.: Ft. Stockton Tchrs. Assn. (treas. 1988—89), Ft. Stockton Water Carnival Assn. (pres. 1999—2000), Xi Zeta Lambda (v.p. 1998), Delta Kappa Gama. Baptist. Avocations: gardening, reading, surfing, sports. Home: 400 S Pecas Fort Stockton TX 79735 Office: Alamo Elem Sch 804 S US Hwy 385 Fort Stockton TX 79735

HICKMAN, WILLIAM WAYNE, music educator; b. Enterprise, Ala., Dec. 30, 1945; s. Gaston Wayne and Hazel Ellis Hickman; m. Linda Tucker, June 2, 2001; children: William, Matthew. MS in Edn., Troy State U., 1972. Dir. instrumental music Jordan H.S., Columbus, Ga.; dir. music edn. Midfield (Ala.) City Schs., 1994—. Named Nat. Tchr. of Mo., Channel One TV, 1996; named to, Nat. H.S. Band Dir.'s Hall of Fame, 1995—. Mem.: Music Educators Nat. Conf. Office: Midfield City Schs Park St Midfield AL 35228 Home: 230 Cambrian Ridge Tr Pelham AL 35124 Office Fax: 205-929-0953. Business E-Mail: Bhickman@midfield.k12.al.us.

HICKOK, D. ALICIA, lawyer; b. Whittier, Calif., Oct. 19, 1960; d. Gus J. Gerson, Jr. and Diane E. Gerson; m. Peter K. Hickok, Mar. 16, 1985; children: Samuel, Elonnai, Bennet. BA cum laude, Tex. Christian U., 1979; JD cum laude, U. Pa., 2001. Bar: Pa. 2001, N.J. 2001, U.S. Dist. Ct. (ea. dist.) Pa., U.S. Dist. Ct. N.J., U.S. Ct. Appeals (3rd cir.). Law clk. to hon. M.O. Rendell 3d Cir. Ct. Appeals, 2001—02; atty. Drinker, Biddle & Reath, Phila., 2002—. Tchg. asst. U. Pa., 1999; coach mem. Jessup Internat. Moot Ct. Team, 1999—2000, 2000—01. Assoc. editor: U. Pa. Law Rev., 1999—2000, tech. editor:, 2000—01. Mem.: ABA (antitrust, internat. law and lit. sects.). Avocations: bridge, bread baking. Office: Drinker Biddle & Reath One Logan Sq 18th and Cherry Philadelphia PA 19103 Office Phone: 215-988-3364. E-mail: alicia.hickok@dbr.com.

HICKOK, EUGENE WELCH, former federal agency administrator; b. Jan. 1, 1950; m. Katharine Pauley; 2 children. BA, Hampden-Sydney Coll., 1972; master's, U. Va., 1978, PhD, 1983. Spl. asst. Office Legal Counsel U.S. Dept. Justice, 1986—87; dir. fin. aid Hampden-Sydney Coll., Va.; assoc. dir. dept. polit. sci. Miss. State U.; instr. polit. sci. Dickinson Coll., Carlisle, Pa., dir. Clarke Ctr. Interdisciplinary Study of Contemporary Issues; sec. edn. Commonwealth of Pa. Dept. Edn., Harrisburg, 1995—2001; under sec. US Dept. Edn., Washington, 2001—04, acting dep. sec., 2003—04, dep. sec., 2004—05. Dir. Clarke Ctr. Interdisciplinary Study of Contemporary Issues. Author books; contbr. articles to profl. jours. Mem. Carlisle Area Sch. Bd. Recipient Ganoe Award for Inspirational Teaching, 1985, 1990, Edward C. First Jr. Faculty Achievemet award, 1995, Dickinson Sch. Law; Adj. scholar Heritage Found.*

HICKOX, CHARLES R., library director; b. Clifton, Tex., Nov. 14, 1944; s. Emil Thomas and Florence Jeanette (Kimball) H.; m. Carolyn Kay Ownbey, Jan 14, 1967; children: Justin Scott, Loyd Matthew. BA in English, North Tex. State U., 1969; MLA, East Tex. State U., 1970; postgrad., Fedn. North Tex. Area Univs., 1989—. Asst. dir. libr. N.E. Campus Tarrant County Jr. Coll., Hurst, Tex., 1970-82; owner Bardahl West Tex., San Angelo, 1982-84; edn. specialist Tandy Corp., Dallas, 1985; dir. libr. Dallas Christian Coll., 1986, Kaufman County Campus Trinity Valley Community Coll., Terrell, Tex., 1986-89, Amber U., Garland, Tex., 1989—. Mem. Tex. Libr. Assn., Tex. Jr. Coll. Tchrs. Assn., Friends Irving Pub. Libr., Doctoral Students Assn. East Tex. State U. Mem. Ch. Christ. Avocations: travel, fishing, genealogy, photography, target shooting. Office: Amber U Head Libr 1700 Eastgate Dr Garland TX 75041-5511

HICKROD, GEORGE ALAN KARNES WALLIS, educational administration educator; b. Fort Branch, Ind., May 16, 1930; s. Hershell Roy and Bernice Ethel (Karnes) H.; m. Ramona Dell Poole, 1952 (dec.); m. Lucy Jen Huang, 1964 (dec.); 2 stepchildren, Goren Wallis Liu (dec.), Wayne Liu; m. Marcia D. Escott, 1998; stepchildren: Eric David Escott, Beth Ann Escott Newcommer, Hazel Jane Escott. AB, Wabash Coll., 1954; MA, Harvard U., 1955, EdD, 1966. Asst. prof. ednl. and social scis. Lake Erie Coll., 1962-67; assoc. prof. ednl. adminstrn. Ill. State U., Normal, 1967-71, prof., 1971-83, disting. prof., 1983-95, emeritus disting. prof., 1995—, dir. Ctr. for Study Ednl. Fin., 1974-95. Dir. McArthur/Spencer Ill. Sch. Fin., 1987—92, Joyce Found. Sch. Fin. Study, 1990—92; pres. Coalition for Ednl. Rights Under the Constn., 1989—91, mem. ednl. rights com., 1990—98; editl. writer Pantagraph and Normalite, Bloomington and Normal, Ill., 1997—. With USMC, 1948-52, Korea. Recipient Chgo. Urban League award, 1994, Van Miller Disting. Scholar award U. Ill., 1994; State of Ill. and U.S. Govt. grantee. Mem. Am. Edn. Fin. Assn. (v.p. 1983-84, pres. 1984-85, Disting. Svc. award 1992), Scottish-Am. Soc. Ctrl. Ill. Club (past chief), Clan Wallace Internat. Royal Order of Scotland Masonic, Phi Beta Kappa, Commun Gaidhleach Am., Masons, Elks. Democrat. Unitarian Universalist. Avocations: history, genealogy, travel, cooking, gaelic (albanach) language. Home: 2 Turner Rd Normal IL 61761-4218 E-mail: AlanHickrod@aol.com.

HICKS, ALLEN MORLEY, retired hospital administrator; b. Toronto, Iowa, May 11, 1928; s. Perle and Grace (Mowry) H.; m. Sue Hicks; children by previous ma rriage: David, Dennis, Wendy, Patricia. Student, Long Beach City Coll., 1949-50; BS, U. Iowa, 1952, MS, 1954. Adminstrv. resident St. Lukes Hosp., Davenport, Ia., 1953-54; adminstr. Schmitt Meml. Hosp., Beardstown, Ill., 1954-57, Pekin (Ill.) Meml. Hosp., 1957-63, Ill. Masonic Hosp. and Med. Center, Chgo., 1963-72; pres. Community Hosp., Indpls., 1972-84, Meth. Health Care Systems, Memphis, 1984-85, VHA Enterprises, 1985-90; adminstr. Midwest Med. Ctr., Indpls., 1991-93. Sr. advisor St. Vincent's Hosp. and Health Care Corp.; chmn. bd. Vol. Hosps. Am., 1980-84, Multi-Mut. Ins. Cos. of Bermuda and Cayman Islands; bd. dirs. Am. Coll.

Testing, Ind. Blue Cross, Am. Health Capital, Indpls. Conv. Ctr.; preceptor masters degree program in health and hosp. adminstrn. U. Iowa; chmn. com. extended care Coun. on Assn. Svc., 1963; pres. Chgo. Hosp. Coun., 1970-71. Campaign chmn., bd. dirs., chmn. indsl. div. United Fund, Pekin, Ill., 1959-64; pres. Tazwell County United Cerebral Palsy, 1960-61; chmn. Cancer Crusade, Pekin, 1960-61; service chmn. Tazewell County, 1958-60; chmn. bd. Tomahawk dist. Creve Coeur council Boy Scouts Am., 1963-64, bd. dirs. Crossroads council; bd. dirs. Cancer Soc., Hosp. Research and Devel. Inst., Inc.; pres. Meth. Health Systems Memphis, 1984-85. H, Served with USNR, 1945- 49, 51-52. Recipient Outstanding Young Man of Year award State Ill., 1960; Distinguished Service award Pekin Jr. C. of C., 1960; Boss of Year award Marquette chpt. Nat. Secs. Assn., 1962 Fellow Am. Coll. Health Adminstrn.; mem. Am. Hosp. Assn. (del. 1971—, chmn. com. community relations), Ill. Hosp.Assn. (trustee, chmn. com. personnel relations), Am. Coll. Hosp. Adminstrs., Am. Assn. Maternal and Infant Health, Ill. Welfare Assn., Ill. C. of C., Am. Legion, Am. Vets., 500 Assn., Beta Gamma Sigma. Presbyterian (elder, trustee). Clubs: Mason, Elks, Kiwanis (bd. dirs. Internat. Found. 1981-85, pres. local chpt. 1983). Address: 202 Wellington Rd Irving TX 75063-7201

HICKS, C. FLIPPO, lawyer; b. Fredericksburg, Va., Feb. 24, 1929; s. Robert A. and Nell (Jones) Hicks; m. Patricia DeHardit (dec. 1983); children: Robert, Patricia Shull, J. Flippo(dec.), Paula Mooradian; m. Martha Kent. BS in Commerce, U. Va., 1950, LLB, 1952. Bar: Va. 1952, U.S. Supreme Ct. 1955. Asst. atty. gen. Commonwealth of Va., Richmond, 1953-59; ptnr. Martin, Hicks, Ingles, Ltd., Gloucester, Va., 1959-91; gen. counsel Va. Assn. Counties, Richmond, 1991—2003; pvt. practice Gloucester, 2003—. Presdl. elector, 1968, 1976, 1980; pres. exec. coun. Episcopal Diocese of Va., 1970—71, mem. standing com., 1971—74. Fellow: Am. Bar Found.; mem.: ABA (Leader of the Yr. award gen. practice sect., Constbar Leader of the Yr. 1992), Defenders Commn. Va., Nat. Assn. Counties Civil Attys. (pres. 1999—, bd. dirs.), Va. State Bar (pres. 1990—91). Democrat. Episcopalian. Avocations: gardening, college sports. Office: PO Box 1300 6517 Main St Gloucester VA 23061 E-mail: counsel@vaco.org.

HICKS, HAROLD EUGENE, chemical engineer; b. Mpls., Jan. 20, 1919; s. Julius and Della (Beebe) H.; m. Ruth Esther Nelson, Oct. 4, 1941 (dec. Mar. 1989); children: Barbara H. Young, Charlotte H. Silvia, David H., Douglas E.; m. Virginia C. Hobson, Mar. 31, 1990. B Chem. Engring., U. Minn., 1941; postgrad., U. Del., 1946-47. Chemist Hercules Powder Co., Wilmington, Del., 1941, rsch. chemist, 1941, 46-50, prodn. supr. Hattiesburg, Miss., 1950-64, plant mgr. Chicopee, Mass., 1964-66, Hercules Inc., Franklin, Va., 1966-68, Brunswick, Ga., 1968-76, Louisiana, Mo., 1978-80; tech. advisor Dawood-Hercules, Lahore, Pakistan, 1976-78; vol. exec. Internat. Exec. Svc. Corp., 1986-94; pres. The Book Shop, Inc., Brunswick, 1991—. Bd. dirs. Downtown Devel. Authority, Brunswick. Mem. county cos. Glynn County; dir. St. Mark's Towers, Glynn-Brunswick Navy League of the U.S., Pine Belt Savings & Loan Assn, Hattiesburg, Miss., 1958-64, dir., 1st Nat. Bank of Brunswick, Ga., 1969-76. Maj. U.S. Army, 1941-46, ETO. Mem. AIChE (emeritus), Am. Chem. Soc. (emeritus), Rotary. Episcopalian. Avocations: computers, photography, travel, reading, gardening. Home: 262 Sutherland Bluff Dr Townsend GA 31331-9239

HICKS, IRLE RAYMOND, food service executive; b. Welch, W.Va., Dec. 21, 1928; s. Irle Raymond and Mary Louise (Day) H. BA, U. Va., 1950. Bus. mgr. Hicks Ford, Covington, Ky., 1952-58; acct. Firestone Plantations Co., Harbel, Liberia, 1958-60; auditor Kroger Co., Cin., 1960-66, gen. auditor, 1966-68, asst. treas., 1968-72, treas., 1972—. Bd. dirs. Old Masons' Home Ky. Served with AUS, 1950-52. Mem. Fin. Execs. Inst., Bankers Club, Alpha Kappa Psi, Phi Kappa Psi. Clubs: Mason, Cincinnati. Episcopalian. Home: 454 Oliver Rd Cincinnati OH 45215-2507 Office: 1014 Vine St Cincinnati OH 45202-1141

HICKS, JACK ALAN, library director; b. Ft. Dodge, Iowa, Sept. 14, 1939; s. Thomas D. and Calma J. (Voss) H.; m. Donna Marie Westervelt; children: Maren Lydia, Sarah Marie. BA, Hamline U., 1967; MLS, Rosary Coll., 1972. Librarian Deerfield (Ill.) Pub. Libr., 1972—. V.chmn. Joint Computer Program for Librs., Skokie, Ill., 1988—2001; bd. dir. Ill. Ctr. for the Book. Contbr. articles to profl. publs. Mem. adv. bd. Coll. of Lake County, Highland Park, Ill., 1988-95; fundraiser Girl Scouts U.S., Moraine Coun., 1975—, Historic Pullman Found. Sgt. U.S. Army, 1961-65. Mem. ALA, Ill. Libr. Assn., Ch. and Synagogue Libr. Assn., Deerfield C. of C., Pi Gamma Mu. Episcopalian. Avocations: motorcycles, kayaking. Office Phone: 847-945-3311. Business E-Mail: jhicks@deerfieldlibrary.org.

HICKS, JANET KELTY, language educator; b. Memphis, Jan. 6, 1949; d. Karl C. and Merle M. (McDaniel) Kelty; m. Benjamin P. Hicks (div. 1982); children: Tony, Andy. BA in English, U. Fla., 1971, BS in Nursing, 1973; MS in Nursing, U. Ky., 1985, MA in English, 1997. Staff nurse VA Hosp., Gainesville, Fla., 1973-76; cottage rounds nurse Sunland Instn., Gainesville, 1976-77; office nurse Lexington, Ky., 1977-79; staff nurse U. Ky. Med. Ctr., Lexington, 1978-85; prof. nursing Lexington C.C., 1985—2000, prof. English, 2000—. Mem. panel of content experts Nat. Coun. Licensing Exams., 1992. Vol. Ronald McDonald House, Lexington, 1987-93, Cmty. Kitchen, Lexington, 1982-84, VA Hosp. Alzheimer's Unit, Lexington, 1989-91; senator Ky. C.C., 1990-92, tchg. cons., 1992-99; vol. recorder for blind, 1998—. Mem. Nat. League for Nursing, Sigma Theta Tau. Republican. Methodist. Home: 4316 Southmoor Park Lexington KY 40514-1815 Office: Bluegrass Cmty and Tech Coll Regency Campus Regency Rd Lexington KY 40506-0001

HICKS, JUDITH EILEEN, nursing administrator; b. Chgo., Jan. 1, 1947; d. John Patrick and Mary Ann (Clifford) Rohan; m. Laurence Joseph Hicks, Nov. 22, 1969; children: Colleen Driscoll, Patrick Kevin. BSN, St. Xavier Coll., Chgo., 1969; MSN, U. Ill., Chgo., 1971. Staff nurse Mercy Hosp., Chgo., 1969-70, nursing supr., 1970-73; cons. continuing edn. Ill. Nurses Assn., Chgo., 1974-75; dir. ob-gyn. nursing Northwestern Meml. Hosp., Chgo., 1975-81; v.p. nursing Children's Meml. Hosp., Chgo., 1981-86; pres. Children's Meml. Home Health, Inc., 1986—2001, Children's Meml. Nursing Svcs., 1986—2001. Pres. Allied & Children's Home Health and Nursing Svcs., 1988, CM Healthcare Resources, Inc., 1988—2001, The Pediat. Pl., Inc., 1994—2001, Focused Health Solutions, Inc., 2000—; dir. Near North Health Corp., Chgo., 1982—85; pres. Pediat. Excellence Program Svc.; bd. dirs. Infant Welfare Soc. Chgo., Nat. Breast Cancer Assn., Children's Meml. Med. Ctr., 1985—. Recipient Jonas Salk Leadership award March of Dimes, 1998, Ernst and Young Outstanding Ill. Nurse Leader award, 1999, Ernst and Young Finalist Entrepreneur of Yr., 2004. Mem. Am. Soc. Nursing Adminstrs., Women's Health Exec. Network (1984-85), Ill. Hosp. Assn. (chmn. coun. on nursing 1982-83), Inst. Medicine, Econ. Club of Chgo. Home: 2206 Beechwood Ave Wilmette IL 60091-1508 Office: Focused Health Solutions 1650 Lake Cook Rd Deerfield IL 60015 E-mail: judith.hicks@myway.com.

HICKS, JUDITH KAE, retired educator; b. Grundy Center, Iowa, Feb. 2, 1940; d. Bertram Lyle and Victoria Marie (Smith) Robinson; m. John Richard Hicks, June 15, 1969; children— Jeremy Robinson, Sarah Elizabeth. B.A. in History, Wartburg Coll., 1963; student Colo. State Coll., 1960-61. History tchr. Nokomis Community Dist. 22 (Ill.), 1963-67, 68-69; social studies tchr. Greenview Sch. System (Ill.), 1967-68; tchr. history Webber Twp. H.S., Bluford, Ill., 1978—2001, ret. tchr. history Webber Twp. H.S., 2001; trustee Egyptian Area Schs. Employees Benefit Trust, 1983-85. Mem. AAUW, NEA, Ill. Edn. Assn., Webber Secondary Edn. Assn. (pres. 1983-84), Webber Twp. Edn. Assn. (pres. 1984-85). Methodist. Club: PEO. Home: 1806 Pace Ave Mount Vernon IL 62864-2860 Office: Webber Twp High Sch S St Bluford IL 62814

HICKS, KRISTINA MARIE, music educator; b. Columbus, Ohio, May 26, 1977; d. Edward Allen and Joyce Marie Pack; m. J. Phillip Hicks, May 26, 1977; 1 child, Caleb Andrew. B in Music Edn., U. Okla., 1999. Vocal music dir. Highland West Jr. H.S., Moore, Okla., 1999—2003, Moore H.S., 2003—. Mem.: NEA, Am. Choral Dirs. Assn., Nat. Assn. for Music Educators, Sigma Alpha Iota. Office: Moore High School 300 N Eastern Ave Moore OK 73160 Office Phone: 405-793-3100. Office Fax: 405-793-3140. Business E-Mail: kristinahicks@mooreschools.com.

HICKS, LADAWN ANN, elementary school educator; d. Kenneth Merl and Ima Jean (Coyle) Hicks. BS, S.W. Okla. State U., 1978. Cert. tchr. Okla. State Dept. Edn., 1978. Tchr. Woodward (Okla.) Pub. Schs., 1978—. Bus. coord. First Assembly of God, Woodward, 1981—2005, capt. drive, 1979—2005. Recipient Outstanding Vol. Svc. award, Okla. Dept. Human Svcs., 1999. Mem.: Am. Choral Dirs. Assn., N.W. Okla. Geneal. Soc. (pres. 1999—2000). Republican. Avocations: genealogy, baseball card collecting, stamp collecting/philately, singing, travel. Office: Woodward Public Schools 1610 - 2nd Woodward OK 73801 Office Phone: 580-256-2660. Office Fax: 580-571-6252. Personal E-mail: penguinschool@itlnet.net. E-mail: hicks@woodwardps.net.

HICKS, LANIS L., healthcare educator; d. Elza David Hicks and Verda Lucille Feltenberger. BA, Sch. of Ozarks, 1969; PhD, U. Mo., 1975. Health planning specialist State of Mo., Jefferson City, 1974—76; post-doctorate fellow Harvard U., Boston, 1976—77; lectr. U. Mo., Columbia, 1979—80, asst. prof., 1980—86, assoc. prof., 1986—2001, prof. health econs., 2001—. Cons. UN Devel. Program, Panama City, Panama, 1984—84; faculty Nat. Ctr. for Managed Care, Kansas City, Mo., 1988—98; cons. Pan Am. Health Orgn., Trinidad and Tobago, 1989—89; short-term profl. WHO, Geneva, 2003—. Author: (book) An Economic Approach to Rationing Health Care Resources, 1985, Role of the Nurse in Managed Care (ANA Book of the Yr., 1994); mem. editl. bd.: Nursing Econs., 1983—86; contbr. articles to profl. jours. Mem. Elder Care, Columbia, 2000—03; mem./sec. Mo. State Bd. Registration for Healing Arts, Jefferson City, 1982—87. Recipient Outstanding Prof. award, Grad. Student Assn. Health Mgmt. & Informatics, 1983, 1986—88, 1990, 1993, 1997, 2000—01; fellow Grad. Studies, NSF, 1969—70; grantee, Agy. for Health Care Policy and Rsch., 1995—96, Health Resources and Svcs. Adminstrn., 2003—, Ctrs. for Medicare and Medicaid, 2003—. Mem.: Assn. U. Programs in Health Adminstrn., Internat. Soc. for Pharmacoeconomics and Outcomes Rsch., Internat. Health Econs. Assn. (abstract rev. panel 2003), Nat. Rural Health Assn. (abstract rev. panel 1998—2003, editl. bd./chair 2000, Disting. Rschr. award 1999). Avocations: photography, travel. Home: 1705 Garrison Pl Columbia MO 65203 Office: Univ Missouri 324 Clark Columbia MO 65211 Office Phone: 573-882-8418. Business E-Mail: hicksl@health.missouri.edu.

HICKS, LINDA REONA, elementary school educator; b. Taloga, Okla., Oct. 14, 1949; d. Kenneth Merl and Ima Jean (Coyle) Hicks. BA, Southwestern Okla. State U., 1971, EdM, 1975; Reading Recovery cert., West Tex. A & M U., 2002; postgrad., Ft. Hays State U., 2004—05. Cert. reading specialist. Music and English educator Hardesty (Okla.) Pub. Schs., 1971—74, Tyrone (Okla.) Pub. Schs., 1974—2000; reading recovery educator Unified Sch. Dist. #480 - Lincoln Elem., Liberal, Kans., 2001—05. Chairperson Tyrone Tchrs. Inservice Com., 1996—97; pres. Tyrone Edn. Assn., 1997—99; mem. North Ctrl. Accreditation Steering Com. for Lincoln Elem., Liberal, Kans., 2001—05. Music dir. First Assembly of God, Liberal, 1988—2005, sec. of the bd., 2000—03, 2005. Named Tchr. of the Yr., Tex. County Edn. Assn., 1976, Tyrone Edn. Assn., 1998—99, Tchr. of Today, Mason's Lodge, 1998—99. Mem.: Internat. Reading Assn., Reading Recovery Coun. N.Am. (assoc.), Assn. Am. Educators (assoc.), Am. Choral Dirs. Assn. (life), Delta Kappa Gamma. Republican. Avocations: reading, scrapbooks, singing, playing musical instruments. Office: USD480 Liberal KS 67901

HICKS, MARION LAWRENCE, JR., (LARRY HICKS), lawyer; b. Bethlehem, Pa, Sept. 5, 1945; s. Marion Lawrence and Martha (McCracken) H.; m. Beverly Brickman, Nov. 28, 1970; children: Yale McCracken, Hadley Brook, Kelley Hayden. BA History, Duke U., 1967; JD with honors, U. Tex., 1970. Bar: Tex. 1970. Law clk. 9th cir. US Ct. Appeals, LA, 1970-71; assoc. Thompson, Knight, Simmons & Bullion, Dallas, 1971-77; ptnr., head Dallas office Thompson & Knight, 1977—. Spkr. in field. Editor Tex. Law Review; contbr. articles to profl. jour. Mem. ABA (real property, trust and probate sect.), Am. Coll. Mortgage Atty. (regent), State Bar Tex., Dallas Bar Assn. (past chmn. real property sect., legal aid and legal svc. com.), Coll. State Bar Tex., Order of Coif, Tower Club (bd. gov.), Phi Delta Phi. Avocations: sports, hunting, fishing. Home: 4310 Throckmorton St Dallas TX 75219-2240 Office: Thompson & Knight LLP 1700 Pacific Ave Ste 3300 Dallas TX 75201-4693 Office Phone: 214-969-1627. Business E-Mail: larry.hicks@tklaw.com.

HICKS, SHERMAN GREGORY, pastor; b. Bklyn., June 22, 1946; s. Charles Sr. and Sarah Mae (Rollins) H.; m. Anna Marie Peck, Sept. 12, 1970 (div.); children: Andrea, Geoffrey, Christopher. BA, Wittenberg U., 1968; MDiv, Hamma Sch. Theology, 1973; DD (hon.), Carthage Coll., 1988, Elmhurst Coll., 1989, Wittenberg U., 1990. Ordained to ministry Luth. Ch., 1973. Pastor Concordia Luth. Ch., Buffalo, 1973-77; co-pastor Holy Trinity Luth. Ch., East Orange, N.J., 1977-79; asst. to bishop Ill. Synod, Luth. Ch. Am., Chgo., 1979-87; bishop Met. Chgo. Synod, Evang. Luth. Ch. in Am., Chgo., 1988-95; sr. pastor First Trinity Luth. Ch., Washington, 1996—2003; mission dir. divsn. outreach Evang. Luth. Ch. Am., 2003—. Pres. of bd. Third World Social Svcs., 1998; bd. dirs. Mission Resource Inst. Pres. Interfaith Coun. for Homeless, Chgo., 1988, AIDS Nat. Interfaith Network, 1991; trustee Carthage Coll., Kenosha, Wis., 1988, Nat. AIDS Fund, 1997; bd. dirs. Luth. Social Svcs. Ill., 1988-95, Bethphage, Omaha; mem. Coun. Religious Leaders, Chgo., 1988-95; bd. dirs. Leadership Coun. for Met. Open Cmty., Luth. Housing Svcs., Luth. Svcs. in Am. Named One of Outstanding Young Men in Am., Jaycees, 1974; recipient Alumni Citation, Wittenberg U., 1993. Office: The Luth Ctr 700 Light St Baltimore MD 21230 Office Phone: 410-230-2878. Personal E-mail: doelca8@aol.com, sgreghicks@aol.com. *In my experiences with life I have discovered that there are three very basic questions that we humans have the need to know answers for: (1) Who am I? (2) For what purpose am I here? (3) What am I going to do? Within the context of our faith we can find the answers.*

HICKS, SHIRLEY E., director; b. St. Louis, Nov. 9, 1936; d. Joseph Alonzo and Thelma Elizabeth Hill; m. Sharon Lavert Hicks (div. Aug. 1978); children: Beth Ann Hargrove, Lynne Marie Catching. BA, Notre Dame Coll., Lemay, Mo., 1975; MA, Webster U., 1980. Program specialist/in-house coord. St. Louis Housing Authority; MEGASKILLS regional trainer Cooperating Sch. Dist., St. Louis; pres. S.E. Hicks and Assocs.; spl. svcs. educator Sch. Dist. City of Ladue, St. Louis. Chmn. mktg. and pub. rels. Mo. Coun. Women's Econ. Devel. Tng., State of Mo., 1988—93. Contbr. articles to profl. jours. Mem., com. chmn. Mo. Coun. on Women's Econ. Devel. and Tng., Jefferson City, St. Louis, 1988—93; mem. Grad. Class 13 Coro Found.-Women in Leadership, St. Louis. Recipient Leadership award, Chums, Inc., 1986, Excellence in Tchg. award, Urban League Met. St. Louis, 1993. Mem.: ASCD, Mo. State Tchrs. Assn. (pres. Ladue chpt. 1993—95), Red Hat Ladies Soc. (chap. founder 2005—), Chums, Inc. (nat. pub. rels. officer 1988—90, nat. v.p. 1990—94, Leadership award 1986), Zonta Internat. (St. Louis chpt.), Phi Delta Kappa (pres. 1992—94, Washington U.-Maryville chpt.). Avocations: travel, concerts, painting, reading. Home: Apt 217 3915 Olive St Saint Louis MO 63108-3157

HICKS, TYLER GREGORY, publishing company executive, writer; b. N.Y.C., June 21, 1921; s. Ernest Tyler and Mary B. (O'Brien) H.; m. Saretta M. Gratke, Feb. 23, 1946 (dec. Mar. 1974); children: Gregory T., Barbara L., Steven D.; m. Mary T. Shanley, Aug. 29, 1975. B of Mech. Engring., Cooper Union Advancement Sci., 1948. Engr. Merport Realty Co., 1943-46; design engr. Lockwood-Greene Engrs. Inc., 1946-49; editor in chief Profl. and Reference Books div. McGraw-Hill Co., N.Y.C., 1962-85, pres., chmn. bd. dirs. employees fed. credit union, 1970-95, bd. dirs., 1995—. Instr. Cooper Union, N.Y.C.; owner Internat. Engring. Assocs.; pres. Internat. Wealth Success Inc., Rockville Centre, N.Y.; lectr. in field Author: How To Borrow Your Way to a Great Fortune, 1970, Magic Mind Secrets for Building Riches Fast, 1971, How To Make One Million Dollars in Real Estate in Three Years Starting with No Cash, 2000, Tyler Hicks' Encyclopedia of Wealth-Building Secrets, 1980, How to Borrow Your Way to Real Estate Riches, 1987, Business Capital Sources, 1984, Financial Broker, Finder, Business Broker Complete Success Kit, 1988, Real Estate Riches Success Kit, 1988, Complete Business Borrowers Success Kit, 1988, 101 Ways to 100% Financing of Business and Real Estate, 1997, How to Get Rich on Other People's Money, 1988, Standard Handbook of Engineering Calculations, 1995, Handbook of Mechanical Engineering Calculations, 1998; co-author: Handbook of Electric Power Calculations, 1984, Handbook of Chemical Engineering Calculations, 1984; co-editor: Standard Handbook of Consulting Engineering, 1986, How to Get Rich on Other People's Money, 1988, How to Build A Million Dollar Fortune, 1989, Mail Order Success Secrets, 1990, How to Make Big Money in Real Estate, 2000, 199 Greate Home Businesses You Can Start (and Prosper In), for Under $1,000, 1993, How to Start Your Own Business on a Shoestring and Make Up to $500,000 a Year, 1995, 203 Home-Based Businesses, 1999, Handbook of Civil Engineering Calculations, 2000, Civil Engineering Formulas, 2002, Mechanical Engineering Formulas, 2003, 209 Easy Spare-Time Ways to Build Zero Cash Into 7 Figures A Year in Real Estate, 2004. With U.S. Mcht. Marines, 1936-43. Mem. IEEE, ASME, U.S. Naval Inst., Internat. Oceanographic Found. Clubs: Rockville Links Golf, Huntington Yacht. Home: 24 Canterbury Rd Rockville Centre NY 11570-1310 Office: McGraw-Hill 2 Penn Plz Rm 1500 New York NY 10121-1599 Office Phone: 516-766-5850. E-mail: tyhicks@iwsmoney.com, TYGHicks@aol.com. *The clearest and strongest thought permeating my life is based on my own experience and observation of lives of thousands of people throughout the world. This thought is: Men and women can achieve in life whatever goals they set for themselves if a person combines careful planning and analysis of each objective with mental images of successful achievement. This approach seems to work everywhere— for everyone. Choosing to do what one enjoys also contributes to success because better performance occurs when people like what they're doing. Helping others achieve their goals in life brings great rewards to both the helper and the person assisted.*

HICKS, WAYLAND R., rental company executive; b. 1942; BS, Ind. U. With Xerox Corp., London, from v.p. to group v.p., pres. reprographics bus., 1966-86, exec. v.p., pres. bus products and systems group, 1986-89, exec. v.p. mktg. and customer ops. Stamford, Conn., 1989—; vice-chmn., CEO United Rentals. Lt. USAF. Office: Xerox Corp Long Ridge Rd PO Box 1600 Stamford CT 06904-1600

HICKS, WENDELL, history professor, political scientist, publishing executive; b. Pitts., July 2, 1946; s. John Verris and Juanita H.; m. Patricia Ann Du Hart, Jan. 15, 1976 (div. Jan. 1980); children: Wendell Leon Jr., Gregory Moore. BA, Fayetteville State U., 1971; MA, N.C. Ctrl. U., 1973. Grad. asst. N.C. Ctrl. U., Durham, 1972; instr. St. Augustine's Coll., Raleigh, NC, 1973—74; grad. asst. U. Toledo, 1974-78; prof. history Bowling Green (Ohio) State U., 1978; pub. Azaka Publs., Pitts., 1983—. Author: The Bloody Flux: The World's No. 1 Killing Disease for the Past Six Centuries, 1982, The Ku Klux Klan: A Psychoanalytical and Medical Perspective, 1992, A 2001 Historical Update on Black Holes: The Most Contructive and Destructive Objects in the Universe, 2001. Co-chmn. Operation PUSH, Pitts., 1983; active NAACP, Pitts., Vet. Club, Fayetteville, N.C.; mem. Nat. Campaign Tolerance. With USN, 1965-71. Mem.: AAUP, Phi Alpha Theta (v.p. 1976—77, pres. 1977—78), Pi Gamma Mu. Democrat. Methodist. Avocations: football, track and field, swimming, weightlifting, boxing. Home: 711 Ledlie St Pittsburgh PA 15219-3631 Home and Office: Azaka Publs 715 Mercer St Apt 711 Pittsburgh PA 15219-4146

HICKS, WESTON MILLIKEN, securities analyst; b. Tulsa, Nov. 17, 1956; s. Robert Hamilton and Mary Margaret (Hopkins) H.; m. Ann Deborah Lefkowith, May 30, 1981; children: Zachary Andrew, Jasper Simon. BS in Bus. and Econs., Lehigh U., 1979. CPA, N.Y.; CFA. Sr. acct. Peat, Marwick, Mitchell & Co., N.Y.C., 1979-82; sr. fin. cons. Bank Am. NT & SA, San Francisco, 1982-83, asst. v.p. London, 1983-84, asst. v.p., account officer N.Y.C., 1984-85; 2d v.p. Chase Manhattan Bank, N.Y.C., 1985-86; v.p., assoc. dir. Moody's Investors Svc., N.Y.C., 1986-91; sr. rsch. analyst Sanford C. Bernstein & Co. Inc., N.Y.C., 1991—; pres., dir., CEO Alleghany Corp., N.Y.C. Bd. dirs. Internat. Sch. of Brussels Found., N.Y.C., 1994—. Mem. Assn. Investment Mgmt. and Rsch., N.Y. Soc. Securities Analysts. Avocations: tennis, running. Home: 56 Twin Oak Rd Short Hills NJ 07078-2259 Office: Alleghany Corp 375 Park Ave New York NY 10152 Office Phone: 212-752-1356. Office Fax: 212-759-8149.*

HICKS, WILLIAM ALBERT, III, lawyer; b. Welland, Ont., Can., Apr. 6, 1942; s. William Albert and June Gwendolyn (Birrell) H.; m. Bethany G. Galvin, May 21, 1982; children: James Christopher, Scott Kelly, Alexandra Elizabeth, Samantha Katherine. AB, Princeton U., 1964; LLB, Cornell U., 1967. Bar: N.Y. 1967, Ariz. 1972, U.S. Dist. Ct. Ariz. 1972. Assoc. Seward & Kissel, N.Y.C., 1967-68, Snell & Wilmer LLP, Phoenix, 1972-75, ptnr., 1976—. Instr. Ariz. State U., 1974-75. Mem. U.S. Olympic Fencing Squad, 1964; bd. adv. Casino USA, Inc., 1981-84; bd. dirs. Scottsdale Arts Ctr. Assn., 1984-88, v.p. devel,. 1985-87; bd. dirs. Valley Leadership, Inc., 1987-91, sec., 1988-89, sec.-treas., 1989-90; bd. dirs. Scottsdale Cultural Coun., 1988-97, vice chmn., 1992-95, chmn., 1995-96; active The Luke's Men, 1992-2003, bd. dirs., 1993-97, 99-2002, sec., 1993-94, v.p. 1995-96, pres., 1996-97; adv. bd. Scottsdale Arts Ctr., 1988-91, chmn., 1988-90; bd. dirs., vice chmn. Ariz. Coun. on Econ. Edn., 1999-2000, chmn., 2000—. Capt. JAG Corps, USAF, 1968-72. Decorated DSM. Mem. ABA, Ariz. State Bar Assn., N.Y. State Bar Assn., Nat. Assn. Bond Lawyers (vice chmn. com. on fin. health care facilities 1982-83, chmn. com. on fin. health care facilities 1983-86, securities law and disclosure com. 1994—), Assn. for Govtl. Leasing and Fin., Princeton U. Alumni Assn. Ariz. (pres. 1978-81, 2003—, sec. 1981—2003), Paradise Valley (Ariz.) Country Club, Princeton Club N.Y. Office: Snell & Wilmer LLP One Arizona Ctr Phoenix AZ 85004-2202 Office Phone: 602-382-6303. Business E-Mail: whicks@swlaw.com.

HICKSON, ERNEST CHARLES, financial executive; b. L.A., July 14, 1931; s. Russell Arthur and Marilyn Louise (Mambert) H.; m. Janice Beleal, Sept. 5, 1959; children: Arthur, Jennifer, Barton. BS, U. So. Calif., 1961; postgrad., UCLA Grad. Sch. of Bus. Admin., 1961-63. Lic. real estate broker Calif., 1956. Credit supr. ARCO (Richfield Oil), L.A., 1955-60; asst. v.p. Union Bank L.A., 1960-64; v.p. County Nat. Bank (now Wells Fargo), Orange, Calif., 1964-67; v.p., sr. loan ofcr. City Bank, Honolulu, 1967-70; pres., CEO Shelter Corp. (merged with USF), 1968-72; exec. v.p., dir. U.S. Fin., Inc. NYSE, San Diego, 1970-73, pres., CEO USF Investors, 1971-73; exec. v.p. Sonnenblick Goldman, L.A., 1973-76; pres., CEO First Hawaiian Devel., Honolulu, 1976-82; sr. ptnr. TMH Resources and affiliates, Laguna Niguel, Calif., 1982—. Expert witness in fin. Author: The Developers, 1978; editor: (newsletter) Financial Marketing, 1978-83. Staff sgt. USAF, 1951—54. Recipient Exec. award Grad. Sch. of Credit and Fin. Mgmt., Stanford U., 1964, Assocs. award The Nat. Inst. of Credit, UCLA, 1959. Mem. U. So. Calif. Assocs., U. So. Calif. Pres.'s Circle, Urban Land Inst., Town Hall, Salt Creek Club (charter), Pacific Club (Honolulu), Outrigger Canoe Club (Honolulu), Phi Gamma Delta. Avocations: tennis, walking, writing, swimming. Fax: 948-495-9458. Office Phone: 949-495-9400. Personal E-mail: ernesth541@aol.com.

HICKSON, ROBIN JULIAN, mining company executive; b. Irby, Eng., Feb. 27, 1944; s. William Kellett and Doris Matilda (Martin) H.; m. P. Anne Winn, Mar. 28, 1964; children: Richard, Sharon, Nicholas, Steven. BS in Mining Engring. with honors, U. London, 1965; MBA, Tulane U., 1990. Chartered engr., U.K. and Europe. Mining engr. N.J. Zinc Co., Austinville, 1965-70, divisional mgr. Jefferson City, Tenn., 1970-71; spl. project engr. Kerr McGee Corp., Grants, N.Mex., 1971-72; gen. mgr. Asarco, Inc., Vanadium, N.Mex., 1972-78, Gold Fields Mining Corp., Ortiz, N.Mex., 1978-83, Mesquite, Calif., 1982-86; v.p. Freeport Mining Co., New Orleans, 1986-91, Freeport Indonesia Inc., Irian Jaya, 1991-92; pres. Freeport Rsch. and Engring. Co., New Orleans, 1992-93; sr. v.p. Cyprus Climax Metals Co., Tempe, Ariz., 1993-94; pres. Cyprus Amax Engring. and Project Devel. Co., Tempe, 1994-99; exec. officer Cyprus Amax Minerals Co., 1994-99; sr. v.p.

engring. and project mgmt. Kvaerner Metals, San Ramon, Calif., 2000—02; pres., COO Gabriel Resources Ltd., Toronto, Canada, 2002—03; prin., sr. v.p. McIntosh Engring., Tempe, 2003—. Author (with others): Interfacing Technologies in Solution Mining, 1981, Mineral Processing: Plant Design, Control and Practice, 2002. Recipient Robert Earll McConnell award AIME, 1999. Mem. Instn. Mining and Metallurgy, Am. Inst. Mining and Metallurgy, Mining and Metall. Soc., N.Mex. Mining Assn. (bd. dirs. Santa Fe chpt. 1975-83), Calif. Mining Assn. (bd. dirs. Sacramento chpt. 1982-86), Beta Gamma Sigma. Episcopalian. Avocations: ornithology, travel. Home: 12246 S Honah Lee Ct Phoenix AZ 85044-3455 Office: 4440 S Rural Rd Tempe AZ 85282 Office Phone: 480-831-0310 215. Business E-Mail: rjhickson@mcintoshengineering.com. E-mail: annerobin@worldnet.att.net.

HIDALGO, DAVID ARTHUR, plastic surgeon; b. Hartford, Conn., 1952; BS, BA magna cum laude, Georgetown U., MD cum laude, 1978. Cert. Nat. Bd. Med. Examiners, 1980, Am. Bd. Surgery, 1984, Am. Bd. Plastic Surgery, 1987. Intern in surgery NYU Med. Ctr., NYC, 1978—79, resident in surgery, 1979—83, resident in plastic surgery, 1983—85, fellow in plastic surgery, 1985—86; affiliated with Meml. Sloan-Kettering Cancer Ctr., NYC, 1986—2000, chief plastic surgery, 1992—2000; assoc. attending surgeon Manhattan Eye, Ear & Throat Hosp., 1986—; affiliated with NY-Presbyn. Hosp., 1986—, Southampton Hosp., 2000—; pvt. practice aesthetic plastic surgery NYC, 2000—. Clin. prof. Cornell Med. Ctr., 1999—; lectr., presenter in field; spkr. on panels; vis. prof. Johns Hopkins U., Yale U., U. Pa., U. Chgo., various other coll. and U., Plastic Surgery Ednl. Found., 2002. Contbr. Plastic and Reconstructive Surgery, Annals of Plastic Surgery;, author numerous chpt. in textbooks and other reference publ. in plastic surgery; publr. (videos on plastic surgery technique). Named one of Best Doctors in Am., Northeast Region, Best Doctors in NY, NY Mag.; recipient First Prize, Plastic Surgery Ednl. Found. Nat. Sr. Resident's Conf., 1985, Best Paper of Yr. award to appear in Plastic and Reconstructive Surgery, Am. Soc. Maxillofacial Surgeons, 1989, 2003, Best Surgical Technique Video awards, 1992, Health and Sci. Network, 1990, James Barrett Brown award for Best Sci. Paper of Yr., Am. Assn. Plastic Surgeons, 1991, Clin. Rsch. award, Plastic Surgery Ednl. Found., 2001. Fellow: Am. Coll. Surgeons; mem.: NY Regional Soc. Plastic and Reconstructive Surgery, NY County Med. Soc., NY State Med. Soc., Am. Soc. Maxillofacial Surgeons (ASMS Award 2003), Am. Assn. Plastic Surgeons, Am. Soc. Aesthetic Plastic Surgery, Am. Soc. Plastic Surgeons, Alpha Omega Alpha Med. Honor Soc. Avocations: art, painting. Office: 655 Park Ave Fl 1 New York NY 10021-5937 Office Fax: 212-517-2527. E-mail: info@drdavidhidalgo.com.

HIDALGO, ISMAEL J., pharmaceutical scientist; s. Deciderio and Rafaela Hidalgo; m. Margarita Gantes, Aug. 23, 1979; children: Carlos A., Daniel A. BS in Pharmacy, U. Panama, Panama City, 1978; PhD, U. So. Calif., L.A., 1986. Lab. asst. U. Panama, 1978—80; postdoctoral fellow U. Kans., Lawrence, 1986—88, asst. rsch. scientist, 1989—90; rsch. investigator SmithKline Beecham, King of Prussia, Pa., 1990—91, sr. rsch. investigator, 1991—92; rsch. fellow Rhone-Poulenc Rorer, Collegeville, Pa., 1993—95, sr. rsch. fellow, 1995—97; co-founder, chief sci. officer Absorption Systems, Exton, Pa., 1997—. Named Entrepreneur of the Yr. in the Life Scis. for the Phila. area, Ernst & Young, 2002; fellow, UpJohn Co., 1986—88; scholar, OAS, 1980—82. Mem.: AAAS (assoc.), Am. Assn. Pharm. Scientists (assoc.), Am. Chem. Soc. (assoc.). Roman Catholic. Achievements include patents for device to measure electrical resistance of cell monolayers in side-by-side diffusion apparatus; first to characterizing a cell culture model (Caco-2) of small intestinal permeability. Avocations: golf, travel, music, reading. Office: Absorption Systems LP Ste 300 440 Creamery Way Exton PA 19341 E-mail: hidalgo@absorption.com.

HIDALGO, RICHARD, professional baseball player; b. Caracas, Venezuela, July 2, 1975; Center fielder Houston Astros, 1997—2004, New York Mets, 2004—. Office: c/o NY Mets Shea Stadium 123 01 Roosevelt Ave. Flushing NY 11368-1699 Fax: 713-799-9881.

HIDAY, VIRGINIA ALDIGÉ, sociologist educator; b. New Orleans, Jan. 28, 1939; d. Robert Joseph and Mary Boagni (Anding) A.; m. L.L. Hiday, Sept. 5, 1970 (div. June 2, 1997). AB, U. N.C., 1960, MEd, 1961, PhD, 1973. Asst. prof. U. Colo., Boulder, 1972-75; postdoctoral fellow Duke U. Med. Ctr., Durham, N.C., 1975-76; asst. prof., prof. N.C. State U., Raleigh, 1976—. Vis. prof. U. N.C., Chapel Hill, 1974-75; referee for various sci. jours. in sociology, law, psychiatry; cons. N.C. Divsn. Mental Health, Raleigh, 1986, 89, Nat. Health Svc., London, 1999, Ont. Ministry of Health, Toronto, 2000. Mem. editl. bd. Contemporary Sociology, 1986-91, 98-2000, Rose Monograph Series, 1982-88, Jour. Health and Social Behavior, 2000—, Internat. Jour. Law and Psychiatry, 2000; contbr. numerous articles to profl. jours. Mem., com. AAUP, Boulder, Colo., 1972-75; worker Campaigns for local, state, nat. offices, Chapel Hill, 1966—, Habitat for Humanity, Chapel Hill, 1996-97; bd. dirs. Orange County Mental Health Assn., Chapel Hill, 1995-99. Named NIMH Postdoctoral fellow, Popultion Predoctoral fellow NICHD. Mem. APA, Am. Sociol. Assn. (coun. mem. med. sect., sec., treas. mental health), So. Sociol. Soc. (coun. mem.), Internat. Acad. Law & Mental Health (coun. mem. 1993—), Soc. for Study of Social Problems, Phi Kappa Phi, Sigma Xi. Democrat. Episcopalian. Avocations: tennis, skiing, dance. Office: NC State U Dept Sociology/Anthropology PO Box 8107 Raleigh NC 27695-0001

HIDEN, ROBERT BATTAILE, JR., lawyer; b. Boston, May 8, 1933; s. Robert Battaile Sr. and Clotilda (Waddell) H.; m. Ann Eliza McCracken, Mar. 27, 1956; children: Robert B. III, Elizabeth Patterson, John Hughes. BA, Princeton U., 1955; LLB, U. Va., 1960. Bar: NY 1961, US Ct. Appeals (2d cir.) 1974, US Dist. Ct. (so. dist.) NY 1975, US Supreme Ct. 2005. Assoc. Sullivan & Cromwell, N.Y.C., 1960—67, ptnr., 1968—98, of counsel, 1999—2000, sr. counsel, 2001—. Articles editor and contbr. U. Va. Law Rev., 1959-60; contbr., mem. editl. bd. Futures Internat. Law Letter, 1987-92. Trustee Hampton (Va.) U. and Hampton Inst., 1984—2003; mem. Dillard scholarship com. U. Va. Law Sch., 1984—98, 2001—02; gov. Ramapo (N.J.) Coll. Found., 2002—; commr. Larchmont (N.Y.) Little League, 1964—68; chmn. Larchmont Jr. Sailing Program, 1977—78; vestry, jr. warden St. John's Episc. Ch., Larchmont, 1982—86, 1999—2002. Served to lt. (j.g.) USNR, 1955—57. Mem. ABA, NY State Bar Assn., Assn. of Bar of City of NY, NY County Bar Assn., Am. Judicature Soc., Larchmont U. Club (pres. 1976-77), Larchmont Yacht Club (trustee 1979-85, sec. 1990—), Coral Beach Club (Bermuda), Raven Soc., Order of Coif, Omicron Delta Kappa. Democrat. Avocations: skiing, golf, sailing, tennis. Home: 2 Walnut Ave Larchmont NY 10538-4232 Office: Sullivan & Cromwell 125 Broad St Fl 28 New York NY 10004-2489 Personal E-mail: rbobhiden@aol.com.

HIDSON, PATRICIA DIANE, artist, educator; b. Edmonton, Alta., Can., Nov. 20, 1948; arrived in U.S., 1974; d. Albert John Hidson and Patricia Florence Ryland; m. James Wilfred Brozek, Feb. 14, 1991; m. Brian Peter Bentz, Jan. 16, 1974 (div. Oct. 1985); children: Paul Bentz, Meighan Bentz, Brian Bentz. BA, U. Alta., Edmonton, 1975; postgrad., U. Wis., Milw., 1978—81, Cape Sch. Art, Provincetown, Mass., 1982—84, Milw. Inst. Art and Design, 1983—84. Dir., tchr. The Hidson Art Sch. and Studio, Milw.; prin., owner Pat Hidson Art Gallery, Milw., 2003—. Lectr., spkr. in field; mem. faculty Pa. Art Sch., Door County, Wis. One-woman shows include Regional Art Ctr., LaCrosse, Wis., 1998, Grace Chosy Gallery, Madison, Wis., 1998, 1995, 1993, Gruen Gallery, Chgo., 1997, 1990, Madison U. Med. Hosp., 1993, Tory Folliard Gallery, Milw., 1993, others, exhibited in group shows at Door County, Wis., 2001, Tory Folliard Gallery, 2000, 1999, 1998, Art Resources Gallery, St. Paul, 1998, Edmonton Art Gallery, 1997, Gallerie Stephanie, Chgo., 1995, Wustum Mus., Racine, Wis., 1985—97, Carolyn Ruff Gallery, Mpls., 1993, Banaker Gallery, San Francisco, 1993, San Miguel Allende, Mex., 1993, others, Wis. Artists Biennial, Anderson Art Ctr., Kenosha, 2005, Represented in permanent collections Walt Disney Corp., Quadracci Corp. Collection (Milw.), Associated Bank (Milw.), Marine Bank (Milw.), numerous others; featured and reviewed (numerous publs.). Episcopalian. Avocations: yoga, reading, wildlife rehabilitation. Home: 5730 N river Forest Dr Glendale WI 53209 Office: Hidson Art Sch Studio and Art Gallery 303-133 W Pittsburgh Ave Milwaukee WI 53204 Office Phone: 414-227-0991. E-mail: phidson@wi.rr.com.

HIDY, GEORGE MARTEL, chemical engineer, engineering executive; b. Kingman, Ariz., Jan. 5, 1935; s. John William and Margaret (Coqueron) H.; m. Dana Sexton Thomas, Oct. 15, 1958; children— Anne, Adrienne, John; m. 2d, Doris A. Wilson, Sept. 28, 1990. AB, Columbia U., N.Y.C., 1956, BS, 1957; MSE., Princeton U., N.J., 1958; D.Eng., Johns Hopkins U., Balt., 1962. Asst. dir. chemistry and microphysics Nat. Ctr. Atmospheric Rsch., Boulder, Colo., 1967-69; group leader chem. physics Rockwell Internat. Sci. Ctr., Thousand Oaks, Calif., 1969-73, assoc. dir., 1973-74; gen. mgr. Environ. Rsch. & Tech., West Lake, Calif., 1974-76, v.p., 1976-84; pres. Desert Rsch. Inst., Reno, 1984-87; v.p. Electric Power Rsch. Inst., Palo Alto, Calif., 1987-94; assoc. dir. coll. engring. Ctr. Environ. Rsch. and Technol. U. Calif., Riverside, 1994-96; prin. Aerochem Assocs., Riverside, 1995—; Ala. Indsl. prof. environ. engring. U. Ala., Birmingham, 1996-99; prin. Envair Aerochem, 1999—; interim dir. N.Mex. State U. Carlsbad Ctr. for Environ. Monitoring/Rsch., 2001—02. Commr., Calif. Youth Soccer Assn., L.A., 1982-84; bd. dirs. El Pueblo Health Ctr., 2003—, chmn., 2004—. Fellow AAAS, Air and Waste Mgmt. Assn.; mem. AIChE, Am. Meteorol. Soc., Am. Chem. Soc., Am. Geophys. Union. Home: 6 Evergreen Dr Placitas NM 87043-8903 E-mail: dhidy113@comcast.net.

HIEATT, ALLEN KENT, retired language educator; b. Indpls., Jan. 21, 1921; emigrated to Can., 1968, returned to U.S., 1986. s. Allen Andrew and Violet Rose (Kent) H.; m. Constance Bartlett, Oct. 25, 1958; children by previous marriage: Alice Allen, Katherine Marsh. AB, U. Louisville, 1943; PhD, Columbia U., 1954. Lectr. Columbia U., N.Y.C., 1944-45, instr., 1945-55, asst. prof., 1956-59, assoc. prof., 1960-69; prof. English U. Western Ont., London, 1969-86, emeritus, 1987—; sr. founding editor Spenser Newsletter, London, Ont., 1970-75; ret., 1987. Mem. editorial bd. Duquesne Studies, Pitts., 1976—, Spenser Studies, 1979—; editorial cons. Spenser Ency., 1990; co-editor: College Anthology of British and American Verse, 1964, Poetry in English: An Anthology, 1987; author: Short Time's Endless Monument, 1960, (with C. Hieatt) The Canterbury Tales of Geoffrey Chaucer, 1964, rev. edit., 1981, Spenser: Selected Poetry, 1970, Chaucer, Spenser, Milton, 1975; translator: (with M. Lorch) Lorenzo Valla, On Pleasure, 1977; co-author: (with C. Hieatt) (children's book) The Canterbury Tales of Geoffrey Chaucer, 1961. Cutting fellow, 1946-47; leave grantee Can. Council, Oxford, Eng., 1977-78; research fellow Social Sci. and Humanities Research Council of Can., 1981-82 Fellow Royal Soc. Can.; mem. MLA (chmn. div. English lit. Renaissance 1978-79, William Riley Parker Prize, 1984), Spenser Soc. (pres.), Renaissance Soc. Am. (chmn. north central div. 1973-79) Home: 335 Essex Mdws Essex CT 06426-1526

HIEATT, CONSTANCE BARTLETT, English language educator; b. Boston, Feb. 11, 1928; d. Arthur Charles and Eleonora (Very) Bartlett; m. Allen Kent Hieatt, Oct. 25, 1958. Student, Smith Coll., 1945-47; AB, Hunter Coll., 1953, AM, 1957; PhD, Yale U., 1959. Lectr. City Coll., CUNY, 1959-60; from asst. prof. to assoc. prof. English Queensborough C.C., CUNY, 1960-65; from assoc. prof. to prof. St. John's U., Jamaica, N.Y., 1965-69; prof. English U. Western Ont., London, Can., 1969-93, prof. emeritus, 1993—. Author: (with A.K. Hieatt) The Canterbury Tales of Geoffrey Chaucer, 1964, rev. edit., 1981, Spenser: Selected Poetry, 1970; The Realism of Dream Visions, 1967, Beowulf and Other Old English Poems, 1967, rev. edit., 1983, Essentials of Old English, 1968, The Miller's Tale By Geoffrey Chaucer, 1970; (with Sharon Butler) Pleyn Delit: Medieval Cookery for Modern Cooks, 1976, rev. edit., 1979; (with Brenda Hosington) rev. 2d edit., 1996, Karlamagnus Saga, Vols. I and II, 1975, Vol. III, 1980; (with Sharon Butler) Curye on Inglysch, 1985; An Ordinance of Pottage, 1988; (with Robin F. Jones) La Novele Cirurgerie, 1990; (with Minnette Gaudet) Guillaume de Machaut's Tale of the Alerion, 1994; (with Brian Shaw and Duncan Macrae-Gibson) Beginning Old English, 1994; (with Rudolf Grewe) Libellus de Arte Coquinaria, 2001; also children books (with Hieatt) The Canterbury Tales of Geoffrey Chaucer, 1961, Sir Gawain and the Green Knight, 1967, The Knight of the Lion, 1968, The Knight of the Cart, 1969, The Joy of the Court, 1971, The Sword and the Grail, 1972, The Castle of Ladies, 1973, The Minstrel Knight, 1974. Yale U. fellow, and Lewis-Farmington fellow, 1957-59, Vis. fellow Yale U., 1985-86, 89-93; Can. Council and Social Sci. and Humanities Rsch. Coun. grant. Fellow Royal Soc. Can.; mem. MLA, Medieval Acad. Am., Internat. Soc. Anglo-Saxonists, Can Soc. Medievalists. Episcopalian. Home: 335 Essex Mdws Essex CT 06426-1526 Personal E-mail: constance.hieatt@yale.edu.

HIEBERT, CLEMENT ARTHUR, surgeon, consultant, educator; b. Boston; s. Joelle Cornelius and Susie (Pauls) H.; m. Mary Anne Tremaine, June 10, 1956; children: Timothy, Sarah, Katherine, Amy, John; m. May Cameron, Dec. 9, 1978. AB magna cum laude, Bowdoin Coll., 1947; MD, Harvard U., 1951. Diplomate Am. Bd. Surgery, Am. Bd. Vascular Surgery; lic. MD, Maine. Intern, resident Mass. Gen. Hosp., Boston, 1951-56; rsch. fellow Harvard U., Strangeways Rsch., Cambridge, Eng., 1956-57; chief resident West Surgical Svcs, Mass. Gen. Hosp., Boston, 1957-58; senior registrar in thoracic surgery Frenchay Hosp., Bristol, Eng., 1958-59; dir. surg. clinics Mass. Gen. Hosp., Boston, 1959-60; attending surgeon Maine Med. Ctr., Mercy Hosp., Portland, Maine, 1960—; chmn. dept. surgery Maine Med. Ctr., Portland, 1086-89, chmn. emeritus dept. surgery, 1990—; lic. state of Maine guide Boy Scouts Am. Eagle Scout. Dep. med. dir. voyage IV rotation to W. Africa, Project Hope, 1964; instr. in Thoracic Surgery, Harvard Med. Sch., Mass. Gen. Hosp. Post-Grad course; guest lectr. U. Toronto, ann. refresher course in Gen. Thoracic Surgery; staff surgeon divsn. thoracic surgery, Toronto Gen. Hosp., 1984-85, U. Paris (OSEO), 1984, Curzo Internat. de Actualizacion en Circugia, Madrid, 1984, Medizinische Hochschule, Hannover, Germany, 1985, U. Rio Grande de Norte, Natal, Brazil, 1985; lectr. Royal Coll. Surgeons Can., Meml. U. St Johns, Newfoundland, U. Leuven, Belgium, 1985, 96, U. Conn., 1989, Ctr. Med. de Forcilles, Attilly, Paris, 1991, Kantonspital, Basel, Switzerland, 1993, Dartmouth Med. Sch., Bay State Med. Ctr. U. Mass.; rep. Am. Bd. of Surgery to the inaugural Arab Bd. of Surgery Examinations, Baghdad, Iraq. 1986. Co-editor (with others) 2 vol. textbook in Thoracic Surgery, 1995; contbr. over 60 articles to profl. jours including Annals of Thoracic Surgery, Surgery, JAMA, Am. Jour. of Surgery, World Jour. of Surgery and chpts. in a variety of textbooks, Jour. Thoracic and Cardiovascular Surgery, 2003. Past mem., bd. dirs. Portland Symphony Orch., Opportunity Farm for Boys, New Gloucester, Maine; bd. dirs. World Affairs Coun., Portland, Maine, 1995-98; instr. Maine Handicapped Skiing, 1995. With U.S. Navy, Atlantic Fleet, 1944-46. Recipient Santos Dumont medal of merit, Govt. of Brazil, Brazilian Embassy, Washington, 1086; named Scholar-in-Residence, Rockefeller Found., Lake Como, Italy, 1990, Annual Student Attending Tchg. award, U. Vt., 2002, Student Resident Tchg. award, 2002. Fellow ACS, Am. Coll. Cardiology; mem. Am. Bd. Surgery (sr. mem., bd. dirs.), Soc. of Thoracic Surgeons, Boston Surgical Soc., Internat. Soc., Soc. for Cardiovascular Surgery. Avocations: landscape gardening, photography, skiing. Home: 63 Blueberry Cove Yarmouth ME 04096 Fax: (207) 892-9976. E-mail: hiebert@mymailstation.com.

HIEBERT, RAY ELDON, writer, educator; b. Freeman, S.D., May 21, 1932; s. Peter Nicholas and Helen (Kunkel) H.; m. Roselyn Lucille Peyser, Jan. 30, 1955 (div. Apr. 1985); children: David, Steven, Emily, Douglas; m. Sheila Jean Gibbons, Dec. 21, 1985 BA, Stanford U., 1954; MS, Columbia U., 1957; MA, U. Md., 1961, PhD, 1962. Faculty Am. U., 1958- 67, prof. journalism, chmn. dept. journalism, 1962-67; dir. Washington Journalism Center, 1965-68; head dept. journalism U. Md., College Park, 1968-72; dean Coll. Journalism, 1973-79, prof., 1980-98, prof., dean emeritus, 1998—. Pres. Comm. Rsch. Assocs., 1979—; dir. Am. Journalism Ctr., Budapest, Hungary, 1991-95; acad. adv. U.S. Voice of Am., 1983-91; vice chmn. Montgomery County (Md.) Cable-TV Commn., 1973-77; mem. St. Mary's County Cable-TV Commn., 2001-05. Author: more than 20 books; editor. Fulbright fellow to Africa, 1982; recipient U. Md. Landmark award for Internat. Svc., 2000. Mem. Soc. Profl. Journalists (pres. Md. chpt. 1977-78), Cosmos Club (Washington), Kappa Tau Alpha, Phi Kappa Phi, Omicron Delta Kappa. Home: 38091 Beach Rd Coltons Point MD 20626-0180 Office: 1220 Watergate S 700 New Hampshire Ave NW Washington DC 20037

HIEBNER, AIDA CECILIA, secondary school educator, education educator; b. Quito, Ecuador, Aug. 18, 1946; arrived in U.S., 1975; d. Carlos Humberto Padilla Salazar and Zoila Amada Vallejo Diaz; m. Lauren Wayne, June 2; children: Andrey Johann, Diego Ryan. Elem. edn., Normal for Tchrs., 1965; BA in ESL, Ctrl. U. Quito, 1972, U. Nebr., 1987, MEd, 2001; postgrad., Inst. Children's Lit., 2001. Typist Dept. Civil Registry, Quito, 1965—69; exec. sec. Ecuadorian Ins. Co., Quito, 1969—73; sec. Def. Dept., Quito, 1973—75; tchr. Pvt. Sch., Quito, 1974—75; tchr. aide O'Neill Elem. Sch., Nebr., 1978—80; tchr. Page Pub. Sch., Nebr., 1989—92; tchr. art O'Neill Pub. Sch., 1993—. Tchr. art St. Mary's H.S., O'Neill, 1988—89, tchr. Spanish, 1993—; instr. Spanish I North East C.C., O'Neill, 2000—. Author (poem): Nat. Libr. Poetry, 1998 (Editor's Choice, 1998); Hispanic Art Show, Kearney, Nebr., 1986 (1st Pl., 1986), State Art Clubs, 1988 (Hon. Memtion), Ranchland Art Group, 1981—89 (Best of Show). Mem.: O'Neill Edn. Assn., Nebr. Assn. Art Clubs, Nebr. State Edn. Assn., Alpha Delta Kappa. Avocations: painting, travel, reading, photography, writing. Office: O'Neill Pub Sch PO Box 230 Oneill NE 68763

HIEKEN, CHARLES, lawyer; b. Granite City, Ill., Aug. 15, 1928; s. Samuel and Margaret (Isaacs) H.; m. Donna Jane Clanin, Jan. 6, 1961; children: Tina Jane, Seth Paul. SBEE, SMEE, MIT, 1952; LLB, Harvard U., 1957. Bar: Ill. 1957, Mass. 1958, U.S. Supreme Ct. 1960, U.S. Ct. Customs and Patent Appeals 1961, U.S. Ct. Claims 1963, U.S. Ct. Appeals (fed. cir.) 1982. Patent asst. Lab. Electronics, Boston, 1954-56, Fish, Richardson & Neave, Boston, 1956-57; assoc. Hill, Sherman, Meroni, Gross & Simpson, Chgo., 1957, Joseph Weingarten, Boston, 1957-58, Wolf, Greenfield & Hieken, Boston, 1958-61, ptnr., 1961-70; prin. Charles Hieken Law Offices, Waltham, Mass., 1970-87; ptnr. Fish & Richardson, Boston, 1987-94, prin., 1995—. Mem. Pres. Carter's adv. com. on indsl. innovation, 1979. Mem. pres.'s adv. coun. Bentley Coll., 1993—; mem. coun. Harvard Law Sch. Assn., 1998-02. Served with U.S. Merchant Marine, 1944-47, U.S. Army, 1952-54. Mem.: IEEE (sr.; life), Boston Patent Law Assn. (chmn. pub. rels. com. 1965—66, chmn. antitrust law com. 1966—70, treas. 1970—71, v.p. 1971—72, pres.-elect 1972—73, pres. 1973—74, chmn. antitrust law com. 1978—80), Ill. State Bar Assn. (privileged mem.), Mass. Bar Assn. (chmn. intellectual property com. 1977—80), Boston Bar Assn. (civil procedure com. 1959—), U. Mass. Club (founding bd. govs.), Down Town Club (bd. govs 1988—2003, v.p. gen counsel 2000—03), Tau Beta Pi, Eta Kappa Nu. Home: 193 Wilshire Dr Sharon MA 02067-1561 Office: Fish & Richardson PC 225 Franklin St 31st Fl Boston MA 02110-2804 Business E-Mail: hieken@fr.com.

HIELSCHER, ANDREAS HELMUT, biomedical engineer; b. Bremen, Germany, Feb. 15, 1964; s. Helmut Reinhardt and Inge Hielscher; m. Maria Anagnostopoulou, May 15, 1995; 1 child, Amélie Lukia Inge. BS in Physics, U. Hannover, Germany, 1989; MS in Applied Physics, U. Hannover, 1991; PhD, Rice U., Tex., 1995. Postdoctoral fellow Los Alamos Nat. Lab., N.Mex., 1995—98; asst. prof. SUNY - Downstate Med. Ctr., Bklyn., 1998—2001; adj. prof. Poly. U., 1999—2001; assoc. prof. of biomedical engring. and radiology Columbia U., NYC, 2001—. Contbr. articles to sci. and profl. jours. Recipient Shechao Charles Feng Meml. prize, SPIE Internat. Soc. of Optical Engring., 1997, Young Investigator award, Whitaker Found., 1999; grantee Optical Tomography Diagnosis Joint Diseases, Nat. Inst. Arthritis and Musculoskeletal and Skin Diseases, 1999—, Optical Tomographic Imaging Brain Injuries and Diseases, NYC Coun. Spkrs. Fund Biomed. Rsch., 1999—2003, Model Based Iterative Reconstruction Techniques Optical Tomography, Whitaker Found., 1999—2003, MRI Compatible Diffuse Optical Tomography Sys. for Small Animal Oximetry, Nat. Inst. for Biomedical Imaging and Bioengineering, 2003—; Dirs. Postdoctoral fellow, Los Alamos Nat. Lab., 1995, Dept. Biomed. Engring. and Laser Medicine fellow, Free U. of Berlin, 2003. Mem.: IEEE, SPIE Internat. Soc. of Optical Engring., Optical Soc. of Am. (chair of biomedical optical spectroscopy group 2001—03). Achievements include patents for Characterization of highly scattering media by measurement of diffusely backscattered polarized light, US Patent No. 6, 011, 626; patents pending for Iterative reconstruction scheme for optical tomography based on the equation of radiative transfer; A digital signal processor-based detection system for optical tomography. Office: Columbia Univ 500 W 120th Str MC8904 New York NY 10027

HIER, DANIEL BARNET, neurologist; b. Chgo., Mar. 23, 1947; BA, Harvard U., 1969, MD, 1973. Medical intern Bronx Mcpl. Hosp., N.Y.C., 1973-74; neurology resident Mass. Gen. Hosp., Boston, 1974-77, neurology fellow, 1977-79; neurologist Michael Reese Hosp., Chgo., 1979-89, chmn. neurology, 1987-89; head neurology U. Ill., Chgo., 1989—2003, assoc. prof. neurology, 1989-91, prof., 1991—. Fellow Am. Acad. Neurology, Am. Heart Assn. (stroke council). Home: 1206 Manor Dr Wilmette IL 60091-1029 Office Phone: 312-996-1759. E-mail: dbhier@gmail.com.

HIER, MARSHALL DAVID, lawyer; b. Bay City, Mich., Aug. 24, 1945; s. Marshall George and Helen May (Copeland) H.; m. Nancy Speed Brown, June 26, 1970; children: John, Susan, Ann. BA, Mich. State U., 1966; JD, U. Mich., 1969. Bar: Mo. 1969. Assoc. Peper, Martin, Jensen, Maichel and Hetlage, St. Louis, 1969-76, ptnr., 1976-95; prin. Bertram, Peper and Hier, P.C., St. Louis, 1996—. Bd. dirs. Gateway Ctr. Met. St. Louis, Mercantile Libr. Assn., St. Louis Soc. Blind and Visually Impaired. Contbr. articles to profl. jours. Mem. St. Louis Bar Assn. (editor jour. 1988—), St. Louis Civil Round Table (former pres.). Baptist. Home: 17141 Chaise Ridge Rd Chesterfield MO 63005-4457 Office Phone: 314-621-1988.

HIERONYMUS, EDWARD WHITTLESEY, lawyer; b. Davenport, Iowa, June 13, 1943; BA cum laude, Knox Coll., 1965; JD with distinction, Duke U., 1968. Bar: Calif. 1969, Iowa 1968. Ptnr. O'Melveny & Myers, LA, 1974—96, of counsel, 1996—99. Contbr. articles on law to profl. jours. Exec. sec. Los Angeles Com. Fgn. Relations, 1975-86. Served with Judge Adv. Gen. U.S. Army, 1965-74. Mem. ABA (award for profl. merit 1968), Calif. Bar Assn. (founding co-chair natural resources subsect., real property sect. 1986-88), Los Angeles County Bar Assn., Iowa Bar Assn. Office: O'Melveny & Myers 400 S Hope St Los Angeles CA 90071-2899

HIERS, RICHARD HYDE, lawyer, educator, writer; b. Phila., Apr. 8, 1932; s. Glen Sefton and Mildred (Douthitt) H.; m. Jane Leslie Gale, Jan. 30, 1954; children: Peter Leslie, Rebecca Hathaway. BA magna cum laude, Yale U., 1954, BD cum laude, 1957, MA, PhD, 1959, 61; JD with high honors, U. Fla., 1983. Bar: Fla. 1984, U.S. Dist. Ct. (we. dist.) Tex. 1988, U.S. Ct. Appeals (5th cir.) 1988. Asst. prof. Coll. Liberal Arts and Scis., U. Fla., Gainesville, 1961-66, assoc. prof., 1966-72, prof., 1972—2003, prof. emeritus, 2003—, affiliate prof. law Coll. Law, 1994—2003, affiliate prof. law emeritus, 2003—. Jud. law clk. U.S. Ct. Appeals, Austin, Tex., 1987-88. Author: Trinity Guide to the Bible with Apocrypha, 2001, Contbr. numerous articles to law jours. including Cumberland Law Rev., Jour. Coll. and Univ. Law, Fifth Cir. Reporter, George Mason Civil Rights Law Jour., Jour. of Law and Religion, Southwestern Law Jour., U. Fla. Jour. Law and Pub. Policy, Wayne Law Rev. Recipient Disting. Faculty award, Fla. Blue Key Orgn., 1998. Mem. Am. Acad. of Religion (pres. southeastern region 1969-70), AAUP (pres. U. Fla. chpt. 1972-74), Soc. of Biblical Lit. (pres. southeastern reg. 1982-83), Fla. Bar Assn. (com. on individual rights and responsiblities 1985-87, 90, pub. interest law sect. 1990-), Bar Assn. of 5th Fed. Cir., Danforth Assocs. in Tchg, Order of Coif, Aurelian Honor Soc., Skull and Bones, Phi Beta Kappa (pres. U. Fla. chpt. 1975-76), Phi Kappa Phi (pres. U. Fla. chpt. 1995-96). Democrat. Avocation: hiking. Office: U Fla 107 Anderson Hall Gainesville FL 32611-7410 Business E-Mail: rhiers@law.ufl.edu. *All decisions affecting ourselves, other persons, and other living beings, are basically ethical decisions. And ethical decisions inevitably give expression to our ultimate loyalties and convictions as to the meaning of life that is, ultimately, religious in character.*

HIETALA, VALERIE GRACE, realtor, environmentalist, educator; d. Douglas Waldie Dill; m. Kaarlo John Hietala, July 27, 1999; children: Rachel Anne Rutizer, Kaarlo John, Ingrid Bacher, Amber Nicole Rutizer, Sasha Noel Rutizer. BS in Agrl., U. Wis., 1973; MS, U. Colo., 1991. Cert. edn. Fla., 1998, Fla. Assn. Realtors, 2002. Environ. educator Cheyenne Mountain Zoo, Colorado Springs, Colo., 1984—90; dir. Blue Belly Lizard, Los Olivos, Calif., 1993—96; environ. educator McIntosh Mid. Sch., Sarasota, Fla., 1996—2000; dir. Lucy Spoons Island Outfitters, Holmes Beach, 1998—2002; realtor, real estate sales Re/Max Gulfstream, 2000—. Environ. educator, cons. Butterfly Assn., Bradenton, Fla., 1999—. Jewelry, Non Titled (Longboat Key Art award, 2004). Edn. com. DAR, Anna Maria, Fla., 2003—04. Scholar, Longboat Key Art Ctr., 2004. Mem.: Selby Bot. (assoc.), Ringling Art Musuem (assoc.), DAR (assoc.). Achievements include research in Geneological research for Daughters of the American Revolution. Avocations: travel, swimming, photography, scuba diving, art. Personal E-mail: wawanuky@rwobox.com.

HIGASHIDA, RANDALL TAKEO, radiologist, neurosurgeon, medical educator; b. L.A., Oct. 26, 1955; s. Henry and Alice Higashida; m. Jean Kim, May 17, 1986. BS, U. So. Calif., 1976; MD, Tulane U. Diplomate Am. Bd. Radiology. Intern Harbor UCLA Med. Ctr., 1980-81, resident in radiology, 1981-84, fellow in diagnostic/interventional neuroradiology, 1984-85; asst. prof. radiology UCLA Med. Ctr., 1985-86; assoc. prof. radiology U. Calif. San Francisco Med. Ctr., 1986-94, prof. radiology and neurosurgery, 1994—. Cons. Target Therapeutics Corp., Fremont, Calif., 1989-93, Interventional Therapeutics Corp., Fremont, 1986-93, Cordis Corp., Miami Lakes, Fla., 1993-96; mem. exec. com. stroke rsch. grants Abbott Labs., Chgo., 1994-96. Mem. editl. bd. Jour. Endovasc. Surgery, 1994-96, Jour. Minimally Invasive Neurosurgery, 1994-96; manuscript reviewer Am. Jour. Neuroradiology, 1992—. Recipient rsch. award Am. Heart Assn., Dallas, 1978-79. Mem. AMA, Am. Soc. Neuroradiology (sr. mem., exec. coun. joint section of cerebrovascular neurosurgery), Soc. Cardiovascular and Interventional Radiology, Am. Soc. Interventional and Therapeutic Neuroradiology (exec. com. 1994-96), Internat. Soc. Endovascular Surgery. Republican. Protestant. Avocations: hiking, tennis, biking, photography, travel. Office: UCSF Medical Ctr 505 Parnassus Ave # L352 San Francisco CA 94143-0001

HIGBEE, DALE (STROHE), musician, retired psychologist; b. Proctor, Vt., June 14, 1925; s. Paul Wilbur Higbee and Catherine Ann Strohe; 1 child, Catherine Ann Higbee Mize. AB, Harvard, Cambridge, Mass., 1949; PhD, Univ. Tex. at Austin, Austin, Tex., 1954; studied flute with, Georges Laurent, Arthur Lora, Marcel Moyse; studied recorder with, Carl Dolmetsch. Clin. psychologist SC State Hosp., Columbia, SC, 1954—55, VA Med. Ctr., Salisbury, NC, 1955—87; freelance flutist & recorder player NC, 1954—87; music dir. Carolina Baroque, Salisbury, NC, 1988—. Contbr. articles to profl. jour. Gov. Dolmetsch Found., 1963—. Pfc. 314th reg., 79th divsn., 1943—45. Decorated Combat Infantry badge, Purple Heart. Home and Office: Carolina Baroque 412 S Ellis St Salisbury NC 28144

HIGBEE, DONNA GOOD, writer, researcher; b. Cedar Rapids, Iowa, Feb. 28, 1947; d. Richard Vernon and Freda Lee Good; m. William Higbee, Sept. 23, 1989. BA in Dramatic Arts, Pasadena (Calif.) Playhouse Coll. Theatre Arts, 1967; AA in Psychology, Santa Barbara City Coll., Calif., 1982; BA in religious studies, U. Calif., Santa Barbara, 1985. Cert. clin. hypnotherapist Hypnosis Motivation Inst., 1994. Personal asst. to chancellor U. Calif., Santa Barbara, 1986—90; exec. asst., pub. rels. 2020 Group, Santa Barbara, 1993—94; pres. Daona Promotions, Santa Barbara, 1994—, Contact Encounters Investigation Team, Santa Barbara, 1994—. Freelance writer, lectr., Santa Barbara, 1994—; counselor, lectr. Natural Alternative Medicine, Santa Barbara, 1996—. Author: (films) The Girl Next Door, 2003, Shop Girl, 2003, Mrs. Harris, 2004, In Her Shoes, 2004, Chumscrubber, 2004, The Wedding Crashers, 2004, Serenity, 2004, Monster-In-Law, 2005, (TV pilot) NYPD 2069, 2003, (TV series) Turning Homeward, 2003, Arrested Development, 2004, Wedding Chapel, 2005; contbr. articles to profl. jours. Mem.: AFTRA, SAG, U. Calif. Alumni Assn., Pasadena Playhouse Alumni & Assocs. Avocations: music, dance.

HIGBY, EDWARD JULIAN, safety engineer; b. Milw., June 9, 1939; s. Richard L. Higby and Julie Ann (Bruins) O'Kelly; m. Frances Ann Knoodle, 1959 (div. 1962); 1 child, Melinda Ann Mozader. BS in Criminal Justice, Southwestern U., Tucson, 1984. Cert.: county ct. mediator. Tactical officer Miami Police Dept., Fla., 1967-68; intelligence officer Fla. Divsn. Beverages, 1968-72; licensing coord. Lums Restaurant Corp., Miami, 1972-73; legal asst. Walt Disney World, Lake Buena Vista, Fla., 1973-78; loss control cons. R.P. Hewitt & Assocs., Orlando, Fla., 1978-79; safety coord. City of Lakeland, Fla., 1979-94. Author: Safety Guide for Health Care, 1979. Councilman City of Bay Lake, 1974-76, mayor, 1975-76; active Fla. League of Cities, 1974-76, Tri-County League of Cities, 1974-76, Orange County Criminal Justice Coun., 1974-78, Ctrl. Fla. Safety Coun., 1978-79; bd. dirs. Greater Lakeland chpt. ARC, 1980-86, chmn. bd. dirs., 1983-84, 85-86, chmn. health svcs., 1980-86; budget com. United Way Ctrl. Fla., 1983-85; bd. dirs. Tampa Area Safety Coun., 1983-92, pres., 1990-91; bd. dirs. Imperial Traffic Safety Coun., 1983-89, Employers Health Care Group Polk County, 1987-89, Parent Resources and Info. on Drug Edn., 1989-92; mem. Polk County Disaster Coordination Com., bd. dirs., 1984-92; bd. dirs. ARC Polk County chpt., 1990-92, 94-96, coord. Mass Care, 1994-95, chmn. Health and Safety, 1994-95, chmn. Risk Mgmt., 1995-96; active ARC Disaster Svcs. Human Resources Sys., 1994-99; mem. Fla. Adv. Com. Arson Prevention, Local Emergency Planning Com., State of Fla., 1987-92, 94—, chmn. Dist. 7, 1998—, Fla. Disaster Mortuary Team, 1995—; adv. panel Polk County Industry Cmty., 1997-2002; adv com. Charlotte Harbor Nat. Estuary, 1997-2002, chmn. citizen adv. com., mgmt. com., 1999-2002; bd. dirs. Friends of Charlotte Harbor Estuary, 2000-2002; adv. coun. Kingsford Elem. Sch., 1999—; Fla. Emergency Mgmt. Reservist Program, 2001—. With U.S. Army, 1963-64. Named Vol. of Yr., Greater Lakeland chpt. ARC, 1983-84. Mem. NRA (life), World Safety Orgn., Fla. Sheriffs Assn. (hon. life), Internat. Assn. Identification (life, Fla. divsn., Russian divsn.), Nat. Found. Mortuary Care, Automatic Fire Alarm Assn., Disaster Emergency Response Assn. (life), Environ. Assessment Assn., U. Fla. Nat. Alumni Assn. (life), Fla. Pub. Health Assn., Fla. Fedn. Safety, Am. Soc. Safety Engrs. (regional oper. com. 1983-85, 88-90, profl. devel. conf. com. 1983, 85, chpt. bd. dirs. 1983-87, chpt. pres. 1984-85, v.p. profl. devel. region VIII 1988-90, Safety Profl. of Yr. 1984-85, Albert G. Mowson award 1995-96, Davis Productivity award 2001), Heartland Safety Soc. (life, pres. 1982-83, 94-95), Fla. Citrus Safety Assn. (pres. 1981-83), Nat. Fire Protection Assn., Am. Indsl. Hygiene Assn. (Fla. chpt.), Fire Marshals Assn. N.Am., Soc. Fire Protection Engrs. (bd. dirs. Fla. chpt. 1994-99), So. Health Assn., Fla. Affiliation of Ins. Safety Reps., Internat. Critical Incident Stress Found., Critical Incident Stress Debriefers Fla., Nat. Assn. Search and Rescue, Fla. Funeral Dirs. Assn., Fla. Emergency Preparedness Assn., Fla. Assn. Code Enforcement, Fla. Acad. Profl. Mediators, First Amendment Found., Internat. Assn. Arson Investigators, Fla. Cracker Cattle Assn. (life), Harley Owners Group (life), Am. Motorcycle Assn. (life), Lakeland Rifle and Pistol Club. Republican. Avocations: hunting, fishing. E-mail: ed-valeriehigby@webtv.net.

HIGBY, LAWRENCE, newspaper publishing executive; Exec. v.p., marketing chmn. of Orange County edition Los Angeles Times, Calif.; dir., CEO Apria Healthcare Group. Office: Apria Health 26220 Enterprise Ct Lake Forest CA 92630-8405 Office Phone: 949-639-2000. Office Fax: 949-587-9363.*

HIGBY, MARY A., marketing executive, educator; b. Mt. Clemens, Oct. 2, 1943; d. Clarence Cooper and Mary H.; m. Edward W. Smykay, Aug. 30, 1980 (dec. Sept. 1982). BS in Biology, Mich. State U., 1965, MBA, 1969, MS, 1970, PhD in Bus., 1976. Mktg. planner Amway Corp., Ada, MI, 1970-72; grad. asst. Mich. State U., East Lansing, 1972-76; staff asst. Sears & Roebuck & Co., Chgo., 1976-78; staff mgr. Ill. Bell Tel., Chgo., 1978-79, Chesapeake & Potomac Tel. Co., Silverspring, Md., 1979-81; mktg. mgr. AT&T, N.J., 1981-83; assoc. prof. mktg. Ea. Mich. U., Ypsilanti, 1983-89, U. Detroit Mercy, 1989—2005. Pres. Mindenhall Assocs., Birmingham, Mich., 1982—. Author: Marketing Processes, 1976, An Evaluation of Alternative Channels of Distribution, 1976; contbr. articles to profl. jours. Mem. Am. Mktg. Assn. (bd. dirs. 1987-88), Am. Collegiate Retailing Assn., Acad. Mktg. Sci., Starkweather Soc., Direct Mktg. Assn. Detroit, Adcraft, Beta Gamma Sigma. Office: U Detroit Mercy Coll PO Box 19900 4001 W Mcnichols Rd Detroit MI 48221-3038

HIGBY, WAYNE (DONALD HIGBY), artist, educator; b. Colorado Springs, Colo., May 12, 1943; s. Donald W. and Betty (Bates) H.; m. Donna Claire Bennett, Mar. 12, 1966; children: Austin Myles, Sarah Lark. BFA, U. Colo., 1966; MFA, U. Mich., 1968. Prof. art N.Y. State Coll. Ceramics, Alfred U., 1973—, chair divsn. ceramic art, 1983—91, Robert C. Turner chair ceramic art, 2005—. Panelist Task Force for Individual Artists N.Y. State Coun. Arts, 1980-82, chair, 1978, mem. visual arts panel, 1976, 77; mem. NEA Visual Artists Fellowship/Crafts, 1986, NEA Visual Arts Overview Panel, 1989-90; hon. prof. Shanghai U., 2000, ceramic art Jingdezhen Ceramic Inst, People's Republic of China, 1994; bd. dirs. Intrnat. Acad. Ceramics. One-man exhbns. include Helen Drutt Gallery, 1988, 90, Mus. of Art and Design, Helsinki, Finland, 1999; invitational exhbns. include 8th and 13th Chunichi Internat. Exhbn. Ceramic Art, Nagoya, Japan, 1980, 85, respectively, Everson Mus. Art, Syracuse, N.Y., 1981, 87, 89, Am. Craft Mus., N.Y.C., 1982, 89, Jacksonville (Fla.) Mus. Art, 1982, Nelson-Atkins Mus. Art, Kansas City, 1983, Boston Mus. Fine Arts, 1984, Victoria and Albert Mus., London, 1986, Seoul Olympics Arts Festival, 1988, Nat. Mus. Ceramic Art, Balt., 1989, Kanazawa, Ishibkawa Pref, Japan, 1991, Nat. Mus. Modern Art, Tokyo, 1992-93, Met. Mus. Art, N.Y.C., 1999; public collections include Met. Mus. Art, N.Y.C., Mpls. Mus. Art, Phila. Mus. Art, Everson Mus. Art, Joslyn Mus. Art, Omaha, Am. Craft Mus., Victoria and Albert Mus., Boston Mus. Fine Arts, Bklyn. Mus. Art, L.A. County Mus. Art. Bd. dirs. Haystack Mountain Sch. Crafts, Deer Isle, Maine, 1983—, pres., 1989-92, chmn., 2000—. Howard Found. fellow, 1985-86, 89-90; recipient Master Tchr. award U. Hartford, 1990, Chancellor's award SUNY, 1993, Disting. Educator award James Renwick Alliance, Master of the Media award, 2005, Hon. of Coun. award Nat. Coun. Edn. in Ceramic Art, 2005; named visionary of Am. craft Am. Craft Mus., 1995, Disting. Educator James Renwick Alliance, 2002, 1st Fgn. Citizen of Jingdezhen People's Republic of China, 2004. Mem. Coll. of Fellows Am. Craft Coun. Office: N Y State Coll Ceramics Alfred U Alfred NY 14802-2207 Office Phone: 607-871-2207. E-mail: higbydwdc@infoblvd.net.

HIGDON, LEE, academic administrator; b. Chgo., 1946; married; 4 children. AB in History, Georgetown U., 1968; MBA in Fin., U. Chgo., 1972. Mgr. divsn. global investment banking Salomon Bros., vice chmn., exec. com., 1973; dean grad. sch. bus. U. Va., Charles C. Abbott chair bus. adminstrn.; pres. Babson Coll., Wellesley, Mass., Coll. Charleston, 2001—. Bd. dirs. Crompton Corp., Eaton Vance Corp., Newmont Mining. Contbr. articles to profl. and popular publs. Mem. Peace Corps., Malawi, South Africa. Office: Randolph Hall 66 George St Charleston SC 29424

HIGDON, PAMELA LEIS, writer; b. San Bernardino, Calif., Sept. 2, 1943; d. Stella Doss and Raymond Ellsworth Leis; m. Sherman Robert Higdon Jr., Aug. 29, 1964 (dec.); 1 child, Mary Katherine Christian. BS in Edn., Tex. Technol. U., Lubbock, 1966. Cert. tchr. Tex., 1966. Elem. sch. tchr., sci. coord. for elem. sch., dist. lang. arts com. mem., after sch. computer instr. Arabian Am. Oil Co., Ras Tanura, Saudi Arabia, 1978—86; editor/writer, Bird Talk Mag. and Birds USA Fancy Publications, Irvine, Calif., 1987—90; writer/editor, product developer, project mgr., acquisitions editor Ednl. Insights, Carson, Calif., 1990—94; freelance writer and editor PLH Writing/Editing, Castroville, Tex., 1994—. Author: (children's educational book) Science Notes: How Things Move; author, editor (pet care book) The Essential Cockatiel, The Essential Zebra Finch; editor: (prehospital medical booklet) The Life You Save: Community Defibrillation Programs & the Emergency Care Responder; author: (monthly newsletter Can. Paramedics) Jour. Emergency Med. Svcs.; editor (monthly periodicals) Journal of Emergency Medical Services, Fire Rescue Magazine, Clarity, EMS Insider, EMS M&S, EMS Best Practices, Caring for the Ages-for Long-Term Care Practitioners; author (with Julie Mancini): (bird watching book) Watching Backyard Birds; author: (children's educational book) Pattern Blocks (math series); author, project manager (computerized educational games) Geosafari & Geosafari Jr., assorted; author (with Katherine Christian): (educational book) Third Grade Review; writer, Nat. Wildlife Fedn. (interactive, wildlife, educational) Insects, Exotic Animals, Sea Life, Wild Animals, Dinosaurs; author (with Dr. David McCluggage): (animal care book) Holistic Care for Birds: A Manual of Wellness and Healing; author: (pet care book) Bird Care and Training, (bird care book) Happy Healthy Pets: The Quaker Parrot; writer, editor (pet care book) The Essential African Grey. Vol. writer of cmty. newsletter Mills Br. Village Bd. Dirs., Kingwood, Tex., 1996—2000; vol. writer, designer, pub. town newsletter Castroville, Tex., 2001—03; exec. bd., rec. sec. Meth. Ch., Castroville, 2003—; chair Landmark Hist. Preservation Commn., 2004—. Recipient Cmty. Svc. award, Mills Br. Village Bd. Dirs., 1997. Mem.: Exec. Bd., Meth. Ch., Castroville, Tex., DAR (life), Daughters of the Republic of Tex. (rec. sec. 2002—). Democrat. Avocations: mentoring children, quilting, reading, swimming, birdwatching.

HIGGINBOTHAM, EDITH ARLEANE, radiologist, researcher; b. New Orleans, Sept. 14, 1946; d. Luther Aldrich and Ruby (Clark) H.; m. Terry Lawrence Andrews (div. 1979); m. Donald Temple Ford (div. 1989). BS, Howard U., 1967, MS, 1970, MD, 1974. Diplomate Am. Bd. Radiology, Am. Bd. Nuclear Medicine. Intern St. Vincent's Hosp., N.Y.C., 1974-75, resident in diagnostic radiology, 1975-78, resident in nuclear radiology, 1978-79; asst. prof. radiology, chief nuclear medicine Howard U., Howard U. Hosp., Washington, 1979-82; assoc. prof. clin. radiology, dir. nuclear medicine U. Medicine and Dentistry N.J., Newark, 1982-90; locum tenens radiologist Sterling Med., Cin., 1991-94, Med. Nat., San Antonio, 1990-91; diagnostic radiologist Diagnostic Health Imaging Systems, Lanham, Md., 1994-95; locum tenens radiologist, 1995-97; radiologist, dir. radiology N.E. Wash. Med. Group, Colville, Wash., 1997—99; radiologist Mount Carmel Hosp., Colville, 1997-99, Barstow (Calif.) Cmty. Hosp., 1999, Queen of Peace Hosp., Mitchell, SD, 1999—2002, New Ulm Med Ctr., Minn., 2002—03, dir. radiology, 2003; radiologist Naeve Hosp., Albert Lea (Minn.) Med. Ctr., Mayo Health Sys., 2003—. Cons. Biotech. Rsch. Inst., Rockville, Md., 1989-94; profl. assoc. Ctr. for Molecular Medicine and Immunology, Newark, 1984-90; asst. prof. radiology George Washington U., Washington, 1990; counselor Am. Coll. Radiology, SD, 2001; presenter in field. Contbr. articles to profl. jours. Named Outstanding Working Woman, Glamour mag., 1981, Hon. Dep. Atty. Gen., State of La., 1982. Mem.: SD Med. Assn. (continuing med. edn. com. 2001), Freeborn County Med. Soc. (pres. 2005), Minn. Med. Assn. (continuing med. edn. com. 2005), Soc. Nuclear Medicine, Radiol. Soc. N.Am., Am. Coll. Radiology, Phi Delta Epsilon, Sigma Xi. Roman Catholic. Avocations: aerobics, reading, music, travel. E-mail: ehigginbothammd@charter.net.

HIGGINBOTHAM, EVE JULIET, ophthalmologist, educator; b. New Orleans, Nov. 4, 1953; d. Luther Aldrich and Ruby Edith (Clark) H.; m. Frank Christopher Williams, June 7, 1986. BSChE, MS in Engring., MIT, 1975; MD, Harvard U., 1979. Intern Pacific Med. Ctr., San Francisco, 1979-80; resident La. State U. Eye Ctr., 1980-83; fellow Mass. Eye and Ear Infirmary, Boston, 1983-85; asst. prof. U. Ill., Chgo., 1985-90; assoc. prof. U. Mich., Ann Arbor, 1990-94; prof., chair dept. ophthalmology U. Md., Balt., 1994—. Co-editor: Management of Difficult Glaucoma, 1994, Clinician's Guide to Comprehensive Ophthalmology, 1998; contbr. articles to profl. jours; mem. editl. bd. Jour. of Glaucoma, 1990-93, Archives of Ophthalmology, 1994—; sect. editor: Glaucoma in Principles and Practice of Ophthalmology. Bd. dirs. Prevent Blindness Am., Schaumburg, Ill., 1990-97, chair publs. com., 1990-95, chair scientific adv. com., 1995—. Fellow Am. Acad. Ophthalmology (trustee 1992-95); mem. Women in Ophthalmology (bd. dirs. 1990-99), Assn. Univ. Profs. Ophthalmology, Assn. in Rsch. in Vision and Ophthalmology, Inst. Medicine, Md. Soc. Eye Physicians and Surgeons (v.p. 1997-99, pres. 2000—), Balt. City Med. Soc. (treas. 1999-00, v.p. 2000—). Avocations: golf, piano. Office: U Md 419 W Redwood St Baltimore MD 21201-1734

HIGGINBOTHAM, JOAN E., astronaut; b. Chgo., Aug. 03; BSEE, So. Ill. U., 1987; M in Mgmt., Fla. Inst. Tech., 1992, M in Space Sys., 1996. Payload elec. engr. divsn. ele. and telecomm. sys. NASA, Kennedy Space Ctr., Fla., 1987, lead orbiter experiments space shuttle Columbia, 1987, exec. staff asst. to dir. shuttle ops. and mgmt., backup orbiter project engr. space shuttle Atlantis, lead orbiter project engr. space shuttle Columbia; astronaut, mission specialist NASA, Johnson Space Ctr., Houston, 1996—. Named Disting. Alumni, Fla. Inst. Tech., 1997, So. Ill. U.; named one of 50 Disting. Scientists and Engrs., Nat. Tech. Assn.; recipient Key to City of Cocoa, Fla., Key to City of Rockledge, Presdl. Sports award in bicycling and weight training, Outstanding Woman of Yr. award, Exceptional Svc. Medal, NASA. Mem.: Links, Inc., Bronze Eagles, Delta Sigma Theta. Avocations: weightlifting, bicycling, music, motivational speaking. Office: Astronaut Office/CB NASA Johnson Space Ctr Houston TX 77058

HIGGINBOTHAM, JOHN TAYLOR, lawyer; b. St. Louis, Feb. 10, 1947; s. Richard Cann and Jocelyn (Taylor) H.; m. Lauren Flint Totty, Aug. 9, 1975 (div. 1979). BA, UCLA, 1969; JD, Columbia U., 1972. Bar: N.Y. 1975, Calif. 1976. Assoc. Kirlin, Campbell & Keating, N.Y.C., 1972-74; atty. Nat. Bank of N.Am., N.Y.C., 1974-76, Bank of Am., 1977; assoc. Barger & Wolen, L.A., 1977-78, Halperin, Shivitz, Scholer, Schneider & Eisenberg, 1978-79; atty., dir. real estate Korvettes, Inc., N.Y.C., 1979-82; assoc. Leon Katz, Bklyn., 1983-84, Finley, Kumble, Wagner, Heine, Underberg, Manley & Casey, N.Y.C., 1984-86; assoc. regional counsel HUD, N.Y.C., 1986-88; assoc. Fink, Weinberger, Fredman, Berman, Lowell & Fensterheim, N.Y.C., 1988—89; atty. First Sterling Capital Resources, Inc., Manhasset, NY, 1989—93; counsel Willkie, Farr & Gallagher, N.Y.C., 1993. Editor: Safe Deposit Decisions and Practice, 1977—. Mem. NARAS, NATAS, Acad. Motion Picture Arts and Scis., League Am. Theatres and Prodrs. Inc.

HIGGINBOTHAM, KENNETH JAMES, finance company executive; b. Phila., Aug. 3, 1942; s. James V. and Elizabeth R. (Roebus) H.; m. Ruth M. Schaffer, Apr. 12, 1969; children: Jennifer K., Scott G. BA, Rutgers U., 1971; MBA, Drexel U., 1973. Cert. sr. advisor. Fin. analyst, discount window Fed. Res. Bank Phila., 1972—77; cons. corp. cash mgmt. First Pa. Bank NA, Phila., 1977—79; cons. EFT Control Data Corp., Mpls., 1979—84; dist. rep. Aid Assn. for Luths., Appleton, Wis., 1984—94; reg. rep. Lincoln Fin. Advisors, Richboro, Pa., 1994—2000; prin. Ind. Retirement Planners LLC, Richboro, 2000—. Adj. faculty LaSalle U., Phila., 1977—. Bd. dirs. Mallard Creek Condominium Assocs. With USN, 1963-67. Mem. AAUP, Fin. Planning Assn., Bucks County Estate Planning Coun. (officer, past pres.), Northampton Twp. Bus. and Profl. Assn. Office: Independent Retirement Planners LLC Mallard Creek Village 130 Almshouse Rd Ste 201 B Richboro PA 18954-1917 Office Phone: 215-357-0911. Personal E-mail: plannerken@aol.com.

HIGGINBOTHAM, PATRICK ERROL, federal judge; b. McCalla, Ala., Dec. 16, 1938; Student, U. Ala., 1956, Arlington State Coll., 1957, North Tex. State U., 1958, U. Tex., 1958; BA, U. Ala., 1960, LLB, 1961; LLD (hon.), So. Meth. U., 1989. Bar: Ala. 1961, Tex. 1962, U.S. Supreme Ct. 1962. Assoc. to ptnr. Coke & Coke, Dallas, 1964—75; judge U.S. Dist. Ct. (no. dist.) Tex., Dallas, 1976—82, U.S. Ct. Appeals (5th cir.), Dallas, 1982—. Adj. prof. So. Meth. U. Law Sch., 1971—, adj. prof. constl. law, 1981—, U. Tex. Sch. Law, 1998; M.D. Anderson pub. svc. prof. in residence Tex. Tech. U. Sch. Law, 1999; John Sparkman jurist-in-residence U. Ala. Sch. Law, 1995, 97, 99; conferee Am. Assembly, 1975, Pound Conf., 1976; bd. suprs. Inst. Civil Justice Rand. Contbr. articles to profl. jours. With JAG USAF, 1961—64. Named Outstanding Alumnus, U. Tex., Arlington, 1978, One of Nation's 100 Most Powerful Persons for the 80's, Next Mag.; recipient Dan Meador award, U. Ala., Samuel E. Gates Litigation award, Am. Coll. Trial Lawyers, 1997, A. Sherman Christensen award, 2002. Fellow: Am. Bar Found.; mem.: ABA, Ctr. for Am. and Internat. Law (bd. dirs. 1998—, chmn.), Am. Inns of Ct. Found. (pres. 1996—2000), Farrah Law Soc., Dallas Inn of Ct., Nat. Jud. Coun. State and Fed. Cts., Am. Judicature Soc., Am. Law Inst., Dallas Bar Found., Dallas Bar Assn., Bench and Bar, Order of Coif (hon.), Omicron Delta Kappa. Office: US Ct Appeals Rm 400 903 San Jacinto Blvd Austin TX 78701

HIGGINBOTHAM, WENDY JACOBSON, legislative staff member, writer; b. Salt Lake City, Oct. 23, 1947; d. Alfred Thurl and Virginia Lorraine (LaCom) Jacobson; m. Keith Higginbotham, July 12, 1969; children: Ann Elizabeth Morley, Ryan Keith, Laura Carol Hoopes. Student, Occidental Coll., 1965—66, U. Grenoble, France, 1967; BA cum laude with highest honors, Brigham Young U., 1969. Tchg. instr. Brigham Young U., Provo, Utah, 1969-70, editor univ. press, 1970-71; freelance editor Camarillo, Calif., 1971-78; freelance newspaper writer Vienna, Va., 1983-85; mem. profl. staff U.S. Senate Labor Com., Washington, 1985-86; exec. asst. U.S. Senator Orrin G. Hatch, Washington, 1986-88, legis. dir., 1988-91, chief of staff/adminstrv. asst., 1991-94, chief policy adviser, 1994-95; polit. adviser, freelance writer Washington, 1996—. Mem. Profl. Rep. Women, Phi Kappa Phi. Republican. Mem. Lds Ch. Avocations: travel, hiking. Home: 2022 Willow Branch Ct Vienna VA 22181-2972

HIGGINBOTTOM, SAMUEL LOGAN, retired air transportation executive; b. North Lawrence, Ohio, Oct. 5, 1921; s. Samuel Bradlaugh and Vera Abbie (Gutchess) H.; m. Fair Steinschneider, Aug. 30, 1947 (dec. May 1997); children: Samuel Logan, Marie Fair, Michele Rowan Maclaren; m. Janaina Dornelles, Aug. 4, 1998. BS in Civil Engring, Columbia, 1943; grad. Advanced Mgmt. Program, Harvard U. Design engr. Parsons, Brinckerhoff, Hogan & McDonald, N.Y.C., 1945-46; v.p. engring., flight, test and inspection Trans World Airlines, Inc., 1946-64; v.p. engring. and maintenance Eastern Air Lines, Inc., 1964-67, v.p. operations group, 1967-69, sr. v.p., 1969, exec. v.p., 1969-70, pres., chief operating officer, 1970-73; chmn., pres., chief exec. officer Rolls-Royce Inc., N.Y.C., 1974-86. Bd. dirs. Heico Corp. Emeritus chmn. bd. trustees Columbia U.; mem. adv. bd. Taub Inst. Capt. USAAF, WWII, ETO. Decorated hon. comdr. Order Brit. Empire; recipient Egleston medal Columbia U. Engring. Sch., 1977 Fellow AIAA; mem. Soc. Automotive Engrs., Conquistadores del Cielo, Wings Club (pres.1980-81), Deering Bay Yacht and Country Club, Tau Beta Pi, Psi Upsilon, Theta Tau. Roman Catholic. Office: 95 Merrick Way Ste 520 Miami FL 33134-5311

HIGGINS, BRIAN, congressman; b. Buffalo, Oct. 6, 1959; m. Mary Jane Hannon; children: John, Maeve. BA, MA, Buffalo State Coll.; MPP, Harvard U. John F. Kennedy Sch. of Govt., 1996. N.Y. state rep., 1998—2004; mem. U.S. Ho. Reps., 109th Congress, 27th Dist. NY, 2005—. Recipient Forty Under Forty award, Bus. First newspaper; scholar Judge John D. Hillary Scholarship award; Inaugural Western N.Y. Harvard Grad. Fellowship, 1995. Democrat. Roman Catholic. Office: 431 Cannon House Office Bldg Washington DC 20515-3227 Office Phone: 202-225-3306.*

HIGGINS, BRIAN ALTON, art gallery owner, artist; b. Brookline, Mass. s. Gerald and Catherine (Walsh) H.; m. Jane Edgington, July 1, 1975; children: Brenda, Belinda, Devon. Ops. mgr. Sta. WMTW-TV, Portland, Maine, 1965-68; v.p., gen. mgr. Sta. WSMW-TV, Worcester, Mass., 1974-84; pres. Brian Edgington Collection Am. Art, 1974—. Pastel exhbns. include Danforth Mus. Art, For Pastels Only, Pastel Soc. Am., Land, Sea, Earth, San Francisco (PSA sanctioned), 1997, Art on Paper, 21st Ann. (Maryland Fedn. of Art), Pastel Painters' Soc. of Cape Cod, Ann. Exhibition Award, Internat. Assn. of Pastel Socs., 1998, Pastel Soc. of the Southwest, 18th Ann., Renaissance in Pastel, Conn. Pastel Soc., 1999, Art of Northeast, 50th Ann. award; shows Lindenberg Gallery, N.Y.C., Gallery 214, Montclair, N.J., 2000, Ann. Exhbn. Conn. Acad. Fine Arts, Slater Mus., 2000, 01, 02, Reading Between the Lines: A National Exhbn., Constn. Sq. Hist. Site, Ky. (Purchase award 2000), 2000, Pastel Painters of Maine, 2000 (The Merit award 2000), Nat. Pastel Exhbn., Impact Artists Gallery, Buffalo, N.Y., 2000 (award 2000), 50th Nat. Exhbn. Contemporary Realism in Art, Acad. Artists Assn., 2000, 2001, 2002, 2003, 2004, 13th Ann. Exhbn. Pastel Soc., Oreg., 2000, Good and Evil, Fredericksburg Ctr. for Creative Arts, Va. Mus. Fine Arts, 2000, 20th Anniversary Miniature Juried Show, Colorado Springs, 2001, Edward Hopper Ctr., N.Y., 2001, Pastel Nat., Wichita, Kans., 2002, Mass Gen. Hosp., 2003, 68th Exhbn., Cooperstown, N.Y. (Grumbacher Gold medal 2003), San Diego (Calif.) Art

Inst., 2004. Chmn. bd. Ctrl. Mass. Symphony Orch., 1979—, Ctrl. Mass. chpt. Am. Heart Assn.; bd. dirs. Ctrl. Mass. chpt. ARC; mem. coun. YMCA, Worcester Art Mus.; past vice-chmn. Maine Project Hope. Recipient numerous civic awards. Mem. Degas Pastel Soc., Pastel Soc. Am., Conn. Acad. Fine Arts, United Pastelists Am., Acad. Artists Assn. Republican. Home: Ridge Rd West Brookfield MA 01585 Office: PO Box 1011 West Brookfield MA 01585-1011 Personal E-mail: brianhiggins@charter.net, jebahiggins@yahoo.net.

HIGGINS, DANIEL B., lawyer; b. Willcox, Ariz., Oct. 14, 1948; BA with distinction, Stanford U., 1973; JD magna cum laude, U. Santa Clara, 1977. Bar: Calif. 1977. Atty. McCutchen, Doyle, Brown & Enersen, San Francisco; ptnr. Paul, Hastings, Janofsky & Walker LLP, San Francisco, mem. policy com., chmn. healthcare practice group. Comment editor: U. Santa Clara Law Rev., 1976-77; contbr. articles to profl. jours. Mem. ABA (mem. healthcare and antitrust sects.), Am. Acad. Healthcare Attys., Nat. Health Lawyers Assn., Healthcare Fin. Mgmt. Assn., Phi Beta Kappa. Office: Paul Hastings Janofsky & Walker LLP 55 Second St Twenty-Fourth Floor San Francisco CA 94105 Office Phone: 415-856-7052. Office Fax: 415-856-7152. Business E-Mail: danhiggins@paulhastings.com.

HIGGINS, E. TORY, psychology professor, research scientist; b. Montreal, Que., Can., Mar. 12, 1946; s. Benjamin H. Higgins and Agnes C. Quamme; m. Robin S. Wells; 1 child, Kayla. PhD, Columbia U., 1972. Prof. psychology NYU, N.Y.C., 1981—89, Columbia U., N.Y.C., 1989—. Chair sci. awards com. APA; co-founder Ontario Symposium on Personality and Social Psychology; assoc. editor Social Cognition; mem. spl. com. on social psychology and aging Nat. Inst. of Aging Task Force; exec. com. Soc. Exptl. Social Psychology; mem. com. on sci. rev. restructuring NIH; mem. basic behavioral sci. task force NIMH; chair dept. psychology Columbia U., 1994—2001. Author over 15 edited books and monographs, over 50 book chpts.; contbr. numerous articles to profl. jours. Named Stanley Schachter Prof. Psychology, Columbia U., 2001, Univ. Lectr., 2001; recipient Donald T. Campbell award, Soc. for Personality and Social Psychology, 1996, Thomas M. Ostrom award for outstanding contbns. to social cognition, Social Cognition Soc., 1999, William James Fellow award, Am. Psychol. Soc., 2000, award for disting. sci. contbns., Am. Psychol. Assn., 2000, MERIT award, NIMH, 1989; fellow, Ctr. for Advanced Study in the Behavioral Scis., 1986. Office: Columbia U 116th St New York NY 10027

HIGGINS, EDWARD ALOYSIUS, retired newspaper editor; b. St. Louis, Aug. 22, 1931; s. Edward Aloysius and Elsie (Gummersbach) H.; m. Mary Suzanne Vallar, May 15, 1954; children— Nancy Elizabeth, David Francis, Carol Marie. AB, St. Louis U., 1953; Stanford Journalism fellow, Stanford U., 1968-69. Gen. assignment reporter St. Louis Post-Dispatch, 1953-67, editorial writer, 1967-84, editor Commentary Page, 1984-87, asst. editor editorial page, 1986-87, editor editorial page, 1987-97; ret., 1997. Home: 15340 Braefield Dr Chesterfield MO 63017-1832 E-mail: edwhiggins@msn.com.

HIGGINS, EDWARD JOSEPH, dean; b. Phila. s. Edward Joseph and Cleta Donahue Higgins. BA, Cath. U. Am., 1996; MEd, Boston Coll., 2004. Solemn vows Order of Friars Minor, Holy Name of Jesus, 1997. Hist. tchr. Paterson Cath. H.S., Paterson, NJ, 1996—2000; tchr., campus min. Cath. Meml. Sch., West Roxbury, Mass., 2000—03; dean of studies Cardinal Hayes H.S., 2003—. Mem.: KC. Roman Catholic. Avocations: music, theater, walking. Office: Cardinal Hayes High Sch 650 Grand Concourse Bronx NY 10451 Business E-Mail: ehiggins@cardinalhayes.org.

HIGGINS, GEORGE EDWARD, sculptor; b. Gaffney, SC, Nov. 13, 1930; BA, U. N.C. Instr. sculpture Parsons Sch. Design, N.Y.C., 1961-62. Vis. prof. Cornell U., 1968, U. Wis., 1968-69, U. Ky., 1969-70, Sch. Visual Arts, N.Y.C., 1964-72 One man shows, Leo Castelli Gallery, N.Y.C., 1960, 63, 66, Richard Feigen Gallery, Chgo., 1964, Mpls. Inst. Art, 1964, exhibited group shows Art, USA, 1959, Detroit Inst. Art, 1959-60, Carnegie Inst., 1961, Mus. Modern Art, N.Y.C., 1961, 63, Martha Jackson Gallery, N.Y.C., 1960, Andrew Dickson White Gallery, 1960, Bernard Gallery, Paris, France, 1960, Whitney Mus., N.Y.C., 1964, 66, Documenta, Kassel, Germany, 1968, Art Inst. Chgo., Brandeis U., Tate Gallery, London, Phila. Mus. Arts, New Sch. Art Center, N.Y.C., Smithsonian Instn., numerous others; represented in permanent collections, Whitney Mus., N.Y.C., Guggenheim Mus., N.Y.C., Albright-Knox Gallery, Buffalo, Houston Mus. Fine Arts, Mus. Modern Art, N.Y.C., Albright Art Gallery, Chase Manhattan Bank, N.Y.C., others. Address: 2655 Henley Rd Sanford NC 27330-7549

HIGGINS, GINA O'CONNELL, psychologist, writer; b. Bklyn. d. Paul Bernard Patrick Joseph and Virginia Payne (Conrad) O'Connell; m. James T. Higgins, Aug. 5, 1972 (div. June 1997); children: Caitlin, Taryn; m. R.D. Norton, June 13, 1998; children: Maya, Elias. BA magna cum laude, Tufts U., 1972, MEd, 1974; EdD, Harvard U., 1985. Lic. psychologist, Mass. Diagnostician, med. edn. and evaluation clinic North Shore Children's Hosp., 1982-87; psychotherapist, intake diagnostician, case cons. Mental Health Ctr., North Shore Children's Hosp., 1982-86; fellow Clin. Devel. Inst., Belmont, Mass., 1990—2002; staff psychologist Mass. Gen. Hosp., Boston, 1993—2001; pvt. practice psychotherapy and psychodiagnosis, Salem, Mass., 1993—2002. Lectr. Middlesex C.C., Bedford, Mass., 1974-75, Eliot Pearson dept. child study Tufts U., 1974-75; lectr. Lesley Grad. Sch., Cambridge, Mass., 1974-76, asst. prof., 1976-81; clin. assoc. Harvard Med. Sch./Mass. Gen. Hosp., Boston, 1994-2002. Author: Resilient Adults: Overcoming a Cruel Past, 1994. Recipient scholarship and fellowships. Mem APA, Mass. Psychol. Assn. Office: One Salem Green Ste 555 Salem MA 01970 Office Phone: 978-741-3459.

HIGGINS, HARRIET PRATT, investment advisor; b. Cortland, N.Y., Dec. 18, 1950; d. Edward Frances and Adeline (Bostelmann) Higgins; children from previous marriage: John Higgins MacDonald, Peter Brewster MacDonald. BA, Wells Coll., 1972; MA, Middlebury Coll. Grad. Sch. Langs., 1973; MBA, Columbia U., 1977. Corp. fin. officer Bank Am., N.Y.C., 1978-80; asst. v.p. J. Henry Schroder Bank and Trust Co., N.Y.C., 1980-82; mgr. Royal Bank Can., N.Y.C., 1982-84, sr. mgr., 1984-94; v.p. pvt. client svcs. TCW Group, N.Y.C., 1994-99; mng. dir. Auda Advisor Assocs. LLC, 1999—2000; mgr., CEO Alyssa LLC, 1999—2000; pres. Mayflower Capital, 2000—04; mng. dir., ptnr. Fin. Net Boston, 2001—04; rep. Winston, Evans & Crocher, Boston, 2001—; investment advisor Smith Barney/Citigroup, N.Y.C., 2005—. Adj. prof. econs. Pace U., N.Y.C., 1979—80, NYU, N.Y.C., 1983—84; chmn., CEO, pres. McGraw, NY, 1987—95; alumni bd. Columbia Bus. Sch., 1982—87; trustee, chair investment com. Wells Coll., 1998—. Trustee Boston Police Found.; mem. Commonwealth of Mass. Ctrl. Artery and Tunnel Commn.; vol., contbr. Rep. Nat. Com., N.Y.C., 1980—; trustee Boys and Girls Club, Newport County, 2000—. Fellow Carnegie Found., 1974—75. Mem.: Fin. Womens Assn., Preservation Soc. Newport County, Newport Hist. Soc., Desc. of the Mayflower Soc. Republican. Episcopalian. Avocations: skiing, tennis, violin. Office: Smith Barney/Citigroup 31 W 52d St 23 Fl New York NY 10019: Easton's View 236 Eustis Ave Newport RI 02840 Office Phone: 212-603-6151. Business E-Mail: harriet.p.higgins@smithbarney.com.

HIGGINS, ISABELLE JEANETTE, retired librarian; b. Evanston, Ill., Dec. 13, 1919; d. Frank LeRoy and Ada Louise (Wilcox) Heck; m. George Alfred Higgins, Jan. 23, 1945 (dec. Sept. 1994); children: Alfred Clinton, Donald Quentin, Heather Higgins Aanes, Laura Higgins Palmer, Carol Higgins. BS, Northwestern U., 1940; MLS, U. Md., 1971. Cert. libr., Md. With Liebermann Waelchli Co., Tokyo, 1940-41, Shanghai Evening Post, 1941-42; editl. asst. Newsweek mag., N.Y.C., 1944; wire editor FBIS/FCC, Washington, 1944-46; rsch. and analysis China desk CIA, Washington, 1946-49; supr. library vols. Westbrook Sch., Bethesda, Md., 1965-69; reference libr. Montgomery County Pub. Librs., Bethesda, 1969-83; libr. Brooks Inst. Photography, Santa Barbara, Calif., 1984-96, ret., 1996. Treas. Friends of Santa Barbara Pub. Libr., 1987-88. Mem. AAUW (bd. dirs. Santa Barbara br. 1988-94, del. nat. conv. 1989), Spl. Librs. Assn., Calif. Libr. Assn., Santa Barbara Little Gardens Club (pres. 1987-89), Floriade Garden Club (pres. 1990-91). Congregationalist. Avocations: reading, swimming, gardening. Home: 3775 Modoc Rd Apt 203 Santa Barbara CA 93105-4467 E-mail: higginsij@aol.com.

HIGGINS, JAMES HENRY, III, marketing executive; b. Providence, May 8, 1940; s. James Henry Jr. and Betty (Hall) H. AB, Brown U., 1962. Mem. faculty Gov. Dummer Acad., Byfield, Mass., 1964-66; rsch. assoc. Entelek Inc., 1966-69; mgr. sch. svc. group Sterling Inst., 1969-72; v.p. Vickerman and Schultz, Inc., Washington, 1985-87; sr. v.p. Complete Comm., Inc., Washington, 1987-90; dir. devel. The Brit. Consortium, Washington, 1990—. Mktg. cons. Time Life Video, NYC, 1972-73, Longman Group Ltd., Eng., 1973-74, McGraw-Hill Publ. Co., NYC, 1975-85. Lectr., contbr. articles to boating publ. Mem. mgmt. com. A.S.K. Brown Mil. Collection, Brown U., 1990-2000; pres. City TavernPreservation Found., 2000. Mem. Am. Soc. Assn. Execs., Naval War Coll. Found. (assoc.), Mystic Seaport Mus. (yachting com. 1986-2000), Antique and Classic Boat Soc. (pres., v.p., bd. dirs. 1978-94), Lake Placid Inst. (bd. dirs. 1996-2001, adv. bd. 2002—), Adirondack Archtl. Heritage (bd. dirs. 2000—), City Tavern Club (bd. govs. 1998-2000, sec. 1998-2000), Agawam Hunt Club, Hope Club, St. Regis Yacht Club. Home: 2807 O St NW Washington DC 20007-3130 Office: 1101 30th St NW Ste 500 Washington DC 20007-3708

HIGGINS, JANE EDGINGTON, secondary school educator; b. London, Eng., Sept. 1, 1955; came to U.S., 1966; d. John Herbert and Dorothy Ann (Bjork) Edgington; m. Brian Alton Higgins, July 1, 1975; 1 child, Devon. BA in Art Edn., Framingham State Coll., 1977; MS in art Edn., Mass. Coll. Art, 1996. Cert. tchr. art K-12, Mass. Registrar Danforth Mus. of Art, Framingham, Mass., 1979-85; dir. dept. art David Prouty H.S., Spencer, Mass., 1987—, audio visual dir., 1997—. Coord. ann. portfolio art shows Spencer Art Shows, 1992-94; dir. Projects Fair and exhbns., 1995—; dir. Summer Arts, Town of West Brookfield, 1996—; set design and prodn. com. Prouty Players, David Prouty H.S., Spencer, Mass., 1987-94, faculty advisor sch. newspaper, 1993-2004, faculty advisor yearbook, 2004—; judge ann. art show Mass. Art Guild, 2004 Illustrator: (cover) The Onyx, 1973, Choomia Contemporary Poetry, 1977, (textbook) The Physically Handicapped Child, 1976. Recipient 1st prize Friends of Marlboro Libr. Ann. Juried Show, 1979. Home: PO Box 1011 West Brookfield MA 01585-1011 Office: David Prouty HS 302 Main St Spencer MA 01562-1841

HIGGINS, JAY F., diversified financial services company executive; b. Gary, Ind., June 25, 1945; s. J. Francis and Veronica (Conroy) H.; m. Gail Marie Joy, Nov. 23, 1979; children: Maura Ellis, Kerry Elizabeth, Erin Leigh, Conor Francis. AB, Princeton U., 1967; MBA, U. Chgo., 1970. With Salomon Bros., N.Y.C., 1970-92, v.p., 1976, gen. ptnr. mergers and acquisitions dept., 1978, head corp. fin. dept., 1986, vice chmn., head global investment banking, 1987-92; mng. ptnr. Cloverleaf Ptnrs., Inc., Greenwich, Conn., 1992—98; chmn. Bengal Partners, LLC, North Palm Beach, Fla., 1998—. With USAR, 1967. Mem. Knights of Malta. Roman Catholic. Office: Bengal Partners LLC 701 US 1 Ste 401 North Palm Beach FL 33408 Home: 2818 Old Cypress North Jupiter FL 33410

HIGGINS, KATHRYN O'LEARY, consulting firm executive; b. Sioux City, Iowa, Oct. 11, 1947; d. Paul C. and Mary Kathryn (Callaghan) O'Leary; widowed; children: Liam James, Kevan Paul. BS, U. Nebr., 1969. Manpower specialist U.S. Dept. Labor, Washington, 1969-78; asst. dir. employment policy White House Domestic Policy, Washington, 1978-81; staff dir. minority U.S. Senate Labor & Human Resources Com., Washington, 1981-86; chief of staff U.S. Representative Sander Levin, Washington, 1986-93, Sec. of Labor Robert Reich, Washington, 1993-95; cabinet sec. White Ho. Cabinet Affairs, Washington, 1995-97, dep. sec. of labor, 1997-99; v.p. pub. policy Nat. Trust for Hist. Preservation, Washington, 1999—2003; pres. TATC Cons. Firm, 2004—. Bd. dirs. Charles Carroll House, Surface Transp. Dept. Policy Project Bd.; cabinet mem. Balt. Basilica; bd. dirs. Londontown Found.; bd. dirs. project children young leaders U. Md. Sch. Pub. Affairs; bd. dirs. Bridges to Peace Ignatian Lay Vol. Corps, Video Action; adv. coun. Historic Annapolis. Democrat. Roman Catholic. Avocations: cooking, antiques, book club. Home: 151 Duke Of Gloucester St Annapolis MD 21401-2504 Office: TATC Consulting 2409 18th St NW Washington DC 20009

HIGGINS, M. EILEEN, management consultant, educator; b. Dayton, Ohio, Apr. 4, 1943; d. Harold Elwood and Esther Marie (Kelly) Benjamin; m. James Edward Higgins (div.); children: Joseph Benjamin, James Timothy; m. Edward William Lavine, Jan. 1, 2002. BA in Psychology, Pa. State U., 1965; MBA, Frostburg State U., 1985; postgrad., U. Md., 2004—. Editl. asst. Signal Mag., Washington, 1965—66; publ. editor Nat. Coun. on Radiation Protection and Measurements, Washington, 1966—67; pvt. practice Montgomery Village, Md., 1967—78; sr. mng. editor Aspen Publ., Rockville, Md., 1978—88; instr. Frostburg (Md.) State U., 1989—. Trainer Georgetown U., Washington, 2000—; cons. in field; deans adv. panel, students adv. bd. U. Md., 2001—03. Editor: Editl. Experts, 1969—78; contbr. articles to profl. jours. Dir. publ. Am. Soc. for Enternal and Parenteral Nutrition, Silver Spring, 1990—91. Mem.: Internat. Acad. Bus. Disciplines, Mgmt., Spirituality and Religion (sec.-treas. 2003—05), Frederich County C. of C. (spkrs. bur.), Am. News Women's Club. Avocations: reading, travel, yoga, hiking. Home: PO Box 383 Libertytown MD 21762 Office: Frostburg State Univ Frostburg MD 21532

HIGGINS, MARGARET ANN, medical/surgical nurse; b. Plattsburgh, NY, Nov. 10, 1949; d. Joseph Alexander and Gertrude Jane (Grogan) Gosselin; m. Richard L. Chellis, Aug. 19, 1971 (div. Nov. 13, 1981); children: Tracey Lynn, Terry Lee; m. Michael F. Higgins, Sept. 27, 1985. LPN, AT&T Ctr., Plattsburgh, 1967; AAS in Nursing, Adirondack C.C., 1969; cert. family support facilitator, U. Vt. Cert. bereavement facilitator Am. Acad. Bereavement. ICU staff nurse Champlain Valley Physician's Hosp. Med. Ctr., Plattsburgh, 1967, oper. rm. staff nurse, 1969—74, St. Luke's Hosp., Denver, 1974—77, Med. Ctr. Hosp. Vt., Burlington, 1977—83; staff nurse, mgr. Profl. Nurses Svc., Winooski, Vt., 1983—. Adv. bd. Traumatic Brain Injury, Vt.; conf. planning com. Parent to Parent Vt. Author: (workbook) These Days of Divorce, 1997. Mem. We Abenaki Elder's Coun., New Eng.; vol. grief councilor CVU HS, Hinesburg, Vt. Democrat. Roman Catholic. Avocations: Native crafts, Native Am. dance and singing, reading, music. Home: 312 Turkey Ln Panton VT 05491 Office: Profl Nurses Svc Inc PO Box 188 96 W Canal St Winooski VT 05404

HIGGINS, MARY CELESTE, lawyer, researcher; b. Chgo., Feb. 9, 1943; d. Maurice James and Helen Marie (Egan) H. AB, St. Mary-of-the-Woods Coll., Ind., 1965; JD, DePaul U., 1970; LLM, John Marshall Law Sch., Chgo., 1976; postgrad., Harvard U., 1981—82, MPA, 1982; MPhil, U. Cambridge (Eng.), 1983. Bar: Ill. 1970, U.S. Dist. Ct. (no. dist.) Ill. 1970. Pvt. practice, Chgo., 1970—72, 1979—80; atty. corp. counsel dept. Continental Bank, Chgo., 1972—76; asst. sec., asst. counsel Marshall Field & Co., Chgo., 1976—79; sr. atty. Mattel, Inc., Hawthorne, Calif., 1980—81; rsch. in revitalization and adjustment U.S. Industries in U.S. and World Mkts., 1981—83; legal cons., 1983—85; Midwest regional officer Legal Svcs. Corp., 1985—87, assoc. dir., 1986, acting dir. office of field svcs., 1986—87, dir., 1987—89, Meridian One Corp., Alexandria, Va., 1990—. Recipient Am. Jurisprudence award, 1966—70. Mem.: Ill. Bar. Assn. Home: 203 Yoakum Pky Apt 508 Alexandria VA 22304-3711 E-mail: mhiggins@meridianone.com.

HIGGINS, MARY ELLEN See HAWKINS, MARY ELLEN HIGGINS

HIGGINS, PAUL ANDREW TWISTINGTON, research scientist; b. Ann Arbor, Mich., Apr. 4, 1971; s. Ian Thomas Twistington and Millicent W Higgins. BS, U. of Mich., 1989—93; MS, Stanford U., 1994—96, PhD, 1999—2004. Rsch. assoc./chemist NIH, Bethesda, Md., 1993—94; rsch. assoc./dir., co2 project field site U. of Mich., 1998—99; rsch. fellow U. of Calif., 2003—; congl. sci. fellow Am. Meteorol. Soc., U. Corp. for Atmospheric Rsch., & AAAS, Washington, 2005—. Grad. Rsch. Environ. fellowship, Dept. of Energy, Global Change Edn. Program, 1999—2003. Mem.: Am. Meteorol. Soc., AAAS, Am. Geophys. Union, Ecol. Soc. of Am. Office: Univ of Calif 151 Hilgard Hall Berkeley CA 94720-3110 Office Phone: 510-717-4088. Personal E-mail: phiggins@globalecology.stanford.edu. E-mail: phiggins@nature.berkeley.edu.

HIGGINS, ROBERT (ROBERT WALTER HIGGINS), career officer, physician; b. Uniontown, Wash., Nov. 9, 1934; s. Nelson Leigh and Abbie Elizabeth (Rowe) H.; m. Barbara Jean Wright, Aug. 19, 1956 (dec. Feb. 2002); m. Judith Ellen Glenn, Nov. 15, 2003; children: Fred, Colleen, Jay. BS in Pharmacy, Wash. State U., 1957; MD, U. Wash., 1965. Pharmacist Wenatchee (Wash.) Thrifty Drugs, 1957-59; owner Higgins Drug Store, Pullman, Wash., 1959-61; intern L.A. County Harbor Gen. Hosp., Torrance, 1965-66; commd. lt. USN, 1966; ships surgeon USS Tutuila, Vietnam, 1966-68; ptnr. Ludwick, Zook & Higgins Family Medicine, Wenatchee, 1968-72; commd. lt. comdr. USN, 1972, advanced through grades to rear adm., 1988; chmn. dept. family medicine Naval Hosp., Charleston, S.C., 1972-78, Camp Pendleton, Calif., 1978-80, Bremerton, Wash., 1980-86, comdg. officer Camp Pendleton, 1986-87; med. officer USMC Washington, 1987-89; dep. surgeon gen. USN, 1989-93. Specialty advisor surgeon gen. USN, Washington, 1973-86. Contbg. author: Behavioral Disorders, 1984, 90; contbr. articles to profl. jours. Scoutmaster Boy Scouts Am., Charleston, 1974-78, Camp Pendleton, 1978-80; trustee Family Health Found. Am., Wash. State U. Found., 1992-98; bd. visitors Wash. State U. Coll. Pharmacy, 1998—, pres., 2002-05. Decorated Disting. Svc. medal, Legion of Merit, Meritorious Svc. medal, Navy Commendation medal; recipient Alumni Achievement award Wash. State. U., 1988, Disting. Alumnus award U. Wash. Sch. Medicine, 1996; bd. regents disting. alumnus award, Wash. State U., 2002. Fellow: Am. Acad. Family Physicians (pres. 1984—85, alt. del. to AMA 1985—91, del. 1992—2000, John G. Walsh award 2001), Philippine Acad. Family Physicians (hon.); mem.: World Orgn. Family Medicine (v.p. 1986—95, pres.-elect 1995—98, pres. 1998—2001), Uniformed Svcs. Acad. Family Physicians (pres. 1974—76), Masons. Avocations: bird watching, fly fishing, model airplanes, stamp collection, jogging. Home and Office: 2303 Highland Dr Anacortes WA 98221-3143 E-mail: rhigginsmd@aol.com.

HIGGINS, ROBERT ARTHUR, electrical engineer, educator, consultant; b. Watertown, SD, Sept. 5, 1924; s. Arthur C. and Nicoline (Huseth) H.; m. Barbara Jeanne Fagerlie, 1958; children— Patricia Suzanne, Daniel Alfred, Steven Robert BEE with honors, U. Minn., 1948; MSEE, U. Wis., 1964; PhDEE, U. Mo., 1969. Registered profl. engr. Engr. Schlumberger Well Survey Corp., Tex., 1948-57; rsch. technologist Mobil Rsch. and Devel. Corp., Tex., 1958-61; rsch. engr. United Aircraft Rsch. Labs., Conn., 1965; staff specialist Remote Sensing Inst., SD, 1969-71; asst. prof. elec. engring. SD State U., 1969-74, assoc. dir. Engring. Expt. Sta., 1973-77, prof. elec. engring., 1974-79; cons. Mankato State U., 1980; prin. engr. Sperry Univac, 1981-85; prof. elec. engring. St. Cloud (Minn.) State U., 1985-95, prof. emeritus, 1995—. Cons. Control Data Corp., 1977-80, Lawrence Livermore Lab., 1971-73, USAF Office Sci. Rsch., Fla., 1976, NCR-Comten, 1988-90, FMC Corp., 1991-92, Ontrack Computer Sys., 1993-98; project dir., cons. NSF, 1973-80, 87-89. Contbr. articles to profl. jours. Bd. dirs. Eden Prairie Bd. Edn., Minn., 1982-85, Nat. Storage Industry Consortium, 1995-98. With CE, AUS, 1943-46. NASA fellow, 1966-68; grantee NSF, 1966, 72, 74, 86, AEC, 1971-73, Office Water Resources Rsch., 1971-74 Mem. IEEE (sr., life), Am. Soc. Engring. Educators, Sigma Xi, Eta Kappa Nu. Home: 11260 Windrow Dr Eden Prairie MN 55344-4055 E-mail: rahiggins@ieee.org.

HIGGINS, ROBERT J., retail entertainment executive; Founder Trans World Entertainment Corp., Albany, N.Y., 1972, pres., CEO, 1995-2000, chmn., CEO, 2000—. Former chmn., bd. mem. exec. com. Albany Med. Ctr. Office: Trans World Entertainment Corp 38 Corporate Cir Albany NY 12203*

HIGGINS, DAME ROSALYN, judge of international court of justice; b. June 2, 1937; d. Lewis Cohen and F. Inberg; m. Terence L. Higgins, 1961; 2 children. Student, Cambridge U., Yale U. Intern Office Legal Affairs UN, 1958; Commonwealth Fund fellow, 1959; vis. fellow Brookings Inst., Washington, 1960; jr. fellow internat. studies L.S.E., 1961-63, vis. fellow, 1974-78; staff specialist internat. law Royal Inst. Internat. Affairs, 1963-74; prof. internat. law U. Kent, Canterbury, England, 1978-81, L.S.E., 1981-95; judge Internat. Ct. Justice, The Hague, Netherlands, 1995—. Mem. com. human rights UN, 1985-95; vis prof. Stanford U., 1975, Yale U., 1977; v.p., Brit. Inst. Internat. Comparative Law, 2002—, Queen's Counsel, 1986—. Author: The Development of International Law through the Political Organs of the United Nations, 1963, Conflict of Interests, 1965, The Administration of the United Kingdom Foreign Policy through the United Nations, 1966, UN Peacekeeping: Documents and Commentary; editor: (with James Fawcett) Law in Movement—Essays in Memory of John McMahon, 1974, Problems & Process, 1994, Terrorism & International Law, 1997; contbr. articles to profl. jours. Mem. Ordre Palmes Academiques. Avocations: sports, cooking. Office: Internat Ct Justice Peace Palace 2517KJ The Hague Netherlands

HIGGINS, ROXANNE SNELLING, educational consultant; b. Ft. Eustis, Va., Aug. 17, 1954; d. William Rodman and Anne Louise (Kurtz) Snelling; m. Robert K. Higgins, June 16, 2001; m. Vincent James Elliott, Oct. 3, 1983 (div.); children: Brian William Elliott, Lauren Elizabeth Elliott. BA, Denison U., 1976; MBA, Syracuse U., 1978. Internat. loan officer First Pa. Bank, Phila., 1978—82; ins. assoc. Ind. Sch. Mgmt., Wilmington, Del., 1982—83, dir. mgmt. insts., 1983—87, cons., exec. dir. consortium, 1984—, v.p., 1986—90, pres., 1990—. Office: Ind Sch Mgmt 1316 N Union St Wilmington DE 19806-2594

HIGGINS, SHAUN BRIAN, beverage company executive; b. Mt. Vernon, N.Y., Jan. 18, 1950; s. Joseph Lincoln and Alma Delores (Horan) H.; m. Lois Jane Anelli, April 7, 1973; children: Emily Jane, Elizabeth Jane. BBA magna cum laude, Pace U., 1972. CPA, N.Y. Sr. auditor Arthur Young & Co., N.Y.C., 1972-76; acctg. mgr. Joyce Beverages Inc., New Rochelle, N.Y., 1976-79, controller, 1979-81, v.p., 1981-84, CFO, 1984-86; v.p., CFO Coca-Cola Bottling Co. NY, sr. v.p., CFO; CFO Coca-Cola Beverages, Ltd., Canada, 1993—95, pres., COO, 1995—98; corp. v.p., European group pres. Coca-Cola Enterprises Inc., 1999—2003, sr. v.p. & chief strategy planning officer Atlanta, 2003—04, exec. v.p., CFO, 2004—05, pres., European Group, 2005—. Mem. Arthur Young Bus. Assn., Am. Inst. CPA's, N.Y. State Soc. CPA's. Clubs: Westchester Country (Harrison, N.Y.). Republican. Roman Catholic. Avocations: golf, squash, jogging, marathon running. Office: Coca-Cola Enterprises Inc 2500 Windy Ridge Pkwy Atlanta GA 30339*

HIGGINS, SISTER THERESE, literature educator, former college president; b. Winthrop, Mass., Sept. 29, 1925; d. James C. and Margaret M. (Lennon) Higgins. AB cum laude, Regis Coll., 1947; MA, Boston Coll., 1959, DHL, 1993; PhD, U. Wis., 1963; DHL, Emmanuel Coll., 1977, Lesley Coll., 1991; postgrad. in lit. and theology, Harvard U., 1965-66; LLD (hon.), Northeastern U., 1982, Bentley Coll., 1992, Regis Coll., 1994. Joined Congregation of Sisters of St. Joseph, Roman Cath. Ch., 1947; asst. prof. English, Regis Coll., Weston, Mass., 1963-65, asst. prof., 1965-67, assoc. prof. English lit., 1968—, pres., 1974-92, also trustee, v.p. devel., 2003—. Book reviewer Boston Globe, 1965—. Trustee Waltham (Mass.) Hosp., 1978—85, Cardinal Spellman Philatelic Mus., 1976—92; mem. Mass. Gov.'s Commn. on Status Women, 1977—79. U. Wis. rsch. grantee Eng. Mem. Nat. Cath. Ednl. Assn., AAUW, MLA, AAUP, Assn. Ind. Colls. and Univs. Mass. (exec. com.), New Eng. Colls. Fund, NEASC (commn.). Office: Regis Coll 235 Wellesley St Weston MA 02493-1505 E-mail: therese.higgins@regiscollege.edu.

HIGGINS, VALERIE JAN, lawyer; BA in History with honors, UCLA, 1978; JD, Glendale U., 1981; diploma, Inst. Internat. & Comparative Law, Paris, 1981; cert., Hague Acad. Internat. Law, The Netherlands, 1985; diploma, Inst. Internat. Law, Dublin, Ireland, 1993; LLM in Govt. Law and Pub. Policy (hon.), U. Pacific, 2003. Bar: Calif. 1982, U.S. Dist. Ct. (ctrl. and no. dists.) Calif. 1982, U.S. Ct. Appeals (9th cir.) 1982. Legal rsch. asst. civil default and law and motion depts. L.A. Mcpl. Ct., 1980—; ptnr., atty. Law Offices of Higgins and Higgins, San Francisco, 1982—. Settlement conf. judge pro tem San Francisco Superior Ct., 1985—, arbitrator, 1985—; arbitrator San Francisco Mcpl. Ct., 1995—; arbitrator Nat. Arbitrator Forum, 1999—; adj. prof. U. Pacific, 2003—; mediator in field. Mem. State Bar Calif., PEO Sisterhood. Avocations: equestrienne, music, writing. Office: Law Offices of Higgins and Higgins 700 Larkspur Landing Cir Ste 199 Larkspur CA 94939

HIGGINS, WALTER M., III, electric power industry executive; b. 1945; BS in Nuclear Sci., U.S. Naval Acad., 1966; student, U.S. Nuclear Power Tng. Program, 1966-68, U. Idaho, 1979; MBA, George Washington U., 1975-77. Commd. USN, 1966, advanced through grades; nuclear engr. Charleston Navy Shipyard, until 1974; sr. nuclear engr. Bechtel Power Corp., Washington, 1975; with U.S. Nuclear Regulatory Commn., Washington, 1975-77; various mgmt. and exec. positions Portland (Oreg.) Gen. Electric Co., 1977-91; pres., COO Louisville Gas and Electric Co., 1991—93; chmn., pres. CEO Sierra Pacific, 1993—98, AGL Resources Inc., Atlanta, 1998—2000, Sierra Pacific Resources, Reno, 2000—. Office: Sierra Pacific Resources 6100 Neil Rd Reno NV 89511

HIGGINS, WILLIAM WOODS, painter, art educator; b. St. Paul, Feb. 19, 1947; s. John Russell-William Higgins and Helen Catherine Woods; children: Alexander, Catherine. MA, U. Toledo, 1971. Painter, 1972—; lectr. art, theology, and philosophy Geologengasse, Vienna, 1987—. Exhibits include Longboat Key (Fla.) Art Ctr., 1973, 75, Sarasota (Fla.) Art Ctr., 1977, 79, Whitney Mus., N.Y.C., 1979, Coconut Grove (Fla.) Art Festival, 1987, 88, 89, 92, Coconut Grove Playhouse, 1988, Spoleto Festival, Charleston, S.C., 1991, 92, 97, 98, XIII Internat. Congress of Vedanta, Oxford, Ohio, 2002. Avocations: swimming, chess, writing screenplays. Office: Geologengasse 8/6 A-1030 Vienna Austria Personal E-mail: utchateye@lowcountry.com.

HIGGINSON, CARLA JEAN, lawyer; b. Snoqualmie, Wash., Jan. 27, 1955; d. William Hollis and Jean Marie (Landahl) H.; m. Jack (A. John) Wuebker, Feb. 14, 1987; 1 stepchild, Cody Wuebker. BA cum laude, Western Wash. U., 1976; JD, U. Wash., 1979. Bar: Wash. 1980, U.S. Dist. Ct. (we. dist.) Wash. 1980, U.S. Supreme Ct. 1987. Assoc. Gaddis & Fox, Seattle, 1979, Francis, Lopez & Ackerman, Seattle, 1980-81; pvt. practice Friday Harbor, Wash., 1980—. Judge Town of Friday Harbor, 1981-89. Mem. ABA, San Juan County Bar Assn., Wash. State Bar Assn.

HIGGINSON, JOHN, retired career officer; b. St. Louis, Oct. 24, 1932; s. John and Clara Elizabeth (Lindemann) H.; married; children: Robert, Mark, Patrick, Paul. BA, St. Mary's U., 1954; BS, Naval Postgrad. Sch., 1966; MS, George Washington U., 1968. Ensign USN, advanced through grades to Rear Adm., ret.; comdr. Helicopter Anti-submarine Squadron 2, 1973-74, Helicopter Anti-submarine Squadron 10, 1976-78, USS Inchon, 1979-80, Amphibious Squadron 7, 1981-83, Amphibious Group 3, 1985, Naval Surface Group, Long Beach, 1986, ret., 1990-92; pres. Long Beach C. of C. Prof. mgmt. Naval War Coll., Newport, R.I. Co-author: Sea and Air, The Marine Environment, 1968, 2nd. edit., 1973. Bd. dirs. United Way, LA, Long Beach Symphony, Long Beach Youth Activities, DARE, Inc., Leadership Long Beach, St. Mary's Med. Ctr.; trustee Long Beach City Coll. Found.; dir. Internat. City Theater, Arts Coun. for Long Beach; exec. bd. Long Beach coun. Boy Scouts of Am.; trustee The Pacific; exec. coun. Industry-Edn. Coun. Calif.; former chmn. LA Combined Fed. Campaign; pres., CEO Am. Gold Star Manor Charitable Trust, 1993-. Mem. Navy Helicopter Assn. (former pres.), Fed. Exec. Bd. (former chmn.), Rotary (commr. Calif., mem. Vets. Meml. Commn.). Home: 5341 Las Lomas Park Estates Long Beach CA 90815 Office Phone: 562-426-7654. Business E-Mail: jhigginson@mpicomputers.com.

HIGGISON, PEYTON, artist; b. N.Y.C., Mar. 6, 1955; s. Peyton and Merle (Izard) Higgison; m. Chake Kavookjian; children: Hunter, Skyler. BFA, Maine Coll. Art, 1979. New Eng. dir. Telemark. Exhibited in group shows at Greenhut Galleries, 1981 (Best in Show award, 1981), Allentown Arts Festival (Best in Show award, 1987, 1989); music CDs include Out of Time But Still in Step, 1993, Snippits, 2003. Home: 613 River Rd Brunswick ME 04011-7117

HIGGS, CRAIG DEWITT, lawyer; b. Coronado, Calif., Mar. 19, 1944; s. DeWitt Alexander and Florence (Fuller) Higgs; m. Cynthia Aaron, May 19, 1993; children: Marisa DeWitt, Alexander Craig. BS, U. Redlands, 1966; JD, U. San Diego, 1969. Bar: Calif. 1971, U.S. Dist. Ct. (so. dist.) Calif. 1971. Dep. city atty. San Diego, 1970—71; assoc. Higgs, Fletcher & Mack, San Diego, 1971—76, ptnr., 1976—. Del. 9th Cir. Jud. Conf., 1992—94; dir. San Diego Law Ctr., 1983—89. Bd. visitors U. San Diego Sch. Law, 1983—. Fellow: Am. Coll. Civil Trial Mediators, Internat. Acad. Mediators; mem.: San Diego County Bar Assn. (pres. 1984), State Bar Calif. (chmn. commn. on jud. nominees evaluation 1981), San Diego Inn of Cts. (pres. 1993), Am. Bd. Trial Advocates (pres. 1955), San Diego Bar Found. (bd. dirs. 1983—89). Democrat. Home: 12686 Crest Knolls Ct San Diego CA 92130-2411 Office: Higgs Fletcher & Mack 401 W A St Ste 2600 San Diego CA 92101-7913

HIGGS, JOHN H., lawyer; b. Balt., Mar. 10, 1934; s. E. Homer and Josephine (Doughty) H.; m. Helen Platt, Aug. 25, 1956; children: Sarah, Anne, Julia, Susan. AB, Dartmouth Coll., 1956; LLB, U. Pa., 1960. Bar: N.Y. 1961. Founder Higgs Pavements Co., Milford, Conn., 1953-56; assoc. Sullivan & Cromwell, N.Y.C., 1960-61, 62-68, Wickes, Riddell, Bloomer, Jacobi & McGuire, N.Y.C., 1968, ptnr., 1969-79, Morgan, Lewis & Bockius, LLP, N.Y.C., 1979-97, ret.; ptnr. Skyport Indsl. Park, Newark, N.J. Sec. Ea. States Bankcard Assn., Lake Success, N.Y., 1970-88; bd. dirs. Indsl. Bank Japan Trust Co. (now Mizuho Corp.), N.Y., 1974—, Mizuho Found. Inc., N.Y., 1989—; mem. staff adv. com. on comml. bank supervision State N.Y., 1965-66. Contbr. articles to profl. jours. Mayor Village of Pelham Manor, N.Y., 1979-81. Home: John's Island 45 Wax Myrtle Way Vero Beach FL 32963-3721

HIGH, DAVID ROYCE, lawyer; b. Oklahoma City, Aug. 28, 1950; s. Jack Eugene and Harriett Ann High; m. Charlotte Anne Bonsteel, Dec. 28, 1975; 1 child, Katie McKenzie. BA, U. Okla., 1973; JD, Oklahoma City U., 1978. Bar: Okla. 1978, U.S. Dist. Ct. (we. dist.) Okla. 1978, U.S. Ct. Appeals (10th cir.) 1990. Assoc. Tomerlin & High, Oklahoma City, 1978-80; ptnr. Tomerlin, High & High, Oklahoma City, 1980-92, pvt. practice law, 1992—. Legal counsel The Children's Ctr., Bethany, Okla., 1978—, Oklahoma City Beautiful Inc., 1982-89. Mem. ABA, Okla. Bar Assn. (gov. 1988-91), Oklahoma County Bar Assn. (bd. dirs. 1981-91, v.p. 1984-85, Outstanding Oklahoma County Young Lawyer award 1981). Avocation: tennis. Office: Tomerlin High & High 3601 N Classen Blvd Ste 203 Oklahoma City OK 73118-3269

HIGH, S. DALE, construction executive; b. Lancaster, Pa., May 2, 1942; s. Sanford H. and Erma (Denlinger) H.; m. Sadie S. Horst; children from previous marriage: Steven D., Gregory A., Suzanne M. BSBA, Elizabethtown Coll., 1963, LDH (hon.), 1993; LDH (hon.), Thaddeus Stevens Coll. Tech., 2002. Exec. v.p. High Steel Structures, Inc., Lancaster, 1963-77; ptnr. High Properties, Lancaster, 1963—; chmn., pres. High Industries, Inc., Lancaster, 1977—. Bd. dirs. High Investors, Ltd., Lancaster, High Food Svcs., Ltd., Lancaster, High Hotels Ltd., Lancaster, Pa. Chamber, Inc., 1995—, Penn Sq. Gen. Corp., chmn.; chmn. bd. dirs. Sageworth Holdings, Inc., 2000—; mem. panel of judges Ctrl. Pa. Entrepreneur of the Yr. Award Program, 1994—95, chmn., 1996; bd. dirs. Educators Mutal Life Ins. Co., 1979—2002. Trustee The High Found., Lancaster, 1980—, Elizabethtown Coll., Pa., 1974—99, Lancaster Gen. Hosp., 1976—84, Lancaster County Cmty. Found., 1985—, chmn., 2004—; judge Ea./Ctrl. Pa. Entrepreneur of Yr. Program, 2004; mem. coun. Pa. Soc.; mem. Pa. State Rep. com., Harrisburg, 1985; co-chmn. fin. Lancaster County Rep. Com., 1985—88; chmn. Pa. Chamber PAC, 2002; mem. adv. com. Friends of Better Govt. PAC, 2000—, chmn., 2000—02; bd. dirs. United Way Lancaster County, 1975—78, Lancaster County Rev. Commn., 1984—86, Pa. Chamber of Bus. and Industry, Harrisburg, 1991—, vice-chair, 2000—02, chmn., 2003—04; bd. dirs. Modern Transit Partnership, 1998—2002, Team Pa. Found., 2003—. Named Outstanding Young Man, Lancaster Jaycees, 1977, Disting. Pennsylvanian, Phila. C. of C., 1981; recipient Exemplar award Lancaster C. of C. and Industry, 1995, Disting. Bus. Alumni award Elizabethtown Coll., 1995, Jr. Achievement Spirit Achievement award, 1997, Pa. Dutch Coun./BSA Disting. Citizen award, 1999; named Ctrl. Pa. Master Entrepreneur of Yr. Ernst & Young, 1999, Pa. Chamber of Bus. and Industry Outstanding Bus. Leader, 1999, Nat. Entrepreneur of Yr., Real Estate, Ernst and Young, 1999, Centennial medal Elizabethtown Coll., 2000, Cmty. Svc. award Lancaster Rotary Club, 2000, Educate for Svc. award Elizabethtown Coll., 2000, Bus. Achievement award West Shore C. of C., 2001, Family Bus. of Yr. award Wharton Enterprising Families Initiative, 2002, Disting. Alumni award Lampeter Strasburg Sch. Dist., 2003. Mem. World Pres.'s Orgn., Lancaster C. of C. (bd. dirs. 1976-82, chmn. 1981), Newcomen Soc. U.S., Hamilton Club, Lancaster Country Club Republican. Presbyterian. Avocations: reading, bicycling, hiking, travel. Office: High Industries Inc PO Box 10008 1853 William Penn Way Lancaster PA 17601-6713

HIGH, TIMOTHY GRIFFIN, artist, educator, curator, writer; b. Memphis, Tenn., Mar. 10, 1949; s. Warren Barrett and Jo Ellen (Wise) H.; m. Cynthia Spikes, Aug. 10, 1973. BFA, Tex. Tech U., 1973, MA, 1975; MFA, U. Wis., 1976. Assoc. prof. U. Tex., Austin, 1976—. Visual artist drawings, serigraphs, papermaking, monoprints, monotypes, water-media painting, installation and papier maché sculpture; free-lance writer. Over 225 solo, invitational and gallery group shows since 1976, including Amarillo (Tex.) Art Mus., 1993, Martin-Rathburn Gallery, San Antonio, 1997, Tarrytown Gallery, Austin, 2001, Gallery W, Sacramento, 2002, U. Gallery, La. State U., Baton Rouge, 2005; group exhbns. include Adair Margo Gallery, El Paso, Tex., 1996, 177th Ann. Exhbn. of NAD, Mus. Visual Art, N.Y.C., 2002; represented in permanent collections including Art Inst. Chgo., Bklyn. Mus., Mus. Fine Art, Boston, Met. Mus. Art, N.Y.C., Fogg Mus., Cambridge, Mass., Mus. Fine Art, Houston, Milw. Mus. Art; curator group invitational exhbns., Tex. Prints, 2001, Tex. Xpress-I, 2001, Border Crossings, 2001, Three Aces, 2002, Bread Upon the Water, 2003, Contemporary Am. Serigraphs, 2004—. Travel fellow Ford Found., Peruvian Andes, 1978; individual artist fellow Nat. Endowment Arts, 1989. Mem. So. Graphics Coun. (conf. coord. 1989, 2001, nominating com. 2005—), Mid-Am. Coll. Art Assn. (1998 conf. spkr.), Nat. Assn. Scholars (panelist conv. 1993), Tex. Fine Arts Assn., Christians in Visual Art, CIVA Printmakers Network (chair 2003). Avocations: travel, photography, backpacking, fly fishing, reading. Address: care/Terra Rosa Studio 2308 Lawnmont Ave Austin TX 78756-1915 Office: Univ of Tex Austin Dept Art & Art History Austin TX 78712 Office Phone: 512-467-2123.

HIGHAM, CHARLES, author; b. London, Feb. 18, 1931; came to U.S., 1971; s. Charles Frederick and Josephine (Webb) H. Educated English pub. schs. Book columnist Sydney (Australia) Morning Herald, 1958-62; poet, critic, biographer, historian, playwright, 1958—; entertainment and lit. editor The Bulletin, Sydney, 1963-68; Regents prof. Commonwealth lit. U. Calif., Santa Cruz, 1970; feature writer N.Y. Times, Hollywood, Calif., 1971-81. Cons. Simon Wiesenthal Ctr. of Holocaust Studies, 1985—. Author: (poetry) A Distant Star, Spring and Death, The Earthbound, Noonday Country, The Voyage to Brindisi, (true-crime) Murder in Hollywood: Solving a Silent Screen Mystery, 2004; (biographies) Cecil B. DeMille, Ziegfeld, Ava, Kate: The Life of Katharine Hepburn, Charles Laughton: An Intimate Biography, The Adventures of Conan Doyle, Marlene: The Life of Marlene Dietrich, Errol Flynn: The Untold Story, Bette: The Life of Bette Davis, The Romantic Life of Merle Oberon, The Duchess of Windsor: The Secret Life, Audrey: The Life of Audrey Hepburn, Orson Welles, Brando: The Unauthorized Biography, (with Roy Moseley) Princess Merle, Elizabeth and Philip, Howard Hughes, Rose (Kennedy), (politics) Trading With the Enemy, American Swastika, (film history) The Art of the American Film, (with Joel Greenberg) Hollywood in the Forties, The Celluloid Muse, (anthology) Penguin Australian Writing Today, (collections) Celebrity Circus: Interviews for the New York Times, (novel) The Midnight Tree, (criticism) The Films of Orson Welles, (plays) His Majestry Jr. Kean, Murder by Moonlight, (adaptation) The Moon and Sixpence, Vicious Circle, others; contbr. articles to various profl. jours., mags. and newspapers. Recipient Jr. Poetry prize Poetry Soc. of London, 1952, Sydney Morning Herald Verse prize, 1956, Prix des Créateurs, Academie Francaise, 1976. Mem. Dramatists Guild, Pan Am. Theatrical Assn. (Cesar award 1988). Address: care Jay Harris 909 3rd Ave New York NY 10022-4731

HIGHAM, ROBIN, historian, editor, publisher; b. London, June 20, 1925; came to U.S., 1940, naturalized, 1954; s. David and Margaret Anne (Stewart) H.; m. Barbara Davies, Aug. 5, 1950; children: Peter (dec.), Susan Elizabeth (dec.), Martha Anne, Carol Lee. AB cum laude, Harvard U., 1950, PhD, 1957; MA, Claremont Grad. Sch., 1953. Instr. Webb Sch. Calif., 1950-52; grad. asst. in oceanic history Harvard U., 1952-54; instr. U. Mass., 1954-57; asst. prof. U. N.C., Chapel Hill, 1957-63; assoc. prof. history Kans. State U., 1963-66, prof., 1966—79; historian Brit. Overseas Airways Corp., 1960-66, 76-78; editor Mil. Affairs, 1968-88, emeritus; editor Aerospace Historian, 1970-88, emeritus, 1989—; editor, pub. Jour. of the West, 1977—2004; adv. editor Tech. and Culture, 1967-85; founder, pres. Sunflower Univ. Press, 1977—2004; mil. adv. editor Univ. Press Ky., 1970-75. Cons. Epic of Flight, Time/Life Books, 1980-82; lectr. in field; mem. publs. com. Conf. Brit. Studies, 1965-93; advisor Core Collection for Coll. Librs., 1971-72; pres., cons. com. Revue Internat. d'Histoire Militaire, 1976-85, mem. mil. archives com., 1990—, acting pres., 1996-2000, sec. gen., 2002-2003; founder, organizer Conf. Historic Aviation Writers, 1982-98. Author: Britain's Imperial Air Routes, 1918-39, 1960, The British Rigid Airship, 1908-31, 1961, Armed Forces in Peacetime: Britain 1918-39, 1963, The Military Intellectuals in Britain: 1918-1939, 1966, (with David H. Zook) A Short History of Warfare, 1966, Hebrew edit., 1970, Chinese edit., 1985, The Compleat Academic (Macmillan Book Club choice), 1975, Air Power: A Concise History (selection Mil. Book Soc., History Book Club, Flying Book Club), 1973, 2d enlarged edit., 1984, 3d enlarged edit., 1988, The Bases of Air Strategy, 1998, (with Mary Cisper & Guy Dresser) A Brief Guide to Scholarly Editing, 1982, Diary of a Disaster: British Aid to Greece, 1940-41, 1986; editor: Bayonets in the Streets, 1969, 89, Civil Wars in the Twentieth Century, 1972, A Guide to the Sources of British Military History, 1971, A Guide to the Sources of U.S. Military History, 1975, (with Donald J. Mrozek) supplements, 1981, 86, 93, 99 (with Carol Brandt) The U.S. Army in Peacetime: Essays in Honor of the Bicentennial, 1975, Intervention or Abstention, 1975, (with Jacob W. Kipp) Soviet Aviation and Air Power, 1977, Garland Military History Bibliographic Series (with Jacob W. Kipp), 1978-92, Flying Combat Aircraft (with A. T. Siddall) vol. 1, 1975, (with Carol Williams) vol. 2, 1978 and vol. 3, 1981; editor (with George E. Ham) The Rise of the Wheat State: a History of Kansas Agriculture, 1861-1986, 87, (with Thanos Veremis) The Metaxas Dictatorship: Aspects of Greece, 1936-1940. (with John T. Greenwood and Von Hardesty) Russian Aviation & Air Power, 1998, A Handbook of Air Ministry Organization, 1998; ed. Writing Official Military History, 1999, Official Military History, 2 vols., 2000, The Bases of Air Strategy, 2000, (with Frederick W. Kagan) A Military History of Russia, A Military History of the Soviet Union, 2002, (with David A. Graff) A Military History of China, 2002, Research on World War I: A Handbook, 2003, 100 Years of Air Power and Aviation, 2003, Flying American Combat Aircraft of World War I, 2004, II, 2005; sr. advisor on Ency. of U.S. Mil. History, Acad. Mil. Scis., Beijing, 1988—; advisory editor Ency. of USAF, 1988-92; mem. aviation editl. adv. bd. Smithsonian Instn. Press, 1989-92; adv. Greenwood Press, 1992—; mem. editl. bd. Defence Analysis, 1984—; cons., contbr.: Dictionary of Business Biography, 1980-86, Encyclopedia of the American Military, 1994; contbr. Oxford, 1994-2002; contbr. articles to profl. jours. Trustee U.S. Commn. on Mil. History, 1993-2000; mem. Kans. State Aviation Adv. Com., 1986-95, sec., 1992-95. Vol. res. RAF. Named Disting. Grad., Faculty Kans. State U., 1971; recipient Victor Gondos award Am. Mil. Inst., 1983, Samuel Eliot Morison award for disting. scholarship Am. Mil. Inst., 1986, Stamey Tchg. award, 1996, Aviation Honors award Gov. Kans., 2000; Social Sci. Rsch. Coun. nat. security policy rsch. fellow, 1960-61. Mem. AIAA (standing com. history 1973—), Soc. History Tech., Am. Aviation Hist. Soc., RAF Hist. Soc., Friends of RAF Mus. (life), Burma Star Assn. (life), Air Force Hist. Found. (trustee 1984-98), Soc. Army Hist. Rsch. (corr. mem. coun. 1980-98), Am. Mil. Inst., WWII Studies Assn. (dir. 1973-75, 79-82, 83-2001, archivist 1977-2003), Am. Aviation Hist. Soc., Am. Air Mus. in Britain (founding), Nat. D-Day Mus (charter mem.), U.S. Commn. on Mil. History, Riley County Hist. Soc. (past dir., chmn. long-range planning com. 1980-97).Hist. Book Club, 2003 Home: 2961 Nevada St Manhattan KS 66502-2355 E-mail: marolync@flinthills.com.

HIGHAM, SCOTT, reporter; BA in History, SUNY Stony Brook; M in Journalism, Columbia U. Reporter Allentown Morning Call, Miami Herald, Balt. Sun, Washington Post, 2000—. Recipient Pulitzer prize for investigative reporting, 2002. Office: Washington Post 1150 15th St NW Washington DC 20071 Office Phone: 202-334-7947.

HIGHBY, DENNIS, retail executive; With Cabela's Inc., Sidney, Nebr., 1976—, v.p., 1996—2003, pres., CEO, 2003—. Bd. dirs. Cabela's Inc., 2003—. Office: Cabela's Inc One Cabela Dr Sidney NE 69160

HIGHET, MAC, travel company executive; Exec. v.p. fin. & ops. Reed Travel Group, Secaucus, N.J., 1998; exec. v.p. corp. devel. Reed Elsevier, N.Y.C., 1996-98; pres., COO RezSolutions, 1998-99, CEO, 1999—2000. Office: Pegasus Solutions #100 14000 N Pima Rd Scottsdale AZ 85260-3603

HIGHFILL, PHILIP HENRY, JR., retired language educator; b. Petersburg, Va., Aug. 12, 1918; s. Philip Henry and Grace (Jones) H.; m. Annabelle Hollowell (Molly), 1943; children: Mary Hollowell, Philip Henry III. BA, Wake Forest Coll., 1942; postgrad., Middlebury Coll., 1946; MA, U. N.C., 1948, PhD, 1950. Reporter Daily Advance, Elizabeth City, N.C., 1942, 46, Shreveport (La.) Times, 1942; instr. U. Rochester, N.Y., 1950-53, asst. prof., 1953-55; assoc. prof. George Washington U., Washington, 1955-61, prof., 1961-89, prof. emeritus, 1989. Cons. lit. Folger Shakespeare Library, Washington, 1964-68. Co-author: (with Kalman A. Burnim and Edward A. Langhans) A Biographical Dictionary of Actors, Actresses, Musicians, Dancers, Managers and Other Stage Personnel in London, 1660-1800, 16 vols., 1973-93; (with George Winchester Stone) In Search of Restoration and 18th-Century Theatrical Biography, 1976, (with Kalman A. Burnim) John Bell, Patron of Theatrical Portraiture, 1998; editor: Shakespeare's Craft, 1982; contbr. numerous articles and revs. to scholarly jours. With U.S. Army, 1942—46. Grantee Huntington Library, 1959, NEH, 1967-68, 70-71, 74-76, 84-87; fellow John Simon Guggenheim Found., 1959-60, Folger Shakespeare Library, 1968, Theodore Stewart fellow Nat. Library Scotland, 1975; fellow Washington Evening Star, 1963; recipient George Freedley award Theatre Library Assn., 1980. Mem. MLA, South Atlantic MLA, Soc. for Theatre Rsch. (Eng.), Am. Soc. Theatre Rsch. (spl. award 1994), Am. Soc. for 18th Century Studies, Am. Handel Soc. (bd. dirs. 1986-93), Lit. Soc. Washington (v.p. 1991, pres. 1992-93), Wafflers Club, Cosmos Club (v.p. 1979, pres. 1980, bd. dirs. 1976-81) Avocations: travel, music, cooking. Home: 5105 Westpath Ct Bethesda MD 20816-2319

HIGHLANDER, RICHARD WILLIAM, communications executive; b. Beckley, W.Va., Feb. 17, 1940; s. Ronald William and Lucille Bernice (Bland) Highlander; m. Ida Mae Canterbury, June 26, 1965; 1 child, Alison Renee. BA, Rutgers U., 1963; MA, U. Ga., 1972. Commd. 2d lt. U.S. Army, 1963, advanced through grades to lt. col., 1979, ret., 1984; dir. communications, def. systems group FMC Corp., Santa Clara, Calif., 1984-94; v.p. comm. United Def. LP, San Jose, Calif., 1994-99; dir. pub. rels. Calpine, San Jose, 1999—2003, v.p., 2003. Contbr. articles to profl. jours. Trustee San Jose Repertory Co., 1985, pres. bd. trustees, 1998—2005. Decorated Legion of Merit with bronze oak leaf cluster, Bronze Star with two bronze oak leaf clusters, Purple Heart; recipient Rex Harlow award for Lifetime Achievement in Pub. Rels., Arthur W. Page Soc., Freedom Found. award, 1966, 1981. Mem.: PRSA (accredited), Calif. Mfrs. Assn. (bd. dirs. 1985, chmn. bd. dirs. 1993), Internat. Assn. Bus. Communicators, San Jose Met. C. of C. (bd. dirs. 1989—95), Rotary, Chi Psi. Republican. Methodist. Avocations: racquetball, golf. Home: 5906 Gleneagles Cir San Jose CA 95138-2370

HIGHLEN, LARRY WADE, music educator, piano rebuilder, tuner; b. Warren, Ind., Oct. 31, 1936; s. Lawrence Wade and Anna Belle (Dungan) H.; m. Camille Pence (div. 1975); children: Laurel, Wade, Jennifer, Tanna. Student, Niles Bryant Coll., 1967, Ivy Tech. Coll., Kokomo, Ind., 1975-76, Ivy Tech. Coll., Ft. Wayne, Ind., 1983-84. Pvt. piano tchr., Kokomo, 1967-85; piano tchr. Barbara Martin Piano Svc., Indpls., 1985-88, 1990—, Van Wezel Performing Arts Hall, Sarasota, Fla., 1988-90. Author: Piano Abstract, 1981. Fellow Ancient and Mystical Order Rosae Crucis. Avocation: building experimental musical instruments. Home and Office: 1912 W Defenbaugh St Kokomo IN 46902-6032 Office Phone: 765-452-3103.

HIGHSMITH, SHELBY, federal judge; b. Jacksonville, Fla., Jan. 31, 1929; s. Isaac Shelby and Edna Mae (Phillips) H.; m. Mary Jane Zimmerman, Nov. 25, 1972; children: Holly Law, Shelby. AA, Ga. Mil. Coll., 1948; BA, JD, U. Kansas City, 1958. Bar: Fla. 1958. Trial atty., Kansas City, Mo., 1958-59, Miami, Fla., 1959-70; circuit judge Dade County, Fla., 1970-75; sr. ptnr. Highsmith, Strauss, Glatzer & Deutsch, P.A., Miami, 1975-91; judge U.S. Dist. Ct. (so. dist.) Fla., Miami, 1991—. Chief legal adviser Gov.'s War on Crime Program, 1967-68; spl. counsel Fla. Racing Commn., 1969-70; mem. Inter-Agy. Law Enforcement Planning Coun. Fla., 1969-70. Served to capt. AUS, 1949-55. Decorated Bronze Star; recipient Outstanding Alumni Achievement Law award, U. Mo., 1998, Korean War Svc. medal, Pres. South Korea on 50th Anniversary of Korean War, Disting. Alumnus award, Ga. Mil. Coll., 2002. Fellow Internat. Soc. Barristers; mem. ABA, Dade County Bar Assn., Bench and Robe, Torch and Scroll, Miccosukee Golf and Country Club, Wildcat Cliffs Country Club, (Highlands, N.C.), Omicron Delta, Phi Alpha Delta. Republican. Roman Catholic. Office: Fed Justice Bldg 99 NE 4th St Rm 1027 Miami FL 33132-2138 Office Phone: 305-523-5170. Business E-Mail: shelby_highsmith@flsd.uscourts.gov.

HIGHSTEIN, JENE ABEL, sculptor; b. Balt., June 16, 1942; s. Gustav and Ada Abel Highstein; m. Alanna Heiss (div.); 1 child, Lokke Abel; m. Katharine Duane; children: Alex, Jesse. BA, U. Md., 1963; postgrad., U. Chgo., 1963—65, NY Studio Sch., 1966, Royal Acad. Sch., London, 1967—70. Vis. artist Emily Carr Coll. Art, Vancouver, B.C., Can., 1979, Tyler Sch. Art, Phila., 1990, RI Sch. Design, Providence, 1991, Vt. Studio Ctr., Johnsonville, Vt., 1993, Brandeis U., Waltham, 1995; instr. Sch. Visual Arts, NY, 1974, NYU, NYC, 1984-86, Parsons Sch. Design, NY, 1983; vis. prof. UCLA, 1987, Cranbrook Acad. Art, Bloomfield Hills, Mich., 1990; vis. lectr. Harvard U., Cambridge, Mass., 1995-96. One-man shows include Baumgartner Galleries, Washington, 1993, Ace Contemporary Exhbns., LA, 1993, Portland (Oreg.) Art Mus., 1993, St. Gauden's Meml., Cornish, NH, 1993, Secca, Winston-Salem, NC, Ace Gallery NY, Art Space, Seoul, 1996, Stark Gallery, NY, 1997, Hill Gallery, Birmingham, Mich., 1998, 5501 Columbia Arts Ctr., Dallas, 1998, Anders Tornberg Gallery, Sweden, 1998, Todd Gallery, London, 1998, Crosby St. Project Space, 1999, Auchincloss Gallery, 1999, Grant Selwyn Fine Art, 2000, U. Hartford Joseloff Gallery, 2000, Anthony Grant Gallery, 2005; group shows include Kunstmuseum, Passau, Germany, 1992, Rhona Hoffman Gallery, Chgo., 1992, Anders Tornberg Gallery, Lund, Sweden, 1993, Bklyn. Mus., 1993, Portland Art Mus., 1993, Andre Emmerich Gallery, NYC, 1993, Galerie Art 4, Galerie de l'Esplanade, Paris, 1993, Werkstaat Kollerschlag, Austria, 1993, Kunst Halle Krems, Austria, 1993, Caldas Da Rainha, Portugal, 1993, Drawing Ctr., NYC, 1993, Baumgartner Galleries, Washington, 1994, Neuberger Mus. Art, Purchase, NY, 1994, Michael Klein Gallery, NYC, 1995, Galerij S 65, Aalst, Belgium, 1995, Bilboa Guggenheim, Spain, "Snow Show", Rovaniemi, Finland, others; represented in permanent collections at Balt. Mus. Art, Bklyn. Mus., Collection Panza di Biumo, Varese, Italy, Dallas Art Mus., Detroit Inst. Arts, Musee Pleine Aire, Paris, Met. Mus. Art, NYC, Mus. Contemporary Art, NYC, Mus. Modern Art, NYC, New Mus. Contemporary Art, NYC, NY Pub. Libr., Portland Art Mus., Rose Art Mus., Brandeis U., Waltham, Mass., San

Diego Mus. Contemporary Art, La Jolla, Calif., David and Alfred Smart Art Mus., Chgo., Solomon R. Guggenheim Mus., NYC, Victoria and Albert Mus., London, LA County Mus., Harvard U. Mus., Yale Art Mus., others. Grantee Change Inc., 1974, Creative Artists Pub. Svc., 1975, Theo Doran award Ninth Paris Beinnale, 1975, Nat. Endowment for Arts, 1976, 77, 78, 84, 94, Creative Artists Pub. Svc., 1979; recipient John Simon Guggenheim award, 1980, St. Gauden's Meml. prize, 1992. Office: 515 W 36th St New York NY 10018-1100 Office Phone: 212-594-2479.

HIGHT, B. BOYD, lawyer; b. Lumberton, N.C., Feb. 15, 1939; s. B. Boyd and Mary Lou (Lennon) H.; m. Mary Kay Sweeney, Mar. 31, 1962; children: Kathryn, Kevin. BA, Duke U., 1960; LLB, Yale U., 1966; diploma in comparative law, U. Stockholm, 1967. Assoc. O'Melveny & Myers, Los Angeles, 1967-74, ptnr., 1974-79, 81-84, 89—; dep. asst. sec. trans. and telecommunications U.S. Dept. State, Washington, 1979-81; exec. v.p., gen. counsel Sante Fe Internat. Corp., Alhambra, Calif., also bd. dirs. Bd. dirs. Planned Parenthood L.A., 1986-95, pres., 1992-94; mem. bd. overseers Rand Ctr. Russian and Eurasian Studies, 1987-2000, chair, 1994-2000; trustee Am. U. Cairo, 1987—, chmn., 2004—, Autry Nat. Ctr., 2002—; bd. dirs. Calif. Supreme Ct. Hist. Soc., 1993-2001; bd. overseers The Huntington, 1996—. Mem. Coun. Fgn. Rels., Pacific Coun. on Internat. Policy, Calif. Club (pres. 2005—), Los Angeles Country Club. Democrat. Office: O'Melveny & Myers 400 S Hope St Los Angeles CA 90071-2899 E-mail: bhight@omm.com.

HIGHT, ORIAN LANGLEY, retired education educator; d. Vernon Arthur Langley and Ida Mae Langley/Fitzgerald; m. Adolph Aubrey Hight, Dec. 14, 1957; children: James Emmett II, Bryan Keith. BS in Chemistry, Hampton U., 1955; MS in Chemistry, Syracuse U., 1959; PhD in Math. Edn., U. Md., 1993. Postgrad. profl. tchrs. cert. Va., cert. tchr. Mass., N.C., advanced profl. tchrs. cert. Md. Middle sch. and H.S. math.-sci. tchr. various pub. sch. systems, 1955—86; math. rsch. asst. U. Md., College Park, 1989—90, math. counseling asst., 1990—93; instr. grad. edn. Trinity Coll., Washington, 1994; asst. prof. Prince George's CC, Largo, Md., 1994—97, assoc. prof., 1997—; ret., 2000. Workshop presenter in field. Compiler: Transparency Masters to Accompany Mary Kay Beaver's Essential Mathematics, 1997. Fund-raising vol. Am. CAncer Soc., New Bedford, Mass., 1964, March of Dimes, Woodbridge, Va., 1973, The Kidney Found., Woodbridge, 1975, March of Dimes, Olney, Md., 1984, Am. Lung Assn., Olney, 1994, Am. Heart Assn., Williamsburg, Va., 1999, 2000. Scholar, Hampton U., 1951—55; GE Chemistry summer fellow, Union Coll., 1956, NSF Summer fellow, Syracuse U., 1957, 1959, NSF fellow, 1958—59, Patricia Roberts Harris fellow, U. Md., 1986—89, Other Race Grant fellow, 1989—90. Mem.: Nat. Sci. Tchrs. Assn., Assn. for Women in Math., Am. Math. Soc., Math. Assn. Am., Nat. Coun. Tchrs. Math., Delta Sigma Theta. Democrat. Baptist. Achievements include wrote proposal, designed, developed and implemented a federally funded grade 9 remedial math program at Gar-Field Senior High School, Woodbridge, Virginia; conducted a survey on the study skill habits of students enrolled in freshman biology and chemistry courses at University Maryland, College Park. Avocations: reading, sewing, gardening, walking. Home: 3484 Frances Berkeley Williamsburg VA 23188

HIGHTOWER, JACK ENGLISH, retired judge, congressman; b. Memphis, Tex., Sept. 6, 1926; s. Walter Thomas and Floy Edna (English) H.; m. Colleen Ward, Aug. 26, 1950; children— Ann, Amy, Alison. BA, Baylor U., 1949; JD, 1951; LLM, Univ. Va., 1992. Bar: Tex. 1951. Since practiced in, Vernon; mem. Tex. Ho. of Reps., 1953-54; dist. atty. 46th Jud. Dist. Tex., 1955-61; mem. Tex. Senate, 1965-75, pro tempore, 1971; mem. 94th-98th Congresses from 13th Tex. Dist., 1975-85; 1st asst. atty. gen. State of Tex., 1985-87; justice Texas Supreme Ct., Austin, 1988-95; ret., 1996. Mem. Tex. Law Enforcement Study Commn., 1957; del. White House Conf. Children and Youth, 1970; alt. del. Dem. Nat. Conv., 1968; bd. regents Midwestern U., Wichita Falls, Tex., 1962-65; trustee Baylor U., 1972-81, acting gov., 1971; trustee Wayland Bapt. U., Plainview, Tex., 1991-2001, Bapt. Children's Home, 1959-62, Tex. Scottish Rite Hosp. Children, 1991—, chmn., 2002—; trustee Human Welfare Commn.; bd. dirs. Bapt. Std., 1959-68; mem. Nat. Commn. on Librs. and Info. Sci., 1999—. With USNR, 1944-46. Named Outstanding Dist. Atty, Tex., Tex. Law Enforcement Found., 1959, Disting. Alumnus, Baylor U., 1978; recipient Knapp-Porter award Tex. A&M Univ., 1980. Mem. Tex. Dist. and County Attys. Assn. (pres. 1958-59), Scottish Rite Ednl. Assn. Tex. (exec. com. 1990—), Tex. Supreme Ct. Hist. Soc. (pres. 1991-98), Tex. Bar. Found. (fellow 1992), SAR, U.S. Supreme Ct. Hist. Soc., Tex. State Hist. Assn. (exec. coun. 1998-2002), Masons (grand master Tex. 1972), Lions (pres. Vernon 1961), Scottish Rite Freemasonry (sovereign grand inspector gen. 1992-).

HIGHTOWER, JOHN BRANTLEY, arts administrator, educator; b. Atlanta, May 23, 1933; s. Edward A. and Margaret (Kimzey) H.; m. Martha Ruhl, Feb. 25, 1984; children: Amanda, Matthew. BA in English, Yale U., 1955; DFA, Calif. Coll. Arts and Crafts. Asst. to pub. Am. Heritage Pub. Co., Inc., NYC, 1961-63; exec. asst. NY State Coun. Arts, NYC, 1963-64, exec. dir., 1964-70; dir. Mus. Modern Art, NYC, 1970-72; pres. Am. Coun. Arts, NYC, 1972-74, South St. Seaport, 1977-83; dir., vice chmn. So. St. Seaport, 1983-84; exec. dir. Richard Tucker Music Found., 1977-89, Maritime Ctr. at Norwalk, 1984-89; dir. planning and devel. for the arts U. Va., 1989-93; pres., CEO The Mariners' Mus., Newport News, Va., 1993—. Exec. com. WHRO, Norfolk, 1996-99; vice chmn., Newport News Pub. Art Found., 2000—; founder, chmn. Adv. for Arts, 1974-77; instr. arts mgmt. Wharton Sch., U. Pa., 1976-77, New Sch., 1976-77; cultural advisor Rockefeller Mission to Latin Am., 1969; vis. critic in arts adminstrn. Grad. Sch. Drama, Yale U., 1972-77; chmn. Planning Corp. for Arts, Urban Arts Corps. Bd. dir. NY State Coun. on Arts, Poets and Writers. Capt. USMCR, 1955-63. Fulbright fellow; recipient NY State award, 1970. Mem. Century Assn. (NYC), 1805 Club (London). Home: 101 Museum Pkwy Newport News VA 23606-3635 E-mail: jhightower@mariner.org.

HIGHTOWER, PAULINE PATRICIA, retired elementary school educator; b. Lewisburg, Tenn., May 13, 1941; d. Floyd L. Tidwell and Celestine (Hill) Tidwell-Walker; m. Bennie Fisher, Oct. 1961 (div. 1966); 1 child, Patricia Denise Fisher Wilcox; m. Charles Hightower, Jan. 1968 (div. Apr. 1998). BS Elementary Edn., Tenn. State U., 1963; MS in Spl. Edn./Learning Disabilities, Calif. Luth. Coll., 1980. Cert. elem. tchr. Tenn., N.D., Nebr., Calif. Tchr. Jones Sch., Lewisburg, Tenn., 1964-65, Cornersville (Tenn.) Sch., 1965-66, Buena Vista Elem. Sch., Nashville, 1966-70, Westmeade Elem. Sch., Nashville, 1970-71, Twining Elem. Sch., Grand Forks, ND, 1971-76, Fillmore Elem. Sch., Lompoc, Calif., 1979-80, Ft. Crook Elem. Sch., Omaha, 1980-83; tchr. learning disabled Vogelweh Elem. Sch., Kaiserslautern, Germany, 1984-86; tchr. pre-sch. and severely handicapped Bowie Spl. Edn. Ctr., Wichita Falls, Tex., 1987; tchr. Ft. Crook Elem. Sch., Omaha, 1987—2005; ret., 2005. Mem. tchr. assistance team Ft. Crook Elem. Sch., 1989—94, mentor tchr., 1990—2000, team leader, 1995—2005. Mem.: Bellevue Edn. Assn. Republican. Ame. Avocations: reading, sewing, museums, hiking, collecting stuffed animals. Home: 2536 Mose Ave Bellevue NE 68147-2060 Office: Ft Crook Elem Sch 12501 S 25th St Bellevue NE 68123-1599 E-mail: pthightower@aol.com.

HIGHTOWER, SUZIE, writer; b. Little Rock, Mar. 30, 1954; d. Harriett Ann David and Joe Donald Sims, David Michael Pottorff (Stepfather) and Sybil Lee Jones (Stepmother). BS in Bus. Edn., La. Tech U., 1976. Dir. of govt. rels. S & A Restaurant Corp., Dallas, 1979—87; mgr. of investor rels. Amtech Corp., Dallas, 1989—91; dir. of regional and govt. rels. Promotional Products Assocs. Internat., Irving, Tex., 1992—96; bus. adminstr. Ark. Cardiovasc. Surgery Assocs., P.A., Little Rock, 1997—2003. Cons. Ark. Cardiovasc. Surgery Assocs., P.A., Little Rock, 1996—97. Author: Working Together: Diversity As Opportunity, 1998, Intuition At Work: Pathways to Unlimited Possibilities, 1996, The Gifts, 2002. Mem.: Inst. of Noetic Scis. Personal E-mail: suzie@suziehightower.com.

HIGLEY, BRUCE WADSWORTH, orthodontist; b. Iowa City, Dec. 1, 1928; s. Lester Bodine and Harriet (Wadsworth) H.; m. Marta Beatriz Velasco, Sept. 23, 1966. D.D.S., State U. Iowa, 1952, MS, 1953; student, Grinnell Coll., 1946-48, orthodontic certificate, 1953. Diplomate Am. Acad. Pain Mgmt. Research, instr. Iowa Dental U., 1952-53; practice dentistry, specializing in orthodontics South Miami, Fla., 1955—; Owner, chmn. bd. M.B.H. Enterprises, Inc., Miami, Fla., 1960—. Vice chmn. dist. coun. Boy Scouts Am., 1959-62; Mem. Personnel Bd., South Miami, 1959. Served as 1st lt. Dental Corps AUS, 1953-55. Fellow Internat. Coll. Cranio-Mandibnlar ORthopaedics, World Fedn. Orthodontists; mem. Am. Assn. Orthodontics, Fla. Orthodontic Soc., So., Miami socs. orthodontists, Fla., Am. socs. dentistry for children, Fla., Fla. East Coast, Miami dental socs., Am., S. Dade dental assns., Fedn. Dentaire Internat., English Royal Acad., C. of C. (past dir., sec., treas.), Psi Omega, Omicron Kappa Upsilon. Presbyn. (deacon). Clubs: Rotarian (pres. 1961-62), Elk, Coral Reef Yacht, Coral Gables Country, Royal Palm Tennis; Bankers, Executive (Miami); Army-Navy. Home: 2000 Brickell Ave Miami FL 33129-1721 Office: 7210 S Red Rd Miami FL 33143-5321 Office Phone: 305-666-8781, 305-607-5738. Personal E-mail: drhigley@higleyorthodonticspecialist.com.

HIGNITE, MICHAEL ANTHONY, computer information systems educator, researcher, writer, consultant; b. Baxter Springs, Kans., Jan. 23, 1954; s. Denver and Goldie Beatrice (Farris) H.; m. Lisa Jo Barger, May 15, 1976; 1 child, Anna. BS in Bus. Adminstrn., Okla. State U., 1976, MS in Bus., 1979; PhD in Bus. Edn., U. Mo., 1990. Computer programmer Atlantic Richfield Co., Dallas, 1979-80, 85-86, programmer, analyst Tulsa, 1980-82, systems analyst Anchorage, 1982-85, cons., 1987-88; asst. prof. S.W. Mo. State U., Springfield, 1990-95, assoc. prof., 1995—2003, prof., 2003—. Adj. prof. computer sci. Anchorage C.C., 1982-85. Mem. Am. Assn. for Higher Edn., Delta Sigma Pi, Beta Gamma Sigma. Republican. Methodist. Avocations: reading, running, collecting antiques, kayaking. Home: 4760 S Connor Ave Springfield MO 65804-7518 Office: Southwest Mo State U 901 S National Ave Springfield MO 65804-0088 E-mail: mah985f@smsu.edu.

HIGUCHI, SHIRLEY A., lawyer; Grad., Georgetown U., 1984. Atty. Epstein, Becker & Green, PC; asst. exec. dir. legal and regulatory affairs APA, Washington. Mem.: Asian Pacific Am. Bar Assn. (bd. dirs.), D.C. Bar Assn. (treas. 1993, bd. govs. 1994—2000, pres. 2003—04, pub. svc. activities com., co-chair health law sect.'s steering com.). Office: Am Psychol Assn 750 First St NW Washington DC 20002

HIJLEH, MARK, composer, educator; b. Wilmington, Del., Oct. 23, 1963; s. Ali Taher and Sondra Hijleh; m. Kelley Ruth Hijleh, Aug. 25, 1990; children: Hannah Sondra, Noah Daniel. BS, William Jewell Coll., Liberty, Mo., 1985; MusM, Ithaca Coll., N.Y., 1987; D in Musical Arts, Peabody Conservatory, Balt., 1991. Music instr. Inst. of Notre Dame, Balt., 1990—93; prof. of composition and conducting Greatbatch Sch. of Music, Houghton Coll., NY, 1993—. Founder and pres. Christian Fellowship of Art Music Composers, Houghton, NY, 1994—; music dir. and condr. Houghton Philharmonia Orch., NY, 1995—. Composer: (song cycle) O Ignis Spiritus (Winner, NATS Vocal Composition Award, 2002), (orchestral work) Open the Door, (piano solo) Homage to Messiaen, (string quartet) String Quartet #1: Offering for a New Creation, (wind ensemble) Sacrae Symphoniae (Hon. Mention (last movement), ASCAP, 1993); author: (book) The Music of Jesus: From Composition to Koinonia, 2001. Choir dir. Houghton Wesleyan Ch., Houghton, NY, 2000—02. Recipient ASCAP Std. Award, ASCAP, Anually since 1995. Mem.: Soc. of Composers, Inc., Am. Composers Forum, Pi Kappa Lambda. Avocations: chess, computers. Office: Houghton College 1 Willard Ave Houghton NY 14744 Personal E-mail: mark.hijleh@houghton.edu.

HILARIS, BASIL S., radiation oncologist, educator; b. Athens, Greece, 1928; MD, Athens U., 1955. Diplomate Am. Bd. Radiology - Therapeutic Radiology, Am. Bd. Radiology - Nuc. Medicine. Asst. in surgery Gen. State U., Athens, Greece, 1955; intern Alexian Bros. Hosp., Elizabeth, NJ, 1956; resident pathology St. Peter's Hosp., New Brunswick, NJ, 1956—57; resident radiology Meml. Hosp., N.Y.C., 1957—59, fellow, 1959—64; chief brachytherapy Meml. Sloan-Kettering Cancer Ctr., N.Y.C., 1991—; prof., chmn. radiation medicine N.Y. Med. Coll., N.Y.C., 1988—; dir. radiology Our Lady of Mercy Med. Ctr., N.Y.C., 1991—; prof. radiation medicine Cornell U. Med. Coll. Mem. med. adv. bd. Photoelectron Corp., Lexington, Mass., 1998—2002; reviewer Jour. Radiation Oncology Biology, Physics and Oncology, 1988—. Fellow, Am. Cancer Soc., 1963. Fellow: Am. Coll. Radiology, Am. Urol. Assn.; mem.: European Soc. Stereotactic and Functional Neurourgery (mem. sci. com. 1997—), Am. Bracytherapy Soc., Am. Coll. Radiation Oncology (bd. dirs. 1981, mem. practice accrediation com. 1994—). Office: Our Lady Mercy Med Ctr 600 E 233 St Bronx NY 10466 Office Phone: 718-920-9204. E-mail: bshilaris@aol.com.

HILBERS, MARY ELIZABETH, elementary school educator; b. Norfolk, Nebr., Apr. 15, 1967; d. Lambert and Marion Rita (Koch) Podany; m. Gary Marvin Hilbers, Dec. 29, 1989, children: Brett Gehrig Hibers, Blaire Leone Hilbers BFA, Wayne State Coll., 1989; MusM, U. Mo., 1994, postgrad., 1998. Dir. vocal music Bergan High Sch., Fremont, Nebr., 1989-92; music specialist Fremont (Nebr.) Pub. Schs., 1992—. Adj. prof. Wayne (Nebr.) State Coll., 1992-96; founder, dir. Piano Prodigy Camp., Wayne, 1994-97, staff mem. Wayne State Music Camp, 1987-97; presenter in field. Choir dir. St. Paul's Ch., Winside, Nebr., 1986-88; choir conductor Fremont Elem. Festival, 1995-98; conductor St. John's Centennial, Petersburg, Nebr., 1996; ch. organist St. Pat's Ch., Fremont, 1989-96; founder, dir. Piano Tchr. workshop, Wayne, 1996-97. Bd. Trustees scholar Wayne State Coll., 1985-89, Chancellor's Exceptional Merit scholar U. Mo., Kansas City, 1994-97. Mem. NEA, Music Tchrs. Nat. Assn., Nebr. State Edn. Assn., Fremont Edn. Assn. (head rep. 1997-98), Phi Kappa Lambda. Republican. Roman Catholic. Avocations: piano, cooking, needlecrafts, reading, interior design. Office: Fremont Pub Schs 957 N Pierce St Fremont NE 68025-3949

HILBERT, RICHARD ANDREW, sociologist, educator; b. Glendale, Calif., Oct. 31, 1947; s. Louis William and Beth Cordelia (Pendell) Hilbert; m. Susan Gravelin, Sept. 30, 1990. BA in sociology, SD State U., 1969; MA in sociology, U. Calif., 1974, PhD in sociology, 1978; postdoctoral in psychiat. epidemiology, UCLA, 1983. Prof. sociology, dept. chair Gustavus Adolphus Coll., St. Peter, Minn., 1978—. Cons., adj. prof. Union Inst. Grad. Sch., Cin., 1996—2001; assoc. editor Social Problems, 1987—94, 2002—; adv. editor Sociological Quarterly, 1991—; assoc. editor Sociological Theory, 1993—95; organizer Roundtable meetings, Midwest Sociological Soc., St. Louis, 1994; participant Symposium, Reconsidering Social Constructionism, U. Wis., 1992; guest lectr. U. Wis., Madison, Wis., 1980. Author: The Classical Roots of Ethnomethodology, 1992; editor: (papers) Faculty-R, Gustavus Adolphus Coll., 2001; contbr. chapters to books various profl. reference books, articles various profl. jours.; author: Jackpot for Tornado Victims, 1998. Mem.: Soc. for the Study of Social Problems, Midwest Sociological Soc., Assn. for the Study of Dreams, Am. Sociological Assn. Avocations: piano, photography, films. Office: Gustavus Adolphus Coll Sociology Anthropology Dept Saint Peter MN 56082 Office Phone: 507-933-7248.

HILBERT, RITA L., librarian; b. Orange, N.J., Nov. 1, 1942; d. Ralph P. LaSalle and Arlene (Julian) Strobel; children: Toby Gayle Buchanan, Stacey Giordano, Joseph, Matthew. AA, NYU, 1988, BA, 1990; MLS, Rutgers U., 1992. Merchandising rsch. analyst Burrelle's, Livingston, N.J., 1975-82; teaching asst. Montessori Sch., Millburn, N.J., 1982-84; outreach specialist Rockwood Meml. Libr., Livingston, 1984-90, head spl. svcs., 1990-92; libr. dir. Lincoln Park (N.J.) Pub. Libr., 1992-94, Mount Olive Township Pub. Libr., 1994—. Mem. Adult Sch. Bd., Livingston, 1990—, Lincoln Pk. Bd. of Edn., 1995-98, chair policy com., 1997-98, negotiations com., 1997-98. Member Livingston Adv. Com. for the Handicapped, 1985—, Livingston Coun. for Sr. Citizens, 1985—, Region III Com. for Svcs. to Spl. Populations, sec., 1987-88; elected mem. Lincoln Park Bd. Edn., 1995-98, chair policy and negotiations coms., 1995-98; trustee Lincoln Park Libr., 1997-98. Recipient Founder's Day award NYU, 1990. Mem.: AAUW (scholarship 1987), ALA, Morris Automated Info. Network (sec. 1993—94, v.p. 1995, pres. 1996, rep. planning coun. 2004), NJ Assn. Libr. Assts. (pres. 1989—90, scholarship in her name 1994), NJ Libr. Assn. (scholarship 1990), Mt. Olive C. of C. (rec. sec. 2002—05, bd. dirs. 2005, Bus. Person of Yr. 2005), Mt. Olive Twp. Hist. Soc. (founding and charter mem.), Kiwanis (bd. dirs. 1999—), Alpha Sigma Lambda. Avocations: walking, painting, travel. Office: 202 Flanders-Drakestown Rd Flanders NJ 07836 Office Phone: 973-691-8686.

HILBERT, ROBERT S(AUL), optical engineer; b. Washington, Apr. 29, 1941; s. Philip G. and Bessie (Friend) H.; m. Angela Cinel Ferreira, June 19, 1966; children: David M., Daniel S. BS in Optics, U. Rochester, 1962, MS in Optics, 1964. Optical design engr. Itek Corp., Lexington, Mass., 1963-65, supr. lens design sect., 1965-67, asst. mgr. optical engr. dept., 1967-69, mgr. optical engring. dept., 1969-74, dir. optics, 1974-75; v.p. engring. Optical Rsch. Assocs., Pasadena, Calif., 1975-84, sr. v.p., 1985-91, pres., COO, 1991-2000, pres., CEO, 2000—, also bd. dirs. Lectr. Northeastern U., Burlington, Mass., 1967-69; mem. trustees vis. com. Sch. Engring. and Applied Sci., U. Rochester, 1995-97. Patentee in lens systems. Recipient Future Scientist of Am. award, 1957; Am. Optical Co. fellow U. Rochester, 1962. Fellow Soc. Photo-Optical Instrumentation Engrs. (chmn. fellows com.); mem. Optical Soc. Am. (engring. coun. 1990-92, mem. Fraunhofer award com. 1997-98), Lens Design Tech. Group (chmn. 1975-77). Jewish. Avocations: reading, the cinema. Home: 863 San Vicente Rd Arcadia CA 91007 Office: Optical Rsch Assocs 3280 E Foothill Blvd Pasadena CA 91107-3103 Office Phone: 626-795-9101 306. Business E-Mail: bob@opticalres.com.

HILBRECHT, NORMAN TY, lawyer; b. San Diego, Feb. 11, 1933; s. Norman Titus and Elizabeth (Lair) H.; m. Mercedes L. Sharratt, Oct. 24, 1980. BA, Northwestern U., 1956; JD, Yale U., 1959. Bar: Nev. 1959, U.S. Supreme Ct. 1963. Assoc. counsel Union Pacific R.R., Las Vegas, 1962; ptnr. Hilbrecht & Jones, Las Vegas, 1962-69; pres. Hilbrecht, Jones, Schreck & Bernhard, 1969-83, Hilbrecht & Assocs, 1983—, Mobil Transport Corp., 1970-72; gen. counsel Bell United Ins. Co., 1986-94; mem. Nev. Assembly, 1966-72, minority leader, 1971-72; mem. Nev. Senate, 1974-78; legis. commn., 1977-78; oper. mem. Corp. Svcs. Group, 1998—; pres. Corp. Svcs. Co., 1998—, Nev. Incorporating Co., 1998—; mng. mem. Amcorp LLC., 1999—. Asst. lectr. bus. law U. Nev., Las Vegas. Author: Nevada Motor Carrier Compendium, 1990, Nevada Corporation Handbook, 1999. Labor mgmt. com. NCCJ, 1963; mem. Clark County (Nev.) Dem. Ctrl. Com., 1959-80, 1st vice chmn., 1965-66; del. Western Regional Assembly on Ombudsman; chmn. Clark County Dem. Conv., 1966, Nev. Dem. Conv., 1966; pres. Clark County Legal Aid Soc., 1964, Nev. Legal Aid and Defender Assn., 1965-83; assoc. for justice Nat. Jud. Coll., 1993-96. Capt. AUS, 1952-67. Named Outstanding State Legislator Eagleton Inst. Politics, Rutgers U., 1969. Mem. ABA, ATLA, Am. Judicature Soc., Am. Acad. Polit. and Social Sci., State Bar Nev. (chmn. adminstrv. law com. 1991-94, chmn. sect. on adminstrv. law 1996), Nev. Trial Lawyers (state v.p. 1966), Am. Assn. Ret. Persons (state legis. com. 1991-94), Literary Soc. Las Vegas, Las Vegas Social Register, Rotary, Las Vegas Rotary Found. (pres. 2004-05), U. Nev.-Las Vegas Found., Elks, Phi Beta Kappa, Delta Phi Epsilon, Theta Chi, Phi Delta Phi. Lutheran. Office: 723 S Casino Center Blvd Las Vegas NV 89101-6716 Office Phone: 702-384-1036. E-mail: hilbrecht@lvcm.com.

HILBURN, JOHN CHARLES, geologist, geophysicist; b. Dallas, Sept. 16, 1946; s. William Grant and Catherine (Thorwald) H.; 1 child, John C. Jr. BS in Geol. Scis., U. Tex., Austin, 1978. Mfg. mgr. Scorpio, Inc., Austin, 1972-74; rsch. engr., scientist U. Tex., Austin, 1974-78; corp. v.p. Reeves, Inc., Houston, 1978-79; mgr. acquisitions S.AM. Western Geophys. Corp., Houston, 1979-80; sr. mktg. geophysicist GECO Geophys. Co., Inc., Houston, 1980-85; pres. John Hilburn & Assocs., Inc., Austin, 1985—. Mem. Soc. Exploration Geophysicists, European Assn. Exploration Geophysicists, Can. Soc. Exploration Geophysicists, Am. Assn. Petroleum Geologists, Geol. Soc. Am. Avocations: gem cutting, stamp collecting/philately, skiing, scuba diving, cooking. Home and Office: 6302 Mountainclimb Dr Austin TX 78731-3908

HILD, HEIDI, public policy consultant; b. Denver, Dec. 25, 1961; d. Leonard Gene and Marilyn Ann (Handrock) Hild; m. Samuel Ralph Boyer, Dec. 27, 1992 (div. 2004); children: Elliott Gene Boyer, Ryan Stuart Boyer. BA, Colo. State U., 1985. Sr. ptnr. H. Earhart & Assocs., Denver, 1987-90; dir. comm. Colo. Assn. Commerce and Industry, Denver, 1990; dir. legis. affairs Rocky Mountain Farmers Union, Denver, 1990-93; pres. Colo. Capitol Preservation Fund, Denver, 1995-98; state fin. dir. Norton for Gov., Denver, 1997-98; sr. ptnr. Sq. Root Gardens, 2002—. Rsch. assoc. Gov.'s Unified Housing Task Force, Denver, 1987; cons. Planned Parenthood Rocky Mountains, 1988, Gov.'s Task Force on Homeless, 1989; exec. dir. Denver Archtl. Found., 2004-05. Press sec. Sci. and Cultural Facilities Dist. Campaign, Denver, 1994; vol. Make-A-Wish Found., 1995-2000; mem. steering com. Colo. Open Lands, 1998—. Recipient Denver Post/Am. Newspaper Publs. Assn. Scholastic Journalist award, 1980. Mem. LWV, Inst. Internat. Edn., Colo. State U. Devel. Coun., Kappa Alpha Theta. Avocations: gardening, skiing, reading, travel.

HILD, MATTHIAS, finance educator; b. Oberscheld, Hessen, Germany, Aug. 16, 1968; s. Karl Heinz and Edith Hild; m. Anastasia Dakouri-Hild, July 29, 2000. DPhil, Oxford (Eng.) U., 1997. Jr. rsch. fellow Christ's Coll., Cambridge, England, 1997—2000; rsch. fellow Ctr. for Interdisciplinary Rsch., Bielefeld, Germany, 2000; sr. rsch. fellow Calif. Inst. of Tech., Pasadena, 2000—02; Adam Smith vis. chair Bayreuth (Germany) U., 2001—02; asst. prof. of bus. adminstrn. Darden Grad. Sch. of Bus. Adminstrn., Charlottesville, Va., 2002—. Rschr. in astrobiology Jet Propulsion Lab., Pasadena, Calif., 2000—02. Business E-Mail: matthias@hild.org.

HILDEBRAND, ARTHUR ANTHONY, music educator; b. Chgo., Dec. 6, 1946; s. Walter V. and Louise M. Hildebrand. MusB. in Edn., Vandercook Coll. Of Music, 1969; MEd, Ea. Ill. U., 1972. Tchr. Piper City Ill. Comm. Unit, 1969—72, Kings County Amalgamated Sch. Bd., Kentville, Canada, 1972—78, Biddeford (Maine) Sch. Dept., 1979—92, Meredosia-Chambersburg (Ill.) Cu. Dist. #11, 1994—95, North Chgo. Ill. Sch. Dist. 187, 1995—. Instr. Acadia U. Summer Music Camps, Wolfville, Canada, 1974—79. Contbr. articles to profl. jours. Dir. Italian Heritage Concert Band, Portland, Maine, 1990—94, Painchaud's Cmty. Band, Biddeford, Maine, 1982—90. Mem.: Ill. Music Educators Assn., Music Educators Nat. Conf. Avocations: model railroads, sailing, bicycling, acting. Home: 208 E Skokie Road Lake Bluff IL 60044 Office: North Chicago School District #187 Lewis And Argonne Street North Chicago IL 60064

HILDEBRAND, JOHN FREDERICK, columnist, educator; b. Chgo., Dec. 23, 1940; s. Paul Hedden and Harriet L. (Cummins) H.; m. Vasana Lohitkoopt, June 24, 1972; children: Marisa Cummins, Shana Victoria, Brent Daniel. B Journalism, U. Mo., 1965; MS in Journalism, Columbia U., 1966. Reporter Poplar Bluff (Mo.) Daily Am. Republic, 1963, Joplin (Mo.) Globe, 1964, AP, Jefferson City and Kansas City, Mo., 1965; fgn. svc. officer U.S. Info. Svc., Washington and Bangkok, 1966-70; reporter Newsday, Melville, N.Y., 1970-74, asst. city editor, 1974-76, edn. writer, 1976—. Adj. prof. journalism Chulalongkorn U., Bangkok, 1967; pres. Lloyd Neck (N.Y.) Holding Corp., 1988-91, bd. dirs., 1986-95. Vestryman St. John's Episcopal Ch., Cold Spring Harbor, N.Y., 1992-98. Recipient citation Adelphi U., Garden City, N.Y., 1987, citation Kappa Delta Pi, Oakdale, N.Y., 1988, citation Phi Delta Kappa Suffolk County Chpt., 1999, Newsday Pub.'s. Spl. Achievement award, 1997. Mem. Edn. Writers Assn. (1st prize opinion article 1978, 1st prize article series 1982, 97, 1st prize article package 1992), Phi Gamma Delta (sec. Chi Mu chpt. 1964). Home: 23 Target Rock Dr Huntington NY 11743-1464 Office: Newsday Inc 235 Pinelawn Rd Melville NY 11747-4250 Office Phone: 516-843-2956. Business E-Mail: john.hildebrand@newsday.com.

HILDEBRAND, JOHN G(RANT), neuroscientist, educator; b. Boston, Mar. 26, 1942; s. John G. and Helen S. Hildebrand; m. Gail Deerin Burd, July 24, 1982. AB, Harvard U., 1964; PhD, Rockefeller U., 1969; Laurea Honoris Causa, U. Cagliari, Italy, 2000. Instr. neurobiology Harvard U. Med. Sch., Boston, 1970-72, asst. prof., 1972-77, assoc. prof., 1977-80, vis. prof.,

1980-81; prof. biol. scis. Columbia U., N.Y.C., 1980-85; prof. neurobiol., biochemistry, molecular biophysics and cellular biology, entomology U. Ariz., Tucson, 1985—, Regents prof., 1989—, dir. div. neurobiology, 1985—. Assoc. behavioral biology Harvard U. Mus. Comparative Zoology, Cambridge, Mass., 1980-97; trustee Marine Biol. Lab., Woods Hole, Mass., 1981-89, mem. exec. com., 1981-88; Jan de Wilde lectr. U. Wageningen, The Netherlands, 1992; King Solomon lectr., Hebrew U., Jerusalem, 1995; K.D. Roeder lectr. Tufts U., 1995; Felix Santschi lectr. U. Zurich, Switzerland, 1995; Grandpierre Meml. lectr. Columbia U., 2002; Padydula lectr. Wellesley Coll., 2003; Cajal lectr. Cajal Inst., Madrid, 2004. Co-editor: Chemistry of Synaptic Transmission, 1974, Receptors for Neurotransmitters, Hormones, and Pheromones in Insects, 1980, Molecular Insect Science, 1990; devel. neurosci. sect. editor Jour. Neurosci., 1983-88; co-editor Jour. Comparative Physiology A, 1990—; mem. editorial bd. various other jours. Trustee Rockefeller U., N.Y.C., 1970-73. Recipient Javits Neurosci. award Nat. Isnt. Neurol. and Communicative Disorders and Stroke, NIH, 1986-94, Merit award Nat. Inst. Allergy and Infections Diseases, NIH, 1986-97, R.H. Wright award Simon Fraser U., B.C., Can., 1990, Max Planck Rsch. award Max Planck Gesellschaft and Alexander von Humboldt-Stiftung of Germany, 1990, Founder's Meml. award Entomol. Soc. Am., 1997, Humboldt rsch. award, 1997, Manheimer Lectureship award, Monell Chem. Senses Ctr., 2005; Helen Hay Whitney Found. fellow, 1969-72, A.P. Sloan Found. fellow, 1973-77. Fellow: AAAS, Royal Entomol. Soc. UK; mem.: Ariz. Arts, Scis. and Tech. Acad. (chmn., founding fellow), Am. Acad. Arts and Sci., Norwegian Acad. Sci. and Letters, Deutsche Akademie der Naturforscher Leopoldina, Internat. Soc. Chem. Ecology (pres. 1998—99), Soc. Integrative and Comparative Biology, Internat. Soc. Neuroethology (pres. 1995—98), Soc. for Neurosci. (treas. 1993—94), Assn. for Chemoreception Sci. (pres. 2002—03, IFF Innovative Rsch. award 1997), Am. Soc. Biochemistry and Molecular Biology. Avocations: music, lower brass instruments. Home: 629 N Olsen Ave Tucson AZ 85719-5136 Office: U Ariz ARL Div Neurobiology PO Box 210077 Tucson AZ 85721-0077 Business E-Mail: jgh@neurobio.arizona.edu.

HILDEBRAND, PHILLIP J., insurance company executive; b. Prineville, Oreg., 1952; Attended, Northern Ariz. U., 1974. Sr. v.p. New York Life Ins. Co., N.Y.C., 1997—2001, exec. v.p., 2001—, chief dist. officer, life annuity, 2001—. Office: NY Life Ins Co 51 Madison Ave New York NY 10010

HILDEBRAND, ROGER HENRY, astrophysicist, physicist; b. Berkeley, Calif., May 1, 1922; s. Joel Henry and Emily (Alexander) H.; m. Jane Roby Beedle, May 28, 1944; children: Peter Henry, Alice Louise, Kathryn Jane, Daniel Milton. AB in Chemistry, U. Calif., Berkeley, 1947, PhD in Physics, 1951. Physicist, U. Calif., 1942-51; physicist Tenn. Eastman Corp., Oak Ridge Nat. Lab., 1945; asst. prof. dept. physics Enrico Fermi Inst., U. Chgo., 1952-55, asso. prof., 1955-60, prof., 1960—, prof. dept. astronomy and astrophysics, 1978—. Samuel K. Allison Disting. Service prof., 1985—, chmn. dept. astronomy and astrophysics, 1984-88; dir. Enrico Fermi Inst., 1965-68, dean coll., 1969-73. Assoc. lab. dir. for high energy physics Argonne (Ill.) Nat. Lab., 1958-64; chmn. sci. policy com. Stanford (Calif.) Linear Accelerator Ctr., 1962-66; mem. physics adv. com. Nat. Accelerator Lab., 1967-69; mem. sci. and ednl. adv. com. Lawrence Berkeley Lab., 1972-80; chmn. com. to rev. U.S. medium energy sci. AEC and NSF, 1974; chmn. airborne obs. users group NASA, 1983-84; chmn. sci. cons. group Stratospheric Obs. for Infrared Astronomy (SOFIA), NASA, 1985-89, mem. sci. working group, 1995-97, sci. coun., 1997—; mem. space astronomy and astrophysics Space Sci. Bd., 1987-90; mem. coun. Columbus Project, 1987-88; mem. sci. and tech. adv. panel for the submillimeter array Harvard/Smithsonian Ctr. for Astrophysics, 1989-95; mem. astronomy and astrophysics survey com. NAS Panel for Infrared Astronomy, 1989-90; chmn. Dannie Heineman prize com. Am. Inst. Physics, 1990; mem. sci. and tech. adv. group Large Millimeter Telescope, 1995—; mem. obs. vis. com. Assn. Univs. for Rsch. in Astronomy, 1993-96, chmn. Stratospheric Obs. Infrared Astronomy sci. coun., 1997—; mem. NASA review panel for Small Explorer (SMEX) Proposals, 2000; mem. NASA/JPL bd. for Planck High Frequency Instrument Detectors, 2000-02; mem. faculty Canary Islands Winter Sch. Astrophysics, 2000. Guggenheim fellow, 1968-69, Alfred P. Sloan Found. fellow, 1975. Fellow Am. Phys. Soc., Am. Acad. Arts and Scis.; mem. Am. Astron. Soc., Internat. Astron. Union, Midwestern Univs. Rsch. Assn. (dir. 19956-58, 62-68), Phi beta Kappa, Sigma Xi; chair adv. com. 2001-2003, assoc. mem. 2003-, NSF Ctr. for Cosmological Physics. Office: U Chgo Enrico Fermi Inst 5640 S Ellis Ave Chicago IL 60637-1433

HILDEBRAND, VERNA LEE, human ecology educator; b. Dodge City, Kans., Aug. 17, 1924; d. Carrell E. and Florence (Smyth) Butcher; m. John R. Hildebrand, June 23, 1946; children: Carol Ann, Steve Allen. BS, Kans. State U., 1945, MS, 1957; PhD, Tex. Women's U., 1970. Tchr. home econs. Dickinson County H.S., Chapman, Kans., 1945-46; tchr. early childhood Albany (Calif.) Pub. Schs., 1946-47; grad. asst. Inst. Child Welfare U. Calif., Berkeley, 1947-48; tchr. kindergarten Albany Pub. Schs., 1948-49; dietitian commons and hosp. U. Chgo., 1952-53; instr. Kans. State U., Manhattan, 1953-54, 59, Okla. State U., Stillwater, 1955-56; asst. prof. Tex. Tech U., Lubbock, 1962-67; from asst. prof. to prof. Mich. State U., East Lansing, 1967-97, prof. emeritus, 1997—. Legis. clk. Kans. Ho. of Reps., Topeka, 1955. Author: Introduction to Early Childhood Education, 1971, 6th edit., 1997, Guiding Young Children, 1975, 7th edit., 2004, Parenting and Teaching Young Children, 1981, 90, Management of Child Development Centers, 1984, 5th edit., 2002, Parenting: Rewards and Responsibilities, 1994, 2d edit., 1997, 6th edit., 2002, tchrs. annotated edit., 2003; co-author: China's Families: Experiment in Societal Change, 1985, Knowing and Serving Diverse Families, 1996, 2d edit., 1999. Mem. Nat. Assn. for the Edn. Young Children (task force 1975-77), Am. Home Econs. Assn. (bd. dirs., Leader award 1990), Women in Internat. Devel., Nat. Assn. Early Childhood Tchr. Edn. (award for meritorious and profl. leadership 1995).

HILDEBRANDT, FREDERICK DEAN, JR., management consultant; b. Upper Darby, Pa. m. Marjorie Louise Smith, July 27, 1968; children: Frederick Dean III, Elizabeth Florence. AB magna cum laude, Dartmouth Coll., 1954, MS, 1955. Engr. Eastman Kodak Co., Rochester, N.Y., 1957-60; systems mgr. J.T. Baker Chem. Co., Phillipsburg, N.J., 1960-63; assoc. Booz, Allen & Hamilton Inc., N.Y.C., 1963-72, v.p., 1972-78; sr. v.p. Am. Ins. Assn., N.Y.C., 1978-81; v.p. Travelers Ins. Cos., Hartford, Conn., 1981-89; pres. Dean Hildebrandt & Assocs., Simsbury, Conn., 1989—. Adminstr. Ins. Rsch. Coun., 1979, bd. dirs., 1982-88; vice chmn. bd. dirs. Workers Compensation Rsch. Inst., 1987-88 With U.S. Army, 1955-57. Mem. Inst. Mgmt. Cons. (cert. mgmt. cons.), Phi Beta Kappa.

HILDEBRANDT-WILLARD, CLAUDIA JOAN, banker; b. Ingelwood, Calif., Feb. 12, 1942; d. Charles Samual and Clara Claudia (Palumbo) Hildebrandt; m. I. LeRoy Willard, Nov. 5, 1993 (dec. Oct. 2001). BBA, U. Colo. Head teller First Colo. Bank & Trust, Denver, 1969—70; asst. cashier First Nat. Bank, Englewood, Colo., 1975—79, asst. v.p., 1979—83, v.p., 1983—92; owner CJH Enterprises, Inc., Breckenridge, Colo., 1980—, Garden Tea Shop, Georgetown, Colo., The Gifted Swan, Georgetown, Colo., 1982—92, Laudiac, Inc., Breckenridge, 1993—, Mgmt. for Ministry, 1993—. Mem.: Am. Inst. Banking, Am. Soc. Pers. Adminstrn., Fin. Women Internat. (pres.-elect 1989—92), Nat. Assn. Bank Women, Mile High Group. Roman Catholic. Home: PO Box 665 Georgetown CO 80444-0665 Office: 410 3d St Georgetown CO 80444

HILDERLEY, JERIANN GERTRUDE, novelist, educator; b. Saginaw, Mich., July 17, 1937; d. Clifton Tabor and Gertrude (Volz) Hilderley. Student, Smith Coll., 1955-57; BA, U. Calif., Berkeley, 1959; MA, U. Mich., 1961; M Spl. Edn., CUNY, 1988. Lic. spl. edn. tchr., N.Y. Dir. cmty.-based theaters Burning City Theater and Women's Ritual Theater, N.Y.C., 1962-74; dir. Sea Wave Record Co., N.Y.C., 1978-81; coord. data conversion BRS Med. Inc., N.Y.C., 1982-83; exec. sec. Nat. Coun. Chs., N.Y.C., 1983-84; tchr., curriculum developer, grants writer N.Y.C. Pub. Sch. 721, 1994—. Juror in music C.A.P.S., N.Y.C., 1979-80; cons. Computer Arts Mgmt., N.Y.C., 1994—. Author: Mari, 1990; contbr. articles to profl. publs. Fundraiser, mem. Upper West Side Dem. Party, N.Y.C., 1986—; mem. adv. bd. Soho Women Artists, N.Y.C., 1992—; mem. West End Ave. Block Assn., N.Y.C., 1991—. Grantee N.Y. coun. Arts, 1971-73, CEC, Impact, Am. Heart Assn., 1985-89, N.Y. Found. for Arts, 1991-93, Art Ptnrs. Dewitt Wallace grantee N.Y. Fund for Pub. Edn., 1991-93. Fellow Blue Mountain Artists Ctr. (writer in residence 1994), Va. Creative Ctr. Arts (writer in residence 1993), Cummington Cmty. of Arts (writer in residence 1992); B.M.I. (composer, reviewer 1979—), Lady Slipper Inc. (contbg. composer 1979-84). Avocations: musician, composing, performing. Home: 711 W End Ave # Ggn New York NY 10025-6821

HILDING, JEREL LEE, music and dance educator, retired dancer; b. New Orleans, Sept. 24, 1949; s. Oscar William and Loeta Dana (Boldra) H.; m. Krystyna Zofia Jurkowski, July 1, 1978; children: Dennis Jozef, Kristopher Jay. BA, La. State U., New Orleans, 1971. Prin. dancer Joffrey Ballet, N.Y.C., 1975-89; dir. arts in edn. N.J. Ballet, 1989-90; assoc. prof., dir. dance U. Kans., 1990—. Avocations: piano, sports. Office: U of Kansas Dept Music and Dance 460 Murphy Hall 1530 Naismith Dr Lawrence KS 66045-0001

HILDRETH, EUGENE A., physician, educator; b. St. Paul, Mar. 11, 1924; s. Eugene A. V. and Lila K. (Clator) Hildreth; m. Dorothy Anne Myers, Mar. 23, 1946; children: Jeffrey Reed, William Myers, Anne Sarver, Katherine Clator. BS, Washington Jefferson Coll., 1943; MD, U. Va., 1947. Diplomate Am. Bd. Internal medicine, Am. Bd. Allergy and Immunology. Intern Johns Hopkins, 1947—48; resident in medicine Hosp. U. Pa., 1948—49, USPHS Postdoctoral Research fellow in cardio-vascular disease, 1949—51, chief resident in medicine, 1953—54, fellow in allergy and immunology, 1954—58, faculty, 1954—69, faculty, 1971—; instr. medicine U. Pa., Phila., 1953—54, asso. medicine, 1954—55, asst. prof. medicine, 1955—60, assoc. prof., 1960—69; assoc. dean U. Pa. (Sch. Medicine), 1964—69, prof. clin. medicine, 1971—90, prof. emeritus, 1990—, acting chmn. dept. research medicine, 1960—64. Chmn. dept. medicine Reading (Pa.) Hosp. and Med. Ctr.; cons. project site visitis USPHS, 1965—70; cons. VA Hosp. Phila., 1955—; nat. adv. com. Medic Alert Found. Internat., 1964—83; cons. Citizens' Com. to Study Grad. Med. Edn., 1966; Am. Bd. Med. Spltys. rep. of subsplty. Bd. Allergy and Immunology of Am. Bd. Internal Medicine, 1969—72; mem. Am. Bd. Internal Medicine, 1969—72, 1975—82, cons., com. mem., 1972—75, chmn. certifying exam. com., 1978—81, mem. core exam. com., 1986—87, mem. exec. com., 1978—82, chmn., 1981—82; founding com. Am. Bd. Allergy and Immunology, 1970, mem., 1970—72, 1st co-chmn.; mem. rep. Am. Bd. Med. Spltys., 1976—83, chmn. nominating com., 1979—80; mem. med. adv. bd. Lupus Found. Del. Valley, 1979—; chmn. Federated Coun. Internal Medicine; appeals bd. liaison Coun. of Grad. Med. Edn., 1980—. Co-author: Low Fat Diet, 1953; mem. editl. bd.: Annals Internal Medicine, 1960—68, Postgrad. Medicine, 1969—75, Jour. Berks County Med. Soc., 1969—73, Internal Medicine Digest, 1971—75; contbr. chapters to books, articles to profl. jours. With USNR, 1943—45, with USNR, 1951—53. Grantee, USPHS; scholar John and Mary R. Markle scholar in acad. medicine, 1958—63. Master: ACP (mem. bd. regents 1985—92, chmn. bd. regents 1989—91, pres. 1991—92, immediate past pres. 1992—, mem. ethics com. 1986—90, chmn. com. to delineate privileges of med. procedures, mem. nominating 1997—); fellow: Am. Clin. and Climatologic Assn., Acad. Medicine of Singapore (hon.); mem.: ACGME (mem. residency rev. com. internal medicine), AAAS, Working Group on Disability of U.S. Presidents, Royal Soc. Medicine, Federated Coun. Internal Medicine, Am. Acad. Allergy, Inst. Medicine of NAS (mem. nominating com. 1982—84, mem. coun. 1986—90, chmn. nominating com. for coun. memberships 1989—90, mem. fin. com. 1988—90), N.Y. Acad. Scis., Fedn. AM. Socs. for Exptl. Biology, Peripatetic Soc., Phila. Art Mus. Home: 5285 Sweitzer Rd Mohnton PA 19540-8140

HILDRETH, JAMES ROBERT, retired air force officer; b. Pine Bluff, Ark., May 4, 1927; s. William Wilson and Martha Leah (Chidester) H.; m. Beth Dixon Baker, July 12, 1955; children: John Baker, William Reid, Margaret Leah, Mark Dixon, Amy Beth. BA cum laude, La. Poly. Inst., 1952. Commd. 2d lt. USAF, 1952, advanced through grades to maj. gen., 1976; ret., 1981; comdr. 1st Air Commando Sqdn., 1967; comdr. 4th Tactical Fighter Wing, 1970—72; dep. dir. ops. Office of Joint Chiefs of Staff, 1972—73; dep. comdr. 13th Air Force, 1973—75; sr. Air Force rep. Weapons Systems Evaluation Group, Office of Sec. Def., 1975—76; comdr. Tactical Fighter Weapons Center, 1976—79; comdr. 13th Air Force, 1979—81. Pres. So. Nev. Fed. Exec. Agy., 1975-76; mem. adv. bd. United Way, Las Vegas, Nev., 1975-79; bd. dirs. Las Vegas C. of C., 1976-79; dist. chmn. Boy Scouts Am., 1979-81. Decorated D.S.M. (2), Silver Star, Legion of Merit (3), D.F.C. (3), Bronze Star, Air medal (14), Def. Superior Svc. medal, Meritorious Svc. Medal, Air Force Commendation medal (3), Purple Heart, Cross of Gallantry (Vietnam), Rep. Phillipines Legion of Honor. Mem. Kappa Sigma, Phi Kappa Phi, Omicron Delta Kappa, Sigma Tau Delta. Clubs: DAV. Methodist. Home: 315 E Branch St PO Box 897 Spring Hope NC 27882-0897 Office: 9070 Edgerton Rd Spring Hope NC 27882-8916 Personal E-mail: cbhild@aol.com.

HILDRETH, RICHARD G., law educator, lawyer; b. 1943; BSE, Univ. Mich., 1965, JD, 1969; diploma in law, Oxford Univ., 1969, Univ. Stockholm, 1973. Bar: Calif. 1969. Atty. Steinhart & Falconer, San Francisco, 1969—78; prof. Univ. Oreg. Sch. Law, 1978—; dir. Environ. & Natural Resources Ctr., Univ. Oreg.; co-dir. Ocean & Coastal Law Ctr, Univ. Oreg. Mem. editl. adv. bd. Coastal Mgmt., Ocean Development & Internat. Law. Co-author: Coastal & Ocean Law: Cases & Materials, Coastal & Ocean Mgmt. Law in a Nutshell, Ocean & Coastal Law. Office: Ocean and Coastal Law Center School of Law 1221 University of Oregon Eugene OR 97403-1221

HILEMAN, BETTE JO, journalist; b. Akron, Ohio, Mar. 4, 1937; d. Francis Matthew and Elsie Josephine Buresh; m. Stephen Caswell Clapp, Sept. 25, 2004; m. Samuel Palmer Hileman, June 20, 1963 (div. Mar. 27, 1978); children: Milena Lee, Charles Warren, Frank Stafford. AB, Mt. Holyoke Coll., 1959. H.S. tchg., sci, math. Va., 1974. H.s. tchr. Brimmer and May Sch., Chestnut Hills, Mass., 1960—61, Bath County H.S., Warm Springs, Va., 1972—73, Clifton Forge H.S., Clifton Forge, Va., 1974—75; head of sci. dept. Stuart Hall Sch., Staunton, Va., 1978—81; assoc. editor Environ. Sci. & Tech., Pub. by Am. Chem. Soc., Washington, 1981—84; sr. editor Chem. & Engring. News, Weekly Newsmagazine of Am. Chem. Soc., 1984—. Contbr. articles to profl. jours. Chair Hist. Dist. Commn., East New Market, Md., 1994—2001. Recipient Phi Beta Kappa, Phi Beta Kappa Soc., 1959. Mem.: New Dominion Chorale. Avocations: singing, swimming, hiking, skiing. Home: 17267 Banbury Ct Jeffersonton VA 22724 Office: Chem & Engring News 1155 16th St NW Washington DC 20036 Office Phone: 202-872-4583. Business E-Mail: b_hileman@acs.org.

HILER, BRUCE A., lawyer; b. Watervliet, MI, 1952; BA magna cum laude, U. Notre Dame, 1974; JD with honors, U. Mich., 1977. Bar: Ill. 1977, DC 1995. Staff atty. US Securities and Exchange Commn., Divsn. Enforcement, Washington, 1978—80, spl. coun., 1981, branch chief, 1981—85, asst. dir., 1985—90, assoc. dir., 1990—94; instr. civil procedure, legal asst. program George Washington U., 1987; adj. prof. securities law Georgetown U. Law Sch., 1992—98; ptnr. O'Melveny & Myers LLP, Washington; chair securities enforcement and regulatory counseling practice. Adj. prof. securities law, LLM program Georgetown U., 1992—98; lectr. and spkr. at various legal profession & bus. conventions & continuing edn. seminars. Author articles in prof. jours.; mem. advisory bd. Securities Regulation Law Jour. Mem.: ABA (mem. task force SEC settlements, mem. fed. regulations of securities com., bus. law sect.). Office: O'Melveny & Myers LLP 1625 Eye St NW Washington DC 20006 Office Phone: 202-383-5372. Office Fax: 202-383-5414.

HILER, EDWARD ALLAN, agricultural and engineering educator; b. Hamilton, Ohio, May 14, 1939; s. Earl and Thelma (Kolb) H.; m. Patricia Burke; children: Karen, Richard, Scott. BS in Agrl. Engring., MS in Agrl. Engring., Ohio State U., 1963, PhD in Agrl. Engring., 1966. Registered profl. engr., Tex. Asst. prof. Tex. A&M U., College Station, 1966-69, assoc. prof., 1969-73, prof., 1973—, head dept. agrl. engring., 1974-88, dep. chancellor for acad. program planning and rsch., 1989-91, interim chancellor, 1991, exec. dep. chancellor, 1991, dep. chancellor for acad. and rsch. programs, 1991-92; vice chancellor, dean agrl. and life scis., dir. Tex. Agrl. Expt. Sta., 1992—2004; dir. Tex. Coop. Ext., 1998—2002, Ellison chair in internat. floriculture, depts. hort. scis. and biol. and agrl. engring., 2005—. Cons. on water conservation, environ. quality, energy and biol. processes and future agrl. engring. Office Tech. Assessment, U.S. Congress, Office of Water Rsch. and Tech., Dept. Interior, others. Contbr. over 100 articles to profl. jours. Recipient numerous ednl. and rsch. awards. Fellow AAAS, Instn. Agrl. Engrs. Eng., Am. Soc. Engring. Edn., Am. Soc. Agrl. Engrs. (bd. dirs., pres. 1991-92, trustee Found.); mem. NAE. Presbyterian. Avocations: golf, professional reading novels. Business E-Mail: e-hiler@tamu.edu.

HILES, BARBARA LYNN, retired elementary school educator; b. Independence, Mo., Nov. 24, 1936; d. Olien Kendall and Jennie Lucinda (Bowen) Peters; m. Sylvester Scott Hiles, June 27, 1955; children: Kenneth, Ronald. BS in Edn., Cen. Mo. State U., 1975, MS in Reading, 1977, EdS, 1979. Cert. elem. edn. and reading tchr., Mo. Kindergarten tchr. Blue Springs (Mo.) R-IV Sch. Dist., 1975-76, elem. tchr., 1976-80, 1995—2000, reading tchr., 1980—95; ret., 2000; pvt. reading tutor, 2000—. Adult edn. tchr., 1983—. Mem. Internat. Reading Assn. (pres. Mo. State Coun. 1990-91, state coord. 1997—, Literacy award 1988), Blue Springs Ret. Educators Assn. (pres. 2002-04), Delta Kappa Gamma (pres. Beta Phi chpt. 1984-88). Home: 312 Gingerbread Ln Blue Springs MO 64014-3611 E-mail: bhiles24@msn.com.

HILES, BRADLEY STEPHEN, lawyer; b. Granite City, Ill., Nov. 11, 1955; s. Joseph J. and Betty Lou (Goodman) H.; m. Toni Jonine Failoni, Aug. 12, 1977; children: Eric Stephen, Nina Catherine, Emily Christine. BA cum laude, Furman U., 1977; JD cum laude, St. Louis U., 1980. Bar: Mo. 1980, U.S. Dist. Ct. (ea. dist.) Mo., 1980, Ill. 1981. From assoc. to ptnr. Blackwell Sanders Peper Martin, St. Louis, 1980—. V.p., sec., gen. counsel Miss. Lime Co., 1992. Editor-in-chief St. Louis Univ. Law Jour., 1979-80; contbr. articles to profl. jours. Mem. Bar Assn. of Met. St. Louis (chmn. environ. and conservation law com. 1993-94). Republican. Baptist. Avocations: gospel singing, bicycling. Home: 34 Meditation Way Ct Florissant MO 63031-6535 Office: Blackwell Sanders Peper Martin 720 Olive St Fl 24 Saint Louis MO 63101-2338 Office Phone: 314-345-6489. E-mail: bhiles@blackwellsanders.com.

HILEY, DAVID, academic administrator; BA in History, Auburn U., 1966; MA in Philosophy, U. Ga., 1969, PhD in Philosophy, 1972. From asst. prof. to prof. philosophy, mem. grad. faculty U. Memphis, 1972—89; prof. philosophy, mem. grad. faculty Auburn U., 1989—92, assoc. dean for rsch. Coll. Liberal Arts, 1989—91, acting dean Coll. Liberal Arts, 1991—92; prof. philosophy, mem. grad. faculty, pub. policy faculty, affiliate mem. women's studies Va. Commonwealth U., 1992—, dean Coll. Humanities and Scis., 1992—96, interim vice provost for acad. affairs, dean Coll. Humanities and Scis., 1995—96, vice provost for acad. affairs, 1996—99; prof. philosophy, provost, v.p. acad. affairs U. N.H., Durham, 1999—. Chair dept. philosophy U. Memphis, 1982—85, founding dir. Ctr. for the Humanities, 1987—89. Author: Philosophy in Question: Essays on a Pyrrhonian Theme, 1988; editor (with James Bohman and Richard Shusterman): The Interpretive Turn: Philosophy, Science and Culture, 1991; contbr. articles to profl. jours. Fellow, Fulbright Found., Korea, NEH. Fellow: Assn. Am. Colls.; mem.: Phi Kappa Phi. Office: U NH Office of Provost and VP Acad Affairs Durham NH 03824

HILFERTY, BRYAN CAREY, public relations specialist; b. Arlington, Mass., Aug. 10, 1960; s. Walter Gerard and Ruthe (Hughes) H.; m. Shawna LaNaye Patton, Aug. 16, 1990. BA, U. Mass., 1987; MA, Colo. State U., 1996. Commd. 2d lt. U.S. Army, 1984, advanced through grades to lt. col., 2002; asst. prof. English U.S. Mil. Acad., West Point, N.Y., 1996-99; pub. affairs officer U.S. Army, Alaska, 1999—2001, pub. affairs officer 10th Mountain divsn., Afghanistan Ft. Drum, NY, 2001—; pub. affairs officer Dept. Army, 2004—. Contbr. articles to profl. jours. Decorated Bronze Star medals (3). Mem. Pub. Rels. Soc. Am., Assn. U.S. Army, VFW, Rotary. Roman Catholic. Avocations: chess, boating. Home: 1910 Rampart Dr Alexandria VA 22308 Office Phone: 703-693-0295. E-mail: bhilferty@cox.net.

HILFIGER, TOMMY (THOMAS JACOB HILFIGER), fashion designer; b. Elmira, New York, Mar. 24, 1951; m. Susie Hilfiger, 1980 (div. 2000); 4 children. Designer, owner People's Place, NY, to 1979; pres. Tommy Hilfiger Corp., 1982—89, head designer now prin. designer, 1984—, dir., 1992—, hon. chmn. bd., 1994—. Host (TV series) the Cut, 2005—; actor: (films) The Intern, 2000, Zoolander, 2001; (TV series) Rich Girls, 2003, (TV) The Beatles Revolution, 2000; voice (TV series) Frasier, 1994, guest appearances (TV) VH1 Fashion Awards, 1997, ESPN Sports Century, 2000; guest appearances Pulse, 2004. Founder Tommy Hilfiger Corp. Found., 1995—; mem. Martin Luther King Jr. Nat. Mem. Project Found., Anti-Defamation League; dir. Fresh Air Fund, Race to Erase MS, 1994—. Recipient From the Catwalk to the Sidewalk award, VH1, 1995, Designer of the Year award, GQ, 1998, Parson's Sch. Design, 1998, International Designer of the Year award, GQ, 2002, Future of Am. award, Drug Abuse Resistance Education (D.A.R.E.), 2002. Mem. Coun. Fashion Designers Am. (Menswear Designer of Yr. 1995). Address: Tommy Hilfiger Corp 25 W 39th St New York NY 10018 Office: Tommy Hilfiger Corp 9 F Novel Industrial Blvd 850-870 Lai Chi Kok Rd Cheung Sha Wan Hong Kong Office Phone: 212-840-8888, 852 2216 0668.

HILGENBERG, JOHN CHRISTIAN, corporate financial executive, consultant; b. Balt., Sept. 6, 1941; s. Carl R. and Elizabeth (Rianhard) Hilgenberg; m. Evelyn Brantley Handy, Apr. 1, 1971; children: Rodney, Crady. BA, Yale U., 1963; MBA, U. Va., 1965. With internat. lending divsn. Md. Nat. Bank, Balt., 1970-75; v.p., dir. fin. svcs. S.M. Hyman Co., Balt., 1975-78; v.p. fin. Eastmet Corp., Balt., 1978-85. Trustee Harbor Hosp. Ctr., 1975—2002, Harbor Hosp. Found., 2002—; v.p., treas., dir. Sky Alland Rsch. Corp., 1986, 1989—90; pres., bd. dirs. Ski Tech. Holdings, Inc., 1987—89, CADS USA, Inc., 1987—89; mng. ptnr. Eager St. Group, Inc., Balt., 1991—; cons., investor in early-stage cos.; bd. dirs. Synthecell Corp., pres., 1992—95; bd. dirs. Cyto Pulse Scis., Inc., Salar, Inc. Lt. USNR, 1965—70. Mem.: Balt. Choral Arts Soc. (dir. 1975—2004), Bachelors Cotillon, Md. Club, Elkridge Club. Republican. Episcopalian. Address: PO Box 338 2705 Greenspring Valley Rd Stevenson MD 21153 Office Phone: 888-828-1400. Personal E-mail: jhilgenberg@eagerstreet.com.

HILGERS, JOHN JACK WILLIAM, management and transportation consultant; b. Carmel-by-the-Sea, Calif., Nov. 17, 1934; s. Rudolph Joseph and Eleanor Maude (King) H.; m. Sharon Ann Hilgers, Dec. 15, 1968; children; Jon Marc, John Jack William Jr. BA in Psychology, San Jose State U., 1956; BA in Criminology, U. Calif., Berkeley, 1963; MS in Sys. Mgmt., U. So. Calif., 1984; MS in Urban Studies, Old Dominion U., 1995, PhD in Urban Svcs., 1998. Enlisted USMC, 1957, advanced in grades to col., ret. Norfolk, 1988; rsch. asst. Bur. Rsch. Old Dominion U., Norfolk, 1988-90, program mgr. Coll. Bus. and Pub. Adminstrn., 1991-98, assoc. dir. Internat. Maritime Ports and Logistics Inst., 1993—98; exec. asst. Va. Legislature, 1999—. Dir., mem. exec. com. Atlantic Rim Network, Boston, 1995-2001; exec. sec. Maritime Adv. Coun., Norfolk, 1991—; mem. tech. com. Met. Planning Orgn., Hampton Roads, Va., 1996-98; internat. maritime com. chmn. Conf. of World Regions, 1997-03. Editor (newsletter) Bullets and Cannonballs, 1993-98, (mag.) Bus. and Econ. Quar., 1992-96. Divsn. dir. United Way, Norfolk, 1996, 97, Virginia Beach Sister City Group, 1995-2000; trustee Old Dominion U., 1998-2002, Old Dominion U. Rsch. Found. Bd., 2001--. Recipient Va. Commerce Builder award, 1999, Va. Patrick Henry award, Commonwealth of Va., 2001. Mem.: ASPA (exec. com. transp. policy and adminstrn. com. 1997—2001), Internat. Bus. Coun., Econs. Club (Hampton Roads), Propeller Club U.S. (dir. Port of Norfolk 1996—2003), Pepper Lovers Club Va. Internat. (dir. 1994—96), Hampton Roads Fgn. Commerce Club (pres. 1996), Rotary (pres. Sunrise Norfolk chpt 1997—98, asst. gov. Dist. 7600 2002—04, Paul Harris fellow 1996, 2002), Phi Alpha Alpha, Phi Kappa Phi. Avocation: antique and classic automobiles. Home and Office: 1309 Lakeview Dr Virginia Beach VA 23454 Office Phone: 757-490-8383. E-mail: jackhilgers@earthlink.net.

HILL, ALAN GORDON, sociologist, educator; b. Greenville, SC, Jan. 25, 1945; s. Arthur G. Hill, Bonta Bush Hill; m. Toyo Murono; 1 child, Arthur. M.Phil., MA, Columbia University, New York, NY, 1967—76; BA, Furman University, Greenville, 1963—67. Chair, Dept. of Sociology Delta College, University Center, MI, 1987—2002; Sociology Instructor Furman University, Greenville, SC, 1979—87. Executive Officer Michigan Sociological Association, MI, 2000—02. Author: (Book) Discovering Society, 1999 (Distinguished Contribution to Instruction, Computers and Sociology Section, American Sociological Assn., 2000). Moderator New Hope Baptist Church, Bay City, MI, 2001—02; Vice President Michigan Region of the American Baptist Churches, E. Lansing, MI, 1996—97; President Delta Chapter of AAUP, University Center, MI, 2002—02. Sergeant Army Medical Service Corps, 1969—75, various. Mem.: Michigan Sociological Association (Past President), Michigan Sociological Association (Executive Officer 2000—02), American Sociological Association (Distinguished Contribution to Instruction (listed above) 2000). Baptist. Home: 3637 Monitor Road Bay City MI 48706-9219 Office: Delta College 1961 Delta Road University Center MI 48710 Office Phone: 989-686-9369. Business E-Mail: aghill@alpha.delta.edu.

HILL, ALFRED, law educator; b. N.Y.C., Nov. 7, 1917; m. Dorothy Turck, Aug. 12, 1960; 1 dau., Amelia. BS, Coll. City N.Y., 1937; LL.B., Bklyn. Law Sch., 1941, LL.D., 1986; S.J. D., Harvard U., 1957. Bar: N.Y. State bar 1943, Ill 1958. With SEC, 1943-52; prof. law So. Meth. U., 1953-56, Northwestern U., 1956-62, Columbia U., 1962-75, Simon H. Rifkind prof. law, 1975-87, Simon H. Rifkind prof. law emeritus, 1988—. Contbr. articles on torts, conflict of laws, fed. cts. constl. law to legal jours. Mem. Am. Law Inst. Home: 79 Sherwood Rd Tenafly NJ 07670-2734 Office: Columbia Law Sch New York NY 10027

HILL, ALICE LORRAINE, historian, researcher, genealogist; b. Moore, Okla., Jan. 15, 1935; d. Robert Edward and Alma Alice (Fraysher) H.; children: Debra Hrboka, Pamela Spangler (dec.), Eric Shiver, Lorraine Styczinski. BS in Bus. and Acctg., Ctrl. State U., 1977; student, U. Okla., 1977-78; postgrad., Calif. Luth. U., 1988; ed. Sch. Edn., UCLA, 1990. Cert. cmty. coll. life instr. acctg., bus. and indsl. mgmt., computer and related techs., and real estate, Calif.; real estate broker, Wash., Calif. Former model, 1990-95; with L.A. Unified Sch. Dist., 1990-95; real estate broker Shiver Realty, Oxnard, Calif., 2003—; tchr. mentor K-12 Asuza (Calif.) Pacific U., 2005—. Founder Los Artistas for creative activities for young people, 1975. Author: America, We Love You (Congl. Record Poem, made into World's 1st Internat. Patriotic song), 1975, Land of Lands (now world's first internat. patriotic song); author: (lyrics) Come Listen to the Music, 2004, Someday John, 1996. Named hon. grad., Patricia Stevens Modeling Sch., Fla.; recipient Hon. recognition, Okla. State Bd. of Regents for Higher Edn., 1977, Presdl. citations for Pres. Ford, 1975, 1976, Admired Woman of the Decade award, 1994, Lifetime Achievement award, 1995, Most Gold Record award, 1995, Key award for rsch., Woman of Yr. award, 1995, The Alice Lorraine Hill Poet of Yr. medallion, The Famous Poets Soc., 2003; scholar Leadership Enrichment Program, Okla., 1977. Mem.: AAUW, Freedom Force Internat., Internat. Poetry Soc. (disting., internat. hall of fame 1996, Best Poets of 20th Century). Home: 1646 Lime Ave Oxnard CA 93033-6897 Office Phone: 805-488-6412. E-mail: alice.hill@dock.net.

HILL, ALLEN EDWARD, transportation services executive; b. Decatur, Ala., Sept. 9, 1955; BA, David Lipscomb U., Nashville, 1977; JD, Nashville Sch. Law, 1984. Bar: Tenn. 1984. Joined as package loader and sorter UPS, Inc., 1976, joined legal dept., 1988, v.p., dept. mgr. corp. legal group, 1995—2003, sr. v.p. legal and pub. affairs, gen. counsel, corp. sec., 2004—. Bd. vis. Ga. State U. Coll. Law. Mem.: ABA, Tenn. Bar Assn., Am. Corp. Counsel Assn. Office: United Parcel Svc Inc 55 Glenlake Pkwy NE Atlanta GA 30328

HILL, ANTONY J., headmaster, history educator; BA with honors, Sydney U.; MEd, Boston U. Lawyer, Sydney, Australia; teacher Narrabeen Girls' High Sch.; asst. head of sch. then head of sch. King's Sch., Sydney; head of sch. Christ Church Grammar, Perth, Melbourne Grammar, Melbourne, St. Mark's Sch., Boston, 1994—. Mem. Nat. Bd. of Employment, Edu. & Training, Schools Council, Australia. Mem.: AISV, AISWA, NCISA, AHISA, HMC, Australian Coll. of Edu., Phi Delta Kappa. Office: St Mark's Sch 25 Marlborough Rd Southborough MA 01772*

HILL, BARBARA BENTON, healthcare executive; b. Balt., May 28, 1952; d. George Stock and Charlotte (Russ) Benton; m. Charles David Hill, June 4, 1970 (dec. Oct. 1980); children: Gregory George, Douglas Charles; m. Ancelmo E. Lopes, May 9, 1987. BA, John's Hopkins U., 1973, MS, 1976. Counselor Planned Parenthood of Md., Balt., 1975-76, Hillcrest Clinic, Balt., 1977, dir. community rels., 1977-78, adminstr., 1978-80, exec. dir., 1980-83; pres. Hill & Ward Constrn. Co., Balt., 1980-81; exec. dir. East Balt. Med. Plan, Balt., 1983-84; v.p. John's Hopkins Health Plan, Balt., 1984-85, pres., 1985-91, Hopkins Preferred Network, Balt., 1986-91; v.p. mid-atlantic group ops. Prudential Ins. Co., Balt., 1991-93, v.p. health care policy Newark, 1993-94; pres. Aetna Health Plans of Midwest, Chgo., 1994-96, Rush Prudential Health Plans, Chgo., 1996—. Treas. Greater Balt. com., 1993-94, bd. dirs., 1991-94; mem. Mayor's Econ. Adv. Coun., 1993-94. Named Businessperson of the Yr., Balt. Bus. Jour., 1989. Mem. Ill. Assn. HMOs (v.p. 1994-96, pres. 1996—), Md. C. of C. (bd. dirs. 1993-94), Phi Beta Kappa. Office: Rush Prudential Health Plans 233 S Wacker Dr Ste 3900 Chicago IL 60606-6324

HILL, BARON PAUL, former congressman; b. Seymour, Ind., June 23, 1953; s. Edwin Merrill and Edith Goen Hill; m. Betty Jean Schepman, 1972; children: Jennifer, Cara, Elizabeth. BS in History, Furman U., 1975. Fin. analyst Merrill Lynch; mem. U.S. Congress from 9th Ind. dist., 1999—2005. Mem. Agr., Armed Forces coms., Blue Dog Dems., New Dem. Coalition, Joint Econ. Com., Com. Veterans Affairs. Mem., Ind. Ho. Reps., 1982-90; appointed by Speaker of the House to serve as chmn. House Rules Com.; asst. whip for Dem. Caucus, as chmn. Ind. House Campaign Com. from 1985-89; exec. dir. State Student Assistance Commn., 1992. Democrat.

HILL, BARRY MORTON, lawyer; b. Wheeling, W.Va., Sept. 13, 1946; m. Jacqueline Sue Jackson, Aug. 12, 1967 (div. Mar. 1988); children: Jackson Duff, Brandy; m. Lisa C. Wien, Jan. 7, 1989; 1 child, Gabriel Hunter. BS in Journalism, W.Va. U., 1968, JD, 1977. Bar: W.Va. 1977, U.S Dist. Ct. (no. and so. dists.) W.Va. 1977, Ohio 1978, U.S. Dist. Ct. (no. dist.) Ohio 1978, U.S. Ct. Appeals (3d, 4th, 6th and D.C. cirs.) 1984, U.S. Supreme Ct. 1984, U.S. Ct. Appeals (2d and 11th cirs.) 1986, Pa. 1986, U.S. Ct. Appeals (5th, 7th and 10th cirs.) 1988; cert. civil trial specialist Nat. Bd. Trial Adv., med. profl. liability trial specialist Am. Bd. Profl. Liability Attys. Ptnr. Hill Toriseva & Williams, Wheeling, W.Va. Spl. asst. atty. gen., State of W.Va., for antitrust and consumer protection litigation; chmn. W.Va. std. med. malpractice jury instrn. com., 2000; adj. prof. Saba U. Sch. of Medicine, 1994-96. Founding sponsor Civil Justice Found. Served to 1st lt. U.S. Army, 1969—71. Mem.: ATLA (chmn. propulsid litigation group 2000—, chmn. Baycol litigation group 2002—04), So. Trial Lawyers Assn. (bd. govs. 1988—), W.Va. Trial Lawyers Assn. (pres. 1987—88, ct. apptd. state liaison propulsed multi-dist. litig. US Dist. Ct. 2001—05, Outstanding mem. 1984), Pa. Trial Lawyers Assn., Ohio Acad. Trial Lawyers, Am. Bd. Profl. Liability Attys. (Risperdal/Duragesic and Celebrex/Bextra Consumer Protection litig. 2003—05, diplomate, spl. asst. atty. gen. State of W.Va., sects. banking litig., Visa/Mastercard Antitrust litig., augmentin/Relafen/Paxil Antitrust li). Democrat. Avocations: scuba, tennis, travel, writing, golf. Office: Hill Torisev & Williams 89 12th St Wheeling WV 26003-3266 Office Phone: 304-233-4966. Business E-Mail: bhill@htwlaw.us.

HILL, BONNIE GUITON, consulting company executive; b. Springfield, Ill., Oct. 30, 1941; d. Henry Frank and Elizabeth (Newman) Brazelton; m. Walter Hill Jr.; 1 child, Nichele Monique. BA, Mills Coll., 1974; MS, Calif. State U., Hayward, 1975; EdD, U. Calif., Berkeley, 1985. Adminstr. asst. to pres.'s spl. asst. Mills Coll., Oakland, Calif., 1970-71, adminstrv. asst. to asst. v.p., 1972-73, student svcs. counselor, adv. to resuming students, 1973-74, asst. dean of students, interim dir. ethnic studies, lectr., 1975-76; exec. dir. Marcus A. Foster Ednl. Inst., Oakland, 1976-79; adminstrv. mgr. Kaiser Aluminum & Chem. Corp., Oakland, 1979-80; v.p., gen. mgr. Kaiser CTR Inc., Oakland, 1980-84; vice chair Postal Rate Commn., Washington, 1985-87; asst. sec. for vocat. and adult edn. Dept. Edn., Washington, 1987-89; sec. State and Consumer Svcs. Agy. State of Calif.; spl. adv. to Pres. for Consumer Affairs, dir. U.S. Office Consumer Affairs, 1989-90; pres., CEO Earth Conservation Corps, Washington, 1990-91; sec. State and Consumer Svcs. Industry, State of Calif., 1991-92; dean McIntire Sch. Commerce U. Va., Charlottesville, 1992-97; v.p. The Times Mirror Co., 1997-2000; pres. B. Hill Enterprises, LLC, 2001—; COO Iconblue, Inc., LA Times, 2001—. Sr. v.p. comm. and pub. affairs L.A. Times, 1998—2001; pres., CEO The Times Mirror Found., 1997—2001; bd. dirs. The Home Depot Co., Hershey Foods Corp., AK Steele Corp., Yum Brands, Inc., Albertsons Inc., Calif. Water Svc. Co. Office: B Hill Enterprises LLC Ste 600 5670 Wilshire Blvd Los Angeles CA 90036 Office Phone: 323-634-5312.

HILL, BRIAN, professional basketball team coach; b. East Orange, N.J., Sept. 19, 1947; m. Kay Hill; children: Kimberly, Christopher. BS in Phys. Edn., Kennedy Coll., 1969. Basketball coach Clifford Scott High Sch., 1970-72; asst. coach Montclair State U., 1972-74, Pa. State U., 1983-86, Lehigh U., 1974, head coach, 1975-83; asst. coach Atlanta Hawks, 1986-90, Orlando (Fla.) Magic, 1990-93, head coach, 1993-97, 2005—, Vancouver Grizzlies, 1997-99. Head coach NBA Ea. Conf. All-Stars, 1995. Office: Orlando Magic 8701 Maitland Summit Blvd Orlando FL 32810*

HILL, BRUCE MARVIN, statistician, educator; b. Chgo., Mar. 13, 1935; s. Samuel and Leah (Berman) H.; m. Linda Ladd, June 18, 1958; children—Alec Michael, Russell Andrew, Gregory Bruce; m. Anne Edith Gardiner Bruce, Aug. 5, 1972. BS in Math., U. Chgo., 1956; MS in Stats., Stanford U., 1958, PhD in Stats., 1961. Mem. faculty U. Mich., Ann Arbor, 1960—, assoc. prof. stats. and probability theory, 1964-70, prof., 1970—. Vis. prof. bus. Harvard U., 1964-65; vis. prof. systems engring. U. Lancaster, U.K., 1968-69; vis. prof. stats. U. London, 1976; vis. prof. econs. U. Utah, 1979; vis. prof. math. U. Milan, U. Rome, 1989. Author: Hill Tail index estimator; editor Jour. Am. Statis. Assn., 1977-83, Jour. Bus. and Econ. Stats., 1982—; contbr. articles to profl. jours., chpts. to books on stats, encys. Grantee NSF, 1962-69, 81-86, 89—, USAF, 1971-73, 87-89. Fellow Am. Statis. Assn. (pres. Ann Arbor chpt. 1986-91), Inst. Math. Stats.; mem. AAUP, Am. Math Assn., Rsch. Club U. Mich., Psi Upsilon, Sigma Chi. Office: U Mich Dept Stats Ann Arbor MI 48109-1027 Home: 1645 Polipoli Rd Kula HI 96790-7524 Personal E-mail: bhill@prodigy.net.

HILL, CAMILLE CRUNELLE, music educator; b. Chgo., Nov. 1, 1938; d. Lawrence D. and Helen (Doft) Crunelle; m. J. Robert Hill, June 28, 1963; children: Anne, Yvonne. BMus, Northwestern U., 1960, MusM, 1962; BME, Wis. State U. Stevens Point, 1961; PhD, U. Ky., 1996. Instr. Music, French Lindsey Wilson Coll., Columbia, Ky., 1962—66, Elizabethtown C.C., Elizabethtown, Ky., 1966—86, assoc. prof., prof. music, chmn. divsn. arts and humanities, 1986—. Choir dir. First Presbyn. Ch., Elizabethtown, 1970—88. Chair Program Artists VSA Arts, Elizabethtown, 1985—. Mem.: Am. Assn. Tchr. French, Am. Assn. Tchr. of Fgn. Langs., Music Educators Nat. Conf., Am. Choral Dirs. Assn., Am. Musicol. Soc. Democrat. Office: Elizabeth Cmty and Tech Coll 600 College Street Rd Elizabethtown KY 42701 Office Phone: 270-706-8448. Business E-Mail: camille.hill@kctcs.edu.

HILL, CAROL KOELLING, library director; BS, Mo. Western State, 1974; MLS, Emporia State U., 1980. Libr. dir. City of Fort Walton Beach, Fla., 1995—. Office: 185 Miracle Strip Pkwy SE Fort Walton Beach FL 32548-6614 E-mail: chill@fwb.org.

HILL, CAROLYN JO, art educator; b. Raleigh, NC, Nov. 12, 1964; d. George Floyd and Martha Ellis Hill. BA, Meredith Coll., 1987; BFA, East Carolina U., 2003; student, Barton Coll., 2004. Graphic designer Meredith Coll., Raleigh, NC, 1987—93; part-time assessment specialist, art instr. Wayne C.C., Goldsboro, NC, 1993—2004; art instr. Wayne County Day Sch., Goldsboro, NC, 2005—. Part-time instr. McKimmon Ctr. NC State U., Raleigh, 1993; part-time instr. Project Enable Wayne C.C., 1993—94. One-woman shows include Kinston Cmty. Coun. Arts, 2003. Vol. 150 mile bike tour Nat. Multiple Sclerosis Soc., Newbern, NC, 2003, 2004. Recipient Best in Show photo divsn., Wayne County Agrl. Fair, Goldsboro, 2003, 3d Pl. award portrait photo, Woman's Club NC, State Conference, 2004. Mem.: Nat. Art Educators' Assn., Goldsboro Jr. Woman's Club (corr. sec. 2004, bd. dirs., Kitty Askins Newcomer's award 2003—04). Avocations: photography, computer art, swimming, walking, reading.

HILL, CATHARINE B., economics professor, provost; BA, Williams Coll., 1976; BA with 1st class honors, Oxford U., 1978; PhD, Yale U., 1985. Former Arthur Okun Rsch. fellow Brookings Instn., Washington; formerly with Econ. Devel. Inst., Ministry of Fin., Zambia, World Bank; former chair dept. econs. and Ctr. for Devel. Econs. Williams Coll., Williamstown, Mass., provost, John J. Gibson prof. econs. Contbr. articles to profl. jours.; co-editor: Public Expenditure in Africa. Grantee, NSF, Coun. on Fgn. Rels., Am. Coun. Learned Socs. Office: Williams Coll Provost Office 880 Main St Hopkins Hall 3d Fl Williamstown MA 01267

HILL, CATHERINE PARHAM, school psychologist; b. Fort Chaffee, Ark., July 2, 1951; d. Aubrey Brunson and LaVerne O'Neal Parham; children: Leslie Hill Crow, Lucas Parham, Andrew Cleveland. BS, La. Tech U., 1973, MS, 1974, U. La., 2003. Nationally Certified School Psychologist Nat. Sch. Psychology Certification Bd., 2004, Certified School Psychologist State of La., 2003, Certified Secondary Teacher State of La., 1974. Tchr. Richland Parish Sch. Sys., Mangham, La., 1973—2000; sch. psychologist Tangipahoa Parish Schools, Amite, La., 2002—. La. at-large bd. mem. Ozark Soc., Little Rock, 1999—. Mem.: NASP (assoc.), La. Sch. Psychologist Assn. (assoc.), Am. Canoe Assn., Ozark Soc., Ark. Canoe Club, Psi Chi, Phi Kappa Phi, Pi Mu Epsilon, Omicron Delta Kappa. Office: Tangipahoa Parish Pupil Appraisal 1745 SW Railroad Ave Ste 302 Hammond LA 70403 Office Phone: 985-310-2128.

HILL, CHARLES GRAHAM, JR., chemical engineering educator; b. Elmira, N.Y., July 28, 1937; s. Charles Graham and Ethel Mayburn (Pfleegor) H.; m. Katharine Mertice Koon, July 11, 1964; children: Elizabeth, Deborah, Cynthia. BS, MIT, 1959, MS, 1960, ScD, 1964. Asst. prof. MIT, Cambridge, 1964-65, U. Wis., Madison, 1967-71, assoc. prof., 1971-76, prof. chem. engring., 1976—, John T. and Magdalen L. Sobota prof. chem. engring., 1995—, prof. food sci., 1989—, chmn. dept. chem. engring., 1989-92. Cons. A.D. Little, Cambridge, 1964-65, Joseph Schlitz Brewing Co., Milw., 1973-76, Nat. Bur. Stds., 1979-95. Author: Introduction to Chemical Engineering Kinetics and Reactor Design, 1977; contbr. articles to profl. jours. Capt. U.S. Army, 1965-67. Gen. Motors Nat. scholar, 1955-59; NSF fellow, 1959-62, Ford Found. fellow, 1964-65, Fulbright Sr. fellow, 2000. Fellow AIChE; mem. Am. Chem. Soc., Inst. Food Technologists, Am. Oil Chemists Soc., Soc. Biological Engring, Sigma Xi, Tau Beta Pi, Phi Lambda Upsilon. Republican. Presbyterian. Office: U Wis Dept Chem Engring 1415 Engineering Dr Madison WI 53706-1607 Office Phone: 608-263-4593. Business E-Mail: hill@engr.wisc.edu.

HILL, CHRISTOPHER R., federal agency administrator, former ambassador; b. Little Compton, R.I. BA in Econs., Bowdoin Coll., Brunswick, Maine, 1974; MS, Naval War Coll., 1994. Vol. Peace Corps, Cameroon; with Sr. Fgn. Svc., Class of Minister-Counselor; sr. country officer for Polish affairs US Dept. State, US amb. to Macedonia Skopje, 1996—99; sr. dir. S.E. European affairs NSC, Washington, 1999—2000; amb. to Poland US Dept. State, Warsaw, 2000—04, amb. to Republic of Korea Seoul, 2004—05, asst. sec. East Asian & Pacific Affairs Washington, 2005—. Recipient Robert S. Frasure award for Peace Negotiations, Dept. State, Disting. Svc. award for Bosnian peace negotiations. Office: US Dept State Harry S Truman Bldg 2201 C St NW Rm 6205 Washington DC 20520

HILL, CLARA EDITH, psychologist, educator; b. Shivers, Miss., Sept. 13, 1948; d. Fletcher Von and Anna (Teich) H.; m. James Gormally, May 25, 1974; children: Kevin, Katherine. BA, So. Ill. U., 1970, MA, 1972, PhD, 1974. Lic. psychologist, Md. Asst. prof. dept. psychology U. Md., College Park, 1974-78, assoc. prof. dept. psychology, 1978-85, prof. dept. psychology, 85—. Author: Therapist Techniques and Client Outcomes, 1989, Working with Dreams in Psychotherapy, 1996, Helping Skills: The Empirical Foundation, 2001, Helping Skills: Facilitating Exploration, Insight and Action, 1999, Helping Skills: Facilitating Exploration, Insight and Action 2d edit., 2004, Dream Work in Therapy: Facilitating Exploration, Insight and Action, 2004; editor: Jour. Counseling Psychology, 1994—99, Psychotherapy Rsch., 2004—. Grantee NIMH, 1983-92. Fellow APA (Leona Tyler award, divsn. 17 2002, Disting. Psychologist award, divsn. 29, 2003); mem. Soc. Psychotherapy Rsch. (pres. N.Am. chpt. 1990, pres. internat. orgn. 1994-95), Assn. Study of Dreams, Soc. Exploration of Psychotherapy Integration. Avocations: reading, dining out, walking. Office: U Maryland Dept Psychology College Park MD 20742-0001 Business E-Mail: Hill@psyc.umd.edu.

HILL, CLINTON, artist; b. Payette, Idaho, Mar. 8, 1922; s. Samuel Edgar and Iva Marie (Horn) H. BS U. Oreg., 1947; postgrad., Bklyn. Mus. Sch., 1949-51, Academie de la Grande Chaumiere, Paris, France, 1951, Instituto d'Arte Statale, Florence, Italy, 1951-52. Prof. Queens Coll., N.Y.C., 1968-87, now prof. emeritus. One-man shows include Marilyn Pearl Gallery, N.Y.C., 10 shows 1979-92, Montclair Mus., N.J., 1981, Galleria Blu, Milan, Italy, 1984, Worcester Mus., Mass., 1992, Andre Zarre Gallery, N.Y.C., 1993-2001; represented in permanent collections Mus. Modern Art, N.Y.C., Met. Mus., N.Y.C., Phila. Mus., Albright Knox Gallery, Buffalo, Nat. Gallery Australia, Canberra, Bklyn. Mus., Phoenix Art Mus., Whitney Mus., N.Y.C., Brit. Mus., London, Fogg Mus., Harvard U., Princeton (N.J.) U. Libr. Rare Books Divsn., Godwin-Ternbach Mus. Queens Coll., N.Y., others. Served to lt. (j.g.) USN, 1943-47. Fulbright grantee India, 1956; Creative Artists Pub. Service grantee, 1975; Nat. Endowment for Arts grantee, 1976, 80*

HILL, DARLENE, newscaster; b. Cleve. m. Bernard Murray, 1996; 2 children. B, Ohio State U. Gen. assignment reporter CBS affiliate, Monterey, Calif.; anchor and reporter KJRH-TV, Tulsa, Okla., WFLD-TV, Chgo., 1994—. TV Journalist The Expt. in Black and White, 2002 (Nat. Emmy award cmty. svc., regional Emmy award, AP award, Edward R. Murrow award, Scripps Howard Found. award, Nat. Assn. Black Journalists award, Soc. Profl. Journalists award). Mem.: Chgo. Assn. of Black Journalists, Nat. Assn. of Black Journalists, Alpha Kappa Alpha. Office: WFLD-TV 205 N Mich Ave Chicago IL 60601

HILL, DAVID, broadcast executive; b. Australia; V.p. of Sports Nine Network, Australia, 1977—88; head Eurosport, England, 1988—91, Sky Sports, England, 1991—93; pres. Fox Sports, Los Angeles, 1993—; CEO Fox Sports Network, 1996—; chmn., CEO Fox TV, 1996—. Office: Fox Sports PO Box 900 Beverly Hills CA 90213-0900 also: 575 Amalfi Dr Pacific Palisades CA 90272-4504*

HILL, DAVID ALLAN, electrical engineer; b. Cleve., Apr. 21, 1942; s. Martin D. and Geraldine S. (Yoder) H.; m. Elaine C. Dempsey, July 9, 1971. BSEE, Ohio U., 1964, MSEE, 1966; PhD in Elec. Engring., Ohio State U., 1970. Vis. fellow Coop. Inst. for Rsch. Environ. Sci., Boulder, Colo., 1970-71; rsch engr. Inst. for Telecommunication Scis., Boulder, 1971-82; sr. scientist Nat. Inst. Stds. and Tech., Boulder, 1982—. Adj. prof. U. Colo., Boulder, 1980-. Editor Geosci. and Remote Sensing Jour., 1980-84, Antennas and Propagation Jour., 1986-89; contbr. over 150 articles to profl. jours., chpts. to books. Recipient award for best paper Electromagnetic Compatability Jour., 1987, 2003. Fellow IEEE (chpt. chmn. 1975-76, editor 1986-89); mem. Electromagnetic Soc. (bd. dirs. 1980-86), Internat. Union Radio Sci. (nat. com. 1986-89), Colo. Mountain Club (Boulder), Sierra Club. Office: Nat Inst Stds & Tech 813-02 325 Broadway St Boulder CO 80305-3337 Business E-Mail: dhill@boulder.nist.gov.

HILL, DAVID LAWRENCE, lawyer, real estate agent; b. Balt., Mar. 21, 1945; s. Albert Lawrence and Thelma Jane (Pierson) H.; m. Carol Lee Cato, Feb. 12, 1966 (div.); children: Dave Jr., Brian L., Martha J.; m. Pamela Ann Haddad, Mar. 02, 2000. AB, W.Wv. U., 1969, MA, 1971; JD, Wake Forest U., 1974. Bar: N.C. 1974, U.S. Dist. Ct. (mid. dist.) N.C. 1974, W.Va. 1976, U.S. Dist. Ct. (so. dist.) W.Va. 1976. Pvt. practice, Winston-Salem, N.C., 1974-75; hearing officer N.C. Bd. Alcohol Control, Raleigh, N.C., 1975-78; pvt. practice Hurrican, W.Va., 1978—. Mem. mental hygiene com., 1986—. Mem. B'nai Brith. Mem. Masons, Rotary, Shriners, Scottish Rite. Home: PO Box 506 Hurricane WV 25526-0506 Office: 210 Midland Trl Hurricane WV 25526-1429

HILL, DAVID R., federal agency administrator, lawyer; b. 1963; m. Kristina Hill; 3 children. BA, U. Mo., 1985; JD, Northwestern U. Law clk. to Judge James K. Logan U.S. Ct. Appeals (10th cir.); assoc. counsel com. on agriculture U.S. Ho. of Reps., Washington; ptnr. Wiley, Rein, & Fielding, LLP, Washington, Blackwell Sanders Peper Martin, LLP, Kansas City, Mo.; dep. gen. counsel for energy policy U.S. Dept. Energy, Washington, 2002—05, gen. counsel, 2005—. Office: US Dept of Energy Forrestal Bldg 1000 Independence Ave SW Rm 6A 245 Washington DC 20585-1000 Office Phone: 202-586-5281. Office Fax: 202-586-1499.*

HILL, DAVID WARREN, lawyer; b. Taunton, Mass., May 27, 1946; s. Warren Witherell and Frances Robbins (Allen) H.; m. Jane Leslie Shields, June 14, 1969; children: Trevor Campbell, Ainsley Shields. BS in Engring., U.S. Mil. Acad., 1969; MSBA, Boston U., 1974; JD, George Washington U., 1977, LLM with highest honors, 1981. Bar: D.C. 1977, Va. 2003. Commd. 2d lt. U.S. Army, 1969, advanced through grades to maj., 1976, ret., 1990; tech. advisor U.S. Ct. Customs and Patent Appeals, Washington, 1976-77; assoc. Finnegan, Henderson, Farabow, Garrett & Dunner, Washington, 1977-83, ptnr., 1983—. Chmn. bd. 1st Ch. of Christ Scientist, Alexandria, Va., 1985, McLean, Va., 1993-94, 2d reader, 1998-2001; bd. dirs. Reps. Abroad, Tokyo, 1988; scoutmaster troop 51 Boy Scouts Am., Tokyo, 1988-89. Mem. Am. Intellectual Property Law Assn. (com. chmn. 1980-85, 95-97, 2000-2002), Licensing Execs. Soc., U.S. Trademark Assn., Bar Assn. D.C. (coun. Patent Trademark Copyright sect. 1985-87), D.C. Bar Assn. (officer intellectual property law sect. 1985-86, 91-97), Va. State Bar (bd. govs. intellectual property sect. 2003—), Am. C. of C. in Japan (com chmn. 1987-89), Army and Navy Club, Tokyo Am. Club. Republican. Office: Finnegan Henderson Farabow Garrett & Dunner Two Freedom Sq 11955 Freedom Dr Reston VA 20190-5675 Office Phone: 571-203-2735. Business E-Mail: david.hill@finnegan.com.

HILL, DEBORA ELIZABETH, writer, journalist, screenwriter; b. San Francisco, July 10, 1961; d. Henry Peter and Madge Lillian (Ridgeway-Aarons) H. BA, Sonoma State U., 1983. Talk show host Rock Jour. Viacom, San Francisco, 1980-81; interviewer, biographer Harrap Ltd., London, 1986-87; editor North Bay Mag., Cotati, Calif., 1988; guest feature writer Argus Courier, Petaluma, Calif., 1993-95; concept developer BiblioBytes, Hoboken, N.J., 1994-95; feature writer The Econs. Press, 1996-97; film cons., editor United Film Prodns. Internat., 2003—. Assoc. prodr. White Tiger Films, 1995—2003; concept developer Star Trek: Voyager and Star Trek: Deep Space Nine, 1997—98; mem. MedioCom, 2001—03; script cons. Shadowhawk Prodns., Ireland, 2003—. Author: CUTS from a San Francisco Rock Journal, 1982, Punk Retro, 1988, Gale Research-Resourceful Woman, 1994, St. James Guide to Fantasy Writers, 1996, St. James Guide to Famous Gays and Lesbians, 1997; co-writer, cons. prodr. The Danger Club; author: A Ghost Among Us, 2002, A Wizard By Any Other Name, 2004, (sequel) Jerome's Quest, 2003, numerous poems, short stories; contbr. articles to profl. jours.;

contbr.: Unconditional Love: Pet Tales By the Humans Who Love Them, 2004, Celebrations: Letter to my Mother, 2004, Letter to my Pet, 2004, Letters to my Father, 2004, featured in anthologies: Resourceful Woman, 1994, The St. James Guide to Fantasy Writers, 1996, The St. James Guide to Famous Gays and Lesbians, 1997, Spectacle: Women on Popular Culture, 1997, Poets of 2000, Poets of 2001, Poets of 2002, Poets of 2004, Between Darkness and Light, 2000, Eyes of the World, 2001, Hidden Frontiers, 2001, The Colors of Life, 2003; author: Love Letters to Mothers, 2003, Love Letters to Pets, 2003, Love Letters to Fathers, 2004. Named Best Poet, Internat. Biographical Ctr., Cambridge, 2003. Democrat. Avocations: clothing design, cooking, internet, reading, interior design. Home and Office: Lost Myths Ink LLC 8312 Windmill Farms Dr Cotati CA 94931-4570 Office Phone: 707-792-7918. Personal E-mail: debhill@att.net.

HILL, DEBORAH NIXON, elementary school educator, minister; b. Norfolk, Va., Apr. 8, 1955; d. Joe Dancy and Gladys Jones Nixon; m. Fred Eugene Hill, July 4, 1975; children: Marcus Donnell, Calvin Dwayne, Alexis Evon. BS in Bus. Adminstrn. and Fin., Norfolk State U., 1973; M in Elem. Edn., Regent U., 1998. Operator/trainer AT&T Co., Norfolk, Va., 1978—92; tchr., child care coord. Norfolk Pub. Schs., 1992—. Lang. art tchr./coord. HOST, 1995—99; mem. Norfolk Pub. Sch. Tchr. Mentor Corp., Norfolk, 1998; site coord. Comer-Zigler, 1998—2003; mem. adv. bd. Ida Gray Yes 2 Children-Before/After Sch. Care, Norfolk, 2003. Mem.: NEA, Va. Edn. Assn. (state del. 2001—02), Internat. Reading Assn. (chaplain Alpha Chi chpt.), Nat. Coun. Negro Women, Iota Phi Lambda. Democrat. Apostolic. Avocations: reading, singing, walking. Home: 2121 Burnside Pl Chesapeake VA 23325 Office: Norfolk Pub Schs 1300 Marshall Ave Norfolk VA 23504

HILL, DEBRA S., lawyer; b. Dennison, Ohio, Apr. 21, 1957; d. Richard A. and Shirley L. (Delcoma) Hill. BA, Kent State U., 1983, MA, 1986; JD, Case Western Reserve U., 1991. Bar: Ohio 1991, Fla. 1998. Gen. counsel Arthur Treachers, Inc., Jacksonville, 1994—97; vis. asst. prof. Fla. Costal Sch. of Law, Jacksonville, 1997—2001; shareholder Debra S. Hill, PA, Jacksonville, 2000; pres. Saculla Hill & Co., Inc., Jacksonville, 2001—02; mng. ptnr. Smith Hill Law Firm, Jacksonville, 2002—. Office: Smith Hill Law Firm 8810 Goodby's Executive Dr Ste C Jacksonville FL 32217 Office Phone: 904-346-0140. E-mail: dhill@fdn.com.

HILL, DONALD DEE, management consultant, educator, writer; b. Moultrie, Ga. s. Thomas Dee and Vivan Mae (Monk) H. BCE, Ga. Inst. Tech. Registered Engr., Ala., Ga. Structural engr. Patchen & Zimmerman Cons. Engrs., Augusta, Ga.; asst. dir. F.S.D. Am. Plywood Assn., Tacoma; mng. dir., CEO ASME Internat. Gas Turbine Inst., Atlanta. Lectr. and spkr. in field; cons., lectr. to Czech Republic, 1996; lectr., Vietnam, 1997; lectr. advanced mgmt. course for vis. Asian execs. Kennesaw State U. Columnist Convene Mag. V.p. Letterman's Club; 1st lt. U.S. Army. Named Eagle of the Acropolis, Palais de Congres, Nice, France; named to Coll. of 17 Gentlemen, Netherlands Congress Bur.; named Ark. Traveler, Gov. of Ark.; recipient R. Tom Sawyer Gas Turbine award ASME, 1996. Mem.: Ga. Tech. Alumni Assn., Meeting Profls. Internat., Am. Soc. Assn. Execs., Kappa Sigma. Avocation: weightlifting. Home and Office: 5108 Parkside Dr Roswell GA 30075-7654

HILL, DONALD RAYMOND, anthropologist, educator; b. Long Beach, Calif., Nov. 21, 1939; s. Lowell Reed and Rosamond (Martin) Hill; m. Blanche Olivia Taylor, June 11, 1962; 1 child, Anthony Alan. BA, Pomona Coll., Claremont, Calif., 1961; MA, San Francisco State U., Calif., 1968; PhD, Ind. U., Bloomington, 1973. Junior College Teaching Credential San Francisco State U., 1968, cert. Jr. Coll. Tchg. Credential Calif., 1968. Instr. in phys. anthropology San Quentin Prison and San Mateo Jr. Coll., San Quentin, Calif., 1967; lectr. in anthropology San Francisco State U., San Francisco, 1967—67; tchg. asst. Ind. U., Bloomington, 1968—69; asst. curator of edn. Am. Mus. of Natural History, New York, NY, 1973—76; asst. prof. anthropology Hunter Coll. & City U. Ctr. of NY, New York, NY, 1976—78; prof. africana/latino studies and anthropology SUNY, Oneonta, NY, 1978—. Dir. minority tng. program Am. Mus. Natural History, co-founder Margaret Mead Film Festival; adj. prof. Anthropology and Mus. Studies NYU, 1975; adj. prof. Hartwick Coll., Oneonta, NY, 1986; cons. in field. Author: Calypso Calaloo (Cowinner U. Chgo. Folklore Prize, Finalist for Assn.Recorded Sound Collections ethnic music category., 1994); prodr.: (CD) Calypso Pioneers, 1989, Arkansas Songs and Tunes of the Ozarks, 1997, 'Goodnight Ladies and Gents': The Creole Music of Lionel Belasco, 1999; mem. editl. bd.: Am. Mus. of Natural History, 1973, Humanities Rev. Jour., 2002—; contbr. photographs to popular mags., articles to profl. jours. Parent rep. Com. on Handicapped Children, Oneonta, NY, 1978—85. With U.S. Army, 1961—64. Fulbright-Hays Grad. Rsch. grant, US Govt., 1970. Mem.: Carriacou Hist. Soc. (assoc.). Democrat. Avocations: swimming, travel, walking. Office: State Univ New York Ravine Parkway Oneonta NY 13820 Office Phone: 607-436-2018. Personal E-mail: hilldr@oneonta.edu.

HILL, DONALD S., state commissioner; married; 2 children. BS cum laude, U. N.H., 1971; MBA, Plymouth State Coll., 1983. Acct. I, II, III N.H. Dept. Edn., Concord, 1971-76, bus. adminstr. III, 1976-82, chief of bus. mgmt., 1982-83; sr. bus. supr. N.H. Dept. of Adminstrv. Svcs., 1983-88, asst. commr., budget officer, 1988-96, commr., 1996—. Budget com. Town of Pembroke, N.H., 1981-87, town treas., 1981-84, bd. of selectman, 1972-81. Office: NH Adminstrv Svcs Dept State House Annex - Rm 120 25 Capitol St Concord NH 03301-6312*

HILL, DONNA MARIE, writer, retired librarian; d. Clarence Henry and Emma Charlotte (Wirthlin) Hill. Student, Phillips Gallery Art Sch., 1940—43; BA, George Washington U., 1948; MS, Columbia U., 1952. Code clk. U.S. Embassy, Paris, 1949—51; asst. to librarian NY Pub. Libr., N.Y.C., 1952—59; instr. Hunter Coll., CUNY, N.Y.C., 1970—75, head tchrs. ctrl. lab., 1974—84, asst. prof., 1975—79, assoc. prof., 1980—84, prof. emeritus, 1984—. Established Donna Hill Collection Marriott Libr., U. Utah, Salt Lake City, 1994. Author: First Your Penny, 1985, Murder Uptown, 1992, Shipwreck Season, 1998 (Christopher award, 99); Exhibited in group shows at Paris, Washington, world tour, 1950—51. Recipient Cert. of Distinction, Alumni Assn. Ctrl. H.S., 1984. Mem.: Women's Nat. Book Assn. (membership chmn. N.Y.C. chpt. 1991—93), Am. Recorder Soc. (nat. sec. 1959—61, editor-in-chief 1962—63), Delta Kappa Gamma (Ruth Mack Havens award 1991), Phi Beta Kappa. Mem. Lds Ch. Avocations: opera, Baroque music, recorder playing, drawing, painting.

HILL, DRAPER, editorial cartoonist; b. Boston, July 1, 1935; s. L. Draper and Jean Hutchins (Thompson) H.; m. Sarah Randolph Adams, Apr. 22, 1967; children: Jennifer Randolph, Jonathan Draper. BA magna cum laude, Harvard U., 1957; postgrad, Slade Sch. Fine Arts, Univ. Coll., London, Eng., 1960-63. Reporter and cartoonist Quincy (Mass.) Patriot Ledger, 1957-60; editorial cartoonist Worcester (Mass.) Telegram, 1964-71, Comml. Appeal, Memphis, 1971-76, The Detroit News, 1976-99; contbg. cartoonist Oakland Press, Pontiac, Mich., 2003—04. Dir. Play of Month Guild, N.Y.C., 1958-82; instr. drawing Worcester Art Sch., 1967-71; lectr. Thomas Nast, Garibaldi, Beerbohm, Gillray, and others. Author: Mr. Gillray, The Caricaturist, 1965, Fashionable Contrasts, 1966, (with James Roper) The Decline and Fall of the Gibbon, 1974, The Satirical Etchings of James Gillray, 1976, (essay) Cartoons & Caricatures in Ency. of Collectibles, 1978, Political Asylum: Editorial Cartoons by Draper Hill, 1985; also catalogs; one-person shows include Art Gallery of Windsor (Ont.), 1985-86, Detroit Hist. Mus., 1996, Detroit Artists Market, 2005. Mem. Egyptians, Memphis, 1972—76, Club Odd Vols., 1965—2000; mem. adv. bd. Swann Found. for Caricature and Cartoon, N.Y.C., 1980—93, 1998—. Winner Thomas Nast prize for editorial cartooning Landau-in-der-Pfalz, Fed. Republic Germany, 1990. Mem.: Witagemote Soc., Assn. Am. Editl. Cartoonists Notebook (2d v.p. 1972—74, 1st v.p. 1974—75, pres. 1975—76, author quar. column History Corner Assn. Notebook 1974—99), Prismatic Club. Home: 368 Washington Rd Grosse Pointe MI 48230-1616

HILL, EDWARD JEFFREY, family life educator; b. Santa Cruz, Calif., Apr. 7, 1953; s. Edward Eyring and LaDean Jones Hill; m. Juanita Ray, May 5, 1976; children: Sarah Ray Allred, Seth Joshua, Jeffrey Ray, Aaron Thomas, Abigail LaDean, Hannah Ray, Heidi Ehtlyn, Emily Ray, Amanda Ray. BA in Comm., Brigham Young U., 1977, M Orgnl. Behavior, 1984; PhD in Family and Human Devel., Utah State U., 1995. Industry specialist office products divsn. IBM, Tacoma, 1977—84, rsch. assoc. SW mktg. divsn. Atlanta, 1984—86, acct. sys. engr. mktg. divsn. Phoenix, 1986—90, project mgr./sr. acct. rep. global employee rsch. divsn. Armonk, NY, 1990—98, part time sr. human resources profl., 2000—02; assoc. prof. home and family living Brigham Young U., Provo, Utah, 1998—. Contbr. articles to profl. jours. Bishop 10th Ward LDS Ch., Logan, Utah, 1995—98, mem. high coun. Orem (Utah) Canyon View stake, 2000—03; bd. dirs. Westhaven Inst., West Haven, Utah, 1995—2003. Recipient Helping Hands award, Utah Non-Profits Assn., 2000. Mem.: APA, Soc. Indsl. and Orgnl. Psychologists, Nat. Coun. Family Rels. (cert. family life educator). Mem. Lds Ch. Avocations: backpacking, jogging, walking. Home: 964 E 930 N Orem UT 84097-3456 Office: Brigham Young U 1042 SWKT Provo UT 84602-5524 Office Phone: 801-422-9091. Personal E-mail: ejhill22@aol.com. Business E-Mail: jeff_hill@byu.edu.

HILL, EDWIN D., trade association administrator; b. Center Township, Pa., Aug. 11, 1937; m. Rosemary Hill; children: Michele Hill, Toni Hill, Edwin Jr. Hill. Pres., co-founder Internat. Brotherhood Elec. Workers Credit Union, 1964—70, bus. mgr., 1970—82; mem. exec. com. & council Penn. AFL-CIO, 1976—97; internat. rep. 3d Dist. Internat. Brotherhood Elec. Workers, 1992—94, v.p. 3d Dist., 1994—97, internat. sec., 1997, internat. sec.-treas., 1998, pres., 2001—. V.p., COPE chmn. Beaver County Central Labor Council, 1972—77; treas., v.p., COPE chmn. Beaver County Building Trades Council, 1970—78. Active with March of Dimes, YMCA, United Way. Office: Internat Brotherhood Elec Workers 1125 15th St NW Washington DC 20005 Office Phone: 202-833-7000.

HILL, ELIZABETH ANNE, academic administrator, lawyer; b. NYC, Dec. 29, 1942; d. Harry Gerald and Grace Marie (Byrne) H. BA, St. Joseph's Coll., Bklyn., 1964; MA, Columbia U., 1965; JD, St. John's Law Sch., Jamaica, N.Y., 1978. Bar: N.Y. 1979, U.S. Dist. Ct. (ea. dist.) N.Y. 1979; cert. tchr. English and social studies K-12, N.Y. HS tchr. Acad. St. Joseph, Brentwood, NY, 1967-70, Bishop Kearney HS, Bklyn., 1970-71; co-dir. formation program Sisters of St. Joseph, Brentwood, 1971-76; atty. Cath. Migration Office, Bklyn., 1978-80; exec. asst. to pres. St. Joseph's Coll., Bklyn., 1980-97, pres., 1997—. Mem. bd. dirs. LI Assn., Commn. Independent Colls. and Univs., Ind. Savings Found., Myrtle Ave. Revitalization Project, Bklyn. C.of C.; mem. bd. trustees LI Reg. Adv. coun. Higher Edn. Mem. Bishop's Commn. on Pub. Policy, Bklyn., 1978-81; mediator Diocesan Mediation and Arbitration Panel, Bklyn., 1981—; bd. dirs. Independence Cmty. Found., Fort Greene Strategic Neighborhood Action Partnership, Fair Media Coun Mem. Nat. Assn. Coll. and Univ. Attys., Bklyn. C. of C. (bd. dirs.). Office: St Joseph's Coll 245 Clinton Ave Brooklyn NY 11205-3602 Business E-Mail: sehill@sjcny.edu.

HILL, ELIZABETH MARIE, research scientist; b. Tuscaloosa, Ala., Oct. 26, 1954; d. William Taylor and Kathleen (Jordan) H. AB in Psychology, U. Mich., 1977; MS in Exptl. Psychology, Tulane U., 1979, PhD in Exptl. Psychology, 1983; MS in Biometry, La. State U., 1986. Instr. dept. psychology Furman U., Greenville, S.C., 1981-82; rsch. fellow dept. psychiatry Albert Einstein Coll. Medicine, N.Y.C., 1982-84; rsch. fellow dept. biometry and genetics La. State U. Med. Ctr., New Orleans, 1985-87; rsch. fellow dept. psychiatry U. Mich., Ann Arbor, 1987-88, asst. rsch. scientist dept. psychiatry, 1990-97; assoc. prof. dept. psychology U. Detroit Mercy, 1997—. Dir. data mgmt. and analysis U. Mich. Alcohol Rsch. Ctr., Ann Arbor, 1989—97. Contbr. articles to profl. jours. Grantee Nat. Inst. on Alcoholism and Alcohol Abuse, 1995, 96. Mem. Rsch. Soc. on Alcoholism, Human Behavior and Evolution Soc. (treas. 1989-90, newsletter editor 1992-97), Animal Behavior Soc. Avocations: sports, enjoying nature. Office: Univ Detroit Mercy Dept Psychology Rm 216 Reno Hall 4001 W McNichols Rd Detroit MI 48221-3038 Office Phone: 313-578-0405.

HILL, ELIZABETH STARR, writer; b. Lynn Haven, Fla., Nov. 4, 1925; d. Raymond King and Gabrielle (Wilson) Cummings; m. Russell Gibson Hill, May 28, 1949 (dec. 1999); children: Andrea van Waldron, Bradford Wray. Student, Finch Jr. Coll., 1941-42, Columbia U., 1970-73. Freelance writer. Past dir. Princeton Creative Ctr.; tchr. writing Princeton Adult Sch. Author: (juvenile books) The Wonderful Visit to Miss Liberty, 1961, The Window Tulip, 1964, Evan's Corner, 1967, 91 (ALA Notable Book for Children), Master Mike and the Miracle Maid, 1967, Pardon My Fangs, 1969, Bells: A Book to Begin On, 1970, Ever-After Island, 1977, Fangs Aren't Everything, 1985, When Christmas Comes, 1989, The Street Dancers, 1991, Broadway Chances, 1992 (ABA Pick of the Lists), The Banjo Player, 1993, Curtain Going Up!, 1995, Bird Boy, 1999 (Outstanding Achievement in Children's Books award Parent's mag. 1999); contbr. articles to mags. including Reader's Digest, many others. Mem. Authors Guild Am., Authors League Am., Univ. Club Winter Park. Office: c/o Harold Ober Assocs Inc 425 Madison Ave New York NY 10017-0940

HILL, ELSA N., headmaster, literature and language educator; m. Anthony Hill. AB, Smith Coll., Northampton, Mass.; MAT, Harvard U.; LIB, U. New S. Wales, Kensington, Australia. Head of sch. St. Mark's Sch., Southborough, Mass., 1994—. Office: St Mark's Sch 25 Marlborough Southborough MA 01772*

HILL, EMITA BRADY, academic administrator, consultant; b. Balt., Jan. 31, 1936; d. Leo and Lucy McCormick (Jewett) Brady; children: Julie Beck, Christopher, Madeleine Vedel. BA, Cornell U., 1957; MA, Middlebury Coll., 1958; PhD, Harvard U., 1967. Instr. Harvard U., 1961-63; asst. prof. Western Reserve U., 1967-69; from asst. prof. to v.p. Lehman Coll. CUNY, Bronx, N.Y., 1970-91; chancellor, grad. faculty Ind. U., Kokomo, Ind., 1991-99, chancellor emerita, 1999—. Vis. advisor Salzburg Seminar Univs. Project; cons. in field. Trustee Am. U. in Central Asia; mem. Women's Forum of NY. Mem.: Internat. Assn. Univ. Pres., Phi Beta Kappa. Avocations: music, scuba diving, tennis. Business E-Mail: ehill@indiana.edu.

HILL, EMMA, apparel executive; b. Eng. Grad., Ravesnbourne Coll. Design and Comm., London. Accessories designer Marc Jacobs; sr. designer for men's and women's accessories Calvin Klein, N.Y.C.; accessories designer Burberry, London; v.p. men's and women's accessories The Gap, Inc., San Francisco, 2002—. Office: Gap Inc Two Folsolm St San Francisco CA 94105

HILL, EMMA LEE, education educator; b. Crane, Tex., Jan. 13, 1949; d. Howard Lee and Eddie Marie (Gill) H. BS, Hardin-Simmons. U., 1970; MEd, Abilene Christian U., 1974, postgrad., 1979. Cert. provisional elem. mentally retarded, lang./learning disabilities, bilingual tchr., profl. supr., profl. midmgmt., tchr. appraiser, Tex. Tchr. Kileen (Tex.) Ind. Sch. Dist., Harker Heights, 1970-71, Winters (Tex.) Ind. Sch. Dist., 1971-73, Abilene (Tex.) Ind. Sch. Dist., 1973—. Bldg. rep. Supt.'s Task Force on Schs. 5-Yr. Plan, Abilene, 1990-91; tchr. leader/dir. Coll. Connections, McMurray U., 1991—; sch. rep. Cleannn/Pond program. Illustrator: (book) Richard the Great, 1967. Mem. local election com. Tex. Tchrs. for Gov., Abilene, 1988; sec. Abilene PTA, 1980-82, Tex. PTA, 1980-82. Scholar Abilene C. of C., 1967-69. Mem. Assn. for Supervision and Curriculum Devel., Internat. Reading Assn., Tex. Assn. Bilingual Educators (pres. Abilene 1988-89), Tex. Classroom Tchrs. Assn., Assn. Tex. Profl. Educators (bldg. rep. 1980—, Outstanding Tchr. award 1989), AAUW, Internat. Soc. Poets (life), Nat. Honor Soc., Delta Kappa Gamma (treas. Abilene 1990-91). Avocations: watching professional sports, playing basketball and baseball, running, walking, movie classics. Home: PO Box 266 Tye TX 79563-0266 Address: 801 G Ave E Apt 3 Alpine TX

HILL, FAITH, musician; b. Jackson, Miss., Sept. 21, 1967; d. Ted and Edna Perry; m. Daniel Hill, 1988 (div. 1991); m. Tim McGraw, Oct. 6, 1996; children: Gracie, Maggie, Audrey. Grad., McLaurin H.S. With Warner Bros. Records, 1993—. Musician: (recordings) Take Me As I Am, 1993, It Matters To Me, 1995, Faith, 1998, Breathe, 1999 (ACM Video of YR., 2000, Billboard Hot 100 Airplay Track of Yr., 2000, Best Female Country Vocal Performance Grammy, 2001, Best Country Album, 2001, Top Selling Album, Can. Country Music Assn., 2001), Cry, 2002 (Best Female Country Vocal Performance Grammy, 2003, Hottest Female Video of Yr., CMT Flameworthy Video Music Awards, 2003); contbr. to sound tracks: Pearl Harbour, How the Grinch Stole Christmas, Prince of Egypt, Practical Magic, Maverick, contbr. to TV sound track: King of the Hill; actor: (films) The Stepford Wives, 2004. Founder Faith Hill Family Literacy Project, 1996. Named New Female Vocalist of Yr., ACM, 1993, Top Country Female Artist, Billboard, 1994, Female Star of Tomorrow, TNN/MCN, 1995, Female Vocalist of Yr., ACM, 1999, TNN/MCN, 2000, Female Country Artist of Yr., Country Weekly, 2000, Hot 100 Singles Female Artist of Yr., Billboard, 2000, Favorite Female Artist Country Music, AMA, 2001, Favorite Pop-Rock Female Artist, 2001, Female Vocalist of Yr., ACM, 2001, TNN/CTM Country Weekly Music Awards, 2001, Favorite Female Artist Country Music, AMA, 2002; recipient Single of Yr., Song of Yr., Video of Yr. for It's Your Love, ACM, 1998, Video of Yr. for This Kiss, CMA, 1998, Single of Yr. for This Kiss, ACM, 1999, Video of Yr. for This Kiss, 1999, Vocal Event of Yr. for Just To Hear You Say You Love Me, 1999, GNN/MCN, 1999, Song of Yr. for Just to Hear You Say That You Love Me, TNN/MCN, 1999, Sigle of Yr. for This Kiss, 1999, Video of Yr. for This Kiss, 1999, Best Country Collaboration with Vocals for Let's Make Lofe, Grammy Awards, 2001, Favorite Female Mus. Performer, People's Choice Awards, 2001, Favorite Country Album, AMA, 2001, 5 Platinum awards, Can. Rec. Industry Assn., 2001, Favorite Female Artist Country, AMA, 2003, Favorite Female Mus. Performer, People's Choice Awards, 2002, 2003. Office: c/o Creative Artists Agy 3310 West End Ave 5th Fl Nashville TN 37203

HILL, G. RICHARD, lawyer; b. Chapel Hill, N.C., Oct. 22, 1951; BA magna cum laude, U. Minn., 1973, MA, 1975; JD, Yale U., 1978. Bar: Wash. 1978. Atty. McCullough Hill, Seattle. Adj. prof. law U. Wash., 1987-88; co-founder Pacific Real Estate Inst. Editor: Regulatory Taking: The Limits of Land Use Controls. Mem. ABA (mem. urban, state and local govt. law sect., chair 1995-96, mem. exec. com. 1992-95, chmn. land use planning and zoning com. 1990-92, co-chmn. subcom. hazardous waste and mcpl. liability 1984-86, chmn. subcom. on land use litigation and damages 1986-88). Office: McCullough Hill 2025 1st Ave # 1130 Seattle WA 98121-2100 Office Phone: 206-448-1818. E-mail: rich@m6law.com.

HILL, GARY D., lawyer; b. Eugene, Oreg., Apr. 7, 1952; s. Virgil R. and Doris H.; m. Patricia L. Hill, July 10, 1976. BA, Linfield Coll., McMinnville, Oreg., 1974; JD, Northwestern Sch. of Law, Portland, 1981. Bar: Oreg. 1982. News anchor KPTV, Portland, Oreg., 1976-92; pvt. practice Portland, Oreg., 1981-84, 88-92; atty. Hergert & Assocs., Oregon City, Oreg., 1992—. Vol. Oreg. Rep. Party, Portland, 1996, Oregon Dole-Kemp presdl. campaign, 1996. Recipient Am. Juris Prudence award, Lawyers Coop. Pub. Co., 1981; recognized for participation in CLE Oreg. State Bar, 1985, 91. Mem. Oreg. State Bar Assn. (law related edn. com. 1996-97, chair-elect small firm and sole practitioner sect. 1997-98, chair 1998-99, Juvenile and Family Law Sect. 1992—, Oreg. Assn. of Family Law Practitioners. Avocations: golf, sailing, fishing. Office: Hergert & Assocs 1001 Molalla Ave Ste 201 Oregon City OR 97045-3768 E-mail: garyh@hergertlaw.com.

HILL, GEORGE JAMES, physician, educator; b. Cedar Rapids, Iowa, Oct. 7, 1932; s. Gerald Leslie and Essie Mae (Thompson) H.; m. Helene (Zimmermann), July 16, 1960; children: James Warren, David Hedgcock, Sarah, and Helena Rundall. BA, Yale U., 1953; MD, Harvard U., 1957; MA, Rutgers U., 1999; DLitt, Drew U., 2005. Intern N.Y. Hosp., 1957-58; fellow and resident in surgery Peter Bent Brigham Hosp. and Harvard Med. Sch., 1958-61, 63-66; clin. assoc. NIH, Bethesda, Md., 1961-63; instr. surgery U. Colo., 1966-67, asst. prof., 1967-72, asso. prof., 1972-73; prof. Washington Univ., 1973-76; prof., chmn. Marshall Univ., 1976-81; prof., dir. surg. oncology U. of Medicine and Dentistry of N.J., N.J. Med. Sch., Newark, 1981-96; adj. prof. surgery Uniformed Svcs. U. of Health Scis., Bethesda, Md., 1989—; Am. Cancer Soc. prof. clin. oncology U. Medicine and Dentistry N.J., N.J. Med. Sch., Newark, 1989-92; pres. faculty N.J. Med. Sch., Newark, 1991-92; interim pres. Sterling Coll., Craftsbury Common, Vt., 1996; prof. emeritus U. of Medicine and Dentistry of N.J., N.J. Med. Sch., Newark, 1997—; rsch. coord. St. Barnabas Med. Ctr., Livingston, NJ, 1997-99. Adj. prof. history Kean U., Union, N.J., 2000-2001; hon. mem. med. sch. staff St. Barnabas Med. Ctr., 1999—; chmn. clin. cancer edn. com. Nat. Cancer Inst., 1978-80; vis. fellow in molecular biology, Princeton U., 1988; clin. prof. surgery Sch. Medicine Mt. Sinai U., 1999—. Author: Leprosy in Five Young Men, 1970, paperback edit., 1979; Outpatient Surgery, 1973, 3d edit., 1988; Clinical Oncology, 1977; contbg. 150 articles to med. journals. Nat. dir. at large Am. Cancer Soc., 1989—96, mem. nat. exec. com., 1990—91, hon. life mem., 1996—, pres. W.Va. divsn., 1980—81; pres. Tri State Area coun. Boy Scouts Am., Huntington, W.Va., 1980—82; mem. N.J. State Commn. on Cancer Rsch., 1983—84; v.p. Essex coun. Boy Scouts Am., 1983—89; trustee Frost Valley YMCA, 1986—, NJ State Opera, 2004—; pres. N.J. divsn. Am. Cancer Soc., 1987—89; chmn. nat. health career exploring com. Boy Scouts Am., 1987—92; pres. Hill Family Trust, 1989—; trustee Sterling Coll., Craftsbury Common, Vt., 1990—2002, sec., 1993—96, interim pres., 1996; commr. No. N.J. coun. Boy Scouts Am., 1998, v.p. no. N.J. coun., 2000—05; emeritus trustee Sterling Coll., Craftsbury Common, Vt., 2003—; vestry Ch. of the Holy Innocents, 1994—96, 2002—05, warden, 2003—05. Capt. M.C. USNR, active duty USN, 1990—91, ret., 1992. Named Jerseyan of Week, Newark-Star Ledger, 1987, 1993; recipient Damon Runyon fellowship, 1957—58, Lederle Med. Faculty award, 1970, Civic Actions medal, Republic South Vietnam, 1972, Silver Beaver award, Boy Scouts Am., 1981, Silver Antelope award, 1998, Disting. Eagle award, 2005, Am. Cancer Soc. Nat. Divisional award, St. George medal, 1992, Gorgas medal, Assn. Mil. Surgeons U.S., 1991, Outstanding Svc. medal, Uniformed Svcs. U. Health Scis., 1992, Meritorious Svc. medal, USN, 1993, Nat. William Spurgeon III award, Boy Scouts Am., 1994, N.J. Disting. Svc. medal, 2001, Disting. Eagle award, Boy Scouts Am., 2005. Fellow: Royal Soc. Medicine, Explorers Club; mem.: SAR (pres. N.J. Soc. 2001—02, nat. trustee 2002—03, v.p. gen. 2005—), ACS (com. on cancer 1987—93), AAUP (pres. chpt. 1988—89), N.J. Med. Club (pres. 1999—2001), Med. Soc. N.J. (chmn. com. cancer control 1985—94, sec. 1995—96), Essex County Med. Soc. (pres. 1995—96), Med. History Soc. N.J. (v.p. 2000—02), Am. Assn. Cancer Rsch., Oncology Nursing Soc. (hon.), Am. Assn. Cancer Edn. (pres. 1985—86, Edwards medal 1994), Ctrl. Surg. Assn., Soc. Surg. Oncology (exec. coun. 1985—88), Soc. Univ. Surgeons, Acad. Medicine NJ (pres. 1992—93), Huguenot Soc. Am., Order Crown Charlemagne, Soc. War of 1812, Soc. Sons of the Revolution (trustee N.J. state soc. 2004—), Order Founders and Patriots of Am. (dep. gov. N.J. state soc. 2003—05, gov. 2005—), Soc. Mayflower Descs. (bd. dirs. NJ state soc. 2002—), Soc. of Colonial Wars (sec. N.J. state soc. 2003—05, dep. gov. 2005—), Soc. of the Cin., Naval Res. Assn. (v.p. 3d dist. 2004—), Army and Navy Club, Harvard Clubs N.Y.C. and Boston, Alpha Omega Alpha, Sigma Xi (chpt. pres. 1986—87). Republican. Episcopalian. Address: 3 Silver Spring Rd West Orange NJ 07052-4317 Office Phone: 973-736-0738.

HILL, GRACE LUCILE GARRISON, education educator, consultant; b. Gastonia, NC, Sept. 26, 1930; d. William Moffatt and Lillian Tallulah (Tatum) Garrison; m. Leo Howard Hill, July 24, 1954; children: Lillian Lucile, Leo Howard Jr., David Garrison. BA, Erskine Coll., 1952; MA, Furman U., 1966; PhD, U. S.C., 1980. Lic. sch. psychologist, S.C. Tchr. Bible, Clinton (S.C.) Pub. Schs., 1952-53; tchr. English Parker High Sch., Greenville, S.C., 1953-55; elem. tchr. Augusta Circle Sch., Greenville, 1955-57; tchr. homebound children Greenville County Sch. Dist., Greenville, 1961-64, psychologist, 1966-77; adj. prof. grad. studies in edn. Furman U., Greenville, 1977—, U. S.C., Columbia, 1982—; ednl. cons. Ednl. Diagnostic Svcs., Greenville, 1980—. Exec. dir. Camperdown Acad., Greenville, 1986-87; cons. learning disability program Erskine Coll., Due West, S.C., 1978—; Disting. lectr. Erskine Coll., 1999. Contbr. articles to profl. jours. Pres. Lake Forest PTA, Greenville, 1970-71; pres. of Women A.R. Presbyn. Ch., Greenville, 1973-75, adult Bible tchr., 1978—; sec. bd. trustees Erskine Coll., 1982-88; bd. dirs. Children's Bur. S.C., Columbia, 1981-87, YWCA, Greenville, 1984-88; bd. advisors for adoption S.C. Dept. Social Svcs., Columbia, 1987-92. Recipient Order of the Jessamine, Greenville News award, 1994—95, Sullivan award, Erskine Coll., 2000, Chmns. award, 2005. Mem. Am. Edn. Rsch. Assn. (southeastern rep. 1982-84, editor newspaper for SIG group 1982-83), Jean Piaget Soc., Assn. for Supervision and Curriculum Devel., Orton Dyslexia Soc. (pres. Carolinas br. 1984-88), Ea. Ednl. Rsch. Assn., S.C. Psychol. Assn., Order of the Jessamine, 21st Century Learning Initiative, Delta Kappa Gamma. Democrat. Avocations: travel, writing. Home and Office: 28 Montrose Dr Greenville SC 29607-3034 *Where did we get the idea that for children to succeed we must set them up to fail? Poverty, crime, and abuse beget poverty, crime, and abuse--not success and achievement. When will America wake up?.*

HILL, GRANT, professional basketball player; b. Dallas, Oct. 5, 1972; s. Calvin and Janet Hill. BA in History, Duke U., 1994. Forward Detroit Pistons, 1994—99, Orlando Magic, Fla., 2000—. Mem. Dream Team III U.S. Olympic Team, 1996. Named Co-Rookie of Yr., 1994; named to Eastern Conf. All-Star team, 2005. Achievements include mem. NCAA Champion Duke Blue Devils, 1991, 1992. Avocation: African-Am. art collector. Office: Orlando Magic 8701 Maitland Summit Blvd Orlando FL 32810*

HILL, HAROLD NELSON, JR., lawyer; b. Houston, Apr. 26, 1930; s. Harold Nelson and Emolyn Eloise (Geeslin) H.; m. Betty Jane Fell, Aug. 16, 1952; children: Douglas, Nancy. BS in Commerce, Washington and Lee U., Lexington, Va., 1952; PhD, Washington & Lee U., 1981; LL.B., Emory U., 1957, PhD, 1986. Bar: Ga. 1957. Assoc., then partner firm Gambrell, Harlan, Russell, Moye & Richardson, 1957-66; asst. atty. gen. Ga., 1966-68; exec. asst. atty. gen., 1968-72; partner firm Jones, Bird & Howell, 1972-74; assoc. justice Supreme Ct. Ga., 1975-82, chief justice, 1982-86; ptnr. Hurt, Richardson, Garner, Todd & Cadenhead, Atlanta, 1986-92, Judicial Resolutions Inc., Atlanta, 1993-94; of counsel Long, Aldridge & Norman, Atlanta, 1994-95. Served with AUS, 1952-54. Fellow Am. Bar Found.; Mem. Am. Law Inst., State Bar Ga., Lawyers Club Atlanta, Old War Horse Lawyers Club. Methodist.

HILL, HARRY HOFFMAN, JR., musician, educator; b. Atlanta, Jan. 11, 1956; s. Harry Hoffman and Pauline (Duncan) Hill; m. Karen Leigh Farah, Mar. 1, 1986; children: Stephen Michael, Gabriel Farah, Nathaniel Hoffman. MusB, Ga. State U., 1979; MusM, U. Mich., 1981; D in Musical Arts, U. S.C., 1999. Prin. clarinetist Asheville (S.C.) Symphony Orch., 1985—; prof. Limeston Coll., Gaffney, SC, 1985—. Mem. bd. overseers Master Works Festival, Winona Lake, Ind., 2000—. Founder, coord., clarinetist: Arbor Wind Trio, 1984—. Mem. exec. bd. Cherokee County/Limestone Coll. Arts Coun., Gaffney, 1995—; mem. Christian Performing Artists' Fellowship, Winona Lake, 1997—, bd. dirs., 2004—. Recipient Fullerton Found. Tchg. award, Fullterton Found./Limestone Coll., 1991, 1995, 1999. Mem.: Coll. Music Soc., Internat. Clarinet Assn. Avocations: bicycling, gardening, cooking, camping. Office: Limestone Coll 1115 College Dr Gaffney SC 29340 Office Phone: 864-488-4507.

HILL, HENRY ALLEN, physicist, researcher; b. Port Arthur, Tex., Nov. 25, 1933; s. Douglas and Florence Hill. BS, U. Houston, 1953; MS, U. Minn., 1956, PhD, 1957; MA (hon.), Wesleyan U., 1966. Research asst. U. Houston, 1952-53; teaching asst. U. Minn., 1953-54, research asst., 1954-57; research assoc. Princeton U., 1957-58, instr., then asst. prof., 1958-64; assoc. prof. Wesleyan U., Middletown, Conn., 1964-66, prof. physics, 1966-74, chmn. dept., 1969-71; prof. physics U. Ariz., Tucson, 1966-95, prof. emeritus, 1995—. Chmn. bd. Zetetic Inst., 1992—; researcher on nuclear physics, relativity, astrophysics, and optics. Contbr. articles to profl. jours. Sloan fellow, 1966-68 Fellow Am. Phys. Soc.; mem. AAAS, SPIE, Am. Astron. Soc., Optical Soc. Am., Am. Geophys. Union. Office: Zetetic Inst 1665 E 18th St Ste 206 Tucson AZ 85719-6809

HILL, HOWARD DARNELL, retired academic administrator; b. May 4, 1942; s. Howard Jr. and Della Mae (Williams) H.; m. Clemmie Faye Coulter, Dec. 24, 1963; children: Ray Darnell, Edith Renee (dec.). BA in Social Studies, Philander Smith Coll., 1964; MSE in Secondary Sch. Adminstrn., Ark. State U., 1968; PhD in Curriculum and Instrn., Kans. State U., 1973; postdoctoral study in ednl. adminstrn., U. S.C., 1983—85. Secondary sch. tchr. Jonesboro Pub. Sch., Ark., 1964-66; supr. instrn. Marion Sch., Ark., 1966-69; asst. prin. West Memphis (Ark.) Schs., 1969-70; secondary sch. tchr. Tunica Pub. Sch., Miss., 1970-71; asst. prof. edn. U. Houston, 1973-77; assoc. prof. Miss. Valley State U., Itta Bena, 1977-78; prof., chmn., program coord. dept. edn. S.C. State U., Orangeburg, 1978-87; dir. chpt. programs Phi Delta Kappa Hdqs., Bloomington, Ind., 1987-97; dean Sch. Grad. Studies S.C. State U., 1997-98, dir. doctoral program, chair ednl. leadership/counselor edn., 1998—2001; v.p. acad. affairs Claflin U., Orangeburg, SC, 2001—05. Cons. Nat. Ednl. Svc., Bloomington, Ind., bd. mem. Regional Med. Found., Orangeburg Contbr. articles to profl. jours. and books. Bush-Hewlett scholar Harvard U., 2002. Mem. ASCD, John Dewey Soc., Am. Assn. Colls. Tchr. Edn., Nat. Coun. Social Studies, Nat. Alliance Black Sch. Educators, Coun. of Grad. Sch. Deans, Assn. Tchr. Educators, Nat. Assn. Secondary Sch. Prins., SC Assn. of Sch. Administrators, Orangeburg County C. of C. (v.p. 2001-2002), Rotary Club (pres. 2001-2002, scholarship programs com. Dist. 7770 2000—, coord. vocat. awareness 2003—), Phi Delta Kappa. Home: 1186 Pruitt Dr NW Orangeburg SC 29118-4024 Office Phone: 803-535-5401. Personal E-mail: educationconsultant@sc.rr.com.

HILL, JACQUELYN LOUISE HARRISON, secondary school educator; b. Summerville, S.C., July 26; d. Joe and Pearl Geneva (Tucker) Harrison; m. George Rutledge Hill, Jr., Sept. 28, 1969; children: George Rutledge III, Brian Desmond Harrison. BS in Biology, Benedict Coll., 1969; MEd in Elem. Edn., Coll. of Charleston, 1978; EdS in Adminstrn., The Citadel, 1989; postgrad., Nova U., 1993—. Tchr. biol. R.B. Stall High Sch., Charleston, SC, 1969-70; tchr. sci. and math. Givhans Elem. Sch., 1970—2003; tchr. sci. DuBose Mid. Sch., Summerville, 1985—. USDA summer food coord. Berkely, Dorchester and Colleton County Community Action Agy., summers 1977, 79; tchr. biology Morningside Mid. Sch., Charleston, summer 1986; tchr. adult edn. Garrett High Sch., 1991. Lay speaker Murray Meth. Ch., Summerville, pres. United Meth. Women, 1988-91, now v.p., mem. stewardess bd., 1989—; layman Bethel A.M.E. Ch., 1988-91. Music scholar Benedict Coll. 1965-68. Mem. NEA, S.C. Edn. Assn. (Outstanding Pres. award 1983), Summerville Edn. Assn. (pres. 1988-89), Zeta Phi Beta (pres. Lambda Nu Zeta chpt. 1985-91, coor.d S.C. Archotte 1991—). Avocations: assisting and volunteering with elderly, writing articles for community newspapers and newsletters, sewing, physical fitness. Home: 307 S Railroad Ave Ridgeville SC 29472-6306

HILL, JAMES CLINKSCALES, federal judge; b. Darlington, SC, Jan. 8, 1924; s. Albert Michael and Alberta (Clinkscales) H.; m. Mary Cornelia Black, June 7, 1946; children: James Clinkscales, Albert Michael. BS in Commerce, U. S.C., 1948; JD, Emory U., 1948. Bar: Ga. 1948, U.S. Supreme Ct. 1969. Assoc. Gambrell, Russell, Killorin & Forbes, Atlanta, 1948—55, ptnr., 1955—63, Hurt, Hill & Richardson, Atlanta, 1963—74; judge U.S. Dist. Ct. (no. dist.) Ga., 1974—76, U.S. Cir. Ct. (5th cir.), Atlanta, 1976—81, U.S. Cir. Ct. (11th cir.), Atlanta, 1981—89; sr. U.S. cir. judge U.S. Ct. Appeals, Atlanta, 1989—. Past chmn. com. on appellate ednl. programs Fed. Jud. Ctr.; mem, com. on intercir. assignments Jud. Conf. U.S., 1990—. With USAF, 1943—45. Fellow: ACTL; mem.: ABA, Am. Judicature Soc., Atlanta Bar Assn., State Bar Ga., World Assn. Judges, Am. Law Inst., Am. Bar Found. (life), Old War Horse Lawyers, Lawyers Club Atlanta (life). Republican. Baptist. Office: US Ct Appeals PO Box 52598 Jacksonville FL 32201-2598 also: Elbert P Tuttle US Ct Appeals Bldg 56 Forsyth St NW Atlanta GA 30303 E-mail: JCHretreat@aol.com.*

HILL, JAMES SCOTT, lawyer; b. Boston, Mar. 21, 1924; s. Benjamin B. and Dorothy (Scott) H.; m. Sally C. Foss, June 28, 1945; children: Richard B., Chessye F., Cynthia C., Michael O. BA magna cum laude, Williams Coll., 1947; JD, Columbia U., 1949. Bar: N.Y. 1949, N.J. 1958. Assoc. Baldwin, Todd & Lefferts, N.Y.C., 1949-50; corp. sec., atty. Johnson & Johnson, N.J., 1950-66; v.p., sec., gen. counsel Celanese Corp., N.Y.C., 1966-74; v.p., gen. counsel, dir. Liggett & Myers, Durham, N.C., 1974-76; v.p. law and govt. affairs CBS Inc., N.Y.C., 1976-78; group pres. law and regulatory affairs Am. Hosp. Supply Corp., Evanston, Ill., 1978-81; of counsel Shanley & Fisher, 1981-88, Smith, Stratton, Wise, Heher & Brennan, Princeton, N.J., 1988—. Judge Princeton (N.J.) Twp., 1959-65 Treas. N.J. Republican Fin. com., 1965-70; trustee John Seward Johnson Sr. Charitable Trusts, Princeton Med. Ctr., N.J. State Aquarium, Trinity Counselling Svc., Princeton, N.J.; chmn. Williams Coll. Devel. Coun.; chmn. Boyden Soc.-Deerfield Acad.; bd. dirs. Friends of Channel 13; mem. exec. com. Friends of the Inst. for Advanced Study, Princeton. Served to 1st lt. USAAF, 1943-46. Fellow Am. Coll. Trust and Estate Counsel (mem. charitable planning and exempt orgn. com.); mem. Assn. Gen. Counsel, Met. Club (Washington), Princeton Club (N.Y.C.), Mid-Ocean Club (Bermuda), Bedens Brook Club (bd. govs. 1995—), Springdale Club, Nassau Club (trustee 1993-96), Jasna Polana Golf Club (Princeton), Chi Psi. Republican. Episcopalian (warden). Home: 155 Lambert Dr Princeton NJ 08540-2306 Office: care Smith Stratton 2 Research Way Princeton NJ 08540-6628 Office Phone: 609-987-6670. Office Fax: 609-987-6670. Business E-Mail: jhill@smithstratton.com.

HILL, JAMES STANLEY, computer company executive, consultant; b. Merrickville, Ont., Can., July 24, 1914; m. Doris C. Huelster, 1938; children: George, Janice, Mary, Beverly, Richard. With Minn. Life Ins. Co., 1930-69; sr. v.p., 1966-69; pres. Digiplan, Inc., White Bear Lake, Minn., 1969—, Red Oak Press, 1994—. Bd. dirs., chmn. audit com. Hadco Inc., 1981-98; pub. spkr., 1994—. Author: Confessions of an 80 Year Old Boy, 1994, Almost Immortal, 1996. Treas. Minn. State H.S. Math. League, 1984-2004; bd. dirs. United Hosp., 1972-99. Fellow Soc. Actuaries (bd. govs., v.p.). Home and Office: Digiplan Inc 5011 Lake Ave Apt 205 Saint Paul MN 55110-2655 *To live each day free from guilt, worry and fear, with opportunities to serve and love others and to exercise both mind and body vigorously— with these goals (and it's taken me over 60 years to come even close), the other things (money, recognition, love from others, and appreciation) come automatically. Christ and others have said it better, but the important thing is: It Works.*

HILL, J(AMES) TOMILSON, investment banker; b. Westbury, N.Y., May 24, 1948; s. James Tomilson Jr. and Dorothy H. (Kutcher) H.; m. Janine A. Wolf, Feb. 2, 1980; children: Margot Langdon, Astrid Tomilson. BA, Harvard U., 1970, MBA, 1973. Vice pres. mergers and acquisitions 1st Boston Corp., N.Y.C., 1973-79; sr. v.p. Smith Barney, Harris Upham & Co. Inc., N.Y.C., 1979-82; mng. dir., dir. mergers and acquisitions, co-head investment banking div. Shearson Lehman Bros. Inc., N.Y.C., 1982-90; vice-chmn., co-chief exec. officer Lehman Bros., N.Y.C., 1990-93; also bd. dirs. Shearson Lehman Bros. Holdings, Inc., co-pres., co-chief operating officer, 1993; co-chief exec. officer Lehman Bros., 1993, Shearson Lehman Bros., 1993, SLB Asset Mgmt., 1993; vice chmn., mem. investment and mgmt. com. Blackstone Group, N.Y.C., 1993—; pres., CEO Blackstone Alternative Asset Mgmt., 1995—. Bd. dirs. Allied Waste. Contbr. articles to profl. publs. Chmn. Hirshhorn Mus. and Sculpture Garden; vice chmn. Lincoln Ctr. Theater; bd. dirs. Milton Acad., Nightingale-Bamford Sch. Named one of 200 Top Collectors, ARTnews mag., 2004. Mem. Coun. Fgn. Rels. (chmn. investment subcom. of fin. and budget com.), Piping Rock Club, Meadow Brook Club, Links Club, River Club, Knickerbocker Club. Avocation: Collector postwar Am. and European art. Office: Blackstone Group 345 Park Ave Ste New York NY 10154-0004 Office Phone: 212-583-5809. Business E-Mail: hill@blackstone.com.

HILL, JERRY DEAN, secondary school educator; b. Stuart, Va., June 27, 1952; s. Walter Doyle and Doris Gracie Hill. AA in Liberal Arts, Bluefield Coll., 1972; BA in Religious Edn., Gardner-Webb U., 1974; MD in Christian Edn., So. Bapt. Theol. Sem., 1978. Ednl. dir., Martinez Bapt. Ch., Augusta, Ga., 1978—80; farmer Lawsonville, NC, 1980—84; tchr. Martinsville (Va.) City Schs., 1984—89; music dir. Bethany Christian Ch., Roanoke, Va., 1986—89; fine and performing arts chair Newport Sch., Kensington, Md., 1989—2001; tchr. Arlington (Va.) County Pub. Schs., 2001—04, Prince George's County Pub. Schs., Md., 2004—. Mem. accreditation teams Middle States & Assn. Ind. Md. Schs., 1996—2000; mem. profl. devel. com. Assn. Ind. Md. Schs., Md., 1997—2001; liaison Nat. Assn. Music Educators, Reston, Va., 2000. Avocations: piano, photography, travel. Office Phone: 703-931-4755. Personal E-mail: jdeanhill@aol.com.

HILL, JESSE HOYT, economics and business educator, training specialist; b. Memphis, Mar. 3, 1950; s. James Richard and Mary Althea (Ruby) H.; m Sheri Loree Robinson, July 17, 1970; children: Christ Corrine, Jesse Jaron. BS, U North Tex., 1975; MS, Amber U., 1986; EdD, Nova Southeastern U., 1996. Provisional tchr. cert., Tex., 1975. Tng. specialist City of Dallas, 1972—; tchr. econs. and bus. mgmt. Grad. SCh. Amber U., 1999—. Adj. faculty No. Lake Coll., Irving, Tex., 1987-94, No. Ctrl. Tex. Coll., Gainesville, 1995-96, U. Dallas, Irving, 1996—. Deacon First Presbyn. Ch., Grapevine, Tex., 1984-87; pres., bd. dirs. First Presbyn. Pre-Sch., Grapevine, 1985-88; referee U.S. Soccer Fedn. Recipient award Jaycee of the Yr., 1985. Mem: Tex. Jr. Coll. Tchrs. Assn., Tex. Assn Coll. Tech. Educators. Avocations: little league coach, painter. Home: 3719 High Dr Grapevine TX 76051-4553 Office: City Dallas 1500 Marilla St # 6 Dallas TX 75201-6390

HILL, JIMMIE DALE, retired federal agency administrator; b. Fort Worth, Tex., Dec. 28, 1933; s. William Haden and Myrtle Maude H.; m. Martha Lee Hoad, May 26, 1956; children: William, Loretta, Carol, Patricia. Student, DelMar Coll., 1955-57, U. Okla., 1957-58, U. Wichita, 1963-64. Enlisted in U.S. Air Force, 1951, advanced through grades to maj., 1974; comptroller for space systems acquisition Los Angeles, 1963-70; adv. CIA, 1970-73; ret., 1974; spl. asst. to undersec. Air Force, Washington, 1974-78; dir. Office of Space Systems, Dept. Air Force, 1978-82; dep. undersec. Air Force Space Systems, 1982-96; dep. dir. Nat. Reconnaissance Office, 1982-96. Scoutmaster Boy Scouts Am., 1971-76. Decorated Legion of Merit; recipient Disting. Civilian Svc. medal Dept. Def., 1974, 76, 87, 96, Presdl. Rank award of Meritorious Exec., 1980, 88, Presdl. Rank of Disting. Exec., 1981, 91, Air Force sr. exec. award, 1982-87, 89, 90, 92, 93, 94, 95, Air Force Exceptional Civilian Svc. award, 1987, 96, Nat. Intelligence Disting. Svc. medal, Ctrl. Intelligence Agy. Disting. Intelligence medal, Disting. Svc. medal NASA, Goddard Meml. Trophy, Nat. Space Club, 1996, Goddard Astronautics award AIAA, 1998. Mem. Air Force Assn. Methodist. Home: 7920 Lewinsville Rd Mc Lean VA 22102-2407 E-mail: jimmiehill@aol.com. *Choose an occupation or profession because you like it, not for recognition and reward. For if you're happy in your work, with loyalty, dedication and hard work, ample recognition and reward will follow.*

HILL, JOHN HOWARD, retired lawyer; b. Pitts., Aug. 12, 1940; s. David Garrett and Eleanor Campbell (Musser) H. BA, Yale U., 1962, JD, 1965. Bar: Pa. 1965, US Dist. Ct. (we dist.) Pa. 1965, US Ct. Appeals (3d cir.) 1965, US Supreme Ct. 1982. Assoc. Reed, Smith, Shaw & McClay, Pitts., 1965-75, ptnr., 1975-90; of counsel Jackson Lewis LLP, Pitts., 1991—2004, ret., 2004. Bd. dirs. Travelers Aid Soc., Pitts., 1972-99, treas., 1982-87, pres., 1987-90; bd. dirs. Pitts. Opera, Pitts. Symphony Soc. Mem.: ABA, Allegheny County Bar Assn., Pa. Bar Assn., Pa. Soc., Hosp. Assn. Pa., Rolling Rock Club, Duquesne Club, Fox Chapel Golf Club, Phi Gamma Delta. Republican. Presbyterian. Home: 4722 Bayard St Pittsburgh PA 15213-1708 Office: Jackson Lewis LLP One PPG Pl 28th Fl Pittsburgh PA 15222-5414 Personal E-mail: sedgewycke@aol.com.

HILL, JOHN LUKE, JR., lawyer, judge; b. Breckenridge, Tex, Oct. 9, 1923; s. John Luke Hill; m. Elizabeth Ann Graham, 1946; children: Melinda, Graham, Martha. LLB, U Tex., 1947. Sole practice, Houston, 1947—73; sec. of state State of Tex., Austin, Tex., 1966—68, atty. gen., 1973—78; ptnr. Hughes & Hill, Austin, Tex., 1979—85; chief justice Supreme Ct. Tex., Austin, Tex., 1985—89; sr. ptnr. Locke, Liddell & Sapp, LLP, Houston, 2003—. Lt. USN, 1943—45. Office: Locke Liddell & Sapp LLP 3400 Chase Tower 600 Travis Houston TX 77002 Business E-Mail: jhill@lockeliddell.com.

HILL, JOHN SYLVESTER, allergist; b. Charleston, W.Va., 1948; MD, U. W.Va., 1974. Diplomate Am. Bd. Allergy and Immunology, Am. Bd. Internal Medicine. Intern Charleston (W.Va.) Area Med. Ctr., resident in internal medicine; fellow in allergy and immunology Virginia Mason Clinic, Seattle; now with St. Joseph Hosp., Lexington, Ky. Mem. Ky. Med. Assn. Address: Kaplan Hill PSC 2370 Nicholasville Rd Ste 102 Lexington KY 40503-3014 Office Phone: 606-276-1452.

HILL, KENT RICHMOND, federal agency administrator; b. Nampa, Idaho, May 24, 1949; s. Double E. and Helen Louise (Robertson) H.; m. Janice Elaine Hurn, June 12, 1972; children: Jennifer Lynn, Jonathan Kent. BA in History, N.W. Nazarene Coll., 1971; diploma for basic Russian lang., Def. Lang. inst., 1972; postgrad., Georgetown U., 1973-74; MA in Russian and East European Studies, U. Wash., 1976, PhD in History, 1980. Teaching asst. in history N.W. Nazarene Coll., Nampa, Idaho, 1969-71; Russian translator U.S. Army, 1972-74; teaching asst. in history of Christianity U. Wash., Seattle, 1980, asst. prof. history, 1980-85; assoc. prof. history Seattle Pacific U., 1985-86; pres. Inst. on Religion and Democracy, Washington, 1986-92, Ea. Nazarene Coll., Quincy, Mass., 1992—2001; asst. adminstr. bur. for Europe and Eurasia USAID, Washington, 2001—, acting asst. adminstr. for global health, 2005—. Interviews, speaker, presenter in field. Author: The Puzzle of the Soviet Church: An Inside Look at Christianity and Glasnost, 1989, Turbulent Times for the Soviet Church, 1991, The Soviet Union on the Brink, 1991; contbr. articles to profl. publs. Bd. dirs. Peter Deyneka Russian Ministries, 1991-2001, Keston Coll., 1985-2001; mem. nat. exec. bd. World Without War Coun., Berkeley, Calif., 1986-2001; bd. advisors Inst. on Religion and Democracy, 1984-86, bd. dirs., 1993-2001; mem. ch. bd. 1st Ch. of Nazarene, Seattle, 1980-85; bd. trustees Russian-Am. Christian U., Moscow, 1998-2000; bd. dirs. Quincy Hist. Soc., 1997-2000. Named Alumnus of Yr., N.W. Nazarene Coll., 1988, to Presdl. Leadership list John Templeton Found., 1999; presented with Key to City, Mayor of City of Nampa, 1983; named Prof. of Yr. Seattle Pacific U., 1986; grantee Seattle Pacific U., 1981-82, 82-83, 84, 85, U. Wash., 1979-80; Nat. Def. Fgn. Lang. fellowship, 1976-77, Earhart fellow Internat. Rsch. and Exchs. fellow, 1978; recipient Pushkin award for Outstanding Scholarship, Def. Lang. Inst., 1972. Office: USAID Bur for Europe and Eurasia RRB 1300 Pennsylvania Ave NW Washington DC 20523

HILL, LABAN CARRICK, writer; b. 1960; Tchr. Columbia U., Baruch Coll., St. Michaels' Coll., Vt. Author: Harlem Stomp! A Cultural History of the Harlem Renaissance, 2004 (Nat. Book Award finalist, 2004); co-author: Bugged Out!, 1997, Watch Out for Room 13, 1997, The Evil Pen Pal, 1998, Welcome to Horror Hospital, 1998, Spy Survival Handbook, 2004.

HILL, LARKIN PAYNE, jewelry designer, manufacturer; b. Oct. 30, 1954; d. Max Lloyd and Jane Olivia (Evatt) H. Student, Coll. Charleston, 1972-73, U. N.C., 1973. Lic. real estate broker, N.C. Sec., property mgr. Max L. Hill Co., Inc., Charleston, S.C., 1973-75, sec., data processor, 1979-82, v.p. adminstrn., 1982—, Mt. Pleasant, SC, 2004—; ops. mgr. Shorline Internat. Real Estate, 2003—04; pres., jewelry designer and mfr. Pearl, LLC, 2004—. Resident mgr. Carolina Apts., Carrboro, N.C., 1975-77; sales assoc., Realtor, Southland Assocs., Chapel Hill, N.C., 1977-78; jewelry designer Pearl, LLC, pres.; cons. specifications com. Charleston Trident Multiple Listing Service, 1985. Bd. dirs. Charleston Area Arts Coun., 1992-93; co-chair Beaux Arts Ball, Sch. Arts. Mem. Royal Oak Found., Scottish Soc. Charleston (bd. dirs. 1989-91), Preservation Soc., Charleston Computer Users Group, N.C. Assn. Realtors, Spoleto Festival USA (chmn. auction catalog com. 1990-92). Republican. Methodist. Avocations: reading, crossword puzzles, American Staffordshire Terriers. Home: 7 Riverside Dr Charleston SC 29403-3217 Office: Max L Hill Co INc 824 Johnnie Dodds Blvd Mount Pleasant SC 29464 also: Pearl LLC PO Box 22813 Charleston SC 29413 Office Phone: 843-853-3947. E-mail: info@pearlllc.com.

HILL, LAURYN, vocalist, actress; b. South Orange, N.J., May 25, 1975; Student, Columbia U. Teamed with Prakazrel "Pras" Michel and Wyclef Jean as the Fugees while still in H.S.; trio produced 2 albums: Blunted on Reality, 1994, and The Score, 1996 (17 million copies sold). Solo albums: The Miseducation of Lauryn Hill, 1998, MTV Unplugged No. 2.0, 2002; wrote and produced On That Day for gospel artist CeCe Winans; wrote A Rose is Still a Rose for Aretha Franklin album, also directed song's accompanying video. Actress: (films) Sister Act 2: Back in the Habit, 1993, King of the Hill, 1993, Rhyme & Reason, 1997, Hav Plenty, 1997, Restaurant, 1998; television appearances As the World Turns, 1991, Daddy's Girl, 1997. Founder non-profit The Refugee Youth Camp Youth Project. With Fugees received 2 1996 Grammy awards--Best Rap Album for The Score and Best R&B Performance by a Duo or Group With Vocal (Killing Me Softly). Recipient 1999 Grammy awards for Album of Yr., Best New Artist, Best R&B Song, Best R&B Album, Best Female R&B Vocal Performance. Nominated for several awards at 13th Annual Soul Train Music Awards in L.A. Recipient 4 awards (Outstanding New Artist, Outstanding Female Artist, Outstanding Album and NAACP President's award) 30th Annual NAACP Image Awards, Pasadena, Calif., 1999. Other awards include Favorite New Soul/R&B Artist (26th Annual Am. Music Awards), Best New Artist (Danish Grammy Awards), Entertainer of Yr. (Entertainment Weekly), #1 Album of Yr. (Time mag., N.Y. Times), Best R&B Album of 1998 (USA Today), Artist of Yr. (Spin mag.), Artist of Yr. (Details mag.), 3 Rolling Stone Music Awards.

HILL, LAWRENCE SIDNEY, finance educator; b. Gary, Ind., Nov. 10, 1923; m. Evelyn Honig, Mar. 22, 1964; 1 child, Robert J. BSE, Purdue U., 1947; cert. in Indsl. Hygiene, Ga. Inst. Tech., 1948; MBA, U. So. Calif., 1960, MSIE, 1962, Engr., 1965, PhD, 1968. Registered profl. engr., Calif. Asst. indsl. engr. USX Corp., Gary, 1947, indsl. engr., 1951—52; engr. indsl. hygiene Ill. Dept. Pub. Health, Chgo., 1948—51; sr. engr. Nat. Safety Coun., Chgo., 1953; sr. indsl. engr. Martin Marietta Co., Balt., 1953—55; group head McDonnell Douglas Co., Santa Monica, Calif., 1955—57; sr. mem. staff Rand Corp., Santa Monica, 1957—71; prof. mgmt. sci, Calif. State U., L.A., 1969—97; cons., prin. engr. Ralph M. Parsons Co., Pasadena, Calif., 1973—82; v.p. Calif. Tech. Sys., Inc., Pasadena, 1979—82; cons., sr. mem. tech. staff TRW Inc., Redondo Beach, Calif., 1982—90; cons., environ. mgr. USN, Long Beach, Calif., 1991—94. Lectr. U. So. Calif., 1964—70; vis. lectr. Ops. Rsch. Soc. Am./Inst. Mgmt. Scis., 1973—95; expert witness in safety, mgmt., 1986—. Contbr. articles to profl. jours., chapters to books. Mem.: Alpha Iota Delta, Alpha Pi Mu. Avocation: sports. Home: 3653 Oceanhill Way Malibu CA 90265-5637 Office Phone: 310-454-2782.

HILL, LEDA KATHERINE, librarian; b. Bklyn., Feb. 16, 1952; d. David and Leda Louise (Jones) H. BA, Bklyn. Coll., 1974, MS in Edn., 1989; MLS, Queens (N.Y.) Coll., 1995. New bus. coord. INAC Corp., Cranford, N.J., 1974-80; paralegal Orgn. Women for Legal Awareness, Inc., East Orange, N.J., 1980-83; tchr. Roselle (N.J.) Bd. Edn., 1983-84; libr., tchr. N.Y.C. Bd. Edn., Bklyn., 1985—. Mem. ALA, Bklyn. Reading Coun., N.Y.C. Sch. Librs. Assn., N.Y. Libr. Assn., Am. Assn. Sch. Librs. Office: Middle School 2 655 Parkside Ave Brooklyn NY 11226-1505 Office Phone: 718-462-6992. E-mail: lhill4@nycboe.net.

HILL, LEWIS REUBEN, horticulturist, nursery owner, writer; b. Greensboro, Vt., July 1, 1924; s. Alvah Aaron and Grace Gibson (Towle) H.; m. Nancy May Davis, May 4, 1969. High sch. grad., Greensboro, Vt. Owner, mgr. Hillcrest Nursery, Greensboro, 1947-82, Vermont Daylilies, Greensboro, 1982-93, Berryhill Nursery, Greensboro, 1993—. Author: Fruits and Berries for the Home Garden, 1977, Pruning Simplified, 1979, Cold Climate Gardening, 1981, Secrets of Plant Propagation, 1985, Yankee Summer, 2000; co-author (with Nancy Hill): Country Living, 1987, Successful Perennial Gardening, 1988, Christmas Trees, 1989, Fetched Up Yankee, 1990, Daylilies, The Perfect Perennial, 1991, Bulbs-Four Seasons of Beautiful Blooms, 1994, Pruning Made Easy, 1997, Lawns, Grasses & Groundcovers, 1995, The Lawn and Garden Owners Manual, 2000, The Flower Gardener's Bible, 2003; (with others) Berries, 1991, Vines, 1992, Wise Garden Encyclopedia, 1997, 1990 edit., Vermont Voices, 1991, others; contbr. numerous articles to gardening publs. Del. State Rep. Conv. twice; various town offices and coms. Recipient Disting. Svc. award for youth work Vt. Edn. Assn., 1967, Gov's Commn. on Children and Youth, Montpelier, Vt., 1970; 4-H citation Nat. Extension Svc., Washington, 1974; cert. of appreciation Ea. Nurserymen's Assn., Montpelier, 1982; Lit. Excellence award Greensboro Libr., 1990, Vt. Horticulture Achievement award Vt. Profl. Horticulturists, 1993, Quill and Trowel award Garden Writers of Am., 1995. Mem. League Vt. Writers, Vt. Profl. Horticulturists (bd. dirs., pres.),Internat. Ribes Assn. Mem. United Ch. Avocations: photography, skiing, motorcycling, nature. Home and Office: Hillcrest Farm 353 Hillcrest Rd Greensboro VT 05841 E-mail: hillnl@vtlink.net. *Nancy and I think having a goal, and always keeping it in mind, is important, whether it is developing a new plant or a book.*

HILL, LORIE ELIZABETH, psychotherapist; b. Buffalo, Oct. 21, 1946; d. Graham and Elizabeth Helen (Salm) H. Student, U. Manchester, Eng., 1966-67; BA, Grinnell Coll., 1968; MA, U. Wis., 1970, Calif. State U., Sonoma, 1974; PhD, Wright Inst., 1980. Instr. English U. Mo., 1970-71; adminstr., supr. Antioch-West and Ctr. for Ind. Living, San Francisco, Berkeley, 1975-77; dir. tng. Ctr. for Edn. and Mental Health, San Francisco, 1977-80, exec. dir., 1980-81; pvt. practice Berkeley and Oakland, Calif., 1976—; instr. master's program in psychology John F. Kennedy U., Orinda, Calif., 1985, 94—. Founder group of psychotherapists against racism; spkr. on cross-cultural psychology; creater Jump Start, a violence prevention and unlearning racism program for youth; trainer for trainers 3rd Internat. Conf. Conflict Resolution, St. Petersburg, Russia; sr. facilitator Color of Fear. Organizer against nuc. war; founding mem. Psychotherapists for Social Responsibility; psychologist Big Bros. and Big Sisters of the East Bay, 1986—88; vol. instr. City of Oakland Youth Skills Devel. Program; founder, dir. Providing Alternatives to Violence; creator JumpStart program; active Rainbow Coalition for Jesse Jackson's Presdl. Campaign, Ron Dellums Re-election Com.; campaigner for Clinton-Gore; co-founder Wellstone Progressive Dem. Club, 2003, East Bay Votes!. Mem. Calif. Psychol. Assn. (chair pub. interest divsn. 1997, Helen Margulies Mehr Pub. Svc. award 1996, chair social issues 1996—, Silver Psi award 1999), Wellstone Dem. Renewal Club (co-founder), East Bay Votes (co-founder). Democrat-Socialist. Avocations: sports, travel, music, reading. Office: 2955 Shattuck Ave Berkeley CA 94705-1808 Office Phone: 510-644-0922, 510-486-8088. E-mail: loriepav@aol.com.

HILL, LOUIS ALLEN, JR., former university dean, consultant; b. Okemah, Okla., May 18, 1927; s. Louis Allen and Gladys Adelia (Dietrich) Hill Wise; m. Jeanne Rose Murray, June 14, 1951; children: Dawn, David, Dixon. BA, Okla. State U., 1949, BSC.E., 1954, MSC.E., 1955; PhD, Case Inst. Tech., 1965. Registered profl. engr., Okla., Ariz. Engr. Lee Hendricks Engring., Tulsa, 1955-57, Hudgins, Thompson, Ball & Assocs., Oklahoma City, 1957-58; asst. prof. civil engring. Ariz. State U., 1958-66, assoc. prof., 1966-70, prof., 1970-74, chmn. dept. civil engring., 1974-81; dean Coll. Engring. U. Akron, 1981-88, assoc. v.p. rsch. and grad. studies, 1988. Chmn. Ohio Engring. Dean's Council, 1983-85; trustee Engring. Found. of Ohio, 1985-88; staff engr. Salt River Project, Ariz., 1962; cons. in field. Author: Fundamentals of Structures, 1975, Compendium of Structural Aids, 1975, Structured Programming in Fortran, 1981; contbr. numerous articles to profl. jours.; designer numerous bridges, hwys. Ch. leader-tchr. 1st Bapt. Ch., 1971-88, Scottsdale Presbyn. Ch., 1990—. Served to capt. C.E., U.S. Army, 1945-47, 51-53, The Philippines, Japan. Recipient Disting. award Akron Coun. Engring. and Sci. Socs., 1987, commendation Minorities in Mainstream Tech. Com., 1990, Disting. Svc. award U. Akron Coll. Engring., 1994; named Educator of Yr., Inroads N.E. Ohio, Inc., 1986, Sr. Svc. award Presbytery of Grand Canyon, 2001; Louis A. Hill Jr. Ann. Faculty award established and endowed in his honor Qua Tech., 1987, Louis A. Hill Jr. scholarship established in his honor Minorities in Mainstream Tech. Com., 2004, Mayor Plusquellic proclaimed April 23, 1997 as Dr. Louis A. Hill Day in City of Akron; fellow Continental Oil Co., 1955, faculty fellow NSF, 1963. Fellow ASCE (life); mem. NSPE (sec., profl. engr. in edn. 1986-88), Am. Soc. Engring. Edn. (life, Western Electric Fund award 1967), Sigma Xi, Tau Beta Pi, Omicron Delta Kappa. Republican. Home and Office: 3208 N 81st Pl Scottsdale AZ 85251-5800

HILL, LOWELL DEAN, agricultural marketing educator; b. Delta, Iowa, Apr. 27, 1930; s. Frederick Carl and Harriet Jane (Atwood) H.; m. Betty Elaine Carpenter, Dec. 9, 1951; children: Rebecca Elaine, Brent Howard. BS in Agrl. Edn., Iowa State U., 1951; MS in Agrl. Econs., Mich. State U., 1961, PhD in Agrl. Econs., 1963. Asst. prof., then assoc. prof. dept. agrl. econs. U. Ill., Urbana, 1963-72, prof., 1972-77, L.J. Norton prof. agrl. mktg., 1977-98, L.J. Norton prof. emeritus, 1998—. Cons. Office Tech. Assessment, Washington, 1986-88, South Am. and Europe, 1995, FAO, Rome, 1978-80, U.S. AID, 1983, World Bank, Washington, 1989-90, 92-93, Argentina, Colombia, Chile, 1989-94, U.S. Feed Grains Coun., Venezuela, Japan, Korea, 1990-93, USDA, Russia, 1993-96; mem. adv. com. Fed. Grain Inspection Svc., USDA, 2000-2003. Author: Grain Grades and Standards: Historical Issues, 1990; editor: Role of Government in a Market Economy, 1982, Corn Quality in World Markets, 1985. Cpl. U.S. Army, 1952-54. Fellow East West Ctr.; recipient Quality of Comm. award, 1980, 88, Disting. Policy Contbr. award 1988, Extension Programs award, 1989, Disting. Svc. award USDA, 1989, Internat. Mktg. Support award Am. Soybean Assn., 1989, Faculty award for rsch. excellence, 1991; Univ. scholar, 1992. Fellow: Am. Agrl. Econ. Assn.; mem.: Coun. Agrl. Sci. and Tech. (chmn. 1989—90), Rotary. Office: Univ Ill Mumford Hall 1301 W Gregory Dr Urbana IL 61801-9015 E-mail: l-hill3@uiuc.edu.

HILL, LUTHER LYONS, JR., lawyer; b. Des Moines, Aug. 21, 1922; s. Luther Lyons and Mary (Hippee) H.; m. Sara S. Carpenter, Aug. 12, 1950; children— Luther Lyons III, Mark Lyons. BA, Williams Coll., 1947; LLB, Harvard U., 1950; LLD (hon.), Simpson Coll., 1979. Bar: Iowa 1951. Law clk. to Justice Hugo L. Black U.S. Supreme Ct., 1950-51; assoc., ptnr. Henry & Henry, Des Moines, 1951-69; mem. legal staff Equitable Life Ins. Co. of Iowa, 1952-87, exec. v.p., 1969-87, gen. counsel, 1970-87; of counsel Nyemaster, Goode, McLaughlin, Voigts, Wiest, Hansell O'Brien, Des Moines, 1992—. Counsel, adminstr. Iowa Life and Health Ins. Guaranty Assn. Bd. dirs., past pres. United Comty. Svcs. Greater Des Moines; past trustee, past chmn. Simpson Coll., Indianola, Iowa. Capt. M.I., AUS, WWII, ETO. Mem. ABA, Iowa Bar Assn., Polk County Bar Assn., Assn. Life Ins. Counsel, Des Moines Club, Wakonda Club. Republican. Avocation: walking in the Swiss mountains. Office: Ste 1600 700 Walnut St Des Moines IA 50315-3929 Office Phone: 515-283-3163.

HILL, MACK C., career officer; b. Tampa, Fla. Commd. officer U.S. Army, advanced through grades to brig. gen.; comdg. gen. Madigan Army Med. Ctr./Western Regional Med. Command, Tacoma, 1998-99; chief Med. Svc. Corps, Office Surgeon Gen. U.S. Army, Falls Church, Va., 1999—. Office: Office Surgeon Gen US Army 6 Skyline Pl 5109 Leesburg Pike Falls Church VA 22041-3208

HILL, MARC LAMONT, educational researcher, writer; s. Leon Melvin and Hallean Adkins Hill; 1 child, Anya Tai Coleman-Hill. Ph.D., U. of Pa., Philadelphia, Pennsylvania, 2001—05; MS in Edn., U. of Pa., Philadelphia, PA, 2001—05; BS in Edn., Temple U., Philadelphia PA, 1998—2000. Anthropology Am. Anthrop. Assn., 2001. Asst. prof. Temple U. Coll. Edn., Phila., 2005—; cultural critic, music journalist PopMatters Mag., Evanston, Ill., 2002. Curriculum cons. Sch. Dist. of Phila., 2002—. Author: (book) Vocab: Dictionary of Hip-Hop Slang; editor: New Dilemmas of the Black Intellectual, Media, Learning, and Sites of Possibility. Recipient Top Black Leaders Under 30, Ebony Mag., 2005. Mem.: Am. Studies Assn., Am. Anthrop. Assn., Am. Ednl. Rsch. Assn., Most Worshipful Prince Hall Grand Lodge. Independent. Achievements include first to Ebony Magazine's Top Leaders Under 30 Award. Avocations: basketball, music (percussion). Office: Temple University 1301 Cecil B Moore Philadelphia PA 19122 Office Phone: 215-203-4173. Personal E-mail: marclhill@aol.com.

HILL, MARIE See DAVIS, MAGGIE

HILL, MARTHA N., community health nurse; b. Boston, July 14, 1943; d. Paul Lawrence Norton and Margaret M. Hagerty; m. Gary S. Hill, June 18, 1966; children: Paul, Justin. Diploma, Johns Hopkins Hosp., Balt., 1964; BSN, The Johns Hopkins U., 1966, PhD, 1987; MSN, U. Pa., 1977. From instr. to assoc. prof. Johns Hopkins Hosp. Sch. Nursing, Balt.; nurse specialist in hypertension Hosp. of U. Pa., Phila.; dean Johns Hopkins Univ. Sch. of Nursing, Balt., 2002—. Contbr. articles to profl. jours. Recipient Malcolm Alderfer Schweiker award, 1985, Ruth B. Freeman award 1987; fellow Am. Acad. Nursing, 1989. Mem. ANA (rep. to NIH high blood press coord. com.), Am. Heart Assn. (vice chmn. coun. cardiovasc. nursing 1989-91, pres. 1997-98), Inst. of Medicine.

HILL, MELVIN JAMES, retired oil industry executive; b. Santa Ana, Calif., May 19, 1919; s. Albert Frederick and Alice Lucile (Moody) H.; m. Daphne G. Langston, Mar. 1, 1947; children: Patricia Michalek, Candace A. AB, U. Calif., Berkeley, 1941. With Western Gulf Oil Co., Calif., 1941-56, Gulf Rsch. & Devel. Co., Harmarville, Pa., 1956-63, Gulf Oil Corp., Pitts., 1963-75, v.p., 1971-74, sr. v.p., 1974-75, exec. v.p., 1981-84; ret., 1984; pres. Gulf Energy and Minerals Co.-Internat., Houston, 1975-78, Gulf Exploration & Prodn. Co., Pa., 1978-81. Mem. Am. Petroleum Inst., Am. Assn. Petroleum Geologists, Am. Inst. Profl. Geologists, Geol. Soc. Am., Soc. Exploration Geophysicists, Am. Geophys. Union. Home: 970 Aurora Ave Apt F201 Boulder CO 80302 E-mail: hill.melvin@comcast.net.

HILL, MILLICENT E., English educator; b. Nashville, Mar. 23, 1940; d. Jeremiah W. and Mildred Moore; m. Ezekiel H. Hill Jr. (div.); children: Caroll E. Hill-Goldsmith, David E. BA, Fisk U., 1962; postgrad., U. So. Calif., 1990. Cert. tchr. Calif. Englisht chr. L.A. Unified Sch. Dist., 1966—99; dir. edn. Huio St. Enterprises Inc., L.A., 1999—2000; acad. advisor Unity T.W.O. Satellite House, L.A., 1999—. Author: (anthology) Timothy & Friends, 1999, Love Letters in Silence, 2000. Founder Martin Luther King Jr. Mus., L.A., 1986—99. Named one of Tchrs. Who Make A Difference, John Walsh Show, 2002; recipient Tchr. of Yr. award, NAACP, 1989, Outstanding Svc. award, Mayor Richard Riordan, 1999, Congresswoman Maxine Waters, 1999, Proven Achievers award, Channel 5 News, KJLH, 2003. Avocations: singing, piano, poetry, reading. Home: 755 E 92d St Los Angeles CA 90002 Office: Mama Hill's Help Inc 755 E 92d St Los Angeles CA 90002 Office Phone: 323-969-6910. Office Fax: 323-305-1661. E-mail: hllmllcnt@aol.com.

HILL, NED CROMAR, dean, finance educator, consultant; b. Salt Lake City, Dec. 18, 1945; s. Richard G. Sharp and Bettie (Cromar) Hill; m. Claralyn Martin, Nov. 26, 1968; children: Evan M., Jonathan C., Aaron R., Joseph B., Alison. Student, Brigham Young U., 1967; BS in chemistry, U. Utah, 1969; MS in chemistry, Cornell U., Ithaca, NY, 1971, PhD in fin., 1976. Cert. cash mgr. Asst. prof. fin. Cornell U., 1976-77, Ind. U., Bloomington, 1977-81, assoc. prof. fin., 1981-87; Joel C. Peterson prof. fin. Brigham Young U., Provo, Utah, 1987-96, asst. to pres., 1996-98, dean, Marriot Chair Bus. Mgmt., Marriott Sch. Mgmt., 1998—. Cons. Hill Fin. Assocs., Bloomington, 1978—; bd. dirs. Beneficial Life Ins. Co., Morgan Stanley Bank, Pete Suazo Bus. Ctr. Author: Essentials in Cash Management, 1984, Short-Term Financial Management, 1987; co-founder Jour. Cash Mgmt., 1981, EDI Forum: Jour. Electronic Commerce, 1987. Mem. Utah Info. Tech. Commn., 1993-97; stake pres. Ch. Jesus Christ of the Latter Day Saints, 1982-87, 2000—; fin. v.p. Boy Scouts Hoosier Trails Council, Bloomington, 1980-86. With U.S. Army, 1971—72. Named Outstanding Faculty Mem., Marriott Sch. Mgmt., Brigham Young U., 1992. Mem. Fin. Mgmt. Assn. (bd. dirs. 1986-88), Phi Beta Kappa, Phi Kappa Phi. Republican. Avocations: vocal music, birding. Office: Brigham Young U Marriott Sch of Mgmt 730 TNRB Provo UT 84602 Office Phone: 801-422-4122. Business E-Mail: ned_hill@byu.edu.

HILL, NILS ARVID, artist, educator; b. NYC, July 7, 1949; s. Frederick Alexander and Edith M. (Meyer) Hill; m. Ivy Dachman, June 19, 1977; m. Judith Gregory (div.); 1 child, Ian Wesley. MFA, Ind. U., 1971—73; BFA, Phila. Coll. of Art, 1967—71. Permanent Certification, Art NY State Edn. Dept., 1991. Tchr. of art BOCES So. Westchester, North White Plains, NY, 1988—. One-man shows include Noho Gallery, NYC, 1981-82, 1985; exhibited in group shows at The Beautiful Object, Phila. Coll. Art, 1976, Noho Gallery, NYC, 1980, Nine Artists, 1982, Tenth Anniversary Exhbn., 1985, No. Westchester Ctr. for the Arts, Golden Bridge, NY, 1986, Pamela Stockwell Gallery, NYC, 1988, Berkshire Art. Mus., Pittsfield, Mass., 1989, Ossining Area Artists, Rye Art Ctr., NY, 1989, 95, Brandreth Studios, Plus Two, Old Libr. Art. Ctr., Westport, Conn. 1989, Neo Geo in Peekskill, Paramont Ctr. for the Arts, NY, 1991, Waterside Art Studios, Stamford, Conn., 1992, Krasdale Foods Gallery, White Plains, NY, 1992, Garrison Art Ctr., NY, 1992, Gallery at Hastings-on-Hudson, NY, 1994, Katonah Mus. Art, NY, 1995, Pace U., Pleasantville, NY, 1996, Soho 20, NYC, 1998, Arts Exchange, White Plains, NY, 2000, The Size Show, 2001, Art Northeast Silvermine Guild Arts Ctr., New Canaan, Conn., 2004, Halle Meml. Libr., Pound Ridge, NY, 2004, Gallery 128, NYC, 2005. Fellow Position of Assoc. Instr., Fine Arts Dept., Ind. U., 1972-1973. Home: 8 1/2 Narragansett Ave Ossining NY 10562 Personal E-mail: arvid@aol.com.

HILL, PATRICIA FRANCINE, information technology executive, educator; b. Buffalo, Jan. 9, 1955; d. Walter W. and M. Phyllis (Jones) H. BA in Math., BS in Engring., Swarthmore Coll., 1977; MS in Computer Engring., U. Mich., 1980; MBA, Harvard U., 1990. Tech. staff AT&T Bells Labs., Middletown, NJ, 1980-86; sr. systems analyst Internat. MarketNet (IMNET), N.Y.C., 1986, Marine Midland Bank, N.Y.C., 1987-88; sr. bus. cons. Kraft Gen. Foods, Skokie, Ill., 1990—92; dir. support svcs. Hyatt Hotel Corp., Chgo., 1993-94; mng. prin. Oracle Corp., 1995-96; cons. Ameritech, Chgo., 1996—2003; analyst Motorola Corp., Ill., 2003—04, Talk Am., 2004—. Cons. McDonald's Corp., Oakbrook, Ill., 1992-93; lectr. in field. Active various charitable orgns. Mem. Nat. Assn. Negro Bus. and Profl. Women, Nat. Tech. Assn. Democrat. Mem. Ch. of Christ. Avocation: athletics.

HILL, PETER WAVERLY, lawyer; b. White River Junction, Vt., June 24, 1953; s. Richard Bert and Elaine Etta (Kimball) H.; m. Eileen Winderman, Aug. 27, 1994; 1 stepchild, Marshall Jackson Miller. BA in Philosophy and Govt., U. Ariz., 1975, JD, 1978. Bar: Ariz. 1978, U.S. Dist. Ct. (no. dist.) N.Y. 1979, N.Y. 1980, U.S. Ct. Appeals (2d cir.) 1982. Staff atty. Legal Aid Soc. Mid N.Y., Utica, 1978-79, Oneonta, 1979-83; assoc. Law Offices of Paternoster & O'Leary, Walton, N.Y., 1983-84; pvt. practice, Oneonta, 1985—. Contbr. articles to profl. jours. Mem. N.Y. State com. Socialist Party, Syracuse. Mem. Nat. Lawyers Guild, Nat. Orgn. Social Security Claimants Reps., N.Y. State Bar Assn., Otsego County Bar Assn., Delaware County Bar Assn., Injured Workers' Bar Assn., Inc. Unitarian Universalist. Office: 384 Main St Oneonta NY 13820-1930

HILL, PHILIP BONNER, lawyer; b. Charleston, W.Va., May 1, 1931; AB, Princeton U., 1952; LLB, W.Va. U., 1957. Bar: W.Va. 1957, Iowa 1965. Assoc. Dayton, Campbell & Love, Charleston, 1957—61; ptnr. Porter, Hill, Thomas, Williams & Hubbard, Charleston, 1961—65; v.p. Thomas & Hill, Charleston, 1961—65; assoc. counsel Equitable Life Ins. Co. of Iowa, Des Moines, 1965—68, counsel, 1968—75; ptnr. Riemenschneider, Hanes & Hill, Des Moines, 1975—79, Austin & Gaudineer, Des Moines, 1979—82, Snyder & Hassig, Sistersville and New Martinsville, W.Va., 1982—96, of counsel, 1997—99, Bowles Rice McDavid Graff & Love, LLP, Martinsburg, W.Va., 2000—. Mem. staff W.Va. Law Rev., 1955-57; contbr. articles to profl. jours. Lt. USNR, 1952-54. Fellow W.Va. Bar Found.; mem. ABA (exec. coun. young lawyers sect. 1966-67), W.Va. State Bar (chmn. jr. bar sect. 1961-62, bd. govs. 1989-92), W.Va. Bar Assn. (pres. 1998-99), Iowa State Bar Assn., Assn. Life Ins. Counsel, Am. Land Title Assn., Am. Judicature Soc., Phi Delta Phi. Office: Bowles Rice McDavid Graff & Love LLP PO Drawer 1419 101 S Queen St Martinsburg WV 25402-1419 Office Phone: 304-213-0833. Business E-Mail: phill@bowlesrice.com.

HILL, RANDALL WILLIAM, information technology manager, director; b. Killeen, Tex., Aug. 30, 1956; s. Randall William and Geraldine Thomas Hill; m. Marianne Haver Hill, May 27, 1957; children: Austin Randall Haver-Hill, Aria Joy Haver-Hill. BS, U.S. Mil. Acad., 1978; MS, U. So. Calif., 1987, PhD, 1993. Mem. tech. staff Jet Propulsion Lab., Pasadena, Calif., 1984—94, supr. tech. group, 1994—95; from rsch. computer scientist Info. Scis. Inst. to dir. U. So. Calif., Marina del Rey, Calif., 1995—2004, dir. applied rsch. and transition Inst. Creative Tech., 2004—. Chmn. conf. Innovative Applications of Artificial Intelligence, Menlo Park, Calif., 2003—04. Capt. M.I. U.S. Army, 1978—84. Mem.: Am. Assn. Artificial Intelligence (licentiate). Protestant. Achievements include research in critical leadership analysis system; virtual human project. Office: USC Institute for Creative Technologies 13274 Fiji Way Marina del Rey CA 90292-7008 Office Phone: 310-574-7815. E-mail: hill@ict.usc.edu.

HILL, RAYMOND JOSEPH, packaging company executive; b. Chanute, Kans., May 4, 1935; s. Raymond Joseph and Emma Leona (Arthurs) Hill; m. Bettie Anne Handshumaker, Mar. 2, 1957; children: David, Dianne, Todd, Scott, Jennifer. A in Engring., Coffeyville (Kans.) Coll., 1955; MBA, U. Denver, 1977. Field engr. Phillips Petroleum Co., Bartlesville, Okla., 1957—59; design engr. Thiokol Chem. Corp., Brigham City, Utah, 1959—60; tech. supr. Hercules Chem. Corp., Salt Lake City, 1960—68; project mgr. aerospace div. Ball Corp., Boulder, Colo., 1968—70, plant mgr. and v.p. mfg. metal container div. Findlay, Ohio and Denver, Colo., 1970—78, pres. agrl. systems div. Westminster, Colo., 1978—85, 1990—93; exec. v.p. food plastics N.Am.; pres. Chesnee Assocs., Inc., Internat. Cons., 1993—97; exec. v.p. The PopStraw Co., also bd. dirs.; bd. dirs. Navaho Agrl. Products Industries, United Energy Devel., Packaging Adv. Coun., Flex Packing Assn., The Hallmark Group, Packaging Ptnrs., Classic Signatures, Inc., PopStraw Co.; mem. policy adv. com. to Office of U.S. Trade Rep., 1980—. Mem.: Irrigation Assn., Soc. Tool Engrs., Nat. Food Processors Assn., Am. Ordnance Assn., Rotary. Republican. Episcopalian. Home: 889 Turnbridge Cir Naperville IL 60540-8342 Office: Chesnee Assocs Inc 2010 E Algonquin Rd Ste 210 Schaumburg IL 60173-4168

HILL, RICHARD (RICK) ALLAN, former congressman; b. Grand Rapids, Minn., Dec. 30, 1946; m. Betti Christie, June 10, 1983; children: Todd, Corey, Mike. BA in Econs. and Polit. Sci., St. Cloud State U., 1968; JD, Concord U. Sch. Law, 2005. Surety bonding businessman, owner InsureWest, 1968-90; real estate and investment ptnr., 1983—; committeeman State Rep. Party, 1990-94; legis. liaison to Gov. Marc Racicot, Mont., 1993; mem. 105th-106th Congress from Mont. dist. U.S. Ho. Reps., Washington, 1997-2001, mem. banking and fin. svcs. com., mem. resources com., mem. small bus. com. Fin. chair State Rep. Party, 1989-91, state chair, 1991-92. Bd. dirs. Mont. Sci. and Tech. Alliance, 1992, Blue Cross Blue Shield Mont., 2003-. Republican. Home: PO Box 4717 Helena MT 59604-4717

HILL, RICHARD DEVEREUX, retired banker; b. Salem, Mass., Nov. 6, 1919; s. Robert W. and Grace (Dennis) H.; m. Polly Bergstedt, Sept. 13, 1947; children: Steven D., Johanna Hill Simpson, Richard Devereux. AB, Dartmouth Coll., 1941; MCS, Amos Tuck Sch. Adminstrn. and Finance, 1942; postgrad. in banking, Rutgers U., 1951; LLD (hon.), Babson Coll.; LLD, Northeastern U., Salem State Coll.; D in Bus. Adminstrn. (hon.), Boston Coll., Tufts U. With The First Nat. Bank of Boston, 1946-84, loan officer, 1948-51, asst. v.p., 1951-55, v.p., 1955-65, exec. v.p., 1965-66, pres., 1966-71, chmn. bd., chief exec., 1971-83, chmn. exec. com., 1983-84, chmn. bd., chief exec. officer, 1971-83, Bank of Boston Corp., 1971-83, chmn. exec. com., 1983-84. Pres. fed. adv. coun. Fed. Res. System, 1977; chmn. Inst. Internat. Fin. Inc., 1983-86. Former chmn. transp. com. New Eng. Coun.; mem. vis. com. Sloan Sch. Mgmt., MIT, 1967-70; mem. Greater Boston adv. bd. Salvation Army; mem. bd. visitors Fletcher Sch. Internat. Law and Diplomacy, 1980—2002; trustee Dartmouth Coll., 1981-83, chmn. trustees 1981-83, trustee emeritus, former mem. investment com.; pres. emeritus, hon. trustee Mus. Fine Arts, Boston; former trustee Boston Urban Found.; hon. mem. Corp. Woods Hole Oceanographic Instn.; former overseer Crotched Mountain Found.; former chmn. Bus. Coun. for Internat. Understanding. Recipient Acad. Disting. Bostonians award Greater Boston C. of C., Christian A. Herter award World Affairs Coun., Lifetime Achievement award Boston Coll., 2005. Mem. Internat. Monetary Conf. (hon.; past pres.), Transp. Assn. Am. (bd. dirs., past chmn. investor panel), Assn. Res. City Bankers (hon.; past pres.), Am. Inst. Banking (adv. com. Boston chpt. 1967-82), Dartmouth Alumni Assn. Boston (past v.p.), New Eng. Exeter Alumni Assn. (past pres.), Mass. Hist. Soc., Masons, Comml. Club (Boston), Eastern Yacht Club (Marblehead), Royal Bermuda Yacht Club, Riddell's Bay Golf and Country Club (Bermuda), Coral Beach and Tennis Club (Bermuda), Sigma Nu. Republican. Congregationalist. Home: Sargent Rd Marblehead MA 01945 Office: 100 Federal St Boston MA 02110-1802 Office Phone: 617-434-2180. Personal E-mail: rdhill00@comcast.net.

HILL, RICHARD EARL, academic administrator; b. Clintonville, Wis., Mar. 30, 1929; s. Lyle Earl and Gladness Josephine (Love) H.; m. Marilyn Jean Thompson, June 5, 1951; children: Mark R., Kenneth L., Richard Earl, Joy A., Sarah J. BA, Carroll Coll., Waukesha, Wis., 1951, L.H.D., 1974; M.Div., McCormick Theol. Sem., 1956. Ordained to ministry Presbyterian Ch., 1956; pastor chs. in Wis., 1955-62; pastor Frame Meml. Presbyn. Ch., Stevens Point, Wis.; also univ. pastor U. Wis., Stevens Point, 1962-69; asst. to pres. Carroll Coll., 1969-74; pres. Huron (S.D.) Coll., 1974-77, Lakeland Coll., Sheboygan, Wis., 1977-89, pres. emeritus, 1991—, chancellor, 1989-91. Pres. S.D. Fedn. Pvt. Colls., 1977; exec. com. Colls. Mid-Am., 1975-77; mem. 6th Congl. Dist. Acad. Selection Com., 1978-89; v.p. Wis. Found. Ind. Colls., 1983-85, pres., 1985-86. Mem. Am. Assn. Colls., Council Advancement and Support Small Colls., Council Advancement and Support Edn., Wis. Assn. Ind. Colls. and Univs. (pres. 1980-83), Am. Mgmt. Assn., Sheboygan Econ. Club (pres. 1985), Pi Kappa Delta, Pi Gamma Mu. Clubs: Rotary. Address: 23033 Westchester Blvd Apt C-404 Port Charlotte FL 33980

HILL, RICHARD LEE, lawyer; b. Spanish Fork, Utah, May 17, 1951; s. Von and Maxine (Chambers) H.; m. Kathryn Smith, July 10, 1980; children: Natalie Kathryn, Nicole Charlene, Kristina Michelle, Kara Alexandra, Alexis Marie. BS cum laude, Brigham Young U., Hawaii, 1976; JD, Brigham Young U., 1979. Bar: Utah 1979, U.S. Dist. Ct. (cen. dist.) Utah 1979, U.S. Supreme Ct. 1979. Ptnr. Parker, McKeown, McConkie, Salt Lake City, 1979-82, Hill, Johnson, Schmutz, & P.C., Provo, Utah, 1982—. Mem. Utah Arts Coun., 1994—; bd. dirs. Provo Theatre Co., 1987—. Mem. Utah Bar Assn., Riverside Country Club. Mem. Lds Ch. Avocation: acting. Office: Hill Johnson & Schmutz 3319 N University Ave Provo UT 84604-4484

HILL, RICHARD S., manufacturing executive; BSE, U. Ill., 1974; MBA, Syracuse U., 1981. With GE, Motorola, Hughes Aircraft; v.p., gen. mgr. oscilloscope group Tektronix, Inc., 1990—91, pres., test & measurement group, 1991—93; CEO Novellus Systems, Inc., San Jose, Calif., 1993—, chmn., 1996—. Mem.: bd. dirs., Novellus Systems, Inc., 2003-. Office: Novellus Systems Inc 4000 N First St San Jose CA 95134

HILL, RONALD CHARLES, surgeon, educator; b. Parkersburg, W.Va., Sept. 4, 1948; s. Lloyd E. and Margaret (Pepper) H.; m. Lenora Jane Rexrode, June 12, 1971; children: Jeffrey, Mandy. BA, W.Va. U., 1970, MD, 1974. Diplomate Diplomate Am. Bd. Surgery, Am. Bd. Thoracic Surgery. Intern dept. of surgery Duke U. Med. Ctr., Durham, NC, 1974—75; resident surgery Duke U., Durham, 1974—85, rsch. assoc., 1976—79, tchg. scholar, 1984—85; asst. prof. surgery W.Va. U., Morgantown, 1985—90, assoc. prof., 1990—96, prof. surgery, 1996—, clin. prof. surgery Sch. Osteopathic Medicine, 1999—. Cons. VA Med. Ctr., Clarksburg, W.Va., 1985—; dir. surg. rsch. dept. surgery W.Va. U., 1986—88, student coord. dept. surgery, 1986—97; mem. adh hoc com. merit rev. bd. for cardiovasc. studies VA,

Washington, 1988—90; mem. Surg. Edn. and Self-Assessment Programs; chmn. instnl. rev. bd. Protection Human Subjects, 1994—2004, program chmn. dept. surgery, 1998—2003, dir., thoracic surgery program, 2005—. Contbr., co-contbr. numerous book chpts. and articles to profl. publs. Mem.-at-large adminstrv. bd. Drummond Chapel United Meth. Ch., Morgantown, 1987—89, 1993—95, fin. com., 1994—96, lay del. to ann. conf., 1995—97, chmn. coun. on evangelism, 1999—2001. Recipient Lange Med. Book award, 1971, 1973, 1974, Roche Med. award, 1972, Merck Med. Book award, 1974, Sowers award, Founders Soc. Duke U., 1992. Fellow ACS (coun. W.Va. chpt. 1999-2001, sec.-treas. 2001-2002, 2d v.p. 2002-2003, 1st v.p. 2003-2004, pres. 2004—, chmn. com. on applicants dist. 1 W.Va.), Southeastern Surg. Congress, Assn. Acad. Surgery, Sabiston Soc., Am. Coll. Cardiology, Am. Coll. Chest Physicians, So. Thoracic Surg. Assn. (program chmn. 1995-96, coun. 1999-2000), Soc. Thoracic Surgeons; mem. Am. Heart Assn., (v.p., pres. elect, pres. W. Va. affiliate 1994-96), Soc. Univ. Surgeons, Am. Assn. Thoracic Surgery, Internat. Surg. Soc., Assn. Programs Dirs. in Surgery, Assn. Surg. Edn., So. Surg. Assn., W.Va. Med. Assn., Mended Hearts, Lakeview Country Club, Pines Country Club, Phi Beta Kappa, Alpha Omega Alpha, Alpha Epsilon Delta, Profl. Assn. Diving Instrs. Soc. (cert. master scuba diver). Republican. Avocations: fishing, photography, scuba diving, shell collecting. Home: 10 Flegal St Morgantown WV 26505-2240 Office: WVa U Med Ctr Dept Surgery Medical Center Dr Morgantown WV 26506 Office Phone: 304-293-2541. Business E-Mail: rhill@hsc.wvu.edu.

HILL, RUTH BEEBE, editor, writer; b. Cleve., Apr. 26, 1913; d. Herman C. and Flora M. (Frantz) Beebe; m. Borroughs R. Hill, Oct. 17, 1940 (dec. 1982); 1 child, B. Reid. AB, Case Western Res. U., 1935, MA, 1937; HHD (hon.), Oglethorpe U., 1993. Lectr. dept. geology U. Miss., Oxford, 1937-39; head bridal cons. May Co., Denver, 1940-41, Filene's, Boston, 1941-43; founder, owner Gull Hill Elem. Sch., New Orleans, 1946-49; mag. columnist Horse and Rider, L.A., 1967-68; freelance editor, lectr. L.A., 1979—. Lectr. Leigh Bur., L.A., 1979-82. Author: Hanta Yo, 1979 (Pulitzer prize nominee, Overseas award 1979, Ohioana award 1979, Booksellers award for excellence in writing 1979, Nat. Heritage award 1979, honoree Am. Acad. Achievement 1979). Mem. DAR (San Juan Islands chpt.), Nat. Writers (bd. dirs.). Republican. Presbyterian. Avocations: censusing grizzlies, animal studies. Home: PO Box 788 Friday Harbor WA 98250-0788

HILL, SEAN CHRISTOPHER, psychology professor; b. Chgo., Oct. 23, 1973; s. Charley and Eloise (Green) H. BA, Anderson U., 1996; MA, Slippery Rock U., 1998; PhD, Loyola Univ., Chgo., 2005. Rsch. asst. Ctr. for Urban Rsch. and Learning, Univ. of Chgo., 1998—2000; adj. instr. gen. edn. Northwestern Bus. Coll., 2001—02; asst. prof. psychology Lewis and Clark C.C., 2002—; adj. instr. edn. Greenville Coll., 2004. Mem. APA, Am. Ednl. Rsch. Assn., Assn. for Moral Edn., Am. Sociological Assn., Assn. of Black Psychologists. Avocations: exercise, reading. E-mail: shill@lc.edu.

HILL, SUSAN BEASLEY, recreational therapist; b. Hattiesburg, Miss., June 16, 1944; d. William Lee Beasley, Jr. and Alice Odelle (Taylor) Beasley; 1 child, Susannah Odelle. BA in English, Speech and DRama, Greensboro Coll., 1966; MSW, U. N.C., 1982. Tchr., prin. John Umstead Hosp., Butner, NC, 1967—70; crisis counselor, co-founder Dial Help, Salisburg, NC, 1970—71; social worker Rowan County Dept. Social Svc., Salisburg, 1970—71; sales mgr./pub. rels. Beasley Lumber Co., Scotland Neck, NC, 1971—80; bus. owner, mgr. Repeat Performances, Raleigh, 1976—78; co-dir., counselor, tchr. Project Redirection Wake County Pub. Schs., Raleigh, 1978—79; clin. social worker, therapist Orange-Person-Chatham Mental Health Ctr., Chapel Hill, NC, 1980—81; clin. social worker, therapist Adult Outpatient Group Clinic N.C. Meml. Hosp., Chapel Hill, 1981—82; clin. social worker/family advisor Divsn. for Disorders of Devel. and Learning U. N.C., Chapel Hill, 1982; pvt. counselor, ednl. tchr. Harnett County, NC, 1982—; dir. Learning Ctr. Acads. Plus, Dunn, NC, 1993—95; activity profl. Dunn (N.C.) Rehab. and Nursing Ctr., 1998—. Shut-in and nursing home ministry Gospel Tabernacle Ch., Dunn, 1982—90. Author: (newspaper series) Aegism: A Six Party Study, 1981. Mem. women's bd. Gospel Tabernacle Ch., 1987, active, 1988—. Republican. Avocations: cooking, painting, politics, cats. Home: 106 Greenwich Ct Dunn NC 28334 Office: Dunn Nursing and Rehab Ctr 711 Susan Tart Rd Dunn NC 28334

HILL, TAMMY YVONNE, elementary school educator; b. Columbus, Ohio, Nov. 26, 1967; d. James Carl and Barbara Virginia Birney; m. Jeffrey Scott Hill, June 22, 1991. BSc in Edn., Ohio U., 1991; MA in Tchg., Marygrove Coll., 1998. Cert. tchr. Ohio, 1998. Tchr. grade 4 Brook Elem. Sch., Byesville, Ohio, 1992—93, tchr. kindergarten, 1996—; tchr. grade 6 Meadowbrook Mid. Sch., Byesville, 1993—96. Mem. budget com. Brook Elem. Sch., 1996—, calendar com. rep., 2000—. Sec. Mt. Zion Ladies Aide Ch., Pleasant City, Ohio, 1997—. Mem.: NEA, Ohio Edn. Assn., Rolling Hills Edn. Assn. (bldg. rep. 1996—), Ea. Ohio Angus Assn. (sec. 2004—, treas. 2004—). Avocations: walking, reading, volleyball. Home: 5450 Wintergreen Rd Senecaville OH 43780-9603 Office: Brook Elem Sch 58601 Marietta Rd Byesville OH 43723

HILL, TERRELL LESLIE, chemist, researcher, biophysicist; b. Oakland, Calif., Dec. 19, 1917; s. George Leslie and Ollie (Moreland) H.; m. Laura Etta Gano, Sept. 23, 1942; children: Julie Lisbeth Eden, Carolyn Jo (Mrs. Gary Lineburg), Ernest Evan. AB, U. Calif. at Berkeley, 1939, PhD, 1942; postgrad., Harvard U., 1940. Instr. chemistry Western Res. U., 1942-44; rsch. assoc. radiation lab. U. Calif. at Berkeley, 1944-45; rsch. assoc. chemistry, then asst. prof. chemistry U. Rochester, 1945-49; chemist U.S. Naval Med. Rsch. Inst., 1949-57; prof. chemistry U. Oreg., 1957-67, U. Calif. at Santa Cruz, 1967-71, adj. prof., 1977-89, prof. emeritus, 1989—, vice chancellor for scis., div. natural scis., 1968-69; research chemist NIH, Bethesda, Md., 1971-88, scientist emeritus, 1988—. Mem. biophysics study sect. USPHS, 1954-57; chemistry panel NSF, 1961-64 Author: Statistical Mechanics, 1956, 87, Statistical Thermodynamics, 1960, 86, Thermodynamics of Small Systems, vol. I, 1963, 94, 2002, vol. II, 1964, 94, 2002, Matter and Equilibrium, 1965, Thermodynamics for Chemists and Biologists, 1968, Free Energy Transduction in Biology, 1977, Cooperativity Theory in Biochemistry, 1985, Linear Aggregation Theory in Cell Biology, 1987, Free Energy Transduction and Biochemical Cycle Kinetics, 1989, 2005, also rsch. papers. Guggenheim fellow Yale, 1952-53; recipient Arthur S. Flemming award U.S. Govt., 1954; Distinguished Civilian Service award U.S. Navy, 1955; award Washington Acad. Scis., 1956; Disting. Service award USPHS, 1981; Disting. Service award U. Oreg., 1983; Sloan Found. fellow, 1958-62 Mem Nat. Acad. Scis., Am. Chem. Soc. (Kendall award 1969), Biophys. Soc., NAACP, ACLU, Phi Beta Kappa. Home: 3400 Paul Sweet Rd Apt C220 Santa Cruz CA 95065

HILL, TESSA, non profit environmental group executive; BA in Edn., Park Recreation Adminstrn., U. Minn., 1968. Tchr. elem. schs., 1970; founder Kids For Saving Earth Worldwide, Mpls., 1989—. Adv. com. U.S. Environ. Protection Agy., Dept. Health Human Svcs. Agy. Toxic Substances Disease Registry. Editor CHEC Report, Kids for Saving Earth News/Programs. Bd. dirs. Children's Health Environ. Coalition, Nat. Coalition Against Misuse Pesticides. Home and Office: Kids for Saving Earth Worldwide 5425 Pineview Ln N Minneapolis MN 55442-1704 Business E-Mail: KSEWW@aol.com.

HILL, THOMAS ALLEN, lawyer; b. Salem, Ohio, Mar. 29, 1958; s. Charles Spencer and Dorothy Jane (Allen) H. BA magna cum laude, Hiram Coll., 1980; JD, George Washington U., 1984. Bar: Ohio 1984, Pa. 1987, D.C. 1988, U.S. Supreme Ct. 1989, Tex. 1990, Okla. 1991, U.S. Dist. Ct. (no. dist.) Ohio, 2004. Legis. intern Office of Hon. John Conyers, Jr., Washington, 1979; asst. to dean campus Life for Housing, conf. dir. Hiram (Ohio) Coll., 1980-81; corp. counsel Capital Oil & Gas Inc., Austintown, Ohio, 1984-93; gen. counsel, sec. North Coast Energy, Inc., Cleve., 1987-2001, Trinity Oil & Gas, Inc. subs. North Coast Energy Inc., Warren, Ohio, 1990-93; gen. counsel Eric Petroleum Corp., Canfield, Ohio, 2001—. Mem. mini-task force on notices of violation Ohio Div. Oil and Gas, Columbus, 1988-90; part-time fin. analyst Primerica Fin. Svcs., Inc., 1997-2000; corp. sec. Peake Energy, Inc., Ravenswood, W.Va., 2000-01. Mem. ABA, Ohio Bar Assn., Mahoning County Bar Assn., Pa. Bar Assn., Okla. Bar Assn., D.C. Bar Assn., State Bar Tex., Trumbull County Bar Assn., Ohio Oil and Gas Assn., Christian Legal Soc., Energy Bar Assn., Ohio Land Title Assn., Ohio Geneal. Soc., Mahoning Valley Hist. Soc., Austintown Hist. Soc., Gen. Soc., War of 1812, SAR, Order of Arrow, Kappa Delta Pi, Pi Gamma Mu. Republican. Avocations: local history, study of amaranth. Home: 4841 Westchester Dr Apt 102 Youngstown OH 44515-2548 Office: Eric Petroleum Corp 4206 1/2 Boardman-Canfield Canfield OH 44406 Office Phone: 330-533-1828. *Motto: I Peter 1: 23-25.*

HILL, THOMAS CLARK, lawyer; b. Prestonsburg, Ky., July 17, 1946; s. Lon Clay and Corinne (Allen) H.; m. Barbarie Friedly, June 13, 1968; children: Jason L., Duncan L. BA, Case Western Reserve U., 1968; JD, U. Chgo., 1973. Bar: Ohio 1973, U.S. Supreme Ct. 1976. Assoc. atty. Taft, Stettinius & Hollister LLP, Cin., 1973-81, ptnr., 1981—. Author: Monthly Meetings in North America: A Quaker Index, 4th edit., 1998. Trustee, treas. Wilmington (Ohio) Coll., 1982-94, 99—, sec., 2002—; treas. Ams. sect. Friends World Commn. for Consultation, 1990-95, presiding clk., 1995-99, ctrl. exec. com., presiding clk., London, 2000—; trustee Wilmington Yearly Meeting of Friends (Quakers), 1986-98, Friends United Meeting, 1999—2004, presiding clk. trustees, 2002—04. Mem. ABA, Ohio State Bar Assn., Cin. Bar Assn., Friends Hist. Assn. (bd. dirs. 1994-95). Republican. Mem. Soc. Of Friends. Avocation: Quaker history. Office: 425 Walnut St Ste 1800 Cincinnati OH 45202-3948 E-mail: hill@taftlaw.com.

HILL, THOMAS QUINTON, communication specialist, graphics designer; b. Talladega, Ala., June 27, 1959; s. Sandy and Maude Verdell (Griggs) H. Student, San Francisco Art Inst., 1978-79, Acad. of Art, San Francisco, 1993-94; BS in Bus. Mgmt., U. Phoenix, 1997; MA in Orgnl. Devel., U. San Francisco, 2001. Comms. coord. Sedgwick, San Francisco, 1990-92; comm. cons. Sedgwick Noble Lowndes, San Francisco, 1992-97; prin. Graphic Details Design, San Francisco, 1993—; sr. comm. analyst Kaiser Permanent, Oakland, Calif., 1997-99; sr. comm. cons. Bank of Am., 1999-2000; sr. comm. specialist Nat. Semiconductor Corp., 2000—. Creative cons. Sedgwick Proposal Com., San Francisco, 1996-97; design cons. Francisco Med. Soc., San Francisco, 1993—; part-time instr. Graphic Arts Inst., San Francisco, 1998. Vol. Alzheimer's Svcs. Orgn., Berkeley, Calif., 1994, Leukemia Soc. Am., San Francisco, 1994, United Way, San Francisco, 1994—; mem. bd. dirs. Calif. divsn. Am. Cancer Soc., Off the Leash arts orgn, 2000—. Recipient Award of Appreciation, Leukemia Soc. Am., 1994, Pinnacle of Success award Am. Assn. Med. Soc. Execs., 1995. Mem. Internat. Assn. Bus. Communicators (chpt. pres. 1998, exec. bd. 2000—, judge blue ribbon panel 1998, Cert. Appreciation 1997), Am. Inst. Graphic Arts (outreach com. 1993—), Commonwealth Club of Calif., Coun. Comm. Mgmt. Avocations: health and fitness, music, theater, films. Office: Nat Semiconductor 1130 Kifer Rd San Francisco CA 94086

HILL, THOMAS WILLIAM, JR., lawyer, educator; b. N.Y.C., Dec. 25, 1924; s. Thomas William Sr. and Marion (Bond) H.; m. Elizabeth Rowe, June 18, 1949; children: Gretchen P., Catharine B., Thomas William III. BS, U. Pa., 1948; MBA, NYU, 1950; JD, Columbia U., 1953. Bar: N.Y. 1953, D.C. 1954, U.S. Supreme Ct. 1958, Fla. 1989; CPA N.Y. Sr. tax acct. Hurdman & Cranstoun, 1949-50; asst. U.S. atty. So. Dist. N.Y., 1953-54; assoc. Cahill, Gordon, Reindel & Ohl, 1954-58; sr. ptnr. Spear & Hill, 1958-75; ptnr. Sidley & Austin, 1981-86; pres. Belco Petroleum Co., N.Y.C., 1962-63; legal adviser Sultanate of Oman, 1972-76. Adj. prof. law U. Miami, 1986-97. Contbr. articles to profl. jours. Vice chmn., pres., trustee Internat. Coll., Beirut, Lebanon, 1978-91. 1st lt. AUS, 1943-46. Decorated Bronze Star, Purple Heart, Medal of Oman (Sultanate of Oman), Order of Homayun (Iran). Mem. ABA, Assn. of Bar of City of N.Y., IBA, Racquet and Tennis Club (N.Y.C.), Mayacoo Golf Club, Taconic Golf Club, Phi Delta Phi, Kappa Sigma. Home: 1967 Breakers Pointe Way West Palm Beach FL 33411-5119 Office Phone: 501-793-4031. Personal E-mail: twhilljr@aol.com.

HILL, VERNON W., II, bank executive; b. San Francisco, Aug. 18, 1945; m. Shirley Hill, 1973; 4 children. BA in Economics, U. Pa. Wharton Sch., 1967. Founder Site Development Inc.; founder, chmn. Commerce NJ, Marlton, NJ, 1973; chmn., pres. Bancorp, 1982, Commerce Bancorp, Inc., Cherry Hill, NJ; chmn. Commerce Pa., 1984—86, Commerce Shore, 1989, Commerce No., 1989—, Commerce Delaware, 1999—, Commerce NYC, 2002, Commerce Long Island, 2002. Founder Galloway Nat. Golf Club. Bd. trustees U. Pa. Recipient Community Banker of the Year, American Banker, 2000. Office: Commerce Bancorp Inc Commerce Atrium 1701 Route 70 E Cherry Hill NJ 08003-2390*

HILL, VICTOR ERNST, IV, mathematics professor, musician; b. Pitts., Nov. 3, 1939; s. Victor Ernst III and Lois Kathryn (Rahenkamp) H.; m. Christi Deanne Adams, Aug. 12, 1967 (div. 1981); children: Victoria Christina Hill Resnick, Christopher Andrew Michael. BS, Carnegie-Mellon U., 1961; MA, U. Wis.-Madison, 1962; PhD, performer's cert. in harpsichord, U. Oreg., 1966. Asst. prof. math. Williams Coll., Williamstown, Mass., 1966-72, assoc. prof, 1972-78, prof., 1978-89, Thomas T. Read prof. math. Vis. prof. math. Ga. Inst. Tech., 1987-88, 91-92, artist-in-residence, 1987-88; vis. prof. music U. Oreg., 1967; concert organist, harpsichordist, 1964—; editor Tudor Choral Works Broude Bros. Author: Groups, Representations, and Characters, 1975, Groups and Characters, 2000; composer organ and choral works. Reader Rec. for Blind and Dyslexic, Inc., Williamstown, 1971—, bd. trustees Berkshire unit, 1996-99; organist-choirmaster St. John's Episcopal Ch., Williamstown, 1972-96. Mem. Assn. Anglican Musicians (archivist 1982—, editl. bd. 1996—, bd. review 1998—), Am. Guild Organists (dean Berkshire chpt. 1982-84, exec. bd. 1995-98), Assn. Christians in Math. Scis., Soc. of St. Margaret (assoc.). Home: PO Box 11 Williamstown MA 01267-0011

HILL, VIRGIL LUSK, JR., academic administrator, military officer; b. Shelby, N.C., Apr. 2, 1938; s. Virgil Lusk and Ellen (Dilling) H.; m. Mary Kimberly Jordan, Jan. 11, 1964; children: James S., Katherine E. BS in Naval Sci., U.S. Naval Acad., 1961. Commd. ensign USN, 1961, advanced through grades to rear adm. (upper half), 1989; served on USS Thomas Jefferson, Groton, Conn., 1968-70; material officer COMSUBRON 18, Charleston, S.C., 1970-73; exec. officer USS L. Mendel Rivers, Charleston, 1973-75; comdg. officer USS Hammerhead, Norfolk, Va., 1976-80; dir. spl. projects Office Chief Naval Ops., Washington, 1980-83; comdr. Submarine Devel. Squadron 12, Groton, 1983-85; dir. attack submarine divsn. Office of Chief Naval Ops., Washington, 1985-87; comdr. Submarine Group 5, San Diego, 1987-88; supt. U.S. Naval Acad., Annapolis, Md., 1988-91; comdr. operational test and evaluation forces USN, Norfolk, 1991-93; pres. Valley Forge (Pa.) Mil. Acad. and Coll., 1993-2000; sr. fellow Villanova U., 2002—. Bd. dirs. Greater Main Line br. ARC, Southeastern Pa. chpt. Decorated Distinguished Svc. medal with gold star, Legion of Merit with 3 gold stars, Meritorious Service medal with 3 gold stars, Navy Commendation medal with 1 gold star; recipient Admiral David Glasgow Farragut award Naval Order of U.S. 1996, Robert Morris award Boy Scouts Am., 1996, Order of Magna Charta, 1996. Mem. Assn. Mil. Colls. and Schs. of the U.S. (former pres.), United Svcs. Orgn. of Phila. (bd. dirs.), Assn. Ind. Colls. and Univs. Pa. (bd. dirs.), Nat. Assn. Ind. Colls. and Univs. (pub. rels. commn.), Pa. Assn. Colls. and Univs., Pa. Assn. Ind. Schs., Nat. Assn. Ind. Schs., U.S. Naval Inst., Naval Order of the U.S., Mil. Order of Fgn. Wars, U.S. Navy League, Naval Submarine League, World Affairs Coun. of Phila., Sunday Breakfast Club of Phila., Penn Club of Phila., Union League of Phila. (bd. dirs.), St. David's Golf Club (Wayne, Pa.), others. Office Phone: 215-591-3875. Personal E-mail: virgilhill@aol.com.

HILL, WALTER, film director, writer, producer; b. Long Beach, Calif., Jan. 10, 1942; Student, Mexico City Coll., Mich. State U. Screenplays include Hickey and Boggs, 1972, The Getaway, 1972, 1994, The Thief Who Came to Dinner, 1973, The Mackintosh Man, 1973, The Drowning Pool, 1975, The Warriors, 1979; writer, dir.: Hard Times, 1975, The Driver, 1978, The Warriors, 1979, Southern Comfort, 1981, 48 Hrs., 1982, Streets of Fire, 1984, Wild Bill, 1995, Last Man Standing, 1996; producer: Alien, 1979, Blue City, 1986; writer, prodr. (with Gordon Carroll and David Giler) Aliens, 1986, Alien 3, 1992; dir.: The Warriors, The Long Riders, 1980, Brewster's Millions, 1985, Crossroads, 1986, Extreme Prejudice, 1987, Johnny Handsome, 1989, Another 48 Hrs., 1990, Tresspass, 1992, Geronimo, 1993 (also prodr.), Supernova, 2000, Undisputed, 2002, The Phophecy, 2002, Deadwood, 2004 (Emmy award Outstanding Directing for a Drama Series, 2004). Office: William Morris Agy c/o J Burnham 151 S El Camino Dr Beverly Hills CA 90212-2704

HILL, WILLIAM U., state supreme court justice, former state attorney general; b. Montgomery, Ala., 1948; BA, U. Wyo., 1970; JD, U. Wyo. Coll. of Law, 1974. Bar: Wyo. 1974. Asst. atty. gen. State of Wyo., Cheyenne, Wyo., 1974—77; atty. priv. practice, Riverton, Wyo., 1977—80, Seattle, 1977—80; chief of staff, chief counsel Sen. Malcolm Wallop, Wash., DC, 1980—89; atty. priv. practice, Cheyenne, Wyo., 1989—91; asst. U.S. atty., 1991—95; atty. gen. State of Wyo., Cheyenne, Wyo., 1995—98; justice Wyo. Supreme Ct., Cheyenne, 1998—2002, chief justice, 2002—. Mem.: Wyo. State Bar Assn. Office: Wyoming Supreme Court 2301 Capitol Ave Cheyenne WY 82001-3656

HILLARD, JAMES RANDOLPH, psychiatry educator; b. Ft. Smith, Ark., Mar. 15, 1951; s. James Milton and Louise (Winzenried) H.; m. Aingeal Grehan, Sept. 18, 2001; children by previous marriage: Miriam Elena, Ian James Adams, Nathaniel Kenneth. BA, U. N.C., 1973; MD, Stanford U., Palo Alto, Calif., 1977. Diplomate Am. Bd. Psychiatry and Neurology; lic. psychiatrist, N.C., Va., Ohio. Intern Duke U. Med. Ctr., Durham, N.C., 1977-79, resident, 1979-81; psychiatrist dept. student health U. Va., 1981, asst. prof. dept. behavioral medicine and psychiatry, 1981-84; dir. psychiat. emergency svc. dept. psychiatry U. Cin., 1984-89, prof., chmn. dept. psychiatry, 1989—. Pres. U. Cin. Med. Assocs., 1993—, exec. assoc. dean for clin. affairs, 1997—. Editor Current Psychiatry; contbr. articles to profl. jours., chpts. to books. Mem. Am. Assn. Emergency Psychiatrists (pres. 1988-90), Am. Assn. Chmn. Dept. Psychiatry, Cin. Psychiat. Assn., Mental Health Assn. Office: U Cin Coll Medicine Dept Psychiatry Ml 559 Cincinnati OH 45267-0001 Home: 3046 Ononta Ave Cincinnati OH 45226-2015 Office Phone: 513-558-4274. Business E-Mail: Hillarjr@email.uc.edu.

HILLE, BERTIL, physiology educator; b. New Haven, Oct. 10, 1940; s. C. Einar and Kirsti (Ore) H.; m. Merrill Burr, Nov. 21, 1964; children: Erik D., J. Trygve. BS, Yale U., 1962; PhD, Rockefeller U., 1967. H.H. Whitney fellow Cambridge U., 1967-68; asst. prof. U. Wash., Seattle, 1968-71, assoc. prof., 1971-74, prof. physiology, 1974—. Vis. prof. U. Saarland, Hamburg, Germany, 1975-76. Author: Ion Channels of Excitable Membranes, 3d edit., 2001; mem. edit. bd.: Jour. Gen. Physiology, 1971—, Am. Jour. Physiology, 1984—87, Jour. Neurosci., 1984—87, Neuron, 1987—, Curr. Opinion Neurobiol., 1990—99, Procs. of NAS, 1996—99; contbr. articles to profl. jours. Recipient Alexander von Humboldt Sr. Scientist award, 1975, Bristol-Myers Squibb award, 1990, (with Dr. Clay Armstrong) Louisa Gross Horowitz prize for biology or biochemistry Columbia U., 1996, (with Drs. Clay Armstrong and Roderick MacKinnon) Albert Lasker Basic Med. Rsch. award, 1999; co-recipient Gairdner Found. 2001 Internat. award, 2001. Mem. NAS, Biophys. Soc. (K.S. Cole award 1975), Am. Acad. Arts and Sci., Inst. of Medicine, Soc. Neurosci. Home: 10630 Lakeside Ave NE Seattle WA 98125-6934 Office: U Wash Box 357290 Seattle WA 98195-7290 E-mail: hille@u.washington.edu.

HILLEARY, (WILLIAM) VAN, former congressman, lawyer; b. Rhea County, Tenn., June 20, 1959; s. Bill and Evelyn Hilleary; m. Meredith Brown, June 3, 2000. BS in Bus. Adminstrn., U. Tenn., 1981; JD, Samford U., 1990. Bar: Tenn. With SSM Industries, Inc., Spring City, Tenn., 1984—86, dir. planning and bus. devel., 1992—94; mem. US Congress 4th Tenn. Dist., 1995—2002; mem. fin. services com.; mem. edn. and the workforce com.; of counsel, pub. law & policy strategies group Sonnenschein Nath & Rosenthal LLP, Washington, 2003—. Served USAF, 1981-1982, USAFR, 1982—; served in Persian Gulf. Decorated 2 US Air Medals, Nat. Svc. medal, Kuwaiti Liberation Medal. Mem. Am. Legion, Sigma Chi. Republican. Presbyterian. Office: Sonnenschein Nath & Rosenthal LLP Ste 600, E Tower 1301 K St NW Washington DC 20015 Office Phone: 202-408-9182. Office Fax: 202-408-6399. Business E-Mail: vhilleary@sonnenschein.com.*

HILLEL, ZAHARIA, anesthesiologist; BS in Physics, City Coll. (CUNY), 1971; PhD in Biophysics, Albert Einstein Coll. Med., 1977; MD, U. Miami, 1981. Diplomate Am. Bd. Anesthesiology, Nat. Bd. of Echocardiography. Resident in anesthesia Mount Sinai Med. Ctr., N.Y., 1982-84, fellowship in cardiothoracic anesthesia, 1984-85; prof. clin. anesthesiology Coll. of Physicians and Surgeons, Columbia U. Office: St Luke's Roosevelt Hosp Ctr St Luke's Hosp Dept Anesth 1111 Amsterdam Ave New York NY 10025-1716 Fax: 212-523-3930. Office Phone: 212-523-2500. E-mail: zh2@columbia.edu.

HILLENBRAND, BARRY RICHARD, journalist; b. Chgo., Sept. 30, 1941; s. George C. and Mary (Traut) H.; m. Phuong Nga Nguyen, Sept. 21, 1974; 1 child, Kim. BS in Humanities, Loyola U. Chgo., 1963; postgrad., NYU, 1965-67. Corr. Time Mag., L.A., 1970-72, S.E. Asia corr. Saigon, Vietnam, 1972-74, Rio Bur. chief Rio de Janeiro, 1974-78, corr. Chgo., 1978-81, Boston bur. chief, 1981-83, Persian Gulf bur. chief Manama, Bahrain, 1983-86, Tokyo bur. chief, 1986-92, London bur. chief, 1992-99, internat. corr. Washington, 1999—. Peace Corps vol., Ethiopia, 1963-65. Mem. Assn. of Am. Corr. in London (pres. 1995). Home: 3344 Upland Ter NW Washington DC 20015 Office: Time Magazine 555 12th St NW Washington DC 20004-1400 E-mail: barryhillenbrand@aol.com.

HILLENBRAND, DAVID M., museum administrator; s. Martin J. Hillenbrand; m. Georgianna Hillenbrand; children: Stuart, Joseph. With Mobay Chem., 1980—88; sr. v.p., gen. site mgr. Miles Inc., Elkhart, 1991—94; pres., CEO Canadian Ops. Bayer Inc., 1994—2002; exec. v.p Bayer Polymers, 2002—03; pres. Carnegie Museums of Pitts., 2005—. Dir. Koppers, 1999—. Office: Carnegie Museums 4400 Forbes Ave Pittsburgh PA 15213-4080 Office Phone: 412-622-3333.

HILLENBRAND, LAURA, writer; b. Fairfax, Va., 1967; Student, Kenyon Coll. Editor: Equus Mag., 1989—; contbr. articles to mags.; author: Seabiscuit: An American Legend, 2001 (finalist Nat. Book Critics Cir. award). Office: Ballantine Books Random House 1745 Broadway New York NY 10019

HILLENBURG, STEPHEN, writer, television producer, animator; b. Fort Sill, Okla., Aug. 21, 1961; m. Karen Hillenburg; 1 child. BS in Marine Biology, Humboldt State U., 1984; MFA in Experimental Animation, Calif. Inst. of Arts, 1992. Marine sci. instructor Orange County Ocean Inst., Dana Point, Calif., 1985—87. Creator, writer, prodr., dir. & storyboard artist (TV series) Rocko's Modern Life, 1993—96, creator, writer, exec. prodr. SpongeBob SquarePants, 1999—2004 (Emmy nom. for outstanding children's program, 2002, Emmy nom. for outstanding animated program, 2003, 2004), creator, animator (films) The Green Beret and Wormholes, dir., prodr., writer, actor, composer & storyboard artist The SpongeBob SquarePants Movie, 2004 (Annie award nom. for dir., 2005). Recipient Princess Grace award in film, 1992, Walk the Talk award, Heal the Bay, 2001, Princess Grace Statue award, 2002.*

HILLENMEYER, HENRY REILING, JR., restaurant company executive; b. Temple, Tex., Nov. 13, 1943; s. Henry Reiling and Lucy Carolyn (Taylor) H.; m. Sallie Long Sigler, Oct. 30, 1976; children: Henry Reiling, Edward Ferriday, Taylor Jennings, Morgan Andrew, Hunter Taverner. BA, Yale U., 1965. Trainee Kanawha Valley Bank, Charleston, W.Va., 1965-67, asst. sec., 1967-68; v.p. CBM, Inc., Cleve., 1968-70, pres., 1970-72, chmn., dir., 1972-74; pres., dir. Ireland's Restaurants, Inc., Nashville, 1974-78; exec. v.p. Womco, Inc., Nashville, 1978-82; pres., dir. So. Hospitality Corp., Nashville, 1983-89, chmn., pres., dir., 1989-94; chmn., CEO, dir. Skillsearch Corp., Nashville, 1995-99, Cooker Restaurant Corp., 1999—2004; cons., 2004—. Bd. dirs. Jr. Achievement, Nashville, 1985—, chmn., 1991-92, 97-99; bd. dirs. Tenn. Spl. Olympics, Nashville, 1986-90; trustee Harding Acad.,

Nashville, 1985-90; nat. assoc. Boys Clubs of Am., N.Y.C., 1986-90. Mem. World Pres. Orgn., Belle Meade Country Club, Scroll and Key Soc., Fence Club, Yale Club of Middle Tenn. (pres. 1983-88). Republican. Episcopalian. Home and Office: 8 Foxhall Close Nashville TN 37215-1808 Office Phone: 615-292-4687. Personal E-mail: hilly615@bellsouth.net.

HILLER, ARTHUR, motion picture director; b. Edmonton, Alta., Can., Nov. 22, 1923; Ed., U. Toronto and U. B.C., Alta., Toronto and B.C.; F.V.Ch.C., Victoria Coll., Glasgow, 1967; MA in Psychology; LHD, London Inst. Applied Research, 1973; DFA (hon.), U. Victoria, 1995; LLD, U. Toronto, 1995. Dir. TV prodns. Matinee Theatre, Playhouse 90, Alfred Hitchcock Presents, Route 66, Naked City; dir. films Americanization of Emily, 1965, Out of Towners, 1970, Love Story, 1970, Plaza Suite, 1971, Hospital, 1971, Man of La Mancha, 1972, The Man in the Glass Booth, 1975, Silver Streak, 1976, The In-Laws, 1979, Making Love, 1982, Teachers, 1984, Outrageous Fortune, 1987, The Babe, 1992. Decorated comdr. Internat. Order Sursam Corda; doctor laureate Imperial Order Constantine Brussels, 1972; recipient Can. radio awards, 1951, 52; awards for edn. by radio Ohio U., 1952, 53; best dir. nomination Nat. Acad. TV Arts and Scis., 1962; best dir. nomination Acad. Motion Picture Arts and Scis., 1970; Golden Globe award for best dir., 1970; Dir.'s award nomination Dirs. Guild Am., 1970; Best Dir. award N.Y. Fgn. Press, 1970; Jean Hersholt Humanitarian award Acad. Motion Picture Arts and Scis., 2002. Mem. Directors' Guild of Am. (pres. 1988-92), Acad. Motion Picture Arts and Scis. (pres. 1993-97), Nat. Film Preservation Bd. of Libr. Congress.

HILLER, DAVID DEAN, publishing executive; b. Chgo., June 12, 1953; AB, Harvard U., 1975, JD, 1978. Bar: Ill. 1981. Law clk. to Hon. Judge Malcolm Wilkey US Ct. Appeals DC Cir., 1978-79; law clk. to Hon. Justice Potter Stewart US Supreme Ct., 1979-80; spl. asst. to Atty. Gen. William French Smith US Dept. Justice, 1981—82, assoc. dep. atty. gen., 1982—83; assoc. Sidley & Austin, Chgo., 1983—86, named ptnr., 1986; v.p., gen. counsel Tribune Co., Chgo., 1988—93, sr. v.p., gen. counsel, 1993, sr. v.p. devel., 1993—2000, pres. interactive, 2000—04, sr. v.p. pub., 2003—04; pres. & pub. Chgo. Tribune, 2004—. Bd. dirs. CareerBuilder, Classified Ventures, CrossMedia Services. Editor Harvard Law Rev., 1977-78. Bd. trustees Roosevelt U., Chgo. Hist. Soc.; bd. dirs. Chgo. Tribune Found., McCormick Tribune Found. Mem. ABA, Chgo. Coun. Fgn. Rels, Econ. Club Chgo. (bd. dirs.). Office: Chicago Tribune 435 N Michigan Ave Chicago IL 60611 E-mail: dhiller@tribune.com.*

HILLERMAN, TONY, writer, journalist, educator; b. Sacred Heart, Okla., May 27, 1925; s. August Alfred and Lucy Mary (Grove) Hillerman; m. Marie Elizabeth Unzner, Aug. 16, 1948; children: Anne, Janet Hillerman Grado, Anthony Jr., Monica Hillerman Atwell, Steven, Daniel. Student, Okla. State U., 1942-43; BA, U. Okla., 1948; MA in English, U. N.Mex., 1965, LittD (hon.), 1990, Ariz. State U., 1991. Police reporter Borger (Tex.) News-Herald, 1948; reporter, city editor constn. Morning Press, Lawton, Okla., 1949-50; polit. reporter UP, Oklahoma City, 1950-52, bur. mgr. Santa Fe, 1952-54; reporter, then city editor and editor The New Mexican, Santa Fe, 1954-62; prof. journalism U. N.Mex., Albuquerque, 1965-87, asst. to pres., 1963-65, 81-84. Author: (novels) The Blessing Way, 1970, The Fly on the Wall, 1971, The Boy Who Made Dragonfly, 1972, Dance Hall of the Dead, 1973 (Edgar Allen Poe award, 1973), Listening Woman, 1986, People of Darkness, 1986, The Dark Wind, 1986, The Ghostway, 1986, Skinwalkers, 1986 (Anthony award, 1987), A Thief of Time, 1988 (Macavity award Mystery Readers Internat., 1988, Dept. Interior award, 1990), Talking God, 1988 (Media award Am. Anthrop. Assn., 1990), The Joe Leaphorn Mysteries, Coyote Waits, 1990, Sacred Clowns, 1993, Finding Moon, 1995, The Fallen Man, 1996, The First Eagle, 1998, Hunting Badger, 1998, The Wailing Wind, 2002, Sinister Pig, 2003, Skeleton Man, 2004, (non-fiction) The Great Taos Bank Robbery, 1996, New Mexico, 1996, Rio Grande, 1996, The Spell of New Mexico, 1996, Indian Country, 1996, The Best of the West, 1996, The Oxford Book of American Detective Stories, 1996, Seldom Disappointed, 2001, Kilroy Was There, 2005; contbr. articles, audio recs.; editor: The Mysterious West, 1994. With inf. U.S. Army, 1943—45, ETO. Decorated Bronze Star, Silver Star, Purple Heart; recipient Golden Spur award, Western Writers Am., 1987, Spl. Friend of Dineh award, Navajo Tribal Coun., 1987, Grand Prix de Littérature Policière award, France, 1992, Amb. award, Ctr. for the Indian, 1992. Mem.: Internat. Crime Writers Assn., Mystery Writers Am. (pres. 1988, Grand Master award 1991, Robert Keroch Lifetime Achievement award 2005). Democrat. Roman Catholic. Avocation: trout fishing.

HILLEY, MARY KAY, music educator; b. Ft. Valley, Ga., Oct. 31, 1963; d. John Dunham and G. Joan (Baker) Warner; m. Harry Quinton Dunlap (div.); 1 child, John Quinton Dunlap; m. Daniel Grover Hilley, Sept. 15, 2001. AA in Music, Darton Coll., 1996; BS in Music Edn., Ga. Southwestern State U., 1999. Tchr. Wheeler Piano Studio, Americus, Ga., 1997—2000; pvt. piano tchr. Leesburg, Ga., 1999—. Organist 1st Presbyn. Ch., Albany, Ga., 1998—2000; pianist, choir dir. Northgate Presbyn. Ch., Albany, 2000—. Mem.: Nat. Guild Piano Tchrs. Avocations: reading, bicycling, sewing, camping. Home and Studio: 129 Lee Dr Leesburg GA 31763 Office Phone: 229-446-6179. E-mail: dmjhilley@netzero.net.

HILL-FOSTER, IALINE, retired secondary school educator; b. Houston, Apr. 13, 1936; d. Charlie B. and Alice Bernice Burch; m. James Willie Foster. BA, Dallas Bapt. Coll., 1975. Educator Dallas Ind. Sch. Dist., 1970—96. He Called Our Name, 2001 (Editor's Choice Award, 2002); author: Keep Looking Li'l Girl, 2001 (Internat. Poet of Merit Award, 2001). Recipient Outstanding Svc. and Dedication award, Disabled Am. Verterans, 2001. Mem.: AARP, Internat. Soc. of Poets (Disting. Mem. Award 2001), Parent Tchr. Assn. (life Outstanding Vol. Svc. Award). Avocation: reading, gardening, cooking, writing, collecting antiques.

HILLGREN, SONJA DOROTHY, journalist; b. Sioux Falls, SD, May 17, 1948; d. Ralph Oliver and Priscilla Adaline (Mannes) Hillgren; m. Ralph Lee Hill (dec.). BJ, U. Mo., 1970, MA, 1972; postgrad., Harvard U., 1982—83. Washington corr. Ohio-Washington News Svc., 1972-73; reporter UPI, Annapolis, Md., 1974-76, reporter, editor Washington, 1976-78, farm editor, 1978-88; Washington corr. Knight-Ridder, Washington, 1988-90; Washington editor Farm Jour., 1990-95, editor, 1995—2004, sr. v.p., 2000—. Exec.-in-residence U. Mo., 1997; campaign steering com. U. Mo. Sch. Journalism, 2003—. Chair bd. dirs. Nat. Press Bldg. Corp., 1997; bd. dirs. Winrock Internat., Philabundance, 2000—. Named Old Master, Purdue U., 1992, Agrl. Communicator of Yr., Nat. Agri-Mktg. Assn., 1996; recipient J.R. Russell award, Newspaper Farm Editors Am., 1985, Reuben Brigham award, Agrl. Comms. in Edn., 1988, Oscar in Agr. for Excellence in Agrl. Reporting, U. Ill., 1998, Recognition of Excellence in Print Media award, Ill. Soybean Assn., 2002, Prodr. Comms. award, United Soybean Bd., 2003; Nieman fellow, Harvard U., 1982—83, Woodrow Wilson vis. fellow, 1993—94. Mem.: Coun. on Fgn. Rels., Farm Found., Nat. Agri-Mktg. Assn., Am. Agrl. Editors' Assn., Am. Soc. Mag. Editors, N.Am. Agrl. Journalists (pres. 1987—88), Congl. Country Club, Nat. Press Club (bd. govs. 1991—96, chair 1993—94, v.p. 1995, pres. 1996), Alpha Zeta, Pi Beta Phi (Carolyn Helman Lichtenberg Crest award 1999). Lutheran. Avocations: sports, reading. Home: 315 S 18th St Philadelphia PA 19103-6619 Office: Farm Jour 1818 Market St Fl 31 Philadelphia PA 19103-3654 Business E-Mail: shillgren@farmjournal.com.

HILLHOUSE, ROBERT EARL, music educator; b. Water Valley, Miss., Apr. 16, 1951; s. Garlan and Lucile Hillhouse; m. Margaret Mary Davis, Aug. 28, 1976; children: Brian, Elizabeth. BA in Music Edn., Chgo. State U., 1977. Music educator, chorus dir. Chgo. Pub. Schs., 1991—. Cub Scout leader Boy Scouts Am., Evergreen Park, Ill., 1995—2001. Democrat. Roman Catholic. Avocations: golf, swimming, running. Home: 9524 S Trumbull Evergreen Park IL 60805

HILLIARD, ANDREA LEIGH, writer; b. Columbus, Ohio, Feb. 23, 1973; d. Robert Matthew and Maryanne Feeney; m. Jason William Hilliard, July 20, 1996; children: Maxwell Robert, Quinn Michael. Telemarketer, auditor TruGreen-Chemlawn, Westerville, Ohio, 1989, customer svc. adminstr., 1989—94, bus. analyst Memphis, 1994—96, office mgr. Florence, Ky., 1996—97, customer svc. adminstr. Columbus, Ohio, 1997—98, ops. asst. Westerville, 1998—99. Author: Tales of the Eventide and Other Dark Matter, 2004, The Colors of Life, 2003, (poetry) Suburban Fall - The Best Poems and Poets of 2003, The Chronicles of Night. Home: 317 Kenbrook Dr Columbus OH 43085

HILLIARD, ANN J., retired academic administrator; b. Chgo., Nov. 5, 1933; d. Wesley Norman and Clara Anna (Long) Jackson; children: Colette, Sharon. BA, Ohio Wesleyan U., 1966; MA, U. Tampa, 1976. Tchr. DeSoto County Schs., Arcadia, Fla., 1966—68; head dept. Hillsborough Sch. Dist., Plant City, Fla., 1968—76; coord. Fresno (Calif.) County Schs., 1976—94, Fla. Keys C.C., Key West, 1994—98; ret., 1998. Mem.: Order Eastern Star, Phi Delta Kappa. Episcopalian.

HILLIARD, DAVID CRAIG, lawyer, educator; b. Framingham, Mass., May 22, 1937; s. Walter David and Dorothy (Shortiss) H.; m. Celia Schmid, Feb. 16, 1974. BS, Tufts U., 1959; JD, U. Chgo., 1962. Bar: Ill. 1962, U.S. Supreme Ct. 1966. Mng. ptnr. Pattishall, McAuliffe, Newbury, Hilliard & Geraldson, Chgo., 1983—2002, sr. ptnr., 2003—. Adj. prof. law Northwestern U., 1971—, chmn. Symposium Intellectual Property Law and the Corp. Client, 1987—; lectr. in advanced trademark law and info. regulation U. Chgo. Law Sch., 1999—. Author: Unfair Competition and Unfair Trade Practices, 1985, Trademarks, 1987, Trademarks and Unfair Competition, 1994, 6th edit., 2005, Trademarks and Unfair Competition Deskbook, 2001, 2d edit., 2003, online edit., 2005; editor-in-chief Chgo. Bar Record, 1978-81. Trustee Art Inst. Chgo., 1980—, vice-chmn., 1998-2000, exec. com., 1994-2000, chmn. sustaining fellows, 1981-85, chmn. adv. com. dept. architecture, 1981—, pres. aux. bd., 1977-79, chmn. exhbns. com., 1993—, chmn. bd. govs. of the sch., 1997-2000; trustee Newberry Libr., 1983—, exec. com., 1987—; trustee Robert Allerton Trust, 2002—; pres. Lawyers Trust Fund Ill., 1985-88; vis. com. DePaul U. Law Sch., U. Chgo. Sch. of Law, chmn., 1987-88, Northwestern U. Assocs., 1985—; profl. adv. bd. Atty. Gen. Ill., 1982-84; mem. Ill. Commn. on Rights of Women, 1983-85; bd. dirs. Ill. Inst. Continuing Legal Edn., 1980-82; pres. Planned Parenthood Assn. Chgo., 1975-77. Lt. JAGC, USN, 1962-66. Recipient Maurice Weigle award, 1974, Chgo. Coun. Lawyers award for jud. reform, 1983. Fellow Am. Coll. Trial Lawyers (chmn. courageous adv. com. 1995-97); mem. ABA (chmn. trademark divsn. 1986-87, mem. coun. 1991-95, intellectual property law sect.), Ill. Bar Assn., Chgo. Bar Assn. (pres. 1982-83, founding chmn. young lawyers sect. 1971-72), Internat. Trademark Assn. (bd. dirs. 1989-91, CPR disting. panel of neutrals 1994—), Arts Club, Chgo. Club, Econ. Club, Grolier Club, Lawyers Club, Legal Club (pres. 1989-90), Univ. Club, Casino, Wayfarers Club (pres. 1994-95). Home: 1320 N State Pkwy Chicago IL 60610-2118 Office: Pattishall McAuliffe Newbury Hilliard & Geraldson 311 S Wacker Dr Ste 5000 Chicago IL 60606-6631 Office Phone: 312-554-8000. E-mail: dhilliard@pattishall.com.

HILLIARD, EARL FREDERICK, congressman, lawyer; b. Apr. 9, 1942; s. Mary Franklin Hilliard; m. Iola H. Hilliard, June 9, 1967; children: Alesia, Earl F. BA, Morehouse Coll., 1964; JD, Howard U., 1967; MBA, Atlanta U., 1970. Rsch. asst. Howard U., 1965-67; instr. Miles Coll., 1967-68; asst. to pres. Ala. State U., 1968-70; ptnr. Hilliard, Jackson, Little & Stansel, Birmingham, 1974-78; pvt. practice Birmingham; pres. Am. Trust Life Ins. Co.; mem. Ala. Ho. of Reps., 1974-80, chmn. Black legis. caucus, 1975; mem. Ala. Senate, 1980-93, U.S. Congress from 7th Ala. dist., 1993—2002; ptnr. Hillard, Smith & Hunt, Birmingham, 2003—. Reginald Herber Smith Comty. Lawyer fellow, 1970-71. Mem. NAACP (life), Nat. Bar Assn. (life), Ala. Black Lawyers Assn., Morehouse Coll. Alumni Assn. (life), Alpha Phi Alpha (life). Democrat. Baptist. Home: 1625 Castleberry Way Birmingham AL 35214-4867 Office: Hilliard Smith & Hunt PO Box 12445 Birmingham AL 35202-2445 Office Phone: 205-326-8844. E-mail: earlhilliard@bellsouth.net.

HILLIARD, LANDON, banker; b. Norfolk, Va., Apr. 13, 1939; s. Landon and Irene (Bernard) H.; m. Mary Warfield Eichert, May 28, 1960 (div. Nov. 1980); children: Landon, IV., David Shelburne; m. Mary Cary Myers, Dec. 6, 1980; children: Harrison Carter; stepchildren: Mary Cary Morrison, R. Hamilton Morrison BA in Econs., U. Va., 1962. V.p. Morgan Guaranty Trust Co. of N.Y., N.Y.C., 1962-74; ptnr. Brown Bros. Harriman & Co., N.Y.C., 1974—. Bd. dirs. Owens-Corning, Toledo, Norfolk So. Corp., Western World Ins. Co., Franklin Lakes, NJ, Russell Reynolds Assocs. Inc., N.Y.C.; dir., mem. trustee Provident Loan Soc., N.Y.C., 1975—, chmn., 1992—; trustee Episcopal H.S., Va., 2001—; bd. dirs. Jefferson Scholars Found, 2001, The Nat. Found. for Tchg. Entrepreneurship, N.Y.C., 2000—. Mem. Econ. Club of N.Y. (sec. 1988—), Nat. Golf Links of Am. (Southampton, N.Y.), The Links, The Brook, Racquet and Tennis Club, Piping Rock Club (Locust Valley, N.Y.), Meadow Brook Club (Jericho, N.Y.). Avocations: skiing, golf. Office: Brown Bros Harriman & Co 140 Broadway New York NY 10005-1101

HILLIARD, ROBERT GLENN, insurance company executive, lawyer; b. Anderson, S.C., Jan. 18, 1943; s. Baz Robert and Louise (Holcombe) H.; m. Heather Ann Prevost, Apr. 1, 1966; children: Kathryn Louise Stuart, Nancy Ann, Mary Elizabeth Glenn. BA, Clemson U., 1965; JD, George Washington U., 1968. Bar: S.C. 1969. Gen. counsel Liberty Life Ins. Co., Greenville, S.C., 1965-82, 1975-82; v.p., gen. counsel, sec. Liberty Life Ins. Co., Greenville, S.C., 1975-82; pres., chief exec. officer Liberty Life; pres. Liberty Life Ins. Co., Greenville, S.C., 1982-88, chmn. bd., 1988-89; dir. Liberty Corp., 1982-89; pres., CEO, Security Life of Denver ING Americas, Atlanta, 1989—92, pres., CEO ING America Life, 1992—93, CEO, pres., chmn., 1993—2003; non-exec. chmn. Conseco, Carmel, Ind., 2003—04, chmn., 2004—. Bd. dirs. Carolina First Corp., Security Life; founder, chmn. emeritus Foothills Trail Conf.; chmn. Netherlands Ins. Co., ING Can., N.Am. Investment Centre, NN Fin. Bd. dir. Piedmont Hosp., Atlanta; vice chmn., fin., High Mus.; chmn. investment com., Clemson Univ. Found.; former chmn. bd. dirs. S.C. Gov.'s Sch. for Arts, Perception, Inc. Recipient Jim Kern award Am. Hiking Soc. Mem. ABA, S.C. Bar Assn., Am. Coun. Life Ins., Assn. Life Ins. Counsel, INternat. Ins. Soc., Org. for Internat. Investment, Internat. Bus. Fellows, Bare Minimum Track Club (co-founder, bd. dirs.), Greenville Country Club, Poinsett Club (S.C.), Colo. Concern, Colo. Forum, Denver Athletic Club, Univ. Club. Presbyterian. Office: Conseco 11825 N Pennsylvania St Carmel IN 46032*

HILLIARD, ROBERT L., communications educator; b. N.Y.C., June 25, 1925; children: Mark, Mara. BA, U. Del., 1948; MA, Western Res. U., 1949, MFA, 1950; PhD, Columbia U., 1959; postgrad., Tchrs. Coll., 1959-60. Profl. in theatre, radio and TV, newspaper reporter, editor, 1943-64; instr. Bklyn. Coll., 1950-56; asst. prof. Adelphi U., Garden City, N.Y., 1956-60; assoc. prof. U. N.C., Chapel Hill, 1960-64; chief Ednl./Pub. Broadcasting Br., FCC, Washington, 1964-80; chmn. Fed. Interagency Media Com., Washington, 1965-78; dean grad. studies Emerson Coll., Boston, 1980-84, prof., 1984—. Cons. and lectr. in field. Author: Surviving the Americans: The Continued Struggle of the Jews After Liberation, 1997, Global Broadcasting Systems, 1996; (with Michael Keith) The Broadcast Century, 1992, 2d edit., 1997, The Federal Communications Commission, 1991, Writing for Television and Radio, 6th edit., 1996, Television Station Operations and Management, 1989, Television and Adult Education, 1986, Radio Broadcasting, 3d edit., 1985, others; contbr. articles to profl. jours. Pres. adv. congress Cambridge (Mass.) Cmty. Cable TV, 1986-90, bd. dirs., 1986-90; bd. dirs. Armstrong Meml. Rsch. Found., 1994—, Joda Inst., 1996—; trustee New Eng. Inst. for Peace, 1987-90; del. Mass. Dem. conv., 1986; active Mass. Telecomm. Commn., 1981-92. With U.S. Army, 1944-46. Decorated Purple Heart; Goethe Inst. fellow; recipient award Ohio Med. Edn. Network, Broadcast Preceptor award Kappa Delta Pi, World Comm. Yr. award Phi Delta Kappa, Ann. award Cambridge Cmty. TV, also nat. playwriting awards. Mem. AFTRA, Nat. Instrs. TV Fixed Svc. Assn. (bd. dirs.), Actors Equity Assn., Internat. Univ. Comm. (founder, 1st pres.). Home: 38 Essex St Cambridge MA 02139-2646 Office: Emerson Coll 120 Boylston St Boston MA 02116-4624

HILLIARD, RUSSELL F., lawyer; BS, Rensselaer Poly. Inst., 1973; JD, Cornell U., 1976; ML in Taxation, Boston U., 1985. Bar: N.H. 1976. Ptnr. Upton & Hatfield, LLP, Concord, NH. Mem. N.H. Bd. Bar Examiners, 1981—90, N.H. Legis. Ethics Commn., 1991—97. Fellow: Am. Coll. Tiral Lawyers; mem.: Merrimack County Bar Assn., Am. Arbitration Assn. (panel of arbitrators), N.H. Bar Assn. (pres.-elect 2001—02, pres. 2002—03), ABA. Office: Upton and Hatfield LLP PO Box 1090 10 Centre St Concord NH 03302-1090

HILLIARD, SAM BOWERS, geography educator; b. Hart County, Ga., Dec. 21, 1930; s. Asa Farris and Flora Elizabeth (Bowers) H.; m. Joyce Collier, June 4, 1955; children— Steven Glen, Anita Joy. AB, U. Ga., 1960, MA, 1962; MS, U. Wis., 1963, PhD, 1966. Electrician Savannal River Valley plant Dupont Co., Aiken, S.C., 1954-59; teaching asst. U. Wis., 1961-65, instr. Milw., 1965-67; asst. prof. geography So. Ill. U., 1967-71; prof. La. State U., Baton Rouge, 1971-82, alumni prof., ret., 1983-93, chmn. dept. geography, 1976-79, 85-86, dir. Sch. Geosci., 1977-79. Columnist The Hartwell Sun newspaper; historian Hart County. Author: Hog Meat and Hoecake: Food Supply in the Old South, 1972, An Atlas of Antebellum Southern Agriculture, 1984; co-author: Louisiana: Its Land and People, rev. edit., 1987, The South Revisited: Forty Years of Change, 1992, Vignettes of Hart, vol. 1, 2001, vol. 2, 2002, A Century of Rural Education: Hart County, 1860-1960, A Calling of Churches: Sketches of Hart County Churches, 2003; contbr. articles to profl. jours. County historian, 1998. Served with U.S. Navy, 1950-54. Mem. Nat. Geog. Soc., Agrl. History Assn.

HILLIER, ASHLEIGH JANE, psychology professor; arrived in U.S., 2000; d. Roger James Hillier and Gillian Rosemary Waller; m. David Andrew Hutchinson, May 28, 2003. BSc with honors in Psychology, U. Lincoln, England, 1995, PhD in Psychology, 2000. Lectr. U. Lincoln, 1996—99, Westminster U., London, 1999—2000; vis. asst. prof. Ohio U., Athens, 2000—01; fellow Ohio State U., Columbus, 2001—04, adj. asst. prof., 2004—. Contbr. articles to profl. jours. Founder, dir. Aspirations, Columbus, Ohio, 2003—. Grantee, White Castle Found., 2004; scholar, Ohio State U., 2003. Mem.: Autism Soc. Am., Cognitive Neurosci. Soc., Soc. Neurosci. Avocation: travel. Office: Ohio State Univ 1654 Upham Dr Columbus OH 43210

HILLIER, JAMES, technology management executive, researcher; b. Brantford, Ont., Can., Aug. 22, 1915; came to U.S., 1940; s. James Sr. and Ethel Anne (Cooke) H.; m. Florence Marjory Bell, Oct. 24, 1936 (dec. 1992); children: James Robert, William Wynship (dec.). BA, U. Toronto, 1937, MA, 1938, PhD, 1941, DSc (hon.), 1978, N.J. Inst. Tech., 1981; LLD (hon.), Wilfrid Laurier U., 2002. Rsch. asst. Banting Inst. U. Toronto Med. Sch., 1938-40; head electron microscope rsch. RCA Labs., Camden and Princeton, N.J., 1940-53; adminstrv. engr. corp. rsch. and engring. RCA Corp., Princeton, 1954-55, chief engr. comml. electronic products Camden, 1955-57, gen. mgr. labs. Princeton, 1957-58, v.p. labs., 1958-68, v.p. corp. rsch. and engring. N.Y.C., 1968-69, exec. v.p. rsch. and engring., 1969-76, exec. v.p., sr. scientist, 1976-77, ret., 1977; dir. corp. rsch. Westinghouse Air Brake Co., Pitts. and Alexandria, Va., 1953-54. Mem. higher edn. study com. Gov.'s Office, State of N.J., 1963-64; mem. commerce tech. adv. bd. U.S. Dept. Commerce, Washington, 1964-70; chmn. adv. coun. dept. elect. engring. Princeton U., 1963-65; mem. adv. coun. Coll. Engring., Cornell U., Ithaca, N.Y., 1966-99; mem. joint consultative com. U.S. AID/Egyptian Acad. Sci. Rsch. and Tech., Cairo, 1978-84. Co-author: Electron Optics and the Electron Microscope, 1945; co-contbr.: Medical Physics, 1944, vol. II, 1950, Colloidal Chemistry, vol. VI, 1946; contbr. Ency. Britannica, 1948. Pres., founder James Hillier Found., Inc., 1996—. Decorated officer Order of Can; inducted into Nat. Inventors Hall of Fame, 1980, N.J. Inventors Hall of Fame, 1992; recipient James Loudon Gold medal U. Toronto, 1937, Albert Lasker award APHA, 1960, Commonwealth award, 1980, Presdl. award Microbeam Analysis Soc., 1989; mem. Can. Sci. and Engring. Hall of Fame, 02. Fellow AAAS (chmn. nomination com. sect. M 1965), IEEE (David Sarnoff award 1967, Founders medal 1981), Am. Phys. Soc. (mem. at large, governing bd. 1964-65); mem. Microscope Soc. Am. (pres. 1944, Disting. Scientist award 1977), Indsl. Rsch. Inst. (bd. dirs. 1960-65, pres. 1964, Inst. medal 1975), Nat. Inventors Hall of Fame Found., Inc (bd. dirs. 1992—, Lifetime Achievement award 2002), Nat. Acad. Engring. (coun. 1971), Rotary (bd. dirs. 1988-91), Nassau Club, Sigma Xi. Achievements include 41 patents in field; co-design of first successful electron microscope in North America, of first commercially available electron microscope in North America; discovery of principle of Stigmator for correcting astigmatism of electron microscope objective lenses; invention of electron microprobe microanalyser; first to picture tobacco mosaic virus, bacterial viruses and ultra-thin section of a single bacterium. Home: 22 Arreton Rd Princeton NJ 08540-1402 Personal E-mail: drjhillier@aol.com.

HILLIER, J(AMES) ROBERT, architect; b. Toronto, Ont., Can., July 24, 1937; came to U.S., 1941, naturalized, 1961; s. James and Florence (Bell) H.; m. Barbara Ann Weinstein, Apr. 7, 1986; 1 child, Jordan Rebecca Hillier; children by previous marriage-Kimberly (dec.), James Baldwin. BA, Princeton U., 1959, MFA, 1961; MBA (hon.), Bryant Coll., 1992. Project designer J. Labatut, Princeton, N.J., 1961-62; project mgr. Fulmer & Bowers, Princeton, 1961-66; prin. J. Robert Hillier, Princeton, 1966-72; pres. The Hillier Group, Princeton, 1972-87, chmn. bd., 1987—. Adj. faculty mem. Sch. Arch. Princeton U. Prin. works include Bryant Coll. campus, Smithfield, R.I., 1969, Peddie Campus Bldgs., 1970—, Rutgers U. Athletic Center, Piscataway, N.J., 1977, Butler Hosp, Providence, 1978, N.J. State Justice Complex, Trenton, 1985, Harbor Island Design, Tampa, Fla., 1981, Beneficial Corp. Complex, 1982, Merritt Tower, 1985, Wharton Sch. Exec. Ctr., 1986, N.J. Aquarium, 1991, Am. Home Products Corp. Headquarters, 1992, Sprint World Hqrs., 1997, Glaxo Smith Kline Hdqrs., 1998, Capital One Corp. Hdqrs., 2002, Restoration Supreme Ct. Bldg., Washington, D.C., 2003. Trustee Peddie Sch., Hightstown, N.J., 1981—, McCarter Theatre, Princeton, 1983-89, Bryant Coll., Smithfield, R.I., 1993-96, Edison Coll. Found., Milton Hershey Sch., 1997-2002; bd. overseers N.J. Inst. Tech. Recipient over 250 design awards from archtl. assns., 1966—; Architect of Yr. award N.J. Contractors Assn., 1976, 87, 92, 97, Disting. Svc. award Internat. Assn. Conf. Ctrs., 1988, Award of Excellence N.J. Bus. and Industry Assn., 1988, N.J. Entrepreneur of Yr., 1989, Community Svc. Human Rels. award, 1992, Da Vinci award Profl. Svc. Mgmt. Assn., 2002. Fellow AIA (v.p. N.J. chpt. 1974); mem. Nat. Coun. Archtl. Registration Bds., Princeton Quadrangle Club, Nassau Club, Princeton Club, Lookaway Golf Club. Avocations: running, swimming, golf. Home: 2846 River Rd New Hope PA 18938-9527 Office: The Hillier Group 500 Alexander Rd Princeton NJ 08540-6002 Office Phone: 609-452-8888. Business E-Mail: jrhillier@hillier.com.

HILLIKER, DONALD BECKSTETT, lawyer; b. Dixon, Ill., Jan. 6, 1944; s. Donald Herschel and Bernadette (Welch) H.; m. Carolyn Ann Beckstett, Dec. 16, 1972; children: Carrie Ford,Sarah Dillon. BS, Loyola U., Chgo., 1966; JD, Northwestern U., 1969. Bar: Ill. 1969, U.S. Dist. Ct. (no. dist.) Ill. 1969, U.S. Ct. Appeals (7th cir.) 1971, U.S. Ct. Appeals (6th cir.) 1988, U.S. Supreme Ct. 1989. Lawyer, legal aid bur. United Charities Chgo., 1969-70; assoc. Isham, Lincoln & Beale, Chgo., 1970-74, ptnr., 1976-79, Coin, Crowley, Nord & Hilliker, Chgo., 1979-81, Phelan, Pope & John, Ltd., Chgo., 1981-90, Pope & John, Ltd., Chgo., 1990-95; ptnr., chmn. pro bono com. McDermott, Will & Emery, Chgo., 1995—. Vis. asst. prof. law, asst. dean Sch. Law, Northwestern U., Chgo., 1975-76; mem. com. on profl. responsibility Ill. Supreme Ct., 1978-95; bd. dirs. Legal Assistance Found., pres., 2002-2004; adj. prof. law Northwestern U., Chgo., 1993—. Co-author: Law Journal Seminars Press, 1980, 84; contbr. articles to numerous legal jours.; editorial bd. Northwestern U. Law Rev., 1969-70. Pres. sch. bd. St. Clement Sch., Chgo.,1984-87; nat. chmn. ann. fund drive Northwestern U. Sch. Law, 1986-88, mem. visitors com., 1988-94, treas. Alumni Assn., 1997—. Reginald Heber Smith fellow, 1969-70. Mem. ABA (co-chair ethics: beyond the rules task force 1994-98, co-chair comml. and banking litigation com. 1997-98, standing com. ethics and profl. responsibility 1997-2003, chair, 2001-03, litigation sect. coun. mem. 1998—, chair sect./divsn. com. on ethics and professionalism, co-chair pro bono and pub. interest com., mem. commn. rev. model rules jud. conduct, 2003-, chair coordinating coun. ctr. profl. responsibility, 2005-), Chgo. Bar Assn. (chair large law firm com. 1998-2000, mem. profl. responsibility com.), Chgo. Coun. Lawyers (legal counsel 1981-83), Am. Law Inst., Ctr. for Ethics and Corp. Policy (bd. dirs. 1991-94), Order of Coif. Democrat. Roman Catholic. Office: McDermott Will & Emery LLP 227 W Monroe St Ste 3100 Chicago IL 60606-5096 Office Phone: 312-984-7610. Office Fax: 312-984-7700. Business E-Mail: dhilliker@mwe.com.

HILLILA, BERNHARD HUGO PAUL, retired education educator; b. Gwinn, Mich., May 21, 1919; s. Hugo Mathias and Hannah Maria (Mattonen) H.; m. Esther Pauline Halttunen, June 28, 1944; children: Esther Pauline Nelson, Sarah Christine Lewis, Martin Bernhard. Grad., Suomi Coll., Hancock, Mich., 1938, Suomi Theol. Sem., 1941; AB, Boston U., 1943; MA, Western Res. U., 1945, postgrad., 1945-46; EdD, Columbia U., 1955. Ordained to ministry Luth. Ch., 1941; pastor Maynard, Mass., 1941-43, Fairport Harbor, Ohio, 1943-46, Bklyn., 1946-49, 52-57; instr. Wagner Coll., S.I., 1948-49; pres. Suomi Coll. and Theol. Sem., 1949-52; pastor Warren, Ohio, 1957-60; dean, prof. practical theology Hamma Sch. Theology, Wittenberg U., 1960-64, dir. grad. div., 1961-63; dean Calif. Luth. U., Thousand Oaks, Calif., 1964-68; prof. edn. Valparaiso (Ind). U., 1968-84, prof. emeritus, 1984—; lectr. Purdue U., 1969-73. V.p. Finnish Evang. Luth. Ch. Am., 1955-60; mem. Joint Commn. Luth. Unity, 1956-62, Inter-Luth. Consultation Commn., 1962-66; councillor Nat. Luth. Coun., 1962-66; del. Luth. World Fedn. Assembly, 1957; mem. Mich. TB Sanatorium Commn., 1950-52 Editor: The Lutheran Counselor, 1942-44; author: The Sauna Is, 1979, The Riches of Prayer (translated from Finnish), 1985, History of the Indiana-Kentucky Synod, Lutheran Church in America, 1970-87, 1988, The Haven: New Poetry, 1988, A Fly on the Swatter: Poems, 1990, About Time to Pray (translated from Finnish), 1991, Cutting Edge, (poems) 1996 Finn Fun, 1997, The Finnish Line: More Finn Fun, 2002; project dir. Public Art and Porter County, 1977-78, Civilsation, 1981, The Shock of the New, 1984. Hon. chmn. bd. dir. Fair Havens Rest Home, Middleboro, Mass. Named Performer of Yr., Finlandia Found., 1997. Mem. Word Weavers, Porter County Arts Commn., Poets and Patrons Chgo., Acad. Am. Poets, Poets Club Chgo., Poetry Soc. Am. Home: 3715 Chimney Hill Dr Valparaiso IN 46383-0513 Business E-Mail: Bernhard.Hillila@valpar.edu.

HILLINGER, CHARLES, journalist, writer; b. Evanston, Ill., Apr. 1, 1926; s. William Agidious H. and Caroline Bruning; m. Arliene Otis, June 22, 1948; children: Brad, Tori. BS in Polit. Sci., UCLA, 1951; degree (hon.), Marymount Coll., Rancho Palos Verdes, 1997. Circulation mgr., columnist Park Ridge (Ill.) Advocate, 1938-41; copy boy, libr., feature writer Chgo. Tribune, 1941-43; reporter, feature writer, syndicated columnist L.A. Times, 1946-92, ret., 1992. Author: California Islands, 1957, Bel-Air Country Club, A Living Legend, 1993, Charles Hillinger's America, 1996, Charles Hillinger's Channel Islands, 1998, Hillinger's California, 1997, California Characters, 2002, (audiobooks) Charles Hillinger's America, 1999, California Characters, 2001, California, 2003. Mem. adv. bd. Santa Cruz Is. Found., Santa Barbara, Calif., 1992—; treas. 8-Ball Welfare Found. Greater L.A. Press Club, 1992—. With USN, 1943-46. Mem. Greater L.A. Press Club (sec. 1978-88, v.p. 1988-90, pres. 1990-92), Dutch Treat Club W. Avocations: tennis, golf, hearts. Home: 3131 Dianora Dr Rancho Palos Verdes CA 90275 Personal E-mail: chxlat@aol.com.

HILLIS, JOHN DAVID, broadcast executive, television producer, newswriter; b. Washington, Dec. 28, 1952; s. Willard E. and Holly M. Hillis; m. Catherine H. McQuaig, Nov. 21, 1975; children: Faith Courteney, David Esten, Elizabeth Nicole. AB in Journalism, U. Ga., 1975. Film editor Sta. WSB-TV, Atlanta, 1973-74, asst. producer, 1974-76, news producer, 1976; exec. news producer Sta. KOTV-TV, Tulsa, 1976-79; news producer Sta. WRAL-TV, Raleigh, N.C., 1979-80, Cable News Network, Inc., Atlanta, 1980-81, exec. producer, Newswatch, 1981-83, exec. producer, 1983-84, spl. events producer, 1984; news dir. Cablevision Systems Corp., Woodbury, N.Y., 1984-86; gen. mgr. Rainbow News 12 Co., Woodbury, 1986-89; pres., CEO Allnewsco, Inc., Washington, 1989—2002, Newschannel 8 Cable Svc., Springfield, Va., 1991—2002; pres., prin. Equinox Media Internat., LLC, Fairfax, Va., 2002—. Contbr. articles to profl. jours. Mem. strategic com. Greater Washington Bd. of Trade; bd. dirs. Va. Cmty. Found. Recipient Radio Newscast award Ga. AP Broadcasters, 1973, TV Newscast award Okla. AP Broadcasters, 1978, TV Series award News Acad. Cable Programming, 1985, Washington Region Emmy award, 1997, Cable Ace awards, 1996, 97, 98, Cmty. Spirit award NCTA, 1999, Scripps-Howard award, 1999. Mem. NATAS (Bd. of Govs. award Washington chpt.), Soc. Profl. Journalists (disting. svc. award 1998), Radio TV News Dirs. Assn., Nat. Press Club, Assn. Regional News Channels (founder, chmn. 1993), Nat. Cable TV Assn. (satellite network com.). Methodist. E-mail: mail@equinox-media.com.

HILLIS, WILLIAM DANIEL, biology professor; b. Paris, Ark., June 12, 1933; s. Charles Raymond Hillis and Carra Elizabeth (Daniel) Coffee; m. Argye Idell Briggs, Dec. 23, 1952; children: William Daniel Jr., David Mark, Argye Elizabeth Trupe. BS, Baylor U., 1953; MD, Johns Hopkins U., 1957. Lic. in medicine and surgery Md., Tex. Asst. prof. pathobiology Johns Hopkins U. and Sch. Hygiene and Pub. Health, Balt., 1965-68, assoc. prof., 1968-72; asst. prof. Johns Hopkins U. Sch. Medicine, Balt., 1972-76, assoc. prof., 1976-82; prof., chmn. dept. biology Baylor U., Waco, Tex., 1982-85, Cornelia Marshall Smith prof. biology, 1985-98, disting. prof. biology, 1995—, exec. v.p., 1985-89, v.p. student affairs, 1989-98. Cons. Nat. Cancer Inst., Bethesda, Md., 1965-68, Nat. Heart and Lung Inst., Bethesda, 1977-82; dir. Health Professions Rsch. Tng. Program, Balt., 1979-82, Out-Patient Clin. Rsch. Ctr., Balt., 1975-82. Contbr. articles to profl. jours. Pres. Bapt. Home Md., Balt., 1972-81; Md. rep. exec. com. So. Bapt. Conv., NAshville, 1977-82; bd. dirs. Food for Hungry, Glendale, Calif., 1972-82, Caritas, Waco, Tex., chair, 1989-95. Col. USAF, 1960-65, USAFR, 1965-85. Named Outstanding Prof., Baylor U., 1985; recipient Louis Livingston Seaman award, Assn. Mil. Surgeons U.S., 1978, Disting. Alumnus award, Baylor U., 1998. Mem. Am. Assn. Immunologists, Soc. for Exptl. Biology and Medicine, Am. Soc. for Microbiology, N.Y. Acad. Sci., McLennan County Med. Soc., Waco C. of C. (bd. dirs. 1987), Johns Hopkins Soc. of Scholars, Mortar Bd., Phi Beta Kappa, Alpha Omega Alpha, Omicron Delta Kappa. Clubs: Brazos (Waco); Johns Hopkins (Balt.). Democrat. Avocations: vocal music, drama, gardening, carpentry, stamp collecting/philately. Home: 3640 Alta Vista Dr Waco TX 76706-3741 Office: Baylor Univ PO Box 97388 Waco TX 76798-7388 Office Phone: 254-710-2091.

HILLJE, BARBARA BROWN, lawyer; b. Carlisle, Pa., Dec. 18, 1942; d. R. Morrison and Gladys M. (Lauver) Brown; m. John W. Hillje, Mar. 23, 1968. AB, Vassar Coll., 1964; BS in Edn., Ind. U. Pa., 1965; MA, Temple U., 1971, ABD, 1977; JD, Villanova U., 1984. Bar: Pa. 1984, U.S. Dist. Ct. (ea. dist.) Pa. 1984, N.J. 1985, U.S. Dist. Ct. N.J. 1985, U.S. Supreme Ct. 1990. English tchr. Council Rock Sr. High Sch., Newtown, Pa., 1965-68; assoc. Harry J. Agzigian and Assocs., Levittown, Pa., 1985-87; pvt. practice Langhorne, Pa., 1987—. Contbr. articles to profl. jours. Bd. dirs., pres. bd. Children of Aging Parents, Levittown, 1985-93; mem. facility ethics com. Statesman Health & Rehab. Ctr., Levittown, Pa., 1996—; bd. dirs. D'Youville Manor, 2001—. Recipient Women Helping Women award Soroptimists of Indian Rock, Inc., 1995; named Woman of Yr., Lower Bucks AAUW, 1985, Neshaminy BPW, 1987, Legal Humanitarian of Yr., Bucks County United Way, 1994, Consumer Connection award, 1996. Mem. AAUW (bd. dirs. 1978—, legis. cons. Pa. divsn. 1990-92), Middletown-Newtown LWV (bd. dirs. 1983-89, citizen campaign watch adv. panel 1992, 94, 96), Pa. Bar Assn., Nat. Acad. Elder Law Attys., Older Women's League (legis. chair 1984-94, Women of Worth award 1993). Office: 506 Corporate Dr W Langhorne PA 19047-8011 Office Phone: 215-579-9440.

HILLMAN, ALAN L., internist, educator, researcher; b. NYC, July 12, 1956; s. Herman David and Edith (Geilich) H.; children: Jennifer, Abigail. BA cum laude, Cornell U., 1978, MD, 1981; MBA with distinction, U. Pa., 1986. Intern in internal medicine N.Y. Hosp., 1981-82, asst. resident in internal medicine, 1982-84; dir. clin. programs Hosps. of U. of Pa., Phila., 1986-90, med. dir. Health Pass, 1987-90; assoc. dir. med. group U. Pa., Phila., 1987-90, sr. scholar clin. epidemiology, 1990—, dir. Ctr. for Health Policy, 1990-98, mem. comprehensive cancer ctr., 1992—98; assoc. prof. health care Wharton Sch., U. Pa., Phila., 1993—96, prof. health care mgmt., 1996—; assoc. prof. medicine Sch. of Medicine, U. Pa., Phila., 1993—96, prof. medicine, 1996—; assoc. dean health svcs. rsch. U. Pa., Phila., 1995-98. Asst. instr. dept. medicine N.Y. Hosp.-Cornell Med. Ctr., 1981—84; mem. Inst. for Human Gene Therapy, U. Pa. Med. Ctr., Phila., 1995—96; mem. drug use effects com. Hosp. of U. Pa., 1990—91; mem. admissions and awards com. health care mgmt. dept. Wharton Sch., 1990—92; mem. exec. com. Leonard Davis Inst. Health Econs., 1990—, sr. fellow, 1984—; co-dir. Health of the Pub. program Sch. Medicine U. Pa., 1991—92, mem. com. on jud. ethics, 1993—99, mem. ctr. for bioethics adv. com., faculty senate Sch. Medicine, 1994—2000, mem. master's program in med. ethics adv. com. Coll. Arts and Scis., 1995—99, mem. com. on health svcs. rsch. Sch. Medicine, 1995—99, mem. com. on multiculturalism in rsch. Inst. on Aging, 1995—99, mem. info. sys. strategic planning steering com. Sch. Medicine, 1996; cons. Solvay Pharms., Marietta, Ga., U. Mo. Sch. Medicine, Columbia, 1994, UNISYS Corp., Blue Bell, Pa., 1993, Prudential Ins. Co., Atlanta, 1993—99, PACC Bd. Dirs., Clackamas, Oreg., 1993, Gate Pharms., Kulpsville, Pa., 1994—95, Exogen Co., Princeton, NJ, 1994—99, Forest Labs., N.Y.C., 1994—99, VidaMed Corp., Palo Alto, Calif., 1993—95, Health Industry Mfrs. Assn., Washington, 1993—94, Procter & Gamble, Morris Plains, NJ, 1993, Syntex, 1993—, Eli Lilly Corp., Indpls., 1993—95, Amgen, Thousand Oaks, Calif., 1993—, Rhone-Poulenc Rorer, Antony Cedex, France, 1992—, Abbott Labs., Abbott Park, Ill., 1991—99, others; lectr. in field. Contbr. over 150 articles to profl. jours. and newspapers, chpts. to books. Recipient Article of the Year award Assn. for Health Svcs. Rsch., 1990, Young Investigator's award, 1993. Fellow ACP, Am. Bd. Internal Medicine; mem. Internat. Soc. Tech. Assessment in Health Care, Soc. Gen. Internal Medicine, Phila. Coll. Physicians, Internat. Soc. for Pharm. Outcome Rsch., Am. Fedn. for Clin. Rsch., Assn. for Health Svcs. Rsch., Physicians for Social Responsibility, Soc. Gen. Internal Medicine, Am. Soc. for Clin. Investigation, Alpha Omega Alpha, Gamma Beta Sigma. Office: U Pa Sch Medicine Divsn Gen Internal Med Blockley Hall 6021 423 Guardian Dr Philadelphia PA 19104-6021

HILLMAN, BARBARA HALL, retired elementary school educator; b. Summit, N.J., Dec. 5, 1947; d. Ralph Charles and Dorothy Jane (Young) Hall; m. Robert John Hillman, Dec. 21, 1969; children: Eric, Greg. BA in Elem. Edn., Kean Coll., 1974. Cert. elem. and early childhood tchr., N.J. Tchr. St. Rose of Lima Sch., Freehold, N.J., 1968-73, Wall Twp. Bd. Edn., Wall, NJ, 1974—2001, whole lang. tchr. trainer, 1989—. Whole lang. tchr. trainer Manalapan (N.J.)-Englishtown Bd. Edn., 1992, 93. Mem. Sea Girt (N.J.) Recreation Commn., 1991-96—; cub scout pack master Boy Scoutm., Sea Girt, 1984-91; treas. West Belmar PTA, Wall, 1982-92—; active Sea Girt Sh. PTO, 1982-94. Wall Found. for Ednl. Excellence grantee, 1993, 95; named Life Mem., PTA, 1991. Mem. NEA, Internat. Reading Assn., Monmouth County Reading Assn., N.J. Edn. Assn., Monmouth County Edn. Assn., Wall Twp. Edn. Assn. Avocations: children's literature, reading, travel, family. Home: 411 Chicago Blvd Sea Girt NJ 08750-2010

HILLMAN, CHARLENE HAMILTON, public relations executive; b. Akron, Ohio; d. Charles Edward and Maeron (Anderson) Hamilton; m. Robert Edward Hillman; 1 child, Robert Edward (dec.). Student, Youngstown Coll., Ind. U. Extension. Various positions Bob Long Assocs., Indpls., 1959-62; pub. rels. dir. Paul Lennon Advt. Agy., Indpls., 1962-63, Clowes Meml. Hall, Indpls., 1963-84; owner, pres. Charlene Hillman, Pub. Rels. Assocs., Indpls., 1964-75; sr. v.p. pub. rels. Caldwell-van-Riper, Inc., Indpls., 1975-90, also bd. dirs., 1975-90; editor Hoosier Ind. (quar. mag.), Indpls., 1966-95. Recipient Frances Wright award 1984. Mem. Pub. Rels. Soc. Am. (pres. Hoosier chpt. 1967, nat. bd. dirs. 1974-74, inducted to coll. fellows 1992), Home and Office: 612 Allens Way Columbia SC 29205-2843 Fax: (317) 879-9584.

HILLMAN, GILBERT ROTHSCHILD, medical educator; b. New Haven, Conn., May 1, 1943; s. Jacob D. and Clara (Rothschild) H.; m. Rachel Read, Aug. 27, 1965; child: Laura. BA, Harvard, 1965; PhD, Yale, 1969. Asst. prof. Brown U., 1970-76; assoc. prof. U. Tex. Med. Br., Galveston, 1976-82, prof., 1982—. Contbr. articles to profl. jours. Grantee NIH, NSF, 1976—. Office: U Tex Med Br Dept Of Pharmacology Galveston TX 77555-0001 E-mail: gil.hillman@utmb.edu.

HILLMAN, HENRY L., investment company executive; b. Pitts., Dec. 25, 1918; s. J.H. (Jr.) and Juliet Cummins (Lea) H.; m. Elsie Mead Hilliard, May 12, 1945; children: Lea, Audrey, Henry, William. AB, Princeton U., 1941. Chmn. exec. com. Hillman Co. Emeritus mem. exec. com. Allegheny Conf. on Cmty. Devel.; chmn. Hillman Found., Inc.; trustee emeritus Carnegie Inst. Lt. USNR, 1942—45. Mem.: Duquesne (Pitts.), Pitts. Golf, Fox Chapel Golf, Rolling Rock (Ligionier, Pa.) (hon. gov.), Laurel Valley Golf (Ligionier, Pa.), Links (N.Y.C.). Home: Morewood Heights Pittsburgh PA 15213 Office: Hillman Co 330 Grant St Pittsburgh PA 15219-2202

HILLMAN, HOWARD BUDROW, writer, editor, publishing executive, consultant; b. Hollywood, Calif, Dec. 8, 1934; s. Donald Edward and Rebecca (Budrow) H. BA, Calif. State U.-Long Beach, 1959; MBA, Harvard U., 1961. Pres. Nat. Acad. Sports, N.Y.C., 1961, Howard Hillman Co., N.Y.C., 1966—; editor, pub. Howard Hillman Publs., N.Y.C., 1982—; pres. Customer Satisfaction Inst., N.Y.C., 1986—; editor, pub. Quality Digest, N.Y.C., 1987—. V.p. Am. Film Theatre, N.Y.C., 1972-74; internat. lectr. and cons. in field Author: Hillman's Insiders Guide to New York Restaurants, 1969, The Ins and Outs of Living in New York, 1970, New York at a Glance, 1971, San Francisco at a Glance, 1971, Chicago at a Glance, 1971, Hawaii at a Glance, 1972, Washington at a Glance, 1972, Boston at a Glance, 1972, Florida at a Glance, 1972, The Complete New Yorker, 1972, The Art of Winning Foundation Grants, 1975, The Art of Winning Government Grants, 1977, The Diner's Guide to Wine, 1978, The Book of World Cuisines, 1979, The Art of Winning Corporate Grants, 1980, The Art of Writing Business Reports and Proposals, 1980, The Cook's Book, 1981, Kitchen Science, 1981, Great Peasant Dishes of the World, 1983, The Gourmet Guide to Beer, 1983, The Art of Dining Out, 1984, The Macmillan Complete Computer Buyer's Checklist, 1984, The Computer Log, 1985, Avoiding Computer Nightmares, 1985, Public Domain Software on File for the Apple, 1985, Hillman's Restaurant Ratings, 1986, Public Domain Software on File for the IBM, 1986, New Kitchen Science, 1989, The Educated Palate, 1991, Quality Digest, 1992, The Art of Satisfying Customers, 1993, Quality Consensus, 1994, The CSI Critique Book, 1995, The Art and Psychology of Pleasing Diners, 1996, Hillman Travel Wonders of the World, 1998, Hillman Wonders, 2000, New Kitchen Science, 2003; contbr. articles to various mags., newspapers and jours.; guest radio, TV talk shows. Served with U.S. Army, 1954-56. Mem.: Harvard (N.Y.). Episcopalian. Home and Office: 220 E 63rd St New York NY 10021-7660

HILLMAN, JENNIFER ANNE, commissioner, ambassador, trade association administrator, lawyer; b. Toledo, Jan. 29, 1957; d. Charles Winchell and Anne Sylvia (Mossberg) H.; m. Mitchell Rand Berger, Oct. 20, 1990; children: Benjamin Stanley Berger, Daniel Charles Berger. BA, Duke U., 1978, MEd, 1979; JD, Harvard U., 1983. Bar: D.C., U.S. Ct. Internat., U.S. Mil. Appeals. Asst. to chancellor Duke U., Durham, N.C., 1979-80; freshman Proctor Harvard U., Cambridge, Mass., 1981-83; assoc. Patton, Boggs & Blow, Washington, 1983—; legis. asst. Senator Terry Sanford, Washington, 1987-88, legis. dir., 1988-92; dep. cluster coord. for fin. instns. U.S. Presdl. and Vice Presdl. Transition Team, Washington, 1992-93; ambassador, chief textile negotiator Office of U.S. Trade Rep., Exec. Office of Pres., Washington, 1993-95; gen. counsel Office of the U.S. Trade Rep., 1995-97; commr. Internat. Trade Commn., Washington, 1998—; vice-chmn. U.S. Internat. Trade Commn., 2002—04. Trustee Duke U., 1977-80. Adviser Terry Sanford for Senate Campaign, 1986, 1992; Trinity Coll. bd. visitors Duke U., 1999—; commr. Stoddert Youth Soccer, 2000—; mem. Selection Panel on Truman Scholars, 2000—; pres. Trade Policy Forum, 2001—04; mem. N.C. Dems., Raleigh, 1986—, Georgetown Presbyn. Ch., 1988—; tchr. adult learning Sacred Heart, Washington, 1983—92. Mem. Coun. on Women's Studies Duke U., Phi Beta Kappa. Avocations: running, scuba diving, travel, reading. Office: Internat Trade Commn 500 E St NW Washington DC 20436-0003

HILLMAN, KATHY ROBINSON, librarian; b. Sonora, Tex., Aug. 5, 1951; d. Thomas Payne and Mary Allie (Barton) Robinson; m. John Royce Hillman, Dec. 22, 1973; children: John Marshall, Michael Thomas, Holly Michelle-Marie. BA summa cum laude, Baylor U., 1973, postgrad., 1976-80; MLS, U. North Tex., 1976. Cert. tchr., Tex. Tchr./libr. Eldorado (Tex.) H.S., 1974-76; asst. acquisitions libr. Baylor U., Waco, Tex., 1976-79, assoc. prof. acquisitions libr., 1980—. Co-author: Devotions from the World of Sports, 1998, Devotions from the World of Women's Sports, 2000; contbr. articles to profl. jours. Adv. bd. Heart O' the Hills Camp, Hunt, Tex., 1993—, Camp Stewart for Boys, Hunt, 1993—; bd. dirs. Paisano Bapt. Encampment, Alpine, Tex., 1996—; vol. Jr. League, Waco, 1985-89, 92—; bd. dirs. Baylor Bear Found., 1995-96; promotional v.p. Tex. Woman's Missionary Union, Dallas, 1988-92, pres., 2000-04; v.p. Woman's Missionary Union SBC, 2000-04, rec. sec., 2004—; mem. com., house bd. Hist. Waco Found., 1976—; mem. Waco Symphony Coun., 1988—. Named Outstanding Alumni Mortar Bd., 1989, Outstanding Young Alumni, Baylor U., 1989. Mem. Tex. Libr. Assn. (life, chair acquisitions roundtable 1984-85), Am. Libr. Assn., So. Bapt. Libr. Assn. (rec. sec. 1996-98, v.p. 1999-2000, pres. 2000-01), Baylor Alumni Assn. (life, sec. Class of 1973, 1973—), Waco Alumnae Panehllenic (pres. 1986-87), Delta Delta Delta. Avocations: writing, spectator sports, drama, photography. Home: 8505 Oakdale Dr Waco TX 76712-3557 Office: Baylor Univ PO Box 97151 Waco TX 76798-7151 Office Phone: 254-710-6684. E-mail: kathy_hillman@baylor.edu.

HILLMAN, LEON, electrical engineer; b. NYC, July 31, 1921; s. Harry and Jennie (Gartenberg) H.; m. Rita Katchen, July 18, 1948; children: David, Deborah. BEE, NYU, 1950. Registered profl. engr., N.J. Radio engr. Communication Devel. Co., Newark, 1940-42; head elec. sect. U.S. Army Engring. Lab., Ft. Monmouth, n.J., 1942-45; rsch. assoc. Elec. Engring. Dept., NYU, N.Y.C., 1946-51; v.p., chief engr. Prodn. Rsch. Corp., Thornwood, N.Y., 1951-56; pres. Automation Dynamics Corp., Northvale, N.J., 1957-71, ADCO Aerospace Inc., Closter, N.J., 1971—. Electronics cons. Johnson Controls, Milw., 1949-69; lectr. in field. Contbr. articles to profl. jours. Chmn. United Jewish Appeal, Englewood, N.J., 1960, Demarest, N.J., 1978. Sgt. USAAF, 1945-46. Named Hon. Citizen, State of Md., 1957. Mem. IEEE, Am. Phys. Soc., Sigma Xi, Eta Kappa Nu. Achievements include patents for meteorological instruments, industrial controls and water sterilization; design of instruments used in space flight and lunar landing; invention of electronic controlled water treatment system. Office Phone: 201-768-9200. Personal E-mail: leon_hillman@hotmail.com.

HILLMAN, PETER N., lawyer; b. NYC, Mar. 19, 1953; BA magna cum laude, with highest honors, Williams Coll., 1975; JD, Columbia U., 1978. Bar: NY 1979, US Dist. Ct. (So. Dist.) NY 1979, US Dist. Ct. (DC) 1979, US Ct. Appeals (11th Cir.) 1981, US Supreme Ct. 1982, US Ct. Appeals (6th Cir.) 1982, US Ct. Appeals (9th Cir.) 1984, US Dist. Ct. (Ea. Dist.) NY 1986, US Dist. Ct. (Conn.) 1989, US Ct. Appeals (2nd Cir.) 1992, US Dist. Ct. (No. Dist.) NY 1998. Mem. Chadbourne & Parke LLP, NYC, 1978—, ptnr., 1986—, chmn., Employment Law. Contbr. articles to profl. jour.; lectr. in field. Harlan Fiske Stone Scholar. Mem.: ABA (Tort & Ins. Practice Sect., Labor & Employment Law Sect.), NY State Bar Assn., Phi Beta Kappa. Office: Chadbourne & Parke LLP 30 Rockefeller Plz New York NY 10112 Office Phone: 212-408-1010. Office Fax: 212-541-5369. Business E-Mail: phillman@chadbourne.com.

HILLMAN, RITA, investor; b. N.Y.C., May 16, 1912; d. Rudolf and Bertha (Goodman) Kanarek; m. Alex L. Hillman, Aug. 23, 1932 (dec. 1968); children: Richard Alan (dec.), Alex L. Student, NYU, 1929-32. Mem. Met. Mus. Art (mem. vis. com. 20th century art dept.), Am. Friends Israel Mus. (exec. com.), Bklyn. Acad. Music (mem. exec. com.), Internat. Ctr. Photography (hon. chmn.), Alex Hillman Family Found. (pres.). Home: 895 Park Ave New York NY 10021-0327 Office: 630 5th Ave New York NY 10111-0100

HILLMAN, ROBERT ANDREW, lawyer, educator, retired dean; b. N.Y.C., Dec. 23, 1946; s. Herman D. and Edith N. (Geilich) H.; m. Elizabeth Hall Kafka, Aug. 24, 1969; children: Jessica H., Heather D. BA, U. Rochester, 1969; JD, Cornell U., 1972. Bar: N.Y. 1973, Iowa 1976. Law clk. to judge U.S. Dist. Ct., N.Y.C., 1972-73; assoc. Debevoise & Plimpton, N.Y.C., 1973-74; prof. law U. Iowa, Iowa City, 1975-82, Cornell U., Ithaca, N.Y., 1982—, acad. dean, 1990-97, Edwin Woodruff prof. law. Author or co-author: Common Law and Equity Under the UCC, 1985, Law: Its Nature, Functions, and Limits, 1986, Contract and Related Obligation: Theory, Doctrine, and Practice, 1987, 4th edit., 2001, The Richness of Contract Law, 1997, Modern American Contract Law, 2000, Principles of Contract Law, 2004; reporter Am. Law Inst. Prins. of The Law of Software Contracts; contbr. articles to profl. jours. Mem. Am. Law Inst. Avocations: tennis, bicycling. Office: Cornell U Law Sch Myron Taylor Hall Ithaca NY 14853 E-mail: rah16@cornell.edu.

HILLMAN, SANDRA SCHWARTZ, public relations executive, marketing professional; b. Chester, Pa., 1941; m. Robert S. Hillman, Apr. 1964; children: Pamela Hillman Loeb, Allison Buchalter. BA, Pa. State U., 1962. Assoc. editor McFadden-Bartell Pub., N.Y.C., 1963-64; pub. rels. account exec. Edward M. Meyers & Assocs., N.Y.C., 1964-66; info. officer Nat. Tchr. Corps, U.S. Office Edn., Washington, 1966-68, Balt. Dept. Housing and Cmty. Devel., 1968-71; prin., CEO Trahan, Burden & Charles, Inc., 1984—. Mktg., pub. rels. cons. to cities of Pitts., San Diego, Buffalo, Niagara Falls, N.Y., N.Y.C., Miami, Milw., Curacao, Netherlands Antilles, Charleston, Chattahooga, Edinburg; mem. bd. Gov.'s Tourism Task Force; presenter, lectr. in field. Bd. dirs. Balt. Symphony Orch., World Trade Ctr. Inst., Balt. City Found., Boy Scouts Am., Md. Film Commn., The Nat. Aquarium, Jr. League Cmty. Coun., Urban League; pres. Balt. Ctr. for Performing Arts, 1976-92. Recipient Lifetime Achievement award Balt. Pub. Rels. Soc., 1996. Fellow Pa. State U. (Disting. 1991); mem. Gov.'s World Trade Ctr. Inst. (mem. bd., coms.), Md. C. of C. (strategic planning com.), Children's Theater Assn.

HILLMER, MARGARET PATRICIA, library director; b. Cirencester, Gloucestershire, Eng., Mar. 17, 1936; came to U.S., 1960; naturalized, 1973; d. John Albert and Margaret Evelyn (Richardson) Hall; m. Max Lorraine Hillmer, Mar. 24, 1962; children: Felicity Margaret, Jennifer Anne. ALAM, London Acad. Music Dram. Art, London, 1955; AB magna cum laude, Heidelberg Coll., 1976; AM in Libr. Sci., U. Mich., 1977. Cert. libr. Ohio. Speech and ballet tchr., Cirencester, 1955-58; governess Australia, 1959—60; ballet instr., choreographer Heidelberg Coll., Tiffin, Ohio, 1969-73, adminstrv. asst. pub. rels. Water Quality Lab., 1978-79; head reference dept. Tiffin-Seneca Pub. Libr., 1979-80, libr. dir., 1980—. Contbr. articles to profl. publs. Chair Take Our Daughters to Work Day, 1993-2000; bd. dirs. Tiffin-Seneca Teen Ctr., 1992—; mem. Tiffin City Schs. Bd. Edn., 1991-2003, pres., 1995-96; mem. Seneca County Dept. Human Svcs. Bd., 1984-91, pres., 1987-89. Recipient Liberty Bell award Seneca County Bar Assn., 1990, People's Law Sch. award Ohio Acad. Trial Lawyers, 1993, Athena award Tiffin Area C. of C., 1999; named Ohio Libr. of Yr., 2004. Mem. ALA, AAUW, LWV (pres. Tiffin chpt. 1980-82, chair internat. rels. Ohio 1975-76), Ohio Libr. Assn. (legislation com. 1985-89, chair legis. network 1989-93, chair awards and honors com. 1995-96, seminar spkr. 1985—), Pub. Libr. Assn., Freedom to Read Assn., Tiffin Rotary Club (pres. 2001-02), Beta Phi Mu. Democrat. Episcopalian. Avocations: reading, theater, classical music. Home: 25 Southview Pl Tiffin OH 44883-3312 Office: Tiffin-Seneca Pub Libr 77 Jefferson St Tiffin OH 44883-2339 Office Phone: 419-447-3751. Business E-Mail: hillmepa@oplin.org.

HILLOCKS, GEORGE, JR., language educator, researcher; b. Cleve., June 15, 1934; s. George and Ina Ternan Hillocks; m. Jo Anne Bruce, 1957 (div. 1998); children: Marjorie Anne, George McInnes. BA, Coll. of Wooster, 1956; MA, Case Western Res. U., 1958; diploma in English Studies, U. Edinburgh, 1959; PhD, Case Western Res. U., 1970. English tchr. Euclid (Ohio) Pub. Schs., 1956-58, 59-65; English instr. Bowling Green (Ohio) State U., 1965-70, asst. prof. English, 1970-71; asst. prof. Edn. U. Chgo., 1971-75, assoc. prof. Edn., 1975-85, prof. Edn. and English, 1985—2003. Dir. MA program in tchg. English U. Chgo., 1971-2002; vis. Thomas R. Watson disting. prof. U. Louisville, 2000. Author: Research on Written Composition: New Directions for Teaching, 1986, Teaching Writing as Reflective Practice, 1995 (David H. Russel award 1997), Ways of Thinking, Ways of Teaching, 1999, The Testing Trap: How Statewide Writing Assessments Control Learning, Choice: Outstanding Academic Work, 2002; co-author: The Dynamics of English Instruction, 1971. Fellowship Ctr. for Advanced Study in Behavioral Scis., 2000—01. Fellow Nat. Conf. Rsch. Lang. and Literacy (pres. 2000—); mem. Nat. Acad. Edn., Nat. Coun. Tchrs. English (chair Assembly for Rsch. 1986, Disting. Svc. award, 2004), Am. Ednl. Rsch. Assn. Avocations: reading, writing, bagpipes. Home: 2012 W 110th St Chicago IL 60643 Office Phone: 773-429-0119. Business E-Mail: ghillock@uchicago.edu.

HILL-PALMER, STEPHANIE L., special education educator; b. Englewood, N.J., Oct. 13, 1962; d. Raymond Eugene and Jean Carole (Jacocks) Hill; m. William Palmer, Jr., Aug. 8, 1987; children: Janée, Jilian. BA, Jersey City State Coll., 1984; MA, Columbia U., 1986; postgrad., U. Madrid. Cert. spl. edn. tchr., N.Y., N.J. Tchr. spl. edn. Englewood Pub. Sch. System, 1984-85, Elizabeth (N.J.) Pub. Sch. System, 1985-87, Buffalo Pub. Sch. System, 1987-90; cognitive therapist Head Injury Day Treatment Program, Pa., 1990-91; child care dir. YMCA, 1991—. Mem. NEA, ASCD, Buffalo Tchrs. Fedn. (del.).

HILLS, AUSTIN EDWARD, vineyard executive; b. San Francisco, Oct. 13, 1934; s. Leslie William and Ethel (Lee) H.; m. Erika Michaela Brunar, May 20, 1978; children: Austin, Justin. AB, Stanford U., 1957; MBA, Columbia U., 1959. Chmn. bd. dirs. Hills Bros. Coffee, Inc., San Francisco, 1976, Grgich Hills Cellar, Rutherford, Calif., 1977—. Pres. Hills Vineyards, Inc., Rutherford, 1975-97; pres. Pacific Coast Coffee Assn., San Francisco, 1975-76, Hills Vineyard, Inc., 1999—. Pres. San Francisco Soc. for Prevention of Cruelty to Animals, 1972-78, No. Calif. Soc. for Prevention of Cruelty to Animals, 1972-78. With Air N.G. Mem. Am. Soc. Enologists. Libertarian. Office: 490 Post St Ste 1049 San Francisco CA 94102-1301 E-mail: hillsa@pacbell.net.

HILLS, CARLA ANDERSON, lawyer, former federal official; b. Los Angeles, Jan. 3, 1934; d. Carl H. and Edith (Hume) Anderson; m. Roderick Maltman Hills, Sept. 27, 1958; children: Laura Hume, Roderick Maltman, Megan Elizabeth, Alison Macbeth. AB cum laude, Stanford U., 1955; student, St. Hilda's Coll., Oxford (Eng.) U., 1954; LLB, Yale U., 1958; hon. degrees, Pepperdine U., 1975, Washington U., 1977, Mills Coll., 1977, Lake Forest Coll., 1978, Williams Coll., 1981, Notre Dame U., 1993, Wabash Coll., 1997. Bar: Calif. 1959, DC 1974, US Supreme Ct. 1965. Asst. US atty. civil divsn., LA, 1958-61; ptnr. Munger, Tolles, Hills & Rickershauser, LA, 1962-74; asst. atty. gen. civil divsn. Justice Dept., Washington, 1974-75; sec. HUD, 1975-77; ptnr. Latham, Watkins & Hills, Washington, 1978-86, Weil, Gotshal & Manges, Washington, 1986-88; US trade rep. Exec. Office of the Pres., 1989-93; chmn., CEO Hills & Co. Internat. Cons., 1993—. Chair Nat. Com. for US-China Rels.; bd. dir. Inst. for Internat. Econ., CSIS, Am. Internat. Group, Time Warner, Lucent Tech., Inc., Chevron Corp., TCW Group, Inc.; mem. adv. bd. Calif. Coun. on Criminal Justice, 1969—71; adj. prof. Sch. Law UCLA, 1972; mem. corrections task force LA County Sub-Regional; mem. standing com. discipline US Dist. Ct. for Ctrl. Calif., 1970—73; mem. Adminstrv. Conf. US, 1972—74; bd. councillors U. So. Calif. Law Ctr., 1972—74; mem. at large exec. com. Yale Law Sch., 1973—78; mem. exec. com. law and free soc. State Bar Calif., 1973; trustee Pomona Coll., 1974—79; mem. com. on Law Sch. Yale U. Coun.; mem. Sloan Commn. on Govt. and Higher Edn., 1977—79, Internat. Found. for Cultural Cooperation and Devel., 1977—89, Am. Com. on East-West Accord, 1977—79, Trilateral Commn., 1977—82; mem. adv. com. Princeton U., Woodrow Wilson Sch. of Pub. and Internat. Affairs, 1977—80; mem. Fed. Acctg. Std. Adv. Coun., 1978—80; Gordon Grand fellow Yale U., 1978; trustee Brookings Instn., 1985, Am. Productivity and Quality Ctr., 1988; coun. mem. Calif. Gov. Coun. Econ. Policy Adv., 1993—98, Coun. Fgn. Rels., 1993—; mem. Trilateral Commn., 1993—; vice-chair bd. dir. Inter-Am. Dialogue, 1999—; vice chair Coun. Fgn. Rels., 2001—. Co-author: Federal Civil Practice, 1961; co-author, editor: Antitrust Adviser, 1971, 3d edit., 1985; contbg. editor: Legal Times, 1978-88; mem. editorial bd. Nat. Law Jour., 1978-88. Trustee U. So. Calif., 1977-79, Norton Simon Mus. Art, Pasadena, Calif., 1976-80; trustee Urban Inst., 1978-89, chmn., 1983-89; co-chmn. Alliance to Save Energy, 1977-89; vice chmn. adv. coun. on legal policy Am. Enterprise Inst., 1977-84; bd. visitors, exec. com. Stanford U. Law Sch., 1978-81; bd. dir. Am. Coun. for Capital Formation, 1978-82; mem. exec. com. Inst. for Internat. Econ., 1993—; mem. adv. com. MIT-Harvard U. Joint Ctr. for Urban Studies, 1978-82. Fellow Am. Bar Found.; mem. Am.'s Soc. (bd. dir.), LA Women Lawyers Assn. (pres. 1964), ABA (chair publ. com. antitrust sect. 1972-74, council 1974, 77-84, chair 1982-83), Fed. Bar Assn. (pres. LA chpt. 1963), LA County Bar Assn. (fed. rules and practice com. 1963-72, chair issues and survey 1963-72, chair sub-com. revision local rules for fed. cts. 1966-72, jud. qualifications com. 1971-72), Am. Law Inst., Am.-China Soc. (bd. dir. 1995-), Am. Soc. (bd. trustees 1996-2002), Asia Soc. (bd. trustees 1996-2002), Yale of So. Calif. Club (bd. dir. 1972-74), Yale Club. Clubs: Yale of So. Calif. (dir. 1972-74); Yale (Washington). Office: Hills & Co 901 15th St NW Ste 400 Washington DC 20005 Office Phone: 202-822-4700.

HILLS, FREDERIC WHEELER, editor, publishing executive; b. East Orange, N.J., Nov. 26, 1934; s. Frederic Wheeler and Mildred Chambers (Hood) H.; m. Patricia Schulze, Jan. 17, 1958 (div. Dec. 1973); children: Christina, Bradford; m. Kathleen Matthews, Apr. 21, 1980; children: Gregory, Teddy. BA, Columbia U., 1956; MA, Stanford U., 1959. Editor F.W. Dodge Corp., San Francisco, 1959-60, N.Y.C., 1960-61; editor McGraw-Hill Book Co., N.Y.C., 1961-68, editor-in-chief Coll. divsn., 1968-72, editor-in-chief Gen. Books divsn., 1972—79; mem. editorial bd. Simon & Schuster Book Co., N.Y.C., 1979—, v.p., 1981—. With AUS, 1958. Mem. PEN, Assn. Am. Pubs., Shelter Island Yacht Club, N.Y. Athletic Club. Home: 218 Monterey Ave Pelham NY 10803-2310 also: PO Box 1061 Shelter Island Heights NY 11965-1061 Office: Simon & Schuster Book Co 1230 Ave of the Americas New York NY 10020-1586 Business E-Mail: fred.hills@simonandschuster.com.

HILLS, JOHN MERRILL, educational association administrator, consultant, public relations executive, researcher; b. Wethersfield, Conn., May 6, 1944; s. Merrill Clarke and Elizabeth (Tarrant) H.; m. Irene Jeanne Lavallee, Oct. 7, 1974 (div.); children: John M. Jr., Sara Clarke. Student, U. Hartford, 1963; BBA, Nichols Coll., 1969; postgrad., U. Md., 1976. Salesman Peter A Frasse and Co., Inc., Hartford, Conn., 1963-64; dir. alumni relations, asst. dir. admissions Nichols Coll., Dudley, Mass., 1969-72; regional dir. Georgetown U., Washington, 1972-74; dir. devel. cen. adminstrn. U. Md., College Park, 1974-77; v.p. Roanoke Coll., Salem, Va., 1977-86, The Brookings Instn., Washington, 1986-98; pres. JMH Assocs., 1998—. Pres. J.M.H. Assocs., Washington, 1979—; cons. Am. Assn. Univ. Cons., Inc., Washington, 1975-77; mgmt., pub. relations and fund raising cons. Trustee, mem. exec. com. Nichols Coll., Dudley, Mass., 1993-2000, Higher Edn. Roundtable, Lamplighters; judge U.S. Steel Alumni Award, Pitts., 1979-86; bd. dirs. Mill Mountain Theater, Roanoke, 1983-86, Roanoke ARC, 1984-86, Roanoke Valley C. of C., 1983-86; mem. adv. bd. Phoenix Soc. Georgetown U. Sch. Law.; mem. Little Theater of Alexandria. With U.S. Army, 1965-67, N.G. Recipient Alumni Achievement award Nichols Coll., 1991; named one of Outstanding Young Men Am., U.S. Jaycees, 1980, Outstanding Nat. Advisor, Pi Lambda Phi, Conn., 1983, 86. Mem. Nat. Soc. Fund Raiser Execs., Coun. for Advancement and Support of Edn. (faculty chmn.), Alexandria Sportsman's Club (mem. exec. com.), Hunting Hills Club, Jefferson Club (Roanoke), Met. Club Washington, Paul Hill Choral Soc. (mem. corp. bd.). Roman Catholic. Avocations: sailing, jogging. Home (Summer): 17 Josephine St Rehoboth Beach DE 19971-2017 Office: JMH Assocs 5801 Bayview Dr Fort Lauderdale FL 33308 also: JMH Assocs 429 R St NW Washington DC 20001 Office Phone: 954-267-9155. Personal E-mail: jackhills@jackhills.com.

HILLS, PATRICIA GORTON SCHULZE, curator; b. Baraboo, Wis., Jan. 31, 1936; d. Hartwin A. Schulze and Glennie Gorton Baker; m. Frederic W. Hills, Jan. 17, 1958 (div. Feb. 1974); children: Christina, Bradford; m. Guy Kevin Whitfield, Jan. 3, 1976; 1 child, Andrew. BA, Stanford U., 1957; MA, Hunter Coll., 1968; PhD, NYU, 1973. Curatorial asst. Mus. Modern Art, N.Y.C., 1960-62; guest curator Whitney Mus. Am. Art, 1971-72, assoc. curator 18th and 19th Century art, 1972-74; vis. asst. prof. art dept. Hunter Coll., 1973; adj. assoc. prof. fine arts Inst. Fine Arts NYU, 1973-74; assoc. prof. fine arts and performing arts York Coll. CUNY, 1974-78; assoc. prof. dept. art history Boston U., 1978-88, prof., 1988—, chmn. dept., 1995-97. Adj. assoc. prof. Grad. Sch. Arts and Scis., Columbia U., 1974—75; adj. curator Whitney Mus. Am. Art, 1974—87. Author: Eastman Johnson, 1972, The American Frontier: Images and Myths, 1973, The Painters' America: Rural and Urban Life, 1810-1910, 1974, Turn-of-Century America: Paintings, Graphics, Photographs, 1890-1910, 1977, Alice Neel, 1983, Social Concern and Urban Realism: American Painting of the 1930s, 1983, John Singer Sargent, 1986, Stuart Davis, 1996, Modern Art in the USA: Issues and Controversies of the 20th Century, 2001, May Stevens, 2005; co-author: The Figurative Tradition and the Whitney Mus. Am. Art, 1980, Jacob Lawrence: Thirty Years of Prints: 1963-1993, Eastman Johnson: Painting America, 1999. Danforth Found. grad. fellow for women, 1968-72, John Simon Guggenheim Meml. Found. fellow, 1982-83, Charles Warren Ctr. for Studies in Am. History fellow, 1982-83, W.E.B. DuBois Inst. for Afro-Am. Rsch. fellow, Harvard U., 1991-92, NEH fellow, 1995. Mem. Coll. Art Assn., Women's Caucus for Arts, Am. Studies Assn., Am. Assn. Mus. Home: 238 Putnam Ave Cambridge MA 02139-3767 Office: Boston U Dept Art History Boston MA 02215 Office Phone: 617-353-2520. Business E-Mail: pathills@bu.edu.

HILLS, REGINA J., journalist; b. Sault Sainte Marie, Mich., Dec. 24, 1953; d. Marvin Dan and Ardithanne (Tilly) H.; m. Vincent C. Stricherz, Feb. 25, 1984. BA, U. Nebr., 1976. Reporter UPI, Lincoln, Nebr., 1976-80, state editor, bur. mgr., 1981-82, New Orleans, 1982-84, Indpls., 1985-87; asst. city editor Seattle Post-Intelligencer, 1987-99, online prodr., 1999—2001, mng. prodr., 2001—. Panelist TV interview show Face Nebr., 1978-81; vis. lectr. U. Nebr., Lincoln, 1978, 79, 80; columnist weekly feature Capitol News, Nebr. Press Assn., 1981-82. Mem.: U. Nebr. Alumni Assn., Zeta Tau Alpha. Office: Seattle Post Intelligencer 101 Elliott Ave W Ste 200 Seattle WA 98119-4295 Office Phone: 206-448-8000.

HILLS, ROBERT O., retired pharmaceutical company executive; b. Bklyn., Apr. 13, 1946; s. Harry Stith and Elaine H.; m. Charlene Rose Cummins, Dec. 31, 1998; children: Alexander Winston, Jonathan Harry. AB, Princeton U., 1967; JD, U. Pa., 1971. Atty. Kelly Drye & Warren, N.Y.C., 1971-74, Merck Rsch. Labs., Rahway, N.J., 1974-76; sr. atty., dir. licensing, exec. dir. strategic planning Merck Sharpe & Dohme, West Point, Pa., 1976-90; v.p. mktg. human health divsn. Merck & Co., Whitehouse Station, N.J., 1991-93, sr. v.p. Merck-Medco divsn. Mahwah, N.J., 1994. Co-author: Price Controls and the Auto Industry, 1973. Bd. dirs. Planned Parenthood Assn. Bucks County, Solebury Hist. Soc.

HILLS, RODERICK M., lawyer, former government official; b. Seattle, Mar. 9, 1931; s. Kenneth Maltman and Sarah B. (Love) H.; m. Carla Helen Anderson, Sept. 27, 1958; children: Laura, Roderick Jr., Megan, Allison. BA in History, Stanford U., 1952, LLB, 1955. Bar: Calif. 1957, U.S. Supreme Ct. 1960, D.C. 1977. Law clk. to Justice Stanley F. Reed U.S. Supreme Ct., 1955-57; assoc. Musick, Peeler & Garrett, L.A., 1957-62; ptnr. Munger, Tolles & Hills, L.A., 1962-75; chmn. Republic Corp., L.A., 1971-75; counsel to Pres. U.S., 1975; chmn. SEC, 1975-77; chmn., CEO Peabody Coal Co., St. Louis and Washington, 1977-79; ptnr. Latham, Watkins & Hills, Washington, 1978-82; chmn. Sears World Trade, Inc., Washington, 1982-84; chmn., mng. dir. The Manchester Group, Ltd. (renamed Hills Enterprises, Ltd.), Washington, 1984—; mng. ptnr. Donovan, Leisure, Rogovin, Huge & Schiller, Washington, 1989-92; chmn. internat. practice group Shea & Gould, Washington, 1992-94; ptnr. Mudge Rose Guthrie Alexander & Ferdon, Washington, 1994-95, Hills & Stern, Washington, 1995—. Vis. prof. law Harvard U., 1969—70; lectr. law Stanford U., 1960—69; disting. faculty fellow in internat. fin. Yale U. Sch. Mgmt., 1986—89; bd. dirs., vice chmn. Oak Industries, 1990—2000, Feg. Mogul Corp., 1977—2003, chmn., 1996; bd. dirs. Regional Market Makers, Chiquita Brands Internat.; chmn. Hills Governance Program, CSIS, 2001—; bd. dirs. Certus, Inc., 2004. Bd. editors, comment editor: Stanford Law Rev, 1953-55. Trustee Com. Econ. Devel., 1978—; dir. U.S.-ASEAN Bus. Coun., Inc., 1982—, chmn., 1986-90, vice chmn., 1990—; mem. Bretton Woods Com. Fellow Am. Bar Found.; mem. ABA, U.S. Supreme Ct. Bar Assn., L.A. County Bar Assn., State Bar Calif., Order of Coif, Chancery Club, Chevy Chase Club, Phi Delta Phi. Republican. Episcopalian. Avocations: tennis, golf, history. Home: 3125 Chain Bridge Rd NW Washington DC 20016-3411 Office: Hills Enterprises Ltd 1200 19th St NW Washington DC 20036-2412 Office Phone: 202-822-1611. E-mail: rmhills@hillsandstern.com.

HILLS, STEPHEN P., publishing executive; b. Oscar and Carol Hills; m. Joslyn Hills; 2 children. Grad., Yale U., 1981; MBA, Harvard Bus. Sch., 1987. Dir. advt. and mktg. ITB, Inc., Emeryville, Calif., 1981—82; co-founder The Bay City Bus. Jour., Emeryville, 1982; bus. intern The Washington Post, 1986—87, advt. sales rep., 1987, various positions in advt. and mktg., 1987—93, named v.p. advt., 1993, v.p. sales & mktg., 2001—02, pres. & gen. mgr., 2002—. Dir. Greater Washington Bd. Trade; mem. sales adv. com. Nat. Newspaper Network. Office: The Washington Post 1150 15th St NW Washington DC 20071*

HILLSMAN, JOAN RUCKER, music educator; b. Anderson, S.C., Mar. 25, 1943; d. William Isaiah and Elizabeth Gilliard Rucker; m. Horace Jerome Hillsman (dec. Mar. 2002); 1 child, Quentin Jerome. B in Music Edn., Howard U., 1964, M in Music Edn., 1969; PhD in Musicology, Union Inst., 1978. Music tchr. St. Mary's County Pub. Schs., Leonardtown, Md., 1964—67, D.C. Pub. Schs., Washington, 1967—88, supr. music, 1988—96; ret.; prof. music Bowie (Md.) State U., 1996—. Owner, music cons., talent promoter Joan Hillsmans Music Network, Suitland, Md., 1996—; adj. music prof. Union Inst., Cin., Shenandoah Conservatory and Union Inst. Cmty. and Civic awards; organizer nation's Capitol 1st Gospel Homeless Choir. Author: Gospel: An African American Art Form, 1990, 1992, poetry. Vol. music for the elder various nursing homes, 2000—; vol. Prince George County Dems., 2002. Recipient Key to City of Detroit; Joan Hillsman's Day in the Nation's Capital named in her honor. Mem.: Gospel Music Workshop Am. (scholarship chair), Coll./Univ. Assn., Music Educators Nat. Conf. (D.C. pres. 1996—2000, Outstanding Educator award 1996), Nat. Coun. Univ. Women, Black Urban League, Top Ladies Orgn., Sigma Alpha Iota, Phi Delta Kappa, Alpha Kappa Alpha. Baptist. Avocations: music, poetry, bowling, research. Home: 3706 Stonecliff Rd Suitland MD 20746 Office: Bowie State Univ Fine and Performing Arts 14000 Jericho Park Rd Bowie MD Personal E-mail: jrhillsman@comcast.net.

HILLSTROM, THOMAS PETER, engineering executive; b. Lakewood, Ohio, Apr. 20, 1943; s. Harry Edward and Mary Pauline (Mauss) H.; m. Jean Elizabeth Greenfield; children: Edward, Mary. BS in Mech. Engring., Northwestern U., Evanston, 1966; MBA, Northwestern U., Chgo., 1977. Design engr. Internat. Harvester, Hinsdale, Ill., 1966-74, project engr., 1974-78, product safety engr., 1978-82; mgr. engring. Fire Apparatus Div., FMC, Tipton, Ind., 1982-85; mgr. contract engring. FMC Naval Systems Div., Mpls., 1985-87, program mgr., 1987-90, mgr. splty. engring., 1990-91; program mgr. United Def., L.P., Mpls., 1985—. Patentee in field. Mem. Soc. Automotive Engrs., Am. Soc. Agrl. Engrs., System Safety Soc., Boy Scouts Am. Order of the Arrow. Republican. Home: 17955 39th Pl North Plymouth MN 55446 Office: United Def LP 4800 E River Rd Minneapolis MN 55421-1402

HILLYARD, IRA WILLIAM, retired pharmacologist, retired educator; b. Richmond, Utah, Mar. 23, 1924; s. Neal Jacobsen and Lucille (Duce) H.; m. Venice Lenore Williams, July 10, 1945 (dec.); children: Christine, Kevin, Eric; m. Norma Larsen, May 1, 1970. BS, Idaho State U., 1949; MS, U. Nebr., 1951; PhD, St. Louis U., 1957. Pharmacologist Mead Johnson Co., Evansville, Ind., 1957-59; sr. pharmacologist, sect. leader Warner-Lambert Research Inst., Morris Plains, N.J., 1959-69; assoc. prof. pharmacology Idaho State U. Coll. Pharmacy, Pocatello, 1969-73, 77-79, dean, 1979-87, prof. pharmacology, 1979-91, prof. emeritus, 1991—; ret., 1991. Dir. pharmacology and toxicology ICN Pharms., Irvine, Calif., 1973-77, cons., 1977-80; cons. Pennwalt Pharm. Co., Rochester, N.Y., 1978-83 Contbr. articles to profl. jours. Served with USN, 1943-45, 51-53. Decorated Purple Heart. Fellow Am. Found. Pharm. Edn.; mem. Western Pharmacology Soc., Am. Assn. Colls. Pharmacy, Am. Soc. Pharmacology and Exptl. Therapeutics, N.Y. Acad. Scis., Sigma Xi, Rho Chi, Phi Delta Chi. Lodges: Rotary. Home: 594 S 800 W Mapleton UT 84664-4313 *I firmly believe that we make individual contributions to the welfare and progress of mankind only if every action is based on truth. If we remain honest and open-minded in our approach, truth will always be recognized and those challenging decisions which must precede every action, will be correctly made even though each decision may not always be agreeable to us or to others. In the end, however, if truth prevails, progress will be made because we will all recognize the correctness of what is said or done.*

HILPERT, DALE W., retail shoe company executive; BS, U. Wyo., 1966; MBA, U. Denver, 1970. With Dayton Hudson Corp., Mpls., 1970-76, Cook United, Inc., Cleve., 1976-78, May Dept. Stores, St. Louis, 1978-80, Volume Shoe Corp., Topeka, 1980-92, chief fin. officer, sr. v.p., 1980-81, exec. v.p., 1981-82, now chmn., chief exec. officer, dir., 1982-92; pres., COO Venator Group Inc., N.Y.C., 1995—99, pres., CEO, 1999-2000; chmn., CEO Foot Locker Inc. (formerly Venator Group Inc.), N.Y.C., 2000—01; CEO Williams-Sonoma, Inc., 2001—03; chmn., pres., CEO Footstar, Inc., West Nyack, NY, 2004—. Bd. dirs. Signet Group plc. Office: Footstar Inc 1 Crosfield Ave West Nyack NY 10994

HILPERT, EDWARD THEODORE, JR., lawyer; b. Frazee, Minn., Apr. 29, 1928; s. Edward Theodore Sr. and Hulda Gertrude (Wilder) H.; m. Susan Hazelton, May 5, 1973. AB, U. Wash., 1954, JD, 1956. Bar: Wash. 1956, U.S. Dist. Ct. (we. dist.) Wash. 1956, U.S. Tax Ct. 1959, U.S. Ct. Appeals (9th cir.) 1959, U.S. Supreme Ct. 1970. Law clk. to Hon. George H. Boldt U.S. Dist. Ct. (we. dist.) Wash., Tacoma, 1956-58; assoc. Ferguson & Burdell, Seattle, 1958-63, ptnr., 1963-91; sr. ptnr. Schwabe, Williamson, Ferguson & Burdell, Seattle, 1992—. Exec. com. 9th cir. Jud. Conf., San Francisco, 1987—90. Judge pro tem Seattle Mcpl. Ct., 1971-80. Capt. USAR, 1946-49, 50-52, Korea. Mem.: ABA, Mensa, The Rainer Club, Seattle Tennis Club, Broadmoor Golf Club, Sea Pines Country Club. Republican. Lutheran. Home: 10405 - 192nd Ave NE Redmond WA 98053 Office: Schwabe Williamson Ferguson & Burdell US Bank Ctr 1420 5th Ave Ste 3010 Seattle WA 98101-2393 Home: 26 Twin Pines Rd Hilton Head Island SC 29928

HILSBERG, DONALD CHARLES, elementary school educator; b. Austin, Tex., Sept. 21, 1954; s. Donald Karl and Ruth Ione (Fowler) H. B Music Edn., U. Denver, 1979; MusM, Manhattan Sch. Music, N.Y.C., 1983. Elem. tchr. gen. music Aurora (Colo.) Pub. Schs. Prin. harpist Denver Chamber Orch., Arapahoe Philharm., Englewood, Colo.; staff harpist Denver Ctr. for Performing Arts. Fellow Manhattan Sch. Music. Mem. Music Educators Nat. Conf., Am. String Tchrs. Assn., Chamber Music Am.

HILSMAN, ROGER, political scientist, educator; b. Waco, Tex., Nov. 23, 1919; s. Roger and Emma (Prendergast) H.; m. Eleanor Willis Hoyt, June 22, 1946; children— Hoyt R., Amy, Ashby, Sarah. BS, U.S. Mil. Acad., 1943; MA, Yale U., 1950, PhD, 1951. Commd. 2d lt. U.S. Army, 1943, advanced through grades to maj., 1951; with (Merrill's Marauders), Burma, 1944; comdg. officer (OSS guerrilla group in), Burma, 1944-45; asst. chief Far East intelligence operations, Hdqrs. OSS, Washington, 1945-46; spl. asst. to exec. officer CIA, 1946-47; planning officer NATO affairs, Joint Am. Mil. Adv. Group, London, Eng., 1950-52; internat. politics br. Hdqrs. U.S. European Command, 1952-53; resigned, 1953; research fellow Center Internat. Studies, Princeton, 1953-54, research asst., 1954-55; research assoc., lectr. Woodrow Wilson Sch.; lectr. internat. relations Columbia, 1958; research asso. Washington Center Fgn. Policy Research, lectr. internat. affairs Sch. Advanced Internat. Studies, Johns Hopkins, 1957-61. Chief fgn. affairs div., legislative reference service Library Congress, 1956-58, dep. dir. for research, 1958-61; dir. bur. intelligence and research State Dept., 1961-63; asst. sec. state Far Eastern affairs, 1963-64; prof. govt. Columbia U., 1964-89, prof. emeritus, 1990—; lectr. Nat. War Coll., Air U., Army War Coll., Indsl. Coll. Armed Forces.; Fulbright Disting. lectr., India, 1985; USMC Found. chair mil. affairs, 1991. Author: Strategic Intelligence and National Decisions, 1956, To Move a Nation, 1967, The Politics of Policy Making in Defense and Foreign Affairs, 1971, The Crouching Future: International Politics and U.S. Foreign Policy— A Forecast, 1975, To Govern America, 1979, The Politics of Governing America, 1985, The Politics of Policy Making: Conceptual Models and Bureaucratic Politics, 1987, 90, 92, American Guerrilla: My War Behind Japanese Lines, 1990, George Bush vs Saddam Hussein: Military Success! Political Failure?, 1992, The Cuban Missle Crisis, The Struggle Over Policy, 1996, From Nuclear Military Strategy to a World Without War, A History and Proposal, 1999; co-author: Military Policy and National Security, 1956, Alliance Policy in the Cold War, 1959, NATO and American Security, 1959, Foreign Policy in the Sixties, 1965, The Superpowers and Revolution, 1986, Nuclear Strategy and Arms Control, 1986, A Layman's Guide to the Universe, the Earth, Life on Earth, and the Migrations of Mankind, 2003. Rockefeller fellow, 1958. Home: 317 W Main St #2105 Chester CT 06412-1057

HILST, GLENN RUDOLPH, environmental services administrator, researcher; b. May 1, 1923; s. William Frederick and Lola Katherine (Cordes) H.; m. Lorraine Virginia Pilke, June 2, 1949 (div. 1976); children: Randolph Glenn, Elizabeth Ann, Katherine Louise; m. Zenobia R. Scoggins, June 21, 1986. SB, MIT, 1948, SM, 1949; PhD, U. Chgo., 1957. Rsch. assoc. Argonne Nat. Labs. Chgo., 1952-54; mgr. atmospheric physics GE Co., Richland, Wash., 1954-60; exec. v.p. Travelers Rsch. Corp., Hartford, Conn., 1960-70, 74-76; v.p. Aero Rsch. Assocs. of Princeton, Inc., N.J., 1970-74; sr. program mgr. Electric Power Rsch. Inst., Palo Alto, Calif., 1977-87; ret., 1987. Cons., 1976-77; sr. sci. advisor Battelle N.W. labs., 1988-93; mem. com. NAS, NAE. Author: Air Pollution, 1968, Toward a National Urban Policy, 1971, Encyclopedia of Physical Science and Technology, 1987; contbr. articles to profl. jours. Task force mem. State of Conn., 1967; commr. Conn. Air Pollution Control Commn., 1968. With USAF, 1941-46. Fellow AAAS (sec. 1979-82), Am. Meteorol. Soc. (councilor 1967-70, Charles F. Brooks award 1973, Cleveland Abbe award 1995), Explorers Club; mem. Nassau Club (Princeton), Sigma Xi Home: 11725 N Kathy Ln Spokane WA 99218-2726 E-mail: ghilst@aol.com.

HILT, MARY LOUISE, artist; b. Muskegon, Mich., May 17, 1947; d. Jack Lyle and Martha Campbell (Van Epps) H.; m. Randolph Allen Austill, March 3, 2000. Student, Milw. Inst. Design and Art, 1966—68. Art tchr. for spl. needs adults Kelliher Ctr., Arlington, Mass., 1994-96. One-woman shows include Harvard Law Sch., Cambridge, 1987, Armenian Genocide Collection, Mass. State House, Boston, 1995, Armenian Libr. and Mus. Am., Watertown, Mass., 1995-96, 99, Mass. Audubon Habitat Edn. Ctr. and Wildlife Sanctuary, Belmont, Mass., 2004; two-person show Fruenthal Ctr. for Performing Arts, Muskegon, 1989; exhibited in group shows at Bravos Gallery, Georgetown, Mass., 1987, 90-92, 94, 96, 2002, Nat. Arts Club, NYC, 1997, Fed. Res.

Bank, Boston, 1998, Art and Cultural Ctr., Fallbrook, Calif., 2000, others. Mem.: Copley Soc. Boston. Episcopalian. Office: Hilt Studio 7 Central St Ste 205 Arlington MA 02476-4816 Office Phone: 617-489-0985. E-mail: hiltstudio@pobox.com.

HILT, THOMAS HARRY, minister; b. Phila., May 19, 1947; s. Francis Joseph and Alice Elizabeth (Flanagan) H.; m. Carolyn Louise Poulsen, Aug. 23, 1969; 1 child, Tamara Leah. BA, Tusculum Coll., Greeneville, Tenn., 1969; grad., Missionary Tng. Sch., Long Beach, Calif., 1974; M Ministry, Internat. Sem., Plymouth, Fla., 1983, D Ministry, 1984; PhD, Carolina U. of Theology, 1992. Ordained min. of Gospel, Okinawa, Japan, 1979. Mem. staff Christians in Action, Long Beach, 1974-77, missionary Okinawa, Japan, 1977-79; founder Christians in Action Evang. Ch., Guam, 1979-81; founder, dir. Micronesian Evang. Mission, Barrigada, 1981—; founder, adminstr. Evang. Christian Acad., Chalan Pago, Guam, 1982—2003; sr. pastor Ch. of the Cross, Sarasota, Fla., 2001—02; pres. SonHaven Ministries Internat., Sarasota, 2001—; founder, adminstr. SonHaven Prep. Acad., Sarasota, 2002—. Founder, dir. Family Counseling Ministries, 1990-2001; mem. Nat. Bible Week-Guam Com., 1988-92; advisor Guam chpt. Women's Aglow Fellowship Internat., 1987-90; chaplain Guam Fire Dept., 1992-2000; chmn. bd. Guam Critical Incident Stress Mgmt. team, 1997-2000. Mem. Guam Gov.'s Social Svcs. Adv. Bd., 1981-83; mem. standards of licensing com. child welfare task force Guam Dept. Pub. Health and Social Svcs., 1982-83; mem. Blue Ribbon Commn. on Edn., 1991-93; minister Cmty. Care Faith Presbyterian Ch., Sarasota, Fla., 2005—. With U.S. Army, 1970-73. Recipient award Ancient Order of Chamorri, 1983, lst place award Guam Press Club, 1985. Fellow Am. Acad. Experts in Traumatic Stress; mem. Am. Acad. Experts in Traumatic Stress, Guam Ministerial Assn. (sec.-treas. 1980-81, pres. 1983-84, 86-88, v.p. 1991-92), Bible Soc. Micronesia (pres. bd. dirs. 1989-90, v.p. bd. 1991-92, 99-2000). Home: 5351 Avant Ave Sarasota FL 34235 Office: Po Box 50517 Sarasota FL 34232-0304 Office Phone: 941-360-2000. E-mail: thilt@earthlink.net. *It has been my experience that God does not grant us special favors, but rather special grace.*

HILTON, ANDREW CARSON, investment company executive, retired manufacturing executive, management consultant; b. D'Lo, Miss., Nov. 20, 1928; s. A.C. and Pearl (Walters) H. BA, U. Md., 1952; MA, George Washington U., 1953; PhD, Western Res. U., 1956. Former research asso. Personnel Research Inst., Western Res. U.; cons. Psychol. Corp., N.Y.C.; dir. personnel relations Raytheon Co.; then dir. personnel Internat. Tel.& Tel. Corp.; sr. v.p. adminstrn. Coltec Industries Inc., N.Y.C., 1963-83, exec. v.p., 1983-91, vice chmn., 1991-94, also bd. dirs.; vice chmn. Coltec Industries Inc, 1991-94; proprietor Hilton Mgmt. Enterprises, 1994—. Contbr. articles to profl. jours. Mem. APA, N.Y. Acad. Scis. Clubs: University (N.Y.C.), Aspetuck Valley Country Club, Weston, Conn. Office: Hilton Mgmt Enterprises Inc 147 E 48th St New York NY 10017-1223

HILTON, BARRON, hotel executive; b. Dallas, 1927; s. Conrad Hilton. DHL, U. Houston, 1986. Founder, pres. San Diego Chargers, Am. Football League, until 1966; v.p. Hilton Hotels Corp., Beverly Hills, Calif., 1954, pres., CEO, 1966—96, chmn., 1979—, also dir.; chmn. Hilton Equipment Corp, Beverly Hills. Mem. gen. adminstrv. bd. Mfrs. Hanover Trust Co., N.Y.C.; bd. dirs. Conrad N. Hilton Found., So. Calif. Visitors Coun. and Exec. Coun. on Fgn. Diplomats. Named to, Culinary Inst. Am. Hall of Fame, 1986; recipient Am. Spirit award, Nat. Bus. Aircraft Assn., 1995, Chevalier of Confrerie de la Chaine Des Rotisseurs, Magestrial Knight, Sovreign Mil. Order Malta. Mem.: Peace Found. Coun., Conouistadares del Cielo. Office: Hilton Hotels Corp 9336 Civic Center Dr Beverly Hills CA 90210-3604*

HILTON, JEAN BULL, musician; b. Northampton County, Va., Sept. 29, 1926; d. Charles Russell and Margret Davis Bull; m. Ellis Baker Hilton Jr., July 3, 1948 (dec. Mar. 1988); children: Jeffery Allan, Ellis Baker, William Russell, Andrew Douglas. BA, Randolph-Macon Woman's Coll., 1947; MSc, Old Dominion U., 1974. Music tchr. Norfolk Pub. Schs., Norfolk, Va., 1947—48, Radford Pub. Sch., Radford, Va., 1948—49; minister of music First Luth. Ch., Portsmouth, 1951—91; tchr. Portsmouth Pub. Sch., Portsmouth, Va., 1961—68, music supr., 1969—91; minister of music First Luth. Ch., 1998—. Composer songs. Recipient 1st Place award, Va. Fedn. Music Clubs, 2000. Mem.: AAUW, Va. Gateway Ctr. for the Arts, Portsmouth Cmty. Concerts, Inc., Va. Fedn. Music Clubs, Nat. Fedn. Music Clubs, Va. Music Educators Conf., Music Educators Nat. Conf., Daughters of Am. Revolution, Jamestowne Soc., Delta Kappa Gamma (Gamma chpt.). Lutheran. Avocations: reading, geneology, exercise.

HILTON, NICKY (NICHOLAI OLIVIA HILTON), apparel designer; b. Oct. 5, 1983; d. Rick and Kathy Hilton; m. Todd Andrew Meister, Aug. 15, 2004 (annulled Nov. 9, 2004). Designer Samantha Thavasa, Tokyo, 2001—. Actor: (films) Wishman, 1991. Contbr. Free Arts for Abused Children Found. Achievements include appeared on cover of numerous mag. including Maxim, GQ, FHM, Vanity Fair, others; heiress and great-grand daughter of Conrad Hilton, founder of Hilton Hotel Chains; modeled for Anand Jon.

HILTON, PARIS, actress; b. NYC, Feb. 17, 1981; d. Rick and Kathy Hilton. Student, U. Ariz. Designer Samantha Thavasa, Tokyo, 2001—. Actor: (films) Wishman, 1991, Sweetie Pie, 2000, Zoolander, 2001, QIK2JDG, 2002, Nine Lives, 2002, Wonderland, 2003, The Cat in the Hat, 2003, L.A. Knights, 2003, Raising Helen, 2004, The Hillz, 2004, House of Wax, 2005; co-star: (TV series) The Simple Life, 2003; The Simple Life 2: Road Trip, 2004; The Simple Life: Interns, 2005; actor(guest appearances): Saturday Night Live, 2003, Las Vegas, 2003, The O.C., 2003; author: (novels) Confessions of an Heiress: A Tongue-in-Chic Peek Behind the Pose, 2004 (Publishers Weekly Bestseller list, 2004). Contbr. Toys for Tots. Achievements include appeared on cover of numerous mag. including Maxim, GQ, FHM, Vanity Fair, others; heiress and great-grand daughter of Conrad Hilton, founder of Hilton Hotel Chains; modeled for designers March Bouwer and Catherine Malandrino; worked on ad campaign for Italian label Iceberg.*

HILTON, PETER JOHN, mathematician, educator; b. London, Apr. 7, 1923; s. Mortimer and Elizabeth (Freedman) H.; m. Margaret Mostyn, Sept. 14, 1949; children: Nicholas, Timothy. MA, Oxford (Eng.) U., Eng., 1948; PhD, Oxford (Eng.) U., 1950, Cambridge (Eng.) U., Eng., 1952; HHD (hon.), No. Mich. U., 1977; DSc (hon.), Meml. U. Nfld., Can., 1983, U. Autonoma Barcelona, Spain, 1989. Lectr. Manchester U., Eng., 1948-52, sr. lectr., 1956-58; lectr. Cambridge U., 1952-55; Mason prof. pure math. Birmingham U., Eng., 1958-62; prof. math. Cornell U., 1962-71, U. Wash., 1971-73; Beaumont prof. Case Western Res. U., 1973-82; disting. prof. SUNY, Binghamton, 1982-93, emeritus, 1993—; disting. prof. U. Ctrl. Fla., Orlando, 1993—. Guest prof. Swiss Fed. Inst. Tech., Zurich, 1966—67, Zurich, 1981—82, Zurich, 1988—89, Courant Inst. Math. Scis., NYU, 1967—68, Ohio State U., 1977, U. Autonoma, Barcelona, 1989, U. Lausanne, 1996; Erskine fellow U. Canterbury, 2001, 02; Mahler lectr. Australian Math. Soc., 1997; vis. fellow Battelle Seattle Rsch. Ctr., 1970—71, fellow, 1971—; co-chmn. Cambridge Conf. on Sch. Math., 1965; chmn. com. applied math. tng. NRC, 1977—; chmn. U.S. Commn. on Math. Instrn., 1979—80; sec. Internat. Commn. Math. Instrn., 1979—82. Author: Homotopy Theory, 1953, (with S. Wylie) Homology Theory, 1960, Homotopy Theory and Duality, 1966, (with H.B. Griffiths) Classical Mathematics, 1970, General Cohomology Theory and K-Theory, 1971, (with U. Stammbach) Course in Homological Algebra, 1971, 2d edit., 1997, Le Langage des Categories, 1973, (with Y.C. Wu) Course in Modern Algebra, 1974, (with G. Mislin and J. Roitberg) Localization of Nilpotent Groups and Spaces, 1975 (with J. Pedersen) Fear No More, 1982, Nilpotente Gruppen und Nilpotente Räume, 1984, (with J. Pedersen) Build Your Own Polyhedra, 1987, (with J. Pedersen) College Preparatory Mathematics, 1992, (with D. Holton and J. Pedersen) Mathematical Reflections, 1997, 2d edit., 2001, (with D. Holton and J. Pedersen) Mathematical Vistas, 2002; editor: Ergebnisse der Mathematik, 1964—, Ill. Jour. Math., 1962-68, Jour. Pure and Applied Algebra, 1970-75, Topics in Modern Topology, 1968, Miscellanea Mathematica, 1991; contbr. articles to profl. jours. Recipient Silver medal U. Helsinki, Finland, 1975, Centenary medal John Carroll U., 1985. Mem. Am. Math. Soc., Math. Assn. Am. (1st v.p. 1978-80), Can. Math. Soc., Math Soc. Belgium (hon.), London Math. Soc., Cambridge Philos. Soc., Brazilian Acad. Scis. (hon.). Home: 29 Murray St Binghamton NY 13905-4504 Office: SUNY Dept Math Scis Binghamton NY 13902-6000 Office Phone: 607-777-4867. Business E-Mail: marge@math.binghamton.edu.

HILTON, RONALD, international relations educator; b. Torquay, Eng., July 31, 1911; came to U.S., 1937, naturalized, 1946; s. Robert and Elizabeth Alice (Taylor) H.; m. Mary Bowie, May 1, 1939; 1 dau., Mary Alice Taylor. BA, Oxford U., Eng., 1933, MA, 1936; student, Sorbonne, Paris, 1933-34, U. Madrid, 1934-35, U. of Perugia, Italy, 1935-36. Dir. Comité Hispano-Inglés Library, Madrid, 1936; asst. prof. modern langs. U. B.C., 1939-41; assoc. prof. Romanic langs. Stanford U., 1942-49, prof., 1949-75, prof. emeritus humanities and scis., 1975—. Dir. Inst. Hispanic Am. and Luso-Brazilian studies; hon. prof. U. de San Marcos, Lima, Peru; vis. prof. U. Brazil, 1949; cultural dir. U. of Air, KGEI, San Francisco.; founder, pres. World Assn. Internat. Studies; vis. fellow Hoover Instn., 1973—. Author: Campoamor, Spain and the World, 1940, Handbook of Hispanic Source Materials in the U.S, 1942, 2d edit., 1956, Four Studies in Franco-Spanish Relations, 1943, La America Latina de Ayer y de Hoy, 1970, The Scientific Institutions of Latin America, 1970, The Latin Americans, Their Heritage and Their Destiny, 1973; assoc. editor: Who's Who in America; editor: The Life of Joaquim Nabuco, 1950, The Movement Toward Latin American Unity, 1969, World Affairs Report, 1970—, Spain. From Monarchy to Civil War, 1990, La Legende Noir, 1995. Decorated officer Cruzeiro do Sul (Brazil); Commonwealth Fund fellow U. Calif., 1937-39. Mem. Am. Assn. Tchrs. Spanish and Portuguese, Hispanic Soc. of Am., Am. Acad. Franciscan History. Office: World Assn Internat Studies Hoover Instn Stanford CA 94305-6010 E-mail: hilton@stanford.edu.

HILTON, STANLEY GOUMAS, lawyer, educator, writer; b. San Francisco, June 16, 1949; s. Lukas Stylianos and Effie (Glafkides) Goumas; m. Raquel Estrella Villalba, Feb. 25, 1996; children: Loucas, Angelika, Karmen (triplets). BA with honors, U. Chgo., 1971; JD, Duke U., 1975; MBA, Harvard U., 1979. Bar: Calif. 1975, U.S. Dist. Ct. Calif. 1975, U.S. Ct. Appeals (9th cir.) 1983, U.S. Supreme Ct. 1985. Libr. asst. Duke U. Libr., Durham, N.C., 1972-75, Harvard U. Libr., Cambridge, Mass., 1977-79; minority counsel U.S. Senator Bob Dole, Washington, 1979-80; adminstrv. asst. Calif. State Senate, Sacramento, 1980-81; pvt. practice San Francisco, 1981—; CEO Froggg, Inc., 1999—, San Francisco Landlords Union, 1999—. Adj. assoc. prof. Golden Gate U., San Francisco, 1991—; profl. spkr.; polit. writer; CEO Taxpayers of U.S., 2001—; pres. Fair Play In the Middle East Com., 2002—; tutor Harvard U., 1978—79; chair Vegetarians World Unite, 2001—, 911 Victims Fund, 2004—; founder, pres. Cicero-Aristotle Sch. Rhetoric, 2004—. Author: Bob Dole: American Political Phoenix, 1988, Senator for Sale, 1995, Glass Houses, 1998 (Best writer 1998), To Pay or Not to Pay, 2003. Pres. Com. to Stick With Candlestick Park, San Francisco, 1992-96, Value Added Tax Now, San Francisco, 1994—, Save the 4th Amendment, San Francisco, 1995—, 911 Truth Movement, 2001—; pres., CEO Animalism, Inc., San Francisco Landlord's Union, 2001—; pres. Save the Cows, 2004; CEO Fountain of Youth; alt. mem. San Mateo County Dem. Ctrl. Com., 2002--; Dem. candidate for Gov. Calif. spl. recall election, 2003. Mem. Calif. State Bar, Abolish the Fed. Res. Bank Assn. (pres. 1999—), Hellenic Law Soc., Bechtel Toastmasters Club (pres.), Rhinoceros Toastmasters Club, Ams. For Better Congress (pres. 2003—), Debtors United (chmn. 2004—) Democrat. Avocations: stamp collecting/philately, photography, classical music, ancient greek and roman history. Office: 580 California St Ste 500 San Francisco CA 94104-1000 Office Phone: 415-378-6142. Personal E-mail: loucasloukas@yahoo.com, frog727@aol.com.

HILTON, STEVEN J., real estate executive; Project mgr. Premier Cmty. Homes; co-founder Monterey Homes (merger Homeplex Mortgage Investment Co.), 1985, treas., sec., 1985-96; pres., co-CEO, Meritage Corp., Plano, Tex., 1996-98, co-chmn, co-CEO, 1998—. Mem. Nat. Homebuilders' Assn., Nat. Bd. Realtors, Ctrl. Ariz. Homebuilders' Assn., Scottsdale Bd. Realtors. Office: Meritage Corp 4050 W Park Blvd Plano TX 75093-3839*

HILTON, THEODORE CRAIG, computer scientist, Internet company executive; b. Oakland, Calif., June 14, 1949; s. Theodore Caldwell and Maxine (Donnelly) Hilton; m. Peggy Estes, May 21, 1990; children: Christopher, Kelly, Clark, Lisa, Trey, Veronique. BS in Internat. Rels., Occidental Coll., 1972; BS, Calif. Inst. Tech., 1972; MS in Computer Sci., N.Y. Inst. Tech., 1980; DSc in Computer Studies (hon.), Buxton U., 1995. Ptnr., founder Ctrl. Data Corp., L.A., 1971—, CEO, 1988—; engr. RSK, L.A., 1972-73; prof. Lake (Fla.) Coll., 1981-85, dept. chmn., 1983-85; prin. rsch. invest. U.S. Dept. Def., L.A., 1985-88; chmn. Access LLC, 1996—; chmn., CEO E-City Corp., 1996—99; chmn. WEB Holdings Corp., 1998. Creator computer sys. E-City, 1956, Broadcast Mgmt. Sys., 1972, ICSS, 1974, EBook, 1993, Quality Assurance Sys., 1994, Nat. Curriculum Clearinghouse Sys., 2002; U.S. presenter SOLE Internat. Conv., 1991; CALS presenter, 95; adv. bd. Accurate Rsch. Corp., 2000; bd. dirs. TBS S.A., Carolina Access LLC, S.E. Data Comms., Nat. Scholar Corp., LW Industries. Author: (book) Web Databases & PHP3, 1999, Web Databases & PHP3, Japanese edit., 2000, Web Databases & PHP3, Polish/Russian edits., 2002, Data-Base Development, 1999, Web Databse, 2000; contbr. articles to profl. jours. Named SC Bus. Man of Yr., 1999, Wall St. Businessman of Yr., 2000, NC Businessman of Yr., 2001—02; recipient Congl. medal Distinction, 2001. Mem.: IEEE, N.Y. Acad. Scis., Data Processing Mgmt. Assn., Logistics Engrs. Soc., Am. Mgmt. Assn., IEEE Computer Soc., Rotary (Paul Harris fellow). Achievements include patents for ultra-wide band voting system; autonomous network smart labels; filterable digital advertising; internet database management system; image system and public network exchange system; medical measurement devices; others. Office: Cen Data Corp 145 N Church St Ste 402 Spartanburg SC 29306-5163 E-mail: chilton@upstate.net.

HILTY, JAMES WALTER, historian, educator, media consultant; b. Columbus, Ohio, May 22, 1939; s. Robert Burns and Henrietta Isabel Hilty; m. Shirley Brown, Jan. 1963 (dissolved June 1975); children: Carolyn Marland, Robert; m. Kathleen Griffin Hilty, Oct. 19, 1979; 1 child, Maura. BS, Ohio State U., 1965, MA in Edn., 1966, MA in History, 1967; PhD in History, U. Mo., 1973. Prof. history Temple U., Phila., 1970—, assoc. dean Grad. Sch., 1978—80, acting dean Grad. Sch., 1980—81, asst. v.p. acad. affairs, 1982—82, dir. planning, 1982—85, asst. to pres., 1985—88, chair dept. history, 1988—94. Trustee Atwater Kent Mus., Phila., 1985—2002; cons. NBC News, N.Y.C., 1993, A&E Biography, N.Y.C., 2002. Author: JFK: Idealist Without Illusions, 1976, Robert Kennedy: Brother Protector, 1998; contbr. articles to profl. jours. Pres. Ogontz Vol. Fire Co., Montgomery County, 1980—85; bd. mem. Fire Adv. Bd., Montgomery County, Pa., 1979—94, ARC, Phila., 1985—95. With USMC, 1958—62, PTO. Recipient Disting. Tchg. award, Lindback Found., 2001. Mem.: Orgn. Am. Historians. Democrat. Avocations: golf, gardening. Office: History Dept 11th and Berks Sts Philadelphia PA 19122 Office Phone: 215-204-5581. Business E-Mail: jhilty@temple.edu.

HILTZ, ARNOLD AUBREY, retired chemist; b. Can., July 31, 1924; arrived in U.S., 1953; s. Aubrey Claremont and Fannie Mae (Bryanton) H.; m. Margery Jane (Beer), July 17, 1946; children: Sharon Lynne, Deborah Jane. BS in Chemistry, Acadia U., Wolfville, N.S., Can., 1947; PhD in Phys. Chemistry, McGill U., Montreal, Que., Can., 1952; LLD honoris causa (hon.), U. Prince Edward Island, 2004. Ordained deacon and priest Episc. Ch., 1976. Rsch. sci. officer Def. Rsch. Bd. Can., Quebec City, 1951—53; rsch. chemist Am. Viscose Corp., Phila., 1953—59, group leader, 1959—60, Avisun Corp., Phila., 1960—65; rsch. chemist Borden Chem. Co., Phila., 1965—66; sr. scientist GE, Phila., 1966—79, mgr. materials applications, 1979—91. Tutor math. and sci. Rose Tree Media, Pa. Sch. Dist., 1958-74. Contbr. articles to profl. journals; patentee in field. Docent Phila. Mus. Art, 1988—; sch. dir. Rose Tree Media Sch. Dist., 1969—74; bd. dirs., treas. Middletown (Pa.) Free Libr., 1964—69; vol. gallery guide Art Gallery N.S., 2004—; treas. Halifax County Condo. Corp., 2004—; bd. dirs. Sheepscot Island co., MacMahan Island, Maine, 1983—85. Recipient Silver medal Gov. Gen. Can. 1942, Can. Def. medal, Can. Vol. Svc. medal, Claspto CVSM, War medal 1939-45, Gen. Svc. badge, Can. Overseas medal 1945, Frank J. Sensebrenner fellow McGill U., 1949-51. Mem.: Am. Chem. Soc. (chem. abstractor 1958—79, sci. lectr. 1958—), Hebrides Home Owners Assn. (pres. 1999—2001, bd. dirs. 1999—2001, treas. 2002—). Republican. Episcopalian. Avocations: art, music, reading, gardening, golf. Home: 40 Regency Pk Dr # 607 B3S 1L4 Halifax NS Canada E-mail: aandmhiltz@aol.com.

HILTZ, STARR ROXANNE, sociologist, educator, writer, consultant, computer scientist; b. Little Rock, Sept. 7, 1942; d. John Donald and Mildred V. Smyers; m. Murray Turoff, 1985; children: Jonathan David, Katherine Amanda. AB, Vassar Coll., 1963; MA, Columbia U., 1964, PhD, 1969. Prof. sociology Upsala Coll., 1969-85; info. sys. N.J. Inst. Tech., 1985-93, disting. prof. computer sci., 1993—. Cons. social impacts of computer systems. Author: Creating Community Services for Widows, 1976, (with M. Turoff) The Network Nation, 1978, 2d edit., 1993, (with E. Kerr) Computer-Mediated Communication, 1982, Online Communities, 1984, The Virtual Classroom, 1994, (with L. Harasim, L. Teles and M. Turoff) Learning Networks, 1995, (with Ricki Goldman) Learning Together Online, 2004. Recipient N.J. Woman of the Millennium for Ednl. Tech., 2000. Mem.: Assn. for Info. Sys., Assn. Computing Machinery. Unitarian Universalist. Home: 19 Meadowbrook Rd Randolph NJ 07869-3808 Office: NJ Inst Tech Info Systems Newark NJ 07102

HILTZIK, MICHAEL, journalist; b. NYC, Nov. 9, 1952; s. Harold & Bernice (Rothman) Hiltzik; m. Deborah Ibert, 2 children, Andrew, David. BA English, Colgate U., 1973; MS Journalism, Columbia U. Grad Sch Journalism, 1974. Journalist Buffalo Courier-Express, Buffalo, 1974-78, bureau chief, 1976-78; staff writer Providence Journal-Bulletin, Providence, 1979-81; finan. writer L.A. Times, 1981-83, N.Y. fin. corr. NYC, 1982-88, Nairobi bur. chief Nairobi, Kenya, 1988-93, Moscow corr. Moscow, 1993-94, fin. staff writer/editor, columnist LA, 1994—. Author, non-fiction: A Death in Kenya, 1991, Dealers of Lightning: Xerox PARC and the Dawn of the Computer Age, 1999, The Plot Against Social Security: How the Bush Plan is Endangering Our Financial Future, 2005. Co-recipient Pulitzer prize for Beat Reporting, 1999, recipient, ABA Silver Gavel award, Overseas Press Club citation for coverage of E. Africa. Office: Golden State Columnist Los Angeles Times Times Mirror Sq Los Angeles CA 90001 E-mail: golden.state@latimes.com.*

HILYARD, JAMES EMERSON, manufacturing executive; b. New Castle, Pa., Feb. 15, 1941; m. Roberta Smoker, Mar. 14, 1964; children: Todd James, Sharon Lee. BSChemE, Carnegie Mellon U., 1963; MBA, Case Western Res., 1970; Exec. Program, Columbia U., 1977, Dartmouth U., 1988. V.p. materials mgmt. Sherwin Williams, Chgo., 1979-81, mgr. of mfg., 1981-83; plant mgr. CertainTeed Corp., Chicago Heights, Ill., 1983-84, v.p. so. region Savannah, Ga., 1984-85, v.p. ea. region, 1985-86; v.p. mfg. Roofing Div. CertainTeed, Valley Forge, Pa., 1986-87, v.p. ops., 1987-88, v.p., gen. mgr., 1988-90, pres., 1990—. Bd. dirs., vice-chmn. Ludowici-Celadon, Inc., New Lexington, Ohio, 1990-2002, Air Vent Inc., Peoria, Ill., 1988-90; bd. dirs. Nat. Coun. Housing Industry, Bird Corp., Norwood, Mass., 1998; pres. Ludowici Roof Tile, Inc., New Lexington, 1994-2002, Celadon, New Lexington, 1994-2002, G S Roofing Co., 1999. Admissions counselor Carnegie Mellon U., Pitts., 1967—; mem. Phila. Coun. on World Affairs, 1992-2000, Industry Commn. Savannah Chamber, 1985; chmn. Race Rels. Com., Isle of Hope Meth. Ch., Savannah, 1985; v.p. CertainTeed Found., Norton Co. found., 1998-2001; sr. advisor St. Gobain, 2003. Named Boss of the Yr., Savannah Sec.'s Club, 1985. Mem. Am. AICE, Am. Prodn. Control Soc., Asphalt Roofing Mfrs. Assn. (bd. dirs., treas. 1997-99, v.p. 1999-2001, pres. 2001-03, mem. exec. com. 1997-2003, chmn. exec. com. 2004-), Nat. Tile Roofing Mfrs. Assn., Nat. Roofing Contractors Assn., Castle Harbor Yacht Club (fleet capt. 1993, commodore 1994, bd. dirs. 1995), Chesapeake Bay Yacht Clubs Assn. (del. 1994-95), Found. for Architecture. Avocations: boating, cross country skiing. Home: 122 Cloverly Ln West Chester PA 19380-3874 Office: CertainTeed Corp PO Box 860 750 E Swedesford Rd Valley Forge PA 19482

HILZENDEGER, LAURA KAYE, business and marketing educator; d. Leo and Carol Hilzendeger. BA in Edn., Ctrl. Wash. U., 1989, MEd in Mktg. Edn., 1995. Vocat. Certification in Bus. and Mktg. Edn. Wash., 1989, Continuing Teaching Certificate in Business, Marketing, & Traffic Ed. Office of Supt. of Pub. Instrn., 1989. Substitute tchr. AC Davis H.S., Yakima, Wash., 1990, Yakima Valley OIC, 1990; tchr. bus. edn. Port Angeles H.S., 1990—92; instr. bus. Peninsula C.C., 1991—92; tchr. bus. edn. Collins H.S., Buckley, 1993—94, Enumclaw H.S., 1994—2000; instr. bus. Green River C.C., Auburn, 1997—2000; tchr. bus. & mktg. edn. Fife H.S., Tacoma, 2000—. Rsch. asst. Ctrl. Wash. U., Ellensburg, 1983; legal asst. Menke & Jackson, Atty. Law, Yakima, 1989. Textbook reviewer E-Commerce Marketing. Bd. mem. Milton Hollow Homeowners Assn., 2003. Recipient Tchr. Recognition award, City of Fife, 2002, Bus. Edn. award Merit H.S. Level, Wash. State Bus. Edn. Assn., 2002. Mem.: NEA (assoc.), Fife H.S. Adv. Com. (assoc.; chair 2000—03), Assn. Career & Tech. Edn. (assoc.; region V awards chair 2002—05), Wash. Assn. Career & Tech. Edn. (assoc.; pres.-elect, pres., past pres. 2001—04), Wash. State Bus. Edn. Assn. (assoc.; bd. rep. 1995—97, treas. 1997—98, pres.-elect, pres., past pres 1998—2001, bd. rep. 2000—02), Nat. Bus. Edn. Assn. (assoc.), Delta Pi Epsilon (assoc.; v.p., pres. 1996—98). Roman Catholic. Avocations: reading, travel, music, shopping. Office: Fife High Sch 5616 20th St E Tacoma WA 98424 Office Phone: 253-517-1100.

HIMELFARB, RICHARD JAY, investment company executive; b. Balt., Feb. 3, 1942; s. Jacob and Jennie (Willen) H.; m. Margaret Conn, Sept. 7, 1969; children: Elizabeth Jayne, Michael Ross. BA, Johns Hopkins U., 1962; LLB, Yale U., 1965. Bar: Md., 1965. Assoc., then ptnr. Weinberg & Green (now Saul Ewing LLC), Balt., 1967-83; exec. v.p. Legg Mason, Inc., Balt., 1983—, also bd. dirs. Bd. dirs. Center Stage, Inc., Balt., 1984-2002, Balt. Goodwill Industries, 1984-93, Kennedy Krieger Inst., 1993—, Bryn Mawr Sch., 1991-94; mem. bd. visitors U. Md., Balt., 1990-96, chmn., 1996-2000; chmn. U. Md. Balt. Found., 2000—; bd. visitors Inst. of Human Virology, 1997—; bd. dirs. Balt. Devel. Corp., 1997-2003, UMB Rsch. Park Corp., 2003—. Capt. U.S. Army, 1965—67. Mem. Phi Beta Kappa. Home: 116 Taplow Rd Baltimore MD 21212-3312 Office: Legg Mason Inc 100 Light St Baltimore MD 21202-1099

HIMELRICK, RICHARD G., lawyer; b. Detroit, Nov. 6, 1949; s. Richard G. and Mildred R. Himelrick; m. Shirley A. Himelrick, June 4, 1975 (dec. Apr. 2003); 1 child, Richard Todd. BA, Oakland U., 1971; JD, Wayne State U., 1974. Bar: Ariz. 76, U.S. Dist. Ct. Ariz. 76, U.S. Ct. Appeals (9th cir.) 77. Ptnr. Byrnes, Rosier & Himelrick, P.C., Scottsdale, Ariz., 1990—96, Tiffany & Bosco, P.A., Phoenix, 1997—. Contbr. articles to profl. jours. Mem.: ATLA, Pub. Investors Arbitration Bar Assn. Democrat. Avocations: reading, running, skiing. Office: Tiffany & Bosco PA 2525 E Camelback Rd Third Fl Phoenix AZ 85016 Office Phone: 602-255-6021. E-mail: rgh@tblaw.com.

HIMELSTEIN, MORGAN YALE, language educator; b. Lebanon, Conn., Sept. 19, 1926; s. Max Abraham and Dorothy Judith (Malkin) H.; m. Libby June Rosenfeld, Dec. 21, 1958; children: Andrew Louis, Bruce Philip. BA, Wesleyan U., 1947; AM, Columbia U., 1948, PhD, 1958. Instr. English Univ. Rochester, N.Y., 1948-50, Adelphi Univ., Garden City, N.Y., 1957-60, asst. prof. English, 1960-64, assoc. prof. English, 1964-68, dir. grad. studies in English, 1965-74, prof. in English, 1968—, summer chair in English, 1965-86. Cons. various publs., 1970—, various opera theatres, 1980—. Author: Drama Was A Weapon, 1963, 1976; translator: La Grande Duchesse De Gerolstein, 1977, La Perichole, 1982, Orphee Aux Enfers, 1985, Die Fledermaus, 1990; contbr. articles to profl. jours. Trustee Garden City (N.Y.) Jewish Ctr., 1965—, pres., 1981-83. Cpl. U.S. Army, 1950-52. Recipient Winchester fellowship Wesleyan Univ., Middletown, Conn., 1948-49; honoree United Jewish Appeal, Garden City, 1978. Mem. Modern Lang. Assn., Wesleyan Alumni Schs. Com., Phi Beta Kappa. Avocations: gardening, travel. Home: 37 Maxwell Rd Garden City NY 11530-1844 Office: Adelphi Univ South Ave Garden City NY 11530

HIMES, DIANE ADELE, buyer, fundraiser, actress, lobbyist; b. San Francisco, Aug. 11, 1942; d. L. John and Mary Louise (Young) H. BA, San Francisco State U., 1964. Rep. west coast home furnishings Allied Stores, nationwide; gift buyer Jordan Marsh, Miami; buyer The Broadway Stores; west coast sales mgr. Xmas divsn. Vincent Lippe Corp., L.A.; midwest sales mgr. Vincent-Lippe Chgo. Actress Nine 'O Clock Players, 1995, short film The Traveling Companion, 1998. Statewide co-chair Californians Initiative No On #102, 1988; founding co-chair Life AIDS Lobby, 1985—88; mem. Beverly Hills rent control bd., 1984; co-chair Californians Against Proposition #64, 1986; co-chmn. Mcpl. Elections Com., L.A.; bd. dirs. L.A. Women's Shakespeare Group, 1992—94. Named Woman of Yr. of L.A., ACLU, 1987, Christopher Street West, 1988. Avocations: acting, appearing in short films.

HIMES, JAMES ALBERT, retired veterinary medicine educator; b. Lucas, Ohio, Aug. 12, 1919; s. Albert Merle and Nina Grace (Galleher) H.; m. Ruth Naomi Banks, Apr. 26, 1958 (div. 1973); children: Leslie Jo, Jillyn Alicia; m. Genia Lee, May 10, 1973 (div. 2000). BS, Muskingum Coll., 1941; postgrad., U. Nebr., 1941-42, 46; VMD, U. Penn., 1950; PhD, Cornell U., 1965. Veterinarian, Tenn., Va., Fla., 1950-62; rsch. asst. Cornell U., Ithaca, N.Y., 1962-65; from asst. prof. to assoc. prof. U. Fla., Gainesville, 1965-76, dir. vet. medicine edn., 1975-77, prof., 1976-90; from asst. dean to assoc. dean U. Fla. Coll. Vet. Medicine, Gainesville, 1977-90; prof. emeritus U. Fla., Gainesville, 1990—. Editor: Part X, Spontaneous Animal Models of Human Disease, 1979. Sgt. U.S. Army, 1942-45. Mem. AVMA, Fla. Vet. Med. Assn. (Vet. of Yr. 1987, Exec. Disting. Svc. award 1992), Alachua Vet. Med. Assn. (sec.-treas. 1973-74, pres. 1995), Marion County Vet. Assn. Avocations: reading, music, walking, jogging, cooking. Home: 2841 SW 37th Pl Apt 59F Gainesville FL 32608-3122 Business E-Mail: himesJ@mail.vetmed.ufl.edu.

HIMES, JOHN HARTER, medical researcher, educator; b. Salt Lake City, July 25, 1947; s. Ellvert Hiram and Mildred Anna (Harter) H.; children: Rachel Anne, Matthew Hiram, Sarah Elizabeth; m. LaVell Gold. BS, Ariz. State U., 1971; PhD, U. Tex., 1975; MPH, Harvard U., 1982. Rsch., sr. scientist Fels Rsch. Inst., Yellow Springs, Ohio, 1976-79; Fels asst. prof. Wright State U. Sch. Medicine, Dayton, Ohio, 1977-79; sr. analyst, project dir. Abt Assocs., Cambridge, Mass., 1979-82; assoc. prof. CUNY, Bklyn., 1982-87; from assoc. prof. to prof. U. Minn. Sch. Pub. Health, Mpls., 1992—, dir. nutrition coord. ctr., 1995—. Expert com physical status WHO, Geneva, Switzerland, 1991-94, expert adv. panel nutrition, 1994—; mem. tech. working groups Ctrs. for Disease Control, Washington and Atlanta, 1988-97. Author: Parent-specific Adjustment for Assessment of Recumbent Length & Stature, 1981, Anthropometric Assessment of Nutritional Status, 1991; contbr. articles to profl. jours. Recipient Nathalie Masse Meml. prize Internat. Children's Ctr., Paris, 1979. Fellow Human Biology Coun.; mem. APHA, N.Am. Assn. Study Obesity, Internat. Assn. Human Auxology, Pan Am. Health Orgn. (tech. adv. nutrition 1994—2000, Nat. Ctr. Health Stats. (tech. working group 1994-97), Am. Soc. Nutritional Scis., Soc. for Study Human Biology, Sigma Xi, Phi Kappa Phi, Delta Omega. Business E-Mail: himes@epi.umn.edu.

HIMMA, KENNETH EINAR, philosophy educator; BA, U. Ill., Chgo., 1985; MA, UCLA, 1987; JD, U. Wash., 1990, PhD, 2001. Bar: Wash. 1992, Calif. 1990. Lectr. philosophy, info. scis. and law U. Wash., Seattle, 2001—04; assoc. prof. philosophy Seattle Pacific U., 2004—. Contbr. more than 80 articles to profl. jours. Mem. steering com. Jubilee NW, Seattle, 2004—05. Mem.: Golden Key Nat. Honor Soc., Phi Kappa Phi, Phi Beta Kappa. Office: Seattle Pacific U 3307 Third Ave West Seattle WA 98119 Office Phone: 206-281-2038. Office Fax: 206-281-2335. E-mail: himma@spu.edu.

HIMMEL, ETHEL EILEEN, library consultant; b. Peoria, Ill., May 6, 1943; d. Clifford Paul and Eleanor Elizabeth (Penn) Bleichner; m. Clark Eldon Himmel, June 4, 1964 (div. July 1980); children: Erich Brian, Karen Lynn; m. William James Wilson, Mar. 17, 1990. BA, U. Ill., Urbana, 1964; MLS, U. Wis., 1970, PhD, 1992. Head pub. svcs. LaCrosse (Wis.) Pub. Libr., 1978-83; dep. dir., LaCrosse pub. libr. Winding Rivers Libr. Sys., 1984-87; rsch. asst. Wisconsin Interlibr. Svcs., Madison, 1987-91; prin. ptnr. Himmel and Wilson Libr. Cons., 1987—. Contributions (books) Keeping the Books, 1992, Encyclopedia of Library History, 1994. Mem.: Assn. Specialized and Coop. Libr. Agys., Assn. Specialized Coop. Libr. Agys. (pres. 2000—03, chair standards rev. com. 1996—2000), Wis. Libr. Assn. (pres. 1994), Info. Futures Inst, Spl. Librs. Assn., ALA. Democrat. Avocations: gardening, reading, travel. Office: Himmel & Wilson Libr Cons 417 E High St Milton WI 53563-1501

HIMMELBERG, CHARLES JOHN, III, mathematics professor, researcher; b. North Kansas City, Mo., Nov. 12, 1931; s. Charles John and Magdalene Caroline (Batliner) H.; m. Mary Patricia Hennessy, Jan. 27, 1962; children: Charles, Ann, Mary, Joseph, Patrick. BS, Rockhurst Coll., 1952; MS, U. Notre Dame, 1954, PhD, 1957. Assoc. analyst Midwest Rsch. Inst., Kansas City, Mo., 1957-59; asst. prof. math. U. Kans., Lawrence, 1959-65, assoc. prof., 1965-68, prof., 1968—, chmn. dept. math., 1978-99. Mem. editorial bd. Rocky Mountain Jour. Math, 1972-88; contbr. articles to profl. jours. Mem. Am. Math. Soc., Math. Assn. Am. Roman Catholic. Office: U Kans Dept Math Lawrence KS 66045-7523 Business E-Mail: himmelberg@ku.edu.

HIMMELBERG, ROBERT FRANKLIN, historian, educator; b. Kansas City, Mo., July 16, 1934; s. Alexander Franklin and Genevieve Fay (Leonard) H.; m. Josephine Ann Boone, Dec. 27, 1958; children: Thomas A., Robert A., Juliana Ruth. BA, Rockhurst Coll., 1956; MA, Creighton U., 1958; PhD, Pa. State U., 1963. Instr. Am. history Fordham U., Bronx, N.Y., 1961-63, asst. prof., 1963-68, assoc. prof., 1968-77, prof., 1977—, chmn. dept., 1969-72, pres. faculty senate, 1989-92, dean Grad. Sch. Arts and Scis., 1993-2000. Hoover Presdl. Library fellow, 1984-85, grantee, 1993. Author: The Origins of the National Recovery Administration: Business, Government and the Trade Association Issue, 1921-1933, 1976, revised edit., 1994; editor: Business and Government in America Since 1870, 1994; co-editor: Historians and Race: Autobiography and the Writing of History, 1996, The Great Depression and the New Deal, 2000; contbr. articles to profl. jours. Grantee, Am. Philos. Soc., 1978. Mem.: Orgn. Am. Historians. Republican. Roman Catholic. Office: Fordham Univ Dept History Bronx NY 10458 E-mail: himmelberg@fordham.edu.

HIMMELBLAU, DAVID MAUTNER, chemical engineer; b. Chgo., Aug. 29, 1923; s. David and Roda (Mautner) H.; m. Betty H. Hartman, Sept. 1, 1948; children: Andrew, Margaret Ann. BS, MIT, 1947; MBA, Northwestern U., 1950; PhD, U. Wash., 1957. Cost engr. Internat. Harvester Co., Chgo., 1946-47; cost analyst Simpson Logging Co., Seattle, 1952-53; mgr. Excel Battery Co., Seattle, 1953-54; teaching asst., instr. U. Wash., Seattle, 1955-57; successively asst. prof., asso. prof., prof. chem. engring. U. Tex., Austin, 1957—, chmn. dept., 1973-77. Pres. RAMAD Corp.; Univ. Fed. Credit Union, 1964-68; exec officer CACHE Corp. of Mass., 1984-2000. Author: Basic Principles and Calculations in Chemical Engineering, 1962, 7th edit., 2004, Process Analysis and Simulation, 1968, Process Analysis by Statistical Methods, 1970, Applied Nonlinear Programming, 1974, Optimization of Chemical Processes, 1989, 2d edit., 2000; contbr. articles to profl. jours. Served with U.S. Army, 1943-46, 51-52. Grantee, NSF, 1953—94, NATO Sci. Com., 1969. Mem. Am. Inst. Chem. Engrs. (dir. 1973-76), Am. Chem. Soc., Am. Math. Soc., Ops. Research Soc. Am., Soc. Indsl. and Applied Mathematics, Sigma Xi, Delta Mu Delta. Clubs: Headliners (Austin). Home: 4609 Ridge Oak Dr Austin TX 78731-5211 Office: Univ Texas Coll Engring Austin TX 78712 Office Phone: 512-471-7445. Business E-Mail: himmelblau1@che.utexas.edu.

HIMMELFARB, GERTRUDE (MRS. IRVING KRISTOL), writer, educator; b. N.Y.C., Aug. 8, 1922; d. Max and Bertha (Lerner) H.; m. Irving Kristol, Jan. 18, 1942; children— William, Elizabeth. BA, Bklyn. Coll., 1942; MA, U. Chgo., 1944, PhD, 1950; L.H.D. (hon.), R.I. Coll., 1976, Kenyon Coll., 1985, Adelphi U., 1989, Boston U., 1987, Yale U., 1990; Litt. D. (hon.), Smith Coll., 1977, Lafayette Coll., 1978, Jewish Theol. Sem., 1978, Williams Coll., 1989; LLD (hon.), Union Coll., 1989. Distinguished prof. history Grad. Sch., CUNY, 1965-88, prof. emeritus, 1988—. Author: Lord Acton: A Study in Conscience and Politics, 1952, Darwin and the Darwinian Revolution, 1959, Victorian Minds, 1968, On Liberty and Liberalism— The Case of John Stuart Mill, 1975, The Idea of Poverty, 1984, Marriage and Morals Among the Victorians, 1986, The New History and the Old, 1987, Poverty and Compassion: The Moral Imagination of the Late Victorians, 1991, Untimely Thoughts on Culture and Society, 1994, The De-Moralization of Society: From Victorian Virutes to Modern Values, 1995, The Road to Modernity: The British, French, and American Enlightenment, 2004; editorial bd.: Am. Scholar, First Things. Trustee Nat. Humanities Ctr.; bd. Woodrow Wilson Internat. Ctr., Brit. Inst. of U.S., Inst. Contemporary Studies; mem. council scholars Library of Congress; mem. council acad. advisors Am. Enterprise Inst.; assoc. scholar Ethics and Pub. Policy Ctr. Recipient Rockefeller Found. award, 1962-63, 63-64, 80-81, Nat. Humanities Presdl. medal, 2004; Guggenheim fellow, 1955-56, 57-58; sr. fellow NEH, 1968-69; Am. Council Learned Socs. fellow, 1972-73; Phi Beta Kappa vis. scholar, 1972-73; Woodrow Wilson Ctr. fellow, 1976-77 Fellow British Acad., Am. Philos. Soc., Royal Hist. Soc., Am. Acad. Arts and Scis., Soc. Am. Historians; mem. Am. Hist. Assn., Conf. on Brit. Studies.

HIMMELFARB, JOHN DAVID, artist; b. Chgo., June 3, 1946; s. Samuel and Eleanor (Gorecki) H.; m. Mary Louise Day. AB, Harvard U., 1968; MA, Grad. Sch. Edn., 1970. One-man shows include Ill. Arts Coun., Chgo., 1974, Graphics I&II, Boston, 1974, Ill. Center, Chgo., 1975, U. Nebr., Omaha, 1976, Dorothy Rosenthal Gallery, Chgo., 1976, Ill. State Mus., Springfield, 1978, Albrecht Mus. Art, St. Joseph, Mo., 1978, Ball State U., 1978, 89, Sheldon Meml. Art Gallery, 1978, Ill. Wesleyan U., 1979, Terry Dintenfass Inc., N.Y.C., 1979, 83, 86, 89, 91, Gallery 72, Omaha, 1979, 83, 85, 87, 90, 92, 94, 96, 99, 2001, 03, Fountain Gallery, Portland, Oreg., 1980, Hull Gallery, Washington, 1980, Barbara Balkin Gallery, Chgo., 1982, Area X Gallery, NYC, 1985, Brody's Gallery, Washington, 1985, 90, Sioux City Art Ctr., 1985, 2000, Davenport Mus., 1986, John Nichols, NYC, 1986, Blanden Art Mus., 1987, Evanston Art Ctr., 1987, 96, Fundacio Josep Artigas, Barcelona, Spain, 1989, Kalamazoo Inst. Arts, 1989, Miami U. Art Mus., 1990, Ark. Art Ctr., 1990, Madison Art Ctr., 1990, Huntington Mus. Art, 1990, Cissie Peltz Gallery, 1991, Anchor Graphics, 1992, U. No. Iowa, 1993, Gallery 1756, Chgo., 1995, Chgo. Cultural Ctr., 1995, Spaightwood Gallery, Madison, Wis., 1996, 99, Jean Albano Gallery, Chgo. 1996, 98, 2000, 2002, 2005, William Havu Gallery, Denver, 2002, 04, Ind. U. N.W., 2002, Ctr. for Contemp. Art, Christchurch, New Zealand, 2001, 03, Coll. Lake County, Grays Lake, Ill., 2005, Phyliss Stigliano Gallery, Bklyn., 2005, Salena Gallery, L.I. U., Bklyn., 2005, others; exhibited in group shows at Minn. Mus. Art, Total Mus. Contemporary Art, Seoul, Korea, Bklyn. Mus., Indpls. Mus. Art, Art Inst. Chgo., Walker Art Ctr., Nat. Mus. Am. Art; represented in permanent collections: Art Inst. Chgo., Indpls. Mus. Art, Nat. Mus. Am. Art, Fogg Mus. Art, Cleve. Mus. Art, Mpls. Inst. Art, Portland Mus. Art, Ill. State Mus., Bklyn. Mus., Balt. Mus. Art, Des Moines Art Center, High Mus. Art, Atlanta, Toledo Mus. Art, Univs. Wis., Minn., Oreg., Iowa, Total Mus. Contemporary Art, Seoul, Korea, Brit. Mus., others. NEA fellow in painting, 1982, in drawing, 1985, Ill. Arts Council fellow, 1986, 02, Pollock-Krasner fellow, 2002. Studio: 2400 S Oakley Ave Chicago IL 60608-4902 Office Phone: 733-376-0366. Business E-Mail: johnhimmelfarb@mac.com.

HIMMELFARB, MILTON, retired editor; b. Bklyn., Oct. 21, 1918; s. Max and Bertha (Lerner) H.; m. Judith Siskind, Nov. 26, 1950; children: Martha, Edward, Miriam, Anne, Sarah, Naomi, Dan. BA, CCNY, 1938, MS, 1939; B.Hebrew Lit., Jewish Theol. Sem. Coll., 1939; diplôme, U. Paris, 1939; postgrad., Columbia U., 1942—47. Dir. information and research Am. Jewish Com., N.Y.C., 1955-86; editor Am. Jewish Year Book, N.Y.C., 1959-86; contbg. editor Commentary mag., N.Y.C., 1960-86. Vis. prof. Jewish Theol. Sem., N.Y.C., 1967-68, 71-72; vis. lectr. Yale, 1971; vis. prof. Reconstructionist Rabbinical Coll., Phila., 1972-73. Author: The Jews of Modernity, 1973. Mem. U.S. Holocaust Meml. Coun., 1986-89. Personal E-mail: braflam@juno.com.

HIMMELRIGHT, ROBERT JOHN, JR., rubber company executive; b. Canton, Ohio, Mar. 29, 1926; s. Robert John and Katherine Dewees (Nusly) H.; m. Suzanne Hadley, Mar. 11, 1950; children: Robert John III, Christina S., George H., Anne D. BA, U. N.Mex., 1951; LLD (hon.), Kenyon Coll., 1987. With Teledyne Monarch Rubber Co., Hartville, Ohio, 1950-84, asst. to pres., then v.p., 1955-62, pres., 1963-84; chmn. Monarch South Seas Ltd., Delray Beach, Fla., 1984—. Alt. del. Rep. Nat. Conv., 1972, 76; trustee Kenyon Coll., Gambier, Ohio. With USNR, 1944-46, 50-51. Lutheran. Home and Office: 200 N Ocean Blvd Delray Beach FL 33483-7126 Personal E-mail: redhjr@aol.com.

HINCH, STEPHEN WALTER, telecommunications industry executive; b. Seattle, July 13, 1951; s. Harlan Delmer and Ivy Roslyn (Thrush) h.; m. Nicolette Constance Obritsch, Sept. 11, 1976; children: Gregory P., Juliana G. BS, MS in Engring., Harvey Mudd Coll., 1974. Mfg. engr. Hewlett-Packard Co., Santa Rosa, Calif., 1974-78, mfg. engring. mgr. Rohnert Park, Calif., 1978-84, corp. SMT program mgr. Palo Alto, Calif., 1984-88, Santa Rosa, Calif., 1988-90, rsch. and devel. mgr., 1988-90; R&D mgr. Agilent Techs., Santa Rosa, 1990—. Instr. Inst. Interconnection and Packaging of Electronic Circuits, Lincolnwood, Ill., 1985-93. Author: Handbook of Surface Mount Technology, 1988, Guide to State Parks of Sonoma Coast and Russian River, 1998; contbr. chpts. to books, tech. articles to profl. jours.; patentee in field. Mem. Bennett Valley Sch. Bd. Trustees, 1994-98, pres. 1996-97. Mem. IEEE, Telecomms. Industries Assn. Avocations: freelance writing, photography. Office: Agilent Techs 1400 Fountain Grove Pkwy Santa Rosa CA 95403-1738

HINCHEY, JOHN WILLIAM, lawyer; b. Knoxville, Tenn., June 18, 1941; s. Roy William and Ruth (Ownby) H.; m. Sherie Paulette Archer, May 12, 1968; children: Paul William, Meredith Marie, John Oliver. AB, Emory U., 1964, LLB, 1965; LLM, Harvard U., 1966; MLitt., Oxford U., 1980. Bar: Ga. 1965, U.S. Dist. Ct. (no., mid. and so. dists.) Ga. 1968, U.S. Ct. Appeals (11th cir.) 1968, U.S. Supreme Ct. 1970. Asst. atty. gen. State of Ga., Atlanta, 1968-72; ptnr. McConaughey & Hinchey, Decatur, Ga., 1972-76, Phillips & Mozley, Atlanta, 1976-84, Phillips, Hinchey & Reid, Atlanta, 1984-92, King and Spalding, Atlanta, 1992—. Contbr. articles to profl. jours. Mem.: ABA (chair Forum on Constrn. Industry), Am. Arbitration Assn. (constrn. arbitration master panel 2004—), CPR Inst., Alternative Dispute Resolution Counsel, Chartered Inst. Arbitrators, London Ct. Internat. Arbitration, Atlanta Bar Assn. (chair constrn. law sect. 1999—2000), Ga. Bar Assn., Am. Coll. Constrn. Lawyers (bd. govs. 2001—04, sec. 2005—), Druid Hills Golf Club. Republican. Methodist. Office: King & Spalding LLP 191 Peachtree St SW Atlanta GA 30303-1763 Office Phone: 404-572-4922. E-mail: jhinchey@kslaw.com.

HINCHEY, MAURICE D., congressman; b. N.Y.C., Oct. 27, 1938; s. Maurice D. and Rose (Bonack) H.; m. Ilene Marder; children: Maurice Scott, Josef L., Michelle R. BA, SUNY, New Paltz, 1968, MA, 1970. Mem. N.Y. State Assembly, 1974-93, U.S. Congress from 22d N.Y. dist., 1993—; mem. appropriations com., agr. subcom., interior subcom., joint econ. com. Chmn. N.E. Task Force Food & Farm Policy & Assembly Environ. Conserv. Comm., Higher Ednl. Rules & Racing & Wagering Comm., Joint Legis. Comm. Solid Waste Mgmt., Interstate Coun. on Migrant Edu., N.Y. Urban Cultural Parks Adv. Coun.; bd. visitors, house minority legions whip U.S. Mil. Acad. Author: (with others) Organized Crime and the Solid Waste Industry, 1986; N.Y. City Water Supply, A History, 1988. Hudson River Greenway Coun.; bd. dirs. Children's Rehab. Ctr., WAMC Nat. Pub. Radio. Recipient of Legislator of the Yr. award, Environ Planning Lobby, 1975, 1979, N.Y. State Bar Assn. Environ award, 1989. Mem. Saugerties Dem. Club (founding mem.), N.Y. State Dem. Commn. (vice-chmn.). Democrat. Roman Catholic. Office: US Ho of Reps 2431 Rayburn Hob Washington DC 20515-3222*

HINCKLEY, GORDON B., religious organization administrator; b. Salt Lake City, June 23, 1910; s. Bryant S. and Ada (Bitner) H.; m. Marjorie Pay, Apr. 29, 1937; children: Kathleen Hinckley Barnes Walker, Richard G., Virginia Hinckley Pearce, Clark B., Cynthia Jane Hinckley Dudley. Ordained 15th pres., prophet LDS Ch., 1995. Asst. Coun. of Twelve Apostles LDS Ch., Salt Lake City, 1958-61, mem. Coun., 1961-81, mem. Quorum Twelve Apostles, 1961—95, counselor in 1st presidency Salt Lake City, 1981-81, 2d counselor in 1st presidency, 1982-85, 1st counselor in 1st presidency, 1985-95, pres. of ch., 1995—. Proselyting mission Brit. Isles LDS Ch. Named One of most admired men in world 2d consecutive yr., ann. survey Ams., 2001. Mem. Lds Ch. Office: First Presidency LDS Ch 47 E South Temple Salt Lake City UT 84150-9701 Address: LDS Ch Office of Pres 47 E South Temple Salt Lake City UT 84150

HINCKLEY, GREGORY KEITH, software industry executive; b. San Francisco, Oct. 3, 1946; s. Homer Clair and Josephine F. (Gerrick) H. BS in Math. and Physics, Claremont Men's Coll., 1968; MS in Applied Physics, U. Calif., San Diego, 1970; MBA, Harvard U., 1972. CPA, Ill. Second v.p. Continental Bank, Chgo., 1972—78; dir. fin ITEL Corp., San Francisco, 1978—79; group contr. Raychem Corp., Menlo Park, Calif., 1979—83; v.p. fin., CFO Bio-Rad Labs., Richmond, Calif., 1983—89; sr. v.p. fin., CFO Crowley Maritime Corp., San Francisco, 1989—91; sr. v.p., CFO VLSI Tech. Inc., 1992—97; pres. Mentor Graphics Corp., Wilsonville, Oreg., 1997—, also bd. dirs. Bd. dirs. Amkor Tech., West Chester, Pa., Oreg. Mus. Sci. and Industry, Portland, Arcsoft, Inc., Fremont, Calif., Unova Inc., Everett, Wash. Bd. dirs. Portland Opera. Fulbright fellow, Eng., 1968. Mem. AICPAs. Home: 2417 SW 16th Ave Portland OR 97201-2308

HIND, HARRY WILLIAM, pharmaceutical company executive; b. Berkeley, Calif., June 2, 1915; s. Harry Wyndham and B.J. (O'Connor) H.; m. Diana Vernon Miesse, Dec. 12, 1940; children: Leslie Vernon Hind Daniels, Gregory William. BS, U. Calif., Berkeley, 1939, LLD, 1968; DSc (hon.), U. Scis. Phila., 1982. Founder Barnes-Hind Pharms., Inc., Sunnyvale, Calif., 1939—. Pres. Hind Health Care, Inc. Contbr. articles to profl. jours.; designer ph meter and developer of ophthalmic solutions. Recipient Ebert award for pharm. rsch., 1948, Eye Rsch. Found. award, 1958, Helmholtz Ophthalmology award for rsch., 1968, Carbert award for sight conservation, 1973, Alumnus of Yr. award U. Calif. Sch. Pharmacy, 1965, Disting. Svc. award U. Calif. Proctor Found., 1985, Commendation by Resolution State of Calif., 1987, Pharmaceutical Achievements commendation State of Calif. Assembly, Hon. Recognition award Contact Lens Mfrs. Assn., 1990. Fellow AAAS; mem. Am. Pharm. Assn., Am. Optometric Assn. (Man of Yr. award Pharmacist's Planning Svc. 1987), Contact Lens Soc. Am. (Hall of Fame 1989), Am. Assn. Pharm. Scientists, Am. Chem. Soc., Calif. Pharm. Assn., NY Acad. Scis., Los Altos Country Club, Sigma Xi, Rho Chi, Phi Delta Chi. Office Phone: 650-948-2919.

HINDEMITH, PAUL, music educator, musician; b. Omaha, Nebr., Feb. 10, 1976; s. Dennis F. Hindemith and Agnes M. Hindemith (nee McCann). MusB in Music Performance (Voice), So. Meth. U., 1999; postgrad., U. of Md., 2002—. Cert. tchr. Nebr. Vocal music tchr. Omaha Pub. Schs., North H.S., 1999—; on-air host & programmer Classical 90.7, KVNO, Omaha, 1999—. Pvt. voice instr., Omaha, 1999—; singer Omaha Chamber Singers, 2001—02; quartet mem. The Canterbury Singers of the Nebr. Shakespeare Festival, Omaha, 2001—02; numerous concert, stage, and other solo performances. Singer: (voice recital with jimmy emery, piano) I Will Sing New Songs, 2001. Recipient Encouragement award, Met. Opera Guild - Nebr. Dist., 2000, Golden Key / Peat Marwick Outstanding Sr. Scholar award, Golden Key, 1997. Mem.: Am. Choral Directors Assn., Music Educators Nat. Conf., Nebr. Music Educators Assn., Pi Kappa Lambda. Roman Catholic. Avocations: travel, computers. Personal E-mail: lyricbaritone@yahoo.com.

HINDEN, STANLEY JAY, newspaper editor; b. N.Y.C., Jan. 27, 1927; s. Edward I. and Rose (Kroshinsky) H.; m. Sara Leopold, May 24, 1953; children: Alan, Lawrence, Pamela. BA, Syracuse U., 1950. Reporter, polit. editor, editor editl. pages, nat. corr. Washington Newsday, Garden City, NY, 1952-71; exec. editor, editor Nat. Jour., Washington, 1971-73; editl. page features editor, editor Dist., Md. and Va. weekly sects., fin. reporter, columnist Washington Post, 1973-96, fin. writer column Washington Investing. Author: How to Retire Happy, 2001; contbr. polit. column Inside Politics, Newsday, 1955-65, Retirement Jour. column Washington Post, 1996-2003. Served with AUS, 1945-46. Home: Apt 630 3310 N Leisure World Blvd Silver Spring MD 20906-5664 Office: 1150 15th St NW Washington DC 20071-0001 Personal E-mail: stanjh@aol.com.

HINDERAKER, IVAN, retired political science professor; b. Hendricks, Minn., Apr. 29, 1916; s. Theodore and Clara (Hanson) H.; m. Evelyn Birkholz, June 7, 1941 (dec. June 17, 2004); 1 child, Mark (dec. Feb. 23, 2004). BA, St. Olaf Coll., 1938; MA, U. Minn., 1942, PhD, 1949. Mem. faculty UCLA, 1948—, prof. polit. sci., 1956—, chmn. dept., 1960-62; vice chancellor acad. affairs U. Calif.-Irvine, 1962-64; chancellor U. Calif.-Riverside, 1964-79, chancellor emeritus, 1979—; ret., 1979. Mem. Minn. Ho. of Reps., 1941-43; mem. Calif. Transp. Commn., 1978-84, chmn., 1982. Served to 1st lt. USAAF, 1943-46. Home: 19191 Harvard Ave #919 Irvine CA 92612

HINDERLITER, RICHARD GLENN, electrical engineer; b. Tulsa, Apr. 9, 1936; s. Robert Verl and Aileen (Burton) H.; m. Leila Ratzlaff, June 8, 1958; children: Daniel Scott, Susan Paige, Alison Ann, Matthew Glenn. BSEE with honors, U. Kans., 1958; MSEE, NYU, 1960, PhD in Ops. Rsch., 1973. Staff mem. Bell Labs., Murray Hill, NJ, 1958-62; dept. head Bell Labs., Holmdel, NJ, 1962-72, Whippany, NJ, 1972-82; divsn. mgr. AT&T, N.Y.C., 1982-83, Bellcore, Morristown, NJ, 1984-91. Contbr. articles to Internat. Conf. on Communications, Computer Mag., Internat. Symposium on Subscriber Loops, Internat. Teletraffic Conf. Chmn. Zoning Bd. of Adjustment, Chatham Twp., N.J., 1992-99; scoutmaster Boy Scouts Am., Kansas City, Mo., Chatham Twp., Red Bank, N.J., Wichita, Kans., 1956—; v.p. Stonebrooke Estates Howeowners Assn.; treas. Kansas City Northland Art League, 2004—. Recipient Silver Beaver award Morris-Sussex coun. Boy Scouts Am., 1988, Eagle Scout Hall of Fame, 1998, Outstanding Vol. award with spl. recognition Vols. of Morris County; James E. West fellow Boy Scouts Am. Fellow AAAS; mem. IEEE (sr.), N.Y. Acad. Scis., Inst. for Ops. Rsch. and the Mgmt. Scis., Meth. Friday Niters Fellowship Soc. (pres.), Methodist Inquirers Fellowship (pres.), Kiwanis (treas. Chatham, pres. North Kansas City, Mo. chpt., George F. Hixson fellow), Tau Beta Pi, Sigma Tau (v.p.), Theta Tau (vice regent), Eta Kappa Nu (pres.), Alpha Phi Omega, Pi Mu Epsilon, Sigma Pi Sigma. Methodist. Achievements include application of ops. rsch. techniques to large software systems. Personal E-mail: hondolite@prodigy.net.

HINDERS, EILEEN, education educator; b. Chgo., Sept. 3, 1948; d. Frank J. and Mary M. Murphy; m. Eugene T. Hinders, Aug. 21, 1971; children: Daniel, Leanne, John. BA, Siena Coll., Memphis, 1971, MA, U. Memphis, 1982, postgrd. Cert. tchr., Tenn. Secondary sch tchr. various schs., Chgo. and Memphis, 1971-88; editor East Shelby Rev., Arlington, Tenn., 1989-95; prof. Lambuth U., Jackson, Tenn., 1993-98, U. Memphis, 1989-93,98—. Evaluator ETS Testing, 1991—; seminar leader ASCD, 1994; spkr. in field; leader ann. group tour to Europe. Contbr. acad. essays to Tenn. English Jour. Mem. Assn. for Preservation of Tenn. Antiquities (pres. 1998—), Kappa Delta Pi (v.p. 1999—), Omicron Phi Tau.

HINDERY, LEO JOSEPH, JR., former communications executive; b. Springfield, Ill., Oct. 31, 1947; s. Leo Joseph and E. Marie (Whitener) H.; m. Deborah Diane Sale, Feb. 20, 1980; 1 child, Robin Cook. BA, Seattle U., 1969; MBA, Stanford U., 1971. Asst. treas. Utah Internat., San Francisco, 1971-80; treas. Natomas Co., San Francisco, 1980-82; exec. v.p. fin. Jefferies & Co., LA, 1982-83; CFO A.G. Becker Paribas, NYC, 1983-85; chief officer planning and fin. Chronicle Pub. Co., San Francisco, 1985-88; mng. gen. ptnr. InterMedia Ptnrs. (merged with ATT Broadband/Internet Svcs.), San Francisco, 1988-97; pres. Tele-Communications, Inc., 1997—99; pres., CEO

AT&T Broadband and Internet Services, 1999; chmn., CEO GlobalCenter Global Crossing Ltd., 1999—2000, chmn., CEO, 2000, YES Network, 2001—04; supporter John Kerry presdl. campaign, 2004. Bd. dirs. GT Group Telecom Inc., Tanning Tech. Corp., TD Waterhouse Group Inc., VerticalNet, Inc. Mem. adv. coun. Stanford Bus. Sch.; bd. trustees Hampton U.; bd. dirs. Daniels Fund; vice chmn. Mus. of TV and Radio. With U.S. Army, 1968—70. Avocation: golf.

HINDI, RIYADH, engineering educator, researcher; b. Mosul, Nainava, Iraq, Aug. 7, 1966; s. Nafea Hindi and Monera Naoom; m. Luma Kutaimi, Dec. 3, 1975; children: Lourdes S., Noah B. BSc in Civil Engring., U. Baghdad, 1988, MSc in Structural Engring., 1992; PhD in Structures, U. B.C., 2001. Registered profl. engr., Assn. Profl. Engrs. and Geoscientists, B.C. Structural designer Hindi Engring., Victoria, Canada, 1995—97; rsch. asst. U. B.C., Vancouver, 1997—2001; bridge designer McElhanney Engring., Surrey, 1999—2001; asst. prof. Bradley U., Peoria, Ill., 2001—. Faculty advisor Bradley U., Peoria, Ill., 2001—, dir. structural lab., 2001—. Contbr. articles to profl. jours. Recipient Outstanding faculty award, Bradley U., 2004. Mem.: ASCE (assoc.), Earthquake Engring. Rsch. Inst. (assoc.), Am. Concrete Inst. (assoc.), St. Sharbel Ch. (assoc.), St. Vincent de Paul Ch. (assoc.). Roman Catholic. Achievements include patents for Using opposing spirals to confine reinforced concrete members to enhance strength and ductility. Home: 1118 W Pembrook Dr Peoria IL 61614 Office: Bradley U 1501 W Bradley Ave Peoria IL 61625 Office Phone: 309-677-2945. Office Fax: 309-677-2867. Personal E-mail: rhindi@hotmail.com. E-mail: hindi@bradley.edu.

HINDMAN, LARRIE C., lawyer; b. Meservey, Iowa, Mar. 30, 1937; s. Marvin C. and Fredona E. (Lemke) H.; m. Jeannie Carol Richey, June 18, 1961; children: Bryant C., Derek Cory. BS, Iowa State U., 1959; JD, U. Iowa, 1962. Bar: Mo. 1963, Kans. 1975. Ptnr. Stinson Morrison & Hecker LLP, Kansas City, Mo., 1962-2000. Contbr. legal articles to profl. jours. Mem.: Am. Land Title Assn. (lender counsel), Am. Coll. Real Estate Lawyers, Club at Porto Cima. Office: Stinson Morrison & Hecker LLP 1201 Walnut Ste 2800 Kansas City MO 64106-2150 Home: 1186 Grand Cove Rd Sunrise Beach MO 65079 Office Phone: 816-842-8600. Personal E-mail: ljhindman@earthlink.net.

HINDMAN, LESLIE SUSAN, auction company executive; b. Hinsdale, Ill., Dec. 1, 1954; d. Don J. and Patricia (de Forest) H. Student, Pine Manor Coll., 1972-74, U. Paris, 1974-75, Ind. U., 1975-76. Mgr. Sotheby Parke Bernet, Chgo., 1978—82; pres. Leslie Hindman Auctioneers, Chgo., 1982—97, Salvage One Archtl. Artifacts, Chgo., 1986—2002; former co-owner Chgo. Antiques Ctr.; pres. Sotheby's, Chgo., 1997—99; chmn. Leslie Hindman Enterprises, 1999—; founder, pres. Eppraisals.com, 1999—2001, Leslie Hindman Auctioneers, Chgo., 2003—, AntiquesChicago, 2003—. Bd. mem. MB Fin. Bank. Host HGTV's At the Auction and The Appraisal Fair, 1995—2003; author: Adventures at the Auction, 2001; columnist: What's It Worth?, 1999—2003. Bd. mem. Children's Meml. Hosp., The Goodman Theatre, Chgo. Pub. Libr. Found., The Arts Club Chgo. Mem. Com. of 200, Internat. Women's Forum, Young Pres's. Orgn., Arts Club Chgo. Clubs: Women's Athletic (Chgo.) (bd. dirs. 1988—). Office: 122 N Aberdeen Chicago IL 60607

HINDO, WALID AFRAM, radiology educator, researcher; b. Baghdad, Iraq, Oct. 4, 1940; arrived in U.S., 1966, naturalized, 1976; s. Afram Paul and Laila Farid (Meshaka) H.; m. Fawzia Hanna Batti, Apr. 20, 1965; children: Happy, Rana, Patricia, Heather, Brian MB, ChB, Baghdad U., 1964. Diplomate Am. Bd. Radiology. Instr. radiology Rush Med. Coll, Chgo., 1971-72; asst. prof. Northwestern U., Chgo., 1972-75; assoc. prof. medicine and radiology Chgo. Med. Sch., 1975-80, prof., chmn. dept. radiology, 1980-90, prof. dept. radiology, 1990—, dir. radiology rsch. program, 1990-94; cons. UtiliMed, Northbrook, Ill., 1994—96; pres. Northbrook Inst. for Rsch. and Devel., 1992—. Dir. radiology rsch. program VA Med. Ctr., North Chicago, Ill., 1990-94; cons. Ill. Cancer Coun. Contbr. articles on cancer treatment, imaging and managed care to profl. jours. Bd. dirs. Lake County div. Am. Cancer Soc., Ill., 1975-80. Served to lt. M.C., Iraq; Army, 1965-66 Recipient Golden Apple award, The Chgo. Med. Sch., 1994; named Prof. of Yr., Chgo. Med. Sch., 1981, 82, 83, 85, 86. Mem. Radiology Soc. North Am., Am. Soc. Acad. Radiologists. Republican. Roman Catholic. Office: Northbrook Inst for R&D Ste 119 1955 Raymond Dr Northbrook IL 60062-6732 Office Phone: 847-753-9149.

HINDS, C. ROBERT (BOB), retired writer; children: Karen Hinds Foster, Cynthia Hinds Wehmer, Kelly Andrew, Sandra Lynn. BS in Agr., U. Mo., 1953; grad., Reich Sch. Auctionnering, 1958. Field supr. Vets. Agr., Willow Springs, Mo., 1947—51; agr. cons. Export Corp., Japan, Taiwan, Bolivia, Germany, 1972—77. Spkr. in field; bd. dirs. Nat. Hampshire Swine Reg., Peoria, Ill.; pres. Prodrs. Creamery, Cabool, Mo., 1955—57. Author: College the Easy Way, 1998, Ozark Pioneer, 1999, Ozark Laughter, 1999, Train Your Own Stock Dog, 1999, Double Your Church Attendance, 1999, Arthritis, 1999, Computer Short Cuts, 1999, Solving the Mysteries of Dating, 1999, Ozark Attractions, 2000, Ozark Recipes, 2002. Recipient Disting. Svc. resolution, Mo. Stat Legis., 1982. Mem.: Lions Club, Gamma Sigma Delta. Avocations: fishing, hunting. Home: PO Box 100 Willow Springs MO 65793

HINDS, EDWARD DEE, insurance and investment professional, financial planner; b. Madera, Calif., May 13, 1949; s. Edward Dee Jr. and Donna (Parker) H.; m. Olga P. Hinds; children: Sarah, Stephen, Rebekah. Grad., Life Underwriting Tng. Coun., 2002. CLU; ChFC; registered fin. cons.; fellow Life Underwriter Tng. Coun. Sr. acct. agt. Allstate, Lemoore, Calif., 1983—90; gen. agt. various cos. Paso Robles, Calif., 1990—; gen. ptnr. Edward D. Hinds, Ins. and Fortress Fin. Strategies, Paso Robles, 1990—, Edward D. Hinds, Ins., 1995—; founder, gen. ptnr. Fortress Fin. Strategies, A Registered Investment Adviser, 1995—97; founder, gen. mgr. Hinds Fin. Group, LLC, 1998—. Benefits cons. U-Haul Dealers, Ctrl. Calif., 1992—, KOA, Calif., 1997. Mem.: Nat. Assn. Alternative Benefit Cons., Nat. Assn. Health Underwriters, Million Dollar Roundtable, Nat. Assn. Estate Planners and Couns., Nat. Assn. Ins. and Fin. Advisors, Soc. Fin. Profls. Office Phone: 805-239-7443. Business E-Mail: dhinds@hindsfinancial.com.

HINDS, LEONARD DALE, educator; b. Detroit, Mich., Jan. 6, 1966; s. David Lee and Lillian Adriana Hinds; life ptnr. George E. Barker. BA, Univ. Mich., Ann Arbor, Mich., 1989; PhD, Emory Univ., Altanta, Ga., 1995. Vis. asst. prof. Emory Univ., Atlanta, 1996; asst. prof. Ind. Univ., Bloomington, Ind., 1996—2003. Author: Narrative Transformations, 2002. Mem.: Modern Language Assn. (reg. del. 2000—02). Office: Ind Univ 1530 North Harlem Ave #2N River Forest IL 60305-1242 Home: 470 N Austin Blvd #2 Oak Park IL 60302

HINDS, RENE KATHRYN, artist; b. N.Y.C., July 4, 1947; d. Andrew and Maria (Lofaso) Raffa; children: Abby, Khari. BFA cum laude, Fordham U., 1982; postgrad., N.Y. Inst. Tech., 1983-85. Cert. profl. fine artist; lic. massage therapist, N.Y. Cons. Morin Miller Galleries, N.Y.C., 1986-90. Contbg. artist Bklyn. Sch. to Work Partnership, 1996; coord. Westside Arts Coalition, N.Y.C., 1984-86. Visual artist (book) Best of Oil Paintings, 1997, N.Y. Art Review, 1987, (mag.) Women of Power, 1986, Cover Mag., Outlook Mag., Forum Mag., 1993. Mem. NOW, Artist's Equity. Home: 733 Amsterdam Ave New York NY 10025-6330

HINE, ROBERT VAN NORDEN, JR., historian, educator; b. Los Angeles, Apr. 26, 1921; s. Robert Van Norden and Elizabeth (Bates) H.; m. Shirley M. McChord, June 24, 1949; 1 child, Allison. BA, Pomona Coll., 1948; MA, Yale U., 1949, PhD, 1952. From instr. history to prof. emeritus U. Calif., Riverside, 1954—90, prof. emeritus, 1990—, prof. recalled Irvine, 1990—. Author: California's Utopian Colonies, 1953, California's Utopian Colonies, rev. edit., 1983, Edward Kern and American Expansion, 1962, Edward Kern and American Expansion, rev. edit., In the Shadow of Fremont, 1982, Bartlett's West: Drawing the Mexican Boundary, 1968, The American Frontier: Readings and Documents, 1972, The American West: An Interpretive History, 1973; author: (with John Mack Faragher) The American West: A New Interpretive History, 3d edit., 2000 (Wrangler award Cowboy and Western Heritage Mus., Caughey award, Western Hist. Assn.); author: Community on the American Frontier: Separate But Not Alone, 1980, California Utopianism: Contemplations of Eden, 1981; editor: William Andrew Spalding, Los Angeles Newspaperman, 1961, Soldier in the West: Letters of Theodore Talbot, 1972, Josiah Royce: West As Community in Writing Western History, 1991, Josiah Royce: From Grass Valley to Harvard, 1992 (Commonwealth Club award, 1992), Second Sight, 1993 (N.Y. Times Notable Book of 1993); contbr. articles to profl. jours. Recipient Harbison award for disting. teaching Danforth Found., 1968, Wagner Meml. award Calif. Hist. Soc., 1986; Huntington Libr. fellow, 1953, 60, Guggenheim fellow, 1958, 68, Nat. Endowment for Humanities sr. fellow, 1977, Calif. Coun. for Promotion of History award, 1994. Mem.: Western History Assn. (life hon. 1990, Award of Merit 1996), Phi Beta Kappa. Home: 19191 Harvard Ave # 233 Irvine CA 92612-4670 E-mail: rvhine@uci.edu.

HINELINE, CURT ROY, lawyer; b. 1959; BS in Bus. Adminstrn., Univ. Neb., Lincoln, 1982; JD magna cum laude, Univ. Puget Sound, 1986. Bar: Wash. 1986, US Ct. Appeals (9th, 8th cir.) 1988, US Dist. Ct., Oreg. Dist. 1991. Mem. Bogle & Gates PLLC, Seattle; ptnr., trial, regulatory, tech. practice group Dorsey & Whitney LLP, Seattle, 1999—, and co-chair, securities, fin. inst. litig. practice group. Named a Super Lawyer, Wash. Law and Politics, 2003. Mem.: ABA, Wash. State Bar Assn., Oreg. State Bar Assn., Phi Delta Phi. Office: Dorsey & Whitney LLP Ste 3400 US Bank Ctr 1420 Fifth Ave Seattle WA 98101-4010 Office Phone: 206-903-8853. Office Fax: 206-903-8820. Business E-Mail: hineline.curt@dorsey.com.

HINERFELD, NORMAN MARTIN, manufacturing executive; b. N.Y.C., May 17, 1929; s. Benjamin B. and Anne (Blitz) H.; m. Ruth Jean Gordon, Dec. 25, 1952; children— Lee Ann, Thomas Benjamin, Joshua Gordon. AB, Harvard U., 1951, MBA, 1953. Security underwriter, underwriting dept. Goldman Sachs & Co., 1953; asst. to pres. Julius Kayser & Co., 1955-56, Catalina, Inc., 1956-57, v.p. mfg., 1957-64, sr. v.p., 1964-67; v.p. Kayser-Roth Corp., 1967—74, exec. v.p., 1967-74, mem. exec. com., 1972—85, pres., COO, 1974-76, dir., 1958-85, chmn. exec. com., 1976-85; chmn., CEO Wingspread Corp., 1985—88; chmn. Pandora Industries, Inc., N.Y.C., 1988—, Tica Industries, Inc., N.Y.C., 1990—; chmn., CEO The Delta Group, 1993—; cons. to non-profit orgns., 2004—. Sec.-treas. Thermacon Industries Inc., New Hyde Park, N.Y., 1989—2003; chmn. Care Anyware LLC, 1999—; bd. dirs. Supermarkets Gen. Corp.; chmn. coun. Ctr. for Study Democratic Instns.; mem. U.S.A.-BIAC to OECD, 1978—; mem. exec. com. Dist. Export-Coun. U.S. Dept. Commerce, 1978—; mem. adv. coun. on Japan-U.S. Econ. Rels., 1980—; adjucator Mass Tort Life Ins. Settlement, 1999-2001. Author: (with D. Moross) Automation-Challenge to Management, 1953; patentee self-programmed automatic machinery. Bd. overseers NYU Sch. Bus., 1984-88; chmn. Metro N.Y.-Bus. Execs. for Nat. Security, 1990—, mem. exec. com., 1992—; chmn. fin. com. Animal Med. Ctr., N.Y.C., 1999—. lst lt. U.S. Army, 1953-55. Mem. Am. Arbitration Assn. (chmn. bd. 1984-90, exec. com., bd. dirs. 1969—), Am. Apparel Mfrs. Assn. (bd. dirs., past pres., mem. exec. com.), Internat. Apparel Fedn. (past pres.), Nat. Knitted Sportswear Assn. (exec. com., bd. dirs.), U.S. C. of C. (chmn. export policy com. 1979-89). Home: 11 Oak Ln Larchmont NY 10538-3917 Office: Reelan Industries LLC 623 Stewart Ave Ste 201 Garden City NY 11530 Personal E-mail: Norcomp@aol.com.

HINERFELD, ROBERT ELLIOT, lawyer; b. N.Y.C., May 29, 1934; s. Benjamin B. and Anne (Blitz) H.; m. Susan Hope Slocum, June 27, 1957; children: Daniel Slocum, Matthew Ben. AB, Harvard U., 1956, JD, 1959. Bar: Calif. 1960. Asst. U.S. atty So. Dist. Calif., 1960-62; assoc. Leonard Horwin, Beverly Hills, Calif., 1962-66; mem. Simon, Sheridan, Murphy, Thornton & Hinerfeld, L.A., 1967-74, Murphy, Thornton, Hinerfeld & Cahill, 1975-83, Murphy, Thornton, Hinerfeld & Elson, 1983-85, Manatt, Phelps & Phillips LLP, 1985-2000, sr. of counsel, 2000—05, solo practitioner as arbitrator and expert witness, 2005—; arbitrator bus. panel L.A. Superior Ct., 1979-82; assoc. ind. counsel (diGenova), 1993-95. Judge pro tempore Beverly Hills Mcpl. Ct., 1967-74; clin. lectr. U. So. Calif. Law Ctr., 1980-81, guest lectr., 1993-96; expert witness, 1988—, legal affairs on-air guest spkr. sta. KCRW-FM, Santa Monica, Calif., 1998-99. Contbr. articles to profl. jours. Trustee Westland Sch., L.A., 1970—75, Pacific Hills Sch., 1971—72. Fellow: Am. Bar Found. (life); mem.: ABA, Calif. Acad. Appellate Lawyers (membership com. 1983—88, 2d v.p. 1985—87, 1st v.p. 1987—88, pres. 1988—89), Am. Arbitration Assn. (arbitrator comml. panel 1966—, mem. large complex case panel 2003—), State Bar Calif. (mem. disciplinary investigation panel dist. 7 1977—80, hearing referee State Bar Ct. 1981—83, exec. com. litig. sect. 1983—85, referee rev. dept. 1984—87, civil litig. adv. group 1985—88, mem. Jud. Nominees Evaluation Commn. 2000—04, mem. com. on criminal law and procedure, chmn. spl. com. revision fed. criminal code), L.A. County Bar Assn. (spl. com. jud. evaluation 1978—82, arbitration com. 1981—83, spl. com. on appellate elections evaluation 1996—2000, settlement officer 2d appellate dist. appellate case project 1996—2005), Ctr. for Profl. Responsibility, Assn. Profl. Responsibility Lawyers, Harvard Club N.Y.C., Harvard Club So. Calif. (dir. 1974—83, sec. 1978—80, mem. prize book com. 1992—94). Home and Office: 371 24th St Santa Monica CA 90402-2517 Office Phone: 310-394-4902. Personal E-mail: rhinerfeld@mac.com.

HINERFELD, RUTH G., civic organization executive; b. Boston, Sept. 18, 1930; m. Norman Hinerfeld, children: Lee, Thomas, Joshua. AB, Vassar Coll., 1951; grad. Program in Bus. Adminstrn., Harvard-Radcliffe Coll., 1952. With LWV, 1954—, UN observer, 1969-72, chairperson internat. rels. com., 1972-76, 1st v.p. in charge legis. activities, 1976-78, pres., 1978-82. Dir. LWV Overseas Edn. Fund, 1975-76, trustee, 1975-86; chair LWV Edn. Fund, 1978-82; mem. White House Adv. Com. Trade Negotiations, 1975-82; sec. UN Assn. US, 1975-78, bd. govs., 1975—, vice chmn., 1983—, mem. econ. policy coun., 1976-93; bd. dirs. Overseas Devel. Coun. 1974-00; trustee, vice chair Inst. of Internat. Edn., 1997—; mem. U.S. del. auspices of Nat. Com. on U.S.-China Rels. and Chinese People's Inst. Fgn. Affairs, 1978. Mem. coun. Nat. Mcpl. League, 1977-80, 83-86; del.-at-large Internat. Women's Yr. Conf., Houston, 1977; mem. exec. com. Leadership Conf. on Civil Rights, 1978-82; trustee Citizens Rsch. Found., 1978-2000; mem. Nat. Petroleum Coun., 1979-82; mem. U.S. del. to World Conf. on UN Decade for Women, 1980; mem. adv. com. Nat. Inst. for Citizen Edn. in the Law, 1981-91; mem. North South Roundtable, 1978-88; mem. nat. gov. bd. Common Cause, 1984-90; vice chmn. U.S. com. UNICEF, 1986-90, treas., 1990-91; mem. vis. com. Harvard U. Bus. Sch., 1984-90; bd. dirs. Com. for Modern Cts., 1993-96. Recipient Disting. Citizen award Nat. Mcpl. League, 1978; Outstanding Mother award Nat. Mother's Day Com., 1981; Aspen Inst. Presdl. fellow, 1981. Mem. Coun. on Fgn. Rels., Phi Beta Kappa. Office: 11 Oak Ln Larchmont NY 10538-3917

HINES, ALIDA N., marketing professional, researcher; d. Roosevelt Delano Hines and Verdell Lett Dawson. Student, Duke U., 1994—95; BA magna cum laude in Econs., Spelman Coll., 1998; MA with hons. in Mktg. Rsch., U. of Ga., 2000. Bus. rsch. intern Eastman Kodak Co., Atlanta, 2000, bus. rsch. analyst, 2001—03; market rsch. analyst The Home Depot, Atlanta, 2003—. Tutor Mt. Olivet Bapt. Ch., Rochester, NY, 2001—02; mentor Big Brothers Big Sisters, Atlanta, 2003—. Recipient, Nat. Merit Scholarship Corp., 1994; scholar, Armstrong World Industries, 1994, Motorola, 1997, UNCF scholarship, Quaker Oats Co., 1997, Coca-Cola Found., 1999—2000. Mem.: Nat. Assn. Female Execs. Office: The Home Depot 2455 Paces Ferry RD Atlanta GA 30329 E-mail: alida_hines@homedepot.com.

HINES, ANDREW HAMPTON, JR., utilities executive; b. Lake City, Fla., Jan. 28, 1923; s. Andrew Hampton and Louise Dixie (Howland) H.; m. Ann Groover, June 28, 1947' children: Andrew Hampton III, Elizabeth Renee, John Bradford, Daniel Howland. BME with high honors, U. Fla., 1947; degree (hon.), Stetson U., 1987, U. South Fla., 1989, Rollins Coll., 1989, Fla. So. Coll., 1994. Registered profl. engr., Fla. With R&D depts. GE, 1947-51; pres. Fla. Power Corp., 1972-82; chmn. bd. Fla. Progress Corp., St. Petersburg, 1982-91, Precise Power Corp., Bradenton, Fla., 1990-97. Cons. Triangle Cons. Group; past chmn. N.Am. Electric Reliability Coun.; exec.-in-residence Eckerd Coll., 1990-2001. Trustee Asbury Theol. Sem.; bd. dirs. U. Fla. Found., Sunday sch. tchr. Christian Missionary Alliance Ch.; chmn. Pinellas County Cmty. Reuse Orgn., 1994-97; chmn. No Casinos in Fla., Inc., 1994-1998. 2d lt. USAAF, 1943-45. Decorated Air medal, Prisoner of War medal. Fellow ASME; mem. U.S. Energy Assn., Blue Key, St. Petersburg Yacht Club, Sigma Tau, Phi Kappa Phi, Tau Beta Pi, Beta Gamma Sigma. Office Phone: 727-864-9656. Personal E-mail: ahh@tampabay.rr.com. *You cannot out give God. If you cast your bread upon the waters it will come back buttered.*

HINES, ANGUS IRVING, JR., petroleum marketing executive; b. Suffolk, Va., Aug. 7, 1923; s. Angus Irving and Lois E. (Howell) H.; m. Genevieve Hopkins McCollum, Nov. 24, 1949 (div. 1977); children: Ann Russell Hines Mauer, Marilyn N. Hines Stulb, A. McCollum, Angus Irving III. Pres. Angus I. Hines, Inc., Suffolk, 1945—; Angus Hines, Inc., Svc. Gas Co., Inc. Served with U.S. Maritime Service, 1943-45; ETO. Mem. Va. Petroleum Jobbers Assn. (past pres.), Rotary (past pres.), Quiet Birdmen. Methodist. Office: Angus I Hines Inc PO Box 1080 1426 Holland Rd Suffolk VA 23439-1080 Office Phone: 757-539-2358. E-mail: angushines@aol.com.

HINES, CHERYL, actress; b. Miami Beach, Sept. 21, 1965; m. Paul Young, Dec. 30, 2002; 1 child, Catherine Rose. BA in radio and TV, U. Cent. Fla. Mem. The Groundlings Theater, star Cheryl Hines' One Woman Show; actor: (TV series) Curb Your Enthusiasm, 2000— (Emmy nomination best supporting actress, 2003), (voice) Father of the Pride, 2003,: (TV films) Double Bill, 2003; (films) Cheap Curry and Calculus, 1996, Along Came Polly, 2004, Our Very Own, 2005, Lucky 13, 2005, Herbie: Fully Loaded, 2005, (guest appearances): (TV series) Unsolved Mysteries, 1997, Suddenly Susan, 1998, Wayans Brothers, 1998, Friends, 2000, Everybody Loves Raymond, 2002, Reno 911, 2003. Office: Internat Creative Mgt 8942 Wilshire Blvd Beverly Hills CA 90211-1934 Office Phone: 310-550-4000.*

HINES, EDWARD FRANCIS, JR., lawyer; b. Norfolk, Va., Sept. 5, 1945; m. Elaine Geneva Carroll, Aug. 21, 1971; children: Jonathan Edward, Carolyn Adele. AB, Boston Coll., 1966; JD, Harvard U., 1969. Bar: Mass. 1969. Assoc. Choate Hall & Stewart, Boston, 1969-77, ptnr., 1977-2001, mng. ptnr., 1983—87; ptnr. Hines & Corley LLC, Lexington, Mass., 2001—. Bd. dirs. Boston Med. Ctr., Boston Med. Ctr. Ins. Co., Cayman Islands, Chase Corp., Investors Fin. Svcs. Corp.; trustee Merrimac Fund Complex, 1996—2003. Trustee, treas. World Heart Fedn., Geneva, 2003—; trustee Social Law Libr., 1993—98; bd. dirs. Cath. Charities, 2002—, Assoc. Industries Mass., 1990—, chmn., 1996—98; bd. dirs. Am. Heart Assn., Dallas, 1984—86, 1991—2000, chmn., 1998—99; bd. dirs. Mass. Taxpayers Found., 1987—93, Carroll Ctr. for the Blind, 1983—89, 1990—96, chmn., 1994—96. With USAR, 1969—75. Recipient Boston Coll. H.S. St. Ignatius award, 1998, Gold Heart award, Am. Heart Assn., 2003. Fellow: Am. Coll. Trust and Estate Counsel; mem.: Mass. CLE (pres. 1985—87), Accion Internat. (bd. dirs. 1999—2005), Supreme Jud. Ct. Hist. Soc. (trustee 1989—96), Am. Coll. Greece (Athens bd. dirs., vice chmn. 1988—97), Boston Bar Found. (pres. 1995—97), Boston Bar Assn. (pres. 1988—89), Allen Harbor Yacht Club, Boston Coll. Club, North Andover Country Club. Office: Hines & Corley LLC Ste 3200 55 Hayden Ave Lexington MA 02421 Business E-Mail: efh@hinesandcorley.com.

HINES, EMME LARRAINE, director; b. Spartanburg, S.C., Jan. 10, 1977; d. Larry Curtis and Linda Haneline Hines. BA Instrumental Music Edn., Converse Coll., Spartanburg, S.C., 1999. Cert. Music Edn. SC., Ga., 2003. Band dir. Thomson H.S., Thomson, Ga., 2002—, Hartsville Jr. H.S., Hartsville, SC, 1999—2002. Oboist Savannah River Winds, Augusta, Ga., 2002—05; pvt. instr., Thomson, Ga., 2002—. Home: 430 Johns Road Thomson GA 30824 Office: Thomson HS 1160 Whiteoak Rd Thomson GA 30824 Office Phone: 706-597-2520 4334. Personal E-mail: elhrr@comcast.net. Business E-Mail: hinese@mcduffie.k12.ga.us.

HINES, GERALD D., architectural firm executive; BSME, Purdue U., 1948, D of Engring. (hon.), 1983. Chmn. Fed. Res. Bank Dallas; co-owner, CEO, founder, chmn., mem. exec. com. Hines Leadership. Prin. works include Galleria shopping, office and hotel complex, Dallas, Pennzoil Place, Houston, 101 California St., San Francisco, Columbia Square, Washington, Norwest Ctr., Mpls. U. Houston's Coll. Arch. renamed in his honor Office: Gerald D Hines Interests 2800 Post Oak Blvd Houston TX 77056-6100

HINES, JOHN MADISON, educational association administrator; b. Lancaster, Pa., Dec. 12, 1958; s. Emmett Womack and Blanche Hines; m. Lynn Ann Follen; children: Kelly Ann, Matthew James. BA, Western Md. Coll., 1981; MBA, George Wash. U., 1983. Exec. dir. Congl. Youth Leadership Coun., Washington, 1987—96; CEO Envision EMI, LLC, Washington, 1996—. Mem. Sandy Spring (Md.) Friends Sch., 2002—. Home: PO Box 125 WW Sandy Spring MD 20860-0125 Office: Envision EMI LLC Ste 300 1110 Vermont Ave Washington DC 20005 Office Phone: 202-777-4011. Home Fax: 202-318-2402; Office Fax: 202-318-2402. Personal E-mail: john@thehinesfamily.com. E-mail: jhines@envisionemi.com.

HINES, MARSHALL, construction engineering company executive; b. Chgo., Dec. 29, 1923; s. Herbert Waldo and Helen (Gartside) H.; m. Janet Young, July 28, 1945; children: Karen Lynn, Keith Douglas, Dori Hines Alton. BCE, Mich. State U., 1947, MCE, 1948. Registered profl. engr., Mich. Project engr. The Christman Co., Lansing, Mich., 1948-55, supt., 1955-70, gen. supt., 1971-83, exec. v.p., 1983—96, ret. cons., 1996—. With U.S. Army, 1943-45. Mem. NSPE, Mich. Soc. Profl. Engrs. (bd. dirs. 1986, Constrn. Engr. Yr. 1990, Engr. of Yr. award 1994), Builders Exch. of Lansing (pres. 1988), Rotary (bd. dirs. Lansing club 1986-87). Republican. Methodist. Home: 1137 Rebecca Rd East Lansing MI 48823-5210 Office: The Christman Co 408 Kalamazoo Plz Lansing MI 48933-1990

HINES, N. WILLIAM, law educator, dean; b. 1936; AB, Baker U., 1958; LLB, U. Kans., 1961; LLD, Baker U., 1999. Bar: Kans. 1961, Iowa 1965. Law clk. U.S. Ct. Appeals 10th cir., 1961-62; tchg. fellow Harvard U., 1961-62; asst. prof. law U. Iowa, 1962-65, assoc. prof., 1965-67, prof., 1967-73, J.F. Rosenfield disting. prof., 1973—, dean, 1976—2004, dean emeritus, Joseph F. Rosenfield Prof., 2004—. Vis. prof. Stanford U., 1974—75. Editor (notes and comments): Kans. Law Rev. Founder, pres. Johnson County Heritage Trust. Fellow, Harvard U., 1961—62. Fellow: Iowa State Bar Found., ABA Found.; mem.: Assn. Am. Law Schs. (exec. com. 2004—, pres. 2005), Environ. Law Inst. (assoc.), Order of Coif. Office: U Iowa Coll Law Iowa City IA 52242-0001 Office Phone: 319-335-9236. Business E-Mail: n-hines@uiowa.edu.

HINES, PRESTON HARRIS, state supreme court justice; b. Atlanta, Sept. 6, 1943; s. James Reuben and Edith (Hawkins) Hines; m. Helen Holmes Hill; children: Mary Margaret, James Harris. AB in Polit. Sci., Emory U., 1965, JD, 1968. Bar: Ga. 1968, U.S. Dist. Ct. Ga. 1973. Law clk. Civil Ct. Fulton County, 1968-69; pvt. practice Marietta, Ga., 1969-74; judge State Ct. of Cobb County, 1974-82, Superior Ct. of Ga., 1982—95; justice Ga. Supreme Ct., 1995—. Chmn. attys. divsn. Cobb County United Appeal, 1972; participant Leadership Ga., 1975, Leadership Atlanta, 1978-79; pres. YMCA Cobb County, 1976; co-treas. Cobb Landmarks Soc., 1976-77; former bd. dirs. Cobb County Emergency Aid Assn., Cobb-Marietta Girls Club, Ga. chpt. Leukemia Soc. Am., Cobb County Children's Ctr., Met. Atlanta Red Cross, First Presbyn. Day Kindergarten; mem. cmty. adv. com. Marietta-Cobb County LWV; bd. dirs. Kennesaw Coll. Found.; trustee Cobb Cmty. Symphony. Named Outstanding Young Man of Yr., Ga. Jaycees, 1975, Boss of Yr., Cobb County Legal Secs. Assn., 1975-76, 83-84. Mem. ABA, State Bar Ga. (chmn. Law Day com. 1975, mem. exec. com. younger lawyers sec. 1974-76), Cobb Jud. Cir. (sec. 1972-73, chmn. Law Day com. 1972), Joseph Henry Lumpkin Inn of Ct. Ga., Atlanta Lawyers Club, Kiwanis (bd. dirs. Marietta chpt., chmn. Key Club com., past chmn. spiritual aims com., past pres.), Cobb County C. of C., Sigma Alpha Epsilon (Atlanta and Marietta chpts.). Office: Supreme Court 244 Washington St Atlanta GA 30334*

HINES, THOMAS SPIGHT, historian, educator, architecture critic; b. Oxford, Miss., Oct. 28, 1936; s. Thomas S. and Polly M. Hines; children: Tracy Odessa, Taylor Spight. BA, U. Miss., 1958; PhD, U. Wis., 1971. Prof. history and architecture UCLA, 1968—; Ruth Carter Stevenson prof. U. Tex., 2003—04. Vis. prof. Sch. Architecture and Am. studies program U. Tex., Austin, 1974-75, Ruth Carter Stevenson chair, 2003-04; Fulbright prof. Am. studies U. Exeter, Eng., 1984-85; vis. prof. Sch. Arch. Columbia U., 2004. Author: Burnham of Chicago: Architect and Planner, 1974, Richard Neutra and the Search for Modern Architecture: A Biography and History, 1982, The Architecture of Richard Neutra: From International Style to California Modern, 1982, William Faulkner and the Tangible Past: The Architecture of Yoknapatawpha, 1996, Irving Gill and the Architecture of Reform, 2000; hist. advisor, co-author film Frank Lloyd Wright, 1985; hist. advisor Robert Moses: Urban Planner for WGBH, 1988; contbr. chpts. to books, articles to profl. jours. 1st lt. U.S. Army, 1960—63. Recipient John H. Dunning prize Am. Hist. Assn., 1976; NEH fellow, 1978-79; Fulbright fellow, 1984-85; Guggenheim fellow, 1987-88; Getty scholar, 1996-97. Mem.: Am. Acad. Arts and Scis. Democrat. Episcopalian. Office: UCLA Dept Architecture Perloff Hall 405 Hilgard Ave Los Angeles CA 90095-9000

HINES, WALTER JAMES, stock exchange executive; b. Providence, Nov. 14, 1947; s. Walter Joseph and Marguerite Ann (Adams) H.; m. Karen Janice Ness, June 27, 1970. BA in Modern Langs., Providence Coll., 1969. With GE, Plainville, Conn., 1973-77; contr. GE Precision Protective Devices Inc., Palmer, 1977-79, GE Midwest Electric Products Inc., Makato, Minn., 1979-83; corp. contr. Modular Computer Systems Inc., Ft. Lauderdale, Fla., 1983-87; corp. v.p. fin. and adminstrn. AEG Corp., Somerville, N.J., 1987-88; sr. v.p. fin. and adminstrn. Coffee, Sugar and Cocoa Exch. Inc., N.Y.C., 1989; sr. v.p., CFO New York Bd. Trade. CFO NY Exchs. Hdqrs. Project, NYC, 1991; treas. Commodities Exch. Ctr., NYC, 1992. 1st lt. U.S. Army, 1969-72. Avocations: running, landscaping. Office: NY Bd Trade One North End Ave 13th Fl New York NY 10282

HINES, WILLIAM EUGENE, banker; b. N.Y.C., July 5, 1914; s. William J. and Alice M. (Callahan) H.; m. Dorothy H. Moore, June 4, 1949; children: Alice M., Dorothy H., Margaret M., William J., Elizabeth A., Robert J. Student, Columbia U.; grad., Rutgers U. Grad. Sch. Banking, 1948. With Bankers Trust Co., N.Y.C., 1950—, asst. v.p., 1958-63, v.p., 1963—. Instr. Am. Inst. Banking, 1948—64, Am. Youth Hostels, 1954—65, former chmn., now dir. Chmn. planning bd. Village of Quogue, N.Y., 1991-2003, mem. bd. trustees, 2005—; trustee Quogue Libr., 1993-2000, pres. 1994-96, treas., 2001—. Mem. N.Y. Soc. Security Analysts, Accts. Club N.Y.C., Nat. Assn. Mental Health (nat. treas., dir. 1966, nat. trustee, adminstrv. com.), Quogue Assn. (pres. 1994-96, trustee 1992-2000), Shinnecock Yacht Club (commodore 1974-76, treas. 1980-94). Office: PO Box 5035 21 Quaquanantuck Ln Quogue NY 11959

HINES-MARTIN, VICKI PATRICIA, nursing educator, researcher; b. Louisville, Aug. 18, 1951; d. William Adolphus Hines and Mary Iris Bailey; m. Kenneth Wayne Martin, Dec. 30, 1978; 1 child, Michelle Hines Martin. BSN, Spalding Coll., 1975; MA in Edn., Spalding U., 1983; MSN, U. Cin., 1986; PhD, U. Ky., 1994. Cert. clin. specialist in adult psychiat. mental. Staff nurse Norton Hosp., Louisville, 1978-81; instr. critical care Sts. Mary & Elizabeth Hosp., Louisville, 1981-82; asst. chief nursing svcs. VA Med. Ctr., Cin., 1983-85; nursing instr. Jefferson Community Coll., Louisville, 1985-87; head nurse mgr. VA Med. Ctr., Louisville, 1987-88; asst. prof. nursing Ind. U. S.E., New Albany, 1989-95, U. Ky., Lexington, 1995-98; assoc. prof. U. Louisville, 1998—. Bd. dirs. Seven Counties Mental Health Svcs., 1995-2000; mem. steering com. on practice parameters Ky. Health Policy Bd., 1996. Contbr. articles to profl. jours. Chmn. bd. dirs. West Louisville Area Health Edn. Ctr., 1997-2000; mem. African-Am. Health Edn. Leadership Program com. Jefferson County Health Dept., 1997-98, African-Am. Health Initiative, African-Am. Strategic Planning Group, 1998-2000; bd. dirs. Ky. Nurses Found., 1998-2001. Nurses scholar/fellow, Lucy Zimmerman scholar, 1982, Estelle Massey Osborne Meml. scholar, 1983-84, trainee U. Cin., 1983, grad. scholar, 1983; named to Outstanding Young Women of Am., 1986; Elizabeth Carnagie scholar, 1991, Am. Nurses Found. scholar, 1992; U. Ky. fellow, 1988, grad. fellow, 1992; recipient Rsch. award Ky. Nurses Found., 1992, Nursing Excellence award Jefferson County Ky., 1995, Psychiat. Mental Health Nurse of Yr., Ky. Nurses Assn., 1995, Rsch. in Minority Health award So. Nursing Rsch. Soc., 1999, Emerging Nursing Star Health Disparities Rsch. award Howard U. Sch. Nursing, 2004, Nurse of Yr. in Rsch., Kynna Black Nurses of Ky., 2005; ANA Ethnic Minority postdoctoral fellow in health policy, 1996; Louisville Courier Jour. Forum fellow, 1997; fellow U. Pa. Health Disparities Rsch. Inst., 2005 Mem.: ANA (minority clin. fellow 1991—93, ethnic racial minority fellow 1997), Internat. Soc. Psychiat. Nurses (mem. rsch. coun., chair diversity task force, divsn. dir.), So. Nurses Rsch. Soc., Nat. Black Nurses Assn., Kyanna Black Nurses Inc. (co-founder, past pres.), Ky. Nurses Assn. (mental health coun. sec. 1986—88, editl. bd. 1994—97), Am. Psychiat. Nurses Assn. (chair coun. African Am. nurses 2000—02), Sigma Theta Tau. Office: Univ Louisville 3038 Bldg K 555 S Floyd St Louisville KY 40202-3801 Office Phone: 502-852-8515. Business E-Mail: vphine01@louisville.edu.

HING, BARBARA LIM, elementary school educator, assistant principal, data processing executive; b. Jan. 06; arrived in U.S., 1973; d. Amado K. H. and Bee-chu Tan Lim; m. Y. Ray Hing, Oct. 11, 1975; children: Abigail Hing Wen, Byron Lim, Colleen Lim. BA, Maryknoll Coll., Quezon City, The Philippines, 1971; MA, Ea. Mich. U., 1975; prin. cert., Cleve. State U., 1994. Cert. tchr. Ohio, Ill., adminstr. Ohio, Ill. Inst. St. Claire Coll., Windsor, Canada, 1975; substitute tchr. Shawnee Local Schs., Lima, Ohio, 1980-84, Solon (Ohio) City Schs., 1984-86; tchr. Cleve. Pub. Schs., 1986-95, title I tchr., 1995—2000; asst. prin. Buhrer Elem. Sch., Cleve., 2000—02, data mgr., 2003—04. Contbr. strategic planning com. Solon Schs., 1989—91; chairperson Fundraising Com., Cleve., 1995—98, Attendance Com., Cleve., 1995—. Author: (book) Joy the Spider, 1975; writer, editor, pub.: Harvey Rice Attendance Newsletter, 1996—99, Harvey Rice Newsletter, 1999—2000. Mem., supporter Heritage Found., Washington, 1991—, Cmty. Action Team, 1993—94, Concord Coalition, Washington, 1996; chairperson scholarship com. Solon Acad. Boosters Club, 1995—97; sustaining mem. Rep. Nat. Com., Washington, 1994—. Named Outstanding Leader, Health Den, Mentor, Ohio, 1999; recipient Outstanding award, Charities of Choice, Cleve., 1995—97. Mem.: Orgn. Chinese Ams. Greater Cleve. (supporter, v.p. 1998—2003, bd. dirs. 1999—, Outstanding Citizen award 1999, 2002), Chinese Women Assn. Cleve. (founder, treas. 1999—2001, pres. 2005—). Personal E-mail: chiuma@sbcglobal.net.

HINGLE, PAT, actor; b. Miami, Fla., July 19, 1924; s. Clarence M. and Marvin (Patterson) H.; m. Julia Wright, Oct. 25, 1979; children— Jody, Billy, Molly. BFA, U. Tex., 1949; PhD (hon.), Otterbein Coll., 1974. Numerous acting roles on stage, screen and TV, including End as a Man, 1953, On the Waterfront, 1953, The Long Grey Line, 1954, Festival, 1954, Cat on a Hot Tin Roof, 1955, 83, 93, Girls of Summer, 1956, The Strange One, 1956, Dark at the Top of the Stairs, 1957, No Down Pavement, 1957, J.B., 1958, The Deadly Game, 1960, Macbeth, 1961, Troilus and Cressida, 1961, Strange Interlude, 1963, Blues for Mr. Charlie, 1964, A Girl Could Get Lucky, 1964, Invitation to a Gunfighter, 1964, The Glass Menagerie, 1965, The Odd Couple, 1966, Nevada Smith, 1966, Johnny No-Trump, 1967, Hang 'Em High, 1968, The Price, 1968, Bloody Mama, 1969, Child's Play, 1970, Norwood, 1970, Wusa, 1970, The Selling of the President, 1972, That Championship Season, 1973, Super Cops, 1973, Hazel's People, 1973, Running Wild, 1973, The Lady from the Sea, 1976, Independence, 1976, The Gauntlet, 1977, Norma Rae, 1979, When You Comin' Back, Red Ryder, 1979, Thomas A. Edison, Reflections of a Genius, 1978, A Life, 1980, Running Brave, 1982, Sudden Impact, 1983, Falcon and the Snowman, 1984, Brewster's Millions, 1985, Blue Skies, 1988, Rescue of Jessica McClure, 1989, Batman, 1989, The Kennedys of Massachusetts, 1989, The Grifters, 1990, Moon for the Misbegotten, 1990, The Habitation of Dragons, 1991, Gunsmoke III, 1991, Batman Returns, 1992, Citizen Cohn, 1992, Simple Justice, 1992, Will and Bart Show, 1992, Cheers, 1993, In the Heat of the Night, 1993, Lightnin' Jack, 1994, The Quick and the Dead, 1994, Friendly Suit, 1994, One Christmas, 1994, Batman Forever, 1995, Truman, 1995, Wings, 1996, Larger Than Life, 1996, Bastard Out of Carolina, 1996, A Thousand Acres, 1996, Batman and Robin, 1997, The Shining, 1997, 1776, 1997-98, Touched By an Angel, 1999, Morning, 2000, The Angel Doll, 2000, Road to Redemption, 2000, The Runaway, 2000, Our Town, 2002, Goodbye to Eddie Hart, 2003; command performances at White House, 1965, Libr. of Congress, 1984. Served with USNR, 1942-46, 51-52.

HINGORANI, ANIL PRIBHU, surgeon; b. Rome, N.Y., Sept. 20, 1967; s. Pribhu Gopaldas and Savitri Hingorani; m. Renu Anil Karamchardani-Hingorani, Dec. 16, 1968; children: Amrit, Aarthi Hangorani. BS, Rensselaer Polytech. Inst., 1986; MD, Albany Med. Coll., 1990. Intern, resident St. Lukes Roosevelt Hosp. Ctr.; vascular surgeon Maimondes Med. Ctr., Bklyn., 1998—. Office: Maimondes Med Ctr Divsn Vascular Surgery 4802 10th Ave Brooklyn NY 11219

HINGSON, RALPH W., medical educator; b. July 21, 1948; BA in Internat. Rels., Johns Hopkins U., 1969, ScD, 1974; MPH, U. Pitts., 1970. Prof. dept. social behavior sci. Boston U. Sch. Pub. Health, 1986—; dir. divsn prevention and epidemiology Nat. Inst. on Alcohol Abuse and Alcoholism. Cons., Nat. Ctr. for Substance Abuse Prevention, Nat. Trans. Rsch. Bd., others; nat. bd. advs. MADD,; former v.p. Pub. Policy; pres.-elect Internat. Coun. Alcohol Drugs and Traffic Safety. Contbr. numerous articles to profl. jours. Named one of America's 10 Outstanding Young Men, U.S. Jaycees, 1984; recipient Hero award, MADD, 1995, Innovators Combating Substance Abuse award, Robert Wood Johnson Found., 2001, Widmark award, Internat. Coun. Alcohol Drugs and Traffic Safety, 2002, Ralph W. Hingson Rsch. in Practice Presdl. award, MADD, 2003. Home: 4 Louisburg Sq Boston MA 02108-1203 Office: Boston U Sch Medicine Sch Pub Health 715 Albany St Boston MA 02118-2526 Office Phone: 301-443-1274. Business E-Mail: rhingson@mail.nih.gov.

HINICH, MELVIN JAY, government and economics educator; b. Pitts., Apr. 29, 1939; s. Joseph and Sara (Rubinstein) Hinich; m. Sonje Gregg, Sept. 14, 1966; 1 child, Amy Sara. BS, Carnegie Inst. Tech., 1959, MS in Math, 1960; PhD in Statistics, Stanford, 1963. Asst. prof. indsl. adminstrn. Carnegie Inst. Tech., 1963-68; assoc. prof. indsl. adminstrn., statistics, 1968-70; prof. statistics, polit. economy Carnegie Mellon U., 1970-73; prof. econs. dept. Va. Poly. Inst. and State U., Blacksburg, 1973-82; prof. govt. and econs. U. Tex., Austin, 1982—, Frank Erwin prof. govt., 1984-86, Mike Hogg prof. govt. and econs., 1986—, with Applied Rsch. Labs., 1985—. Fairchild disting. scholar Calif. Inst. Tech. Inc., Pasadena, 1975-76; cons. Teledyne-Isotopes, Inc., Internat. Research & Tech., Inc., FDA, Air Pollution Control-Allegheny County Health Dept., U.S. Naval Coastal Systems Center, Tracor Applied Scis., Inst. Macroeconomics, Fed. Res. Bank of Mpls.; cons. task force on regulatory reform U.S. Senate Govt. Ops. Com., NATO Saclant Research Ctr., La Spezia, Italy, devel. program UN. Author: Introduction to Continuous Probability, 1969, Consumer Protection Legislation and the U.S. Food Industry, 1980, The Spatial Theory of Voting: An Introduction, 1984, Advances in the Spatial Theory of Voting, 1990, Political Economy: Institutions, Competition and Representation, 1993, Ideology and the Theory of Political Choice, 1994, Analytical Politics, 1997, Empirical Studies in Comparative Politics, 1998; assoc. editor: Macroeconomic Dynamics; contbr. articles to profl. jours. Fellow: Am. Statis. Assn., Pub. Choice Soc. (pres. 1992—94), Inst. Math. Stats.; mem.: Sigma Xi. Home: 3902 Cresthill Dr Austin TX 78731-3808 Office: U Tex Burdine Hall Austin TX 78712-1087 Office Phone: 512-232-7270. E-mail: hinich@mail.la.utexas.edu.

HINIKER, LUANN, management consultant, educator, researcher, grants consultant; b. Mankato, Minn., Sept. 30, 1956; d. Christopher Joseph Hiniker and Phyllis C. Krier; m. Donald George Olson, June 27, 1992. AS, Minn. State U., 1985, BS in Spanish summa cum laude, 1991, MS in Edn. Adminstrn., 1995; PhD in Work Force Edn. and Devel., So. Ill. U., 2002. Admissions recruiter Minn. State U., Mankato, 1979-91, coord. Rsch. Enterprise, 1991-93, rsch. adminstr., 1991-96, dir. Info. Scis. Inst., 1997—; dist. dir. U. Minn. Ext. Svc. Heintz Ctr., Rochester, Minn., 2003—. Rsch. adminstr. Minn. State U., Mankato, 1991-96; mem. adv. coun. S. Ctrl. Minn. Tech. Coun., 1993-96, Region Nine Small Bus. Devel. Ctr., 1993-96; grants cons. Housing Authority Murray State U., 1998-99; instr. multimedia devel. Workforce Edn. and Devel. So. Ill. U., Carbondale, 1999-2000, rschr. videoconferencing technologies, 1999-2000; mem. bd. dirs. Minn. Tech., Inc., 1991-96. Presdl. scholar Minn. State U., 1994-95. Mem. AAUW, NAFE, Am. Ednl. Rsch. Assn., Phi Kappa Phi, Phi Delta Kappa, Omicron Tau Theta. Avocations: guitar, parrots, scuba diving, gardening. Office: U Minn Ext Svc Heintz Ctr Rochester MN 55904 Home: 39 Sunnydale Ln SE Rochester MN 55904-4965 E-mail: luannh@umn.edu.

HINING, MICHAEL LYNN, music educator, conductor; b. St. Petersburg, Fla., May 5, 1962; s. Verdus L. and Kathryn R. Hining. MusB, No. Ill. U., 1985, MusM, 1987, cert. in Performing, 1989. Musician Rockford (Ill.) Symphony, 1982—94, Elgin (Ill.) Symphony, 1986—98; co-founder Ill. Valley Youth Symphony, La Salle, Ill., 1987—92, condr.; founder The Violin and Viola Studio, Oak Park, Ill., 1987—, tchr., 1987—. Founder The Windy City String Ensemble, Oak Park, Ill., 1994—, condr., 1994—; vis. prof. violin and viola Ill. Wesleyan U., Bloomington, 1999—2004. Composer: Rhapsody on Themes of Rachmoninoff, 2002 (award, 2002), Elegy on Palestian and Hebrew Themes, 2003; condr. Windy City String Ensemble, Carnegie Hall, N.Y., 2003. Mem. campaign com. Michelle Harton for Sch. Bd., Oak Park, 2003; fund raiser Cmty. Response Aids Care, Oak Park, 1998, Amity Sch. Childes Aid, Oak Park, 2000, Oak Park (Ill.) Animal Care League, 2000. Named Outstanding Tchr., Musicians Union, 1999; recipient Gold medal, Sydney (Australia) Internat. Music Festival, 1999, Bloomfield award, Ea. Music Festival, 1981. Mem.: Oak Park (Ill.) Area Arts Coun., Am. String Tchrs. Assn. (tchr. 1998—), Suzuki Assn. Am. (tchr. 1998—, mem. outstanding outreach group 2000). Avocations: animal rights, dogs. Office Phone: 708-383-2025. Personal E-mail: fugacci@aol.com.

HINKLE, BARTON LESLIE, retired electronics company executive; b. Miami Beach, Fla., Nov. 2, 1925; s. Frank Leslie and Kathryn Barton (Paddock) H.; m. Christine Smith, Aug. 22, 1949 (dec. Aug. 1955); m. Sabrena Sanford, Apr. 4, 1959; children— Karen, Douglas, Jean, Maria, Elizabeth. BS in Chem. Engring, Purdue U., 1949; MS, Inst. Textile Tech., 1951; PhD, Ga. Inst. Tech., 1953. Research asst. Ga. Inst. Tech. Exptl. Sta., Atlanta, 1951-53; research engr. E.I. duPont de Nemours & Co., Inc., Richmond, Va., 1953-55, research supr., 1955-57, tech. supt., 1957-61, mfg. supt., 1961-62, asst. plant mgr., 1962-64, plant supt. Clinton, Iowa, 1964-69, product mgr. Wilmington, Del., 1969-71, lab. mgr., 1971-75, adminstrv. and planning asst., 1976-77, personnel mgr., 1977-84; v.p. human resources Electromagnetic Scis., Inc., Norcross, Ga., 1984-87, cons. human resources, 1987—. Patentee in field aerosol electrification, viscous polymers, cellophane. Sr. warden, vestryman St. Davids Episcopal Ch., 1975-78. Served with AUS, 1944-46, ETO. Republican. Home: 9399 Colvincrest Dr Mechanicsville VA 23116-2909 E-mail: blhink@comcast.net.

HINKLE, BETTY RUTH, retired academic administrator; b. Atchison, Kans., Mar. 18, 1930; d. Arch W. and Ruth (Baker) Hunt; m. Charles L. Hinkle, Dec. 25, 1950 (div.); children: Karl, Eric. BA, U. Corpus Christi, 1950; MS, Baylor U., 1956; MA, U. North Colo., 1972, EdD, 1979. Cert. tchr., Tex., Mass., Colo.; cert. adminstr., Colo. Tchr. Alice (Tex.) Ind. Sch. Dist., 1950, Waco (Tex.) Ind. Sch. Dist., 1951-52, 53-58, Hawaii Pub. Schs., Oahu, 1952-53, Newton Pub. Schs., Newtonville, Mass., 1962-63, Colorado Springs (Colo.) Pub. Schs., 1966—75; cons., exec. dir. spl. project unit Colo. State Dept. Edn., Denver, 1975—95, asst. commr., 1995, ret., 1995, rep. fed. rels. Office Commr. Edn., 1995-96, ret., 1996. Pvt. cons., 1997-2001; pres. BH Cons., Colorado Springs, 1997-2001; mem. cabinet Colo. Dept. Edn., mem. Quality Coun., fed. liaison rep. to chief state sch. officers, Washington, chmn. 1996; alt. foreman Denver Grand Jury, 1983; mem. state exec. fellowship program Instn. Ednl. Leadership, Coun. Chief STate Sch. Officers and U.S. Dept. Edn., 1985. Vol. for Colo. Mountain Reclamation Projects, 2001—. Recipient Dept. Edn. Specialists award Colo. Assn. Sch. Execs., 1979, Employee Yr. award Colo. Dept. Edn., 1986, Fed. Ednl. Program Adminstrv. Coun. ann. award for Distinctive Svc. to Colo. Children, 1988; named an Outstanding Secondary Educator of Am., 1974. Mem. Am. Assn. Sch. Adminstrs., Colo. Assn. Sch. Execs. (coord. coun. 1976-79, v.p. dept. edn. specialists 1974-75, pres. 1975-76), Colo. Assn. Sch. Execs., Phi Delta Kappa. Home: 1011 N 18th St Colorado Springs CO 80904-2852 Personal E-mail: b3h@adelphia.net.

HINKLE, CHARLES FREDERICK, lawyer, educator; b. Oregon City, Oreg., July 6, 1942; s. William Ralph and Ruth Barbara (Holcomb) H. BA, Stanford U., 1964; MDiv, Union Theol. Sem., N.Y.C., 1968; JD, Yale U., 1971. Bar: Oreg. 1971; ordained to ministry United Ch. of Christ, 1974. Instr. English, Morehouse Coll., Atlanta, 1966-67; assoc. Stoel Rives LLP (formerly Stoel, Rives, Boley, Jones & Grey), Portland, Oreg., 1971-77, ptnr., 1977—. Adj. prof. Lewis and Clark Law Sch., Portland, 1978-2001; bd. govs. Oreg. State Bar, 1992-95. Oreg. pres. ACLU, Portland, 1976-80, nat. bd. dirs., 1979-85; bd. dirs. Kendall Cmty. Ctr., 1987-93, Youth Progress Assn., 1994-98, Portland Baroque Orch., 1999-2000; mem. pub. affairs com. Am. Cancer Soc., 1994-99; mem. Oreg. Gov.'s Task Force on Youth Suicide, 1996. Recipient Elliott Human Rights award Oreg. Edn. Assn., 1984, E.B. MacNaughton award ACLU Oreg., 1987, Wayne Morse award Dem. Com. Oreg., 1994, Tom McCall Freedom of Info. award Women in Comm., 1996, Civil Rights award Met. Human Rights Commn., 1996, Pub. Svc. award Oreg. State Bar, 1997. Fellow Am. Bar Found.; mem. ABA (ho. of dels. 1998-2000), FBA, Multnomah County Bar Assn., City Club Portland (pres. 1987-88). Democrat. Home: 14079 SE Fairoaks Way Milwaukie OR 97267-1017 Office: Stoel Rives 900 SW 5th Ave Ste 2600 Portland OR 97204-1268 Office Phone: 503-294-9266. E-mail: cfhinkle@stoel.com.

HINKLE, DOUGLAS PADDOCK, retired languages educator; b. Stamford, Conn., June 9, 1923; s. Frank Leslie and Kathryn B. Paddock Hinkle; m. Rose-Marie Hecker, Apr. 14, 1966; children: Anthony Barton, Monica Kathryn. BA, U. Va., 1952, MA, 1954. Lic. law enforcement officer, Ohio. Tchr. English Va. Pub. Schs., Nelson County, 1948-49; dir. binat. ctr. U.S. Info. Svc., La Paz, Bolivia, 1955-57, Caracas, Venezuela, 1958; asst. prof. Spanish and French Sweet Briar Coll., Amherst, Va., 1958-62, Southwestern U., Memphis, 1962-63; coll. editor modern langs. D.C. Heath & Co., Boston, 1963-65; assoc. prof. modern langs. Ea. Ky. U., Richmond, 1965-67; sr. lectr. modern langs. Ohio U., Athens, 1967-93, prof. emeritus modern langs., 1994—; forensic artist LETN-TV, Dallas, 1990-91. Program evaluator NEH, Washington, 1975-78. Author: (books) Faces of Crime, 1989, Mug Shots, 1990, (book of poetry) Poetry Is You, 1977, (slideshow/video program) Remembering Faces, 1990; mem. editl. bd. NAMES, 1968-74; contbr. numerous articles to profl. jours. Chmn. drug abuse com. Kiwanis Club, Athens, Ohio, 1983-87; cert. aux. Athens Police Dept., 1982-87, forensic artist, 1981-87; bd. dirs. Cen. Va. Crime Clinic, Richmond, 1994-97. Cpl. U.S. Army, 1943-46. Recipient Caballero, Order of Condor award Republic of Bolivia, 1957, Citizenship award Athens Bar Assn., 1983. Mem. Portrait Soc. Am., Am. Soc. Marine Artists, Ctrl. Va. Crime Clinic (bd. dirs. 1995-98), Va. Mus. Fine Arts, Fraternal Order of Police (hon. permanent mem.), Raven Soc., Va. Hist. Soc., Phi Beta Kappa. Republican. Roman Catholic. Avocations: painting, writing, historical linguistics, marksmanship. Home: 6413 Poplar Rd Quinton VA 23141 E-mail: mrhdph@aol.com.

HINKLE, JANET, psychologist; b. Groton, Conn., Mar. 26, 1958; d. David Randall and Muriel (Nelson) Hinkle; m. Richard Alden Wilcox, Oct. 1, 1983 (div. Mar. 1991); 1 child, Lillian Marie. AA in Fashion Design cum laude, Endicott Jr. Coll. Women, Beverly, Mass., 1978; BA in Psychology, Conn. Coll., 1981; MBA, Rensselaer Poly. Inst., 2004. Project leader Sonalysts, Inc., Waterford, Conn., 1983—. Coporator Lawrence and Meml. Hosp., New London, Conn., 1995—, mem. planned giving com., 1998—99; mem. gift com. adv. Cmty. Found., New London, 1998—; mem. curriculum com. planned sci. and tech. Magnet HS, 2003—; bd. dirs. United Way SECT. Named to Outstanding Young Women of Am., 1997. Mem.: Thames Club. Republican. Avocations: training horses, ballet, tennis, skiing, painting. Home: 221 Elm St Stonington CT 06378-1165 Office: Sonalysts Inc 215 Parkway N Waterford CT 06385-1209 E-mail: jlhinkle@sonalysts.com.

HINKLE, MURIEL RUTH NELSON, naval warfare analysis company executive; b. Bayonne, N.J., Mar. 17, 1929; d. Andrew and Florence Martha Ida (Nuber) Nelson; m. David Randall Hinkle, June 5, 1954; children: Valerie Nelson, Janet Lee, Sally Ann. Student, Md. Coll. for Women, 1947-49; BA, U. Md., 1951. Mgr. Wildacres Thoroughbred Horse Farm, Waterford, Conn., 1960-70; illustrator naval warfare predictions/computer simulated naval engagements Analysis & Tech., Inc., North Stonington, Conn., 1970-73; pres. Sonalysts, Inc., Waterford, Conn., 1973-88, 94-98, CEO, 1973-2001, pres., CEO emerita, 2001—; also founder, past dir. Command Engring. & Tech. Svcs. Co.; pres., CEO, chmn. Stonington Farms Inc. (now Mystic Valley Hunt Club), 1983. Adv. bd. Conn. Nat. Bank, 1988-92; chmn., CEO Angiers Assocs., 1989-96, S.I. Devel. Corp., 1989-2001; cons. Def. Nuclear Agy. for Tactical Nuclear Effects in anti-submarine warfare, 1974-75; spl. edn. substitute tchr. Waterford Pub. Schs., 1968-74; bd. dirs. Sonalysts, Inc. Co-author: Scope of Acoustic Communications Systems in Naval Tactical Warfare, 1974, Non-Acoustic Anti Submarine Warfare, 1974, Nuclear Weapons Effects in Anti Submarine Warfare, 1974, Measures of Effectiveness, Naval Tactical Communications, 1975, Destroyer ASW Barrier, 1977. Bd. trustees Thames Sci. Ctr., 1979-82. Recipient commendation for svcs. to submarine force Comdr. Submarine Squadron Ten, 1973, SBA New Eng. Contractor of Yr. award, 1986, SBA Adminstr.'s award for excellence, 1985, 86, bus. assoc. of yr. award Naval Inst., 1999, Disting. Cmty. Svc. award Mitchell Coll., 2001, William Crawford Disting. Svc. award C. of C., 2002. Mem. Am. Horse Shows Assn., Nat. Audubon Soc., Submarine Devel. Group Two Wives Club (pres. 1968), Sigma Kappa (pres. Senesk chpt. 1987-89), Navy Wives Club. Republican. Baptist. Home: 9 Cove Rd Stonington CT 06378-2304 Office: Sonalysts Inc PO Box 280 215 Parkway N Waterford CT 06385-1209 Office Phone: 860-326-3670.

HINKLE, WADE P., political scientist; b. Alexandria, Va., Feb. 28, 1955; s. Charles Wade and Emily (Trevillian) H.; m. Katherine Lynn Rhyne, Aug. 14, 1977 (div. Oct. 21, 1995); m. Mary Denise LaMorte, Aug. 22, 1998. BA, U. Va., 1977, MA, 1980; PhD, U. Md., 1990. Assoc. dir. United Way, Charlottesville, Va., 1977-79; presdl. mgmt. intern Dept. Def., Arlington, Va., 1980-82; ops. rsch. analyst Office of Sec. Def., Arlington, 1982-91, dir. policy planning, 1991-94; rsch. staff mem. Inst. Def. Analyses, Alexandria, 1994—. Adj. prof. U. Md., College Park, 1989-93, George Mason U., Fairfax, Va., 2000—03; adj. faculty George C. Marshall Ctr. European Security Studies, Garmisch, Germany, 1994-2002; instr. CIA, 1998-2000; vis. faculty Cornell U., Ithaca, N.Y., 1999-2000, Air War Coll., Montgomery, Ala., 2001; spkr. in field. Contbr. articles to profl. jours. Bd. dirs. Louisa County Intergrity Coun., Va., 1978-79, Nelson County, 1978-79. MacArthur fellow U. Md., 1989-90. Mem. Mil. Ops. Rsch. Soc., Pa. R.R. Tech. & Hist. Soc., U.S. Naval Inst., Air Force Assn., Assn. U.S. Army, Phi Kappa Phi. Episcopal. Avocations: railroads, historical wargames, typography. Home: 4200 Cordell St Annandale VA 22003 Office: Inst Def Analyses 4850 Mark Center Dr Alexandria VA 22311 E-mail: whinkle@ida.org.

HINKLEY, DEBORAH ANN, physician; b. Flushing, NY, July 1, 1961; d. Paul Kenneth and Carol Ann Hinkley; m. Douglas E. Krebs, May 26, 1996. BS cum laude in biology, Coll. Mt. St. Vincent, 1983; MD, NY Med. Coll., 1989; MPH, Tulane U., 2004. Diplomate bd.cert. Am. Bd. Family Practice, lic. NY, Utah. Basic surgery intern Naval Hosp., Oakland, Calif., 1989—90; student naval flight surgeon Naval Aerospace Med. Inst., Pensacola, Fla., 1990—91; flight surgeon Commander Tra wing six, Pensacola, Fla., 1991—94, HSL-40, Mayport, Fla., 1994—97; intern to resident, family medicine Naval Hosp., Jacksonville, Fla., 1997—2000, staff physician Oak Harbor, Wash., 2000—03; resident Naval Aerospace Medicine Inst., Pensacola, Fla., 2004—; asst. prof. Manhattan Coll., Coll. Mt. St. Vincent,

1983—84. Author: (The New Phytologist) Seed protein quantities of field-grown soybeans exposed to simulated acidic rain, 1984. Instr. Basic Life Support, 1991—, Advanced Cardiac Life Support, 2000—, Pediatric Advanced Life Support, 2003. Cdr. USN, 1989—. Fellow: Aerospace Med. Assn. (assoc.); mem.: Am. Acad. of Family Physicians, Naval Inst. (life), Am. Med. Assn. (life), Soc. US Naval Flight Surgeons (life), Uniformed Svcs. Acad. of Family Physicians, Beta Beta Beta (life), Pi Mu Epsilon (life), Sigma Xi (life), Delta Omega (life). Republican. Cath. E-mail: debhinkley@att.net.

HINKLEY, EVERETT DAVID, JR., physicist; b. Augusta, Maine, Nov. 19, 1936; s. Everett David and Julina Margaret Hinkley; m. Christine Marie, June 18, 1960; children: Anne, Mark, Kristin, David. Student, Rensselaer Poly. Inst., 1954-56; BS in Engring. Physics, Washington U., St. Louis, 1958; MS in Physics, Northwestern U., 1961, PhD in Physics, 1963. Mem. rsch. staff Gen. Telephone Labs., Northlake, Ill., 1958-59; rsch.-teaching assoc. Northwestern U., Evanston, Ill., 1960-63; mem. tech. staff MIT Lincoln Lab., Lexington, Mass., 1963-76; v.p. Laser Analytics, Inc., Lexington, 1976-77; sect. mgr., program mgr., sr. rsch. scientist Calif. Inst. Tech. Jet Propulsion Lab., Pasadena, 1976-86; chief electronics scientist Lockheed Aero. Rsch. Lab., Valencia, Calif., 1986-87; chief scientist Hughes Aircraft Co., El Segundo, Calif., 1987-89; chief scientist, global change initiative TRW Space & Tech. Group, Redondo Beach, Calif., 1989-92; v.p., chief scientist Bainbridge Tech. Group, Ltd., L.A., 1992-93; sr. scientist, mgr. Sci. and Tech. Corp., 1993—. Sr. rsch. fellow Ctr. for Internat. Rels., UCLA, 1991-94, mem. physics dept. adv. coun., 1993-95, chmn. atmospheric scis. adv. coun., 1991-98; mem. space systems and tech. adv. com. NASA, 1991-94. Author, editor: Laser Monitoring of the Atmosphere, 1976; contbr. articles to tech. jours., chpts. to books. Mem. Pasadena Lung Assn., 1980—86. Fellow Optical Soc. Am. (co-chmn. Conf. on Lasers and Electro-Optics 1986); mem. IEEE (sr., chmn. aerospace policy com. 1993-96, co-chmn. spaceborne photonics conf. 1991, co-chmn. combined optical-microwave earth and atmospheric sensing conf. 1993), IEEE Lasers and Electro-Optics Soc. (sec.-treas. 1987-89, bd. govs. 1987—), Washington U. Alumni Coun., Sigma Xi, Tau Beta Pi. Avocations: racquetball, music.

HINMAN, ALAN RICHARD, health facility administrator, epidemiologist; b. New Orleans, Mar. 23, 1937; s. E. Harold and Katharine Ellen (Fradenburgh) H.; m. Donna Virgene Graham, Dec. 21, 1959 (div. 1962); m. Lucy Winkler Householder, May 30, 1965; children: Johanna Mary, Katharine Emily. BA, Cornell U., 1957; MD, Western Res. U., 1961; MPH, Harvard U., 1969. Intern Cleve. Met. Hosp., 1961—62, resident in internal medicine, 1962—64, chief resident, 1964-65; with USPHS, 1965-70, 77-96; advanced through grades to asst. surgeon gen., 1988; epidemic intelligence svc. officer Ctr. for Disease Control, Calif. State Dept. Health, 1965-66; regional evaluation officer malaria eradication program Ctrs. for Disease Control, Atlanta, 1966-67, San Salvador, El Salvador, El Salvador, 1967-68, asst. chief viral diseases br. epidemiology program Atlanta, 1969-70; dir. Bur. Epidemiology, N.Y. State Dept. Health, Albany, 1970-71, asst. commr. epidemiology and preventive health svcs., 1971-75; asst. commr., dir. Bur. Preventive and Med. Svcs., Tenn. Dept. Pub. Health, Nashville, 1975-77; dir. divsn. immunization Ctr. for Prevention Svcs., Ctrs. for Disease Control, Atlanta, 1977-88; coord. nat. vaccine program Office of Asst. Sec. for Health, 1987-90; asst. surgeon gen. USPHS, 1988-96; dir. Nat. Ctr. for Prevention Svcs. Ctrs. for Disease Control, 1988-95; sr. advisor to dir. Ctrs. for Disease Control and Prevention, 1995-96; coord. CDC World Bank collaboration on immunizations Task Force Child Survival and Devel., Atlanta, 1996-2000, sr. pub. health scientist, 1996—; prin. investigator All Kids Count, Atlanta, 2000—04; coord. PARTNERS TB ctrl. program, Atlanta, 2001—02. Adj. asst. prof. preventive and cmty. medicine Albany Med. Coll., Union U., 1970-75; adj. asst. prof. pub. health Rensselaer Poly Inst., 1971-75; assoc. clin. prof. dept. preventive medicine Vanderbilt U., 1975-77; clin. asst. prof. dept. cmty. medicine Divsn. Healthcare Svcs., U. Tenn., 1975-77; clin. asst. prof. dept. family and cmty. health Meharry Med. Coll., 1975-77; clin. assoc. prof. dept. preventive medicine-cmty. health Emory U. Sch. Medicine, Atlanta, 1978-90; vis. prof. Case Western Res. U. Sch. Medicine, 1984; adj. prof. Emory U. Sch. Pub. Health, 1990—; vis. lectr. Shanghai 1st Med. Coll., 1981; sr. cons. for pub. health programs, The Task Force for Child Survival and Devel., 1996—. Contbr. over 300 articles to profl. jours. Decorated D.S.M.; recipient Indian Health Svc. Dir. Spl. Excellence award, 1992. Fellow ACP, APHA (mem. gov. coun. 1975-77, mem. program devel. bd. 1984-86, mem. nominating com. 1984-86, chair 1985-86, chair-elect epidemiology sect. 1985-87, chair sect. 1987-89, past chair 1989-91, mem. exec. bd. 1991-95, spkr. governing coun. 1995—), Am. Acad. Pediat., Am. Coll. Epidemiology (mem. exec. bd. 1990-94, v.p. 1991-92, pres. 1992-93), Am. Coll. Preventive Medicine (regent 1974-75, 77-81, v.p. for pub. health 1975-76); mem. AMA, Am. Epidemiol. Soc., Am. Soc. Tropical Medicine and Hygiene, Am. Venereal Disease Assn. (bd. dirs. 1972-75, sec.-treas. 1975-77), Assn. Tchrs. Preventive Medicine, Infectious Diseases Soc. Am., Internat. Epidemiol. Assn., Physicians for Social Responsibility, Soc. Epidemiol. Rsch., Soc. Med. Decision Making. Home: 2194 Creek Park Rd Decatur GA 30033-2714 Office Phone: 404-687-5636. Business E-Mail: ahinman@taskforce.org.

HINMAN, FRANK, JR., urologist, educator; b. San Francisco, Oct. 2, 1915; s. Frank and Mittie (Fitzpatrick) H.; m. Marion Modesta Eaves, Dec. 3, 1948. AB with great distinction, Stanford U., 1937; MD, Johns Hopkins U., 1941. Diplomate Am. Bd. Urology (trustee 1979-85). Intern Johns Hopkins Hosp., 1941-42; resident Cin. Gen. Hosp., 1942-44, U. Calif. Hosp., 1945-47; pvt. practice San Francisco, 1947-85; assoc. clin. prof. urology U. Calif., San Francisco, 1954-62, clin. prof., 1962—; urologist-in-chief Children's Hosp., 1957-85. Adv. council Nat. Inst. Arthritis, Diabetes, Digestive and Kidney Diseases, 1983-86 Lt. USNR, 1944-46. Named Disting. Alumnus, Johns Hopkins U., 1995. Fellow ACS (regent 1972-80, vice-chmn. 1978-79, v.p. 1982-83), Royal Coll. Surgeons (hon., Eng.); mem. Am. Urol. Assn. (hon.), Am. Assn. Genito-Urinary Surgeons (hon., pres. 1981, Keyes medalist 1998), Clin. Soc. Genito-Urinary Surgeons (pres. 1979), Internat. Soc. Urol. (pres. Am. sect. 1980-84), Am. Assn. Clin. Urologists, Am. Fedn. Clin. Research, Soc. Pediatric Urology (founding mem., pres. 1971), Soc. Univ. Urologists (founding mem., pres. 1973), Am. Acad. Pediatrics (pres. urology sect. 1986), Urodynamics Soc. (founding mem., pres. 1980-82), Genito Urinary Reconstructive Soc. (founding mem.), Pan Pacific Surg. Assn. (v.p. 1980-83), Internat. Continence Soc., Brit. Assn. Urologic Surgeons (hon.) (St. Paul Medalist 1991), Soc. Française d'Urologie, Australasian Soc. Urologic Surgeons (hon.), Phi Beta Kappa, Alpha Omega Alpha. Clubs: Bohemian, St. Francis Yacht, San Francisco Yacht. Home: 1000 Francisco St San Francisco CA 94109-1127 Office: U Calif Med Ctr San Francisco CA 94143-0738 Office Phone: 415-476-1611. Business E-Mail: fhinman@urol.ucsf.edu. *Devoting two afternooons each week to research, teaching and other academic pursuits, uninterrupted by surgery and clinical practice, can result in advances.*

HINMAN, GEORGE WHEELER, physics educator; b. Evanston, Ill., Nov. 7, 1927; s. Norman Seymour and Bess (Bryan) H.; m. Mary Louise Cauffield, June 19, 1952; children: Norman Field, Lydia Hinman, Nancy Wheeler. BS in Physics and Math., Carnegie Mellon U., 1947, MS in Physics, 1950, DSc in Physics, 1952. Asst. prof., then assoc. prof. physics Carnegie Mellon U., Pitts., 1952-63; chmn. physics Gen. Atomic Co. subs. Gulf Oil Corp., San Diego, 1963-69; prof. physics, dir. Applied Energy Studies Wash. State U., Pullman, 1983—97; dir. N.Mex. Energy Research & Devel. Inst., Santa Fe, 1982-83; chair environ. sci. & regional planning, 1989-97. Cons. Los Alamos (N.Mex.) Nat. Lab., 1976-90, GAO, 1977—, Nat. Nuclear Accreditation Bd., 1992-98. Author: Dictionary of Energy, 1983; contbr. articles to profl. jours. Grantee NSF, others. Fellow Am. Phys. Soc.; mem. Am. Nuclear Soc., AAAS, Am. Soc. Engring. Edn. Democrat. Avocation: fishing. Home: 925 SW Fountain St Pullman WA 99163-2132 Office: Wash State U Troy Hl Rm 305 Pullman WA 99164-4430 Office Phone: 509-335-8689. Personal E-mail: ghimman@insightful.net.

HINMAN, HARVEY DEFOREST, lawyer; b. May 7, 1940; s. George Lyon and Barbara H.; m. Margaret (Snyder), June 23, 1962; children: George, Sarah, Marguerite. BA, Brown U., 1962; JD, Cornell U., 1965. Bar: Calif., 1966. Assoc. Pillsbury, Madison, and Sutro, San Francisco, 1965—72, ptnr., 1973—93; v.p., gen. counsel Chevron Corp., San Francisco, 1993—2002; of counsel Pillsbury, Winthrop, Shaw, Pittman LLP, San Francisco, 2004—. Bd. dirs. Legal Aid Soc., San Francisco, 1994—; pres. Brazil Ranch Environ. Ctr., 2004, bd. dirs., 2004—. Bd. dirs., sec. Holbrook Palmer Park Found., 1977—86; trustee Castillija Sch., 1988—89; bd. govs. Filoli Ctr., 1988—, pres., 1994—95; bd. dirs. Phillips Brooks Sch., 1978—84, pres., 1983—84. Fellow: Am. Bar Found.; mem.: ABA, San Francisco Bar Assn. Office: 50 Fremont St San Francisco CA 94105

HINMAN-BICKHAM, CHERYLL D., music educator, consultant; d. Nelson N. and Pauline L. Hinman; m. William L. Bickham, Mar. 24, 1985; children: Stephen Matthew Bickham, Ryan Edward Bickham. Diploma, tchg. cert., Am. Coll. Music, Austin, Tex., 1984; student, Stetson U., 1988; A in Bus. Adminstrn., ICS, Scranton, Pa., 1992. Elem. tchr., K-12 music tchr. Lakeland (Fla.) Bapt. Acad., 1977—81, Way of Life Bapt. Sch., Titusville, Fla., 1982—83; tchr. Merritt Island (Fla.) Christian Sch., 1983—84; music tchr. K-8 Park Ave. Bapt. Sch., Titusville, 1984—87; home sch. tchr. Deland, Fla., 1987—89; mgr. Band Aid Shop, Bellefontaine, Ohio, 1990—98; missionary music tchr. Oneida (Ky.) Bapt. Acad., 1998—2000. Co-founder, past pres., trustee West Ctrl. Ohio Cmty. Concert Band, Bellefontaine, 1991—; cons. Calvary Christian Sch., Bellefontaine, 2004—; mem. Brevard Youth Symphony, 1970—71, Nashville Youth Symphony, 1971—72, Palm Beach (Fla.) Symphony Orch., 1973—74, Jackson Symphony Orch., 1974—76, Lakeland Symphony Orch., 1977—83, Gift of Music Ministries Orch., 1984—88, Brevard Cmty. Band, 1983—87. Vol. music missionary Bapt. Assn., Jackson Center, Ohio, 1989—95; music dir. West Ctrl. Bapt. Assn., Jackson Center, 1989—95; handbell choir dir. 1st United Presbyn. Ch., Bellefontaine, 2000—04. Mem.: West Ctrl. Ohio Cmty. Concert Band (charter, pres. 1995—98, Founders' award 1998), Am. Guild English Handbell Ringers, Nat. Guild Piano Tchrs. (chmn. 1993—98, founder Bellefontaine chpt. 1993—). Republican. Avocations: gardening, reading, dogs, lanscape theme design. Home and Office: Ladybug Music Svcs 7322 Foster St Russells Point OH 43348

HINNANT, HILARI ANNE, elementary school educator, consultant; b. Coral Gables, Fla., Mar. 23, 1953; d. William Walker and Margaret Elizabeth (Ennis) H.; m. M. Greg Miller. BS in Edn., U. Ga., 1974; MS in Edn., Fla. Internat. U., 1976. Art tchr. Banyan Elem. Sch. Dade County, Miami, 1974-79; tchr. Hilliard (Fla.) Sr. H.S., 1979-80, Callahan (Fla.) Jr. H.S., 1980-81, Duval County Pub. Schs., Jacksonville, Fla., 1981-83, The Am. Sch., Hamburg, West Germany, 1983-84, Brevard County Pub. Schs., Rockledge, Fla., 1984-86; clin. experience facilitator U. Wis., LaCrosse, 1987-88; tchr. Sarasota (Fla.) County Pub. Sch., Sarasota, Fla., 1988-90; asst. dir., exploratorium specialist Ednl. Rsch. Ctr. for Child Devel. U. South Fla., Tampa, 1990-91; dir. cen. and VA brs. YMCA Child Care, Milw., 1991-92; ednl. coord. Portage (Wis.) Project transition grant Coop. Edn. Svc. Agy. # 5, 1992-93; project transition grantee Coop. Svc. Agy. # 5, 1992-93; instr. child care & devel. Madison (Wis.) Area Tech. Coll., 1993-94; ednl. cons., 1994—; tchr. Bedford County Pub. Schs., 1994-96, Prince William Pub. Schs., 1996—99, Fairfax (Va.) Pub. Schs., 1999—2000, Alexandria (Va.) City Pub. Schs., 2000—. Illustrator, writer Brevard County Maths. Curriculum Guide Rockledge; presenter Va. Assn. Early Childhood Edn. Conf., 1998, Va. Social Studies Educators Conf., 2004; presenter and cons. in field. Author poems; contbr. articles to profl. jours. Selby grantee, l989, tchg. tolerance grantee So. Poverty Law Ctr., 1997-98, grantee Nat. Tree Trust, 1998—, Va. Arts Coun., 1999, Washington Post, 2002, 03, Phi Delta Pi, 2000, Kappa Delta Pi Innovative Practices, 2003; Va. Govs. Physical Fitness award, 2004 Mem. Nat. Assn. for Edn. Young Children, So. Early Childhood Assn., Midwest Assn. for Edn. Young Children (conf. presenter 1992, 93), Kappa Delta Pi (presenter internat. convocation 1988), Phi Delta Kappa (past pres. Sarasota-Bradenton chpt. 1989, rsch. grantee 1996), Delta Gamma. Democrat. Roman Catholic. Avocations: running, poetry, painting. Home: 7357 Mallory Cir Alexandria VA 22315-4709 Office Phone: 703-824-6970. Business E-Mail: hilarihinnant@acps.k12.va.us.

HINOJOSA, FEDERICO GUSTAVO, JR., judge; b. Edinburg, Tex., Apr. 16, 1947; s. Federico Gustavo and Zulema (Trevino) H.; m. Yolanda Silva, 1970 (div. 1977); children: Cynthia, Zelda Cassandra; m. Magdalena Garza, Oct. 30, 1992. BA, Pan Am. U., 1969; JD, U. Houston, 1977. Bar: Tex. 1977, U.S. Dist. Ct. (so. dist.) Tex. 1977, U.S. Ct. Appeals (5th cir.) 1980, U.S. Supreme Ct. 1980. Assoc. Clark, Lowes & Carrithers, Houston, 1977-79; ptnr. Clark & Hinojosa, Houston, 1979-81; child support atty. Tex. Dept. Human Resources, McAllen, 1981-83; asst. dist. atty. Hidalgo County, Edinburg, 1983-84; assoc. Atlas & Hall, McAllen, 1984-87; ptnr. Lewis, Pettitt & Hinojosa, McAllen, 1987-91; justice Tex. Ct. Appeals for 13th Dist., Corpus Christi, 1991—. Sgt. USAF, 1970—74. Fellow Tex. Bar. Found.; mem. State Bar Tex., Mexican-Am. Bar Tex., Mexican-Am. Bar Assn. Coastal Bend (dir. 1993-94), Hidalgo County Bar Assn. (dir. 1986-90). Democrat. Office: 13th Ct Appeals 100 E Cano St Edinburg TX 78539-4548 Business E-Mail: fghinojosa@courts.state.tx.us.

HINOJOSA, JUAN LORENZO, not-for-profit developer, theologian, consultant; b. Cochabamba, Bolivia, June 24, 1946; s. Eduardo and Matilde Hinojosa; m. Sarah Elizabeth Toomer, May 16, 1971; children: Sabrina Clare, Christin Maria, Monica Raven, Damien John, Mateo Juan. PhD, Grad. Theol. Union, Berkeley, Calif., 1984. Founder, exec. dir. Lay Ministry Inst., San Antonio, 1986—92, Ctrl. Tex. Pastoral Ctr., Austin, 1986—92; cons. Incarnate Word Health Sys., San Antonio, 1991—94; founder, exec. dir. Ctr. for Spirituality and Work, Austin, Tex., 1992—94; exec. dir. Hillenbrand Inst., Mundelein, Ill., 1994—2000, Solidarity Bridge, Inc., Evanston, Ill., 1998—; cons. Ctr. for Sport, Spirituality and Character Formation, Aston, Pa., 1998; dir. Chgo. Cath. Med. Mission, Evanston, Ill., 1999—2005, Chgo. Cath. Enterprise Mission, Evanston, Ill., 2001—; founder, mng. ptnr. Dharma Merc., San Anselmo, Calif. Cons. St. Norbert Coll., DePere, Wis., 1999—, Ctr. for Sport, Spirituality and Character, Aston, Pa., 2000—00. Contbr. articles to profl. jours. Cons. Nat. Conf. of Cath. Bishops, Washington, 1991—93; seminar mem. Common Root - Chgo. Cath./Evang. Dialog, 1999—2003; bd. dirs. Communitarian Network, Washington, 1995—99; bd. chair and vice chair Solidarity Bridge, Inc., Evanston, Ill., 1998; bd. sec. Youth Employment Svcs., Austin, Tex., 1988—90; bd. dirs. Austin Comes Together, Tex., 1993—94, Ill. Fatherhood Initiative, Chgo., 1996—2000. Roman Catholic. Personal E-mail: gsusml@aol.com.

HINOJOSA, RICARDO H., federal judge; b. Rio Grande City, Tex., 1950; BA, U. Tex., 1972; JD, Harvard U., 1975. Judge U.S. Dist. Ct. (so. dist.) Tex.; law clk. Tex. Supreme Ct., 1975-76; assoc. Ewers & Toothaker, McAllen, Tex., 1976-79, ptnr., 1979-83; judge U.S. Dist. Ct. (so. dist.) Tex., McAllen, 1983—. Mem. Pan Am. U. Bd. Regents, 1979—83, chmn., 1981—83; mem. US Sentencing Commn., 2003—, chmn., 2004—; adj. prof. U. Texas Sch. Law. Recipient Disting. Svc. award, Pan-Am. U. Alumni Assn., 1986, Disting. Alumnus award, U. Texas Ex-Students Assn., 2001. Office: US Dist Ct So Dist Tex 1701 W Bus Hwy 83 Ste 1028 Mcallen TX 78501*

HINOJOSA, RUBEN, congressman; b. Edcouch, Tex., Aug. 20, 1940; m. Martha Lopez; 5 children. BBA, U. Tex., Austin, 1962; MBA, U. Tex.-Pan Am., 1980. Pres., CFO H & H Foods; mem. U.S. Congress from 15th Tex. dist., 1997—; mem. edn. and workforce com., fin. svcs. com., resources com. Mem. Tex. State Bd. Edn, 1974-84.; Tex. Higher Edn. Named Hispanic Man of the Yr. Rio Grande Valley, 1994; recipient Lifetime Achivement award Hispanic Bus. Mag. Democrat. Office: 2463 Rayburn House Washington DC 20515-4315*

HINOJOSA, TISH (LETICIA HINOJOSA), vocalist; b. San Antonio, Dec. 6, 1955; d. Felipe and Maria H.; m. Craig Barker, 1982; children: Adam, Maria, Christina. Singer Mel Tillis Prodn. Co., Nashville, 1983-85. Performer locally and on radio, 1973, gubernatorial inauguration Ann Richard's, 1991, presdl. inauguration Bill Clinton, 1993. Albums: Taos to Tennessee (self-released cassette), 1985, Homeland, 1989, Aquella Noche, 1991, Memorabilia Navidenia, 1991, Culture Swing, 1992, Destiny's Gate, 1994, Frontéjas, 1995, Dreaming from the Labyrinth, 1996, Cada Nino, 1996, Sonar Del Labertino, 1997, Sign of Truth, 2000, From Texas for a Christmas Night, 2003; TV appearances include CBS This Morning, 1993; radio appearances include Prairie Home Companion, All Things Considered, 1994. Recipient First prize Kearville Folk Festival, 1979. Office: Manazo Music Mgmt PO Box 3304 Austin TX 78764-3304

HINOJOSA-SMITH, ROLAND, language educator, writer; b. Mercedes, Tex., Jan. 21, 1929; s. Manuel Guzman and Carrie Effie (Smith) H.; children: Clarissa Elizabeth, Karen Louise, Robert Huddleston. BS, U. Tex., 1953; AM, N.Mex. Highlands U., 1963; PhD, U. Ill., 1969. Chmn. dept. modern langs. Tex. A&I U., Kingsville, 1970-74, dean Coll. Arts and Scis., 1974-76, v.p. acad. affairs, 1976-77; prof. English U. Minn., Mpls., 1977-81; Ellen Clayton Garwood prof. English U. Tex., Austin, 1985—, Mari Sabusawa Michener chair, 1989-93, dir. Tex. Ctr. for Writers, 1989-93, prof. dept. Spanish and Portuguese, 1993—. Juror Pulitzer Prize Novel, 1994; USIA cons., Panama, Mexico, Iraq, France; lectr. in field. Author: Estampas del Valle, 1973 (Quinto Sol 1973), Klail City, 1976 (Casa de las Americas 1976), Korean Love Songs, 1978, The Valley, 1983, Dear Rafe, 1985, Partners in Crime, 1985, Fair Gentlemen of Belken County, 1986, We Happy Few, 1986, Klail City, 1987, Becky and Her Friends, 1990, Los Amigos de Becky, 1991, Korea Liebes Lieder, 1992, The Useless Servants, 1993, Ask a Policeman, 1998, My Dear Rafe/Mi Querido Rafa, 2005; guest editor Am. Short Fiction, 1993-94. Illini (U. Ill.) Comback Guest, 1996. Named Disting. Alumnus, U. Ill., 1998, U. Tex.-Brownsville, 1998, Celebrity Author, Scott Foresman, 1999—2001, Disting. Vis. Prof., U. Kans., summer, 1994, Marshal, U. Tex., 1995—2001; recipient Outstanding Latino faculty mem., Hispanic Caucus Am. Assn. Higher Edn., Disting. Achievement award, U. Ill., 1998, Pulitzer Prize, 2003—04; fellow, Ford Found., 1979. Fellow Soc. Spanish and Spanish Am. Studies, The Hispanic Soc. (assoc.); mem. MLA, Academia Real de la Lengua. Democrat. Roman Catholic. Office: U Tex Dept English Austin TX 78712 E-mail: rorro@mail.utexas.edu.

HINSHAW, ADA SUE, dean, nursing educator; b. Arkansas City, Kans., May 20, 1939; d. Oscar A. and Georgia Ruth (Tucker) Cox; children: Cynthia Lynn, Scott Allen Lewis. BS, U. Kans., 1961; MSN, Yale U., 1963; MA, U. Ariz., 1973, PhD, 1975; DSc (hon.), U. Md., 1988, Med. Coll. of Ohio, 1988, Marquette U., 1990, U. Nebr., 1992, Mount Sinai Med. Ctr., NY, 1993, U. Medicine and Dentistry N.J., 1995, Grand Valley State U., 1995, U. Toronto, Can., 1996, St. Louis U., 1996, Georgetown U., 1998. Instr. Sch. Nursing U. Kans., 1963-66; asst. prof. U. Calif., San Francisco, 1966-71; prof. U. Ariz., Tucson, 1975-87; dir. nursing rsch. U. Med. Ctr., Tucson, 1975-87; dir. Nat. Inst. Nursing Rsch. Pub. Health Svc., Dept. Health and Human Svcs., NIH, Washington, 1987—94; dean, prof., Sch. Nursing U. Mich., Ann Arbor, 1994—. Contbd. articles to profl. jours. Recipient Kay Schilter award U. Kans., 1961, Lucille Petry Leone award Nat. League for Nursing, 1971, Wolanin Geriatric Nursing Rsch. award U. Ariz., 1978, Alumni of the Yr award Sch. Nursing U. Kans., 1981, Disting. Alumni award Sch. Nursing Yale U., 1981, Alumni Achievement award U. Ariz., 1990, Disting. citation Kans. Alumni Assn., 1992, Health Leader of the Yr. award Pub. Health Svc., 1993, Centennial award Columbia Sch. Nursing, 1993, Presdl. Meritorious Exec. Rank award, 1994. Mem. ANA (Nurse Scientist of Yr. Award 1985, Salute to Nurses award 1994), Inst. Medicine Coun., Coun. Nurse Rschrs. (Nurse Scientist of Yr. Award 1985), Md. Nurses Assn., Western Soc. for Rsch. in Nursing, Am. Acad. Nursing, Inst. Medicine, 1989-, Sigma Xi, Sigma Theta Tau (Beta Mu Chpt. award of Excellence in Nursing Edn., 1980, Elizabeth McWilliams Miller Excellence in Rsch. Award, 1987), Alpha Chi Omega. Avocations: hiking, camping, bicycling. Office: U Mich Sch Nursing 400 N Ingalls St Ann Arbor MI 48109-2003

HINSHAW, BARBARA CARPENTER, chemistry educator; b. Murray, Utah, Mar. 19, 1944; d. Maurice O. and Audrey G. (Christensen) Carpenter; m. Jerald C. Hinshaw, June 16, 1967 (div. Oct. 1983); children: Janna, Aaron. BA, Westminister Coll., 1966; MS, U. Utah, 1969. Rsch. asst. U. Utah, Salt Lake City, 1969-70, Brigham Young U., Provo, Utah, 1983-84, asst. mgr., 1984-87, chem. mgr. officer, 1987-90, assoc. tchg. prof. chemistry, 1990—. Mem. Am. Chem. Soc., Internat. Campus Safety Assn.,LDS. Mem. Lds Ch. Office: Brigham Young U Provo UT 84602

HINSHAW, CARROLL ELTON, economics professor; b. Texarkana, Ark., Aug. 2, 1936; s. Curtis Tillman and Loma Dean (Roberts) H.; m. Jane A. Simpson, Aug. 11, 1957; children: Stephen, Rebecca, Carroll. BBA, Baylor U., 1958; PhD, Vanderbilt U., 1966. Assoc. prof. La. Coll., 1962-64; from prof. econs. to prof. emeritus Vanderbilt U., Nashville, 1966—2000, prof. emeritus, 2000—, asst. dean Coll. Arts and Sci., 1970-72, assoc. dean, 1972-74. Vis. asst. prof. Getulio Vargas Found., Rio de Janeiro, Brazil, 1967-69; CEO Shiloh Paper, Inc.; CFO Farmhouse Foods, Inc.; cons. in field. Author: Forecasting and Recognizing Business Cycle Turning Points, 1968; Contbr. articles to profl. jours. H.B. Earhart fellow, 1965-66 Mem. Am. Econ. Assn. (sec. 1976-93, treas. 1988-96, sec., treas. emeritus, 2000), Beta Alpha Psi, Omicron Delta Epsilon. Baptist. Home: 4400 Belmont Park Ter Apt 113 Nashville TN 37215-6272 Office: Am Econ Assn 2014 Broadway Ste 305 Nashville TN 37203-2425 also: Dept Econs Vanderbilt Univ Nashville TN 37232-0001

HINSHAW, CHESTER JOHN, lawyer; b. Sacramento, Mar. 10, 1941; s. Chester Edward and Gertrude Lorraine (Miller) H.; m. Karen Forbes Breakey, Feb. 19, 1977. AB, Stanford U., 1963; JD, U. Calif., Berkeley, 1966. Bar: Calif. 1966, U.S. Dist. Ct. (no. dist.) Calif. 1967, U.S. Ct. Appeals (9th cir.) 1967, N.Y. 1968, U.S. Dist. Ct. (so. dist.) N.Y. 1972, U.S. Dist. Ct. (ea. dist.) N.Y. 1974, U.S. Ct. Appeals (2d cir.) 1974, U.S. Dist. Ct. (no. dist.) N.Y. 1980, U.S. Dist. Ct. (ea. dist.) Mich. 1982, U.S. Dist. Ct. (no. dist.) Tex. 1983, Tex. 1984, U.S. Ct. Appeals (5th cir.) 1984, U.S Supreme Ct. 1991. Assoc. Chadbourne & Parke, N.Y.C., 1967-74, ptnr., 1974-83, Jones, Day, Reavis & Pogue, Dallas, 1983-99. Lectr. U. Calif. Berkeley, 1966. Mem. ABA, Tex. Bar Assn., Calif. Bar Assn. Home: 5510 Park Ln Dallas TX 75220-2158

HINSHAW, EDWARD BANKS, retired broadcast executive; b. Aurora, Ill., Feb. 27, 1940; s. Lorenzo M. and Emily (Roach) H.; m. Victoria Leone Biggers, Jan. 16, 1965; children: Eric, Brian. Student, Harvard Coll., 1958-59, U. Minn., 1959-62. Announcer Sta. KSTP-Radio-TV, Mpls., 1959-64; announcer Voice of America, Washington, 1964-65; reporter, anchorman Jour. Broadcast Group, Inc. (formerly Sta. WTMJ, Inc.), Milw., 1965-70, editorialist, 1970-74, editorial dir., 1974—, mgr. public affairs, 1979-90, mgr. pers. and editorial affairs, 1990-94, v.p. human resources, 1994—2002. Instr. broadcast journalism U. Wis., Whitewater, 1976, 79, 86. Trustee Nat. First Amendment Congress, 1980-83; chair Wis First Amendment Congress, 1985; bd. chair Milw. Urban League, 1987; bd. dirs. Children's Outing Assn., 1987-90, Ko-Thi Dance Co., 1992-99, pres., 1994-96; bd. dirs. Richard and Ethel Herzfeld Found., 1997—, Pabst Theater, 2002—, Riverworks Devel. Corp., Milw. Ctr. for Independence, 2004—, Lionel's House, 2003—, Donors Fourm of Wis., 2004—. Recipient DuPont-Columbia Citation in Broadcast Journalism, 1978; Abe Lincoln Merit award So. Baptist Radio-TV Commn., 1978; NCCJ Gold Media Medallion, 1977; named to Wis. Broadcasters Hall of Fame, 2002. Mem.: Milw. Press Club (bd. dirs. 1990—95, pres.-elect 1992, pres. 1993, Knight of the Golden Quill, Hall of Fame 2002), Wis. Broadcasters Assn. Found. (treas. 2000—), Nat. Broadcast Editl. Assn. (pres. 1980—81), Nat. Conf. Editl. Writers (life), Sigma Delta Chi (Disting. Svc. award 1977, Excellence in Journalism award 1988, Freedom of Info. award 1994). Business E-Mail: ehinshaw@wi.rr.com.

HINSHAW, ERNEST THEODORE, JR., private investor, retired Olympic team official, retired finance company executive; b. San Rafael, Calif., Aug. 26, 1928; s. Ernest Theodore and Ina (Johnson) H.; m. Nell Marie Schildmeyer, June 24, 1952; children: Marc Christopher, Lisa Anne, Jennifer, Amy Lynn. AB, Stanford U., 1951, MBA, 1957. Staff asst. to pres. Capital Research and Mgmt. Co., Los Angeles, 1957-58, dir. planning, 1967-68; fin. analyst Capital Research Co., Los Angeles, N.Y.C., 1958-68, v.p., 1962-71, mgr. N.Y.C. office, 1962-66; dir., exec. v.p. Am. Funds Service Co., Los Angeles, 1968-69, pres., 1969-72, chmn. bd., 1972-82; dir. pres. Capital Data

Systems, Inc., Los Angeles, 1971-73, chmn., 1973-79; v.p. Capital Group, Inc., Los Angeles, 1973-83; sr. v.p. Growth Fund Am., 1973-74, pres., 1974-76, chmn. bd., 1976-82, dir., 1974-96; sr. v.p. Income Fund Am., 1973-74, pres., dir., 1974-76, chmn. bd., 1976-82, dir., 1974-96; commr. yachting 1984 Olympic games Los Angeles Olympic Organizing Com., 1980-84. Dir. Capital Research & Mgmt. Co., 1972-83; mem. guest faculty Northwestern U. Transp. Center, 1965-66; mem. ops. com. Investment Co. Inst., 1970-74 Bd. dirs. Newport Harbor Nautical Mus., 1989-92, Girl Scout Coun. Orange County, 1993—2002, chair fin. com., 1996-97, treas., 1998-01; trustee Friends of Girl Scouts Trust; mem. investment com. Hoag Hosp. Found., 1992-97. Served to 1st lt. USMC, 1951-53. Mem. Soc. Airline Analysts (sec. 1965-66), Nat. Kite Class (pres. 1968-69), Lido 14 Internat. Class Assn. (pres. 1978-79), Assn. Orange Coast Yacht Clubs (commodore 1976), So. Calif. Yachting Assn. (commodore 1979), B.O.A.T., Inc. (dir. 1977-81), Pacific Coast Yachting Assn. (dir. 1979-80), U.S. Yacht Racing Union (dir. 1980-81), U.S. Sailing Ctr. Long Beach, Calif. (adv. coun. mem.). Clubs: Lido Isle Yacht (Newport Beach, Calif.) (commodore 1973), Stanford U. Sailing (trustee 1984-96), St. Francis Yacht (San Francisco), Ft. Worth Boat Democrat. Home: 729 Via Lido Soud Newport Beach CA 92663-5530

HINSHAW, MARK LARSON, architect, urban planner; b. Glendale, Calif., Aug. 17, 1947; s. Lerner Brady and Alice Elaine (Larson) H.; m. Caryl Ann Kunsemuller, Dec. 21, 1968 (div. 1982); 1 child, Erica; m. Marilyn Kay Smith, June 18, 1983 (div. 1997); children: Lindsay, Christopher. BArch magna cum laude, U. Okla., 1970; M in Urban Planning, CUNY, 1972. Registered arch., Wash. Sr. planner Planning Dept., Anchorage, 1976-77; project planner TRA, Seattle, 1977-82; urban designer City of Bellevue, Wash., 1982-90; ind. cons., 1991-97; dir. urban design LMN Archs., Seattle, 1997—. Arch.-in-the-sch. Seattle Sch. Dist., 1979. Columnist on architecture, urban design: Seattle Times, 1993—2004; author: Citistate Seattle: Shaping a Modern Metropolis, 1999—; contbg. editor: Landscape Architecture Mag.; contbr. articles to profl. jours. and books. Mem. Urban Beautification Commn., Anchorage, 1975, Design Jury, Hemet (Calif.) Civic Ctr. Competition, Seattle Design Commn., 1990-91; mem. Downtown Seattle Design Rev. Bd., 1996-. 1st lt. USAF, 1972-76. NEA grantee, 1975; recipient merit award for Hist. Preservation, City of Seattle, 1983. Fellow AIA (pres. Seattle chpt. 1992-93), Am. Inst. Cert. Planners (mem. nat. bd. 1994-98); mem. Am. Planning Assn. (sec. Wash. chpt. 1982, v.p. 1983-85, pres. 1987-89). Office: 801 2nd Ave Fl 5 Seattle WA 98104-1576 Office Phone: 206-682-3460. Business E-Mail: mhinshaw@imnarchitects.com.

HINSHAW, VIRGINIA, academic administrator; BA in Lab. Tech., MS in Microbiology, Auburn U., 1967, PhD in Microbiology, 1972. Clin. and rsch. microbiologist Med. Coll. Va., 1967—68; rsch. virologist U. Calif., Berkeley, 1974; rsch. assoc. divns. virology St. Jude Children's Rsch. Hosp.; assoc. prof. virology dept. patho-biol. scis. U. Wis., Madison, 1985—88, prof., 1988—92, interim assoc. dean for rsch. and grad. studies Sch. Vet. Medicine, 1992—93, assoc. vice-chancellor, 1994—95, vice chancellor for rsch., dean Grad. Sch., sr. rsch. officer, 1995—2001; provost, exec. vice chancellor U. Calif., Davis, 2001—. Office: Univ Calif Davis One Shields Ave Davis CA 95616

HINSON, BOBBY D., lawyer; b. Lancaster, SC, Mar. 14, 1962; AB magna cum laude in Economics and Polit. Sci., Duke U., 1984; JD, U. Va., 1987. Bar: NC 1987, SC 1989, US Ct. Appeals 4th Cir. Assoc. Kennedy Covington Lobdell & Hickman LLP, Charlotte, NC, 1987—94; mem. Womble Carlyle Sandridge & Rice PLLC, Charlotte, NC, 1994—, leader real estate develop. practice group. Bd. dirs. Habitat for Humanity, Charlotte, NC, Jackson Park Ministries. Mem.: SC Bar Assn. (real property sect.), NC Bar Assn. (real property sect.), Mecklenburg County Bar Assn. Office: Womble Carlyle Sandridge & Rice PLLC One Wachovia Ctr Ste 3500 301 S College St Charlotte NC 28202-6037 Office Phone: 704-331-4918. Office Fax: 704-338-7803. Business E-Mail: bhinson@wcsr.com.

HINSON, CYNTHIA THOMAS, minister; b. Charlotte, N.C., Jan. 26, 1951; d. Frealon Ed Thomas and Frances Elizabeth Love; m. Yancy Gerald Hinson, Dec. 22, 1973; children: Y. Jerry Hinson, III, William Thomas, Elizabeth Anne. BA in English Linguistics, U. Houston, 1994; MDiv cum laude, So. Meth. U., 1998; Beeson Doctoral fellow in Ministry, Asbury Theol. Sem., 2001—. Lic. pastor The United Meth. Ch., Houston, Tex., 1996, ordained deacon The United Meth. Ch., Houston, Tex., 1997, ordained elder The United Meth. Ch., Houston, Tex., 2000, cert. pastoral care specialist Krist Samaritan Ctr. for Couseling and Edn., Clear Lake, Tex., 2000; lic. real estate broker Real Estate Licensing Bd., North Carolina, 1971. Guitar instr. YWCA, Charlotte, NC, 1966—72; lab. technician The ARC, Charlotte, 1972—74; mgr. Headen and Co., Charlotte, 1974—76, Jetero Properties, Houston, 1977—79; property mgr. Krupp Co., Houston, 1979—81; english tchr. Houston Ind. Sch. Dist., Bellaire, Tex., 1994—95; sr. pastor St. Paul United Meth. Ch., Conroe, Tex., 1995—. Registrar com. on ordained ministry Houston (Tex.) North Dist. United Meth. Ch., 2001—; divsn. of edn. Tex. Ann. Conf. United Meth. Ch., Houston, 2000—, mentor pastor Com. Rules and Structure, 2000—; bd. of trustees Montgomery County Interfaith Hospitality Network, Conroe, Tex., 2000—02; spiritual dir. Houston North Emmaus Cmty., Tex., 1999—; page Gen. Conf. 2000 of the UMC, Cleveland, Ohio, 2000—00; v.p. Friends of Bellaire (Tex.) Parks, 1985—92; faith-based initiative Montgomery Co. Dept. of Corrections and St. Paul United Meth. Ch., Conroe, 2001—; instr. Lay Spkr. Sch. United Meth. Ch., Houston, 1996—2002; spkr. in field. Russ Pitman Park Playground. Supervising pastor Clowns for Christ, Conroe, 1999—2003; trustee Mont. County Interfaith Hospitality Network, Conroe, 2000—02. Recipient Vision award, Friends of Bellaire (Tex.) Pks., 1996; fellow, Beeson Internat. Sch. for Bibl. Preaching, Asbury Theol. Sem., 2001—. Mem.: Renewal Network, Sam Houston State U. Parents' Assn. (bd. dirs.), Houston Emmaus Cmty. (spiritual dir. 1999—), The Confessing Movement United Meth. Ch., Ea. Star, Sigma Tau Delta. Republican. United Meth. Office: St Paul United Methodist Church 1100 W Semands / P O Box 506 Conroe TX 77305 Office Phone: 936-756-5442.

HINSON, H. DOUGLAS, lawyer; b. Staunton, Va., June 27, 1960; s. Harold D. and Betty M. (Morris) H.; m. Michelle R. Olsen, Aug. 9, 1986. BA magna cum laude, Emory U., 1982; JD cum laude, Georgetown U., 1986. Bar: Ala. 1986, Ga. 1989, U.S. Dist. Ct. (no. and so. dists.) Ala. 1986, U.S. Ct. Appeals (11th cir.) 1987, U.S. Dist. Ct. (no. dist.) Ga. 1989. Assoc. Bradley, Arant, Rose & White, Birmingham, Ala., 1986-88; assoc. Alston & Bird, Atlanta, 1988-94, ptnr., litig., 1994—. Active Salvation Army. Mem. Phi Beta Kappa. Avocations: golf, travel. Office: Alston & Bird 1 Atlantic Ctr 1201 W Peachtree St NW Atlanta GA 30309-3424 Office Phone: 404-881-7590. Office Fax: 404-881-7777. Business E-Mail: dhinson@alston.com.

HINSON, JACK ALLSBROOK, research toxicologist, educator; b. Mullins, S.C., Aug. 18, 1944; s. Layton Liston and Will (Allsbrook) H.; m. Joanne Edwards Kidd; children: Edward Thomas, Richard William. BS, Coll. of Charleston, 1966; MS, U. S.C., 1968; PhD, Vanderbilt U., 1972. Postdoctoral fellow Nat. Inst. of Health, Bethesda, Md., 1972-75, sr. staff fellow, 1975-80; rsch. toxicologist Nat. Ctr. Toxicological Rsch., Jefferson, Ark., 1980-90, chief biochem. mechanisms br., 1989-90; adj. prof. U. Ark. Med. Sci., Little Rock, 1980-90, prof., dir. div. toxicology. Dir. interdisciplinary toxicology program U. Ark. Med. Sci., 1990—; chmn. Ark. Toxicology Symposium, 1992-99; adj. assoc. prof. U. Tenn. Ctr. for Health Scis., Memphis, 1982-90; vis. fellow Middlesex Hops. Med. Sch., London, 1982; vis. prof. U. Leiden, The Netherlands, 1986. Editor Drug Metabolism Revs., 1997—, mem. editl. bd., 1995-97; mem. editl. bd. Toxicology and Applied Pharmacology, 1980-89, 96—, Jour. Toxicology and Environ. Health, 1991—; contbr. chpts. to books and articles to profl. jours. Mem. Soc. Toxicology (pres. South Ctrl. chpt. 1990-92), Am. Soc. Pharmacology and Exptl. Therapeutics, Internat. Soc. for Study of Xenobiotics. Episcopalian. Home: 8 Piedmont Ln Little Rock AR 72223-2232 Office: U Ark Med Sci Divsn Toxicology 4301 W Markham St # 638 Little Rock AR 72205-7101 Business E-Mail: HinsonJackA@uams.edu.

HINSON, ROBERT WAYNE, education educator; b. Charlotte, N.C., Oct. 24, 1949; s. Selkirt Alexander and Sally (Helms) H.; m. Sandra Rowell (div. Aug. 1988); 1 child, Jennifer AnnaBeth; m. Linda Ritchie. BA in English, U. N.C., Charlotte, 1972, MEd in English Edn., 1986, CAS in English Edn., 1989; EdS in Ednl. Adminstrn., Winthrop Coll., 1989; PhD in English, Union Grad. Sch., Cin., 1993. Cert. sch. adminstr., postgrad. in ednl. adminstrn., prin., supr., secondary tchr., S.C. Tchr. English and reading Marlboro County Sch. Dist., Bennettsville, S.C., 1981-93; Charlotte (N.C.)-Meck Schs., 1993—; writing cons. Marlboro County Sch. Dist., Bennettsville, S.C., 1986—; prof. English and writing Wingate (N.C.) Coll., 1989—. Author: (poetry) Winds of the World, 1975, Fear Years, 1978, Route Reflections, 1986, Journal of Pauley's Island, 1987, (novella) Fairfield Plantation, 1982, Individual Therapy Journal Writing, 1989. Chmn. Union County Rep. Com., 1973; chmn. steering com. campaign for N.C. gov., 1974. Ednl. Found. Pee Dee grantee, 1988. Mem. N.C. English Tchrs. Assn., S.C. English Tchrs. Assn., North and S.C. Reading Assn., Palmetto State Tchrs. Assn., Writers Workshop Asheville (co-founder). Methodist. Avocation: writing. Home: 6238 Old Monroe Rd Indian Trail NC 28079-5343 E-mail: hhinsonrw@aol.com.

HINSON, ROBERT WILLIAM, advertising executive, consultant; b. Neptune, N.J., Nov. 30, 1944; s. Herbert William and Bernice (Stadelhofer) H. AB in Econs. and Sociology, Boston Coll., 1966. Media planner Benton & Bowles, Inc., N.Y.C., 1968-70; v.p., assoc. media dir. SSC&B: Lintas Worldwide, N.Y.C., 1970-74, sr. v.p., dir. media ops., 1976-80; v.p., assoc. media dir. Foote Cone & Belding, Inc., L.A., 1974-76; exec. v.p., chmn. mgmt. com., chmn. ops. com., dir. media svcs. Rosenfeld, Sirowitz & Lawson, Inc., N.Y.C., 1980-85, exec. v.p., dir. mktg. and media svcs., chief adminstrv. officer, 1986-87; pres., chief exec. officer Hinson and Assocs., Inc., N.Y.C., 1987-91. Cons. in field, 1991—. Author: Media Leverage, 1985. Media dir. Tuesday Team, Reagan-Bush '84 campaign, 1984; sustaining mem. Rep. Nat. Com.; mem. Ronald Reagan Presdl. Libr. Found., Monmouth County (N.J.) Rep. Orgn.; bd. dirs. Monmouth (N.J.) Symphony Orch.; mem. nat. campaign com. Boston Coll. Mem. NATAS, Internat. Assn. TV, Arts and Scis., Internat. Radio and TV Soc., Media Dirs. Industry Coun., Am. Assn. Advt. Agys. (media policy com. 1980-87), Am. Rsch. Found. (media com. coun. 1983-86), Boston Coll. Alumni Assn., Wagner Soc. N.Y., Monmouth County Hist. Soc., Alliance Francaise of Monmouth County (N.J.), Alliance Francaise of Ft. Lauderdale, Nature Conservancy, Nat. Trust for Hist. Preservation, Vieux Carre Property Owners Assn., N.Y. Athletic Club, Deal (N.J.) Golf and Country Club, Allenhurst (N.J.) Beach Club, Coral Ridge (Fla.) Country Club. Roman Catholic. Home: 133 N Pompano Beach Blvd Pompano Beach FL 33062-5728 also: 921 Chartres St New Orleans LA 70116-3227

HINTERBUCHNER, CATHERINE N., rehabilitative medicine educator, physician; b. Greece, Nov. 22, 1926; m. Ladislav P. Hinterbuchner, Dec. 10, 1955. MD cum laude, Nat. & Kapodistriakon U., Athens, Greece, 1951; DS (hon.), New Med. Coll., 2002. Intern St. Luke's Hosp., 1953-54; resident in internal medicine French Hosp., 1954-55, Kingsbrook Jewish Med. Ctr., 1955-56, fellow in phys. medicine and rehab., 1956-57, N.Y. Med. Coll., 1956-57, N.Y. Med. Coll. and Met. Hosp. Ctr., 1959-60; acting cmn. dept. rehab. medicine N.Y. Med. Coll., Valhalla, 1970-71, prof., chmn. dept. rehab. medicine, 1971—2004; chief rehab. medicine, attending physician Met. Hosp. Ctr., N.Y.C., 1964—2004; chief rehab. medicine Lincoln Med. and Mental Health Ctr., 2001—04. Fellow ACP, N.Y. Acad. Medicine, Am. Acad. Phys. Medicine and Rehab.; mem. AMA, N.Y. State Med. Soc., N.Y.C. Med. Soc., Am. Congress Rehab. Medicine, N.Y. Acad. Scis.

HINTHORN, MICKY TERZAGIAN, retired executive secretary; b. Jersey City, July 5, 1924; d. Bedros H. and Aznive (Hynelian) Terzagian; m. Wayne L. Hinthorn, Aug. 11, 1957. BS in Occupational Therapy, U. So. Calif., 1953; MBA, Notre Dame de Namur U., Belmont, Calif., 1984. Registered occupational therapist. Gen. office worker Drake Secretarial Coll., Jersey City, 1941-42; sec., expediter Western Electric Co., Kearny, N.J., 1943-45; sec. div. edn. CBS, NYC, 1945-46; sec. to v.p. sales Simon and Schuster, Inc., NYC, 1947-51; gen. office worker in Sch. of Edn. U. So. Calif., L.A., 1951-52; occupational therapist Palo Alto (Calif.) Clinic, 1954-55; chief occupational therapist Children's Health Coun., Palo Alto, 1954-56; sec. to chief mil. engr. Lenkurt Electric Co., San Carlos, Calif., 1956-58; sr. sec. re-entry program Bank of Am., Redwood City, Calif., 1979-80; ret., 1980. Organizer occupational therapy dept. Children's Health Coun., Palo Alto, Calif., 1954, chief 1954-56. Author: editors profl. newsletters. Charter mem., membership chair U. So. Calif. Pres. Cir., San Francisco, 1978-80; treas. North Peninsula chpt. San Francisco Opera Guild, San Mateo, Calif., 1979; vol. pub. info. chair re-election San Mateo County Supr., Redwood City, Calif., 1978; founder, charter pres. Friends of Belmont (Calif.) Libr., 1974-75; mem. Coastside Fireworks Com., 1989-94, chair corp. sponsorship, 1992-93. Recipient Hon. Mem., Friends of San Francisco Pub. Libr., 1974, 1990-1995, Assoc. Mem. Half Moon Bay Coastside Chamber Comm. (chair Bus. Edn. scholarships 1992, 93), Recognition Award 1993. Mem. AAUW (hon. life, pres. San Mateo br. 1976-77, chair local scholarships Half Moon Bay br. 1992, historian 1992-94, corr. sec. 1995-97, scholarship com. 1999-2000, edn. found. com. 1999-2003, name grant honoree Edn. Found. Jodi Gordon Endowment 1991-92), U. So. Calif. Alumni Assn. (life), Notre Dame de Namur U. Alumni Assn., Friends of Filoli, Friends of Half Moon Bay Libr., Coastside Women's Club (scholarship com. 1999-2003, com. for scholarships and charities 2003—). Avocations: photography, walking, reading, writing, attending performing arts events. Home: PO Box 176 Half Moon Bay CA 94019-0176

HINTIKKA, JAAKKO, philosopher, educator; b. Helsinginpitäjä, Finland, Jan. 12, 1929; s. Toivo Juho and Lempi J. (Salmi) H.; m. Merrill Bristow Provence, Feb. 11, 1978 (dec.); m. Ghita Holmström, Dec. 19, 1987. Grad. in Philosophy, U. Helsinki, Finland, 1952, PhD, 1956; postgrad., Harvard U., 1954; Doctorate (hon.), U. Liège, 1984, Jagiellonian U., 1995, Uppsala U., 2000, U. Oulu, 2001, U. Turku, 2003. Jr. fellow Soc. Fellows, Harvard U., 1956-59; prof. philosophy U. Helsinki, 1959-70; rsch. prof. Acad. Finland, 1970-81; prof. philosophy Fla. State U., Tallahassee, 1978-90, McKenzie prof., 1986-90, also prof. computer sci., 1986-90; prof. Boston U., 1990—. Vis. prof. Brown U., 1962, U. Calif., Berkeley, 1963, Hebrew U. Jerusalem, 1974; part-time prof. philosophy Stanford U., 1964-82, Immanuel Kant lectr., 1985; John Locke lectr. Oxford (Eng.) U., 1964; fellow Ctr. for Advanced Study in Behavioral Scis., 1970-71; Hägerström lectr. U. Uppsala, 1983; co-chair Am. organizing com. Twentieth World Congress Philos., 1998. Author: Knowledge and Belief, 1962, 2d edit., 2005, Models for Modalities, 1969, Tieto on valtaa, 1969, Logic, Language-Games and Information, 1973, Time and Necessity, 1973, Knowledge and the Known, 1974, (with U. Remes) The Method of Analysis, 1974, The Intentions of Intentionality, 1975, The Semantics of Questions and the Questions of Semantics, 1976, Aristotle on Modality and Determinism, 1977, The Game of Language, 1983, (with J. Kulas) Anaphora and Definite Descriptions, 1985, (with Merrill B. Hintikka) Investigating Wittgenstein, 1986, (with Martin Kusch) Kieli ja maailma, 1988, (with Merrill B. Hintikka) The Logic of Epistemology, 1989, Intentionnalite et mondes possibles, 1989, (with James Bachman) What If? Toward Excellence in Reasoning, 1990, (with Gabriel Sandu) On the Methodology of Linguistics, 1991, Eseje Logiczno-Filozoficzne, 1992, Fondements d'une theorie du langage, 1994, The Principles of Mathematics Revisited, 1996, Ludwig Wittgenstein: Half-truths and One-and-a-Half Truths, 1996, Lingua Universalis vs. Calculus Ratiocinator, 1996, Language, Truth and Logic in Mathematics, 1997, Paradigms for Language Theory, 1997, El Viaje Filosófico más Largo, 1998, Inquiry as Inquiry, 1999, On Goedel, 2000, On Wittgenstein, 2000, Filosofian Koyhyys ja Rikkaus, 2001, Aspects of Aristotle, 2004; contbr. over 300 articles to profl. jours.; editor-in-chief: Internat. Jour. Synthese, 1965-76, 82-2002; editor: Synthese Libr., 1965-2002 Acta Philosophica Fennica, 1973-79, Synthese Lang. Libr., 1976-84, (with Patrick Suppes) Aspects of Inductive Logic, 1966, Philosophy of Mathematics, 1969, (with Donald Davidson) Words and Objections, 1969, (with Patrick Suppes) Information and Inference, 1970, (with others) Approaches to Natural Language, 1973, Rudolf Carnap, Logical Empiricist, 1976, (with others) Essays on Wittgenstein in Honor of G.H. von Wright, 1976, (with Robert Butts) Procs. 5th Internat. Congress Logic, Methodology and Philosophy of Science (4 vols.), 1977, (with Lucia Vaina) Cognitive Constraints on Communication, 1984, (with S. Knuuttila) The Logic of Being, 1986, (with Leila Haaparanta) Frege Synthesized, 1987, Aspects of Metaphor, 1994, From Dedekind to Gödel, 1995. Decorated comdr. Order of the Lion of Finland, 1st class, 1987; recipient Wihuri Internat. prize, 1976, E.J. Nyström prize Soc. Scientiarum Fennica, 1988, Suomen Kulttuurirahasto grand prize, 1989, Schock prize, 2005; Guggenheim fellow, 1979-80. Mem. Assn. Symbolic Logic (v.p. 1968-70), Internat. Inst. Philosophy (v.p. 1993-96, pres. 1999-2002), Internat. Union History and Philosophy Sci. (v.p. 1971-75, pres. 1975), Finnish Acad. Sci. and Letters (coun. 1972-79), Philosophy of Sci. Assn. (governing bd. 1970-72), Societas Scientiarum Fennica, Internat. Fedn. Philos. Socs. (governing bd. 1978-88, 93-98, v.p. 1993-98), Am. Philos. Assn. (v.p. Pacific divsn. 1974-75, pres. 1975-76), Am. Acad. Arts and Scis., Norwegian Acad. Sci., C.S. Peirce Soc. (pres. 1997), Russian Acad. of Scis. (fgn. mem.), Hungarian Acad. Scis., Phi Beta Kappa (hon.). Home: 38 Flint Dr Marlborough MA 01752-6701 Office: Boston U Dept Philosophy Boston MA 02215-4701 also: U Helsinki Inst Philosophy PO Box 9 FIN 00014 Helsinki Finland Business E-Mail: hintikka@bu.edu.

HINTON, FLOYD, retired lawyer; b. Olympia, Wash., Sept. 11, 1923; s. Irma (Yost) Ness.; married; children: Denise C. Hinton Maaranen, Stefan V., Bradford R. BS, U. Org., 1948; LLB, Northwestern Law Sch., Portland, Oreg., 1958. Bar: Oreg. 1958, U.S. Dist. Ct. Oreg. 1959, U.S. Ct. Appeals (ith cir.) 1980. Sole practitioner, Portland, 1958-61; ptnr. Deich Hinton & Meece and predecessors, Portland, 1961-88; in house counsel Oreg. Ctrl. Credit Union, 1988—99; ret., 1999. Chmn. supervisory com. Oreg. Cen. Credit Union. Active in fin. devel. Oreg. Lung Assn., Portland, 1982-85; bd. dirs. N.W. Native Am. Arts Coun., 1985—. SErved with U.S. Army, 1943. Mem. Oreg. State Bar (author ins. and creditor rights for continuing legal edn. com.), Multnomah County Bar Assn., Oreg. Trial Lawyers Assn., Am. Arbitration Assn., Portland Art Assn., Portland City Club (mem. study groups), Viking Athletic Assn. (bd. dirs. 1985), Elks (trustee). Home: 1472 Glenwood Dr Brookings OR 97415-8135

HINTON, JAMES FORREST, JR., lawyer; b. Gadsden, Ala., Nov. 19, 1951; s. James Forrest Sr. and Juanita Grey (Weems) H. BA, Vanderbilt U., 1974; JD, U. Ala., 1977. Bar: Ala. 1977, D.C. 1979, U.S. Dist. Ct. (so. dist.) Ala. 1979, U.S. Ct. Appeals (5th cir.) 1980, U.S. Ct. Appeals (11th cir.) 1981, La. 1982, U.S. Dist. Ct. (ea. and mid. dists.) La. 1982, U.S. Dist. Ct. (no. dist.) Ala 1982, U.S. Supreme Ct. 1982, U.S. Dist. Ct. (we. dist.) La. 1983, U.S. Dist. Ct. (no. dist.) Ohio 1983, U.S. Ct. Appeals (D.C. cir.) 1984, U.S. Ct. Appeals (fed. cir.) 1985, U.S. Dist. Ct. (so. dist.) Tex. 1987, U.S. Dist. Ct. (no. dist.) Tex. 1991, Tex. 1992, Tenn. 1992, U.S. Dist. Ct. (ea. and we. dists.) Ark. 1992, U.S. Ct. Appeals (6th and 8th cirs.) 1992, U.S. Dist. Ct. (ea. and we. dists.) Tex. 1993, U.S. Dist. Ct. (mid. dist.) Ala. 1993, U.S. Dist. Ct. (ea. and mid. dist.) Tenn. 1994, U.S. Dist. Ct., Colo. 2000. Law clk. to chief judge U.S. Dist. Ct. (so. dist.) Ala., Mobile, 1977-79; ptnr. Darby, Myrick & Hinton, Mobile, 1979-82; dir. McGlinchey Stafford Lang, New Orleans, 1982-93; ptnr. Adams & Reese, New Orleans, 1993-97; shareholder Berkowitz, Lefkovits, Isom & Kushner, Birmingham, 1997—2003, Baker, Donelson, Bearman, Caldwell & Berkowitz, 2003—. Contbr. articles to profl. jours. Mem. ABA (antitrust, intellectual property, litigation sects.), FBA, La. Assn. Def. Counsel, Order of Coif, Phi Beta Kappa. Office: Baker Donelson Bearman Caldwell & Berkowitz PC 420 20th St N Ste 1600 Birmingham AL 35203-5200 Office Phone: 205-250-8332. E-mail: fhinton@bakerdonelson.com.

HINTON, KATHERINE CH'IU, foundation administrator; b. Chengdu, China; d. Rui-fu Ch'iu, Lan-Ying Chao; children: May Lyle, Lorin Lyle. MPH, Columbia U., 1978—80; PhD, U. Hawaii, 1983—88. East asian specialist Yale U., New Haven, 1962—64; rsch. asst. Nat. Common Maternal Child Health, 1965—66; info scientist Population Coun., NYC, 1967—79; field rep. in China Rockefeller Found., NYC, 1980—87, rsch. scientist, 1987—89; program officer for China UNICEF, NYC, 1989—94, country rep. for Mongolia, 1994—99. Cons. U.S. Nat. Inst. Health, Wash., DC, 1973—74; hon. mem. Peking Union Med. Coll. Hosp., Beijing, 1986. Author: (book) China's Resources, 1977, Internat. Family Planning Program, 1978; editor: (e-book) Programme Operation (UNICEF), 1999. Chair NY Quarterly Meeting, NYC, 2003—; trustee Friends Seminary, 1976—79. Recipient Rsch. award, PURC US Acad. Sci., 1979, Rockefeller Found., 1979—80; scholarship, PEO Internat. Peace, 1961—63. Mem.: NY Acad. Sci. Home: 90 La Salle St Apt 15E New York NY 10027 Personal E-mail: ktqiu65@yahoo.com.

HINTON, NORMAN WAYNE, retired information services executive; b. Maysville, Ky., Mar. 8, 1944; s. Eugene Fay and Julia Lafelle (Dalton) H.; m. Juanita Ann Smith, Nov. 16, 1968; children: Janis Renee Proctor, Brian Wayne. BA in Bus. Adminstrn., Centre Coll. Ky., 1966. ordained elder. Programmer, systems analyst Union Cen. Life Ins., Cin., 1966-70, Electronic Data Systems Corp., Dallas, 1970-99; ret., 1999; realtor Century 21 Park One Realtors, Allen, Tex., 1999—. Bd. dirs. S.E. La. chpt. ARC, New Orleans, 1991-92, Orleans Svc. Ctr., 1990-92; chmn. emergency svcs. commn. Info. and Referral Ctr. of Collin County, 1994-97, vice-chmn., 1995-96, chmn., 1996-97; adv. bd. Tulane U. Coll. Bus., New Orleans, 1989-92; Dallas-Ft. Worth Ch. coun. Ch. of God Internat., 1994-96, treas., 1995, pres., 1996; bd. dirs. Christian Ednl. Ministries, 2000-04; chmn., bd. dirs. Christian Ednl. Ministries Festival Assn., 1999-2002. Fellow Life Office Mgmt. Assn., Am. Mgmt. Assn.; mem. Assn. Ky. Cols., Rotary Club of Allen (bd. dirs. 2002—, chmn. program com. 2002-03, 05—, chmn. internat. com. 2003-05, chmn. program com., 2005-), Sigma Alpha Epsilon Avocations: quarterhorses, golf, travel.

HINTON, PAULA WEEMS, lawyer; b. Gadsden, Ala., Dec. 5, 1954; d. James Forrest and Juanita (Weems) H.; m. Steven D. Lawrence, Mar. 31, 1984; 1 child, David Hinton Lawrence. BA in Polit. Sci. magna cum laude, U. Ala., 1976, MPA, JD, U. Ala., 1979. Bar: Ala. 1979, U.S. Dist. Ct. (so. dist.) Ala. 1980, U.S. Dist. Ct. (so. dist.) Tex. 1981, U.S. Ct. Appeals (5th and 11th cirs.) 1981, Tex. 1982, U.S. Dist. Ct. (no. dist.) Tex. 1988, U.S. Dist. Ct. (ea. and we. dists.) Tex. 1989, U.S. Dist. Ct. (no. and mid. dists.) Ala. 1993, U.S. Supreme Ct. 1998. Law clk. to magistrate U.S. Dist. Ct. Ala., Mobile, 1979-80; assoc. Vinson & Elkins, LLP, Houston, 1981-88; ptnr. Akin Gump Strauss Hauer & Feld, L.L.P., Houston, 1989—2001, Vinson & Elkins, Houston, 2001—. Mem. Supreme Ct. Gender Bias Reform Implementation Com., 1998—, co-chair, 2000—, chair, 2002—; mem. faculty Tex. Coll. Judicial Studies, 2004; panel arbitrators Am. Arbitration Assn., 1989—97; spkr. in field. Contbr. articles to profl. jours. Mem. women's initiative cabinet United Way Tex. Gulf Coast; mem. adv. bd. Sch. Law Found. U. Houston; bd. dirs. Planned Parenthood Houston and S.E. Tex., Inc., 2000—03. Named a Tex. Super Lawyer, Tex. Monthly and Law and Politics, 2003, 2004; Rotary fellow, U. Sevilla, Spain, 1980—81. Fellow: Tex. Bar Found. (nominating co-chair 2002, co-chmn. nominating com. 2002—03, chair new fellows com. 2003, liaison to bd. 2003—05), Houston Bar Found. (life; bd. dirs. 1994—96, chmn. 1996—97, bd. dirs. 2002—); mem.: ATLA, ABA (mem. litigation sect., internat. law and practice sect., bus. law sect., women and the law sect., women's adv. com. on corp. counsel, commn. on women's Margaret Brent League), Am. Bar Found., Surpeme Ct. Hist. Soc., Am. Law Inst., Am. Inns of Ct., Tex. Assn. Def. Counsel, Coll. State Bar Tex., Tex. Assn. Def. Counsel, Internat. Assn. Def. Counsel, Am. Law Inst., Tex. Ctr. for Legal Ethics and Professionalism, Tex. Exec. Women, London Ct. of Internat. Arbitration, Internat. Bar Assn. Section on Bus. Law (sect. bus. law, barristers & advocates forum), Houston Bar Assn. (minority opportunities in legal profession com. 1997, civil justice ctr. com. 1997—98), Greater Houston Partnerships, Exec. Women's Partnership (steering com. 2002—03), U. Houston Law Found. (adv. bd), State Bar Tex. (chair women in the profession com. 1996—98, ad hoc com. to select minority dirs. 1997, local grievance com. 1998, mem. disciplinary rules of profl. conduct com. 2000—01, bd. dirs. 2002—05, vice chair spl. pattern jury charge oversight com. 2003, exec. com. 2003—04, mem. disciplinary rules of profl. conduct com. 2004—05, mem. litigation sect., internat. law sect., antitrust and bus. litigation sect., alternative dispute resolution sect., women and law sect., women and the sect. Ma'at Justice award 2003, Woman on Move award 2004), Alexis de Tocqueville

Soc., Am. Inns of Ct., Supreme Ct. Hist. Soc., Phi Delta Phi, Omicron Delta Kappa, Pi Sigma Alpha. Office: Vinson and Elkins LLP First City Tower 1001 Fannin St Ste 2300 Houston TX 77002-6760 Business E-Mail: phinton@velaw.com.

HINTON, VELECIA ANN, social welfare administrator; b. St. Louis, Nov. 12, 1957; d. Grady, Sr. and Clara B. (Gardner) Blunt; m. Rodney B. Patterson, Mar. 8, 1980 (div. May 1991); children: Islandia E. McIntyre, Amber T. Patterson, Osha L. Patterson; m. Elbert J. Hinton, Aug. 21, 1994. AA in Biblical Theology, Internat. Bible Coll. and Seminar, 1987; BA in Social Svcs., Lael Coll. & Grad. Sch., 1992; MMin, Christian Bible Coll. & Seminary, 2000; DMin in Christian Edn., Patriot U., 2004. Cert. Christian counseling therapist Christian Bible Coll. and Sem., 2000. Child care adminstr. St. Louis Pub. Schs., 1989—99; sr. support coord. Coun. for Extended Care, St. Louis, 1999—2002; classified acct. exec. Good News Christian Herald Newspaper, St. Louis, 2002; edn. coord. Our Lady's Inn Shelter, St. Louis, 2002—03, family specialist, 2003—; sr. svcs. coord. Adams Park Cmty. Ctr., St. Louis, 2003; pastor Footsteps of Jesus Christ Apostles' Doctrine Ch., Inc., St. Louis, 1994—; adminstr. Footsteps of Jesus Christ Coll., St. Louis, 2003—. Adv. bd. mem. Black African-Am. Christian Counselors, Detroit, 2000—04. Author: Preach the Word, 7 vol. set, 1999—2004. Dist. sec. Full Gospel Assembly Ch., Pine Lawn, Mo., 1993—. Avocations: bowling, writing, singing, teaching, preaching. Home: 9916 Castle Dr Moline Acres MO 63136 Office Phone: 314-922-7289. E-mail: FOJCCollege@aol.com.

HINZ, CARL FREDERICK, JR., immunologist, educator; b. Cleve., Apr. 9, 1927; s. Carl Frederick and Marie (Jones) H.; m. Joan Herndon, June 5, 1953; children— Elizabeth, Richard, Catherine, Gretchen. BS, Western Res. U., 1948, MD, 1951. Faculty dept. medicine Western Res. U. Sch. Medicine, Cleve., 1953-67, asst. prof., 1961-67, research asso. div. research in med. edn., 1964-67; prof., asso. dean U. Conn. Sch. Medicine, 1967-92, acting head dept. medicine, 1979-80, emeritus, 1992—. Mem. Conn. Med. Exam. Bd., 1976-80 Chmn. bd. dirs. blood svcs. Conn. region ARC, 1993-95, chair coun. of chairs North Atlantic area, 1995-98. Markle scholar, 1959-64; scholar-in-residence Inst. Medicine, Nat. Acad. Sci., 1987-88. Fellow ACP; mem. Am. Soc. Clin. Investigation, Am. Assn. Immunologists, Am. Soc. Hematology, Central Soc. Clin. Research, Am. Fedn. Clin. Research, Conn. Med. Soc., Hartford County Med. Assn. (dir. 1976-92, pres. 1986-87), Conn. Lung Assn. (pres. 1979-81) Home: 11 Highwood Dr Avon CT 06001-2411

HINZ, DOROTHY ELIZABETH, writer, editor, corporate communications specialist; b. N.Y.C. AB, Hunter Coll.; student, Columbia U. Asst. to dir. devel. Columbia U., N.Y.C., 1953-55; mng. editor, econs. rschr.-analyst, writer speeches, position papers, mgr. pubs. W.R. Grace & Co., N.Y.C., 1955-64; staff writer Oil Progress, fgn. news media, speeches, films, internat. petroleum ops., pub. rels. dept. Caltex Petroleum Corp., N.Y.C., 1964-69; fin. editor Merrill Lynch, Pierce, Fenner & Smith, 1969-74; mgr. publs., mgr. speakers' bur., assoc. speech writer mktg. and corp. comm. dept. Mfrs. Hanover Corp., N.Y.C., 1974-88; mem. Internat. Seminars, Columbia U., N.Y.C., 1988—. Contbr. articles on multinat. corps., developing nations, trade and fin. to various publs.; researcher of policy proposals for J.P. Grace's book, It's Not Too Late in Latin America. Mem. The Ams. Found. Mem. N.Y. Press Club, Americas Soc., Bolivarian Soc. (sec., bd. dirs.), Fgn. Press Assn., Coun. of Ams. Home and Office: 600 W 115th St Apt 104 New York NY 10025-7720

HINZ, THEODORE VINCENT, architect; b. June 5, 1933; s. Theodore V. and Lillian (Adolph) H.; m. Louise R. Symmons; 1 child, Linda. BArch, Pratt Inst., 1956. Registered arch., N.Y., N.J., Va., Md., Conn., Ill. Draftsman, designer Muller & Ash Archs., N.Y.C., 1956-59; designer Urban, Brayton & Burrows, N.Y.C., 1959; designer, project arch. Goldstone & Dearborn, N.Y.C., 1959-66, assoc., 1966-70; ptnr. Goldstone, Dearborn & Hinz, N.Y.C., 1970-73, Goldstone & Hinz, N.Y.C., 1973—. Capt. C.E., U.S. Army, 1956-57. Recipient cert. Merit for Excellence in Design for Greenacre Park, 1972, Good Neighbor award Volvo Hdqs. N.J. Mfg. Assn., 1973, Bus. Friend of Arts award, 1988, Lumen citation Illumination Engring. Soc., 1990, Spl. Recognition award Concrete Industry Bd., 1993, Build N.Y. award Gen. Bldg. Contractors of N.Y., 1993. Mem. AIA, N.Y. Soc. Archs., N.Y. State Assn. Archs., Constrn. Specifications Inst., Bayside Hist. Soc. (trustee 1975-77, 81-83, v.p. 1977-79, pres. 1979-81), Queens Hist. Soc. (trustee 1980-87). Office: Goldstone & Hinz Architects PC 104 E 40th St Rm 803 New York NY 10016-1838

HINZE, VICKI KAY, writer, educator; b. Denver, Mar. 10, 1954; d. Victor Harry Sampson and Edna Mae Martin-Sampson; m. Lloyd H. Hinze, July 3, 1976; children: Raymond, Michael, Kristen. Undergrad., Miss. Gulf Coast Jr. Coll., 1973; undergrad in bus., Our Lady Holy Cross Coll., 1975; MBA in Creative Writing, LaSalle U., New Orleans, 1996; PhD in Philosophy, Theocentric Bus. and Ethics, Am. Coll., 1999. Lectr. in field. Author: Mind Reader, 1993 (Five Star Gold award Heartland Critiques), Maybe This Time, 1996 (Five Star Gold award Gothic Jour., Laurel Leaf award), Beyond the Misty Shore, 1996, Festival, 1997, Upon a Mystic Tide, 1997, Shades of Gray, 1998 (Top Pick award Romantic Times, Best Contemporary Suspence Novel of the Yr. Romantic Times), Duplicity, 1999 (Golden Quill award, Top Pick award Romantic Times), Acts of Honor, 1999 (Laurel Leaf award of excellence, Maggie award of excellence, Silver Star award Romance Communications, Gold Medal award Romantic Times, Top Pick award Romantic Times), All Due Respect, 2000 (Daphne de Maurier award, RT Book Club Top Pick award), Lady Liberty, 2002 (Daphne de Maurier award, Romantic Times Gold medal and Top Pick awards, Best Romantic Intrigue, 2003), War Game Series: Body Double, 2004;: Lady Justice, 2004, Double Vision, 2005, Double Care, 2005, Smokescreen, 2005, (anthology) Seeing Fireworks!, 1998, A Message From Cupid, 1999, All-About Writing to Sell, 2001; contbr. articles to profl. jours. Recipient SARA award for svc. and faithful support romance genre, 2000. Mem.: Internat. Thriller Writers Am., Novelists Inc., Authors Guild, Mystery Writers Am., Romance Writers Am. (cons., com. mem., Nat. Svc. award 1995). Avocations: reading, home remodeling, painting. Office: PO Box 235 Niceville FL 32588

HIOTT, WILLIAM DAVID, SR., historian, curator, educator; b. Lancaster, SC, Dec. 21, 1961; s. Sherrill Craig Sr. and Dorothy Craig Hiott; m. Susan Margaret Giaimo, Oct. 21, 1962; children: William David Jr., Nathaniel Arthur, Daniel Edward. BA, U. SC, 1983, MA, 1986; postgrad., Clemson U., 1990—2004. Cert. tchr. SC. Mus. educator Historic Columbia (SC) Found., 1983—86; exec. dir. Spartanburg (SC) County Hist. Assn., 1986—87, Oaklands HIstoric House Mus., Murfreesboro, Tenn., 1988—89; dir. historic properties Fort Hill and Hanover House U. SC, Clemson, 1990—. Profl. devel. com. SC Fedn. Mus., Columbia, 1994—98; past tourism adv. com. City of Clemson; cons. in field. Contbr. articles to profl. jours. Chmn. bd. dirs. SC Heritage Corridor Ragion I, 1993—94. Grantee, Inst. Mus. and Libr. Svcs., 1989, SC Humanities Coun., 1992, SC Dept. Archives and History, 1993—94, 1996, Inst. Mus. and Libr. Svcs., 1993, 1999, Historic Am. Bldgs. Survey, 1997, Nat. Park Svc., 2002. Mem.: Am. Assn. for State and Local History, Am. Assn. Mus., Nat. Trust for Historic Preservation, Alpha Phi Omega (life). Home: 145 Briarcliff Rd Central SC 29630-9424 Office: Clemson Univ 101 Fort Hill St Clemson SC 29634-5615 Office Fax: 864-656-1026. Personal E-mail: forthill@innova.net. Business E-Mail: hiottw@clemson.edu.

HIPFEL, STEVEN J., lawyer; Grad., U.S. Army Command and Gen. Staff Coll., 1998; LLM in Environ. Law, George Washington U., 2000. Head internat. environ. law br. Internat. and Operational Law Divsn. Office of Judge Advocate Gen. of Navy, Pentagon, 1997—99; acting ocean affairs asst. Under Sec. of Def. for Policy, Pentagon, 1998; environ. counsel to commdr. Navy Region S.W., 2000—03, chief naval ops. environ. coun., 2003—. Contbr. articles to profl. jours.; article submissions editor: Environ. Lawyer, 1999—2000, bd. editors: Free Speech Yearbook, 1997—2000. Address: 6035 Wilmington Dr Burke VA 22015 Office Phone: 703-602-6843. E-mail: shipfel@aol.com.

HIPP, WILLIAM HAYNE, broadcast executive; b. Greenville, S.C., Mar. 11, 1940; s. Francis Moffett and Mary Matilda (Looper) H.; m. Anna Kate Reid, June 14, 1963; children: Mary Henigan, Francis Reid, Anna Hayne. BA, Washington and Lee U., 1962; MBA, U. Pa., 1965. With Met. Life Ins. Co., 1965-69; v.p. Liberty Life Ins. Co., Greenville, S.C., 1969-74, exec. v.p., 1977-79, chmn. bd. dirs., 1979—; chief exec. officer Liberty Corp., Greenville, 1979—, also bd. dirs. Bd. dirs. Wachovia Corp., SCANA Corp., S.C. Rsch. Authority, Trustee, vice-chmn. Nat. Urban League, 1979-89; trustee Com. Econ. Devel., N.Y., 1988—, Episcopal H.S., Alexandria, Va., 1982-88; chmn. Greenville Urban League, 1978, Greenville YMCA, 1979; trustee Greenville County Sch. Sys., 1975-76, Washington and Lee U., Lexington, Va., 1985-[illegible] Greenville C. of C., 1985; trustee, chmn. Alliance for Quality Edn., 1986-[illegible], Greenville Hosp. Sys., 1989-95; bd. dirs. Am. Coun. Life Ins., 1995—, S.C. State Devel. Bd., 1980-85, and others. Mem. Greenville C. of C. (chmn. 1985). Office: Liberty Corp PO Box 789 2000 Wade Hampton Blvd Greenville SC 29615-1037

HIPPEAU, ERIC, book publishing executive; b. Paris, Aug. 16, 1951; came to U.S., 1986; Student, Sorbonne Univ., Paris. V.p. computer publs. IDG, N.Y.C.; pub. IDG Info World; pub. Computer World Ziff-Davis, N.Y.C., 1989—90, exec. v.p., 1990—91, pres., COO, 1991, chmn., CEO, 1991—93, Ziff Comms. Co., N.Y.C., 1993—2000; pres., exec. mng. dir. Softbank Intl. Ventures, 2000—. Dir. Yahoo!, Inc., 1996—. Office: Ziff-Davis Inc 28 E 28th St New York NY 10016-7900

HIPPEE, WILLIAM H., JR., lawyer; b. Des Moines, 1946; BS, U. Pa., 1968; JD, Stanford U., 1972. Bar: Minn. 1972. Ptnr. Dorsey & Whitney LLP, Mpls., 1972—. Office: 40 H Endrlives Inl Ste 2300 120 S 6th Ave Minneapolis MN 55402

HIPPLE, WALTER JOHN, language educator; b. Chgo., Mar. 14, 1921; s. Walter John and Emilie (Scheu) H.; m. Anne Ruth Poier, Nov. 27, 1962; children: Heidi Kristina, Ethan John; m. Kay F. Moomaw. BA, U. Chgo., 1947, MA, 1948, PhD, 1954; postdoctoral, U. London, 1957, Cambridge (Eng.) U., 1961-62; LittD, Shimer Coll., 1977. Lectr. Roosevelt U., Chgo., 1948; instr. U. Chgo., 1948-50, U. Ark., 1951-52; asst. prof. U. Fla., Gainesville, 1952-56; assoc. prof. Cornell Coll., Mt. Vernon, Iowa, 1957-61; prof. U. Pacific, Calif., 1962, Idaho State U., 1963, U. So. Calif., 1963; prof., chmn. dept. humanities Ind. State U., Terre Haute, 1963-72; dean Shimer Coll., Mt. Carroll, Ill., 1972-76; acad. v.p. West Chester (Pa.) State Coll., 1976-77; prof. philosophy West Chester (Pa.) U., 1977-91, assoc. to pres., 1977-79, dir. honors, 1979-91, prof. emeritus, 1991; prof. English Heilongjiang (People's Republic of China) U., Harbin, 1991-92. Chmn. Com. on Humanities in Secondary Schs. Ind., 1965-69; prof. univs. and insts. in Peoples Republic of China, 1986-92; guest prof. U. Autonomous Region Caribbean Coast Nicaragua, 1997, U. Guyana, 2001, Ginling Coll., Nanjing Normal U., Peoples Republic of China, 2004-05. Author: The Beautiful, the Sublime and the Picturesque in Eighteenth Century British Aesthetic Theory, 1957; editor, author introduction: Alexander Gerard, An Essay on Taste, 1963; contbr. articles to profl. jours. With U.S. Army, 1943-45. Guggenheim fellow, 1961-62. Home: 328 S Darlington St West Chester PA 19382-3341 Business E-Mail: whipple@wcupa.edu.

HIPPS, KERRY WAYNE, chemistry professor, researcher; b. El Paso, Tex., Mar. 16, 1948; s. Manson J. and Amaline (Nabhan) H.; m. Ursula Mazur, July 12, 1979; children: Autumn, Lorry. BS, U. Tex., El Paso, 1970; PhD, Wash. State U., 1976. Lectr. U. Mich., Ann Arbor, 1976-78; asst. prof. Wash. State U., Pullman, 1978-81, assoc. prof., 1981-84, prof. chemistry, 1984—, prof. material sci., 1991—, chmn. materials sci. program, 2005—. Lectr. 68th Disting. Faculty Conf., Wash. State U. Co-author: Tunneling Spectroscopy, 1982; contbr. over 130 artcles to sci. publs. Named Tchr. of Yr., Wash. State Tchrs. Assn., 1987; Alfred P. Sloan Found. fellow, 1982, NSF energy-related postdoctoral fellow, 1976; grantee NSF, 1979—, Petroleum Rsch. Fund, 1981—. Mem. Am. Chem. Soc. (chmn. N.W. regional chpt. 1983, organizer summer sch.), Am. Phys. Soc., Materials Rsch. Soc., Sigma Xi, Phi Lambda Upsilon (faculty advisor 1979-86). Achievements include the development of inelastic electron tunneling spectroscopy of electronic transitions; exited state metal complex structure determination through vibronic structure analysis; observation of resonant tunneling in M-I-M diodes and in the STM, spectroscopy of buried interfaces, scanning tunneling microscopy studies of molecular and sub-molecular conductivity; organizer Physical Chemistry on the Nanometer Scale; development of sub-molecular imaging of electron transfer processes in molecules, single molecule electronic spectroscopy. Office: Wash State U Dept Chemistry Pullman WA 99164-0001 Business E-Mail: hipps@wsu.edu.

HIPWELL, ARTHUR P., lawyer, managed health care company executive; b. 1949; BBA, U. Notre Dame; JD, U. Louisville. Bar: 1976. Tax counsel Humana, Inc., 1979—90, v.p., assoc. gen. counsel, 1990—92, sr. v.p., gen. counsel, 1992—93, 1994—99, 1999—, Galen Health Care, Inc., 1993—94. Office: Humana Inc 500 W Main St Louisville KY 40202

HIRABAYASHI, KEITH COOKE, actor, martial arts instructor; b. Seattle, Sept. 17, 1959; Attended, U. Wash., Seattle. Founder, martial arts instructor Champions Martial Arts, Los Angeles, 1995—. Actor: (films) Picasso Trigger, 1988, China O'Brien, 1990, China O'Brien II, 1991, Born to Ride, 1991, The King of the Kickboxers, 1991, Heatseeker, 1995, Mortal Kombat, 1995, Beverly Hills Ninja, 1997, Mortal Kombat: Annihilation, 1997, Lost Time: The Movie, 2001, National Security, 2003, Red Trousers: The Life of the Hong Kong Stuntmen, 2003. Named Grand Champion, US World Karate Tournament, US Open Karate Tournament; named to Black Belt Mag. Hall of Fame, 1985. Office: Champions Martial Arts 137 S Barrington Pl Los Angeles CA 90049*

HIRAHARA, PATTI, public relations executive; b. Lynwood, Calif., May 10, 1955; d. Frank C. and Mary K. Hirahara; m. Terry K. Takeda, Sept. 1995. AA, Cypress Coll., 1975; BA, Calif. State U., Fullerton, 1977. Pub. affairs dir. United TV, L.A., 1977-80; v.p. Asian Internat. Broadcasting Co., L.A., 1980-81; mktg. cons. Disneyland, Anaheim, Calif., 1982; pub. rels. agt. Japan External Trade Orgn., L.A., 1982-86, 87-92; owner, pres. Prodns. By Hirahara, Anaheim, 1982—. Comml. photographer Hirahara Photography, Anaheim, 1977-83; publicist Tokyo Met. Govt., 1981, World Trade Week So. Calif., 1997, 98, 99; advisor State Colo. Trade Mission to Japan, 1986, State Ariz. Trade/Investment Mission to Japan, 1987, County Riverside, Calif. for Japanese trade, investment, tourism, 1986-88; coord. JETRO's Bus. Study Series, L.A., 1988; advisor Japan External Trade Orgn., 1987-88, TV Prodr./Host: Images, 1980, Expressions, 1994; reader panel Callaway Mag., 2005. Mem. reader panel Golf for Women Mag., Callaway Golf Mag., 2005. Bd. dirs. Nisei Week Japanese Festival, L.A., 1980-81; mem. Anaheim H.S. 20 Yr. Reunion Com., 1993. Nat. scholar Seventeen Mag. Youth Adv. Coun., 1973; named Orange County Nisei Queen, Suburban Optimist Club, Buena Park, Calif., 1974, nat. semi-finalist Outstanding Working Women Competition Glamour Mag., 1975; recipient svc. award Suburban Optimist Club of Buena Park, 1975. Mem. NAFE, Soc. Profl. Journalists (bd. dirs. 1980-81), World Trade Ctr. Assn. Orange County, Japanese Am. Citizens League, Am. Women in Radio and TV (bd. dirs. So. Calif. chpt. 1980-82, vice-chair western conf. 1981), So. Calif. Golf Assn., Pub. Rels. Soc. Am. (Orange County chpt. 1990), Adelaide Price Elem. Sch. (30 yr. reunion chair 1997), Suburban Optimist Club of Buena Park (bd. dirs. 1993-96, chairperson 30th Anniversary Celebration 1996, Optimist of Yr. 1995-96), Anaheim (Calif.) Hills Women's Golf Club (bd. dirs. 2005), Alpha Gamma Sigma.

HIRAI, CRAIG KAZUO, accountant; b. Honolulu, Jan. 3, 1949; s. Ralph and Tamie (Matsuo) H.; m. Linda Kuulei Goto, Oct. 12, 1980; children: Susan, Midori. BS, U. So. Calif., 1970; MS, MBA, U. Pa., 1971, 72; JD, U. Calif., Hastings, 1978; LLM in Taxation, NYU, 1979. Bar: Hawaii 1978, U.S. Dist. Ct. Hawaii, 1978, U.S. Tax Ct. 1979, U.S. Ct. Appeals (9th cir.) 1982; CPA, Hawaii, lic. real estate broker, Hawaii. Assoc. Fong & Miho, Honolulu, 1980-82; from assoc. to dir. Torkildson, Katz, Fonseca, Jaffe, Moore & Hetherington, Honolulu, 1982—2004; dir. Bowen Hunsaker Hirai, CPAs, APC, Honolulu, 2004—. Mem. 1st taxation dist. Hawaii Bd. of Taxation Rev., 1988-92; chmn., vice chmn. Hawaii Rental Housing Trust Fund Commn., 1992-98. Deacon Ctrl. Union Ch., Honolulu, 1988-92, trustee, 1992-95; chmn. Hawaii Rental Housing Trust Fund Adv. Commn., 1998-2001, Hawaii Tax Rev. Commn., 2001-03; dir. Housing and Cmty. Devel. Corp. Hawaii, 1998-2000. Mem. ABA, AICPA, Hawaii Bar Assn., Hawaii Soc. CPAs (chmn. tax com. 1986-87, vice chmn., then chmn. ethics com. 1994-95, 99—), Hawaii Assn. Realtors (chmn. taxation/fin. subcom. 1988-2001, vice-chmn. legis. com. 1992-93, 96-99, 2004-05) Democrat. Home: 802 Puuikena Dr Honolulu HI 96821-2500 Office: Bowen Hunsaker Hirai CPAs APC 733 Bishop St Ste 2020 Honolulu HI 96813 Office Phone: 808-526-2020. E-mail: craig@bhhcpa.net.

HIRAI, DENITSU, surgeon; b. Yokkaichi, Mie, Japan, July 27, 1943; came to U.S. 1969; s. Denyomu and Shizuo (Tanaka) H.; m. Fumiko Hada, June 14, 1969; 1 child, R. Lisa. MD, U. Tokyo, 1968; MBA, U. So. Calif., 2003. Diplomate Am. Bd. Surgery, Am. Bd. Quality Assurance and Utilization Rev. Physicians, Am. Bd. Surg. Critical Care; cert. nutrition support physician; cert. wound care specialist. Intern and residency Waterbury (Conn.) Hosp., 1969-74; fellow Mt. Sinai Hosp., 1974-75; asst. chief surgery VA Med. Ctr., Lincoln, Nebr., 1975-80, chief surgery, 1981-2000; asst. clin. prof. surgery Creighton U., Omaha, 1982-84, asst. prof. surgery, 1984-2000; clin. instr. U. Nebr., Omaha, 1986-88, clin. asst. prof. surgery, 1988-2000; assoc. prof. clin. surgery, mem. surgery staff Sch. Medicine U. So. Calif., L.A., 2000—. Author: Brain Ticklers (Japanese), 1983. Fellow ACS, Am. Coll. Critical Care Medicine; mem. AAAS, AMA, ACS, Am. Soc. Parenteral and Enteral Nutrition, Soc. Am. Gastrointestinal Endoscopic Surgeons, Southwestern Surg. Congress, Soc. Critical Care Medicine, Assn. VA Surgeons. Avocations: photography, braille transcription, karate. Office: LAOPC 351 E Temple St Los Angeles CA 90012 Personal E-mail: dhirai@usc.edu.

HIRAMOTO, JUDY MITSUE, artist; b. Tokyo, July 28, 1951; came to U.S., 1952; m. Richard T. and Lily Y. (Hirayanagi) H. BA, Antioch U., 1973; MFA, San Francisco State U., 1992. Ceramic instr. U.S. Embassy, Tokyo, 1979-81; asst. dir. Japanese Cultural Ctr., Los Altos Hills, Calif., 1988; artist in residence Creative Growth Art Ctr., Oakland, Calif., 1988-91; instr. Acad. of Art Coll., San Francisco, 1991—. Lectr. U. Calif., Santa Cruz, 1994. One-woman shows include Himovitz/Salomon Gallery, 1988, Purdue U., 1986, Am. Club, Tokyo, 1980, Seibu Dept. Store, Fujisawa, Japan, 1980, U. Calif., Santa Cruz, 1994. Fellow Sigma Omnicron Pi, 1989; Kuwahara Creative Art grant Japanese Am. Citizens League, 1986, Visual Arts grant Barbara Deming Meml. Fund, 1989. Mem. AAUW (fellowship 1990), Asian Am. Women Artists Assn., Coll. Art Assn. Home: 316 Naylor St San Francisco CA 94112-4513

HIRANO, ASAO, neuropathologist; b. Tomioka, Gunma, Japan, Nov. 26, 1926; s. Yoshiro and Miyoe Hirano; m. Keiko Okubo, May 23, 1959; children: Michio, Ikuo, Yoko, Shigeo MD, Kyoto U., 1952. Chief resident neurology Montefiore Hosp., Bronx, 1957-58; vis. scientist NIH, 1959-65; head div. neuropathology Montefiore Med. Ctr., Bronx, 1965—, Harry M. Zimmerman prof. neuropathology, 1995—; prof. pathology Albert Einstein Coll. Medicine, 1971—, prof. neurosci., 1974—. Vis. prof. Kansai Med. U., Osaka, Japan, 1985, Nippon Med. Sch., Tokyo, 1993. Author: Atlas of Neuropathology, 2d rev. edit., 1974, A Guide to Neuropathology, 1976, 2d edit., 1986, 3d edit., 1992, 4th edit., 2003, English edit., 1981, German edit., 1983, Metastatic Tumors of the Nervous Systems, 1982, Color Atlas of Neuropathology, 1980, 2d edit., 1988, English 1st edit., 1988, French edit., 1981; editor: Neuropsychiatric Disorders in the Elderly, 1983, Patholoy of the Myelinated Axon, 1985, Amyotrophic Lateral Sclerosis, Progress and Perspectives in Basic Research and Clinical Application, 1995; mem. internat. editl. bd. Sec. 5 Excerpta Medica, 1976-; mem. editl. com. Neurol. Medicine, 1978-; mem. adv. bd. Jour. Neuropathology and Exptl. Neurology, 1971-81, mem. editl. bd., 1981-84; mem. editl. bd. Progress in Computerized Tomography, 1978-, Annals of Neurology, 1983-89, Acta Neuropathologica, 1991-2004, Amyotrophic Lateral Sclerosis and Other Motor Neuron Disorders, 1999-2004; mem. cons. editor Human Cell; mem. adv. bd. Clin. Neuropathology, 1982—, Neuropathology and Applied Neurobiology, 1983—; hon. editor Brain Tumor Pathology, 1993—, Neuropathology, 1994-2003; mem., neuropathology cons. Surg. Neurology, 1996—; mem. internat. adv. bd. Med. Electron Microscopy, 1997-; mem., cons. editor Human Cell. Recipient Billings Silver medal AMA, 1959, Key to Osaka City, Japan, 1977, Royal Coll. Lectr. award Can. Assn. Neuropathologists, Royal Coll. Physicians and Surgeons Can., 1980, 1st Jack Prichard Meml. Lectr. award Queen's U., Belfast, 1981, 1st Endowment Lectr. of Neuropathology in memory of Mrs. Rajan Bharati and 150th Yr. Celebration of Madras Med. Coll., 1984, Commendation award Hon. Ben Blaz, 1992, Plaque, U.S. Ho. Reps., 1992, Order of Rising Sun, Gold Rays with Rosette, Govt. of Japan, 2001. Mem.: World Fedn. Neurology (rsch. com. 1978), Brit. Neuropathol. Soc. (assoc. 1982—2000), Japanese Soc. Neuropathology, Internat. Soc. Neuropathology, Am. Soc. Cell Biology, Assn. for Rsch. in Nervous and Mental Diseases, Am. Assn. Neuropathologists (pres. 1977—78, Weil award 1968, award for meritorious contbn. to neuropathology 1995), Australian and New Zealand Soc. Neuropathology (hon.), Western Pacific Neurol. Soc. (hon.), Am. Neurol. Assn. (hon.), Japanese Soc. Neurosurgery (sr.), Am. Acad. Neurology (sr.). Office: Montefiore Med Ctr 111 E 210th St Bronx NY 10467-2401 Office Phone: 718-920-4447. Business E-Mail: ahirano@montefiore.org.

HIRASAKI, GEORGE JIRO, chemical engineer, educator; b. Beaumont, Tex., Sept. 26, 1939; s. Tokuzo and Toki (Kishi) H. BSChemE with honors, Lamar U., 1963; PhDChemE, Rice U., 1967. With Shell Devel. Co., Houston, 1967-93; A.J. Hartsook prof. in chem. engrg. Rice U., Houston, 1993—. Prof. Rice U., Houston, 1993—. Contbr. articles to profl. jours.; patentee in field. Mem. NAE, Am. Chem. Soc., AIChE, Soc. Petroleum Engrs. (Lester C. Uren award 1989), Soc. Core Analysts, SIAM. Avocations: windsurfing, skiing, mountain climbing. Office: Rice U Dept Chem Engring 6100 Main St Houston TX 77005-1892

HIRAYAMA, EIJI, psychologist, educator; b. Tokyo, Sept. 13, 1955; s. Gosai and Shizuko Hirayama; m. Atsuko Hanaoka; three children. BA, Aoyamagakuin U., Tokyo, 1979, Rikkyo U., 1981; MA, Kyushu U., Fukuoka, Japan, 1986, PhD, 1996. Cert. clin. psychologist. Chief Psychol. Clinic, Kyushu U., Fukuoka, 1989-90; counselor Student Counseling Ctr., Fukuoka U., 1990-96; assoc. prof. Matsuyama (Japan) Shinonome Coll., 1996-99, Aoyamagakuin U., Tokyo, 1999—2004; vis. scholar UCLA, 2004—. Author: Clinical Psychology Today: On Mental Health, 1994, Encounter Group and the Process of Personal Growth, 1998, Group Approach in Psychotherapy, 2004; contbr. articles to profl. jours. Mem. APA, Japan Psychoanalytical Assn., Assn. Japanese Clin. Psychology (The Most Disting. Sci. award 1999). Office: UCLA 1285 Franz Hall Los Angeles CA 90095-1563 Home: 555 Levering Ave 305 Los Angeles CA 90024 Business E-Mail: hirayama@psych.ucla.edu.

HIRES, WILLIAM LELAND, psychologist, consultant; b. South Orange, N.J., July 5, 1918; s. Harrison Streeter and Christine B. (Leland) H.; m. Karen Reynolds Perrott, July 12, 1975; 1 child, Jennifer Leland. BS, Haverford Coll., 1949; PhD, U. Pa., 1972. Asst. to dean of admissions, asst. dir of scholarships U. Pa., 1952-55; supr. psychol. svcs., spl. classes, asst. supt. Office Supt. Chester County (Pa.) Schs., 1956-59; assoc. prof. West Chester Coll., 1960-61; adminstrv. asst. Office of Pres., asst. to sec. U. Pa., 1961-64; assoc. Edward N. Hay & Assocs., 1964-65; asst. supt. pub. schs. Chester County, 1966-68, pvt. cons., 1968-75; dir. diagnostic and consultative svc. Chester County Intermediate Unit, 1975-76, pvt. practice psychology, 1976-78; dir. pupil svcs. Upper Darby (Pa.) Sch. Dist., 1978-81; dean acad. studies Curtis Inst. Music, Phila., 1981-86; ptnr. Hires Assocs., Phila., 1987—. With USMC, 1942—46, with U.S. Army, 1941—42, with U.S. Army, 1950—52, lt. col. AUS, 1978—, col. hon. Pa. Army N.G. ret. Mem. AAAS, APA, Soc. of Cin., Welcome Soc., Hist. Soc. Pa., 1st Troop Phila. City Cavalry (hon.), Soc. Colonial Wars Pa. (hon. gov.), Phila. Club, Franklin Inn Club, Merion Cricket Club, Harvard-Radcliffe Club of Phila., The Rabbit.

HIRNING, FREDRIC CARL, pharmacist; b. Lodi, Calif., Aug. 20, 1947; s. Clarence Christian Reuben and Gertrude (Hoff) H.; m. Marilyn Kay Truitt, Aug. 31, 1968; children: Lindsay Ann, Katherine Erin, John Michael. BS in Pharmacy cum laude, U. of the Pacific, 1970, PharmD cum laude, 1972; cert. pharmacy mgmt., U. N.C., 1989; cert. health care mgmt., U. So. Calif., 1991. Registered pharmacist, Calif. From pharmacist to dir. pharmacy Mercy Hosp., Sacramento, 1970-76; dir. pharmacy St. Josephs Med. Ctr., Stockton, 1976-80, pharmacist, 1980-82; dir. pharmacy svcs. Sutter Davis (Calif.) Hosp., 1983-85; pharmacist Relief Pharmacy Svc., Stockton, 1985-87; dir. pharmacy svcs. Drs. Hosp. Manteca, Calif., 1987—. Adj. prof. U. of the Pacific Sch. Pharmacy, Stockton, 1987-89, new dean search com., 1994-95; instr. chemical dependency studies Calif. State U., Sacramento, 1991-95; instr. drug & alcohol counselor cert. program U. of the Pacific, Stockton, 1993-95, bd. dirs. pharmacy assoc., 1990-97; field monitor Occupl. Healthcare Svcs., Larkspur, Calif., 1988-93; chmn. Calif. Vet. Diversion Com., 1993-95; vice-chmn. Calif. Nursing Diversion Com., 1992-94; cons. and presenter in field. Co-author: Purchasing and Inventory Control, 1992, Points of Light, A Guide for Helping..., 1996; contbr. articles to profl. jours. Active Bishops Adv. Com. on Drug and Alcohol, Fresno, 1987—, Partners in Prevention/Parents Who Care, Stockton, 1987-95, Pharmacists Against Drug Abuse, 1986—, Calaveras County Drug Abuse Task Force, San Andreas, Calif., 1986-87, Leadership, Manteca, 1989-90; asst. scoutmaster Boy Scouts Am., Stockton, 1991-97; bd. dirs. PALS-Drug Treatment Program, Stockton, 1993-95; coun. mem. Lincoln H.S., Stockton, 1991-93. Recipient Geigy Leadership award Sacramento Valley Soc. Hosp. Pharmacists, 1976, Commendation award San Joaquin County Sheriff, 1982, Appreciation award Boy Scouts Am., 1990, Nat. Cmty. Svc. award U.S. Pharmacist jour., 1993; named Disting. Pharmacist, Roerig Pharmaceuticals, 1989, Disting. Alumni, U. of the Pacific Alumni Assn., 1997; named to Lodi Sports Hall of Fame, 1994. Fellow Am. Pharm. Assn. (del. 1990-95); mem. Internat. Pharmacy Fedn., Acad. Pharmacy and Practice & Mgmt. of Am. Pharm. Assn. (edn. standing com. 1993-94, vice-chmn. awards standing com., sect. chmn. 1994-95, Merit award 1999), Am. Soc. Health-Sys. Pharmacists, Calif. Pharmacists Assn. (editl. rev. com. 1993-99, edni. found. adv. com. 1997-99, Bowl of Hygeia award 1991), Am. Inst. for the History of Pharmacy, Christian Pharmacists Fellowship Internat., Internat. Pharmacists Anonymous, Am. Pharm. Assn. Found., Am. Soc. Health-Sys. Pharmacists Found., Internat. Coalition Addiction Studies Educators, Acad. Hosp. Pharmacists (bd. dirs. 1994-96, Quality Commitment award 1995), San Joaquin Pharmacists Assn. (bd. dirs. 1989-94, pres. 1993), Cen. Valley Soc. Hosp. Pharmacists (bd. dirs. 1988-93, pres. 1992, Pharmacist of Yr. 1992), San Francisco Zool. Soc., U.S. Holocaust Meml. Mus. Assn., Nat. Eagle Scout Assn., Rho Chi. Republican. Episcopalian. Avocation: travel. Office: Drs Hosp Manteca 1205 E North St Manteca CA 95336-4932

HIRONAKA, HEISUKE, mathematics professor, academic administrator; b. Yamaguchi-ken, Japan, Apr. 9, 1931; DPhil, Kyoto U., 1963; PhD, Harvard U., 1960. Pres. Yamaguchi U., Yamaguchi, Japan, 1996—2001; prof. math. Harvard U. Recipient Fields medal Internat. Congress Nice, 1970, Order of Culture, Japan, Ordre National de la Legion d'Honneur, 2004. Achievements include proof of the theorem concerning the resolution of singularities on an algebraic variety for all dimensions. Office: Harvard U Dept Math One Oxford St #35 Cambridge MA 02138

HIRONO, MAZIE KEIKO, former lieutenant governor; b. Fukushima, Japan, Nov. 3, 1947; arrived in U.S., 1955, naturalized, 1959; d. Laura Chie (Sato) H. BA, U. Hawaii, 1970; JD, Georgetown U., 1978. Dep. atty. gen., Honolulu, 1978-80; Shim, Tam, Kirimitsu & Naito, 1984-88; mem. Hawaii Ho. of Reps., Honolulu, 1980-94; lt. gov. State of Hawaii, 1994—2002. Bd. dirs. Nat. Asian Pacific Am. Bar Assn.; chair Hawaii Policy Group, Nat. Commn. on Tchg. and Ams. Future, Govs. Task Force on Sci. and Tech. Dep. chair Dem. Nat. Com., 1997; bd. dirs. Nuuanu YMCA, Honolulu, 1982—2004, Moiliili Cmty. Ctr., Honolulu, 1984—, Blood Bank of Hawaii. Mem. U.S. Supreme Ct. Bar, Hawaii Bar Assn., Phi Beta Kappa. Democrat. E-mail: hirono@hawaii.rr.com.

HIROSE, AKIRA, physics professor, researcher; b. Kijimadaira, Nagano, Japan, Aug. 16, 1941; came to Can., 1971; s. Genji and Katsuyo (Yamada) H.; m. Kimiko Yamamoto, Feb. 4, 1969; children: Tadashi, Kyoko. B Engring., Yokohama (Japan) Nat. U., 1965, M Engring., 1967; PhD, U. Tenn., 1969; DSc, U. Sask., 1994. Mem. rsch. sect. Oak Ridge (Tenn.) Nat. Lab., 1969-71; rsch. scientist U. Sask., Saskatoon, Can., 1971-77, assoc. prof., 1977-79, prof. physics, 1979—. Corr. Plasma Phys. Controlled Fusion, 1984—; chmn. Internat. Conf. on Plasma Sci., Saskatoon, 1986; vis. prof. FOM Inst. Plasmafysica, The Netherlands, 1989, Tokyo Met. Inst. Tech., 1996; disting. fgn. rschr. Japan Atomic Energy Rsch. Inst., 1995. Author: Introduction to Wave Phenomena, 1985; contbr. numerous articles to profl. jours. Recipient IEEE Merit award Nuclear and Plasma Scis. Soc., 1993, Disting. Rschr.'s award U. Sask., 1995, Plasma Sci. and Applications award IEEE Nuclear Plasma Sci. Soc., 1998, Can. Rsch. Chair, 2001; Fulbright scholar, 1967; Nat. Sci. Engring. Rsch. Coun. grantee, 1977; Japan Soc. Promotion Sci. rsch. fellow, 1984. Fellow: IEEE (assoc. editor Trans. Plasma Sci. 1983—), European Acad. Sci., Acad. Sci. Royal Soc. Can., Am. Phys. Soc. (divsn. assoc. editor Phys. Rev. Letter 1999—2002); mem.: Can. Assn. Physicists (chmn. divsn. plasma physics 1981—82, 1994—95). Home: 2914 East View Saskatoon SK Canada S7J 3H9 Office: U Sask Dept Physics & Engring Phys Saskatoon SK Canada S7N 5E2 E-mail: akira.hirose@usask.ca.

HIROSE, TERUO TERRY, surgeon, educator; b. Tokyo, Jan. 20, 1926; arrived in U.S., 1959; s. Yohei and Seiko (Ogushi) H.; m. Tomiko Kodama, June 1, 1976; 1 son, George Philamore. BS, Tokyo Coll., Japan, 1944; MD, Chiba U., Japan, 1948, PhD, 1958. Diplomate Am. Bd. Surgery, Am. Bd. Thoracic Surgery. Intern Chiba U. Hosp., Japan, 1948-49, resident in surgery, 1949-52; practice medicine specializing in surgery Chiba, Japan, 1952-53; resident in surgery Am. Hosp., Chgo., 1954; resident in thoracic surgery Hahnemann Med. Coll., Phila., 1955-56; chief of surgery Tsushimi Hosp., Hagi, Japan, 1958-59; tchg. fellow surgery NY Med. Coll., NYC, 1959-60; rsch. fellow advanced cardiovasc. surgery Hahnemann Hosp., Phila., 1959; asst. prof. surgery Chiba U., Japan, 1959; instr. NY Med. Coll., NYC, 1961-62, resident in thoracic surgery, 1961-62; sr. attending surgeon St. Barnabas Hosp., NYC, 1965-81; pvt. practice NYC, 1965-89, NJ, 1965-89; chief vascular surgery Union Hosp., Bronx, NY, 1966-67; attending surgeon Flower and Fifth Ave Hosp., NYC, 1973-80; clin. prof. surgery NY Med. Coll., NY, 1974-89; dir. cardiovasc. lab. St. Barnabas Hosp., NYC, 1975-84; attending surgeon Jewish Hosp. Med. Center, Bklyn., 1976-80, St. Vincent Hosp., NYC, 1976-88, Mamonides Hosp., Bklyn., 1976-78, Passaic Gen. Hosp., 1977-88, Westchester County Hosp., NY, 1977-78, Yonkers Profl. Hosp., NY, 1978-79, Westchester Sq. Hosp., 1978-84, Yonkers Gen. Hosp., Yonkers, NY, 1980-89, St. Joseph Hosp., Yonkers, NY, 1980-89; dir. KPMG Health Care, Japan, 1997—2001; chmn., prof. dept. head, health care admin. Shumei U., Tokyo, 1999; chmn., pres. Japanese Assn. for Healthcare Adminstrs., 2002—. Author: (in Japanese) A Chaos of American Medicine, 1987, Japanese Doctor, 1987, Where American Medicine Is Going, 1988, Major Surgery Without Blood Transfusion, 1990, Problems and Solutions of American Medicine, 1991, Warning for Modern Medical Science (New Medical Ethics), 1992, Comparative Studies of Medical System in the World, 1992, The Changing Face of Geriatrics, 1994, Monologue of Japanese American Physician, 1995, Environmental Medicine, 1998, Japan! Do Not Follow American Health Care System, 1998, Quality of Life in Modern Medicine, 1998, Medicine About Life and Death, 1998, 99, Why AIDS Can Not Be Conquered, 1999, Mechanism of Human Body, 2000, Comparison of Healthcare Systems Between U.S.A. and Japan, 2000, Medicine of Death, 2000, Lifestyle Related Medicine and Cutting Edge Technique, 2001, Alternative Medicine, 2001, Thanatology, 2000, Protect Japanese Health Care System By Health Care Reform, 2002, Basic and Practice of Health Care Administration, 2002, Better Understanding of Physician and Hospital, 2003, What Can We Learn from Medical Education System in USA, 2003, How Should We Take Care of Aged Population, 2004; editor Japanese Med. Planner Ltd.; contbr. over 900 articles to profl. jours. Recipient Hektoen Bronze medal, AMA, 1965, Gold medal, 1971. Fellow: NY Acad. Medicine, Internat. Coll. Surgeons, Am. Coll. Cardiology, Am. Coll. Chest Physicians, Am. Coll. Angiology; mem.: Soc. Vascular Surgery, Japanese Assn. Health Care Adminstrs. (chmn., pres.), Japan PEN Club, Am. Writers Assn., Am. Fedn. Clin. Rsch., Am. Geriatric Soc., Internat. Cardiovasc. Soc., Pan Pacific Surg. Assn., NY Soc. Thoracic Surgery, Am. Assn. Thoracic Surgery. Achievements include invention of single pass low prime oxygenator; pioneer aortocoronary direct bypass surgery, open heart surgery without blood transfusion. Personal E-mail: coronarybypass@earthlink.net. *One should respect another's religion or creed and offer assistance regardless of whether or not one is in agreement with the other's belief, provided that belief harms no other.*

HIRREL, LEO P., historian, retired military officer; b. Alexandria, Va., Dec. 31, 1952; s. Michael A. and Evelyn L. Hirrel. BA, Loyola Coll., Balt., 1974; MA, Univ. Va., Charlottesville, Va., 1981, PhD in History, 1989; MLS, Cath. Univ. of Am., Washington, 2000. Hist. cons., Gaithersburg, Md., 1995—98; libr. asst. Cath. Univ. of Am., Washington, 1998—99; hist. US Army Ctr. & Mil. History, Washington, 1999—2002, US Joint Forces Command, Norfolk, Va., 2002—. Project dir. Am. Religious Experience, Morgantown, W.Va., 1998—. Author: Children of Wrath: New School Calvinism and Antebellum Reform, 1998, Response to Terrorism: US Joint Forces Command of 11 September, 2003. Lt. col. USAR, 1974—2002. Mem.: Soc. Hist. Am. Republic. Home: 5020 Cypress Point Cir Virginia Beach VA 23455 Office: US Joint Forces Command 1562 Mitscher Ave #200 Norfolk VA 23551 Office Phone: 757-836-6369. Personal E-mail: leohirrel@aol.com.

HIRSCH, ANTHONY TERRY, physician; b. N.Y.C., Jan. 29, 1940; s. Robert S. and Minna Hirsch; m. Barbara Hershan, July 8, 1961; children: Deborah, Kenneth, Steven. BS cum laude, Tufts U., 1961, MD, 1965. Diplomate Am. Bd. Pediatrics, Am. Bd. Allergy-Immunology. Pvt. practice pediatrics Children's Med. Group, L.A., 1973-84; chair dept. pediatrics, dir. residency tng. program in pediatrics White Meml. Med. Ctr., L.A., 1984—. Capt. USAF, 1969-71. Fellow Am. Acad. Pediatrics (chair access task force Calif. br., mem. nat. access task force, chair coun. on pediatric practice), Am. Acad. Allergy-Immunology. Avocation: sailing. Office: White Meml Med Ctr Dept Pediat 1701 Cesar Chavez Ave # 456 Los Angeles CA 90033-2410

HIRSCH, BARRY, lawyer; b. NYC, Mar. 19, 1933; s. Emanuel M. and Minnie (Levenson) H.; m. Myra Seiden, June 13, 1963; children: Victor Terry II, Neil Charles Seiden, Nancy Elizabeth. BSBA, U. Mo., 1954; JD, U. Mich., 1959; LL.M., N.Y. U., 1964. Bar: N.Y. bar 1960. Assoc., then partner firm Seligson & Morris, N.Y.C., 1960-69; v.p., sec., gen. counsel dir. B.T.B. Corp., 1969-71; v.p., sec., gen. counsel Loews Corp. (and subsidiaries), 1971-86, sr. v.p., sec., gen. counsel, 1986—2003. Bds. dirs. Neuberger Berman Funds. Served to 1st lt. AUS, 1954-56. Mem. ABA, Assn. of Bar of City of N.Y., N.Y. State Bar Assn., Zeta Beta Tau, Phi Delta Phi. Home: 1010 5th Ave New York NY 10028-0130 Office Phone: 212-737-4371. Personal E-mail: barry@hotmail.com. Business E-Mail: bhirsch@loews.com.

HIRSCH, BETTE G(ROSS), academic administrator, language educator; b. N.Y.C., May 5, 1942; d. Alfred E. and Gladys (Netburn) Gross; m. Edward Raden Silverblatt, Aug. 16, 1964 (div. Feb. 1975); children: Julia Nadine Silverblatt Young, Adam Edward Silverblatt; m. Joseph Ira Hirsch, Jan. 21, 1978; stepchildren: Hillary, Michelle, Michael. BA with honors, U. Rochester, 1964; MA, Case Western Res. U., 1967, PhD, 1971. Instr. and head French dept. Cabrillo Coll., Aptos, Calif., 1973-90, 2003—04, divsn. chair fgn. langs. and comms. divsn., 1990-95, interim dir. student devel., 1995-96, dean of instrn., transfer and distance edn., 1996—2003, emerita and adj. instr. French, 2004—. Mem. steering com. Santa Cruz County Fgn. Lang. Educators Assn., 1981-86; mem. liaison com. fgn. langs. Articulation Coun. Calif., 1982-84, sec., 1983-84, chmn., 1984-85; workshop presenter, 1982—; vis. prof. French Mills Coll., Oakland, Calif., 1983; mem. fgn. lang. model curriculum stds. adv. com. State Calif., 1984; instr. San Jose (Calif.) State U., summers 1984, 85; reader Ednl. Testing Svc. Advanced Placement French Examination, 1988, 89; peer reviewer for div. edn. programs, NEH, Washington, 1990, 91, 93; grant evaluator, NEH, 1995; mem. fgn. lang. adv. bd. The Coll. Bd., N.Y.C., 1986-91. Author: The Maxims in the Novels of Duclos, 1973; co-author (with Chantal Thompson) Ensuite, 1989, 93, 98, 2003, 05, Moments Litteraires, 1992 (with Chantal Thompson and Elaine Phillips) Mais Oui! workbook, lab. manual, video manual, 1996, 2000, 04; contbr. revs. and articles to profl. jours. Pres. Loma Vista Elem. Sch. PTA, Palo Alto, Calif., 1978-79; bd. dirs. United Way Stanford, Palo Alto, 1985-90, mem. allocations com., 1988, bd. dirs. Cabrillo Music Festival, 1996-2003, sec., 1998, v.p., 2000-2002; bd. dirs. Cmty. TV of Santa Cruz County, 1997-99, vice chair, 1997-98. Grantee NEH, 1980-81, USIA, 1992; Govt. of France scholar, 1982, 2003. Mem.: MLA (mem. adv. com. on fgn. langs. and lits. 1995—2000, chair 1999—2000, com. on info. tech. 2001—, chair 2003—, mem. com. on cmty. colls. 2004—), Am. Assn. Tchrs. of French, Assn. Depts. Fgn. Langs. (exec. com. 1985—88, pres. 1988), Assn. Calif. C.C. Adminstrs. Democrat. Jewish. Avocations: travel, reading, antique collecting, gourmet eating and cooking. Home: 4149 Georgia Ave Palo Alto CA 94306-3813 Office: Cabrillo College 6500 Soquel Dr Aptos CA 95003-3194 Business E-Mail: behirsch@cabrillo.edu. *Treat life like a work of art in progress. Strive for the creative, the exceptional. Do it all with style.*

HIRSCH, CHARLES S., city health department administrator; b. Chgo., 1937; m. Claude Hirsch; 1 child, Sophie. BS, U. Ill., Urbana, 1958; MD, U. Ill., Chgo., 1962. Internist U. Hosp., Cleve., 1962—63; resident, pathology Case Western Reserve U. Inst. Pathology, Cleve., 1963—65; resident, neurol. pathology Md. State Med. Examiner's Office, Balt., 1965—66, resident, forensic pathology, 1966—67; dep. coroner Cayuga Co., Ohio, 1976—79; dir., forensic pathology Hamilton Co., Ohio, 1979—85; prof., forensic pathology SUNY Med. Sch., Stony Brook; med. examiner Suffolk Co., NY, 1985—89; prof., forensic medicine and pathology, chmn. NYU Sch. Medicine, N.Y.C.; chief med. examiner N.Y.C. Dept. Health and Mental Hygiene, 1989—. Recipient Disting. Alumnus award, U. Ill., Chgo., 2003. Office: Office of the Chief Medical Examiner 520 First Ave New York NY 10016

HIRSCH, DANA S, music educator; b. Queens, NY, July 9, 1964; d. Alan Leonard and Victoria Sokoloff; m. Bradley Jay Hirsch, Aug. 7, 1997. BFA, State U. of NY at Buffalo, 1982—86; MSc, LI U at CW Post, 1988—90. Music tchr. Patchogue-Medford Public Sch., 1986—87, Pub.Sch. No. Bellmore, 1987—. Pvt. music tchr., 1984—; wedding entertainer, 1990—. Active fundraiser Lupus Found. of LI, 1998—. Recipient Irving Cheyette Music Ednl. award, Buffalo U. Music Dept., 1986. Mem.: NY State United Teachers, Music Educators Nat. Conf., Nassau Music Educators Assn. Avocations: singing, crafts. Home: 3543 Stephen Lane Wantagh NY 11793

HIRSCH, DAVID L., lawyer; BA, Pomona Coll., 1959; JD, U. Calif., Berkeley, 1962. Bar: Calif. 1963. Dir. real estate, constrn. and property mgmt. svcs. and risk mgmt. coun. Metaldyne/NI Industries, Inc., Taylor, Mich., 1966—; pres. NI Industries, Inc., Taylor, Mich., 2004—. V.p. mem. commn. on Govt. Procurement for U.S. Congress, 1971. Mem. editl. bd. Bur. Nat. Affairs' Fed. Contracts Report. Fellow Am. Bar Found.; mem. ABA (life fellow of fellows, chair emerging issues com. sect. pub. contract law, sec. pub. contract law sect. 1977-78, mem. council 1978-80, chmn. 1981-82), Calif. Bar (bd. advisors pub. law sect.), Los Angeles County Bar Assn., Fed. Bar Assn., Nat. Contract Mgmt. Assn. (nat. bd. advisors), Fin. Exec. Inst. (legal advisor com. on govt. bus.). Office: Masco Tech Corp/NI Industries Inc 21001 Van Born Rd Taylor MI 48180-1340

HIRSCH, EDWARD MARK, language educator; b. Chgo, Jan. 20, 1950; s. Kurt and Irma (Ginsburg) H.; m. Janet Landay, May 29, 1977. BA, Grinnell Coll., 1972; PhD, U. Pa., 1978. Asst. prof. Wayne State U., Detroit, 1978-82, assoc. prof., 1982-85, U. Houston, 1985-87, prof. English, 1987—; pres. John Simon Guggenheim Meml. Found., 2003—. Author: (poems) For the Sleepwalkers, 1981 (Lavan Younger Poets award 1985), Wild Gratitude, 1986 (Nat. Book Critics Cir. award), The Night Parade, 1989, Earthly Measures, 1994, On Love, 1998, Lay Back the Darkness, 2003; (prose) How to Read a Poem and Fall in Love with Poetry, 1999, Responsive Reading, 1999, The Demon and the Angel: Searching for the Source of Artistic Inspiration, 2002; editor: Transforming Vision: Writers on Art, 1994; co-editor: A William Maxwell Portrait, 2004, Theodore Roetlke: Selected Poems, 2005. Nat. Endowments for Arts Creative Writing fellow, 1982, Guggenheim fellow, 1985; recipient Tex. Inst. of Arts and Letters award, 1987, Lit. award Am. Acad. Arts Letters, 1998; recipient Prix de Rome, 1988, Lyndhurst prize, 1994-96; MacArthur fellow, 1998. Office: John Simon Guggenhaim Meml Found 90 Park Ave New York NY 10016 Office Phone: 212-687-4470.

HIRSCH, ERIC DONALD, JR., language educator; b. Memphis, Mar. 22, 1928; s. Eric Donald and Leah (Aschaffenburg) H.; m. Mary Monteith Pope, June 15, 1958; children: Eric, John, Frederick, Elizabeth. BA, Cornell U., 1950; MA, Yale U., 1955, PhD (Fulbright fellow), 1957; LittD (hon.), Williams Coll., 1989, Rhodes Coll., 1993, Rollins Coll., 1994, Marietta Coll., 1997. Instr. Yale, 1956-61, asst. prof. English, 1961-64, assoc. prof., 1964-66; prof. U. Va., Charlottesville, 1966—, chmn. dept. English, 1968-71, 81-83, dir. composition, 1971—, Kenan prof. English, 1973—, Linden Kent prof. English Charlottesville, 1989-94, Univ. prof. edn. and humanities, 1994; founder, pres. Core Knowledge Found., Charlottesville, 1986—. Bd. dirs. U. Press; lectr. in field; supervising com. English Inst., 1972-74; mem. nat. adv. coun. N.Y. Regent's Competency Tests in Writing, 1979; advisor Nat. Coun. Ednl. Rsch., 1983; bd. dirs. Founds. Literacy Project, 1985—; pres. Cultural Literacy Found., 1987, Core Knowledge Found., 1990; dir. Albert Shanker Inst., 1997—. Author: Wordsworth and Schelling: A Typological Study of Romanticism, 1960, Innocence and Experience: An Introduction to Blake, 1964 (Explicator award), Validity in Interpretation, 1967, The Aims of Interpretation, 1976, The Philosophy of Composition, 1977, Cultural Literacy: What Every American Needs to Know, 1987; co-author: A Dictionary of Cultural Literacy, 1993, 2002; editor: A First Dictionary of Cultural Literacy, 1989, 2004, The Core Knowledge Series, Book I: What First Graders Need to Know, 1991, Book II: What Second Graders Need to Know, 1991, Book III: What Third Graders Need to Know, 1992, Book IV: What Fourth Graders Need to Know, 1992, Book V: What Fifth Graders Need to Know, 1993, Book VI: What Sixth Graders Need to Know, 1993, The Schools We Need and Why We Don't Have Them, 1996; mem. adv. bd. Jour. Basic Writing, Blake Studies, Critical Inquiry, Genre New Lit. History, Lit. in Performance; contbr. articles to profl. jours. Pres. Coalition for Core Curriculum, 1989—, 1989—. Served with USNR, 1950—52. Recipient Fordham award 2003; Morse fellow, 1961-62, Guggenheim fellow, 1964-65, sr. fellow NEH, 1971, 80-81, fellow Center for Humanities Wesleyan U., 1973, fellow Council Humanities Princeton U., 1976, fellow Center for Advanced Study in Behavioral Scis., 1980-81, fellow Humanities Research Ctr., Australian Nat. U., 1982; Bateson lectr. Oxford U., 1983 Fellow: Internat. Acad. Edn. in Royal Acad. Sci. Lit. and Arts (Brussels); mem.: MLA, Am. Fedn. Tchrs. (Biennial Quest award 1997), Am. Acad. Arts and Scis. (supervisory com. 1981—86), Byron Soc. Home: 2006 Pine Top Rd Charlottesville VA 22903-1233 Personal E-mail: edh9k@aol.com. Business E-Mail: edh9k@virginia.edu.

HIRSCH, FAYE, editor, art critic; Sr. editor Print Collector's Newsletter; founding editor Art on Paper; sr. editor Art in Am., NYC. New prints selection com. Internat. Print Ctr. NY, 2000. Lectr., writer in field, curator Color Detour exhibit, 1997, guest curator Calif. Abstract Expressionists, Internat. Print Ctr. Chelsea Gallery, NYC, 2003. Office: Art in America Brant Art Publications 575 Broadway New York NY 10012 Office Phone: 212-941-2800. Office Fax: 212-941-8885.

HIRSCH, GEORGE AARON, publishing executive; b. NYC, June 21, 1934; s. George J. and Sylvia (Epstein) H.; m. Shay Yandell Scrivner; children: David Aaron, William George; stepchildren: Ian Gregory Scrivner, Sean Gabriel Scrivner. AB magna cum laude, Princeton U., 1956; MBA, Harvard U., 1962. With Time-Life Internat., 1962-67; founding pub., pres. New York Mag., N.Y.C., 1967-71; chmn., pres., CEO New Times Comm. Corp., N.Y.C., 1973-79; founding pub. New Times mag., N.Y.C., 1973-79, The Runner Mag., N.Y.C., 1978-87; v.p., pub. Runner's World Mag., 1987—2000, worldwide pub., 2000—02, worldwide pub. emeritus, 2003—04; group pub. Rodale Active Network, 1987—97; pub. dir. Men's Health mag., 1987—2002; dir. internat. mags. Rodale Press, 1995—2002. Host "The Runner's Corner", ESPN Sports Ctr., 1983—84; TV sports commentator Olympic Games, 1984, 88, 92; bd. dirs. Salon Media Group Inc., N.Y. Roadrunners. A founder NYC Marathon, 1976; Dem. candidate for 15th Congl. Dist., NY, 1986; del. Dem. Nat. Conv., 1988. With USNR, 1957-60. Mem. Mag. Pubs. Assn. (chmn. internat. com. 2000-04), Century Assn. Club. Personal E-mail: georgehirsch1@hotmail.com.

HIRSCH, GILAH YELIN, artist, writer; b. Montreal, Que., Can., Aug. 24, 1944; came to US, 1963; d. Ezra and Shulamis (Borodensky) Y. BA, U. Calif., Berkeley, 1967; MFA, UCLA, 1970. Prof. art Calif. State U., Dominguez Hills, L.A., 1973—. Adj. prof. Internat. Coll., Guild of Tutors, LA, 1980-87, Union Grad. Sch., Cin., 1990. 50 solo exhbns., mus. collections, 15 publs. Founding mem. Santa Monica (Calif.) Art Bank, 1983-85; bd. dir. Dorland Mountain Colony, Temecula, Calif., 1984-88. Named artist-in-residence, RIM Inst., Payson, Ariz., 1989—90, Tamarind Inst. Lithography, Albuquerque, 1973, Rockefeller Bellagio Ctr., Italy, 1992, Tyrone Guthrie Ctr. for Arts, Annamahkerrig, Ireland, 1993, Internat. Sympat., Slovakia, 2004, 2005; recipient Disting. Artist award, Calif. State U., 1985, Found. Rsch. award, 1988—89, 1997—98, Creative Rsch. award, Sally Canova Rsch. Scholarship and Creative Activities awards program, 1997—99, 2003; grantee Nat. Endowment for the Arts, 1985, Class Found., 2003, Calif. State U., Dominguez Hills, 2005; Dorland Mountain Colony fellow, 1981—84, 1983, 1984, 1992, 1995, 2003, Banff Ctr. for the Arts fellow, Can., 1985, MacDowell Colony fellow, N.H., 1987. Office: Calif State Univ Dominguez Hills 1000 E Victoria St Carson CA 90747-0001 Office Phone: 310-243-3966. Personal E-mail: gilah@linkline.com.

HIRSCH, HARVEY STUART, psychiatrist; b. NYC, Nov. 3, 1950; s. Leoanrd Samuel and Roberta Joan (Dreyer) H.; m. Linda Karen Green, Sept. 27, 1981; children: Daniel, Carly. BA, Columbia U., 1972; MD, Mt. Sinai Med. Sch., N.Y.C., 1976. Diplomate Am. Bd. Psychiatry and Neurology, Nat. Bd. Med. Examiners, 1976. Intern Mt. Sinai Hosp., N.Y.C., 1976, attending physician, 1979—; clin. instr. Mt. Sinai Med. Sch., N.Y.C., 1979—; resident Mt. Sinai Hosp., N.Y.C., 1977-79, chief resident, 1979—. Recipient Ams. Top Psychiatrists, Consumers Rsch. Coun. of Am., Wash., D.C., 2003. Mem. Am. Psychiat. Assn., Cum Laude Soc., Le Club (N.Y.C.), Phi Beta Kappa. Avocations: tennis champion, swimming champion. Office: 1185 Park Ave New York NY 10128-1308 Office Phone: 212-828-2213. Personal E-mail: hirschharvey@yahoo.com.

HIRSCH, HORST EBERHARD, metal products executive, consultant; b. Woelsendorf, Fed. Republic Germany, July 26, 1933; came to U.S., 1984; s. Albert and Emilie (Eberhardt) H.; m. Helga G. Gruber, May 2, 1961; children: Manon K., Fabiane M., Erin A. Diploma in chemistry, Tech. U. Karlsruhe, Fed. Republic Germany, 1959, D in Chem. Tech., 1961. Postdoctoral fellow NRC of Can., 1961-62; research and devel. engr., mgr. Cominco Ltd., Trail, B.C., Can., 1962-84; pres., CEO Cominco Electronic Materials Inc., Spokane, Wash., 1984-88; pres. Johnson Matthey Electronics N.Am., Spokane, 1989-91, MSM (Metals and Semiconductor Materials), 1991—; vis. exec. IESC (Internat. Exec. Svc. Corps), 1992, field assoc., 1993—; co-founder, CM, HT Metals LLC, 2001—. Mem. bd. mgmt. B.C. Rsch. Coun., Vancouver, 1980-84; senate U. B.C., Vancouver, 1981-85; mem. adv. com. Wash. Tech. Ctr., 1992-94. Contbr. articles on chemistry and metallurgy to profl. publs., chpts. to books; patentee in field. Recipient Excellence in Innovation award Fed. Govt. Can., 1985. Mem. Soc. German Mining and Metall. Engrs. Lutheran. Avocations: reading, skiing, swimming, golf. E-mail: zollegeg@aol.com.

HIRSCH, IRVING B., lawyer; b. NYC, Mar. 15, 1954; BA, CUNY, 1975; JD, Bklyn. Law Sch., 1978. Bar: NY 1979. Joined Manhattan dist. atty.'s office, NYC, 1978, asst. dist. atty., dep. bur. chief trial bur., chief spl. projects bur., chief narcotics eviction program; ptnr. Wilson, Elser, Moskowitz, Edelman & Dicker LLP, NYC. Mem.: NY County Lawyers Assn., NY State Bar Assn. Office: Wilson Elser Moskowitz Edelman & Dicker LLP 23rd Fl 150 E 42nd St New York NY 10017-5639 Office Phone: 212-490-3000 ext. 2411. Office Fax: 212-490-3038. Business E-Mail: hirschi@wemed.com.

HIRSCH, JEFFREY ALLAN, lawyer; b. Chgo., June 14, 1950; m. Lennie Sue Henderson, June 16, 1979; children: Lea, Ashley. BSBA, U. Fla., 1972, JD with honors, 1975. Bar: Fla. 1975, U.S. Dist. Ct. (so. and mid. dists.) Fla. 1975. Assoc. Swann & Glass, Coral Gables, Fla., 1975-76, Glass, Schultz, Weinstein & Moss, Coral Gables, 1976-80; ptnr. Holland & Knight, Ft. Lauderdale, Fla., 1980-93; prin. shareholder Greenberg, Traurig, P.A., Ft. Lauderdale, Fla., 1993—. Exec. dir. Govtl. Research Ctr., Gainesville, Fla., 1975. Active Leadership Broward, Ft. Lauderdale, 1986—, Leadership Fla., 1994—. Mem. ABA, Fla. Bar Assn., Broward County Bar Assn. Avocations: reading, travel. Office: Greenberg Traurig PA 401 E Las Olas Blvd Ste 2000 Fort Lauderdale FL 33301-2278 Office Phone: 954-765-0500. E-mail: hirschj@gtlaw.com.

HIRSCH, JEROME S., lawyer; BA in Econs., SUNY, Binghamton, 1970; JD, Fordham U., 1974. Bar: N.Y. Ptnr. Skadden, Arps, Slate, Meagher & Flom, N.Y.C., 1982—. Mem. ABA, N.Y. State Bar Assn., Assn. Bar City of N.Y. Office: Skadden Arps Slate Meagher & Flom 4 Times Sq New York NY 10036-6595

HIRSCH, JUDD, actor; b. NYC, Mar. 15, 1935; s. Joseph Sidney and Sally (Kitzis) H. BS in Physics, CCNY, 1960. Broadway appearances in Barefoot in the Park, 1966, Knock Knock, 1976 (Drama Desk award for best featured actor), Chapter Two, 1977-78, Talley's Folly, 1980 (Tony nomination), I'm Not Rappaport, 1985-86, (Tony award for best actor in play 1986, Outer Critics Circle award, 1986), Conversations with My Father, 1992 (Tony award for best actor in play 1992, Outer Critics Circle award, 1992), A Thousand Clowns, 1996, Art, 1998, I'm Not Rappaport, 2002, Sixteen Wounded, 2004; off-Broadway appearances in On the Necessity of Being Polygamous, 1963, Scuba Duba, 1967-69, King of the United States, 1972, Mystery Play, 1972, Hot L Baltimore, 1973, Prodigal, 1973, Knock Knock, 1975, Talley's Folly, 1979 (Obie award), The Seagull, 1983, I'm Not Rappaport, 1985, Below the Belt, 1996; regional appearances include Theater for Living Arts, Phila., Line of Least Existence, Harry Noon and Night, The Recruiting Officer, 1969-70, Annenberg Ctr., Phila., Hough in Blazes, 1971, Seattle Repertory, Conversations with My Father, 1991, Scarborough, Eng., 1994, London, 1995, Chapel Hill, NC, Death of a Salesman, 1994, Long Wharf Theater Robbers, 1995, Manitoba Theatre Ctr., Winnipeg and Royal Alexandra Theatre, Toronto, Death of A Salesman, 1997, Art, London, 1999, 2001; stock and tours A Thousand Clowns, Threepenny Opera, Fantastiks, Woodstock, NY, 1964, Peterpat, Houston and Ft. Worth, 1970, Harvey, Chgo., 1971, And Miss Reardon Drinks a Little, Palm Beach, Fla., 1972, I'm Not Rappaport, nat. tour, 1986-87, Conversations With My Father, Doolittle Theatre, LA, 1993, Art, nat. tour, 1999-2000; TV series include Delvecchio, 1976-77, Rhoda, 1977, Taxi, 1978-83 (Emmy award for best actor in a comedy series, 1981, 1983), Dear John (Golden Globe award 1988), 1988-92, George and Leo, 1997, Regular Joe, 2003, Numbers, 2004; TV movies include The Law, 1974, Fear on Trial, 1975, The Legend of Valentino, 1975, The Halloween That Almost Wasn't, 1979, Sooner or Later, 1979, Marriage Is Alive and Well, 1980, First Steps, 1985, Brotherly Love, 1985, The Great Escape-Untold Story, 1988, She Said No, 1990, Betrayal of Trust, 1993, Color of Justice, 1997, Rocky Marciano, 1999; films include King of the Gypsies, 1978, Ordinary People (nominated Acad. Award), 1980, Without a Trace, 1983, Teachers, 1984, The Goodbye People, 1984, Running on Empty, 1988, Independence Day, 1996, Man On the Moon, 1999, A Beautiful Mind, 2001, Zeyda and the Hitman, 2004; dir. Squaring the Circle, 1962, Not Enough Rope, 1973, Talley's Folly, 1981, Art, 2000-01. Mem. Acad. Motion Picture Arts and Scis., Acad. TV Arts and Scis., Actors Equity Assn., SAG, AFTRA, SSDC.

HIRSCH, JULES, physician, researcher; b. N.Y.C., Apr. 6, 1927; Student, Rutgers U., 1943—45; MD, U. Tex., 1948; DSc (hon.), SUNY, 1988. Intern pathology and medicine Duke Hosp., NC, 1948—50; from asst. resident to resident coll. medicine SUNY, Syracuse, 1950—52; asst. prof., assoc. physician Rockefeller U., N.Y.C., 1954—60, assoc. prof., physician, 1960—67, prof., sr. physician, 1967—98. Sherman Fairchild prof. Rockefeller U., 1988—98, emeritus, 1998—; sr. physician Rockefeller U. Hosp., 1967—, physician-in-chief, 1992—96, emeritus, 1996—. Recipient Robert H. Herman award, 1994, McCollum award, 1984. Fellow: ACP, Royal Coll. Physicians Edinburgh; mem.: Harvey Soc., Am. Fedn. Clin. Rsch., Assn. Am. Physicians, Am. Soc. Clin. Nutrition, Am. Soc. Clin. Investigation, Inst. of Medicine of NAS, AAAS, Assn. for Patient Oriented Rsch. (founding mem.). Achievements include research in obesity, human behavior, internal medicine, biochemistry and physiology of lipids, lipid metabolism and nutrition. Office: Rockefeller U 1230 York Ave New York NY 10021-6399 Business E-Mail: hirsch@mail.rockefeller.edu.

HIRSCH, LARRY JOSEPH, retired retail executive, lawyer; b. Boston, July 1, 1938; s. Samuel and Anne (Rossman) Hirsch; m. Kay Pollock, Mar. 15, 1974. BA, Syracuse U., 1962; JD, Suffolk U., Boston, 1968; grad. gemologist, Gem Inst. Am., Los Angeles, 1981. Bar: Mass. 1968, R.I. 1968, Fla. 1970. Mgr. Vality Dept. Store, Groton, Conn., 1962—63; asst. area dir. Am. Jewish Com., Miami, 1968—69; asst. city atty. City of Miami, 1969—71; atty. Feuer and Feuer, Miami, 1971—74, Turano and Turano, Westerly, RI, 1974—78; asst. town solicitor Town of Westerly, RI, 1975—76; pres. Westerly Jewelry Co. Inc., RI, 1978—2000; ret. RI, 2000—; atty. RI, 1974—. Adv. bd. Fleet Bank, Westerly, 1984-90; chmn. adv. group Westerly Edn. Endowment Fund, 2000-01, dir., 2001; bd. dir. Washington Trust Bancorp, Inc., 1994- Pres. Chariho Westerly Animal Rescue League, 1976—; trustee Ctr. for the Arts, Westerly, RI, 1984, Westerly (R.I.) Hosp., 1984—94, mem. human resources com., 1998—2000; mem. fin. com. Cmty. Hosp. of Westerly, RI, 1984—2001, incorporator, 1985—; v.p. Westerly Heart Assn., RI, 1986; bd. gov. Cmty. Hosp. of Westerly, RI, 1995—2002; incorporator Westerly Pub. Libr., RI, 1997—; pres. Local Devel. Corp., 1998—; mem. site planning group West H.S., RI, 1998—2000; treas. Dante Italian Heritage Soc., 2004—; mem. student handbook com. West H.S., 1999—2000; v.p. Cmty. Hosp. of Westerly, RI, 1999—2002; dir. Chariho Westerly Animal Rescue League, RI, 2001—; v.p. Stand Up for Animals, RI, 2002—, Congregation Sharon Zedek, 2004—; dir. Stand Up for Animals, Key West, Fla., 2004—; bd. dir. Chariho Westerly Animal Rescue League, 1976—, Joint Devel. Task Force, Westerly, RI, 1988—; mem. Charter Revision Com. Westerly, RI, 1985—89; v.p. Joint Devel. Task Force, Westerly, RI, 1994—99, dir., 2001—, pres., 1999—2000; bd. dir. Animal Rescue League of So. R.I., 1988—94; mem. adv. coun. Westerly Integrated Social Svc. Program, RI, 1996, chmn., 1997—2000; bd. dir. Am. Heart Assn., Westerly, RI, 1986—93; mem. salary rev. and benefits com. Westerly Fire Dist., RI, 1996—2002. Served in U.S. Army, 1958—60. Larry Hirsch Day named in his honor, Town of Westerly, 1980; recipient Someone Spl. Award, Channel 26 WTWS TV, New London, Conn., 1987, Sam Walton Bus. Leadership Award Westerly Pawcatuck C. of C., 2000; named Columbus Citizen of Yr., Golden Key Club, Westerly, 1989, Citizen of Yr., Westerly Pawcatuck C. of C., 2000. Mem.: Gemological Inst. Am., Am. Gem Soc. (cert. gemologist), New Eng. Appraiser Assn., Nat. Assn. Jewelry Appraisers, Dante Italian Heritage Soc. (treas. 2004—), Fraternal Order of Police (assoc.; scholar com.), Westerly Track Club (pres. 1976, bd. dir. 1976—95), Elks (Larry Hirsch Run 1980—95). Avocations: long distance running, humane treatment of animals. Personal E-mail: larryjhirsch@cox.net.

HIRSCH, LAURENCE ELIOT, construction executive, investment banker; b. N.Y.C., Dec. 19, 1945; s. S. Richard and Lillian (Avenet) H.; m. Susan Judith Creskoff, Dec. 23, 1967; children: Daria Lee, Bradford Richard. BS in Econs., U. Pa., 1968; JD cum laude, Villanova U., 1971; MS in Internat. Pub. Policy, Johns Hopkins Sch. Internat. Studies, 2005. Bar: Pa. 1972, Tex. 1973. Assoc. Wolf, Block, Schorr & Solis Cohen, Phila., 1971-73, Bracewell & Patterson, Houston, 1973-76, ptnr., 1976-78; pres. Southdown, Inc., Houston, 1977-85, CEO, 1984-85; pres. Centex Corp., Dallas, 1985-88, CEO, 1988—2004, also chmn. bd. dirs., 1991—2004; chmn. Eagle Materials, Inc., Dallas, 1994—; sr. adv. Ctr. European Policy Analysis, 2005—. Bd. dirs. Belo Corp., Luminex Corp., dir. Heidelberger Zement, A.G.; trustee U. Pa.; chmn. Highlander Ptnrs., L.P. Mem. bd. cons. Villanova U. Law Sch. With USAR, 1968—75. Office: Eagle Materials Inc 3811 Turtle Creek Blvd Ste 1100 Dallas TX 75219 Office Phone: 214-245-5000. Business E-Mail: lhirsch@eaglematerials.com, lhirsch@highlander-partners.com.

HIRSCH, LAWRENCE LEONARD, physician, retired educator; b. Chgo., Aug. 20, 1922; m. Donna Lee Sturm; children: Robert, Edward, Sharon. BS, U. Ill., 1943; MD, U. Ill., Chgo., 1950. Diplomate: Am. Bd. Family Medicine. Intern. Ill. Masonic Med. Ctr., Chgo., 1950-51; practice medicine specializing in family medicine Chgo., 1951-70; dir. ambulatory care Ill. Masonic Med. Ctr., Chgo., 1970-71, dir. family practice residency program, 1971-75; prof., chmn. dept. family medicine Chgo. Med. Sch., 1975-89, prof. emeritus, 1989—. Mem. med. licensing bd. State of Ill., 1982-94, chmn., 1988-94, hosp. licensing bd., 1994-2004; bd. dirs. Ill. Coun. for continuing Med. Edn., 1981-85, pres., 1986-87; cons. recombinant DNA Abbott Labs., 1980-87; lectr. in field; staff pres. Ill. Masonic Med. Ctr., 1970. Book rev. editor: Soc. of Tchrs. Family Medicine, 1979-89; book reviewer: Jour. AMA, 1969-; contbr. articles to profl. jours. Bd. dirs. Mid-Am. chpt. ARC, Chgo., 1978-88; nat. pres. Alpha Phi Omega, Kansas City, Mo., 1974-78; exec. com. Chgo. Found. Med. Care and PSRO, 1977-84, Ill. State Inter-Ins. Exchange, 1975-; bd. dirs. Crescent Counties Found. for Med. Care, 1985-91; commr. Northbrook (Ill.) Park Dist., 1987-91, pres., 1990—; mem. Village of Northbrook Planning Commn., 1987-89. With U.S. Army, 1943—46. Recipient Silver Beaver award Boy Scouts Am., 1963; recipient Silver Antelope award Boy Scouts Am., 1967, Disting. Eagle award Boy Scouts Am., 1969, Brotherhood award Lakeview Interfaith Council, 1968, Physician Speaker award AMA, 1981; inducted into City of Chgo. Sr. Citizens Hall of Fame, 1991. Fellow AAAS, Am. Acad. Family Physicians (mem. congress of dels.); mem. Chgo. Med. Soc. (pres. 1979, Pub. Svc. award 1990), Ill. Acad. Family Physicians (pres. 1977), Assn. Depts. Family Medicine (exec. com.), Masons, Shriners, Kiwanis (dir. local club). Democrat. Unitarian Universalist.

HIRSCH, MARTIN, dentist; m. Noreen Hirsch; 2 children. BS, CUNY, 1968; DMD, U. Pa., 1972; splty. in prosthondontics, U. Iowa, 1975; splty. in maxillofacial prosthetics, U. Chgo., 1976. Dental extern Coatsville Hosp., Pa., 1971—72; dental intern Mt. Sinai Hosp., N.Y.C., 1972—73; resident VA Hosp., Iowa City, 1973—75, U. Chgo. Hosp. and Clinics, 1975—76; asst. prof. dept. otolaryngology Abraham Lincoln Sch. Medicine U. Ill. Med. Ctr., Chgo., 1976—77; dir. maxillofacial prosthetics clinic Ctr. for Craniofacial Anamolies U. Ill. Med. Ctr., Chgo., 1976—77; asst. prof. U. Ill. Coll. Dentistry, Chgo., 1977—93; staff dept. dentistry U. Ill. Hosp. Med. Ctr., Chgo, 1979—83; staff dept. surgery dental sect. Cuneo Hosp., Chgo., 1979—87; staff dept. surgery dental section Cabrini Hosp., Chgo., 1979—92; staff dept. dentistry Ill. Masonic Med. Ctr., Chgo., 1979—, mem. head and neck treatment ctr., 1981—; sr. staff dept. dental surgery Columbus Hosp., Chgo., 1979—98; pvt. practice gen., cosmetic and prosthetic dentistry Chgo., 1979—; attending Cath. Health Ptnrs., Chgo., 1998—2001, Resurrection Health Care St. Joseph's Hosp., 2001—. Adj. instr. U. Chgo. Hosps. and Clinics, 1975—76; spkr. dental confs., symposiums, seminars; presenter to lay audiences on radio and TV. Spkr. Am. Cancer Soc., Chgo., 1981—87, chmn. profl. edn. com., 1981—85, mem. oral cancer com., 1982—86. Mem.: ADA, Chgo. Dental Soc., Ill. Dental Soc. Avocations: swimming, reading. Office: 2800 N Sheridan Rd Chicago IL 60657-6156 Office Phone: 773-248-6140.

HIRSCH, MARTIN STANLEY, internist, epidemiologist, researcher; b. Cortland, N.Y., Apr. 16, 1939; s. Hans and Grete (Lipper) H.; m. Corinne Becker, Oct. 18, 1964; children: Tera Gretchen, Michael Edward. AB, Hamilton Coll., 1960; MD, Johns Hopkins U., 1964; MA, Harvard U., 1990. Diplomate Am. Bd. Internal Medicine, Am. Bd. Internal Medicine and Infectious Diseases. Intern in medicine U. Chgo. Clinics and Hosp., 1964-65, resident in medicine, 1965-66; fellow in virology Ctr. for Disease Control, Atlanta, 1966-68; fellow Nat. Inst. for Med. Rsch., London, 1968-69; fellow in infectious diseases Harvard U., Boston, 1969-71, asst. prof., 1971-76, assoc. prof., 1976-88, prof. medicine, 1988—; assoc. physician MGH, Boston, 1981-87; physician Mass. Gen. Hosp., Boston, 1988—. Mem. sci. adv. bd. AM Found. for AIDS Rsch., 1987—; chmn. AIDS program adv. com. NIH, Bethesda, Md., 1989-92. Contbr. 147 chpts. to books, more than 233 articles to profl. jours.; editor-in-chief: Jour. of Infectious Diseases, 2002—. Surgeon USPHS, 1966-68. Fellow Infectious Disease Soc. Am.; mem. Am. Soc. Clin. Investigation, Am. Soc. Virology, Assn. Am. Physicians, Phi Beta Kappa, Alpha Omega Alpha. Achievements include first isolation of HIV-1 from genital secretions, central nervous system and blood monocytes; pioneering treatment of human Herpes virus and HIV infections with agents used singly or in combination. Office: Mass Gen Hosp Infectious Disease Unit 65 Landsdowne St Cambridge MA 02139

HIRSCH, PAUL J., orthopedist, surgeon, health facility administrator, medical educator; b. Bklyn., Oct. 12, 1937; s. Morris M. and Dorothy (Wolitzer) H.; 1 child, Jeremy S. BA in English, Roanoke Coll., 1957; MD, U. Va., 1961. Diplomate Am. Bd. Orthopedic Surgery. Intern NYU-Bellevue Med. Ctr., N.Y.C., 1961-62, resident, 1964-68; chief orthop. surgery Raritan Valley Hosp., Green Brook, N.J., 1969-71; pvt. practice orthop. surgery Bridgewater, N.J., 1971—; clin. prof. orthop. surgery Seton Hall Sch. Grad. Med. Edn. Vice chmn., bd. dirs. MIIX Group, Inc.; pres., med. dir. InterMedix, Lawrenceville, N.J.; emeritus staff, orthop. svc. Somerset (N.J.) Med. Ctr.; courtesy staff Robert Wood Johnson U. Hosp., New Brunswick, N.J.; clin. asst. prof. orthop surgery Rutgers Med. Sch., 1971-79; clin. instr. orthop. surgery NYU-Bellevue Med. Ctr., 1969-79; clin. assoc. prof. orthop. surgery N.J. Med. Sch., 1980—; clin. prof. orthop. surgery Seton Hall Sch. Postgrad. Medicine; chmn., bd. trustees Jour. Bone and Joint Surgery, 1999; mem. practicing physicians adv. group Nat. Com. Quality Assurance, 1996-98. Chmn. publs. com. Jour. Med. Soc. N.J., 1980-85; contbr. articles, editor profl. jours.,; mem. editl. bd. N.J. Medicine; editor-in-chief N.J. Medicine. Chmn. N.J. Com. for Quality Orthop. Care; trustee Rutgers Prep. Sch., pres. bd. trustees, 1983—86; trustee Raritan Valley C.C., 1986—; bd. dirs. N.J. Med. Polit. Action Com., 1983—; bd. trustees Orthop. Rsch. and Edn. Found., 1989—94. Mem.: N.J. State Med. Underwriters, Inc. (bd. dirs. 1990—99, vice chmn. bd. dirs. 1991—99), Med. Inter-Ins. Exch. N.J. (bd. govs. 1987—90), Ind. Sch. Chmn. Assn., N.J. Assn. Med. Splty. Socs. (pres. 1979—80, dir. 1981—85), N.J. Hosp. Assn. (trustee 1986—89), N.J. Health Scis. Group (treas. 1982—83), Internat. Soc. Orthop. Surgery and Traumatology, Am. Trauma Soc. (pres. ctrl. Jersey unit 1977—81), Acad. Medicine of N.J. (chmn. orthop. sect. 1975—78, trustee 1978—91, pres.-elect 1982—83, pres. 1983—84), Somerset County Med. Soc. (bd. trustees), Med. Soc. N.J. (chmn. orthop. sect. 1977—78, ho. of dels. 1976—, treas. 1982—86, 2d v.p. 1986—87, 1st v.p. 1987—88, pres.-elect 1988—89, pres. 1989—90, trustee 1982—91), N.J. Orthop. Soc. (pres. 1979—80), Ea. Orthop. Assn. (trustee 1981—84), Am. Coll. Physician Execs., Am. Acad. Orthop. Surgeons (bd. councilors 1982—88), Am. Orthop. Assn., AMA, ACS. Office: Green Knoll Profl Park #720 US Hwy 202-206 Bridgewater NJ 08807-1746

HIRSCH, RAYMOND ROBERT, chemicals executive, lawyer; b. St. Louis, Mar. 20, 1936; s. Raymond Winton and Olive Frances (Gordon) H.; m. Joanne Therese Dennis, Jan. 30, 1960; children: Amy Elizabeth, Thomas Christopher, Timothy Joseph, Mary Patricia. LL.B., St. Louis U., 1959. Bar: Mo. 1959. With Treasury Dept., 1960-62, Petrolite Corp., St. Louis, 1962—, sec., 1971—, v.p., gen. counsel, 1973-82, sr. v.p., gen. counsel, 1982-92; of counsel Guilfoil, Petzall & Shoemake, St. Louis, 1992-2000. Mem. Pub. Defender Commn., Mo. Mcpl. judge City of Bridgeton, Mo., 1970-73; mem. City of Des Peres Planning and Zoning Commn., 1974-78; mem. bd. edn. Spl. Sch. Dist. St. Louis County, 1981-83; mem. Mo. Air N.G., 1959-60; trustee Childhaven. Mem. ABA, Am. Soc. Corp. Secs., Mo. Bar Assn., Bar Assn. St. Louis, Mo. Athletic Club. Roman Catholic. Home: 3 W Walinca Walk Saint Louis MO 63105-2007 Office: Guilfoil Petzall & Shoemake 100 S 4th St Saint Louis MO 63102-1800 Office Phone: 314-241-6890. E-mail: rrhirsch@charter.net.

HIRSCH, (WILLIAM) REECE, lawyer; b. Dallas, Tex., Jan. 4, 1960; BS, Northwestern U., 1982; JD, U. So. Calif., 1990. Bar: Calif. 1990. Assoc. Davis Wright Tremaine LLP, San Francisco, 1994—98, ptnr., 1998—2002, Sonnenschein Nath & Rosenthal LLP, San Francisco, 2002—. Mem. editl. adv. bd. BNA's Health Law Reporter, Healthcare Informatics, HIPAA Security Compliance Insider, Internet Healthcare Strategies, TIPS on Managed Care. Mem.: ABA (mem. health law sect.), Healthcare Fin. Mgmt. Assn., Am. Health Lawyers Assn., Calif. Soc. Healthcare Attorneys. Office: Sonnenschein Nath & Rosenthal 685 Market St, 6th Fl San Francisco CA 94105 Office Phone: 415-882-5040. Office Fax: 415-543-5472. Business E-Mail: rhirsch@sonnenschein.com.

HIRSCH, ROBERT LOUIS, energy analyst, consultant; b. Evanston, Ill., Mar. 6, 1935; s. Louis Aaron and Dorothy Jean (Block) H.; m. Evelyn Podhouser, Feb. 1, 1959 (div. 2000); children: Allen, Lauri, Scott. BS, U. Ill., 1958, PhD, 1964; MS, U. Mich., 1959. Rsch. engr. Atomics Internat., 1959-60; physicist, later dir. ITT Indsl. Labs., Fort Wayne, Ind., 1964-68; sr. physicist controlled thermonuclear rsch. AEC (now Dept. Energy), Washington, 1968-72, divsn. dir., 1972—76; asst. adminstr. solar, geothermal and advanced energy sys. ERDA (presdl. appointment), 1976-77; dep. mgr. sci. and tech. dept. Exxon Corp., 1977; gen. mgr. exploratory petroleum rsch. Exxon Rsch. and Engring. Co., 1977-80, mgr. Synthetic Fuels Rsch. Lab. Baytown, Tex., 1980-83; v.p., mgr. rsch. and tech. svcs. dept. Arco Oil and Gas Co., Dallas, 1983-91; CEO ARCO Power Techs., Inc., 1986-91; v.p. Washington office Electric Power Rsch. Ins., 1991-94; cons. in tech. and mgmt., 1994—; exec. advisor Advanced Power Technologies, Washington, 1997—2001; pres. The Energy Tech. Collaborative, Inc., 1995-97; sr. energy analyst Rand, 2001—02; chmn. bd. on energy and environ. sys. NRC, 1996—2003; sr. energy program advisor SAIC, 2003—. Mem. bds. Annapolis Ctr. and Fusion Power Assocs.; participant in Atlantic Coun. Studies; mem. LDRD Bd. Lawrence Livermore Nat. Lab., 1993-95; mem. U.S.-USSR Joint Commn. on Peaceful Uses of Atomic Energy, 1970s; chmn. U.S. del. U.S.-USSR Joint Fusion Power Coord. Com., 1970s; mem. Internat. Fusion Rsch. Coun., 1970s, Dept. Energy Rsch. adv. bd., 1980s; vice chmn. com. on sci., engring. and tech. Fed. Coord. Coun. for Sci. Engring. and Tech., 1976; adv. bd. Princeton Plasma Physics Lab., 1980s, Oak Ridge Nat. Lab., 1993-97; rsch. coord. coun. Gas Rsch. Inst., 1980s. Contbr. articles to profl. jours; patentee in field. Elected nat. assoc. Nat. Acads., 2001. Recipient Meritorious award William Jump Found., 1971, Disting. Svc. award AEC, 1974, spl. achievement award Fusion Power Assocs., 1982, spl. Achievement award ERDA, 1976, 77, commendation NASA, 1982, merit award U. Mich. Engring. Alumni Soc., 1997; AEC Spl. fellow, 1960-63. Fellow AAAS; mem. Am. Nuc. Soc. (chmn. fusion tech. group, dir. 1975-76, 78-79, outstanding tech. achievement award 1983), Tau Beta Pi (U. Ill. Alumni Honor award), Phi Epsilon Pi. Home and Office: 122 Princess St Alexandria VA 22314 E-mail: rlhirsch@comcast.net.

HIRSCH, ROBERT MAURICE, hydrologist; b. Highland Park, Ill., June 6, 1949; s. James C. and Constance (Klauber) H.; children: Jacob R., Benjamin A. BA, Earlham Coll., 1971; MS, U. Wash., 1972; PhD, Johns Hopkins U., 1976. Hydrologist U.S. Geol. Survey, Reston, Va., 1976-88, asst. chief hydrologist, 1988-93, acting dir., 1993-94, chief hydrologist, 1994—. Author: Statistical Methods in Water Resources, 1992. Recipient Meritorious Svc. award U.S. Dept. Interior, Washington, 1988, Disting. Svc. award, 1994, Water Mgmt. Achievement award Interstate Coun. Water Policy, Washington, 1996. Fellow AAAS; mem. ASCE, Am. Goephys. Union, Am. Water Resources Assn. Office: USGS 409 Nat Ctr Reston VA 20192-0001 Business E-Mail: rhirsch@usgs.gov.

HIRSCH, ROSEANN CONTE, publisher; b. N.Y.C., Feb. 5, 1941; d. Frank and Anna (Burzycki) Conte; m. Barry Jay Hirsch, Oct. 1, 1967; children: Brian Christopher, Nicholas Benjamin, Jonathan Alexander. Student, Boston U., 1958-61; BA, Columbia U., 2004. Editorial asst. Grolier, Inc., 1962-64; editor Ideal Pub. Corp., N.Y.C., 1968-74; editorial dir. Sterling's Mags., Inc., N.Y.C., 1975-78, Hearst Spl. Publs., Hearst Corp., N.Y.C., 1978-84; v.p. Ultra Communications, Inc., N.Y.C., 1984-89; pub., pres. Dream Guys, Inc., N.Y.C., 1986-93; pres. Lamppost Press, Inc., N.Y.C., 1989—. Author: Super Working Mom's Handbook, 1986; editor: Young & Married Mag., 1976-77, 100 Greatest American Women, Good Housekeeping's Moms Who Work; contbr. articles to various mags. Home and Office: Lamppost Press Inc 870 United Nations Plaza 10E New York NY 10017 Office Phone: 212-750-0706.

HIRSCHBERG, JOSEPH GUSTAV, physicist, educator; b. Chgo., Apr. 13, 1921; s. Joseph Gustav and Lillian Hirschberg; m. Delores Dietrich, Jan. 1944 (div. Apr. 1946); m. Ginette Henriette Tetard, Apr. 26, 1947 (dec. Aug. 1992); children: Dorothy Jean Pixomatis, Joseph Gerald, Anne Marie Tumarkin, Lynn Susan Sontag; m. Judith Klausner Mintz, Apr. 2, 1996. AB, Dartmouth Coll., 1943; MS, U. Wis., 1951, PhD, 1952. Rsch. assoc. U. Wis., 1953—57; head optical group, rsch. physicist Plasma Physics Lab., Princeton, 1958—65; prof. d'Echange U. Paris, 1963; prof. physics U. Miami, Fla., 1965—85, chmn. dept., 1965—72, dir. optical physics lab., 1968—, prof. emeritus physics, 1986—. Pres. Fed. Engring. Corp., 1953—58; contractor Langley Rsch. Ctr., NASA, 1966—69; vis. rsch. faculty Oak Ridge Nat. Lab., Tenn., 1966; vis. rsch. physicist Princeton U., NJ, 1976, sr. rsch. faculty, 1986—89; leader solar eclipse expdns., Mexico, 1970, Canada, 72, Kenya, 73; vis. astronomer Sacramento Peak Obs., 1977; vis. scientist Inst. de Pathologie Cellulaire, Paris, 1980, Chercheur d'Echange, Mus. d'Histoire Naturel, Paris, 1983, Chercher d'Echange, Hosp. Henri Mondor, Creteil, France, 1985; vis. sr. scientist Max Planck Inst. Biophys. Chemistry, Göttingen, Germany, 1996, Göttingen, 97, Göttingen, 2002. Served to capt. USAAF, 1943—47. Fellow: Papanicolaou Cancer Rsch. Inst., European Acad. Scis., Arts and Letters, Optical Soc. Am., Am. Phys. Soc.; mem.: AAAS, Fla. Acad. Scis., Am. Soc. Photobiology, Sigma Xi, Phi Beta Kappa, Omega Delta Kappa, Sigma Pi Sigma. Achievements include co-discoverer telluric sodium absorption in solar radiation; invention of optical spectroscopic devices; infrared turbidity meter; Brillouin laser ocean probe; non-linear optical interference microscope; microfluorospectrometers; x-ray microscopy; solar and tidal energy systems; compact triangular interferometer; hydrogen economy devices; photoacoustic microscope. Home: 1046 Alfonso Ave Coral Gables FL 33146-3302 Office Phone: 305-284-2323. E-mail: jhirshberg@aol.com.

HIRSCHFELD, MICHAEL, lawyer; b. Bronx, July 4, 1950; s. Lawrence John and Ida (Miller) H.; m. Heidi P. Greenspan, June 17, 1973; children: Adam Lawrence, Philip Richard. BEE summa cum laude, CCNY, 1972; JD cum laude, U. Pa., 1975; LLM in Taxation, NYU, 1980. Bar: N.Y. 1976, U.S. Dist. Ct. (so. and ea. dists.) N.Y. 1976, U.S. Tax Ct. 1978. Assoc. Shearman and Sterling, N.Y.C., 1975-80, Roberts and Holland, N.Y.C., 1980-83, Carro, Spanbock, Kaster and Cuiffo, N.Y.C., 1983-85, ptnr., 1985-88, Winstown & Strawn, N.Y.C., 1988-98, Dechert LLP, N.Y.C., 1998—. Lectr. NYU, Assn. of Bar of City of New York, Fundamentals of Internat. Taxables, 2001-03, ABA, ALI-ABA, PLI, Syracuse U., U. Tex., Tulane U., Georgetown U.; chmn. NYU Inst. Real Estate Taxation; co-chmn. 49th, 50th, 52d, 53d and 54th ann. Fed. Income Taxation Confs.; 11th-23d ann. NYU Confs. on Fed. Taxation of Real Estate Taxations: mem. nat. edn. bd., Business Entities (RIA publ.) Real Estate Tax Digest, Jour. of Internat. Tax, Tax. Mgmt. Real Estate Jour.; mem. adv. bd. Tax Mgmt. Real Estate, Inst. Fed. Tax. Co-author: Real Estate Limited Partnerships, 3rd edit., 1991; bd. editors Real Estate Tax Digest, BNA Tax Mgmt.; editl. adv. bd. NYU Real Estate Adv. Bd. Mem.: Am. Tax Policy Inst. (treas. 2004—), Am. Coll. Tax Counsel, Internat. Tax Assn., Assn. of Bar of City of N.Y. (mem. com. on taxation of bus. entities), N.Y. State Bar Assn. (exec. com. 1987—97, lectr., co-chmn. coms. on income from real property tax sect. 1988—91, co-chmn. com. on preferences and minimum tax 1991—92, co-chmn. com. on individuals 1992—93, co-chmn. com. U.S. activities of fgn. taxpayers 1993—96, co-chmn. com. on real property 1996—98, co-chmn. tax accts. 1997—98, com. on internat. mems.), Am. Law

Inst. (lectr.), ABA (tax sect. vice chmn. ACRS depreciation recapture subcom. 1983—85, task force pres.'s tax reform proposals minimum tax subcom. 1985—86, chmn. syndications subcom. 1985—87, chmn. real estate tax problems com. 1989—91, co-chmn. govt. subcom. 1992—94, vice chmn. gov. submission com. 1992—95, chmn. govt. subcom. 1994—97, coun. 1997—2000, coun. dir. tax sect. internat. com. 1997—2000, vice chmn. individual income taxpayers com. 2000—02, vice chair com. ops. 2001—04, lectr. taxaction sect., chair 911 task force). Avocation: music (drum). Office: Dechert LLP 30 Rockefeller Plz Fl 22 New York NY 10112-2200 Fax: (212) 698-3599. Office Phone: 212-698-3635. E-mail: michael.hirschfeld@dechert.com.

HIRSCHFIELD, ALAN JAMES, entrepreneur; BS, U. Okla.; MBA, Harvard U. V.p. Allen & Co., Inc., 1959-67; v.p. fin., dir. Warner Bros. Seven Arts, Inc., 1967-68; with Am. Diversified Enterprises, Inc., 1968-73; pres., CEO Columbia Pictures Industries, N.Y.C., 1973-78; vice chmn., COO 20th Century-Fox Film Corp., L.A., 1979-81, chmn. bd., CEO, 1981-85; cons., investor entertainment industries, L.A., 1985-89; mng. dir. Wertheim Schroder & Co., L.A., 1990-92. Co-CEO, co-chair Data Broadcasting Corp., 1990-2000; bd. dirs. Cantel Med. Corp., Interactive Data Corp., Carmike Cinemas, Inc., Peregrine Sys., Leucadia Nat. Corp. Bd. dirs. Cmty. Found. Jackson Hole; trustee Dana Farber Cancer Inst, 2002. Office: PO Box 7443 Jackson WY 83002-7443

HIRSCHHORN, AUSTIN, lawyer; b. Detroit, Feb. 20, 1936; s. Herman and Dena Grace (Ufberg) H.; m. Susan Carol Goldstein, June 30, 1963; children: Laura Elsie, Carol Helen, Paula Gail. BA with honors, Mich. State U., 1957; JD, Wayne State U., 1960. Bar: Mich. 1961. Assoc. Arnold M. Gold Law Offices, Detroit, 1960-63; ptnr. Gold & Hirschhorn, Detroit, 1963-65; pvt. practice Detroit, 1965-68; ptnr. Boigon, Hirschhorn & Winston, Detroit, 1968-69, Boigon & Hirschhorn, Detroit and Southfield, 1969-78; pvt. practice Southfield, 1979-80; ptnr. Zemke & Hirschhorn (P.C.), Southfield, Mich., 1980-83, Austin Hirschhorn, P.C., Southfield, 1983-91; of counsel Rubenstein, Isaacs, Haroutunian & Sobel, P.C., Southfield, 1991-92; pvt. practice Austin Hirschhorn, P.C., Birmingham, Mich., 1992-96, Troy, Mich., 1996—. Lectr. Inst. Continuing Legal Edn., Mich. Trustee The Internat. Sch., Farmington Hills, Mich. With AUS, 1960-62. Mem. ABA, Fed. Bar Assn., Mich. Bar Assn., Oakland County Bar Assn., Am. Bankruptcy Inst., Comml. Law League Am. Jewish. Home: 26903 York Rd Huntington Woods MI 48070-1361 Office: 101 W Big Beaver Rd #1050 Troy MI 48084-5299 E-mail: austinh@ix.netcom.com.

HIRSCHHORN, CHARLES, media company executive; Grad., Harvard U., 1980. Employee Sack Theatres (now Sony Theaters), 1980—83; v.p. devel. Fox Broadcasting Co., 1986—89; v.p. prodn. Hollywood Pictures The Walt Disney Co., 1989—95, exec. v.p., 1995—96; pres. Disney Telefilms, 1996—97, Walt Disney TV and TV Animation, 1997—99; exec. v.p. prodn. Walt Disney Motion Pictures Group, 1997—99; founder Fountain Prodns.; founder, CEO G4 Media Inc., West L.A., 2002—. Developer, prodr.: (theatrical motion picture) The Joy Luck Club; Quiz Show; The Santa Clause; developer: (TV series) In Living Color; assoc. prodr.: (films) Bull Durham; exec. prodr.: (films) Dirty Rotten Scoundrels; exec. prodr.: (films) Herbie: Fully Loaded. Bd. mem. Nat. Multiple Sclerosis Soc., Harvard Coll. Office of the Arts, Berklee Coll. Music. Arts Mgmt. fellow, Nat. Endowment Arts. Office: G4 Media Inc 12312 W Olympic Blvd West Los Angeles CA 90064

HIRSCHHORN, ERIC LEONARD, lawyer; b. N.Y.C., Apr. 28, 1946; m. Leah Wortham, Oct. 31, 1981; children: Alexander, Elizabeth, Anne. BA, U. Chgo., 1965; JD, Columbia U., 1968. Bar: N.Y. 1968, U.S. Supreme Ct. 1972, D.C. 1973. Reginald Heber Smith Community Lawyer fellow MFY Legal Svcs., N.Y.C., 1968-71; counsel Dem. Study Group N.Y. State Assembly, Albany, 1971; legis asst. to Rep. Bella Abzug, U.S. Ho. of Reps., Washington, 1971-73; assoc. Cadwalader, Wickersham & Taft, N.Y.C., 1973-75; chief counsel subcom. on govt. info. and individual rights U.S. Ho. of Reps., Washington, 1975-77; dep. assoc. dir. internat. affairs & trade U.S. Office Mgmt. & Budget, Washington, 1977-80; dep. asst. sec. for export adminstrn. U.S. Dept. Commerce, Washington, 1980-81; ptnr. Winston & Strawn LLP (formerly Bishop, Cook, Purcell & Reynolds), Washington, 1981—. Exec. sec. Industry Coalition on Tech. Transfer, Washington, 1986—. Author: The Export Control and Embargo Handbook, 2000, 2d edit., 2004; contbr. articles to profl. jours. Mem. Assn. Bar City N.Y., Thurgood Marshall Am. Inn of Ct., D.C. Bar (legal ethics com. 1997-98, 99-2005, vice-chmn. 2001-03, chmn. 2003-05, rules of profl. conduct rev. com. 2004—). Office: Winston & Strawn LLP 1700 K St NW Washington DC 20006 Office Phone: 202-282-5706.

HIRSCHHORN, JOEL, lawyer; b. Bklyn., Mar. 13, 1943; s. Leo S. and Thelma (Bassin) H.; m. Evelyn Ruth Finkelstein, Jan. 29, 1966; children: Bennett K., Douglas K. BA, U. Conn., 1964; JD, U. Wis., 1967. Bar: Fla. 1967, Wis. 1967, U.S. Ct. Appeals (1st, 2d, 3d, 4th, 5th, 6th, 7th, 8th, 9th, 10th and 11th cirs.), U.S. Tax. Ct. Pvt. practice, Miami, Fla., 1967—69; assoc. Wilson, Abramson & Rosenthal, Miami, 1970—72; pvt. practice Miami, 1972—89; sr. ptnr., head litig. dept. Broad & Cassel, Miami, 1989—90; pvt. practice Miami, 1990—99; ptnr. Hirschhorn & Bieber, PA, Coral Gables, Fla., 2000—. Lectr. in field. Mem. bd. dirs. Hope Ctr., Miami, 1974-82, bd. trustees, 1982-84, hon. trustee, 1984—; exec. bd. mem. Greater Miami chpt. Am. Jewish Com., 1968-76, v.p., 1972-76, chmn. nat. legal com., 1989-90; chmn. Dade County Alliance for Safer Cities, 1972-73; former bd. dirs., sec. Concern Unltd., Inc.; former bd. dirs., v.p. Advocate Program, Inc.; mem. Dade County Cmty. Rels. Bd., 1978-81; bd. trustees Freedom to Read Found., 1997-2001, 2002-04, treas., 1999-2005. Fellow Am. Bd. Criminal Lawyes (pres. 2003), Internat. Acad. Trial Lawyers; mem. ABA, ATLA (exec. com. Criminal Law sect.), Nat. Assn. Criminal Def. Lawyers (bd. dirs. 1979-86, chmn. Fair Trial/Free Press and Televised Criminal Trials com. 1977-79, cert. for work in criminal def. 1979, for work regarding opposition to cameras in courtrooms 1980), First Amendment Lawyers. Assn. (pres. 1974-75), Fla. Bar Assn. (chmn. fed. practice com. 1983, ethics com. criminal law sect. 1986-87, pres., non resident lawyers divsn. 2005, bd. govs. 2004-), Dade County Bar Assn. (cert. of appreciation 1975), Fla. Criminal Def. Lawyers Assn., Acad. Fla. Trial Lawyers, Wis. Law Found., State Bar Wis. (bd. govs., 2004—). Democrat. Jewish. Office: Penthouse 1 2600 S Douglas Rd Coral Gables FL 33134-6143 Office Phone: 305-445-5320.

HIRSCHHORN, KURT, pediatrics educator; b. Vienna, May 18, 1926; arrived in U.S., 1940, naturalized, 1945; s. Emanuel and Helen (Mayberger) Hirschhorn; m. Rochelle Reibman, Dec. 20, 1952; children: Melanie D., Lisa R., Joel N. Student, U. Pitts., 1944; BA, NYU, 1950, MD, 1954, MS, 1958. Intern Bellevue Hosp., N.Y.C., 1954—55, resident, 1955—56; fellow NYU, 1956—57, U. Uppsala, Sweden, 1957—58; instr. NYU Sch. Medicine, 1956—58, asst. prof., 1958—63, assoc. prof., 1963—66; Arthur J. and Nellie Z. Cohen prof. genetics and pediat. Mt. Sinai Sch. Medicine, CUNY, 1966—76, Herbert H. Lehman prof., chmn. pediat., 1977—95, prof. pediat., human genetics and medicine, 1995—. Adj. prof. biology NYU, 1966—74; established investigator Am. Heart Assn., 1960—65; career scientist N.Y.C. Health Rsch. Coun., 1965—75. Author numerous sci. publs.; editor (with Harry Harris): Advances in Human Genetics, 1969—95; mem. editl. bd.: 16 sci. jours. Mem. coun. Village Cmty. Sch., 1968—73, chmn., 1972—73. Served with U.S. Army, 1944—47. Recipient Rudolph Virchow medal, 1974, Alumni Achievement award, NYU Sch. Medicine, 1982, Jacobi medal, Mt. Sinai Med. Ctr., 1993, William Allan award, Am. Soc. Human Genetics, 1995, J. Lester Gabrilove award for significant contbns. to medicine, Mt. Sinai Sch. Medicine, 2001; Bergquist fellow, NYU, 1958. Fellow: AAAS, N.Y. Acad. Medicine, Am. Acad. Pediat.; mem.: Am. Cancer Soc. (coun. 1989—92), Am. Soc. Pediatric Chmn. (coun. 1983—86), Environ. Mutagen Soc. (coun. 1969—76), Genetics Soc. Am., Harvey Soc. (v.p. 1979—80, pres. 1980—81, coun. 1981—84), Am. Assn. Immunologists, Am. Soc. Human Genetics (pres. 1969, dir. 1964—65, 1968—71, Human Genetics Edn. Excellence award 2002), Am. Pediatric Soc., Am. Assn. Physicians, Am. Soc. Clin. Investigation, Am. Coll. Med. Genetics, Inst. Medicine of NAS, Pediatric Travel Club, Alpha Omega Alpha, Sigma Xi, Phi Beta Kappa. Home: 29 Washington Sq W New York NY 10011-9180 Office: Mt Sinai Sch Medicine 1 Gustave L Levy Pl New York NY 10029-6500 Office Phone: 212-241-4305. Business E-Mail: kurt.hirschhorn@mssm.edu.

HIRSCHHORN, ROCHELLE, genetics educator; b. Bklyn., Mar. 19, 1932; d. Hyman and Anna Reibman; m. Kurt Hirschhorn; children: Melanie D., Lisa R., Joel N. BA, Barnard Coll., 1953; MD, NYU, 1957. Intern NYU-Bellevue Med. Divsn., N.Y.C., 1958—59; rsch. fellow, teaching asst. NYU Sch. Medicine, N.Y.C., 1963—65, assoc. rsch. scientist, 1965—66, instr. medicine, 1966—69, asst. prof. medicine, 1969—74, assoc. prof. medicine, 1974—79, prof. medicine, 1975—, head divsn. med. genetics, 1984—, prof. medicine and cell biology, 1996—. Hon. fellow Galton Lab. Human Genetics & Biometry Univ. Coll., London, 1971—72; assoc. attending physician in medicine Beffevue Hosp., N.Y.C., 1969—80, Univ. Hosp., NYU Sch. Medicine, 1974—81; attending physician Bellevue Hosp., 1980—, Univ. Hosp., 1981—; mem. numerous coms. & study sects. NIH, 1973—; vis. prof. Harvard U., 1995, U. Calif., San Francisco, 1995. Trustee AIDS Med. Found./AMFAR; judge Westinghouse Nat. Sci. Talent Search; founding mem. Village Cmty. Sch.; senator NYU Senate, mem. pediatrics search com., 1987—89, human subjects instl. rev. bd., 1989—94, co-dir. second year med. genetics course, 1989—93, NYU appts. and promotions com., 1995—2002. Named Disting. Alumna, Barnard Coll. Master: Am. Coll. Rheumatology; fellow: AAAS, Hero Arthritis Found., Am. Coll. Med. Genetics (founder); mem.: Inst. of Medicine of NAS, Harvey Soc. (coun. 1989—92), Soc. for Inherited Metabolic Diseases, Peripatetic Soc., Interurban Clin. Club (pres. 1987—88), Am. Soc. Human Genetics (cert. 1987), Am. Assn. Immunologists, Assn. Am. Physicians, Am. Soc. for Clin. Investigation, Alpha Omega Alpha (councillor Delta of N.Y. 1982—2002). Achievements include elucidation of pathophysiologic mechanisms, delineation of molecular and biochemical defects of genetic disorders including adenosine deaminase and glycogen storage disease type II. Office: NYU Med Ctr 550 1st Ave CD612 New York NY 10016-6402 Office Phone: 212-263-6276. Business E-Mail: hirscr01@med.nyu.edu.

HIRSCHHORN, SIDNEY, accountant, educator; b. NYC; s. Benjamin Hirschhorn and Pauline Schechter. BBA, CUNY, 1946; MA in Bus. Edn., NYU, 1948, PhD in Edn., 1991. CPA N.Y.; cert. sch. adminstr. and supr. N.Y., tchr. acctg. and bus. practice in secondary schs. N.Y. Tchr. English and citizenship for fgn.-born adults N.Y.C. Bd. Edn., 1952—55, tchr. common br. subjects, 1954—56, tchr. spl. edn., 1956—57, tchr. acctg., 1957—68, guidance counselor, 1968—91, instr. multi-cultural counseling strategies course for practicing guidance counselors, 1986. Tchr. bus. law, bookkeeping, and comml. arithmetic, summer and evening pub. H.S. Bd. Edn., N.Y.C., 1955—64; adj. instr. acctg. Mercy Coll., 1977—79, Bergen C.C., Paramus, NJ, 1979—80; interim acting HS asst. prin. Bd. Edn., NYC, 1978; instr. mandated workshop for tchrs. recently lic. NYC Bd. Edn., 1985—86, supr. of tchrs., 1987, instr. human rels., 1988—89. Donor archival materials concerning bus. edn., acctg., and bus. law in N.Y.C. pub. high schs. Columbia U. Tchrs. Coll., 2003. Recipient cert. of merit, Pres. of Borough of the Bronx. Mem.: AICPA, N.Y. State Soc. CPAs. Avocations: reading, movies, theater, opera, museums.

HIRSCHMAN, BARRY H., human resources specialist; b. Perth Amboy, NJ, Dec. 21, 1972; s. Monroe and Susan Hirschman (Stepmother); m. Randi Joy Lipkin, Aug. 31, 2003. BA, Bowling Green State U., 1994; postgrad., Rutgers U., 2004—. Cert. human resources profl. Sr. recruiter, acct. mgr., Princeton, NJ; group human resources mgr. Mistras Holdings Group, Princeton Junction, NJ, 1999—. Bd. dirs. Princeton East Condo. Assn., East Windsor, NJ. Sgt. U.S. Army. Mem.: Soc. Human Resources. Office: Mistras Holdings Group 195 Clarksville Rd Princeton Junction NJ 08550 E-mail: bhirschman@pacndt.com.

HIRSCHMAN, CHARLES, JR., sociologist, educator; b. Atlanta, Nov. 29, 1943; s. Charles Sr. and Mary Gertrude (Mullee) H.; m. Josephine Knight, Jan. 29, 1968; children: Andrew Charles, Sarah Lynn. BA, Miami U., Oxford, Ohio, 1965; MS, U. Wis., 1969, PhD, 1972. Vol. Peace Corps, Malaysia, 1965-67; prof. Duke U., Durham, N.C., 1972-81, Cornell U., Ithaca, N.Y., 1981-87, U. Wash., Seattle, 1987—, chair dept. sociology, 1995-98, Boeing internat. prof., 1999—. Cons. Ford Found., Malaysia, 1974-75; chair social scis. and population study sect. NIH, Washington, 1987-91; vis. scholar Russell Sage Found., 1998-99. Author: Ethnic and Social Stratification in Peninsula Malaysia, 1975; editor: The Handbook of International Migration: The American Experience, 1999; contbr. articles to profl. jours. Fellow Ctr. Advanced Study in the Bahavioral Scis., Stanford, Calif., 1993-94. Fellow AAAS (chair sect. K on social, econs. and polit. scis. 2004-), Am. Acad. Arts and Scis.; mem. Assn. for Asian Studies (bd. dirs. 1987-90), Population Assn Am. (bd. dirs. 1992-94, v.p. 1997, pres. 2005). Office: U Wash Dept Sociology PO Box 353340 Seattle WA 98195-3340 Office Phone: 206-543-5035. Business E-Mail: charles@u.washington.edu.

HIRSCHMAN, KAREN L., lawyer; b. York, Pa., Dec. 15, 1952; BA, U. Del., 1973; MA, U. Tex., 1980, JD with honors, 1983. Bar: Tex. 1983, DC 2002, NY 2003. Ptnr., co-head Litig. Sect. Vinson & Elkins LLP, Dallas. Fellow: Tex. Bar Found.; mem.: ABA, Am. Law Inst. Office: Vinson & Elkins LLP Trammell Crow Ctr 2001 Ross Ave, Ste 3700 Dallas TX 75201 Office Phone: 214-220-7795. Business E-Mail: khirschman@velaw.com.

HIRSCHMAN, SHALOM ZARACH, physician; b. Troy, N.Y., Aug. 5, 1936; s. Meyer and Anne Hirschman; divorced; children: Orin, Raquel, Doritte, Benyamin; m. Frances E. Neumann Ron, 1995. BA, Yeshiva U., 1957; MD, Albert Einstein Coll. Medicine, 1961; PhD equivalent, NIH Grad. Sch., 1966. Intern medicine Mass. Gen. Hosp., Harvard Med. Sch., 1961-62, resident, 1962-63; research assoc. NIH, Nat. Insts. Arthritis, Metabolic and Digestive Diseases, 1963-65, sr. investigator, 1965-66; NIH fellow in medicine Columbia-Presbyn. Med. Center, N.Y.C., 1966-67; sr. investigator Nat. Cancer Inst., NIH, 1967-69; instr. medicine George Washington U. Sch. Medicine, 1963-65; assoc. prof. medicine, dir. div. infectious diseases Mt. Sinai Sch. Medicine, CUNY, 1969-71, prof. medicine, dir. div. infectious diseases, 1971—, vice chmn. dept. medicine, 1972-75; attending physician Mt. Sinai Hosp., N.Y.C., 1971—; dir. emeritus divsn. infectious diseases Mt. Sinai Med. Ctr., 1996—. Mem. merit rev. bd. VA, 1976-79; mem. virology and microbiology exec. bd. Am. Cancer Soc., 1981-86; pres., CEO Advanced Viral Rsch. Corp., 1996—; scientific dir. Advanced Viral Rsch. Inst., 1998—. Founder, trustee Touro Coll., Touro Law Sch., N.Y.C., 1970. Served with USPHS, 1963-69. NIH fellow, 1964; research grantee, 1970—. Fellow ACP, Am. Soc. Infectious Diseases (councillor N.Y. chpt. 1995-96), Am. Coll. Clin. Pharmacology, Royal Coll. Hygiene and Tropical Medicine; mem. AAAS, Am. Biophys. Soc., Am. Soc. Microbiology, Soc. Gen. Virology, Am. Soc. Liver Diseases, Soc. Exptl. Biology and Medicine, Am. Soc. Clin. Investigation, Assn. Am. Physicians, Am. Fedn. Clin. Rsch., Am. Fedn. Med. Rsch., N.Y. Acad. Scis. (chmn. microbiology sect. 1975), Harvey Soc. Office: 200 Corporate Blvd S Ste 145 Yonkers NY 10701-6805 E-mail: shirschman@adviral.com.

HIRSCHMANN, RALPH FRANZ, chemist; b. Fuerth, Bavaria, Germany, May 6, 1922; came to U.S., 1937; s. Carl and Alice (Buchenbacher) H.; m. Lucy Marguerite Aliminosa, Mar. 9, 1951; children— Ralph F., Carla M. Hirschmann Hummel AB, Oberlin Coll., 1943, D.Sc. (hon.), 1969; MA, U. Wis., 1948, PhD, 1950, DSc (hon.), 1996. Asst. dir. Merck Sharp & Dohme Research Labs., Rahway, N.J., 1964-68, dir., 1968-71, sr. dir. West Point, Pa., 1972-74, exec. dir., 1974-76, v.p. Rahway, 1976-78, sr. v.p., 1978-87; research prof. chemistry U. Pa., Phila, 1987—; prof. biomed. research Med. U. S.C., Charleston, 1987-97; Makineni prof. bioorganic chemistry U. Pa., Phila., 1994—. Mem. N.J. Gov.'s Commn. on Sci. and Tech., 1984; mem. adv. com. NSF, 1985; mem. com. to survey opportunities in chem. scis. NRC, 1982; Romanes lectr. U. Edinburgh, Eng., 1985; Charles D. Hurd lectr. Northwestern U., 1985; Shell Disting. lectr., 1994, Monsanto lectr. Purdue U., 1996; mem. com. on chem. and pub. affairs Am. Chem. Soc. Contbr. numerous articles to profl. jours.; patentee in field Trustee Oberline Coll., 1986-93. Served with U.S. Army, 1943-46, PTO. Recipient Nichols medal, 1988, Chem. Pioneer award Am. Inst. Chemists, 1992, Gold medal Max Bergman Kreis, 1993, Alfred Burger award Am. Chem. Soc., 1994, Padmavathy and Noth Guthikonda Meml. award, 1996, Dr. Josef Rudinger award European Peptide Soc., 1996, Rsch. Achievement award in medicinal and natural products chemistry Am. Assn. Pharm. Scientists, 1996, Nat'l Acad. Sci. award for Industrial Application of Science, 1999, Arthur C. Cope Medal, 1999, Ed Smissman Bristol-Meyers Squibb award, 1999, Nat'l Medal of Science, 2000, Williard Gibbs Medal, 2002. Fellow AAAS, ACS (Medicinal Chemistry award 1986, Carothers award Del. sect. 1994); mem. Am. Acad. Arts and Scis., Am. Soc. Biol. Chemists, NAS; sr. fellow, Institutes of Medicine. Home: Meadowood 711 Radcliff Ct Lansdale PA 19446 Office: U Pa Dept Chemistry 231 S 34th St Philadelphia PA 19104-3803 Office Phone: 215-898-7398.

HIRSCHOWITZ, BASIL ISAAC, physician; b. Bethal, South Africa, May 29, 1925; came to U.S., 1953, naturalized, 1961; s. Morris and Dorothy (Drieband) H.; m. Barbara L. Burns, July 6, 1958; children: David E., Karen, Edward A., Vanessa. BSc, Witwatersrand U., Johannesburg, 1943, MB.BCh, 1947, MD, 1954; MD (hon.), Gothenburg (Sweden) U., 2004. Intern, resident Johannesburg Gen. Hosp., 1948-50; house physician Postgrad. Med. Sch., London, Eng., 1950; registrar Central Middlesex Hosp., London, 1951-53; instr., asst. prof. U. Mich., 1953-56; asst. prof. Temple U., 1957-59; assoc. prof. medicine U. Ala. Med. Center, Birmingham, 1959-64; prof. medicine U. Ala. Med. Ctr., 1964-95, emeritus prof., 1995; prof. physiology U. Ala. Med. Center, 1970—; Disting. faculty lectr. U. Ala., 1988; chmn. faculty coun. U. Ala. Sch. Medicine, 1989-90; dir. div. gastroenterology U. Ala. Hosp. and Clinics, 1959-87; chmn. exec. com. U. Ala. Hosp., 1986-88. Named U. chair in honor, 1997; named to, Ala. Acad. Honor, 1991, Ala. Health Care Hall of Fame, 2002; recipient Charles F. Kettering prize, GM Cancer Found., 1987, Seale Harris award, So. Med. Assn., 1992, Markowitz award, Am. Soc. Surg. Rsch., 1999, Pioneer in Endoscopy award, Soc. Am. Gastrointestinal Surgeons, 2003. Master ACP (Laureate award 1989); fellow AAAS, Assn. Am. Physicians, Royal Coll. Physicians (Edinburgh), Royal Coll. Physicians (London), Royal Soc. Medicine (hon.), Royal Philatelic Soc., (London); mem. AMA, South African, Brit., Ala. Med. Assns., Med. Rsch. Soc. Gt. Britain, Am. Fedn. Clin. Rsch., So. Soc. Clin. Investigation, Am. Physiol. Soc., Biophys. Soc., Am. Gastroent. Assn. (Friedenwald medal 1992), Am. Soc. Gastro-Intestinal Endoscopy (Schindler medal 1974, Disting. lectr. 1994), Am. Coll. Gastroenterology (Disting. Sci. Achievement award 1982), Brit. Soc. Gastro-Intestinal Endoscopy (hon.), Brit. Soc. Gastroenterology (Hurst lectr. 1966, Found. lectr. 1988, Astra internat. lectr. 1997), Italian Soc. Gastroenterology corr.), William Beaumont Soc. (Eddy Palmer award for contbns. to endoscopy 1976), Soc. Exptl. Biology and Medicine, Sigma Xi, Alpha Omega Alpha. Office: U Ala Med Ctr Birmingham AL 35294-0001 Business E-Mail: bih@uab.edu.

HIRSCHY, GORDON HAROLD, real estate broker, auctioneer; b. Sturgis, Mich., Jan. 28, 1942; s. Harold L. and Clara L. (Roy) H.; m. Alice Ann Grossman, Aug. 8, 1964 (dec. 1983); m. Sarah Lee Gerber, Nov. 20, 1994; children: Daniel, Benjamin, Matthew, Kurtt, Lori, Hannah, Nichole, Caitlyn, Sarah, Josh. BS in Gen. Agriculture, Purdue U., 1964; degree in auctioneering sci. and mgmt., Am. Acad. Auctioneers, 1990. FIC, LUTCF. State nitrogen engr., constrn. supr. Smith-Douglass Fertilizer Co., Indpls., 1965-67; asst. mgr. LaGrange County (Ind.) Farm Bur. Corp., 1967-72; county office mgr., agt. LaGrange County Farm Bur. Ins., 1972-80; owner, operator Community Ins. Svcs., Inc., LaGrange, 1980-88; ins. agt. Ins. Market Place, Inc., LaGrange, 1988-89; dist. rep. Modern Woodmen of Am., Inc., Rock Island, Ill., 1989-91; auctioneer Century 21 Fairfield Real Estate, Fort Wayne, Ind., 1999, Hirschy Real Estate & Auctioneering, 1999—. Named one of Outstanding Young Men Am., 1972, Rookie of Yr. Mich. Football Ofcls. Assn., 1988. Mem. N.E. Ind. Assn. Life Underwriters (pres. 1983, Mem. of Yr. 1982), Ind. Life and Health Ins. Leaders Club (exec. dir., sec. 1978-91), Nat. Auctioneers Assn., Ind. Auctioneers Assn., Nat. Assn. Realtors, Ind. Assn. Realtors, Am. Soc. Farm Equipment Appraisers, Gideons Internat., Ind./Mich. Football Ofcls. Athletic Assns. Republican. United Methodist. Avocations: football officiating, auctioneering. Office: 6110 Bluffton Rd Ste 117 Fort Wayne IN 46809 Office Phone: 260-478-7755. E-mail: hrareal@verizon.net.

HIRSH, ALLAN T., III, book publisher; b. Balt., Feb. 5, 1949; s. Allan T. Jr. and Eleanor (Rosenthal) H.; m. Lisa S. Hirsh, Sept. 23, 1972; children: Jessica Deanne, Alison Elizabeth. Attended, Balt. City Coll., 1967; BS in Commerce, U. Va., 1971. V.p. Ottenheimer Pubs., Inc., 1971—82, exec. v.p., CEO, 1982—87, pres., CEO, 1987-95, 1999—2003, pres., 1995—99; CEO, pres. Creative Horizons, LLC/Jesali, Inc., Balt., 1995—2001; mng. mem. Ottenheimer Properties, LLC, 2003—. Guest lectr. in field. Mem. organizing com. Balt. Hebrew Congregation Day Sch., 1990-93, treas., 1993-95, first v.p., 1995-97, pres., 1997-99; chmn., mem. many standing and ad hoc coms. Balt. Hebrew Congregation, 1971-02, chair resource devel. com., 1996-00, vice-chair strategic planning com., 1998-00, v.p., 1998-00, chair synagogue Task Force Worship Transformation, 2000-, sec., 2000-02, first v.p. (pres.-elect), 2002-04, pres., 2004-; mem. bd. pres Union for Reform Judaism, 2003-, Life Long Learning Coun., 2003-, exec. mem. bd., 2003-, chmn. press. pub. com., 2004-, Fulltime Edn. Com., 2004-; mem. bd. Mid-Atlantic Coun. Union for Reform Judaism, 1977-79, 03-, chair camp com., 1978-81, 04-, asst. treas., 1979-81; mem. bd. Progressive Assn. Reform Day Schs., 2000-02, v.p., 2002-03, chmn., 2003-; bd. dirs. The Associated (Jewish Charities Balt.) Jill Fox Meml. Fund, 1994-. Mem. Am. Book Prodrs. Assn. (bd. mem. 1984-90, v.p. 1987-88, pres. 1988-90, host Ann. Am. Book Prodrs. Seminar 1990-98, guest spkr. many industry seminars), Suburban Club Balt. County (chmn. food and svc. com. 1990-96, first v.p. 1994-96, pres.-elect 1996-97, pres. 1997-99). Home: 7903 Ivy Ln Baltimore MD 21208-3019 Office: Creative Horizons 10 Church Ln Baltimore MD 21208-3708

HIRSH, ALLAN THURMAN, JR., publishing executive; b. Cumberland, Md., Aug. 19, 1920; s. Allan Thurman and Ellinor Goldsmith (Ottenheimer) H.; m. Eleanor R. Rosenthal, June 17, 1944; children: Helene, Allan III, Eleanor. BS in Econs., Johns Hopkins U., 1941. CPA, Md. Acct. Burke Landsberg Gerber, Balt., 1941-42; pres. Ottenheimer Pubs., Inc, Balt., 1946-89, chmn. bd., 1989—; v.p. Allan Pubs., Inc., Balt., 1980—2003, Creative Horizons (formerly Ottenheimer Creations Inc.), Balt., 1994—2003, Thurman House, Hong Kong, 1994—2003; ptnr. Ottenheimer Properties LLC, 2003—. Bd. dirs. Balt. Hebrew Congregation, 1960-63, 83-86, 11 Slade Apt. Corp., 1985-88, 98-2003, pres., 1987-88, treas., 1998-2002, Lincoln Towers, West Palm Beach, Fla., 2005—; assoc. Jewish Charities, Balt., 1972-79; pres. Forest Park H.S. PTA, 1968, Balt. City Coll. PTA, 1971; bd. dirs. Hebrew Burial and Social Service Soc., 1946, pres. 1972-79; mem. adv. coun. on aging Johns Hopkins, 2004—. With USN, 1942-46. Mem.: Suburban (Balt.) (dir. 1974-79, v.p. 1976-79); Presidents (West Palm Beach, Fla.). Democrat. Jewish. Home: Apt 710 11 Slade Ave Baltimore MD 21208 Personal E-mail: allanhirsh@aol.com.

HIRSH, CRISTY J., principal; b. Dallas, Oct. 3, 1952; d. Bernard and Johanna (Cristol) H. BS in Early Childhood and Elem. Edn., Boston U., 1974; MS in Spl. Edn., U. Tex., Dallas, 1978; MEd in Counseling and Student Svcs., U. North Tex., 2001. Cert. counselor, sch. counselor; lic. profl. counselor, Tex.; cert. tchr., Tex., Mass.; cert. prin., Tex. Dir., learning specialist Specialized Learning, Dallas, 1981—93; counselor, mem. adj. faculty Eastfield Coll., Mesquite, Tex., 1992—95; counselor Grapevine-Colleyville Ind. Sch. Dist., Tex., 1995—2000, alternative sch. prin., 2000—. Mem. adj. faculty Richland Coll., Dallas, 1991—92. Mem. ACA, ASCD, Am. Sch. Counselor Assn., Coun. for Exceptional Children, Coun. for Children with Behavior Disorders, Tex. Assn. for Alternative Edn., Pi Lambda Theta, Phi Delta Kappa. Avocations: travel, theater, film, cooking, reading. Office: VISTA Alternative Campus 3051 Ira E Woods Ave Grapevine TX 76051-3817

HIRSH, THEODORE WILLIAM, lawyer; b. Gary, Ind., Nov. 16, 1934; s. Phillip and Libby (Krieger) H.; m. Beatrice Elaine Given, Aug. 28, 1955; children: Robert, Margo, Elizabeth, Irwin. AB, Ind. U., 1954, JD, 1957. Bar: Ind. 1957, Ill. 1958, Md. 1965. Atty. Montgomery Ward & Co., Chgo., 1958;

pvt. practice Gary, 1958-60; trial lawyer, chief counsel IRS, Chgo., 1960-65; ptnr. Venable, Baetjer & Howard, Balt., 1965-76, Miles & Stockbridge, Balt., 1978-86; prin. Sussman & Hirsh, P.A., Balt., 1976-78; ptnr. Melnicove, Kaufman, Weiner, Smouse & Garbis, P.A., Balt., 1986-89, Miles & Stockbridge, Balt., 1989-96; with Law Offices of Peter G. Angelos, P.C., Balt., 1996-99, Ballard, Spahr, Andrews & Ingersoll, LLP, Balt., 1999—. Office: Ballard Spahr Andrews & Ingersoll LLP 300 E Lombard St Ste 1800 Baltimore MD 21202-6739 Office Phone: 410-528-5568. Business E-Mail: hirsht@ballardspahr.com. E-mail: twhirsh@aol.com.

HIRSHBERG, JENNEFER, public affairs executive; BA, Cornell U., 1965; attended, Harvard U., UCLA; grad., Calif. State U., Los Angeles. Former dir., corp. comm. Bendix Automation; former dir., pub. affairs FTC; former press secretary First Lady Nancy Reagan; former asst. dir., office of mgmt. and budget for comm. and pub. liaison The White House; former sr. v.p., corp. strategic comm. Ogilvy & Mather Pub. Affairs; former exec. v.p. Kaufman Pub. Relations; with Capitoline Internat. Group, 1992—98, mng. dir. pub. relations then pres., CEO, 1999; pres. Capitoline Comm.; ptnr. Alcalde & Fay, 2000—, co-chair, edu. practice group. Bd. dirs. Multiple Sclerosis Soc., Girls Inc., Am. Woman's Economic Develop. Corp.; mem. President's Council of Cornell Women; mem. adv. com. Washington Race for the Cure. Office: Alcalde & Fay 400 N Capitol St NW Ste 475 Washington DC 20001*

HIRSHFIELD, LOUIS RUSSELL, music educator, musician; s. Jay L. Hirshfield and Marjorie M. Hirschfield; m. Leila Larijani, June 23, 2004. MusB, Eastman Sch. Music, 1988; MusM, Boston (Mass.) U., 1990; MusD, U. Colo., 1996. Instr. U. Colo., Boulder, Colo., 1993—95; asst. prof. Northwestern State U., Natchitoches, La., 1996—2000, We. Conn. State U., Danbury, Conn., 2000—05, assoc. prof., 2005—. Vis. prof. State U. Campinas, Brazil, 1997—98. Musician: various piano performances throughout the world. Mem.: AAUP, Coll. Music Soc., Music Tchrs. Nat. Assn. Office: Music Dept Western Conn State Univ 181 White St Danbury CT 06810 Office Phone: 203-837-8356.

HIRSHFIELD, PEARL, artist; b. Chgo., July 5, 1922; d. Louis and Anna (Nissenson) Belly; m. Myman J. Hirshfield, Dec. 17, 1944; children: Leslie, Laura, Deborah, Jo-Anne. AA, Herzl Jr. Coll., 1944; BA, Chgo. Sch. Art Inst., 1979; student, Northwestern U. Curator Midwest Artists for Peace, Chgo., 1967; co-curator art works Peace March, 1982; organizer Midwest Arts Festival, Chgo.; presenter Nat. Sculpture Conf., Cin., 1987, Found. Auschwitz, Brussels, 1997. Author: Conspiracy The Artist as Witness, 1972; film coord., Peace Prodns., 1983; creator, organizer Godine Press Art Portfolio, 1972; contbr. articles to jours. and newsletters; art exhibits include Nat. Sculpture Conf./Works by Women, Cin., 1987, Am. Internat. Archs. Hdqrs., San Francisco, 1987, Peace Mus., Chgo., 1988, 93, Holocaust Meml. Mus., Skokie, Ill., 1988, Internat. Conf. Ctr., Hiroshima, Japan, 1989, Archi-Center Gallery, Chgo., 1989, Lafayette Mus. Art, Ind., 1990, Franklin Furnace Mus., N.Y., 1991, Palais de Congres, Montreaux, Switzerland, 1992, Arthur Woods Gallery, Embach, Switzerland, 1992, Met. Mus. & Art Ctr., Coral Gables, Fla., Aurora U. Gallery, Ill., 1994, No. Ill. Art Mus., Chgo., 1996, Nat. Mus. Women in Arts, Washington D.C., 1996, Orange Ctr. for Contemporary Art, Santa Ana, Calif, 1997, Woman Made Gallery, Chgo., 1999, Witness and Legacy: Contemporary Art About the Holocaust, Minn. Mus. Am. Art, St. Paul, 1995, Columbus Mus. Art, Ohio, 1995, Finegood Gallery Art, West Hills, Calif., 1996, Aurora Pub. Art Commn., 1997, Blaffer Gallery, Houston, 1997, Knoxville Mus. Art, 1998, Tampa Bay Holocaust Mus., 1998, N.J. State Mus., Trenton, 1999, Oklahoma City Art Mus., 1999, Telfair Mus., Savannah, Ga., 1999, DeCordova Art Mus., Lincoln, Mass., 2000, Huntsville Mus. Art, Ala., 2000, Tucson Art Mus., 2000-01, South Bend Reg. Mus. Art, 2001, Frye Mus., Seattle, 2001-02; installation "Shadows of Auschwitz" on three year loan to Fla. Holocaust Mus., 2002-; Ill. Women Artists: The New Millenium, Ill. State Mus., Chgo., 1999, Nat. Mus. Women in Arts, 1999, Lakeview Mus. Arts & Scis., Ill, 2000, So. Ill. State U., 2000, So. Ill. Art Gallery, 2000, The Galleries, Ill. State U., 2000, Rockford Art Mus., 2001, Parkland Art Gallery, 2001, Quincy Art Ctr., 2001, Lodz Biennale, Poland, 2004, Michell Art Mus., Mount Vernon, Ill., 2004, Peoria Art Guild, 2004, Fla. Holocaust Mus., 2005; permanent pub. collections include Flaxman Libr., Sch. of Art Inst. Chgo., The Peace Mus., Chgo. Organizer, Peace Ctr., Evanston, 1958, bd. mem., 1958-60; co-chmn., organizer, Peace Walk, 1982; coord. Peace March, N.Y.C., 1982; mem. planning com., Art for a Nuclear Freeze, Chgo., 1983; cons. Art in Chgo., Mus. Contemporary Art, Chgo., 1997; mem. com. Paul Robeson 100th Birthday, Chgo., 1997. Recipient prize Whirlpool Found. Sculpture Competition, 1986, Nat. Holocaust Memorial Competition finalist, 1988, visual arts award Citizens Alert Bill of Rights, 1991, Task Force Against Police Brutality, 1993, Best 3 Dimensional Art award Baer Competition, 1998, Ill. Arts Coun. Visual Arts award, 1993; scholar Columbia Coll., 1940; grantee Ill. Art Coun. tech. assistance grant, 1983, Sculpture grant, 1984, Puffin Found., 1996; fellow Ill. Arts Coun., 1986. Mem. AAUW, Nat. Mus. Women in Arts (charter), Chgo. Artists' Coalition, Women's Caucus for Art, Physicians for Social Responsibility. Home and Office: 1333 Ridge Ave Evanston IL 60201-4131

HIRSHFIELD, STUART, lawyer; b. N.Y.C., Dec. 31, 1941; s. William Louis and Anne H.; m. Susanne Drucker, Jan. 22, 1967; children: Matthew S., Edward R. BA, Syracuse U., 1963, JD, 1966. Bar: N.Y. 1966, U.S. Dist. Ct. (so. and ea. dists.) N.Y. 1968, U.S. Ct. Appeals (2nd cir.) 1968. Assoc. Krauss & Krauss, N.Y.C., 1966-67; atty. N.Y. Cen. RR, N.Y.C., 1967-69; assoc. Blum, Haimoff, Gersen, Lipson & Szabad, N.Y.C., 1969; atty. CIT Fin., N.Y.C., 1970-72; assoc. Shea & Gould, N.Y.C., 1972-77, ptnr., 1977-88; ptnr., chmn. bankruptcy practice group Dewey Ballantine, N.Y.C., 1988—2003; ptnr., co-head bankruptcy and bus. reorgn. dept. Ropes & Gray LLP, NYC, 2003—. Bd. dirs. 565 Tenants Corp. Contbr. Asset Based Financing--A Transactional Guide, 1985. Assn. atty. Allenwood Civic Assn., Great Neck, N.Y., 1984; bd. advisors Syracuse U. Coll. Law, 1990—, exec. com., 1991-96; trustee The Colonial Theatre, 2004—. With USAR, 1966-72. Fellow Am. Coll. Bankruptcy (2d cir. admissions coun. 1994-2001, chair 1998-2001, bd. regents 1998-2001, bd. dirs. 2002—), Am. Bar Found.; mem. ABA (com. on bankruptcy 1983—), N.Y. Bar Assn., Assn. Bar City N.Y. (corp. reogn. com. 1975-78, 82-85), Assn. Comml. Fin. Attys. (dir. 1980-93), Am. Coll. Bankruptcy Found. (bd. dirs. 2002—), Rockefeller Ctr. Club, Phi Delta Phi. Office: Ropes & Gray LLP 45 Rockefeller Plaza New York NY 10111 Office Phone: 212-841-0682. Office Fax: 212-841-5725. Business E-Mail: stuart.hirshfield@ropesgray.com.

HIRSHMAN, HAROLD CARL, lawyer; b. Durham, N.C., Apr. 22, 1945; s. Morry and Florence Miriam (Goldman) H.; m. Linda Redlick, Dec. 21, 1966 (div. May 1984); 1 child, Sarah Anne; m. Lorie Chaiten, Feb. 19, 1989; children: Samuel David, Emma Lillian, Jacob Edwin. BS, Cornell U., 1966; JD, U. Chgo., 1969. Bar: Ill. 1969, U.S. Supreme Ct. 1976. Ptnr. Sonnenschein, Nath & Rosenthal, Chgo., 1969—. Author: (with others) Commercial Damages, 1986—. Bd. dirs. Lawyers Com. for Civil Rights, Chgo., Am. Jewish Congress Midwest Region; bd. dirs. Chgo. Opera Theatre, 1983-90. Mem. ABA, ACLU (past mem. bd. dirs. Chgo. chpt.), Chgo. Bar Assn., Chgo. Coun. Lawyers. Democrat. Office: Sonnenschein Nath Et Al 233 S Wacker Dr Ste 8000 Chicago IL 60606-6491 Office Phone: 312-876-8025. E-mail: hhirshman@sonnenschein.com.

HIRSHON, JON MARK, physician, educator; m. A. Cecilia Hirshon. MD, U. So. Calif., L.A., 1990; MPH, Johns Hopkins Sch. Pub. Health, 1994. Bd. cert. Am. Bd. Emergency Medicine, 1994, Am. Bd. Preventive Medicine, 2002. Asst. prof. Johns Hopkins U., Balt., 1996—2000, U. Md., Balt., 2001—04, assoc. prof., 2004—. Office: U Md 701 W Pratt St Rm 524 Baltimore MD 21201 Office Phone: 410-328-7474. E-mail: jhirs001@umaryland.edu.

HIRSHON, ROBERT EDWARD, lawyer; b. Portland, Maine, Apr. 2, 1948; s. Selvin and Gladys (Wein) H.; m. Roberta Lynn Miller, Aug. 16, 1969; children: Todd, Sara, Jason, Miriam. BA, U. Mich., 1970, JD, 1973. Bar: Maine 1973, U.S. Dist. Ct. Maine 1973, U.S. Ct. Appeals (1st cir.) 1977, U.S. Supreme Ct. 2000. Shareholder Drummond, Woodsum & MacMahon P.A., Portland, Maine, 1973—2003; CEO Tonkon Torp LLP, Portland, 2003—. Adj. prof. law U. Maine Law Sch. Contbr. articles to profl. jours. Chairperson Breakwater Sch Bd., Portland, 1978-85; mem. Zoning Bd. Appeals, Cape Elizabeth, Maine, 1983-90. Mem. ABA (mem. Ho. of Dels. 1992—, chair standing com. lawyers pub. svc. responsibility 1990-93, chair steering com. pro bono ctr. 1991-96, chair torts and ins. practice sect. 1996-97, chair standing com. on membership 1997-2000, pres. 2001-02), Maine Bar Assn. (pres. 1986, chair continuing legal edn. com. 1975-83), Cumberland County Bar Assn., Maine Bar Found. (pres. 1990), Multromah Bar Assn. Avocations: reading, tennis, skiing. Home: 3 Oakhurst Rd Cape Elizabeth ME 04107 Office: Tonkon Torp LLP 1600 Pioneer Tower 888 SW Fifth Ave Portland OR 97204 Business E-Mail: bobh@tonkon.com.

HIRSHON, SHELDON IRA, lawyer; b. Bklyn., Mar. 27, 1947; s. Jay and Jeanne (Benk) H.; m. Claudia Glenn Barasch; children: Ariel, Yaniv, Jessica. BS, NYU, 1968, JD, 1972, LLM, 1978. Bar: N.Y. 1972. Assoc. Graubard, Moskovitz, McGoldrick, Dannett & Horowitz, N.Y.C., 1972-76, Windels, Marx, Davies & Ives, N.Y.C., 1976-78, Krause, Hirsch & Gross, N.Y.C., 1978-80; assoc., ptnr. Stroock & Stroock & Lavan, N.Y.C., 1980-87; ptnr. Proskauer, Rose LLP, N.Y.C., 1987—. Mem. ABA, N.Y. Bar Assn., Assn. Bar City N.Y. Office: Proskauer Rose LLP 1585 Broadway Fl 27 New York NY 10036-8299 Office Phone: 212-969-3270. Business E-Mail: shirshon@proskauer.com.

HIRSHOWITZ, MELVIN STEPHEN, lawyer; b. N.Y.C., Dec. 11, 1938; s. Samuel Albert and Lillian Rose (Minkow) H.; m. Susan Bonnie Brezel, June 19, 1983; children: Lauren Allison, Emily Sara. BA with hons., Cornell U., 1960; LLB cum laude, Harvard U., 1963; MA in Biology, CUNY, 1977. Bar: N.Y. 1963, N.J. 1987, U.S. Dist. Ct. (so. dist.) N.Y. 1969, (ea. dist.) N.Y. 1977, N.J. 1993, U.S. Ct. Appeals (2d cir.) 1978, U.S. Supreme Ct. 1994. Assoc. atty. SEC, N.Y.C., 1963-65; sole practitioner Melvin Hirshowitz Law Office, N.Y.C., 1968-76, 87--; of counsel Hyman Bravin Law Offices, N.Y.C., 1976-87. *Over 35 years of experience in civil litigation and appeals in New York State and New York Federal Courts. Areas of concentration include commercial and fraud, litigation in estate lawsuits including will contests.* Author: (manual) Proof of an Over the Counter Manipulation, 1964. Vice chmn. N.Y. Libertarian Party, 1970-72, candidate for surrogate ct. judge and ct. of appeals judge. Mem. N.Y. County Lawyers Assn. (com. on profl. ethics 1986-92, com. fed. legislation 1986-88), Assn. of Bar of City of N.Y. (com. on the civil ct. 1986-89), N.Y. State Bar Assn., Harvard Club of N.Y.C., Phi Beta Kappa, Pi Delta Epsilon. Republican. Jewish. Avocations: bird watching, art, tennis. Office: 630 3rd Ave New York NY 10017-6705 Office Phone: 212-867-9595. Personal E-mail: mshlawoffices@aol.com.

HIRSHSON, STANLEY PHILIP, history educator; b. Bklyn., June 8, 1928; s. Morris M. and Rose (Gallant) H.; m. Claire Shibin, Nov. 21, 1965; 1 son, Mark Robert; m. Janet N. Feldman, Mar. 4, 1974; 1 son, Scott Garad. AB, Rutgers U., 1950; MA, Columbia U., 1951, PhD, 1959. Lectr. history Seton Hall U., South Orange, N.J., 1957-59; asst. prof. Paterson (N.J.) State Coll. (now William Paterson Coll.), 1959-62; asso. prof. Queens Coll., City U. N.Y., Flushing, 1963-66, prof., 1966—. Author: General Patton; A Soldier's Life, 2002, The White Tecumseh: A Biography of General William T. Sherman, 1997, The Lion of the Lord, A Biography of Brigham Young, 1969, Grenville M. Dodge, Soldier, Politician, Railroad Pioneer, 1967, Farewell to the Bloody Shirt, Northern Republicans and the Southern Negro, 1962, My History Is Holy, A Biography of Mary Baker Eddy. Served with AUS, 1946-47, 53-55. Am. Coun. Learned Socs. fellow, 1962-63, Guggenheim fellow, 1966-67, Rockefeller Found. fellow, 1981-82, Andrew W. Mellon fellow Huntington Libr., 1993. Home: 59 Wilson Pl Closter NJ 07624-2321 Office: Queens Coll Dept History Flushing NY 11367

HIRT, F. WILLIAM, insurance company executive; BA, Wittenberg Univ., 1947. CPCU. With Erie Indemnity Co. (Erie Ins. Group), Erie, Pa., 1947—, v.p., 1967—76, pres., 1976—81, CEO, 1981—90, chmn., 1981—. Co-trustee H.O. Hirt Trusts. Office: Erie Indemnity Co 100 Erie Insurance Place PO Box 1699 Erie PA 16530*

HIRT, JANET ROSE, law educator, law librarian; b. Meadville, Pa., Mar. 14, 1942; d. Ira George and Gladys Gertrude (McLaren) H. AB in English, Eastern Coll., St. Davids, Pa., 1964; MA in English, Allegheny Coll., Meadville, Pa., 1969; MA in Counseling, Villanova (Pa.) U., 1973, JD, 1987; MS in Info. Sci., Drexel U., Phila., 1977; postgrad., Oxford U., 1970, Sussex U., 1977. Bar: Pa. 1987, U.S. Dist. Ct. (ea. dist.) Pa. 1988, U.S. Ct. Appeals (3d cir.) 1988), U.S. Ct. Appeals (D.C. cir.) 1989; cert. tchr., Pa. Copy editor Am. Bapt. Bd. Publs., Valley Forge, Pa., 1964; tchr. English Springfield High Sch., Pa., 1964-73, 76-85, guidance counselor, 1973-75; evening and weekend supr. reader svcs., reference librarian Villanova U. Sch. Law, 1985; legal rschr. Schnader, Harrison, Segal & Lewis, Phila., 1986-87; reference rsch. libr. Widener U. Sch. Law, Wilmington, Del., 1987-89, assoc. dir. Law Libr. Wilmington and Harrisburg, Pa., 1989-95; dir. Law Libr., assoc. prof. law U. Orlando, Fla., 1995-96; libr., lectr. law Vanderbilt U., Nashvile, 1997—. Liaison Coun. on Internat. Edn., Springfield H.S. and Bexhill (Eng.) Grammar Sch.; cons. acad. law libr. evaluation for schs. seeking ABA approval; rschr. small law firms. Contbg. editor An Internet Guide for Tennessee Lawyers, 1998. Mem. ABA (bus. law sect., tax sect., sect. on legal edn.), ALA (Am. Coll. and Rsch. Librs. Divsn.), Godort Roundtable, Libr. Adminstrn. and Mgmt. Assn., Nat. Coun. Tchrs. English (life), Am. Assn. Law Librs. (acad. librs. spl. interest sect., editor newsletter 1994-96, mem. standing com. on copyright 1989-91, adv. com. indexing periodical lit. 2003-04, chair 2004-2005), Pa. Bar Assn. (unauthorized practice of law com. 1994—, local ct. rules com. 1989-91, com. on professionalism 1998—), Greater Phila. Law Libr. Assn. (newsletter prodr. 1990-91, mem. planning com. (copyright inst. 1992), exec. bd. 1989-91), S.E. Assn. Law Librs. (placement com. 2000-02, membership com. 2002—, local arrangements ann. meeting 1999, 2002) Home: 3818 West End Ave Nashville TN 37205 Office: Alyne Queener Massey Law Libr Vanderbilt U Nashville TN 37203 Office Phone: 615-343-0208. Business E-Mail: janet.hirt@law.vanderbilt.edu.

HIRTH, JOHN PRICE, metallurgical engineering educator; b. Cin., Dec. 16, 1930; s. John Willard and Betty Ann (Price) H.; m. Martha Joan Davis, Nov. 28, 1953; children: John Marcus, Laura Ellen, James Gregory, Christina Louise. B. Metall. Engring., Ohio State U., 1953; MS, Carnegie-Mellon U., 1953, PhD, 1957; DSc (hon.), Ohio State U., 1995. Asst. prof. metall. engring. Carnegie-Mellon U., Pitts., 1958-61; Mershon prof. Ohio State U., 1961-67; vis. prof. Stanford, 1967-68; prof. Ohio State U., Columbus, 1967-88, Wash. State U., Pullman, 1988—. Aizen vis. prof. Nat. U. Mex., Mexico City, 1976; cons. in field; bd. overseers Acad. for Contemporary Problems, 1971-76. Author: Condensation and Evaporation, 1964, Theory of Dislocations, 1968, 82; editor: Scripta Metallurgica, 1974-94. Served with USAF, 1953-55. Fulbright fellow Bristol U., Eng., 1957-58 Fellow AAAS, TMS (Hardy medal 1960, Mehl medal 1980, Mathewson medal 1982), Am. Soc. Engring. Edn. (McGraw award 1967), Am. Soc. Metals (Stoughton award 1964, Campbell lectr. 1972, White award 1989, Gold medal 1994, Sauveur Achievement award 1998); mem. NAS, NAE, ASME (Nadai medal 1999), Norwegian Acad. Scis. and Letters, AIME (hon.), Sigma Xi. Home: 114 E Ramsey Canyon Rd Hereford AZ 85615-9614 Personal E-mail: jphmdh1@cox.net.

HIRX, JOHN WILLIAM, conservator; b. Mineola, N.Y., Jan. 4, 1962; s. Robert Louis Hirx and Karen Lydia Schroeder. BA, Hunter Coll., 1985, MA, 1987; diploma in Conservation, NYU, 1992. Assoc. objects conservator L.A. (Calif.) County Mus. Art, 1999—2000, head objects conservator, 2000—. Co-author: (appendix) Technical Study: The Glazed Press-Molded Tiles of the Takht-I Sulaiman; contbr. articles to profl. jours. Grantee, Barakat Found., 2001. Mem.: Am. Inst. Conservation (assoc.; chmn. rsch. and tech. studies subcom. 2002—03). Avocation: ceramics. Home: 4338 Wawona Street Los Angeles CA 90065 Office: Los Angeles County Museum of Art 5905 Wilshire Blvd Los Angeles CA 90036 Office Phone: 323-932-5860. Office Fax: 323-857-4754. Personal E-mail: jhirx@lacma.org.

HISADA, MICHIE, physician, epidemiologist; MD, Keio U., Tokyo, 1988; MPH, Harvard U., 1993, ScD, 1998; PhD, Keio U., 2000. Diplomate Japan, 1988. Investigator Nat. Cancer Inst., Rockville, Md., 1998—. Office: Nat Cancer Inst 6120 Executive Blvd EPS 8008 Rockville MD 20852

HISCAVICH, MICHELLE, music educator, consultant; b. Suffern, N.Y., July 14, 1962; d. Lawrence John and Rose Marie Hiscavich. MusB, U. Miami, 1984; MEd, U. Mo.-Columbia, 1986; Sixth Yr. Degree in Ednl. Leadership, So. Conn. State U., New Haven, 1994. Cert. initial educator adminstr./supr. Conn., profl. educator music preK-12 Conn. Orch. dir. Ridgefield Pub. Sch., Conn., 1987—88, Newtown Pub. Sch., Conn., 1988—, dir. music, 1995—. Asst. condr. Ridgefield Youth Orch., Conn., 1988—91. Bd. dirs. Danbury Music Ctr., Conn. Mem.: ASCD, Music Educators Nat. Conf., Kappa Delta Pi. Avocations: music, outdoor activites. Office Phone: 203-426-7646. E-mail: hiscavichm@newtown.k12.ct.us.

HISCOCK, RICHARD CARSON, marine safety investigator; b. Washington, Dec. 18, 1944; s. Earle Francis and Alice Morgan (Carson) H.; m. Nancy Lynn Schafer, Oct. 12, 1968 (div. Jan. 1986); m. Virginia Murray Brierley, July 6, 1996. Student, Am. U., 1964-66. Fisherman F/V Benjo, Chatham, Mass., 1977-78; asst. harbormaster Town of Chatham, 1977—87; exec. dir. U.S. Lifesaving Mfrs. Assn., North Chatham, Mass., 1984-86; investigator Marine Safety Cons., Fairhaven, Mass., 1987-91; pres. ERE Assoc. Ltd., 1991—2002. Instr. hypothermia, cold water survival, emergency rescue equipment and fishing vessel safety, 1979—; mem. Comm. Fishing Industry Vessel Adv. Com., 1991-98; mem. Cape Cod Coastal Zone Mgmt. Adv. Com., 1977-92, chmn., 1986-91; mem. Barnstable County Coastal Resources Com., 1992-93; mem., chmn. Chatham Waterways Adv. Com., 1983-87; founder, bd. dirs. Marine Safety Found., Inc., Mass., 1993, v.p., 1999—; mem. Chatham Fin. Com., 1993-95; mem. Chatham Bylaw Rev. Com., 1995-97; industry advisor USCG Fishing Vessel Casualty Task Force, 1999. Contbr. articles to profl. jours. Mem. planning commn., Waitsfield, Vt., 2003—. Recipient Pub. Svc. Commendation, USCG, 1984, Cert. of Merit, USCG, 1998, Meritorious Team Commendation, USCG, 1999. Mem. Soc. Naval Architects and Marine Engrs., U.S. Marines Safety Assn., Mass. and Vt. Soc. Mayflower Descendents, Mad River Path Assn. (bd. dirs. 2003, v.p. 2003-04, pres. 2004—). Achievements include drafting a bill to establish crew licensing, inspection and additional safety requirements of certain fishing industry vessels; rsch. on comml. fishing, uninspected vessel safety, fishing vessel safety and hypothermia. Home: 2257 E Warren Rd Waitsfield VT 05673 E-mail: richard@offsoundings.com, rch@gmavt.net.

HISCOX, FRANK S., lawyer; b. 1952; BA in English with honors, Univ. Calif., Santa Barbara, 1974; MA in English with honors, Univ. Calif., 1977; PhD candidate in English, Univ. Tex., Austin; JD with honors, Univ. San Francisco, 1982. Bar: Calif. 1982. Ptnr., intellectual property and trademark, copyright, and brand mgmt. practice groups Dorsey & Whitney LLP, Palo Alto, Calif. Named one of Best Lawyers in Silicon Valley, 2000—02. Mem.: Santa Clara County Bar Assn., Silicon Valley Intellectual Property Assn., Internat. Trademark Assn. Office: Dorsey & Whitney LLP Ste 200 850 Hansen Way Palo Alto CA 94304-1017 Office Phone: 650-494-8700. Office Fax: 650-494-8771. Business E-Mail: hiscox.frank@dorsey.com.

HISE, MARK ALLEN, dentist; b. Chgo., Jan. 17, 1950; s. Clyde and Rose T. (Partipilo) Hise. AA, Mt. San Antonio Coll., Walnut, Calif., 1972; BA with highest honors, U. Calif., Riverside, 1974; MS, U. Utah, 1978; DDS, UCLA, 1983. Instr. sci. NW Acad., Houston, 1978-79; chmn. curriculum med. coll. prep program UCLA, 1980-85; instr. dentistry Coll. of Redwoods, Eureka, Calif., 1983; pvt. practice Arcata, Calif., 1983—2001, Scotia, Calif., 2002—. Numerous radio and TV appearances; spkr. in field. Editor: Preparing for the MCAT, 1983—85; contbr. articles to profl. jours. Named Best Dentist on North Coast, Times-Std. Newspaper, 2002; recipient awards for underwater photography; fellow, NIH, 1975—79; Henry Carter scholar, U. Calif., 1973, Regents scholar, 1973, Calif. State scholar, 1973—74. Mem.: ADA, AAAS, Nat. Soc. Med. Rsch., Acad. Gen. Dentistry, Calif. Dental Assn., North Coast Scuba Club. Roman Catholic. Avocation: underwater photography. Office: PO Box 68 Scotia CA 95565 Office Phone: 707-764-5300. Personal E-mail: mhise@aol.com.

HISE, RANDALL TODD, music educator, department chairman, choral educator; b. Denver, Mar. 31, 1974; s. Kathleen Alice Hise. MusB in Music Edn., Colo. State U., Ft. Collins, 1995; MA in Music Edn., U. No. Colo., Greeley, 2005. Cert. ORFF tchr. levels I & II 1997, 1998. Music specialist K-6 Thomson Elem., Arvada, Colo., 1995—2000; creative dramatics co-tchr. Mt. Evans Outdoor Edn. Lab. Sch., Evergreen, Colo., 1997—; head choral dir., music dept. chair Standley Lake Sr. HS, Westminster, Colo., 2000—. Mem.: Am. Choral Dirs. Assn. Home: 12267 W New Mexico Pl Lakewood CO 80228-3934 Office: Jefferson County Schs R-1 SLHS 9300 W 104th Ave Westminster CO 80021 E-mail: rtommyh@aol.com.

HISE, RICHARD TODD, marketing professional, educator, consultant; b. Washington, D.C., July 10, 1937; s. Theodore Richard and Lenor Mary (Parry) H.; m. Carol Lee Zeigler, Dec. 20, 1964; children: Richard William (dec.), Amy Caroline, Emily Carol. BA, Gettysburg Coll., 1959; MBA, U. Md., 1961, DBA, 1970. Instr. Elizabethtown (Pa.) Coll., 1962-64, Mich. State U., East Lansing, 1964-65, U. Md., College Park, 1965-70; assoc. prof., prof., head bus. adminstrn. Shippensburg (Pa.) State Coll., 1970-74; assoc. prof., dir. MBA program Va. Commonwealth U., Richmond, 1974-77; prof., holder Foley's professorship in retailing and mktg. Tex. A&M U., College Station, 1977—. Cons. IBM, Color Tile, Harley Davidson, Hotel Sofitel, Rosewood Properties, Mary Kay Cosmetics, Fleetwood Enterprises, OI Corp. Author: Quantitative Techniques for Marketing Decisions, 1973, Product/Service Strategy, 1977, Basic Marketing: Concepts and Decisions, 1979, Effective Salesmanship, 1980, Cases in Marketing Strategy, 1984, Basic Marketing: Concepts, Decisions, and Strategies, 1986, Millennial Marketing: Strategies for Success in the 21st Century and Beyond, 2001; contbr. more than 75 articles to profl. jours. including Jour. Mktg., Jour. Advt., Jour. Advt. Rsch., Jour. Global Mktg., Jour. Product Innovation Mgmt., Jour. Tchg. Internat. Bus., Mgmt. Acctg., Jour. Retailing, Jour. Acad. Mktg. Sci., among others. Sustaining mem. Rep. Nat. Com., 2001. Mem. Am. Mktg. Assn., Acad. Internat. Bus., Internat. Mgmt. Devel. Assn., Am. Legion, Pi Lambda Sigma, Beta Gamma Sigma, Phi Kappa Phi. Republican. Baptist. Avocations: international travel, impressionism art. Home: 1107 Merry Oaks Dr College Station TX 77840 Office: Tex A&M U Dept Mktg College Station TX 77843 E-mail: dick-hise@tamu.edu.

HISERT, GEORGE A., lawyer; b. Schenectady, NY, Sept. 18, 1944; BS summa cum laude, MS, Brown U., 1966; JD cum laude, U. Chgo., 1970. Bar: Calif. 1971. Law clk. to Hon. Sterry R. Waterman U.S. Ct. Appeals (2nd cir.), 1970-71; ptnr. McCutchen, Doyle, Brown & Enersen, San Francisco, 1977-93, Brobeck, Phleger & Harrison, San Francisco, 1993—2003; now ptnr. Bingham McCutchen LLP. Mem. editl. bd. Chgo. Law Rev., 1969-70; ABA sect. on bus. law liaison to UCC Permanent Editl. Bd. Mem. ABA (subcom. letter of credit, subcom. secured trans. of uniform comml. code com. bus. law sect., subcom. on syndications and loan participations of comml fin. svc. com., bus. law sect.), Internat. Bar Assn. (banking law com., bus. law sect.), State Bar Calif. (uniform comml. code com. bus. law sect., vice-chair 1992-93, chair 1993-94), Am. Coll. Comml. Fin. Lawyers, Order of Coif, Sigma Xi. Office: Bingham McCutchen LLP Three Embarcadero Ctr San Francisco CA 94111 Office Phone: 415-393-2577. Business E-Mail: george.hisert@bingham.com.

HISKES, DOLORES G., language educator; b. Chgo. d. Leslie R. and Dagmar (Brown) Grant; m. John R. Hiskes; children: Robin Caproni, Grant. Student, U. Ill., Chgo. Tutoring programs cons.; presenter in field. Author, illustrator: Phonics Pathways, Pyramid, The Short-Vowel Dictionary (5 nat. 1st pl. awards); developer ednl. games: The Train Game, Blendit!, Wordworks. Recipient 5 nat. awards for Best Phonics Program in U.S. Mem. Internat. Reading Assn., Assn. Am. Educators, Assn. Ednl. Therapists, Calif.

Assn. of Res. Specilaists, Orton Dyslexia Soc., Learning Disabilities Assn., Nat. Right to Read Found., The Calif. Reading Assn., Pubs. Mktg. Assn., Calif. Watercolor Soc., Commonwealth Club of Calif., Bay Area Ind. Pubs. Assn. Avocations: watercolors, travel, reading, exercise. Office: Dorbooks PO Box 2588 Livermore CA 94551-2588 Office Phone: 925-449-6983. Business E-Mail: dor@dorbooks.com.

HISS, TONY, writer; b. Washington, Aug. 5, 1941; s. Alger and Priscilla Harriet (Fansler) H.; m. Lois Cynthia Metzger, Feb. 22, 1986; 1 child, Jacob. AB, Harvard Coll., 1963. Staff writer The New Yorker, N.Y.C., 1963—; vis. scholar Taub Urban Rsch. Ctr. NYU, N.Y.C., 1994—. Regents' lectr. landscape architecture dept. U. Calif., Berkeley, Davis, 1992. Author: Laughing Last, 1977, The Experience of Place, 1990, The View from Alger's Window, 1999; co-author: All Aboard With E.M. Frimbo, 1974, 97, A Region at Risk, 1996, Disarming the Prairie, 1998, Prairie Passage: The I&M Canal Corridor, 1998, Building Images: Seventy Years of Photography at Hedrich Blessing, 2000; illustrator: The Bird Who Steals Everything Shining, 1987. Cons. Hudson River Greenway Coun., Albany, N.Y., 1990; juror Rudy Bruner Found., N.Y.C., 1991; trustee Conservancy Hist. Battery Pk, 1995; bd. dirs. Village Alliance, 1998; adv. bd. Scenic Am., Inc., 1999. Recipient best content article in non-geog. periodical award Nat. Coun. for Geog. Edn., 1990, Nat. Lit. award Nat. Recreation and Park Assn., 1995, George S. Lewis award Am. Inst. Archs. (local chpt.); Guggenheim fellow, 1994. Mem. Pen Am. Ctr., N.Y. Inst. Humanities. Avocations: train travel, hiking, rafting. Home: 22 E 8th St New York NY 10003-5920 Office: NYU Taub Urban Rsch Ctr 269 Mercer St Fl 2 New York NY 10003-6687 E-mail: tony.hiss@wagner.nyu.edu.

HITCHCOCK, BION EARL, lawyer; b. Muscatine, Iowa, Oct. 9, 1942; s. Stewart Edward and Arlene Ruth (Eichelberger) H. BSEE, Iowa State U., 1965; JD, U. Iowa, 1968. Bar: Iowa 1968, Okla. 1968, U.S. Ct. Customs and Patent Appeals 1973, U.S. Ct. Appeals (fed. cir.) 1982. Atty. Phillips Petroleum Co., Bartlesville, Okla., 1968-69, 73-76; mgr. licensing Phillips Petroleum Co. Europe-Africa, Brussels, 1977-80; sr. patent counsel Phillips Petroleum Co., Bartlesville, 1980-84, assoc. gen. patent counsel, 1984-2000; asst. gen. counsel intellectual property Chevron Phillips Chem. Co., LP, Houston, 2000—02; pvt. practice Sugar Land, Tex., 2002—. Bd. dirs. Bartlesville Symphony Orch., 1973-77, 80-91, pres., 1975-77, 82-84; bd. dirs. Bartlesville Allied Arts and Humanities Coun., 1976-77, 80-86, 1st v.p., 1982-83; mem. Govt. and Fin. Goals for Bartlesville Com., 1974-75; bd. dirs. Bartlesville Cmty. Concert Assn., 1982-90, Okla. Assn. Symphony Orchs., 1983-88. Lt. JAGC, USN, 1969-73. Mem. ABA, Okla. Bar Assn. (dir. patent trademark and copyright sect. 1980-86, sec. 1982-83, vice chmn. 1983-84, chmn. 1984-85), Iowa Bar Assn., Washington County Bar Assn. (pres. 1981-82), Am. Intellectual Property Law Assn., Am. Judicature Soc., Fed. Cir. Bar Assn., Licensing Execs. Soc., Eta Kappa Nu. Home: 1227 Misty Lake Ct Sugar Land TX 77478-5613 Office: 1227 Misty Lake Ct Sugar Land TX 77478-5613

HITCHCOCK, FREDERICK E., JR., (FRITZ HITCHCOCK), automotive company executive; CEO, owner Hitchcock Automotive Resources, City of Industry, Calif., 1980—. Recipient All Star Dealer Award, Sports Illus., 1988, 1995, Quality Dealer Award, Time Mag., 1993. Mem.: State of Calif. New Motor Vechicle Bd. (pres.), NADFC (ambassador), NADA (chmn. Gov. Rel. Com.). Office: Hitchcock Automotive Resoure 17340 Gale Ave La Puente CA 91748-1512

HITCHCOCK, JANE STANTON, playwright, novelist; b. NYC, Nov. 24, 1946; d. Robert Tinkham Crowley and Joan (Alexander) Stanton; m. William Mellon Hitchcock, Oct. 10, 1975 (div. Jan. 1991); m. Jim Hoagland, July 14, 1995. BA, Sarah Lawrence Coll., Bronxville, 1964-68. Author: Grace, 1982, Trick of the Eye, 1992 (Edgar award nominee, Hammett prize nominee), The Witches' Hammer, 1994, Social Crimes, 2002, One Dangerous Lady, 2005; screenwriter Our Time, 1974, First Love, 1976; producer Stalking Immortality (documentary) 1978; playwright Grace, 1981, Bhutan or Black Tie in the Himalayas, 1983, The Custom of the Country, 1986, Vanilla, 1990. Mem. PEN, The Dramatists' Guild, The Writers' Guild. Avocations: weightlifter, medieval literature, book collecting.*

HITCHCOCK, JOANNA, publisher; b. London; BA, Oxford (Eng.) U., 1960, MA in Modern History, 1965. Asst. publicity dept. Oxford U. Press, London, 1962-66; asst. promotion mgr. Princeton (N.J.) Univ. Press, 1966-68, advt. and exhibits mgr., 1968-69, staff editor, 1970-72, mng. editor, 1972-80, exec. editor, 1980-84, asst. dir., 1985-87, exec. editor for humanities, 1988-92; dir. U. of Tex. Press, Austin, 1992—. Mem. Princeton U. Libr. Coun., 1986-95; adv. com. Tex. Book Festival, 1996-. Mem. Am. Assn. Univ. Presses (bd. dirs. 1984-87, chair equal opportunities com. 1985-86, ann. program planning com. 1986-87, pres. 1997-98, past pres. 1998-99). Home: 1507 Preston Ave Austin TX 78703-1903 Office: Univ of Texas Press PO Box 7819 Austin TX 78713-7819

HITCHCOCK, KAREN RUTH, biology professor, dean, academic administrator; b. Feb. 10, 1943; d. Roy Clinton and Ruth (Wardell) H. BS in Biology, St. Lawrence U., 1964; PhD in Anatomy, U. Rochester, 1969. Postdoctoral fellow in pulmonary cell biology Webb-Waring Inst. Med. Rsch., 1968-70; asst. prof. dept. anatomy Tufts U. Sch. Medicine, Boston, 1970-75, assoc. prof. dept. anatomy, 1975-80, assoc. prof., acting chmn. dept. anatomy, 1978-80, prof., chmn. dept. anatomy and cellular biology, 1980-82, George A. Bates prof. histology, 1982-85, chmn. dept. anatomy and cellular biology, 1982-85; prof. dept. cell biology and anatomy Tex. Tech. U. Health Scis. Ctr.; assoc. dean Tex. Tech. U. Sch. Medicine, Lubbock, 1985-87; vice chancellor rsch., dean grad. coll. U. Ill., Chgo., 1987-91, prof. cell biology, anatomy and biol. scis., 1987-91; v.p. acad. affairs, prof. biol. scis. U. at Albany, SUNY, 1991-95, interim pres., 1995-96, pres., 1996—. Mem. nat. adv. rsch. resources coun. NIH, 1992-96, Nat. Bd. Med. Examiners, 1987-95; bd. dirs. N.Y. Capital Region Ctr. Econ. Growth, 1996—; mem. steering com. Assn. Colls. & Univs. State N.Y., 1995—; mem. N.Y. State Senate Higher Edn. com. adv. com., 1995—; pres., bd. dirs. Capital Region Info. Svc., N.Y., 1995—; bd. dirs. Charter One Bank F.S.B., 1999. Mem. exec. com. Gov.'s Sci. Adv. Com., Ill., 1991; pres. Albany-Colonie C. of C., 1999. Mem. Am. Assn. Anatomists (exec. com. 1981-85, v.p. 1986-88, pres. 1990-91), Nat. Assn. for Biomed. Rsch. (bd. dirs. 1990-92), Nat. Assn. State Univs. and Land-Grant Colls. (chair coun. acad. affairs com. 1994-95), Ill. Soc. Med. Rsch. (pres. 1988-91). Home: 5 Englewood Pl Albany NY 12203-1042 Office: U at Albany Office of Pres Room UAB 430 1400 Washington Ave Albany NY 12222-0100

HITCHCOCK, KEN, professional hockey coach; b. Edmonton, Alta., Can., Dec. 17, 1951; m. Nancy; children: Emily, Alex, Noah. Student, U. Alta., Edmonton, Can. Head coach Kamloops Blazers, 1984-90; asst. coach Phila. Flyers, 1990-93; head coach Kalamazoo Wings, 1993-94; coach All-Star Games IHL, 1993-94, 94-95; head coach Dallas Stars, 1996—2002, Phila. Flyers, 2002—. Named Coach of Yr. Minor Hockey, 1982-83, Alta. Minor Hockey Assn., 1983-84, WHL, 1986-87, 89-90, top coach Canadian Major Jr. Hockey, 1989-90. Office: c/o Phila Flyers First Union Ctr 3601 S Broad St Philadelphia PA 19148

HITCHCOCK, WALTER ANSON, retired educational consultant; b. Shelton, Wash., Dec. 9, 1918; s. Paul H. and Hazel (Boyington) H.; m. Helen Nadine Rainbolt, Mar. 13, 1944; children: Paul H., Walter Anson, Larry W. BABA, Wash. State U., 1940, BEd, 1941, MA in Edn., 1948; postgrad., U. Okla., 1943-44, summer 1946; EdD, Wash. State U., 1966. Tchr. bus. subjects Omak (Wash.) Sr. High Sch., 1941-42; counselor Weatherwax Sr. High Sch., Aberdeen, Wash., 1946-47; prin. Wilbur (Wash.) High Sch., 1947-49; supt. schs. Nespelem, Wash., 1949-50, Wilbur, 1950-55, Moxee, Wash., 1955-59, West Valley schs., Spokane, 1959-66, Kennewick schs., 1966-69; dep. supt. Spokane city schs., 1969-72, supt., 1972-80; assoc. Interpacific Investors Services, 1980-85; pres. Skookum Investments, 2004—. Mem. adv. com. on tchr. edn. Ea. Wash. State U., 1959-63, ednl. imperatives com., 1984-86; adminstrv. adv. com. State Sch. Supt., mem. spl. edn. com., 1976-79; mem. Wash. State Ednl. TV Adv. Com., 1972-74; mem. spl. edn. adv. com. Cen. Wash. State U., 1975-79. Mem. Tri-Cities United Cmty. Svcs., 1967-69, v.p., 1968; active Benton-Franklin Govtl. Conf., 1968-69; bd. dirs. Expo 74, 1972-75, United Way, Spokane County, 1972-79, Inland Empire Red Cross, Inland Empire Coun. Boy Scouts Am., Spokane Area Youth Com., OK Boys Ranch sponsored by Olympia Kiwanis, 1993-94; panel mem. Eastern Wash. Area Agy. on Aging, 1984-85. Served with AUS, 1942-45. Mem. Am. Assn. Sch. Adminstrs. (mem. SASA-AASA rels. com. 1971-74), NEA, Wash. Edn. Assn. (bd. dirs. dept. adminstrn. and supervision 1968-69), Inland Empire Edn. Assn. (pres. 1972-73), N,.W. Regional Sch. Adminstrs. (chmn.), Yakima Valley Sch. Adminstrs. (chmn.), Spokane Area Supts. Assn. (pres.), Lincoln-Adams Bi-County Activities Assn. (pres.), Wash. Assn. Sch. Adminstrs. (pres. 1969-70, mem. exec. com.), Wash. State Sch. Retirees Assn. (del. 1986-99, 2001—, mem. fin. com. 1994—, chmn. 1996-97, 99—, actuarial study com. 1998-2000, facility need com. 1999-2000), Thurston County Sch. Retirees Assn. (bd. dirs. 1986-95, 97, 99-2002, found. com. 1996-2002), Phi Kappa Phi, Alpha Kappa Psi, Phi Delta Kappa, Sigma Phi Epsilon. Presbyterian. (trustee 1957-59, ruling elder). Clubs: Lion, Wilbur Commercial (pres. 1952-54), Kiwanis (trustee 1961-63, 67-69, 72-76). E-mail: whitchcock@juno.com.

HITCHENS, CHRISTOPHER, columnist; b. Portsmouth, Eng., 1949; Degree in Philosophy, Politics, Econs., Oxford (Eng.) U., 1970. Social sci. corr. The Times Higher Edn. Supplement, London, 1974-80; rschr., reporter Weekend World (London TV), 1974-80; fgn. corr. Daily Express, London, 1974-80; writer New Statesman, London, 1974-80; "Am. Notes" columnist Times Lit. Supplement, London, 1982—; Washington columnist The Spectator, 1981-86; contbg. editor The Nation, NYC, columnist. Author: For the Sake of Argument: Essays and Minority Reports, 1993, The Missionary Position: Mother Teresa in Theory and Practice, 1995, Letters to a Young Contrarian, 2001, Why Orwell Matters, 2002, Blood Class and Empire: The Enduring Anglo-American Relationship, 2004, Love, Poverty and War: Journeys and Essays, 2005; other books. Office: The Nation 72 5th Ave Fl 5 New York NY 10011-8046

HITCHENS, ROBERT JOSEPH, minister, college president; b. Milford, Del., Mar. 2, 1942; s. Bradford and Pearl Elizabeth (Scott) H.; m. Charlotte Roberta Shiflett, Feb. 1, 1964. Bible diploma, BRE, Prairie Bible Inst., Three Hills, Alta, Can., 1971; MA in Theology, Immanuel Bapt. Coll., Atlanta, 1979; DMin, Clarksville Sch. Theology, 1982. Ordained to ministry Bapt. Ch., 1971; cert. Evang. Tchr. Tng. Assn. Assoc. pastor Maranatha Bapt. Ch., Elkton, Md., 1971—; acad. dean Md. Bapt. Bible Coll., Elkton, 1973-90, pres., 1990—. Served with U.S. Army, 1959-67. Mem. Archaeol. Inst. Am., Md. Coalition of Bible Insts., Colls. and Seminaries (pres. 1985), Smithsonian Assocs., Citizens for Republic, U.S. Senatorial Club, NRA. Republican. Home: 3228 Old Elk Neck Rd Elkton MD 21921-6840 Office: PO Box 66 Elkton MD 21922-0066 Office Phone: 410-398-6667. E-mail: rjhitchens@juno.com.

HITCHENS, WILLIAM RANDOLPH (RANDY HITCHENS), healthcare executive; b. Logansport, Ind. s. William T. and Alberta J. Hitchens; m. Katherine J. Hitchens, Oct. 8, 1977; children: Cyrena, Chase, Carin. BS in Pharmacy, Purdue U., 1976; MBA, Ind. U., 1983. Pharmacist, mgr. Revco Drug, Ft. Wayne, Ind., 1977—83; assoc. product mgr. Boehringer Mannheim, Indpls., 1983, account mgr., 1984, product mgr., 1984—87, group mktg. mgr., 1987—90, sr. group product mgr., 1990—92, regional bus. mgr., 1992—94, nat. accounts managed care, 1994—97, dir. corp. partnership, 1997—98; corp. accts. dir. Roche, Indpls., 1998, nat. dir. corp. accounts, 1998—2004, dir. sales and mktg., 2004—05, area bus. dir., 2005—. Ofcl. U.S. Swimming, 1996-2004. Mem. Acad. Managed Care Pharmacists (legis. com. 1997-98, strategic mtkg. com. 1999). Presbyterian. Avocations: running, travel. Office: Roche 9115 Hague Rd Indianapolis IN 46256-1045

HITCHINS, KEITH ARNOLD, historian, educator; b. Schenectady, N.Y., Apr. 2, 1931; s. Henry Arnold Hitchins and Lillian Mary Turrian. AB, Union Coll., 1952; AM, Harvard U., 1953, PhD, 1964; D (hon.), U. Cluj, Romania, 1991, U. Sibiu, 1993, U. Alba Iulia, 2001. Instr., asst. prof. History Wake Forest U., Winston-Salem, NC, 1958—65; asst. prof. History Rice U., Houston, 1965—67; assoc. prof., prof. History U. Ill., Urbana-Champaign, 1967—. Cons. Coun. for Internat. Exch. Scholars, 1970—79; cons. Joint com. on Ea. Europe ACLS and SSRC, 1982—89. Author: Rumanian Nat. Movement in Transylvania 1780-1849, 1969, Orthodoxy and Nationality, 1977, Rumania 1866-1947, 1994, The Romanians, 1774-1866, 1996, A Nation Discovered, 1999, A Nation Affirmed, 1999, The Identity of Romania, 2003; editor: Rumanian Studies, 1970—86, Studies in East European Social History, 1977—81, Jour. of Kurdish Studies, 1995—; cons.: Caucasian Studies-Ency. Iranica. Recipient Nat. Order for Merit, Pres. Romania, 2000. Mem.: Romanian Acad. (hon.). Home: 117 W Delaware Ave Urbana IL 61801 Office: Univ Illinois Dept History 309 Gregory Hall 810 S Wright St Urbana IL 61801 Office Phone: 217-333-9891.

HITES, BECKY E., financial executive; b. Oceanport, NJ, Sept. 24, 1964; d. Robert William and Beatrice Everitt (Beck) Hites. BBA in Econs., U. West Ga., 1986; MBA in Fin., Ga. State U., 1992. Pers. asst. The Robinson-Humphrey Co., Inc., Atlanta, 1986-88, rsch. asst., 1988-89, analyst asst., 1989-92, sr. analyst asst., 1992-95, fin. analyst, 1995-96; mergers and acquisitions Kurt Salmon Assocs., Atlanta, 1996-98; corp. fin. BT Alex Brown, 1998-99; v.p. M. Hecht & Assocs., N.Y.C., 1999-2001; equity rschr. Salomon Smith Barney, Chgo., 2001—02; dir. World Steel Dynamics, 2003—. Guest lectr. MBA program Ga. State U., 1995, U. West Ga., 1998-2000, 05 Patron Ga. Shakespeare Festival, 1986—2000, Shakespeare in the Park, 2001—; vol. Com. to Elect Paul Coverdell, 1992; vol. Rep. Nat. Conv., 2004, Freedom Flyer Ministries, 2002—03. Mem. CFA Inst. (program com. ann. conf. 1996), Inst. Chartered Fin. Analysts (Cert. of Achievement 1993-95), Assn. of Women in Metal Industries (program chair Atlanta chpt. 1995-96, treas. 1997-98, co-chair conf. 1998), NY Soc. Security Analysts, Wildlife Conservation Soc., Met. Mus. Art, NY Botanical Garden, Am. Mus. Natural History, Beta Gamma Sigma, Omicron Delta Kappa Baptist.

HITES, RONALD ATLEE, ecologist, educator, chemist; b. Jackson, Mich., Sept. 19, 1942; s. Wilbert T. and Evelyn J.H.; m. Bonnie Rae Carlson, Dec. 26, 1964; children: Veronica, Karin, David. BA in Chemistry, Oakland U., 1964; PhD in Analytical Chemistry, MIT, 1968. NAS fellow Agrl. Rsch., Peoria, Ill., 1968-69; mem. rsch. staff, dept. chemistry MIT, Cambridge, 1969-72, asst. prof. chem. engring., 1972-76, assoc. prof., 1976-79; prof. Ind. U., Bloomington, 1979-89, Disting. prof. pub. and environ. affairs and chemistry, 1989—, dir. Environ. Sci. Rsch. Ctr., 2001—. Cons. EPA, 1974—. Assoc. editor Environ. Sci. Tech., 1990—; mem. editorial bd. Chemosphere, 1979-99; contbr. articles to prof. jours. Grantee NSF, 1974—, EPA, 1974—, Dept. Energy, 1977-95. Fellow AAAS; mem. Am. Chem. Soc. (award in environ. sci. 1991), Am. Soc. for Mass Spectrometry (pres. 1988-90, mem. editl. bd. 1990-96), Soc. Environ. Toxicol. Chemistry (bd. dirs. 1997-2000, Founders award 1993), Sigma Xi. Office: Ind U Sch Pub and Environ Affairs 410H Bloomington IN 47405 Office Phone: 812-855-0193. Business E-Mail: hitesr@indiana.edu.

HITLIN, DAVID GEORGE, physicist, researcher; b. Bklyn., Apr. 15, 1942; s. Maxwell and Martha (Lipetz) H.; m. Joan R. Abramowitz, 1966 (div. 1981); m. Abigail R. Gumbiner, 1982 (div. 1998); m. Martha Mann Slagerman, 2000. BA, Columbia U., 1963, MA, 1965, PhD, 1968. Instr. Columbia U., NYC, 1967-69; rsch. assoc. Stanford (Calif.) Linear Accelerator Ctr., 1969-72, asst. prof., 1975-79, mem. program com., 1980-82; asst. prof. Stanford U., 1972-75; assoc. prof. physics Calif. Inst. Tech., Pasadena, 1979-85, prof., 1985—. Mem. adv. panel U.S. Dept. Energy Univ. Programs, 1983; mem. program com. Fermi Nat. Accelerator Lab., Batavia, Ill., 1983—87, Newman Lab., Cornell U., Ithaca, NY, 1986—88; mem. rev. com. U. Chgo., Argonne Nat. Lab., 1985—87; chmn. Stanford Linear Accelerator Ctr. Users Orgn., 1990—93; mem. program com. Brookhaven Nat. Lab., Upton, NY, 1992—95; spokesman BABAR Collaboration, 1994—2000; mem. high energy physics adv. panel DOE/NSF, 2001—04; mem. Univs. Rsch. Assn. Fermilab Bd. Overseers, 2003—. Contbr. numerous articles to profl. jours. Fellow Am. Phys. Soc. Achievements include research in elementary particle physics. Office: Calif Inst Tech Dept Physics 356-48 Lauritsen Pasadena CA 91125-0001 Office Phone: 626-395-6694. Business E-Mail: hitlin@hep.caltech.edu.

HITT, DAVID HAMILTON, SR., retired health facility administrator; b. Tuscaloosa, Ala., May 14, 1925; m. Lola McKinney, Mar. 12, 1999 (dec.); m. Frances Ford, Aug. 12, 1949 (dec.); children: David Hamilton, Kathryn Ann; m. Mary Chesser, July 10, 2004. BS, MS in Commerce and Bus. Adminstrn, U. Ala.; MHA, U. Minn., 1952. Hosp. adminstr. U. Ala. Hosp., 1947-50; various positions, including chief exec. officer Baylor U. Med. Center, 1952-79; sr. v.p. James A. Hamilton Assocs. (hosp. consultants), Dallas, 1979-84; pres., chief exec. officer Meth. Hosps. of Dallas, 1984-96, also bd. dirs., pres. emeritus; chmn. bd. dirs. Am. Rubber Tech. Inc., Jacksonville, Fla. Dir. emeritus Bapt. Med. Ctr., Jacksonville, Fla., Dallas Meth. Hosps. Found.; pres. Dallas Hosp. Coun., 1959; mem. adminstrv. bd. Coun. Tchg. Hosps. of Assn. Am. Med. Colls., 1972-79; assoc. clin. prof. Washington U., St. Louis, 1961-96; adj. assoc. prof. Trinity U., San Antonio, 1964-96. Contbr. numerous articles to profl. jours. Mem. exec. bd. council Boy Scouts Am.; v.p. Community Council Greater Dallas. Recipient Earl M. Collier award Distinguished Hosp. Adminstrn. Tex., 1973, Dean Conley award, Silver Beaver award Boy Scouts. Fellow Am. Coll. Healthcare Execs. (Gold medal award for excellence in healthcare mgmt. 1990, past regent, editl. bd. Frontiers Health Svcs. Mgmt. 1991-93); mem. Am. Hosp. Assn. (life, Citation for Meritorious Svc. 1987, Disting. Svc. award 1992, trustee, past chmn. coun. financing), Tex. Hosp. Assn. (trustee, treas., v.p., pres., chmn. ho. of dels. 1967), Am. Protestant Hosp. Assn. (past trustee), Alumni Assn. U. Minn. Program Hosp. Adminstrn. (past pres.), Marine Corps Assn., Exch. Club East Dallas (pres. 1957), Rotary (Dallas) (bd. dirs., dist. Ethics Bus. award 1993). Home: 6255 W Northwest Hwy # 209 Dallas TX 75255 Personal E-mail: twintree75@yahoo.com.

HITT, LEO RICHARD, retired mathematician, educator; b. Washington, June 19, 1950; s. Joel Reuben Hitt and Evelyn Quinn Eddleman; m. Linda Joan Turpin; children: Derek Jordan, Teagan Renee. BS, Fla. State U., 1972, MS, 1975, PhD, 1977. Asst. prof. of math. U. South Ala., Mobile, 1977—81, assoc. prof. of math., 1981—92, prof. of math., 1992—2003, prof. emeritus of math., 2005—. Contbr. articles to profl. jours. Recipient Faculty Svc. and Devel. awards, U. South Ala., 1985, 1995; Rsch. Trainee fellowship, NSF, 1972-1975, Equipment grant, Sun Microsystems, Inc., 1990, Instrumentation and Lab. Improvement grant, NSF, 1990-1993, Grad. Fellowship Program in Math. grant, US Dept. of Edn., 1994-1997, Patricia Roberts Harris fellowship, 1994-1996. Mem.: Math. Assn. of Am., Am. Math. Soc. Avocations: racquetball, flute playing. Home: 800 Founders Pointe Blvd Franklin TN 37064

HITTLE, RICHARD HOWARD, gas industry executive, oil industry executive, consultant; b. Columbus, Nebr., Apr. 30, 1923; s. Arthur Howard and Frieda Margaret (Poppe) H.; m. Catherine Louise Dethlefsen, May 11, 1951; children: Ann-Louise, Thomas Woodford, Bradley Arthur. Student, Cambridge (Eng.) U., 1945; BS, U. Denver, 1950, LLB, 1951; MBA, Harvard U., 1955. With Conoco Inc., 1955-87, mgr. internat. acquisitions, 1964-75; pres. Continental Overseas Oil Co., N.Y.C. also Stamford, Conn., 1969-75; gen. mgr., v.p. internat. govt. affairs Conoco, Inc., Stamford, 1975-83, Wilmington, Del., 1983-87. Bd. govs. Dorset Field Club; bd. advisors Merck Forest and Farmland Ctr., Rupert, Vt. Served with AUS, 1943-46, USAF, 1951-53. Mem. Dorset Nursing Assn. (bd. trustees), Harvard Club (N.Y.C.), Stanwich Club, Dorset Field Club (Vt.), Met. Club (Washington), Dorset Field Club (bd. dirs.), Merck Forest and Farmland Ctr. (bd. advisors). Clubs: Harvard (N.Y.C.); Stanwich (Greenwich, Conn.); Dorset Field. (Vt.); Metropolitan (Washington). Republican. Congregational. Home and Office: PO Box 325 Dorset VT 05251-0325 Personal E-mail: rhkh@adelphia.net.

HITTNER, DAVID, federal judge; b. Schenectady, N.Y., July 10, 1939; s. George and Sophie (Moskowitz) H.; children: Miriam, Susan, George. BS, NYU, 1961, JD, 1964. Bar: N.Y. 1964, Tex. 1967. Pvt. practice, Houston, 1967-78; judge Tex. 133d Dist. Ct., Houston, 1978-86, U.S. Dist. Ct. (so. dist.) Tex., Houston, 1986—2004, sr. judge, 2004—. Author 2 books; contbr. articles to profl. jours. Mem. Nat. coun. Boy Scouts Am. Capt. inf., paratrooper U.S. Army, 1965-66. Recipient Silver Beaver award Boy Scouts Am., 1974, Silver Antelope award Boy Scouts Am., 1988, Samuel E. Gates award Am. Coll. Trial Lawyers. Mem. ABA (Merit award), State Bar Tex. (Outstanding Lawyer in Tex. award), Houston Bar Assn. (Pres.'s and Dirs.' award), Am. Law Inst., Masons (33d degree), Order of Coif (hon.). Office: US Courthouse 515 Rusk St Ste 8509 Houston TX 77002-2603 Office Phone: 713-250-5711.

HITZ, FREDERICK PORTER, public and international affairs educator; b. Washington, Oct. 14, 1939; s. Frederick Porter and Elizabeth (Hume) H.; m. Mary Buford Bocock, Sept. 7, 1963; 1 child, Eliza. AB, Princeton U., 1961; JD, Harvard U., 1964. Bar: Mass. 1965, Va. 1966, D.C. 1976, U.S. Supreme Ct. 1988. Asst. lectr., law dept. U. IFE, Ibadan, Nigeria, 1964-65; fgn. svc. officer U.S. Dept. State, Abidjan, Ivory Coast, 1967-73, congl. rels. officer Washington, 1974-75; dep. asst. sec. legis. affairs U.S. Dept. Def., Washington, 1975-77; mem. energy policy and planning staff Exec. Office of Pres., Washington, 1977; dir. congl. affairs U.S. Dept. Energy, Washington, 1977-78; legis. counsel CIA, Washington, 1978-81; ptnr. Schwabe, Williamson & Wyatt, Washington, 1982-90; inspector gen. CIA, Washington, 1990-98; lectr. in pub. and internat. affairs Woodrow Wilson Sch., Princeton U., 1998—, Weinberg prof. of pub. policy, 1999—; sr. fellow Butler Coll., 2000—. Mem. Coun. Fgn. Rels., 2003—; lectr. U. Va. Sch. Law, 2004—. Author: The Great Game: The Myth and Reality of Espionage, 2004. Trustee Potomac Sch., McLean, Va., 1989-95, chmn. bd. trustees, 1992-94; vestry St. Paul's Ch., Alexandria. Mem. ABA, Wash. Nat. Cathedral, Protestant Episcopal Cathedral Found., Deer Isle Yacht Club (Maine), Met. Club (Washington, bd. govs. 1994-99, sec. 1995-96, pres. 1998-99), Ivy Club (Princeton, N.J., grad. bd. 2001-). Democrat. Episcopalian. Avocations: sailing, skiing, squash. Office: Princeton U Woodrow Wilson Sch Bendheim Hall Princeton NJ 08540 Personal E-mail: fphitz@aol.com.

HIXON, ANDREA KAYE, health science association administrator; b. Clifton Forge, Va., Jan. 15, 1955; d. Leon Malcolm and Mary Ruth (Bowyer) Whitmer; m. Charles L. Hixon Jr., Sept. 11, 1976. ADN, Frederick (Md.) Community Coll, 1974; BSN, George Mason U., Fairfax, Va., 1981; MS, U. Md., Balt., 1986; PhD, Kennedy We. U., Calif., 2005. Cert. profl. for healthcare quality, 1993. With VA Med. Ctr., Martinsburg, W.Va., 1974—82, nursing home adminstr., 1982—86; quality assurance coord. nursing James A. Haley VA Hosp., Tampa, Fla., 1987-93; coord. med. ctr. CQI Program, Fla., 1993—2002. Examiner Malcolm Baldrige Nat. Quality Program; appraiser ANA Magnet Nursing Svcs. Program, ANA Magnet Recognition Program. Mem. Nat. Assn. for Healthcare Quality. Home: 2254 Woods and Water Ct Sebring FL 33872

HIXON, EMILY EARL, artist, educator; b. Auburn, Ala., July 30, 1919; d. Charles Robert and Hassie Earl (Terrell) Hixon; m. Paul David Sturkie, June 19, 1940 (div. Oct. 1962); children: David Paul Sturkie, Margaret Anne (Sturkie) Mitchell; m. Frank Beasley Gunter, July 4, 1974 (dec. July 1979); m. George Arthur Taplin, Aug. 15, 2001. BA, Auburn U., 1940, MA, Rutgers U., 1966. Illustrator Ala. Ext. Svc., Auburn, 1942-44; art dir. Rutgers Prep., Somerset, NJ, 1961-74; founding, exhibiting mem. Amos Eno Gallery, NYC, 1974—. One-woman shows include, Edinburgh, Scotland, Princeton, NYC, New Brunswick, NJ, exhibited in group shows, Coburg, Germany, Windsor, Can., Phila., exhibitions include exhibitions, Boston, exhibited in group shows, Calif., Chgo., East Hampton, Sag Harbor, Montclair Coll., NJ, Montclair Mus., NJ State Mus., Trenton, NJ, Represented in permanent collections Bristol-Meyers Squibb, Johnson & Johnson, Rutgers U., Monmouth Coll., Himalayan Inst. Mem. HS Task Force, Franklin Twp., NJ, 1968, mem. human rels. commn., 1968—72; bd. dirs. Hamilton Pk. Youth Devel., Franklin Twp., 1970—74, Intercounty Cmty. Devel. Corp., Franklin Twp.,

1975—82. Recipient 1st prize in oils, Monmouth Coll., 1964, Printmaker's prize, NJ Painters and Sculptor's Soc., 1965, Purchase prize, Monmouth Coll., 1973. Mem.: Amos Eno Gallery, Parrish Art Mus., Guild Hall, Artists Alliance East Hampton. Democrat. Avocations: playing piano, cats.

HIXON, KAREN J., art and environmental patron; d. J. Lee Johnson III and Ruth Carter Stevenson; m. George C. (Tim) Hixon. Supporter of numerous environ. organizations; bd. trustees Amon Carter Mus., Ft. Worth. Named a Texas Legend of Conservation, Nat. Fish and Wildlife Found., 2004. Office: Amon Carter Mus 3501 Camp Bowie Blvd Fort Worth TX 76107-2695*

HIXON, ROBIN RAY, food service executive, writer; b. Vancouver, Wash., May 4, 1954; s. Charles Donovan and Leona Margaret (Teske) Hixson. Exec. chef, Am. Culinary Fedn., 1972-77; BA in Bus., Purdue U., 1992. Cert. Am. Restaurant Assn., 1992. Apprentice Redlion Inns, Vancouver, 1972-77, exec. chef, 1977-80, Hilton Hotel, Baton Rouge, 1981; chief steward Delta Queen Steamboat Co., New Orleans, 1981-86, gen. mgr., 1986-88; exec. chef Icicle Seafoods Inc., Seattle, 1989-92, Sea Spirit Cruise Lines, Inc., 1992-93, Petersburg Fisheries, Inc., Alaska, 1993-96; dir. ops. The Calzone-Co. Inc., Duncan & Ptnrs., Pete's Pizza Inc., Spokane, Wash., 1996-97; writer, layout coord. Dream Works, Seattle, 1997—. Cons. RSVP Travel Prodns., Inc., Mlps., 1992—, Arctic Storm, Inc., Seattle, 1998—. Author: American Regional Cuisines, 1987; contbr. articles to profl. jours. Mem. Nat. Trust for Hist. Preservation, 1982-92, Wash. Hist. Preservation, 1990-92, Oreg. Pub. Broadcating, 1990-92, N.Y. Met. Opera, 1973-80; performer Peruvian Singers, 1972-74, A Chorus-Line, 1975-76, Spokane's Mens Chorus, 1996-97. Mem. Am. Culinary Fedn. (writer 1985-91), Chefs De Cuisine Soc. Oreg. (sgt. at arms 1974-80), N.Y.C. Acad. Theatre and Dance, Am. Film Inst. Democrat. Home: 1701 Broadway St # 262 Vancouver WA 98663-3436

HIXSON, ELMER L., retired engineering educator; Prof. emeritus dept. elec. engring. U. Tex., Austin. Recipient Fellow Mems. award Am. Soc. Engring. Educators, 1992. Fellow Acoustical Soc. Am.; mem. IEEE (life), Inst. for Noise Control Engring. (founding mem.). Office: U Tex Dept Elec & Computer Engring Austin TX 78712 E-mail: ehixson@mail.utexas.edu.

HIXSON, HARRY F., JR., health products executive; BSChemE, Purdue U.; MBA, U. Chgo.; PhD in Phys. Biochemistry, Purdue U. Pres., COO Amgen, Inc., 1985—91; pres., CEO GeneSys Therapeutics, Inc., 1991—92; CEO, chmn. bd., pres. Elitra Pharms., Inc., San Diego, 1998—. Dir. Signal Pharms., Inc. Office: Elitra Pharmaceuticals Inc 10410 Science Center Dr San Diego CA 92121-1119

HIXSON, KATHRYN, art critic; Studio graduate, Sch. of the Art Inst. Chgo. Curator, contemporary art; tchr., contemporary art and conceptual art theory, dept. art criticism, history, and theory Sch. of the Art Inst. Chgo. Writer, art criticism, Chgo., 1985—, New Art Examiner, Arts Magazine, NY, Flash Art, Milan, Italy, writer (of catalogue essays for galleries and mus.), former editor New Art Examiner. Mem.: Chgo. Art Critics Assn. Address: 900 Grove St Evanston IL 60201 E-mail: kathrynhixson@earthlink.net.*

HIXSON, WENDELL MARK, lawyer; b. Oklahoma City, Dec. 6, 1966; s. Wendell Dee and Mary Theresa (Landgraf) H.; m. Shaa Marie Green, June 22, 1996. BA, Conception Sem. Coll., 1989; JD, U. Okla., 1992. Bar: Okla. 1992, U.S. Dist. Ct. (we. dist.) Okla. 1992, U.S. Dist. Ct. (ea. and no. dists.) 1993, U.S. Ct. Appeals (10th cir.) 1993, U.S. Supreme Ct. 1995. Assoc. Stan Chatman, P.C., Yukon, Okla., 1992-94, Bill James, Yukon and Oklahoma City, 1994-96; pvt. practice Yukon, 1996—. Spl. mcpl. judge, Oklahoma City, 1997—2002; juvenile defender, City of Yukon, 1994—; indigent defender Okla. Indigent Def. Sys., Norman, 1994—. Mem. troop com. Boy Scouts Am., Oklahoma, 1992-97. Fellow: Okla. Bar Found. (benefactor); mem.: Canadian County Bar Assn. (pres. 1997—98, legal ethics com.), Okla. Bar Assn. (chmn. 2003, litig. sect., sec. 1998—99, 2001, treas. 2000—01, family law sect., mem., vice chmn. criminal law com. 2002, rules of profl. conduct com., del. ho. of dels. 1996, 1997, 1998, alternate del. 1999—2002, strategic planning com., legal ethics com. 2003, Outstanding Young Lawyer 1998), Cath. Lawyers Guild of Archdiocese of Oklahoma city, Okla. Criminal Def. Lawyers Assn., U.S. Supreme Ct. Hist. Soc. Republican. Roman Catholic. Office: 800 W Main Yukon OK 73099-1040 E-mail: wmhixson@ykn66law.com.

HJERPE, EDWARD ALFRED, III, finance and banking executive; b. Worcester, Mass., Jan. 25, 1959; s. Edward Alfred Jr. and Nancy Ann (O'Connor) H.; m. Macrina Goody, Aug. 17, 1985; children: Christine G., Edward A. IV, Catherine Ann. BA in Econs. and Bus., St. Anselm Coll., 1981; MA in Econs., U. Notre Dame, 1984, PhD in Econs., 1985. Industry economist Commodity Futures Trading Commn., Washington, 1985-86; fin. economist Fed. Home Loan Bank Bd., Washington, 1986-88; v.p., chief economist Fed. Home Loan Bank, Boston, 1988-89, sr. v.p., 1989-92, exec. v.p., CFO, 1992-97; sr. v.p., treas., CFO First Fed. Am. Bancorp, Inc., Fall River, Mass., 1997—98, exec. v.p., COO, CFO Swansea, Mass., 1998—. Bd. dirs. Dentaquest Ventures, 2003—. Contbr. articles to profl. jours. Bd. trustees St. Anselm Coll., 1992—, chmn. fin. com., mem. exec. com.; chmn. fin. com. Medway Town, 1995-98; bd. trustees Roger Williams Med. Ctr., Providence, 2000—, chmn., 2004—; bd. dirs. United Way Fall River, Mass, 2001—. Recipient A. Schmitt Dissertation fellowship. Mem. Am. Econ. Assn., Omicron Delta Epsilon, Delta Epsilon Sigma, Pi Gamma Mu. Roman Catholic. Home: One Great Rd Barrington RI 02806-1579 Office: First Fed Savs Bank Am One First Park Swansea MA 02777

HJORT, HOWARD WARREN, economist, consultant; b. Plentywood, Mont., Dec. 20, 1931; BS, Mont. State U., 1958, MS, 1959; postgrad., N.C. State U. Staff economist Office of Sec. Agr., Washington, 1963-65, spl. asst. to under sec., 1965; dir. staff for program planning and analysis Office of Sec., 1965-69; planning and mgmt. adviser with Ford Found., India, 1969-72; dir. Office of Econs., Policy Analysis and Budget, 1977-81; co-founder Schnittker Assocs. (agrl. cons.), Washington, 1972-77; ptnr. EPI (McLean), Va., 1981-84; dir. policy analysis div. FAO, Rome, 1984-90, dir. liaison office for N.Am. Washington, 1990-91, dep. dir. gen. Rome, 1992-97; cons., 1998—. Office: 1910 Franklin Ave Mc Lean VA 22101-5307 Office Phone: 703-536-1810. Personal E-mail: howardhjort@aol.com.

HJORTSBERG, WILLIAM REINHOLD, writer; b. N.Y.C., Feb. 23, 1941; s. Helge Reinhold and Anna Ida (Welti) H.; m. Marian Souidee Renken, June 2, 1962 (div. 1982); children: Lorca Isabel, Max William.; m. Sharon Leroy, July 21, 1982 (div. 1985). BA, Dartmouth Coll., 1962; postgrad., Yale U., 1962-63, Stanford U., 1967-68. Ind. author, screenwriter, 1969—. Adj. prof. media and theatre arts Mont. State U., 1991—. Author: Alp, 1969, Gray Matters, 1971, Symbiography, 1973, Toro! Toro! Toro!, 1974, Falling Angel, 1978, Tales & Fables, 1985, Nevermore, 1994, Odd Corners, 2004, (films): Thunder and Lightning, 1977, Legend, 1986, Angel Heart, 1987; co-author TV film: Georgia Peaches, 1980; contbg. editor Rocky Mountain Mag., 1979; contbr. fiction to Realist, Playboy, Cornell Rev., Penthouse, Oui, Sports Illustrated; contbr. criticism to N.Y. Times Book Rev. Recipient Playboy Editorial award, 1971, 78; Wallace Stegner fellow, 1967-68; Nat. Endowment Arts grantee, 1976. Mem. Authors Guild, Writers Guild Am. Avocations: fly fishing, skiing, collecting modern first editions, art, antique toys. Home: 2586 Boulder Rd Mc Leod MT 59052 Office: care Harold Matson Co Ste 714 276 Fifth Ave New York NY 10001 Office Phone: 212-679-4490.

HLATKY, MARK ANDREW, cardiologist, medical researcher; b. Windber, Pa., June 4, 1950; s. George Andrew and Rose Annette (Gonnella) H.; m. Donna Marie Alvarado, May 12, 1984; 1 child, Nicholas Michael. BS, MIT, 1972; MD, U. Pa., 1976. Diplomate Am. Bd. Internal Medicine, Am. Bd. Cardiovasc. Disease; lic. physician, Calif. Intern, resident U. Ariz., Tucson, 1976-79; Robert Wood Johnson clin. scholar U. Calif., San Francisco, 1979-81; fellow in cardiology Duke U., Durham, N.C., 1981-83, asst. prof. medicine, 1983-89; assoc. prof. health rsch. and policy, assoc. prof. medicine Stanford (Calif.) U., 1989-96, prof. health rsch. and policy, prof. medicine, 1996—. Attending physician, cardiovasc. medicine svc. Stanford U. Med. Ctr., 1989—; mem. Health Care Tech. Study sect. NIH, Rockville, Md., 1992-96. Contbr. over 175 articles to profl. jours. Sloan scholar, 1972. Fellow Am. Coll. Cardiology; mem. Am. Heart Assn. (fellow coun. on clin. cardiology), Phi Beta Kappa. Achievements include research in outcomes after coronary surgery, coronary angioplasty, acute myocardial infarction, and cardiac arrhythmias. Home: 168 Rinconada Ave Palo Alto CA 94301-3725 Office: Stanford U Sch Medicine HRP Redwood Bldg Rm 150 Stanford CA 94305 Business E-Mail: hlatky@stanford.edu.

HLAVAC, DANA PAUL, lawyer, consultant; b. Bayshore, NY, Jan. 24, 1960; s. Raymond Zetterberg and Violet Hlavac; m. Rosanne M. Swinnich, May 29, 1982 (div. June 1995); children: Matthew, Nicole, Kelsey; m. Patty S. Herrman, Oct. 11, 1998. BA, Syracuse U., 1981; JD, U. Denver, 1988. Bar: Colo. 1988, Ariz. 1996. Pres., CEO Credit Systems Design, Inc., Colorado Springs, Colo., 1989-90; dep. dist. atty. 4th Jud. Dist. Atty. Office, Colorado Springs, 1990-92; owner, pres. Creative Strategies, Ltd., Colorado Springs, 1989—; pvt. practice, Colorado Springs, 1992-99; asst. dist. atty. 3d Jud. Dist., 1999-2001; pub. defender Mohave County, Kingman, Ariz., 2001—. Bd. dir. Cerebral Palsey Assn., Colorado Springs, 1989-95, pres. 1994-95; treas. Citizens to Elect David Stiver, Colorado Springs, 1996; pres. bd. dirs. Spl. Kids-Spl. Families, Inc. Capt. U.S. Army, 1981-85. Mem. Ariz. Bar Assn., Colo. Bar Assn., Ariz. Pub. Defender Assn. (dir., treas, 2001-04, v.p., 2004—), Nat. Assn. Criminal Def. Lawyers, Nat. Legal and Defender Assn., Am. Coun. Chief Defenders, Mohave County Bar Assn (dir., 2001-05, pres., 2005-). Office: Law Offices of Mohave County Pub Defender PO Box 7000 Kingman AZ 86402-7000 Office Phone: 928-753-0734. Business E-Mail: dana.hlavac@co.mohave.az.us.

HLAVACEK, ROY GEORGE, publishing executive; b. Chgo., Sept. 17, 1937; s. George Louis and Lillian Barbara (Vasovic) H.; m. Nancy Elaine Wroblaski, Aug. 3, 1963; children: Carrie Lee Felix, Alexander Michael. BS, U. Ill., 1960; MBA, U. Chgo., 1969. Project engr. R&D Ctr., Swift & Co., Chgo., 1960-65; v.p., editor, pub. Food Processing mag., Foods of Tomorrow mag. Food Publs. div. Putman Pub. Co., Chgo., 1965-92; v.p., group pub. Food Group, Delta Comms. Inc., Chgo., 1992-2001; v.p. comms. Inst. Food Technologists, 2001—. Adv. com. dept. food sci. U. Ill., Urbana-Champaign, 1988-93. Patentee in field. Commr. Oak Park (Ill.) Landmarks Commn., 1972-79, chmn., 1976-79; treas. Oak Park Bicentennial Commn., 1973-76, Ernest Hemingway Found. of Oak Park, 1983-2000. Mem. ASME, Food Processing Machinery and Supplies Assn. (dir. 1987-91), Inst. Food Technologists (councilor 1975-81, chmn. Chgo. sect.), Pi Tau Sigma, Sigma Tau. Home: 904 Forest Ave Oak Park IL 60302-1310 Office: Inst Food Technologists 525 W Van Buren Chicago IL 60607 Business E-Mail: rghlavacek@ift.org.

HLAVAY, JAY ALAN, financial analyst; b. Pitts., Sept. 30, 1956; s. Joseph and Margaret Marie (Danjou) H.; m. Cayce Avril Martin, Sept. 26, 1992; children: Joseph Martin, Christopher Jay. Student, Rutgers U., 1979; BS in Geology magna cum laude, U. Pitts., 1983, MBA, 1989. Geologist RSC Energy Corp., New Philadelphia, Ohio, 1983-85; dist. geologist Carless Resources Inc., New Philadelphia, 1985-89; gen. mgr. What on Earth, Pitts., 1989-90; prin. OPUS Energy Cons. Svcs., Coraopolis, Pa., 1990-92; exploration fin. analyst Union Pacific Resources, Ft. Worth, 1991-92, Austin chalk analyst, 1992-93, contr. Gulf of Mexico/Other Profit Ctr., 1993-95, contr. Gulf Coast Profit Ctr., 1996, project mgr. fin. ops., 1996-97, mgr. compensation, people dept., 1997-98, fin. advisor, 1998—2000; mgr. strategic and bus. analysis Food Lion, LLC, Salisbury, NC, 2000—03; dir. fin. and acctg. Kash n Karry/Sweetbay Supermarkets, Tampa, Fla., 2003—. Navy ROTC scholar, 1974; recipient Appreciation award Tuscarawas Valley Desk and Derrick Club, 1985, 86, 87; recipient West Allegheny Sch. Dist. Disting. Alumni award, 1988. Mem. Am. Assn. Petroleum Geologists (co-chmn. fin. com. S.W. sect. ann. conv. 1993), Sigma Gamma Epsilon. Office: Sweetbay/Kash n' Karry Supermarkets 3801 Sugar Palm Dr Tampa FL 33619 Office Phone: 813-620-1139 ext. 444. Business E-Mail: jhlavay@kashnkarry.com.

HLEDE, KORIE, professional basketball player; b. Mar. 29, 1975; BS in Psychology and Comm., Duquesne U. Guard Montig, Croatia; guard Detroit Shock WNBA, 1998—99, guard Utah Starzz, 1999—. Named 1995 Atlantic 10 Rookie of the Yr., 1997-98 Atlantic 10 Player of the Yr. Achievements include becoming first athlete in Duquesne history to have jersey number retired; ranks second in Atlantic 10 history in career points; Duquesne's all-time leading scorer, male or female, with 2,631 points. Avocations: tennis, travel, reading.

HNATYSZYN, HARRY JAMES, health products executive, research scientist; b. Saskatoon, Can., Oct. 10, 1967; arrived in U.S., 1992; s. Harry Elia and Joan Iris Hnatyszyn; m. Terri Lynn Lewis Hnatyszyn, Aug. 14, 1993. BS in Anatomy with honors, U. Saskatoon, 1989; PhD in Pathology, UCLA, 1995; postgrad., U. B.C., 1989—91. Fellow U. Calif., San Diego, 1995—96; rschr. U. Miami, 1996—98, asst. prof., 1998—2002; prin. staff scientist, mgr. sci. and clin. affairs Bayer Healthcare, Berkeley, Calif., 2002—04, prin. staff. scientist diagnostics, 2004—, head mktg. devel., 2004—, head Bayer Inst. Clin. Investigation, 2004—. Adj. asst. prof. U. Miami, 2002—; presenter in field, 1990—. Co-author: McGraw-Hill Yearbook of Science and Technology, 1996; contbr. articles to numerous profl. jours.; ad hoc reviewer: Jour. Coin. Microbiology. Fundraising, pub. awareness activities Am. Cancer Soc., Juvenile Diabetes Found., Am. Humane Soc., World Wildlife Found. Recipient Pilot Project award, Sylvester Comprehensive Cancer Ctr., 1999—2000, U. Miami, 2001—02; grantee, Dept. of Def., 1997—2000, Leukemia and Lymphoma Soc. Am., 1998—2001, U. Miami, 1999, AmFAR, 1999—2000, NIH, 2000—02, 2000—02, Am. Cancer Soc., 2001—02, GTX, Inc., 2002—03, NCI CTEP, 2002—. Master: Leukemia and Lymphoma Soc. (bd. dirs. Fla. divsn. 2000—02); mem.: AAAS, U.S. Lacrosse, Alcatraz Criminal Lacrosse Club, Miami Makos Lacrosse Club (Rookie of Yr. 2002, Most Improved Player of Yr. 2002), Am. Canyon Motorcycle Club, UCLA Alumni Assn. Achievements include research in disease-related genetic markers; gene interference technologies including antisense, ribozymes, RNase P EGS and RNAi; innate immunity; rapid and sensitive detection and diagnostic systems for infectious diseases and human malignancies; counter-bioterrorism programs; immunotherapy and vaccine strategies; pathogenesis and epidemiology of infectious diseases; primate models for infectious disease research; targeted drug and gene delivery systems. Avocations: lacrosse, hockey, motorcycling. Office: Bayer Healthcare Diagnostics Divsn 725 Potters St 94702 Office Phone: 510-705-5845. Office Fax: 510-705-5718. Business E-Mail: james.hnatyszyn.b@bayer.com.

HO, BETTY JUENYÜYÜLIN, physiological educator, researcher; b. Nanking, China, Nov. 20, 1930; came to U.S., 1947; d. William Tien-Hu and Gwei-Hsin (Wang) Ho; m. Lajos Rudolf Elkan, Feb. 27, 1958 (div. Aug. 1967); children: Amanda, Anita, Julien (dec.), Raoul. Student, Western Coll., Oxford, Ohio, 1947-48; BS, Columbia U., 1952; postgrad., Lausanne U., 1955—56, piano studies with Maurice Perrin, Lausanne, Switzerland, 1956-58, CCNY, 1966-67, 72-74. Lab. technician Columbia U., N.Y.C., 1953-54; ct. report typist Palais de Justice, Lausanne, Switzerland, 1956-57; pianist, accompanist Ecole de Ballet Mara Dousse, Lausanne, Switzerland, 1958-60; English tchr. Montcalme Inst., Lausanne, Switzerland, 1960-61; piano tchr. Le Manoir Inst., Lausanne, Switzerland, 1960-61, N.Y.C., 1964-65. Rsch. dir. Juvenescent Rsch. Corp., N.Y.C., 1963—. Author: The Living Function of Sleep, Life & Aging, 1967, The Origin of Variation of Races of Mankind & The Cause of Evolution, 1969, A Scientific Guide to Peaceful Living, 1972, A Chinese and Western Guide to Better Health and Longer Life, 1974, How to Stay Healthy A Lifetime Without Medicines, 1979, A Chinese & Western Daily Practical Health Guide, 1982, Immediate Hints to Health Problems, 1991, 101 Ways to Live 150 Years Young and Healthy, 1993, A Unique Health Guide for Young People, 1994, How To Live a Long Life, 2004 Named Citizen of Yr. Principality of Hutt River Province, Queensland, Australia, 1994, awarded royal patronage status for life, 1995, XXth Century Achievement award; recipient Internat. Order of Merit, 1999. Mem.: The Order Internat. Fellowship (life). Achievements include patents for infant feeding method. Home and Office: Juvenescent Research Corp 807 Riverside Dr Apt 1F New York NY 10032-7352 Office Phone: 212-795-2292.

HO, CHUNGWU, mathematician, educator; arrived in U.S., 1960; s. Chenghsien Wu; m. Yinhsin Ho, June 20, 1964; children: Minnie, Ronald. MS, U. Wash., 1965; PhD, MIT, 1970. Asst. prof. So. Ill. Univ., Edwardsville, Ill., 1970—74, assoc. prof., 1974—78, prof., 1978—2000, chmn. dept. math., 1988—94, prof. emeritus, 2000—; prof. math. Evergreen Valley Coll., San Jose, Calif., 2001—. Hon. prof. Hangzhou Tchr. Coll., China, 1992—, Hefei Ednl. Inst., China, 1985—. Contbr. articles to profl. jours., poems to lit. publs. Grantee, NSF, 1988—90. Mem.: Acad. Am. Poets, Math. Assn. Am., Am. Math. Soc., NY Acad. Scis. Avocations: writing, Chinese opera. Home: 3261 Falls Creek Dr San Jose CA 95135-2352 Office: Evergreen Valley Coll 3095 Yerba Buena Rd San Jose CA 95135 Personal E-mail: hoc@alum.mit.edu.

HO, DAVID D., research physician, virologist; b. Taichung, Taiwan, Nov. 3, 1952; arrived in U.S., 1964; s. Paul and Sonia Ho; m. Susan Kuo Ho; children: Kathryn, Jonathan, Jaclyn. Student, MIT; BS summa cum laude, Calif. Inst. Tech., 1974; MD, Harvard, 1978. Resident internal medicine UCLA Sch. Medicine, 1981, chief resident, 1982; clin. and rsch. fellow Infectious Disease Unit Mass. Gen. Hosp., 1982—85; rsch. fellow medicine Harvard U., 1982—85; physician, rsch. scientist divsn. infectious diseases, dept. medicine Cedars-Sinai Med. Ctr., 1986—90; dir. Ctr. for AIDS Rsch. NYU, 1994—96, prof. medicine and microbiology, co-dir., 1990—96; dir. Diamond AIDS Rsch. Ctr., N.Y.C., 1990—. Assoc. prof. medicine in residents UCLA, 1986—89, assoc. prof., 1989. Contbr. articles to profl. jours. Named 1996 Man of Yr., Time Mag.; recipient Mayor's award (N.Y.C.) for Excellence in Sci. and Tech., Sci. award, Chinese Am. Med. Soc. Fellow: AAAS (Ernst Jung prize in medicine); mem.: NIH vaccine working group, Com. of 100 (Chinese Am. leadership orgn.), AmFAR (bd. dirs. sci. bd.). Office: Aaron Diamond AIDS Rsch Ctr 455 1st Ave Fl 7 New York NY 10016-9121

HO, DOREEN WOO, bank executive; b. Australia; married; 3 children. BA, Smith Coll.; MA, Columbia U. Corr. Time Mag., Phnom Penh, Democratic Peoples Republic of Korea, 1972—73; various sr. level positions Citibank, 1973—98; pres. nat. home equity Wells Fargo Home Mortgage, Inc., San Francisco, 1998—. Mem. exec. com. Wells Fargo Diversity Coun. Bd. dir. San Francisco (Calif.) Opera. Office: Wells Fargo Home Mortgage Inc 420 Montgomery St San Francisco CA 94163

HO, JEFFREY C., banker; b. Singapore, Dec. 7, 1957; arrived in U.S., 1978; s. Jimmy and Betty Ho; children: Brian, James. BS, Calif. Poly Coll., 1981; MBA, Calif. Poly. Coll., 1985. Credit officer Wedbuth Morgan Securities, L.A., 1983—88; securities specialist Union Bank, 1989—90; acctg. analyst Countrywide, Pasadena, 1990—94; trust adminstr. First Interstate Bank, L.A., 1994—97; team leader Bank N.Y. Trust Co., 1997—. Vol. Materials Regent Facility Task Force, Walnut, Calif., 1994. Mem.: Sierra Club, Calif. Mountaineering Club. Avocations: mountain climbing, travel, bicycling, photography. Office: 700 S Flower St Ste 200 Los Angeles CA 90017

HO, RALPH TINGHAN, radiologist; BS in Biochemistry, Cornell U., 1991; MD, Northwestern U. Intern, OB/GYN then resident, diagnostic radiology Wayne State U., 1995—2000; trauma radiology fellow U. Wash., 2000—01; asst. prof. trauma and body imaging U. Tenn., vascular and interventional radiology fellow, 2002—03; interventional radiologist Mid-South Imaging and Therapeutics, Memphis, 2003—. Mem. Asian Young Professionals Group. Mem.: AMA, Am. Coll. of Radiology, Soc. of Interventional Radiology, Am. Soc. of Emergency Radiology, Am. Roentgen Ray Soc. Office: Mid-South Imaging & Therapeutics 6305 Humphreys Blvd Memphis TN 38120*

HO, REGINALD CHI SHING, medical educator; b. Hong Kong, Mar. 30, 1932; came to U.S., 1940; s. Chow and Elizabeth (Wong) Ho; m. Sharilyn Dang, Nov. 14, 1964; children: Mark, Reginald, Gianna Masca, Timothy. Student, St. Louis U., 1954, MD, 1959. Diplomate Nat. Bd. Med. Examiners, Am. Bd. Internal Medicine. Rotating intern U. Cin. Hosps., 1959-60, resident in internal medicine, 1960-62; fellow in hematology and oncology Barnes Hosp./Washington U., St. Louis, 1962-63; assoc. clin. prof. medicine JAB Sch. Medicine U. Hawaii, Honolulu, 1972-77, clin. prof. medicine, 1977—; attending physician dept. hematology and oncology Straub Clinic and Hosp., Honolulu, 1973—. Prin. investigator Hawaii Cmty. Clin. Oncology Program, Honolulu, 1983-86; adj. prof. clin. sci. Cancer Rsch. Ctr. Hawaii, 1989—, mem. various coms. Contbr. articles to med. jours. Bd. dirs. Cath. Svcs. for Families, 1987-91. Mem. AMA, ACP, Am. Cancer Soc. (divsn. del. 1982-93, del. dir. 1983-92, exec. com. 1989—, chair med. and sci. exec. com. 1991-92, past officer dir. 1994—, v.p. 1991-92, pres. 1992-93, immediate past pres. 1993-94, bd. dirs. Hawaii divsn. 1968—, pres. 1976-77, chmn. bd. dirs. 1977-78, hon. life mem. 1989—, bd. dirs.), Hawaii Med. Assn. (Hawaii cancer commn. 1980-85, chair cancer com. 1981-90), Honolulu County Med. Assn. (del. to Hawaii Med. Assn. 1969-72), Exptl. Med. Care Rev. Orgn. (exec. com., chair ambulatory care edn. audit com. 1972), Alpha Omega Alpha. Roman Catholic. Avocation: tennis. Office: Straub Clinic Hosp 888 S King St Honolulu HI 96813-3083 Office Phone: 808-522-4313.

HO, TEH CHUNG, chemical engineer, researcher; b. Kaohsiung, Taiwan, June 25, 1949; arrived in U.S., 1973; s. Shih Lung and Hsiu Teh Ho; m. Wei Wei Hsu, June 24, 1978. BS, Tunghai U., Taichung, Taiwan, 1971; PhD, U. Del., Newark, 1976. Rsch. scientist Halcon R & D Corp., Little Ferry, NJ, 1976—80; head, hydroprocessing catalysis group Exxon (now ExxonMobil) Rsch. & Engring. Co., Annandale, NJ, 1983—86, head, applied math. group, 1990—95, sr. engring. assoc. Bd. dirs. Jour. Applied Catalysis A: Gen. Mem. editl. bd.: Jour. Applied Catalysis A: Gen.; contbr. articles to profl. jours. Platoon leader, 2d lt. Taiwan Marine Corps, 1971—73. Recipient Catalysis and Reaction Engring. Practice award, AIChE, 2002, R.H. Wilhelm award, 2004, Thomas Alva Edison Patent award, State of NJ, 2002. Mem.: N.Y. Catalysis Soc. (bd. dirs. 1999—2002, pres. 1998—99), Chinese Am. Chem. and Chem. Engring. Soc. (pres. 2004—05). Achievements include patents in field; research in commercialization of new-generation oil refining technologies.

HO, YIK HONG, colon and rectal surgeon; b. Singapore, Apr. 21, 1956; s. Peng Yoke Ho and Mei Yiu (Lucy) Fung; m. Chui Wah Ludmilla Tung, Sept. 13, 1984; 1 child, Elaine Jo-Lan. MBBS with honors, U. Queensland, 1980, MD, 2001. Intern Princess Alexandra Hosp., Brisbane, Australia, 1980-81, resident, 1981-82; med. officer Sai Ying Pun Hosp./Tang Shiu Kin Hosp., Hong Kong, 1982-83; registrar U. Surg. Unit Queen Mary Hosp., Tung Wah Hosp., Hong Kong, 1983-89; sr. registrar Singapore Gen. Hosp., 1989-93, cons., 1993-98, dir. Pelvic Floor Lab., 1996—2002, sr. cons., 1998—2002; vis. staff sr. cons. surg. oncology Nat. Cancer Centre, 1999—2002; clin. sr. lectr. Nat. U. Singapore, 2001—02; prof., head dept. surgery James Cook U. Sch. Medicine, 2002—; coord. North Queensland Ctr. for Cancer Rsch., Australian Inst. Tropical Medicine, 2004—. Rsch. fellow U. Hosp U. Nottingham, England, 1989; part-time clin. lectr. Nat. U. Singapore, 1990—2001; dep. chmn. Electronics Med. Records Workgroup Singapore Gen. Hosp., 1994—2002; head North Queensland Ctr. Cancer Rsch., Australian Inst. Tropical Medicine. Mem. editl. rev. com. Annals of Acad. of Medicine, 1994-2002, mem. editl. com., 2000-2002; mem. editl. com. Singapore Gen. Hosp. Procs., 1995-99, assoc. editor, 1995-98, editor, 1999-2002; mem. editl. bd. Internat. Surgery, 2002—, World Gastroenterology Jour.; contbr. articles to profl. jours. Scholarship Australian Kidney Found., 1977. Fellow Royal Australasian Coll. Surgeons, Royal Coll. Surgeons (Edinburgh), Royal Coll Physicians and Surgeons (Glasgow), Internat. Coll. Surgeons (Singapore sect. com. mem. 1994-96, 98-99, treas. 97-99, sec. 1999, pres. 2000-2002, world additional gov. 1999-2000, additional v.p. 2001—); mem. Singapore Soc. Continence (v.p. 1993-2002), Biomed. Rsch. and Exptl. Therapeutics Soc. Singapore (hon. sec. 1993-95, pres. 1995-97), Internat. Soc. Surgery (nat. rep. 1999-2002), Am. Soc. Colon-Rectal Surgeons (mem. internat. adv. com. 2000). Avocations: exercise, computer, photography, swimming, tai-chi. Office: James Cook U Dept Surgery Sch Medicine Queensland 4811 Australia Office Phone: 617-47961417. Home Fax: 0438080575. Business E-Mail: yik-hong.ho@bigpond.com.

HOAG, DAVID GARRATT, retired aerospace engineer; b. Boston, Oct. 11, 1925; s. Alden Bomer and Helen Lucy (Garratt) H.; m. Grace Edward Griffith, May 10, 1952; children— Rebecca Wilder, Peter Griffith, Jeffrey Taber, Nicholas Alden, Lucy Seymour. BS, MIT, 1946, MS, 1950. Staff engr. instrumentation lab. MIT, Cambridge, 1946-57; tech. dir. Polaris Missile Guidance, 1957-61; tech. dir., program mgr. Apollo Spacecraft Guidance, 1961-72; advanced system dept. head C.S. Draper Lab., Inc., Cambridge, 1972-86; ret., 1990. Recipient Pub. Svc. award NASA, 1969, Spl. award Royal Inst. Navigation, Britain, 1970, Laurels, Aviation Week, 1970. Fellow AIAA (Louis W. Hill Space Transp. award 1972, chmn. New Eng. sect. 1979-80); mem. Nat. Acad. Engring., Inst. Navigation (Thurlow award 1969, pres. 1978-79), Internat. Acad. Astronautics (assoc. editor ACTA Astronautica 1973-79) Home: 116 Winthrop St Medway MA 02053-2310

HOAG, MARGARET JANE, special education educator; b. Rochester, N.Y., Aug. 19, 1947; d. David Asa Hoag and Jane Louise Fox; children from previous marriage: Lori, Michele, Danielle. BS in Psychology, SUNY, Brockport, 1991; M in Reading, Nazareth U., Rochester, 1996. Cert. elem. spl. edn. and reading N.Y. Tchr. spl. edn. Greece Arcadia HS, Rochester, 1993—. Recipient Golden Apple award, Greece Tchr. Assn., 2002. Republican. Avocations: scrapbooks, travel, embroidery. Home: 69 White Oaks Dr Rochester NY 14616 Office: Greece Arcadia HS 120 Island Cottage Rd Rochester NY 14612

HOAG, TAMI, writer; b. 1959; Author: McKnight in Shining Armor, 1988, The Trouble with J.J., 1988, Straight from the Heart, 1989, Mismatch, 1989, Man of Her Dreams, 1989, Rumor Has It, 1989, Magic, 1990, Tempestuous, 1990, The Rainbow Chasers: Heart of Gold, 1990, The Rainbow Chasers: Keeping Company, 1990, The Rainbow Chasers: Reilly's Return, 1990, Heart of Dixie, 1991, Sarah's Sin, 1991, Magic, 1991, The Restless Heart, 1991, The Last White Knight, 1992, Taken by Storm, 1992, Lucky's Lady, 1992, Still Waters, 1992, Cry Wolf, 1993, Dark Paradise, 1994, Night Sins, 1995, Guilty as Sin, 1996, A Thin Dark Line, 1997, Ashes to Ashes, 2000, Dust to Dust, 2002, Lucky's Lady, 2003, Dark Horse, 2004, Kill the Messenger, 2004. Office: Andrea Cirillo Jane Rotrosen Agency 318 East 51st St New York NY 10022

HOAGLAND, DONALD WRIGHT, lawyer; b. NYC, Aug. 16, 1921; s. Webster Comley and Irene (Wright) H.; m. Mary Tiedeman, May 14, 1949; children: Peter M., Mary C., Sara H., Ann W. BA, Yale U., 1942; LLB, Columbia U., 1948. Bar: N.Y. 1948, Colo. 1951. Assoc. firm Winthrop, Stimson, Putnam & Roberts, N.Y.C., 1948-51; ptnr. Davis, Graham & Stubbs, Denver, 1951-63, 66-87, of counsel, 1987—; with AID, 1964-66, asst. adminstr. devel. finance and pvt. enterprise, 1965-66, cons., 1967-75. Lectr. U. Denver Sch. Law, 1971-75; chmn. bd. Bi-Nat. Devel. Corp., 1968-70; dir. Centennial Fund, Inc., 2d Centennial Fund, Inc., Gryphon Fund, Inc., 1959-63; mem. Colo. Supreme Ct. Grievance Com., 1992-98. Mem. Denver Planning Bd., 1955-61, 67-70, chmn., 1959-61; bd. dirs., v.p. Denver Art Mus., 1959-63, 72-76, 79-82; bd. dirs. Colo. Urban League, 1960-63, 66-72, chmn. bd., 1968-72; adv. bd. Vols. Tech. Assistance vice-chmn. bd. Denver chpt. ARC, 1959-61; bd. dirs. Legal Aid Soc. Colo., 1972-84, pres., 1975-79; trustee Phillips Exeter Acad., 1960-67, Colo. Rocky Mountain Sch., 1981-84, Am. U., Washington, 1982-85; chmn. bd. dirs. Legal Aid Found., Colo., 1983-87; bd. dirs. Colo. Bus. Coalition for Health, 1988-89, Colo. Found. for Ednl. Excellence, 1998-2004; exec. dir. Ctr. for Health Ethics and Policy U. Colo., Denver, 1987-91; chmn. Colo. Health Data Commn., 1986-88, Gov. Romer's panel health advisors, 1992-94, Social Sci. Found. Denver U., 1975—; mem. Caring for Colo. Found., 1999-2002, chmn., mem. program com., 2003—; chmn. Colo. Pub. Health Edn. and Rsch. Adv. Com., 2002—; pres. Colo. Found. Pub. Health and Environment, 1995-98, bd. dirs., 1995—; ethics com. Nat. Jewish Med. and Rsch. Ctr., 1993-2005. With USNR, 1943-45. Decorated Air medal with oak leaf cluster. Mem. ABA, Colo. Bar Assn., Denver Bar Assn. Home: 355 Garfield St Denver CO 80206-4509 Office: Davis Graham & Stubbs 1550 17th St Ste 500 Denver CO 80202 Office Phone: 303-892-9400.

HOAGLAND, JIMMIE LEE, newspaper editor; b. Rock Hill, S.C., Jan. 22, 1940; s. Lee Roy and Edith Irene (Sullivan) H.; m. Jane Stanton Hitchcock, July 14, 1995; children: Laura Lee (dec.), Lily Hue, Lee Clayton. AB in Journalism, U. S.C., 1961; student, U. Aix-en-Provence, France, 1961-62, Columbia U., 1968-69. Reporter Evening Herald, Rock Hill, 1960; copy editor N.Y. Times Internat. Edit., Paris, France, 1964-66; reporter Washington Post, 1966-69, Africa corr., 1969-72, Middle East corr., 1972-75, Paris corr., 1975-77, fgn. editor, 1979-81, asst. mng. editor, 1981-86, assoc. editor, chief fgn. corr., 1986—. Author: South Africa: Civilizations in Conflict, 1972. Ford Found. fellow Columbia U., 1968-69; recipient Pulitzer prize internat. report, 1970; Overseas Press Club award internat. reporting, 1977; Pulitzer prize for commentary, 1991; Eugene Meyer Career Achievement award, 1994. Mem. Coun. on Fgn. Rels., Phi Beta Kappa, Pi Kappa Alpha. Office: Washington Post 1150 15th St NW Washington DC 20071-0002 Business E-Mail: jimhoagland@washpost.com.

HOAGLAND, KARL KING, JR., lawyer; b. St. Louis, Aug. 21, 1933; s. Karl King and Mary Edna (Parsons) H.; m. Sylvia Anne Naranick, July 13, 1957; children: Elisabeth Parsons, Sarah Stewart, Karl King III, Alison T. BS in Econs., U. Pa., 1955; LLB, U. Ill., 1958. Bar: Ill. 1958, U.S. Dist. Ct. (so. dist.) Ill. 1958. V.p., gen. counsel, sec. Jefferson Smurfit Corp., St. Louis, 1960-92, Container Corp. Am., St. Louis, 1986-92; of counsel Hoagland, Fitzgerald, Smith & Pranaitis, Alton, Ill., 1987—. Chmn. bd. dirs. Millers' Mut. Ins. Assn. Ill., 1989-92. Asst. editor: U. Ill. Law Forum, 1957-58. Trustee, treas. Monticello Coll. Found., 1965—. 1st lt. USAF, 1958-60. Mem. Ill. Bar Assn., Madison County Bar Assn., Alton-Wood River Bar Assn., Lockhaven Country Club, Mo. Athletic Club, Crystal Lake Club, Orcas Tennis Club, Order of the Coif, Beta Gamma Sigma. Episcopalian. Avocations: tennis, skiing, hunting, fishing, golf. Home (Summer): PO Box 1454 Eastsound WA 98245 Home (Winter): PO Box 130 Alton IL 62002

HOAGLAND, MAHLON, biochemist, educator; b. Boston, Oct. 5, 1921; s. Hudson and Anna (Plummer) H.; m. Olley Virginia Jones, Jan. 10, 1961; children from previous marriage: Judith, Mahlon, Robin. Student, Williams Coll., 1940-41, Harvard U., 1941-43, MD, 1948; Sc.D. (hon.), Worcester Poly. Inst., 1973, U. Mass., 1984. From rsch. fellow to asst. prof. medicine Med. Sch. Harvard U. at Mass. Gen. Hosp., 1948-60; assoc. prof. bacteriology and immunology Med. Sch. Harvard U., 1960-67; prof. biochemistry, chmn. dept. Med. Sch. Dartmouth, 1967-70; pres., sci. dir. Worcester Found. for Biomed. Rsch., Shrewsbury, Mass., 1970-85, pres. emeritus, 1985—. Rsch. assoc. Carlsberg Labs., Copenhagen, 1951-52, Cavendish Labs., Cambridge, Eng., 1957-58; cancer rsch. scholar Am. Cancer Soc., 1953-58; founder, spokesman Del. for Basic Biomed. Rsch., 1978-85. Author: 6 Books; contbr. over 65 articles to profl. jours. Recipient Franklin medal, 1976; 2 book awards Am. Med. Writers Assn., 1982, 96. Fellow Am. Acad. Arts and Scis.; mem. NAS. Achievements include discovery of mechanism of amino acid activation and (with P.C. Zamecnik) transfer ribonucleic acid. Home: PO Box 183 Academy Rd Thetford VT 05074-0183 Office Phone: 802-785-2233.

HOAGLAND, TONY, writer; b. Ft. Bragg, N.C., 1953; Prof. U. Pitts.; prof. grad. writing program U. Houston. Author: (poetry) Sweet Ruin, 1992 (Brittingham prize in poetry, Zacharis award Emerson Coll.), Donkey Gospel, 1998 (James Laughlin award), What Narcissism Means to Me, 2003. Fellow, Provincetown Fine Arts Work Ctr.; grantee, Nat. Endowment for the Arts.

HOAGLIN, THOMAS E., savings and loan association executive; b. Charleston, W.Va., 1949; BA in Econs., Denison U.; MBA, Stanford U. Pres. Huntington Bancshares Inc., Columbus, Ohio, 2001—, chmn., 2001—, CEO, 2001—. Pres., chmn., CEO Huntington Nat. Bank, Columbus; bd. dirs. Denison U., The Columbus (Ohio) Partnership, Columbus (Ohio) Downtown Devel. Corp., Columbus (Ohio) Coll. Art and Design, Ohio Ctr. Sci. and Industry; bd. dir. Capital South Corp., The Gorman-Rupp Co., Mansfield, Ohio; bd. trustees Ohio Health. Bd. dir. Greater Columbus (Ohio) C. of C., Ohio Bus. Roundtable. Mem.: The Fin. Svcs. Roundtable, World Pres. Org. Office: Huntington Bancshares Inc Huntington Ctr 41 South High St Columbus OH 43287*

HOAGLUND, SUSAN ELIZABETH, music educator; b. Worcester, Mass., Apr. 16, 1957; d. Robert Holdsworth and Janesse Audrey Hoaglund. BM, Boston U., 1980; diploma, Goethe Inst., Munich, Germany, 1986; MA, U. Pa., 1995. Violin and viola tchr. Stadtische Musikschule, Dusseldorf, Germany, 1980-84; tchr., head dormitory St. Paul's Sch., Concord, N.H., 1984-94; violin and viola tchr. Settlement Music Sch., Phila., 1994-98; head performing arts dept., music tchr. The Shipley Sch., Bryn Mawr, Pa., 1996—. Adj. prof. music Chestnut Hill Coll., Phila., 1997—; various adminstrv. jobs Boston U., Tanglewood Inst., 1982-92; site dir. Ctr. for Talented Youth, Johns Hopkins U., Balt., summers 1994-69, creative writing tchr., 1995-96. Adminstrv. asst. vol. Bath Festival Phila., 1994-2000; sponsor Save the Children, 1998—; mem. Phila. Reads, 2000—; mem. Save the Bay, 1984—. Mem. Pa. Music Educators Assn., Music Educators Nat. Assn. Episcopalian. Avocations: playing in handbell choir, travel, reading, writing, tutoring children in reading. Office: The Shipley Sch 814 Yarrow St Bryn Mawr PA 19010 Home: 654 Dayton Rd Bryn Mawr PA 19010-3802

HOAK, JONATHAN S., SR., lawyer; b. Eugene, OR, July 1949; BA, U. Colo., 1971; postgrad., Exeter (Eng.); JD, Drake U., 1977. With Heritage Comms., Des Moines, 1971-74; assoc. Sidley & Austin, 1979-85, ptnr., 1985-90; gen. atty. fed. sys. divsn. AT&T, 1990-93; sr. v.p., gen. counsel NCR Corp., Dayton, Ohio, 1993—. Bd. counselors Drake U. Law Sch., U. Dayton Sch. Law Adv. Coun. Mem. ABA, Fed. Cir. Bar Assn., Ohio Bar Assn. Office: NCR Corp 1700 S Patterson Blvd Dayton OH 45479-0002 Home: 116 W Thruston Blvd Dayton OH 45419

HOANG, DUC VAN, pathologist, educator; b. Hanoi, Vietnam, Feb. 17, 1926; came to U.S. 1975, naturalized 1981; s. Duoc Van and Nguyen Thi (Tham) H.; m. Mau-Ngo Thi Vu, 7 children. MD, Hanoi U. Sch. Medicine, Vietnam, 1952; DSc, Open Internat. U., Sri Lanka, 1989. Dean Sch. Medicine Army of the Republic of Vietnam, Saigon, 1959-63; dean Minh-Duc U. Sch. Medicine, Saigon, 1970-71; clin. prof. theoretical pathology U. So. Calif. Sch. Medicine, L.A., 1978—. Adj. prof. Emperor's Coll. Traditional Oriental Medicine, Santa Monica, Calif., 1988-91; initiator of attitudinal immunology. Author: Towards an Integrated Humanization of Medicine, 1957; The Man Who Weights the Soul, 1959; Eastern Medicine, A New Direction?, 1970; also short stories; author introdn. to work of Marie Noël, Vietnamese transl. of La Rose Rouge; translator: Pestis, introduction to the work of Albert Camus, Vietnamese translation of La Peste; editor: The East (co-founder); jour. Les Cahiers de l'Asie du Sud-Est. Founder, past pres. Movement for Fedn. Countries S.E. Asia; co-founder, past v.p. Movement for Restoration Cultures and Religions of Orient; mem. The Noetic Inst., 1988—, Internat. Found. for Homeopathy, 1987; founder, pres. Intercontinental Found. for Electro-Magnetic Resonance Rsch., 1989—; coord. Unity and Diversity World Health Coun., 1992—. Named hon. dean, The Open Internat. U. of Complementary Medicines, Sri Lanka, 1989; Unity-and-Diversity World Coun. fellow, 1990—. Mem. AAUP, Assn. Clin. Scientists, Am. Com. for Integration Eastern and Western Medicine (founder), Assn. Unitive Medicine (founder, pres.), U. So. Calif. Faculty Member Club (L.A.). Roman Catholic. Home: 3630 Barry Ave Los Angeles CA 90066-3202 E-mail: hoangvduc@yahoo.com.

HOANG, LOC BAO, electrical engineer; b. Saigon, Vietnam, Feb. 26, 1964; came to U.S., 1980; s. Chau Van Hoang and Quy Thi Bui; m. Tracy Phuong-Nga Doan, Dec. 7, 1990; children: Kimberly Bao, Christopher Dang-Khoa. BSEE, U. Calif., Berkeley, 1988; MSEE, San Jose State U., 1993. Design engr. Xicor, Inc., Milpitas, Calif., 1989-90; sr. design engr. Nat. Semiconductor Corp., Santa Clara, Calif., 1991-93, Silicon Storage Tech., Inc., Sunnyvale, Calif., 1993-94; design mgr. Winbond Memory Lab., San Jose, Calif., 1994-97; dir. design Winbond Electronics Corp. Amer., San Jose, Calif., 1997—. Presenter Internat. Symposium on VLSI Tech., 1993. Mem. IEEE. Achievements include patent for Row Decoder and Driver with Switched-Bias Bulk Regions; semiconductor mem. device with dataline undershoot detection and reduced read access time, electrically byte selectable and byte alterable mem. arrays, flash cell having self-timed programming, memory device and method of operation, semiconductor memory device with reduced read disturbance, semiconductor memory array with buried drain lines and method therefore, semiconductor memory array partitioned into memory blocks and sub-blocks and method of addressing, and other patents; patent pending for notable findings of methods and design techniques to improve performance and/or reliability of non-volatile semiconductor memories. Office: Winbond Electronics Corp Am 2727 N 1st St San Jose CA 95134-2029 E-mail: locbaohoang@yahoo.com.

HOARE-TEMPLE, PIERS HOWARD, building maintenance executive; b. London, Mar. 5, 1946; s. Euan Temple and Margot Carol Blaut Temple Hoare; m. Jane Evelyn Montague Browne, Aug. 19, 1978; 1 child, Guy Arthur Anthony. Salesman Va. Oak Tannery, Luray, 1965-67; barrister The English Bar, London, 1972-87; chmn. bd., majority shareholder Blaut Verwaltung & Grundstücks GmbH & Co., Neu Isenburg, Germany, 1987—, Heritage Restoration Ltd., Jersey, Channel Islands, 1991—, Heritage Restoration GmbH, Dusseldorf, Germany, 1992—2003; owner Reisebüro Engels, Friedberg, Germany, 1987-94. Cons. Riverside (Great Stour Ltd.), Canterbury, Eng., 1994, dir. Canterbury Leisure Devel. Ltd., 1993—. Mem. mgmt. com., trustee Hearing Rsch. Trust, London, 1988—; chmn. Richmond Legal Advice Svc., London, 1973—. Lt. comdr. Naval Res. Decorated Reserve Decoration, Her Majesty the Queen, 1985. Mem. Criminal Bar Assn., Conservative Lawyers Assn., Pres.'s Res. Officers' Assn. (com. mem.), Royal Howal Res. Officer Dining Club (v.p.), Naval Club London (counselor bd.), Old Pauline Club (com. mem.). Ch. of Eng. Avocations: travel, wining and dining, swimming, socializing. Office: Blaut Verwaltung und Grundstucks GMBh & Co Dornhofstrasse 89 Neu Isenburg 63263 Germany Office Phone: 0049 6102 25265.

HOART, GLADYS GALLAGHER, English language educator; b. N.Y.C., June 27, 1914; d. Martin and Edna (Parker) Gallagher; m. Francis Xavier Hoart, June 25, 1939; children: Robert, Helen, Andrew. AB cum laude, NYU, 1967, MA, 1970; MA in Liberal Studies, New Sch. for Social Rsch., 1975. Cert. mem. N.Y. Stock Exchange. Adj. prof. English Nassau C.C., Garden City, N.Y., 1970—. Dir. Career Seminars for Teenage Girls, Flushing, N.Y., 1963-64; tutor Black Studies Program, Manhasset, N.Y., 1968-69. Pres., co-founder Broadway Homeowners' Assn., Flushing, N.Y., 1964-65; committeewoman Dem. Party, Manhasset, N.Y., 1970; organizer Parkchester (N.Y.) Golden Age Club, 1953; trustee Dalcroze Sch. of Music, 1998—, treas., 2001. Mem. AAUW, Alliance Floor Brokers, Musicians Club (bd. dirs. 1993—, v.p. 2001). Roman Catholic. Avocations: architecture, equitation, gardening, music.

HOBBIE, RUSSELL KLYVER, physics professor; b. Albany, N.Y., Nov. 3, 1934; s. John Remington and Eulin Pomeroy (Klyver) H.; m. Cynthia Ann Borcherding, Dec. 28, 1957; children: Lynn Katherine, Erik Klyver, Sarah Elizabeth, Ann Stacey. BS in Physics, Mass. Inst. Tech., 1956; A.M., Harvard U., PhD, 1960. Research asso. U. Minn., 1960-62, mem. faculty, 1962—, prof. physics, 1972-98, prof. physics emeritus, 1998—, assoc. dean, 1984-95, dir. Space Sci. Ctr., 1978-84. Author: Intermediate Physics for Medicine and Biology, 1978, 3d edit. 1997. Mem. Am. Assn. Physics Tchrs. (exec. bd. 1980-83), Am. Phys. Soc., Am. Assn. Physicists in Medicine, AAAS., IEEE. Home: 2151 Folwell Ave Saint Paul MN 55108-1306 E-mail: hobbie@tc.umn.edu.

HOBBINS, ROBERT LEO, lawyer; b. Des Moines, June 5, 1948; s. Leo Michael and Margaret Ellen Hobbins; m. Carmela Theresa Tursi, Dec. 27, 1974; children: Brian, Patrick, Edward. BA magna cum laude, Creighton U., 1970; JD, NYU, 1973. Bar: Minn. 1973. Assoc. Dorsey & Whitney, Mpls., 1973-78; ptnr., labor, employment law practice Dorsey & Whitney LLP, Mpls., 1979. Adj. faculty U. St. Thomas Sch. Law, 2002—. Root-Tilden scholar; Named a Super Lawyer, Minn. Law & Politics and Mpls. St. Paul Mag. Mem. ABA (labor sect., EEO law com.), Minn. State Bar Assn., Hennepin County Bar Assn., Creighton U. Alumni Assn. (v.p. 1994). Office: Dorsey & Whitney 50 S 6th St Ste 1500 Minneapolis MN 55402-4502 Office Phone: 612-340-2919. Office Fax: 612-340-2868. E-mail: hobbins.robert@dorseylaw.com.

HOBBINS, WILLIAM T., career officer; BS in Bus. Fin., U. Col., 1969; grad., Squadron Officer Sch., Maxwell AFB, Ala., 1976; MA in Bus. Adminstr., Troy State U., 1977; grad., Armed Forces Staff Coll., Norfolk, Va., 1981, Air War Coll., Maxwell AFB, 1985; grad. Jt. Flag Officer Warfighting, Maxwell AFB, 1997; grad., Joint Force Air Cmdrs., 1999; postgrad., Syracuse U., 2000. Cert. command pilot. Commd. 2d. lt. USAF, 1969, advanced through grades to Lt. Gen., 2001; pilot trng. Laredo AFB, Tex., 1970-70; instr. pilot 3389th Pilot Training Squadron, Keesler AFB, Miss., 1970-73; instr. pilot, class commander 29th Flying Trng. Wing, Craig AFB, Ala., 1973-74; At-28 fight pilot/chief 1131st Spl. Activity Squadron, Udorn Royal Thai AFB, Thailand, 1974-75; chief 29th Flying Tng. Wing, Craig AFB, Ala., 1975-77; flight comdr., instr. pilot, opers. officer 7th Tactical Fighter Squadron, 49th Tactical Fighter Wing, Holloman AFB, N.Mex., 1977-80; F-15 ops. monitor, chief weapons sys. br., program element monitor Hdrs. USAF, Washington, 1981-84; chief wing inspections 33rd. Tactical Fighter Wing, Eglin AFB, Fla., 1985-87; dep. comdr. opers. 12th Flying Trng. Wing, Randolph AFB, Tex., 1987-88; vice commander, then commdr. Air Forces Iceland, Keflavik Naval Air Sta, Iceland, 1988-90; vice comdr., then comdr. 405th Tactical Tng. Wing, Luke AFB, Ariz., 1990-91; vice comdr. 58th Fighter Wing, Luke AFB, Ariz., 1991-92; J-3 US forces Yokota Air Base, Japan, 1992-94; comdr. 18th Wing, Kadena AFB, Japan, 1994-96; dir. plans and policy (J-5) U.S. Atlantic Command, Norfolk, Va., 1996-98; dir. ops. Hdqs. USAF in Europe, Ramstein Air Base, Germany, 1998-2000; comdr. 12th Air Force and U.S. So. Command Air Force, 2000—03. Nat. security leadership course, Syracuse U., 2000. Decorated Disting. Svc. Medal with oak leaf cluster, Def. Superior Svc. medal with oak leaf cluster, Legion of Merit, Meritorious Svc. medal with four oak leaf clusters, Joint Svc. Commendation medal Air Force Commendation medal with oak leaf cluster, Order of the Rising Sun with Gold Rays, Star of Armed Forces in grade of Star of Mil. Merit (Ecuador), Aeronautical Merit Medal (Uruguay), Medal of Merit 1st class, (Honduras), Meritorious Air Cross Medal (Chile), Air Force Medal (Guatemala), comdr. Armed Forces Order of Aero. Merit (Bolivia), gt. officer Air Force Cross of Aero. Merit (Columbia), Legion of Merit Sys. Cooperation Am. Air Forces; recipient Khmer Aviation citation, Air Force Assn. citation. Office: HQ USAF/XI 1800 Air Force Pentagon Washington DC 20330-1800

HOBBS, ANN S., lawyer; b. Washington, Nov. 20, 1945; BS, U. Md., Coll. Park, 1968; PhD in Biophysics, U. Md., Balt., 1973; JD with honors, U. Md. Sch. of Law, 1991. Bar: Md. 1991, US Ct. of Appeals, Federal Circuit 1992, DC 1993, US Patent and Trademark Office. Former rsch. scientist NIH, Md.; former faculty mem. U. Md. Sch. of Medicine; former patent advisor/atty. Office of Tech. Transfer, NIH; atty. priv. practice; ptnr., patent prosecution & intellectual property litigation Venable LLP, Washington, 2005—. Mem.: ABA, DC Bar Assn., Am. Soc. for Biochemistry and Molecular Biology, NY Acad. of Sci. Office: Venable LLP 575 7th St NW Washington DC 20004 Office Phone: 202-344-4651. Office Fax: 202-344-8300. Business E-Mail: ashobbs@venable.com.

HOBBS, C. FREDRIC, artist, filmmaker, writer; b. Phila., Dec. 30, 1931; s. Robert Frederic and Gertrude (Madison) H.; children: Leslie Newbold, Mary Alison. Grad., Menlo Sch.; BA, Cornell U., 1953; grad., Academia de San Fernando de Bellas Artes, Madrid, 1955-56. Pres. Fredric Hobbs Films, Inc., 1975; chmn., chief exec. officer Virginia City (Nev.) Restoration Corp., 1978-85. Writer, dir., producer 4 feature films, (TV series) Taiwan, The Other China, 1988-90, (TV/multimedia series) Fastfuture, 2000—; author: The Richest Place on Earth, 1978, Eat Your House: Art Eco Guide to Self Sufficiency, 1980, The Spirit of the Monterey Coast, 1990, and others; also articles.; one-man shows include, Calif. Palace Legion of Honor, San Francisco, 1958, Mus. Sci. and Industry, Los Angeles, 1976, San Francisco Mus. Modern Art, 1980-81, Sierra Nevada Mus. Art, 1984; maj. mus. exhbns. include Concurso Internat. Palacio de la Virreina, Barcelona, Spain (17 countries), Art USA, Madison Sq. Garden, N.Y., Pa. Acad. Fine Arts., Phila, Internat. Drawing Competition II, Nat. Fine Arts Collection, Smithsonian Inst., Washington, Drawings USA 63" II Biennial, St. Paul Art Ctr., Minn., Ann. Sculpture-Painting Exhbns., SFAI, San Francisco Mus. Art, III and V Invitationals, Finch Coll. Mus. Art., N.Y.C., Gallery Modern Art., N.Y.C., Nat. Gallery Art, Washington, Reed Coll., Portland, Oreg., U. Pacific, Stockton, Calif., San Diego Mus. Art., Mills Coll., Oakland, Calif., Touring Am. Mus., Ebert Gallery, 1994, 95, 97, others; permanent collections include Mus. Modern Art, N.Y.C., Met. Mus. Art, N.Y.C., Spencer Meml. Ch., N.Y.C., Calif. Palace Legion of Honor, Finch Coll. Mus. Art, St. Paul Art Gallery, San Francisco Mus. Modern Art, Fine Arts Mus. San Francisco, Sierra Nevada Mus. Art, Reno, Stanford (Calif.) U. Mus. Art., San Francisco State Coll., U. Calif. Media Ctr., San Jose (Calif.) Mus. Art., Oakland (Calif.) Mus. Art., Johnson Mus., Cornell U., Penn Treaty Pk. Pl., Phila., Pa., others; galleries include Twentieth Century West Galleries, N.Y.C., Braunstein Gallery, San Francisco, Heritage Gallery, L.A.; represented by Ebert Gallery, San Francisco. 1st lt. USAF, 1953-55. Mem. Film Arts Found. Democrat. Episcopalian. Home and Office: The Madison Hobbs Studio PO Box 223759 Carmel CA 93922 *To create a work of art is an act of faith in the human spirit and in God. Art must always transcend materialist values and monuments to success. It is often the work of fools and children yet it is the ultimate reality.*

HOBBS, CASWELL O., III, lawyer; b. Sherman, Tex., Aug. 25, 1941; s. Caswell Owen II and Marie Elizabeth (Bloomfield) H.; m. Anne Louise Simpson, June 7, 1968; children: Elizabeth Ellen, Emily Jane. BS, U. Kans., 1963; LLB, U. Pa., 1966. Bar: D.C. 1967, U.S. Ct. Appeals (4th cir.) 1975, U.S. Supreme Ct. 1972. Asst. to chmn., dir. Office of Policy Planning and Evaluation, FTC, Washington, 1970-73; assoc. Morgan Lewis & Bockius, Washington, 1973-76, ptnr., 1976—, chmn. Washington office mgmt. com., 1987-89, mem. governing bd., 1989-92, 95-99; lectr. Conf. Bd., ABA. Author: Antitrust Strategies for Mergers, Acquisitions, Joint Ventures and Strategic Alliances, 2000; contbr. articles to profl. jours. Trustee Legal Aid Soc. D.C., 1982-92, pres., 1989-91, pres. coun., 1991—. Served to capt. JAGC, USAR, 1966-72. Fellow ABA (chair antitrust sect. 1994-95, officer 1991-96, co-chair task force on competition policy 1993, mem. commn. to study the FTC, 1988); mem. Am. Law Inst. E-mail: cohobbs@morganlewis.com. Office: Morgan Lewis and Bockius LLP 1111 Pennsylvania Ave NW Washington DC 20004-2541

HOBBS, CHARLES RODERICK BRUCE, JR., retired geologist; b. Englewood, N.J., Dec. 24, 1929; s. Charles Roderick Bruce and Kathryn Sue (Warner) Hobbs; m. Anne Pierce, June 2, 1962. BS, Va. Poly., 1952, MS, 1954, PhD, 1957. Geologist B, geologist C Va. Divsn. Mineral Resources, Charlottesville, 1957—70, asst. state geologist, asst. commr. mineral resources, 1970—80, dep. state geologist, dep. commr. mineral resources, 1980—91; ret. Mem.: Geol. Soc. Am. (emeritus), Am. Assn. Petroleum Geology. Home: 250 Pantops-Mtn Rd #3 Charlottesville VA 22911

HOBBS, DAVID ELLIS, mechanical engineer; BA in Engring. Sci., Dartmouth Coll., 1963; BSME, Case Inst. Tech., 1964; MSME, Rensselaer Poly. Inst., 1967, PhD in Mech. Engring., 1983. With turbine component design group Pratt & Whitney, East Hartford, Conn., 1964-67, with turbine analysis and tech. devel. group, 1967-77, with compressor analysis and tech. devel. group, 1977-94; gas turbine design sys. cons. FTS Cons., Inc., East Hartford, Conn., 1995-2000, TurboVision Cons. Group, Miami, Fla., 1995—. Contbr. articles to profl. jours. Recipient Horner citation United Technologies Corp.,

1993. Fellow AIAA (assoc., chmn. Conn. sect. 2001-04); mem. ASME (gas turbine turbomachinery com., axial compressor panel, Gas Turbine award 1988). Home: 20 Bayberry Trl South Windsor CT 06074-3809 E-mail: dehobbs@cox.net.

HOBBS, GARY G, music educator; b. Portland, Oreg., Nov. 7, 1948; s. Lawrence Nordstrom and Johanna Marie Hobbs; m. Marcia B Brown, Apr. 23, 1952; 1 child, Britta Marie. AA, Mt. Hood C.C., 1969—71. Profl. musician(drums) Stan Kenton Orch., Los Angeles, Calif., 1975—77; band dir. Prairie H.S., Battle Ground, Wash., 1995—97; drummer Woody Herman Orch., Miami, 2001, Bud Shank Band, Port Townsend, Wash., 1998—, Tom Grant Band, Portland, Oreg., 1980—, Gary Hobbs Bands, Vancouver, 1982—; clinician performing artist Yamaha Drum Co., Buana Park, Calif., 1980—, Zildjian Cymbal Co., Norwell, Mass., 1975—; drumset instrn. U. Of Oreg., 1997—, Whitman U., Walla Walla, Wash., 1996—2000. Musician: (albums) (record) Stan Kenton Orchestra:, Jim Widner Big Band: Rides Again, Mike Vax Big Band: I Remember You, Mike Vax Big Band: Live On The Road, Tom Grant: You Hardly Know Me, Tom Grant: Tom Grant, Tom Grant: Big Fun, Dan Siegel: Night Ride, Dan Siegel: Reflections, Richard Cole: The Forgotten, Gary Hobbs: Low Flight Through Valhalla, Stan Kenton Orchestra: Journey To Capricorn, Stan Kenton Orchestra: Live In Europe, Stan Kenton Orchestra:Live In Cologne, Stan Kenton Orchestra: Artistry In Symphonic Jazz, Dave Frishberg: Quality Time, Nancy King and Glen Moore: Cliff Dance, Jim Widner Big Band: Yesterdays And Today, Jim Widner Big Band: Body And Soul. Lutheren. Avocations: running, bicycling, cars. Office: 200 W37th St Vancouver WA 98660 Business E-Mail: tubmanbeat@hotmail.com.

HOBBS, GREGORY JAMES, JR., state supreme court justice; b. Gainesville, Fla., Dec. 15, 1944; s. Gregory J. Hobbs and Mary Ann (Rhodes) Frakes; m. Barbara Louise Hay, June 17, 1967; children: Daniel Gregory, Emily Mary Hobbs Wright. BA, U. Notre Dame, 1966; JD, U. Calif., Berkeley, 1971. Bar: Colo. 1971, Calif. 1972. Law clk. to Judge William E. Doyle 10th U.S. Cir. Ct. Appeals, Denver, 1971-72; assoc. Cooper, White & Cooper, San Francisco, 1972-73; enforcement atty. U.S. EPA, Denver, 1973-75; asst. atty. gen. State of Colo. Atty. Gen.'s Office, Denver, 1975-79; ptnr. Davis, Graham & Stubbs, Denver, 1979-92; shareholder Hobbs, Trout & Raley, P.C., Denver, 1992-96; justice Colo. Supreme Ct., Denver, 1996—. Counsel No. Colo. Water Conservancy, Loveland, Colo., 1979-96. Contbr. articles to profl. jours. Vol. Peace Corps-S.Am., Colombia, 1967-68; vice chair Colo. Air Quality Control Com., Denver, 1982-87; mem. ranch com. Philmont Scout Ranch, Boy Scouts Am., Cimarron, N.Mex., 1988-98; co-chair Eating Disorder Family Support Group, Denver, 1992—. Recipient award of merit Denver Area Coun. Boy Scouts, 1993, Pres. award Nat. Water Resources Assn., Washington, 1995. Fellow Am. Bar Found.; mem. ABA, Colo. Bar Assn., Denver Bar Assn. Avocations: backpacking, fishing, poetry. Office: Colo Supreme Ct 2 E 14th Ave Denver CO 80203-2115*

HOBBS, GUY STEPHEN, financial executive; b. Lynwood, Calif., Feb. 23, 1955; s. Franklin Dean and Bette Jane (Little) H.; m. Laura Elena Lopez, Jan. 6, 1984; 1 child, Mariah Amanda. BA, U. Calif., Santa Barbara, 1976; MBA, U. Nev., 1978. Sr. rsch. assoc. Ctr. for Bus. and Econ. Rsch., Las Vegas, Nev., 1978-80; pvt. practice mgmt. cons. Las Vegas, 1979-82; mgmt. analyst Clark County, Las Vegas, 1980-81, sr. mgmt. analyst, 1981-82, dir. budget and fin. planning, 1982-84, comptroller, dir. fin., chief fin. officer, 1984-96; pres. Hobbs, Ong & Assocs., Inc., 1996—. Lectr. in mgmt. Coll. Bus. and Econs., U. Nev., Las Vegas, 1977-88; pres. Pacific Blue Ent., 1991—; mem. Interim Legis. Com. Infrastructure Fin., 1993-94; mem. Interim Legis. Com. Studying Laws Relating to the Distbn. of Taxes in Nev., 1995-96, 97—; mem. fiscal rev. com. Henderson State Coll., 2001, County Mgrs.'s orgnl. rev. com., 2001; chmn. Gov.'s Task Force on Tax Policy in Nev., 2001-02; mem. exec. adv. bd. Dept. Econs. U. Nev., Las Vegas, 2004—; mem. growth task force Clark County, 2004—; prodr. game day U. Nev., Las Vegas, 2004. Author publs. in field. Instr. Las Vegas Baseball Acad., 1998—2001; mem. exec. bd. Miss Nev. USA and Miss Nev. Teen USA, 1996—2002; head coach Silver State Girls Soccer League, 1998—2001; pres. U.S. Youth Soccer-Nev., 2003—; exec. prodr. WUSA exhbn. game between San Diego Spirit and San Jose Cyber Rays, 2002, WUSA exhbn. game between Boston Breakers and San Jose Cyber Rays, 2003; exec. producer Las Vegas Soccer spectacular; gen. mgr. Las Vegas Tabagators of Women's Premier Soccer League, 2004—. Mem. Am. Soc. Pub. Adminstrn. (Pub. Adminstr. of Yr. 1987), Govt. Fin. Officers Assn. (Fin. Reporting Achievement award 1984-95, Disting. Budget Presentation, award 1993-96), Nev. Taxpayers Assn. Republican. Avocations: sports, photography, travel. Office: Hobbs Ong & Assocs Inc 3900 Paradise Rd Ste 152 Las Vegas NV 89109-0928 Office Phone: 702-733-7223.

HOBBS, IRA, federal agency administrator; b. Tallahassee, Fla. BA in Polit. sci., Fla. A&M U., 1976; MPA, Fla. State U., 1977. Presdl. mgmt. intern Dept. Agr., Washington, 1978-80, pers. mgmt. specialist Human Resources Divsn., 1980-83, from br. chief to dep. dir. Adminstrv. Svcs. Divsn., 1983-88, dir. Info. Sys. and Comms. Divsn. Animal and Plant Health, 1989-94, dir. Office of Ops., 1994-97, dep. chief info. officer, 1997—2004. Spkr. in field; co-chair Fed. Chief Information Officer (CIO) Coun. Workforce and Human Capital for IT Com.; bd. dirs. Dept. Agr. Grad. Sch. of Bus., Washington. Mem. Pres.'s Com. for Purchasing from the Blind and Severely Disabled, Leadership Washington, 1996. With US Army. Mem. ASPA, Conf. Minority Pub. Adminstrs., Leadership Wash., Class of 1996 Office: Dept Treasury 1750 Pennsylvania Ave NW 12th Fl Washington DC 20220-0001 Office Phone: 202-622-1200. Office Fax: 202-622-2224.

HOBBS, J. TIMOTHY, SR., lawyer; b. Yakima, Wash., Sept. 23, 1941; s. Leonard M. and Virginia (Snider) H.; m. Barbara J. Hatfield, June 14, 1964; children: Amy Elizabeth, J. Timothy Jr. BA in Polit. Sci., U. Wash., 1964; JD, Am. U., 1968. Bar: D.C. 1969, U.S. Ct. Supreme Ct. 1973, U.S. Ct. Appeals Fed. Crct. 1982, U.S. Ct. Appeals (11th cir.) 1986, U.S. Ct. Appeals (5th cir.) 1989, U.S. Ct. Appeals (6th cir.) 1996. Assoc. Mason Fenwick & Lawrence, Washington, 1969-76, ptnr., 1977-82, sr. ptnr., 1982-91; ptnr., head intellectual property dept. Dykema Gossett, 1991-99; ptnr. Wiley, Rein & Fielding, Washington, 1999—. Author chpt. on copyright law, West's Federal Practice Manual, 1983. Pres. Arlington Outdoor Edn. Assn., 1990-92. Mem.: D.C. Bar (chmn. trademark com. 1982—84), Internat. Trademark Assn. Forums (spkr. 1988). Office: Wiley Rein & Fielding 1776 K St NW Washington DC 20006-2304 Home: 46424 276 Ave SE Enumclaw WA 98022 Office Phone: 202-719-7105. Business E-Mail: thobbs@wrf.com.

HOBBS, JAMES BEVERLY, business administration educator, writer, academic administrator; b. Topeka, Sept. 9, 1930; s. Kenneth Beverly and Ida (Burkholder) H.; m. Peggy Genevieve Whitney, Nov. 2, 1957; children: David Beverly, Nancy Ruth. AB, Harvard U., 1952; MBA, U. Kans., 1957; DBA, Ind. U., 1962. Fin. analyst Hotpoint divsn. GE, Chgo., 1957-60; asst. prof. mgmt. and acctg. Kans. State U., 1962-66, assoc. dean, 1964-66; assoc. prof. mgmt. and acctg. Lehigh U., 1966-70, prof., 1970-79, Frank L. Magee Disting. prof. bus. adminstrn., 1979-91, Frank L. Magee Disting. prof. bus. adminstrn. emeritus, 1991—, chmn. dept. mgmt., fin., mktg. and law, 1970-75, chmn. dept. mgmt., fin. and mktg., 1982-83, dir. MBA program, 1986-89, co-chmn. mgmt. dept., 1989-90, assoc. dean Coll. Bus. and Econ., 1993, assoc. dean Coll. Arts and Scis., 1993-95, chmn. art and architecture dept., 1996, assoc. dean emeritus Coll. Arts & Scis., 1999—. Vis. prof. acctg. U. Canterbury, New Zealand, 1976, Mich. Technol. U., 1975; vis. prof. mgmt. U. Edinburgh, Scotland, 1984, Ecole Superieure Commerce de Poitiers, France, 1990, Acad. Ednl. Devel., Bishkek, Kyrghystan, 1999; participant mission to Ulan Bator, Mongolia, UN Devel. Program, 1992; participant missions to Ternopil, Ukraine, Vladivostok, Russia, Bratislava, Slovak Republic and Kishnev, Moldova, Internat. Exec. Svc. Corps, 1993, 95, 97, 98, mission to Skopje, Macedonia, U.S. Energy Assn., 1997; acad. cons. Author: Financial Accounting, 1984, Corp. Staying Power, 1987, Homophones & Homographs, 1999. Served as naval aviation cadet USN, 1952, as regtl. sgt. maj. U.S. Army, 1952-54, Korea. Mem. Mensa, Phi Beta Kappa, Phi Kappa Phi, Beta Gamma Sigma, Beta Alpha Psi, Sigma Iota Epsilon, Omicron Delta Epsilon, Omicron Delta Kappa, Delta Mu Delta, Phi Beta Delta. Unitarian Universalist. Home: 1915 Black River Rd Bethlehem PA 18015-8920 Office Phone: 610-758-3439. E-mail: jbh1@lehigh.edu.

HOBBS, LEWIS MANKIN, astronomer; b. Upper Darby, Pa., May 16, 1937; s. Lewis Samuel and Evangeline Elizabeth (Goss) H.; m. Jo Ann Faith Hagele, June 16, 1962; children: John, Michael, Dara. B of Engring. Physics, Cornell U., 1960; MS, U. Wis., 1962, PhD in Physics, 1966. Jr. astronomer Lick Obs., U. Calif., Santa Cruz, 1965-66; faculty U. Chgo., 1966—, prof. astronomy and astrophysics, 1976—2003, prof. emeritus, 2003; dir. Yerkes Obs. Williams Bay, Wis., 1974-82. Bd. dirs. Assn. Univs. for Rsch. in Astronomy, Washington, 1974-85; mem. Space Telescope Inst. Coun., 1982-87; astronomy com. of bd. trustees Univs. Rsch. Assn., Inc., Washington, 1979-83, chmn., 1979-81; bd. govs. Astrophys. Rsch. Consortium, Inc., Seattle, 1984-91; mem. Users Com. for Hubble Space Telescope, NASA, 1990-94; mem. telescope allocation com. Nat. Optical Astronomy Obs., 1998-2000. Contbr. articles to profl. jours. Bd. dirs. Mil. Symphony Assn. of Walworth County, 1972-88. Alfred P. Sloan scholar, 1955-60. Mem.: Internat. Astron. Union, Am. Phys. Soc., Am. Astron. Soc. Office: U Chgo Yerkes Observatory Williams Bay WI 53191 Office Phone: 262-245-5555.

HOBBS, MARCUS EDWIN, retired chemistry professor; b. Chadbourn, N.C., Aug. 11, 1909; s. Julius Charles and Maude Elizabeth (Player) H.; m. Sarah Ferguson Blanchard, July 3, 1937; children: Sarah Lillian, Joan Elizabeth. AB, Duke U., 1932, MA, 1934, PhD, 1936. Indsl. rsch. fellow tobacco Duke, 1931-33, instr. chemistry, 1936, asst. prof., 1942, assoc. prof., 1945, prof., 1950—, univ. disting. svc. prof. emeritus, 1978—, chmn. dept. chemistry, 1951-54; dean Duke (Grad. Sch. Arts and Scis.), 1954-58, dean of univ., 1958-64, vice provost, 1960-64, provost, 1969-71, charge spl. courses in chemistry of explosives, 1941-42. Research assoc. Nat. Def. Rsch. Com., George Washington U., 1942-45; civilian cons. Nat. Def. Rsch. Com., George Washington U. (divsn. 2), 1942-44, Nat. Def. Rsch. Com., George Washington U. (divsn. 3), 1943-45; adviser Office Ordnance Rsch., 1951-61, chief scientist, acting, 1951-52; Dir. N.C. Blue Cross and Blue Shield, Inc., 1967-81, chmn. exec. com., 1978-81; mem. adv. coun. Army Rsch. Office, 1970-76; mem. adv. com. jr. sci. and humanities symposia Dept. Army, 1974-77, adviser, 1980-85; mem. NSF adv. panel U.S.-Japan Coop. Svc. Program, 1963-65; adv. com. utilization R & D, USDR, 1964-70; mem. N.C. Bd. Sci. and Tech., 1963-75; chmn. exec. com. Rsch. Triangle Inst., 1958-68, 71-98, disting. gov. emeritus, 2000. Contbr. articles to profl. jours. Recipient Army-Navy Cert. of Merit sci. work with OSRD during World War II, 1945; Outstanding Civilian Svc. medal Dept. of Army, 1959; Cigar Industry Rsch. award, 1959, U. medal Disting. Meritorious Svc. Duke U., 1989, Archie K. Davis award, 1999. Fellow AAAS; mem. Am. Chem. Soc. (chmn. N.C. sect. 1946), AAUP, Rotary (pres. Durham 1978-79, Marcus E. Hobbs award named in his honor 1981), Phi Beta Kappa, Sigma Xi, Phi Lambda Upsilon, Sigma Pi Sigma, Sigma Chi. Home: 2701 Pickett Rd Apt 4009 Durham NC 27705-5652

HOBBS, MICHAEL EDWIN, broadcasting company executive; b. Washington, Nov. 26, 1940; s. Robert Boyd and Barbara Alberta (Davis) H.; m. Ann Reed, Sept. 16, 1989. AB cum laude, Dartmouth Coll., 1962; JD, Harvard U., 1965. Bar: Mass. 1966. Staff counsel, asst. to gen. mgr. Sta. WGBH Ednl. Found., Boston, 1966-67; exec. asst. ednl. TV stas. Nat. Assn. Ednl. Broadcasters, Washington, 1967-70; sec. PBS, Washington, 1970-87, gen. counsel, 1970-71, dir. adminstrn., 1970-73, v.p., 1973-76, sr. v.p., 1976-87, sr. v.p. for policy and planning, 1987-91; sr. fellow Hartford Gunn Inst., Alexandria, Va., 1991—. Active Alexandria Rep. City Com., 1997—, chmn. 1998-2000; bd. dirs. Old Town Civic Assn., 2001—, pres., 2004—; bd. dirs. Agenda: Alexandria, 2005—. Mem.: ABA (intellectual property law sect.), Nat. Acad. TV Arts and Scis., Mass. Bar Assn., George Town Club, Phi Beta Kappa. Home and Office: Hartford Gunn Inst 419 Cameron St Alexandria VA 22314-3221 Personal E-mail: mhobbs27@comcast.net.

HOBBS, PATRICK ESMOND, dean, law educator; m. Joanne Hobbs; children: Patrick, John, Alexandra. BS magna cum laude, Seton Hall U., 1982; JD, U. NC, Chapel Hill, 1985; LLM in Taxation, NYU Sch. Law, 1988. Assoc. Hannoch Weisman, P.C., Roseland, NJ, 1985—87, Shanley & Fisher, P.C., Morristown, 1987—90; asst. prof. law Seton Hall U. Sch. Law, 1990—93, assoc. prof., 1993—97, prof., 1997—, assoc. dean fin., 1995—99, dean, 1999—. Contbr. articles to law jours. Mem. Legal Edn. Task Force, 1996; project dir. Newark in 21st Century Commn., 1997; mem. N.J. Commn. on Professionalism, 2000—; bd. mem. N.J. Inst. Continuing Legal Edn., 2000—, Beth Israel Med. Ctr., 2002—; mem. Newark Arena Commn., 2002—. Mem.: ABA, Essex County Bar Assn., N.J. State Bar Assn., Am. Bar Fellows. Office: Seton Hall U Sch Law One Newark Ctr Newark NJ 07102 E-mail: hobbspat@shu.edu.

HOBBS, SYDONNA GINN, music educator; b. Maysville, Ky., May 11, 1955; d. Howard Russell and Faye Dixon Ginn; 1 child, Davonna Faye. B in music edn., Morehead State U., 1975, MA, 1977. Music tchr. Pikeville H.S., Ky., 1976—78, Greenup County H.S., 1978—2004. Dist. choral chair Ky. Music Edn. Assn., 1985—86; head fine arts dept. Greenup H.S., 1983—87, 1991—95. Recipient Tchr. of the Yr., Dist. 8, 1990. Mem.: Ky. Music Educators Assn. Avocations: antiques, piano, reading. Home: 29 Toni Dr Flatwoods KY 41139

HOBBS, TRUMAN MCGILL, federal judge; b. Selma, Ala., Feb. 8, 1921; s. Sam F. and Sarah Ellen (Greene) H.; m. Joyce Cummings, July 9, 1949; children— Emilie C. Reid, Frances John Rose, Dexter Cummings, Truman McGill. AB, U. N.C., 1942; LL.B., Yale U., 1948. Bar: Ala. 1948. Practiced in, Montgomery, 1951-80; law clk. U.S. Supreme Ct., 1948-49; ptnr. Hobbs, Copeland, Franco & Screws, 1951-80; U.S. dist. judge Montgomery, 1980—; now sr. judge. Chmn. Ala. Unemployment Appeal Bd., 1952-58 Pres. United Appeal Montgomery; pres. Montgomery County Tb Assn.; v.p. Ala. Com. for Better Schs.; Chmn. Montgomery County Exec. Democratic Com., 1970. Served to lt. USNR, 1942-46, ETO, PTO. Decorated Bronze Star medal. Fellow Am. Coll. Trial Lawyers; mem. Internat. Acad. Trial Lawyers, Ala. Plaintiffs Lawyers Assn. (past pres.), Ala. Bar Assn. (pres. 1970-71), Montgomery County Bar Assn. (past pres.) Home: 2301 Fernway Dr Montgomery AL 36111-1603

HOBBY, WILLIAM PETTUS, retired broadcast executive; b. Houston, Jan. 19, 1932; s. William Pettus and Oveta (Culp) H.; m. Diana Poteat Stallings, Sept. 11, 1954; children: Laura Poteat Beckworth, Paul William, Andrew Purefoy, Katherine Pettus Gibson. BA, Rice U., 1953. Pres. H & C Communications, Inc., 1979-83, chmn. bd., chief exec. officer, 1983-96; lt. gov. Tex., 1973-91; chancellor Univ. of Houston Sys., 1995-97. Sid Richardson prof. Lyndon B. Johnson Sch. Pub. Affairs, U. Tex., Austin, 1990-97; Radoslav Tsanoff prof. Rice U., Houston, 1991—. Served to lt. (j.g.) USNR, 1953-57. Office: Hobby Comm LLC 2131 San Felipe Houston TX 77019-5620 Office Phone: 713-521-0960.

HOBERMAN, MARY ANN, author; b. Stamford, Conn., Aug. 12, 1930; d. Milton and Dorothy (Miller) Freedman; m. Norman Hoberman, Feb. 4, 1951; children: Diane, Perry, Charles, Meg. BA, Smith Coll., 1951; MA, Yale U., 1984. With advt. dept. Gimbel's Dept. Store, N.Y.C., 1951-52; newspaper reporter Harrisburg, Pa., 1952; editor N.Y. Graphic Soc., Greenwich, Conn., 1963-64. Poetry cons.; lectr. in field; program coord. C.G. Jung Ctr., N.Y.C., 1981; adj. prof. Fairfield (Conn.) U., 1980-83; instr. Yale U., New Haven, 1989; founder, mem. The Pocket People, 1968-75; founder, performer Women's Voices, 1983-93. Author: All My Shoes Come in Two's, 1957, How Do I Go?, 1958, Hello and Good-by, 1959, What Jim Knew, 1963, Not Enough Beds for the Babies, 1965, A Little Book of Little Beasts, The Raucous Auk, 1973, The Looking Book, 1973, Nuts to You and Nuts to Me, 1974, I Like Old Clothes, 1976, Bugs, 1976, A House Is a House for Me, 1978, Yellow Butter, Purple Jelly, Red Jam, Black Bread, 1981, The Cozy Book, 1982, Mr. and Mrs. Muddle, 1988, A Fine Fat Pig and Other Animal Poems, 1991, Fathers, Mothers, Sisters, Brothers, 1991; editor: My Song is Beautiful, 1994, The Cozy Book, 1995, The Seven Silly Eaters, 1997, One of Each, 1997, Miss Mary Mack, 1998, The Llama Who Had No Pajama, 1998, And to Think that We Thought We Would Never Be Friends, 1999, The Cozy Book, 1999, The Eensy Weensy Spider, 2000, the Two Sillies, 2000, Michael Finnegan, 2001, It's Simple, Said Simon, 2001, You Read to Me, 2001, The Looking Book, 2002, The Marvelous Mouse Man, 2002, Right Outside My Window, 2002, Bill Grogan's Goat, 2002, Mary Had a Little Lamb, 2003, You Read to Me, I'll Read to You II, 2003, Whose Garden Is It?, 2003, Yankee Doodle, 2003, You Read to Me, I'll Read to You III, 2005. Bd. dirs. Greenwich Libr., 1988-91, Literacy Vols., 1997-2003, Conn. Ctr. for the Book, 2003—. Recipient Nat. Book award, 1984, Poetry for Children award Nat. Coun. Tchrs. of English, 2003. Mem. Authors Guild. Avocations: dance, gardening, hiking, tennis. Home: 98 Hunting Ridge Rd Greenwich CT 06831-3134

HOBEROCK, CHRISTOPHER, lawyer; b. Neosho, Mo., May 24, 1951; s. Lawrence and Teresa B. (Gornick) H.; m. Susan Carol Henry, Aug. 30, 1974; children: Jared, Grant, Meredith. BBA in Fin. and Banking, U. Ark., 1973; JD with distinction, U. Mo., Kansas City, 1978. Bar: Mo. 1978, U.S. Dist. Ct. (we. dist.) Mo. 1978. Ptnr. Ewing & Hoberock, Nevada, Mo., 1978—. Pres. Sunny Days Pre-Sch. and Child Care Ctr., Nevada, 1981, United Community Funds of Vernon County, Nevada, 1982; past pres. Nevada Country Club; council mem. St. Mary's Cath. Ch., Nevada, 1986. 2d lt. U.S. Army, 1973-75. Mem. Order of Bench and Robe., Lions (pres. Nevada chpt. 1982). Roman Catholic. Home: 155 Country Club Dr Nevada MO 64772-3026 Office: Ewing & Hoberuck PO Box 287 223 W Cherry St Nevada MO 64772-3361

HOBEROCK, LAWRENCE LINDEN, mechanical engineer, educator; b. Wichita, Kans., Oct. 21, 1939; s. Lawrence H. and Teresa B. (Gornick) H.; m. Judith L. Anderson, June 6, 1964; children: Michael Jo, Barbara T., Timmothy M. BSME, U. Mo., Rolla, 1961, MSME, 1963; PhD, Purdue U., 1966. Registered profl. engr., Tex., Okla. Asst. prof., then assoc. prof. U. Tex., Austin, 1968-78; rsch. assoc. Amoco Prodn. Co., Tulsa, 1978-81, rsch. supr., 1981-85; v.p. rsch. Derrick Mfg. Corp., Buffalo, 1985-86; pvt. practice engring. cons. Buffalo, 1986-87; prof., head mech. and aero. engring. Okla. State U., Stillwater, 1987—. Cons. Amoco Prodn. Co., 1977-78, 88, Shell Devel. Co., Houston, 1989-91, Conoco, Ponca City, Okla., 1990, Cagle Oilfield Svcs., Tulsa, 1990. Contbr. articles to profl. pubs. Capt. U.S. Army, 1966-68. Fellow ASME (dedicated svc. award, chair dynamic sys., v.p. sys. and design, assoc. editor); mem. AIAA, IEEE, IEEE Control Sys. Soc., Soc. Petroleum Engrs. (assoc. editor), Am. Soc. Engring. Edn. Avocations: carpentry, bird watching, wines, upland bird hunting. Office: Okla State U Sch Mech and Aero Engring 218 En Stillwater OK 74078-5016 Office Phone: 405-744-5900.

HOBGOOD, EARL WADE, college chancellor; b. Wilson, N.C., June 28, 1953; s. Max Earl and Mary (Carpenter) H.; m. Dianne Bland, Apr. 24, 1977; children: Courtney, Heather. BFA, E. Carolina U., 1975, MFA, 1977; postgrad., Am. Inst. for Philanthropic, Studies, 1995, Harvard U. Inst. Ednl. Mgmt., 1997, Sashakawa Fellowship/AACSCU, 1998. Asst. prof. art Ark. State U., Jonesboro, 1977-78; design dir. and asst./assoc. prof. art Western Carolina U., Cullowhee, N.C., 1978-84; chmn., assoc. to full prof. art and design Winthrop U., Rock Hill, S.C., 1984-88, acting chmn. dept. music, 1991-92, assoc. dean and prof. Coll. Visual and Performing Arts, 1988-92; dean Coll. of Fine Arts, Stephen F. Austin State U., Nacogdoches, Tex., 1992-93; dean Coll. of Arts, Calif. State U., Long Beach, 1993-2000; chancellor N.C. Sch. of the Arts, Winston-Salem, 2000—05; cons. U. of Del., 2004. Sr. evaluator Nat. Assn. Schs. of Art and Design, 1987-99; presenter Global Arts Conf., New Zealand, 1999; evaluator/cons. Arts Edn. Partnership Grants, Ky. Arts Coun., 1992; evaluator/panelist Challenge grants, NEA, 1991, correspondent/cons. Arts Edn. Rsch. Briefing, 1991; mem. bd. advisors First Wachovia Bank, 2003—. Bd. dirs. Winston-Salem Alliance, 2001—, Davidson Coll. Friends of the Arts, Brenner Children's Hosp., 2002—, Forsyth County Tourism Devel. Authority, 2002—, So. Arts Fedn., 2002—, Winston-Salem Symphony, 2002-05; chair bd. dirs. Kenan Inst. for the Arts, 2000-2005. Mem. Winston-Salem/Forsyth C. of C. (bd. dirs. 2001—). Office: NC Sch of the Arts PO Box 12189 Winston Salem NC 27117-2189 Office Phone: 336-770-3200. E-mail: wh@ncarts.edu.

HOBLITZELL, JOHN REED, lawyer; b. Parkersburg, W.Va., June 24, 1948; s. John Dempsey and Charlotte (Reed) H.; m. Sara Pickett Ziebold, May 10, 1975; children: John, William, Mark. BS in Econs., W.Va. U., 1970, JD, 1973. Bar: W.Va. 1973, U.S. Dist. Ct. (s. and no. dists.) W.Va. 1973, U.S. Ct. Appeals (4th cir.) 1973. Assoc. Kay, Casto & Chaney, Charleston, W.Va., 1973-77; ptnr. Kay Casto & Chaney PLLC, Charleston, 1978—. Mem. W.Va. Legislature, Charleston, 1985-88. Mem. W.Va. Higher Edn. Policy Commn., 2000—04, chmn., 2000—02; trustee Charleston Area Med. Ctr., 2004—, U. W.Va. Sys., Charleston, 1989—2000, chmn., 1993—95. Mem. W.Va. U. Alumni Assn. (pres. 1988-89). Republican. Episcopalian. Avocations: reading, skiing, golf. Office: Kay Casto Chaney PLLC 1500 Bank One Plz Charleston WV 25301-2722

HOBSON, BURTON HAROLD, publishing company executive; b. Galesburg, Ill., Apr. 16, 1933; s. Burt and Geneva (Sornberger) H.; m. Maxine C. Meyer, Aug. 9, 1953; children: Alice L., Andrew J., Mark R. BA, U. Chgo., 1953; LHD honoris causa, Johnson & Wales U., 2002. Mgr. collector's coin dept. Marshall Field & Co., Chgo., 1953-61; sales mgr. Sterling Pub. Co., Inc., N.Y.C., 1961-66, v.p. sales, 1966-72, exec. v.p., 1972-79, pres., 1979-95, chmn., 1995—2003, dir., 1966—2003; pres. Pub. Adv. Svc., 2003—. Author: (with Fred Reinfeld) Manual for Coin Collectors and Investors, 1963, Picture Book of Ancient Coins, 1963, U.S. Commemorative Coins and Stamps, 1964, Catalogue of the World's Most Popular Coins, 1965, What You Should Know about Coins and Coin Collecting, 1965, Hidden Values in Coins, 1965, International Guide to Coin Collecting, 1966, Coins You Can Collect, 1966, Coin Identifier, 1966, Coin Collecting As a Hobby, 1967, (with Robert Obojski) Illustrated Encyclopedia of World Coins, 1970, Catalogue of Scandinavian Coins, 1970, Historic Gold Coins of the World, 1971, Coin Collecting for Beginners, 1970, Stamp Collecting for Beginners, 1970, Coins and Coin Collecting, 1971; editor: The Benenson Restaurant Guide, 1985; pub. Gastronome mag., 1993—. Recipient Robert Friedberg award for numismatic lit., 1972 Mem. Am. Numismatic Soc., Confrérie des Chevaliers du Tastevin, Confrérie de la Chaine des Rôtisseurs (nat. pres.), Culinary Inst. Am. (trustee), Am. Acad. Chefs (hon. trustee), Univ. Club of N.Y., Delta Upsilon. Home and Office: 600 Harbor Blvd Unit 833 Weehawken NJ 07086-6748 Personal E-mail: burtonhh@msn.com.

HOBSON, DAVID LEE, congressman, lawyer; b. Oct. 17, 1936; m. Carolyn Alexander; children: Susan Marie, Lynn Martha, Douglas Lee. BA, Ohio Wesleyan U., 1958; JD, Ohio State Coll. Law, 1963; hon. degree, Ctrl. State U., Wittenberg U. Former resident counsel Kissell Co., Springfield, Ohio; former atty. Union Ctrl. Life Ins. Co., Cin.; mem. Ohio Senate, 1982-90, majority whip, 1986-88, pres. pro tem, 1988-90; mem. U.S. Congress from 7th Ohio dist., Washington, 1991—; mem. house appropriations com., def. subcom., VA, HUD and Ind. Agys. subcom., chmn. mil constrn. subcom. House coms. appropriations, budget, standards of ofcl. conduct. Former trustee Wilberforce U., Ohio, Urbana U.; trustee Ohio Wesleyan; bd. dirs. Ohio. Mem. ABA, AMVETS, Ky. Bar Assn., Ohio Bar Assn., Springfield Bd. Realtors, Springfield Area C. of C. (past bd. dirs.), Non-Commissioned Officers Assn., Masons (32 degrees), Am. Legion, VFW, Moose, Elks, Rotary, Shrine Club. Republican. Office: US Ho of Reps 2346 Rayburn Hob Washington DC 20515-3507*

HOBSON, GEORGE DONALD, retired geophysicist; b. Hamilton, Ont., Can., Jan. 8, 1923; s. Robert Charles and Agnes Hamilton (Mathieson) H.; m. Arletta Louise Russell, May 21, 1948; children: Robert, Linda, Douglas, Donna. BA, McMaster U., 1946, DSc (hon.), 1991; MA, Toronto U., 1948. Registered profl. geophysicist, Can. Party chief, ptnr. Heiland Exploration Can. Ltd., Calgary, Alta., 1948-55; geophysicist Can. Fina Oil Co., Calgary, 1955-56; chief geophysicist Merrill Petroleums Ltd., Calgary, 1956-57; geophysicist Pacific Petroleums Ltd., Calgary, 1957-58; chief seismic sect.

Geol. Survey Can., Ottawa, Ont., 1958-69, chief geophysics div., 1969-71; dir. Polar Shelf Project, Ottawa, 1972-88, sr. advisor, 1988-90; rsch. assoc. Nunavut Rsch. Inst., Iqaluit, NWT, Can., 1997—. Author or co-author over 200 articles in field. Recipient No. Sci. award and Centennial medal Dept. Indian and No. Affairs, Can., 1991, Ind. Achievement award Am. Soc. Mech. Engrs., Massey Medal, 1991, Royal Can. Geog. Soc., Queen Elizabeth Goldn Jubilee medal 2002. Fellow Exploration Geophysicists India, Royal Can. Geog. Soc. (bd. govs. 1987-94, Massey medal 1991, Camsell award 1998, The Queen's Golden Jubilee Medal), Arctic Inst. N.Am. (bd. govs. 1984-91); mem. Sci. Inst. N.W. Territory (bd. govs. 1990-93), Soc. Exploration Geophysicists (v.p. 1968), Assn. Profl. Engrs., Geologists, Geophysicists Alta., Can. Soc. Exploration Geophysicists. Mem. United Ch. Can. Avocations: genealogy, barbershop singing. Home: PO Box 161 5428 Long Island Rd Manotick ON Canada K4M 1A3

HOBSON, JAMES RICHMOND, lawyer; b. Atlanta, Sept. 13, 1937; s. Richmond Pearson and Alice Chambers (Carey) H.; m. Nancy Hulbert Saussy, Nov. 29, 1963; children: Kathleen Hunter, Caroline Richmond, Susan Saussy. BA in English, Cornell U., 1959; MA in Govt., Georgetown U., 1963; JD, U. San Francisco, 1971. Bar: Calif. 1972, U.S. Ct. Appeals (9th cir.) 1972, U.S. Dist. Ct. (no. dist.) Calif. 1972, D.C., 1973, U.S. Ct. Appeals (D.C. cir.) 1973, U.S. Dist. Ct. D.C. 1973. Staff writer Charlotte (N.C.) Observer, 1963; rschr., writer Rep. Nat. Com., Washington, 1964-65; Washington editor Med. Econs. Mag., 1965; info. officer Hoover Instn., Stanford, Calif., 1966-72; atty., mgr. FCC, Washington, 1972-78; asst. v.p. GTE Svc. Corp., Washington, 1978-81; Washington counsel GTE Corp., Washington, 1982-91; v.p. Donelan, Cleary, Wood & Maser, PC, Washington, 1991-95, prin., 1995—, pres., 2000—; of counsel Miller & Van Eaton, PLLC, 2000—. Co-editor: The Communications Act: A Legislative History of the Major Amendments, 1935-1996, 1999. Bd. dirs. Mid-Peninsula Citizens for Fair Housing, Palo Alto, Calif., 1971-72; sr. warden Immanuel Ch. on the Hill, Alexandria, Va., 1977, 90, jr. warden, 1976, 88; traffic and parking bd. City Alexandria, 1980-82; mem. Alexandria Libr. Co., 1991—, pres., 1995-96; mem. panel arbitrators Am. Arbitration Assn., 1994-97; adv. bd. Inst. for Conflict Analysis and Resolution, George Mason U., 1989—, chmn., 1995-98; bd. trustees Goodwin House, Inc., 1996—, exec. com., 1998—. Mem. ABA, Fed. Comm. Bar Assn. (exec. com. 1984-87, 94-96), Met. Club. Washington, Sigma Alpha Epsilon. Episcopalian. Home: 3613 Trinity Dr Alexandria VA 22304-1840 Office Phone: 202-785-0600. E-mail: jhobson@millervaneaton.com.

HOBSON, JOHN ALLAN, psychiatrist, researcher, educator; b. Hartford, Conn., June 3, 1933; s. John Robert and Anne Barnard (Cotter) H.; m. Joan Merle Harlowe, June 18. 1956 (div. Jan. 1993); children: Ian, Christopher, Julia; m. Lia Cesarea Silvestri, May 19, 1995; children: Andrew, Matthew. BA, COnn. Wesleyan U., 1955; MD, Harvard U., 1959. Diplomate Am. Bd. Psychiatry and Neurology; lic. physician, Mass. Intern Bellevue Hosp., N.Y.C., 1959-60; resident in psychiatry Mass. Mental Health Ctr., Boston, 1960-61, 64-66; NIMH spl. fellow dept physiology U. Lyon, France, 1963-64; rsch. assoc. dept. physiology Harvard Med. Sch., Boston, 1964-67, instr. psychiatry, 1966-67, assoc. in psychiatry, 1967-69, asst. prof., 1969-74, 74-78, prof. psychiatry, 1978—, prof. psychiatry (neurosci.), 1983—. Sr. psychiatrist Mass. Mental Health Ctr., Boston, 1965-67, dir. lab. neurophysiology, 1967, prin. psychiatrist, 1967—, dir. group therapy tng. program, 1972-80; lectr. psychiatry Brown U., Providence, 1972-74; clin. assoc. NIMH, Bethesda, Md., 1961-63; vis. scientist, lectr. U. Bordeaux, France, 1973; Sandoz lectr. U. Edinburgh, Scotland, 1975; lectr. Italian Nat. Health Rsch. Inst., Rome, 1978; vis. prof. Instituo di Psicologia, U. degli Studi, Rome, 1983; participant internat. confs.; mem. sci. adv. bd. NIMH Intramural program, NIH, Bethesda, 1981-84, Max Planck Inst. Psychiatry, Munich, 1985—; scholar in residence Rockefeller Study Ctr., Bellagio, Italy, 1987; Decade of the Brain lectr. Soc. Neurosci., 1991, Am. Acad. Neurology, 1993; Joseph P. Erlanger Disting. lectr. Am. Physiol. Soc. Author: The Dreaming Brain, 1988, Sleep, 1989, The Chemistry of Conscious States, 1994, Consciousness, 1998, Dreaming as Delirium, 1999; mem. editl. bd. Jour. Cellular and Molecular Neurobiology, 1980—, Archives Itallienes de Biologie, 1983—; contbg. editor Sleep Revs., 1970-72, assoc. editor, 1972-73, editor-in-chief, 1973-74, book rev. editor, 1975-76; sect. editor Neuroreport, 1990—, Psychophysiology, 1993—; assoc. editor Dreaming; contbr. articles to profl. jours. Recipient Sleep Rsch. Soc. Disting. Scientist award, 1998, Disting. Investigator award Sleep Rsch. Soc., 1999; Olin scholar, 1951. Mem. AAAS, Assn. Psychophysiol. Study of sleep, soc. Neurosci. (program com. 1974-76, chmn. mus. adv. group 1976), Boylston Med. Soc., Mind-Body Network, John D. and Catherine T. MacArthur Found., Sigma Xi, Thursday Club. Office: Harvard Med Sch 74 Fenwood Rd Boston MA 02115-6113

HOBSON, KATHERINE JILL, school system administrator; d. Charles David and Patricia Ohnich Hobson. BEd in English Edn., U. Ga., 1991; MEd in Leadership and Supervision, Ga. State U., 1995. Cert. tchr. Ga., 1991, Ga., 1991, in Ednl. Leadership Ga., 1995. Tchr. Barrow County Schs, Winder, Ga., 1991—98; specialist instrnl. tech. Vickery Creek Mid. Sch. Forsyth County Schs., Cumming, Ga., 1998—2001, coord. instrnl. tech., 2001—. Coord. Metro Atlanta Instrl. Tech. Network, Atlanta, 2004—; chmn. conf. Digital Schoolhouse, Cumming, 2004—; presenter in field. Mem. adv. bd. Kennesaw (Ga.) State U., 2004. Mem.: Assn. Supervisors and Curriculum Dirs. (assoc.), Burts Crossing Homeowners Assn. (sec. 2004). Office: Forsyth County Schools 1120 Dahlonega Highway Cumming GA 30040 Office Phone: 770-887-2461. Office Fax: 770-888-3474. E-mail: jhobson@forsyth.k12.ga.us.

HOBSON, MELLODY, investment company executive; b. Chgo., Apr. 3, 1969; BA, Woodrow Wilson Sch. Internat. Rels., Princeton U., 1991. Joined mktg. team Ariel Capital Mgmt., Inc., 1991—94, sr. v.p., dir. mktg., 1994—2000, pres., 2000—. Bd. mem. Tellabs, Inc., 2002—; fin. corr. ABC's Good Morning Am. Bd. dir. Chgo. Pub. Edn. Fund, Chgo. Pub. Libr., Field Mus.; bd. trustees Princeton U. Named a Global Leader Tomorrow, World Econ. Forum, Davos, Switzerland, 2001; named one of 30 Leaders of Future, Ebony, 40 under 40, Crain's Chgo. Bus. Office: Ariel Capital Mgmt LLC 200 E Randolph Dr Ste 2900 Chicago IL 60601 Office Phone: 312-726-0140. Office Fax: 312-612-2702.

HOBSON, STEPHEN GILBERT, conductor, music educator; b. Mason City, Iowa, Jan. 18, 1946; s. Stephen and Lee Hobson; m. Sharon Lee Williams, June 15, 1968; children: Lisa Hobson-McMahon, Stephen. BS in Edn., Ctrl. Mich. U., Mount Pleasant, Mich., 1970; MusM in Conducting, Mich. State U., East Lansing, Mich., 1980. Dir. orch. Traverse City Jr. High, Traverse City, Mich., 1970—74, Traverse City H.S., Traverse City, Mich., 1974—83; music dir. and condr. Omaha Area Youth Orch., Omaha, 1983—93; orch. condr. & string dept. chairperson U. Nebr., Omaha, 1983—86; dir. orch. Evanston Twp. H.S., Evanston, Ill., 1993—2001, Highland Pk. H.S., Highland Pk., Ill., 2001—. Mem., bd. dirs. and u.s. rep. World Fedn. of Amateur Orch., Toyohashi, Japan, 1998—2005; advisor, minority recruitment com. Chgo. Civic Orch., Chgo., 1998—98; guest lectr. Northwestern U., Evanston, Ill., 1998—99; orch. condr. Music Inst. of Chgo., Winnetka, Ill., 1994—98. Contbr. articles pub. to profl. jour. Nominee Tchr. of the Yr., Mich. Sch. Band & Orch. Assn., 1982, 1983. Mem.: Ill. Music Educators Assn. (pres., dist. vii orch. directors 1998—2000), Music Educators Nat. Conf., Am. String Teachers Assn. (nebr. state pres. 1988—90). Achievements include Guest Conductor, Blue Lake Internat. Orch. 1982, 1983; Guest Conductor for Orch. Festivals throughout the U.S; Conducted orch. on concert tours in Norway, Sweden, Denmark, Netherlands, Germany, Austria, China, Mexico, England, Canada; Conducted Carnegie Hall concerts in 1990, 2001; Conducted Omaha Youth Orch. at Midwest Internat. Band & Orch. Clinic, 1988; Guest Conductor, Blue Lake Fine Arts Camp, 1976-1983. Office: Highland Pk H S 433 Vine Ave Highland Park IL 60035 Office Phone: 224-765-2166. Business E-Mail: shobson@dist113.org.

HOBURG, JAMES FREDERICK, electrical engineering educator; b. Pitts., Dec. 30, 1946; s. William Lawrence and Virginia (Stewart) H.; m. Margaret Jean Ryan, Mar. 4, 1978 BS, Drexel U., 1969; SM, MIT, 1971, PhD in Elec. Engring., 1975. Instr. MIT, Cambridge, Mass., 1973-75; asst. prof. elec. engring. Carnegie-Mellon U., Pitts., 1975-80, assoc. prof. elec. engring., 1980-84, prof. elec., computer engring., 1984—, assoc. head, dept. elec., computer engring., 1985-91. Cons. rsch. devel. orgns. Contbr. articles to profl. jours. Fellow IEEE; mem. Electrostatics Soc. Am., Am. Soc. Engr. Edn., Sigma Xi, Tau Beta Pi, Eta Kappa Nu Avocations: long distance running, walking, mountain climbing. Home: 1000 Oak Creek Ln Baden PA 15005-2856 Office: Carnegie-Mellon U Dept Elec and Computer Engring Schenley Park Pittsburgh PA 15213-3830

HOCH, ANNE Z., physiatrist, researcher, medical educator; b. Escanaba, Mich., Mar. 21, 1965; d. Byron K. and Betty A. Zeni; m. Stephen D. Hoch; 1 child, Hannah Anne. BS, Marquette U., Milw., 1987; DO, Mich. State U., East Lansing, 1992. Bd. cert. phys. medicine and rehab. Med. dir. sports rehab. dept. phys. medicine and rehab. Med. Coll. of Wis., Milw., 1997—2002, asst. prof. dept. phys. medicine and rehab. and orthop. surgery, 2002—, assoc. prof. dept. orthop. surgery, 2003—. Adj. prof. health edn. Wis. Luth. Coll., Milw., 1999—2001; adj. prof. dept. biomechanical engring. Marquette U., 2000—; rsch. comm. Strategic Health Initiative Am. Coll. SportsMedicine, 2001—; dir. women's sports medicine program Froedtert Hosp. Med. Coll. Wis., Milw., 2002—, mem. women's faculty coun.-comm., 2001—03. Author: Medicine and Sci. in Sports and Exercise, 2003 (ERF Best Rsch. Paper award, 2003), 1998 (Sarah Baskin Rsch. Paper Writing award, 1997); contbr. articles to profl. jours. (Best Rsch. Paper by Physiatrist, JAMA, 1996). Contbr. Wis. Humane Soc., Milw., 2000—; vol. physician Mt. Mary Coll., 2000—; vol. team physician Divine Savior Holy Angels H.S., 2001—; pres. Wis. Women's Sports Found., 2001—. Recipient First prize poster, Passor-Midwest Regional Meeting, 1995; grantee phys. medicine and rehab., Med. Coll. of Wis., 2001, gen. clin. rsch. ctr., 2002—03, 2003—04. Fellow: Am. Acad. of Phys. Medicine and Rehab., Am. Coll. of Sports Medicine, Am. Coll. of Medicine; mem.: Acad. of Academic Physiatrists. Avocations: triathalon, kayaking, hiking, travel, reading. Office: Dept Orthop Surgery FEC 5th Fl 9200 W Wis Ave Milwaukee WI 53226 Office Phone: 414-805-7461.

HOCH, BENJAMIN, lawyer; b. N.Y.C., June 6, 1963; BS, Bklyn. Coll., 1985; JD, Harvard Univ., 1988. Bar: N.Y. 1989, US Dist. Ct. (so. N.Y.). Ptnr. & co-chmn. corp. reorganization & bankruptcy group Dewey Ballantine LLP, N.Y.C. Mem.: ABA, N.Y. State Bar Assn., Am. Bankruptcy Inst., Turnaround Mgmt. Assn. Office: Dewey Ballantine LLP 1301 Ave of the Americas New York NY 10019-6092 Office Fax: 212-259-6928, 212-259-6333. Business E-Mail: bhoch@dbllp.com.

HOCH, DAVID ALLEN, athletic director; b. Northampton, Pa., July 26, 1946; s. Sterling Palmer and Evelyn Mae (McCallister) H.; m. Diane Duffy, June 18, 1977; children: Matthew David, Jennifer Lynn. AB in German, Grove City (Pa.) Coll., 1968; MEd in Phys. Edn., The Coll. N.J., 1972; EdD in Phys. Edn., Temple U., 1989. Tchr., coach Washington Twp. H.S., Sewell, N.J., 1968-71, Upper Dublin H.S., Ft. Washington, Pa., 1972-78, Ramsey (N.J.) H.S., 1978-79, Germantown Acad., Ft. Washington, 1981-89; instr., coach Pa. State U., Altoona, 1979-80; instr. phys. edn., basketball coach U. Pitts., Bradford, 1989-93; athletic dir. Eastern Tech. H.S., Balt. County, 1994—2003, Loch Raven H.S., Balt. County, 2003—. Presenter in field. Mem. editl. adv. bd. Athletic Bus. mag., 1999-, pub. com. NFHS Coaches Quar., 2002—; contbr. articles to profl. jours., chpts. in books. Mem. AAHPERD, NEA, Nat. H.S. Athletic Coaches Assn. (Regional Athletic Dir. of Yr. award 1999), Nat. Interscholastic Athletic Adminstrs. Assn. (state award of merit for Md. 2002, Nat. Dist. Svc. award, 2004), Nat. Fedn. Coaches Assn. (Md. state dir. 2000—), Md. State Athletic Dirs. Assn. (v.p. 1999-2003, pres. 2003-2005, Athletic Dir. of Yr. 2000), Md. Assn. for Health, Phys. Edn., Recreation and Dance (v.p. athletics, 2000-01), Md. State Coaches Assn. (pres. 2002-03, newsletter editor and membership dir. 2001—), Nat. Assn. Sports Pub. Address Announcers (Md. state rep). Presbyterian. Avocations: running, marathons, gardening, photography. Home: 1207 Peachtree Rd Fallston MD 21047-1804 Office: Loch Raven HS 1212 Cowpens Ave Towson MD 21286 E-mail: dhoch@bcps.org.

HOCH, EDWARD DENTINGER, writer; b. Rochester, N.Y., Feb. 22, 1930; s. Earl George and Alice Mary (Dentinger) Hoch; m. Patricia Ann McMahon, June 5, 1957. Student, U. Rochester, 1947-49. Rsch. asst. Rochester (N.Y.) Pub. Libr., 1949-50; circulation asst. Pocket Books, N.Y.C., 1952-54; pub. rels. writer Hutchins Advt. Co., Rochester, 1954-68. Author: (novels) The Shattered Raven, 1969, The Judges of Hades, 1971, The Transvection Machine, 1971, The Spy and the Thief, 1972, City of Brass, 1972, Fellowship of the Hand, 1973, The Frankenstein Factory, 1975, The Thefts of Nick Velvet, 1978, The Monkey's clue and the Stolen Sapphire, 1978, The Quests of Simon Ark, 1984, Leopold's Way, 1985, The Night My Friend, 1991, Diagnosis: Impossible, 1996, The Ripper of Storyville, 1997, The Velvet Touch, 2000, The Night People, 2001, The Old Spies Club, 2001, The Iron Angel, 2003, More Things Impossible, 2005; editor Dear Dead Days, 1972, All But Impossible, 1981, Murder Most Sacred, 1989, (book) The Best Detective Stories of the Year, 1976—81, Year's Best Mystery and Suspense Stories, 1982—95, Twelve American Detective Stories, 1997. Trustee Rochester Pub. Libr., 1981—98. With U.S. Army, 1950—52. Mem.: Crime Writers Assn. (Eng.), Authors Guild, Sci. Fiction Writers Am., Mystery Writers Am., Inc. (dir., pres. 1982, Edgar award 1967, Edgar scroll 1980, Grand Master 2001). Roman Catholic. Home and Office: 2941 Lake Ave Rochester NY 14612-5529 Office Phone: 585-865-1179. Personal E-mail: edhoch@frontiernet.net. *After publishing over 900 short stories and 50 books, I have to admit that I write primarily to entertain. But I've yet to decide whether it's more to entertain the reader or myself.*

HOCH, FREDERIC LOUIS, medical educator; b. Vienna, Apr. 14, 1920; came to U.S., 1922, naturalized, 1928; s. Samuel and Dore (Glinert) H.; m. Martha Louise Ludwig, Apr. 8, 1961. BS, CCNY, 1939; MD, N.Y. U., 1943; MS, M.I.T., 1951. Intern Michael Reese Hosp., Chgo., 1943; resident in pathology Tufts Med. Sch., Boston, 1947; research asso. in biology MIT, 1948-51; research fellow in biochemistry Mass. Gen. Hosp., Boston, 1951-53; research asso., asst. prof. medicine Harvard Med. Sch., Boston, 1953-66; jr. asso., sr. asso. medicine Peter Brent Brigham Hosp., Boston, 1953-66; asso. prof. internal medicine and biol. chemistry U. Mich. Med. Sch., Ann Arbor, 1967-77, prof. internal medicine and biol. chemistry, 1977-86, prof. emeritus internal medicine, biol. chemistry, 1987—. Author: Energy Transformations in Mammals: Regulatory Mechanisms, 1971. Served to capt. M.C. U.S. Army, 1944-46. Fellow Baruch Found., 1948, NIH, 1949-51, Jane Coffin Childs Found., 1951-53, Howard Hughes Med. Inst., 1957-64. Mem. AAAS, Am. Chem. Soc., Biochem. Soc. (London), Am. Soc. Biol. Chem. Molecular Biology, Phi Beta Kappa, Sigma Xi. E-mail: fredhoch@umich.edu.

HOCH, IVO, former library director; b. Slany, Czech Republic, Aug. 14, 1950; s. Antonín Hoch and Helena (Šlapáková) Hochová; m. Eva Šelová, June 20, 1975; 1 child, Dana. PhD, Charles U., Prague, Czech Republic, 1979. Libr. Czech Nat. Libr., Prague, 1969-71; info. specialist Teplotechna, 1971-90; libr. dir. CAFL, Prague, 1990—2001; libr. analysis specialist Nat. Libr. Czech Republic, Prague, 2002—. Contbr. articles to profl. jours. Mem. IAALD, Sdružení knihovníku a inf. pracovníku. Avocations: cultural activities, travel. E-mail: ihoch@nkp.cz.

HOCHBERG, BAYARD ZABDIAL, retired lawyer; b. NYC, May 16, 1932; s. Abraham and Sonia (Pincus) Hochberg; m. Arlene Beethoven, Feb. 15, 1953; children: Ronny Mark, Randy Jean, Elizabeth Joyce. BA, CCNY, 1953; LLB, U. Va., 1958, JD, 1958. Bar: Md. 1958, Va. 1958. Law bailiff to Hon. Joseph Allen Supreme Bench Balt., 1958-59; asso. law office Paul Berman, Esq., Balt., 1959-68; ptnr. Levin, Hochberg & Chiarello, Balt., 1968-82; sr. ptnr. Hochberg, Chiarello & Costello, Balt., 1983-2000, Hochberg, Costello & Baron, Balt., 2001—02, of counsel, 2002—, ret. Mem. editl. bd. Va. Law Rev., 1956—58; editor: Law Weekly DICTA. Served to maj. USAR, 1953—75. Fellow: Md. Bar Found. (emeritus fellow), Am. Coll. Trial Lawyers; mem.: ATLA, ABA (Md. del. standing com. state legis. 1970—73, mem. tort and ins. practice sect. 1979—2002), Md. Trial Lawyers Assn. (co-chmn. com. legis. 1970—72, bd. govs. 1970—76, v.p. Balt. 1975, mem. Amicus brief com. 1979—81), Balt. County Bar Assn. (mem. family law com.), Balt. Bar Assn. (chmn. legis. com. 1968—69, bd. govs. 1969—70, mem. jud. adminstrn. com. 1980—86, mem. family law com. 1985—88), Md. Bar Assn. (chmn. ins., negligence and workmens compensation section 1973, mem. exec. bd., mem. state-city medicolegal com. 1979—91, chmn. 1983—86, mem. ct. appeals rules com. 1993—2002), Cavalier King Charles Spaniel Club (bd. dirs. 1993—2001, v.p. 1998—2001, chair ethics com. 1993—2002), Order of Coif. Home: 1978 Shadybrook Trail Charlottesville VA 22911 Office Phone: 410-823-2922. Personal E-mail: arlbob@earthlink.net.

HOCHBERG, FAITH S., US district court judge; BA summa cum laude, Tufts U., 1972; JD magna cum laude, Harvard U., 1975. Law clk. to Hon. Spottswood W. Robinson III U.S. Ct. Appeals (D.C. cir.), 1975-76; pvt. practice Washington, Boston, Roseland, N.J., 1977-83; asst. U.S. atty. Dist. N.J., Newark, 1983-87; ptnr. Cole, Schotz, Bernstein, Meisel & Forman, Hackensack, NJ, 1987-90; sr. dep. chief counsel Office Thrift Supervision, U.S. Treasury Dept., Jersey City; dep. asst. sec. law enforcement U.S. Treasury Dept., Washington; U.S. Atty. Dist. of N.J., 1994-99; judge U.S. Dist. Ct., 1999—. Office: US Courthouse and PO Bldg Newark NJ 07102

HOCHBERG, RONALD MARK, lawyer; b. Bklyn., Apr. 3, 1955; s. Fred S. and Adele (Gunsberg) H.; m. Sharon A. Berg, Aug. 11, 1985; children: Rachel, Sarah. BA, Rutgers U., 1977; JD, Bklyn. Law Sch., 1980; LLM, U. Miami, 1982. Assoc. Klatsky & Klatsky, Red Bank, N.J., 1980-81, Fuerst, Singer & Yusem, Somerville, N.J., 1982-83, Law Offices of Steven Schanker, Melville, N.Y., 1983-86; ptnr. Schanker & Hochberg, Attys., Huntington, N.Y., 1986—. Frequent lectr. on estate planning; instr. Adelphi U., 1984-93. Columnist Financial World Mag., 1993-97; contbr. articles to profl. publs. Mem. ABA, N.Y. State Bar Assn., Estate and Tax Planning Coun. Avocations: skiing, sailing. Office: Schanker & Hochberg 27 W Neck Rd PO Box 1905 Huntington NY 11743-2618 Office Phone: 631-424-5400. Business E-Mail: mark@schankerhochberg.com.

HOCHFELD, WILLIAM SIDNEY, construction executive, consultant; b. Bklyn., May 10, 1933; s. Louis and Sadie Hochfeld; m. Joyce Oster Hochfeld, Dec. 10, 1955; children: Elise Gayle, Marla Beth, Eric David. Cert., Rantoul (Ill.) Sch. Meteorology, 1952, Cert., 1955, Inst. Design and Constrn., Bklyn., 1956—57, Pohs Inst. Real Estate, Jamaica, NY, 1964—65. Lic. real estate sales NY. Exec. adminstr. Goodrich Bldg. Corp., N.Y.C., 1968—71; cons., owner's rep. 1410 Bedford Ave. Corp., Bklyn., 1971—75; v.p./constrn. analyst Nat. Westminster Bank USA, N.Y.C., 1975—85; constrn. cons. William Cons. Svcs., Oceanside, NY, 1985—92; archtl. cons. D.E. Leibowitz, Architects, N.Y.C., 1992—96; developers cons. Temple Beth Torah, Melville, NY, 1996—98; arch./cons. D.E. Leibowitz/ LiRo, N.Y.C., NY, 2000—. Mem. exec. com., bd. dirs. 1410 Bedford Ave. Corp., Bklyn., 1971—75; bd. dirs., mem. real estate com. Nat. WestBank USA, N.Y.C., 1975—85; bd. dirs., mem. exec. com. Temple Beth Torah, Melville, 1996—98. Author, editor Architects Prison Surveys & Investigations (Fin., 1995); author: (book of poetry) The Arc, Family History. S/Sgt. USAF, 1952—56, U.S., Japan, Korea. Named Ky. Col., 1967. Mem.: Mortgage Bankers Assn., Odd Fellows. Achievements include design of acousti-shell ceiling tile (w. Barry Oster); General & specific designs; interior design innovations & new products; worked on WTC, prisons (Riker's Island, Manhattan, Bronx), sch. cons. authority renovations, Sperry Rand Bldg; listed with father Louis & brother Stanley on Military Wall of Honor, East Meadow, LI, NY. Avocations: history, carpentry, genealogy, theater, puzzles.

HOCHFIELD, SYLVIA, arts editor; Assoc. editor ARTnews Mag., NYC, editor-at-large. Author: Beautiful Loot: Soviet Plunder of Europe's Art Treasures, 1995, Stolen Treasure: The Hunt for the World's Lost Masterpieces, 1995. Office: ARTnews Magazine 48 W 38th St New York NY 10018 Office Phone: 212-398-1690. Office Fax: 212-819-0394.

HOCHHALTER, GORDON RAY, advertising communications executive; b. Jerome, Idaho, Oct. 3, 1946; s. Ralph R. and Evelyn (McClellan) H. BA, Brigham Young U., 1972. Asst. promotion supr. Armstrong World Industries, Lancaster, Pa., 1972-74, promotion supr., 1974-76, sr. promotion supr., 1976; asst. advt. mgr. R.R. Donnelley & Sons Co., Chgo., 1976-79, asst. mgr. advt., sales promotion, 1979-81, advt. mgr., 1981-84, group mgr. mktg. com., creative devel., 1984-86, dir. mktg. com., creative dir., 1986-91; v.p., gen. mgr., creative dir. Mobium Corp. Design & Comm., Chgo., 1991-96, v.p., creative dir. design and conceptual devel., 1996-97; chief creative officer Mobium Creative Group, Chgo., 1998-99, mng. ptnr. creativity, strategy, technology, 2000—04; mng. ptnr. creativity strategy connectivity Mobium Creative Group Colle & McVoy, 2004—. V.p., creative cons. Caviale Fashions, NYC, 1987—; mem. internet adv. bd. B2B Works, bd. dirs., Design Industry Found. Fighting Aids (Chgo.), 2003-, Literacy Chgo. Bd. Dirs., 2000-02. Author: Strategies for a New Age of Bus. Comm., 1998, New Media in a New Age of Bus. Comm., 1998, Creative Leverage in a New Age of Bus. Comm., 1999, Hugging Your Customers in the Face of Bus. Comm. Change, 2002, Leveraging the Paradigm Shifts that are Changing Bus. Comm., 2001, Increasing Your Brandwidth in the Face of Bus. Comm. Change, 2002, Interactivating Your Messages in the Face of Bus. Comm. Change, 2002, others; monthly columnist Integrated Mktg. and Promotion Mag.; contbr. to profl. jour. and Libr. of Congress. Recipient London Internat. Advt. awards, 1987, One Show, Type Dirs. Club, Clio awrds, Art Dirs. Club awards, Andy awards, Addy awards, Internat. Advt. Festival AIGA awards, ProCom awards, Ace awards, Chgo. Tower awards, 1987-2005, Am. Bus. Media CEBA awards, 2002-03, Am. Bus. Press Objective and Results award, 1992, Cresta Internat. Advt. award, 1993, Sawyer award Bus. Mktg. Mag., 1993, Marcom High-Tech. Advt. award, 1994-96, Pinnacle award, 1994, Icon award Bus. Week Mag., 1994-95, 98-2000, Creativity, 2000. Mem. Am. Ctr. for Design, Am. Advt. Fedn., Chgo. Advt. Fedn., Bus. Mktg. Assn.(bd. dir. Chgo. chpt. 1998-2000), NY Art Dir. Club. E-mail: ghochhalter@mobium.com.

HOCHHAUSER, RICHARD MICHAEL, marketing professional; b. N.Y.C., Aug. 25, 1944; s. Stanley and Rita (Weingarten) H.; m. Carole Beth Wasserstein, Sept. 6, 1969; children: Jonathan, Jennifer. BS, Carnegie Mellon U., 1966; MBA, Columbia U., 1968. Systems engr. U.S. Dept. of Navy, Washington, 1968-70; v.p. market research Quayle Plesser & Co., N.Y.C., 1970-75; pres. research RMH Research, Inc. subs. Harte-Hanks Communications, Fort Lee, N.J., 1975-80; pres. mktg. services Harte Hanks Inc., Fairlawn, N.J., 1980-84, pres. direct mktg. N.Y.C., 1984-95, exec. v.p., 1996—, COO, 1998—, pres., 1999—. Faculty NYU. Mem. Direct Mktg. Assn. (exec. com., bd. dirs., chmn.). Avocations: horticulture, antique watches. Home: 1025 5th Ave # 9dn New York NY 10028-0134 Office: Harte Hanks Inc 55 Fifth Ave New York NY 10003

HOCHHEISER, MARILYN, writer, actress; b. LA, Sept. 3, 1935; d. Froman Jackson and Ann Nemerofsky; m. Sidney Ralph Hochheiser, Feb. 28, 1959 (dec. Sept. 1995); children: Glenda, Sharon, Steven. LVN, L.A. Trade Tech., 1959; cert. writing instr., Calif. Luth. Coll., Thousand Oaks, 1979. ordained to ministry, Glory House Ministries (Full Gospel), 1990. Instr. creative writing Simi Valley (Calif.) Adult Edn., 1976-89; editor poetry Ventura (Calif.) County Woman, 1985-87; minister Glory House Ministries, Simi Valley, 1992—; actress Am. Broadcasting Network, Hollywood, Calif., 1996—2002. Freelance writing cons., 1975—; prodr., moderator videos Inglewood, Calif., 1999-2000. Founder, moderator Simi Poetry Series, 1975-96; author: A View Through The Thicket, 1977; contbg. poet (anthology) So Luminois the Wildflowers, 2003; editor Verve mag., 1989-99; lyricist Call Me Eddie, 2001, You Touched My Life, 2005; author numerous poems; contbr. articles to mags. Recipient 1st place Ark. Benton County Sesquicentennial, 1986, 2d place Chgo. Libr. Poetry, 1993. Mem.: ASCAP, First Stage, Poets and Writers, Nat. League Am. Pen Women (Woman of Achievement award 1992—94, Disting. Svc. award 1994). Avocations: yoga, movies, plays, nature. Home: 5406 E Los Angeles Ave Simi Valley CA 93063

HOCHLERIN, DIANE, pediatrician, educator; b. N.Y.C., Feb. 4, 1942; d. William J. and Bertha Hochlerin. BS, U. City of N.Y., 1958; MD, Med. Coll. Pa., 1966. Diplomate Am. Bd. Pediats. Intern Albert Einstein Hosp., Phila., 1966-67; resident Phila. Gen. Hosp., 1967-69; attending pediatrician St. Luke's Roosevelt Hosp., N.Y.C., 1969—; clin. assoc. prof. pediats. Columbia U., N.Y.C., 1969—; asst. attending physician Cath. Med. Ctr., N.Y.C., 1993-99. Faculty advisor Adelphi U., N.Y.C., 1994. Fellow Am. Acad. Pediats.; mem. N.Y. State Med. Soc., County Med. Soc. Home: 305 E 86th St New York NY 10028

HOCHMAN, KENNETH GEORGE, lawyer; b. Mt. Vernon, N.Y., Nov. 12, 1947; s. Benjamin S. and Lillian (Gilbert) H.; m. Carol K. Hochman, Apr. 8, 1979; children: Brian Paul, Lisa Erin. BA, SUNY, Buffalo, 1969; JD, Columbia U., 1972. Bar: Ohio 1973, Fla. 1977, N.Y. 1979. Assoc. Jones Day, Cleve., 1972-79, ptnr., 1980—, chmn. wealth mgmt., ptnr. adminstn. Cleve. (Ohio) office. Trustee Katharine Kenyon Lippitt Found., Cleve., 1988, Kenridge Fund, Cleve., 1989, Bolton Found., Cleve., 1990, Elisha-Bolton Found., Cleve., 1993, Menteliore Found., 2005; bd. dirs. Parkwood Corp. Trustee United Way of Cleve., 2002—04. Harlan Fiske Stone scholar Columbia U., 1971, 72. Fellow Am. Coll. Trusts and Estate Counsel; mem. Phi Beta Kappa, Oakwood Club (Cleve.) (trustee 1997, officer 2000). Office: Jones Day North Point 901 Lakeside Ave E Cleveland OH 44114-1190 Business E-Mail: kghochman@jonesday.com.

HOCHMAN, M. SETH, neurologist; b. N.Y.C., Aug. 17, 1942; s. Max and Bessie Hochman: m. Zella Ostrower, Aug. 14, 1965; children: Michael Cory, Ian Kenneth, Kevin Daniel. BA, NYU, 1964; MD, U. Pa., 1968. Diplomate Am. Bd. Psychiatry and Neurology. Med. intern Albert Einstein Coll. Medicine, Bronx, N.Y., 1968-69, jr. resident neurology, 1969-70, sr. resident, chief resident, 1972-74; clin. assoc. USPHS, NIH Gerontology Rsch. Ctr., Balt., 1970-72; clin. investigator Phase III Pharm. Trials, 1996—; neurologist Miami (Fla.) Ctr. Neurol. Diseases, 1974—. Rsch. trainee dept. neurology USPHS, U. Pa., 1966; guest worker Lab. Neurochemistry, NIH, Nat Inst. Neurol. Disease and Blindness, Bethesda, Md., 1967; clin. asst. prof. neurology U. Miami Sch. Medicine, 1977-82, clin. assoc. prof., 1982-97, clin. prof., 1997—: vis. physician Balt. City Hosps., 1970-72; neurol. cons. Miami Dolphins Football Team, 1977-89; neurol. cons. Hurricane football team, Coral Gables, 1998—. Contbr. articles to profl. jours. Lt. comdr. USPHS, 1970-72. Fellow ACP, Am. Acad. Neurology, Royal Soc. Medicine; mem. Am. EEG Soc., Am. Epilepsy Soc., Am. Assn. Electromyography and Electrodiagnosis, Peripheral Neurol. Inst., N.Am. Spine Soc., Stroke Coun. Am. Heart Assn., Fla. Soc. Neurology, Phi Beta Kappa, Alpha Omega Alpha. Avocations: tennis, writing. Office: Miami Ctr Neurol Diseases 8600 SW 92nd St Ste 107 Miami FL 33156-7377

HOCHMAN, NAOMI LIPSON, special education educator, consultant; b. Bklyn. d. William Lipson and Tillie Silverstein-Beech Lipson; m. Elihu Hochman (div. Mar. 1978); children: Richard, Lisa, Lauren. BA cum laude, Bklyn. Coll., 1956; MA, William Paterson U., 1973. Cert. spl. edn. tchr., N.Y., learning disability cons., N.J. Tchr. Bd. Edn., N.Y.C., 1956-58, spl. edn. tchr. Wayne, N.J., 1968-73; instr. edn. William Paterson U., Wayne, N.J., 1973-74; learning disability cons. Wayne Bd. Edn., 1973-2000; cons. Assocs. Ednl. Consulting, 2000—. Mem. Thorough & Efficient Steering Com., N.J., 1975-80, Adv. Panel Spl. Edn., 1985-93; spkr. Literacy Vols. N.J. Passaic C.C., 1991—; bd. dirs. Wayne Counseling Youth, 1987-90. Mem. LWV, Wayne, 1965-73, Wayne Arts League, 1968-72. Recipient Honors Edn. award Bklyn. Coll., 1956, Anita McKeon award, 1998, N.J. Sch. Psychologists award, 2004. Mem. N.J. Edn. Assn., Profl. Svcs. Coun. N.J., N.J. Assn. Learning Cons. (pres. 1989-91). Avocations: tennis, dollhouses. Home: 201 Zeppi Ln West Orange NJ 07052-4130 Office: Assocs Ednl Cons PO Box 1829 Clifton NJ 07015-1829

HOCHMUTH, GEORGE J., horticultural educator; b. Balt., Mar. 31, 1953; married; 2 children. BS in Horticulture, U. Md., 1975; PhD in Plant Breeding and Plant Genetics, U. Wis., 1980. Staff Hochmuth Farms, Mardela Springs, Md., 1974; entomology technician U. Md. Vegetable Rsch. Farm, Salisbury, Md., 1972, summer vegetable rsch crew leader, 1973, 74; with USDA Vegetable Rsch. Lab., Beltsville, Md., 1974, 75; rsch. asst. dept. horticulture U. Wis., 1975-80; asst. prof. plant and soil scis. U. Mass., Amherst, 1980-84; asst. prof. and extension vegetable specialist, Vegetable Crops Dept. U. Fla., Gainesville, 1984-88, assoc. prof. and extension vegetable specialist, Horticultural Scis. Dept., 1988-93, prof. and extension vegetable specialist, Horticultural Scis. Dept., 1993—. Contbr. over 350 articles to scientific jours. Recipient Extension Publ. award So. Region Am. Soc. for Hort. Sci., 1989, 1994, Extension Edn. Aids award Am. Soc. for Hort. Sci., 1994, Extension Divsn. Excellence award, 1994, Outstanding Extension Educator award, 1995. Fellow: Am. Soc. Hort. Sci. Office: U Fla NFREC 155 Research Rd Quincy FL 32351-5677 Office Phone: 850-875-7116. E-mail: gjh@ifas.ufl.edu.

HOCHSCHILD, ADAM, commentator, writer, journalist; b. NYC, Oct. 5, 1942; s. Harold K. and Mary (Marquand) H.; m. Arlie Russell, June 26, 1965; children: David, Gabriel. AB cum laude (hon. nat. scholar 1960-61), Harvard U., 1963. Reporter San Francisco Chronicle, 1965-66; writer, editor Ramparts mag., 1967-68, 73-74; commentator Nat. Pub. Radio, 1982-83. Regents lectr. U. Calif.-Santa Cruz, 1987; lectr. Grad. Sch. Journalism U. Calif., Berkeley, 1992—; Fulbright lectr., India, 1997-98. Author: Half the Way Home: A Memoir of Father and Son, 1986 (Notable Book of Yr. ALA and N.Y. Times Book Rev.), The Mirror at Midnight: A South African Journey, 1990, The Unquiet Ghost: Russians Remember Stalin, 1994 (Notable Book of Yr. N.Y. Times Book Rev. and Libr. Jour., Madeline Dane Ross award Overseas Press Club Am., Gold medal Soc. Am. Travel Writers), Finding the Trapdoor: Essays, Portraits, Travels, 1997 (PEN/Spielvogel-Diamonstein award for the Art of the Essay), King Leopold's Ghost: A Story of Greed, Terror and Heroism in Colonial Africa, 1998 (finalist Nat. Book Critics Circle award, Mark Lynton History prize, Gold medal Calif. Book awards, Lionel Gelber prize, Duff Cooper prize), Bury the Chains: Prophets and Rebels in the Fight to Free an Empire's Slaves, 2005; freelance writer nat. mags.:, co-founder, editor: Mother Jones mag., 1974—81, commentator: Pub. Interest Radio, 1987—88, included in: Best American Essays, 2001. Recipient Cert. of Excellence, Overseas Press Club, NYC, 1981, Spann prize Eugene V. Debs Found., 1984, Thomas Storke Internat. Journalism award World Affairs Coun. No. Calif., 1987, award for mag. reporting Soc. Profl. Journalists, 1999. Mem. PEN, Nat. Writers Union, Nat. Book Critics Circle.

HOCHSCHILD, ROGER C., investment company executive; BA, Georgetown U.; MBA, Amos Tuck Sch. Bus. Sr. exec. MBNA Am. Bank, 1994—98; exec. v.p. diversified fin. services Morgan Stanley, 1988—2001, exec. v.p., chief adminstrv. officer, chief strategic officer, 2001—04, pres., COO, Discover Financial Services, 2004—. Office: Morgan Stanley 2500 Lake Cook Rd Riverwoods IL 60015 Office Phone: 224-405-0900. Office Fax: 224-405-2009.*

HOCHSTADT, HARRY, mathematician, educator; b. Vienna, Sept. 7, 1925; s. Samuel and Amalie (Dorn) H.; m. Pearl Schwartzberg, Mar. 29, 1953; children— Julia Phyllis, Jesse Frederick. B.Chem. Engring., Cooper Union, 1949; MS, N.Y. U., 1950, PhD, 1956. Rsch. engr. W. L. Maxson Corp., N.Y.C., 1951-57; mem. faculty Poly. U., 1957—; prof. math. Poly. Inst. Bklyn., 1961-92, head dept., 1963-90, dean arts and scis., 1974-76, dir. inst. rels., 1976-80, prof. emeritus, 1992—. Author: Special Functions of Mathematical Physics, 1961, Differential Equations, A Modern Approach, 1964, The Functions of Mathematical Physics, 1971, Integral Equations, 1973; Translation editor: Linear Equations of Mathematical Physics (Mikhlin), 1967; adv. editor: Wiley-Intersci. Series on Pure and Applied Mathematics. Served with inf. AUS, 1943-45. Decorated Bronze Star, Combat Inf. badge. Mem. Am. Math. Soc., Math. Assn. Am., Soc. Indsl. and Applied Math., Sigma Xi, Tau Beta Pi. Home: 126 Joralemon St Brooklyn NY 11201-4008 Personal E-mail: hochstadt@etaccess.net.

HOCHSTEDLER, LISA INEZ, educational association administrator; b. El Dorado Springs, Mo., Oct. 25, 1970; d. Gary Lee and Barbara Helene Messick; m. Bernard LeRoy Hochstedler, Aug. 16, 1989; children: Garren Machquade, Gunnar Levi. AS, Drury U., 2002; B of Psychology, Druru U., 2005. Child devel. assoc. Wash. Vol. West Ctrl. Mo. Cmty. Action Agy., Head Start, Stockton, Mo., 1996—98; substitute West Ctrl. Mo. Cmty. Action Agy., Head Start, Stockton, Mo., 1998—2000, co-tchr./driver, 2000—03; ctr. dir. Head Start West Ctrl. Mo. Cmty. Action Agy., El Dorado Springs, Mo., 2003—. Treas. Jerico Springs Picnic Com., Mo., 2003—; mem. Open Initiative Program. Christian. Avocations: cooking, sports, scrapbooks. Home: 307 East Logan Jerico Springs MO 64756 Office: El Dorado Springs Head Start 210 E Fields Blvd El Dorado Springs MO 64744 Office Phone: 417-876-5895. Personal E-mail: latergator647562000@yahoo.com.

HOCHSTER, HOWARD S., oncologist; b. Mpls., Dec. 30, 1953; MD, Yale U., 1980. Diplomate Am. Bd. Med. Oncology, Am. Bd. Hematology. Intern NYU-Bellevue Hosp., N.Y.C., 1980—81, resident, 1981—83; fellow NYU Med. Ctr., 1983—85; Fulbright fellow Jules Bordet Inst., Brussels, 1985—86; oncologist NYU Med. Ctr., N.Y.C., 1986—. Assoc. prof. medicine NYU Sch. Medicine, 1995—2002, prof., medicine, 2002—; dir., clin. trials NYU Cancer Inst., 2003—. Office: 160 E 32d St New York NY 10016

HOCHSTETLER, DONALD DEE, librarian; b. Kokomo, Ind., Nov. 2, 1946; s. Alvin and Lulua (Borntrager) H.; m. Jeanne Elizabeth Felton Sarber, Feb. 8, 1950; children: Grant Sarber, Katharine Sarber, Julia Sarber. BA in History, Ind. U., 1969, MA in History, 1972, MLS, 1984; PhD in History, Mich. State U., 1981. Teaching asst. history dept. Mich. State U., East Lansing, 1975-79, 79-80, instr. humanities dept., 1980, vis. asst. prof. history dept., 1982; instr. history dept. U. Mich., Flint, 1981-83; pub. svcs./govt. documents libr. Ctrl. Meth. Coll., Fayette, Mo., 1984-87; coord. pub. svcs. Mo. Western State Coll., St. Joseph, 1987-89; dir. libr. Marian Coll., Indpls., 1989—. Author: A Conflict of Traditions, 1992. With U.S. Army, 1969-71. Recipient Scholarships, West German Fulbright Commn., U. Tübingen, 1978-79. Mem. ALA, Medieval Acad. Am., Ind. Libr. Fedn. Mennonite. Office: Marian Coll Libr 3200 Cold Spring Rd Indianapolis IN 46222-1960

HOCHSTETTLER, THOMAS JOHN, academic administrator, historian; b. Bryan, Ohio, July 23, 1947; s. Hugh Donavon and Martha Lucille Taylor Hochstettler; m. Marcia Della Glas, Jan. 4, 1975; children: William Cameron Glas-Hochstettler, Taylor David Glas-Hochstettler, Benjamin Joseph Glas-Hochstettler. BA, Earlham Coll., 1969; MA, U. Mich., 1970, PhD, 1978. From lectr. history to sr. planning assoc. Stanford (Calif.) U., 1978—86, sr. planning assoc. and staff economist, 1986—87; lectr. history Bowdoin Coll., Brunswick, Maine, 1987—92, dean planning and gen. adminstrn., 1987—92, acting treas., 1990—92; dir. planning U. Houston Sys., 1992—96; assoc. provost Rice U., Houston, 1996—2002, adj. asst. prof. history, 1998—2000; vis. prof. history Internat. U. Bremen, Germany, 1999—2002, v.p. academic affairs, 1999—2004; pres. Lewis & Clark Coll., Portland, Oreg., 2004—. Mem. bd. trustees New Eng. Regional Computing Consortium, 1987—92; bd. dir. Oreg. Ind. Colls. Found. Moderator First Congl. Ch., Houston, 1992—94; bd. dirs. Midcoast Maine Red Cross, Brunswick, Maine, 1987—91, United Way of Midcoast Maine, Brunswick, 1987—92. Fellow, Woodrow Wilson Found., 1969—70, Horace H. Rackham Doctoral fellowship, U. Mich., 1973—74, Stanford U. Dept. of History, 1978—80; grantee, Deutsche Akademische Austauschdienst, 1975—76. Mem.: Rotary Club of Bremen Germany (youth svc. officer. mem., exec. com. 2000—04), Rotary Club Houston. Achievements include founding of International University Bremen, the first comprehensive private research university to be established on the European Continent following World War II. Office: Lewis & Clark College 0615 SW Palatine Hill Road Portland OR 97219-7899 Office Phone: 503-768-7680. Business E-Mail: pres@lclark.edu.

HOCHSTRASSER, DONALD LEE, cultural anthropologist, community health and public administration educator; b. Taylorsville, Ky., June 10, 1927; s. Emil John and Mary E. (Schad) H.; m. Marie Emlen, Apr. 9, 1960; 1 child, Letitia Cope; stepchildren: Eloise Q. Hatch, Laura A. Hatch. BA, U. Ky., 1952, MA, 1955; postgrad. (univ. fellow) Northwestern U., 1955-56; PhD in Anthropology, U. Oreg., 1963; MPH, U. Calif.-Berkeley, 1969. Rsch. asst. dept. rural sociology U. Ky., Lexington, 1954-55, instr. dept. anthropology, 1956-57, 1959-60, instr. dept. cmty. medicine, 1961-63, asst. prof., 1963-66, assoc. prof., 1966-73, prof., 1973-80, assoc. dir. Ctr. Devel. Change, 1970-73, prof. cmty. health Coll. Allied Health, prof. anthropology Coll. of Arts and Scis., prof. pub. adminstrn. Grad. Ctr. Pub. Adminstrn., 1980-93, prof. emeritus dept. health svcs., 1993—; tchg. fellow dept. anthropology U. Oreg., Eugene, 1957-58, instr., 1958-59, NSF rsch. fellow, 1960-61; USPHS spl. rsch. fellow Sch. Pub. Health, U. Calif.-Berkeley, 1968-69; chmn. state family planning rev. com. Ky. State Comprehensive Health Planning Coun., 1972-74; mem. state family planning task force Coun. Health Svcs., Ky. State Dept. Human Resources, 1974-78; cons., adv. numerous orgns.; vis. scholar dept. adminstrv. and social health scis. Sch. Pub. Health, U. Calif.-Berkeley, 1979; dir. Bluegrass Regional Birth Planning Coun., Inc., Lexington, 1978-81, Lexington Planned Parenthood, Inc., 1982-89; mem. adv. coun. Ctr. of Creative Living/Adult Care Program of Lexington-Fayette County Health Dept., 1989. Mem. Union of Concerned Scientists, Am. Farmland Trust, Wilderness Soc. Served with USN, 1946-47. Grantee pub. health, family planning, sickle cell anemia, Tb control and occupl. health-risk factors. Fellow Am. Anthrop. Assn., Soc. Applied Anthropology; mem. Soc. Med. Anthropology (founding), Am. Pub. Health Assn. (founding mem. population sect.), Assn. Tchrs. Preventive Medicine, AAAS, AAUP, Phi Beta Kappa, Sigma Xi, Alpha Kappa Delta, Delta Omega. Democrat. Clubs: Univ. Faculty, Alumni. Contbr. numerous articles to profl. publs. Home: 953 Holly Springs Dr Lexington KY 40504-3119 Office: Univ Ky Med Ctr 208A Annex 2 Lexington KY 40536-0001

HOCK, MORTON, entertainment advertising executive; b. NYC, June 24, 1929; s. Louis and Grace Dora (Solomon) H.; m. Anita Zagerman, Nov. 8, 1959; children— Jennifer, Jonathan With Blaine Thompson Co., N.Y.C.; acct. supr. David Merrick Productions, 1954-60; advt. mgr. Paramount Pictures, N.Y.C., 1960-63, v.p., 1967-71; dir. advt. United Artists Corp., N.Y.C., 1963-67; exec. v.p. Charles Schlaifer & Co., Inc., N.Y.C., 1972-83; exec. v.p. entertainment div. DDB Needham Worldwide, N.Y.C., 1983—; pres. Mort Hock Assocs., 2002—. Mgmt. supr. Universal Pictures Account, United Artists Theatres Account, Gramercy Pictures Account. Contbr. articles to Variety. Mem. adv. com., bd. dirs. Will Rogers Found., 1983— . Named Showman of Yr. Nat. Assn. Theatre Owners; recipient Nat. Screen Svc. award for best theatre trailer. Mem. Acad. Motion Picture Arts and Scis. (bd. dirs.), Motion Picture Pioneers. Clubs: Variety of N.Y. (pres. 1979-80); Friars (admission com.). Lodges: B'nai Brith (trustee cinema unit 1980—). Avocations: sports, music, reading, travel. Home: 400 E 56th St #29p New York NY 10022-4147

HOCK, RANDOLPH EDWARD, chemistry professor, writer; b. Chestertown, Md., Dec. 11, 1944; s. Arthur Sayers and Anna Smith Hock; m. Linda Eileen King, 1968 (div. 1978); m. Pamela Ann Pope, July 23, 1983; children: Matthew Evan, Stephen Arthur, Elizabeth Alice. BS, Salisbury State Coll., 1962—66; MLS, U. of Md., 1970—71; MA, Temple U., 1974—76, PhD, 1974—78. Chemistry tchr. Annapolis Sr. H.S., Annapolis, Md., 1962—66; chemistry libr. Massachsetts Inst. of Tech., Cambridge, Mass., 1971—73; data services libr. U. of Pennsylvania, Philadelphia, Pa., 1973—74; regional rep. DIALOG Info. Services, NYC, 1978—82, regional dir. Boston, 1982—92, Knight-Ridder Info. Services, Arlington, Va., 1992—96; prin. Online Strategies, Vienna, Va., 1996—. Author: Yahoo! to the Max, 2005, The Extreme Searcher's Guide to Web Search Engines, 1999 (About.com Search Engine Book of the Yr., 1999), 2d edit., 2001, The Extreme Searcher's Internet Handbook, 2004; author: (columnist) CyberSkeptic's Guide to Internet Research, 1997—. Troop com. mem., etc. Boy Scouts of Am., Vienna, Va., 1993—2005. Recipient Eagle Scout, Boy Scouts of Am., 1961. Mem.: Assn. of Ind. Info. Professionals, Am. Soc. for Info. Sci. and Tech (bd. dirs. 1989—91). Democrat. Avocation: genealogy. Home: 9919 Corsica St Vienna VA 22181 Office: Online Strategies 9919 Corsica St Vienna VA 22181 Office Phone: 703-242-6078. Personal E-mail: ran@onstrat.com. E-mail: ran@onstrat.com.

HOCKEIMER, HENRY ERIC, engineering executive; b. Winzig, Germany, Apr. 3, 1920; came to U.S., 1946, naturalized, 1951; s. Erich and Gertrude (Masur) H.; m. Margaret Feeny, May 26, 1956; children: Ellen Patricia, Henry Eric. Student, RCA Insts., 1946—47; electronics and bus. mgmt., NYU, 1948—51. With Philco-Ford Corp., Phila., 1947—, gen. mgr. communications and tech. services div., 1962-63, corp. v.p., 1963-72; v.p., gen. mgr. refrigeration products div. Connorsville, Ind., 1972-75; pres. Ford Aerospace & Communications Corp., Dearborn, Mich., 1975-85; v.p. Ford Motor Co., 1981-85; cons. USIA, Washington, 1985, dep. dir. TV and film service, 1986-87, asst. dir., 1987-88, assoc. dir. for mgmt., 1988-91, cons., 1991—; commr. RIAS, 1991—. Mem. Engring. Soc. Detroit, Smithsonian, Univ. Club Washington, Washington Arts Soc. Personal E-mail: hhockeimer@aol.com.

HOCKENBERG, HARLAN DAVID, lawyer; b. Des Moines, July 1, 1927; s. Leonard C. and Estyre M. (Zalk) H.; m. Dorothy A. Arkin, June 3, 1953; children: Marni Lynn, Thomas Leonard, Edward Arkin. BA, U. Iowa, 1949, JD, 1952. Bar: Iowa 1952. Assoc. Abramson & Myers, Des Moines, 1952-58, Abramson, Myers & Hockenberg, Des Moines, 1958-64; sr. ptnr. Davis, Hockenberg, Wine, Brown, Koehn & Shors, Des Moines, 1964-95; shareholder, dir. Sullivan & Ward, P.C., Des Moines, 1995—. Bd. dirs. West Des Moines State Bank, Rep. Jewish Coalition, Smoother Sailing Found. Mem. bd. editors U. Iowa Law Review. Mem. Citizens for Ind. Cts., Internat. Rels. and Nat. Security Adv. Coun., Rep. Nat. Com., 1978; chmn. Coun. Jewish Fedns., Small Cities Com., 1970-71; mem. exec. com. Am. Israel Pub. Affairs Com.; pres. Wilkie House, Inc., Des Moines, 1965-66, Des Moines Jewish Welfare Fedn., 1973-74; mem. Presdl. Commn. on White House Fellowships, 1988-92; mem. Holocaust Meml. Coun., 2003—. With USNR, 1945-46. Mem. Iowa State Bar Assn. (past chair professionalism com.), Des Moines C. of C. (pres. 1986, chmn. bur. econ. devel. 1979, 80, bd. dirs. 1986), Des Moines Club, Pioneer Club, Delta Sigma Rho, Omicron Delta Kappa, Phi Epsilon Pi Office: Sullivan & Ward PC 801 Grand Ave Ste 3500 Des Moines IA 50309-8005 Office Phone: 515-247-4721. Business E-Mail: bhockenberg@sullivan-ward.com.

HOCKENBERRY, E'RENA, music educator; b. Tilden, Ill., Oct. 28, 1927; d. Clarence and Frances Terry, Cecil B. and Mrs. Hatch; m. Charles E. Hockenberry, Mar. 17, 1946; children: Coreen Hockenberry Grogan, Ted D. BS, cert., Colo. State Coll., 1946; MA, U. No. Colo., 1972. Elem. educator Greeley (Colo.) Pub. Sch.; music educator Jeff County Pub. Sch., Colo. Mem.: Colo. Music Educators (past historian, past pres.). Democrat. Avocation: golf. Home: 6527 W 34th Ave Wheat Ridge CO 80033

HOCKER, JOHN ROBERT, non-profit foundation executive; b. Elwood, Ind., Aug. 11, 1935; s. Joseph Eugene and Helen Margaret (Benedict) H.; m. Barbara Siemers, Aug. 11, 1962; children: Constance Lynn, Guy Albert. BS in Engring., U.S. Mil. Acad., 1957; MS in Applied Math., U. Freiburg, Germany, 1965; M of Mil. Arts and Sci., U.S. Army Command and Gen. Staff Coll., 1971; student, French War Coll., Paris, 1976-78. Commd. 2d lt. U.S. Army, 1957, advanced through ranks to Col., 1978, co-comdr. 1st Calvary divsn., 1966-67; assoc. prof. dept. math. U.S. Mil. Acad., West Point, NY, 1967-70; insp. Infantry Airborne/Spl Units for Mil Equipment Delivery Team, Phnom Penh, Cambodia, 1971-72; comdr. 2d bn. 325th airborne infantry 82d airborne divsn. U.S. Army, Fort Bragg, NC, 1972-75; joint exercise dir. Orgn. of Joint Chief of Staff, Washington, 1975-76; policy dir. Hdqrs. U.S. European Command, Stuttgart, Germany, 1978-80; spl. asst. to Supreme Allied Comdr. Supreme Hdqrs. Allied Powers Europe, Belgium, 1980-82; chief of staff Def. Mobilization Systems Planning Activity, Washington, 1982-84; ret. U.S. Army, 1984; dir. bus. devel. Info. Systems Group Martin Marietta, Bethesda, Md., 1984-91, dir. tech. ops., 1991-95; dir. engring. edn. Lockheed Martin Corp., 1995; exec. dir. Nat. Sci. and Tech. Medals Found., Washington, 1995—. Decorated Bronze Star, Def. Superior Svc. Medal; recipient Sec. of Army Outstanding Civil Svc. medal, 2002; Olmsted Found. scholar, 1963. Mem. Assn. Fund Raising Profls., Internat. Congress of Dist. Awards. Avocations: travel, golf. Home: 6112 Goldtree Way Bethesda MD 20817-5839 Office: Nat Sci and Tech Medals Found 1818 N St NW Ste 600 Washington DC 20036-2476 E-mail: nstmf@asee.org.

HOCKETT, BETTY MAY, writer, educator; b. Caldwell, Idaho, Nov. 13, 1930; d. Edgar Lincoln Street and Leela Bertha Pearson; m. Milo Gene Hockett, Sept. 7, 1951. BA, George Fox Coll., 1952. Christian edn. curriculum planner Evang. Friends Internat., Newberg, Oreg., 1972—84; sec. Evan. Friends Christian Edn. Commn., 1973—82; freelance writer, 1968—; writing tchr. Chemeketa C.C., McMinnville, Oreg., 1996—2003, Monmouth, Oreg., 2003—05. Author: (book) From Here to There and Back Again, 1984, What Will Tomorrow Bring?, 1985, Down A Winding Road, 1985, Happiness Under the Indian Trees, 1986, Catching Their Talk In A Box, 1987, Mud On Their Wheels, 1988, Whistling Bombs and Bumpy Trains, 1989, Keeping Them All in Stitches, 1990, No Time Out, 1991, Outside Doctor on Call, 1992, More Than Empty Dreams, 1988, Eight of a Kind, 1988, Looking Through the Window, 1995 (noteworthy book in C.S. Lewis medal competition, 1996), Come What May, 1998. Vol. Pub. Libr., Newberg; mem. George Fox U. Alumni Bd., 2004—. Finalist Helen Kelts award for writer of the yr., Ore. Christian Writers, 1991; recipient Christian Svc. award, George Fox U. Alumni Assn., 2003, Yammy award for video documentary, Liberty Cable Television, 1984. Mem.: Oregon Christian Writers. Republican. Evang. Friends. Avocation: reading. Home: 1301 E Fulton #413 Newberg OR 97132

HOCKEY, CHRISTOPHER LAWRENCE, academic administrator; b. Syracuse, N.Y., May 7, 1979; s. Sharlene Marie and Dennis Charles Spina (Stepfather). BSc, SUNY, Oswego, N.Y., 2002; MSc, Syracuse (N.Y.) U., 2005. V.p. Student Assn. SUNY, Oswego, 2001—02; assoc. mgr. Discovery Channel Stores, Victor, NY, 2002; resident dir. Utica (N.Y.) Coll., 2002—, coord. orientation staff, 2002—04, instr. first yr. seminar, 2004—. Adv. Alpha Omega Phi, Utica, 2004—; presenter in field. Named Senator of the Yr., SUNY Oswego Student Assn., 2002; Teachers and Adminstr. scholarship, Baldwinsville Ctrl. Sch. Dist., 1997. Mem.: Nat. Orientation Dirs. Assn., Nat. Assn. Student Pers. Administrs., Am. Coll. Pers. Assn., Coll. Student Pers. Assn. N.Y. State, Inc., Omicron Delta Kappa. Democrat. Methodist. Avocations: reading, camping, weightlifting. Home and Office: Utica College 1600 Burrstone Rd Utica NY 13502 Office Phone: 315-792-3285. Home Fax: 315-792-3715; Office Fax: 315-792-3715. Personal E-mail: chockey@utica.edu.

HOCKFIELD, SUSAN, academic administrator, medical educator; d. Thomas and Elizabeth Byrne; m. Thomas Byrne; 1 child, Elizabeth Hockfield Byrne. BA in Biology, U Rochester, 1973; PhD in Anatomy & Neuroscience, Georgetown U, 1979; MA (hon.), Yale U, 1994. NIH Post-Doc Fellow Dept. of Anatomy and Neuroscience Program, U of Calif., San Francisco, 1979—80; jr. staff investigator Cold Spring Harbor Lab, Cold Spring Harbor, NY, 1980—82, sr. staff investigator, 1982—85; asst. prof. Sect. of Neurobiology Yale U Sch. of Med., New Haven, 1985—89, assoc. prof. (term) Sect. of Neurobiology, 1989—91, assoc. prof. (tenure) Sect. of Neurobiology, 1991—94, prof. Dept. of Neurobiology, 1994—2004; dean, Grad. Sch. of Arts and Sci. Yale U., 1998—2002, provost, 2003—04; pres. MIT, Cambridge, 2004—. Mem. Nat. Adv. Neurological Disorders and Stroke Council (NIH), 2002—; mem. at large AAAS, Sect. on Neuroscience, 2000—04; bd. trustees Cold Spring Harbor Lab., Cold Spring Harbor, NY, 1998—; Brain Cancer Adv. Panel James S. McDonnell Found., 1997—2002; bd. dir. Haskins Lab., 1988—2002; U Adv. Council Yale-New Haven Tchrs. Inst., 1998—2002; elected mem. of the bd. Council of Grad. Sch., 2002; neuroscience adv. bd. Astra Pharmaceuticals, 1997—99; program dir. Summer Neurobiology Program Cold Spring Harbor Lab., Cold Harbor Springs, NY, 1985—97; councilor Soc. for Neuroscience, 1992—96; sci. adv. bd. Hereditary Disease Found., 1991—95, 1996—2000; mem. NIH Study Section

(Visual Sci. B), 1988—92; chair Gordon Plasticity, 1997; participant, mem. of bd. several orgns., studies and soc. Contbr. articles, in numerous profl. jours., chapters to books co-authored chapters in numerous books, book Molecular Probes of the Nervous System: Selected Methods for Antibodies and Nucleai Acid Probes Cold Spring Harbor Lab. Press, 1993. Recipient PHS Post-doctoral Rsch. Award, NIH, 1980, Grass Traveling Sci. Award, Soc. for Neuroscience, 1987, Charles Judson Herrick Award, Am. Assoc. of Anatomists, 1987, William Edward Gilbert Prof. of Neurobiology, Yale U., 2001; grantee Esther A. and Joseph Klingenstein Fellowship in the Neurosciences, NSF, NIH, 1985. Fellow: American Acad. Arts & Scis. (elected); mem.: FASEB, Soc. for Devel., Am Assn. for Advancement of Sci. (assoc.; mem.-at-large, Section on Neuroscience 2000—), Am. Assoc. of Anatomists (Charles Judson Herrick Award 1987), Soc. for Neuroscience (Grass Traveling Scientist 1987). Achievements include three patents in field of neuroscience. Office: Off of Pres Rm 3-208 MIT 77 Massachusetts Ave Cambridge MA 02139-4307*

HOCKIN, ROBERT J., management consultant, educator; BA in Psychology and History, Moravian Coll., Bethlehem, Pa.; MA in Sociology, PhD, U. Minn., Mpls.; cert. in Bus. Admnstrn., Wharton Sch. Bus., Phila. Cert. mktg. exec. Sales and Mktg. Execs. Internat., mgmt. cons. Inst. Mgmt. Cons., healthcare profl. Acad. Managed Healthcare. Dir. and practice leader nat. accounts Blue Cross Blue Shield of Minn., Inc., 1995—97; v.p. ops. and bus. devel. Stratis Health, 1997—2000; key account consulting prin. pub. sector IBM Global Svcs., 2001—02; v.p. strategic sales and bus. devel. JZM Rsch., Inc., 2004—. Adj. faculty sch. bus. Capella Learning, 1994—; assoc. prof. sch. bus. Kaplan Coll.; adv. bd. exec. coaching program Corp. Coach U. Internat.; nat. examiner Malcom Baldridge Nat. Quality Awards; sr. examiner and judge Minn. Quality Awards; editl. rev. bd. Acad. Entrepreneurship Jour.; mentor Carlson Sch. Mgmt. U. Minn.; cons. and mgmt. course designer; presenter in field. Trainer Minn. Literacy Coun., bd. dir., v.p. orgnl. devel. Mem.: Am. Soc. Quality (editl. rev. bds.), Inst. Mgmt. Cons. (v.p. pub. rels.), Sales and Mktg. Execs. Internat., Am. Mktg. Assn. (v.p. programming). Address: 3712 Sparrow Pond Ln Raleigh NC 27606

HOCKING, JOE C., JR., music educator; b. Texas City, Tex., Nov. 15, 1956; s. Joe C. Hocking, Sr. and Ruby Joyce Hocking; m. Sara Lynn Seglem, Mar. 4, 1989; children: Elizabeth Joyce, Ian Doyle. MusB in Edn., U. Ctrl. Okla., 1982; MusM in Choral Conducting, U. Okla., 1988, MusD in Choral Conducting, 1995. Choral dir. Midwest City (Okla.) H.S., 1982—86, Conrad Mid. Sch., Wilmington, Del., 1991—98; tchr. John Dickinson H.S., Wilmington, 1998—2002, 2003—, Moore (Okla.) H.S., 2002—03. Grantee, MBNA Found., 2004—05; Michael Schaffer scholarship, U. Okla., 1987, 1989. Mem.: Brandywine Hundred Choral Soc. (co-founder 1997, condr. 1997—2000), Music Educators Nat. Conf., Am. Choral Dirs. Assn. (chmn. mid.sch. and jr. H.S. choirs 1995—97, pres. 1997—99). Baptist. Home: 1215 New Street Wilmington DE 19808 Office: John Dickinson High School 1801 Milltown Road Wilmington DE 19808 Office Phone: 302-992-5500. Home Fax: 302-992-5506; Office Fax: 302-992-5506. Personal E-mail: joe.hocking@redclay.k12.de.us.

HOCKLESS, MARY FONTENOT, educational consultant; b. New Iberia, La., July 23, 1954; d. Gill B. and Thelma Fontenot; m. Jospeh W. Hockless; children: Kellie, Amie, Marcus. BA in Speech Pathology, U. La., 1978, EdM, 1984, postgrad., 2003—. Cert. speech pathology, early intervention guidance & counseling K-12, family svc. coord. Speech therapist Iberia Sch. Dist., New Iberia, La., 1977, presch. tchr., early interventionist; coord. La. Dept. Edn., 1992, regional coord., 1992—2000; rsch. U. Ark., Little Rock, 2000—03; pvt. practice First Steps Referral and Cons. LLC, New Iberia, 2003—. Contbr. articles to profl. jours.; author: (manual) Challenging Behavior Support, 2002, Perfect Rhythm, 2003. Named Tchr. of Yr., Jaycees, New Iberia, 1985, Outstanding Alumni, U. Southwestern La., 2003. Home: PO Box 12213 New Iberia LA 70562 Office: First Steps Referral & Cons LLC 810 Center St New Iberia LA 70560

HOCKMAN, LORRAINE FRANCES, music educator; d. Murrell Francis and Eileen Lorraine (Barnes) Stevens; m. Arthur Francis Hockman, May 13, 1978; children: Shannon, Christina, Hockman. BA in Piano, Bob Jones U., 1972. Pianist, singer, sec. Life Action Revival Ministries, Buchanan, Mich., 1972—76; tchr. piano, organist Thomas Road Bapt. Ch. and Sch., Lynchburg, Va., 1976—79; pianist, singer Light Ministries, Redding, Calif., 1979—81; asst. pianist South Sheridan Bapt. Ch., Denver, 1982—95; pvt. piano tchr. Denver, 1982—; pianist Colo. Advs. for the Home Sch. Arts, Colo. Homeschool Arts, Denver, 1997—2002, Woodside Bapt. Ch. and Sch., Denver, 1995—2002. Judge Rocky Mt. Accordian Soc., Denver, 1972, 95, 99. Author: (albums) We Will Serve the Lord - Wilds, 2000. Singer Liberty Singers Rep. Conv., 1980; leader caucus, del. Rep. Party, Denver, 1985—92. Mem.: Heart of Am. Accordian Soc., Rocky Mountain Accordian Soc. (various awards), Nat. Guild Piano Tchrs. (chmn. ctr. 1989—2005, tchr. 1982—2005, judge 1988—2005). Republican. Baptist. Avocations: music, sewing, board games. Home: 5230 Eagle St Denver CO 80239 Office Phone: 303-916-0242. Personal E-mail: artman-5@juno.com.

HOCKNEY, DAVID, artist; b. Bradford, Yorkshire, Eng., July 9, 1937; s. Kenneth and Laura Hockney. Student, Bradford Coll. Art, 1953—57, Royal Coll. Art, London, 1959—62, hon. degree, 1992; D (hon.), U. Aberdeen, 1988. Lectr. U. Iowa, 1964, U. Colo., 1965, U. Calif., Berkeley, 1967, UCLA, 1966, hon. chair of drawing, 1980. One-man shows include Kasmin Gallery, 1963-89, Mus. Modern Art, N.Y.C., 1964, 68, Stedelijk Mus., Amsterdam, Netherlands, 1966, Whitechapel Gallery, London, 1970, Andre Emmerich Gallery, N.Y.C., 1972-96, Musee des Arts Decoratifs, Paris, 1974, Museo Tamayo, Mexico City, 1984, LA Louver, Calif., 1986, 89, 95, 98, 05, Nishimura Gallery, Tokyo, 1986, 89, 90, 94, Met. Mus. Art, 1988, L.A. County Mus. Art, 1988, 96, Tate Gallery, London, 1988, 92, Royal Acad. Arts, London, 1995, 99, Hamburger Kunsthalle, 1995, Nat. Mus. Am. Art, Washington, 1997, 98, Mus. Ludwig, Cologne, 1997, MFA, Boston, 1998, Centre Georges Pompidou, Paris, 1999, Musee Picasso, Paris, 1999, Mus. Contemparty Art, L.A., 2001, Kunst-Und Ausstellung Halle, Bonn, 2001, La. Mus Mod. Art, Copenhagen, 2001, Annely Juda Fine Art, London, 1997, 99, 2003, Richard Gray Gallery, NY, 1992, 99, 02, 04, Nat. Portrait Gallery, London, 2003, Whitney Biennial, NY, 2004, others; designer: Rake's Progress, Glyndebourne, Eng., 1975; sets for Magic Flute, Glyndebourne, 1978, Parade Triple Bill, Stravinsky Triple Bill, Met. Opera House, 1980-81, Tristan und Isolde, Los Angeles Music Ctr. Opera, 1987; Turandot, Lyric Opera, Chgo., 1992—, San Francisco Opera, 1993, Die Frau Ohne Schatten, Covent Garden, London, 1992, L.A. Music Ctr.Opera, 1993; author: David Hockney by David Hockney, 1976, David Hockney: Travels with Pen, Pencil and Ink, 1978, Paper Pools, 1980, David Hockney Photographs, 1982, Cameraworks, 1983, David Hockney: A Retrospective, 1988, Hockney Paints the Stage, 1983, That's the Way I See It, 1993, David Hockney's Dog Days, 1998, Hockney on Art, 1999, Secret Knowledge: Rediscovering the Lost Techniques of the Old Masters, 2001, Hockney's Portraits and People, 2003, Hockney's Pictures, 2004; illustrator: Six Fairy Tales of the Brothers Grimm, 1969, The Blue Guitar, 1977, Hockney's Alphabet, 1991. Recipient Guinness award and 1st prize for etching, 1961, Gold medal Royal Coll. Art, 1962, Graphic prize Paris Biennale, 1963, 1st prize 8th Internat. Exhbn. Drawings Lugano, Italy, 1964, 1st prize John Moores Exhbn. Liverpool, Eng., 1967, German award of Excellence 1983, 1st prize Internat. Ctr. of Photography, N.Y., 1985, Kodak photography book award for Cameraworks, 1984, Praemium Imperiale Japan Art Assn., 1989, 5th Ann. Gov. Calif. Visual Arts award, 1994, Charles Wollaston award Royal Acad. Arts London, 1999; named Companion of Honour, Her Majesty, the Queen of Eng., 1997. Office: 7508 Santa Monica Blvd Los Angeles CA 90046-6407

HOCKNEY, DEAN WESLEY, editor, writer; b. Kokomo, Ind., Sept. 11, 1967; s. Daniel William and Sherri Lynne Hockney. Notary pub. Ind., 2001. Assoc. editor Indy Sports Mag., Indpls., 1988—89; fuels journeyman USAF, 1990, advance through grades to staff sgt., ret., 1999; sports editor Kokomo (Ind.)Perspective, 1999—2001; mng. editor Kokomo (Ind.) Perspective, 2001—. Author: Kats with a K: The 100 Year History of Kokomo Wildkat Boys Basketball. Ofcl. track and field judge Ind. H.S. Athletic Assn., 1999—2002; sound dir. Lamplighter Christian Dinner Theater, Kokomo, 2000—03; ofcl. scorer Kokomo H.S., 2001—02; key bank achieve anything award judge United Way, Kokomo, 2001—03; football coach Police Athletic League, Kokomo, 2001—03; cmty. rels. com. YMCA, Kokomo, 2002—03; founder, pres. Howard County Sports Hall of Fame, Kokomo, 2002—03; baseball coach Kokomo Parents Babe Ruth League, 2002—03; founding dir. Kokomo Derby of the All-American Soap Box Derby, 2003—04; minor league dir. Southside Youth Baseball League, Kokomo, 1988—90; bd. dirs. Kokomo 16-18 Baseball League, 2000—02; v.p. UCT Youth Baseball League, Kokomo, 2001—02. Decorated NATO medal, Southwest Asia Svc. medal with campaign star, Nat. Def. medal, Achievement medal with 3 Oak Leaf Clusters USAF, Armed Forces Svc. medal, Armed Forces Expeditionary medal; named one of Top 10 People of Yr. in Howard County, Kokomo Perspective, 2001, 2003. Mem.: Am. Legion (baseball mgr. 2000—03), Kiwanis (sec. 2001—03, chairperson Howard County girls basketball banquet 2002—03, del. 2003, sgt. at arms 2003, pres. 2004—, Perfect Attendance 2001-2002, 2002-2003), FOP (assoc.). Avocations: coaching, travel. Home: PO Box 1285 Kokomo IN 46903-1285 Office: Kokomo Perspective 209 N Main St Kokomo IN 46901 Office Phone: 765-452-0055.

HOCUTT, MAX OLIVER, retired philosophy educator; b. Berry, Ala., July 3, 1936; s. Harry Juell and Edith Pauline (Skelton) H.; m. Dorothy Lois Etheredge, Nov. 22, 1957; children: James Max, Cassandra Diane. BA in Philosophy with honors, Tulane U., 1957, MA, 1958; PhD, Yale U., 1960. Instr. U. South Fla., Tampa, 1960-62, asst. prof., chmn. dept. philosophy, 1962-65; assoc. prof. U. Ala., 1965-70, prof., 1970—2001, chmn. dept., 1978-91; ret., 2001. Vis. fellow Princeton U., 1979, St. Andrews U., 1987; bd. dirs. ACLU, University, 1969. Author: The Elements of Logical Analysis and Inference, 1979, First Philosophy, 1980, Grounded Ethics, 2000; editor: Behavior and Philosophy, 1992-96; contbr. articles to profl. jours. Honors scholar, Tulane U., 1957, So. Fellowships Career Tchg. fellow, Yale U., 1960. Mem. Ala. Philos. Soc. (pres. 1967), So. Soc. Philosophy and Psychology, Am. Philos. Assn., Phi Beta Kappa. Home: 5510 Golden Pond Ave Northport AL 35473-1529 Office: U Ala Dept Philosophy Tuscaloosa AL 35487-0001

HODAKIEVIC, JAMES JOSEPH, retired secondary education educator; b. Cleve., Aug. 21, 1947; s. Joseph Edward and Genevieve Sophie (Chodakowski) H.; m. Johanna Rita Dolphin, Feb. 15, 1969; children: Peter James, Bethany Nanette. BS in Edn., Bowling Green State U., 1969, MEd, 1972; postgrad., Kent State U., 1980-82. Cert. edn., Ohio. Driver edn. tchr. Lakota Local Schs., Kansas, Ohio, 1969; tchr., coach Western Res. HS, Warren, Ohio, 1969-71; instr., football coach Bowling Green (Ohio) State U., 1971-72; tchr., head football coach West Holmes HS, Millersburg, Ohio, 1972-75, Defiance (Ohio) HS, 1975—79; tchr. Bedford (Ohio) HS, 1979—2004, head football coach, 1982—2004; atheletic dir. Archbishop Hoban HS, Akron, 2004—. Guest lectr. Bowling Green State U. Athletics, 1975-77; staff dir. Ozzie Newsome Football Camp, Cleve., 1987, Tim Manoa Sports Performance Clin., 2004; spkr. Youngstown (Ohio) State U. Athletics, 1994; staff Ohio State Summer Football Camp, 1997, Pa. State Summer Football Camp, 1997, 2000. Recipient Dr. Lee Tressel Meml. Coaching award Cleve. Touchdown Club, 1994; named Coach of Yr., Coshocton (Ohio) Tribune, 1974, Greater Cleve. Conf., 1993, Lake Erie League Erie Divsn., 1998, 99, 2001, NFL HS Coach of the Yr. finalist, 2000, Bedford Schs. Atheletic Hall of Fame, 2005 Mem. Nat. Fedn. Interscholastic Coach, Am. Football Coaches Assn. (assoc., spkr. Wis. State, 2004), Ohio HS Football Coaches Assn., Greater Cleve. Football Coaches Assn. (pres., league dir., Golden Deeds award 1997). Avocation: golf. Home: 907 School Ave Cuyahoga Falls OH 44221-4113 Office: Archbishop Hoban HS One Holy Cross Blvd Akron OH 44306

HODAL, MELANIE, public relations executive; Pres., CEO Dennis Davidson Assocs., Inc., L.A. Office: Dennis Davidson Assoc Inc 8491 W Sunset Blvd #470 West Hollywood CA 90069-1911

HODAN, PATRICK JOHN, lawyer; b. San Francisco, Aug. 8, 1962; s. Theodore and Mary Francis (Vidas) H.; m. Kerry Hickey, Aug. 25, 1990; children: Patrick Jr., Bridget, Colleen. B of Bus. Adminstrn. summa cum laude, Georgetown U., 1985; JD cum laude, Marquette U., 1990. Bar: Wis. 1990, U.S. Dist. Ct. (ea. and we. dists.) Wis. 1990. Ptnr. Reinhart Boerner Van Deuren, Milw., 1990—. Pub. spl. prosecutor Milw. County Dist. Atty.'s Office, 1995. Mem. Wis. Acad. Trial Lawyers, Milw. Bar Assn. Office: Reinhart Boerner Van Deuren Norris & Rieselbach 1000 N Water St Ste 2100 Milwaukee WI 53202-3197 Office Phone: 414-298-8333. E-mail: phodan@reinhartlaw.com.

HODARA, SUSAN MINA, writer; b. Washington, Nov. 7, 1953; d. Bernard and Selma Wenesky Rubin; m. Paul Sterling Hodara, Oct. 9, 1983; children: Sofie Elana, Ariel Marissa. BFA, Harvard U., 1975; MFA, Columbia U., 1979. Editor in chief Big Apple Parent, N.Y.C., 1991—2000; consulting editor Westchester Parent, No. White Plains, NY, 2000—; freelance writer. Tchr. Young Writers Workshop, Chappaqua, NY, 1997—, Gilda's Club, White Plains, NY, 2002—03, No. Westchester Ctr. for the Arts, Mt. Kisco, NY, 2003—04; pub. reader Hudson Valley Writers Ctr., Sleepy Hollow, NY, 2001, Borders Books, N.Y.C., 2005. Author: Animation: The Art and The Industry, 1984; contbr. articles to profl. jours. and mags. Recipient Editl. Excellence award, Parenting Publs. Am., 1993. Home and Office: 204 Croton Ave Mount Kisco NY 10549 Office Phone: 914-666-6704. E-mail: hodara@earthlink.net.

HODEL, MARY ANNE, library director; b. St. Louis, Aug. 12; d. William George and Florence Marie (Betz) H.; children: Courtney Hodel Denham, Christian Hodel Denham. BA, U. Wis., 1972; MLS, Catholic U., 1973. Project libr. TRACOR-JITCO, Rockville, Md., 1973-74; from project mgr. to database mgr. Nat. Resources Libr. U.S. Dept. of Interior, Washington, 1974-77; cataloger USAF Base Libr., Ramstein, Germany, 1977-79; from project libr. to automation libr. Law Libr. Georgetown U., Washington, 1984-85, automation libr. Law Libr., 1985-91; chief state libr. resource ctr. Enoch Pratt Free Libr., Balt., 1991-95; dir. Ann Arbor (Mich.) Dist. Libr., 1995—2001, Orange County (Fla.) Libr. System, 2002—. Network coord. Coun. Md. Librs., 1991-95; mem. Sailor Implementation group, 1992-95, grants and devel. task force liaison, 1993-95; v.p. Mich. Libr. Consortium, 1998-99, bd. pres., 1999-2000, bd. dirs. Mem. exec. com. Ann Arbor Hands On Mus., 1998—2001. Recipient Libr. of Yr. award Libr. Jour., 1997-98. Mem.: ILAMA, ALA, ALA (local arrangements chmn. ann. conf. Orlando 2004, Libr. of Yr. award 1997—98), Law Librs. Soc. Washington (pres. acad. spl. interest sect. 1988—89, program coord. 1989, chair innovative interfaces users workshop 1989, rec. sec. 1989—91, program coord. 1990), Md. Libr. Assn. (del. to ALA legis. day 1992, conf. planning com. 1993, co-chair tech. interest group 1994, conf. planning com. 1994, program coord. 1994), Md. Assn. Profl. Libr. Adminstrs., Pub. Libr. Assn. (sys. sect. v.p./pres.-elect 1994—95, pres. 1995—, chair Leonard Wertheimer award com. 2000—01), Mich. Libr. Consortium (v.p. 1999, pres. 1999—2000), Am. Assn. Law Librs. (program coord. ann. meeting 1987, chair innovative interfaces users com. 1988—89, editor innovative interfaces users com. 1989), Mich. Libr. Assn. (chair pub. libr. divsn. 2001—). Avocations: travel, photography. Home: 9152 Pinnacle Cir Windermere FL 34786 Office: 101 Central Orlando FL 32801 Office Phone: 407-835-7601.

HODES, ALLEN L., retired psychologist, educator; s. Joseph and Florence Hodes; m. Ina R. Glickfield; children: Marc S., Wendy F. Elverson. BA, Vanderbilt U., 1955; MEd, Rutgers U., 1964; PhD, Fordham U., 1973. Tchr. Kearny Pub. Schs., NJ, 1960—67, sch. counselor, 1967—74, sch. psychologist, 1974—82. Adj. prof. Seton Hall U., South Orange, NJ, 1967—85, Union County Coll., Cranford, NJ, 1987—; evaluator assessment programs Fordham U., NY, 1972; stats. cons., Springfield, NJ, 73, Metuchen Pub. Schs., Metuchen, NJ, 1980, Weehawken Pub. Sch.s, NJ, 1980. Baseball coach Springfield Twp., 1978. 1st lt. U.S. Army, 1955—57, Germany. Democrat. Jewish. Avocations: reading, opera, football, computers. Home: 19 N Derby Rd Springfield NJ 07081 Office: Union County Coll 1033 Springfield Ave Cranford NJ 07016

HODES, BARNEY, artist; b. Englewood, NJ; s. George and Margaret Hodes; m. Frances Hodes; 1 child, Georgia. AB, Columbia Coll., 1964; MFA, U. NC, 1966. Adj. lectr. art history, sculpture Fairleigh Dickinson U., 1970—72; instr., art history, sculpture Friends Seminary, 1971—72; adj. lectr. Bklyn. Coll., 1977—84; assoc. prof. St. John's U., Notre Dame Coll., Staten Is., NY, 1977—84; sculpture chmn. Bklyn. Mus. Art Sch., 1974—80; co-founder, dir. New Bklyn. Sch., 1979—83, NY Acad. Art, 1983—86; instr. sculpture Nat. Acad. Design, NYC, 2000—, Art Students League, NYC, 1986—; lectr. art history, design U. NC, 1968—70. Solo exhibition, Suffolk County Cmty. Coll., 2000, exhibitions include Audubon Artists, Salmagundi Club, 2003, Denise Bibro Gallery, 1999, Art Students League, 1998, Mayfair Festival, Allentown, Pa., 1998, First Street Gallery, 1995, Francesca Anderson Pine Art, Concord, Mass., 1994, Audubon Artists, Nat. Arts Club, 1992, Carlson Gallery, U. Bridgeport, 1991, Art 54, 1989; contbr. articles to publs.; Represented in permanent collections Art Students League Portrait Commn., U. Richmond, U. NC, Francis Cunningham et. al. Recipient Art Students League award, Audubon Artists, 2003. Avocation: Karate. Home: 4 High St Cold Spring NY 10516 Office Phone: 347-837-1727.

HODES, RICHARD J., federal agency administrator, immunologist, researcher; b. N.Y.C., Dec. 31, 1943; BA, Yale U., 1965; MD, Harvard U., 1971. Diplomate Am. Bd. Internal Medicine. Clin. investigator Nat. Cancer Inst. NIH, Bethesda, Md., dep. chief, acting chief immunology br. Nat. Cancer Inst., dir. Nat. Inst. Aging, 1993—. Program coord. U.S.-Japan Coop. Cancer Research Program, 1982; mem. adv. bd. Cancer Research Inst., 1992; mem. The Dana Alliance for Brain Initiatives, 1995—. Editor scholarly jours. including Jour. Exptl. Medicine and Therapeutic Immunology; contbr. numerous rsch. papers to profl. publs. Fellow: AAAS; mem.: NAS, Inst. of Med. Office: Nat Inst on Aging 31 Center Dr Bldg 31 Rm 5c35 Bethesda MD 20892-0001

HODES, ROBERT BERNARD, lawyer; b. Bklyn., Aug. 25, 1925; s. James and Florence (Cohen) H.; m. Florence R. Rosenberg, Dec. 22, 1946 (div. Nov. 1984); 1 child, Paul; m. Cecilia Mendez, Dec. 18, 1984; children: James, Maria Paz. AB, Dartmouth Coll., 1946; LLB, Harvard U., 1949. Bar: N.Y. Supreme Ct. 1950, U.S. Dist. Ct. (so. dist.) N.Y. 1951, U.S. Tax Ct. 1955, U.S. Claims Ct. 1957, U.S. Ct. Appeals (2d cir.) 1959. Assoc. Willkie Farr & Gallagher, N.Y.C., 1949-56, ptnr., 1956-95, co-chmn., 1982-95, counsel, 1995—. Bd. dirs. LCH Investments N.V., Loral Space & Telecomm., Ltd., Mueller Industries, Inc., RV1 Guaranty Co., Ltd. Active Cremer Found., Beaver Dam Sanctuary, Inc., Nat. Philanthropic Trust. Home: 860 United Nations Plz New York NY 10017-1810 Office: Willkie Farr & Gallagher Equitable Ctr 787 7th Ave New York NY 10019-6099 Office Phone: 212-728-8538. Business E-Mail: rhodes@willkie.com.

HODES, SCOTT, lawyer; b. Chgo., Aug. 14, 1937; s. Barnet and Eleanor (Cramer) H.; m. Maria Bechily, 1982; children— Brian Kenneth, Valery Jane, Anthony Scott. AB, U. Chgo., 1956; JD, U. Mich., 1959; LLM, Northwestern U., 1962. Bar: Ill. 1959, D.C. 1962, N.Y. 1981. Assoc. Arvey, Hodes, Costello & Burman, Chgo., 1959-61, ptnr., 1965-91, Ross & Hardies, Chgo., 1992—2003, Bryan Cave LLP, Chgo., 2004—. Bd. dirs. First Investors Life Ins. Co. NY, Richardson Electronics, Ltd., State Ill. Savs. and Loan Bd., Expressions of Culture, Inc. Author: The Law of Art and Antiques, 1966, What Every Artist and Collector Should Know About the Law, 1974; Assoc. news editor: Fed. Bar News, 1963-70; co-editor: Conf. Mut. Funds, 1966, Legal Rights in the Art and Collectors' World, 1986; Contbr. articles to profl. jours. Chmn. Philippine Exch. Nurses award com., 1966; nat. chmn. Lawbooks U.S.A., 1962-73; chmn. Mut. Funds and Investment Mgmt. Conf., 1966-75; co-chmn. Chgo. World Friendship Day, 1967; mem. Ill. Arts Coun., 1973-75; Committeeman Ill. 9th Dist. Dem. Com., 1970-82; bd. dirs. Michael Reese Hosp. Rsch. Inst., 1965-73, Found. of Fed. Bar Assn., 1970—, United Cerebral Palsy Chgo., 1976-84; governing bd. Chgo. Symphony Soc., 1978-1999; governing mem. Art Inst. Chgo., 1980—; com. on internat. investment and tech. Dept. State, 1980-83; bd. dirs. Chgo. Neighborhood Theatre Found., 1980-92, Harold Washington Found., 1988-2000; exec. com. Anti Defamation League, 1990-98; chmn. Mayor's Task Force on Neighborhood Land Use, 1986-88; chmn. Navy Pier Devel. Authority, 1988-89; mem. Ill. Atty. Gen. adv. com., 1991-95; spl. counsel Art in Embassies Program, Dept. State, 1992-94; co-chmn. Private Enterprise Rev. and Adv. Bd., Ill., 1992-94; pres. Lawyers Creative Arts, 2000-04; dir. Mex. Fine Arts Ctr. Mus., 2003—. Capt. JAGC, AUS, 1962-64. Decorated Army Commendation medal; named one of Chicago's ten outstanding young men Jr. Assn. Commerce and Industry, 1968, Chgo. Artist's award for Support of Visual Arts, 1996, Disting. Svc. award Lawyer's for the Creative Arts, 1997. 02169408, Fed. Bar Assn. (chmn. council financing 1966-71, chmn. younger lawyers div. 1963-64, nat. council 1965—, Distinguished Service award 1971, 75, 86, Earl Kintner award for Outstanding Service, 1998), Ill. Bar Assn., Chgo. Bar Assn., Chgo. Art Inst. (life), Chgo. Hist. Soc. (life), Judge Adv. Gens. Assn. (life), Zeta Beta Tau, Tau Epsilon Rho. Clubs: Standard, Econ. (Chgo.), Mid-Day. Lodges: Masons (32 degree). Jewish. Home: 1540 N Lake Shore Dr Chicago IL 60610-6684 Office: Bryan Cave 161 N Clark St Ste 4800 Chicago IL 60601-7567 Business E-Mail: scott.hodes@bryancave.com.

HODES, SUZANNE RUTH, artist; b. NYC, May 2, 1939; d. Charles and Helen (Nadell) Hodes; m. Henry Linschitz, Aug. 28, 1964; 1 child, Joseph Linitz. Student, Radcliffe Coll., 1956-58; BFA, Brandeis U., 1960; MFA, Columbia U., 1962. Artist Impressions Workshop, Boston, 1968-71, Hodes Studio, Waltham, Mass., 1964-80, Artist West Studios, Waltham, 1980—. Juror on art panel Tufts Med. Sch., Waltham, 1989-93; tchr. art Francis Cabot Lowell Mill, Waltham, 1990-93; co-founder Artists West Studios, Waltham, 1980, pres., 1985-89; co-founder Artists for Survival, Waltham, 1982; tchr. painting Lesley Coll., 2004-05 One-woman shows include Revel Gallery, N.Y.C., 1963, Verle Gallery, Hartford, Conn., 1965, Weeden Gallery, Boston, 1968, Radcliffe Inst., 1971, Weizmann Inst., Israel, 1972, Harvard Grad. Sch. Design, 1972-73, Wellesley (Mass.) Coll., 1974, Phoenix Gallery, N.Y.C., 1976, 78, Clark Gallery, Lincoln, Mass., 1978, Allport Assocs. Gallery, San Francisco, 1979, Newton (Mass.) Arts Mus., 1980, Artists West Open House, 1981-91, Zionist House, Boston, 1984, Rockefeller U., N.Y.C., 1984, Julia Saul Gallery, Sudbury, Mass., 1987, Hess Gallery, Pine Manor Coll., Chestnut Hill, Mass., 1989, Common Space Gallery, Artists West, Waltham, Mass., 1990, 92, 93, Eliza Spencer Gallery, Newton, 1991, Beacon Constrn. Co., Boston, 1992, Charles Webb Furniture Showroom, Cambridge, 1993, Tofias Gallery, Reservoir Place, Waltham, 1993, Lightwater Gallery, Wellfleet, Mass., 1994, Bunting Inst., Radcliffe Coll., Cambridge, 1996, Cove Gallery, Wellfleet, Mass., People and Places Schlesinger Libr. at Radcliffe, Cambridge, Mass., 2002-03, New York Reflections Joan Whalen Fine Art, N.Y.C., 2002-03, Collage and Memory:Paintings of Social Commentary Perkins Gallery Striar JCC, Stoughton, Mass., 2003, Artana Gallery, Brookline, Mass., 2004, Judi Rotenberg Gallerly, Boston; exhibited in group shows at Boston Pub. Libr., 1986, 94, DeCordova Mus., 1986, Newport (R.I.) Art Mus., 1988, Straus Gallery, N.Y.C., 1990, Boston Printmakers, 1986-94, Copley Soc., 1988, 93; represented in permanent collections at Fogg Mus., Rose Art Mus., Bank of Am., Boston, Cabot Corp., Hale and Dorr, Duxbury Art Complex Mus., DeCordova Mus., Boston Pub. Libr., Rockefeller U., Combined Jewish Philanthropies, also pvt. collections. Mem. Mayor's Commn. for Cultural Affairs, Waltham, 1986-89; mem. exec. com. Internat. Save Life on Earth Project, Cambridge, 1984-88. Fulbright Commn. fellow, Paris, 1963-64, Bunting Inst. fellow Radcliffe Coll., Cambridge, Boston, Israel, 1970-72; recipient award in painting Kokoschka Sch., City of Salzburg, Austria, 1959. Mem.: Boston Visual Artists Union, Copely Soc. Boston, Monotype Guild New England, Boston Printmakers, Artists Against Racism and War. Avocations: reading, sailing, political activism. Home: 35 Riverside Dr Waltham MA 02453-2409 Office: Artists West Studio 144 Moody St Waltham MA 02453-5332 Office Phone: 781-899-4124.

HODESS, ARTHUR BART, cardiologist; b. N.Y.C., Jan. 15, 1950; s. Samuel and Dora (Rosenkrantz) H.; m. Carol Yasuna, Aug. 31, 1969 (div. May 1985); children: Joshua David, Jeremy Scott; m. S. Christina Ellsworth, Dec. 23, 1987; children: Jonathan Ellsworth, Jason Dorian, Jordan Gottier. BA, Boston U., 1970; MD, Columbia U., 1974. Intern Hosp. of U. Pa., Phila.,

1974-75, resident in medicine, 1975-77, fellow in cardiology, 1977-79; asst. instr. dept. medicine Hosp. U. of Pa., Phila., 1974-79; instr. physiology, dept. animal biology U. Pa., Sch. Veterinary Medicine, Phila., 1977-78; clin. assoc. dept. medicine U. Pa., Phila., 1979-81; attending cardiologist Brandywine Hosp., Coatesville, Pa., 1979—, dir. critical care, 1989—, chief of cardiology, 1990—, chmn. dept. medicine, 1991-95; pres. Brandywine Valley Cardiovascular Assocs., Thorndale, Pa., 1991—. Contbr. articles to profl. jours. V.p. Chestnut Hollow Homeowners Assn., West Chester, Pa., 1990-94, bd. dirs. 1995; bd. dirs. Beth Israel Congregation, Chester County, 1991-96. Fellow Clin. Coun. Cardiology Am. Heart Assn. Fellow: ACP, Am. Heart Assn., Am. Coll. Chest Physicians, Am. Coll. Cardiology; mem.: Soc. Critical Care Medicine, Cardiac Electrophysiology Soc., Am. Soc. Echocardiography. Office: Brandywine Valley Cardio 3025 Zinn Rd Thorndale PA 19372-1131 Office Phone: 610-384-2211.

HODGDON, TIMOTHY JOHN, historian, educator; BA summa cum laude, Macalester Coll., 1982; PhD, Ariz. State U., 2002. Vis. asst. prof. St. Thomas U., Fredericton, Canada, 2002—03; Mellon fellow Duke U., Durham, NC, 2003—. Bd. dir. Communal Studies Assn., 2002—; assoc. dir. pubs. U. Writing Program, Duke U., Durham, NC, 2004—. Contbr. articles to profl. jours. Recipient Dissertation Prize, Ctr. for Communal Studies, U. of So. Ind., 2003, Phi Beta Kappa, Epsilon of Minn., 1982. Mem.: Internat. Communal Studies Assn., Communal Studies Assn., Oral History Assn., Am. Hist. Assn. Office: Box 90025 Duke Univ Duke University Durham NC 27708

HODGE, ANN LINTON, artist; b. Long Beach, Calif., Aug. 24, 1934; d. Mills Schuyler and Irma Jean (Linn) Hodge; m. Quentin Conitz Becker, Dec. 19, 1968 (dec. May 1978); children: Susan Jean Becker Pedersen, Kathryn Ann Becker Michlitsch, Deborah Rena Becker Lippert, Naomi Ruth, David Mills, Sharon Elizabeth Becker Glutting. Student, U. So. Calif., Long Beach, Carroll N. Jones Jr.'s Sch. Fine Arts, Stowe, Vt., 1990-92. Fine arts portrait artist individual commns., Whittier and Long Beach, Calif., 1958-68; mural artist for local businesses, 1958-68; fine arts portrait artist individual commns. Mandan & Bismarck, N.D., 1968—; instr. basic drawing and advanced portraiture The Renaissance Palette Sch. Fine Arts, Mandan, 1970—; adj. prof. basic drawing Bismarck State Coll., Mandan, 1996. Ofcl. state portrait artist Rough Rider Hall of Fame, N.D. State Capital, Bismarck, 1994—; judge art show Glen Ullin (N.D.) Art Assn., 1995; guest lectr. art Shiloh Christian Sch., Bismarck, 1988, Hughes Jr. H.S., Bismarck, 1996. Portraits on display on Internet, 1995—; two-woman show at Bismarck Arts and Gallery, late 1960's - early 1970's. Bible tchr., Bismarck, 1980's. Avocations: building furniture, bible teaching, poetry, reading, making christmas decorations. Address: The Renaissance Palette 1008 6th Ave NW Mandan ND 58554-2407

HODGE, ANTHONY THOMAS, criminologist, evangelist, private investigator; s. Arthur and Ruth Diggs Hodge; m. Carmen Maria Giraud, Feb. 29, 1980 (div. Feb. 1982). BS in Sociology/Criminology, Ctrl. State U., Xenia, Ohio, 1976; AA, Grace Meml. Inst. Holistic Parapsychology, L.A., 1978; JD, Northrup Sch. Law, 1980; MA in Sociology, Ohio State U., 1998. Chmn., acting dir. Hodge Found., Inc., Columbus, 1976—77; program dir. United Way, L.A., 1978—79; chief, pres. A.T.H. Hodge Private Investigation, Collection & Protection Agy., Columbus, 1981—; asst. dir. pub. rels. Jack Lewellyn Coles and Assocs., Columbus, 1983—85; pub. rels. agt. Tom Davis and Assocs., Cleve., 1985—87; founder, min., dir. Earth Temple, Inc., Columbus, 1991—. Author: The Story Must Be Told, 1995, Tina to Tiná, 1998, Trisexuality, 2000; prodr.: (pub. access TV) Godbrother, Earth Temple Speaks. Mem. Ame Ch. Address: PO Box 272100 Columbus OH 43227

HODGE, BOBBY LYNN, mechanical engineer, manufacturing executive; b. Yadkinville, NC, Oct. 14, 1956; s. Robert Henry and Betty Jean (Martin) H.; m. Robin Mayhue Renegar, June 8, 1979; children: Andrew, Adam. AAS with honors, Forsyth Tech. Inst., Winston-Salem, N.C., 1976; BS in Engring. Tech., U. N.C., Charlotte, 1978. Design engr. Clark/Gravely Corp., Clemmons, N.C., 1978-79, project engr., 1979-80; design engr. Ingersoll-Rand, Davidson, N.C., 1980-83, devel. engr., 1983-85; sr. applications engr. INA Bearing Co., Ft. Mill, S.C., 1985-87, mgr. automotive driveline engring. group, 1987-88, mgr. automotive applications engring., 1988-89, dir. automotive applications engring., 1989-96, dir. automotive engring., 1996-99; v.p. engring./product devel. The Setco Group, Cin., 1999—2002, v.p. engring/quality, 2002—. Internat. spkr. on design and application of rolling element bearings and machine tool spindles. Contbr. articles to profl. jours.; inventor, 9 patents in field. Mem. adv. coun. U. N.C.-Charlotte Coll. Engring. Mem. ASME, SAE, Soc. Mfg. Engrs., Soc. Tribologists and Lubrication Engrs., Am. Soc. Metals. Republican. Baptist. Avocations: golf, hunting, woodworking. Home: 1518 Jolee Dr Hebron KY 41048-9514 Office: The Setco Group 5880 Hillside Ave Cincinnati OH 45233-1599 Personal E-mail: hodge1518@aol.com. Business E-Mail: bhodge@setcousa.com. *One of the most important tasks anyone can undertake is to establish a vision for their life. Without a vision there can not be direction. Without direction, any success or achievement comes merely by accident.*

HODGE, ELIZABETH ELAINE, secondary school educator; b. Buffalo, Jan. 21, 1947; d. Edmund and Florence Monczynski; m. William Robert Hodge, July 10, 1971; children: Cheryl Elizabeth, William Edmund. Bachelor, SUNY, Buffalo, 1968, Master, 1971. Tchr. Medina H.S., NY, 1968—69, Lancaster Ctrl. Schs., NY, 1969—. Leader Lancaster Girl Scouts, NY, 1982—85, neighborhood dir., 1986—89. Named Tchr. of Yr., N.Y. State English Tchrs., 1995. Mem.: Zonta. Avocation: horseback riding. Office: Lancaster HS 1 Forton Dr Lancaster NY 14086

HODGE, GAMEEL BYRON, surgeon; b. Spartanburg, SC, Sept. 16, 1917; s. Charles B. and Mary (Bargoot) H.; m. Katie Adams, Sept. 22, 1943; children: Susan, Byron, John Adams. BS, Wofford Coll., 1938; MD, Vanderbilt U., 1942, D Pub. Service (hon.), U. SC, 1982; DSc (hon.) Wofford Coll., 2003. Diplomate Am. Bd. Surgery. Intern Duke U. Med. Sch. and Hosp., Durham, NC, 1942-43, asst. resident, 1943-47, chief resident surgeon, 1947-48; attending surgeon Spartanburg Gen. Hosp.; cons. surgeon St. Luke's Hosp., Tryon, NC, 1948-58, Cherokee County (SC) Meml. Hosp., 1948-74; thoracic surgeon Spartanburg County Tb Hosp., 1948-69; chief surgery Mary Black Meml. Hosp., 1969-72; assoc. clin. prof. surgery Med. U. SC, Spartanburg, 1970—. Contbr. articles to profl. jours. Chmn. Spartanburg County Commn. for Higher Edn., 1967—; trustee Spartanburg Day Sch., 1958—. With M.C., USAR, 1942-53. Recipient Disting. Svc. award U. SC Ednl. Found., 1991. Fellow Am. Coll. Chest Physicians, Internat. Acad. Proctology, NY Acad. Sci., Am. Fedn. Clin. Rsch., Indsl. Medicine Assn.; mem. Am. Heart Assn., SC Med. Assn., SC Surg. Soc., SC Vascular Surg. Soc., AMA, Spartanburg Med. Soc., Am. Geriatrics Soc., Deryl Hart Surg. Soc., Duke U. Med. Alumni Assn. (past pres.), Spartanburg Area C. of C. (past pres., Neville Holcombe Disting. Service award 1988), Kiwanis (Citizenship of Yr. award 1969), Omicron Delta Kappa, Order of Palmetto, Phi Beta Kappa, Phi Beta Pi. Episcopalian. Clubs: Piedmont, Carolina Country. Home: 2500 Old Knox Rd Spartanburg SC 29302-3427 Office Phone: 864-583-1504. Personal E-mail: daffodilkatie@msn.com.

HODGE, JAMES LEE, German language educator; b. Harrisburg, Pa., Sept. 18, 1935; s. Earl Henry and Catherine Margaret (Ferber) M.; m. Janice Ellen Dunn, June 21, 1958; children: Geoffrey Lee, Stephen Charles. AB, Tufts U., 1957; A.M., Pa. State U., 1960, PhD, 1961. Grad. asst. Pa. State U., 1957-60; instr. German Bowdoin Coll., Brunswick, Maine, 1961-63, asst. prof., 1963-68, assoc. prof., 1968-74, prof., 1974—2004, prof. emeritus, 2004—, George Taylor Files prof. modern langs., 1977, chmn. dept. German, 1974—93, 1999—2002. Mem. IIE Fulbright Screening Com., 1973, 91. Author: Portable German Tutor, 1970; editor: (with Buehne and Pinto) Helen Adolf Festschrift, 1968; editor: (with T. Beebee and S. Cerf) The Speech of Richard von Weizsacker on May 8, 1985; editorial staff German Quar, 1976-83; contbr. articles to profl. jours. and reference works. Cubmaster Pine Tree council Boy Scouts Am., Brunswick, 1974. NDEA grantee, 1966-67; Bowdoin Mellon grantee, 1977, 84 Mem. AAUP, Am. Assn. Tchrs. German, MLA. Independent. Home: 37 Meadowbrook Rd Brunswick ME 04011-3421 Office: Bowdoin Coll Dept German Brunswick ME 04011 E-mail: jhodge@bowdoin.edu.

HODGE, KATHLEEN O'CONNELL, academic administrator; b. Balt., Dec. 26, 1948; d. William Walsh and Loretto Marie (Wittek) O'Connell; m. Vern Milton Hodge, Apr. 8, 1972; children: Shea, Ryan. BS, Calif. State U., Fullerton, 1971, MS, 1975; EdD, U. So. Calif., 2002; postgrad., U. Calif., Irvine, 1977-84. Cert. marriage and family therapist. Counselor Saddleback Coll., Mission Viejo, Calif., 1975-87, prof. of psychology, speech, 1975—2002, dean of continuing edn., cmty. svcs., dean emeritus inst., 1987-95, vice chancellor, 1995—, acting chancellor, 1998-99. Accreditation liaison officer Saddleback Coll., 1986; mem. adv. bd. Nat. Issues Forum, Calif., 1985, 87, Saddleback Coll. Community Services, 1984, Access and Aspirations U. Calif., Irvine, 1979. Author: (workbook) Assessment of Life Learning, 1978; editor emeritus: Flavors in Time Anthology of Literature, 1992. Mem. Calif. Community Coll. Counselors Assn. (region coord. 1987), Calif. Tchrs. Assn., Am. Assn. Women Community and Jr. Colls., Assn. Marriage Family Therapists, C.C. Educators of Older Adults (pres. 1990-92). Democrat. Roman Catholic. Avocations: skiing, reading, political advocacy. Home: 4011 Calle Juno San Clemente CA 92673-2616 Office: South Orange County C C Dist 28000 Marguerite Pky Mission Viejo CA 92692-3635

HODGE, LINDA M., former educational association administrator; m. Bob Hodge; 3 children. Pres. Hawaii State PTA; chair Resource Develop., Bylaws, Tech./Safety, and Membership coms. Nat. PTA, region 7 dir. Alaska, Hawaii, Idaho, Mont., Oreg., Wash., Wyo., v.p. programs, 1999—2001, pres. elect, 2001—03, pres., 2003—05. Former mem. Exec., Budget, Elections, Leadership, and Nominating Coms., IOD Cultural Arts Subcommittee; com. mem. Nat. Rsch. Coun., NAS; nat. adv. bd. mem. Neag Sch. Edn., U. Conn. Recipient Hon. Svc. Award, Calif. PTA, Continuing Svc. Award, Vallejo Sch. Dist. Award. Office: Nat PTA Ste 1300 541 N Fairbanks Ct Chicago IL 60611-3396 also: 1090 Vermont Ave NW, Ste 1200 Washington DC 20005-4905 Office Phone: 312-670-6782, 202-289-6790. Office Fax: 312-670-6783, 202-289-6791.*

HODGE, PHILIP GIBSON, JR., mechanical and aerospace engineering educator; b. New Haven, Nov. 9, 1920; s. Philip Gibson and Muriel (Miller) H.; m. Thea Drell, Jan. 3, 1943; children: Susan E., Philip T., Elizabeth M. AB, Antioch Coll., 1943; PhD, Brown U., 1949. Rsch. asst. Brown U., 1947-49, asso., 1949; asst. prof. math. UCLA, 1949-53; assoc. prof. applied mechanics Poly. Inst. Bklyn., 1953-56, prof., 1956-57; prof. mechanics Ill. Inst. Tech., 1957-71, U. Minn., Mpls., 1971-91, prof. emeritus, 1991—. Russell Severance Springer vis. prof. U. Calif., 1976; vis. prof. emeritus Stanford U., 1993—; sec. U.S. nat. com. Theoretical and Applied Mechanics, 1982-2000. Author: 5 books, the most recent being Limit Analysis of Rotationally Symmetric Plates and Shells, 1963, Continuum Mechanics, 1971; also numerous rsch. articles in profl. jour.; tech. editor Jour. Applied Mechanics, 1971-76. Recipient Disting. Service award Am. Acad. Mechanics, 1984; Karman medal ASCE, 1985. NSF sr. postdoctoral fellow, 1963 Mem. NAE, ASME (hon., Worcester Reed Warner medal 1975, ASME medal 1987, Daniel C. Drucker medal 2000), Internat. Union Theoretical and Applied Mechanics (del. 1982-2000, asst. treas. 1984-92, mem. at large 2000—). Home: 580 Arastradero Rd Apt 701 Palo Alto CA 94306-3948 E-mail: phodge1@stanford.edu.

HODGE, RAY, lawyer; b. Jonesboro, Ark., Oct. 18, 1930; s. Charles R. and Neva Hodge; m. Betty M. Hodge, Nov. 25, 1959; children: Ryan, Raylene, Ronnie, Renee, Ricky, Roxann. BA, Wichita State U., 1964; JD, Oklahoma City U., 1967; postgrad., U. Nev., 1978. Bar: Kans. 1967, U.S. Dist. Ct. Kans. 1967, U.S. Ct. Appeals (10th cir.) 1969, U.S. Supreme Ct. 1970, U.S. Dist. Ct. (we. dist.) Mo. 1998, D.C. 1999. Capt. Sedgwick County Sheriff, Wichita, Kans., 1962—68; commd. officer/pilot USAR/Kans. N.G., 1965—86, col., 1986—91, ret., 1991; pvt. practice Wichita, Kans., 1967—77; spl. agt. Kans. Atty. Gen., Topeka, 1971—75; dist. judge State of Kans., Wichita, 1977—89; atty. Ray Hodge & Assocs., Wichita, 1989—. Bd. governours Kans. Trial Lawyers, Topeka; mcpl. ct. judge pro tem City of Wichita, United States. Decorated Legion of Merit, Meritorious Svc. medal. Mem.: Wichita Bar Assn. (life; mem. ethics com.), Reserve Officers Assn. (life). Home: 105 S Breezy Pointe Cir Wichita KS 67235

HODGE, RAYMOND DOUGLAS, minister; b. Charlotte, N.C., Dec. 5, 1951; s. George Washington Hodge and Mary (Allen) Maloy; m. Gale Lynn Baldwin, Aug. 11, 1972; children: Raymond Douglas Jr., Randolph Daniel. Student, Carson-Newman Coll., 1968, Lee Coll., 1970-71; MA, Ch. of God Sch. Theology Seminary, 1992; DMin, Grad. Theol. Found., 2003. Ordained to ministry Ch. of God., 1979. Evangelist Ch. of God in S.C., Mauldin, 1972-73; pastor Chs. of God, N.C. and Tenn., 1974-79, Dandridge (Tenn.) Ch. of God, 1979-84, Paragon Mills Ch. of God, Nashville, 1984-85, South Haven Ch. of God, Maryville, Tenn., 1985-94, Spring Creek Ch. of God, East Ridge, Tenn., 1994-98; state dir. evangelism and home missions Ch. of God in Tenn., Chattanooga, 1998—2000, adminstrv. coord., 2000—. Bd. dirs. State Bd. Evangelism, Chattanooga, State Bd. Youth and Christian Edn., Chattanooga; chmn. Ministerial Exam. Bd., Nashville, 1984-85; spkr. on daily radio program Life in the Spirit, 1978; adj. faculty Lee Coll., Cleveland, Tenn., 1992-98; mem. Tenn. state coun. Ch. of God, 1994-96, chmn., 1996-98. Recipient Merit award Vision Found., 1978. Republican. Office: Tenn Ch of Got State Office 7428 Old Lee Hwy Chattanooga TN 37421-1141 Home: 4018 Banner Crest Dr Ooltewah TN 37363-8371 *One must stand on the Scriptures, lead by serving others, pray without failing, love sincerely, understand if at all possible, be joyful in Christ always. Then life will be a pleasure and not a task.*

HODGE, ROBERT JOSEPH, retail executive; b. St. Louis, July 5, 1937; s. Joseph Edward and Alberta Marie (Oehler) H.; m. Carmen Maria Villalobos, Sept. 1, 1960; children: Ralph, Robert, Carmen. BS in Indsl. Relations, St. Louis U., 1959. Meat dept. merchandiser Kroger Co., Cleve., 1972-74, corp. v.p. deli/bakery Cin., 1981-83, v.p. Atlanta div., 1983-85, meat merchandiser St. Louis, 1977-80, v.p. gateway region, 1985-87; v.p. meat ops. Ralph's Grocery Co., Los Angeles, 1974-77; gen. mgr. Super X Drug, Melbourne, Fla., 1980-81; sr. v.p. Dillon Co., Hutchinson, Kans., 1987-89; sr. v.p. merchandising, manufacturing Kroger Co., Cin., 1989-92, pres. Cin./Dayton mktg. area, 1992—. Sgt. U.S. Army, res., 1959-66. Avocations: golf, skiing. Home: 614 Watchcove Ct Cincinnati OH 45230-3777 Office: Kroger Co 150 Tri County Pkwy Cincinnati OH 45246-3246

HODGE, VERNE ANTONIO, judge; b. St. Thomas, V.I., Nov. 16, 1933; s. John Wesley Hodge and Idalia Victoria Stout; children: Verne Jr., Bridget, Teresa. BS magna cum laude, Hampton U., 1956; JD cum laude, Howard U., 1969. Bar: V.I. 1969, D.C. 1969, U.S. Ct. Appeals (3d cir.) 1970, U.S. Supreme Ct. 1973. Internal auditor, internal revenue agt. V.I. Govt., 1958-61; pub. accountant, comptroller Mannassah Busline, Inc., St. Thomas, 1961-65; bus. mgr., personnel dir. V.I. Dept. Pub. Works, 1965-66; private practice law V.I., 1969-73; atty. gen., 1973-76; chief judge V.I. Territorial Ct., St. Thomas, 1976-99, ret., 1999. Past chmn. Eastern region Nat. Assn. Attys. Gen.; Mem. V.I. Indsl. Incentive Bd., 1963-64, V.I. Bd. Elections, 1964-66 Author: The Need for Constitutional Courts in U.S. Territories, 1968, The Mirror Theory and Its Effects, 1969. Served to 1st lt., inf. U.S. Army, 1956-58. Recipient Am. Jurisprudence awards in state, local and fed. taxation, 1968-69, certificate in advanced income tax law Internal Revenue Service, 1960, award of merit 9th Inf. Div. U.S. Army, 1958 Mem. Am. Judges Assn., Am., Nat., V.I. bar assns. Democrat. Lutheran. *Nothing is so complicated that it cannot be simplified by hard work.*

HODGELL, MURLIN RAY, university dean; b. Mankato, Kans., Jan. 6, 1924; s. Ray Darius and Lora Henrietta (Overman) H.; m. Billie RoJean Seward, July 20, 1947; children— Janet, Kristen, Kevin. BS, Kans. State U., 1949; MS, U. Ill., 1952; M.R.P., Cornell U., 1956, PhD, 1959. Licensed architect, engr. and planner. Prof. U. Ill., 1950-54, Kans. State U., 1957-63; chmn. dept. city and regional planning Rutgers U., 1963-64; dir. Sch. Architecture, U. Nebr., 1964-69; dean Coll. Environ. Design, U. Okla., 1969—, dean emeritus; prin. Hodgell Assocs. in Architecture, Engring. and Planning. City planning dir., Manhattan, Kans., 1957-58, planning commr., 1959-63; dir. Kans. State U. Center Community Devel., 1959-63 Author: Contemporary Farmhouses, 1956, Forgotten Millions, 1959, Zoning, 1957. Trustee Weigal Found., Leonard Bailey Found. Served to lt. (j.g.) USNR, 1943-45. Named Kan. Outstanding Young Man of Yr. Kans. Jr. C. of C., 1959, Man of Yr. Manhattan, Kans., 1960; recipient citation distinguished community service Lane-Bryant Found., 1960 Fellow AIA, ASCE; mem. Am. Inst. Cert. Planners, Am. Soc. Planning Ofcls., Assn. Collegiate Schs. Architecture, Asso. Schs. Constrn. Home: 14151 Travis St Overland Park KS 66223-4810

HODGEN, MAURICE DENZIL, management consultant, retired education educator; b. Timaru, New Zealand, Aug. 7, 1929; s. William Arnold and Lindsey Frances (Neill) H.; m. Rhona Brandstater, June 20, 1951; children: Philip Denzil, Victoria Anne. Student, Avondale Coll., Cooranbong, Australia, 1948-50; BS, Pacific Union Coll., 1953; MA, Columbia U., 1956, Ed.D., 1958. Asst. prof. La Sierra Coll., Riverside, Calif., 1958-64; lectr. Solusi Coll., Bulawayo, Zimbabwe, 1964-66; dir. tchr. edn. Helderberg Coll., Somerset W., S. Africa, 1966-68; assoc. prof. Sch. Edn., Loma Linda U., Calif., 1968—72, prof. Calif., 1972—84, dean Grad. Sch., 1978—87, coop. faculty, 1985—88; devel. officer Claremont (Calif.) Grad. U., 1987-93; mgmt. cons., 1999—. Exec. dir. Cmty. Found. of Riverside County, 1993-99. Served with U.S. Army, 1953-55.

HODGES, ANN, retired video editor, columnist; b. McCamey, Tex., Sept. 7, 1928; d. Ernest Cornelius and Margaret Isabel (Wood) Haynes; m. Cecil Ray Hodges, July 2, 1954 (div. Nov. 1974); children: Craig McNeley, Elizabeth Ann. BJ, U. Tex., 1948. Reporter Houston Chronicle, 1948-51; soc. editor The News, Mexico City, 1951-52, TV editor, columnist, TV critic, 1962—2003; ret., 2003. Mem. adv. bd. U. Miami TV Ctr. for Advancement of Modern Media, 1994—; U.S. juror Banff TV Festival, 1995. Mem.: Houston Press Club (pres. 1967), TV Critics Assn. (founder, exec. bd., v.p., pres.), Critics Consensus (dir. 1965—75).

HODGES, ANN, actress, singer, dancer; b. Elizabethtown, Ky., June 24; d. Henry Lavely and Margaret Rhodes (Lewis) H.; m. Richard Angeline; 1 child, Michael Christian Angeline; m. Barry C. Tuttle, Sept. 16, 1969 (div. 1972). Cert., registered yoga alliance tchr.; ordained min. Congl. Ch. Practical Theology. Yoga instr., Tampa, St. Petersburg, Safety Harbor, Clearwater, Fla., Under the Live Oak, Casa Bella Vista. Pvt. instr. Yoga, Fla. Appeared in (Broadway shows) No Strings, The Rothschilds, Heathen, (off-Broadway shows) The Boys From Syracuse, There Goes The Old Ballgame, Bella, (TV shows) The Jackie Gleason Show, The Steve Allen Show, The Ed Sullivan Show, Bell Telephone Hour, Ellery Queen, Omnibus, The Vic Damone Show, The Big Record, (TV spls.) Once Upon A Mattress, The G.M. Spectacular, The Esso Spectacular, (motion pictures) The Cardinal, The New Life Style, Oldsmobile, (plays) Applause, The Best Little Whorehouse in Texas, Gypsy,(leading roles in plays) Hello Dolly!, Sugar Babies, Chicago, Can Can, Sweet Charity, Mame, Damn Yankees, See How They Run, Catch Me If You Can., Legends!, I Ought to Be in Pictures, How the Other Half Loves, Pajama Tops, The Last of the Red Hot Lovers, Pal Joey, Cole Porter Reveiw, Gone with the Wind (role of Belle Watling in American Premiere Production), The Greenwich Village Scandals of 1923; also many commls., voice overs and indsls.; performer numerous charities including Am. Cancer Soc., Am. Heart Assn., Handicapped, Abused Wives and Children; star performer Gasparilla Coronation, 1991, guest performer Fla. Orch. at Clearwater Jazz Festival. Yoga instr. Safety Harbor Spa, Don CeSar, Harbour Island Athletic Club, Casa Bella Vista. Named the Queen of Mus. Theatre by the Press, one of Tampa Bay's top achievers. Mem.: Suncoast Yoga Tchrs. Assn. (past pres., bd. dirs.). Avocations: yoga, swimming, horse back riding, piano playing, embroidery.

HODGES, BRIAN W., consumer products company executive; Various supr. and engring. positions Honeywell, Inc., Tex. Instruments; dir. ops., various sr. mgmt. positions Brunswick Tech. Group, 1987-95; v.p. Intellitec, 1997—; pres. Advanced Tech. Products, Ind., Deland, Fla., 1997—. Office: Advanced Tech Products Inc 2000 Brunswick Ln Deland FL 32724-2001

HODGES, DAVID ALBERT, electrical engineering educator, dean; b. Hackensack, N.J., Aug. 25, 1937; s. Albert R. and Katherine (Rogers) H.; m. Susan Spongberg, June 5, 1965; children: Jennifer, Alan. B.E.E., Cornell U., 1960; MS, U. Calif., Berkeley, 1961, PhD in Elec. Engring, 1966. Mem. tech. staff Bell Telephone Labs., Murray Hill, N.J., 1966-69, head system elements research dept. Holmdel, N.J., 1969-70; asso. prof. dept. elec. engring. and computer scis U. Calif., Berkeley, 1970-74, prof., 1974-98, chmn. dept., 1989-90, dean Coll. Engring., 1990-96, prof. Grad. Sch., 1998—. Contbr. articles to profl. jours.; patentee in field. Fellow AAAS, IEEE.; mem. NAE. Office: Univ Calif Coll Engring 516 Cory Hl Berkeley CA 94720-1700

HODGES, DEBORAH, investment company executive; BA, Princeton U.; MBA, Kellogg Grad. Sch. Mgmt. With Capital Mgmt. Group Bankers Trust; COO DB Capital Ptnrs., 2000; COO, ptnr. MidOcean Ptnrs. Office: MidOcean Ptnrs 320 Park Ave Ste 1700 New York NY 10022 Office Phone: 212-497-1400.

HODGES, DEWEY HARPER, aerospace engineer, educator; b. Clarksville, Tenn., May 18, 1948; s. Plummer Maxwell Sr. and Etha Maude (Harper) H.; m. Margaret Elin Jones, Aug. 14, 1971; children: Timothy, Jonathan, David, Philip, Benjamin. BS in Aerospace Engring., U. Tenn., 1969; MS in Aero. and Astronautical Engring., Stanford U., 1970, PhD in Aero. & Astronautical Engring., 1973. Rsch. scientist U.S. Army Aeroflight Dynamics Directorate, Ames Rsch. Ctr., Moffett Field, Calif., 1970-80, sr. rsch. scientist, theoretical group leader, 1980-86; prof. aerospace engring. Ga. Inst. Tech., Atlanta, 1986—. Instr. No. Calif. Bible Coll., San Jose, 1974-86; lectr. Stanford U., 1980-86; guest rsch. scientist DLR Inst. Structural Mechanics, Braunschweig, Fed. Republic of Germany, 1984. Contbr. more than 260 articles to profl. jours. and conf. procs., chapters to books. Elder Christian Comty. Ch., San Jose, 1980-86, Mt. Paran Ch., Atlanta, 1992-94, Chalcedon Presbyn. Ch., Cumming, Ga., 2003—. Fellow AIAA, Am. Helicopter Soc., Am. Acad. Mechanics; mem. ASME, Sigma Xi, Tau Beta Pi, Pi Tau Sigma Republican. Presbyterian. Achievements include patents for hingeless helicopter rotor with improved stability; real-time missile guidance system. Home: 1172 Branch Water Ct Atlanta GA 30338-4026 Office: Ga Inst Tech Sch Aerospace Engring Atlanta GA 30332-0001 Office Phone: 404-894-8201. Business E-Mail: dewey.hodges@ae.gatech.edu. *We know about the wise men who sought the Lord Jesus at His birth. I believe that wise men still seek Him and that His promise of abundant life to those who follow Him is still being fulfilled today.*

HODGES, DIANE MITCHELL, creative arts therapist, bereavement counselor; b. Cleve., Sept. 19, 1954; d. John Andrew Mitchell and Leah Abbie Ashbrook; m. Ralph Emerson Hodges, Sept. 21, 1980. BA in Psychology, Wittenberg U., 1976; MA in Art Edn., Ohio State U., 1985. Cert. bereavement counselor. Child life specialist Children's Hosp., Columbus, Ohio, 1978—80; art therapist, poetry therapist Ohio State U., Columbus, 1980—85, Parkside Med. Ctr., Columbus, Ohio, 1986—88, Delaware County Cultural Arts Ctr., Ohio, 1989—96; art therapist, bereavement counselor Hospice at Grady Meml. Hosp., Delaware, Ohio, 1989—. Contbr. articles to profl. jours. Mem. exec. bd. Ctrl. Ohio Symphony, Delaware County Cultural Arts Ctr., New World Theatre, Nat. Coalition for Arts in Therapy, The Arts Farm; coord. Painted Concrete Horse Project, Delaware, Ohio, 2000—. Mem.: Nat. Poetry Therapy Assn. (exec. bd.), Buckeye Art Therapy Assn. (exec. bd.), Nat. Art Edn. Assn., Nat. Assn. Poetry Therapy (registered poetry therapist), Am. Art Therapy Assn. (registered art therapist), Mid-Ohio Dressage Assn. (exec. bd.). E-mail: dhogdes@wchins.net.

HODGES, JENNEFER RAE, sculptor; b. Bay City, Tex., Feb. 14, 1973; d. Bobby Owens and Ygerne Roxanne Michalec Hubbell; m.Craig Jefferson Hodges, May 17, 2003; children: Lexis DeVoe Beauford, Madison Nicole. Student, Richland Jr. Coll., 1991, 92; BFA with honors, U. Ctrl. Ark., 1998; MFA, U. Ark. Little Rock, 2001. Intern, apprentice Richard Hunt Studios, Chgo., 1997; tech. asst. Chgo. Fine Art Foundry, 1997, Hunt Studios, Chgo., 1997; sculptor disability svcs. U. Ctrl. Ark., Conway, 1998; tchr. Assn. Retarded Citizens, Little Rock, 1999, U. Ala.-Little Rock Share Am. Cmty. Outreach Program, 2001—; tchr. sculpture Gallery B, 2002; prof. sculpture and Intro to Art U. Ark., Little Rick, 2003—05, prof. intro. to art, 2005—. Mem. com. Kramer Artist Coop., Little Rock, 1997; v.p. Kramer Sch. Artist Coop. Moon Meditation, 1997, exhibited in group shows at U. Ctrl. Ark., Conway, 1997, 1998, Woman's City Club, 1999, Ctrs. Youth and Family, 1999, Art Found., Hot Springs, 1999, 2000, Youth Home Inc. Eggshibition, 2002. Scholar U. Ctrl. Ark., 1998. Mem. Art History Assn. (v.p. 1997). Democrat. Avocations: painting with oil, watercolors, acrylic, camping, canoeing, swimming, figure drawing. Home: 2403 N Grant Little Rock AR 72207 Personal E-mail: jennefer@sbcglobal.net.

HODGES, JIM, artist; b. Spokane, Wash., 1957; BFA, Fort Wright Coll., Wash., 1980; MFA, Pratt Inst., 1986. One-man shows include A Diary of Flowers, CR Gallery, NY, 1994, States, Fabric Workshop & Mus., Phila., 1996, yes, Marc Foxx, Santa Monica, Calif., 1996, every way, Mus. Contemporary Art, Chgo., 1999, this and this, CR Gallery, NY, 2002, colorsound, Addison Gallery Am. Art, Phillips Acad., Mass., 2003, Returning, Art Pace, San Antonio, 2003, Don't be Afraid, Worcester Art Mus., Mass., 2004, Heaven & Earth, Centro Galego de Arte Contemporanea, Santiago de Compostello, Spain, 2005, exhibited in group shows at Selections From The Artists File, Artists Space, NY, 1988, Partnership for the Homeless with Aids, Christie's, NY, 1990, Our Perfect World, Grey Art Gallery, NY, 1993, Ethereal Materialism, Apex Art, NY, 1994, It's how you play the game, Exit Art/The First World, NY, 1994, New Works, Feigen Gallery, Chgo., 1995, Poetics of Obsession, Linda Kirkland Gallery, NY, 1997, Age of Influence: Reflections in the Mirror of Am. Culture, Mus. Contemporary Art, Chgo., 2000, Gardens of Pleasure, John Michael Kohler Arts Ctr., Sheboygan, Wis., 2000, CAMERA WORKS: The Photographic Impulse in Contemporary Art, Boesky Gallery, NY, 2001, Life Death Love Hate Pleasure Pain, Mus. Contemporary Art, Chgo., 2002, In Full View, Andrea Rosen Gallery, NY, 2003, Treble, Sculpture Ctr., Long Island City, NY, 2004, Whitney Biennial, Whitney Mus. Am. Art, 2004, Visual Music: 1905-2005, Mus. Contemporary Art, LA, 2005, Landscape Confection, Wexner Ctr. Arts, Columbus, Ohio, 2005. Recipient, Mid Atlantic Arts Found., NEA, 1992, Albert Ucross Prize, 2001; grantee Louis Comfort Tiffany Found., 1995; Regional Fellowship, Paper & Works on Paper, 1992, Penny McCall Found. Grant, 1994, Wash. State Arts Commn., 1999, Artist-in-Residence, Calif. Coll. Arts & Crafts, 2000. Mailing: c/o CR Gallery 535 West 22nd St 3rd Floor New York NY 10011*

HODGES, JOSEPH GILLULY, JR., lawyer; b. Denver, Dec. 7, 1942; s. Joseph Gilluly Sr. and Elaine (Chanute) H.; m. Jean Todd Creamer, Aug. 7, 1971; children: Ashley E., Wendy C., Elaine V. BA, Lake Forest Coll., 1965; JD, U. Colo., 1968. Bar: Colo. 1968, U.S. Dist. Ct. Colo. 1969, U.S. Ct. Mil. Appeals 1969. Assoc. Hodges, Kerwin, Otten & Weeks, Denver, 1969-73, Davis, Graham & Stubbs, Denver, 1973-76, ptnr., 1976-86; pvt. practice, Denver, 1986—. Bd. dirs. Arapahoe Colo. Nat. Bank, Littleton, Colo., 1971-90, Cherry Creek Improvement Assn., Denver, 1979-91; bd. trustees Lake Forest (Ill.) Coll., 1977-87; pres. Colo. Arlberg Club, Winter Park, Colo., 1984-85; treas. St. Johns Episcopal Cathedral, Denver, 1981-96; chmn. bd. Spalding Cmty. Found., 1995—. Capt. USAR, 1969-74. Named Best Lawyers in Am., Woodward/White, N.Y.C., 1994-95. Fellow Am. Coll. Trust and Estate Counsel (state chmn. 1991-96); mem. ABA (chmn. probate divsn. G-2 Tech. 1990-95, coun. mem. real property, probate and trust law sect. 1996—), Am. Judicature Soc., Colo. Bar Assn. (chair probate coun. 1981-82), Denver Bar Assn., Denver Estate Planning Coun., Colo. Planned Giving Roundtable (bd. 1991-94), Rotary Club Denver, Kappa Sigma, Phi Alpha Delta. Republican. Avocations: skiing, hiking, fishing, photography, computers. Office: 3300 E 1st Ave Ste 600 Denver CO 80206-5809 Home: 2552 E Alameda Ave Unit 5 Denver CO 80209-3324

HODGES, JOT HOLIVER, JR., retired lawyer, corporate financial executive; b. Archer City, Tex., Nov. 16, 1932; s. Jot Holiver and Lola Mae (Hurd) H.; m. Virginia Cordray Pardue, June 11, 1955; children: Deborah, Jot, Darlene. BS, BBA, Sam Houston State U., 1954; JD, U. Tex., 1957. Bar: Tex. 1958, U.S. Dist. Ct. (so. dist.) Tex. 1958, U.S. Ct. Appeals (5th cir.) 1958. Asst. atty. gen. State of Tex., Austin, 1958—60; chmn. bd. Presidio Devel. Corp., Missouri City, Tex., 1971. Organizer, founder 3 banks, several corps. and ltd. partnerships; residential and comml. real estate developer. Contbr. articles to profl. jours. Capt. U.S. Army. Mem. Houston Club, Quail Valley Country Club. Home: 3527 Thunderbird St Missouri City TX 77459-2445

HODGES, KATHLEEN MCGILL, art educator; b. Mpls., Oct. 9, 1964; d. John Michael and Marilyn (Gore) McGill; m. Garry Allen Hodges, Dec. 28, 1991. BFA, U. North Tex., 1987; MEd, Tex. Woman's U., 1991. Elem. art specialist Garland (Tex.) Ind. Sch. Dist., 1988—. Illustrator Cooper Inst. Aerobics Rsch., Dallas, 1995—98, Garland ISD, 1988—, Med. Health Group Credit Union, 1988, Tex. Assn. Landscape Contractors, 1996; campus improvement team Walnut Glen Acad., Garland, 1991—2003, creator pet patrol, 1995—. Art and design com. Dallas Area Rapid Transit, 2000; creator ann. paper towel drive Rogers Wildlife Rehab. Ctr., Hutchins, Tex., 1996—; mem. PTA, Garland, 1988—, hon. life mem., 2003—. Named Tchr. of Yr., Wal-Mart, 2001; grantee, Garland Ind. Sch. Dist., 2001. Mem.: Tex. Art Edn. Assn., Nat. Art Edn. Assn., Pi Beta Phi. Avocations: skiing, antiques, travel. Office: Walnut Glen Acad Excellence 3101 Edgewood Dr Garland TX 75042

HODGES, MARGARET MOORE, writer, educator; b. Indpls., July 26, 1911; d. Arthur Carlisle and Anna Marie (Mason) Moore; m. Fletcher Hodges, Jr., Sept. 10, 1932; children: Fletcher III, Arthur Carlisle, John Andrews. AB with honors, Vassar Coll., 1932; MLS; Carnegie Libr. Staff scholar, Carnegie Inst. Tech., 1958. Lectr. U. Pitts. Grad. Sch. Library and Info. Services, 1964-68, asst. prof., 1968-72, assoc. prof., 1972-75, prof., 1975-77, emeritus, 1977— (Children's libr., radio and TV storyteller) Carnegie Library Pitts., 1953—64, (story specialist) Pitts. Pub. Schs., 1964—68, (storyteller) WQED Schs. Svcs. Dept NIT network., 1965—; author: (juvenile books) One Little Drum, 1958, What's for Lunch Charley?, 1961, Club Against Keats, 1962, Tell It Again, 1963, Secret in the Woods, 1963, Wave, 1964, Hatching of Joshua Cobb, 1967, Constellation, a Shakespeare Anthology, 1968, Sing Out, Charley!, 1968, Lady Queen Anne, 1969, Making of Joshua Cobb, 1971, Gorgon's Head, 1972, Hopkins of the Mayflower, 1972, Fire Bringer, 1972, Persephone and the Springtime, 1973, Baldur and the Mistletoe, 1974, Freewheeling of Joshua Cobb, 1974, Knight Prisoner, The Tale of Sir Thomas Malory and His King Arthur, 1976, The High Riders, 1980, The Little Humpbacked Horse, 1980, The Avenger, 1982, If You Had a Horse, 1984, Saint George and the Dragon, 1984, Making a Difference, 1989, The Voice of the Great Bell, 1989, The Arrow and the Lamp, 1989, The Kitchen Knight, 1990, Buried Moon, 1990, Brother Francis and the Friendly Beasts, 1991, Saint Jerome and the Lion, 1991, Hauntings, 1991, Don Quixote and Sancho Panza, 1992, Of Swords and Sorcerers, 1993, St. Patrick and the Peddler, 1993, The Hero of Bremen, 1993, Hidden in Sand, 1994, Gulliver in Lilliput, 1995, Comus, 1996, Molly Limbo, 1996; co-editor: Elva S. Smith's The History of Children's Literature, 1980, The True Tale of Johnny Appleseed, 1997, Silent Night, the Song and Its Story, 1997, Up the Chimney, 1998, Joan of Arc, the Lily Maid, 1999, The Boy Who Drew Cats, 2002, The Legend of St. Christopher, 2002, Merlin and the Making of the King, 2004. Mem. ALA (Newbery-Caldecott com. 1960), Pa. Library Assn., Am. Assn. Library Schs., Pitts. Bibliophiles, Zonta Internat., Distinguished Daus. Pa. Republican. Episcopalian. Home: Longwood at Oakmont 0-229 Verona PA 15147 Office: U Pitts Bellefield Ave Pittsburgh PA 15260

HODGES, NORMAN, retired district judge; b. Silver City, N. Mex., Aug. 5, 1925; s. Joseph William and Eva Irene H.; m. Tressie Lee Murdock Weiland, Oct. 5, 1963; 1 stepchild, William V. Weiland. BA, U. N. Mex., 1947, BS, 1948, LLB, 1951, JD, 1968. Bar: N. Mex. 1951, U.S. Dist. Ct. N. Mex. 1952, U.S. Ct. Mil. Appeals 1960, U.S. Supreme Ct. 1960. Ptnr. Hodges, Hodges & Hodges, Attorneys, Silver City, 1951-52; assoc. H. Vearle Payne, Lordsburg, N. Mex., 1952-56; dist. attorney Grant, Luna, Hidalgo Counties, Silver City, 1957-63; dist. judge 6th Judicial Dist., Silver City, 1963-86, retired, 1986—. Mem. N. Mex. Supreme Ct. Children's Ct. Rules com., Albuquerque, 1970-73. Capt. USN, 1942-99. Recipient Judge of Yr. award N. Mex. State Bar Assn., Albuquerque, 1982. Mem. VFW, Ret. Officers Assn., Am. Legion, Silver City Mus. (bd. dirs.), Copper Crest Country Club (bd. dirs. 1965-69), Elks Club, Sigma Chi (pres. 1944). Democrat. Protestant. Avocations: books, Southwestern America. Home: PO Box 390 Silver City NM 88062-0390 Office Phone: 505-538-3646.

HODGES, ROBERT STANLEY, biochemist, educator, biotechnologist, researcher; b. Saskatoon, Sask., Can., Dec. 30, 1943; s. Bert and Frances H.; children: Sherylynn June, Clinton Jeffrey; m. Phyllis Hodges. BS in Biochemistry with honors, U. Sask., 1965; PhD in Biochemistry, U. Alta., Edmonton, Can., 1971. Postdoctoral and rsch. assoc. Rockefeller U., N.Y.C., 1971-74; asst. prof. dept. biochemistry U. Alta., Edmonton, 1974-77, assoc. prof. dept. biochemistry, 1977-84, prof., 1984—2001; prof. dept. biochemistry and molecular genetics U. Colo. Health Scis. Ctr., Aurora, 2001—, dir. program in biomolecular structure, John Stewart chair in peptide chemistry, 2001—. Mem. Med. Rsch. Coun. Group in Protein Structure and Function, Edmonton, 1974—2001; pres. Alta. Peptide Inst., 1985—2002, Synthetic Peptides Inc., 1986-94; network leader protein engring. network Ctr. Excellence, 1994—2000. Author: (with others) Calmodulin Antagonists and Cellular Physiology, 1985, HPLC of Biological Macromolecules: Methods and Applications, 1990, Computer-Assisted Method Development for High-Peformance Liquid Chromatography, 1990, HPLC of Proteins, Peptides and Polynucleotides, 1991, High Peformance Liquid Chromatography of Peptides and Proteins: Separation, Analysis and Conformation, 1991; editor Peptide Rsch., 1988—, Peptides: Chemistry Structure and Biology, 1994; editl. adv. bd. Protein and Peptides Letters, Jour. Peptide Sci., Biomed. Peptides, Proteins and Nucleic Acids; contbr. numerous articles to scholarly and profl. jours. Competitor in speed skating Winter Olympics, Grenoble, France, 1968, Sapporo, Japan, 1972; mgr. Can. speed skating team Winter Olympics, Lake Placaid, N.Y., 1980; vice chmn. speed skating, Winter Olympics, Calgary, Alta., 1988. Recipient honors scholarship U. Sask., 1964, Med. Rsch. Coun. studentship, Edmonton, 1969-71, postdoctoral fellowship, N.Y.C., 1971-73, Spl. Recognition for Contbns. to Biotechnology, Govt. Alta., 1986, Disting. MRC Scientist award, 1995, Alberta Sci. and Tech. award, 1995. Fellow Royal Soc. Can.; mem. Can. Biochem. Soc. (Boehringer-Mannheim Can. prize 1995), Protein Soc., Am. Peptide Soc. (pres. 1995-99, Vincent Du Vigneaud award 2002), N.Y. Acad. Scis. Achievements include a patent for Synthetic Psuedomonas aeruginosa Pilin Peptide and Related Vaccines and Diagnostics; research in synthetic peptides and proteins, de novo design of proteins, high performance liquid chromatography and capillary electrophoresis of peptides and proteins, synthetic vaccines and antibody therapeutics, antibacterial peptides, role of coiled-coils in protein function and self assembly. Office Phone: 303-734-3253. E-mail: robert.hodges@uchsc.edu.

HODGES, SHARON GREEN, editor, consultant, writer; b. Miami, Fla., Aug. 16, 1944; d. Charles Purrington and Ruth Mary (Hall) Green; m. William Clark Hodges, June 22, 1966; children: Michael David, Matthew Ryan. BA, U. Miss., 1966; postgrad., San Diego State U., 1969, Fla. Atlantic U., 1988—90. Writer, Deerfield Beach, Fla., 1980—84; tchr. Deerfield Beach H.S., 1988—90; rsch. asst. Fla. Atlantic U., Boca Raton, 1989—90; writer The Apelian-DuBois Group, Boca Raton, 1997—98; editl. dir. Backbone Celebrity Classic, Miami Lakes, Fla., 2001—02; editor-in-chief The BACKBONE Chronicles, 2002. Editl. cons. Horses and the Handicapped, Boca Raton, 1982—85, Boy Scouts Am., Miami Lakes, 1984—, Broward County Schs., Ft. Lauderdale, Fla., 1986—90, Aid to Victims of Domestic Abuse, Inc., Delray Beach, Fla., 1994—97, Jr. Achievement South Fla., Inc., Pompano Beach, 1996—98, Broward Sheriff's Office, Ft. Lauderdale, 1997—99, Patrons of the Arts of the Vatican Mus., Vatican City, 1999, South Fla. Forensic Assn., Ft. Lauderdale, 1999. Designer, editor: newsletter The Scouter, 1997—2000 (award of excellence Fla. Printing Assn., 1998), author, designer, project dir.: Champions of Free Enterprise, 1996—98, author, designer: One Summer Evening, 2003, author, designer, project dir.: A Place of Our Own, 1999, A Call to Greatness, 2000, As Far as the Eye Can See, 2001, A Matter of Importance, 2001, A Mission of Love, 2002, The Samaritan Fund, 2000 (Best Booklet, Fla. Printing Assn., 2000), The Disciple Fund, 2000 (Judges' award Fla. Printing Assn., 2000); author, designer, project dir. To the Mountain, 2003, A Sanctuary for Life, 2005, A New Day - A New Beginning, 2005. Mem. Boy Scouts of America's James E. West Soc., 2003—; chmn. Learning Disabilities Early Identification Program Broward County Schs., Ft. Lauderdale, 1976—77; co-founder Second Chance Club, North Ridge Med. Ctr., Ft. Lauderdale, 1977; treas., pres. Middle Sch. Band Parents Assn., Deerfield Beach, 1984—85; adult leader South Fla. Coun. Boy Scouts Am., Miami Lakes, 1979—94, exec. bd. mem., 1985—; bd. trustees South Fla. Coun.-Boy Scouts Am., Miami Lakes, 1998—; v.p. South Fla. Coun. Boy Scouts Am., Miami Lakes, 1997—2000; pres. Friends of the Libr., Deerfield Beach, 1984—86; sec. High Sch. Band Parents Assn., Deerfield Beach, 1987—89; chmn. Libr. Adv. Bd., Deerfield Beach, 1988—89; prin. mem. textbook evaluation com. Broward County Schs., Ft. Lauderdale, 1988—89; pub. rels. Poinciana Women's Rep. Club of Fla. Fedn. Rep. Women, Boca Raton, 1994—98; adv. bd. mem. Broward County Schs., Ft. Lauderdale, 1996—98; mem. campaign com. City Mayoral Election, Boca Raton, 1997, Gubernatorial Election, Boca Raton, 1997; South Fla. Council, BSA Honoree Eagle Class of 2002 - 2003, 2003; prin. sect. mem. Chancel Choir, St. Jerome Cath. Ch., 2002—; prin. sect. mem. South Fla. based internat touring choir, 2004—. Named to Soc. Golden Eagles, South Fla. Coun., Boy Scouts Am., Miami Lakes, 2000—; recipient Spl. Commendation, City of Deerfield Beach, 1982, Award of Merit, South Fla. Coun. Boy Scouts Am., Miami Lakes, 1982, Spl. Commendation, United Way Broward County, Ft. Lauderdale, 1988, Outstanding Vol. award, Broward County Schs., Ft. Lauderdale, 1989, Silver Beaver award, Boy Scouts Am., Irving, Tex., 1994, Commendation, Broward Sheriff's Office, Ft. Lauderdale, 1997, Pres. award for best mktg. strategy, Boy Scouts Am., Irving, 1998, Good Turn award, South Fla. Coun. Boy Scouts Am., Miami Lakes, 2002, U Scholar, Dean's List, Panhellenic Council, U Miss., Pres. List, Coll., of Edn. Dean's Adv. Bd., Fla. Atlantic U. Mem.: Nat. Med. Musicians Group, Alpha Omicron Sorority (life; v.p. 1962—66). Republican. Roman Catholic. Avocations: reading, sports, travel.

HODGES, VERNON WRAY, mechanical engineer; b. Roanoke, Va., Dec. 26, 1929; s. Charlie Wayne and Kathleen Mae (Williams) Hodges; m. Lorraine Patricia Smart, Apr. 1, 1955 (div. 1966); children: Vernon Wray Jr.(dec.), Gregory Elmer, Michelle Lynn; m. Linda Lou Wall, Feb. 3, 1967 (dec. Apr. 1997); children: Kenneth Wray, Kelly Diane; m. Emily Louise Tinsley, Aug. 19, 2000; children: John Keith Tinsley, Karen Denise Tinsley. BS in Mech. Engring., Va. Poly. Inst. and State U., 1951; MS in Systems Mgmt., U. So. Calif., 1979. Registered profl. engr., Kans., Wash., Calif. Commd. 2d lt. USAF, 1951, advanced through grades to major, 1964, ret., 1965; flight test engr. Boeing Co., Wichita, Kans., 1966-71, sr. engr. Seattle, 1971-76; systems test engr. Rockwell Internat., Edwards AFB, Calif., 1976-77, sr. engr. El Segundo, Calif., 1981—84, Palmdale, Calif., 1984—90, Hughes Helicopters, Inc., Culver City, Calif., 1977-81, Computer Scis. Corp., Edwards AFB, 1990-93. Comml. pilot, 1953—; asst. prof. air sci. Boston U., 1958—61. Active Rep. Party, Sacramento, 1977—, Rep. Nat. Com., Washington, 1977—; elder, deacon Presbyn. Ch. USA, Lancaster, 1981—. Recipient Letters of Commendation, USAF. Mem. ASME, NSPE (sec. 1972-75), Air Force Assn., Masons (50 yr. mem.), Shriners, Elks. Home: 2915 W Ave J-4 Lancaster CA 93536 E-mail: vwhodges0819@verizon.net.

HODGES, WILLIAM TERRELL, federal judge; b. Lake Wales, Fla., Apr. 28, 1934; s. Haywood and Clara Lucy (Murphy) H.; m. Peggy Jean Woods, June 8, 1958; children: Judson, Daniel, Clay. BSBA, U. Fla., 1956, JD, 1958, LLD (hon.). Bar: Fla. 1959. Mem. firm Macfarlane, Ferguson, Allison & Kelly, Tampa, 1958-71; instr. bus. law U. South Fla., Tampa, 1961-66; judge U.S. Dist. Ct. (mid. dist.) Fla., Tampa, 1971—82, 1989—99, chief judge, 1982—89, sr. judge, 1999—. Mem. com. on ops. jury system Jud. Conf., 1982-87, cir. coun., 11th cir., 1981-86; mem., adv. com. on criminal rules procedure and evidence Jud. Conf., 1987-93, chmn., 1990-93; ad hoc com. on habeas corpus reform; chmn., bench book com. Fed. Jud. Ctr., 1987-93; chmn., Ad Hoc Com. of the Jud. Conf. to study relations within the Fed. Jud. Ctr., 1997-98; chmn., US Jud. Panel on Multidistrict Litig., 2000-. Exec. editor, U. Fla. Law Rev., 1957-58. Mem. Am., Tampa-Hillsborough County bar assns., Fla. Bar (chmn. grievance com. 1967-70, chmn. uniform comml. code com. 1970-71), Dist. Judges Assn. 5th Circuit (co-chmn. com. on pattern jury instrn. 1977-81), Dist. Judges Assn. 11th Circuit (chmn. jury instrns. com. 1982—, pres. 1981-82) Am. Judicature Soc. Office: US Dist Ct 207 NW 2nd St Rm 337 Ocala FL 34475-6666

HODGINS, BEATRICE DAVIS, elementary school educator, primary school educator; b. Bangor, Maine, Dec. 8, 1932; d. Ralph Wilson and Pauline Lucille (Davis) H. BS Early Childhood Edn., Framingham State Coll., 1983. Bank bookkeeper First Nat. Bank Boston, 1950-54; tchr., co-owner Humpty Dumpty Kindergarten and Nursery Sch., Framingham, Mass., 1954-78; real estate broker Century 21, Framingham, Mass., 1978-81; pvt. home health care Newton, Mass., 1980-83; dir., tchr., owner Humpty Dumpty Kind and Nursery Sch., Framingham, 1983—. Distbr. Ecoquest Internat., 1999—. Republican. Avocation: writing fiction for children. Home and Office: 11 Warren Rd Framingham MA 01702-6344 Office Phone: 508-872-4401. E-mail: hodgi5@aol.com.

HODGKIN, DOUGLAS IRVING, political science educator; b. Lewiston, Maine, May 11, 1939; s. Clayton Pierce and Laura Marion (Meade) H.; m. Phyllis June Sherman, June 30, 1962; children: Andrew Clayton, Deanna Louise Hodgkin Mao, Valerie Ruth Hodgkin Trantanella. BA, Yale U., 1961; MA, Duke U., 1964, PhD, 1966. Govt. instr. Bowdoin Coll., Brunswick, Maine, 1964-66; vis. lectr. polit. sci. Bates Coll., Lewiston, Maine, 1966-68, asst. prof. polit. sci., 1968-73, assoc. prof. polit. sci., 1973-79, prof. polit. sci., 1979—2002, chmn. polit. sci., 1980-90, prof. emeritus, 2002—. Mem. adv. com. Maine Supreme Jud. Ct. on Rules of Profl. Responsibility, 2003—. Author: Lewiston Memories, 1994, (with others) Interest Group Politics in the Northeastern States, 1993, The Grange at Crowley's Junction, 2004, Fractured Family: Fighting in the Maine Courts, 2005; editor: Records of Lewiston, Maine, Vol I: Town Records Prior to 1852, 2001, Vol. II: Town Records 1852-1963 Vital Records Prior to 1865, 2002. Mem. exec. com. Lewiston Bicentennial Com., 1991-96; newsletter editor, bd. dirs. Androscoggin Hist. Soc., Auburn, Maine, 1990—; mem. Lewiston Hist. Preservation Rev. Bd., 1996—, Lewiston/Auburn Together Commn., 1996; mem. Maine Rep. Second Congl. Dist. Com., 1968-84, 86-90, 94-96, 2000-2004, chmn., 1972-76. Mem. Northeastern Polit. Sci. Assn. (exec. coun. 1983-88, program chair 1985-86, pres. 1986-87). Avocations: running, singing tenor, genealogy, politics. Home: 9 Sutton Pl Lewiston ME 04240-5210 Business E-Mail: dhodgkin@bates.edu.

HODGKIN, JOHN E., pulmonologist; b. Portland, Oregon, Aug. 22, 1939; s. Williard E. and Dorothy (Rigsby) H.; m. Jeanie (Walker), Sept. 6, 1980; children: Steve, Kathryn, Carolyn, Jonathan, and Jamie. BS, Walla Walla Coll., Wash., 1960; MD, Loma Linda U., Calif., 1964. Fellow pulmonologist Mayo Clinic, Rochester, Minn., 1970-72; chief pulmonary sect. Loma Linda U., Calif., 1974-80; clin. prof. medicine U. Calif., Davis, 1983—. Med. dir. respiratory care St. Helena Hosp., Deer Park, Calif., 1983—, med. dir. pulmonary rehab., 1983—, med. dir. ctr. for health promotion, 1983-96, asst. to pres., 1994—, med. dir. smoking cessation program, 2003—; med. dir. Adventist Health No. Calif., Roseville, Calif., 1995-98, Calif. Med. Found., 1995-98; med. dir. pulmonary rehab., Redbud Hosp., Clearlake, Calif., 2003— Editor: Chronic Obstructive Pulmonary Disease: Current Concepts in Diagnosis and Comprehensive Care, 1979, Respiratory Care: A Guide to Clin. Practice, 1977, 4th rev. edit. 1997, Pulmonary Rehabilitation: Guidelines to Success, 1984, 3d rev. edit., 2000, Fundamentals of Lung and Heart Sounds, 1988, 3d rev. edit., 2004. Decorated bronze star U.S. Army, 1968. Fellow Am. Assn. Cardiovas. and Pulmonary Rehab. (pres. 1995-96), Am. Coll. Chest Physicians, Am. Coll. Physicians, Am. Thoracic Soc., Nat. Assn. Med. Direction of Respiratory Care, Am. Assn. Respiratory Care (bd. med. advisors). Avocations: tennis, softball, skiing. Home: 1330 Crestmont Dr Angwin CA 94508-9634 Office: St Helena Hosp Lloyd Bldg Ste 502 Deer Park CA 94576 E-mail: drjohn@napanet.net.

HODGKINS, CANDACE CLARK, healthcare educator; d. Jane Emer LeVine; m. Don Anthony Boselli, Sr., Jan. 2, 1971 (div. 1983); children: Don Anthony Boselli Jr., Jennifer Anne Wright, Michael Francis Boselli; m. Frederick Crie Hodgkins, Mar. 23, 1990. BA, Gonzaga U., Spokane, Wash., 1967—71; MA, U. Colo., Boulder, 1983—85; PhD, U. Fla., Gainesville, 1998—2003. Lic. Mental Health Counselor State of Fla., 1999, cert. Counselor Nat. Bd. Cert. Counselors, 1994, lic. Profl.Counselor State of Colo., 1993. Clinician Colo. W. Mental Health Ctr., Vail, 1986—95, program dir., 1995—97; program adminstr., adolescent residential Gateway Cmty. Svcs., Inc., Jacksonville, Fla., 1997—99, assoc. v.p., residential svcs., 1999—2000, chief adminstrn. officer, 2000—02, chief of profl. svcs., 2002—03, sr. v.p., adminstrn., 2003—. Cons. for program evaluation, Jacksonville, Fla., 2002—05. Bd. co-chairperson The Eagle Family Ctr. Bd., Colo., 1996—97; bd. mem. Head Start and CPP Health Adv. Coun., Avon, Colo., 1996—97, N.E. Fla. Coun. for Alcohol and Drug Abuse, Jacksonville, 1998—2000. Recipient Outstanding Practitioner in the Doctorate Program, Chi Sigma Iota, 2001, Individual Commitment to Lifelong Learning, Excellence in Tng. & Employee Devel. Awards, U. N. Fla., 2003. Mem.: Fla. Mental Health Counselors Assn., Am. Mental Health Counselors Assn., Am. Counselors Assn. Avocations: travel, golf, hiking, skiing. Office: Gateway Community Svcs Inc 555 Stockton St Jacksonville FL 32204 Office Phone: 904-387-4661. Office Fax: 904-387-4706. E-mail: chodgkins@gatewaycommunity.com.

HODGKINS, DANIEL THOMAS, music educator; b. New Britain, Conn., Oct. 19, 1979; s. Donald and Diane Hodgkins. BS magna cum laude, Ctrl. Conn. State U., 1997—2001. Lic. Music Pre K - 12 Conn., 2001. Music tchr. Torrington Pub. Schools, Conn., 2001—. Dir. of bands Torrington Pub. Schools, Conn., 2001—. Mem.: CMEA. Avocations: hiking, jazz.

HODGKINS, DOUGLAS WENDELL, music educator; b. Winchester, Mass., Apr. 18, 1965; s. Wendell W. and JoAnn M. Hodgkins; m. Pamela Jean Dalton. MusB in Edn., U. Mass., 1987. Music tchr. Bishop Fenwick HS, Peabody, Mass., 1989—91, Sharon (Mass.) HS, 1991—92, Sandwich (Mass.) HS and Oak Ridge Elem. Sch., 1992—97, Lynnfield (Mass.) HS, 1997—. Organist Christ Meth. Ch., Malden, Mass., 1989—2001, choir dir., 1989—2001; organist Ctr. Congl. Ch., Lynnfield, 2001—, choir dir., 2001—. Mem.: Am. Choral Dirs. Assn., Mass. Music Educators Assn., Music Educators Nat. Conf. Avocations: baseball, basketball, football. Office: Lynnfield High School 275 Essex Street Lynnfield MA 01940

HODGKINS, WILLIAM F., career officer; BS in Secondary Edn., Auburn U., 1970, M in Edn. Adminstrn., 1973; grad., Squadron Officer Sch., 1974, USAF Fighter Weapons Sch., 1982, Air Command and Staff Coll., 1983, Can. Forces Command and Staff Coll., 1986; student, Air War Coll., 1995; student program for execs., Carnegie-Mellon U., 1997. Commd. 2d lt. USAF, 1974, advanced through grades to maj. gen., 1998; student, undergraduate navigator tng. Mather AFB, Calif., 1974; student and outstanding grad. Strategic Air Command Combat Crew Tng. Sch., Castle AFB, Calif., 1974—75; EC-135 and RC-135 navigator 2nd Airborne Command Control Squadron and 343rd Strategic Reconnaissance Squadron, Offutt AFB, Nebr., 1975—77; student and outstanding grad., undergraduate pilot tng. Williams AFB, Ariz., 1977—78; student and outstanding grad., F-15 upgrade tng. Luke AFB, Ariz.,

1978—79; F-15 aircraft comdr., instr. pilot 33rd Tactical Fighter Wing, Eglin AFB, Fla., 1979—83, standardization and evaluation pilot, 1979—83, unit weapons and tactics officer, 1979—83; F-15 student US Air Force Fighter Weapons Sch., Nellis AFB, Nev., 1982; F-15 instr. pilot, wing weapons and tactics officer 18th Tactical Fighter Wing, Kadena AFB, Japan, 1983-85; air ops. joint staff officer various weapons programs Can. Forces Nat. Def. Hdqs., Ottawa, Canada, 1986-88; chief weapons and tactics div. 1st Tactical Fighter Wing, Langley AFB, Va., 1988-89; chief, weapons and tactics divsn., chief spl. programs div., dep. chief staff ops. Hdqs. Tactical Air Command, Langley AFB, 1989-92; dep. chief staff ops. Hdqs. 17th Air Force, Sembach Air Base, Germany, 1992-93; comdr. 32d Fighter Group, Soesterberg Air Base, Netherlands, 1993-94; chief war plans and mobilization divsn., directorate of plans, dep. chief of staff for plans and ops. Hdqs. USAF, Washington, 1995, chief, regional plans & issues divsn., and mem., US & Can. permanent joint bd. for defense, directorate of plans, dep. chief of staff plans & ops., 1995—96, exec. officer to the dep. chief of staff for plans & ops., 1996—97; dir. ops. J-3 US Forces Japan, Yokota Air Base, 1997-98; dep. comdr. Can. NORAD, Winnipeg, Canada, 1998—2000; comdr. 325th Fighter Wing, Tyndall AFB, Fla., 2000—02; dep. comdr. CAOC 7, Air South, Strategic Command Europe, NATO, Larissa, Greece, 2002—04; dir. plans N. Am. Aerospace Defense Command, Peterson AFB, Colo., 2004—. Decorated Legion of Merit with oak leaf cluster, Def. Superior Svc. medal with oak leaf cluster, Meritorious Svc. medal with three oak leaf clusters, Air Force Commendation medal with oak leaf cluster, Air Force Achievement medal, Combat Readiness medal with oak leaf cluster; named USAF Tactical Deception Officer of Yr., 1984; recipient Chennault award, Outstanding USAF Aerial Warfare Tactician, 1985. Office: CAN/DCR Aircom Hq Box 17000 Station Forces Winnipeg Manitoba Canada R35 3Y5

HODGKINSON, GRETA, dancer; b. Providence, R.I. Grad., Nat. Ballet Sch., 1990. Mem. Nat. Ballet of Can., Toronto, Canada, 1990—96, prin. dancer, 1996—. Dancer (ballets) Swan Lake, 1999, Romeo and Juliet, The Merry Widow, The Sleeping Beauty, Onegin, The Taming of the Shrew, La Bayadère, Giselle, Manon, The Four Seasons, Herman Schmerman Pas de Deux, Sphinx, the Rubies Variation; internat. guest artist Can., U.S., Europe, Australia and Russia. Office: Walter Carsen Ctr Nat Ballet of Canada 470 Queens Quay West Toronto ON Canada M5V 3K4

HODGKINSON, WILLIAM JAMES, publishing executive; b. July 31, 1939; s. William James and Augusta Anne (Botka) H.; m. Virginia Evelyn Humphreys, Sept. 7, 1963; 1 child, Elizabeth Anne. AB, Bucknell U., 1961; MBA, Columbia U., 1963. Mktg. rsch. analyst Singer Co., N.Y.C., 1963-66; asst. adminstrn. writing paper divsn. Am. Paper Inst., N.Y.C., 1966-67; market rsch. mgr. Diners Club, N.Y.C., 1967-68; with Dun & Bradstreet Cos., Inc., 1968-92, mgmt. cons. William E. Hill Co. divsn. N.Y.C., 1971-73, mgr. fin. svcs. group Donnelly Mktg. divsn. Stamford, Conn., 1973-86, v.p., 1987-92; COO Career Sys., Inc., Fairfield, Conn., 1993-97; pres. Marketview Pub. Corp., Fairfield, 1997—. Contbr. articles to profl. jours. Bd. dirs. Bklyn. Pub. Libr. br., 1974-79, Enlightenment Together, Inc., 1971-76; rsch. coord. Presdl. Task Force on Improving Small Bus., 1969-70; v.p., trustee Montessori Sch. Bklyn., 1975-79; trustee Greens Farms Congl. Ch., 1983-85; co-chmn. Save Fairfield Com., 1984—; bd. deacons Episc. ch., 1971-78, pres., 1977-78. With U.S. Army, 1963. Recipient Brotherhood award Bucknell U., 1960; grantee Columbia U., 1962-63. Mem. Bank Mktg. Assn., Am. Mktg. Assn., Direct Mail Mktg. Assn., Princeton Club (N.Y.C.), Phi Lambda Theta. Home: 4454 Black Rock Tpke Fairfield CT 06824

HODGSON, ERNEST, toxicology educator; b. Durham, Eng., July 26, 1932; arrived in U.S., 1955; s. Ernest Victor and Emily (Moses) H.; m. Mary Kathleen Devlin, Dec. 21, 1957 (dec.); children: Mary Elizabeth, Audrey Catherine, Patricia Emily Devlin, Ernest Victor Felix. B.Sc. with honors, Kings Coll. U. Durham, Eng., 1955; PhD, Oreg. State U., 1959. Rsch. fellow Oreg. State U., Corvallis, 1955-59, U. Wis., Madison, 1959-61; asst. prof. N.C. State U., Raleigh, 1961-63, assoc. prof., 1963-65, prof. toxicology, 1965—, William Neal Reynolds prof., 1977—, chmn. toxicology dept., 1982-97, Disting. Alumni Rsch. prof., 1987-90. Mem. adv. panel U.S. EPA, Washington, 1982-85; mem. toxicology study sect. NIH, Washington, 1985-89, mem. NIEHS study sect., 1992-96, chmn. 1994-96; pres. Toxicology Comm., Raleigh, 1982—; vis. scientist U. Wash., Seattle, 1975. Author, editor: Introduction to Biochemical Toxicology, 1980, 3d edit., 2000, Modern Toxicology, 1987, 3d edit., 2004, Dictionary of Toxicology; editor: Reviews in Biochemical Toxicology, 1979-, Reviews in Environmental Toxicology, 1984-, Jour. Biochemical and Molecular Toxicology; mem. editorial bd. Chemico-Biol. Interactions; contbr. articles to profl. jours. Chmn. policy rev. com. Gov.'s Waste Mgmt. Bd., Raleigh, 1984. Grantee NIH, 1962—, U.S. Army, 2000—. Mem. AAAS, Soc. Toxicology (edn. com. 1984—, Edn. award 1984, Merit award 1994, pres. mechanisms sect. 1991-92, pres. N.C. chpt. 1984-85), Am. Soc. Pharmacology (drug metabolism com. 1981-84), Am. Chem. Soc. (Burdick and Jackson Internat. award in pesticide chemistry, Sterling Hendricks award USDA, 1997), Internat. Soc. Study Xenobiotics (coun. 1986-89, sec.-elect 1990-92, sec. 1992-94, pres.-elect 1996-97, pres. 1998-99), Sigma Xi (chpt. pres. 1974). Democrat. Avocations: history, writing, travel. Office: NC State U Dept Toxicology PO Box 7633 Raleigh NC 27695-0001 E-mail: ernest_hodgson@ncsu.edu.

HODGSON, HARRIET W., non-fiction writer; b. Flushing, N.Y., Sept. 27, 1935; d. Alfred Earnst and Mabel Clifton Weil; m. C. John Hodgson, Aug. 10, 1957; children: Helen Anne, Amy Jeanne. BS in Early Childhood Edn., Wheelock Coll., 1957; MA in Art Edn., U. Minn., 1960. Former tchr. (12 yrs.). Author: Smart Aging: Taking Charge of Your Physical and Emotional Health, 1999, The Alzheimer's Caregiver: Dealing with the Realities of Dementia, 1998, Alzheimer's: Finding the Words, a Communication Guide for Those Who Care, 1995, Heart Surgery and You: An Activity Book for Preschoolers, Heart Surgery and You: An Activity Book for Gradeschoolers, Heart Surgery and You: a Guide for Teens, Powerplays: How Teens Can Pull the Plug on Sexual Harassment, 1993, Powerplays Leader's Guide, When You Love a Child, 1992, Rochester: City of the Prairie, 1989, Parents Recover Too: When Your Child Comes Home from Treatment, 1988, A Parent's Survival Guide: How to Cope When Your Kid is Using Drugs, 1986, Contraptions, Toyworks, Gameworks, Artworks, My First Fourth of July Book, 1987, "I Made It Myself!", E is for Energy, M is for Me, Just for You, Food Label Detective: An Activity Book, 2002; co-author: Catching the Exercise Thief: A Game Book for Kids, 2004; co-author: (with Lois Krahn) Smiling Through Your Tears: Anticipating Grief, 2005; contbr. articles to websites, reports, columns, and profl. jours.; editor: Scope newsletter of the Minn. Med. Assn. Mem. Walden Hill Vocal Ensemble; vol. McGruff House; past mem. regional devel. bd. Minn. Pub. Radio; mem. Minn. Takes Action for Healthy Kids, Adolescent Health Com., Zumbro Valley Med. Soc., Minn. Med. Assn. Commn. Com. Mem.: AAUW, Assn. Health Care Journalists, Wing of the Aerospace Med. Assn. (past pres., chair mktg. com.), Zumbro Valley Med. Assn. Alliance (bd. dirs., past pres., v.p., sec., newsletter editor), Am. Med. Assn. Alliance, Minn. Manx Assn., N.Am. Manx Assn., The Study Club. Avocations: cooking, art projects. Home and Office: 1107 Foxcroft Ln SW Rochester MN 55902

HODGSON, JAMES STANLEY, antiquarian bookseller; b. Detroit, Apr. 26, 1942; s. Norman Thomas and Marion Phyllis (Konat) H.; m. Nancy Irons Mercer, Aug. 10, 1968 (div. Feb. 1996); children: Emily Harcourt, William Mercer. AB, Brown U., 1964; MS, Simmons Coll., 1967. Acquisitions librarian Fogg Art Mus. Harvard U., Cambridge, Mass., 1968-83, librarian, 1983-84, chief librarian faculty Grad. Sch. of Design, 1984-90; pres. James Hodgson Books, Inc., Boston, 1990—. Mem. adv. bd. Boston Archtl. Ctr., Boston, 1984—. Contbr. numerous articles to profl. jours. Trustee Rotch House and Garden Mus., New Bedford, 1984—; v.p. Coalition for Buzzard's Bay, 1994—. Mem. Art Libraries Soc. N.Am. Home and Office: 39 Chestnut St South Dartmouth MA 02748-3508

HODGSON, JANE ELIZABETH, obstetrician, gynecologist, consultant; b. Crookston, Minn., Jan. 23, 1915; d. Herbert and Adelaide (Marin) H.; m. Frank Walter Quattlebaum, Feb. 22, 1940; children: Gretchen, Nancy. BS, Carleton Coll., 1934, DSc (hon.), 1994; MD, U. Minn., 1939, MS in Ob-gyn., 1947. Diplomate Am. Bd. Ob-gyn. Fellow Mayo Clinic, Rochester, Minn., 1941-44; pvt. practice in ob-gyn. St. Paul, 1947-72; med. dir. Preterm Clinic, Washington, 1972-74; med. dir. fertility control clinic St. Paul Ramsey Med. Ctr., 1974-79; med. dir. Planned Parenthood Minn., St. Paul, 1980-82, Midwest Health Ctr. Women, Mpls., 1981-83, Women's Health Ctr., Duluth, Minn., 1981-84, mem. staff, 1986—, also bd. dirs.; ostetrician/gynecologist Project Hope, Grenada, West Indies, 1984; vis. prof. ob-gyn. project hope Zheijiang Med. Sch., Hangzhou, China, 1985-86; clin. assoc. prof. ob-gyn. U. Minn., Mpls., 1986—. Vis. med. educator Project Hope, Cairo, 1979-80; vis. prof. dept. ob-gyn. U. Calif., San Francisco, 1983. Editor: Abortion & Sterilization, 1981; contbr. numerous articles to profl. jours. Bd. dirs. Genesis II Women, Mpls., 1988—, Pro Choice Resources, Mpls., 1991—, Wellstone Alliance, Mpls., 1992—; bd dirs. Ctr. for Reproductive Rights, N.Y.C., 1995-2004, hon. trustee, 2004—. Recipient Ann. Humanitarian award Nat. Abortion Fedn., 1981, Woman Physician of Yr. award Med. Women Minn. Med. Assn., 1983, Ann. Jane Hodgson Reproductive Freedom award Nat. Abortion Rights Action League, 1989, Hanah G. Solomon award Nat. Coun. Jewish Women, 1990, Margaret Sanger award Planned Parenthood Fedn. of Am., 1995, Harold Swanberg award Am. Med. Writer's Assn., 1996. Fellow Am. Coll. Ob-Gyn. (founding); mem. Am. Med. Women's Assn. (E. Blackwell award 1992, Reproductive Health award 1994), Minn. Ob-Gyn. Soc. (pres. 1967), Minn. Med. Assn. (So. Minn. Med. award 1952), Minn. Women's Polit. Caucus (16th Ann. Founding Feminist award 1988), Mayo Clinic Alumni Assn. Home and Office: 211 2nd St NW Apt 1405 Rochester MN 55901-2895 Office Phone: 507-536-9338.

HODGSON, JOHN C., manufacturing executive; m. Lynda Hodgson; 2 children. BS in indsl. mgmt., U. Tenn. X-ray sales DuPont Co., New Orleans, Okla. City, N.Y.C, Wilmington, 1966—79, bus. mgr., electronic materials-Europe Geneva, 1979—82, bus. dir., diagnostic sys. - Europe, 1982—84, global bus. dir., diagnostic sys. Wilmington, Del., 1984—89, global bus. dir., microcircuit materials, 1990—94, mng. dir., gen. mgr., electronic materials Triangle Park, NC, 1994—96, v.p., gen. mgr., photopolymer and electronic materials Wilmington, Del., 1996—2000, group v.p., gen. mgr.- DuPont iTechnologies, 2000—02, exec. v.p., 2002—04, sr. v.p., 2004—. Mem.: Am. Chemistry Coun. (mem. exec. com.). Office: DuPont DuPont Bldg 1007 Mkt St Wilmington DE 19898

HODGSON, KEITH O., chemistry professor; b. 1947; m. Britt Hedman. BS, U. Va., 1969; PhD, U. Calif., Berkeley, 1972. Prof. chemistry Stanford U., 1984—. Dep. dir. synchrotron divsn. Stanford Linear Accelerator Ctr., divsn. dir. synchrotron divsn., 1998; chair DOE Biol. and Environ. Rsch. Adv. Com.; mem. NIH Nat. Ctr. Rsch. Resources Adv. Coun. Co-author: more than 200 sci. publ. Recipient Sidhu award for contbn. to x-ray diffraction, 1978, Ernest Oliver Lawrence award, US Dept. Energy, 2002; fellow, Alfred P. Sloan Found., 1976—78; NATO Postdoctoral Fellow, E.T.H., Zurich, 1972—73. Office: Stanford Synchrotron Radiation Lab SLAC 2575 Sand Hill Rd MS 69 Menlo Park CA 94025

HODGSON, PAUL EDMUND, surgeon, department chairman; b. Milw., Dec. 14, 1921; s. Howard Edmund and Ethel Marie (Niemi) H.; m. Barbara Jean Osborne, Apr. 22, 1945; children: Ann, Paul. BS summa cum laude, Beloit Coll., 1943; MD cum laude, U. Mich., 1945. Diplomate: Am. Bd. Surgery. Intern U. Mich. Hosp., 1945-46, resident in surgery, 1948-52; mem. faculty dept. surgery U. Mich., 1952-62, assoc. prof., 1956-62; prof. surgery U. Nebr. Coll. Medicine, Omaha, 1962-88, prof. emeritus, 1988—, asst. dean for curriculum, 1966-72, chmn. dept. surgery, 1972-84. Trustee Beloit Coll., 1977-80 Served to capt. M.C. U.S. Army, 1946-48. Mem. A.C.S., Frederick A. Coller Surg. Soc., Soc. Univ. Surgeons, Central Surg. Assn., Soc. Surgery Alimentary Tract, Am. Assn. Surgery Trauma, Western Surg. Assn., Am. Surg. Assn. Presbyterian. Office: Dept Surgery Med Ctr 983280 Nebraska Medical Center Omaha NE 68198-3280

HODGSON, W(ALTER) JOHN (BARRY HODGSON), surgeon; b. Middlesborough, Eng., Sept. 17, 1939; came to U.S., 1975; s. Walter Aggett and Constance Lillian (Nelson) H.; m. Jean C. Morgan, Apr. 20, 1967; children: Sean, Russell, Miranda. MB, BS, Charing Cross Med. Sch., London, 1964; M of Surgery, London U., 1976. Rotating intern, resident London U., 1964-75; surgeon Bronx (NY) VA Med. Ctr., 1975-78, asst. chief surg. svc., 1977-82; pvt. practice specializing in surgery Mt. Sinai Hosp., NYC, 1978-81; chief gastrointestinal surgery Westchester Med. Ctr., Valhalla, NY, 1981-94; dept. surg. Montefiore Med. Ctr. and Einstein Hosp., Bronx, 1997—; prof. surgery NY Med. Coll., Valhalla, 1987-98, course organizer for laparoscopic surgery, 1990-92, prof. cell biology and anatomy, 1993—; clin. prof. surgery NYU, 1995—; prof. surgery Albert Einstein Coll. Medicine, 1998—. Contbr. articles to profl. jours.; editor: Liver Tumors: Multidisciplinary Management, 1987; inventor cavitron surg. technique for livor tumor surgery. Organizer, coach Larchmont (NY) Jr. Soccer League, 1977; mem. Larchmont Rep. Com., 1985. Cavitron Co. grantee, 1978, Cavitron Lasersonics grantee, 1987, Ethicon grantee, 1999. Fellow ACS, Am. Coll. Gastroneterology; mem. NY Surg. Soc. for Acad. Surgery, Am. Assn. Clin. Anatomists, Am. Soc. Colon & Rectal Surgery, Soc. Am. Gastroendoscopic Surgery, Larchmont Yacht Club. Episcopalian. Avocations: sailing, hill walking, skiing. Office: Montefiore Med Park Dept Surgery 1575 Blondell Ave Dept Surgery Bronx NY 10461-2660 Office Phone: 718-405-8239. E-mail: wjbhodgson@optonline.net.

HODKINSON, SYDNEY PHILLIP, composer, educator, musician; b. Winnipeg, Man., Can., Jan. 17, 1934; s. Ernest and Irene (Pilgrim) H.; m. Elizabeth Jane Deischer, July 22, 1955; children: Mark, Scott, Grant. MusB, U. Rochester, 1957, MusM, 1958; D of Mus. Arts, U. Mich., 1968. Mem. faculty U. Va., 1958-63, Ohio U., Athens, 1963-66, U. Mich., Ann Arbor, 1968-73; prof. composition, chair conducting and ensembles Eastman Sch. Music, Rochester, N.Y., 1973-98. Artist-in-residence, Mpls.-St.Paul, 1970-72; Meadows chair composition So. Meth. U., Dallas, 1984-86; vis. prof. composition U. Western Ont., London, Can., 1990, Aspen Music Festival, 1998—, Ind. U., 2002, Duke U., 2003; Almand chair composition Stetson U., 2004—. Composer numerous works for brass, woodwinds, strings and percussion, 1958—, also for orch., chorus, stage, opera, wind and chamber ensembles; artist various recs. Guggenheim fellow, 1978-79; grantee U. Va., 1961, Ohio U., 1964, Can. Coun., 1966, 69, 77-78, Danforth Found., 1966-68, U. Mich., 1969, 70-73, Ford Found., 1976, Nat. Endowment for Arts, 1975-76, 78, 83-84, 90-91, Martha Baird Rockefeller Found., 1976. Mem. Broadcast Music Inc., Am. Composers Alliance, Am. Music Ctr., Phi Mu Alpha Sinfonia. Home: 2589 John Anderson Dr Ormond Beach FL 32176-2417

HODNIK, DAVID F., retail company executive; b. 1947; Grad., Western Ill. U., 1970. Sr. auditor Paul Pettengill & Co., 1969-72; with Ace Hardware Corp., Hinsdale, Ill., 1972—, acct., 1972-74, mgr. acctg., 1974-76, controller, 1976-80, v.p., treas., 1980-82; v.p. fin., treas. ACE Hardware Corp., Oak Brook, Ill., 1982-88, sr. v.p., 1988-90, exec. v.p., 1990-93, exec. v.p., COO, 1993-95, pres., COO, 1995-96, pres., CEO, 1996—. Office: ACE Hardware Corp 2200 Kensington Ct Oak Brook IL 60523-2100 E-mail: hodnik@acehardware.com.*

HODOSH, RICHARD M., neurosurgeon; b. Providence, 1946; BS, Brown U.; MD, U. Cin. Diplomate Am. Bd. Neurol. Surgery. Intern Parkland Meml. Hosp.-U. Tex. Health Scis. Ctr., Dallas, 1972—73; resident in neurol. surgery U. Tex. Health Scis. Ctr., Dallas, 1973—78; fellow in neurol. radiology Nat. Hosp. Neurol. Diseases, Queen Sq., London, 1975; fellow in cerebrovascular surgery Kantonsspital, U. Zurich, Switzerland; attending physician Overlook Hosp., Summit, 1980—, Morristown (N.J.) Meml. Hosp., 1980—; dir. Neuroscience Ctr., Overlook Hosp., Summit, NJ; dir., cerebrovascular surgery Atlantic Health Sys. Dir. neuroscis. Atlantic Health Sys., Summit; clin. prof. neurosurgery U. Medicine and Dentistry N.J. Med. Sch., Newark. Named one of Top Drs. in N.Y. Metro Area, Castle Connolly, Top Drs. 2003, N.J. Monthly Mag.; recipient Top Drs. 2004, N.Y. Mag., 2004. Mem.: Am. Heart Assn. (pres., Heritage Affiliate, mem. adv. bd.), Acoustic Neuroma Assn. Office: Atlantic Brain and Spine Inst 99 Beauvoir Ave Summit NJ 07902 Office Phone: 908-522-4979. Office Fax: 908-522-5377. Business E-Mail: richard.hodosh@ahsys.org.*

HODOUS, ROBERT POWER, lawyer; b. Zanesville, Ohio, July 29, 1945; s. Robert Frank and Nancy Aurelia (Power) H.; m. Susan Cottrell Birkhead, Feb. 1, 1969; children: Robert Everett, Shannon Alycia. BA, Miami U., Oxford, Ohio, 1967; JD, U. Va., Charlottesville, 1970. Bar: Va. 1970. Assoc. firm McGuire, Woods & Battle, Charlottesville, 1970-71; asst. trust officer Nat. Bank & Trust Co., Charlottesville, 1971-72, trust officer, 1972-75, sec., 1975-79, Jefferson Bankshares, Inc. (formerly NB Corp.), Charlottesville, 1979-91, v.p., sec., 1985-91, sr. v.p., sec., 1987-91; asst. to pres. Jefferson Nat. Bank, Charlottesville, 1987-91; pvt. practice law Charlottesville, 1991-92; mem. firm Payne & Hodous, L.L.P., Charlottesville, 1992—. Author: Let's Really Change Taxes, 1998. Chmn. profl. div. Thomas Jefferson Area United Way, 1973, vice-chmn., 1978-79, campaign chmn., 1979-80, v.p. planning, 1981, pres., 1983; bd. dirs. Central Va. chpt. ARC, 1972-78, treas., 1972-75, chmn., 1975-77; commr. Charlottesville Redevel. and Housing Authority, 1974-78; mem. Region X Cmty. Mental Health and Retardation Svcs. Bd., 1973-79, chmn., 1974-76, mem. exec. com., 1976-78; v.p. Soccer Orgn. of Charlottesville-Albemarle, 1985-86, pres., 1986-88; co-pres. Greenbier Sch. PTA, 1985-86; chmn. recreation precinct Charlottesville City Dem. Com., 1971, Rep. com., 1992—; chmn. City Rep. Com., 2000—; bd. dirs. Charlottesville-Albemarle Cmty. Found., 1987-2000, chmn. devel. com., 1991-93, mem. exec. and fin. coms., 1991-2000, chmn. fin. com., 1997-2000; bd. dirs. Free Enterprise Forum, 2002-. Mem.: Charlottesville C. of C. (govt. affairs com. 1996—, co-chair 2002—04), Computer Law Assn., Va. Bankers Assn. (com. drafted Va. Trust Subs. Act 1973, trust com. 1974—77, legal affairs com. 1986—91, large bank legis. coord. 1987—91), Va. State Bar, Charlottesville-Albemarle Bar Assn., Va. Bar Assn., Fairview Club (Charlottesville) (pres. 1974—75). Roman Catholic. Home: 1309 Lester Dr Charlottesville VA 22901-3143 Office: 412 E Jefferson St Charlottesville VA 22902-5109 *To me success is indicated by feelings of personal peace and satisfaction, not by external possessions. My goals are to do my best in contributing to the success of endeavors in which I become involved and to remember that the people involved in activities are the most important part of the activities. I feel my family is my most important endeavor. I hope never to become so involved in activities that I cannot enjoy my family, my surroundings and people I meet, or that I cannot spend the time necessary to do well those activities in which I am involved.*

HODSOLL, FRANCIS SAMUEL MONAISE, government official; b. LA, May 1, 1938; s. Frank and Adelaide (Monaise) H.; m. Margaret Mimi McEwen, Aug. 18, 1963; children— Lisa-Monaise, Francis Hamill McEwen BA, Yale U., 1959; MA, LLB, Cambridge U., 1963; JD, Stanford U., 1964; Fgn. Svcs. econ. course, Washington, 1972; DFA (hon.), Pratt Inst., 1983, U. Mass., 1986. Assoc. Sullivan & Cromwell, N.Y.C., 1965-66; fgn. service officer Adminstrv. Office Am. embassy, Belgium, 1966-68; asst. polit. advisor SHAPE, Belgium, 1968-69; controlling dir. Warner, Barnes & Co., Manila, 1964-71; oceans policy officer State Dept., Washington, 1969-71; spl. asst. chmn. Council on Environ. Quality, Washington, 1972-73; spl. asst. adminstr. EPA, Washington, 1973-74; dir. energy conservation div. Commerce Dept., Washington, 1974, staff dir. cabinet work edn. task force, 1974, exec. asst. to undersec., 1974-76, dept. asst. sec. commerce for energy and strategic resources, 1976-77; dir. Office of Law of Sea Negotiation State Dept., Washington, 1977, dep. U.S. spl. rep. for nonproliferation, 1978-80; mem. White House transition team Exec. Office Pres., Washington, 1980-81; dep. asst. to Pres. and dep. to chief of staff White House, Washington, 1981; chmn. Nat. Endowment for Arts, Washington, 1981-89; exec. assoc. dir., CFO U.S. Govt. Office Mgmt. and Budget, Exec. Office of Pres., Washington, 1989-91; dep. dir. for mgmt. Office Mgmt. and Budget, Exec. Office of Pres., Washington, 1991-93. Chair, bd. dirs. Ctr. for Arts & Culture, Washington, 2001—; sr. cons. Logistics Mgmt. Inst., 2001—, Gene Rouleau & Assocs., 2002—03; co-chmn. Sally Mae Edn. Svcs. Coun., 1995—96, Am. Assembly Arts and the Pub. Purpose, 1996—97; co-chair, CEO Southwest Colo. Data Ctr., 1994—97; CEAR reviewer Assn. Govt. Accts., 2003—; mem. performance consortium oversight com. Nat. Acad. Pub. Adminstrn., 2003—; cons. in field; mem. U.S. Nat. Commn. for UNESCO, 2004—. Chmn. bd., commissioners Ouray County, 2000—01; vice chair Nat. Assn. Counties Geospatial Data com., 1998—99; review com. New Century Colo., 1999—2000, com. mem., 1999—2000; mem. Nat. Assn. Counties Rural Leadership Caucus and Chair Rural Telecom. Task Force, 1999—2001; vice chair steering com. Nat. Assn. Counties Telecom and Tech., 2000—01; co. chmn. Am. Assembly Arts, Tech. and Intellectual Property, 1999—2002; chmn. bd. dirs. Ctr. for Arts and Culture, 2001—; prin. coun. Excellence in Govt., 1993—; chmn. Ouray County (Colo.) Rep. com., 1995—96; commr. Ouray County, 1997—2001; mem. Gen. Govt. Transition Team Colo. Gov. elect Bill Owens, 1998—99; dir. Colo. River Water Conservation Dist., 1997—2001. Mem. Nat. Assn. Counties (presdl. transition team), N.Y. State Bar Assn., Stanford U. Alumni Assn., Yale Club, Met. Club, Zeta Psi. Republican. Episcopalian. Personal E-mail: fhodsoll@cox.net.

HODSON, CYNTHIA LOU, elementary school educator; b. Independence, Mo., June 7, 1954; d. Arthur L and Maryan R Welch; m. Ken L. Hodson, Aug. 17, 1973; 1 child, Jon L.; 1 child, Kenny L. BS in Edn., William Jewell Coll., Liberty, Mo., 1986; MA in Curriculum and Instrn., U. Mo., Kansas City, 1991, Ednl. Specialist Degree in Curriculum and Instrn., 1996. State of Missouri Public School Teacher's Certificate Mo. State Bd. of Edn., 1986. 5th grade tchr. Raytown (Mo.) C-2 Sch. Dist., 1987—. Tech. lead tchr. Raytown C-2 Sch. Dist., 2002—. Recipient Tchr. of the Yr., Spring Valley Elem., 1991, Innovative Tchg., Third Internat. Conf. on Innovations in Edn., 1991. Mem.: RCTA (assoc.), ASCD (assoc.). Avocations: travel, photography. Home: 6609 Sterling Ave Raytown MO 64133 Personal E-mail: lou2412@comcast.net.

HODSON, ROY GOODE, JR., retired logistician; b. Enon, Ala., July 22, 1927; s. Roy Goode and Ilda Fern (Jinks) H.; m. Mildred Bernice Parlier, Dec. 3, 1966 (dec. July 1992); children: Joan Hodson Bash, Scott Daniel, Jayne Clymer. Student, San Diego Jr. Coll., 1947-49, San Diego Vocational, 1947-49, San Diego State Coll., 1949-50. Security officer US Naval CB Ctr. (Civil Service), Port Hueneme, Calif., 1950-52; logistician Gen. Dynamics, San Diego, 1952-64, GTE Govt. Systems, Inc., Mt. View, Calif., 1964-89. Bd. dirs. San Jose Civic Light Opera Assn., 1988-95; advisor San Jose Children's Musical Theater, 1995-2002; mem. Boys and Girls Club. With U.S. Army, 1945-47. Recipient Bravo award Silhoutte mag., 1988, Ginny award, 1989. Mem.: Wildlife Land Trust, Cornell Lab. of Ornithology, Nat. Audubon Soc., Archaeol. Inst. Am., Am. Indian Relief Coun., Am. Indian Edn. Found., Am. Birding Assn., Humane Soc. Limestone County, Ind. Sheriffs Assn., Nat. Humane Edn. Soc., Spiceland Hist. and Tourism Soc., Nat. Pks. and Conservation Assn., Am. Philatelic Soc., Internat. Platform Assn., Internat. Freelance Photographers Orgn., Nature Conservancy, Nat. Svc. Found., Easter Seals Found., Nat. Arbor Day Found., Am. Legion, Humane Soc. U.S., Am. Film Inst., Am. Assn. Ret. Persons, AMVETS, Athens C. of C., Am. Image Press Club. Democrat. Mem. Church of Christ. Avocations: photography, lapidary, geneaology, music. Home: 17266 Seven Mile Post Rd Athens AL 35611-8457

HOEBEL, BARTLEY GORE, psychologist, educator; b. N.Y.C., May 29, 1935; s. Edward Adamson and Frances (Gore) H.; m. Cynthia A. Eney, June 22, 1962; children— Valerie, Carolyn, Brett. AB, Harvard, 1957; PhD, U. Pa., 1962; PhD (hon.), U. Cath. Louvain, 1991. Mem. faculty psychology dept. Princeton, 1962—, prof, 1970—. Founder, pres. Delaware River Steamboat Floating Classroom, Inc., 2000—. Contbg. author: Handbook of Psychopharmacology, 1977, S.S. Stevens Handbook of Experimental Psychology, 1988, Handbook of Obesity, 1997, 2004; contbr. articles to tech. jours. and books. Fellow AAAS, APA (pres. physiol. and comparative psychol. divsn. 1994), Am. Psychol. Soc.; mem. Soc. Neurosci., Soc. Study Ingestive Behavior (pres. 1995), Ea. Psychol. Assn. (pres. 1997). Unitarian Universalist. Home: 207 Hartley Ave Princeton NJ 08540-5615 Office: Dept Psychology Princeton Univ Princeton NJ 08544 Office Phone: 609-258-4463. Business E-Mail: hoebel@princeton.edu.

HOECKER, THOMAS RALPH, lawyer; b. Chicago Heights, Ill., Dec. 14, 1950; s. William H. and Norma M. (Wynkoop) H.; m. V. Sue Thornton, Aug. 28, 1971; children: Elizabeth T., Ellen T. BS, No. Ill. U., 1972; JD, U. Ill., 1975. Bar: Ill. 1975, Ariz. 1985. Assoc. Davis and Morgan, Peoria, Ill., 1975-80, ptnr., 1980-84; assoc. Snell and Wilmer, Phoenix, 1984-86, ptnr., 1987—. Mem. steering com. Western Pension Conf., Phoenix, 1986-92, pres., 1991-92. Fellow Am. Coll. Employee Benefits Coun. (charter), Ariz. Bar Found.; mem. ABA (chair tax sect. employee benefits com. 2002-03, co-chair legis. and adminstrv. subcom. of labor sect. employee benefits com. 1994-96), Ariz. Bar Assn., Ill. Bar Assn., Marciopa County Bar Assn., (mem. investment com. 1988-94). Avocation: fly fishing. Office: Snell Wilmer 1 Arizona Ctr Phoenix AZ 85004 Business E-Mail: thoecker@swlaw.com.

HOEFFLIN, RICHARD MICHAEL, lawyer, judicial administrator; BS in Acctg., Calif. State U., Northridge, 1971; JD, Loyola U., L.A., 1974. Bar: Calif. 1974, U.S. Dist. Ct. (cen. dist.) Calif. 1974, U.S. Tax Ct. 1976, U.S. Dist. Ct. (no. and so. dists.) Calif. 1976, U.S. Supreme Ct. 1982, cert.: (mediator). With Lewitt, Hackman, Hoefflin, Shapiro, Marshall & Harlan, 1974—2000, ptnr., 1977—2000; prin. Hoefflin & Assocs., ALC, 2000—. Judge pro tem L.A. Superior Ct., 1982—, Ventura County Superior Ct., 1991—, Fee Dispute Resolution Svcs. for L.A. County Bar. Co-founder Ventura County Homeowners for Equal Taxation, Westlake Village, Calif., 1978—79; pres., gen. counsel Westlake Hills Homeowners Assn., 1975—77; chmn. Celebrity Love Match Tennis Tour for John McEnroe United Cerebral Palsy/Spastic Children Found., 1990—96; bd. dirs. Michael Hoefflin Found., 1996—, No. Ranch Country Club, 2000—03, Alliance for Arts, 2000—. Mem.: ABA, Westlake Hills Owners Assn. (pres. 1977—78), San Fernando Valley Bar Assn. (co-chair bus. and real estate sect. 1995—97), Ventura County Bar Assn., L.A. Bar Assn., North Ranch Country Club (pres. tennis asn. 1984—85, sec. 2000—03). Office: 2659 Townsgate Rd #232 Westlake Village CA 91361 Office Phone: 805-497-8605. Business E-Mail: rmhoefflin@hoefflinlaw.com.

HOEFFLIN, STEVEN M., plastic surgeon; b. Seattle, Wash., Feb. 7, 1946; MD, UCLA, 1972; BA, Calif. St. U. Intern UCLA Med. Ctr., 1972—73, resident, 1973—77; plastic surgeon Santa Monica (Calif.) Hosp.; assoc. clin. prof. UCLA. Co-author: Ethnic Rhinoplasty, 1998. Mem.: Amer. Bd. Plastic Surgery. Office: 1530 Arizona Ave Santa Monica CA 90404-1208

HOEFLE, ANDREW H., musician, educator; MusM, No. Ill. U., Dekalb, 1984—85. Band dir. Orangeville H.S., Ill., 1979—82, Lanark H.S., Ill., 1982—84; dir., instrumental music Highland Coll., Freeport, Ill., 1983—96; band dir., music dept. chair S. Suburban Coll., South Holland, Ill., 1997—. Guest condr. S. Suburban Coll., South Holland, Ill., 1990—; artist, clinician Custom Music Corp., Ferndale, Mich., 1993—; euphonium Millar Brass Ensemble, Evanston, Ill., 1996—. Chair Internat. Assn. for Jazz Edn., Manhattan, Kans., 1991—93. Recipient Outstanding C.C. Tchr. of the Yr., Ill. C.C. Bd., 1989. Mem.: Am. Fedn. Tchrs., Ill. Music Educators Assn., Internat. Assn. for Jazz Edn., Music Educators Nat. Conf. Office: S Suburban Coll 15800 S State St South Holland IL 60473 Office Phone: 708-596-2000. E-mail: ahoefle@southsuburbancollege.edu.

HOEFLE, H. FREDERICK, lawyer; b. Cin., Apr. 7, 1938; s. Henry Alfred and Norma (Lambeck) H.; m. Joyce Ann Dreier, Aug. 21, 1965 (dec. Jan. 19, 1996); children: Jennifer, Meredith. AB with high honors, U. Cin., 1960; JD, Chase Coll. Law, Cin., 1965. Bar: Ohio 1965, U.S. Supreme Ct. 1971, U.S. Ct. Appeals (D.C., 5th and 6th cirs.), U.S. Dist. Ct. (so. dist.) Ohio, U.S. Dist. Ct. (ea. dist.) Ky. Assoc. Shea & McKay, Norwood, Ohio, 1966-71; asst. atty. gen. State of Ohio, Cin., 1971-79; pvt. practice, Cin., 1971—; sr. trial counsel Hamilton County Pub. Defender, Cin., 1979-90. Mem. death penalty task force U.S. Ct. Appeals (6th cir.). Contbg. author: Ohio Death Penalty Manual, 1981; Ohio Appellate Manual, 1983. Mem. Ohio Death Penalty Task Force, Columbus, 1981—. Mem. Cin. Bar Assn. (exec. com. 1976, spl. award of merit 1978), Ohio State Bar Assn., Stewart Inn of Ct. (Courageous Advocate award), Cin. Criminal Def. Lawyers Assn. (Pres.'s award 1996), Order of Curia, Phi Beta Kappa, Phi Delta Theta. Democrat. Unitarian Universalist. Home: 4532 Runningfawn Dr Cincinnati OH 45247-7530 Office: 630 Vine St Ste 415 Cincinnati OH 45202-2437

HOEFLE, PAUL RYAN, lawyer; b. Aurora, Ill., July 25, 1956; s. Ronald Anthony and Shirley Ann Hoefle; m. Mary Beth Wredling, June 25, 1983; children: Mary Elyse, Mitchell, Matthew. BS in Fin. summa cum laude, U. Ill., 1978; JD, U. Mich., 1981. Bar: Wis., U.S. Dist. Ct. (ea. and we. dists.) Wis. Assoc. Frisch, Dudek & Slattery, Milw., 1981-86, shareholder, 1986-88, Slattery, Hausman & Hoefle, Waukesha, Wis., 1988-98; shareholder, mng. ptnr. Bode, Carroll, McCoy, Hoefle & Mihal, Waukesha, 1998—2001; ptnr. Laufenberg & Hoefle, SC, Milw., 2002—. Bd. dirs. Wildlife in Need, Oconomowoc, Wis., 1998-2000. Mem. State Bar Wis., Milw. Bar Assn., Waukesha Bar Assn., Wis. Acad. Trial Lawyers (bd. dirs. 1988—, exec. com. 1997—), Waukesha Rotary Club. Avocations: outdoor activities, children's activities. Office: Laufenberg & Hoefle SC 115 S 84th St Ste 330 Milwaukee WI 53214 E-mail: prh@lauflaw.com.

HOEFLICH, CHARLES HITSCHLER, banker; b. Phila., Apr. 4, 1914; s. Llewellyn Ashbridge and Mary Ann (Osterheldt) H. BS in Econs., U. Pa., 1936; cert. in banking, Rutgers U., 1949; cert. in bank mktg., Northwestern U., 1955; LLD, Okla. Christian U., 1972. V.p. Phila. Nat. Bank, 1951-62; pres. Union Nat. Bank & Trust Co., Souderton, Pa., 1962-76, chmn. bd. dirs., 1976-84, chmn. exec. com., 1984-86; chmn. Univest Corp. Pa., Souderton, 1973-86, chmn. emeritus, 1986—. Sec.-treas. Intercollegiate Studies Inst., Wilmington, Del., 1955—; trustee Okla. Christian U., Oklahoma City, 1974—; founder Penn Found. for Mental Health, 1955—, now dir. emeritus, Adult Total Care Svcs., non-dir. emeritus; bd. dirs. The Lamb Found., Eisenhower Commn., 2002; life mem. Rep. presdl. task force, 1981-92, 2000—; chmn. Bedminster Zoning Bd. Recipient Presdl. citation USAAF, 1946, Citizen of Yr. award Fed. Bar Assn., 1960, Lifetime Achievement award Intercoll. Studies Inst., 2000. Mem. Bank Mktg. Assn. (pres. 1964-65), Am. Bankers Assn., Union League Club (Phila.), Indian Valley Country Club (Telford, Pa.), The Exec. Com. (assoc.), Heritage Found., Intercollegiate Studies Inst. Republican. Avocations: collecting americana antiques and art, painting, horticulture. Office: Univest Corp Pa Main And Broad St Souderton PA 18964 Fax: 215-7212433.

HOEFLICH, MICHAEL HARLAN, law educator, department chairman; b. N.Y.C., Jan. 11, 1952; s. Sterling Martin and Barbara Su (Junger) H.; m. Karen Nordheden, Sept. 13, 1986. BA, MA in Canon Law, Haverford (Pa.) Coll., 1973; MA, Cambridge (Eng.) U., 1976; JD, Yale U., 1979; PhD, Cambridge (Eng.) U., 2001. Bar: N.Y. 1980. Rsch. fellow Cambridge U., 1975-77; tax assoc. Cravath, Swaine & Moore, N.Y.C., 1978-79, 79-81; asst. prof. law U. Ill., Champaign, 1981-84, assoc. prof., 1984-86, prof., univ. scholar, dir. rsch. on legal history, 1986-88; prof. law and history Syracuse (N.Y.) U., 1988-94, dean coll. law, 1988-94; dean sch. law U. Kans., Lawrence, 1994-2000, John M. and John H. Kane Disting. prof., 1997—. Author: Roman and Civil Law, and the Development of Anglo-American Jurisprudence, 1997; co-author: Cases and Materials on Federal Taxation of Deferred Compensation, 1989; co-editor Property Law and Legal Education, 1988; editor The Gladsome Light of Jurisprudence, Learning the Law in England and the United States in the 18th and 19th Centuries, 1988, Lex & Romanities, Essays for Alan Watson, 2000.; legal columnist Lawrence Jour.-World, 1994—; contbr. numerous articles to profl. publs. Housing commr. Champaign County Housing Authority, 1987-88; host weekly radio show on sta. WILL-AM, Champaign, 1986-88; bd. dirs. U. Ill. Libr. Friends, Champaign, 1988-90. Recipient Surrency Prize Am. Soc. Legal History, 1985. Fellow Am. Bar Found., Am. Philos. Soc. (Phillips); mem. Onondaga County Bar Assn. (bd. dirs. 1991-93), N.Y. State Bar Assn. (com. on professionalism 1988-94), Am. Law Inst. (advisor restatement, property, security and mortgages coms. 1989-93), Fund for Modern Cts. (bd. dirs. 1988-90), Kans. Bar Assn. Office: U Kansas Sch Law Green Hall Lawrence KS 66045-7577 E-mail: mhoeflich@ukans.edu.

HOEFLIN, RONALD KENT, philosopher, writer; b. Richmond Heights, Mo., Feb. 23, 1944; s. William Eugene and Mary Elizabeth (Dell) Hoeflin. Student, Calif. Inst. Tech., 1962-63, U. Calif., Berkeley, 1966-67, U. N.C., 1970-71; BA, U. Minn., 1968, Shimer Coll., 1974; MLS, Ind. U., 1970; MA, New Sch. Social Rsch., 1979, PhD, 1987. With various librs., 1969-85; publisher, editor Triple Nine Soc., N.Y.C., 1979-81, 85-89; publisher, editor, founder Top One Percent Soc., N.Y.C., 1989—, One-in-a-Thousand Soc., N.Y.C., 1992—. Designer Mega Test, 1985, Titan Test, 1990, Ultra Test, 1995, Hoeflin Power Test, 1996; author: The Encyclopedia of Categories: A Theory of Categories and Unifying Paradigm for Philosophy, 2 vols., 2005. Mem.: Am. Philos. Assn. (Fifth Ann. Rockefeller prize 1988), Prometheus Soc. (founder 1982), Mega Soc. (founder 1982), Mensa. Office: PO Box 539 New York NY 10101-0539 E-mail: Ronaldk31415@aol.com.

HOEFT, MARJORIE CLAIRE, librarian; b. Vancouver, B.C., Can., Feb. 26, 1938; came to U.S., 1947; d. Leonard Neil and Jessie R. R. (McKinnon) Osgood; m. Robert Dean Hoeft, Dec. 19, 1959; children: Melissa Kathryn, Eric Von. BA, U. Oreg., 1960, MA, 1964. Tchr., libr. Creswell (Oreg.) High Sch., 1961; tchr. Agana (Guam) High Sch., 1961-63; cataloging libr. Umatilla County Library, Pendleton, Oreg., 1965, Blue Mountain Community Coll., Pendleton, 1966—2003. Mem. Alpha Psi Omega, Phi Beta Kappa. Republican. Avocations: travel, reading, gardening. Home: 4242 Clayton Rd Ashland OR 97520-9046

HOEFT, ROBERT GENE, agricultural studies educator; b. David City, Nebr., May 21, 1944; s. Otto O. Hoeft and Lula (Barlean) Pleskac; m. Nancy A. Bussen, Sept. 1, 1990; children: Jeffrey, Angela. BS, U. Nebr., 1965, MS, 1967; PhD, U. Wis., 1972. Asst. prof. S.D. State U., Rapid City, 1972-73, U. Ill., Urbana, 1973-77, assoc. prof., 1977-81, prof., 1981—, head dept. crop scis., 2005—. Author: Modern Corn Production, 1986, Modern Corn & Soybean Production, 2000; editor Jour. Prodn. Agr., 1986-92. Recipient Funk award U. Ill., 1990, Robert E. Wagner award Potash and Phosphate Inst., 1998. Fellow Soil Sci. Soc. Am., Am. Soc. Agronomy (pres. 2002-03, CIBA-Geigy award 1978, Agronomic Extension award, grantee 1988, Agronomic Achievement award-soils 1995, Werner Nelson award for diagnosis of yield limiting factors 1996); mem. Coun. for Sci. and Tech. Office: U Ill 1102 S Goodwin Ave Urbana IL 61801-4730 Business E-Mail: rhoeft@uiuc.edu.

HOEG, DONALD FRANCIS, chemist, consultant, research and development company executive; b. Bklyn., Aug. 2, 1931; s. Harry Herman and Charlotte (Bourke) H.; m. Patricia Catherine Fogarty, Aug. 30, 1952; children— Thomas Edward, Robert Francis, Donald John, Mary Beth, Susan Catherine. BS in Chemistry summa cum laude, St. John's U., N.Y., 1953; PhD in Chemistry, Ill. Inst. Tech., 1957. Fellow in chemistry and chem. engring. Armour Research Found., 1953-54; grad. research asst. Ill. Inst. Tech., 1954-56; research chemist W.R. Grace & Co., 1956-58, sr. research chemist, 1958-61; group leader addition polymer chemistry Roy C. Ingersoll Research Center, Borg-Warner Corp., Des Plaines, Ill., 1961-64, mgr. polymer chemistry, 1964-66, assoc. dir., head chem. research dept., 1966-75, dir., 1975-88; pres. DFH Assocs., 1988—. Former mem. solid state scis. adv. bd. NAS; bd. overseers Lewis Coll. Scis. and Letters of Ill. Inst. Tech., 1980-91; bd. dirs. Ill. Inst. Tech. Alumni, 1979-82, Mt. Prospect Combined Appeal, 1963-65 Bd. editors: Research Mgmt. Mag, 1979-82; contbr. numerous articles tech. publs., chpts. in books; patentee in field. TaPing Lin scholar, 1955-56; AEC asst., 1954; Armour Research Found. fellow, 1953-54; Ill. Inst. Tech. Achievement award, 1983 Mem. Am. Chem. Soc., AAAS, N.Y. Acad. Scis., Dirs. Indsl. Research, Am. Mgmt. Assn. (v.p. council 1984-88), Research Dirs. Assn. Chgo. (pres. 1977-78), Indsl. Research Inst. (bd. dirs. 1986-88), Sigma Xi. Office Phone: 847-577-5951. E-mail: dfh1931@aol.com. *I've counseled myself that all ideas and concepts, no matter how seemingly difficult, are products of man's mind, and, therefore fundamentally understandable.*

HOEG, MATTHEW, lawyer; b. Oceanside, NY, 1960; AB with honors, Coll. William & Mary, 1982; JD, U. Houston, 1985. Bar: Tex. 1985. Ptnr., Labor/Employment Sect. Andrews Kurth LLP, Houston, mem. mgmt. com. Editor: Houston Law Rev., 1983—85. Mem.: ABA, State Bar Tex., Houston Young Lawyers Assn., Houston Bar Assn., Order of Barons. Office: Andrews Kurth LLP 600 Travis St Ste 4200 Houston TX 77002 Office Phone: 713-220-4012. Office Fax: 713-238-7328. Business E-Mail: matthewhoeg@andrewskurth.com.

HOEGLER, JEAN SANDBERG, artist, art educator, computer programmer, analyst; b. Chgo., July 14, 1929; d. Leonard Raymond and Dessa Katherine (Olson) Sandberg; m. Robert F. Gerstung, Sept. 9, 1951 (dec. 1957); children: Daniel Robert, Susan Barbara; m. Fred C. Hoegler, Dec. 26, 1959 (div.); children: Frederick Craig, Jeanette Lynn. BA, Wheaton Coll., 1951; MEd, Nat. Louis U., Wilmette, Ill., 1976; student in programming, Control Data, Chgo., 1982. Adminstrv. asst. Associated Aviation Underwriters, Chgo., 1979-81; programmer, analyst No. Ill. Gas, Aurora, 1982-93; ret., 1993. Vis. lectr. art, Trinity Coll., Deerfield, Ill., 1971-79. Group show portrait in wood, Chicago, 2000. Mem. Am. Soc. Portrait Artists. Avocation: dress design. Home: 319 W School St Villa Park IL 60181-2548

HOEHN, ELMER LOUIS, lawyer, educator, state agency administrator, consultant, federal agency administrator; b. Memphis, Ind., Dec. 19, 1915; s. Louis and Agnes (Goss) H.; m. Frances Cory, June 10, 1943; children: Kathleen Gillmore, G. Patrick. BS, Canterbury Coll., 1936, Northwestern U., 1937; JD, U. Louisville, 1940. Bar: Ky. 1940, D.C. 1969, U.S. Supreme Ct. 1969, U.S. Ct. Appeals 1970, Ind. 1981. Prof. bus. and law Jeffersonville High Sch., Ind., 1937-41, IUS, 1940-41; with legal and personnel div. Am. Barge Lines, 1942-44; realtor Ind., 1949—; apptd. dir. by Gov. Ind. Oil and Gas, 1949-53; apptd. adminstr. by Pres. U.S. Oil Import Adminstrn., Nat. Security Agy., Crude Oil, Petroleum Products & Petrochem. Feedstocks, 1965-69; sec.-treas. Am. Assn. Oil Well Drilling Contractors, 1956-60; exec. sec. Ind. Oil Producers and Land Owners Assn., 1953-64; pvt. practice law Washington, 1969-91, Indiana, 1981—. ADR civil mediator, Ind., 1993; gov.'s rep. Interstate Oil & Gas Compact Commn., 1949—53, 1961—65; apptd. commr. by gov. Ohio River Greenway Devel. Commn., 1994; cons. petroleum, natural resources, energy and environment; chmn. Clark County Redevel. Commn., 1996—, Charlestown Ammo INAAP Reuse Authority, 1997—. Mem. Ind. Gen. Assembly, 1945- 49, minority floor leader, 1947, chief clk., 1949, Democratic chmn., Clark County, Ind., 1945-52; Ind. del. Dem. Nat. Conv., 1964, chmn. 8th Congl. Dist., 1952-58; mem. Ind. Dem. Exec. Com., 1952-58, Ind. and Midwest campaign mgr., LBJ campaign for president, 1960. Named Hon. Citizen, Ind. and Ky., Citoyen Honneur, Soufflenheim, France, Ambassador, Clark County, Ind., Disting. Benefactor, Clark Meml. Hosp. Interfaith Ctr.; recipient Humanitarian award, ARC, 2003, Chancellor's Medallion award, IUS, 2003, Helping Hand award, Haven House Svcs., Lewis & Clark Bicentennial Commemoration, Falls of the Ohio, Ea. Legacy, 2003—. Mem. ABA, Fed. Bar Assn., Ky. Bar Assn. (Disting. sr. counselor 1990), D.C. Bar Assn., Ind. Bar Assn. (Disting. Sr. Counselor 1990), Coop. Oil and Gas Assns. (liason com. Washington 1969-91), Am. Inn of Ct., Univ. Club (Louisville), Sigma Delta Kappa. Clubs: Nat. Lawyers, Nat. Press (Washington); Ind. Legislators (Indpls.); Filson (Louisville), Elks Country (Jeffersonville). Roman Catholic. Home: 2105 Utica Pike Jeffersonville IN 47130-5005 Personal E-mail: ehoehn@watertowersquare.com.

HOEHN, MARGARET MAIER, neurologist; b. San Francisco, Nov. 24, 1930; d. Peter Paul and Eva Till Maier; children: Robert Anthony Till, Margaret Eve Maier Hanan. BA, U. Sask., Saskatoon, Can., 1950; MD, U. B.C., Vancouver, Can., 1954; postgrad., U. B.C. and Nat. Hosp. Neurol. Diseases, London, 1954—60. Asst. in neurology Boston U., 1961-62; asst. prof. Columbia U., NYC, 1963-70; clin. prof. U. Colo., Denver, 1970—, dir. Parkinson's disease and movement disorder clinic, 1984—. Clin. rschr. Parkinson's Disease and other movement disorders; cons. in clin. rsch., lectr. in field. Contbr. over 100 articles to profl. jours.; developer Hoehn and Yahr Scale as a measure of severity of Parkinson's disease. Fellow ACP, Royal Coll. Physicians Can., Am. Acad. Neurology; mem. Am. Neurol. Assn., Movement Disorder Soc., Colo. Soc. Clin. Neurology, Alpha Omega Alpha. Avocations: travel, bridge, swimming, reading, theater. Office: 3851 S Xanthia St Denver CO 80237-1602 Office Phone: 303-843-9624.

HOEHN, ROBERT GUTHRIE, science educator; b. San Jose, Calif., Jan. 31, 1937; s. George Vermando and Laura Pearl Hoehn; m. Peggy Louise Piert, Aug. 10, 1958; children: Valerie, Susan, James. BA, San Jose State U., 1963. Cert. gen. secondary life (K-12), spl. health and safety life, adminstrv. svcs. Tchr. Roseville Joint Union HS Dist., Calif., 1963—. Cons. editor Sci. Activities Magazine, 1985—; mentor Roseville Union HS Dist. Recipient Excellence award, Independence HS, 2003, 2004, Roseville Area Outstanding Tchr. award, Roseville HS Dist., 2005. Mem.: NEA, Calif. Sci. Tchrs. Assn., Calif. Tchrs. Assn. Republican. Methodist. Avocations: fishing, hiking, writing. Home: 5016 Deerpark Cir Fair Oaks CA 95628

HOEKSTRA, PETER, congressman, manufacturing executive; b. Groningen, The Netherlands, Oct. 30, 1953; m. Diane M. Johnson; children: Erin, Allison, Bryan. BA, Hope Coll., 1975; MBA, U. Mich., 1977. Furniture exec. Herman Miller, Inc., 1977-92, project mgr., product mgr., dir. product mgmt., dir. dealer mktg., v.p. dealer mktg., 1988-92, v.p. product mgmt., 1992-93; mem. U.S. Congress from 2d Mich. dist., 1993—, mem. edn. and the workforce com., chmn. select edn. subcom. edn. and the workforce com., 2001, mem. permanent select com. on intelligence, 2001—, chmn., 2004—, mem. com. on transp. and infrastructure, mem. subcom. on C.G. and maritime transp., mem. subcom. on hwys., transit and pipelines. Chmn. edn. and the workforce ctr. subcom. on oversight and investigations. Contbr. to project devel. Equa Chair, recognized as outstanding product of 1980s by Time Mag. Recipient Deficit Hawk award, Concord Coalition, 1996, Disting. Alumni award, Hope Coll. Alumni Assn., 2001, Pub. Policy award, Volunteer Ctr. Nat. Network Coun., 2003, Pub. Svc. award, Friends of Libraries USA and American Libraries Assn., 2003. Republican. Office: US Ho Reps 2234 Rayburn House Office Bldg Washington DC 20515-2202 E-mail: tellhoek@mail.house.gov.*

HOEL, DAVID GERHARD, statistician, science educator; b. L.A., Nov. 18, 1939; s. Paul Gerhard and Hazel Bessie (Helvig) H.; m. Nancy Carolyn Keller, Sept. 3, 1961; children: Erik Gerhard, Brian David, Christian Paul. AB, U. Calif., Berkeley, 1961; PhD, U. N.C., Chapel Hill, 1966. Postdoctoral fellow Stanford U., Calif., 1966-67; sr. mathematician Westinghouse Rsch. Labs., Pitts., 1967-68; statistician Oak Ridge (Tenn.) Nat. Lab., 1968-70; adj. prof. dept. biostats. U. N.C., Chapel Hill, 1970—. Math. statistician Nat. Inst. Environ. Health Scis., Research Triangle Park, N.C., 1970-73, chief biometry br., 1973-81, acting sci. dir., 1977-79, dir. div. biometry and risk assessment, 1981-93; prof., chair Med. U. S.C., Dept. Biometry and Epidemiology, 1993-97, disting. univ. prof., 1997—; mem. coun. fellows Collegium Ramazzini, 1987; vis. scientist Radiation Effects Rsch. Found., Hiroshima, Japan, 1979-80, dir., 1984-86; mem. NAS sci. bd. on toxicity and environ. health hazards, Washington, 1981-85, NAS com. on biol. effects of ionizing radiation, 1986-89, NAS com. to provide interim oversight of Dept. Energy nuclear weapons complex, 1988-90, NAS com. on environ. epidemiology, 1990, NAS com. on epidemiology and vets. affairs, 1990—; NAS com. on applied and theoretical stats, 1991-94, NAS com. on the health effect of mustart gas, 1991-92, NAS com. on radiol. safety in the Marshall Islands, 1992—, chmn. NAS com. to study the mortality of mil. pers. present at atmospheric tests of nuc. weapons, 1993-94; chmn. NCRP sci. com. on extrapolation of risks from non-human exptl. systems to man; mem. sci. adv. bd. Nat. Ctr. for Toxicological Rsch., 1977-80, EPA Radiation Com., 1993-94, Environ. Health Found., 1994—. Contbr., co-contbr. articles to profl. publs.; co-editor workshop, conf. proceedings. Recipient NIH Dir. award, 1977, Mortimer Spiegelman Gold medal award APHA, 1977; Pub. Health Svc. Supr. Svc. award USPHS, 1980, Disting. Scientist award S.C. U. Rsch. and Edn. Found., 1993, Ramazzini award Collegium Ramazzini and the Town of Carpi, 1994; named Sr. Exec. Svc., Bonus Nat. Inst. Environ. Health Scis., 1983, 87-91. Fellow AAAS, Am. Statis. Assn. (sec. biometrics sect. 1979); mem. NAS Inst. Medicine, Internat. Statis. Inst., Royal Statis. Soc., Radiation Rsch. Soc., Health Physics Soc., Biometric Soc., Soc. for Risk Analysis (coun. mem. 1982-85). Home: 36 S Battery St Charleston SC 29401-2327 Office: 135 Cannon St Ste 302 PO Box 250835 Charleston SC 29425-0551

HOEL, LESTER A., civil engineering educator, department chairman; b. Bklyn., Feb. 26, 1935; s. Johannes and Julia (Michelsen) Hoel; m. Unni Sonja Blegen, Jan. 24, 1959; children: Julie Britt Bryan, Sonja Leslie, Lisa Hoel Rafael. B.C.E., City Coll., N.Y., 1957; MS in Civil Engring, Bklyn. Poly. Inst., 1960; D.Eng., U. Calif. at Berkeley, 1963. Registered profl engr, Calif, Pa, Va. Asst. prof. engring. San Diego State Coll., 1962-64; Fulbright research scholar Inst. Transport Economy, Oslo, 1964-65; prin. engr. Wilbur Smith & Assoc., San Francisco, 1965-66; faculty Carnegie-Mellon U., Pitts., 1966-74, prof. civil engring., 1970-74; assoc. dir. Transp. Research Inst., 1966-74; Hamilton prof. dept. civil engring. U. Va., 1974-99, chmn. dept., 1974-89, L.A. Lacy Disting. prof., 1999—; dir. Ctr. Transportation Stud., 2002—. Author: (book) Traffic and Highway Engineering, 3d edit., 2002; editor: Public Transportation, 1979, Public Transportation, rev 2d ed, 1992; mem. editl. bd.: transp. jours.; contbr. technical papers, books and articles. Recipient Alumni Award in Civil Eng, Col City NY, 1957, Stanley W Gustafson Leadership Award, Hwy Users Fedn, 1989, S S Steinberg Educ Award, Am Rd and Transp Builders, 1991, Disting. Faculty award, Coun. Univ. Transp. Ctrs., 2002, Jack H. Dillard Best Paper award, Va. Transp. Rsch. Coun., 2003; grantee Fulbright Travel, 1964—65. Fellow: ASCE (Huber Research Prize 1976, Frank Masters Award 1990, James Laurie Prize 1999), Inst Transp Engrs (Wilbur S Smith Dinsting Educator Award 2001), Nat Acad Eng; mem.: Am Soc Eng Educ, Transp Research Bd (chmn exec comt 1986, chmn comt tranps profl needs, truck weight study, Pyke Johnson Award 1977), Tau Beta Pi, Chi Epsilon, Sigma Xi. Home: 1340 Sunset Cir Charlottesville VA 22901 Business E-Mail: LAH@virginia.edu.

HOELSCHER, KATHLEEN STAR, elementary school educator; b. Orange, Calif., July 24, 1943; d. Samuel Cecil Celum and Mary Catherine Twibell; m. Cyril Mark Hoelscher, Sr., Dec. 12, 1937; children: Cyril Jr., Grace Ann, Paul, Donald, Douglas. AA, Victoria (Tex.) Coll., 1982; BS in Edn. magna cum laude, U. Houston, 1985. Tchr. 4th grade Calhoun County Ind. Sch. Dist., Pt. Lavaca, Tex., 1986, tchr. 1st grade, 1986—87, tchr. 2d and 3d grade, 1988—91, tchr. combined grades, 1991—93, tchr. 3d grade, 1993—94, tchr. 2d grade, 1994—95, tchr. 3d grade, 1995—. Facilitator Math Camp of Calhoun Ind. Sch. Dist., Pt. Lavaca, 1998—2003, Calhoun County Ind. Sch. Dist., Montgomery, Tex., 1992. Lector Our Lady of Gulf Ch., Pt. Lavaca, 1975—; educator GED Program, Pt. Lavaca, 1985—87. Named Tchr. of Yr., Jackson-Roosevelt, 1997, 2005, Educator of Yr., Calhoun County Ind. Sch. Dist., 2005; scholar, U. Houston. Mem.: Jackson-Roosevelt PTA, Internat. Reading Assn., Mid-Coast Reading Assn. (treas. 1996). Roman Catholic. Avocations: sewing, quilting, reading, crafts. Office: Jackson Roosevelt Calhoun County Ind Sch Dist 1512 Jackson Port Lavaca TX 77979

HOELSCHER, ROBERT JAMES, lawyer; b. Cleve., July 5, 1952; s. Max W. and Lorraine A. (Bass) H.; m. Constance J. Fiske, Sept. 20, 1986; children: Ann, Carol. BA, Pa. State U., 1974; JD, Harvard U., 1977. Bar: Pa. 1977, N.J. 1992, U.S. Dist. Ct. (ea. dist.) Pa. 1978, U.S. Ct. Appeals (3d. cir.) 1983, U.S. Dist. Ct. N.J. 1992. Law clk. Supreme Ct. Pa., Pitts., 1977—78; assoc. Drinker Biddle & Reath, Phila., 1978—86; ptnr. Drinker, Biddle & Reath, Phila., 1986—97; counsel CoreStates Fin. Corp. (now Wachovia Corp.), Phila., 1997—. Articles editor Harvard Jour. on Legislation, 1977. Trustee Old Pine St. Ch., Phila., 1984-87, sec. bd. trustees, 1990-93; trustee Friends of Old Pine St., 1999—; elder First Presbyn. Ch., Ardmore, Pa., 1995-2001, 03—. Mem. Phi Beta Kappa. Presbyterian. Office: Wachovia Corp Legal Divsn PA4840 123 S Broad St Philadelphia PA 19109 Office Phone: 215-670-6877.

HOENACK, AUGUST FREDERICK, architect; b. N.Y.C., Apr. 1, 1908; s. Hugo H. and Hulda (Kilian) H.; m. Mary Margery Course, June 14, 1939; children— Stephen A., Judith (Mrs. Paul Schultz), Francis A., August Jeremy. B.Arch., Pratt Inst., 1938; student, Columbia, 1930-31; postgrad., George Washington U., 1940-41. Architect PBA, Washington, 1938-41; asso. architect hospital facilities USPHS, Washington, 1942-46, asst. chief, 1946-55, chief architecture, engring. equipment br., 1955-68; v.p. firm Jensen & Halstead (Architects, Engrs. & Consultants), Chgo., 1968-73; asso. Dalton, Dalton, Little, Newport, Bethesda, Md., 1973-80. Contbr. profl. jours. Recipient Superior Service award HEW, 1967, Outstanding Alumnus award Pratt Inst., 1968 Fellow AIA (mem. health environment com. 1960-67), Am. Assn. Hosp. Planning (Distinguished Service to Hosp. Design award 1967), Am. Hosp. Assn., Internat. Hosp. Fedn. Home: 119 Ridgewood Ave Madison CT 06443-2713 E-mail: phoenack@ix.netcom.com.

HOENIG, STEVEN LAWRENCE, chemist; b. Queens, N.Y., June 18, 1957; s. William Frederick and Emily Alice (Montag) H. BS, Polytechnic Inst. N.Y., 1985; MS, L.I. U., 1985. Chemist U.S. Customs Svc., N.Y.C., 1986-91, electronic specialist, 1988-91; chemist DEA, N.Y.C., 1991—. Mem. ASTM, N.Y. Acad. Scis. Home: 1862 Himrod St Flushing NY 11385-1539 Office: Drug Enforcement Adminstrn Northeast Lab 99 10th Ave Ste 721 New York NY 10011-4713

HOENIGSWALD, S(USAN) ANN, conservator; b. West Chester, Pa., June 25, 1950; d. Henry Max and Gabriele Lina (Schoepflich) Hoenigswald; m. Nicholas Thorner, Oct. 5, 1979; children: Daniel Richard Thorner, Samuel Peter Thorner. BA, U. Pa., Phila., 1968—72; MA, Oberlin Coll., Ohio, 1974—77. Cert. in conservation Intermus. Conservation Assn., Oberlin, Ohio, 1977. Conservator Hist. Soc. Pa., Phila., 1972—74; sr. conservator of paintings Nat. Gallery Art, Washington, 1977—. Contbr. articles to profl. jours. Fellow, Ctr. for the Advanced Study in the Visual Arts, 1998—99; Robert H. Smith fellow, Nat. Gallery Art, 1994, 2002. Fellow: Internat. Inst. for Conservation; mem.: Am. Inst. for Conservation. Office: Nat Gallery of Art 6th and Constitution Aves Washington DC 20565

HOEPNER, THEODORE JOHN, banker; b. Redwood Falls, Minn., June 28, 1941; s. John W. and Lenore Theodora (Gandrud) H.; m. Barbara Jo Vierling, Dec. 26, 1964; children: Theodore J. Jr., Jennifer. BA, Carleton Coll., Northfield, Minn., 1963; AMP, Harvard U., 1983. Asst. sec. Irving Trust Co., N.Y.C., 1963-68; exec. v.p. Flagship Nat. Bank of Miami Beach, Fla., 1968-77; chmn., pres., chief exec. officer Flagship Nat. Bank of Jacksonville, Fla., 1977-83; chmn., chief exec. officer Sun Bank (merger), Miami, 1983-90; chmn., pres., CEO Sun Bank, N.A., Orlando, Fla., 1990-95, SunTrust Banks of FL Inc., 1995—. Dir. Poe and Brown, Inc., 1994. Founding co-chmn. Beacon Coun., Miami, 1985; trustee U. Miami, 1987-90; chmn. United Way, Orlando, 1993, campaign chair, 1992; trustee Rollins Coll., 1993—. Named Bus. Leader of Yr., Miami News, 1987. Mem. Young Pres. Orgn., Greater Miami C. of C. (chmn. 1988—, Forty-Niners, Country Club Orlando. Republican. Presbyterian. Avocations: hunting, fishing. Office: SunTrust Bank of FL Inc 200 S Orange Ave Orlando FL 32801-3410

HOEPPNER, DAVID WILLIAM, mechanical engineering educator; b. Waukesha, Wis., Dec. 17, 1935; s. William Frank and Lillian Hulda (Rosche) H.; m. Sue Ellen McFarlane, June 13, 1959; children: Laura Anne, Lynne Susan, Amy McFarlane. BME, Marquette U., 1958; MS, PhD, U. Wis., 1963. Asst. prof. metall. engring. U. Wis., Madison, 1963-64; rsch. metallurgist Battelle Meml. Inst., Columbus, 1964-69; group leader Lockheed Calif. Co., Burbank, 1969-74; prof. U. Mo., Columbia, 1974-78; Cockburn prof. U. Toronto, Ont., Can., 1978-85; prof., chmn. dept. mech. engring. U. Utah, Salt Lake City, 1985-92, prof. mech. engring., 1992—. Cons. Rolls Royce, Derby, Eng., 1973-95, Pratt and Whitney of Can., Longueuil, Que., 1978-2003, Lockheed Aircraft (1976, 1985-2003), Boeing, 1992-95; pres. Faside Internat. Inc., Salt Lake City, 1978—. Author: (with Wallace) Case Studies in Aircraft Corrosion, 1986; editor: Effect of Environment and Complex Load History on Fatigue, 1970, Fracture Prevention, 1974, Fatigue of Weldments, 1977; co-editor: Fretting Fatigue, Current Technology and Practice, 2000, Fretting Fatigue, Advances in Basic Understanding and Applications, 2003. Internat. senator Jaycees, Santa Paula, Calif., 1973; mem. city planning commn., Santa Paula, 1972-74. Mem. AIAA, ASME, ASTM (chmn. subcom. 1969-79, co-editor fretting fatigue, 1999, 2003), Am. Soc. Metals, Am. Soc. Engring. Edn., Soc. Automotive Engrs., Sigma Xi. Avocations: gardening, reading, skiing, hiking. E-mail: hoeppner@eng.utah.edu.

HOERNEMAN, CALVIN A., JR., economics educator; b. Youngstown, Ohio, Sept. 30, 1940; s. Calvin A. and Lucille A. (Leiss) H.; m. Cheryl L. Morand, Aug. 10, 1973; children: David, Jennifer, Christina. BA, Bethany Coll., 1962; MA, Mich. State U., 1964, postgrad., Cambridge U. Mem. faculty, Delta Coll., University Center, Mich., 1966—, prof. econs., 1976—; cons. Prentice-Hall, Acad. Press, Goodyear Pub., Random House Pub., Forbes Econ. Survey Panel, 2001-02; econ. expert witness; mem. Forbes mag. Econ. Survey Panel. Author: Poverty, Wealth and Income Distribution, 1969; co-author: "Caper" Principles of Economics Software Study Guide; contbr. articles to various publs. Recipient Recognition award AAUP, 1972, Bergstein award Delta Coll. Grad. Class, 1972, Competition for Excellence award IBM and the League for Innovation, 1988. Mem. AAUP, Am. Econ. Assn., Midwest Econ. Assn., Nat. Assn. Forensic Economists. Home: 5712 Lamplighter Ln Midland MI 48642-3137 Office: Delta Coll Dept Econs University Center MI 48710-0001

HOERNER, ROBERT JACK, lawyer; b. Fairfield, Iowa, Oct. 12, 1931; s. John Andrew and Margaret Louise (Simmons) Hoerner; m. Judith Chandler, Apr. 21, 1954 (div. Feb. 1975); children: John Andrew II, Timothy Chandler, Blayne Marie Hoerner Murray, Michelle Margaret Hoerner Smith; m. Mary Paolano, June 3, 1989. BA, Cornell Coll., 1953; JD, U. Mich., 1958. Bar: Ohio 1960, US Supreme Ct 1964, US Ct Appeals (6th cir) 1972, US Ct Appeals (fed cir) 1990. Law clk. to hon. Chief Justice Earl Warren U.S. Supreme Ct., Washington, 1958-59; assoc. Jones, Day, Reavis & Pogue, Cleve., 1959-63, 65-66; chief evaluation sect. antitrust divsn. Dept. Justice, Washington, 1963-65; ptnr. Jones, Day, Reavis & Pogue, Cleve., 1967-93. Contbr. articles to profl jours; editor (editor-in-chief): (journal) Mich Law Rev. Trustee New Orgn Visual Arts, Cleveland, Ohio, 1976—80, 1987—90. With Counter Intelligence Corps U.S. Army, 1953—55. Mem.: ABA (antitrust sect, patent sect), Fed. Bar Assn., Cleve. Intellectual Property Law Assn., Greater Cleve. Bar Assn., Ohio Bar Assn., Leland Mich. Country Club, Order of Coif, Phi Beta Kappa. Democrat. Home: 360 Darbys Run Bay Village OH 44140-2968 Office: Jones Day 901 Lakeside Ave E Ste N-335 Cleveland OH 44114-1190 Office Phone: 216-586-7168. Business E-Mail: rjhoerner@jonesday.com.

HOERTH, KENNETH D., music educator; b. Eureka, SD, Sept. 16, 1948; s. Walter E. and Elizabeth Hoerth; m. Debora M. Krueger, June 9, 1978; children: Victoria, Kayla, Chris. BS Composite music, Valley City State U, Valley City, ND, 1971. Dir. Streeter HS, Streeter, ND, 1971—73, Hosmer HS, Hosmer, SD, 1973—76, Lakota HS, Lakota, ND, 1976—. Musician Aristocrats (prof. dance band), Devils Lake, ND, 1985—, Shriners Band, Grand Forks, ND, 2000—. Mem. Elks, Devil's Lake, ND, 1985—, Masons, Grand Forks, ND, 2000—, Shriners, Grand Forks, ND, 2000—. Recipient 30 yr., Music Ed. Nat. Conf., 2001, Citation of Excellence award, ND chpt. Nat. Band Assn., 2003, Cert. of Merit, Valley City State Univ., 2003. Mem.: Nat. Band Assn. (sec. treas., N.D. chptr.), Lakota Ed. Assoc., NEA, Am. Choral Dir. Assoc., Phi Beta Mu (charter mem.). Democrat. Lutheran. Achievements include first to Lakota Music program deemed 100 best places to live in America for music education in 2002 and 2004. Avocations: umpiring, softball, walking, bicycling, performing. Home: 618 W2 Box 131 Lakota ND 58344-0131 Office Phone: 701-247-2992.

HOESLI, HANNA, dentist; BS in Biology, UCLA, 1978; DDS, U. So. Calif, 1982. Pvt. practive, LA, 1982—; clin. prof. U. So. Calif Sch. Dentistry. Recipient Am. Assn. Dental Anesthesiology Sr. Recognition award. Mem.: Am. Dental Assn., Calif. Dental Soc., LA Dental Soc., U. So. Calif. Dental Sch. Alumni Assn., Acad. Gen. Dentistry, Phi Betta Kappa Alumni. Office: 7060 Hollywood Blvd #400 Hollywood CA 90028 also: U So Calif Sch Dentistry 925 W 34th St DEN 235 Los Angeles CA 90089 E-mail: drhanna@flash.net.

HOESLY, EILEEN M., academic administrator, educator; b. Portland, Oreg., Jan. 16, 1947; d. Ferdinand J. Hoesly and Nancy Jane Whitmore; m. Heracles J. Petropakis, June 5, 1975; children: Janeka Petropakis, Christina Petropakis. BA, Portland State U., 1969, MBA, 1974, postgrad., 1985—86. Video program adminstr. Ctrl. Tex. Coll., Athens, Greece, 1976—83; lectr. U. Md., Athens, Greece, 1974—90; mktg. asst. AT&T, Pacific N.W. Bell, Portland, Oreg., 1974; prof. fin., mgmt. U. LaVerne, Athens, Greece, 1977—2004, CFO, 1995—2004. Acct. Uniwest Inc., Portland, Oreg., 1969—72; mgmt. cons. Eli Lilly, Athens, Greece, 1980—83; vis. prof. Imperial Coll., London, 1995—96, U. LaVerne, Calif., 1990—91; pres. bd. edn. Am. Cmty. Schs., Athens, Greece, 1999—. Mem.: AAUP. Home: 15409 SE Oatfield Rd Milwaukie OR 97267

HOESLY, KURT D., music educator; b. Ladysmith, Wis., Jan. 14, 1970; s. Clarence and Nancy Hoesly. BA in Music, St. Olaf Coll., Northfield, Minn., 1989—93; MMus in Edn., VanderCook Coll. Music, Chgo., 2002. Band tchr. Alleman H.S., Rock Island, Ill., 1995—97; orch. tchr. Sch. Dist. 6-1, Aberdeen, SD, 1997—99, Mount Pleasant Area Schs., Iowa, 1999—2000; band & Spanish tchr. Winner Schs., SD, 2000—02; orch. tchr. Roosevelt H.S., Sioux Falls, SD, 2002—03, Ind. Sch. Dist. 742, Saint Cloud, Minn., 2003—. Dist. dir., music & performance Barbershop Harmony Soc., 2005—. Mem., chpt. officer Barbershop Harmony Soc., 1997—; mem. Quad Cities Music Guild, Moline, Ill., 1997—2003, Winner Cmty. Theater, SD, 2000—05. Mem.: NRA (life), Mensa. Avocation: sports official. E-mail: kurt.hoesly@isd742.org.

HOESSLE, CHARLES HERMAN, zoological park administrator, director; b. St. Louis, Mar. 20, 1931; m. Marilyn Mueller, Jan. 5, 1952; children: Maureen, Kirk, Tracy, Bradley. AA, Harris Tchrs. Coll., 1951; student, Am. Assn. Zool. Parks and Aquariums Zoo Mgmt. Sch., 1976-77; LLD (hon.), Maryville Coll., 1986, St. Louis U., 1990, U. Mo., St. Louis, 1994. Reptile keeper St. Louis Zoo, 1963, asst. curator, 1964, curator reptiles and curator edn., 1968-69, gen. curator and dep. dir., 1969-82, dir., 1982—2002, dir. emeritus, 2002—. Adj. prof. dept. biology St. Louis U., 1973-74, 81-82, 83; owner, operator Exotic Pet Shop, St. Louis; host St. Louis Zoo Show, 1968-78 Chmn. Reptile Study Merit Badge counselors, St. Louis; mem. adv. bd. Mo. Coalition for Environment, 1997; state chmn. UN Day, 1982; mem. St. Louis County Counts; bd. dirs. Harris-Stowe State Coll. Found., City Mus.; mem. Bd. Regents Harris-Stowe State Coll. Recipient Disting. Alumnus award Harris-Stowe State Coll., 1987. Mem. Internat. Union Dirs. Zool. Gardens, Am. Zoo and Aquarium Assn. (bd. dirs. 1977-79, 85-87, v.p. 1988, pres. 1990-91, past pres. 1991-92, rep. to species survival commn. Internat. Union for Conservation Nature and Natural Resources), St. Louis Naturalists Club, St. Louis Ctr. for Internat. Rels. (bd. dirs. 1993—), St. Louis Mus. Collaborative (pres. 1993), Animal Protective Assn. (bd. dirs.), Internat. Friendship Alliance St. Louis County (chmn. cultural com.), Explorers, St. Louis Herpetological Society, Hawthorne Soc., St. Louis Rotary Club, St Louis Ambassadors Club (bd. dir.). Home: 10814 Forest Circle Dr Saint Louis MO 63128-2007

HOEVEN, JOHN, governor; b. Bismarck, N.D., Mar. 13, 1957; m. Mical (Mikey); children: Marcela, Jack. B in history and econ., Dartmouth Coll., 1979; MBA, J.L. Kelloge Grad. Sch. Mngmt., Northwestern U., 1981. Exec. v.p. First Western Bank, Minot, N.D., 1986-93; pres. and CEO Bank of N.D. (BND), 1993-2000; gov. N.D., 2000—. Econ. adv. N.D. Univ.; trustee Bismarck State Coll.; regent Minot State U, chmn, Midwestern Gov. Conf. Cmty. chair Mo. Slope Areawide Campaign, 1998; chair Minot Chamber Commerce AFB Retention com., Minot Area Devel. Corp.; dir. Minot Kiwanis Club, Souris Valley Humane Soc, State Fair Adv. com.; mem. bd. dirs. First Western Bank and Trust, N.D. Bankers Assn., State Bank Bd., N.D. Small Bus. Investment Co., Prairie Pub. Broadcasting, N.D. Econ. Devel. Assn., Bismarck YMCA, Harold Schafer Leadership Ctr. Republican. Roman Catholic. Office: Gov Office 600 E Blvd Ave Bismarck ND 58505-0001*

HOFBAUER, JOHN D., ophthalmologist; BA, U. Chgo., 1971; MD, Columbia U., 1975. Lic. physician Calif., N.Y., diplomate Am. Bd. Ophthalmology, Nat. Bd. Med. Examiners. Intern Harbor Gen. Hosp., Torrance, Calif., 1975—76; resident Montefiore Hosp. and Med. Ctr., Albert Einstein Coll. Medicine, 1976—79; fellow in corneal and external diseases Jules Stein Eye Inst., 1979—80; pvt. practice ophthalmology Beverly Hills, Calif., 1980—. Asst. clin. prof. Jules Stein Eye Inst., dir. 1st yr. resident surg. tng. program; cons. ABC's Extreme Makeover; med. adv. com. Specialty Surg. Ctr. Bd. dirs. Calif. Mus. Ancient Art. Mem.: Pediat. Keratoplasty Assn., Calif. Assn. Ophthalmology (bd. dirs. 1991—95), Eye Bank Soc. Assn., Internat. Soc. Refractive Surgery, Castroviejo Soc. Corneal Surgeons, Ocular Microbiology Immunology Group, Calif. Cornea Soc., L.A. County Med. Assn., Am. Acad. Ophthalmology. Office: 416 N Bedford Dr #300 Beverly Hills CA 90210

HOFEDITZ, KEVIN PAUL, performing arts educator, associate dean; b. Alton, Ill., Jan. 25, 1955; s. Clarence Ferdinand and Cleo Betzold Hofeditz; m. Patricia Mary Hazen, Dec. 18, 1976; children: Sara Katherine, Jordan Hazen. MFA, U. Mo., Kansas City, 1982. Prof., chair, assoc. dean U. Nebr., Lincoln, 1983—98; prof., assoc. dean So. Meth. U., Dallas, 1998—. Elder North Park Presbyn. Ch., Dallas, 2003—05. Mem.: Actors Equity Assn., Phi Kappa Phi, Navy of the Gt. State of Nebr. (life; adm. 1998). Democrat. Home: 12530 Pleasant Valley Dr Dallas TX 75243 Office: So Meth U Meadows Sch of Arts PO Box 750356 Dallas TX 75275-0356 Fax: 214-768-3272. Office Phone: 214-768-3947. Personal E-mail: hofeditz@smu.edu.

HOFELDT, JOHN W., retired lawyer; b. Elkhart Lake, Wis., Sept. 6, 1920; s. Johann Heinrich and Matilda A. (Kuester) H.; m. Marion Ruth Meyer, Nov. 27, 1943; children: Nancy R. Hofeldt Werley, William A., Mark R. Ph.B., U. Wis.-Madison, 1943, LL.B. (editor Law Rev. 1946-47), 1947. Bar: Wis. 1947, Ill. 1948. Since practiced in, Chgo.; ptnr. Haight & Hofeldt (and predecessors), 1955—89; ret., 1989. Lectr. John Marshall Grad. Sch., Chgo., 1971-91. Mem. Ill. Sch. Dist. 194 Bd. Edn., 1964-72. Served with USN, 1943-46. Mem. Am., Wis., Ill. bar assns., Patent Law Assn. Chgo. Clubs: Masons (Chgo.), Shriners (Chgo.), Union League (Chgo.). Republican. Home: 5555 Tancho Dr Madison WI 53718-1920

HOFER, ROY ELLIS, lawyer; b. Cin., Oct. 10, 1935; s. Eric Walter and Elsie Katherine (Ellis) H.; m. Suzanne Elizabeth Sturtz, June 6, 1956 (div. 1974); m. Cynthia Ann Corson, June 5, 1981; children: Kimberly, Tracy, Eric. BChemE, Purdue U., 1957; JD, Georgetown U., 1961. Patent examiner U.S. Patent & Trademark Office, Washington, 1957-59; patent agt. Exxon Corp., Washington, 1959-61; ptnr. Brinks Hofer Gilson & Lione, Chgo., 1961—, pres., 1995-99. Adv. com. No. Dist. Ill., 1991-95. Contbr. articles to profl. jours. Bd. dirs. Chgo. Lung Assn., 1982-83, Ctr. for Conflict Resolution, 1983-88, 90-91, pres., 1991-97; bd. dirs. Union League Club Chgo., 1984-88, Boys and Girls Club, Chgo., 1985-89, Ill. Inst. CLE, Chgo., 1986-88. Mem. ABA (dir. litigation sect. 1982-87), Fed. Cir. Bar Assn. (pres. 1993-94), Chgo. Bar Assn. (pres. 1988-89), Intellectual Property Law Assn. Chgo., Am. Intellectual Property Law Assn., Legal Club Chgo., Phi Eta Sigma, Tau Beta Pi, Omega Chi Epsilon. Republican. Office: Brinks Hofer Gilson & Lione Ste 3600 455 N Cityfront Plaza Dr Chicago IL 60611-5599 Office Phone: 312-321-4204. Business E-Mail: rhofer@usebrinks.com.

HOFER, RYAN KEITH, music educator; b. Sioux Falls, S.D., Nov. 9, 1975; s. Harlow Dale and Michal Ann Hofer; 1 child, Morgan Jane Dresch. BA in Music Edn., Augustana Coll., 1998. Dir. of bands Dell Rapids (S.D.) H.S., 1998—99, Roosevelt H.S., Sioux Falls, 1999—2000, Sioux Falls Sch. Dist., 2000—. Mem., sec., treas., libr. Sioux Falls Mcpl. Band, 1995—2000; owner, musician Spooncat!, Sioux Falls, 1996—. Mem.: Nat. Fedn. Interscholastic Music Activities, S.D. Bandmasters Assn., Music Educators Nat. Conv. Office: Whittier Middle Sch 930 E 6th St Sioux Falls SD 57103 Home: 609 N Bahnson Ave Sioux Falls SD 57103-6662

HOFER, STEPHEN ROBERT, lawyer; b. Anderson, Ind., July 25, 1950; s. Robert E. and Maxine (Hert) H.; m. Cheryl A. Stiles, Aug. 27, 1994; children: Victoria Sloane, Morgan BrynRose. AB, Ind. U., 1976; JD, Northwestern U., 1980. Bar: Calif. 1980, U.S. Dist. Ct. (ctrl. dist.) Calif. 1980, U.S. Ct. Appeals (9th cir.) 1980, U.S. Dist. Ct. (ea., no., and so. dists.) Calif. 1982, U.S. Supreme Ct. 1995. Mng. editor Daily Herald-Tel., Bloomington, Ind., 1972-74; asst. city editor Miami Herald, Ft. Lauderdale, Fla., 1976-77; atty. Gibson Dunn & Crutcher, L.A., 1980-84; venue press chief L.A. Olympic Organizing Com., 1983-84; v.p., gen. counsel Am. Golf Corp., Santa Monica, Calif., 1984-92; of counsel Bailey & Marzano, Santa Monica, 1992-98; ptnr., chair corp. and transactional dept. Bailey & Ptnrs., Santa Monica, 1998—. Instr. law U. So. Calif., L.A., 1983-84, lectr. aviation law Calif. State U., L.A. Sec., bd. dirs. Mus. of Flying, Santa Monica, 1986-89; bd. dirs. L.A. Philharmonic Assn., 1992-95, Santa Monica Symphony Assn., 1999-2000; pres. L.A. Philharmonic Bus. and Profl. Assn., 1992-95. Mem.: SAR, Sons of Union Vets. of Civil War, Jamestowne Soc. Democrat. Avocations: symphonic music and jazz, mountain climbing, travel, genealogy, photography. Office: Bailey & Ptnrs 2d Fl 2828 Don Douglas Loop N Santa Monica CA 90405-2959 E-mail: SHofer@baileypartners.com.

HOFERER, PAUL R., rail transportation executive, lawyer; BA, Ctrl. Mo. State U., 1972; JD, Washburn U. Sch. Law, 1975. Mem. law dept. Burlington Northern Santa Fe, Fort Worth, Tex., 1975—89, gen. atty., 1989—94, asst. gen. counsel, 1994, asst. v.p., 1995—98, gen. counsel, 1999—2002, v.p., gen. counsel, 2002—. Bd. govs. Washburn U. Sch. Law. Mem.: Nat. Assn. Railroad Trial Counsel (pres.). Office: Burlington No Santa Fe Corp PO Box 961039 2500 Lou Menk Dr AOB-9 Fort Worth TX 76161-0059 Office Phone: 817-352-2332. Business E-Mail: paul.hoferer@bnsf.com.

HOFERT, JACK, consulting company executive, lawyer; b. Phila., Apr. 6, 1930; s. David and Beatrice (Schatz) H.; m. Marilyn Tukeman, Sept. 4, 1960; children: Dina, Bruce. BS, UCLA, 1952, MBA, 1954, JD, 1957. Bar: Calif. 1957; CPA, Calif. Tax supr. Peat, Marwick Mitchell & Co., L.A., 1959-62, tax mgr., 1974-77; v.p. fin. Pacific Theaters Corp., L.A., 1962-68; freelance cons. L.A., 1969-74; tax mgr. Lewis Homes, Upland, Calif., 1977-80; pres. Di-Bru, Inc., L.A., 1981-87, Scolyn, Inc., L.A., 1988-95; bus. cons., 1995—. Dir. Valley Fed. Savs. and Loan Assn., 1989-92. Mem. UCLA Law Rev., 1956-57; contbr. articles to tax, fin. mags. Served with USN, 1948-49. Avocation: tennis. Home and Office: 2479 Roscomare Rd Los Angeles CA 90077-1812 Personal E-mail: jhofert90077@yahoo.com.

HOFF, BENJAMIN LLOYD, writer, scriptwriter; b. Portland, Oreg., Nov. 27, 1946; s. Lloyd Henry and Clementine Catlin (Elmer) Hoff; m. Deborah Alysoun Pratt, May 1, 1993; 1 stepchild, Joel Orion Newman. BA in Asian Art, Evergreen State Coll., 1973. Author: The Tao of Pooh, 1982 (NY Times Bestselling Paperback Authors, 1994), The Singing Creek Where the Willows Grow: the Rediscovered Diary of Opal Whiteley, 1986 (Am. Book award), The Te of Piglet, 1992, N.Y. Times Bestselling Paperback Authors, 1994, The Singing Creek Where the Willows Grow: the Mystical Nature Diary of Opal Whiteley, 1995. Avocations: landscape photography, classical guitar, fine pruning, tennis.

HOFF, GERHARDT MICHAEL, lawyer, insurance company executive; b. Vienna, June 12, 1930; came to U.S., 1951, naturalized, 1955; s. Erich Theodor and Vilma (Frank) Klockenhoff; m. Lisa Decristoforo, June 1, 1970; children: Michael, Elisabeth, Anne-Christine. Student, U. Munich Law Sch., Germany, 1948-51, Columbia U., 1951-52; LL.B., NYU, 1958; LL.M. in Taxation, Emory U., 1982; C.L.U., 1961. Bar: Mass. 1959, D.C. 1968, Ga. 1984. With Mass. Mut. Life Ins. Co. and Variable Annuity Life Ins. Co., 1958-67; v.p. Variable Annuity Life Ins. Co. Am., Washington, 1967-68; mem. staff fin. services group ITT Corp., 1968-69; pres. ITT Hamilton Life Ins. Co., also ITT Variable Annuity Ins. Co., St. Louis, 1970-72, Sun Life Ins. Co. Am., Balt., 1972-78, 81-83, chief exec. officer, 1972-83; pres. Sun Life Group Am., Inc., Atlanta, 1978-83. Chmn. law practice Bus. Planning Corp. Am., Atlanta, 1983—; founder (with Lisa Hoff) Cities in Color, Inc., 1985—. Served with AUS, 1955-57. Decorated Commendation ribbon with pendant. Mem. Am. Soc. C.L.U.'s, ABA Clubs: Capital City (Atlanta). Presbyterian. Office: 12 Braemore Dr NW Atlanta GA 30328-4845 Office Phone: 404-255-1185. E-mail: gmhoff2@aol.com. *We'll get along better with others if we recognize their right to be hard or easy on themselves, depending on their own choice of priorities.*

HOFF, JOHN SCOTT, lawyer; b. Des Moines, Jan. 2, 1946; s. John Richard and Valetta R. (Scott) H.; m. Susan Murial Felver, June 21, 1972 (div. 1975); m. Shirley Jo Ward, June 21, 1975; children: Jennifer Jo, John Baron. BSBA, Drake U., 1967; MBA, Calif. State U., Fullerton, 1971; postgrad., Oxford (Eng.) U., 1973; JD, Southwestern U., L.A., 1975; MA in Mil. History, Am. Mil. U., 1995. Bar: Iowa 1976, Ill. 1977, Calif. 1980, Nebr. 1983, D.C. 1983, Wis. 1984, N.Y. 1995, Minn. 1996, U.S. Ct. Claims 1976, U.S. Ct. Customs and Patent Appeals 1976, U.S. Ct. Mil. Appeals 1976, U.S. Dist. Ct. (no. dist.) Ill. 1977, U.S. Ct. Appeals (7th cir.) 1979, U.S. Supreme Ct. 1982, U.S. Dist. Ct. (so. dist.) Iowa 1987, U.S. Ct. Appeals (9th and 10th cirs.) 1988, U.S. Dist. Ct. Ariz. 1990, U.S. Ct. Appeals (6th cir.) 1990, Mich. 1991, U.S. Ct. Appeals (8th cir.) 1991, U.S. Dist. Ct. (cen. dist.) Ill. 1996; CPCU; chartered cost analyst; FAA comml. pilot; cert. flight instr., instrument and mult-eng ratings. Staff atty. FAA Hdqrs., Washington, 1975-76; assoc. Lord, Bissell & Brook, Chgo., 1976-81; ptnr. Lapin, Hoff, Slaw & Laffey, Chgo., 1981-92, John Scott Hoff & Assocs., P.C., Chgo., 1992—; adj. prof. aviation law John Marshall Law Sch., Chgo., 1993—. Real estate broker Ill. Dept. Profl. Regulation, Springfield, 1980— Contbr. articles to profl. jours. Bd. dirs. USO of Ill., 1996—. Col. USAF, 1967—98. Decorated Legion of Merit. Mem. ABA, Aviation Ins. Assn. (dir. 1988-1990, v.p. 1990-92, pres. 1992-94), Air Force Assn. (v.p., pres. 1980-93), Internat. Soc. Air Safety Investigation (v.p.), Nat. Aero. Assn., Gen. Aviation Pilots' Assn., Res. Officers Assn., Mil. Officers Assn., Chgo. Bar Assn., Lawyers-Pilots Bar Assn., NTSB Bar Assn., Aircraft Owners and Pilots Assn., Exptl. Aircraft Assn., Nat. Assn. Flight Instrs., Aero. Club Chgo. Republican. Presbyterian. Avocations: flying, military history. Office: Hoff Collins & Cook 20 S Clark St Ste 2210 Chicago IL 60603-1816 Office Phone: 312-346-8111. Business E-Mail: jsh@aviationattorney.com.

HOFF, JONATHAN M(ORIND), lawyer; b. Chgo., July 4, 1955; s. Irwin S. and Ida (Indritz) H. AB, U. Calif., Berkeley, 1978; JD, UCLA, 1981. Bar: Calif. 1981, U.S. Dist. Ct. (no. and cen. dists.) Calif. 1981, N.Y. 1982, U.S. Dist. Ct. (so. dist.) N.Y. 1982, U.S. Ct. Appeals (4th, 5th, 7th, 8th, 9th, 10th cirs.) 1982. Ptnr. Weil, Gotshal & Manges, N.Y.C., 1981-98, Cadwalader, Wickersham & Taft, N.Y.C., 1998—. Comment editor UCLA Law Rev., 1980-81; contbr. articles to law jours. Mem. ABA, Calif. Bar Assn. Office: Cadwalader Wickersham & Taft LLP 100 Maiden Ln New York NY 10038-4818

HOFF, JULIAN THEODORE, neurosurgeon, educator; b. Boise, Idaho, Sept. 22, 1936; s. Harvey Orval and Helen Marie (Boraas) H.; m. Diane Shanks, June 3, 1962; children— Paul, Allison, Julia. BA, Stanford U., Calif., 1958; MD, Cornell U., N.Y.C., 1962. Diplomate Am. Bd. Neurol. Surgery. Intern N.Y. Hosp., N.Y.C., 1962-63, resident in surgery, 1963-64, resident in neurosurgery, 1966-70; asst. prof. neurosurgery U. Calif., San Francisco, assoc. prof. neurosurgery, 1974-78, prof. neurosurgery, 1978-81, U. Mich., Ann Arbor, 1981—, head sect. neurosurgery, 1981—. Sec. Am. Bd. Neurol- Surgery, 1987-91, chmn., 1991-92; mem. bd. sci. councillors Nat. Inst. Neurol. Diseases and Stroke-NIH, 1993-97, nat. adv. coun., 1999—. Editor: Practice of Neurosurgery, 1979-85; Current Surgical Management of Neurological Diseases, 1980; Neurosurgery: Diagnostic and Management Principles, 1992, Mild to Moderate Head Injury, 1989; co-editor: Neurosurgery: Scientific Basis of Clinical Practice, 1985, 3rd edit., 1999; contbr. articles to profl. jours. Served to capt. US Army, 1964-66. Recipient Tchr.-Investigator award, NIH, 1972—77, Javits Neurosci. Investigator award, 1985—99, Macy Faculty scholar, London, 1979. Fellow: ACS (2d v.p.-elect 1998—99); mem.: Soc. Neurol. Surgeons (pres. 1999—2000, Grass prize 2001), Cen. Neurosurg. Soc. (pres. 1985—86), Am. Acad. Neurosurgeons (treas. 1989—92, sec. 1992—, pres. 1996—), Congress Neurol. Surgeons (v.p. 1982—83, Honored Guest 2003), Am. Surg. Assn., Am. Assn. Neurol. Surgeons (v.p. 1991—93, pres. 1993—94, Cushing medal 2001), Inst. Medicine NAS. Republican. Presbyterian. Home: 2120 Wallingford Rd Ann Arbor MI 48104-4563 Office: U Mich Hosp TC 2128 Ann Arbor MI 48109 Office Phone: 734-936-5020.

HOFF, PETER SLOAT, academic administrator, educator; m. Dianne L. Balzer; children: Marc, Jay, Lara. BA in English with honors, U. Wis., 1966; MA in English and Humanities, Stanford U., 1968, PhD in English and Humanities, 1970. Prof., faculty devel. leader U. Wis., 1970—87, adminstr.; acad. vice chancellor Ind. U. S.E., 1987—90, Univ. Sys. of Ga., 1990—93, Calif. State U., 1993—97; pres. U. Maine, Orono, 1997—2004, univ. sys. prof., 2004—. Contbr. articles on nineteenth and twentieth century Brit. fiction. Player French horn in orchs. Mich., Wis., Ind., Ga., Calif., Maine. Mem. Phi Kappa Phi, Phi Beta Kappa. Office Phone: 207-581-2722. E-mail: peterhoff@umaine.edu.

HOFF, RENO R., academic administrator; b. 1937; BS, Western Bapt. Bible Coll.; MS, Oreg. Coll. Edn.; LLD (hon.), Western Bapt. Coll. Bus. mgr. Western Bapt. Coll., Salem, Oreg., chair, bus. mgmt. dept., prof., v.p. adminstrn., 1991—97, exec. v.p., provost, 1998—99, pres., 1999—. Office: Western Baptist Coll 5000 Deer Park Dr SE Salem OR 97301 Business E-Mail: rhoff@wbc.edu.

HOFFA, HARLAN EDWARD, retired university dean, art educator; b. Kalamazoo, June 23, 1925; s. Leolan William and Pearl (Foster) H.; m. Marian Perko, Aug. 10, 1946 (div. 1971); children: Kathryn Jane, Thomas Scott; m. Suzanne Aldridge Dudley, Sept. 11, 1971. BS, Wayne U., 1948, MEd, 1949; EdD, Pa. State U., 1959. Tchr. Evanston (Ill.) Pub. Schs., 1949-51; instr. art edn. Ohio State U., 1951-53; asst. prof. art State U. Coll. at Buffalo, 1953-59; assoc. prof. fine arts and edn. head dept. Boston U., 1959-65; art edn. specialist U.S. Office Edn., 1964-67; prof. edn. and fine arts, chmn. art edn. program Ind. U., 1967-70; prof., head dept. art edn. Pa. State U., 1970-76, head div. art and music edn., 1976-79, acting dir. Sch. Visual Arts, 1979-80, 84-85, assoc. dean for research and grad. studies Coll. Art and Architecture, 1985-90, ret., 1990, prof. emeritus, 1990—. Assoc. dir. Ctr. Policy Studies in the Arts, 1989; Fulbright sr. lectr./researcher, Helsinki, Finland, Jan.-Jun., 1987. With AUS, 1943-45. Mem. Nat. Art Edn. Assn. (pres. 1971-73) Home: 1343 Penrose Cir State College PA 16803-3255 E-mail: hxh11@psu.edu.

HOFFA, JAMES P., labor union administrator; b. Detroit, May 19, 1941; s. Josephine and James R. Hoffa. m. Virginia Harris; children: David, Geoffrey. Degree in Economics, Mich. State U., 1963; JD, U. Mich., 1966. Former labor lawyer, Detroit; teamster laborer Internat. Brotherhood Teamsters, Detroit and, Alaska, 1960—68, atty., 1968-93, exec. asst. to pres. Mich. Joint Coun. 43, 1993-98, gen. pres., 1999—. Mem. Pres. Council on the 21st Century Workforce, 2002, Secretary of Energy Adv. Bd., 2002. Avocations: fishing, hunting, golf. Office: Internat Brotherhood Teamsters Office of the Gen Pres 25 Louisiana Ave NW Washington DC 20001-2130

HOFFBERG, DAVID LAWRENCE, retired lawyer; b. N.Y.C., Jan. 8, 1932; m. Gwendolyn Dounce; children: Kevin, Claudia, Eric. AB, Cornell U., 1953; LL.B., NYU, 1955. Bar: N.Y. 1956. Ptnr. Nixon & Peabody, LLP (and predecessors), Rochester, N.Y., 1965-2000, chmn. litigation/adminstrv. law sect., 1990-92; ret., 2000. Mem. Com. to Advise N.Y. State Conf. on Civil Practice Law and Rules, 1968-70; instr. profl. ethics SUNY, Brockport, 2000—. Bd. dirs. GeVa Theatre, 1978-87, 97—, chmn. bd., 1980-82; bd. dirs. YMCA of Rochester and Monroe County, 1979-84, Rochester Area Crimestoppers, Inc., 1984-89, Arts for Greater Rochester, 1991-94; mem. Brockport Coll. Comty. Adv. Group, 1986-94; treas. Monroe County Dem. Com., 1978-82; pres. bd. dirs. Family Svc. of Rochester, 1970-73; mem. judicial screening com. Sen. Daniel Patrick Moynihan, 1983-2000; chmn. SUNY Brockport Coun., 1995-2001, chmn. presdl. search com., 1996-97; bd. dirs. Brockport Coll. Found., 2000—. Fellow Am. Coll. Trial Lawyers, Am. Bar Found., N.Y. Bar Found.; mem. Monroe County Bar Assn. (chmn. judiciary com. 1973-76, trustee 1977-78, 82-84, pres. 1983), Monroe County Bar Found. (bd. dirs. 1982-90, pres. 1987-89). E-mail: dlhoffberg@aol.com.

HOFFENBERG, MARVIN, retired political science professor; b. Buffalo, July 7, 1914; s. Harry and Jennie Pearl (Weiss) H.; m. Betty Eising Stern, July 20, 1947; children: David A., Peter H. Student, St. Bonaventure Coll., 1934—35; BSc, Ohio State U., 1939, MA, 1940, postgrad., 1941. Asst. chief divsn. interindustry econs. Bur. Labor Statistics, Dept. Labor, 1941-52; cons. U.S. Mut. Security Agy., Europe, 1952, Statistik Sentralbyra, Govt. of Norway, Oslo, 1955; dir. rsch., econ. cons. dept. deVegh & Co., 1956-58; economist RAND Corp., 1952-56; staff economist Com. Econ. Devel., 1958-60; project chmn. Rsch. Analysis Corp. (formerly Johns Hopkins U. Ops. Rsch.), 1960-63; dir. cost analysis dept. Aerospace Corp., 1963-65; rsch. economist Inst. Govt. and Pub. Affairs, UCLA, 1965-67, prof.-in-residence polit. sci., 1967-85, prof. emeritus, 1985—; dir. M.P.A. program, co-chmn. Interdepartmental Program in Comprehensive Health Planning UCLA, 1974-76. Author: (with Kenneth J. Arrow) A Time Series Analysis of Inter-Industry Demand, 1959; editor: (with Levine, Hardt and Kaplan) Mathematics and Computers in Soviet Economics, 1967; contbr. articles to profl. jours., chpts. to books. Mem. bd. advisers Sidney Stern Meml. Trust; bd. dirs. L.A. chpt. Am. Jewish Com.; foreman L.A. County Grand Jury, 1990-91; commr. L.A. County Economy and Efficiency Commn., 1991-92. C.C. Stillman scholar Ohio State U.; Littauer fellow Harvard U., 1946; recipient Disting. Svc. award Coll. Adminstrv. Scis., Ohio State U., 1971. Mem.: AAAS (life fellow 1957). Jewish. Home: 1365 Marinette Rd Pacific Palisades CA 90272 Office Phone: 310-825-4331. Personal E-mail: hoffen@ucla.edu.

HOFFENBLUM, ALLAN ERNEST, political consultant; b. Vallejo, Calif., Aug. 10, 1940; s. Albert A. and Pearl Estelle (Clarke) H. BA, U. So. Calif., 1962. Mem. staff L.A. County Rep. Com., 1967-71; staff dir. Rep. Assembly Caucus Calif. legislature, Sacramento, 1973-75; polit. dir. Rep. Party of Calif., L.A., 1977-78; owner Allan Hoffenblum & Assocs., L.A., 1979—. Pub. Calif. Target Book, 1994—. Capt. USAF, 1962-67, Vietnam. Decorated Bronze Star medal. Mem.: Am. Assn. Polit. Cons. Jewish. Office: PO Box 691068 Los Angeles CA 90069 Office Phone: 310-205-8811.

HOFFER, J. LEE, health facility administrator, medical educator; BS, LeTourneau U., 1955; PhD, U. N.C., MD, 1976. Diplomate Am. Bd. Anesthesiology, Am. Bd. Quality Assurance. Rotating intern in anesthesiology U. N.C. Hosps.; dir. anesthesiolgy rsch., prof. anesthesiology Scott & White Regional Clinics, Temple, Tex., prof. engineergin. Chmn. libr. com., Scott & White Regional Clinics, mem. quality assurance com., coord. CPI, mem. instnl. rev. bd., mem. tenure and faculty promotion com. Office: 2401 S 31st St Temple TX 76508

HOFFERT, MARTIN IRVING, aerospace scientist, educator; b. Bklyn., July 1, 1938; s. Solomon and Ceil (Hyman) H.; m. Linda Epstein, Sept. 4, 1960; 1 child, Eric; m. 2d, Iris E. Fierst, Jan. 29, 1965. BS in Aero. Engring., U. Mich., 1960, MS in Astronautics, 1964; PhD in Astronautics, Poly. Inst. Bklyn., 1967; MA in Liberal Studies, New Sch. for Social Research, 1969. Sr. scientist Gen. Applied Sci. Labs., Westbury, N.Y., 1962-67; research scientist NYU, 1967-68; sr. research scientist Advanced Tech. Labs., Westbury, 1968-69; mem. research staff Riverside Research Inst., N.Y.C., 1969-72; sr. research assoc. Goodard Inst. for Space Studies NASA, N.Y.C., 1972-74; sr. research scientist NYU, 1974-76, assoc. prof. applied sci., 1976-83, prof. applied sci., 1983-94, chmn. applied sci., 1984-91, prof. physics, 1995—2005, prof. emeritus, 2005—. Mgmt. ops. working group in planetary atmosphere NASA, Washington, 1986-90; bilateral coop. working group VIII U.S. Del. Joint U.S.-USSR Commn., 1986-92; cons. Exxon Rsch. & Engring., Annandale, N.J., 1986-95, Lawrence Livermore Nat. Lab., 1990—. Contbr. over 65 articles to profl. jour. and chpts. to books. Fellow AAAS; mem. AAIA, Am. Geophys. Union, Am. Metereol. Soc., Aspen Global Change Inst. (adv. bd.). Democrat. Jewish. Avocations: bicycling, hiking, boating. Home: 12 Oak Dr Great Neck NY 11021 Office: NYU Dept Physics New York NY 10003 Office Phone: 212-998-3747. E-mail: marty.hoffert@nyu.edu.

HOFFERT, PAUL WASHINGTON, surgeon; b. N.Y.C., Feb. 22, 1923; s. Charles and Rose (Isaacs) H.; m. Rosolyn Sheiman, Apr. 20, 1947; children: Marvin Jay, Renee Beth, Deborah Susan. AB with honors, Columbia U., 1942; MD cum laude, Yale U., 1945. Diplomate Am. Bd. Surgery, Am. Bd. Abdominal Surgery. Intern New Haven (Conn.) Hosp., 1945-46; fellow radiology Hosp. U. Pa., 1948-49; resident surgery VA Hosp., Bronx, NY, 1949-53; pvt. practice medicine specializing in gen./vascular surgery Yonkers, NY, 1953—. Attending surgeon Yonkers Gen. Hosp., 1953—, chief of surgery, 1987—; sr. gen. and vascular surgeon St. Joseph's Hosp., 1953—; assoc. vascular surgeon Montefiore Hosp., 1965—; asst. prof. surgery Albert Einstein Coll., 1955—. Contbr. articles to profl. jours. Capt. U.S. Army Med. Corps, 1946-48. Fellow Am. Coll. Surgeons (pres. Westchester, N.Y. chpt.), Am. Coll. Angiology, N.Y. Acad. Medicine, Westchester Acad. Medicine (charter), Clin. Soc. N.Y. Diabetes Assn.; mem. N.Y. Surgical Soc., N.Y. Soc. Cardiovascular Surgery, Zionist Orgn. Am. (life, past pres. Lincoln Park, Yonkers region), Phi Beta Kappa, alpha Omega Alpha, Phi Delta Epsilon, Masons. Home: 5068 E S Regency Cir Tucson AZ 85711

HOFFHEIMER, DANIEL JOSEPH, lawyer; b. Cin., Dec. 28, 1950; s. Harry Max and Charlotte (O'Brien) Hoffheimer; m. Elizabeth Lee Hoffheimer; children: Rebecca, Rachel, Leah. Grad., Phillips Exeter Acad., 1969; AB cum laude, Harvard Coll., 1973; JD, U. Va., 1976. Bar: Ohio 1976, U.S. Dist. Ct. (so. dist.) Ohio 1976, U.S. Ct. Appeals (6th cir.) 1977, U.S. Ct. Appeals (D.C. and fed. cir.) 1986, U.S. Ct. Internat. Trade 1986, U.S. Tax Ct. 1992, U.S. Supreme Ct. 1980, cert.: (Specialist Estate Planning Trust and Probate Law). Assoc. Taft, Stettinius & Hollister, Cin., 1976-84, ptnr., 1984—. Lectr. law Coll. Law, U. Cin., 1981-83; trustee Judges Hogan & Porter Meml. Trust; mem. adv. bd. Ohio Dist. Ct. Rev., Greater Cin. Chinese Music Soc., 2004—; state counsel Ohio, John Kerry for Pres. Com., 2004. Editor-in-chief U. Va. Jour. Internat. Law, 1975-76; co-author: Practitioners' Handbook Ohio First District Court Appeals, 1984, 2d edit., 1991, Federal Practice Manual, U.S. 6th Circuit Court of Appeals, 1999, Manual on Labor Law, 1988; mem. editl. bd. Probate Law Jour. Ohio, 2000—; contbr. articles to profl. jours. Mem. Cin. Symphony Bus. Rels. Com., 1977-86, Cin. Composers Guild, 1988-93, Ohio Supreme Ct. Com. Racial Fairness, 1993-2000; trustee Underground R.R. Freedom Ctr., 1995—, presiding co-chair, 2004—; mem. adv. bd. Consumer Protection, Cin., 1978-80, Hoxworth Blood Ctr. Univ. Cin. Hosp., 1994-99; mem. bd. Hebrew Union Coll. Jewish Inst. Religion, 1994—, WGUC-FM Pub. Radio, 1988—, vice chmn., 1993-96, chmn., 1996-98; trustee Cin. Chamber Orch., 1977-80, Seven Hills Sch., Cin., 1980-86, Internat. Visitors Ctr., Cin., 1980-84, Friends Coll. Conservatory of Music, Cin., 1985-86, Cin. Symphony Orch., 1988-94, 96—, sec., 1996-99, vice chair 1999-2000, chair, 2001—04, Children's Psychiat. Ctr., Cin., 1986-89, treas., 1987-89; vice chmn. Jewish Hosp., Cin., 1989-92; Leadership Cin., 1989-90; sec., trustee Cin. Symphony Musicians Pension Fund, 1989-99, Jewish Cmty. Rels. Coun., 1990-98, v.p., 1996-98; sec. Nat. Conf. Commn. Justice, 1992-99, treas. 1999-2000, trustee emeritus, 2000—; counsel Cin. AIDS Commn., 1991—, Cin. Inst. Fine Arts Govt. Affairs Com., 1993-94, B'nai B'rith Nat. Coun. Legacy Devel., 1996-97; trustee Nat. Underground R.R. Freedom Ctr., 1995—, presiding co-chair, 2004—. Named Outstanding Young Man, U.S. Jaycees, 1984, 98. Life fellow Am. Bar Found., Ohio Bar Found.; fellow Am. Coll. Trust and Estate Counsel; mem. ABA, Internat. Bar Assn., Internat. Trade Bar Assn., Internat. Arbitration Assn. (comml. arbitrator 1991-95), Fed. Bar Assn. (treas. 1984, sec. 1985, v.p. 1986-87, pres. 1987-88), Ohio State Bar Assn. (bd. govs. Est. Pl. Trust and Probate Law sect. 1996—), Cin. Bar Assn. (trustee 1988-93, v.p. 1990-91, pres. 1992-93, chair Cin. Acad. Leadership for Lawyers 1998-2000), Harvard Club of Cin. (bd. dirs. 1980-88, v.p. 1983-86, pres. 1986-87). Democrat. Avocations: music, tennis, chinese and japanese art. Home: 1 Forest Hill Dr Cincinnati OH 45208-1953 Office: 425 Walnut St Ste 1800 Cincinnati OH 45202-3923 Office Phone: 513-381-2838. Business E-Mail: hoffheimer@taftlaw.com. *The elusive meaning and joy of life is really at our fingertips: to make life better for others.*

HOFFHEIMER, MICHAEL HARRY, law educator; b. Cin., Dec. 21, 1954; s. Harry Max and Charlotte (O'Brien) H.; m. Luanne Buchanan; children: Joseph Allen, Jean Sarah. BA with gen. honors, Johns Hopkins U., 1977; MA, U. Chgo., 1978, PhD in History, 1981; JD cum laude, U. Mich., 1984. Bar: Ohio 1984, U.S. Dist. Ct. (ea. dist.) Ky. 1984, U.S. Ct. Appeals (6th cir.) 1984, U.S. Dist. Ct. (so. dist.) Ohio 1985, D. C. Ct. Appeals 1985, U.S. Supreme Ct. 1987, U.S. Ct. Appeals (5th cir.) 1987. Intern Office of State Appellate Defender, Ottawa, Ill., summer-fall 1982; summer assoc. Frost & Jacobs, Cin., 1983, assoc., 1984-87; asst. prof. law U. Miss., Oxford, 1987-90, assoc. prof. law, 1990-97, prof. law, 1997—. Miss. Def. Lawyers Assn. Disting. lectr., 1998—. Adj. faculty U. Cin. Coll. Law, 1985-87; panel mem. Hamilton County Pub. Defender, Cin., 1985-87. Author: Justice Holmes and the Natural Law, 1992, Eduard Gans and the Hegelian Philosophy of Law, 1995, Directory of Law Reviews, 5th edit., 2004, Fiddling for Viola, 2000; articles editor U. Mich. Jour. Law Reform, 1983; contbr. articles to profl. jours. Kunstader fellow U. Chgo., 1978-79. Office: U Miss Law Ctr Oxford MS 38677

HOFFINGER, ADAM STEVEN, lawyer; b. N.Y.C., Oct. 22, 1956; s. Jack S. and Bernice Claire (Green) Hoffinger; m. Elizabeth Katherine Ramage, Aug. 4, 1985; children: Katherine, William, Margaret. BA, Trinity Coll., Hartford, Conn., 1978; JD, Fordham U., 1982. Bar: NY 1983, DC 1992, admitted to practice: US Supreme Ct. 1992, US Dist. Ct. (So. Dist.) NY 1983, US Dist. Ct. (Ea. Dist.) NY 1983, US Ct. Appeals (2nd Cir.) 1986, US Ct. Appeals (DC Cir.) 1990, US Dist. Ct. Md. 1996. Assoc. Anderson, Russell, Kill & Olick, N.Y.C., 1982-85; asst. U.S. Atty. So. Dist. N.Y., N.Y.C., 1985-90; prin. Schwalb, Donnenfeld, Bray & Silbert, Washington, 1990—98; ptnr. DLA Piper Rudnick Gray Cary, Washington, 1998—, head DC litigation, 1998—, chmn. White Collar practice group. Instr. Georgetown Univ. Law Ctr., George Mason Univ. Law Sch., Fed. Judicial Ctr. Editor: Fordham Urban Law Jour.; contbr. articles to profl. jour. Bd. dir. NY Ave. Found., Washington, 1993—. Named one of Top Lawyers in Washington, Washingtonian mag., Legal Times, 75 Best Lawyers in Washington, Washingtonian mag., 2002. Mem.: DC Bar, Assn. Bar City NY, ABA (white collar crime com.). Democrat. Jewish. Office: DLA Piper Rudnick Gray Cary 1200 19th St NW Washington DC 20036-2412 Office Phone: 202-861-6253. Office Fax: 202-223-2085. Business E-Mail: adam.hoffinger@dlapiper.com.

HOFFLEIT, ELLEN DORRIT, astronomer; b. Florence, Ala., Mar. 12, 1907; d. Fred and Kate (Sanio) H. AB, Radcliffe Coll., 1928, MA, 1932, PhD, 1938; DSc (hon.), Smith Coll., 1984, Ctrl. Conn. State U., 1998. From research asst. to astronomer Harvard Coll. Obs., 1929-56; mathematician Ballistic Research Labs., Aberdeen Proving Ground, Md., 1943-48; tech. expert, 1948-62; lectr. Wellesley Coll., 1955-56; mem. faculty Yale U., 1956—, sr. research astronomer, 1974—. Dir. Maria Mitchell Obs., Nantucket, Mass., 1957—78; mem. Hayden Planetarium Com., N.Y.C., 1975—90; editor Meteoritical Soc., 1958—68. Author: Some Firsts in Astronomical Photography, 1950, Yale Bright Star Catalogue, 4th edit., 1982, Astronomy at Yale, 1701-1968, 1992, (autobiography) Misfortunes as Blessings in Disguise, 2002; also rsch. papers. Recipient Caroline Wilby prize Radcliffe Coll., 1938, Grad. Soc. medal, 1964, cert. appreciation War Dept., 1946, alumnae recognition award Radcliffe Coll., 1983, George van Biesbroeck award U. Ariz., 1988, Glover award Dickinson U., 1995, Maria Mitchell Women in Sci. award, 1997; asteroid Dorrit named in her honor, 1987, Anni Mirabiles Symposium in hon. of 90th birthday Yale U., 1999; inducted into Conn. Women's Hall of Fame, 1998. Fellow AAAS, Meteoritical Soc.; mem. Internat. Astron. Union, Am. Astron. Soc. (Annenberg award 1993), Am. Geophys. Union, Astron. Soc. New Haven (hon.), Am. Assn. Variable Star Observers (hon., William Tyler Olcott Disting. Svc. award 2002), Am. Def. Preparedness Assn., N.Y. Acad. Scis., Conn. Acad. Arts and Scis., Nantucket Maria Mitchell Assn. (hon.), Nantucket Hist. Soc., Yale Peabody Mus. Assocs., Astron. Soc. Pacific, Phi Beta Kappa, Sigma Xi, Harvard Club of So. Conn. Office Phone: 203-432-3032. Business E-Mail: hoffleit@astro.yale.edu. *The guiding motto of my life has been: Work for the work's sake and it will become a part of you. Work for the sake of worldly gain and you sell your soul to the Devil. Love for research and boundless perseverance have enabled me to achieve, not all that I might have wished, but far more than I would ever have dared to expect on the basis of mediocre high school grades.*

HOFFLUND, PAUL, lawyer; b. San Diego, Mar. 27, 1928; s. John Leslie and Ethel Frances (Cline) H.; m. Anne Marie Thalman, Feb. 15, 1958; children: Mark, Sylvia. BA, Princeton (N.J.) U., 1950; JD, George Washington U., 1956. Bar: D.C. 1956, U.S. Dist. Ct. D.C. 1956, U.S. Ct. Appeals (D.C. cir.) 1956, Calif. 1957, U.S. Dist. Ct. (so. dist.) Calif. 1957, U.S. Ct. Mil. Appeals 1957, U.S. Ct. Claims 1958, U.S. Ct. Appeals (9th cir.) 1960, U.S. Supreme Ct. 1964, U.S. Tax Ct. 1989. Assoc. Wencke, Carlson & Kuykendall, San Diego, 1961-62; ptnr. Carlson, Kuykendall & Hofflund, San Diego, 1963-65, Carlson & Hofflund, San Diego, 1965-72; Christian Sci. practitioner San Diego, 1972-84; arbitrator Mcpl. Cts. and Superior Ct. of Calif., San Diego, 1984-99; pvt. practice San Diego, 1985—. Adj. prof. law Nat. U. Sch. Law, San Diego, 1985-94; judge pro tem Mcpl. Ct. South Bay Jud. Dist., 1990-99; disciplinary counsel to U.S. Tax Ct., 1989-2003; asst. U.S. atty. U.S. Dept. of Justice, L.A., 1959-60, asst. U.S. atty. in charge, San Diego, 1960-61, spl. hearing officer, San Diego, 1962-68; asst. corp. counsel Govt. of D.C., 1957-59. Author: (chpt. in book) Handbook on Criminal Procedure in the U.S. District Court, 1967; contbr. articles to profl. jours. Treas. Princeton Club of San Diego; v.p. Community Concert Assn., San Diego; pres. Sunland Home Found., San Diego, Trust for Christian Sci. Orgn., San Diego; chmn. bd. 8th Ch. of Christ, Scientist, San Diego; chmn. Christian Sci. Com. on Instnl. Work in Calif., 2004—. With USN, 1950-53, comdr. JAGC, USNR, 1953-72, ret. Mem. ABA, San Diego County Bar Assn. Phi Delta Phi. Democrat. Avocations: theater, classical music, bridge, fine art, biblical study. Home and Office: 6146 Syracuse Ln San Diego CA 92122-3301 *Decisions should be based on divine direction rather than human determination. Pray first; then act. A life devoid of spirituality lacks dimension. The steps of a good man are ordered by the lord: And he delighteth in his way.*

HOFFMAN, ALAN CRAIG, lawyer, consultant; b. Chgo., Oct. 1, 1944; s. Morris Joseph and Marie E. Hoffman; m. Pamela Hoffman. BA, Carthage Coll., 1968; JD, John Marshall Law Sch., 1973. Bar: Fla. 1973, Ill. 1973, U.S. Dist. Ct. (no. dist.) Ill. 1974, U.S. Dist. Ct. (mid. dist.) Fla. 1981, U.S. Ct. Appeals (7th cir.) 1975, U.S. Ct. Appeals (5th and 11th cirs.) 1981, U.S. Supreme Ct. 1977. Staff atty. Cook County Legal Assistance Found., Brookfield, Ill., 1973-74, Patient Legal Svcs., Chgo., 1974; pvt. practice law Chgo., 1973—, River Grove, Ill., 1973-86, Oak Brook, Ill., 1980-87, Hinsdale, Ill., 1987-93; with assocs., 1980—. Spl. asst. atty. gen. Ill. Criminal Justice Divsn., Chgo., 1977—79, Ill. Condemnation Divsn., Chgo., 1980—87; pres. Almar, Ltd., 1986—91; v.p. Marach, Ltd., 1986—89, Hoffman Realty, 1978—; pres., dir. North Shore Greenview Bldg. Corp., 1978—2002; asst. prof. Lewis U., 1974—79; vis. prof. Coll. Law Paraprofl. Ctr., 1974—76, adj. prof., 1979—80; adj. prof. law Health Law Inst. Loyola U., Chgo., 2000—; assoc. prof. No. Ill. U., 1979—80; v.p. Adv. Svc., Inc.; cons. Med-Legal Cases, 1982—. Author (with F. Lane and D. Birnbaum): Lane's Medical Litigation Guide, 1981; contbr. Med. Trial Technique Quar. Mem. Oak Park Twp. (Ill.) Mental Health Bd., 1975—80, v.p., 1975, chmn. program com., 1975—77, pres., 1978; mem. governing bd. Women In Need Growing Stronger, 1993—96; bd. govs. Jewish Fedn. Chgo., Coun. for Elderly, 1995—98; co-chair Rainbow House Bread and Roses Ann. Fundraiser, 1997—98; bd. dirs. Cary Pk. Dist. Found., 2004—. Fellow: Am. Coll. Legal Medicine (editl. bd. med. and legal textbook com. 1987—, textbook update com. 1988, program com. 1988—, legal com. 1988—, profl. devel. com. 1990—98, student awards com. 1992—, moot ct. competition com. 1992—98, co-chair com. violence and abuse in the family 1993); mem.: ATLA, ABA (civil procedure and evidence com. 1993—, comml. tort com. 1993—), Chgo. Acad. Law and Medicine, West Suburban Bar Assn., DuPage Bar Assn., Chgo. Bar Assn., Ill. State Bar Assn. (vice chmn. standing com. on mentally disabled 1975—77, chmn. 1977—78), Fla. Bar Assn. (health law com. 1983—84, out-of-state practitioner com. 1988—91), Ill. Trial Lawyers Assn. (profl. negligence com. 1982), Am. Soc. Law and Medicine, Mensa, Phi Alpha Delta. Office Phone: 312-855-0000.

HOFFMAN, ALAN JAY, lawyer; b. Phila., Aug. 31, 1948; s. Heinz Julius and Sylvia (Wise) H.; m. Julie Goldman; children: Jennifer, Lauren, Allison. BBA, Temple U., 1970; JD, Villanova U., 1973. Bar: Pa. 1973, U.S. Dist. Ct. (ea. dist.) Pa. 1973, U.S. Dist. Ct. Del. 1973, U.S. Ct. Appeals (3rd cir.) 1973, Del. 1977, U.S. Supreme Ct. 1984, D.C. 1990. Asst. U.S. atty. U.S. Dept. Justice, Wilimington, Del., 1973-78; ptnr. Dilworth, Paxson, Kalish & Kauffman, Phila., 1979-92, mem. exec. mgmt. com., 1989-90, chmn. new bus. com., 1990-91; ptnr. Blank Rome LLP (formerly Blank, Rome, Comisky and McCauley), Phila., 1992—, adminstrv. ptnr. in charge Wilmington, Del., 1996—2002, chmn. litigation and dispute resolution dept., 1996—, mem. exec. mgmt. com. Phila., 1998—, co-chmn. atty. recruiting com., 1998—. Lectr. Widener Del. Law Sch., Wilmington, 1974, Mealy's Conf. on Toxic Torts, 1999—, Mealy's Conf. on MTBE pollution, 2000. Contbg. co-editor Villanova Law Rev., 1972-73; contbr. articles to profl. jours. Bd. dirs. Men's Club Temple Adath Israel, Merion, Pa., 1993-94; pres. Villanova Law Sch. Inn of Ct., 1999—. Recipient Atty. Gen.'s Spl. Commendation U.S. Dept. Justice, Washington, 1977. Fellow Am. Bar Found.; mem. ATLA, ABA, Pa. Bar Assn., Fed. Bar Assn., Phila. Bar Assn., Del. Bar Assn., Del. Trial Lawyers Assn., Pa. Trial Lawyers Assn., White Manor Country Club (pres. 1993—, 1st v.p. 1990-93, bd. dirs. 1988-90, admissions chmn. 1989—), J. Willard O'Brien Villanova Law Sch. Inn of Ct. (pres. 1999—). Avocation: golf. Office: Blank Rome LLP One Logan Sq Philadelphia PA 19103-6998 Office Phone: 215-569-5500. Business E-Mail: hoffman@blankrome.com.

HOFFMAN, ALAN JEROME, mathematician, educator; b. N.Y.C., May 30, 1924; s. Jesse and Muriel (Schrager) H.; m. Esther Atkins Walker, May 30, 1947 (dec. July 1988); children: Eleanor, Elizabeth Hoffman Perry; m. Elinor Klausner Hershaft, Sept. 2, 1990. AB, Columbia U., 1947, PhD, 1950; DSc (hon.), Technion U., 1986. Mem. Inst. Advanced Study, Princeton, N.J., 1950-51; mathematician Nat. Bur. Standards, Washington, 1951-56; sci. liaison officer Office Naval Research, London, 1956-57; cons. Gen. Electric Co., N.Y.C., 1957-61; rsch. staff mem. IBM Rsch. Ctr., Yorktown Heights, NY, 1961—2002, fellow, 1978—2002, fellow emeritus, 2002—. Vis. prof. Technion, Haifa, Israel, 1965, Stanford U., 1980-91, Rutgers U., 1990-96, Ga. Inst. Tech., 1992-93; adj. prof. CUNY, 1965-76, Yale U., 1976-85; Phi Beta Kappa lectr., 1989-90. With U.S. Army, 1943-46, ETO, PTO. Recipient von Neumann prize Ops. Rsch. Soc. and Inst. Mgmt. Sci., 1992, Founder's award Math. Programming Soc., 2000. Fellow Inst. for Ops. Rsch. and Mgmt. Sci., N.Y. Acad. Sci., Am. Acad. Arts and Scis.; mem. NAS, Am. Math. Soc. (coun. 1982-84). Office: IBM TJ Watson Rsch Ctr PO Box 218 Yorktown Heights NY 10598-0218 Office Phone: 914-945-2270.

HOFFMAN, ALFRED, JR., real estate developer; BS, US Military Acad., West Point; MBA, Harvard Univ. Pvt. developer, Tampa Bay, 1975—85; CEO, chmn. Fla. Design Communities, 1985—89, 1993—94; CEO, dir.

Watermark Communities LP, 1995—2005, chmn., 2005—; and CEO, chmn. Courtyards at Sun City Ctr., Inc. and Sun City Ctr. Office Plz. Inc. Bd. dir. Aston Care Sys. Inc. Fighter pilot USAF. Office: WCI 24301 Walden Ctr Dr Bonita Springs FL 34134*

HOFFMAN, ALICE, writer; b. NYC, Mar. 16, 1952; m. Tom Martin; children: Jake, Zack. BA, Adelphi U., 1973; MA, Stanford U., 1975. Author: Property of, 1977, The Drowning Season, 1979, Angel Landing, 1980, White Horses, 1982, Fortune's Daughter, 1985, Illumination Night, 1987, At Risk, 1988, Seventh Heaven, 1990, Turtle Moon, 1992, Second Nature, 1994, Practical Magic, 1995, Local Girls, 1999, Fireflies: A Winter Tale, 1999, Horsefly, 2000, The River King, 2000, Blue Diary, 2001, Aquamarine, 2001, Indigo, 2002, Green Angel, 2003, The Probable Future, 2003, Blackbird House, 2004, The Ice Queen, 2005, (screenplay) Independence Day, 1983. Mirelles fellow Stanford U., 1975, Breadloaf fellow, 1976. Office: c/o Putnam Berkley 200 Madison Ave New York NY 10016-3903

HOFFMAN, ALLAN SACHS, chemical engineer, educator; b. Chgo., Oct. 27, 1932; s. Saul A. and Frances E. (Sachs) H.; m. Susan Carol Freeman, July 29, 1962; children: David, Lisa. BSChemE, MIT, 1953, MSChemE, 1955, ScDChemE, 1957. Instr. chem. engring. MIT, Cambridge, 1954-56, asst. prof., 1958-60, assoc. prof., 1965-70; research engr. Calif. Research Corp., Richmond, 1960-63; asso. dir. research Amicon Corp., Cambridge, 1963-65; prof. bioengring. and chem. engring. U. Wash., Seattle, 1970—; asst. dir. Center for Bioengring., 1973-83. Cons. to various govtl., indsl. and acad. orgns., 1958—; UN adviser to Mexican govt., 1973-74. Author: (with W. Burlant) Block and Graft Copolymers, 1960; author numerous articles and book chpts. on chem. engring. and biomaterials; patentee in field. Kimberly Clark fellow, 1954-55, Visking fellow, 1955-56, Fulbright fellow, 1957-58, Battelle fellow, 1970-72; Festschrift in honor of 60th birthday 8 issues of Jour. Biomaterials Sci., Polymer Edn., 1993. 94. Mem. AIChE, Nat. Acad. Engring., Am. Chem. Soc., Am. Soc. for Artificial Internal Organs, Internat. Soc. Artificial Internal Organs (trustee, bd. dirs. 1987-1990), Soc. for Biomaterials (pres. 1983-84, Clemson award for biomaterial sci. lit., 1985, Founder's award, 2000), Controlled Release Soc. (Excellence in Guiding Grad. Rsch. award 1989, 98), Japan Biomaterials Soc. (Biomaterials Sci. prize 1990, Symposium in honor of 70th birthday 2002). Home: 10616 Riviera Pl NE Seattle WA 98125-6938 Office: U Wash Mail Box 352255 Seattle WA 98195-2255 Office Phone: 206-543-9423. Business E-Mail: hoffman@u.washington.edu.

HOFFMAN, BARRY PAUL, lawyer; b. Phila., May 29, 1941; s. Samuel and Hilda (Cohn) H.; m. Mary Ann Schrock, May 18, 1978; children: Elizabeth Barron, Hayley Rebecca. BA, Pa. State U., 1963; JD, George Washington U., 1968. Bar: Pa. 1972, Mich. 1983. Asst. U.S. Senator Wayne Morse, Oreg., Washington; spl. agt. FBI, Washington; asst. dist. atty. Phila. Dist. Atty.'s Office; exec. v.p., gen. counsel Valassis Communications, Inc., Livonia, Mich., also bd. dirs. 1st lt. U.S. Army, 1963-65, Korea. Home: 49933 Standish Ct Plymouth MI 48170-2882 Office: Valassis Communications Inc 19975 Victor Pkwy Livonia MI 48152-7001 E-mail: hoffmanb@valassis.com.

HOFFMAN, BRENDA JOYCE, gastroenterology educator; b. Madisonville, Ky., Sept. 4, 1957; d. John Willis and Lavada Fae (Baxter) H. BS, Murray State U., 1979; MD, U. Ky., 1983. Diplomate Am. Soc. Gastroenterology and Internal Medicine. Resident Med. U. S.C., Charleston, 1983-86, chief med. resident, 1986-87, gastroent./internal medicine fellow, 1987-89, therapeutic fellow, 1989-90, clin. instr. medicine, 1990-91, asst. prof. medicine, 1991-95, assoc. prof. medicine, 1995-2000, prof. medicine, 2001—, chief endosonography, clin. dir., 1993—. Contbr. articles to profl. jours. Fellow ACP, Am. Coll. Gastroenterology; mem. Am. Gastroent. Assn., Am. Soc. Gastrointestinal Endoscopy. Avocations: soccer, sailing, reading. Office: Med U SC 171 Ashley Ave Charleston SC 29425-0001

HOFFMAN, CARL H., lawyer; b. St. Louis, May 28, 1936; s. Carl Henry and Anna Marie (Remlinger) H.; m. Pamela L. Polk, May 8, 1971 (div. Novl 1982); children: Kurt M., Jennifer K. BS, St. Louis U., 1958; postgrad., U. Mex., Mexico City, 1958, U. Nev., 1960—61, Tex. Technol. Coll., 1961—62; JD, Washington U., St. Louis, 1966. Bar: Mo. 1966, Fla. 1969, U.S. Supreme Ct. 1970; cert. civil trial adv. Nat. Bd. Trial Advocacy. Pilot Eastern Airlines, Inc., Miami, Fla.; assoc. Spencer & Taylor, Miami, Fla., 1969—70; pvt. practice Miami, 1970—80; ptnr. Hoffman & Hertzig, P.A., Coral Gables, Fla., 1980—. Capt. USAF, 1958-63. Mem. AIAA, ABA, ATLA, SAE Internat., Fla. Bar (cert. civil trial lawyer, cert. bus. litigation lawyer, chmn. aviation law com. 1997-98), Fla. Acad. Trial Lawyers, Am. Jurisprudence Soc., Greater Miami C. of C. (trustee). Office: Hoffman & Hertzig PA 901 Ponce De Leon Blvd Ste 500 Coral Gables FL 33134-3073 Office Phone: 305-445-3100 104. Business E-Mail: chh@hoffhertz.com.

HOFFMAN, CHARLES E., information technology executive; m. Maureen Hoffman; 4 children. BS, MS, U. Mo. Various sr. mgmt. positions SBC Comm., pres., gen. mgr. Cellular One ops., mng. dir. wireless; pres. NE region Sprint PCS; CEO Rogers AT&T, 1998—2001; pres., CEO Covad Comm., 2001—. Bd. dirs. Wysdom Inc., Cellular Telecom. Internet Assn., Canadian Wireless Telecomm. Assn., Cibernet, Inc. Office: Covad Comm Group Inc 110 Rio Robles San Jose CA 95134-1813

HOFFMAN, CHRISTINA MARIE, special education educator; b. Wilkes-Barre, Pa., Feb. 4, 1979; d. Catherine Ann Shulna and James Horchos; m. Cory Edward Hoffman, June 14, 2003; 1 stepchild, Sky Marie. BA in Elem. Edn., BA in Spl. Edn., Coll. Misericordia, Dallas, Pa., 2001. Cert. Profl. Tchrs. Pa., 2001. Autistic support tchr. Capital Area Intermediate Unit, Upper Dauphin, Pa., 2002—03; learning support tchr. 9-12 Newport Sch. Dist., Newport, Pa., 2003—. Co-advisor youth ministry Newport H.S., Newport, Pa., 2004—. Recipient Dean's List, Coll. Misericordia, 2000-2001; scholar Helen McAndrew O'Connor Scholarship, O'Connor Family, 2001; Kappa Delta PI, Coll. Misericordia, 2000-2001, Coun. for Exceptional Children, 2001-2002. Home: 215 Maple Ln New Bloomfield PA 17068 Office: Newport Sch Dist Newport PA 17074 Office Phone: 717-567-3806.

HOFFMAN, DANIEL (GERARD), literature educator, poet; b. N.Y.C., Apr. 3, 1923; s. Daniel and Frances (Beck) H.; m. Elizabeth McFarland, May 22, 1948; children: Kate, Macfarlane. BA, Columbia U., 1947, MA, 1949, PhD, 1956; DHL, Swarthmore Coll., 2005. Instr. English Columbia U., 1952-56; vis. prof. Am. Lit. Faculté des Lettres, Dijon, France, 1956-57; asst. prof. to prof. English Swarthmore Coll., 1957-66; prof. English U. Pa., 1966-83, poet-in-residence, 1978-93, Felix E. Schelling prof. English lit., 1983-93, prof. emeritus, 1993—. Fellow Ind. U. Sch. Letters, 1959; George Elliston lectr. poetry U. Cin., 1964; lectr. 6th Internat. Sch. Yeats Studies, Sligo, Ireland, 1965; poetry cons. Libr. of Congress, 1973-74, hon. cons. in Am. letters, 1974-77; poet-in-residence Cathedral Ch. of St. John the Divine, 1988-99; vis. prof. English, King's Coll. London, 1991-92. Author: (poetry) An Armada of Thirty Whales, 1954, A Little Geste and Other Poems, 1960, The City of Satisfactions, 1963, Striking the Stones, 1968, Broken Laws, 1970, The Center of Attention, 1974, Able Was I Ere I Saw Elba, 1977, Brotherly Love, 1981, Hang-Gliding from Helicon, 1988, Middens of the Tribe, 1995, Darkening Water, 2002, Beyond Silence: Selected Shorter Poems, 2003, MAkes You Stop and Think: Sonnets, 2005; (poetry transl.) A Play of Mirrors by Ruth Domino, 2002; (criticism) Paul Bunyan: Last of the Frontier Demigods, 1952, The Poetry of Stephen Crane, 1957, Form and Fable in American Fiction, 1961, Barbarous Knowledge, 1967, Poe Poe Poe Poe Poe Poe Poe, 1972, Faulkner's Country Matters, 1989, Words to Create a World, 1993; (memoir) Zone of the Interior, 2000; editor: The Red Badge of Courage, 1957, American Poetry and Poetics, 1962, Ezra Pound and William Carlos Williams, 1983; editor, contbr.: (criticism) Harvard Guide to Contemporary American Writing, 1979. Served to 1st lt. USAAF, 1943-46. Decorated Legion of Merit; recipient U. Chgo. Folklore prize, 1949, Poetry Center Introductions prize, 1951, Yale Series of Younger Poets award, 1954, Ansley prize, 1956, Lit. award Athenaeum of Phila., 1963, 83, medal for excellence Columbia U., 1964, Nat. Inst. Arts and Letters award in poetry, 1967, meml. medal Hungarian PEN, 1980, Hazlett Meml. award for lit., 1984, Paterson Poetry prize, 1989, 2005, Aiken Taylor award for Modern Am. Poetry, 2003, Arthur Rense Poetry prize, 2005; poetry grantee Ingram Merrill Found., 1971-72; fellow Am. Council Learned Socs., 1961-62, 66-67, NEH, 1975-76, Guggenheim Meml. Found., 1983-84. Mem. MLA, Assn. Literary Scholars and Critics, Acad. Am. Poets (chancellor 1973-97, chancellor emeritus 1997—), Authors Guild (council). Clubs: Century (N.Y.C.); Franklin Inn (Phila.).

HOFFMAN, DANIEL STEVEN, lawyer, educator; b. N.Y.C., May 4, 1931; s. Lawrence Hoffman and Juliette (Marbes) Ostrov; m. Beverly Mae Swenson, Dec. 4, 1954; children: Lisa Hoffman Ciancio, Tracy Hoffman Cockriel, Robin Hoffman Black. BA, U. Colo., 1951; LLB, U. Denver, 1958. Bar: Colo. 1958. Assoc., then ptnr. Fugate, Mitchem, Hoffman, Denver, 1951—55; mgr. of safety City and County of Denver, 1963—65; ptnr. Kripke, Hoffman, Carrigan, Denver, 1965—70, Hoffman, McDermott, Hoffman, Denver, 1970—78; of counsel Hoffman & McDermott, Denver, 1978—84; mem. Holme Roberts & Owen, LLC, Denver, 1984—94; dean Coll. Law, U. Denver, 1978—84, dean emeritus, prof. emeritus, 1984—; ptnr. McKenna & Cuneo LLP, Denver, 1994—2000, Hoffman Reilly Pozner & Williamson LLP, 2000—. Chmn., mem. Merit Screening Com. for Bankruptcy Judges, Denver, 1979—84; chmn. subcom. Dist. Atty.'s Crime Adv. Commn., Denver, 1984—; chmn. Senator Wirth's jud. nomination rev. com., Cong. DeGette's jud. nomination rev. com.; mem. jud. ethics adv. com. Colo. Supreme Ct., 2004—. Contbr. chpts. to books Mem. Rocky Mountain region Anti-Defamation League, Denver, 1985; bd. dirs. Colo. chpt. Am. Jewish Com., 1985, Legal Ctr., Denver, 1985—; mem. adv. com. Samaritan Shelter, Denver, 1985; chmn. Rocky Flats Blue Ribbon Citizens Com., Denver, 1980-83; mem. bd. visitors J. Reuben Clark Law Sch. Brigham Young U., 1986-88. With USAF, 1951-55. Recipient Am. Jewish Com. Nat. Judge Learned Hand award, 1993, Humanitarian award Rocky Mountain chpt. Anti-Defamation League, 1984, Alumni of Yr. award U. Denver Coll. Law, 1997, Lifetime Achievement award Colo. Trial Lawyers Assn., 2001. Fellow: Am. Bar Found., Colo. Bar. Found., Am. Coll. Trial Lawyers (state chmn. 1975—76), Internat. Soc. Barristers; mem.: Am. Judicature Soc. (bd. dirs. 1977—81), Assn. Trial Lawyers Am. (nat. com. mem. 1962—63), Colo. Trial Lawyers Assn. (pres. 1961—62, Lifetime Achievement award 2001), Colo. Bar. Assn. (pres. 1976—77, Young Lawyer of Yr. award 1965), Order of Coif (hon.). Democrat. Jewish. Avocation: tennis. Office: Hoffman Reilly Pozner & Williamson LLP Kittredge Bldg 511 16th St Ste 700 Denver CO 80202-4248 Office Phone: 303-893-6100. Business E-Mail: dhoffman@hrpwlaw.com.

HOFFMAN, DARLEANE CHRISTIAN, chemistry professor; b. Terril, Iowa, Nov. 8, 1926; d. Carl Benjamin and Elverna (Kuhlman) Christian; m. Marvin Morrison Hoffman, Dec. 26, 1951; children: Maureane R., Daryl K. BS in Chemistry, Iowa State U., 1948, PhD in Nuclear Chemistry, 1951; D (hon.), U. Bern, Switzerland, 2001; PhD (hon.), Clark U., 2000. Chemist Oak Ridge (Tenn.) Nat. Lab., 1952—53; staff radiochemistry group Los Alamos (N.Mex.) Sci. Lab., 1953—71, assoc. leader chemistry-nuclear group, 1971—79, leader chem.-nuclear divsn., 1979—82, leader isotope and nuclear chem. divsn., 1982-84; prof. chemistry U. Calif., Berkeley, 1984—91, prof. emeritus, 1991—93, prof. grad. sch., 1993—; faculty sr. scientist Lawrence Berkeley Lab., 1984—; dir.'s fellow Los Alamos Nat. Lab., 1990—; dir. Lawrence Livermore Nat. lab., G.T. Seaborg Inst. for Transactinium Sci., 1991—96. Spkr. in field; subcom. on nuclear and radiochemistry NAS-NRC, 1978—81, chmn. subcom. on nuclear and radiochemistry, 1982—84, bd. on radioactive waste mgmt., 1994—99; titular mem. commn. on radiochem. and nuclear techniques Internat. Union of Pure and Applied Chem., 1983—87, sec., 1985—87, chmn., 1987—91, assoc., 1991—93; organizer of symposiums in field; com. mem. Internat. Symposium on Nuclear and Radiochemistry, 1988; organizing com. Actinides, 1993, nat. adv. com., 2001; planning panel Workshop on Tng. Requirements for Chemists in Nuclear Medicine, Nuclear Industry, and Related Fields, 1998; radionuclide migration peer rev. com., Las Vegas, 1986—87; steering com. Advanced Steady State Neutron Source, 1986—90; steering com., panelist Workshop on Opportunities and Challenges in Rsch. with Transplutonium Elements, Washington, 1983; energy rsch. adv. bd. cold fusion panel Dept. Energy, 1989—90, nuclear energy rsch. adv. com, 2000—01; separations subpanel of separations tech. and transmutation systems panel NAS, 1992—94; mem. steeering com. Accel. Transmutation Waste Roadmapping Study, 1999; mem. ANTT subcom. NERAC, 2002—06; Welch Found. lectr. Tex. univs., 2000; mem. NAS-NRC BRWM, 1994—99, NAS-NRC BRWM Joint US/Russian Commn., 2001—02, 2004—05. Author: The Transuranium People, 2000; contbr. articles to profl. jours. Named Disting. Lectr., Inst. Phys. Rsch and Tech., Ames Lab., 1998, Welch Found. Conf. lectr., 1991; named to Women in Tech. Internat. Hall of Fame, 2000; recipient Alumni Citation of Merit, Coll. Scis. and Humanities, Iowa State U., 1978, Disting. Achievement award, Iowa State U., 1986, Welch Found. Conf. lectr., 1997, Berkeley Citation, U. Calif., 1996, US Nat. Medal Sci., 1997, Leonard A. Ford Lectureship, Mankato State U., 1998, Frontiers Sci. award, Soc. Cosmetic Chemists, 1998; fellow, Guggenheim Found., 1978—79; Sr. postdoc.fellow, NSF, 1964—65. Fellow: AAAS (coun. mem. 1995—97), Am. Acad. Arts and Scis., Am. Phys. Soc., Am. Inst. Chemists (pres. N.Mex. chpt. 1976—78); mem.: Radiochem. Soc. (Lifetime Achievement award 2003), Norwegian Acad. Sci. and Letters, Am. Chem. Soc. (John Dustin Clark award 1976, Nuc. Chemistry award 1983, Francis P. Garvan-John M. Olin medal 1990, Priestley medal 2000, Mosher award 2001), Sigma Xi (Procter prize for sci. achievement 2003), Alpha Chi Sigma (Hall of Fame 2002), Sigma Delta Epsilon, Pi Mu Epsilon, Iota Sigma Pi (nat. hon. mem. 1993), Phi Kappa Phi. Methodist. Home: 2277 Manzanita Dr Oakland CA 94611-1135 Office: Lawrence Berkeley Nat Lab MS70R0319 NSD Berkeley CA 94720 Business E-Mail: Hoffman@lbl.gov.

HOFFMAN, DARNAY ROBERT, management consultant; b. N.Y.C., Nov. 25, 1947; s. Bill and Toni (Darnay) H.; m. Jennifer Lea Sheppard, Aug. 20, 1984; children by previous marriage: Brandon, Brett; m. Sydney Biddle Barrows, May 14, 1994. BA, SUNY, 1977; MBA, CUNY, 1980; JD, Yeshiva U., 1982. Bar: N.Y. 1995, U.S. Dist. Ct. (so., ea., we. and no. dists.) N.Y. 1995, U.S. Ct. Appeals (fed. cir.) 1995, U.S. Tax Ct. 1995, U.S. Ct. Internat. Trade 1995, U.S. Dist. Ct. Colo. 2000, U.S. Dist. Ct. (no. dist.) Ga. 2000, U.S. Ct. Appeals (fed. cir.). Pres., mgmt. cons. Darnay Hoffman Assocs., Inc., 1969—; mgmt. cons. Hoffman Rsch. Group Inc., N.Y.C., 1977—; rsch. assoc. Baruch Coll., 1977-79. Bd. dirs. Hobton Realty Corp.; dir. Nat. Conf. Law Historians Am., 1987—. Author: Murder in the Wilderness, 1989, Allen Contact, 1989, (pamphlet) Products in Decline, 1980. Mem. ABA, ATLA, Am. Mgmt. Assn., Am. Mktg. Assn., Acad. Mgmt. Scis., Nat. Assn. Criminal Def. Attys., N.Y. State Bar Assn., N.Y. County Lawyers Assn., Assn. Bar of City of N.Y., N.Y. State Trial Lawyers Assn., Player's, Beta Gamma Sigma, Alpha Delta Sigma. Office Phone: 212-712-2766. Personal E-mail: darnayh@aol.com.

HOFFMAN, DAVID JOHN, physiologist, ecotoxicologist; b. New London, Conn., Sept. 22, 1944; s. John Leslie and Margaret Amy (Stokes) H.; m. Suzanne Elizabeth O'Clair, Aug. 20, 1966; children: Michael David, James Stephen. BS, McGill U., 1966; PhD, U. Md., 1971. Instr. in genetics, embryology U. Md., College Park, 1968-71; postdoctoral fellow/NIH Oak Ridge Nat. Lab., Oak Ridge, Tenn., 1971-73; faculty, biology dept. Boston Coll., Newton, Mass., 1973-74; sr. staff physiologist Health Effects Rsch. Lab/U.S. EPA, Cin., 1974-76; rsch. physiologist Patuxent Wildlife Rsch. Ctr./USDI, Laurel, Md., 1976—. Adj. prof. U. Md., 1992—. Mem. editl. bd. Archives of Environ. Contamination and Toxicology Jour., 1986—, Jour. Toxicology and Environ. Health, 1989-96, Environ. Toxicology and Chemistry, 1990-92, Oecologia Montana, 1992—, Current Topics in Ecotoxicology and Environ. Chemistry, 1995—, Current Topics in Toxicology, 1996—; editor: Handbook of Ecotoxicology, 1995, 2d edit., 2003; contbr. over 200 chpts. to books, articles to profl. jours. and symposia. Recipient dissertation fellowship U. Md., College Park, 1970, spl. achievement award USDI, 1990, 94, 96, 2003, Honor award, 1995. Mem. AAAS, Teratology Soc., Soc. Environ. Chemistry and Toxicology (editoral bd. 1990—), Soc. Exptl. Biology and Medicine, Soc. Toxicology, Nature Conservancy, Nat. Audubon Soc., Phi Sigma Soc. Avocations: distance swimming, adult fitness swimming, fishing, boating, birdwatching. Home: 25 New Boston Rd Amherst NH 03031-1804 Office: Patuxent Wildlife Rsch Ctr USDI Laurel MD 20708 Office Phone: 301-497-5712. Business E-Mail: david_hoffman@usgs.gov.

HOFFMAN, DONALD ALFRED, lawyer; b. Milw., May 4, 1936; s. Harry Gustav and Emily Frances (Schwartz) H.; m. Louise Hardie Chapman, June 8, 1963; children: Donald Hardie, Richard Rainey. BBA, U. Wis., 1958, JD, 1968. Bar: La. 1969, U.S. Supreme Ct. 1972, U.S. Ct. Appeals (5th cir.) 1973, U.S. Dist. Ct. (ea., mid. and we. dists.) La. Assoc. Lemle & Kelleher, New Orleans, 1968-73; ptnr. Lemle, Kelleher, Kohlmeyer, Matthews & Schumacher, New Orleans, 1973-75, McGlinchey, Stafford, Mintz & Hoffman, New Orleans, 1975-78; city atty. City of New Orleans, 1978-79; dir. Carmouche, Gray & Hoffman, New Orleans, 1979-82; sr. dir. Hoffman, Siegel, Seydel, Bienvenu & Centola, New Orleans, 1982—2000, Hoffman Seydel LLC, New Orleans, 2004. Fellow Am. Bar Found., La. Bar Found.; mem. Am. Bd. Trial Advocates (pres. La. chpt.), French-Am. C. of C. (chmn. La. chpt.). Presbyterian. Home: 1524 4th St New Orleans LA 70130-5918 Office: Hoffman Seydel LLC Ste 3770 701 Poydras St New Orleans LA 70139 Office Phone: 504-587-0900 ext. 102. Business E-Mail: dhoffman@hoffmanseydel.com.

HOFFMAN, DONALD DAVID, cognitive and computer science educator; b. San Antonio, Dec. 29, 1955; s. David Pollock and Loretta Virginia (Shoemaker) H.; m. Geralyn Mary Souza, Dec. 13, 1986; 1 child from previous marriage, Melissa Louise. BA, UCLA, 1978; PhD, MIT. MTS and project engr. Hughes Aircraft Co., El Segundo, Calif., 1978-83; rsch. scientist MIT Artificial Intelligence Lab, Cambridge, Mass., 1983; asst. prof. U. Calif., Irvine, 1983-86, assoc. prof., 1986-90, prof., 1990—. Cons. Fairchild Lab. for Artificial Intelligence, Palo Alto, Calif., 1984; panelist MIT Corp. vis. com., Cambridge, 1985, NSF, Washington, 1988; conf. host IEEE Conf. on Visual Motion, Irvine, 1989, Office of Naval Rsch. Conf. on Vision, Laguna Beach, Calif., 1992; vis. prof. Zentrum für Interdisziplinäre Forschung, Bielefeld, Germany, 1995-96, cons. Sextant Tech. Inc., Irvine, Calif., 2000-05. Author: Visual Intelligence, 1998; co-author: Observer Mechanics, 1989; mem. editl. bd. Cognition, 1991-2002, Psychol. Rev., 1995-96; contbr. articles to profl. jours. Vol. tchr. Turtle Rock Elem. Sch., Irvine, 1988-90. Recipient Distinguished Scientific award, Am. Psychol. Assn., 1989, Troland Rsch. award U.S. Nat. Acad. Scis., 1994; grantee NSF, 1984, 87, 2001. Mem.: Am. Psychol. Soc., Assn. for Sci. Study of Consciousness, Assn. Sci. Study Consciousness. Avocations: running, swimming, racket sports, ice skating.

HOFFMAN, DONALD M., lawyer; BS, UCLA, 1957, LL.B., 1960. Bar: Calif. 1961. Pvt. practice, L.A. County, 1961—; ptnr. firm Greenwald, Hoffman, Meyer & Montes, 1964—. Pres. L.A. Estate Planning Council. Served to 2d lt. U.S. Army. Mem. Am., Los Angeles County bar assns., Phi Alpha Delta, Beta Gamma Sigma. Office: 500 N Brand Blvd Ste 920 Glendale CA 91203-1923 Office Phone: 818-507-8100. Business E-Mail: dmboftman@ghmm.com.

HOFFMAN, DUSTIN LEE, actor; b. L.A., Aug. 8, 1937; s. Harry and Lillian Hoffman; m. Anne Byrne, May 4, 1969 (div.); children: Karina, Jenna; m. Lisa Gottsegen, Oct. 21, 1980; children: Jacob, Rebecca, Max, Alexandra. Student, Santa Monica City Coll., Pasadena Playhouse; studied with, Barney Brown, Lonny Chapman & Lee Strasberg. Stage debut: Sarah Lawrence Coll. prodn. of Yes Is for a Very Young Man; Broadway debut: A Cook for Mr. General, 1961; appeared in Endgame, The Quare Fellow, In The Jungle of Cities, A Country Scandal, The Dumbwaiter, The Room, Waiting for Godot, Picnic on the Battlefield, Dirty Hands, The Cocktail Party, All Theatre Company of Boston, Three Men on a Horse, 1964, Harry, Noon and Night, 1965, The Journey of the Fifth Horse (Obie award 1966), 1966, Fragments, 1966, Eh? (Drama Desk award 1967, Verna Rice award 1967, Theatre World award 1967), 1966, Jimmy Shine, 1968, Death of a Salesman, 1984, The Merchant of Venice, 1989; recorded: Death of a Salesman on Caedmon Records (Drama Desk award 1984); appeared in films: The Tiger Makes Out, 1967, The Graduate, 1967 (Acad. award nom. best actor 1968, BAFTA award best actor 1969, Golden Globe award most promising newcomer 1968), El Millón de Madigan, 1969, Sunday Father, 1969, Midnight Cowboy, 1969 (Acad. award nom. best actor 1970, BAFTA award best actor 1970), John and Mary, 1969 (BAFTA award best actor 1970), Little Big Man, 1970 (BAFTA award nom. best actor 1972), Who Is Harry Kellerman and Why Is He Saying Those Terrible Things About Me?, 1971, Straw Dogs, 1971, Alfredo, Alfredo, 1972, Papillon, 1973, Lenny, 1974 (Acad. award nom. best actor 1975, BAFTA award nom. best actor 1976), All the President's Men, 1976 (BAFTA award nom. best actor 1977), Marathon Man, 1976 (BAFTA award nom. best actor 1977), Straight Time, 1978, Agatha, 1979, Kramer vs. Kramer, 1979 (Acad. award best actor, 1980, BAFTA award nom. best actor 1981, Golden Globe award best actor 1980), Tootsie, 1982 (Acad. award nom. best actor 1983, Golden Globe award best actor 1983, BAFTA award best actor 1984), Ishtar, 1987, Rain Man, 1988 (Acad. award best actor 1989, BAFTA award nom. best actor 1990, Golden Globe award best actor 1989), Family Business, 1989, Dick Tracy, 1990, Billy Bathgate, 1991, Hook, 1991, Hero, 1992, Outbreak, 1995, American Buffalo, 1996, Sleepers, 1996, Mad City, 1997, Wag the Dog, 1997 (Acad. award nom. best actor 1998), Sphere, 1998, Messenger: The Story of Joan of Arc, 1999, Tuesday (voice), 2001, Moonlight Mile, 2002, Confidence, 2003, Runaway Jury, 2003, I Heart Huckabees, 2004, Finding Neverland, 2004, Meet the Fockers, 2004, Lemony Snicket's A Series of Unfortunate Events, 2004, (voice) Racing Stripes, 2005; appeared in TV movies: Journey of the Fifth Horse, 1966, The Star Wagon, 1967, The Point (voice), 1971, Death of a Salesman, 1985 (Emmy award best actor 1986, Golden Globe award best actor 1986), A Wish for Wings That Work, 1991; TV series: Liberty's Kids (voice), 2002; prodr. films: Straight Time, 1978, A Walk on the Moon, 1999, The Furies, 1999; exec. prodr. TV movie: The Devil's Arithmetic, 1999. Decorated officer Order of Arts and Letters (France), 1995, Golden Globe lifetime achievement award, 1997, AFI Life Achievement award, 1999. Office: Creative Artists Agy 9830 Wilshire Blvd Beverly Hills CA 90212

HOFFMAN, E. LESLIE, lawyer; b. Charleston, W. Va., Aug. 8, 1947; s. E. Leslie and Mary Jane (Lively) H.; m. Susan Sandy, Sept. 9, 1967 (div. 1983); children: Melissa North, Marc Clayton. BA Polit. Sci., West Va. U., 1969, JD, 1972. Bar: W.Va. 1972, U.S. Dist. Ct. (no. and so. dists.) W.Va. 1972, U.S. Ct. Appeals (4th crct.) 1973, U.S. Ct. Appeals (9th crct.) 1984. Asst. atty. gen. State W. Va., Charleston, 1972-76; asst. U.S. Atty. so. dist. W. Va., Charleston, 1976-81; asst. dir. atty. gen's. advocacy inst. U.S. Dept. Justice, Washington, 1982, trial atty. fraud sect., 1983-86; dep. sect. chief fraud sect. U.S Dept. Justice, Washington, 1987-88; counsel Pettit & Martin, Washington, 1988-90, ptnr., 1991-95, Piper Marbury Rudnick & Wolfe, Washington, 1995—2002, Jackson & Kelly PLLC, Washington, 2002—. Mem. ABA. Democrat. Episcopalian. Office: Jackson & Kelly PLLC 2401 Pennsylvania Ave NW Washington DC 20037 E-mail: phoffman@jacksonkelly.com.

HOFFMAN, ELIZABETH, political science professor; b. Bryn Mawr, Pa. BA in history, Smith Coll., 1968; MA in history, U. Pa., 1969, PhD in history, 1972; PhD in econs., Calif. Inst. of Tech., 1979. Academic and adminstrv. positions U. Fla., Northwestern U., Purdue U., U. Wyo., U. Ariz., Iowa State U.; prof. econs., history, polit. sci., psychology U. Ill., Chgo., 1997—2000, prof. Inst. of Govt. and Pub. Affairs, 1997—2000, provost and vice chancellor, 1997—2000; pres. U. Colo. Sys., Boulder, Colo., 2000—05; prof. Grad. Sch. Pub. Affairs U. Colo., Denver, 2005—. Appointee Nat. Sci. Bd., 2002. Author books; contbr. articles to profl. jours. Named one of 100 women making a difference, Today's Chgo. Woman, 1999, 25 Most Powerful People, Colo. Biz Mag., 2004; recipient Ronald H. Coase prize, Electronic Intelligence citation, ANBAR. Office: U Colo Grad Sch Pub Affairs PO Box 173364 - Campus Box 142 Denver CO 80217-3364

HOFFMAN, ELLENDALE MCCOLLAM, psychologist, pastoral counselor; b. Alexandria, La., Apr. 3, 1951; d. William and Hope Flower (Joffrion) McCollam; m. Charles L. Hoffman, Nov. 27, 1976. AA, Briarcliff Coll., 1971; BA, Manhattanville Coll., 1973; MDiv, Episcopal Div. Sch., 1976; DMin, Andover Newton Theol. Sch., 1978. Ordained priest Episcopal Ch., 1977, deacon, 1976; lic. psychologist, Mass.; cert. marriage and family therapist, Conn. Clin. supr. Pastoral Inst. Tng. and Alcohol Problems, Cambridge, Mass., 1976-78; dir. growth and learning ctr. Marion (Mass.) Ctr. for Human Svcs., 1978-79; clin. dir. Cape Counseling Ctr., Hyannis, Mass., 1979-82; pvt. practice psychology and pastoral counseling Falmouth, Mass., 1976-88, Old Saybrook, Conn., 1988—. Author course Driver's Alcohol Education Curriculum. Chairperson commn. on today's famlies Diocese of Mass., 1980-82; pastoral assoc. Grace Episc. Ch., 1989—. Roothbert fellow, 1976-78; Epis. Women's scholar, 1976-78. Fellow Am. Assn. Pastoral Counselors (profl. concerns com.); mem. Am. Psychol. Assn., Am. Assn. Marriage and Family Therapists (clin.), LWV. Home and Office: 8 Sharon Ln Old Saybrook CT 06475-2037

HOFFMAN, ESTHER, pianist, educator; b. Toronto, Ont., Can., Sept. 30, 1922; d. Sidney and Annie (Wiseman) H.; m. Gerald Wexler, July 26, 1968. Grad. assoc. Toronto Conservatory Music, U. Toronto, 1939; diploma, Hebrew Union Coll., 1952. Faculty Toronto Conservatory of Music, 1941-44; piano faculty Mannes Coll., N.Y.C., 1962—. Recitalist Can. Broadcasting Corp.; recital and orch. appearances in Can. and the U.S. Mem. Music Tchrs. Nat. Assn. (cert.), Associated Music Tchrs. League (mem. exec. bd.), Piano Tchrs. Congress. Home: 124 W 79th St New York NY 10024-6446

HOFFMAN, FAITH LOUISE, social worker; b. Buffalo, June 7, 1944; d. William George Hoffman, Louise Caroline Hoffman; children: Donald Louis, Louis William, Christopher Robert. BS magna cum laude, Medaille Coll., 1983—87; MSW, SUNY, Buffalo, 1991—93. LCSW 1993. Case mgr. N.Y. Crime Victim's Assistance Program, Buffalo, 1987—88; dir. domestic violence program YWCA of Tonawanda's, 1988—90; dir. family support program Concerned Ecumenical Ministry, Buffalo, 1990—92; social worker Dept. Veteran's Affairs Med. Ctr., Buffalo, 1993—95, women veteran's program mgr., 1995—. Adj. prof. U. Buffalo Grad. Sch. Social Work, 2004—; dir., founder Hopegivers, Buffalo, 1991—; dir. VA Domestic Violence Program, Buffalo, 1995—; field faculty SUNY, Buffalo, 1996—; domestic violence cons. Erie County Dept. Health, Buffalo, 2000—02; spkr. in field. Named cmty. hero, torchbearer Western N.Y. Olympic Torch Relay, Atlanta Olympic Com., 1996—96; recipient Svc. to Mankind award, Sertoma Greater Buffalo, 1998—98, ann. leadership award, YWCA Western N.Y., 2001—01, Joan A. Levine award, Woman Focus, 2002, Fed. Woman of Yr. award, Buffalo (N.Y.) Fed. Exec. Bd., 2003, Person of Yr. award, Jewish War Vets. Am.-Buffalo Frontier Post 25, 2004. Office: VA Western NY Healthcare Sys 3495 Bailey Ave Buffalo NY 14215 Office Phone: 716-862-8771. Business E-Mail: faithhoffman@med.va.gov.

HOFFMAN, FRED L., human resources specialist; b. Wauseon, Ohio, Mar. 13, 1953; s. Lowell Max and Annabell (Whitmire) Hoffman; m. Diane Patricia Pope, Sept. 19, 1975; 1 child, Brandon C. BSBA, Bowling Green U., 1975. Asst. mgr. indsl. rels. Colonial Press div. Sheller-Globe Corp., Clinton, Mass., 1975-76, dir. human resources Leece-Neville div. Gainesville, Ga., 1976-88; v.p. human resources, staff ops. Golder Assocs., Atlanta, 1988—, also bd. dirs. Bd. dirs. Hoffman-Rettig Foods, Inc., Maquoketa, Iowa. Guest columnist: BG News, 1971—75. Lt. col. aide-de-camp gov.'s staff Gov. Joe Frank Harris, Atlanta, 1983—91; state dir. pub. rels. Ohio League Coll. Reps., Columbus, 1974, 1975. Recipient Disting. Svc. award, Bowling Green State U., 1975. Mem.: Soc. Human Resources Mgmt., Antaen Soc. (pres. 1974—75), Atlanta C. of C., Atlanta Athletic Club, Pres.'s Club Bowling Green State U., Phi Delta Theta, Omicron Delta Kappa. Home: 235 Parian Run Duluth GA 30097-2418 Office: Golder Assocs Corp 3730 Chamblee Tucker Rd Atlanta GA 30341-4414 Office Phone: 770-496-1893. Personal E-mail: hoffmandp@yahoo.com.

HOFFMAN, GILBERT L., information technology executive; Sr. v.p. & chief info. officer Maritz, Inc., St. Louis. Named a Premier 100 IT Leader, Computerworld mag., 2001; named named one of top tech. innovators, Info. Week mag., 2004. Office: SVP & CIO Maritz Inc 1375 N Hwy Dr Fenton MO 63099

HOFFMAN, HOWARD STANLEY, experimental psychologist, educator; b. N.Y.C., May 23, 1925; s. Melvin Leo and Henrietta (Rosenthal) H.; m. Alice Marie Cruikshank, June 7, 1961; children: Randall, Gwendolyn, Russell, Franklin, Daniel, Martha. BA, New Sch. for Social Research, N.Y.C., 1952; MA, Bklyn. Coll., 1953; PhD, U. Conn., 1957. Rsch. fellow in auditory perception U. Conn., 1953-56, instr. dept. stats., 1956-57; asst. to prof. psychology Pa. State U., 1957-70; prof. psychology Bryn Mawr Coll., 1970-92, prof. emeritus, 1992—. Bd. editors: Jour. Exptl. Analysis Behavior, 1966-69, Jour. Exptl. Psychology, Animal Behavior Processes, 1974-84; reviewer: Jour. Comparative and Physiol. Psychology. Served with AUS, 1943-45. Fellow AAAS, Am. Psychol. Assn., Am. Psychol. Soc.; mem. Eastern Psychol. Assn., AAUP, Sigma Xi, Phi Kappa Phi, Psi Chi. Home: 3300 Darby Rd Apt 3211 Haverford PA 19041-1070 Office: Bryn Mawr Coll Dept Psychology Bryn Mawr PA 19010 Personal E-mail: hshoffman@comcast.net.

HOFFMAN, IRWIN, orchestra conductor; b. N.Y.C., Nov. 26, 1924; s. Harry and Augusta (Cohen) H.; m. Esther Glazer, Feb. 21, 1946 (div. 1990); children: Joel H., Gary, Toby, Deborah; m. Maria Lourdes Lobo, 1990. Student, Juilliard Sch. Music, 1942-43, 45-48; MusD (hon.), U. Tampa, 1984. Dir. music Orquesta Sinfonica de Chile, 1994-97. Condr. Phila. Orch. at Robin Hood Dell, summer 1942, Bronx (N.Y.) Symphony, 1948-52, Yonkers (N.Y.) Philharm., 1950-52, Westchester (N.Y.) Chamber Orch., 1950-52, for Martha Graham Dance Co., 1949-50; condr., mus. dir. Vancouver (B.C., Can.) Symphony Orch., 1952-64; assoc. condr. Chgo. Symphony Orch., 1964-68, acting music dir., 1968-69, condr., 1969-70, prin. condr. Grant Park, Chgo., 1965-73; permanent condr. Belgian Radio and TV Symphony Orch., 1973-76; music dir. Fla. Orch., 1968-87, music dir. laureate, 1987-95; music dir. Flagstaff (Ariz.) Festival of Arts, 1983-95; condr. St. Louis Little Symphony, summers 1959-64, lectr., condr., U. B.C., State Coll. Wash., 1958, guest condr. Toronto, Vancouver, Chgo., Israel Philharm., 1960, Dallas Symphony, 1962, Brazil, 1962, 78, St. Louis Symphony Orch., 1963, Miami and Tampa symphonies, 1967, protege of Serge Koussevitzky, Tanglewood, 1948-50, guest condr. BBC Symphony, Manchester, Eng., 1968, Brussels (Belgium), Radio Orch., 1968, Strasbourg (France) Radio Orch., 1968, BBC Welsh, 1969-82, BBC Scottish, 1971-82, BBC No. Orch., 1971-82, Orch. Nat., France, 1970, Orch. Philharmonique, France, 1970, Orch. Nat., Peru, 1970, Philharmonia Orch., Eng., 1971, Chgo., Vancouver symphonies, 1971, N.J., Denver, Costa Rica, 1977-78, Chgo., 1977, Montevideo (Uruguay) Nat., 1979, Buffalo symphonies, 1980-81, New Orleans Philharm., 1981, Winnipeg Symphony, 1985, Pitts. Symphony, 1986, Colorado Springs Symphony, 1989, Kitchener-Waterloo Symphony, 1989, music dir. Nat. Symphony Orch. of Costa Rica, 1987-2001; guest condr. Israel Chamber Orch., 1990, Jalapa Symphony, Mex., 1990, Phoenix Symphony, 1991, UNAM Mex., 1991, Orch. Symphonique Francaise, 1991, Orquesta Sinfonica, Caracas, 1992, 93, 94, Orquesta Sinfonica De Chile, 1992, 93, 94, music dir. 1995-97; guest condr. Orquesta Sinfonica de San Luis, Argentina, 1994, Orquesta de Sodre, Montevideo, Uruguay, 1994, Orquesta de Concepcion, Chile, 1995, Orquesta Sinfonica de Buenos Aires, 1996, 98, Taipei Symphony Orch., 1997, 98, 99, 2000, Orquesta Sinfonica de Bogotá, 1998, 99, Fla. Orch., 1999, Nat. Symphony Guatemala, 1998, Orquestra Sintonica Panama, 1999; music dir. Orquesia Sinfonica-De Bogota, Colombia, 2000-03, Filarmonica Orq de Bogota, 2004—, Beijing Symphony Orch., 2004-05, Cali Symphony Orch., 2005, Taipei Nat. Orch., 2005, Budapest Conger Orch., 2005, ORQ, Sinfonica de Venezuela, 2005; composer two string quartets, violin sonata, Orquesta Filarmónica of Bogotá, Columbia, 1997, 98, others; collector autography music manuscripts, mus. memorablia. Served with AUS, 1943-45. Juilliard fellow, 1948. Home and Office: Apdo 818-1260 Plaza Colonial Escazu San José Costa Rica

HOFFMAN, JAMES PAUL, lawyer; b. Waterloo, Iowa, Sept. 7, 1943; s. James A. and Luella M. (Prokosch) Hoffman; 1 child, Tiffany K. BA, U. No. Iowa, 1965; JD, U. Iowa, 1967. Bar: Iowa 1967, U.S. Dist. Ct. (no. dist.) Iowa 1981, U.S. Dist. Ct. (so. dist.) Iowa 1968, U.S. Dist. Ct. (so. dist.) Ill. 1971, U.S. Tax Ct. 1971, U.S. Ct. Appeals (8th cir.) 1970, U.S. Supreme Ct. 1974. Sr. mem. James P. Hoffman, Law Offices, Keokuk, Iowa, 1967—. Author: The Iowa Trial Lawyers and the Use of Hypnosis, 1980. Chmn. bd. Iowa Inst. Hypnosis. Fellow: Am. Inst. Hypnosis; mem.: ATLA, ABA, Lee County Bar Assn., Iowa Trial Lawyers Assn., Ill. Trial Lawyers Assn., Iowa Bar Assn. Democrat. Roman Catholic. Home and Office: Middle Rd PO Box 1087 Keokuk IA 52632-1087 Office Phone: 319-524-4441.

HOFFMAN, JERRY IRWIN, retired dental educator; b. Chgo., Nov. 20, 1935; s. Irwin and Luba Hoffman; m. Sharon Lynn Seaman, Aug. 25, 1963; children: Steven Abram, Rachel Irene. Student, DePaul U., 1953-56; BS in Biology and Chemistry, Roosevelt U., 1956; DDS, Loyola U., Chgo., 1960; M of Health Care Adminstrn., Baylor U., 1972. Certificate, General Practice Residency, U.S. Army, 1978. Commd. officer U.S. Army, 1960 (served to 1962, returned 1964), advanced through grades to col., 1978, hdqrs. rep. local dental tng. confs. Europe Garmisch, Fed. Republic Germany, 1965-67; cons. to Comdg. Gen. U.S. Army Med. Research and Devel. Command, Washington, 1972-76; cons. Office of Surgeon Gen. U.S. Army, Washington, 1972-76, liaison rep. to Nat. Adv. Council and Oral Biology and Medicine Study Sessions of the Nat. Inst. Dental Research and NIH, 1973-76, resident in Gen. Practice Residency, 1976-78; comdg. officer U.S. Army Dental Activity, Fort Monmouth, N.J., 1979-82; ret., 1982; pvt. practice dentistry Chgo., 1962-64; assoc. prof. operative dentistry Loyola U. Sch. Dentistry, Maywood, Ill., 1982-93, dir. gen. practice residency, 1982-85, coordinator extramural dental resources, 1983-85, assoc. dean for clin. affairs, 1985-93; dir. sci. programs Chgo. Dental Soc., 1993—2002, ret., 2002. Staff dentist Silas B. Hayes Army Hosp., Fort Ord, Calif., 1976-79, Patterson Army Hosp., Ft. Monmouth, 1979-82; lectr., presenter seminars in field. Contbr. articles to profl. jours. Decorated Legion of Merit, Meritorious Svc. Medal with oak leaf cluster. Fellow: Am. Coll. Dentists, Internat. Coll. Dentists, Odontographic Soc.; master: Acad. Gen. Dentistry; mem. ADA, Ill. Dental Soc., Chgo. Dental Soc., Am. Assn. Dental Schs., Am. Soc. Assn. Execs., Assn. Healthcare Execs., Profl. Conv. Mgmt. Assn., Omicron Kappa Upsilon.

HOFFMAN, JOEL ELIHU, lawyer; b. N.Y.C., Sept. 23, 1937; s. Samuel S. and Flora (Pasachoff) H.; m. Sandra Joyce Stone, June 3, 1962 (div. June 1985); children: Susanna Beth, Alexander Laurence, Jeremy Andrew; m. Katherine Louise Joss, Feb. 15, 1986. BA, NYU, 1957; LLB, Yale U., 1960. Bar: N.Y. 1960, D.C. 1963. Trial atty. antitrust div. U.S. Dept. Justice, Washington, 1960-63; assoc. Wald, Harkrader and Ross, Washington, 1963-68, ptnr., 1968-85, Sutherland, Asbill and Brennan, Washington, 1985-99, of counsel, 1999—. Adj. prof. law Franklin Pierce Law Sch., 1997-2003, Law Sch. George Mason U., 1998—. Mem. editorial adv. bd. Food Drug and Cosmetic Law Jour., 1981-89; contbr. articles to profl. jours. Mem. ABA (chmn. food and drug com. adminstrv. law sect. 1976-82, 95-99, vice chmn. consumer product regulation com. 1976—, coun. mem. 1973-76). Office: Sutherland Asbill & Brennan 1275 Pennsylvania Ave NW Washington DC 20004-2415 Office Phone: 202-383-0100.

HOFFMAN, JOHN FLETCHER, lawyer; b. N.Y.C., May 22, 1946; s. George Fletcher and Helen (Gilbert) H.; m. Coralie Tallman, June 29, 1969; children: Julie Gilbert, William Delano. BS, St. Lawrence U., 1969; JD, Washington and Lee U., 1975. Bar: N.Y. 1976, U.S. Dist. Ct. (so. dist.) N.Y. 1976, U.S. Dist. Ct. (ea. dist.) N.Y. 1978, U.S. Supreme Ct. 1980, U.S. Ct. Appeals (2d cir.) 1982, U.S. Dist. Ct. (no. dist.) Tex. 1988, U.S. Ct. Appeals (11th cir.) 1991, U.S. Ct. Appeals (fed. cir.) 1999. Assoc. Cadwalader, Wickersham & Taft, N.Y.C., 1975-83, ptnr., 1983-94; v.p., assoc. gen. counsel Schering-Plough Corp., Kenilworth, NJ, 1995—2005. Trustee First Unitarian Congl. Soc. Bklyn., 1980-83; v.p. fin. Unitarian Universalist Congregation of Monmouth County, 2002-04, sr. v.p., 2004—; trustee, treas. Bklyn. Children's Mus., 1985-95. Mem.: ABA, Order of Coif, Omicron Delta Kappa. Office: Schering Plough Corp 2000 Galloping Hill Rd Kenilworth NJ 07033-1328

HOFFMAN, JOHN RALEIGH, physicist; b. Evansville, Ind., July 7, 1926; s. John Henry and Ruth Margaret (Bryant) H.; m. Phyllis Christine Reindel, July 5, 1950; children: John Russell, Gary Paul. BS, U. Richmond, 1949; MS, U. Fla., 1951, PhD, 1954. Rsch. asst. U. Fla., 1950—54; rsch. scientist Sandia Corp., Albuquerque, 1954—57; supr. project Kaman Nuc. Co., Colorado Springs, 1957—68; v.p. Kaman Scis. Corp., Colorado Springs, 1968—86, sr. v.p., 1986—90, exec. v.p., 1990—92; gen. mgr. Kaman Instrumentation Corp., 1989—90; ret. Kaman Scis Corp., 1992; tech. and mgmt. cons., 1992—. Mem. nominating com. Colo. Supreme Ct., 1998-2004; bd. dirs. Red Spot Paint and Varnish Co., U. Club U. Colo., Colo. Springs Served with USNR, 1944-46. Mem. IEEE, Am. Phys. Soc. Republican. Presbyterian. Home and Office: 5020 Lyda Ln Colorado Springs CO 80904-1008 E-mail: JRaleighHo@aol.com.

HOFFMAN, JOHN RAYMOND, lawyer; b. Rochester, N.Y., July 24, 1945; s. Raymond Edward and Ruth Emily (Karnes) H.; m. Linda Lee Moore, Aug. 22, 1970; 1 child, Heather Anne. BA, Washburn U., 1967; JD, U. Mo.-Kansas City, 1971. Bar: Mo. 1972, Tenn. 1976, Kans. 1980, U.S. Supreme Ct. 1975. Law clk. United Telecom, Kansas City, Mo., 1967-70, gen. atty., 1970-75; gen. counsel, sec. United Telephone Sys.-S.E. Group, Bristol, Tenn., 1975-80; v.p., gen. counsel United Telephone Sys. Inc., Kansas City, Mo., 1980-84; sr. v.p. legal, dir. US Telecom, Inc., Kansas City, Mo., 1984-86; sr. v.p. external affairs Sprint Corp., Kansas City, Mo., 1986-99, ret., 2000; chmn. FCC N.Am. Numbering Coun., 1999—2000. Bd. dirs. United Telephone Co. of N.W., 1990-98. Author: That Was a Pin? The History of Sprint Corp., 2000. Bd. dirs. Ctr. Pub. Utilities, N.Mex. State U., 1989—90, Kansas City Area Econ. Devel. Coun., 1988—89, Trinity Luth. Hosp., Kansas City, 1984—89, Bishop Miege H.S. Found., 1990—92, 1999—2001, Health Initiatives, Inc., Kansas City, 1985—89, pres., 1986—89; bd. dirs. Kansas City Young Audiences, 1981—85, Johnson County Fire Dist., Prairie Village, Kans., 1982—86, Kansas City/Coro Found., 1983—84, Friends of the Zoo, Kansas City, 2000—01. Mem. ABA, Mo. Bar Assn., Tenn. Bar Assn., Kans. Bar Assn., Kansas City Bar Assn., Competitive Telecommunications Assn. (chmn. 1986-88), Ind. Telephone Pioneers Assn., Phi Delta Phi. Club: Optimist. Home: 17960 S Bond Ave Bucyrus KS 66013 Personal E-mail: john_r_hoffman@yahoo.com.

HOFFMAN, JOY LYNN, educational association administrator; b. Seoul, Rep. of Korea, Nov. 21, 1967; d. Clifton Hale and Isabel Jeanette (Jones) Stuewe; m. John Louis Hoffman, May 26, 2002; 1 child, Hanna Elizabeth Alexander; 1 child, Clifton John Alexander. BA in liberal Studies, Coll. Irvine, 1980; MEd in coll. student affairs, Azusa Pacific U., 2002. Tchr. Concordia Luth. Sch., Cerritos, Calif., 1990—94; dir. student life Concordia U., Irvine, Calif., 1994—2001; dir. multi ethnic programs Azusa Pacific U., Azusa, Calif., 2001—. Sexual violence prevention and intervention independent, 1999—2003. Chair, social and networking Asian Pacific Islander Knowledge Cmty., 2005—; v.p. Concordia U. Alumni Bd., 2003—04; mentor Minority Undergrad. Fellows Program, 2004—05. Recipient Alumni award for svc. and support, Concordia U., 2001. Mem.: Nat. Assn. Student Personnel Adminstr. Independent. Luth. Avocation: football. Office: Azusa Pacific U Multi Ethnic Program PO Box 7000 Azusa CA 91702-7000 E-mail: jhoffman@apu.edu.

HOFFMAN, JUDY GREENBLATT, preschool director; b. Chgo., June 12, 1932; d. Edward Abraham and Clara (Morrill) Greenblatt; m. Morton Hoffman, Mar. 16, 1950 (div. Jan. 1983); children: Michael, Alan, Clare. BA summa cum laude, Met. State Coll., Denver, 1972; MA, U. No. Colo., 1976, MA in Spl. Edn. Moderate Needs, 1996. Cert. tchr., Colo. Pre-sch. dir. B.M.H. Synagogue, Denver, 1968-70, Temple Emanuel, Denver, 1970-85, Congregation Rodef Shalom, Denver, 1985-88; tchr. Denver Pub. Schs., 1988—. Bilingual tchr. adults in amnesty edn. Denver Pub. Schs., 1989-90. Author: I Live in Israel, 1979, Joseph and Me, 1980 (Gamoran award), (with others) American Spectrum Single Volume Encyclopedia, 1991. Coord. Douglas Mountain Therapeutic Riding Ctr. for Handicapped, Golden, Colo., 1985—; dir. Mountain Ranch Summer Day Camp for Denver Pub. Schs., 1989-91. Mem. Nat. Assn. Temple Educators. Democrat. Avocations: riding, writing, music. E-mail: jhoff3@earthlink.net.

HOFFMAN, JULIEN IVOR ELLIS, pediatrician, educator, cardiologist; b. Salisbury, Southern Rhodesia, July 26, 1925; arrived in U.S., 1957, naturalized, 1967; s. Bernard Isaac and Minrose (Bermant) H.; m. Kathleen (Lewis), 1986; children: Anna, Daniel. BS, U. Witwaterstrand, Johannesburg, South Africa, 1944, BSc (hon.), 1945, MB, BCh, 1949, MD, 1970. Intern, resident internal medicine, South Africa, 1950-56; rsch. asst., postgrad. Med. Sch., London, 1956-57; fellow pediatric cardiology Boston Children's Hosp., 1957-59; fellow Cardiovasc. Rsch. Inst., San Francisco, 1959-60; asst. prof. pediat., internal medicine Albert Einstein Coll., N.Y.C., 1962-66; assoc. prof. pediat. U. Calif., San Francisco, 1966-70, prof., 1970-94, prof. physiology, 1981-88, prof. emeritus, 1994—. Sr. mem. Cardiovasc. Rsch. Inst. U. Calif., San Francisco, 1966—; mem. bd. examiners, sub-bd. pediat. cardiology Am. Bd. Pediat., 1973—78, sub-bd. pediat. intensive care, 1985—87; chmn. Louis Katz Award Com., Basic Sci. Coun., Am. Heart Assn., 1973—74, George Brown Meml. lectr., 1977; George Alexander Gibson Meml. lectr. Royal Coll. Physicians (Edinburgh), 1978; Lilly lectr. Royal Coll. Physicians (London), 1981; Isaac Starr lectr. Cardiac Systems Dynamics Soc., England, 1982, John Keith lectr., 85; Disting. Physiology lectr. Am. Coll. Chest Physicians, 1985; Nadas lectr. Am. Heart Assn., 1987; 1st Donald C. Fyler lectr. Children's Hosp., Boston, 1990; 1st MacDonald Dick lectr. U. Mich., Ann Arbor; Kreidberg lectr. Med. Sch. Tufts U., 2004; Tebarzruk lectr. Mt. Sinai Hosp., Balt., 2005. Co-editor: Rudolph's Pediatrics, 1982—96, Coronary Circulation, 1990, Recent Advances in the Coronary Circulation, 1993, Pediatric Cardiovascular Medicine, 2000. Recipient Bayer Cardiovasc. Mentor award, 1989. Fellow Royal Coll. Physicians; mem. World Congress Pediat. Cardiology and Cardiac Surgery (hon. joint pres. Paris 1993), Am. Physiol. Soc., Am. Pediatric Soc., Soc. Pediatric Rsch. Achievements include extensive research into congenital heart disease and coronary blood flow. Home: 925 Tiburon Blvd Belvedere Tiburon CA 94920-1525 Office Phone: 415-476-9313. Business E-Mail: jiehoffman@yahoo.com.

HOFFMAN, KARLA LEIGH, mathematician, educator; b. Paterson, NJ, Feb. 14, 1948; d. Abe and Bertha (Guthaim) Rakoff; m. Allan Stuart Hoffman, Dec. 26, 1971; 1 child, Matthew Douglas. BA, Rutgers U., 1969; MBA, George Washington U., 1971, DSc in Ops. Rsch., 1975. Ops. rsch. analyst IRS, Washington, 1970-72; rsch. asst. George Washington U., 1972-75, assoc. profl. lectr., 1978-85; NSF postdoctoral rsch. fellow NAS, Washington, 1975-76; assoc. prof. sys. engring. dept. George Mason U., Fairfax, Va., 1985-86, assoc. prof. ops. rsch. and applied stats., 1986-89, prof. ops. rsch., 1990—, disting. prof., 1989, interim dept. chmn., 1996-97, chmn., 1997-98, chmn. sys. engring. and ops. rsch., 1998—2000. Mathematician Nat. Bur. Stds., Washington, 1976—84; vis. assoc. prof. ops. rsch. U. Md., 1982; mng. ptnr. Optimization Software Assocs.; cons. Govt. Agys., Airline, Telecom. and Def. Industries. Assoc. editor Internat. abstracts of Ops. Rsch., 1991—96, The Math. Programming Jour., Series B, 1987—, The Ops. Rsch. Soc. Jour. on Computing, 1991—96, Jour. Computational Optimization and Applications, 1992—98, mem. editl. bd. Annals of Ops. Rsch., 2000—; contbr. articles to profl. jours. Recipient Applied Rsch. award, Nat. Inst. Stds. and Tech., 1984, Silver medal, U.S. Dept. Commerce, 1984, Disting. Prof. award, 1989, Kimball medal, Inst. Ops. Rsch. & Mgmt. Svc., 2005. Fellow: Inst. Ops. Rsch. and Mgmt. Sci. (treas. 1995—96, exec. com. 1995—99, pres. 1998); mem.: Math. Programming Soc. (editor newsletter 1979—82, chmn. com. algorithms 1982—85, coun. 1985—88, exec. com., chmn. membership com. 1988—89), Ops. Rsch. Soc. Am. (sec.-treas. Computer Sci. Tech. sect. 1979—80, vis. profl. lectr. 1980—, vice chmn. sect. 1981, chmn. sect. 1982, chmn. tech. sect. com. 1983—86, coun. 1985—88, chmn. Lanchester Prize com. 1989, treas. 1993—94). Home: 6921 Clifton Rd Clifton VA 20124-1525 Office Phone: 703-993-1679. Business E-Mail: khoffman@gmu.edu.

HOFFMAN, KENNETH CARY, lawyer; b. Miami, Fla., Oct. 17, 1958; s. Larry J. and Deborah (Alexander) H.; m. Hillary Hoffman, Sept. 21, 1958; children: Julian, Andrew, Kevin, Gregory. BA, Tulane U., 1980; JD, U. Miami Law Sch., 1983. Shareholder, group head aviation practice group Greenberg Traurig LLP, Miami. Dir. Venture Coun. Forum, Miami, Fla., 1989-91. Dir. Bakehouse Art Complex, Miami, Fla., 1988-91. Office: Greenberg Traurig LLP 1221 Brickell Ave Miami FL 33131-3224 Office Phone: 305-579-0809. Office Fax: 305-579-0717. Business E-Mail: hoffmank@gtlaw.com.

HOFFMAN, KENNETH MYRON, mathematician, educator; b. Long Beach, Calif., Nov. 30, 1930; s. Myron Grant and Madge (Harrison) H.; children: Donna, Laura, Robert; m. Alicia C. Coro, Mar. 1997. AA, John Muir Coll., 1950; AB, Occidental Coll., 1952; MA, UCLA, 1954, PhD, 1956. Instr. math. MIT, Cambridge, 1956-59, asst. prof., 1959-61, assoc. prof., 1961-63, prof., 1963-96, prof. emeritus, 1996—, chmn. pure math., 1968-69; chmn. Commn. on Edn., 1969-71, head dept. math., 1971-79; exec. dir. Commn. on Resources for Math. Sci., NRC, 1981-85, Math. Scis. Edn. Bd. NRC, Washington, 1989-91; assoc. exec. officer for edn. NRC, Washington, 1991-94; pres. MSTE.NET, Madison, Md., 1996—. Chmn. adv. com. NSF Sci. and Engring. Edn. Directorate, 1984-85; cons. Math. Scis. Edn. Bd. NRC, 1985-89; head, Office Govtl. and Pub. Affairs, Joint Policy Bd. for Math., 1984-89; chmn. Md. Math. & Sci. Coalition, 1996—; pres. Nat. Alliance State Sci. and Math. Coalitions, 1997-2002, sr. counsel, 2002--. Author: (with Ray Kunze) Linear Algebra, 1961, Fundamentals of Banach Algebras, 1962, Banach Spaces of Analytic Functions, 1962, Analysis in Euclidean Space, 1975; Contbr. (with Ray Kunze) articles to profl. jours. Mailing. Fellow Alfred P. Sloan Found., 1964-66 Fellow AAAS (coun.); mem. Am. Math. Soc. (past mem. coun.), Math. Assn. Am., Nat. Coun. Tchrs. Math., Phi Beta Kappa. Office: MSTE net 909 Parsons Dr Madison MD 21648 E-mail: ken@mste.net.

HOFFMAN, KENNETH R., lawyer; b. Washington, Aug. 1, 1952; BS, Frostburg State Coll., 1974; JD, U. Md. Sch. of Law, 1977. Bar: Md. 1977, DC 1998. Law clerk to Judge C. Awdry Thompson Ct. of Special Appeals, Md., 1977—78; ptnr., employee benefits & taxation Venable LLP, Washington. Mem. Comptroller's Task Force on Tax Reform, 1985—86; pres. Pro Bono Resource Center of Md., Inc., 1997—99; adjunct prof. U. Balt.; mem., tax advisory com. Congressman Benjamin Cardin. Sec. & trustee Nat. Aquarium in Balt. Found., Inc; bd. dirs & past pres. CollegeBound Found., Inc. Mem.: ABA (mem. employee benefits com.), DC Bar Assn., Md. Bar Assn. (chair taxation section 1991—92, mem. special pro bono com. 1995—97). Office: Venable LLP 575 7th St NW Washington DC 20004 Office Phone: 202344. Office Fax: 202-344-8300. Business E-Mail: krhoffman@venable.com.

HOFFMAN, LARRY J., lawyer; b. NYC, Aug. 20, 1930; s. Max and Pauline (Epstein) H.; m. Deborah E. Alexander, Oct. 2, 1954; children: Lisa, Ken, Heidi, Mark. AA, U. Fla.; JD, U. Miami. Bar: Fla. 1954. Chmn. Greenberg, Traurig, PA, Miami, 1968—. Mem. ABA, Fla. Bar Assn., Dade County Bar Assn. Avocations: art, computers, photography, golf. Office: Greenberg Traurig LLP 1221 Brickell Ave Miami FL 33131-3224 Business E-Mail: hoffmanl@gtlaw.com.

HOFFMAN, LINDA M., chemist, educator; b. N.Y.C., Dec. 18, 1939; d. Theodore and Esther Weiss; m. Robert G. Hoffman, Feb. 2, 1958; 1 child, Samuel A. BS in Chemistry, Queens Coll., 1959; MS, NYU, 1967, PhD in Organic Chemistry, 1970. Rsch. assoc. Kingsbrook Jewish Med. Ctr., N.Y.C., 1973-77; asst. prof. Baruch Coll., CUNY, N.Y.C., 1977-79, assoc. prof., 1979-82, prof., 1982—, chair dept. natural scis., 1995-98. Reviewer grant proposals NIH. Contbr. articles on Tay-Sachs disease and glycosphingolipids to profl. jours. Mem. edn. com. UN Internat. Sch., N.Y.C., 1981-84; bd. dirs. Forest Hills Gardens Corp., 1993-2000. Recipient Moore award Am. Soc. Neuropathologists, 1981, 84, Founders Day award NYU, 1971, 112th Precinct Cmty. Coun. award, 1993; postdoctoral fellow Sloan Kettering Inst. Cancer Rsch., N.Y.C., 1972-73. Mem. AAAS, Am. Chem. Soc., Sigma Xi. Office: Baruch Coll Dept Natural Scis One Bernard Baruch Way New York NY 10010-5518 E-mail: linda_hoffman@baruch.cuny.edu.

HOFFMAN, LINDA R., social services administrator; b. New Haven, July 23, 1940; d. Bernard Harry and Sylvia (Paul) Rosenfield; m. Peter A. Hoffman, Sept. 25, 1965; 1 child, Tracie Hoffman Cohen. BA, Russell Sage

Coll., 1962; MSW, Columbia U., 1968. Cert. social worker NY. Case worker Conn. Dept. Welfare, New Haven, 1962-63, NYC Bur. Child Welfare, NYC, 1963-65, supr., 1965-66; asst. to commr. program planning NYC Dept. Social Svcs., NYC, 1968-70; spl. asst. to commr. NYC Spl. Svc. for Children, NYC, 1972-79; pres. NY Found. Sr. Citizens, NYC, 1979—. Cons. USIA, Teheran, Iran, 1975; adj. prof., mem. dean's adv. coun. Columbia Sch. Social Work. Mem. Cmty. Bd. # 8, NYC, 1982—, YWCA/NYC Acad. Women Achievers, 1995—; mem. Grosvenor Neighborhood House, 2003—, Women's Forum, 1998—; bd. mem. West Side YMCA, 2004-. Recipient, Presdl. Recognition award for Community Svc., 1983, East Manhattan C. of C., award for Disting. Civic Svc., 1990, The Mcpl. Art Soc. of NY award, 1997; named to Columbia U. Sch. Social Work Hall of Fame, 2000. Mem. Nat. Assn. Social Workers (cert.), Women's City Club of NY Avocations: boating, fishing, and thoroughbred race horses. Office: NY Found Sr Citizens Ste 1416 11 Park Pl Rm 1416 New York NY 10007-2801

HOFFMAN, LISA R., mathematics educator; b. St. Louis, June 10, 1972; d. Richard K. and M. Kay Evans; m. Scott C. Hoffman, June 24, 1995; children: Roelyn, Dalton. BS in Edn., U. Mo., 1994; M in Curriculum and Instrn., Nat. Louis U., 1999. Educator math. Troy Buchanan High Sch., Mo., 1995—. Coach cheerleading Troy Buchanan High Sch., 1995—. Mem.: Mo. Cheer Coaches Assn., Mo. State Tchrs. Assn. Avocations: quilting, gardening. Home: 394 Shepard Farm Rd Truxton MO 63381 Office: Troy Buchanan High Sch 1190 Old Cap Au Gris Rd Troy MO 63379

HOFFMAN, LLOYD ALAN, plastic surgeon; b. N.Y.C., Apr. 16, 1952; MD, Northwestern U., Evanston, Ill., 1978. Diplomate Am. Bd. Plastic Surgery with subspecialty in hand surgery, Am. Bd. Surgery. Intern N.Y. Hosp., N.Y.C., resident in gen. surgery; resident in microsurgery NYU, N.Y.C., resident in plastic surgery, fellow in hand surgery; chief divsn. plastic surgery N.Y. Hosp./Cornell U., N.Y.C., 1987—98; chief combined plastic surgery program Cornell and Columbia Univs., N.Y.C., 1998—, assoc. prof. plastic surgery. Office: NY Hosp-Cornell U Med Ctr Box 115 525 E 68th St New York NY 10021-4873

HOFFMAN, M. KATHY, graphic designer, packaging designer; b. Sidney, Nebr., Aug. 30, 1956; d. Norman and Irline (Dillon) Barnica; m. Jeffrey W. Hoffman, Apr. 16, 1988. BA, U. Nebr., Kearney, 1978, BFA, 1984, MA, 1987. Product quality assurance Baldwin Filters, Kearney, Nebr., 1978-88, product technician, 1988-90, product devel. technician, 1990-92, product identification coord., 1992—93, packaging and graphics designer, 1993—. Mem. Inst. Packaging Profls., Assn. Corel Artists and Designers, Women in Packaging. Avocations: collect cat figures, reading, movies. Office: Baldwin Filters 4400 Highway 30 E Kearney NE 68847-0724

HOFFMAN, MARGUERITE STEED, former art gallery director; m. Robert Kenneth Hoffman; 1 child, Katherine. Positions with Dallas Mus. Art; former dir. Gerald Peters Gallery. Bd. trustees Dallas Mus. Art, 1999—, chmn. bd.; bd. dirs. Tex. Freedom Network; mem. coun. Dallas Women's Found.; donated $150 contemporary art collection and a $20 million endowment Dallas Mus. Art, 2005. Named one of Top 200 Collectors, ARTnews mag., 2004. Avocation: Collector postwar Am. and European art, Chinese monochromes. Office: Dallas Mus Art 1717 N Harwood Dallas TX 75201*

HOFFMAN, MARIAN RUTH, singer, voice educator; m. Warren Marlyn Hoffman, Aug. 13, 1955; children: Mark Edward, Paul Stephen, Jeffrey Brian, Thomas Warren. MusB, U. Dubuque, 1955; MFA, U. Minn., 1973. Tchr. music Darlington Pub. Schools, Wis., 1955—58; instr. voice Inver Hills C.C., Minn., 1973—75, Home Studio, St. Paul, 1973—; profl. soloist Westminster Presbyn. Ch., Mpls., 1974—2004; instr. voice Normandale C.C., Bloomington, 1974—86, Bethel U., St. Paul, 1981—91. Pres., v.p., editor Thursday Musical, Mpls., 1974—; bd. mem. Schuessler Vocal Arts Ctr., 1990—; v.p. Young People's Symphony Concert Assn., 2005—. Singer: (recitals and concerts) 10-15 Appearances Yearly; singer: (various roles) (operas) Rape of Lucretian, Madame Butterfly, Savitri, Riders of the Sea, Tender Land, Wise Women; singer: (anna, mother superior, singer) (musical theater) King and I, Sound of Music, West Side Story, Oliver. Parish leader Westminster Presbyn. Ch., Mpls., 1990. Mem.: Am. Guild Organists (sec. 1967—68), Nat. Assn. Tchrs. Singing (sec. 1978—80, emeritus 2002), Sigma Alpha Iota (life; v.p. 2000—05, Sword Honor, Alumni Distinction 2000, 2003). Avocations: travel, walking, knitting, gardening.

HOFFMAN, MARK, broadcast executive; b. LA; B, Univ. Calif., Berkeley; M in Journalism, Univ. Mo. News assoc. KNX Radio, LA, 1981—82; prodr. KMGH-TV, Denver, WNEV-TV, Boston; exec. prodr. to mng. editor WLS-TV, Chgo.; asst. news dir. WABC-TV, NYC; news dir. WAGA-TV, Atlanta, WBBM-TV, Chgo.; v.p., news KNBC-TV, LA, 1993; v.p., gen. mgr. KDNL-TV, St. Louis; exec. prodr./develop. WarnerBrothers/Telepictures; exec. prodr. CNBC, LA, 1997—98, v.p./mng. editor, 1999—2000, v.p., editor, bus. develop., 2001; interim pres. CNBC Europe, 2000—01; pres. CNBC, LA, 2005—; pres., gen. mgr. WVIT-NBC, Hartford, Conn., 2001—05. Office: CNBC #C296 3000 W Alameda Ave Burbank CA 91523*

HOFFMAN, MARTIN JOSEPH, artist, illustrator; b. St. Augustine, Fla. s. William Arthur Hoffman and Bernice Ethyl Braddock; m. Gail Coleen Dougherty (div.); children: Marsha, Mark, Marlan, Marisa, Athena-Marie. BA, Fla. State Univ., Tallahassee, Fla., 1955; MA, Univ. Miami, Fla., 1967. Art dir. The Miami News, Miami, Fla., 1956—62, Graphic Arts Inc., Miami, Fla., 1962—70, Steiner & Wall Advt., Coral Gables, Fla., 1965—67; tchg. Univ. Miami, Miami, Fla., 1967—70. Exhibitions include Mus. of Modern Art, N.Y. Cultral Ctr., Vassar Coll. Mus., State Univ, Potsdam Sidney Janis Gallery, Frank and Jeff Lavaty, State Mus., Andy Warhol, N.Y., Univ. Miami, Lowe Mus., Coral Gables, Fla. State Univ., Miami Mus. of Modern Art, Fla., Yves Saint Laurent, Paris, Charles Saatchi, London, L'Uomo Vogue, Milan, Paramount Pictures, Hollywood, numerous collections; contbr. pub. to profl. jour. Proposal New World Trade Ctr., 2002, Libr. of Congress, 2002. Rotc USNR, 1951—61, Miami. Avocations: music, writing, philosophy, nature studies. Home: 1840 Waterford Dr #2 Vero Beach FL 32966-8039

HOFFMAN, MARY CATHERINE, retired nurse, anesthetist; b. Winamac, Ind., July 14, 1923; d. Harmon William Whitney and Dessie Maude (Neely) Hoffman. RN, Meth. Hosp., Indpls., 1945; cert. obstet. analgesia and anesthesia, Johns Hopkins Hosp., 1949; grad., Cleve. Sch. Anesthesia, 1952. Staff nurse Meth. Hosp., 1945-49; rsch. asst., then staff anesthetist Johns Hopkins Hosp., 1949-62; staff anesthetist Meth. Hosp., 1962-64, U. Chgo. Hosps., 1964-66; chief nurse anesthetist Paris (Ill.) Cmty. Hosp., 1966-80; staff anesthetist Hendricks County Hosp., Danville, Ind., Ball Meml. Hosp., Muncie, Ind., 1981-86; ret. Mem. Am. Assn. Nurse Anesthetists, Am. Heart Assn., Ind. Fedn. Bus. and Profl. Women's Clubs (Ill. dist. chmn. 1977-78, state found. chmn. 1978-79, Found. award 1979). Republican. Presbyterian. Home: 1700 N Maddox Dr Muncie IN 47304-2674

HOFFMAN, MATHEW, lawyer; b. Bklyn., Mar. 9, 1954; s. S. David and Naomi B. (Brosterman) H.; m. Bracha Hoffman; children: Ari, Gavriel, Shelhevet, Miri, Shira, Tova, Elisheva, Adina. BA, U. Mich., 1974; JD, Columbia U., 1977. Bar: N.Y. 1978, U.S. Dist. Ct. (so. and ea. dists.) N.Y. 1978, U.S. Ct. Appeals (2d and 7th cirs.) 1980, U.S. Dist. Ct. (we. dist.) Mich., 2003; ordained rabbi, 1988. Atty. Proskauer, Rose, N.Y.C., 1978-80, Gordon, Hurwitz, N.Y.C., 1980-85; ptnr. Koether, Harris & Hoffman, N.Y.C., 1985-89, Keck Mahin & Cate, N.Y.C., 1989-94, Rosen & Reade, N.Y.C., 1994-96; ptnr., head of litigation Todtman, Nachamie, Spizz & Johns, P.C., N.Y.C., 1997—. Arbitrator Wuhan Arbitation Commn., 2004—. Contbr. articles to profl. jours. Mem. Jewish Flame (trustee 1979—). Home: 62 Rosehill Ave New Rochelle NY 10804-3615 Office: Todtman Nachamie Spizz & Johns PC 425 Park Ave New York NY 10022-3506 Office Phone: 212-754-9400. Business E-Mail: mhoffman@tnsj-law.com.

HOFFMAN, MERLE HOLLY, political activist, social psychologist, author; b. Phila., Mar. 6, 1946; d. Jack Rheins and Ruth (Dubow) H.; m. Martin Gold, June 30, 1979. BA magna cum laude in Psychology, Queens Coll., 1972; postgrad., CUNY, 1972-75. Founder, pres. Choices Women's Med. Ctr., Long Island City, N.Y., 1971—; family planning cons. Health Ins. Plan, N.Y.C., 1973-85; founder, pres. Ctr. for Comprehensive Breast Svcs., N.Y.C., 1979-82, Merle Hoffman Enterprises, N.Y.C., 1986—, Choices Mental Health Ctr., 1993—. Speaker, debator on women's rights and polit. issues; founder, pres. Nat. Liberty Com., 1981; active Choices East Project, Moscow, 1992—; provider of Project Liberty Svc., Sept. 11, 2001; bd. mem. Vet. Feminists Am. Cons. editor Female Health Topics and Diagnostic Reporter, 1979-81; editor, pub. On The Issues: The Progressive Woman's Quarterly; contbr. articles in field to various publs.; producer documentary film Abortion A Different Light; founder N.Y. Pro-Choice Coalition; host cable TV series MH: On the Issues, 1986. Recipient Women's Equality award, L.I. NOW, N.Y., 1995, Woman of Power and Influence award, N.Y. Chpt. NOW, 1998, Lifetime Svc. award, Vet. Feminists Am., 2000. Mem. APPA (bd. dirs.), Nat. Assn. Abortion Facilities (co-founder, pres. 1976-77), Nat. Abortion Fedn. (co-founder, sec. 1977-78), Vet. Feminists of Am., Nat. Adv. Bd., Phi Beta Kappa, Achievements include papers in Sallie Bingham Ctr. Women's History, Duke U. Office: Choices Women's Med Ctr Inc 29-28 41st Ave Long Island City NY 11101-3303 Office Phone: 718-349-9100 x 880. Personal E-mail: Mhoti@aol.com.

HOFFMAN, MICHAEL BRUCE, music educator, composer; b. Glen Cove, N.Y., Aug. 23, 1955; s. Edwin Bennett Hoffman and Muriel Beatrice Boland. PhD, NYU, 1999. Cert. tchr. N.Y., 1987. Music educator Mercy Coll., Dobbs Ferry, NY, 1983—90; mgr. of orch. dept. and rental divsn. C. F. Peters Music Publishers, N.Y.C., 1989—96; music educator Scared Heart U., Stanford, Conn., 1998—99, Queensborough C.C., N.Y.C., 1999—2000, Kean U., Union, NJ, 1999—2000, Bucks County C.C., Newtown, Pa., 2000—. Composer: (music composition) Waterfall in a Cloud, 6 Jazz Portraits For Solo Trumpet, Isle of Devils, Suite: 3 Jazz Spirals, .As the Crow Flies. Composer's Asssistance grant, Am. Music Ctr., 2005. Mem.: Internat. Assn. of Jazz Educators, Broadcast Music Inc., Soc. of Composers, Am. Music Ctr. Office: Bucks County CC 275 Swamp Rd Newtown PA 18940 Office Phone: 215-504-8595. Personal E-mail: mikhof@verizon.net. Business E-Mail: hoffmanm@bucks.edu.

HOFFMAN, MICHAEL J., manufacturing executive; BA in Mktg. Mgmt., Univ. St. Thomas, St. Paul, Min.; MBA, Univ. Minn. Sales, svc., mktg. positions Toro Co., Mpls., 1977—89, various mgmt. positions, 1989—97, v.p., gen. mgr., comml. bus., 1997—2000, v.p., gen. mgr. consumer bus., 2000—01, group v.p., consumer and landscape contractor bus., 2001—02, group v.p., consumer, landscape contractor, internat. businesses, 2002—04, COO, 2004—05, pres., 2004—, CEO, 2005—. Office: Toro Co 8111 Lyndale Ave S Minneapolis MN 55420 Office Phone: 952-888-8801.*

HOFFMAN, MICHAEL JEROME, humanities educator, educator; b. Phila., Mar. 13, 1939; s. Nathan P. and Sara (Perlman) H.; m. Margaret Boegeman, Dec. 27, 1988; children by previous marriage: Cynthia, Matthew. BA, U. Pa., 1959, MA, 1960, PhD, 1963. Instr. Washington Coll., Chestertown, Md., 1962-64; asst. prof. U. Pa., Phila., 1964-67; from asst. prof. to prof. U. Calif., Davis, 1967—2001, asst. vice chancellor acad. affairs, 1976-83, chmn. English dept., 1984-89, dir. Davis Humanities Inst., 1987-91, coord. writing programs, 1991-94, undergrad. coord., 1994-95, grad. advisor, 1995-98, dir. honors program, 1992-99. Chmn. joint projects steering com. U. Calif.-Calif. State U., 1976-87; chmn. adv. bd. Calif. Acad. Partnership Program, 1985-87; dir. Calif. Humanities Project, 1985-91. Author: The Development of Abstractionism in the Writings of Gertrude Stein, 1965, The Buddy System, 1971, The Subversive Vision, 1972, Gertrude Stein, 1976, Critical Essays on Gertrude Stein, 1986, Essentials of the Theory of Fiction, 1988, 2d rev. edit., 2005, Critical Essays on American Modernism, 1992. With USAR, 1957-61. Nat. Def. Edn. Act fellow U.S. Govt., 1959-62. Mem. Modern Lang. Assn. (Am. lit. group). Democrat. Jewish. Avocation: tennis. Home: 4417 San Marino Dr Davis CA 95616-5012 Office: U Calif Dept English Davis CA 95616 Business E-Mail: mjhoffman@ucdavis.edu.

HOFFMAN, MICHAEL WILLIAM, lawyer, accountant; b. Bowling Green, Ohio, Feb. 5, 1955; s. Oscar William and Marie Louise Hoffman; m. Lynne Ellen Steele, Aug. 31, 1975; children: Megan, Jessica, Kristine, Robert. BA in Acctg. summa cum laude, Bowling Green State U., 1976; JD, U. Toledo, 1981. Bar: Ohio 1981, Ga. 1983; CPA, Ga., Ohio. Acct. Ernst & Whinney, Toledo, 1976—81; acct., ptnr. Touche Ross & Co., Atlanta, 1981—86; v.p. Profl. Svcs. Network Inc., Atlanta, 1986; assoc. Chamberlain, Hrdlicka, White, Johnson & Williams, Atlanta, 1986—89; ptnr. Somers & Altenbach, Atlanta, 1989—91; chmn., CEO Hoffman & Assocs., Attys. at Law, LLC, Atlanta, 1991—. Organizing dir. Paces Bank & Trust Co., Atlanta; spkr. in field. Author: RIA's U.S.A. News for the Inbound Investor, 1983. Treas. Friendship Force Internat., 1984; Eagle scout Boy Scouts Am.; mem. parish coun. Holy Family Ch., 2004—, coach youth basketball and baseball. Recipient Leadership award Boy Scouts Am., 1986. Mem.: AICPA, ABA, Estate Planning Coun. of North Ga., Ga. Soc. CPAs (chmn. Tax Forum Com. 1990—92, chmn. Estate Gift & Trust Sect. 1997—2000, Disting. Chair award 1998—99, v.p. mgmt. com. 2000—01, bd. dirs. 2000—01), Am. Assn. Atty.-CPA, State Bar Ga. (fiduciary law sect., tax sect.), Bowling Green State U.-Atlanta Alumni Assn. (parents adv. coun. 1999—2000), Atlanta Country Club (bd. dirs. 1998—2001). Republican. Avocations: golf, tennis, hiking, reading, fishing. Home: 535 Willow Knoll Dr Marietta GA 30067-4647 Office: # 300 6100 Lake Forrest Dr NW Atlanta GA 30328-3845 Office Phone: 404-255-7400. E-mail: hoff_law@bellsouth.net.

HOFFMAN, MURRAY STANLEY, internist, educator, cardiologist; b. Denver, Apr. 15, 1924; s. Harry and Rose (Tokarsky) H.; m. Eleanor Cynara Reeves, Dec. 23, 1962; children: Eric, Rachel, Hugh. BA, U. Denver, 1944; MD, U. Colo., 1947; MS, U. Minn., 1953. Diplomate Am. Bd. Internal Medicine, Am. Bd. Cardiovascular Disease. Intern Cin. Gen. Hosp., 1947-48, resident, 1948-49; fellow Mayo Found., Rochester, Minn., 1949-51; mem. attending staff Univ. Hosp./Colo. Health Scis. Ctr., Denver, 1993—, assoc. clin. prof. medicine, 1993-97, clin. prof. medicine, 1997—. Fellow Am. Coll. Cardiology (trustee 1972-77), Coun. on Clin. Cardiology, Am. Heart Assn.; mem. AMA, Nat. Mayo Clinic Alumni Assn. (pres. 1970-72), Colo. Heart Assn. (pres. 1968-69). Home: 501 S Harrison Ln Denver CO 80209-3516 Office: U Colo Health Scis Ctr Campus Box B120 4200 E 9th Ave Denver CO 80262-0001 Personal E-mail: mshoffman@earthlink.net.

HOFFMAN, NANCY, art gallery director; b. N.Y.C., 1944;, Wellesley Coll., 1964, Columbia U., 1966. Asst. registrar Asia House Gallery, N.Y.C., 1964-69; dir. Contemporary Gallery French & Co., N.Y.C., 1969-72; owner, pres. Nancy Hoffman Gallery, N.Y.C., 1972—. Lectr., jury exhibitor throughout U.S. Contbr. chpt. to text. Office: Nancy Hoffman Gallery 429 W Broadway New York NY 10012-3799 Office Phone: 212-966-6676. Business E-Mail: nancyhoffmangallery@hotmail.com.*

HOFFMAN, NATHANIEL A., lawyer; b. Cin., Mar. 4, 1949; s. Ralph H. and Betty (Goldfarb) H.; m. Sara Naomi Fishman, Aug. 3, 1980; children: Joshua, Rebecca, Esther, David. BA, Yale U., 1971; JD, U. Mich., 1975. Bar: Calif. 1975, Wis. 1983. Assoc. McDonough, Holland & Allen, Sacramento, 1975—78, Herz, Levin, Teper, Sumner & Croysdale, Milw., 1982—85; ptnr. Michael, Best & Friedrich, Milw., 1985—2004, Whte Hirschboeck Dudek SC, Milw., 2005—. Atty. N.Y.C. Pub. Devel. Corp., 1980-82. Mem. ABA, State Bar Wis., Milw. Bar Assn., State Bar Calif. Home: 3258 N 51st Blvd Milwaukee WI 53216-3236 Office: Whyte Hirschboeck Dudek SC 555 E Wells St Ste 1900 Milwaukee WI 53202 Office Phone: 414-978-5634. Business E-Mail: nhoffman@whdlaw.com.

HOFFMAN, OSCAR ALLEN, retired forest products company executive; b. Newark, Feb. 4, 1920; s. Ernest Benjamin and Edith Marie (Myers) H.; m. Carolyn Ruth Layman, May 10, 1947 (div.); children: Peter Miles, Jared Mark; m. Geri McReynolds, Aug. 21, 1956. AB, Drew U., 1943; MS, Syracuse U., 1945; PhD, Stanford U., 1948; postgrad., U.S. Naval War Coll., 1953. Sect. leader MIT-Naval Ops. rsch. group, Washington, 1948-54; mgr. ops. rsch. AMF, Greenwich, Conn., 1954-58; v.p., spl. asst. to pres. Champion Internat. Corp., Stamford, Conn., 1958-85; commr. fin. City of Stamford, 1978—82. Chief ops. research Turkish Gen. Staff, Ankara, summer 1956. Episcopalian. Home: 1546 Georgetowne Ln Sarasota FL 34232-2014 Personal E-mail: hoff1546@aol.com.

HOFFMAN, PATRICIA DICKINSON, academic administrator, volunteer; b. Phila., Apr. 3, 1943; d. Gordon Hobart Dickinson and Ruth Evelyn Coombe; m. David Dale Hoffman, June 15, 1963; children: Lee Dickinson, Kurt Andrew. AB, Muhlenberg Coll., 1964; MEd, Lehigh U., 1971. Cert. reading specialist, elem. tchr. Elem. tchr. Allentown (Pa.) Sch. Dist., 1964-68; literacy instr. Lehigh Carbon C.C., Allentown, 1986-98, coord., 1998—. Peer trainer Pa. Dept. of Edn., Harrisburg, 1998—. Bd. dirs., pres. Allentown Sch. Bd., 1987—; allocation panel United Way of the L.V., Bethlehem, Pa., 1996—; bd. dirs. Habitat for Humanity of the Lehigh Valley, 2002—, Carbon-Lehihg Intermediate Unit #21, Schnecksville, Pa., 1988—, Soc. of the Arts-Allentown Art, 1968—. Recipient Outstanding Vol. Soc. of the Arts-Allentown Art Mus., 1973, Jr. League of the Lehigh Valley, 1984, Alumni Achievement award Alumni Coun. Muhlenberg Coll., 1983, WELD bowl Women's divsn. United Way, 1988. Mem. AAUW, Jr. League of Lehigh Valley (treas. 1982-84), Bd. of Assocs. of Muhlenberg Coll., Pa. Sch. Bds. Assn., Nat. Sch. Bds. Assn., Pa. Assn. of Adult Continuing Educators. Republican. Presbyterian. Avocations: travel, reading, fishing. Home: 806 N 30th St Allentown PA 18104-3804

HOFFMAN, PAUL EVERETT, history professor; b. Balt., Apr. 5, 1943; s. Louis Frederick and Ella C. Hoffman; m. Barbara Anne Shuman, Dec. 21, 1966; children: Philip Louis, Stephen Andrew. BA, Eckerd Coll., 1964; MA, U. Fla., 1965, PhD, 1969. Asst. prof. U. Wyo., Laramie, 1969—72; from asst. prof. to prof. La. State U., Baton Rouge, 1972—2001, Paul W. and Nancy W. Murrill disting. prof., 2001—. Hist. cons. St. Augustine Restoration Found. Inc., Fla., 1972—80; cons. in field. Author: The Spanish Crown and the Defense of the Indies 1535-1585, 1980, A History of Louisiana Before 1813, 1985, Spain and the Roanoke Voyages, 1987, A New Andalucia and a Way to the Orient: The American Southeast During the Sixteenth Century, 1990, Luisiana, 1992, Florida's Frontiers, 2002, The Louisiana Purchase and Its Peoples: Perspectives From the New Orleans Conference, 2004; co-author (with Charles E. Pearson): The Last Voyage of El Nuevo Constante: The Wrech and Recovery of an Eighteenth Century Spanish Ship Off the Louisiana Coast, 1995. Recipient William H. Kadel Career Achievement award, Eckerd Coll., 1993. Mem.: La. Hist. Assn. (pres. 2000—01), Conf. L.Am. History, Am. Hist. Assn. Presbyterian. Avocations: stamp collecting/philately, fly fishing, fishing. Office: La State U Dept History Baton Rouge LA 70803 Office Fax: 225-578-4909. E-mail: hyhoff@lsu.edu.

HOFFMAN, PAUL FELIX, geologist, educator; b. Toronto, Ont., Can., Mar. 21, 1941; s. Samuel and Dorothy Grace (Medhurst) Hoffman; m. Erica Jean Westbrook, Dec. 4, 1976; 1 child, Guy Samson. BS, McMaster U., 1964; MA, Johns Hopkins U., 1965, PhD, 1970. Lectr. Franklin & Marshall Coll., Lancaster, Pa., 1968-69; rsch. scientist Geol. Survey Can., Ottawa, Ont., 1969-92; lectr. U. Calif., Santa Barbara, 1971-72; prof. U. Victoria, B.C., Can., 1992-94; Sturgis Hooper prof. geology Harvard U., Cambridge, Mass., 1994—. Lectr. U. Calif., Santa Barbara, 1971—72; mem. Internat. Union Geol. Scis., Commn. Precambrian Stratigraphy, 1976; vis. prof. U. Tex., Dallas, 1978, Columbia U., 1990; dir. lectr. Am. Assn. Petroleum Geologists, 1979—80; adj. prof. Carleton U., 1989—92; associated with Can. Inst. Advanced Rsch., 1994—, NASA Astrobiology Inst., 1999—, Tectonics Spl. Studies Ctr., 2002—. Recipient Bownocker medal, Ohio State U., 1989, Henno Martin medal, Geol. Soc. Namibia, 2000, Wegener medal, European Un. Geosci., 2001; scholar Fairfield Found. vis., Calif. Inst. Tech., 1974—77. Fellow: Geol. Soc. Am., Geol. Assn. Can. (Past Pres.' medal 1976, Logan medal 1992), Royal Soc. Can. (Willet G. Miller medal 1997); mem.: NAS U.S. (assoc.), Can. Soc. Petroleum Geologists (R. J. W. Douglas Meml. medal 1991), Am. Geophys. Union, Am. Acad. Arts and Sci. (hon.). Home: 1 Waterhouse St Apt 45 Cambridge MA 02138-3610 Office: Harvard U Dept Earth/Planetary Sci 20 Oxford St Cambridge MA 02138-2902 E-mail: hoffman@eps.harvard.edu.

HOFFMAN, PAUL SHAFER, lawyer; b. Harrisburg, Pa., Dec. 12, 1933; s. Paul and Lucy Rose (Shafer) H.; m. Patricia Ann Rudisill, 1958; children: Eric, Kathryn, Julia, Margot. AB in Physics, Gettysburg Coll., 1957; JD, Harvard U., 1962. Bar: N.Y. 1963, U.S. Patent Office 1963, U.S. Dist. Ct. (so. dist.) N.Y. 1977, U.S. Ct. Appeals (2d cir.) 1977, U.S. Supreme Ct. 1977. Assoc. Kenyon & Kenyon, N.Y.C., 1962-63; application analyst IBM-ASDD, Yorktown, N.Y., 1963-66; dir. tech. research Matthew Bender Co., N.Y.C., 1966-68; v.p. Bowne and Co., Inc., N.Y.C., 1968-77; sole practice Croton-on-Hudson, N.Y., 1977—. Mem. Croton Sch. Bd., 1972-75, pres., 1974-75; trustee Village Croton-on-Hudson, 1977-81, acting village justice, 1991—; bd. dirs. Croton Caring Com., Inc., 1982—. Served to cpl. U.S. Army, 1952-54. Mem. N.Y. State Bar Assn. (assoc. editor-in-chief N.Y. State Bar jour. 1991-98), Westchester County Bar Assn., Computer Law Assn. (bd. dirs. 1984-94, 96-2001). Clubs: Harvard (N.Y.C.). Lodges: Masons. Republican. Lutheran. Office: 139 Grand St Croton On Hudson NY 10520-2306

HOFFMAN, PHILIP EDWARD, legislative consultant; b. Jackson, Mich., Nov. 10, 1951; s. Ralph Jacob Jr. and Nancy Joan (Vanantwerp) H.; m. Dennise Fitzgerald, Jan. 29, 1977; children: R. Jacob, Benjamin, Philip. BS, Ferris State U., 1974; postgrad. in edn., Mich. State U., 1975. Undercover narcotics investigator Region II Metro Squad, 1974-77; deputy sheriff Jackson County Sheriff's Dept., Jackson, 1974-82; mem. Mich. Ho. of Reps., Lansing, 1982-93, Mich. Senate from 19th dist., Lansing, 1993—2002; v.p. pro tempore Mich. Senate, Lansing; founder, prin. Hoffman Legis. Cons. LLC, 2002—. Chmn. Transportation Com., State Police Com., Military Affairs Com. Hunting, Fishing, Fishing. Forestry Com.; mem. Reapportionment Com.; bd. trustees Jackson (Mich.) C.C., 2004—. Mem. Rep. Exec. Com.; pres. Great Sauk Trail coun. Boy Scouts Am., 1995-96, v.p. 1992-95; past pres. Land O'Lakes Coun., 1992-94; lifelong mem. NAACP; co-chmn. Mich. Fire Svcs. Caucus, 1993—. Named Outstanding Legislator of Yr., Mich. Assn. Chiefs Police, 1993, Legis. Conservationist of Yr., Mich. United Conservation Clubs, 1994, Guardian of Small Bus., Nat. Fedn. Ind. Bus., 1996, Legis. of Yr., Mich. Sheriff's Assn., 1997; Federalism Summit, 1995; Toll fellow, 1995; Fleming fellow, 1994, 95, fellow Coun. State Govts., Ctr. for Policy Alternatives; recipient Silver Beaver award Boy Scouts Am., 1997, Advocate of Yr. award Mich. Mfrs. Assn., 1998, Flame Leadership award Ferris State U., 1998, Star award Dep. Sheriff's Assn. Mich., 1999, Legis. Leadership award Mich. Soft Drink Assn., 1999, Disting. Svc. award Ind. Colls. and Univs. of Mich. Assn., 2000; Am. Legion Legislative award, 2000, Disting. Svc. medal Mich Dept. Mil. and Vets Affairs, 2001, Legis. Leadership award Internat. Brotherhood Elec. Workers and Mich. Chpt. Nat. Elec. Contractors Assn., 2001, Disting. Citizen of Yr. award, Boy Scouts Am., 2001, Legislator of Yr. award, Police Officers Assn. Mich., 2001, Adjutant Gen. Patriot award Mich. Dept. Mil. and Vets. Affairs, 2001, Presdl. Citation award Mich. Sheriff's Assn., 2002, others. Mem. NAACP (life), Am. Legis. Exch. Coun. (Outstanding Legis. Mem. of Yr. 1992, chmn. telecom. task force, 1992-95, bd. dirs. 1996), Jackson C.C. Alumni Assn. (Disting. Svc. award 1987), Ferris State U. Alumni Assn. (Disting. Alumnus 1990), Mich. Jaycees (1 of 10 Outstanding Young People in Mich. 1985), Eagles, Moose, Ducks Unltd., Pheasants Forever, Alpha Sigma Chi. Republican. Roman Catholic. Office: 721 N Capitol Ave Ste 3 Lansing MI 48906 Office Phone: 517-371-3333. E-mail: phil@hoffmanlc.com.

HOFFMAN, PHILIP GUTHRIE, former university president; b. Kobe, Japan, Aug. 6, 1915; s. Benjamin Philip and Florence (Guthrie) H. (Am. citizens); m. Mary Elizabeth Harding, Aug. 31, 1939; children: Philip Guthrie, Mary Victoria Hoffman Cobb, Ruth Ann Hoffman Cabler, Jeanne Hoffman Camp. Student, George Washington U., 1936-37; AB, Pacific Union Coll., 1938; MA, U. So. Calif., 1942; PhD, Ohio State U., 1948; H.H.D.

(hon.), Jacksonville U.; LL.D. (hon.), U. Americas, U. Akron; L.H.D. (hon.), Pikeville Coll., Marshall U., U. Houston, 1987; D.L. (hon.), Kyung Hee U., Korea; D.H.C. (hon.), Autonomous U., Guadalajara (Mex.); Litt.D. (hon.), U. St. Thomas, 1979. Credit mgr. Harding Sanitarium, Worthington, Ohio, 1938-40; instr. history Ohio State U. Columbus, 1946-49; asst. prof. history U. Ala., Tuscaloosa, 1949-51, assoc. prof., 1951-53, dir. arts and scis. extension services, 1949-53; dean, assoc. prof. history gen. extension div. Oreg. System Higher Edn., Portland, 1953-55; prof. history Portland State Coll., Oreg., 1955-57, dean faculty, 1955-57; v.p., dean faculties, prof. history U. Houston, 1957-61, pres., 1961-79, pres. emeritus, 1979—. Cons. Mitchell Energy and Devel. Corp., Houston, 1980-81; pres. Tex. Med. Ctr. Inc., Houston, 1981-85; dir. Fed. Res. Bank Dallas Mem. Nat. Commn. on Accrediting; mem. Am. Council on Edn., Coll. Entrance Exam. Bd. Lt. (j.g.) USNR, 1943-45. Recipient Centennial Achievement award Ohio State U., 1970, Merit award U. So. Calif., 1975. Mem. Tex. Hist. Assn., Gulf Hist. Assn., Am. Hist. Assn., Assn. Tex. Coll. and Univs. (pres.), Assn. Urban Univs. (pres. 1965-66), Nat. Assn. State Univs. and Land-Grant Colls. (dir. 1971-75), So. Univ. Conf. (pres. 1976-77), Phi Kappa Phi, Phi Alpha Theta (nat. pres. 1952-54), Omicron Delta Kappa Clubs: Petroleum (Houston), Torch (Houston); Houston; River Oaks (Houston). Lodges: Rotary. Home: 2929 Buffalo Speedway Unit 2208 Houston TX 77098-1711

HOFFMAN, RANDY MICHAEL, automotive executive; b. Bklyn., Sept. 9, 1965; s. Sheldon and Lois (Wolff) Hoffman; m. Randi Marie Rosenson, Oct. 18, 1987. Grad. HS, North Miami Beach, Fla. Store mgr. Club 2000 Ltd., North Miami Beach, 1981—83, Chess King, Inc., Hialeah, 1983—84; dist. sales mgr. Electronic Concept, Inc., Miami, 1984—85; wholesale retail distbr. Impulse Distbrs., Inc., North Miami Beach, 1985—; owner Blue Ribbon Food Svc., Inc., Oakland Park, Fla., 1986—88; bus. mgr. Maroone Chevrolet, Pembroke Pines, 1988—93; sr. dir. sales tng., fin. and ins. Ed Morse Automotive Group, 1994—. Vice-chmn. econ. devel. bd. City of Pembroke Pines, Fla. Mem.: Assn. Fin. and Ins. Profls., Distributive Edn. Clubs Am. (pres. 1982—83, treas. 1981—82), Rotary (charter). Democrat. Jewish. Avocations: coin collecting/numismatics, photography, sports. Office: Impulse Distbrs Inc PO Box 820283 South Florida FL 33082-0283 Office Phone: 954-646-8500. E-mail: rhoff10337@aol.com, randy_hoffman@edmorse.com.

HOFFMAN, RICHARD BRUCE, lawyer; b. Columbus, Ohio, June 8, 1947; s. Marion Keith and Ruth Eileen (McLear) Hoffman; m. Sandra Kay Schenkel, July 26, 1975; children: Kipp Hunter, Tyler Blake. BS in Gen. Engring., U. Ill., 1970; JD, DePaul U., 1973; LLM, John Marshall Sch. of Law, 1981. Bar: Ill. 1973, U.S. Dist. Ct. (no. dist.) Ill. 1973, U.S. Patent and Trademark Office 1973, U.S. Ct. Appeals (7th cir.) 1979, U.S. Ct. Appeals (fed. and 9th cirs.) 1982. Assoc. McCaleb, Lucas & Brugman, Chgo., 1973-76, ptnr., 1976-84, Tilton, Fallon, Lungmus & Chestnut, Chgo., 1984-2001, Marshall, Gerstein & Borun LLP, Chgo., 2001—. Mem.: ABA, Intellectual Property Law Assn. Chgo., Internat. Trademark Assn., Am. Intellectual Property Law Assn., Chgo. Bar Assn., Ill. Bar Assn., Union League Club of Chgo., Lawyers Club Chgo. Office: Marshall Gerstein & Borun 6300 Sears Tower 233 S Wacker Dr Chicago IL 60606-6357 Office Phone: 312-474-6300. Business E-Mail: rhoffman@marshallip.com.

HOFFMAN, RICHARD M., lawyer; b. N.Y.C., Oct. 22, 1942; s. Simon and Pearl (Lancet) H.; children: Mark, Michael Grad., CCNY, 1964; LL.B., Bklyn. Law Sch., 1967. Bar: N.Y. 1968. Law clk. to U.S. Dist. Judge U.S. Dist. Ct. (ea. dist.) N.Y., N.Y.C., 1967-69; assoc. Kramer, Lowenstein, Nessen & Kamin, N.Y.C., 1969-73; various positions legal dept. Gen. Instrument Corp., N.Y.C., 1973-81, v.p., gen. counsel, 1981-86, v.p. gen. counsel, sec., 1986-91; pvt. practice, N.Y.C., 1991-94; sr. v.p., gen. counsel Coltec Industries Inc., N.Y.C., 1994-95; of counsel Rubin, Baum, Levin, Constant & Friedman, N.Y.C., 1995-99; ptnr. Friedman Kaplan Seiler & Adelman and predecessor firm, N.Y.C., 1999—. Mem. ABA, N.Y.C. Bar Assn. (com. corp. law depts. 1981-84). Home: 60 Brite Ave Scarsdale NY 10583-2328

HOFFMAN, RICHARD WILLIAM, retired banker; b. Rice Lake, Wis., Feb. 8, 1918; s. William A. and Anna (Amundson) H.; m. June M. Weink, June 27, 1948; children: William H., Stephen C. BA, U. Wis., 1939; MBA, 1954; postgrad., Grad. Sch. Banking, U. Wis., 1952, BAI Sch. for Bank Auditors and Comptrollers, 1957; grad. certificate, Am. Inst. Banking, 1960. With First Wis. Nat. Bank Milw., 1939-83, asst. v.p., asst. comptroller, 1959-63, v.p., comptroller, 1963-70, 1st v.p., 1970-83; v.p. First Wis. Corp., 1965-83; instr. Duke U., 1943-45, Army Finance Sch., Ft. Benjamin Harrison, 1945, Am. Inst. Banking, 1946-62, U. Wis., 1946-62, BAI Sch. Bank Adminstrn., 1956-77. Mem. Polit. Edn. and Action League, 1962-68; adv. com. Pub. Expenditure Survey Wis., 1963-83; asso. div. chmn. Milw. County United Fund, 1960-63; mem. Milw. Am. Revolution Bicentennial Commn., 1975-76; exec. v.p. army fin. K.I.T., 1979—. Served to maj., Finance Corps AUS, 1941-46, served to lt. col. USAR, 1946-84 Mem. Am. Inst. C.P.A.s, Am. Legion, Fin. Execs. Inst., Nat. Alumni Assn. Bank Adminstrn. Inst., Res. Officers Assn., Wis. Econ. Devel. Assn., Soc. Ret. U.S. Army Fin. Officers, Ala. Soc. CPA's, Beta Alpha Psi, Beta Gamma Sigma. Clubs: Wisconsin Alumni. Home: 3801 Oak Grove Dr Apt 107 Montgomery AL 36116-1169

HOFFMAN, ROBERT KENNETH, restaurant owner, former beverage company executive; b. Oklahoma City, July 18, 1947; s. Edmund M. and Adelyn Hoffman; m. Marguerite Steed; 1 child, Katherine; children: Hannah, Augusta. Grad., Harvard U., 1970, MBA, 1972. Co-chmn. Coca-Cola Bottling Group SW, until 1998; co-owner Abacus restaurant, Dallas, 1999—. Co-founder National Lampoon, 1969, mng. editor, 1970. Founding chmn. The Dallas Plan; donated $150 million contemporary art collection and a $20 million endowment to Dallas Mus. Art, 2005. Named one of Top 200 Collectors, ARTnews mag., 2004; recipient Inst. Human Relations Award, Am. Jewish Com., 1995, Gertrude Shelburne Humanitarian Award, Planned Parenthood of Dallas and N.E. Tex., 1996, Linz Award, Zale Corp. & Dallas Morning News, 1996. Avocation: Collector postwar Am. and European art, Chinese monochromes. Office: Abacus 4511 McKinney Ave Dallas TX 75205 Office Phone: 214-559-3111. Office Fax: 214-559-3113.*

HOFFMAN, RONALD, historian, educator; b. Balt., Feb. 10, 1941; s. Emanuel and Ethel (Lubin) H.; m. Sandra Zalma Rudman, Aug. 28, 1965; children: Maia, Barak. AA, Balt. C.C., 1963; BA, George Peabody Coll., 1964; MA, U. Wis., 1965, PhD, 1969. Asst. prof. history U. Md., College Park, 1969—74, assoc. prof., 1974—92, prof., 1992—95; dir. Omohundro Inst. Early Am. History and Culture, Williamsburg, Va., 1992—; prof. Coll. William and Mary, Williamsburg, 1993—. Cons. Office Sec. Def., Washington, 1975—; symposia dir. U.S. Capitol Hist. Soc., Washington, 1977-93. Author: A Spirit of Dissension, 1973, Princes of Ireland, Planters of Maryland: A Carroll Saga, 1500-1782, 2000, (winner Libr. Va. Book Literary award non-fiction, So. Hist. Assn. Frank L. and Harriet C. Owsley award for disting. book in So. history, Md. Hist. Soc. book prize 2002); co-author: The Pursuit of Liberty: A History of the American People, 1983; editor: Dear Papa, Dear Charley: The Papers of Charles Carroll of Carrollton, 3 vols.; co-editor: Diplomacy and Revolution, 1971, Sovereign States in an Age of Uncertainty, 1982, Slavery and Freedom in the Age of the American Revolution, 1983, Arms and Independence: The Military Character of the American Revolution, 1983, An Uncivil War: The Southern Backcountry during the American Revolution, 1985, Peace and Peacemakers: The Treaty of 1783, 1985, The Economy of Early America: The Revolutionary Period, 1763-1790, 1989, We Shall Overcome: Martin Luther King, Jr., and the Black Freedom Struggle, 1990, To Form a More Perfect Union: The Critical Ideas of the Constitution, 1992, Religion in a Revolutionary Age, 1994, Of Consuming Interests: The Style of Life in the Eighteenth Century, 1994, The Transforming Hand of Revolution, 1996, Launching the Extended Republic: The Federalist Era, 1996, The Bill of Rights: Government Proscribed, 1997, Native Americans and the New Republic, 1999; contbr. articles to hist. publs. 3d class petty officer USNR, 1959-61. Fellow Ford Found., 1967, Eleutherian Mills-Hagley Found., 1978; grantee NEH, 1977, 2004, Nat. Hist. Publs. and Records Commn., 1979-. Mem. Am. Hist. Assn., Orgn. Am. Historians, Assn. Documentary Editing, So. Hist. Assn., Va. Hist. Soc., Md. Hist. Soc. Democrat. Jewish. Home: 201 Palace Green St Williamsburg VA 23185-4238 Office: Omohundro Inst Early Am History and Culture PO Box 8781 Williamsburg VA 23187-8781 Business E-Mail: ieahc1@wm.edu.

HOFFMAN, RONALD BRUCE, biophysicist, consultant, life scientist; b. Balt., Mar. 29, 1939; s. Marvin Lionel and Edna Mildred (Fillman) H.; m. Carolyn Jean Phillips, July 6, 1969; children: Christine B., David A., Matthew T. BS in Physics, U. Md., 1962; MA in Psychology, U. Houston, 1971, PhD in Biophys. Sci., 1974. Cert. human factors engring. profl. Assoc. engr. Douglas Aircraft Co., Inc., Santa Monica, Calif., 1962-64; aerospace engr. NASA Johnson Space Ctr., Houston, 1964-67, 68; sr. rsch. analyst Northrop Svcs., Inc., Houston, 1974; NRC-NASA rsch. assoc. NRC, Washington, 1975-77; rsch. scientist, mgr. life scis. GE/MATSCO, Houston and Moffett Field, Calif., 1977-80; site mgr. Tech. Inc., Washington, 1980-82; sr. project mgr. GE, Washington, 1982-85; mgr. biotech. Advanced Tech. Inc., Reston, Va., 1985-87; lead scientist MITRE Corp., McLean, Va., 1987-95, sr. human factors engr., 1995-96; lead human factors engr. Mitretek Systems (formerly with MITRE Corp.), McLean, 1996—2001; sr. rsch. psychologist Sci. Applications Internat. Corp., McLean, 2001—04; discipline scientist Neurosciences Wyle Lab., 2004—. Co-investigator Apollo-Soyuz Test Project exptl. team NASA, Houston, 1974-75; mem. govt. industry adv. group for man systems integrated standards, Houston, 1988; life sci. cons. Mitsui and Co., Ltd., Biosystems Internat., Tokyo, 1985-86. Fellow AIAA (assoc., USAF space ops. workshop Colorado Springs, Colo. 1984-85, chmn. life scis. and sys. tech. com. 1989-91, chmn. human factors engring. working group 1991-96, dep. group dir. space and missiles group 1993-96), Aerospace Med. Assn., Aerospace Human Factors Assn.; mem. Soc. for Neurosci., Human Factors and Ergonomics Soc. (pres. Potomac chpt. 1997), Southwestern Psychology Assn., Am. Soc. Gravitational and Space Biology, Sigma Xi (rsch. fellow 1974), Phi Kappa Phi. Avocations: photography, scuba diving. Office: Wyle Lab Life Sci Sys and Svcs 1290 Hercules Dr Houston TX 77058 Office Phone: 281-461-2764. Business E-Mail: rhoffman@wylehou.com.

HOFFMAN, RONALD L., manufacturing executive; m. Cynthia Hoffman. BS, Okla. State U. With Allis Chalmers, 1970—72, Vickers, 1972—85; pres. Tulsa Winch, Okla., 1985—96; joined Dover (acquired Tulsa Winch), NYC, 1996—; exec. v.p. Dover Resources, Inc., 2000—02, pres., 2002—03, Dover Corp., NYC, 2003—05, COO, 2003—05, pres., CEO, 2005—. Lifetime mem. Collinsville Edn. Found. Office: Dover Corp 280 Park Ave New York NY 10017-1292*

HOFFMAN, S. DAVID, lawyer, engineer, educator, artist, military officer; b. N.Y.C., June 16, 1922; s. Joseph and Ida Hoffman; m. Naomi Barbara Brosterman, June 30, 1946; children: Mathew E., Robert Adam. BE in Elec. Engring., Yale U., 1945; JD, St. John's U., N.Y.C., 1955; postgrad., Sch. Naval Justice, Newport, R.I., 1950. Bar: N.Y. 1955, U.S. Supreme Ct. 1960, U.S. Ct. Mil. Appeals 1961, U.S. Patent Office 1964, Ill. 1981. Engr. Western Electric Co., N.Y.C., Newark, 1946-49; head elec. engring. Am. Nat. Stds. Inst., N.Y.C., 1949-66, resident legal counsel, 1955-66, dir. contracts and cert., 1955-66; v.p., gen. counsel Underwriters Labs. Inc., Northbrook, Ill., 1966-88, cons. counsel to the pres., 1988-90; arbitrator Lake and Cook County (Ill.) Cts., 1989—. Sec. U.S. nat. com. Internat. Electrotech. Commn., 1955-66; vol., cons. multimedia resource, visual arts asst. Highland Park (Ill.) H.S., 1990—; adj. prof. divsn. of indsl. and systems engring. dept. mech. engring. U. Ill., Chgo., 1974-92; vol. Internet tutor Highland Park Libr., 1996—; U.S. Presdl. Exec. Interchange program mgr. tech. activities Nat. Bur. Stds. for U.S. Consumer Products Safety Commn., 1970-71. Contbr. numerous articles to profl. jours. Mem. indsl. adv. bd. U. Ill., Chgo., 1974-95; commr. City of Highland Park (Ill.) Telecomms. Commn., 1998-2000; on-line instr. Sr. Net, 1998—; lic. amatuer radio operator, 1981—; mem. U.S. Navy-Marine Military Affiliate Radio Svc., 1991—. With USNR, 1942-46, 50-52, ret. comdr. JAG Corp. Recipient Achievement award U.S. Pres. Commn. on Exec. Interchange, 1973-74, Merit awards (2) Am. Nat. Stds. Inst., Joint award ASTM-Stds. Engring. Soc., Robert J. Painter Meml. award, 1977, Stds. Engring. Soc. Leo B. Moore medal 1980, Margaret Dana award ASTM, 1989. Fellow IEEE (life), Stds. Engring. Soc. (life mem.). Personal E-mail: dhoffman49@comcast.net.

HOFFMAN, SHARON LEAH, technical journalist, educator, editor; b. Danville, Pa., May 21, 1957; d. Joseph and Colina Levina Jordan; m. Russell David Hoffman, Aug. 31, 1977. Student, Pa. State U., 1974, 76-77, Computer Processing Inst., Bridgeport, Conn., 1981. Jr. programmer Real-Time Computer Sys., Bridgeport, 1981-82; instr. Computer Processing Inst., Bridgeport, 1981-83; cons. What-If? Software, Greenwich, Conn., 1983-84; project leader DAPREX, Inc., Stamford, Conn., 1984-91; sr. programmer analyst CIT Group, N.Y.C., 1991-92; editor Midrange Computing, Carlsbad, Calif., 1992-96, editor-in-chief, 1996-97; sr. tech. editor iSeries Network, Loveland, Colo., 1997—. Spkr., mem. curriculum team COMMON, Chgo., 1985—. Author: DB2/400 Design Concepts, 1996; editor newsletter The AS/400 Strategist, 1997-99; internet columnist The AS/400 Obs., 1997-2001; mag. columnist The AS/400 Strategist, 1999-2004 Recipient Disting. Svc. award COMMON, 1992. Avocation: mountain biking. Office: iSeries Network PO Box 1936 Carlsbad CA 92018-1936 Personal E-mail: shoffman@techreflections.com.

HOFFMAN, SHARON LYNN, adult education educator; b. Chgo. d. David P. and Florence Seaman; m. Jerry Irwin Hoffman, Aug. 25, 1963; children: Steven Abram, Rachel Irene. BA, Ind. U., 1961; M Adult Edn., Nat.-Louis Univ., 1992. High sch. English tchr. Chgo. Pub. Schs., 1961-64; tchr. Dept. of Def. Schs., Braconne, France, 1964-66; tchr. ESL Russian Inst., Garmisch, Fed. Republic Germany, 1966, 67; tchr. adult edn. Monterey Peninsula Unified Schs., Ft. Ord, Calif., 1977-79; tchr. ESL MAECOM, Monmouth County, N.J., 1979-80; lectr., tchr. adult edn. Truman Coll./Temple Shalom, Chgo.; tchr. homebound Fairfax County Pub. Schs., Fairfax, Va., 1976; entry operator Standard Rate & Data, Wilmette, Ill., 1986-87; rsch. editor, spl. projects editor Marquis Who's Who, Wilmette, 1987-92; mem. adj. faculty Nat.-Louis U., Evanston and Wheeling, Ill., 1993-99, tutor coord., then coord. learning specialist, 1993-99; pres. Cultural Transitions, Pebble Beach, Calif., 1992—. Mem.: TESOL, ASTD, Nat. Coun. Tchrs. English. Personal E-mail: culturaltrans1@aol.com.

HOFFMAN, STANLEY MARC, composer, editor; b. Cleve., 1959; BMus in Music Composition cum laude, Boston Conservatory of Music, 1981; MMus in Music Composition, New Eng. Conservatory of Music, 1984; PhD in Music Composition/Theory, Brandeis U., 1993. Engraver Scores Internat., Boston, 1990-98; chief editor ECS Pub., Boston, 1998—. Vocalist Temple B'nai Torah High Holiday Choir, 1997—; condr. Temple Israel High Holidays Choir, Swampscott, Mass., 1988-96, Temple Emmanuel Choir, Newton, Mass., winter 1983. Composer: There Is a Flower (oboe and piano), 1980, rev., 2000, Three Short Piano Pieces, 1980, Two-part Invention (piano), 1980, The Man in the Street (cello), 1981, Romance for Orchestra (in C minor), 1982, Rondino (wind quintet), 1983, Little Sea Nocturne (orch.), 1982, String Sextet (2 violins, 2 violas, 2 cellos), 1984, rev. 2000, Cycles (piano), 1985, Thirteen Ways of Looking at a Blackbird (BMI award 1984-85, mezzo soprano, string quartet), 1984, rev., 1993, Of All the Souls that Stand Create (baritone, piano), 1985, rev., 1993, Anim Zemiros (acapella choir), 1985, rev., 1993, String Quartet, 1987, rev., 1993, Poem and Lamentations (violin, piano), 1987, Piano Piece, 1986, Hymn of Glory (violas, cellos), 1988, rev., 1994, Rain (a cappella choir), 1988, rev., 1993, Nocturne for Nine Players (2 flutes, oboe, clarinet, bassoon, 2 horns, harp, percussion), 1992, Veshameru (cantor, choir, organ), 1993, Moulded Clay-Chiselled Rock (instrument in C, piano), 1994, Bagatelle (bassoon or bass trombone), 1994, A Song Without Words (horn), 1994, A Psalm Beyond the Silences (choir, piano), 1994, Lord of the World (a cappella choir, 1994, A Pacific Prelude (brass quintet), 1995; There Is a Name (children's choir, guitar) 1995, Trio in One Movement (clarinet, viola, cello), 1995, Psalm 23 (a cappella choir), 1998, Psalm 1 (a cappella choir), 1998, Psalm 121 (a cappella choir), 1998, The Writing of Autumn (choir, piano), 1999, Psalm 130 (a cappella choir), 1999, Psalm 146 (a cappella choir), 1999, Three Miniatures (a cappella treble choir), 1999, Intermezzo, Organ, 1999, Psalm 67 (choir, organ), 1999, She Gave Him All Her Heart, 2000, Psalm 117 (a cappella male, treble or mixed choir), 2000, A Lovely Summer Night (alto saxophone and piano), 2000, Behold, God Is My Salvation (choir, organ), 2001, Yih'yu l'ratzon (May the words of the mouth) (a cappella), 2001, A Prayer for Chanukah, (choir, piano), 2001, Grant Us Peace (a cappella choir), 2002, FantasyPiece (cello, bass), 2001, Land of Crystal Dreams (choir), 2002, Yism'chu (soprano, choir), 2003, A Prayer for the World (choir), 2003, Mi y'maleil (Who Can Recount) (choir, piano), 2005. Office: ECS Pub Co 138 Ipswich St Boston MA 02215-3534

HOFFMAN, STEVEN A., performing arts association administrator; s. Jerry I. Hoffman; life ptnr. Jason D. Brunz. BA in Speech Comm., U. Ill., Champaign-Urbana, 1988; MA in Arts Adminstrn., U. Wis., 1992. Ops. mgr. Goodman Theatre, Chgo., 1989—90; mktg. dir. univ. prodsn. U. Mich., Ann Arbor, 1992—94; program dir. Huntington (N.Y.) Arts Coun., 1994—97; exec. dir., CEO Wash. Pavilion Arts and Sci., Sioux Falls, SD, 1997—. Grant reviewer Inst. Mus. and Libr. Svcs., Washington, 2003—04; guest lectr. in field. Stakeholder Sioux Falls Tomorrow, 2003—05; adv. bd. mem. Bolz Ctr. for Arts Adminstrn., U. Wis., Madison, 2001—04; bd. mem. Sioux Empire Arts Coun., Sioux Falls, 1997—2005. Mem.: NY State Task Force on Partnerships in Dance, SD Dance-on-Tour Consortium, Plains Presenters, John F. Kennedy Ctr. for the Performing Arts - Partnership in Edn. Program, Am. Assn. Museums, Assn. Performing Arts Presenters, Triangle Frat. Office: Washington Pavilion of Arts and Science 301 S Main Ave Sioux Falls SD 57104 Office Phone: 605-367-7397. Personal E-mail: hoffmanwpmi@hotmail.com.

HOFFMAN, SUSAN L., lawyer; b. Montreal, Que., Can., Oct. 28; BA, UCLA, 1969; PhD, Stanford U., 1974; JD, Yale U., 1979. Note editor Yale Law Jour., New Haven, 1978—79; shareholder Tuttle & Taylor, LA, 1979—91; ptnr. Bingham McCutchen, 1991—. Mem.: Assn. Bus. Trial Lawyers, Securities Industry Assn. Legal Compliance Divsn. Avocations: skiing, bicycling, photography. Office: Bingham McCutchen 355 S Grand Ave 4400 Los Angeles CA 90071 Office Phone: 213-680-6454. Office Fax: 213-680-6499. Business E-Mail: susan.hoffman@bingham.com.

HOFFMAN, THOMAS EDWARD, dermatologist; b. L.A., Oct. 14, 1944; s. David Maurice and Ann (Corday) H.; m. Donna Madsen, 1973 (div. 1977); m. Linda L., Feb. 20, 1979; children: David, Jay. AB, U. So. Calif., 1966; MD, Tulane U., 1970. Intern U. So. Calif. USC Med. Ctr., 1970-71; residency dermatology Stanford (Calif.) U., 1973-76, fellow dermatopathology, 1973-74; dermatologist pvt. practice, Menlo Park, Calif., 1976—. Clin. assoc. prof. Stanford (Calif.) U., 1981-97, clin. prof. dermatology, 1997. With USPHS, 1971-73. Recipient Achievement award Tulane U., 1970. Fellow Am. Coll. Physicians, Am. Acad. Dermatology, Am. Soc. Dermatopathology, Am. Soc. Dermatologic Surgery, Am. Soc. Laser Medicine & Surgery, San Francisco Dermatologic Soc. (pres. 2000—). Avocations: tennis, skiing. Office: Menlo Dermatology Med Group 888 Oak Grove Ave Menlo Park CA 94025-4432 Office Phone: 650-325-1511. E-mail: mnma@mnma.com.

HOFFMAN, TILLIAN ANGIE, accountant; b. Indpls., Feb. 22, 1965; arrived in US, 1966; d. Chuck and Mary Watson; m. Jason Hoffman, Apr. 12, 1990; 1 child, Emily. BS in Acct., Fla. Atlantic U., 1984; MS in Acct., Kean U., 1986. CPA 1986. Tax specialist H&R Block, Toms River, NJ, 1985—86; jr. staff acct. Morgan Stanley, NYC, 1986—90; staff acct. Withum, Meriks & Barney Assocs., Shrewsbury, NJ, 1990—95, jr. assoc., 1995—99, ptnr. Graysville, Ala., 1999—. Contbg. editor: Accountants Anonymous, 2000—03. Vol. taxation worker State NY for World Trade Ctr. disaster, NYC, 2001—02. Recipient Ptnr. of Yr., Withum, Meriks & Barney Assocs., 2005. Mem.: AICPA (sec. 1988—90, treas. 1990—93, Influence award 1992), Accts. of Am. Assn. Republican. Presbyterian. Avocations: Karate, softball, swimming. Home: 152 Laurel Ave Graysville AL 35073 Office: Withum Meriks & Barney Assocs 662 Windsor Dr NE Graysville AL 35073-1231 Office Phone: 585-798-6400. Business E-Mail: tah@wmbassociates.com.

HOFFMAN, VALERIE FORMAN, education educator, researcher; b. Woodbury, NJ, Nov. 5, 1974; d. Phillip Robert and Kathie Jean Forman; m. Christopher Alan Hoffman, Apr. 19, 2003. BA, Lehigh U., 1996; MPH, Yale U., 1999; PhD, Johns Hopkins U., 2002. Behavioral rschr. Pics, Inc., Reston, Va., 2002; assoc. dir. K30 program U. Iowa, Iowa City, 2002—, asst. prof., 2004—; co-investigator Iowa City VA, 2004—. Cons. in field. Active North Liberty (Iowa) Telecomm. Commn., 2003—; bd. dirs., vice-chair Free Med. Clinic, Iowa City, 2003—. Grantee, Nat. Inst. Aging, 2005, U. Iowa, 2005. Mem.: Am. Pub. Health Assn., Soc. Behavioral Medicine. Avocations: baseball, exercise, reading, cooking. Office: Univ Iowa Coll Medicine SE-611GH 200 Hawkins Dr Iowa City IA 52242

HOFFMAN, VALERIE JANE, lawyer; b. Lowville, NY, Oct. 27, 1953; d. Russell Francis and Jane Marie (Fowler) H. Student, U. Edinburgh, Scotland, 1973-74; BA summa cum laude, Union Coll., 1975; JD, Boston Coll., 1978. Bar: Ill. 1978, U.S. Dist. Ct. (no. dist.) Ill. 1978, U.S. Ct. Appeals (3rd cir.) 1981, U.S. Ct. Appeals (7th cir.) 1983. Assoc. Seyfarth Shaw LLP, Chgo., 1978—87, ptnr., 1987—. Adj. prof. Columbia Coll., 1985. Contbr. articles to legal publs. Dir. Remains Theatre, Chgo., 1981-95, pres., 1991-93, v.p., 1993-95; dir. The Nat. Conf. for Cmty. and Justice, Chgo. Region, 1993-2004, nat. trustee, 1995-2004; trustee bd. advisors Union Coll., 1996-99, trustee, 1999—, trustee and sec., Grad. Coll. Union U., 2003—; dir. AIDS Found. of Chgo., 1997-2004, exec. com., 1999-2003. Mem. ABA, Chgo. Bar Assn., Univ. Club Chgo. (bd. dirs. 1984-87), Phi Beta Kappa. Office: Seyfarth Shaw 55 E Monroe St Ste 4400 Chicago IL 60603-5713 Office Phone: 312-346-8000.

HOFFMAN, WAYNE MELVIN, retired airline official; b. Chgo., Mar. 9, 1923; s. Carl A. and Martha (Tamillo) H.; m. Laura Majewski, Jan. 26, 1946; children— Philip, Karen, Kristin. BA cum laude, U. Ill., 1943, JD with high honors, 1947. Bar: Ill. bar 1947, N.Y. bar 1958. Atty. I.C. R.R., 1948-52; with N.Y.C. R.R. Co., 1952-57, exec. asst. to pres., 1958-60, v.p. freight sales, 1960-61, v.p. sales, 1961-62, exec. v.p., 1962-67; chmn. bd. N.Y. Central Trans. Co., 1960-67, Flying Tiger Line, Inc. and Tiger Internat., Inc., 1967-86. Trustee McCallum Theatre, Palm Desert, Calif., Eisenhower Med. Ctr., Rancho Mirage, Calif. Served to capt. inf. AUS, World War II. Decorated Silver Star, Bronze Star with oak leaf cluster, Purple Heart with oak leaf cluster; Fourragere (Belgium). Mem. Bohemian Club (San Francisco), Vintage Club (Indian Wells), Phi Beta Kappa. Home: 74-435 Palo Verde Dr Indian Wells CA 92210-7367 Office: 2450 Montecito Rd Ramona CA 92065-1644

HOFFMAN, WILLIAM, writer; b. Charleston, W.Va., May 16, 1925; s. Henry William and Margaret Julia (Beckley) H.; m. Alice Richardson, Nov. 13, 1924; children: Ruth Beckley, Margaret Kay. BA, Hampden-Sydney Coll., 1949, DLitt (hon.), 1980; postgrad., Washington and Lee U., 1949-50, DLitt (hon.), 1995; postgrad., State U. Iowa, 1950-51; DLitt (hon.), Sewanee, U. of South, 1999—. Prof. English lit. Hampden-Sydney (Va.) Coll., 1952-59, writer-in-residence, 1964-71. Bd. dirs. The Kay Co., Charleston. Author: The Trumpet Unblown, 1955, Days in the Yellow Leaf, 1958, A Place for My Head, 1960, The Dark Mountains, 1963, Yancey's War, 1966, A Walk to the River, 1970, A Death of Dreams, 1973, The Land That Drank the Rain, 1982, Godfires, 1985, Furors Die, 1990, Tidewater Blood, 1998, Lies, 2005, (short stories) Virginia Reels, 1978, By Land, by Sea, 1988, Follow Me Home, 1994, Best American Short Stories: Prize Stories The O. Henry Awards, Doors, 1999. With U.S. Army, 1943-46, ETO. Recipient Emily Clark Balch prize Va. Quar. Rev., 1988, Andrew Lytle prize The Sewanee Rev., 1989, Goodheart prize The Arthur and Margaret Glasgow Endowment Com., Washington and Lee U., 1989, Dos Passos prize, 1993, Hillsdale prize for fiction Fellowship So. Writers, 1995, Hammett award Internat. Assn. Crime Writers, 1998; named Cultural Laureate, State of Va., 1986; NEA fellow, 1976. Mem. Authors Guild, Fellowship of So. Writers. Republican. Presbyterian.*

HOFFMAN, WILLIAM YANES, plastic surgeon; b. Rochester, N.Y., 1952; MD, U. Rochester, 1977. Plastic surgeon U. Calif. San Francisco Med. Ctr.; also prof. plastic surgery U. Calif., San Francisco. Office: UC San Francisco Plastic Surgery 350 Parnassus Ave Ste 509 San Francisco CA 94117-3608 also: Prof & Chief Plastic Surgery Univ Calif San Francisco Box 0932 San Francisco CA 94143-0932 Office Phone: 415-353-4287.

HOFFMANN, CARL KONRAD, lawyer; b. Plant City, Fla., Mar. 10, 1929; s. Virginia Pauline (Randolph) H.; m. Patricia Ray Shepard, Mar. 18, 1961; children: Debra, Sandra, David, William. BS, Northwestern U., 1951; JD, Yale U., 1957. Bar: Fla., Va., D.C. Ptnr. Kimbrell & Hamann PA, Miami, Fla., 1970—93, mng. dir., 1990—94. Lt. USN, 1951-54, Korea. Mem. Nat. Soc. SAR (pres. gen. 1997-98). Presbyterian. Avocations: stamp collecting/philately, historical research, travel. Home: PO Box 4332 Anna Maria FL 34216-4332

HOFFMANN, CHRISTOPH LUDWIG, lawyer; b. Elsterwerda, Germany, Oct. 9, 1944; came to U.S., 1965; s. Gunther and Ruth (Hornschuh) H.; m. Susan Magnuson, June 18, 1983. Student, Freie U. Berlin, 1964-65; BA, U. Wis., 1966; JD, Harvard U., 1969. Bar: Mass. 1969, R.I. 1977. Assoc. Bingham, Dana & Gould, Boston, 1969-76; asst. gen. counsel Textron Inc., Providence, 1976-83; v.p., gen. counsel, sec. Pneumo Corp., Boston, 1983-85; sr. v.p., gen. counsel, sec. Pneumo Abex Corp., Boston, 1985-91; v.p., sec., gen. counsel Raytheon Co., Lexington, Mass., 1991-94, sr. v.p. law, human resources and corp. adminstrn., sec., 1994-95, exec. v.p. law and corp. adminstrn., sec., 1995-98; ltd. ptnr. Carlisle 1999, L.P., 1998—. Bd. dirs. Med. Web Techs., Inc., Info. Mng., Inc.; chmn., trustee Beth Israel Deaconess Hosp., Needham, 1994—; mem. adv. bd. eLaw Forum Corp., 1999—. Mem. ABA, Mass. Bar Assn., R.I. Bar Assn., Assn. Gen. Counsel.

HOFFMANN, CHRISTOPHER ALLEN, priest; b. Milw., 1960; s. Kenneth Arthur Hoffmann and Elizabeth Jane Wiktorek. BSc, Marquette U., 1982; MDiv, St. Mary's Sem., 1987. Ordained priest Diocese of Orlando, 1987. Assoc. pastor Epiphany Cath. Ch., Port Orange, Fla., 1987—89, Holy Redeemer Cath. Ch., Kissimmee, Fla., 1989—91; sch. pastor Father Lopez H.S., Daytona Beach, Fla., 1991—94, Bishop Moore H.S., Orlando, Fla., 1994—95; pastor St. Clare Cath. Ch., Deltona, Fla., 1995—2001, Blessed Sacrament Cath. Ch., Clermont, Fla., 2001—03, St. Ann Cath. Ch., Haines City, Fla., 2003—. With Cath. Campus Ministry Stetson U., Deland, Fla., 1993—2001; dir. diocesan Campus Min. Diocese Orlando, 1997—. Co-chmn. Faith Orgn., Daytona Beach, 1995—2001. Republican. Roman Catholic. Home: 1265 E Robinson Dr Haines City FL 33844 Office: St Ann Catholic Church PO Box 1285 Haines City FL 33845 Office Phone: 863-422-4370. E-mail: frchris@stannhc.org.

HOFFMANN, DONALD, architectural historian; b. Springfield, Ill., June 24, 1933; s. George C. and Ines (Catron) H.; m. Theresa Cecelia McGrath, Apr. 12, 1958; children— George, Alan, Eric, Michael, Valerie. Student, U. Chgo., 1949-53, U. Kansas City, Mo., 1958. Mem. staff Kansas City (Mo.) Star, 1956-90, art critic, 1965-90. Mem. journalism adv. com. Fulbright Scholarship Program, 1968-70. Editor: The Meanings of Architecture-Buildings and Writings by John Wellborn Root, 1967; author: The Architecture of John Wellborn Root, 1973, Frank Lloyd Wright's Fallingwater, 1978, 2d rev. edit., 1993, Frank Lloyd Wright's Robie House, 1984, Frank Lloyd Wright: Architecture and Nature, 1986, Frank Lloyd Wright's Hollyhock House, 1992, Understanding Frank Lloyd Wright's Architecture, 1995, Frank Lloyd Wright's Dana House, 1996, Frank Lloyd Wright, Louis Sullivan and the Skyscraper, 1998, Frank Lloyd Wright's House on Kentuck Knob, 2000; asst. editor Jour. Soc. Archtl. Historians, 1970-72; contbr. articles to profl. jours. Younger Humanist fellow NEH, 1970-71; Art Critic's fellow-grantee Nat. Endowment for Arts, 1974. Mem. Soc. Archtl. Historians (bd. dirs. 1968-70), Art Inst. Chgo. (life) Home: 6441 Holmes St Kansas City MO 64131-1110 Office Phone: 816-333-0355. E-mail: donhoff@homerelay.net.

HOFFMANN, FRANCES PORTER, librarian, development coordinator; b. Louisville, Dec. 27, 1927; d. Robert Hugh and Frances (Pfeffer) Porter; m. John F. Hoffmann, Sept. 14, 1948; children: Frances H. Stains, Amy H. Veeneman BA in History, Trinity U., San Antonio, 1949; MSLS, Our Lady of the Lake U., San Antonio, 1978. Office mgr. acad. libr. St. Mary's U., San Antonio, 1975-77, library assoc., 1977-79, tech. svcs. librarian, 1979-84; coord. tech. svcs. & automated systems Palo Alto Coll., San Antonio, 1986-90, spl. project librarian, 1990-95; devel. coord. I Care San Antonio, 1995—. 1st v.p. Nueces County Pharm. Assn. Auxiliary, Corpus Christi, Tex., 1965; chaplain Tom Brown Middle Sch. PTA, Corpus Christi, 1966; troop leader Girl Scouts of Am., Corpus Christi, 1960-65; docent San Antonio Mus. Assn., 1968-69; v.p. Tech. Svcs. Int. Group, 1992-93; pres. Coun. Rsch. Acad. Librs., 1993-94; devel. coord. I Care San Antonio, 1998. Mem. ALA, Nat. Soc. Daughters of the Am. Revolution Presbyterian. Avocations: genealogical research, collecting pre-1950 fashion jewelry, needlecrafts, family activities, travel.

HOFFMANN, FRANK WILLIAM, library science educator, writer; b. Geneva, N.Y., May 2, 1949; s. Frank Anton and Lydia Mae (Mayer) H.; m. Lee Ann Black, Jan. 5, 1980. BA, Ind. U., 1971, MLS, 1972; PhD, U. Pitts., 1977. Libr. Memphis Pub. Libr., 1972-74; grad. asst. Grad. sch. Libr. & Info. Sci. U. Pitts., 1974-77; libr. Woodville State Hosp., Carnegie, Pa., 1976-78; prof. Sam Houston State U., Huntsville, Tex., 1979—. Part-time reference libr. Carlow Coll., Pitts., 1974-76, Northland Pub. Libr., Pitts., 1976-78; adj. prof. La. State U., 1980, U. Houston, 1985-88, U. Tex., Brownsville, 1996-97; editor Haworth Press, Binghamton, N.Y., 1990—, ABC-Clio, 1997. Author: The Literature of Rock, vol. 1, 1981 (Best Acad. Book, Choice Mag. N.Y.C. 1981), vol. 2, 1986, vol. 3, 1995, Popular Culture and Libraries, 1984, Intellectual Freedom & Censorship, 1988 (Best Acad. Book, Choice Mag. N.Y.C. 1988), Encyclopedia of Fads, vol. 1, 1990, vol. 2, 1991, vol. 3, 1992, vol. 4, 1993, American Popular Culture, 1995, Library Collection Development Policies, 1996, Guide to Popular U.S. Government Publication, 5th edit., 1998, Grantmanship for Schools and Public Libraries, 1998, Intellectual Freedom Bibliography, 1998; editor: Popular Culture in Libraries, 1993-96, Popular Culture Sourcebooks, 1990—; reviewer jours. in field; editor (book series) Popular Culture, 1977—; contbr. articles to profl. jours. Bd. trustees Montgomery County Pub. Libr. Sys., Conroe, Tex., 1990—; lay rep. Houston Area Librs., 1990—; automation consortium mem. North Harris C.C.-Montgomery Librs., Houston, 1994—. Mem. ALA, Spl. Libr. Assn. (Tex. chpt. bd. dirs. 1979-89), Popular Culture Assn., Beta Phi Mu. Democrat. Avocations: record collecting, weightlifting, bicycling, reading. Home: 30 E Shadowpoint Cir The Woodlands TX 77381-5142 Office: Sam Houston State U Dept Libr Sci PO Box 2236 Huntsville TX 77341-2236

HOFFMANN, INGE SCHNEIER, psychologist, educator; b. Vienna, Jan. 16, 1929; came to U.S., 1940; d. Josef Michael Schneier and Szerena Susan Löffelholz; m. Stanley Harry Hoffmann, Oct. 6, 1963. BA, Bard Coll., 1950; MA, Harvard U., 1953. Lic. clin. psychologist, Mass. Lectr., asst. to dir. Social Sci. Found. U. Denver, 1953-54; rsch. assoc., assoc. dir. rsch. AIR, Inc., 1954-56; rsch. assoc. Ctr. for Internat. Studies, MIT, 1956-59; lectr. Harvard Coll., 1970-76; lectr. psychology, dept. psychiatry Harvard U. Med. Sch., Cambridge Hosp., 1976—, group dir. study of violence, 2004—. Faculty assoc. Currier House, Harvard U., 1970—, mem. group on study of violence Med. Sch.; affiliate Ctr. for European Studies, Harvard U., 1994—; presenter in field Co-author: Coercive Persuasion, 1961, DeGaulle, Artiste de la Politique, 1973; contbr. articles to profl. jours.; patentee design of art fabrics. Active in mediating Palestinian-Israeli conflict, 1976—; mem. Lifton Study Group on Violence, 2004—. Recipient painting awards Mus. of Modern Art, others; Bard scholar Schepp Found., N.Y., 1947, 48, 49, 50; Radcliffe Inst. scholar Harvard U., 1970, 71, 72. Mem. Cambridge Art Assn., Harvard U. Shop Club, Boston Psychoanalytic Inst. (friend, collaborator 1972-89), Internat. Soc. Polit. Psychology (founding mem. 1987—). Avocations: lieder singing, painting. Office: 91 Washington Ave Cambridge MA 02140-2716

HOFFMANN, JANE ELIZABETH, secondary school educator; b. Milw., Sept. 6, 1923; d. Peter Nickolas and Anna Marie (Schumacher) H. BS, Cardinal Stritch Coll., 1951; MA, U. Minn., 1967. Cert. tchr., Ariz., Wis. Tchr. elem. sch. St. Dominic Sch., Sheboygan, Wis., 1944-50, St. Bruno (Calif.) Sch., 1950-53; instr. The Edn. Clinic, Boston, 1953-54; asst. prin. Assumption High Sch., Granger, Iowa, 1954-58; prin. St. Ann's Elem. Sch., Chicago Heights, Ill., 1958-65; mem. faculty, dept. chmn. St. Mary's Acad., Milw., 1965-86; mem. faculty, chmn. dept. Xavier Coll. Preparatory H.S., Phoenix, 1987—; adj. faculty mem. Rio Salado C.C., Phoenix, 1888—1996, Phoenix annex of Chapman Coll., 1987—. Grantee NSF, 1970. Mem. Sisters of St. Francis of Assisi, Coun. of Religions (com. mem. 1987—), Saint Mary's Acad. Alumnae Assn. (com. mem. 1966-86), Omicron Nu. Roman Catholic. Avocations: creative sewing, house plants, gourmet cooking.

HOFFMANN, JOAN CAROL, retired academic dean; b. Cedarburg, Wis., Feb. 20, 1934; d. Frank Ernst and Althea Wilhelmina (Behm) H. Nursing diploma, Michael Reese Hosp., 1955; BS in Zoology, U. Wis., Madison, 1959; PhD in Physiology, U. Ill., Chgo., 1965. RN, Wis., Ariz. Sci. instr. Michael Reese Hosp., Chgo., 1959-62; USPHS trainee U. Ill., Chgo., 1962-64; NSF postdoctoral fellow Coll. de France, Paris, 1964-65; asst. prof. U. Rochester, N.Y., 1965-70; assoc. prof., prof. U. Hawaii, Honolulu, 1970-83; dean of students U. Mass. Med. Sch., Worcester, 1983-94; ret., 1994. Chmn. anatomy U. Hawaii, 1973-80. Contbr. articles to sci. jours. NIH rsch. grantee, 1966-75. Mem. Endocrine Soc., Soc. for Study of Reprodn., Am. Assn. Anatomists, Women in Endocrinology (sec. 1978-79, pres. 1987-88), Am. Coun. Edn. (bd. dirs., Mass. chpt., network identification program 1993-94), Phi Beta Kappa, Sigma Xi. Avocations: gardening, needlecrafts, wood turning, reading. Home: 3525 Cass Ct #416 Oak Brook IL 60523-3707

HOFFMANN, LEONARD A, church administrator, director; b. St. Louis, Mo., Apr. 5, 1949; s. Leonard C and Joyce E Hoffmann; m. Susan Cathy Kleist, Mar. 24, 1972; 1 child, Bethany Terese. D in ministry, Luther Northwestern Sem., 1993. Cons. Walsh and Assoc., Kairos, Baldwin, Wis., 1995—99; v.p. Luth. Social Svcs., Natick, Mass., 1999—2005; sr. pastor Trinity Luth. Ch., Rockford, Ill., 2005—. Sr. pastor Gethsemane Luth. Ch., Baldwin, Wis., 1991—94. Contbr. articles Ministers Annual Manual for Preaching/Clergy Jour. Bd. Luth. Social Svcs. New Eng. Found., Natick, Mass., 2001, Learning Ctr., Inc.; Trinity House, Inc. Mem.: Assn. of Luth. Devel. Execs. D-Conservative. Lutheran. Avocations: travel, politics. Office: Trinity Luth Ch 200 N First St Rockford IL 61107

HOFFMANN, LOUIS GERHARD, immunologist, educator; b. Bloemendaal, Netherlands, July 12, 1932; arrived in U.S., 1950; s. Gerhard Hendrik and Louise Gertrude (Tobi) Hoffmann; m. Georgianna Grace Stracke, Nov. 4, 1955; children: Julianna Tobi, Eugenie Claire. BA with honors, distinction, Wesleyan U., 1953; MSc in Hygiene, Johns Hopkins U., 1958, ScD, 1960. Diplomate Am. Bd. Sexology. NSF postdoctoral fellow U. Calif., Berkeley, 1960-62; from instr. to asst. prof. microbiology Johns Hopkins U., Balt., 1962-64; asst. prof. U. Iowa, Iowa City, 1964-67, assoc. prof., 1967-74, prof., 1974-96; ret., 1997; pvt. practice sex therapy team, 1978—. Contbr. articles to profl. jours. Mem. Dem. Ctrl. Com., Johnson County, Iowa, 1966—76. Fellow, NIH, 1962—63; grantee, 1964—67, 1980—83, NSF, 1968—74, Iowa Heart Assn., 1969—72, 1977—79, Damon Runyon Meml. Fund, 1972—74. Home: 4 Timberwick Rd Santa Fe NM 87508 E-mail: annilou2@earthlink.net.

HOFFMANN, MARK R., physical chemist, educator; b. St. Paul, Minn., Oct. 3, 1958; s. Gerhard R. and Heidi B. Hoffmann; m. Cathy Hacking, June 22, 1993. BA, Northwestern U., Evanston, Ill., 1980; PhD, U. Calif., Berkeley, 1984. Post doctoral rsch. assoc. U. Chgo., 1985—86; postdoctoral rsch. assoc. U. Utah, Salt Lake City, 1986—88; asst. prof. U. ND, Grand Forks, 1988—94, assoc. prof., 1994—2000, prof., 2000—, chmn. dept. chemistry, 2003—. Author: Low-lying Potential Energy Surfaces, 2002; contbr. scientific papers. Grantee, Am. Chem. Soc., 1992, Office of Naval Rsch., 1996-1999, NSF, 1999-2003, 2003—, DOE, 2004—. Mem.: Am. Phys. Soc., Am. Chem. Soc. Achievements include research in new methods of molecular electronic structure theory. Avocation: photography. Office: Univ ND Dept of Chemistry Grand Forks ND 58202-9024 Office Phone: 701-777-2742. E-mail: mhoffmann@chem.und.edu.

HOFFMANN, MARTIN RICHARD, lawyer; b. Stockbridge, Mass., Apr. 20, 1932; m. Margaret Ann McCabe; children: Heidi H. Slye, William, Bern. AB, Princeton U., 1954; LLB, U. Va., 1961. Bar: D.C. 1961. Law clk. U.S. Ct. Appeals (4th cir.), 1961-62; asst. U.S. atty. Washington, 1962-65; minority counsel com. on judiciary Ho. of Reps., Washington, 1965-67; legal counsel to Senator C. Percy, U.S. Senate, Washington, 1967-69; asst. gen. counsel Univ. Computing Co., Dallas, 1969-71; gen. counsel AEC, Washington, 1971-73; spl. asst. to sec. and dep. sec. def. Washington, 1973-74; gen. counsel Dept. Def., Washington, 1974-75; sec. Dept. Army, Washington, 1975-77; mng. ptnr. Gardner, Carton & Douglas, Washington, 1977—89; v.p., gen. counsel, sec. Digital Equipment Corp., Maynard, Mass., 1989-93; sr. vis. fellow Ctr. for Policy, Tech. and Indsl. Devel., MIT, Cambridge, 1993—95; of counsel Skadden, Arps, Slate, Meagher & Flom, Washington, 1996-2000. Bd. dirs. Castle Energy, Phila., Sea Change Corp., Maynard, Mass. Maj. USAR, 1954-73. Mem. Met. Club. Home: 1546 Hampton Hill Cir Mc Lean VA 22101 Personal E-mail: mrhoffmann101@aol.com.

HOFFMANN, MICHAEL RICHARD, lawyer; b. Des Moines, Apr. 26, 1947; s. Robert Wyman and Margaret Inez Wagner (stepmother) H. and Patricia Hilliard; m. Amy Marie Gales; children: Kurt Michael, Kristen Elaine, Kevin Richard. BS in Chemistry and Zoology, U. Iowa, 1969; JD, Drake U., 1972; LLM in Patent and Trade Regulation, George Washington U., 1973. Bar: Iowa 1972, U.S. Ct. Customs and Patent Appeals 1972, U.S. Patent and Trademark Office 1973, U.S. Dist. Ct. (so. and no. dists.) Iowa 1974, U.S. Ct. Appeals (8th cir.) 1976, U.S. Supreme Ct. 1977. Clerk Jones, Hoffmann & Davison, Des Moines, 1970-73; assoc. Bacon and Thomas, Arlington, Va., 1973-74; assoc. Jones, Hoffmann & Davison, Des Moines, 1974-79, ptnr., 1979-83; pres. Michael R. Hoffmann, P.C., Des Moines, 1983-95; pvt. practice, 1995-2002; atty. Hoffmann Law Firm, P.C., 2002—; del. U.S./Japan Bilateral Session: A New Era in Legal and Econ. Relations, Tokyo, 1988; mem. Iowa Def. Counsel, Def. Research Inst., Inc. Recipient Am. Jurisprudence award Bancroft-Whitney Co. and Lawyers Coop. Pub. Co., 1970-72. Mem. Iowa State Bar Assn., ABA (sci. and tech. sect.), Iowa Patent Bar Assn. (charter mem.), Am. Patent Law Assn., Am. Judicature Soc., Polk County Bar Assn., Iowa Assn. Workers' Compensation Lawyers, Internat. Assn. Indsl. Accident Bds. and Commns., Prairie Club (pres. Des Moines chpt. 1993-94), NRA (Washington). Office: 3708 75th St Des Moines IA 50322-3002 Office Phone: 515-270-8899. Business E-Mail: hlf@hoffmannlawfirm.com.

HOFFMANN, PETER CONRAD WERNER, historian, educator; b. Dresden, Germany, Aug. 13, 1930; came to Can., 1970; s. Wilhelm and Elfriede Frances (Müller) H.; m. Helga Luise Hobelsberger, July 22, 1959. Student, U. Stuttgart, 1953-54, U. Tübingen, 1954-55, U. Zurich, 1955, Northwestern U., 1955-56; PhD, U. Munich, 1961. William Kingsford prof. history McGill U., Montreal, Que., Can. Author: Die diplomatischen Beziehungen zwischen Württemberg und Bayern im Krimkrieg und bis zum Beginn der Italienischen Krise (1853-1858), 1963, Widerstand, Staatsstreich, Attentat: Der Kampf der Opposition gegen Hitler, 1969, Die Sicherheit des Diktators: Hitlers Leibwachen, Schutzmassnahmen, Residenzen, Hauptquartiere, 1975, The History of the German Resistance 1933-1945, 1977, Hitler's Personal Security, 1979, Widerstand gegen Hitler, 1979, La résistance allemande contre Hitler, 1984, German Resistance to Hitler, 1988, Claus Schenk Graf von Stauffenberg und seine Brüder, 1992, Tedeschi contro il nazismo: La Resistenza in Germania, 1994, Stauffenberg: A Family History, 1905-1944, 1995, Stauffenberg und der 20. Juli 1944, 1998. Mem.: German Studies Assn., Royal Soc. Can., Can. Hist. Assn., Württembergischer Geschichts- und Altertumsverein, Deutsche Schillergesellschaft, Can. Com. History of 2d World War, Sigma Alpha Epsilon.

HOFFMANN, RICHARD JOHN, science educator; b. Ames, Iowa, Nov. 8, 1946; s. Edward John and Dorothy Lois (Carrothers) H.; m. Vicki Wetherington, June 14, 1969; children: Erin, Christopher. BS, Coll. of William & Mary, 1969; PhD, Stanford U., 1974. Postdoctoral scholar Woods Hole (Mass.) Oceanographic Instn., 1974-75; asst. prof. U. Pitts., 1975-79; assoc. prof. Iowa State U., Ames, 1980-87, prof., 1987—, assoc. dean liberal arts and scis., 1993—. Prin. investigator Marine Biol. Lab., Woods Hole, 1978-81, Mt. Desert Island Biol. Labs., Salsbury Cove, Maine, 1983-89, trustee, 1989-90. Contbr. articles to profl. jours. Woodrow Wilson Found. fellow, 1969, NSF fellow, 1989-90; grantee NIH, NSF. Fellow AAAS; mem. Soc. for the Study of Evolution. Achievements include research in biochemical and evolutionary genetics, population biology of clonal organisms and mitochondrial genome evolution. Office: Iowa State U Coll Liberal Arts And Scis Ames IA 50011-0001

HOFFMANN, RICHARD KARL, composer, educator; b. Vienna, Apr. 20, 1925; arrived in U.S., 1947; s. Richard and Emanuela Hoffmann; m. Joan Alfhild Flint, Dec. 21, 1957; children: Paul, Anna, Peter. MusB, U. New Zealand, 1945; student, U. Calif., L.A., Calif., 1949—51; studied with Arnold Schoenberg, L.A., Calif., 1947—51. Prof. Oberlin (Ohio) Coll. Conservatory Music, 1954—2004. Vis. prof. U. Calif., Berkeley, Calif., 1965—66, Victoria U., Wellington, New Zealand, 1968, Harvard U., Cambridge, Mass., 1970, U. Iowa, Iowa City, 1976, Vienna (Austria) U., 1984, Columbia U., 1988—92; lectr. in field. Co-editor: Schoenberg Gesamtausgabe, 1961; editor: Von haute auf morgen, 1961—; composer: numerous songs dating from 1944 including most recently, (songs) Ruckert, 1990, Percussion 1,2 and String Trio, 1991, Monopoly, 1994, Notturno, 1995, Die Heimkehr, 1997, (recordings) String Quartet #6, 1998; musician: (albums) String Trio, 1963, Orchestra Piece, 1961, in memoriam patris, 1976; contbr. articles to profl. jours. Recipient Huntington Hartford prize, 1950, award, Music Found. Commn., 1960, Nat. Inst. Arts and Letters, 1966, Ehrenzeichen fur Kunst und Kultur award, 1991; fellow, Deutscher Akademische Austauschdienst, 1968; grantee, NEA, 1976, 1978, 1979, Fulbright Found., 1984—85; scholar, Auckland Centennial, 1943—45; Huntington Hertford fellow, 1953—56, Huntington Hartford fellow, 1959, Guggenheim fellow, 1970—71, 1977—78. Avocations: classic automobiles, classic motorcycles, travel, cooking. Home: 11 Shipherd Cir Oberlin OH 44074

HOFFMANN, ROALD, chemist, educator; b. Zloczow, Poland, July 18, 1937; arrived in U.S., 1949, naturalized, 1955; s. Hillel and Clara (Rosen) Safran, Paul Hoffmann (Stepfather); m. Eva Börjesson, Apr. 30, 1960; children: Hillel Jan, Ingrid Helena. BA, Columbia U., 1958; MA, Harvard U., 1960, PhD, 1962; D Tech. (hon.), Royal Inst. Tech., Stockholm, 1977; D.Sc. (hon.), Yale U., 1980, Columbia U., 1982, Hartford U., 1982, CUNY, 1983, U. P.R., 1983, U. Uruguay, 1984, U. La Plata, 1984, SUNY, Binghamton, 1985, Colgate U., 1985, Lehigh U., 1989, Carleton Coll., 1989, Ben Gurion U. of the Negev, 1989, U. Md., 1990, U. Athens, 1991, U. Thessaloniki, Greece, 1991, U. Ariz., 1991, U. Cen. Fla., 1991, Bar Ilan U., 1991, U. St. Petersburg, Russia, 1991, U. Barcelona, 1992, Ohio State U., 1993; D.Sc., Northwestern U., 1996, The Technion, 1996, Brandeis U., 1997, Georgetown U., 2000, Durham U., 2000, Luther Coll., 2001. Jr. fellow Soc. Fellows Harvard U., 1962—65; assoc. prof. Cornell U., Ithaca, NY, 1965—68, prof., 1968—74, John A. Newman prof. phys. sci., 1974—96, Frank T. Rhodes prof. humane letters, 1996—. Tage Erlander prof. Swedish Rsch. Coun. Author (with R.B. Woodward): Conservation of Orbital Symmetry, 1970; author: Solids and Surfaces, 1988; author: (with V. Torrence) Chemistry Imagined, 1993; author: (poetry) The Metamict State, 1987, Gaps and Verges, 1990, (non-fiction) Soliton, 2002, (poetry) Memory Effects, 1999, The Same and Not the Same, 1995; author: (with S. Leibowitz Schmidt) Old Wine, New Flasks, 1997; author: (drama, with C. Djerassi) Oxygen, 2000; author: Soliton, 2002, Catalista, 2002. Recipient award in pure chemistry, Am. Chem. Soc., 1969, Arthur C. Cope award, 1973, Fresenius award, Phi Lambda Upsilon, 1969, Harrison Howe award, Rochester sect. Am. Chem. Soc., 1970, ann. award, Internat. Acad. Quantum Molecular Scis., 1970, Guggenheim Fellowship, 1978, Pauling award, 1974, Nobel prize in Chemistry, 1981, inorganic chemistry award, Am. Chem. Soc., 1982, Nat. medal of Sci., 1983, Priestley medal, 1990, Centennial medal, Harvard U., 1994, Jawarharlal Nehru Birth Centenary award, 1998, Pergamon Press Fellowship in Lit., 1988. Mem.: NAS (award in chem. scis. 1986), Finnish Acad. Arts and Letters, Royal Swedish Acad. Scis., Indian Nat. Sci. Acad., Royal Soc. (fgn. mem.), Internat. Acad. Quantum Molecular Scis., Russian Acad. Scis. (N.N. Semenov Gold medal), Am. Acad. Arts and Scis. Avocation: poetry. Office: Dept Chemistry and Chem Biology 222A Baker Laboratory Cornell Univ Ithaca NY 14853-1301 Office Fax: 607-255-4137. Business E-Mail: rh34@cornell.edu.

HOFFMANN, THOMAS RUSSELL, business management educator; b. Milw., Sept. 10, 1933; s. Alfred C. and Florence M. (Morlock) H.; m. Lorna G. Gruenzel, Aug. 31, 1957; 1 child, Timothy Jay. BS, U. Wis., 1955, MS, 1956, PhD, 1959. Engring. trainee Allis-Chalmers Mfg. Co., 1956-59; asst. prof. U. Wis. Sch. Commerce, 1959-63; mem. faculty U. Minn. Sch. Mgmt., Mpls., 1963-99, prof., 1965-99, chmn. dept. mgmt. scis., 1969-78; dir. West Bank Computer Center, 1971-87. Cons. to industry. Author: Production Management and Manufacturing Systems, 2 edit., 1967-71, (with others) Fortran 77: A Structured, Disciplined Style, 1978, 83, 88, Production and Inventory Management, 1983, 2d edit., 1991, Production and Operations Management, 1989; editor-in-chief Jour. Ops. Mgmt., 1993-95; contbr. articles to profl. jours. Chmn. long range planning com. Luth. Ch., 1971, pres., 1974, 89, treas., 1977-82, 93-98. Mem. Am. Prodn. and Inventory Control Soc. (pres. Twin Cities chpt., 1970-71, internat. pres. 1998). Home: 4501 Sedum Ln Edina MN 55435-4051 Office: U Minn Carlson Sch Mgmt Minneapolis MN 55455 Business E-Mail: thoffmann@csom.umn.edu.

HOFFMEISTER, JANA MARIE, cardiologist; MD, SUNY Upstate Med. Ctr., Syracuse, 1976. Diplomate Am. Bd. Internal Medicine, Am. Bd. Cardiovascular Diseases. Intern Albany (N.Y.) Med. Ctr., 1976-78, resident, 1978-80, fellow div. cardiology, 1981-83, Emory U., Atlanta, 1984; fellow coronary angioplasty and interventional cardiology Emory U. Hosp., 1985-86. Presenter numerous cardiology confs. Contbr. numerous articles to profl. jours. Mem. ACP, AMA, Cardiac Soc. Upstate N.Y., N.Y. State Soc. Internal Medicine, Am. Soc. Cardiovascular Intervention. Home: PO Box 11049 Albany NY 12211-1632

HOFFMEYER, WILLIAM FREDERICK, lawyer, educator; b. York, Pa., Dec. 20, 1936; s. Frederick W. and Mary B. (Stremmel) H.; 1 child, Louise C. AB, Franklin and Marshall Coll., 1958; JD, Dickinson Sch. Law, 1961. Bar: Pa. 1962, U.S. Dist Ct. (mid. dist.) Pa. 1981, U.S. Supreme Ct. 1983. Pvt. practice law, 1962-81; sr. ptnr. Hoffmeyer & Semmelman, 1982—. Adj. prof. real estate law York Coll. Pa., 1980-92, real estate law, paral legal program Pa. State U., 1978-2000. Autor: Abstractor's Bible, 1981, Pennsylvania Real Estate Installment Sales Contrct Manual, 1981, Real Estate Settlement Procedures, 1982, Contracts of Sale, 1984, How to Plot a Deed Description, 1985; author, lectr., moderator and course planner numerous Pa. Bar Inst. CLE Programs. Recipient Disting. Svc. award Gen. Alumni Assn. Dickinson Sch. Law, 1993, Pa. Bar medal, 1997. Mem. ABA, Pa. Bar Assn. (co-chmn. unauthorized practice of law com.), York County Bar Assn. (chmn. continuing legal edn. com. 1992-96), Am. Coll. Real Estate Lawyers, Lions (past pres. East York club), York Area C. of C. (chair small bus. support network 1997-99), Masons, Shriners (past pres. York County). Address: 30 N George St York PA 17401-1214 Office Phone: 717-846-8846.

HOFFNER, JOHN F., food service executive; m. Jean Hoffner; children: John, Robert. BS in Indsl. Mgmt., Purdue U., 1970; MBA, Xavier U., 1974. With Procter & Gamble; asst. contr. Federated Dept. Stores; contr., dir. fin. svcs. Mervyn's Divsn. of Dayton Hudson Corp.; v.p., CFO Pic N Save Stores; sr. v.p. fin. and adminstrn. Wherehouse Entertainment Inc.; exec. v.p., CFO Sweet Factory, Inc.; exec. v.p. adminstrn., CFO, sec. Cost Plus, Inc., 1998—2001; exec. v.p., CFO Jack in the Box, Inc., San Diego, 2001—. Office: Jack in the Box Inc 9330 Balboa Ave San Diego CA 92123

HOFFNER, MARILYN, university administrator; b. N.Y.C., Nov. 16, 1929; d. Daniel and Elsie (Schulz) H.; m. Albert Greenberg, May 29, 1949; children: Doren Roe, Peter Cooper. BFA, Cooper Union. Art dir. Printers' Ink mag., N.Y.C., 1953-63, Print Mag., N.Y.C., 1960-62; corp. art dir. Vision, Inc., L.Am., 1963-75, 92-95; dir. alumni rels. and devel. Cooper Union, 1974-96, exec. dir. instnl. advancement, 1996-99, cons., 1999-2001; pres. Alumni Assn., 1999-2001. Project dir. Nat. Graphic Design Archives, 1990-97; bd. dirs. Art Dirs. Club N.Y., 1973-75, 79-82, exec. sec., 1973-75, exec. treas., 1979-82. Contbg. editor Print mag., Art Direction, Graphis mag.; designer mags., advt., books and exhbns. Mem. Citizens Adv. Cultural Arts Com. Dutchess County, 1978-80. Recipient Gold medal Art Dirs. Club, 1979, N.Y. State Coun. of the Arts award, 1995; named Alumnus of the Yr., Cooper Union, 1968. Mem. Cooper Union Alumni Assn. (editor-in-chief 1971-74, 1st v.p. 1974-75), Coun. Advancement and Support of Edn., Type Dirs. Club (numerous awards), Nat. Arts Club (Exhbn. com.). Home: 51 5th Ave New York NY 10003-4320 E-mail: cu1948@aol.com.

HOFFSCHNEIDER, GERTRUDE DELORES, pre-school educator; d. Gustoph Henry Steffen and Anne Ida Ebert; m. Dale Wilbur Hoffschneider, July 15, 1956; children: Fred Philip, Charles William, Joel Thomas, Jonathan Andrew. BS, Concordia U., 1957; MA, NYU, 1969. Educator various elem. schs., Calif., 1953—64, 1953—64, 1953—64, 1953—64, NYC Bd. Edn., Bklyn., 1970—73; educator early childhood Ironwood Area Schs., Mich., 1973—90; site mgr. L.A. County Head Start, Maywood, 1991—93; substitute tchr. L.A. Unified Sch. Dist., 1993—96, Oxnard Sch. Dist., 1996—2000, Ft. Wayne Cmty. Schs., Ind., 2000—05. Fellow, NYU, 1969—70. Mem.: Am. Orff. Schulwerk Assn., Orgn. Am. Koda'ly Educators, Am. Guild Organists (mem.-at-large 2004—). Democrat. Lutheran. Avocations: music, reading, piano, gardening.

HOFKIN, ANN GINSBURGH, photographer, poet; b. Holyoke, Mass., Dec. 20, 1943; d. Albert and Fruma (Winer) G.; m. Michael Gary Hofkin, June 30, 1966; children: Daniel, Benjamin. AB, Mt. Holyoke Coll., 1965; MSS, Bryn Mawr Coll., 1967. One-woman shows include Unicorn Galleries, Mpls., 1980, Warm Gallery, Mpls., 1982-85, 87-88, 90, 96, 98, St. Mary's Coll., Winona, Minn., 1986, U. Wis., Meml. Union, 1993, Bladin Found., 1990, Phipps Ctr. for the Arts, Wis., 1994, So. Light Gallery, Tex., 1994-95, MC Gallery, Mpls., 1986, 89, 91-92, 94, 97, Bethany Luth. Coll., Minn., 1999, Hoyt Inst. Fine Arts, 1999, Pietra di Luna Gallery, Fla., 2000, Coll. St. Benedict's, Minn., 2002, Bet Gabriel, Israel, 2003, Jerusalem Theatre, Israel, 2003, Alliance Francaise de Mpls./St.Paul, 2003, Mount Holyoke Coll, 2004, Tel Aviv Opera Ho., 2004; group shows include Gallery Triangle, Washington, 1996, Pindar Gallery, N.Y., 1987, Phinney Ctr., Seattle, 1987, Print Club, Phila., 1988, U. Minn., 1988, Plains Art Mus., 1988, U. Minn., 1989, Durango Arts Ctr., Colo., 1989, Northfield Arts Guild, Minn., 1982, 90, Mich. Friends of Photography, 1992, Jewish Cmty. Ctr., Houston, 1990, 92, Hennepin History Mus., 1992, LaGrange (Ga.) Coll., 1992, Chautauqua Art Assn., N.Y., 1992, Edn. Testing Svc., N.J., 1992, Slocumb Galleries, Tenn., 1993, Barrett House Galleries, N.Y., Erector Sq. Gallery, Conn., 1993, McPherson Coll., Ks., 1993, Middle (Tenn.) State U., 1993, Sioux City Art Ctr., Iowa, 1987, 89, 93, Mpls. Coll. Art and Design, 1987, 89, 94, Lubbock (Tex.) Fine Arts Ctr., 1995, Shoestring Gallery, N.Y., 1993, 94, 95, Phila. Art Alliance, 1995, Murray (Ky.) State U., 1996, Ctrl. Mo. State U., 1996, Stephen Austin State U. Tex., 1996, Houston Ctr. for Photography, 1995, 96, Perry House Galleries, Va., 1996, 97, U. S.D., Vermilion, 1994, 97, Nebr. Wesleyan U., 1997, U. No. Iowa, 1997, ekliktikos gallery, Washnigton, 1997, Chuck Levitan Gallery, N.Y., 1997-98; group exhibitions: Mpls. Inst. Arts, 85, 86, 2000, Minnesota State Fair, 1986-93, 95-97, 99-2000, U. Wisconsin, Green Bay, 1988, 94, 98, Coll. St. Catherine, MN, 1997, 99, Mpls., Jewish Community, Ctr., 1997, 99, Phipps Ctr. For the Arts, WI, 98, 99, Bausch & Lomb, Rochester, NY, 1998, Texas Nat., 1998, 2000, Savannah COll. of Art & Design, 1998, St. John's U., MN, 1999, Pentimenti Gallery, PA, 2000, Euro Galleries, MN, 2000, GOCAIA Gallery, AZ, 2000, San Diego Art Inst., CA, 2000, Wellington B Gray Gallery, NC, 2001, Rehab Inst. Chgo., 2003, Weisman Art Mus., U. Minn., 2003, Plains Art Mus., Fargo, 1988, 2001, 2003, Michael Lord Gallery, WI, 2003, FLATFILE, Chgo., 2001, 02, 03, Icebox Gallery, MN, 2004, Sande Webster Gallery, Phila., 2004; represented in permanent collections Dana Farber Cancer Inst., Fidelity Investments, Mass. Gen. Hosp., Hennepin History Mus., Savannah Coll. Art & Design, Minn. Ctr. Environ. Advocacy, Valley Hosp. Finalist Jerome Foundation, Erector Square Gallery, Warm Land Mark Print Project, Northfield Arts Guild; recipient Qualex award, Wellington B. Gray Gallery; fellow Rimon Cultural Arts. Home: 1422 Tamarack Dr Long Lake MN 55356 E-mail: aghofkin@aol.com.

HOFKIN, GERALD ALAN, gastroenterologist; b. Balt., July 4, 1936; m. Phyllis Hofkin, Aug. 23, 1959; children: Leah, Stephen, Karen. AB, MA, Johns Hopkins U., 1957; MD, U. Md., 1961; MBA, Johns Hopkins U., 2003. Diplomate Am. Bd. Internal Medicine, Am. Bd. Gastroenterology. Intern U. Md. Hosp., Balt., 1961, resident in medicine, 1962-63, 64-65, Sinai Hosp., Balt., 1963-64, 65-66; resident in gastroenterology Letterman Hosp., San Francisco, 1966-67; pvt. practice Balt., 1969-91; staff Sinai Hosp., Balt., 1991-99; part-time pvt. practice Woodholme Gastroenterology Assocs., Balt., 1999—. Chmn. med. exec. com. Sinai Hosp. Med. Staff, Balt., 1989, pres., 1992-93. Contbr. articles to profl. jours. Maj. U.S. Army, 1966—69. Decorated Army Commendation medal. Fellow ACP, Am. Coll. Gastroenterology; mem. Am. Soc. Gastroenterol. Endoscopy, Md. Soc. Gastrointesinal Endoscopy (pres. 1995-97), Balt. Amateur Radio Club (v.p. 1978-79), Balt. Radio Amateur TV Soc., Alpha Omega Alpha. Avocations: amateur radio, computers, bridge. Office: Woodholme Gastroenterology Assoc 2411 W Belvedere Ave Baltimore MD 21215-5229 Office Phone: 410-367-9600. Personal E-mail: ghofkin@pol.net.

HOFMAN, ELIZABETH ELVERETTA, retired mathematics educator, guidance counselor, dean; b. South Bend, Ind., Feb. 27, 1917; d. Curtis Hamilton and Ossie Marie (Meissner) Vernon; m. Raphael B. Hofman, June 10, 1942 (dec.). Diploma, Mich. County Normal Tng. Sch., Alpena, 1936—37; attended, Huntington Coll., Ind., 1941—42; BS, Western Res. U., Cleve., 1947, MA in Edn., 1948. Cert. HS math. tchr. Western Res. U., 1947, in pupil personnel svcs. Western Res. U., 1964. Tchr. grades K-8 Alpena County Schs., 1937—41; math. tchr. grades 4-8 Warrensville Heights Jr. HS, Ohio, 1945—63, math. tchr. jr. and sr. HS, advisor math., 1963—72, part time guidance counselor, 1960—64, 1963—72, tchr. math. grades 11 and 12, 1960—64, dean of girls, 1968—72, ret., 1972. Mem.: NEA, Ohio Ret. Tchrs. Assn., Nat. Ret. Tchrs. Assn. Home: 700 Brittany O Delray Beach FL 33446-1073

HOFMANN, ALAN FREDERICK, biomedical researcher, educator; b. Balt., May 17, 1931; s. Joseph Enoch and Nelda Rosina (Durr) Hofmann; m. Marta Gertrud Pettersson, Aug. 15, 1959 (div. 1976); children: Anthea Karin, Cecilia Rae; m. Helga Katharina Aicher, Nov. 3, 1978. BA with honors, Johns Hopkins U., 1951, MD with honors, 1955; MD, U. Lund, Sweden, 1965; MD (hon.), U. Bologna, Italy, 1988. Intern, resident dept. medicine Columbia Presbyn. Med. Ctr., N.Y.C., 1955-57; clin. assoc. clin. ctr. Nat. Heart Inst., NIH, Bethesda, Md., 1957-59; postdoctoral fellow, dept. physiol. chemistry U. Lund, Sweden, 1959-62; asst. physician Hosp. Rockefeller U., N.Y.C., 1962-64, assoc. physician, 1964-66; outpatient physician N.Y. Hosp., N.Y.C., 1963-64; cons. in medicine, assoc. dir. gastroenterology unit Mayo Clinic, Rochester, Minn., 1966-77; prof. medicine, attending physician Med. Ctr. U. Calif., San Diego, 1977-98, emeritus prof., 1998—. Asst. prof. dept. medicine Rockefeller U., N.Y.C., 1964—66; assoc. prof. medicine and biochemistry U. Minn. Mayo Grad. Sch., 1966—69, assoc. prof. medicine and physiology, 1969—70, prof., 1970—73, Mayo Med. Sch., 1973—77; cons. physiology Mayo Clinic, Rochester, 1975—77; adj. prof. pharmacy U. Calif., San Francisco, 1986—94; vis. prof. U. Mich., Ann Arbor, 1980—85. Contbr. articles to profl. jours., chapters to books. Co-recipient Eppinger prize, Falk Found., 1976; recipient Travel award, Wellcome Trust, 1961—63, NSF, 1964, Sr. Scientist award, Humboldt Found., Fed. Rep. Germany, 1976, 1991, Disting. Achievement award, Modern Medicine mag., 1978, Chancellor's Rsch. Excellence award, U. Calif., 1986, Disting. Alumnus award, Mayo Found., 2001, Disting. Mentor award, Found. Digestive Health Nutrition, 2004; Sr. fellow, NIH, 1986. Fellow: AAAS, Royal Soc. Medicine, Royal Coll. Physicians (hon.); mem.: Am. Gastroent. Assn. (chmn. biliary diseases coun. 1991—92, Disting. Achievement award 1970, co-winner Beaumont prize 1979, Friedenwald medal 1994), Am. Physiol. Soc. (Horace Davenport medal 1996), Am. Liver Found. (chmn. sci. adv. bd. 1986—91), Serbian Soc. Medicine (hon.), Royal Flemish Acad. Medicine (hon.; fgn. corr. mem.), Chilean Soc. Gastroenterology (hon.), Soc. Gastrointestinal Radiology (hon.), Swedish Soc. Gastroenterology (hon.), Gastroent. Soc. Australia (hon.), Brit. Soc. Gastroenterology (hon.), German Soc. Digestive and Metabolic Disease (hon. Siegfried Thannhauser medal 1996), Assn. Am. Physicians, Am. Soc. Clin. Investigation, Am. Assn. Study Liver Disease (pres. 1984, numerous coms., Disting. Achievement award 1997), Sigma Xi, Phi Beta Kappa, Omicron Delta Kappa, Alpha Omega Alpha. Achievements include description and modelling of the enterohepatic circulation of bile acids; clarification of the multiple physiological roles of bile acids; conjugated bile acid replacement therapy for bile acid deficiency in short bowel syndrome; discovery of new vertebrate bile acids; structure-function relationships of bile acids; therapeutic uses of bile acids in liver, biliary and intestinal disease. Home: 5870 Cactus Way La Jolla CA 92037-7069 Personal E-mail: hofmannaf@cs.com. Business E-Mail: ahofmann@ucsd.edu.

HOFMANN, GEORGE W., artist, educator; b. Jamaica, N.Y., May 22, 1938; s. George Hofmann and Margarete Vogl; 1 child, David E. Student, Akademie d.Bildenden Kuenste, Nuremberg, Germany, 1958—61. Instr. Pratt Inst., Bklyn., 1967—68; prof. Hunter Coll., CUNY, 1967—2002. Dir. Francis J. Greenburger Found., N.Y.C., NY, 1986—88. Painting, After Tiepolo (Purchase, Institute of History and Art, Albany, NY, 2001). Judge N.Y. Found. for Arts, N.Y.C., 1995—2002. Fellow Visual Arts, NEA, 1976.

HOFMANN, HEATH FRED, electrical engineer; s. Clifford Fred and Brenda Williams Hofmann. PhD in Elec. Engring., U. Calif., Berkeley, 1998. Grantee "Flywheel Tech. Devel. for Small Satellite Applications, NASA Glenn Rsch. Ctr., 2001—03, "Modelling and Control of ARCP in Power and Dr. Sys., ", Office of Naval Rsch., 1999—2002, "Harvesting Electric Energy During Walking with a Backpack: Physiol., Ergonomic, Biomechanical and Electromechanical Materials, Devices and Syste, 2003—04, "Investigation of Ultrahigh Power Density Machine Designs, NASA Glenn Rsch. Ctr., 2001. Mem.: IEEE. Achievements include patents pending for Self-Sensing Thermoacoustic Refrigerator Drive. Home: 355 McBath St State College PA 16801 Office: Pa State Univ 121 Electrical Engineering East University Park PA 16802 Office Phone: 814-865-2229. Office Fax: 814-865-7065. Personal E-mail: heath_hofmann@yahoo.com. E-mail: hofmann@ee.psu.edu.

HOFMANN, HERBERT C., diversified financial services company executive; BA, Cornell U.; degree, Program Mgmt. Devel., Harvard U. Various mgmt. positions with subs. Loews Corp., 1966—81, v.p., oper. planning, 1976—92, sr. v.p., 1992—; COO Bulova Corp., 1981—89, pres., CEO, 1989—. Office: Bulova Corp One Bulova Ave Woodside NY 11377*

HOFMANN, JOHN RICHARD, JR., retired lawyer; b. Oakland, Calif., June 24, 1922; s. John Richard and Esther (Starkweather) H.; m. Mary Macdonough, Feb. 6, 1954; children: John Richard III, Gretchen Hofmann, Sarah Worthington Hack, Joan Macdonough Alexander. AB, U. Calif., Berkeley, 1943; JD, Harvard U., 1949. Bar: Calif. 1950. Assoc. Pillsbury, Madison & Sutro, San Francisco, 1949-58, ptnr., 1959-92, of counsel, 1992-96, ret., 1996—; exec. v.p. MPC Ins., Ltd., 1988-96. City atty. City of Belvedere, Calif., 1958. Mem. County of Marin (Calif.) Aviation Commn., 2001—05, chmn., 2003—05. Office: Pillsbury Winthrop Shaw Pittman LLP PO Box 7880 San Francisco CA 94120-7880 Office Phone: 415-983-1522.

HOFMANN, MARIE-CLAUDE, cell biologist, educator, research scientist; b. Lausanne, Switzerland; BS in Biology, U. Lausanne, 1979, PhD, 1988. Postdoctoral fellow Burnham Inst., La Jolla, Calif., 1989—95; asst. prof. U. Dayton, Ohio, 1995—2001, assoc. prof., 2001—. Contbr. articles to profl. jours. Grantee, NIH, 1998—, Lance Armstrong Found., 2002. Achievements include establishment of the first mammalian male germ line cell line. Office: U Dayton 300 College Park Dayton OH 45469 E-mail: marie-claude.hofmann@notes.udayton.edu.

HOFMANN, PAUL BERNARD, healthcare consultant; b. Portland, Oreg., July 6, 1941; s. Max and Consuelo Theresa (Bley) H.; m. Lois Bernstein, June 28, 1969; children: Julie, Jason. BS, U. Calif., Berkeley, 1963, MPH, 1965, DPH, 1994. Research assoc. in hosp. adminstrn. Lab. of Computer Sci., Mass. Gen. Hosp., Boston, 1966-68, asst. dir., 1968-69; asst. adminstr. San Antonio Community Hosp., Upland, Calif., 1969-70, assoc. adminstr., 1970-72; dep. dir. Stanford (Calif.) U. Hosp., 1972-74, dir., 1974-77; exec. dir. Emory U. Hosp., Atlanta, 1978-87; exec. v.p., chief ops. officer Alta Bates Corp., Emeryville, Calif., 1987-91, cons., 1991-92, Alexander & Alexander, San Francisco, 1992-94; disting. vis. scholar Stanford (Calif.) U. Ctr. for Biomed. Ethics, 1993-97; sr. fellow Stanford (Calif.) U. Hosp., 1993-94; sr. cons. strategic healthcare practice Alexander & Alexander Cons. Group, San Francisco, 1994-97; sr. v.p. strategic healthcare practice Aon Cons., San Francisco, 1997-99; pres. The Hofmann Healthcare Group, San Francisco, 2000-01; with Provenance Health Ptnrs., Moraga, Calif., 2001—. Instr. computer applications Harvard U., 1968-69; lectr. hosp. adminstrn. UCLA, 1970-72, Stanford U. Med. Sch., 1972-77; assoc. prof. Emory U. Sch. Medicine, Atlanta, 1978-87. Author: The Development and Application of Ethical Criteria for Use in Making Programmatic Resource Allocation Decisions in Hospitals, 1994; co-editor: Managing Ethically: A Guide for Executives, 2001, Mistakes in Healthcare Management: Identification, Prevention and Correction, 2005; contbr. articles to profl. jours Served with U.S. Army, 1959. Fellow Am. Coll. Hosp. Adminstrs. (recipient Robert S. Hudgens meml. award 1976); mem. Am. Hosp. Assn., U. Calif. Grad. Program in Health Mgmt. Alumni Assn. (Disting. Leadership award 2004). Business E-Mail: phofmann@provenancehealth.com.

HOFMANN, POLLY A., physiologist, science educator; b. Dixon, Ill., July 8, 1960; married; 1 child. BS in Biology, U. Ill., 1982; PhD in Physiology, U. Pitts., 1987. Postdoctoral fellow dept. physiology U. Wis., Madison, Wis., 1987; asst. prof. dept. physiology and biophysics U. Tenn., Memphis, 1991—97, assoc. prof. dept. physiology, 1997—. Mem. prof. search com. Dept. Physiology and Biophysics, U. Tenn., 1991—92, grad. program tng. com., 1992—93, 1993—; student progress and promotions com. biomed. sci. Coll. of Medicine, U. Tenn., 1992—96; chmn. search com. Dept. Preventive Medicine, U. Tenn., 1993—94; Alma and Hal Reagan fellowship seletion com. Coll. Grad. Health Scis., U. Tenn., 1994—; mem. conflict resolution coun. of student mistreatment program Coll. of Medicine, U. Tenn., 1995—. Ad hoc reviewer Am. Jour. Physiology, Jour. Pharmacology and Exptl. Therapeutics; contbr. articles to profl. jours. Recipient Dave McClain Rsch. award, Am. Heart Assn., 1988, Established Investigator award, 1995; fellow predoctoral fellow, NIH, 1983—87, postdoctoral fellow, 1989—92, Am. Heart Assn., 1988—89; grantee, NIH, 1992—, Am. Heart Assn., 1992—93. Mem.: Internat. Soc. Heart Rsch. (Upjohn Young Investigator award 1990), Biophys. Soc., Am. Physiol. Soc. (career opportunities in physiology com. 1995—), Sigma Xi. Office: U Tenn 894 Union Ave Ste 426 Memphis TN 38163-0001 Office Phone: 901-448-7348. Office Fax: 901-448-7126. Business E-Mail: phofmann@physiol.utmem.edu.

HOFMANN, THEO, biochemist, educator; b. Zurich, Switzerland, Feb. 20, 1924; emigrated to Can., 1964, naturalized, 1969; s. Edwin and Hedwig (Moos) H.; m. Doris Topham Forbes, July 15, 1953; children: Martin Ian, Tony David, Peter Adrian. Diploma chem. engring., Swiss Fed. Inst. Tech., Zurich, 1947, Dr. Sc. Tech., 1950. Research asst. U. Aberdeen, Scotland, 1950-52; sci. officer Hannah Dairy Research Inst., Ayr, Scotland, 1952-56; lectr. Sheffield (Eng.) U., 1956-64; prof. biochemistry U. Toronto, Ont., Can., 1964-89, emeritus prof. biochemistry, 1989—. Vis. assoc. prof. U. Wash., 1962-63; vis. scientist Commonwealth Sci. and Indsl. Research Orgn., Sydney, Australia, 1971-72; vis. prof. divsn. natural scis. U. Calif.-Santa Cruz, 1981; vis. prof. physical chemistry, U. Lund, Sweden, 1987. Asso. editor: Can. Jour. Biochemistry, 1968-71; Contbr. numerous articles to profl. jours. Med. Rsch. Coun. (Can.) grantee, 1964-94. Mem. Can. Soc. Biochemistry and Molecular and Cellular Biology, Am. Soc. Biochemistry and Molecular Biology, Biochem. Soc. Achievements include rsch. in function and evolution of enzymes. Home: 199 Arnold Ave Thornhill ON Canada L4J 1C1 Office: U Toronto Dept Biochemistry Toronto ON Canada M5S 1A8 Office Phone: 416-978-2683. Business E-Mail: theo@hera.med.utoronto.ca.

HOFMANN, THOMAS W., petroleum company executive; BS, U. Del., 1973; MS, Villanova U., 1994. With Coopers & Lybrand, Sun Co. Inc. (now Sunoco, Inc.), Phila., 1977—; comptroller Sun Co. Inc., Phila., 1990-91, dir. tax adminstrn., 1991-94, dir. performance analysis, 1994-95, comptroller, 1995-98, v.p., CFO, 1998—2002, sr. .vp., CFO, 2002—, also bd. dirs. V.p. fin. Helios Capital Corp. subs. Sun Co. Inc., 1987. Office: Sunoco Inc 10 Penn Ctr 1801 Market St Philadelphia PA 19103-1699

HOFMANN, WALTER D., psychiatrist, writer; b. Valley Home, Calif., Dec. 18, 1927; s. Karl F. and Berta A. Hofmann; 7 children. BA, Pacific Union Coll., 1949; MD, Loma Linda U., 1953. Diplomate Am. Bd. Psychiatry, Am. Bd. Forensic Psychiatry. Intern San Diego Navy Hosp., San Diego, 1953; residence Ohio State U. Psychiatry, 1959—61; owner Hofmann Clinic, Glendale, Calif., 1961—81; head forensic psychiatry L.A. Superior Ct., 1981—95. Chief psychiatry Glendale Adv. Med. Ctr., 1965—75. Author: (health column) Ask Dr. David, 2002—05. Served on grand jury San Diego Superior Ct., 2004—05. Lt. comdr. USN, 1953—57. Office: 1740 El Cam Teatro La Jolla CA 92037 Home: 438 Rosemont St La Jolla CA 92037

HOFSOMMER, DONOVAN LOWELL, history professor; b. Ft. Dodge, Iowa, Apr. 10, 1938; s. Vernie George and Helma J. (Schager) H.; m. Sandra Louise Rusch, June 13, 1965; children: Kathryn Anne, Kristine Beret, Knute Lars. BA, U. Northern Iowa, 1960, MA, 1966; PhD, Okla. State U., 1973. Tchr. Fairfield (Iowa) High Sch., 1961-65; instr. U. Northern Iowa, Cedar Falls, 1965-66, Lea Coll., Albert Lea, Minn., 1966-70; teaching asst. Okla. State U., Stillwater, 1970-73; assoc. prof. and dept. head Wayland Coll., Plainview, Tex., 1973-81; corp. historian So. Pacific Co., San Francisco, 1981-85; hist. cons. Burlington No. Inc., Seattle, 1985-87; vis. prof. U. Mont., Missula, 1986-87; exec. dir. ctr. Western studies Augustana Coll., Sioux Falls, S.D., 1987-89; prof. history St. Cloud (Minn.) State U., 1989—. Cons. Dyanelectron and Dynarail, Pueblo, Colo., 1979-81, Grand Trunk Corp., Detroit, 1988-95; mem. editl. bd. annals of Iowa, Iowa City, 1975-94, R.R. history, Akron, Ohio, 1975—. Author: Prairie Oasis, 1975, Katy Northwest, 1976, Southern Pacific 1901-1985, 1986; co-author: History of Great Northern Railway, 1988, Quanah Route, 1991, Grand Trunk Corp., 1995, The Tootin' Louie, 2004, History of Minneapolis & Saint Louis, 2004, Steel Trails of Hawkeye Land, 2005; editor: Lexington Group Transport History, 1975—; mem. editl. bd. Annals of Iowa, Iowa City, 1975-92, R.R. History, Akron, Ohio, 1975—. With U.S. Army, 1960-66. Mem. Okla. Hist. Soc. (Wright Heritage award 1979), Ry. and Locomotive Hist. Soc. (Book award 1988, Sr. Achievement award 1995), Western History Assn., Orgn. Am. Historians, State Hist. Soc. Iowa, Am. Assn. for State and Local History. Episc. Home: 1803 13th Ave SE Saint Cloud MN 56304-2231 Office: St Cloud State U Dept History Saint Cloud MN 56301

HOFSTEAD, JAMES WARNER, laundry machinery company executive, lawyer; b. Jackson, Tenn., Feb. 3, 1913; s. Harry Oliver and Agnes Lucile (Blackard) H.; m. Ellen Frances Bowers, Dec. 27, 1940 (dec.); 1 child, Eda Lucile. AB, Vanderbilt U., 1935, LLB, 1938. Bar: Tenn. Pvt. practice law; v.p., bd. dirs. United Tel. Co., Nashville, 1969—, emeritus; ret.; pres., bd. dirs. Wishy Washy, Inc., Nashville, 1946—, Wishy Sales Inc., Nashville, 1959—, pres. emeritus. Capt. USMC, 1942-45. Mem. SAR (nat. committeeman, state pres. emeritus, nat. trustee), SCV, Vanderbilt Bar Assn. (pres. emeritus), So. Srs. Golf Assn., Soc. of Cincinnati, English Spkg. Union (emeritus, chmn.), Soc. Colonial Wars (past gov. Tenn., past dep. gov. gen.), Nashville C. of C., Belle Meade Country Club, 200 Club, Exch. Club, Eccentric Club (London), Gasparilla 48 Club, Cumberland Club (charter), Sigma Chi. Home: 504 Elmington # 406 Nashville TN 37205 Office: 3729 Charlotte Pike Nashville TN 37209-3734

HOGABOOM, MAURINE HOLBERT, cultural organization administrator; b. Wichita Falls, Te., Feb. 3, 1912; d. Joseph Eggleston Holbert and Ada Viola Davis; m. Robert Edward Hogaboom, July 16, 1982 (dec. Nov. 1993). BA summa cum laude, Fordham U., 1976; MA, Goddard Coll., 1979; postgrad., U. of the South, 1992—95. Actor, dir., tchr., N.Y.C., 1955—57; founder Chrysalis Rsch. Ctr. for the Arts, N.Y.C., 1979—83; founder, co-dir. Synthesis Ctr. St. Mary's, 1990—. Founding mem., performer Arts Alliance, St. Mary's Coll., 1983—; active Trinity Episcopal Ch., St. Mary's City, Md., 2001—. Avocations: gardening, yoga.

HOGAN, BRIAN JOSEPH, editor; b. Aberdeen, S.D., Apr. 11, 1943; s. Arthur James and Magdalena (Frison) H.; m. Jamie Isabelle Schwingel, June 21, 1987. BS in Aerospace and Mech. Engring., U. Ariz., 1965, BS in Geophysics-Geochemistry, 1968; MS in Journalism, U. Utah, 1972. Rsch. asst. U. Va. Rsch. Labs for Engring. Scis., Charlottesville, 1965-66; exploration geophysicist Anaconda Co., Tucson, 1968-71; assoc. editor Benwill Pub. Co., Brookline, Mass., 1973-74; asst. editor Design News, Boston, 1974-75, midwest editor Chgo., 1975-87, sr. editor Newton, Mass., 1987-89, mng. editor, 1989-97; chief editor Mfg. Engring.-Soc. Mfg. Engrs., Dearborn, Mich. Author stage plays The Young O'Neil, 1983, Awakening, 1984. Precinct worker Cook County Rep. Com., Oak Park, Ill., 1986-87; interpreter Frank Lloyd Wright Home and Studio Found., Oak Park, 1981-87. Recipient numerous awards Am. Soc. Bus. Press Editors, Soc. Tech. Communication, Aviation Space Writers Assn. Mem. Am. Soc. Bus. Press Editors, Am. Hist. Print Collectors Soc. Republican. Roman Catholic. Avocations: photography, print collecting, bicycling, hiking. Office: Mfg Engring 1 SME Dr PO Box 930 Dearborn MI 48121-0930 Office Phone: 313-425-3252. Business E-Mail: bhogan@sme.org.

HOGAN, BRIGID L., molecular biologist; b. England, Aug. 28, 1943; BA, U. Cambridge, 1964, PhD, 1968. NATO rsch. fellow dept. biology MIT, 1968-70; lectr. biochemistry U. Sussex, England, 1970-74; sci. staff Imperial Cancer Rsch. Fund, Mill Hill, England, 1974-84; head lab. molecular embryology Nat. Inst. Med. Rsch., Mill Hill, England, 1985-88; prof. cell biology Vanderbilt Med. Sch., Nashville, 1988—2002; chair, dept. cell biology Duke U. Med. Ctr., 2002—. Hortense B. Ingram chair molecular oncology Howard Hughes Med. Inst., 1993-2002; vice chair Basement Membrane Gordon Conf., 1994, chair, 1996; co-chair sci. human embryo rsch. panel NIH, 1994; Jenkinson meml. lectr. U. Oxford, 1995; Margaret Pittman lectr. NIH, 1996. Mem. Br. Soc. Cell Biology (com. 1982-86), Br. Soc. Devel. Biology (com. 1984-88), NAS Inst. Medicine, European Molecular Biology Orgn. Office: Duke U Med Ctr 388 Nanaline Duke Bldg, Box 3709 Durham NC 27710

HOGAN, CLARENCE LESTER, retired electronics executive; b. Great Falls, Mont., Feb. 8, 1920; s. Clarence Lester and Bessie Hogan; m. Audrey Biery Peters, Oct. 13, 1946; 1 child, Cheryl Lea. BSChemE, Mont. State U., 1942, Dr. Engring. (hon.), 1967; MS in Physics, Lehigh U., 1947, PhD in Physics, 1950, D in Engring. (hon.), 1971; AM (hon.), Harvard U., 1954; Doctorate (hon.), Mont. State U., 1968; D in Sci. (hon.), Worcester Poly. U., 1969. Rsch. chem. engr. Anaconda Copper Mining Co., 1942-43; instr. physics Lehigh U., 1946-50; mem. tech. staff Bell Labs., Murray Hill, N.J., 1950-51, sub-dept. head, 1951-53; assoc. prof. Harvard U., Cambridge, Mass., 1953-57, Gordon McKay prof., 1957-58; gen. mgr. semi-conductor products divsn. Motorola, Inc., Phoenix, 1958-60, v.p., 1960-66, exec. v.p., dir., 1966-68; pres., CEO Fairchild Semicondr. (formerly Fairchild Instruments), Mt. View, Calif., 1968—74, vice chmn. bd. dirs., 1974-85. Gen. chmn. Internat. Conf. on Magnetism and Magnetic Materials, 1959, 60; mem. materials adv. bd. Dept. Def., 1957-59; mem. adv. coun. dept. electrical engring. Princeton U.; mem. adv. bd. sch. engring. U. Calif., Berkeley, 1974—, adv. bd. dept. chem. engring. Mont. State U., 1988—; mem. nat. adv.

bd. Desert Rsch. Inst., 1976-80; mem. vis. com. dept. electric engring. and computer sci. MIT, 1975-85; mem. adv. coun. div. electrical engring. Stanford U., 1976-86; mem. sci. and ednl. adv. com. Lawrence Berkeley Lab., 1978-84; mem. Pres.'s Export Coun., 1976-80; mem. adv. panel to tech. adv. bd. U.S. Congress, 1976-80. Chmn. Commn. Found. Santa Clara County, Calif., 1983—85; mem. vis. com. Lehigh U., 1966—71, trustee, 1971—80, also life trustee; trustee Western Electronic Edn. Fund; dir. Computer History Mus., 1982—86; mem. governing bd. Maricopa County Jr. Coll.; bd. regents U. Santa Clara. Lt. (j.g.) USNR, 1942—46. Recipient Community Svc. award NCCJ, 1978, Medal of Merit Am. Electronics Assn., 1978, Berkeley Citation U. Calif., 1980; named Bay Area Bus. Man of Yr. San Jose State U., 1978, One of 10 Greatest Innovators in Past 50 Yrs. Electronics Mag., 1980, chair (hon.) Computer Sci. and Engring. U.C. Berkeley, 1997. Fellow AAAS, IEEE (Frederick Philips gold medal 1976, Edison silver medal Cleve. Soc. 1978, Pioneering medal for microwave theory and tech. 1993), Inst. Elec. Engrs. (hon.); mem. NAE, Am. Phys. Soc., Menlo Country Club, Masons, Sigma Xi, Tau Beta Pi, Phi Kappa Phi, Eta Kappa Nu, Kappa Sigma. Democrat. Baptist. Achievements include patentee in field; inventor microwave gyrator, circulator, isolator. Avocations: woodworking, computer programming. Home: 36 Barry Ln Atherton CA 94027-4023

HOGAN, CURTIS JULE, labor union administrator, industrial relations specialist, consultant; b. Greeley, Kans., July 25, 1926; s. Charles Leo and Anna Malene (Roussello) H.; m. Lois Jean Ecord, Apr. 23, 1955; children: Christopher James, Michael Sean, Patrick Marshall, Kathleen Marie, Kerry Joseph. BS in Indsl. Rels., Rockhurst Coll., 1950; postgrad., Georgetown U., 1955, U. Tehran, Iran, 1955-57. With Gt. Lakes Pipeline Co., Kansas City, Mo., 1950-55; with Internat. Fedn. Petroleum and Chem. Workers, Denver, 1955-85, gen. sec., 1973-85; pres. Internat. Labor Rels. Svcs., Inc., 1976—. Cons. in field; lectr. Rockhurst Coll., Kansas City, 1951-52. Contbr. articles to profl. publs. Served with U.S. Army, 1945-46. Mem. Internat. Indsl. Rels. Assn., Indsl. Rels. Rsch. Assn., Oil Chem. and Atomic Workers Internat. Union. Office: Internat Fed Petroleum Chem Workers 435 S Newport Way Denver CO 80224-1321

HOGAN, DANIEL BOLTEN, management consultant; b. Lawrence, Mass., Sept. 20, 1943; s. Daniel Edward and Gisela (Bolten) H.; m. Jean Elizabeth Haley, Jan. 25, 1979 (div. Jan. 2002); children: Matthew Pollard, Sarah Elizabeth, Haley Elizabeth; m. Jean Kilbourne, Oct. 5, 2002; 1 stepchild, Claudia Lux. BA, Yale U., 1965; EdM, Boston U., 1971; JD, Harvard U., 1972, PhD, 1983. Lic. psychologist; bar: Mass., U.S. Dist. Ct. Mass. Rural community devel. worker U.S. Peace Corps, Butha-Buthe, Lesotho, 1967-69; mgmt. cons. Wayland, Mass., 1972-76; rsch. and teaching fellow Dept. Psychology and Social Rels., Harvard U., Cambridge, Mass., 1976-81; clin. fellow and instr. psychology Harvard Med. Sch., Boston, 1981-85; asst. in psychology McLean Hosp., Belmont, Mass., 1982-83, asst. psychologist, 1983, asst. attending psychologist, 1984-86; mgmt. cons. Weston, Mass., 1986-90; v.p. and dir. R & D McBer & Co., Boston, 1990; pres. The Apollo Group, Concord, Mass., 1991—2001; assoc. dept. psychology Harvard U., 1996-98; assoc. Stratin Cons., Maynard, Mass., 2001—. Bd. dirs. Standex Internat. Corp., Salem, N.H., also mem. compensation com., 1986—; trustee, sr. rsch. assoc. Nat. Ctr. for Study of Professions, Washington, 1976-83; mem. com. on use of human subjects in rsch. Harvard U. Faculty Arts and Scis., 1980-81. Author: The Regulation of Psychotherapists: A Study in the Philosophy and Practice of Professional Regulation, vol. I, 1979, The Regulation of Psychotherapists: A Handbook of State Licensure Laws, vol. II, 1979, The Regulation of Psychotherapists: A Review of Malpractice Suits in the United States, vol. III, 1979, The Regulation of Psychotherapists: A Resource Bibliography, vol. IV, 1979; guest editor (spl. double issue) Law and Human Behavior, 1983, cons. editor, 1985-91; contbr. articles to profl. jours., chpts. books. Trustee, mem. exec. com., chair com. on trustees, chair leadership gifts Fenn Sch., Concord, 1993-96; trustee Cambridge Ctr. for Behavioral Studies, chair nominating comm., 1985-91; bd. dirs. New Eng. Tng. Inst., Stonington, Conn., 1976-78, Phillips Exeter Acad. Alumni Coun., Exeter, N.H., 1986-92; trustee Cmty. Change, Inc., Boston, 1972-79, adv. bd., 1979—; pres., chmn. bd. dirs. Triangle Conservation Coalition, 1996-2000; chmn. transp. plan com. Town of Concord, 1996-99. Maurice Falk Med. Fund. grantee, 1976-78. Fellow APA, Am. Psychol. Soc., Am. Assn. Applied Preventive Psychology, Am. Orthopsychiatric Assn.; mem. Am. Psychology Law Soc. (dir. 1982-84), Internat. Orgn. Devel. Assn., Mass. Psychol. Assn. (bd. profl. affairs 1980-83), Mass. Bar Assn., Nat. Register of Health Svc. Providers in Psychology, Mensa. Avocations: squash, tennis, music, computers. E-mail: dan.hogan@stratin-consulting.com.

HOGAN, EDWARD ROBERT, financial services executive; b. Yonkers, NY, Mar. 21, 1939; s. John J. and Blanche (Corradi) H.; m. Linda Carroll, Sept. 25, 1959 (div. Oct. 1975); children: Linda Hogan Benya, Edward R. Jr., Barbara Hogan Comblo; m. Sandra Lesperance, Sept. 17, 1993. Dist. mgr. New Eng. Life, Thornwood, N.Y., 1962-64; pres. Profl. Employment Svcs., Scarsdale, N.Y., 1964-66, Royal Transport & Distbn. Inc., Yonkers, N.Y., 1966-71; v.p. Fin. Ins. Group, NYC, 1971—74, Franklin United Life Ins. Co., Garden City, N.Y., 1974-79; sr. v.p. Adv. Svcs. Corp., White Plains, N.Y., 1979-83; pres. Faculty Svcs. Corp., Wappingers Falls, N.Y., 1983—, FSC Adminstrv. Svcs. Corp., Wappingers Falls, N.Y., 1986—. Registered prin. Cadaret, Grant & Co., Inc., Syracuse, N.Y., 1989—. Pres. Yonkers Young Rep. Orgn., 1960-64; v.p. Westchester County Young Reps., White Plains, 1961-63; candidate 1st Assembly Dist. State Assembly, Yonkers, 1962; Westchester County campaign dir. U.S. Sen. James L. Buckley, 1968. With USN, 1957-59. Mem. Nat. Tax Shelter Annuity Assn. Avocations: boating, flying, skiing. Office: Faculty Svcs Corp PO Box 1635 Wappingers Falls NY 12590-8635 Office Phone: 845-297-0300. Personal E-mail: facultysc@optonline.net.

HOGAN, ELWOOD, lawyer; b. Augusta, Ga., Mar. 4, 1929; s. William Elwood and Geneva Isabell H.; m. Myrtle Elizabeth McCall, June 15, 1957; children: Martha Elizabeth Ondrejcak, Darrell William Hogan. BBA, U. Ga., 1954; JD, Stetson U., 1958. Bar: Fla. 1958, U.S. Ct. Appeals (6th circuit) Fla. 1958, U.S. Dist. Ct. Fla. 1959, U.S. Ct. Appeals (11th circuit) 1959, U.S. Tax Ct. 1965, U.S. Supreme Ct. 1973; cert. circuit ct. mediator. Assoc. Wolfe & Bonner Attys., Clearwater, Fla., 1958—63; ptnr. Wolfe, Bonner & Hogan, Clearwater, 1964—75; pres. Bonner & Hogan P.A., Clearwater, 1985—99, McFarland, Gould, Lyons, Sullivan & Hogan, P.A., Clearwater, 2000—. Prosecutor Mcpl. Ct., Clearwater, 1966-68, judge, 1968-74; bd. trustees Morton Plant Hosp., Clearwater, 1981-86, chmn., 1984-86; pres. Fla. Mcpl. Judges Assn., 1972; Fla. Circuit Ct. mediator. Vice chmn. Clearwater Hist. Com., 1974; mem. Clearwater Hist. Soc.; past mem. adv. bd. Clearwater (Fla.) Salvation Army; deacon Calvary Bapt. Ch., 1958—; founder The Presential Prayer Team, 2001—04; past bd. dirs. Girls Clubs Pinellas County, Inc. With U.S. Army, 1947—48. Recipient Businessman of Yr. award, Fla. Rep. Com. Bus. Adv. Coun., 2003—04. Mem. ABA, Fla. Acad. Profl. Mediators, Kiwanis Club (dist. gov. Fla. dist. 1979-80), Clearwater Bar Assn. (pres. 1972-73), Phi Alpha Delta (life). Avocations: swimming, tennis, fishing. Office: McFarland Gould Lyons Sullivan & Hogan 311 S Missouri Ave Clearwater FL 33756-5833 Office Phone: 727-461-1111. Business E-Mail: hogan@mcfarlandgouldlaw.com.

HOGAN, FELICITY, artist; b. England; m. Michael Clark, Dec. 1995. Co-dir. Mus. Contemporary Art, Washington, 1996—. Exhibitions include Clark & Hogan: Paintings & Collaborations, Barry Gallery, 2002—03, Mus. Contemporary Art, 1997—, Clark in Context: Day of the Revolutionary, 2003. Office: Mus Contemporary Art 1054 31st St Washington DC 20007 E-mail: felicityhogan@aol.com.*

HOGAN, FRANK W., III, lawyer, manufacturing executive; b. Lowell, Mass., July 16, 1960; BA, Boston (Mass.) U., 1982, JD, 1987. Assoc. Winthrop, Stimson, Putnam & Roberts (now Pillsbury Winthrop LLP), 1988—95, ptnr., 1995—97; v.p., gen. counsel, sec. Silgan Holdings, Stamford, Conn., 1997—2002, sr. v.p., 2002—, gen. counsel, 2002—, sec., 2002—. Mem.: ABA. Office: Silgan Holdings Ste 400 4 Landmark Sq Stamford CT 06901*

HOGAN, JAMES D., bank executive; Contr. Star Bank, 1987—93; exec. v.p., contr. Firstar Corp. (formerly Star Bancorp), 1993—2001; CFO Sovereign Bancorp, Phila., 2001—, exec. v.p., 2002—. Office: Sovereign Bancorp 1500 Market St Philadelphia PA 19102

HOGAN, JEREMY ROBERT, photojournalist; b. Porterville, Calif., Sept. 3, 1972; s. Jerry Wayne Hogan and Kathleen Marie Dodd. BS in Journalism, San Jose State U., 1997. Staff photographer Bloomington (Ind.) Herald-Times, 1997—. Recipient Photo of the Yr. award Hoosier State Press Assn., 1998. Mem. Nat. Press Photographers Assn., Ind. Press Photographers Assn. Avocations: travel, writing, reading, astrophotography, bicycling. Office: 1900 S Walnut St Bloomington IN 47401-7720 E-mail: Hoganj8@aol.com.

HOGAN, JOHN, broadcast executive; Sr. v.p. Clear Channel Radio, San Antonio, pres., COO, 2001—02, pres., CEO, 2002—. Named Radio Group Exec. of Yr., Industry Achievement Awards, Radio & Records. Office: Clear Channel Comm Inc 200 E Basse Rd San Antonio TX 78209

HOGAN, JOHN DONALD, retired college dean, finance educator; b. Binghamton, N.Y., July 16, 1927; s. John D. and Edith J. (Hennessy) H.; m. Anna Craig, Nov. 26, 1976; children: Thomas P., James E. AB, Syracuse U., 1949, MA, 1950, PhD, 1952. Registered prin. Nat. Assn. Securities Dealers. Prof. econs., chmn. dept. Bates Coll., Lewiston, Maine, 1953-58; dir. edn. fin. research State of N.Y., 1959, chief mcpl. fin., 1960; staff economist, dir. research Northwestern Mut. Life Ins. Co., Milw., 1960-68; sr. v.p. Nationwide Ins. Cos., Columbus, Ohio, 1968-76; dean Sch. Bus. Adminstrn. Central Mich. U., Mt. Pleasant, 1976-79; v.p. Am. Productivity Ctr., Houston, 1979-80; pres., chmn., chief exec. officer Variable Annuity Life Ins. Co., Houston, 1980-83; sr. v.p. Am. Gen. Corp., Houston, 1983-86; dean, prof. fin. Coll. Commerce U. Ill., Champaign, 1986-91; dean, prof. fin. and econs. Coll. Bus. Adminstrn. Ga. State U., Atlanta, 1991-97, prof. fin. and econs., 1998—2001, dean and prof. emeritus, 2002—. Bd. dirs. Sinfonia da Camera, Champaign, Ga. Coun. on Econ. Edn., Pvt. Industry Coun., World Trade Ctr., Atlanta; vis. prof. fin. Poznan (Poland) U. Econs., Caucasus Sch. Bus., Tbilisi, Georgia; cons. in field. Author: American Social Legislation, 1965, U.S. Balance of Payments and Capital Flows, 1967, School Revenue Studies, 1959, Fiscal Capacity of the State of Maine, 1958, American Social Legislation, 1973; editor: Dimensions of Productivity Research (2 vols.), 1981; contbr. articles to jours., abstracts to profl. meetings. Bd. dirs. Goodwill Industries, Columbus, 1972-76, chmn. capital fund drive, 1974-75; mem. Houston Com. on Fgn. Rels., 1980—, Chgo. Coun. on Fgn. Rels., 1986—, Chgo. com., 1987—; mem. dean's coun. Maxwell Grad. Sch., Syracuse U., 2003—. Served with U.S. Army, 1944-46, ETO; capt. (ret.) USAR. Maxwell fellow Syracuse U., 1950-52; recipient Best Article award Jur. Risk and Ins., Alumni Appreciation award U. Ill., 1991, 1964, Medal of Merit Poznan U., Poland, 1999; Maxwell Centennial lectr. Maxwell Grad. Sch., Syracuse U., 1970. Mem.: Inst. Rsch. in Econs. of Taxation (dir. 1984—), Nat. Tax Assn. (dir. 1981—85, treas., exec. com. 1988—2001), Nat. Assn. Bus. Economists, Inst. Mgmt. Scis., Am. Econ. Assn., Acad. Mgmt., Columbus C. of C. (chmn. econ. policy com. 1972—76), World Trade Club (Atlanta, bd. dirs. 1993—99), Columbus Athletic Club, Heritage Club (Houston), Commerce Club (Atlanta), Lincolnshire Fields Country Club (Champaign), Univ. Club (Chgo.), Beta Gamma Sigma, Phi Kappa Phi. Office: Ga State U Coll Bus Adminstrn Univ Plaza Atlanta GA 30303-3083 also: 3892 Byrnwyck Pl NE Atlanta GA 30319-1654

HOGAN, JOHN PAUL, chemistry researcher, consultant; b. Lowes, Kentucky, Aug. 7, 1919; s. Charles F. and Alma (Wyman) H.; m. Glenda M. (Moultrie), 1943; children: E. Fay, Hogan Sweney, Kenneth B., Susan G., Hogan Lair. Attended, U. Redlands, 1940-41; BS in Chemistry and physics, Murray State U., 1942, ScD (hon.), 1971. Tchr. Mayfield High Sch., Ky., 1942-43; physics instr. Okla. State U., Stillwater, 1943-44; rsch. chemist Phillips Petroleum Co., Bartlesville, Okla., 1944-48, group leader, 1948-60, polymer sci. sect. mgr., 1960-77, polymer sci. sr. research assoc., 1977-85, cons., 1985-86, Bartlesville, Okla., 1986—. Chmn. N.E. Okla. sect. Am. Chem. Soc., 1970. Patentee in field; contbg. chapters to books. Recipient Creative Invention Award, Am. Chem. Soc., 1969; Pioneer Chemists Award, 1972; Perkin medal, Soc. Chem. Industry, 1987; Heros in Chemistry Award Am. Chem. Soc., 1998; named Disting. Alumnus, Murray State U., 1972; Inventor of Yr., Okla. Bar Assn. Copyright and Patent Sect., 1976; Polymeric Materials Man of Yr., Soc. Plastics Engr., 1981; Paul Harris fellow Rotary Found., 2000; named to Hon. Order of Ky. Col., 1972; inductee Nat. Inventor Hall of Fame, 2001, Okla. Inventors Hall of Fame, 2002. Fellow Am. Inst. Chemists. Republican. Baptist. Avocations: Ch. work, fly fishing, chess, gardening. Home: 1049 S E Greystone Ave Bartlesville OK 74006-5010

HOGAN, JOHN W., JR., lawyer; b. New Haven, Conn., Feb. 22, 1939; BA, Coll. Holy Cross, 1961; JD, Conn. U., 1964. Bar: Conn. 1964. Sr. prin. Hogan & Rini, PC, New Haven. Mem. Nahley Mediation Panel, 1989—90; mng. trustee The David T. Langrock Found. Class gifts and bequests chair Coll. of the Holy Cross; chair New Haven Devel. Commn.; dir. The New Haven Regional Leadership Coun.; trustee Hosp. St. Raphael; dir., sec. and counsel The Found. of the Greater New Haven C. of C. and The Greater New Haven C. of C.; dir. Friends of Legal Svcs., New Haven; dir., sec. Shubert Performing Arts Ctr.; dir. The New Haven Land Trust; pres., dir. Vis. Nurse Assn. Greater New Haven. Recipient Citizen of Yr. award, Conn. Cts. of Probate, 1989. Mem.: Conn. Bar Assn. (clients' security fund 1973—91, ho. dels. 1978—83, exec. com. banking law sect. 1981—98, chair clients' security fund 1985—91, chair awards com. 1996—2000, v.p. 2001—02, pres.-elect 2002—03, pres. 2004, John Eldred Shields Meml. Disting. Profl. Svc. award). Office: Berchem Moses & Devlin PC 75 Broad St Milford CT 06460

HOGAN, JOSEPH M., health products executive; b. Mar. 7, 1957; m. Lisa Hogan; children: Tyler, Jason, Nicolas. BS in Bus. Adminstrn., Geneva Coll.; MBA, Robert Morris U., 1984. Sales, mktg. in plastics G.E., 1985—98; pres., CEO G.E. Fanuc Automation N. Am., 1998—2000; exec. v.p., COO G.E. Med. Sys., 2000; pres., CEO G.E. Healthcare Technologies, 2000—. Office: GE Medical Sys 3000 N Grandview Blvd Waukesha WI 53188*

HOGAN, MICHAEL, academic administrator; BA, U. No. Iowa; MA, PhD in History, U. Iowa. Chair dept. history Ohio State U., 1993—99, dean Coll. Humanities, 1999—2003, exec. dean Colls. Arts and Scis., 2001—04; provost U. Iowa, Iowa City, 2004—. Cons. in field. Author, editor: nine books; contbr. articles to profl. jours. Recipient Bernath Lecture prize, 1984; fellow, Harry S. Truman Libr. Inst., Woodrow Wilson Internat. Ctr. for Scholars. Office: Univ Iowa Office of the Provost 111 Jesup Hall Iowa City IA 52242

HOGAN, MICHAEL F., state official; married; 3 children. BA, Cornell U.; PhD, Syracuse U. With Mass. Dept. of Mental Health, 1976—84; dep. commr. Conn. Dept. of Mental Health, 1984—87, commr., 1987—91; dir. OH Dept. of Mental Health, 1991—; chair President's New Freedom Commn. on Mental Health, 2002—. Mem. Nat. Adv. Mental Health Coun., 1994—98, Nat. Assn. of State Mental Health Program Dirs. Rsch. Inst., 1989—99, pres. Mem.: McArthur Found. Network on Mental Health Policy Rsch. Office: OH Dept Mental Health 30 E Broad St 8th Fl Columbus OH 43215-3430

HOGAN, NEVILLE JOHN, mechanical engineering educator, consultant; b. Dublin, Feb. 11, 1949; came to U.S., 1970; s. Walter Henry and Edna Constance (Liller) H.; m. Sara Jane Seiden; children: Alexandra, Brian, Amanda, Victoria. Diploma in engring. with honors, Coll. Tech., Dublin, 1970; MS in Mech. Engring., MIT, 1973, mech. engring. degree, 1976, PhD in Mech. Engring., 1977; D (hon.), Tech. U. Delft, 1997, Dublin Inst. Tech., 2004. Product devel. and design engr. Donnelly Mirrors Ltd., Nass, Ireland, 1977-78; prof. MIT, Cambridge, 1978—; dir. Newman Lab., 1992—. Cons. in phys. systems modeling, design and control and in biomed. engring. Contbr. numerous articles to profl. jours. TRW Found. fellow, Whitaker Health Scis. Fund fellow; recipient Silver medal Royal Acad. Medicine, Ireland, 2004. Mem.: ASME, AAAS, Neural Control of Movement Soc., Soc. Neuroscience, Sigma Xi. Office Phone: 617-253-2277.

HOGAN, RANDALL J., manufacturing executive, electronics executive; BS in Civil Engring., MIT; MBA, U. Tex. Cons. McKinsey & Co.; with Gen. Electric; with Pratt & Whitney divsn. United Techs., pres. carrier transicold divsn.; exec. v.p. and pres. of elec. and elec. enclosures group Pentair, Inc., Golden Valley, Minn., 1998—99, pres. and COO, 1999—2001, pres. and CEO, 2001—02, chmn. and CEO, 2002—. Office: Pentair Inc Ste 800 5500 Wayzata Blvd Golden Valley MN 55416

HOGAN, ROBERT HENRY, trust company executive; b. N.Y.C., Apr. 12, 1926; s. Frederick Avertus and Carrie (Cronhardt) H.; m. Katherine Ann Wilkes, Feb. 9, 1957; children: Robert Wilkes, Mary Katherine, Margaret Ann, John William. Student, CCNY, 1943-44. Field rep. Moral Re-Armament, Inc., various locations, 1947-65, dir. N.Y.C., 1965-68; portfolio mgr. U.S. Trust Co., N.Y.C., 1969-72, asst. sec., 1972-78, asst. v.p., 1978-82, v.p., 1982-85, sr. v.p., 1985-2000. Mem. advisory bd. Uncommon Friends Found., Ft. Myers, Fla. M/Sgt. U.S. Army, 1944-46, ETO. Mem. CFA Inst. (formerly Assn. Investment Mgmt. and Rsch.), N.Y. Soc. Security Analysts. Republican. Episcopalian. Avocations: stamp collecting/philately, antiquarian books, fishing.

HOGAN, STEVEN L., lawyer; b. LA, Aug. 31, 1953; s. Kenneth Carlton Hogan and Ninon Michelle Kingsley; m. Debra Karen Garshfield, June 27, 1975; children: Rebecca Sarah, Cheryl Lee. AB magna cum laude, UCLA, 1975; JD, U. So. Calif., 1978. Bar: Calif. 1978, U.S. Ct. Appeals (9th cir.) 1979,U.S. Dist. Ct. (cen. dist.) Calif. 1979, U.S. Supreme Ct. 2000, U.S. Ct. Appeals (3d cir.) 2002, U.S. Dist. Ct. (so. dist., ea. dist., no. dist.) Calif. 1985. Assoc. Anderson, McPharlin & Conners, L.A., 1978-80; ptnr. Bryan Cave, L.A., 1980-95; shareholder Lurie, Zepeda, Schmalz & Hogan, Beverly Hills, CA, 1995—. Mem. Los Angeles County Bar Assn., Order of Coif, Phi Beta Kappa, Phi Gamma Mu. Office: Lurie Zepeda Schmalz & Hogan 9107 Wilshire Blvd Ste 800 Beverly Hills CA 90210-5533 Office Phone: 310-274-8700. Business E-Mail: shogan@lurie-zepeda.com.

HOGAN, TERRENCE JAMES, academic administrator, consultant; b. Cleve., May 22, 1955; s. Joseph Patrick and Mary Catherine Hogan; m. Deborah Susan Haas, Feb. 18, 1955; children: Connor O'Rourke, Olivia Haas. BSc in Radio/TV, Ohio U., 1977, MA in Orgnl. Comm., 1983, PhD in Higher Edn., 1992. Dean of students Ohio U., Athens, 1998—2004, sr. assoc. v.p., dean of students, 2004—. Bd. dirs. N.Am. Interfraternal Found., Indpls. Exec. officer, mem. Athens Civitan Club, 1986—95; chair, vol. O'Bleness Hosp. Fund Dr., Athens, 2001—04; mem. Team Athens County, 1999; exec. officer, mem. HAVAR, Inc., Athens, 1985—2001, Athens Youth Hockey Assn., 1995—2001. Named Disting. Pres., Civitan Internat., 1992; grantee Internat. Student Vol. Program, Nat. Assoc for Fgn. Student Affairs, 1990, Appalachian Access, Corp. for Nat. and Cmty. Svc., 1993—96, Integrating Service-Learning, Ohio U. Found. 1804 Fund, 1993, Ohio AppalCorps AmeriCorps Program, Corp. for Nat. Svc., 1996—99, Monday Creek Restoration Project, Ohio Campus Compact, 1996, HealthCorps, Corp. for Nat. Svc., 1996, Learn and Serve Ohio U., 1997—99. Mem.: Am. Coun. on Edn., Am. Assn. for Higher Edn., Am. Coll. Pers. Assn., Nat. Assn. Student Pers. Administrators (nat. chair fraternity/sorority affairs knowledge cmty. 2002—04). Avocations: golf, basketball, youth sports. Home: 30 Elmwood Pl Athens OH 45701 Office: Ohio University 202 Baker Univ Center Athens OH 45701 Office Phone: 740-593-1800. Office Fax: 740-593-0223. Personal E-mail: hogan@ohio.edu.

HOGAN, THOMAS FRANCIS, federal judge; b. Washington, May 31, 1938; s. Bartholomew W. and Grace (Gloninger) H.; m. Martha Lou Wyrick, July 16, 1966; 1 son, Thomas Garth. AB, Georgetown U., 1960, JD, 1966; postgrad., George Washington U., 1960-62. Bar: Md. 1966, U.S. Dist. Ct. D.C. 1967, D.C. 1967, U.S. Ct. Appeals (D.C. cir.) 1972, U.S. Dist. Ct. Md. 1973, U.S. Supreme Ct. 1973. Law clk. to presiding judge US Dist. Ct. DC, 1966-67; counsel Nat. Commn. on Reform of Fed. Criminal Laws, Washington, 1967-68; ptnr. McCarthy & Wharton, Rockville, Md., 1968-75, Kenary, Tietz & Hogan, Rockville, 1975-81, Furey, Doolan, Abell & Hogan, Chevy Chase, Md., 1981-82; judge US Dist. Ct. DC, Washington, 1982—2001, chief judge, 2001—. Asst. prof. Potomac Sch. Law, Washington, 1977-79; adj. prof. law Georgetown Law Ctr., 1985—; mem. U.S. Jud. Conf., 2001—, mem. specialties com., 2001—. Pub. mem. Officer Evaluation Bd. U.S. Fgn. Service, 1973; chmn. Christ Child Inst. for Disturbed Children, 1975; bd. dirs. Providence Hosp., Washington, 1984-86. Recipient cert. recognition and appreciation for vol. services Montgomery County Govt., 1976; recipient cert. appreciation Christ Child Soc., 1976; St. Thomas More fellow Georgetown U. Law Ctr., 1965-66 Mem. ABA (Md. chmn. Drug Abuse Edn. Program, Young Lawyers sect. 1970-73, mem. Litigation sect.), Bar Assn. D.C. (mem. com. on D.C. cts.), Md. State Bar Assn. (Litigatin sect.), Montgomery County Bar Assn. (chmn. legal ethics com. 1973-74, lawyer referral service com. 1974-75, adminstrn. justice com. 1979-82, bd. govs. 1977-78), Nat. Inst. for Trial Advocacy Assocs., Def. Research Inst., Md. Assn. Def. Trial Counsel, Md. Trial Lawyers Assn., Georgetown U. Alumni Assn., Smithsonian Assocs., John Carroll Soc., Knights of Malta. Clubs: Barristers, Chevy Chase, Lawyers. Office Phone: 202-354-3420.*

HOGAN-CROSS, CINDY, computer engineer; d. Ed Hogan and Jeannie White; m. Adam Cross, June 23, 2001; children: Holly Biernacki, Heidi Biernacki. BS, Tex. Woman's U., Denton, 1989—96. Tech. support rep. IBM, Dallas, 1989—96; software engr. BancTec Inc., 1996—2000, IBM, 2000—.

HOGANS, MACK L., paper company executive; BS in Forestry, U. Mich.; MS in Forest Resources, U. Wash. Forester, govt. affairs mgr. Weyerhaeuser Co., Tacoma, Wash., 1979-90, v.p. govt. affairs, 1990-95, sr. v.p. corp. affairs, 1995—. Chair Weyerhaeuser Co. Found.; bd. dirs. Wash. Coun. Internat. Trade. Bd. dirs. U. Puget Sound, Zion Preparatory Acad., Pub. Affairs Coun., Discovery Inst., Nature Conservancy. Office: Weyerhaeuser Co PO Box 9777 Federal Way WA 98063-9777

HOGBERG, CARL GUSTAV, retired metal products executive; b. Escanaba, Mich., July 19, 1913; s. Claus Emil and Anna C. (Franson) H.; m. June Loraine Evans, June 10, 1935 (dec. Aug. 1991); children: David K., Janet H. (Mrs. Nicholas A. Matwiyoff). BS in Metall. Engring., Mich. Coll. Mining and Tech., 1935; DEng (hon.), Mich. Tech. U., 1968. Blast-furnace apprentice South Chgo. works Carnegie-Ill. Steel Corp., 1935, various operating positions blast-furnace dept., 1935—38, sec. blast-furnace and coke-oven com. Pitts., 1939—41; asst. chmn. blast-furnace com. U.S. Steel Corp., Pitts., 1942—54; asst. to v.p. Mich. Limestone divsn., Detroit, 1955, asst. v.p., 1956, v.p., 1957—60, pres., 1960—63, v.p. raw materials svc., parent co., 1964; pres. Orinoco Mining Co. subs., Caracas, Venezuela, 1965—70; v.p. internat. U.S. Steel Corp., 1970—73; ret., 1973. Contbr. tech. articles to trade publs. Mem. AIME (J.E. Johnson, Jr. award 1945), Assn. Iron and Steel Inst., Ea. Western States Blast Furnace and Coke Assns. Home: 263 Norman Dr Cranberry Township PA 16066-4205

HOGE, FRANZ JOSEPH, accounting firm executive; b. N.Y.C., Apr. 2, 1944; s. Albert and Sophie (Hutter) H.; m. Margaret Ann Hoefling, Oct. 11, 1969; children: Joanne Curoe, Susan Glennon, Daniel. BBA, CCNY, 1966. CPA, N.Y., Ohio. Staff acct. Coopers and Lybrand, N.Y.C., 1968-70, in-charge acct., 1970-73, mgr., 1973-77, ptnr., 1977-80, mng. ptnr. Dayton, Ohio, 1980-97, Ohio unit leader, 1993-97, middle market industry leader, 1993-97; ret., 1997. Chmn. bus. adv. bd. Wright State U., 1986-2001, Dayton Pub. Schs.; chmn. bd. The Fund for Dayton Urban Children and Schs., 1997-2003; bd. dirs. Nat. Ctr. Indsl. Competitiveness, Premier Health Ptnrs., Athenaeum of Ohio; chmn. bd. Good Samaritan Hosp., 1989-99, chmn. Montgomery County Human Svc. Levy Coun., 2001—. Co-author two audit and acctg. guides, 1978, 79. Bd. dirs. Dayton Mus. Natural History, pres. 1983-90, Dayton Opera Assn., pres. 1983-92, Maria Joseph Living Care Ctr., chmn.

1984-95; chmn. bd. dirs. NCCJ, 1999-2002, chmn., Kettering Children's Choir; v.p. Assn. for Corp. Growth, Hipple Cancer Rsch. Ctr., Dayton, 1981-87, Big Bros./Big Sisters Found., Dayton, 1983-87, Dayton Performing Arts Fund, 1983-87; bd. dirs. Wright State U. Found., 1996-2001 Named Montgomery County Citizen of the Yr. 2003. Mem. Moraine Country Club. Republican. Roman Catholic. Home: 939 Laurelwood Rd Dayton OH 45419-1228 E-mail: hoge939@msn.com.

HOGE, WARREN M., editor; b. NYC, Apr. 13, 1941; s. James F. Hoge and Virginia (McClamroch) Barber; m. Olivia Larisch, Nov. 21, 1981; 1 child, Nicholas; stepchildren: Christina, Tatjana. BA, Yale U., 1963; postgrad., George Washington U., 1964-65. Reporter Washington Star, 1964-66; bur. chief N.Y. Post, Washington, 1966-69, city editor, asst. mng. editor N.Y.C., 1970-75; dep. met. editor N.Y. Times, N.Y.C., 1976-78, fgn. corr. Rio de Janeiro, 1979-83, fgn. editor N.Y.C., 1984-87, asst. mng. editor, 1987-90; asst. mng. editor and editor N.Y. Times Mag., N.Y.C., 1991-92, asst. mng. editor for culture, style, book rev., and recruitment of writers, 1993-96; chief London Bur., N.Y. Times, 1996—2003; fgn. affairs corr. UN, N.Y.C., 2004—. Baptist. Home: 325 East 57 New York NY 10022 Office: NY Times Fgn Desk 229 W 43rd New York NY 10036

HOGEN, KATHRYN ANN, secondary school educator; b. Milw., Mar. 21, 1952; d. Darell George Anthony and Genevieve Kathryn Hilleshiem; m. Richard Orvin Hogen, May 30, 1975; children: Kristina Kathryn Schwartz, John Richard. AA, Mesa C.C., 1973; BA, Ariz. State U., 1975; M, No. Ariz. U., 1992. Tchr. home econs. McClintock High Sch., Tempe, Ariz., 1977—78, Seton Cath. Sch., Chandler, 1978—79, Marcos de Niza High Sch., Tempe, 1979—86, Tempe High Sch., 1985, Corona del Sol High Sch., Tempe, 1985; tchr. specialist/family and consumer sci. Hendrix Jr. High Sch., Mesa, 1985—. Mem.: ASCD, Nat. Sci. Tchrs. Assn. Democrat. Roman Catholic. Office: Hendrix Jr High Sch 1550 W Summit Pl Chandler AZ 85224

HOGEN-ESCH, THIEO E., chemistry professor; b. Terneuzen, The Netherlands, Feb. 22, 1936; came to U.S., 1968; s. Jan Jogen-Esch and Elisabeth Wietje Roelofs; m. Chryl E. McCafferty, Nov. 19, 1966 (div. 1991); children: John, Thomas, Christopher. BSc, Leiden State U., The Netherlands, 1958, MSc, 1961, PhD, 1967. Adv. technologist Shell, Rotterdam, The Netherlands, 1966-68; postdoctoral SUNY, Syracuse, 1968-70; asst. prof. chemistry U. Fla., Gainesville, 1970-75, assoc. prof. chemistry, 1975-79, prof. chemistry, 1979-88, U. So. Calif., L.A., 1988—. Vis. prof., U. Bordeaux, France, 1991. Editor: Recent Advances in Anionic Polymerization, 1987; contbr. 200 articles to profl. chem. and polymer jours.; mem. editl. bd., Polymer Internat., 1997—, Designed Monomers and Polymers, 1997—. Fellow Japanese Soc. Advancement of Sci.; mem. AAAS, Am. Chem. Soc.

HOGENKAMP, HENRICUS PETRUS CORNELIS, biochemistry researcher, educator; b. Doesburg, Gelderland, The Netherlands, Dec. 20, 1925; came to U.S., 1958; s. Johannes Hermanus and Maria Margaretha J. (Abeln) H.; m. Lieke Ter Haar, Apr. 25, 1953; children: Harry Peter, Derk John, Margaret Angelina. BSA, U. B.C., Vancouver, 1957, MSc, 1958; PhD, U. Calif., Berkeley, 1961. Rsch. biochemist U. Calif., Berkeley, 1961—62; assoc. scientist Fisheries Rsch. Bd. Can., Vancouver, 1962—63; asst. prof. U. Iowa, Iowa City, 1963—67, assoc. prof., 1967—71, prof., 1971—76; prof., head dept. biochemistry U. Minn., Mpls., 1976—92, prof. dept. biochemistry, 1992—2002, prof. emeritus, 2002. Vis. prof. Australian Nat. U., Canberra, Australia, 1966-67, Philipps U., Marburg, Fed. Republic of Germany, 1986-87, 1988, 1990; guest scientist U. Calif. Los Alamos (N.Mex) Sci. Lab., 1974-75. Sgt. Royal Netherlands Army, 1946-50, Indonesia. Recipient Alexander von Humboldt-Stiftung award Philipps U.-Fachbereich Microbiology, Marburg, Fed. Republic of Germany, 1986-87; named to Minn. Acad. Medicine,Mpls., 1980-; Guggenheim fellow U. Iowa, Iowa City, 1974-75. Mem. Am. Chem. Soc., Am. Soc. Biochemistry and Molecular Biology (mem. pub. affairs com. 1986-91), Assn. Med. Sch. Depts. Biochemistry, Internat. Union Biochemists (chmn. U.S. nominating com. 1988). Home: 2211 Marion Rd Saint Paul MN 55113-3805 Office: U Minn BMBB Dept Ste 6-155 321 Church St SE Minneapolis MN 55455 Office Phone: 612-625-4471.

HOGFOSS, ROBERT E., lawyer; b. Glenwood, Minn., Jan. 15, 1952; BA, Univ. Chgo., 1980; JD, Lewis & Clark Univ., 1986. Law clk., Hon. Diarmuid F. O'Scannlain 9th Cir. Ct. of Appeals, 1986—87; ptnr., Resources, Regulatory, Environ. Law Hunton & Williams LLP, Atlanta, and mem. exec. com. Articles editor Environ. Law Rev., Lewis & Clark Univ., 1986. Named one of top Ga. Environ./Land Use Super Lawyers, Atlanta Mag., 2004, Ga. Super Lawyers Mag., 2005. Mem.: ABA, State Bar Ga. Office: Hunton & Williams Bank of Am Plz Ste 4100 600 Peachtree St NE Atlanta GA 30308-2216 Office Phone: 404-888-4042. Office Fax: 404-888-4195. Business E-Mail: rhogfoss@hunton.com.

HOGG, DAVID CLARENCE, physicist; b. Vanguard, Sask., Can., Sept. 5, 1921; came to U.S., 1953, naturalized, 1964; s. Francis Sandison and Frances Katherine (Gadsby) H.; m. Jean E. MacMillan, Feb. 15, 1947; children—David Randal, Rebecca Jean. BSc, U. Western Ont. (Can.), London, 1949; MSc, McGill U., Montreal, Que., Can., 1951, PhD, 1953. With Bell Telephone Labs., 1953-77, head atmospheric physics research, 1966-72, head antenna and propagation research Holmdel, N.J., 1972-77; chief environ. radiometry wave propagation lab. Environ. Research Lab., NOAA, Boulder, Colo., 1977-83, chief radio meteorology, 1983-86; lectr., adj. prof. U. Colo., Boulder, 1984—, lectr. ECE dept, 1989—; sr. scientist Colo. Inst. Research Environ. Scis., U. Colo., Boulder, 1986-89. Research, numerous publs. on microwaves, optics, satellite communications and remote sensing; patentee microwave antennas; composer vocal, choral, strings and piano classical music. Served with Can. Army, 1940-45. Recipient Silver medal U.S. Dept. Commerce, 1983, Composer's award Colo. Music Educators Assn., 1992. Fellow IEEE (founder Jersey Coast sect., Disting. Achievement award 1984); mem. NAE, Union Radio Scientifique Internat., Am. Music Ctr. Episcopalian. Home: 4978 Carter Ct Boulder CO 80301-3895 Office Phone: 303-530-3770.

HOGG, JAMES HENRY, JR., retired education educator; b. Pleasantville, Pa., Aug. 15, 1926; s. James Henry and Carrie Ethel (Swan) H.; m. Elizabeth Beatrice George, Sept. 8, 1945 (dec. Feb. 1988); children: Carolyn Elizabeth, James Henry III; m. Reva Rowene Heffernan, Jan. 1, 1992. BA, Houghton Coll., 1951; MA, Allegheny Coll., 1961; EdD, Pa. State U., 1971. Cert. secondary tchr., Pa. Tchr. English and social studies Meadville (Pa.) Sr. H.S., 1962-67; instr. in secondary edn. Pa. State U., University Park, 1968-71, asst. prof., 1971-77, assoc. prof., 1977-91; ret., 1991. Trustee Houghton Coll., 1964-67; Pa. State Adv. Bd., Mid. States Assn. Colls. and Schs., 1984-91 (chmn. evaluation teams, 1983-91). Contbr. articles to profl. jours. Councilman Cooperstown Borough, 1993-98, 2000—. With U.S. Army, 1944-46, ETO. Named participant in 2d Inst. Am History Pa. State U., 1966, Assn. Tchr. Educators LaureATE, 1989; recipient cert. of appreciation U.S. House Reps. Page Sch., 1985. Mem. Nat. Assn. Tchr. Educators, Pa. Assn. Tchr. Educators, Phi Delta Kappa, Alpha Tau. Republican. Methodist. Avocations: hunting, fishing, bowling, chess. Home: 148 Lakeview Dr Cooperstown PA 16317 E-mail: jameshg@csonline.net.

HOGG, JAMES STUART, lawyer; b. N.Y.C., Aug. 5, 1952; s. John S. and Rosalie (Smith) H.; m. Kathleen Anne Rhoades, May 20, 1978; children: John S., Robert W., Elizabeth A. BA, Kalamazoo Coll., 1974; JD, U. Mich., 1977. Bar: N.Y. 1978, Ohio 1985. Assoc. Brown, Wood, Ivey, Mitchell & Petty, N.Y.C., 1977-80, Carter, Ledyard & Milburn, N.Y.C., 1980-83; sr. counsel The Standard Oil Co., Cleve., 1983-87; asst. gen. counsel GenCorp Inc., Fairlawn, Ohio, 1987-88; v.p. law GenCorp Automotive, Akron, Ohio, 1989-93; of counsel Ulmer & Berne, LLP, Cleve., 1994-96; prin. Cowden, Humphrey, Nagorney & Lovett Co., L.P.A., Cleve., 1996—. Mem. ABA, Cleve. Bar Assn., Ohio Bar Assn. Republican. Episcopalian. Avocations: golf, tennis. Office: Cowden Humphrey Nagorney & Lovett Co LPA 1414 Terminal Tower Cleveland OH 44113 E-mail: jamie@cowdenlaw.com.

HOGG, JESSE STEPHEN, lawyer; b. Whitesburg, Ky., Dec. 24, 1931; s. Doyle and Crystal (Eversole) H.; m. Lorella Joyce Graham, Jan. 26, 1957 (div. 1978); children: Laura Ellen, Stephen Graham. BSBA, Morehead State U., 1953; JD, U. Ky., 1958. Bar: Ky. 1958, Fla. 1962, U.S. Dist. Ct. (no., middle and so. dists.) Fla., U.S. Ct. Appeals (2d, 4th, 5th, 6th, 11th cirs.), U.S. Supreme Ct. Pvt. practice, Winchester, Ky., 1958-62; assoc. Fowler, White, Collins, Gillan, Humkey and Trenam, Tampa, Fla., 1962-65, ptnr., 1965-68, head dept. labor law, 1968-69; sr. ptnr. Hogg, Allen, Ryce, Norton and Blue P.A., various locations, Fla., 1969—2000, Hogg, Ryce & Spencer, Coral Gables, Fla., 2000—. Served with U.S. Army, 1954-55. Mem. ABA (lab law sect. 1962—), Fla. Bar Assn. (labor law com. 1962—), Ky. Bar Assn. Clubs: Cocoplum Yacht Club. Republican. Avocations: golf, boating, sport fishing. Home: 7701 Erwin Rd Miami FL 33143-6249 Office: Hogg et al 7701 Erwin Rd Miami FL 33143 Office Phone: 305-665-5526. Personal E-mail: jayessh@aol.com.

HOGG, JUDITH E., neurologist, educator; b. Binghamton, N.Y. d. Edwin Charles and Virginia Anne (Pettinato) H. AB, MD, Boston U., 1970. Diplomate Am. Bd. Psychiatry and Neurology. Intern Lenox Hill Hosp., N.Y.C., 1970-71, resident in internal medicine, 1971-72; resident in neurology Mt. Sinai Hosp., N.Y.C., 1972-75; pvt. practice, 1975-77; neuro-epidemiology rschr. NIH, Bethesda, Md., 1977-79; asst. clin. prof. neurology George Washington U., Washington, 1979-88; staff neurologist Santa Clara Valley Med. Ctr., San Jose, Calif., 1988-91; assoc. prof. sch. medicine Tex. Tech. U., Lubbock, 1991-98; pvt. practice, 1998—. Mem. AMA, Greenville County Med. Soc., Am. Acad. Neurology, Am. Assn. Electrodiagnostic Medicine (assoc.), Phi Beta Kappa.

HOGG, RICHARD, process engineer; b. Redcar, England, Jan. 6, 1938; married. BSc, U. Leeds, 1963; MS, U. Calif., Berkeley, 1965; PhD in Mineral Tech., U. Calif., 1970. From asst. prof. to assoc. prof. Pa. State U., 1969-79, prof. mineral processing, 1979-2000, prof. emeritus mineral processing and geo-environ. engring., 2000—. Asst. specialist mineral tech. U.Calif., Berkeley, 1966-69; mem. com. Comminution & Energy Consumption NAS, 1978-80. Recipient Antoine M. Gaudin award Soc. for Mining, 1994, Metallurgy & Exploration, 1994, Arthur F. Taggart award, 1997. Mem.: Am. Fitration & Separations Soc., AIME. Achievements include research in fundamental basis of mineral processing operations; colloid and surface chemistry; mixing, segregation and flow of particulate solid materials; fine grinding processes. Office: Pa State Univ Mineral Procg Sect 213 Hosler Bldg University Park PA 16802-5000 Address: 1232 S Garner St State College PA 16801-6326 E-mail: rxh19@psu.edu.

HOGG, ROBERT VINCENT, JR., mathematical statistician, educator; b. Hannibal, Mo., Nov. 8, 1924; s. Robert Vincent and Isabelle Frances (Storrs) H.; m. Carolyn Joan Ladd, June 23, 1956 (dec. June 1990); children: Mary Carolyn, Barbara Jean, Allen Ladd, Robert Mason; m. Ann Burke, Oct. 15, 1994. BA, U. Ill., 1947; MS, U. Iowa, 1948, PhD, 1950. Asst. prof. math. U. Iowa, Iowa City, 1950-56, assoc. prof., 1956-62, prof., 1962-65, chmn. dept. stats., prof. stats., 1965-83, 92-93, Hanson prof. mfg. productivity, 1993-95, prof. emeritus, 2001—. Co-author: Introduction to Mathematical Statistics, 1959, 6th edit., 2005, Finite Mathematics and Calculus, 1974, Probability and Statistical Inference, 1977, 7th edit., 2005, Applied Statistics for Engineers and Physical Scientists, 1987, 2d edit., 1992; assoc. editor Am. Stats., 1971-74; contbr. articles to profl. jours. Vestryman local Episc. ch., 1958-60, 66-68, 91-92, 2001-03. With USNR, 1943-46. Grantee NIH, 1966-68, 75-78, NSF, 1969-74; Disting. Alumni Award, U. Iowa, 2003. Fellow Inst. Math. Stats. (program sec., bd. 1968-74), Am. Statis. Assn. (pres. Iowa sect. 1962-63, coun. 1965-66, 73-74, vis. lectr. 1965-68, 77-85, chmn. tng. sect. 1973, assoc. editor jour. 1978-80, pres.-elect 1987, pres. 1988, past pres. 1989, Founders award 1991, Noether award 2001); mem. Math. Assn. Am. (pres. Iowa sect. 1964-65, 95-96, bd. govs. 1971-74, visa. lectr. 1976-81, Outstanding Tchg. award 1993), Internat. Statis. Inst., Rotary (pres. Iowa City 1984-85), Sigma Xi (pres. Iowa dist. chpt. 1970-71), Pi Kappa Alpha. Home: 30130 Trails End Buena Vista CO 81211 Office: U Iowa Dept Statis Acturial Sci Iowa City IA 52242 E-mail: bhogg@starband.net.

HOGG, STACY LORENE, elementary school educator; b. Joplin, Mo., June 8, 1963; d. John Orbin Delmont Jr. and Eleanor Mae (Fry) Moncrief. Student, Northeastern Okla. A&M Coll., 1982; BS in Edn., Pittsburg (Kans.) State U., 1986; MA in Ednl. Adminstrn., Calif. Luth. U., 1992. Elem. tchr. Bakersfield (Calif.) City Sch. Dist., 1986-91, Panama Buena Vista Union Sch. Dist., 1991—. Joyce and George Hudiburg scholar, 1986. Mem. Kappa Delta Pi (scholar 1986). Avocations: reading, bicycle riding. Home: 19620 Brimhall Rd Bakersfield CA 93314 Office: PBVUSD 4200 Ashe Rd Bakersfield CA 93313

HOGGARD, LARA GULDMAR, conductor, educator; b. Kingston, Okla., Feb. 9, 1915; s. Calvin Peter and Eva Lillian (Smith) H.; m. Mildred Mae Teeter, Sept. 11, 1943; 1 dau., Susan. BA, Southea. Tchrs. Coll., 1934; MA, Columbia U., 1940, EdD, 1947. Supr. music Durant (Okla.) Pub. Schs., 1934-39; dir. choral activities, opera and oratorio U. Okla., 1940-43; assoc. founder, prin. instr. Waring Summer Choral Workshops, 1948-52; co-editor Shawnee Press, Del. Water Gap, Pa., 1946-52; dir. music and music edn. rsch. Indian Springs Sch., Ala. Edn. Found., Birmingham, 1955-60; founder Nat. Young Artist Competition, Midland-Odessa, 1962—; William Rand Kenan prof. music U. N.C., Chapel Hill, 1967-80, founder Carolina Choir, 1967—; founder N.C. Collegiate Choral Festival, 1969—; Fuller E. Callaway prof. music Columbus Coll., U. Ga., 1981-82. Condr. NBC-USN Navy Hour, 1945, assoc. condr. Waring's Pennsylvanians, 1946—52, condr., dir. (nat. touring concert group) Civic Music and Nat. Concert Artists Corp., Festival of Song, 1952—53; dir.: N.C. Summer Insts. in Choral Art, 1953—83; founder, condr., musical dir. Midland-Odessa (Tex.) Symphony Orch. and Chorale, 1962—67, condr. numerous music festivals, Am., Europe, artistic dir., prin. condr. Festival of Three Cities, Vienna-Budapest-Prague, 1973, Internat. Jugendmusikfest in Wien, 1973, 1974, guest lectr. and condr. univs. and conservatories in Am. and Europe, condr. several music premieres, including Behold the Glory (Talmage Dean) with Louisville Orch., 1964, Light in the Wilderness (Dave Brubeck), Chapel Hill, 1968, new edit. Ein deutsches Requiem (Brahms) with N.C. Symphony, 1986, numerous others; author: Improving Music Reading, 1947, Exploring Music, 1967; editor: an oratorio Light in the Wilderness (Dave Brubeck), 1968; composer, arranger, editor 37 choral publs.; editor: new English transl. and corr. orch. score and parts Ein deutsches Requiem (Brahms), 1983—89; composer: Le Jongleur, 1951. Served to lt. (j.g.) USN, 1943-45, PTO. Recipient award for outstanding svc. to music in Ala., Ala. Fine Arts Festival, 1958, citation for outstanding svc. to fine arts in Tex., Tex. Senate and Gov., West Texan award, 1967, Tanner award U. N.C., 1972, Ten Best Profs. award, 1978, Order Long Leaf Pine Gov. N.C., 1980, Disting. Alumnus award Southeastern Okla. State U., 1981, Lara G. Hoggard endowed professorship named in his honor U. N.C., 1993. Mem. Music Educators Nat. Conf. (life; Master Builder), Am. Choral Dirs. Assn. (life, award for contbn. to music in N.C. 1976, citation for contbn. to music in Am., divsn. 5, 1986, award for excellence and lifelong commitment So. divsn. 1998), AAUP, N.C. Music Educators Assn. (hon. life), N.C. Lit. Soc. (life), Rotary, Phi Mu Alpha Sinfonia (nat. hon. life). Democrat. Presbyterian. Office Phone: 919-544-4062. *Creativity within the individual is our best weapon against total conformity and robotism. The arts challenge and elevate both the intellect and the spirit. Sensitivity and respect for the true, the good and the beautiful, stand in defiance of three attitudes which must not prevail, if civilization is to survive:- bigotry, arrogant ignorance, and acceptance or approval of mediocrity.*

HOGLE, ANN MEILSTRUP, painter, art educator; b. San Francisco, Sept. 23, 1927; d. Carlton Fredrick Meilstrup and Lillian (Hackney) Meilstrup Willer; m. Richard Raymond (div.); children— Timothy, Megan, Catherine; m. George H. Hogle, Aug. 29, 1966. Student U. Oreg., 1945-47, Marylhurst Coll., 1949-50; B.F.A., Calif. Coll. of Arts and Crafts, 1976, M.F.A., 1978. One-person shows include Stanford U., Calif., 1966, Palo Alto Cultural Ctr., Calif., 1976, William Sawyer Gallery, San Francisco, Butters Gallery, Portland, 1993, Menlo Pk. Libr., Menlo Pk., Calif., 1994, Smith Andersen Gallery, Palo Alto Calif., 1995, Bolinas Gallery, Bolinas, Calif., 1995, de Saisset Mus., Santa Clara, Calif., 1998, Fresno Art Mus., Fresno, Calif., 1998, Vorpal Gallery, San Francisco, 1999, Commonweal, Bolinas, Calif., 1999, John Natsoulas Gallery, Davis, Calif., 2001, guest artist Marin Agricultural Land Trust, Point Reyes Sta., Calif., 2003; exhibited in group shows at Portland Art Mus., Janus Gallery, Los Angeles, Richmond Art Ctr., William Sawyer Gallery, San Francisco, 84, Purdue U., Ind., Penninsula Mus., Monterey, Calif., 1993; represented in permanent collections Kemper Ins. Cos., St. Francis Meml. Hosp., Dysan Corp., First Interstate Bank. Portland Mus. Recipient Phelan awards exhibit Legion of Honor, 1965. Personal E-mail: ghogle711@earthlink.net. Business E-Mail: hogle@artistforum.com.

HOGLUND, J. DAVID, architectural firm executive; b. 1964; BArch, U. Ill. Ptnr. Perkins Eastman Archs. PC, Pitts. Author: Housing for the Elderly: Privacy and Independence, 1997; co-author: Building Type Basics for Senior Living, 2004. Fellow: AIA (pres. Pitts. (Pa.) chpt.). Office: Perkins Eastman Architects PC 1100 Liberty Ave Pittsburgh PA 15222

HOGNESS, JOHN RUSTEN, internist, educator, academic administrator; b. Oakland, Calif., June 27, 1922; s. Thorfin R. and Phoebe (Swenson) Hogness. Student, Haverford Coll., 1939—42, DSc (hon.), 1973; BS, U. Chgo., 1943, MD, 1946; DSc (hon.), Med. Coll. Ohio at Toledo, 1972; LLD, George Washington U., 1973; DLitt, Thomas Jefferson U., 1980. Diplomate Am. Bd. Internal Medicine. Intern Presbyn. Hosp., N.Y.C., 1946—47, asst. resident, 1949—50; chief resident King County Hosp., Seattle, 1950—51; asst. U. Wash. Sch. Medicine, 1950—52, Am. Heart Assn. research fellow, 1951—52, mem. faculty, 1954—64, prof. medicine, 1964—71, med. dir. univ. hosp., 1958—63, dean, chmn. bd. health scis., 1964—69, exec. v.p., 1969—70; dir. Health Scis. Ctr., 1970—71; pres. Inst. Medicine, Nat. Acad. Scis., 1971—74; prof. medicine George Washington U., 1972—74; pres. U. Wash., Seattle, 1974—79, pres. emeritus, 1979—, prof. medicine, 1974—79; pres. Assn. Acad. Health Ctrs., 1979—88. Disting. professorial lectr. dept. medicine Georgetown U., 1983—88; prof. U. Wash. Sch. Pub. Health, 1989—92; provost Hahnemann U., 1992—93; commr.'s adv. com. on exempt orgns. IRS, 1969—71; adv. com. for environ. scis. NSF, 1970—71; adv. com. to dir. NIH, 1970—71; mem. Nat. Cancer Adv. Bd., 1972—76, Nat. Sci. Bd., 1976—82; selection com. for Rockefeller pub. svc. awards Princeton U., 1976—82; chmn. med. injury compensation study steering com. Inst. Medicine NAS, chmn. com. to evaluate the artificial heart, 1990—91; council for biol. scis. U. Chgo. Pritzker Sch. Medicine, 1977—89; chmn. adv. panel on cost-effectiveness of med. techs. Office Tech. Assessment, U.S. Congress, 1978—80; chmn. study sect. for health care tech. assessment Nat. Ctr. for Health Svcs. Rsch. and Health Care Tech. Assessment, 1985—88; pres. Sun Valley Forum on Nat. Health, 1986—94; dir. Inst. for Health Policy Edn. and Rsch., U. Tex. Health Sci. Ctr., Houston, 1988; council health care tech. HEW; adv. panel for study fin. grad. med. edn. Dept. Health and Human Svcs., 1980—87. Contbr. articles to profl. jours. Trustee Case Western Res. U., 1972—73. With U.S. Army, 1947—49. Recipient Disting. Svc. award, Med. Alumni Assn. U. Chgo., 1966, Profl. Achievement award, Alumni Assn. U. Chgo., 1973, Convocation medal, Am. Coll. Cardiology, 1973, Cartwright medal, Columbia U. Coll. Physicians and Surgeons, 1978, Carel C. Koch Meml. award, Am. Acad. Optometry, 1986; Centennial scholar, Johns Hopkins U., 1976. Master: ACP (regent 1987—2000); fellow: AAAS, Am. Acad. Arts and Scis. (v.p. 2001—04); mem.: Assn. Am. Med. Colls., Assn. Am. Physicians, Assn. Am. Med. Colls. (chmn.-elect coun. of deans 1968—69, exec. coun.), Assn. Am. Physicians, Inst. Medicine NAS, Alpha Omega Alpha.

HOGUE, JOE R., music company executive, composer; b. Plant City, Fla., May 9, 1965; s. Joseph Randolph and Nancy Lee Hogue; life ptnr. Sean R. Petersen; 1 child, Caden Joseph. Prodr. Joe Hogue Prodn., Sun Valley, Calif., 1986—. Composer 615 Prodn., Nashville, 1993—97; ptnr. THC Entertainment LLC, Franklin, Tenn., 1997—2001. Composer (prodr.): (theme) A&E Biography (Emmy award, 1995); prodr.(writer): (musical recording) DCTalk Free At Last (Grammy award, RIAA cert. Platinum, 1991); musician (arranger): (album) Handel's Soulful Messiah (Grammy award, 1992); prodr.: (compilation recording) Generation to Generation (GMA Dove award), (musical recording) Carman's Addicted To Jesus (RIAA cert. Gold, 1991). Mem.: Am. Fedn. Musicians (assoc.). D-Liberal. Avocations: music, movies, swimming. Home: 9966 Roscoe Blvd Sun Valley CA 91352 Office: Joe Hogue Prodn 9966 Roscoe Blvd Sun Valley CA 91352 Office Phone: 818-653-7800. Personal E-mail: jojoho@aol.com.

HOGWOOD, CHRISTOPHER JARVIS HALEY, music educator; b. Nottingham, Eng., Sept. 10, 1941; s. Haley Evelyn and Marion Constance (Higgott) Hogwood. BA, Cambridge (Eng.) U., 1964, MA, 1969; postgrad., Charles U., Prague, Czechoslovakia, 1964-65; DMus (hon.), Keele (Eng.) U., 1991. Founding mem. Early Music Consort London, 1965—76; dir. The Acad. Ancient Music, London, 1973—; music faculty Cambridge U., 1975—, hon. prof. music, 2002—. Artistic dir. Handel & Haydn Soc., Boston, 1986—2001, condr. laureate, 2001—; hon. prof. music Keele U., 1986—90; dir. music St. Paul Chamber Orch., 1987—92, prin. guest condr., 1992—98; internat. prof. early music performance Royal Acad. Music, London, 1992—; vis. prof. dept. music King's Coll., London, 1992—96; artistic dir. Summer Mozart Festival Nat. Symphony Orch. USA, 1993—2001; assoc. dir. Beethoven Academie, Antwerp, 1998—2002; prin. guest condr. Kammerorchester Basel, 2000, Orquesta Ciudad de Granada, 2001—04, Orch. Sinfonica di Milano Giuseppe Verdi, 2003—. Author: (book) Music at Court, 1977, The Trio Sonata, 1979, Haydn's Visits to England, 1980, Handel, 1984; editor: Music in Eighteenth Century England, 1983, Holmes' Life of Mozart, 1991, The Keyboard in Baroque Europe, 2003. Decorated Comdr. of the Brit. Empire; named Freeman, Worshipful Co. Musicians, London, 1989, Christopher Hogwood Historically Informed Performance Fellowship in his honor, Handel & Hadyn Soc.; recipient Wilson Cobbett medal, Worshipful Co. Musicians, London, 1986, Disting. Musician award, Inc. Soc. Musicians, 1997, Martinu medal, Bohuslav Martinu Found., Prague, 1999; Hon. fellow, Jesus Coll., Cambridge, 1989—, Pembroke Coll., Cambridge, 1992—. Home and Office: 10 Brookside Cambridge CB2 1JE England

HOHENBERGER, PATRICIA JULIE, fine arts and antique appraiser, consultant; b. Holyoke, Mass. d. Ambrose Harrington and Irene Leo (Ducharme) Reynolds; m. John H. Hohenberger, June 27, 1953; children: Lisa Maria, Julie Suzanne, John Henry, James Reynolds, Patricia Antonia. BA in English, Coll. of New Rochelle, N.Y., 1950; MA in Folk Art Studies, NYU, 1983. Cert. elem. edn. tchr., Mass. Tchr. Hadley (Mass.) Pub. Schs., 1950-52, Springfield (Mass.) Pub. Schs., 1952-54; owner, dir. The Brown House Nursery Sch., Williamstown, Mass., 1962-64; tchr. Coindra Hall, Huntington, N.Y., 1970-71, St. Edward the Confessor, Syosset, N.Y., 1971-81; pres. Patricia Reynolds Hohenberger Appraisals, Northport, N.Y., 1983—. Cons. O'Toole-Edwald Art Assn., Inc., N.Y., 1984-91, Alexander-Benwood Co., Inc., Huntington, N.Y., 1991—; lectr. Symposium-Gen. Accident Ins., N.Y., 1994. Author: (monograph) Gentle Reminders of the Past, 1984. Recipient Recognition for Achievement award Alexander-Benwood Co., Inc., Huntington, N.Y., 1995. Mem. Nat. Trust for Historic Preservation, Nat. Mus. Women in the Arts (charter), New England Appraisers Assn. Roman Catholic. Avocations: collecting american decorative arts and antiques, photography. Home: 72 Burt Ave Northport NY 11768-2046 E-mail: prhohen@aol.com.

HOHENDAHL, PETER UWE, German language and literature educator; b. Hamburg, Fed. Republic Germany, Mar. 17, 1936; came to U.S., 1964; s. Wilhelm and Emilie (Uelschen) H.; m. Iky Maria Zoetelief, July 2, 1965; children: Deborah, Gwendolyn. Student, U. Bern, Switzerland, 1955, U. Hamburg, 1955-57, 59-63, PhD, 1964; postgrad., U. Goettingen, Fed. Republic Germany, 1958. Asst. prof. Pa. State U., 1965-68; assoc. prof. Washington U., St. Louis, 1968-69, prof., 1970-77, head dept., 1972-77; prof. comparative and German lit. Cornell U., Ithaca, N.Y., 1977—, chmn. dept. German, 1981-86, Schurman prof. German and Comparative lit., 1985—, dir. Inst. for German Cultural Studies, 1992—. Merton vis. prof. Berlin U., 1976; disting. vis. prof. Ohio State U., 1987; supr. Studien zur Literatur des 19, Jahrhunderts, 1993, sr. fellow Am. Inst. Contemporary German Studies,

Washington, 2000, corr. fellow Inst. Germanic Studies, U. London-Sch. Advanced Study, London, 2001-; Passagen, Festschrift fuer Peter Uwe Hohendahl zum 65. Geburtstag, Weidler Buchverlag, Berlin, Germany, 2001, Am. Acad. Arts & Scis., 2003. Author: Literaturkritik und Oeffentlichkeit, 1974, Der Europaeische Roman der Empfindsamkeit, 1977, The Institution of Criticism, 1982, Literarische Kultur im Zeitalter des Liberalismus, 1985, A History of German Literary Criticism, 1988, Building a National Literature, 1989, Reappraisals: Shifting Alignments in Postwar Critical Theory, 1991, Heinrich Heine and the Occident: Multiple Identities, Multiple Receptions, 1991, Geschichte, Opposition, Subversion, Studien zur Literatur des 19. Jahrhunderts, 1993, Prismatic Thought: Theodor W. Adorno, 1995, (with R.A. Berman, K. Kenkel and A. Strum) Oeffentlichkeit: Geschichte eines kritischen Begriffs, 2000, others; mem. editl. bd. Studies in 20th Century Lit., 1979—, German Quar., 1983-88. Fellow Harvard U., 1964-65, fellow Ctr. for Interdisciplinary Rsch., Bielefeld, 1981, 87, Guggenheim Found., 1983-84. Mem. MLA, Am. Assn. Tchrs. German, N.Am. Heine Soc. (exec. coun. 1982—, pres. 1986-90), Zeitschrift fuer Germanistik (bd. dirs. 1990—). Home: 81 Genung Rd Ithaca NY 14850-9602 Office: Cornell U Dept of German Studies Ithaca NY 14853 Office Phone: 607-255-8353. Business E-Mail: puh1@cornell.edu.

HOHENEMSER, CHRISTOPH, physics educator, researcher; b. Berlin, May 29, 1937; came to U.S., 1947; s. Kurt H. and Katherine (Dietrich) H.; m. Anne S. Holland, June 20, 1960; children: Lisa, Julia. BA with honors, Swarthmore Coll., 1958; PhD, Washington U., St. Louis, 1963. Research assoc. Washington U., St. Louis, 1963-64; instr., asst. prof. Brandeis U., Waltham, Mass., 1964-71; assoc. prof. physics Clark U., Worcester, Mass., 1971-76, prof., 1976—2002, prof. emeritus, 2002—, chmn. dept. physics, 1979-83, chmn. sci., tech. and society program, 1971-84, chmn. environ., tech. and society program, 1984-92, dir. Ctr. for Tech., Environ. and Devel, 1983-84. Vis. scientist U. Groningen, Netherlands, 1973-74, 78-79, U. Konstanz, Fed. Republic Germany, 1986, U. Calif., Berkeley, 1990-91. Co-author: Corporate Management of Health and Safety Hazards, 1988; co-editor: Risk in Technological Society, 1982, Perilous Progress, 1985; contbr. over 140 articles and chpts. on physics and tech. assessment to jours. and books. Recipient Bronze medal UN Environ. Programme, 1982; NSF research grantee, 1971-91. Fellow Am. Phys. Soc., Soc. Risk Analysis; mem. AAAS, Sigma Xi, Phi Beta Kappa. Home: 146 Mill Rd Littleton MA 01460-1548 Office: Clark U Dept Physics 950 Main St Dept Physics Worcester MA 01610-1477 E-mail: chohenemser@clarku.edu.

HOHMAN, ANDREW, music educator; b. Lima, Ohio, Sept. 21, 1979; s. Gary and Beatrice Hohman; m. Jennifer Lynn Raftery, Aug. 6, 2005. MusB in Edn., Cedarville U., 2002; MusM, Bowling Green State U., 2003. Lic. tchr. Ohio. Vocal music tchr. Temple Christian Sch., Lima, Ohio, 2002—03; grad. asst. Bowling Green State U., Ohio, 2002—03; vocal music dir. Cuyahoga Valley Christian Acad., Cuyahoga Falls, Ohio, 2003—. Mem.: Am. Choral Dirs. Assn. (assoc.), Ohio Music Educators Assn. (assoc.).

HOHN, DAVID, physician; b. Tucson, 1942; BS cum laude, U. Ill., 1964, MD, 1970. Intern Rush-Presbyn. St. Luke's Hosp., Chgo., 1970—71; resident in gen. surgery U. Calif., San Francisco, 1971—78, asst. prof. surgery, 1978—84, assoc. prof. surgery, 1984—87, U. Tex. Med. Sch., M.D. Anderson Cancer Ctr., 1987—90; prof. surgery U. Tex. Med. Sch., 1990—97; v.p. patient care M.D. Anderson Cancer Ctr.-U. Tex., Houston, 1993—97; pres., CEO Roswell Park Cancer Inst., 1997—. Deans coun. Univ. Buffalo Sch. Med. Mem.: Soc. of Surg. Oncology, Surg. Infection Soc., Surg. Infection Soc., Am. Assn. for Cancer Rsch., Am. Soc. for Clin. Oncology, Am. Fedn. for Clin. Rsch., Am. Coll. Physiciam Execs., Assn. for Acad. Surgery. Office: Roswell Park Cancer Inst Elm And Carlton St Buffalo NY 14263-0001*

HOHN, HARRY GEORGE, retired insurance company executive, lawyer; b. N.Y.C., Mar. 1, 1932; s. Harry George and Violia (Meehan) H.; m. Janet Jean LaRosa, June 19, 1954; children: Cynthia, Jennifer, Nancy, Patricia. BS, NYU, 1953, LLM, 1959; JD, Fordham U., 1956. Bar: N.Y. 1956, U.S. Supreme Ct. 1976. With N.Y. Life Ins. Co., N.Y.C., 1956-2000, sr. v.p., gen. counsel, 1977-82, exec. v.p., gen. counsel, 1982-83, exec. v.p., 1983-86, CEO, 1990-97, also chmn. bd. dirs., past vice chmn. bd. dirs., 1997—, ret. chmn., CEO, 1997. Bd. dirs. Life and Health Ins. Med. Rsch. Fund, Million Dollar Roundtable Found.; chmn. bd. dirs. Life Ins. Coun. N.Y.; past chmn. Am. Coun. Life Ins.; mem. internat. adv. bd. Credit Comml. de France; trustee Mainstay Funds. Editor: Fordham Law Rev, 1955-56. Trustee Am. Coll., Com. Econ. Devel.; trustee emeritus Found. Ind. Higher Edn.; chmn., bd. trustees Nat. AIDS Fund; bd. govs. United Way of Tri-State; mem. adv. bd. North Fork Environ. Coun., Bowery Mission; chmn. bd. advisors Resurrection Sch. in Harlem, N.Y.C. Fellow Am. Bar Found. (life); mem. Assn. Life Ins. Counsel (bd. govs.), Bus. Roundtable. Republican. Roman Catholic. Office: NY Life Ins Co 51 Madison Ave New York NY 10010-5077 Office Phone: 212-576-5077.

HOHNHORST, JOHN CHARLES, judge; b. Jerome, Idaho, Dec. 25, 1952; m. Raelene Casper; children: Jennifer, Rachel, John. BS in Polit. Sci./Pub. Adminstrn., U. Idaho, 1975, JD cum laude, 1978. Bar: Idaho 1978, U.S. Dist. Ct. Idaho 1978, U.S. Ct. Appeals (9th cir.) 1980, U.S. Ct. Claims 1983, U.S. Supreme Ct. 1987. Adminstrv. asst. to Sen. John M. Barker Idaho State Senate, 1975; ptnr. Hepworth, Lezamiz & Hohnhorst, Twin Falls, Idaho, 1978—2001; dist. judge 5th Jud. Dist. Ct., Twin Falls County, Idaho, 2001—. Contbr. articles to profl. jours. Mem. planning & zoning commn. City of Twin Falls, 1987-90. Mem. ABA, ATLA, Idaho State Bar (commr. 1990-93, pres. 1993), Am. Coll. Trial Lawyers, Idaho Trial Lawyers Assn. (regional dir. 1985-86), 5th Dist. Bar Assn. (treas. 1987-88, v.p. 1988-89, pres. 1989-90), Am. Acad. Appellate Lawyers, Greater Twin Falls C. of C. (chmn. magic valley leadership program 1988-89, bd. dirs. 1989-92), Phi Kappa Tau (Beta Gamma chpt., Phi award 1988). Office: Theron Ward Jud Bldg 427 Shoshoe St N PO Box 126 427 Twin Falls ID 83303-0126 Office Phone: 208-736-4047.

HOI, SAMUEL CHUEN-TSUNG, academic administrator; b. Hong Kong, Mar. 25, 1958; came to U.S., 1975; JD, Columbia U. Bar: N.Y. 1983. Dir.-Paris Campus Parsons Sch. Design, 1988—91; dean Corcoran Coll. Art & Design, Washington, 1991—2000; pres. Otis Coll. Art & Design, LA, 2000—. Mem., bd. dirs. Leadership Washington, 1996. Mem. Assn. Ind. Colls. of Art and Design, Nat. Assn. Schs. Art and Design (bd. dirs.). Office: Office of the President Otis Coll Art & Design 9045 Lincoln Blvd Los Angeles CA 90045*

HOIBY, LEE, composer, concert pianist; b. Madison, Wis., Feb. 17, 1926; s. Henry Bjorn and Violet Ethel (Smith) H. MusB, U. Wis., 1947; MA, Mills Coll., Oakland, Calif., 1952; cert., Curtis Inst., Phila., 1952; DFA (hon.), Simpson Coll., Indianola, Iowa, 1985. Composer (operas) The Scarf, 1955, Piano Concerto 1, 1957, A Month in the Country, 1964, Summer and Smoke, 1970, Something New for the Zoo, 1979, The Italian Lesson, 1980, The Tempest, 1985, This Is the Rill Speaking, 1992, (ballet) After Eden, 1967, (cantatas) Hymn of the Nativity, 1960, For You O Democracy, 1993, (oratorio) Galileo Galilei, 1975, Piano Concerto 2, 1979, (baritone and orch.) The Tides of Sleep, 1960, I Have A Dream, 1988, Serenade for Violin and Orch., 1987, Flute Concerto, 1994, (opera) Romeo and Juliet, 2003, (organ and chorus) Song of Songs, 2004, also chamber, choral, vocal, theatre music. Recipient Am. Acad. Arts and Letters award, 1957; fellow Fulbright Found., 1952, Guggenheim Found., 1958, Nat. Endowment for the Arts, 1980, Rockefeller Found. grantee, 1979. Mem. ASCAP, Am. Guild Organists (hon.) Home: 9807 County Hwy 28 Long Eddy NY 12760 Office Phone: 845-887-4321. E-mail: aquarius@catskill.net.

HOIDAL, DAVID, health facility administrator; B in Psychology, U. Nebr.; M in Health Adminstrn., U. Mo., Columbia. With HCA Penninsula Hosp., Hampton, Va., 1985, CEO, 1989—93, HCA DePaul Hosp., New Orleans, 1993—97; sr. v.p. COO Tulane U. Hosp. and Clinic, New Orleans, 1997—2000; exec. dir. The Kirklin Clinic UAB, Birmingham, Ala., 2000—02; pres. Callahan Eye Found. Hosp. UAB Health Sys., Birmingham, 2002; interim CEO U. Ala. Hosp. UAB Health Sys., 2004—. Office: Univ Ala Hosp at Birmingham 619 19th St S Birmingham AL 35249

HOIE, CLAUS, artist; b. Stavanger, Norway, Nov. 3, 1911; came to U.S., 1924, naturalized, 1942; s. Claus and Marie (Foss) H.; m. Helen Hunt Bencker, Nov. 17, 1956. Student, Pratt Inst., 1930-33, Ecole des Beaux Arts, Paris, 1945. Art dir., designer, illustrator various advt. and pub. firms in, N.Y.C., 1933-41, 46-62, painter, graphic artist, 1962—; exhibited in one man shows at Denver Art Mus., 1943, Saltpeter Gallery, N.Y.C., 1962, 63, Monmouth (N.J.) Art Ctr., 1970, Benson Gallery, Bridgehampton, N.Y., 1972, 77, 80, 86, Southampton Coll., 1972, Guild Hall Mus., East Hampton, N.Y., 1973, Norwegian-Am. Mus., 1975, U. Minn. Galleries, Mpls., 1976, Akershus Mus., Oslo, 1982, Vered Gallery, 1987, 88, East Hampton, 1984, 85, 86, 89; group shows at Chgo. Art Inst., 1946, NAD, 11 shows 1956-89, Am. Water Color Soc., 1960-80, 82, 89, L.I. Painters, 1972, 75, Nat. Inst. Arts and Letters, 1975, Am. Watercolor Soc., 1985, 88, Mexico City Mus. Watercolor, 1989, numerous others; represented in permanent collections Bklyn. Mus., Norfolk Mus., Okla. Mus. Art, Butler Inst., East Hampton Guild Hall Mus., Akershus Mus., Oslo, U. Minn., Centre Coll. Ky., Norwegian-Am. Mus., Brigham Young U. Contbr. articles to profl. jours. Served with AUS, 1942-45, ETO. Decorated Bronze Star medal; recipient Nat. Inst. Arts and Letters award for painting, 1975, Adolph and Clara Obrig prize NAD, 1985, John Pike Meml. award NAD, 1989, Audubon Artists Ann. Exhbn. award, 1990, Marine Environ. Wildlife award, Mystic Seaport Mus., 1998. Mem. N.A.D., Soc. Illustrators, Am. Watercolor Soc. (v.p. 1960-62, Gold medal of honor 1962) Clubs: Devon Yacht (East Hampton). Episcopalian. Mailing: c/o Maritime Gallery at Mystic Seaport 75 Greenmanville Ave PO Box 6000 Mystic CT 06355*

HOISINGTON, STEVEN H., industrial engineer; b. Aberdeen, Md., Dec. 3, 1953; s. Beverly Ann and James Ellis Hoisington; 1 child, Lenny James. Student, U. Wis., Menomonie, 1976—78; AA in Mech. Engring. Tech., Rochester C.C., 1976; MBA, Winona State U., 1984. Cert. mech. engring. tech., Minn., Six Sigma Black Belt, Wis. From engr. to dir. quality and customer satisfaction IBM, Rochester, Minn., 1979—99; v.p. quality Johnson Controls, Inc., Milw., 1999—2005; sr. v.p. orgnl. excellence and quality Exel, Hayward, Calif., 2005—. *Currently, the Senior Vice President of Organizational Excellence and Quality for Exel, PLC in Bracknell, England. Responsible for defining a global continuous improvement, productivity, operational efficiency, and quality strategy to guide Exel operations worldwide to excellent levels of productivity, efficiency, and operational performance. Responsibilities under this strategy include performance measurement and management, deployment of continuous improvement initiatives including Six Sigma and Lean, ISO 9000 and global agency registration, customer satisfaction management and measurement, global process definition and deployment, and reduction in waste and variation. Former Vice President of Quality at Johnson Controls, Inc. in Milwaukee, Wisconsin, where he held a similar role.* Co-author: Customer Centered Six Sigma: Linking Customers, Process Improvement, and Financial Results, Implementing Strategic Change; author: Six Sigma in Corporate Real Estate; contbr. chapters to books, articles to profl. jours. Malcolm Baldrige Nat. Quality award examiner US Dept. Commerce, Nat. Inst. Sci. and Tech., Gaithersburg, Md., 1993—; chmn. bd. dirs. Wis. Forward (Quality) Award, Madison, 1999—. Mem.: Inst. Indsl. Engrs. (v.p.), Am. Soc. for Quality (cert. mgr.), Am. Legion, VFW (life; chaplain). Achievements include patents for minimum contamination during mfr. of disk drives. Office: Exel 4120 Point Eden Way Ste 200 Hayward CA 94545 Office Phone: 510-731-3436, 510-731-3434. Business E-Mail: steven.hoisington@us.exel.com.

HOIVIK, THOMAS HARRY, military educator, international consultant; b. Mpls., June 6, 1941; s. Tony Horace and Helen Lenea (Carlsen) H.; m. Judith Lisa Kohn; children: Todd, Gregory. BA, U. Minn., 1963; grad. with distinction, Naval Test Pilot Sch., 1969; MS with distinction, Naval Postgrad. Sch., 1973; grad. with distinction, Naval War Coll., 1976; MA, Salve Regina U., 1988. Cert. exptl. test pilot, air transport pilot, jet aircraft, helicopter, glider single and multi-engine. Commd. ensign USN, 1963, advanced through grades to capt., 1963-91; test pilot Naval Air Test Ctr., Patuxent River, Md., 1968-71; program mgr. H-53 aircraft Naval Air Systems Command, Washington, 1976-78; comdg. officer Helicopter Mine Countermeasure Squadron 14, Norfolk, Va., 1978-80; dir. U.S. Naval Test Pilot Sch., Patuxent River, 1980-82; fed. exec. fellow Ctr. for Strategic and Internat. Studies, Washington, 1982-83; chair tactical analysis Naval Postgrad. Sch., Monterey, Calif., 1983-85; comdg. officer Naval Air Sta., Willow Grove, Pa., 1985-87; chair applied systems analysis Naval Postgrad. Sch., Monterey, 1987-91, prof. acquisition mgmt. and ops. rsch., 1991—; ret. capt. USN, 1991; dir. test and evaluation sr. level curriculum Defense Acquisition U., 1993—. Mem. U.S. Congrl. Study Group on Nat. Strategy, Washington, 1982-83, World Economy, 1982-83; cons. U.S., Internat. Govt. Orgns., 1990—; founder, pres. Lysonics Rsch. Internat., 1993, Inst. for In-Flight Rsch., 1996; flight demonstration pilot Paris Internat. Air Show, 1967 Contbr. articles to profl. jours. Bd. dirs. Vocat. Edn. Bd., Montgomery County, Pa., 1985-87, Congrl. Svc. Acad. Appointment Bd., Phila., 1985-87; youth leader, counselor YMCA, St. Paul, 1955-61. Recipient Legion of Merit Pres. of U.S., 1987, Outstanding Youth Leadership award YMCA, 1960; established U.S. Helicopter Speed Record, 1966. Mem. AIAA, Soc. of Exptl. Test Pilots, Internat. Test and Evaluation Assn. (Internat. Test and Evaluation Cross award 1997), Nat. Contract Mgmt. Assn., Ops. Rsch. Soc. Am., Mil. Ops. Rsch. Soc., U. Minn. "M" Club, Disable Am. Vets, Sigma Alpha Epsilon. Avocations: tennis, music composition. Office: Naval Postgrad Sch Monterey CA 93943

HOJAHMAT, MARHABA, research scientist; b. 1966; d. Hojahmat Yunus and Rehima Yusup; 1 child, Yifutehaer Nijiati. M in engring., Tokyo U. Sci., 1997, PhD, 2000. Post-doctoral rschr. U. Ky., Lexington, 2000—02, rsch. assoc., 2002; rsch. scientist Yaupon Therapeutics Inc., Lexington, 2002—. Contbr. articles to profl. jours. Japanese Govt. scholarship, Ministry of Edn., Sci. and Culture of Japan, 1996—2000, ITOCHU award, ITOCHU Co., Japan, 1995, STTR, NIH, 2002. Mem.: Soc. Silicon Chemistry, Japan, Chem. Soc. Japan, Am. Chem. Soc., Am. Assn. Pharm. Scientists. Home: 175 Malabu Dr Apt 33 Lexington KY 40503 Office: Yaupon Therapeutics Inc Univ Ky A169 ASTeCC Bldg Lexington KY 40506 Office Phone: 859-257-2300. Office Fax: 859-257-2489. E-mail: mhoja2@uky.edu.

HOJILLA-EVANGELISTA, MILAGROS PARKER, research chemist, research scientist; b. Quezon City, Philippines, Mar. 7, 1960; d. Hector Biaco and Carmen Felisa Parker Hojilla; m. Roque Lagman Evangelista, Apr. 20, 1985; children: Roderick Hojilla Evangelista, Mylene Hojilla Evangelista. BS Food Tech. cum laude, U. Philippines, Los Banos, 1980, MS in Food sci., 1984; PhD in Food Tech., Iowa State U., 1990. Instr. Inst. of Food Sci. and Tech., U. Philippines, Los Banos, 1980—86; postdoctoral rsch. assoc. dept. food sci. and human nutrition Iowa State U., Ames, 1990—94, asst. scientist, 1994—97; rsch. chemist plant polymer rsch. USDA-ARS Nat. Ctr. Agrl. Utilization Rsch., Peoria, Ill., 1997—. Assoc. editor Jour. of the Am. Oil Chemists' Soc., Champaign, Ill. Contbr. articles to profl. jours. Pres. Filipino Assn. at Iowa State U., Ames, 1989—92; newsletter assoc./layout editor Filipino-Am. Soc. of Ctrl. Ill., Peoria, 2001—03. Recipient Outstanding Paper in Cereal Chemistry award, Am. Assn. of Cereal Chemists-Corn Refiners' Assn., 1990, Archer Daniels Midland-Protein Divsn. Best Paper award, Am. Oil Chemists Soc., 1993, 2003; scholarship, S.E. Asian Regional Ctr. for Grad. Study and Rsch. in Agr., 1982-1984. Mem.: Am. Chem. Soc., Am. Oil Chemists' Soc. (sec./treas. 2000—02, vice-chairperson protein divsn. 2002—04, chairperson protein divsn. 2004—), Gamma Sigma Delta, Phi Kappa Phi, Phi Beta Delta (v.p. 1991—92). Roman Catholic. Achievements include research in development of formulation for soybean flour-based foamed plywood adhesive (now used commercially); Co-developed the Sequential Extraction Process for corn, an alternative corn milling process that uses ethanol for extracting oil and protein and generates novel value-added co-products; Identified the major protein fractions in the protein co-product from the Sequential Extraction Process, determined their functional properties and evaluated their potential applications. Avocations: travel, reading. Office: USDA ARS NCAUR 1815 N University St Peoria IL 61604 Office Phone: 309-681-6350. Office Fax: 309-681-6691. Business E-Mail: hojillmp@ncaur.usda.gov.

HOJNOWSKI, JULES AUSTIN, entrepreneur; b. Elmira, N.Y., Nov. 3, 1959; m. Michael Q. Hojnowski, Sept. 4, 1994. BS, Elmira Coll., 1985, MS, 2001. Profl. spinner of exotic fibers, 2000—. Author: Mark Twain's in-law's - the Langdons, Mark Twain's Three Medieval Books Made into Curriculums with the Use of Multiple Intelligences and Activities, 2005; contbr. articles to profl. jours. Mem.: So. Atlantic MLA (corr.; spkr.), Elmira, Mark Twain Soc. (assoc.; student asst. 1982—2000), Mark Twain Boyhood Assn. (assoc.), Mark Twain Forum (corr.), Mark Twain Club (assoc.; pres. 1976—77). Home: 1690 Trumansburg Rd Ithaca NY 14850-9213 Personal E-mail: jah@twcny.rr.com.

HOKANA, GREGORY HOWARD, engineering executive; b. Burbank, Calif., 1944; s. Howard Leslie and Helen Lorraine H.; m. Eileen Marie Youell, 1967; children: Kristen Marie, Kenneth Gregory. BS in Physics, UCLA, 1966. Design engr. Raytheon Co., Oxnard, Calif., 1967-74; staff engr. Bunker Ramo Corp., Westlake Village, Calif., 1974-84; mgr. analog engring. AIL Systems, Inc., Westlake Village, 1984-91; mgr. product devel. Am. Nucleonics Corp., Westlake Village, 1991-93; tech. mgr. Litton Data Sys., Agoura Hills, Calif., 1994-2000; sr. tech. staff Litton Guidance and Control Sys., Woodland Hills, Calif., 2000—01; tech.mgr. Northrop Grumman Nav. Systems Divsn., Woodland Hills, 2001—. Mem. IEEE, Assn. Old Crows. Democrat. Methodist. Avocations: golf, swimming, photography. Office: Northrop Grumman Navigation Systems Divsn 21240 Burbank Blvd Woodland Hills CA Office Phone: 818-715-4241. Business E-Mail: greg.hokana@ngc.com. E-mail: ghokana@adelphia.net.

HOKANSON, SCOTT FRANCIS, SR., insurance agent; b. Boston, Mass., Apr. 12, 1972; s. Herbert Howard Hokanson, Jr. and Barbara Murray Hokanson; m. Ann Marie Sullivan Sullivan, Dec. 30, 1995; children: Elizabeth Mary, Scott Francis Jr., Andrew Sullivan. BBA, Marquette U., Milw., 1994. Employee benefit broker Employee Benefit Adminstr., Pembroke, Mass., 1994—. Continuing edn. provider: ins. brokers Commonwealth of Mass., Pembroke, Mass., 2000—; continuing edn. provider: cpas Employee Benefit Adminstrs., Pembroke, Mass., 2004—. Youth group coord. St. Bonaventure Youth Group, Plymouth, Mass., 1999—2004. Recipient Top 25 Employee Benefit Brokerage Firm, Boston Bus. Jour., 2001-2004, Inc. 500 Award, Inc. Mag., 1999. Mem.: Nat. Assn. of Life Underwriters (pres. coun. 2001, 2002, Million Dollar Round Table 2004), Mass. Assn. of Health Underwriters, Self Ins. Inst. of Am., Internat. Found. of Employee Benefit Plans, Nat. Assn. of Health Underwriters (Golden Eagle 2003, 2004, Golden Eagle Award 2003). Office: Employee Benefit Adminstr Inc 64 Schoosett St Pembroke MA 02360 Office Phone: 781-826-1177 365. Fax: 781-826-3264. Business E-Mail: scotth@employeeben.com.

HOKE, MOLLY ELIZABETH, chemist, research scientist; b. Camp Hill, Pa., Oct. 19, 1972; d. Suzanne Beck and Keith Allen Hoke. BS, Gettysburg Coll., 1995; PhD, U. Md., 2001. Sr. rsch. scientist II Wyeth Rsch., Princeton, NJ, 2000—. Office: Wyeth Rsch CN-8000 Rm 2001 Princeton NJ 08543 Office Phone: 732-274-4172. Office Fax: 732-274-4505. E-mail: hokem@wyeth.com.

HOKE, S. CANDICE, lawyer, educator; b. Raleigh, N.C., Sept. 5, 1955; m. George H. Taylor. BA in Polit. Philosophy, Hollins Coll., 1977; postgrad., U. Chgo., 1978—79; JD, Yale U., 1983. Bar: Mass. 1984, U.S. Ct. Appeals (1st cir.) 1987. Law clk. to judge U.S. Ct. Appeals (1st cir.), Boston, 1983—85; assoc. Hill and Barlow, Boston, 1985—87; asst. prof. law U. Pitts., 1987—93; vis. assoc. prof. law Case We. Res. U., Cleve., 1993—94, Cleve. State U., 1994—95, assoc. prof. law, 1995—. Acting dir. Ctr. for Election Integrity; mem. N.C. Drug Commn., 1973-77. Contbr. to profl. jours. Acting dir. Ctr. Election Integrity. Mem. ABA. Avocations: gardening, mystery novels. Office: Cleveland-Marshall Coll Law Cleve State U 2121 Euclid Ave Cleveland OH 44115-2223

HOKE, SHEILA WILDER, retired librarian; b. Greensboro, N.C. d. Herbert Bruce Wilder and Virginia Dare (Caylor) Wilder-Dell; m. Robert Edward Hoke, Nov. 22, 1958 (dec.); children: Raymond Fellow, Philip Wilder. Student, Montclair Coll., 1948; BA in History, U. Kans., 1950, postgrad., 1951, BS in Edn., 1952; postgrad., John Hopkins U., 1955; MLS, U. Wis., 1955; MS in Edn., Southwestern Okla. State U., 1977; postgrad., Johns Hopkins U., Montclair State Coll. Tchr. history Fredonia (Kans.) High Sch., 1952-54; student asst. U. Wis., Madison, 1954-55; children's libr. BR Enoch Pratt Libr., Balt., 1955-58; libr. dir. U.S. Army Spl. Svcs., Bavaria, Fed. Republic Germany, 1958-59; libr. U.S. Army Dependent Schs., Straubing, Fed. Republic Germany, 1959-60; cataloger Southwestern Okla. State U. Libr., Weatherford, 1963-69, libr. dir., 1969-93; ret., 1993. Mem. spl. projects com. Okla. Dept. Edn., 1974, adv. com. Okla. State Regents Libr., 1975-77. Mem. Okla. State Regents for Higher Edn. Libr. Networking, 1989-93; mem. sr. citizens choir 1st Bapt. Ch., Weatherford; vol. with children Agape Med. Clinic; reading tutor to 1st grade student Weatherford Pub. Schs.; vol. helper for home-bound; active sr. citizens groups. Mem. AAUW (pres., state bd. dirs. 1980, Weatherford br. 1981-83), Nat. Assn. Ret. Fed. Employees, Okla. Libr. Assn. (chmn. tech. svcs. divsn. 1969-70, chmn. coll. and univ. divsn. 1972-73, chmn. adminstrs. workshop 1973, chmn. libr. edn. divsn. 1975-76, chmn. recruitment com. 1978, archives com. 1980), Okla. Ret. Tchrs. Assn., Weatherford C. of C. (edn. com. 1974-75, cert. meritorious achievement from Gov. Nigh 1985), Custer County Hist. Soc., western Okla. Hist. Soc., Higher Edn. Alumni Coun. Okla., Delta Kappa Gamma (pres. Lambda chpt. 1980-82), Phi Alpha theta, Kappa Kappa Iota (pres. Lambda chpt. 1984-85, 2005—). Republican. Baptist. Avocation: travel. E-mail: shoke@itlnet.net.

HOKENSON, DAVID LEONARD, secondary school educator; b. Mpls., Nov. 9, 1950; s. Raymond Leonard and Barbara Jean (Hooker) H.; m. Cynthia Jane Luehmann, July 28, 1979. BA, St. Olaf Coll., 1972; postgrad., U. Minn., 1977, 78, 82. Lic. secondary sch. social studies and history tchr., Minn. Social studies tchr. Preston (Minn.)-Fountain Pub. Schs., 1972-93, Fillmore Ctrl. H.S., Harmony, Minn., 1993-95; Fillmore Ctrl. Mid. Sch., Preston, Minn., 1995—. Mem. team evaluation State Dept. Edn., St. Paul, 1981, 83, 91, 98. Mem. Nat. Trust for Hist. Preservation; treas. Preston-Fountain Edn. Assn., 1987—93, negotiator, 1993—94; treas. Edn. Minn. Fillmore Ctrl., 1994—; mem. evaluation team North Ctrl. Accreditation Assn., 1994; participant Project 120, 1995; mem. Minn. Hist. Soc.; precinct chair Dem.-Farmer-Labor Party, Preston, 1990—2004; pres. Christ Luth. Ch., 2001—02. Recipient scholarship Minn. Inst. for Advancement of Teaching, St. Paul, 1992, 97. Mem. Nat. Geog. Soc., Am. Scandinavian Found., Am.-Swedish Inst., Smithsonian Instn., Minn. Hist. Soc., Libr. of Congress. Office: Fillmore Ctrl Schs PO Box 50 Preston MN 55965-0050 Business E-Mail: david.hokenson@isd2198.k12.mn.us, d.hokenson@mchsi.com.

HOKENSTAD, MERL CLIFFORD, JR., social work educator; b. Norfolk, Nebr., July 21, 1936; s. Merl Clifford and Flora Diane (Christian) H.; m. Dorothy Jean Tarrell, June 24, 1962; children: Alene Ann, Laura Rae, Marta Lynn. BA summa cum laude, Augustana Coll., 1958; Rotary Found. fellow, Durham (Eng.) U., 1958-59; MSW., Columbia U., 1962; PhD, Brandeis U., 1969, Inst. Ednl. Mgmt., Harvard U., 1977. With Lower East Side Neighborhood Assn., N.Y.C., 1962-64; community planning assoc. United Community Services, Sioux Falls, S.D., 1964-66; instr. Augustana Coll., Sioux Falls, 1964-66; research assoc. Ford Found. Project on Community Planning for Elderly, Brandeis U., Waltham, Mass., 1966-67; prof., dir. Sch. Social Work, Western Mich. U., Kalamazoo, 1968-74; prof., dean Sch. Applied Social Scis., Case Western Res. U., Cleve., 1974-83, Ralph and Dorothy Schmitt prof., 1983—, chmn. PhD program, 1990-94; prof. internat. health Sch. of Medicine, 1994—. Vis. prof. Inst. Sociology, Stockholm U., 1978, Fulbright lectr., 1980; vis. prof. Nat. Inst. Social Work, London, 1981, Sch. Social Work, Stockholm U., 1982-86, Eotvos Lorand U., Budapest, Hungary, 1992,

95, 96, London Sch. Econs., 1994; Fulbright rsch. scholar Inst. Applied Social Rsch., Oslo, 1989; fellow U. Canterbury, Christchurch, New Zealand, 1994; mem. UN tech. com. World Assembly on Aging, 2000-02; mem. U.S. delegation UN World Assembly on Aging, 2002. Author: Participation in Teaching and Learning: An Idea Book for Social Work Educators; editor: Meeting Human Needs: An International Annual, Vol. V, Linking Health Care and Social Services: International Perspectives; editor-in-chief Internat. Social Work Jour., 1985-87; co-editor: Profiles in Internat. Social Work, 1992, Issues in International Social Work, 1997, Models of International Exchange, 2003, Lessons from Abroad: International Social Welfare Innovations, 2004; (internat. issue) Jour. Gerontol. Social Work, 1988, Jour. Sociology and Social Welfare, 1990, Jour. Social Policy and Administration, 1993, Jour. Aging Internat., 1994, Jour. Applied Social Scis., 1996; contbr. articles to profl. jours., chpts. to books. Mem. alcohol tng. rev. com. Nat. Inst. Alcoholism and Alcohol Abuse, 1974-78; workshop leader Am. Assn. State Colls. and Univs., 1974; chmn. U.S. com. XVIII Internat. Congress Schs. Social Work, 1976; chmn. Kalamazoo County Cmty. Mental Health Svcs. Bd., 1971, vice chmn., 1972; mem. edn. and tng. task force Mich. Office Drug Abuse and Alcoholism, 1972-73; mem. Mich. Assn. Mental Health Bds., 1972; bd. dirs. Cleve. United Way Svcs., 1982-84, del. assembly, 1974-82, mem. periodic rev. oversight com., 1982, mem. leadership devel. com., 1978, cmty. resources com., 1988—; bd. dirs. Kalamazoo United Way, 1968-72; trustee Cleve. Internat. Program for Youth Workers and Social Workers, chmn. program com., 1985-87; mem. program devel. com. Cleve. Center on Alcoholism, 1976; trustee Alcoholism Services Cleve., Inc., 1977-86, v.p., 1982-85; trustee Cmty. Info./Vol. Action Ctr., 1982-88, chmn. leadership devel. com., 1984-86, chmn. unmet needs com., 1986-88, exec. com., 1985-88, v.p., 1986-88; exec. com. Western Reserve Geriatric Edn. Ctr., 1995—; mem. adv. com. Coun. for Internat. Exch. Scholars, 1991-93, Fedn. for Cmty. Planning Coun. on Older Persons, 1991—, vice chmn., 2005—, chmn. caregiver support program initiative, 1995-96; mem. adv. coun. Cuyahoga County Dept. Sr. and Adult Svcs., 1998—2003, chair, 2001—03; bd. dirs. Western Res. Area Agy. on Aging, 2004—; mem. task force of social transition in Soviet Union, U.S. State Dept. Bur. Human Rights and Humanitarian Affairs; mem. UN NGO Com. on Aging, 1996—; co-chmn. U.S. Com. for Internat. Yr. of Older Persons, 1999. Named Outstanding Alumnus, Augustana Coll., 1980, Ohio Soc. Worker of the Yr., 1992; Fulbright Research fellow; NIMH trainee, 1960-62; Vocat. Rehab. trainee, 1966; Gerontology trainee, 1967; Rotary Found. fellow, 1958-59; recipient Golden Achievement Award, Golden Age Ctr., 2003. Mem. NASW (internat. com. 1989-93, chmn. 1992-93, Found. Pioneer 2003—), Acad. Cert. Social Workers, Internat. Assn. Schs. Social Work (exec. bd. 1978-92, 98—, treas. 1978-86, v.p. N.Am. 1988-92, membership sec. 1996-2000, Katherine Kendall award 2004), Internat. Coun. on Social Welfare (dir. U.S. com. 1982-92), Coun. on Social Work Edn. (del. 1972-75, 77-83, chmn. ann. program meeting 1973, chmn. com. on nat. legis. and adminstrv. policy 1975-79, nominating com. 1978-81, internat. com. 1980-86, 96—, chmn. com. 1982-84, dir. 1979-82, exec. com. 1986-89, pres. 1986-89, Lifetime Achievement award 2002), Nat. Conf. on Social Welfare (bd. dirs. 1978-80, chmn. sect. V program com. 1977-78), World Future Soc. (area coord. 1972-74), Fulbright Assn. (v.p. N.E. Ohio chpt. 1990-91), Nat. Coun. on Aging (bd. dirs. 1991-97, internat. com. 1991-97, pub. policy com. 1992-97). Democrat. Episcopalian. Home: 2917 Weymouth Rd Cleveland OH 44120-2234 Office: Case Western Res U 10900 Euclid Ave Cleveland OH 44106-1712 Office Phone: 216-368-2323. Business E-Mail: mch2@cwru.edu.

HOKIN, LOWELL EDWARD, biochemist, educator; b. Chgo., Sept. 20, 1924; s. Oscar E. and Helen (Manfield) H.; m. Mabel Neaverson, Dec. 1, 1952 (dec. Aug. 2003); children: Linda Ann, Catherine Esther (dec.), Samuel Arthur; m. Barbara M. Gallagher, Mar. 23, 1978 (div. July 1998); 1 child, Ian Oscar. Student, U. Chgo., 1942-43, Dartmouth Coll., 1943-44, U. Louisville Sch. Medicine, 1944-46, U. Ill. Sch. Medicine, 1946-47; MD, U. Louisville, 1948; PhD, U. Sheffield, Eng., 1952. Postdoctoral fellow dept. biochemistry McGill U., 1952-54, faculty, 1954-57, asst. prof., 1955-57; mem. faculty U. Wis., Madison, 1957—, prof. physiol. chemistry, 1961-68, prof. pharmacology, 1968-99, prof., chmn. pharmacology, 1968-93, prof. emeritus, 1999—. Contbr. numerous articles to tech. jours., chpts. to numerous books on phosphoinositides, biol. transport, the pancreas, the brain and lithium in manic-depression. With USNR, 1943—45. Mem.: AAAS, N.Y. Acad. Scis., Am. Soc. Pharmacology and Exptl. Therapeutics, Biochem. Soc. (U.K.), Am. Soc. Biochemistry and Molecular Biology. Achievements include discovery of phosphoinositide signaling system. Home: 4021C Monona Dr Monona WI 53716 Office: U Wis Med Sch Dept Pharm 1300 University Ave Madison WI 53706-1510 Office Phone: 608-224-2190. Business E-Mail: lehokin@wisc.edu.

HOLABIRD, JOHN AUGUR, JR., retired architect; b. Chgo., May 9, 1920; s. John Augur and Dorothy (Hackett) H.; m. Donna Katharine Smith, Nov. 25, 1942 (div. 1969); children: Jean, Katharine, Polly, Lisa (dec.); m. Marcia Stefanie Fergestad, June 28, 1969 (dec. Mar. 1994); children: Ann, Lynn; m. Janet Nothhelfer Connor, May 7, 1996. BA, Harvard U., 1942, MArch, 1948. Archtl. designer Holabird & Root, Chgo., 1948-49, 55-64, assoc. firm, 1964-70, ptnr., 1970-87. Tchr. drama Francis Parker Sch., Chgo., 1949-55; stage designer NBC-TV, 1955 Major: archtl. works include Francis Parker Sch, Chgo., Ravinia Stage and Restaurant, Highland Park, Ill., 1970, Bell Telephone Labs, Naperville, Ill., 1975, Canal Bldg, Chgo., 1974. Pres. Park West Community Assn., 1962; dir. Lincoln Park Conservation Assn., 1960-64, Corlands, 1979-85; mem. Chgo. Commn. on Historic and Archtl. Landmarks, 1981-85; bd. dirs. Lincoln Park Community Conservation, 1964; trustee Francis Parker Sch., Ravinia Festival Assn., Ill. Inst. Tech., 1980-86. Served with U.S. Army, 1942-45. Decorated Silver Star, Bronze Star; Fourragère (Belgium); Order of William (The Netherlands). Fellow AIA (pres. Chgo. chpt. 1977-78); mem. Tavern Club, Harvard Club (dir. 1974-78), Phi Beta Kappa. Democrat. Home: 200 E Pearson St Apt 3W Chicago IL 60611-2352 Office: Holabird & Root 300 W Adams St Chicago IL 60606-5101

HOLADAY, ALLAN GIBSON, language educator; b. Grand Ledge, Mich., Jan. 16, 1916; s. Robert Clayton and Effie (Hooks) H.; m. Ruby Roxane Lees, Sept. 30, 1945; children— Allan Scott, Bruce Lees. BA, Miami U., Oxford, Ohio, 1938; MA (Grad. fellow), Cornell U., 1939; PhD (Grad. Council fellow), George Washington U., 1943. Instr. English U. Ill. at Urbana, 1942-47, asst. prof., 1947-53, asso. prof., 1953-57, prof., 1957-80, emeritus, 1980—. Author, editor: Thomas Heywood's The Rape of Lucrece, 1950, The Plays of George Chapman, 1970; co-editor: The Life of Lazarillo de Tormes, 1955; editor: Illinois Studies in Language and Literature; gen. editor: George Chapman's Tragedies, 1987; contbr. articles profl. jours. Mem. Modern Lang. Assn., Modern Humanities Research Assn., Cambridge Bibliog. Soc., Am. Assn. U. Profs., Phi Beta Kappa, Phi Eta Sigma, Delta Phi Alpha. Home: PO Box 343 Culver IN 46511-0343

HOLBA, MARIE ANN, elementary school educator; b. Perry, Okla., Mar. 23, 1954; d. Edward Eugene and Elsie Marie (Hollingsworth) Lee; m. James Melton Holba, May 17, 1974; children: Amie L., Michelle D., Amanda G. BS, Okla. State U., 1976. Lic. elem. tchr. Tchr. Billings (Okla.) Elem. Sch. Dist., 1983—. Sponsor Billings 4-H Club, 1989-92, 7th and 8th grades, FCCLA. Mem. Cimmaron Reading Coun. (treas. 1987-88), Noble County Rural Tchrs. Assn. (treas. 1987-92), Ceres Ladies Aid. Democrat. Mem. Christian Ch. Avocations: crafts, roller skating, basketball, going to livestock shows. Office: Billings Sch PO Box 39 Billings OK 74630-0039

HOLBECK, RICHARD ALAN, music educator; b. Two Harbors, Minn., July 3, 1968; s. Michael Aaron and Diane Rae Holbeck; m. Susan Jeanne Jackowell, July 28, 2000; children: Kyle Scott, Eva Marie, Lilia Rose. BS, Bemidji State U., 1993; MS, Southwest State U., 2002. Music tchr. Carlton Pub. Sch., Carlton, Minn., 1993—95; asst. mgr. REPP Big and Tall, Inc., Eden Prairie, Minn., 1995—96; sales cons. DeGrood's Inc., Mankato, Minn., 1996—97, Lager's Inc., St. Peter, Minn., 1997—99; music tchr. Mesabi East Pub. Sch., Aurora, Minn., 1999—2001, Eveleth-Gilbert Pub. Schs., Eveleth-Gilbert, Minn., 2001—. Music dir. Aurora Hoyt Lakes City Band, Aurora, Minn., 1999—, Mesabi Cmty. Theater, Eveleth, 2002—05. Fellow: Edn. Minn. Independent. Meth. Avocations: golf, beer brewing, music composition and arranging. Home: 702 Summit St. Aurora MN 55705 Office: Eveleth Gilbert Schs 801 Jones St Eveleth MN 55734 Office Phone: 218-744-7782. E-mail: r.holbeck@mchsi.com.

HOLBERG, AMBER MARIE, structural engineer; b. Casper, Wyo., Oct. 4, 1975; d. Robert and Anita Lynn Kuhlman; m. Lukas Donald Holberg, Jan. 6, 1996; 1 child, Lucille Olivia. BS in Archtl. Engring., U. Wyo., 1998, MSCE, 2000. EIT Wyo. Structural engr. CTA Inc., Billings, Mont., 2000—. Mem.: Am. Inst. Steel Constrn., Tau Beta Pi. Republican. Lutheran. Avocations: piano, knitting, volleyball.

HOLBERT, KEITH EDWIN, engineering educator; s. William T. and Marjorie S. Holbert; m. Cecilia B. Holbert; 1 child, Kara E.; m. Elizabeth K. Patterson (div.). BS, U. Tenn., 1984, MS, 1986, PhD, 1989. Registered profl. engr., Ariz., 1997. Engr. AMS Corp., Knoxville, Tenn., 1984—87; asst. prof. Ariz. State U., Tempe, Ariz., 1989—95, assoc. prof., 1995—, assoc. chair, 1997—2004. Vis. scientist Los Alamos (N.Mex.) Nat. Lab., 2004—. Author: Electrical Energy Conversion and Transport: an interactive computer-based approach, 2004; co-author: Innovations: World Innovations in Engineering Education and Research, 2004, Encyclopedia of Electrical and Electronics Engineering, 1999; contbr. articles to profl. jours. Recipient Tchg. Excellence award, Fulton Sch. Engring., 1996—97; fellow, Inst. Nuc. Power Ops., 1984—85, U.S. Dept. Energy, 1985—86. Mem.: IEEE (chmn. student activities 2001—05, Spl. Chair award 2003), Am. Soc. Engring. Edn., Am. Nuc. Soc. Office: Arizona State University Electrical Engineering Department Tempe AZ 85287-5706 Office Phone: 480-965-3424. E-mail: holbert@asu.edu.

HOLBERT, KELLY MCKAY, exhibition coordinator, art historian; b. Wash., Feb. 27, 1967; d. John McKay and Sara (Hedekin) Holbert. BA in History of Art cum laude, Princeton U., NJ, 1989; MA, Yale U., New Haven, Conn., 1991, MPhil, 1993, PhD, 1995. Carol Bates grad. fellow Walters Art Gallery, Balt., 1995—96, rsch. assoc. medieval art, 1996—98; asst. curator medieval art Walters Art Mus. (formerly known as Walters Art Gallery), Balt., 1998—2002; exhbn. coord. Smith Coll. Mus. Art, Northampton, Mass., 2002—. Lectr. in field. Contbr. articles to profl. jours., chapters to books; contbg. author Medieval Art, 1997, Manuscripts and Rare Books, 1997, volume editor (collection catalogue) Ethiopian Art: The Walters Art Museum, 2001. Sumner McK. Crosby grant, 1992, 1993—94, Andrew W. Mellon Dissertation fellowship, 1994—95. Mem.: Medieval Acad. Am., Internat. Ctr. Medieval Art, Coll. Art Assn., Am. Assn. Museums. Office: Smith Coll Mus Art Elm St at Bedford Ter Northampton MA 01063 Business E-Mail: kholbert@smith.edu.

HOLBERTON, PHILIP VAUGHAN, entrepreneur, educator; b. N.Y.C., Sept. 29, 1942; s. Robert Maynard and Charlotte Metcalf (Stone) H.; m. Gale Russell, May 16, 1970 (div. 1980); children: Matthew Russell, Alexandra; m. Anne Meigs Blodget, June 6, 1987; 1 child, Philip Vaughan Jr., Tod. AB in Acctg., Franklin and Marshall Coll., Lancaster, Pa., 1964. CPA, N.Y. Auditor Hurdman and Cranstoun CPAs, N.Y.C., 1964-72; mgr. audit svcs. Peat Marwick CPAs, N.Y.C., 1975-79; investment profl. McDonald & Co., N.Y.C., 1972-75; asst. contr. Becton Dickinson & Co., Franklin Lakes, N.J., 1979-81, group contr. Paramus, N.J., 1981-85; v.p. fin. Gen. Cinema Theatres, Chestnut Hill, Mass., 1985-91; v.p. fin. and adminstrn., CFO, Cambridge, Neuroscience, Inc., Cambridge, Mass., 1991-95; founder Holberton Group, Inc., Lincoln, Mass., 1995—. Outside dir. Mgmt. Decision Lab., NYU, 1981-84; adj. faculty Northeastern U., Brandeis U., Babson Coll.; bd. dirs. Barbour Stockwell, Inc. Chmn. strategic planning panel United Way of Bergen County, Paramus, 1983-85; dir. Poppenhusen Inst., College Point, N.Y., 1981-83; sr. warden St. Anne's in the Fields, Lincoln, Mass., 1994-96. Mem. AICPA, Fin. Execs. Inst. (pres. bd. dirs. Boston chpt. 1995-96), Nat. Spkrs. Assn., New Eng. Spkrs. Assn. (bd. dirs. 1998-2002). Office: Holberton Group Inc PO Box 254 Lincoln MA 01773-0254 Office Phone: 781-259-9719. Business E-Mail: pholberton@holberton.com.

HOLBIK, KAREL, economics professor; b. Czech Republic, Sept. 9, 1920; came to U.S., 1948, naturalized, 1952; s. Karel and Catherine (Krouzel) H.; m. Olga Rehackova, Sept. 10, 1956; 1 son, Thomas. JD, Charles U., Prague, 1947; MBA, U. Detroit, 1949; PhD, U. Wis., 1956. Researcher Bank of Am., San Francisco, 1951-53; teaching asst. in banking U. Wis., 1953-55; asst. prof. econs. Lafayette Coll., Easton, Pa., 1955-58; prof. econs. Boston U., 1958-86, prof. econs. emeritus, 1986—. Cons. U.S. Naval War Coll., Newport, R.I., 1963-64, lectr., 1964-73; vis. prof. U. Brussels, 1969-70; vis. faculty Harvard U., 1981-98; chief sect. for devel. fin. instns. UN, 1976-80; Fulbright sr. scholar U. Tunis, 1983-84; internat. fin. cons., 1986—. Author: Italy in International Cooperation, 1959, Postwar Trade in Divided Germany, 1964, The United States, The Soviet Union and the Third World, 1968, West German Foreign Aid 1956-1966, 1968, American-East European Trade, 1969, Contemporary American Economic Problems, 1970, Trade and Industrialization in the Central American Common Market, 1972, Monetary Policy in Twelve Industrial Countries, 1973, Industrialization and Employment in Puerto Rico, 1975; others. Mem. Am. Econ. Assn., Am. Fin. Assn. Home: 313 Country Club Rd Newton MA 02459-3148 *It appears that America, more than any other country, challenges human capabilities and permits individual dreams to come true.*

HOLBROOK, CONNIE C., lawyer; b. 1946; BA, Brigham Young U.; JD, U. Utah. Bar: 1974. Asst. sec. Mountain Fuel Supply Co., staff attty., v.p., sec.; sr. v.p. gen. counsel, corp. sec. Questar Corp., Salt Lake City, 1993—. Bd. dirs. United Way, Salt Lake City. Mem.: ABA, Am. Soc. Corp. Secs. Office: Questar Corp 180 East 100 S PO Box 45433 Salt Lake City UT 84145-0433 Office Phone: 801-324-5215. Office Fax: 801-324-5483. E-mail: connie.holbrook@questar.com.

HOLBROOK, JAY MACK, publishing company executive; b. Chesterfield, Idaho, Jan. 12, 1937; s. Lawrence E. and Mary Marjorie Holbrook; m. DeLene Clark, Dec. 20, 1962; children: Jalene, Lanae, Marinda, Danelle. BS, Utah State U., 1961; MA, Georgetown U., 1967, U. Wis., 1970. Contract adminstr. Dept. Navy, Washington, 1962-66; instr., asst. prof. Edgewood Coll., 1969, Brigham Young U., 1970-71, Utah State U., 1971-72, Nichols Coll., 1972-74, Cen. N.E., 1979-83, Mt. Wauchussett Community Coll., 1979-80; pub. Holbrook Rsch. Inst., Oxford, Mass., 1975—, Archive Pub., Oxford, 1990—. Sr. trainer Applicon, Burlington, Mass., 1983-84, Apollo, Chelmsford, Mass., 1984-85; bd. dirs. Holbrook Rentals, Oxford, Micro Tech Supply, Oxford, Archive Pub., Oxford. Author numerous publs. on Mass. vital records, census and demographic reconstrn. of colonial New Eng. Mem. Oxford Fin. Com., 1989-96, pers. bd., 1999-2003, cable adv. com., 1999-2003. Home and Office: 1462 W 1970 N Provo UT 84604-1153

HOLBROOK, JEFFREY, art educator, secondary school educator; b. Columbus, Ohio, Oct. 24, 1975; s. Jerry Lee and Rose Marie Holbrook. BS Education, Ashland U., Ohio. Art tchr., Bucyrus, Ohio, 2000—. Coach football Buycrus H.S, 2000—. Avocation: weightlifting. E-mail: holbrookj@wynford.kiz.oh.us.

HOLBROOK, KAREN ANN, academic administrator, biologist; b. Des Moines, Nov. 6, 1942; married, 1973; 1 child. BS, U. Wis., 1963, MS, 1966; PhD in Biol. Structure, U. Wash., 1972. From instr. to assoc. prof. U. Wash. Sch. of Medicine, Seattle, 1971-79, vice chmn. dept. biol. structure, 1981—93, prof., 1984—93, assoc. dean sci. affairs, 1985—93; sr. v.p. & prof. U. Ga., Athens, Ga., 1993—98; pres. Ohio State U., Columbus, Ohio, 2002—. Instr. biology Ripon Coll., 1966-69; NIH trainee, 1969-72, trainee, sr. fellow dermatology, 1976-78, mem. study sect. gen. medicine; adj. assoc. prof. med. dermatology, U. Wash., 1979-84; mem. spl. study sect. Nat. Inst. Arthritis & Metabollic Diseases, Nat. Inst. Arthritis, Diabetes & Digestive Kidney Diseases, 1985-88; adj. prof. med. dermatology, 1984-93. Named Disting. Woman Physician/Scientist, 1996; recipient Kung Sun Oh Mem prize, 34th Annual Mation Spencer Fay Nat. Bd. award, Disting. Contribn. to Rsch. Admin. award. Mem. AAAS, Am. Assn. Anatomists, Am. Soc. Cell Biology, Soc. Invest Dermatology, Soc. Pediat. Dermatology, Am. Assn. Of Univ., Nat. Assn of State Univ & Land Grant Coll., Assn of Am. Med. Coll. Commn on Higher Edn.; bd. dir. ACT, Am. Coun. On Edn., Nat. Merit Scholarship Corp, Nat. Coun. For Sci. .and Environment, Huntington Bancshares, Reservoir Venture Ptnrs., Columbus Tech. Coun., Columbus Ptnrshp., Ctr. of Sci. & Industry, Columbus Downtown Dev. Corp., Ctrl. Ohio United Negro Coll. Fund, United Way of Ctrl. Ohio, Greater Columbus Area C. of C., CEOs for Cities, Columbus Sch. For Girls; Sigma Xi; trustee, Cap. So. Urban Redev. Corp. Achievements include research in fine structural & biochemical analysis of human skin including development of the human epidermis and dermis in vivo prenatal diagnosis of inherited skin diseases, structural abnormalities of the dermis in individuals with inherited disorders of connective tissue metabolism, epidermis in inherited disorders of keratinization. Office: Off of the Pres Ohio State Univ Columbus OH 43210*

HOLBROOKE, RICHARD CHARLES ALBERT, former ambassador, investment banker, writer; b. N.Y.C., Apr. 24, 1941; s. Dan and Trudi (Moos) H.; children: David Dan, Anthony Andrew. BA, Brown U., 1962; postgrad., Princeton, 1969-70. Joined Fgn. Service, 1962; served in Vietnam, 1963-66; mem. White House staff, 1966-67; assigned State Dept.; staff Paris (France) peace talks on Vietnam, 1968-69; dir. Peace Corps, Morocco, 1970-72; mng. editor Fgn. Policy mag., 1972-77; cons. Commn. Orgn. Govt. for Conduct of Fgn., 1974-75; contbg. editor Newsweek Internat., 1976; asst. sec. for East Asian and Pacific affairs Dept. State, Washington, 1977-81; v.p. Public Strategies, Washington, 1981-85; sr. advisor Lehman Bros., 1981-84, mng. dir., 1985-93; U.S. amb. Federal Republic of Germany, 1993-94; asst. sec. state European and Can. affairs Dept. State, Washington, 1994-96; vice chmn. Credit Suisse First Boston, N.Y.C., 1996-99; U.S. amb. to U.N. N.Y.C., 1999—2001; vice chmn. Perseus LLC, N.Y.C., 2001—; pres. Global Bus. Coalition on HIV/AIDS, 2001—. Chief negotiator Dayton Peace Accords, Bosnia, 1995; spl. presdl. emissary to Cyprus; mem. Trilateral Commn., chmn., Asia Society, 2002-. Author: vol. The Pentagon Papers, 1967, To End a War, 1998; contbr. numerous articles to N.Y. Times, Washington Post, Wall St. Jour., Atlantic, other mags. and jours.; co-author: Counsel to the President, 1991. Bd. dirs. Internat. Rescue Com.; chmn. Refugees Internat. Mem. Am. Acad. Berlin, Coun. Fgn. Rels., Inst. Strategic Studies; bd mem., Amer. Museum Nat. History, Nat. Endowment for Democracy, Human Genome Sciences; Fellow, Am. Acad.of Arts and Sci., 2004 Office: Coun Fgn Rels 58 E 68th St New York NY 10021*

HOLBROW, GWENDOLYN JANE, artist, writer; b. N.Y.C., Aug. 22, 1957; d. Charles Howard and Mary Ross Holbrow; m. Mark Joseph Kacvinsky; children: Hilary, Charles, Giles, Felicity. BA with honors, U. Wis., 1980; BA, Framingham State Coll., 2001. Cert. fluency in German as fgn. lang. Goethe Inst. Freelance writer, 1997—; instr. Danforth Mus. Sch., Framingham, Mass., 2001—. Freelance editor, graphic designer, desk-top pub., Frankfurt am Main, Germany, 1990—98; contbg. author Main City, Frankfurter Allgemeine Zeitung, Frankfurt am Main, 1997—98, Middlesex Beat, Groton, 2001—; lectr. Framingham State Coll., 2002—, AAUW, 2002; author, rev. artsMedia, Boston, 2002—. Mixed-media installation, The Throne Of The Queen Of The Universe and Her Handmaidens, 2000, mixed-media fountain with barbie doll, Keep It Clean, 2000 (First prize Concord Art Assn., 2000), acoustic copper sculpture, Gravity Chimes, 2001 (Juror's Choice award Cambridge Art Assn., 2001), poster, Universal Applicaton, 2002; author: (essay) Louse Bourgeois: Bridging the Chasm Between Self and Other, 2001 (Cheryl di Mento Art History Essay award Framingham State Coll., 2001). Town meeting mem. Town Meeting, Framingham, 2001—01. Named winner, Artists' Valentine Grant Competition, 2003; recipient Silver medal, Mass. Hort. Soc., 2002, 2005, Gold medal, 2004, Best of Show for Queen Kong sculpture, Cambridge Art Assn., 2004. Mem.: New Eng. Sculptors Assn., Concord Art Assn., Cambridge Art Assn., Internat. Sculpture Ctr., Framingham Artists' Guild. Unitarian Universalist. Avocation: singing in choirs and opera. Business E-Mail: holbrow@hotmail.com.

HOLBROW, KATHERINE A., conservator; b. Madison, Wis., Mar. 8, 1962; d. Charles Howard and Mary Louise (Ross) Holbrow. AB in History, Fine Arts, Amherst Coll., 1984; MA in Art History, U. Mass., 1990; MS in Art Conservation, U. Del., 1994. Intern objects conservation Nat. Mus. Am. History, Washington, 1990—91; art objects conservator, Mellon fellow Nat. Gallery Art, Washington, 1994—97; conservator, dept. head Williamstown Art Conservation Ctr., Mass., 1998—. Mem.: Am. Inst. for Conservation (assoc.). Office: Williamstown Art Conservation Ctr 225 South St Williamstown MA 01267

HOLCH, GREGORY JOHN, editor, writer; b. Tokyo, Nov. 19, 1952; (parents Am. citizens); s. Arthur Everett and Ellen Constance (O'Keefe) Holch; m. Rhonda Lyn Brauer, Sept. 7, 1989; children: Jillian Brauer, Justin Brauer. BA in English, Manhattanville Coll., 1974; MA in Am. Civilization, NYU, 1984. Editl. asst. Globe Comm., Greenwich, Conn., 1977-78, Random House Student Book Clubs, N.Y.C., 1978-80, Bantam Books, N.Y.C., 1981-83; assoc. editor Scholastic, N.Y.C., 1983-85, editor, 1985-94, sr. editor, 1994—. Guest editor Mademoiselle mag., 1974. Author: (novels) The Things with Wings, 1998; co-author: Jungle Jokes, 1979; author: short stories; contbr. photographs to mags. Mem.: Soc. Children's Book Writers and Illustrators, Am. Radio Relay League (life). Avocations: amateur radio, photography. Office: Scholastic Inc 557 Broadway New York NY 10012-3919

HOLCOM, FLOYD EVERETT, international business consultant; b. Astoria, Oreg., Jan. 19, 1964; s. Edward Everett and Esther Jean (Wilkinson) H.; m. Sheryl Plagata, Dec. 1994; children: Nathaniel, Victoria Elizabeth. BA in Bus. Adminstrn., Oreg. State U., 1989; MBA, Portland State U., 1991. Sr. spl. ops. engr. Joint Spl. Forces Commd. Dept. Def.; dir. internat. trade field study program Internat. Trade Inst., Portland, Oreg.; internat. dir. The IBIS Group, 1991—; with Peratrovich, Nottingham & Drage Inc., Engring. Cons., Astoria, Oreg., 1997—. Cons. Nike, Inc., 1991-93; spl. envoy State of Oreg. rep. to Fujian Provincial Govt., China, 1990; ind. retail co. with Unocal, 1979-89. Responsible for 1st U.S. comml. shipment to Vietnam since 1975, 1992. Adv. coun. Internat. Bus. Degree program Linfield Coll.; adv. bd. Open U. of Ho Chi Minh City, Vietnam. With U.S. Army, 1981-86, spl. forces res., 1986-94, spl. forces N.G., 1994—. Mem. Assn. Internat. Trade Specialists (past v.p., bd. dirs.), Japan-Am. Soc. Oreg., Pacific N.W. Internat. Trade Assn., Suzhou-Portland Sister City Assn. (bd. dirs.), N.W. Regional China Coun. (past chmn. fgn. hospitality com.), Soc. Am. Mil. Engrs., Army Engr. Assn., Spl. Forces Assn., World Affairs Coun. Oreg., World Trade Ctr. Portland, Columbia River Maritime Mus. Assn., Am. Philatelic Soc., Clatsop County Hist. Soc. (bd. dirs. 1998—). Republican. Episcopalian. Home: 652 Alameda Ave Astoria OR 97103-5945

HOLCOMB, DONALD FRANK, physicist, academic administrator; b. Chesterton, Ind., Nov. 8, 1925; s. Roger L. and Ethel (Frank) H.; m. Barbara Page, Aug. 26, 1950; children: Douglas Page, Jane D., Nancy M. AB, DePauw U., 1949; MS, U. Ill., 1950, PhD, 1954. Instr. U. Ill., 1954; mem. faculty Cornell U., 1954—, prof. physics, 1962—, dir. lab. atomic and solid state physics, 1964-68, chmn. dept. physics, 1969-74, 82-86, trustee, 1976-81. Cons. Corning Glass Research Lab., 1959-64, Central Inst. Indsl. Research, Oslo, Norway, 1962 Contbr. profl. jours. Served with USNR, 1944-46. Sr. vis. fellow NATO, 1962; Guggenheim fellow, 1968-69; Sci. Research Council sr. fellow, 1978 Fellow Am. Phys. Soc., AAAS; mem. Am. Assn. Physics Tchrs. (pres. 1987, Oersted medal 1996), Sigma Xi. Presbyterian. Achievements include spl. rsch. solid state physics, chem. physics, coll. physics course devel. Home: 385 Savage Farm Dr Ithaca NY 14850-6505

HOLCOMB, GRANT, III, museum director; b. San Bernardino, Calif., Sept. 30, 1944; BA, UCLA, 1967; MA, U. Del., 1970, PhD, 1972. Asst. prof. Mt. Holyoke Coll., South Hadley, Mass., 1972-80, SUNY, Stony Brook, 1980-81; curator San Diego Mus. Art, 1981-83; assoc. dir. Timken Art Mus., San Diego, 1983-85; dir. Meml. Art Gallery, Rochester, N.Y., 1985—. Author: (exhibit catalogue) John Sloan, The Gloucester Years, 1980, Wake of the

Ferry, 1984; editor: Voices in the Gallery: Writers on Art, 2001; contbr. articles to pofl. jours. Bd. dirs. BOA edits., 1991—, Conv. Vis. Bur., 1990—, Friends of Ganondagan, 1994—; former bd. dirs. Rochester Contemp., coun. advs. Kress fellow Nat. Gallery Art, 1972; Am. Council Learned Socs. grantee, 1980. Mem.: Arts Cultural Coun. Rochester, Aesthetic Edn. Inst. (bd. dirs. 1985—), Arts and Cultural Coun. of Greater Rochester (bd. dirs. 1985—), Assn. Art Mus. Dirs. Office: Meml Art Gallery 500 University Ave Rochester NY 14607-1414 Office Phone: 585-473-7720 Ext 3002.

HOLCOMB, JEFFREY G., lawyer; b. Hamilton, Ohio, Dec. 16, 1971; s. John Frederick and Judith Ellen Holcomb; m. Brandi L. Holcomb, July 13, 2001. BA in History, Xavier U., Cin., 1994; JD, U. Toledo, Ohio, 1998. Bar: Ohio 1998, U.S. Dist. Ct. (so. dist.) Ohio 1999. Law clk. Holcomb & Hyde LLP, Hamilton, Ohio, 1995, County Ct. Common Pleas, 1996—97; legal intern City of Maumee Prosecutor's Office, Ohio, 1998; atty. Holcomb & Hyde LLP, Hamilton, 1998—2000, John A. Garretson Co., LPA, Hamilton, 2000—. Mem.: ABA, Ohio Acad. Trial Lawyers, Butler County Bar Assn., Ohio State Bar Assn. Office: John A Garretson Co LPA PO Box 1166 Hamilton OH 45012

HOLCOMB, LYLE DONALD, JR., retired lawyer; b. Miami, Fla., Feb. 3, 1929; s. Lyle Donald and Hazel Irene (Watson) H.; m. Barbara Jean Roth, July 12, 1952; children: Susan Holcomb Davis, Scott H. (deceased), Douglas J., Mark E. BA, U. Mich., 1951; JD, U. Fla., 1954. Bar: U.S. Ct. Appeals (5th and 11th cirs.) 1981, U.S. Supreme Ct. 1966. Ptnr. Holcomb & Holcomb, Miami, 1955-72; assoc. Copeland, Therrel, Baisden & Peterson, Miami Beach, Fla., 1972-75; ptnr. Therrel, Baisden, Stanton, Wood & Setlin, Miami Beach, Fla., 1976-85, Therrel, Baisden & Meyer Weiss, Miami Beach, Fla., 1985-93; pvt. practice Tallahassee, Fla., 1993-95. Organizing pres. So. Fla. Migrant Legal Svcs. Program (now Fla. Rural Legal Svcs.), 1966-68. Exec. bd. So. Fla. coun. Boy Scouts Am., 1958-93; past pres., past counselor Miami chpt. Huguenot Soc. Fla. With USNR, 1947-53. Recipient Silver Beaver award, So. Fla. coun. Boy Scouts Am., 1966. Fellow Am. Coll. Trust and Estate Counsel, 1980-94, Acad. Fla. Probate and Trust Litigation Attys., 1980-95; mem. Dade County Bar Assn. (dir. 1960-71, sec. 1963-71), Miami Beach Bar Assn. (pres. 1980), Estate Planning Coun. Greater Miami, Soc. Mayflower Descs. (past pres. Miami club, past counselor state soc.), SAR (past pres. Miami chpt.), Univ. Yacht Club. Republican. Mem. United Ch. Of Christ. Home: 3538 Killarney Plaza Dr Tallahassee FL 32309-3491 Personal E-mail: lholcomb23@aol.com.

HOLCOMB, MILDRED GENEVA COMRIE, elementary school educator; b. New London, Conn., Sept. 22, 1941; d. Wendell Silas and Florence Marjorie (Gallup) Comrie; m. Michael Alan Holcomb, Dec. 22, 1973. BS, Ea. Nazarene Coll., 1963; MA, U. Conn., 1968; MS, U. Houston, Clear Lake, Tex., 1983; EdD, Nova S.E. U., 2002. Cert. elem. edn. tchr., Tex. Tchr. 2d grade Ledyard (Conn.) Sch. Dist., 1963-68; tchr. 1st and 2d grades Mt. Vernon (Ohio) Sch. Dist., 1968-72; tchr. 4th grade Sheldon Ind. Sch. Dist., Houston, 1972-75; tchr. K-2d Pasadena (Tex.) Ind. Sch. Dist., 1976-83; tchr. kindergarten and 1st grade Sheldon Ind. Sch. Dist., Houston, 1985—. Vol. Nixon polit. campaign, Houston, 1972; organist Open Fellowship Ch. of the Nazarene, Houston, 1987-88, Broadway Ch. of the Nazarene, Houston, 1988-89, Pasadena Ch. of the Nazarene, 1980-81, Crosby Ch. of the Nazarene, 1994—; v.p. Pasadena Ind. Sch. Dist. PTO, 1979-80; pres. Parkway Elem. Sch. PTO, Houston, 1993-94; founder Parkside C.H.A.T.S. miniworkshops, 1990—. Named Tchr. of Yr., Parkway Elem. Sch., 1990-91. Mem. Assn. Tchrs. and Profl. Educators, Sheldon Educators Assn. Republican. Avocations: organ, reading, photography, gardening, travel.

HOLCOMB, RICHARD DENNIS, lawyer; BA in Polit. Sci., Hampden Sydney Coll. Va., 1976; JD, U. Richmond, 1979. Chief staff U.S. Reps. John Linder, D. French Slaughter, Jr., Craig T. James, 1989-94; commr. Va. Dept. of Motor Vehicles, Richmond, 1994—2001; gen. counsel, sr. v.p. law and regulatory affairs Am. Trucking Assns., Alexandria, Va., 2001—. Office: Am Trucking Assns 2200 Mill Rd Alexandria VA 22314-4677

HOLCOMB, RITA, landscape architect; b. Bonham, Tex., Aug. 29, 1948; d. Guy M. and Marie (Moore) Ownby; m. Darrell Holcomb, July 29, 1972; 1 child, Stuart. A in Fine Arts, Grayson County Coll., Denison, Tex., 1974, A in Bus. Adminstrn., 1991. Owner Holcomb Miniatures, Sherman, Tex., 1980-90; sales Breathco/Mediserv, Sherman, 1990-94; owner Plants on the Move, Sherman, 1994—. Pres. bd. dirs. Red River Hist. Mus., Sherman, 1997, Sherman Cmty. Players Theater Guild, 1989; active Sherman City Coun., 1999—2000; co-chair Conv. and Visitors Coun., 2002; bd. dirs. Texoma Coun. Govts., 1999—2000, LWV Sherman/Grayson County, Tex., 2001—02, Grayson County Tri-County Nutrition, 1998—, Sherman Preservation League, 1995—97, 2000—01. Avocations: theater, miniatures, Tae Kwan Do, genealogy.

HOLCOMBE, JOSEPH STEVEN, academic administrator, educator; b. Charlotte, NC, Oct. 2, 1950; s. Joseph and Lois Inez Holcombe; m. Suzanne Camille Keller, June 24, 1972; 1 child, Allison Camille. BS in Indsl. Mgmt., Clemson U., 1972; MBA, Clemson-Furman U., 1979; MS in Indsl. Mgmt., Clemson U., 1991. Mgr. comml. tufted plans Bigelow-Sanford, Inc., Greenville, SC, 1972—88; indsl. engr. Asten, Inc., Clinton, SC, 1993—2000; asst. dir. of faculty svcs. So. Wesleyan U., Central, SC, 2002—03, dir. faculty svcs., 2003—04, dir. bus. programs/adult and grad. studies, 2004—. Mem. adj. faculty Furman U., Greenville, SC, 1991—93; adj. prof. So. Wesleyan U., Central, 2002—; vis. instr. Clemson U., 1991—93. Vol. builder Habitat for Humanity, Greer, SC, 2000—; learn-to-swim instr. Upstate S.C. chpt.ARC, Greenville, 2001—02, first aid/cardiopulmonary instr., 1999—, first aid/safety com., 2001—; Sunday sch. tchr. Brushy Creek Bapt. Ch., Taylors, SC, 1990—; deacon Brushy Creek Bapt., Taylors, SC, 1990—2002. Named New Vol. of the Yr. Runner-up, Upstate S.C. chpt. of the ARC, 2001. Mem.: Am. Prodn. and Inventory Control Soc. (assoc.; cert. prodn. and inventory mgmt. 1992, cert. integrated resource mgmt. 1995, Instr. of the Yr. Indsl. Crescent chpt. 2001). Southern Baptist. Avocations: jogging, reading historical fiction, travel. Office: So Wesleyan U 907 Wesleyan Dr Central SC 29630 Office Phone: 864-644-5336. Business E-Mail: sholcombe@swu.edu.

HOLCOMBE, RANDALL GREGORY, economics professor; b. Bridgeport, Conn., June 4, 1950; s. Lynn Montanye Holcombe and Gloria Gabriel (Rita) Ledbetter; m. Lora Hunt Pritchett, June 18, 1983. BS, U. Fla., 1972; MA, Va. Tech., 1974, PhD, 1976. Asst. prof. Tex. A&M U., College Station, 1975-77; prof. Auburn (Ala.) U., 1977-88, Fla. State U., Tallahassee, 1988—. Sr. fellow James Madison Inst., Tallahassee, 2004-, mem. rsch. adv. com., 1987-2004, chmn., 1991-2004; mem. editl. bd., Rev. Austrian Econs., 1987-97, Pub. Fin. Rev., 1995-2003, Quar. Jour. Austrian Econs., 1998-, Pub. Choice, 2004—; adj. scholar Ludwig Von Mises Inst., 1982-; mem. Fla. Gov.'s Coun. Econ. Advisors, 2000-; contbg. editor Independent Rev., 2004—. Author: Public Finance and the Political Process, 1983, An Economic Analysis of Democracy, 1985, Economic Models and Methodology, 1989, The Economic Foundations of Government, 1994, Public Policy and the Quality of Life, 1995, Public Finance: Government Revenues and Expenditures in the United States Economy, 1996, (with R. Sobel) Growth and Variability in State Tax Revenue, 1997, Writing Off Ideas, 2000, From Liberty to Democracy: The Transformation of American Government, 2002; contbr. articles to profl. jours. Scaife Found. fellow, 1972-73, H.B. Earhart Found. fellow, 1973-75; research grantee Earhart Found., 1979-80, 83, 89, 90, 98. Mem. Am. Econ. Assn., Pub. Choice Soc., So. Econ. Assn., Western Econ. Assn. Home: 3514 Limerick Dr Tallahassee FL 32309-3139 Office: Fla State U Dept Econs Tallahassee FL 32306 Business E-Mail: holcombe@garnet.acns.fsu.edu.

HOLCROFT, NANCY ELIZABETH, elementary school educator; b. Plattesburg, N.Y., Mar. 14, 1947; d. James S. and Elizabeth Holcroft. AA, Reedley (Calif.) Coll., 1967; BA, Calif. State U., Fresno, 1969, MA, 1984. Cert. reading specialist Calif. Tchr. Kings Canyon Unified Sch. Dist., Reedley, 1969—. Mem. Sierra Club, Fresno, 1975—, Audubon Soc., Fresno, 1990—2003. Mem.: Kings Canyon Edn. Assn. (tchr. rep., mem. exec. bd.). Democrat. Methodist. Avocations: hiking, reading. Home: 43775 Brookside Miramonte CA 93641 Office: Gt Western Elem Sch 5051 S Frankwood Ave Reedley CA 93654

HOLDAWAY, RONALD M., retired federal judge; b. Afton, Wyo. m. Judy Janowski, Dec. 1958; children: Denise, Georgia. BA, U. Wyo., 1957, JD, 1959. Bar: Wyo. 1959, U.S. Dist. Ct. (Wyo.), U.S. Ct. Mil. Appeals, 1960, U.S. Army Ct. Mil. Rev., U.S. Supreme Ct., 1967. Commd. 2nd lt. U.S. Army., 1960, advanced through grades to brig. gen., 1989; legal staff officer U.S. Army, Ft. Lewis, Washington, 1960-63, legal staff Hawaii, 1963-66, instr. criminal law, Judge Advocate Gen.'s Sch. Charlottesville, Va., 1966-69, staff judge advocate 1st cav. divsn. Vietnam, 1969-70, chief govt. appellate divsn. Washington, 1971-75, chief of pers., 1975-77, staff judge advocate Stuttgart, Germany, 1978-80, exec. to judge advocate gen. Washington, 1980-81, asst. judge advocate gen., 1981-83; judge advocate U.S. Army Europe, Heidelberg, Germany, 1983-87; chief judge Ct. Mil. Review U.S. Army, Washington, 1987-89; judge U.S. Ct. Vets. Appeals, Washington DC, 1990—2002; ret., 2002. Decorated Bronze Star, Legion of Merit, Disting. Svc. medal with Oak Leaf Cluster, Meritorious Svc. medal with Oak Leaf Cluster, Air medal, Nat. Def. Svc. medal, Vietnam Campaign medal with 4 campaign stars, Vietnam Svc. medal, Overseas medal (3). Mem. Wyo. State Bar Assn., Assn. U.S. Army, Army Navy Club.

HOLDEMAN, JOSHUA, art appraiser; BA in Art History, MA in Painting, Bates Coll., Maine. Head, photography dept. Phillips de Pury & Luxembourg; photograph expert Robert Miller Art Gallery; head, photography dept. Christie's, NYC, head, 20th Century decorative arts dept., internat. dir. Exhibit curator Hotel de Sully, Paris, Victoria & Albert Mus., London. Office: Christie's 20 Rockefeller Plz New York NY 10020 Office Phone: 212-636-2330. Office Fax: 212-492-5718. Business E-Mail: jholdeman@christies.com.

HOLDEN, BETSY D., former food products company executive; b. Lubbock, Tex., 1956; BA, Duke U.; MA in edn., Northwestern U., MBA, 1982. Asst. product mgr. desserts Gen. Foods Corp., 1982—84; brand mgr., venture div. Kraft Foods Inc., 1984—85, brand mgr., Miracle Whip Northfield, Ill., 1985—87, group brand mgr., confections & snacks, 1987—90, v.p. new product devel. and strategy Northfield, Ill., 1990—91, v.p., mktg., dinners, & enhancers, 1991—93, pres. Tombstone Pizza Northfield, Ill., 1993—95, exec. v.p., gen. mgr. cheese divsn., 1995—97, pres. cheese divsn., 1997—98, exec. v.p., ops., procurement, research & devel., consumer insights and E-commerce, 1998—2000; pres., CEO Kraft Foods North America, 2000—01; co-CEO Kraft Foods Inc., 2001—03, pres., global mktg. & category devel., 2004—05. Mem., bd. dirs. Kraft Foods, Tribune Co., Tupperware Corp. Pres. Chicago's Off the Street Club; mem., bd. Grocery Manufacturers of Amer., Evanston Northwestern Healthcare.

HOLDEN, CAROL H., county official; b. Boston, Nov. 6, 1942; m. Donald B. Holden; 4 children. BA, Trinity Coll., 1964; MAT, Boston Coll., 1965. Intern U.S. Senate, 1963-64; mem. N.H. Ho. of Reps., 1984-97, vice chair children, youth and juvenile justice com.; mem. state-fed. rels. com.; asst. majority leader, 1996. Vice chair Hillsborough County Bd. Commrs., 1997—; mem. Amherst Ways and Means Commn., 1983-86; tchr., vol. coord. Del. N.H. Constl. Conv., 1984; pres. Amherst Women's Rep. Club, 1986-88; v.p. N.H. Fed. Rep. Women's Club, 1989-94, pres., 1994-95; mem. Amherst Sch. Dist. Mod., 1990—; dir. N.H. Ptnrs. in Edn., 1987—, sec., 1989—, vice chair, 1990—, chair, 1992—; mem. Gov.'s Steering Com. on Volunteerism, 1991-96; mem. N.H. Alliance for Effective Schs., 1991-96; v.p. N.H. Congress Parents and Tchrs., 1984-86, 90-92; trustee N.H. Childrens Trust Fund, 1991-98; treas. Nat. Conf. County Rep. County Officials, 2004-; bd. dirs. Nashua Cmty. Coun., 2002. Mem. Nat. Assn. of Counties (v.p.), Trinity Coll. Alumni Assn. (bd. dirs. 1980-87, sec. bd. dirs. 1994-97, 2d v.p. 1997-98), N.H. Assn. of Counties (1st v.p. 1999—2001, pres. elect, 2001-03, pres. 2003), Nat. Assn. of Counties (steering com. labor and employment 1999—, bd. dirs. 2002—), Boston Coll. Club of N.H. (pres. 1999-2001), Vesta Roy Series (v.p. 2002—). Avocations: travel, sailing, tennis, skiing, reading. Home: PO Box 13 Amherst NH 03031-0013 Office: Bd Commrs 329 Mast Rd Ste120 Goffstown NH 03045 Office Phone: 603-624-1129. Business E-Mail: ccommish@rcn.com.

HOLDEN, DONALD, artist, writer; b. L.A., Apr. 22, 1931; s. Mack and Miriam (Epstein) H.; m. Wilma Shaffer, Jan. 10, 1954; children: Wendy, Blake. BA, Columbia U., 1951; MA, Ohio State U., 1952; LLD (hon.), Maine Coll. Art, 1986. Teaching asst. Ohio State U., Columbus, 1951-52; dir. pub. rels. Phila. Coll. Art, 1953-55; dir. pub. rels. and personnel Henry Dreyfuss, N.Y.C., 1956-60; assoc. mgr. pub. rels. Met. Mus. Art, N.Y.C., 1960-61; art cons. Fortune mag., N.Y.C., 1962; editorial dir. Watson-Guptill Publs., 1963-79, Am. Artist mag., N.Y.C., 1971-75. Lectr. in field; mem. faculty, mem. artist adv. bd. Scottsdale Artists Sch., Ariz. Author: Art Career Guide, 1961, rev. edits., 1967, 73, 83, Whistler Landscapes and Seascapes, 1969 (selected for inclusion in White House Libr. by Assn. Am. Pubs. 1975), Donald Holden Watercolors, 2004; under pseudonym Wendon Blake: Acrylic Watercolor Painting, 1970, Complete Guide to Acrylic Painting, 1971, Creative Color: A Practical Guide for Oil Painters, 1972, Landscape Painting in Oil, 1976, The Watercolor Painting Book, 1978, The Acrylic Painting Book, 1978, The Oil Painting Book, 1979, The Portrait and Figure Painting Book, 1979, The Drawing Book, 1980, The Color Book, 1981, Complete Guide to Landscape Painting in Oil, 1981, Painting in Alkyd, 1982, Creative Color for the Oil Painter, 1983, The Complete Painting Course, 1984, The Complete Oil Painting Book, 1989, The Complete Acrylic Painting Book, 1989, The Complete Watercolor Book, 1989, Getting Started in Drawing, 1991, The Artist's Guide to Using Color, 1992; contbr. articles to profl. publs.; editorial cons., Watson-Guptill Publs., 1979-87; sculpture, watercolors, and drawings in numerous group and one-man exhbns., including retrospective watercolor exhbn. at Butler Inst. Am. Art, Youngstown, Ohio, 1999, Contemporary Art Ctr. Va., 2000, Portland (Maine) Mus. Art, 2004, Springfield (Mo.) Art Mus., 2004, Round Top Ctr. Arts, Damariscotta, Maine, 2004; represented in collections Century Assn., N.Y., Ga. Mus. Art, U. Ga., Athens, Hickory (N.C.) Mus. Art, New Britain (Conn.) Mus. Am. Art, Springfield (Mo.) Art Mus., Wichita Art Mus., Kans., Fine Arts Museums of San Francisco, Met. Mus. Art, N.Y.C., New Orleans Mus. Art, Victoria and Albert Mus., London, Yale U. Art Gallery, New Haven, Ark. Arts Ctr., Little Rock, Ashmolean Mus., Oxford, Eng., Corcoran Gallery, Washington, Meml. Art Gallery, Rochester, N.Y., Farnsworth Mus., Rockland, Maine, Nelson-Atkins Mus. Art, Kansas City, Mo., Columbus (Ohio) Museum Art, Nat. Park Found. (Washington), Ogunquit (Maine) Mus. Am. Art, Portland (Maine) Mus. Art, Art Students League N.Y., Delaware Art Mus., Wilmington, Phila. Mus. Art, Spencer Mus. Art, U. Kans., Lawrence, Bates Coll. Mus. Art., Brit. Mus., London, Ulster Mus., Belfast, No. Ireland, Neuberger Mus. SUNY, Purchase, NAD, N.Y.C., U. N.H. Art Gallery, Durham, Albright-Knox Gallery, Buffalo, Nat. Gallery Art, Washington, Phillips Collection, Washington, Syracuse (N.Y.) U. Libr., Fitzwilliam Mus., Cambridge (Eng.) U. James A. Michener Art Museum, Doylestown, Penn, Munson Williams Proctor Inst., Utica N.Y., Butler Inst. Am. Art, Youngstown, Ohio, Palmer Mus. Art Pa. State U., University Park, U.S. Dept. State, Washington, D.C., Smithsonian Am. Art Mus., Washington, D.C., Nev. Mus. Art, Reno, Nev Recipient Adolph & Clara Obrig Prize, Nat. Acad. Design 176th Ann. Exhbn., 2001; Florsheim Art Fund grant, 1999. Mem. NAD, Artists Equity Assn., Nat. Art Edn. Assn., Maine Coast Artists, Century Assn., Salmagundi Club Office Phone: 914-591-8253.

HOLDEN, FLORENCE CUDWORTH, retired cultural organization administrator; b. Brattleboro, Vt., Apr. 20, 1923; d. William Henry and Edith Lane Cudworth; children: Gwen, Russell, Robin, Bruce, Mark, Sandra, Jody. BA, U. Vt. Pres. Franklin Pierce Brigade, Concord, NH, 1964—2004, Bistate Home Health Care Assocs., 1970—74; trustee Concord Hist. Soc., 2000—. Pres. Concord Hosp. Assocs.; pres. univ. alumni U. Vt., 1960—64, trustee, 1979—87. Served with USN, 1942—45. Recipient Disting. Svc. award, U. Vt., 1962. Home: PO Box 169 Concord NH 03302

HOLDEN, FREDERICK DOUGLASS, JR., lawyer; b. Stockton, Calif., Nov. 21, 1949; s. Frederick Douglass and Sarah Frances (Young) H.; m. Patricia Brierton, June 25, 1988; children: Elizabeth, Andrew. BA, U. Calif., Santa Barbara, 1971; JD, U. Calif., Davis, 1974. Bar: Calif. 1974, D.C. 1996, U.S. Dist. Ct. (no., cen., ea. and so. dists.) Calif. 1974, U.S. Ct. Appeals (9th cir.) 1974, U.S. Ct. Appeals (fed. cir.) 2004, U.S. Dist. Ct. D.C. 1996, U.S. Supreme Ct. 2001. Assoc. Brobeck, Phleger & Harrison LLP, San Francisco, 1974-81, ptnr., 1981—2003; chair bench-bar liaison com. U.S. Bankruptcy Ct. No. Dist. Calif., 2001—02; ptnr. Orrick, Herrington & Sutcliffe, LLP, 2003—. Mem. faculty Practising Law Inst., 1990; spkr. Nat. Conf. Bankruptcy Judges, 1987, 91, Banking Law Inst., 1986, Calif. Continuing Legal Edn. of Bar, Calif., 1983-85, Calif. State Bar, 1993; bd. dirs. Bay Area Bankruptcy Forum. Mng. editor U. Calif. Davis Law Rev., 1974. Fellow Am. Coll. Bankruptcy; mem. ABA (bus. bankruptcy com., spkr. 1991, 95), Calif. Bar Assn. (commendation 1983), San Francisco Bar Assn. (cert. appreciation 1985, 88, 90, 95, chair 2004), Turnaround Mgmt. Assn. (dir., sec. 1994-96), Am. Bankruptcy Inst., Marin Audubon Soc. (bd. dirs. 2003—), San Francisco Yacht Club, Sigma Pi (pres. 1970). Democrat. Avocations: triathlons, skiing, sailing, surfing. Home: 140 Bella Vista Ave Belvedere CA 94920-2466 Office: Orrick Herrington & Sutcliffe LLP The Orrick Bldg 405 Howard St San Francisco CA 94105-2669 Office Phone: 415-773-5985. Business E-Mail: fholden@orrick.com.

HOLDEN, GEORGE FREDRIC, brewing company executive, public policy specialist, author; b. Lander, Wyo., Aug. 29, 1937; s. George Thiel Holden and Rita (Meyer) Zulpo; m. Dorothy Carol Capper, July 5, 1959; children: Lorilyn, Sherilyn, Tamilyn. BSChemE, U. Colo., 1959, MBA in Mktg., 1974. Adminstr. plastics lab. EDP, indsl chems. plant, prodn. process engrng., tool control supervision, aerospace (Minuteman, Polaris, Sparrow), Parlin, NJ, Salt Lake City, Cumberland, Md., 1959-70; by-product sales, new market and new product devel., resource planning and devel. and pub. rels. Adolph Coors Co., Golden, Colo., 1971-76; dir. econ. affairs corp. pub. affairs dept., 1979-84, dir. pub. affairs rsch., 1984-86; owner Phoenix Enterprises, Arvada, 1986—; dep. treas. Jefferson County Colo. Fin. Analysis and Comm., 2003—; mgr. facilities engrng. Coors Container Co., 1976-79; instr. brewing, by-products utilization and waste mgmt. U. Wis.; cons., spkr. in field. Mem. bd. economists Rocky Mountain News, 1990-95; mem. Heritage Found. Ann. Guide to Pub. Policy Expert, 1987—, Spkrs. Bur., Commn. on the Bicentennial US Constn., 1991-93; del. Colo. Rep. Conv., 1976—; adv. Cost of Govt. Day; bd. dirs. Colo. Pub. Expenditures Coun., 1983-86, Nat. Spkrs. Assn., 1982-97, Colo. Spkrs. Assn. (bd. dirs. 1982-97, 1987-90, 91-93 bus economist, 1982-90), Nat. Assn. Bus. Economists, 1982-97, Colo. Assn. Commerce and Industry Execs. Ednl. Found. Sr. fellow budget policy Independence Inst. Colo. "ThinkTank", 1990-95, fiscal policy, 2003—. Mem. congregation coun., Arvada's King of Glory Luth. Ch., 1975-79, 2004-, pres. 2004-); Mem. US Brewers Assn. (chmn. by-products com. 1973-76, ednl. found. 1974-75, Hon. Gavel, 1975), Colo. Ind. Pubs. Assn. (bd. dirs. 2000-2003), Am. Inst. Indsl. Engrs. (dir. 1974-78), Washingtons Am. for Tax Reform Found.; Author: The Phoenix Phenomenon, 1984, Total Power of One in America, 1991 new edit., 2001; Co-author: Secrets of Job Hunting, 1972; contbr. articles to Chem. Engring. mag., 1968-76, over 400 published articles, white papers in field; over 1100 speeches, 640 appearances on radio talk shows nationwide. Home: 6463 Owens St Arvada CO 80004-2732 Office: Phoenix Enterprises PO Box 1900 Arvada CO 80001-1900

HOLDEN, MICHAEL JOHN, lawyer; b. Sheboygan, Wis., Sept. 29, 1955; s. John Robert and Hilda H.; m. Mary Louise Turkovich, Apr. 9, 1983; children: John, Anne. AB, U. Mich., 1977; JD, Duke U., 1980. Bar: Ariz. 1980, U.S. Dist. Ct. Ariz. 1980, U.S. Ct. Appeals (9th cir.) 1980. Assoc. Lewis and Roca, Phoenix, 1980-85, ptnr., 1985-2000, Holden Walker PLC, Phoenix, 2000—. Mem. ABA, Am. Subcontractors Assn. Ariz. (bd. dirs. 1993), Associated Gen. Contractors Ariz. (assoc.), Ariz. State Bar (chmn. constrn. law sect. 1987-89). Office: Holden Brodman PLC 2425 E Camelback Rd Ste 1050 Phoenix AZ 85016-4208 E-mail: mholden@holdenbrodman.com.

HOLDEN, ROBERT (BOB HOLDEN), former governor; b. Kansas City, Mo., Aug. 24, 1949; s. Lee Holden and Wanda Laird; m. Lori Hauser, 1983; children: Robert, John. BS in Polit. Sci., Southwest Mo. State, 1973; Degree Kennedy Sch. Govt. for Public Execs. and Flemming Fellow Leadership Inst., Harvard U. Asst. to state treas. State of Mo., 1976—83; mem. Mo. Ho. of Reps., 1983-89; adminstrv. asst./liaison to U.S. Rep. Richard Gephardt US Ho. Reps., St. Louis, 1989—91; state treas. State of Mo., Jefferson City, 1993—2000, gov., 2001—05. Chmn. gen. approations com.; co-sponsor Excellence in Edn. Act; mem. Bd. Fund Commrs., Mo. State Employees Retirement System, Mo. Bus. Coun., Mo. Rural Opportunities Coun.; past chmn. Mo. Housing Devel. Commn. Dean Am. Legion Mo. Boy's State Legislative Sch.; mem. Holden Scholarship Fund, Leadership St. Louis; former mem. Confluence's Edn. Implementation, Tower Grove Hgts. Neighborhood Assn., Save the Children's Program; mem. Mo. Coun. Econ. Edn., Coun. State Govts.; vice-chair Mo. Cultural Trust. Mem. Nat. Assn. State Treas. (legis. chair). Democrat.

HOLDEN, ROBERT WATSON, radiologist, educator, dean; b. Brazil, Ind., Mar. 31, 1936; s. John William and Naomi Ellen (Watson) H.; m. Miriam Ann Bognanno, June 20, 1964; children: Anne, Robert II, Jennifer. BS in Pharmacy, Purdue U., 1958; MD, Ind. U., 1963. Diplomate Am. Bd. Radiology. Intern L.A. County Gen. Hosp., 1963-64; resident radiology Vanderbilt U., Nashville, 1970-73; asst. prof. Ind. U. Sch. Medicine, Indpls., 1973-77, assoc. prof., 1977-82, prof., 1982—, prof., chmn. dept. radiology, 1991-95, dean, 1996—2000; ret., 2000. Chief vascular and interventional radiology Wishard Meml. Hosp., Indpls., 1973-79, chief radiology, 1977-91; counselor NIH, 1990-94. Contbr. over 100 articles to profl. jours. Chmn. bldg. com. 1st United Meth. Ch., Mooresville, 1988-95. Capt. U.S. Army, 1964-66. Recipient Gold medal Assn. Univ. Radiologists, 1999, Gold medal Am. Roentgen Ray Soc., 2000; named Disting. Alumnus, Purdue U. Sch. Phharmacy, 1992. Fellow Soc. Cardiovascular and Interventional Radiology, Am. Coll. Radiology (counselor, Gold medal 2005), Radiologic Soc. N.Am. (counselor), Ind. Roentgen Soc. (past pres.). Republican. Avocations: forestry, agriculture, tennis. Office: Ind U Sch Medicine fH 302 1120 South Dr Rm 302 Indianapolis IN 46202-5135 Home: 2171 Gulf Shore Blvd N Apt 101 Naples FL 34102-4625 Office Phone: 317-274-7109. Business E-Mail: rholden@iupui.edu.

HOLDEN, SUSAN M., lawyer; BA magna cum laude, St. Cloud State Univ., 1984; JD cum laude, William Mitchell Coll. of Law, 1988. Cert.: civil trial specialist. Law clerk Sieben, Grose, Von Holtum & Carey, Mpls., 1985—88, atty., 1988—93, ptnr., bd. dir., 1993—. Fellow: Am. Bar Found.; mem.: ABA, Nat. Conf. of Bar Presidents, Assn. of Trial Lawyers of Am., Minn. Trial Lawyers Assn., Minn. Women Lawyers, Hennepin County Bar Assn. (pres. 1999—2000), Minn. State Bar Assn. (treas. 2003, pres.-elect 2004), Phi Alpha Delta. Office: Sieben Grose Von Holtum & Carey East Bldg 800 Marquette Ave Minneapolis MN 55402

HOLDEN, TIM, congressman, protective official; b. St. Clair, Pa., Mar. 5, 1957; s. Joseph F. and Catherine Siney H.; m. Gwen Kieres. BA in Sociology, Bloomsburg State Coll., 1980. Ins. broker/real estate agent; probation officer Schuylkill County, Pa.; sgt.-at-arms Pa. Ho. of Reps.; sheriff Schuylkill County, Pa., 1985-93; mem. U.S. Congress from 17th Pa. dist., Washington, 1993—; mem. agr. com., transp. and infrastructure com.; mem. Blue Dog Coallition. Democrat. Roman Catholic. Office: US Ho of Reps 2417 Rayburn Ho Office Bldg Washington DC 20515-0001*

HOLDEN, WILLIAM, food service executive; b. Pawtucket, R.I. m. Bea Holden; 1 child. A in Bus. Adminstrn., Johnson & Wales U., 1966. Gen. mgr. mdse. Sysco Corp., Miami, 1980—81, dir. mktg. Norton, Mass., 1981—83, v.p. mktg., 1983—84, exec. v.p., 1984—96, pres., CEO, 1996—97, sr. v.p. ops., 1997—2002, sr. v.p. food svc. ops., 2002—. Office: Hallsmith Sysco Food Svcs 380 S Worchester St Norton MA 02766

HOLDEN, WILLIAM WILLARD, insurance executive; b. Akron, Ohio, Oct. 5, 1958; s. Joseph McCullem and Lettitia (Roderick) H.; m. Kim Homan, Aug. 31, 1985; 1 child, Jennifer Catharine. BA, Colgate U., 1981. Crime ins. trainee Chubb & Son, Inc., N.Y.C., 1981-82, exec. protection dept. mgr. San Jose, Calif., 1982-85, Woodland Hills, Calif., 1986-91; sr. v.p., mgr. Fin. Svcs. Group, Inc., Rollins, Hudig, Hall, Aon Fin. Svcs. Group, L.A., 1991-2000; tng. analyst Chubb & Son, Inc., Warren, N.J., 1985-86; exec. v.p. USI of So. Calif. Ins. Svcs., Woodland Hills, 2000—. Co-author manual: Chubb Claims Made Training, 1985; contbr. articles to Colgate alumni mag. Mgr., coach Campbell (Calif.) Little League, 1983-85; coach Simi Valley Girls Softball, 1995-2005; pres. Le Parc Homeowners Assn., Simi Valley, Calif., 1987-89; mem. Community Assn. Inst., L.A., 1986-2004; bd. dirs. Friends of the Vols. for L.A. Unified Sch. Dist., 2001-03, chmn., 2001-03. Mem. Profl. Liability Underwriting Soc. (L.A. steering com.), Forum for Corp. Dirs. Republican. Avocations: golf, reading, hiking, swimming, skiing. Office: USI of So Calif Ins Svcs Inc 21600 Oxnard St 8th Flr Woodland Hills CA 91367 Office Phone: 818-251-3093. E-mail: william.holden@usi.biz.

HOLDER, ANGELA RODDEY, law educator; b. Rock Hill, S.C., Mar. 13, 1938; d. John T. and Angela M. (Fisher) Roddey; 1 child, John Thomas Roddey Holder. Student, Radcliffe Coll., 1955-56; BA, Newcomb Coll., 1958; postgrad., Faculty of Law-King's Coll., London, 1957-58; JD, Tulane U., 1960; LLM, Yale U., 1975. Bar: La. 1961, S.C. 1960, Conn. 1981. Counsel Roddey, Sumwalt & Carpenter, Rock Hill, S.C., 1960-91; atty. criminal div. New Orleans Legal Aid Bur., 1961-62; counsel York County Family Ct., S.C., 1962-64; asst. prof. polit. sci. Winthrop Coll., Rock Hill, 1964-74; research assoc. Yale U. Law Sch., 1975-77, exec. dir. program in law, sci. and medicine, 1976-77; lectr. dept. pediatrics Yale U. Sch. Medicine, 1975-77, asst. clin. prof. pediatrics and law, 1977-79, assoc. clin. prof., 1979-83, clin. prof., 1983-2001; prof. practice of med. ethics Duke U. Med. Ctr., Durham, NC, 2001—, interim dir. Ctr. for Study of Med. Ethics and Humanities, 2004—. Trustee Am. Bd. Pediatrics, 2003—; mem. com. on pediat. palliative care Inst. Medicine, 2001—02, mem. com. on clin. rsch. with children, 2002—04. Author: The Meaning of the Constitution, 1968, 3d edit., 1997, Medical Malpractice Law, 1975, 2d edit. 1978, Legal Issues in Pediatrics and Adolescent Medicine, 1977, 3d edit., 1997; contbg. editor: Prism mag.; contbg. editor., AMA; mem. editl. bd.: IRB, 1976-2000, Medicine and HealthCare, 1978-2000, Jour. Philosophy and Medicine; contbr. articles to profl. jours. Mem. Rock Hill Sch. Bd., 1967—68; chmn. bd. dirs. Family Planning Clinic, 1970—73; bd. trustees Ednl. Commn. for Fgn. Med. Grads., 1990—97, exec. com., 1997; bd. dir. Conn. Planned Parenthood, 1993—99, exec. com., 1996—99; mem. lawyers' rev. group Health Care Task Force, The White House, 1993; bd. trustees Cushing/Whitney Med. Libr. at Yale U., 1996—2001; ethics com. Leeway AIDS Hospice, New Haven, 1996—2001; alumnae bd. visitors Nat. Cathedral Sch., Washington, 2000—; cons. Artificial Reproductive Techs. Com., Ct. Ho. of Reps.; mem. adv. bd., grad. health programs Sarah Lawrence Coll., 2004—. Mem. ABA, S.C. Bar Assn. (medico-legal com. 1973—), La. Bar Assn., New Haven County Bar Assn., Am. Soc. Law and Medicine (treas. 1981-83, sec. 1983-85, pres. 1986-88, bd. dirs. 1977-91). Democrat. Episcopalian. Home: 3408 Hope Valley Rd Durham NC 27707 Office: Ctr for Study of Med Ethics and Humanities Duke U Med Ctr Box 3040 108 Seeley G Mudd Bldg Durham NC 27710 Office Phone: 919-668-9010. E-mail: angela.holder@duke.edu.

HOLDER, CALVIN BERESFORD, history professor; b. Barbados, Sept. 28, 1946; s. Clifford Beresford and Beryl Leotta (Smith) H.; divorced; children: Aisha Margaret, Oshun Doris. AB, CCNY, 1970; AM, Harvard U., 1971, PhD, 1976. Prof. history Coll. of S.I., CUNY, N.Y., 1975—. Office: Coll SI CUNY Dept History 2800 Victory Blvd Staten Island NY 10314

HOLDER, DONALD, lighting designer; b. Y; Grad., Yale Sch. of Drama. Lighting designer (Broadway) The Lion King (Tony, Drama Desk, Outer Critics Cir. awards), Juan Darien (Tony, Drama Desk nominations), Hughie (Am. Theatre Wing nomination), Eastern Standard, Holiday, Solitary Confinement, Little Shop of Horrors, 2004 (Touring Broadway awards, best prodn. design, lighting, 2005), All Shook Up, 2005, (Off-Broadway) Most Fabulous Story Ever Told, Sight Unseen, Three Days of Rain, All My Sons, Communicating Doors, Caucasian Chalk Circle (Drama Desk nomination), Spunk, Avenue K, Fit to be Tied, From Above, Richard II/III, Titus Andronicus, The Green Bird (Am. Theater Wing nomination), The Changeling, Jeffrey, Maiden's Prayer, Pterodactyls, Birdie Blue, 2005, many others, (include Operas) Salome, (regional therater includes) Hartford Stage, Long Wharf, Mark Taper Forum, La Jolla Playhouse, American Repertory Theatre, Center Stage, many others, (archtl. lighting includes) Sony Plaza, Swiss Ctr. in N.Y., Jitney, 2000. Recipient Tony award for Lion King lighting design. Mailing: c/o Palace Theatre 1564 Broadway New York NY 10036*

HOLDER, DOUGLAS, editor, writer; b. N.Y.C., July 5, 1955; s. Lawrence Jay and Rita Holder; married, July 9, 1994. BA, SUNY, Buffalo, 1977; MA, Harvard U., 1997. Founder Ibbetson St. Press, Somerville, Mass., 1998—; arts editor Somerville News, 2000—; dir. Newton (Mass.) Libr. Poetry Series, 2002—. Mem. faculty adv. bd. Wilderness House Lit. Retreat, Littleton, Mass., 2004—. Contbr. poems to lit. anthologies. Mem. adv. bd. New Renaissance lit. mag., 2003—; pres. Stone Soup Poets, Boston, 2000. Recipient poetry award, Lucid Moon Poetry.com, 2003, award, State of Maine, 2000. Achievements include interviews with contemporary poets housed at Lamont Library poetry room Harvard University. Home: 25 School St Somerville MA 02143 Office Phone: 617-628-2313. E-mail: dougholder@post.harvard.edu.

HOLDER, ERIC H., lawyer, former federal agency administrator; b. NYC, Jan. 21, 1951; s. Eric H. and Miriam R. (Yearwood) H.; m. Sharon Malone; 3 children. BA, Columbia U., 1973, JD, 1976. Bar: NY 1977, DC 1980. Law clerk NAACP Legal Def. Fund, Criminal Divsn., Dept. Justice; trial atty. pub. integrity sect. US Dept. Justice, 1976-88; assoc. judge Superior Ct., Washington, 1988-93; US atty. DC US Dept. Justice, Washington, 1993-97, US dep. atty. gen., 1997—2001, acting atty. gen., 2001; ptnr. Covington & Burling, Washington, 2001—. Bd. dirs., mem. MCI; mem. ad hoc adv. group US Sentencing Commn.; chmn. external diversity adv. panel Eastman Kodak. Meyer Found.; See Forever Found. Mem. Concerned Black Men. Democrat. Office: Covington & Burling 1201 Pennsylvania Ave NW Washington DC 20004-2401 Business E-Mail: eholder@cov.com.

HOLDER, HAROLD DOUGLAS, SR., investor, hotel executive; b. Anniston, Ala., June 25, 1931; s. William Chester and Lucile (Kadle) H.; m. Anna Maria Yaccarino, 1996; children: Debra Holder Carnaroli, Harold Douglas Jr., Charlie Kadle. Student, Anniston Bus. Coll., 1949, Jacksonville State U., 1954-57, Druitt Sch. Speech, 1962. Dept. mgr. Sears, Roebuck & Co., Anniston, 1954-57, merchandising mgr. Atlanta, 1957-59, dir. coll. recruiting, 1959-61, dir. exec. devel. program, 1961, asst. personnel dir., 1962-63, store mgr. Cocoa, Fla., 1965-67, Ocala, Fla., 1963-65, opers. zone mgr. Atlanta, 1967-68, asst. gen. mgr. mdse., 1968-69, sales promotion mgr. So. area, 1968; pres., bd. dirs. Cunningham Drug Stores, Inc., Detroit, 1969-70; v.p. Interstate Stores, 1971; pres., bd. dirs. Rahall Communications Corp., 1971-73; chmn. bd., chief exec. officer, dir. Am. Agronomics Corp., 1973-86; pres. Harold Holder Leasing; mng. dir. The Holder Group, Inc., 1987—. CEO, bd. dirs. Cutler Mfg. Corp., 1989-2000, Atlas Aircraft Corp., 1987-2000; mem. exec. com., bd. dirs. Coastland Corp., Fla., 1979-84; pres., bd. dirs. Golden Harvest, Inc., 1976-88; bd. dirs., treas. Dome Products, Inc., 1989-2000; CEO Casino Mgmt. Svcs. Internat., 1999—; chmn., CEO The Holder Hospitality Group, Inc.; CEO Silver Club Hotel Casino, El Capitan Resort Casino, Sharkey's Nugget Casino, Sundance Casino, Model "T" Resort Casino, Charlie Holder's Casino, Fernley Truck-Inn and Casino; chmn. New Dawn Resorts, Ltd., Accra, Ghana. Author: Don't Shoot, I'm Only a Trainee, 1975. Chmn., bd. dirs. Miracle, Inc., Brevard County; chmn. United Appeal, Ocala, Fla., 1964, Cocoa, Fla., 1966; bd. dirs. United Way Hillsborough County (Fla.); chmn. Heart Fund Drive, Ocala, 1964, Marion (Fla.) Com. of 100; bd. dirs. So. Coll. Placement Assn., Am. Acad. Achievement; bd. dirs. Marion chpt. ARC, Opera Arts Assn.; exec. com. Share, U. Fla.; bd. trustees U. Tampa; chmn. bd. trustees, trustee emeritus Eckerd Coll. With USMC, 1950-53. Named Harold D. Holder chair of Internat. Bus. and Fin., Eckerd Coll., Nev. Hotelier of the Yr., 2004; recipient Disting. Svc. award, Marion County 4-H Club, 1965, Golden Plate award, 1983, Champion of Higher Edn. award, 1982, Fla. NAACP Humanitarian award, 1984. Mem.: Young Pres. Orgn. (past chmn. Fla. chpt.), C. of C. (chmn. beautification com., retail bus. com.), Chief Execs. Forum, Omicron Delta Kappa. Episcopalian. Office: The Holder Hospitality Group Inc 1040 Victorian Ave Sparks NV 89431-4923 Office Phone: 775-358-4771.

HOLDER, JANICE MARIE, state supreme court justice; b. Canonsburg, Pa., Aug. 29, 1949; d. Louis V. and Sylvia (Abraham) H.; m. George W. Loveland II, June 5, 1976 (div. Mar. 1987). Student, Allegheny Coll., 1967-68, Sorbonne, 1970; BS summa cum laude, U. Pitts., 1971; JD, Duquesne U., 1975. Bar: Pa. 1975, Tenn. 1979, D.C. 1988. Sr. law clk. to chief judge U.S. Dist. Ct. for Western Dist. Pa., Pitts., 1975-77; assoc. Catalano & Catalano, P.C., Pitts., 1977-79, Holt, Batchelor, Spicer & Ryan, Memphis, 1980-82; pvt. practice Memphis, 1982—87; assoc. James S. Cox & Assocs., Memphis, 1987-89; pvt. practice law Memphis, 1989-90; judge 30th Jud. Dist., Memphis, 1990-96; justice Tenn. Supreme Ct., 1996—. Solicitor Borough of McDonald (Pa.), 1978-79. Bd. dirs. Alliance for Blind and Visually Impaired, Memphis, 1985—94, Midtown Mental Health Ctr., 1995—97; trustee Memphis Bot. Garden Found., 1995—2002; mem. state coordinating coun. Tenn. Task Force Against Domestic Violence, 1994—96. Fellow: Tenn. Bar Found. (trustee 1995—99); mem.: ABA, Tenn. Trial Judges Assn. (exec. com. 1994—96), Tenn. Lawyers' Assn. for Women, Memphis Trial Lawyers Assn. (bd. dirs. 1988—90), Am. Inns Ct., Tenn. Jud. Conf. (treas. 1993—94, exec. com. 1993—96), Assn. for Women Attys. (treas. 1989, v.p. 1991, Marion Griffin-Frances Loring award 1999), Memphis Bar Assn. (bd. dirs. 1986—87, 1993—94, editor Memphis Bar Forum 1987—91, 1993—94, sec. 1993, treas. 1994, Sam A. Myar award 1990, Judge of Yr. divorce and family law sect. 1992, Chancellor Charles A. Rond award Outstanding Jurist 1992), Tenn. Bar Assn., Am. Bar Found. Office: Tenn Supreme Ct 119 S Main St Ste 310 Memphis TN 38103-3678

HOLDER, LAWRENCE EDWARD, radiologist, educator; b. N.Y.C., Mar. 25, 1943; s. Emanuel E. and Ann I. (Isenberg) H.; m. Nancy Ann Kaufman, Aug. 20, 1966; children: Elizabeth, David, Anne. BA, Vanderbilt U., 1964; MD, Washington U., St. Louis, 1968. Diplomate Am. Bd. Radiology, Am. Bd. Nuclear Medicine. Chief nuclear medicine Union Meml. Hosp., Balt., 1975-92, chief radiology, 1991-93, Children's Hosp., Balt., 1988-93; prof. radiology, dir. nuclear medicine U. Md., Balt., 1993—. Author: Primer of Sectional Anatomy with MR and CT Correlation, 1990, 2d edit., 1994; contbr. articles to profl. jours. Bd. dirs. Stella Maris Hospice; bd. Jewish Hist. Soc. Jewish Community Ctr., Balt. Comdr. USPHS, 1969-71. Fellow Am. Coll. Radiology (commr. 1993—, commn. nuclear medicine 1993—, expert panel urologic imaging 1993—), Am. Coll. Nuclear Physicians; mem. Md. Radiol. Soc. (pres. 1991-93, counselor 1993—), Soc. Nuclear Medicine (treas. mid. east chpt. 1982-84), Md. Soc. Nuclear Medicine (pres. 1978-80). Jewish. Avocations: golf, fishing, photography. Home: 2331 Old Court Rd Apt 212 Baltimore MD 21208-3426 Office: U Md Med Sys Dept Diag Rad Divsn Nuclear Medicine 22 S Greene St Baltimore MD 21201-1544

HOLDER, ROSE MARY FANNIN, retired elementary school educator; b. Montgomery, Ala., June 23, 1954; d. Bill Frank and Mae (Hudson) Fannin. BA, Huntingdon Coll., Montgomery, Ala., 1975; MA, Troy State U., 1976, 87, AA, 1979. Tchr. Montgomery Bd. Edn., 1975—; ret. Named one of Outstanding Young Women of Yr., 1985. Mem. NEA, Montgomery County Edn. Assn. (elections com. 1977-79, budget com. 1979), Ala. Edn. Assn., Montgomery Tchr. Ctr. (master tchr. 1977). Republican. Methodist. Avocations: reading, swimming, hand sewing. Home: 26672 US Highway 331 Lapine AL 36046-7122

HOLDER, ROY CECIL, music educator; b. Nashville, Tenn., Oct. 27, 1948; s. John Ray and Doris Lorene Holder; m. Doris June Horner, June 5, 1971; children: Jessie Marie, Jani Noel. BS in music edn., U. Tenn., 1970; MS in music edn., 1985. Tchr. Alcor City Sch., 1970—77, Knox County Sch., 1977—84, Cobb County Sch., 1984—85, Fairfax County Sch., 1985—. Contbr. articles to profl. jours. Recipient Super Flag of Honor, John Philip Sousa Soc., 1994, Citation of excellence, Nat. Band Assn., 1990, Va. Govt. Sch. for Gifted and Talented, 2004, Cert. recognition, Fairfax County Bd. Supervisors, 2004. Mem.: Nat. Band Assn., Am. Bandmaster Assn., Phi Beta Mu. Avocations: camping, fishing, travel. Home: 6947 Confederation Dr Springfield VA 22153 Office: Lake Braddock Sec Sch 9200 Burke Lake Rd Burke VA 22015 Office Phone: 703-426-1072. Business E-Mail: roy.holder@fcps.edu.

HOLDER, THOMAS LEE, lawyer; b. Bklyn., Feb. 15, 1956; s. Howard Martin and Joan Roslyn (Geffner) H.; m. Laura Mary Mantrone, Sept. 13, 1987. Student, U. Lancaster, Eng., 1975-76; BA, Case Western Res. U., 1977; JD, Emory U., 1981. Bar: Ga. 1981; U.S. Dist. Ct. (no. dist.) Ga. 1981; U.S. Ct. Appeals (11th cir.) 1981. Assoc. Appel, Strickland & Robins, Atlanta, 1981-84, Siler & Jonap, Atlanta, 1984-86; ptnr. Long & Holder, Atlanta, 1986—. Vice-chmn. Young Careers Group High Mus. of Art, Atlanta, 1986-87. Named to Outstanding Young Men of Am., 1986. Mem. Atlanta Bar Assn. (chmn. workers compensation sect. 1987-89), State Bar of Ga. (chmn. worker's compensation sect. 2000-01), Ga. Trial Lawyers Assn. (exec. com., workers compensation sect. 1992—), Assn. of Trial Lawyers of Am., Inman Pk. Neighborhood Assn. (pres. 1996-98). Avocations: basketball, running, reading. Home: 1124 Alta Ave NE Atlanta GA 30307-2515 Office: Long & Holder LLP 127 Peachtree St NE Ste 1515 Atlanta GA 30303-1809 Office Phone: 404-523-6100. Business E-Mail: tom@longandholder.com.

HOLDORF, HARRY HULBERT, health facility administrator; b. Jamestown, N.Y., May 1, 1958; s. John A. and Louise Holdorf; m. Cynthia L. Baron, Aug. 28, 1982; children: Christopher, Nicholas. AS in Radiol. Tech., Union County Coll.; BA in Environ. Scis., Stockton State Coll.; MPA, Kean U.; PhD in Health Svcs. Adminstrn., Southwest U. Lic. radiologic technologist Am. Registry Radiologic Technologists N.J., N.Y., med. sonographer Am. Registry Diagnostic Med. Sonographers. Radiol. technologist Elizabeth Gen. Med. Ctr., NJ, 1983—86, St. Barnabas Med. Ctr., NJ, 1986—87; splty. technologist Dover Hosp., NJ, 1987—88; staff ultrasonographer Overlook Hosp., NJ, 1988; staff ultrasonographer Elizabeth Gen. Med. Ctr., 1988—89, coord. ultrasound program, 1989—92, mem. faculty sch. radiol. scis., 1988—97, dir. ultrasound program, 1992—97, mgr. radiology, 1997—2000; quality assurance coord., mgr. med. imaging svcs. Irvington Gen. Hosp., NJ, 2001—. Cons. Schs. Med. Imagery and Med. Scis. Muhlenberg Regional Med. Ctr., 2000—03, adminstrv. dir. med. imaging svcs. Schs. Med. Imagery and Med. Scis., 2001—03; program dir. diagnostic med. sonography Schs. Nursing, Med. Imaging and Therapeutic Scis., 2003—; site visitor Joint Rev. Com. on Edn. in Diagnostic Med. Sonography. Mem. Am. Soc. Diagnostic Med. Sonographers, Soc. Vas. Ultrasound, Am. Soc. Radiol. Technologists, Am. Soc. Notaries, State of NJ Notary Public Commn., Pi Alpha Alpha. Home: 532 Woodland Ave Mountainside NJ 07092-2524 Office: Schs Nursing Med Imaging and Therapeutic Scis Park Ave and Randolph Rd Plainfield NJ 07062 Office Phone: 908-668-2884. Business E-Mail: hholdorf@solarishs.org.

HOLDREN, JAMIE LYNN, music educator; b. Cin. d. Dallas E. Harper and Marlene Kirby; m. William P. Holdren; children: Nicholas J., James D. MusB in Edn., Georgetown (Ky.) Coll., 1982; MEd in adminstrn. and supervision, Xavier U., 1989. Gen. music tchr. Oak Hills Sch. Dist., Cin., 1982—83; choral and gen. music tchr. Princeton Jr. H.S., Cin., 1983—89, Robert E. Lucas Intermediate Sch., Cin., 1989—95; choral dir. Princeton H.S., Cin., 1993. Asst. dist. music coord. Princeton City Schs., Cin., 1995—2000. Dir.: A Prayer, 2000, 13th Annual Intermountain Choral Festival, 2003 (2d Pl. award, 2003), I Know A Song; contbr. articles to profl. jours. Musician Mt. Carmel Bapt. Ch., Cin., 1978—2003. Mem.: Ohio Choral Dir.'s Assn., Ohio Music Educators Assn., Music Educators Nat. Conf. (Young Composer award 2000), Am. Choral Dir.'s Assn. (assoc.), Delta Kappa Gamma. Avocations: genealogy, reading, travel, gardening. Office: Princeton High School 11080 Chester Road Cincinnati OH 45246 E-mail: jholdren@princeton.k12.oh.us.

HOLDREN, JOHN PAUL, physicist, educator, writer; b. Sewickley, Pa., Mar. 1, 1944; s. Raymond Andrew and Virginia June (Fuqua) H.; m. Cheryl Edgar, Feb. 5, 1966; children: John Craig, Jill Virginia SB, MIT, 1965, SM, 1966; PhD, Stanford U., 1970; ScD (hon.), U. Puget Sound, 1975; D Engring. (hon.), Colo. Sch. Mines, 1997; DSc (hon.), Clark U., 2003. Aerodyn. engr. Lockheed Missiles & Space Co., Sunnyvale, Calif., 1966-67; theoretical physicist Lawrence Livermore Lab., Calif., 1970-71; sr. research fellow Calif. Inst. Tech., Pasadena, 1972-73; asst. prof. energy and resources U. Calif.-Berkeley, 1973-75, assoc. prof. energy and resources, 1975-78, prof. energy and resources, 1978-96, Class of 1935 prof. energy, 1991-96, chmn. grad. degree prog. in energy and resources, 1983-84; Teresa and John Heinz prof. environ. policy Harvard U., Cambridge, Mass., 1996—, dir. sci., tech. and pub. policy prog., Kennedy Sch., prof. environ. sci. and pub. policy, dept. of earth and planetary scis. Cons. in fusion energy Lawrence Livermore Labs., 1974—; sr. investigator Rocky Mountain Biol. Lab., Crested Butte, Colo., 1974-88; vis. fellow East-West Ctr., Honolulu, 1979-80, Max-Planck-Gesellschaft, Starnberg, Fed. Republic Germany, 1987; vis. fellow arms control program MIT, 1988; vis. prof. physics U. Rome tor Vergata, 1987; vis. scientist Woods Hole Rsch. Ctr., 1992—; mem. Fusion Energy adv. com. Sec. of Energy, 1991-94; chaired studies for the White House; mem. Pres. Clinton's Com. of Advisors on Sci. and Tech. (PCAST), 1994-2001. Co-editor: Man and the Ecosphere, 1971, Strategic Defences, 1987, The Cassandra Conference, 1988; co-author: Energy, 1971, Human Ecology, 1973, Ecoscience, 1977, Management and Disposition of Excess Weapon Plutonium, 1994, The Future of U.S. Nuclear Weapons Policy, 1997; co-editor: Earth and the Human Future, 1986, Conversion of Military R & D, 1999; bd. editors Bull. of Atomic Scientists, Chgo., 1984-86; contbr. to articles and rsch. papers in the field. Mem. exec. com. Pugwash Confs. on Sci. and World Affairs, London and Geneva, 1982-97, chmn., 1987-97; chmn. U.S. Pugwash Com., Cambridge, Mass., 1983-95; mem. coun. Smithsonian Instn., 1988-91; bd. dirs. McArthur Found., 1991—; mem. Pres.'s Com. Advisors on Sci. and Tech., 1994-2000. Recipient Gustavsen lectureship U. Chgo., 1978; MacArthur Prize fellow MacArthur Found., Chgo., 1981-86; recipient Volvo Environ. Prize, 1993, leadership award Fusion Power Assocs., 1998, award for excellence Kaul Found., 1999, Tyler Environment prize, 2000, Heinz prize in Public Policy, 2001. Fellow AAAS (pres.-elect 2005, co-chair nat. commn. on energy policy 2002—), Am. Acad. Arts and Scis. (vice chmn. com. on internat. security 1983—, Kistiakowsky Meml. Lectureship 1986-87), Calif. Acad. Scis.; mem. NAE, NAS (com. internat. security and arms control 1992-2004, chmn. 1993-2004), Fedn. Am. Scientists (council, treas. 1979-80, vice chmn. 1981-84, chmn. 1984-86, bd. sponsors, 1986—, Pub. Service award 1979), Am. Phys. Soc. (Forum award 1995). Democrat. Office: Harvard U Kennedy Sch Govt BelferCtr for Sci & Internat Affairs 79 John F Kennedy St Littauer-370 Cambridge MA 02138-5801 Office Phone: 617-495-1464. Office Fax: 617-495-8963. E-mail: john_holdren@harvard.edu.

HOLDRIDGE, BARBARA, book publisher; b. N.Y.C., July 26, 1929; d. Herbert L. and Bertha (Gold) Cohen; m. Lawrence B. Holdridge, Oct. 9, 1959; 2 children. AB, Hunter Coll., 1950. Asst. editor Liveright Pub. Corp., N.Y.C., 1950-52; co-founder Caedmon Records, Inc., N.Y.C., 1952, ptnr., 1952-60, pres., 1960-62, treas., 1962-70, pres., 1970-75; founder Stemmer House Pubs. Inc., Owings Mills, Md., 1975, pres., 1975—2003; founder Stemmer House, Inc., Owings Mills, 2003, pres., 2003—. Co-founder, v.p. Shakespeare Rec. So., Inc., N.Y.C., 1960-70, Theatre Rec. Soc., Inc., N.Y.C., 1964-70, BEDE Prodns., 1984, History Rec. Soc., Inc., N.Y.C., 1964, pres., 1964-70; lectr. on Ammi Phillips, 1959—; lectr. on book pub., 1992—; adj. prof. writing media Loyola Coll., Balt., 1987-91. Author: Ammi Phillips, 1968, Aubrey Beardsley Designs from the Age of Chivalry, 1983, Chinese Cut-Out Designs of Costumes, 1989; articles on Am. paintings. Named to Hunter Coll. Hall of Fame, 1972, Nat. Women's Hall of Fame, 2001; recipient Am. Shakespeare Festival award, 1962, N.Y.C. cert. of appreciation, 1972, Lifetime Achievement award, Audio Pubs. Assn., 2001. Mem. 14 West Hamilton Street Club, Phi Beta Kappa Alumni Assn. of Greater Balt. (bd. dirs.). Office: 2627 Caves Rd Owings Mills MD 21117-2919 Office Phone: 410-363-3690. Personal E-mail: stemmerhouse@comcast.net.

HOLDSCLAW, CHAMIQUE SHAUNTA, professional basketball player; b. Flushing, N.Y., Aug. 9, 1977; Grad., U. Tenn., 1999. Basketball player Washington Mystics, 1999—. Named Sports Illustrated and Sporting News Nat. Women's Player of Yr., 1999, Naismith finalist, AP Women's Basketball Player of Yr., 1997—98, 1998—99, N.Y.C. Player of Yr., Rawlings/WBCA Player of Yr., Player of Yr., Columbus, Ohio Touchdown Club, 1995, Rookie of the Yr., WNBA, 1999; named one of 12 female athletes selected as inspirational role models, Women's Sports and Fitness mag., 1998; named to Kodak 25th Anniversary Team, Women's Basketball Jour., Street & Smith All-Am., three-time, USA Today All-Am., WNBA All-Star Team, 1999, 2000, 2003, All-WNBA Team, 2000, 2001; recipient Sullivan award, Gold medal, 1998 World Championships, 1997 World Qualifying Tournament, 1995 Olympic Festival, USA Basketball Player of Yr. award, 1997, ESPY's for Female Athlete of Yr. award, second consecutive Women's Basketball Player of Yr. award, 1999, Naismith award, Atlanta's Tip-Off Club, 1995, Gold medal, U.S. Olympic Team, 2000. Office: Washington Mystics MCI Center 601 F St NW Washington DC 20004-1605

HOLDSWORTH, JANET NOTT, women's health nurse; b. Evanston, Ill., Dec. 25, 1941; d. William Alfred and Elizabeth Inez (Kelly) Nott; children: James William, Kelly Elizaveth, John David. BSN with high distinction, U. Iowa, 1963; M of Nursing, U. Wash., 1966. RN, Colo. Staff nurse U. Colo. Hosp., Denver, 1963-64, Presbyn. Hosp., Denver, 1964-65, Grand Canyon Hosp., Ariz., 1965; asst. prof. U. Colo. Sch. Nursing, Denver, 1966-71; counseling nurse Boulder PolyDrug Treatment Ctr., Boulder, 1971-77; pvt. duty nurse Nurses' Offcl. Registry, Denver, 1973-82; cons. nurse, tchr. parenting and child devel. Teenage Parent Program, Boulder Valley Schs., Boulder, 1980-88; bd. dirs., treas. Nott's Travel, Aurora, Colo., 1980—; nurse Rocky Mountain Surgery Ctr., 1996—. Instr., nursing coord. ARC, Boulder, 1979-90, instr., nursing tng. specialist, 1980-82. Mem. adv. bd. Boulder County Lamaze Inc., 1980-88; mem. adv. com. Child Find and Parent-Family, Boulder, 1981-89; del. Rep. County State Congl. Convs., 1972-96, sec. 17th Dist. Senatorial Com., Boulder, 1982-92; vol. Mile High ARC, 1980; vol. chmn. Mesa Sch. PTO, Boulder, 1982-92, bd. dirs., 1982-95, v.p., 1983-95; elder Presbyn. Ch. Mem. ANA, Colo. Nurses Assn. (bd. dirs. 1975-76, human rights com. 1981-83, dist. pres. 1974-76), Coun. Intracultural Nurses, Sigma Theta Tau, Alpha Lambda Delta. Republican. Home: 1550 Findlay Way Boulder CO 80305-6922 Office: Rocky Mountain Surgery Ctr 1630 30th St # 153 Boulder CO 80301-1014

HOLE, RICHARD DOUGLAS, lawyer; b. Auburn, N.Y., Aug. 23, 1949; s. Robert B. and Barbara (Swift) H.; m. Deborah Elizabeth Muldoon, Jan. 8, 1972; children: Emily, Brian, Jeffrey. BA, Hamilton Coll., 1971; JD, Syracuse (N.Y.) U., 1975. Bar: N.Y. 1976, U.S. Dist. Ct. (no. dist.) N.Y. 1976, U.S. Dist. Ct. (we. dist.) N.Y. 1980. Assoc. Bond, Schoeneck & King, Syracuse, 1976—83, ptnr., 1984—. Pres. N.Y. Employee Benefits Conf., Rochester, 1987-88. Pres. Fayetteville-Manlius (N.Y.) Little League, Inc., 1988-93; pres. Eye Rsch. Inst. of Ctrl. N.Y., Syracuse, 1988-93; bd. dirs. Cystic Fibrosis Found., Syracuse, 1988-93; pres., bd. trustees United Ch. of Fayetteville, 1990-95, 98—; bd. dirs. Syracuse Symphony, 1995-2001; pres. Ctrl. N.Y. Alumni Coun. Hamilton Coll., 1999—. Mem.: Nat. Assn. Coll. and Univ. Attys., Onondaga County Bar Assn., NY State Bar Assn. Republican. Presbyterian. Office: Bond Schoeneck & King 18th Fl One Lincoln Ctr Syracuse NY 13202

HOLEMAN, LORA WHITE, music educator; b. Oklahoma City, Jan. 11, 1964; d. Marvin E. and Lora Edith White; m. Gerald E. Holeman, Jr., July 25, 1999. MusB in Edn., U. Ctrl. Okla., 1987, MusM in Edn., 1990. K-12 License

Okla. State Dept. of Edn., 1987. Instr. piano, voice, Oklahoma City, 1982—90; instr. music Jefferson State Coll., Birmingham, Ala., 1991—94. Ind. voice & piano instr., Oklahoma City, 1982—90; adj. instr. music Birmingham-So. Coll., Ala., 1990—94. Founder, pres. BIG Options, Oklahoma City, 2003—. Mem.: Ctrl. Okla. Music Tchrs. Assn., Okla. Music Tchrs. Assn., Music Tchrs. Nat. Assn., Music Educator's Nat. Conf., Nat. Assn. Advance Fat Acceptance (founder chpt.). Avocations: medical arts, cats. Office: BIG Options PO Box 30094 Oklahoma City OK 73140 E-mail: bigoptions4u@aol.com.

HOLEMAN, RUSSELL KENT, civil engineer; b. Lexington, Mo., Oct. 23, 1957; s. E.G. and Joyce Lynette (Bredehoeft) H.; m. Linda Lea Cameron, May 23, 1981; children: Jared Tyler, Chelsea Paige. BSCE, Tex. Tech. U., 1979. Registered profl. engr., Tex. Civil engr. U.S. Army Facilities Engrs., Fort Hood, Tex., 1979-81, U.S. Army Corps Engrs., Fort Hood, 1981-83, chief, office engring., 1983-85, chief, contract adminstrn. Amarillo, Tex., 1985-87, area engr., 1987-95, dir. mil. project mgmt. Tulsa, 1995—2000, asst. chief engring. and constrn., 2000—02, chief hydrology, 2002—. Facilitator U.S. Army, Ctr. for Army Leadership, Ft. Leavenworth, Kans., 1989-2001; spec. assignment for reconstruction of Iraqi oil system, 2003, 05 Co-developer: (software) Construction Office Contract Administrator, 1983-86. Pres. Tex. Panhandle Fed. Exec. Assn., 1994; v.p. Prince of Peace Luth. Ch., Amarillo, 1988; major acct. exec. govt. sector, United Way, Amarillo, 1991, vice chmn., 1992, chmn., 1993; vice chmn. Tulsa combined fed. campaign, 1997; asst. scoutmaster Boy Scouts Am., 1996—, vice chmn. outer limits com., 1997—, venturing tng. chmn., 2002—, advisor Boy Scout Explorer Post 2001, 1998—, Boy Scout dist. commr. 2005-. Recipient Engr. of Yr., Tulsa Dist., 1990, Leadership award Tulsa Dist., 1993, Comdr.'s award for civilian svc., 1998, Venturing Leadership award Boy Scouts Am., 1999, Meritorious Civilian Svc. award, 2003, Customer Care Employee of Yr., 2003. Mem. NSPE, Tex. Soc. Profl. Engrs., Tex. Panhandle Fed. Exec. Assn. (sec., treas. 1991-92, v.p. 1992-93, pres. 1993-94). Avocations: softball, skiing, backpacking, camping. Office Phone: 918-669-7302. E-mail: russell.holeman@us.army.mil.

HOLEN, NORMAN DEAN, retired art educator, artist; b. Cavalier, ND, Sept. 16, 1937; s. Alvin C. and Norma H. Holen; m. Ilene Gronaas, Sept. 3, 1960; children: Peter John, Alisa Ilene. BA, Concordia Coll., 1959; MFA, State U. Iowa, 1962; postgrad., U. Minn., 1972. Instr. Northwestern Coll., Orange City, Iowa, 1962-63, Concordia Coll., Moorhead, Minn., 1963-64; prof. Augsburg Coll., Mpls., 1964—2002; ret., 2002. Contbr. articles to profl. jours. Mem.: Allied Artists Am. (Rachel L. Armour award 1980, 1982, In Memorium award 1983), Nat. Sculpture Soc. (Bronze medal 1980, Joel Meisner award 1983), Soc. Minn. Sculptors, Artist Equity Assn. (v.p. Minn. chpt. 1973—74, chpt. pres., nat. exec. bd. 1974—75). Republican. Lutheran. Avocations: playing classical guitar, inventing tools and splints for my physically challenged students. Home: 7332 12th Ave S Minneapolis MN 55423-3343

HOLFORD, THEODORE RICHARD, biostatistician, educator; b. Columbus, Ohio, May 19, 1947; s. Charles Richard and LaVern Lucille (Lukens) H.; m. Maryellen Hutchinson Holford, Dec. 21, 1969; children: Matthew Edwin, Lesley Erin. BA in Math and Chemistry, Andrews U., 1969; PhD in Biometry, Yale U., 1973. Rsch. staff Yale U., New Haven, 1972-73, asst. prof., 1974-79, assoc. prof., 1979-89, prof., 1989—, head divsn. biostatistics, 1990-97, 2003—, dir. grad. studies, 1997—2002, acting dean pub. health, 2001. Dir. cancer biostats. tng. NCI. Editor: Statistical Methods in Medical Research, 1992—; assoc. editor Am. Jour. Epidemiology, 1989-97, Biometrics, 1984-88; contbr. articles to profl. jours. Mem. Consensus Devel. Conf. on Health Implications of Smokeless Tobacco, Washington, 1986, Epidemiology & Disease Control Study Section, Washington, 1986-89, Epidemiology Adv. Subcom. Oak Ridge (Tenn.) Assn., 1988-93. Elinor Roosevelt Cancer fellow, 1981-82; recipient Wakeman award, 1990, numerous NIH grants. Fellow Am. Coll. Epidemiology, Am. Statis. Assn.; mem. Am. Statis. Assn., 1973—, Biometric Soc., 1973—, Soc. for Epidemiologic Rsch., 1978—. Avocations: trumpet, hiking, photography. Office Phone: 203-785-2838. Business E-Mail: theodore.holford@yale.edu.

HOLGATE, STEVEN MARK, music educator; s. Mark A. and Dorothy C. Holgate; m. Jonna Holgate, Dec. 27, 2003. BS Music Edn., Ind. U. Pa., Ind., Pa., 1992; MM Music Performance Tuba/Conducting, Ill. State U., Normal, Ill., 1999. Cert. Music Educatio Pa., 1992. Tchg. asst. / grad. student Ill. State U., Normal, Ill.; music tchr. Gov. Mifflin SD, Shillington, Pa., 1999—. Brass instr. Reading Buccaneers Drum and Bugle Corps, Reading, Pa., 1999—2005; brass tchr. Cmty. Sch. of Music and Arts, Reading, Pa. Mem.: Music Educators of Berks County (assoc.), Music Educators Nat. Conf. (assoc.), Nat. Band Assn. (assoc.), Tau Beta Sigma (assoc.), Phi Sigma Pi (assoc.). Independent-R. Bible Fellowship. Avocations: fishing, hunting, shooting sports, coin collecting/numismatics, computers. Home: 370 Sunset Rd West Reading PA 19611-1345 Office: Gov Mifflin SD 10 South Waverly St Shillington PA 19607 Office Phone: 610-775-5089. Personal E-mail: sholgate@comcast.net. Business E-Mail: sholgate@gmsd.k12.pa.us.

HOLGUIN, GABRIEL, psychologist; b. Laredo, Tex., Aug. 31, 1972; s. Jesus and Sylvia Holguin; m. Patricia Ann Dominguez, June 30, 2001; children: Carina Isabelle, Carissa Alejandra. BA, U. Tex., Austin, 1993; PhD, U. Nebr., Lincoln, 1998—2002. Lic. profl. psychologist Tex. State Bd. Examiners Psychologists, 2004. Practicum counselor Stop Child Abuse & Neglect, Inc., Laredo, Tex., 1997; intern U.S. - Mex. Border Health Program, Bethesda, Md., 1998; intern counselor Children's Internat. Advocacy Ctr. of Webb County, Laredo, Tex., 1998; fgn. lang. consulting psychologist State of Nebr., Lincoln Regional Ctr., 1999—2001; clin. psychology extern Nebr. Dept. Correctional Svcs., Lincoln, 1999—2000; clin. therapist Project SAFE, Lincoln, Nebr., 1999—2001; clin. psychology extern Psychol. Consultation Ctr., U. Nebr., Lincoln, 1999—2001; forensic psychology asst. Forensic Mental Health Svcs. - Lincoln Regional Ctr., Nebr., 2000—01; clin. psychology extern Bryan LGH Med. Ctr. West, Lincoln, Nebr., 2000—01; clin. psychology resident USAF, Andrews AFB, Md., 2001—02, chief, psychol. svcs. Kirtland AFB, N.Mex., 2002—; forensic psychologist USAF Legal Office, 2003—. Behavioral/psychol. cons. USAF Office of Spl. Investigations, 2001—; hostage negotiations cons. USAF, Kirtland AFB, N.Mex., 2004—; cert. behavioral cons. USAF Aircraft Mishap Investigation Bds., 2004—; bd. of directors Legal FACS, Albuquerque, 2004—. Contbr. articles to profl. jours. Disaster response mem. ARC, Albuquerque, 2004; mem. League of United Latin Am. Citizens, Albuquerque, 2003; vol. coach Spl. Olympics, Laredo, Tex., 1989—91, USTA, Laredo, Tex., 1989, Little League Baseball, Laredo, Tex., 1988—90; vol. Rio Grande Internat. Study Ctr., Laredo, Tex., 1993—94; task force mem. Higher Edn. Initiative Task Force, Kirtland AFB, N.Mex., 2003; mem. Albuquerque Hispano C. of C., 2004; mentor Thresholds Adult Reinitegration Mentoring Project, Albuquerque, 2002; bd. mem. Legal FACS, Albuquerque, 2004; nat. mil. rep. Am. Group Psychotherapy Assn., Inc., N.Y.C., 2003; legislative & fed. advocacy com. mem. N.Mex. Psychol. Assn., Albuquerque, 2004. Capt. USAF, 2001, Kirtland AFB. Decorated Nat. Def. Medal USAF, Achievement Medal - Operation Iraqi & Enduring Freedom, Expeditionary Ribbon - Operation Iraqi & Enduring Freedom, Global War on Terrorism Medal - Operation Iraqi & Enduring Freedom, Outstanding Unit Medal - Kirkuk, Iraq - Operation Iraqi & Enduring Freedom; recipient Minority Academic Achievement Award, U. Tex., Austin, 1991—93. Mem.: APA, Military Officers Assn. Am., U. Tex. at Austin Alumni Assn. Conservative. Roman Catholic.

HOLIDAY, EDITH ELIZABETH, former presidential adviser, cabinet secretary; b. Middletown, Ohio, Feb. 14, 1952; d. Harry Jr. and Kathlyn (Watson) H.; m. Terrence B. Adamson, June 8, 1985; children: Kathlyn Holiday Adamson, Elizabeth Holiday Adamson; 1 stepchild, Terrence Morgan Adamson. Student, Miami U., Oxford, Ohio, 1970-71; BS with honors, U. Fla., 1974, JD, 1977. Bar: Fla. 1977, D.C. 1978, Ga. 1984. Assoc. Read Smith Shaw & McClay, Washington, 1977-83, Dow Lohnes & Albertson, Atlanta, 1983-84; exec. dir. Commn. on Exec. Legis. and Jud. Salaries, Washington, 1984-85; spl. counsel polit. action com. Fund for Am. Future, Washington, 1985-87; dir. ops. George Bush for Pres., Inc., Washington, 1987-88; chief counsel, nat. fin. and ops. dir. Bush-Quayle 88, Washington, 1988; with legal svcs. staff George Bush for Pres. Compliance Com., Washington, 1988; asst. sec. for pub. affairs and pub. liaison, counselor to sec. Departmental Offices, U.S. Dept. Treasury, Washington, 1988; gen. counsel U.S. Dept. Treasury, Washington, 1989-90; asst. to U.S. pres., sec. of cabinet Washington, 1990-93. Legis. asst. to U.S. Sen. Nicholas F. Brady, Washington, 1982—83; bd. dirs. Amerada Hess Corp., H.J. Heinz Co., Beverly Enterprises, Inc., Franklin Templeton Group Funds, RTI Internat. Metals, Inc., Canadian Nat. Railway Co.; oper. trustee TWE Holdings I, II Trusts, 2002—. Recipient Alexander Hamilton award Sec. of Treasury, 1991, spl. citation John Marshall Bar Assn. Mem. Phi Delta Phi, Kappa Tau Alpha. Republican.

HOLIFIELD, LEONARD CLEVE, security firm executive, educator; b. Johnstown, Pa., Jan. 5, 1960; s. Cleveland and Ruth Holifield; m. Ena Herminia Faulkner, May 22, 1996; 1 child, Cameron Seth. PhD in Martial Sci., Am. Coll. Martial Sci., 2002. Cert. advanced exec. protection Exec. Security Internat. Chief combatives instr. US Army, NC, 1988—97, advanced through grades to E6 staff sgt., 1996; chief instr./owner/founder Sikaron Karate Fedn., Montgomery, Ala., 1980—; exec. security officer / cert. protection specialist, dep. marshal Ala. Supreme Ct., Montgomery, 2000—. Dean homeland security Am. Coll. Martial Sci., 2003; pres., founder Internat. Acad. Exec. Protection Agts. Author: Close Quarter Combat, 1997; video artist: Close Quarter Fighting Series, 1994. Exec. v.p. World Martial Arts Hall Fame, Cleve., 1991—2002. Recipient Authorship award, Soldiers Mag., 1990, Army Trainers Mag., 1992, 1994, Grandmaster of the Yr. award, Wa No Michi-Ryu Kai Internat., 1998, Meritorious Svc. Award (U.S Army JROTC), 1995, Spl. Recognition award, U.S. Congress, 1991, award of excellence, U.S. Army, 1995, more than 200 Letters of Commendation. Mem.: World Martial Arts Hall of Fame (exec. v.p. 1995—2002, Instr. of the Yr. 1998, Head Founder of the Yr. award 1999, Exec. Valor award 1997), Phi Theta Kappa (life). Achievements include founding system of CETA close-engagement-target-acquisition; holding 10th dan black belt in Sikaron Karate. Avocations: classical music, exercise, martial arts, classic movies, self improvement. Office: Found for Moral Law 2005 N Country Club Dr Montgomery AL Personal E-mail: holifieldcps@aol.com.

HOLIFIELD, MARILYN J., lawyer; b. Tallahassee, June 17, 1948; BA, Swarthmore Coll., 1969; JD, Harvard U., 1972. Bar: NY 1973, Fla. 1980. Law clerk, Hon. Paul H. Roney US Fifth Cir. Ct. of Appeals; gen. coun. NY State Divsn. for Youth; asst. counsel NAACP Legal Def. and Edn. Fund, NYC; ptnr., gen. litig. Holland & Knight, Miami, and co-leader, Caribbean Initiative. Bd. dirs. Harvard Alumni Assn.; pres. Harvard Law Sch. Assn. Fla., 1986—88; mem. Swarthmore Coll. Alumni Coun., 1987—89; mem. bd. mgrs. Swarthmore Coll., 1993—; mem. Fed. Magistrate selection panel So. Dist. Fla., 1989—90. Named one of America's Top Lawyers, Black Enterprise Mag., 2003. Fellow: Am. Bar Found.; mem.: ABA, Fla. Acad. Trial Lawyers, Am. Judicature Soc., Am. Law Inst., Nat. Bar Assn. Office: Holland & Knight 701 Bricknell Ave Ste 3000 Miami FL 33131 Office Phone: 305-788-7730. Office Fax: 305-789-7799. Business E-Mail: marilyn.holifield@hklaw.com.*

HOLIFIELD, MARK, retail executive; BBA, U. Tex., Austin; MBA, Baylor U. Various logistics positions H-E-B Grocery Co., 1977—86; mem. staff in logistics Frito-Lay Pepsico, 1986—88; supply chain sys. positions Dallas Sys. Corp., 1988—94; dir. transp Office Depot, Inc., Delray Beach, Fla., 1994—96, v.p., transp., logistics, 1996—97, sr. v.p., supply chain, 1997—2003, exec. v.p. supply chain, 2003—. Office: Office Depot Inc 2200 Old Germantown Rd Delray Beach FL 33445*

HOLIFIELD, PEARL KAM (KAM HOLIFIELD, MOMI KAM HOLIFIELD), poet; b. Honolulu, Dec. 13, 1916; d. Albert Tin Kam and Helen Wo Soon Lyau; m. Harold Desmond Holifield, 1947; children: Wallace Grant, Harry. BA, U. Hawaii, 1944; MA, U. Calif., Berkeley, 1945; postgrad., U. Wash., 1946—47. Univ. libr. U. Hawaii, Honolulu, 1945—46; children's libr. N.Y. Pub. Library, N.Y.C., 1948—80; haiku poet N.Y.C., 1978—. Author: Workshop Poems, 1989. Mem.: Spring St. Haiku Workshop, Haiku Soc. Am. Avocations: gardening, singing, hula. Home: 85-190 Ala Hema St Apt E Waianae HI 96792-2426

HOLL, JAMES ANDREW, prehospital care administrator; b. Jersey City, Sept. 15, 1961; s. Charles J. Jr. and Alice M. (Kearney) H. AS in Nursing, Atlantic C.C., 1986; BA in Nursing Mgmt., Stockton State Coll., 1991; postgrad. flight nurse prog., USAF Sch. Aerospace Medicine, 1993. Cert. emergency nurse, flight nurse, paramedic, NJ Coll. Dentistry/Medicine 1981. Lieutenant, EMT instr. Brigantine (N.J.) Fire Dept., 1979—, firefighter, instr. dep. coord emergency mgmt., 1987—; paramedic mobile intensive care West Jersey Health System, 1982-83, Underwood Meml. Hosp, 1980—; forensic med. investigator Atlantic County Med. Examiners Office, 1982-86; nurse dept. intensive care, emergency Shore Meml. Hosp., 1986-97; sr. flight nurse, 2000; asst. chief nurse, 2003. Mem. 714th Aeromed. Squad USAF, 1991—. Decorated USAF Commendation medal, 1997, Air medal, 2004; recipient citation Senator Dan Dalton. Mem. Nat. Flight Nurses Assn., Nat. Registry Emergency Med. Technicians, N.J. State Emergency Med. Technician Instrs., Emergency Nurses Assn., Emergency, Internat. Assn. Firefighters, Atlantic County Firefighters Assn. Office: 1417 W Brigantine Ave Brigantine NJ 08203-2147 Address: PO Box 164 Brigantine NJ 08203-0164

HOLL, JOHN WILLIAM, engineering educator; b. Danville, Ill., Feb. 20, 1928; s. William Benjamin and Anna Marie (Waldo) H.; m. Antoinette Fillhouer, Aug. 20, 1950; children— Jessica, Vanessa, Melissa, Cassandra, Alyssa, Nathan, Zachary. BS in M.E, U. Ill., 1949, MS in M.E, 1951; PhD in M.E, Pa. State U., 1958, B of Music, 1996. Rsch. asst. in mech. engring. Engring. Experiment Sta. U. Ill., Urbana, 1949-51; rsch. assoc. Applied Rsch. Lab. Pa. State U., 1951-54, 56-58, asst. prof. engring. rsch., 1958-59, asso. prof. aerospace engring., 1963-67, prof., 1967-91, prof. emeritus, 1991—. Asso. prof. mech. engring. U. Nebr., Lincoln, 1959-63; cons. in field Mem. Lincoln Symphony Orch., 1960-63; mem. Nittany Valley Symphony Orch., State College, Pa., 1969—, State Coll. Mcpl. Band, 1977—; Trustee Unitarian Ch., Lincoln, 1961-62. Served with U.S. Army, 1955-56. Fellow ASME (R.T. Knapp award 1970, 91, Melville medal 1970, Centennial medallion 1980, dedicated service award 1985); assoc. fellow AIAA; mem. Internat. Clarinet Assn., Golden Key Nat. Honor Soc., Sigma Xi, Phi Mu Alpha Sinfonia, Pi Kappa Lambda. Home: 1108 Mayberry Ln State College PA 16801-6952 Office: Pa State U Aerospace Engring 227 Hammond Bldg University Park PA 16802

HOLL, KRISTI DIANE, writer, educator; b. Guthrie Center, Iowa, Dec. 8, 1951; children: Jennifer Marie Vogtlin, Laurel Renee, Jacqueline Dawn Sharrow. BA in Elem. Edn., U. No. Iowa, 1974. Author: (24 novels, 3 nonfiction books) for titles, check www.KristiHoll.com or amazon.com (children's choice award Md., 1990). Tchr. Campus Crusade Mil. Ministry, San Antonio, Tex. Mem.: Soc. Children's Book Writers and Illustrators. Baptist. Avocations: quilting, reading, classic movies, travel. Home: 7667 Callaghan Rd #1102 San Antonio TX 78229 Personal E-mail: kristi@kristiholl.com.

HOLL, STEVEN MYRON, architect; b. Bremerton, Wash., Dec. 9, 1947; s. Myron Leroy and Helen May Holl; B.A. cum laude, U. Wash., 1971; postgrad. in Rome and London. Architect, tchr. archtl. design U. Wash., Seattle, 1979; individual practice architecture, San Francisco, 1974-76, N.Y.C., 1977—; prof. Grad. Sch. Architecture, Columbia U, 1981—. Recipient Nat. Endowment for Arts award, 1982, Progressive Architecture award, 1978, 82, 84, 86-87, 90, AIA award 1985-86, 89-90, Arnold W. Brunner prize in architecture Am. Acad. and Inst. of Arts and Letters, 1990, Cooper Hewitt Nat. Design award in arch. Smithsonian Instn., 2002, NY AIA Project award for Loisium Visitors' Ctr., Langenlois, Austria, 2003, Nat. AIA award for Design Excellence for Simmons Hall, MIT, 2003, award of excellence for best design of a parking facility Internat. Parking Inst., Nelson Atkins Mus. Art, Kansas City, Mo., 2004; named America's Best Arch., Time Mag., 2001; Archtl. fellow N.Y. State Coun. on Arts., 1979; grantee NEA, Grahame Found., NYSCA, 1988. Exhibited in Mus. Modern Art, N.Y.C., 1989, Harvard Grad. Sch. Design; author: The Alphabetical City, 1980, Urban and Rural House Types in North America, 1983, Within The City, 1988, Anchoring, 1989; mem. NCARB, AIA, Am. Assn. Mus., Hon. Whitney Cir., Alvar Aalto Found. Office: 11th Fl 450 W 31st St New York NY 10001 Office Phone: 212-629-7262. Business E-Mail: mail@stevenholl.com.

HOLL, WALTER JOHN, architect, interior designer; b. Richardton, ND, May 14, 1922; s. John and Rose Mary Holl; m. Eleanor Mary Triervieler, Jan. 23, 1943; children: Mark Walter (dec. 2001), Michael John, Randolph Gregory, Linda Michelle, Timothy James, John Walter. Student, Internat. Corr. Schs., 1946-47, 59; student in interior design, U. Nebr., 1976; student, student in photography, Clarke Coll., 1981. Licensed arch., Calif., interior designer, Ill.; cert. Nat. Coun. for Interior Design Qualifications. Steel detailer, estimator E.J. Voggenthaler Co., Dubuque, Iowa, 1941-42; engr., also methods developer Marinship Corp., Sausalito, Calif., 1942-44; ptnr. Holl & Everly, Dubuque, Iowa, 1946-47; prin. Holl Designing Co., also W. Holl & Assocs., Dubuque, San Francisco, 1947-87, Walter J. Holl, Arch., Burlingame, Calif., 1987, 89, San Diego, Calif., 1989—. Cons. Clarke Coll. Art Students, Dubuque, 1953-61; commd. arch., interior designer, constructor renovations and hist. preservation Dubuque County Courthouse, 1978-85; mem. convoy USCG Ofcl. Presdl. Security Patrol, 1979; oral exam commr. Calif. Bd. Archtl. Examiners, 1994-96; cert. mem. Calif. State Office Emergency Svc.; participant The Brit. Coun.-Archs. Study Tour, Belfast, No. Ireland, 1995; juror Nat. Coun. for Interior Design Qualification, 1996, 98. Chmn. Dubuque Housing Rehab. Commn., 1976-77. With AUS, 1944-46, ETO. Decorated 2 bronze stars; recipient Nat. Bldg. Design awards, 1968, 69, 73, 94. Mem. AIA (bd. dirs. 1993-99, pres.-elect north county sect. San Diego chpt. 1995, pres. 1996, bldg. codes and stds. com. San Diego chpt. 1998-99), USCG Aux. (comdr. 1975-78), Am. Soc. Interior Designers (profl.), Am. Arbitration Assn. (panel arbitrators), Inst. Bus. Designers (profl. Chgo. chpt.), Dubuque Golf and Country Club (bldg. commn. 1953-54), Julien Dubuque Yacht Club (commodore 1974-75), Mchts. and Mfrs. Club (Chgo.). Roman Catholic. Achievements include patent for castered pallet. Home: 27545 Sun City Blvd Sun City CA 92586

HOLLADAY, WILHELMINA COLE, interior designer, museum director; b. Elmira, N.Y., Oct. 10, 1922; d. Chauncy E. and Claire Elizabeth (Strong) Cole; m. Wallace Fitzhugh Holladay, Sept. 27, 1946; children: Wallace Fitzhugh, Scott Cole. BA, Elmira Coll., 1944; postgrad. art history, U. Paris, 1953—54, U. Va., 1960—61; PhD (hon.), Moore Coll. Art, 1988, Mt. Vernon Coll., 1988, Elmira Coll., 1994. Exec. sec. Howard Ludington, Rochester, N.Y., 1944-45, Chinese Embassy, Washington, 1945-48; staff Nat. Gallery of Art, Washington, 1957-59; dir. interior design div. Holladay Corp., Washington, 1970-95. Dir. Adams Nat. Bank, 1978-86, chmn., 1978-86; founder, chmn., bd. dirs., creator art collection by women (Renaissance through contemp.), Nat. Mus. Women in Arts, 1982—. Founder Archival Libr. of Periodicals, Books, Exhbn. Catalogs on Women's Art for Rsch. Purposes; bd. dirs. Am. Field Svc., 1964-80, Internat. Student House, 1973—, Leeds Castle Found.; mem. coun. friends of Folger Shakespeare Libr., 1978-82; mem. world svc. coun. YWCA; trustee Corcoran Gallery of Art, 1980-90, The Fund for Endowment of Diplomatic Reception Rms.; mem. Mayor's Blue Ribbon Com., The Year of Visual Arts Com., Am. Acad. Rome; mem. adv. council The Girl Scouts of US; pres. Langley Sch. Decorated Order of Merit Norwegian Govt.; named laureate, Washington Bus. Hall of Fame, Washingtonian of Yr., Washingtonian Mag., 1987, Woman of Achievement, Washington Ednl. TV Assn., 1984, Woman of Distinction, Coun. Ind. Colls., 1987, Hon. Citizen, State of Tex., 1992, Hon. Athenian, Mayor of Athens, 2002; named one of 21 Leaders for 21st Century, Women's eNews, 2005; named to Women of Distinction, Birmingham So. Coll., 1991, Nat. Women's Hall of Fame, 1996; recipient Thomas Jefferson award, Am. Soc. Interior Designers, Horizon's Theatre award, 1986, Disting. Woman's award, Northwood Inst., 1987, award, Anti-Defamation League, 1987, Disting. Achievement award, Nat. League Am. Pen Women, 1991, Women Achievers award, Internat. Alliance, 1991, Key to City of Kansas City, 1991, Hon. Citizen award, State Tex., 1992, Women First award, YWCA, 1993, Women as Leaders award, The Wash. Ctr., Sears, 1994, Fellow award for disting. svc. to arts, New Orleans Mus. Art, 1997, Disting. Washingtonian award in lit. and the arts, Univ. Club Washington, 1998, Gold medal honor award, Nat. Inst. Social Scis., 2000, Honoree, Historic Georgetown Club, 2000, Leadership award, Pine Manor Coll., 2002, Nat. Women Arts award, Phoenix Art Mus. League, 2003. Mem. Am. Assn. Mus., Am. Fedn. Art, Women's Caucus for Arts, Mus. Modern Art, Art Librs. N.Am., Coll. Art Assn., Archives Am. Art, Art Table, Smithson Soc., Internat. Women's Forum, Nat. Women's Econ. Alliance (bd. dirs. 1984—, Soaring Eagle award 1988), Internat. Women's Forum (Woman That Makes a Difference award, 1991), Women's Caucus for Art (honors, 2001), The Smithsonian Soc., Golden Circle Kennedy Ctr., Am. News Women's Club., Capital Speakers Club. Episcopalian. Home: 3215 R St NW Washington DC 20007-2941 Office: Nat Mus Women Arts 1250 New York Ave NW Washington DC 20005 *You haven't failed until you quit trying.*

HOLLAND, BARBARA, artist, educator; b. Bury, Eng., Sept. 29, 1939; came to U.S., 1990; d. William Arthur and Hilda (Woodhead) Goodwin; m. Marshall Robert Holland Jr., Sept. 21, 1963; children: William, Kathleen. BA in Art Edn., Leicester (Eng.) U., 1961; MA, U. North Tex., 1968. Tchr. art Bartholomew Sch., Eynsham, Eng., 1961-63; artist, designer Susan Crane Packaging Co., Dallas, 1964-66; grad. rsch. asst. U. North Tex., Denton, 1966-68; tchr. Holy Trinity Ch. of Eng. H.S., Halifax, Eng., 1969-70; art tchr. in charge Reath Park Girls Sch., Romford, Essex, Eng., 1970-72; tchr., head of art Unsworth Comprehensive Sch., Bury, 1972-79; tchr., head design faculty Parrenthorn H.S., Prestwich, Eng., 1979-90; instr. children's art and continuing edn. Kilgore (Tex.) Jr. Coll., 1992—; adj. instr. Tyler (Tex.) Jr. Coll., 1992—99, instr. art, 2000—. Moderator for art N.W. Exam. Bd., Eccles, Eng., 1978-81; team rep. N.W. Funded Curriculum Design, Bury, 1986-88; mem. curriculum working com. Nat. Tech. Vocat. Edn. Initiative, Manchester, Eng., 1988-90; instr. study in Eng., North Tex. Cmty. and Jr. Coll. Consortium affiliate Am. Inst. Fgn. Study, Denton, summer 1998. Contbr. illustration to: Industrial Archeology Review, Vol. 2, 1978, Vol. 14, 1979; artwork included in: (book) Colored Pencil 3, 1996. Awards include Hon. Mention and Purchase award West Bank Guild for World Trade Ctr., New Orleans, 1991, Citation and Spl. awards East Tex. Fine Art Assn., Longview, 1992, 93, 95, 2nd pl. nat. juried exhbn. Navarro Arts Coun., Corsicana, 1995, Hon. Mention, TJC Faculty Exhbn., TMA, 1997, NISOD medal for tchg. excellence U. Tex., 2001. Mem. Nat. Soc. for Edn. in Art and Design (life), Upper Level Artists Gallery. Episcopalian. Avocations: reading, listening to classical music, tap dancing, gardening, knitting. Home: 104 Janet Kay Dr Longview TX 75605-8004 Office: Tyler Jr Coll PO Box 9020 Tyler TX 75711-9020

HOLLAND, BETH, actress; b. N.Y.C. d. Samson and Florence (Liebman) Hollander; m. Louis L. Friedman, Aug. 28, 1953; children: Ellen Lynn, Cathy Jayne. Pvt. studies in acting, voice tng. Arts funding cons. N.Y. State Senate, 1974-89. Appeared in various roles on TV, film and theatre, also comedy video Your Favorite Jokes, 1988; cabaret debut, N.Y.C., 2004. Pres. Sonia Alden Found. Inc.; bd. dirs. Fla. Opera Soc., Symphony of Americas. Recipient Carbonell performance award, Theatre League of South Fla., 1996. Mem. AFTRA (pres. N.Y. chpt. 1989-91, bd. dirs., trustee Health and Retirement Funds, past treas.), SAG, English Speaking Union, N.Y. TV Acad. (past bd. dirs.), Actors Equity Assn., Twelfth Night Club, Episcopal Actors Guild (first women pres.), Players Club (libr. bd.), Lambs Club, Tower Club, Friars Club. Avocations: travel, politics, arts. E-mail: bethholland146@aol.com.

HOLLAND, BRENT ANDREW, art educator, painter; b. Springfield, Mo. s. Sam and Barbara Holland; m. Erica Abell, July 24, 2004. BFA, Mo. State U., Springfield, 2001; MFA, U. Wash., Seattle, 2004. Instr. of record U. Wash., Seattle, 2003—04; faculty Seattle Acad. Fine Art, 2004—; asst. prof. Iowa State U., Ames, 2005—. Vis. lectr. U. Wash., Seattle, 2004; painter. Recipient

Juror's Choice award, Ark. Arts Ctr., 2000, Grad. Rsch. award, U. of Wash., 2003, Spl. Recognition award, Gonzales Scholarship, 2003, Gonzales Excellence in Tchg. award, U. Wash., 2004; scholar Art and Design, Mo. State U., 2000; Lasallion Internat. Art and Cultural Ctr. assistantship, Royalty Rsch. Scholar assistantship. Mem.: Coll. Arts Assn. Office Phone: 206-240-3511.

HOLLAND, BRIAN JOSEPH, corporate financial executive; s. Michael Francis and Louise Grace Holland. BA, Vanderbilt U., Nashville, 1985—89, MBA, 1990—92. Equity analyst First Albany Corp., N.Y.C., 1992—94; sr. portfolio mgr. Bankers Trust N.Y./Deutsche Bank, N.Y.C., 1994—99; rsch. dir. Boyd Watterson Asset Mgmt., Cleve., 2000—. Mem. Cleve. Soc. Security Analysts, 2001—. Bd. mem. Easter Seals, Cleve., 2001—03; ptnr. Playhouse Partners, Cleve., 2002—. Mem.: Assn. Investment Mgmt. Rsch., Cleve. Soc. Securty Analysts, Cleve. 20/30 Club (assoc.), Cleve. Athletic Club (assoc.). Democrat. Methodist. Avocations: running, travel, tennis, golf. Home: 598 S Court St Medina OH 44256 Office: Boyd Watterson Asset Mgmt 1801 E 9th St Ste 1400 Cleveland OH 44114 Business E-Mail: bholland@boydwatterson.com.

HOLLAND, CHARLES JOSEPH, lawyer; b. Ottumwa, Iowa, Oct. 6, 1949; m. Nancy Jo Daniels, Aug. 29, 1970; children: Tyler, Emily, Clare. BA, U. Iowa, 1971, JD (with high honors), 1977. Bar: Iowa 1977, U.S. Dist. Ct. (so. dist., no. dist.) Iowa 1977. Assoc. Hayek, Hayek & Hayek, Iowa City, 1977-81; ptnr. Hayek, Hayek, Holland & Brown, Iowa City, 1981—92; pvt. practice, 1992—2000; ptnr. Holland & Anderson LLP, 2000—. Mem. exec. coun. Nat. Conf. Bar Pres., 2003—. Dir. Iowa City Downtown Assn., 1988-92. Mem. Iowa Coun. Sch. Bd. Attys. (chair 2004-), ABA, Iowa Bar Assn.(pres. 2001-2002), Johnson County Bar Assn. Office: 300 Brewery Sq 123 N Linn St PO Box 2820 Iowa City IA 52244-2820 Office Phone: 319-354-0331.

HOLLAND, CHARLES R., career military officer; BS in Aero. Engring., USAF Acad., 1968; grad., Squadron Officer Sch., 1974, Air Command and Staff Coll., 1975; MS in Bus. Mgmt., Troy State U., 1976; nat. security mgmt. course, 1982; grad., Indsl. Coll. of Armed Forces, 1986; program for sr. ofcls. in nat. security, Harvard U., 1990. Commd. 2d lt. USAF, 1968, advanced through grades to gen., 1997; air ops. staff officer directorate of airlift Hdqs. U.S. Air Forces in Europe, Ramstein Air Base, West Germany, 1974-76; joint tng. exercise plans officer Mil. Airlift Ctr. Europe, Ramstein Air Base, 1976-77; chief space shuttle flight ops. br., exec. to comdr. L.A. Air Force Sta., 1979-83; comdr. 21st Tactical Airlift Squadron, Clark Air Base, The Philippines, 1983-85; dep. chief airlift and tng. divsn., mil. dep. acquisition Office of Asst. Sec. of Air Force, Washington, 1986-87, chief airlift and tng. divsn., mil. dep. acquisition, 1987-88; vice comdr., comdr. 1550th Combat Crew Tng. Wing, Kirtland AFB, N.Mex., 1988-91; comdr. 1st Spl. Ops. Wing, Hurlburt Field, Fla., 1991-93; dep. comdg. gen. Joint Spl. Ops. Command, Ft. Bragg, N.C., 1993-95; comdr. Spl. Ops. Command, Pacific, Camp H.M. Smith, Hawaii, 1995-97, Air Force Spl. Ops. Command, Hurlburt Field, 1997-99; vice comdr. Hdqs. U.S. Air Forces in Europe, Ramstein Air Base, Germany, 1999—2000; comdr. U.S. Spec. Ops. Command, MacDill AFB, Fla., 2000—03. Decorated Def. Superior Svc. medal with 2 oak leaf clusters, Legion of Merit with oak leaf cluster, D.F.C., Meritorious Svc. medal with 2 oak leaf clusters.

HOLLAND, DAVID THURSTON, former editor; b. Phila., May 26, 1923; s. Rupert Sargent and Margaret Currier (Lyon) H. BA, Harvard, 1944, MA, 1946. Vice consul U.S. Fgn. Svc., Budapest, Hungary, 1945; teaching fellow Harvard U., Cambridge, Mass., 1946-49; coll. traveller Oxford U. Press, N.Y.C., 1953-54; asst. editor Harcourt Brace, N.Y.C., 1955-59; asst. editor Ency. Internat. Grolier Inc., N.Y.C., 1959-62, assoc. editor Ency. Americana, 1962-65, sr. editor, 1965-85; exec. editor, 1985; editor in chief Ency. Americana Grolier Inc., Danbury, Conn., 1985-91; ret., 1991. Democrat. Episcopalian.

HOLLAND, ELLEN C., music educator; b. Washington, Nov. 6, 1960; d. Theodore R. and Frances W. Creel. BMus cum laude, East Carolina U., 1983; MMus, U. S.C., 1985. Music tchr. Virginia Beach City Pub. Schs., Va., 1986—, coord. dept., 2002—03; accompanist First Bapt. Ch. Virginia Beach, 2004—. Music tchr. Holland Studio of Piano, 1986—95. Sec. Virginia Beach Chorale, 1988—92, audition com., 1988—98. Mem.: Virginia Beach Edn. Assn., Va. Music Educators Assn. (co-chair dist. chorus II 1999—2000, chair dist. chorus II 2000—01), Smart Stockers Investment Club (founder/treas. 1990—). E-mail: opy1dopy@cox.net.

HOLLAND, GENE GRIGSBY (SCOTTIE HOLLAND), artist; b. Hazard, Ky., June 30, 1928; d. Edward and Virginia Lee (Watson) Grigsby; m. George William Holland, Sept. 22, 1950; 3 children. BA, U. So. Fla., 1968; studied with, Ruth Allison, Talequah, Okla., 1947—48, Ralph Smith, Washington, 1977, Clint Carter, Atlanta, 1977, R. Jordan, Winter Park, Fla., 1979; student, Cedric Baldwin Egeli Workshop, Charleston, SC, 1984. Various clerical and secretarial positions, 1948-52; news reporter, photographer Bryan (Tex.) Daily News, 1952; clk. Fogarty Bros. Moving and Transfer, Tampa and Miami, Fla., 1954-57; tchr. elem. schs., Hillsborough County, Fla., 1968-72; salesperson, assoc. real estate, 1984-2000; owner, operator antique store, 1982-87. One-woman and group shows include Tampa Woman's Clubhouse, 1973, Cor Jesu, Tampa, 1973, Bank, Monks Corner, SC, 1977, Summerville Artists Guild, 1977-78, Apopka (Fla.) Art and Foilage Festival, 1980, 81, 82, Fla. Fedn. Women's Clubs, 1980, 81, 82; numerous group shows, latest being Island Gifts, Tampa, 1980-82, Brandon (Fla.) Sta., 1980-81, Holland Originals, Orlando, Fla.; represented in permanent and pvt. collections. Vol. ARC, Tampa, 1965-69, United Fund Campaign, 1975-76; pres. Mango (Fla.) Elem. Sch. PTA, 1966-67; pres. Tampa Civic Assn., 1974-75; vol. Easter Seal Fund Campaign, 1962-63; art chmn. Apopka Art & Foilage Festival, 1990; deaconness Ctrl. Christian Ch. Orlando, 1992-94, chmn. bible study, 1993-94; deaconness First Christian Ch. Tampa, 1996-99. Recipient numerous art awards, 1978-82. Mem. AARP (parlimentarian Apopka chpt.), Internat. Soc. Artists, Coun. Arts & Scis. for Ctrl. Fla., Fedn. Women's Clubs (pres. Tampa Civic 1974-75), Meth. Women's Soc. (sec. 1976-77), Nat. Trust Hist. PReservation, Nat. Hist. Soc., Fla. Geneal. and Hist. Soc., Am. Guild Flower Arrangers, The Nat. Grigsby Family Soc. (assoc. sec. 1991-92, corp. sect. 1992-96, dir. 1995-97, 99-2001, S.W. chpt. dir. 1997-2000), Internat. Inner Wheel Club (past chmn. dist. 696, pres. Tampa 1972-73), Friday Morning Musicale Club (1st v.p. bd. incorporators Tampa 1974-75, bd. dirs.), Gen. Fedn. of Fla. Clubs Apopka Woman's Club (pres. 1981-82, bd. dirs. 1983-85, Woman of Yr. 1991-92), Apopka Tennis Over 50's Group Club (pres. 1988-90), Federated Garden Club Plant City Fla. (conservation chmn.), South Bay Geneal. Soc., Tampa PC User Group, Computer Club Inc. of Sun City Ctrs., Lexington Geneal. Assn. Home: 231 Mooring Ln Lexington SC 29072-9106

HOLLAND, GEORGE EDISON, JR., (ED HOLLAND), lawyer; b. Rutherfordton, NC, Dec. 2, 1952; m. Elizabeth Bird; children: Laura E., Caroline S. BA, Auburn U., 1975; JD, U. Va., 1978. Bar: Fla. 1978, US Dist. Ct. No. Dist. Fla. 1978, US Ct. Appeals 11th Cir. 1981, US Ct. Appeals 5th Cir. 1986, US Ct Appeals DC Cir. 1988, US Supreme Ct. 1990. Joined So. Co., Atlanta, 1992, sys. compliance officer; v.p. power generation/transmissions, corp. counsel Gulf Power subsid., Pensacola, Fla.; pres, CEO Savannah Electric subsid., Savannah, Ga., 1997—2001; exec. v.p., general counsel So. Co., Atlanta, 2001—. Mem.: Escambia-Santa Rosa Bar Assn. (pres. 1987—98), Fla. Bar (mem. adminstrv. law sect.), ABA (mem. pub. utility law sect.). Office: So Co 170 Peachtree St NW Ste 1400 Atlanta GA 30303

HOLLAND, GEORGE FRANK, II, investment company executive; b. N.Y.C., Jan. 19, 1931; m. Elizabeth R. Hardy, Aug. 31, 1957; children: Steven Todd, William Eric, Roger Hardy, Ellen. AB, Ind. U., 1953, MBA, 1957. Asst. v.p. Am. Fletcher Nat. Bank, Indpls., 1957-70; exec. v.p., dir., sec. Traub Co. Inc., Indpls., 1970-97; v.p. investment David A. Noyes & Co., Indpls., 1998—. Contbr. articles to profl. jours. Lt. col. USAFR, 1953-77. Mem. Indpls. Soc. Fin. Analysts (past pres.), Res. Officers Assn., Ret. Officers Assn., Ind. U. Alumni Assn., Carmel Breakfast Sertoma Club (past pres.), Indpls. Stock & Bond Club, Am. Legion, Scottish Rite, Shriners, Sigma Chi Alumni Assn. Republican. Episcopalian. Home: 20 Wildwood Dr Carmel IN 46032-1416 Office: David A Noyes & Co 111 Monument Cir Ste 300 Indianapolis IN 46204-5110

HOLLAND, HOWARD WALTER, mechanical engineer, engineering executive; b. Balt., Feb. 5, 1945; s. Howard Allison and E. Carlyn (Lynch) H.; m. Toni Gene Kozuch, Aug. 14, 1971; children: William, Sean, Megan. BSME, Drexel U., Phila., 1968; MSME, Stanford U., 1969. Registered profl. engr., Pa., Tex., Calif., Ohio, Hawaii. Constrn. coord. Mobil-Joliet (Ill.) Refinery, 1971-72; sr. project nuclear engr. Pa. Power and Light, Allentown, 1972-80; engring. mgr. Brown & Root, Houston, 1980-87; asst. engring. mgr. and power divsn. mgr. Stone & Webster, Houston, 1987-90; dir. project devel. Transco Power Co., Houston, 1990-92; v.p. Enron Engring. & Constrn. Co., Houston, 1992—. N.Am. coord./tech. coord. Internat. Gas Turbine Inst., Atlanta, 1992-93; BWRtech.r ev. post TMI Industry Com., Allentown, 1979-80. Editor ASME Cogen Turbo Power, 1992, 93 (Plaque 1992-93, cert. 1996); contbr. articles to profl. jours. Coach basketball/baseball, Houston, 1984-86, soccer, 1986-92; v.p. Houston Civic Assn., 1988-90. With U.S. Army, 1969-71. Recipient Cert. Am. Boiler Mfrs. Assn., 1996. Mem. ASME, Am. Nuclear Soc., Am. Welding Soc., Internat. Gas Turbine Inst. Avocations: swimming, tennis, soccer, hiking, camping. Home: 11954 Fawnview Dr Houston TX 77070-2702 Office: 333 Clay St Ste 1500 Houston TX 77002-4000

HOLLAND, JAMES F., medical educator; b. May 16, 1925; AB, Princeton U., 1945; MD, Columbia U., 1947; DSc (hon.), SUNY, Buffalo, 1997. Intern, resident Presbyn. Hosp., N.Y.C., 1947—49; fellow Francis Delafield Hosp., N.Y.C., 1951—53; dir. Derald H. Ruttenberg Cancer Ctr. Mt. Sinai Sch. Medicine, N.Y.C., 1973—94, chmn. dept. neoplastic diseases, 1973—94, disting. prof. neoplastic diseases, 1994—. Chmn. Cancer and Leukemia Group B Internat. Rsch. Group, 1963-81; chmn. N.Y. State Health Rsch. Sci. Bd., 1998-2000. Editor: Cancer Medicine, 1972, 6th edit., 2003; contbr. over 600 articles to med. and cancer jours. Office: Mt Sinai Sch Medicine 1 Gustave L Levy Pl New York NY 10029-6500 Office Phone: 212-241-4495. E-mail: james.holland@mssm.edu.

HOLLAND, JAMES R., real estate company officer; b. St. Louis, Feb. 20, 1944; s. Randolph and Thelma (Robinson) Holland; m. Helen M. Devine, Feb. 18, 1972; children: Danielle, James Randolph, Eric Marc. Student, Principia Coll., 1962—64; BFA, Ohio U., 1966; postgrad., U. Mo. Sch. Journalism, 1966. Photog. intern Nat. Geog. Soc., Washington, 1966, contract photographer for mag., 1967-68; film prodr. Christian Sci. Ctr., Boston, 1969-74; real estate developer, pres. Brownstone Properties, Inc., Boston, 1975-77; real estate broker Street & Co., Inc., Boston, 1978-82; pres. A Bit of Boston Real Estate, Inc., Boston, 1982—. Author: The Amazon, 1971, Mr. Pops-Arthur Fiedler, 1972, Tanglewood, 1973; illustrator, photographer Continental and Colonial Currency of Colonical America; co-author: Photojournalism-Principles and Practice, 2d edit., 1980; contbr. articles photographs to publs., video games, textbooks; prodr.: Twinkle Toes Videos; Represented in permanent collections Truman Libr., JFK Libr., Boston Pub. Libr. Active Neighborhood Assn. Back Bay, 1972—, Boston Home and Property Owners Assn., Small Property Owners Assn., 2000—; assoc. Boston Pub. Libr.; active Friend of Beverly Hills (Calif.) Pub. Libr., Dickerson Pk. Zoo, Mus. Ozarks History, Boston Athenaeum; sponsor Babe Ruth Baseball League Team, 1992—; league sponsor Bck Bay, Beacon Hill and North End Little League Teams, 1999—; 10th anniversary com. Boston U. Photographic Resource Ctr. Named AAU Nat. Karate Champion, 1989; recipient World Press Competition award, 1967, Newsweek/Bolex Documentary Film award, 1969, Indls. Photography Film Competition award, 1970, Bronze medal, Internat. Film and TV Festival N.Y., 1971, 6th national ranking in weapon's form, Reeves Sport Karate Ratings, 1989. Mem.: N.Am. Sport Karate Assn. (various awards), Nat. Press Photographers (award 1966, 1967, 1968), Am. Soc. Mag. Photographers, Samuel Fletcher and Angeline Drury Soc. Achievements include broadcast of film work on NBC, ABC, CBS, PBS, BBC, Travel Channel. Home: 208 Commonwealth Ave Boston MA 02116-2534 Office: A Bit of Boston Real Estate Inc 5 Brimmer St Boston MA 02108-1001

HOLLAND, JAMES TULLEY, retired plastics company executive; b. Pikeville, Ky., May 24, 1940; s. Thomas Joseph and Mary Alta (Tulley) Holland; m. Susan Ellen Joy; children: James Christopher, Kathleen Holland Wiesel. BA in Econs., U. Va., 1962; MBA, Am. U., 1969. With br. banking ops. United Va. Bank, Alexandria, 1965-67; with Booz Allen & Hamilton, Washington, 1967-76; treas., chief fin. officer O'Sullivan Corp., Winchester, Va., 1976-84, exec. v.p., COO, 1984-86, pres., COO, 1986—95, CEO, 1995-98, ret., 1998, also bd. dirs. Bd. dirs. Va. Nat. Bank-Winchester Region, Valley Health Sys., Valley Regional Enterprises; adv. bd. Liberty Mut. Ins. Co. Trustee Glass Glen Burnie Found. Capt. U.S. Army, 1963—65. Mem. Winchester Country Club, Farmington Country Club (Charlottesville, Va.), Belle Haven Country Club (Alexandria). Roman Catholic. Avocations: golf, reading, writing. Home: 261 Merrifield Ln Winchester VA 22602-2306 E-mail: jimholland@adelphia.net.

HOLLAND, JEFFREY R., religious organization administrator; b. St. George, Utah, Dec. 3, 1940; s. Frank D. and Alice (Bentley) H.; m. Patricia Terry, June 7, 1963; children: Matthew, Mary, David. BS, Brigham Young U., 1965, MA, 1966; PhD, Yale U., 1973. Dean religious instrn. Brigham Young U., 1974-76; commr. Latter Day Saints Ch. Ednl. System, 1976-80; pres. Brigham Young U., 1980-89; gen. authority, mem. 1st Quorum of the 70 LDS Ch., 1989-94; Apostle Quorum of the Twelve, 1994—. Dir. Deseret News Pub. Co., Key Bank of Utah, Key Bancshares of Utah, Inc. Author: (books) However Long & Hard the Road, 1993, Christ & the New Covenant: The Messianic Message of the Book of Mormon, 1997, Shepherds, Why This Jubilee?, 2000, Of Souls, Symbols & Sacraments, 2001, Trusting Jesus, 2003; co-author (with Patricia T Holland): On Earth as It Is in Heaven, 1993. Mem. Am. Assn. Presidents of Ind. Colls. and Univs. (past pres.), Nat. Assn. Ind. Colls. and Univs. (former bd. dirs.), Am. Council Edn., Phi Kappa Phi. Office: LDS Church 50 E South Temple Salt Lake City UT 84150-0001

HOLLAND, JIMMIE C., psychiatrist, educator; b. Forney, Tex., Apr. 9, 1928; m. James F. Holland; 5 children. BA, Baylor U., 1948, MD, 1952. Diplomate Am. Bd. Psychiatry, Am. Bd. Neurology. Instr. to prof. SUNY, Buffalo, 1956-73; assoc. prof., assoc. attending physician to asst. dir. cons.-liaison psychiatry Albert Einstein Coll. Medicine and Montefiore Med. Ctr., Bronx, 1973-77; chair dept. psychiatry and behavioral scis., Wayne E. Chapman chair in psychiat. oncology Meml. Sloan Kettering Cancer Ctr., NYC, 1997—2003. Prof. dept. psychiatry Weill Med. Coll., N.Y.C., 1977—; cons. NIMH-USSR joint schizophrenia study Psychiat. Rsch. Inst., Moscow, 1972-73, NIMH, Rockville, Md., 1973-75; chmn. psychiatry com. Cancer and Leukemia Group B Clin. Trials, Brookline, Mass., 1976-2001. Editor: Handbook of Psycho-oncology: Psychological Care of the Patient with Cancer, 1989, Psychooncology, 1998; co-editor Jour. Psycho-oncology; author, co-author: The Human Side of Cancer, 258 jour. articles, book chpts., monographs. Bd. dirs. Cancer Care, Inc., 1979-81. Recipient Disting. Alumna award Baylor U., Waco, Tex., 1982; Am. Cancer Soc. Medal of Honor, 1994 Fellow Inst. Medicine, Am. Coll. Psychiatrists, Am. Psychiat. Assn., Acad. Psychosomatic Medicine (founding pres.), Internat. Psycho-Oncology Soc. (founding pres.), Am. Psychosocial Oncology Soc., Am. Psychosomatic Soc., Am. Soc. Clin. Oncology. Office: Meml Sloan-Kettering Cancer Ctr 1275 York Ave New York NY 10021-6094 Office Phone: 212-639-3904. Business E-Mail: hollandj@mskcc.org.

HOLLAND, JOHN ADAMS, lawyer; b. Sacramento, Aug. 18, 1952; s. Alfred Earl and Laura Ruth (Adams) H.; m. Claudia Ayers, Aug. 1, 1981 (div. Mar. 1989); children: Jesse Whitney, Meredith Ayers; m. Cathie Andrews, Nov. 24, 1991; 1 child, Cameron Tinh. BA, U. Mont., 1975; MA, U. Calif., Santa Barbara, 1976; JD, U. Pacific, 1982. Bar: Calif. 1982, U.S. Dist. Ct. (ea. and no. dists.) Calif. 1982, U.S. Ct. Appeals (9th cir.) 1984. Assoc. Law Offices Jos. Van den Berg, Sacramento, 1982-83, Martorana Law Corp., Sacramento, 1984-85, Law Offices Steven A. Lewis, Sacramento, 1985-86; pvt. practice, Sacramento, 1983-84, 86-98; atty. Office of Spill Prevention and Response, Dept. Fish & Game, Sacramento, 1998—. Bd. dirs. Save the American River Assn., Sacramento, 1981-86, pres., 1984-86; mem. slalom kayaking team Summer Olympics, Munich, 1972; mem. U.S. world championship teams for whitewater slalom kayaking, Bourg St. Maurice, France, 1969, Skopje, Yugoslavia, 1975, Spittal, Austria, 1977. Mem. ABA, Calif. Bar Assn., Sacramento Bar Assn. Avocation: whitewater kayaking. Office: Office Spill Prevention and Response 1700 K St Ste 250 Sacramento CA 95814 E-mail: jholland@ospr.dfg.ca.gov.

HOLLAND, JOHN BEN, clothing manufacturing company executive; b. Scottsville, Ky., Mar. 26, 1932; s. Elbridge Winfred and Lou May (Whitney) H.; m. Margaret Irene Pecor, Jan. 31, 1954; children: John Sandra, Robert. BS in Acctg., Bowling Green U., 1959. With Union Underwear Co., Inc., Bowling Green, Ky., 1961—2001, v.p. adminstrn., 1972-74, vice chmn., 1975, chmn., chief exec. officer, 1976-96; ret., 1996; cons., 1996—99; pres., CEO Fruit of the Loom, Inc., 2002—. Bd. dirs. Dollar Gen. Corp., Farmers Nat. Bank. Bd. dirs. Ky. Coun. Econ. Edn., Louisville, 1981-90, Ky. Advocates for Higher Edn. Inc., 1985-93, Ky. C. of C., 1987-88, Camping World Inc., 1985-97, Associated Industries of Ky., Ireland-Am. Econ. Adv. Bd., Tech. Corp. Inc.; chmn. corp. coun. Western Ky. U., devel. steering com., 1985-96; vice-chmn. West Point Pepperial, Inc., 1989-92; chmn. Intermodal Transp. Authority, 1998-2000. Mem. Bowling Green-Warren County C. of C. (bd. dirs. 1981-85), Am. Arbitration Assn. (panel 1985-93). Office: Fruit of the Loom Inc PO Box 90015 Bowling Green KY 42102-9015

HOLLAND, JOHN MADISON, retired family practice physician; b. Holden, W.Va., Oct. 7, 1927; s. Ophia I. and Lou V. (Elliott) H.; m. Mary Louise Bourne, Sept. 2, 1950; children— David, Stephen, Nancy BS, Eastern Ky. State U., Richmond, 1949; MD, U. Louisville, 1952. Diplomate Am. Bd. Family Practice, Am. Bd. Hospice and Palliative Medicine. Intern St. Joseph Infirmary, Louisville, 1952-53; gen. practice family medicine Physicians Group, Springfield, Ill., 1955-80; med. dir. St. John's Hosp., Springfield, 1971-94, St. John's Hospice, 1995—; clin. prof. family practice So. Ill. U., Springfield, 1978—. Served to capt. USAF, 1953-55 Mem. Am. Acad. Family Physicians, Am. Acad. Hospice/Palliative Medicine. Baptist. Home: 2131 Lindsay Rd Springfield IL 62704-3242 Office Phone: 217-544-6464.

HOLLAND, JOSEPH JOHN, financial executive; b. New Brunswick, N.J., Nov. 7, 1927; s. Thomas Clifford and Ruth Elizabeth (Feaster) Holland; m. Bernice T. Kearns, July 1, 1984; 1 child, Wayne Joseph. BS magna cum laude, Mount St. Mary's Coll., 1952; MBA, Rutgers U., 1955. CPA N.J., N.Mex., Tex. Sr. acct. Peat, Marwick, Mitchell & Co., Newark, 1952—61; plant contr., ops. auditor Crane Co., N.Y.C., 1961—65; fin. contr. Ingersoll-Rand Co., U.K., 1965—68; v.p., contr. PPD Corp., Newark, 1968—73; v.p. fin., treas. Edgcomb Steel & Aluminum Corp., Hillside, NJ, 1973—76; cons. in field North Brunswick, NJ, 1978; v.p. fin., dir. Berry Solar Products, Edison, NJ, 1978—86; dir. fin. control Berger Industries, Maspeth, NY, 1986—88; cons. Milltown, NJ, 1988—96; ret. Mem. adv. coun. Rutgers U. Acad. for Life Long Learning. With USN, 1946—48. Mem.: AICPAs, Exchange Club (New Brunswick), Sales Execs. Club of N.J. (chmn. disting. salesman award 1978), Elks.

HOLLAND, KATHLEEN, psychologist, educator; b. San Jose, Calif., Oct. 12, 1949; d. Raymond Eugene and Veronica Jane Holland, Carol Holland (Stepmother); m. Jerry Lee LaRose, Feb. 5, 1969 (dec. 1975); children: Dustin Tierney, Nathan LaRose. BA with honors, San Jose State U., 1973, MS, 1975; D degree, Newport U., 1999. Lic. edn. psychologist, Calif. Sch. psychologist Lindsay (Calif.) Unified Schs., 1975-77, Sonoma County Office Edn., Santa Rosa, Calif., 1977-84; psychology instr. various colls. for U.S. Mil. Hawaii, 1985-86; sch. psychologist Brisbane (Calif.) Schs., 1998—. Pvt. practice, Santa Rosa, 1983, 99; expert test and item reviewer Calif. Bd. Behavioral Sci., Sacramento, 1999. Exhibited glass art. Vol. various youth groups, Calif., 1965—85. Mem. APA, Am. Psychol. Soc., Am. Coll. Forensic Examiners, Am. Acad. Experts in Traumatic Stress, Am. Bd. Disability Analysis, Calif. Assn. Sch. Psychologists, Psi Chi. Republican. Avocations: art, gardening, music, sewing, crafts.

HOLLAND, KATHLEEN, political science professor; b. Burbank, Calif., Feb. 25, 1960; f. Robert and Lenore Gates; m. David Holland, Sept. 18, 1982. B, Calif. State U., 1990, M, 1993. Instr. L.A. Pierce Coll., Woodland Hills, Calif., 1996—, Glendale (Calif.) C.C., 1999—, L.A. Trade Tech., 1999—. Author: Instructor's Manual for Democracy Under Pressure, 2001. Mem. exec. bd. AFT Guild, Local 1521, L.A., 2000—. Mem. Am. Polit. Sci. Assn., Faculty Assn. Calif.'s Cmty. Colls. (com. mem. 2000—). Democrat. Roman Catholic. Office: LA Pierce Coll 6201 Winnetka Ave Woodland Hills CA 91371-0002 Fax: 818-710-8944. Office Phone: 818-710-4494 5265. E-mail: kdholland@earthlink.net.

HOLLAND, LYMAN FAITH, JR., lawyer; b. Mobile, Ala., June 17, 1931; s. Lyman Faith and Louise (Wisdom) H.; m. Leannah Louise Platt, Mar. 6, 1954; children: Lyman Faith III, Laura. BS in Bus. Adminstrn, U. Ala., 1953, LLB, 1957. Bar: Ala. 1957, U.S. Supreme Ct. 1992. Assoc. Hand, Arendall & Bedsole, Mobile, 1957-62; ptnr. Hand, Arendall, Bedsole, Greaves & Johnston, 1963-94, mem., 1995, Hand Arendall LLC, 1996—. Mem. Mobile Jr. C. of C. (Jaycees), 1957-1968, bd. dirs., 1963-68; mem. Mobile Hist. Devel. Com., 1965-69, v.p., 1967-68; bd. dirs. Mobile Azalea Trail, Inc., 1963-68, chmn. bd., 1963-65; bd. dirs. Mobile Mental Health Ctr., 1969-76, v.p., 1972, pres., chmn. bd., 1973; bd. dirs. Mobile chpt. ARC, 1969-97, vice-chmn., 1975-77, exec. vice-chmn., 1978-80, chmn., 1980-82, life bd. dirs. emeritus, 1997—; bd. dirs. Deep South coun. Girl Scouts U.S., 1965-71, Gordan Smith Ctr. Inc., 1973, Bay Area Coun. on Alcoholism, 1973-76, Cmty. Chest Coun. Mobile County, Inc., 1976-81, Greater Mobile Mental Health-Mental Retardation Bd., Inc., 1975-81, pres., 1975-77; active Mobile Estate Planning Coun., 1981—, exec. com., 1988-97, pres., 1994-95. Lt. col. USAF, ret. Mem.: ABA, Ala. Law Found., Ala. Law Inst. (coun. 1978—), Am. Coll. Trust and Estate Counsel Found. (bd. dirs. 1990—96), Am. Coll. Trust and Estate Counsel, Am. Counsel Assn., Mobile County Bar Assn., Ala. State Bar (chmn. sect. corp., banking and bus. law 1978—80), Camellia Club of Mobile, Bienville Club, Country Club of Mobile, Athleston Club (Mobile), Lions, Phi Delta Phi, Pi Kappa Alpha. Baptist (deacon, ch. trustee 1968-73, chmn. trustees 1971-73). Home: 3606 Provident Ct Mobile AL 36608-1534 Office: Hand Arendall LLC PO Box 123 Mobile AL 36601-0123 Office Phone: 251-432-5511.

HOLLAND, MICHAEL EDWARD, archivist, educator; b. Oklahoma City, Aug. 8, 1954; s. Michael R. and Dorothy Victorene Holland; m. Deborah Kay Crosley, Nov. 18, 1980; 1 child, Nicholas Luther. BS, Okla. State U., 1976, MA, 1978. Cert. archivist Acad. Cert. Archivists, 1989. Archivist Okla. Dept. Librs., Oklahoma City, 1980—84; univ. archivist, records mgmt. officer Appalachian State U., Boone, NC, 1984—85; asst. dir. local recs. divsn. Tex. State Libr. and Archives, Austin, 1986—89; univ. archivist, recs. officer Oreg. State U., Corvallis, 1989—96; univ. archivist U. Mo., Columbia, 1997—. Recipient David B. Gracy II award, Soc. Ga. Archivists, 1990. Mem.: Acad. Cert. Archivists (vice pres., pres. elect 2004—05, pres. 2005—, regent cert. maintenance 1997—2002), Jefferson Club U. Mo. Achievements include Early pioneer in the delivery of archival finding aids via the Internet. Avocations: travel, writing. Office: U Mo Archives 706 Lewis Hall Columbia MO 65211-4320 Office Phone: 573-882-4602. Office Fax: 573-884-0027. Personal E-mail: ezrachurch@aol.com. E-mail: hollandm@missouri.edu.

HOLLAND, MICHAEL FRANCIS, investment company executive; b. Cleve., July 8, 1944; s. Joseph Thomas and Mary Louise H.; m. Louise Grace, Aug. 20, 1966; children: Brian, Thomas, Joseph, Daniel, John, Michael Jr. AB, Harvard U., 1966; MBA, Columbia U., 1968. With Morgan Guaranty Trust Co., N.Y.C., 1968-80, investment mgr., 1972-80, v.p., 1975-80; sr. v.p. investments Reliance Group, Inc., also Reliance Ins. Co., N.Y.C., 1980-83;

pres. Holland & Co., Inc., 1983-84; pres., chief exec. officer First Boston Asset Mgmt. Corp., 1984-89; dir., chmn. bd. dirs., chief exec. officer Global Growth and Income Fund, Inc., 1986-89; chmn., CEO Salomon Bros. Asset Mgmt., Inc., 1989-92; vice chmn. Oppenheimer & Co. Inc., 1992-94; dir. The China Fund, Inc., 1992—, Reaves Utility Fund, Inc., 2004—; gen. ptnr. The Blackstone Group, 1994-95; chmn. Holland & Co. L.L.C., 1995—; dir., chmn. State St. Master Funds Inc., 2003—. Dir. The Latin Am. Investment Fund, Inc., 1990-92. Panelist: Louis Rukeyser's Wall Street, 1990—. Vice chmn. Harvard Coll. Fund Assoc. Program, 1998—; mem. com. on univ. resource, com. on faculty selection Harvard U.; trustee Vanguard Charitable Endowment Program, 1997—; mem. bd. fin. Town of New Canaan, Conn., 1997—2003; trustee Harvard Club N.Y.C. Found., 2001—. Mem. Harvard Club of N.Y.C. (bd. mgrs. 1998-2001). Clubs: Racquet & Tennis; Country of New Canaan, Winter (New Canaan); Harvard of Fairfield County. Home: 1 Greenley Rd New Canaan CT 06840-3513 Office: Holland & Co LLC 375 Park Ave Ste 1903 New York NY 10152-1994

HOLLAND, MICHAEL JAMES, computer services administrator; b. N.Y.C., Nov. 20, 1950; s. Robert Frederick and Virginia June (Wilcox) H.; m. Anita Garay, Jan. 5, 1981 (Aug. 1989); 1 child, Melanie. BA in Comparative Lit., Bklyn. Coll., 1972. Enlisted USN, 1975, advanced to CPO, 1989; field med. technician 3rd Marine Divsn., Okinawa, Japan, 1976-77, 1st Marine Divsn., Camp Pendleton, Calif., 1978-79; clin. supr. Naval Hosp. Subic Bay, Philippines, 1979-81; dept. head Tng. Ctr. USMCR, Johnson City, Tenn., 1981-84; clin. supr. No. Tng. Area, Okinawa, 1984-85, 3rd Marine Air Wing, Camp Pendleton, 1985-88; cons. Naval Regional Med. Command, San Diego, 1988-90; system analyst Naval Med. Info. Mgmt. Ctr. Detachment, San Diego, 1990-92; computer svcs. adminstr. U.S. Naval Hosp., Guam, 1993-95; ret., 1995; svc. rep. SBC Calif., 1997—. Mem. Fleet Res. Assn., Comm. Workers Am., Nat. City C. of C. (com. 1989-91).

HOLLAND, NORMAN NORWOOD, critic; b. N.Y.C., Sept. 19, 1927; s. Norman Norwood and Harriette (Breder) H.; m. Jane Kelley, Dec. 17, 1954; children: Kelley, John. BS, MIT, 1947; LLB, Harvard U., 1950, PhD, 1956; cert. in psychoanalysis, Boston Psychoanalytic Inst. From instr. to assoc. prof. MIT, Cambridge, 1955-66; McNulty prof. English SUNY, Buffalo, 1966-83; assoc. prof. U. Paris, 1971-72, 85; Marston-Milbauer eminent scholar U. Fla., Gainesville, 1983—. Cons. various pubs., 1960—, Pres.'s Coun. on Obscenity, 1971, Can. Coun., 1980. Author: The First Modern Comedies 1959, The Shakespearean Imagination, 1964, Psychoanalysis and Shakespeare, 1966, The Dynamics of Literary Response, 1968, Poems in Persons: An Introduction to the Psychoanalysis of Literature, 1973, rev. edit., 2000, 5 Readers Reading, 1975, Laughing: A Psychology of Humor, 1982, The I, 1985, The Brain of Robert Frost: A Cognitive Approach to Literature, 1988, Holland's Guide to Psychoanalytic Psychology and Literature-and-Psychology, 1990, The Critical I, 1992, Death in a Delphi Seminar, 1995. Am. Couns. Learned Socs. fellow, 1974-75, Guggenheim Found. fellow, 1979-80. Mem. Am. Acad. Psychoanalysis (sci. assoc.), Boston Psychoanalytic Soc., Modern Lang. Assn. (div. exec. com. 1975-81). Democrat. Avocation: movies. Office: U Fla Dept English Gainesville FL 32611

HOLLAND, PATRICIA CHRISTINE, music educator, musician; b. Ann Arbor, Mich., Apr. 19, 1957; d. William Franklin Jewell, III and Joan Lorey Jewell; m. Daniel Olin Holland, June 26, 1982. BA, U. Mich., 1979; MusM, Mich. State U., 1990; MusD, U. Mich., 1996. Prin. bassoon Jackson Symphony Orch., 1981—94; prof. music U. Wis., Stevens Point, 1994—. Bassoon instr. Hillsdale Coll., Mich., 1988—94; adj. instr. Jackson C.C., 1993—94; aux. bassoon Grand Rapids Symphony Orch., Mich., 1989—94; prin. bassoon Fox Valley Symphony Orch., Appleton, Wis., 1999—; contra bassoon Peninsula Music Festival, Fish Creek, Wis., 1999—. Contbr. articles to profl. jours. Mem.: Coll. Music Soc., Am. Fedn. Musicians, Internat. Double Reed Soc., Phi Kappa Phi, Pi Kappa Lambda. Office: Univ Wis Stevens Point Stevens Point WI 54481 Office Phone: 715-346-3119.

HOLLAND, PHILLIP KENT, aerospace engineer; b. Wichita, Kans., Oct. 10, 1959; s. Phillip Norman and Lafreda Louise (Davenport) H.; m. Linda Kay Rosenbaum, June 27, 1980 (div. Dec. 1987); m. Delaine Marie Thompson, Mar. 17, 1989. BS in Aerospace Engring., Wichita State U., 1993. Seating engr. Raytheon Aircraft, Wichita, 1979-93; R&D group engr. Interiors and Seating Group Bombardier Learjet Inc., Wichita, 1993-99; pres. Millennium Concepts Inc., Wichita, 1999—. Mem. AIAA, Soc. Aerospace Engrs., (mem. AS8049 ad hoc com. 1990-97, vice chmn. SAE seat com. 1997-2001), GAMA (seat working group 1994-2000), Aviation Rulemaking Adv. Com. (AC25.562-1 seat working group 1994-96). Republican. Greek Orthodox. Achievements include design and certification engr. on aircraft seats and interiors. Home: 4206 Spyglass Cir Wichita KS 67226-3354 Office: Millennium Concepts Inc 9050 W Monroe Cir Wichita KS 67209 Office Phone: 316-821-9300. E-mail: pholland@millennium.aero.

HOLLAND, RANDY JAMES, state supreme court justice; b. Elizabeth, NJ, Jan. 27, 1947; s. James Charles and Virginia (Wilson) H.; m. Ilona E. Holland, June 24, 1972 BA in Econs., Swarthmore Coll., 1969; JD cum laude, U. Pa., 1972; LLM, U. Va., 1998; Doctorate (hon.), Widener U. Sch. Law, 2001. Bar: Del. 1972. Ptnr. Dunlap, Holland & Rich and predecessors, Georgetown, Del., 1972-80, Morris, Nichols, Arsht & Tunnell, Georgetown, Del., 1980-86; justice Del. Supreme Ct., Georgetown, Del., 1986—. Mem. Del. Bar Examiners, 1978-86; mem. Gov.'s Jud. Nominating Commn., 1978-86, sec., 1982-85, chmn., 1985-86; mem. Del. Supreme Ct. Consol. Com., 1985-86; pres. Terry-Carey Inn of Ct., 1991-94; v.p. Am. Inns of Ct., 1996-2000, pres., 2000—; co-chair Racial and Ethnic Task Force, 1995—; adj. prof. Widener U. Sch. Law, 1991—, U. Pa. Sch. Law, 1993-94, U. Iowa Sch. Law, 1997—, Vanderbilt Law Sch., 2000—; co-chair Del. Cts. Planning Com., 1996; chair nat. jud. adv. com. fed. Office of Child Support Enforcement; Jud. Ethics Adv. Commn., 1994—; del. Code Jud. Conduct Rev. Commn., 1991-94; del. Bar Bench Media Conf., 1990—; dir. Appellate Judges' Edn. Inst., 2003—. Mem. editorial bd. Del. Lawyer Mag., 1981-85; contbr. chpt. Del. Appellate Handbook, 1985—; author Delaware Supreme Court: Golden Anniversary, 2001, The Delaware Constitution: A Reference Guide, 2002; co-editor The Delaware Constitution of 1897: The First One Hundred Years. Pres. adminstrv. bd. Ave. United Meth. Ch., Milford, Del. Bar Found.; hon. chmn. History of the Del. Bar in 20th Century, 1992—; active Rhodes Scholarship com., 2003—; bd. mgrs. U. Pa. Law Alumni Soc., 2004—; adv. com. US Judicial Conf., State judge mem., 2004. Recipient Henry C. Loughlin prize for legal ethics U. Pa. 1972, St. Thomas More award, 1999, Alumni award of merit U. Pa. Sch. Law, 2002; named Judge of the Yr. Nat. Child Support Enforcement Assn., 1992, Hon. Master of the Bench, Lincoln's Inn, London, 2004, Judge James L. Latchum Professionalism award, 2004. Mem. ABA (standing com. on lawyer competence, nat. jud. coll. adv. commn. model rules jud. disclosure enforcement 1996, appellate judge's conf. exec. com. 2001—, chmn. joint com. on lawyer regulation 2002—), Am. Judicature Soc. (nat. trustee 1992—, ctr. for jud. ethics, 1994, chair 1997—, Herbert Harley Award 2003), Appellate Judges Edn. Inst. (bd. dirs. 2003—), Am. Inns of Ct. Found. (trustee 1992—, nat. trustee 1996—, v.p. 1996-2000, nat. pres. 2000-04), Am. Law Inst., Del. Bar Found. Republican. Avocations: tennis, swimming. Office: Del Supreme Ct 34 The Circle Georgetown DE 19947-1500

HOLLAND, REBECCA LLOYD, publishing executive; b. N.Y.C., Nov. 29, 1964; d. John Sheperson Lloyd and Elizabeth Lee Holland; m. David Marten Miller, Apr. 26, 2003; children: Sarah Lloyd Holland Miller, Matthew Leigh Holland Miller. BA, NYU, Binghamton, 1986. Prodn. editor Henry Holt, N.Y.C., 1990—92; prodn. mgr. Pine Forge Press, Sage Pubs., Inc., Thousand Oaks, Calif., 1993—96; mng. editor Broadway Books, N.Y.C., 1997—2002; pub. dir./exec. mng. editor Doubleday Broadway Pub. Group, Random Ho., Inc., N.Y.C., 2002—. Democrat-Npl. Avocations: ballet, music, violin. Home: 43 Beverley Rd Montclair NJ 07043 Office: Random House Inc 1745 Broadway 23-3 New York NY 10019 Office Phone: 212-782-8350. E-mail: rholland@randomhouse.com.

HOLLAND, ROBERT, JR., food products executive; b. 1940; Married; 3 children. BSME, Union Coll.; MBA in Internat. Mktg., Baruch Coll. Assoc. McKinsey & Co., 1968-81; chmn., CEO Rokher-J, White Plains, N.Y. and, Mich., 1984-87, 91-95; chmn. Gilreath Mfg., 1987-91; pres., CEO Ben & Jerry's Homemade, Inc., Waterbury, Vt., 1995—96; CEO WorkPlace Integrators, 1997—2001. Bd. dirs. Lexmark Internat. Inc., 1998-,Olin Corp., Mut. N.Y., TruMark Mfg. Co., Middlesex Mut. Ins. Co., MONY Group Inc., Mazaruni Granite Products, Carver Fed. Bank, UNC Ventures, Yum Brands!, Inc. Chmn. bd. trustees Spelman Coll.; trustee Atlanta Univ. Ctr.; dir. Lincoln Ctr. Theater, Harlem Jr. Tennis Program. Office: 740 New Circle Rd NW Lexington KY 40550

HOLLAND, ROBERT CAMPBELL, anatomist, educator; b. Bushnell, Ill., Aug. 16, 1923; s. Harvey Howard and Lois Sarah (Campbell) H.; m. Hilda P. Burgi, Sept. 26, 1946 (dec. 1980); children: Jonathan Robert, Heather, Judith Ashley. BS, U. Wis., 1948, MS, 1949, PhD, 1955. Instr. Dental Sch. Northwestern U., 1949-51; asst. prof. anatomy Sch. Medicine U. N.D., 1955-60; assoc. prof. Sch. Medicine U. Ark., 1960-66; prof. chmn. dept. anatomy Mahidol U., Bangkok, 1966-76; prof., chmn. dept. anatomy Morehouse Sch. Medicine, Atlanta, 1976-90, prof. emeritus dept. anatomy, 1990—. Mem. staff Rockefeller Found., 1966-76; vis. prof. UCLA Sch. Medicine, 1976. Author research pubs. on the brain. With M.C., U.S. Army, 1943-46. Fellow Wis. Alumni Rsch. Found., 1951-54, Nat. Found. Infantile Paralysis, 1957-58; grantee NIH, 1959-88. Mem. Am. Assn. Anatomists, Am. Acad. Neurology, Soc. Exptl. Biology and Medicine, Soc. Neurosci., Sigma Xi

HOLLAND, ROBERT CARL, economist; b. Tekamah, Nebr., Apr. 7, 1925; s. Carl Luther and Gretchen (Thompson) H.; m. DeEtte Harriet Hedlund, Sept. 7, 1947; children: Joan DeEtte Holland Geltz, Nancy Gretchen Holland Kerr, Timothy Robert. Student, U. Nebr., 1942-43, 46; BS in Fin., U. Pa., 1948, MA in Econs., 1949, PhD in Econs., 1949. Instr. money and banking U. Pa., 1948-49; with Fed. Res. Bank Chgo., 1949-61, v.p., 1959-61; with bd. govs. Fed. Res. System, 1961-76; mem. bd. govs. FRS, 1973-76, sec. of bd., 1968-71, exec. dir., 1971-73, sec. to fed. open market com., 1966-73; pres. Com. for Econ. Devel., Washington, 1976-90, sr. econ. cons., 1990-96. Sr. fellow, bd. dirs. SEI Ctr. for Advanced Studies in Mgmt., U. Pa., 1990—; sr. fellow dept. Legal Studies, U. Pa., 1992—. With AUS, 1943-45. Mem. Am. Econ. Assn., Nat. Acad. Pub. Adminstrn., Internat. Soc. of Bus. Econs. and Ethics, Cosmos Club, Kenwood Country Club (Bethesda, Md.), Beta Theta Pi. Home: 5508 Cromwell Dr Bethesda MD 20816-2006 Home Fax: 301-229-5205. Personal E-mail: r.c.holland@worldnet.att.net.

HOLLAND, ROBERT JAMES, retired lawyer; b. Dayton, Ohio, Jan. 8, 1936; s. John Edward and Alma Naomi (Himes) Holland; m. Barbara Jane Drake, Aug. 27, 1960; children: Robert Jr., Duncan, Wendolyn, Justin. BA, Yale U., 1958; JD, Ohio State U., 1963. Bar: Ohio 1963, U.S. Supreme Ct. 1972. Assoc. Chester & Rose, Columbus, Ohio, 1963—67; gen. counsel Banc Ohio Corp., Columbus, 1967—71; city atty. City of Upper Arlington, Ohio, 1976—86; ptnr. Bodiker & Holland, Columbus, 1971—97; pres. Mid-Ohio Regional Planning Commn., Columbus, 1970—71, gen. counsel, 1971—85; gen. counsel, bd. dirs. Servinat, Inc., N.Y.C., 1976—2001; ret., 2001. Founder, bd. dirs. 1st Cmty. Bank. Co-author: (book) Ohio Taxation: Truth in Lending, 1969. Bd. dirs. Wellington Sch., Columbus, 1979—89; pres., bd. dirs. Ctrl. Ohio Transit Authority, Columbus, 1971—74. Served to lt. USNR, 1958—60. Named to Ten Outstanding Men, Columbus Jaycees, 1970. Mem.: ABA, Columbus Bar Assn. (chmn. law insts. com. 1968—70, chmn. unauthorized practice 1973—74, mem. ethics com. 1973—77), Ohio State Bar Assn., Internat. Food and Wine Soc., Union League (Chgo.), Scioto Club, Athletic Club. Home: 907 Cheyenne Ct Box 3007 Ketchum ID 83340

HOLLANDER, ANNE, writer; b. Cleve., Oct. 16, 1930; d. Arthur and Jean Hill (Bassett) Loesser; m. John Hollander, June 15, 1953 (div. 1977); children: Martha, Elizabeth; m. Thomas Nagel, June 26, 1979. BA, Barnard Coll., 1952. Author: Seeing Through Clothes, 1978, Moving Pictures, 1989, Sex and Suits, 1994, Feeding the Eye, 1999, Fabric of Vision, 2002. Guggenheim fellow, 1975. Fellow N.Y. Inst. for the Humanities (interim dir. 1995-96); mem. Costume Soc. Am., College Art Assn., PEN Am. Ctr. (pres. 1995-96), Century Assn.

HOLLANDER, DANIEL, gastroenterologist, medical educator; b. Mar. 3, 1939; Student, UCLA, to 1960; MD, Baylor U., 1964. Diplomate Am. Bd. Internal Medicine, Am. Bd. Gastroenterology. Intern Phila. Gen. Hosp., 1964-65; resident in internal medicine Med. Ctr., U. Kans., Kansas City, 1965-67; NIH rsch. fellow in gastroenterology U. Wash., Seattle, 1967-69; asst. prof. medicine Albany (N.Y.) Med. Coll., Union U., 1971-73, assoc. prof., 1973; assoc. prof. medicine, head div. gastroenterology Wayne State U., Detroit, 1973-77, prof. medicine, head div. gastroenterology, 1977—94, U. Calif., Irvine, 1978-94, prof. physiology and biophysics, 1981-94, assoc. dean for rsch. and program devel. Coll. Medicine, 1984-85, assoc. dean for acad. affairs, 1985-89, sr. assoc. dean for clin. affairs, 1989-91, chief gastroenterology Irvine Med. Ctr., 1979-94; exec. dean Sch. of Medicine U. Kans., Kansas City, 1994—96; chief med. officer Sierra Pacific Network, San Francisco, 1996-98; prof. medicine U. Calif., San Francisco, 1996-98; pres., CEO Harbor-UCLA Rsch. and Edn. Inst., 1998-2001; prof. medicine UCLA, 1998—, dir. inflammatory bowel disease grants broad med. rsch. program for Eli and Edythe L. Broad Found., 2001—. Attending physician, attending gastroenterologist Albany Med. Ctr. Hosp., 1971-73; chief gastroenterology svc., attending physician Harper Hosp., Detroit, 1973-78; cons. in gastroenterology Children's, Detroit Gen. and VA hosps., 1973-78; chief gastroenterology VA Med. Ctr., Long Beach, Calif., 1978-80; chmn. Gastrointestinal Gerontology Rsch. Group, 1988-89; vis. scientist dept. molecular medicine U. Auckland, New Zealand, 1990-91; vis. prof., invited speaker numerous other univs., profl. meetings, confs. Author: (with G. Gitnick, N. Kaplowitz, I.M. Samloff, L.J. Schoenfield) Principles and Practice of Gastroenterology and Hepatology, 1988, (with A. Tarnawski) Gastic Cytoprotection—A Clinician's Guide, 1989, (with Porro G. Bianchi) Treatment of Digestive Disease with Sucralfate, 1989; mem. editl. bd., reviewer Can. Jour. Gastroenterology; contbr. numerous articles, revs. to profl. jours., book chpt. With USAF, 1969-71. Calif. Heart Assn. rsch. fellow, 1960; Fogarty Sr. Internat. fellow Oxford (Eng.) U., 1984-85; grantee NIH, Nat. Inst. on Aging, Nat. Insts. Arthritis, Metabolism and Digestive Diseases, Skillman Found., VA, Goldsmith Found., Internat. Pharm. Products. Mem. ACP (A. Blaine traveling scholar 1973), Am. Fedn. for Clin. Rsch. (pres. Midwestern sect. 1979-80), Am. Gastroent. Assn., Am. Physiol. Soc., Am. Soc. for Clin. Investigation, Orange County Gastroenterology Assn. (pres. 1986-87), Brit. Soc. Gastroenterology, European Assn. Gastroenterology, Western Assn. Physicians, Western Gut Club (pres. 1981-82), Alpha Omega Alpha. Office: The Eli and Edythe L Broad Found 10900 Wilshire Blvd 12th Fl Los Angeles CA 90024-6532 E-mail: dhollander@broadmedical.org.

HOLLANDER, DAVID J., lawyer; b. Bklyn., Mar. 11, 1951; s. Ernest and Fay Hollander; m. Laurie Hope Casten, Aug. 19, 1953; children: Joshua, Zachariah. BA in Philosophy, BA in Judaic Studies, Bklyn. Coll., 1973; JD, Bklyn. Law Sch., 1976. Bar: N.Y. 1977, U.S. Dist. Ct. (so. and ea. dists.) N.Y. 1977, Oreg. 1978, U.S. Dist. Ct. Oreg. 1979, U.S. Ct. Appeals (9th cir.) 1979, U.S. Ct. Appeals (10th cir.) 1998. Assoc. Jack Taube P.C., Bklyn., 1976-78, Galton, Popick & Scott, Portland, 1979-82; pvt. practice Portland, 1982-85; ptnr. Harper, Leo & Hollander, Portland, 1985-87; sr. ptnr. Hollander & Lebenbaum, Portland, 1987-91, Hollander, Lebenbaum & Gannicott, Portland, 1991—. Office: Hollander Lebenbaum & Gannicott Ste 700 1500 SW 1st Ave Portland OR 97201-5825

HOLLANDER, GERALD MARTIN, physician; b. N.Y.C., June 28, 1947; s. Emanuel and Miriam Hollander; m. Barbara Sarah Hollander, Jan. 26, 1975; children: Aviva, Shani, Nahva. BS, CCNY; MD, SUNY, Bklyn. Resident in medicine Brookdale Hosp. Med. Ctr., Bklyn., 1973-75, fellow in cardiology, 1976-78; dir. cardiac ICU Maimonides Med. Ctr, Bklyn., 1978—, dir. cardiology, 1994-99, dir. clin. cardiology, 1999—; assoc. prof. clin. medicine SUNY Health Sci. Ctr., Bklyn., 1994—. Contbr. articles to profl. jours. Bd. dirs. Hebrew Acad. of Long Beach, N.Y., 1986—. Fellow Am. Coll. Cardiology, Am. Coll. Physicians, Am. Coll. Chest Physicians; mem. Phi Beta Kappa. Office: Maimonides Med Ctr 4802 10th Ave Brooklyn NY 11219-2844

HOLLANDER, JOHN, humanities educator, poet; b. N.Y.C., Oct. 28, 1929; s. Franklin and Muriel (Kornfeld) H.; m. Anne Helen Loesser, June 15, 1953 (div. 1977); children: Martha, Elizabeth; m. Natalie Charkow, Dec. 15, 1981. AB, Columbia U., 1950, AM, 1952; PhD, Ind. U., 1959; DLitt (hon.), Marietta Coll., 1982; LHD (hon.), Ind. U., 1990; DFA (hon.), Maine Coll. of Art, 1993; DHL (hon.), CUNY, 2001; DHL (hon.), New Sch. U., 2003. Jr. fellow Soc. Fellows, Harvard, 1954-57; lectr. English Conn. Coll., New London, 1957-59; instr. English Yale, 1959-61; asst. prof. English, fellow Ezra Stiles Coll., 1961-64, assoc. prof., 1964-66; prof. Hunter Coll., CUNY, 1966—77; prof. English Yale U., New Haven, 1977—, A. Bartlett Giamatti prof., 1987—, Sterling prof., 1995—2002, prof. emeritus, 2002. Vis. prof. Linguistic Inst., Inc. U., 1964; faculty Salzburg Seminar in Am. Studies, 1965; Christian Gauss seminarian Princeton U., 1962; Clark lectr. Trinity Coll., Cambridge, Eng., 2000. Author: A Crackling of Thorns, 1958, The Untuning of the Sky, 1961, Movie-Going and Other Poems, 1962, Various Owls, 1963, Visions from the Ramble, 1965, The Quest of the Gole, 1966, Types of Shape, 1968, 2d edit., 1991, Images of Voice, 1970, The Night Mirror, 1971, Town and Country Matters, 1972, The Head of the Bed, 1973, Tales Told of the Fathers, 1975, Vision and Resonance, 1975, Reflections on Espionage, 1976, 2d edit., 1999, Spectral Emanations, 1978, In Place, 1978, Blue Wine, 1979, The Figure of Echo, 1981, Rhyme's Reason, 1981, 2d edit., 1989, 3rd edit., 2000, Powers of Thirteen, 1983, (with Saul Steinberg) Dal Vero, 1983, In Time and Place, 1986, Some Fugitives Take Cover, 1988, Harp Lake, 1988, Melodious Guile, 1988, Tesserae, 1993, Selected Poetry, 1993, The Gazer's Spirit, 1995, The Work of Poetry, 1997, The Poetry of Everyday Life, 1998, Figurehead and Other Poems, 1999, Picture Window, 1993; editor: Poems of Ben Jonson, 1961, (with Harold Bloom) The Wind and the Rain, 1961, (with Anthony Hecht) Jiggery-Pokery, 1966, Poems of Our Moment, 1968, Modern Poetry: Essays in Criticism, 1968, American Short Stories Since 1945, 1968, (with Frank Kermode) The Oxford Anthology of English Literature, 1973, (with Reuben A. Brower and Helen Vendler) For I.A. Richards: Essays in His Honor, 1973, (with Irving Howe and David Bromwich) Literature as Experience, 1979, The Essential Rossetti, 1990, Animal Poems, 1994, Garden Poems, 1996, Committed to Memory, 1997, Marriage Poems, 1997, War Poems, 1999, Sonnets, 2001, (with Joanna Weber) A Gallery of Poems, 2001, American Wits, 2003, Selected Poems of Emma Lazarus, 2005, Poems Haunted and Bewitched, 2005; contbg. editor: Harper's mag, 1969-71, Word and Image, 1985-91, Literary Imagination, 1999-; Art and Lit., 1985—, Lit., 1989—; assoc. for poetry Partisan Review, 1959-65; mem. poetry bd. Wesleyan U. Press, 1959-62; author numerous poems. Recipient Yale Younger Poets award, 1958, Poetry Chap Book award, 1962, award in lit. Nat. Inst. Arts and Letters, 1963, Levinson prize, 1974, Bollingen prize, 1983, Mina P. Shaughnessy award, 1963, Melville Cane award, 1990, Ambassador Book award, 1994, Gov.'s Arts award State of Conn., 1997, Robert Penn Warren-Cleanth Brooks award, 1998; Overseas fellow Churchill Coll., Cambridge (Eng.) U., 1967-68, sr. fellow NEH, 1973-74, Guggenheim fellow, 1979-80, MacArthur Found. fellow, 1990-95. Mem.: Am. Acad. Arts and Scis., Am. Acad. Arts and Letters (sec. 2000—03), Am. Assn. Lit. Scholars and Critics (pres. 2000—01), Century Assn. (N.Y.C.), Phi Beta Kappa. Office: Yale U Dept English PO Box 208302 New Haven CT 06520-8302 Office Phone: 203-432-4566. E-mail: john.hollander@yale.edu.

HOLLANDER, LAWRENCE JAY, marketing executive; b. Chgo., Feb. 15, 1940; s. Harry and Ann Blanche Hollander; m. Sallie Sue Mines, June 21, 1964 (div. Aug. 1999); children: Marla, Amy, Rebecca. BSBA, Roosevelt U., 1963. Dir. Far East ops. Indsl. & Sci. Conf. Mgmt., Chgo., 1972-77; dir. mktg. Far East ops. Clapp & Poliak, Inc., NYC, 1978-81; pres. Expoconsul Internat. Inc., Princeton, NJ, 1981-95, EI Mktg., Inc., Princeton, 1987-94, Ctr. for Tech. Concepts, Inc., Princeton, 1988-92, Expoconsul Mktg. Group, Inc., Princeton, 1992-94; dir. corp. fin. J.S. Holdings Group, Inc., Bay Head, NJ, 1996; shareholder, investment banker J.S. Securities, Inc., Bayhead, 1995-96; pres. Entrepreneurial Mgmt. Group, Inc., Princeton, 1996—. Bd. dirs. Congregation Beth Chaim, West Windsor, NJ, 1984, Jewish Cmty. Ctr., of Delaware Valley, Ewing, NJ, 1987-96, v.p. 1990-92, pres. 1993-94; bd. dirs. Jewish Fedn. Mercer and Buck Counties, NJ, Pa., 1988-95, v.p., 1989-90; mem. planning bd. West Windsor Twp., NJ, 1997-2002. Mem.: Rotary Club of the Princeton Corridor (charter mem. 1986—, sec. 1990—91, sgt.-at-arms 1991—92, bd. dirs. 1992—93, 1996—2005, sgt.-at-arms 1997—98, v.p. 2001—02, pres.-elect 2002—03, pres. 2003—04). Republican. Jewish. Avocations: weight-lifting, walking, tennis. Office: Entrepreneurial Mgmt Group Inc 202 Sayre Dr Princeton NJ 08540 E-mail: ljhceo@aol.com.

HOLLANDER, ROBERT B., JR., Romance languages educator; b. N.Y.C., July 31, 1933; s. Robert B. and Laurene (McGookey) H.; m. Jean Haberman, Apr. 23, 1964; children: Cornelia Vanness, Robert B. III. AB, Princeton U., 1955; PhD, Columbia U., 1962. Tchr. Latin and English, Collegiate Sch., N.Y.C., 1955-57; instr. English Columbia U., N.Y.C., 1958-62; mem. faculty dept. Romance langs. Princeton (N.J.) U., 1962—, prof. European lit., 1974—, chmn. comparative lit., 1994-98. Mem. Nat. Coun. on Humanities, 1974-80, 87-92, vice chmn., 1978-80; mem. N.J. Com. for Humanities, 1980-86; dir. Dartmouth Dante Project, 1982—, Princeton Dante Project, 1997—; v.p. Assn. Internat. Studi di Lingua et Lett. Italiana, 1985-94; trustee La Scuola d'Italia, N.Y.C., 1986-92, Collegiate Sch., 1990-96, vice pres. bd., 1994-96, pres. bd., 98-2001; mem. adv. bd. Ctr. for Electronic Texts in the Humanities, 1991-98, pres., 1993-98; pres. Internat. Dante Seminar, 1992-2003, bd. mem., 2003—. Author: Allegory in Dante's Commedia, 1969, Boccaccio's Two Venuses, 1977, Studies in Dante, 1980, Il Virgilio dantesco, 1983, Boccaccio's Last Fiction: Il Corbaccio, 1988, Dante's Epistle to Cangrande, 1993, Boccaccio's Dante and the Shaping Force of Satire, 1997, Dante Alighieri, 2000, Dante, 2001; editor and translator: (with T. Hampton and M. Frankel) Amorosa Visione, 1986; co-editor: L'Espositione di Bernardino Daniello da Lucca sopra la Comedia di Dante, 1989, (with Jean Hollander) Dante Alighieri, Inferno, 2000, Purgatorio, 2003, 2004—. Trustee Nat. Humanities Ctr., 1981—, chmn. bd. trustees, 1988-91. Guggenheim fellow, 1970-71; NEH fellow, 1974-75, 82-83; recipient Gold medal of the City of Florence for work on behalf of Dante, 1988, Bronze medal of the City of Tours, 1993, John Witherspoon award in the Humanities, Com. for the Humanities, N.J., 1988, Internat. Nicola Zingarelli prize for Dantean philology and criticism, 1999; named Disting. Alumnus, Collegiate Sch., 2003; hon. citizen Certaldo, Italy, 1997. Mem. Am. Acad. Arts and Scis., Dante Soc. Am. (mem. council 1976-85, pres. 1980-85, founding editor-in-chief Electronic Bull. 1995-2004, editor 1996—, assoc. editor 2004—, Charles T. Davis award 2005), Am. Boccaccio Assn. Clubs: Cosmos (Washington). Republican. Office: Princeton U Dept French and Italian E Pyne Princeton NJ 08544-0001 Business E-Mail: bobh@princeton.edu.

HOLLANDER, SAMUEL, economist, educator; b. London, Apr. 6, 1937; s. Jacob and Rachel-Leah (Bornstein) H.; m. Perlette Kéroub, July 20, 1959; children: Frances, Isaac. BSc in Econs, London Sch. Econs., 1959; MA, Princeton U., 1961, PhD, 1963; LLD, McMaster U., 1999. Asst. in instrn. Princeton U., 1962-63; asst. prof. econs. U. Toronto, Ont., Can., 1963-66, assoc. prof., 1966-70, prof., 1970-84, univ. prof., 1984-98, univ. prof. emeritus, 1998—; rsch. dir. U. Nice (CNRS), France, 1999—2000; prof. Ben Gurion U., Israel, 2000—. Author: The Sources of Increased Efficiency, 1965, The Economics of Adam Smith, 1973, The Economics of David Ricardo, 1979, The Economics of J.S. Mill, 1985, Classical Economics, 1987, Ricardo: The 'New View'-Collected Essays I, 1995, The Economics of Thomas Robert Malthus, 1997, The Literature of Political Economy-Collected Essays II, 1998, John Stuart Mill on Economic Theory and Method-Collected Essays III, 2000, Jean-Baptiste Say and the Classical Canon in Economics, 2005. Decorated officer Order of Can.; Guggenheim fellow, 1968-69, Killam sr. fellow, 1973-75, Connaught sr. fellow, 1984-85. Fellow Royal Soc. Can. Jewish. Home: 2 Rehov Sapir 89066 Arad Israel Office Phone: 972-8-647 2305. Personal E-mail: sholland@bgumail.bgu.ac.il.

HOLLANDER, TOBY EDWARD, education educator; b. Queens, N.Y., June 21, 1931; s. David and Eve (Shroot) H.; m. Harriet Goldberg, June 14, 1953; children: Marc, Deborah. BS cum laude, NYU, 1952, MBA, 1953; PhD, U. Pitts., 1960. Instr. econs. U. Pitts., 1957-58; asst. prof. Duquesne U., 1958-59; prof. Baruch Coll., CUNY, 1963-67, dean, 1967-69, vice chancellor, 1969-71; dep. commr. higher edn. N.Y. State Edn. Dept., 1971-77; chancellor N.J. Dept. Higher Edn., Trenton, 1977-90; prof. Rutgers U., 1990—. Author books in field; contbr. articles to profl. jours. Served with U.S. Army, 1953-55. Mem. State Higher Edn. Exec. Officers Assn. (pres. 1977-78). Office: Rutgers U Sch Bus 180 University Ave Newark NJ 07102-1818 Office Phone: 973-353-5226. Business E-Mail: tholland@andromeda.rutgers.edu. E-mail: tedwardhollander@msn.com.

HOLLANDSWORTH, PHYLLIS W., marriage and family therapist; b. Storm Lake, Iowa, Aug. 7, 1938; d. Lloyd Earl and Hildegarde Elaine (Uken) Williamson; m. James Richard Hollandsworth, Sept. 5, 1959; children: Michael, Mark. AA, Brewton-Parker Coll., 1984; BS, Valdosta State Coll., 1987, MS, 1988; cert. in marriage & family therapy, Voldosta State Coll., 1995; PhD in Human Sexuality, Maimonides U., 2004. Lic. marriage & family therapist Fla., 1996, cert. sex therapist Fla., 2002. Counselor Ga. Dept. Corrections, Albany, 1989—91; therapist, emergency screener North Fla. Mental Health, Lake City, Fla., 1992—96; therapist ACT Corp., Daytona Beach, Fla., 1996—2000; intake coord., therapist Children's Home Soc., Daytona Beach, Fla., 2000—02; therapist Fla. Health Care Plans, Daytona Beach, Fla., 2002—; pvt. practice Daytona Beach, Fla., 2000—. Mem.: Am. Acad. Clin. Sexologists (diplomate), Am. Psychotherapy Assn. (diplomate), Am. Assn. Marriage and Family Therapists (clin. mem.). Office: 1635 S Ridgewood Ave Rm 216 South Daytona FL 32119 Business E-Mail: hollyphyll@netzero.net.

HOLLANS, IRBY NOAH, JR., retired trade association administrator; b. Christiansburg, Va., Nov. 3, 1930; s. Irby Noah and Annie May (Lester) H.; m. Frances Jo Cox, June 21, 1957; children: Susan Frances, Carol Leigh, Irby Neil. BS in Gen. Bus. Adminstrn., Va. Poly. Inst. and State U., 1953. Mgr. promotion Sta. WRVA-Radio, Richmond, Va., 1956-64, editor bus. news, 1956-64; dir. travel devel. Va. State C. of C., 1964-70, asst. exec. dir., 1970-72; exec. dir. Optical Labs. Assn., Washington, 1972-96. Instr. bus. Va. Commonwealth U., Richmond, 1965-71 Mem. Dulles (Va.) Internat. Airport Devel. Commn., 1968-76; mem. Va. Nat. Capital Airports Acquisition Study Commn., 1968-76; bd. dirs. Va. Thanksgiving Festival Inc., 1965-70, Keep Va. Beautiful, Inc., 1965-73, Central Va. Ednl. TV, 1970-72, Va. Travel Coordinating Com., 1964-72. Served to maj. USAF, 1953-72, Korea. Recipient Service award Va. Profl. Photographers Assn., 1966; Nat. award Profl. Photographers Assn. Am., 1970 Mem. Am. Soc. Assn. Execs. (cert.), Va. Pub. Rels. Conf., Nat. Assn. Wholesaler-Distbrs.-Pros Group, Am. Nat. Stds. Inst. (med. devices stds. mgmt. bd. 1973-80), Washington Soc. Assn. Execs., Va. C. of C., Vienna (Va.) Photog. Soc. (pres. 1990-92), Greater Washington Coun. Camera Clubs (exec. v.p. 1988-93), Rotary Internat. (exec. dir. 1996—). Home and Office: 5339 Cristfield Ct Fairfax VA 22032-3809 Office Phone: 703-503-9788. E-mail: ihollans@earthlink.net.

HOLLARAN, CAROLYN RADA, writer, small business owner; b. Rome, Ga., Mar. 15, 1950; d. James Donald and Mabel Ree Hollaran. Student, Okla. Christian Coll. Pres. and owner Celebrity Tours, Nashville, 1983—97. Cons. country music bus., 1997—2004. Author: Your Favorite Country Music Stars, 1975, Meet the Stars of Country Music, 1977, Brightest Stars in Country Vol. 1, 1979, Brightest Stars in Country Vol. 2, 1979, Really Cookin with Stella Parton, How to Achieve Stardom in Country Music, Country Music Stars Reveal What It Takes to Get a Break, 2004. Office: A Hollaran Book Box 336 Lafayette CO 80026 Office Phone: 720-771-6807. Business E-Mail: askcarolyn@usa.net.

HÖLLDOBLER, BERTHOLD KARL, zoologist; b. Erling-Andechs, Germany, June 25, 1936; came to U.S., 1973; s. Karl and Maria (Russmann) H.; m. Friederike Probst, Feb. 9, 1980; children: Jakob, Stefan, Sebastian. Dr. rer. nat., U. Wurzburg, 1965; Dr. habil., U. Frankfurt a.M., 1969; D (hon.), U. Konstanz, 2000. Prof. zoology U. Frankfurt a.M., 1971-72; prof. biology Harvard U., Cambridge, Mass., 1973-90, Alexander Agassiz prof. zoology, 1982-90; prof. U. Wurzburg, Germany, 1989—. Adj. prof. U. Ariz., Tucson; rsch. assoc. Harvard U.; Andrew D. White prof. at large Cornell U., 2002—; Found. prof. Ariz. State U., Tempe, 2004—. Author: (with Edward O. Wilson) The Ants, 1990 (Pulitzer Prize for gen. non-fiction 1991), (with E.O. Wilson) Journey to the Arts, (Shortlisted for the Rhone-Poulenc Sci. Book prize, 1995, Phi Beta Kappa prize, 1995). John Simon Guggenheim fellow, 1980; recipient Sr. Scientist award Alexander von Humboldt Found., 1986-87, Gottfried Wilhelm Leibniz prize, 1989, Phi Beta Kappa prize (with E.O. Wilson) 1995, Karl Ritter von Frisch medal and Sci. prize, German Zool. Soc., 1996, Körber-prize for European Sci., 1996, Benjamin Franklin, Wilhelm v. Humboldt Prize of the German Amer. Acad. Coun. (GAAC), 1999, Werner Heisenberg medal Alexander v. Humboldt Found., Alfried Krupp Sci. prize, 2004; named to Bavarian Maximilian Order, 2003. Fellow AAAS, Am. Animal Behavior Soc.; mem. Nat. Acad. of Sci. (fgn. mem.), Am. Acad. Sci., German Acad. der Naturforscher Leopoldina, Bayerische Acad. der Wissenschaften, Acad. Europaea, Berlin-Brandenburgische Acad., Am. Philos. Soc. (fgn. mem.), Bundesverdienstkrenz (Nat. Merit medal Germany 2000). Office: Biozentrum Am Hubland D-97074 Würzburg Germany

HOLLE, REGINALD HENRY, retired bishop; b. Burton, Tex., Nov. 21, 1925; s. Alfred W. and Lena (Nolte) H.; m. Marla Christianson, June 16, 1949; children: Todd, Joan. BA, Capitol U., 1946, DD (hon.), 1979; MDiv, Trinity Luth. Sem., 1949; D of Ministry, Ohio Consortium Religious Stdy, 1977; DD (hon.), Wittenberg U., 1989. Ordained minister Evang. Luth. Ch. Am., then bishop. Assoc. pastor Zion Luth. Ch., Sandusky, Ohio, 1949-51; sr. pastor Salem Meml. Luth. Ch., Detroit, 1951-72, Parma Luth. Ch., Cleve., 1973-78; bishop Mich. dist. Am. Luth. Ch., Detroit, 1978-87; bishop NW Lower Mich. Synod Evang. Luth. Ch., Lansing, 1988-95. Bd. dirs. Aubsburg Fortress Pub. House, Wittenberg U. Author: Planning for Funerals, 1978; contbr. to Augsburg Sermon Series. Bd. dirs. Ronald McDonald House Ctrl. Mich., 1995—, Planned Giving Luth. Social Svcs. Mich., 1995—. Recipient Pub. Svc. citation Harper Woods City Coun., 1976, Recognition for Community Svc., Detroit Pub. Schs., 1974. E-mail: rholle@juno.com.

HOLLEB, DORIS B., urban planner, economist; b. N.Y.C., Oct. 26, 1922; m. Marshall M. Holleb, Oct. 15, 1944; children: Alan, Gordon, Paul. BA magna cum laude, Hunter Coll., 1942; MA, Harvard U., 1947; postgrad., U. Chgo., 1959-60, 65-66. Economist Fed. Res. Bd., Washington, 1943—44; freelance journalist, 1945-63; econs. cons. Chgo. Dept. City Planning, 1963-64; rsch. assoc. Ctr. Urban Studies U. Chgo., 1966-78, sr. rsch. assoc., 1978-88; dir. Met. Inst., 1973-84, professorial lectr., 1979—2004, professorial lectr. emerita, 2004—. Chmn. ednl. coun. Francis W. Parker Sch., 1963-80; cons., 1980-92; adv. coun. Ctr. for the Study Democratic Instns., 1975-79; nat. adv. com. White House Conf. on Balanced Nat. Growth and Econ. Devel., 1978; mem. Northea. Ill. Planning Commn., 1973-77; mem. Chgo. Met. Area Transp. Coun., 1980-84; adv. coun. to Nat. Ctr. Rsch. on Vocat. Edn., U.S. Dept. Edn., 1979-82, U.S. Dept. State adv. com. internat. investment, tech. and devel., 1979-81; mem. Chgo. Plan Commn., 1986—, Nat. Coun on Humanities, 1998-2003. Author: Social and Economic Information for Urban Planning, 1968, Colleges and the Urban Poor, 1972; mem. editl. bd. Ill. Issues, 1977—; contbr. articles to profl. jours Fellow: Nat. Phi Beta Kappa Soc. (bd. dirs.).

HOLLEMAN, VERNON DAUGHTY, internist, educator; b. Brownwood, Tex., Oct. 1, 1931; s. Vernon Edgar and Olene Nollie (Reece) H.; m. Shirley Eyvonne Roberts, April 26, 1961; children: Richard, Joel, Douglas. BA in Chemistry and Biology, Howard Payne Coll., Brownwood, 1953; MD, Baylor U., 1958. Mem. med. staff Santa Fe Meml. Hosp, 1962-83; pres. med. staff Santa Fe Meml. Hosp., 1979-83; mem. med. staff Scott and White Hosp., 1962—; asst. chief physician Santa Fe Employees Hosp. Assn., 1962-85, med. dir., 1985—; intern Scott and White Clinic and Hosp., Temple, Tex., 1958-59, resident in internal medicine, 1959-62; dir. div. gen. internal medicine Santa Fe Ctr., Temple, Tex., 1985—; assoc. prof. internal medicine Tex. A&M Coll. Medicine, Temple, 1982—. Adj. faculty clinician Ohio Coll. of Podiatric Medicine, Cleveland, 1982-86; med. dir. Consol. Assns. Railroad Employees, 1997—. Illustrator: Aesculapian, 1957, So. Bapt. Student Union Projects, 1954-58; illustrator ltd. edit. lithographs Baylor U. Lettermans Assn., 1994; contbr. photography to books, including Colorados Biggest Bucks and Bulls, Boone and Crocket Books, Awesome Antlers, Records of North American Mule Deer; author: articles on health, preventive medicine, and numerous others. Bd. dirs Santa Fe Meml. Found.; hon. chmn. physicians adv. bd. Tex. Nat. Rep. Congl. Com. Art Instrn., Inc. scholar, 1952; recipient Centennial award Santa Fe Meml. Found., 1991. Mem. AAAS, Nat. Assn. Ret. and Vet. Railway Employees (hon. life), AMA, ACP, Am. Coll. Phys. Execs., Am. Soc. Internal Medicine, Tex. Med. Assn. (Vernon D. Holleman-Lewis M. Rampy Soctt and White Centennial chair gerontology 1999), Tex. Med. Found., Am. Heart Assn. (cardiopulmonary coun.), Am. Assn. Ry. Physicians, World Med. Assn., Tex. Diabetes and Endocrine Soc., N.Y. Acad. Scis., So. Med. Assn. (life), Am. Coll. Occupl. Medicine, Am. Pain Soc., Am. Acad. Pain Mgmt. (diplomate), Am. Soc. Pain Educators (charter), Internat. Soc. Phys. Activity in Prevention of Osteoporosis (charter), Boone and Crockett Club, Tex. Taxidermy Assn., Nat. Safari Club (life), Alpha Chi, Phi Chi. Baptist. Avocations: medical history, art, hunting, photography, conservation. Office: Scott and White Clinic 600 S 25th St Temple TX 76504-5227

HOLLEN, ROBERT B., art educator; b. Akron, Ohio, Sept. 1, 1955; s. Charles W. and Helen L. Hollen; m. Sandra (Sonie) E. Hollen, Dec. 22, 1979; children: Carrie J., Shaun D. BS, Findlay Coll., 1977; MA, Mary Grove, Detroit, 2002. Art tchr. Granville (Ohio) HS, 1977—. Mem.: Ohio Assn. Tracked Cross Country Coaches (pres. 2001—03). Home: 193 Field Point Rd Heath OH 43056 Office: Granville HS 248 New Burg St Granville OH 43023-1033

HOLLENBACH, DWYANE L., music educator; b. Sellersville, Pa., June 12, 1963; m. Emily Erika Hollenback, May 23, 2003; 1 child, Julianna Mae. MusB, Manhattan Sch. Music, 1986, MusM, 1987; cert. in tchg., U. Nev., 1996. Lic. tchr. N.Y., cert. Nev. Band dir. McQueen H.S., Reno, 1996—97, Huntington (N.Y.) H.S., 1997—2001, Reno H.S., 2001—04, Edward C. Reed H.S., Sparks, Nev., 2004—. Adj. tchr. Youth Edn. in Arts, Allentown, Pa., 1996—; Nev. state chair Tri-M Music Honor Soc., 2002—. Musician (trumpet): Reno Philharmonic, Reno Jazz Orch. Mem.: NEA, Music Educators Nat. Conf., Internat. Trumpet Guild. Mem. Lds Ch. Home: 3290 Dana Way Sparks NV 89431 also: Edward C Reed High Sch 1350 Baring Blvd Sparks NV 89434

HOLLENBAUGH, H(ENRY) RITCHEY, lawyer; b. Shelby, Ohio, Nov. 12, 1947; m. Diane Robinson Nov. 21, 1973 (div. 1989); children: Chad Ritchey, Katie Paige; m. Rebecca U., Aug. 8, 1995. BA, Kent State U., 1969; JD, Capital U., 1973. Bar: Ohio 1973, U.S. Dist. Ct. (so. dist.) Ohio 1974, U.S. Ct. Appeals (6th cir.) 1976, U.S. Supreme Ct. 1978. Investigator Ohio Civil Rights Com., Columbus, Ohio, 1969-72; legal intern City Atty.'s Office, Columbus, Ohio, 1972-73, asst. city prosecutor, 1973-75, sr. asst. city atty., 1975-76; ptnr. Hunter, Hollenbaugh & Theodotou, Columbus, Ohio, 1976-85, Delligatti, Hollenbaugh, Briscoe & Milless, Columbus, Ohio, 1985-91, Climaco Seminatore Delligatti & Hollenbaugh, Columbus, 1991-93, Delligatti, Hollenbaugh & Briscoe, Columbus, 1993-95, Draper, Hollenbaugh, Briscoe, Yashko & Carmany, 1996-99, Carlile Patchen & Murphy, Columbus, 1999—. Mem. Ohio Pub. Defender Commn., 1988-94; chmn. Franklin County Pub. Defender Commn., 1986-92. Treas. The Gov's. Com., 1987-96, Friends With Celeste, Friends of Gov's. Residence, 1987-92, Participation 2000, 1987-91, Ohio Legal Assistance Found., 1998—. Fellow ABA Found. (chair commn. on advt. 1993-97, ho. of dels. 1993—, chair nat. conf. lawyers and reps. of media 2000—); mem. Ohio State Bar Assn. (bd. govs. 1989-94, pres. 1992-93), Columbus Bar Assn. (pres. 1987-88), Nat. Conf. Bar Pres., Nat. Assn. Criminal Def. Lawyers, Capital Club, Brookside Golf and Country Club. Democrat. Methodist. Avocations: golf, politics. Home: 8549 Glenalmond Ct Dublin OH 43017-9737 Office: Carlile Patchen & Murphy 336 E Broad St Columbus OH 43215-3202 Office Phone: 614-228-6135. Business E-Mail: hrh@cpmlaw.com.

HOLLENBECK, KAREN FERN, foundation consultant; b. Snover, Mich., Mar. 30, 1943; d. Glenn Lee and Ada Gertrude (Robinson) Roberts; m. Marvin Allen Hollenbeck, June 18, 1966. AA, Kellogg Community Coll., 1980; BSBA, Nazareth Coll., 1987. Dir. fellowships W.K. Kellogg Found., Battle Creek, Mich., 1979-85, asst. v.p. adminstrn., 1985-88, v.p. adminstrn., 1988—98; cons., 1999—. Bd. dirs. Cutting Edge Designs, Denver, 1993-96. Editor: Marco Messenger, 1999—2004. Bd. dirs. Arc Ministries, Allegan, Mich., 1982—, Vol. Bur., Battle Creek, 1984-86, ARC, Calhoun County, Mich., 1985-96, Emerging Young Leaders, 1996-2000; pres. com. Marco Presbyn. Ch., 2002—; trustee Ind. Wesleyan U., 2001—. Recipient Outstanding Young Women of Am. award. Mem. Am. Mgmt. Assn., Soc. Human Resources Mgmt. Avocations: knitting, music, drama activities. Home and Office: 1060 Borghese Ln #502 Naples FL 34114 Office Phone: 239-285-1230. E-mail: karenmi@earthlink.net.

HOLLENBERG, PAUL FREDERICK, pharmacology educator; b. Phila., Sept. 18, 1942; s. Frederick Henry and Catherine (Dentzer) H.; m. Emily Elizabeth Vanootighem, May 6, 1967; children: Kathryn Mary, David Paul. BS in Chemistry, Wittenberg U., 1964; MS in Biochemistry, U. Mich., 1966, PhD in Biochemistry, 1969. Postdoctoral fellow U. Mich., Ann Arbor, 1969, U. Ill., Urbana, 1969-72; asst. prof. Northwestern U., Chgo., 1972-81, assoc. prof., 1981-84, prof. pathology and molecular biology, 1984-87; prof. pharmacology, chmn. dept. Wayne State U. Sch. Medicine, Detroit, 1987-94, U. Mich. Med. Sch., Ann Arbor, 1994—. Mem. pharmacology test com. Nat. Bd. Med. Examiners; mem. Chem. Pathology Study Sect. NIH, 1987-91. Co-founder, assoc. editor Chem. Rsch. in Toxicology, 1988—; assoc. editor Jour. Pharmacology and Exptl. Therapeutics; mem. editl. bd. Drug Metabolism and Disposition, British Jour. Pharmacology. Schweppe Found. research fellow, 1974-77; NIH research grantee, 1974—. Mem. Am. Chem. Soc., Am. Soc. Biochemists and Molecular Biologists, Am. Soc. Pharmacology and Exptl. Therapeutics (sec./treas. 1998-99, pres.-elect 2001-02, pres. 2002-03), Am. Assn. for Cancer Rsch., Soc. Toxicology, Internat. Soc. for Study of Xenobiotics. Avocations: reading, running, golf. Home: 1968 Woodlily Ct Ann Arbor MI 48103-9728 Office: Univ Mich 2301 MSRB III Sch Medicine 1150 W Medical Center Dr Ann Arbor MI 48109-0632 Office Phone: 734-764-8166. Business E-Mail: phollen@umich.edu.

HOLLENCAMP, GREG, architectural firm executive; BArch, U. Minn. Registered Minn. Pres. KKE Archs., Mpls., bd. dir. Mem.: AIA, Nat. Assn. Office and Indsl. Pks., Internat. Coun. Shopping Ctrs. Office: KKE Architects 300 First Ave North Minneapolis MN 55401

HOLLENDER, LARS GÖSTA, dental educator; b. Veinge, Sweden, Oct. 22, 1933; arrived in U.S., 1984; s. Gunnar Yngve and Astrid Margareta (Andersson) H.; m. Gunnel Charlotta Bergdahl, May 19, 1956 (div. 1975); children: Peter, Marie, Lena, Stefan; m. Sheridan Ellen Houston, Apr. 8, 1989; 1 child, Ashley Ellen. DDS, Sch. Dentistry, Malmö, Sweden, 1958, PhD, 1964. Diplomate Am. Bd. Oral and Maxillofacial Radiology. Assoc. prof. Sch. Dentistry, Malmö, 1964-68, prof., chair Göteborg, Sweden, 1969-87; prof., dir. U. Wash. Sch. Dentistry, Seattle, 1988—. Sec. gen. Internat. Assn. Dentomaxillofacial Radiology, 1974-85; vis. prof. UCLA Sch. Dentistry, 1980-82, U. Wash. Sch. Dentistry, 1984-87; sec./treas. Am. Bd. Oral and Maxillofacial Radiology, 1992-94, pres., 1995, councillor, 1996—. Editor-in-chief Odontologist Revy, 1964-69; contbr. over 100 chpts. to books and articles to profl. jours. Recipient Rsch. prize South Swedish Dental Soc., 1964, Rsch. prize Swedish Dental Assn., 1965, Elander Rsch. prize Gothenburg Dental Soc., 1976. Fellow Am. Acad. Oral and Maxillofacial Radiology (pres. 1997-98); mem. ADA (mem. review com. for OMFR commn. on dental accreditation 1999—), Internat. Assn. Dental and Maxillofacial Radiology (hon.), Australian Maxillofacial Radiology Soc. (hon.), Wash. State Dental Assn., King County Dental Assn. Avocations: reading, golf, cooking, travel, music. Office: Univ Wash Sch Dentistry PO Box 356370 Seattle WA 98195-6370 E-mail: larsholl@u.washington.edu.

HOLLER, MANFRED JOSEPH, economics professor; b. Munich, July 25, 1946; s. Joseph and Rosalie Holler; m. Barbara Klose Ullman, Nov. 18, 1995; 1 child, Michael. Diploma, U. Munich, 1971, PhD, 1975, Dr. rer. pol. habil., 1983. Asst. prof. U. Munich, 1974-85; assoc. prof. U. Aarhus, Denmark, 1986-91; prof. econs. U. Hamburg, Germany, 1991—. Founding editor: European Jour. of Polit. Economy, Homo Oeconomicus; editor volumes for sci. jours. Mem. Internat. Acad. Sci. (dir. edn.), Gesellschaft Integrierte Studien (bd. dirs.). Office: Inst Econs U Hamburg Von-Melle-Park 5 20146 Hamburg Germany E-mail: holler@econ.uni-hamburg.de.

HOLLERBACH, SERGE, artist; b. Pushkin, Russia, Nov. 1, 1923; came to U.S., 1949, naturalized, 1955; s. Lew and Ludmila (Agapov) H. Ed., Acad. Fine Arts, Munich, Germany, Art Students League. Tchr. art. Exhibited in group shows, Drawings, U.S.A., 1961, Met. Mus. Art, N.Y.C., 1966, Childe Hassam Fund Exhbn., Am. Acad. Arts and Letters, 1968; works represented in ann. exhbns., N.A.D., Am. Watercolor Soc., Audubon Artists, Nat. Arts Club; painter, designer, book illustrator. Recipient Gold medal Nat. Arts Club, 1963; prize N.A.D., 1965; Adolph and Clara Obrig prize, 1971, 76; Silver medal Am. Watercolor Soc., 1978; Gold medal Am. Watercolor Soc., 1983, Bronze medal of honor, Am. Watercolor Soc., 2002; medal and purchase Butler Inst. Am. Art, 1977; also numerous purchase awards and prizes. Mem. NAD; Mem. Am. Watercolor Soc., Audubon Artists, Nat. Soc. Painters in Casein, Allied Artists Am.*

HOLLERMAN, CHARLES EDWARD, retired pediatrician; b. Turtle Creek, Pa., Apr. 22, 1929; s. Harry R. and Lena F. H.; m. Catharine, Aug. 22, 1953; children: James, Karen, Jeffrey, Pamela. BS in Chemistry, Allegheny Coll., 1951; MD, Cornell U., 1955; student, U.S. Navy Sch. Aviation Medicine, 1957. Lic. pediatrician Pa. Intern York County (Pa.) Hosp., 1955-56; pvt. practice Cochranton, Pa., 1959-60; resident in pediat. Children's Hosp., Buffalo, 1960—62; fellow in clin. nephrology SUNY, 1962-65, instr. pediatrics, 1965-66; from asst. prof. to prof. pediat. Georgetown U., 1966—75; prof. pediat. U. S.D., Vermillion, 1976—82, asst. dean clin. services; acting dean, exec. dean U. S.D. Sch. Medicine, 1977-79, dean, 1979-82, v.p. health affairs, 1979-82; chmn. dept. pediatrics Mercy Hosp., Pitts., 1982-86, v.p. med. affairs, 1985-92; chief divsn. Pediat. Nephrology Mercy Childrens Med. Ctr., Pitts., 2000—; v.p. med. affairs St. Joseph's Mercy Hosps., Clinton Twp., Mich., 1992-95; regional v.p. physician and clin. integration Mercy Health Ptnrs. Southwest Ohio, Cin., 1995-99. Author: Pediatric Nephrology-Medical Outline Series, 1979; contbr. in field. Served with USN, 1956-59. Fellow Am. Coll. Physician Execs. (cert. physician exec.); mem. AMA, Am. Acad. Pediats., Phi Beta Kappa (cert. pediatrician, pediat. nephrologist, med. mgr.). Home: 4550 Nature Trail Dr Allison Park PA 15101-1131

HOLLEY, CYRUS HELMER, management consulting service executive; b. Chgo., June 14, 1936; s. Cyrus Howell and Elizabeth Fay (Helmer) H.; m. Shirley Marquitta Cannon, Aug. 31, 1957; children— Barrett Cannon, Russell William BS in Chem. Engring., Tex. A&M U., 1957; LLD (hon.), Bloomfield (N.J.) Coll., 1998. Registered profl. engr. Vice pres. indsl. chems. BASF Wyandotte Corp., Parsippany, N.J., 1976-79; sr. v.p. minerals & chem. div. Engelhard Corp., Edison, N.J., 1979-81, v.p., exec. v.p., 1981-83, v.p., pres., chief operating officer metals div., 1983-84, sr. v.p., pres. chem. div., 1984-85, exec. v.p., chief operating officer, 1985-91; pres. Mgmt. Cons. Svcs., 1991—. CEO Oakmont Enterprises, Inc., 1993—, Hanna Properties, LLC, 2002-. Contbr. articles to profl. jours. Trustee Bloomfield (N.J.) Coll., 1988-97, trustee emeritus, 1997—; dir. Nat. Assn. Ptnrs. in Edn., 1990-95, 99-02, Tex. Assn. Ptnrs. in Edn., 1991-99, 2001-03, N.J. Assn. Ptnrs. in Edn., 1991-99, Tex. Bus. & Edn. Coalition, 1992-96; chair Ind. Coll. Fund. N.J., 1990-92; bd. dirs. Tex. Ind. Coll. Fund, 1998-2001. Mem. AIChE. Republican. Presbyterian. Avocations: reading, golf, music. Office: Mgmt Cons Svcs 120 Oakmont Dr Trophy Club TX 76262

HOLLEY, IRVING BRINTON, JR., historian, educator; b. Hartford, Conn., Feb. 8, 1919; s. Irving B. and Mary L. (Sharp) H.; m. Janet Carlson, Oct. 9, 1945; children: Janet Turner Holley Wegner, Jean Carlson Holley Schmidt, Susan Sharp Holley. BA cum laude, Amherst Coll., 1940; MA (Brooker scholar), Yale U., 1942, PhD, 1947; student, Oxford U., summer, 1937. Instr. dept. history Duke U., Durham, N.C., 1947-51, asst. prof., 1952-54, asso. prof., 1955-61, prof., 1962-89, prof. emeritus, 1989—; vis. prof. U.S. Mil. Acad., 1974-75, Nat. Def. U., 1978-79; cons. to Army Research Office, 1963-73; mem. U.S. Commn. on Mil. History, 1974—. Occasional lectr. Army War Coll., USAF Acad., Inf. Sch., Air War Coll., Command and Gen. Staff Coll.; chmn. adv. com. on history Sec. Air Force, 1970-79; mem. adv. com. on history NASA, 1974-81 Author: Ideas and Weapons, 1953, Buying Aircraft, 1964, Development of Aircraft Gun Turrets in the AAF, 1917-1944, Evolution of the Liaison Type Airplane, 1917-1944, 1946, An Enduring Challenge: The Problem of Air Force Doctrine, 1974, General John M. Palmer, Citizen Soldiers, and the Army of a Democracy, 1982, Technology and Military Doctrine, 2004; contbr. articles on mil. history to scholarly publs.; editor: The Transfer of Ideas: Historical Essays, 1968, editorial adviser various jours. Trustee Air Force Hist. Found., 1973—. With USAAF, 1942—47, capt. USAAF, 1947—81, reserves, maj. gen. USAF, 1981, reserves. Decorated D.S.M., Legion of Merit; recipient Outstanding Civilian Service to the Army medal, 1975, Exceptional Civilian Service to the Air Force medal., 1979 Fellow AIAA (assoc.); mem. Am. Hist. Assn., Soc. History of Tech., Soc. Mil. History, Phi Delta Theta. Episcopalian. Home: 2701 Pickett Rd Apt 3028 Durham NC 27705-5651 Office: Duke Univ Dept History Durham NC 27708 Office Phone: 919-684-2103. E-mail: ibholley@duke.edu.

HOLLEY, KATHLEEN, secondary school educator; b. Dallas, Mar. 3, 1958; d. William Morris and June Elizabeth McGee. BS in Biochemistry, U. Tex., Arlington, 1980; MA in Elem. Edn., Tex. Woman's U., Denton, 1991. Cert. tchr., Tex. Sch. health specialist Edn. Svc. Ctr. Region XI, Ft. Worth, 1986-91; sci. tchr. Lamar H.S., Arlington, Tex., 1990-91, Gunn Jr. H.S., Arlington, 1991; adj. instr. Tarrant County Coll., Ft. Worth, 1993-98; A.P. sci. tchr. Grand Prairie (Tex.) H.S., 1992-95, Crowley (Tex.) H.S., 1995-98, North Crowley H.S., Ft. Worth, 1998—2004, chair sci. dept., 2000—04; sci. tchr. Upper Sch., The Oakridge Sch., Arlington, Tex., 2004—. Sponsor, founder Masters of the Universe Sci. Demo Team, Arlington, 1993—, Active Sci. Unltd., Inc., Arlington, 1997—. Contbg. author Macmillan Ency. of Chemistry, 1996. Mem. Ft. Worth Civic Orch., 1985—, also past pres.; mem. Arlington Cmty. Band, 1989—, pres., 2000-02. Named Outstanding Sci. Tchr., Tex. Med. Assn., 1995, Tex. Chemistry Tchr. of Yr., 2003-2004; Tandy Tech. scholar, 1996. Mem. Am. Chem. Soc., Sci. Tchrs. Assn. Tex., Assn. Tex. Profl. Educators, Nat. Mole Day Found., Phi Delta Kappa. (rec. sec.). Avocations: playing flute, computers, electronics, pyrotechnics. Office: Oakridge Sch 5900 W Pioneer Pkwy Arlington TX 76013

HOLLEY, PAMELA SPENCER, retired librarian; b. Mpls., July 31, 1944; d. Boyd Edgar Gustafson, Jane Lenore Gustafson; m. Richard Howard Holley; m. Arthur Snow Spencer (dec. Oct. 24, 1996). BS Biology and Secondary Edn., Longwood Coll., 1965; MS, Coll. William and Mary, 1970; MLS, U. Md., 1973. Cert. libr. Va., 1973. Tchr. sci. Stephen Foster Intermediate/Fairfax County Pub. Schs., Alexandria, Va., 1965—72; libr. Lake Braddock Secondary Sch., Burke, 1973—75, Mount Vernon H.S., Alexandria, 1975—86; media specialist Area I Office, 1986—87; libr. Thomas Jefferson H.S. for Sci. and Tech., 1987—94; libr. program specialist Chapel Sq. Ctr., Annandale, 1994—96; coord. librs. FCPS, 1996—98; ret., 1998. Chair film series com. Virginia Beach Pub. Libr. Friends Bd., Va., 2000—02, v.p., 2002—03; mem. editl. adv. bd. Voice of Youth Advocates Mag., Lanham, 2000—; chair adv. com. Am. Econoclad Svcs., Topeka, 1988—95; host, co-host Cable 21 Ednl. Channel, Annandale, 1992—97; editl. adv. bd. Booklist Mag., Chgo., 1988—90; bd. dirs. Libr. Friends, v.p., 2002—03. Author: What Do Young Adults Read Next? (continuing series),

1993, Audiobooks, It Is!, 2002—, Column, VOYA, 2002—. Mem.: ALA (bd. dirs. divsn. young adult libr. svcs. assn. 1990—93, councilor 1995—99, v.p. 2004—05, pres. 2005—), Beta Phi Mu. Episcopalian. Avocations: kayaking, exercise, travel, reading, needlepoint. Home: PO Box 9 Assawoman VA 23302 Personal E-mail: pamsholley@aol.com.

HOLLEY, RICK, paper company executive; BA, San Jose State Univ. With GE, 1974, Burlington No. Inc., 1983—85. With World Forestry Ctr., Seattle Children's Hospital. Mem.: Am. Forest Found. (mem. bd.), Am. Forest & Paper Assn. (mem. bd.). Office: Plum Creek Timber Ste 4300 999 Third Ave Seattle WA 98104*

HOLLEY, ROBERT WILLIAM, sales executive, minister; b. Phila., Pa., Dec. 11, 1948; s. Robert John and Grace Mildred Holley (Stepmother), Evelyn Holly and Charles Hague Mavian (Stepfather); m. Patricia Ruth Meluzio, Dec. 26, 1970; 1 child, Jephthah David. BS in Bible, Phila. Coll. Bible, 1974; MDiv, Bibl. Sch. Theology, Hatfield, Pa., 1977; STM, Bibl. Theol. Sem., Hatfield, Pa., 1978. Saint Stephen's Course in Orthodox Theology Antiochian Orthodox Christian Archdiocese N.Am., 1999. Author: How Do I Choose the Right Partner for Life?, 2003, The Myth of Teenaged Problems. Mem. com. on marriage and family Antiochian Orthodox Christian Archiocese, 2000—. Staff sgt. USAF, 1967—70, Viet Nam. Republican. Avocations: writing, language study, bible study. Home: 431 Portola Ave La Habra CA 90631-5463 Office: McCrometer Incorporated 3255 W Stetson Ave Hemet CA 92545-7799 Office Phone: 562-691-3894. Home Fax: 1-562-691-8394. Business E-Mail: bobh@mccrometer.com.

HOLLEY, STEVEN LYON, lawyer; b. Ft. Wayne, Ind., Apr. 5, 1958; s. Wesley Lewis and Cornelia Alice (Reeder) H. BA in History/Polit. Sci., Ind. U., 1980; JD, NYU, 1983. Bar: N.Y. 1984, U.S. Dist. Ct. (so. and ea. dist.) N.Y. 1985, U.S. Dist. Ct. (no. dist.) N.Y. 1988. Law clk. Hon. Jose' A. Cabranes, Hartford, Conn., 1983-84; assoc. Sullivan & Cromwell, N.Y.C., 1984-90, ptnr., 1991—. Mem. Assn. Bar City of N.Y. (sec. com. on profl. and jud. ethics 1988-90). Democrat. Home: 832 Broadway New York NY 10003-4813 Office: Sullivan & Cromwell 125 Broad St Fl 34 New York NY 10004-2498 Office Phone: 212-558-4737. Business E-Mail: holleys@sullcrom.com.

HOLLI, MELVIN GEORGE, history professor; b. Ishpeming, Mich., Feb. 22, 1933; s. Walfred and Sylvia (Erickson) H.; m. Betsy Biggar, Aug. 12, 1961; children: Susan, Steven. Student, Suomi Coll., 1952-54; BA, North Mich. U., 1957; MA, U. Mich., 1958, PhD, 1969. Curator manuscripts Bentley Libr., U. Mich., Ann Arbor, 1962-64; asst. prof., assoc. prof. history U. Ill., Chgo., 1965, prof., 1975—, chmn. dept., 1991-94. Fulbright prof. U. Finland, 1978, 89-90. Author: Reform in Detroit, 1969, Detroit, 1975, Ethnic Chicago, 1981, 3d edit., 1995 (nonfiction prize Soc. Midland Authors 1985, Best book award Ill. Polit. Sci. Assn. 1985), Bashing Chicago Traditions, 1989, Restoration: Chicago Elects a New Daley, 1991, The Mayors: The Chicago Political Tradition, 1995, 3d edit., 2005, The American Mayor: The Best and Worst Big City Leaders, 1999; (with Paul M. Green) From Mid Century to Millennium: A View From Chicago's City Hall, 1999, (with F. Beuttler and R. Remini) The University of Illinois at Chicago: A Pictorial History, 2000, The Wizard of Washington: Emil Hurja Franklin Roosevelt and the Birth of Public Opinion Polling, 2002, (with Green) World War II Chicago, 2003; bd. editors Urban Affairs Quar., 1992-95; editor: U. Ill. Press Ethnic History in Chicago book series. Bd. dirs. Scandinavian Ctr., North Park Univ., Chgo., 1997—. Woodrow Wilson fellow, 1957-58; recipient Disting. Alumni award No. Mich. U., 1985. Mem. Am. Hist. Assn., Orgn. Am. Historians, Swedish Am. Hist. Soc. (mag. bd. 1990-93), Soc. Midland Authors (bd. dirs. 1989-93, 94—), Finnish-Am. Soc. of the Midwest (bd. dirs.). Home: 1311 Ashland Ave River Forest IL 60305-1029 Office: Dept History U Ill Chicago IL 60607-7109 Office Phone: 312-996-2232. E-mail: mholli@uic.edu.

HOLLIDAY, BARBARA JOYCE, reference librarian, minister; b. Savannah, Ga. d. John Willie and Eula Mae Holliday. BSc, Savannah State Coll.; MSc in Libr. Sci., Clark Atlanta U. Cataloging libr. Tex. So. U. Law Libr., Houston, 1976—79; pharmacy libr. Tex. So. U. Pharmacy Libr., Houston, 1979—81; asst. ref. libr. Tex. So. U. Robert James Terry Libr., Houston, 1981—93; ref. libr. Tex. So. U., 1993—. Recipient Nurse of the Yr., Miracle House of Prayer, Inc., 1984. Mem.: ALA. Democrat. Avocations: reading, writing, poetry. Office: Tex So U 3100 Cleburne St Houston TX 77004 Office Phone: 713-313-4424. Business E-Mail: holliday_bj@tsu.edu.

HOLLIDAY, CHARLES O., JR., chemical company executive; b. Nashville, Mar. 9, 1948; s. Charles O. Sr. and Ann (Hunter) H.; m. Ann Blair, June 27, 1970; children: Scot, Chad. BS in Indsl. Engring., U. Tenn., 1970; DSc (hon.), Washington Coll., Chesterton, Md., 1988; Dsc (hon.), Polytechnic U. Registered profl. engr., Tenn. From engr. to CEO DuPont, Nashville, 1970—98, CEO, 1998—, chmn., 1999—. Chmn. World Bus. Coun. Sustainable Devel., World Bus. Coun., Catalyst; mem. Singapore-U.S. Bus. Coun. Vice chmn. John F. Kennedy Ctr. Performing Arts; active Alliance Global Sustainability, Del. Bus./Pub. Edn. Coun., U. Tenn., Winterthur Mus. Mem. Japan Am. Soc. Del., Soc. Chem. Industry, Inst. Indsl. Engrs. (sr.), Soc. Chem. Inter-Am. Sect. Office: Dupont 1007 Market St D9000 Wilmington DE 19898

HOLLIDAY, GUY D. "DOC", publishing executive; BS in Orgnl. Leadership, U.S. Mil. Acad., 1986; MS in Quality Sys. Mgmt. with honors, Nat. Grad. Sch., 2002. Ops. mgr. Kimberly Clark Corp., 1992—94; gen. supr. finishing ops., ops. mgr., project coord., engr. Lukens Steel, 1994—96; asst. plant mgr. N.Y. Times printing plant N.Y. Times, Edison, NJ, 1996—2000, dir. engring. and maintenance ops. N.Y.C., 2000—04, v.p. advt. sales, 2004—. Capt. U.S. Army, 1986—92, maj. U.S. Army, 2003—04. Office: NY Times 229 W 43rd St New York NY 10036-3959

HOLLIDAY, JENNIFER MARGARET, music educator; b. Beckley, W.Va., Dec. 19, 1977; d. Theodore Jennings and Lois Bailess Holliday. BS in Music Edn., Bob Jones U., Greenville, SC, 2000, MusM in Edn., 2002. Cert. in music edn. SC, Kindermusik educator Kindermusik Internat. Asst. to music tchrs. Bob Jones Elem. and Jr. HS, Greenville, 1998—2002; home sch. band dir. Pecknel Music Co., Greenville, 2000; music educator Berean Bapt. Music Acad., Lilburn, Ga., 2002—. Asst. coord. S.C. Cello Choir and Masterclass, Greenville, 2001—01. Mem.: Am. Coll. Musicians. Personal E-mail: cellomujer@aol.com.

HOLLIDAY, KENT ALFRED, music educator; b. St. Paul, Mar. 9, 1940; s. Robert Daniel Holliday and Sylvia Suel; m. Barbara Jane Gilbert (div.); children: Cheryl Galloway, Stephen. BA, Hamline U., 1962; MA, U. Minn., Mpls., 1964, PhD, 1968. Music tchr. So. Colo. State Coll., Pueblo, 1965—77, Colo. State U., Ft. Collins, 1972—74, Va. Tech., Blacksburg, 1974—. Author: Reproducing Pianos Past and Present, 1989. Recipient Competition award, Va. Music Tchrs. Assn., 1983, 1996, 1998, Del. New Music Competition, U. Del., 1996. Avocations: photography, tennis.

HOLLIDAY, PATRICIA A., elementary school educator; b. Delta City, Miss., May 7, 1965; d. Benny Hopson and Alma Ruth Garner; m. Robert R. Holliday, July 21, 1985; children: Tatiana Moniqe, Tierra Jecolia, Crystal Angelique. BA, Northeastern U., Chgo., 1999, MA, 2002. Cert. elem. and secondary sch. tchr. Ill. State Bd. of Edn. Sr. billing/credit rep. Xerox Corp., Park Ridge, Ill., 1990—99; tchr. Chgo. Pub. Schs., Chgo., 2000—. Author: (novels) Turning Pain Into Power. Pastor Faith Deliverance Temple, Chgo., 1999—2004. Grantee, Chgo. Found. for Edn. Pentecostal Assemblies Of The World. Office: Lovett Elem Sch 6333 W Bloomingdale Chicago IL 60639 Office Phone: 773-534-3130. Personal E-mail: pah5540@sbcglobal.net.

HOLLIDAY, PATRICIA RUTH MCKENZIE, evangelist; b. Jacksonville, Fla., Nov. 17, 1935; d. Robert Irving and Leona Adele (Bell) McKenzie; m. Jan. 20, 1965; children: Connie, Katheryn, Alexander. Student, Massey Bus. Coll., 1969, Luther Rice Sem., 1976; DD, Southeastern Theol. Sem., 1986, ThD, 1989, PhD, 1992. Sec. Delta Drug Corp., Jacksonville, 1965—; pres. Microfilm Ctr., Jacksonville, 1974—, Miracle Outreach Ministry, Jacksonville, 1974—; pastor Miracle World Outreach, Jacksonville; prof. Southeastern Theol. Sem., Jacksonville, 1992—; with Internat. Evang. Miracle Outreach, 2000—. Author: Holliday for the King, 1978, Be Free, 1979, Only Believe, 1980, Born Anew, 1981, The Walking Dead, 1982, Anointing Power, 1982, Signs, Wonders and Reactions, 1984, Dealing with Heresies, 1986, Marriage Answers, 1992, Solitary Satanist, 1993, Entertaining Angels of Light, 1993, The Plan: Ascended Masters, 1994, The New World Aftershock, 1994, Can. Women Preach?, 1995, New Creations, 1995, From Curses to Blessings Vols. 1, 2 & 3, 1995, Angel Fire, 1995, Can Witches Be Saved, 1996, Spirit of Idolatry, 1996, Is Halloween Pagan?, 1996, Gods of the Stars, Astrology, 1997, Gifts of the Holy Spirit, 1997, Baptism of the Holy Spirit, 1997, Deliverance Manuals, Vols. 1, 2 & 3, 1997, Spiritual Welfare Army, 1997, Spiritual Warfare - Weapons, 1997, Healing & Miracles, 1998, The Spiritual Armor of God, 1998, Children of the New Age, 1998, Prayer Warriors, 1998, Battling Territorial Spirits, 1998, New Age Inner Healing, 1999, Demons Tremble, 1999, Transference of Spirits, 1999, Experiencing Jesus, 2001, Witch Doctor and the Man-Fourth Generational Witch Doctor Finds Christ, 2001, Satan's Romper Room, 2002, Never, Never Land, 2003, The Fallen Prince, 2003, others; columnist Christian Courier. Sec. Four Found., Inc.; Rep. candidate Fla. Ho. of Reps., 1972; mem. Fla. Rep. Com., 1976-80; lobbyist Fla. Legislature, 1978-80; hostess Pat Holliday TV Show, Jacksonville. Recipient Rep. Gold Medal award, Nat. Rep. Congl. Com., 2004. Mem. Minutewomen of Fla. Club (founder) Univ. Women Club, Ponte Vedra Women's Club. Home: 9252 San Jose Blvd Apt 2804 Jacksonville FL 32257-9205 Personal E-mail: hollidaypat@hotmail.com.

HOLLIDAY, ROBERT KELVIN, retired state legislator, publishing executive; b. Logan, W.Va., Feb. 11, 1933; s. James Kelvin and Helen Kathleen (Harris) Holliday; children: Kelvin, Kathleen Eddy, Stephen, Robert L., Jeffrey, Tracey, Brandon. BA, W.Va. U. Tech., 1954; MA, Marshall U., 1955. Co-owner, editor Montgomery (W.Va.) Herald, 1955—85; co-owner, editor The Fayette Tribune, 1955—85, Fayette Tribune, 1955—85, Meadow River Post, Rainelle, W.Va., 1966—85; with W.Va. Divsn. Corrections, 2001—03. Mem. W.Va. Ho. of Dels., 1963-68, W.Va. Senate, 1968-72, 80-94; adj. polit. sci. instr. W.Va. U. Inst. Tech., 1994, 99, 2000, 02-05, W.Va. State Coll., 1997-98, Bluefield State Coll., 1996, Greenbrier C.C., 1995, Glenville State Coll., 1997. Author: Tests of Faith, 1966, About Montgomery, 1956, Our Chat, 1956, A Portrait of Fayette, 1960, Politics in Fayette County, 1958. Mem. W.Va. State Dem. Exec. Com., 1978-80; pres. Fayette Needy Assn., 1960-68; elder Presbyn. Ch. With U.S. Army. Recipient Gov.'s Living Dream award Martin Luther King Jr., 1988, Outstanding Leadership award W.Va. NAACP, 1988, award Kanawha-Fayette Cmty. Svc., Inc., 1985-2005; named Outstanding Legislator, W.Va. Trial Lawyers Assn., 1988, 92. Mem.: W.Va.Rehab Assn. (Structural Barriers award 1988), W. Va. Edn. Assn. (Pearl S. Buck award 1982), W. Va. Mental Health Assn. (past dir.), New Rivers Nat. River (founder), Shriners, Masons (32 degree), Pi Sigma Alpha. Presbyterian.

HOLLIDAY, ROBERT LEE, civil engineer; b. Charleston, W.Va., Nov. 18, 1950; s. Lee Carrington and Mildred Spitzer Holliday; m. Maria Josefa Sequeira; children: Sean Robert, Jason Lee, Ian Robert D. BSCE, W.Va. U. Inst. Tech., 1972; lic. in engring., U. Costa Rica, San Jose, 1975. Lic. profl. engr., Fed. Coll. Engrs. and Archs. Costa Rica. Dir. field ops. DelMonte-Pineapple Devel. Corp., Buenos Aires, 1980—82; owner, operator Brasil Bloque S.A, San Jose, 1982—85; chief field engr. Fishbach and Moore Internat., San Jose, 1985—88; resident field mgr., U.S. embassy to San Salvador, Embassy Task Group, Sverdrup Corp., San Salvador, 1988—91, sr. constrn. mgr. St. Louis, 1992—95; dep. gen. dir. Centreacademstroi, Menatep Bank, Moscow, 1995—96; sr. project mgr. Parsons Internat. Corp., Moscow, 1996—98; dir. project mgmt. U. Chgo., 1999—. Honored presenter Chgo. Bldg. Congress, 2003; presenter in field. V.p., bd. dirs. Hyde Park Neighborhood Club, Chgo., 2000—04; bd. dirs. Blue Gargoyle Youth Ctr., Chgo., 2000—04. Recipient Cert. of Appreciation, U.S. Dept. of State, 1992, Contbn. to Cmty. Pres.'s citation, African Am. Contractors Assn., 2004. Mem.: NSPE, KC. Roman Catholic. Avocations: travel, foreign languages. Office: U Chgo 5555 S Ellis Ave Chicago IL 60637 Office Phone: 773-834-2714.

HOLLIDAY, RONALD STURGIS, lawyer; b. Wichita, Kans., Dec. 11, 1947; s. Robert Dwight and Mary Irene (Smith) H.; m. Deborah June Winship, Aug. 29, 1975; children: Brian Joseph, Kathryn June. BA with honors, U. Kans., 1969; JD magna cum laude, U. Mich., 1972. Bar: Mich. 1972, U.S. Dist. Ct. (ea. dist.) Mich. 1972, U.S. Dist. Ct. (we. dist.) Mich. 1977, U.S. Ct. Appeals (6th cir.) 1982, Fla. 1986, U.S. Dist. Ct. (mid. dist.) Fla. 1987. Assoc. Dykema Gossett, Detroit, 1972-80, ptnr., 1980; mng. ptnr. Tampa off. DLA Piper Rudnick Gray Cary. Served to lt. JAGC, USN, 1973-76. Recipient Leadership Detroit award Greater Detroit C. of C., 1980. Fellow Mich. State Bar Found. (mem. antitrust law sect.); mem. ABA, Mich. Bar Assn., Detroit Bar Assn., Fla. Bar Assn., Sarasota County Bar Assn., Hillsborough County Bar Assn. Office: DLA Piper Rudnick Gray Cary Ste 2000 101 E Kennedy Blvd Tampa FL 33602-5149 Office Phone: 813-222-5926. Office Fax: 813-229-1447. Business E-Mail: ronald.holliday@dlapiper.com.

HOLLIDAY, THOMAS EDGAR, lawyer; b. Ft. Hood, Tex., July 3, 1948; s. William Lamont and Eileen (Fiebig) H.; m. Linda Loudon, May 7, 1988; children: Devon M., Trey S. BA, Stanford U., 1971; JD, U. So. Calif., 1974. Bar: Calif. 1974. Assoc. Gibson, Dunn & Crutcher LLP, L.A., 1974-81; ptnr. Gibson, Dunn & Crutcher, L.A., 1981—. Editor: (book, desk edition) Antitrust and Trade Regulations. Trustee S.W. Mus., L.A., 1981-98, bd. pres., 1995-97; trustee Found. for People, L.A., 1985-90, Clarkson U., 2000—; mem. L.A. Police Dept. Meml. Found. Bd. Fellow Am. Coll. Trial Lawyers; mem. Fed. Bar Assn. (exec. com. L.A. chpt. 1990, pres. 1998). Avocation: collecting southwestern art. Office: Gibson Dunn & Crutcher LLP 333 S Grand Ave Ste 4400 Los Angeles CA 90071-3197

HOLLIEN, HARRY FRANCIS, communications scientist; b. Brockton, Mass., July 16, 1926; s. Henry Gregory and Alice Bernice (Coolidge) H.; m. Patricia Ann Milanowski, Aug. 26, 1969; children: Karen Ann, Kevin Amory, Keith Alan, Brian Christopher, Stephanie Ann, Christine Ann. BS, Boston U., 1949, MEd, 1951; MA, U. Iowa, 1953, PhD, 1955. Asst. prof. Baylor U., 1955-58, U. Wichita, 1958-62; assoc. prof. speech U. Fla., Gainesville, 1962-68, prof., 1968-98, prof. linguistics, 1976-98, prof. criminal justice, 1979-98, assoc. dir. comm. scis. lab., 1962—65, dir. comm. scis. lab., 1968—75, dir. Inst. Advanced Study Comm. Processes, 1975—84; prof. emeritus, rsch. scientist Inst. Advanced Study of Communication Processes, 1998—, assoc. dir. linguistics, 1989-91; founding dir. Inst. Advanced Study Comm. Processes U. Fla., 1984—. Vis. prof. Inst. Telecomm. and Acoustics, Wroclaw Tech. U., Poland, 1974; adj. prof. Juilliard Sch. Music, N.Y.C., 1973-84; rsch. assoc. Gould Rsch. Lab., 1958; vis. sci. Speech Transmission Lab., Royal Inst. Tech., Stockholm, 1970; Fulbright prof. U. Trier, Germany, 1987; fencing coach U. Iowa, 1953-55; mem. comm. sci. study sect. NIH, 1963-67; mem. neurobiology merit rev. bd. VA, 1969-74; pres. Hollien Assocs., 1966—; cons. in field. Author: Current Issues in Phonetic Sciences, 1978, Acoustics of Crime, 1990, Forensic Voice Identification, 2002; assoc. editor Jour. Speech and Hearing Rsch., 1967-69, Jour. Voice, 1987—; editor The Phonetician, 1975-92; mem. edtl. bd. Jour. Comm. Disorders, 1980-91, Jour. Rsch. in Singing, 1980-83, Jour. Phonetics, 1982-85, Studia Phonetica Posnan, 1985—, Speech, Language and the Law, 1993-2002. Chmn. bd. Unitarian Fellowship, Waco, Tex., 1956-58; chmn. bd. Wild Animal Retirement Village, 1981-90. Served with USN, 1944-46; with USNR, 1946-75. Recipient Garcia/Sandoz prize Internat. Assn. Logopedics and Phoniatrics, 1971, Gould award Wm. and Harrett Gould Found., 1975, Gutzmann medal Union European Phoniatrists, 1980, Professorial Excellence award U. Fla., 1996; NIH career fellow, 1965-70, Fulbright scholar, 1987. Fellow AAAS, Am. Speech and Hearing Assn., Acoustical Soc. Am., Internat. Soc. Phonetic Scis. (pres. 1989-98, sec.-gen. 1975-89, exec. v.p. 1983-89, Kay Elemetrics prize 1987, S. Smith prize 1991, Soc. Honors 1998, hon. pres. 1999—), Am. Acad. Forensic Sci. (John R. Hunt award 1988), Inst. Acoustics; mem. SAR (pres. local chpt. 2001-03, regional v.p. 2000-04. sr. v.p. 2004-2005, pres. 2005—, state rec. sec. 2001-03, Patriot medal, 2003), Am. Assn. Phonetic Scis. (pres. 1973-75, editor 1976-79, exec. com. 1979-82), Japan Soc. Phonetic Scis. (hon. v.p. 1989-97), World Congress Phoneticians (permanent coun.), Voice Found. (sci. bd., merit awards 1981, 93), Internat. Assn. Forensic Phonetics, Mayflower Descs. (gov. local chpt. 2002-2005, capt. state soc. 1999-2002), Order Found. Patriots (chaplain, state soc. 2004—), Sigma Xi. Republican. Achievements include patent for apparatus using radiation sensitive switch for signalling and recording data. Home: 229 SW 43rd Ter Gainesville FL 32607-2270 Office: U Fla Inst Advanced Study Comm Processes 46 Dauer Hall Gainesville FL 32611 Office Phone: 352-392-2046 x229. Business E-Mail: Hollien@Grove.ufl.edu.

HOLLIEN, PATRICIA ANN, small business owner, researcher; b. N.Y.C., May 11, 1938; d. Leon and Sophia (Biernacki) Milanowski; m. Harry Hollien, Aug. 26, 1969; children: Brian, Stephanie, Christine. AA, Sante Fe Jr. Coll., 1969; ScD (hon), Marian Coll., 1983; student, U. Fla., 1977—. Rsch. asst. Marineland Rsch. Labs., 1965-69; co-owner, exec. v.p. Hollien Assocs., 1969—; owner, dir. Forensic Comm. Assocs., Gainesville, Fla., 1981—, The Eden Group, Gainesville, 1995-97. Vis. assoc. Royal Inst. Spl. Transmission Lab., Stockholm, 1970, Wroclaw Tech. U., Poland, 1974; asst. in research Inst. Advanced Study Communication Scis. U. Fla., 1977-83, assoc. in research, 1983—; adj. asst. prof. Communication Sci. Lab., N.Y., 1982—. Co-author: Current Issues in the Phonetic Sciences, 1979; editor The Phonetician, 1991-98; contbr. articles to profl. jours. Treas. Soc. Son's of the Am. Revolution, 2001—; bd. dirs. Ann. Retirement Village, Waldo, Fla., 1981—93. Fellow Am. Acad. Forensic Scis., Internat. Soc. Phonetic Scis. (coun. reps. 1983—, Honors of the Assn. for 1995, 1997); mem. Am. Assn. Phonetic Scis., Acad. Forensic Application of the Comm. Sci., Internat. Assn. Forensic Phonetics (sec. gen. 7th ann. congress 1995), Ladies Aux. Fla. Soc. SAR (treas. 2003-05, pres. 2005—), Ladies Aux., Fla. Soc. Son's Am. Revolution (pres., 2005—, treas, 2002-2005). Home: 229 SW 43d Ter Gainesville FL 32607-2270 Office: Forensic Comm Assocs PO Box 12323 Gainesville FL 32604-0323 Office Phone: 352-377-8622. E-mail: fca@forcomm.com.

HOLLIER, LARRY HAROLD, vascular surgeon, hospital administrator; b. Crowley, Louisiana, Apr. 18, 1943; s. Villere Joseph and Agnes (Guidry) H.; m. Diana Gayle Johnson, Jan. 25, 1964; children: Larry Jr., Michelle Ann. BS, La. State U., 1965, MD, 1968. Diplomate Am. Bd. Surgery, spl. qualifications in vascular surgery. Intern Charity Hosp. La., New Orleans, 1968-69, gen. surgery resident, 1969-75; vascular surgery fellow Baylor U. Med. Ctr., Dallas, 1973-74; chief vascular surgery La. State U. Med. Sch., New Orleans, 1975-80, Mayo Clinic, Rochester, Minn., 1980-87; chmn. dept. surgery Ochsner Clnic, New Orleans, 1987-93; med. dir. HCI Internat. Med. Centre, Glasgow, Scotland, 1993—96; Julius H. Jacobson II MD prof. surgery Mount Sinai Sch. Medicine, NYC, 1996—2003, chmn. dept. surgery, 1996—2003; surgeon-in-chief Mount Sinai Med. Ctr., NYC; pres. The Mount Sinai Hosp., NYC, 2002—03; dean, Sch. Medicine La. State U. Health Sci. Ctr., New Orleans, 2004—. Founder divsn. vascular surgery Mayo Clinic, Rochester, 1983; bd. mgmt. Ochsner Clinic, New Orleans, 1989-93. Editor: Vascular Surgery - Basic Science in Clinical Correlations, 1994, Haimovici's Vascular Surgery, 1995. Maj. USAF, 1970-72. Fellow ACS (young surgeons rep. 1979, pres. La. chpt. 1989); mem. Soc. Vascular Surgery (chmn. membership com. 1985-86), Soc. Clin. Vascular Surgery (pres. 1995), So. Assn. Vascular Surgery (pres. 1995), Midwestern Vascular Soc. (pres. 1988). Avocations: sailing, scuba diving. Office: LSU Med Sch 533 Bolivar, Suite 362 New Orleans LA 70112 Office Phone: 504-568-4009. Business E-Mail: lhholl@lsumsc.edu.

HOLLIGER, FRED LEE, oil company executive; b. Kansas City, Mo., Feb. 4, 1948; s. Ronald and Margorie (Klein) H.; m. Susan Lynn Harris, Oct. 6, 1972; children: Meredith, Allison, Lauren. BS in Petroleum Engring., U. Mo., Rolla, 1970; postgrad., U. Mich., 1978. Petroleum engr. Transok Pipeline Co., Tulsa, 1971; reservoir engr. No. Natural Gas Co., Omaha, 1972-73, project mgr. Lyons, Kans., 1974-76, area mgr. Great Bend, Kans., 1977-79, gen. mgr. mktg. Omaha, 1980-83, v.p. gas supply, 1984-85, v.p. mktg., 1986, pres., COO, 1987-88; sr. v.p. Giant Industries, Scottsdale, Ariz., 1989, exec. v.p., COO, 1989—2002, chmn., CEO, 2002—. Dir. Giant Industries. Mem. Nat. Petroleum Refining Assn. (dir. 1990—), Desert Highlands Golf Club. Office: Giant Industries 23733 N Scottsdale Rd Scottsdale AZ 85255*

HOLLIMAN, W. G. (MICKEY), JR., furniture manufacturing executive; Founder, pres., CEO Action Industries subs. Furniture Brands Internat., 1970-96; pres., chmn., CEO, Furniture Brands Internat., St. Louis, 1996—. Office: Furniture Brands Internat Ste 1900 101 S Hanley Rd Saint Louis MO 63105-3493

HOLLINGER, MORTON, small business owner, artist; b. Port Chester, N.Y. s. Max and Anna Hollinger; m. Myrna Rachel Hollinger, Mar. 30, 1958; children: Nancy Samson, Steven. BA, Syracuse U., 1949; studied with William Arrowsmith, prin. oboist, Met. Opera; studied painting with Louis Di Valentin. Pres. M.H. Pierce & Co., Stamford, Conn., 1958—. Oboist Westchester Symphony, White Plains, N.Y., 1982-85, Bronx (N.Y.) Symphony, 1986-89. Author: Paintings of Morton Hollinger, 1998; exhibitions include Studio Soto Gallery, Boston, 2004. Pres. Jr. C. of C., Port Chester, N.Y., 1957. Recipient Stamford Mus. award for oil painting, 1968, Windsor-Newton award for oil painting, 1990. Mem. Stamford Art Assn. Avocations: clarinet, oboe, english horn, painting. Home: 11 Ledge Terr Stamford CT 06905 Office Phone: 203-327-2970. Personal E-mail: m.hollinger@sbcglobal.net.

HOLLINGER, PAULA COLODNY, state legislator; b. Washington, Dec. 30, 1940; d. Samuel and Ethel (Levy) Colodny; m. Paul Hollinger, Sept. 16, 1962; children: Ilene, Marcy, David. RN, Mt. Sinai Hosp. Sch. Nursing, N.Y.C., 1961. RN NY. Pub. health sch. nurse, resident camp nurse Balt. County Dept. Health; Myasthenia Gravis specialist Acute Stroke Unit U. Md. Hosp.; clin. instr. psychiat. nursing Tuskegee Inst.; head nurse surgery intensive care unit Mt. Sinai Hosp., N.Y., night charge nurse emergency rm.; Carter del., 1976; mem. Md. Ho. of Dels., Annapolis, 1978-86, Md. Senate, Annapolis, 1987—, majority whip, 2000—, vice chair senate edn. health and environ. affairs com., 1995—, senate chair joint com. on health care delivery and financing, 1995—, chair senate econ. and environ. affairs health subcom., 1988—, chair edn., health and environ. affairs com., 2003—, majority whip, 2000—03. Chmn. adminstrv., exec., legis. rev. com., health subcom. Md. Senate, Annapolis, 1987, chmn. 1991-95, chmn. joint com. health care delivery and financing, 1995, chmn. joint com. fed. rels., 1987-90, vice-chair econ. and environ. affairs com.,1995, mem. exec. nominations com., 1995—; vice-chair health com. Nat. Conf. State Legis., 1990-91, chair health com., 1991-92, chair sci. and resources tech. com., 1984, com. long term care, 1985, chmn. women's network, 1993, vice chmn. 1992, 96, chmn., 1992, rep. assembly fed. issues; mem. joint oversight com. on health care cost containment, Medicaid joint com.; chmn. joint protocol com. Md. Gen. Assembly, 1998—; alt. mem. So. Legis. Conf. Coun. State Govts. Human Svcs. And Pub. Safety Com.; mem. Gov.'s Task Forces to Study: Nursing Crisis, Uses of Methlphenidate, 1997—, Class Size Reduction Programs in Md., 1998—, Alternative Methods of Coll. Financing, Joint Legis. Task Force on Organ and Tissue Donation, 1997-98, Task Forces on Violence and Extremism, Quality of Care in Nurising Facilities, 1999, AIDS; mem. Gov.'s adv. coun. on AIDS; mem. Gov.'s com. nursing issues in Md.; mem. Gov.'s commns. black and minority health, black males, chmn. health subcom.; mem. interagy. Coordinating coun. for infants and toddlers; mem. exec. com. Nat. Assn. Jewish Legislators, 1997—; mem. state adv. com. Office for Children, Youth and Families; mem. state adv. coun. organ and tissue donation awareness, 1998—; pres. Women Legislators of Md., 1986-88, v.p., 1985; lectr., spkr., guest panelist in field. Bd. dirs. Nat. Coun. Jewish Women, Safety First, 1990, Jewish Family Svcs., 1995—, Progress Unlimited, Inc., Juvenile Diabetes Assn. (hon.); adv. to bd. dirs. United Way Cmty. Partnership Balt.; adv. bd. Second Step, Inc., Md. Organ procurement Ctr., Inc.; bd. trustees Transplant Resource Ctr. Md., Inc., 1997—, Group for Independent Learning Disabled; grad. adv. coun. Notre Dame Coll.; mem. com. adolescent drug and alcohol abuse Md. Bar Assn., Environ. Matters Com.; faculty assoc. U. Md. Sch. Nursing, 1998—. Recipient Murry Guggenheim award, 1961, Bramson award Women's American ORT, 1981, Legis. award Mental Health Assn., 1983, Legislator of Yr. award Md. Nurse's Assn., 1984, Human Svc. award Constant Care Med. Ctr. 1984, Outstanding Contbns. to Edn. award Tchr.'s Assn. Balt. County, 1984, Outstanding Commitment and Dedication to Treatment of Alcoholic award Pilot House, 1984, Dedication and Commitment to Health and Environ. award Ctrl. Md. Health Sys. Agy., Edith Rosen Strauss award, 1987, Outstanding Svc. award Md. Psych. Assn., 1987, Pres.' award Md. Assn. Non-Profit Homes for Aging, 1987, Humanitarian award, Liberty Rd. Cmty. Coun., 1987, Leadership Laurel award Safety 1st Club Md., 1987, Outstanding Legis. Leadership award On Our Own Md., 1988, Outstanding Support and Devel. Rehab. Programs award Johns Hopkins Dept. Rehab., Md. Health Care Found., 1988, Legis. Honor Roll award Md. Assn. Psychosocial Svcs., 1988, Spl. award leadership Pikesville revitalization Pikesville Cmty. Growth Corp., 1988, Pres.' award Md. Assn. Home Care, 1988, Verda Welcome award for outstanding polit. achievements and pub. svc., 1989, Cmty. Svc. award Balt. Hebrew U., 1990, Physician's Asst. Appreciation award, 1991, Leadership and Commitment award Walbrook H.S. Primary Health Care Ctr., 1991, Betty Tyler Pub. Affairs award Planned Parenthood, 1992, 93, Excellence in Social Work Legislation award Md. Social Work Coalition, 1993, award Chesapeake Bay Found. Environ. Leadership, 1994, Policy Maker Leadership award Adv. for Youth, 1995, Ann. Leadership award Md. State Sch. Health Coun., 1996, Legis. award Legis. and Pub. Info. Com. Balt. County Commn. Disabilities, 1997, Legis. award Md. Retired Tchrs., 1997, award Md./D.C. Soc. Respiratory Care, 1997, Dedication and Support award Nat. Kidney Found. Md., 1998, Legis. award Md. Assn. Counseling and Devel., 1998, Sch. Health Advocacy award Sch. Nurse Inst., 2000, Outstanding Svc. award Md. Psychol. Assn., 2000, Pres.'s award Md. Nat. Capitol Home Care Assn., 2000, Presdl. award of Recognition Md. Occupl. Therapy Assn., 2001, Legis. of Yr. award, Mental Health Assn. Md., 2001, Pacesetter award Nat. Women Legis.'s Lobby, 2001, Distin. Leadership award Abilities Network and Epilepsy Found. of Chesapeake Region, 2002; named Woman of Yr., Women Realtors Anne Arundel County, 1988, Pikesville C. of C., 1989, Sen. of Yr., Md. Assn. Psychiat. Support Svcs., 1993, Oustanding Legislator, Md. Speech, Lang., Hearing Assn., 1993, Most Disting. Alumnus, Mt. Sinai Hosp. Sch. Nursing Alumnae Assn., 1998, Md.'s Top 100 Women, Daily Record, 1999, 2001, 03, Legislator of Yr. AHA, 1999, Chesapeake Bay Bound., 2004. Mem. Am. Assn. Marriage and Family Therapy (Mid Atlantic Divsn., hon., hon. licensure), B'nai Brith Women, Hadassah, Na'Amat, Orgn. for Rehab. Tng. (Bramson award 1981), Chi Eta Phi (hon.). Office: Miller Senate Bldg Annapolis MD 21401-1991

HOLLINGHEAD, JUANITA GREEN, elementary school educator; b. Leakesville, Miss., Sept. 4, 1963; d. Jacob F. Jr. Ruth Illadean (Herring) Green; m. William A. Hollinghead, Aug. 15, 1982; children: Andrew Jacob, Paige Janean. BS, U. So. Miss., 1984; MS in Elem. Edn., William Carey Coll., Hattiesburg, Miss., 1990; student, Jones County Jr. Coll., Ellisville, Miss., 1981. Ednl. adminstrn. endorsement Miss., 1996. 2nd grade tchr. Cen. Elementary Sch., Lucedale, Miss.; 4th grade tchr. Leakesville (Miss.) Elementary Sch.; 6th grade tchr. Leaksville Jr. HS. Alderman Town of Leakesville, 1997—2005. Mem. NEA, Miss. Assn. Educators, Miss. Assn. Math. Tchrs., Nat. Coun. Tchrs. Math., Phi Theta Kappa, Kappa Delta Pi. Home: 1416 Alabama St Leakesville MS 39451-5587

HOLLINGS, FRITZ (ERNEST FREDERICK HOLLINGS), former senator; b. Charleston, SC, Jan. 1, 1922; s. Adolph G. and Wilhelmine D. (Meyer) H.; m. Rita Louise Liddy, Aug. 21, 1971; children by previous marriage— Michael Milhous, Helen Hayne, Patricia Salley, Ernest Frederick III. BA, The Citadel, 1942, LL.D. (hon.), 1960; LL.B., U. S.C., 1947, LLD (hon.), 1980. Bar: S.C. 1947, U.S. Supreme Ct. 1952, U.S. Ct. Appeals (D.C.) 1989. Mem. S.C. Ho. of Reps., 1948-54, speaker pro tem, 1951-54; lt. gov. State of S.C., 1955-59, gov., 1959-63; pvt. practice Charleston, SC, 1963-66; U.S. senator from S.C., 1966—2005; chmn. Senate commerce, sci. and transp. com., 1987—95, 2001—03; sr. mem. Senate appropriations com., 1971—2005; chmn. commerce, justice, state, judiciary and related agencies subcoms.; sr. mem. Senate com. on the budget, 1974—2005; chmn. Senate com. on the budget, 1980—81. Mem. Hoover Commn. on Intelligence Activities, 1954—55, Pres.'s Adv. Commn. on Intergovtl. Rels., 1959—63, Pres.'s Adv. Commn. on Federalism, 1981; chmn. Legis. Coun., 1955—59, Regional Adv. Coun. on Nuclear Energy; mem. adv. com. Nat. River and Harbors Congress; del. Law of Sea Conf.; mem. Senate Dem. Policy Com., Senate Dem. Tech. and omms. om. Author: The Case Against Hunger: A Demand for a National Policy, 1970. Served to capt. U.S. Army, 1942-45, ETO, NATOUSA. Recipient Founders award S.C. Com. for Tech. Edn., 1963, Nat. Vet. award, 1968, Friend of Edn. award S.C. Edn. Assn., 1974, Neptune award Am. Oceanic Orgn., 1978, James Woodruff award Assn. U.S. Army, 1980, Nat. Future award Am. Space Found., 1984, S.C. Disting. Pub. Svc. award, 1983, Consumer Fedn. of Am. Disting. Pub. Svc. award 1985, Govt. Social Responsibility award Martin Luther King Jr. Ctr., 1986, Golden Bulldog award Watchdogs of the Treasury, 1988, Outstanding Leadership award Nat. Assn. Black-owned Broadcasters, 1988, Disting. Health Svcs. award, 1988, The Sound Dollar award, 1988-90, Hall of Leaders award Nat. Travel Industry, 1990, Disting. Svc. award Nat. Assn. Ind. Colls. and U., 1990, Nat. Security Indsl. Assn., 1990, Congl. award Nat. Coalition for Cancer Rsch., 1992, Sgt. Jasper Freedom award S.C. C. of C., 1992, No. 1 Govtl. Friend of Tourism, SE Tourism Soc., 1993, Spl. Health Recognition award N.H. Assn. Cmty. Health Ctrs., 1994; named one of Ten Outstanding Young Men U.S. Jr. C. of C., 1954, and numerous other awards. Mem. ABA, Charleston County Bar Assn., S.C. Bar Assn., Assn. Citadel Men, Hibernian Soc., Am. Legion, Univ. S.C. Law Fedn., St. Andrews Soc. Lodges: Elks, Masons. Democrat. Lutheran.

HOLLINGSWORTH, ABNER THOMAS, finance educator; b. Wilmington, Del., Mar. 19, 1939; s. Abner and Dorothy Elizabeth (Dunn) H.; m. Jacqueline Manning, Mar. 19, 1966; 1 child, Alexander Thomas. BSin BA, U. Del., Newark, 1964; MBA, Mich. State U., 1966, PhD, 1969. Asst. prof. mgmt. So. Ill. U., Carbondale, 1969-71, Fla. Atlantic U., 1971-73; assoc. prof. mgmt. U. S.C., 1973-77, prof. mgmt., 1977-80, U. Petroleum and Minerals, Dhahran, Saudi Arabia, 1980-82; prof. mgmt., chmn. mgmt. dept. U. N.C., Asheville, 1983-87; dean Sch. Bus. Adminstrn. Monmouth Coll., 1987-88, prof. mgmt., 1988; prof. mgmt. and dir. Bus. Rsch. Inst. St. John's U., 1988-90; prof. mgmt. Fla. Inst. Tech., Melbourne, 1990—, dean Coll. Bus., 1990—2005. Cons. in field; conductor numerous tng. programs. Author: (with Richard Hodgetts) Readings in Basic Management, 1975, (with H. hand) A Practical Approach to the Management of Small Business, 1979, Readings in Small business Management, 1979, Supervisory Behavior, 1974, (with R. Howell and R. Hodgetts) A Reader, Study Guide in Basic Management, 1979, others; assoc. editor Jur. Bus. Rsch., 1984-87; editorial bd. Jour. Mgmt., 1977-79, book reviewer for Acad. Press, Bus. Pubs., Inc., Wiley/Hamilton, many others; contbr. articles to profl. jours. Bd. dirs. Holmes Regional Med. Ctr. & Health First, Inc., Melbourne, Jr. Achievement of Ea. Ctrl. Fla., United Way. Rsch. grantee, Inst. Pub. Utilities, Mich. State U., 1967, Fla. Atlantic U., 1972, U. S.C., 1975, Social Security Adminstrn., 1977, others. Avocations: scuba diving, sailing, reading. Office: Fla Inst Tech Coll Bus 150 W University Blvd Melbourne FL 32901-6982 Office Phone: 321-674-7327. Business E-Mail: aholling@fit.edu.

HOLLINGSWORTH, BOBBY G., career officer; BS in Elec. Engring., La. State Univ. Flight line officer Marine Attack Squadron 331, Beaufort, S.C.; embarkation officer Marine Attack Squadron 223, Chu Lai, South Vietnam; landing signal officer Marine Aircraft Group 12, Chu Lai, South Vietnam; asst. divsn. air officer 3rd Marine Divsn., Phu Bai, South Vietnam; combat tactics instr. Marine Training Squadron 103, Yuma, Ariz.; asst. ops. officer Marine Fighter Squadron 112, Dallas; exec. officer Marine Aircraft Group 42, Alameda, Calif.; commander Marine Attack Squadron 133, Alameda, Calif.; asst. chief of staff 4th Marine Aircraft Wing, New Orleans; chief of staff II Marine Expeditionary Brigade, Camp Lejeune, N.C.; commanding gen. Marine Corps Res. Support Command, Kans. City, Mo., Fourth Force Svc. Support Group, New Orleans; deputy commander Jt. Task Force, Saudi Arabia; vice commander Marine Forces Pacific, Camp Smith, Hawaii; exec. dir. Nat. Com. Employer Support of Guard and Res., 1999—. Advisor to Asst. Sec. Def. for Res. Affairs U.S. Armed Forces. Decorated Legion of Merit, Distinguished Flying Cross, Def. Meritorious Svc. medal, Air Medal with numeral 5, Combat Action Ribbon, Presdl. Unit Citation with Bronze Star, Meritorious Unit Commendation, Select Marine Corps. Res. medal with Silver Star, Nat. Def. Medal with Bronze star, Armed Forces Expiditionary medal, Vietnam Svc. medal with two Bronze Stars, Navy and Marine Corps Overseas Svc. Ribbon with two Bronze Stars, Armed Forces Res. medal with hourglass Device, Rep. of Vietnam Unit Citation, Rep. Vietnam Campaing medal with 1960 Deivce. Home: 12404 Grantley Ct Woodbridge VA 22192-2367

HOLLINGSWORTH, BRENDA JACKSON, employment consultant; b. Roxboro, N.C., Aug. 12, 1958; d. John Vanstory and Effie Clayton Jackson; children: Brandy Effie, William (Denzel). BS, St. Augustine's Coll., Raleigh, N.C., 1981. Income maintenance caseworker Social Svcs., Durham, N.C., 1987-89, fraud investigator Roxboro, 1990-92; youth counselor Job Tng. Partnership Act, Roxboro, 1992-94; employment cons. Employment Security Commn., Roxboro, 1997—. Avocations: volleyball, poetry, aerobics. Home: 95 Gatesworth Rd Roxboro NC 27573

HOLLINGSWORTH, DIANE LUCILE, language educator; b. Memphis, Mar. 5, 1952; d. Claude Eston and Claudia Lucile (Waren) H. BA, U. Pitts., 1974, MA, 1976; student, U. Bonn, W. Germany, 1975, U. Munich, 1979. ESL, German Instr. Benedict-Schule, Cologne, Germany, 1980-83, Frontistirio Skouras, Xanthi, Greece, 1983-84, Frontistirio Tsoi, Athens, Greece, 1984-88, Gaston Coll., Dallas, N.C., 1989-93; German instr. Belmont Abbey Coll., Belmont, NC, 1990—95; transl. Inst. Sci. Info., Phila., 1996—2005. Author: Sprechen Sie Deutsch? A First Course in German, 1990; contbr. articles to profl. jours. Avocations: jazz piano, radio production, amateur theater. Home: 4716 Hazel Ave Philadelphia PA 19143-2023 E-mail: dochdoch42@yahoo.com.

HOLLINGSWORTH, DONALD KEITH, JR., mechanical engineer, educator; b. Clinton, N.C., Jan. 24, 1958; s. Donald Keith and Doris Elaine Hollingsworth; m. Patricia Ann Tomanek, Sept. 2, 1995. BSME, NC State U., 1980, MSME, 1982; PhD in Mech. Engring., Stanford U., 1989. Registered profl. engr., Tex. Project engr., project mgr. N.C. Alternative Energy Corp., Research Triangle Park, 1982—84; asst. prof. mech. engring. U. Houston, 1989—95, assoc. prof., 1995—. Recipient Faculty Achievement award, El Paso Energy Corp. Found., 2001. Mem.: ASME (Herbert Allen award for outstanding tech. achievement South Tex. sect. 1993, Warren M. Rohsenow prize gas turbine and heat transfer divsns. 1999). Office: U Houston Engring Bldg One Houston TX 77204-4006 Office Phone: 713-743-4534. Business E-Mail: hollingsworth@uh.edu.

HOLLINGSWORTH, JACK WARING, mathematics professor; b. South Haven, Kans., Mar. 3, 1924; s. Virgil Braxton and Ethel (Waring) H.; m. Nancy Lee Harris, Sept. 14, 1950; children: Joel, Priscilla, Seth (dec.). BS in Engring. Physics, U. Kans., 1948, BA, 1949; MS, U. Wis., 1951, PhD, 1954. Teaching asst. U. Kans., 1947-49, U. Wis., 1949-50, computing asst., 1950-54; gen. sci. aide U.S. Naval Ordnance Lab., 1950; mathematician Gen. Electric Co., 1954-57; mem. faculty Rensselaer Poly. Inst., 1957-79, prof. math., 1961-79, supr. computer lab., 1957-70, chmn. interdisciplinary com. computer sci., 1967-73; prof. Sch. Computer Sci. and Tech./Rochester Inst. Tech., NY, 1979-86, dir., 1980-82; prof. math. Rochester Inst. Tech., 1986-96, prof. emeritus, 1996—. Mem. Bd. Coop. Ednl. Services, Saratoga-Warren Counties, 1970-79 Served to 1st lt. USAAF, 1943-45. Decorated D.F.C., Air medal with 4 oak leaf clusters, Purple Heart; Jack Hollingsworth Prize in Computer Sci. established in his honor Rennselaer Poly. Inst. Mem. Assn. Computing Machinery (treas. spl. interest group of univ. computing centers 1964-70), Am. Math. Soc., Soc. Indsl. and Applied Math., Math. Assn. Am., Sigma Xi, Tau Beta Pi, Omicron Delta Kappa, Kappa Eta Kappa. Mem. Reformed Ch. (elder). Home and Office: 55 Crestview Dr Pittsford NY 14534-2242

HOLLINGSWORTH, JOE GREGORY, lawyer; b. Indpls., Mar. 3, 1949; s. Don Roy and Marilyn Ann (Gregory) H.; m. Nancy Elaine Bartlett, Jan. 21, 1971; children: Gregory Bartlett, Grant Wagner, Brooke Ann. BA, De Pauw U., 1971; JD, Georgetown U., 1974. Bar: DC, 1975, DC Ct. of Appeals, 1975, US Ct. of Appeals Ninth Circuit, 1978, Fed. Circuit, 1982, Eleventh Circuit, 1985, Third Circuit, 1987, First Circuit, 1988, Second Circuit, 1989, Fourth Circuit, 1991, Sixth Circuit, 1993, Tenth Circuit, 1995, Seventh Circuit, 2001, Eighth Circuit, 2002. From assoc. to ptnr. McKenna, Conner & Cuneo, Washington, 1974-82; ptnr. Spriggs & Hollingsworth, Washington, 1982—. Mem. Product Liability Advisory Council, 2004—; mem. constitutional & adminstrv. law com. U.S. Chamber of Commerce Nat. Litigation Ctr. Mem.: Kenwood Country Club (Bethesda, Md.), Fed. City Club (Washington), Met. Club. Presbyterian. Avocations: tennis, running, golf, hunting, mountain climbing. Office: Spriggs & Hollingsworth 1350 I St NW Washington DC 20005 Office Phone: 202-898-5800. Office Fax: 202-682-1639. Business E-Mail: jhollingsworth@spriggs.com.

HOLLINGSWORTH, JOHN ALEXANDER, retired science and mathematics educator, writer, consultant; b. Owego, N.Y., Sept. 25, 1925; s. John Alexander Sr. and Florence Eve (Haley) W.; m. Winifred Louise Stoelting Hollingsworth. BS in Agr., N.C. A&T State U., 1950, MS in Adult Edn., 1985; MS in Biology, N.C. Ctrl. U., 1960; postgrad., Cornell U., 1962-63. Staff sgt. U.S. Army, 1943-46, advanced through grades to capt., 1949-57; tchr. sci. Fayetteville (N.C.) City Schs., 1959-73, coord. sci., 1968-83, coord. math., 1973-83; cons., author, artist Cherokee Village, Ark., 1985—. Dir. Emergency Sch. Assistance Act Pilot Project, Fayetteville, 1972-80; grants writer Title I and Emergency Sch. Assistance Act Pilot Project, Fayetteville, 1972-80. Co-author: (booklet) The Improvement of High School Research Through the Research Participation Program, 1968. Active Ecology Action/Common Ground, Willits, Calif.; active, charter mem. Nat. Mus. of the Am. Indian. Mem. NEA (life), Nat. Ret. Tchrs. Assn., N.C. Sci. Tchrs. Assn. (state pres. 1971-73), N.C. Assn. Educators (pres. Fayetteville unit 1970-71), N.C. Ret. Sch. Pers., N.C. Ret. Govtl. Employees Assn., Inst. Noetic Scis., Nat. Assn. Black Vets. (life). Avocations: watercolor painting, genealogy, gardening. Home: 61 Otalco Dr Cherokee Village AR 72529

HOLLINGSWORTH, JOHN MARK, lawyer; b. Dallas, May 5, 1951; BA, Rhodes Coll., 1973; JD, So. Meth. U., 1977. Bar: Tex. 1976. Sr. counsel John E. Mitchell Co., Dallas, 1978-83; corp. counsel Keycon Industries, Inc., Dallas, 1983-85; asst. sec., gen. counsel Valhi, Inc., Dallas, 1985—97, v.p., gen. counsel, 1997—. Office: Valhi Inc Three Lincoln Ctr 5430 LBJ Fwy Ste 1700 Dallas TX 75240-2697

HOLLINGSWORTH, MARTHA SCHMIDT, lawyer; b. Indpls., Oct. 6, 1944; s. Paul W. and Clara M. Schmidt. AB, Ind. U., 1966, JD magna cum laude, 1972. Bar: Ind. 1972, Fla. 1973, U.S. Supreme Ct. 1979, U.S. Dist. Ct. (no. and so. dists.) Ind. 1972, U.S. Dist. Ct. (so. dist.) Fla. 1973. Ptnr. Bingham, McHale LLP, Indpls., 1974—. Recipient Maynard K. Hine award Ind. U. Alumni Assn., 1991, Disting. Alumni Svc. award Ind. U.-Indpls. Sch. Law, 1992, award of recognition Ins. Inst. Ind., 1997; diplomat Ind. Def. Trial Counsel, 1995. Mem. Ind. Def. Laywers Assn. (bd. dirs. 1988—, Ind. Def. Lawyer of Yr. 1997), Indpls. Bar Assn. (bd. dirs., sec., v.p., 1985-86, 87), Underground Storage Tank Fin. Assn. (bd. dirs. 1988—, chair 1992-96), Ind. U. Sch. of Law Alumni Assn. (bd. dirs., pres. 1987-88). Baptist. Office: Bingham McHale LLP 2700 Market Tower 10 W Market St Ste 2700 Indianapolis IN 46204-4900

HOLLINGSWORTH, SAMUEL HAWKINS, JR., bassist; b. Birmingham, Ala., June 29, 1922; s. Samuel Hawkins and Bennie Louise (Brown) H.; m. Patricia Ann Patton, Apr. 1, 1957 (div. 1967); children: Priscilla P., Samuel Hawkins III; m. Elizabeth Mary Malezi, Dec. 31, 1974. Student, Juilliard Sch. Music, N.Y.C., 1940-42, George Peabody Coll. Tchrs., Nashville, 1953-54. Prin. bassist Nashville Symphony, 1946-65, Chamber Symphony of Phila., 1966-68, Dallas Symphony, 1968-70, Pitts. Symphony, 1970-92, prin. emeritus, 1992-95; retired, 1995. Mem. governing bd. dirs. Nashville Symphony Orch., 1960-63; chmn. Dallas Symphony Orth Players, 1969-70. Home: 1111 Pinewood Dr Pittsburgh PA 15243-1809

HOLLINGTON, RICHARD RINGS, JR., lawyer; b. Findlay, Ohio, Nov. 12, 1932; s. Richard Rings and Annett (Kirk) H.; m. Sally Stecher, Apr. 4, 1959; children: Florence A., Julie A., Richard R. III. Peter S. BA, Williams Coll., 1954; JD, Harvard U., 1957. Bar: Ohio 1957. Ptnr. Marshman, Hornbeck & Hollington, Cleve., 1958-67, McDonald, Hopkins, Hardy & Hollington, Cleve., 1967-69; law dir. City of Cleve., 1971-72; sr. ptnr. Baker & Hostetler, Cleve., 1969-71, 73—. Vice chair Sky Fin. Group, 1998-2004, lead dir., 1999-2003; dir. The Ohio Bank, 1958-2001; mem. adv. com. on banking policy FDIC, 2002-; mem. Ohio Banking Commn., 2001—, fin. dir. Hunting Valley, 2004-. Mem. Ohio Gen. Assembly, 1967-70, Cuyahoga County Rep. Ctrl. Com., 1962-66; exec. com. Ohio Rep. Fin. Com., 1971-98, Cuyahoga County Rep. Orgn., 1968-98, Geauga County Rep. Orgn., 1998—; trustee Cleve. State U., 1970-73, Greater Cleve. Hosp. Assn., 1976-82, Cleve. Mus. Natural History, 1969-81, Cleve. Zool. Soc., 1970-99, N. E. Ohio Regional Sewer Dist., 1972-73, Cuyahoga County Hosp. Found., 1968-73, Cleve. 500 Found., 1990-95, U. Findlay, 1991—; mem. bds. commrs. grievance and discipline Ohio Supreme Ct., 1993-95, mem. unauthorized practice of law com., 2005—. Mem. ABA, Ohio Bar Assn., Greater Cleve. Bar Assn., Sixth Cir. Jud. Conf. (life), Eighth Dist. Ohio Jud. Conf. (life), Ct. Nisi Prius, Union Club (Cleve.), The Country Club (Pepper Pike), Pepper Pike Club, Roaring Gap (N.C.) Club, Rolling Rock (Pa.) Club. Home: 13792 County Line Rd Chagrin Falls OH 44022-4008 Office: Baker & Hostetler 3200 National City Ctr 1900 E 9th St Ste 3200 Cleveland OH 44114-3475 Office Phone: 216-861-7623.

HOLLINRAKE, JOHN D., JR., lawyer; b. 1957; BSBA with high distinction, Univ. Ariz., 1980; JD magna cum laude, Univ. Houston, 1987. CPA 1982; bar: Wash. 1987. Ptnr., co-chair tax group Dorsey & Whitney LLP, Seattle. Named a Leading US West Coast Lawyer, Euromoney Legal Group, Super Lawyer, Wash. Law & Politics. Mem.: Seattle Internat. Tax Roundtable (chmn. 1992—93), Seattle Tax Group, Canadian Tax Found., Wash. State Bar Assn., Phi Kappa Phi, Beta Gamma Sigma, Beta Alpha Psi. Office: Dorsey & Whitney LLP Ste 3400 US Bank Ctr 1420 Fifth Ave Seattle WA 98101-4010 Office Phone: 206-903-8812. Office Fax: 206-903-8820. Business E-Mail: hollinrake.john@dorsey.com.

HOLLINS, MITCHELL LESLIE, lawyer; b. N.Y.C., Mar. 11, 1947; s. Milton and Alma (Bell) H.; m. Nancy Kirchheimer, Mar. 27, 1977 (div. 1999); m. Jan C. Philipsborn, Oct. 24, 1999; children: Herbert K. II, Dorothy Ann, Betsy Ann Mizell. BA, Case Western Res. U., 1967; JD, NYU, 1971. Bar: Ill. 1971, U.S. Dist. Ct. (no. dist.) Ill. 1971. Editor NYU Jour. Internat. Law and Politics, 1970—71; assoc. Sonnenschein Nath & Rosenthal, Chgo., 1971—78, ptnr., 1978—2000, Piper Rudnick, Chgo., 2000—02; COO, gen. counsel Meadow Ptnrs. LLC, Chgo., 2003—04; v.p., chief legal officer, sec. Oak Brook Bank, Ill., 2004—. Asst. sec., asst. gen. counsel Jr. Achievement Chgo., 1980-2004, dir. 1980—; bd. dirs. Young Men's Jewish Coun., 1973-75; bd. dirs. young people's divsn. Jewish United Fund Met. Chgo., 1972-76; bd. dirs. Med. Rsch. Inst. Coun., mem. exec. com., 1979-92, sec., 1981-82, gen. counsel, 1983-86, vice chmn., 1987-92, chmn. jr. bd., 1978-79. Mem. ABA, Lake Shore Country Club (mem. bd. govs. 1984-92, sec. 1985-92), Lawyers Club. Republican. Home: 265 Wentworth Ave Glencoe IL 60022-1931 Office: Oak Brook Bank 1400 16th St Oak Brook IL 60523 Office Phone: 630-990-2265 ext. 252.

HOLLINSHEAD, ARIEL CAHILL, oncologist, educator; b. Allentown, Pa., Aug. 24, 1929; d. Earl Darnell and Gertrude Loretta (Cahill) H.; m. Montgomery K. Hyun, June 12, 1957; children: William C., Christopher C. Student, Swarthmore Coll., 1947-48; AB, Ohio U., 1951, DSc (hon.), 1977; MA, George Washington U., 1955, PhD, 1957, MD, 1977. Asst. prof., fellow in virology Baylor U. Med. Ctr., 1958-59; asst. prof. pharmacology George Washington Med. Ctr., 1959-61, asst. prof. medicine, 1961-64, assoc. prof. medicine, head lab. virus and cancer rsch., 1964-73, prof., dir. lab. virus and cancer rsch., 1974-89; on sabbatical leave 1990, prof. medicine emeritus, 1991—; rschr. HI Virus and Cancer Rsch., 1991—2002. Bd. dirs. Neogenix; clin. rschr. trials in oncology and virology; cons. to biotech. cos.; panelist FDA and NIH. Contbr. over 270 articles on active immunotherapy and immunochemotherapy of cancer and virus diseases to sci. jours. Bd. dirs. Nat. Women's Econ. Alliance, Ohio U., Med. Coll. Pa., 1980-2003, Women's Inst., 1995-97. Named Bicentennial Med. Woman of Yr., Joint Bd. Am. Med. Colls., 1976, one of Outstanding Woman of Am., 1987, Outstanding Alumnus of Yr., Ohio U., 1990; recipient Cert. Merit Med. Coll. Pa., 1975-76, Marion Spencer Fay Med. Woman of Year award Med. Coll. Pa.; decorated Star of Europe, 1980. Fellow AAAS (med. sci. com. 1993-96, 99—), Washington Acad. Sci. N.Y. Acad. Scis.; mem. Grad. Women in Sci. (nat. pres. 1985-86, bd. dirs. 1986-92, nat. liaison to Washington, 1992—), Internat. Soc. Preventive Oncology, Nat. Soc. Exptl. Biology and Medicine (Disting. Scientist award 1985, Disting. Scientist emeritus award for Outstanding Career in Tchg. and Rsch. in Medicine 1996, past pres. Greater Washington chpt.), Am. Soc. Microbiology, Am. Assn. Cancer Research, Am. Assn. Immunologists, Women in Cancer Rsch., Vet. Females Am., Clin. Immunology Soc., Internat. Soc. Antiviral Research, Am. Soc. Clin. Oncology, Internat. Assn. Study Lung Cancer, Internat. Union Against Cancer, Am. Med. Writers Assn., Soc. of the Emeriti, Kenwood Country Club, Blue Ridge Mountain Country Club, Twin Isles Country Club, Washington Forum (pres. 1987, 91), Phi Beta Kappa (alumnus 1990). Achievements include being first to purify, develop and test cancer gene products, including peptides and to study activities; first to invent field called proteomics; peptides were studied and identified for the ability to induce long-lasting cell-mediated immunity; developed proteomics technology and pioneered clinical testing and monitoring epitope activity during seventeen clinical trials; patentee in field. Home: 23465 Harborview Rd #622 Punta Gorda FL 33980-2162 *The Latin phrase "Carpe diem", meaning seize the day, or, guard the moment: my first discovery for effective viral disease treatment was the use of purine, pyrimidine and sulfur-containing analogues, one of which was used to attenuate virulent polioviruses; another discovery was the first non virion antigen to block virus-induced animal tumors; my first discovery for effective cancer immunotherapy was the separation and identification of active peptides from cell membranes and the first proof of their efficacy in tumor prevention in animals and in man. Phase I, II or III clinical trials were conducted with individual tumor-related peptides selected for nineteen forms of human cancer. I discovered that little pieces of these active proteins (called epitopes) not only were useful for monitoring tumor progression U.S. patent received but were the oncogene products for even better polyvalent therapies in the future. With Dr. T.H.M. Stewart, established the first identification of induced dormancy in human lung cancer patients in USA and Canada receiving our vaccines and, greater than 12 year survival free of lung cancer.*

HOLLINSHEAD, EARL DARNELL, JR., lawyer; b. Pitts., Aug. 1, 1927; s. Earl Darnell and Gertrude (Cahill) H.; m. Sylvia Antion, June 29, 1957; children: Barbara, Kim, Earl III, Susan. AB, Ohio U., 1948; LLB, U. Pitts., 1951. Bar: Pa. 1952, U.S. Ct. Mil. Appeals 1954, U.S. Dist. Ct. (we. dist.) Pa. 1955, U.S. Supreme Ct. 1956, U.S. Ct. Appeals (3d cir.) 1959, U.S. Dist. Ct. (ea. dist.) Ohio 1978. Sole practice, Pitts., 1955-70; ptnr. Hollinshead and Mendelson, Pitts., 1970-89, Hollinshead, Mendelson, Bresnahan & Nixon, P.C., Pitts., 1990-97; sole practitioner Pitts., 1997—. Mem. Pitts. Estate Planning Coun. Contbr. articles to profl. jours. Served to lt. USNR, 1951-55. Fellow Pa. Bar Found. (life); mem. Pa. Bar Assn. (chmn. real property divsn. 1983-85, real property, probate and trust sects. 1985-86), Allegheny County Bar Assn. (chmn. real property sect. 1975-76), Pa. Bar Inst. (lectr., planner, bd. dirs. 1988-94), Am. Coll. Real Estate Lawyers. Home: 2535 Windgate Rd Bethel Park PA 15102-2730 Office: Regional Enterprise Tower 425 Sixth Ave Ste 2490 Pittsburgh PA 15219-1819

HOLLIS, CHARLES EUGENE, JR., finance company executive; b. Daytona Beach, Fla., Sept. 14, 1948; s. Charles Eugene and Betty Lou (Beech) H.; m. Carol Repass, Mar. 20, 1971 (div. Nov. 1993); children: Stephanie Dyane, Charles Preston, Robin Jene. AA, Dayton Beach Jr. Coll., 1968; BA, U. South Fla., 1972. CPA Fla. Asst. Deloitte Haskins & Sells, Tampa, Fla., 1972—73, sr. asst., 1973—75, sr., 1975—78, mgr., 1978—82; audit mgr. Jack Eckerd Corp., Clearwater, Fla., 1982—85; v.p. fin., contr. Freedom Savs. and Loan Assn., Tampa, 1985—87, sr. v.p., CFO, treas., 1987—88, exec. v.p., 1988—89, CenTrust Fed., Miami, Fla., 1990; supervisory fin. instn. specialist Resolution Trust Corp., Atlanta, 1990—95; exec. v.p. Beech Mgmt. Group, Inc., 1996—2000; portfolio mgr. GMAC Comml. Mortgage Corp., 2000—. Chmn. fin. and taxation com. Fla. League Cities, Tallahassee, 1979—81; mem. fin. com. Nat. League Cities, Washington, 1980—86; code enforcement bd. City of Temple Terrace, 1986—91; trustee Univ. Community Hosp., 1987—91; charter mem., treas. Northeast Sertoma, 1989—90; City councilman City of Temple Terrace, Fla., 1976—86, vice mayor, 1981—82; treas. Christ Our Redeemer Luth. Ch., 1984—86, pres., 1987—88; treas. Fla. Synod-Evangelical Luth. Ch. in Am., 1988—92. Recipient Disting. Service award, U. South Fla. Coll. Bus., 1972, Outstanding Alumnus award, Beta Alpha Psi, 1983. Mem.: Tampa C. of C. (Leadership Tampa 1987—88), Fin. Mgrs. Soc., Fla. Soc. CPAs, Am. Inst. CPAs, Beta Alpha Psi. Republican. Home and Office: 985 Gardendale Dr Columbia SC 29210-4906 Office Phone: 404-654-2366. Business E-Mail: charles_hollis@gmaccm.com.

HOLLIS, DONALD ROGER, management consultant; b. Warren, Ohio, Mar. 4, 1936; s. Louis and Lena (Succo) Hollis; m. Marilyn G. Morganti, Aug. 23, 1958; children: Roger, Russel Kirk, Gregory, Heather. BS, Kent State U., 1959. Regional mgr. Glidden Corp., San Francisco, 1959-65, dir. mgmt. info. svcs. Cleve., 1965-68; dir. mgmt. info. services SCM Corp., N.Y.C., 1968-71; v.p. Chase Manhattan Bank, N.Y.C., 1971-81; sr. v.p. First Chgo. Corp., 1981-85, exec. v.p., 1986-95, head sys., data processing, cash mgmt. and security products and quality programs, 1986-95; pres., CEO DRH Strategic Cons., Chgo., 1995—. Bd. dirs. S2 Corp., Quickstream, Wausau Fin. Sys., OptiPay; Life Trustee III Inst. Tech. Office: c/o Diamond Cluster Internat 875 N Michigan Ave Ste 2800 Chicago IL 60611 Office Phone: 312-255-6975.

HOLLIS, KATHERINE MARY, information scientist, consultant; d. Albert George and Rosalyn Mary Duren; m. David Martin Hollis, Aug. 25, 1990; children: Kent David Miller, Jason Randolph Miller; children: Brittany Frances, David Christopher. MS in Nat. Security Strategy, Nat. War College, 1999; B in Polit. Sci., U. Minn., 1983. Dir. resource mgmt. installation support modules program Program Exec. Office - STD. Mgmt. Info. Sys., Ft. Belvoir, Va., 1989—93; program mgr. electronic commerce/electronic data interchange Def. Info. Sys. Agy., Falls Chruch, Va., 1993—96, spl. asst. to the dep., pub. key infrastructure program mgmt. office, 1999—2000; dep. dir. electronic processes initiatives coun. task force Office of the Deputy Sec. of Def., Rosslyn, Va., 1996—98; deputy dir. dept. def. Y2K office Office of the Sec. of Def., Crystal City, Va., 1998—99; dir. global info. assurance solutions Electronic Data Sys., Herndon, Va., 2000—. Adv. com. Fed. Electronic Commerce Coalition, Falls Church, Va., 1999—; chair smart card integrated process team Def. Info. Sys. Agy., 1999—2000; spkr. in field. Vol. educator Prince William County Schools, Manassas, Va., 2001. Recipient Commanders award, Dept. of the Army, Dept. of Def., 1989, Federal 100 award, Federal Computer News, 1998. Avocations: archaeology, Egyptology, travel, writing. Office: Electronic Data Sys 13600 EDS Dr (A2S-D49) Herndon VA 20171

HOLLIS, MARTHA, director, educator; m. Anthony Scaggs. BA, Coll. William and Mary, 1970; MBA, George Wash. U., 1973; PhD, Ariz. State U., 1976; MS in Clin. Psychology, Capella U., 2001. Faculty dir. rsch. Capella U., Minnesota, 2000—; founding pres. SearchWrite, Ramsey. Freelance writer www.classicalgolf.com; rsch. and statis. cons. Author: High Tech Hits Home, The International Breakfast Book, Cooking With the Young and the Restless, Culinary Secrets of Great Virginia Chefs, Culinary Trends. Grantee, NSF. Mem.: Inst. for Ops. Rsch. and Mgmt. Sci., Am. Edn. Rsch. Assn., Acad. of Mgmt. Achievements include research in Fiscal Impact Budgeting systems for local governments; Business Research methodologies. Avocations: chef, midi music, master gardener, sociologist. Office: Capella University 225 So 6th St 9th Fl Minneapolis MN 55402 Office Phone: 888-CAP-ELLA. Business E-Mail: mhollis@capella.edu.

HOLLIS, REGINALD, archbishop; b. Eng., July 18, 1932; emigrated to Can., 1954; s. Jesse Farndon and Edith Ellen (Lee) H.; m. Marcia Crombie, Sept. 7, 1957; children— Martin, Hilda, Aidan. BA, Cambridge U., Eng., 1954; MA, Cambridge U., 1958; BD, McGill U., Montreal, 1956; DD (hon.), U. South, 1977, Montreal Diocesan Theol. Coll., 1975. Ordained to ministry Anglican Ch. as deacon, 1956, as priest, 1956. Chaplain Montreal Diocesan Theol. Coll.; also chaplain to Anglican students McGill U., 1956-60; asst. St. Matthias Parish, Westmount, Que., 1960-63; incumbent St. Barnabas Ch., Roxboro, Que., 1963-66, rector, 1966-71, Christ Ch., Beaurepaire, Que., 1971-74; dir. parish and diocesan services Diocese Montreal, 1974-75, bishop, 1975-90; archbishop of Montreal Met. of the Ecclesiastical Province of Can., 1989-90; asst. bishop Diocese of Ctrl. Fla., Orlando, 1990-94; episc. dir. Anglican Fellowship of Prayer, 1990-94; rector St. Paul's Ch., New Smyrna Beach, Fla., 1994-97; ret., 1997. Author: Abiding in Christ, 1987. Anglican. Home: 1175 Newport Ave Ste 303 Victoria BC Canada V8S 5E6

HOLLIS, SHEILA SLOCUM, lawyer; b. Denver, July 15, 1948; d. Theodore Doremus and Emily M. (Caplis) Slocum (dec.); m. John Hollis; 1 child, Windsong Emily Hollis. BS in Journalism with honors, BS in Gen. Studies cum laude, U. Colo., 1971; JD, U. Denver, 1973. Bar: Colo. 1974, D.C. 1975, U.S. Supreme Ct. 1980. Trial atty. Fed. Power Commn., Washington, 1974-75; assoc. firm Wilner & Scheiner, Washington, 1975-77; dir. office enforcement Fed. Energy Regulatory Commn., Washington, 1977-80; pvt. practice, 1980—; ptnr. Vinson & Elkins, Washington, 1987-92; sr. ptnr. Metzger, Hollis, Gordon & Alprin, Washington, 1992-97; mng. ptnr. Washington office Duane Morris LLP, 1997—2004, chair Washington office, 2004—; mem. exec. com. firm ptnrs. bd. Duane Morris LLP, 2003—. Professorial lectr. in energy law George Washington U., 1980—2000; bd. dirs. U.S. Energy Assn. Co-author: Energy Decision Making, 1983, Energy Law and Policy, 1989; mem. editl. bd. Oil and Gas Reporter, Pub. Utility Fortnightly; contbr. articles to profl. publs. Established and developed enforcement program Fed. Energy Regulatory Commn.; mem. adv. bd. Pub. Utility Ctr. N.Mex. State U., 1986—94; mem. adv. bd. N.Am. Energy Stds. Bd., 1998—; pres. Women's Coun. Energy and Environment, 1997—2003; bd. dirs. Found. for Vets. Health Care., Wyo. State Soc., 2001—03, Am. Friends of Royal Soc. U. Denver scholar, 1972-73; named Woman of Yr. Women's Coun. Energy and Environment, 2003, One of 50 Key Women in Energy-Global, Commodities Now Mag., 2004. Fellow: ABA (chair coord. group energy law 1989—92, 1995—97, chair standing com. environ. law 1997—2000, mem. bd. editors ABA Jour. 2000—, chair sect. environ., energy and resources 2001—02, standing com. fed. judiciary 2002—05, mem. ho. dels. 2004—); mem.: Womens Fgn. Policy Group, Fed. Bar Assn., John Carroll Soc., Women's Bar Assn. D.C., D.C. Bar Assn., Colo. Bar Assn., Internat. Legal Edn. Ctr. (trustee), Oil and Gas Ednl. Inst., Energy Bar Assn. (pres. 1991—92), Am. Law Inst., Internat. Bar Assn., Comml. Bar of Eng. and Wales (hon.), Sir Thomas More Soc. Am. (pres. 2003—), Cosmos Club, Nat. Press Club, Dame of Malta of the Am. Assn. Roman Catholic. Office: Duane Morris LLP 1667 K St NW Ste 700 Washington DC 20006-1608 Office Phone: 202-776-7810. Business E-Mail: sshollis@duanemorris.com.

HOLLIS, SUSAN TOWER, history professor; b. Boston, Mar. 17, 1939; d. James Wilson and Dorothy Parsons (Moore) Tower; m. Allen Hollis, Nov. 10, 1962 (div. Feb. 1975); children: Deborah Durfee, Harrison. AB, Smith Coll., 1962; PhD, Harvard U., 1982. Cert. C.C. instr. history and humanities. Asst. prof. Scripps Coll., Claremont, Calif., 1988—91; prof. Coll. of Undergrad. Studies Union Inst., L.A., 1991—93; dean coll., prof. humanities Sierra Nev. Coll.-Lake Tahoe, Incline Village, Nev., 1993—95; ind. scholar, cons. Reno, 1995—96; ctr. dir., assoc. dean Ctrl. N.Y. Ctr. SUNY Empire State Coll., Syracuse, 1996—99, assoc. prof. Rochester, 1999—, coord. we. region MA in Liberal Studies program, 2000—. Convener hist. studies Empire State Coll. of SUNY, 2000—03; co-chair acad. policies and learning programs com. Empire State Coll. SUNY, 2003—04, mem. academic policies and learning program com., 2001—05. Author: The Ancient Egyptian "Tale of Two Brothers", 1990; editor: Hymns, Prayers and Songs: Anthology of Ancient Egyptian Lyrics & Poetry (by John L. Foster), 1996; co-editor: Feminist Theory and the Study of Folklore, 1993; contbr. articles to profl. jours, encys. Music vol. Open Readings, Belmont, Mass., 1982—88; vol. Sierra Club, 1988—; problem capt. Odyssey of the Mind, Nev., 1994—95, judge, 1997—98; crew chief Tahoe Rim trail, 1994—96; active Masterworks Chorale, NY, 1996—99. Mem.: N.Y. State Network for Women Leaders in Higher Edn. (bd. dirs., assoc. coord. 1999—2000, coord. 2000—03), N.Y. Acad. Scis., Egyptological Soc. N.Y., Soc. Bibl. Lit. (co-chair Egyptology and Ancient Israel group 1995—96, chair Egyptology and Ancient Israel group 1996—, convenor Ancient Near East Consortium 1998—, Outstanding Svc. in Mentoring award 2003), Soc. for Study Egyptian Antiquities, Internat. Assn. Egyptologists, Am. Rsch. Ctr. Egypt, Am. Oriental Soc., Am. Folklore Soc., Am. Assn. Higher Edn., Am. Acad. Religion, Am. Recorder Soc., Incline Village/Crystal Bay C. of C. (sec., bd. dirs. 1994—95), Ka-na-wa-ke Canoe Club (bd. dirs. 1998—2000), Adirondack Mountain Club, Appalachian Mountain Club (co-leader 1987—88). Democrat. Home: 7 New Wickham Dr Penfield NY 14526-2703 Office: Empire State Coll of SUNY 1475 Winton Rd N Rochester NY 14609-5803 Office Phone: 585-224-3246. Business E-Mail: susan.hollis@esc.edu.

HOLLIS, TIMOTHY MARTIN, bank executive; b. Marietta, Ga., Nov. 13, 1962; s. Milton Joel and Mary Sylvia (Skanner) Hollis. BSBA in Mgmt., Shorter Coll., 1986. Desk supr. front desk Wyndham Hotel Co., Atlanta, 1986-87; personal banker C&S/Sovran Corp., Atlanta, 1987-90, sr. personal banker, 1990-91; asst. br. mgr., banking officer NationsBank Ga., N.A., Atlanta, 1991-92, banking ctr. mgr., 1992-95; sales mgr. Wachovia Bank, NA (formerly First Union Nat. Bank Ga.), Atlanta, 1995—97; fin. specialist, v.p. Wachovia Diversity Coun.-Ga. Gen. Bank, 1999—2003. Treas., mktg. chair, mem. fin. com., trustee Choral Guild Atlanta, 1991; bd. dirs. Artcare, Inc., Atlanta, 1991—94; docent, vol. mem. Friends of Zoo Atlanta; mem. steering com. First Night Atlanta, 1993—99, 1994 Class Atlanta Midtown Leadership Program, Atlanta Midtown Alliance, 1992—, Human Rights Campaign Fund, 1992—, GAPAC, 1993—95, AIDS Walk Atlanta, 1995—97; mem. adv. bd. Atlanta Exec. Network, 1993—96, co-chair young profls., 1996—98; mem. adv. bd. Joining Hearts Inc., 1994—99; bd. dirs. Positive Impact, 1996—97, Pets are Lovin Support, Inc., 1997—99; conf. chair First Night Internat., 1998; bd. dirs. AIDS Treatment Initiative, 1997—99, pres., 1998—99; mem. Buckhead Young Reps., Atlanta, 1989—92. Mem.: Atlanta Track Club (vol.). Methodist. Avocations: running, singing, exercise, volunteering. Home: 28 Finch Trail NE Atlanta GA 30308-2418 Office: Wachovia Bank NA 1605 Monroe Dr NE Atlanta GA 30324-5003 Personal E-mail: timhollis@bellsouth.net.

HOLLIS-SAWYER, LISA ANN, psychologist, gerontologist, researcher; d. Dale Eugene and Patricia Ann Hollis; m. Thomas Paul Sawyer, Aug. 9, 1997; 1 child, Joshua Thomas Sawyer. PhD in Indsl. Gerontol. Psychology, U. of Akron, 1996. Assoc. prof. of psychology and gerontology, gerontology program coord. Northeastern Ill. U., Chgo., 1998—. Editor (author): (book) Intersections of aging: Readings in Social Gerontology, 2000; author: (coll. textbook and instr.'s guide) Exercises in Psychological Testing Laboratory Manual, 2002, (book chpt.) Social Inequities, Health, and Healthcare Delivery, vol. XX; contbr. articles various to profl. jours. Acad. advisor Met. Family Svcs. - Seniorcare Adv. Coun., Chgo., 2000—02. Recipient Found. Faculty Rsch. and Scholarly Project grant. Mem.: Gerontol. Soc. of Am. (assoc.), Sigma Phi Omega (life 4 Faculty Excellence awards). Avocations: travel, photography, writing children's books, volunteering, painting. Office: Northeastern Ill U Dept Psychology 5500 N Saint Louis Ave Chicago IL 60625 Office Phone: 773-442-5846. Business E-Mail: l-hollissawyer@neiu.edu.

HOLLISTER, ARTHUR CLAIR, JR., epidemiologist, consultant, retired public health service officer; b. New Orleans, May 9, 1918; s. Arthur Clair Hollister and Cora Preston Odom; m. Olivia Ewing, Aug. 2, 1942; children: Arthur III, Olivia Corinna. BS, Tulane U., 1938, MD, 1941; MPH, Johns Hopkins U., 1948. Diplomate Am. Bd. Preventive Medicine and Pub. Health. Intern So. Bapt. Hosp., New Orleans, 1941-42; pub. health med. officer Calif. State Dept. Health, Berkeley, Sacramento, 1946-48, med. epidemiologist, 1946-83; cons. Ctr. Disease Control and NIH, Atlanta, Washington, Calif., 1950-70; lectr. UCLA Sch. Pub. Health, Berkeley, 1950-65; cons. epidemiologist Contra Costa County Social Svcs., Martinez, Calif., 1992—. State epidemiologist, chair Bur. Communicable Diseases, Calif., 1950—58; various other offices, 1958—83; mem. health svcs. study sect. NIH, Bethesda, Md., 1968—73; mem. chair health com. Adv. Coun. Aging, Martinez, 1986—, chair longterm care com., 1992—; mem. workgroup Calif. Coun. Longterm Care Integration, 2001—; apptd. sr. rep. Calif. 10th congl. dist. Nat. Silver Haired Congress, 2004—. Contbr. sci. reports and articles to profl. jours. Active City of Pleasant Hill (Calif.) Commn. Aging, 1987—92; vestry, choir mem. St. Stephen's Episc. Ch., Orinda, Calif., 1954—. Capt. USAAF, 1942—46, maj. USAR, 1946—51, surgeon USPHS Res., 1954—70, med. dir. USPHS ret. Fellow: APHA (past chair epidemiology sect., governing coun.), Am. Coll. Preventive Medicine; mem.: ACLU, Health Care for All Californians, Physicians for Nat. Health Program, Calif. Physicians Alliance, Am. Epidemiol. Soc., Gray Panthers, Ret. Pub. Employees Assn., U. Calif.-Berkeley Faculty Club, Alpha Kappa Kappa, Kappa Sigma, Delta Omega. Democrat. Avocations: classical and popular piano, jazz, classic cars, real and model railroads. Home and Office: 14 Boies Ct Pleasant Hill CA 94523 Personal E-mail: magikcats@earthlink.net.

HOLLISTER, ROBINSON GILL, JR., economics professor; b. Newark, Oct. 11, 1934; s. Robinson Gill and Jean Ackerman Hollister; m. Valerie Dutton, Oct. 10, 1964; children: Arusha Alexandra, Matissa Nicole. BA, Amherst Coll., 1956; PhD, Stanford U., 1965. Asst. prof. Williams Coll., Williamstown, Mass., 1962-64; rschr. Orgn. for Econ. Cooperation and Devel., Paris, 1964-65; dir. rsch. and planning OEO, Washington, 1966-67; assoc. prof. econs. U. Wis., Madison, 1967-70; prof. econs. Swarthmore (Pa.) Coll., 1971—. Chair com. on youth employment programs NAS, Washington, 1983-85; rsch. adv. com. Pub./Pvt. Ventures, Phila., 1988—; internat. expert Prime Mins. Planning Unit, Govt. Malaysia, Kuala Lumpur, 1979-80; cons. labor markets in Near East, U.S. AID, Washington, 1992-93. Co-author: Labour Market Policy and Unemployment, 1991, Labor Markets in Near East, 1994; co-author, editor: The National Supported Work Demonstration, 1984, Youth Employment and Training Programs, 1985. Bd. dirs. Chester (Pa.) Cmty. Improvement Project, 1990-2002. Fulbright scholar U.S. Govt., London, 1962, resident scholar Rockefeller Found., Bellagio, Italy, 1992, 2005, vis. scholar Russell Sage Found., NYC, 1992-93. Mem. Am. Econ. Assn., Assn. for Pub. Policy and Mgmt., Econometrics Soc. Avocations: tennis, swimming, skiing. Home: Hollister PO Box 256 Swarthmore PA 19081-0256 Office: Swarthmore Coll Dept Econs 500 College Ave Swarthmore PA 19081 E-mail: rhollis1@swarthmore.edu.

HOLLISTER, WINSTON NED, pathologist; b. Milw., Mar. 23, 1942; s. Harold Arthur and Jeannette Clara (Gastrav) H.; m. Carol Jean Potter, Dec. 7, 1963 (div. May 1978); children: Timothy Carl, David Andrew; m. Margaret Ravenel Papen, Oct. 29, 1988; children: Charles Davis, Margaret Ravenel. BS in Physics, U. Wis., 1964; MD, Med. Coll. Wis., 1971. Diplomate Am. Bd. Internal Medicine, Am. Bd. Pathology. Staff pathologist St. Joseph's Hosp., Milw., 1976—; pres., CEO Franciscan Shared Lab, Wauwatosa, Wis., 1988-90; med. dir., chmn. bd. dirs. Med. Sci. Labs., Wauwatosa, 1989—2003. Cons. in field. Contbr. articles to profl. jours. Vestry mem. St. Paul's Episcopal Ch., Milw., 1978-83. Lt. USN, 1964-67. Recipient Houghton & Houghton award Med. Soc. Wis., 1971. Fellow Coll. Am. Pathologists (clin. practice com. 1984-87); mem. ACP, Am. Pathology Found. (pres. 1994-96), River Tennis Club (bd. dirs., pres. 1978-98), Univ. Club Milw. Republican. Episcopalian. Avocations: sailing, skiing, tennis, travel, music. Home: 4940 N Maple Lane Nashotah WI 53058 Office: Med Sci Labs 11020 W Plank Ct Wauwatosa WI 53226-3279

HOLLOMON, FREDERICK SHELTON, retired minister; b. Dawson, Ga., May 25, 1925; s. Shelton Augustus and Mattie Milbrey Hollomon; m. Patricia Agnes Maas, May 31, 1975; children: Judy, Cathy, Becky, Cay Lynn, John, Billy, Dona, Kristi, Suzanne. BS in Bus. Adminstrn., U. Ala., 1949; M in Religious Edn., S.W. Bapt. Theol. Sem., 1953, MDiv, 1956. Bookkeeper Merchants and Planters Bank, Montevallo, Ala., 1949—51; pastor So. Bapt. Conv., Nashville, 1952—2002; ret. Adminstrv. asst. Kans. State Legis., Topeka, 1975—78; chaplain Kans. Senate, Topeka, 1979—82, Topeka, 1986—. Lt. (j.g.) USN, 1943—46. Walter Pope Bunns fellow, William Jewll Coll., 1993. Mem.: Kans.-Nebr. So. Bapt. Conv. (v.p. 1966), Kiwanis (chmn. spirtual aims com. 2004). Republican. Baptist. Avocations: reading, writing, walking. Home: 4758 SW 17th Terr Topeka KS 66604 Personal E-mail: fshollomon@aol.com.

HOLLORAN, THOMAS EDWARD, business educator; b. Mpls., Sept. 27, 1929; s. Edward Francis and Florence G. (Loftus) H.; m. Patricia M. Holloran, June 26, 1954; children: Mary Patricia Harley, Anne Florence. BS, U. Minn., 1951, JD, 1955. Bar: Minn. 1955, Fed. 1955. Ptnr. Wheeler and Fredrikson, Mpls., 1955-67; exec. v.p. Medtronic, Inc., Mpls., 1967-73, pres., 1973-75; chmn., chief exec. officer Inter-Regional Fin. Group, Inc. (renamed Dain Rauscher Corp), Mpls., 1976-85; prof. U. St. Thomas, St. Paul, 1985—2002, prof. emeritus, 2002—, sr. disting. fellow Sch. Law, 2003—. Bd. dirs. Flexsteel Industries, Inc., Dubuque, Iowa; dir. emeritus Medtronic, Inc. Spl. judge Mcpl. Ct. of Shorewood, Excelsior, Tonka Bay, Greenwood and Deephaven, Minn., 1961-65; Mayor, City of Shorewood, 1971-74; chmn. Urban Coalition, Mpls., 1977-78, City of Mpls. Task Force on Tech., 1983-84; mem. Mpls.-St. Paul Met. Airports Commn., 1974-82, vice chmn., 1976-82, chmn., 1989-91; bd. trustees Coll. St. Scholastica, 1971-81, chmn., 1979-81; trustee Coll. St. Thomas, 1979-88, U. Minn. Found., 1983-85, Bush Found., 1982—2000, chmn. 1991-96; trustee Mpls. Art Inst., 1986-93, Mpls. Children's Health Ctr., 1983-84; pres. Upper M.W. Coun., Mpls., 1978-80; bd. dirs. InterStudy, Excelsior., 1975-85, Minn. Press Coun., 1982-87, mem. corp. bd. Cath. Archdiocese Mpls. and St. Paul, 1990—. With USN, 1952-54, Korea. Mem. ABA, Minn. State Bar Assn. Roman Catholic.

HOLLOWAY, BARBARA JEAN CHAMBERS, retired secondary school educator; b. Pensacola, Fla., June 23, 1938; d. Colon and Annie Bell (Mickles) Chambers; m. John Frederick Holloway Jr., May 11, 1962; Frederick Dwayne, Deloris Jeanette. BS, Bishop Coll., 1960; MEd, Cleve. State U., 1979; student, Kent State U., 1980-81. Sec. Horace Mann Jr. High Sch., Omaha, 1960-62; svc. rep. Northeastern Bell Tel. Co., Omaha, 1963-65; tchr. Pennsauken (NJ) HS, 1969-72, Sawyer Bus. Coll., Cleve., 1972, John Adams HS, Cleve., 1972-73; tchr., coord. Bedford (OH) HS, 1973—89; chmn. bus. edn. dept. Bedford (Ohio) HS, 1983—2000; ret., 2000. Part-time tchr. Cuyahoga Cmty. Coll., Warrensville, OH, 1975-85; spkr. Vocat. Edn. Div. OH Edn. Dept., 1978-79, Kent (OH) State Bus. Edn. Conf., 1979, AM Cleve. Talk Show, 1979, Bedford Rotary, 1979; bd. dirs. Saunder Office Computer Products, Inc., Solon, OH, Datalink Sys., Chagrin Falls, OH. Mem. Jay-cettes, Willingboro, NJ, 1971-72, Orange Bd. Edn. Task Force, Orange Village, OH, 1982-83; coord. Vocat. Bus. Edn. Drive-In Conf. Cleve. State U., 1974-75. Recipient Disting. Svc. award Cory United Meth. Ch., 1980. Mem. Northeastern OH Bus. Tchrs. Assn. (Tchr. of Yr. 1979, 86), Cleve. Area Bus. Tchrs. (bd. dirs., sec. 1978-80), OH Office Edn. Assn. (regional adviser 1975-78), Bus. Profls. Am., Am. Bus. Women's Assn., Pi Lambda Theta, Alpha Kappa Alpha, Phi Delta Kappa. Clubs: Couples, Funchasers Camping. Avocations: sewing, bowling, reading, golf, camping. Office: Bedford Sch Dist 475 Northfield Rd Cleveland OH 44146-2201 Home: 7060 Rampart Way Pensacola FL 32505 Personal E-mail: bjch23@bellsouth.net.

HOLLOWAY, CHARLES ARTHUR, public and private management educator; b. Whittier, Calif., May 28, 1936; s. Heber H. and Theodosia S. (Stephens) H.; m. Christina Ahlm, July 11, 1959; children: Deborah, Susan, Stuart. BSEE with honors, U. Calif., Berkeley, 1959; MS, UCLA, 1963, PhD in Bus. Adminstrn. with distinction, 1969. Sr. engr. Bechtel Corp., San Francisco, 1964-65; tchg. fellow UCLA, 1965-66; asst. prof. to prof. Stanford (Calif.) U., 1968—, Herbert Hoover prof. pub. and pvt. mgmt., 1980-91, assoc. dean acad. affairs Grad. Sch. Bus., 1980-87, 90-91, Kleiner Perkins Caufield and Byers prof. mgmt., 1991—. Bd. dir. SRI Internat.; co-chair Stanford Ctr. Entrepreneurial Studies; co-chair Stanford Ctr. Entrepreneurial Studies, 1995—. Author: Decision Making Under Uncertainty: Models and Choices, 1979, Perpetual Enterprise Machine: Seven Keys to Corporate Renewal, 1994. Bd. dir. Save Redwoods League. With USN, 1959-63. Fellow Ford Found., 1966-68. Mem. Inst. Mgmt. Sci., Ops. Rsch. Soc. Am., Stanford Integrated Mfg. Assn. (co-chair 1991-95). Home: 730 Santa Maria Ave Palo Alto CA 94305-8438 Office: Stanford U Grad Sch Bus Stanford CA 94305 Business E-Mail: holloway_chuck@gsb.stanford.edu.

HOLLOWAY, CHRISTOPHER MATTHEW, brokerage house executive; b. Portsmouth, Va., Jan. 23, 1973; s. Marc Vincent and Mabel Lurlene H.; m. Susan Janrae Spears Holloway, June 26, 1999; 1 child, Erin Angela. BS in Bus. Adminstrn., Old Dominion U., Norfolk, Va., 1995, MBA, 1998. Regis. Series 4 NASD Options Prin., Series 7 Rep. N.Y. Stock Exchange, Series 24 NASD Gen. Securities Prin., Series 55 OTC Equity Trader, Series 63 NASD Uniform State Law, Series 65 NASD Regis. Investment Adv., Series 27 Fin. and Ops. Prin., Series 53 MSRB Prin. Trend analyst The Finance Co., Norfolk, Va., 1993-96; fin. analyst TFC Enterprises, Inc., Norfolk, Va., 1996-98; v.p. of ops. and compliance Investors Security Co., Inc., Suffolk, Va., 1998—. Dir. Investors Security Co., Inc., Suffolk, Va., 1998—; ops. mgr. Old Dominion Investors Trust, Inc., Mutual Fund, Suffolk, Va., 1998-2004. Recipient 6 All Am. Scholar awards, U.S. Achievement Acad., 1991-95; named Outstanding Jr. Phi Kappa Phi, Norfolk, Va., 1994, Univ. Scholar Old Dominion U., Norfolk, Va., 1995, Outstanding Mgmt. Acctg. Student of Yr., Inst. of Mgmt. Acctg./Old Dominion U. Mgmt., Norfolk, Va., 1998. Mem. Inst. Mgmt. Accts., Golden Key Nat. Hon. Soc., Beta Gamma Sigma, Phi Kappa Phi. Republican. Avocations: coin collecting/numismatics, travel, auto enthusiast, antiques. Office: Investors Security Co Inc Ste 101 127 E Washington St Suffolk VA 23434 Office Fax: 757-925-4353. Business E-Mail: cholloway@investorssecurity.com.

HOLLOWAY, DAVID JAMES, political science educator; b. Dublin, Oct. 13, 1943; came to U.S., 1983; s. James Joseph and Gertrude Mary (Kennedy) H.; m. Arlene Jean Smith, June 12, 1976; children: James, Ivor. MA, PhD, Cambridge (Eng.) U., 1964. Asst. lectr. U. Lancaster, Eng., 1967-69; rsch. assoc. Inst. for Strategic Studies, London, 1969—70; lectr. U. Edinburgh, Scotland, 1970—84, reader, 1984—86; prof. Stanford (Calif.) U., 1986—, co-dir. Ctr. Internat. Security and Arms Control, 1991—97, Raymond A. Spruance prof. in internat. history, 1997—, assoc. dean humanities and scis., 1997—98, dir. Inst. for Internat. Studies, 1998—. Dir. internat. rels. program Stanford U., 1989-91. Author: The Soviet Union and the Arms Race, 1983, Stalin and the Bomb, 1994; co-author: (with S. Drell and P. Farley) The Reagan Strategic Defense Initiative, 1985. Bd. dirs. Ploughshares Found., San Francisco, 1989—. Mem. Am. Polit. Sci. Assn., Am. Assn. for the Advancement of Slavic Studies. Avocations: opera, reading. Home: 710 Torreya Ct Palo Alto CA 94305-4160 Office: Stanford U Inst Internat Studies Encina Hall Stanford CA 94305-6055

HOLLOWAY, DIANE ELAINE, psychotherapist, consultant, writer; b. Tulsa, Oct. 19, 1937; d. Lawrence Lynn and Helen May (Six) Hatcher; m. 1961; children: Brian, Kathleen; m. 2d, Bob Cheney, 1980. BS, Tex. Woman's U., 1972, MA, 1974, PhD, 1979. Lic. psychotherapist, Tex. Brit. rep. Study Abroad, Inc., London, 1957-59; psychologist Presbyn. Hosp., Dallas, 1970-75, dir. psychol. svcs., assoc. dir. continuing edn. psychiatry, 1976-78; mental health/mental retardation cons. Drug Rehab. and Law Enforcement Offices, Dallas County, 1975-77; psychotherapist in pvt. practice Dallas, 1978-89; assoc. Pain Therapy Assn., Dallas, 1979-81; pres. Security & Mgmt. Sys., Dallas, 1979-81, Mental Health Profl. Group, Dallas, 1980-89; drug cood. Dallas Office of Mayor, 1989-92; vis. prof. various univs., 1993—. Author: Before You Say I Quit, 1990, The Mind of Oswald, 2000, Dallas and the Jack Ruby Trial, 2001, Analyzing Leaders, Presidents and Terrorists, 2002; contbr. newsletter, articles to profl. jours.:, editor internet sites. Hogg Found. grantee,

Southwestern Med. Sch., 1972-73. Mem. APA, Am. Med. Writers Assn., Internat. Assn. Chiefs of Police, Archaeol. Inst. Am., Soc. Police and Criminal Psychology, Mensa. Office: 20402 N 150th Dr Sun City West AZ 85375-5765

HOLLOWAY, DONALD PHILLIP, lawyer; b. Akron, Ohio, Feb. 18, 1928; s. Harold Shane and Dorothy Gayle (Ryder) Holloway. BS in Commerce, Ohio U., Athens, 1950; JD, U. Akron, 1955; MA, Kent State U., 1962. Bar: Ohio 1955. Title examiner Bankers Guarantee Title & Trust Co., Akron, 1950-54; acct. Robinson Clay Product Co., Akron, 1955-60; libr. Akron-Summit Pub. Libr., 1962-69, head fine arts and music divsn., 1969-71, sr. libr., 1972-82; pvt. practice Akron, 1982—. Payroll treas. Akron Symphony Orch., 1957-61; treas. Friends Libr. Akron and Summit County, 1970-72. Mem. ABA, ALA, Ohio Bar Assn., Akron Bar Assn., Ohio Libr. Assn., Nat. Trust Hist. Preservation, Music Libr. Assn., Soc. Archtl. Historians, Coll. Art Assn., Art Librs. N.Am. Republican. Episcopalian. Avocations: art and architecture, music, travel. Home: 293 Delaware Pl Akron OH 44303-1275 Office Phone: 330-867-6147.

HOLLOWAY, EDWARD OLIN, human services manager; b. Rochester, N.Y., July 3, 1944; s. Charles Robert and Chrystal Gertrude (Darling) Holloway; m. Hama Elizabeth Farris, Dec. 23, 1967. AA, Palm Beach Jr. Coll., 1964; BA, Lenoir Rhyne Coll., 1967; MS in Pub. Health, U. N.C., 1975. From sanitarian I to sanitarian supr. I Palm Beach County Health Dept., West Palm Beach, Fla., 1969—73; from coord. emergency med. svcs. to exec. dir. dist. IX Health Planning Coun., Inc., West Palm Beach, 1975—89; sr. health and human svcs. planner bd. county commrs. Palm Beach County Dept. Cmty. Svcs., West Palm Beach, 1989—2000. Mem. faculty Pub. Health Physician Residency Program, 1990—2002, apptd. spl. advisor, 2002—; mem. accreditation five yrs. U. Miami, 1999—2004; mem. steering com. Fla. Atlantic U. Inst. Govt., 1992—2000, vice chmn., 1994—99, apptd. spl. adv., 2000—. Vol. planning staff fed. govt., 2004; chmn. dist. 9 adv. coun. Dept. Health and Rehab. Svcs., West Palm Beach, 1990—92; pres. Fla. Assn. Health Planning Agys., Inc., 1984—89; mem. planning unit steering com. Leadership Palm Beach County, 1991; mem. Palm Beach County data collection com. Health and Human Svcs. Planning Assn., 1992—98; mem. Interagy. Planning Group, 1994—2000; mem. sch. adv. com. Palm Beach Gardens Cmty. HS, 1994—, vice chair, 2000—03, mem. membership safety com., 2000—, mem. budget com., 2001—; appointee for customer svc. West Palm Beach VA Med. Ctr., 1997—; mem. Palm Beach County Partnership for Aging program United Way, 1998—; apptd. ex officio mem., spl. advisor Palm Beach County Citizens Adv. Com. on Health and Human Svc., 2000—; vol. State of Fla. Dept. Health, 2000—, vol. staff, chair planning implementing and evaluation needed health and human svc. sys. improvements Guiding Principles and Ops. Comm., 2002—; vol. mem team to evaluate quality of care and customer svc. provided at local VA Med. Ctr. Fed. Insp. Gen.'s Office, 2002. With U.S. Army, 1967—69, Vietnam. Decorated Bronze Star, Purple Heart, Army Commendation medal, Cross of Gallantry (Vietnam); recipient Cert. Appreciation, Wall Soc. of the Vietnam Veterans Memorial Fund, Letters of Commendation, CDC, 1980, Outstanding Svc. award, Fla. Assn. Health Planning Agys., 1989, Outstanding Achievement award, Bd. County Commrs., Palm Beach County Citizens Adv. Com. on Health and Human Svcs., 1995, Letters of Commendation, State of Fla., Lawton Chiles, 1998, Cert. of Merit, Rep. Nat. Com., 2001, Cert. Appreciation, Americans Disabled for Life Meml., 2003, Cert. Honor, Pres. 2004 Team, 2004, Cert. Commendation, Mus. US Army, 2004, Cert. of Unanimous Inclusion in Rep. Presdl. Honor Roll, Nat. Rep. Congressional Com., 2005; grantee State Fla. Dept. Transp. planning grantee, Regional Emergency Med. Svcs., 1975. Mem.: DAV, APHA, ASPA (chpt. 102 coun. 1989—98), Fla. Environ. Health Assn., Neuropathy Assn., Nat. Alliance for Mentally Ill, Nat. Environ. Health Assn., Am. Coll. Grad. Med. Edn., Am. Legion, U. N.C. Sch. Pub. Health Alumni Assn. (bd. dirs. 1994—2001), Paralyzed Vets. Am. (life), Vietnam Vets. Am., Commanders Club. Republican. Lutheran. Avocations: reading, target and skeet shooting, machairology. Home and Office: 104 Vision Ct Palm Beach Gardens FL 33418-3859 Office Phone: 561-622-8495. Personal E-mail: holl1543@bellsouth.net.

HOLLOWAY, ERNEST LEON, university president; b. Boley, Okla., Sept. 12, 1930; m. Jan. 19, 1957; children: Ernest L., Reginald, Norman. BS, Langston U., 1952; MS, Okla. State U., 1955; EdD, U. Okla., 1970. Tchr., prin. Boley H.S., 1952-62; with Langston U., 1963—, profl. sci. higher edn., 1978—, v.p. adminstrn., 1975-77, acting pres., 1977-78, pres., 1979—. Mem. bd. advisors pres. Bush's Historically Black Colls. and Univs.; cons. in field. Elected to Okla. Afro-Am. Hall of Fame, 1987, Okla. Educators Hall of Fame, 1996; inducted into Okla. Higher Edn. Hall of Fame, 1999, Okla. State U. Alumni Assn.'s Hall of Fame, 2001; recipient Thurgood Marshall Schoolarship Fund Edn. award, 2002, Career Achievement award, U. Okla. Mem. Okla. Higher Edn. Alumni Coun., Nat. Assn. State Univs. and Land-Grant Colls., Nat. Assn. Equal Opportunity in Higher Edn., Langston U. Alumni Assn., Alpha Phi Alpha, Phi Delta Kappa, The Lions Club, Imperial Coun. of Shriners. Office: Langston U PO Box 907 Langston OK 73050-0907 Office Phone: 405-466-3201. E-mail: elholloway@lunet.edu.

HOLLOWAY, GORDON ARTHUR, lawyer; b. Wichita, Kans., July 27, 1938; s. George Arthur and Margurite (Bondurant) H.; m. Carol H. Criss, Sept. 1, 1960; children: Gregory Arthur, Suzanne Criss, Garrett Austin. BBA, U. Tex., 1960, JD, 1963. Bar: Tex. 1963, Colo. 1993. Assoc. McGregor, Sewell, Junell & Riggs, Houston, 1963-71; ptnr. Sewell and Riggs, Houston, 1971-93, Holloway & Rowley, 1994—. Staff sgt. Air N.G., 1964-71. Mem. Am. Bd. Trial Advocates (diplomate), Nat. Assn. Railroad Trial Counsel, Internat. Assn. Defense Counsel, Tex. Bd. Legal Specialization (cert. personal injury, civil trial law, qualified atty.-mediator), Houston Club, Intertel. Office: Holloway & Rowley P C 1415 Louisiana St Ste 2550 Houston TX 77002-7378 Office Phone: 713-751-0055. E-mail: gordonholloway@swbell.net.

HOLLOWAY, JACQUELINE, county commissioner; b. Knoxville, Tenn., Mar. 16, 1935; d. Clyde Herbert and Ernestine Cooper; m. George Rudolph Holloway, July 21, 1951; children: Lynda, George Jr., Michelle, Cheryl, Ingrid. AA in Bus., Cooper Inst., Knoxville, 1961; cert., U. Tenn. Ctr. Govt. Tng., 1990. Cert. pub. adminstr. U. Tenn. Biol. technician Oak Ridge (Tenn.) Nat. Lab., 1963—96; county commr. Anderson County, Clinton, Tenn., 1990—2002. Chmn. Families First Coun., 1997—; vice chair Am.'s Promise, 1999—; bd. dirs. Anderson County Health Coun., 2000—, chmn., 2002, Quality Childcare Initiative, Tenn. Nutrition and Consumer Edn. Program; v.p. Coalition Oak Ridge Ret. Employees, 2000—03; v.p. cmty. problem solving United Way Anderson County; mem. Anderson County Headstart Policy Coun.; mem. exec. com. Anderson County Dems.; pres. Dem. Women, Tenn., 1996—98; v.p. Dem. Fedn., Tenn., 1996—2003; bd. dirs. Clinch River Home Health. Mem. Tenn. County Commn. Assn. (bd. dirs. 1991-2002), Tenn. County Svcs. Assn. Methodist. Home and Office: 102 Artesia Dr Oak Ridge TN 37830-7817 E-mail: G32284@aol.com.

HOLLOWAY, JAMES LEMUEL, III, foundation executive, retired military officer; b. Charleston, S.C., Feb. 23, 1922; s. James Lemuel and Jean Gordon (Hagood) H.; m. Dabney Hix Rawlings, Dec. 14, 1942; children: Lucy Dabney Lyon, Jane Meredith. BSEE, Naval Acad., Annapolis, 1942. Cert. naval aviator, naval nuclear reactor operator. Commd. ensign USN, 1942, served in destroyers, WWII Atlantic and Pacific Atlantic, Pacific World War II, 1942-45, carrier jet fighter pilot, Korean War Republic of Korea, 1951—53; comdr. jet squadron USS Valley Forge Lebanon Landings Quemon-Matsu Def., 1958-59; comdr. 1st nuclear carrier Enterprise USN, Vietnam, 1965-67, advanced through grades to adm., 1973; comdr. carrier striking force U.S. 6th fleet Syrian invasion Jordan, 1970; comdr. U.S. 7th fleet USN, Vietnam, 1971-73, vice chief naval ops., 1973-74, mem. Joint Chiefs of Staff, Dept. Def., 1974-78, chief naval ops., 1974-78, ret., 1978; pres. Coun. Am.-Flag Ship Operators, Washington, 1981-88, Naval Hist. Found., Washington, 1982-98, chmn., 1998—. Def. and fgn. policy cons. Paine Weber, Inc., 1980-88; chmn. Dept. of Def. Spl. Rev. Group investigating Iranian hostage rescue, 1981; exec. dir. Presdl. Task Force on Combatting Terrorism, 1985; spl. envoy V.P. Bush to Middle East, 1986; commr. Presdl. Blue Ribbon Commn. on Def. Mgmt., 1985, congl. Commn. on Mcht. Marine and Def., 1987-88, Presdl. Commn. on Long Term Integrated Strategy, 1987-88; U.S. rep. to South Pacific Commn., 1990-94. Tech. advisor: (film) Top Gun, 1985; contbr. articles to mags. Trustee St. James Sch., Md., 1962—, pres., 1989—, chmn. 1996, chmn. emeritus, 2001; bd. dirs. Olmsted Found., Washington, 1978-2000; mem. bd. advisors The Citadel, 1981-86; chmn. academic adv. bd. U.S. Naval Acad., 1983-91; chmn. Hist. Annapolis Found., Inc., 1986-96, chmn. emeritus, 1996—; pres., chmn. Naval Acad. Found., 1994-2001, chmn. emeritus, 2001—; trustee George Marshall Found., 1988-96; dir. Atlantic Coun., 1987-96; bd. visitors and govs. St. John's Coll., 1995, Bd. Mariners Mus., Newport News, Va., 1995-97, dir. emeritus. Decorated Bronze Star, Air medals (3), Legion of Merit (2), DFC, Def. DSM with 2 oak leaf cluster, Navy DSM with 4 oak leaf clusters, Order of Rising Sun (Japan), Grand Cross (Fed. republic Germany), Legion of Honor (France), Rank of Commandeur, 31 others; recipient Triennial Modern Patriot award SAR, 1994, Disting. Pub. Svc. award Navy League, 1996, Disting. Patriot award SAR, 1999, Disting. Grad. award U.S. Naval Acad., 1999, 2000; elected Nat. Wrestling Hall of Fame, 1998; named to Naval Aviation Hall of Honor, 2004. Mem. Assn. Naval Aviation (pres. 1982-91, chmn. 1991-96, chmn. emeritus 2004), Met. Club (Washington gov. 1988—, pres. 1992), Golden Eagles, Brook Club (N.Y.C.), N.Y. Yacht Club (N.Y.C.), Md. Club (Balt.), Annapolis Yacht Club, Soc. Cin., Alfalfa Club (Washington). Republican. Episcopalian. Avocation: sailing. Office Phone: 202-678-4333. Personal E-mail: xcocvan65@aol.com.

HOLLOWAY, JEROME KNIGHT, publisher, retired foreign services officer, former military strategy educator; b. Phila., May 8, 1923; s. Jerome Knight and Emily Margaret (Ennis) H.; m. Gertrud Harms, Apr. 16, 1953 (dec. Jan. 1976); children— Jerome Knight III, Karen M., Nicholas H. AB, Cath. U., 1947; MA, U. Mich., 1959; lang. student, Tokyo, Japan, 1958-60; fellow, Harvard, 1968-69. Joined U.S. Fgn. Service, 1947, ret., 1975; 3d sec. Rangoon, Burma, 1947-49; vice-consul Shanghai, China, 1949-50, Bremen, Germany, 1950-52; consul Hong Kong, 1952-57; 2d sec. Tokyo, 1960-61; assigned State Dept., Washington, 1961-64, 69-70; 1st sec. Stockholm, Sweden, 1964-65; counselor, 1965-68; consul gen. Osaka-Kobe, Japan, 1970-74; state dept. adviser to pres. U.S. Naval War Coll., Newport, R.I., 1974-75, prof. strategy, 1976-90; pub. Hanlin Press, Newport, R.I., 1990—. Served to lt. (j.g.) USNR, 1942-46. Mem. U.S. Naval Inst., Assn. Asian Studies.

HOLLOWAY, JOHN THOMAS, physicist, consultant; b. Cape Girardeau, Mo., June 19, 1922; s. Herbert Henry and Addie Mae (Cahill) H.; m. Kay Vickers, Nov. 11, 1965; children: Linda, Kim (dec. Jan. 1999). AB, Millikin U., Decatur, Ill., 1943; PhD, Iowa State U., 1957. With nuclear physics br. Office Naval Research, Washington, 1946-53, head br., 1951-52; research asst. Ames Lab., AEC, Iowa, 1954-57; with Office Dir. Def. Research and Engring., Washington, 1958-61; dep. dir. Office of Sci. Dir. Def. Research and Engring., 1959-61; with NASA, 1961-68, dep. dir. grants and research contracts, 1961-67, chief advanced programs and tech., space applications div., 1967-68; dir. Nat. Hwy. Safety Research Center, Dept. Transp., 1968-69; v.p. research Ins. Inst. Hwy. Safety, 1969-72; asso. dir. ops. Interdisciplinary Communications Program, Smithsonian Instn., 1972-77, program mgr. internat. program population analysis, 1972-77, research and devel. cons. in hwy. safety, biomed. electronics, energy conservation, 1977-78; sr. staff officer bd. on radioactive waste mgmt. Nat. Acad. Scis.-NRC, 1978-85; cons. on radioactive waste mgmt., hwy. safety, 1985—. Mem. conf. com. Nat. Conf. Advancement Research, 1971-75 Author papers in field; adviser documentary films. Served with USNR, 1944-46. Mem. Am. Phys. Soc., Sigma Xi. Clubs: Cosmos (Washington); Army-Navy Country (Arlington, Va.). Home: 2220 Cathedral Ave NW Washington DC 20008-1504

HOLLOWAY, PAUL FAYETTE, retired aerospace transportation executive; b. Hampton, Va., June 7, 1938; s. Eldridge Manning and Minnie Powell H.; m. Barbara Jane Menetch, June 23, 1956; children: Paul Manning (dec.), Eric Scott. BS, Va. Poly. Inst. and State U., 1960; postgrad., U. Va., 1961, Coll. William and Mary, 1962-63; grad. advanced mgmt. program, Harvard U., 1988; PhD (hon.), Old Dominion U., 1994. With NASA Langley Rsch. Ctr., Hampton, Va., 1960-97, aerospace technologist, 1960-69, space shuttle task group, 1969, chief space sys. divsn., 1972-75; acting dep. assoc. adminstr. Office Aeronautics and Space Tech., 1977, dir. for space, 1975-85, dep. dir., 1985-91, dir., 1991-96, acting dep. adminstr., 1992-93, ret., 1997. Cons. in field. Mem. editl. bd. Jour Spacecraft and Rockets, 1972-77, editor in chief, 1978-80; contbr. articles to profl. jours. Mem. Poquoson (Va.) Planning Commn.; v.p. local PTA; mem. coll. bd. Thomas Nelson C.C., 1997-2001. Recipient Outstanding Leadership medal NASA, 1980, Exceptional Svc. medal, 1981; Presdl. Rank award for meritorious exec., 1981, Presdl. Rank award for disting. exec., 1987, 93, Equal Opportunity medal, 1992, Disting. Svc. medal, 1992; named Peninsula Engr. of Yr., Peninsula Engrs. Club, 1996; elected to Va. Tech. Acad. Engring. Excellence, 2002. Fellow AIAA (v.p. publs. 1991-94), Am. Astronautical Soc.; mem. Internat. Acad. Astronautics, Sigma Gamma Tau. Methodist. Home: 16 N Westover Dr Poquoson VA 23662-1424 E-mail: pholloway@erols.com.

HOLLOWAY, RALPH LESLIE, anthropology educator; b. Phila., Feb. 6, 1935; s. Ralph L. and Marguerite (Grugan) H. BS in Geology, U. N.Mex., Albuquerque, 1959; PhD in Anthropology, U. Calif., Berkeley, 1964. Asst. prof. anthropology Columbia U., N.Y.C., 1964-69, assoc. prof., 1969-73, prof., 1973—. Author: Brain Endocasts: The Paleoneurological Evidence, vol. 3 of Human Fossil Record, 2004; editor: Primate Aggression, Territoriality and Xenophobia: A Comparative Perspective, 1974; contbr. numerous articles to profl. jours. Recipient Ctr. for Rsch. into the Anthrop. Found. Tech., Ind. U. Ann. award for Outstanding Rsch., Craft award, 2002, Wilton Krogman award for disting. achievement in biol. anthropology U. Pa., 2004; Guggenheim Found. fellow, 1974; NSF grantee, 1984. Fellow AAAS, N.Y. Acad. Sci.; mem. Am. Anthrop. Assn., Am. Assn. Phys. Anthropologists, Soc. for Neurosci., Sigma Xi, Phi Beta Kappa. Office: Columbia U Dept Anthropology New York NY 10027 Office Phone: 212-854-4570. Business E-Mail: rlh2@columbia.edu.

HOLLOWAY, ROBERT CHARLES, musician, composer; b. Balt. s. George Albert and Edna Mildred (Smith); m. Leslee R. Seymour, June 4, 1960; children: Bruce, Collin, Christy, Heather, Deven, Duana. Arranger, orchestrator Alvin Ailey Dance Co., 1987; pres. Chelsea Music Svc., Inc., N.Y.C., 1990-92. V.p. St. Croix Records. Arranger, orchestrator for ABC-TV, CBS Radio, NBC Tonight Show, Radio City Music Hall, Children's TV Workshop Sesame Street, USN Band, Boston Pops Orch., PS Classics, San Antonio Symphony, Denver Symphony, Pacific N.W. Ballet; orchestrator Le Ballet de Coeurs commd. by San Francisco Ballet, (film) Edith Piaf: Her Story...Her Songs; (Broadway musicals) Odyssey, Barnum, Peter Pan, Dancin', Sophisticated Ladies, On Your Toes, Jerome Robbins Broadway; (performers) Skitch Henderson, Enrique Madriguera, Richard Hayman, Tommy Tune, Betty Carter, Eddie Fisher, Caterina Valente, Connie Francis, Raquel Bitton, Philip Chaffin, Vt. Jazz Ensemble, Jazz Experience; composer: Prelude, Busybody, Southern Suite, Improvisations in Jazz, Celebration, Wildcat, Bone Fracture Mem. ASCAP, Am. Soc. Music Arrangers, Am. Fedn. Musicians. Avocation: boxing. Home: 1079 Forest Rd Alstead NH 03602 E-mail: bobholloway@cheshire.net.

HOLLOWAY, ROBERT ROSS, archaeologist, educator; b. Newton, Mass., Aug. 15, 1934; s. Charles Thomas and Mildred Evelyn (Guthrie) H.; m. Nancy Jane Degenhardt, May 21, 1960; children: Anne Lovelace Studholme, Susannah Porter Hollers. AB summa cum laude, Amherst Coll., 1956; AM, U. Pa., 1957; MA, PhD, Princeton U., 1960; LHD (hon.), Amherst Coll., 1976; MA (hon.), Brown U., 1967; D honoris causa, U. Louvain, Belgium, 1997. Asst. prof. U. N.C., Chapel Hill, 1963-64; mem. faculty Brown U., Providence, 1964—, prof. archaeology, 1970—; dir. Ctr. for Archaeology and Art, 1978—87, 1994—2001. Cons. curator ancient art Mus. Art, RISD, 1971—; del. Centro Internat. di Studi Numis., Naples, Italy, 1973—, pres., 1980-86. Author: The Thirteen Months Coinage of Hieronymos of Syracuse, 1969, Satrianum, 1970, Buccino, 1973, A View of Greek Art, 1973, Influence and Styles in the Late Archaic and Early Classical Greek Sculpture of Sicily and Magna Graecia, 1978, Italy and the Aegean, 1981, The Archeology of Ancient Sicily, 1990, The Archeology of Early Rome and Latium, 1994, Catalogue of Ancient Greek Coins Museum Art, 1998, Constantine and Rome, 2004; co-author: Terina, 1983, Ustica I, 1995, Ustica II, 2001; editor catalogue of classical collection Mus. Art, RISD, 1965. Grantee, Am. Philos. Soc., 1962; NEH rsch. grantee, 1972, 80, 82, 83, sr. fellow, 1977; Am. Coun. Learned Soc. fellow, 1969, Gold medal Archaeol. Inst. Am., 1995. Fellow Am. Numis. Soc., Royal Numis. Soc., Am. Acad. Rome; mem. Assn. Field Archaeology (pres. 1975-77), Archaeol. Inst. Am. (Gold medal for archaeol. achievements 1995), Royal Belgian Numis. Soc. (hon.), Nat. Inst. Etruscan and Italic Studies (Italy; hon.), Inst. Prehist. Studies (Florence, Italy), German Archaeol. Inst. (corr.), Soc. Art Historians (Rome; corr.), Soc. War of 1812 (Md., Conn.), Soc. Colonial Wars (Md., R.I.), Bristol Yacht Club, Providence Art Club, Phi Beta Kappa. Home: 185 Elmgrove Ave Providence RI 02906-4240

HOLLOWAY, ROBERT WESTER, radiochemist; b. Morrilton, Ark., Jan. 3, 1945; s. Otho and Bessie Vance (Woolverton) H.; m. Mary Ella Hamel, Dec. 31, 1970 (div.); children: David, Jason; m. Marina Borovik, March 28, 2003 BS, Harding Coll., 1967; postgrad., U. Okla., 1968; PhD, U. Ark., 1977. Asst. prof. U. Ark., Pine Bluff, 1976-79; research chemist DuPont Corp., Aiken, S.C., 1979-81; supervisory chemist EPA, Las Vegas, 1981-94; pres. Nev. Tech. Assocs., Inc., 1994—. Contbr. articles to profl. jours. Served to capt. USAF, 1967-72. Mem. Am. Chem. Soc., Health Physics Soc., Toastmasters, Optimists. Republican. Avocation: sailing. Office: Nev Tech Assocs Inc PO Box 90748 Henderson NV 89009-0748 Personal E-mail: holloway3@aol.com. Business E-Mail: roberth@ntanet.net.

HOLLOWAY, ROY LEE, JR., music educator; b. Toledo, Ohio, Dec. 14, 1970; s. Roy Lee Holloway, Sr. and Sandra LaVonne Holloway; 1 child, Jonathan. BS, Bowling Green State U., 1994. Cert. Music Education K-12 2002. Elem. music edn. tchr. South Morrison Elem. Sch., Newport News, Va., 1999—2001; choral dir. Passage Mid. Sch., Newport News, Va., 2001. Music tech. tchr. C. Waldo Scott Ctr., Newport News, Va., 2000—02. Composer: (choral arrangement) Sometimes I Feel Like a Motherless Child, 1997. Recipient Three Cheers for Tchrs. award, Sylvan learning Centers/WTKR 3 (CBS Affiliate), 2000. Mem.: Alpha Phi Alpha Frat. Inc. Home: 491 Nelson Dr Apt 4 Newport News VA 23601 Office: Newport News Pub Schs 12465 Warwick Blvd Newport News VA 23606 Personal E-mail: rhol2@hotmail.com.

HOLLOWAY, SYBIL LYMORISE, psychologist, writer; b. New York, NY, Apr. 16, 1967; d. Thomas Carvin and Bannie Lymorise Holloway. BA, Smith Coll., Northampton, Mass., 1989; MA, Ind. Univ. of PA, Ind., Pa., 1991, D in Psychology, 1994. Lic. psychologist Pa. Coun. intern Univ. of Calif., Santa Barbara, Calif., 1993—94; psychol. coun., asst. prof. Bloomsburg Univ., Bloomsburg, Pa., 1999—. Bd. of dir. Smith club of Long Is., Long Is., NY, 1998—99. Recipient Fin. Aid Success Story, Nat. Assoc. of Student Fin. Aid Admin./Wash., D.C., 2000, Vol. Svc. Award, Alice Paul House/Ind., Pa., 1992, Alumnae Scholarship, Smith Coll./Northampton, Mass., 1989; fellow IUP Found. Fellowship, Ind. Univ. of Pa./Ind., Pa., 1989. Mem.: APA, AAUW, Pennwriters, Nat. Acad. Adv. Assoc., Assoc. for Women in Psychol., Pa. Psychol. Assoc. Avocations: writing, reading, tap, TV watching, stamp collecting/philately. Office: Bloomsburg Univ 400 E 2nd St (240 SSC) Bloomsburg PA 17815

HOLLOWAY, WANDA KAYE, psychotherapist, consultant; b. Mansfield, Mo., Sept. 10, 1960; d. Thomas McDonald and Patsy Jorene Smith; m. David Leigh Holloway, Sept. 7, 1996. BS, Coll. of the Ozarks, 1979—82; MEd, Univ. Ark., 1986—87; PsyD, Forest Inst. of Prof. Psychology, Springfield, Mo., 1995—2000. Vol. supr. of occupl. therapy Ozark Guidance Ctr., Springdale, Ark., 1983; outpatient counselor Decision Point, Springdale, Ark., 1983—88; therapist Charter Vista Hosp., Fayetteville, Ark., 1986—87; dir. substance abuse Burrell Behavioral Health, Springfield, Mo., 1988—99, intern, resident, 1999—2001, provisional lic. Psychologist, 2001—; therapist cons. Cox Med. Ctr., Springfield, Mo., 2003—. Mem.: Health Psychology Divsn., Am. Psychological Assn. Republican. Assembly Of God. Avocations: outdoor activities, bicycling, skeet shooting, target shooting, skiing, reading. Office: Burrell Behavioral Health 1300 Bradford Pky Springfield MO 65804 Office Phone: 417-269-5400.

HOLLOWAY, WILLIAM JIMMERSON, retired education educator; b. Smithfield, Va., May 6, 1917; s. Arnett Jimmerson and Lucy Pernell (White) H.; m. Julia Naomi Edmundson, June 17, 1944; children: Wendell, Arnett, Lynn. BS with honors, Hampton Inst., 1940; MA, U. Mich., 1946; Ed.D., U. Ill., 1961; postgrad., Harvard U., 1950. Prin. Union Sch., Hampton, Va., 1946-47; dean students Savannah State Coll., 1947-55; prin. Ligon High Sch., Raleigh, N.C., 1956-57; counselor N.C. Central U., Durham, 1959-61; supt. Va. State Sch., Hampton, 1961-65; edn. program officer U.S. Office Edn. Washington, 1965-70; vice provost Ohio State U., Columbus, 1970-78, prof. edn., 1970-82, prof. emeritus, 1982—; dir. Nigerian edn. program, Ohio State U., 1980-82; pres. Internat. Ednl. and Service Inst., Inc., Raleigh, N.C., 1981-88; disting. prof. edn. St. Augustine's Coll., Raleigh, 1983-87. Author: The Education of Blacks in Virginia Before the Civil War, 1619-1860, 1993, The Odyssey of a North American Educator, 2001; mem. editl. bd. The Negro Educational Review, 1972, editor-in-chief, 1995; editor-in-chief emeritus, 1999; chief cons. Insight Enterprises African Am. Disability Program, 1998. Trustee Freedoms Found., 1974, St. Augustines Coll., 1968-77. Recipient Freedoms Found. medal, 1954, Superior Accomplishment award HEW, 1968, Disting. Alumni award Hampton Inst., 1970, award Nat. Press Inst., 1972, Outstanding Citizen award Ohio Gen. Assembly, 1978, Outstanding Achievement award Ohio State U., 1978, Disting. Service award Ohio State U., 1984, Community Leadership award Capital U., 1978, Nat. Disting. Service award United Negro Coll. Fund, 1979, Excellence in Internat. Edn. award Govt. of Nigeria, Disting. Career award Negro Ednl. Rev., 1984, Outstanding Achievement award U. Mich., 1987, Negro Ednl. Rev. Golden Anniversary Disting. Svc. award, 2000; Harvard Far Eastern Studies fellow, 1956, Disting. Svc. award Insight Enterprises Emmet H. Scott, 1998.; named to Ohio State U. Coll. Edn. Hall of Fame, 2002. Mem. Am. Assn. Higher Edn., Am. Personnel and Guidance Assn., Alpha Kappa Delta, Phi Delta Kappa, Kappa Delta Pi. Democrat. Presbyterian (elder). Clubs: Lions (pres. 1975); Cosmos (Washington). Avocations: duplicate bridge, saltwater fishing. Home: 3618 Littledale Rd Ste 213 Kensington MD 20895 *As an educator I have worked to develop sensitivity to the needs, hopes, and aspirations of all people, particularly those at the bottom of the socio-economic ladder. With youth and adults I have labored to kindle sparks of brotherhood leading to harmony. I feel that our survival on this planet is linked with our capacity to use cultural differences in creative and constructive ways.*

HOLLOWAY, WILLIAM JUDSON, JR., federal judge; b. 1923; AB, U. Okla., 1947; LLB, Harvard U., 1950; LLD (hon.), Oklahoma City U., 1991. Ptnr. Holloway & Holloway, Oklahoma City, 1950—51; atty. Dept. Justice, Washington, 1951—52; assoc., ptnr. Crowe and Dunlevy, Oklahoma City, 1952—68; judge U.S. Ct. Appeals (10th cir.), Oklahoma City, 1968—84, chief judge, 1984—91, sr. judge, 1992—. Mem.: FBA, ABA, Oklahoma County Bar Assn., Okla. Bar Assn. Office: US Ct Appeals 10th Cir PO Box 1767 Oklahoma City OK 73101-1767

HOLLYFIELD, JOHN SCOGGINS, lawyer; b. Harlingen, Tex., Aug. 20, 1939; m. Penny Pounds, Dec. 27, 1962; children: Jon Scott, Courtney. Bar: Tex. 1968. Assoc. Fulbright & Jaworski, Houston, 1968—75, ptnr., 1975—2001, of counsel, 2001—. Lt. USNR, 1961-65. Recipient Pres.'s award Houston Bar Assn., 1986. Mem. ABA (coun. real property sect. 1986-93, sec. 1993-94, vice chair real property divsn. 1994-96, chair 1997-98, ho. of dels. 1999—2004), Am. Coll. Real Estate Lawyers (pres. 1990-91), Anglo-Am. Real Property Inst. (chair 2001). Office: Fulbright & Jaworski LLP 1301 Mckinney St Houston TX 77010-3095 Office Phone: 713-651-3717. Business E-Mail: jhollyfield@fulbright.com.

HOLM, BRUCE ALLEN, academic administrator, researcher; b. Waterloo, Iowa, Jan. 20, 1959; s. Howard Laverne and Bernita Clara Holm; m. Allison Leslie Wishner, June 10, 1989; children: Alexander Nathan, Christopher Isaac. BS in biochemistry, U. of Iowa, Iowa City, IA, 1977—81; MS in biophysics, Unviersity of Rochester Sch. of Medicine, 1982—83; PhD, U. of Rochester Sch. of Medicine, 1982—86. Perinatology fellow Children's Hosp., Buffalo, 1988—89; assoc. prof. of pediat. SUNY at Buffalo, 1991—95, sr. assoc. dean of medicine, 1993—98, prof. of pediat., ob/gyn, and pharmacology, 1996—, sr. assoc. v.p. of health sciences, 1998—2002, sr. vice provost, 2002—. Sci. dir. ONY, Inc., Amherst, NY, 1988—; cons. Forest Pharmaceuticals, New York, 2000—; dir. STAR Ctr. for Therapy Discovery, Buffalo, 2001—. Editor: (book series) Clinics in Perinatology, (book) Acute Lung Injury. Bd. mem. CUBRC, Buffalo, 1999—2002; pres. Health Care Industries Assn., Buffalo, 1999—2002; bd. mem. Women & Children's Health Rsch. Found., Buffalo, 1993—2002. Recipient Tech./Discovery award, Health Care Industries Assn., 1998, 2000, Merit Scholar, U. of Iowa, 1977, Harold C. Hodge award, U. of Rochester, 1987, Alpha Omega Alpha Med. Honor Soc., U. at Buffalo, 1997, George Thorn award, 1999, Chancellor's Award for Rsch. in Scinece and Medicine, SUNY, 2001, Chancellor's Award for Entrepreneurial Activity, State Unviersity of NY, 2002; grantee Rsch. of Diseases in Infants and Newborns, Nat. Instituties of Health, 1991-2005; Predoctoral fellowship, NIH, 1982—87, Rsch. Career Devel. award, NIH: Heart, Lung and Blood Inst., 1991—96, Genomics and Proteomics, Howard Hughes Med. Inst., 1999—2003, Microbial Pathogenesis Ctr., Lucille P. Markey Charitable Trust, 1996—2001. Mem.: AAAS, NY Acad. of Sci., Am. Physiol. Soc., Am. Thoracic Soc., Perintal Rsch. Soc. D-Liberal. Lutheran. Achievements include patents for lung surfactant replacements drugs; research in molecular therapies in inflammatory lung disease; treatments for congenital anomalies in newborn infants; first to surfactant deficiencies in lung disease. Home: 1425 Clover St Rochester NY 14610 Office: State University of New York at Buffalo 562 Capen Hall Buffalo NY 14260 E-mail: baholm@buffalo.edu.

HOLM, DANIEL THOMAS, education educator; b. Redwood City, Calif., Oct. 6, 1954; s. John Otto and Patricia (Gee) H.; m. Lois Garibotti, Sept. 25, 1981; children: Amy Shivers, Andrew Shivers, Matthew Shivers, Katherine Joy Holm. BA, U. of the Pacific, 1976, MA, 1980. Tchr. elem. San Lorenzo Valley Sch. Dist., Felton, Calif., 1976-89, 91—; intermittent tchr. Calif. Youth Authority, Santa Cruz, 1988-89; instr. U. Ariz., Tucson, 1989-91. Program evaluator Summer Bridge/New Start, Tucson, 1990-91. Inst. LRC, Tucson, 1990-91. Mem. Am. Ednl. Rsch. Assn., Nat. Reading Conf., Internat. Reading Assn., Ariz. Reading Assn., Tucson Tchrs. Applying Lang. Home: 12690 East St Boulder Creek CA 95006-9116 Office: SLV Unified Sch Dist 6134 Highway 9 Felton CA 95018-9704

HOLM, SIR IAN, actor; b. Sept. 12, 1931; s. James Harvey and Jean (Wilson) Cuthbert; m. Lynn Mary Shaw, 1955 (div. 1965); m. Sophie Baker, 1982 (div. 1986); m. Penelope Wilton, 1991 (div. 2001); m. Sophie de Stempel, Oct. 25, 2003. Student, Royal Acad. Dramatic Art, 1950-53; LittD (hon.), U. Sussex, 1999. Actor with Shakespeare Mem. Theatre, 1954-55; in repertory, 1956; toured in Titus Andronicus, 1957; numerous roles Royal Shakespeare Co. including Henry V, Romeo and Richard III, 1958-67; plays include Moonlight, 1993, Landscape, 1994, King Lear, 1997 (Evening Std. award for Best Actor, Olivier award Best Actor and Critics Cir. award, 1998); film appearances include Young Winston, Alien, Chariots of Fire (named Best Supporting Actor, Cannes Film Festival, 1981, Brit. Acad. Film and TV Arts, 1982, Acad. Award nomination Best Supporting Actor, 1982), Greystoke, Brazil, Dance With A Stranger, 1985, Wetherby, 1985, Dreamchild, 1985, Another Woman, 1988, Henry V, 1990, Hamlet, 1990, Kafka, 1991, The Naked Lunch, 1992, Blue Ice, 1992, Hour of The Pig, 1993, The Madness of King George, 1994, Lochness, 1994, Mary Shelley's Frankenstein, 1995, Big Night, 1995, Night Falls on Manhattan, 1995, The 5th Element, 1996, A Life Less Ordinary, 1996, The Sweet Hereafter, 1996 (Genie Best Actor award), Existenz, 1998, Simon Magus, 1998, The Match, 1998, Esther Kahn, 1999, Joe Gould's Secret, 1999, Beautiful Joe, 1999, From Hell, 2000, Lord of the Rings: The Fellowship of the Ring, 2001, The Lord of the Rings: The Return of the King, 2003, The Day After Tomorrow, 2004, Garden State, 2004, The Aviator, 2004, The Treatment, 2005, The Lord of War, 2005, Beyond Friendship, 2005, Pulse, 2005, Strangers With Candy, 2005; TV appearances include The Lost Boys (Best Actor award Royal TV Soc., 1979), Strike, 1981, (miniseries) Game, Set and Match, 1988, The Last Romantics, 1991, (series) The Borrowers, 1992-93, others; TV appearances include Landscape, BBC, 1995, King Lear, BBC, 1997, Alice Through the Looking Glass, Channel 4, 1998, The Last of the Blonde Bombshells, 2000, The Emperor's New clothes, 2000. Awarded Knighthood by Queen of Eng.; recipient Tony award for Best Supporting Actor, 1967, Evening Std. award, 1967, 93, 97, Genie award, 1997, Olivier award, 1998.

HOLM, JOY ALICE, goldsmith, psychology professor, artist, art educator; b. Chgo., May 21, 1929; d. Alvin Herbert and Willette Eugenia (Miller) Holm. BFA, U. Ill., 1952; MS in Art Edn. Inst. Design, Ill. Inst. Tech., 1956; PhD in Edn., U. Minn., 1967. Tchr. art, Eng. West Chgo. H.S., 1952—54; instr., tchr. art J.S. Morton H.S. and Jr. Coll., Cicero, Ill., 1954—65; asst. prof. art & design Mankato (Minn.) State U., 1965—66; asst. prof. art Ill. State U., Normal, 1966—69; assoc. prof. art & design So. Ill. U., Edwardsville, 1969—71; assoc. prof. art, art edn. Winona (Minn.) State U., 1971—75; assoc. prof., chmn. dept. art St. Mary's Coll. of Notre Dame, Ind., 1975—76; assoc. prof. art & design, secondary, continuing edn. U. Wis., Eau Claire, 1976—78; assoc. prof. art & design Sch. Art & Design Kent (Ohio) State U., 1978—80; lectr. Jungian studies C.G. Jung Inst., Chgo., 1980—82; adj. assoc. prof. art edn. Sch. Art and Design, Sch. Edn. U. Ill., Chgo., 1981—82; lectr. U. Calif. Ext., Santa Cruz, 1983—; adj. prof. art edn., design San Jose (Calif.) State U., 1983—84; owner bus. designer-goldsmith Oak Park, Ill., 1980—82, Carmel, Calif., 1982—87, Atelier XII, Winona, 1988—. Curriculum cons. North Ctrl. Assn. Accreditation Team State of Ill., Edwardsville, 1970; regional cons. Supt. Pub. Instrn., Springfield, Ill., 1970; juror exhbns.; panelist, spkr., presenter confs., meetings. Contbr., cons. Alternative Medicine: A Definitive Guide, 1994; contbg. author: Living Science, 2003; contbr. articles to profl. jours; one-woman shows at J. Sterling Morton HS & Jr. Coll., 1963, Russell Art Gallery, Bloomington, 1968, Owatonna (Minn.) Art Ctr., 1980, 86; exhbns. include La Grange (Ill.) Art League (Best of Show, 1st Place award prints), 1963-64, Minn. Mus. Art, 1974-75, Craft & Folk Art Mus., L.A., 1978, The Gallery Kent State U., 1978-79, Saenger Nat. Small Sculpture and Jewelry Exhibit, 1978, Diamonds Internat., NY, 1978, Inst. Design Alumni, 1988, Internat. Biographical Ctr. Congress Exhbn., Edinburgh, Scotland, 1994, others. Fellow World Lit. Acad.; mem. AAUP, Nat. Art Edn. Assn. (rep. Wis. Women's Caucus Houston Conf. 1978, higher edn. divsn. 1961—), Am. Assn. Higher Edn., Coll. Art Assn., Soc. N.Am. Goldsmiths, Gemological Inst. Am., C.G. Jung Inst. (Chgo.), Hon. Soc. Illustrators (hon.), Internat. Soc. Study of Subtle Energies and Energy Medicine, Inst. Noetic Scis., Order of Internat. Fellowship, Alpha Lambda Delta (hon.), Phi Kappa Phi (hon.). Methodist. Office: Atelier XII PO Box 183 Winona MN 55987-0183

HOLMAN, ARTHUR STEARNS, artist; b. Bartlesville, Okla., Oct. 25, 1926; s. Newton Davis and Barbara (Hendry) H. BFA, U. N.Mex., 1951; postgrad., Hans Hofmann Sch., 1951, Calif. Sch. Fine Arts, San Francisco, 1953. One-man shows include Esther Robles Gallery, L.A., 1960, David Cole Gallery, San Francisco, 1962, 80, De Young Mus., San Francisco, 1963, San Francisco Mus., 1963, Gumps Gallery, San Francisco, 1964-66, 69, 87, Marin Civic Ctr. Gallery, 1970, 95, William Sawyer Gallery, San Francisco, 1971, 73, 74, 76, John Bolles Gallery, Santa Rosa, Calif., 1982, Braunstein, Quay Gallery, San Francisco, 1992, The Art Foundry, Sacramento, Calif., 2003; exhibited in group shows at San Francisco Mus., 1960-76, Downey Mus., L.A., 1961, 50 Calif. Artists, Whitney Mus., N.Y.C., Walker Art Ctr., Albright-Knox Gallery, Des Moines Art Ctr., 1962, U. N.C. Annual, 1965, Smithsonian Instn., Washington, 1977, Coll. of Marin, 1983, Hall of Flowers, San Francisco, 1985, 86, 20th Century Landscape Drawings, De Young Mus., San Francisco, 1989, Jan Holloway Gallery, San Francisco, 1989, Bolinas (Calif.) Mus., 1997, San Francisco Art Inst., 2001, Marin Civic Ctr. Gallery, 2005; represented in permanent collections, San Francisco Mus., Oakland Mus., Mills Coll., Stanford U., Eureka Coll., Achenbach Found., San Francisco. With USAAF, 1945-46. Address: PO Box 72 Lagunitas CA 94938-0072

HOLMAN, BUD GEORGE, lawyer; b. NYC, June 30, 1929; s. Harry and Fannie Abrams (Bass) H.; m. Kathleen Barbara McLean, Sept. 1, 1961; children: Jennifer Jean, Wayne George. BBA, CCNY, 1950; LLB, Yale U., 1956. Bar: N.Y. 1956, Conn. 1979, D.C. 1982. Law sec. to judge N.Y. Ct. Appeals, 1956-58; practice in N.Y.C., 1958—; ptnr. Kelley Drye & Warren (and predecessor firms), 1965—. Pres., chmn. bd. dirs. Sixty Sutton Corp., 1969-97; lectr. Practising Law Inst., Wage Price Inst., Young Pres. Orgn. Editor: The Bar, 1949-50, Yale Law Jour., 1955-56. Trustee U.S. Naval Acad. Found., 1978—85; bd. dirs. USO Met. N.Y., 1978—2004. Mem. Naval Res. Assn. (pres. 3d naval dist. chpts. 1973-75, mem. nat. adv. coun. 1975-94), Am. Arbitration Assn. (bd. dirs., mem. exec. com. 1991-2003), Navy League (bd. dirs. coun. N.Y. chpt. 1979-99), Yale U. Law Sch. Assn. (mem. exec. com. 1987-90, 93-96, bd. dirs.), Yale Law Sch. Assn. N.Y.C. (bd. dirs.), Met. Club, Yale Club, Beta Gamma Sigma. Democrat. Office: Kelley Drye & Warren LLP 101 Park Ave New York NY 10178-0002 Home: 60 Sutton Pl S New York NY 10022 Office Phone: 212-808-7729. Personal E-mail: holmanbg@aol.com. Business E-Mail: bholman@kelleydrye.com.

HOLMAN, DONALD REID, retired lawyer; b. Astoria, Oreg., Jan. 30, 1930; s. Donald Reuben and Hattie Laveda (Card) H.; m. Susan Muncy Morris, Aug. 31, 1956; children: Donald Reid, Laura Morris Holman O'Brien, Douglas Edward. BA, U. Wash.-Seattle, 1951, JD, 1958; postgrad., U. Oreg.-Eugene, 1955-57. Bar: Oreg. Assoc. Miller Nash LLP, Portland, 1958-63, ptnr., 1963-93, mng. ptnr., 1987-90, sr. counsel, 1994-2001, ret., 2001. Lt. (j.g.) USN, 1951-55; capt. JAGC USNR, 1977-90, ret. Fellow Am. Bar Found.; mem. Order of Coif, Multnomah Athletic Club (trustee 1983-85, v.p. 1985-86), Waverley Country Club, Phi Delta Phi. Republican. Avocations: tennis, golf, squash. Home: 8040 SW Broadmoor Ter Portland OR 97225-2121 E-mail: holmor@comcast.net.

HOLMAN, HALSTED REID, medical educator, physician; b. Cleve., Jan. 17, 1925; s. Emile Frederic and Ann Peril (Purdy) H.; m. Barbara Marie Lucas, June 26, 1949 (div. July 9, 1982); children: Michael, Andrea, Alison; m. Diana Barbara Dutton, Aug. 10, 1985; 1 child, Geoffrey. Student, Stanford U., 1942-43, UCLA, 1943-44; MD, Yale U., 1949. Med. resident Montefiore Hosp., N.Y.C., 1952-55; staff physician Rockefeller Inst., N.Y.C., 1955-60; prof. medicine Stanford (Calif.) U., 1960—, chmn. dept. medicine, 1960-71, co-chief, divsn. family and cmty. medicine, 1987-2001, dir. clin. scholar program, 1969-97, dir. Multipurpose Arthritis Ctr., 1977-97, co-chief, divsn. immunology and rheumatology, 1997-2000, dir. Stanford Program for Mgmt. of Chronic Disease, 1997—. Pres. Midpeninsula Health Svc., Palo Alto, Calif., 1975-80; mem. adv. bd. Calif Health Facilities Commn., Sacramento, 1978-81, Office Tech. Assessment, U.S. Congress, 1979-81, Inst. Advancement of Health, N.Y.C., 1982-90; Guggenheim prof. medicine, 1960—. Author 2 books; assoc. editor Arthritis and Rheumatism, 1995-2000; co-editor Chronic Illness, 2004—; contbr. articles to profl. jours. Recipient Bauer Meml. award, Arthritis and Rheumatism Found., N.Y., 1964, John W. Gardner Vision award, Pathways Found., 2003. Master: Am. Coll. Rheumatology (Presdl. Gold medal 2001); fellow: AAAS (coun. 1974—79), ACP (Laureate award no. Calif. chpt. 1994, John Phillips Meml. award 2004); mem.: Improving Chronic Illness Care-R.W. Johnson Found. (Vision award 2001), Arthritis Found. (Hero Overcoming Arthritis 1998, Engalitcheff award 1999, McGuire Educator award 2000), Western Assn. Physicians (pres. 1966), Am. Soc. Clin. Investigation (pres. 1970), Assn. Am. Physicians. Democrat. Home: 747 Dolores St Stanford CA 94305-8427 Office: Stanford U Divsn Immunol and Rheumatol 1000 Welch Rd Ste 203 Palo Alto CA 94304-1808 E-mail: Holman@Stanford.edu.

HOLMAN, JAMES, allergist; b. Jacksonville, Tex., Aug. 13, 1921; MD, U. Tex. Southwest, 1945. Diplomate Am. Bd. Allergy and Immunology. Intern Parkland Meml. Hosp., Dallas, 1945-46; resident in allergy U. Va., Charlottesville, 1947-48; fellow in medicine U. Tex. Southwest, Dallas, 1946-47, 48-50; with Presbyn. Hosp., Dallas, 1966—. Asst. clin. prof. pharmacology U. Tex. Southwest Med. Sch., 1950-83, clin. assoc. prof. internal medicine, 1981-88. Fellow Am. Acad. Allergy, Asthma and Immunology, Am. Coll. Allergy, Asthma and Immunology, Am. Coll. Clin. Pharmacology and Chemotherapy. Office: Presbyn Prof Bldg 8210 Walnut Hill Ln Ste 818 Dallas TX 75231-4421 Office Phone: 214-369-1901.

HOLMAN, JAMES J., lawyer; b. Chester, Pa., Mar. 21, 1964; BA summa cum laude, Allentown Coll. of St. Francis de Sales (now DeSales U.), 1986; JD, Villanova U., 1989. Bar: NJ 1989, Pa. 1989, US Dist. Ct. Ea. Dist. Pa., US Dist. Ct. Dist. NJ, Supreme Ct. Pa., Supreme Ct. NJ. Assoc. Duane Morris LLP, Phila., 1989—99, ptnr., 1999—, hiring ptnr. Mem. Phila. Vol. Lawyers for the Arts, Amnesty Internat. Mem.: ABA (bus. law sect.), Phila. Bar Assn., Pa. Bar Assn. Office: Duane Morris LLP One Liberty Pl Philadelphia PA 19103-7396 Office Phone: 215-979-1530. Office Fax: 215-979-1020. Business E-Mail: jjholman@duanemorris.com.

HOLMAN, JAMES LEWIS, financial consultant, management consultant; b. Chgo., Oct. 27, 1926; s. James Louis and Lillian Marie (Walton) Holman; m. Elizabeth Ann Owens, June 18, 1948 (div. 1982); children: Craig Stewart, Tracy Lynn, Mark Andrew, Bonnie Gwen(dec.); m. Geraldine Ann Wilson, Dec. 26, 1982. BS in Econs. and Mgmt., postgrad., U. Ill., 1950, Northwestern U., 1954—55. Traveling auditor, then statistician, asst. controller parent buying dept. Sears, Roebuck & Co., Chgo., 1951—54; asst. to sec.-treas. Hanover Securities Co., 1954—65; asst. to controller chem. ops. divsn. Montgomery Ward & Co., Inc., 1966—68; controller Henrotin Hosp., 1968; bus. mgr. Julian, Dye, Javid, Hunter & Najafi Associated, 1969—81, cons., 1981—84. Vol. cons., adminstrv. asst. Fiji Sch. Medicine, Suva, 1984—86, cons., 1987—89; vol. bus. cons. U.S. Peace Corps, Honduras, 1989, cons., 1989—; cons., dir., sec.-treas Comprehensive Resources Ltd., Glenview, Ill., 1982, Wheaton, 82, Walnut Creek, Calif., 82; sec.-treas. Medtran, Inc., 1980—83; sec. James C. Valenta, P.C., 1979—82; sponsored project adminstr. Northwestern U., Evanston, Ill., 1984. Sec. B.R. Ryall YMCA, Glen Ellyn, Ill., 1974—76; treas. DuPage Symphony, 1955—58; trustee Gary Meml. United Meth. Ch., Wheaton, 1961—69, 1974—77; bd. dirs. B.R. Ryall YMCA, 1968—78, DuPage Symphony, 1954—58, Goodwill Industries, Chgo., 1978—79. With USN, 1944—46. Mem.: Kiwanis (bd. dirs. Chgo. 1956—60, bd. dirs. youth found. 1957—60, pres. 1958—60). Baha'I. Home and Office: 1571 Burr Oak Ct Wheaton IL 60187-2709

HOLMAN, J(OHN) LEONARD, retired manufacturing corporation executive; b. Moose Jaw, Sask., Can., Aug. 30, 1929; s. Charles Claude and Lillian Kathleen (Haw) H.; m. Julia Pauline Benfield, July 18, 1953; children: Nancy Jane, Sally Joan. BS in Civil Engring., U. Alta., 1953. Pres. Consolidated Concrete Ltd., Calgary, Canada, 1969-72; dir., pres. BACM Industries Ltd., Calgary, 1972-76; exec. v.p. Genstar Corp., Calgary, 1976-79, San Francisco, 1980-87, dir. several subs. cos.; pres., CEO CBR Cement Corp., San Mateo, Calif., 1986-88, chmn. bd., 1988-89, ret., 1990. Bd. dirs., officer several nat. trade assns. Mem. Assn. Profl. Engrs. Alta. (life), Calgary Exhbn. and Stampede (hon., life, dir.), Calgary Golf and Country Club. Home: 111 Country Club Estates 111-5555 Elbow Dr SW Calgary AB Canada T2V 1H7 Personal E-mail: johnlholman@shaw.ca.

HOLMAN, KAREN MARIE ANDERSON, purchasing agent; b. Anchorage, Sept. 6, 1962; d. Joseph Willie and Rose Millicent (Watson) Anderson; m. Robert L. Holman Jr., Nov. 27, 1982. AA in Bus. Adminstrn., Anchorage Community Coll., 1984; BA in Orgnl. Adminstrn., Alaska Pacific U., 1991; postgrad., Concord U., 2003—. Cert. purchasing mgr.; accredited purchasing practitioner. masters cert. gov. contracting, George Washington U. 1996. Sr. office clk. Bur. of the Census, Anchorage, 1980; premium audit clk. Providence Wash. Ins., Anchorage, 1981-82; info. systems clk. G.A Ltd., Anchorage, 1982-83; purchasing agt. State of Alaska, Anchorage, 1984-89, U. Alaska, Anchorage, 1989-92, ATU Telecommunications, 1992—97; purchasing sys. mgr. Am. Airlines, Ft. Worth, 1999—2002, sr. commodity mgr., 1997—, 2002—; co-woner Holman & Assocs. real estate rentals, 1984—. Del. Dem. Group State Caucuses, Anchorage, 1989; state dir. pub. rels. Alaska Ecclesiastical Jurisdiction; bd. dirs. Alaska Women's Resource Ctr., 1989-91, chmn. bd., 1999-2001, 1st v.p., 2002-03; chair bd. dirs. Greater Ft. Worth chpt. Sickle Cell Disease Assn., Ft. Worth, 2003—. Mem. Nat. Assn. Purchasing Mgmt. Home: 12543 Basque Pl Woodbridge VA 22192-3134

HOLMAN, LARRY DEAN, health care administrator; b. Lincoln, Nebr., Nov. 1, 1940; s. Clarence Woodford and Ethel Elizabeth (Remmenga) H.; m. Setsuko Umekawa, Dec. 5, 1960 (div. Aug. 1978); children: Lori Akiko, Yuko Donna; m. Debbie Joan Berkowitz, Dec. 8, 1980; children: Andrew Joseph, Jodi Michelle, Matthew Jacob. AA, Palomar Community Coll., San Marcos, Calif., 1971, C.C. of Phila., 1999; BS, George Washington U., 1974; MBA, LaSalle U., 1989, MS, 1990. Enlisted USN, 1958, advanced through grades to lt. comdr., ret., 1982, hosp. corpsman, 1958-71; with USN Med. Service Corps, 1971-82; purchasing dir. St. Francis Country House, Darby, Pa., 1982-85; bus. mgr. Stapeley Hall, Phila., 1985-86; bus., program mgr. Seaman's Ch. Inst., Phila., 1986-87; buyer Grad. Hosp., Phila., 1988-89, Grad. Health System, Phila., 1989; purchasing agt. Shriners Hosps., Phila., 1989-91; purchasing mgr. Jeanes Hosp., Phila., 1991-98; Y2K project site coord. Temple U. Health Sys., Phila., 1998-2000; asst. dir. purchasing Temple U., Phila., 2000—. Mem.: AMVETS, VFW (life), Internat. Chief Petty Officers Assn., CEC/Seabee Hist. Found., Nat. Assn. Medics and Corpsmen, Am. Mil. Soc., Nat. Assn. of Purchasing Mgrs., Jewish War Vets. U.S. (past comdr. Post 706, legis. chair Phila. County Coun., nat. vice chair Vietnam vets., newsletter editor 2004), Vets. Vietnam War, Naval. Res. Assn., Vietnam Era Seabees, Fleet Res. Assn., Non-Commd. Officers Assn., Am. Assn. Navy Hosp. Corps, Am. Soc. Mil. Compts., Nat. Assn. Uniformed Svcs. (life), Am. Mil. Retirees Assn. (life), Mil. Officers Assn. Am. (life), Navy Seabee Vets. Am. (life), Navy League U.S. (life), Vietnam Vets. Am. (life), Assn. Mil. Surgeons U.S. (life), Friends of Pennypack Pk. (life), Navy Club USA, Am. Legion. Jewish. Avocations: reading, counseling. Home: 6746 Souder St Philadelphia PA 19149-2208 Office: Temple U 1601 N Broad St Philadelphia PA 19122-6099 Office Phone: 215-204-2745. E-mail: lholman@prodigy.net.

HOLMAN, LESLIE ANN, lawyer; b. N.Y.C., Feb. 10, 1962; d. Martin and Agnes Eve Ehrenreich; m. Andrew Keith Holman, June 14, 1990; children: Amanda, Zachary. BA in Psychology, Clark U., 1983; JD with distinction, Hofstra U., 1987. Bar: N.Y. 1988, Vt. 1997. Assoc. Rivkin Radler Dunne & Byan, Uniondale, NY, 1987—90, Milgrim, Tomajan & Lee, N.Y.C., 1990—91, Pierez, Ackerman & Levine, Great Neck, NY, 1991—92, Wilson Powell Lang & Faris, Burlington, Vt., 1996—99, Bothfeld & Volk, Burlington, 1999—2000; pvt. practice Burlington, 2000—. Mem. Flynn Theater Programming Com., 2001—. Mem.: Vt. Bar Assn. (mem. internat. law com.), Am. Immigration Lawyers Assn. (Vt. INS liaison N.E. chpt. 2001—). Avocations: dance, skiing. Office: 1 Lawson Ln Burlington VT 05401 E-mail: lholman@immigrationvt.com.

HOLMAN, MAUREEN, lawyer; b. Mpls., Jan. 30, 1952; BA, U. Nebr., 1973; JD, U. N.D., 1983. Bar: N.D. 1983, Minn. 1983. Atty. Serkland Law Firm, Fargo, ND. Mem.: ABA, Order of Coif, State Bar Assn. N.D. (bd. govs. 1995—97, joint task force on family law 1995—, disciplinary bd. Supreme Ct. 1997—), Cass County Bar Assn., Minn. State Bar Assn. (pres.-elect 2002—03), Phi Delta Phi, Phi Beta Kappa. Office: Serkland Law Firm PO Box 6017 10 Roberts St Fargo ND 58108-6017

HOLMAN, RALPH THEODORE, retired biochemistry professor, nutritionist; b. Mpls., Mar. 4, 1918; s. Alfred Theodore and May Carlia Anna (Nilson) Holman; m. Karla Calais, Mar. 26, 1943; 1 child, Nils Teodore. AA, Bethel Jr. Coll., 1937; BS, U. Minn., 1939; MS, Rutgers U., 1941; PhD, U. Minn., 1944. Instr., div. of biochemistry U. Minn., Mpls., 1944-46; NRC-Nat. Acad. Scis. fellow Med. Nobel Inst., Stockholm, Sweden, 1946-47; Am. Scandinavian Found. fellow U. Uppsala, Sweden, 1947; assoc. prof. biochemistry and nutrition Tex. A&M U., College Station, 1948-51; assoc. prof. biochemistry Hormel Inst., U. Minn., Austin, 1951-56, prof., 1956-88, exec. dir., 1975-85, emeritus prof., 1988—; also adj. prof. of biochemistry Mayo Med. Sch., Rochester, Minn., 1977—. Mem. nutrition study sect. NIH, 1959-63; pres., organizer Golden Jubilee Internat. Congress on Essential Fatty Acids and Prostaglandins, 1980; mem. adv. bd. Deul. Conf. on Lipids, 1960-86; Sinclair Meml. lectr. Third Internat. Congress on Essential Fatty Acids and Eicasanoids, Adelaide, 1992. Founding editor Progress in Lipid Research, 1951—; editor Lipids, 1974-85; mem. editl. bd. Jour. Nutrition, 1962-66; contbr. 400 publs. on nutritional biochemistry of lipids; initiated omega 3 and omega 6 nomenclature for essential fatty acids, 1963; current rsch. on essentiality of omega 3 fatty acids. Pres. Mower County Coun. Churches., Austin, 1953-57; mem. Hormel Found., Austin, 1979-86. Recipient Fachini award Italian Oil Chemists, Milan; named Disting. Alumnus Bethel U., 1998. Fellow Am. Inst. Nutrition (Borden award 1966); mem. NAS, Am. Chem. Soc., Am. Oil Chemists Soc. (pres. 1974-75, Lipid Chemistry award 1979, Baldwin Disting. Svc. award 2001), Am. Soc. Biol. Chemists, Am. Orchid Soc. (rsch. com. 1980-85), Am. Heart Assn. (bd. dirs. Minn. affiliate 1991-93). Democrat. Congregationalist. Achievements include original research on essential nature of omega 3 polyunsaturated fatty acids. Home: 1403 2nd Ave SW Austin MN 55912-1609 Office: U Minn Hormel Inst 801 16th Ave NE Austin MN 55912-3679 Office Phone: 507-437-8804.

HOLME, HOWARD KELLEY, lawyer; b. Denver, May 5, 1945; s. Peter Hagner Jr. and Lena (Phillips) H.; m. Barbara Lynn Shaw, June 16, 1968; children: Timothy Peter, Lisa. AB in history with distinction and honor, Stanford U., 1967; JD, Yale U., 1972. Bar: Colo. 1972, U.S. Dist. Ct. Colo. 1972, U.S. Ct. Appeals (10th cir.) 1972, U.S. Supreme Ct. 1984. Staff Denver U. Law Sch., 1969—71; assoc. Fairfield & Woods, Denver, 1972—77; ptnr., dir. Fairfield & Woods, PC, Denver, 1977—98; pres. Bandwidth Market Ltd., Denver, 1998—. Cons. Fryingpan-Ark. Project, Southeastern Colo. Water Conservation Dist., 1976-98. Editor: National Water Resources Regulation: Where is the Environment Pendulum Now?, 1994; contbr. articles to profl. jours. Bd. dirs. nat. legal adv. com. Planned Parenthood Fedn. Am., N.Y.C.; active Colo. Supreme Ct. law com., Denver. Mem. Colo. Bar Assn., Denver Bar Assn., Denver Law Club, Colo. Yale Assn. (pres.), Assn. Yale Alumni (del.), Cactus Club (pres.). Home: 5833 Montview Blvd Denver CO 80207-3923 Office: Bandwidth Market Ltd 1700 Lincoln St Ste 2400 Denver CO 80203-4524 Office Phone: 303-355-0179. Office Fax: 415-329-1651. Business E-Mail: hholme@bandwidthmarket.com.

HOLME, RICHARD PHILLIPS, lawyer; b. Denver, Nov. 6, 1941; s. Peter Hagner Jr. and Lena (Phillips) H.; m. Barbara June Friel, July 17, 1944; children: Daniel Friel, Robert Muir. BA, Williams Coll., Williamstown, Mass., 1963; JD, U. Colo., 1966. Bar: Colo. 1966, U.S. Dist. Ct. Colo. 1966, U.S. Ct. Claims 1990, U.S. Ct. Appeals (10th cir.) 1966, U.S. Ct. Appeals (1st cir.) 1980, U.S. Dist. Ct. D.C. 1988, U.S. Ct. Appeals (D.C. cir.) 1988, U.S. Ct. Appeals (4th cir.) 1989, U.S. Ct. Appeals (fed. cir.) 1995, U.S. Supreme Ct. 1975. Assoc. Davis, Graham & Stubbs, Denver, 1966-68, ptnr., 1972-87, 91—, mng. ptnr., D.C. office, 1987-91; dep. Denver Dist. Atty., 1969-71. Grievance com. Colo. Supreme Ct., Denver, 1979-85, civil rules com., 1994—, civil justice com., 1998—. Fellow Am. Bar Found.; mem. ABA, ABA Found., Colo. Bar Found., Colo. Bar Assn. (bd. govs. 1974-76, 85-87, 95-99, 2001-03), Denver Bar Assn. (trustee 1977-80, 1st v.p. 1997-98), Order of Coif. Presbyterian. Home: 3944 S Depew Way Denver CO 80235-3105 Office Phone: 303-892-9400.

HOLMEN, REYNOLD ALGOTT EMANUEL, chemist; b. Essex, Iowa, Oct. 23, 1916; s. John Algott and Clara Amelia (Christensen) H.; m. Betty Jane Heginbottom, June 20, 1942 (dec. 1990); children: Karen C., John R., Robert C.; m. Johnnie Mae Leak, Nov. 20, 1993 (dec. 2000). AB, Augustana Coll., Ill., 1936; MS, U. Mich., 1937, PhD, 1949. Rsch. chemist DuPont Co., Phila., also Flint, Mich., 1937-46; sr. rsch. chemist ctrl. rsch. dept. 3M Co., St. Paul, 1948-55, sect. mgr. tech. info. and patient liaison, 1955-57, sect. mgr. inorganic sect., 1957-62, organic scouting mgr., 1959-62, mgr. R&D Lab.,

Reflective Product divsn., 1962-71, lab. mgr. R&D spl. enterprises dept., 1971-82; v.p. R&D KEMSERCH, Inc., Onamia, Minn., 1984-96; ret. Author: Kasimir Fajans: The Man and His Work, 1990. With med. corps. U.S. Army, 1941. Rackham scholar U. Mich., 1936-37; named to Wisdom Hall of Fame. Mem. Am. Chem. Soc., Phi Lambda Upsilon, Sigma Gamma Epsilon. Lutheran. Achievements include 20 U.S. patents; development of first catalytic dehydration of lactic acid to acrylic acid, first catalytic dehydrochlorination of alpha-chloropronic acid to acrylic acid, (with other) first sealed polycellular cube-corner retroreflective sheet, first conterfeit-resistant driver's license adopted by a state, development of first binary packaging film from two disparate solid films joined sans adhesive, improved authenticatable document construction. Home: 240 East Ave Apt 317 Mahtomedi MN 55115-2295 E-mail: reholmen@aol.com.

HOLMER, ALAN FREEMAN, former trade association executive; b. N.Y.C., July 24, 1949; s. A. Freeman and Marcia K. (Wright) H.; m. Joan Mary Ozark, June 30, 1973; children— Scott, Joy AB, Princeton U., 1971; JD, Georgetown U., 1978. Bar: D.C., Oreg. Adminstrv. asst. Senator Bob Packwood, Washington, 1972-78; assoc. Steptoe & Johnson, Washington, 1978-81; dep. asst. to pres. for intergovtl. affairs The White House, Washington, 1981-83; dep. asst. sec. for import adminstrn. Dept. Commerce, Washington, 1983-85; gen. counsel Office of U.S. Trade Rep., Washington, 1985-87; amb. Dep. U.S. Trade Rep., Washington, 1987-89; ptnr. Sidley & Austin, Washington, 1989-96; pres., CEO, Pharm. Rsch. and Manufacturers of Am., Washington, 1996—2005. Adj. prof. Georgetown U. Law Ctr., Washington, 1990; amb. and chmn. U.S. del. to Bonn Econ. Conf., 1990. Author: (with Judith H. Bello) The Antidumping and Countervailing Duty Laws: Key Legal and Policy Issues, 1987, Guide to the U.S.-Canada Free-Trade Agreement, 1990; contbr. numerous articles to profl. jours. Mem. Svcs. Policy Adv. Com., 1991-94; mem. adv. coun. Korea Econ. Inst. Am., 1992-96; trustee Met. D.C. chpt. Cystic Fibrosis Found., 1984-96, pres., 1991-94); bd. dirs. Coun. on Family Health, 1996—, Friends of the Nat. Libr. of Medicine, 1996—, Nat. Health Coun., 1999—. Recipient Disting. Cmty. Svc. award, Princeton Club Washington, 1992, Marriott Lifetime Achievement award, Arthritis Found., 2001. Mem. Internat. Fedn. of Pharm. Mfrs. (mem. coun. 1996—), Coun. Fgn. Rels. Republican.

HOLMES, ANN HITCHCOCK, journalist; b. El Paso, Apr. 25, 1922; d. Frederick E. and Joy (Crutchfield) H. Student, Whitworth Coll., 1940, So. Coll. Fine Arts, 1944. With Houston Chronicle, 1942—, fine arts editor, 1948-89, critic-at-large, 1989-98. Author: Presence, The Transco Tower, 1985, Joy Unconfined—Robert Joy in Houston: A Portrait of Fifty Years, 1986, Alley Theater: Four Decades in Three Stages, 1986. Mem. Houston Mcpl. Art Commn., 1965-74; mem. fine arts adv. coun. U. Tex., Austin, 1967—; bd. dirs. Rice Design Alliance, Houston, 1988-91, Alliance Francaise, Houston, 1989-93, Bus. Arts Fund, Houston, 1993-96. Recipient Ogden Reid Found. award for study of arts in Europe, 1953; Guggenheim fellow, 1960-61; recipient Ford Found. award, 1965, John G. Flowers award archtl. writing Tex. Soc. Architects, 1972, 74, 77, 80 Mem.: Am. Theater Critics Assn. (founding mem. 1974, exec. com. 1975—, co-chmn. 1987—88). Home and Office: 10807 Beinhorn Rd Houston TX 77024-3008 Personal E-mail: annhholmes@aol.com.

HOLMES, ANNA-MARIE, ballerina, ballet mistress; b. Mission City, B.C., Can., Apr. 17, 1942; arrived in U.S., 1981; d. George Henry and Maxine Marie (Botterill) Ellerbeck; m. David Holmes; 1 child, Lian-Marie. Diploma, Royal Conservatory of Music. Lectr. in field. Dancer (ballets) Swan Lake, Cinderella, Romeo and Juliet, Sleeping Beauty, Bayadere, Laurencia, Paquita, Graduation Ball, Les Sylphides, Prince Igor, Giselle, Nutcracker, Firebird, Raymonda, Kirov Ballet, Leningrad, 1963, (films) Tour En L'Air, Ballet Adagio, Don Juan, Chinese Nightingale, numerous appearances on European N.Am. TV, Don Quixote, 1989—; co-dir.: (ballets) Massimo Opera Theatre, 1993; prodr.(film documentation): Kirov Vagonova Tchg. Sys.; choreographer Swan Lake, Tokyo, 1991, Norwegion Nat. Ballet, 1998, Sleeping Beauty Act III, Boston Ballet, 1991, Giselle, 1991, Sleeping Beauty, Boston Ballet, 1993, 1996, Tokyo, 1996, Le Corsaire, Boston Ballet, Am. Ballet Theatre, 1998, Great Performances, 1999, Met. Opera House, N.Y.C., 1999, Don Quixote, Boston Ballet, 2000; co-prodr.: Raymonda Finnish Nat. Ballet, 2003, Premier Am. Ball Theater, 2004; artistic dir. La Bayadere, Flanders-Antwerp Belgium, 2004. Recipient Emmy award, 2000. Office: Carnegie House 100 W 57th St Ste 11-O New York NY 10019 Office Phone: 917-365-5311. E-mail: Aellerbeck@aol.com.

HOLMES, ARTHUR S., manufacturing executive; m. Christy Holmes. BS, MS, Pa. State U.; MBA, Northwestern U. Founder, chmn., CEO Chart Industries, Inc., Cleve., 1989—; chmn. ALTEC Internat. Ltd. Partnership. Bd. dirs. 1st Bank Milw. Mem. bd. advisors Biterbo Coll.; mem. La Crosse Area Devel. Com.; mem. sch. adv. bd. U. Wis. Named Pa. State Disting. Engring. Alumnus, 1993; recipient Pope John XXIII award Viterbo Coll., 1999. Office: Chart Industries 5885 Landerbrook Dr Ste 205 Cleveland OH 44124-4031 Fax: 440-753-1491.

HOLMES, BARBARAANN KRAJKOSKI, secondary school educator; b. Evansville, Ind., Mar. 21, 1946; d. Frank Joseph and Estella Marie (DeWeese) Krajkoski; m. David Leo Holmes, Aug. 21, 1971; 1 child, Susan Ann Sky. BS, Ind. State U., 1968, MS, 1969, specialist cert., 1976; postgrad., U. Nev., 1976-78. Acad. counselor Ind. State U., 1968-69, halls dir., 1969-73; dir. residence halls U. Utah, 1973-76; sales assoc. Fidelity Realty, Las Vegas, Nev., 1977-82; cert. analyst Nev. Dept. Edn., 1981-82; tchr. Clark County Sch. Dist., 1982-87, computer cons., adminstrv. specialist, instrnl. mgmt. sys., 1987-91, chair computer conf., 1990-92, adminstrv. specialist K-6, 1990-93; dean of student summer sch. site adminstr. Eldorado H.S., 1991-96; asst. prin. Garrett Mid. Sch., Boulder City, Nev., 1997-1999, So. Nev. Vocat. Tech. Ctr. Magnet H.S., 1999—. Mem. leadership design team Clark County Sch. Dist., 1996—98, 2001—02. Named Outstanding Sr. Class Woman, Ind. State U., 1969; recipient Dir.'s award U. Utah Residence Halls, 1973, Outstanding Tchr. award, 1984, Dist. Excellence in Edn. award, 1984, 86, 87, 88. Mem. AAUW, Am. Assn. Women Deans, Adminstrs. and Counselors, Am. Pers. and Guidance Assn., Nat. Assn. Sch. Adminstrs. (Clark County sch. adminstrv. sec., 2002-05), Clark County Assn. Secondary Sch. Prin. (sec. 2003-05, treas. 2005—), Am. Coll. Pers. Assn., Alumnae Assn. Chi Omega (treas. Terre Haute chpt. 1971-73, pres., bd. officer Las Vegas 1977-81, state rush info. chair, 1997—), Clark County Panhellenic Alumnae Assn. (pres. 1978-79), Computer Using Educators So. Nev. (sec. 1983-86, pres.-elect 1986-87, pres. 1987-88, state chmn. 1988-89, conf. chmn. 1989-92, sec. 1994-96, Hall of Fame 1995), Job's Daus. Club (guardian sec. 1995-99, dir. music 1999-2001,assisting Supreme Dep. 2001—, world youth v.p. 2004—), Order Eastern Star (worthy matron 2003-04, grand chaplin 2004-05), Phi Delta Kappa (Action award 1990-96, newspaper editor 1992-93). Achievements include developing personal awareness program U. Utah, 1973-76. Home: 1227 Kover Ct Henderson NV 89015-9017 Office: So Nev Vocat Tech Magnet HS 5710 Mountain Vista St Las Vegas NV 89120-2310 Office Phone: 702-799-7500 x 4201.

HOLMES, BERT OTIS E., JR., retired editor; b. Milan, Tenn., Sept. 20, 1921; s. Otis E. and Mary (Lassiter) H.; m. Marian Bush, June 10, 1942 (dec. Nov. 1964); children: Bert Otis E., Richard Bush; m. Helen Hankins, July 24, 1965; children: Chris, David. AA, Magnolia A. and M. Jr. Coll., 1940; BS, So. Meth. U., 1942. Successively copy reader, makeup editor, state editor, city staff reporter, city editor Dallas Times Herald, 1946-56, news editor, 1956-60, asst. mng. editor, 1960-64, exec. editor, 1964-65, assoc. editor, 1965-90. Pres. Family Svc. Agy., 1963-68, Tex. United Community Svcs., 1970-72, Sr. Citizens of Greater Dallas, 1995-96; bd. dirs. Dallas United Fund, Dallas Community Coun.; mem. City of Dallas Sr. Affairs Commn., 2005. With AUS, 1942-46, PTO. Mem. Dallas Assembly, Sigma Delta Chi, Dallas Press Club (pres. 1957, 78-79) Methodist. Home: 4515 W Lawther Dr Dallas TX 75214-1935

HOLMES, BROOX GARRETT, lawyer; b. Mobile, Ala., Nov. 15, 1932; s. Williams Coghlan and Philomene (Boogaerts) H.; m. Laura Claire Hays, Feb. 21, 1955 (dec. 2000); children: Broox Garrett, Dupree Hays, Williams Coghlan II; m. Elsie Crain Lyons, June 5, 2004. BA, U. Ala., 1954, JD, 1960. Bar: Ala. 1960. Since practiced in, Mobile; mem. firm Armbrect Jackson LLP, 1960—. Trustee St. Paul's Episcopal Sch., chmn. bd., 1980-83. Capt. USMCR, 1954-58. Fellow Am. Coll. Trial Lawyers (state chmn. 1991-92), Am. Bar Found.; mem. ABA, Ala. State Bar (bd. commrs. 1987-93, chmn. litigation sect. 1991, pres. 1994-95), Ala. Bar Found., Mobile Bar Assn. (exec. com. 1987-93), Nat. Assn. R.R. Trial Counsel, Internat. Assn. Def. Counsel, Am. Law Inst., Ala. Law Inst., Ala. Def. Lawyers (pres. 1977-78, named one of Best Lawyers in Am. bus. and personal injury litigation), Mobile Country Club (pres. 1983-84), Mobile Touchdown Club, Athelstan Club, Delta Kappa Epsilon, Phi Delta Phi. Episcopalian. Home: 5 Holland Park Mobile AL 36608 Office: Armbrecht Jackson LLP PO Box 290 Mobile AL 36601-0290 Office Phone: 251-405-1300. Business E-Mail: bgh@ajlaw.com.

HOLMES, CALVIN VIRGIL, mathematician, educator; b. New Hebron, Miss., Oct. 21, 1924; s. Norvel Virgil Holmes and Maud May Rester; m. Alvene Ione Hull, Sept. 2, 1956; children: Michael Lewis, Julie Ann Rolfing. BA, U. Miss., Oxford, 1947, MA, 1948; MS, U. Ill., 1952; PhD, U. Kans., 1955. From instr. to asst. prof. Murray (Ky.) State U., 1948—51; mathematician Northrop Aircraft, Hawthorne, Calif., 1955—56; asst. prof. San Diego State U., 1956—60, assoc. prof., 1960—64, prof., 1964—92, prof. emeritus, 1992—. Lt. USN, 1943—63. Mem.: Math. Assn. Am.

HOLMES, DALE ARTHUR, optics scientist; b. Biwabik, Minn., Dec. 31, 1937; s. Arthur Emil Holmes and Saima Amanda Luoma; m. Joan Christine Cawthon, May 4, 1962 (dissolved July 1996); children: Kevin, Camille. BEE, Purdue U, 1960; MS, Carnegie Inst. Tech., 1961, PhD, 1965; MS, U Rochester, 1969. Asst. prof. EE Carnegie Inst. Tech., Pitts., 1965—66; officer USAF Weapons Lab, Albuquerque, 1966—74; optical engr. Boeing, Canoga Park, Calif., 1974—2003. Contbr. articles profl. jour. Capt. USAF, 1966—74. Decorated R&D award USAF. Republican. Christian. Achievements include patents in field. Avocations: pistol shooting, fishing. Home: 27904 Doubletree Way Castaic CA 91384

HOLMES, DALLAS SCOTT, judge, educator; b. L.A., Dec. 2, 1940; s. Donald Cherry and Hazel (Scott) H.; m. Patricia McMichael, Aug. 21, 1965; children: Mark Scott, Tobin John. AB cum laude, Pomona Coll., 1962; MS, London Sch. Econs., 1964; JD, U. Calif., Berkeley, 1967. Bar: Calif. 1968. Assoc. Best, Best & Krieger, Riverside, Calif., 1968-74, ptnr., 1974-96; mem. Calif. Jud. Coun., 1995-96; adj. prof. Hastings Coll. Law U. Calif., San Francisco, 1990; exec. asst. to Assembly majority fl. leader, Calif. State Legislature, Sacramento, 1969-70; asst. adj. prof. Grad. Sch. Mgmt., U. Calif.-Riverside, 1977-88; lectr. UCLA Ext., 1987-2002; Superior Ct. judge, 1996—; chair Riverside Superior Ct. Jury Com., 1997-2003, 2005—; chair Calif. jud. coun. task force jury sys. improvements, 1998-2003; mem. bd. trustees, U. Calif., Riverside Found., 1983-; city atty. City of Corona, Calif., 1976-96; lectr. local govt. and univ. ext. groups. Pres., Pomona Coll. Alumni Coun., 1973-74, Century Club, Riverside, 1974-76, Citizens Univ. Com., 1983-85, Downtown Riverside Assn., 1987-88, Torchbearers Pomona Coll., 1995-96; chmn. legal affairs com. Assn. Calif. Water Agys., 1985-91. Mem. bd. govs. State Bar Calif., 1990-93, v.p. 1992-93. Named Man of Yr., Riverside Press-Enterprise, 1962, Young Man of Yr., Riverside Jr. C. of C., 1972. Mem. Riverside County Bar Assn. (pres. 1982), Calif. State Bar Assn. (exec. com. pub. law sect. 1983-86), Am. Judicature Soc. (jury ctr. adv. com.), Riverside Rotary Club. Republican. Presbyterian. Contbr. articles on mass transit, assessment of farmland in Calif., exclusionary zoning and environ. law to profl. jours.; author proposed tort reform initiative for Calif. physicians. Office: Riverside Superior Ct 4050 Main St Riverside CA 92501-3702 Office Phone: 951-955-1482.

HOLMES, DAVID LYNN, religion educator; BA in English, Mich. State U.; MA in English, Columbia U.; MA, PhD in Religion, Princeton U.; postgrad., Columbia U., Union Theol. Sem., N.Y.C., Duke U. Div. Sch.; DHL (hon.), Lycoming Coll., 2000. Prof. religious studies Coll. of William and Mary, Williamsburg, Va., 1965—, Walter G. Mason prof. religious studies, 2005—. Instr. Carnegie-Mellon U.; vis. prof. U. Va. Author: A Brief History of the Episcopal Church, 1993, Devereux Jarratt: An Autobiography, 1995, A Nation Mourns, 1999, The Religion of the Founding Fathers, 2003, others; ch. revs. editor: Anglican and Episcopal History; contbr. articles to profl. jours. Exec. bd. dirs. Coun. for America's First Freedom. Mem. Am. Soc. Ch. History (mem. exec. coun.), Hist. Soc. Episcopal Ch. (exec. bd. dirs.), Ptnrs. for Sacred Places, Episcopal Guild of Scholars, Bishop James Madison Soc., Phi Beta Kappa. Democrat. Episcopalian. Office: Coll William and Mary Dept Religious Studies Sir Christopher Wren Bldg Williamsburg VA 23187-8795 Office Phone: 757-221-2177. Business E-Mail: dlholm@wm.edu.

HOLMES, DWIGHT ELLIS, architect; b. Ashville, N.C., Nov. 8, 1938; s. John Dwight and Leymon (Butler) H.; m. Mary Rose Speer; children—Sheryl, John, Scott BS in Architecture, Ga. Inst. Tech., 1960; B.Arch., N.C. State U., 1962. Registered architect, Fla. Architect Mark Hampton, Architect, Tampa, Fla., 1961-72; architect Rowe Holmes Assocs. Architects, Inc., Tampa, Fla., 1972-84, The Design Arts Group, Inc., Tampa, 1984-85, Rowe Holmes Hammer Russell Architects, Inc., Tampa, 1986-92, Holmes, Hepner & Assocs. Architects, Tampa, 1992—. Contbr. articles to profl. jours. Mem. State of Fla. Smart Schs. Clearinghouse, 1997—. Recipient numerous awards Am. Assn. Sch. Adminstrs., Am. Plywood Assn., Archtl. Record, Council Ednl. Facilities Planners, Fla. Concrete and Products Assn., Inc., Fla. Growers' Assn., Hillsborough County Planning Commn., Owens Corning Co., Fla. Solar Energy Ctr., Hillsborough County Hist. Preservation Bd., State of Fla. Fellow AIA (medal of honor Fla. Central chpt. 1980, award of honor Fla./Caribbean region 1982, numerous other awards) Clubs: University, Tampa Yacht and Country. Republican. Roman Catholic. Home: 5800 S Gordon Ave Tampa FL 33611-4768 Office: Holmes Hepner & Assocs Architects 109 N Brush St Tampa FL 33602 Office Phone: 813-229-0614. E-mail: holmes@holmeshepner.com.

HOLMES, EDWARD WARREN, dean, physician, medical educator; b. Winona, Miss., Jan. 25, 1941; s. Edward and Mary (Hart) H.; m. Judith L. Swain, Jan. 25, 1980. BS, Washington and Lee U., 1963; MD, U. Pa., 1967. Intern Hosp. of U. Pa., 1967-68; resident in medicine Duke U. Med. Ctr., Durham, NC, 1970—71, 1973—74, fellow in metabolism, 1971—73; prof. medicine and biochemistry Duke U. Sch. Medicine, Durham, NC, 1974-91, chief divsn. metabolism, endocrinology and genetics, 1983—91; investigator Howard Hughes Med. Inst., 1974-87; prof., chmn. dept. medicine U. Pa., Phila., 1991-97; sr. assoc. dean rsch. Stanford U. Sch. Medicine, 1997-2000; dean Duke U. Sch. Medicine, Durham, 1999—2000; vice chancellor academic affairs Duke U. Med. Ctr., Durham, 1999—2000; vice chancellor health scis., dean sch. medicine U. Calif., San Deigo, 2000—. Reviewer in molecular medicine. With USPHS, 1968-70. Grantee NIH. Mem. Am. Soc. Clin. Investigation, Assn. Am. Physicians. Office: Univ Calif Sch Medicine 1313 Basic Sci Bldg 9500 Gilman Dr La Jolla CA 92093-0602

HOLMES, FREDERICK FRANKLIN, retired medical educator, physician, researcher; b. Tacoma, Wash., Oct. 16, 1932; s. Allan Russell and Margaret A. (Beistel) H.; m. Grace Elinor Foege, June 26, 1955; children: Heidi, Cynthia (dec.), Lisa, Theodore, Julia, Andrew. BA, Coll. Puget Sound, 1953; MD, U. Wash., 1957. Diplomate Am. Bd. Internal Medicine. Intern U. Kans. Med. Ctr., Kansas City, 1957-58, resident, 1963-65, fellow hematology, 1965-66; med. missionary Luth. Ch. Clinic, Menglembu, Malaysia, 1959-63; chief medicine Kilimanjaro Christian Med. Centre, Moshi, Tanzania, 1970-72; asst. prof. U. Kans. Med. Ctr., Kansas City, 1966-70, from assoc. prof. to prof., 1978-82, Edward Hashinger disting. prof., 1982-2000. Contbr. articles to profl. jours., chpts. to books. Vol. Am. Cancer Soc., Topeka, 1972—, nat. del., 1988. Recipient Humanitarian award U. Wash. Sch. Medicine, 1995; named Alumnus Cum Laude U. Puget Sound, 1985, Hon. Prof. Henan Med. U., 1989. Fellow ACP, Royal Soc. Medicine; mem. AAAS, AMA, Am. Fedn. for Aging Rsch., Am. Geriatrics Soc., Royal Soc. for Asian Affairs, Soc. for the Preservation and Encouragement of Barbershop Quartet Singing in Am. Lutheran. Avocation: music. Business E-Mail: fholmes@kumc.edu.

HOLMES, HARRY DADISMAN, health facility administrator; b. Houston, Aug. 8, 1944; s. Harry Newton and Ruth Eleanor (Dadisman) H.; m. Jaleea George, May 15, 2004; children: Colin George, Hillary Hunt, Ashley Elizabeth. BA, Rice U., 1966; MA, La. State U., 1968; PhD, U. Mo., 1973. Asst. prof. urban devel. U. Tenn., Knoxville, 1973—76; asst. to exec. v.p. Tex. Med. Ctr., Inc., Houston, 1976—80; dir. govt. affairs, orgnl. liaison U. Tex. System Cancer Ctr., Houston, 1980—90; asst. to pres. U. Tex. Sys. Cancer Ctr., Houston, 1981—90; v.p. govt. rels. U. Tex. M.D. Anderson Cancer Ctr., Houston, 1990—. Pres., bd. dirs. City of Houston Higher Edn. Fin. Corp., 1985-; mem. Cancer Ctrs. Adminstrs. Forum, 1994—; mem. select com. on pub. issues Greater Houston Hosp. Coun., 1983-94; mem. exec. adv. bd. White, Petrov and McHone, 1987-95; mem. pub. rels. adv. coun. Tex. Med. Ctr., 1985—; founder Houston Biotech. Assn., 1986; mem. exec. com. Nat. Comprehensive Cancer Networks, 1998—; chair public issues com. Assn. Am. Cancer Insts., 1999-; mem. govt. rels. com. Am. Hosp. Assn., 1999-2000; govt. rels. com., vice chmn. Tex. Healthcare and Biosci. Inst., 2005; pres. bd. dirs. City of Houston Health Facilities Corp., City of Houston Indsl. Devel. Corp., Nat. Coalition Cancer Rsch., 2005. Mem. adminstrv. bd. St. Luke's Meth. Ch.; mem. Mayor's Task Force on Pvt. Sector Initiatives for Houston, 1981-82, Houston C.C. Found. Bd., 1992—, Greater Houston Partnership State and Fed. Com., 1989—; mem. U. Tex. Tex./Mex. Border Health Task Force, 1989-2003, exec. com., 1989-2001; pres. Houston Health Facilities Corp., 2000—, Houston Indsl. Devel. Corp., 2000—; mem. Rice U. Fund Coun., 1991-94, Nat. Cancer Ctrs. Task Force, 1991—; mem. steering com. Tex. Colorectal Cancer Plan; mem. exec. bd. Leadership Houston, 1983-86, Houston Ctr. for Humanities, 1983-86; mem. govt. rels. com. Greater Houston Hosp. Coun., 1985-95; mem. com. Instnl. Task Force on Oncology in Chile, 1986-87; exec. com. Instnl. Strategic Planning Com., 1986-95; divsn. chmn. United Way of Houston, 1983. White fellow U. Mo., 1972. Office: U Tex MD Anderson Cancer Ctr 1515 Holcombe Blvd Houston TX 77030-4009 Home: 4203 Coleridge St Houston TX 77005 Office Phone: 713-792-8209. Business E-Mail: hholmes@mdanderson.org.

HOLMES, HENRY ALLEN, diplomat; b. Bucharest, Romania, Jan. 31, 1933; (parents Am. citizens); s. Julius Cecil and Henrietta (Allen) H.; m. Marilyn Janet Strauss, July 25, 1959; children: Katherine Anne, Gerald Allen. AB, Princeton U., 1954; Woodrow Wilson fellow, U. Paris, 1958. Intelligence rsch. analyst Dept. State, Cameroon, 1958-59, commd. fgn. svc. officer, 1959, assigned to Am. Embassy Yaoundé, Cameroon, 1959—61, Rome, 1963-67, counselor polit. affairs Am. embassy Paris, 1970-74, sr. exec. Seminar in Fgn. Policy Washington, 1974-75; assigned as dir. Office NATO and Atlantic polit. mil. aff. Bur. European Affairs, Washington, 1975-77; dep. chief mission U.S. Embassy Dept. State, Rome, 1977-79, prin. dep. asst. sec. state for European and Can. affairs Washington, 1979-82, amb. Am. embassy Portugal, 1982-85, asst. sec. Bur. Politico Mil. Affairs Washington, 1985-89, amb. at large for burdensharing, 1989-93, asst. sec. def. for spl. ops. and low-intensity conflict, 1993-99; adj. prof. Georgetown U., 2000—. Served as capt. USMC, 1954-57. Mem. Am. Fgn. Svc. Assn., Coun. Fgn. Rels., Am. Acad. Diplomacy, Washington Inst. Fgn. Affairs, Metro Club (Washington). Episcopalian. Personal E-mail: hallenholmes@aol.com.

HOLMES, JACK EDWARD, political science professor; b. Wichita, May 16, 1941; s. Herbert Paul and Marguerite Elizabeth (Duerr) H.; m. Linda Sue Pacheco, Dec. 28, 1996; stepchildren: Valerie, Cynthia, Jacqueline, Elizabeth. BA, Knox Coll., 1963; MA, U. Denver, 1967, PhD in Internat. Studies, 1972. Asst. prof. Hope Coll., Holland, Mich., 1969-72; dist. asst. Congressman Don Brotzman, Denver, 1973-75; asst. prof. Hope Coll., Holland, 1975-76, assoc. prof., 1976-87, prof., 1987—, chmn. dept. polit. sci., 1988—95, 1999—2004. Author: Mood/Interest Theory of American Foreign Policy, 1985; co-author: American Government Essentials and Perspectives, 1991, 94, 98. Campaign chmn. Ottawa County Reps., Holland, 1978, 82-96, chmn., 1997-2002, Ottawa County Bush for Pres, 2000, 2004; del. Rep. Nat. Conv., 2000; chmn. 2d Congl. Dist. Rep. Party, 2003—. Capt. U.S. Army, 1967-69. Named to Mich. Model UN Hall of Fame. Mem. Internat. Studies Assn., Am. Polit. Sci. Assn., Holy Cross Wilderness Def. Fund. Presbyterian. Avocations: backpacking, fishing. Office: Hope Coll 210 Lubbers Hall Holland MI 49422-9000 Office Phone: 616-395-7543. E-mail: holmes@hope.edu.

HOLMES, JAMES HILL, III, lawyer; b. Birmingham, Ala., Sept. 10, 1935; s. Houston Eccleston and Celia Lindsey (Wearn) Holmes; m. Julia (Judy) Ryman, Aug. 17, 1963; children: James H. IV, Randell Ryman, Tucker Malone. BBA, So. Meth. U., 1957, LLB, 1959. Bar: Tex. 1959, U.S. Ct. Mil. Appeals 1960, U.S. Dist. Ct. (no. dist.) Tex. 1963, U.S. Dist. Ct. (ea. dist.) Tex. 1966, U.S. Dist. Ct. (we. dist.) Tex. 1979, U.S. Ct. Appeals (5th and 11th cirs.) 1981, U.S. Supreme Ct. 1974. Ptnr. Burford & Ryburn, Dallas, 1962—. Mock trial participant Tex. Nurses Assn., 1978—86; spkr. State Bar Tex. Profl. Devel. Program, 1987—2002; co-chair adv. com. professionalism Supreme Ct. Tex., 1989—90. Contbr. articles to profl. jours. Past mem. University Park (Tex.) Bd. Adjustment; chmn. University Park (Tex.) Planning and Zoning Commn., 1988—94; numerous other offices in civic orgns.; city councilman City of University Park, 1994—2000, 2002—04, mayor pro tem, 1998—2000, mayor, 2004—; past dir. Child Guidance Clinic; past bd. dirs. Park Cities Town North YMCA; trustee Tex. Ctr. Legal Ethics & Professionalism, 2001—03; vice chmn. adminstrv. Tex. Ctr. Legal Ethics and Professionalism, 2001—03; past dir., past pres. All Sports Assn., Dallas, 1977; pres. Univ. Pk. Cmty. League, 1987—88. With USAF, 1959—62. Named one of Tex. Super Lawyers, Tex. Monthly, 2003, 2004, 2005; recipient Presdl. Citation, State Bar of Tex., 1995, Judge Sam Williams Local Bar Leadership award, 2001, Professionalism award, Coll. of the State Bar Tex., 1999, Morris Harrell Professionalism award, Dallas Bar Assn. and Tex. Ctr. for Ethics and Professionalism, 2000, Lola Wright Found. award, 2002, Jo Anna Moreland Outstanding Com. Chair award, DBA, 2003, Disting. Alumni award atty. in pvt. practice, So. Meth. U. Law Sch., 2004, 2005. Fellow: Tex. Bar Found., Am. Coll. Trial Lawyers; mem.: Dallas Bar Found., Patrick E. Higginbotham Am. Inn of Ct. (master 1989—95), Am. Bd. Trial Advocates (pres. Dallas chpt. 2000, named Tex. and Dallas chpts. Trial Lawyer of Yr. 2004), Tex. Bar Assn., Dallas Bar Assn. (numerous coms.), Def. Rsch. Inst. (state chmn. 1994), Internat. Assn. Def. Counsel, Assn. Def. Trial Attys., Tex. Assn. Def. Counsel (pres. 1992—93, Founder's award 1997), Dallas Assn. Def. Counsel (chmn. 1975), Blue Key, Phi Delta Theta, Phi Alpha Delta. Episcopalian. Avocations: jogging, spectator sports, outdoors. Home: 3804 Lovers Ln Dallas TX 75225 Office: Burford & Ryburn LLP 3100 Lincoln Pla 500 N Akard St Dallas TX 75201-6697 Office Phone: 214-740-3114.

HOLMES, JEAN LOUISE, real estate investor, humanities educator; b. Butler, Mo., Dec. 9, 1943; d. Victor Julius and Helen Emilia (Knapheide) Witte; m. Eugene Philmore Carter Jr., Aug. 21, 1965 (div. Aug. 1992); children: Kristin, Lance; m. Reed M. Holmes, Jan. 26, 1993. AA, Graceland Coll., Lamoni, Iowa, 1963; BA, Iowa State U., 1965; postgrad., U. Paris, 1965, Tufts U., 1973; MA in Judaic Studies magna cum laude, Hebrew Coll., Brookline, Mass., 1989; postgrad., Ratisbonne Ctr. of Judaic Studies, Jerusalem, 1993-95, Hebrew U./Yad Vashem, 1992, 95, Yad Vashem/Poland, 1998. Lic. bldg. constrn. supr. Mass. Tchr. French, Iowa, Mass., 1966-69; tchg. English lang. and lit., 1966-67; real estate broker Carter Realty, Pepperell, Mass., 1975—; pres., mgr. Viewpax Mondiale, Independence, Mo., 1982—; pres. Keshet Hashalom, Jerusalem, 1989—. Propr., Holmes Mgmt., 1997—; clk. Ctrl. Middlesex Multiple Listing Svc., Concord, Mass., 1980-81, v.p., 1982, pres., 1983; lectr. Remembering for the Future II, Berlin, 1994, Internat. Holocaust Scholars Conf., Mpls., 1996; dir., adj. prof. student intercultural travel to Israel, Jordan, Egypt, Park U., Mo., Graceland U., 1982—. Co-author: The Forerunners, 2003. Adv. bd. Peace Ctr., Independence, 1989-91; interfaith rels. com. Cmty. of Christ, Independence, 2000—; dir. Maine Friendship House, 2003—; exec. com. Nat. Christian Leadership Conf. for Israel, 2001—. Recipient Friendship award Israel Ministry of Tourism, Jerusalem, 1992, Maine Preservation award, 1866 Maine Friendship House, Jaffa Am. Colony, 2004. Avocations: photography, archaeology, adventure travel, literature. Home: PO Box 680 Pepperell MA 01463-0680 Office: Holmes Mgmt 125 Littleton Rd Apt 9 Ayer MA 01432-1733 Office Phone: 978-772-5797. Personal E-mail: jeanreed@mindspring.com.

HOLMES, JEANNE OWEN, horticulture educator; b. Hereford, Tex., Feb. 18, 1953; d. Jack Weldon and Helen Tietjens Owen; m. Tony Alan Holmes, Aug. 8, 1952; children: Nicolaus Alan, Susannah Lea, Martha Margarete. BS in Horticulture, U. Mo., Columbia, 1975; MS in Adult & Occupl Edn., Kans. State U., Manhattan, 1980. Horticulture instr. Paola Pub. Schs., Kans., 1975—79, Labette C.C., Parsons, Kans., 1980—82; horticulture prof. East Ctrl. Coll., Union, Mo., 1988—2001; horticulture instr. Mineral Area Coll., Park Hills, Mo., 2001—. Bd. dirs. Nat. Postsecondary Agr. Students, Indpls. Mem.: Mo. Assn. Colls. and Tchrs. of Agr. (assoc.; state coord. 2003—05). Home: 115 Southpark Dr Bonne Terre MO 63628 Office: Mineral Area Coll PO Box 1000 Park Hills MO 63601 Office Phone: 573-518-2323. Personal E-mail: tholmes001@charter.net. Business E-Mail: jholmes@mineralarea.edu.

HOLMES, JENNIFER SMITH, political scientist, educator; b. Edina, Minn., Aug. 15, 1971; d. Theodore Gerald and Carolyn April Smith; 1 child. BA in Polit. Sci., U. Chgo., 1993; PhD in Polit. Sci., U. Minn., 1998. Vis. asst. prof. govt. and politics U. Tex. at Dallas, Richardson, 1998—2000, asst. prof. govt. and politics and polit. economy, 2000—. Author: (book) Terrorism and Democratic Stability, 2001, New Approaches to Comparative Politics: Insights from Political Theory, 2003; contbr. articles to profl. jours. Mem. Dallas Com. on Fgn. Rels., 2000. Mem.: Southwestern Polit. Sci. Assn., Asociacion de Colombianistas, Latin Am. Studies Assn., So. Polit. Sci. Assn., Am. Polit. Sci. Assn. Democrat. Office: Univ Tex at Dallas GR 31 PO Box 830688 Richardson TX 75083-0688 Business E-Mail: jholmes@utdallas.edu.

HOLMES, JOHN LEONARD, chemistry professor; b. London, Nov. 29, 1931; came to Can., 1958; s. Leonard Thomas and Jessie Ethel (Doble) H.; m. Una Jane Watts, Dec. 12, 1958 (div. 1993). children: Susan P., Jonathan B.; m. Sheila Jean Robertson, Apr. 13, 1994; stepchildren: John Fergus, Isobel Clare. BSc, London U., 1954, PhD, 1957, DSc, 1983. Postdoctoral fellow NRC, Ottawa, Can., 1958-60; I.C.I. fellow Edinburgh U., Scotland, 1960-61, lectr., 1961-62; asst. prof. U. Ottawa, 1962-65, assoc. prof., 1965-73, prof., 1973-97, emeritus prof., 1997—. Nuffield vis. prof. U. Ghana, 1971, Overbeek vis. prof. U. Utrecht, The Netherlands, 1979, Disting. vis. scholar U. Adelaide, Australia, 1984; vis. fellow Australian Nat. U., Canberra, 1993, 2000; internat. sci. exchange fellow U. Bern, 1993. Editor Organic Mass Spectrometry Jour., 1976-93, European Mass Spectrometry jour., 1994-2001; contbr. over 280 articles to profl. jours. Recipient Barringer Rsch. award Can. Spectroscopy Soc., 1980, Herzberg award Can. Spectroscopy Soc., 1990, F.P. Lossing award Can. Mass Spectrometry Soc., 2000. Fellow Chem. Inst. Can. (medal 1989), Royal Soc. Can.; mem. Am. Soc. Mass Spectrometry, Brit. Soc. Mass Spectrometry (life), Internat. Yacht Racing Union (judge 1986-99), Can. Yachting Assn., Royal Yachting Assn. Clubs: Britannia Yacht (Ottawa). Home: 121 Buell St Unit 58 Ottawa ON Canada K1Z 7E7 Office Phone: 613-562-5118. E-mail: jholmes@science.uottawa.ca.

HOLMES, KAREN ANDERSON, lawyer; b. Arcadia, Calif., Nov. 7, 1957; d. Harold F. and Maureen L. Anderson; m. Richard N. Holmes, June 25, 1988; 1 child, Haley E. BA in Polit. Sci., San Diego State U., 1979; JD, Calif. Western Sch. of Law, 1983. Bar: Calif. 1983, U.S. Dist. (so. dist.) Calif. 1983, U.S. Ct. Appeals (9th cir.) 1984. Assoc. Alford & MacLeod, San Diego, 1983-86; from assoc. to ptnr. Edwards, Sooy & Byron (formerly Edwards, White & Sooy), San Diego, 1986-99; ptnr. Jaroszek, Roth & Kennedy, San Diego, 1999—. Bd. dirs., pres. San Diego State Alumni, 19889-91. Mem. So. Calif. Def. Lawyers, Def. Rsch. Inst. (chair constrn. law com. 2000-01), San Diego Def. Lawyers (bd. dirs., pres. 1991-95), San Diego County Bar Assn. (chair constrn. sect. 1997-99). Office: Jaroszek Roth & Kennedy 1230 Columbia St 600 San Diego CA 92101 E-mail: kahjrk@aol.com.

HOLMES, KATIE (KATHERINE NOELLE HOLMES), actress; b. Toledo, Ohio, Dec. 18, 1978; d. Martin and Kathy Holmes. Actor: (films) The Ice Storm, 1997, Disturbing Behavior, 1998, Go!, 1999, Teaching Mrs. Tingle, 1999, Wonder Boys, 2000, The Gift, 2000, Phone Booth, 2002, Abandon, 2002, The Singing Detective, 2003, Pieces of April, 2003, First Daughter, 2004, Batman Begins, 2005; (TV series) Dawson's Creek, 1998—2003. Office: c/o BWR Pub Rels 9100 Wilshire Blvd West Tower 6th Fl Beverly Hills CA 90210*

HOLMES, KING KENNARD, medical educator; b. St. Paul, Sept. 1, 1937; AB, Harvard Coll., 1959; MD, Cornell U., 1963; PhD in Microbiology, U. Hawaii, 1967. Diplomate Am. Bd. Internal Medicine, infectious diseases. Resident U. Wash., Seattle, 1967-68, chief resident, 1968-69, from instr. to assoc. prof. medicine, 1969-78, vice chmn. dept. medicine, 1984-89, prof. medicine, 1978—, dir. Ctr. AIDS and Sexually Transmitted Diseases, 1989—. Head divsn. pulmonary diseases USPHS Hosp., Seattle, 1969-70, asst. chief dept. medicine, 1969-83, head divsn. infectious diseases, 1970-83; dir. Sexually Transmitted Disease Clinic, Harborview Med. Ctr., 1972-79, chief med., 1984-89; mem. numerous adv. coms. Nat. Inst. Allergy & Infectious Diseases, NIH, USPHS, WHO, NAS; prin. investigator NIH, Nat. Cancer Inst., Nat. Inst. Allergy & Infectious Diseases, Nat. Inst. Child Health & Human Devel., Ctrs. Disease Control, 1983—. With USN, 1965-67. Recipient Squibb award Infectious Disease Soc. Am., 1978, Thomas Parran award Am. Veneral Disease Assn., 1983. Fellow ACP, Royal Coll. Physicians Eng.; mem. AMA, Inst. Medicine-NAS, Assn. Am. Physicians, Am. Epidemiol. Soc., Am. Fedn. Clin. Rsch. Office: U Wash Str AIDS & STDs Harborview Med Ctr 325 9th Ave MS# 359931 Seattle WA 98104-2420 Fax: 206-731-3694.*

HOLMES, LARRY, JR., retired professional boxer; b. Cuthbert, Ga., Nov. 3, 1949; s. John and Flossie Holmes; children: Listy, Lisa. Ed. public schs. Formerly worked in car wash, quarry, rug mill, foundry; profl. boxer, 1973—. Owner, founder Larry Holmes Enterprises, Larry Holmes Ringside Restaurant. Author: (autobiography) Against All Odds; subject: (documentaries) In the Arena. Heavyweight champion World Boxing Council, 1978-83, Internat. Boxing Fedn., 1983-85. Achievements include winning 19 of 22 amateur fights. Undefeated for a record 13 years. Office: Larry Holmes Enterprises 91 Larry Holmes Dr Ste 200 Easton PA 18042

HOLMES, LEONARD GEORGE, psychologist; b. Roanoke, Va., May 31, 1954; s. George Washington and Mary Maxine (Templeton) H.; m. Susan Rose Tankersley, June 19, 1976; children: Allison Gayle, Mary Kathleen. BA in Psychology and Religious Studies with high distinction, U. Va., 1976; MS in Clin. Psychology, Fla. State U., 1979, PhD, 1981. Lic. clin. psychologist, Va. Psychology intern William S. Hall Psychiat. Inst., Columbia, S.C., 1980-81; lectr., clin. psychologist Ctr. for Psychol. Svcs., Coll. of William and Mary, Williamsburg, Va., 1981-88, asst. dir., 1984-88; pvt. practice in clin. psychology Williamsburg, 1984—. Adj. asst. prof. psychology Coll. William and Mary, 1991—; cons. V.A. Med. Ctr., Hampton, 1985-90, coord. behavioral physiology lab., 1990—, dir. chronic pain program, 1992—; psychologist Sentara Psychol. Group, Newport News, Va., 1988-90; clin. psychologist Behavioral Medicine Inst., 1990-98; clin. psychologist Family Psychiat. Svcs., Hampton, 1998-2000; adj. asst. prof. Ea. Va. Med. Sch., 1995—; webmaster Netpsychology, 1996—, About.com Mental Health Guide, 1997—, Healing Sites Network. Univ. fellow Fla. State U., 1977-78, 79-80. Mem.: Am. Psychol. Soc. Avocations: gardening, computers, fishing, hiking. Home: 102 Barlows Run Williamsburg VA 23188-9326 Office: VA Med Ctr 116B Hampton VA 23667 Office Phone: 757-722-9961 2215. E-mail: leonard.holmes@gmail.com.

HOLMES, LORENE BARNES, academic administrator; b. Mineola, Tex., July 27, 1937; d. William Henry and Jessie Mae (Kelly) Barnes; m. Charles Murphy Holmes, Sr., Feb. 9, 1960 (dec.); children: Charles Murphy, Jr., James Henry, Jessyca Yvette. BS, Jarvis Christian Coll., 1959; M in Bus. Edn., U. North Tex., 1966, EdD, 1970. Dir. fin. aid Jarvis Christian Coll., Hawkins, Tex., 1966-68, asst. prof. bus., 1969-70, acting chair social and behavioral sci. divsn., 1970-71, chair social and behavioral sci. divsn., 1971-75, chair social sci. and bus. divsn., 1975-81, chair bus. adminstrn. divsn., 1981-96, exec. asst. to pres., 1996—. Nat. treas. Nat. Alumni Assn., Hawkins, 1960; exec. asst. to pres., 1996-98, 98-99; dir. alumni rec. profl., 1999-2000; dir. career mgmt., 2000-. Editorial reviewer Communication in Business, 1989; contbr. articles to profl. jours. Bd. dirs. Hawkins Helping Hands, 1987-93, Allen Meml. Pub. Libr., Hawkins, 1988-94. Recipient Recognition plaque Nat. Urban League, N.Y.C., 1989, T.A. Abbott Teaching award Christian Ch., Indpls., 1988; inductee Pioneer Hall of Fame, Jarvis Christian Coll., 1994; honored by Nat. Alumni Assn. Dallas chpt. at Heritage Scholarship Banquet. Mem. AAUW, Nat. Bus. Educators Assn., Tex. Bus. Educators Assn. (Bus. Tchr. of Yr. award Dist. 8), Jarvis Christian Coll. Alumni and Ex-Students Assn. (life, Dist. Alumni Educator of Yr. award), Top Ladies of Dist. Inc. (Lady of Yr. award), Hawkins C. of C. (charter), Delta Sigma Theta (Golden life mem., S.W. Gen. Educator of Yr. award 1991), Delta Pi Epsilon (life). Democrat. Mem. United Methodist Ch. Avocations: reading, writing, sewing, Scrabble. Home: PO Box 858 Hawkins TX 75765-0858 Office: Jarvis Christian Coll PO Drawer G Hawkins TX 75765

HOLMES, LOUIS IRA, physician assistant, educator, photojournalist; b. L.A., July 16, 1943; s. Louis Issac and Mabel Jane (Walsh) H.; m. Krystal Ladda Premchaona, Nov. 16, 1991 (separated); children: Jonathan Joseph, Kimberly Ellen, Louis Boon. AA, El Camino Coll., Torrance, Calif., 1972; cert. physician asst., U. So. Calif., 1978. Cert. Nat. Commn. Cert. Physician Assts.; cert. ACLS. Resident in surgery Norwalk Hosp.-Yale U. Sch. Medicine, 1980; nursing staff emergency dept. South Bay Dist. Hosp., Redondo Beach, Calif., 1970-75; nursing staff trauma and surg. intensive care Harbor Gen. Hosp.-UCLA Med. Ctr., Torrance, 1976-77; physician asst. Gen. Med. Corp., L.A., 1979; physician asst., divsn. thoracic surgery City of Hope Med. Ctr., Duarte, Calif., 1980-81; sr. physcian asst. thoracic and cardiovascular surgery Bert Meyer MD, et al, L.A., 1981-91; sr. physician asst. cardiothoracic surgery, instr. postgrad. cardiothoracic surgery residency program Cedars-Sinai Med. Ctr., L.A., 1991-95; asst. prof. clin. surgery and family medicine U. So. Calif., L.A., 1995—, phys. asst. in cardiothoracic surgery, 1995—. Vis. surg. instr., China; examiner Nat. Commn. on Cert. of Physician Assts., 1981—92; mem. program planning com. Masters Degree program in Health Sci. for Physician Assts., Calif. State U., Dominguez Hill, 1991—95; adj. faculty physician asst. program U. So. Calif., 1982—90, mem. adv. com., 1983—84, mem. long-range planning com., 1988—90; spkr., cons., expert witness in field; contbr. numerous color photographic images The Green Berets: Weapons and Equipment (Hans Halberstadt), 1989; bd. dirs. TV Parade Mag., 1991—2001. Contbr. articles to profl. jours. and chpts. to books; mem. editl. bd. Clinician Reviews, 1990-96, Physician Asst. Jour., 1987-90; med. tech. advisor, appeared in (feature film) City of Angles, TV program on History Channel. Instr. ACLS, Am. Heart Assn., 1980-96. With Spl. Forces, U.S. Army, 1964-70; with Calif. Army N.G., 1976-83, U.S. Army Res., 1984-91. Recipient 21 mil. decorations, including awards from U.S., Vietnam, Thailand, Outstanding Svc. award Physician Asst. Jour., 1989. Fellow Soc. Critical Care Medicine (bd. dirs. Calif. chpt. 1995), Am. Acad. Physician Assts. (ho. of dels. 1982-87, vice chair surg. coun. 1985-87, conf. planning com. 1986-88, vets. caucus chair 1986-88, advisor to bd. dirs. 1989-91), Calif. Acad. Physician Assts. (chmn. govt. affairs 1984-86, pres. 1985, Presdl. Leadership award 1986, 88), Am. Assn. Surgeons Assts. (v.p. 1988), Assn. Physician Assts. Cardiovascular Surgery (pres. 1989-91), Mil. Order World Wars, Mil. Surgeons of the U.S., VFW, Spl. Forces Assn., Spl. Ops. Assn. Republican. Buddhist. Avocations: photo journalism, running, military history. Office: Cardiothoracic Surgeons Inc 50 Bellefontaine St Ste 403 Pasadena CA 91105 Home: 24 Country Ridge Rd Pomona CA 91766-4815

HOLMES, MARK V., judge; b. New York, 1960; BA, Harvard Coll., 1979; JD, Univ. Chicago Law Sch., 1983. Bar: New York, D.C., U.S. Supreme Ct., D.C. second, fifth, ninth circuit, Ct. of Fed. Claims. Clerk Hon. Alex Kozinski, Ninth Circuit, 1985—87; counsel to commissioners U.S. Internat. Trade Commn., Washington, 1991—96; counsel Miller & Chevalier, 1996—2001; dep. asst. atty. gen. tax divsn. US Dept. Justice, Washington, 2001—03; judge U.S. Tax Ct., Washington, 2003—. Mem. Am. Bar Assoc., Tax Division. Office: US Tax Court 400 Second St NW Washington DC 20217*

HOLMES, MELVIN ALMONT, insurance company executive; b. West New York, N.J., Jan. 2, 1919; s. Edward L. and Sarah J. (Brown) H.; m. Clare G. White, May 30, 1943; children: Clare Ann, Karen, Joan, Patricia, Catherine, Donald, Jacqueline. Student in bus. adminstrn., NYU; L.H.D. (hon.), Coll. of Ins., 1976. C.P.C.U., 1955. With Frank B. Hall & Co., Inc., Briarcliff Manor, N.Y., 1937-84, asst. mgr. liability dept., 1945-52, asst. v.p., 1952-56, v.p., 1956-68, chief exec. officer, pres., 1968-73, vice chmn., 1973-79, cons., dir., 1979-84. Chmn. bd. trustees Coll. of Ins., 1974-76 Hon. trustee Valley Hosp., Ridgewood, N.J. Served to capt. C.E., U.S. Army, 1941-46. Recipient Good Scout award Boy Scouts Am., 1975; Free Enterprise award Ins. Fedn. N.Y., 1975 Mem. Nat. Assn. Ins. Brokers (past pres.), Ins. Soc. N.Y., Soc. CPCUs (Eugene A. Toale Meml. award 1976), Ins. Inst. Am., Am. Inst. Property and Liability Underwriters Inc. (past trustee), Ins. Fedn. N.Y. (past pres.), Tequesta Country Club. Home: 605 Universe Blvd Apt T100 Juno Beach FL 33408-2449

HOLMES, MICHAEL, performing company executive, performing arts educator; b. Palestine, Tex., June 29, 1939; s. George Washington and Marion Rebecca Holmes. Student, U. Tex. Austin, 1957—60. Tchr. Debbie Reynolds Studio, N. Hollywood, Calif., 1979—87; artistic dir. The Chandler Studio, N. Hollywood, Calif., 1988—. Prof. UCLA, 1989—93; pres., CEO Action/Reaction Theater Corp., L.A., 1994—, artistic dir., 1994—, Glendale, Calif., 2003—. Actor(adapter - director): (play) Acting: The First Six Lessons (3 Drama-Logue Awards, 1990, LA Times Outstanding prodn. of the yr. in smaller theater, 1988); author (director - producer): (play) Ryder (L. A, Valley Theater League, Best Play; Best Dir., 1992), The Ring (4 Drama-Logue Awards; Valley Theater League Best Dir., Best Play, 1994, L.A. Times Recognition of the 10 Most Memorable Prodns. of the Yr., 1995), The Cleaning Man (Critics Choice: The LA Times, 2000). Dir. summer theater Glendale Hist. Soc., 2001—04. Recipient Pick of the Week: Infinite Cages, Hollywood Complex, The L.A Weekly, 2000, Drama-Logue award, Drama - Logue Industry newspaper, 1990—96, Artistic Dir. awards, The Valley Theater League, 1992—95, Pick of the Week: Infinite Cages, Hollywood Complex, The LA Weekly, 2002. Mem.: AFTRA, SAG, Actors Equity Assn. Achievements include Many articles in the Los Angeles Times and other publications including a picture and story on the front page of the Los Angeles Times; featured on Broadway, films and television. Home: 13000 Burbank Blvd Sherman Oaks CA 91401 Office: The Chandler Studio 12443 Chandler Blvd North Hollywood CA 91607 Office Phone: 818-786-1045. Home Fax: 818-780-6516 ext 7. Personal E-mail: mholmes@dslextreme.com.

HOLMES, MICHAEL GENE, lawyer; b. Longview, Wash., Jan. 14, 1937; s. Robert A. and Esther S. Holmes; children: Helen, Peyton Robert. AB in Econs., Stanford U., 1958, JD, 1960. Bar: Oreg. 1961, U.S. Dist. Ct. Oreg. 1961, U.S. Ct. Appeals (9th cir.) 1961, Temp. Emergency Ct. Appeals 1976, U.S. Supreme Ct. 1976. Assoc. Spears, Lubersky, Bledsoe, Anderson, Young & Hilliard, Portland, 1961-67, ptnr., 1967-90, Lane Powell Spears Lubersky, Portland, 1990-95, of counsel, 1995. Mem. Oreg. Joint Com. of Bar, Press & Broadcasters, 1982-85, sec., 1983-84, chmn. 1985. Author Survey of Oregon Defamation and Privacy Law, ann., 1982-95. Trustee Med. Rsch. Found. Oreg., Portland, 1985-94, exec. com., 1986-94; hon. trustee Oreg. Health and Sci. Univ. Found., 1995—; trustee Portland Civic Theatre, 1962-66. Mem. Oreg. Bar Assn., Phi Beta Kappa.

HOLMES, MICHAEL L., career officer; m. Viola Holmes; children: Jared, Justin, Michael Jason. Diploma in Math., Pembroke State U., 1972. Commd. ensign USN, 1973, advanced through ranks to rear adm.; various assignments to aircraft comdr. Patrol Squadron 24, Jacksonville; comdr. Patrol Wings, U.S. Pacific Fleet, Pearl Harbor, Hawaii. Office: PSC 817 Box 2 FPO AE 09622-0002 E-mail: mlholmes@aol.com.

HOLMES, MIMI, artist, educator; b. New Orleans, Nov. 10, 1956; d. O. Louis and Barbara Ann (Trastour) H. BA in Art and Theater, Agnes Scott Coll., 1978; MFA in Studio Art, Fla. State U., 1984. Asst. dir. Acad. Theatre, Atlanta, 1978-80; actess, dir. A Co. of Players, Jacksonville, Fla., 1980-81; artist-in-edn. Ala. State Coun. on the Arts, Haleyville, Florence, Ala., 1984-88; asst. prof. Art Cornell Coll., Mt. Vernon, Iowa, 1988-92; freelance artist, educator Sacred Heart Prodns., Mpls., 1992—. Sculptor Fear of Developing Desires, 1988-92, Guardians of My Heart's Desires, 1991-92, Guilt for the Death of One I Loved, 1993. Blue Mountain Ctr. fellow, 1986, 87, 97, Ucross Found. fellow, 1984, Ala. State Coun. on Arts fellow, 1987. Mem. Women's Caucus for Art (chpt. liaison 1991-93, bd. dirs.). Avocations: folk dancing, longsword, storytelling. Home: 630 4th St NE Minneapolis MN 55413-2017

HOLMES, MIRIAM H., publisher; b. Bavaria, Germany, June 2, 1951; came to U.S., 1952; d. Max J. and Mala (Rosenwasser) H.; m. Stephen H. Gelb, June 25, 1995. BA, Queens Coll., 1972; JD, Yeshiva U., 1987. Bar: N.Y. 1988. Pres. Holmes & Meier Pub., N.Y.C., 1990—. Mem. Assn. Jewish Book Coun. (bd. dirs.), Pubs. Mktg. Assn. Office: PO Box 943 Teaneck NJ 07666 Office Phone: 201-833-2270. Business E-Mail: info@holmesandmeier.com.

HOLMES, NANCY ELIZABETH, pediatrician; b. St. Louis, Aug. 3, 1950; d. David Reed and Phyllis Anne (Hunger) Holmes; m. Arthur Erwin Kramer, May 15, 1976; children: Melanie Elizabeth Kramer, Carl Edward Kramer. BA in Psychology, U. Kans., 1972; MD, U. Mo., 1976. Diplomate Am. Acad. Pediatrics. Intern., resident in pediatrics St. Louis Children's Hosp., Washington U., St. Louis, 1976-81; pediatrician Ctrl. Pediatrics, St. Louis, 1981—. Sch. physician Sch. Dist. Clayton, Mo., 1985—92; asst. prof. clin. pediats. Washington U., St. Louis, 1993—2000, assoc. prof., 2000—; cons. 1st Congregational Preschool, Clayton, 1984—86, Jewish Hosp. Daycare Ctr., St. Louis, 1993—97, Flynn Park EArly Edn. Ctr., University City, Mo., 1994—; cmty. outpatient experience Preceptor Hosp., St. Louis Children's Hosp., 1991—93, 1994—; mem. med. exec. com. St. Louis Children's Hosp., 1992—94. Vol. reading tutor Flynn Park Sch., University City, 1992—98, cub scout leader, 1993—98; mem. com. Troop 493 Boy Scouts Am., 2000—; elder Trinity Presbyn. Ch., University City, 1989—92, 1996—2001; bd. dirs. Children's Hosp. Care Group. Fellow Am. Acad. Pediatrics; mem. AMA, Mo. State Med. Assn., St. Louis Metro. Med. Soc, St. Louis Pediatric Soc. Presbyterian. Avocations: reading, gardening, photography, travel. Office: Ctrl Pediatrics Inc 8888 Ladue Rd Ste 130 Saint Louis MO 63124-2056 Office Phone: 314-862-4002.

HOLMES, NATHANIEL J., surgeon; MD, Robert Wood Johnson Med. Sch., 1987. Diplomate Am. Bd. Surgery, 1996. Intern Robert Wood Johnson Med. Sch., Piscataway, NJ, 1987—89, resident in surgery, 1989—93; fellow in colon, rectal surgery St. Vincent Health Ctr., Erie, Pa., 1993—94; physician divsn. gen. surgery Robert Wood Johnson U. Med. Group, New Brunswick, NJ, 1994—2005; dir. colon and rectal surgery, dir. colorectal cancer program Atlantic Health System, Montclair, NJ, 2005—. Asst. prof. surgery Robert Wood Johnson Med. Sch. U., New Brunswick, NJ, 1995—. Office: Ambulatory Pavilion 1 Bay Ave Ste 3 Rm 271 Montclair NJ 07042 Office Phone: 973-429-6689. E-mail: nate.holmes@ahsys.org.

HOLMES, PAUL LUTHER, political scientist, educational consultant; b. Rock Island, Ill., Mar. 7, 1919; s. Bernt Gunnar and Amanda Sophia (Swenson) H.; m. Ardis Ann Grunditz, Nov. 1, 1946; children: Mary Ann, David Stephen. BA, U. Minn., 1940; MA, Stanford U., 1949, George Washington U., 1964; EdD, Stanford U., 1968. Career officer USN, 1941-64, ret. at capt.; adminstr. Laney Coll., Oakland, Calif., 1965-70; dean Contra Costa Coll., San Pablo, Calif., 1970-71; pres. Coll. Alameda (Calif.), 1971-75, prof. polit. sci., 1975-80; dir. doctoral studies program Nova U., No. Calif., 1975-80. Cons. higher edn. Gig Harbor, Wash., 1981—; regent Calif. Luth. U., 1973-76. Decorated with medals. Mem. Stanford U. Alumni Assn., Rotary, Phi Delta Kappa. Lutheran.

HOLMES, PRIEST, professional football player; b. Fort Smith, Ark., Oct. 7, 1973; children: De'Andre, Jekovan, Corion. Postgrad in Sport Mgmt., U. Tex. Running back Balt. Ravens, 1997—2001, Kansas City Chiefs, 2001—. Spokesperson Md. Dept. Edn. Gear Up Program, McDonald House Charities; contbr. Dr. Ben Carson Scholarship Fund, Children's Miracle Net.; spkr. Ray Kroc youth achievement awards McDonald's Corp.; spkr. Youth Explosion, 2000, Urban Youth Min.; mem. Fellowship Christian Athletes. Named NFL Offensive Player of Yr., 2002, NFL All-Pro, 2002; named to Am. Football Conf. Pro Bowl Team, 2001—03. Achievements include mem. Super Bowl XXXV Champion Balt. Ravens, 2001. Office: 1 Arrowhead Dr Kansas City MO 64129*

HOLMES, RANDALL KENT, microbiology educator, academic administrator, internist, epidemiologist; b. Muskegon, Mich., Nov. 7, 1940; s. Scott Travis and Helen Marie (Rosell) H.; m. Kathryn Louise Voelker, June 16, 1962; children: Rebecca Kathryn, Elisabeth Marie. AB, Harvard U., 1962; MD, PhD in Microbiology, NYU, 1968. Diplomate Am. Bd. Internal Medicine, Am. Bd. Infectious Diseases. Intern, then resident Beth Israel Hosp., Boston, 1968-70; rsch. assoc. NIH, Bethesda, Md., 1970-72; instr. medicine U. Tex. Southwestern Med. Sch., Dallas, 1972-73, asst. prof., 1973-75, assoc. prof., 1975-76; prof., chmn. microbiology and immunology Uniformed Svcs. U. Health Scis., Bethesda, 1976-95, assoc. dean for acad. affairs, 1984-93, acting chmn. biochemistry, 1993-95; prof., chmn. microbiology U. Colo. Sch. Medicine, Denver, 1995—. Adv. com. vaccines and related biol. products Nat. Ctr. for Drugs and Biologics, Bethesda, 1983-87; cholera panel NIH, 1987-92, bacteriology and mycology 1 study sect., 1993-95, microbiology and infectious disease rsch. com., 2000-2005, chair, 2003-2005; chair VA-DOD Rsch. Program on Mechs. of Emerging Pathogens Rev. Panel, 1997; steering com. postdoc. rsch. assoc. program in infectious diseases and pub. health microbiology ASM/Nat. Ctr. for Infectious Disease, 1993-2002, chair, 1996-2002. Contbr. articles to profl. jours. Served to surgeon USPHS, 1968-70. Recipient Rsch. Career Devel. award NIH, 1975-76. Fellow ACP, Infectious Diseases Soc. Am.; mem. Am. Acad. Microbiology (bd. govs. 1992-95, com. on awards 1995—, chair 2002—), Am. Soc. for Clin. Investigation, Am. Soc. for Microbiology (editl. bd. Infection and Immunity 1978-86, Microbiol. Revs. 1983-88), Nat. Bd. Med. Examiners (microbiology test com. 1984-93, chair 1987-93, US med. licensing exam. step I com. 1990-92, US med. licensing exam. composite com. 1992-95), Coun. Acad. Socs. of Assn. Am. Med. Colls. (adminstrn. bd. 2004—), Phi Beta Kappa, Alpha Omega Alpha. Republican. Avocations: reading, hiking, camping, swimming. Office: Univ Colo Sch Medicine Dept Microbiology Mail Stop 8333 PO Box 6511 Aurora CO 80045 Business E-Mail: randall.holmes@uchsc.edu.

HOLMES, RICHARD BROOKS, mathematical physicist; b. Milw., Jan. 7, 1959; s. Emerson Brooks Holmes and Nancy Anne Schaffter; m. Sandra Lynn Wong, June 27, 1998. BS, Calif. Inst. Tech., 1981; MS, Stanford (Calif.) U., 1983. Sr. sys. analyst Comptek Rsch., Vallejo, Calif., 1982-83; staff scientist Western Rsch., Arlington, Va., 1983-85; sr. scientist AVCO Everett (Mass.) Rsch. Lab., 1985-88; prin. rsch. scientist North East Rsch. Assocs., Woburn, Mass., 1988-90; sr. mem. tech. staff Rocketdyne divsn. Rockwell Internat., Canoga Park, Calif., 1990-95; sr. staff scientist Lockheed Martin Rsch. Labs., Palo Alto, Calif., 1995-98; pres. Nutronics, Inc., Cameron Park, Calif., 1998—, Gen. Nutronics, Inc., Milpitas, Calif., 2001—. Cons. North East Rsch. Assocs., 1990. Contbr. Matched Asymptotic Expansions, 1988; contbr. articles to Phys. Rev. Letters, Phys. Rev., Jour. of the Optical Soc. Am. and IEEE Jour. of Quantum Electronics. Mem. No. Calif. Scholarship Founds., Oakland, 1977; mem. Wilderness Soc., Washington, 1989. Stanford fellow Stanford U., 1982; fellow MIT, 1990; recipient Presdl. Medal of Merit, 1992. Mem.: SPIE (conf. organizer 1995—99), AAAS, Optical Soc. Am., Am. Phys. Soc. Achievements include patents for means for photonic communication, computation, and distortion compensation; discovery of spin-two phonons. Office: Gen Nutronics Inc 238 Caribbean Drive Sunnyvale CA 94089 Office Phone: 408-891-0265. Personal E-mail: rholmes001@aol.com.

HOLMES, RICHARD DALE, history consultant; b. Sandown, N.H., Sept. 6, 1945; s. John B. Jr. and Marjorie A. (Andrews) H.; m. Carol A. Martineau, Dec. 19, 1970; children: John B. III, Leah K. BEd, Keene (N.H.) State Coll., 1968; MA, Rivier Coll., Nashua, N.H., 1980. Cert. tchr., N.H. Tchr. social studies Pelham (N.H.) Meml. Sch., 1968-2000, chmn. dept., 1975-2000. Hist. cons., rschr. Sandown Mus., 1980-88, Chester (N.H.) Hist. Soc., 1989—. Author: View from Meeting House Hill, 1988, Derry, 1995, Derry Revisited, 2005, Chester Revisited, 1997,. Pres. Old Meeting House Assn., Sandown, 1987—; dir. Derry Mus., 2001—; mem. Derry Hist. Dist. Commn., 1988—, chmn. 1998—. With U.S. Army, 1969-71, Vietnam. Decorated Cross of Gallantry with palm, Civic Action medal 1st class (Vietnam). Mem.: NEA, Derry Hist. Soc., Sandown Hist. Assn. (hist. cons., rschr. 1980—88, pres. 1986—87), N.H. Hist. Soc., Pelham Edn. Assn. (v.p. 1976—77), N.H. Guide Dog Users Assn., Nat. Fedn. Blind. Congregationalist. Avocations: collecting books, public speaking, research. Home: 33 Hillside Ave Derry NH 03038-2215 Office: Town Hall 48 E Broadway Derry NH 03038 Fax: 603-432-6131. Office Phone: 603-434-1247. E-mail: rholmes33@comcast.net.

HOLMES, ROBERT ALLEN, former lawyer, law educator, consultant, educator; b. Sewickley, Pa., Dec. 12, 1947; s. Lee Roy John and Nellie Ann (Kupits) H.; div.; children: Wesley Paige, Ashley Reagan. BA in Bus. Adminstrn., Coll. William and Mary, 1969, JD, 1972. Bar: Md. 1972, U.S. Dist. Ct. Md. 1972, Va. 1973, U.S. Dist. Ct. (ea. dist.) Va. 1973, U.S. Dist. Ct. (no. dist.) Ohio 1988, U.S. Ct. Appeals (6th cir.) 1988. Assoc. Ober, Grimes & Shriver, Balt., 1972-73, Kellam, Pickrell & Lawler, Norfolk, Va., 1973-75; ptnr. Holliday, Holmes & Inman, Norfolk, 1975-77; asst. prof. law Bowling Green State U., Ohio, 1977-82, assoc. prof., 1982-2001. Dir. Purchasing Law Inst., 1979—, EEO-Affirmative Action Rsch. Group, 1978—; lectr. in field. Author: (with others) Computers, Data Processing and the Law, 1984; numerous manuals on discrimination and affirmative action law, corp. purchasing law and internat. bus. law; contbg. editor, monthly columnist Midwest Purchasing, 1983-84. Recipient Outstanding Young Man award William and Mary Soc. Alumni, 1973. Mem. Md. Bar Assn., Va. Bar Assn., Am. Bus. Law Assn., Am. Soc. Pers. Adminstrs., Nat. Assn. Purchasing Mgmt., Mensa. Republican. Home: 1030 Conneaut Ave Bowling Green OH 43402-2118

HOLMES, ROBERT EUGENE, legislative staff member, journalist; b. Shelbyville, Ind., June 5, 1928; s. Eugene Lowell and Sarah Lucinda (Hughes) H.; m. Retha Carolyn Richey, June 27, 1955 (div. Sept. 1966); 1 child, Enid Adair Offley. Staff reporter Elkhart, Ind. Truth, 1954-57; city editor, investigative editor Press-Enterprise, Riverside, Calif., 1957-70; sr. cons. Calif. State Senate Dem. Caucus, Sacramento, 1971-74, dep. dir., 1978-79; press sec. Lt. Gov. of Calif., Sacramento, 1975-77; project dir. Border Area Devel. Study, U.S. Econ. Devel. Adminstrn., Sacramento, 1978; chief cons. Joint Legis. Ethics Com., Calif. Legislature, Sacramento, 1981-82; staff dir. Joint Com. on Prison Constrn. and Ops., Legislature, Sacramento, 1983-94. Rsch. cons. Calif. Rsch. Bur., Calif. State Libr., Sacramento, 1991-92; cons. Calif. Hist. State Capitol Commn., 1995-96. Author, editor rschr. legis. reports; contbg. editor creative writing quar. Noah's Hotel, Inverness, Calif., 1991—; contbr. articles to mags., short stories. Media dir. Lt. Gov. Campaign, Sacramento and L.A., 1974. Sgt. USMC, 1952-53. Recipient Silver Gavel award ABA, 1969, 1st Place media award Calif. State Bar Assn., 1968, 1st Place award Calif. Newspaper Pubs. Assn. Best Series, 1969, 70, 71; Am. Polit. Sci. Assn. Ford Found. fellow Stanford U., 1970, Jack Anderson award Calif. Correctional Peace Officers Assn., 1993. Mem.: ACLU, Common Cause. Democrat. Avocations: bicycling, tennis, world travel, short story writing. Home: 416 Florin Rd Sacramento CA 95831-2007

HOLMES, ROBERT M., minister, counselor, educator; b. Mitchell, S. Dak., May 4, 1925; s. Merrill Jacob and Carrie Rowena (McFadon) Holmes; m. Pauline Leigh Mudge, Aug. 31, 1951; children: Stephen Merrill, Tim Edmund, Krys Leigh. BA, Illinois Wesleyan U, Bloomington, Ill, 1948; MDiv, Garrett Evangelical Sem., Evanston, Ill, 1951; MA, Northwestern U, Evanston, Ill, 1956; ThD, Pacific Sch./ Rel., Berkeley, Calif., 1965. Min. to mil. pers. First Meth. Ch., Rapid City, SD, 1951—53; pastor United Meth. Ch., Canyon Lake, Rapid City, SD, 1953—61; chaplain, asst. prof. Rocky Mountain Coll., Billings, Mont., 1965—81; pastor St. Paul's United Meth. Ch., Helena, Mont., 1981—88; instr., part time Pacific Sch. of Religion, Stockton, Calif., 1962—64. Chaplain (vol) Helena Police Dept., Helena, Mont., 1986—, Sherrif Dept., Lewis and Clark County, Helena, Mont., 1986—; preacher Nat. Protestant Hour, Atlanta, 1986—2004, Atlanta, 2002. Author: (book) The Academic Mysteryhouse", 1970, (book of sermons) Why Jesus Never Had Ulcers, 1986. Lt. (JG) USN, 1943—46, Pacific. Recipient Angel Award, Religion in Media, for Protestant Hour Series, 1986—87, Francis Asbury Award, United Meth. Ch. (higher ed.), 1999. Home: 822 Breckenridge Helena MT 59601

HOLMES, RUPERT, playwright, singer, writer; b. Northwich, Cheshire, Eng., Feb. 24, 1947; m. Liza Holmes, 1968. Grad., Manhattan Sch. Music. Piano player for bands Cuff Links and Buoys; producer (albums) for Sparks, the Sailors, Barbra Streisand; singer (albums) Widescreen, 1974, Rupert Holmes, The Singles, Pursuit of Happiness, Partners in Crime (including Escape: The Piña Colada Song and Him), Adventure, Full Circle; (plays) The Mystery of Edwin Drood, 1986 (recipient: Tony awards for book, music and lyrics), Accomplice (Edgar award), Solitary Confinement, (playwright) Goosebumps, Thumbs, Swango, Say Goodnight Gracie (Carbonell award for Best Play of 2000); (television) Remember WENN; (author) Where the Truth Lies, 2003, Swing, 2005. Office: The Holmes Line Ste 114 717 White Plains Rd Scarsdale NY 10583 Business E-Mail: email@rupertholmes.com.

HOLMES, STEPHEN T., law educator; b. 1948; BA, Denison U., 1969; MA, Yale U., 1974, MPhil, 1975, PhD in Philosophy, 1976. From asst. to assoc. prof. dept. govt. Harvard U., 1979-85; prof. polit. sci. and law U. Chgo., 1985-96, dir. Ctr. for Study of Constitutionalism in Ea. Europe; prof. polit. sci. Princeton U., 1997—2000; prof. law NYU Sch. Law, 1997—, now Walter E. Meyer prof. law. Mem. Wissenschaftskolleg, Berlin, 1991. Author: Benjamin Constant and the Making of Modern Liberalism, 1984, Anatomy of Antiliberalism, 1993, Passions and Constraint: The Theory of Liberal Democracy, 1995; co-author (with C. Sunstein): The Cost of Rights, 1998. Guggenheim Fellowship, 1988. Office: NYU Sch Law Vanderbilt Hall Rm 506 40 Washington Sq S New York NY 10012-1099 Office Phone: 212-998-6357. E-mail: stephen.holmes@nyu.edu.*

HOLMES, SUSAN G., music educator; b. Kansas City, Mo., Mar. 7, 1955; d. Burton E. and Gloria A. (Spencer) H. BA, U. Kans., Lawrence, 1980. Cert. music therapy, education. Tchr. Dade County Schs., Miami, Fla.; music therapist, tchr. ESOL Miami, Fla.; tchr., music therapist The Palace Retirement Cmty.; tchr. ESOL Miami-Palmetto (Fla.) Adult Edn. Ctr., Korean cmty., Miami, Fla.; instr. GED writing lab. Miami Dade C.C., Miami, Fla. Tchr. ESOL to newly-arrived immigrants. Recipient Honor for TV series CBS News. Mem. Nat. Orgn. for Exec. Women. Avocations: writing, music composition.

HOLMES, SUZANNE MCRAE, nursing supervisor; b. Birmingham, Ala., June 23, 1952; d. Paul Bickman and Mabel E. (Tyler) McRae; m. Bryan Thomas Holmes, Jan. 14, 1989; 1 child, Meredith Rae. ADN, Jefferson State Coll., Birmingham, 1988. RN, Ala.; cert. BCLS instr.; cert. asthma educator, Am. Lung Assn. Staff nurse burn unit The Children's Hosp., Birmingham, 1988-89; staff nurse dept. medicine The Kirklin Clinic at U. Ala.-Birmingham, 1989-90, head nurse gen. medicine clinic, 1990-91, head nurse allergy clinic, 1991—, head nurse for pulmonary/allergy clinic, 2002—, head nurse for pulmonary/allergy, PFT, Gastroenterology and Endoscopy Clinic, 2004. Facilitator and spkr. on nursing at asthma workshops Aventis Pharms., Collegeville, Pa., 1994—; mem. faculty Genecom, N.Y.C., 1994—; operator 1-800 Allergy Info. Svc., 1991—92. Editor Allergy Update, 1991-92. Leader Girl Scouts Am., 1998—2004. Mem. Am. Coll. Allergy and Immunology, Am. Acad. Allergy, Asthma and Immunology,mem. Am. Lung Assn. (cert. asthma educator), Asthma and Allergy Found. Am. (charter bd. dirs. Ala. chpt.), Assn. Asthma Educators. Methodist. Avocations: baking, sewing, gardening. Office: The Kirklin Clinic Allergy Clinic 4th Fl 2000 6th Ave S Birmingham AL 35233-2110

HOLMES, SVEN ERIK, federal judge, educator; b. Grand Junction, Colo., Feb. 13, 1951; s. Clifford Newton and Ruth (Bradley) Holmes; m. Lois Romano, Oct. 31, 1983; children: Kristen Elizabeth Romano, Virginia Morgan Romano. AB, Harvard U., 1973; JD, U. Va., 1980; LLM, Georgetown U., 1987. Bar: Okla. 1980, DC 1985, admitted to practice: US Dist. Ct. (DC) 1985, US Dist. Ct. (No. Dist.) Okla. 1985, US Dist. Ct. (Ea. Dist.) Okla. 1985, US Dist. Ct. (We. Dist.) Okla. 1985, US Ct. Appeals (10th Cir.) 1985, US Ct. Appeals (DC Cir.) 1985, US Tax Ct. 1985, US Ct. Claims 1985, US Supreme Ct. 1994. Campaign coord. David L. Boren for Gov., Oklahoma City, 1975; adminstrv. asst. to gov. State of Okla., Oklahoma City, 1975-77; law clk. to judge US Dist. Ct. (No. Dist.) Okla., Tulsa, 1980-81; assoc. Doerner, Stuart, Saunders, Daniel & Anderson, Tulsa, 1981-83; exec. dir. Dems. for "80's", Washington, 1983-85; from assoc. to ptnr. Williams & Connolly, Washington, 1985-87, 89-95; designated liaison staff mem. Senate Select Com. on Secret Mil. Assistance to Iran, Washington, 1987; gen. counsel, staff dir. Senate Select Com. on Intelligence, Washington, 1987-89; judge US Dist. Ct. (No. Dist.) Okla., Tulsa, 1995—, chief judge. V.p. Balt. Orioles, Md., 1989—93; adj. prof. constl. law U. Tulsa Sch. Law. Mem.: DC Bar Assn., Okla. Bar Assn. Lutheran. Avocations: reading, tennis. Office: US Dist Ct 411 US Courthouse 333 W 4th St Tulsa OK 74103-3839*

HOLMES, WILLARD, museum director; b. Saskatoon, Sask., Canada, 1949; Grad. in art history, U. B.C., 1972. With Fine Arts Gallery, U. B.C.; head of exhbns. Nat. Gallery of Can.; curator Vancouver Art Gallery; dir. Pender St. Gallery, from 1975; chief curator, dir. Charles Scott Gallery, head curatorial studies program Emily Carr Coll., 1976-87; chief curator, interim dir., then dir. Vancouver Art Gallery, 1987-93; dep. dir., CEO Whitney Mus. Am. Art, NYC, 1994—2003; dir. Wadsworth Atheneum Mus. Art, Hartford, Conn., 2003—. Office: Wadsworth Atheneum Mus Art 600 Main St Hartford CT 06103*

HOLMES CHUSTEK, CHERILYN ALISA, music educator; b. Bellmore, NY, Apr. 15, 1978; d. Chester E. Holmes, Jr. and Rose Holmes; m. David Stuart Chustek, Aug. 31, 2003; 1 child, Steven Andrew. BS in Music Edn. cum laude, Hofstra U., 2000, MA in Elem. Edn. with distinction, 2002. Music tchr. East Meadow Sch. Dist., 2000—02; tchr. music Kings Pk. Ctrl. Sch. Dist., 2002—. Middle sch. marching band dir. Kings Pk. Ctrl. Sch. Dist., 2004—; dir. marching band Newsday Marching Band Festival, 2003. Performance grant, Hofstra U., 1996. Mem.: NY State Sch. Music Assn., Music Educators Nat. Conf., Suffolk County Music Educators Assn. Avocations: dance, trumpet, travel.

HOLMGREN, JANET L., college president; b. Chgo., Dec. 1, 1948; d. Kenneth William and Virginia Ann (Rensink) H.; m. Gordon A. McKay, Sept. 7, 1968 (div. 1990); children: Elizabeth Jane, Ellen Katherine. BA in English summa cum laude, Oakland U., Rochester, Mich., 1968; MA in Linguistics, Princeton U., 1971, PhD in Linguistics, 1974. Asst. prof. English studies Federal City Coll. (now U. D.C.), Washington, 1972-76; asst. prof. English U. Md., College Park, 1976-82, asst. to chancellor, 1982-88; assoc. provost Princeton (N.J.) U., 1988-90, vice-provost, 1990-91; pres. Mills Coll., Oakland, Calif., 1991—. Mem. external adv. bd. English dept. Princeton U. Bay Area Biosci. Ctr. Author: (with Spencer Cosmos) The Story of English: Study Guide and Reader, 1986, Narration and Discourse in American Realistic Fiction, 1982; contbr. articles to profl. jours. Faculty rsch. grantee U. Md., 1978; fellow NEH, 1978, Princeton U., 1968-69, 70-72, NSF, 1969-70; recipient summer study aid Linguistic Soc. Am., Ohio State U., 1970. Mem. Assn. Ind. Caif. Colls. and Univs. (exec. com.), Nat. Assn. Ind. Colls. and Univs., Am. Coun. on Education (chair office of women in higher edn.), Calif. Acad. Sci. (coun.). Democrat. Episcopal. Avocations: travel, swimming, reading. Office: Mills Coll Office Pres 5000 Macarthur Blvd Oakland CA 94613-1301

HOLMGREN, MIKE, professional football coach; b. San Francisco, June 15, 1948; m. Kathy Holmgren; children: Gretchen, Emily, Jenny and Calla (twins). BS in Bus. Fin., U. So. Calif., 1970. Coach Lincoln High Sch., San Francisco, 1971-72, Sacred Heart High Sch., 1972-74, Oakgrove High Sch., 1975-80; quarterbacks coach, offensive coord. San Francisco State U., 1981-82; quarterbacks coach Brigham Young U., 1982-85, San Francisco 49ers, 1985-89, offensive coord., 1989-92; head coach Green Bay Packers, 1992-98, Seattle Seahawks, 1999—. Office: Seattle Seahawks Kingdome 11220 NE 53rd St Kirkland WA 98033-7595*

HOLMGREN, MYRON ROGER, social sciences educator; b. Willmar, Minn., Mar. 19, 1933; s. Alfred and Cleora Victora (Scott) H.; m. Ellen Mary Shaheen, June 9, 1957; children: Brian, Mary Jo Haas. BA, Mankato State U., 1958; MA, No. Colo. State U., 1959. Instr. Grinnell (Iowa) H.S., 1959-62, Joliet (Ill.) Jr. Coll., 1962-66; instr., fin. advisor Am. Express Fin. Advisors, Joliet, 1966-72; instr. Benedictine Coll., Atchison, Kans., 1973, Moraine Valley C.C., Palos Hills, Ill., 1974-75, Minooka (Ill.) H.S., 1974-93, dept. chmn., 1984-87, dir., coach Scholastic Bowl Team, 1976-93. Local dir. Exrox Award in Humanities, 1988=93; chmn. philosophy and goals North Ctrl. Accreditation, 1987-88. Author: Profitable Pricing Techniques, 1973; contbr. articles to profl. jours. Block chmn. March of Dimes, Am. Cancer Soc., 1989, 92-93; treas. bd. dirs. The Family Counseling Agy. of Will and Grundy Counties, 1996-99; mem. vestry St. Edward's Episcopal Ch., 2002—. Grantee, Asian Found., 1962. Mem. Internat. Platform Assn. Republican. Avocations: reading, writing, travel, gourmet cooking, market analysis. Home: 1314 Douglas St Joliet IL 60435-5814

HOLMQUEST, DONALD LEE, nuclear medicine physician, lawyer, retired aerospace engineer; b. Dallas, Apr. 7, 1939; s. Sidney Browder and Lillie Mae (Waite) H.; m. Ann Nixon James, Oct. 24, 1972. BS in Elec. Engring., So. Meth. U., 1962; MD, Baylor U., 1967, PhD in Physiology, 1968; JD, U. Houston, 1980. Student engr. Ling-Temco-Vought, Dallas, 1958-61; electronics engr. Tex. Instruments, Inc., Dallas, 1962; intern Meth. Hosp., Houston, 1967-68; pilot tng. USAF, Williams AFB, Ariz., 1968-69; scientist-astronaut NASA, Houston, 1967-73; research assoc. MIT, 1968-70; asst. prof. radiology and physiology Baylor Coll. Medicine, 1970-73; dir. nuclear medicine Eisenhower Med. Ctr., Palm Desert, Calif., 1973-74; assoc. dean medicine, assoc. prof. Tex. A&M U., College Station, 1974-76; dir. nuclear medicine Navasota (Tex.) Med. Ctr., 1976-84, Med. Arts Hosp., Houston, 1977-85; ptnr. Wood Lucksinger & Epstein, Houston, 1980-91, Holmquest & Assocs., Houston, 1991—2004; v.p. legal affairs N.Am. Med. Mgmt., Inc., Nashville, 1995-96; practice leader profl. svcs. group McKesson Info. Solutions, San Francisco, 2002—. Asst. prof. internal medicine Baylor Coll. Medicine, Houston, 1999—. Contbr. articles to med. jours. Mem. Soc. Nuclear Medicine, Am. Coll. Nuclear Physicians, Tex. Bar Assn., Am. Fighter Pilots Assn., Sigma Xi, Alpha Omega Alpha, Sigma Tau. Home and Office: 263 Princeton Rd Menlo Park CA 94025-5217

HOLMQUIST, THOMAS N, elementary school educator, farmer; b. Salina, Kans., Aug. 18, 1954; s. Darrel N and Mary L Holmquist; m. Marlysue L Esping, Aug. 2, 1980; children: Ryan, Majkin, John. BS, Bethany Coll., 1976; MA, Emporia State U., 1999. Farmer/stockman Holmquist Farm, Smolan, Kans., 1976—; tchr. Marquette H.S., 1976—84, Marquette Elem. Sch., Kans., 1976—. Author: (history book) Pioneer Cross, 1995, (book) Bluestown, 2001. Fireman Saline County Rural Fire Dist. 6, Smolan, Kans., 1972—92. Fulbright Meml. Fund scholar, 2000, Horizon grant, Saline County, 1998. Office: Marquette Elem Sch 310 Swedonia Marquette KS 67464 Business E-Mail: tholmquist@smdeyvalley.org.

HOLNESS, GORDON VICTOR RIX, engineering executive, mechanical engineer; b. London, Sept. 6, 1939; arrived in US, 1969, naturalized, 1989; s. Ernest Arthur and Ivy A. (Rix) H.; m. Susan F. Sage (dec.); m. Audrey A. Bezz, Apr. 18, 1984. Cert., Croydon Tech. Coll., Surrey, Eng., 1962; diploma in environ. engring., Nat. Coll., London, 1964. Registered profl. engr. Mich., Minn., Tex., Conn., Calif., Kans., Colo., Fla., Ariz., N.Y., D.C., Ala., N.C., Ky., Ohio, Mo., Tenn., Ill., Ont., Can. Design engr. West Sussex County Coun., Chichester, Sussex, Eng., 1956-59, C. McKechnie Jarvis & Ptnrs., London, 1959-64, Barlow Leslie & Ptnrs., Croydon, 1964; sr. engr. R. J. Tamblyn & Ptnrs., Toronto, Ont., Can., 1964-66; asst. chief engr. Giffels Assocs., Windsor, Ont., Can., 1966-69; from asst. chief engr. to chmn. and CEO, bd. dirs. Albert Kahn Assocs. Inc., Detroit, 1969—2001, also bd. dirs.; ret. chmn. emeritus, 2001. Contbr. articles to profl. jours. Bd. dirs. YMCA, Mt. Clemens, Mich., 1980-82; commr. Grosse Pointe Shores Planning Commn.; trustee Grosse Pointe Shores Improvement Found. Fellow ASHRAE (chmn. energy mgmt. com. 1987, chmn. govt. affairs com. 1989,chmn. bd. policy com., bd. dirs. 2002-04, v.p. 2004-); mem. NSPE, Am. Cons. Engrs. Coun., Chartered Inst. Bldg. Svcs. of Eng., Engring. Soc. Detroit, Mich. Soc. Profl. Engrs. (v.p. 1986, fellow 1998), Detroit Econ. Club (bd. dirs.). Republican. Presbyterian. Avocations: golf, tennis, racquetball, chess, sailing. Home: 55 S Edgewood Dr Grosse Pointe Shores MI 48236-1226 Office: Albert Kahn Assocs Inc 7430 2nd Ave Ste 800 Detroit MI 48202-2798 Personal E-mail: gholness@comcast.net.

HOLONYAK, NICK, JR., electrical engineering educator; b. Zeigler, Ill., Nov. 3, 1928; s. Nick and Anna (Rosoha) Holonyak. BS, U. Ill., 1950, MS, 1951, PhD (Tex. Instruments fellow), 1954; DSc (hon.), Northwestern U., 1992; DEng. (hon.), Notre Dame U., 1994. Tech. staff Bell Telephone Labs., Murray Hill, NJ, 1954—55; physicist, unit mgr., mgr. advanced semiconductor lab. Gen. Electric Co., Syracuse, NY, 1957—63; prof. elec. engring. and materials research lab. U. Ill., Urbana, 1963—, John Bardeen chair prof. elec. & computer engring. & physics, 1993—; mem. Center Advanced Study, 1977—. Author (with others): Semiconductor Controlled Rectifiers, 1964, Physical Properties of Semiconductors, 1989. With U.S. Army, 1955—57. Recipient Cordiner award GE, 1962, John Scott medal, City of Phila., 1975, GaAs Conf. award with Welker medal, 1976, Monie A. Ferst award, Sigma Xi, 1988, Nat. Medal Sci., NSF, 1990, Indsl. Application Sci., NAS, 1993, Centennial medal, ASEE, 1993, 50th Ann. award, Am. Elec. Assn, 1993, Japan prize, 1995, Nat. Medal of Tech. award, 2002, Internat. Global Energy prize, 2003, Lemelson-MIT prize, 2004, MRS Von Hippel award, 2004. Fellow: AAAS, IEEE (life Morris Liebmann award 1973, Jack A. Morton award 1981, Edison medal 1989, medal of honor 2003, Third Millennium medal), Internat. Engring. Consortium, Am. Phys. Soc., Am. Acad. Arts and Scis., Am. Phys. Soc., Optical Soc. Am. (Charles H. Townes award 1992, Frederic Ives medal 2001); mem.: NAS (Indsl. Application of Sci. award 1993), NAE, Lincoln Acad. Ill. (laureate 2005), We. Soc. Engrs. (Washington award 2004), Ioffe Inst. (hon.), Math. Assn. Am., Russian Acad. Scis. (fgn. mem.), Minerals, Metals and Materials Soc. (John Bardeen award 1995), Math. Assn. Am., Electrochem. Soc. (Solid State Sci. and Tech. award 1983), Tau Beta Pi (Outstanding Alumnus award 1999), Eta Kappa Nu (eminent mem. 1998, Karapetoff Eminent Mems. award 1994, eminent mem. 1998). Home: 2212 Fletcher St Urbana IL 61801-6915 Office: U Ill Dept Elec/Computer Engring 1406 W Green St Urbana IL 61801-2918

HOLOUBEK, MAKAYLA SIBLEY, history educator; d. Tommy Joe Sibley and Joy Wilson Shaw; m. Charles Gilbert Holoubek, Dec. 5, 1998; 1 child, Jackson Sibley. BA in Polit. Sci., La. State U., 1998; MS in Environ. Law, Vt. Law Sch., 2001; MA in History, La. Tech. U., 2003. Rsch. asst. Dartmouth Coll., Hanover, NH, 1999—2000; social studies tchr. Franklin (N.H.) H.S., 2004—. Presenter in field. Active mem. N.H. Dem. Party, Concord, 2004—; mem. Amnesty Internat., Washington, 2004—. McGinty fellow, La. Tech. U., 2002—03. Mem.: Am. Hist. Assn., Phi Alpha Theta (v.p. La. tech. chpt. 2002—03), Omicron Delta Kappa. Democrat. Roman Catholic. Avocations: travel, reading.

HOLQUIST, JAMES MICHAEL, literature educator, department chairman; b. Rockford, Ill., Dec. 20, 1935; s. Leonard and Billye Alverta (Appleby) H.; m. Lydia Landis, July 30, 1960 (div. Dec. 1972); children: Peter Isaac, Benjamin Michael, Joshua Appleby; m. Katerina Clark, Apr. 15, 1974 (div. May 1999); children: Nicholas Manning, Sebastian; m. Elise Snyder, Nov. 6, 1999. BA with highest honors, U. Ill., 1963; PhD, Yale U., 1968; PhD honoris causa, U. Stockholm, Sweden, 2001. Asst. prof. Yale U., New Haven, 1968-72, assoc. prof., 1972-75; assoc. prof., dept. chmn. U. Tex., Austin, 1976-78, prof., 1978-80; prof. Slavic langs. and lit. dept., chmn. Ind. U., Bloomington, 1981-85; prof. comparative lit., dir. lit. major Yale U., 1986-91, chmn. coun. on Russian and East European studies, 1992-98, chmn. dept. comparative lit., 1998—2003, Northrop Frye prof. lit. theory, 2000. Co-owner Loire Wines, LLC; Christian Gauss lectr. Princeton U., 1991; NEH exchangee Soviet Acad. Scis., 1983; mem. exec. com. and editl. bd. PMLA. Author: (with Kernan and Brooks) Man and His Fictions, 1973, Dostoevsky and the Novel, 1977, reprinted, 1986; editor: (co-translator) The Dialogic Imagination: Four Essays by M.M. Bakhtin, 1981, (with Katerina Clark) Mikhail Bakhtin, 1984, Dialogism: The World of Mikhail Bakhtin, 1990, 2d edit., 2003, Philosophy of the Act, 1993; editor-in-chief: Tex. Slavic Studies, 1980; co-editor: Ind. Soviet Studies, 1982; editorial bd.: Yearbook of Comparative and Gen. Lit., 1982, Slavic Rev., 1983. Served with U.S. Army, 1958-61. Recipient Burnes-Sewall prize for excellence in tchg. Yale Coll., 2004; Rockefeller Humanities fellow, 1983; vis. scholar Phi Beta Kappa, 1984-85; grantee NEH, 1979, Morse fellow Yale U., 1970. Mem. MLA, Am. Assn. Advancement of Slavic Studies, Internat. Bakhtin Soc. (newsletter editor 1982—), Internat. Dostoevsky Soc., Am. Assn. Tchrs. Slavic and East European Langs., Grotesque Club, Mory's Assocs., Elizabethean Club. Democrat. Home: 180 Linden St Apt H3 New Haven CT 06511-2459 E-mail: michael.holquist@yale.edu.

HOLSAPPLE, CLYDE WARREN, decision and information systems educator; b. Raleigh, N.C., Nov. 1, 1950; s. Van Warren and Jeanne (Rickert) H.; m. Carol Eades; children: Christiana, Claire. BS in Math., Purdue U., 1972, MS in Computer Sci., 1975, PhD in Mgmt., 1977. From asst. prof. to assoc. prof. bus. adminstrn. U. Ill., Urbana, 1978-83; vis. asst. prof. mgmt. Purdue U., West Lafayette, Ind., 1977-78, from assoc. prof. to prof. mgmt., 1983-89; prof. decision sci. and info. systems U. Ky., Lexington, 1988—, Rosenthal endowed chair in mgmt. info. systems, 1988—, chmn. dept. decision sci. and info. systems, 1993-94. Adj. prof. U. Tex., Austin, 1989—. Co-author: Foundations of Decision Support Systems, 1981, Micro Database Management, 1984, Manager's Guide to Expert Systems, 1986, The Information Jungle, 1988, Operations Research and Artificial Intelligence, 1994, Decision Support Systems: A Knowledge-Based Approach, 1996; editor: Handbook on Knowledge Management, 2003; editor Jour. Orgnl. Computing and Electronic Commerce, Erlbaum Corp., Mahwah, N.J., 1990—; assoc. editor Mgmt. Sci., Providence, 1991-98; area editor Decision Support Systems, Amsterdam, 1992—; contbr. over 100 articles to profl. jours. Recipient Pres.'s Acad. award Purdue U., 1970, 71, 72, Computer Educator of Yr. award Internat. Assn. for Computer Info. Systems, 1993. Recipient Chancellor's award for Outstanding Tchr., 1995, R&D Excellence Program award, Ky. Sci. and Engring. Found., 2002. Mem. IEEE, Internat. Soc. for Decision Support (co-founder, co-dir. 1989—), Assn. for Computing Machinery, Inst. for Operations Rsch. Mgmt. Scis., Assn. for Info. Systems, Decision Sci. Inst., Phi Beta Kappa, Phi Kappa Phi. Office: U Ky Gatton Coll Bus & Econs Lexington KY 40506-0034 Office Phone: 859-257-5236. Business E-Mail: cwhols@uky.edu.

HOLSAPPLE, LINDA HARRIS, editor; b. New Rochelle, N.Y., Nov. 20, 1948; d. Herbert Barney and Elizabeth (Curren) Harris; m. Earle Taylor Holsapple III; children: Elizabeth, John. Grad., Loyola Rome Ctr., 1970; BS in Intermediate Edn., Loyola U., Chgo., 1971; MA in Higher Edn. Adminstrn., Cath. U., 1973; Diploma di Merito in Italiano, 2000; diploma, Scola Leonardo Da Vinci, 2002. Admissions counselor various colls., 1971—75; mktg., comm. specialist, editor Rutgers Cmty. Health Plan, New Brunswick, NJ, 1978-85; dir. bus. devel. SciTech Devel., Detroit, 2002—. Leader, cons. Warren (N.J.) Girl Scouts, 1987-96; leader Warren Cub Scouts, 1993-97. Avocation: nature hiking. Home: 281 Kercheval Ave Grosse Pointe Farms MI 48236-3105

HOLSCHER, WILLIAM A., information scientist; BS in Computer Info. Sys., Mercy Coll., 2004; post grad., Capella U., 2004—. Cert. CMM level 2. Sys. ops. Danneman Fabrics, Dover, Del., 1975—77; sr. R&D programmer and analyst Corstar Bus. Computing Co., White Plaines, NY, 1978—80, Battery Products Divsn. Union Carbide Corp., Eastview, NY, 1980—81; pres. and owner Software and Sys. Svcs., White Plains, NY, 1981—85; chief apps. arch. and project mgr. Info. Sys. Svcs., Inc., 1981—85; mgmt. and IT cons., project mgr., sys. integrator, chief apps. arch. WAH Internat., 1985—98; dir. tech. arch. group, project mgr. and sr. apps. arch. John Hancock Fin. Svcs., Inc., Boston, 1998—2001. Team leader sys. devel. and support Battery Products Divsn. Union Carbide Corp., Eastview, NY, 1980—81. With Sys. Ops. USAF, 1973—77. Address: 30 George Waterman Rd Johnston RI 02919

HOLSCHUH, JOHN DAVID, federal judge; b. Ironton, Ohio, Oct. 12, 1926; s. Edward A. and Helen (Ebert) H.; m. Carol Eloise Stouder, May 25, 1952; 1 child, John David Jr. BA, Miami U., 1948; JD, U. Cin., 1951. Bar: Ohio 1951, U.S. Dist. Ct. (so. dist.) Ohio 1952, U.S. Ct. Appeals (6th cir.) 1953, U.S. Supreme Ct. 1956. Atty. McNamara & McNamara, Columbus, Ohio, 1951-52, 54; law clk. to Hon. Mell. G. Underwood U.S. Dist. Ct., Columbus, 1952-54; ptnr. Alexander, Ebinger, Holschuh, Fisher & McAlister, Columbus, Ohio, 1954-80; judge U.S. Dist. Ct. (so. dist.) Ohio, 1980—, chief judge, 1990-96. Adj. prof. law Ohio State U. Coll. Law, 1970; mem. com. on codes of conduct Jud. Conf. U.S., 1985-90. Pres. bd. dirs. Neighborhood House, Columbus, 1969-70; active United Way of Franklin County, Columbus. Fellow Am. Coll. Trial Lawyers; mem. Order of Coif, Phi Beta Kappa, Omicron Delta Kappa. Home and Office: US Dist Ct 109 US Courthouse 85 Marconi Blvd Rm 109 Columbus OH 43215-2823 Office Phone: 614-719-3310.

HOLSCHUH, JOHN DAVID, JR., lawyer; b. Columbus, Ohio, Dec. 21, 1955; s. John D. and Carol Elouise (Stouder) H.; m. Wendy G. Ellis, Sept. 22, 1984; children: Heather Elyse, John David III, Jacob Alexander. BS, Miami U., Oxford, Ohio, 1977; JD, U. Cin., 1980. Bar: Ohio 1980, U.S. Dist. Ct. (so. dist.) Ohio 1980, U.S. Ct. Appeals (6th cir.) 1986, U.S. Supreme Ct. 1986, U.S. Dist. Ct. (ea. dist.) Ky. 1987, Ky. 1991. Assoc. Santen, Shaffer & Hughes, Cin., 1980-87, ptnr., 1987-89, Santen & Hughes, Cin., 1989—. Pros. atty. City of Loveland, Ohio, 1987-92, magistrate, 1992—; magistrate Village of Fairfax, Ohio, 1999—; mem. faculty Nat. Inst. Trial Advocacy, 1990, 91, 96, 2005; participant Pretrial Civil Litigation Skills Workshop, 1991. Author: Medical Malpractice, 1986, Tort Reform Pleading, 1987, Civil Procedure, 1986, rev. edit., 1989, Damages for Plaintiff and Defense Attorneys in Ohio, 1990, 2d edit., 1991, Tort Reform Update, 1990, Masters in Trial, 2004. Recipient merit award Ohio Legal Ctr. Inst., 1986. Mem.: ATLA, Order of Barristers, Potter Stewart Inns of Ct. (emeritus mem.), Cin. Bar Found. (trustee 2001—), Cin. Bar Assn. (chmn. common pleas ct. 1991—93, trustee 1995—2004, co-chmn. bench-bar conf. 1997—98, sec. 1999—2000, v.p. 2000—01, pres.-elect 2001—02, pres. 2002—03), Hamilton County Trial Lawyers (pres. 1990—92), Ohio State Bar Assn., Ohio Acad. Trial Lawyers (trustee 1991—95, 1998—2000), Am. Bd. Trial Advs., 6th Cir. Jud. Conf. (life; del. 1983—88). Avocations: sports, travel. Office: Santen & Hughes 312 Walnut St Ste 3100 Cincinnati OH 45202-4044 Office Phone: 513-721-4450. E-mail: jdh@santen-hughes.com.

HOLSCLAW, JASON SCOTT, financial analyst; b. Lexington, Ky., Aug. 29, 1977; s. Dennis Scott and Teresa Louise Holsclaw; m. Abby Alissa Hughes, May 12, 2001. BA, Ouachita U., 1999; MPA, U. Ky., 2001. Legis. asst. Lexington-Fayette (Ky.) Urban County Govt., 2001—02; analyst U.S. GAO, Washington, 2002—. Liberal. Bapt. Avocations: softball, reading, singing, travel, exercise.

HOLSEN, JAMES NOBLE, JR., retired chemical engineer; b. Palo Alto, Calif., June 20, 1924; s. James N. and Esther (Giltrud) H.; m. Nancy Schwankhaus, Feb. 24, 1950 (div.); children— James Noble III, David Edwards; m. Margot Meyer Best, Nov. 11, 1977; stepchildren— Victoria, Christopher, John BS, Princeton U., 1948; D.Sc., Washington U., St. Louis, 1954. Registered profl. engr., Mo. Chem. engr. Olin Mathieson Chem. Corp., 1954-55; asst. prof. chem. engring. Washington U., 1955-58, assoc. prof., 1958-61, prof., 1961-73; prof. chem. engring. U. Mo.-Rolla, 1973-74, vis. prof. engring. mgmt., 1974-75; program mgr. McDonnell Douglas Corp., St. Louis, 1977-92; ret., 1992. Cons. chem. engring. and aerospace scis.; vis. prof. engring. Kabul U., Afghanistan, 1963-64, 69-73; mem. U.S. Engring. Team, Kabul, 1963-64, 69-73 Served with AUS, 1942-46 Fellow AIAA (assoc.); mem. Am. Inst. Chem. Engrs. (chmn. St. Louis sect. 1962), Am. Chem. Soc., Am. Soc. Engring. Edn., AAAS, Ethical Soc. Sigma Xi, Tau Beta Pi Clubs: Princeton Quadrangle. Achievements include research on gas phase reaction kinetics, gaseous transport properties, materials processing in space, satellite components and structure, thermodynamics. Active in environmental affairs with St. Louis Audubon Soc. Home: 419 E Argonne Dr Kirkwood MO 63122-4523 Personal E-mail: jholsen@mindspring.com.

HOLSINGER, CANDICE DOREEN, lawyer; b. Pitts., June 9, 1955; d. Edward P. and Myrtle-Jane (Atwood) H.; m. Barry Alan McClune, Nov. 23, 1984. BA, Westminster Coll., 1977; JD, Duquesne U., 1981. Bar: Pa., U.S. Dist. Ct. (we. dist.) Pa., U.S. Ct. Appeals (3d cir.), U.S. Supreme Ct.; CPA 2002. Law clk. Child Advocacy Assn., Pitts., 1981; assoc. Tarasi & Tighe, Pitts., 1982-84, Metz, Cook, Hanna, Welsh Bluestone & Beamer, Pitts., 1984-87, Hyatt Legal Svcs., Pitts., 1987-94, Karlowitz & Cromer, 1994; pvt. practice Wilmerding, 1994—97; assoc. Kramer Thompson & Assoc, Pitts., 1997—. With H&R Block, 1997. Mem.: Am. Inst. Cert. Pub. Accountants, Pa. Inst. Cert. Pub. Accounts, Allegheny County Bar Assn. Home: 225 Welsh Ave Wilmerding PA 15148-1216 Office: Kramer Thompson & Assoc 875 Greentree Rd Bldg 7 Ste 175 Pittsburgh PA 15220

HOLSINGER, JAMES WILSON, JR., physician; b. Kansas City, Kans., May 11, 1939; s. James Wilson and Ruth Leona (Reitz) H.; m. Barbara Jenn Craig, Dec. 28, 1963; children: Anna Elizabeth, Martha Ruth, Sarah Frances, Rachel Catherine. Student, Duke U., 1957-60, MD, 1964, PhD, 1968; MS, U. S.C., 1981; BA, U. Ky., 1997; DS (hon.), Pikeville Coll., 1996. Intern Duke U. Hosp., Durham, N.C., 1964, resident in surgery, 1965, fellow in thoracic surgery, 1966, fellow in anatomy, 1966-68; resident in surgery U. Fla., Gainesville, 1968-70, fellow in cardiology, 1970-72; with VA, 1969-94; chief of staff VA Med. Ctr., Augusta, Ga., 1978-81, dir. Richmond, Va., 1981-90, Lexington, Ky., 1993-94; chief med. dir. Dept. Vets. Affairs, Washington, 1990-93, under sec. health, 1992-93; prof. medicine and anatomy Med. Coll. Ga., Augusta, 1978-81; prof. med. and health admin. Med. Coll. of Va., Richmond, 1981-93; asst. v.p. health scis. VA Commonwealth U., Richmond, 1985-90; chancellor U. Ky. Med. Ctr., Lexington, 1994—2003, Wethington chair in health scis., 2001—, chancellor emeritus, 2003—; prof. medicine, surgery and anatomy U. Ky. Coll. Medicine, 1994—; profl. health care adminstrn. U. Ky. Coll. Allied Health Profls., 1994—; sr. v.p. U. Ky., Lexington, 2001—03; sec. Cabinet Health and Family Svcs. Commonwealth of Ky., Frankfort, 2003—. Mem. com. evangelism N. Ga. conf. United Meth. Ch., 1980-81, com. 80, World Meth. Coun., 1981—, bd. discipleship Va. conf., 1982-86, lay mem., 1984-93, assoc. dist. lay leader, 1983-84, dist. lay leader, 1984-86, conf. lay leader, 1986-92, conf. chmn. health and welfare ministries, Ky., 1996-2000, Ky. conf. lay mem., 1996-00, del. gen. conf., 1988, 92, 96, 2000, del. S.E. jurisdictional conf., 1988, 92, 96, 2000; exec. com. World Meth. Coun., 1986—. treas., 1993—, gen coun. on ministries United Meth. Ch., 1988-2000, Gen. Bd. Pubs., 1992-96, bd. dirs. United Meth. Pub. House, 1996-2000, jud. council, 2000—, pres. 2004—; commr. Joint Commn. on the Accreditation of Healthcare Orgns., 1996-2002. Contbr. articles to profl. jours. Major gen. M.C., USAR, 1989-92. Master ACP; fellow Am. Coll. Cardiology, Am. Coll. Healthcare Execs. (Gold medal award 1993); mem. Am. Assn. Anatomists, Am. Heart Assn. (fellow clin. coun.), Soc. Med. Adminstrs., Internat. Brotherhood Magicians (order of Merlin), Ky. Inst. Medicine, Ret. Officers Assn. (bd. dirs. 1998-2000). Republican. Office: Cabinet Health and Family Svcs 275 E Main St Frankfort KY 40621-0001

HOLST, RUTH MARY, medical librarian; b. Fond du Lac, Wis., Sept. 22, 1947; d. Delmar and Marie (Daun) H.; m. Robert Peter Thiel, May 7, 1977; 1 child, Alexandra. BS, U. Wis., 1970, MS, 1973. Med. libr. Columbia Hosp., Milw., 1970-82, dir. libr. svcs., 1983—2002; assoc. dir. nat. network libr. medicine U. Ill., Chgo., 2002—. Adj. asst. prof. U. Wis. Milw. Sch. Libr. and Info. Sci., 1981-90; dir. women's health Columbia Hosp., 1988-91, mgr. coordinated care, 1994-98; biomed. libr. rev. com. Nat. Libr. Medicine, Bethesda, Md., 1996-2000. Editor: Hospital Library Managament, 1983; mem. libr. adv. bd. New Eng. Jour. Medicine; contbr. articles to profl. jours. Bd. dirs. Friends of Golda Meir Libr., Milw., 1985-89. Grantee Nat. Libr. Medicine, 1990. Fellow Med. Libr. Assn. (bd. dirs. 2001-04, sec., 2002-04, editor The Med. Libr. Assn. Guide to Managing Health Care Librs. 2000); mem. Coun. Wis. Librs. (bd. dirs. 1993-97), Spl. Librs. Assn., Columbia History Medicine Club (sec.), Acad. Health Info. Profls., Milw. Acad. Medicine Avocations: reading, cooking, singing. Office: Univ Ill at Chgo Libr Health Scis 1750 W Polk St Chicago IL 60612 Business E-Mail: rholst@uic.edu.

HOLSTAD, CHRISTIAN, artist; b. Anaheim, Calif., 1972; BFA, Kans. City Art Inst., 1994. One-man shows include Sand Day: A Show of Artifacts, Absentia Art Gallery, Williamsburg, NY, 2002, one-man shows include with Chris Verene The Self-Esteem Salon: The Baptism Series, Deitch Projects, NY, 2003, one-man shows include Life is a Gift, Daniel Reich Gallery, 2002, Sonnenaufgang, Aurel Scheibler Gallery, Germany, 2003, Sonnenuntergang, Daniel Schmidt Gallery, Germany, 2003, The Birth of Princess Middlefinger, Prague Biennial, 2003, The Housekeepers, Daniel Reich Gallery, NY, 2003, Am. Express, Galeria Massimo de Carlo, Milan, Italy, 2004, Moving toward the Light, Daniel Reich Gallery, 2004, Innocent Killers, P.S. 1 Contemporary Art Ctr., Queens, NY, 2004, Gaity; Discovering the Lost Art, Kunsthalle, Zurich, Switzerland, 2004, exhibited in group shows at Midwest Bound, Chorus Gallery, Mpls., 1995, Sauna Hut Available, 1996, Cult of Claude, Here Arts Gallery, NY, 1997, exhibited in group shows, Fleshy Juggler, Brownies, NY, 1998, exhibited in group shows, Car Show, Reported Injuries Art Space, Bklyn., 1999, Slide Show, John Michael Kohler Art Ctr., Sheboygan, Wis., 2000, Zeek Sheck Collaboration, Knitting Factory, NY, 2001, Bathroom Group Show, Daniel Reich Gallery, NY, 2002, Now Playing, D'amelio Terras, NY, 2003, Calif. Earthquakes, Daniel Reich Gallery, NY, 2004, Whitney Biennial, Whitney Mus. Am. Art, 2004. Mailing: c/o Daniel Reich Gallery 537 A West 23 St New York NY 10011*

HOLSTEAD, JOHN BURNHAM, retired lawyer; b. Dallas, Mar. 5, 1938; s. J.B. and Maurice (Cook) H.; m. Marilyn Morris, Nov. 23, 1963; children: Will, Rand, Scott. BA, La. Tech. U., 1959; LL.B., U. Tex.-Austin, 1962. Bar: Tex., U.S. Dist. Ct. Tex. 1965, U.S. Ct. Appeals (5th cir.), U.S. Ct. Appeals (10th cir.), U.S. Supreme Ct. 1974. Briefing clk. Tex. Sup. Ct., 1962-63; assoc. Vinson & Elkins, Houston, 1965-72, ptnr., 1972; ret., 2001. Mem. bd. advisors Biology of Info. Ctr., Baylor Coll. Medicine; spkr. on civil litigation and bus. disputes. Bd. dirs., trustee Goodwill Industries Houston, Inc. Named Centennial Outstanding Alumni, La. Tech. U., 1998. Fellow Internat. Soc. Barristers, Houston Bar Found., Tex. Bar Found.; mem. ABA, Tex. Bar Assn., Houston Bar Assn., River Oaks Country Club, Houston Club Episcopalian. Office: Vinson & Elkins 3200 First City Tower 1001 Fannin St Ste 3300 Houston TX 77002-6706 E-mail: jholstead@velaw.com.

HOLSTEIN, WILLIAM KURT, business administration educator; b. Stamford, Conn., Nov. 19, 1936; s. Kurt Edward and Doris Christiana (Werner) H.; m. Audrey Louise Bedford, Aug. 15, 1959; children: Kurt Edward II, William Kurt Jr., Catherine Louise. BChE, Rensselaer Poly. Inst., Troy, N.Y., 1958; MS in Indsl. Mgmt., Purdue U., 1959, PhD in Econs., 1964. Instr., then asst. prof. indsl. mgmt. Purdue U., 1959-64; asst. prof., then assoc. prof. Harvard U. Grad. Sch. Bus. Adminstrn., 1964-72; prof. SUNY, Albany, 1972-99, disting. svc. prof., 1991-99, dean sch. of bus., 1972-81, 86-87, exec. dir. Inst. for Study of Info. Sci., 1988-96; dir. Ctr. for Pvt. Enterprise Devel., Budapest, Hungary, 1991-93; D. Hollins Ryan prof. bus. adminstrn. Coll. William and Mary, Williamsburg, Va., 1999—; prof. Grad. Sch. Bus. Adminstrn., Zurich, 1996—. Dir. exec. devel. programs in Singapore, Taiwan, Argentina, Switzerland, Eng. and Ctrl. Am., 1969—, cons. to industry and govt.; vis. prof. IMEDE, Lausanne, Switzerland, 1983-85. Co-author: Production Planning and Control, 1963, Casebooks in Production Management, 1968, BASIC: Concepts and Applications, 1987; author articles in field. Trustee Upsala Coll., 1969-72; mem. accreditation com., editorial adv. com., visitation teams Am. Assembly of Collegiate Schs. of Bus., 1972-81; mem. exec. com. Middle Atlantic Assn. Schs. Bus. Adminstrn., 1976-81, pres., 1980; bd. dirs. Albany Symphony Orch., 1976-99, Seagle Music Colony, 1998—; bd. dirs., treas., v.p. adminstrn. Parsons Child and Family Center, Albany, 1977-94, pres., 1989-92; chmn. Metro 2000 Project, 1979; mem. com. on computer-aided mfg. Nat. Acad. Scis., 1980-83. Mem. Inst. Mgmt. Scis., Am. Prodn. and Inventory Control Soc. (hon.), Delta Sigma Pi, Beta Gamma Sigma. Lutheran. Home: 3104 Parkside Ln Williamsburg VA 23185-7696 Office: Coll William and Mary Sch Bus Adminstrn Williamsburg VA 23187-8795 E-mail: holstein@albany.edu.

HOLSTI, KALEVI JACQUE, political scientist, department chairman; b. Geneva, Apr. 25, 1935; s. Rudolf Woldemar and Liisa Anniki (Franssila) H.; children: Liisa, Matthew, Karina. BA, Stanford U., 1956, MA, 1958, PhD, 1961. Mem. faculty U. B.C., Vancouver, Canada, 1961—, U. Killam prof. polit. sci. Canada, 1997—. Vis. prof. McGill U., Montreal, Can., 1972, Kyoto (Japan) U., 1977, Hebrew U., Jerusalem, 1978, Internat. U. Japan, 1988, 92, 94; vis. fellow Australian Nat. U., 1983; cons. in field. Author: International Politics: A Framework for Analysis, 7th edit., 1994, Why Nations Realign, 1982, The Dividing Discipline: Hegemony and Pluralism in International Theory, 1985, Peace and War: International Order and Armed Conflict, 1648-1989, 1991, Change in the International System: Essays on the Theory and Practice of International Relations, 1991, The State, War, and the State of War, 1996, Taming the Sovereigns: Institutional Change in International Politics, 2004; editor: Internat. Studies Quar., 1970-75; co-editor: Can. Jour. Polit. Sci., 1978-81. Recipient Killam Rsch. prize, 1992; Fulbright scholar, 1959-60; Can. Coun. leave fellow, 1967, 72, 78, Can. Coun. Killam Rsch. fellow, 1987-89. Fellow Royal Soc. Can.; mem. Internat. Studies Assn. (pres. 1986-87), Can. Polit. Sci. Assn. (pres. 1984-85), Finish Acad. Scis. & Letters (fgn. mem.). Office: U BC Dept Polit Sci Vancouver BC Canada V6T 1Z1 Office Phone: 604-822-3607. Business E-Mail: holsti@interchange.ubc.ca.

HOLSTI, OLE RUDOLF, political scientist, educator; b. Geneva, Aug. 7, 1933; came to U.S., 1940, naturalized, 1954; s. Rudolf Waldemar and Liisa (Franssila) H.; m. Ann Wood, Sept. 20, 1953; children: Eric Lynn, Maija. BA with highest honors, Stanford U., 1954, PhD, 1962; MAT., Wesleyan U., Middletown, Conn., 1956. Instr., asst. prof. polit. sci., research coordinator Stanford U., 1962-67; assoc. prof. U. B.C., Vancouver, Can., 1967-71, prof., 1971-74; George V. Allen prof. polit. sci. Duke U., 1974—, chmn. dept. polit. sci., 1977-83; prof. Dept. Polit. Sci. U. Calif., Davis, 1978-79. Mem. adv. com. on hist. diplomatic documentation U.S. Dept. State, 1983-86; mem. oversight com. NSF, 1981-84; co-dir. Triangle Univs. Security Sem. Duke U., 1983-98. Author (with D.J. Finlay and R. R Fagan): Enemies in Politics, 1967; author: Analysis of Communication Content: Development in Scientific Theories and Computer Techniques, 1969, Content Analysis for Social Sciences and Humanities, 1969, Crisis Escalation War, 1972, Unity and Disintegration in International Alliances: Comparative Studies, 1973, Change in the International System, 1980, American Leadership in World Affairs: The Vietnam and Breakdown of Consensus, 1984, Pub. Opinion and Am. Fgn. Policy, 1996, 2004; co-author: International Crises, 1972, Content Analysis: Handbook with Application for the Study of Internat. Crisis, 1963, Political Science Annual, 1975, Thought and Action in Foreign Policy, 1975, The Behavior of Nations, 1976, World Politics, 1976, Diplomacy, 1979, Challenges to America, 1979, Containment, 1986, Behavior, Society and Nuclear War, 1989, Soviet-American Relations after the Cold War, 1991, Explaining the History of American Foreign Relations, 1991, 2d edit., 2004, Psychological Dimensions of War, 1991, Diplomacy, Force and Leadership, 1993, Encyclopedia of US Foreign Relations, 1997—, Pondering Postinternationalism, 2000, The New International Studies Classroom, 2000, Soldiers and Civilians: The Civil-Military Gap and American National Security, 2001, Millennial Reflections on International Studies, 2002, On The Cutting Edge of Globalization, 2005; contbg. author numerous books including The United States and Human Rights, 2000; co-prodr.: American Democracy Promotion, 2000, Eagle Rules?: Foreign Policy and American Primacy in the 21st Century, 2001; assoc editor Western Polit. Quar., 1970—79, Jour. Conflict Resolution, 1967—72, bd. editors Computer Studies in the Humanities and Verbal Behavior, 1968—76, Am. Jour. Polit. Sci, 1975—80, Internat. Interaction assoc., Am. Review of Politics, editor then bd. editors Internat. Studies Quar., 1970—, Jour. Politics, 1991—, Internat. Studies Perspectives, 1999—, adv. bd. Univ. Press Am., 1976—, corr. editor Running Jour, —, corr. Racing South, —; contbr. mumerous articles to profl. jours. Served with AUS, 1956-58. Recipient Nevitt Sanford award, 1988, Disting. Tchrs. award Howard Johnson, 1990, Runner of Yr. award CGTC, 1985, Alumni Disting. Undergrad. Tchg. award, 1995, All-Am. award U.S. Masters Track & Field, 2000, 02; GE Found. Owen D. Young fellow, 1960-61, Haynes Found. Rsch. fellow, 1961-62, Can. Coun. Leave fellow, 1970-71, Ctr. Advanced Study in Behavioral Sci. fellow, 1972-73, Ford Found. Faculty Rsch. fellow, 1972-73, Guggenheim fellow, 1981-82, Pew Faculty fellow Harvard U., 1990; grantee Can. Coun. Rsch., 1969, NSF, 1975-77, 79-81, 83-85, 88-90, 92-95, 96-98; mem. Nat. Champion Cross Country Team (men 50-59), 1985, 88, champion, 1988; champion Tar Heel Running Tour, 1987, champion, Triple Crown Race, 1992-93; named Runner Yr., 1993, Carolina Godiva Track Club. Mem. Internat. Studies Assn. (pres. west region 1969-70, south region 1975-77, nat. pres. 1979-80, Tchr.-Scholar award Internat. Studies Assn. 2000), Internat. Soc. Polit. Psychology (coun. 1990-92, v.p. 1993-95, Nev. H. Sanford award 1988), Internat. Peace Sci. Soc. (pres. so. sect. 1975-76), Am. Polit. Sci. Assn. (coun. 1982-84, adminstrn. com. 1982-85, Disting. Lifetime Achievement award 1999, Best Fgn. Policy Paper award 2004), Can. Polit. Sci. Assn., Western Polit. Sci. Assn. (exec. coun. 1971-74), USA Track and Field (N.C. Racewalk chair 1999-2002), Phi Beta Kappa, Duke Master Runners Club, Carolina Godiva Track Club (Runner of Yr. award 1985, 93). Home: 608 Croom Ct Chapel Hill NC 27514-6706 Office: Duke U Dept Polit Sci PO Box 90204 Durham NC 27708-0204 Office Phone: 919-660-4348. Business E-Mail: holsti@duke.edu.

HOLSTON, A. FRANK, retired commentator, communications educator; b. Balt., Feb. 25, 1928; s. Arthur F. Sr. and Sara A. Holston; m. Marianne B. Holston, Dec. 27, 1953; children: William Carroll, Sara Anne, Jeanne Marie. BS, U. Ala., 1951; MA, Mich. State U., 1962. Radio and TV broadcaster, sports dir., Balt., 1944-72; announcer ABC-TV, ESPN, N.Y.,Conn., 1974-88; prof. comm. C.C. Balt., 1956-88; ret., 1988. Chmn. faculty senate exec. com., Balt., 1969—70; gen. mgr. Liberty Campus, Balt., 1968—69, WBJC-FM, 1968—69; pres., bd. dirs. Shearwater, Inc., 1996—98; track ofcl. U.S. Naval Acad., 1998—; spkr. in field. Bd. dirs. Annapolis (Md.) Bur. Recreation, 1993—, Broadcast Edn. Assn., Washington, 1985-89, Ecumedia, Balt., 1975-76; v.p. Rep. Ctrl. Com., 1991-97, pres., 1995-97; chmn. '51 reunion U. Ala., 2001; pres. Feddayes, Boumi Temple Shrine, 1967-68. With USN, 1945, USNR. Ford Found. scholar, Northwestern U., 1958, News Am. fellow, Syracuse U., 1960. Mem.: Shriners (pres. Annapolis club 1960—61). Presbyterian. Home: 2B1 Spa Creek Landing Annapolis MD 21403 Office Phone: 410-974-9221.

HOLSWORTH, DOUGLAS MITCHELL, music educator, department chairman, director; b. Ft. Dix, N.J., Oct. 3, 1962; s. Francis Charles and Janet (Russo) Holsworth; m. Kathryn Lee Potter, May 5, 1985; children: Samantha, Benjamin Douglas. BS in Music Edn., U. Ala., 1985. Cert. tchr. music Fla. Dir. bands DeSoto County HS, Arcadia, Fla., 1992—95; dir. bands, music dept. head Escambia HS, Pensacola, Fla., 1995—. Music dir.: (plays) Annie, 2000 (Crystal award); actor, dir. Smoke on the Mountain, 2002 (Crystal award). Vol. tech. crew, vol. actor Pensacola Little Theater, 1995—. Capt. aviation/intelligence U.S. Army, 1985—91. Mem.: Fla. Bandmasters Assn., Fla. Music Educators Assn. Avocations: guitar, painting, acting. Office: Escambia HS 1310 N 65th Ave Pensacola FL 32506

HOLT, BERTHA MERRILL, state legislator; b. Eufaula, Ala., Aug. 16, 1916; d. William Hoadley and Bertha Harden (Moore) Merrill; m. Winfield Clary Holt, Mar. 14, 1942; children: Harriet Wharton Holt Whitley, William Merrill, Winfield Jefferson. AB, Agnes Scott Coll., 1938; postgrad., U. N.C. Law Sch., 1939-40; LLB, U. Ala., 1941; grad., Sch. Creative Leadership, Greensboro, N.C., 1992. Bar: Ala. 1941. With Treasury Dept., Washington, 1941-42, Dept. Interior, Washington, 1942-43. Mem. N.C. Ho. of Reps. from 22d Dist., 1975-80, 25th Dist., 1980-94, chmn. select com. govtl. ethics, 1979-80, chmn. constl. amendments com., 1981, 83, mem. joint commn. govtl. ops., 1982-88, chmn. appropriation com. justice and pub. safety, 1985-88, co-chair House appropriation sub-com. transp., 1991-92, co-chair appropriation sub-com. Justice and Pub. Safety, 1993-94. Pres., Democratic Women of Alamance, 1962, chmn. hdqrs., 1964, 68; mem. N.C. Dem. Exec. Com., 1964-75, 95—; pres. Episcopal Ch. Women, 1968; mem. coun. N.C. Episcopal Diocese, 1972-74, 84-87, 95-98; chmn. budget com. 1987; chmn. fin. dept., 1973-75, parish grant com., 1973-80, mem. standing com., 1975-78; mem. Episcopal Diocese Ecclesiastical Ct., 1998-2002; vestry mem. Ch. of Holy Comforter, 2005—; chmn. Alamance County Social Svcs. Bd., 1970; mem. N.C. Bd. Sci. and Tech., 1979-83; chair Legis. Women's Caucus, 1991-94; past bd. dirs. Hospice N.C.; bd. dirs. State Coun. Social Legis., pres. SCSL 1996-97, State Conf. Social Work, N.C. Epilepsy Assn., N.C. Pub. Sch. Forum, 1989, U. N.C. Sch. Pub. Health Adv. Bd., Salvation Army Alamance County, N.C., Nursing Found., 1989, Epilepsy Found., 1989; bd. Alternatives for Status Offenders Burlington, N.C., Sch. Pub. Health Adv. Bd.; bd. dirs. N.C. ACLU, Partnership For Children (N.C.), 1993-98. Recipient Outstanding Alumna award Agnes Scott Coll., 1978, Legis. award for svc. to elderly Non-Profit Rest Home Assn., 1985, health, 1986, ARC, 1987, Faith Active in Pub. Affairs award N.C. Coun. of Chs., 1987, Ellen B. Winston award State Coun. For Social Legis., 1989, N.C. Disting. Women's award in gov., 1991, Disting. Svc. award Alamance County, 1992, Chi Omega award Women in Leadership, 1st ann. Hallie Ruth Allen Dem. Women award Alamance County, 1992, Disting. Svc. award Chi Omega, 1996, Svc. award Triennial Conv., Episcopal Ch. Women of U.S., 1997, Outstanding Alumna award U. N.C.-Chapel Hill, 1998, Gwyneth B. Davis award N.C. Assn. Women Attys., 1998, Outstanding Svc. award N.C. Assn. Women Attys., 1998, Disting. Alumna award U. N.C.-Chapel Hill, 1999, numerous others; named One of 5 Disting. Women of N.C. (Govt.), 1991; award established Bertha B. Holt award, NC Bar Juvenile Justice Sect., first recepient, 2004; AAUW award for Edn. and Equity for Women and Girls, 2004. Mem. AAUW, NOW, N.C. Women's Forums, Law Alumni Assn. U. N.C. Chapel Hill (bd. dirs. 1978-81, 1994-99), N.C. Bar Assn. (bd. dirs. sr. lawyers sect., constnl. rights sect. 1998-2004, juvenile justice and children's rights 1999-, chair 2002-03), English Speaking Union, N.C. Hist. Soc., Soc. Wine Educators, Les Amis du Vin, Pi Beta Phi, Phi Kappa Gamma, Delta Kappa Gamma, Phi Theta Kappa, Century Club. Address: PO Box 1111 Burlington NC 27216-1111

HOLT, DONALD A., agronomist, consultant, researcher, retired academic administrator; b. Minooka, Ill., Jan. 29, 1932; s. Cecil Bell and Helen (Eickoff) H.; m. Marilyn Louise Jones, Sept. 6, 1953; children: Kathryn A. Holt Stichnoth, Steven Paul, Jeffrey David, William Edwin. Grad., Joliet Jr. Coll., 1952; BS in Agrl. Sci., MS in Agronomy, U. Ill.; PhD in Agronomy, Purdue U. Farmer, Minooka, Ill., 1956-63; instr., asst. prof., assoc. prof. then prof. agronomy Purdue U., West Lafayette, Ind., 1964-82; prof., head dept. agronomy U. Ill., Urbana-Champaign, Ill., 1982-83, dir. Ill. Agr. Expt. Sta., assoc. dean Coll. Agr., 1983-96, sr. assoc. dean Coll. Agr., cons. environ. sci., 1996-2002, ret., 2002, prof. emeritus, 2003—; interim dir. Nat. Soybean Rsch. Lab., 2003—03. Cons. Deere and Co., Ottumwa, Iowa, 1978, NASA, Houston, 1979, Control Data Corp., Mpls., 1978-79, EPA, Corvallis, Oreg., 1981-90. Town Bd. commr., Otterbein, Ind., 1972-76. Fellow AAAS, Am. Soc. Agronomy (pres. 1988), Crop Sci. Soc. Am.; mem. Agrl. Rsch. Inst. (pres. 1991), Am. Forage and Grassland Coun., Ill. Forage and Grassland Coun., Gamma Sigma Delta (internat. pres. 1974-76). Republican. United Methodist. Home: 1801 Moraine Dr Champaign IL 61822-5261 Office: U Ill 170 N5RC 1101 W Peabody Dr Urbana IL 61801-4723 Office Phone: 217-244-1706. Business E-Mail: d-holt@uiuc.edu.

HOLT, FRIEDA M., nursing educator, retired academic administrator; BSN with honors, U. Colo., Boulder, 1956; MS in Cmty. Health Nursing, Boston U., 1969, EdD, 1973. RN, Ariz., Calif., Colo., Mass., Md., Pa., Wash., Liberia, W. Africa. Instr., dir. of nursing Cuttington Coll., Liberia, Africa, 1964-67; teaching fellow sch. of nursing Boston U., 1969, asst. prof. sch. of nursing, 1969-74; assoc. prof., assoc. dean for grad. studies sch. of nursing U. Md., 1975-77, dean's dep. sch. of nursing, 1975-86, prof., assoc. dean for grad. studies sch. of nursing, 1977-86, acting dean sch. of nursing, 1978, acting asst. dean sch. of nursing, 1981-82, acting chmn. sch. of nursing, 1983-84, acting dean sch. of nursing, 1986-87, prof., assoc. dean for grad. studies, dean's dep. sch. of nursing, 1987-88, prof., exec. assoc. dean. sch of nursing, 1988-89, acting dean, prof. sch. of nursing, 1989-90, prof. sch. of nursing, 1990-91, prof., dir. sch. of nursing, 1992—94; dir. grad. programs Pa. State Sch. Nursing, 1994—2000; ret., 2000. Project dir. Primary Care Adult Nurse Practitioner Leadership grant, 1976-82, Preparation for Tchrs. in Maternal Child Nursing, judge U. Md. grad. sch. rsch. awards, 1979-84; author, project dir. Pa. State PhD Nursing Program Grant; NLN vis. for Accreditation of Baccalaureate and Masters Nursing Program, SREB/SCCEN Task Force on Grad. Edn., presenter seminars, confs., workshop. Contbr. articles to profl. jours. Bd. dirs. Md. Nurses Found. (v.p., 1988—). Recipient VA Commendation award, 1990, Charter Trustee award Found. for Nursing of Md., 1990, Martin Luther King, Jr. Humanitarian award, 1990; named Pa. Nurse Educator of Yr., 1998. Mem. ANA, ANA (coun. nurse rschrs.), APHA, AAUP, Nat. League for Nursing, Am. Edn. Rsch. Assn., Am. Edn. Rsch. Assn., Md. Assn. for Higher Edn., Soc. for Rsch. in Nursing Edn., Sigma Theta Tau. Home: 151 Woodpecker Ln Port Matilda PA 16870 Personal E-mail: 814-fmh.3@adelphia.net.

HOLT, GLEN EDWARD, editor; b. Abilene, Kans., Sept. 14, 1939; s. John Wesley and Helen Laverne (Schrader) H.; m. Leslie Edmonds, Jan. 29, 1994; children from previous marriage: Kris, Karen, Gordon. BA, Baker U., 1960; MA, U. Chgo., 1965, PhD, 1975. From instr. to asst. prof. Wash. U., St. Louis, 1968-82; dir. honors div. Coll. Liberal Arts, U. Minn., 1982-87; exec. dir. St. Louis Pub. Libr., 1987—2004; editor Pub. Libr. Quar., 2004—; nonprofit planning and policy cons. Cons. Chgo. Hist. Soc., 1976-79, Mo. Hist. Soc., St. Louis, 1979-87, Buffalo-Erie County Pub. Libr., 1997-98; mem. Online Computer Libr. Ctr. Pub. Libr. Adv. Com., 1991-95. Co-editor: St. Louis, 1975; co-author: Chicago, A Guide to the Neighborhoods, 1979. Recipient Cmty. Svc. award Commerce Bank, 2001; named Woodrow Wilson Found. fellow, 1963-64, Danforth fellow, 1963-68. Mem. ALA, Pub. Libr. Assn. (Charlie Robinson award 2001). Avocation: photography. Home: 4954 Lindell Blvd Apt 4W Saint Louis MO 63108-1520 E-mail: leholt@aol.com.

HOLT, HELEN, librarian, consultant, former government official; b. Gridley, Ill., Aug. 16, 1913; d. William Edward and Edna (Gingerich) Froehlich; m. Rush Dew Holt, June 19, 1941 (dec. Feb. 1955); children: Helen Jane (Mrs. David Seale), Rush Dew Holt Jr. AA, Stephens Coll., Columbia, Mo., 1932; BA, Northwestern U., 1934, MS, 1938; postgrad., U. Mo., U. N.C., George Washington U. Sci. librarian, instrl. asst. Stephens Coll., 1934—37; instr. biology Nat. Park Coll., Forest Glen, Md., 1938—41; instr. sci. Greenbrier Coll., W.Va., 1955—58; mem. W.Va. Ho. of Dels., 1955—57; sec. of state W.Va., 1957—59, asst. commr. pub. instns., 1959—60; spl. asst. to commr., dir. mortgage ins. program for constrn. long term care facilities FHA, 1960—70; asst. to sec., dir. elderly programs Dept. Housing and Urban Devel., 1970—84; mem. adv. bd. Small Bus. Adminstrn., 1986—90. Cons. in field. Contbr. articles to profl. jours. Del.-at-large, vice chmn. platform com. State of W.Va. Rep. Nat. Conv., 1958; sr. citizen vol. Rep. Nat. Com., 1984; elder local Presbyn. Ch., 1975—, bd. trustees 1968-74, 80-86, bd. deacons, 1988-94; bd. dirs. Thompson Markward Hall, Nat. Alliance Sr. Citizens, Nat. Safety Council, exec. com. Women's div. 1975-87, chmn. 1987. NSF fellow, 1956; recipient Community Svc. Human Rights award, UN Assn., 1985, Stephens Coll. Alumnae award. Fellow Am. Coll. Health Care Adminstrs. (Community Svc. award 1978); mem. Am. Health Care Assn., Nat. League Am. PEN Women (br. pres., nat. chaplain), Washington Forum, Potomac Bus. and Profl. Women (pres. 1983, Woman of the Yr. 1978), Gen. Fedn. Women's Clubs (state v.p. 1989—, other offices), Washington Forum (pres.), The Washington Club, Sigma Delta Epsilon, Sigma Xi, Delta Delta Delta (dist. pres.), Zeta Mu Epsilon (nat. pres.). Lodges: Zonta (bd. dirs.). Republican. Presbyterian. Home and Office: 2500 Virginia Ave NW Apt 1107 Washington DC 20037-1901 Personal E-mail: hfholt@aol.com.

HOLT, HOMER ANTHONY, JR., urologist, educator; b. Ashland, Ky., July 6, 1938; s. Homer A. Holt; m. Virginia Cayce, Nov. 22, 1962; children: Kathryn Holt Kerpestein, Kimberly Holt Cochran, Homer A. III. BA, Vanderbilt U., 1960; MD, U. Louisville, 1965. Diplomate Am. Bd. Urology. Straight surg. intern U. Louisville Sch. Medicine, 1965-66, resident in gen. surgery, 1966-68, resident in urology, 1969-72, chief resident in urology, 1971-72, clin. prof. surgery (urology), 1972—; pvt. practice, Louisville, 1972—. Cons. dept. surgery (urology) VA Med. Ctr., Louisville; active staff Norton Healthcare Sys.; courtesy staff Kosair Children's Hosp., Bapt. Hosp. East; pres. med. staff Meth. Evang. Hosp., 1989-90 Contbr. articles to med. jours. Capt. M.C. USAF, 1967—69. Fellow ACS (com. on applicants for Ky. 1982-98, chmn. com. 1988-98); mem. Am. Urol. Assn., Southeastern Sect. Am. Urol. Assn., Am. Lithotripsy Soc., Ky. Med. Assn., Ky. Urol. Assn. (pres. 1979-80), Jefferson County Med. Soc. (editor bull. 1978-79, treas. found. bd. 1984-86, v.p., 2004-05) Office: Gray Street Med Bldg 210 E Gray St Ste 1000 Louisville KY 40202-3906 Home: 5808 Brittany Woods Cir Louisville KY 40222-5908

HOLT, JONATHAN TURNER, public relations executive; b. New Haven, Jan. 8, 1949; s. Frederick Burton and Thelma (Turner) H. BA, Drew U., 1971. Chief adminstrv. officer Office of Policy and Analysis, FEA, Washington, 1973-76; chmn. bd. dirs. Holt, Ross Inc., Gladstone, NJ, 1977—2003; ptnr. Holt Mulroy & Germann, LLC, Trenton, NJ, 1999—. Cons. U.S. Dept. Energy Regional polit. dir. Pres. Ford Com., Washington, 1976, sec./treas. Worldcom Pub. Relations Group, Inc., 2000—. Vice-chmn. Westfield (N.J.) Town Rep. Com., 1980-84; mem. Delaware River Basin Water Resources Assn., 1979—; chmn. bd. visitors, Drew U., 1998—. NSF fellow, 1971. Mem. N.J. State C. of C., Am. Water Works Assn., N.J. Audubon Soc., Am. Assn. Polit. Cons., Pub. Rels. Soc. Am. (bd. dirs. N.J. chpt.), Nature Conservancy (trustee N.J. chpt.), Conservation Resources (dir. 2004—). Republican. Office: Holt Mulroy & Germann LLC 172 W State St Trenton NJ 08608 Office Phone: 609-656-0225. Business E-Mail: jholt@hmgpa.com.

HOLT, KAREN ANITA YOUNG, language educator; b. Waltham, Mass., Oct. 23, 1949; d. Rexford Vernon and Linia Virginia (Duke) Young; m. Robert Jackson Holt, Dec. 30, 1974 (div. Sept. 1984). BA in English and French, Southwestern Okla. State U., 1971; MA in English, Okla. State U., 1973, postgrad., 1973-77, 86, Cen. State U., 1986. Cert. tchr., Okla. Instr. Okla. State U. Tech. Br., Oklahoma City, 1977-87; arts in edn. coord. Putnam City Schs., Oklahoma City, 1985-87; prof. Rose State Coll., Midwest City, Okla., 1987—. Dir. Righting Writing, Midwest City, 1989-91; coord. Poetry at Rose, Midwest City, 1988—, Students' Poetry, 1992—; chairperson long-range planning Cross Timbers Arts and Humanities Coun., Midwest City, 1990-91; cons. Excellence in the Arts project Kennedy Found. Sch. Bd., 1988, Okla. Writing Project, 1995. Editor: Chapbook, 1971; contbr. poetry to various publs.; poet An Evening with Oklahoma Poets, U. Okla., 1991, City Arts Conversations with the Book, 1997. Charter mem. Carpenter Sq. Theatre Vols., Oklahoma City, 1986—; mem. Rose State Coll. Speakers' Bur., Midwest City, 1990—, senator humanities divsn. faculty, 1991-94, faculty senate treas., 1993-94. Recipient honorable mention poetry award Red Dirt Press, 1988, Outstanding Prof. of Yr. award Phi Theta Kappa, 1993, keynote spkr., 1997; Adult Inst. for Arts scholar Okla. Arts Inst., 1990-92, Regents scholar, 1992-94; Project AIM grantee Nat. Endowment for Arts, 1986-87. Mem. Okla. Alliance for Arts Edn., Okla. Assn. Cmty. and Jr. Colls. (English chairperson 1989-90), Okla. Coun. Tchrs. of English, Rose State Coll. Faculty Assn., Rose State Coll. Founders Club, Okla. Arts Inst. Alumni Assn. Republican. Methodist. Avocations: reading, dance, film history, photography, flute. Office: Rose State Coll 6420 SE 15th St Oklahoma City OK 73110-2704 Home: 2257 NW 52nd St Oklahoma City OK 73112-8053

HOLT, LEON CONRAD, JR., lawyer, chemicals executive; b. Reading, Pa., June 19, 1925; s. Leon Conrad and Elizabeth (Bright) H.; m. June M. Weidner, June 30, 1947; children: Deborah Holt Weil, Richard W. BS cum laude in Metall. Engring, Lehigh U., 1948; JD, U. Pa., 1951. Bar: N.Y. 1952. With firm Mudge, Stern Williams & Tucker (attys.), N.Y.C., 1951-53; atty. Am. Oil Co. (and predecessor co.), N.Y.C., 1953-57; gen. atty. Air Products & Chems., Inc., Allentown, Pa., 1957-61, v.p., 1961-76, v.p. adminstrn., 1976-78, gen. counsel, 1961-78, vice chmn. bd., chief adminstrv. officer, 1978-90, also dir., mem. exec., finance, pub. policy coms. Bd. dirs. VF Corp., exec. fin. and audit coms., 1983-98. Vice chmn. Lehigh Centennial Fund, 1964-65; chmn. Allentown Bd. Ethics, 1970-74; bd. dirs. Lehigh County United Fund, 1971-83, mem. exec. com., 1971-74, campaign chmn., 1972; bd. dirs. Allentown YMCA, 1965-69, trustee, 1972-79; trustee Allentown Art Mus., pres., 1988-92; mem. Allentown Sch. Dist. Authority, 1978-86; trustee Mfrs. Alliance for Productivity and Innovation, 1981-91; mem. adv. bd. Inst. Law and Econs., U. Pa., bd. overseers Law Sch., 1985-94; trustee Dorothy Rider-Pool Health Care Trust, 1982-96, chmn., 1990-96; trustee Rider-Pool Found., Com. Econ. Devel., Holt Family Found.; dir. Pa. chpt. Nature Conservancy, 1991-2004, Pocono Lake Preserve; co-chmn. Partnership for Comty. Health, 1991-94. Lt. (j.g.) USNR, 1943-46. Mem. ABA, Pa. Soc., Assn. Bar NYC, Allentown C. of C. (gov. 1965-68), Tunkhannock Creek Assn. (pres.), Alpha Tau Omega, Lehigh Country Club (bd. govs. 1970-77). Republican. Episcopalian. Home: 3003 Parkway Blvd Allentown PA 18104-5384 Office: 1611 Pond Rd Ste 300 Allentown PA 18104-2258

HOLT, LESLEY LEA, music educator; b. Crossville, Tenn., May 5, 1956; d. James Harold and Wilma Jean Kirby; m. Terry Jay Holt, Dec. 31, 1980; children: Jay Kirby, Abbi Leigh Holt Dunford. BS in Edn., Austin Peay State U., Clarksville, Tenn., 1978; degree in music, Roane State CC, Nashville, 1988. Tchr. Marshall Elem. Sch., Ft. Campbell, Ky., 1978—80, Fentress County Schs., Jamestown, Tenn., 1980, 1986—98, York Inst. HS, Jamestown, 1998—. Dir. music, pianist 1st United Meth. Ch., Jamestown, 1981—, Sunday sch. tchr., 1987—, youth dir., 1994—2002, v.p. women's group, 2004—; dir. Cumberland G.A.P. Mission, Jamestown, 1998—. Avocations: sewing, gardening, cooking. Home: 1008 Lincoln Rd Jamestown TN 38556 Office: York Inst PO Box 70 Jamestown TN 38556-0070

HOLT, MARJORIE SEWELL, lawyer, retired congresswoman; b. Birmingham, Ala., Sept. 17, 1920; d. Edward Rol and Juanita (Felts) Sewell; m. Duncan McKay Holt, Dec. 26, 1946; children: Rachel Holt Tschantre, Edward Sewell, Victoria. Grad., Jacksonville Jr. Coll., 1945; JD, U. Fla., 1949. Bar: Fla. 1949, Md. 1962. Pvt. practice, Annapolis, Md., 1962; clk. Anne Arundel County Circuit Ct., 1966-72; mem. 93d-99th Congresses from 4th Dist. of Md., 1973-86; armed svcs. com., vice-chair Office Tech. Assessment, 1977; chair Rep. Study com., 1975-76; of counsel Smith, Somerville & Case, Balt., 1986-90. Supr. elections Anne Arundel County, 1963-65; del. Rep. Nat. Conv., 1968, 76, 80, 84, 88; mem. Pres.'s Commn. on Arms Control and Disarmament, Gov.'s Commn. on Carefirst, 2003; mem. ind. commn. USAR; bd. dirs. Annapolis Fed. Savs. Bank; adv. bd. Crestar; co-chair George W. Bush Presdl. campaign, Md., 2000. Co-author: Case Against The Reckless Congress, 1976, Can You Afford This House, 1978. Bd. dirs. Md. Sch. for the Blind, Hist. Annapolis Found. Recipient Disting. Alumna award U. Fla., 1975, Trustees award U. Fla. Coll. Law, 1984, Alumnae Outstanding Achievement award, 1997. Mem. ABA, Md. Bar Assn., Anne Arundel Bar Assn., Phi Kappa Phi, Phi Delta Delta. Presbyterian (elder 1959).

HOLT, MILDRED FRANCES, educator; b. Lorain, Ohio, July 30, 1932; d. William Henry and Rachel (Pierce) Daniels; B.S., U. Md., 1962, M.Ed., 1967, Ph.D., 1977; m. Maurice Lee Holt, Sept. 11, 1949 (dec.); children— Claudia, Frances, William, Rudi. Tchr. spl. edn. St. Mary's (Md.) County Public Schs., 1962-64, coordinator Felix Johnson Spl. Edn. Center, 1964-66; demonstration tchr. spl. edn. U. Md., College Park, summer 1970, instr. spl. edn. dept. Coll. Edn., 1969-73; supr. spl. edn. Calvert and St. Mary's (Md.) Counties, 1968-69; asso. prof. spl. edn. W. Liberty (W.Va.) State Coll., 1973-75; asst. prof. Eastern Ill. U., Charleston, 1975-77; supr. spl. edn. Warren County Public Schs., Front Royal, Va., 1977-85; spl. edn. tchr. Dallas Ind. Sch. Dist., 1985— . Mem. NEA, Warren County Edn. Assn., Council Exceptional Children, Assn. for Gifted, Assn. Supervision and Curriculum Devel., Va. Edn. Assn., Va. Council Exceptional Children, Blue Ridge Orgn. Gifted and Talented, Assn. Children with Learning Disabilities, Nat. Assn. Gifted Children, Phi Theta Kappa, Kappa Delta Pi. Contbr. articles to profl. jours.; author: Reach Guidebook, 1979. Home: 2916 Sidney Dr Mesquite TX 75150-2253 E-mail: mholt@texas.net.

HOLT, PETER M., professional sports team executive, agricultural products executive; b. Peoria, Ill. s. B.D. Holt; m. Julianna Hawn. Former investment banker, restaurateur, Calif.; pres., CEO Holt Machinery Co., San Antonio, 1983—; owner, chmn. bd., CEO San Antonio Spurs, 1996—. Commr. Tex. Dept. Parks & Wildlife; bd. dir. Free Trade Alliance-San Antonio, San Antonio Econ. Devel. Found.; corp. bd. mem. Chase Bank, San Antonio. Past chmn. United Way, San Antonio; chmn. bd. St. Mary's Hall Sch. Served to sgt. E5 U.S. Army, Vietnam. Decorated Purple Heart, Silver Star, three Bronze Stars; named to Texas Bus. Hall of Fame, 2004. Mem.: World Presidents' Orgn. Office: San Antonio Spurs 100 Montana St San Antonio TX 78203-1031*

HOLT, PETER ROLF, gastroenterologist, educator; b. Berlin, Sept. 8, 1930; s. Arthur and Ruth H.; m. Joyce Weil, May 15, 1979; children: Rachel Janna, Shawn David, Tamara Naomi. BSc, U. London, 1949, MB, BS with honors, 1954. Intern London Hosp., 1954-55; asst. resident in medicine St. Luke's Hosp. Center, N.Y.C., 1957-59; tng. fellow in medicine Mass. Gen. Hosp., Boston, 1959-61; chief gastroenterology med. Service St. Luke's Hosp. Center, N.Y.C., 1961-96, attending physician, 1971—, Presbyn. Hosp., N.Y.C., 1988; chief gastroenterology St. Luke's-Roosevelt Hosp. Ctr., N.Y.C., 1996-2000; sr. scientist Inst. for Cancer Prevention, N.Y.C., 2000—04, dir. James E. Olson Cancer Prevention Program, 2004—, sr. scientist Strang Cancer Prevention Ctr., 2004—. Adj. sr. scientist Strang Cancer Ctr., NY, 2000—03; rsch. collaborator Brookhaven Nat. Lab., Upton, NY, 1973—79; mem. faculty dept. medicine Coll. Physicians and Surgeons Columbia U., N.Y.C., 1961—, prof., 1975—2000, prof. emeritus, 2000—, mem. Bio-engring. Inst., 1975—2000, Inst. Human Nutrition, 1978—2000, Comprehensive Cancer Ctr.; mem. 12th work group on clin. rsch. Nat. Commn. on Digestive Disease, 1977—79; mem. nat. sci. adv. com., nat. rev. com. Nat. Found. for Ileitis and Colitis, 1976—88, also chmn. rsch. tng. awards com.; vis. investigator Meml. Sloan-Kettering Cancer Ctr., 1988—89; vis. assoc. physician Rockefeller U., 2001—, adj. prof., 2004—; Trevor Howell lectr. Brit. Geriat. Soc., 1992; Dorothy Ewerson lectr. U. Pisa, 1999; adj. sr. sci. Rockefeller U., 2003—. Author, contbr. chpts. to books, articles to med. jours. Served to maj. Brit. Royal Army M.C., 1955-57. Recipient William H. Rorer award in Gastroenterology, 1965, Jannsen Lifetime Achievement award in Digestive Diseases, 2002, Internat. Solvay Nutrition award, 2002; named one of Best Doctors in Am., Castle Connoly Guide, 2002-05, Best Doctors in N.Y., N.Y. Mag., 1980-2005; NIH grantee. Fellow: ACP (gov.'s com. 1978—81); mem.: Am. Gastroenterology Assn. (pres. 1971, chmn. com. rsch. 1973—74, chmn. com. on aging 1982—86, chmn. admissions com. 1985—86, ethics com. 1997—2000, manpower and tng. com. 2001—04, internat. com.), Orgn. Mondiale de Gastro-Enterologie (chair nominating com. 1990—94, nomenclature com. and rsch. com.), Gerontol. Soc. Am., N.Y. Acad. Sci., Am. Soc. Cancer Rsch., Am. Soc. Clin. Nutrition, Am. Soc. Clin. Investigation, Am. Physiol. Soc., Am. Assn. Study of Liver Diseases, Intersoc. Com. Clin. Investigation in Digestive Disease (chmn. 1975—79). Office: Theobald Smith Hall Ste 210 Rockefeller U 1230 York Ave New York NY 10021 Office Phone: 212-734-0567 x207. E-mail: pholt@chpnet.org.

HOLT, RICHARD B., toy company executive; Dir. acctg. ops. Hasbro Inc., 1976—80, corp. controller, 1980—92, v.p., controller, 1987—92, sr. v.p., controller, 1992—2003, sr. v.p., chief audit and fiscal compliance officer, 2003—. Office: Hasbro Inc 1027 Newport Ave Pawtucket RI 02862

HOLT, ROBERT EZEL, data processing executive; b. Red Bay, Ala., May 8, 1957; s. Robert E. Sr. and Ruby (Weathers) H.; m. Elizabeth Ann Simmons, May 19, 1978; children: Robert E. III, James Michael. AA, N.E. Community Coll., 1977; BS, Miss. State U., 1980. Operator, programmer Watkins, Ward & Stafford, CPA, West Point, Miss., 1978-81; computer programmer Gen. Tire Corp., Inc., Columbus, Ohio, 1981-83; programmer, analyst Arvin Industries, Inc., Starkville, Miss., 1983-84; analyst, data processing mgr. Data Systems Mgmt., Inc., Columbus, Miss., 1984—. Data processing cons., West Point, 1983. Deacon, chmn. Calvary Bapt. Ch., West Point, 1990-91; mem. West Point Follies, 1991. Recipient Deacon Cert., Calvary Bapt. Ch., West Point, 1986. Democrat. Baptist. Avocations: golf, hunting, fishing, gardening. Home: 1190 Lone Oak Park West Point MS 39773-9792 Office: Data Systems Mgmt Inc Ste 300 200 6th St N Columbus MS 39703 Office Phone: 662-329-1222. E-mail: reh9773@lycos.com.

HOLT, ROBERT THEODORE, political science professor, educator, dean; b. Caledonia, Minn., July 26, 1928; s. Oscar Martin and Olga Linnea (Mattson) H.; m. Shirley J. Russell, Dec. 14, 1957; children: Susan Jane, Ann Carol, Sharon Linnea. AB magna cum laude, Hamline U., 1950; MPA, Princeton U., 1952, PhD, 1957. Instr. dept. polit. sci. U. Minn., Mpls., 1956-57, asst. prof., 1957-60, assoc. prof., 1960-64, prof., 1964-2001, prof. emeritus, 2001—, chmn. dept., 1978-81, dir. Ctr. for Comparative Studies in Tech. Devel. and Social Change, 1967-80, dir. rsch. devel. Coll. Liberal Arts, 1975-78, dean Grad. Sch., 1982-91, chair rsch. exec. coun., 1988-91, interim dean Coll. Liberal Arts, 1996, prof. emeritus, 2001. Bd. dirs. Coun. Grad. Schs., 1984-90, chair, 1989-90; mem. Assembly Social and Behavioral Scis., NAS, 1972-75. Author: Radio Free Europe, 1958, (with F.W. Van de Velde) Strategic Psychological Operations, 1960, The Soviet Union: Paradox and Change, 1962, (with J.E. Turner) The Political Basis of Economic Development, 1966, The Methodology of Comparative Research, 1970, Political Parties in Action, 1971, (with Turner and Chase) American Government in Comparative Perspective, 1979 With U.S. Army, 1953-55. Fellow Ctr. for Advanced Studies in Behavioral Scis., 1961-62. Mem. Am. Polit. Sci. Assn., Internat. Studies Assn., Mid West Polit Sci. Assn., Assn of Grad. Schs. (exec. com. 1985-88, chair grad. student fin. assistance com. 1986-91), 39er's Club. Episcopalian. Office: U Minn Polict Sci Dept 1414 Social Sci Tower 267 19th Ave S Minneapolis MN 55455-0499 Business E-Mail: rholt@polisci.umn.edu.

HOLT, RUSH DEW, congressman, physics educator, researcher, consultant; b. Weston, W.Va., Oct. 15, 1948; s. Rush Dew and Helen (Froelich) H.; m. Margaret Lancefield, 1985. BA, Carleton Coll., 1970; MS, NYU, 1975, PhD, 1981. Am. Phys. Soc. Congl. fellow U.S. Congress, Washington, 1982-83; vis. scientist High Altitude Obs., Boulder, Colo., 1984; asst. prof. physics dept. Swarthmore (Pa.) Coll., 1980-88; sci. analyst U.S. Dept. State, 1987-89; asst. dir. Plasma Physics Lab. Princeton (N.J.) U., 1989-98; mem. U.S. Congress from 12th N.J. dist., 1999—; intelligence com., budget com., edn. and workforce com., former mem. resources com. Patentee in field. Mem.: Sigma Xi, AAAS, Am. Assn. Physics Teachers, Am. Phys. Soc. Democrat. Achievements include being a five time winner on "Jeopardy". Office: Ho of Reps 1019 Longworth Hob Washington DC 20515-0001: 50 Washington Rd Princeton Junction NJ 08550*

HOLT, SIDNEY CLARK, journalist; b. St. Louis, Sept. 7, 1955; s. Noel Clark and Rosalee (Powell) H.; m. Jill Brodsky, Nov. 16, 1991; children: Elizabeth Summers, Victoria Edmunds. BA, Columbia U., 1979. Editor Simon & Schuster Inc., N.Y.C., 1979-84; asst. editor Rolling Stone, N.Y.C., 1984-85, assoc. editor, 1985-87, sr. editor, 1987-89, asst. mng. editor, 1989-90, mng. editor, 1990-97; editl. dir. US mag., N.Y.C., 1995-97; v.p. Wenner Media, Inc., N.Y.C., 1996-97; exec. v.p., editor-in-chief Ad Week Mags., N.Y.C., 1998—2005; editl. dir. VNU Bus. Media, N.Y.C., 2005—. Editor: The Rolling Stone Interviews: The 1980s, 1989. Bd. dirs. Fedn. Protestant Welfare Agys., N.Y.C., 1994—. Recipient Nat. Mag. award for gen. excellence, 1998. Mem. Am. Soc. Mag. Editors, Columbia Club N.Y. Democrat. Methodist. Home: 680 Titicus Rd North Salem NY 10560-2106 Office: VNU Business Media 770 Broadway New York NY 10003 Office Phone: 646-654-5245.

HOLT, STEPHEN S., astrophysicist; b. N.Y.C., May 17, 1940; s. Aaron J. and Faye E. (Schwartz) Holtz; m. Carol Ann Weissman, June 3, 1961; children: Peter David, Eric Lawrence, Laura Kimberly. BS, NYU, 1961, PhD in Physics, 1966. Instr. physics NYU, 1964—66; astrophysicist Goddard Space Flight Center, Greenbelt, Md., 1966-2000; chief high energy astrophysics NASA Hdqrs., 1980-81; dir. Lab. for High Energy Astrophysics Goddard Space Flight Ctr., Greenbelt, Md., 1983-90, dir. space scis., 1990-2000; prof. Physics Olin Coll., Needham, Mass., 2000—; prof., dir. natural scis. Babson Coll., Wellesley, Mass., 2000—. Lectr. physics U. Md., 1967-87, adj. prof. astronomy, 1988— Contbr. articles to profl. jours. Recipient medal for exceptional sci. achievement NASA, 1977, 80, medal for outstanding leadership, 1991, 2000, Presdl. meritorious exec. award, 1992, John C. lindsay Meml. award outstanding sci. achievement, 1993, NASA Disting. Svc. medal, 2000, COSPAR Internat. Coop. medal, 2004. Fellow AAAS, Am. Phys. Soc. (chair divsn. exec. com.); mem. Am. Astron. Soc. (chair div.), Internat. Acad. Astronautics, COSPAR (chair div.), Sigma Xi, Tau Beta Pi, Sigma Pi Sigma. Home: 77 Pond Ave Apt 1202 Brookline MA 02445-7115 Office: Olin Coll Olin Way Needham MA 02492-1245 E-mail: steve.holt@olin.edu. *The most important intrinsic requisites for success in experimental science are probably imagination and diligence. Very few individuals possess these in sufficient quantities to dominate the extrinsic variables which shape their careers in research, however. I consider myself fortunate to have been able to capitalize on whatever talent I possess by having my research interests aligned with funding priorities, and by being blessed with the cooperation of unselfish and stimulating colleagues.*

HOLT, THADDEUS, lawyer; b. Birmingham, Ala., Nov. 26, 1929; s. Thad and Sarah Ames (Oliver) H.; m. Waring Inge, Dec. 1, 1956 (dec. 2002); children: Sarah, Harrison. B.A., U. of South, 1951; M.A., Yale U., 1952; B.A. (Rhodes Scholar), Oxford U., 1954; LL.B., Harvard U., 1956. Bar: Ala. 1956, D.C. 1959, U.S. Supreme Ct. 1960, N.Y. 1969, Pa. 1985. Assoc. Cabaniss & Johnston, Birmingham, 1956-58; assoc. Covington & Burling, Washington, 1958-65; dep. undersec. Dept. Army, Washington, 1965-67; pres. Leacock Pennebaker Inc., NYC, 1968-69; sec. Corp. for Pub. Broadcasting, N.Y.C. and Washington, 1970-71; ptnr. Breed, Abbott & Morgan, Washington and N.Y.C., 1972-86; sole practice, Washington, Carlisle, Pa., Point Clear, Ala., 1986—. Author: The Deceivers: Allied Military Deception in the Second World War, 2004; contbr. articles to MHQ, N.Y. Times Book Rev., other mags. Recipient decoration for Disting. Civilian Service U.S. Army, 1967. Mem. Am. Law Inst., Wahington Inst. for Fgn. Affairs, Met. Club (Washington). Episcopalian. Address: PO Box 440 Point Clear AL 36564

HOLT, WILLIAM E., lawyer; b. Phila., Aug. 31, 1945; BBA, U. Iowa, 1967, JD with distinction, 1970. Bar: Iowa 1970, Wash. 1971. Law clk. to Hon. William T. Beeks U.S. Dist. Ct. (we. dist.) Wash., 1970-71; mem., chmn. Gordon, Thomas, Honeywell, Malanca, Peterson & Daheim, Tacoma, 1999, 2000. Adj. prof. U. Puget Sound Law Sch., 1974-75. Note editor Iowa Law Rev., 1969-70. Mem. ABA, Wash. State Bar Assn. (exec. com. real property, probate and trust sect. 1987-89), Phi Delta Phi. Office: Gordon Thomas Honeywell Malanca Peterson & Daheim PO Box 1157 Ste 2100 Tacoma WA 98401-1157 Office Phone: 253-620-6412. E-mail: holtw@gth-law.com.

HOLT, WILLIAM HENRY, physicist, researcher; b. San Antonio, Aug. 5, 1939; s. Joseph Marion and Mildred Louise (Ragsdale) H.; m. Margaret Ann Harrell, June 21, 1963; children: Benjamin, Andrew. BS cum laude, St. Mary's U., San Antonio, 1960; MA, U. Tex., 1962, PhD, 1967. Postdoctoral fellow, lectr. U. Man., Winnipeg, Can., 1966-69; rsch. physicist Naval Surface Warfare Ctr., Dahlgren, Va., 1969—. Patentee; contbr. articles and papers to numerous sci. jours. and revs. Past tchr. Sunday sch. St. Matthias United Meth. Ch., Fredericksburg, Va.; past co-chmn. edn., past lay leader, past mem.

pastor-parish rels. com., past chmn. coun. on ministries. Mem. Am. Phys. Soc., Can. Assn. Physicists, Materials Rsch. Soc., Sigma Xi, Sigma Pi Sigma, Lions. Office: Naval Surface Warfare Ctr Dahlgren VA 22448-5100 Office Phone: 540-653-8687.

HOLTAN, RAMER B., JR., lawyer; b. Wilmington, Del., Oct. 20, 1944; AB, Harvard U., 1966; JD cum laude, U. Ill., 1972; postgrad., U. Freiburg, West Germany. Bar: Wash. 1973. Mem. Perkins Coie, Seattle. Articles editor U. Ill. Law Rev., 1971-72. Mem. Order of the Coif. Office: Perkins Coie 1201 3rd Ave Fl 40 Seattle WA 98101-3029 Office Phone: 206-359-8400. Business E-Mail: rholtan@perkinscoie.com. E-mail: rholtan@comcast.net.

HOLTBY, KENNETH FRASER, retired manufacturing executive; b. Escanaba, Mich., May 18, 1922; s. David William and Nina Kate (Hemenway) H.; m. Bettie Roberts, June 11, 1943; children— Michael Earle, Tracy Linda Meilleur, Jeffrey Thomas, Kristen Ann Buren, Matt Fraser. BSME, Calif. Inst. Tech., 1947; SM in Indsl. Mgmt., MIT, 1961. Aerodynamicist Boeing Co., Seattle, 1947, various mgmt. positions, 1953-82, sr. v.p., 1982-87; ret. Found. mem. Pacific Sci. Ctr., Seattle, 1974—. Served to lt. USAF, 1943-46. Fellow: AIAA (hon. Aircraft Design award 1984, Laureate Bagnou prize), Brit. Royal Aero. Soc.; mem.: U.S. Nat. Acad. Engring., NRC. Avocations: tennis, skiing, sailing. Address: 6346 So Chinook Dr Clinton WA 98236

HOLTE, DEBRA LEAH, investment company executive, financial analyst; b. Madison, Wis. d. Daniel Kennseth and Marian Anne Reitan. BA, Concordia Coll., Moorhead, Minn., 1973. Chartered Fin. Analyst, Cert. Divorce Planner. Capital markets specialist 1st Bank Mpls., 1981-83; v.p. Allison-Williams Co., Mpls., 1983-86; exec. v.p. Hamil & Holte Inc., Denver, 1986-93; pres. Holte & Assocs., Denver, Taos, N.Mex., 1993—. Active Denver Jr. League, Western Pension Com., 1986—; bd. dirs. Denver Children's Home, 1987—, treas., 1987-91, chmn. fin. com., 1987-91, v.p., 1990—, chmn. nominating com., 1991—, pres.-elect, 1994-95, bd. pres., 1995—; adv. bd. Luth. Social Svcs., 1987; co-chair U.S. Ski Team Fundraiser; bd. dirs. Minn. Vocat. Edn. Fin., Mpls., 1984-86; bd. dirs. Colo. Ballet, 1988-93, chair nominating com., 1991-93, v.p., 1992-93, chmn. bd., 1993; mem. Fin. Analyst Nat. Task Force in Bondholder Rights, 1988-90; bd. dirs. Ctrl. City Opera Guild, 1994-95, Western Chamber Ballet, 1994-96, Taos Humane Soc., 1997—; social co-chmn. The Arapahoe Fox Hunt, 1993-94; bd. dirs., mem. steering com. Denver Dumb Friends League, 2001—. Mem. Fin. Analysts Fedn., Denver Soc. Security Analysts (bd. dirs. 1990-97, chair ethics and bylaws com. 1987—, chair edn. com. 1988, chair membership com. 1989, rec. sec. 1990, sec. 1991, treas. 1992, program chair 1993, pres. 1994-95, dir. 1995-96).

HOLTER, ARLEN ROLF, cardiothoracic surgeon; b. Sullivan's Island, SC, Feb. 1, 1946; s. Arne and Helen (Soderberg) H.; m. Elizabeth Anne Reid, Nov. 9, 1974; children: Matthew Arlen, Peter Reid, Andrew Douglas. BS, Stanford U., 1968; MS, U. Ill., Chgo., 1971, MD, 1973. Diplomate Am. Bd. Thoracic Surgery, Am. Bd. Surgery. Intern Mass. Gen. Hosp., Boston, 1973-74, resident in surgery, 1974-78; sr. registrar in cardiac surgery South Hampton Chest Hosp., 1978; resident in cardiac surgery Yale U., New Haven, 1978-80; pvt. practice Mpls., 1980—. Instr. surgery Yale U., 1979-80. Contbr. articles to profl. jours. Recipient Franklin McLean rsch. award U. Chgo., 1973. Fellow: ACS; mem.: Mpls. Acad. Medicine, Am. Heart Assn., Soc. Thoracic Surgeons, US Triathlon Assn. (Iron Man finisher). Lutheran. Avocations: skiing, photography, triathlons. Office: Cardiac Surg Assocs Ste 258 2356 University Ave W Saint Paul MN 55112 Office Phone: 651-917-6160. Personal E-mail: arholter@aol.com.

HOLTER, KATHY ANN, elementary school educator, music educator; b. Viborg, S.D., July 10, 1952; d. LaVerne Wayne Frick and Dorothy Miranda Ekern; m. David Warren Holter, Feb. 6, 1971; children: Chad, Todd, Lisa. B, S.D. State U., 1973; M in Edn., St. Scholastica, 1999; B in Mid. Sch. Sci. and History, U. Sioux Falls, 2000, cert. in med. sch., 2001. GED and CLEP tchr. U.S. Army, Germany, 1974—76; elem. tchr. 4th Bapt. Sch., Columbus, Ga., 1980—82, LaCrosse (Wis.) Christian, LaCrosse, 1984—87, Grace Christian Sch., Eau Claire, Wis., 1988—2000, Oscar Howe Elem. Sch., Sioux Falls, 2001—02, Garfield Elem. Sch., Sioux Falls, 2002—. Author: Teaching Children to Read, 1999. Vice chairperson Sioux Reading Coun., 2002—, v.p., 2003—; vol. Rep. party, Eau Claire, 1996—2000, vol. phone tree Sioux Falls, 2001—; Awana dir. 1st Bapt. Ch., Chippewa Falls, SD, 1988—2000; mem. music dept. Cross Pointe Bapt., Sioux Falls, 2000—, Awana leader, 2000—. Recipient Tchr. of Yr., 1996, Vol. Tchr. of Sioux Falls, 2005. Republican. Avocations: sewing, reading, singing, piano. Home: 28448 SD Hwy 11 Canton SD 57013 Office: Garfield Elem Sch 2421 W 15th St Sioux Falls SD 57104

HOLTER, ROBERT M., federal judge; b. Williston, N.D., Mar. 13, 1927; BS, U. Mont., JD, 1954. Bar: Mont. 1954. Legal practice, Bozeman, from 1956; county atty. Gallatin County, 1961-62; judge Mont. Dist. Ct. (19th dist.), from 1977; magistrate judge U.S. Dist. Ct. Mont., Great Falls. Chmn. Mont. Criminal Jury Instrn. commn., 1980-92, Mont. Child Support Enforcement Commn., 1985-87, Mont. Dist. Ct. Com., 1979-85; mem. faculty Nat. Jud. Coll., 1985-88. Served with U.S. Army, 1945-46, 1st lt. USAF, 1954-56. Recipient Nat. Patrolman award, Nat. Ski Patrol. Mem. State Bar Mont., Mont. Judges Assn. (pres. 1986-87), Rotary Club, Masons. Episcopalian. Avocations: skiing, antique collecting, flying, golf. Address: PO Box 2386 Great Falls MT 59403-2386 E-mail: b.l.holter@bresnan.net.

HOLTFRETER, LILLIAN SCHLEPPI, music educator, consultant; b. Columbus, Ohio, Sept. 16, 1923; d. George Leroy and Effie Elizabeth Schleppi; m. Fred R. Holtfreter, Jan. 20, 1946 (dec. Feb. 18, 1981); children: Paul, Timothy, Jonathan, Kathryn, David. MusB in Piano Performance, Capitul U., 1944; cert. in Music Tchg., U. Mich., 1962, MusM in Edn., 1981. Pvt. piano tchr., Columbus, Ohio, 1942—44, Euclid, Ohio, 1944—48, Pitts., 1957—61; dir. children and youth choirs St. John Luth. Ch., Pitts., 1957—61; dir. children and Youth Choirs Zion Luth. Ch., Ann Arbor, 1961—66, dir. handbell choirs, 1999—, dir. Zion Singers Sr. Chorus, 1996—; vocal music tchr. Ann Arbor (Mich.) Pub. Schs., 1966—89; freelance nat. cons. Washington, 1987—. Chmn. Mich. Music Edn. Multicultural Com., Ann Arbor, 1982—2000; dir. Zion Singers Sr. Chorus, Ann Arbor, 1989—. Author: A Sequential Approach to Teaching Elementary Vocal Music Combining Orff & Kodaly Approach, 1981; prodr., dir.: (films) Flowing Waters, Ind. Gamelan, 1990. Adv. Evang. Luth. Ch. Am., Detroit, 1990—93. Mem.: Mich. Music Educators Assn. (multicultural adv. 1981—90), Music Educators Nat. Conf. Home: 1525 Barnard Rd Ann Arbor MI 48103

HOLTKAMP, JAMES ARNOLD, lawyer, educator; b. Albuquerque, Apr. 4, 1949; s. Clarence Jules and Karyl Irene (Roberts) H.; m. Marianne Coltrin, Dec. 28, 1973; children: Ariane, Brent William, Rachel, Allison, David Roberts. BA, Brigham Young U., 1972; JD, George Washington U., 1975. Bar: Utah 1976, U.S. Dist. Ct. Utah 1977, U.S. Ct. Appeals (10th cir.) 1979, Colo. 1995. Mem. staff U.S. Senate Watergate Com., Washington, 1974; atty.-advisor Dept. Transp., Washington, 1975; atty. Dept. Interior, Washington, 1975-77; assoc. Van Cott, Bagley, Cornwall & McCarthy, Salt Lake City, 1977-81, ptnr., 1981-89, Davis, Graham & Stubbs, Salt Lake City, 1989-92, Stoel Rives, Salt Lake City, 1992-97, LeBoeuf, Lamb, Greene & MacRae, Salt Lake City, 1997—2003, Holland & Hart, Salt Lake City, 2003—. Adj. prof., Law Sch. Brigham Young U., Provo, Utah, 1979—2002; adj. prof. Coll. Law U. Utah, 1995—. Co-author: Utah Environmental and Land Use Permits and Approvals Manual, 1981; contbr. articles to legal jours. Missionary LDS Ch., 1968-70; active Gt. Salt Lake coun. Boy Scouts Am., 1977—; trustee Coalition for Utah's Future, 1996-2001. Mem. ABA (vice-chmn. air quality commn. 1985-89), Utah State Bar (chmn. energy and natural resources sect. 1984-85, chmn. pub. utilities law com. 1990-93, energy and natural resources sect., Lawyer of Yr. award 1981, Disting. Svc. award 2002), Utah Mining Assn. (bd. dirs. 1999—), Rocky Mtn. Mineral Law Found. (trustee 1999-2002, sec. 2002-2003), Utah Petroleum Assn., George Washington Law Assn. (nat. bd. dirs. 1999—). Home: 7990 Deer Creek Rd Salt Lake City UT 84121-5752 Office: Holland & Hart 60 E South Temple Ste 2000 Salt Lake City UT 84111-1031

HOLTON, CARLOTTA, editor-in-chief, writer; d. Michael George and Dorothy Victoria (Sydlo) Gulvas; m. James W. Holton, Sept. 15, 1996; m. Edward J. Swarden, June 28, 1969 (dec. Feb. 22, 1995); 1 child, Mark Edward Michael. BA in Edn., Kean U., 1969, MA in Humanities, 1974. Cert. tchr. nursery, K-8 N.J. Dept. Edn. Writer The Daily Jour., Elizabeth, NJ, 1985—89; editor, travel writer North Jersey Media Group, Hackensack, NJ, 2000—03; editor-in-chief Chiropractics Monthly, Mountainside, NJ, 2003—. Adj. faculty Union County Coll., Cranford, NJ, 1991—95, Coll. St. Elizabeth, Convent Station, NJ, 1992—98, Gibbs Coll., Montclair, NJ, 1999. Author: Getting Out of Limbo, 2000 (award N.J. Press Women, 2001); contbr. columns in newspapers including Star Ledger, N.Y. Times. Mem. adv. bd. Internat. ChildrensSay, Summit, NJ, 2002. Recipient Excellence Cardiovasc. Reporting award, Am. Heart Assn., 1990. Mem.: N.J. Press Women (v.p., 46 Writing awards 1989—2000), Nat. Fedn. Press Women (3 Writing awards 1990). Avocations: swimming, boating, travel. Home: 1 Ironia Rd Flanders NJ 07836 Office: Chiropractor Monthly 1136 Rte 22 W Mountainside NJ 07092 Office Phone: 908-789-1960.

HOLTON, GERALD, physicist, educator, science historian; b. Berlin, May 23, 1922; s. Emanuel and Regina (Rossmann) H.; m. Nina Rossfort, Sept. 12, 1947; children: Thomas, Stephan. Nat. certificate elec. engring., Sch. Tech., Oxford, Eng., 1940; BA, Wesleyan U., 1941, MA, 1942, D.H.L. (hon.), 1981; MA, Harvard U., 1946, PhD, 1948; D.Sc. (hon.), Grinnell Coll., 1967, Kenyon Coll., 1977, Bates Coll., 1979; LL.D. (hon.), Duke U., 1981. Instr. Wesleyan U., 1941-42, Brown U., 1942-43; staff, officers radar course and OSRD Harvard, 1943-45, various faculty positions, 1947—; rsch. prof. physics and history of sci. Harvard-Leningrad U., 1962; vis. mem. Inst. Advanced Study, Princeton, 1964; fellow Center Advanced Study in Behavioral Scis., Stanford, 1975-76. Vis. prof. MIT, 1976-94; Herbert Spencer lectr. Oxford U., 1979; Jefferson lectr. in humanities, 1981; John Simon Guggenheim fellow, 1980-81; mem. com. scholarly comm. with People's Republic of China, NAS, 1967-72, mem. com. conduct of sci., NAS, 1989-91, mem. office on pub. understanding sci., NAS, 1995-2001; mem. U.S. Nat. Commn. on UNESCO, 1975-80, U.S. Nat. Commn. of IUHPS, 1982-89, Coun. of Scholars, Libr. of Congress, 1980-95, U.S. Nat. Commn. on Excellence in Edn., 1981-83; mem. adv. com. for sci. and engring. edn. NSF, 1985-93, chair, 1986-89; mem. selection bd. Albert Einstein Peace Prize, 1980—; mem. German Am. Acad. Coun. Kuratorium, 1997-2000; mem. com. interdisciplinary rsch. NAS, 2003—. Author: Introduction to Concepts and Theories in Physical Science, 1952, 2d edit., 1985, (with D.H.D. Roller) Foundations of Modern Physical Science, 1958, Science and the Modern Mind, 1958, Science and Culture, 1965, (with others) The Project Physics Course, 1970, 75, 81, The 20th Century Sciences: Studies in Intellectual Biography, 1971, Thematic Origins of Scientific Thought: Kepler to Einstein, 1973, 2d edit., 1988, The Scientific Imagination: Case Studies, 1978, 98, (with others) Limits of Scientific Inquiry, 1979, Albert Einstein, Historical and Cultural Perspectives, 1982, 97, The Advancement of Science and Its Burdens, 1986, 98, Science and Anti-Science, 1993, Einstein, History and Other Passions, 1996, (with Gerhard Sonnert) Gender Differences in Science Careers: The Project Access Study, 1995, Who Succeeds in Science? The Gender Dimension, 1995, (with Stephen Brush) Physics, The Human Adventure, 2001, (with Gerhard Sonnert) Ivory Bridges: Connecting Science and Society, 2002, (with David Cassidy and James Rutherford) Understanding Physics, 2002, Victory and Vexation in Science: Einstein, Bohr, Heisenberg and Others, 2005; founding editor-in-chief Daedalus, 1957-61; mem. editl. com., editl. adv. bd. The Collected Papers of Albert Einstein, 1980-1995; contbr. articles to profl. jours. Recipient J.D. Bernal prize Soc. Social Studies Sci., 1989. Fellow AAAS (bd. dirs. 1967-71), Am. Philos. Soc., Am. Acad. Arts and Sci. (editor 1957-63, exec. bd. 1970-78, coun. 1991-95), Am. Phys. Soc. (chmn. divsn. history of physics 1992-93), Internat. Acad. History of Sci. (v.p. 1981-89), Deutsche Acad. Naturforscher-Leopoldina, Internat. Acad. Philosophy of Sci.; mem. NAS (assoc.), Am. Inst. Physics (governing bd. 1968-74, Andrew Gemant award 1989), Am. Assn. Physics Tchrs. (Robert A. Millikan medal 1967, Oersted medal 1979), History Sci. Soc. (pres. 1983-84, George Sarton medal 1989, Joseph H. Hazen Edn. prize 1998). Office: Harvard U Jefferson Phys Lab Cambridge MA 02138 Business E-Mail: holton@physics.harvard.edu.

HOLTON, GRACE HOLLAND, accountant; b. Durham, NC, Sept. 14, 1957; d. Samuel Melanchthon and B. Margaret (Umberger) Holton. BS in Math., Univ. N.C., Greensboro, 1978; MBA, Univ. N.C., Chapel Hill, 1984; M.Acctg. Sci., U. Ill., 1993. CPA NC, cert. mgmt. acct., internal auditor. Indsl. engr. Burlington Industries, Inc., Mayodan, NC, 1978-79, plant indsl. engr. Stoneville, NC, 1979-80; methods indsl. engr. Blue Cross and Blue Shield of N.C., Durham, 1980-82; fin. analyst R.J. Reynolds, Inc., Winston-Salem, NC, 1984-85; accounting cons. Ryder Truck Rental, Inc., Miami, Fla., 1985-88; contr. Ryder Jacobs (divsn. Ryder Distbn. Resources), Jessup, Md., 1988-90; grad. asst. in acctg. U. Ill., Urbana, 1990-93; contr. Salem NationaLease, Winston-Salem, 1993-94; fin. officer Chapel Hill-Carrboro City Schs., 1994-99; mgr. benefits and payroll Ryder Pub. Transp. Svcs., Cin., 1999-2000; exec. dir. budget and evaluation Charlotte-Mecklenburg Schs., 2000—02; acctg. instr. Alamance C.C., Graham, NC, 2003—. Scholar KPMG-Peat Marwick scholar, 1991—92. Mem.: AICPA, Inst. Internal Auditors, N.C. Soc. CPA, Inst. Mgmt. Accts. Democrat. Methodist.

HOLTON, J(ERRY) THOMAS, concrete company executive; b. Middletown, Ohio, June 7, 1932; s. Joseph Walton and Elizabeth (Fagaly) H.; m. Annie Lou Dearborn, Sept. 26, 1958; children: Elizabeth, Luanne, Ruth, Catherine, J. Thomas Jr. BSE, Princeton U., 1954; MBA, Harvard U., 1959. V.p. Sherman Concrete Pipe Co., Birmingham, Ala., 1959-66, pres., 1966-74, Sherman Industries, Birmingham, 1974-84; pres., chmn. Sherman Internat. Corp., Birmingham, 1984—. Bd. dirs. Fed. Res. Bank Atlanta, Robin-Morton Corp., KSA, Inc., Sciotoville, Ohio, The Shaw Group Ltd., Halifax, N.S., Stockham Valve & Fittings Co. Inc. Pres. coun. U. Ala. Birmingham, 1984-92; mem. exec. bd. Boy Scouts Am., Birmingham, 1985—; chmn., Salvation Army, Birmingham; elder Briarwood Presbyn. Ch., Birmingham, 1968—. Lt. comdr. Civil Engring. Corp. USN, 1954-57. Mem. Birmingham Country Club, Shoal Creek, The Club, Summit Club. Home: 10 Ridge Dr Birmingham AL 35213-3632 Office: Sherman International Inc 402 Office Park Dr Ste 100 Birmingham AL 35223-2435 Personal E-mail: jtholton@aol.com.

HOLTON, LISA, writer, editor, researcher; BS in Journalism, Northwestern Univ., 1981; student med. editing, writing cert. program, Univ. Chgo., 2003. Reporter, editor Chgo. Sun-Times, 1981—96, bus. editor, 1992—93; founder Card Mktg., 1996—97; editor Business Journalist newsletter, 1998—99; founder The Lisa Co., Evanston, Ill., 1998—. Author: How to Be a Value Investor, 1999, Essential Dictionary of Real Estate, 2003. Mem.: Am. Med. Writers Assn., Am. Soc. Journalists & Authors, Internat Assn. Bus. Communicators. Office: The Lisa Co 2327 Brown Ave Evanston IL 60201 Office Phone: 847-869-7106. Business E-Mail: Lisa@TheLisaCo.com.*

HOLTON, LISA, publishing executive; Graduate cum laude, Colgate Univ. Asst., spl. sales to mgr. sub rights, dir., prod. devel. Frederick Warne, dir. mktg., Puffin Books Viking Penguin, 1984—90; v.p., dir. mktg., merchandise devel. to v.p., assoc. pub., editor-in-chief HarperCollins Children's Books, 1990—96; v.p., pub. Hyperion Books for Children, Disney Press, 1996—99; group pub. Disney Children's Books, 1999—2001; sr. v.p., pub. Global Disney Books, 2001—05; pres. book fairs and trade, exec. v.p. Scholastic Inc., NYC, 2005—. Office: Exec VP Scholastic Inc 555 Broadway New York NY 10012 Office Phone: 212-343-6100.*

HOLTON, ROBERT PAGE, publishing executive; b. St. Paul, Jan. 18, 1938; s. Robert Henry and Grace (Page) H.; m. Sandra Janice Heyl, July 16, 1960. BS in Indsl. Distbn., Clarkson Coll., 1960. Asst. editor McGraw-Hill Indsl. Distbn., N.Y.C., 1960-61, dist. mgr. Chgo., 1963-65, McGraw-Hill-Textile World, Phila., 1965-71, McGraw-Hill-Chem. Engring., Pitts., 1971-76, mktg. service dir. N.Y.C., 1976-81; sr. v.p., pub., Marine Engring./Log Simmons-Boardman, N.Y.C., 1981-85; pres. Robert Holton Assocs., 1994—; pub. PennWell Publ.-Computer Graphics World mag., 1985-94. Group pub. Computer Graphics World, Computer Artist, Computer Graphic World Buyers Guide, Computer Graphics World-Asia Pacific, Electronic Pub., Color Pub., 1991-94. Assoc. pub., advt. dir. USA Lawyers Weekly Pubs., 1997-98; contbr. articles to profl. jours. Recipient Order of Merit Boy Scouts Am., 1969; recipient Silver Beaver Boy Scouts Am., 1975 Mem. Assoc. Bus. Pubs. (pub. com. 1989-92).

HOLTON, SUSAN A., communications educator; b. Columbus, Ohio, Apr. 24, 1948; d. William C. and Mary (Floyd) H.; 1 child, Christopher L. Holton-Jablonski; m. Joe Snyders, Aug. 4, 1991; stepchildren: John, Mark. BS, Miami U., Oxford, Ohio, 1970; MA, Case Western Res. U., 1973, PhD, 1976. Cert. mediator. Dir. Gabriel Ames Assocs., Taunton, Mass., 1975—; asst. to pres., asst. prof. Bridgewater (Mass.) State Coll., 1984-88, dept. chair., assoc. prof., 1988-90, prof., 1990—, asst. to pres., 1991-92. Bd. dirs. Profl. Orgn. in Higher Edn.; coord. Mass. Faculty Devel. Consortium, 1988-90; chair. nominating com. Unitarian Universalis Assn., Boston, 1987-89; cons. Alban Inst., 1989-93; mem. faculty Am. Coun. Edn programs, others. Author: The Mad Madonna, 1987, Under the Influence of Life, Conflict Management in Higher Education, 1995, Mending the Cracks in the Ivory Tower: Strategies for Conflict Management in Higher Education, 1998; editor, author over 60 chpts. in books; contbr. articles to profl. jours. Dir. Ch. the Larger Fellowship, Boston, 1987-91; founder FOCUS on Gifted and Talented, Framingham, Mass. Mem. Speech Communication Assn., Boston Area Assn. Psychol. Type (founder), N.E. Assn. Psychol. Type, Ea. Communications Assn., Communications Assn. Mass., Am. Assn. for Higher Edn., Assn. Conflict Resolution. Avocations: reading, writing, walking. Office: Bridgewater State Coll Maxwell Libr Bridgewater MA 02325-0001 Office Phone: 508-531-1750. Business E-Mail: sholton@bridgew.edu.

HOLTON, WALTER CLINTON, JR., lawyer; b. Winston-Salem, N.C. s. Walter Clinton and Mabel (Hartsfield) H.; m. Lynne Rowley. BA in Polit. Sci., U. N.C., 1977; JD, Wake Forest U., 1984. Bar: N.C. 1984, U.S. Dist. Ct. (mid. dist.) N.C. 1986, U.S. Ct. Appeals (4th cir.) 1990, U.S. Supreme Ct., 1996. Asst. dist. atty. Office 21st Jud. Dist. Atty., Winston-Salem, 1985-87; assoc. White & Crumpler, Winston-Salem, 1987-88; pvt. practice Winston-Salem, 1989; ptnr. Holton & Menefee, Winston-Salem, 1989-92, Tisdale, Holton & Menefee, PA, Winston-Salem, 1992-94; U.S. atty. Office U.S. Atty. Mid. Dist. N.C., Greensboro, N.C., 1994-2001; pvt. practice Grace Holton Tisdale & Clifton PA, Winston-Salem, 2001—. Democrat. Office: Grace Holton Tisdale & Clifton 301 N Main St Ste 100 Winston Salem NC 27101 Fax: (336) 721-1176. Office Phone: 336-777-3480. E-mail: wholton@ghtclaw.com.

HOLTON, WILLIAM, artist; b. Knoxville, Tenn., 1966; Student, U. Ariz., 1987—88; BFA, Atlanta Coll. Art, 1991. Intern Rolling Stone Press, Atlanta, 1989; asst. Atlanta Arts Festival, 1991. One-man shows include Anthony Ardavin Gallery, Atlanta, TVUUC Gallery, Knoxville, 1999, two-person shows include, Anthony Ardavin Gallery, 1995, 1997, 1999, exhibited in group shows, 1993, Atlanta Coll. Art Gallery, 1993, Southeastern Ctr. Contemporary Art, Winston-Salem, 1997, Zoe Gallery, Louisville, 1998, 1999; contbg. artist Drawing, Space, Form and Expression, 1988. Recipient Merit award, Magic City Arts Festival, 1991, Best of Show award, ARTFEST, 1994; grantee Regional Visual Arts fellow, Southeastern Arts Fedn., Nat. Endowment Arts, 1996. Home: 499 Fort Washington Ave Apt 6H New York NY 10033-4609

HOLTON, WILLIAM COFFEEN, electrical engineering executive; b. Washington, July 24, 1930; s. William B. and Esther (Coffeen) H.; m. Mary Schaeffer, Aug. 5, 1953; children: Elizabeth Ashe, William Andrew, Sarah Anne. BS in Physics, U. N.C., 1952; PhD in Physics, U. Ill., 1960. Tech. staff corp. rsch. lab. Tex. Instruments, Dallas, 1960-65, mgr. quantum electronics, 1965-72, dir. advanced components lab., 1972-78, dir. R & D semicondr. group, 1978-82, mgr. strategic planning, 1982-83; dir. Semiconductor Rsch. Corp., Research Triangle Park, N.C., 1984-88, sr. dir., 1989-90, v.p., 1990-95; prof. NC State U., Raleigh, 1996—, U. NC, Chapel Hill, 2004—. Lt. (j.g.) USN, 1952-54. Union Carbide fellow, 1959; recipient Dept. of Energy award, 1997. Fellow IEEE (mem. awards bd. 1999—, Phillips award 1998), Am. Phys. Soc., Electron. Device Soc. of IEEE (governing bd. 1975-98, chmn. internat. electron device meeting 1975); mem. Phi Beta Kappa, Phi Eta Sigma. Presbyterian. Home: 601 Brookview Dr Chapel Hill NC 27514-1401 Office: NC State Univ Box 8617 234B Engring Grad Rsch Ctr Raleigh NC 27695-8617 Business E-Mail: holton@eos.ncsu.edu.

HOLTON, WINFRED BYRON, III, writer; b. N.Y.C., May 13, 1925; s. Winfred Byron Holton Jr. and Elizabeth Holton; m. Mary Macneil Chittenden, Aug. 18, 1956; children: Michael, Scott, Catharine, John. Gen. mgr. Yal Towne, N.Y.C., 1950—63; v.p. Dexter, Ind., Grand Rapids, Mich., 1963—68; pres. Holton Co., Stamford, Conn., 1968—75, Winjon, Stamford, 1975—85, Budco, Pelham, NY, 1985—95. Author: An Embezzelors Story, Betrayed. With USN, 1943—66. Republican. Avocations: golf, fishing.

HOLTSCHNEIDER, DENNIS H., academic administrator, priest; b. Detroit, Jan. 14, 1962; BA, Niagara U., 1984; MDiv, ThM, Mary Immaculate Sem., Northampton, Pa., 1989; EdD, Harvard U., 1997. Ordained priest Roman Cath. Ch., 1989. Assoc. dean, asst. prof. St. John's U., NYC, 1996-99; exec. v.p., COO, Niagara U., Niagara Falls, NY, 2000—04; pres. DePaul U., Chicago, Ill., 2004—. Mem. N.Y. Acad. Pub. Edn. (life). Office: DePaul U 1 E Jackson Chicago IL 60604

HOLTZ, DIANE, retail executive; Divsnl. v.p. Bloomingdale's; v.p. career merchandise and tops Ann Taylor, mgr. gen. merchandise, sr. v.p.; v.p. spl. projects design svcs. Limited Brands, Inc., 2000—02; pres. Limited Stores, Limited Brands Inc., 2002—. Office: Limited Stores Three Ltd Pkwy Columbus OH 43230*

HOLTZ, GILBERT JOSEPH, steel company executive; b. NYC, Jan. 23, 1924; s. Al S. and Carrie (Schindler) H.; m. Carla Kahn, July 18, 1848; children: Steven J., Robert A. Student, NYU, 1940-42. V.p. Hanger Svc. Co., Yonkers, N.Y., 1946-48; owner Economy Sales Co., Yonkers, 1948-50; v.p. Belvedere Space Saving Products, Inc., 1951-72; pres. Walnut Metal Industries, Inc., Yonkers, 1955-72, Belvedere Home Products Inc. (formerly 411 Walnut St. Corp.), 1962—, Holtz Realty Corp., 1962—, Walnut Assn. Inc., 1961—, Belvedere Internat. Ltd., 1970—. Patentee in field. Ward leader 2d Ward Republican County Com., Yonkers. Served with AUS, 1943-46. Decorated Bronze Star; recipient Conspicuous Svc. Cross, N.Y. State. Mem. Rotary. Home: 182 Tibbetts Rd Yonkers NY 10705-2646 Office: 937 Saw Mill River Rd Yonkers NY 10710-3230

HOLTZ, LAURENCE, artisan, photographer; b. Spangler, Pa., Jan. 9, 1949; s. Paul Omer and Helen Zita (McCombie) H.; m. Priscilla Suzanne Adsit, May 17, 1981 (div. Apr. 2005); 1 child, Samara Adsit BA, LaSalle Coll., Phila., 1974. Hand weaver, Hardwick, Vt., 1987—. Contbr. Vt. Arts Coun. Spl. Exhbn., Montpelier, Vt., fall 2000. Exhibited at Wood Gallery and Arts Ctr., Vt. Coll., Montpelier; contbr. short story and poetry to Coldspot, 1998; contbr. poetry to Exit 1, 2003; instrumental guitarist, vocalist First Night, St. Johnsbury, Vt., 2005. Mem. Ctrl. Vt. Regional Planning Commn., Montpelier, 1982, Plainfield (Vt.) Planning Commn., 1982; vol. Vt. Dept. Corrections Northeast Regional Correctional Facility, St. Johnsbury, 1998-2002; mem. Reparative Probation Bd., Barre Office, 1998-2000. Mem. New England Antiquities Rsch. Assocs., Vt. Weaver's Guild, Hardwick Area Writer's Group, Handweavers Guild Am., Alliance for Prison Justice (workshop panelist 2002). Zen Buddhist. Avocations: instrumental music, creative writing.

HOLTZ, SARA, marketing consultant; b. L.A., Aug. 7, 1951; BA, Yale U., 1972; JD, Harvard U., 1975. Bar: D.C. 1975, Calif. 1982. Assoc. Brownstein, Zeidman & Schomer, Washington, 1975-77; dep. asst. dir. FTC, Washington, 1977-82; divsn. counsel Clorox Co., Oakland, Calif., 1982-90; v.p., dep. gen. counsel Nestle U.S.A., Inc., San Francisco, 1990-94; prin. Client Focus, 1996—. Mem. Am. Corp. Counsel Assn. (bd. dirs. 1986-95, chmn. 1994-95). Office: 5320 Olive Tree Ct Granite Bay CA 95746-9484

HOLTZ, TRACY LYNN, music educator; b. Menomonie, Wis., Apr. 28, 1965; d. Eldin Roy and Marilyn Jean (Davis) Stevens; m. Wesley Adam Holtz, July 18, 1992; children: Arianna Lynn, Seth David. B of Music Edn., Wartburg Coll., 1987. Cert. tchr. K-12 band, 5-12 gen. music, Minn. Tchr. gen. music, choir, band Stewart (Minn.) Pub. Schs., 1987-91, tchr. vocal and gen. music, band, 1991-92; tchr. gen. music, band McLeod West Jr. H.S., Stewart, 1992-94, tchr. gen. music, band, choir, 1994-97. Advisor Danceline, McLeod West, Stewart, 1991-92, 94-95, 95-96. Sec. Stewart Fedn. Tchrs., 1990-91, v.p., 1993-94, pres., 1994-95. Lutheran. Avocations: crocheting, animals, crafts. Office: McLeod West Jr High Sch 301 Main St Stewart MN 55385-8420

HOLTZEN, MARK WAYNE, elementary school educator; b. Fort Huachuca, Ariz., July 21, 1968; s. Dennis Wayne and Marilyn Louise Holtzen; m. Carolyn Mockett, Feb. 25, 1974. BS in Graphic Design, Oreg. State U., Corvallis, 1986—90; BA in Elem. Edn., MA in Readi and Elem. Edn., Boise State U., Idaho, 1997—99. Cert. tchr. Idaho, Calif., 1999. Asst. tchr. The Cmty. Sch., Sun Valley, Idaho, 1994—96; 3d grade tchr. Burton Valley Elem., Lafayette, Calif., 1999—2005. Reading club tchr. Burton Valley Elem., Lafayette, Calif., 2002—04. Mem.: NEA, Calif. Tchr.'s Assn., Phi Kappa Phi. Office Phone: 925-284-7046. Personal E-mail: mholtzen@mac.com.

HOLTZER, ALFRED MELVIN, chemistry educator; b. Bklyn., Feb. 22, 1929; s. Abraham and Miriam (Brecher) H.; m. Joanne Rappaport, Feb. 6, 1954 (dec. Nov. 1967); children— Esther Rachel, Dan Robert; m. Marilyn Frances Emerson, June 24, 1969. AB, Washington U., St. Louis, 1950; PhD, Harvard, 1954. Instr. chemistry Yale, 1954-57; asst. prof. chemistry Washington U., 1957-59, asso. prof., 1959-65, prof., 1965—2000; prof. emeritus, 2000. Mem. Am. Chem. Soc., Am. Soc. Biol. Chemists. Home: 6636 Pershing Ave Saint Louis MO 63130-4642

HOLTZMAN, DAVID MICHAEL, neurologist; b. St. Louis, July 31, 1961; BS in Med. Edn., Northwestern U., 1983, MD, 1985. Bd. cert. neurology. Intern/resident U. Calif., San Francisco, 1985—89, postdoctoral rsch. tng. William C. Mobley Lab., 1989—94; lab. dir. Washington U., 1994, Charlotte and Paul Hagemann assoc. prof. neurology, 2001—, prof. molecular biology and pharmacology, 2002—; Andrew and Gretchen Jones chmn. dept. neurology Washington U. Sch. Medicine, St. Louis, 2003—. Asst. prof. U. Calif., San Francisco, 1991—94. Recipient Paul Beeson Physician Faculty Scholar award in aging rsch., MetLife award for promising rsch. on Alzheimer's disease, 2002, Potamkin prize, Am. Acad. Neurology, 2003. Office: Washington Univ Sch Medicine Dept Neurology 660 S Euclid Ave Saint Louis MO 63110

HOLTZMAN, DEANNA, psychoanalyst, psychologist; b. Chgo. m. David B. Holtzman; children: Susan, Karen, Daniel. BA cum laude, U. Mich., 1965; MA, Wayne State U., Detroit, 1969; PhD, Wayne State U., 1975; grad., Mich. Psychoanalytic Inst., 1982. Cert. psychoanalyst Am. Psychoanalytic Assn. Assoc. in psychiatry Wayne State U., Detroit, 1975—76, dept. psychiatry, 1977—80, adj. asst. prof. dept. psychiatry, 1976—88, adj. assoc. prof., 1989—; tng. and supervising analyst Mich. Psychoanalytic Inst., 1987—. Adj. prof. psychology U. Detroit, 1980—. Author: Nevermore: The Hymen and the Loss of Virginity, 1996; contbr. articles to profl. jours. Trustee Sigmund Freud Archives, 1988—. Recipient Faculty award, Mich. Psychoanalytic Inst., 1992, Outstanding Faculty, Candidates Mich. Psychoanalytic Inst., 1996, Excellence in Tchg. award, 2002. Mem.: Mich. Psychol. Assn. (clin. essay award 1999), Am. Psychoanalytic Assn., APA. Office: 1400 Ardmoor Dr Bloomfield Hills MI 48301

HOLTZMAN, ELIZABETH, lawyer; b. Bklyn., Aug. 11, 1941; d. Sidney and Filia Holtzman. AB magna cum laude, Radcliffe Coll., 1962; JD, Harvard U., 1965; L.D.S., Regis Coll., 1975, Skidmore Coll., 1980, Simmons Coll., 1981, Smith Coll., 1982. Bar: N.Y. 1966. Assoc. Wachtell, Lipton, Rosen, Katz & Kern, N.Y.C., 1965-67; asst. to mayor N.Y.C., 1968-69; assoc. Paul, Weiss, Rifkind, Wharton & Garrison, 1970-72; mem. 93d-96th Congresses from 16th dist., N.Y.; vis. prof. Law Sch. and Grad. Sch. Pub. Adminstrn. NYU, 1981; dist. atty. Kings County, Bklyn., 1982-89; comptr. City of N.Y., 1990-93. Mem. Am. Jewish Commn. on the Holocaust, Nazi and Japanese War Criminal Records Interagency Working Group, 1999—; Dem. nominee U.S. Senate, 1980; N.Y. State Dem. committeewoman, 1970—72; mem. Pres.'s Nat. Commn. on U.S. Observance Internat. Women's Yr., Helsinki Watch Com., 1981—88, Select Com. on Immigration Policy, 1979—80; bd. overseers Harvard U., 1976—82; trustee Radcliffe Coll., 1999, Bklyn. Acad. Music Endowment Trust, 1999—; mem. Lawyers Com. Internat. Human Right, 1981—88. Recipient Nat. Coun. Jewish Women's Faith and Humanity award, YWCA Elizabeth Cutter Morrow award, Maccabean award N.Y. Bd. Rabbis, Alumni recognition award Radcliffe Coll. Alumnae Assn., 1973, N.J. and L.A. ACLU awards for contbns. to def. of Constn. and preservation of civil liberties, 1981, Athena award N.Y.C. Commn. on Status of Women, 1985, Woman of Yr. award N.Y. League Bus. and Profl. Women, 1985, Jan Korzak award 5th Ann. Kent State Holocaust Conf., 1986, Outstanding and Meritorious Svc. award Jewish War Vets. of U.S., 1986, Award of Remembrance Warsaw Ghetto Resistance Orgn., 1987, Gates of Freedom award State of Israel Bonds, 1987; Award of Honor United Jewish Appeal, 1988, Deed of Tzedakah award, 1991. Fellow N.Y. Inst. Humanities; mem. Assn. of Bar of City of N.Y., Nat. Women's Polit. Caucus (Outstanding Svc. award 1987), Phi Beta Kappa. Office: Herrick Feinstein LLP 2 Park Ave New York NY 10016-9302 Office Phone: 212-592-1400.

HOLTZMAN, GARY YALE, retired diversified financial services company executive; b. N.Y.C., Aug. 7, 1936; s. Abram and Pearl (Kashetsky) H.; m. Alice A. Lang, Sept. 5, 1958; children: Bruce, Sheri, Michele. BBA, CCNY, 1958. Buyer, ops. mgr. Bloomingdale's, N.Y.C., 1966; exec. v.p. control and ops. Jordan Marsh Co., Miami, Fla., 1967-87; sr. v.p. ops. and stores L. Luria & Sons Inc., Miami, 1987-93; exec. dir. Mar Jewish Community Ctr., Greater Miami, Fla., 1993-95; agt. Social Security Adminstrn.-TSR, 1995—2002; ret., 2002. Bd. advisers Universal Nat. Bank. Bd. dirs. Dade County Safety Coun., Miami, 1978-85, Jewish Cmty. Ctr. Greater Miami, 1983-88, Fla. Bus. Roundtable, 1975-80, Anti-Defamation League of B'nia B'rith, 1983-87; bd. advisers Opportunities Industrialization Ctr., 1982-84; pres. Michael Ann Russell Jewish Cmty. Ctr., 1984-86, bd. dirs., 1980—; life bd. dirs. Temple Beth Torah Adath Yeshurun, 1969-94, Temple B'nai Aviv, 1994-98; mem. fin. com. Temple Dor Dorim, 1999—; active Jewish Fedn. Broward County and Greater Miami, Miami Jewish Fedn.; com. chmn. United Way of Dade County. Lt. U.S. Army, 1958-59; capt. USAR, 1959-67. Recipient Americanism award Anti-Defamation League, 1983; recipient Adath Yeshurun Man of Yr. award, 1978 Mem. Greater Miami C. of C., Fla. Retail Fedn. Democrat. Home: 2019 Cove Ln Weston FL 33326-2336 E-mail: algari@bellsouth.net.

HOLTZMAN, LISA A., school psychologist; b. Irwin, Pa., July 18, 1974; d. Catherine Sherbondy; m. Christopher J. Holtzman, July 6, 2002; 1 child, Christopher J. BA, Calif. U. Pa., 1997, MS, 1998. Cert. sch. psychology. Behavior specialist, cons. Northwestern Human Svcs., Greensburg, Pa., 1997—2000; sch. psychologist Holy Family Inst., Pitts., 2000—01, Intermediate Unit *, Somerset, 2001—04, Intermediate Unit 7, Greensburg, 2005—. Mem.: Nat. Assn. Sch. Psychologists. Roman Catholic. Avocations: photography, scrapbooks, crafts. Home: 101 Mohican Dr Greensburg PA 15601 Office: Westmoreland Intermediate Unit 7 RR 12 Box 205 Donahue Rd Greensburg PA 15601

HOLTZMAN, MARC LAWRENCE, catalog chain executive; b. Wilkes-Barre, Pa., Mar. 1, 1960; s. Seymour and Evelyn (Krohn) H. BA in Econs., Lehigh U., 1983. Exec. dir. Pa. Reagan-Bush Campaign, Phila., 1979-80; asst. to sec.-designee U.S. Dept. Transp., 1980-81; chief staff Lt. Gov.'s Office, State of Pa., Harrisburg, 1981-82; exec. dir. Citizens for Am., Washington, 1983-85; pres. Holtzman & Assocs., Inc., pub. affairs, Washington, 1986-88, Jewelcor Jewelers and Distbrs., Inc., Wilkes-Barre, 1988—, Jewelcor Travel, Inc., Wilkes-Barre, 1988—. Bd. dirs. SH Holdings, Inc., Wilkes-Barre; exec. asst. to sec.-designee U.S. Dept. Transp., Washington, 1980-81; guest lectr. numerous bus., civic orgns. and colls. throughout U.S. and fgn. countries. Mem. Presdl. Electoral Coll., 1984; bd. dirs. N.E. Pa. Econ. Devel. Coun., 1989—; bd. advisors Ctr. for Security Policy, Washington, 1989—; mem. nat. adv. coun. Peace Corps, Washington, 1989—. Republican. Home: 33 Sahara Dr Wilkes Barre PA 18704-5311 Office: Jewelcor Jewelers-Distbrs Box J Wilkes Barre PA 18773

HOLTZMAN, MICHAEL, alcohol abuse professional; b. Chgo. s. Bernard and Juanita (Good) H.; m. Elaine Cyr, Apr. 11, 1967; children: Michael (dec.), Jed, Ann. Student, U. Internat. Studies, Rome. V.p. mktg. Container Corp. Am., 1955-62; pres. Blair Graphics, Chgo., 1962-70; co-founder, dir. Indemnified Cap. Invest. Anglo Am. Commodity Invest. Program, Buenos Aires and London, 1970-77, founder, pres. London, 1980-98; ret., 1998. Arbitrator Am. Arbitration Assn., Coral Gables, Fla., 1980—. Trustee Coll. Rome, 1975-95; mem. exec. com. Found. Educative Pro Deo, Rome, 1980-95; chmn. steering com. Ill. Drug Free Program, Chgo., 1995—; sr. mem. Pres. Coun. on Alcohol:Drug Abuse, 1971—; pres. Sr. Corp Ret. Exec. (SBA), Kankakee, Ill., 1998—; pres. Kankakee Symphony, 1998—; presenter high schs. seminars on alcoholism, Ill., 1995—. Capt. infantry, 1952-55. Mem. Am. Arbitration Assn. (sr. arbitrator 1985—), Am. Club (Buenos Aires), Brit. Army and Navy Club (London), Kankakee County Upstairs Bridge Club. Avocations: golf, bridge, trap shooting, gardening. Home: 160 W Dixie Hwy Saint Anne IL 60964-5400

HOLTZMAN, ROBERT ARTHUR, lawyer; b. L.A., July 17, 1929; s. Ruben and Bertha (Dembowsky) H.; m. Barbara Polis, June 26, 1954 (dec. 1985); children: Melinda, Mark, Bradley; m. Liliane Gurwith Endlich, July 6, 1986. BA, UCLA, 1951; LLB, U. So. Calif., 1954. Bar: Calif. 1955, U.S. Dist. Ct. (ctrl. dist.) Calif. 1955, U.S. Ct. Appeals (9th cir.) 1958. Assoc. Gang, Tyre & Brown, L.A., 1954, Loeb and Loeb, L.A., 1956-63, ptnr., 1964-95, of counsel, 1996—. Judge pro tem Mcpl. Ct. L.A. Jud. Dist.; lectr. Calif. Continuing Edn. of Bar. Contbr. articles to legal publs. With U.S. Army, 1954-56. Mem. ABA (dispute resolution sect., vice-chmn. arbitration com.), Calif. Bar Assn. (chmn. com. on adminstrn. of justice 1984-85), L.A. County Bar Assn., Am. Arbitration Assn. (panel arbitrators 1974—, panel mediators 1992—, arbitrator large complex case program 1993—). Office: Loeb & Loeb LLP 10100 Santa Monica Blvd Ste 2200 Los Angeles CA 90067-4164 Office Phone: 310-282-2280. Business E-Mail: rholtzman@loeb.com.

HOLTZMAN, ROBERTA LEE, French and Spanish language educator; b. Detroit, Nov. 24, 1938; d. Paul John and Sophia (Marcus) H. AB cum laude, Wayne State U., 1959, MA, 1973, U. Mich., 1961. Fgn. lang. tchr. Birmingham (Mich.) Sch. Dist., 1959-60, Cass Tech. H.S., Detroit, 1961-64; from instr. to prof. French and Spanish, Schoolcraft Coll., Livonia, Mich., 1964-84, chmn. French and Spanish depts., 1984—2004; ret., 2004; adj. prof. French Schoolcraft Coll., Livonia, Mich., 2004—. Trustee Cranbrook Music Guild, Ednl. Community, Bloomfield Hills, Mich., 1976-78. Fulbright-Hays fellow, Brazil, 1964. Mem. AAUW, NEA, MLA, Nat. Mus. Women in Arts (co-founder 1992), Am. Assn. Tchrs. of Spanish and Portuguese, Am. Assn. Tchrs. of French, Mich. Edn. Assn. Avocations: swimming, book collecting, photography, travel. Office: Schoolcraft Coll 18600 Haggerty Rd Livonia MI 45152-2696 Business E-Mail: rholtzma@schoolcraft.edu.

HOLTZMAN, WAYNE HAROLD, psychologist, educator; b. Chgo., Jan. 16, 1923; s. Harold Hoover and Lillian (Manny) H.; m. Joan King, Aug. 23, 1947; children: Wayne Harold, James K., Scott E., Karl H. BS, Northwestern U., 1944, MS, 1947; PhD, Stanford U., 1950; LHD (hon.), Southwestern U., 1980. Asst. prof. psychology U. Tex., Austin, 1949-53, assoc. prof., 1953-59, prof., 1959—2003, dean Coll. Edn., 1964-70, Hogg prof. psychology and edn., 1964—2003, prof. emeritus, 2003—. Assoc. dir. Hogg Found. Mental Health, 1955-64, pres., 1970-93, spl. counsel, 1993-2003; dir. Social Sci. Rsch. Coun., 1957-63, Centro de Investigationes Sociales, Mex., 1960-70; cons. USAF, sci. adv. bd., 1969-71; basic rsch. com. NRC, 1968-71; behavioral sci. study sect. USPHS, 1957-59, mem. mental health study sect., 1960, chmn. personality and cognition rsch. rev. com., 1968-72; rsch. adv. panel Soc. Security Adminstrn., 1961-62; L.Am. adv. bd. IBM, 1985-89; dir. WHO Collaborating Ctr. in Mental Health for Tex. and Mex., 1993-2003; pres. Austin Project, 2001-03; bd. dirs. Menninger Clinic, The Learning Initiative. Author: (with B.M. Moore) Tomorrow's Parents, 1964, Computer Assisted Instruction Testing and Guidance, 1971, (with R. Diaz-Guerrero and J. Swartz) Personality Development in Two Cultures, 1975, Introduction to Psychology, 1978; (with K.A. Heller and S. Messick) Placing Children in Special Education, 1982, (with T. Bornemann) Mental Health of Immigrants and Refugees, 1990, School of the Future, 1992, Holtzman Inkblot Technique Research Guide, 1999, (with M.R. Rozenweig, Michel Sabourin and David Belanger) History of the International Union of Psychological Science, 2000; editor: Jour. Ednl. Psychology, 1966-72. Trustee Ednl. Testing Service, Princeton, 1972-74, 77-80, 83-86, J.W. and Cornelia Scarborough Found., 1977-82, Ctr. for Applied Linguistics, 1978-80, Salado Inst. Humanities, 1980-85, Population Inst., 1979-85, Menninger Atel, 1982--2003, bd. dir., 1986-, Population Resource Ctr., 1980—, chmn. bd. dirs.; dir. Sci. Rsch. Assocs., 1975-88; pres., bd. dirs. S.W. Ednl. Devel. Lab., 1974-75; mem. adv. com. computing activities NSF, 1970-73; mem. computer sci. and engring. bd. NAS, 1971-73, chmn. panel on selection and placement of mentally retarded students, 1979-82; chmn. interdisciplinary cluster on social and behavioral devel. Pres.'s Biomed. Research Panel, 1975-76; bd. dirs. Found.'s Fund for Rsch. in Psychiatry, 1973-77, chmn., 1976-77; dir. Conf. of S.W. Found., 1976-84, pres., 1978-79; mem. nat. adv. mental health coun. Alcohol, Drug Abuse, and Mental Health Adminstrn., 1978-81; mem. acad. info. sys. adv. coun. IBM, 1982-85. Commd. ensign USNR, 1944, Northwestern U. NROTC, anti-aircraft gunnery officer USNR, Pacific, lt. (jg.) USNR, 1945, flag lt. to admiral oscar badger to admiral roper USNR. Faculty Rsch. fellow, Social Sci. Rsch. Coun., 1953—54, Ctr. Advanced Study Behavioral Scis., 1962—63. Fellow APA, AAAS; mem. Tex. Psychol. Assn. (pres. 1957), S.W. Psychol. Assn. (pres. 1958), Am. Statis. Assn., InterAm. Soc. Psychology (pres. 1966-67), Am. Ednl. Rsch. Assn., Internat. Union Psychol. Scis. (sec.-gen. 1972-84, pres. 1984-88, exec. com. 1972-92), Philos. Soc. Tex. (pres. 1982-83), Sigma Xi. Methodist. Avocations: photography, gardening, travel, swimming. Home: 3300 Foothill Dr Austin TX 78731-5823 E-mail: wayne.holtzman@mail.utexas.edu.

HOLTZMANN, HOWARD MARSHALL, lawyer, judge; b. NYC, Dec. 10, 1921; s. Jacob L. And Lillian (Plotz) H.; m. Anne Fisher, Jan. 14, 1945 (dec. Aug. 1967); children: Susan Holtzmann Richardson, Betsey; m. Carol Ebenstein Van Berg, Dec. 23, 1972. AB, Yale Coll., 1942, JD, 1947; LittD (hon.), St. Bonaventure U., 1952; LLD (hon.), Jewish Theol. Sem., NYC, 1990. Bar: NY 1947. Atty. Colorado Fuel & Iron Corp., Buffalo, 1947-49; ptnr. Holtzmann, Wise & Shepard, NYC, 1949-95; judge Iran-U.S. Claims Tribunal, The Hague, Netherlands, 1981-94; arbitrator, sr. claims judge, 1994—; sr. claims judge Claims Resolution Tribunal for Dormant Accounts, Zurich, Switzerland, 1998—2002. U.S. del. UN Commn. on Internat. Trade Law, 1975—, Hague Conf. on Pvt. Internat. Law, 1985; advisor U.S.A. Arbitration agreements with USSR, Russian Fedn., China, Hungary, Bulgaria, Czechoslovakia, Poland and German Dem. Republic. Author, editor: A New Look at Legal Aspects of Doing Business with China, 1979; co-author: A Guide to the Unicitral Model Law on International Commercial Arbitration-Legislative History and Commentary, 1988 (cert. of merit Am. Soc. Internat. Law 1991); contbr. chpts. to books and articles to law jours. Mem. governing coun. Downstate Med. Sch. SUNY, Bklyn., 1961-78; trustee St. Bonaventure U., Olean, NY, 1968-90, trustee emeritus, 1990—; chmn. bd. Jewish Theol. Sem., NYC, 1983-85, hon. chmn., 1985—; trustee Inst. Internat. Law, Pace U. Sch. Law, 1992—; mem. bd. advisors Lighthouse Internat. Decorated comdr. Swedish Royal Order of Polar Star; assoc. fellow, Pierson Coll., Yale, 2005—. Mem. ABA (chmn. com. code ethics comml. arbitrators 1973-77), Internat. Coun. for Comml. Arbitration (hon. vice chmn.), Am. Arbitration Assn. (hon. chmn., Gotshal Internat. Arbitration award 1980), Internat. C. of C. (vice chmn. arbitration commn. 1979-2001), Stockholm Arbitration Inst. (adv. bd.), Am. Bar Found., NY County Lawyers Assn., Internat. Law Assn., Am. Fgn. Law Assn. (v.p. 1995-2003), Internat. Bar Assn., NY State Bar Assn., Assn. Bar City of NY, Am. Soc. Internat. Law (cert. merit 1991), Soc. Profls. in Dispute Resolution, Indsl. Rels. Rsch. Assn., NY Law Inst., Am. Judicature Soc., Am. Assn. for Internat. Commn. of Jurists. Office: Ste 2000 630 Fifth Ave New York NY 10111-0100 Office Phone: 212-332-7140. E-mail: holtzmannh@cs.com.

HOLTZSCHUE, KARL BRESSEM, lawyer, author, educator; b. Wichita, Kans., Mar. 3, 1938; s. Bressem C. and Josephine E. (Landsittel) H.; m. Linda J. Gross, Oct. 24, 1959; children: Alison, Adam, Sara. AB, Dartmouth Coll., 1959; LLB, Columbia U., 1966. Bar: N.Y. 1967, U.S. Dist. Ct. (so. and ea. dists.) N.Y. 1968. Assoc. Webster & Sheffield, N.Y.C., 1966-73, ptnr., 1974-88; ptnr., head real estate dept. O'Melveny and Myers, N.Y.C., 1988-90; pvt. practice N.Y.C., 1990—. Adj. prof. Fordham U. Law Sch., 1990—2003; adj. prof. Bus. Sch. Columbia U., 1990—96, Law Sch., 1991. Author: Holtzschue on Real Estate Contracts, New York Practice Guide: Real Estate, Vol. 1 on Purchase and Sale, Real Estate Transactions: Purchase and Sale of Real Property, Lexis Nexis Answer Guide: New York Real Property; editor: NYSBA's Res. R.E. Forms on Hot Docs.; mem. editl. bd. Warren's Weed New York Real Property, 2003—. Trustee Soc. of St. Johnland, 1980-86, Ensemble Studio Theatre, 1986-88; bd. dirs. The Bridge, 1990—, pres., 1992-95; mem. alumni bd. Dartmouth Ptnrs. in Cmty. Svc., 1994—, chmn., 1994-99. Lt. (j.g.) USN, 1959-62. Mem.: ABA (com. on legal opinions in real estate transactions 1990—2003), Tri Bar (opinions com. 1990—99), Am. Coll. Real Estate Lawyers (opinions com. 1989—2003, vice chmn. 1992—95), Assn. Bar City N.Y. (com. on real property law 1977—80, chmn. 1987—90, 1995—98, com. Ctrl. and East Europe 1998—99), N.Y. State Bar Assn. (com. on attys. opinions 1992—2003, co-chmn. com. on title and transfer 1998—2004, exec. com. real property sect. 1998—, vice chair exec. com. real property sect. 2005—). Episcopalian. E-mail: kholtzschue@nyc.rr.com.

HOLUB, MARTIN, architect; b. Prague, Czechoslovakia, Dec. 11, 1938; arrived in U.S., 1970, naturalized, 1977; s. Jan and Miloslava (Jerabkova) Holub. MS, Czech Tech. U., 1963, Acad. Art, Prague, 1966. Registered arch., N.Y., N.J., Tenn., Fla., Conn. Designer Konstruktiva, Prague, 1963-67; asst. arch. Greater London Coun., 1967-68; sr. designer R. Seifert and Ptnrs., London, 1968-69, Kahn and Jacobs, N.Y.C., 1970-71; prin. Martin Holub Archs. and Planners, N.Y.C., 1971—, br. office Prague, 1990—. Prin. works include Rokeby Apts., Nashville (Design award, 1976), Patricia Lane Ho. (1st prize Am. Soc. Registered Archs. Design Awards probram, 2001), Dominican Chapel, Sparkill, N.Y. (Design award Am. Soc. Registered Archs., 2002). Mem.: AIA, Archtl. League N.Y., Am. Arbitration Assn. Home: 500 E 77th St Apt 1529 New York NY 10162-0019 Office: 116 W 72nd St Fl 16 New York NY 10023-3338 Office Phone: 212-787-7644.

HOLUB, ROBERT FRANTISEK, nuclear chemist, physicist; b. Prague, Czechoslovakia, Sept. 19, 1937; came to U.S., 1966; s. Stanislav and Marie (Prochazkova) H.; m. Johnna S. Thames, Dec. 27, 1977; children: Robert M., John F., Elisabeth J. BS, Charles U., Prague, 1958, MS, 1960; PhD, McGill U., 1970. Rsch. assoc. Fla. State U., Tallahassee, 1970-73; tchg. intern U. Ky., Lexington, 1973-74; rsch. physicist Bur. Mines, U.S. Dept. Interior, Denver, 1974-95; prof. dept. physics and dept. environ. sci. and engring. Colo. Sch. of Mines, Golden, 1995—. Cons. IAEA, Vienna, Austria, 1984-89, key participant radon metrology program, 1990-97; faculty affiliate Colo. State U., Ft. Collins, 1982—. Patentee continuous working level exposure apparatus; contbr. articles to sci. jours. NRC Can. scholar, 1967-70. Mem. Am. Phys. Soc., Health Physics Soc., Am. Assn. for Aerosol Rsch. Office Phone: 303-384-2068. E-mail: rholub@mines.edu.

HOLWAY, DAVID, labor union administrator; b. Cambridge, Mass. 3 children: Shalie, Allei, John Conor. Attended, Boston Coll. Dep. commr. State Dept. Corrections, Mass.; chmn. Union's Health and Welfare Trust Fund; CFO Norfolk County Hospital; legis. dir., chief contract negotiator State employees Mass. Nat. Assn. Govt. Employees, pres., 2002—. Candidate St. Senate, Mass., 1986. Mem.: Mass. Dem. Com. (former chmn.), Dem. Nat. Com. (deleg. st. & nat. Dem. Conv.). Office: Nat Assn Govt Employees 159 Burgin Pkwy Quincy MA 02169 Office Phone: 617-376-0220.

HOLWAY, ELLEN TWOMBLY HAY, primary education educator; b. Summit, N.J. d. Allan and Ellen Clark (Twombly) Hay; m. William Crocker Holway III; children: Julie Ellen, Suzanne Clark, Cammy Twombly, Amy Hay, Daniel Hitchcock, Joanna Howland. AB in Psychology cum laude, Colby Coll., 1953; MEd, U. Lowell, 1975; postgrad., U. Mass., Lowell, 1987—, Boston U., 1978, Cen. New Eng. Coll., 1987. Cert. elem. tchr. and prin., perceptually handicapped, gen. supr., supt./asst.supt., Mass.; asst. psychologist, psychometrist, child welfare worker, pub. assistance caseworker, Maine. Asst. psychologist, acting dept. head Pineland Hosp. and Tng. Ctr., 1953-55; elem. tchr., specialist Odenton, Md., 1955-57; primary tchr., prof. devel. team leader Horace Mann, Maynard, Mass., 1972—; elem. asst. prin. Green Meadow Sch., 1994-97, elem. prin., 1997-99; MPS facilitator 21sth century initiatives K-12, 1999—2000; freelance edn. adminstrn. cons. K-12, 2000—. Freelance edn. adminstrv. cons. K-12, 2000—; MPS facilitator 21st century initiatives K-12, 1999-2000; mem. adj. faculty dept. bus. and career edn. Boston U. Grad. Sch. Edn.; freelance editor, cons. pilot program liaison D.C. Heath Pub. Co.; developer, coord. Acton-Boxborough Student Activities Fund, numerous others; cons. Technol. R & D Corp.; mem. Mass. Math. Adv. Com., Mass. Sci. Adv. Com.; lead tchr. New Standards Project. Chmn. Acton and Acton-Boxborough Regional Sch. Com., Acton 250th Celebration; mem. MASC Assessment Com.; charter mem., bd. dirs., mem. pub. rels. com. Acton Hist. Soc.; jr. leader, coord. summer camp Girl Scouts U.S.A.; counselor citizenship badge, Eagle advisor Boy Scouts Am., Acton and Maynard; tchr., supr. ch. sch., numerous others. Mem. NEA, ASCD, Am. Ednl. Rsch. Assn., Nat. Sch. Bd. Assn., Nat. Career Edn. Assn (charter), Mass. ASCD, Mass. Assn. Sch. Coms., Mass. Tchrs. Assn., Maynard Edn. Assn., LWV (charter, v.p., chmn. pub. rels.), Yarmouth Hist. Soc. (life), Phi Beta Kappa, Pi Lambda Theta, Pi Gamma Mu. Office: Maynard Pub Schs 12 Bancroft St Maynard MA 01754-1702

HOLWELL, PETER, management consultant; b. Mar. 28, 1936; s. Frank and Helen (Howe) H.; m. Jean Patricia Ashman, 1959; 2 children. BSc in Econ., London Sch. Econs. Articled clk. Arthur Andersen & Co., 1958-61, mgmt. cons., 1961-64; head univ. computing O & M unit U. London, 1967-77, sec. for acctg. & adminstrv. computing, 1977-82; clk. of the ct., 1982-85; prin. U. London, 1985-97, dir. sch. exams coun., 1988-97; mgmt. cons. Prince of Wales' Inst. Architecture, 1998-99, Chatham Hist. Dockyard Trust, 1999-2000, Leeds Castle Found., 2001. Mem. U. London Exams and Assessments Coun., 1991-96. Mem. Samuel Courtauld Avd. Bd., 1985—98; chmn. City of East London Family Health Svcs. Authority, 1994—96; trustee Leeds Castle Found., 2001—03; mem. N.E. Thames Regional Health Authority, 1990—94; chmn. St. Marks Rsch. Found. and Ednl. Trust, 1995—2000; vice chmn. coun. Wye Coll., U. London, 1995—2000, mem. coun. Sch. Pharmacy, 1996—2001; mem. Edexcel Found. Coun., 1996—97. ACA Ltd. (dir.), 1998—. Home: Hookers Green Bishopsbourne Canterbury Kent CT4 5JB England

HOLWELL, RICHARD J., federal judge; b. NYC, July 2, 1946; married; 2 children. BA, Villanova U., 1967; JD cum laude, Columbia Law Sch., 1970; Diploma in Criminology, Cambridge U., 1971. Bar: N.Y. 1972. Assoc. litigation atty. White & Case LLP, 1971—79, ptnr., 1971—2003; judge U.S. Dist. Ct. (So. Dist. NY), 2003—. Chairperson Panel NY State Supreme Ct. Departmental Disciplinary Com. Mem. ABA, N.Y. State Bar Assn. Office: 500 Pearl St New York NY 10007*

HOLYDAY, DOUGLAS CHARLES, city councillor; b. Etobicoke, Ont., Can., July 31, 1942; s. Arthur John and Anne H.; m. Franca Palma Pellizzari, Aug. 16, 1969; children: Stephen, David. Formerly ward 6 councillor Etobicoke City Coun.; past chmn. Etobicoke Bd. Health; mayor City of Etobicoke, 1994-97; councillor City of Toronto, 1997—. Former pres., owner Holyday Ins. Brokers, Inc., Etobicoke. Founding chair Etobicoke Lakeshore Oldtimers Hockey Tournament; bd. dirs. mcpl. sect. Can. Nat. Exhbn. Assn. Avocations: golf, hockey, reading. Office: City Hall 2d Fl 100 Queen St W Toronto ON Canada M5H 2N2 Office Phone: 416-392-4121. Business E-Mail: councillor_holyday@toronto.ca.

HOLYER, ERNA MARIA, adult education educator, writer, artist; b. Weilheim, Bavaria, Germany, Mar. 15, 1925; d. Mathias and Anna Maria (Goldhofer) Schretter; m. Gene Wallace Holyer, Aug. 24, 1957 (dec. 1999). AA, San Jose Evening Coll., 1964; student, San Mateo Coll., 1965—67, San Jose State U., 1968—69, San Jose City Coll., 1980—81; DLitt, World U., 1984; DFA (hon.), The London Inst. Applied Rsch, 1992. Freelance writer under pseudonym Ernie Holyer, 1960—; tchr. creative writing San Jose (Calif.) Met. Adult Edn., 1968—. Exhibited in group shows at Crown Zellerbach Gallery, San Francisco, 1973-4, 76-77; I.B.C. Gallery, San Francisco, 1978 (medal of Congress, 1988, 89, 92, 94, Congress Challenge trophy, 1991), L.A., 1981, Cambridge, Eng., 1992, Cambridge, Mass., 1993, San Jose, Calif., 1993, Edinburgh, 1994, San Francisco, 1996; author: Rescue at Sunrise, 1965, Steve's Night of Silence, 1966, A Cow for Hansel, 1967, At the Forest's Edge, 1969, Song of Courage, 1970, Lone Brown Gull, 1971, Shoes for Daniel, 1974, The Southern Sea Otter, 1975, Sigi's Fire Helmet, 1975, Reservoir Road Adventure, 1982, Wilderness Journey, Golden Journey, California Journey, 1997, Self-Help for Writers: Winners Show You How, 2002, Dangerous Secrets: A Young Girl's Travails Under the Nazis, 2003, Survival: An Electrifying Tale, 2004; contbr. articles to mags. and newspapers Recipient Woman of Achievement Honor cert. San Jose Mercury-News, 1973, 74, 75, Lefoli award for excellence in adult edn. instr. Adult Edn. Senate, 1972, Women of Achievement awards League of Friends of Santa Clara County Commn., San Jose Mercury News, 1987, various art awards. Mem. N.L.A.P.W. Inc., World Univ Roundtable (doctoral). Home and Office: 1314 Rimrock Dr San Jose CA 95120-5611 Personal E-mail: holyerE@aol.com.

HOLYFIELD, EVANDER, retired professional boxer; b. Atlanta, Oct. 19, 1962; Winner unanimous decision vs. Ray Mercer, 1995; defeated Mike Tyson to win WBC Heavyweight Title, 1996; defended title successfully winning over Lennox Lewis, 1999. Performer/competitor (TV series) Dancing with the Stars, ABC network, 2005. Recipient Bronze medal, 1984 Summer Olympics, World Boxing Assn. cruiserweight title, 1986, Internat. Boxing Fedn. cruiserweight title, 1987, World Boxing Coun. cruiserweight title, 1988, Internat. Boxing Fedn. heavyweight championship, 1997, undisputed heavyweight world champion, 1990—92, 1993—94, loss titles to Lennox Lewis, 1999. Office: 794 Evander Holyfield Hwy Fairburn GA 30213*

HOLZ, CARL WAYNE, retired theologian; s. Harold Otto and Gwendolyn Dee Holz; m. Rebecca Joy Osterhout, Sept. 16, 1972; 1 child, James Michael. BA, Cedarville U., Ohio, 1973; MDiv cum laude, Grace Theol. Sem., Winona Lake, Ind., 1976; ThM, Princeton Theol. Sem., N.J., 1988; PhD, Pensacola Christian Coll., Fla., 1995; DLitt (hon.), Sofia Bible U., Sofia, Bulgaria, 2000; Dr.Religious Letters (hon.), Ctrl. Christian U., 2001; DD (hon.), South Fla. Bible Coll. and Sem., Deerfield Beach, 2004. Lic. preacher Conservative Bapt. Assn./Ind., 1974, ordained minister Gen. Assn. of Regular Bapt. Churches/Mich., 1975. N.Am. dir. for libr. acqusitions Sofia Bible U., Sofia, Bulgaria, 2000—02; writer/editor U.S. Army, Ft. Monmouth, NJ, 1989; humanitarian evangelist Bapt. Mid-Missions, Monrovia, Liberia, 1972. Trustee Sofia Bible U., Sofia, Bulgaria, 2000—02; cons. The Prudent Trader, Inc., N.Y.C., 2001—03. Capt. U.S. Army, 1977—86. Decorated Silver Star Medal U.S. Army, Bronze Star Medal, Purple Heart U.S Army, Air Medal US. Army, Cross of Galantry Vietnam, 4 Army Commendation Medals Army; recipient Presdl. Cert. of Appreciation, Whitehouse, Wash. D.C., 1971. Fellow: Christian Fellowship Internat. (hon.).

HOLZ, GEORGE G., IV, medical educator, research scientist; b. Santa Monica, Calif., May 8, 1953; s. George G. and Mignon M. (Kiproff) Holz. BS, Cornell U., 1975; PhD, U. Ill., 1984. Rsch. fellow Tufts U. Med. Sch., Boston, 1984—89; rsch. assoc. Howard Hughes Med. Inst., Boston, 1990—93; instr. medicine Mass. Gen. Hosp.-Harvard Med. Sch., Boston, 1990—93, asst. prof. medicine, 1994—98; assoc. prof. physiology and neurosci. NYU Med. Sch., N.Y.C., 1998—; rsch. fellow Marine Biology Lab., Woods Hole, Mass., 2000—. Corp. mem. Marine Biol. Lab., Woods Hole, Mass. Mem. All-Sectional Gymnastics Team N.Y., 1971. Recipient Rsch. award, Am. Diabetes Assn., 1996, 2000; grantee rsch. grantee, NIH; scholar N.Y. State Regents scholar, Cornell U., 1971—75. Mem.: AAAS, Am. Diabetes Assn., Soc. Gen. Physiologists, Endocrine Soc., Soc. for Neurosci. Office Phone: 212-263-5434. E-mail: holzg01@popmail.med.nyu.edu.

HOLZ, HARRY GEORGE, lawyer; b. Milw., Sept. 13, 1934; s. Harry Carl and Emma Louise (Hinz) H.; m. Nancy L. Heiser, May 12, 1962; children: Pamela Gretchen, Bradley Eric, Erika Lynn. BS, Marquette U., 1956, LLB, 1958; LLM, Northwestern U., 1960. Bar: Wis. 1958, Ill. 1960. Tchg. fellow Northwestern U. Sch. Law, 1958-59; assoc. Sidley & Austin, Chgo., 1960; ptnr. Quarles & Brady, Milw., 1968—2002, of counsel, 2002—. Lectr. law securities regulation U. Wis. Law Sch., 1971—74; adj. prof. Marquette U. Sch. Law, 1976—91; faculty program on antitrust law Wis. State Bar Sems., 1975—82, 1989, 93; bd. dirs., sec. Creative Sharp Presentations Inc.; lectr. PLI 33rd Antitrust Inst.; lectr., spkr. in antitrust field. Bd. visitors Marquette U. Sch. Law, 1990, 93; moderator First Congl. Ch., Warnator. Capt. C.E. U.S. Army, 1960-67. Fellow: Am. Bar Found.; mem.: ABA (lectr. nat. antitrust program 1997, Robinson-Patman com., corp. counsel com., antitrust litigation com.), Marquette U. Law Alumni Assn. (bd. dirs.), Milw. Bar Assn., Wis. Bar Assn. (chmn. bus. law com. 1978—79, bd. dirs. 1978—83, chair 180 standing rev. com. 2001—, standing com. bus. law), Marquette U. Sch. Law Woolsack Soc. (bd. dirs., past pres.), Western Racquet Club, Phi Delta Phi, Beta Gamma Sigma. Office: Quarles & Brady 411 E Wisconsin Ave Ste 2550 Milwaukee WI 53202-4497 Business E-Mail: hgh@quarles.com.

HOLZ, ROBERT KENNETH, retired geography educator; b. Kankakee, Ill., Nov. 3, 1930; s. Harry H. and Margaret (Conway) H.; m. Joyce F. Harpin, May 19, 1951; 1 child, Eric R. BA in Zoology, So. Ill. U., 1958, MA in Geography, 1959; PhD in Geography, Mich. State U., 1963. Asst. prof. U. Tex., Austin, 1962-67, assoc. prof., 1967-72, prof., 1972—, dir. ctr. for Middle Eastern Studies, 1991-99, Eric W. Zimmerman Regents prof., 1991-99, Eric W. Zimmerman Regents prof. emeritus, 1999—; ret., 1999. Cons. in field. Co-author: Mendes I, 1980; author, editor: The Surveillant Science, 2d edit., 1985. Staff sgt. USAF, 1951-55. Recipient Group Achievement award NASA, 1974, Urban Achievement award L.B.J. Sch. Pub. Affairs, 1984. Mem. Assn. Am. Geographers (chmn. remote sensing specialty group 1980-82, chmn. southwest div. 1971-72, medal for outstanding contbns. to remote sensing Remote Sensing Specialty Group 1998), Am. Soc. Photogrammetry, Tex. Assn. Coll. Tchrs., Am. Congress of Surveying and Mapping. Roman Catholic. Avocations: hunting, fishing, squash. Home: 2610 Fiset Dr Austin TX 78731-5614 Office: U Tex Dept Geography Austin TX 78712 Personal E-mail: holzrj@aol.com.

HOLZBACH, RAYMOND THOMAS, gastroenterologist, educator, writer; b. Salem, Ohio, Aug. 19, 1929; s. Raymond T. and Nelle A. (Conroy) H.; m. Lorraine E. Cozza, May 26, 1956; children: Ellen, Mark, James. BS, Georgetown U., 1951; MD, Case Western Res. U., 1955. Diplomate Nat. Bd. Med. Examiners, Am. Bd. Internal Medicine. Intern, asst. resident U. Ill. Research and Edn. Hosps., Chgo., 1955-56; sr. asst. resident medicine Cleve. Met. Gen. Hosp., 1959-60; asst. chief gastroenterology Case Western Res U., 1961-63; physician Gastroenterology Unit U. Hosps. of Cleve., 1961-63; instr. medicine Case Western Res. U. Sch. Medicine, Cleve., 1961-64, clin. instr. medicine, 1964-71; head gastrointestinal research unit, assoc. physician div. medicine St. Luke's Hosp., Cleve., 1967-73, dir. div. gastroenterology, 1970-73; head gastrointestinal research unit dept. medicine Cleve. Clinic Found., 1973—. Vis. prof. numerous instns. including Mayo Med. Sch., 1974, U. Calif., San Diego, 1977, U. Heidelberg, 1978, U. Pa., 1979, U. Zurich, 1980, U. Munich, 1982, U. Minn. Med. Ctr., 1985, med. ctrs., numerous Japanese univs., 1985, 92, Karolinska Inst., 1986, Royal Soc. London, 1987, Pa. State U. Sch. Med., U. Helsinki, RWTH-Aachen, Düsseldorf, Fed. Republic of Germany, U. Groningen, Utrecht, U. Amsterdam, The Netherlands, 1989, U. Perugia, Italy, Va. Commonwealth U.-Med. Coll. Va., Richmond, Christ Ch. Sch. Medicine, U. Otago, New Zealand, SUNY, Buffalo Sch. Medicine, 1990, Pontifical/Cath. U. Chile Sch. Medicine, 1991, Hiroshima U. Sch. Medicine, 1992, Kyoto U. Sch. Medicine, 1992, Sch. Medicine U. Jikei, Tokyo, 1992, Tel Aviv U., Israel Sch. Medicine, 1995, U. Leipzig, Germany, 1996, U. Heidelberg, Germany, 1996; lectr. in field. Mem. editl. bd. Gastroenterology jour., 1984-89; contbr. revs. and articles to med. jours. Served to capt. USAF, 1957-59. Recipient Alexander von Humboldt Found. Spl. Program award, 1978, 82. Fellow ACP; mem. ABA, Am. Gastroent. Assn. (rsch. com. 1976-79), Ctrl. Soc. Clin. Rsch., Am. Assn. for Study of Liver Diseases, AAAS, Am. Soc. Biol. Chemists, Am. Physiol. Assn., Biophys. Soc., Internat. Assn. Study of Liver, Am. Fedn. Clin. Rsch., Midwest Gut Club, Am. Soc. Clin. Nutrition, Ohio State Med. Assn., Sigma Xi. Unitarian Universalist. Home: 39251 Lander Rd Chagrin Falls OH 44022-2146 Office: Cleve Clin Found 9500 Euclid Ave Cleveland OH 44195-0001 Personal E-mail: tomholzbach@adelphia.net.

HOLZER, EDWIN, advertising executive; b. June 22, 1933; MusB, Yale U., 1954, MusM, 1955; postgrad., Ind. U., 1956. Acct. exec. Benton & Bowles Inc., N.Y.C., 1959-62; account supr. William Esty Co., N.Y.C., 1962-66, Grey Advt. Inc., N.Y.C., 1966-68, mgmt. supr., 1968-70; exec. v.p. Grey Inc., N.Y.C., 1970-73; pres., CEO, COO Grey-North Inc., Chgo., 1973-85; chmn., CEO, Grey Chgo. (name changed to LOIS/GGK 1988), 1988; chmn., CEO LOIS/EJL (formerly Lois/USA), Chgo., from 1988; chief marketing officer CornerDrugstore.com, 2000—.

HOLZER, HAROLD, public information officer, historian, writer; b. Bklyn., Feb. 5, 1949; s. Charles and Rose (Last) H.; m. Edith Spiegel, Feb. 27, 1971; children: Remy, Meg. BA, CUNY, Queens, 1969; diploma (hon.), Lincoln Meml. U., 1988, Lincoln Coll., 1992. Editor Manhattan Tribune, N.Y.C., 1969-73; dir. spl. projects Dept. Civic Affairs, City of N.Y., 1973-75; press sec. to Congresswoman Bella Abzug N.Y.C., 1975-77; communications specialist Sec. of State office, N.Y., 1978; dir. pub. affairs Sta. WNET (PBS), N.Y.C., 1978-84; v.p. pub. affairs Javits Conv. Ctr., N.Y.C., 1984-85; exec. v.p. pub. affairs Urban Devel. Corp., State of N.Y., 1985-92; chief comm. officer Met. Mus. Art, N.Y.C., 1992-96, v.p. comm., 1996-2001, v.p. comm. and mktg., 2001—05, sr. v.p. external affairs, 2005—. Co-author: The Lincoln Image, 1984, Changing the Lincoln Image, 1985, The Confederate Image, 1987, The Lincoln Family Album, 1990, Lincoln on Democracy, 1990, Mine Eyes Have Seen the Glory: The Civil War In Art, 1993, The Union Preserved, 1999, The Lincoln Forum, 1999, The Union Image, 2000; author: The Lincoln-Douglas Debates, 1993, Washington and Lincoln Portrayed, 1993, Dear Mr. Lincoln: Letters to the President, 1993, Witness to War: The Civil War, 1996, The Civil War Era, 1996; The Lincoln Mailbag: America Writes to the President, 1998, Lincoln As I Knew Him, 1999, Abraham Lincoln, The Writer, 2000, Lincoln Seen and Heard, 2000, Prang's Civil War, 2001, State of the Union, 2002; Rediscovering Abraham Lincoln: The Lincoln Forum, 2002, The President is Shot!, 2004, Lincoln at Cooper Union: The Speech that Made Abraham Lincoln President, 2004; contbr. over 350 articles on Lincoln and the Civil War to popular mags., scholarly jours. and newspapers; contbr. chpts. in books; columnist Antique Trader, 1985-95; contbg. editor: Americana Mag., 1991-93; writer various pamphlets on Abraham Lincoln; contbg. historian various CD-ROMS, TV spls. on C-SPAN, A&E, The History Channel, NBC, ABC, CBS, PBS. Lectr. on Lincoln and Civil War before various hist. groups; co-organizer 4 exhbns. on Lincoln and Civil War; trustee N.Y. State Archives Partnership Trust, 1994—; mem. U.S. Lincoln Bicentennial Commn. (appointed by Pres. Clinton), 2000, co-chmn., 2001--. Recipient Barondess/Lincoln award Civil War Round Table of N.Y., 1984, 91, 94, 2005, George Washington medal Freedom Found. Valley Forge, 1988, Writer of Distinction award Internat. Reading Assn., 1989, award Manuscript Soc. Am., 1996, Newman Book award Am. Hist. Print Collectors' Soc., 2000, Nevins-Freeman award, CWRT/Chgo., 2002 Mem. Abraham Lincoln Assn. (bd. dirs. 1988-95, Achievement award 1991, Lincoln prize, 2005), Lincoln Group of N.Y. (v.p. 1979-90, pres. 1990-96, Achievement award 1988, 93, 05), State Coun. for Humanities (bd. dirs. 1991-93), Ulysses S. Grant Assn. (bd. dirs. 1996—), The Lincoln Forum (vice chmn. 1996—). Office: Met Mus of Art 1000 Fifth Ave New York NY 10028-0113 E-mail: harold.holzer@metmuseum.org.

HOLZER, JENNY, artist; b. Gallipolis, Ohio, July 29, 1950; d. Richard Vornholt and Virginia (Beasley) H.; m. Michael Andrew Glier, May 21, 1984; 1 child. Student, Duke U., 1968-70, U. Chgo., 1970-71; BFA, Ohio U., 1973, DA (hon.), 1994; MFA, R.I. Sch. Design, 1977; postgrad., Whitney Mus. Am. Art, 1977; DFA (hon.), Williams Coll., 2000. One-woman shows include Rüdiger Schöttle Gall, Münich, 1980, Barbara Gladstone Gallery, NYC, 1983, 86, 94, Kunsthalle, Basel, Switzerland, 1984, Des Moines Art Ctr., 1986, MIT, Cambridge, 1986, Mus. Contemporary Art, Chgo., 1987, Inst. Contemporary Art, London, 1988, Bklyn. Mus., NYC, 1988, DIA Art Found., NYC, 1989, Guggenheim Mus., NYC, 1989, Am. Pavilion, 44th Biennale, Venice, Italy, 1990, La. Mus., Humlebaek, Denmark, 1991, Albright-Knox Art Gallery, Buffalo, 1991, Walker Art Gallery, Mpls., 1991, Ydessa Hendeles Art Found., Toronto, 1992, Dallas Mus. Art, 1993, Haus der Kunst, Munich, 1993, Bergen Mus. Art, Norway, 1994, Art Tower Mito, Japan, 1994, Williams Coll. Mus. Art, Williamstown, Mass., 1995, Kunstmus. des Kantons Thurgau, Kartouse Ittingen, Warth, Switzerland, 1996, Contemporary Art Mus., Houston, 1997, Cheim & Read, NY, 1997, Yvon Lambert Gallery, Paris, 1998, 2004, Inst. Cultural Itau, São Paulo, Brazil, 1998, Centro Cultural Banco do Brasil, Rio de Janeiro, 1999, BALTIC Ctr. Contemporary Art, Gateshead, 2000, Neue Nat. Galeri, Berlin, 2001, Mus. Contemporary Art, Bordeaux, France, 2001, Monterrey, Mex., 2001, Mönahehaus Mus., Goslar, Germany, 2002, Monika Spruth Philomerie Magers, 2002, 04, Kunsthaus Bregenz, Austria, 2004, N.Y.C., N.Y., 2005, others; exhibited in group shows at Documenta 7, Kassel, Germany, 1982, Contemporary Arts Ctr., Cin., 1984, Mus. Art Carnegie Inst., Pitts., 1985, Israel Mus., Jerusalem, 1986, Frankfurter Kunstverein, Frankfurt, Germany, 1986, Europa/Amerika Mus. Ludwig, Koln, 1986, Sonsbeck, Arnhem, The Netherlands, 1986, Whitney Mus. Am. Art, NYC, 1989, Mus. Contemporary Art, LA, 1989, Mus. Modern Art, NYC, 1988, 90, 96, Documenta 8, Kassel, 1987, Ctrl. Mus., Utrecht, The Netherlands, 1991, Kunsthalle, Basel, 1992, Guggenheim Mus., Soho, NYC, 1993, 96, Lenbachhaus, Munich, 1994, SITE Santa Fe, 1995, Pompidou Ctr., Paris, 1996, Biennale di Florence, Italy, 1996, Joseph Helman Gallery, NY, 1997, Kunsthalle Wien, Vienna, Austria, 1998, Nat. Gallery Australia, Canberra, 1998, Rhona Hofman Gallery, 1998, Oslo Mus. Contemporary Art, 2000; represented in permanent collections Ujazdowski Castle, Warsaw, Poland, Black Garden, Nordhorn, Germany, Erlauf (Austria) Peace Monument, Guggenheim Mus., Bilbao, Bundestag, Berlin, U. So. Calif., LA, Ludwig Mus., Aachen, Germany, Neue Nat. Galerie, Berlin, Toyota Mclpl. Mus. Art, Hamburg Kunstalie, US Fed. Courthouse, Sacramento, Allentown, Pa., Telenor Hdqr., Norway. Recipient Golden Lion award 44th Venice Biennale, 1990, Skowhegan medal for installation Skowhegan Sch. Painting and Sculpture, N.Y., 1994, Crystal award World Econ. Forum, Cologny-Geneva, Switzerland, 1996, BMW Art car, BMW, Munich, 1999, Kaiserring award City of Goslar, Germany, 2002. Fellow Am. Acad., Berlin, 2000. Avocation: reading. E-mail: studio@jennyholzer.com, gallery@cheimread.com.

HOLZER, LINDA RUTH, music educator, pianist; b. Chgo., Aug. 9, 1963; d. Robert and Ruth (Rechtoris) Holzer; life ptnr. Peggy Harstvedt. MusB, Northwestern U., 1985; MM, U. NC, 1987; MusD, Fla. State U., 1995. Artist-in-residence Wake Tech. CC, Raleigh, NC, 1988—90, Catawba Valley CC, Hickory, NC, 1990—92; asst. prof. of music U of Ark., 1995—2001, assoc. prof. of music, 2001—. Musician: (concerto soloist) Rachmaninoff Concerto #2; contbr. articles to profl. jours. (Article of Yr., Am. Music Tchr. Mag., 2003). Mem.: Internat. Alliance for Women in Music, Chamber Music Am., Coll. Music Soc., Music Teachers Nat. Assn., Pi Kappa Lambda. Office: UALR Music Dept 2801 S University Ave Little Rock AR 72204 Business E-Mail: lrholzer@ualr.edu.

HOLZER, MARC, public administrator educator; b. Feb. 28, 1945; s. Philip and Ann Lee (Blinder) H.; m. Madeleine Fuchs, Aug. 31, 1969; children: Matthew, Benjamin. BA in Polit. Sci., U. Rochester, 1966; MPA, U. Mich., 1967, PhD of Polit. Sci., 1971. Asst. prof. govt. and pub. adminstrn. John Jay Coll. CUNY, 1971-74, assoc. prof., 1975-79, prof., 1980-89; prof. I pub. adminstrn. Rutgers U., Newark, 1989—2002, prof. II pub. adminstrn., 2002—, chair grad. dept. pub. adminstrn., 2000—. Founder, exec. dir. Nat. Ctr. for Pub. Productivity, 1975—; founder, chmn. Internat. Productivity Network, 1988—; cons. internat. and fed. depts. agys., city, state and county agys.; dir. numerous funded projects in field; mem. Croton-Harmon Bd. Edn., 1984-87, pres. 1986-87; adv. acad. bd./bd. trustees Campus Arts & Scis., Athens. Author: (with others) Managing for Improved Productivity, 1981, (with Arie Halachmi) Public Sector Productivity, 1988, (with Virginia Cherry) Public Administration Research Guide, 1991, (with Kathe Callahan) Government at Work, 1998; editor: Productivity in Public Organizations, 1976, Public Productivity Handbook, 1991, (with K. Morris and W. Ludwin) Literature in Bureaucracy: Readings in Administrative Fiction, 1979, (with Ellen D. Rosen) Current Cases in Public Administration, 1981, (with Stuart Nagel) Productivity and Public Policy, 1984, (with Arie Halachmi) Strategic Issues in Public Sector Productivity, 1986, Competent Government, 1995, (with Vatche Gabrielian) Case Studies in Productive Public Management, 1995, (with Kathe Callahan and Joseph DeIorio) Reinventing New Jersey, 1995, Public Service: Callings, Commitments and Contributions, 2000, (with Byong-Joon Kim) Building Good Governance, 2002, (with Mengzhong Zhang) Chinese Public Administration in Exploration, 2002, Economic Globalization and Strategies of Chinese Public Administration, 2003, Piblic Productivity Handbook, 2d edit., 2004, Research Resources in Public Administration, 2005; founder, editor-in-chief Public Productivity and Mgmt. Rev., 1975—, Pub. Voices, 1994—, Chinese Pub. Adminstrn. Review, 2002—, ASPA Classics Series, 1997—, (with Jay Shafritz) Selections from the International Encyclopedia of Public Adminstration, 2001; assoc. editor Internat. Ency. Pub. Policy and Adminstrn.; assoc. editor Ency. of Pub. Adminstrn. and Pub. Policy, 2002; mem. editl. bd. Internat. Jour. Pub. Adminstrn., Pub. Adminstrn. Quar., Pub. Budgeting and Fin. Mgmt., The Pub. Mgr. (formerly The Bureaucrat), Jour. Non-Profit and Pub. Sector Mktg., Jour. Mgmt. History, Internat. Jour. Orgnl. Theory and Behavior, ASPA Classics, Internat. Rev. Pub. Adminstrn., Pub. Adminstrn. Rev., Pub. Adminstrn. and Mgmt.; contbr. numerous chpts. in books, articles to profl. jours. Founder, co-chairperson Pub. Adminstrn. Tchg. Roundtable, 1980—. Recipient Nat. Excellence in Tchg. award, Nat. Assn. Schs. Pub. Affairs & Adminstrn., 1998, Bd. Trustees award for Excellence in Rsch., Rutgers U., 2001, Southeastern Conf. Pub. Adminstrn. Sen. Peter Boorsma award, 2001, Bd. Trustees Pub. Svc. award, Rutgers U., 2002, Excellence award, Chinese Pub. Adminstrn. Soc., 2002, Human Dignity award, Rutgers U., 2004, Acad. award, Internat. City Mgmt. Assn., 2005; fellow Rockefeller Inst. Govt., 1986—87, World Acad. Productivity Sci., 2001—. Mem.: ASPA (chmn. nat. tng. com. 1981—82, 1983—84, nat. coun. 1982—85, chairperson mgmt. sci. sect 1981—82, 1989—90, pres. N.Y. Met. chpt. 1978—79, 0799—1980, chairperson sect. humanistic, artistic and reflective expression 1993—95, chair publs. com. 1993—94, nat. v.p. 1998—99, nat. pres.-elect 1999—2000, nat. pres. 2000—01, N.Y. Met. Outstanding Acad. award 1985, N.J. Outstanding Achievement award 1992, Donald C. Stone award 1994, Charles H. Levine award 2000, Mosher award Best Article (with Patricia Julnes) 2001, Wholey Disting. Scholarship award (with Patricia Julnes) 2001). Home: 4 Giglio Ct Croton On Hudson NY 10520-2005 Office: Rutgers U Hill Hall 7th Fl 360 King Blvd Newark NJ 07102-1801 E-mail: mholzer@rutgers.edu, mholzer@pipeline.com.

HOLZKAMP, JANE STRAUSS, business owner; b. Chgo., July 3, 1944; d. Joseph Loeb and Leanore (Purvin) Strauss; m. Muller Davis, Dec. 28, 1963 (div. July 1998); children: Melissa Muller, Muller Davis Jr., Joseph; m. Robert B. Holzkamp, Oct. 17, 1998. BA with honors in Am. Culture, Northwestern U., 1980, postgrad. studies in Am. History, 1980-81. With residential sales Kenneth Friend Realty, Winnetka, Ill., 1971-74, J.H. Kahn Realty, Glencoe, Ill., 1974-77; v.p. personal trust dept. Harris Trust & Savs. Bank, Chgo., 1983-89; v.p. Bankers Trust Co. Pvt. Bank, Chgo., 1989-90; founder Jane Davis Connections, Chgo., 1991—, Connections Next Step, 1993—, Young Chgo. Authors, 1992-95, Charlotte.Com, Inc., Chgo., 1996—. Founder Charlotte Com, Inc.; dir. Met. Family Svcs. Mem. woman's bd. Rush-Presbyn.-St. Luke's Med. Ctr., Chgo., 1978—; co-chmn. med. rsch. campaign Michael Reese Med. Ctr., Chgo., 1982-96; mem. costume com. Chgo. Hist. Soc., 1980-90; mem. campaign for gt. tchrs. Northwestern U., Evanston, Ill., 1988-90, mem. vis. com., 1989—, mem. coun. of 100; mem. Chgo. Symphony Orch. Woman's Assn., 1990-98; mem. coun. Children's Meml. Hosp. Med. Rsch. Inst., 1991-98; mem. Coun. of 100, The Chgo. Bd.; chmn. 50th anniversary day celebration Roosevelt U., Chgo., 1995, co-chmn. Itzhak Pearlman concert, 1996; mem. Tree of Life Min. Mission, 1996—, Leadership Broward Found. Class XVIII; mem. exec. steering com. Nova Southeastern U. Cir. of Friends, 1999-2001; bd. dirs. SOS Children's Village, Fla., 2000—, Bonnet House, Asbury Theol. Sem.; founder J and B Mktg. Connections, 2000. Methodist. E-mail: flgal650@aol.com.

HOLZMAN, D. KEITH, management consultant, record company executive, consultant; b. NYC, Mar. 22, 1936; s. Jacob Easton and Minnette Cathryn (Sternberger) H.; m. Jo Susan Handelman, Nov. 16, 1971; children: Susanne Carla, Lucas Jon, Rebecca Leigh. BA, Oberlin (Ohio) Coll., 1957; MFA, Boston U., 1959. Asst. to gen. mgr. and stage mgr. N.Y.C. Light Opera, 1959, 62-64; dir. prodn. Elektra Records, N.Y.C., 1964-70; v.p. prodn. and mfg. Elektra/Asylum/Nonesuch Records, Los Angeles, 1970-81, sr. v.p. prodn. and mfg., 1981-84; pres. ROM Records, 1987—2000; producer, arts cons. Treasure Trove, Inc., 1984—2000; mng. dir. Discovery Records, Santa Monica, Calif., 1991-98; prin. Keith Holzman Solutions Unltd., 1998—. Pres. Treasure Trove Inc.; dir. Nonesuch Records, 1980-84; music supr. Witches of Eastwick, Warner Bros., LA, 1986; bd. dirs. Plumstead Theatre Soc., LA, 1985—, Early Music Acad., LA, 1983-86, Assn. Classical Music, NYC, 1983-86, Wizard Music. Author: The Complete Guide to Starting a Record Company, 2004. Served with AUS, 1960-62. Mem. Audio Engring. Soc., Early Music Acad. (bd. dirs.) Nat. Acad. Rec. Arts and Scis., Assn. Classical Music (bd. dirs.), Plumstead Theatre Co. (bd. dirs.). Avocation: flying.

HOLZMAN, JAMES L(OUIS), lawyer; b. Bklyn., Jan. 7, 1949; s. Robert Conrad and Muriel Claire (Smith) H.; m. Jonnie Irene Frisbie; children: James Casey, Meredith Claire, Jon Carroll. BA, John B. Stetson U., 1970; JD, U. Fla., 1972. Bar: Fla. 1973, Del. 1973, U.S. Dist. Ct. Del. 1974, U.S. Dist. Ct. (so. dist.) Fla 1973, U.S. Tax Ct. 1973, U.S. Ct. Appeals (3d.cir.) 1976, U.S. Ct. Appeals (fed. cir.) 1983, U.S. Ct. Appeals (2d cir.) 2001, U.S. Supreme Ct. 2002. Assoc. Prickett, Ward, Burt & Sanders, Wilmington, Del., 1973-77, ptnr., 1977-79, Prickett, Jones, Elliott, Kristol & Schnee, Wilmington, Del., 1979—, mng. ptnr., 1986-90. Author Rev. Devel. Corp. Law. Mem. ABA (sect. bus. law, chair revenue com. 2001—, chair bus. and corp. litigation com. 1996-2000, chair coun. fin. com. 2004-05, section liaison, presdl. task force on atty. client privilege, co-chair judge's task force, mem. task force litigation reform and rules revision, mem. corp. governance com., mem. editl. bd. The Bus. Lawyer), Del. State Bar Assn. (mem. corp. law sect. coun. 1998—), Assn. of Bar of City of N.Y., Fla. Bar, Fed. Bar Assn., Wilmington Club (trusteeTower Hill Sch., pres. 2000-03). Home: 3213 Fordham Rd Wilmington DE 19807-3117 Office: Prickett Jones & Elliott 1310 N King St Wilmington DE 19801-3220 Office Phone: 302-888-6509.

HOLZMAN, ROBERT STEPHEN, physician; b. N.Y.C., Apr. 13, 1940; s. Stanford and Shiffie (Mirkin) H.; m. Clare Gottfried, June 30, 1963; children; Daniel, Diane. BA, Rutgers U., 1961; MD, Johns Hopkins U., 1965. Intern NYU Med. Ctr., N.Y.C., 1965-66, resident, 1968-70, fellowship, 1970-73; asst. hosp. epidemiologist Bellevue Hosp., N.Y.C., 1973-80; asst. prof. NYU

Sch. Medicine, 1973—80; hosp. epidemiologist Bellevue Hosp., N.Y.C., 1980—, assoc. prof., 1980—2000, prof. medicine and environ. medicine, 2000—, acting chief divsn. immunology and infectious diseases, 2000—02. Treas. Com. for the Promotion of Med. Rsch., N.Y.C., 1980—. Contbr. over 100 articles to profl. jours. Sr. asst. surgeon USPHS, 1966-68. Fellow ACP. Office: NYU Med Ctr 550 1st Ave New York NY 10016-6497 Office Phone: 212-263-6402.

HOLZNER, BURKART, sociologist, educator; b. Tilsit, Germany, Apr. 28, 1931; came to U.S., 1957, naturalized, 1965; s. Hans Otto and Brigitte (Prenzel) H.; children by previous marriage: Steven, Daniel, Claire; m. Leslie Salmon-Cox; stepchildren: Sara Ruth Salmon-Cox, Weir Becket Strange. Student, U. Munich, 1949—52, U. Wis., 1952—53, postgrad., 1967—69; student, U. Munich, 1953—54; Diploma Psychology, U. Bonn, 1957, Dr.Phil., 1958. Grad. asst., acting instr. U. Wis., 1958—60; asst. prof. U. Pitts., 1960—63, assoc. prof., 1963—65, prof., chmn. sociology dept., 1966—80, dir. bd. visitors field staff Learning R&D Ctr., 1964—66, 1971—78, dir. Univ. Ctr. for Internat. Studies, 1980—2000, prof. Univ. Ctr. for Internat. Studies, 1998—, disting. svc. prof. internat. studies, 1999—2003, sr. rsch. assoc., prof. emeritus, 2003—. Assoc. sociologist, assoc. dir. Social Sci. Rsch. Inst., U. Hawaii, 1965-66; vis. prof. sociology, dir. Social Rsch. Centre, Chinese U. of Hong Kong, 1969-70, external examiner in sociology, 1995-98; vis. prof. U. Augsburg, 1977, Chinese Acad. Social Scis., Beijing, 1979, 80; cons. Nat. Inst. Edn., Westinghouse Electric Corp.; mem. exec. com. Pa. Coun. for Internat. Edn., 1980-89, chmn., 1980-83, 88-89. Author: Amerikanische und deutsche Psychologie, 1958, Völkerpsychologie, 1960, Reality Construction in Society, rev. edit, 1972, (with John Marx) Knowledge Application: The Knowledge System in Society, 1979; editor: (with Roland Robertson) Identity and Authority, Explorations in the Theory of Society, 1980, (with Jiri Nehnevajsa) Organizing for Social Research, 1981, (with Zdenek Suda) Directions of Change: Modernization Theory, Research and Reality, 1981, (with Andrew Dinniman) Education for International Competence in Pennsylvania, 1988; co-editor Knowledge: Creation, Distribution, Utilization, 1985, Knowledge in Society, 1987-89. Mem. dist. export council U.S. Dept. Commerce. Recipient Philip R.A. May award for internat. svc., 1991; named hon. citizen of Johnstown, Pa., hon. mem. U. Augsburg, 1990. Mem. Am. Sociol. Assn., North Central Sociol. Assn., Pa. Sociol. Assn., Sociol. Rsch. Assn., Sozialwissenschaftlicher Studienkreis für Internationale Probleme, Internat. Soc. for Comparative Study of Civilizations (mem. U.S. coun., v.p. 1977-79), Assn. Internat. Edn. Adminstrs. (exec. com. 1986—, pres. 1990-91, Charles Klasek award for career achievement in internat. edn. 2000, sr. counselor 2001—), World Federalist Assn. Pitts. (pres. 1996-2001). Home: 1700 Grandview Ave Apt 801 Pittsburgh PA 15211-1006 Office: U Pitts Dept Sociology Univ Ctr Internat Studies 4116 Posvar Hall Pittsburgh PA 15260 E-mail: holzner@ucis.pitt.edu.

HOLZWORTH, DONALD A., lab administrator; BS in Sys. Analysis, MS in Environ. sci., Miami U., Oxford, Ohio; grad. tng. in Biostats., N.C. State U. Biostatistician Battelle Meml. Inst., Washington, 1977—81, prin. rsch. scientist, 1981; v.p. Program Resources, Inc., 1981—83; gen. mgr. DynCorp, 1990—91; co-founder, dir. Constella Group, 1983—91, exec. v.p., 1991—95, owner, pres., CEO, 1995—. Co-founder, inaugural CEO Expression Analysis, Inc., chmn., bd. dirs. Finalist Entrepreneur of Yr., Ernst & Young. Office: Constella Group Inc 2605 Meridian Pkwy Durham NC 27713

HOM, DAVID BRIAN, surgeon; b. San Diego, 1956; s. James and Evelyn Hom; m. Lorraine Hom, 1984. BA summa cum laude, U. Calif., San Diego, 1978; MD, UCLA, 1982. Diplomate Am. Bd. Otolaryngology and Facial Plastic and Reconstructive Surgery. Gen. surg. resident U. Calif., Irvine, 1983-84; otolaryngology, head and neck surgery resident U. Mich., Ann Arbor, 1984-88; facial plastic fellow Am. Acad. Facial Plastic Surgery, Birmingham, Ala., 1988-89; asst. prof. dept. otolaryngology, head and neck surgery U. Minn., Mpls., 1989-96, assoc. prof., 1996—. Mem. otolaryngology expert adv. panel U.S. Pharmacopia Conv., Washington, 1994—; bd. dirs. Am. Bd. Facial Plastic and Reconstructive Surgery. Editor: Wound Healing for the Otolaryngologist-Head and Neck Surgeon, 1995; contbr. numerous articles to profl. jours., chpts. to books. Med. cons. NCAA, Mpls., 1996-97. NIH Rsch. grantee, 1996-2002. Fellow ACS, Am. Acad. Otolaryngology, Head and Neck Surgery (Nat. Percy Meml. Rsch. award 1991), Am. Acad. Facial Plastic and Reconstructive Surgery (chmn. rsch. 1997-2000, bd. dirs. 2005—, Nat. Ben Shuster Rsch. award 1988); mem. AAAS, Minn. Acad. Otolaryngology-Head and Neck Surgery (pres. 2005). Avocations: fishing, kayaking. Office: Univ Minn Dept Otolaryngology Box 396 420 Delaware St SE Minneapolis MN 55455

HOMAN, J. MICHAEL, library administrator; b. Portland, Oreg., Aug. 16, 1947; s. Gerald B. and Beverly J. Homan. BA, Lewis and Clark Coll., 1969; MA, U. Chgo., 1971; cert. advanced study, UCLA, 1972. MEDLARS analyst UCLA, 1972-74, head info. svcs., 1974-79, Upjohn Co., Kalamazoo, Mich., 1979-88; asst. univ. libr. scis. U. Calif., Irvine, 1988-94; dir. libs. Mayo Found./Mayo Clinic, Rochester, Minn., 1994—. Author: (book chpts.) Management of Scientific and Technical Libraries, 1986, Introduction to Reference Sources in the Health Sciences, 1984. USPHS fellow U. Chgo., 1969-71, UCLA, 1971-72. Mem. ALA, Med. Libr. Assn. (pres. 2000-01, bd. dirs. 1987-89, editor jour. 1996-2000, mng. editor of books 1990-96), Assn. Acad. Health Sci. Libr. Dirs. (bd. dirs. 1991-94, pres. 2001-2005), Spl. Librs. Assn., Am. Med. Informatics Assn., Coalition for Networked Info. (rep.), Assn. Coll. and Rsch. Librs., Libr. Adminstrn. and Mgmt. Assn. Episcopalian. Avocations: music, opera, travel, reading. Office: Mayo Clinic Mayo Med Libr 200 1st St SW Rochester MN 55905-0002 E-mail: homan@mayo.edu.

HOMAN, MICHELE ANNETTE, language educator; b. Coldwater, Ohio, Aug. 15, 1967; d. Ronald F. and Maryann P. Homan. BA in Bilingual Multi-cultural Elem. Edn., U. Findlay, Findlay, Ohio, 1990; MA in Reading, Western Mich. U., Kalamazoo, Mich., 2000. Bilingual-ESL kindergarden-2d grade tchr. Mars Elem. Sch., Berrien Springs (Mich.) Pub. Schs., 1992—. Mem.: MABE (Mich. Assn. for Bilingual Edn.), MEA (Mich. Edn. Assn.), BSEA Berrien Springs Edn. Assn. (treas. 1994—2005). Avocations: singing, horseback riding, rubber stamping, walking. Home: 406 South Main St Berrien Springs MI 49103 Office: Berrien Springs Pub Schs - Mars One Sylvester Ave Berrien Springs MI 49103 Office Phone: 269-471-1836. Personal E-mail: mhoman@remc11.k12.mi.us.

HOMAN, RALPH WILLIAM, finance company executive; b. Wilkes-Barre, Pa., June 7, 1951; s. Norman Ryan and Adelaide Bernice (Sandy) H.; m. Donna Marie Webb, Jan. 25, 1975. BS in Acctg., Wheeling Coll., 1977; MBA in Mktg., Nat. U., 1986. Paymaster Dravo Corp., Pitts., 1974-75; tax preparer H&R Block, Wheeling, W.Va., 1977; fin. services exec. NCR Credit Corp., Sacramento, 1977-84; leasing exec. CSB Leasing, Sacramento, 1984-85; pres. Convergent Fin. Svcs., Colorado Springs, Colo., 1985—. Bd. dirs. Concord Coalition, Colorado Springs. Cons. Jr. Achievement, 1990—. Co-winner Name the Plane Contest Pacific Southwest Airlines, 1984; recipient Businessperson of Yr. award, Colo. Springs chpt. Future Bus. Leaders Am., 1995, 2000. Mem. The 30/40 Something Social Club (founder, pres. Sedona chpt.), Am. Assn. Boomers (pres. Pikes Peak chpt. 1992-93), Toastmasters (treas. Oak Creek chpt. 1988-89), Kiwanis (sec. 1988-89, founder, chmn. adult soccer league), Concord Coalition (bd. dirs., pres. Colorado Springs chpt.). Avocations: photography, camping, off-road motorcycling, woodworking. Home and Office: Convergent Fin Svcs 29 Mount Hope Dr Twin Lakes CO 81251-9705 Office Phone: 800-338-5999. Business E-mail: cfssolutions@earthlink.net.

HOMBURGER, THOMAS CHARLES, lawyer; b. Buffalo, Sept. 16, 1941; s. Adolf and Charolotte E. (Stern) H.; m. Louise Paula Shemin, June 6, 1965; children: Jennifer Anne, Richard Ephraim, Kathryn Lee. BA, Columbia U., 1963, JD, 1966. Bar: Ill. 1966, U.S. Dist. Ct. (no. dist.) Ill. 1966. Assoc., ptnr. Sonnenschein, Carlin, Nath & Rosenthal, Chgo., 1966—86, Bell, Boyd & Lloyd LLC, Chgo., 1986—. Chmn. real estate John Marshall Law Sch., Chgo., 1986—2003, adj. prof., 1989—. Contbr. articles to profl. jours. Chmn. Chgo. regional bd. Anti-Defamation League, B'nai Brith, 1986-88; chmn. nat. exec. com. Anti-Defamation League, 2000-2003; pres. Anti-Defamation League Found., 2003—; mem. Glencoe (Ill.) Bd. Edn., 1984-89. Mem.: ABA (real property divsn., probate & trust law sect., fin. subcom.), Chgo. Mortgage Attys. Assn. (pres. 1975—77), Am. Coll. Real Estate Lawyers (bd. govs. 2000—03), Chgo. Bar Assn. (chmn. real property law com. 1984—85), Ill. Bar Assn. (real property sect.), Std. Club, Law Club Chgo., Lambda Alpha Internat. Home: 20 East Cedar St Apt 2F Chicago IL 60611-1149 Office: Bell Boyd & Lloyd 70 W Madison St Ste 3100 Chicago IL 60602-4284 Office Phone: 312-807-4267. E-mail: tc@homburger.cnchost.com, thomburger@bellboyd.com.

HOMER, WILLIAM INNES, art history educator, art expert, writer; b. Merion, Pa., Nov. 8, 1929; s. Austin and Evelyn (Innes) H.; 1 child, Stacy Innes; m. Christine D. Hyer, Aug. 24, 1986. AB, Princeton U., 1951; postgrad., N.Y.U., 1952-53; MA, Harvard U., 1954; PhD, 1961. Instr. dept. art and archeology Princeton (NJ) U., 1955-59, lectr., 1959-61, asst. prof., 1961-64; assoc. prof. history of art Cornell U., 1964-66; prof. U. Del., Newark, 1966-99, chmn. dept. art history, 1966-81, 86-93; dir. index of dissertations and theses in Am. art Archives of Am. Art, Washington; vis. fellow Princeton U., 1972-73; assoc. fellow Ctr. for Advanced Studies, Nat. Gallery of Art, 1980-81. Mem. Del. Arts Coun., 1969-70, New Castle County Beautification Bd., 1967-70; adv. screening com. (overseas) Fulbright-Hays Fellowship Awards, 1970-72, chmn., 1971-72; mem. sr. fellowship panel Nat. Endowment for Humanities, 1970; mem. exhbn. com. Del. Art Mus., 1968-73, chmn. accessions com., 1974-78 Author: Seurat and the Science of Painting, 1964, Robert Henri and His Circle, 1969, Alfred Stieglitz and the American Avant-Garde, 1977, The Photographs of Gertrude Käsebier, 1979, Alfred Stieglitz and the Photo-Secession, 1983, Pictorial Photography in Philadelphia, 1984; co-author Albert Pinkham Ryder: Painter of Dreams, 1989, Thomas Eakins, His Life and Art, 1992, The Language of Contemporary Criticism Clarified, 1999, Stieglitz and the Photo-Secession, 1902, 2002; mem. editl. bd. Am. Art Jour., 1970—, Winterthur Portfolio, 1978-80; sr. editor Am Art Rev., 1992—. Mem. adv. com. Am. Studies Inst., Lincoln U., 1967-76; mem. corp. Mus. Am. Art, Ogunquit, Maine, 1958-92; regional adv. com. Archives Am. Art, 1979—; trustee Am. Friends Nat. Portrait Gallery, London, 1995—, Sewell C. Biggs Mus. Am. Art, 1994-97; bd. dirs. Ctr. Advanced Studies in Visual Arts Nat. Gallery Art, 1994-98. Coun. of Humanities fellow Princeton U., 1962-63; Am. Coun. Learned Socs. fellow, 1964-65; Guggenheim fellow, 1972-73; Nat. Endowment for Humanities fellow, 1980-81; Ctr. for Advanced Study U. Del. fellow, 1985-86 Fellow Royal Soc. Arts (London), New Pictorialist Soc. (dir. 1981—); mem. Coll. Art Assn. Am., Pictorial Photographers Am., Royal Photog. Soc., Welcome Soc. of Pa., Princeton Club (N.Y.C.), Nat. Arts Club, Cosmos Club, Phi Kappa Phi. Home: PO Box 4195 Greenville DE 19807 Office: U Del Dept Art History Newark DE 19716

HOMESTEAD, SUSAN E. (SUSAN FREEDLENDER), psychotherapist; b. Bklyn., Sept. 20, 1937; d. Cy Simon and Katherine (Haas) Eichelbaum; m. Robert Bruce Randall, 1956 (div. 1960); 1 child, Bruce David; m. George Gilbert Zanetti, Dec. 13, 1962 (div. 1972); m. Ronald Eric Homestead, Jan. 16, 1973 (div. 1980); m. Arthur Elliot Freedlender, Apr. 1, 1995. BA, U. Miami-Fla., 1960; MSW, Tulane U., 1967. Diplomate Am. Bd. Clin. Social Work; Acad. Cert. Social Workers, 1971, LCSW, Va., Calif. Psychotherapist, cons., Richmond, Va., 1971—, Los Altos, Calif.; pvt. practice Homestead Counseling, Richmond, Piedmont Psychiatric Ctr., P.C. (formerly Psychol. Evaluation Rehab. Cons., Inc.), Lynchburg, Va., 1994-97; cons. Family and Children's Svcs., Richmond, 1981—, Richmond Pain Clinic, 1983-84, Health Internat. Va., P.C., Lynchburg, 1984-86, Franklin St. Psychotherapy & Edn. Ctr., Santa Clara, Calif., 1988-90; pvt. practice, 1971—, Santa Clara County Children's Svc., 1973-75, 86-88. Co-dir. asthma program Va. Lung Assn., Richmond, 1975-79, Loma Prieta Regional Ctr.; chief clin. social worker Med. Coll. Va., Va. Commonwealth U., 1974-79; field supr. 1980 Census, 1981-87. Contbr. articles to profl. jours. Active Peninsula Children's Ctr., Morgan Ctr., Coun. Cmty. Action Planning, Cmty. Assn. for Retarded, Comprehensive Health Planning Assn. Santa Clara, Mental Health Commn., Children and Adolscent Target Group Calif., Women's Com. Richmond Symphony, Va. Mus. theatre; mem. adv. com. Va. Lung Assn.; mem. steering com. Am. Cancer Soc.(Va. divsn.), Epilepsy Found., Am. Heart Assn. (Va. divsn.), Ctrl. Va. Guild for Infant Survival; mem. fin. com. Robb for Gov. Mem. NASW, Va. Soc. Clin. Social Work, Inc. (charter mem., sec. 1975-78), Internat. Soc. Communicative Psychoanalysis & Psychotherapy, Am. Acad. Psychotherapists, Internat. Soc. for the Study of Dissociation, Am. Assn. Psychiatric Svcs. for Children. Fax: 650-965-7301. E-mail: SueEF@aol.com.

HOMMEL, KEVIN ARTHUR, psychologist; b. Washington, June 22, 1974; s. William L. and Barbara E. Hommel. BA, U. Ctrl. Okla.; PhD, Okla. State U., Stillwater, 2002. Clin. psychologist Cin. Children's Hosp. Med. Ctr., 2001—04, The Children's Hosp. Phila., 2004—. Contbr. articles to profl. jours. Leadership scholar, Psi Chi, 1997. Mem.: APA, Soc. Pediat. Psychology (Rsch. award 2002).

HOMMO, HARUMI, accountant; b. Kameda-machi, Niigata, Japan; came to U.S., 1990; BA, Tokyo U., 1980; MS in acct., Pace U., 1995. CPA. Sr. translator Goldman Sachs, Tokyo, 1985-86, Nat. West County Securities, Tokyo, 1986-89, Morgan Stanley, Tokyo, 1989-90, Daiwa Inst. Rsch., N.Y.C., 1990-97; acct. Ernst & Young, N.Y.C., 1998, Arthur Andersen LLP, N.Y.C., 1999; tax acct. Indsl. Bank Japan, N.Y.C., 2000—01; prin., owner HH Fin. Svcs., N.Y.C., 2002—. Mem. Am. Translators Assn. Avocations: readings, movies, travel, music, light sports. Home: 280 Park Ave S Apt 11D New York NY 10010-6130 Office Phone: 212-748-9133.

HOMSLEY, DENISE LOUISE, music educator; b. Nampa, Idaho, Sept. 9, 1949; d. Lewis Griffith and Eileen Innes Davis; m. Jon Mark Homsley, June 23, 2001; m. David Karl Stoehr, Sept. 12, 1969 (div. Jan. 4, 1982); children: Melissa Dawn (Stoehr) Joseph, Justen David Stoehr Blackburn, Regan Karl Stoehr. BA in Music, Boise State Coll., 1972. Nat. Cert. Tchr. Music Music Tchrs. Nat. Assn., 2003. Music tchr. Ind., Boise, Idaho, 1966—75; owner, operator Stoehr Orchards, Wilder, Idaho, 1982—85; receptionist Farm Bur. Ins., Nampa, Idaho, 1997—99, Ackerley Outdoor Advt., Portland, 1999—2002; music tchr. Denise Homsley Piano Studio, Portland, 1999—2003, Jacksonville, Fla., 2003—05, 2005—; dir. Bravo! Music Camp, 2004—. Hotline referral admintr. Oreg. Music Tchrs. Assn., Portland, 2001—03. Children's leader Bible Study Fellowship, Caldwell, Idaho, 1992—99; pianist Happy Valley Bapt. Ch., Portland, 2001—03, adjudicator, 2005—. Mem.: Jacksonville Music Tchrs. Assn. (bd. cmty. svc. 2004, co-chair Multi-Piano Festival 2005, v.p. 2005), Fla. State Music Tchrs. Assn., Nat. Fedn. of Music Clubs, Music Tchrs. Nat. Assn. Evangelical Free. Avocations: travel, gourmet cooking, couture sewing. Home and Studio: 12546 SE Blackstone Ave Clackamas OR 97015 Office Phone: 503-223-0499. Business E-Mail: dh88redrose@aol.com.

HON, JOHN WINGSUN, physician; b. Canton, China, Aug. 21, 1947; s. Yuen-Pak and Yuk-Ying (Zhang) Hon. BA, Hunter Coll., 1972; MA, SUNY, Buffalo, 1975; DO, Kirksville Coll. Medicine, 1979. Diplomate Am. Bd. Emergency Physicians, bd. cert. emergency medicine and family practice. Enlisted U.S. Army, 1975, advanced through grades to capt., 1979; intern, resident Tripler Army Med. Ctr., Honolulu, 1979-80; gen. med. officer U.S. Army Med. Corps, Honolulu, 1979-80; intern Tripler Army Med. Ctr., Honolulu, 1979-80; gen. med. officer U.S. Army Med. Corps, Korea, Republic of Korea, 1980-81, U.S. Mil. Acad., West Point, 1981-83; attending physician Woodhull Hosp., Bklyn., 1983-86; pvt. practice Woodside, NY, 1983—2002, Elmhurst, NY, 1993—, Flushing, NY, 2002—. Attending physician Bronx Lebanon Hosp., 1987—91, Mt. Sinai Hosp., Queens, 1983—, St. John Hosp., Elmhurst, NY, 1992—, N.Y. Hosp. Dept. Medicine, 1996, Elmhurst Hosp., 1999—; clin. asst. prof. family practice N.Y. Med. Coll. Fellow: Am. Coll. Emergency Physicians; mem.: N.Y. State Osteo. Med. Soc., Chinese Am. Med. Soc. (life), Am. Osteo. Assn. Avocation: photography. Home: 10 West St Apt 33A New York NY 10004 Office: 132-07 41st Rd Flushing NY 11355 also: 86-08 Elmhurst Ave Elmhurst NY 11373 E-mail: hon8song@yahoo.com.

HONAMAN, J. CRAIG, health facility administrator; b. Montclair, N.J., June 15, 1943; s. Richard Karl and Gloria (McElwain) H.; m. Dee Dee Toerpe, Dec. 31, 1971; children: Justin Craig Jr., Garman Grayson. BS, N.C. State U., 1965; MS, U. Ala., Birmingham, 1971. Sr. v.p. Bapt. Hosp., Pensacola, Fla., 1970-79; exec. v.p. Tallahassee (Fla.) Meml. Hosp., 1979-89; adminstr. Quorum Health Resources/Leesburg (Fla.) Regional Med. Ctr., 1989-91; v.p., adminstrn. home health care Meth. Med. Ctr., Jacksonville, Fla., 1991-92; pres. Kellogg Healthcare, Inc., Jacksonville, 1992-93, KNH Healthcare, Jacksonville, 1993-95; exec. dir. HomeCare Alliance of Ga., Inc., Atlanta, 1994-98; sr. v.p. Haney & Assocs., Atlanta, 1998—2001; prin. H&H Cons. Ptnrs., LLC, Atlanta, 2001—. Cons. in field, Atlanta, Ga., 1991—. Contbr. articles to profl. jours. Active Boy Scouts Am., ARC, Am. Cancer Soc., Ronald McDonald House. Capt. U.S. Army, 1966-69, Vietnam. Recipient Nat. Golden Hour award MBB Helicopter, 1988, Pub. Benefit Flying award Nat. Aeronautic Assn., 2004. Fellow Am. Coll. Healthcare Execs. (cert. health care mgr.; regent for north Ga.), Rotary. Methodist. Avocations: golf, running. Office: H&H Cons Ptnrs LLC 560 Cambridge Way NE Ste 101 Atlanta GA 30328-1007 Personal E-mail: Careerdir1@aol.com.

HONAN, MAUREEN ANN, special education educator; b. New Haven, Conn., July 12, 1954; d. Timothy and Mary Honan. BA, St. Joseph Coll., West Hartford, Conn., 1976; MS, So. Conn. State Coll., 1979. Spl. edn. and elem. tchg. cert. Conn., edn. leadership cert. Conn. 5th grade tchr. Region 15-Rochambeau Sch., Southbury, Conn., 1976—79; spl. edn. tchr. Region 15-Pomperaug H.S., Southbury, Conn., 1979—2002, spl. edn. resource tchr. and 504 coord., 2002—. Mem. evaluation com. Region 15, Southbury, 1978—, profl. devel., 1978—; co-chair stds. com. Pomperaug H.S., Southbury, 2002—; evaluator New Eng. Assn. Schs. and Colls., Bedford, Mass., 1985—2000. Author: A Teacher's Guide to Performance-Based Learning and Assessment. Vol. Columbus Ho., New Haven, 2000—05; mem. substance abuse task force Conn. Edn. Assn., Hartford, 2000—05, dir. NEA, 2005—, New Haven County dir., 1999—2005, sec., 2000—04; Conn. dir. NEA, Washington, 2005—. Recipient Susan Rogers award, Pomperaug H.S., 1980, 1988, Michael's Jewelers award, 1990. Mem.: ASCD, Pomperaug Edn. Assn. (sec. 1981—2005), Phi Delta Kappa (sec. 2003—). Home: 1230 Ridge Rd North Haven CT 06473-4408 Office: Pomperaug HS 234 Judd Rd Southbury CT 06488 Office Phone: 203-262-3236. Office Fax: 203-262-6806. Personal E-mail: maureenh@att.net. E-mail: mhonan@region15.org.

HONDA, MICHAEL M., congressman; b. Walnut Creek, Calif., June 27, 1941; m. Jeanne (dec. 2004); children: Mark, Michelle. BS in Biol. Sci., San Jose St. Univ., 1970, BA in Spanish, MA in Edn., San Jose St. Univ., 1973. Sci. tchr., Sunnyvale; prin. pub. sch.; mem. San Jose Planning Commn., 1971—81, San Jose Unified Sch. Bd., 1981—89, Santa Clara County Bd. of Supervisors, 1990—96, Calif. Assembly, 1997—2000, US Congress from 15th Calif. dist., 2001—. Conducted ednl. rsch. at Stanford; elected Reg. Whip, vice chair Congl. Asian Pac. Am. Caucus, Transp. com., Sci. com. Congress, Calif. 15th dist. Mem. edn. com. Calif. Assembly. Served Peace Corps, 1965-67. Named High Tech Legislator Yr., Am. Electronics Assn. Democrat. Office: 1713 Longworth House Office Bldg Washington DC 20515-0515*

HONEA, FLOYD FRANKLIN, lawyer; b. Dallas, May 20, 1950; s. Floyd Franklin and Gloria Anne H. BS, North Tex. State U., 1973; JD, U. Tex., 1976. Bar: Tex. 1976, U.S. Supreme Ct., U.S. Ct. Appeals (5th and 10th cirs.), U.S. Ct. Claims, U.S. Dist. Ct. (no., ea. and we. dists.) Tex. Ptnr. Payne & Vendig, Dallas, 1976-97; shareholder Winstead Sechrist & Minick, P.C., Dallas, 1997—. Mem. Dallas Hist. Soc., 1978—; mem. Rep. Nat. Com. Rep. party Tex., 1979—; Keeton fellow, mem. dean's coun. U. Tex. Sch. Law; active Dallas Zool. Soc., 1986—, Dallas Symphony Assn.; sponsor Kimbell Art Mus., Smithsonian Inst., WMS Civic Trust, Dallas Mus. Art. Mem. ABA, State Bar Tex., Dallas Bar Assn., The 500, Inc., Crescent Club Dallas. Baptist. Home: 8865 Flint Falls Dr Dallas TX 75243-7542 Office: 5400 Republic Nat Bank Towe Dallas TX 75201

HONEGGER, FEDERICO, artist; b. Milan, Sept. 11, 1926; s. Carlo and Maria Antonia (Casiraghi) H.; m. Lucia Serafina Carminati, Apr. 30, 1959; children: Carlo, Marco, Andrea, Anna. Baccalaureat, Coll. St. Michel, 1945; law degree, Cath. U., 1952. Textile practice Vereinigte Seidenwebereien AG, Krefeld, Germany, 1950-51; with Gaspare Honegger, Milan, Italy, 1946-59; buying mgr. Carminati Industrie Tessili SpA, Milan, 1960-82. Author: The Digital Outlook, 1984, (art project) The Ke'nosis Project, 1986 (award), Jacobs Ladder, 1989, The Eye of the Needle, 1992, Portraits, 1992, Cromatic Alphabets, 1993, Constellations, 1993, Adam's Rib, 1994, Metaphysical Alphabets, 1994, The Signs-Number of Image, 1996, The Universe of Fragments, 1996, The Profecy of Ezechiele, 1998, God All in Everybody, 1999, Soul and Body, 1999, El Shadday-The Primary Numbers, 1999, The Background, Place of Dialogue Between Thou (two) and Innumerable, 2000, Your Voice, My Voice, Our Voice: The Wise Men and the Star, 2000, From One to Two and From I to Thou, 2000, Glory, Grace and Liberty, 2001, Equal and One, 2002, Straight and Curved, 2002, Reasoned Catalogue of Works, Art Projects and Form from 1975 to 2003, 2004, The Lord Said Unto My Lord (PS. 107-108)- Birth of Heavens, 2005. Recipient Silver Palette City of Milan, 1979, Top 70 Winner Art '95 N.Y. Internat. Competition, 1995. Mem. Symbolicum Art Group (co-founder). Home and Office: Via Annunciata 23/2 20121 Milan Italy Office Phone: 0039-02-6597056. Office Fax: 0039-02-6590687. E-mail: federico.honegger@fastwebnet.it.

HONEMANN, DANIEL HENRY, lawyer; b. Balt., Oct. 20, 1929; s. Henry Letcher and Maude Elizabeth (Wilson) H.; m. Rose Ann Clark, Mar. 23, 1974; children by previous marriage: Deborah, Dori, Daniel, Donna. AB, Western Md. Coll., Westminster, 1951; JD, U. Md., 1956. Bar: Md. 1956. Practice law, Balt.; partner firm Clapp, Somerville, Honemann & Beach, 1962-85, Whiteford, Taylor & Preston, 1986—; asst. U.S. atty. Dist. Md., 1960-61. Author: (with others) Robert's Rules of Order Newly Revised, 10th edit. Served to 1st lt. inf. AUS, 1951-53. Decorated Bronze Star, Combat Inf. badge. Fellow Am. Coll. Trust and Estate Counsel, Md. Bar Found.; mem. ABA (ho. of dels. 1978-80), Md. Bar Assn. (sec. 1977-84, bd. govs. 1975-84), Balt. Bar Assn. Home: 2318 Harcroft Rd Lutherville Timonium MD 21093-2638 Office: 7 Saint Paul St Ste 1400 Baltimore MD 21202-1654 Personal E-mail: dhonemann@comcast.net. Business E-Mail: dhonemann@wtplaw.com.

HONEY, RICHARD CHURCHILL, retired electrical engineer; b. Portland, Oreg., Mar. 9, 1924; s. John Kohnen and Margaret Fargo (Larrison) H.; m. Helen Waugaman, June 8, 1952 (div. Feb. 1980); children: Leslie, Steven, Laura, Janine; m. Jo Anne Kipp, Jan. 11, 1993. BS, Calif. Inst. Tech., 1945; EE, Stanford U., 1950, PhD, 1953. Research asst. Stanford U., 1948-52; sr. research engr. microwave group Stanford Research Inst., 1952-60; tech. program coordinator Electromagnetic Techniques Lab., 1960-64, lab. dir., 1964-70, staff scientist, 1970-89, sr. prin. scientist, 1989—; 86. Dir. ILC Tech.; mem. Army Sci. Bd., 1978-84. Contbr. articles to books, encyc., profl. jours.; patentee in field. Served with USN, 1943-46. Fellow IEEE, Optical Soc. Am.; mem. Optical Soc. No. Calif., Coyote Point Yacht Club, Sigma Xi. Office: SRI Internat 333 Ravenswood Ave Menlo Park CA 94025-3453

HONEY, SANGEET, molecular biologist; b. Sirsa, Haryana, India; s. Dharam Pal; married. MSc, Kurukshetra (India) U., 1986; postgrad. degree, Panjab U., Chandigarh, India, 1987; PhD, Postgrad. Inst. Med. Edn. Rsch., 1993. Sr. rsch. fellow Postgrad. Inst. Med. Edn. and Rsch., 1992-95; rsch. assoc. SUNY, Buffalo, 1995-97; postdoctoral fellow Cold Spring Harbor (N.Y.) Lab., 1997-2000; sr. rsch. scientist SUNY, Stony Brook, 2000-01. Contbr. articles to profl. jours., including Jour. Nucleic Acids Rsch., Trace Elements in Exptl. Medicine, Aquatic Toxicology, Molecular and Cellular Biochemistry, others. Cultural sec. Assn. Basic Med. Scientists, Chandigarh, 1989-90. Sr. rsch. fellow Coun. Sci. and Indsl. Rsch., New Delhi, 1992, Young Scientist travel fellow Dept. Sci. and Tech, New Delhi, 1995. Mem. AAAS, Am. Assn. Cancer Rsch., N.Y. Acad. Scis. Office: Cold Spring Harbor Lab 1 Bungtown Rd Cold Spring Harbor NY 11724 Office Fax: 631-632-9717. E-mail: shoney@ms.cc.sunysb.edu.

HONEYCHURCH, DENIS ARTHUR, lawyer; b. Berkeley, Calif., Sept. 17, 1946; s. Winston and Mary Martha (Chandler) H.; m. Judith Ann Poliquin, Oct. 5, 1969; children: Sean, James, Thomas. BA, UCLA, 1968; JD, U. Calif., San Francisco, 1972. Bar: Calif. 1972, U.S. Dist. Ct. (no. dist.) Calif. 1972, U.S. Ct. Appeals (9th cir.) 1972. Dep. pub. defender Sacramento County Calif., Sacramento, 1973-75; supervising asst. pub. defender Solano County, Fairfield, Calif., 1975-78; ptnr. Honeychurch & Finkas and predecessor firm, Fairfield, 1978—. Bd. dirs. Fairfield-Suisun Unified Sch. Dist., Fairfield, 1979-83, Solano Coll., Fairfield, 1985—; chmn. bd. dirs. Downtown Improvement Dist., Fairfield, 1980-82; mem. Dem. Ctr. Com. Solano County, 1994-98. Mem. ABA, Nat. Assn. Criminal Def. Lawyers, Calif. Attys. Criminal Justice, Calif. Pub. Defenders Assn., Solano County Bar Assn. (pres. 1991), Calif. Bd. Legal Specialization (cert.), Nat. Bd. Trial Advocacy (cert.). Democrat. Office: Honeychurch & Finkas 823 Jefferson St Fairfield CA 94533-5591 Office Phone: 707-429-3111.

HONEYCUTT, BRENDA, secondary school educator; Tchr. sci. Fort Mill (S.C.) Middle Sch.; chmn. sci. dept. Rep. Nat. Mid. Sch. Conf. Recipient hon. mention Outstanding Earth Sci. Tchr. award Nat. Assn. of Geology Teachers, 1992, S.C. Earth Sci. Tchr. Yr., 1992. Office: Fort Mill Middle Sch 200 Highway 160 Byp Fort Mill SC 29715-8746 E-mail: honeycuttb@fort-mill.k12.sc.us.

HONEYCUTT, GEORGE LEONARD, retired photographer; b. High Point, N.C., Jan. 5, 1936; s. Leonard Franklin and Pearl (Reynolds) H.; m. Sandra Spencer, Mar. 29, 1955; children: George Keith, Stephen Kurt, Kevin Spencer. Student, Sch. Modern Photography, N.Y.C., 1954. Photographer Charlotte (N.C.) News, 1959-62; Staff photographer Houston Chronicle, 1963, dir. photography, 1963-97, retired, 1997. Served with AUS, 1955-57. Recipient awards AP, awards UP, awards Headliners; 4-time winner Profl. Football Hall of Fame Mem. Nat. Press Photographers Assn. (named Nat. Newspaper Photographer of Yr. 1962) Methodist. Office: 801 Texas St Houston TX 77002-2904

HONEYCUTT, JANICE LOUISE, nurse; b. Plainfield Twp., Pa., Feb. 8, 1943; d. Mortimer Singer and Mary Irene (Chase) Purdy; m. Billie B. Honeycutt, Aug. 8, 1987; 1 child, Jason G. ThB, Penns Creek (Pa.) Bible Sch., 1972; ADN, Westark C.C., 1985. Bd. cert. in gerontology and gen. nursing practice. Clinic dir. Highlands, Papua, New Guinea, 1973-76; case mgr. Kimberly Quality Care, Amarillo, Tex., 1988-95; asst. dir. of nursing Olsen Manor Nursing Home, 1995; case mgr. Casha Resource, 1996, quality assurance rep. Amarillo, 1997—; dir. profl. improvement VIP Home Care, Amarillo, 1998-2000; charge nurse Country Club Manor, Amarillo, Tex., 2000—01, Plum Creek Specialty Hosp., Amarillo, 2001—. Author: The Lighthouse, 1975; contbr. articles to profl. jours. Local st. campaign leader Arthritis Found., Amarillo, 1996. Mem. NGNA. Avocations: water color painting, crafts, sewing. Office Phone: 806-351-1000.

HONEYCUTT, VAN B., computer company executive; b. Va., 1945; BS in Bus. Adminstrn., Franklin U.; grad. exec. program, Stanford U., 1984. With Computer Scis. Corp., El Segundo, Calif., 1975—, corp. v.p. and pres., 1987, COO, 1993—, pres. industry svcs. group, 1993—2001, chmn., CEO, 1995—. Bd. dir. Beckman Coulter Inc., Tenet Healthcare Corp. Office: Computer Sci Corp 2100 E Grand Ave El Segundo CA 90245-5024

HONEYSTEIN, KARL, lawyer, media specialist; b. N.Y.C., Jan. 10, 1932; s. Herman and Claire (Rosen) H.; m. Buzz Halliday, Sept. 14, 1965 (div. Dec. 1978); 1 child, Gail; m. Shauna Wood Trabert, Jan. 24, 1995. BA, Yale U., 1953; JD, Columbia U., 1959. Bar: N.Y. 1959. Assoc. Greenbaum, Wolff & Ernst, N.Y.C., 1959-62; v.p. Ashley Famous Agy., N.Y.C., 1962-69, Internat. Famous Agy., N.Y.C., 1969-71; exec. v.p. The Sy Fischer Co., N.Y.C. and L.A., 1971-80; exec. v.p., chief operating officer The Taft Entertainment Co., Los Angeles, 1980-88; pres. K.H. Strategy Corp., Los Angeles, 1988—. Dir. Rhythm & Hues, Inc.; lectr. law Bklyn. Law Sch., N.Y.C., 1973-75; mem. adv. group Wood Warren, Investment Bankers. Served to lt. j.g. USNR, 1953-56 Mem.: Internat. Acad. TV Arts and Scis., Friars Club. Office Phone: 310-273-0696.

HONG, BAOMING, research scientist, engineer; b. Taizhou, China, Jan. 1, 1964; arrived in U.S., 1996; s. Mafa Hong and Linge Wang. BS, Zhejiang U., Hangzhou, China, 1986; MS, Beijing Inst. Tech., 1992; PhD, U. Mass., Dartmouth, 2002. Rsch. asst., lectr. Beijing Inst. Tech., 1986—96; rsch. asst. U. Mass., North Dartmouth, 1996—2000; sr. scientist Motion TV Inc., Campbell, Calif., 2000—01; sr. R&D engr. Media Motion Inc., Santa Clara, Calif., 2001—02; rsch. fellow Hartford (Conn.) Hosp. Inst. Living, 2003—04; rsch. scientist Yale U., New Haven, 2004—. Contbr. chpt. to book. Recipient sci. tech. award, 1992. Mem.: SPIE (mem. program com. 2001), IEEE (mem. program com. 2005). Achievements include research in semi-physical simulation technique for radio fuses. Avocations: skiing, tennis, swimming. Office: Yale U 333 Cedar St New Haven CT 06520 Office Phone: 203-785-2829. Business E-Mail: baoming.hong@yale.edu. E-mail: baoming_hong@yahoo.com.

HONG, CHENG, radiologist, researcher; m. Fang Zhu. MD, Huazhong U. Sci. and Tech. (former Tongji Med. U.), 1992; PhD, U. Munich, 2001. Cert. radiologist Chinese Med. Assn. Rsch. scientist Wash. Univ. Sch. of Medicine, St. Louis, 2001—; rsch. fellow U. Munich, Germany, 1999—2001. Health-care advisor Gerson Lehrman Group, New York, 2003—. Author: (scientific paper) Radiology. Mem.: Radiol. Soc. N.Am. (assoc.). Achievements include research in Radiology - cardiac imaging. Office: Washington Univ Sch Medicine 4525 Scott Ave Ste 3357 Saint Louis MO 63110

HONG, JAE-DONG, industrial engineering educator; b. Daegu, South Korea, Mar. 20, 1954; arrived in U.S., 1981; s. Hyun-Tae and Kyung-Hee (Kim) H.; m. Bong-Sun Lee, Sept. 25, 1981; children: Thomas, Christina, James. BS, Korea U., Seoul, 1979; MS, Pa. State U., 1985, PhD, 1988. Quality and process engr. Daewoo Heavy Indsl., Anyang, South Korea, 1979-81; from asst. prof. to assoc. prof. indsl. engring. tech. S.C. State U., Orangeburg, 1988-97; prof., Gov.'s disting. prof. S.C. State U. Sch. Engring. Tech. and Scis., Orangeburg, 1997—. Contbr. articles to profl. jours. Named Disting. prof., Gov. S.C., 1993. Home: 106 Fox Run Ct Orangeburg SC 29118-9791 Office: SC State U 102 Lewis Lab Orangeburg SC 29117-7722 Office Phone: 803-536-8861. E-mail: jdhong@earthlink.net.

HONG, KUHN, nuclear medicine physician; b. Seoul, Republic of Korea, Aug. 27, 1946; s. Tae Joon Hong and Moon Young Ahn; married; children: Timothy, Joseph, David, Sarah. Student, Seoul Nat. U., 1964-66, MD, 1970. Diplomate Am. Bd. Radiology, Am. Bd. Nuclear Radiology, Am. Bd. Nuclear Medicine. Intern Gottlieb Meml. Hosp., Melrose Park, Ill., 1973-74; resident in radiology Mercy Hosp., Chgo., 1974-77; fellow in nuclear medicine Rush Presbyn.-St. Luke Med. Ctr., Chgo., 1977-79; dir. nuclear medicine, dept. radiology Little Co. of Mary Hosp., Evergreen Park, Ill., 1979—. Trustee No. Bapt. Theol. Seminary, Lombard, Ill., 1998—. Mem. AMA, Am. Coll. Radiology, Soc. Nuclear Medicine, Radiol. Soc. N.Am., Chgo. Med. Soc. (coun. 1990, continuing med. edn. com., profl. liability com., com. for internat. med. grads., past pres., v.p., treas., sec. southwest br.), Ill. State Med. Soc. (del. 1996), Christian Med. and Dental Soc. (coun. mem. Chicagoland area 1999—). Avocations: painting, drawing, downhill skiing, Judo, stamp collecting/philately. Office: Little Co Mary Hosp 2800 W 95th St Evergreen Park IL 60805-2795 E-mail: KuhnHong@aol.com.

HONG, MEI, chemistry professor; BA, Mt. Holyoke Coll., 1992; PhD, U. Calif. Berkeley, 1996. NIH postdoctoral fellow Mass. Inst. Tech., Cambridge; rsch. prof. U. Mass., Amherst; assoc. prof. chemistry Iowa State U., Ames, Iowa, 1999—. Mem. editl. bd.: Jour. Magnetic Resonance. Recipient Beckman Young Investigator award, 1999, Rsch. Corp. Innovation award, 2000, Career award, NSF, 2001, Pure Chemistry award, Am. Chem. Soc., 2003; Alfred P. Sloan Fellow, 2002. Achievements include development and application of solid-state NMR spectroscopy to investigate the structure and dynamics of membrane and insoluable fibrous proteins. Office: Dept Chemistry 1605 Gilman Hall Iowa State Univ Ames IA 50011-3111 Office Phone: 515-294-3521. E-mail: mhong@iastate.edu.

HONG, PENGYU, biologist; PhD, U. Ill., Urbana-Champaign, 2001. Post-doctoral fellow Harvard U., Cambridge, Mass., 2002—04, Stanford U., Calif., 2004—05; asst. prof. Brandies U., 2005—. Office Phone: 617-384-8361.

HONG, RAN-E, literature educator; b. Seoul, Republic of Korea, May 20, 1960; arrived in U.S., 1996; d. Iel Hong and Hae-Sook Kim; 1 child, Rhee-Soo. BA, Ewha Woman's U., Seoul, 1981, MA, 1983; PhD 3d cycle, U. Paris-Sorbonne, 1987; PhD, Brown U., 2000. Adj. faculty Ewha Woman's U., Seoul, 1987—93, Hongik U., Seoul, 1992—93, Hankook U. Fgn. Studies, Seoul, 1993—95, Konkuk U., Seoul, 1994—96; asst. prof. Rivier Coll., Nashua, NH, 2000—01, Grand Valley State U., Allendale, Mich., 2001—04. Author: L'Impossible Social Selon Moliere, 2002; contbr. articles to profl. jours. Mem.: MLA, Assn. Internat. des Etudes Francaises, N.Am. Soc. 17th Century French Lit. Avocations: reading, movies, travel. Home: 3293 Park Ridge Ln NE Grand Rapids MI 49525 Personal E-mail: rh522@hotmail.com.

HONG, RANI JENELLE, real estate broker; b. Kottamam, Kerala, India, May 4, 1972; arrived in U.S., 1979; d. Chacko and Alia Konukudy, Nelle Jean Clark; m. Trong Moc Hong, Aug. 8, 1992; children: Andrew James, Tyler Moc, Samantha Jenelle, Nathan Daniel. AA, South Puget Sound C.C., 1993. Real estate cons. Tronie Corp., Olympia, Wash., 1997—. Activist Shared Hope Internat., Vancouver, Wash., 2004; U.S. spkr. specialist U.S. Dept. Of State, Washington, 2003; activist Wash. State Task Force Against Human Trafficking, Olympia, 2002. Recipient medal, Deputados Da 51A Legislatura, 2003, Inspirational Spkr. grant, U.S. Dept. of State, 2003—. Republican. Avocations: travel, kids and family interaction, researcher, sports, camping. Office: 1705 Yelm Hwy SE Olympia WA 98501 Personal E-mail: rani@troniehomes.com.

HONG, SANGJIN, engineering educator, researcher; m. Juhee Lee, June 6, 1992; children: Frederick, Ashley. BS, U. Calif., 1985, MS, 1992; PhD, U. Mich., 2000. Sys. engr. Ford Aerospace and Comm. Corp., Sunnyvale, 1985—88; cad sys. programmer U. of Calif., Berkeley, 1988—89; tech. cons. Samsung Electronics, Inc, Seoul, Republic of Korea, 1991; exec. officer Darim Systems, Seoul, Korea (South), 1991—92; rsch. fellow U. of Mich., Ann Arbor, Mich., 2000; asst. prof. Stony Brook U., Stony Brook, NY, 2000—. Tech. cons. Samsung Electronics, Inc., Seoul, Republic of Korea, 1991. Grantee, NSF. Mem.: IEEE Tech. Confs. (chair), IEEE, Eta Kappa Nu (life). Office: Stony Brook Univ Dept Elec and Computers Stony Brook NY 11794 Office Fax: 631-632-8494. Business E-Mail: snjhong@ece.sunysb.edu.

HONG, SUK JIN, neuroscientist; b. Seoul, Republic of Korea, July 20, 1969; s. Myoungki Hong and Chungja Choi; m. Jaeyoen Yoon, July 22, 2000; 1 child, Mae Jin. BS Cum Laude, KAIST, Taejon Korea, 1991, PhD, 1999. Postdoctoral rschr. UCLA, L.A.; rsch. assoc. Dept. of Veterans Affairs Med. Ctr. West LA, L.A., 1999—2000; postdoctoral fellow Johns Hopkins U., Balt., 2000—04, rsch. assoc., 2004—. Faculty Johns Hopkins U., Balt., 2004—. Author: An animal being forgotten, Leech, Designing the Science; contbr. chapters to books, articles pub. to profl. jour. Vol. Calvery Ch., Balt., 1999—2000. Mem.: Soc. for Neuroscience. Achievements include patents for Elastase inhibitor and process for preparing the same; development of cDNA libr. screening method - DAzLE; patents for Guamerin derived synthetic protease inhibitor; Artificial feeding of blood-sucking leeches; Guamerin: New elastase inhibitor from korean blood-sucking leech. Office: Johns Hopkins Univ 733 N Broadway St Ste731 Baltimore MD 21205 Office Phone: 443-287-5605. Personal E-mail: sukjin_h@yahoo.com. Business E-Mail: shong5@jhmi.edu.

HONG, SUZI, biomedical researcher; d. Sung-Dai Hong and Cheong Lee; m. Randolph Lahmeyer Brooks, Nov. 30, 2002. PhD, U. Ga., 2000. Rschr. U. Calif., San Diego, 2000—04, rsch. faculty, 2004—. Gen. clin. rsch. ctr. flow cytometry core lab. mgr. U. Calif., 2003—. Grantee, UCSD Gen. Clin. Rsch. Ctr. Clin. Rsch. Feasibility Fund Jr. Faculty, 2004; scholar, Hankuk Yuri/ Ewha Woman's U., 1989—92. Mem.: Psychoneuroimmunology Rsch. Soc., Am. Psychosomatic Soc., Am. Coll. Sports Medicine. Achievements include research in Actively Conducting And Publishing Research In The Area Of The Interactions Between The Nervous System And The Immune System. Avocations: martial arts, piano, travel. Office Phone: 619-543-5832.

HONG, WAUN KI, medical oncologist, clinical investigator; b. Kyung gi Do, South Korea, Aug. 13, 1942; naturalized Sept. 17, 1976; s. Sung Ku and Bok Young; m. Mi Hwa Yoo, Sept. 9, 1969; children: Edward, Burton James. Student, Yon-Sei U., 1963, MD, 1967. Diplomate Am. Bd. Internal Medicine in Medical Oncology. Rotating intern Bronx-Lebanon Hosp., N.Y.C., 1970-71; jr. med. resident Boston Vets. Affairs Med. Ctr., 1971-72, sr. med. resident, 1972-73, chief of medical oncology, 1975-84, program dir. hematology/oncology tng. program, 1982-84; teaching assoc. Sch. Medicine Boston U., 1971-73, asst. prof. medicine, 1975-79, assoc. prof. medicine, 1980-84; clin. instr. medicine Cornell U., 1973-75; attending physician in medicine Boston City Hosp., 1978-84; clin. assoc. prof. pharmacology Northeastern U., Boston, 1980-84; internist, prof. medicine M.D. Anderson Cancer Ctr., U. Tex., Houston, 1984—, chief sect. thoracic med. oncology, 1987-88, chief sect. head, neck and thoracic med. oncology, 1988-92, chmn. dept. thoracic/head and neck med. oncology, 1993—, Charles A. LeMaistre Disting. Chair in thoracic oncology. Mem. sci. adv. bd. U. Ala. Birmingham Comprehensive Cancer Ctr., 1998—, Roy Castle Lung Cancer Found., 1997—, U. Calif. San Diego Cancer Ctr., 1997—, Shanghai (China) 2d Med. U. Joint Ctr. Clin. Rsch., 1997—, Fox Chase Cancer Ctr. Population Sci. Program, 1997, Kimmel Found. on Cancer Rsch., 1996—, Yale Cancer Ctr., 1996—, Vanderbilt Cancer Ctr., Seoul Nat. U. Cancer Ctr., 1996—; Baylor Coll. Medicine SPORE program, 1995—, The Cancer Inst. of N.J., 1993-98, The San Antonio Cancer Inst., 1993—; cons. Battelle Pharms., 1997—, Taiho Pharms., 1997—, Trilex Pharms., 1996—, Sequus Pharms., 1996—, Ho-En Ctrl. Rsch. Inst., 1996—, Ilex Oncology, 1995—; Houston Vet. Affairs Med. Ctr., 1992—; adj. prof. medicine Baylor Coll. Medicine, Houston, 1991—; vis. prof. Meml. Sloan-Kettering Cancer Ctr., 1998, Boston U. Cancer Ctr., 1997, Boston VA Med. Ctr., 1997, Nat. Cancer Inst. Intramural Program, 1996, U. Minn. Cancer Ctr., 1994, Tufts U. Sch. Medicine, 1993, Dana-Farber Cancer Ctr., 1993, Johns Hopkins Oncology Ctr., 1993, Tex. Tech. U. Sch. Medicine, 1992; lectr. in medicine Tufts U., 1975-84; Am. Cancer Soc. clin. rsch. prof., 1996—; Gen. Motors Found. vis. prof. Editor: (with others) Chemoimmuno Prevention of Cancer, 1991, The Biology and Prevention of Aerodigestive Tract Cancer, 1992, Advances in the Diagnosis and Therapy of Lung Cancer, 1993, Retinoids in Oncology, 1993, Early Detection of Cancer: Molecular Markers, 1994, Head and Neck Cancer: Basic and Clinical Aspects, 1995, Head and Neck Cancer: A Multidisciplinary Approach, 1996, Lung Cancer, 2d edit., 1998, Internat. Jour. Oncology, 1996—; dep. editor Clin. Cancer Rsch., 1996—; sr. editor Clinical Cancer Research, 1994—, Jour. Molecular and Cellular Differentiation, 1992—, Cancer Rsch., 1993-97; mem. editl. bd. The Cancer Jour., 1998—, Cancer Therapeutics, 1997—, PDQ Screening and Prevention, NCI, 1993-95, Annals of Surg. Oncology, 1993—, Cancer Rsch. Therapy and Ctrl., 1993-96, Jour. Clin. Oncology, 1992-95, Cancer Prevention, 1990-93; mem. editl. adv. bd. Cancer Epidemiology, Biomarkers and Prevention, 1994-96, Jour. Nat. Cancer Inst., 1990—. Served as flight surgeon South Korean Air Force, 1967-70. Recipient AACR 17th Ann. Richard and Hinda Rosenthal Found. award, 1993, pres. citation Am. Soc. for Head and Neck Surgery, 1991; Jr. Med. Oncology fellow Meml. Sloan-Kettering Cancer Ctr., 1973-74, Sr. Med. Oncology fellow Cornell U., 1974-75, ACS Disting. Svc. award, 1993, ACS 3d Ann. Am. Cancer Soc. lectureship award, 1995, Ho-Am prize in medicine Sam-Sung Found., 1994—, M.D. Anderson faculty achievement award in cancer prevention, 1993, Milken Family Found. Cancer Rsch. award, 1990, Cancer Rsch. and Prevention Found. award for Excellence in Cancer Prevention Rsch., Am. Assn. Cancer Rsch., 2003, numerous others; also numerous federal, industry, and found. grants. Fellow AAAS; mem. AMA, ACP, Am. Radium Soc., Am. Fedn. Clin. Rsch., Assn. Am. Physicians, Am. Assn. Cancer Rsch. (bd. dirs. 1996—, publs. com. 1996—, mem. program com., subcom. on clin. investigations 1993-94, cancer prevention 1993-94, mem. task force clin. investigations 1990—, chmn. com. on clin. cancer rsch. 1995, pres.), Am. Cancer Soc. (clin. rsch. prof. 1996—, mem. med. affairs adv. group on professorships in clin. oncology, mem. nat. conf. clin. trials 1992, profl. edn. subcom. on profs. clin. oncology 1990, chmn. 1991), Am. Soc. Clin. Oncology (vice chair cancer prevention and control com. 1995-96, mem. cancer edn. com. 1995-96, mem. edn. com. 1994-96, chmn. cancer prevention and ctrl. com. 1994), Nat. Cancer Inst. (mem. adv. com. to dir. 1997—, extramural bd. sci. advisors 1996—, cancer ctrs. rev. working group 1995-96, mem. pres.'s cancer panel 1994, mem. interim combined ad hoc bd. sci. counselors 1995), Tex. Med. Assn., Radiation Therapy Oncology Group (mem. med. oncology com. 1989—, head and neck com. 1989—), Harris County Med. Soc., Soc. Head and Neck Surgeons. Office: U Tex MD Anderson Cancer Ctr 1515 Holcombe Blvd Houston TX 77030-4009

HONG, YONGMIAO, economics professor, statistician; s. Zai Hong and Xiang Wei; m. Xin Wang, Sept. 24, 1988. PhD, U. Calif., San Diego, 1993. Asst. prof. economics Cornell U., Ithaca, NY, 1993—98, assoc. prof. economics & stats., 1998—2001, prof. economics & stats., 2001—. Office: Dept of Econ Uris Hall 492 Cornell Univ Ithaca NY 14853-7601 Office Phone: 607-255-5130. Home Fax: 607-255-2818; Office Fax: 607-255-2818. Business E-Mail: yh20@cornell.edu.

HONG DUC, DUONG, economic development company executive; b. Vietnam; BA in Ed., History and Geography, U. Saigon; attended, Am. Economic Develop. Inst., U. Okla., Govt. Exec. Inst., U. Md., Coll. Park. Former dir. Refugee Resettlement Program, Wash., 1975—77; asst. dir. Montgomery County Dept. of Economic Develop., 1977—98; founder, pres. DDI Associates Inc., 2001—. Bd. mem. & chmn. Nat. Alliance of Vietnamese Am. Svc. Agencies. Founder Industry Networks and Md. Bioscience Alliance, Techn. Council of Md., Suburban Md. Internat. Trade Assn., 1979, Md. Vietnamese Mutual Assn., 1979; bd. mem. Nat. Asian Pacific Ctr. on Aging, Regional Lourie Ctr. for Infants and Young Children. Mem.: Monte Jade Sci. & Techn. Assn. Office: 1010 Wayne Ave Ste 310 Silver Spring MD 20910*

HON GOH, CHAN, dancer; b. Beijing; Student, Goh Ballet Acad., Vancouver. Mem. Nat. Ballet Co., Toronto, Canada, 1988—, prin. dancer, 1994—. Guest artist Royal Danish Ballet, Singapore Dance Theatre, Hong Kong Ballet, Washington Ballet. Odette/Odile (ballets) Swan Lake, title role Giselle, Tatiana Onegin, Nikiya La Bayadère, Katherina The Taming of the Shrew, Juliet Romeo and Juliet, dancer Jewels, Désir, Forgotten Land, Now and Then, La Ronde. Office: Walter Carsen Ctr Nat Ballet of Canada 470 Queens Quay West Toronto ON Canada M5V 3K4

HONHART, FREDERICK LEWIS, III, academic director; b. San Diego, Oct. 29, 1943; s. Frederick Lewis Jr. and Rossiter (Hyde) H.; m. Barbara Ann Baker, Aug. 27, 1966; children: David Frederick, Stephen Charles. BA, Wayne State U., 1966; MA, Case-Western Res. U., 1968, PhD, 1972. Cert. archivist. Field rep. Ohio Hist. Soc., Columbus, 1972-73; asst. dir. univ. archives & hist. collections Mich. State U., East Lansing, 1974-79, dir., 1979—. Mem. adv. bd. Mich. Nat. Hist. Publs. & Records Commn., Lansing, 1979—; cons. in field. Creator: (microcomputer sys.), MicroMARC:amc, 1986 (Coker prize 1988), MicroMARC for Integrated Format, 1995; contbr. articles to profl. jours. Mem. Internat. Coun. Archives (steering com. sci. and univ. archives sect. 2000-2004, pres. univ. archives sect. 2004—), Soc. Am. Archivists, Mich. Archival Assn. (pres. 1984-86), Midwest Archives Conf. (chair program com. 1982, 94, chair Author Awards com. 2001). Avocations: reading, sports, flying. Office: Mich State U 101 Conrad Hall East Lansing MI 48824-1327 Office Phone: 517-355-2330.

HONICKMAN, HAROLD, food manufacturing company executive; b. Phila., June 10, 1933; Grad., Widener U., 1955. CEO Honickman Affiliates, Pennsauken, N.J.; chmn. bd. Pepsi Cola, Canada Dry of N.Y. Bd. dirs. Technion Soc., B'nai B'rith, Inst. Contemporary Art, The Aperture Found. Office: Honickman Affiliates 8275 N Route 130 Pennsauken NJ 08110-1435*

HONIG, ARNOLD, physics professor, researcher; b. N.Y.C., Feb. 28, 1928; s. Ralph and Margaret (Gershman) Honig; m. Alice Sterling, Oct. 3, 1947 (div. Nov. 1977); children: Lawrence, Madeleine, Jonathan; m. Dolly Komar, Jan. 6, 1979; stepchildren: Anne, Tanya. BA, Cornell U., 1948; MS, Columbia U., 1950, PhD, 1953. Research asst. microwave spectroscopy Columbia U., N.Y.C., 1951-53; research physicist solid state physics U. Calif.-Berkeley, 1953-54; research fellow molecular physics Ecole Normale Superieure, Paris, 1954-56; asst. prof. physics Syracuse U., N.Y., 1956-59, assoc. prof., 1959-62, prof., 1962—. Cons. ITT Labs., 1960—63, Gen. Atomics, 1993—96, Oxford Instruments, 1997—; ptnr., owner Sci.-Art Sys. Co., N.Y.C., 1968—78; vis. prof. Hebrew U., Jerusalem, 1962; vis. scientist Com. a l'Energie Atomique, Saclay, France, 1965. Contbr. articles to profl. jours. Pres. Oran Meml. Pk. Assn., NY, 1981—83. Recipient Glover Meml. award, Dickinson Coll., 1966, Chancellor's citation for exceptional acad. achievement, 1999; grantee, NSF, Dept. Energy, others. Mem.: AAAS, Fedn. Am. Scientists, Am. Phys. Soc. Achievements include patents for infrared image transducer; matrix piano keyboard; production spin-polarized fuels; multi-chronal fluorescence microscope; bulk production and usage of hyperpolarized 129 Xenon; non-invasive susceptibility-based in-vivo iron measurement and imaging utilizing MRI and ESR. Avocations: music, farming. Office: Syracuse U Dept Physics Syracuse NY 13244-0001 Business E-Mail: honig@phy.syr.edu.

HONIG, ETHELYN, artist; b. N.Y.C., July 9, 1933; d. Samuel and Sophie (Brody) Blinder; m. Lester Jerome Honig, July 29, 1955 (dec. July 1992); children: Hillary Wynn Honig Ensminger, Deirdre Lynn Honig. Attended, Bennington Coll.; BA, Sarah Lawrence Coll., Bronxville, N.Y. Chair adv. bd. Sculpture Ctr. Battery Park Maritime Bldg., N.Y.C., 1987; curator art exhbn. for patients Manhattan Psychiatric Ctr., N.Y.C.; pub. Art Editions, Kenneth Noland Sol Lewitt, Chgo. 7 Portfolio. One person exhbns. include Benson Gallery, Bridgehampton, L.I., N.Y., 1968, 55 Mercer Gallery, N.Y.C., 1972, 74, 83, 84, 85, 86, 87, 89, 91, 94, 96, 2001, 03, Franklin Furnace Archive, N.Y.C., 1977, Mus. of Modern Art, 1974, 75, Rosa Esman Gallery, N.Y.C., 1975, South East Mus., Brewster, N.Y., 1978, Katonah (N.Y.) Gallery, 1981; group exhbns. include 55 Mercer Gallery, N.Y.C., 1975, 76, 78, 91, 93, U. Ariz. Mus., Tucson, 1980, So. Allegheny Mus. Art, 1981, Keene Coll. Art Gallery, Union, N.J. Foxworth Gallery, N.Y.C., 1985, Kenkelaba Gallery, N.Y.C., 1985, Somerstown Gallery, Somers, N.Y., 1985, Katonah (N.Y.) Gallery, 1987, Art Initiatives at Tribeca 148 Gallery, 1994, 95, Paula Cooper Gallery, N.Y.C., 1970, represented in permanent collections Mus. Modern Art, N.Y.C., Wadsworth Atheneum Mus., Patrick Lannon Found., Citi-Corps, Smith Coll. Mus., Northampton, Mass.; patentee in field. Founder and chairperson Clozapine Family Info. for the Alliance for the Mentally Ill, N.Y.S., 1990-96. Recipient Svc. awards Alliance for the Mentally Ill N.Y.S., Albany, 1990, Friends and Advocates for the Mentally Ill, 1990-91. Mem. Art Students League, 55 Mercer Artists (founding mem., pres. 1997-98). Avocations: amateur archaeology, swimming, bicycling, photography. Home: 137 E 95th St New York NY 10128-1723

HONIG, GEORGE RAYMOND, pediatrician; b. Chgo., May 5, 1936; s. Joseph C. and Raymonde S. (Moses) Honig; m. Karen R. Jacobson, Dec. 18, 1960 (dec.); children: Sharon, Debra, Robert; m. Olga M. Weiss, May 24, 1998. BS in Liberal Arts and Sci., U. Ill., 1959, MD, MS in Pharmacology, U. Ill., 1961; PhD in Biochemistry, George Washington U., 1966. Diplomate Am. Bd. Pediatrics, Nat. Bd. Med. Examiners. Intern Johns Hopkins Hosp., Balt., 1961-62, fellow in pediatrics, 1961-63, asst. resident in pediatrics, 1962-63; rsch. assoc. Nat. Cancer Inst. NIH, 1963-66; fellow in pediatric hematology U. Ill., Chgo., 1966-68, from asst. prof. to assoc. prof. pediat., 1968—74, prof., 1974-75, 1984—2003, prof. emeritus, 2004—, attending physician, 1968-75, dir. pediatric hematology svc., 1972-75, head dept. pediat. Coll. Medicine, 1984—2003. Attending physician, dir. divsn. hematology Children's Meml. Hosp., Chgo., 1975—83; prof. emeritus U. Ill. Coll.

Medicine, 2004—. Contbr. articles to profl. jours. Mem.: AAUP, Soc. Pediatric Rsch., Am. Pediatric Soc., Am. Soc. Hematology, Am. Soc. Biochemistry and Molecular Biology, Am. Assn. Cancer Rsch., Am. Acad. Pediat., Alpha Omega Alpha. Office: U Ill Coll Medicine 840 S Wood St Chicago IL 60612-7317 Office Phone: 312-996-1788. Business E-Mail: ghonig@uic.edu.

HONIGBERG, CAROL CROSSMAN, lawyer; b. Salina, Kansas, Sept. 23, 1955; d. Robert Denfield and Barbara Jane (Eckberg) Crossman; m. Paul Mark Honigberg, Aug. 18, 1979; children: Michael, Margaret Ann. BA, Duke U., 1977; JD, Vanderbilt U., 1980. Bar: Va., 1980. Assoc. Hazel and Thomas, P.C., Alexandria, Va., 1980—86; propr. Hazel and Thomas, P.C., Falls Ch., Va., 1986—99; ptnr. Reed Smith LLP (formerly Reed, Smith, Hazel, and Thomas, LLP), Falls Ch., 1999—, mem. exec. com. Mem. ABA (mem. real property, probate and trust sect.), Va. State Bar (mem. real property sect.), CREW Network (pres. North Va. chpt. 1998-99, nat. del. 2000-01), Urban Land Inst. (mem. urban devel. and mixed use coun.). Office: Reed Smith LLP 3110 Fairview Park Dr Ste 1400 Falls Church VA 22042 Office Phone: 703-641-4220. Office Fax: 703-641-4340. Business E-Mail: chonigberg@reedsmith.com.

HONMA, KOICHI, pathologist, researcher; b. Shiroishi, Miyagi, Japan, Mar. 28, 1955; s. Tsuneo and Mieko (Isago) Honma; m. Kiyomi Fukuda, Nov. 27, 1986; children: Shiko, Seiji, Shino. BM, Tohoku U., 1979; MD, Dokkyo U., 1986. Instr. Dokkyo U. Sch. Medicine, Tochigi, Japan, 1981-84, asst. prof., 1984-92, assoc. prof., 1992—. Mem. sci. com. No. 9 ILO Conf., Kyoto, 1995—97; organizer internat. workshops on occupl. lung diseases, 1996—. Contbr. Founder, diplomatic counselor London Diplomatic Acad., 2000—. Mem.: European Soc. Pathology, Pulmonary Pathology Soc., Am. Thoracic Soc., European Respiratory Soc., Deutsche Gesellschaft fur Pathologie. Avocations: music, sports. Home: Tomatsuri 3-6-45 Utsunomiya Tochigi 320-0056 Japan Office: Dokkyo U Sch Medicine Dept Pathology Kitakobayashi 880 Mibu Tochigi 321-0293 Japan Fax: 81-282-86-5171. Office Phone: 81-282-87-2129. Business E-Mail: honma@dokkyomed.ac.jp.

HONNOLD, JOHN OTIS, law educator; b. Kansas, Ill., Dec. 5, 1915; s. John Otis and Louretta (Wright) H.; m. Annamarie Kunz, June 26, 1939; children: Carol Honnold Davidon, Heidi Honnold Spencer, Edward. BA, U. Ill., 1936; JD, Harvard U., 1939; LLD (hon.), Capitol U., 1991, Pace U., 1997. Bar: N.Y. 1940, Pa. 1953, U.S. Supreme Ct 1953. Atty. firm Wright, Gordon, Zachry & Parlin, N.Y.C., 1939-41, SEC, 1941; chief ct. rev. br. OPA, 1942-46; mem. faculty U. Pa. Law Sch., 1946-69, 74-84, prof. law, 1952-69, 74-84, prof. emeritus, 1984—; Arthur Goodhart prof. sci. of law. U. Cambridge, Eng., 1982-83. Mem. vis. faculty U. Beijing, 1984, U. Hawaii, 1986, U. Fla., 1988; Canterbury vis. fellow, N.Z., 1986; lectr. UN seminar, Moscow, 1990, U. Stockholm, 1990; chief internat. trade law br. UN; sec. UN Commn. on Internat. Trade Law, 1969-74; mem. faculty law sessions Salzburg (Austria) Seminar Am. Studies, 1960, chmn., 1963, 66; chief counsel Miss. Office, Lawyer's Com. for Civil Rights under Law, 1965; U.S. del., mem. drafting com. diplomatic conf. preparing uniform law for internat. sales of goods, The Hague, Holland, 1964; U.S. del UN Commn. Internat. Trade Law, 1969, 77; U.S. del. diplomatic confs. Conv. Carriage of Goods by Sea, Hamburg, 1978, Contracts for Internat. Sale of Goods, Vienna, 1980; gen. reporter 12th Internat. Congress Comparative Law, 1986 Author: (with C. Mooney, S. Harris, C. Reitz) Sales and Secured Financing, 6th edit., 1993, The Life of the Law, 1964, (with others) Commercial Law, 5th edit., 1993, Uniform Law for International Sales under the 1980 UN Convention, 1982, 3rd edit., 1999, 1991, (with others) United Nations Legal Order, 1995; contbr. articles to profl. jours. Guggenheim fellow, 1958; Fulbright sr. research scholar U. Paris, 1958; recipient Theberge award for contbn. to Pvt. Internat. Law, ABA, 1986; Lincoln Laureate, 1992.

HONOUR, LYNDA CHARMAINE, research scientist, psychotherapist, educator; d. John Henry, Jr. and Evelyn Helena Roberta (Pietrowski) H. BA, Boston U.; MA, Calif. State U., Fullerton, UCLA; PhD, U. So. Calif. Lic. marriage, family and child psychotherapist and psychologist, Calif. Rschr. neuroendocrinology and behavioral neurosci., Calif., 1976—; pvt. practice psychotherapy Carslbad Village, 1991—. Vis. and clin. prof. Pepperdine U., 1989—, Malibu, Calif. Sch. Profl. Psychology, Calif. State U., Long Beach, Northridge; condr. rsch. Neuropsychiat. Inst., Brain Rsch. Inst., Mental Retardation Rsch. Ctr., UCLA, Tulane U. Med. Sch., V.A. Med. Ctr., New Orleans, Salk Inst. Biol. Studies; rsch. cons. U. Calif. Med. Ctr., Irvine; cons. in rsch. or psychotherapy, 1976—; guest expert on safety issues regarding magnetic imaging Premiere Radio Network, 2001; condr. rsch. Neuropsychiat. Inst., Brain Rsch. Inst., Mental Retardation Rsch. Ctr., UCLA, Tulane U. Med. Sch., V.A. Med. Ctr., New Orleans, Salk Inst. Biol. Studies; rsch. cons. U. Calif. Med. Ctr., Irvine, Salk Inst.; cons., ad hoc reviewer (textbooks) Wadsworth/Brooks-Cole, Thomson Internat. Pub., Pacific Grove, Calif.; cons., reviewer Allyn & Bacon Pub., Boston; hon. chmn., Bus. Adv. Coun. Nat. Rep. Congl. Com. Contbr. articles to profl. jours.; musician. Rsch. grantee Organon Internat. Rsch. Group, Netherlands, 1984-88. Mem. APA, Soc. for Neurosci., Internat. Behavioral Neurosci. Soc., Internat. Brain Rsch. Orgn., Calif. Assn. Marriage and Family Therapists, Sons and Daus. of Pearl Harbor Survivors, Psi Chi, Salk Inst. Alumni. Roman Catholic. Achievements include identification of a peptide which facilitates and another peptide inhibits learning and memory task performance permanently in a developmental paradigm in mice; and facilitation peptide can permanently reverse induced learning/memory deficit, with implications for mental retardation and other learning/memory deficit treatment; member of research team which ultimately isolated and characterized corticotropic hormone releasing factor, urocortin; delineated various effects of peptides on behavior including bipolar disorders, endogenous depression, mania and others; human research involving interface between cognition/mind and physiological processes/disease; research in risks associated with MRI exposure; established new N.E. US swimming records in the 1960's. Avocations: metaphysics, art, swimming. Office Phone: 760-720-9665. Business E-Mail: DrLyndaHonour@cs.com.

HONSA, VLASTA, retired librarian; b. Žilina, Czechoslovakia, Sept. 1, 1924; came to U.S., 1951; d. František Petr and Marie (Širkova) Petrova; m. Vladimir Honsa, June 26, 1948; children: Patricia, Eva Honsa-Hogg. BA, Charles U., Prague, 1947; MLS, Ind. U., 1968. Gifts libr. Ind. U. Libr., Bloomington, 1968-70; head reference dept. Clark County Libr., Las Vegas, Nev., 1970-80, asst. adminstr., 1980-94; ret., 1994. Coord. Found. Collection, part of the Found. Ctr.'s Cooperating Collections network, Clark County Libr., 1979-94. Author: Nevada Foundation Directory, 1984, 2d edit., 1989, 3rd edit., 1994. Bd. dirs. So. Nev. Musical Arts Soc., Las Vegas, 1989-92; organized and presented fundraising workshops for cmty. fund raisers sponsored by Las Vegas-Clark County Libr. Dist., 1979-94. Recipient Ind. U. grant-in-aid to conduct rsch. of publs. in cen. Am. univs. and nat. librs., 1970, Champion award Las Vegas-Clark County Libr. Dist., 1985. Mem. ALA, AAUW, Nev. Libr. Assn., Univ. Nevada Las Vegas Faculty Club. Roman Catholic. Avocations: reading, music, arts, travel. Home: 2680 Congress Ave Las Vegas NV 89121-1316 E-mail: honsa@worldnet.att.net.

HOOD, ANTOINETTE FOOTE, dermatologist; b. Honolulu, 1941; MD, Vanderbilt U., 1967. Cert. dermatology. Intern Vanderbilt Affiliated Hosps, 1967-68; fellow dermatology Harvard U., 1973-75, resident dermatology, 1975-76; resident dermatology-pathology Mass. Gen. Hosp., Boston, 1976-78; exec. dir. American Board of Dermatology, Detroit, 2001—. Office: Henry Ford Health System 1 Ford Place Detroit MI 48202

HOOD, BARBARA W., musician, educator; b. Oskaloosa, Iowa, May 8, 1930; d. Herbert E. and Gladys (Lockwood) Wolf; m. Fred Warren Hood, Sept. 2, 1950; children: Victoria Lynn Simpson, Christina Elizabeth Adair. Student, U Chattanooga, 1948—50; BMus Ga. State U, 1967—70. Dir. Children's Choir First Bapt. Choir, Chattanooga, 1948—50; prof. mem. violinist Chatanooga Symphony, 1948—53; billing clerk Profident Ins. Co., Chattanooga, 1950—51; sec., file clerk TVA, Chattanooga, 1951—53; sec. Highland Jr. H.S., Louisville, 1956—57; pvt. music tchr. Pvt. Practice, Moultrie, Ga., 1958—63; tchr. strings Marietta Sch. Sys., 1967—73; pvt. music tchr. pvt. practice, Marietta, Ga., 1963—67, 1973—76; tchr. music Weatherly Heights Bap. Ch., Huntsville, Ala., 1977—83; dir. youth orch. Huntsville(Ala.) Youth Orch. Assn., 1979—83; music tchr. pvt. practice, Huntsville, 1976—83; violinist Huntsville (Ala.) Symphony Orch., 1976—83; music tchr. Sea Pines Montessori, Hilton Head, SC, 1984—87; musician pvt. practice, Hilton Head, 1983—97; dir. music Winters Chapel United Meth. Ch., Atlanta, 1987—90; sec, EPA, Atlanta, 1988—90; music tchr. Fayette County Pub. Sch., Tyrone, Ga., 1990—96; dir. music Nat. Heights Bapt. Ch., Fayetteville, Ga., 1997—2003; pvt. tchr. strings Pvt. Practice, Fayetteville, 1996—; prof. performing group Ensemble pour deux pvt. practice, Fayetteville, 1997—. Dir. childrens choir First Bapt. Ch., Marietta, 1963—76; vol. music tchr. Happiness Hill Sch. for Spl. Needs, Marietta, 1966; dir. childrens choir Weatherly Heights Bapt. Ch., 1976—83, First Bapt. Ch., 1983—87; vol. music activities Seabrook Nursing Home, Hilton Head, 1986—87; founding mem. Hilton Head Orch., 1984—87, string quartet, 1986—87; vol. string tchr. Sams Sch. for Spl. Needs, Fayetteville, 2003. Composer: Hilton Head Prep, 1986, Sea Pines Montessori, 1986, "Chaconne", 1989, For Wheeler H.S., 1989, "Lament", 1990. Mem.: Music Edn. Nat. Conventioni, Am. String Assn. (assoc.), Ga. Music Edn. Assn. (assoc.). Avocation: composing, arranging. Home: 445 Cornwallis Way Fayetteville GA 30214 Office: Private Studio 445 Cornwallis Way Fayetteville GA 30214 Personal E-mail: barbarahood377@bellsouth.net.

HOOD, CARRA LEAH, literature educator; d. Paul Fudicker and Mary Willene Hood. BA, CUNY, 1986; MA, Yale U., 1988, Ph.D, 1998. Prof. So. Conn. State U., New Haven, 1999—2004, La. State U., Baton Rouge, 2004—05, Richard Stockton Coll., NJ, 2005—. Editor: (art book) Survival in Writing and Art 2001: Testaments to Healing through Creativity; contbr. articles to profl. jours. Dir. publs. and pub. rels. Conn. Trauma Coalition, New Haven, 1995—. Rockefeller Humanities grantee. Mem.: Internat. Soc. for Traumatic Stress Studies, Coll. Composition and Comm., Nat. Coun. Tchrs. English, NE Popular Culture Assn., Internat. Comparative Lit. Assn., Am. Comparative Lit. Assn., Modern Lang. Soc.

HOOD, DONALD CHARLES, academic administrator, psychologist, educator; b. Merrick, N.Y., June 2, 1942; s. David and Jessie Theresa (Vetter) H.; m. Nancy Ellen Epstein, Nov. 27, 1978. BA, Harpur Coll.-SUNY, Binghamton, 1965; MS, Brown U., 1968, PhD, 1970. Asst. prof. Columbia U., N.Y.C., 1969-73, assoc. prof., 1973-78, prof. psychology, 1978—, James F. Bender prof. psychology, 1990—, v.p. arts & sci., 1982-87, chmn. psychology dept., 1975-78. Contbr. articles to profl. jours. Trustee Smith Coll., 1989—99, vice chair, 1991—99; trustee Harry Guggenheim Found., 1996—; trustee (fellow) Brown U., 2002—; trustee Assn. Rsch. Vision and Ophthalmology, 2004—. USPHS fellow, 1967—69, N.Y. State Coll. teaching fellow, 1965—67. Fellow: Optical Soc., Soc. Exptl. Psychology; mem.: Ea. Psychol. Assn., Assn. Rsch. Vision and Ophthalmology (trustee 2004—). Home: 450 Riverside Dr New York NY 10027-6801 Office: 415 Schernerhorn Hall 116th St And Broadway New York NY 10027 Office Phone: 212-854-4587. Business E-Mail: dch3@columbia.edu.

HOOD, EDWARD EXUM, JR., retired electronics executive; b. Boonville, N.C., Sept. 15, 1930; s. Edward Exum and Nellie (Triplett) H.; m. Kay Transou, Dec. 30, 1950; children: Lisa Kay, Molly Ann. MS in Nuclear Engring., N.C. State U., 1953. Registered profl. engr., Ariz. Powerplant design engr. Gen. Electric Co., 1957-62, mgr. supersonic transport engine project, 1962-67, v.p., gen. mgr. comml. engine div., from 1968, v.p., group exec. internat. group, 1972-73, v.p., group exec., power generation group, 1973-77, sr. v.p., sector exec. tech. systems and materials sector, from 1977, vice-chmn. and exec officer, 1979-93, also bd. dirs. Served with USAF, 1952-56. Fellow AIAA; mem. Nat. Acad. Engring., Aerospace Industries Assn. (chmn. 1981) Home: 11674 Lake House Ct North Palm Beach FL 33408-3318

HOOD, ERNEST ALVA, SR., pharmaceutical company executive; b. East St. Louis, Ill., July 10, 1910; s. Orestes Rasmus and Daisy Ernestine (Eslick) H.; m. Taeko Haruta; children: Ernest Jr., Dharathula (Hood) Harris, Daisy. CEO Cophtra Ltd., N.Y.C., 1950—; power maintainer Con Edison, N.Y.C., 1952-72; N.Y. rep. Coastal Pharm. Co. Ltd., Norfolk, Va., Ghana, 1974-76, cons. Bklyn., Ghana, 1976—. Cons. Uchi Ichi Shoji Ltd., Japan, 1946—, Jaiama Tayorma Natural Scrap Exch., Freetown, Sierra Leone, Lome Natural Scrap Exch., Lome, Togo, 1994—, Abua Farms and Industries, Ashanti, 1996—, Buckberra Trading Co., Okyere Bour & Co., Ashanti, Two Worlds Mfg. Co.; advisor Cophtra Ltd. Author: (autobiography) Hoodisan-1910-1994. Bd. dirs., Cen. Bklyn. Coord. Coun. 1st lt. U.S. Army. Recipient Ulchii award, Republic South Korea. Mem. VFW, Vets. Assn. Home: 8025 Hickory Ave Gary IN 46403-2265 Office: Cophtra Ltd 550 Green Ave Brooklyn NY 11216-5710

HOOD, GLENDA E., state official; m. Charles M. Hood III; 3 children. BA in Spanish, Rollins Coll.; postgrad., Harvard U., Ga. State U. Commr. City of Orlando, Fla., 1982-92, mayor, 1992—2002; sec. of state Florida, 2003—. Pres. Glenda E. Hood & Assocs., Inc. Vice chmn. mcpl. planning bd. City of Orlando, mem. nominating bd., chmn. task force bd. and commn. restructure; past chmn., founding mem. bd. dirs. Found. Orange County Pub. Schs.; co-chmn. Orlando Fights Back-Coalition for a Drug-Free Cmty.; bd. dirs. U. Ctrl. Fla. Found., Met. Orlando Urban League; past pres. exec. bd. Ctrl. Fla. Coun. of Boy Scouts; bd. overseers Rollins Coll. Crummer Grad. Sch. of Bus.; mem. adv. bd. Valencia C.C., Fla.- Costa Rica Inst.; past co-chmn. United Negro Coll. Fund; pres. Jr. League Orlando-Winter Park, Vol. Svc. Bur.; mem. Orange County Commn. on Children. Named Mcpl. Leader of Yr., Am. City and County Mag., 1992, one of Ten Outstanding Young Americans, U.S. Jaycees, one of Seven Outstanding Youth Floridians, Fla. Jaycees, Woman of Yr., Downtown Orlando Inc., one of Ten People to Watch, Fla. Trend, one of 100 Young Women of Promise, Good Housekeeping; recipient Willie J. Bruton award for cmty. svc. Met. Orlando Urban League, Summit award Women's Resource Ctr., Svc. to Mankind award Leukemia Soc. Am. Ctrl. Fla. chpt. Mem. Nat. League of Cities (past pres.), Fla. League of Cities (past pres.), Fla. C. of C. (past pres.), Greater Orlando C. of C. (past v.p.). Republican. Episcopalian. Office: Florida Dept of State R A Gray Bldg 500 S Bronough Tallahassee FL 32399-0250

HOOD, HENRY J., lawyer, energy executive; b. 1960; AB, Duke U., 1982; JD, U. Okla., 1985. Bar: 1985. With Watson & McKenzie, 1987—92; assoc. White, Coffey, Galt & Fite, 1992—95; v.p. land and legal Chesapeake Energy Corp., Okla. City, Okla., 1995—97, sr. v.p. land and legal, 1997—. Cons. Chesapeake Energy Corp., 1995—97. Mem.: Tex. Bar Assn., Okla. Bar Assn. Office: Chesapeake Energy Corp PO Box 18496 Oklahoma City OK 73154-0496

HOOD, JAMES CALTON, lawyer; b. Panama Canal Zone, Oct. 29, 1947; s. Robin Calton and Eleanor (Marquard) H.; m. Elise Joan Gregory, Aug. 16, 1969; children: Jamie, Molly. BA, U. N.H., 1969; JD, Georgetown U., 1972. Bar: NH 1972. Assoc. and dir. McLane, Graf, Raulerson & Middleton, PA, Manchester, NH, 1972—95; ptnr. Nixon Peabody LLP, Manchester, 1995—. Chmn. NH internat. trade adv. com. to gov. Dept. Resources and Econ. Devel. Bd. dirs. Manchester YMCA, 1982, Chmn., 1986-88; trustee St. Paul's Meth. Ch., Manchester 1985. Served to lst lt. U.S. Army, 1972-73. Mem. ABA, NH Bar Assn. (chmn. corp. sect. 1985), U. NH Alumni Assn. (bd. dirs. 1986-93, pres. 1992-93), Phi Beta Kappa, Phi Kappa Phi. Home: 154 Shaw St Manchester NH 03104-2760 Office: Nixon Peabody 889 Elm St Manchester NH 03101-2019 Office Phone: 603-628-4051. Office Fax: 603-628-4040. E-mail: jchood@nixonpeabody.com.

HOOD, JAMES MICHAEL, lawyer; b. Des Moines, Mar. 27, 1945; s. James Vincent and Maybl (Rayburn) H.; m. Sherrie Elaine Lazar, Apr. 16, 1973; children— James Michael, Grace. B.A., Drake U., 1967, J.D., 1970. Bar: Iowa 1970, U.S. Dist. Ct. (so. dist) Iowa 1970, U.S. Dist. Ct. (no. dist.) Iowa 1972, U.S. Dist. Ct. (so. dist.) Ill. 1978, U.S. Supreme Ct. 1978. Sole practice, Davenport, Iowa, 1970— . Served with USN, 1970-72. Mem. ABA, Iowa Bar Assn., Scott County Bar Assn., Assn. Trial Lawyers Iowa, Assn. Trial Lawyers Am., Iowa Assn. Worker Compensation Lawyers. Home: 2213 Fairhaven Rd Davenport IA 52803-2334 Office: 302 Union Arcade Bldg Davenport IA 52801 Office Phone: 563-323-5255. E-mail: james@jameshood.com.

HOOD, JASON P., lawyer; 2 children. BA cum laude with honors in internat. studies, Rhodes Coll., 1987; JD, U. Tenn., 1994. Bar: Tenn. 1994, U.S. Dist. Ct. (we. dist.) Tenn. 1995. Asst. strategic planning Buckman Labs. Internat., Inc., Memphis, 1987—89, mgr. human resources devel., 1989—91; atty. Glankler Brown PLLC, Memphis, 1994—97; employee benefits atty. Sedgwick Noble Lowndes, Memphis, 1997—98; corp. counsel Wright Med. Tech., Inc., Arlington, Tenn., 1998—98, gen. counsel and sec., 1998—2002; v.p., gen. counsel and sec. Wright Med. Tech., Inc. and Wright Med. Group, Inc., Arlington, 2002—. Exec. bd. mem. Boy Scouts of Am., Chickasaw Coun., Memphis, 1990. Named one of Outstanding Young Men of Am., 1988; named to Order of the Barristers, 1994. Mem.: FBA (pres. Memphis/mid-south chpt. 2001—02), ABA, Def. Rsch. Inst., Assn. Corp. Counsel, Am. Soc. Corp. Secretaries, Memphis Bar Assn., Tenn. Bar Association. Office: Wright Medical Technology Inc 5677 Airline Rd Arlington TN 38002 Office Phone: 901-867-4743.

HOOD, JIM, state attorney general; m. Debbie Hood; 3 children. BA, U. Miss., JD, 1988. Asst. atty. gen. State of Miss., Jackson, Miss.; dist. atty. Third Circuit Ct Dist., N. Miss.; atty. gen. State of Miss., 2003—. Recipient Justice Achievement award, Crime Victim's Compensation Program, 2003. Democrat. Baptist. Achievements include prosecuted (with Dist. Atty. Mark Duncan) Edgar Ray Killen for the 1964 triple murders of civil rights workers Andrew Goodman, James Chaney and Michael Schwerner, June 2005. Office: Miss Atty Gen Off 450 High St PO Box 220 Jackson MS 39205

HOOD, LEROY EDWARD, molecular biologist, educator; b. Missoula, Mont., Oct. 10, 1938; s. Thomas Edward and Myrtle Evylan (Wadsworth) H.; m. Valerie Anne Logan, Dec. 14, 1963; children: Eran William, Marqui Leigh Jennifer. BS, Calif. Inst. Tech., 1960, PhD in Biochemistry, 1968; MD, Johns Hopkins U., 1964. Med. officer USPHS, 1967-70; staff scientist Pub. Health Svc., Bethesda, Md., 1967-70; sr. investigator Nat. Cancer Inst., 1967-70; asst. prof. biology Calif. Inst. Tech., Pasadena, 1970-73, assoc. prof., 1973-75, prof., 1975-92, Bowles prof. biology, 1977-92, chmn. div. biology, 1980-89; Gates prof. molecular biotech., chmn. bd. U. Wash. Sch. Medicine, Seattle, 1992—2000; pres., dir. Instit. for Systems Biology, Seattle, 2000—. Dir. NSF Sci. and Tech. Ctr. for Molecular Biotech., 1989-2001. Author: (with others) Biochemistry, a Problems Approach, 1974, Molecular Biology of Eukaryotic Cells, 1975, Immunology, 1978, Essential Concepts of Immunology, 1978, The Code of Codes: Scientific and Social Issues in the Human Genome Project, 1992; co-editor: Advances in Immunology, 1987, Genetics: From Genes to Genomics, 1999. Co-recipient, Albert Lasker Basic Medical Research Award, 1987, recipient Scientist of the Year Award, 1993, R&D Magazine, Kyoto Prize, 2002, Lemelson prize MIT, 2003. Mem. NAS, Am. Assn. Immunologists, Am. Assn. Sci., Am. Acad. Arts and Scis., Sigma Xi, Am. Philosophical Soc., Inst. Medicine, 2004. Achievements include invention of automated gene sequencer. Avocations: mountain climbing, rock-climbing, photography. Office: Inst for Systems Biology 1441 34th St Seattle WA 98103-8904

HOOD, MARY DULLEA, law librarian; b. Fargo, N.D., Jan. 3, 1947; d. Maurice Eugene and Rosemary (Melican) Dullea; m. Michael L. Hood, May 26, 1974; children: David Patrick, Michelle Marie. BA, U. Santa Clara, 1970, JD, 1975; MLS, San Jose State U., 1979. Bar: Calif. 1976. Libr. asst. Law Libr., U. Santa Clara, Calif., 1970-75, reference libr., 1975-78; instr. legal rsch. Paralegal Inst., 1976-84; head pub. svcs. U. Santa Clara, Calif., 1978-87, assoc. dir., 1987—, mem. univ. automation task force, 1986-91, mem. adj. faculty advanced legal rsch. Law Sch., 1998-99, 2001, acting dir., 2001. Mem. Santa Clara CSC, 1976-78. Mem. Am. Assn. Law Librs. (placement com. 2000-02, awards com. 2002-04), No. Calif. Assn. Law Librs. (pres. 1982-83), U. Santa Clara Law Sch. Alumni Assn. (treas. 1983-85). Avocations: needlepoint, reading, stained glass. Office: Santa Clara U Law Libr 500 El Camino Real Santa Clara CA 95053-0430 E-mail: mhood@scu.edu.

HOOD, PHYLLIS ILENE, special education educator; d. James H Brown and Viola Mae Riggle, Brown, Jones; m. James Richard Morris, May 27, 1954 (div. Mar. 6, 1986); m. Charles Gary Hood, Feb. 18, 1988 (div. Nov. 8, 1993); children: Stacy Lynn Gebhardt, James Richard Morris, Teresa Rene Thompson, Vilas Lester Morris, Ruth Ilene Owens, Richard Hayden Morris. BS in edn., NW Mo. State U., 1985—89, MS in edn., 1989—96. Elem. Edn. NW Mo. State U., 1989, Learning Disabled NW Mo. State U., 1989, Mentally Handicapped NW Mo. State U., 1991, Reading NW Mo. State U., 1996, Mild/Moderate Behavior Disorder U. of Ctrl. Ark., 2000. Spl. edn. and reading tchr. North Andrew R-VI Elem. Sch., Bolkow, Mo., 1989—90; spl. edn. tchr. Nodaway-Holt R-VII H.S., Graham, Mo., 1990—92, Camdenton R-III Sch. Dist., Camdenton, Mo., 1992—98, Spl. Sch. Dist., Town and Country, Mo., 1998—. Cheerleader sponsor Nodaway-Holt R-VII Sch. Dist., Graham, Mo., 1991—92, Camdenton R-III Sch. Dist., Camdenton, Mo., 1992—94, Hazelwood Sch. Dist., St. Louis, 2000—01; sponsor Big Bros./Big Sisters, St. Louis, 2001—. Ladies aux. Mo. Army N.G., Maryville, Mo., 1989—96; club mem. Optimist Club of Camdenton, Mo., 1992—98, pres., 1997—98; club mem. Optimist Club of O'Fallon, O'Fallon, Mo., 1999—2003, pres., 2000—01. Named a Honor Pres., Optimist Internat. -East Mo. Dist., 2000—01; named Disting. Pres., Optimist Internat.-West Mo. Dist., 1997—98; recipient Cert. of Appreciation, Optimist Internat. -East Mo. Dist., 2001—02. Mem.: Coun. for Exceptional Children (corr.). D-Liberal. Christian. Avocations: dance, travel, swimming, walking, gardening. Office: Hazelwood East High School 11300 Dunn Rd Saint Louis MO 63138

HOOD, RONALD CHALMERS, III, historian, writer; b. Florence, Ala., Apr. 2, 1947; s. Ronald Chalmers II and Elizabeth Woods (Craig) H.; m. Lucile O'Connor, Dec. 20, 1969; children: Ronald Chalmers IV, Reed Cathleen. BS, U.S. Naval Acad., 1969; MA, U. Maine, Orono, 1972; PhD, U. Md., 1979. Commd. 2d lt. USMC, 1969, advanced through grades to capt., 1973, resigned, 1982; historian, writer Johns Hopkins U., Balt., 1982—, George Mason U., Fairfax, Va., 1982—, U. Md., College Park, 1982—, Mary Washington Coll., 1999—. Lectr. Smithsonian Instn., Washington, 1988; speaker Conf. on Strategic Studies, Washington, 1985; co-chair Muscle Shoals Revisited Conf. on Future of Tenn. Valley, 1993; theatre and arts critic The Daily Jour. Author: (history monograph) Royal Republicans, 1985; co-author: (mil. history) Military Effectiveness, 1987, Body, Mind, Spirit: 75 Years of Camp Hazen YMCA, 1995; contbg. author Internat. Ency. for Military History; contbr. editorial columns to Washington Post, Richmond Times-Dispatch, Potomac News, articles to profl. jours. Asst. scoutmaster Boy Scouts Am., Woodbridge, Va., 1989—; advisor Va. State Bd. Edn., 2003-; instr. ARC, Prince William County, 1982—. Samuel Eliot Morison fellow U. Maine, Orono, 1971-72, Grad. Sch. fellow U. Md., 1975, fellow Am. Philos. Soc., 1998, sr. fellow to France Am. Coun. Learned Societies, 2000-2001. Mem. AAUP, Writers' Ctr., Smithsonian Instn., Nat. Geographic Soc. Avocations: travel, acting, bike riding, aquatic activities, cross country skiing. Home and Office: 12317 Oakwood Dr Woodbridge VA 22192-1911

HOOD, SANDRA DALE, librarian; b. Edmond, Okla., Nov. 28, 1949; d. Rufus Gustav and Hope Louvica (Hutton) Farber; m. Frank D. Hood Jr., May 17, 1971; 1 child, Charles Richard. BA, U. Okla., 1971, MLS, 1972; MA in Bicultural Bilingual Studies, U. Tex., San Antonio, 1996. Libr. South Oklahoma City Jr. Coll., 1973, Daus. of Republic of Tex. Libr. at the Alamo, San Antonio, 1980—88; acad. outreach prof., automation and libr. sys. libr. Palo Alto Coll. Learning Resources Ctr., San Antonio, 1988—. Pres. Palo Alto Coll. Faculty Sen., 2001—02, parliamentarian, 2004—. Featured (TV game show) Jeopardy, 2004. Pres. tech. svcs. spl. interest group Coun. Rsch. and Acad. Librs., San Antonio, 1991-92, chmn. circulation and interlibr. loan spl. interest group, 1997—; sec., mem. exec. bd. Timberwood Park Property Owners Assn., San Antonio, 1991-94. Recipient NISOD award, 2003. Mem. ALA, Tex. Libr. Assn. (conf. planning com. 1992-93, 97-98, 2002-04), Tex.

Accelerated Libr. Leader 1997, disaster relief com. 2002—), Bexar Libr. Assn. (exec. bd., dir. editor 1988-90), Tex. Cmty. Coll. Tchrs. Assn. Democrat. Lutheran. Achievements include contestant on Jeopardy, Apr. 2004. Avocations: travel, reading, computers. Home: 27030 Foggy Meadows St San Antonio TX 78260-1822 Office: Palo Alto Coll Learning Resources Ctr 1400 W Villaret Blvd San Antonio TX 78224-2417 Office Phone: 210-921-5062. Business E-Mail: shood@accd.edu.

HOOD, THOMAS GREGORY, minister; b. Stamford, Conn., Mar. 26, 1948; s. George E. and Shirley W. (Brundage) H.; m. Esther A. Whitcomb, July 1, 1967; children: Thomas G., Sarah D. BA, Johnson State Coll., 1984; MDiv, Covington Sem., Rossville, Ga., 1986, PhD in Counseling, 1988. Ordained to ministry Fellowship of Christian Assemblies, 1969, Am. Bapt. Chs. in U.S.A., 1984. Asst. pastor Bethel Full Gospel Ch., Barton, Vt., 1968-71; pastor Lyndonville (Vt.) Full Gospel Ch., 1969-71, Sheffield (Vt.) Fed. Ch., 1971-74, Sutton (Vt.) Bapt. Ch., 1972-84, Adams Center (N.Y.) Bapt. Ch., 1984—. Del. Am. Bapt. Conv., N.Y., 1984—. Author: The Lord's Prayer, 1986, A Theology of Victory, 1987, Biblical Principles, 1988; composer religious songs. Mem. Am. Bapt.Mins. Coun. Republican. Home: 13463 US Rt 11 Adams Center NY 13606 *It is impossible to forgive ourselves for our failures if we are unwilling to forgive others theirs. The rule we use to judge others will always reflect back on ourselves.*

HOOD, WILLIAM BOYD, JR., cardiologist, educator; b. Sylacauga, Ala., Mar. 25, 1932; s. William Boyd and Katherine Elizabeth (Anderson) H.; m. Katherine Candace Todd, May 5, 1972; 1 son, Jefferson Boyce. BS summa cum laude, Davidson Coll., 1954; MD, Harvard U., 1958. Intern Peter Bent Brigham Hosp., Boston, 1958-59, resident in internal medicine, 1959-60, 62-63; from asst. prof. to assoc. prof. medicine Harvard U., 1967-71; from assoc. prof. to prof. medicine Boston U., 1971-82; chief cardiology Boston City Hosp., 1973-82; prof. medicine U. Rochester (N.Y.), 1982-98; head cardiology unit Strong Meml. Hosp., Rochester, 1982-98; emeritus prof. medicine U. Rochester, 1998—. Cons. NIH, 1975—, NASA, 1994—; clin. prof. medicine U. Wash. Sch. Medicine, Seattle, 2000—. Mem. editorial bd. New Eng. Jour. Medicine, 1974-81, Circulation, 1980-83, Circulation Research, 1982-89, Jour. Clin. Investigation, 1984-89, Cochrane Collaboration Heart Group, 1997—; contbr. articles, revs. and editorials on cardiovascular physiology to profl. jours., chpts. to books. Served to capt. USAF, 1963-65. Research grantee NIH, 1971-98; grantee Am. Heart Assn., 1971-76. Fellow ACP; mem. Am. Soc. Clin. Investigation, Assn. Am. Physicians, Am. Heart Assn., Am. Physiol. Soc., Assn. Profs. Cardiology (past pres.), N.Y. Cardiol. Soc. (past pres.), Phi Beta Kappa, Alpha Omega Alpha. Achievements include studies on experimental and clinical myocardial ischemia and infarction, and congestive heart failure.

HOO FATT, MICHELLE STEPHANIE, engineering educator, mechanical engineer; b. Kingston, Jamaica, July 11, 1964; d. Lascelles Charles and Ethel Dorothy Hoo Fatt. BS, MIT, 1987, MS, 1990, PhD, 1992. Lectr., rschr. U. Calif., Berkeley, 1992—93; rschr. MIT, Akron, Mass., 1993—95; assoc. prof. mech. engring. U. Akron, Ohio, 1995—. Author: (research paper) Journal of Composite Structures. Grantee, NSF, 2003—04. Mem.: ASME. Achievements include patents pending for tensile impact apparatus. Office: Univ Akron Dept Mech Engrg Akron OH 44325-3903 Office Phone: 330-972-6308. Home Fax: 330-972-6027; Office Fax: 330-972-6027. E-mail: hoofatt@uakron.edu.

HOOGASIAN, SETH H., electronics executive, lawyer; b. Worcester, Mass., Apr. 18, 1954; BS with distinction, Cornell U., 1976; JD with distinction, Duke U., 1979. Bar: D.C. 1979, Md. 1989, Mass. 1993. Gen. counsel Thermo Electron Corp., Waltham, Mass., 1992—, v.p., 1996—, sec., 2001—. Mem. ABA, Mass. Bar Assn., Tau Beta Pi. Office: Thermo Electron Corp PO Box 9046 81 Wyman St Waltham MA 02451-1223*

HOOGENBOOM, GERRIT, agricultural engineer; b. Monster, Netherlands, Dec. 19, 1955; came to U.S., 1981; s. Gerrit and Christina Margaretha (van Duijker) H.; m. Carol Jo Wilkerson, Dec. 16, 1984. MSc, Agrl. U., Wageningen, Netherlands, 1981; PhD, Auburn U., 1985. With Scottish Horticultural Rsch. Inst., 1977-78; vis. scientist Volcani Ctr., Bet Dagan, Israel, 1979; grad. rsch. asst. Auburn (Ala.) U., 1981-85; postdoctoral rsch. assoc. U. Fla., Gainesville, 1985-89; asst. prof. dept. biol. and agrl. engring. U. Ga., Griffin, 1985-95, assoc. prof., 1995-2000, prof., 2000—. Cons. Winrock Internat., New Delhi, India, 1990, FAO, Beijing, 1997. Co-editor: Understanding Options for Agricultural Production; assoc. editor Agronomy Jour.; contbr. articles to Can. Jour. Forest Rsch., Agrl. Sys., Agronomy Jour., Agr. and Fgn. Meteorology, Trans. Am. Soc. Agrl. Engrs. Mem. Am. Soc. Agrl. Engrs., Crop Sci. Soc. Am., Soil Sci. Soc. Am., Am. Soc. Agronomy (Step award 1984), Soc. Computer Simulation (sr.), Sigma Xi. Episcopalian. Achievements include co-design of a computer model which simulates root growth and water uptake, ROOTSIMU, and of a computer model which stimulates growth, development and yield of soybean, peanut, dry bean, and chickpea (CROPGRO). Linkage of crop simulation models and Geographic Information Systems. Management of an automated environmental monitoring network for the state of Georgia. Home: 142 Rabbit Run Rd Dandridge TN 37725-5876 Office: U Ga 1109 Experiment St Griffin GA 30223-1797 E-mail: gerrit@griffin.peachnet.edu.

HOOK, HAROLD SWANSON, former management consulting executive; b. Kansas City, Mo., Oct. 10, 1931; s. Ralph C. and Ruby (Swanson) H.; m. Joanne T. Hunt, Feb. 19, 1955; children: Karen Anne, Thomas W., Randall T. BS in Bus. Adminstrn., U. Mo., 1953, MA in Acctg., 1954; grad., So. Meth. U. Inst. Ins. Mktng., 1957; postgrad., NYU, 1967-70; LLD (hon.), U. Mo., 1983, Westminster Coll., 1983. CLU, FLMI. Mem. faculty U. Mo. Sch. Bus., 1953-54; asst. to pres. Nat. Fidelity Life Ins. Co., Kansas City, Mo., 1957-60, dir., 1959-66, adminstrv. v.p., 1960-61, exec. v.p., investment com., 1961-62, pres., exec. com., 1962-66; sr. v.p. U.S. Life Ins. Co., N.Y.C., 1966-67, dir., 1967-70, exec. v.p., mem. exec. com., 1967-68, pres., 1968-70, Calif.-Western States Life Ins. Co., Sacramento, 1970-75, chmn., 1975-79, sr. chmn., 1979-91, also bd. dirs.; mem. exec. com. Am. Gen. Corp., Houston, 1975-97, pres., 1975-81, chmn., chief exec. officer, 1978-96, also bd. dirs., chmn., 1996-97. Founder, pres. Main Event Mgmt. Corp., Houston, 1971—; bd. dirs. Duke Energy Corp.,Charlotte, N.C., Sprint Corp., Kansas City, Mo., Cooper Industries, Inc., Houston, Chase Manhattan Corp., N.Y.C., Chase Manhattan Bank, N.Y.C., Chase Bank ofTex., Houston. Founder, mem. Naval War Coll. Found.; trustee, Baylor Coll. Medicine, Houston; coun. overseers Jesse H. Jones Grad. Sch. Adminstrn., Rice U., Houston; pres. nat. exec. bd. Boy Scouts Am., 1988-90, now mem. nat. adv. coun. Boy Scouts Am., mem. adv. bd. Sam Houston Area coun.; past pres. Houston Commerce, bd. dirs., Greater Houston Partnership (formerly Houston C. of C.), Director Emeritus. Recipient Citation of Merit U. Mo. Alumni Assn., 1965, Faculty-Alumni award U. Mo., 1978; Silver Beaver award Boy Scouts Am., 1974, Disting. Eagle Scout award, 1976, Silver Antelope award, 1989, Silver Buffalo award, 1990; Chief Exec. Officer award Fin. World mag., 1979, 82, 84, 86; named Man of Yr., Delta Sigma Pi, 1969, Outstanding Chief Exec. Officer in Multiline Ins. Industry, Wall Street Transcript, 1981-87. Fellow Life Mgmt. Inst.; mem. Mgmt. Exec. Soc., Philos. Soc. Tex., Tex. Assn. Taxpayers (bd. dirs.), Nat. Assn. Life Underwriters, Houston Assn. Life Underwriters, Forum Club (bd. govs. 1983-93), River Oaks Country Club, Petrolum Club, Econ. Club N.Y.C., Eldorado Country Club, Rotary, Beta Gamma Sigma (dirs. table 1976, nat. honoree 1984). Presbyterian. Office: Main Event Mgmt Corp PO Box 3665Pky Houston TX 77253-3665

HOOK, JERRY B., pharmaceutical consultant; b. Elk City, Okla., Sept. 7, 1937; m. Jacqueline H. Smith; children: Bruce, Marilyn. BS, B in Pharmacy with honors, Wash. State U., Pullman, 1960; MS, U. Iowa, 1964, PhD, 1966; DSc (hon.), John Jay Coll. Criminal Justice, CUNY, 1989. Diplomate Am. Bd. Toxicology. Assoc. prof. pharmacology Mich. State U., East Lansing, 1971-75, prof. of pharmacology, 1975-78, prof. pharmacology and toxicology, 1978-83, dir. ctr. for environ. toxicology, 1980-83; v.p. preclin. R & D Smith Kline & French Labs. Phila., King of Prussia, Pa., 1983-87, v.p. preclin. R & D worldwide, 1987-88, v.p. devel., R & D, 1988-89, SmithKline Beecham Pharms., King of Prussia, 1989-90, sr. v.p., dir. devel. R & D, 1990-93; pres., chief exec. officer Lexin Pharm. Corp., Horsham, Pa., 1993-96; pres., CEO Sparta Pharm., Inc., Horsham, Pa., 1996-98, chmn., pres., CEO, 1998-99. Burroughs-Wellcome vis. prof. U. N.D., 1981; vis. scientist Fed. Am. Soc. for Exptl. Biology Vis. Scientists for Minority Instns. Program, U. P.R. Med. Sch., 1984, Herbert H. Lehman Coll. of City U., 1985, Calif. State U., 1988, Pembroke State U., 1989; mem. adv. com. to bd. sci. counselors Nat. Toxicology Program, 1982-86; chmn. peer rev. panel of experts Nat. Toxology Program; vis. scientist John Jay Coll. Criminal Justice CUNY, 1987, mem. adv. bd. Toxicology Rsch. and Tng. Ctr., 1986-93. Author 225 publs. peer-reviewed lit., 60 book chpts., published symposia, reviews, symposia presentations. Bd. dirs. Montgomery County Community Coll. Found., 1987-89. Fellow Am. Coll. Clin. Pharmacology (hon.); mem. AAAS, Am. Soc. for Pharmacology and Exptl. Therapeutics, Internat. Union of Pharmacology (vice chmn. toxicology sect. 1987-90, chmn. toxicology sect. 1990-94), Internat. Union of Toxicology (1st v.p. 1989-92), Mid-Atlantic Chpt. Soc. of Toxicology, Soc. of Toxicology (councillor 1983-85, v.p. elect 1985-86, v.p. 1986-87, pres. 1987-88, past pres. 1988-89, IUTOX councillor). E-mail: jhook0937@aol.com.

HOOK, JOHN BURNEY, investment company executive; b. Franklin, Ind., Sept. 6, 1928; s. Burney S. and Elsie C. (Hubbard) H.; m. Georgia Delis, Feb. 8, 1958; children— David, Deborah. BS, Ind. U., 1956, MBA, 1957. CPA, Ohio.; cert. fin. analyst. Store mgr. Goodman-Jester, Inc., Franklin, Ind., 1949-50; auditor Ernst & Ernst, Indpls., 1953-56; financial analyst Eli Lilly & Co., Indpls., 1957-59; gen. ptnr. Ball, Burge & Kraus, Cleve., 1966-72; pres., dir. Cuyahoga Mgmt. Corp., 1966-81; mng. ptnr. Hook Ptnrs., Cleve., 1984—96. Mem. AICPA, Am. Inst. CFAs, Union Club (Cleve.), Westwood Country Club, Ironwood Country Club (Palm Desert, Calif.). Republican. Methodist. Home: 73233 Ribbonwood Palm Desert CA 92260

HOOK, RALPH CLIFFORD, JR., business educator; b. Kansas City, Mo., May 2, 1923; s. Ralph Clifford and Ruby (Swanson) H.; m. Joyce Fink, Jan. 20, 1946; children: Ralph Clifford III, John Gregory. BA, U. Mo., 1947, MA, 1948; PhD, U. Tex., 1954. Instr. U. Mo., 1947-48; asst. prof. Tex. A&M U., 1948-51; lectr. U. Tex., 1951-52; co-owner, mgr. Hook Buick Co., also Hook Truck & Tractor Co., Lee's Summit, Mo., 1952-58; assoc. prof. U. Kansas City, 1953-58; dir. Bur. Bus. Rsch. and Svcs., Ariz. State U., 1958-66, prof. mktg., 1960-68; dean Coll. Bus. Adminstrn., U. Hawaii, 1968-74; prof. mktg. U. Hawaii, 1974-96, prof. mktg. emeritus, 1996—. Vis. Disting. prof. N.E. La. U., 1979; dir. Hook Bros. Corp Author: (with others) The Management Primer, 1972, Life Style Marketing, 1979, Marketing Service, 1983; contbr. (with others) monograph series Western Bus. Roundup; founder, moderator Western Bus. Roundup radio series, 1958-68. Bd. dirs. Samaritan Counseling Ctr. of Hawaii and Waikiki Health Ctr. 1st lt. F.A., AUS, 1943-46; col. Res. Recipient alumni citation of merit U. Mo. Coll. Bus. and Pub. Adminstrn., 1969; Disting. Svc. award Nat. Def. Transp. Assn., 1977, God and Svc. award United Meth. Ch./Boy Scouts Am., 1986, Hawaii Jefferson award, 2004; named to Faculty Hall Fame Ariz. State U. Coll. Bus. Assn., 1977, Hawaii Transp. Hall of Fame, 1986, Hawaii Bus. Hall of Fame, 2000; named Educator of Yr., Western Mktg. Educators' Assn., 1998, . Fellow Internat. Coun. for Small Bus. (pres. 1963); mem. Am. Mktg. Assn. (v.p. 1965-67, pres. Ctrl. Ariz. chpt. 1960-61, pres. Honolulu chpt. 1991-92, Wayne A. Lemberg award for disting. svc. 1995), Western Assn. Collegiate Schs. Bus. (pres. 1972-73), Sales and Mktg. Execs. Internat. (life), Nat. Def. Transp. Assn. (life, Hawaii v.p. 1978-82), Newcomen Soc. N.Am. (Hawaii chmn.), Pi Sigma Epsilon (v.p. for edn. programs 1990-94), Mu Kappa Tau (pres. 1996-98), Beta Gamma Sigma, Omicron Delta Kappa, Beta Theta Pi, Delta Sigma Pi (gold coun.). United Methodist. Home: 311 Ohua Ave Apt 1104D Honolulu HI 96815-3636 Office: U Hawaii Coll Bus Adminstrn 2404 Maile Way Bldg C Honolulu HI 96822-2223 Office Phone: 808-923-7462.

HOOK, WILLIAM FRANKLIN, retired radiologist; b. Williston, N.D., May 26, 1935; s. Charles Ellis and Ann (Franklin) H.; m. Margo Joanne Booth, June 21, 1958 (div. Sept. 1968); children: William, Christopher, Paul; m. Merry Jean Schimke, Nov. 26, 1968 (div. 1987); 1 child, Kari Ann; m. Linda Marie Rohrich, Aug. 18, 1988. AB, Stanford U., 1957; MD, Jefferson Med. Coll., 1961. Diplomate Am. Bd. Radiology, Am. Bd. Nuc. Medicine. Staff radiologist O&R Clinic, Bismarck, ND, 1969-74, dir. nuc. radiology, 1983-98, chmn. dept. radiology, 1990-98; chief dept. radiology Bismarck Hosp., 1970-74; dir. dept. radiology Mandan (ND) Hosp., 1974-81; staff radiologist Meth. Hosps., Dallas, 1981-83, Med. Ctr. One, 1984-98; co-dir. Regional MRI Ctr., Bismarck, 1987-92. Asst. clin. prof. U. ND, 1978—. Author: Common Sense and Modern First Aid, 1967, (CD-Rom) X-Ray Film Reading Made Easy, 2001. Lt. USNR, 1961-64, col. Res. ret.; comdr. USAR hosp., Persian Gulf, 1991-92. Mem.: AMA (Physicians Recognition award 1983—86, 1986—92), 6th Dist. Med. Soc., N.D. State Radiol. Soc., Radiol. Soc. N.Am., Soc. Nuc. Medicine, Am. Coll. Radiology. Lutheran. Avocations: hunting, golf, aviation. Address: PO Box 2424 36636 N Mule Train Carefree AZ 85377 E-mail: wfhook@aol.com.

HOOKER, JAMES TODD, manufacturing executive; b. Ashland, Ohio, Dec. 21, 1946; s. Melvin Todd and Harriet (Lutz) Hooker; m. Sallie Foulkrod Utz, Feb. 22, 1975; 1 child, Stephanie Rae. BSBA magna cum laude, Ashland U., 1973. From advt. mgr. to v.p. gen. mgr. Gorman-Rupp Co., Mansfield, Ohio, 1974—2003, v.p. gen. mgr. Bellville, Ohio, 2003—. Solicitor United Way, Mansfield; chmn. bd. trustees Richland County Leadership Unlimited; mem. Heritage Found.; plank owner USN Meml. Found.; chmn. bd. dirs. Mansfield Richland County Chamber Edn. Found.; moderator, bd. deacons Presbyn. Ch., 1988—89, elder, mem. Session. Decorated Vietnamese Gallantry Cross; named Ohio State Water Ski Champion, 2002. Mem.: Omicron Delta Epsilon. Republican. Home: 1090 Trout Dr Mansfield OH 44903-9144 Office: Gorman Rupp Industries 180 Hines Ave Bellville OH 44813

HOOKER, JOSEPH DAVID, writer, minister; b. Westover Air Force Base, Mass., May 28, 1955; s. Joseph David and Alice Jane Hooker; m. Connie Ann Richmond, Apr. 4, 1973; children: Montana Crago, Heidi Marie Maurer, Josie Ann, Casandra Jo. DD (hon.), Ministry of Salvation. Ordained min. Gen. Assn. Regular Baptists, 1980. Self employed freelance writer, 1979—; youth min. Garrett (Ind.) 1st Bapt. Ch., 1996—. Supr. youth ministry Garrett 1st Bapt. Ch., 1996—. Contbr. articles to mags. Republican. Baptist. Avocations: fishing, hunting, canoeing, horses, reading. Home: 3673 Cr 1 Kendallville IN 46755 Office: Hooker's Farms 3673 Cr 1 Kendallville IN 46755 Personal E-mail: jdhooker@zwallet.com.

HOOKER, OLIVIA J., psychologist, educator; b. Muskogee, Okla., Feb. 12, 1915; d. Samuel David and Anita Juliette (Stigger) H. BS, Ohio State U., 1937; MA, Columbia U., 1947; PhD, U. Rochester, N.Y., 1962. Cert. sch. psychologist, N.Y. Elem. tchr. Columbus (Ohio) Pub. Schs., 1937-45; clin. psychologist dept. mental hygiene State of N.Y., Albion, 1948-51, Bedford Hills, 1951-57, Rochester, 1955-57, research psychologist dept. mental hygiene Letchworth Village, 1957-61; sch. psychologist Bur. Child Guidance, N.Y.C., 1951-52; psychologist Kennedy Child Studies Ctr., N.Y.C., 1961-64, dir. psychol. svcs., 1964-83; assoc. prof. Fordham U., Bronx, N.Y., 1974-85. Cons. St. Benedicts's Day Care Ctr., N.Y.C., 1976—, Fred S. Keller Sch., Yonkers, N.Y., 1987-99. Trustee Terence Cardinal Cooke Health Svcs. Coun., N.Y.C., 1984-96; mem. adv. bd. Child Life program Westchester County Med. Ctr., Valhalla, N.Y., 1985-99; v.p. White Plains NAACP, 1985-87, White Plains Sr. Pers. Employment Coun., 1987-96; tutor Literacy Vols. Am., 1987—; bd. dirs. White Plains Child Day Care Assn., 1988-2000, Vis. Nurse Assn. Westchester, 1988-94; chmn. adminstrv. bd. Trinity United Meth. Ch., 1985-87. Served with women's res. USCG, 1945-46. U. Rochester fellow, 1955-56; recipient Women's award Women's History Assn., 1986. Fellow APA (div. on devel. disability), Am. Assn. Mental Retardation. Avocations: creative writing, gardening, music. Office: Fordham U Dept Psychology Bronx NY 10458

HOOKER, RENÉE MICHELLE, perinatal and perianesthesia nurse; b. Kansas City, Mo., June 26, 1965; d. Roland Edward and Loretta Mae (Rathbun) Woods; m. Joel Thomas Hooker, Sept. 17, 1988; children: Andrew, Catherine, Rebekah. BSN, U. Kans., 1987. RN, Tex., Calif.; cert post anesthesia nurse, inpatient obstetric nurse ANCC; cert. ACLS, neonatal resuscitation; cert. BLS instr. Am. Heart Assn. Staff med.-surg. nurse Desert Hosp., Palm Springs, Calif., 1987-88; staff nurse neonatal ICU Santa Rose Children's Hosp., San Antonio, 1988; staff obstetrics nurse, post anesthesia care unit McKenna Meml. Hosp., New Braunfels, Tex., 1988-00, pre-post anesthesia care nurse mgr., 1999; staff nurse St. Joseph Health Ctr. Pain Clinic, Kansas City, Mo., 2001—05; clin. nurse educator surg. svcs. Liberty (Mo.) Hosp., 2001—05. Mem. Assn. Women's Health, Obstet. and Neonatal Nursing, Tex. Assn. Post Anesthesia Nurses, Am. Soc. Post Anesthesia Nurses. Avocations: reading, cooking, travel, child advocacy.

HOOKER, ROBERT WRIGHT, journalist; b. New Haven, July 11, 1947; s. Charles Wright and Elma (Black) Hooker; m. Ellen Ann McMackin, Apr. 13, 1974; 1 child, Matthew Wright. BA in History, Davidson (N.C.) Coll., 1969; MA in History, Vanderbilt U., 1971. Reporter St. Petersburg (Fla.) Times, 1971-78, polit. editor, 1978, night city editor, 1979, projects editor, 1979-87, Tampa city editor, 1987, state editor, 1987-90, bus. editor, 1990-96, met. editor, 1996, asst. mng. editor, 1997-2001, dep. mng. editor, 2001—. Author: The Times and Its Times: 1884-1984, 1984. 1st lt. USAR, 1971. Recipient Nat. Edn. Reporting award, Edn. Writers Am., 1983, Best Investigative Reporting award, Am. Sports Editors Assn., 1983. Home: 2982 60th Ave S Saint Petersburg FL 33712-4524 Office: Saint Petersburg Times PO Box 1121 Saint Petersburg FL 33731-1121 Business E-Mail: hooker@sptimes.com.

HOOKER, VAN DORN, architect, artist; b. Carthage, Tex., Sept. 22, 1921; s. Van Dorn and Anne (Wylie) H.; m. Marjorie Mead, June 14, 1947; children: Ann, Van Dorn III, John Hardy. Student, Coll. of Marshall, Tex., 1938-40; BArch, U. Tex., 1947; postgrad., U. Calif.-Berkeley, 1950-51. Registered architect, N.Mex., Tex. Architect, ptnr. McHugh & Hooker-Bradley P. Kidder & Assocs., Santa Fe, 1956-63; univ. architect U. N.Mex., Albuquerque, 1963-87, univ. architect emeritus, 1987—, assoc. prof. architecture, 1971-87; assoc. prof. architecture emeritus, 1987—. Architect numerous bldgs.; one-man show, Bradywine Gallery, Albuquerque, 1973, group shows include, Mus. of N.Mex., 1963, 1979; represented permanent collection, Mus. N.Mex.; author: Centuries of Hands, 1996, Only in New Mexico, 2000; contbr. articles to various publs. Trustee Albuquerque Acad., 1972-82; bd. dirs. Corrales Land Trust, 1991—. Recipient Regents medal U. N.Mex., Fergusson award U. N.Mex. Alumni Assn., 2000. Fellow AIA (pres. Albuquerque chpt. 1971, Silver medal We. Mountain region), Assn. Univ. Architects (pres. 1971); mem. N.Mex. Architecture Found. (pres. 1987), Santa Fe Chamber Music Festival (bd. dirs.), N.Mex. Soc. Architects (honor and merit awards, pres. 1973, Appreciation award 1987). Address: PO Box 2942 Corrales NM 87048-2942

HOOKER, WADE STUART, lawyer; b. Brockton, Mass., Sept. 23, 1941; s. Wade S. and Eleanor T. Hooker; m. Susan M. Levine, May 20, 1984; children: Thomas A., Richard P. BA, Harvard Coll., 1963; LLB, U. Va., 1966. Bar: N.Y. 1969. Assoc. Casey, Lane & Mittendorf, N.Y.C., 1968-77; ptnr. Burlingham Underwood LLP, N.Y.C., 1979—2001; ind. practice, 2002—. Spkr. in field. Editor-in-chief Va. Jour. Internat. Law, 1965-66; contbr. articles to profl. jours. Maxwell fellow Syracuse U., Resident scholar Indian Law Inst., New Delhi, 1966-67. Mem. ABA, Assn. Bar City of N.Y. (chair aeronautics com. 2001-04), Computer Law Assn., Inc., Internat. Bar Assn., Maritime Law Assn. U.S. (chair com. maritime regulation and promotion 1990-94), Mensa. Office: 211 Central Park W New York NY 10024 Office Phone: 212-362-2696. Business E-Mail: wadehooker@post.harvard.com.

HOOKS, AUBREY, ambassador; b. Mullins, SC, May 18, 1948; m. Jean Wilkinson; 6 children. AA, Brevard Coll., 1968; BA, U. SC, 1970; MA in econ., U. Mich., 1984. Sr. sem. 38th class US Govt.; joined Fgn. Svc., 1971—; jr. off. trainee Am. Embassy, Tel Aviv, 1971—73, econ. consular officer Warsaw, 1973—76; cultural affairs off. US Dept. of State, Washington, 1976—78; econ. off. Am. Embassy, Ankara, Turkey, 1979—83, dir. econ. sec. Port-au-Prince, Haiti, 1984—87, econ. counselor Warsaw, 1992—95; amb. to Republic of Congo US Dept. State, Brazzaville, 1996—99; charge d'Affaires Am. Embassy, Bangui, Central African Republic, 1998—99; spl. coord. for the African Crisis Response Intiative US Dept. State, 1999—2001, amb. Dem. Rep. of Congo Kinshasa, 2001—04, amb. Cote d'Ivoire Abidjan, 2004—. Mem. US Delegation to the Conf. on Security & Cooperation in Europe, Helsinki, Finland, 1992. Office: Am Embassy Abidjan 2010 Abidjan Pl Washington DC 20521-2010

HOOKS, EARL J., art educator, sculptor; b. Balt., Aug. 2, 1927; Student, Howard U.; B in Art Edn., Cath. U. Cert. Rochester Inst. Tech., NY. Instr. ceramics and drawing Shaw U., Raleigh, NC, 1953—54, Ind. U., Gary, 1967—67; instr., art cons. Gary Pub. Schs., Ind., 1959—68; assoc. prof. sculpture and ceramics, chmn. dept. art Fisk U., 1968—. Exhibitions include DePauw U., Greencastle, Ind., Harmon Found., NY, City of Gary, Ind., State of Tenn. Arts Commn., Howard U. Invitational, 1961, 21st Syracuse Biennial Traveling Exhbn., Smithsonian Instn., 1961—62, Inst. Minerals & Chemicals, Skokie, Ill., 1966, exhibited in group shows at Art Inst. Chgo., 1967, Ball State Mus., Muncie, Ind., 1969, Two Centuries of Black Am. Art, LA County Mus. Art, 1976, Dallas Mus. Fine Arts, 1977, High Mus., Atlanta, 1977, Bklyn. Mus., 1977, prin. works include ceramic sculpture, State Gift to Gov. Ray Blanton, Tanzania, 1977; co-author: Extended Services in Museum Science Training, 1972, Ben Jones, 1977. Recipient Second Prize, Arts & Crafts, John Herron Art Sch., 1959, Purchase Prize, Dedication of Art Bldg., Howard U., 1960, Cert. of Honor, Internat. Festival of Lagos, Nigerian Govt., 1977.

HOOKS, GEORGE BARDIN, state legislator, insurance and real estate company executive; b. Americus, Ga., May 9, 1945; s. Thomas Bardin III and Rose Mary (Fay) H.; m. Gail Ann Goen, Aug. 30, 1975; children: George Bardin Jr., Mary Ann. BA, Auburn U., 1970; postgrad., Princeton U.; LLD, Mercer U. V.p. southeast region Alliance of Am. Insurers, Atlanta, 1972-77; pres. Hooks Agy. Inc., Americus, Ga., 1977—; rep. State of Ga. House Reps., 1980-90; sen. State of Ga. Senate, 1990—. Floor leader for Gov. Ga. House Reps., 1988-90, chair rules com., 1992-93, chair appropriations com., 1993—. Active bd. dirs. Ft. Valley State U., 1992—, Mercer U., 1997—. Named Legislator of Yr., Mcpl. Assn., 1992, County Com. Assn., 1993. Mem. Ga. Assn. Ins. Agts. (bd. dirs. 1978-80. legis. dir. 1974, Pres. Citation 1974, 80), Ga. C. of C. (leadership Ga. 1982), Americus C. of C. (legis. chmn.), Rotary, Kappa Alpha. Democrat. Baptist. Home: 145 Taylor St Americus GA 31709-4056 Office: PO Box 928 Americus GA 31709-0928 Office Phone: 229-924-2924. Business E-Mail: ghooks@legis.state.ga.us.

HOOKS, JAMES DARWIN, school librarian; b. Kittanning, Pa., Sept. 14, 1942; s. Roy Winfield and Edna Ruth Hooks. BS in Edn., Clarion U., 1964; MLS, U. Pitts., 1966; cert. in libr. sci., U. Pitss., 1971; PhD, U. Pitts., 1979. Libr. Fox Chapel (Pa.) H.S., 1964, Hampton Twp. Sr. H.S., Allison Park, Pa., 1964—70; libr. Armstrong campus IUP, Kittanning, Pa., 1970—. Co-author: Implementing Online Union Lists of Serials: The Pennsylvania Union List of Serials Experience, 1989. Mem.: ALA, Train Collectors Assn., Am. Guild Organists. Democrat. Lutheran. Avocations: train collecting, travel. Office: Armstrong Campus IUP 704 N McKean St Kittanning PA 16201

HOOKS, VENDIE HUDSON, III, surgeon; b. Metter, Ga., Nov. 1, 1948; s. Vendie Hudson Jr. and May (Jones) H.; m. Carolyn Anderson Braithwaite, Nov. 1, 1974; children: Hudson, Susanna, David, Katherine. BS, U. Ga., 1970; MD, Med. Coll. Ga., 1974. Diplomate Am. Bd. Surgery, Am. Bd. Colon and Rectal Surgery (chmn. recertification exam). Intern surgery Med. Coll. Ga. Hosps., Augusta, 1974-75, resident gen. surgery, 1975-78, chief resident gen. surgery, 1978-79; G.I. surgery fellow gen. infirmary U. Leeds (Eng.), 1979-80; colon and rectal surgery fellow U. Minn. Hosps., 1982-83; asst. prof. surgery, asst. chief sect. GI surgery Med. Coll. Ga., Augusta, 1980-85, dir. colon/rectal surgery clinic, 1980-85; attending in surgery VA Hosp., Augusta, 1980-85; from asst. clin. prof. surgery to assoc. clin. prof. Med.

Coll. Ga., Augusta, 1985-2001, clin. prof., 2001—; staff surgeon Univ. Hosp., Augusta, 1985—, St. Joseph Hosp., Augusta, 1985—; attending colon/rectal surgery endoscopy Univ. Hosp., Augusta, 1986—. Dir. Southeastern Familial Polyposis Registry; bd. dirs. Richmond-Columbia County unit Am. Cancer Soc., v.p. medicine, 1985-91; mem. Ethicon Colon and Rectal Adv. Panel, 1988, Panel Specialist-Surgery, Vocat. Rehab., 1980—; mem. interview com. for med. sch. admissions Med. Coll. Ga., 1981-82, 84-85, mem. tissue com., 1983-85; chmn. familial polyposis registry com. U. Hosp. Augusta, 1986—; assoc. examiner Am. Bd. Colon and Rectal Surgery, 1995-98, mem., 1998—, v.p., 2005. Contbr. articles to profl. jours.; book reviewer and abstractor in field; reviewer Gastrointestinal Endoscopy, 1985-88. Pres. med. staff U. Hosp., Augusta, Ga., 1999, Richmond County Hosp. Authority, Augusta, 1998—. Recipient Continuing Med. Edn. award Am. Soc. Colon and Rectal Surgeons, 1984, 87, Spl. award for colorectal cancer control Am. Cancer Soc., 1987, Cert. of Appreciation, Am. Cancer Soc., 1991-92, Award of Excellence, Am. Cancer Soc., 1992-93; grantee Am. Soc. Hosp. Pharmacists, 1981, Smith Kline & French Labs., 1981, Merck Sharp & Dohme, 1984. Fellow ACS, Southeastern Surg. Congress, Am. Soc. Colon and Rectal Surgeons; mem. AMA (Physician Recognition award 1984-89, 1990-93, 93-96, 97-00), Med. Assn. Ga., Richmond County Med. Soc. (sec.), So. Med. Assn., Moretz Surg. Soc., Assn. for Acad. Surgeons, Ga. Gastroenterologic and Endoscopy Soc., Am. Soc. for Gastrointestinal Endoscopy, Soc. Am. Gastrointestinal Endoscopic Surgeons, Ga. Surg. Soc., Piedmont Soc. Colon and Rectal Surgeons (pres. 1992-94), Soc. Surgery Alimentary Tract, Phi Beta Kappa, Alpha Omega Alpha, Phi Kappa Phi. Methodist. Avocations: golf, hunting. Office: 1348 Walton Way Ste 6500 Augusta GA 30901-5111 Office Phone: 706-722-2118.

HOOLEY, DARLENE, congresswoman; b. Williston, N.D., Apr. 4, 1939; d. Clarence Alvin and Alyce (Rogers) Olsen; m. John Hooley (div.); children: Chad, Erin. BS in Edn., Oreg. State U., 1961, postgrad., 1963-65, Portland State U., 1966-67. Tchr. Woodburn (Oreg.) & Gervais Sch., 1962-65, David Douglas Sch. Dist., Portland, Oreg., 1965-67, St. Mary's Acad., Portland, 1967-69; mem. West Linn (Oreg.) City Coun., 1976-80; state rep. Oreg. State Ho. of Reps., 1980-87; county commr. Clackamas County (Oreg.) Bd., 1987-96; mem. U.S. Congress from 5th dist. Oreg., 1996—; mem. budget com., fin. svcs. com. Vice-chair Oreg. Tourism Alliance, Portland, 1991—. bd. dirs. Pub. Employees Ret. Bd., Portland, 1989—, Cmty. Corrections Bd., Oregon City, 1990—, Providence Med. Ctr., Portland, 1989—; acting chair Oreg. Trail Found. Bd., Oregon City, 1991—; mem. Urban Growth Policy Adv. Com., Portland, 1991—. Named Legislator of the Year Oreg. Libr. Assn., 1985-86, Oreg. Solar Energy Assn., 1985; recipient Spl. Svc. award Clackamas City Coun. for Child Abuse Prevention, 1989. Mem. LWV, Oreg. Women's Polit. Caucus (Women of the Yr. 1988). Democrat. Office: 2430 Rayburn Bldg Washington DC 20515-3705*

HOOLEY, MARIA RACHEL, secondary school educator; b. Germany, Nov. 25, 1967; d. David and Charlene Shockley; m. Bret Erman, July 15, 1989 (div.); children: Britney Savanna Erman, Zackary Connor Erman; m. Edward Ellis Hooley, Aug. 18, 2001; 1 child, Taylor Maddison. BA, Cameron U., 1990. Educator Elgin Pub. Schs., Okla., 1998—2003; academic advisor Cameron U., Lawton, Okla., 2003—04; tchr. Lawton Pub. Schs., Okla., 2004—. Editor Eagle Systems, Lawton, Okla., 2002—. Author: (chapbook of poetry) A Different Song, 1999. Mem.: Okla. Writers Fedn., Inc.

HOOPER, ANNE DODGE, pathologist, educator; b. Groton, Mass., July 16, 1926; d. Carroll William and Bertha Sanford (Wiener) Dodge; m. William Dale Hooper, June 17, 1952; children: Elizabeth Anne, Joan Elaine, Caroline Mae. AB, Washington U., St. Louis, 1947, MD, 1952. Diplomate in pathologic anatomy, clin. pathology and forensic pathology Am. Bd. Pathology. Rotating intern Virginia Mason Hosp., Seattle, 1952—53; resident in internal medicine St. Francis Hosp., Hartford, Conn., 1953—54; resident in pathologic anatomy and clin. pathology New Britain (Conn.) Gen. Hosp., 1954—57, Presbyn. Hosp., Phila., 1957—58; resident in forensic pathology Office Med. Examiner, Phila., 1958—60; from pathologist to acting chief lab svc. VA Hosp., Coatesville, Pa., 1960—66; dir. lab. St. Albans (Vt.) Hosp., 1966—69, Kerbs Hosp., St. Albans, 1966—71, Williamson Appalachian Regional Hosp., South Williamson, Ky., 1971—73, Beckley (W.Va.) Appalachian Regional Hosp., 1974—76; asst. prof. pathology W.Va. Sch. Osteo. Medicine, Lewisburg, 1977, assoc. prof. pathology, 1978—97, cons. in pathology, 1997—. Lab. accreditation insp. CAP, 1992—, Am. Osteo. Assn., 1986—99; assoc. med. examiner State of W.Va., 1999—; med. missionary Kijabe Hosp., Kenya, 1998; med. missionary, pathologist Pathologists Overseas at SALFA Lab., Madagascar, 2000; med. missionary with Glens Falls NY Med. Missionary Found., Nueva Santa Rosa, Guatemala, 2001. Contbr. articles to profl. jours. Pres. local elem. sch. PTA, St. Albans, 1967-68; pres. Greenbrier unit Am. Cancer Soc., Lewisburg, 1989-93, bd. dirs. W.Va. divsn., Charleston, 1987-94, profl. edn. com. W.Va. divsn., 1982-94; bd. dirs. ARC, Greenbrier County, W.Va., 2002—. Fellow Coll. Am. Pathologists, Am. Acad. Forensic Scis.; mem. AMA, W.Va. Med. Soc., Raleigh County Med. Soc., Am. Soc. Clin. Pathologists, Internat. Acad. Pathologists, Nat. Assn. Med. Examiners, Am. Osteo. Coll. Pathologists (assoc.). Avocation: playing violin and viola. Office: 63 Cedar Knoll Ronceverte WV 24970-9700

HOOPER, BRAD, editor, librarian; b. Vandalia, Ill. s. William George and Elizabeth Canaday Hooper. BA, Ea. Ill. U., 1971, MLS, 1972. Reference librarian Cleve. (Ohio) Pub. Libr., 1972—74; asst. editor Booklist American Libr. Assn., Chgo., 1974—90, assoc. editor Booklist, 1990—2000, adult books editor Booklist, 2000—. Author: Short Story Readers Advisory, 2000, The Fiction of Ellen Gilchrist, 2005. Mem.: Nat. Book Critic's Cir. Avocations: travel, music. Home: 2008 N Fremont St Chicago IL 60614 Office: American Library Association 50 E HuronSt Chicago IL 60611 Office Phone: 312-280-5757.

HOOPER, DANIEL LEE, music educator, composer; b. San Antonio, Tex., May 17, 1947; s. Charles Henry and Mary Eloise (Parks) Hooper. Sacred Music Master, Union Theol. Sem., N.Y.C., 1971; MusB, Juilliard Sch. Music, N.Y.C., 1971. Mem. faculty Millbrook (NY) Sch., 1971—72; organist, choir master Ch. of the Messiah, Rhinebeck, NY, 1972—73, All Saints' Episcopal Ch., Phoenix, 1973—87; mem. music faculty Phoenix Coll., 1990—. Asst. dir. Mid-Hudson Cmty. Mixed Chorus, Poughkeepsie, NY, 1971—73; music dir. Mid-Hudson Opera, Poughkeepsie, NY, 1971—73; music chmn. Episc. Diocese of Ariz., Phoenix, 1975—81; founding dir. Phoenix Girls' Chorus, 1980—85; co-dir. Phoenix Oratorio Choir, 1980—84; assoc. dir. McConnell Singers Women's Cmty. Chorus, Phoenix, 1994—99, dir., 1999—; concert preview lectr. Sun City (Ariz.) Chamber Music Soc., 1999—; dir. Voices of Phoenix Coll., 2003—. Composer, lyricist: Chancel opera Abraham and Issac (Seth Bingham Composition Award, 1971); composer: (choral anthem) Festive Welcome (First Ariz. ACDA Composition Award, 2003). Asst. accompanist Phoenix Police Honor Chorus, Phoenix, Ariz., 2002—05. Recipient Outstanding Young Musician award, San Antonio Optimists, 1962, Outstanding Pianist award, Sewanee Summer Music Ctr., 1965; scholar Joske Music scholar, Joske's Dept. Store and San Antonio Symphony, 1959, Juilliard Sch. Music, 1966—67. Mem.: ASCAP, Am. Choral Dirs. Assn., Nat. Assn. Tchrs. Singing, Am. Guild Organists (regional conv. co-chairman 1993—96). Independent. Episcopalian. Avocations: power walking, travel, knitting. Office: Phoenix Coll 1202 West Thomas Phoenix AZ 85013 Office Phone: 602-285-7297.

HOOPER, EDWIN BICKFORD, physicist; b. Bremerton, Wash., June 18, 1937; s. E.B. and Elizabeth (Patrick) H.; m. Virginia Hooper, Dec. 28, 1963; children: Edwin, Sarah, William. SB, MIT, 1959, PhD, 1965. Asst. prof. applied sci. Yale U., New Haven, 1966-70; physicist, dep. program leader FE Lawrence Livermore (Calif.) Nat. Lab., 1970—2003, flex term physicist, 2003—. Adv. com. Fusion Energy Bruning Plasmic Program, 2003—; mem. program adv. com. Virtual Lab. Fusion Tech., 2002—. Contbr. articles to profl. jours. Pres. Danville (Calif.) Assn., 1982-84; pres. Friends Iron Horse Trail, 1984-86; v.p. San Ramon Valley Edn. Found., 1989-90; dir. Leadership, San Ramon Valley, 1990-92; mem. adv. com. East Bay Regional Pk., 2002—. Fellow Am. Phys. Soc. (bd. dirs. div. Plasma Physics 1990-91); mem. AIAA (sr.), AAAS. Office: Lawrence Livermore Nat Lab L-637 Livermore CA 94550-4436 Office Phone: 925-423-1409.

HOOPER, HENRY OLCOTT, retired academic administrator, physicist; b. Washington, Mar. 9, 1935; s. Olcott Lorin and Eleanor (Drew) H.; m. Donna Faulkingham, June 10, 1956 (div. 1992); children: Deborah, Bruce, Katherine, Michael, Andrew; m. Jeanne Riley Hughes, Mar. 2, 1996. BS in Engring. Physics, U. Maine, 1956; MS in Physics, Brown U., 1959, PhD, 1961. Asst. prof. Brown U., Providence, 1961-64; asst. prof. physics Wayne State U., Detroit, 1964-66, assoc. prof., 1966-70, prof., 1970-73; prof., chmn. dept. physics U. Maine, Orono, 1973-76, dean Grad. Sch., 1977-80, v.p. acad. affairs, 1979-80; assoc. v.p. acad. affairs, dean Grad. Coll. No. Ariz. U., Flagstaff, 1981-97, interim v.p. acad. affairs, 1993-95, assoc. provost rsch. and grad. studies, 1995-96, prof. physics, dir. Bilby Rsch. Ctr., 1997-2000; dir. sci. and math. Learning Ctr., 1998-2000; ret., 2000; pres. John and Sophie Ottens Found., 2001—. Cons. NASA, Huntsville, Ala., 1967-68; mem. rev. panel div. ednl. programs Argonne (Ill.) Nat. Lab., 1982-84; mem. exec. bd. Assoc. Western Univs., 1991-97, chair 1995-96; v.p. Nat. Coun. Univ. Rsch. Adminstrs., 1991-92, pres., 1992-93. Author: College Physical Science, 3d edit., 1974, Physics and the Physical Perspective, 1977, 2d rev. edit., 1980; editor: Conf. Procs. Amorphous Magnetism, 1973. Fellow Am. Phys. Soc.; mem. AAAS, Am. Assn. Physics Tchrs. E-mail: hoh@independence.net.

HOOPER, IAN (JOHN DEREK GLASS), retired marketing communications executive; b. London, Sept. 8, 1941; came to U.S., 1979; s. John Desmond Glass and Moira Elizabeth (White) H. Student, Coll. Distributive Trades, London, 1960-62, 65-67, Harvard U., 1979. With S. H. Benson, London, 1960-62, 65-67, Nairobi, Kenya, 1962-64; with McCann-Erickson Advt., London, 1967-79; sr. v.p., group account dir. McCann-Erickson, N.Y.C., 1979-85; exec. v.p., mng. dir. McCann Direct, N.Y.C., 1985-90; sr. v.p., worldwide account dir. Young & Rubicam, N.Y.C., 1990-91; sr. v.p., account dir. Brouillard Communications, N.Y.C., 1991-94; sr. v.p., mktg. dir. DeVries Pub. Rels., N.Y.C., 1994-2000, COO, 2000—04; ret., 2004. Home: 180 Stony Kill Rd Canaan NY 12029 E-mail: hooperi@aol.com.

HOOPER, JOSH, advertising executive, writer, director; b. Pa., 1952; s. Henry Lloyd and Mary Katherine H.; m. Cynthia Yeiser; children: Spencer, Mason. BA, Franklin & Marshall Coll., 1974. Tchr. Lower Dauphin Sch. Dist., Hummelstown, Pa., 1974-76; prodn. mgr. Sta. WLYH-TV, Lebanon, Pa., 1976-79; producer PM Mag. Sta. WTVH-TV, Syracuse, N.Y., 1979-80; co-host, producer PM Mag. Sta. WGAL-TV, Lancaster, Pa., 1980-83; pres. Josh Hooper Prodns., Inc., Harrisburg, Pa., 1983-94; actor-dir., pres. A Different Look, L.A., 1983-92; broadcast advt. dir. The Bon Ton, York, Pa., 1992-94; pres., creative dir. Zero Gravity Mktg. and Advt., Harrisburg, Pa., 1994—; v.p. creative direction Panoramic Visions, 2000—02. Theater dir., N.Y., Pa., Calif., 1974—; co-host Sta. WITF Auction, Hershey, Pa., 1982, 83, Easter Seals Telethon, Harrisburg, 1983, Children's Miracle Network, Lancaster, 1983; directing fellow Am. Film Inst., L.A., 1988-89; improv comedian L.A. Connection, 1989, Public Nuisance, L.A., 1989-92. Producer, dir. (TV program) Suite 10:15, 1977; exec. producer (TV kids mag.) Thresholds, 1978; actor (play) Waiting for Godot, 1985, The Winter's Tale, 1986 (film) Station to Freedom, 1987, (TV film) Lucy and Desi: Before The Laughter, 1991; dir. (short film) Collared, 1988, The Point, 1989, Bumper to Bumper, 1989. Mem. Common Cause, Washington, 1980-90; chmn. comms. Three Mile Island Pub. Interest Resource Group, Harrisburg, 1982-84; comm. chair Fox Ridge Neighbors, 1985-87; active Ctr. for Def. Info.; charter mem. Franklin and Marshall Coll. Pres.'s Farwest Adv. Coun.; bd. dirs. Parent Works Parent Edn. Ctrs.; mem. Envision Capital Region Task Force. Recipient Addy award Am. Advt. Fedn., 1987, Addy award Cen. Pa. Advt. Fedn., 1985, 87, 88, Telly award, 1987, 88, 89, 99, Gold award Creativity '96; Film Grants Panelist NEH, 1990, Vision award, Mobius award, 1997. Mem. Am. Film Inst. Alumni Assn. (past pres.), SAG, Ctrl. Pa. Ad Club (bd. dirs. 1994, 95), Capital Area Assn. for the Edn. Young Children, Success by Six. Democrat. Unitarian. Avocations: running, swimming, bicycling, boating.

HOOPER, ROBERT ALEXANDER, television producer, international educator; b. Annapolis, Md., Apr. 13, 1947; s. P. Alexander and Louise (Hickey) H.; m. Virginia L. Gordon; 1 child, Julie Alexandra. BA in Econs., U. Calif., San Diego, 1969; JD, U. Calif., Davis, 1974; MFA in Motion Picture and TV, UCLA, 1982. Bar: Calif. 1975. Film prodr. Scripps Inst. of Oceanography, La Jolla, Calif., 1978-79, EPA, Washington, 1979-81; ind. film prodr. with ABC-TV and CBC, Del Mar, Calif., 1981-84; tv prodr. Sta. KUAC-TV, Fairbanks, Alaska, 1984-86; asst. prof. comm. Boston U., 1986-87; assoc. prof. comm. Loyola Marymount U., L.A., 1987-98; exec. prodr. KPBS-TV, San Diego, 1997—2001; assoc. prof. Calif. State U., 2000—. Vis. assoc. prof. U. Calif., San Diego, 1993, 96, UCLA, 2000; cons. CBC, Toronto, 1982-83, Radio-TV Malaysia, 1998, Fiji TV, 1996; cons. Asia-Pacific Inst. for Broadcasting Devel., 1998-99, course dir., 1998—; Fulbright sr. scholar comm. program U. Sains Malaysia, Penang, 1989-90, U. South Pacific, Fiji, 1994, U. Indonesia, 2001; tng. adviser Am. Samoa Govt.-Sta. KVZK-TV, 1992—; acad. specialist U. Papua New Guinea, 1995; Eisenhower fellow, Malaysia, 1996; Fulbright sr. specialist, Malaysia, 2002-04; U.S. Dept. State Spkr., Laos, 2003-05, Bangladesh, 2003-05 Prodr., dir. (documentaries) Voices From Love Canal, 1978, Decisions at 1000 Fathoms, 1981, Battle at Webber Creek, 1985 (Press Club award), Alaska's Killer Whales, 1989 (Cine Golden Eagle and Silver Apple award); segment prodr. (ABC 20/20) The Deep, 1983; exec. prodr. Nature's Classic, 1998 (Press Club award, four Emmy nominations), Afoot and Afield, 1998, The Impossible Railroad, 1999 (Press Club award, Telly award, Emmy award); cons. prodr. Skin Stories (PBS), 2003; op.-editor writer, L.A. Times, San Diego Union-Tribune, 1999. Recipient Hennessy trophy, Internat. Environ. Film Festival, France, 1983. Mem. NATAS, Calif. Bar Assn., Eisenhower Fellows Assn., Fulbright Sr. Specialists Roster, Sigma Delta Chi. Democrat. Avocations: underwater photography, equestrian endurance riding. Office Phone: 310-243-2865. Personal E-mail: rahooper@hotmail.com.

HOOPER, ROGER FELLOWES, retired architect; b. Southampton, N.Y., Aug. 18, 1917; s. Roger Fellowes and Justine Van Rensselaer (Barber) H.; m. Patricia Bentley, Aug. 10, 1946; children: Judith Bayard Teresi, Rachel Bentley Zingg, Roger Fellowes III. AB, Harvard U., 1939, MArch, 1948. Ptnr. Malone & Hooper, San Francisco, 1949-60; ptnr., pres. Hooper Olmsted & Emmons, San Francisco, 1964-79; chmn. Hooper Olmsted & Hrovat, San Francisco, 1980-94, retired, 1994. Bd. mgr. Marin YMCA, San Rafael, Calif.; bd. dirs., pres. Marin Conservation League, San Rafael. Lt. comdr. USNR, 1941-45, WWII. Mem. AIA.

HOOPER, ROY B., lobbyist; b. Lawton, Okla., Mar. 19, 1947; s. Roy Basil and Frances (Castle) H.; m. Lawanna Sue James, Aug. 2, 1969; children: Blake, Mark. BS, Cameron U., 1971. Registered lobbyist 1995-. Real estate broker, Lawton, 1968-90; rep. State of Okla., Lawton, 1974-86, senator, 1986-94; ins. broker Lawton, 1966—; dir. managed care Southwestern Med. Ctr., Lawton, 1994-99, HealthBack, Oklahoma City, 1999-2000; adminstr. Okla. State and Edn. Employees Group Ins. Program, 2000—01. Pres. Cameron Former Students Assn., Lawton, 1974, Lawton Crimestoppers Orgn., 1996, S.W. chpt. Am. Heart Assn., 1995-96, Lawton Pub. Sch. Found., 1998; v.p. Lawton Bd. Realtors, 1974, KTRO, Pres.'s Ptnrs. Cameron U., Lawton Crimestoppers/Drugbusters; councilman Ward 2, Lawton, 1972-74. Sgt. USAR, 1968-74. Democrat. Baptist. Avocations: hunting, fishing, golf, horse back riding, gardening. Office: Hooper Cons 1114 Laird Lawton OK 73507 Office Phone: 405-826-9429.

HOOPER, WAYNE NELSON, retired clergy member; b. Toronto, Ont., Can., May 25, 1944; s. Earl Edward and Ruby Evelyn (Nelson) H.; m. Diane Elizabeth, Aug. 24, 1968; children: Tanya Joy, Craig Nelson. BA, McMaster U., 1967; MDiv, Gordon-Conwell Theol. Sem., 1970. Ordained to ministry Baptist Ch., 1970. Asst. pastor Emmanuel Bapt. Ch., Cambridge, Mass., 1967-68, First Bapt. Ch., Braintree, Mass., 1968-70; pastor Uxbridge (Ont.) Bapt. Ch., Can., 1970-73; founding pastor Credit Valley Bapt. Ch., Mississauga, Ont., Can., 1973-79; sr. pastor First Bapt. Ch., Orillia, Ont., Can., 1979-83, Avenue Rd. Bapt. Ch., Cambridge, Ont., Can., 1986-98; asst. sec. dept. Can. Missions Bapt. Conv. Ont. and Que., 1983-86; sr. pastor First Baptist Ch., Dartmouth, Canada, 1998—2003, Westview Bapt. Ch., London, Canada, 2003—05; ret., 2005. Contbr. articles to profl. jours. Mem. recruitment com. Bapt. Conv. Ont. and Que., 1973-75, mem. planning com., 1978-80, mem. coun., 1976-82, mem. exec. com., 1977-78; conv. staff rep. Ottawa and N.W. Assns., 1983-86; Bapt. Conv. Ont. and Que. rep. to Inter-Church Regional Planning Assn., 1983-86; mem. Canadian Baptist Ministries Coun., 1995-98. Mem. Can. Bapt. Fedn. (v.p. 1988-91, pres. 1991-94). Baptist. Avocations: sports, boating, stamp collecting/philately, tennis, golf. Home: 67 Parks Edge Crescent London ON Canada N6K 3P5

HOOPIS, HARRY PETER, insurance executive, entrepreneur; b. Providence, May 14, 1947; s. Peter Harry and Angela Rose (Taraborelli) H.; m. Demetra Psilopoulos, Feb. 20, 1972; children: Krina Angela, Peter Harry. BS in Acctg., U. R.I., 1969. CLU; chartered fin. cons. Coll. agt. Northwestern Mut. Life Ins. Co., Kingston, R.I., 1968-69, spl. agt. Providence, 1969-71, dist. agt. Wakefield, R.I., 1971-74, asst. supt. manpower devel. Milw., 1974-77, gen. agt. Evanston, Ill., 1977—. Cons., speaker ins. industry, U.S. and Can., 1977—, Purdue Mgmt. Inst., Lafayette, Ind., 1987-88; pres. Gama Internat., 1996-97; founder Hooper Mgmt. Inst., 1985. Author: (with others) Sales Focus Workbook, 1985, Fixed Activity Commitment, 1980, Managing Sales Professionals, 1993, Essentials of Management Development, 1999. Named to GAMA Internat. Hall of Fame, 2003. Mem. Nat. Gen. Agts. and Mgrs. Assn. (pres. 1989-90, Yates Meml. award 1988, named Master Agy. Builder, 1983-97, sec., bd. dirs. 1989—), Am. Soc. CLUs, Chgo. Assn. CLUs (bd. dirs. 1978-81), Gama Internat. (pres. 1997). Republican. Avocations: skiing, golf. Office: Hoopis Fin Group 5215 Old Orchard Rd Ste 1200 Skokie IL 60077 E-mail: harry.hoopis@nmfn.com.

HOORT, STEVEN THOMAS, lawyer; b. Grand Rapids, Mich., Sept. 18, 1949; s. Allard Hoort and Margaret J. (Vanderkooy) Koens; m. Nancy E. Redmon, Mar. 18, 1978; 1 child, Kendra. BA with high honors, Grand Valley State Coll., Allendale, Mich., 1972; JD magna cum laude, U. Mich., 1975. Bar: Mich. 1977, Colo. 2002, US Dist. Ct. (ea. dist.) Mich. 1977, Mass. 1978, US Dist. Ct. Mass. 1978, US Ct. Appeals (1st cir.) 1978, US Dist. Ct. (we. dist.) Mich. 1993. Law clk. U.S. Dist. Ct. (ea. dist.) Mich., Bay City, Mich., 1975-78; assoc. Ropes & Gray LLP, Boston, 1978-84, ptnr., 1984--, co-head bankruptcy & bus. restructuring dept. Mem. ABA (bus. law sect.), Boston Bar Assn., Am. Bankruptcy Inst., Order of Coif. Office: Ropes & Gray LLP 1 International Pl Fl 4 Boston MA 02110-2624 Office Phone: 617-951-7470. Office Fax: 617-951-7050. Business E-Mail: steven.hoort@ropesgray.com.

HOOTMAN, HARRY EDWARD, educator, retired nuclear engineer, consultant; b. Oak Park, Ill., June 5, 1933; s. Merle Albert and Rachel Edith (Atkinson) H.; m. Linda P. Smith, Nov. 23, 1963; children: David, Holly, John. BS in Chemistry, Mich. Technol. U., 1959, MS in Nuc. Engring., 1962; LLB, LaSalle Ext. U., 1971, MA in English Lit., U. SC, 1999, PhD in English and Am. Lit., 2004. Registered profl. engr., SC Rsch. assoc. Argonne (Ill.) Nat. Lab., 1959-62; process engr. Savannah River Plant, Aiken, SC, 1962-65; rsch. assoc. reactor physics group, nuclear engring. div. Savannah River Lab., Aiken, 1965-87; with New Reactor Devel. Group, 1987-92, adv. engr. Planning, Studies and Analysis, 1992-95; ret., 1995; cons. transuranic waste disposal and incineration, radioisotope prodn., separation and shielding; instr. dept. math. and engring. U. SC, Aiken, 1979-80, 90-94, instr. dept. English, 2004—. Author: Index to British Literary Annuals and Giftbooks 1823-1861; Inventor alpha waste incinerator. Bd. dirs. Central Savannah River Area Sci. and Engring. Fair, Inc., Augusta, Ga., 1972-91. Sgt. USAF, 1953-57. Mem. Am. Acad. Environ. Engrs., NSPE (local chmn. 1978-79), Am. Nuclear Soc. (local chmn. 1979-80), Am. Phys. Soc., Sigma Xi, Sigma Tau Delta, Phi Lambda Upsilon. Baptist Home: 820 Brandy Rd SE Aiken SC 29801-7281 Personal E-mail: hhootman@bellsouth.net.

HOOTON, ELIZABETH CAPASSO, literature and language professor; b. Derby, Conn., Mar. 14, 1943; d. James Joseph Jr. and Anne Catherine Tisi Capasso; m. Richard Joseph Hooton Jr., Feb. 27, 1965; children: Anne Catherine, Richard Joseph III, Joshua Matthew. BA in English, East Carolina U., 1988, MA in English, 1991. Stewardess Am. Airlines, N.Y.C., 1963—65; lectr. dept. English East Carolina U., Greenville, NC, 1990—94; adj. instr. U. West Fla., Pensacola, 1994—. Mem. Blue Ribbon Libr. Task Force, Pensacola, 2004—; sous chef for non-profit Appetite for Life, Inc.; bd. dirs. Friends of Libr., 2004—. Recipient 1st pl. award, N.C. Am. Mothers Lit. Contest, 1993. Home: 6510 Scenic Hwy Pensacola FL 32504

HOOTON, JAMES G., academic administrator; m. Marilyn Hooton; children: Stephanie, Joyce Ann. BA, Tex. A&M U., 1966, MBA, 1967. With Arthur Andersen, Chgo., 1976—2002, head, acctg. and audit practice, 1989, CFO, mng. partner, 2001—02; exec. vice chancellor fin. Tex. A&M Univ. Sys., 2005—. Office: Off of Exec Vice Chancellor Fin Tex A&M Univ Sys 200 Technology Way, Ste 2043 College Station TX 77845-3424 Office Phone: 979-458-6047. E-mail: jhooton@tamu.edu.*

HOOVER, DWIGHT WESLEY, history educator; b. Oskaloosa, Iowa, Sept. 15, 1926; s. Homer Samuel and Ruth (Hull) H.; m. Janet Mae Holmes; children: Polly Ruth, Sara Adeline, Elizabeth Anne. AB, William Penn Coll., 1948; MA (T. Wistar Brown fellow), Haverford Coll., 1949; PhD, State U. Iowa, 1953. Prof., head social sci. dept. Bethune-Cookman Coll., Daytona Beach, Fla., 1953-55, 58; asst. prof. gen. studies dept. Kans. State U., 1958-59; mem. faculty Ball State U., Muncie, Ind., 1959-91, assoc. prof. history, 1963-67, prof., 1967—, dir. Ctr. Middletown Studies, 1981-91. Fulbright prof. Hungary, fall 1988, 1991-92; sr. cons. Middletown Film Project, 1977-81; vis. prof. Doshisha U., Kyota, Japan, 1992-93; spl. lectr. Kansai Gaidai, Oskaka, Japan, 1996-97; adj. prof. U. South Fla., Sarasota, 1994-96. Author: Understanding Negro History, 1968, Henry James, Sr. and the Religion of Community, 1969, A Teacher's Guide to American Urban History, 1971, The Red and the Black, 1976, Cities: A Multimedia Bibliography, 1976, A Pictorial History of Indiana, 1980, Magic Middletown, 1986, Middletown: An Annotated Bibliography, 1988, Middletown Revisited, 1990, A Three Family Tale, 1990, Middletown: The Making of A Documentary Film Series, 1992; co-author: American Society in the 20th Century, 1972; contbg. author: All Faithful People; co-editor: Conspectus on History, 1975, 76, 77, 78, 79, 80, 81. Served to lt. USNR, 1955-58 Mem. AAUP, Am. Hist. Assn., Orgn. Am. Historians, Am. Studies Assn., Pi Gamma Mu, Phi Alpha Theta., Soc. Friends. Home: 11 Sunset Dr Apt 203 Sarasota FL 34236-5544

HOOVER, EDDIE LEE, cardiothoracic surgeon, educator; b. Charlotte, N.C., Sept. 16, 1944; s. Arthur John and Geneva (Phifer) H. BA, U. N.C., 1965; MD, Duke U., 1969. Diplomate Nat. Bd. Med. Examiners, Am. Bds. Surgery and Thoracic Surgery. Intern Duke U., Durham, N.C., 1969-70, resident in gen. surgery, 1970-71, N.Y. Hosp. Cornell U., N.Y.C., 1973-75, resident in cardiothoricic surgery, 1976-78; asst. prof. surgery Cornell U. Med. Ctr., N.Y.C., 1978-80; assoc. prof. surgery SUNY, Bklyn., 1980-87; prof. surgery Meharry Med. Coll., Nashville, 1987-90; prof., chmn. surgery SUNY, Buffalo, 1990—. Author surg. sci. manuscripts. Bd. mem. Urban League, Buffalo, 1991—. Lt. comdr. USNR, 1971-73; PTO. Mem. Nat. Med. Assn. (editor-in-chief Jour.), Am. Surg. Assn., Soc. Univ. Surgeons, Am. Assn. Thoracic Surgery, Sigma Pi Boule. Home: 7557 Greenbush Rd Akron NY 14001-9719 Fax: 716-898-5029. Office Phone: 716-862-6078. E-mail: eddie.hoover@med.va.gov.

HOOVER, GARY LYNN, banker; b. Tipton, Ind., Oct. 20, 1937; s. Carmel Wayne and Virginia Ruth (Mitchell) H.; m. Virginia Maxine James Monet, May 8, 1965 (div. Apr. 1976); m. Laura E. Grigg West, June 25, 1988; children: Devin Page, Melissa Virginia. BS, Purdue U., 1959. Nat. bank examiner Internat. Comptroller of the Currency, Washington, 1962-71; v.p. Am. Fletcher Nat. Bank, Indpls., 1971-81; credit examiner Internat. Farm Credit Adminstrn., Washington, 1981-84; v.p. Nat. Bank for Cooperatives, Englewood, Colo., 1984-95. Dir. Hoover Farms, Inc., Tipton, Ind.; pres. Hoover Fin. Assn., LLC, Highlands Ranch, Colo., 1995—; mem. U. Colo.

Scholarship Fund, Boulder. Mem. pres. coun. Purdue U., West Lafayette, Ind., 1997—. With U.S. Army, 1961—66. Mem. Ind. Bankers Assn. Colo. Republican. Avocations: reading, travel, cartography. Office: Hoover Fin Assocs PO Box 260826 Highlands Ranch CO 80163-0826 Home: PO Box 6424 Vail CO 81658-6424

HOOVER, GEORGE SCHWEKE, architect; b. Chgo., July 1, 1935; s. George Milton and Antoinette (Schweke) H.; children: Sandra Jean, Ranya Sue; m. Mary Elizabeth Benoit, June 6, 1987. BArch., Cornell U., 1958. Registered architect, Colo., Calif., Tex., Minn., Ala., Tenn. Draftsman Holabird Root and Burgee, Chgo., 1957, Designer James Sudler Assocs., Denver, 1961-62; architect Ream, Quinn Assocs., Denver, 1962-65, Muchow Assocs., Denver, 1965-76; prin. Hoover Berg Desmond, Denver, 1976—. Tenured prof. arch. U. Colo. Coll. Arch. and Planning, chmn. dept. arch., 1997—; vis. lectr. U. N.Mex., Okla. State U., Harvard U., Miami U. Prin. works include Douglas County Adminstrn. Bldg., Light of the World Cath. Ch., U. Colo. Bldg., Denver, Denver Diagnostic and Reception Ctr., Labs for Atmospheric and Space Physics, U. Colo., Boulder, Colo. Acad. Master Plan, U. Ariz. Engring. Complex Master Plan, Multipurpose Arena, Nat. Western Stockshow, Nat. Wild Animal Rsch. Ctr., Colo. State U. Conf. Ctr., Storage Tech. Corp., Aerospace & Mech. Engring. Bldg. U. Ariz., Environ. and Natural Resources Bldg. U. Ariz., Master Plan Cummins Power Generation Group Hdqs., Fridley, Minn., Master Plan Fleetguard and Mfg. Plant, Cookeville, Tenn.; finalist Denver Cen. Libr. Competition, 1991; exhbn. Gund Hall Gallery, Grad. Sch. Design, Harvard U., 1986; mem. editl. bd. Avant Garde. Lt. (j.g.) USN, 1958-61. Recipient 1st Design award Progressive Arch., 1972, Citation, 1974, Design award, 1984, 87, Charles Goodwin Sands Medal for excellence in design Tau Beta Pi, Fed. Design Achievement award, 1984, Honor award Interfaith Forum on Religion, Art, and Arch., 1986, Tau Sigma Delta medal, 1991; named Outstanding Young Architect, Archtl. Record, 1974, Fellow AIA (steering com., Pitts. Corning award 1989, Nat. Honor award 1975, 83, 90, Firm of Yr. award Colo. chpt. 1991, Regional Firm of Yr. award 1992, Architect of Yr. award Colo. chpt. 1995), Nat. Acad. Design.; mem. Nat. Com. Design (steering com., chmn. awards task group 1989-92), Nat. Com. Archtl. Edn. (steering com. 1990-92). Episcopalian. Office: Art Hoover Desmond Arch 1645 Grant St Denver CO 80203-1601 also: U Colo 1250 14th St Denver CO 80202-1702 Office Phone: 303-556-5965. E-mail: hoover@ar7.com.*

HOOVER, JOHN ELWOOD, former military officer, consultant, author, United States military history speaker; b. Timberville, Va., Apr. 28, 1924; s. Saylor Cornelius and Ruby Mae (Brill) H.; m. Mary Jo Cox, May 17, 1953; children: M. Kathryn, Holly H. Bullock. Student, Bridgewater (Va.) Coll., 1941-43, Amherst (Mass.) Coll., 1943-44; BS, U.S. Mil. Acad., 1947; MA, Georgetown U., 1955; postgrad., Columbia U., 1955-56, U.S. Army Command and Gen. Staff Coll., Ft. Leavenworth, Kans., 1958-59, U.S. Army War Coll., Carlisle Barracks, Pa., 1962-63. Commd. 2d lt. U.S. Army, 1947, advanced through grades to maj. gen., 1971; with 24th Inf. Div., Japan and Korea, 1948-51, Ft. Gordon, Ga., 1951-53; faculty dept. social scis. U.S. Mil. Acad., 1955-58; bn. comdr. U.S. Army, Fed. Republic of Germany, 1959-60, Hdqrs. U.S. Army Europe, Fed. Republic of Germany, 1961-62; with Office Asst. Sec. Def. for Internat. Security Affairs, Washington, 1963-66; chief communications plans Hdqrs. Pacific Command, Hawaii, 1966-69, group comdr. Vietnam, 1969-70; exec. officer, then dir. communications systems, then dep. asst. chief staff for communication-electronics Hdqrs. Dept. Army, Washington, 1970-73; dep. comdg. gen. U.S. Army Communications Command, Ft. Huachuca, Ariz., 1973-74; dir. Joint Tactical Communications Office, Office Sec. Def., Ft. Monmouth, N.J., 1974-78; ret., 1978. Cons. command, control, communications and mgmt.; historian emeritus U.S. Army Signal Rgt.; author and speaker on U.S. mil. communications history. Decorated D.S.M., Legion of Merit with oak leaf cluster, Bronze Star with oak leaf cluster, Meritorious Svc. medal, Air medal with oak leaf cluster, Joint Svc. Commendation medal, Army Commendation medal, Armed Forces Honor medal Republic of Vietnam; Staff Svc. medal (Republic of Vietnam); Vietnam Gallantry Cross with palm; Meritorious Unit citation, Presdl. Unit citation Republic of Korea Mem. Assn. Grads. U.S. Mil. Acad., Signal Corps Assn., Mil. Heritage Found., Order Mil. Merit, Silver Order Mercoury, Louisville Kiwanis. Home and Office: PO Box 531 Louisville GA 30434-0531

HOOVER, JOHN JOSEPH, education educator; s. Edward A. and Patricia R. Hoover; m. Robin F. Silberg, May 2, 1980; children: Joseph H, Jeremy D, Rachael H. BA in Spl. Edn., Ill. State U., 1973; MA in Spl. Edn., No. Ariz. U., 1978; PhD in Curriculum/Spl. Edn., U. Colo., 1983. Cert. tchr. Ill., Ariz., Colo. Assoc. prof. spl. edn. U. Tex., Tyler, 1984—90; dir., rsch. and evaluation Am. Indian Sci. and Engring. Soc., Boulder, Colo., 1990—96; rsch. assoc., adj. faculty mem. U. Colo., Boulder, 1996—, assoc. dir. BUENO Ctr., 1998—. Author: Curriculum Adaptation for Students with Learning and Behavior Problems, 2005; editor: Current Issues in Special Education, 2005; contbr. articles to profl. publs. Bd. dirs., mem. devel. com. Holy Family H.S., Broomfield, Colo., 1997—2003; bd. dirs. Boulder Little League, 1998—2002; chmn. Boy Scout Troop, Boulder, 2000—02. Sci. and Math Tchr. Tng. Project grantee, Bush Found. of St. Paul, 1993—96, Tech. Tchr. Tng. Project grantee, NASA, 1996—98, Office of English Lang. Acquisition, 1998—2000, Bilingual Spl. Edn. Tchr. Tng. Project grantee, 2002—05, Tchr. Edn. Consortium Project grantee, 2003—. Mem.: Nat. Assn. Bilingual Edn. (assoc.), Am. Ednl. Rsch. Assn. (assoc.), Coun. Exceptional Children (assoc.). Office: U Colorado Boulder UCB 247 Sch Edn Boulder CO 80309 Office Phone: 303-735-2015. Home Fax: 303-492-2883; Office Fax: 303-492-2883. Personal E-mail: john.hoover@colorado.edu.

HOOVER, PAUL, poet; b. Harrisonburg, Va., Apr. 30, 1946; s. Robert and Opal (Shinaberry) H.; m. Maxine Chernoff, 1974; children: Koren, Philip, Julian. BA cum laude, Manchester Coll., 1968; MA, U. Ill., 1973. Asst. editor U. Ill. Press, Champaign, 1973-74; prof. English, Columbia Coll., Chgo., 1974—. Co-founder Poetry Ctr., Sch. of Art Inst. of Chgo., 1974, bd. mem. 1974-87, pres. 1975-78; editor OINK!, 1971-85; co-founder, editor New Am. Writing, 1986. Author: Letter to Einstein Beginning Dear Albert, 1979, Somebody Talks a Lot, 1983, Nervous Songs, 1986, Idea, 1987 (Carl Sandburg award Friends of Chgo. Pub. Libr. 1987), Saigon, Illinois, 1988, The Novel: A Poem, 1990; editor: Postmodern American Poetry, 1994, Viridian, 1997 (Georgia prize 1997), Totem and Shadow: New and Selected Poems, 1999, Rehearsal in Black, 2001, Winter (Mirror), 2002, Fables of Representation: Essays, 2003; contbr. to various periodicals including New Yorker, Partisan Rev., New Directions, Sulfur, Chgo. Rev., Triquarterly, Am. Poetry Rev., New Republic; author: (screenplay) Viridian, 1994. Nat. Endowment for Arts fellow, 1980; Ill. Arts Coun. fellow, 1983, 84, 86; recipient Gen. Electric Found. award for Younger Writers, 1984, Jerome J. Shestack award, 2003. Mem. MLA. Office: Columbia Coll Dept of English 600 S Michigan Ave Chicago IL 60605-1900 Home: 369 Molino Ave Mill Valley CA 94941-2767

HOOVER, R. DAVID, packaging company executive; b. Straughn, Ind., June 21, 1945; BS, DePauw U., Greencastle, Ind., 1967; MBA, Indiana U., Bloomington, 1970; postgrad mgmt. program, Harvard U., 1988. Corp. fin. analyst Eli Lilly & Co., Indpls.; asst. to treas. Ball Corp., v.p., fin. & admin. agrl. sys. divsn., 1980—85, v.p., fin. & admin. aerospace sys. group, 1985—87, asst. treas., 1987—88, v.p. & treas., 1988—92, sr. v.p. & CFO, 1992—96, exec. v.p. & mem. bd. dirs., 1996—98, vice chmn. & CFO, 1998—2000, COO, 2000—01, CEO & pres., 2001—, chmn., 2002—. Bd. mem. Datum, Inc., Maxon Corp. & Energizer Holdings; mem. bd. dirs. & former chmn. Can Manufacturers Inst. Bd. mem. Nat. Food Processors Assn., Boulder Cmty. Found., DePauw U. Bd. Visitors & Bd. Trustees, Indiana U., Kelley Sch. Bus., Dean's Adv. Coun. Office: 10 Longs Peak Dr Broomfield CO 80021-2510*

HOOVER, RICHARD, set designer, art director, actor; Student, U. Oreg. With Mid-Ocean Motion Pictures, Dream Quest Images and the Secret Lab., Sony Pictures Imageworks, Robert Abel & Assocs., 1989. Visual effects supr.: (films) Freejack, 1992; Jungle 2 Jungle, 1997; Armageddon, 1998 (nominee Acad. Award for Best Visual Effects); Inspector Gadget, 1999; Unbreakable, 2000; Reign of Fire, 2002; Darkness Falls, 2003; Seabiscuit, 2003; prodn. designer: (TV) Prime Target, 1989; Teach 109, 1990; Heat Wave, 1990; Twin Peaks, 1990; Family of Spies, 1990; Zooman, 1995; Fail Safe, 2000; Live From Baghdad, 2002 (Emmy, 2003); The Handler, 2003; Entourage, 2004; Blind Horizon, 2004; (films) Feeling 109, 1988; Torch Song Trilogy, 1988; It Takes Two, 1988; Bob Roberts, 1992; Storyville, 1992; Dream Lover, 1994; You So Crazy, 1994; Dead Man Walking, 1995; Panther, 1995; The Blackout, 1997; Nightwatch, 1997; Apt Pupil, 1998; Girl, Interrupted, 1999; Payback, 1999; The Prime Gig, 2000; Twilight: Los Angeles, 2000; Martin Lawrence Live: Runteldat, 2002; The Mothman Prophecies, 2002; art dir. Somewhere Tomorrow, 1983; Girls Nite Out, 1984; The Sure Things, 1985; Miracle Mile, 1988; Checking Out, 1989; Cradle Will Rock, 1999; art dir.: TV Sometimes I Don't Love My Mother, 1982; set decorator: Wisdom, 1986; (TV) Yuri Noshenko, KGB, 1986; In the Mood, 1987; set designer: (films) In the King of Prussia, 1982; Sweet Lorraine, 1987; Lemonade, 1999; (plays) Not About Nightingales, 1999 (Drama Desk award, best set design, nominee, Laurence Olivier Theatre award for Best Set Design, 1998 production, 1999); Twelfth Night, 2000; Bat Boy, 2001; Fifth of July, 2003; Beautiful Child, 2004; Embedded, 2004; Speaking in Tongues; Skreamers; Mephisto; The Seagull; House Arrest; Trojan Women; visual cons.: Ed Wood, 1994; actor: Day by Day: A Director's Journey Part I, 2003, Persistance, 2004. Recipient 1999 Tony award for best set design for Not About Nightingales, Evening Standard award, London Critics' Cir. award, Drama Desk award, Outer Critics Cir. award, Golden Satellite award, 1999, Clio awards. Mem.: IATSE.

HOOVER, ROBERT ALLAN, university president; b. Des Moines, May 9, 1941; s. Claude Edward and Anna Doris H.; m. Jeanne Mary Hoover, Feb. 22, 1968; children: Jennifer Jill Jacobs, Suzanne Hoover Ogden. BS, Ariz. State U., 1967, MA, 1969; PhD, U. Calif., Santa Barbara, 1973. Instr. polit. sci. Utah State U., Logan, 1971-73, asst. prof. polit. sci., 1973-79, assoc. prof. polit. sci., chair polit. sci. dept., 1979-84, prof. polit. sci., 1984-91, dean Coll. Humanities, Arts and Social Scis., 1984-91; v.p. for acad. affairs U. Nev., Reno, 1991-96; pres. U. Idaho, Moscow, 1996—2003, Albertson Coll. Idaho, Caldwell, 2003—. Author: The Politics of MX: A New Direction in Weapons Procurement?, 1982, The MX Controversy: A Guide to Issues and References, 1982, Arms Control: The Interwar Naval Limitation Agreements, 1980. Bd. dirs. United Way, Reno, 1994-96, Channel 5, Reno, 1991-95, St. Scholastica Acad., Canon City, Colo., 1991-96. Avocations: skiing, jogging, camping. Office: Albertson Coll 2112 Cleveland Blvd Caldwell ID 83605-9990 E-mail: rhoover@albertson.edu.

HOPCROFT, JOHN EDWARD, computer scientist, educator; b. Oct. 7, 1939; BS in EE, Seattle U., 1961; MS in EE, Stanford U., 1962, PhD in Elec. Engring., 1964. Asst. prof. Princeton (N.J.) U., 1964-67; assoc. prof. Cornell U., Ithaca, N.Y., 1967-71, prof., 1972—, chmn. computer sci. dept., 1987-92, assoc. dean coll. affairs Coll. Engring., 1992-93, dean Coll Engring., 1994—2001, IBM prof. engring. and applied math., 2004—. Vis. prof. Stanford U., Calif., 1970-71; mem. Info. Sci. and Tech. Office Def. Advanced Rsch. Projects Agy. (DARPA) (chair robotics working group); chmn. adv. bd. NSF, 1987-90; mem. computer sci. and telecomm. bd. NAS/NRC, 1988—, adv. com. for David and Lucille Packard Fellowships in Sci. and Tech., 1991—; mem. sci. adv. bd. USAF, Inst. for Def. Analysis, David and Lucille Packard Found., NSF. Co-author: Formal Languages and Their Relation to Automata, 1969, The Design and Analysis of Computer Algorithms, 1974, Introduction to Automata Theory, Language, and Computation, 1979, Data Structures and Algorithms, 1983, Planning, Geometry and Complexity of Robot Motion, 1987. NSF Grad. fellow, 1961-64. Fellow IEEE, AAAS, Am. Acad. Arts and Scis.; mem. NAE (mem. acad. adv. bd. 1992-95), Nat. Sci. Bd., Inst. for Def. Analysis Supercomputing Rsch. Ctr., Assn. Computing Math. (Turing award 1986), Soc. for Indsl. and Applied Math., Ctr. Excellence Space Data and Info. Sci. (interim dir. 1987-88). Office: Cornell U Dept Computer Sci 5144 Upson Hall Ithaca NY 14853-2201 Business E-Mail: jeh@cs.cornell.edu.

HOPE, CAROL J, pharmacologist, researcher; d. Inabelle Jean and John Finley Payne. BS chem. and petroleum-refining engring., Colo. Sch. of Mines, 1972—76, MS chem. and petroleum-refining engring., 1976—77; MS in biol. sci., U. of Colo. Health Sciences Ctr., 1991—96, BS in pharmacy, 1996—2000, PharmD, 2000—01; Pharmacy Fellowship, Purdue U./Regenstrief Inst., Specialties: Medical Informatics & Health Services Research, 2001—03. Lic. Pharmacist Colo., 2000, Ind., 2001, Miss., 2003. Asst. prof. U. of Miss. Med. Ctr., Schools of Medicine/Pharmacy, 2001—; rsch. pharmacy intern U. Colo. Health Sciences Ctr. IRB, 2001, Veterans Affairs Cooperative Studies Program Clin. Rsch. Pharmacy Coordinating Ctr., Albuquerque, 2000; rsch. pharmacy externship Kaiser HMO, Denver, 1999; rsch. asst. U. of Colo. Health Sciences Ctr., 1999, rsch. project mgr., 1997—98; clin. rsch. asst. Rocky Mountain Soc. for Multiple Sclerosis, Denver, 1996—97; rsch. asst. U. of Colo. Health Sciences Ctr., 1993—96. Grant reviewer Office of Rsch. Integrity, Wash., DC, 2005—; reviewer Am. Soc. of Clin. Pharmacology and Therapeutics, 2003—05; reveiwer Am. Soc. of Health-Systems Pharmacists, 2002. Contbr. articles to profl. jours. Recipient Suicide and Depression Anonymous Humanitarian award, 1995, Suicide and Depression Anonymous Outstanding Vol. award, 1992, On-the-Job Individual Performance award, Lowry AFB, 1990, Outstanding Young Women in Am. award, 1977, Hays award, Chem. Engring. Dept., 1976, AMAX Project Design award, 1976; grant, Drug Info. Assn., 2002—03, Sam and Mytrie Regenstrief Postdoctoral Grant, 2002—03, Colo. Undergraduate Merit scholarship, 1997—99. Mem.: Am. Pharm. Assn., Am. Soc. of Health-System Pharamacists, Am. Coll. of Clin. Pharmacology, Am. Med. Informatics Assn., Am. Soc. for Clin. Pharmacology and Therapeutics (edn. com., adverse drug event symposium steering com. 2003—05). Christian. Achievements include design of new method to detect adverse drug events using non-clinical personnel. Avocations: yoga, reading, needlecrafts. Mailing: 1820 MacKenzie rd Pueblo CO 81001 E-mail: chope@access4less.net.

HOPE, GERRI DANETTE, telecommunications management executive; b. Antelope, Calif., Feb. 28, 1956; d. Albert Gerald and Beulah H. AS, Sierra Coll., Calif., 1977; postgrad., Okla. State U., 1977-79. Instrnl. asst. II San Juan Sch. Dist., Carmichael, Calif., 1979-82; telecomm. supr. Delta Dental Svc. of Calif., San Francisco, 1982-85; telecomm. coord. Farmers Savs. Bank, Davis, Calif., 1987-95; telecomm. officer Sacramento Savs. Bank, 1987-95; telecomm. analyst II contractor dept. ins. State of Calif., Sacramento, 1995—. Owner GDH Enterprises, 1993-97; sr. telecomms. engr. Access Health, Inc., Rancho Cordova, Calif., 1996-97, Any Time Access, Sacramento, 1997-98, GDH Enterprises, North Highlands, 1993-05; employment devel. dept. staff, info. systems analyst specialist State of Calif., 1998—; founder Custom Label Designer, Sacramento, 1993-96; mem. telecomm. adv. panel Golden Gate U., Sacramento; lectr. in toll fraud prevention and voice network security; hon. chmn. Bus. Adv. Coun. Nat. Rep. Congress Com., Calif., 2005. Ministry dir. dinner fellowship Calvary Chapel, Roseville Ch., 2000—. Mem. Telecomm. Assn. (v.p. membership com. Sacramento Valley chpt. 1992-94, v.p. dir. programs 1995-2003, corp. conf. com. programs bd. 1997-99, v.p. pub. rels. bd., dir. edn., webmaster 2002—). Republican. Avocations: writing, computers, stamp collecting/philately, animal behavior, participating in christian ministry. Home: 3025 U St Antelope CA 95843-2513 Office: State Calif EDD ITB Telecom 800 Capital Mall MIC 58-2S Sacramento CA 95814 Office Phone: 916-653-8756.

HOPE, HAKON, research scientist; b. Foerde, Norway, Dec. 15, 1930; s. Harald and Gunhild Hope; m. Sally Pearl Margulies Springer, Feb. 1, 1985; children: Erik Jacob, Mollie Liv. Cand. mag., U. of Oslo, Oslo, Norway, 1950—54; Cand. real., U. of Oslo (and Moscow State U., Moscow), Oslo, Norway, 1954—58. Rsch. asst. U. of Oslo, Oslo, 1958—60, u. fellow, 1961—65; postdoctoral fellow U. of Calif., Los Angeles, Calif., 1961—63; asst. prof. U. of Calif., Davis, Davis, Calif., 1965—68, assoc. prof., 1968—73, prof., 1973—92, prof. emeritus, 1993—. Co-editor Acta Crystallographica, 1984—93; vis. prof. The Weizmann Institue of Sci., Rehovot, Israel, 1978—79, U. of Copenhagen, Copenhagen, 1979—79. Author: (journal articles (about 160) Acta Crystallographica, Journal of the American Chemical Society, Inorganic Chemistry, Journal of Applied Crystallography, and others. Recipient Dr. philos, h. c., U. of Oslo, 1994; Fulbright Fellow, Fulbright Found., 1961-1963. Mem.: Am. Crystallographic Assn. Achievements include research in Developed methods for accurate measurement of electron density in crystals; Developed methods for crystallographic study of proteins at cryogenic temperatures; Developed methods for very rapid structure determination by X-ray crystallography. Avocations: languages; computer programming, gardening; skiing. Office: Department of Chemistry UC Davis One Shields Avenue Davis CA 95616 E-mail: hhope@ucdavis.edu.

HOPE, HENRY WELCKER, lawyer; b. Chattanooga, Tenn., Sept. 11, 1940; s. William Boyd and Eleanor Kate Roberson Hope; m. Sara Elizabeth Bailey, Aug. 5, 1961; children: Eleanor Anne Rooke, Julia Cathleen Falick. BS, U. Tenn., 1962; JD, George Washington U., 1966. Bar: Va. 1966, Tex. 1966, U.S. Patent Office 1966. Assoc. Fulbright & Jaworski, LLP, Houston, 1966-75, ptnr., 1975—. Bd. dirs. Royal Ten Cate (USA), Inc. 1985-, Atlanta, BCM Tech., Inc. 1987-, Houston. Trustee Houston Ballet Found., 1997—, adv. trustee, 2000-01; mem. corp. ptnrs. com. Mus. Fine Arts, Houston, 1997-2004; mem. adv. bd. dirs. Houston Jr. Forum, 1988-91; mem. adminstrv. bd. Meml. Dr. United Meth., Houston. Fellow Tex. Bar Found. (life), Houston Bar Found. (sustaining life); mem. ABA (com. mem. 1966-85), Tex. Bar Assn. (com. mem. 1966-90), Va. Bar Assn., Licensing Exec. Soc. (various chairs 1975-85), MIT Enterprise Forum of Tex. (bd. dirs. 1989-94), Lakeside Country Club (bd. dirs. 1996-2000, pres. 1998-99). Methodist. Avocations: golf, reading, travel. Office: Fulbright & Jaworski LLP 1301 Mckinney St Ste 5100 Houston TX 77010-3031 E-mail: hhope@fulbright.com.

HOPE, MARGARET LAUTEN, retired civic worker; b. NYC; 1 son, Frederick H., III. *Margaret Lauten Hope's maternal grandfather was Henry G.F. Lauten and his wife was Lillie Falls Weiss Lauten, residents of Long Island and Palm Beach. Mrs. Lauten's parents were George Weiss and Elizabeth O'Donnell Weiss of Staten Island. Mr. Lauten wrote the Worth Street Rules that govern the textile industry, was with the cotton textile merchants, and was on the arbitration council. Paternal grandfather Dr. Fritz J. Swanson Sr. resided in Westerly, R.I. at Shelter Harbor. He was knighted by the King of Sweden and given the title, Count of Vasa. Dr. Fritz J. Swanson Sr.'s home, built by Stanford White, was in New York City.* Privately educated. Ball com. various charity fund raising events. Mem. Jr. League NYC; Everglades Club, Palm Beach, Fla.; Women's Nat. Rep. Club (NYC); St. James Club (London). Home: 236 Dunbar Rd Palm Beach FL 33480

HOPE, ROBERTA EDITH, art educator, artist; b. San Rafael, Calif., May 31, 1948; d. Theodore Edward Smith and Pauline Alice Leupold; m. Robert Stein Hope, June 14, 1975; children: Miriam Ruth, Jordan Robert. BA, U. Calif., Davis, 1970; Cert. of Study, Universite Bordeaux, France, 1969. Cert. tchr. Calif. Exec. asst. Arthur Ct. Designs, San Francisco, 1971—79; art and English tchr. Trinity H.S., San Rafael, Calif., 1981—82, Petaluma (Calif.) H.S., 1990—91; art tchr. Rancho Cotate H.S., Rohnert Park, Calif., 1991—, chmn. visual and performing arts dept. Mem. Rancho Cotate Tech. Com., Rohnert Park, 1994—2003; master tchr. student tchr. program Sonoma State U., Rohnert Park, 1988—2003; writer/dist. curriculum com. Cotate-Rohnert Park Unified Sch. Dist., 1989—90; participant,scorer Nat. Bd. for Profession Tchg. Stds., San Francisco, 1994—96; mem. Rancho Cotate Site Coun., Rohnert Park, 2000—04, Rohnert Park, 1994—97. Author: (devotional) The Gospel According to John: An Interactive Study and Devotional, 2004, Women of the Bible, 2005; CD, Flash MX Tutorials and Animations, 2004; editor, dir.: video Sonoma County Water Project, 1996. Host Casa Grande Student Exch., Petaluma, 1996—99; vol. Rancho des Sus Ninos, Tecate, Mexico, 1990—90; tchr. Petaluma Valley Bapt. Ch. Women's Bible Study, Petaluma, 2004—05; tchr. children's missions Adobe Christian Ctr., Petaluma, 1989—95, mem. missions bd., 1995—2000. Recipient Exemplary Visual Arts award, Calif. Art Educators Assn., 1995; Operation Green Eyes grantee, EPA, 1996, State Environ. Edn. grantee, Calif. Bd. Edn., 1995. Avocations: gardening, reading, digital animation, painting, drawing. Office: Rancho Cotate HS 5450 Snyder Ln Rohnert Park CA 94928 Office Fax: 707-792-4758. Personal E-mail: rhope2000@comcast.net.

HOPE, SAMUEL HOWARD, accreditation organization executive; b. Owensboro, Ky., Nov. 5, 1946; s. James Russell and Lorraine (Jones) H.; m. Judy Bucher, June 24, 1978. B.Mus., Eastman Sch. Music, Rochester, N.Y., 1967; M.Music Arts, Yale U., 1970; pupil of, Nadia Boulanger, France, 1966, 67; LHD Marywood U. (hon.), 2001. Dean, composer-in-residence Atlanta Boy Choir Sch. Music, 1970-73, trustee, 1973—2001; vis. instr. Lee U., Cleveland, Tenn., 1973-74; exec. dir. music alumni, asso. dir. grad. profl. programs Campaign for Yale, Yale U., 1974-75; exec. dir. Nat. Assn. Schs. Music, Nat. Assn. Schs. Art and Design, Reston, Va., 1975—, Joint Commn. on Dance and Theatre Accreditation, 1978-83, Nat. Assn. Schs. Theatre, 1980—, Higher Edn. Arts Data Services, 1981—, Nat. Assn. Schs. Dance, 1981—, Working Group on Arts in Higher Edn., 1982—, Coun. of Arts Accrediting Assns., 1980—, Commn. Cmty. and Precollegiate Arts Schs., 2000—. Chmn. assembly of specialized accrediting bodies Council on Postsecondary Accreditation, 1979-82, bd. dirs., 1992-93; bd. dirs. Council Specialized Accrediting Agys., 1978-81, sec.-treas., 1979-81; mem. com. recognition Council Postsecondary Accreditation, 1984-88; chmn. adminstv. com. Found. Advancement Edn. in Music., 1986-90. Composer Piano Sonata I, 1968, II, 1971; motet Solus Ad Victimam Procedis, Domine, 1970, Blessed Be Thou Lord, 1976, Trio for Oboe, Cello and Piano, 1970, Cantata I, 1973, Cantata II, 1975, Symphonia: Psalm 145, 1982, Toccata: Psalm 117 for Organ, 1993; exec. editor Arts Edn. Policy Rev. mag., 1984—. Chmn. govt. relations com. Nat. Music Council, 1976-79, bd. dirs., 1978-84; mem. exec. com. Am. Soc. Univ. Composers, 1977-83; nat. alumni council Eastman Sch. Music, 1975-78, chmn., 1976-77; bd. dirs. Am. Music Conf., 1978-82; trustee Am. Acad. for Liberal Edn., 1997—. Recipient Composition prize Yale U., 1968, 69, 70, disting. svc. award Yale U., 2000, Ohio U., 2000. Mem. Am. Music Ctr., Coll. Music Soc., Music Educators Nat. Conf., Am. Inst. Graphic Artists, Music Tchrs. Nat. Assn., Am. Assn. for Theatre in Higher Edn., Am. Alliance for Theatre and Edn., Nat. Dance Edn. Orgn., Yale Club (N.Y.C.). Anglican. Home: 10717 Rosehaven St Fairfax VA 22030-2826 Office: 11250 Roger Bacon Dr Ste 21 Reston VA 20190-5248

HOPE, WILLIAM DUANE, zoologist, curator; b. Fort Collins, Colo., June 7, 1935; s. William Earl and Lois Howe (Burnett) H.; m. Colleen Bryan, Dec. 23, 1956 (div.); children: Pam Hope Herbert, Karen Hope Van Zandt, Linda Hope Greene. BS, Colo. State U., 1957, MS, 1960; PhD, U. Calif., Davis, 1965. Systematic zoologist. dept. invertebrate zoology Nat. Mus. Natural History, Smithsonian Instn., Washington, 1964—69, curator, 1969—75, chmn. dept., 1976—81. Contbr. articles to profl. jours. Mem. Am. Assn. Zool. Nomenclature, Am. Micros Soc., Biol. Soc. Washington, Helminthological Soc. Washington, Soc. Nematologists, Soc. Systematic Zoology, Internat. Assn. Meiobenthologists. Democrat. Avocations: hiking, biking, flyfishing, bird watching. Office: Smithsonian Instn Natural History Mus Dept Zoology Rm W212 MRC 163 Washington DC 20013-7012 Office Phone: 202-633-1775. Personal E-mail: wdhope@aol.com.

HOPEN, HERBERT JOHN, horticulture educator; b. Madison, Wis., Jan. 7, 1934; s. Alfred and Amelia (Sveum) H.; m. Joanne C. Emmel, Sept. 12, 1959; children: Timothy, Rachel. BS, U. Wis., 1956, MS, 1959; PhD, Mich. State U., 1962. Asst. prof. U. Minn., Duluth, 1962-64; prof. U. Ill., Urbana, 1965-85, prof., acting head, 1983-85; prof. horticulture U. Wis., Madison, 1985-97, prof. emeritus, 1997, chmn. dept. horticulture, 1985-91. Mem. Am. Soc. for Hort. Sci., Weed Sci. Soc. Am., North Ctrl. Weed Sci. Soc., Ygdrasil, Sigma Xi. Avocations: reading, gardening. Office: U Wis Dept Hort 1575 Linden Dr Madison WI 53706-1514 Office Phone: 608-262-1490. Business E-Mail: hjhopen@wisc.edu.

HOPF, FRANK RUDOLPH, retired dentist; b. N.Y.C., Sept. 1, 1920; s. Rudolph Aldridge and Jennie Victoria (Fusco) Hopf; m. Elsie Hedlund, Sept. 10, 1949; children: Christine, Frank, Victoria, William, Robert. BS, Purdue U., 1942; postgrad., Middlesex U. Sch. Medicine, 1943—44; DDS, NYU, 1953, postgrad., 1957—61; MA, Columbia U., 1953, MPH, 1955. Asst. dir.

Bur. Dental Health, NY State Dept. Health, Albany, 1956—57, regional dental dir. White Plains, 1967—90; pvt. practice dentistry specializing in periodontics Rye, NY, 1957—2003; ret., 2003. Rsch. assoc. periodontics NYU Coll. Dentistry, 1958—61; clin. asst. prof. dept. periodontics NJ Coll. Medicine and Dentistry, Jersey City, 1962—67; adj. asst. prof. dept. cmty. dentistry Columbia Sch. Dental and Oral Surgery, N.Y.C., 1971—76; vis. prof. dept. preventive dentistry Pitts. U. Sch. Dentistry, 1967—72. Contbr. articles to profl. publs. Pres. Country Ridge Home Owners Assn., Rye Brook, NY, 1960—62. Served with USNR, 1944—46. Grantee, NIH, 1957. Fellow: APHA, Am. Coll. Dentists, NY Acad. Dentistry, Am. Sch. Health Assn.; mem.: AAAS, ADA, Fedn. Dentaire Internationale, Am. Soc. Dentistry for Children, Westchester Acad. Medicine, North Eastern Soc. Periodontics, Royal Soc. Health, NY State Pub. Health Assn. (pres. 1970—72), Westchester Country Club, Westchester Shore Dental Study Club (pres. 1960—61, Rye, NY), KC (4 deg.). Roman Catholic. Home: 33 Old Field Hill Rd # 7 Southbury CT 06488

HOPFENBECK, GEORGE MARTIN, JR., lawyer; b. N.Y.C., Mar. 1, 1929; s. George Martin and Margaret Spencer (Felt) H.; m. Ruth Elizabeth Allen, June 27, 1953; children: Ann Elizabeth, James Allen. BA, Williams Coll., 1951; JD, Yale U., 1954. Bar: Colo., 1955. Assoc. Davis, Graham & Stubbs and predecessor Lewis, Grant & Davis, Denver, 1954-59, ptnr., 1959-92, of counsel, 1993—. Bd. dirs. Am. Cancer Soc. Inc., Colo. divsn., Denver, 1966-90, chmn., 1975-77; bd. dirs. Colo. Regional Cancer Ctr. Inc., Denver, 1974-81, pres., 1975-77; bd. dirs. Am. Cancer Soc. Inc., Atlanta, 1984-90, Denver Parks and Recreation Found., 1966-75; bd. dirs. Boys and Girls Clubs of Metro Denver, Inc., 1993—, chmn., 1998-2000; mem. Colo. State Pers. Bd., Denver, 1971-75, chmn., 1971-72; mem. Denver Bd. Parks & Recreation, 1961-69; trustee Kent Sch. for Girls, Denver, 1970-73; chmn. campaign com. for Gov. Love, Colo., 1966, campaign com. for McKevitt for Congress, Denver, 1970. Recipient St. George medal Am. Cancer Soc., 1982. Mem. ABA, Colo. Bar Assn., Denver Country Club (bd. dirs. 1967-70, 2002—), University Club (Denver) (bd. dirs. 1973-82). Republican. Episcopalian. Home: 2552 E Alameda Ave 75 Denver CO 80209 Office: 333 Logan St Ste 108 Denver CO 80203-4089

HOPGOOD, HOON-YUNG, state representative; b. Inchon, South Korea, Dec. 8, 1974; BA in Polit. Sci., U. Mich., Ann Arbor, 1996; attending, Northern Mich. U. Intern Office of Congresswoman Lynn Rivers, Washington, 1995; labor coordinator Mich. State AFL-CIO, 1996; with Mich. Ho. Dem. Policy Staff, 1997—99; with legislative office Office of State Repr. Raymond Basham, 1999—2001; mem. Mich. Ho. of Reps., 2002—. Mem. edn., energy and techn. com. & regulatory reform com. Mich. Ho. of Reps.; mem. Steel/Mining Caucus, Children's Caucus, Capitol Speakers Bureau. Mem. adv. bd. Council of Asian-Pacific Am. Mem.: Mich. Dem. Action Network, Dem. Club of Taylor, Mich. Young Dem., Mich. Dem. Party. Office: Mich Ho of Reps S0786 Ho Office Bldg PO Box 30014 Lansing MI 48909-7514*

HOPGOOD, JAMES F., anthropologist, educator; b. Cape Girardeau, Mo., Apr. 18, 1943; s. Finley Marshall and Marjorie Louise (Schneider) Hopgood; m. Esther Berg, Jan. 29, 1966; 1 child, Myka Lynn. BA, U. Mo., 1965, MA, 1969; MPhil, U. Kans., 1971, PhD, 1976. From asst. prof. to prof. anthropology No. Ky. U., Highland Heights, 1973—2003, prof. emeritus, 2003—, chmn. dept. sociology, anthropology and philosophy, 1984-98, dir. Mus. of Anthropology, 1976—2003. Vis. instr. Washburn U., Topeka, 1969; vis. prof. Instituto Tecnologico y de Estudios Superiores de Monterrey, Mexico, 1971, U. Monterrey, 1980; profl. assoc. Asian studies devel. program East-West Ctr. and U. Hawaii, 1991, 93, 94. Author: Settlers of Bajavista: Urban Adaptation in a Mexican Squatter Settlement, 1979; editor, contbr.: The Making of Saints: Contesting Sacred Ground, 2005; mem. editl. bd. Jour. Third World Studies; contbr. articles, reports to profl. jours. Mem. edn. com. Cin. Mus. Natural History, 1992—94. Recipient Strongest Influence award, No. Ky. U. Alumni Coun., 2003, Spl. Recognition award, Ctrl. States Anthrop. Soc., 2005; Jewish Chautauqua Soc. scholar in residence, No. Ky. U., 1988—98, Sasakawa fellow, San Diego State U., 1996. Fellow: Am. Anthrop. Assn. (mem. exec. com. 1996—98); mem.: Ctrl. State Anthropol. Soc. (exec. bd. 1989—92, pres. 1996—97, exec. bd. 1999—2001, editor CSAS Bull. 2001—, Spl. Recognition award in photography 2005), Ky. Acad. Sci. (bd. gov. 1995—98), Sigma Xi, Lambda Alpha. Home: 4918 Corn Row Ct Independence KY 41051-8101 Business E-Mail: hopgood@nku.edu.

HOPKE, PHILIP KARL, chemical engineering educator; b. Sherman, Tex., Mar. 22, 1944; s. George Karl and Dorothy Virginia (Dawson) H.; m. Eleanor Lois Fritz, June 1, 1968; children: Jane Catherine, Frederick Karl. BS, Trinity Coll., 1965; MA, Princeton (N.J.) U., 1967, PhD, 1969. Rsch. assoc. MIT, Cambridge, Mass., 1969-70; asst. prof. SUNY, Fredonia, 1970-74, U. Ill., Urbana, 1974-78, assoc. prof., 1978-82, prof., 1982-89; Robert A Plane prof. Clarkson U., Potsdam, NY, 1989—2001, dean Grad. Sch., 1997-99, Bayard D. Clarkson disting. prof., 2002—, dir. Ctr. for Air Resources Engring. and Sci., 2002—. Chair grant rev. panel on air chemistry and physics EPA, Washington, 1987-92, clean air sci. adv. com., 1995-2000, chair clean air sci. adv. com., 2000—04. Author: Receptor Modeling in Environmental Chemistry, 1985; editor: Radon and It's Decay Products, 1987, Receptor Modeling for Air Quality Management, 1991; editor-in-chief Aerosol Sci. and Tech., 1993-2002; contbr. articles to profl. jours. Mem. Champaign (Ill.) Environ. Adv. Commn., 1977-78; mem., pres. Champaign Community Sch. Bd. of Edn., 1978-81. Grantee U.S. Dept. Energy, EPA, NSF, Ministry of the Enviroment of Ont., N.J. EPA, Calif. Air Resources Bd., N.Y. State ERDA. Mem. Am. Assn. for Aerosol Rsch. (bd. dirs. 1989-94, v.p. 2001-02, pres. 2003-04), Air and Waste Mgmt. Assn. (chair com. 1990-92), Gesellschaft fur Aerosolforschung, Am. Chem. Soc. Achievements include development of multivariate statistical methods for quantitative determination of airborne particle source/receptor relationships; improvement of size measurement methods for ultrafine aerosols; research on physical chemistry of radon and its decay products and homogeneous and heterogeneous nucleation. Office: Clarkson U Ctr for Air Resources Engring & Sci PO Box 5708 Potsdam NY 13699-5708 Office Phone: 315-268-3861. Business E-Mail: hopkepk@clarkson.edu.

HOPKINS, ALBEN NORRIS, lawyer; b. Ripley, Miss., Feb. 14, 1941; s. Lloyd Carter and Reba Genova (Norris) H.; m. Ruth Boyd, May 31, 1963; children: Ashley Anne, A. Norris. BA, Delta State Coll., 1963; JD, U. Miss., 1965; BA, William Carey Coll., 1985; student, Blue Mountain Coll. Bar: U.S. Dist. Ct. (so. dist.) Miss. 1966, U.S. Dist. Ct. (no. dist.) Miss. 1970, U.S. Ct. Appeals (5th cir.) 1972, U.S. Supreme Ct. 1972, U.S. Ct. Appeals (11th cir.) 1981, U.S. Ct. Mil. Appeals 1986. Assoc. Daniel, Coker & Horton, Jackson also Gulfport, Miss., 1965-67, ptnr., 1967-69, resident ptnr., 1969-77; sr. ptnr., mng. ptnr. Hopkins, Crawley, Bagwell & Upshaw, Gulfport, 1977—. Bd. dirs. Delta State U. Found., 1991-94, pres., 1994; bd. dirs. USO, 1974-75, 83—, Gulf Pines Coun. Girl Scouts U.S.A., 1974-82, 85—, United Way Harrison Coutny; bd. dirs., chmn. planned giving com., dist. dir. Am. Heart Assn.; asst. chmn. State Heart Fund, 1983, chmn., 1985; asst. adjutant gen. State of Miss., 1991-95, chief judge Mil. Ct. Appeals, 1996—. Served to maj. gen. U.S. Army N.G., 1965-95, ret. Fellow Miss. Bar Found.; mem. Internat. Assn. Def. Counsel, Fedn. Ins. Counsel, Maritime Law Assn. U.S., Southeastern Admiralty Assn., Hinds County Bar Assn., Harrison County Bar Assn. (v.p. 1976-77), Miss. Bar Assn. (mem. jud. selection com. 1978-79), ABA, Lamar Order, Fed. Bar Assn. (bd. dirs. 1979-82), Kappa Alpha, Pi Kappa Delta, Phi Alpha Delta, Omicron Delta Kappa, Windance Country Club, Gulfport Yacht Club, Univ. Club, Masons, Shriners, YorkRite, others. Republican. Baptist. Office: PO Box 1510 Gulfport MS 39502-1510 E-mail: AHopkins@MsLawyer.com.

HOPKINS, SIR ANTHONY (PHILIP), actor; b. Port Talbot, South Wales, U.K., Dec. 31, 1937; s. Richard Arthur and Muriel Annie (Yeates) H.; m. Petronella Barker, Sept. 1967 (div. 1972); 1 child, Abigail; m. Jennifer Ann Lynton, Jan. 13, 1973 (div. Apr. 30, 2002); m. Stella Arroyave, Mar. 1, 2003. Student, Welsh Coll. Music and Drama, Cardiff, Wales, 1954-56, Royal Acad. Dramatic Art, London, 1961-63; DLitt (hon.), U. Wales, 1988; Fellow (hon.), St. David's Coll., Lampeter, Wales, 1992. Ind. stage, screen, TV actor, 1963—. Made London stage debut in Julius Caesar, 1964; mem. Nat. Theatre Co., 1966-73; appeared in Juno and the Paycock, 1966, A Flea in Her Ear, 1966, Three Sisters, 1967, The Dance of Death, 1967, As You Like It, 1967, The Architect and the Emperor of Assyria, 1971, A Woman Killed with Kindness, 1971, Coriolanus, 1971, The Taming of the Shrew, 1972, Macbeth, 1972, Equus (Best Actor award N.Y. Drama Desk, Best Actor award Outer Critics Circle, Best Actor award Am. Authors Celebrities Forum), N.Y.C., 1974-75, (L.A. Drama Critics award), L.A., 1977, The Tempest, L.A., 1979, Old Times, N.Y.C., 1983, The Lonely Road, London, 1985, Pravda, Nat. Theatre, London, 1985-86 (Olivier award 1985, Stage Actor award Variety Club), King Lear, Nat. Theatre, London, 1986-87, Anthony & Cleopatra, Nat. Theatre, London, 1987, M Butterfly, Shaftesbury Theatre, London, 1989, (also dir.) August, 1994; films include (debut) The Lion in Winter, 1968, Hamlet, 1969, The Looking Glass War, 1969, When Eight Bells Toll, 1971, Young Winston, 1972, A Doll's House, 1973, The Girl from Petrovka, 1974, Juggernaut, 1974, A Bridge Too Far, 1977, Audrey Rose, 1977, International Velvet, 1978, Magic, 1978, The Elephant Man, 1980, A Change of Seasons, 1980, The Bounty, 1984 (Film Actor award Variety Club), The Good Father, 1985, 84 Charing Cross Road, 1986 (Best Actor award Moscow Film Festival 1987), The Dawning, 1988, Silence of the Lambs, 1991 (Acad. award for Best Actor 1992, Best Actor award Chgo. Film Critics 1992, Best Actor award Boston Film Critics 1992, Best Actor award N.Y. Film Critics 1992, Film Actor award Variety Club 1992, Best Film Actor award BAFTA 1992), Freejack, 1992, One Man's War (TV movie), 1991, Spotswood/The Efficiency Expert, 1992, Howard's End, 1992, Bram Stoker's Dracula, 1992, Chaplin, 1992, Remains of the Day, 1993 (Acad. award nominee for Best Actor 1994, Best Actor award L.A. Film Critics Assn. 1993, Best Actor award Nat. Soc. film Critics (U.S.A.) 1993, BAFTA UK best film actor award, Guild of Regional Film Writers UK Best Actor award, Variety Club UK Film Actor award 1993, Japan Critics Best Actor in a Fgn. Film award), Shadowlands, 1993 (Best Actor award Nat. Bd. Rev. 1993, Best Actor award L.A. Film Critics Assn. 1993, Best Actor award Nat. Soc. Film Critics (U.S.A.) 1993), the Trial, 1993, The Road to Welville, 1994, Legends of the Fall, 1994, The Innocent, 1993, Nixon, 1995 (Acad. award nominee for Best Actor 1996), August, 1996, Surviving Picasso, 1996, The Edge, 1997, Amistad, 1997, The Mask of Zorro, 1998, Meet Joe Black, 1998, Instinct, 1999, Titus, 1999, Mission Impossible II, 2000, How the Grinch Stole Christmas (voice), Hannibal, 2001, Hearts in Atlantis, 2001, The Devil and Daniel Webster, 2001, Bad Company, 2002, Red Dragon, 2002, The Human Stain, 2003, Alexander, 2004, Proof, 2005; BBC-TV series War and Peace (Best TV Actor award Soc. Film and TV Arts), 1972; TV shows include A Heritage and Its History, 1968, Vanya, Hearts and Flowers, Three Sisters, The Peasant's Revolt, Dickens, Danton, The Poet Game, Decision to Burn, War and Peace, Cuculus Canorus, Lloyd George, Q.B. VII, 1971, Find Me, A Childhood Friend, Possessions, All Creatures Great and Small, 1975, The Lindbergh Kidnapping Case, 1976 (Emmy award), Victory at Entebbe, 1976, Dark Victory, Mayflower: The Pilgrim's Adventure, 1979, The Bunker, 1980 (Emmy award), Peter and Paul, 1980, Othello, BBC, 1981, Little Eyolf, BBC, 1981, The Hunchback of Notre Dame, 1982, A Married Man, 1984, The Arch of Triumph, CBS, 1984, Hollywood Wives, ABC, 1984, Guilty Conscience, CBS, 1984, Blunt, BBC, 1985, the Tenth Man, CBS, 1988, Across the Lake, BBC, Heartland, BBC, Great Expectations, 1989, Disney Primetime, To Be The Best, 1990, others. Decorated Comdr. of Order of Brit. Empire, 1987, Knights Bachelor, 1993, Comdr. of Order of Arts & Letters, France, 1996; named one of Top 100 Movie Stars of All Time, Empire (U.K.) Mag., 1997; recipient Star on Hollywood Walk of Fame, 2003. Office: Creative Artists Agy 9830 Wilshire Blvd Beverly Hills CA 90212-1804*

HOPKINS, BUDD, artist, writer; b. Wheeling, W.Va., June 15, 1931; s. Elliott Budd and Eleanor Wright (Stewart) H.; m. April Kingsley, Apr. 5, 1973; 1 child, Grace Francesca. BA, Oberlin Coll., 1953; postgrad., Columbia U., 1953-54. One man shows include Poindexter Gallery, N.Y.C., 1956, Zabriskie Gallery, N.Y.C., 1959, Galerie Liatowitsch, Basel, Switzerland, 1974, Lerner-Heller Gallery, N.Y.C., 1977, 78, 80, 82, Marilyn Pearl Gallery, N.Y.C., 1985, 88, Jan Cicero Gallery, Chgo., 1985, Drew U., 1990, Longpoint Gallery, Provincetown, 1994; group shows include Montclair Art Mus., N.J., 1979, Rosa Esman Gallery, N.Y.C., 1980, Contemporary Arts Mus., Houston, 1982; represented in permanent collections Mus. Modern Art, N.Y., Guggenheim Mus. Modern Art, N.Y.C., Whitney Mus. Am. Art, N.Y.C., Bklyn. Mus., Corcoran Gallery Art, Washington, Hirshhorn Mus. and Sculpture Garden, San Francisco Mus. Art; author: Missing Time, 1981 Intruders, 1987; contbr. articles to profl. jours. Named to Wheeling, W. Va. Hall of Fame, 1992. Fellow: NEA, 1976, John Simon Guggenheim, 1976; mem.: Am. Abstract Artists, Provincetown Art Assn. & Mus., Nat. Acad. Design. Democrat.*

HOPKINS, C.J. (CHRISTOPHER JAYNES), playwright; b. Aug. 24, 1961; s. Billie Diane (Latona) and Max Levand Haynes; m. Julia Lee Barclay (div.). BA, U. Miami, 1985. Author (dir.): (play) Horse Country; author: The Position, How To Entertain the Rich, The Installation, Red, How To Go; author: (director) A Place Like This; author: (stage-texts) Texts for Sound Painting, cunnilinguistics, Best of the Adelaide Fringe, 2004. Recipient First of the Fringe Firsts, The Scotsman, Edinburgh, 2002, Fringe First, 2002;, Mabou Mines Ste./Jerome Found., 1995, Developing Artist fellowship, The Drama League of NY, 1994, grant, The Harburg Found., 2000, The Puffin Found. Mem.: The Dramatists Guild of Am. Office: c/o Rosenstone/Wender Ronald Gwiazda New York NY

HOPKINS, DAVID MARK, secondary school educator; b. Neosho, Mo., Aug. 21, 1958; EdM, Lincoln U., Jefferson City, Mo., 2001; specialist in edn., U. Mo., Columbia, 2003. Cert. in Network+ CompTIA. Math instr. McDonald County H.S., Anderson, Mo., 1995—98; tech. instr. North Callaway H.S., Kingdom City, Mo., 1998—. Recipient Educator of Distinction award, Nat. Soc. H.S. Scholars, 2005. Mem.: Mo. Staff Devel. Coun., Nat. Coun. Teachers of Math., Internat. Tech. Edn. Assn. (Presenter at internat. conf. 2005, Greer grant 2005), Tech. Student Assn. (advisor 2003—05, White Star chpt. 2005). Home: 1115B W Broadway Columbia MO 65203 Office: N Callaway HS 2700 Hwy 54 Kingdom City MO 65262 Office Phone: 573-386-3318. Office Fax: 573-386-2403. E-mail: dhopkins@mail.northcallaway.k12.mo.us.

HOPKINS, DEBORAH C., diversified financial services company executive; b. Milw., Nov. 12, 1954; BS, Walsh Coll.; postgrad., U. Pa. With Ford Motor Co., Nat. Bank Detroit, Unisys Corp., v.p. corp. bus., 1991-93, v.p., corp. contr., chief acctg. officer, 1993-95, v.p., gen. mgr. worldwide info. svcs.; gen. auditor GM, 1995-97; v.p. fin., CFO GM Europe, Zürich, Switzerland; sr. v.p., CFO Boeing, Seattle, 1998—2000; CFO, exec. v.p. Lucent Tech., Murray Hill, NJ, 2000—01; sr. ptnr. Marakon Assocs.; chief ops. and tech. officer Citigroup, 2003—. Bd. dirs. E.I. DuPont De Nemours and Co. Bd. dirs. Seattle Symphony. Named one of 50 most powerful women in Am. bus. Fortune Mag., 1999, mgr. to watch in 2000 Bus. Week, 1999. Office: Citigroup 399 Park Ave New York NY 10043

HOPKINS, DONALD J., retired lawyer; b. Long Beach, Calif., Jan. 9, 1947; m. Ellen Colokathis, Aug. 29, 1970; children: Melanie J., Shannon R., Christopher S. AB, Stanford U., 1968; JD, Harvard U., 1971. Bar: Mass. 1971, Colo. 1974, U.S. Dist. Ct. Colo. 1974. Mem. firm Holme Roberts & Owen LLP, Denver, 1973—2004. Fellow: Am. Coll. Trust and Estate Counsel. Home: PO Box 190 9329 US Hwy 50 Howard CO 81233

HOPKINS, DONALD ROSWELL, public health physician; b. Miami, Fla., Sept. 25, 1941; s. Joseph Leonard and Iva (Major) Hopkins; m. Ernestine Mathis, June 24, 1967. BS, Morehouse Coll., 1962; MD, U. Chgo., 1966; MPH, Harvard U., 1970; DSc (hon.), Morehouse Coll., 1988, Emory U., 1994; LHD (hon.), U. Mass., Lowell, 1997; DSc (hon.), Morehouse Coll., 1999. Intern San Francisco Gen. Hosp., 1966—67; resident U. Chgo. Hosps., 1970—72; med. officer program planning and evaluation Ctrs. for Disease Control, Atlanta, 1972—74, dep. chief environ. health svc. divsn., 1974, asst. dir. ops., 1977—80, asst. dir. internat. health, 1980—84, dep. dir., 1984—87; assoc. exec. dir. The Carter Ctr., Inc., 1997—. Asst. prof. tropical pub. health Harvard U., Boston, 1974—77; chmn., advisor on internat. health rsch. Dr. Peter Bourne, White House, Washington, 1977; mem. U.S. del. World Health Assembly, Geneva, 1977—78, Geneva, 1980—86; global adv. group on immunization WHO, Geneva, 1978—79, steering com. epidemiology working group, 1980—83; cons. in field. Author: Princes and Peasants-Smallpox in History, 1983. Decorated knight Nat. Order of Mali, Order of Bifurcated Needle WHO; recipient Commd. Corps Disting. Svc. medal, USPHS, 1986, Joseph Mountin Lecture award, Ctrs. for Disease Control, 1981, John Snow award, APHA, 1997, Medal of Honor of Pub. Health, Govt. of Niger, 2004; fellow MacArthur fellow, 1995. Fellow: Am. Acad. Arts & Scis.; mem.: Inst. Medicine NAS, Am. Soc. Tropical Medicine and Hygiene, Phi Beta Kappa. Democrat. Episcopalian. Office: Carter Presdl Ctr Inc One Copenhill Bldg 453 Freedom Pkwy NE Atlanta GA 30307-1496

HOPKINS, GEORGE MATHEWS MARKS, retired lawyer, engineering executive; b. Houston, June 9, 1923; s. C. Allen and Agnes Cary (Marks) H.; m. Betty Miller McLean, Aug. 21, 1954; children: Laura Hopkins Corrigan, Edith Hopkins Collins. Student, Ga. Inst. Tech., 1943-44; BSChemE, Ala. Poly. Inst., 1944; LLB, JD, U. Ala., 1949; postgrad., George Washington U., 1949-50. Bar: Ala. 1949, Ga. 1954; registered patent lawyer, U.S.; registered profl. engr., Ga.; Can. qualified deep-sea diver. Instr. math. U. Ala., 1947-49; assoc. A. Yates Dowell, Washington, 1949-50, Edward T. Newton, Atlanta, 1950-62; ptnr. Newton, Hopkins and Ormsby (and predecessor), Atlanta, 1962-87; sr. ptnr. Hunt, Richardson, Garner, Todd & Cadenhead, Atlanta, 1987-91; ptnr. Hopkins & Thomas, 1991-95; ret., 1996; spl. asst. atty. gen., 1978; chmn. bd. Southeastern Carpet Mills, Inc., Chatsworth, Ga., 1962-77, Thomas-Daniel & Assocs., Inc., 1981-85, Ea. Carpet Mills, Inc., 1983-87; CEO, Airamar Chem. Engring., Inc., Doraville, Ga., 1997—. Asst. dir. rsch., legal counsel Auburn (Ala.) Rsch. Found., 1954-55; spl. asst. atty. gen. State of Ga., 1978; chmn. bd. S.E. Carpet Mills, Inc., Chatsworth, Ga., 1962-77, Thomas-Daniel & Assocs., Inc., 1981-85, Ea. Carpet Mills, Inc.; dir. Xepol Inc. Served as lt., navigator, Submarine Service USNR, 1944-46, 50-51. Mem. ABA, Ga. Bar Assn. (chmn. sect. patents 1970-71), Atlanta Bar Assn., Am. Intellectual Property Law Assn., Am. Soc. Profl. Engrs., Submarine Vets. World War II (pres. Ga. chpt. 1977-78), Phi Delta Phi, Sigma Alpha Epsilon, Atlanta Lawyers Club, Phoenix Soc., Cherokee Town and Country Club, AtlantaSoc. Episcopalian.

HOPKINS, GERALD FRANK, trade association administrator; b. La Grande, Oreg., Dec. 6, 1943; s. Albert Benjamin and Phyllis Nadine (Munn) H.; m. Mary Martha Abbott, June 9, 1967; children: Angela, Ann. BS, Ea. Mont. Coll., 1966, MS, 1967; advanced Master's degree, U. So. Calif., 1973; EdD, Calif. Coastal Coll., 2002. Grad. asst. Ea. Mont. Coll., Billings, 1966-67; tchr., adminstr. Elysian Schs., Billings, 1967-69; adminstrv. asst. Internat. Schs., Bangkok, 1969-73; prin. Nashua (Mont.) Pub. Schs., 1973-76, Roundup (Mont.) Pub. Schs., 1976-86; owner, operator Town Pump, Billings, 1986-90; exec. dir. La Grande/Union County C. of C., 1990-92; tchr., supt., adminstr. Huntington (Oreg.) Pub. Schs., 1992—. Project coord. Title I, 1996-97. Author: BJ & Boz, 1989, Humor in the Classroom, 1995; contbr. articles to profl. jours. Bd. dirs. Family Crisis Intervention, Roundup, 1983-86, Sr. Citizens Vol. Program, Roundup, 1983-86, State Reading Assn., Roundup, 1986-88, Continuing Edn. Coun., La Grande, 1990, Oreg. Trail Days., Continuing Counsel Higher Edn.; mem. Coop. Community Exch. Coun., 1983-86, hist. validation com Airport Svc. Coun., La Grande, 1991. Recipient State Disting. Title I award, Nat. Disting. Title I program, 1996-97, Oreg. Small Sch. Innovation Program, 1997, 99, Internat. Pres. Humanitarian award, 1998, Salute to Success award Oreg. Sch. Bd. Assn., 2000, 2004, Oreg. Small Sch. award of excellence, 2001, 02, Pioneer award, 2005; invitation to Oxford Edn. Round Table, 2001, 03 Mem. Small Bus. Adminstrn., Nat. C. of C., Elem. Adminstrs. Assn. (dir. ea. dist. 1988-90), Lions (internat. officer 1973-95, Outstanding Achievement award 1986, bd. dirs. La. Grande Club, Roundup of Lion Yr. 1977, 78, 79, 2d Internat. Pres.'s Humanitarian award 1978, Melvin Jones award 2002), Ambs. (assoc.) Home: 68070 Hunter Rd Summerville OR 97876-8133

HOPKINS, GROVER PREVATTE, lawyer; b. Jacksonville, Fla., Sept. 2, 1933; s. John Taylor and Capitola (Prevatte) H.; m. Ann Hutchinson, Oct. 16, 1965 (dec.); children: John, George, James, Corbin; m. Connie Jefferys, June 7, 1973. AB, Fla. State U., 1958; JD, U. N.C., 1971. Bar: N.C. 1971, Fla. 1972, D.C. 1981, U.S. Dist. Ct. (ea. dist.) N.C. 1971, U.S. Ct. Appeals (4th cir.) 1974, U.S. Supreme Ct. 1974; cert. mediator N.C. Cts., 1997. Announcer Sta. WTAL, Tallahassee, 1951-54; pub. rels. dir. Inter-Am. U., San German, P.R., 1958-60; pers. mgr. Northridge Knitting Mills, San German, 1960-62; cons. bus and pers. Mayaguez, P.R., Miami, Fla., 1963-69; mem. Weeks & Muse, Tarboro, N.C., 1971-73, Hopkins & Assocs., Tarboro, 1973—. Served with U.S. Army, 1954-57. Mem. Inter-Am. Bar Assn. (sec. gen. 1989-91). Republican. Office: Hopkins & Assocs 212 N Main St Tarboro NC 27886-5008 Office Phone: 252-823-1156. E-mail: lawyergph@cox.net.

HOPKINS, HENRY TYLER, museum director, art educator; b. Idaho Falls, Idaho, Aug. 14, 1928; s. Talcott Thompson and Zoe (Erbe) Hopkins; children: Victoria Anne, John Thomas, Christopher Tyler. BA, Sch. of Art Inst., Chgo., 1952, MA, 1955; postgrad., UCLA, 1957—60; PhD (hon.), Calif. Coll. Arts and Crafts, 1984, San Francisco Art Inst., 1986. Curator exhbns., publs. LA County Mus. of Art, 1960-68; lectr. art history UCLA Ext., 1960—68; dir. Ft. Worth Art Mus., 1968-74, San Francisco Mus. of Modern Art, 1974-86; chmn. art dept. UCLA, 1991-94, dir. F.S. Wight Gallery, 1991-95, dir. Armand Hammer Mus. Art and Cultural Ctr., 1994-99, prof. art, 1999—2002, prof. emeritus, 2002—. Instr. Tex. Christian U., Ft. Worth, 1968—74; dir. U.S. representation Venice Bienniel, Italy, 1970; dir. art presentation Festival of Two Worlds, Spoleto, Italy, 1970; co-commr. U.S. representation XVI Sao Paulo Biennale, Brazil, 1981; cons. NEA, mem. mus. panel, 1979—84, chmn., 1981; cons., mem. mus. panel NEH, 1976. Contbr. numerous articles to profl. jours. and mus. publs. With AUS, 1952—54. Decorated knight Order Leopold II, Belgium; recipient Spl. Internat. award, Art LA, 1992. Mem.: We. Assn. Art Museums (pres. 1977—78), Am. Assn. Museums, Coll. Art Assn., Assn. Art Mus. Dirs. (pres. 1985—86). Home: 939 1/2 Hilgard Ave Los Angeles CA 90024-3032 Office: UCLA Art Dept 405 Hilgard Ave Los Angeles CA 90095-9000 Office Phone: 310-206-7102. Business E-Mail: hhopkins@ucla.edu.

HOPKINS, HOMER THAWLEY, chemist, researcher, retired chemist; b. Frederica, Del., July 27, 1913; s. Homer Thawley and Lillian Alexander Hopkins, Sr.; m. Victoria Lafferty, Oct. 26, 1940; 1 child, Rebecca. BS, U. Del., 1935; MS, Cornell U., 1939; PhD, U. Md., 1951. Asst. state chemist Bd. Agr., Dover, Del., 1935—37; soil scientist USDA, Washington, 1939—41, Beltsville, Md., 1941—52; chemist FDA, Washington, 1952—76; food scientist NAS, Washington, 1976—77; ret., 1977. Cons. in field; organizer, oper. office fgn. affairs Inst. Applied Agr., U. Md., 1977—82. Contbr. articles to profl. jours. Lt. USN, 1939—42. Republican. Methodist. Avocations: fishing, gardening, reading. Home: Walnut Tree Village 69 Elizabeth Cir Sandy Hook CT 06482

HOPKINS, JAN, journalist, newscaster; b. Warren, Ohio, May 22, 1947; d. Walter Charles and Lois Avelene (Botroff) Reed; m. Walter Hopkins, June 14, 1969 (div. Nov. 1981); m. Richard Trachtman, Nov. 8, 1986. Dir. news Sta. WTCL, Warren, Ohio, 1973-75; reporter, anchor Sta. WERE, Cleve., 1975-77; reporter Sta. WKBN-TV, Youngstown, Ohio, 1977-80; reporter, anchor Sta. WLWT-TV, Cin., 1980-82; assignment editor CBS News, N.Y.C., 1983; reporter, prodr. ABC News, N.Y.C., 1983-84; anchor bus. news CNN, N.Y.C., 1984—. Author: (chapter) Knight Bagehot Guide to Business Journalism, 1990, 2d edit., 2000. Trustee Hiram Coll., 1988—94; adv. bd. Knight Bagehot program journalism Columbia U., N.Y.C., 1994; mem. nat. bd. Girl Scouts USA, 2001—. Recipient Peabody award U. Ga., 1988, Front Page award Newswomen Club N.Y., 1988, Lifetime Achievement award Women's Econ. Roundtable, 2002; Knight Bagehot fellow Columbia U. Sch. Journalism, 1982-83; named to Hall of Excellence Ohio Found. Ind. Colls., 1993, Warren, Ohio, H.S. Disting. Alumni Hall of Fame, 1995. Mem. Econ. Club N.Y. Office: CNN Bus News 5 Penn Plz Fl 20 New York NY 10001-1810 E-mail: jan.hopkins@turner.com.

HOPKINS, JEANNETTE ETHEL, book publisher, editor; b. Camden, N.J., Dec. 7, 1922; d. Carleton Roper and Gladys Eugenia (Hull) H. BA, Vassar Coll., 1944; MS, Columbia Sch. Journalism, 1945. Asst. to Sunday editor New Haven Register, 1945-46; reporter Providence Evening Bull., 1946-50, Oklahoma City Times, 1950-51; sr. editor Beacon Press, Boston, 1951-56, Harcourt Brace, N.Y.C., 1956-64, Harper & Row, N.Y.C., 1964-73; v.p. Met. Applied Res. Ctr., N.Y.C., 1970-72, cons. editor, 1973-80, 89—; dir. Wesleyan Univ. Press, Middletown, Conn., 1980-89. Adj. prof. English Wesleyan U., 1987-89, U. N.H., 1989; propr. Portsmouth Athenaeum, 1991—. Author: Books That Will Not Burn, 1952, 14 Journeys to Unitarianism, 1951, (with K.B. Clark) Relevant War Against Poverty, 1968, Legacy: A History of the South Church Endowment, 1995. Mem. coun. Inst. Religion in an Age of Sci., 1968-72, 80-82, 88-91, mem. adv. bd. 1962-72, 82-94; mem. bd. Unitarian UN Office, 1977-80; mem. Commn. on Appraisal, Unitarian Universalist Assn., 1976-78; bd. dirs. ACLU, 1970-79, mem. nat. adv. coun., 1986—; bd. govs. Comty. Ch. N.Y., 1960-66, Unitarian-Universalist Ch., Portsmouth, 1990-93, lay min., 1991-95; trustee South Ch. Endowment Fund, 1996-99; v.p. Unitarian Fellowship for Social Justice, 1958-62. Louise Hart Van Loon fellow, Vassar Coll., 1944; recipient Disting. Alumni award Columbia Sch. Journalism, 1981. Democrat. Unitarian. Home and Office: 39 Pray St Portsmouth NH 03801-5226

HOPKINS, JEFFREY P., federal judge; b. 1960; JD, Ohio State U., 1985. Bar: Ohio 1985, U.S. Dist. Ct. (so dist.) Ohio 1986, 1986 (Fed.). Law clk. to Hon. Alan E. Norris U.S. Ct. Appeals (6th cir.), 1985-87; assoc. Squire, Sanders & Dempsey, 1987-90; asst. U.S. atty. JPH (so. dist.) Ohio, 1990-96; bankruptcy judge U.S. Dist. Ct. (so. dist.) Ohio, Cin., 1996—. Bd. dir. Fed. Judicial Ctr., mem. edn. com.; adj. prof. Coll. Law U. Cin. Mem.: ABA (mem. bankruptcy law course), Nat. Conf. Bankruptcy Judges (pres. elect 2006—), Sigma Pi Phi. Office: US Bankr Ct So Dist Ohio 221 E 4th Ste 800 Cincinnati OH 45202-4124

HOPKINS, JOHN DAVID, lawyer; b. Memphis, Feb. 8, 1938; s. John and Helen (Sweeney) H.; m. Evelyn Harry, June 8, 1963 (div. Feb. 1985); children: John David III, Katharine Jane, Matthew Foster Joseph; m. Laurie Eileen House, June 3, 1987. BA, Vanderbilt U., 1959; LLB, U. Va., 1965. Bar: Ga. 1966, D.C. 1979. From assoc. to ptnr. King & Spalding, Atlanta, 1965-93; exec. v.p., gen. counsel Jefferson-Pilot Corp., Greensboro, NC, 1993—2003; of counsel Womble Carlyle Sandridge & Rice, PLLC, Atlanta, 2003—. Bd. dirs., mem. exec. com. Rock-Tenn Co., Atlanta, 1989—; mem. bd. visitors Guilford Coll., 1994-2000; bd. dirs. U. N.C. at Greensboro Excellence Found., 1995-2003. Bd. dirs. Atlanta Ballet, 1991-93, Greensboro United Arts Coun., 1994-97, Ea. Music Festival, 1998—2005; mem. alumni coun. U. Va. Law Sch. Alumni Assn., 2000-03; trustee Children's Sch., Inc., Atlanta, 1971-79, 88-89, Nat. Assn. Children's Hosps. and Related Instns., Alexandria, Va., 1973-79. Lt. USN, 1959-62. Mem. Ga. Bar Assn. (chmn. corp. code revision com., corp. and banking sect. 1970-79), D.C. Bar Assn., Cherokee Town and Country Club (Atlanta), Highlands Country Club N.C., Amelia Island Club, Order of Coif, Omicron Delta Kappa. Episcopalian. Office: One Atlantic Ctr 1201 W Peachtree St Ste 3500 Atlanta GA 30309 Office Phone: 404-879-2429. Personal E-mail: jdhopki@yahoo.com.

HOPKINS, JUDITH OWEN, oncologist; b. Norfolk, Va., Sept. 6, 1952; d. Austin and Edythe Owen; m. Marbry Benjamin Hopkins, III; 1 child, Benjamin Owen Hopkins. BS magna cum laude, Westhampton Coll., 1974; D of Medicine, U. Va., 1977. Diplomate Am. Bd. Internal Medicine, Am. Bd. Internal Medicine-Oncology. Resident in internal medicine Bowman Gray Sch. Medicine, N.C. Baptist Hosp., Winston-Salem, 1977-80, oncology fellowship, 1980-82; pvt. practice Winston-Salem, 1984—; clin. asst. prof. medicine Bowman Gray Sch. Medicine, Winston-Salem, 1984-92, asst. prof. medicine, 1982-84, clin. assoc. prof. medicine, 1992—. Contbg. author: Tumors of the Central Nervous System, 1982; contbr. articles to profl. jours. Bd. dirs. Hospice of Winston-Salem/Forsyth County, 1988—92, mem. profl. adv. com., 1982—92; preceptor for alt. curriculum Bowman Gray Sch. Medicine, 1988; mem. spkrs. bur. Am. Cancer Soc., 1982—92, chmn. profl. edn. com., 1982—85; trustee U. Richmond, 2000—04. Mem. ACP, Am. Soc. Internal Medicine, N.C. Soc. Internal Medicine, N.C. Med. Soc., Forsyth-Davie-Stokes County Med. Soc., Am. Soc. Clin. Oncology, Piedmont Oncology Assn., Southeastern Cancer Control Consortium (co-prin. investigator 1995—), N.C. Oncology Soc. (chmn. clin. practices com. 1991-92), Phi Beta Kappa, Alpha Omega Alpha. Episcopalian. Avocations: athletics, religion, coaching track. Home: 313 Susanna Dr Kernersville NC 27284-2161 Office: 1010 Bethesda Ct Winston Salem NC 27103 Office Phone: 336-277-8800. Business E-Mail: jhopkins@phoa.org.

HOPKINS, KAREN BROOKS, performing arts executive; b. 1951; d. Howard and Paula Brooks; divorced; 1 child, Matthew. BA in Theater Arts with honors, U. Md., 1973; MFA, George Washington U., 1980. Mem. group sales staff Am. Theater, Washington, 1973; cmty. rels. dir. Qwindo's Windo Dance Trouing Co., Washington, 1975; theater mgr., asst. dir. Chelm Players Touring Co., 1975-76, prodr., 1975-78; theater dir. Jewish Cmty. Ctr. of Greater Washington, 1976-78; devel. dir. The New Playwright's Theatre, Washington, 1978-79; devel. officer Bklyn. Acad. of Music, 1979-81, v.p. planning and devel., 1981-88, exec. v.p., 1988-98, COO and exec. v.p., 1998-99, pres., 1999—. Adj. prof. program for arts adminstrn. Bklyn. Coll., 1980-84. Author: Successful Fundraising for Arts and Cultural Organizations, 1989, 2d edit., 1997. Fundraising cons. art instns., 1979—; chair Performing Arts Ctrs. Consortium, 1994-96, Cultural Instns. Group, 2003; mem. adv. com. Salzburg Seminar-Alberto Vilar Project of Critical Issues for the Classical Performing Arts; ex-officio mem. N.Y.C. Cultural Affairs Adv. Commn., 2003. Recipient King Olav medal Norwegian Nat. Ballet, 1982, Dramaten medal, 1995. Office: Brooklyn Acad Music 30 Lafayette Ave Brooklyn NY 11217-1430

HOPKINS, KATHRYN CAROL, policy researcher; d. Raymond Frederick and Carol Robinson Hopkins. AB, Brown U., 1996; MA, Stanford U., 2002. Tchg. fellow Dunn Sch., Los Olivos, Calif., 1997—98; environmental tchr. Foothill Horizons, Sonora, 1998—99; field sci. tchr. Headlands Inst., Sausalito, 1999—2001; policy rsch. assoc. John Gardener Ctr., Stanford, 2001—05. Mem. adv. bd. Internat. Sci. Cmty., Swarthmore, Pa., 2000—05. Vol. Dem. Party; bd. mem. Just Think Found., San Francisco, 2004—05. Mem.: Am. Ednl. Rsch. Assn. Avocations: hiking, guitar, tennis, singing.

HOPKINS, KEVIN W., education educator; m. Lori M Hopkins. BA, Greenville Coll., 1983; M, PhD, U. of Ill., 1989. Prof., math. SW Bapt. U., Bolivar, Mo., 1989—. Mem.: Am. Math. Soc., Math. Assn. of Am. Office Phone: 417-328-1675. Business E-Mail: khopkins@sbuniv.edu.

HOPKINS, LAURIE BOYLE, academic administrator; b. Columbia, S.C., Apr. 12, 1951; p. E.C. McGregor and Nancy Ruff Boyle; m. Christie Benet Hopkins, May 25, 1979; children: Alice Benet Hopkins, Thomas Ruff Hopkins; 1 child from previous marriage, Earle Sligh McElveen. BS, U. S.C., 1976, PhD in Math., 1981. Adj. prof. U. S.C., Columbia, 1981-82; asst. prof. Columbia Coll., 1984-89, assoc. prof., 1989-92, prof. math., chmn. dept. math., 1992-98, dir. faculty devel., 1997-98, provost, 1998—. Contbr. articles to profl. jours. Recipient Twin Tribute to Women and Industry Diamond award YWCA, Columbia, 1995, Excellence and Innovation with the use of tech. in collegiate math. award Internat. Conf. on Tech., 1998. Mem. Am. Math. Soc., Math. Assn. Am., Nat. Coun. Tchrs. Math., S.C. Coun. Tchrs. Math. Office: Columbia Coll 1301 Columbia College Dr Columbia SC 29203-5949 E-mail: lhopkins@colacoll.edu.

HOPKINS, LEE BENNETT, writer, educator; b. Scranton, Pa., Apr. 13, 1938; s. Lee Hall and Gertrude (Thomas) H. BA, Kean Coll., 1960, LLD (hon.), 1980; MS, Bank St. Coll., 1964; profl. diploma, Hunter Coll., 1966. Elem. tchr. Fair Lawn (N.J.) Pub. Schs., 1960-66; lang. arts supr. Bank St. Coll., N.Y.C., 1966-68; curriculum specialist Scholastic, Inc., N.Y.C., 1968-75; author Scarborough, NY, 1975—. Cons., vis. prof. various U.S. and Can. colls. and univs.; bd. dirs. Soc. Sch. Librs. Internat.; lit. cons. Random House Achievement Program in Lit.; chmn. Nat. Coun. Tchrs. English poetry award com. Author: Been to Yesterdays: Poems of a Life, 1996 (The Christopher Book award and Golden Kite Honor Book award), numerous children's and junior books, poetry (awards include Nat. Coun. Tchrs. English, Tchrs. Choice award, Pa. Keystone to Reading award, Am. Inst. Graphic Arts award); contbr. articles, texts, and curriculum materials to mags., profl. jours. Recipient Lasting Contbn. to Field Children's Lit. awad U. So. Miss., 1989, Manhattan Coun. Literacy award Internat. Reading Assn., 1983, Ednl. Leadership award Phi Delta Kappa, 1980; named Keystone (Pa.) Author of Yr.; established Lee Bennett Hopkins Poetry award in conjunction with Children's Lit. Coun. Pa. State U., 1993—, Lee Bennett Hopkins Promising Poet award in conjunction with Internat. Reading Assn., 1995—. Avocations: reading, travel. Home and Office: 4923 Agualinda Blvd Cape Coral FL 33914 Personal E-mail: lbhcove@aol.com.

HOPKINS, LEWIS DEAN, architecture educator; b. Lakewood, Ohio, Feb. 20, 1946; s. W. Dean and Harriet (Painter) H.; m. Susan Brewster Cocker, Aug. 24, 1968; children: Joshua, Nathaniel. BA, U. Pa., 1968, postgrad., 1968-69, M of Regional Planning, 1970, PhD, 1975. Asst. prof. landscape arch. Inst. Environ. Studies/U. Ill., Urbana-Champaign, 1972-79, assoc. prof. landscape arch., urban and regional planning, 1979-84, prof., head dept. urban and regional planning, 1984-97, prof. landscape arch., 1984—. Vis. lectr. dept. town and regional planning U. Sheffield, Eng., 1980; coord. grad. program in landscape arch. U. Ill., 1976-79, chair search com. for head dept. landscape arch., 1985, chair com. to evaluate dir. Inst. Environ. Studies, 1990, com. pub. adminstrn. program, 1990, campus budget strategies com., 1991-94, chancellors strategic planning com., 1993-95, campus senate, 1976-79, 82-84, chair ednl. policy com. 1978-79, senate coun. 1978-79, 82-83, budget com. 1984-86; project dir. Ill. Streams Info. sys., 1981-90; fellow Com. Instnl. Coop. Acad. Leadership Program, 1989-90; external site visit team dept. landscape arch. and environ. planning, Ariz. State U., 1990; rsch. adv. com. Ill.-Ind. Sea Grant Program, 1991—; exec. com. Office of Solid Waste Rsch., 1992-95; Fulbright sr. scholar to Nepal, 1997-98. Co-editor: (with Gill-Chin Lim) Jour. Planning Edn. and Rsch., 1987-91; mem. editl. bd. Jour. Planning Lit., Computers, Environment and Urban sys., Urban and Regional Info. Sys. Assn. Jour., Jour. Planning Edn. and Rsch., others; reviewer: European Jour. Ops. Rsch., Geographical Analysis, Internat. Regional Sci. Rev., Landscape Jour., Mgmt. Sci., Transp. Rsch., others; contbr. articles to profl. jours. Fellow Am. Inst. Cert. Planners; mem. AAUP (pres. campus chpt. 1983-84), Am. Planning Assn. (chair nominating com. Ill. chpt. 1988), Assn. Collegiate Schs. of Planning (regional rep. to exec. bd. 1989-91), Inst. Mgmt. Scis., Regional Sci. Assn., Urban and Regional Inf. Sys. Assn. for Planning Accreditation Bd. (chair site visit teams 1988, 92, 94, team mem. 1995, com. on dual degree programs 1992-93), Planning Accreditation Bd. (chair 1997—). Achievements include research in human and computer problem solving processes for incompletely defined spatial problems; land and water resources management, information, and decision support systems; comprehensive planning processes and institutions. Office: U Ill Urbana-Champaign Dept Urban/Regional Plan 611 E Taft Dr Champaign IL 61820-6921

HOPKINS, LILA DYE, retired secondary school educator; b. Las Vegas, N.Mex, May 28, 1929; d. Harold E. and Ina Pearl Dye; m. Charles Richard Hopkins, Aug. 16, 1950; children: Rick, John, Dan, Annette Eaton. BA, Hardin-Simmons U., 1952. Tchr. Calif. Dept. Edn., Alamedia, 1953—54, N.C. Dept. Edn., Aberdeen, 1971—84; ret., 1984. Colunist: Bapt. New Mexican, 1938—40; author: Eating Crow, 1988 (N.C. Juvenile Lit. award, 1988), Talking Turkey, 1990 (N.C. Juvenile Lit. award, 1990), Weave Me a Song, 2002 (Book of the Yr. award), Strike a Golden Chord, 2004 (Book of the Yr. award, 2004). Home: 201 Wilbon Rd Apt 304B Fuquay Varina NC 27526

HOPKINS, MITCHELL SHADE, music educator; s. Mitchell Daniel and Christine Hopkins. BS in Pub. Sch. Music, Morris Brown Coll., 1958; MA, Columbia U., 1962. Cert. Tchg. and Supervising Music Ohio, 1964. Vocal music tchr. Fulton County Schools, Atlanta, 1958—63, Dayton Pub. Schs., Dayton, Ohio, 1964—92; adjudicator Nat. Guild of Piano Tchrs., Austin, Tex., 1987—. Adjudicator Nat. Guild of Piano Tchrs., Ohio, 1987—, Ga., 1987—, Ind., 1987—, Mich., 1987—, Ohio Jr. Fedn. of Music Clubs, Dayton and Springfield, Ohio, 1987—, Dayton Music Club Scholarships, Dayton, Ohio, 1998—2000. Host (radio program) Honoring a former college music professor, chairman (festival) Music Contest (Excellence in Orgn., 1989), member (guide for music instruction) Course of study. Designer Salem Bend Condominium Assn., Trotwood, Ohio, 1998—2001; best decorated home City of Trotwood, Trotwood, Ohio, 2000. Recipient Tchr. of Yr., Fairburn H.S., Fulton County, Ga., 1963, Excellence in Tchg. Award, Ohio Music Edn. Assn., 1983, Svc. Tchg. Award, Dayton Pub. Schools, Dayton, Ohio, 1993. Mem.: Music Educators Nat. Conf., Am. Coll. Musicians (assoc.; faculty mem. 1987—2002), Nat. Guild of Piano Tchrs. (assoc.), Am. Fedn. Musicians (assoc.), Dayton Music Club (assoc.; bd. dirs.), Alpha Phi Alpha (life). Achievements include first to Introduced hand bells to Dayton Public Schools & organized first bell choir in school system, conducted inservice workshops for teachers to learn bell choir techniques. All schools have bell choirs; development of My choral groups and piano students have maintained superior ratings in music contests; first to Organized an annual art/music festival in the Dayton Public Schools at Residence Park Elementary School. Avocations: gardening, interior decorating, fishing, cooking, physical fitness. Office: Am College of Musicians Po Box 1807 Austin TX 78767 Home: 6657 Stranwood Dr Englewood OH 45322-3772

HOPKINS, NANCY H., biology professor; BA, Radcliffe Coll., 1964; PhD, Harvard U., 1971. Asst. prof. MIT, Cambridge, 1973—76, assoc. prof., 1976—82, prof., 1982—, chmn. comm. on women faculty, Sch. Sci., co-chmn. council on faculty diversity, Amgen Inc. prof. molecular and devel. biology. Recipient Laya Wiesner Community Award, 2001, Women's History Month Honoree of NY Academy of Sciences; fellow Amer. Academy of Arts and Sciences. Fellow: Am. Acad. Arts and Scis.; mem.: NAS, Inst. Med. Office: MIT E17-341 77 Massachusetts Ave Cambridge MA 02139-4301 Business E-Mail: nhopkins@mit.edu.

HOPKINS, ROBERT CHARLES, chemistry and biophysics educator; b. Pasadena, Calif., July 23, 1937; s. Fredrick Charles and Maybelle Hopkins; m. Star Martin, Jan. 2, 1965; children: Karen M., Rand C. BS in Chem. Engring., UCLA, 1959; MA in Phys. Chemistry, Harvard U., 1963, PhD in Phys. Chemistry, 1965. Registered profl. engr., Tex. Phys. chemist Shell Devel. Co., Everyville, Calif., 1965-69, staff physicist Houston, 1971-76; special exch. scientist Royal Dutch Shell Co., Amsterdam, The Netherlands, 1969-71; assoc. prof. chemistry U. Houston, 1976-81, prof. chemistry and biophysics, 1981—2002, prof. emeritus, 2002, interim dean Sch. Natural and Applied Scis., 1978-79, 94-95. Vis. prof. chemistry UCLA, 1982, U. Mich., Ann Arbor, 1986. Contbr. articles to profl. jours.; patentee in field. Recipient Bechtel Engring. scholarship UCLA, 1955, Chancellor's Outstanding Rsch. award U. Houston, 1985; NIH predoctoral fellow Harvard U., 1961-65. Mem. Am. Phys. Soc., Biophys. Soc., Internat. Wine and Food Soc. (officer, mem. bd. dirs.), Sigma Xi. Achievements include development of alternative models for DNA structure. Office Phone: 281-283-3770.

HOPKINS, SAMUEL, retired investment banker; b. Highland, Md., Oct. 18, 1913; s. Samuel Harold and Roberta (Smith) H.; m. Winifred Holt Bloodgood, Oct. 15, 1938 (dec. Oct. 1954); children: Samuel, Henry; m. Anne E. Dankmeyer, Oct. 20, 1955; children: Robert, Frederick. BS, Johns Hopkins U., 1934; LL.B., U. Md., 1938. With Fidelity & Deposit Co. of Md., 1934-69, asst. to treas., 1934-50, asst. treas., 1950-54, sec., 1954-67, v.p., sec., dir., 1967-69; dir., mem. trust com. Equitable Trust Co., Balt., 1954-81; sec., dir. Md. Life Ins. Co., 1963-69; gen. partner Alex. Brown & Sons (investment bankers), Balt., 1970-75, ltd. partner, 1976-87. Bd. dirs. Am. Maritime Cases, Inc. Mem. adv. com. housing for elderly U.S. Housing and Fin. Agy., 1956-60; mem. Balt. Bd. Recreation and Parks, 1965-77, pres., 1965-67, 74-77, v.p., 1968-74; Rep. candidate for Congress, 1952; mem. Md. Ho. of Dels., 1950-54; Rep. candidate for mayor, Balt., 1955; del. Rep. Nat. Conv., 1976; trustee Balt. Mus. Art, Peale Mus., Sheppard and Enoch Pratt Hosp., 1972-89; trustee, v.p. State Colls. Md., 1963-70; mem. Balt. City Planning Commn., 1985-95. Lt. USNR, 1942-45. Mem.: ABA, Chartered Security Analysts, Balt. Security Analysts Soc., Md. Hist. Soc. (treas. 1956—69, pres. 1970—75, chmn. bd. trustees 1988—90). Episcopalian. Home: 45 Warrenton Rd Baltimore MD 21210-2924 Personal E-mail: annehopk@mindspring.com.

HOPKINS, STEPHEN, film director, producer; b. Jamaica, 1958; Motion picture dir., prodr. Exec. prodr. film Crossworlds, 1996; prodr., dir. Lost in Space, 1998, Under Suspicion, 2000, (T.V. mini series) Traffic, 2004; dir. films Nightmare on Elm St. 5: The Dream Child, 1989, Predator 2, 1990, Dangerous Game, 1991, Judgment Night, 1993, Blown Away, 1994, The Ghost and the Darkness, 1996, The Life and Death of Peter Sellers, 2004; dir. (T.V. series) Tales from the Crypt, 1989, (also segment writer) Tube Tales, 1999; dir., co-exec. prodr. (TV series) 24, 2001 (nominee Outstanding Directorial Achievement in Dramatic Series Dir.'s Guild Am.). Office: care David Wirtschafter William Morris Agy 151 El Camino Dr Beverly Hills CA 90212

HOPKINS, THOMAS CHARLES, behavior specialist; b. Camden, N.J., Sept. 03; s. Paul Wallace and Rose Helen H.; m. Patricia Ann, June 24, 1972; children: Anthony, Claudia, Joshua, Jason, Thomas. BS, Kans. State U., 1970; MEd, Nat. Louis U., 1994. Tchr. spl. edn. Gloucester Twp. Pub. Sch., Erial, N.J., 1971-74, Bass River Twp. Pub. Schs., New Gretna, NJ, 1974-78, Tuckerton (N.J.) Pub. Sch., 1978-83, Pasco County Pub. Sch., Dade City, Fla., 1983-92; behavior specialist Passo County Pub. Sch., Hudson, Fla., 1992—. Asst. coach Spring Hill (Fla.) Dixie Baseball, 1995, 97. Mem. Coun. Exceptional Children (membership chair 2000—). Democrat. Roman Catholic. Avocation: gardening. Home: 1136 Berger Ave Spring Hill FL 34608

HOPKINS, THOMAS DUVALL, economics professor; b. Spring Valley, Ill., Mar. 10, 1942; s. Joel Willis and Mildred (Duvall) H.; m. Jane Cole Eveleth, Apr. 20, 1968; children: Edward Eveleth, Catherine Chapin Hopkins. BA, Oberlin (Ohio) Coll., 1964; MA, Yale U., 1965, M of Philosophy, 1967, PhD, 1971. Asst. prof. econs. Bowdoin Coll., Brunswick, Maine, 1968-73; cons. Irwin Mgmt. Co., Inc., Columbus, Ind., 1973-75; asst. dir. Coun. on Wage and Price Stability, Washington, 1975-81, acting dir., 1981; dep. adminstr. Office of Mgmt. and Budget, Washington, 1981-84; assoc. prof. U. Md., College Park, 1984-87; assoc. prof. econs. Am. U., Washington, 1987-88; prof. econs., Arthur J. Gosnell prof. Rochester (N.Y.) Inst. Tech., 1988-99, dean coll. of bus., 1999—. Cons. Adminstrv. Conf. U.S., Washington, 1986-88, Office Tech. Assessment, U.S. Congress, 1987-89, Inst. Liberty and Democracy, Lima, Peru, 1986-91, U.S. Regulatory Info. Svc. Ctr., 1990-92, Congl. Budget Office, 1991, U.S. SBA, 1993-95, 2000-02, OECD, Paris, 1994-96; seminar leader Inst. Internat. Edn., Washington, 1987-88; mem. com. on tank vessel design marine bd. NRC, Washington, 1989-91; mem. com. on taxation, fin. and pricing, 1990-93, com. on pub. policy for surface freight transp., 1993-96, com.on fed. role in marine transp. sys., 2003, Transp. Rsch. Bd., NRC; lectr. U.S. Bus. Sch. in Prague, Czech Republic, 1992-98; pub. mem. U.S. Adminstrv. Conf., Washington, 1994-95; adj. fellow Washington U. Ctr. for Study of Am. Bus., St. Louis, 1996-2000; pres. U.S. Bus. Sch. in Prague, Czech Republic, 1999—; mem. regulatory studies program adv. bd. George Mason Univ. Mercatus Ctr., 1999—. Co-author: Tanker Spills: Prevention by Design, 1991. Mem. coun. Eastman House, Rochester, 1991—. Woodrow Wilson Found. fellow, 1964. Fellow NSF; mem. Am. Econs. Assn., Nat. Economists Club. Office: Rochester Inst Tech 107 Lomb Memorial Dr Rochester NY 14623-5608 Office Phone: 585-475-7042. Business E-Mail: thopkins@cob.rit.edu.

HOPKINS, WILLIAM CARLISLE, II, lawyer; b. Mason City, Iowa, Apr. 11, 1945; s. William C. and Dorothy (Purcey) H.; m. Sandra Janssen, Apr. 22, 1978; children: William C. III, Ryan Lee, Leigh Alexandra. BA, S.W. Mo. State U., 1967; JD, U. Mo., Columbia, 1970. Bar: Mo. 1970, U.S. Dist. Ct. (we. and ea. dists.) 1970, U.S. Ct. Appeals (8th cir.) 1970, U.S. Supreme Ct. 1973, Calif. 1983. Assoc. Lathrop Koontz et al., Kansas City, Mo., 1970-75; freelance TV writer Universal, Fox, MTM, L.A., 1975-82; assoc. atty. Mix & Assocs., Redondo Beach, Calif., 1982-83; ptnr. Hubbell Sawyer Peak & O'Neal, Kansas City, 1983-94, Stites McIntosh & Hopkins, Kansas City, 1993-94, Stites Hopkins Fair & Riederer, Kansas City, 1994-99, Stites Hopkins & Miller, Kansas City, 1999—. V.p. Spl. Event Entertainment, L.A., 1975-77. Writer various TV shows including Paper Chase, Lou Grant, Quincy; feature writer The K.C. Counsellor, 1993—. Vol. Head Injury Assn. Greater Kansas City, 1993-94. Mem. ATLA, Mo. Assn. Trial Attys. (com. chair 1983—, chair pub. awareness com. 1994-95, mem. bd. 1994—), Mo. Bar Assn. (Tort Com. coun. 1993), Kansas City Met. Bar Assn., Brain Injury Assn. of Mo. (contributing writer to newsletter The Focus 1993—). Avocations: golf, coaching little league. Office: Stites Hopkins & Miller 1101 Walnut St Ste 1400 Kansas City MO 64106-2182

HOPKINS, WILLIAM HAYES, lawyer, writer; b. Moscow, Idaho, Aug. 5, 1943; s. Bert Earl and Marie Hayes H.; m. Rachel Pomeroy, Aug. 28, 1965; children: Alaa Christina, Elizabeth Anne, Amelia Jeanne, William, Rachel G. BA, Yale U., 1965; JD, Vanderbilt U., 1968. Bar: Conn. 1968, N.H. 1969, U.S. Dist. Ct. N.H. 1969, U.S. Ct. Appeals (1st cir.) 1983. Assoc. atty. Wakefield & Ray, Plymouth, N.H., 1969-75; ptnr. Ray & Hopkins, Plymouth, 1975-88; sr. ptnr. Hopkins & Blaine, Plymouth, 1989-94; pvt. practice Plymouth, 1995—. Vice chmn. N.H. Adult Parole Bd., Concord, 1988-98; chmn. N.H. Wine Law Revision Commn., Concord, 1979-81. Mem. N.H. Bridge Assn. (pres. 1996-98), Plymouth Wine Patrol (guru 1984-93), James Hogan Bridge Club (pres. 1986-98), Yale Club N.H. (pres. 1997-99). Avocations: oenology, skiing, hiking. Home: PO Box 126 Plymouth NH 03264-0126 Office Phone: 603-783-9621. Personal E-mail: hpknslaw@comcast.net.

HOPKINSON, SHIRLEY LOIS, b. Boone, Iowa, Aug. 25, 1924; d. Arthur Perry and Zora (Smith) Hopkinson. Student, Coe Coll., 1942—43; AB cum laude, U. Colo., 1945; BLS, U. Calif., 1949; MA, Claremont Grad. Sch., 1951; EdM, U. Okla., 1952, EdD, 1957. Tchr. pub. sch., Stigler, Okla., 1946—47; tchr. Palo Verde HS., Jr. Coll., Blythe, Calif., 1947—48; asst. libr. Modesto Jr. Coll., Calif., 1949—51; tchr., libr. Fresno, Calif., 1951—52, La Mesa, Calif., 1953—55; asst. prof. librarianship, instrnl. materials dir. Chaffey Coll., Ontario, Calif., 1955—59; asst. prof. librarianship San Jose State Coll., Calif., 1959—64, assoc. prof., 1964—69, prof., 1969—. Bd. dirs. NDEA Inst. Sch. Librs., summer, 1966; mem. Santa Clara County Civil Svc. Bd. Examiners. Author: Descriptive Cataloging of Library Materials, Instructional Materials for Teaching the Use of the Library; editor: Calif. Sch. Libraries, 1963—64; asst. editor Sch. Libr. Assn. of Calif. Bull., 1961—63, book reviewer profl. jours.; contbr. articles to profl. jours. Honnold Honor scholar, Claremont Grad. Sch., 1945—46. Mem.: LWV (bd. dirs. 1950—51, publs. chmn.), AAUW (dir. 1957—58), NEA, ALA, AAUP, Kappa Delta Pi, Alpha Beta Alpha, Calif. Tchrs. Assn., San Diego County Sch. Librs. Assn. (sec. 1945—55), Sch. Librs. Assn. Calif. (com. mem., treas. No. sect. 1951—52), Audio-Visual Assn. Calif., Calif. Library Assn., Bus. Profl. Women's Club, Alpha Lambda Delta, Phi Beta Kappa (scholar 1944), Delta Kappa Gamma (sec. 1994—96, legis. liaison 1996—2002, corr. sec. 2002—), Phi Kappa Phi (disting. acad. achievement award 1981). Office: 1340 Pomeroy Ave Apt 408 Santa Clara CA 95051-3658

HOPMANN, PHILIP TERRENCE, political science educator; b. St. Louis, June 25, 1942; s. Irvin Herman and Loretta (Gerlach) H.; m. Marita Raubitschek, Aug. 24, 1968; children: Alexander Irvin, Nicholas Erich. AB, Princeton U., 1964; MA, Stanford U., 1965, PhD, 1969. Rsch. asst. Stanford (Calif.) U., 1965-67, instr., 1967-68; prof. polit. sci. U. Minn., Mpls., 1968-85, Brown U., Providence, 1985—, dir. program on global security Watson Inst. Internat. Studies, 1993—, dir. Internat. Rels. program, 1985-94. Cons. U.S. Inst. of Peace, 1998—; chmn. faculty exec. com. Brown U., Providence, 1994-95. Author: Unity and Disintergration in International Alliances, 1973, 84, The Negotiation Process and the Resolution of International Conflicts, 1996. Fulbright-Hays fellow Coun. Internat. Ednl. Exch., Belgium, 1975-76, 82-83, Jennings Randolph sr. fellow U.S. Inst. Peace, 1997-98, Fulbright fellow Orgn. Security and Cooperation in Europe, Austria,

1998. Mem. Internat. Studies Assn. (editor 1980-85, v.p. 1991-92), Internat. Polit. Sci. Assn., Arms Control Assn., Am. Polit. Sci. Assn. Democrat. Home: 23 Valerian Ct Rockville MD 20852 Office: Brown U Watson Inst/Internat Studies PO Box 1970 Providence RI 02912-1970

HOPP, ANTHONY JAMES, advertising agency executive; b. Detroit, Jan. 31, 1945; s. William J. and Beverly (Gildea) H.; m. Nancy Jane Dunckel, Nov. 11, 1969; children: Beth, Michael. BA in Advt./Mktg., Mich. State U., 1967, MA in Advt./Psychology, 1968. Asst. account exec. Campbell-Ewald Adv., Warren, Mich., 1968-70; account exec. Lintas Campbell-Ewald, Warren, Mich., 1970-74, account supr., 1974-75, v.p., account supr., 1975-79, sr. v.p., mgmt. supr., 1979-85, group sr. v.p., group mgmt. supr., 1985-88, exec. v.p., account dir., 1988-93, pres., 1993-95, vice chmn., 1995—97, also bd. dirs.; chmn. & CEO Lintas Campbell-Ewald (now Campbell-Ewald), Warren, Mich., 1997—. Bd. dirs. C-E Comm., Warren, Lintas Ams. Recipient Robert E. Healy award Interpublic Group of Cos., 1989. Mem. Adcraft, Hunters Creek, Bloomfield Hills Country Club, Pine Lake Country Club. Avocations: golf, hunting, boating. Office: Lintas-Campbell-Ewald 30400 Van Dyke Ave Warren MI 48093-2368*

HOPP, DANIEL FREDERICK, manufacturing company executive, lawyer; b. Ann Arbor, Mich., Apr. 14, 1947; s. Clayton A. and Monica E. (Williams) H.; m. Maria G. Lopez, Dec. 20, 1968; children: Emily, Daniel, Melissa. BA in English, U. Mich., 1969; JD, Wayne State U., 1973. Bar: Ill. 1974, Mich. 1980. Atty. Mayer, Brown and Platt, Chgo., 1973-79, Whirlpool Corp., Benton Harbor, Mich., 1979-84, asst. sec., 1984-85, sec., asst. gen. counsel, 1985-89, v.p., gen. counsel, sec., 1989-98, sr. v.p., corp. affairs, gen. counsel, 1998—. Bd. dirs. Horizon Bank, Mich. City, Ind. Mem. City of St. Joseph Planning Commn., Mich.; bd. dirs. Horizon Bank, Mich. City, Ind., Lakeland Regional Health Sys., St. Joseph; coun. World Class Cmtys., Benton Harbor, Mich. Served U.S. Army, 1969—71. Mem. Am. Soc. Corp. Secs., Mich. Bar Assn., Ill. Bar Assn., Berrien County Bar Assn. Republican. Mem. Ch. of Christ. Avocation: golf. Office: Whirlpool Corp Adminstrv Ctr 2000 N M 63 Benton Harbor MI 49022-2692

HOPP, GLENN, literature educator; b. St. Louis, July 27, 1954; s. Bill and Marvine Hopp. BA, U. Mo., 1976; MA, So. Ill. U., 1978; PhD, U. Mo., 1986. Prof. English Ctrl. Meth. Coll., Fayette, Mo., 1985—87, Howard Payne U., Brownwood, Tex., 1987—. Author: VideoHound's Epics: Giants of the Silver Screen, 1999, The Pocket Essential Billy Wilder, 2001, Billy Wilder: The Cinema of Wit, 2003. Office: Dept English Howard Payne Univ Brownwood TX 76801 Personal E-mail: glennhopp@msn.com.

HOPP, PHILLIP EDWARD, gifted and talented educator; s. Edward Hopp and Susan Hoffman. BS in History, Portland State U., 2000. Educator Perris (Calif.) Union H.S. Dist., 1999—2001, Val Verde Unified Sch. Dist., Perris, 2002—. Author: Healing and the Laying on of Hands, 2000, I am with You: A Dramatic and Thrilling Account of One Man's Vision of Jesus Christ, 2001; contbr. articles to profl. jours. and mags. Mem.: Mega Found. for Gifted, The Ultranet of the Global Ultra High IQ Cmty. (iq 150+ of the ultranet 2001—03), The Internat. High IQ Soc. (hon.; platinum club 2001—03), Phi Alpha Theta. Avocations: bodybuilding, aerobics, philosophy, theology, bibliophile. Personal E-mail: res06uko@verizon.net.

HOPP, RUSSELL JAMES, pediatrician; s. Ralph Lee and Joann May Hopp; m. Cynthia Lynn Kallweit, Oct. 24, 1998; children: Jennifer Mariae Henningsen, Sara Morin. BS, Creighton U., 1972; DO, Des Moines U., 1975. Diplomate Am. Bd. Asthma, Allergy, and Clin. Immunology, 1985, Am. Bd. Pediat., 1979. Intern Drs. Hosp., Columbus, Ohio, 1975—76; resident U. Mo. Med. Ctr., 1976—78, U. Nebr. Med. Ctr., 1978—80; prof. pediat. and medicine Creighton U., Omaha, 1984—. Contbr. articles;, author chpts. Achievements include research in epidemiolgy of asthma and allergic diseases. Office: Creighton Univ Pediat 601 N 30th St Suite 6820 Omaha NE 68131 Office Phone: 402-280-4580. Business E-Mail: rhopp@creighton.edu.

HOPPE, SHERRY LEE, academic administrator; b. Chickamauga, Ga. BS magna cum laude, U. Tenn., Chattanooga, 1969, MS, 1974; EdD, U. Tenn., Knoxville, 1981. Clk. new accounts Pioneer Bank, Chattanooga, 1965-66; asst. to dir. fin. aid, sec. U. Tenn., Chattanooga, 1966-69; counselor, tchr. Chattanooga Valley High Sch., 1969-77; from coord. vets. affairs to dean Chattanooga State Tech. Community Coll., 1977-87; interim pres. Nashville State Tech. Inst., 1987-88; pres. Roane State Community Coll., Harriman, Tenn., 1988; interim pres. Austin Peay State U., Tenn., 2000—01, pres., 2001—. Contbr. articles to jours. in field. Bd. dirs. Meth. Med. Ctr., Community Devel. Coun., Roane County, Oak Ridge Community Found., Chattanooga Area Am. Heart Assn., Multiple Sclerosis Soc., Sentenga chptr., Jr. Achievement, Chattanooga Venture, Met. Coun., Cherokee Area Coun. Boy Scouts Am., Am. Lung Assn. Southeastern Region, Sovran Bank, Henry Devel. Ctr.; account exec., sect. leader United Way, 1882-84, strategic action com., 1987; Mem. Pub. Rels. Task Force Vision 2000, 1984-85, planning adv. com. Chattanooga-Hamilton County Regional Planning Commn., 1985; chmn. Homecoming '86 Enterprise Com. Greater Chattanooga Area, Made in Chattanooga Exhbn., 1986; participator Leadership Chattanooga, Leadership Roane County. Mem. NEA, Tenn. Edn. Assn., C. of C. (pub. rels. task force 1983), Nat. Coun. Instructional Adminstrs., Am. Assn. Women in Community and Jr. Colls. (participated in Leaders of the '80s 1981), Chattanooga Indsl. Pers. Club, Chattanooga Area Pers. Assn., Rotary. Office: Austin Peay State U Office of Pres BR 125 PO Box 4576 Clarksville TN 37044 Office Phone: 931-221-7567. E-mail: hoppes@apsu.edu.*

HOPPENSTEADT, FRANK CHARLES, mathematician, educator, dean; b. Oak Park, Ill., Apr. 29, 1938; s. Frank Carl and Margaret Hoppensteadt; children: Charles, Matthew, Sarah. BA, Butler U., 1960; MS, U. Wis., 1962, PhD, 1965. Instr. math. U. Wis., Madison, 1965; asst. prof. math. Mich. State U., East Lansing, 1965-68, dean Coll. Natural Sci., 1986-95; dir. sys. sci. engr. rsch., prof. math. and elec. engring. Ariz. State U., Tempe, 1995—2004; assoc. prof. NYU-Courant, N.Y.C., 1968-76, prof., 1976-79, U. Utah, Salt Lake City, 1977-86, chmn. dept. math., 1982-85, sr. vice provost, rsch. prof., 2004—. Author: Mathematical Methods in Population Biology, 1982, An Introduction to Mathematics of Neurons, 1986, 2d edit., 1997, Mathematics in Medicine and the Life Sciences, 1991, Analysis and Simulation of Chaotic Systems, 1993, Weakly Connected Neural Networks, 1997. Mem. Am. Math. Soc. (chmn. applied math. com. 1976-80), Soc. Indsl. and Applied Maths., Sigma Xi. Home: 110 Bleecker St Apt 4B New York NY 10012-2103 E-mail: frank.hoppensteadt@nyu.edu.

HOPPER, ANITA KLEIN, molecular genetics educator; b. Chgo., Sept. 24, 1945; d. Irving and Rose (Warshawsky) Klein; m. James Ernest Hopper, Jan. 3, 1971; 1 child, Julie Victoria. BS, U. Ill., Chgo., 1967; PhD, U. Ill., 1972. Postdoctoral researcher genetics U. Wash., Seattle, 1971-75; asst. prof. microbiology U. Mass. Med. Sch., Worcester, 1975-78, assoc. prof. microbiology, 1978-79; assoc. prof. biochemistry Hershey Med. Sch., Pa. State U., Hershey, 1979-87, prof. biochemistry, molecular biology, 1987—. Genetic biol panel NSF, Washington, 1981—85; mem genetic study sect NIH, Bethesda, Md., 1985—89, mem CDFI study sect, 1997—2000, chair CDFI study sect, 2001—; chair symposia and meetings Pa. State U.; pres. RNA Soc., 2003—04. Editor: Molecular & Cellular Biology, 1989—2000; mem ed bd:, 1986—90, RNA, 1995—97. Fellow Postdoctoral, NIH, 1971—73; grantee NIH, 1979—, Univ Louisville Med Sch, 1989, NSF, 1988—91. Fellow: Am. Acad. Microbiology; mem.: AAAS, Genetics Soc. Am. (sec. 2004—), Am. Assn. Microbiology (chair Eli Lilly award com. 2000—), Am. Assn. Biochemists, Am. Soc. Microbiology (chair genetics and molecular biology divsn. 1988). Office: Pa State U Med Sch Dept Biochemistry & Molec Biol Hershey PA 17033

HOPPER, CAROL, travel company executive; b. Montreal, Que., Can., Apr. 23, 1952; m. Cedric Heimrath; stepchildren: Natasha, Erik. Student, McGill U., 1972; cert., Canadian Inst. Orgnl. Mgmt., 1991. Asst. Ben Fuller Assocs., 1973-89; show dir. Nat. Ski Industries Assn., Montreal, 1989-91, exec. dir., 1991-96, dir. show svcs., 1997-98; project mgr. Chateau Travel, Carlson Mktg. Group, 1998—2002; project leader Vision 2000 Travel Group, 2002—. Mem. adv. com. sporting goods bus. program Sir Sandford Fleming Coll., 1994-98. Mem. Jr. League Montreal (bd. dirs., chmn. coms. 1987-92). Avocations: skiing, golf, reading, travel, sports. Home: 302 Perrault Rosemere PQ Canada J7A 1B9

HOPPER, CELIA ANNE, secondary school educator, writer; b. McKenzie, Tenn., Mar. 9, 1959; d. Ed Lainey and Lucille Johnson Brashear; m. John Lee Hopper. BA, Memphis State U., 1984; MAT, Bethel Coll., 1993. Cert. tchr. secondary English, comms. Tchr. English, comms., broadcast creative writing New Haven (Mich.) H.S. Author: (children's books) Blade, Blade, and the Pearl Princess, 2005, Blade and the Curious Cricket, 2005, (novels) Violets, 2004. Coord. ann. spring festival New Haven H.S., 2001—05, participant DARE show, 2001—05. Named Macomb County Tchr. of Yr., New Haven H.S., 2005; grantee, Bay Haven Coalition, 2002—05. Mem.: Mich. Edn. Assn. Avocations: writing, boating.

HOPPER, DAVID HENRY, theologian, educator; b. Cranford, N.J., July 31, 1927; s. Orion Cornelius and Julia Margaret (Weitzel) H.; m. Nancy Ann Nelson, June 10, 1967 (div. June 1984); children: Sara Elizabeth, Kathryn Ann, Rachel Suzanne. BA, Yale U., 1950; BD, ThM, Princeton Theol. Sem., 1953, ThD, 1959. Ordained Presbyn. minister, 1961. Asst. prof. Macalester Coll., St. Paul, 1959-67, assoc. prof., 1967-73, James Wallace prof. of religion, 1973—2001, prof. emeritus, 2001—. Author: Tillich: A Theological Portrait, 1967 (N.J. Authors award 1968), A Dissent on Bonhoeffer, 1975, Technology, Theology, and the Idea of Progress, 1991. With USN, 1945-46. Recipient Newberry ACM Faculty fellow, 1992-93, Templeton Found. Sci./Religion Course award, 1996. Mem. Internat. Bonhoeffer Soc., Hist. of Sci. Soc., Kierkegaard Soc. Home: 1757 Lincoln Ave Saint Paul MN 55105-1954 E-mail: dhhopper@earthlink.net.

HOPPER, DENNIS, actor, writer, photographer, film director; b. Dodge City, Kans., May 17, 1936; s. Jay and Marjorie Hopper; m. Brooke Hayward, 1961 (div. 1969); 1 child, Marin; m. Michelle Phillips, Oct. 31, 1970 (div. Nov. 8, 1970); m. Doria Halprin, 1972 (div. 1976); 1 child: Ruthana; m. Katherine LaNasa, June 17, 1989 (div. April 1992); 1 child, Henry Lee.; m. Victoria Duffy, Apr. 13, 1996; 1 child. Ed., San Diego pub. schs. Participated in 2002 Whitney Biennial. Numerous TV appearances include Loretta Young Show, 1954; appeared in films: Rebel Without a Cause, 1955, Jagged Edge, 1955, I Died A Thousand Times, 1955, Giant, 1956, The Steel Jungle, 1956, Story of Mankind, 1957, Gunfight at the O.K. Corral, 1957, From Hell to Texas, 1958, The Youngland, 1959, Key Witness, 1960, Night Tide, 1963, The Sons of Katie Elder, 1965, Queen of Blood, 1966, The Trip, 1967, Glory Stompers, 1967, Hang 'Em High, 1968, Cool Hand Luke, 1967, True Grit, 1969, Easy Rider, 1969, The Last Movie, 1971, Kid Blue, 1973, Hex, 1973, The Sky is Falling, 1975, James Dean-The First American Teenager, Mad Dog Morgan, 1976, Tracks, 1976, American Friend, 1978, Apocalypse Now, 1979, Wild Times, 1980, Out of the Blue, 1980, King of the Mountain, 1981, Renacer, 1981, Human Highway, 1981, Rumble Fish, 1983, The Osterman Weekend, 1983, Slagskämpen, 1984, My Science Project, 1985, O.C. & Stiggs, 1985, White Star, 1985, The Texas Chainsaw Massacre Part 2, 1986, Blue Velvet, 1986 (Montreal World Film Festival award 1986), Hoosiers, 1986 (Acad. award nomination 1987), River's Edge, 1987, Black Widow, 1987, Pick-up Artist, 1987, Straight to Hell, 1987, Riders of the Storm, 1988, Let it Rock, 1988, Blood Red, 1989, Flashback, 1990, Motion & Emotion, 1990, Chattahoochie, 1990, Superstar: Life and Times of Andy Warhol, 1990, Backtrack, 1991, Sunset Heat, 1991, Schneeweißrosenrot, 1991, Indian Runner, 1991, Hearts of Darkness, 1991, Paris Trout, 1991, Eye of the Storm, 1991, Super Mario Brothers, 1993, Boiling Point, 1993, True Romance, 1993, Red Rock West, 1993, Speed, 1994, Chasers, 1994, Waterworld, 1995, Search and Destroy, 1995, Carried Away, 1996, Last Days of Frankie the Fly, 1996, Cannes Man, 1996, Basquiat, 1996, Top of the World, 1997, Road Ends, 1997, Good Life, 1997, Star Truckers, 1997, Blackout, 1997, Tycus, 1998, Meet the Deedles, 1998, Sources, 1999, Lured Innocence, 1999, Justice, 1999, Jesus' Son, 1999, Bad City Blues, 1999, EdTV, 1999, Straight Shooter, 1999, Spreading Ground, 2000, Luck of the Draw, 2000, Held for Ransom, 2000, Choke, 2000, Ticker, 2001, Knockaround Guys, 2001, L.A.P.D.: To Protect and to Serve, 2001, Unspeakable, 2002, Leo, 2002, The Keeper, 2003, Out of Season, 2004, House of 9, 2004, Americano, 2005, The Crow: Wicked Prayer, 2005, Land of the Dead, 2005, (narrator) Inside Deep Throat, 2005; writer, dir. Easy Rider 1969 (Cannes Film Festival Best New Dir. award 1969), The Last Movie, 1971, Out of the Blue, 1980, Chasers, 1994, Colors, 1988, The Hot Spot, 1990, Paris Trout, 1991, Double Crossed, 1991, Sunset Heat, 1992, Nails, 1992; TV movies include The Heart of Justice, 1993, Samson and Delilah, 1996, Marlon Brando: The Wild One, 1996, The Last Days of Frankie the Fly, 1996, Jason and the Argonauts, 2000, Firestarter 2: Rekindled, 2002, The Piano Player, 2002, The Groovenians (voice), 2002, Suspense, 2003, Last Ride, 2004; exhibited photographs at Fort Worth Art Mus., Denver Art Mus., Wichita Art Mus., Cochran Art Mus., Spileto Mus., Parco Gallery, Tokyo, Osaka, Kumatomo, Japan; author: (photographic book) Out of the Sixties, 1986. Recipient Best Film award Venice Film Festival, 1971, Best Film award Cannes Film Festival, 1980. Office: Internat Creative Mgmt 8942 Wilshire Blvd Beverly Hills CA 90211*

HOPPER, EDWARD WARREN, language educator; b. Macon, Mo., Sept. 12, 1939; s. Louis Edward Hopper and Kathryn Louise Warren; m. Ruth Elizabeth Thompson, May 12, 1984; children: Thomas Warren, Mary Cagle. BA, N. Tex. State U., 1961; MA, U. Mo., 1964, PhD, 1971. Instr. Spanish U. Mo., Columbia, 1966—67, U. N.C., Charlotte, 1967—71, asst. prof., assoc. prof., 1975—. Home: 633 S Union Concord NC 28025 Office: Univ NC Dept Lang University Blvd Charlotte NC 28223 E-mail: ewhopper@email.uncc.edu.

HOPPER, JACK RUDD, chemical engineering professor; b. Highlands, Tex., May 12, 1937; s. Bonnie Preston and Rosa Mae Hopper; m. Marilyn Joyce Spears, May 30, 1958; children: Connie, Bradley. Student, Lee Coll., 1957; BSChemE, Tex. A&M U., 1959; MChemE, U. Del., 1964; PhD, La. State U., 1969. Rsch. engr. Esso Rsch. and Engring., Baytown, Tex., 1959-67; asst. prof. chem. engring. Lamar U., Beaumont, Tex., 1969-72, assoc. prof. chem. engring., 1972-75, prof. chem. engring., 1975—, chair chem. engring. dept., 1974—99, dir. engring. grad. studies, 1989-99, liaison hazardous waste alternatives ctr., 1987-88; dean coll. engring., 1999—; interim dir Gulf Coast Rsch. Ctr., 1993-94, assoc. dir., 1995-97, dir., 1997-99, Tex. Hazardous Waste Rsch. Ctr., 1993—, Tex. Ctr. Tech. Incubation, 2004—. Cons. J. M. Montgomery, New Orleans, 1991-92, Texaco Chem., Port Arthur, Tex., 1989-90, Star Enterprise, 1990-93, Tex. Internat. Ednl. Consortium, Austin, 1991-93, Mobil Chem., 1993. Mem. editl. bd. Waste Mgmt., 1992-96, co-editor 1996-2001; contbr. articles to profl. publs. Recipient Dow Outstanding Faculty award Am. Soc. for Engring. Edn., 1971, Outstanding Alumni award Lee Coll., 1981. Fellow AIChE; mem. Tex. Soc. Profl. Engs. (Engr. of Yr. award Sabine chpt. 2004). Lutheran. Achievements include inventions in field. Office: Lamar U 4400 MLK Pkwy Beaumont TX 77705

HOPPER, JOHN ALEXANDER, medical educator; BS, U. Mich.; MD, Wayne State U., Detroit, 1985—89. Lic. physician State of Mich., 1994. Intern, resident U. N.C. Hosps., 1989—93; asst. prof. Wayne State U., Detroit, 1994—. Med. dir. Jefferson Ave. Rsch. Clinic, Detroit, 1996—. Office: Wayne State Univ 2761 E Jefferson Detroit MI 48207 Office Phone: 313-993-3977.

HOPPER, NANCY JANE, author; b. Lewistown, Pa., July 25, 1937; d. David Lewis and Joyce Evelyn (Beaver) Swartz; m. James Alvin Hopper, Aug. 20, 1960; children: Christopher James, Jennifer Anne. BA, Juniata Coll., 1959. Tchr. Tyrone (Pa.) High Sch., 1959-60, Freeport (N.Y.) High Sch., 1960-62. Author of over a dozen novels for young people. Vol. Alliance (Ohio) City Schs., 1976-82, Marlington Schs. Alliance, 1987—, Alliance Area Domestic Violence Shelter. Mem. Authors League Am., Authors Guild. Avocations: reading, collecting and identifying shells, travel, bird watching. Home: 181 W Mohawk Dr Malvern OH 44644-9565

HOPPER, PEGGY F., education educator; b. Clarksdale, Miss., Nov. 19, 1955; d. John Hart and Peggy Sue (Foard) Fondren; m. George Martin Hopper, Nov. 23, 1976; children: Benjamin George Hopper, Summer LeMett Hopper. BS in Liberal Arts, Miss. State U., 1977; MS in Curriculum and Instrn., U. Memphis, 1986, EdS, 1991; PhD in Holistic Tchg./Learning, U. Tenn., 1996. Asst. to dir. U. of Memphis Grad. Ctr., Jackson, 1987; tchr. U. Sch. of Jackson, Tenn., 1987-89; coord. for young adult lit. Jackson/Madison County Libr., 1990; instr. Jackson State C.C., 1989-91; prof. Walters State C.C., Morristown, Tenn., 1992—. Adj. instr. U. Tenn., Knoxville, 1996—; adv. bd. Coll. of Edn. Admissions, U. Tenn., 1995-2005. Contbr. articles to profl. jours., articles to profl. newsletters. Pres. Gen. Fedn. of Women's Club - Jr. Chilhowee Club, Maryville, Tenn., 1998; bd. dirs. Blount County Jr. Playhouse, 1997-2001, Boys and Girls' Clubs of Blount County, 1998-99; promotion and tenure task force Tenn. Bd. Regents, 2001-03, acad. auditor, 2005 Grantee Nat. Assn. Developmental Edn., 1997, NEH, 205; recipient Trailblazer award Tenn. Bd. Regents, 2002, Pres.'s Meritorious Leadership award, 2005. Mem. Tenn. Assn. Developmental Edn. (pres. 1996-97), Nat. Assn. Developmental Edn. (liaison 1996-97), Internat. Reading Assn., Phi Lambda Theta, Phi Kappa Phi, Kappa Delta Pi. Avocations: travel, reading. Office: Walters State Cmty Coll 500 S Davy Crockett Pkwy Morristown TN 37813-1908 Home: 1311 Hickory Ln Dandridge TN 37715-6447 Office Phone: 423-585-6927.

HOPPER, RUBY LOU, clergy member; b. Harrison, Ark., May 21, 1950; d. George C. and Ethel M. (Bethany) Eddings; m. Alfred Hopper, Aug. 1, 1970. Diploma, Berean Bible Coll., Springfield, Mo., 1989. Cert. technician class III, Nat. Assn. Radio and Telecomm. Engrs., 1986; ordained minister Evangelistic Messengers, 1986. Youth leader Sycamore Log Ch., Branson, Mo., 1984—; adult Sunday sch. tchr. Branson Ch. of God. Ins. office sec. Mo. Farm Bur., Hollister, 1990-93; sec. Foxen Comm., Hollister, 1993; prodn. dept. Applied Digital, Inc., Branson, 1996; freelance writer, Hollister, 1996. Vol. ARC, Branson, 1986-87; emergency coord. Amateur Radio Emergency Svc., Branson, 1988; adult Sunday sch. tchr. Branson Ch. God, Mo., 2002—. Recipient Vol. Svc. award Pt. Lookout Health Care Ctr., 1991. Mem. Nat. Assn. Female Execs., Nat. Assn. Radio Telecomm. Engrs. (technician class III), Tri-Lakes Amateur Radio Club (v.p. 1984-88). Republican. Pentecostal. Avocations: sports, baseball cards, music, reading, travel. Home and Office: PO Box 332 Hollister MO 65673-0332 Office Phone: 417-335-6692.

HOPPER, STEPHEN RODGER, hospital administrator; b. Chgo., Aug. 28, 1949; s. Rodger Patterson and Dorothy Ann (Newberg) H.; m. Janet Sue Waddill, June 10, 1972; children: Nathan John, Amanda Sue. BA, Ill. Coll., 1971; MHA, U. Minn., 1974. Adminstrv. resident Rochester (Minn.) Meth. Hosp., 1973-74; dir. support svcs. Jennie Edmundson Hosp., Council Bluffs, Iowa, 1974-78; asst. adminstr. Trinity Meml. Hosp., Cudahy, Wis., 1978-83, sr. v.p. med. svcs., 1983-84; pres., chief exec. officer McDonough Dist. Hosp., Macomb, Ill., 1985—. Bd. dirs. Midamerica Nat. Bank, Canton, Ill., chmn bd., 2004—. Bd. dirs. Macomb Area Indsl. Devel., 1985—; Medicine Lodge Dist. com. Illowa coun. Boy Scouts Am., 1997-99. Fellow Am. Coll. Healthcare Execs.; mem. Ill. Hosp. Assn. (past pres. region 1-B, bd. dirs. 1992-95, mem. venture corp. bd. 1999—), Macomb C. of C. (bd. dirs. 1990-94), Rotary (pres.-elect Macomb 1995-96, pres. 1996-97, asst. dist. gov. 2000-03). Avocations: golf, reading, computers, travel. Home: 112 W Totem Trl Macomb IL 61455-1272 Office: McDonough Dist Hosp 525 E Grant St Macomb IL 61455-3318 Business E-Mail: srhopper@mdh.org.

HOPPIN, THOMAS EDWARD, retired transportation executive; b. Bois D'Arc Township, Ill., Aug. 15, 1941; s. Curtiss and Frances (Witt) H.; m. Marvalene Ann Shanks, June 5, 1965; children: Elizabeth Ann, Robert Curtiss. BS, Eastern Ill. U., 1969. Pub. relations exec. Penn Cen. Transp. Co., Phila., 1969-75; media relations coordinator Conrail, 1975-76, dir. media relations, 1976-78, dir. corp. communications, 1978-81; dir. fin. communications CSX Corp., Richmond, Va., 1981-83, asst. v.p. corp. communications, 1983-86, former v.p. corp. communications, 1986-2000. Mem. Nat. Advt. Rev. Bd., 1988-97. Bd. dirs. Boys Club Richmond, 1986-92; bd. dirs. Met. Richmond Pvt. Industry Coun., 1986-91, chmn., 1989-91; bd. dirs. Va. Coll. Fund, 1991-2000, chmn., 1998-2000. Mem. Assn. Nat. Advertisers (corp. comm. com. 1986-93, nat. advt. rev. bd. 1988-97), R.R. Pub. Rels. Assn. (pres. 1986-87, bd. dirs. 1985-88), Willow Oaks Country Club, Bull and Bear Club Richmond, Country Club of Hilton Head, S.C. Avocations: golf, fishing. Home: 7 Carma Ct Hilton Head Island SC 29926-1965

HOPPING, RICHARD LEE, college president emeritus; b. Dayton, Ohio, July 26, 1928; s. Lavon Lee and Dorothy Marie (Anderson) H.; m. Patricia Louise Vance, June 30, 1951; children: Ronald, Debra, Jerrold. Student, Chaffey Coll., 1947-48, U. Dayton, 1948-49, Sinclair Coll., 1948-49; BS, OD, So. Coll. Optometry, 1952, DOS (hon.), 1972; DSc (hon.), SUNY, 1995, DOS (hon.), 2004. Practice optometry, Dayton, Ohio, 1953-73; pres. So. Calif. Coll. Optometry, Fullerton, 1973-97, pres. emeritus, 1997—. Mem. Nat. Acads. of Practice, 1983—; chmn. Nat. Acad. Practice in Optometry, 1985-89; vice chmn. 13th dist. med. quality rev. com., State of Calif. Bd. Med. Quality Assurance, 1985-93; mem. adv. bd. St. Jude Hosp., 1985—2000; nat. spokesperson Better Vision Inst., 1988-2000; cons. in field. Contbr. numerous articles on vision and health care to profl. publs. V.p. Orange County (Calif.) coun. Boy Scouts Am., 1977-79, mem. adv. coun., 1979-94; mem. Coun. Assocs. of Red Cross, North Orange County Svc. Ctr., 1978-80; mem. adv. coun. YWCA, North Orange County, 1984-92. Recipient Orange County Retinitis Pigmentosa award of Excellence in field of vision care, 1988, award of Excellence VisionAmerica, 1991, Dirs. Choice award Optical Labs. Assn., 1995, Leo award of Excellence in Global Eye Care Nat. Eye Rsch. Found., 1995, People of Vision award Prevent Blindness Am., 1997, Lifetime Achievement award So. Coll. Optometry, 1997; named Optimist of Yr., Dayton View Optimists, 1956; named to Nat. Optometry Hall of Fame, 2003. Fellow APHA (Vision Care Disting. Achievement award 1984), Am. Acad. Optometry (chmn. primary care optometry sect. 1973-79, chmn. awards com. 1981-90); mem. Am. Optometric Assn. (pres. 1971-72, chmn. profl. enhancement adv. com. 1982-89, Calif. Optometrist of Yr. 1988, AOA Nat. Optometerist of Yr. 1988, chair industry rels. com. 1989-95, chair nat. edn. summit conf. 1990-91, chair Nat. Optometric Edn. Summit com. 1991-92, chair centennial adv. com. 1996-98, Scope of Optometric Practice Conf. 1992, Dr. Raymond I. Meyers award 1990, Disting. Svc. award 1993), Calif. Optometric Assn. (hon. life, jud. coun., Optometrist of Yr. 1988, Paul Yarwood Meml. award 1997), Assn. Ind. Calif. Colls. and Univs. (trustee 1973-97), Optometric Ext. Programs Found. (hon. life), Assn. Schs. and Colls. of Optometry (pres. 1983-85), Ohio Optometric Assn. (pres. 1964-65, Ohio Optometrist of Yr. 1962, hon. life), Retinitis Pigmentosa Internat. (adv. exec. com. 1984-88), Dayton Jr. C. of C. (Man of Yr.), Lincoln Club of Orange County (chmn. ethics com. 1988-92). E-mail: rhoppingod@aol.com.

HOPSON, EVERETT GEORGE, retired lawyer; b. Stillwell, Ill., Sept. 4, 1922; s. Carman Roy and Adella (George) H.; m. Doris May Hutchins, Aug. 15, 1953 (dec.); children: Christine E., Eugene G. AA, Springfield Jr. Coll., 1942; BS, U. Ill., 1947, JD, 1949; MS in Internat. Affairs, George Washington U., 1967; disting. grad., Air War Coll., 1967. Bar: Ill. 1949, U.S. Ct. Mil. Appeals 1957, U.S. Supreme Ct. 1957. Dep. collector U.S. Treasury, IRS, Carlinville, Ill., 1949-51; commd. officer USAF, 1951, advanced to col., judge advocate, 1951-71; spl. asst. to asst. sec. def. Dept. Def., Washington, 1971; sr. atty. U.S. Postal Svc., Washington, 1972-73; dep. chief gen. law divsn. USAF, Washington, 1973-75, chief gen. law divsn., 1975-94, ret., 1994. Trustee USAF JAG Sch. Found., 2004; trustee ESL immigrant ministries United Meth. Ch. With U.S. Army, 1943—46. Decorated Legion of Merit; recipient Presdl. Rank of Meritorious Exec., USAF, 1981, 87, 92, Freedoms Found. award, 1961, 62, 66. Mem. ABA, Ill. Bar Assn. (sr. counsellor 1999), Fed. Bar Assn., Judge Advocates Assn., Am. Inns of Ct., Phi Alpha Delta. Independent. Methodist. Avocations: coin collecting/numismatics, gardening. Home: 9719 Limoges Dr Fairfax VA 22032-1115 Personal E-mail: eghdmh@aol.com. *Helpful advice and good counsel need to make sense and be reasonable to be effective. In my professional career and in life, I have attempted, with some degree of success, to let common sense prevail and reason rule the land.*

HOPSON, JAMES WARREN, publishing executive; b. St. Louis, May 24, 1946; s. David Warren and Ruth L. (Dierkes) H.; m. Julie Ann Eastlack, Dec. 21, 1968; children: John, Benjamin, Gillian. BJ, U. Mo., 1968; MBA, Harvard U., 1973. Project mgr. Des Moines Register & Tribune, 1973-76, dir. ops., 1976-78, circulation dir., 1978-79; gen. mgr. Corpus Christi (Tex.) Caller Times, 1979-82; pub. Middlesex News, Framingham, Mass., 1982-88; pres. N.E. Group-Harte-Hanks Comms., Framingham, 1984-88; pub. The Press of Atlantic City, N.J., 1989-94; pres. Community Newspaper Co., Boston, 1994-95, Thomson Ctrl. Ohio, Newark, 1995-2000; pub. Wis. State Jour., Madison, Wis., 2000—; v.p. publishing Lee Enterprises, Madison, 2000—. Pres. Vol. Ctr. Atlantic County, 1992—; treas. DeCordova Mus., Lincoln, Mass., 1983-89, dir., 1983-89; sec. Family Health Svc. Ctrl. Ohio, 1997—, treas.; bd. dirs. Audit Bur. of Circulations, 1999—; bd. dirs. Madison Art Ctr., United Way of Dane County. 1st lt. U.S. Army, 1968-73, Vietnam. Mem. New Eng. Newspaper Assn. (chmn. circulation com. 1986-88), Mass. Newspaper Pub. Assn. (dir. 1984-88), Metrowest C. of C. (chmn. 1987-88, dir. audit bur. of circulations 1999—), Greater Madison C. of C. (bd. dirs.) Office: 1901 Fish Hatchery Rd Madison WI 53713-1248

HOPSON, MARK D., lawyer; b. 1958; BA cum laude, Stetson U., 1980; JD summa cum laude, Georgetown U., 1984. Bar: Md. 1985, D.C. 1986, U.S. Supreme Ct. 1988. Ptnr. Sidley Austin Brown & Wood LLP, Washington, 1992—. Office: Sidley Austin Brown & Wood LLP 1501 K Street NW Washington DC 20005

HOPSON, MARY LOUISE CARSTENS, marketing consultant; b. Alexandria, La., Nov. 17, 1956; d. Carl Rand and Sally Randolph (Pitts) Carstens; m. David Carlisle Hopson, Apr. 17, 1982; 1 child, Stuart Randolph. BA in Journalism, La. State U., 1978. Corp. law cert. Inst. for Paralegal Tng., 1978. Corp. legal asst. Tex. Instruments Inc., Dallas, 1979-81; mgr. corp. legal affairs Natural Resource Mgmt. Corp., Dallas, 1981-84; mgr. bus. devel. Haynes & Boone, Dallas, 1984-90; dir. practice devel. Calhoun, Gump, Spillman & Stacy, Dallas, 1990-93; pvt. practice profl. svcs. mktg. cons. Dallas, 1993—; prin. Marketing for the Professions, Dallas, 1993—; freelance writer, editor, 1993—. Lectr. in field. Contbr. articles to profl. jours. Mem. Profl. Svcs. Mktg. Assn. (co-founder 1987, dir. 1987-89, v.p. programs 1997-99), Jr. League Dallas (sustaining mem.) Office: 6142 Sul Ross Ln Dallas TX 75214-2132

HOPWOOD, BRIAN KEITH, music educator, musician; b. Stromsburg, Nebr., July 4, 1956; s. Robert Wayne and Barbara Joann Hopwood; m. Franka Lou Williams, Aug. 5, 1978; children: Brian Joseph, Matthew Robert, Margaret Joann. B of Music Edn., Oral Roberts U., 1978; DipFA, U. Calgary, 1986; M of Music Edn., U. Colo., 1990; D of Music Arts, Ariz. State U., 1998. Lic. profl. tchr. Colo. Dept. Edn., 1978. Dir. bands Florence H.S., Colo., 1978—82, Manitou Springs Dist. 14, 1982—; prin. condr, music dir. Boulder Concert Band, 2000—. Adjudicator DC Festivals, Lubbock, Tex., 2004—, Colo. H.S. Activities Assn., Aurora, 1997—. Recipient Spirit Mustang award, Manitou Springs Sch. Dist. 14, 2002. Mem.: Colo. Music Educators Assn., Colo. Bandmasters Assn., Internat. Trumpet Guild, Music Educators Nat. Conf., Nat. Band Assn., Coll. Band Dirs. Nat. Assn., Pi Kappa Lambda, Phi Beta Mu. Conservative. Avocations: tennis, reading. Office: Manitou Springs High Sch 401 El Monte Pl Manitou Springs CO 80829 Office Phone: 719-685-2645. Office Fax: 719-685-4755. E-mail: bhopwood@mssd14.k12.co.us.

HOPWOOD, HOWARD HOPPY PERRY, military officer; b. Mountain Top, Ark., Mar. 16, 1944; s. Ira Homer Hopwood and Hallie Mae Dunn; m. Mary M. White, Oct. 8, 1945; children: Rebecca Marie McDonell, James Howard. BS in religious Edn., So. Christian U., Montgomery, Ala., 1978. Evangelist, deacon, elder church of Christ, 1969. Sr. master sgt. Hdqs. MAC/LGME USAF, Scott AFB, Ill., 1975—79, chief master sgt. Hdqs. USAFE/LGMA Kiserslautern, Germany, 1981—85. With integrated def. sys. The Boeing Co., Oklahoma City, 1985—. Evangelist, deacon, elder ch. of Christ, Melbourne, Fla., Germany, 1975—2003. Decorated Meritorious Svc. Medal with 3 oak leaf clusters, Air Force Commendation Medal with 31oak leaf clusters, Meritorious Svc. Award. Mem.: Am. Legion (life; KS Post 0062). Conservative. Church Of Christ. Avocations: collecting military memorabilia, history, philosphy, writing, photography. Home: 2318 Ripple Creek Ln Edmond OK 73003 Personal E-mail: hophopwood@aol.com. E-mail: howard.p.hopwood@boeing.com.

HORAHAN, EDWARD BERNARD, III, lawyer; b. Drexel Hill, Pa., Dec. 30, 1951; s. Edward Bernard and Ann Veronica (Schneeweis) H.; m. Rebecca Joy Fusco, Mar. 13, 1976; 1 child, Elizabeth Joy. BA, LaSalle Coll., Phila., 1973; JD, Yale U., 1976. Bar: D.C. 1976. Staff atty. office of gen. counsel SEC, Washington, 1976-78; staff atty. office of solicitor, plan benefits security divsn. U.S. Dept. Labor, Washington, 1978-80; assoc. Arter & Hadden, Washington, 1980-84; ptnr. Parker, Chapin, Flattau & Klimpl, Washington, 1984-88, Stroock & Stroock & Lavan, Washington, 1988-93; pvt. practice Law Offices of Edward B. Horahan III, Washington, 1993-96; counsel Groom Law Group, Washington, 1996-2001, Dechert, Washington, 2001—. Mem. ABA. Office: 1775 Eye St NW Washington DC 20006 E-mail: edward.horahan@dechert.com.

HORAK, BONNIE L., middle school educator; b. Ill., Sept. 3, 1962; d. George and Dorothy Horak. BA, Augustana Coll., 1984; MEd, Tex. A&M U., 1998. Cert. tchr., Tex. Tchr. of the deaf Victoria (Tex.) Ind. Sch. Dist., 1985-89; interpreter for the deaf Bryan (Tex.) Ind. Sch. Dist., 1989-96, tchr. of the deaf, 1989-94, tchr. learning disabled, 1994-98, math. tchr., 1998—2003, resource math tchr., 2003—. Mem. Tex. Classroom Tchrs. Assn., Kappa Delta Pi. Lutheran. E-mail: bhorak@bryanisd.org.

HORAK, JAN-CHRISTOPHER, filmmaker, educator, curator; b. Bad Münstereifel, Fed. Republic Germany, May 1, 1951; came to U.S., 1951; s. Jerome V. and Giselle (Offermanns) H.; m. Martha F. Schirn, May 17, 1988; 1 child, Gianna. BA, U. Del., 1973; MS, Boston U., 1975; PhD, Westfälische Wilhelms-U., Münster, Germany, 1984. Intern Internat. Mus. Photography, Rochester, N.Y., 1975-76, assoc. curator George Eastman House, 1984-87, curator film, 1987-90, sr. curator, 1990-94; asst. prof. film studies U. Rochester, 1985-90, assoc. prof., 1990-93, prof., 1994; dir. Münchner Filmmuseum, Munich, Germany, 1994-98; prof. Hochschule f. Fernsehen u. Film, 1995-98; dir. Archives and Collections Universal Studios, L.A., 1998-00; prof. UCLA, 1999—; curator Hollywood Entertainment Mus., 2000—. Panelist, chmn. film panel N.Y. State Coun. of Arts, N.Y.C., 1986-89; cons. USIA, 1988-90; archivists adv. bd. The Film Found., N.Y.C., 1990-94; v.p., pres. Assn. Moving Image Archivists, 1991-93; exec. com. Internat. Fedn. Film Archives, 1993-95, Kuratorium Junger Deutscher Film, 1995-97. Author: Anti-Nazi Filme der Emigration, 1984, Fluchtpunkt Hollywood, 1986, The Dream Merchants, 1989, Lovers of Cinema: The First American Film Avant-Garde, 1995, Berge, Licht und Traum: Arnold Fanck und der deutsche Bergfilm, 1997, Making Images Move: Photography and Avant-Garde Cinema, 1997; editor: Film und Foto der 20er Jahre, 1979, Helmar Lerski, 1982; founding editor: The Moving Image, 2001—; contbr. articles to profl. jours. Recipient Louis B. Mayer award Mayer Found., Am. Film Inst., 1975; Heinrich Herz Stiftung fellow, 1979-81. Mem.: Internat. Assn. Audio-Visual Media and History, Soc. Exile Studies, Soc. Cinema Studies. Avocations: travel, skiing, swimming. Office: 545 Sierra Vista Ave Pasadena CA 91107 Office Phone: 323-960-4805. Personal E-mail: jchrishorak@aol.com. Business E-Mail: c.horak@hollywoodmuseum.com.

HORCHOW, S(AMUEL) ROGER, marketing consultant; b. Cin., July 3, 1928; s. Reuben and Beatrice (Schwartz) H.; m. Carolyn Pfeifer, Dec. 29, 1960; children: Regen Horchow Fearon, Elizabeth Horchow Routman, Sally Horchow McCauley. BA, Yale U., 1950, DLHD (hon.), 1999. Buyer Foley's, Houston, 1953-60; v.p. Neiman-Marcus, Dallas, 1960-68, 69-71; pres. Design Research, Cambridge, Mass., 1968-69, Kenton Collection, Dallas, 1971-73; chmn. Horchow Collection, Dallas, 1973-90. Author: Elephants in Your Mailbox, 1979, Living in Style, 1981; prodr. Crazy for You, 1991-95; co-prodr. Kiss Me Kate, 1999. Bd. dirs. Jefferson Award for Pub. Svc., Ctr. for Human Nutrition, Yale Art Galley, Com. for Preservation of the White House, Found. Art and Preservation of Embassies. Mem. Yale Club (N.Y.C.), Nantucket Yacht Club, Knickerbocker Club, Birnam Wood Club. Office: 5722 Chatham Hill Rd Dallas TX 75225-3208 Office Phone: 214-692-1954. E-mail: C4U@aol.com.

HORDON, HARRIS EUGENE, economics professor; b. NYC, Dec. 31, 1942; s. Sidney and Betty (Flacks) H.; m. Carole Schulman, July 27, 1969; children: Elana, Robert, Daniel. BA in Econs., Bklyn. Coll., 1963; MA in Econs., NYU, 1965, PhD in Econs., 1968. Instr. econs. Northeastern U., Boston, 1966-69; economist U.S. Dept. of Transp., Washington, 1970-71; chmn. econ. dept., prof. New Jersey City U., 1969—. Fin. cons. in field, 1975—. Author: Introduction to Urban Economics, 1973. Fellowship Brookings Instn., 1970; faculty fellowship Princeton U., 1986. Avocation: boating. Home: 340 East 64th Street Apt 6J New York NY 10021 Office: New Jersey City U 2039 Kennedy Blvd Jersey City NJ 07305-1597 Office Phone: 201-200-3272. Business E-Mail: hhordon@njcu.edu.

HORE, JOHN EDWARD, commodity futures educator; b. Dec. 13, 1929; s. Ernest and Doris Kathleen (Horton) H.; m. Diana King, May 3, 1958; children: Edward John Bruce, Celia Kathleen Hore Milne, Timothy Frank. BA with honors, King's Coll., Cambridge, Eng., 1952, MA, 1957. Chartered fin. analyst. Asst. sales mgr. Borthwicks, London, 1952-54; security analyst Dominion Securities, Toronto, Ont., Can., 1955-57; asst. mktg. mgr. Rio Algom, Toronto, 1957-61; dir. Bell, Gouinlock & Co., Toronto, 1961-75; v.p., dir. futures Can. Securities Inst., Toronto, 1979-94, seminar leader, 1980-2000. Investment edn. cons., 1995—; cons. Can. Dept. Agr., 1993; founding sec. Can. Nuclear Assn.; past v.p. Brit. Can. Trade Assn.; chmn. 1st Can. Internat. Futures Rsch. Seminar, 1985, also editor Proc., 2 vols., 1986; spkr. Can.-Am. Inst. Conf. on Fin. Svcs. at Detroit-Windsor, 1989, compliance seminar Futures Industry Assn. at Alexandria, Va., 1990; chmn. Can. Futures Conf., 1986; chmn. 3d, 4th, 5th and 6th Can. Internat. Futures Conf. and Rsch. Seminars, 1987, 88, 89, 90, mng. editor Selected Papers 1988-91. Author: Trading on Canadian Futures Markets, 1984, 5th edit., 1993; co-author: CFA Inst. Standards of Practice Handbook, 1982 (Pres. Reagan Citation, 1984); co-editor: Canadian Securities Course, 1980—94. Gov. Montcrest Sch., 1970-73; mem. Commodity Futures Adv. Bd., Ont., 1989-95; apptd. mem. internat. com. Futures Industry Assn., Washington, 1988-91, rowing com. Upper Can. Coll., Toronto, 1982-86; pres. St. George's Soc. Toronto, 1978-80, chmn. edn. com., 1987. With Royal Army Ednl. Corps, 1948-49, Singapore. Mem.: CFA Inst. (bd. dirs. investment analysis stds. 1974—85, emeritus 1985), Toronto Soc. Fin. Analysts (bd. dirs. 1968—71), Toronto Round Table (pres. 1999—2001), Royal Overseas League (pres. Ont. chpt. 1992—2004, vice-chmn. 2004—), Hurlingham Club (London), Arts and Letters Club Toronto (exec. com. 2000, treas. 2001—05), Univ. Club Toronto (bd. dirs. 1980—83, v.p. 1982—83), Leander Club (assoc.; Henley-on-Thames). Anglican. Avocations: historical research, squash, choral music, poetry. Office: 185 Carlton St Toronto ON Canada M5A 2K7 Office Phone: 416-922-9227. Personal E-mail: johnhore@aol.com.

HORECKER, BERNARD LEONARD, retired biochemistry professor; b. Chgo., Oct. 31, 1914; s. Paul and Bessie (Bornstein) H.; m. Frances Goldstein, July 12, 1936; children: Doris Colgate, Marilyn Diamond Schnell, Linda Lally. BS, U. Chgo., 1936, PhD, 1939; Laureate honoris causa in Biol. Scis., U. Urbino (Italy), 1982. Rsch. assoc. chemistry U. Chgo., 1939-40; examiner U.S. Civil Svc. Commn., 1940-41; biochemist USPHS, NIH, Bethesda, Md., 1941-59; chief lab. of biochemistry and metabolism Nat. Inst. Arthritis and Metabolic Disease, 1956-59; professorial lectr. enzyme chemistry George Washington U., 1950-57; guest rsch.-worker Pasteur Inst., Paris, 1957-58; prof. microbiology, chmn. dept. NYU Coll. Medicine, 1959-63; prof. molecular biology, chmn. dept. Albert Einstein Coll. Medicine, 1963-72, assoc. dean for sci. affairs, 1971-72; mem. Roche Inst. Molecular Biology, Nutley, N.J., 1972-84, head Lab. Molecular Enzymology, 1977-84; adj. prof. Cornell U. Med. Coll., 1972-84, prof. biochemistry, 1984-89, prof. emeritus biochemistry, 1989, dean Grad. Sch. Med. Sci., 1984-92. Vis. prof. Albert Einstein Coll. Medicine, 1972-84; vis. prof. biochemistry U. Calif., 1954, U. Parana, Brazil, 1960, 63; vis. lectr. U. Ill., 1956; Ciba lectr. Rutgers U., 1962; Phillips lectr. Haverford Coll., 1965; vis. prof. Kyoto (Japan) U., 1967; vis. prof. biochemistry and molecular biology Cornell U., 1965; vis. prof. U. Ferrara, Italy; Reilly lectr. Notre Dame U., 1969; vis. lectr. U. Rotterdam, 1970; prof. honoris causa Fed. U. Parana, Curitiba, Brazil, 1981—; sci. adv. bd. Roche Inst. Molecular Biology, Nutley, NJ, 1967-72, chmn., 1971-72; mem. Rsch. Career Award com. Nat. Inst. Gen. Med. Scis., 1966-70; personnel com. Am. Cancer Soc., 1968-72, sci. adv. com. for biochemistry and chem. carcinogenesis, 1974-78, mem. Coun. for Rsch. and Clin. Investigation Awards, 1984-88; biology divsn. adv. com. Oak Ridge Nat. Lab., 1976-80; mem. Med. Scientist Tng. Program Sect. NIH, 1970-72. Editor Biochem. and Biophys. Rsch. Communications, 1959-89, Current Topics in Cellular Regulation, 1969-89, Archives Biochemistry and Biophysics, 1960-68; chmn. editl. bd. Archives of Biochemistry and Biophysics, 1968-84; contbr. articles to profl. jours. Recipient Paul Lewis Labs. award in enzyme chemistry, 1952, Superior Accomplishment award Fed. Security Agy., 1952, Rockefeller Pub. Svc. award, 1957, Hillebrand prize Am. Chem. Soc., 1954, Award in Biol. Scis., Washington Acad. Scis., 1954, Fulbright Travel award, 1963; Commonwealth Fund fellow, 1967. Fellow AAAS, Am. Acad. Arts and Scis.; mem. NAS, Am. Chem. Soc. (vice chmn. div. biol. chemistry 1975-76, chmn. 1976-77), Biochem. Soc. (Eng.), Swiss Biochem. Soc. (hon. mem.), Spanish Biochem. Soc., hon. mem.), Japanese Biochem. Soc. (hon. mem.), Hellenic Biochem. and Biophys. Soc. (hon. mem.), Am. Soc. Biol. Chemists (pres. 1967-68, chmn. editorial com. 1962-63, Merck award 1981), Virchow-Pirquet Med. Soc. (Neuburg medal 1981), Harvey Soc. (v.p. 1969-70, pres. 1970-71), Brazilian Acad. Sci. (hon.), PanAm. Assn. Biochem. Socs. (vice chmn. 1971, chmn. 1972, mem. exec. com. 1971-78), Indian Nat. Acad. Sci., Argentine Acad. Sci. (corr.), Phi Beta Kappa, Sigma Xi. Home: 16517 Cypress Villa Ln Fort Myers FL 33908-7609 Personal E-mail: blhorecker@comcast.net.

HOREN, JEFFREY HARRY, telecommunications executive; b. Louisville, Oct. 1, 1949; s. H. Solomon and Freda E. (Saphier) H.; m. Susan Alix Chellin, Mar. 4, 1984; children: Melissa, David. BA, U. Mich., 1971; MA, Yale U., 1974, PhD, 1977. Asst. prof. U. Iowa, Iowa City, 1976-83; econ. policy fellow Brookings Instn., Washington, 1980-81; internal cons. AT&T, Basking Ridge, N.J., 1983-87; group mgr. Sprint, Overland Park, Kans., 1987—. Author: Scheduling of Network Television Programs, 1977. Recipient Chester A. Phillips award U. Iowa, 1978; grad. fellow NSF, 1971-74. Home: 12320 Riggs Rd Overland Park KS 66209-4453

HORGAN, CORNELIUS OLIVER, mathematics professor, applied mechanics educator; b. Cork, Ireland, May 16, 1944; m. Myra O'Callaghan; children: Olivia, David. BS, Univ. Coll., Cork, 1964, MS, 1965; PhD, Calif. Inst. Tech., 1970; DSc, Nat. U. Ireland, 1983. Lectr. U. Mich., Ann Arbor, 1970-72; sr. research assoc. U. East Anglia, Norwich, U.K., 1972-74; assoc. prof. U. Houston, 1974-78; prof. applied mechanics and math. Mich. State U., East Lansing, 1978-88; prof. applied math. and applied mechanics U. Va., Charlottesville, 1988-94, Wills Johnson prof., 1994—. Vis. prof. Northwestern U., Evanston, 1977-78, Calif. Inst. Tech., Pasadena, 1984-85, U. Pisa, Italy, 1996, 97, U. Lecce, Italy, 2001, 03, U. Ferrara, Italy, 2001, 03, U. Politecnica de Catalunya, Terrassa, Spain, 2001, 03. Contbr. over 175 publs. in field of theoretical mechanics and applied math. to profl. publs. Fellow ASME (chmn. tech. com. 1981-86), Am. Acad. Mechanics; mem. Am. Math. Soc., Soc. Engring. Sci. (bd. dirs. 1993-99, Eringen Medal 2005), Soc. for Indsl. and Applied Math., Soc. Nat. Phil., Internat. Soc. for the Interaction of Mechanics and Maths. (exec. com. 2000-05). Home: 2820 Meadow Vista Dr Charlottesville VA 22901-9559 Office: U Va Dept Civil Engring Thornton Hall Charlottesville VA 22904 Business E-Mail: coh8p@virginia.edu.

HORGER, EDGAR OLIN, III, retired obstetrics and gynecology educator; b. Eutawville, S.C., May 30, 1937; s. Edgar Olin Jr. and Frances Durant (Jordan) H.; m. Polly Jo Collins, May 29, 1960; children: Edgar Olin IV, David Collins, Patricia Bowen. BS, Furman U., 1959; MD, Med. Coll. S.C., 1962. Intern Med. U. Hosp., Charleston, S.C., 1962-63, resident in ob-gyn, 1963-67; NIH fellow U. Pitts., 1967-68, asst. prof., 1968-69, Med. U. S.C., Charleston, 1969-71, assoc. prof., 1971-76, prof., 1976-90, dir. maternal-fetal medicine, 1973-90; prof. ob-gyn. U. S.C. Sch. Medicine, Columbia, 1990-2001, disting. prof., chmn., 1993-99, disting. prof. emeritus, 2001—. Mem. S.C. Bd. Med. Examiners, 1985-87. Contbr. articles to profl. jours. Adv. bd. Charleston chpt. March of Dimes, 1984-90. Capt. AUS, 1963-66. Recipient Disting. Alumnus award Med. U. S.C., 1995; USPHS fellow, 1967-68. Mem. AMA, S.C. Med. Assn., Am. Coll. Obstetricians and Gynecologists (Outstanding Faculty award dist. IV 1988, vice chmn. S.C. sect. 1993-96, chmn. 1996-98, treas. dist. IV 1997-2000, Outstanding Dist. Svc. award 2001), Coun. Res. Edn. ObGyn, South Ctrl. Ob-Gyn. Soc., South Atlantic Assn. Ob-Gyn. (exec. com. 1983-94, sec. 1987-90, v.p. 1990-91, pres.-elect 1991-92, pres. 1992-93), So. Perinatal Assn. (dir. Mid-Atlantic region 1974-76), Soc. Perinatal Obstetricians (dir. 1977-78), Am. Gynecol. Obstet. Soc., Am. Assn. Ob-Gyn., S.C. Ob-Gyn. Soc. (pres. 1991-92), Columbia Med. Soc., Assn. Profs. Gynecology and Obstetrics (Excellence in Tchg. award 1992), S.C. State Bd. Med. Examiners (bd. dirs. 1985-87), Summit Club, Wild Dunes Club, Alpha Omega Alpha. Home: 125 Holliday Rd Columbia SC 29223-3108 Office: U SC Sch Medicine Dept Ob-Gyn 2 Richland Medical Park Dr Columbia SC 29203-6864

HORI, KEIKO, English literature educator; b. Himeji, Hyogo, Japan, Jan. 18, 1954; d. Takeshi Nishiyama and Fumiko Hori; 1 child, Grace. BA summa cum laude, Osaka (Japan) U., 1976, MA, 1978; postgrad., U. N.H., 1979—80, Osaka (Japan) U., 1978—82. Instr. Osaka Kyoiku U., 1981-82, tenured asst. prof., 1982-87, assoc. prof., 1987-2000, prof., 2000—; instr. Osaka U., Toyonaka, Japan, 1988-90, 92-95. Vis. prof. U. Wyo., Laramie, 1986—87; vis. scholar UCLA, 2001—02. Co-author: Imeji to shite no Toshi: Gakusaiteki Toshi Bunkaron, 1996; annotator: (textbook) American Businessman: Lessons from Life, 1994; co-annotator: (textbook) American and English Ideals, 1991. Recipient Kusumoto award, 1976. Mem. Modern Lang. Assn., English Literary Soc. Japan, Japan Assn. English Romanticism, Japan Assn. Coll. English Tchrs. Home: 7-4-1-3 Umamikita Koryo-cho Kitakatsuragi-gun Nara 635-0831 Japan Office: Osaka Kyoiku U 4-698-1 Asahigaoka Kashiwara Osaka 582-8582 Japan

HORI, YUKIO, engineering educator, scientific association administrator; b. Tokyo, Aug. 22, 1927; s. Kojiro and Yoshi (Saito) H.; m. Noriko Sunabori, May 15, 1965; children: Gen, Jun, Dan. B.Eng., U. Tokyo, 1951, Dr.Eng., 1960. Instr. U. Tokyo, 1953-55, assoc. prof., 1955-65, prof., 1965-88, emeritus prof., 1988—; exec. dir. Japan Soc. for Promotion of Sci., 1988-94; prof., v.p. Kanazawa Inst. Tech., Tokyo, 1994—. Contbr. articles to profl. jours. Recipient Tokyo Metropolis award, 1984, Purple Ribbon medal, 1993. Mem. ASME, Japan Soc. Mech. Engrs. (pres. 1988-89, awards 1960, 74, 89), Japan Soc. Tribologists (pres. 1990-92, award 1982), Japan Fedn. Engring. Soc. (v.p. 1989-93), Engring. Acad. Japan (v.p. 1993-2000, adviser, 2000—). Avocation: music. Home: Kugayama 3-19-19 Suginami-ku Tokyo 168-0082 Japan Office: Kanazawa Inst Tech Akasaka 2-17-41 Minato-ku Tokyo 107-0052 Japan Office Phone: +81-3-3589-2821. E-mail: hori@alum.mit.edu.

HORINKO, MARIANNE LAMONT, former federal agency administrator; b. 1961; BS, U. Md., 1982; JD, Georgetown U., 1986. Staff scientist Nat. Cancer Inst., Bethesda, Md.; atty. Morgan, Lewis, & Bockius, LLP, Washington; atty. advisor, solid wastes & emerg. response EPA, Washington, 1990—93; pres. Clay Assocs., Inc., 1993—2001; asst. adminstr. solid waste and emer. response EPA, 2001—03, acting adminstr., 2003.

HORISZNY, LAURENE HELEN, lawyer; b. Lansing, Mich., Oct. 14, 1955; d. Walter and Jennie Ann (Pellpshen) H.; m. Richard C. Stavoe Jr., June 25, 1983; children: Andrea Kristen, Charles Ross. BA, Mich. State U., 1977; JD, Ohio State U., 1980. Bar: Mich. 1980, U.S. Dist. Ct. (ea. and we. dists.) Mich. 1980. Lawyer Consumers Power Co., Jackson, Mich., 1980-85; corp. counsel Ex-Cell-O Corp., Troy, Mich., 1985-86; sr. lawyer, asst. sec. BorgWarner Automotive, Inc., Troy, 1986—. Exec. bd. Land 'O Lakes coun. Boy Scouts Am., 1984-85. Mem. ABA, Mich. Bar Assn., Nature Conservancy. Avocations: scuba diving, cross country skiing, down-hill skiing, tennis. Office: BorgWarner Inc 6700 181/2 Mile Rd Ste 500 Sterling Heights MI 48311-8022

HORKEY, WILLIAM RICHARD, retired oil industry executive; b. Tulsa, Apr. 22, 1925; s. William Edward and Clara Doris (Rice) H.; m. Barbara Jeanne Williamson, Oct. 18, 1952; children: Elaine Gail, Edward Richard, Ellen Beth. BA, State U. Iowa, 1947; LLB, U. Okla., 1950; grad., Advanced Mgmt. Program, Harvard U., 1962. Bar: Okla. 1950. With Gulf Oil Corp., 1950-51, Skelly Oil Co., 1951-55, Helmerich & Payne, Inc., Tulsa, 1955-90, sec., legal counsel, 1955-64, v.p., 1960-64, exec. v.p., 1964-87, sr. v.p., 1987-90, bd. dirs., 1957-90. Chmn. Grand River Dam Authority, Okla. Ordnance Works Authority, Woolslayer Cos. Inc., EnviroFuels Inc.; bd. dirs. The Great Eastern Shipping Co. London, Asbury Svcs. Inc.; pres. Inverness Village. Bd. dirs. Tulsa United Way, 1978-88; chmn. S.E. Tulsa YMCA, 1970-72; pres. Met. Tulsa YMCA, 1972-73, Tulsa Bus. Health Group 1978-96; chmn. Tulsa chpt. ARC, 1987-88; dir. Tulsa Emergency Med. Authority, 1977-95, chmn., 1981-95; pres. Tulsa Cmty. Found., for Indigent Health Care, 1980—. Mem. ABA, Okla. Bar Assn., Tulsa County Bar Assn., Order of Coif, So. Hills Country Club, Mid-Continent Harvard AMP (Tulsa) (pres. 1969-75), Phi Delta Phi, Phi Delta Theta. Presbyterian (deacon and elder). Home: 3800 W 71st St # 3213 Tulsa OK 74132 E-mail: wrh@invernessvillage.com.

HORLEN, JOE PAUL, law educator, lawyer; b. Burnet, Tex., June 20, 1952; s. Fred Stanley and Evelyn Rose Horlen; m. Becky Lynn Parker, Nov. 28, 1986; 1 child, Dustin James. BS, Tex. A&M U., 1973, MEd, 1977; JD, Baylor U., 1980. Bar: Tex. Atty. pvt. practice, Plano, Tex.; ptnr. Arter & Hadden, Dallas, Harlen Holt & Hollas, College Station; asst. prof. Tex. A&M. U. Chair BCS Econ. Devel., College Station, 2000, Planning & Zoning. Grantee, Tex. Presdl. Comm. Commn., Austin, 2004—05. Avocations: fishing, birdwatching, sports. Office: Tex A&M U 3137 TAMU College Station TX 77843

HORLICK, GARY NORMAN, lawyer, educator; b. Washington, Mar. 12, 1947; s. Reuben S. and Gertrude V. (Cooper) Horlick; m. Kathryn L. Mann, June 1, 1986. AB, Dartmouth Coll., 1968; BA, MA, Diploma in Internat. Law, Cambridge (Eng.) U., 1970; JD, Yale U., 1973. Bar: Conn. 1974, U.S. Ct. Appeals (D.C. cir.) 1975), D.C. 1977, U.S. Supreme Ct. 1977, U.S. Ct. Internat. Trade 1979, U.S. Ct. Customs and Patent Appeals 1980. Asst. to rep. Ford Found., Santiago, Chile, 1973-74, asst. rep. Bogota, Colombia, 1974-76; assoc. Steptoe & Johnson, Washington, 1976-80; internat. trade counsel U.S. Senate Fin. Com., Washington, 1981; dep. asst. sec. U.S. Dept. Commerce, Washington, 1981-83; ptnr. O'Melveny & Myers, Washington, 1983—2002, Wilmer Cutler Pickering Hale and Dorr, LLp, Washington, 2002—. Lectr. law Yale U., New Haven, 1983-86, 2001—, World Trade Inst., U. Berne, 2000—; adj. prof. Georgetown U. Law Ctr., Washington, 1986—; lectr. various orgns.; adv. com. U.S. Ct. Internat. Trade, 1993-97; mem. permanent group of experts World Trade Orgn., 1996-2001, chmn., 1996-97. Author: WTO and NAFTA Rules and Dispute Resolution, 2003. Mem. ABA (chmn. standing com. on customs law 1993), Coun. Fgn. Rels., Internat. Law Assn. (mem. exec. coun. Am. br. 1983—), Internat. Bar Assn. (vice chmn. antitrust and trade law 1987-89), D.C. Bar Assn. (chmn. internat. divsn. 1984-85), Am. Soc. of Internat. Law (exec. coun. 1998-99). Office: Wilmer Cutler Pickering Hale and Dorr LLP 2455 M St NW Washington DC 20037 Office Phone: 202-663-6000. Business E-Mail: gary.horlick@wilmerhale.com.

HORMATS, ROBERT DAVID, economist, investment banker; b. Balt., Apr. 13, 1943; s. Saul and Ruth H. BA, Tufts U., 1965, MA, 1966, MA in Law and Diplomacy, 1967, PhD, 1970. Research asst. Fletcher Sch. of Law and Diplomacy, 1968-69; research assoc. Univ. Coll., Dar-es-Salaam, Tanzania, 1967-68; staff mem. internat. econ. affairs Nat. Security Council, 1969-73, sr. staff mem., 1974-77; sr. dep. asst. sec. for econ. and bus. affairs Dept. State,

1977-79; ambassador and dep. U.S. trade rep., 1979-81; asst. sec. state for econ. and bus. affairs, 1981-82; v.p. Goldman, Sachs and Co., 1982, mng. dir., 1998—; vice chmn. Goldman Sachs (Internat.), 1987—. Guest scholar Brookings Instn., 1973-74; vis. lectr. Princeton U., 1983, 03; mem. internat. capital markets com. N.Y. Stock Exch.; bd. dirs. U.S. Russia Investment Fund, Engelhard Hanovia, Inc., Irvington Inst. Immunological Rsch.; mem. internat. adv. bd. Toyota Motor Corp Author: Making U.S. International Economic Policy, 1984, Reforming the International Monetary System, 1987, Am. Albatross: The Foreign Debt Dilemma, 1988, The Global Economy: America's Role in the Decade Ahead, 1989, International Business in the 21st Century, 1999, The Foreign Policy of the Internet, 2000, The Changing Spectrum in Asia, 2003, Abraham Lincoln and the Global Economy, 2003; mem. editorial bd. Fgn. Policy mag., Internat. Economy mag. Bd. overseers Tufts U.; bd. dirs. Coun. on Fgn. Rels.; mem. dean's adv. coun. John F. Kennedy Sch. of Govt., Harvard U.; mem. internat. adv. coun. Ecole dés Hautes Etudes Commercial, Montreal. Decorated Legion of Honor (France); Shell Oil Co. fellow, 1967-68; Council on Fgn. Relations fellow, 1973-74; Recipient Arthur Flemming award, 1978 Mem. Econ. Club of N.Y., Internat. Longevity Inst. (bd. dirs.). Home: 55 E End Ave Apt 8A New York NY 10028-7935 Office: Goldman Sachs & Co 85 Broad St New York NY 10004-2456 Office Phone: 212-902-5347. Personal E-mail: robert.hormats@gs.com.

HORN, ALAN F., film company executive; MBA with distinction, Harvard U. With Proctor & Gamble, Tandem Productions, T.A.T. Comms., Embassy Comms., 1973—86; pres., COO 20th Century Fox Film Corp., 1986—87; co-founder, chmn., CEO Castle Rock Entertainment, Beverly Hills, 1987—99; pres., COO Warner Bros. Entertainment, Burbank, Calif., 1999—. Bd. dirs. Univision Comm. Bd. dirs. Natural Resources Def. Coun.; vice chmn., bd. trustees Autry Mus. We. Heritage, L.A.; mem. bd. associates Harvard Bus. Sch.; founding mem., bd. dirs. Environ. Media Assn. Capt. USAF. Named one of 50 Most Powerful People in Hollywood, Premiere mag., 2004—05. Mem.: Hollywood Radio and TV Soc., Am. Film Inst., Acad. TV Arts and Scis., Acad. Motion Picture Arts and Scis. Office: Warner Bros 4000 Warner Blvd Burbank CA 91522-0002 Office Phone: 818-954-6000.*

HORN, CARL, III, federal judge; b. 1951; BA with honors, U. Va., 1973; JD, U. S.C., 1976. Bar: N.C. 1976. Assoc. Grier, Parker, Poe, Thompson, Bernstein, Gage & Preston, Charlotte, N.C., 1976-79; legal counsel, instr. Wheaton Coll., 1979-82; spl. asst. civil rights divsn. U.S. Dept. Justice, Charlotte, 1982-83, chief asst. U.S. atty. for western dist. N.C., 1987-93; ptnr. Horn & Conrad and predecessor, Charlotte, 1984-87; U.S. magistrate judge for western dist. N.C., U.S. Magistrate Ct., Charlotte, 1993—2003. Author: Fourth Circuit Criminal Handbook, 1994—, Horn's Federal Criminal Jury Instructions for the Fourth Circuit, 1997, LawyerLife: Finding a Life and a Higher Calling in the Practice of Law, 2003; editor: Michie's Fourth Circuit Criminal Reporter, 1995—; Federal Civil Practice in the Fourth Circuit, 1997, Law for Physicians, 1999, editor: The Battle for Morality in Pluralistic America, 1985; contbr. articles to law jours. Office: 401 W Trade St Ste 238 Charlotte NC 28202-1619 Office Phone: 704-350-7470.

HORN, CHARLES M., lawyer; b. Boston, Sept. 28, 1951; s. Garfield Henry and Alexandra (Matz) H.; m. Jane Charlotte Luxton, May 29, 1976; children: Andrew L., Caroline C. AB magna cum laude, Harvard Coll., 1973; JD, Cornell Law Sch., 1976. Bar: DC 1976, U.S. Dist. Ct. D.C. 1977, U.S. Ct. Appeals (D.C. cir.) 1977, U.S. Supreme Ct. 1980. Atty. U.S. Securities and Exchange Commn., Washington, 1976-82, br. chief divsn. enforcement, 1982-83; asst. dir. securities and corp. practices Office Comptroller of Currency, Washington, 1983-86, dir. securities and corp. practices, 1986-89; ptnr. Stroock & Stroock & Lavan, Washington, 1989-92, Mayer, Brown & Platt, Washington, 1992—2003, Mayer, Brown, Rowe & Maw LLP, Washington, 2003—. Mem. faculty Am. Bankers Assn. Nat. Grad. Compliance Sch., 1991-92, 94, Fed. Fin. Instns. Exam. Coun. (programs off-balance-sheet risk, Trust Exams. Sch.); bd. advisors U. NC Ctr. Banking & Finance, 2004-; lectr. in field. Edit. adv. bd. Bank Acctg. and Fin., 1993—; contbr. articles to profl. jours. Mem. ABA (banking law com., com. fed. regulation securities), D.C. Bar Assn., Washington Golf and Country Club. Home: 1918 Massachusetts Ave Mc Lean VA 22101-4907 Office: Mayer Brown Rowe & Maw LLP 1909 K St NW Washington DC 20006 Office Phone: 202-263-3219. Business E-Mail: chorn@mayerbrownrowe.com.

HORN, D. RALPH, corporate financial executive; BS, Miss. State; completed, Harvard Bus. Sch. Advanced Mgmt. Program. Mgmt. trainee, capital mkts. group First Tenn. Nat. Corp., 1963, exec. v.p., capital mkts. group, CEO, 1994—2002, chmn. of bd., 1996—. Office: First Tenn Nat Corp 165 Madison Ave Memphis TN 38103

HORN, DAVID C., lawyer; b. Cin., Jan. 4, 1952; BA, Yale U., 1974; JD, Vanderbilt U., 1977. Bar: Ohio 1977. Ptnr. Frost & Jacobs (now Frost Brown Todd), Cin.; asst. gen. counsel AK Steel Holdings Corp., Middletown, Ohio, 2000—01, v.p., gen. counsel, 2001—, sec., 2003—, head human resources, 2003—04. Mem.: Butler County Bar Assn., Ohio Bar Assn., Fed. Bar Assn., ABA, Order of the Coif. Office: AK Steel Holding Corp 703 Curtis St Middletown OH 45043

HORN, DONALD HERBERT, lawyer; b. Bronx, NY, Nov. 22, 1945; s. Herbert H. and Alice (Entwistle) H.; m. Marcia Thomas, Oct. 10, 1971. BA cum laude, Queens Coll., 1966; JD, Harvard U., 1969; postgrad. pub. exec., Carnegie-Mellon U., 1981. Bar: N.Y. 1970, D.C. 1975. Sr. trial atty. Bur. Operating Rights CAB, Washington, 1969-76, atty.-advisor Office Gen. Counsel, 1976-80, assoc. gen. counsel for pricing and entry, 1980-84; dep. asst. gen. counsel for internat. law U.S. Dept. Transp., Washington, 1985-88, asst. gen. counsel for internat. law, 1988—. Chmn. transp. Forest Hills Citizens Assn., Washington, 1983-97. Recipient Sec. Transp. Gold medal award Office Internat. Law, 1995, Sec. Transp. award, 1999, 2001, Williams Trophy, Washington Airports Task Force, 1999, Govt. Tech. Leadership award, 1999, Air-21 award FAA, 2000, Code Share Safety award Sec. Transp., 2000, DOT Bronze medal, 2000, award Sec. Transp., 2001. Mem. Fed. Bar Assn., Harvard U. Law Sch. Assn., Queens Coll. Alumni Assn., Phi Beta Kappa, Omicron Delta Epsilon. Office: US Dept Transp 400 7th St SW Washington DC 20590-0001

HORN, DONNA M., pharmacist, medical association administrator; BS in Pharmacy, Mass. Coll. Pharmacy and Allied Health Sci. Mgr. regulatory affairs Brooks Pharmacy, Warwick, RI, 2002—. Pres.-elect Nat. Assn. Bd. Pharmacy, 2003, pres., 2004—. Recipient Ruth Davies Flaherty Svc. award, Lambda Kappa Sigma, 1997, Alumni Achievement award, Mass. Coll. Pharmacy and Health Sci., 2003. Mem.: Boston Druggist Assn., Am. Pharmacists Assn., Mass. Pharmacists Assn. (Nathan Goldberg award 2003), Inst. Safe Medication Practices, Mass. Bd. Registration Pharmacy (bd. pres. 2003—04). Office: Regulatory Affairs Brooks Pharmacy 50 Svc Ave Warwick RI 02886 Office Phone: 401-825-3900.

HORN, HENRY EYSTER, retired minister; b. N.Y.C., May 30, 1913; s. William M. Horn and Marguerite Eyster Jacobs; m. Catherine Hedwig Stainken, June 9, 1939; children: Jean L., Henry S., David J., Charles M., William M., Marguerite E., Richard D., Eleanor A., Michael J., Andrew G. AB with honors, Cornell U., 1933; BD, MST, Luth. Sem., Phila., 1938; DD (hon.), Muhlenberg Coll., 1965; LLD (hon.), Valparaiso U., 1983. Ordained minister, 1936. Pastor Immanuel Luth. Ch., Phila., 1938-43; pres. Marion (Va.) Coll., 1943-49; pastor Luth. Ch. of the Resurrection, Augusta, Ga., 1949-53, Univ. Luth. Ch., Cambridge, Mass., 1953-78, pastor emeritus, 1978—. Lectr. Phila. Luth. Sem., 1981-84, Luther Sem., St. Paul, 1984-86; protestant chaplain Bryn Mawr (Pa.) Coll., 1980-81; chair ch. music com. United Luth. Ch., Phila., 1946-62, mem. bd. deaconess, 1948-62; mem. bd. theol. edn. Luth. Ch. in Am., N.Y.C., 1962-72, chair commn. on liturgy and hymnal, 1964-74. Author: O Sing Unto the Lord, 1956, 62, Christian in Modern Style, 1968, Worship in Crisis, 1972, Lutherans in Campus Ministry, 1972, Models of Ministry, 1989, Thoughts from the Fountainside, 1992. Organizer Friends of the Libr., Augusta, Ga., 1951; active Cambridge Camping Assn., 1950s, Cambridge Econ. Opportunity Com., Cambridge Family Svc. Bd., Cambridge Hosp. Bd., Cambridge Mental Health, Inc., Cambridge Cmty. Svcs., 1960-72; pres. Cambridge Mental Health Assn.; chair Cambridge Somerville Welfare Bd. Recipient Silver Beaver award Boy Scouts Am., Roanoke (Va.) Coun., 1948, Gold medal award for ret. clergymen Religious Heritage of Am., 1990, Christus Lux Mundi award Luther Sem., 2001. Mem. Boston Ministers' Club, Cambridge Club, United Ministry at Harvard (2-time pres.), Phi Beta Kappa Democrat. Avocations: nature, reading, compiling notebooks of quotations, family. Home: 47-1 Trowbridge St Cambridge MA 02138

HORN, HOWARD M., labor union administrator, consultant; b. Bklyn., July 31, 1938; s. Morris Norman and Yetta Horn; m. Carol Evelyn Solomon, Feb. 26, 1961 (dec.); m. Lois Bonnie Pfeffer, Nov. 10, 1997 (dec.); 1 stepchild, Ronald. Post grad. student, Harvard U., 1966. Exec. v.p. Amalgamated Meat Cutters N.Am. Local 627, N.Y.C., 1964—81, UFCW (United Food and Commerercial Workers) Local 50, N.Y.C., 1982—90, UFCW Local 342/50, Mineola, NY, 1991—97, cons., 1997—98. Columnist: On The Truck, 1964—90. Drug counselor N.Y. Ctrl. Labor Coun., Manhattan, 1979—89, referal com., 1975—89; county com. mem. Flushing Dem. Club, NY, 1988—. Pvt. first class U.S. Army, 1961—63. Avocations: phongraph records, history, travel.

HORN, JAMES KENNITH, librarian; b. Erin, Tenn., Oct. 30, 1949; s. James T. and Myrtle A. (Gafford) H.; m. Bonnie Sue Cude, Jan. 13, 1970 (div. 1978); 1 child, Jane Star; m. Sandra Sue Padgett, Mar. 29, 1985. BS in English and Philosophy, Austin Peay State U., 1971; MLS, U. Tenn., 1974, postgrad., 1987—. Cert. librarian, tchr., Tenn. Dir. library service Oak Ridge (Tenn.) Pub. Schs., 1974-76; agt. John Hancock Mt. Ins. Co., Knoxville, Tenn., 1976-78; tchr., librarian Grainger County Schs., Rutledge, Tenn., 1978-80; instr. State Tech. Inst. at Knoxville, 1980; librarian Knoxville City Schs., 1980-87, Knox County Schs., Knoxville, 1982—. Mem. ALA, Am. Assn. Sch. Librarians. Democrat. Avocations: sailing, running. Office: West High Sch 3300 Sutherland Ave Knoxville TN 37919-4544

HORN, JOHN LEONARD, psychology educator, test developer; b. St. Joseph, Mo., Sept. 7, 1928; s. John Leonard and Nellie Rae (Weldon) H.; m. Bonnie Colleen Hoskins (div. May, 1989); children: John Leonard, James Bryan, Julia Lynn, Jennifer Lee.; m. Penelope Keith Trickett, May 28, 1989; stepchildren: Jennifer, Katechen. BA, U. Denver, 1956; postgrad. studies, U. Melbourne, Australia, 1956-58; MA, U. Ill., 1963, PhD, 1965. Asst. prof. U. Denver, 1963-65, assoc. prof., 1965-69, prof., 1969-86; prof., head adult devel. and aging U. So. Calif., L.A., 1986—. Vis. fellow U. Wis., Madison, 1965; vis. prof. U. Calif., Berkeley, 1967-68; rsch. assoc. U. Ill., Urbana, 1964, U. London, Eng., 1972-73, U. Lund, Sweden, 1982; pres. Multivariate Measurement Consultants, Denver, 1969—. Contbr. over 200 articles to profl. jours.; mem. editl. bd. Am. Edn. Rsch. Jour., Am. Psychologist, Applied Pshychol. Measurement, Can. Jour. Behavioral Scis., Developmental Psychology, Internat. Jour. Aging and Human Devel., Jour. Consulting and Clin. Psychology, Jour. Ednl. Measurement, Jour Geontology, Multivariate Behavioral Rsch., Psychol. Bull., Pschometrika, Rsch. on Aging; spkR. at Symposiums, sci. confs., convs. V.p., pres. U. Ill. chpt. NAACP, 1958-59; counselor, mem. bd. trustees East Side Devel. Ctr., Denver, 1967-70; vol. counselor for methadone maintenance and treatment of drug abuse, Five Points Ctr., Denver, 1968-69; mem. Denver City Task Force on Alchoholism, 1973, U. Denver Task Force on Drug Abuse, 1984. With U.S. Army, 1953-56, Korea. Recipient Fulbright fellowship, U. Melbourne, Australia, 1956, Knapp fellowship, U. Wis., 1956 (not accepted); predoctoral rsch. fellowship NIH, 1958-61, predoctoral rsch. fellowship NSF, 1958 (not accepted); U.S. Office Edn. fellowship, 1965, Rsch. Career Devel. award, NIH, 1968-72. Fellow AAAS, Soc. Multivariate Exptl. Psychology (pres. 1976, Ann. prize for disting. publs.,1973, Lifetime Achievement award 1992), Phi Beta Kappa (pres. Gamma of Colo. 1970, triennial rep. 1971, Phi Kappa Phi; grantee: Nat. Inst. Aging, 1989-95, 1991-98; (with P.K. Trickett) Nat. Ctr. for Childhood Abuse and Neglect, 1992-97, Nat. Inst. Mental Health, 1993-98. Home: 3 Plumtree Rd Rncho Pls Vrd CA 90275-5911 Office: U So Calif Psychol Dept Univ Park Campus Los Angeles CA 90089-1060 Office Phone: 213-740-2276. Business E-Mail: jhorn@usc.edu.

HORN, JOYCE ELAINE, music educator; d. Alfred Irving Sette and Elma Louise Robertson; 1 child, Camilla Jeanne VandenBerg. MusB, Grand Rapids Bapt. Coll.; MusM, We. Mich. U, 1972. Assoc. prof. music Cornerstone U, Grand Rapids, Mich., 1962—. Republican. Baptist. Avocations: reading, studying Charles Dickens, music. Home: 7355 Casade Terrace Dr SE Grand Rapids MI 49546 E-mail: jhorn218@aol.com.

HORN, LEE SHAWN, sports analyst; b. Miami, Fla., Feb. 21, 1977; s. Andrew Warren and Melinda F. (Fink) H. Grad. h.s., Miami. Ind. filmmaker, Miami, 1993—; newsroom worker ABC, Miami, 1996; pres. Sports Ltd. Edits. & Memorabilia, 1996—; v.p. Fla. Internat. U., 1999; asst. head football coach St. John Neumann, 2003—. Asst. head coach football team Gulliver Prep., 1997-03; asst. dir. Super Bowl halftime show, 1999; South Fla. dir. Nat. Football Found., Coll. Football Hall of Fame, 2001—. Vol. Atlanta Com. Olympic Games, 1996; chmn. Ted Hendricks Def. End of Yr. award Mem. U. Miami Diamond Darlings, Miami Touchdown Club (bd. dirs.). Democrat. Avocations: football, skiing, fishing, travel. Office Phone: 239-287-5044.

HORN, MARIAN BLANK, federal judge; b. N.Y.C., June 24, 1943; d. Werner P. and Mady R. Blank; m. Robert Jack Horn; 3 children. AB, Barnard Coll., 1962; student, Columbia U., 1965, NYU, 1965-66; JD, Fordham U., 1969. Bar: N.Y. 1970, D.C. 1973, U.S. Supreme Ct. 1973. Asst. dist. atty. Bronx County, N.Y., 1969-72; assoc. Arent, Fox, Kintner, Plotkin & Kahn, 1972-73; project mgr. Am. U. Law Sch. study on alts. to conventional criminal adjudication U.S. Dept. Justice, 1973-75; litigation atty. Fed. Energy Adminstrn., 1975-76; sr. atty. office gen. counsel strategic petroleum res. br. US Dept. Energy, 1976-79, dep. asst. gen. counsel for procurement and fin. incentives, 1979-81; dep. assoc. solicitor div. surface mining US Dept. Interior, 1981-83, assoc. solicitor div. gen. law, 1983-85, prin. dep. solicitor, acting solicitor, 1985-86; judge U.S. Ct. of Federal Claims, 1986—. Adj. prof. law Washington Coll. Law, Am. U., 1973-76, George Washington U. Sch. Law, 1992—. Office: US Ct Fed Claims 717 Madison Pl NW Washington DC 20439-0002*

HORN, PAUL M., information technology executive, crystallographer; b. NYC, Aug. 16, 1946; s. Selig S. and Agnus (Attie) H.; m. Judith Herrick; children: Lisa, Sara. BS, Clarkson Coll. Tech., 1968; PhD, U. Rochester, 1973. Prof., dept. physicis and James Frachk Inst. U. Chgo., 1973-79; mem. rsch. staff T.J. Watson Rsch. Ctr. IBM Corp., Yorktown Heights, 1979, acting dir. phys. scis. dept. T.J. Watson Rsch. Ctr., 1987, dir. phys. scis. dept. T.J. Watson Rsch. Ctr., 1988—90, dir., silicon tech., IBM rsch div., 1990—94, v.p., storage, IBM rsch. div., 1994—96, sr. v.p., dir. rsch., 1996—; dir., advanced semiconductor tech. lab. IBM Semiconductor Rsch. & Devel. Ctr., 1990—94; dir. Almaden Rsch. Ctr., San Jose, Calif., 1994—96. Former assoc. editor Physical Review Letters, published over 85 sci. and tech. papers. Bd. dir. NY Hall of Sci.; mem. Coun. on Competitiveness (Washington based), Gov. U. Industry Rsch. Roundtable; bd. trustee UC Berkeley Indsl. Adv. Bd. NSF fellow; Alfred P. Sloan Rsch. fellow, 1974-78; recipient Bertram Eugene award Am. Crystallographic Assn., 1988, Disting. Leadership award, NY Hall of Sciences, 2000, Hutchinson medal, U. Rochester, 2002, Pake prize, Amer. Physical Soc., 2002. Fellow Am. Phys. Soc. (planning com.); mem. Advanced Photon Source Users Orgn. of Argonne Nat. Labs. (chmn. exec. com.). Office: IBM Corp 1133 Westchester Ave White Plains NY 10604 E-mail: phorn@us.ibm.com.

HORN, ROBERT NELSON, artist, educator; b. Alton, Ill. s. Nelson Mansfield and Marie Kopsie Horn. BA, So. Ill. Univ., Carbondale, Ill., 1969. Painter self employed, Chgo., 1969—2004; tchr. Reanis H.S., Burbank, Ill., 1969—73; artist in residence Wells St. Studios, Chgo., 1977—2004; instr. Lillstreet Art Ctrs., Chgo., 1999—2004, Evanston Art Ctr., Evanston, Ill., 2000—04, Art Inst. of Chgo.; artist in residence Allihies Art Ctr., Allihies, Ireland, 1994—2005. Assoc. dir NAB Gallery, Chgo., 1974—2005. Recipient Palmer Prize, Art Inst. Chgo., 1989; grantee CAAP Grants, City of Chgo., 1986—90, S.T.A.R. Grant, Ill. Art Coun., 1983. Achievements include chief restorer and head of restoration of archl. detail of artists Edgar Miller and Sol Kogan, founders of Chgo. old town.

HORN, RONI, artist; b. NYC, 1955; BFA, RI Sch. Design, 1975; MFA, Yale U., 1978. One-woman shows include Clocktower, Inst. Art & Urban Resources, NY, 1980, Glyptothek Mus., Munich, 1983, Galerie Heinz Herzer, Munich, 1983, Burnett Miller Gallery, LA, 1985, Neuberger Mus., SUNY, 1986, Galerie Maeght Lelong, NY, 1987, Unique Forms of Deviation in Space, Mario Diacono Gallery, Boston, 1988, Paula Cooper Gallery, NY, 1989, Surface Matters, Mus. Contemporary Art, LA, 1990, Mary Boone Gallery, NY, 1991, Jablonka Galerie, Cologne, 1992, 1993, Four Watercolors, Matthew Marks Gallery, NY, 1993, Inner Geography, Balt. Mus. Art, Md., 1994, Gurgles, Sucks, Echoes, Matthew Marks Gallery, NY, 1995, Earths Grow Thick, Wexner Ctr. Arts. Columbus, 1996, You Are the Weather, Fotomuseum Winterthur, Switzerland, 1997, Patrick Painter Gallery, LA, 1998, Pi, Matthew Marks Gallery, NY, 1999, Still Water (The River Thames, for Example), Whitney Mus. Am. Art, NY, 2000, Blah, blah, hair, Blah, blah, your eyes; Blah, blah care, Blah, blah skies, Dia Ctr. Arts, NY, 2001, Clowndoubt, Matthew Marks Gallery, NY, 2002, Galerie Xavier Hufkens, Brussels, 2003, Some Thames, Art Inst. Chgo., 2004, exhibited in group shows, Corning Mus. Glass, NY, 1976, Material Object, Hayden Gallery, MIT, Cambridge, Mass., 1980, Barbara Braatten Gallery, NY, 1984, Lorence-Monk Gallery, NY, 1985, Chris Middendorf Gallery, Washington DC, 1986, Lead, Hirschl & Adler Modern, NY, 1987, Inscribed Image, Lang-O'Hara Gallery, NY, 1988, Non-representation, Anne Plumb Gallery, NY, 1989, Sculptors' Drawings, Balt. Mus. Art, 1990, Whitney Biennial, Whitney Mus. Am. Art, 1991, 2004, Drawn in teh '90s, Ind. Curators Inc., NY, 1992, Drawing the Line Against AIDS, Peggy Guggenheim Collection, Venice, 1993, Photography, Margo Leavin Gallery, LA, 1994, Works on Paper, Matthew Marks Gallery, NY, 1995, Thinking Print: Books to Billboards, 1980-1995, Mus. Modern Art, NY, 1996, Sleight of Mind/Angle of Landscape, Ctr. Curatorial Studies Mus., Bard Coll., NY, 1997, Maverick, Matthew Marks Gallery, NY, 1998, 00, Barbara Gladstone Gallery, NY, 2000, Tenth Anniversary Exhbn., 100 Drawings & Photographs, Matthew Marks Gallery, NY, 2001, Some Chromes, Fogg Art Mus., Harvard U., 2002, Exhbns. of an Exhbn., Casey Kaplan Gallery, NY, 2003, I am the Walrus, Cheim & Read, NY, 2004, Fresh Works on Paper, 5th Anniversary Exhbn., James Kelly Contemporary, Sante Fe, NM, 2004. Recipient Awards Visual Arts, AVA 7, 1988, Moonhole Artists Assn., Bequia, 1996, Alpert Award Arts, 1998; Ford Found. Grant, 1978, Alice Kimball Traveling Fellowship, Yale U., 1978, Humanities Development Grant, Colgate U., 1983, Artist's Fellowship, Nat. Endowment Art, 1984, 1986, 1990, Guggenheim Fellowship, 1990. Mailing: c/o Mattthew Marks Gallery 523 West 24th St New York NY 10011*

HORN, RUSSELL EUGENE, engineering executive, consultant; b. Yoe, Pa., May 4, 1912; s. Eugene M. and Charlotte (Snyder) H.; m. Eleanor B. Baird, Jan. 12, 1934; children: Russell Eugene, Ralph Elliot, Rosalind Emily (Mrs. Lee Kunkel), Robert Errol. BS, Pa. State U., 1933. Foreman Pa. Dept. Hwys. dist. office, York, Pa., 1933-35; draftsman, supr., designer C.S. Buchart, architect, 1935-41; exec. v.p., chief engr. Buchart Engring., 1945-59, pres., chief engr., 1959-61, Buchart-Horn, Inc., 1961-72, chmn. bd. dirs., 1972-2000. Pres. PACE Resources, inc., 1970-87, chmn. bd. dirs. 1970-2001, bd. dirs.; chmn. AAA White Rose Motor Club, 1975-78. Bd. dirs. Auto Club So. Pa.; bd. dirs. emeritus Retirement Homes of Meth. Ch., 1978—. Col. AUS, 1940-45. Mem. NSPE, Soc. Am. Mil. Engrs., Pa. Soc. Profl. Engrs. (pres. Lincoln chpt. 1961), Pa. Assn. Cons. Engrs. (pres. 1965, bd. dirs. 1966), Pa. Hwy Info. Assn. (bd. dirs.), Am. Soc. Hwy. Engrs. (nat. pres. 1962), Tech. Socs. Coun. Southeastern Pa. (chmn. 1963), Engring. Soc. York, Profl. Engrs. Pvt. Practice, Am. Concrete Inst., Assn. Pa. Constructors Assn. Hwy Ofcls. N. Atlantic States, Assn. U.S. Army Res. Officers Assn., ASCE, VFW, Cons. Engrs. Coun., Am. Legion, Pa. State U. Alumni Club (York County), Univ. Club, Lake Club, Exch. Club (Golden Deeds award 1979), Mt. Nittany Soc. Pa. State U., Masons (32 deg., Order of the Double Eagle award 1983, Legion of Freedom award 1986, outstanding engring. alumnus 1987), York County Agrl. Soc. (life), Moose Home: 1270 Brockie Dr York PA 17403-4448 Office: Pace Resources Inc 40 S Richland Ave York PA 17404-3470

HORN, RUSSELL EUGENE, JR., printing company executive; b. York, Pa., Sept. 15, 1934; s. Russell Eugene and A. Eleanor (Baird) Horn; m. Franziska Kathe Kastner (dec. 1995); children: Silvia S., Russell E. III, Monika K., Ursula F., John D.; m. Lilli Maria Funk, 2002. Sgt. lst class U.S. Army Security Agy., 1952-62; sales trainee, sales rep. Print-O-Stat, Inc., York, Pa., 1962-63, mgr., 1970-73, exec. v.p., 1976-77, pres., 1977-96, mr. Towson, Md., 1963-70, v.p. Md., Del., 1973-76; office of pres. PACE Resources, Inc., York, 1987-96, pres., CEO, 1996—2001, chmn., pres., CEO, 2001—. Bd. dirs. Buchart-Horn, Inc., others; mem. adv. bd. Dauphin Deposit Bank-York Region, 1984-98; also officer, advisor, exec. various corps. Bd. dirs. York County chpt. ARC, 2004; active various ednl., charitable activities. Mem. York Area C. of C. Home: 995 Detwiler Dr York PA 17404 Office: PACE Resources Inc 40 S Richland Ave York PA 17404-3470 Personal E-mail: pace40@aol.com.

HORN, SHARON K., government agency administrator; B in Bus. and Econs., U. Ga.; EdM, Tex. A&M U.; PhD in Higher Edn. and Curriculum, U. Tex. Legis. fellow labor and human resources com. US Senate; secondary sch. tchr. of bus., econs. and polit. sci. Tex.; tchr. U. Tex., Tyler, S.W. Tex. State U.; assoc. dir. Program on Ednl. Policy and Orgn. Nat. Inst. Edn., 1982; dir. info. svcs. Office Ednl. Rsch. and Improvement US Dept. Edn., Washington, program officer, dir. Nat. Awards Program for Model Profl. Devel., dir. evaluation and dissemination Office Innovation and Improvement. Office: US Dept Edn FOB-6 Rm 4W332 400 Maryland Ave SW Washington DC 20202*

HORN, SHIRLEY, vocalist, musician; b. Washington, 1934; 1 child, Rainy. Student, Howard U. Albums include Cat on a Hot Fiddle, 1959, Embers And Ashes, 1960, Live at the Village Vanguard, 1961, Loads of Love, 1963, Shirley Horn with Horns, 1963, Travelin' Light, 1965, For Love of Ivy, 1968, A Dandy in Aspic, 1968, Where Are You Going?, 1972, A Lazy Afternoon, 1979, All Night Long, 1982, Violets For Your Ears, 1983, The Sentimental Touch (titled Songbirds in U.S.), 1985, I Thought About You, 1987, Softly, 1988, Close Enough for Love, 1988, Tune in Tomorrow, 1990, You Won't Forget Me, 1991, Dedicated to You-Tribute to Sarah Vaughan with Carmen McRae, 1991, Here's to Life, 1992 (Grammy nomination, Best Jazz Vocal for "Light Out of Darkness", 1994), Violets for Furs, 1994, I Love You Paris, 1994, All Night Long, 1994, (with Charles Ables, Billy Hart) At Northsea, 1996, Jazz Round Midnight, 1998 (Grammy); I Remember Miles, 1998 (Grammy for Best Jazz Vocal Performance); Garden of the Blues, 1998; Violets for Your Eyes, 1998; All Night Long, 1998; Loads of Love, 1998; Ultimate Shirley Horn, 1999; Quiet Now: Come a Little Closer, 1999; You're My Thrill, 2001; May the Music Never End, 2003 (Nat. Endowment for Arts Jazz Master's award 2005). Office: Verve Records 1755 Broadway Fl 3D New York NY 10019-3743 also: Sheila Mathis Enterprises 1007 Tame Ln Charlottesville VA 22901 Office Phone: 434-973-0200. E-mail: sheila@shemetjazz.com.

HORN, STEPHEN, retired congressman, political scientist; b. San Juan Bautista, Calif., May 31, 1931; s. John Stephen and Isabelle (McCaffrey) H.; m. Nini Moore, Sept. 4, 1954; children: Marcia Karen, John Stephen. AB with great distinction, Stanford, 1953, postgrad., 1953-54, 55-56, PhD in Polit. Sci, 1958; M in Pub Adminstrn., Harvard, 1955. Congl. fellow, 1958-59; adminstrv. asst. to sec. labor James P. Mitchell Washington, 1959-60; legislative asst. to U.S. Senator Thomas H. Kuchel, 1960-66; sr. fellow The Brookings Instn., 1966-69; dean grad. studies and research Am. U., 1969-70; pres. Calif. State U., Long Beach, 1970-88, Trustee prof. polit. sci., 1988-93; mem. U.S. Congress from 38th Calif. dist., 1993—2003; mem. govt. reform com., transp. and infrastructure com. Sr. cons., host The Govt. Story on TV, The Election Game (radio series), 1967-69, vice chmn. U.S. Commn. on Civil Rights, 1969-80 (commr. 1980-82); chmn. Urban Studies Fellow Adv. Com., U.S. Dept. HUD, 1969-70; mem. Law Enforcement Ednl. Prog. Adv. Com., U.S. Dept Justice, 1969-70; adv. bd. Nat. Inst. Corrections, 1972-88 (chmn. 1984-87), Author: The Cabinet and Congress, 1960, Unused Power: The Work of the Senate Committee on Appropriations, 1970, (with Edmund Beard) Congressional Ethics: The View from the House, 1975. Active Pres.-elect Nixon's Task Force on Orgn. Exec. Br., 1968, Kutak Found.; vice chmn. Long Beach Area C. of C., 1984-88; co-founder Western U.S. Com. Arts and Scis. for Eisenhower, 1956; chmn. Am. Assn. State Colls. and Univs., 1985-86; mem. Calif. Ednl. Facilities Authority, 1984-93. USAR, 1954-62. Fellow John F. Kennedy Inst. Politics Harvard U., 1966-67. Fellow Nat. Acad. Pub. Adminstrn.; mem. Stanford Assocs., Stanford Alumni Assn. (pres. 1976-77), Phi Beta Kappa, Pi Sigma Alpha. Republican.*

HORN, THOMAS JOSEPH, JR., secondary school educator; b. Albany, Jan. 6, 1953; s. Thomas Joseph and Antoinette (Bologna) H.; m. Dawn Marie Kerr, June 28, 1980 (div. Jan. 1983); children: Thomas Matthew; m. Elizabeth Lynn Chase, Aug. 31, 1993; 1 stepchild, Stephanie Blair. BA, SUNY, 1975, MS, 1982. Clerical, computer FBI, Albany, 1976-83; tchr. computers Mohonasen High Sch., Schenectady, N.Y., 1983-85; coord. computers Fort Edward (N.Y.) Pub. Schs., 1985—. Author: Windows and Nine Applications Made Easy, 1994. Tchr. Sacred Heart Ch., Troy, N.Y., 1985—, Ch. of Immaculate Conception, Schenectady, 1996—. Regents scholar, 1971. Roman Catholic. Avocations: running, computers, music. Home: 23 Blue Barns Rd Rexford NY 12148-1114 Office: Fort Edward Pub Schs 220 Broadway Fort Edward NY 12828-1520

HORN, WADE FREDERICK, federal agency administrator; b. Coral Gables, Fla., Dec. 3, 1954; s. John David and Daisy (Anderson) H.; m. Claudia Blair, Jan. 7, 1977; children: Christiana Watson, Caroline Lindley. BA in Psychology, Am. U., 1975; MA in Clin. Child Psychology, So. Ill. U., 1978, PhD in Clin. Child Psychology, 1981. Rsch. asst. social skills devel. program Carbondale (Ill.) Elem. Schs., 1976-78; behavior analyst, psychol. cons. early childhood program Wabash and Ohio Valley Spl. Edn. Dist., Norris City, Ill., 1978-79; predoctoral intern dept. pediatric psychology Children's Hosp. Nat. Med. Ctr., Washington, 1980-81, postdoctoral clin. psychology fellow behavioral medicine rsch. lab., 1981-82; asst. prof. dept. psychology Mich. State U., East Lansing, 1982-86; vice chairperson dept. pediatric psychology, dir. outpatient psychol. svcs. dept. psychiatry Children's Hosp. Nat. Med. Ctr., Washington, 1987-88; dir. Pediatric Psychology Splty. Clinic, assoc. dir. Psychol. Clinic Mich. State U., East Lansing, 1984-86; attending staff child health care unit St. Lawrence Hosp., Lansing, Mich., 1983-84; assoc. prof. psychiatry, behavioral scis. and child health and devel. Sch. Medicine, George Washington U., 1986-89; mem. presdl. transition team Office of Pres. Elect, Washington, 1988-89; commr. Adminstrn. on Children, Youth and Families, 1989—93; chief Children's Bur., Washington, 1989—93; asst. sec. children & families US Dept HHS, Washington, 2001—. Adj. faculty dept. pediatrics Coll. Human Medicine, Mich. State U., East Lansing, 1983-86, Pub. Policy Ibst., Georgetown U., 1993-2001; mem. Nat. Commn. Childhood Disability, 1994-95; mem. U.S. Adv. Bd. on Welfare Educators, 1996-97. Author: (with G. Greenberg) Attention Deficit Disorder: Questions and Answers for Parents, 1991; contbr. articles to profl. jours. Mem. Health Care Adv. Group for George Bush for Pres. campaign, 1987-88. Mem. Am. Psychol. Assn. (divs. clin. psychology and child clin. psychology), Assn. for Advancement Behavior Therapy, Phi Kappa Phi. Republican. Presbyterian. Office: Dept HHS Admin for Children and Families 370 L'Enfant Promenade SW Washington DC 20447

HORNADAY, RICHARD H., artist, retired art educator; b. Joplin, Mo., Aug. 15, 1927; s. Beecher Hoyt and Zora Hornaday; m. Margaret Ann Gardner, June 29, 1950 (div. Mar. 1972); m. Ruth Mary Miller, Nov. 26, 1972 (dec. Feb. 2002); 1 child, Emily Jane; m. Jenifer Shevis-Packard, Sept. 28, 2002. BFA, U. Iowa, 1950, MFA, 1952; student, Calif. State U., Chico. Cert. art tchr. elem. and secondary schs., Calif. Art instr. Auburn (Calif.) H.S., 1953-54; art supr. elem. sch. dist., Redding, Calif., 1954-67; instr. drawing and painting Shasta Coll., Redding, 1954-68; prof. grad. studies Calif. State U., Chico, 1968-88, chair dept. art, 1972-80, prof. emeritus, 1988—. Judge No. Calif. Art Assn., Crocker Art Mus., Sacramento, 1959. Exhibited works in solo shows at Ruthermore Gallery, San Francisco, 1959-62, Nordness Gallery, N.Y.C., 1962, Henderson Gallery, Monterey, Calif., 1963, Retrospective exhibit Redding (Calif.) Art Mus., 1983, Rosicrucian Mus., San Jose, Calif., 1985, Himovitz Pavillions Gallery, Sacramento, 1992, Watercolor Gallery, Berkeley, Calif., 1985, Vagabond Rose Gallery, Chico, Calif., 1995—; group shows include Mus. Modern Art, N.Y.C., 1962, St. Louis Art Mus., 1963, San Francisco Mus. Art, 1963, 50-Yr. Crocker-Kingsley Retrospective, Sacramento, 1985, Nat. Watercolor Okla., 1994, Nat. Watercolor Exhbn., Concord, Calif., 1996, Visual Arts Ctr. N.E. Fla., Panama City, 1996, Ariz. Aqueous XI Nat., Tubac, 1997, Ga. XVIII Nat. Watercolor Exhbn., Macon, 1997, Taos Nat. Exhbn. Am. Watercolor III, 1997, Gt. Plains Nat., Ft. Hayes, Kans., 1998, Watercolor USA, Springfield, Mo., 1998; works in collections at Shasta Coll., Calif. State U., Chico, Iowa State U., others; subject of articles. Mem. Civic Arts Commn., Redding, 1963-78; art cons. Shasta County Supt. Schs., 1964-67, Creative Arts Ctr., Chico, 1974-75, others. Served with USN, 1945-46, PTO. Recipient awards for art. Home: PO Box 7652 Chico CA 95927-7652

HORNAK, ANNA FRANCES, library administrator; b. College Station, Tex., June 3, 1922; d. Josef and Anna (Drozd) Hornak. BA, U. Tex., Austin, 1944; B.L.S., U. Ill., Champaign-Urbana, 1945; Ed.M., U. Houston, 1956. Children's librarian Schenectady Pub. Library, N.Y., 1945-47; children's librarian Pasadena Pub. Library, Calif., 1947-49; supr. Juvenile Div. Houston Pub. Library, 1949-57, asst. dir., 1957-89, ret., 1989. Named Outstanding Woman, YWCA of Houston, 1977; Outstanding Houston Profl. Woman, Fed. Houston Profl. Women, 1982 Avocations: collecting miniature books, collecting Bohemian red glass, restoring antique furniture. Home: 2217 Woodhead St Houston TX 77019-6820

HORNAK, THOMAS, retired electronics company executive; b. Bratislava, Slovakia, Oct. 14, 1924; came to U.S., 1968; s. Stefan and Elisabeth (Meer) H.; m. Vera Lautner, Mar. 15, 1958; 1 child, Thomas MSEE, Tech U., Bratislava, 1947; PhD in Elec. Engring., Tech U., Prague, Czech Republic, 1966. Sect. mgr. Tesla Radio Research Lab., Prague, 1947-61; sci. advisor Computer Research Inst., Prague, 1962-68; mem. tech. staff Hewlett Packard Labs., Palo Alto, Calif., 1968-73, mgr. research dept., 1973-91, prin. engr., 1991-99, ret., 1999. Contbr. articles to profl. jours. Patentee in field Fellow IEEE (life; assoc. editor Jour. Solid State Cirs. 1986-88, 2001—04, chmn. solid state cirs. and tech. com. 1979-81).

HORNBACH, DANIEL J., academic administrator, biologist, educator; BS in Biology magna cum laude, U. Dayton, 1974, MS in Biology, 1976; PhD in Zoology, Miami U., Ohio, 1980. Asst. prof. dept. biology U. Va., Va., 1980—84, Macalester Coll., St. Paul, 1984—87, assoc. prof. dept. biology, 1987—93, prof. dept. biology, 1993—97, DeWitt Wallace prof. dept. biology, 1998—, chair dept. biology, 1996—99, provost, 1993—95, 1999, provost, dean, 1999—. Mem. faculty Mountain Lake Biol. Sta. U. Va., 1981, 82, 84; team mem. Higginsi Eye Pearly Mussel Endangered Species Recover Team U.S. Fish and Wildlife Svc., 1995—; adj. prof. grad. faculty divsn. water quality dept. fisheries and wildlife U. Minn., 1996—. Assoc. editor: Am. Midland Naturalist, 1995—2001. Recipient Alumni Spl. Achievement award, U. Dayton, 1994; grantee, NSF, 1987, 1988, U.S. Army Corps of Engrs., 1987—90, 1996, Pew Charitable Trusts, 1990, Blandin Found., 1990—91, Minn. Dept. Natural Resources, 1990—91, 1992—93, US EPA, 1991, 1992—96, Wis. Dept. Natural Resources, 1992, 1997—98, U.S. Nat. Pk. Svc., 1993—96, 1997, 1998, 2000—02, 2001—04, 2004—, U.S. Fish and Wildlife Svc., 1994—95, Legis. Commn. on Minn. Resources, 1997—98, 1999—2001. Mem.: N.Am. Benthological Soc., Malacological Soc. London (Sir Charles Maurice Yonge award 2002), Coun. on Undergrad. Rsch., Am. Malacological Union. Office: Macalester College 1600 Grand Ave Saint Paul MN 55105

HORNBACH, MATTHEW JOHN, geophysicist, consultant; b. Cuttyhunk, Mass., July 5, 1975; s. John William and Nancy Lena Hornbach; m. Laura Catherine Schoellkopf, Oct. 29, 2005. BA in Physics, Hamilton Coll., 1998; PhD in Geophysics, U. Wyo., 2004. Intern Conoco Oil Co., Midland, Tex., 2002; rsch. asst. U. Wyo., Laramie, Wyo., 1999—2004; rsch. fellow Inst. for Geophysics U. Tex., Austin, Tex., 2004—. Prin., owner Ground-Truth Geophys., Laramie, 2003—04. Contbr. articles to profl. jours. Scholar, Hamilton Coll., 1994—98; Elihu Root fellowship, 1998. Mem.: Soc. Exploration Geophysicists (assoc.), Am. Geophys. Union (assoc.), Sigma Xi, Phi Beta Kappa. Achievements include invention of a portable multi-channel seismic recording system.

HORNBACK, JOSEPH HOPE, mathematics professor; b. Nevada, Mo., Apr. 20, 1910; s. Joseph Thomas and Geordia (Munn) H. AB, Central Coll., 1932; MA, Harvard, 1933; PhD, U. Ill., 1952; postgrad., U. Chgo., 1933-34, 41-42, 46-49. Tchr. math. Calumet City (Ill.) High Sch., 1934-37, U. Chgo. Lab Sch., 1937-42; asst. prof. math. U. Ala., 1952-57, asso. prof., 1957-63, prof., 1963-80, prof. emeritus, 1980—. Vis. scientist to high schs. for Ala. Acad. Sci. Chmn. gen. bd. 1st Christian Ch., Tuscaloosa, Ala., 1974-76; mem. world outreach com. Christian Chs. of Ala., 1973-75. Served as lt. USNR, 1942-46. Mem. Am. Math. Soc., Math. Assn. Am., Masons, Sigma Xi, Phi Kappa Phi.

HORNBECK, CARRIE L., photographer; BFA, Bard Coll., 1993; MFA, Ind. U., 2000. Assoc. instr. photography Ind. U., Bloomington, 1998—2000; adj. instr. photography Nassau C.C. (SUNY), Garden City, NY, 2004—. Exhibitions include September 11 Photo Project Commemorative Exhibition, New York Public Library (permanent collection), Here is New York, 116 Prince Street, New York, Snapshot, Contemporary Museum, Baltimore, Explicit, Part Two, Kougeas Gallery, Boston, The Passion, Richard Anderson Fine Arts, New York, online exhibition, International Young Art with Art Link, Sothebys.com; photographer (publication (magazine spread) Time Out New York, writer (publication) Public Strategies: Public Art and Public Space, American Photography Institute National Graduate Seminar Proceedings, photographer (exhibition; juror: Ellen Handy) Houston Center for Photography Membership Exhibition, Houston, (exhibition: juror: Debra Wilber) LaGrange National Biennial, Lamar Dodd Art Center, LaGrange GA (Merit award, 2000), (publication; juror: Melissa Harris) The Photo Review, 18th Annual Photography Competition, Langhorne, PA. Fellow, Am. Photography Inst. Grad. Seminar in Photography, NYU, 1998; McIntyre Recruitment fellow, Ind. U., Bloomington, Ind., 1997, Della Fricke Art Tchg. scholar, 1999. Personal E-mail: chornbec@hotmail.com.

HORNBEIN, THOMAS FREDERIC, anesthesiologist; b. St. Louis, Nov. 6, 1930; s. Leonard and Rosalie (Bernstein) Hornbein; m. Gene Schwartz (div. 1968); children: Lia, Lynn, Cari, Andrea, Robert; m. Kathryn Mikesell, Dec. 24, 1971; 1 child, Melissa. BA, U. Colo.; MD, Wash. U. Diplomate Am. Bd. Anesthesiology. Intern King County Hosp., Seattle; resident in anesthesiology Wash. U., St. Louis, USPHS postdoctoral residency, instr. anesthesiology div., 1960—61; asst. prof. U. Wash., Seattle, 1963—67, assoc. prof., 1967—70, prof. anesthesiology, physiology and biophysics, 1970—2002, prof. emeritus, 2002—. Vice chmn. dept. anesthesiology U. Wash., Seattle, 1972—74, asst. chmn. rsch., 1974—77, chmn., 1979—93, rsch. affiliate Primate Ctr., 1980; bd. dirs. Colo. Ctr. for Alternative Medicine and Physiology, 2003—. Author: Everest the West Ridge, 1966 (rated #1 Outside Mag., 2003). Mem. bd. trustees Little Sch., Bellevue, Wash., 1982—89; bd. dirs. Colorado Ctr. Alt. Medicine and Physiology, 2003. Served to lt. comdr. USN, 1961—63. Recipient George Norlin award, U. Colo., Denver, 1970, Alumni Centennial Symposium award, 1975, Disting. Tchg. award, U. Wash., 1982. Fellow: AAAS; mem.: Inst. of Medicine, Soc. Acad. Anesthesia Chmn., Assn. Univ. Anesthetists (treas. 1969—72, pres. 1974—75), Am. Soc. Anesthesiologists (Rovenstine lectr. 1989), Am. Physiol. Soc. (editor 1967—73), Alpha Omega Alpha, Phi Beta Kappa. Avocation: mountain climbing. Office: U Wash Sch Medicine Dept Anesthesiology PO Box 356540 Seattle WA 98195-6540 Office Phone: 206-543-2475. Business E-Mail: hornbnt@u.washington.edu.

HORNBERGER, GEORGE MILTON, environmental science educator; b. Fountain Springs, Pa., June 22, 1942; s. George Vincent and Olive Mae (Delcamp) H.; m. Joan Marie Zackey, Aug. 28, 1965; children: Rachel Joan, George Zackey. BSCE, Drexel U., 1965, MSCE, 1967; PhD, Stanford U., 1970. Asst. prof. U. Va., Charlottesville, 1970-75, assoc. prof., 1975-84, prof., 1984—, disting. prof., 1991—, Ernest H. Ern prof., 1993—, assoc. dean for sci., 2002—. Vis. fellow Australian Nat. U., Canberra, 1977-78; vis. scientist Inst. Hydrology, Wallingford, Eng., 1980, U.S. Geol. Survey, 1990-91; hon. vis. prof. U. Lancaster (Eng.), 1984-85, Stanford U., 1990-91, U. Colo., 1997-98; mem. bd. Radioactive Waste Mgmt. of NAS, 1986-91, chmn. Commn. on Geoscis., Environment and Resources, 1996-2000; chmn. bd. Earth Scis. and Resources of NAS, 2003—, chmn., 2003—; chmn. adv. com. nuclear waste U.S. NRC, 2001-03. Author: Numerical Methods in Subsurface Hydrology, 1971, Elements of Physical Hydrology, 1998; assoc. editor Am. Geophys. Union, 1980-84; N.Am. editor John Wiley & Sons, Eng., 1986-92; editor-in-chief Water Resources Rsch., Am. Geophys. Union, 1993-96. Recipient John Wesley Powell award U.S. Geol. Survey, 1995, First Biennial medal for natural systems Australian Simulation Soc., 1995, Bownocker medal Ohio State U., 1999; elected to NAE, 1996; grantee NSF, Army Rsch. Office, EPA, Nat. Park Svc., NATO, Dept. Energy. Fellow Am. Geophys. Union (pres.-elect hydrology sect. 2004, Robert E. Horton award hydrology sect. 1993, Excellence in Geophys. Edn. award 1999), Assn. for Women in Sci.; mem. NAE, Geol. Soc. Am., Am. Geophys. Union, Sigma Xi. Home: 308 Farm Ln Charlottesville VA 22902-5324 Office: U Va Dept Environ Sci Clark Hall Charlottesville VA 22903-3188 Office Phone: 434-924-3437. Business E-Mail: hornberger@virginia.edu.

HORNBY, DAVID BROCK, federal judge; b. Brandon, Manitoba, Can., Apr. 21, 1944; s. William Ralph Hornby and Retha Patricia (Fox) Sword; m. Helaine Cora Mandel, Oct. 9, 1946; children: Kirstin, Zachary. BA, U. Western Ont., 1965; JD, Harvard U., 1969. Bar: Va. 1973, Maine 1974, U.S. Supreme Ct. 1980. Law clk. U.S. Ct. Appeals, New Orleans, 1969-70; assoc. prof. U. Va. Sch. Law, Charlottesville, 1970-74; ptnr. Perkins, Thompson, Hinckley & Keddy, Portland, Maine, 1974-82; U.S. magistrate Dist. Maine, Portland, 1982-88; assoc. justice Maine Supreme Jud. Ct., Portland, 1988-90; judge U.S. Dist. Ct. Maine, 1990—; chief judge, 1996—2003. Contbr. articles to profl. jours.; editor, officer Harvard Law Rev., 1967-69. Fellow Am. Bar Found.; mem. ABA, Am. Law Inst., Maine State Bar Assn., Maine Bar Found. (bd. trustees 1990-94), Cumberland County Bar Assn. Office: US Dist Ct Edward T Gignoux Courthouse 156 Federal St Portland ME 04101-4152

HORNBY, KENNETH PETER, information technology manager; b. Davenport, Iowa, July 22, 1960; married. Advisor Jr. Achievement, St. Paul, 1983. With U.S. Army, 1985-87. Mem. Twin City Aero Historians (v.p. 1995-98, pres. 2004-05), 2d Cavalry Assn. (life, bd. dirs. 2000), U.S. Cavalry Assn., Am. Air Mus. in Britain, Internat. Plastic Modelers Soc., Am. Legion. Avocations: reading, aviation modeling, historical research and writing, travel, collecting books and militaria.

HORNBY, NICK, writer; b. Maidenhead, Eng., Apr. 17, 1957; s. Sir Derek Hornby; m. Virginia Bovell (div.); 1 child, Danny; 2 children, Lowell and Jesse, with Amanda Posey. Ed., Cambridge U. Author: (essay collection) Contemporary American Fiction, 1992, 31 Songs (pub. in US as Songbook), 2003, (memoir) Fever Pitch, 1992, (novels) High Fidelity, 1995, About a Boy, 1998, How to be Good, 2001 (WH Smith Fiction Award, 2002), A Long Way Down, 2005, (screenplays) Fever Pitch, 1997; editor: My Favourite Year: A Collection of New Football Writing, 1993, Speaking with the Angel, 2001; co-editor (with Nick Coleman): The Picador Book of Sportswriting, 1996; exec. prodr.: Fever Pitch, 2005. Co-founder TreeHouse Trust, London, 1997. Recipient EM Forster Award, AAAL, 1999.*

HORNDESKI, GREGORY WALTER, artist, mathematics educator; b. Cleve., May 14, 1948; s. Walter and Cecile Maria H.; m. Sharon Jo Winklhofer, Apr. 20, 1990. BSc, Washington U., St. Louis, 1970; M in Math, U. Waterloo, Ont., Can., 1971, PhD, 1973. Asst. prof. math. U. Waterloo, Ontario, 1973-78, assoc. prof. math., 1978-82. One-man shows include 20th Century Gallery, Phila., 1984, Alternate Gallery, Dallas, 1984, 86, 88, Cade Gallery, Detroit, 1985, Toni Jones Gallery, Houston, 1985, Gallery 10, Washington, 1985, McIntosh Gallery, Atlanta, 1986, 91, U. Dallas, 1987, Eugene Binder Gallery, 1990, Hooks-Epstein Gallery, Houston, 1991, Dutch Phillips & Co., Dallas, 1994, Harris Gallery, Houston, 1995, Whelan Gallery, Santa Fe, N.Mex., 1998-01, Ezair Gallery, NY, 2003, 05; two-man shows include Alternate Gallery, Dallas, 1985, Plus-Kern Gallerie, Brussels, 1989, Gallery Annext, NYC, 1994, Mulcahy Modern Gallery, Dallas, 1997, Select Art Gallery, Sedona, Ariz., 1997; exhibited in group shows at Groninger (Holland) Mus., 1988, Arlington (Tex.) Mus. Art, 1991; represented in permanent collection Groninger Mus., Dallas Mus. Art, Houston Mus. Fine Art, El Paso Mu. of Art, Mus. of the Southwest, Midland, Tex., Tyler (Tex.) Mus. Art. Home: 2814 Calle Dulcinea Santa Fe NM 87505-6425 Office Phone: 505-438-0484.

HORNE, JOHN R., farm equipment company executive; b. Gary, Ind., 1938; Grad., Purdue U., 1960, Bradley U., 1964. Group v.p., gen. mgr. Navistar Internat. Transp. Corp.; pres., COO, now CEO Navistar Internat. Corp., 1995—, also bd. dirs., 1995—; pres., CEO Navistar Internat. Corp. and Internat. Truck & Engine Corp., 1995—; also chmn. bd. dirs. Navistar Internat. Corp. Mem.Soc. Automotive Engrs. (chmn. fin. com.). Office: Internatl Truck & Engine Corp PO Box 1488 Warrenville IL 60555-7488

HORNE, MARILYN BERNEICE, mezzo-soprano; b. Bradford, Pa., Jan. 16, 1934; d. Bentz and Berneice Horne; m. Henry Lewis, July 1, 1960 (div. 1974); 1 child. Ed., U. So. Calif.; MusD (hon.), Rutgers U., 1970, Jersey City State Coll., 1973, Brown U., 1984, Juillard Sch. Music, 1994; DLitt (hon.), St. Peter's Coll.; LHD (hon.), Kean Coll., 1977. Vocal program dir. Music Acad. of the West, Santa Barbara, Calif., 1995—. Singer: (Operas) (debut) as Hata in The Bartered Bride, 1954, (La Scala debut) Oepidus Rex, 1969, (Met. Opera debut) as Adalgisa in Norma, 1970, (other roles) Rosina in Barber of Seville, Cleonte in The Siege of Corinth, Isabella in L'Italiana in Algieri, Carmen at Met. Opera, 1972—73, Laura in Harvest, Chgo. Lyric Opera, Marie in Wozzeck, San Francisco Opera, (appeared in) Phigenie en Tauride, Semiramide, Samson et Dalila at Met. Opera, 1987, The Ghost of Versailles, 1991, Pelléas et Mélisande, 1995, Venice Festival by invitation of Igor Stravinsky, Am. Opera Soc., N.Y.C., for several seasons, Vancouver Opera, Philharm. Hall, N.Y.C., Paris, Dallas, Houston, Covent Garden, London, roles at La Scala, Italy, Rossini Opera Festival, Pesaro, Italy, Met. Opera, 1987, (recital debuts) Madrid, Dresden, East Berlin, 1987; performer: (at inauguration) of U.S. President Clinton, 1993, ann. recital at Carnegie Hall, European tour with husband for Dept. State, 1963; rec. artist London, Columbia, Deutsche Grammaphon and RCA records, recs. include soundtrack Carmen Jones. Founder Marilyn Horne Found. Named Musician of Yr. Musical Am., 1995, Kennedy Ctr. honoree, 1995; named to Harold C. Schonberg's N.Y. Times' list of 9 All-Time, All-Star Singers in Met. Opera's 100 Years, 1984, Am. Classical Music Hall of Fame, Cin., 1999; recipient Grammy awards, 1964, 1981, 1983, 1994, Handel medallion, 1980, Premio d'Oro, Italian Govt., 1982, Commendatore al merito della Repubblica Italiana, 1983, Gold Merit medal Nat. Soc. Arts and Letters, 1987, Fidelio Gold medal, 1988, George Peabody award, 1989, Silver medal Covent Garden Royal Opera House, 1989, Disting. Dau. of Pa. Silver medal San Francisco Opera, 1990, Nat. Arts medal, 1992. Achievements include having the leading exponent florid vocal style, music of Rossini, Handel, Vivaldi. Office: care Columbia Artists Mgmt Inc Wilford Divsn 165 W 57th St New York NY 10019-2201 also: care Met Opera Assoc Attention: Artistic Dept Lincoln Ctr New York NY 10023 also: BMG Classics/RCA 1540 Broadway New York NY 10036-4039 Office: Music Academy of the West 1070 Fairway Rd Santa Barbara CA 93108-2899*

HORNE, MICHAEL STEWART, lawyer; b. Mpls., May 10, 1938; s. Owen Edward and Adeline (DiGeorgio) H.; m. Martha Brean, Sept. 11, 1965; children: Jennifer, Katherine, Sarah, Owen. BA, U. Minn., 1959; LLB, Harvard U., 1962. Bar: D.C. 1963, U.S. Ct. Appeals (D.C. cir.) 1964, U.S. Supreme Ct. 1968, U.S. Ct. Appeals (6th cir.) 1966, U.S. Ct. Appeals (9th cir.) 1978, U.S. Ct. Appeals (4th cir.) 1979, U.S. Ct. Appeals (5th cir.) 1979, U.S. Ct. Appeals (2d cir.) 1980, U.S. Ct. Appeals (11th cir.) 1983, U.S. Ct. Appeals (8th cir.) 1984, U.S. Ct. Appeals (10th cir.) 1997. Assoc. Covington & Burling, Washington, 1964-71, ptnr., 1971—. Co-author (with T.S. Williamson and A. Herman): The Contingent Workforce, Business and Legal Strategies, 2000. Mem. ABA, D.C. Bar Assn., FCC Bar Assn., Am. Judicature Soc. Democrat. Home: 9008 Levelle Dr Bethesda MD 20815-5608 Office: Covington & Burling 1201 Pennsylvania Ave NW PO Box 7566 Washington DC 20044-7566 Personal E-mail: hornems1@verizon.net. Business E-Mail: mhorne@cov.com.

HORNE, ROBERT LYNN, psychiatrist; BS, Centenary Coll. La., 1971; MD, Washington U., 1975. Diplomate in psychiatry with added qualifications in geriatric psychiatry Am. Bd. Psychiatry and Neurology, adolescent psychiatry Am. Bd. Adolescent Psychiatry, forensic medicine Am. Bd. Forensic Medicine, Am. Acad. Pain Mgmt. Intern Barnes Hosp., St. Louis; resident Hosp. U. Penn., Philadelphia; fellow, Unit Exptl. Psychiatry U. Penn., Philadelphia; med. dir. dept. psychiatry Lake Mead Hosp. Med. Ctr., North Las Vegas, Nev., 1991—; clin. assoc. prof. U. Nev. Sch. Medicine, Las Vegas, 1994—. Pres. Las Vegas Internat. Scouting Mus., 1996. Office: Ste 4 2915 W Charleston Las Vegas NV 89102

HORNE, WILLIAM MCHENRY, finance educator; b. Shreveport, La., Mar. 17, 1921; s. William McHenry and Nora (Kalmbach) H.; m. Joan Spear, Sept. 2, 1950 (div. Oct. 1974); children: Lynellyn D., William McHenry III; m. Alice Hobart, Dec. 28, 1980. BA, DePauw U., 1942; JD, Harvard U., 1949. Bar: Mass. 1949, Ind. 1949, D.C. 1955, Md. 1964. Atty., advisor U.S. Tax Ct., Washington, 1949—50; staff atty. joint com. on taxation U.S. Congress, Washington, 1953—55; assoc. Warner, Stackpole, Stetson & Bradlee, Boston, 1955—57; dir. taxes Olin Mathieson Chem. Corp. (now Olin Corp.), N.Y.C., 1957—64; v.p. Comml. Credit Co., Balt., 1964—70; ptnr. Reed, Smith, Shaw & McClay, Pitts., Washington and Harrisburg (Pa.), 1970—73; sr. v.p., gen. tax counsel Citicorp and Citibank N.A., N.Y.C., 1973—80; lectr. dept. mgmt. and policy Coll. Bus. Adminstrn. U. Ariz., Tucson, 1983—89; vis. prof. DePauw U., Greencastle, Ind., 1989—91. Mem. adv. com. to commr. IRS, 1969-70; past mem. tax and acctg. com. N.Y. Clearing House; past chmn. taxation com. Fin. Execs. Inst.; trustee Fin. Execs. Rsch. Found., 1975-79; fin. cons., 1980-91; bd. dirs. Ariz. Coun. Ct. Apptd. Spl. Advocates, pres., 1997-99; speaker in field. Author: Proceedings of New York University Annual Institute on Federal Income Taxation: Offers in Compromise, 1958; also chpts. to books and articles to profl. jours. Lt. USAAC, 1942-46, PTO; maj. JAGC, USAF, 1950-52. Recipient Disting. Alumni award DePauw U., Greencastle, Ind., 1976; Alfred P. Sloan fellow MIT, Cambridge, 1942. Mem. Tax Execs. Inst. (hon., pres., chmn. bd. dirs. 1968-69), Sigma Chi, Phi Beta Kappa. Avocations: hiking, water activities, travel. Home: 2465 W Tom Watson Dr Tucson AZ 85742-8531 E-mail: wmhorne@comcast.net.

HORNER, ALTHEA JANE, psychologist; b. Hartford, Conn., Jan. 13, 1926; d. Louis and Celia (Newmark) Greenwald; children: Martha Horner Hartley, Anne Horner Benck, David, Kenneth. BS in Psychology, U. Chgo., 1952; PhD in Clin. Psychology, U. So. Calif., 1965. Lic. psychologist NY, Calif. Tchr. Pasadena (Calif.) City Coll., 1965-67; from asst. to assoc. prof. LA Coll. Optometry, 1967-70; supr. Psychology interns Pasadena Child Guidance Clinic, 1969-70; pvt. practice specializing in psychoanalysis and psychoanalytic psychotherapy NYC, 1970-83; supervising psychologist dept. psychiatry Beth Israel Med. Ctr., NYC, 1972-83, coord. group therapy tng.,

1976-82, clinician in charge Brief Adaptation-Oriented Psychotherapy Rsch. Group, 1982-83; assoc. clin. prof. Mt. Sinai Sch. Medicine, NYC, 1977-91, adj. assoc. prof., 1991—; mem. faculty Nat. Psychol. Assn. for Psychoanalysis, NYC, 1982-83; sr. mem. faculty Wright Inst. LA Postgrad. Inst., 1983-85; pvt. practice LA, 1983—2004; clin. prof. dept. psychology UCLA, 1985-95; ret., 2004. Author: (with others) Treating the Neurotic Patient in Brief Psychotherapy, 1985, Object Relations and the Developing Ego in Therapy, 1979, rev. edit., 1984, Little Big Girl, 1982, Being and Loving, 1978, 3rd edit., 2005, Psychology for Living (with G. Forehand), 4th edit., 1977, The Wish for Power and the Fear of Having It, 1989, The Primacy of Structure, 1990, Psychoanalytic Object Relations Therapy, 1991, Working With the Core Relationship Problem in Psychotherapy, 1998, Chrysalis, 1999, Get Over It! Untie Your Relationship Knots and Move On, 2000, Dealing with Resistance in Psychotherapy, 2005; mem. editl. bd. Jour. Humanistic Psychology, 1986—, Am. Jour. Psychoanalysis; assoc. editor Jour. Am. Acad. of Psychoanalysis; contbr. articles to profl. jours Mem. APA, Am. Acad. Psychoanalysis (sci. assoc.), So. Calif. Psychoanalytic Soc. and Inst. (hon.). Office: PMB 256 3579 E Foothill Blvd Pasadena CA 91107-3119 Personal E-mail: altheajane@earthlink.net.

HORNER, ANTHONY ADAM, pediatrician, educator; b. N.Y.C., May 24, 1960; s. Harry and Joan Ruth (Frankel) H. BA in Biochemistry, U. Calif. San Diego, 1983; MD, St. Louis U., 1987. Diplomate Am. Bd. Pediatrics, Am. Bd. Allergy and Immunology. Resident in pediatrics UCLA Med. Ctr., 1990; fellow in pediatric immunology Boston Children's Hosp., 1994; asst. prof. pediatrics med. sch. U. Calif. San Diego, San Diego, 1994—. Co-principle investigator Children's Asthma Mgmt. Program, San Diego, 1994-99. Fellow Am. Acad. Pediatrics, Am. Acad. Allergy and Immunology. Achievements include rsch. in the devel. of DNA-based vaccination strategies for the treatment of disease. Office: U Calif San Diego Med Sch 9500 Gilman Dr # Mc663 La Jolla CA 92093-5004 Office Phone: 858-534-5435. E-mail: ahorner@uosd.edu.

HORNER, CARL MATTHEW, chemistry professor; b. Cicero, N.Y., June 4, 1930; s. Oscar Wendell and Gladys Cecilia (Horner) H. BS, LeMoyne Coll., 1952; MS, Syracuse U., 1958, PhD, 1965. Asst. prof. analytical chemistry SUNY-Oneonta, 1958-61, assoc. prof., 1961-64, prof., 1964—97, prof. emeritus, 1998—. Coord. ann. instrumental chemistry workshops, 1986-95. NSF CAUSE grantee, 1979-82; NSF CSIP grantee, 1986-88; Walter B. Ford Found. grantee, 1980, 83. Mem. AAAS, Am. Chem. Soc., N.Y. Acad. Scis. Achievements include research in infrared spectroscopy and laboratory robotics. Avocations: scuba diving, photography. Home: 24 Suncrest Ter Oneonta NY 13820-4632

HORNER, CLIFFORD R., lawyer; b. June 21, 1963; BS in Bus., Calif. Poly., 1986; JD, U. Calif., San Francisco, 1991. Bar: Calif., U.S. Dist. Ct. (no. dist.) Calif., U.S. Ct. Appeals (9th cir.) 1991. Atty. Zankel & McGrane, San Francisco, 1991-95, Morgan, Miller & Blair, Walnut Creek, Calif., 1995—. Chair MM&B Comml. Real Estate Practice Group, 1999—. Author: Approaching An Action Against A Real Estate Broker, 2001; contbg. author: California Eviction Defense Manual, 1998; cons. California Landlord-Tenant Practice, 1998—; guest editor: Contra Costa Lawyer, 1998. Co-chair Contra Costa (Calif.) Legis. Coun., 1998—. Mem. Hastings Alumni Assn. (Contra Costa chpt. pres. 1998—, bd. govs. 2001—), Walnut Creek C. of C. (dir. 1998—, chair civic affairs com. 1997-99), Contra Costa County Bar Assn. (bd. dirs. real estate sect. 1997—). Office: Morgan Miller & Blair 1676 N California Blvd Ste 200 Walnut Creek CA 94596-4157 E-mail: chorner@mmblaw.com.

HORNER, CONSTANCE JOAN, federal agency administrator; b. Summit, NJ, Feb. 24, 1942; d. David Earl and Cecelia (Murphy) McNeely; m. Charles Edward Horner, May 7, 1965; children: David Bayer, Jonathan Purcell. BA in English Lit., U. Pa., 1964; MA in English Lit., U. Chgo., 1967. Dep. asst. dir. policy planning and evaluation ACTION Agy., Washington, 1981-82, acting assoc. dir. domestic & anti-poverty ops., 1982-83, dep. assoc. dir. for VISTA & service-learning, 1982-83; assoc. dir. for econs. & govt. Office of Mgmt. and Budget, Washington, 1983-85; dir. Office of Pers. Mgmt., Washington, 1985-89; deputy sec. HHS, 1989-91; asst. to pres. and dir. presdl. pers. The White House, Washington, 1991-93; mem. U.S. Commn. on Civil Rights, Washington, 1993-98. Commr. The White House Fellows Commn., Washington, 1985-89; guest scholar The Brookings Inst., Washington, 1993—; vis. faculty Princeton (NJ) U., 1994; fellow, lectr. Johns Hopkins U., 1994-95; mem. adv. com. women in svcs. Dept. Def., 2003; bd. dirs. Pfizer, Inc., Prudential Fin., Inc., Ingersoll-Rand Co. Ltd. Bd. dirs. Annie E. Casey Found., Balt., 1994—. Fellow: Nat. Acad. Pub. Adminstrn.; mem.: Cosmos Club. Republican. Home: 3171 Porter St NW Washington DC 20008-3210

HORNER, DIANE L., dean; BSN, Ohio State U.; MSN in Burn Nursing, U. Cin.; EdD in Adult and Continuing Edn., No. Ill. U.; EdD in Adminstrn. in Higher Edn. Pub. health nurse Cleveland County (Okla.) County Health Dept., Norman, 1964-66; coord. maternal-child health program Dallas (Tex.) County Health Dept., 1966-67; staff nurse Washington Hosp., Fredricksburg, Va., 1968-70; staff nurse, supr. Crittenden Meml. Hosp., West Memphis, Ark., 1970-71, dir. staff devel., 1971-74; instr. U. Cin., 1976-77; asst. prof. Marycrest Coll., Davenport, Iowa, 1977-79; asst., then assoc. prof. Aurora (Ill.) U., 1979-83; dean St. Xavier U., Chgo., 1983-89, U. Miami, Coral Gables, Fla., 1990—. Mem. adv. com. Fla. Pub. Health Nursing, Geriatric Rsch. Edn. and Clin. Ctr., Nursing Spectrum, 1993-97; presenter workshops, confs. in field; mem. VA Deans com., 1990—, Wound Care Inst., 1990-93, U. Fla. acad. dean policy coun., 1990—, long range planning com., 1990—, med. sch. exec. com., 1990-92; bd. dirs. Good News Care Ctr. Contbr. articles to profl. jours. Bd. dirs. Cmty Ptnrship for the Homeless, mem. long range planning com. 1997. Recipient Hurricane Hero award Pts. of Light and Allstate Founds., 1993, Recognition award Transcultural Nursing Soc., 1992. Mem. ANA, Am. Assn. Colls. of Nursing, Am. Orgn. Nurse Execs., Chgo. Nurse Adminstrs. Conf. Group, Fla. Assn. Nurse Execs., Coun. on Grad. Edn. for Adminstrn. in Nursing., Fla. Nurses Assn., Ill. League for Nursing, Ill. Nurses Assn., Ill. Orgn. for Nurse Execs., Nat. League for Nursing (nominating com.), Nat. Orgn. Nurse Practitioner Faculties, Soc. for Rsch. in Nursing Edn. (founder), South Fla. Orgn. Nurse Execs., So. Coun. Collegiate Edn. for Nursing, U. Miami Iron Arrow, Golden Key Soc., Sigma Theta Tau, Kappa Delta Pi. Office: U Miami School of Nursing 5801 S Red Rd Coral Gables FL 33143-2343

HORNER, HARRY CHARLES, JR., sales executive; b. Pitts., Oct. 30, 1937; s. Harry Charles and Sara Marie (Hysong) H.; m. Patricia Ann Hagarty, June 15, 1965 (div. 1981); m. Sharon Kae Wyatt, Dec. 30, 1983; children: Jeffrey Brian, Jennifer Leigh, Mark Gregory. BFA, U. Cin., 1963; postgrad., Xavier U., Cin., 1963-64. Mgr. Retail Credit Co., Atlanta, 1964-68; ops. mgr. Firestone Tire and Rubber Co., L.A., 1968-80; exec. v.p. Romney/Ford Enterprises Inc., Scottsdale, Ariz., 1980-85; sales mgr. Environ. Care Inc., Calabassas, Calif., 1985-93; ops. v.p. Albuquerque (N.Mex.) Grounds Maintenance, Inc., 1993—2002; gen. mgr. and ptnr. Landwork S.W., Phoenix, 2002—; gen. mgr. Mesa Constrn., Landscape and Design, Albuquerque, 2004—. Pres., chief exec. officer The Cons. Group Cos. Ltd., Palm Desert, Calif., 1984—; pres. E. Valley Theatre Co., Chandler, Ariz., 1984-86; bd. dirs. KUNM Radio, Albuquerque. Cons. Ariz. Commn. on Arts, Phoenix, 1983-84. Democrat. Mem. Lds Ch. Avocations: flying, model railroads. Office: PO Box 14912 Albuquerque NM 87191 also: Mesa Construction 514 Pope St NE Albuquerque NM 87107 Office Phone: 505-260-4797. Personal E-mail: harryhorner@comcast.net.

HORNER, JACKIE NEAL, church musician; b. Leeds, Ala., Jan. 7, 1948; s. James Edward and Cleo Gann Horner; m. Gayle Murrah, Apr. 22, 1995; children: Jennifer Leigh, Christian Ryan, Lindsey Marie. B of Music Edn., U. Miss., MusM, 1972. Dir. music Brownsville (Tenn.) Bapt. Ch., 1978—82, St. Luke's United Meth. Ch., Memphis, 1982—90, Auburn (Ala.) United Meth. Ch., 1990—95, First United Meth. Ch., Montgomery, Ala., 1995—. Named Pianist of Yr., U. Miss., 1971, Grad. Student of Yr., 1972. Mem.: Fellowship of United Meths. in Music, Worship and the Other Arts. Avocations: golf, gardening, skiing, running. Office Phone: 334-834-8990.

HORNER, JEFFREY JOHN, lawyer; b. Omaha, Mar. 22, 1958; s. John Edward and Anne Catherine (Evans) H.; m. Laura S. Horner, May 19, 1990; children: Alec, Emily, John Cameron. BA summa cum laude, Vanderbilt U., 1980; JD, U. Va., 1983. Bar: Tex., U.S. Ct. Appeals (5th cir.), U.S. Supreme Ct. Assoc. Bracewell & Patterson, Houston, 1983-91, ptnr., 1991—. Adj. prof. South Tex. Coll. of Law, Houston, 1989—. Editorial adv. com. West Education Law Reporter, Houston, 1989-95; contbr. articles to profl. jours. Mem. Harris County Rep. Party, Houston; bd. dirs. South Tex. Coll. of Law, Houston, 2000—. Fellow Tex. Bar Found.; mem. Houston Bar Assn., Tex. Coun. of Sch. Attys. (pres. 1994-95), Edn. Law Assn. (bd. dirs. 1993-95, v.p. 1996, pres.-elect 1997, pres. 1998, immediate past pres. 1999), NSAA Coun. Sch. Attys. (bd. dirs. 2005-), Houston Club, Sugar Creek Country Club, Vanderbilt Univ. Alumni Club (pres. 1991-92), Phi Beta Kappa, Phi Kappa Psi. Presbyterian. Avocations: golf, basketball, baseball, travel. Office: Bracewell & Patterson Pennzoil Pl 2900 S Tower Houston TX 77002 E-mail: jeffrey.horner@bracepatt.com.

HORNER, JOHN ATLEE, educational association administrator; b. Pitts., Pa., Oct. 7, 1928; s. John Atlee Horner and Dorothy Mae Brandau; m. Mary Alice Miller, Aug. 20, 1955; children: Marilyn Jean Knox, John Atlee III. AB cum laude, Kenyon Coll.; MA in edn. adminstrn., Western Reserve U. Tchr. Blair Acad., Blairstown, NJ, 1950—52, Landon Sch., Wash., DC, 1952—53, U. Sch., Shaker Heights, Ohio, 1953—68; headmaster Harrisburg Acad., Harrisburg, Pa., 1968—78; exec. dir. Cleveland Engring. Soc., Ohio, 1979—85; interim dir. Shaker Lakes Regional Ctr., 1988—89, 1992—93; bd. trustees and pres. Shaker Lakes Regional Nature Ctr., 1985—. Mem. editl. bd. Jour. Ednl. Thought, 1965—68. Chmn. recreation bd. City of Shaker Heights, 1968; chmn. pub. sch. United Fund, 1971. Recipient Lifetime Tchr., State of Ohio. Mem.: SAR (former v.p. gen. 1993—95), Torch Internat. (bd. mem.), Fellowship of Christian Athletes (hon. trustee), Cleve. Alumni of Kenyon Coll. (pres.), Shaker Lakes Nature Ctr. (pres.), Ret. Athletic Dir. and Coaches (pres.), Rotary Club. Avocations: golf, tennis, bridge. Home: 3008 Fontenay Rd Cleveland OH 44120 Personal E-mail: johnmagnolia@aol.com.

HORNER, JOHN ROBERT, paleontologist, researcher, curator; b. Shelby, Mont., June 15, 1946; s. John Henry and Miriam Whitted (Stith) H.; m. Virginia Lee Seacotte, Mar. 30, 1972 (div. 1982); 1 child, Jason James; m. Joann Katherine Raffelson, Oct. 3, 1986 (div. 1994); m. Celeste Claire Roach, Jan. 21, 1995 (div. 2005). DSc (hon.), U. Mont., 1986. Rsch. asst. dept. geology Princeton (N.J.) U., 1975-82; curator paleontology Mus. of the Rockies, Mont. State U., Bozeman, 1982—; Regents prof. paleontology Mont. State U., 2001—. Rsch. scientist Am. Mus. Nat. History, N.Y.C., 1980-82. Co-author: Maia: A Dinosaur Grows up, 1985, Digging Dinosaurs, 1988 (N.Y. Acad. Sci. award 1989), Digging Up Tyrannosaurus Rex, 1993, The Complete T-Rex, 1993, Dinosaur Lives, 1997, Dinosaurs Under the Big Sky, 2001; contbr. articles to profl. jours. With USMC, 1966-68; Vietnam. MacArthur fellow, 1986. Achievements include discovery of a new genus of duckbilled dinosaur, Maiasaura; accomplishments include: the theory of endothermic metabolism in dinosaur development, of parental nurture of new-born hatchlings, that Tyrannosaurus rex was a scavenger; excavator of the Egg Mountain cache of dinosaur nests. Home: 310 Hoffman Dr Bozeman MT 59715-5724 Office: Mont State U Mus Of The Rockies Bozeman MT 59717-0001

HORNER, MATINA SOURETIS, retired academic administrator, corporate financial executive; b. Boston, July 28, 1939; d. Demetre John and Christine (Antonopoulos) Souretis; m. Joseph L. Horner, June 25, 1961; children: Tia Andrea, John, Christopher. AB cum laude, Bryn Mawr Coll., 1961; MS, U. Mich., 1963, PhD, 1968; LLD (hon.), Dickinson Coll., 1973; LLD, Mt. Holyoke Coll., 1973; LLD (hon.), U. Pa., 1975, Smith Coll., 1979, Wheaton Coll., 1979, U. Mich., 1989; LHD (hon.), U. Mass., 1973, Tufts U., 1976, U. Hartford, 1980, U. New Eng., 1987, Bentley Coll., 1989, New Eng. Coll., 1989, Pine Manor Coll., 1989, Am. Coll. Greece, 1990; DLitt (hon.), Claremont U. Ctr. and Grad Sch., 1988, Hellenic Coll., 1990; LHD (hon.), Colby Sawyer Coll., 1991. Teaching fellow U. Mich., Ann Arbor, 1962-66, lectr. motivation personality, 1968-69; lectr. social relations Harvard U., Cambridge, Mass., 1969-70, asst. prof. clin. psychology, 1970-72, assoc. prof. psychology, 1972-89, cons. univ. health svcs., 1971-89; pres. Radcliffe Coll., Cambridge, 1972-89, pres. emerita, 1989—; exec. v.p. TIAA-CREF, NYC, 1989—2003; ret., 2003. Bd. dirs. Neiman Marcus Group, Boston Edison Co.-NSTAR, Black Rock Funds. Co-author: The Challenge of Change, 1983; contbr. psychol. articles on motivation to profl. jours. and chpts. to books. Mem. adv. coun. NSF, 1977-87, chair, 1980-86; bd. trustees Twentieth Century Fund, The Century Found., 1973—, Am. Coll. of Greece, 1983-90, Mass. Eye and Ear Infirmary, 1986-90, Com. for Econ. Devel., 1988—, vice-chmn., 1992-98; bd. trustees Mass. Gen. Hosp., Inst. Health Professions, 1988—, vice chmn., 1994, chair, 1995; bd. dirs. Coun. for Fin. Aid to Edn., 1985-89, Beth Israel Hosp., 1989-95; bd. dirs. Revson Found., 1986-92, chmn., 1992-97; bd. dirs. Women's Rsch. and Edn. Inst., 1979—, chair rsch. com., 1982—; mem. Coun. on Fgn. Rels., 1984—; exec. com. ACE Bus. Higher Edn. Forum, 1984-86; exec. com. New Eng. Colls. Fund, 1980—, 2d v.p., 1984-85, 1st v.p., 1985-88, pres., 1988-89; mem. nat. panel to study declining test scores Coll. Entrance Exam. Bd., 1976-77; exec. com., chair task force Pres.'s Commn. for Nat. Agenda for 1980s, 1979-80; adv. com. Women's Leadership Conf. on Nat. Security, 1982—; exec. com. Coun. on Competitiveness, 1986-89; chair task force on health care Challenge to Leadership Conf., 1987-89; bd. dirs. Greenwall Found., 1997, chair, 2004—; bd. dirs. Fund for City of N.Y., chair, 1997-2003. Recipient Roger Baldwin award Mass. Civil Liberties Union Found., 1982, citation of merit Northeast Region NCCJ, 1982, Career Contbn. award Mass. Psychol. Assn., 1987, Disting. Bostonian award, 1990, Ellis Island medal, 1990. Mem. NOW (nat. corp. adv. bd. of legal def. and edn. fund 1984—), Am. Laryngol. Voice Rsch. and Edn. Found. (pres.), Nat. Inst. Social Scis. (medal for outstanding svc. 1973), Phi Beta Kappa, Phi Delta Kappa, Phi Kappa Phi.

HORNER, RONALD GEORGE, music educator, musician; b. Johnstown, Pa., Mar. 12, 1956; s. Clyde Melvin and Keturah Elizabeth Horner. BS, IN U of Penn., Ind., Pa., 1978; MusM, Duquesne U, Pitts., Pa., 1988, dip. artist, 1992. Cert. profl. instrnl. Pa. Dept. of Ed., 1978. Percussionist Israel Philharm. Orch., Tel-Aviv, Israel, 1978—80; dir. of percussion studies Seton Hill Coll., Greensburg, Pa., 1983—85; sr. lectr. of music Frostburg State U, Frostburg, Md., 1983—; instr. of music U of Pitts., Pitts., 1985—96; percussionist sub. Pitts. Symphony Orch., Pitts., 1989—96; asst. prof. of music Ind. U of Pa., Ind., Pa., 1996—. Music dir. Arion Band of Frostburg, Frostburg, Md., 1995—; condr. Bedford All County Band, Bedford, Pa., 2001; adjudicator Western MD ensemble Festival, Hagerstown, Md., 2002. Instrumentalist soloist (world premier performances) Sonus, 1991, Recitative and Scherzo, 1998, Toccata for Timpani, 2002; arranger: songs Pilgrims Chorus, 1997; author: (music method book) The Tuneful Timpanist, 2000. Mem. Sons of the Am. Rev., Wash., DC, 1998, Nat. Huguenot Soc., Bloomington, Minn., 1998, Soc. of the War of 1812, Phila., 1998. Mem.: Percussive Arts Soc., Phi Mu Alpha Sinfonia, Delta Omicron, Pi Kappa Lambda. Republican. Methodist. Avocations: golf, skiing, classic sports cars. Home: 163 Gilmour Rd Somerset PA 15501 Office: Frostburg State U 209 Performing Arts Ctr Frostburg MD 21532 E-mail: ronhorn@aol.com.

HORNER, SHIRLEY JAYE, columnist, writing and publishing consultant; d. John and Selma (Sosna) Quentzel; m. Robert George Horner (dec. Nov. 1984); children: Charles Bruce, Neil Brian. BA, NYU, 1946; MA, Columbia U., 1948, MPhil, 1976. Instr. English L.I. U., Bklyn., 1948-49, Seton Hall U., Newark, 1949-51, Queens Coll., L.I., 1953-54, Rutgers U., Newark, 1975-76; prodr. preservation experience programs Middlesex County Cultural and Heritage Commn., North Brunswick, N.J., 1980-81; editor fedn. reports Nat. Fedn. State Humanities Couns., Mpls., 1981-84; columnist, writer About Books The N.Y. Times' N.J. Weekly, N.Y.C., 1979—, reporter tri-state regional planning commn., 1979-82. Lectr. for writing workshops Trenton (N.J.) State Coll., 1984, Seton Hall U., South Orange, N.J., 1990-91, N.J. Libr. Assn., Trenton, 1990-93, N.J. Inst. Tech., Newark, 1997; book review panelist WOR-TV, 1986; moderator, panelist Holocaust Rescuers in Italy Day Program, 1995; NEH-funded lectr. Seton Hall U., 1991; reporter Tri-State Regional Planning Commn., The N.Y. Times N.J. Weekly, N.Y.C., 1979-82; founding bd. dirs. N.J. Ctr. for the Book in the Libr. of Congress, 2001—; spkr. in field. Co-editor: Ladies at the Cross-roads, 1978 (AAUW award 1978); editor: Conserving Communities: Urban and Suburban, 1979 (N.J. Inst. Tech. award of excellence 1980), (series of booklets) The Preservation Experience in Middlesex County, 1981 (Middlesex County award of distinction 1981); prodr. (TV program) Political Debate for '79 on Suburban Cable, 1979 (Union County award of achievement 1980); featured author N.J. Lit. Hall of Fame Authors Brunch, 1997; contbg. editor: Ency. N.J., 2004; contbr. articles to profl. jours. Co-chmn. Bicentennial Program for Mountainside, Union County, N.J., 1974-77; del. Union County Rep. Party, Linden, N.J., 1982-88; chmn. evaluation N.J. Com. for Humanities/NEH, New Brunswick, 1979-81; chmn. Union County Planning Bd., 1981-84; mem., publs. advisor N.J. Hist. Commn.; trustee N.J. Lit. Hall of Fame, 1987—, N.J. Ctr. for the Book, Opera at Florham Fairleigh Dickinson U., Madison, N.J., 1992—; mem. historic site com. Soc. Profl. Journalists, 1989; counsellor N.J. Cath. Hist. Records Commn.; publicity cons. Com. Commemorating Heroism of Aristides de Sousa Mendes, 2003. Recipient 1st Pl. Journalism award N.J. Press Women, 1980, 81, award for saving the life of a child Mountainside, N.J., 1968; inducted into N.J. Lit. Hall of Fame, 1987, Notable Twentieth Century N.J. Authors Honor Roll, 2003; NEH grantee, 1980, 90. Mem. Nat. Book Critics Cir. (bd. dirs. 1990-93, judge for NBCC awards), Images '95 Com. N.J. Ctr. for Visual Arts, Nat. Arts Club (literary com. 2000—), Soc. Profl. Journalists (hist. site com. 1989), First Mogilev Podolier Friends Assn. (pres. 1996). Avocations: hiking, archaeological digs. Office: care NY Times NJ Weekly 1575 Brookside Rd Mountainside NJ 07092-1601 Office Phone: 908-232-2804. Personal E-mail: sjhorner@comcast.net. *How empty is the life that has not known love. Treasure the memory.*

HORNER, WINIFRED BRYAN, humanities educator, researcher, consultant, writer; b. St. Louis, Aug. 31, 1922; d. Walter Edwin and Winifred (Kinealy) Bryan; m. David Alan Horner, June 15, 1943; children: Winifred, Richard, Elizabeth, David. AB, Washington U., St. Louis, 1943; MA, U. Mo., 1961; PhD, U. Mich., 1975. Instr. English U. Mo., Columbia, 1966-75, asst. prof. English, 1975-80, chair lower divorce studies, dir. composition program, 1974-80, assoc. prof., 1980-83, prof., 1984-85, prof. emerita, 1985—; prof. English, Radford chair rhetoric and composition Tex. Christian U., Ft. Worth, 1985-93, Cecil and Ida Green disting. prof. emerita, 1993-97. Disting. vis. prof. Tex. Woman's U. Editor: Historical Rhetoric: An Annotated Bibliography of Selected Sources in English, 1980, The Present State of Scholarship in Historical Rhetoric, 1983, Composition and Literature: Bridging the Gap, 1983, Rhetoric and Pedagogy: Its History, Philosophy and Practice, 1995; author: Rhetoric in a Classical Mode, 1987, Nineteenth-Century Scottish Rhetoric: The American Connection, 1993, Life Writing, 1996; co-author Harbrace Coll. Handbook, 11th edit., 1990, 12th edit., 1994, 14th edit., 1998. Named Disting. prof. Tex. Woman's U., 1999, Disting. Alumna, Washington U.; Inst. for the Humanities fellow U. Edinburgh, 1987; NEH grantee, 1976, 87. Mem. Internat. Soc. for History Rhetoric (exec. coun. 1986), Rhetoric Soc. Am. (bd. dirs. 1981, pres. 1987), Nat. Coun. Writing Program Adminstrs. (v.p. 1977-85, pres. 1985-87), Coll. Conf. on Composition and Communication (exec. com.), Modern Lang. Assn. (mem. del. assembly 1981). Home and Office: 1904 Tremont Ct Columbia MO 65203-5467 Business E-Mail: hornerw@missouri.edu.

HORNGREN, CHARLES THOMAS, finance educator; b. Milw., Oct. 28, 1926; s. William Einar and Grace Kathryn (Manning) H.; m. Joan Estelle Knickelbine, Sept. 6, 1952; children: Scott, Mary, Susan, Catherine. BS, Marquette U., 1949, DBA (hon.), 1976; MBA, Harvard U., 1952; PhD, U. Chgo., 1955; LHD (hon.), DePaul U., 1985. CPA, Wis. Instr. U. Chgo., 1952-54, asst. prof., 1954-55, Marquette U., Milw., 1955-56; assoc. prof. U. Wis., Milw., 1956-59, U. Chgo., 1959-63, prof., 1963-65, Stanford U., Calif., 1965—. Bd. dir. ABM Industries, San Francisco. Co-author: Cost Accounting, 12th edit., 2005, Financial Accounting, 5th edit., 2004, Introduction to Management Accounting, 13th edit., 2005, Introduction to Financial Accounting, 9th edit., 2005, Accounting, 6th edit., 2005; editor: Prentice Hall Acctg. Series. With AUS, 1944-46. Recipient Alumni Merit award Marquette U., 1973, Edmund W. Littlefield professorship Stanford U., 1973; named to Acctg. Hall of Fame, 1990. Mem. Am. Acctg. Assn. (dir. research 1964-66, pres. 1976-77, Outstanding Acctg. Educator award 1973), AICPAs (acctg. prins. bd. 1968-73, council 1978-81, Outstanding Educator award 1985), Calif. Soc. CPAs (Faculty Excellence award 1975, Disting. Prof. award 1983), Nat. Assn. Accts. (bd. regents 1981-84), Financial Acctg. Standards Bd. (adv. council 1975-79, trustee 1984-89). Home: 620 Sand Hill Rd # 407C Palo Alto CA 94304-2002

HORNICK, RICHARD BERNARD, physician; b. Johnstown, Pa., Jan. 27, 1929; s. Paul Steven and Gertrude (Cowan) H.; children: Douglas, Thomas, Marcie, Blaine; m. Susan Finnegan. AB, Johns Hopkins U., 1951, MD, 1955. Diplomate Am. Bd. Internal Medicine. Intern Johns Hopkins Hosp., Balt., 1955-56, resident in medicine, 1956-57; faculty U. Md. Med. Sch., 1959-78, head infectious diseases, 1963-78; prof. U. Rochester, N.Y., 1979-87, chmn. dept. medicine, 1979-85, assoc. dean affiliated hosps. and external rels., 1985-87; v.p. med. edn. Orlando (Fla.) Regional Healthcare System, 1988—2000. Cons. WHO, mem. Armed Forces Epidemiol. Bd., 1995-99. Contbr. articles to profl. jours. With U.S. Army, 1957-59. Master ACP (bd. govs., regent); mem,. Am. Fedn. Clin. Rsch., Am. Soc. Clin. Investigation, Am. Clin. and Climatol. Assn., Assn. Am. Physicians, Infectious Disease Soc. (treas.). Home: 75 Palmer Ave Winter Park FL 32789-2529 Office: Orlando Regional Healthcare System 1414 Kuhl Ave Orlando FL 32806-2093 E-mail: rbh@orhs.org.

HORNING, MARKUS, marine biologist, educator, researcher; b. Braunschweig, Germany, Feb. 14, 1960; came to U.S., 1992; s. Hans M. and Ursula Horning. MS, Freiburg (Germany) U., 1988; PhD summa cum laude, Bielefeld (Germany) U., 1992. Biologist Max-Planck-Inst., Seewiesen, Germany, 1989-92; postdoctoral rsch. physiologist Scripps Instn. Oceanography, San Diego, 1992-96; asst. rsch. scientist Tex. A&M U., Galveston, 1996-98, assoc. rsch. scientist, 1998—, dir. Lab. Applied Biotelemetry and Biotech., 2000—. Assoc. prof. marine scis., U. Alaska, Fairbanks, 1999—; sole propr. Ultramarine Instruments, Galveston, 1997—; scientific program com. 1st World Marine Mammal Sci. Conf., Monaco, 1998. Contbr. articles to profl. jours.; inventor in field; assoc. editor Marine Mammal Sci., 1996-98. Recipient U.S. Antarctica medal, NSF, 1981. Mem. AAAS, Ecol. Soc. Am., Am. Physiol. Soc., Animal Behavior Soc., Soc. Marine Mammalogy, Am. Soc. Photogrammetry and Remote Sensing, N.Y. Acad. Sci. Office: Tex A&M U 5007 Avenue U Galveston TX 77551-5926 E-mail: horningm@tamug.tamu.edu.

HORNISH, RONALD FREDERICK, music educator; s. Charles Everett Hornish and Louise Millard-Hornish Virginia. BS in music edn., Duquesne U., 1973—77; MusM, Northwestern U., 1983—84; D of musical arts, U. of Cin. College-Conservatory of Music, 1986—88; MA in supervision and adminstrn., North Ctrl. Coll., 2001—04. Teaching Certification in Music Pa. State Bd. of Edn., 1977, Ill. State Bd. of Edn., 1993, General Administrative Certification Ill. State Bd. of Edn., 2004, Teacher of Music NJ. Bd. of Edn., 1999. Band dir. Keystone Oaks Sch. Dist., Pitts., 1977—80; dir. of instrumental music Solanco H.S., Quarryville, Pa., 1980—83; asst. dir. of bands U. of Nev., 1984—85; dir. of bands Rocky Mountain Coll., Billings, Mont., 1985—86; asst. prof. of music/dir. of bands Bucknell U., Lewisburg, Pa., 1988—90, Grand Valley State U., Allendale, Mich., 1990—93; dir. bands Morton West HS, Berwyn, Ill., 1993—2000; music educator/fine arts tchr./band dir. Downers Grove South HS, Downers Grove, Ill., 2000—. Guest condr., adjudicator and clinician various, 1980—2004. Musician: (professional musician-sax/clarinet) Orchestral, musicals, jazz bands, jazz combos; contbr. panelist (Music Educators Nat. Conf. NW Divsn., 1987); dir.: (director of summer arts program) Flathead Lake Music Camp (Founder and Camp

Dir., 1987). Ward chmn. Dem. Nat. Party, Pittsburgh, Pa., 1988—90. Recipient Outstanding H.S. Educator, U. of Chgo., 1995, Rocky Mountain Coll. Tchr. of the Yr. Finalist, Burlington No. Found., 1986, Citation of Excellence, Nat. Band Assn., 1983, Award for Academic Excellence, Duquesne U., 1977, Pi Kappa Lambda, Northwestern U., 1984, Grammy Signature Sch. Finalist - Morton West HS, NARAS, 1999—2000, Award of Distinction for Notable Contributions to Musical Excellence, Fiesta-Val Arts, 1999, Tchr. of the Month, Morton West H.S., 1998 and 1999, Nominee for Chicagoland Outstanding Music Educator, Quinlan and Fabish, 1995, 1996, 1997, 2001; Grad. scholarship, Northwestern U., 1983—84, Jazz Performance/Cmty. Outreach, Ill. Coun. for the Arts, 2003, Grad. Doctoral scholarship, U. of Cin., 1987—88. Fellow: Pi Kappa Lambda (hon.); mem.: Coll. Band Directors Nat. Assn., Nat. Band Assn. (Pa. state exec. sec. 1980—83, Citation of Excellence 1982), Internat. Assn. of Jazz Educators, Ill. Music Educators Assn., Music Educators Nat. Conf., Mich. Sch. Band and Orch. Assn. (hon. Hon. Life Membership 1993), Phi Mu Alpha Sinfonia - Iota Chpt. Home: 100 Forest Place #P6 Oak Park IL 60301 Office: Downers Grove South High School 1436 Norfolk Downers Grove IL 60301 Personal E-mail: rfhornish@aol.com. E-mail: rhornish@csd99.k12.il.us.

HORNSBY, DAVID MCMILLAN, musician, music educator; b. Fort Worth, Tex., Nov. 14, 1928; s. David Franklin and Anna Estelle Hornsby; m. Lenda Ruth Jones, 1969 (div. 1973); m. Tamara Wilder Dower, 1963 (dec. 1984); 1 child, Michael David. Diploma, Ft. Worth Conservatory, 1945; MusB, Tex. Christian U., 1945—49; MA in Music and Music Edn., Columbia U., 1949—50; postgrad., U. Colo., 1949, postgrad., 1956, postgrad., 1978; studied with, Jeannette Tillett, Ernest von Dohnanyi, Edwin Hughes, Howard Waltz. Piano faculty mem. Ft. Worth Conservatory, 1946—49; ann. piano concerts Chautauqua, Boulder, Colo., 1951—63; music tchr. PR Pub. Schools, PR, 1953—55; music instr. Colorado Pub. Schools, 1955—58; piano instr. Pvt. Piano Studio, Boulder, Colo., 1956—78; music dir. Colegio Bolivar, Cali, Colombia, 1978—79; piano instr. Pvt. Piano Studio, San Antonio, 1980—; music dir. San Antonio Acad. of Tex., 1981—84. Condr., Christmas concert Gov. of PR, 1954; concert performance Polytechnic Inst., San German, PR, 1955; ann. judging tours Nat. Guild of Piano Teachers, 1963—; lectr. Music Teacher's Nat. Conv., Denver, 1975. Co-author: Bassetti Primer; author: (book of poetry) River Scattered Forest. Recipient Piano Guild Hall of Fame, Nat. Guild of Piano Teachers, 1971, Margie B. Boswell Prize for Best Alumni Poem, Tex. Christian U., 1952. Mem.: San Antonio Music Teachers Assn., Tex. Music Teachers Assn., Music Teachers Nat. Assn., The Leschetizky Assn., The Bohemians (N.Y. Musicians Club), Phi Mu Alpha Sinfonia (life). Home and Office: 340 Montclair No 103 San Antonio TX 78209 Office Phone: 210-804-0282.

HORNSTEIN, MARK, financial executive; b. N.Y.C., Dec. 7, 1947; s. Joseph and Anne (Fox) Hornstein. BBA, Pace U., 1969; postgrad., NYU, 1973. Staff acct. PEat, Marwick, Mitchell & Co., N.Y.C., 1969—70; sr. acct. Robert J. Cofini & Co., 1972—74; asst. v.p. United Va. Factors Corp., 1974—77; asst. v.p., adminstrv. head mortgage loan dicsn. James Talcott, Inc., 1977—78; loan adminstrv. officer Aetna Bus. Credit, Inc., East Hartford, Conn., 1978—79; asst. v.p. A.J. Armstrong Co., Inc. (not Bankamerica Bus. Credit, Inc.), N.Y.C., 1979—83; v.p. Leucadia Nat. Corp., 1983—. Treas. Am. Investment Co., St. Louis, 1984—; asst. v.p. Cardiff Equities Corp. (merged with Leucadia Nat. Corp.), La Jolla, Calif., 1984—86; v.p. Charter Nat. Life Ins. Co., St. Louis, 1985—93, PHLCORP, Inc. (formerly Baldwin United Corp.), Phila., 1987—; sec. Bolivian Power Co., Ltd., LaPaz, 1988—94; v.p. Transp. Capital Corp., N.Y.C., 1992—94, chmn., pres., 1994—96. With USNR, 1970—72. Home: 25 Sutton Pl S New York NY 10022-2441 Office: 315 Park Ave S New York NY 10010-3607

HORNTHAL, LOUIS PHILLIP, JR., lawyer; b. Tarboro, N.C., Oct. 16, 1936; s. Louis Phillip and Mildred (Lane) H.; m. Harriett Phillips Lang, Aug. 17, 1963; children: Louis Phillip III, William Lang. AB in History, U. N.C., 1958, LLB, 1963. Bar: N.C. 1963, U.S. Supreme Ct. 1979. Law clk. Justice W.B. Rodman, Jr., N.C. Supreme Ct., Raleigh, 1963-64; staff atty. N.C. Atty. Gen., Raleigh, 1964-65; assoc. LeRoy, Wells & Shaw, Elizabeth City, N.C., 1965-66; ptnr. Hornthal, Riley, Ellis & Maland and predecessor cos., Elizabeth City, 1966—. Bd. dirs. N.C. Lawyers Mutual Ins. Corp., Raleigh, Ga. Lawyers Ins. Co., WCIOLTA; mem. N.C. State Bar Disciplinary Hearing Commn., Raleigh, 1985-92. Vestry, sr. warden Christ Episcopal Ch., Elizabeth City, 1966—; active in past various charitable orgns.; bd. visitors U. N.C., Chapel Hill, 1994—. Fellow Am. Coll. Trial Lawyers; mem. N.C. Bar Assn. (pres. 1996-97, bd. govs. 1986-89), N.C. Assn. Def. Attys. (pres.), Internat. Assn. Ins. Counsel, Assn. Ins. Attys., U. N.C. Chapel Hill Law Alumni Assn. (pres. 1991-92). Democrat. Episcopalian. Avocations: tennis, reading, travel, sports spectator.

HORNUNG, HANS GEORG, aeronautical engineering educator, science administrator; b. Jaffa, Israel, Dec. 26, 1934; came to U.S., 1987; m. Gretl Charlotte Frank, Jan. 29, 1960; children: Ingrid, Karl, Lisa, Jenny. BMechE with honors, U. Melbourne, Australia, 1960, M in Engring. Sci. with honors, 1962; PhD in Aeros., U. London, 1965. Rsch. scientist Aero. Rsch. Labs., Melbourne, 1962-67; lectr., sr. lectr. then reader Australian Nat. U., Canberra, 1967-80; dir. Inst. Exptl. Fluid Mechanics (DLR), Göttingen, Germany, 1980-87; dir. Grad. Aero. Labs. and Clarence Johnson prof. aero. Calif. Inst. Tech., Pasadena, 1987—2005, emeritus, 2005—. Mem. fluid dynamics panel Adv. Group. Aerospace R & D, 1983-88; mem. adv. com. Internat. Shock Tube Symposia, 1979-95; chmn. adv. com. von Kármán Inst. for Fluid Dynamics, 1984-85; mem. German del. Internat. Union Theoretical and Applied Mechanics, 1984-87; Lanchester Meml. lectr. Royal Aero. Soc., London, 1988; hon. prof. U. Göttingen; Prandtl mem. lectr. Ges. Angew. Math. and Mech., Vienna, 1988. Mem. editl. adv. bd. Experiments in Fluids jour., 1987—, Physics of Fluids, 1988-91, Ing. Archiv, 1989-96; contbr. numerous articles to profl. jours. Recipient von Karman award and medal for internat. coop. in aero. Internat. Coun. Aero. Scis.; Humboldt fellow Tech. U., Darmstadt, Germany, 1974-75. Fellow Royal Aero. Soc., Am. Inst. Aero. & Astronautics, AIAA (life); mem. Nat. Acad. of Engring. (fgn. assoc.), Sci. mem. of bd. DLR Germany, Deutsche Gesellschaft für Luft-und Raumfahrt, Gesellschaft für angewandte Mathematik and Mechanik, Am. Phys. Soc., Royal Swedish Acad. Engring. Scis., Ludwig Prandtl Ring German Soc. Aerospace Sci. Achievements include making important contbns. in hypersonic flow theory, exptl. methods and results in real-gas flows, Mach reflection and three-dimensional separation. Office: Calif Inst Tech 1200 E California Blvd Pasadena CA 91125-0001 Business E-Mail: hans@galcit.caltech.edu.

HORNYAK, JOSEPH P., lawyer; b. Silver Spring, Md., Oct. 30, 1964; BS in journalism, U. Md., College Park, 1986; JD, U. Md., 1990. Bar: Md. 1990, DC 1992. Ptnr. Sonnenschein Nath & Rosenthal LLP, Washington. Office: Sonnenschein Nath & Rosenthal LLP Ste 600, E Tower 1301 K St NW Washington DC 20005 Office Fax: 202-408-6399. Business E-Mail: jhornyak@sonnenschein.com.

HORNYAK, ROY ROBERT, music educator, minister; b. St. Joseph, Mo., Nov. 4, 1925; s. Roy and Mildred Gertrude Hornyak; m. Mary Margaret Lewis, Aug. 9, 1953; children: Deborah Margaret Crnkovich, Roy Robert Hornyak, Jr. BA, Ctrl. Meth. U., 1948; MusM, Ind. U., 1950; Ensign, USNR, Naval Midshipmens Sch., 1945; MusD Edn., Ind. U., 1964. Prof. music U. Cin., 1954—86; head music edn. Coll. Conservatory Music, 1967—71, head performance studies, 1976—81, assoc. dean, 1972—75; coord. of campus ministry Am. Bapt. Churches of Ohio, Granville, Ohio, 1988—97; sr. min. Hyde Pk. Bapt. Ch., Cin., 1999—2002; exec. dir. Ohio Campus Ministries, Columbus, 1989—90; music dir. Simon Winds, Cin., 1981—2003; pres. Ohio Campus Ministries, 2003—. Moderator Miami Bapt. Associaton, Cincinnati, Ohio, 1993—96; pres. Am. Bapt. churches of Ohio, Granville, Ohio, 1997—98. Author: Attitudes Toward Contemporary American Music. Chmn. Am. Bapt. Campus Ministry at U. Cin., 1959—86. Lt. comdr. USNR, 1946—71. Recipient Disting. Alumni award, Ctrl. Meth. U., 1976, Newton C. Fedder award, 1995. Mem.: Coll. Band Directors Nat. Assoc., Phi Beta Mu (pres. 1986—88, Mu chpt.), Mil. Order of World Wars (life), Torch Club (pres. 1968—69). Office Phone: 513-922-6241. Personal E-mail: rob.hornyak@juno.com.

HOROSCHAK, MARK J., lawyer; b. Phila., Nov. 15, 1951; BA cum laude in Polit. Sci., U. Va., 1973; JD, Coll. of William and Mary, 1976. Bar: Mich. 1977, Va. 1980, NC 1996, SC 1996, US Ct. Appeals 4th Cir. 1981, US Dist. Ct. Ea. Dist. Mich. 1977, US Dist. Ct. Ea. Dist. Va. 1983, US Dist. Ct. We. Dist. NC 1996. Staff atty. GM, Detroit, 1976—80; assoc. Hunton & Williams, Richmond, Va., 1980—84; with FTC, Washington, 1984—95, atty.-advisor to chmn., 1987—88, asst. gen. counsel, 1988—89, asst. dir. Bur. Competition, 1989—95; mem. Womble Carlyle Sandridge & Rice PLLC, Charlotte, NC, 1995—, leader antitrust practice group, leader health law practice group. Mem.: ABA (vice chair healthcare com. antitrust sect. 1995—95, 1999—), Am. Health Lawyers Assn., NC Bar Assn. (chair antitrust sect. 2001—02). Office: Womble Carlyle Sandridge & Rice PLLC One Wachovia Ctr Ste 3500 301 S College St Charlotte NC 28202-6037 Office Phone: 704-331-4928. Office Fax: 704-338-7844. Business E-Mail: mhoroschak@wcsr.com.

HOROVITZ, ADAM (KING ADROCK), recording artist; b. South Orange, NJ, Oct. 31, 1966; s. Israel and Doris Horovitz; m. Ione Skye, 1991 (div. 1999). Founder, mem. Young and the Useless, 1981—83; mem. The Beastie Boys, 1983—; co-founder, mem. BS2000; co-founder Grand Royal Record Label, 1992—2001. Owner Grand Royal, Grand Royal mag., 1984—. Albums include Licensed to Ill, 1986, Paul's Boutique, 1989, Check Your Head, 1992, 94, Ill Communication, 1994, Some Old Bullshit, 1994, In Sound from Way Out, 1996, Def & Dumb, 1996, (with BS2000) BS2000, 1996, Buddy, 2000, (singles) Jimmy James, 1992, Gratitude, 1992, So What'cha Want, 1992, Sabotage, 1994, Hey Ladies, 1997, Real Men Don't Floss Up, (with BS2000) Simply Mortified, 2001, (extended play singles) Pollywog Stew, 1982, Cooky Puss, 1983, Rock Hard, 1984, Tour Shot, 1994, Sure Shot, 1994, Get It Together, 1994, Root Down, 1995, Aglio E Olio, 1995, (video) Skills to Pay the Bills, 1992, Hello Nasty, 1998, The Sounds of Science, 1999; rap artist Heart of Soul, 1988, Rap's Biggest Hits, 1990, Rap Rap Rap, 1996, Rap: Most Valuable Players, 1996; vocals Rap's Biggest Hits, 1990; prodr. Cb4, 1993, Rebirth of Cool (vol. 3), 1995, Music for Our Mother Ocean, 1996, Rap Rap Rap, 1996, Rap: Most Valuable Players, 1996; (films) Krush Groove, 1985, Tougher than Leather, 1987, Lost Angels, 1989, A Kiss Before Dying, 1991, Long Road Home 1991, Roadside Prophets, 1992, Cityscrapes, 1994, Crossroads, 2002. Office: care Grand Royal Capitol Records 1750 Vine St Los Angeles CA 90028-5209*

HOROVITZ, ISRAEL ARTHUR, playwright; b. Wakefield, Mass., Mar. 31, 1939; s. Julius Charles and Hazel (Solberg) H.; m. Doris Keefe, Dec. 25, 1959 (div. 1974); children: Rachael Keefe, Matthew Keefe, Adam Keefe; m. Gillian Adams, July, 1981; children: Hannah Rebecca and Oliver Adams (twins) Fellow, Royal Acad. Dramatic Art, London, 1961-63; postgrad. in English, CUNY, 1972-77, MA in English, 1977; PhD (hon.), Mass. State, 1991. Am. playwright-in-residence Royal Shakespeare Co., London, 1965; lectr., 1961-75; Fanny Hurst prof. theatre arts Brandeis U., 1974-75; artistic dir. N.Y. Playwrights Lab., 1975—; founder, artistic dir. Gloucester (Mass.) Stage Co., 1980—. Author: (plays) The Comeback, 1958, The Death of Bernard the Believer, 1960, This Play is About Me, 1961, The Hanging of Emanuel, 1962, Jump, 1962, Hop and Skip, 1963, The Killer Dove, 1963, The Indian Wants the Bronx, 1964-66, It's Called the Sugar Plum, 1965, Line, 1967, Rats, 1967, The Honest-to-God Schnozzola, 1968, Chiaroscuro (or Morning), 1968, The World's Greatest Play, 1968, First Season; collection of plays, 1968, Leader, 1969, Morning, Noon and Night, (with others), 1969, Acrobats, 1971, Play for Germs (TV), 1972, Dr. Hero, 1972, Shooting Gallery, 1972, The Wakefield Plays 3 Weeks After Paradise, 2001, Speaking Well of the Dead, 2002, A Mother's Love, 2003, Security, 2003, Cat-Lady, 2004; 7-play cycle including The Alfred Trilogy: Part 1-Alfred the Great, Part 2-Our Father's Failing, Part 3-Alfred Dies, 1972-77 and The Quannapowitt Quartet: Part 1-Hopscotch, Part 2-The 75th, Part 3-Stage Directions, Part 4-Spared, 1971-79; Cappella (novel), 1973; Uncle Snake, 1975, The Great Labor Day Classic, 1979, The Primary English Class, 1975, The Bottom, 1975-76, Mackerel, 1977, Sunday Runners in the Rain, 1979-80, Nobody Loves Me; (novella), 1975, The Reason We Eat, 1976; adaption Ionesco's l'homme aux Valises: Man with Bags, 1977; adaptation from Melville's Bartleby, The Scrivener, 1978; The Former One-On-One Basketball Champion; teleplays Today I Am A Fountain Pen, 1977, A Rosen by Any Other Name, 1979, The Chopin Playoffs, 1978, adaptation from Mailer's The Deer Park, 1979-80; (plays) The Good Parts, 1979—, adaptation from Dickens-Scrooge and Marley, 1980-81, Park Your Car in Harvard Yard, 1980-83, The Widow's Blind Date, 1985-88, Henry Lumper, 1984-87, Year of the Duck, 1984-87, Firebird at Dogtown, 1984-85, North Shore Fish, 1985-87, Faith, 1988, Fighting Over Beverley, 1988-93, Strong-Man's Weak Child, 1988-90, Unexpected Tenderness, 1993-94, Barking Sharks, 1995, The Chips are Down (BBC radio), 1995, Lebensraum, 1996, My Old Lady, 1996, Captains and Courage, 1996, Free Gift, 1996, One Under, 1997, Phone Tag (radio), 1997, Stations of The Cross, 1998, Fast Hands, 1999, Promises.com, 2000, 50 Years of Caddying, 2001, Man in Snow (Radio), 2001; (stage adaptations) Today I Am a Fountain Pen, A Rosen by Any Name, The Chopin Playoffs, 1986; (films) Park Your Car in Harvard Yard, 1991, Fast Eddie, 1980, The Strawberry Statement, 1971, Believe in Me, 1972, Author! Author!, 1982, Fell, 1982-83, Berta, 1982-83, Light Years, 1985-86, Wedlock, 1985-86, (with Diane Kurys) A Man in Love, 1987-88, Payofski's Discovery, 1987-88, The Deuce, 1988-90, The Pan, 1989-91, Letters to Iris, 1989-90, The Quiet Room, 1990, Strong Man, 1991-93, James Dean, 1993—, Without A Word, 1994, A Star is Born (remake), 1994, The Lounge Player, 1995—, The Widow's Blind Date, 1995, North Shore Fish, 1995, Captains and Courage, 1996, (with Istvan Szabo) Sunshine, 1998 (European Film Acad. award 2000, Best Screenplay 2000), 300 Boys, 1999 James Dean, 1999, Sunshine, 2000, The Little Shock, 2003-05, Eager to Die, 2005; contbr. to nat. mags, plays translated, pub. and performed in more than 20 langs. Recipient Vernon Rice award, 1967-68, Drama Desk award, 1967-68, Jersey Jour. best play award, 1968, Obie award, 1967-68, 68-69, French Critics prize, 1974, Christopher award, 1975, Emmy award, 1975, prix Italia-Silver Palm, 1982, L.A. Weekly Critics prize, 1984, 95, Commendation Gov. of Mass., 1984, Eliot Norton prize, 1986, Best Play award Boston mag., 1987, Lifetime Achievement award B'nai Brith, 1996, Washington Coll. Literary prize, 1996, Boston Pub. Libr. Literary Lights award, 1997, Walker Hancock prize City of Gloucester, Mass., 1999, Best Screenwriter award European Film Acad., 2000, Best Screenplay award Writers Guild Can., 2000, Star in Playwrights Sidewalk, N.Y.C., 2000, Sony RAdio award for best drama, 2002; Rockefeller fellow, 1968-69, Nat. Endowment for Arts fellow, 1974, Fulbright fellow, 1975-76, Guggenheim fellow, 1977-78. Mem. Actors Studio, New Dramatists Com., Eugene O'Neill Found., Authors' League Am. (exec. council). Achievements include being a nationally ranked masters track and road runner; most produced Am. playwright in French language. also: MCR-Agence Litteraire Paris France also: Felix Bloch Erben Hardenberg Strasse 6 D-10623 Berlin Germany E-mail: IH1996@aol.com.

HOROWITZ, BARRY ALLAN, music company executive; b. N.Y.C., June 21, 1948; s. Henry and Tania (Aisenfeld) H.; m. Maida Barbara Schwartzberg, Oct. 9, 1977 (dec. Oct. 1994); children: Jessica, Jared. BA, Hofstra U., Hempstead, N.Y., 1971. From sales staff to sr. dir. ops. Sam Ash Music Corp., Hicksville, N.Y., 1971-95, v.p. purchasing and merchandising, 1995—. Avocations: running, skiing, triathlons. Office: Sam Ash Music Corp 278 Duffy Ave Hicksville NY 11801-3605 E-mail: barry@samashmusic.com.

HOROWITZ, BARRY MARTIN, systems research and engineering company executive; b. Bklyn., Apr. 20, 1943; s. Isaac Harry and Clara Fireda (Weintraub) H.; m. Sheryl Robin Lang, Jan. 24, 1965; children: Hillary, Charles. BSEE, CCNY, 1965; MSEE, NYU, 1967, PhDEE, 1969. Asst. project engr. Bendix Corp., 1965-66, sr. project engr., 1967-69; project engr. Gen. Precision, 1966-67; tech. staff MITRE Corp., McLean, Va., 1969-71, group leader, 1971-74, dept. head, 1974-79, dir. spl. studies Bedford, Mass., 1979-80, tech. dir., 1980-84, v.p. strategic programs, 1984-85, v.p. programs, 1985-86, sr. v.p., gen. mgr., 1986, group v.p., gen. mgr., 1986-87, exec. v.p., chief oper. officer, also dir.; CEO Concept Five Tech, McLean, 1996-2000, chmn., 1996—. Cons. sci. adv. bd. USAF, Pentagon, Washington, 1982—, Def. Sc. Bd., Pentagon, 1988—. Contbr. articles to profl. jours. Mem. NAE, IEEE, AIAA, Armed Forces Communications and Electronics Assn. (pres. 1987-88, pres.-elect 1990, Gold medal for Engring. 1990), Ctr. Sci. and Internat. Affairs., Eta Kappa Nu, Tau Beta Pi. Avocation: musician.

HOROWITZ, BEN, health facility administrator; b. Bklyn., Mar. 19, 1914; s. Saul and Sonia (Meringoff) H.; m. Beverly Lichtman, Feb. 14, 1952; children: Zachary, Jody. BA, Bklyn. Coll., 1940; LLB, St. Lawrence U., 1940; postgrad., New Sch. Social Rsch., 1942. Bar: N.Y. 1941. Dir. N.Y. Fedn. Jewish Philanthropies, 1940-45; assoc., ea. regional dir. City of Hope, 1945-50, nat. exec. sec., 1950-53, exec. dir., 1953-85, gen. v.p., bd. dirs., 1985—, bd. dirs. nat. med. ctr., 1980—. Bd. dirs. Beckman Rsch. Inst., 1980—. Mem. Gov.'s Task Force on Flood Relief, 1969-74; bd. dirs., v.p. Hope for Hearing Found., UCLA, 1972-96; bd. dirs. Forte Found., 1987-92, Ch. Temple Housing Corp., 1988-93, Leo Baeck Temple, 1964-67, 86-89, Westwood Property Owners Assn., 1991—. Recipient Spirit of Life award, 1970, Gallery of Achievement award, 1974, Profl. of Yr. award So. Calif. chpt. Nat. Sco. Fundraisers, 1977; Ben Horowitz chair in rsch. established at City of Hope, 1981; city street named in his honor, 1986. Jewish. Formulated the role of City of Hope as pilot center in medicine, science and humanitarianism, 1959. Office: City of Hope 11645 Wilshire Blvd Los Angeles CA 90025-1708

HOROWITZ, CAROLE SPIEGEL, landscape contractor; b. Pitts., Mar. 24, 1940; d. Alvin Duane and Leah (Greenstein) Spiegel; m. Don Roy Horowitz, Jan. 31, 1960; children: Cindy H. Urbach, Thomas Samuel. Student, Carnegie Mellon U., 1958-61. Cert. interior horticulturist, landscape profl. Owner Carole Horowitz Interior Design, Pitts., 1965-72; pres. Plantscape, Inc., Pitts., 1973—. Chmn. U. Pitts. Small Bus. Com., 1986-92; bd. dirs. United Way Allegheny County, Pitts., 1991-94, Jr. Achievment Allegheny County, Pitts., 1985-95, Vocat. Rehab. Ctr., Pitts., 1989-91. Recipient Nat. Landscape award White House and Am. Assn. Nurseryman, 1990, YWCA Entrepreneur Leadership award, 1990; named Entreprenuer of Yr. Ernst & Young & Inc. Mag., 1988, Pitts. Bus. Times Pa.'s Best 50 Women in Bus. award 1997. Mem. Interior Plantscape Assn. (sec., v.p., 1982-85), Associated Landscape Contractor of Am. (cert., chmn. Am. Bd. Govs. 1991-94), Internat. Facility Mgmt. Assn., Westmoreland Country Club, Longboat Key Club, Rotary (sec. Downtown Pitts. chpt.). Jewish. Avocations: travel, golf. Office: Plantscape Inc 3101 Liberty Ave Pittsburgh PA 15201-1400 Office Phone: 412-281-6352. E-mail: ch@plantscape.com.

HOROWITZ, DAVID CHARLES, consumer advocate, radio and television commentator, newspaper columnist, director; b. Bronx, NY, June 30, 1937; s. Marcus Lazar and Dorothy (Lippman) H.; m. Suzanne E. Mc Cambridge, Aug. 26, 1973; children: Victoria, Amanda. BA, Bradley U., 1959; MS in Journalism, Northwestern U., 1961; DHL (hon.), Bradley U., 2002. Editor in chief Tazewell County (Ill.) Newspaper, 1956; reporter Peoria (Ill.) Jour. Star, 1957-60, Lerner Newspapers and Chgo. City News Bur., 1959-60; newscaster Sta. KCCI Radio-TV, Des Moines, 1960-62; newswriter-prodr. ABC Radio Network, NYC, 1963; Far East corr. NBC News, 1963-64; pub. affairs dir. Sta. WMCA, NYC, 1965-66; corr., edn. editor, consumer commentator KNBC News, LA, 1966-92; consumer commentator KCBS News, LA, 1993-95; syndicated columnist Creators Syndicate, LA, 1986-99, eight books syndication, 1999—; creator, host, exec. prodr. syndicated TV show Fight Back! with David Horowitz, LA, 1977-92; pres. Fight Back! Found. Consumer Edn., 1985—; syndicated newspaper, internet commentator Fight Back! Radio Reports, 1989—, Jones-Media Am., 1997—; syndicated consumer talk show Fight Back! Talk Back! Talk Radio Network, 2002—05; commentator Sta. CNBC, 1990-96; CEO Fightback.com, 1996—. Pres. Fight Back! Prodns., 1974—. Author: Fight Back and Don't Get Ripped Off, 1979, Business of Business, 1989, Fight Back! For Your Medical Health, vols. 1-4, 1993, Fight Back! at Work, 1994, five other books, 1976-; host, exec. prodr. Best Defense, 1993; exec. prodr. Fight Back at Work, 1994, (CBS-TV spl.) Frog Girl: The Jennifer Graham Story (Genesis Animal Rights award 1990); spokesperson: Lowermybills.com, 2001-03. Patron LA County Mus. Art; bd. dirs. Nat. Broadcast Editl. Conf., Am. Cancer Soc., City of Hope; bd. advisers LA Jewish Home for Aged, Calif. divsn. Am. Cancer Soc.; mem. adv. bd. Am. Heart Assn., LA County, UCLA Publs., LA County Dist. Atty.; founder Fight Back! Found.; mem. charitable adv. com. City of LA, 1991—; hon. bd. dirs. Caring Inst., Washington, 2000-; hon. mayor Brentwood Cmty., LA, 1991-98; mem. consumer adv. com. FCC, Washington, 2003-; mem. bd. dirs. AFTRA, LA, 2003-, nat. bd. dirs., 2005-. With USNR, 1954-62. CBS fellow Columbia U., 1962-63; recipient LA City and County Pub. Svc. citation, 1979, 80, 81, 82, 83, 89, 92, Calif. State Legislature Pub. Svc. citation, 1980, 81, 82, 83, 91, 92, Spirit of Life award City of Hope, 1979, 1983, Chief US Postal Insp.'s award, 1981, 93, Emmy awards consumer reporting NTAS, 1974, 76-77, 81-86, 89, 90-05, LA Press Club award consumer reporting, 1991, News Reporting award UPI, 1983, 94, Pub. Svc. award Social Security Adminstrn., 1987, NY Internat. Film and TV Festival medal, 1984-86, Golden Mike award, 1986, Armed Forces TV Network Svcs. award, 1988, Toastmasters Internat. Leadership award, 1991, Cmty. Svc. award SBA, 1991, Excellence in Journalism award Nat. Homecare Assn., 1992, Disting. Alumni award Northwestern U., 1994, Cmty. Svc. award UCLA Ctr. Aging, 1995, AP News Reporting award, 1995, Angel award Excellence in Media, 1998, Golden Halo award Motion Picture Coun. So. Calif., 1998, Quality of Life award Proctor Health Care Found., 1998, Lifetime Achievement award Kern County Law Enforcement Found., 1999, Angel award outstanding internet website and pub. svc., 1998, 02; named to Journalism Hall of Achievement, Northwestern U., 1997, LA Press Club Best TV Feature Reporting award, 1986, 94, 97; honored David C. Horowitz Auditorium Bradley U., 2004. Mem. AFTRA, ASCAP, BMI, SAG, Am. Assn. Travel Agts. (Travelers Adv. award 1991), Internat. Radio-TV Soc., Radio-TV News Dirs. Assn., The Guardians, Soc. Consumer Affairs Profls., Nat. Futures Assn. (adv. bd.), Child Passenger Safety Assn., Ill. Broadcasters Assn. (Disting. Svc. award 1986), Newspaper Creator's Assn., Writers Guild Am., Medill Journalism Sch. Alumni Assn. (pres. 1990-98), Friars Club, Overseas Press Club (NYC), Alpha Epsilon Pi, Sigma Delta Chi, Phi Delta Kappa, Omicron Delta Kappa. Avocations: writing, gardening, theater, collecting serious music, collecting contemporary art. Mailing: PO Box 49915 Los Angeles CA 90049-0915 Office Phone: 310-820-1188. E-mail: dhorowitz@fightback.com. *Life is full of compromise, but to compromise principle is to give up your self-respect. I don't want anyone to take me for a sucker, and I don't like to see anyone else taken, either. A lot of things are unfair in life. It's tough; that's the way it is. But, by heaven, if you can do something about it, do it.*

HOROWITZ, DAVID JOEL, author; b. Queens, NY, Jan. 10, 1939; s. Philip and Blanche (Brown) Horowitz; m. Elissa Krauthamer, June 14, 1959 (div.); children: Jonathan, Sarah, Benjamin, Anne; m. April Mullvain. AB, Columbia U., 1959; MA, U. Calif., Berkeley, 1961. Editor Ramparts mag., Berkeley, 1969-74; co-founder, pres. Ctr. for Study of Popular Culture, LA, 1988—; editor Frontpagemag.com; founder Discoverthenetworks.org. Author: Student, 1962, Shakespeare: An Existential View, 1965, The Free World Colossus, 1965, Hemispheres North and South: Economic Disparity Among Nations, 1966, Empire and Revolution: A Radical Interpretation of Contemporary History, 1969, The Enigma of Economic Growth: A Case Study of Israel, 1972, The Fate of Midas, 1973, The First Frontier, 1979; (with Peter Collier) The Rockefellers: An American Dynasty, 1976, The Kennedys: An American Drama, 1984, The Fords: An American Epic, 1987, Second Thoughts: Former Radicals Look Back at the Sixties, 1989, Second Thoughts About Race in America, 1991, Deconstructing the Left: From Vietnam to the Persian Gulf, 1991; (with Peter N. Carroll and David Lee) On the Edge: A History of America From 1890 to 1945, 1990, On the Edge: A New History of America in the Twentieth Century, 1990, Radical Son: A Generational Odyssey, 1997, Sex, Lies & Vast Conspiracies, 1998, Hating Whitey: And Other Progressive Causes, 1999, The Art of Political War And Other Radical Pursuits, 2000, Uncivil Wars: The Controversy Over Reparations for Slavery, 2002, How to Beat the Democrats and Other Subversive Ideas, 2002, Unholy

Alliance: Radical Islam and the American Left, 2004; editor: Containment and Revolution, 1967, Corporations and the Cold War, 1970, Isaac Deutscher: The Man and His Work, 1971; compiler: Marx and Modern Economics, 1968, Radical Sociology: An Introduction, 1971, Counterculture and Revolution, 1972. Co-dir. 2d Thoughts project Nat. Forum Found., Washington, 1986. Office: Ctr for Study of Popular Culture 4th Fl 4401 Wilshire Drive Los Angeles CA 90010*

HOROWITZ, DONALD, lawyer; b. N.Y.C., Nov. 18, 1936; s. Louis and Ethel (Kaplan) H.; m. Rosalind Jean Odrezin Horowitz, Dec. 17, 1967; children: Louis A., Jill, Gary N. BA, Rutgers U., 1958; LLB, Columbia U., 1961. Bar: N.J. 1962, N.Y. 1983, U.S. Dist. Ct. N.J. 1962, U.S. Dist. Ct. (so. dist.) N.Y. 1986, U.S. Dist. Ct. (ea. dist.) N.Y., 1986, U.S. Ct. Appeals (3rd cir.) 1965, U.S. Tax Ct. 1972, U.S. Supreme Ct. 1966, U.S. Ct. Appeals (10th cir.) 1994; cert. civil & criminal trial atty. Supreme Ct. N.J. 1983. Asst. U.S. Atty.'s Office, Newark, 1963-66, asst.-chief criminal divsn., 1966-68, first asst., 1968-69, U.S. atty. dist. of N.J., 1969; spl. dep. atty. gen. State of N.J., 1969-70; ptnr. Cummins, Dunn, Horowitz & Pashman, Hackensack, N.J., 1969-82; sole practice Hackensack, N.J., 1982-85, 89—; ptnr. Horowitz & Jacobs, Hackensack, N.J., 1985-89. Mem. Criminal Justice Adv. Com. Bergen C.C., Paramus, N.J., 1992—. Dem. County Committeeman, Ridgewood, N.J., 1993-98. Staff Sgt. U.S. Army, 1962-68. Mem. ABA, Fed. Bar Assn. (pres. N.J. chpt. 1977-78, 79-80), Nat. Assn. Criminal Def. Lawyers, Assn. Trial Lawyers Am., N.J. State Bar Assn., Assn. Criminal Def. Lawyers of N.J. Jewish. Home: 563 Eastbrook Rd Ridgewood NJ 07450-2114 Office: 24 Bergen St Hackensack NJ 07601-5487 E-mail: dhorowitzesq@earthlink.net.

HOROWITZ, DONALD LEONARD, lawyer, educator, political scientist, arbitrator; b. N.Y.C., June 27, 1939; s. Morris and Yetta (Hibscher) H.; m. Judith Anne Present, Sept. 4, 1960; children: Marshall, Karen, Bruce. AB, Syracuse U., 1959, LLB, 1961; LLM, Harvard U., 1962, AM, 1965, PhD, 1968. Bar: N.Y. 1962, D.C. 1979, U.S. Ct. Appeals (D.C., 6th, 7th and 10th cirs.) 1970, U.S. Supreme Ct. 1969. Law clk. U.S. Dist. Ct. (ea. dist.), Pa., 1965-66; rsch. assoc. Harvard U. Ctr. Internat. Affairs, 1967-69; atty. Dept. Justice, Washington, 1969-71; fellow Coun. on Fgn. Rels./Woodrow Wilson Internat. Ctr. Scholars, Washington, 1971-72; rsch. assoc. Brookings Instn., Washington, 1972-75; sr. fellow Rsch. Inst. on Immigration and Ethnic Studies/Smithsonian, Washington, 1975-81; prof. law and polit. sci. Duke U., Durham, N.C., 1980—, Charles S. Murphy Prof., 1988-93, James B. Duke prof., 1994—. Vis. prof. Charles J. Merriam scholar U. Chgo. Law Sch., 1988; vis. fellow Cambridge U., Eng., 1988; Sticerd Disting. visitor London Sch. Econs., 1998-2000, Centennial prof., 2001; vis. scholar Universiti Kebangsaan Malaysia Law Faculty, 1991; Fulbright sr. specialist, 2002; cons. Ford Found., 1977-82; mem. internat. adv. com. Office of the High Rep., Bosnia, 1998-99; McDonald-Currie Meml. lectr. McGill U., Montreal, 1980; mem. Coun. on Role of Cts., 1978-83; Opsahl lectr. Queen's U., Belfast, 2000. Author: The Courts and Social Policy (Nat. Acad. Public Adminstrn. Louis Brownlow prize for best book in pub. adminstrn. 1977), 1977; The Jurocracy: Government Lawyers, Agency Programs and Judicial Decisions, 1977; Coup Theories and Officers' Motives, 1980, Ethnic Groups in Conflict, 1985, A Democratic South Africa? Constitutional Engineering in a Divided Soc., 1991 (Am. Polit. Sci. Assn. Ralph J. Bunche award for best book in ethnic and cultural pluralism, 1992), The Deadly Ethnic Riot, 2001; mem. editl. bd. Ethnicity, 1974-82, Law and Contemporary Problems, 1983-84, 89-2000, Jour. Democracy, 1993—. V.p. Am. Soc. Polit. and Legal Philosophy, 2004—. Guggenheim fellow, 1980-81; Nat. Humanities Ctr. fellow, 1984; Carnegie scholar, 2001-2002. Fellow Am. Acad. Arts and Scis.; mem. Am. Soc. for Polit. and Legal Philosophy (v.p. 2004—). Office: Duke University School Law Durham NC 27708-0360 Office Phone: 919-613-7058.

HOROWITZ, FRANCES DEGEN, academic administrator, psychology educator; b. Bronx, NY, May 5, 1932; d. Irving and Elaine (Moinester) Degen; m. Floyd Ross Horowitz, June 23, 1953; children: Jason Degen, Benjamin Meyer Levi. BA, Antioch Coll., 1954; EdM, Goucher Coll., 1954; PhD, U. Iowa, 1959. Tchr. elem. sch., Iowa City, 1954-56; grad. rsch. asst. Iowa Child Welfare Sta., U. Iowa, 1956-59; asst. prof. psychology So. Oreg. Coll., Ashland, 1959-61; asst. prof. home econs. U. Kans., Lawrence, 1961-62, USHPS rsch. fellow, 1962-63, assoc. prof. dept. human devel. and family life, 1964-69, prof. dept. human devel. and family life, psychology, 1969—, chmn. dept., 1969-75, rsch. assoc., 1964-75, assoc. dean, 1975-78, vice chancellor rsch., grad. studies and pub. svc., also dean grad. sch., 1978-91, dir. Infant Rsch. Lab., 1964-91; pres. Grad. Sch. and Univ. Ctr. CUNY, 1991—2005, pres. emeritus, 2005—, prof. Grad. Sch. and U. Ctr., 2005—. Bd. dirs. Feminist Press; guest rsch. assoc. Bur. Child Rsch. U. Kans., and Parsons (Kans.) State Hosp. and Tng. Ctr., summer 1960; vis. prof. dept. psychology Tel Aviv U., 1973—74; guest rschr. dept. pediat. Kaplan Hosp., Rehovot, Israel, 1973—74; vis. lectr. dept. psychology Hebrew U., Jerusalem, 1976, cons. rsch. programs in early edn., 1980—; pres. Ctr. for Rsch., Inc., Lawrence, 1978—91; cons. OAS, 1971, U.S. Office Edn., 1969—73, NIMH, 1979; cons. to early infant stimulation program, Caracas, Venezuela, 76; lectr. infant devel., day care to local and regional cmty. groups, 1966—; adv. com. Carolina Inst. on Early Edn. of the Handicapped, 1978—83; reviewer NSF, 1978—91; mem. U. Kans. del. to Peoples Republic China, 1980; exch. scholar Chinese Acad. Scis., China, 1982; mem. Office Sci. Integrity Rev. Adv. Com. PHS, 1991—93; nominating com. Weizmann Women in Sci. award Am. Com. Weizmann Inst. Sci., 1994; mem. Nat. Task Force Grad. Edn., 1994—; workforce devel. subcom. N.Y.C. Partnership, 1994—; mem. U.S. Nat. Com. for the Internat. Union of Psychol. Sci., 1995—97; mem. overseers' com. to visit dept. psychology Harvard U.; mem., founding adv. bd. Sackler Inst. for Human Brain Devel., 1998—; bd. dirs. Nat. Coun. for Rsch. on Women; adv. coun. Nat. Inst. Child Health and Human Devel., 1999—2004; chair nat. adv. bd. Office Child Devel., U. Pitts.; lectr. in field. Editor Memoir Essay, 2002; co-editor science watch sect. Am. Psychologist, 1993—; mem. editl. bd. Jour. Devel. Psychology, 1969-75, Early Childhood Edn. Quar., 1974—, Devel. Rev., 1981—, Infant Behaviour and Devel., 1984—, Contemporary Psychology, 1986-1991; contbr. articles to profl. jours.; TV host Women to Women, 1994—. Trustee Antioch Coll., 1987-91, L.I. Univ., 1992—; bd. dirs. Cmty. Children's Ctr., 1965-68, Douglas County Vis. Nurse Assn., 1968-69; mem. workforce devel. subcom., N.Y.C. Partnership; mem. coun. advisors, Nat. Ctr. for Children in Poverty; mem. commn. on women in higher edn. Am. Coun. on Edn. Ford Found. fellow, 1954, Ctr. Advanced Studies Behavioral Scis. fellow Stanford U., 1983-84, Alumni fellow U. Iowa Coll. Arts and Scis., 2005; recipient Trustees award medal Cherry Lawn Sch., Conn., 1971, Outstanding Educator of Am. award, 1973, Disting. Psychologist in Mgmt. award Soc. for Psychologists in Mgmt., 1993, Rebecca Rice Alumni award Antioch Coll., 1996, Sue Rosenberg Zalk award The Feminist Press, 2003; named to Women's Hall of Fame U. Kans., 1974; Spl. Commendation NYC comptroller's office, 1997, NY Women's Agenda Star award, 2002. Fellow APA (pres. divsn. devel. psychology 1977-78, mem. publs. bd. 1985-91, chief sci. adviser 1989-93, pres. 1991-94, Centennial award 1992), U. Iowa Coll. Arts and Scis. Alumni; mem. AAAS, NY Acad. Scis., Am. Acad. Arts and Scis, Soc. Rsch. in Child Devel. (editor monographs 1976-83, pres. 1997-02), Jewish Cmty. Rels. Coun. (mem. bd. 1999—), Hebrew Free Loan Soc. (mem. bd. 2000—), Am. Assn. on Mental Deficiency, North Ctrl. Accrediting Assn. (bd. commrs. 1977-80), Am. Psychol. Found. (pres. 1991-94), Coun. Rsch. Polic and Grad. Edn. (chair, mem. exec. com.), Assn. Grad. Schs. (mem. exec. com.), N.Y. Women's Forum (bd. dirs. 1995—), Nat. Assn. of State Univs. and Land-Grant Colls. (past chair commn. on human resources and social change, bd. dirs. 1999-02), Sigma Xi, Phi Beta Kappa (hon.). Home: 710 W End Ave 2 New York NY 10025 Office: CUNY Grad Ctr 365 5th Ave New York NY 10016-4309 Office Phone: 212-817-7235. Business E-Mail: fdhorowitz@gc.cuny.edu.

HOROWITZ, GAYLE LYNN, physical education educator; b. Flushing, N.Y., Apr. 29, 1971; d. Robert and Ruth Lois (Brokowsky) H.; m. Chris Topping, Dec. 25, 1993. BS in Physical Edn., Queens Coll., 1993; MS in Physical Edn., Hofstra U., 1993. Lic. tchr. N.Y.C., N.Y.; certified profl. tennis instr., U.S. Nat. Tennis Acad. Teaching asst. Queens Coll., Flushing, N.Y., 1990; team sports activites splst. Pub. Sch. 219, Flushing, 1990-91; health phys. edn. tchr. Franklin K. Lanc HS, Bklyn., 1993-95, William C. Bryant H.S., Queens, 1995-96, John Bowne H.S., Queens, 1996—. Asst. jr. varsity volleyball coach John Bowne HS, Flushing, 1991; guest lectr. circus arts Hofstra U., 1993—, AIDS edn. Franklin K. Lane HS, 1994—. Auxiliary police officer, N.Y.C. Police Dept., Queens, 1988-92; faculty co-advisor Bisexual, Gay, Lesbian Student Union. Mem. United Federation Tchrs., Kissena Cycling Club (sec.). Democrat. Avocations: Judo, bicycling, Aikido, weight training. Office: John Bowne HS 63-25 Main St Flushing NY 11367

HOROWITZ, GEDALE BOB, investment banker; b. N.Y.C., June 13, 1932; s. Abraham and Florence (Bob) H.; m. Barbara Silver, Aug. 17, 1958; children: Ruth Ellen, Seth Robert. AB, Columbia U., 1953, JD, 1955. Bar: N.Y. 1956. With Salomon Bros., N.Y.C., 1955-67, gen. ptnr., 1967-81, mng. dir., 1981-87; exec. v.p., dir. Salomon, Inc., N.Y.C., 1981-97; sr. mng. dir. Salomon Smith Barney, 1997—, Citigroup Global Markets, Inc., 2002—. Vice chmn. bd. trustees Barnard Coll., 1976—; trustee and vice chmn. L.I. Jewish Hosp., 1982-98, chhmn., 1995-98; dir. Mspl. Assistance Corp., City of N.Y., 1989-94; bd. dirs. Jewish Cmty. Rels. Coun. on N.Y., Inc., 1989-2001, pres., 1998-2001; bd. dirs. Statue of Liberty-Ellis Island Found., Inc., 1999—; chmn. N.Y. State Local Govt. Assistance Corp., 1991-94; trustee, chmn. emeritus, exec. com. mem. North Shore/L.I. Jewish Health Sys., 1998—. Served with U.S. Army, 1956-58. Mem. Bond Market Assn. (chm. 1978-79), Securities Industry Assn. (treas. 19 87, chmn. 1991), Mcpl. Securities Rulemaking Bd. (chmn. 1977-78), Mcpl. Bond Club N.Y. (pres. 1982-83), The Bond Club of N.Y., Inc. (pres. 1994-95). Office: Citigroup Global Markets Inc 388 Greenwich St Fl 39 New York NY 10013-2339

HOROWITZ, HERBERT EUGENE, retired diplomat; b. Bklyn., July 10, 1930; s. Max and Jean (Pomerantz) Horowitz; m. Lenore Joan Glasser, Jan. 6, 1963; children: Jason, Richard. BA, Bklyn. Coll., 1952; MA, Columbia U., 1964, Fletcher Sch. Law & Diplomacy, 1965; diploma, Nat. War Coll., 1972. Econ. officer Am. Embassy, Taipei, Taiwan, 1957-62; chief China econ. unit U.S. Consulate, Hong Kong, 1965-69; chief comml. and econ. sect. U.S. Liaison Office, Beijing, 1973-75; dir. Office for Rsch. of East Asia Dept. State, Washington, 1975-78; dir. Office East-West Econ. Policy Dept. Treasury, Washington, 1979-80; consul gen. U.S. Consulate Gen., Sydney, Australia, 1981-84; dep. chief of mission U.S. Embassy, Beijing, 1984-86; amb. to Republic of Gambia, 1986-89. Lectr. history China, cons. Mem.: Am. Fgn. Svc. Assn., Dacor-Bacon Ho. Home and Office: 2737 Devonshire Pl NW # 111 Washington DC 20008-3454

HOROWITZ, IRVING LOUIS, publisher, educator; b. N.Y.C., Sept. 25, 1929; s. Louis and Esther (Tepper) H.; m. Ruth Lenore Horowitz, 1950 (div. 1964); children: Carl Frederick, David Dennis; m. Mary Curtis Horowitz, 1979. BSS, CCNY, 1951; MA, Columbia U., 1952; PhD, Buenos Aires U., 1957; fellow, Brandeis U., 1958-59. Asst. prof. sociology Bard Coll., 1960; assoc. prof. social theory Buenos Aires U., 1955-58; chmn. dept. sociology Hobart and William Smith Colls., 1960-63; from assoc. prof. to prof. sociology Washington U., St. Louis, 1963-69; chmn. dept. sociology Livingston Coll., Rutgers U., 1969-73; prof. sociology grad. faculty Rutgers U., 1969—, Hannah Arendt prof. social and polit. theory, 1979—; Bacardi chair Cuban studies U. Miami, 1992—94. Vis. prof. sociology U. Caracas, Venezuela, 1957, Buenos Aires U., 1959, 61, 63, SUNY, Buffalo, 1960, Syracuse U., 1961, U. Rochester, fall 1962, U. Calif., Davis, 1966, U. Wis., Madison, 1967, Stanford U., 1968-69, Am. U., 1972, Queen's U., Can., 1973, Princeton U., 1976, U. Miami, 1992; vis. lectr. London Sch. Econs. and Polit. Sci., 1962; prin. investigator for numerous sci. and rsch. projects; chmn. bd. dirs., editor-in-chief Transaction/Aldine. Author: Idea of War and Peace in Contemporary Philosophy, 1957, Philosophy, Science and the Sociology of Knowledge, 1960, Radicalism and the Revolt Against Reason: The Social Theories of Georges Sorel, 2d edit., 1968, The war Game; Studies of the New Civilian Militarists, 1963, Historia y Elementos de la Sociologia del Connocimento, 1963, Professing Sociology: The Life Cycle of a Social Science, 1963, The New Sociology: Essays in Social Science and Social Values in Honor of C. Wright Mills, 1964, Revolution in Brazil: Politics and Society in a Developing Nation, 1964, The Rise and Fall of Project Camelot, 1967, rev. edit., 1976, Three Worlds of Development: The Theory and Practice of International Stratification, 1966, rev. edit., 1972, Latin American Radicalism: A Documentary Report on Nationalist and Left Movements, 1969, Sociological Self-Images, 1969, The Knowledge Factory: Masses in Latin America, 1970, Cuban Communism, 1970, 11th edit., 2003, Foundations of Political Sociology, 1972, Social Science and Public Policy in the United States, 1977, Dialogues on American Politics, 1979, Taking Lives: Genocide and State Power, 1979, 5th edit., 2001, Beyond Empire and Revolution, 1982, C. Wright Mills: An American Utopian, 1983, Winners and Losers, 1985, Communicating Ideas, 1987, Daydreams and Nightmares, 1990 (winner best biography Nat. Jewish Book Award), The Decomposition of Sociology, 1993, Behemoth: Main Currents in the History and Theory of Political Sociology, 1999, Veblen's Century: A Collective Portrait, 2002, Tributes: An Informal History of Twentieth Century Social Science. Chmn. bd. Hubert H. Humphrey Inst. Ben Gurion U.; bd. mem. Alexis DeTocqueville Inst., 2003—. Recipient Harold D. Lasswell award Policy Sci. Orgn., Lifetime Achievement award Inter-Univ. Seminar on Armed Forces and Soc., Gerhart Niemeyer Award Disting. Contbns. to Scholarship in Liberal Arts Intercollegiate Studies Assn., 2003, Internat. Humanist award in sci. and pub. svc., 2004, Thomas S. Szasz award for outstanding contbns. to civil liberties Ctr. for Ind. Thought, 2004. Fellow AAAS; founding mem, AAAS Sci and Human Rights Program; mem. AAUP, USIA (bd. advisors), Am. Polit. Sci. Assn., Nat. Assn. Scholars (bd. dirs.), Authors Guild, Ctr. for Study The Presidency, Coun. Fgn. Rels., Internat. Soc. Polit. Psychology (founder), Soc. Internat. Devel., U.S. Gen. Acctg. Office (exec. adv. bd.), U.S. Info. Agy. (exec. adv. bd. Radio and TV Marti), Nat. Assn. Scholars (bd. dirs.), Inst. for a Free Cuba, Raymond Aron Soc. (N.Am. pres. 2004-). Achievements include Subject of Festschrift: The Democratic Imagination, 1994. Home: 1247 State Rd # Rt206 Princeton NJ 08540-1619 Office: Rutgers U Transaction Pubs Bldg 4051 New Brunswick NJ 08903 Office Phone: 732-445-2280. Office Fax: 732-445-3138. Business E-Mail: ihorowitz@transactionpub.com.

HOROWITZ, JACK, biochemistry educator; b. Vienna, Nov. 25, 1931; came to U.S., 1938; s. Joseph and Florence (Gutterman) H.; m. Carole Ann Sager, June 11, 1961; children— Michael Joseph, Jeffrey Frederick. BS, CCNY, 1952; PhD, Ind. U., 1957. Rsch. assoc. Columbia U., N.Y.C., 1957-61; asst. prof. biochemistry Iowa State U., Ames, 1961-65, assoc. prof. biochemistry, 1965-71, prof. biochemistry, 1971-95, Univ. prof., 1995-2000, Univ. prof. emeritus, 2000—, chmn. dept. biochemistry, 1971-74, chmn. molecular, cellular and devel. biology program, 1977-80. Vis. scholar Rockefeller U., N.Y.C., 1968; vis. prof. Yale U., 1974-75; vis. scientist MIT, 1990-91; program dir. biophysics and biochemistry NSF, 1993-94. Contbr. articles to profl. jours. NSF fellow, 1952-54, 57-59; NIH and NSF grantee, 1961—; recipient faculty citation Iowa State U., 1989. Mem. RNA Soc., Am. Soc. Biochemistry and Molecular Biology, AAAS, Phi Beta Kappa, Sigma Xi, Phi Kappa Phi Jewish. Home: 2014 Country Club Blvd Ames IA 50014-7013 Office: Iowa State U Dept Biochemistry Biophys Ames IA 50011-0001 Business E-Mail: jhoro@iastate.edu.

HOROWITZ, JOSEPH IRVING, writer, educator; b. N.Y.C., Feb. 12, 1948; BA, Swarthmore Coll, 1970. Music critic N.Y. Times, 1976-80; program editor, prin. annotator Kaufmann Concert Hall of the 92d St. Y, 1981-94; artistic advisor, exec. dir., exec. prodr. Bklyn. Philharm. Orch., 1992-97; mem. faculty dept. music history and music edn. New Eng. Conservatory of Music, 1998—. Lectr. Bayreuth Festival, summer 1998, also music schs., univs., music festivals, U.S.; spkr. Salzburg Seminar, ann. conv. Am. Musicol. Soc. and Am. Symphony Orch. League; tchr. Mannes Coll. Music; vis. prof. Inst. for Studies in Am. Music at Bklyn. Coll. Author: Conversations with Arrau, 1982 (ASCAP-Deems Taylor award for excellence in writing about music), Understanding Toscanini—How He Became an American Culture-God and Helped Create a New Audience for Old Music, 1987 (one of the most disting. books of yr. Nat. Book Critics Cir.), pub. as paperback edit. Understanding Toscanini-A Social History of American Concert Life, The Ivory Trade—Piano Competition and the Business of Music, 1990, Classical Music in America-A History of its Rise and Fall, 1990, Wagner Nights: An American History, 1994 (Irving Lowens award Sonneck Soc. 1996), The Post-Classical Predicament: Essays on Music and Society, 1995, Classical Music in America, 2005, Dvorak in America: In Search of the New World, 2003; editor 6 Bklyn. Philharm. program books, (ASCAP-Deems Taylor award for excellence in writing on music); dir. (DVD) Dvorak in America, 2003; contbr. articles to profl. publs. Address: 49 W 96th St Apt 6G New York NY 10025-6523 Personal E-mail: horowitz4@juno.com.

HOROWITZ, KENNETH A., communications executive, entrepreneur; b. 1951; AB cum laude, Cornell U., 1973. One of original founders Cellular One; lead investor S. Fla. Soccer, L.L.C., Ft. Lauderdale; owner, operator various cellular phone bus. ventures, U.S.; banking, real estate, comm. and tech. entrepreneur; founder, owner Miami Fusion, 1998—2002. Bd. dirs. pvt. and pub. cos. Achievements include pioneer work in the wireless telephone industry.

HOROWITZ, MARY CURTIS See CURTIS, MARY

HOROWITZ, MARYANNE CLINE, history professor; b. Boston, Mass., June 29, 1945; d. James Edward and Ethel E. Cline; m. Ellis Horowitz, June 23, 1968; children: Pipi R. Diamond, Edward G., Ira. AB cum laude, Brown U., 1965; MAT, Harvard U., 1966; MA, U. Wis., 1968, PhD, 1970. Instr. of govt. Cornell U., Ithaca, NY, 1970—71, rsch. assoc. sci., tech. and society program, 1971—73; asst. prof. politics Ithaca Coll., 1972—73; rsch. assoc. in theology and ch. history Divinity Sch. Harvard U., Cambridge, Mass., 1979—80; reader Warburg Inst. and Inst. Hist. Rsch. U. London, 1997; rsch. assoc. UCLA, 1988—; asst. prof. history Occidental Coll., L.A., 1973—. Mem. advanced placement history design com. Ednl. Testing Svc., Princeton, NJ, 1995—97; founder, chair women's studies adv. com. Occidental Coll., 1977—79, 1982—85, chair history dept., 1988—91; vis. prof. history UCLA, 1992, Title IX officer, 1993—, vis. scholar Ctr. for Study of Women, 2003—04. Author: Seeds of Virtue and Knowledge, 1998 (Jacques Barzun award Am. Philos. Soc., 1999); contbr. articles to profl. jours., chpts. to books; editor (with A.J. Cruz and W.A. Furman): Renaissance Rereadings: Intertext and Context, 1988; editor: (with J. Brink and A. Coudert) Politics of Gender in Early Modern Europe, 1989; editor-in-chief: New Dictionary of the History of Ideas, 2005 (Outstanding Reference Source, ALA, 2005); mem. editl. bd., search com., publ. com. Jour. of History of Ideas, 1976—. Fellow Ford Found., 1968, 1969; grantee NEH, 1971, Haynes Found., 1974, 1977, Mellon Found., 1979, Louis and Hermione Brown Humanities Support Fund, 1995, 1997, Mellon Found., 1998—99, 1999—2000, Louis and Hermione Brown Humanities Support Fund, 1999, Lilly Found., 2003—; Ford Faculty-Student fellow, 1990, 1991. Mem.: 16th Century Studies Conf. (coun. 1977—80, Nancy L. Roelker prize com. 2002, Nancy L. Roelker prize 2002), Renaissance Conf. So. Calif. (v.p. 1982—83, pres. 1983—85, program chair nat. conf. 1985, exec. editl. adv. bd. 1985—88), Internat. Soc. Intellectual History, Am. Hist. Assn. (steering com. 1979—80, coordinating com. for women in hist. profession), Renaissance Soc. Am. (nominating com. 1985—86, exec. bd. 1986—98). Democrat. Jewish. Avocations: horseback riding, tennis, museums, travel. Office: Occidental Coll 1600 Campus Rd Los Angeles CA 90041 Office Phone: 323-259-2583. Business E-Mail: horowitz@oxy.edu.

HOROWITZ, MITCH, editor, writer; b. Manhasset, NY, Nov. 23, 1965; s. Howard and Dacia Horowitz; m. Allison Orr, Apr. 8, 2000. Bachelor's degree, SUNY, Stony Brook, 1988. Exec. editor Tarcher/Penguin, N.Y.C., 2003—, sr. editor, 1997—2003. Sr. editor The Free Press/Simon & Schuster, N.Y.C., 1995—97; vis. fellow Jerusalem Book Fair; panelist N.Y. Open Ctr. Guest editor: Sci. of Mind Mag.; editor: The Secret Teachings of All Ages, 2004; contbr. articles to popular mags. Mem.: Assn. for Rsch. and Enlightenment (sponsoring mem.). Office: Penguin Group (USA) 375 Hudson St New York NY 10014 Office Phone: 212-366-2512. Business E-Mail: mitch.horowitz@us.penguingroup.com.

HOROWITZ, MORRIS A., retired economics professor; b. Newark, Nov. 19, 1919; s. Samuel and Anna (Litwin) H.; m. Jean Ginsburg, July 12, 1941; children— Ruth, Joel. BA in Econs., NYU, 1940; PhD in Econs., Harvard U., 1954. Mem. faculty Northeastern U., Boston, 1956—, prof. econs., chmn. dept., 1959-90, prof. emeritus, 1992—. Vice-chmn. Mass. Joint Labor-Mgmt. Com. for Mcpl. Police and Fire, 1980—; ad hoc labor arbitrator, manpower cons. Home: 1010 Waltham St Apt 341 Lexington MA 02421-8064 Office Phone: 781-861-1153.

HOROWITZ, PHILIP MARTIN, lawyer; b. Newark, Aug. 23, 1946; s. Paul and Louise (Cohen) H.; m. Carol Ruth Weiner, June 28, 1970; children: Jason, Benjamin, Michael. AB magna cum laude, Upsala Coll., 1970; JD, Georgetown U., 1973. Bar: Va. 1973, DC 1973. Assoc. Melrod, Redman & Gartlan, Washington, 1973-79, shareholder-dir., 1979-93, chmn. real estate dept., 1981-93; ptnr. Arter & Hadden, Washington, 1993—2001, chmn. nat. real estate practice group, 1994—2001, mem. exec. com., 1997—2001; ptnr., real estate Venable LLP, Washington, 2002—. Bd. dirs. Washington com. State of Israel Bonds; v.p., bd. dirs. exec. com. Mentors, Inc.; adj. prof. real estate planning Washington Coll. Law, Am. U., 1988—. Mem. exec. coun. D.C. Bldg. Industry Assn. With U.S. Army, 1966-68. Mem. Am. Coll. Real Estate Lawyers (chmn. mem. selection com. 1997-98), D.C. Bar Assn., Va. Bar Assn. Avocations: swimming, basketball, softball. Office: Venable LLP 575 7th St NW Washington DC 20004 Office Phone: 202-344-4746. Office Fax: 202-344-8300. Business E-Mail: phorowitz@venable.com.

HOROWITZ, RAYMOND J., lawyer, director; b. N.Y.C., May 7, 1916; s. Israel S. and Sadye (Freiman) H.; m. Margaret Goldenberg, Sept. 22, 1940; 1 dau., Judith. AB, Columbia U., 1936, LL.B., 1939. Bar: N.Y. 1939. Pvt. practice, N.Y.C., 1939-41; asst. corp. counsel City of N.Y., 1941-43; assoc. Meyer, Wallach & Silverson, N.Y.C., 1943-46; ptnr. McGoldrick, Dannett, Horowitz & Golub and predecessors, N.Y.C., 1946-69; former mem., now of counsel firm Graubard Miller and predecessors, 1969—. Cons. Nat. Housing Agy, 1946-47, Office Housing Expediter, 1947, Temporary State Housing Rent Commn., 1950-51 Author: (with others) Building Regulation in New York City, 1944. Chmn. trustees' vis. com. on Am. paintings and sculpture Met. Mus. Art. Mem. Assn. Bar City N.Y., N.Y. County Lawyers Assn., Phi Beta Kappa. Clubs: Century Assn. Home: 930 Fifth Ave New York NY 10021-2651 Office: Graubard Miller 405 Lexington Ave New York NY 10174-1901

HOROWITZ, SAMUEL BORIS, biomedical researcher, educational consultant; b. Perth Amboy, N.J., Aug. 26, 1927; s. Sol and Lillian (Levine) H.; m. Joan Hughes, June 15, 1956 (div. 1971); m. Marian Sylvia Herman, May 23, 1973 (div. 1986); 1 child, Ann Julia AB, Hunter Coll., N.Y.C., 1951; PhD, U. Chgo., 1956. Research assoc. Eastern Pa. Psychiat. Inst., Phila., 1958-62; vis. investigator Inst. Physiol. and Med. Biophysics U. Uppsala, Sweden, 1962-63; head lab. A. Einstein Med. Ctr., Phila., 1963-72; chief cellular physiology lab. Mich. Cancer Found., Detroit, 1972-93, chmn. dept. biology, 1975-78, chmn. dept. physiology and biophysics, 1981-93. Contbr. articles to profl. jours. Served with U.S. Army, 1946-47 Fellow AAAS; mem. Am. Assn. Cancer Research, Am. Soc. Cell Biology, Sigma Xi. Home and Office: 4159 Woodland Dr Ann Arbor MI 48103-9775 Office Phone: 734-426-2403. E-mail: sbg3210@aol.com.

HOROWITZ, SARA, labor organizer; b. NYC, Jan. 13, 1963; BS, Cornell U., 1984; JD, SUNY, Buffalo, 1992; MPA, Harvard U., 1995. Labor atty. pvt. practice; pub. defender NYC; union organizer Nat. Health and Human Svc. Employees Union, 1199; founder, exec. dir. Working Today, 1995—. Arbitrator Am. Arbitration Assn., Task Force on Restructuring Am.'s Labor Market Institutions, MIT. Contbr. articles to profl. jours. Grantee, fellow Stern Family Fund, Rockefeller Found., Echoing Green. Office: Working Today Ste 710 45 Main St Brooklyn NY 11201 Office Phone: 718-532-1515. Office Fax: 718-222-4440. E-mail: info@workingtoday.org.*

HOROWITZ, STEVE MICHAEL, composer; b. Brooklyn, NY, Oct. 3, 1964; s. Albert and Diane Lee Horowitz; m. Elizabeth Joy Fischer, Jan. 1, 1994; 1 child, Phineas Fischer. Coll., Calif. Inst. of the Arts, 1986—89. Music dir. Calif. Shakespeare Festival, Orinda, 1992—93; audio dir. Nickelodeon Online, NYC, 2000—; pres. The Code Internat. Inc, NYC. Chmn. Interactive Audio Spl. Interest Group, 2002—04. Composer: (chamber music) The Ribbon of Extremes, Amsterdam Suite, (cd) The Code (PONK), The Phycosexual Album, San Francisco Chronicled, 1990 - 1996, The Code International Elevator Culture, (string quartet) Remote Control, Pa Kua, (orchestra) Mix ReMix, (films) Don Gorske Mac Daddy, Super Size Me (Acadamy Award Nomination, 2004), The Re-Taking of Pelham One Two Three, (TV series) Fairly Odd Parents, I Bet You Will, Casino Cinema, Films of Fury, (web) Audio Farm, (web game) Take Blue To School, (web cartoon) Toondirector Series, (video game) Cadillacs and Dinosaurs. Recipient Grammy Award winning Engr., Acad. of Rec. Arts and Sciences, 1996, Webby Award Winning Composer/Sound designer, Internat. Acad. of Digital Arts and Sciences, 2003, Silver Medal Winning Sound designer, Broadcast Design award, 2003. Mem.: ASCAP, Am. Music Ctr., Game Audio Network Guild (founding mem. 2002). Personal E-mail: fluffy@thecopeinternational.com.

HOROWITZ, STEVEN F., cardiologist; MD, N.Y. Med. Coll., 1972. Diplomate in internal medicine and cardiovasc. disease Am. Bd. Internal Medicine. Resident in medicine Beth Israel Med. Ctr., 1972—76; resident in cardiology, fellow in medicine Mt. Sinai Hosp., N.Y.C., 1976—79; attending physician cardiovasc. disease Beth Israel Med. Ctr., N.Y.C., 1988—2002; dir. cardiology Stamford (Conn.) Hosp., 2003—. Clin. prof. medicine and nuc. medicine Albert Einstein Coll. Medicine. Home: 250 Rosedale Ave White Plains NY 10605 Office: PO Box 9317 Shelburne and W Broad St Stamford CT 06904-9317 E-mail: shorowitz@stamhealth.org.

HOROWITZ, STEVEN GARY, lawyer; b. Miami Beach, Fla., Sept. 4, 1950; s. Arthur R. and Bernice (Schwamm) H.; m. Susan Eve Haar, Dec. 7, 1985, children: Jessica Zoe, Benjamin Will, Adam Jedidiah. BA magna cum laude, Yale U., 1972; JD and M in pub. policy cum laude, Harvard U., 1978. Bar: Mass. 1979, U.S. Dist. Ct. Mass. 1979, N.Y. 1988. Asst. planner N.Y.C. Dept. Planning, 1972-74; law clk. to judge U.S. Dist. Ct., Boston, 1978-79, ct. monitor, 1979-81; assoc. Hill and Barlow, Boston, 1981-85; ptnr. Hill & Barlow, 1985-87; of counsel Cleary, Gottlieb, Steen & Hamilton, N.Y.C., 1987-88, ptnr., 1989—. Author: Primer on Transferable Development Rights, 1979, Lender Liability for Cleaning Up Wastes, 1979, Legal Rights and Institutional Reform Litigation: Can The Judiciary Produce Results?, 1988. Bd. dirs. and gen. counsel Arts/Boston, 1983-87; cons. to Mayor of Jerusalem, 1981-83. Mem. Mass. Bar Assn. (pub. law sect. council 1985-87), Boston Bar Assn., N.Y. State Bar Assn. (exec. com. real property law sect. 1989—), Assn. of Bar of City of N.Y. (real property law com.), Am. Coll Real Estate Lawyers, Legal Aid Soc. (dir. 2001—), Anglo-Am. Real Property Inst. Democrat. Jewish. Office: Cleary Gottlieb 1 Liberty Plz New York NY 10006-1404 Office Phone: 212-225-2580. Office Fax: 212-225-3999. Business E-Mail: shorowitz@cgsh.com.

HOROWITZ, WINONA LAURA See RYDER, WINONA

HORRELL, JEFFREY LANIER, library administrator; b. Carbondale, Ill., Sept. 19, 1952; s. C. William and Ettelye M. (Hanser) H. BA, Miami U., Oxford, Ohio, 1975; AM in Libr. Sci., U. Mich., 1976, AM in History of Art, 1978; PhD, Syracuse U., 1995. Libr. intern Nat. Gallery of Art, Washington, 1977; asst. libr. art and architecture U. Mich., Ann Arbor, 1977-80; libr., Sherman Art Libr. Dartmouth Coll, Hanover, NH, 1981-86; Coun. Libr. Resources libr. mgmt. intern Syracuse U. Libr., 1986-87, asst. to univ. libr. for planning, 1987-88; libr., Fine Arts Libr. Harvard Coll., Cambridge, 1992-98, assoc. libr. for collections, 1998—2005; dean of libraries, coll. libr. Dartmouth Coll., Hanover, NH, 2005—. Pres. ARLIS/NA, 1987. Author: Treasures of the Hood Museum of Art, 1985; contbr. articles to profl. publs. Mem. ALA, Coll. Art Assn., Art Libr. Soc. N.Am. (pres. 1987-88), U. Mich. of Info. Studies Alumni Soc. (pres. 1997-98). Avocations: travel, photography. Office: Dartmouth Coll Libr Hanover NH 03755 Office Phone: 603-646-2560.

HORRELL, KAREN HOLLEY, insurance company executive, lawyer; b. Augusta, Ga., July 10, 1952; d. Dudley Cornelius and Eleanor (Shouppe) Holley; m. Jack E. Horrell, Aug. 14, 1976. BS, Berry Coll., 1974; JD, Emory U., 1976. Bar: Ohio 1977. Corp. counsel Great Am. Ins. Co., Cin., 1977-80, v.p., gen. counsel, sec., 1981-85, sr. v.p., gen. counsel, sec., bd. dirs., 1985—; pres. corp. svcs. Great Am. Ins. Property & Casualty Group, 1999—; counsel Am. Fin. Corp., 1980-81; gen. counsel numerous subsidiaries Great Ins. Co.; sec., asst. sec. numerous other fin. and ins. cos. Bd. dirs. Tri-Health, Inc., Bethesda, Inc. Trustee Cmty. Chest, 1987—91, Seven Hills Sch., 1991—2000, v.p., 1995—99; mem. cabinet United Appeal, 1984; bd. dirs. YWCA, 1984—90, v.p. fin., 1986—89; mem. Hamilton County Blue Ribbon Task Force on Child Abuse and Neglect Svcs., 1989—91; trustee Ohio Ins. Inst., 1994—2000, chair, 1996—99, Bethesda Hosp. Inc.; chair Ohio Joint Underwriting Assn., 1992—97; trustee Berry Coll., 1999—; mem. Hamilton County Hosp. Commn., 1999—, vice chair, 2002—; bd. dirs. Children's Home, 2001—. Mem. ABA, Cin. Bar Assn. (admissions com. 1978-91, nominating com. 1987-90). Democrat. Home: 2355 Easthill Ave Cincinnati OH 45208-2608 Office: Great Am Ins Co 580 Walnut St Cincinnati OH 45202-3110

HORRIGAN, BRIAN RICHARD, economist; b. Washington, Sept. 30, 1951; s. William Kienle and Eleanor Gertrude (Ahern) H. BA in Econs., Santa Clara U., 1973; MA in Econs., UCLA, 1975, PhD in Econs., 1980. Economist Fed. Reserve Bank of Phila., Research Dept., Phila., 1980-87; dir. long-term forecasting The WEFA Group, Bala Cynwyd, Pa., 1987-92; sr. economist, v.p. Loomis, Sayles & Co., Boston, 1992-2000, chief economist, 2000—. Bd. dirs. Nat. Assn. for Bus. Econs. Contbr. articles to profl. jours. Mem. Am. Econ. Assn. Office: Loomis Sayles & Co 1 Financial Ctr Fl 34 Boston MA 02111-2660 E-mail: bhorrigan@loomissayles.com.

HORRIGAN, D. GREGORY, packaging products executive; b. Des Moines, Iowa, 1943; Graduate, U. Iowa, Iowa City, 1966. Exec. v.p. Continental Can Co., 1984—87; co-founder, dir. Silgan Holdings Inc., Stamford, Conn., 1987—, co-CEO, 1994—, co-chmn., 2004—. Office: Silgan Holdings Inc Ste 400 4 Landmark Sq Stamford CT 06901*

HORRIGAN, PATRICK E., writer, language educator; b. Reading, Pa., Sept. 18, 1963; s. John F. Jr. and Margaret E. (Ermentrout) H. BA, Cath. U., 1985; PhD, Columbia U., 1994. Tchr. Harvey Milk H.S. for Lesbian and Gay Youth, N.Y.C., 1988-90; prof. English L.I. U., Bklyn., 1993—. Author: Widescreen Dreams: Growing Up Gay at the Movies, 1999; (play) Messages for Gary, 1999. Democrat. Roman Catholic. Avocation: piano. E-mail: pehorrigan@aol.com.

HORROCKS, NORMAN, librarian, educator, editor; b. Manchester, Eng., Oct. 18, 1927; arrived in Canada, 1971; s. Edward Henry and Annie (Barnes) Horrocks; m. Sandra Sheriff, Feb. 3, 1967; children: Julie Carol, Carl Scott, Gina Louise, Anne Patricia, Sarah Helen. Degree, Sch. Libr., Manchester, Eng., 1950, Libr. Assn. Australia, 1957; BA, U. Western Australia, 1960; MLS, U. Pitts., 1964, PhD, 1971. Asst. libr. Manchester Pub. Librs., 1943-45, 50-53; libr. Brit. Coun., Cyprus, 1954-55; tech. libr. State Libr. We. Australia, 1956—63; tchg. fellow U. Pitts., 1963-64, instr., 1964-69, asst. prof., 1969-71; assoc. prof. Sch. Libr. Sci., Dalhousie U., Halifax, 1971-73, prof., 1973-86, dir. sch., 1972-86, dean Faculty Mgmt. Studies, 1983-86, prof. emeritus, 1995—. Vis. lectr. Perth Tech. Coll., 1961—63, U. Hawaii, 1969; ext. lectr. Pa. State Libr., 1966—70; adj. prof. Rutgers U., 1987—95; chmn. Overseas Book Ctr., Halifax, 1980—83; mem. adv. bd. sci. and tech. info. Nat. Rsch. Coun. Can., 1980—86; mem. adv. bd. com. bibliog. svcs. Nat. Libr. Can., 1980—86; v.p. editl. Scarecrow Press, Metuchen, NJ, 1986—95; editl. cons., Lanham, Md., 1995—; mem. promotion and distbn. panel Can. Coun. Editor: N. We. Newsletter, 1952—53, Jour. Edn. Librarianship, 1971—76; assoc. editor: Govt. Publ. Rev., 1973—81; contbr. articles to profl. jours. Bd. visitors Pratt Inst. Rutgers U. With Brit. Army, 1945—48. Recipient Merit award, Atlantic Provinces Libr. Assn., 1979, Disting. Alumnus award, U. Pitts., 1982. Fellow: Libr. Assn. (U.K.) (hon.); mem.: ALA (hon.; coun. 1972—81, exec. bd. 1977—81, coun. 1983—95, various coms., Lippincott award 1995, Forest Press award 2001), Progressive Librs. Guild, N.J. Libr. Assn. (Disting. Svc. award coll. and univ. sect. 1995), Australian Libr. and Info. Assn., Assn. Am. Libr. Schs. (chmn. editl. bd. 1971—76), Assn. Libr. and Info. Sci. Edn. (pres. 1985—86, Svc. award 1990, Profl. Contbns. award 1996), Intelligence Corps Assn. (life), N.S. Libr. Assn. (life), Can. Coun. Libr. Schs. (chmn. 1974—76), Halifax Libr. Assn., Can. Libr. Assn. (2d v.p. 1978—80, various coms., Outstanding Svc. to Librarianship award 1995), Am. Inst. Parliamentarians, Am. Soc. Info. Sci. & Tech. (various coms.), Bibliosmiles, Archons of Colophon (convenor 1992), Beta Phi Mu (pres. 1991—93, Kaula Gold medal 2004). Home: 2 Casavechia Ct Dartmouth NS Canada B2X 3G6 Office: PO Box 440 Dartmouth NS Canada B2Y 3Y5 Office Phone: 902-434-8568. Business E-Mail: norman.horrocks@dal.ca.

HORRY, ROBERT, professional basketball player; b. Aug. 25, 1970; B.A., Univ. Alabama, 1992. Forward Houston Rockets, Tex., 1992—96, Phoenix Suns, Ariz., 1996—97, LA Lakers, Calif., 1997—2003, San Antonio Spurs, Tex., 2003—. Achievements include member, 2005 NBA Nat. Championship Team. Office: San Antonio Spurs One SBC Ctr San Antonio TX 78219

HORSAGER, KENT, stock exchange executive; BS in agrl. econ., U. Minn.; MS in agrl. econ., U. Calif., Davis. Pres. Horsager Trading Co., 1987—2000; bd. dirs. Mpls. Grain Exch., 1991—, bd. chmn., 1996—99, CEO and pres., 2000—. Oilseed and product mcht. Cargill, Inc., Internat. Oilseed Processing Group; econ. lectr. U. Mainz, Germersheim, Germany; mktg. cons. Superior Farming Co., Germersheim, Germany. Office: Mpls Grain Exch 400 S 4th St Minneapolis MN 55415*

HORSBRUGH, PATRICK, architect, educator, environologist; b. Belfast, No. Ireland, June 21, 1920; came to U.S., 1960; s. Charles Bethune and Marion Rose (McQueen) H. Diploma with honors, Archtl. Assn. Sch. Architecture, 1949; diploma city planning, U. London, 1951. With Raglan Squire and Ptnrs., London, 1956-57; vis. critic Harvard Grad. Sch. Design, 1956; with depts. architecture, planning and landscape architecture univs. Ill., N.C., 1957-58; dep. dir., then dir. Hamilton-Wentworth (Ont.) Planning Area Bd., 1958-60. Vis. prof. architecture U. Nebr., 1960-65, U. Tex., 1965-67; prof. architecture U. Notre Dame, 1967-84, prof. emeritus, dir. grad program environic studies, 1970-80; founder, chmn. bd. Environic Found. Internat., Inc., 1970-94; cons. environ. and planning issues, ednl. and design practices; adj. prof. dept. architecture Andrews U., Mich. Designer: High Paddington Project, London, 1951; co-designer: New Barbican Com. Project, London, 1954; contbr: Winston Churchill Meml. in the U.S. commemorating the Iron Curtain Speech given in Fulton, Mo.; author: High Buildings in the United Kingdom, 1952, Pittsburgh Perceived, The Form, Features and Feasibilities of the Prodigious City, 1963; editor: The Texas Conference on Our Environmental Crisis, 1966. Co-chmn. Internat. Earth Day, 1978; v.p. Channel Tunnel Assn., 1974-94; mem. Ind. curriculum adv. coun. Ind. Bd. Edn., 1986; Earth trustee Earth Soc. Found. With Royal Arty., 1938-41; with RAF Vol. Res., 1941-46. Bernard Webb fellow Academica Britannica, Rome, 1950; B.Y. Morrison Meml. lectr. U.S. Dept. Agr., 1969. Fellow AIA (regional and urban design com.), Royal Soc. Arts, Royal Geog. Soc., Brit. Interplanetary Soc., Am. Inst. Cert. Planners; mem. AAAS, Royal Inst. Brit. Architects, Royal Town Planning Inst., Am. Planning Assn., Ancient Monument Soc., Soc. Indsl. Archaeology, Soc. Protection Ancient Bldgs, Georgian Group, Nat. Trust (Gt. Britain), Am. Soc. Landscape Architects (hon.), Am. Soc. Interior Designers (hon.), Irish Georgian soc., Ry. Devel. Soc., Christopher Wren Soc. (founder, London 1995), Ecolesiological Soc., No. Ireland Partnership. Address: 916 Saint Vincent St South Bend IN 46617-1443

HORSBURGH, CHARLES ROBERT, allergist; b. Cleve., 1946; MD, Case Western Res. U., 1977. Intern Mass. Gen. Hosp., Boston, 1977-78; resident in internal medicine U. Colo. Hosps., Denver, 1978-80, resident in infectious diseases, 1980-82; fellow in allergy and immunology Nat. Jewish Hosp., Denver, 1981-83; with Ctrs. for Disease Control, Atlanta. Mem. Am. Soc. Microbiology, Infectious Disease Soc. Am. Address: Pub Health & Med Boston U 715 Albany St Boston MA 02118-2526 Office: Ctrs for Disease Control Mailstop G-29 Atlanta GA 30333

HORSCH, KATHLEEN JOANNE, social services administrator, educator, consultant; b. Mpls., June 27, 1936; d. Clement Nicholas and Delta Jesse (Steckman) Simmer; m. Lawrence Leonard Horsch, Aug. 25, 1956; children: Daniel L., Timothy J., Christopher G., Catherine J., Sarah E. Student, U. Minn., 1967-73. Various positions local, state and nat. levels Am. Cancer Soc., Mpls., 1965—, pres. Hennepin County bd. dirs., 1978, hon. life mem. Hennepin Unit bd., 1992—, chmn. bd. dirs. Minn. divsn., 1984-86, hon. life mem. Minn. divsn., 1993—, sec. nat. bd. N.Y.C., 1982-85, vice-chmn. nat. bd., 1985-87, chmn. nat. bd. Atlanta, 1987-89, past officer, dir. nat. bd., 1992-97, hon. life mem., 1997—, chair Lane W. Adams award com., 1993-98; pres. Dynamics of Vol. Effectiveness, Inc., Mpls., 1985-95. Mem. faculty Met. State U., St. Paul, 1982-94, U.S. Nat. Com./Internat. Union Against Cancer UICC, Washington, 1989-94. Mem. adv. bd. Look Good Feel Better, 1986—2003, Drucker Found. Non-Profit Mgmt., 1992-2003; mem. com. Joint Commn. Health, 1989; bd. govs. United Way Am., 1990-96, St. Croix area United Way, 1996-2002, vice-chair, 1997; bd. govs. Youth for Understanding Internat. Exch., 1992-2001, vice-chair, 1997, chair, 1998-2000; bd. govs. Courage Ctr., 1993-2004, vice-chair, 1996-2000, chair, 2000-02; mem. coun. Internat. Cancer Union, 1990-94, chair campaign orgn. pub. edn. and svc. program, 2990-94; bd. dirs. Josephson Inst. Tehics, 1991-96; pres. Mobilizing the Human Spirit; the Role of Civil Society in America. Recipient Svc. to Mankind award. Mem. Nat. Human Svcs. Assembly (bd. govs. 1995—), Minikahda Club. Avocations: boating, piano, swimming, hiking. Personal E-mail: klhorsch@earthlink.net.

HORSCH, LAWRENCE LEONARD, venture capitalist, corporate financial executive; b. Mpls., Dec. 2, 1934; s. Leonard Charles and Cecilia May (Chamberlain) H.; m. Kathleen Joanne Simmer, Aug. 25, 1956; children: Daniel Lawrence, Timothy John, Christopher Girard, Catherine Jessica, Sarah Elisabeth. BA with honors, Coll. St. Thomas, 1957; MBA, Northwestern U., 1958. Investment banker Paine Webber Jackson & Curtis, Mpls., 1961-67; v.p. N.Am. Fin. Corp., Mpls., 1967-71; pres. Eagle Investment Corp., Mpls., 1971-87; chmn., CEO Munsingwear Inc., Mpls., 1987—90; chmn. bd. Eagle Mgmt. & Fin. Corp., Mpls., 1990—. Chmn. bd. dirs. Sci. Med. Life Sys., Maple Grove, Minn., 1971-94, Med. C.V. Inc., 2003—; bd. dirs. Leuthold Funds, Inc., Gillette Splty. Healthcare. 1st lt. USAF, 1959-61. Mem. Fin. Analysts Fedn., Mpls. Rotary, Minikahda Country Club. Home: 1404 Hilltop Rdg Saint Joseph WI 54082-2013 Office: Eagle Mgmt & Fin Corp PO Box 235 Stillwater MN 55082-0235 Office Phone: 715-549-5294.

HORSEY, DAVID, editorial cartoonist; b. Evansville, Ind., Sept. 13, 1951; m. Nole Ann Ulery; children: Darielle Jean, Daniel Rayden. BA in Comms., U. Wash., 1976; MA in Internat. Rels., U. Kent, Canterbury, Eng., 1986. Formerly govt. reporter, polit. columnist Wash. State Capitol; polit. reporter, columnist, editl. cartoonist Daily Jour.-Am., Bellevue, Wash., 1976-79; editl. cartoonist, columnist, mem. editl. bd. Seattle Post-Intelligencer, 1979—. Syndicated Tribune Media Svcs., 1986-89, 2000—, King Features/N.Am. Syndicate, N.Y.C., 1988-2000; instr. Acad. Realist Art, Seattle, 1998; propr. Horsey--Words and Picturs, Seattle, 1993—. Author: Politics and Other Perversions, 1974, Horsey's Rude Awakenings, 1981, Horsey's Greatest Hits of the '80s, 1989, The Fall of Man, 1994, One Man Show, 1999; co-editor: (anthology) Cartooing AIDS Around the World, 1992; exhibited cartoons at Art Inst. Seattle, 1992, Michael Pierce Gallery, Seattle, 1997, Shoreline C.C., 1999, others. Asst. coach North Ctrl. Little League Baseball, 1992-94; youth coach Woodland Soccer Club, 1989-98; chmn. campaign for excellence St. Benedict Elem. and Mid. Sch., 1991-93, pres. sch. commn., 1993-95. Recipient 1st place Best of the West Journalism Competition, 1995, Environ. Media award, 1995, Global Media award Population Inst., 1991, Berryman award Nat. Press Found., 1998, Pulitzer prize for editl. cartooning, 1999, 2003, numerous others. Mem. Soc. Profl Journalists (12 1st place regional awards, Susan Hutchinson Bosch award 1999), Assn. Am. Editl. Cartoonists (pres.-elect 1999-2000, pres. 2000-01). Office: Seattle Post Intelligencer PO Box 1909 101 Elliott Ave W Ste 200 Seattle WA 98119-4295 E-mail: davidhorsey@seattle-pi.com.*

HORSFIELD, CRAIGIE, artist; b. Cambridge, England, 1949; Exhibitions include, Cambridge Darkroom, England, 1988, Another Objectivity, Inst. Contemporary Arts, London, 1988, Blasphemies, ecstasies, cries, The Serpentine Gallery, London, 1989, Ydesssa Hendeles Found., Toronto, Can., 1990, Frith Street Gallery, England, 1990, A Dialogue about Recent Am. & European Photography in Art, Mus. Contemporary Art, LA, 1991, Carnegie Mus., Pitts., 1994, Epic & the Every day: Contemporary Photography in Art, Hayward Gallery, London, 1994, Carnegie Internat., Carnegie Mus., Pitts., 1995, Barbara Gladstone Gallery, NY, 1996, Monica De Cardenas, Milan, Italy, 1998, El Hierro Conversation, Soundwork 4.1, Documenta 11, Kassel, Germany, 2002, Frith Street Gallery, London, 2003, El Hierro Project, El Hiero, Canary Islands, Spain, 2001—05, and others; co-author: The Lectures, 1992, 1993, Amnesia. Collaboration & Responsibility, 1997, Craigie Horsfield Im Gresprach/Conversation, 1999, Mus. Conversations, 2002, Table book, 2002, El Hierro Conversation, 2003, What Film May Be, 2003—04, and others. Mailing: c/o Barbara Gladstone Gallery 515 West 24th St New York NY 10011*

HORSLEY, JACK EVERETT, lawyer, writer; b. Sioux City, Iowa, Dec. 12, 1915; s. Charles E. and Edith V. (Timms) H.; m. Sallie Kelley, June 12, 1939 (dec.); children: Pamela, Charles Edward; m. Bertha J. Newland, Feb. 24, 1950 (dec.); m. Mary Jane Moran, Jan. 20, 1973; 1 child, Sharon. AB, U. Ill., 1937, LLB, JD, 1939, Med./Legal Doctorate, 2001. Bar: Ill. 1939. Instr. Sch. of the Solder, U. Ill. ROTC, 1934; bd. dirs., chair emeritus Ctrl. Ill. Nat. Bank (now US Bank), 1960—; instr. Sch. of the Solder, U. Ill. ROTC, 1968; adv. cons. Ill. Supreme Ct. Disciplinary Commn., 1976—2003, chmn. rev. bd., 1973—76; temp. prof. law NYU, 1974; instr. Sch. of the Solder, U. Ill. ROTC, 1989; temp. prof. law NYU, 1990; alumni adv. com. U. Ill. Law Forum, 1991—2000, mem. lawyers adv. coun., 1992—2005, chair; Trial Laureate Ill. Trial Lawyers Acad., 1996; instr. Sch. of the Solder, U. Ill. ROTC, 1998; mem. heart diagnostics adv. coun. U. Ill. Law Forum, 1999—2004; temp. prof. law NYU, 1999; instr. Sch. of the Solder, U. Ill. ROTC, 2001, Res. Officer's Assn., 2002—03; temp. prof. law NYU, 2000—05; mem. lawyers adv. coun. U. Ill. Law Forum, 2001—03; adv. dir. Harlan Moore Heart Rsch. Found., 2004; vis. prof. trial practice Fordham Law Sch., N.Y.C., 1989—2002, 1999—2000; vis. prof. U. Berkeley Coll. Law, 1999; Laureata-emeritus Ill. Trial Lawyers Acad., 2000; adv. dir., cons., reviewer Am. Life League, 2001—04; lectr. in field; vis. prof U. Berkeley Coll. Law, 2002; vis. prof. trial practice Fordham Law Sch., 2004—05; chair U. Ill. Law Forum, 2005; asst. treas. Harlan Moore Heart Rsch. Found., 1996—; chmn. emeritus Ill. Supreme Ct. Disciplinary Commn., 2002—. Narrator Poetry Interludes, Sta. WLBH-FM, 1977—2005; author: Trial Lawyer's Manual, 1967, Voir Dire Examinations and Opening Statements, Real Estate Foreclosures, 1968, Inequities to Foreclosure Appraisals, 1997, Current Development in Products Liability Law, 1969, 2d edit., 2005, Illinois Civil Practice and Procedure, 1970, The Medical Expert Witness, 1973, Testifying in Court, 1973, Testifying in Court, 5th edit., 2004, Testifying in Court, supplement 4th edit, 1993, The Doctor and the Law, 1975, The Doctor and Family Law, 1975, The Doctor and Medical Law, 1977, 2d edit., 2004, Anatomy of a Medical Malpractice Case, 1984, Anatomy of a Medical Malpractice Case, 2d edit., 1993, The Doctor and the Law, 1994, Heartstrings of the Mind, 1998, 3d edit., 2002, Trilogy: The Frivolous Law Suit, 2000, Lincoln the Lawyer, 2002, 2d edit, 2004, Lincoln-Circuit Lawyer, 2002, suppl., 2004, Trilogy: Re-Rembrances, Lincoln, Circuit Rider and Thoughts to Ponder, 2005, (municipals) G.O. of Revenue, 1992, World War II, D-Day, 1994, World War II, D-Day, 2d edit., 1998, (co-founder) Life's Challenges Preparation, 1999, (municipals, co-founder) World War II Air Mus, Duxford, Eng., 1999; adv. dir. World War II Air Mus, Duxford, Eng., 2005—; author: (municipals, co-founder) Trial Techniques, 1995, 3d edit., 2003, 4th edit., 2005, Legal Liability Exposure of Trust Co., 1996, Legal Liability Exposure of Trust Co., 2d edit., 1999, On Trust Dept. Guide-lines and Risks, 1996, On Federal Evidence and Examination, 1995—97, 1998—2005, Memories of World War II in the European Theater, 1997, 1999, U.S. Civil War, Its Military Personnel, 2d edit., 2002, (municipals, co-founder) suppl. on post World War II Reserve officer duties in mil. justice, 2000 (USAF Cross, Def. Disting. Svc. WWII Victory medal, 1945, European Theatre Svc. medal, 1943, Judge Advocate Spl. award, 1944, Spl. Svc. medal Rsch. Officer Assn., 1999, Disting. Svc. award USAF Law Dept., 1950), suppl. on post World War II Reserve officer duties, 2d edit., 2001, addendum to 2d edit., 2003, History of the Bar in East Central Illinois, 1997. Remembrances: An Autobiography, 1998, 2d edit., 2000, suppl., 2004, Views of Christianity: Origin of Man, 1999, (pamphlet) A Doctor's Duty: Presciption Care, 1999, The Careless Doctor and Medical Malpractice, Thoughts to Ponder, 2001, Heartstrings of the Mind, 2003; co-author: RN Legally Speaking, 1998, Mathew Bender Forensic Sciences, 1988, suppl., 2005, Litton Bender Forensic Sciences, 3d edit., 2003; editor: Fifty Eight Years as Attorney, 1997, Fifty Eight Years as Attorney: Twelve More Years, 2002; legal cons. Mast-Head, 1972—, RN Mag., Med. Econs., contbr. Forensic Scis. Texts and Treatises, 1981, Forensic Scis. Texts and Treatises, 2d edit., 1999, supplement, 2004, Fed. Evidence Rules, 1996, 1988, 2000, Fed. Evidence Rules, 2d term, 2001, Commission US Judiciary, 1998, Cross-Exam Techniques and Potential Traps, 1996, 2d edit., 2002, Eagle Forum (On Pro-Life), Alton, Ill., 1999, Christianity: The Origin of Man Creationism vs. Darwinism, 1998, Christianity: The Origin of Man and Biblical Legend, U. Ill. Law Rev., 2000, Selected Poems, Interludes of Poetry, 2001, contrb., 2004, cons., reviewer Civil Practice State and Fed. Cts., 1998—2001, Thoughts to Ponder, 2001; author: (pamphlet) 4th edit., 2004, My Brother and I, 1998, My Father and I, 2003, My Grandfather and I, 2003, supplement, 2004, My Great-Grandfather Dr. Arch Sampson, 2005, Prominent Persons, 2005; reviewer Current Developments in Medical Malpractice Law, supplement, 1968, 2d edit., 2004; edit. cons.: Med. Econ., 1969—; author: The Doctor and Business Law, 1976;: 3d edit., 2004. Alt. del. to Rep. Platform Com., 2004; active Senatorial Reelection Com., 1993, 99; mem. exec. com. Ill. Rep. Election Campaign, 1997, 2002, US Supreme Ct. 1963—; founding mem. U.S. Supreme Ct. Hist. Soc., acting regent, 1999; pres. bd. edn. sch. dist. 100, 1946-48; bd. dirs. Harlan Moore Heart Rsch. Found., 1968-91, hon. dir., 1991—; vol. reader in rec. texts Am. Assn. for Blind, 1970-72, 97-98, 2000-05; chmn. exec. com. U. Ill. Law Forum, 1990-91, chair emeritusm 1998-2003; founding mem. Home for Law Alumni Found., Chgo., 1998-99; pres. Res. Officers Assn. East Cen. Ill., 1988-89, 99-2000, 2004-2005, pres. emeritus 2001-2005, chair, bd. dirs., 2000-2002; founder Bertha Newland Horsley award St. John's Coll. Nursing, Springfield, Mary Jane Horsley award trophy Mattoon (Ill.) H.S.; mem. exec. com. Ill. Rep. Election Campaign, 1997, Brig. gen. hon. res., ret., 1997; tournament judge Big Ten Debating Contest, 2001, tech. advisor, 2002, 2004; 4 arguments U.S. Supreme Ct. Bar, 1980-98; chmn. Ill. State Bar Assn. Grievance Com., 1954-55; substitute tchr. Mattoon Meth. Ch., 1988, 1997, Decorated Purple Heart; recipient JAG's Spl. Svc. award, Victory ribbon, ETO Svc. ribbon, Combat Zone Svc. Ribbon ETO, Extended Active Duty ribbon, Disting. Svc. award, U. Ill., 1995. Fellow Am. Coll. Trial Lawyers (co-chair membership commn. 1998, 2000, acting regent 2000-01); mem. ABA, Ill. Bar Assn. (exec. coun. ins. law 1961-63, com. chmn. banking law 1972, lectr. law course for attys. 1962, 64-65, sr. counsellor 1989—, chmn., 1992-99, Disting. Svc. award 1982-83), Assn. of Bar of City of N.Y. (non-residential lic. Ct. Appeals 2005), NY Bar Assn. (non resident mem.), Coles-Cumberland Bar Assn. (v.p. 1968-2000, pres. 1969-70, pres. emeritus 1971—, chmn. com. jud. inquiry 1976-80, chair meml. com. 1989-2000, mem. exec. com. 1998, sr. counsellor 1989, co-author Forensic Scis. Jour. 1991, 2d edit. 1999, Life-time Achievement award 1999), Am. Arbitration Assn. (nat. panel arbitrators, counsel advisor hearing officers in Ill. 1996-97), U. Ill. Law Alumni Assn. (life mem., emeritus mem. 2004, pres. 1966-67, Alumni of Month Sept. 1974, exec. com. 1990-91, Sr. Alumni of Month 2001), Ill. Appellate Lawyers Assn. (editl. cons. 2002), Soc. Legal Scribes (chair emeritus 1995-2004), Ill. Def. Counsel Assn. (pres. 1967-98, chair adv. bd. 1989—, pres. emeritus 1969-2003), Soc.

Trial Lawyers (chmn. profl. activities 1960-61, bd. dirs. 1966-67, 88-94, 2000-04, 2005), Fed. Ct. Hist. Soc. (co-chmn. 1998-2003), Adelphic Debating Soc. (judge of intramural debating U. Ill. 1999), Assn. Ins. Attys., Internat. Assn. Ins. Counsel (hon. pres. 2003), Am. Judicature Soc., Res. Officers Assn. (pres. 1997-98, chair exec. com., pres. emeritus 2002-2004, hon. brig. gen. JAGD 1997), U. Ill. Alumni Assn. (exec. com. 1990-91), Masons (lectr. ceremonial 32 degree Scottish Rite 2000, 03, 33d degree 2004, Sr. Master award 1992), Scabbard and Blade Soc. U. Ill. (pres. 1936, pres. emeritus 1998, bd. dirs. 1997-2003), Delta Phi (exec. com. alumni assn. 1960-61, 67-68, 1999-2003), Sigma Delta Kappa Law Frat. (alumni advisor, 2005). Lutheran. Home: 913 N 31st St Mattoon IL 61938-2271 Office Phone: 217-235-5954. *Time is the stuff of which life is made. To squander it is to squander life.*

HORSLEY, RICHARD DAVID, banker; b. 1942; With FDIC, Washington, 1964-66, Ernst and Ernst, N.Y.C., 1966-72; compt. 1st Ala. Bancshares Inc., Montgomery, 1972-77, v.p., compt., 1977-82; vice chmn., exec. fin. officer Regions Fin. Corp., Birmingham, Ala., 1982—2002, also bd. dirs., 2002—. Office: Regions Fin Corp 417 20th St N Birmingham AL 35203-3203

HORSMAN, DAVID A. ELLIOTT, writer, finance company executive, educator; b. Calvert County, Md., June 28, 1932; s. Alvin W. and Bessie L. (Elliott) H. Student, U. Chgo.; BA, San Francisco State U., 1964; MA, NYU, 1967, PhD, 1970; MDiv, Episc. Div. Sch., 1984. Ordained priest, consecrated bishop Jurisdiction of Orthodox Ch. of Far Isles, 2000. Fl. dir., stage mgr. WTOP-TV, Washington, 1959-61; TV writer/producer Insight, Nat. Coun. Chs., Washington, 1961-62; English master, dir. studies Searing Sch., N.Y.C., 1965-67; asst. prof. humanities Acad. Aeros., Flushing, N.Y., 1967-68; instr. humanities Rensselaer Poly. Inst., Troy, N.Y., 1969-70; assoc. prof., founder and coord. film sequence U. South Fla., Tampa, 1970-80; headmaster All Hallows Acad., Alexandria, Va., 1985-87; pres. Elliott Horsman & Assocs., 1988-89; fin. cons. Shearson Lehman Hutton, Inc., Balt., 1989-91; investment broker RAF Fin. Corp., Atlanta, 1991-92; exec. Josepthal, Lyon & Ross, Atlanta, 1992-93; v.p. Meyers, Pollock & Robbins, Atlanta, 1992-97; pres. Horsman Bros., Inc., 1998—. Chmn. bd. of fellows All Hallows Hall, 1998—; founder Horsman Hedge Fund, 1999 Author: The Liturgy as Communication, 1970, Introduction to Structural Description of Liturgical Dromena, 1979, (novel and screenplay) Pilgrims on Strange Strands, 1979, The Hovering Mercy and the Outstretched Hand, 2003, The Briar Patch, 2003, Christus Via, 2004. With U.S. Army, 1957—59. Recipient Founders Day award NYU, 1971.

HORSMAN, LENORE LYNDE (ELEANORA LYNDE), soprano, educator, actress, voice educator; b. Saginaw, Mich., Apr. 21, 1931; d. George Clark and Gwendolyn (Steele) McNabb; m. Reginald Horsman, Sept. 3, 1955; children: John, Janine, Mara. BS in Music and Piano, Ind. U., 1956, MA in Theatre-Opera, 1958. profl. certs. in voice, Villa Schifanoia, Florence, Accademia Musicale Chigiana, Siena, Accademia Di Virgiliana, Mantua, Italy, Mozarteum, Salzburg. Tchrs: Tito Gobbi, Ettore Campogalliani. Dir. Mt. Clemens Studio of Music, Mich., 1950; tchr. voice, piano and acting for singers Milw. Conservatory of Music, 1964-65; dir., tchr. pvt. voice studio, 1965—; founder, dir., designer Milw. Opera Theater, 1966; vocal coach dept. opera U. Wis., Madison, 1969-70. Dir., performer Cameo Prodn., Milw., 1974, Opera for Two, Milw., 1975, Mu Phi Epsilon Sch. Music, Chgo., 1976-81; dir., tchr. pvt. voice studio, Chgo., 1976-92; voice coach Theatre X, Milw., 1977; tchr. of acting Northshore Theatre, Milw., 1978-80. More than 33 leading roles in opera, operetta, musicals and plays; performances and concerts in US and Italy. Pres. Wis. Women in the Arts, 1973-76; bd. dir. Internat. Women's Yr. Festival, Milw., 1975. Named Women of the Yr., Milw. Panhellenic Assn., 1975; recipient Career Achievement award, 1978, Singers medal of honor Amici della Lirica, Mantua, Italy, 1981, Palcoscenico Music Vocal Silver Stage award, Italy, 1981. Mem. AAUW (v.p. 1999-2000), Nat. Assn. Tchr. Singing, Nat. Opera Assn., Wis. Music Tchr. Assn., Writers' Forum, Guild for Lifelong Learning, Mu Phi Epsilon, Theta Alpha Phi. Avocations: theater, opera, painting, poetry.

HORSNELL, MARGARET EILEEN, retired historian; b. St. Paul, Jan. 3, 1928; d. Kenneth George and Mary Elizabeth (Dowd) Horsnell. BA, U. Minn., 1961, MA, 1963, PhD, 1967. Instr. history U. Minn., 1966-67; mem. faculty Am. Internat. Coll., Springfield, Mass., 1967—, assoc. prof. history, 1976-84, prof., 1984-96, chmn. dept., 1987-96, ret., 1996. Vis. sr. assoc. Mem. Sch. Classical Studies, Athens, 1997—99. Author: Spencer Roane: Judicial Advocate of Jeffersonian Principles, 1986; mem. editl. bd. This Constn., 1986—88; contbr. articles to publs. Mem. adv. panel 500 Yrs. Am. Clothing, 1989—92. Recipient Tozer Found. award, 1966, McKnight Found. award, 1967; Summer grantee, Am. Internat. Coll., 1970, Alt. fellow, AAUW, 1974—75. Mem.: Am. Legal Studies Assn., So. Hist. Assn., Inst. Early Am. History and Culture, Archeol. Inst. Am., Phi Alpha Theta. Home: 15 Atwood Rd South Hadley MA 01075-1601 Office Phone: 413-533-6388.

HORST, BRUCE EVERETT, manufacturing executive; b. Three Rivers, Mich., Feb. 17, 1921; s. Walter and Genevieve (Turner) H.; m. Patricia Kranish, Oct. 4, 1969; children: Michael, Diane, Mark. BS in Bus. and Engring. Adminstrn, Mass. Inst. Tech., 1943. With Barber-Colman Co., Rockford, Ill., 1946-76, pres., 1965-75, vice chmn. bd., 1975-76; pres. Mid-States Screw Corp., 1976—. Bd. dirs. Rockford YMCA, 1964-75, pres., 1965-67. Served to 1st lt. USAAF, 1943-45. Decorated Air medal. Mem. Rotary, Univ. Club (Rockford), Rockford Country Club, Moorings Country Club (Naples), Yacht Club at Lake Geneva (Wis.) Office: Mid-States Screw Corp 1817 18th Ave Rockford IL 61104-7399 Home: 1802 Birchwood Ln Rockford IL 61107 E-mail: msscrewco@aol.com.

HORST, CAROLYN DIANE, accountant; b. Balt., May 20, 1945; d. Norman Kramer and Helen Louise (Gover) Lindner; m. William Earnshaw Horst, Jr., Sept. 7, 1968; children: Michelle L., Cynthia E., Julie A. BS in Acctg. magna cum laude, U. Balt., 1968. Staff acct. J.T. Coughlin, C.P.A., Bel Air, Md., 1968-69; controller GM&W Coal Co., Greencastle, Pa., 1969-77, Crunkleton Elec. Co., Greencastle, 1979-82; acct. pvt. practice, Greencastle, 1982—. Assoc. dir. First Nat. Bank, Greencastle, 1984—, pres. assoc.'s bd., 1986. Pres. Greencastle C. of C., 1984; bd. dirs. Habitat for Humanity, Franklin County, Pa., 2002—. Mem. Nat. Assn. Pub. Accts., Nat. Assn. Tax Practitioners, Jobs Daus. (past Bethel guardian, Bethel 26), Rotary (v.p. Greencaste chpt.). Mem. Christian Ch. (Disciples Of Christ). Avocations: cooking, reading. Home: 13613 Paradise Church Rd Hagerstown MD 21742-2427 Office: Carolyn Horst Acct 32 E Baltimore St Greencastle PA 17225-1202

HORST, DEENA LOUISE, state legislator; b. Sacramento, Feb. 14, 1944; s. Orlo John and Louise Helena (Schultze) Poovey; m. Gordon Lee Horst, 1966; children: Randall, Rebecca. BSE, Emporia State U., 1966, MA, 1972; postgrad., Kans. State U., 1993—. Elem. tchr. Peabody Sch., 1966-68; mid. sch. art tchr., dept. chmn. South Mid. Sch., Unified Sch. Dist. # 305, 1968—; mem. from dist. 69 Kans. State Ho. of Reps., 1995—. Vice chmn. Kans. 2000 com., K-12 edn. com.; chmn. e-govt. com., vice chmn. higher edn. com., vice-chmn. K-12 edn. com., chmn. arts and cultural resources joint com. Kans. House of Reps.; chmn. Kans. Commemorative Coin Commn. State and nat. ofcl. U.S. Jaycee Women, 1968-84; sec. Saline County Rep. Ctrl. Com., Kans., 1992-95. Named Outstanding State Pres., U.S. Jaycee Women, 1979-80; co-recipient Master Tchr. award State of Kans., 1991. Mem. C. of C., Phi Alpha, Alpha Theta Rho, Phi Delta Kappa, Epsilon Sigma Alpha (Zone Outstanding Sister award 1990). Republican. Address: 920 S 9th St Salina KS 67401-4806 Personal E-mail: deena@worldline.net.

HORST, J. ROBERT, lawyer; b. 1943; BA, Case Western Reserve U., 1965; JD, Boston U. Law, 1971. Assoc. gen. counsel Eaton Corp., Cleve., 1991—98, dep. gen. counsel, 1998—99, v.p., gen. counsel, 2000—. Office: Eaton Corp Eaton Ctr 1111 Superior Ave NE Cleveland OH 44114-2584

HORST, PAMELA SUE, medical educator, physician; b. Hershey, Pa., Jan. 23, 1951; d. Ralph H. and Helen (Fry) H.; m. Thomas H. Dennison, Feb. 6, 1982; 1 child, Elizabeth Dennison. BS, Pa. State U., 1972; MD, Pa. State U., Hershey, 1976. Diplomate Am. Bd. Family Practice, Am. Bd. Hospice & Palliative Medicine (cert). Resident in family practice Shadyside Hosp., Pitts., 1979; family physician North Jefferson Health Svcs., Clayton, N.Y., 1979-82; physician emergency rm. Geisinger Med. Ctr., Philipsburg, Pa., 1982-84; asst. prof. family medicine Albany (N.Y.) Med. Coll., 1984-88; assoc. prof. health sci. ctr. SUNY, Syracuse, 1988—. Med. dir. family practice ctr. St. Joseph's Hosp. Health Ctr., Syracuse, 1989—, assoc. residency dir. family practice residency, Syracuse, 1990—; physician Palliative Care Cons. Svc., 1999—, hospice physician, 2002—; chmn. St. Joseph's Health Alliance, 1995-97, SyraHealth, IPA, 1997-98. Author: (with others) Ambulatory Medicine, 1993, Manual of Family Practice, 1996. Mem. Am. Acad. Family Physicians, Soc. Tchrs. Family Medicine, Am. Assn. of Hospice and Palliative Medicine. Avocations: gardening, reading. Office: St Joseph's Health Ctr Family Practice Residency 301 Prospect Ave Syracuse NY 13203-1899

HORSTMANN, JAMES DOUGLAS, retired academic administrator; b. Davenport, Iowa, Oct. 2, 1933; s. Leonard A. and Agnes A. (Erhke) H.; m. Carol H. Griffiths, Sept. 8, 1956; children: Kent, Karen, Diane. BA, Augustana Coll., 1955. C.P.A., Ill., Wis. Staff acct., auditor Arthur Andersen & Co., Chgo., 1955-61; v.p., controller Harry S. Manchester, Inc., Madison, Wis., 1961-65; sr. v.p. fin., treas. H. C. Prange Co., Sheboygan, Wis., 1965-83, also dir.; dir. planned giving Augustana Coll., Rock Island, Ill., 1983-85, v.p. for devel., 1985-93, v.p. planned giving, 1993-98, v.p. emeritus, 1998—; pres. Schonstedt Instrument Co., 1993-95, ret., 1995—. Chmn. Wis. Mchts. Fedn.; bd. dirs. First Wis. Nat. Bank, Fond du Lac, 1975-83; cons. Score, 2004. Chmn. Sheboygan County (Wis.) Rep. Party, 1969-70; vice-chmn. Wis. 6th Congl. Dist., 1972-73, Rock Island County Reps., 2000-02; del. Nat. Rep. Conv., 1976; campaign chmn. Sheboygan United Way, 1977, treas., 1973-75, v.p., 1975-78, pres., 1978-79; bd. dirs. Public Expenditure Survey Wis., 1981-83, Rock Island YMCA, 1986-87, Franciscan Health Care Systems, 1988-92, Christ Luth. H.S. Found., 2000-03, Alternatives for the Older Adult, 2001—, v.p. 2003, pres., 2004—, Marriage and Family Counseling, 2003—, Thrivent for Lutherans, 2003; v.p. Sheboygan Arts Found., 1973-75; v.p., bd. dirs. Sheboygan Retirement Home, 1977-83; bd. dirs. Franciscan Mental Health Ctr., 1984-94, pres., 1985-88; trustee Friendship Manor, 1993-2003, pres., 2000-02; trustee Coun. on Children at Risk, 1989-2001, Franciscan Med. Ctr., 1990-92, Cmty. Found. of the Great River Bend, 2002—, chmn., 2005; trustee Villa Montessori Sch., 1999—, pres. 2000-04; v.p. German Am. Heritage Ctr., 2000-05; treas. Trinity Vis. Nurse/Homemakers Assn., 2001, vice chair, 2004, Pathway Hospice, 2001; bd. dirs. Augustana Hist. Soc., 2001—, Quad Cities Health Initiatives, 2005—. With USN, 1955-57. Named Outstanding Fund Raising Exec. Nat. Soc. Fund Raising Execs., 1992; recipient Outstanding Svc. award Augustana Coll., 1979, Jr. Achievement Free Enterprise Found., 2003. Mem. Am. Heart Assn. (bd. dirs. Quad City chpt. 1999—, pres. 2002-), Am. Cancer Soc. (bd. dirs. Rock Island unit 1992-2001), Wis. Inst. CPAs, Ill. Soc. CPAs, Sheboygan County Assn. CPAs, Fin. Execs. Inst. (dir.), Quad-City Estate Planning Coun., Augustana Hist. Soc. (bd. dirs. 1999—), Augustana Coll. Alumni Assn. (pres. 1970-71), Econ. Club Sheboygan (pres. 1976-77), Kiwanis. Lutheran. Home: 1245 36th Ave Rock Island IL 61201-6022

HORSTMANN, JOHN F., lawyer; b. Phila., June 8, 1951; BA, St. Joseph's U., 1973; JD, Villanova U., 1976. Bar: Pa. 1976, Pa. Supreme Ct., US Dist. Ct. Ea. Dist. Pa., US Bankruptcy Ct. Ea. Dist. Pa. Assoc. Duane Morris LLP, Phila., 1976—84, ptnr., 1984—, chmn. reorganization & fin. sect., 1994—2001, mem. firm partners bd. Mem.: ABA, Turnaround Bus. Mgmt. Assn., Phila. Bar Assn., Pa. Bar Assn. Office: Duane Morris LLP One Liberty Pl Philadelphia PA 19103-7396 Office Phone: 215-979-1504. Office Fax: 215-979-1020. Business E-Mail: horstmann@duanemorris.com.

HORSWILL, C. WEIR, retired obstetrician, retired gynecologist, photographer; b. Madison, Wis., 1924; MD, U. Wis., 1952. Cert. in ob-gyn. Intern Toledo Hosp., 1952-53; resident U. Wis. Hosp., Madison, 1956-60; hon. staff Madison Meriter Hosp.; clin. assoc. prof. ob-gyn. U. Wis. Med. Sch. Fellow ACOG, ACS; mem. Am. Coll. Sports Medicine, Cen. Assn. Obstetricians and Gynecologists.

HORT, MICHAEL, art collector; m. Susan Hort; children: Peter, Andrew, Shoshana, Rema Hort Mann(dec.). Founder Rema Hort Mann Found., NYC, 1995—. Named one of Top 200 Collectors, ARTnews mag., 2004. Avocation: Collector contemporary art. Office: Rema Hort Mann Found 155 Hudson St New York NY 10013*

HORT, SUSAN, art collector; m. Michael Hort; children: Peter, Andrew, Shoshana, Rema Hort Mann(dec.). Founder Rema Hort Mann Found., NYC, 1995—. Named one of Top 200 Collectors, ARTnews mag., 2004. Avocation: Collector contemporary art. Office: Rema Hort Mann Found 155 Hudson St New York NY 10013*

HORTA, JOSÉ CARLOS DE OLIVEIRA SOUSA, civil engineering consultant; b. Homoine, Mozambique, Dec. 16, 1935; s. José Maria de Sousa Horta and Maria do Carmo de Oliveira; children: Viriato, Soahanta Vololona, Maria Carmen, José Daniel. Candidate in Civil Engring., U. Liege, Belgium, 1957; DSc in Earth Scis., U. Algiers, Algeria, 1972, cert. in Applied Geophysics, 1973. Polit. adviser Movimento Popular de Libertação de Angola, 1959-61; geotech. and hwy. engr. Ministry Pub. Works, Algiers, 1966-73; acting dir. Civil Engring. Lab., SONATRACH, Beni Mered, Algeria, 1978-80; sr. hwy. and geotech. engr. Louis Berger Internat. Inc., Paris and East Orange, N.J., 1980-91; project mgr., regional rep. DMJM Internat., Washington, 1991-92; civil engring. cons., Lisbon, 1992—; quality lead engr ExxonMobil, Cameroon, 2000—02. Participant internat. confs. on soils, constrn. materials, road design, constrn. and maintenance, including 5th Internat. Conf. on Low-Volume Roads, Raleigh, N.C., 1991, 2d Internat. Conf. on Roads and Road Transport Problems, New Delhi, 1995. Contbr. articles to profl. jours. and confs., including Engring. Geology, Geotechnique. Mem. ASTM, Indian Roads Congress (life). Avocations: gymnastics, swimming, dance, music, reading. Home: Apt 3F Av Bombeiros Voluntários 42 1495-020 Algés Lisboa Portugal Fax: 351-21-4103515. Office Phone: 351-21-4103515. E-mail: soushort.joyc@mail.telepac.pt.

HORTON, DONALD J., lawyer; b. Palestine, Tex., 1946; BBA, U. Houston, 1969, JD, 1971; LLM in Labor Law, NYU, 1973. Bar: Tex. 1972. Ptnr., Labor Dept. Andrews Kurth LLP, Houston. Asst. prof. law Loyola U., Chgo., 1973—77. Assoc. editor Houston Law Rev., 1971. Mem.: Nat. Employment Law Inst., ABA (Labor Law Sect.), Tex. Bar Assn., Houston Bar Assn., Order of Barons, Phi Alpha Delta. Office: Andrews Kurth LLP 600 Travis St Ste 4200 Houston TX 77002-3090 Office Phone: 713-220-4581. Office Fax: 713-238-4285. Business E-Mail: dhorton@andrewskurth.com.

HORTON, DONALD R., construction executive; Chmn. D.R. Horton, Inc., Fort Worth, Tex., 1991—, pres., 1991—98. Office: 301 Commerce St, Ste 500 Fort Worth TX 76102 Office Phone: 817-856-8200.*

HORTON, FRANK ELBA, academic administrator, geographer, educator; b. Chgo., Aug. 19, 1939; s. Elba Earl and Mae Pauline (Prohaska) H.; m. Nancy Yocom, Aug. 26, 1960; children: Kimberly, Pamela, Amy, Kelly. BA, Western Ill. U., 1963; MS, Northwestern U., 1964, PhD, 1966. Faculty U. Iowa, Iowa City, 1966-75, prof. geography, 1966-75; dir. Inst. Urban and Regional Research, 1968-72, dean advanced studies, 1972-75; v.p. acad. affairs, research So. Ill. U., Carbondale, 1975-80; prof. geography and urban affairs, chancellor U. Wis., Milw., 1980-85; prof. geography, pres. U. Okla., Norman, 1985-88; prof. geography, higher edn. adminstrn., pres. U. Toledo, 1988-98, pres. emeritus, 1999—; prin. Horton & Assocs., Denver, 1999—; interim pres. So. Ill. U., 2000; interim dean coll. biol. scis. UMKC, 2001—02, exec. cons. to provost, 2003—04. Mem. commn. on leadership devel. and acad. adminstrn. Am. Coun. on Edn., 1983-85; mem. presdl. adv. com. Assn. on Governing Bds., 1986-98; dir. 1st Wis. Nat. Bank of Milw., 1980-85, Liberty Nat. Bank, Oklahoma City, 1986-89, Trustcorp. Bank, 1989-90; bd. dirs. Interstate Bakeries, GAC Corp. Author, editor: (with B.J.L. Berry) Geographic Perspectives on Urban Systems - With Integrated Readings, 1970, Urban Environmental Management - Planning for Pollution Control, 1974; editor: (with B.J.L. Berry) Geographical Perspectives on Contemporary Urban Problems, 1973; editorial adv. bd.: (with B.J.L. Berry) Transportation, 1971-78. Co-chmn. Goals for Milw. 2000, 1981-85, Greater Milw. Com., 1980; mem. bus. devel. sub-com. Okla. Coun. Sci. and Tech., 1985-88; mem. Harry S. Truman Library Inst., 1985-88, William Rockhill Nelson Trust, 1985-88; bd. govs. Am. Heart Assn., Wis., 1980-85, Ohio Supercomputer Ctr., 1993-97; mem. exec. com. Okla. Acad. State Goals, 1986-88; trustee Toledo Symphony Orch., 1989-96, Toledo Hosp., 1989-97, Pub. Broadcasting Found. Northwest Ohio, 1989-93, Key Bank, 1990-2000, Ohio Aerospace Inst., 1990-97; chair Inter-Univ. Coun. Pres. of Ohio Public Univs., 1992-93; mem. exec. com. Com. of 100, Toledo, 1989-92. Served with AUS, 1957-60. Mem. AAAs (nat. coun. 1976-78), Assn. Governing Bds. (mem. presdl. adv. commn. 1986-95), Assn. Am. Geographers, nat. Assn. State Univs. and Land Grant Colls. (chair urban affairs div. 1983-85, chmn. Coun. of Pres. 1987-88, exec. com. 1983-88), Nat. Hwy. Rsch. Soc., Okla. Coun. on Sci. and Tech., MidAm. State Univs. Assn. (pres. 1987-88), Ohio Supercomputer Ctr. (bd. govs. 1993), Ohio Aerospace Inst. (trustee 1990—), Okla. Acad. State Goals (pres. 1987-88), Okla. State C. of C. and Industry (v.p. 1987-88), Toledo Area C. of C. (vice chmn. bd. dirs. 1991-93). Home: 288 River Ranch Cir Bayfield CO 81122-8774 Personal E-mail: fehorton@attglobal.net.

HORTON, HENRY HOLLIS, III, lawyer; b. Friona, Tex., Oct. 19, 1955; s. H. Hollis Jr. and Lunell (McFarland) H.; m. Courtney Cannon, Aug. 4, 1979; children: Marriott, Robert. BA, Duke U., 1978; JD, U. Tex., 1980. Bar: Tex. 1981, U.S. Dist. Ct. (ea. dist.) Tex. 1981, U.S. Ct. Appeals (5th cir.) 1981. Assoc. Orgain, Bell & Tucker, Beaumont, Tex., 1981—86, ptnr., 1986—2004; justice 9th Ct. Appeals, 2005. Del. Rep. Party of Tex., 2004; chmn., bd. trustees Trinity United Meth. Ch., 2001—02, chmn. finance com., 2004—05. Named a Tex. Superlawyer, Tex. Monthly, 2003—05. Mem. Jefferson County Young Lawyers Assn. (bd. dirs. 1984). Republican. Methodist. Avocations: reading, computers. Office: 9th Ct Appeals 1001 Pearl Ste 320 Beaumont TX 77701-3552 E-mail: hollishorton@courts.state.tx.us.

HORTON, JAMES WRIGHT, retired lawyer; b. Belton, S.C., Dec. 24, 1919; s. John Aiken and Emmae (Tate) H.; m. Eunice Rice, Nov. 20, 1948; children— James Wright, Max Rice, Rex Rice. BA, Furman U., 1942; JD, Harvard U., 1948. Bar: S.C. 1948. Ptnr. Nettles & Horton, Greenville, S.C., 1948-52; ptnr. Rainey, Fant & Horton, Greenville, S.C., 1952-70, Horton, Drawdy, Marchbanks, Ashmore, Chapman & Brown, Greenville, S.C., 1970-78, Horton, Drawdy, Ward & Black, Greenville, S.C., 1978-91; ret., 1997. Pres. United Fund Greenville County, 1959; mem. Greenville County Sch. Trustees, 1964-70, vice chmn., 1969; pres. Greenville Family and Children's Service, 1954-55, 68-70; bd. dirs. Salvation Army, 1969—, treas., 1970-71; bd. dirs. Family and Children's Service, Greenville Mental Health Clinic, 1956-59, Greater Greenville Community Found., 1981. Col. USMCR, ret. Decorated Silver Star. Mem. Greenville County Bar Assn. (pres. 1981) Baptist (deacon 1964-69, 71-72, 86-88). Home: 2 Osceola Dr Greenville SC 29605-3013

HORTON, JARED CHURCHILL, retired diversified financial services company executive, metal products executive; b. Greenwich, Conn., Oct. 8, 1924; s. Frederic Jared and Marcelene (Churchill) H.; m. Pauline Elizabeth Finn, June 14, 1947; children: Janette Elizabeth Hall, Cynthia Joan Carpenter, Allison Jane, Juliana Ruth. Student, Yale U., 1942; grad., Packard Jr. Coll., 1948. With PM Industries, Stamford, Conn., 1948-54; with Alleghany Corp., N.Y.C., 1954-88, treas., 1956-88, sec., 1959-61, 63-88, v.p., 1967-88. Served to 1st lt. AUS, 1942-46. Episcopalian. Home: Coachlamp Ln Greenwich CT 06830

HORTON, JEANETTE, municipal government official; b. Paterson, N.J., Dec. 1, 1938; d. David and Mary (Carpenter) Potash; m. Troy Horton, Oct. 31, 1958 (dec. May 1990); m. Christos Prousalis, June 29, 1991. Student, Broward C. C., 1970—72, Barry U., 1982, Fla. Atlantic U., 1983—84, Fla. State U., 1985. Cert. master mcpl. clk. Fla. Bookkeeper Fla. Housewares, Miami, 1961—65; asst. to comptr. Gulf Stream Press, Miami, 1965—70; comptr. Chrysler Plymouth, Miami, 1970—75; mcpl. clk., fin. dir. Village of Biscayne Park, Fla., 1975—91, Bal Harbour Village, Fla., 1991—; ret., 2004. Commr. Cooper City, Fla., 1971-73. Mem. Fla. Assn. City Clks. (scholarship 1985-87, scholarship chmn. 1988-89), Am. Bus. Woman of Yr. award 1985, pres., v.p. 1985-87), Dade/Broward City Clks. and Fin. Dirs. (pres. 1992-93), Fla. City and County Mgrs. Assn., Bus. and Profl. Women (pres. 1981), Internat. Mcpl. Clks. Assn., Pers. Mgmt. Assn., Acad. for Advanced of Edn. of Mcpl. Clks. (master mcpl. clk. 2001). Democrat. Roman Catholic. Avocation: reading. Home: 5241 SW Less Davie FL 33312 Office: Village of Bal Harbour 655 96th St Bal Harbour FL 33154-2428 E-mail: retclerkfinder@aol.com.

HORTON, JOSEPH JULIAN, JR., economics and finance educator; b. Memphis, Tenn., Nov. 7, 1936; s. Joseph Julian and Nina (Williams) H.; m. Linda Anne Langley, May 30, 1964; children: Joseph Julian, Anne Adele, David Douglas. AA, Lon Morris Jr. Coll., 1955; BA, N.Mex. State U., 1958; MA, So. Meth. U., 1965, PhD, 1968; postgrad., Harvard U., 1970—71. Claims examiner Social Security Adminstrn., Kansas City, Mo., 1958-60, claims authorizer, 1960-61; with FDIC, Washington, 1967-71, fin. economist, 1967-69, coord. merger analysis, 1969-71; prof., chmn. dept. econs. and bus. Slippery Rock (Pa.) State Coll., 1971-81; vis. fin. economist Fed. Home Loan Bank Bd., Washington, 1978-79; prof., chmn. commerce divsn. Bellarmine (Ky.) Coll., 1981-82, dean W. Fielding Rubel Sch. Bus., 1982—86; dean Sch. Mgmt. U. Scranton, Pa., 1986-96; prof. Coll. Bus. Adminstrn. U. Ctrl. Ark., Conway, 1996—2001, prof. econ. and fin., 2001—. Asst. prof. George Washington U., Washington, 1968-69, U. Md., College Park, 1969-70; pres. Pa. Conf. Economists, Internat. Acad. Bus. Disciplines, Congress of Polit. Economists, U.S.A. Bd. editors Ea. Econ. Jour.; contbr. articles to profl. jours. Recipient Cokesbury award So. Meth. U., 1965; NSF Grad. fellow, 1964-66, Ford Found. Dissertation fellow, 1966-67, Harvard U. Rsch. fellow, 1970-71, Bank Adminstrn. Inst. Clarence Lichtfeldt fellow, 1981, Burk fellow. Mem. Am. Econ. Assn., Am. Fin. Assn., Internat. Acad. Bus. Disciplines (pres.), N.Am. Econs. and Fin. Assn. (bd. dirs., v.p., pres.), Ea. Econ. Assn. (v.p.). Office: U Cen Ark Dept Econ and Fin Coll Bus Adminstrn Conway AR 72035-0001 Office Phone: 501-450-5310. Business E-Mail: jhorton@uca.edu.

HORTON, LAURA M., lawyer; b. Miami, Fla., May 7, 1965; d. Charles Oxford Jr. and Marabel (Hawk) Morgan; m. Mallory McCall Horton, Aug. 5, 1989. BA, Wheaton Coll., 1987; JD, U. Fla., 1990. Bar: Fla. 1990. Ptnr. Charles O. Morgan, Jr. P.A., Miami, Fla., 1990—. Corp. sec. Don Shula Found., Inc., Miami, 1991—. Mem. alumni bd. Miami Country Day Sch., 1990-98. Mem. Christian Legal Soc. (bd. dirs. 1995-98). Office: Charles O Morgan Jr PA 1300 NW 167th St Ste 3 Miami FL 33169-5738

HORTON, LAWRENCE STANLEY, electrical engineer, apartment developer; b. July 25, 1926; s. Gene Leigh and Retta Florene (Abbott) H.; m. Margaret Ann Cowles, Nov. 26, 1946 (dec. 1964); children: Craig, Lawrence Stanley, Steven J.; m. Julia Ann Butler Wirkkula, Aug. 15, 1965; stepchildren: Charles Wirkkula Horton, Jerry Higginbotham Horton. BSEE, Oreg. State U., 1949. Elec. engr. Mountain States power Co., Calif. Oreg. Power Co., Pacific Power and Light Co., 1948-66; mgr. Ramic Corp., 1966-69; cons. elec. engr. Marquess and Assocs., Medford, Oreg., 1969-85, sec., bd. dirs.; pres., owner Medford Better Housing Assn., 1985—; mgr. Horton Properties LLC. Ptnr. Tyee Apts., Julia Ann Apts., T'Morrow Apts., Johnston Manor; mgr. Horton Properties LLC; bd. dirs. People's Bank of Commerce; developer various apt. complexes and retirement cmtys., 1969—, Northwood Apts., Horton Plz., Fountain Plz., Anna Maria Creekside, Terpening Terrace, Tucson Way Retirement, Lynn-Ann Devel. HHAG LLC; grad. instr. Dale Carnegie course, 1955, 56. Contbr. elec. articles to profl. jours. Bd. dirs. Medford Hist.

Commn. Active Medford Planning Commn., Archtl. Rev. Commn., Housing Authority; bd. govs. State of Oreg. Citizens Utility; pres. United Fund, 1963-64. With USN, 1945-46. Named Rogue Valley Profl. Engrs. of Yr., 1969. Mem. IEEE, NSPE, Profl. Engrs. of Oreg., So. Oreg. Rental Owners Assn. (pres.), Rogue Valley Geneol. Soc. (pres.), Medford C. of C. (dir.), Rogue Valley Yacht Club (commodore 1974-75, dir., local fleet capt., champion), Rogue Valley Knife and Fork (past pres.), San Juan 21 Fleet Assn. (western vice commodore, Top Ten San Juan Sailor West Coast 1980), Jackson Toastmasters (founder 1957), Medford Rotary, Kiwanis (life, pres. Crater Golden 1990-91). Republican. Methodist. Office: Medford Better Housing Assn 1118 Spring St Medford OR 97504-6272 Personal E-mail: lhorton25@charter.net.

HORTON, LINDA RAE, lawyer; b. Louisville, Dec. 1, 1946; d. Raymond Thomas and Marcia Bryan Horton; m. Henry Ninghan Ho (dec. Jan. 1987); 1 stepchild, Michael Ho; children: Jonathan Horton, Colleen Horton; m. Carl V. Nelson Jr.; children: Cassandra Nelson, Douglas Nelson. BA, U. Ky., 1968; JD, George Washington U., 1975; LLM, Georgetown U., 1997. Bar: Md. 1975, D.C. 1975, U.S. Supreme Ct. 1980. Mgmt. intern Food and Drug Adminstrn., Arlington, Va., 1968-69; legis. asst. FDA, Rockville, Md., 1970-74, chief legis. br., 1974-75, trial atty., 1975-76, assoc. chief counsel, 1976-79, dep. chief counsel, 1979-93, dir. internat. policy, 1993-99, dir. internat. agreements, 1999—2001, advisor to acting dep. commr, 2001—02; ptnr. Hogan & Hartson LLP, Washington, 2002—04, Brussels, 2004—. Adj. prof. George Washington U. Sch. Law, Washington, 1983-85, Georgetown U. Sch. Law, Washington, 1999—. Chair editl. bd. Food and Drug Law Jour., 1985-86; FDA editl. bd. Commerce Clearing House, 2000—; contbr. chpts. to books and articles to profl. jours. Precinct capt. Dem. Party Ky., Jeffersontown, 1968, del. state pres. conv., Louisville, 1968; PTA fgn. lang. coord. Montgomery County Schs., Potomac, Md., 1986-89; dep. mgr., parent swim team Montgomery Swim League, Rockville, Md., 1988-90. Recipient Disting. Svc. award Dept. Health Human Svc., Washington, 1989, Meritorious Svc. award Am. Nat. Stds. Inst., 1997, Disting. Svc. award Food and Drug Law Inst., 1999, Merit award FDA, 1975, 81, 2001. Mem. ABA, Md. Bar Assn., D.C. Bar Assn., Supreme Ct. Bar, Nat. Cooperation Lab. Accreditation (bd. dirs. 1997-99), Am. Nat. Standards Inst. (bd, dirs 1994-99), Regulatory Affairs Profl. Soc. (bd. dirs. 2001-05) Presbyterian. Avocations: travel, bridge, reading, hiking, writing. Office: rue de l'industrie 26 Brussels Belgium Office Phone: 32 2 505-0931, 322-505-0931. E-mail: lrhorton@hhlaw.com.

HORTON, MICHAEL L., mortgage company executive, publishing executive; b. Pasadena, Calif., Oct. 19, 1961; s. Jerry S. and Mary L. Horton. BA in Bus. Econs., Claremont McKenna Coll., 1983. Lic. real estate broker. Gen. mgr. I.W.S., Pasadena, 1976-80; proprietor NBB Svcs. Orgn., Upland, Calif., 1980-85; regional mgr. Sycamore Fin. Group Inc., Rancho Cucamonga, Calif., 1984-87; CEO, pres. Boulder Fin. Corp., Rancho Cucamonga, 1987—, M.C.M. Pub. Corp., Rancho Cucamonga, 1992—; pres., CEO Sandstone Realty Group, Inc., 1995—; chm. C.H.A.M.P. Inc., 1996—. Author: A Real Estate Professional's Guide to Mortgage Finance, 1985; author Mortgage Fin. Newsletter, 1984—; author fin. workshop. Mem. Rep. State Ctrl. Com., Calif., 1980—, Bldg. and Industry Assn., Rancho Cucamonga, 1988—, Res Publica Soc., Claremont, Calif., 1986—; donor mem. L.A. World Affairs Coun., 1988—. Claremont McKenna Coll. scholar, 1981-83; recipient Dons D. Lepper Meml. award Exec. Women Internat., 1981, So. Calif. Edison Bus. Competition award, 1979, 81. Mem. Nat. Assn. Realtors, Inland Valley Bd. Realtors. Avocations: basketball, racquet sports, water sports. Office: Boulder Fin Corp 494 N Mountain Ave Upland CA 91786-9302

HORTON, PATRICIA MATHEWS, artist, violist and violinist; b. Bklyn., Mar. 6, 1932; d. Edward Joseph and Margaret (Briggs) Mathews; m. Ernest H. Horton Jr., Mar. 6, 1982; 1 stepchild, Carol Horton Tremblay. Student in viola, William Primrose Master Class, 1980; student, Glendale (Calif.) C.C., 1981—90, Glendale (Calif.) CC., 1993, Glendale (Calif.) C.C., 1999—2002, Art Ctr. Coll. Design, Pasadena, Calif., 1988-93; student in painting composition, Peter Liashkov, L.A., 1993-97. Profl. musician on violin and viola, 1951-86; musician on tour, 1952-57. Played with New Orleans Philharm., 1959-61, U.S. Tour of San Francisco Ballet, 1965, L.A. Civic Light Opera, 1974-80, Bolshoi Ballet Co., LA, 1975, Am. Ballet Theatre, 1974-80, N.Y.C. Opera, 1974-80, Royal Ballet of London, 1978, Alicia Alonzo's Cuban Ballet, 1979, Harlem Ballet, 1984, Deutsche Oper Berlin, 1985, also motion picture and TV soundtrack recs.; one-woman shows include Claremont (Calif.) Sch. Theology, 1997, Pasadena First United Meth. Ch., 1997, 99, La Canada Flintridge Libr., 1999. Active Dem. Nat. Com., Women's Caucus for Art. Mem. Am. Fedn. Musicians (life). Avocations: hiking local mountains, desert and beaches, studying classical guitar.

HORTON, PAUL CHESTER, psychiatrist; b. Cin., Jan. 29, 1942; s. Paul Chester, Sr. and Elizabeth Pauline (Rice) Horton; children: Paul Andrey, Alexander Robert. BA, U. Minn., 1964, MD, 1968. Diplomate Am. Bd. Psychiatry and Neurology. Rotating intern U. Cin., 1969; resident in psychiatry Yale U., New Haven, 1972; staff psychiatrist Guidance Clinic of Camden County, West Collingswood, NJ, 1972-74, Milford (Conn.) Family and Child Guidance Clinic, 1974-77; mem. faculty Sch. Medicine Yale U., New Haven, 1974-76; pvt. practice Meriden, Conn., 1974—; cons. psychiatrist Child Guidance Clinic Cen. Conn., Meriden, 1980—94, med. dir., 1994—99. Mem. faculty U. Conn. Sch. Medicine, Farmington, 1978—79; cons. Caring for Children, San Francisco, 1989—; psychiat. cons. Meriden Pub. Schs., 1999—; reviewer Am. Jour. Psychiatry, 1980—. Author: Solace, 1981, paperback edit., 1983, Japanese edit., 1985; sr. editor: The Solace Paradigm, 1988; contbr. articles to profl. jours. Active Big Bros. Orgn., Mpls., 1964—68. Lt. comdr. USN, 1972—74. Mem.: Meriden Wallingford Med. Assn., Am. Psychiat. Assn., Gridiron Club. Office: 234 Hobart St Meriden CT 06450-4380 Office Phone: 203-235-2505. Personal E-mail: phortonmd@aol.com.

HORTON, PETER WILLIAM, actor, director; b. Bellvue, Wash., Aug. 20, 1953; s. William Floyd and Joanne (Munroe) Horton; m. Linda Hamilton, 1979 (div. 1980); m. Michelle Pfeiffer, Oct. 5, 1981 (div. 1988); m. Nicole Deputron, 1995; 1 child. Attended, Principia Coll.; BA in Music Composition, U. Calif., 1976. Acting appearances include (films) Where the River Runs Black, 1985, Side Out, 1989, Singles, 1991, The Baby-sitters Club, 1995, 2 Days in the Valley, 1996, Gun, 1997, The End of Violence, 1997, T-Rex: Back to the Cretaceous, 1998, Thoughtcrimes, 2003, The Dust Factory, 2004, Happy Endings, 2005; (TV movies) Freedom, 1980, Choices of the Heart, 1982; actor, dir. (TV series) Thirtysomething, 1987-91; dir. (TV movies) One Too Many, 1983, Extreme Close-Up, 1990; dir. (TV series) Birdland, 1994, Once and Again, 1999, Grey's Anatomy, 2005. Adv. Earth Island Inst., San Francisco, 1990-91, Tree People, L.A., 1989-91.*

HORTON, PHILIP W., lawyer; b. Apr. 22, 1955; BA summa cum laude, Yale Univ., 1977; JD magna cum laude, Harvard Univ., 1980. Bar: Mass. 1980, D.C. 1983. Ptnr., co-chmn. Pro Bono Com. Arnold & Porter, Washington. Mem. bd. trustees Legal Aid Soc., DC, 1997—, sec., 2001—02, v.p., 2002—. Mem.: Washington Council of Lawyers (bd. dir. 1987—, sec. 1991—94, treas. 1995—). Office: Arnold & Porter 555 Tewlfth St NW Washington DC 20004-1206 Office Phone: 202-942-5787. Office Fax: 202-942-5999. Business E-Mail: philip.horton@aporter.com.

HORTON, ROBERT CARLTON, geologist; b. Tonopah, Nev., July 25, 1926; s. Frank Elijah and Eathel Margaret (Miller) H.; m. Beverly Jean Burhans, Dec. 5, 1952; children: Debra, Robin, Cindy. BS, U. Nev., 1949, DSc (hon.), 1985. Cert. geol. engr., 1966. Assoc. dir. Nev. Bur. Mines, Reno, 1956-66; cons. Reno, 1966-76; dir. geology divsn. Bendix Field Engring. Corp., Grand Junction, Colo., 1976-81; dir. U.S. Bur. Mines, Washington, 1981-87; dir. strategic materials rsch. U. Nev., Reno, 1987-90, assoc. dean MacKay Sch. Mines, 1989-90, assoc. dean emeritus, 1990—. Mem. Nev. Gov.'s Mining Adv. Com., 1966-72. Author: Barite Deposits of Nevada, 1962, Fluorspar Deposits of Nevada, 1963, History of Nevada Mining, 1963. Rep. candidate for Congress from Nev., 1958. Served to lt. USNR, 1944-46, 53-56, PTO. Kennecott scholar, 1948; named Engr. of Yr. Reno chpt., NSPE, 1967; recipient Outstanding Alumnus John Mackay medal, Mackay Sch. Mines, 1991. Mem. AIME (subsect. chmn. Reno 1962-63), Soc. Econ. Geologists, Mining and Metall. Soc. Am. Methodist.

HORTON, SUSAN PITTMAN, bank executive; m. Stan Horton; 1 child, Alexandria Rose. BA in Bus. Adminstrn., Wash. State U., 1984. CPA. Ptnr. McFarland & Alton PS, 1989—99; pres., CEO, chmn. Wheatland Bank, Spokane, Wash., 1999—. Avocations: barrel racing, quarter horses. Office: Wheatland Bank 222 North Wall St Spokane WA 99201

HORTON, THOMAS EDWARD, JR., mechanical engineering educator; b. Houston, Jan. 12, 1935; s. Thomas Edward and Minnie Tolula (Sloan) H.; m. Bobbie Jean Newcomb, June 8, 1963; children— Holly Anne, Thomas Edward. BS, U. Tex., 1957, PhD, 1964; MS (Caterpillar rsch. fellow), Stanford U., 1958. Jr. mech. engr. Shell Devel. Co., Houston, 1957-58; tchg. asst., rsch. asst., rsch. scientist U. Tex., Austin, 1959-62; rsch. engr. Jet Propulsion Lab. Calif. Inst. Tech., Pasadena, 1962, sr. rsch. engr., 1963-66; asso. prof. mech. engring., rsch. engr. U. Miss., 1966-71, prof., rsch. engr., 1971-94, emeritus prof., 1994—. Dir. U.S. Army Laser Sci. Lab., Redstone Arsenal, Ala., 1975-76, Reiton Corp. of Houston; cons. Army Research Office, Jet Propulsion Lab., Marathon Oil Co., Shell Devel. Co., Exxon, Chevron, Mobil, Texaco. Contbr. articles to profl. jours.; patentee in field. Fellow AIAA (assoc.; mem. tech. coms.); mem. ASME (life; mem. tech. coms.), Am. Phys. Soc., Am. Soc. Engring. Edn. (research award Southeastern sect. 1971), Sigma Xi (pres. local chpt.), Tau Beta Pi (student adviser), Pi Tau Sigma, Phi Eta Sigma. Republican. Methodist. Home: 5100 San Felipe Rd 97E Houston TX 77056

HORTON, THOMAS W., telecommunications executive; BBA magna cum laude, Baylor U., 1983; MBA, So. Meth. U., 1985. CPA. With KPMG; v.p., controller AMR Corp., 1985—98, v.p. Europe, 1998—2000, sr. v.p. fin., CFO, 2000—02; sr. v.p., CFO AT&T, 2002—, vice chmn., 2005—. Mem. exec. bd. Cox Sch. of Bus., So. Meth U. Bd. govs. United Way of Tri State. Office: AT&T One AT&T Way Bedminster NJ 07921*

HORTON, WILLIAM RUSSELL, retired utilities executive; b. Toronto, Ont., Can., Aug. 25, 1931; s. Russell Burton and Freda Catherine (Middleton) H.; m. Dorothy Viva Rye, Nov. 27, 1954; children: William Russell, Robert Freeman, Douglas Lloyd, Ronald Edward. BS in Mining Engring., U. Toronto, 1955. Engr. Imperial Oil Ltd., Calgary and Camrose, Canada, 1955-56; engr., mgr. Black Sivalls & Bryson Ltd., Edmonton, 1956—65; v.p. Gamma Engring. Ltd., Edmonton, 1965-68; pres. Horton Engring. Ltd., Edmonton, 1968-2000, chmn., 2000—; mem. Alta. Pub. Utilities Bd., Edmonton, 1973-76, chmn., 1976-83; exec. v.p. Can. Utilities Ltd., Edmonton, 1984-90. Bd. dirs. Akita Drilling Ltd., Atco Utilities Bus. Group; hon. mem. Can. Assn. Members Pub. Utility Tribunals. Mem. Assn. Profl. Engrs. Geologists and Geophysicists Alta. (life). Avocations: sports, music, reading. Home: 17490 Coral Beach Rd Winfield BC Canada V4V 1C1 Office: Can Utilities Ltd 1400-909 11th Ave SW Calgary AB Canada T2R 1N6 Business E-Mail: wrhorton@cablelan.net.

HORTON-TRIPPE, SHELLEY, art association administrator; b. Okla. City, Okla., Mar. 27, 1951; d. Robert Byron and Jean Lyon Horton; 1 child, Bess Murphy. MFA, U. Okla., 1978. Exec. dir. Children's Art Studio Sch., Santa Fe, 1981—87; exec. dir., founder Intercultural Media Forum, Santa Fe, 1991—95; artistic dir. Las Trampas Inst., Santa Fe, 1996—2004. Artist's residency Tagar Gap Sch. of Art, Malta, 1999, Okla. Art Inst., 2005. Salon D'Autumn, Internat. Exhibit, 1983, Venice Dienale, 2000, The Poem Paintings, 1993. Grant, NEA, 1983, 1986, 1993, 2003, Writer Bynner Found. of Poetry, 1996. Home and Studio: 449 Camino Don Biguel Santa Fe NM 87505 E-mail: shelleyhortontrippe@yahoo.com.

HORUZSKO, ANATOLIJ, medical researcher; b. Pinsk, Belarus, Oct. 10, 1953; s. Pavel Horuzsko and Anna Juskevich; m. Vera Portik-Dobos, Mar. 30, 1981; children: Julia Szonja, Daniel David. MD (hon.), Pediat. Med. Sch., Leningrad, Russia, 1976; PhD in immunology and allergy, Inst. of Exptl. Medicine, Russian Acad. of Sci., Leningrad, Russia, 1980; MD, Semmelweis U. of Medicine, Budapest, Hungary, 1986; PhD in clin. immunology and allergy, Hungarian Acad. of Sci., Budapest, Hungary, 1987. Lectr., sr. lectr. Pediatric Med. Sch., Leningrad, Russia, 1979—86; sr. lectr. Nat. Inst. of Hematology and Blood Transfusion, Budapest, Hungary, 1986—92; non-clin. scientist, grade 1 Nat. Inst. for Med. Rsch., London, 1992—95; sr. rsch. scientist Med. Coll. of Ga., Augusta, 1995—98, instr., 1998—2002, asst. prof., 2002—. Author: (over 40 studies) Dealing With Issues In Transplantation Medicine And Immunobiology. Recipient Prize of George Soros, George Soros Found., 1988, Internat. Rsch. award, Wellcome Trust, U.K., 1992—95, Internat. Human Frontier Sci. Program Orgn., Strasbourg, France, 1998, Internat. Union Against Cancer, Geneva, Switzerland, 1999, Roche Organ Transplantation Rsch. Found., Switzerland, 2001. Mem.: European Fedn. for Immunogenetics (assoc.), Hungarian Soc. for Immunology (assoc.), Brit. Soc. for Immunology (assoc.), AAAS (assoc.), Am. Assn. of Immunologists (assoc.). Office: Med Coll of Ga 1120 15th St Augusta GA 30912-2600 Office Phone: 706-721-8736. Personal E-mail: horuzsko@netzero.net. E-mail: ahoruzsko@mcg.edu.

HORVAT, OLGA, artist; b. Belgrade, July 23, 1963; arrived in US, 1989; d. Branko and Ranka (Peasinovic) Horvat; m. Aleksandar Filipovic, June 2, 1990; 1 child, Katharine. BA in Art, Zagreb U., Croatia, 1988; MA in Art Mgmt., Fashion Inst. Tech., 1991. Curator asst. Met. Mus. Art, NYC, 1990—91; art rsch. asst. A.J. Lederman Fine Art, Hoboken, NJ, 1991—92; art dir. Beatrice Design, Inc., NYC, 1992—94, Absolute Image, Inc., NYC, 1994—98; asst. to pres. Basically Kids, NYC, 1998—2001; art dir. Olga Horvat Art, NYC, 2001—. Exhibited in group shows at Khan Mus., Ashfelon, Israel, 2000, CASE Mus., NJ, 2001, Queens Mus. Art, NY, 2002, prin. works include Decorative Fabric Constructions, Digital Photographs, Walt Disney World Co. Recipient Cert. of Excellence, NY Times, 1999. Mem.: Queens Mus. Art, Nat. Mus. Women in the Arts, Nurture Art. Avocations: tennis, aerobics, travel, gardening. Home: 13 Meadowlark Cir Peekskill NY 10566 Office: Olga Horvat Art 457 W 57th St #1704 New York NY 10019 Office Phone: 212-247-7459. E-mail: olgahorvat@artlover.com.

HORVATH, POLLY, writer; b. Kalamazoo, Mich. married; 2 children. Co-author (with Gioia Fiammenghi): (book) An Occassional Cow, 1989; author: No More Cornflakes, 1990, The Happy Yellow Car, 1994, When the Circus Came to Town, 1996, The Trolls, 1999 (Nat. Book award finalist, 1999), Everything on a Waffle, 2001 (Newberry Honor Book), The Canning Season, 2003 (Nat. Book award, 2003), The Vacation, 2005. Office: Books for Young Readers Farrar, Straus & Giroux 19 Union Square West New York NY 10003

HORVATH, VIRGINIA SCHAEFER, academic administrator; b. Buffalo, Dec. 14, 1957; d. Paul Francis and Mary Joyce Schaefer; m. Brooke Kenton Horvath, June 8, 2002; children: Emily Alison Carroll, Caitlin Elizabeth Carroll, Susan Alessandra, Jordan Arianna. BA in English, SUNY, Buffalo, 1978; MA in English, Kent State U., 1979, PhD in English, 1984. Asst. prof. English Kent State U., Ohio, 1985—91, assoc. prof. English, 1991—99, prof. English, 1999—2005, dean acad. and student svcs., 2001—05; v.p. acad. affairs SUNY, Fredonia, 2005—, prof. English, 2005—. Vis. prof. Shimana U., Japan, 1992—93. Fellow: Am. Coun. Edn. Home: 114 Center St Fredonia NY 14063 Office: SUNY Fredonia 818 Maytum Hall Fredonia NY 14063 Office Phone: 716-673-3335. Business E-Mail: Virginia.Horvath@fredonia.edu.

HORVITZ, HOWARD ROBERT, biology professor, researcher; b. Chgo., May 8, 1947; s. Oscar and Mary Horvitz; m. Martha Constantine-Paton, May 2, 1993; 1 child, Alexandra Constantine. BS in Math., BS in Econs., MIT, 1968; MA in Biology, Harvard U., 1972, PhD in Biology, 1974; MD (hon.), U. Rome, 2004. Postdoctoral fellow Med. Rsch. Coun. Lab. Molecular Biology, Cambridge, England; asst. to assoc. prof. biology MIT, Cambridge, 1978-86, prof., 1986—, career devel. assoc. prof. biology, Whitehead Inst., 1982-85, mem. sci. adv. bd. Howard Hughes program in neurosci., 1984-88, investigator Howard Hughes Med. Inst., 1988—, Whitehead prof. biology, 1999-2000, David H. Koch prof. biology, 2000—; with McGovern Inst. for Brain Rsch., 2001—. Investigator Howard Hughes Med Inst., Boston; neurobiologist, geneticist Mass. Gen. Hosp., Boston, 1989—; advisor, dept. biochemistry and molecular biology Harvard U., 1984—90; mem. neurobiology adv. bd. Cold Spring Harbor Lab., 1984—; mem. sci. adv. bd. Hereditary Disease Found., 1987—93, collaborative rsch. group adv. com., 1988—93, cure HD initiative adv. com., 1996—; mem. sci. adv. bd. Jane Coffin Childs Meml. Fund for Med. Rsch., 1989—97; sci. adv. bd. Com. on Scholarly Comm. with People's Rep. of China, U.S. NAS, 1987—93; co-organizer Gordon Conf. on Devel. Biology, 1985; organizer biennial meeting Cold Spring Harbor Internat. Conf., 1985, coms., 81, 87; mem. organizing com. biennial meeting Ea. Coast C. Elegans, Cambridge, 1988, Cambridge, 90; mem. sci. rev. com. Amyotrophic Lateral Sclerosis Assn., 1990—95, co-chair meetings, 1991, 93; lectr. Harvey Soc., 1989; macrofil steering com. spl. programme for esch and tng. in tropical diseases WHO, 1992—95; adv. bd. Umea (Sweden) Ctr. Molecular Pathogenesis, 1993—96; co-chair working group on preclin. models for cancer Nat. Cancer Inst., NIH, 1996—; mem. adv. coun. Nat. Ctr. for Human Genome Rsch., NIH, 1996—; mem. sci. adv. group Sanger Ctr., Cambridgeshire, England, 1994—; chair devel. biology rev. com. Swedish Found. for Strategic Rsch., 1996; mem. sci. adv. bd. Netherlands Cancer Inst. Site Vis. Com., 1998; mem. sci. adv. com. Warren Alpert Found. (prize), 1997—; external rev. bd. dept. molecular, cellular and devel. biology U. Colo., Boulder, 1996; mem. sci. adv. group U. Pa. Med. Ctr. Inst. Aging, 1995—; cons. sci. adv. bd. Idun Pharmaceuticals, Inc., 1993—, Axys Pharms. Inc., 1998—2002, GenPath Pharms., 2003—, Novartis Inst. for Biomedical Rsch., 2003—. Author (with others): (books) The Role of Intercellular Signals: Nav., Encounter, Outcome, 1979, Genetic Maps, 1980, Nematodes as Biol. Models, 1980, Devel. of the Nervous Sys., 1981, Repair and Regeneration of the Nervous Sys., 1982, The Nematode Caenorhabditis elegans, 1988; mem. editl. bd.: Jour. Neurogenetics, mem. editl. bd.: Jour. Neurosci., mem. editl. bd.: Devel. Biology, mem. editl. bd.: Genes and Devel., mem. editl. bd.: Cell, mem. editl. bd.: Trends in Genetics, mem. editl. bd.: Neuron, mem. editl. bd.: The New Biologist, mem. editl. bd.: Genetic Analysis: Techniques and Applications, mem. editl. bd.: Current Opinion in Neurobiology, mem. editl. bd.: Current Biol., mem. editl. bd.: Annual Rev. Genetics, mem. editl. bd.: Cell Death & Differentiation, mem. editl. bd.: Neurobiology of Disease, mem. editl. bd.: Jour. Exptl. Therapeutics and Oncology, mem. editl. bd.: Invertebrate Neurosci., mem. editl. bd.: Devel., mem. editl. bd.: Cancer Rsch., mem. editl. bd.: Procs. of the NAS, mem. editl. bd.: Jour. Cell Biology, mem. editl. bd.: Genome Biology; contbr. numerous articles to profl. jours. Mem. adv. bd. World Health Orgn. Spl. Programme for Rsch. and Tng. in Tropical Diseases, Microfil steering com., 1992-95. Recipient Rsch. Career Devel. award, NIH, 1981—86, Spencer award in Neurobiology, Columbia U., 1986, Warren Triennial prize, Mass. Gen. Hosp., 1986, Molecular Biology award, U.S. Steel Found., 1988, Method to Extend Rsch. in Time award, NIH, 1991, V.D. Mattia award, Roche Inst. Molecular Biology, 1993, Hans Sigrist award, 1994, Charles A. Dana award for pioneering achievements in health and edn., Inst. Medicine NAS, 1995, Ciba-Drew award for biomed. sci., 1996, Rosenstiel award, Brandeis U., 1998, Passano award for the advancement med. sci., 1998, Alfred P. Sloan Jr. prize, GM Cancer Rsch. Found., 1998, Gairdner Found. Internat. award, 1999, Paul Ehrlich and Ludwig Darmstaedter prize, Frankfurt, Germany, 2000, Segerfalk award, 2000, March of Dimes prize in devel. biology, 2000, Charles-Leopold Mayer prize, French Acad. Scis., 2000, Louisa Gross Horwitz prize, 2000, Bristol-Myers Squibb Award for Disting. Achievement in Neuroscience, 2001, Genetics Soc. of Am. Medal, 2001, Genetics prize, Peter Gruber Found., 2002, medal of honor, Am. Cancer Soc., 2002, Wiley prize in biomed. scis., 2002, Nobel Prize in Physiology or Medicine, 2002, Alfred G. Knudson award, Nat. Cancer Inst., 2005; Woodrow Wilson fellow, 1968, NSF predoctoral fellow, 1968—72, Muscular Dystrophy Assn. postdoctoral fellow, 1974—77. Fellow AAAS, Am. Acad. Arts and Scis., Am. Acad. Microbiology, Am. Acad. Microbilogy; mem. Am. Assn. Cancer Rsch., U.S. Nat. Acad. Scis. Inst. Medicine, 2004, Genetics Soc. Am. (membership com. 1984-86, bd. dirs. 1990-92, 94-96, organizer ann. meeting 1989, v.p. 1994, pres. 1995), Soc. Devel. Biology (nominations com. 1989), Soc. Nematologists, Soc. Neurosci. (pub. info. com. 1993-95), Am. Soc. Cell Biology (organizing com. ann. meeting 1992, pub. policy com. 1993-96, joint steering com. pub. policy 1994-97, exec. com. 1995—), Am. Soc. Microbiology, Helminthological Soc. Washington, Inst. Medicine. Achievements include patents in field. Office: MIT Dept Biology 68-425 77 Massachusetts Ave Cambridge MA 02139-4307

HORVITZ, MICHAEL JOHN, lawyer; b. Cleve., Feb. 15, 1950; s. Harry Richard and Lois Joy (Unger) H.; m. Jane Rosenthal, Aug. 25, 1979; children: Katherine R., Elizabeth R. BS in Econs., U. Pa., 1972; JD, U. Va., 1975; LLM in Taxation, NYU, 1980. Bar: Ohio 1975, Fla. 1976. Assoc. Hahn, Loeser, Freedheim, Dean & Wellman, Cleve., 1975-78; counsel Hollywood, Inc., Fla., 1978-79; assoc. Jones & Day, Cleve., 1980-85, ptnr., 1985-2000, of counsel, 2001—. Adv. bd. Kirtland Capital Ptnrs., L.P., 1992—; chmn. Parkland Mgmt. Co., 1992—; vice chmn. Horvitz Newspapers, Inc., 1994—; pres. H.R.H. Family Found., 1992—; chmn. H.R.H. Family Trust, 1992—; bd. dirs. Zephyr Mgmt., Inc.; corp. adv. IMG Worldwide, Inc., 1999-2004, chmn. bd. dirs., 2004. Trustee Jewish Cmty. Fedn. Cleve., 1993-99, 2002-, Case Western Res. U., 1992-2005, Musical Arts Assn., 1992—, Cleve. Ctr. Econ. Edn., 1992-95, Am. Cancer Soc., Cuyahoga County unit, 1989-95, Hathaway Brown Sch., Mt. Sinai Med. Ctr., Cleve. chpt. Am. Jewish Com., 1984-95, Montefiore Home for the Elderly, 1982-90, Health Hill Hosp. for Children, 1982-95, bd. pres., 1987-89; bd. dirs. Cleve. Mus. Art, 1991—, pres. bd., 1996-2001, chmn. bd., 2001—; bd. dirs. U. Va. Law Sch. Found., 1999—, pres., 2002-. Office: Jones Day 901 Lakeside Ave E Cleveland OH 44114-1190 also: Parkland Mgmt Co 1001 Lakeside Ave E Ste 900 Cleveland OH 44114-1172

HORVITZ, PAUL MICHAEL, finance educator; b. Providence, Aug. 6, 1935; s. Abraham and Rose (Gershkoff) H.; m. Carol Broomfield, Nov. 17, 1955; children: Marcia Ellen Cohen, Steven Jay. BA, U. Chgo., 1954; MBA, Boston U., 1956; PhD in Econs., MIT, 1958. Fin. economist Fed. Reserve Bank of Boston, 1957-60; asst. prof. Boston U., 1960-62; sr. economist, compt. of currency Washington, 1963-66; dir. rsch. FDIC, 1967-77; prof. banking and fin. U. Houston, 1977—2001, emeritus, 2001—. Author: Management of Bank Funds, 1981, Monetary Policy & the Financial System, 6th edit., 1987; co-editor Jour. Fin. Svcs. Rsch.; contbr. articles to profl. jours. Mem. Am. Econ. Assn., Am. Fin. Assn., Shadow Fin. Regulatory Com. Home: 150 Sugarberry Cir Houston TX 77024-7244 Office Phone: 713-784-5086. Personal E-mail: paulhorvitz@aol.com.

HORWICH, ALLAN, lawyer; b. Des Moines, Apr. 8, 1944; s. Joseph Maurice and Bernice (Davidson) Horwich; m. Carolyn Ruth Allen, Feb. 28, 1975; children: Benjamin, Diana, Eleanor, Flannery. AB, Princeton U., 1966; JD, U. Chgo., 1969. Bar: Ill. 1969, U.S. Dist. Ct. (no. dist.) Ill. 1969, U.S. Ct. Appeals (7th cir.) 1971, U.S. Supreme Ct. 1976, U.S. Ct. Appeals (10th cir.) 1983, U.S. Dist. Ct. (ctrl. dist.) Ill. 1990, U.S. Dist. Ct. (ea. dist.) Wis. 1995, U.S. Dist. Ct. (ea. dist.) Mich. 1995, U.S. Ct. Appeals (6th cir.) 1996. Assoc. Schiff Hardin LLP, Chgo., 1969-74, ptnr., 1975—, vice-chmn., 1989-95. Adj. prof. law Northwestern U. Sch. Law, 1999—2000, sr. lectr. law, 2000—; mem. adv. bd. Wall St. Lawyer. Contbr. articles to profl. jours. Home: 216 W Concord Ln Chicago IL 60614-5743 Office: Schiff Hardin LLP 6600 Sears Tower Chicago IL 60606 Office Phone: 312-258-5618. Business E-Mail: ahorwich@schiffhardin.com.

HORWICH, ARTHUR L., medical educator; AB, Brown U., 1972, MD, 1975. Prof. genetics and pediat. Yale U., New Haven, investigator Howard Hughes Med. Inst. Recipient Basil O'Connor Rsch. award, Hans Neurath award, Protein Soc., 2001, Gairdner award, Gairdner Found., 2004; John A. Hartford Found. fellow. Mem.: NAS. Office: Dept Genetics Yale U Sch Medicine 333 Cedar St PO Box 208005 New Haven CT 06520-8005

HORWICH, GEORGE, economist, educator; b. Detroit, July 23, 1924; s. Charles and Rose (Katzman) H.; m. Geraldine Lessans, Dec. 27, 1953; children: Ellen Beth, Karen Louise, Robert Lloyd, Susan Jean. Student, Wayne State U., 1942-43, 46, Ind. U., 1943-44; AM, U. Chgo., 1951, PhD, 1954. Lectr. econs. Extension Ctrs. Ind. U., Gar and Calumet, 1949-52, instr. econs. Bloomington, 1952-55; rsch. assoc. Nat. Bur. Econ. Rsch., N.Y.C., 1955-56; from asst. prof. to prof. econs. Purdue U., West Lafayette, Ind., 1956-99, chmn. econs. dept., 1974-78, Burton D. Morgan prof. for study pvt. enterprise, 1981-94, prof. emeritus, 1999—. Sr. rsch. assoc. Brookings Instn., Washington, 1958-62; sr. economist U.S. Dept. Energy, Washington, 1978-80; spl. asst. for contingency planning U.S. Dept. Energy, 1984; adj. scholar Am. Enterprise Inst., 1984—; collaborating scientist energy divsn. Oak Ridge Nat. Lab., 1988-94; mem. U.S. Treasury Cons. Group, Washington, 1969; cons. Fed. Res. Bank, Chgo., 1971; vis. prof. econs. U. Calif., San Diego, 1971-72, People's Univ. of China, Beijing, 1992, Kobe (Japan) U. Commerce, 1996-97; vis. scholar Victoria U., New Zealand, 1997; staff Ind. Coun. Econ. Edn., West Lafayette, 1974—, Ctr. Pub. Policy and Pub. Adminstrn., Purdue U., West Lafayette, 1977—; advisor Econ. Inst. Rsch. and Edn., Boulder, Colo., 1977—; cons. U.S. Dept. Energy, 1980-88, Fortune 500 cos., 1965—, U.S. Dept. State, Washington, 1982, 92, Hudson Inst., 1991; vis. prof. Yokohama (Japan) City U., 2000; lectr. Wabash Area Lifetime Learning Assn, 2003—. Author: Money, Capital and Prices, 1964; (with others) Costs and Benfits of a Protective Tariff on Refined Petroleum Products After Crude Oil Decontrol, 1980, Energy: An Economic Analysis, 1983; (with D.L. Weimer) Oil Price Shocks, Market Response and Contingency Planning, 1984; Responding to International Oil Crises, 1988; editor: Monetary Process and Policy, 1967, (with P.A. Samuelson) Trade, Stability, and Macroeconomics, 1974; (with J.P. Quirk) Essays in Contemporary Fields of Economics, 1981; (with E.J. Mitchell) Policies for Coping with Oil-Supply Disruptions, 1982, Energy Use in Transportation Contingency Planning, 1983; (with G.J. Lynch) Food, Policy and Politics, 1989; contbr. articles to profl. jours. With U.S. Army, 1943-46, ETO. NSF grantee; Fulbright rschr., 1996-97. Mem. Internat. Assn. Energy Econs., Am. Econ. Assn., Midwest Econs. Assn., Mont. Pelerin Soc., Nat. Assn. Scholars, Phila. Soc., Assn. Pub. Policy Analysis and Mgmt. Home: 120 Seminole Dr West Lafayette IN 47906-2116 Office: Purdue U Dept Econs 403 W State St West Lafayette IN 47907-2056 E-mail: ghorwich@purdue.edu.

HORWICH, HARVEY, printing company executive, publishing executive; b. Chgo., Jan. 1, 1929; s. Hy and Lillian Horwich; m. June H. Brounson, Aug. 22, 1948; children: Bruce, amela, Jeffrey, Robert, Paul. BA, UCLA, 1951. Owner, mgr. Lenoir Printing, Long Beach, Calif., 1959—. Councilman City of Torrance, Calif., 1982—; mem. Torrance Planning Commn., Torrance Parks and Recreation Commn.; mem. mgmt. team Spl. Olympics. Named Outstanding Vol., Lions Club, Torrance, 1995, Citizen of Yr., Torrance C. of C., 1997. Mem. Printing Assn. L.A. (past pres.). Home: 5537 Michelle Dr Torrance CA 90503-1836

HORWIN, LEONARD, retired lawyer; b. Chgo., Jan. 2, 1913; s. Joseph and Jennie (Fuhrmann) H.; m. Ursula Helene Donig, Oct. 15, 1939; children: Noel Samuel, Leonora Marie. LLD cum laude, Yale U., 1936. Bar: Calif. 1936, U.S. Dist. Ct. (cen. dist.) Calif. 1937, U.S. Ct. Appeals (9th cir.) 1939, U.S. Supreme Ct. 1940. Assoc. Lawler, Felix & Hall, 1936-39; counsel Bd. Econ. Warfare, Washington, 1942-43; attache, legal advisor U.S. Embassy, Madrid, 1943-47; sole practice Beverly Hills, Calif., 1948—2002. Dir., lectr. Witkin-Horwin Rev. Course on Calif. Law, 1939-42; judge pro tempore Los Angeles Superior Ct., 1940-42; instr. labor law U. So. Calif., 1939-42. Author: Insight and Foresight, 1990, Plain Talk, 1931—; contbr. articles to profl. jours. U.S. rep. Allied Control Council for Ger., 1945-47; councilman City of Beverly Hills, 1962-66, mayor, 1964-65; chmn. transp. Los Angeles Goals Council, 1968; bd. dirs. So. Calif. Rapid Transit Dist., 1964-66; chmn. Rent Stabilization Com., Beverly Hills, 1980. Fellow Am. Acad. Matrimonial Lawyers; mem. ABA, State Bar Calif., Order of Coif, Balboa Bay Club, Aspen Inst., La Costa Country Club. Address: 434 El Camino Dr Beverly Hills CA 90212-4222 E-mail: lhorwin@linkline.com.

HORWITZ, BARBARA ANN, physiologist, educator, consultant; d. Martin Horwitz and Lillian Bloom; m. John M. Horowitz, Aug. 17, 1970. BS, U. Fla., 1961, MS, 1962; PhD, Emory U., 1966. Asst. rsch. physiologist U. Calif., Davis, 1968-72, asst. prof. physiology, 1972-75, assoc. prof., 1975-78, prof., 1978—, disting. prof., 2003—, chair animal physiology, 1991-93, chmn. neurobiology, physiology and behavior dept., 1993-98, vice provost acad. personnel, 2001—. Cons. Am. Inst. Behavioral Rsch., Palo Alto, Calif., 1980, Am. Inst. Rsch., Washington, 1993-99, NSF, Washington, 1981-84, NIH, Washington, 1995-99. Contbr. articles to profl. jours. Named postdoctoral fellow, USPHS, 1966—68, Arthur C. Guyton Physiology Tchr. of the Yr., 1996; recipient Disting. Tchg. award, 1982, U. Calif.-Davis prize for Tchg. and Scholarly Achievement, 1991, Pres.'s award for excellence in fostering undergrad. rsch., 1995. Fellow: AAAS; mem.: Phi Sigma (v.p. Davis chpt. 1983—, nat. v.p. 1989—), Phi Kappa Pi, Soc. Exptl. Biology and Medicine (exec. coun. 1990—94, pres.-elect 1999—2001, pres. 2001—03), N.Am. Assn. for Study of Obesity (exec. coun. 1988—92), N.Y. Acad. Scis., Am. Physiology Soc. (edn. and program coms. coun. 1993—96, pres.-elect 2001—02, pres. 2002—03), Sigma Xi (pres. Davis chpt. 1980—81), Phi Beta Kappa (pres. Davis chpt. 1991—92, 2000—02). Office: U Calif Dept Neurobiology Phys Davis CA 95616 E-mail: bahorwitz@ucdavis.edu.

HORWITZ, BARRY, neuroscientist, researcher; b. St. Louis, Sept. 14, 1942; s. Harold and Edna Horwitz; m. Gloria Claire Greenberg, Dec. 14, 1969; 1 child, Courtney Dina. BA, Wash. U., St. Louis, 1964; PhD in Physics, U. Pa., 1972. Vis. asst. prof. physics Kings Coll., Wilkes-Barre, Pa., 1970—74, Vassar Coll., Poughkeepsie, NY, 1974—76; asst. prof. physics and math. Tex. Woman's U., Denton, 1976—82; sr. staff fellow and rsch. mathematician Lab. Neuroscis. NIA, NIH, Bethesda, Md., 1982—99; sr. investigator lang. sect. NIDCD, NIH, Bethesda, 1999—2002, chief sect. on brainimaging and modeling, 2002—. Mem.: Orgn. Human Brain Mapping, Cognitive Neuroscience Soc., Soc. Neuroscience. Achievements include development of methods for determining brain networks from functional neuroimaging data; computational methods for integrating neural information across multiple spatiotemporal levels; research in brain networks involved in visual and auditory object processing. Office: NIDCD NIH 9000 Rockville Pike Bethesda MD 20892 Office Phone: 301-594-7755. E-mail: horwitzb@mail.nih.gov.

HORWITZ, BERTRAND NATHAN, finance educator; b. Chgo., Mar. 12, 1927; s. Max Solomon and Esther (Green) H.; m. Hertha Ostre Horwitz, Oct. 25, 1952; children: Eve, Neal, Mara. AB, U. Chgo., 1949, MA, 1951; PhD, U. Minn., 1962. Assoc. Russian Rsch. Ctr., Cambridge, Mass., 1960—61; Sloan tchg. fellow MIT, 1962-63; asst. prof. U. Rochester, N.Y., 1964-67; assoc. to full prof. Syracuse (N.Y.) U., 1967-72; prof. Binghamton (N.Y.) U., 1972—. Vis prof. U. Chgo., 1978—79, Nat. Ctr. for Indsl. Sci. and Tech., Mgmt. Devel., China, 1981—82; cons. UN, 1984; vis prof. Nat. Ctr. for Indsl. Sci. and Tech., Mgmt. Devel., China, 1984; vis. prof. U. Internat. Bus. and Econs., Beijing, 1988; vis prof. Chinese U., Hong Kong, 1993—94, City U., Hong Kong, 1994—96, 1998—99, 2000. Co-author: (book) Financial Accounting and Corporate Decisions, 1982; author: (book) Soviet Industrial Accounting, 1969. With USN, 1945-46. Rsch. grantee NSF, 1979, 83; recipient Gov.'s award N.Y. State, 1992, Internat. Edn. and Bus. award U.S. Dept. Edn., 1988-91. Mem. Am. Acctg. Assn., Am. Econ. Assn., Fin. Execs. Inst. Jewish. Avocations: reading, running, foreign languages. Home: 46 Marlborough Rd Asheville NC 28804-1445 E-mail: horwitz@binghamton.edu.

HORWITZ, DAVID A., rheumatologist, educator; BA, U. Mich., 1958; MD, U. Chgo., 1962. Intern, resident Michael Reese Hosp., Chgo., 1966; rheumatology fellow Southwestern Med. Sch. U. Tex., 1969, instr. internal medicine Southwestern Med. Sch. Dallas, 1968-69; from asst. prof. to assoc. prof. medicine Sch. Medicine U. Va., Charlottesville, 1969-79, prof. medicine, 1979-80; prof. medicine and microbiology, chief divsn. rheumatology and immunology sect. Sch. Medicine U. So. Calif., L.A., 1980—. Vis. prof. Clin. Rsch. Ctr., Harrow, Eng., 1976-77; vis. investigator Imperial Cancer Rsch. Fund, London, 1988-89; vis. scientist Nat. Inst. Arthritis, Musculoskeletal and Skin Diseases, NIH, Bethesda, Md., 2001-02. Contbr. more than 100 articles to profl. jours. Recipient James R. Klinnenberg award for rsch., Arthritis Found. Mem.: Am. Rheumatism Assn. (pres. 1985). Achievements include research in elucidation of lymphocytes, cytokines and immunologic circuits involved in the regulation of antibody production, characterization of pathologic abnormalities in immune regulation in subjects with Systemic Lupus Erythematosus; The generation of regulatory T cell subsets ex-vivo, and their potential for the treatment of autoimmune diseases and to prevent graft rejection. Office: Divsn Rheumatology And Immunology 2011 Zonal Ave # 711 Los Angeles CA 90089-0110 Office Phone: 323-442-1946. Business E-Mail: dhorwitz@usc.edu.

HORWITZ, DONALD PAUL, lawyer; b. Chgo., Feb. 5, 1936; s. Theodore J. and Lillian H. (Shlensky) H.; m. Judith Robin, Aug. 23, 1964; children: Terry Robin Kass, Linda Diane, Gail Elizabeth Miller. BS, Northwestern U., 1957; JD, Yale U., 1960. Bar: Ill. 1961, D.C. 1961, U.S. Supreme Ct. 1966; CPA, Ill. With atty. gen.'s honors program Dept. Justice, 1961-63; atty. Gottlieb & Schwartz, Chgo., 1963-66; with Arthur Young & Co. CPAs, Chgo., 1966-72, ptnr., 1971-72; exec. v.p., sec., dir. McDonald's Corp., Oak Brook, Ill., 1972-90; ptnr. Sonnenschein, Nath & Rosenthal, Chgo., 1990—. Lectr. Northwestern U. Law Sch., Grad. Sch. Commerce, DePaul U., Chgo.; bd. dirs. Bernard Tech. Inc., 1997-2004, chmn. bd., 1998-2002; sec. System Capital Corp, 1996—; trustee Evanston Northwestern Healthcare Found., 2003—. Contbr. articles to profl. jours. Trustee Goodman Theatre/Chgo. Theatre Group, 1993—96, Evans Scholars Found., Western Golf Assn., 1984—87; pres., bd. dirs. Briarwood Country Club, 1972—73; caucus nominating com. Village of Glencoe, Ill., 1975—78, vice-chmn., 1988—89; bd. dirs. Northwestern Healthcare Network, 1990—94; vice-chmn., bd. dirs., chmn. bd. Highland Park Hosp., Lakeland Health Ventures and Northwestern Network, bd. govs., 1994—2000; chmn. Midwest region Anti-Defamation League, 1994—95, mem. nat. commn., 1994—2004; exec. com. Yale Law Sch. Assn.; bd. dirs. U.S. com. United Nations Population Fund, 2003—; bd. dirs. Lakeland Health Ventures and Northwestern Network, 1986—94, McDonald's Family Charities, Inc., 2001—, Scholl Sch. Podiatry, 2001—03, Chgo. Med. Sch./Finch U. Health Scis., 1993—2003, Found. for Podiatric Edn., 2002—03. Mem.: ABA, Am. Arbitration Assn. (arbitrator panel 1991—), Chgo. Bar Found. (trustee 1990—97), Chgo. Bar Assn., Northmoor Country Club, Econs. Club, Standard Club. Office Phone: 312-876-8105. E-mail: dhorwitz@sonnenschein.com.

HORWITZ, ELEANOR CATHERINE, public information officer; b. N.Y.C., Dec. 21, 1941; d. Fritz and Hedwig E.F. (Kramer) Jahoda; m. Paul Horwitz, Aug. 15, 1964; children: Gregory Douglas, Catherine Helen, Laura Elizabeth. BA, Swarthmore Coll., 1962; MA, NYU, 1967; MS, Cornell U., 1969; postgrad., Oreg. State U., 1969-70. Sci. tchr. New Lincoln Sch., N.Y.C., 1962-67; coordinator outdoor edn. Lane County Int. Edn. Dist., Eugene, Oreg., 1969-70; staff writer Billerica (Mass.) Banner, 1971-72; instr., writer Mass. Audubon Soc., Lincoln, 1972-75; pub. use specialist U.S. Fish and Wildlife Service, Concord, Mass., 1975; staff writer Soc. Am. Foresters, Washington, 1975-76; mem. Mass. Gov.'s Forestry Rev. Bd., Boston, 1976-77; chief info. and edn. Mass. Div. Fisheries and Wildlife, Westborough, 1977—. Mem. steering com. Sec.'s Adv. Group on Environ. Edn. Exec. Office of Environ. Affairs, Commonwealth of Mass., 1990-2000, co-chair, 1992-97, chair, 1997-98; bd. dirs. Mass. Wildlife Fedn., 1986—, v.p., 1989-94, 95—, pres., 1995-97. Author: Clearcutting, A View from the Top, 1974; author, editor: Ways of Wildlife, 1977 (ACI Book award 1978); editor: (mag.) Massachusetts Wildlife, 1977—; contbr. articles to popular mags. Active Concord Natural Resources Commn., 1976-82, chmn. 1979-80; trustee Concord Land Conservation Trust, 1988—, trustee Holbrook Island Trust, 1995-2000, Bagaduce Music Lending Libr., 2005—; MBA rep. West Concord Union Ch., 1998-2003; deacon West Concord Union Ch., United Ch. of Christ, 2003—; instr. NRA, 2003. Recipient R.E. Dimmick award Oreg. Wildlife Soc., 1970, citation Worcester County League Sportsmen's Clubs, 1987, citation Minutemen chpt. Ducks Unltd., 1987, Conservation award Mahar Fish & Game Assn., 1991, Woman of Yr. award N.E. County Quabbin Anglers Assn., 1991, Sportsman of Yr. New England Outdoor Writers, 1998, Conservation Communicator of Yr. award N.E. Conservation info. and Edn. Assn., 1999, Spl. award for Wildlife edn., Mass. Sportsmen's Coun., 2003, Disting. Svc. award Ducks Unltd., 2003, Lillian Gribbons award, Mass. Sportsmen's Coun., 2005. Mem. Outdoor Writers of Am., New Eng. Outdoor Writers Assn. (membership sec. 1987-90, bd. dirs. 1987—, sec. 1990-93, 2001-2003, v.p. 1993-94, 95—, pres. 1994-95), Am. Forestry Assn. (life), New Eng. Conservation Info. and Edn. Assn. (chmn. 1986-87, 90-91, dir.-at-large 2000—), Mass. Wildlife Fedn., Wildlife Soc. (profl. cert., chmn. edn. com. 1974-76, 84-87, nominating com. 1990-91, Leopold award com. 1996-98, cert. of recognition 1978), Nashoba Sportsmen's Club, Concord Rod and Gun Club, Maynard Rod and Gun Club (hon.), Bucksmills Sportsmans Club. Mem. United Ch. of Christ. Office: Mass Divsn Fisheries and Wildlife Westborough MA 01581 Business E-Mail: ellie.horwitz@state.ma.us.

HORWITZ, JOY A., foundation administrator; b. Apr. 18, 1958; BA in European History and English, Cornell U.; JD, U. Pa. Assoc. Pepper, Hamilton and Scheetz, Phila.; assoc. Environ. program Pew Charitable Trusts, Phila., 1992—98, dir. legal affairs, 1998—. Chair Environ. Commn., Haddonfield, NJ. Office: Pew Charitable Trusts 2005 Market St Ste 1700 Philadelphia PA 19103-7077

HORWITZ, KATHRYN BLOCH, molecular biologist, educator, breast cancer researcher; b. Sosua, Dominican Republic, Feb. 20, 1941; came to U.S., 1952; d. Werner Meyerstein and Olga (Schlesinger) Bloch; m. Lawrence David Horwitz, June 14, 1964; children: Phillip Andrew, Carolyn Anita. BA, Barnard Coll., 1962; MS, NYU, 1966; PhD, U. Tex. Southwestern Med. Sch., Dallas, 1975; postdoctoral, U. Tex. Sch. Medicine, San Antonio, 1978. Instr. U. Tex. Sch. Medicine, San Antonio, 1978-79; asst. prof. U. Colo. Med. Sch., Denver, 1979-84, assoc. prof., 1984-89, prof. of medicine, pathology and molecular biology, 1989—2004, disting. prof., 2004—. Cellular physiology panel NSF, 1985-88; biochem. endocrinology study sect. NIH, 1989-93; mem. Pres.'s Cancer Panel Spl. Commn. on Breast Cancer, 1992, Breast Cancer Task Force, NIH, 1981-84. Author over 150 breast cancer and steroid receptors research papers, books; assoc. editor, editl. bd. for several scientific jours. Chair, sci. adv. bd. Cancer League of Colo., 1987-91; organizer Keystone Symposia on Steroid Receptors, 1996, 98, 2000. Elected fellow AAAS, 2000; recipient Nat. Bd. award Med. Coll. Pa., 1986, Wilson Stone award M.D. Anderson Hosp. and Tumor Inst., 1976, Rsch. Career Devel. award Nat. Cancer Inst., 1981-86, MERIT award NIH, 1992, The U. Helsinki medal and Second Siltavouri lectr. Finland, 1993, William L. McGuire Meml. lectr., 1997, Bicenntenial lectr. U. Louisville, 1998, Disting. Sci. award Clin. Ligand Assay Soc., 2000; grantee NSF, Am. Cancer Soc., Nat. Found. Cancer Rsch. Dept. of the Army, NIH. Fellow AAAS; mem. Endocrine Soc. (program com. 1989-91, nominating com. 1989-91, chair 1991, coun. 1992-95, pres.-elect 1997-98, pres. 1998-99, immediate past pres. 1999-2000, mem. devel. com. 2000—), Am. Fedn. Clin. Rsch., Am. Soc. Cell Biology, Am. Assn. Cancer Rsch. (program com. 1994-95, state legis. com. 1993—), Western Soc. Clin. Investigation, Am. Soc. Biochemistry and Molecular Biology, Fedn. Am. Socs. Exptl. Biology (bd. dirs. 2004). Democrat. Jewish. Avocations: skiing, reading, gardening, travel. Office: U Colo Dept Medicine Endocrinology MS 8106 PO Box 6151 Aurora CO 80045

HORWITZ, MORTON J., law educator; b. 1938; AB, CCNY, 1959; AM, Harvard U., 1962, PhD, 1964, LLB, 1967. Bar: Mass. 1970. Law clk. to Judge Spottswood W. Robinson, III U.S. Ct. Appeals DC Cir., 1967-68; Charles Warren Fellow Harvard Law Sch., Cambridge, Mass., 1968-70, asst. prof. law, 1970-74, prof., 1974—, Charles Warren prof. Am. legal history, 1981—. Vis. prof. Stanford U., 2000—01. Author: The Transformation of American Law, 1780-1860, 1977, The Transformation of American Law, 1870-1960, 1992, American Legal Realism, 1993, The Warren Court and the Pursuit of Justice, 1998. Mem.: Selden Soc., Am. Soc. Legal History Office: Harvard Law Sch 1563 Massachusetts Ave Cambridge MA 02138 Office Phone: 617-495-3164. Office Fax: 617-496-4863. Business E-Mail: horwitz@law.harvard.edu.*

HORWITZ, PAUL, physicist; b. N.Y.C., Dec. 4, 1938; s. Louis David and Sylvia Helen (Laibman) H.; m. Eleanor Catherine Jahoda, Aug. 15, 1964; children: Gregory Douglas Lee, Catherine Helen, Laura Elizabeth. AB, Harvard U., 1960; MS, Columbia U., 1963; PhD, NYU, 1967. Rsch. assoc. Cornell U., Ithaca, N.Y., 1967-69, U. Oreg., Eugene, 1969-71; prin. rsch. scientist Avco Everett Rsch. Lab., Everett, Mass., 1971-79; sr. scientist Bolt, Beranek & Newman Inc., Cambridge, Mass., 1979-91; divsn. scientist Bolt, Branek & Newman Inc., Cambridge, Mass., 1991-94; prin. scientist, 1994-97; sr. scientist The Concord Consortium, 1997—. Contbr. articles to profl. jours. Recipient Founders Day award NYU, 1969, 2 EDUCOM Nat. awards for ednl. software, 1992; Am. Phys. Soc. Congl. fellow, 1975-76; GM Corp. scholar Harvard U., 1960. Mem. Am. Ednl. Rsch. Assn. Office: 10 Concord Crossing Concord MA 01742

HORWITZ, RALPH IRVING, internist, medical educator, epidemiologist; b. Phila., June 25, 1947; s. Sidney and Sara (Altus) H.; m. Sarah McCue, Aug. 5, 1970; 1 child, Rebecca Margaret Taylor. BS, Albright Coll., 1969; MD, Pa. State U., 1973. Diplomate Am. Bd. Internal Medicine. Intern McGill U., Royal Victoria Hosp., Montreal, Que., Can., 1973-75; postdoctoral tng. in epidemiology, clin. scholars program Yale U. Sch. Medicine, New Haven, 1975; sr. resident Harvard U., Mass. Gen. Hosp., Boston, 1977-78; co-dir. clin. scholars program Yale U. Sch. Medicine, New Haven, 1978—2003, asst. prof. medicine, 1978-82, assoc. prof. medicine and epidemiology, 1982-88, prof., 1988—2003, chief gen. internal medicine, 1982-94, vice chmn. internal medicine, 1993-94, chmn. internal medicine, 1994—2003, Harold H. Hines Jr. Prof. Medicine and Epidemiology, 1991—2003; chief Beeson Med. Svc. Yale-New Haven Hosp., 1993—2003; v.p. med. affairs, dean sch. medicine Case Western Res. U., Cleveland, Ohio, 2003—. Mem. nat. selection com. faculty scholar program Henry J. Kaiser Family Found., Menlo Park, Calif., 1987-90; mem. com. allocating resources in biomed. rsch. Inst. Medicine, Washington, 1988-89; mem. profl. standards rev. orgn., Woodbridge, Conn., 1980-82; editorial bd. The Lancet, 1991-96; chmn. bd. dirs. Am. Bd. Internal Medicine. Contbr. over 100 articles to profl. jours. Trustee Am. Bd. Internal Medicine Found. Recipient Faculty Scholar award Kaiser Family Found., 1981-86 Fellow ACP, AAAS, Am. Coll. Epidemiology, Pa. State U. Alumni Assn.; mem. Am. Soc. Clin. Investigation, Assn. Am. Physicians, Am. Epidemiol. Soc., Inst. Medicine, New Haven Lawn Club, Mory's. Jewish. Office: Case Western Res U Sch Medicine 10900 Euclid Ave Cleveland OH 44106-4920

HORWITZ, RONALD M., business administration educator; b. Detroit, June 25, 1938; s. Harry and Annette (Levine) H.; m. Carol Bransky, Mar. 30, 1961; children: Steven, Michael, David, Robert. BS, Wayne State U., 1959, MBA, 1961; PhD, Mich. State U., 1964. CPA, Mich. Prof. fin. U. Detroit, 1963-73, 75-79; healthcare cons., dir. personnel devel. Arthur Young & Co., Detroit, 1974-75; prof. fin., dean Sch. Bus. Adminstrn. Oakland U., Rochester, Mich., 1979-90, acting v.p. for acad. affairs, 1992-93, prof. fin., 1991—2002, prof. emeritus of fin., 2002—. Contbr. articles to profl. jours. Bd. trustees Providence Hosp. and Med. Ctr., 1995—, The Roeper Sch., 1996—; pub. mem. Greater Detroit Health Coun., 1980—; mem. fin. com. Ascension Health, St. Louis, 1998-2001, audit com., 2001—; audit com. Daus. of Charity Nat. Health System, 1988-93; mem. adv. bd. Providence Hosp., Southfield, 1980-95. Stonier fellow Am. Bankers Assn., 1963. Mem. Healthcare Fin. Mgmt. Assn. (bd. dirs. 1976-80), Mich. Assn. CPA's (grantee 1960), Fin. Mgmt. Assn., Acctg. Aid Soc. Detroit (founder), Mich. Bridge Assn. (pres. 1974-76). Avocation: bridge (life master). E-mail: horwitz@oakland.edu.

HORWITZ, SUSAN BAND, molecular pharmacologist; BA, Bryn Mawr Coll., 1958; PhD in Biochemistry, Brandeis U., 1963; PhD (hon.), Universite de la Mediterranee, 2002. Postdoctoral fellow dept. pharmacology, sch. medicine Tufts U., 1963-65, Emory U., 1965-67; rsch. assoc. dept. medicine Albert Einstein Coll. Medicine, N.Y.C., 1967-68, instr. dept. pharmacology, 1968-70, asst. prof. dept. medicine, 1970-75, asst. prof. dept. cell biology, 1973-75, assoc. prof. depts. molecular pharmacology and cell biology, 1980—, co-chair dept. molecular pharmacology, 1985—, Rose C. Falkenstein prof. cancer rsch., 1986—, assoc. dir. cancer rsch. ctr., 1991—. Mem. pharmacology-toxicology rsch. team Nat. Inst. Gen. Med. Sci., 1975-80; adv. com. Irma T. Hirschl Scientist award, 1979-85; bd. scientific counselors divsn. cancer treatment NCI, 1981-86, 87-90, mem. review com. Outstanding Investigators Grant award, 1984—, ad hoc review com. in vitro and in vivo disease-oriented screening project, 1986—; guest reviewer sci. adv. com. Damon Runyon/Walter Winchell Rsch. Fund, 1983, 88; vice chair Gordon Conf. Chemotherapy of Exptl. and Clin. Cancer, 1986, chair, 1987, mem. coun., 1990-93; Sterling Drug vis. prof. dept. pharmacology Boston U., 1987; mem. Charles F. Kettering selection com. Gen. Motors Cancer Rsch. Found., 1988-89, awards assembly, 1991—. Contbr. articles to profl. jours., chpts. to books. Recipient Rsch. Career Devel. award 1970-75, award Pharm. Mfrs. Assn., 1972, Irma T. Hirschl Career Scientists award, 1975-80; grantee Merck, 1970, Nat. Cancer Inst., 1985-92, 92—, Bristol-Myers, 1988-93; named Outstanding Woman Scientist metro N.Y.C. chpt. Assn. Women in Science, Barnard Medal of Distinction, 2003, PhRMA Found. award of Excellence, 2004. Mem. Am. Soc. Pharmacology and Exptl. Therapeutics (com. edn. and profl. affairs 1973-77), Am. Soc. Microbiology (vice chair antimicrobial chemotherapy), Am. Chem. Soc., Am. Assn. Cancer Rsch. (biochem. program com. 1983-84, Clowes award selection com. 1986-87, bd. dirs. 1987-90, spl. confs. com. 1989-92, chmn. Rhoads award selection com. 1990-91, co-chair conf. in cancer rsch. membrane transport in multidrug resistance, devel. and disease, 1991, Cain Meml. award 1992, pres., 2003-), Am. Soc. Cell Biology, Harvey Soc. (mem. coun. 1991—), Amer. Acad. of Arts & sciences, 1994-. Office: A Einstein Coll Medicine Dept Molecular Pharmacology 1300 Morris Park Ave Bronx NY 10461-1926

HORWITZ, WILLIAM J., treasurer; b. St. Louis, Jan. 10, 1946; s. Harold S. and Henrietta B. Horwitz; children: Harris Saul, Pallas Hannah Eleanor. AB, Harvard U., 1967; MPhil, Yale U., 1969, PhD, 1971. Assoc. prof. classics dept. U. Okla., Norman, 1971-79; treas. Bride's House, St. Louis, 1979—. Contbr. articles to profl. jours. Recipient Woodrow Wilson fellowship, 1967, John Harvard Hon. scholarship, 1964, 66. Mem. Harvard Club of St. Louis (v.p. 1988-90, chmn. various coms. 1986-88), Yale Club of St. Louis.

HOSALKAR, HARISH SADANAND, pediatrician, orthopedist, surgeon, consultant; b. Calcutta, India, Sept. 19, 1972; s. Sadanand Ramchandra and Sujata Sadanand Hosalkar; m. Hetal Hosalkar, Mar. 19, 1998; 1 child, Hriday. MB, BChir, U. Mumbai, India, 1995; MS in Orthopedics, U. Mumbai, 1998; DO, Coll. Physicians and Surgeons, Mumbai, 1997. Bd. cert. orthopaedic surgeon specialized in pediat. orthopaedics. Intern K.E.M. Hosp., Mumbai, 1994—95, house officer, 1995, sr. house officer, 1996, registrar, 1996—97, sr. registrar, 1997—98; specialist registrar B.J. Wadia Hosp., Mumbai, 1998—99; lectr. K.B. Bhabha Hosp., Mumbai, 1999—2000; fellow Children's Hosp. Phila., 2000, Valley Children's Hosp., Fresno, Calif., 2000—01, Great Ormond St. Hosp., U. Coll. London, 2001, sr. fellow, 2002—. Dir. orthopaedics Kerkar's Gen. Hosp., Mumbai, 1999—2000; presenter in field. Contbr. articles to profl. jours. Faculty polio surgeon PNR Found., Bhaunagar, 1998—2000; coord. Plague Vaccination Team, Bombay, 1994; cmty. health worker Malavani Village, Mumbai, 1992—93. Named one of Best Citizens of India, 2003; recipient Ranbaxy award for awareness in Aids campaign, 1994, first prize and award, Leprosy Awareness and Mgmt., Ackworth Found., 1994, Dr. Premchand award for cmty. health work, Mumbai, 1995, Rashtriya Gaurav Pride of India award, 2002, Rashtriya Shiromani of India award, 2003. Fellow: Coll. Physicians and Surgeons; mem.: Am. Acad. Orthopaedic Surgeons, Limb Reconstruction Soc. N.Am., Pediat. Orthopaedic Soc. India (life), Maharashtra Orthopaedic Assn. (life), Indian Arthroscopic Assn. (life), Bombay Orthopaedic Soc. (life), Assn. Med. Cons. (life), Indian Med. Assn. (life), Pediat. Orthopedic Soc. N.Am. Avocations: bridge, singing, reading.

HOSANSKY, ANNE, writer; b. N.Y.C., N.Y. d. Abraham and Ada Lichtman; children: Tamar, David. BA in Creative Writing, SUNY. In house editor Weight Watchers Internat., NY, 1973—85. Actor: (off Broadway regional theater); author: Widow's Walk, 1994, Turning Toward Tomorrow, 2002; contbr. articles to publs. Mem.: Am. Assn. Journalists and Authors, Writers Union, Authors Guild.

HOSEK, CHRISTINE MARIE, secondary school educator, art educator; d. David Peter and Janet Marie Stevenson; m. Joseph Edward Hosek, Aug. 1, 1998; children: Katrina, Isabelle. BS, Ill. State U., 1987, MS, 1995. Art tchr. Bradley (Ill.) Bourbomais Cmty. H.S., 1987—. Sponsor art club Bradley (Ill.) Bourbomais Cmty. H.S., 1988—, sponsor class, 1988—2000. Bd. dirs. Kankakee (Ill.) Valley Theatre, 1988—99. Named Most Outstanding Student, Ill. State U., 1987. Avocations: camping, scrapbooks. Office: BBCHS 700 W North St Bradley IL 60915

HOSEK, JOHN JUDE, planning organization executive; b. Cleve., Oct. 1, 1949; s. Norbert James and Elizabeth H.; m. Sharon Marie Hamilton, Nov. 30, 1996; children: Brian Avon, Matthew Avon. BA, Cleve. State U., 1974; MA in Managerial Econs., Case Western Res. U., 1986. Dir. NE Ohio Areawide Coord. Agy., Cleve., 1984—. Adj. faculty Meyers Coll., Cleve., 1984-92. Vol. Normandy Nursing Home, Rocky River, Ohio, 1997; vice chmn. St. Christopher Ch. com., 2000-01. Recipient Greater Cleve. Pub. Works Performance award Cleve. State U., 1994. Mem. Ohio Assn. Regional Couns. (chair transp. com. 1997, 98). Avocations: writing, music, walking, hiking. Home: 16 Pond Dr Rocky River OH 44116-1064

HOSEMANN, C. DELBERT, JR., lawyer; b. New Orleans, June 30, 1947; s. Charles D. and Patricia H.; m. Mary Lynn Lagen; children: Kristen Cullen, Charles Delbert III, Mark Mansfield. BBA, U. Notre Dame, 1969; JD, U. Miss., 1972; LLM in Taxation, NYU, 1973. Assoc. Dossett, Magruder & Montgomery, Jackson, Miss., 1973-78; ptnr. Magruder, Montgomery, Brocato & Hosemann, Jackson, 1978-88, Phelps Dunbar, L.L.P., Jackson, 1988—. Contbr. articles to profl. jours.; speaker in field. Mem. Miss. del. S.E. regional employee benefits liaison com. EP/EO Atlanta, 1986-88, chmn., 1992-93; mem. Leadership Jackson, 1991-92, bd. dirs., 1995-96; pres. Miss. Blood Svcs., Inc., 1994-95; Rep. nominee U.S. Congress 4th Congl. Dist., 1998; trustee Jackson State U. Devel. Found.; chmn. Swedish Am. C. of C. Ctrl. United for So. States., Inc. Mem. ABA (employee benefits com., taxation sect., continuing legal edn. com. budget and fin. com.), Hinds County Bar Assn. (sec. 1980), Miss. State Bar Assn. (dir. young lawyers sect. 1976-78, taxation com.), Jackson Young Lawyers Assn. (pres. 1977-78), First Comml. Bank (bd. dirs.). Office: Phelps Dunbar 200 S Lamar St Ste 500 Jackson MS 39201-4013

HOSHAW, LLOYD, retired historian, educator; b. Benton, Ind., May 9, 1924; s. Walter and Gladys Ethel (Blue) H.; m. Evelyn F. Tyler, Dec. 24, 1954; children: Linda, John, James, Walter, David, Paul. BA, Goshen Coll., 1949; MA, Ind. U., 1951. Tchr. Winamac (Ind.) High Sch., 1952-55; instr. LaSalle(Ill.)-Peru-Oglesby Jr. Coll., 1955-65; history prof., dept. chair Rock Valley Coll., Rockford, Ill., 1965-88, history prof., 1988—2001; ret., 2001. Bd. dirs. Rock River Christian Coll., prof. history. Author: A History of Eastern Civilizations, Vol I., 1994, Vol. II, 1995, 2d edit., 2001. With USN, 1944—45. Mem. VFW (life), Archeol. Inst. Am. (Rockford chpt.), Ill. State Hist. Soc., Rockford Hist. Soc. Baptist. Avocations: photography, travel. Home: 1860 Charlotte Dr Rockford IL 61108-6508

HOSHI, TAKEO, education educator; BA, U. Tokyo, 1983; PhD, MIT, 1988. Asst. prof. U. Calif., San Diego, 1988—94, assoc. prof., 1994—2000, prof., 2000—. Office: Univ Calif San Diego 9500 Gilman Dr La Jolla CA 92093 Office Phone: 858-534-5018.

HOSHINO, YOSHIRO, industrial relations specialist, educator; b. Tokyo-Shi, Tokyo-Hu, Japan, Jan. 13, 1922; s. Teruoki and Matsue Hoshino; m, Kumiko Serizawa, July 7, 1954; children: Syuichiro, Kenjiro, Chieko, Tetsuro. *Father was a Shinto priest. From 1907 through 1942 he held many kinds of festivals in the Tennos' sanctuary attending the Meiji, Taisho, and showa Tennos. Though thoughts differed between father and son, he did not care what his son said or wrote. He was pleased with his child's passionate concern for research and provided much love and tolerance, for which his son is grateful.* B, Tokyo Inst. Tech., 1944, Dr., 1980. Asst. tech. staff Agy. of Tech., Tokyo, 1944-45, critic, 1945-62; prof. Ritsumeikan U., Kyoto, 1962-68, cirtic, 1968-81; prof. indsl. tech. Teikyo U., Tokyo, 1981-97, critic, 1997—. Hon. prof. N.E. U., Shenyang, China, 1985—. Author: Collected Works of Yoshiro Hoshino, 1977-79, Future of Civilization, 1980, Fundamental Problems on Latest Technology, 1986, Technology, Economy and Politics—Japan and China, 1945-1991, 1993, The Origin of Japan's Militarism-Political and Economic Relations among Japan, Korea and China, 1840-1910, 2004. Avocation: driving. Home: 9-8-19 Chiyogaoka Asao-ku Kawasaki-shi Kanagawa 215-0005 Japan

HOSICK, HOWARD LAWRENCE, cell biology professor, academic administrator; b. Champaign, Ill., Nov. 1, 1943; s. Arthur Howard and Eunice Irma (Miller) H.; m. Cynthia Ann Jacobson, June 15, 1968; children: Steven Cameron, Anna Elise, Rachel Victoria. BA, U. Colo., 1965; PhD, U. Calif., Berkeley, 1970. Postdoctoral fellow Karolinska Inst., Stockholm, 1970-72; asst. research biochemist U. Calif., Berkeley, 1972-73; asst. prof. Wash. State U., Pullman, 1973-78, assoc. prof., 1978-83, prof. cell biology, 1983—, chmn. dept. zoology, 1983-87, chmn. dept. genetics and cell biology, 1987-91. Vis. scientist U. Reading, Eng., 1978, B.C. Cancer Ctr., Vancouver, 2003; disting. scientist Aichi Cancer Ctr., Nagoya, Japan, 1986; vis. scholar Cambridge U., 1994; rsch. com. Am. Heart Assn., 1989; grant rev. com. Nat. Cancer Inst., 1993-2000. Rev. editor In Vitro Cellular and Molecular Biology, 1986—97; contbr. articles to profl. jours. Bd. govs. Internat. Assn. Breast Cancer Rsch., 1993-2000. Recipient H.S. Boyce award, 1981, Shell Faculty Devel. award, 1984, Cancer Rsch. awards Eagles Club, 1989-2004, G. and L. Pfeiffer Rsch. Found. award, 1992; fellow NIH, NSF, Am. Cancer Soc., Damon Runyan-Walter Winchell Cancer Fund, Fogarty Internat. Ctr., 1968-2004; grantee NIH, NSF, Am. Cancer Soc., Am. Inst. Cancer Rsch., Pfeiffer Found., 1973-2004, U.S. Army, Internat. Assn. for Cancer Rsch., 2002-. Mem. Am. Soc. Cell Biology, Tissue Culture Assn., Am. Assn. Cancer Research, Internat. Assn. Breast Cancer Research. Lodges: Rotary. Democrat. Buddhist. Avocations: running, woodworking, model aviation. Home: 1185 NE Lake St Pullman WA 99163-3869 Office: Wash State U Sch Biol Scis Pullman WA 99164-4234 Office Phone: 509-335-3035. Business E-Mail: hosick@wsu.edu.

HOSIE, SPENCER, lawyer; BA summa cum laude, U. Calif. Berkeley, 1978; JD, U. Calif. Davis Law Sch., 1981. Law clk. to Hon. Edmond W. Burke, Chief Justice Alaska Supreme Ct., 1981—82; assoc. Heller, Ehrman, White & McAuliffe, San Francisco, 1982—85; ptnr. Hosie, Frost, Large & McArthur, San Francisco, 1985—. Editor: U. Calif. Davis Law Rev. Named one of Top 25 Lawyers Under 45 in Calif., 1993. Mem.: Order of Coif. Office: Hosie Frost Large & McArthur 1 Market Ste 2200 Spear Street Tower San Francisco CA 94105 Office Phone: 415-247-6000. Office Fax: 415-247-6001. E-mail: shosie@hosielaw.com.*

HOSIE, THOMAS WALSH, counselor, educator; b. Buffalo, N.Y. s. Frank and Mary Hosie; m. Denise Joy Hosie; 1 child, Sean Walsh. BA in History, U. Buffalo, 1966, MEd in Counseling, 1970, PhD in Counseling, 1973. Lic. profl. counselor La., 1988, cert. counselor Nat. Bd. of Cert. Counselors, 1999. Asst. prof. N.E. La. U., Monroe, 1973—77; prof., dept. head La. State U., Baton Rouge, 1977—96, Miss. State U., Starkville, 1996—. Sci. and social studies tchr. John F. Kennedy H.S., Cheektowaga, NY, 1966—68; supr. Marine Midland Trust Co. of Western N.Y., Buffalo, 1968—69; supr. of student tchr.s U. Buffalo, 1969—70; sch. counselor Hamburg Ctrl. H.S., NY, 1970—71, 1970—71, Buffalo City Schs. - Woodlawn Jr. H.S., 1970; therapist Suicide Prevention and Crisis Svc., Buffalo, 1971—72. Author: (book chpt.) Historical Antecedents & Current Status of Counselor Licensure, Counselor Education; editor: Jour. of Counseling Svcs.; contbr. articles to profl. jours. Chmn. La. Profl. Counselors Bd. of Examiners, Baton Rouge, 1987—88, mem., 1995—96; v.p. for rsch. Assn. for Humanistic Edn. & Devel., Alexandria, Va., 1978—80; pres., rep. to ACA, treas. Assn. for Counselor Edn. and Supervision, Alexandria, Va., 1989—99; exec. coun. - aces rep. ACA, Alexandria, Va., 1992—95; ACA rep. Coun. for Accreditation of Counseling and Related Ednl. Programs, Alexandria, Va., 1996—99; pres. and v.p. Miss. Assoc. for Counselor Edn. and Supervision, Biloxi, Miss., 1999—2000, La. Sch. Counselors Assn., Baton Rouge, 1976—80; pres. La. Assn. for Counselor Edn. and Supervision, Baton Rouge, 1977—78; pres. and v.p. La. Assn. for Counseling and Devel., Baton Rouge, 1984—88. Recipient Counselor Educator of Yr. award, La. Sch. Counselor Assoc., 1979, Leadership and Achievement award, So. Assoc. for Counselor Edn. and Supervision, 1984, ACES Disting. Svc. award, Assoc. for Counselor Edn. and Supervision, 2002, Herbert M. Handley Outstanding Dissertation Mentor award, Mid-South Ednl. Rsch. Assoc., 2003; Vocat. Rehab. Program by Distance grant, Miss. Dept. of Vocat. Rehab., 1999 - 2003, Exptl. Evaluation of Tutorials in Problem Solving grant, Office of Naval Rsch., 2002, Measurement and Evaluation of Animated Pedagogical Agents grant, 2002, 2003. Mem.: APA, Assn. for Counselor Edn. and Supervision (pres. 1989—90, Rsch. Award & Disting. Profl. Svc. Award 1989 & 2002), Miss. Assn. of Counselor Edn. and Supervision (pres. 2000—01), La. Counseling Assn. (life; pres. 1986—87), Chi Sigma Iota. Avocation: fishing. Office: Miss State Univ PO Box 9727 Mississippi State University MS 39762 Office Phone: 662-325-3426. Office Fax: 662-325-3263. Business E-Mail: hosie@colled.msstate.edu.

HOSING, CHITRA, oncologist, researcher; m. Vic R. Hosing. Diplomate Am. Bd. Internal Medicine, 1996. Asst. prof. MD Anderson Cancer Ctr., Houston, 2001—. Office: M D Anderson Cancer Center 1515 Holcombe Blvd Houston TX 77030 Office Phone: 713-792-8750.

HOSKINS, ALEXANDER L. (PETE HOSKINS), zoological park administrator; b. Woodland, Calif., Sept. 1, 1947; s. Edgar and Betty (Stoner) H.; m. Sharon Paula Barr, May 19, 1990; children: Emily, David, Adam. BA in Polit. Sci., San Jose State U., 1969; MA in Pub. Adminstrn., U. Minn., 1971. Asst. to city mgr. City of Foster City, Calif., 1971-72; mgmt. analyst Mng. Dir.'s Office, City of Phila., 1972-80, exec. dir. Fairmount Park, 1980-88, commr. of streets, 1988-93; pres., CEO, Phila. Zoo, 1993—. Contbr. articles to various publs. Exec. v.p. Chestnut Hill Cmty. Assn., 1974-76; trustee Cmty. Leadership Seminars, 1978-80, Unitarian Soc. Germantown, 1985-87; chmn. Delaware Valley Regional Horticulture Industry Coun., 1985-86, Phila. Independence Marathon, 1985-88 Recipient ann. award for meritorious mcpl. svc. Ctrl. Phila. Devel. Corp., 1986, honor award for restoration and revitalization Pa.-Del. chpt. Am. Soc. Landscape Architects, 1986, govt. svc. award Phila. sect. ASCE, 1990, govt. award for excellence in pub. adminstrn. Phila. regional chpt. ASPA, 1991, award for engring. excellence Cons. Engrs. Coun. N.J., 1991, William V. Donaldson award for civic price PhilaPride, 1992. Mem. Am. Pub. Works Assn. (Delaware Valley exec. com. 1992—). Office: Phila Zoo Garden 3400 W Girard Ave Philadelphia PA 19104-1196

HOSKINS, BOB (ROBERT WILLIAM HOSKINS), actor; b. Bury St. Edmunds, Suffolk, Eng., Oct. 26, 1942; s. Robert and Elsie Lillian Hoskins; m. Jane Livesey 1967 (div. 1978); 2 children: Alex, Sarah; m. Linda Banwell, 1982; 2 children: Jack, Rosa. Student, Stroud Green Sch. Stage debut in Romeo and Juliet, Victoria Theatre, Stoke-on-Trent, 1968; joined Royal Shakespeare Co., 1976; stage appearances include Pygmalion, Albery, Eng., 1974, Aldwych, 1976, The World Has Turned Upside Down, 1978, Has Washington Legs?, 1978, True West, 1989, Guys and Dolls, 1981, Old Wicked Songs, 1996-97, Stage, 1996-97; TV appearances include On The Move, 1976, Pennies From Heaven, 1978, (miniseries) Flickers, 1980, Othello, 1981, The Dunera Boys, 1986, The Changeling, 1993, World War II: When The Lions Roared, 1994, David Copperfield, 1999, Don Quixote, 2000, The Lost World, 2001, Il Papa buono, 2003; film appearances include Zulu Dawn, 1980, The Long Good Friday, 1981, Cotton Club, 1984, Mona Lisa (Best Actor award Cannes Festival, Nat. Soc. Film Critics, 1987), Who Framed Roger Rabbit?, 1988, Mermaids, 1990, Heart Condition, 1990, Shattered, 1990, The Favor the Watch, 1990, The Projectionist, 1990, Hook, 1991, Passed Away, 1991, Super Mario Bros., 1992, Nixon, 1995, Michael, 1996, Cousin Bette, 1996, Twenty-Four/Seven, 1997, 1 Inch Over the Horizon, 1997, Felicias Journey, 1999, Let the Good Times Roll, 1999, Enemy at the Gates, 2001, Maid in Manhattan, 2002, The Sleeping Dictionary, 2003, Vanity Fair, 2004, Beyond the Sea, 2004, Unleashed, 2005, Son of the Mask, 2005 others; (films) actor, writer, director The Raggedy Rawney, 1988; actor, director The Rainbow, 1994; actor, prodr. The Secret Agent, 1995. Avocations: photography, gardening, playgoing. Office: Internat Creative Mgmt Ltd Oxford House 76 Oxford St London W1N 0AX England*

HOSKINS, CAROL NOLL, nursing educator, researcher; b. N.Y.C., Dec. 25, 1932; d. Victor Herbert and Rachel (Perkins) Noll; m. Donald William Hoskins, Dec. 19, 1955; children: Lauren Hoskins Lingley, David William, Bruce Noll. BSN, Cornell U., 1955; MA, NYU, 1973, PhD, 1978; PhD (hon.), U. Athens, Greece, 1998. RN. Pub. health nurse Vis. Nurse Svc. N.Y., N.Y.C., 1955—58; asst. prof. nursing NYU, N.Y.C., 1977—82, assoc. prof. nursing, 1982—87, prof. nursing, 1987—2003, sr. rsch. scientist, 2003—, dir. PhD program in nursing, 1985—90, prin. investigator 3 phase program breast cancer rsch., 1990—. Author (with C.N. Hoskins and C. Mariano): Research in Nursing and Health - Quantitative and Qualitative Methods, 2d ed., 2004; co-author: Breast Cancer: Journey to Recovery, 2001; prin. author: (4-part video series) Journey to Recovery: For Women with Breast Cancer and Their Partners, 2002; contbr. articles to profl. jours. Case mgr. ARC Family Emergency Relief Svcs., 9/11. Recipient Fulbright Sr. Specialist award, 2003; grantee Nat. Inst. Nursing Rsch., Nat. Cancer Inst., 1999—; Sr. Fulbright scholar, 1995. Fellow: Am. Acad. Nursing (award); mem.: ANA, Fulbright Assn., Sigma Theta Tau. Avocations: swimming, skiing, quilting, gardening. Home: 3-24 Parsons Blvd Whitestone NY 11357 Office: NYU Steinhardt Sch Edn 246 Greene St New York NY 10003-6677 Office Phone: 212-998-5326. E-mail: cnh1@nyu.edu.

HOSKINS, DEBBIE STEWART, librarian, artist; b. Bad Kreuznach, Germany, Sept. 24, 1962; d. Jesse Arthur and Rebecca Stewart; married, 2003; 1 child, Jesse. BA, Kent (Ohio) State U., 1984; MS in Libr. Sci., Drexel U., Phila., 1991. Cert. prof. librarian, Mich. Youth svcs. librarian Grand Rapids (Mich.) Pub. Library, 1994-99, youth svcs. specialist, 1999—. Lectr. in field. Reviewer: Sch. Library Jour., 2000—; Remembering Summer, 1999, one-woman shows include Franciscan Life Process Ctr., 2001, 2005. Active church choir Blessed Sacrament Ch., Grand Rapids, Mich., 1998—. Recipient juried art award Festival Regional Arts Exhbn., 2000, Franciscan Life Process Ctr., 1999, 2001, 03, 04, First United Meth. Ch., 2000, 02, 05. Mem. Soc. Children's Book Writers & Illustrators (assoc., adv, com. Mich. 1998—, Mich. illustrator coord. 1999-2001), Am. Library Assn. (life). Roman Catholic. Avocations: music, gardening, balloon animals. Office: PO Box 230271 Grand Rapids MI 49523 Personal E-mail: debbiestudio@yahoo.com.

HOSKINS, DONALD W., medical association administrator; BS, Queens Coll., 1953; MD, Cornell U., 1957. Diplomate Am. Bd. Internal Medicine. Chief med. officer, med. dir., sr. v.p. med. affairs Continuum Health Ptnrs. (Beth Israel), 1997—; assoc. prof. clin. medicine Albert Einstein Coll. Medicine, Bronx, NY. Office: Beth Israel Med Ctr First Ave 16th St New York NY 10003 Office Phone: 212-420-2140. E-mail: dhoskins@chpnet.org.

HOSKINS, JOHN HOWARD, retired urologist, educator; b. Breckenridge, Minn., Mar. 18, 1934; s. James H. and Ruth (Johanson) H.; m. Nancy Weih, Aug. 3, 1957; children: William, James, Laura, Sara. BA in History, U. Iowa, 1956; BS in Medicine, U. S.D., 1959; MD, Temple U., 1961. Diplomate Am. Bd. Urology. Practice medicine specializing in urology, Sioux Falls, S.D., 1966-96; head sect. urology U. S.D. Sch. Medicine, Vermillon, 1977-93; ret., 1997. Maj. M.C. U.S. Army, 1967-69, Vietnam. Fellow: ACS; mem.: Am. Urol. Assn., Augustana Fellows, Rotary, Shriners, Masons. Republican. Methodist. Personal E-mail: jnhoskins@msn.com.

HOSKINS, RICHARD JEROLD, lawyer; b. Ft. Smith, Ark., June 19, 1945; s. Walter Jerold and Emma Gladys Hoskins; children: Stephen Weston, Philip Richard. BA, U. Kans., 1967; JD, Northwestern U., 1970. Bar: N.Y. 1971, Ill. 1976, U.S. Supreme Ct. 1982. Assoc. Davis Polk & Wardwell, N.Y.C., 1970-73; asst. U.S. atty., So. Dist. N.Y., 1973-76; assoc. Schiff Hardin & Waite, Chgo., 1976-77, ptnr., 1978—. Adj. prof. U. Va. Law Sch., 1980-83, Northwestern U. Law Sch., 1992-98, sr. lectr., 1999—. Contbr. articles to profl. jours. Mem. vis. com. U. Chgo. Div. Sch.; chancellor emeritus Episcopal Diocese of Chgo.; bd. visitors and govs. St. John's Coll. Fellow Am. Coll. Trial Lawyers, Am. Bar Found.; mem. ABA, Ill. State Bar Assn., Chgo. Bar Assn., 7th Cir. Bar Assn., Assn. of Bar of City of N.Y., Chgo. Coun. Lawyers, Law Club Chgo., Met. Club (Chgo.), Univ. Club (Chgo.); bd. visitors and govs. St. John's Coll., Office: 6600 Sears Tower Chicago IL 60606 Office Phone: 312-258-5509. Business E-Mail: rhoskins@schiffhardin.com.

HOSKINS, WILLIAM JOHN, obstetrician, educator, gynecologist; b. Harlan, Ky., May 10, 1940; s. Lonnie S. and Joanne (Huff) H.; m. Betty Jean Gay, Sept. 10, 1960 (div. 1985); children: Tonya J., William John Jr.; m. Iffath Abbasi Ahson, Nov. 9, 1985; children: Ahad A., Mariya A. BA, U. Tenn., Knoxville, 1962; MD, U. Tenn., Memphis, 1965. Diplomate Am. Bd. Ob-Gyn., Am. Bd. Gynecol. Oncology. Commd. lt. USN, 1966, advanced through grades to capt.; intern Jacksonville (Fla.) Naval Hosp., 1966-67; med. officer Destroyer Squadron 8 USN, Mayport, Fla., 1967-68; resident in ob-gyn Oakland (Calif.) Naval Hosp., 1968-71; staff dept. ob -gyn Pensacola (Fla.) Naval Hosp., 1971—74; fellow in gynecol. oncology U. Miami, Fla., 1974-76; dir. gynecol. oncology Nat. Naval Med. Ctr., Bethesda, Md., 1976—86; assoc. prof. ob-gyn Uniformed Svcs. U., Bethesda, 1976-86; ret. USN, 1986; assoc. chief gynecology svc. Meml. Sloan-Kettering Cancer Ctr., N.Y.C., 1988-90, chief gynecology svc., 1990—, 1990—; assoc. prof. ob-gyn Cornell U. Med. Ctr., N.Y.C., 1986-90; prof. ob-gyn. Cornell U. Med. Coll., N.Y.C., 1990—2001, vice chmn. protocol com. gynecol. oncology group, 1993-94, vice chmn. gynecologic oncology group, 1993—2002; Avon chair gynecologic oncology rsch. Meml. Sloan-Kettering Cancer Ctr., N.Y.C., 1995-96, dep. physician in chief disease mgmt. teams, 1996—2001; dir. Curtis & Elizabeth Anderson Cancer Ctr. at Memorial Health U. Med. Ctr., Savannah, Ga., 2001—; prof. ob-gyn. Mercer Med. Coll., Macon, Ga., 2001—, sr. assoc. dean Sch. Medicine Savannah, 2004—. Chmn. ovarian com. Gynecol. Oncology Group, Phila., 1984-89; disting. Ga. Cancer scholar, 2001—. Editor: Principles and Practice of Gynecology and Oncology, 1992, 4th edit., 2000, 4th edit., 2004, Cancer of the Ovary, 1993, Cervical Cancer and Perinvasive Peoplasia, 1996, Cancer Management: A Multidisciplinary Approach, 1996, Handbook of Gynecologic Oncology, 2000, 8th edit., 2002, Atlas of Procedures in Gynecologic Oncology, 2003; contbr. over 224 articles to profl. jours., chpts. to books. Fellow Am. Coll. Obstetricians and Gynecologists (v.p. Navy sect. 1982-83), ACS; mem. Am. Gynecol. and Obstet. Soc., Soc. Gynecol. Oncologists (sec.-treas. elect 1992, sec.-treas. 1994—, coun. mem. 1988-91, pres. 1999), Soc. Gynecol. Surgeons, Am. Radium Soc., Am. Assn Cancer Rsch., Internat. Gyn. Cancer Soc. (v.p. 2004—). Republican. Moslem. Office: Anderson Cancer Inst at Meml Health Univ Med Ctr 4700 Waters Ave Savannah GA 31404 Office Phone: 912-350-8337. Business E-Mail: hoskiwi1@memorialhealth.com.

HOSKINS, WILLIAM KELLER, pharmaceutical executive, lawyer, mediator, arbitrator; b. Cin., Feb. 22, 1935; s. John Hobart and Gertrude Louise (Keller) H.; m. Elizabeth Ann Grimm, Aug. 5, 1961; children: Bruce, Andrew, John, Elizabeth, Allison. BA, Yale U., 1956; LLB, Harvard U., 1962. Bar: Ohio 1962, U.S. Dist. Ct. (so. dist.) Ohio 1963, U.S. Tax Ct. 1963, U.S. Ct. Appeals (6th cir.) 1964, N.Y. 1982, Mo. 1983. Assoc. Frost & Jacobs, Cin., 1962-68; gen. counsel Drackett Co., Cin., 1968-71, v.p., gen. counsel, 1971-81; assoc. gen. counsel Bristol Myers Co., N.Y.C., 1981, spl. counsel, 1982; v.p., gen. counsel, sec. Hoechst Marion Roussell (formerly Marion Labs. Inc.), Kansas City, Mo., 1982-97; gen. ptnr. Hoskins Group, Boston, 1998—; pres. Hoskins & Assocs., Boston, 1998—; mng. ptnr. Resolution Coun., LLP, Portland, Oreg., 2002—. Chmn. household div. Soap and Detergent Assn., N.Y.C., 1978-79, chmn. Chem. Spltys. Mfg. Assn., Washington, 1982; bd. dirs. Am. Arbitration Assn., N.Y.C., 1997-2005, Ferrrellgas, Inc., Kansas City, Mo., 2003-. Isotechnika, Inc., Edmonton, 2003-. Mem. Hamilton County Rep. Ctrl. Com., Ohio, 1970-81; sec.-treas. Marion Labs. Polit. Action Com., 1982-89; sec.-treas. polit. action com. Mid-Am. Com. Sound Govt., Lake Quivira, Kans., 1982-86; bd. dirs. Landmark Legal Found., Kansas City, 1995-2003, vice chmn., 2001-2003. Lt. (j.g.) USN, 1956-59. Mem. Mo. Bar Assn., Ohio Bar Assn., N.Y. Bar, Cin. Bar Assn., Harvard Law Sch. Alumni Assn. (bd. dirs. 1991-95). Roman Catholic. Home: 85 E India Row Apt 20B Boston MA 02110-3397 Office Phone: 617-742-8191. E-mail: Bhoskins98@aol.com.

HOSLER, CHARLES LUTHER, JR., meteorologist, educator; b. Honey Brook, Pa., June 3, 1924; s. Charles Luther and Miriam Deichley (Stauffer) H.; m. Gladys Cheesbrough, 1947 (div.); children:Sharon Elizabeth, David Charles, Lynn Rebecca, Peter William; m. Anna R. Stahel, 1971. Student, Bucknell U., 1943-44, MIT, 1944-45; BS, Pa. State U., 1947, MS, 1948, PhD, 1951. Faculty Pa. State U., University Park, 1948—, prof. meteorology, 1960—, head dept., 1961-65, dean Coll. Earth and Mineral Scis., 1965-85, sr. v.p. rsch., dean Grad. Sch., 1985-92. Hydrographer Pa. Dept. Forests and Waters, 1949-59; meteorol. cons., 1950—, vis. prof. colls., lectr. civic and profl. groups; condr. daily TV weather program, 1957-67; spl. rsch. microphysics of clouds; chmn. bd. atmospheric scis. and climate Nat. Acad. Scis., 1984-86; mem. Nat. Sci. Bd., 1985-94; mem. nat. adv. com. on oceans and atmosphere; chmn. bd. trustees Univ. Corp. for Atmospheric Rsch., Boulder, Colo., 1981-85. Contbr. articles to profl. jours. Served to lt. (j.g.) USNR, 1943-46; lt. comdr. Res. Fellow Am. Meteorol. Soc. (councilor, pres. 1976); mem. Nat. Acad. Engring., Am. Geophys. Union Am. Chem. Soc. (regional lectr. 1971-72), AAAS, Sigma Xi (pres. Pa. State U. 1958, nat. lectr. 1972), Tau Beta Pi. Home: 1229 Smithfield Cir State College PA 16801-6426 Office: Pa State U 617 Walker Bldg University Park PA 16802-5014 Office Phone: 814-865-8358. E-mail: hosler@ems.psu.edu.

HOSLER, ELIZABETH, city manager, director; b. Barberton, Ohio, Mar. 1, 1964; d. Ernest Wade and Jean Heath Underwood; m. Michael J. Hosler, Sept. 4, 1950; children: Emilie, Mary Catherine. MBA, U. Dayton, 1993. CPA. Asst. mgr. Rax Restaurants, Columbus, Ohio, 1987-88; clk. The Ltd., Inc., Columbus, 1988-92; dir. bus. mgmt. Solid Waste Authority Cen Ohio, Grove City, Ohio, 2002—. Mem. Nat. Mgmt. Assn. (treas. 1996-98). United Methodist. Avocation: playing pipe organ. Home: 430 E Moler St Columbus OH 43207-1241 Office: Solid Waste Authority Cen Ohio 6220 Young Rd Grove City OH 43123-9518

HOSLEY, MARGUERITE CYRIL, civic worker; b. Houston, July 29, 1946; d. Frederick Willard and Marguerite Estella (Arisman) Collister; m. Richard Allyn Hosley II, July 18, 1968; children: Richard A. III, Sean Frederick, Michelle Cyril. BS in Edn., U. Houston, 1968; postgrad., Tex. A&M U., 1970-71. Cert. tchr., Tex. Tchr. Sharpstown H.S., Houston, 1968-69, Bryan (Tex.) H.S., 1969-71; ins. asst. Farmers Ins., Stafford, Tex., 1981-83; adminstrv. asst., fin. asst. Christ United Meth. Ch., Sugarland, Tex., 1984-92; mem. planning and zoning commn. City of Sugarland, 1995-98; mem. Sugarland City Coun., 1998—; mayor pro tem City of Sugarland, 2000-2001, 2004—. Pres. bd. dirs. Ft. Bend Boys Choir, 1984-85; docent Bayou Bend Collection and Gardens, Houston Mus. Fine Arts, 1994—, day chair, 1997-98, spl. event chmn. 1999-2000, group tour chmn., 2001-2003, program chmn. 2004-05; mem. Ima Hogg Ceramic Cir., 1994—, social chmn., 1997-98; bd. dirs. Am. Cancer Soc., 1990-97; pres. Am. Cancer Soc. League, 1993-94; mem. Lone Star Stomp com. Ft. Bend Mus. Assn., 1991-97; parent vol. Ft. Bend Ind. Schs., 1980-94; raffle chmn. Ft. Bend Drug Alliance Gala, 1989; newsletter chmn. Am. Heart Assn. Guild, 1990-91, v.p., 1992-93; bd. dirs. Sugar Land Cultural Arts Found., 1999—, Battleship Tex. Found., 2001-2002. Named Ft. Bend Outstanding Woman, Ft. Bend County, 1992. Mem. Houston Ladies' Tennis Assn. (team capt.), Ft. Bend Mus., Sweetwater Country Club (bd. govs. 1990-93), Sweetwater Women's Assn. (treas.

1985-87, pres. 1987-88), Friends of Casa (charter mem.), Aggie Moms Club, Chi Omega Alumnae. Republican. Methodist. Avocations: tennis, dance, reading, continuing education classes. Home: 427 W Alkire Lake Dr Sugar Land TX 77478-3527

HOSMAN, SHARON LEE, retired music educator; b. Bisbee, Ariz., Nov. 2, 1943; d. Roy Lee and Virginia Baldwin (Bandel) H. BA, Loretto Heights Coll., 1965; MA, U. No. Colo., 1979. Tchr. Livermore (Calif.) Sch. Dist., 1965-66, Jefferson County Pub. Schs., Golden, Colo., 1966-97; ret., 1997. Faculty rep. North Area Citizens Adv. Com., Arvada, Colo., 1979-81, S.I.P.C., Arvada, 1982-83, North Area Sch. Improvement Process Com., Arvada, 1984-91, North Area Accountability com., 1991-92. Piano accompanist for sch. groups, 1965-97. Mem. NEA, DAR, Jefferson County Edn. Assn., Colo. Edn. Assn., Music Tchrs. Nat. Assn., Colo. State Music Tchrs. Assn., Denver Area Music Tchrs. Assn., Musicians' Soc. Denver, Am. Guild Organists, Hereditary Order of First Families of Mass., Smithsonian, Denver Rescue Mission, Denver Dumb Friends League, St. Luke's Hosp. Aux. (life), The Regis U. Crest Club. Republican. Episcopalian. Avocations: art, music, drama, reading, gardening.

HOSMANE, NARAYAN SADASHIV, chemistry professor; b. Gokarn, Karnatak, India, June 30, 1948; came to U.S., 1976, naturalized citizen, 1993; s. Sadashiv Ganapati and Lalita (Kurse) H.; m. Sumathy Rao, May 6, 1976; children: Suneil Narayan, Nina Narayan. BS, Karnatak U., Dharwar, India, 1968, MS, 1970; PhD, Edinburgh (Scotland) U., 1974. Rsch. asst. Queen's U. of Belfast (No. Ireland), 1974-75; rsch. scientist Lambeg (No. Ireland) Indsl. Rsch. Inst., 1975-76; rsch. assoc. Auburn (Ala.) U., 1976-77, U. Va., Charlottesville, 1977-79; asst. prof. Va. Poly. Inst. and State U., Blacksburg, 1979-82, So. Meth. U., Dallas, 1982-86, assoc. prof., 1986-89, prof., 1989-98, No. Ill. U., 1998—. Chemist cons. Vertically Integrated Tech., Inc., Dallas, 1990-98; invited speaker in field; chmn. 1st Boron-USA (BUSA-I) Workshop, 1988. Author (with others): Boron Chemistry, 1980, Advances in Boron and the Boranes, 1988, Advances in Organometallic Chemistry, 1990, Electron Deficient Boron and Carbon Clusters, 1991, Pure and Applied Chemistry, 1991, Chemical Reviews, 1993; author:, 1997, 2003; author: (with others) (jour.) Cluster Sci.; contbr. articles to profl. jours. Recipient Camille and Henry Dreyfus Scholar award, 1994, Mother-India Internat. Rsch. award for outstanding contbn. to field of chemistry, 1994, Boron in the U.S. award, 1996, Presdl. Rsch. Professorship award, No. Ill. U., 2001, Humboldt Sr. Scientist Rsch. award, 2001; grantee, So. Meth. U., 1983—84, Rsch. Corp., 1983—85, Petroleum Rsch. Fund, 1984—, NSF, 1985—, Tex. Higher Edn. Coordinating Bd., 1994—97, Welch grant, 1985—98. Fellow Royal Soc. Chemistry, Am. Inst. Chemists; mem. Am. Chem. Soc. Soc., Soc. of Sigma Xi (Outstanding Rsch. award 1987). Achievements include synthesis of over 450 main group metallacarboranes of pentagonal bipyramidal geometries and their coordinated complexes; discovery of boron biomolecules for boron neutron capture therapy in cancer treatment; discovery of zirconium-, hafnium-, titanium-, lanthanide- and yttrium-carborane sandwich compounds which are envisioned as potential precursors to Ziegler-Natta catalysts, and of main group metal sandwich compounds of the C2B4-carborane ligands. Home: 663 Teal Ct Dekalb IL 60115-6201 Office: No Ill U Dept Chem and Biochemistry Dekalb IL 60115-2862 Fax: 815-753-4802. Office Phone: 815-753-3556. E-mail: nhosmane@niu.edu.

HOSN, WALLY, plastic surgeon; b. San Diego, Oct. 9, 1966; s. Wally and Janice Paul Hosn; m. Patricia Aida Flores, Mar. 28, 1968. BA magna cum laude, U. Pa., Phila., 1988; MD, Vanderbilt Med. Sch., Nashville, 1992—92. Cert. gen. surgery Cleve. Clinic Found., 1997, plastic surgery Cleve. Clinic Found., 1999, aesthetic cosmetic surgery Aesthetic Cosmetic Surgery Network, 1999, diplomate Am. Bd. Plastic Surgery, 2003. Pvt. practice plastic surgery Wally Hosn, M.D., Beverly Hills, Calif., 2000—, San Luis Obispo, 2002—. Consulting Cedars Sinai Hosp., L.A., 2001—, Sierra Vista Hosp., San Luis Obispo, 2002—, French Hosp., 2002—, surg. quality control, 2004—; presenter at nat. meetings. Contbr. articles to profl. jours. Named Benjamin Franklin scholar, U. Pa., 1989; recipient Am. Inst. Chemistry award, 1998, Resident Tchg. award, Ohio State U., 1998; Surg. Rsch. grant, Diabetes Found., 1990. Mem.: San Luis Med. Soc., Am. Soc. Plastic Surgeons, Phi Beta Kappa. Independent. Achievements include research in glutamine receptors; anatomic description of periorbita; closure of complex chest wounds; ischemic preconditioning of hind limb of rat; effects of glutamine diet on protein metabolism; closure of cranial defect with free muscle transfer. Avocations: hockey, mountain biking, scuba diving, travel, photography. Office: Aesthetic Surgery Ste D 1250 Peach St San Luis Obispo CA 93401 Office Phone: 805-541-0330. Home Fax: 805-474-4218; Office Fax: 805-541-6809.

HOSOKAWA, DAVID, advertising executive; b. 1943; Copy ed, reporter Mpls. Tribune, 1965—67; Staff writer Houston Chronicle, Tex., 1967—68; advt., mktg. consultant, 1968—76; asst mng ed. Albuquerque Journal, 1974—76; asst. pub. Sun Newspapers, Omaha, 1976—79; pres. Sunbelt Pub., 1979—84, David Hosokawa & Assoc, 1984—91; CEO TMP Worldwide, Inc., 1991—97, vice chmn. (ret.) NYC, 1997—98; chmn Voltage Factory, Atlanta, 2000—. Office: Off of Chairman Voltage Factory 400 Perimeter Ctr Terr N Atlanta GA 30346

HOSSAIN, SABIHA HUSNA, project specialist; b. L.A., Nov. 6, 1974; d. Sajid Wahiduddin and Humera Hossain. BSc in Biol. Scis., UCLA, 1997; MSc in Regulatory Scis., U. So. Calif., 2004. Eligibility assoc. Meridian Health Care Mgmt., Thousand Oaks, Calif., 1992—97; clin. lab technician Splty. Laboratories, Santa Monica, Calif., 1997—98; staff rsch. assoc. ii U. of Calif., LA Dept. of Medicine, 1998—2000; rsch. assoc. ii Amgen Inc., Thousand Oaks, Calif., 2000—, project specialist, 2003—. Mem.: Soc. Quality Assurance, Am. Assn. Pharm. Scientists. Office: Amgen Inc One Amgen Center Dr Thousand Oaks CA 91320 Personal E-mail: sabiha_husna@yahoo.com.

HOSSEINI, KHALED, internist, writer; b. Kabul, Afghanistan, Mar. 4, 1965; arrived in Paris, 1976, arrived in San Jose, Calif., 1980; m. Roya Hosseini; children: Haris, Farah. BS in biology, Santa Clara U., 1988; MD, U. Calif. San Diego Sch. Medicine, 1993. Internist, 1996—; now at Kaiser Med. Offices, Mountain View, Calif. Author: The Kite Runner, 2003 (NY Times Best Seller). Office: Riverhead Books 375 Hudson St New York NY 10014*

HOSSLER, DAVID JOSEPH, lawyer, law educator; b. Mesa, Ariz., Oct. 18, 1940; s. Carl Joseph and Elizabeth Ruth (Bills) H.; m. Gretchen Anne, Mar. 2, 1945; 1 child, Devon Annagret. BA, U. Ariz., 1969, JD, 1972. Bar: Ariz. 1972, U.S. Dist. Ct. Ariz. 1972, U.S. Supreme Ct. 1977. Legal intern to chmn. FCC, summer 1971; law clk. to chief justice Ariz. Supreme Ct., 1972-73; chief dep. county atty. Yuma County (Ariz.), 1973-74; ptnr. Hunt, Kenworthy and Hossler, Yuma, Ariz., 1974—. Instr. in law and banking, law and real estate Ariz. Western Coll.; instr. in bus. law, mktg., ethics Webster U.; instr. agrl. law U. Ariz.; co-chmn. fee arbitration com. Ariz. State Bar, 1990—; instr. employee/employer law U. Phoenix. Editor-in-chief Ariz. Adv., 1971-72. Mem. precinct com. Yuma County Rep. Ctrl. Com., 1974-2000, vice chmn., 1982; chmn. region II Acad. Decathalon competition, 1989; bd. dirs. Yuma County Ednl. Found. (Hall of Fame 2000), Yuma County Assn. Behavior Health Svcs., also pres., 1981; coach Yuma H.S. mock ct. team, 1987-94; bd. dirs. friends of U. Med. Ctr., Am. Red Cross, With USN. Recipient Man and Boy award, Boys Clubs Am., 1979, Freedoms Found. award, Yuma chpt., 1988, Demolay Legion of Honor, 1991, Francis Woodward award, Ariz. Pub. Svc., 2000, named Vol. of Yr., Yuma County, 1981—82, Heart of Yuma award, 2000, voted Yuma's Best (atty.), 2001, 2002—03. Mem. ATLA, Am. Judicature Soc., Yuma County Bar Assn. (pres. 1975-76), Navy League, VFW, Am. Legion, U. Ariz. Alumni Assn. (nat. bd. dirs., past pres., hon. bobcat 1996, Disting. Citizen award 1997), Rotary (pres. Yuma club 1987-88, dist. gov. rep. 1989, dist. gov. 1992-93, findings com. 1996, dist. found. chair 1996-2000, co-chmn. internat. membership retention 2000-01, John Van Houton Look Beyond Yourself award 1995, Roy Slayton Share Rotary Share People award 1996, Al Face You Are the Key award 1997, Ted Day Let Svc. Light the Way award 1998, Rotary Found. citation for meritorious svc., Rotary Internat. (dir.), Four Avenues of Svc. award, 2004, Internat. Svc. Above Self award, Cliff Doctorman Real Happiness is Helping Others award, Disting. Svc. award). Episcopalian (vestry 1978-82). Home: 2802 S Fern Dr Yuma AZ 85364-2919 Office: Hunt Kenworthy Hossler 330 W 24th St Yuma AZ 85364-6455 also: PO Box 2919 Yuma AZ 85366-2919 Office Phone: 928-783-0101. E-mail: dhossler@mindspring.com.

HOSTAGE, JOHN BRAYNE ARTHUR, law librarian; b. Hartford, Conn., June 10, 1952; s. John Brayne and Anne (Leonard) H. BA, Columbia U., 1974; MA in German, U. Wis., 1978, MA in LS, 1979. Cataloger U. Ill., Chgo., 1979-82, Harvard U. Law Sch. Libr., Cambridge, Mass., 1982—92; authorities libr. Harvard law Sch., Libr., 1992—. ALA/USIA libr. fellow, Berlin, 1994. Mem. ALA (editor SRRT newsletter 1984-86, coord. SRRT 1987-89); mem. Am. Assn. Law Librs., Internat. Fedn. Libr. Assns. (standing com. on cataloguing 2005—). Office: Harvard Law Sch Libr Langdell Hall Cambridge MA 02138 Office Phone: 617-495-3974. Business E-Mail: hostage@law.harvard.edu.

HOSTETLER, DAVID L., sculptor, educator; b. Beach City, Ohio, Dec. 27, 1926; m. Susan Crehan-Hostetler; children: Jane Palmer, Ann Lampela, Jay. BA, Ind. U.; MFA, Ohio U. Prof. art and sculpture Ohio U., Athens. Vis. prof. San Miguel D'Allande, Mexico, 1958, Kent (Ohio) State U., 1969, U. Ky., Lexington, 1975. Represented in permanent collections Trump Internat. Hotel and Tower, N.Y.C., St. Lawrence U., Canton, N.Y., Mid. Tenn. State U., Murfreesboro, Philharm. Ctr. for the Arts, Naples, Fla., Canton (Ohio) Art Inst., Southeast Psychiat. Hosp., Athens, Ohio, Ahold U.V., The Netherlands, Milw. Mus., So. Ill. U., Edwardsville, Nestle Ltd., Ont., Can., State Tchrs. Retirement Sys., Inc., Columbus, Ohio, SUNY, Fredonia, Kennedy Libr., Boston, Mecom Cos., Houston, City of Reading, Pa., Butler Inst. Am. Art, Youngstown, Ohio, Wauwinet Inn, Nantucket, Mass., W.Va. Wesleyan Coll., Buckhannon, DeCordova Mus. and Sculpture Pk., Lincoln, Mass., Ernst and Young, Inc., Columbus, Marietta (Ohio) Coll., Columbus Mus. Art, T.B.I. Inc., Manchester, N.H., Ohio U., Mus. Fine Arts, Boston, Massillon (Ohio) Mus., U. Minn. Art Gallery, Mpls., Cooper Industries, Houston, Grounds for Sculpture, Hamilton, N.H., Tim Horton Donut Ltd., Ont., Can., Speed Mus., Louisville; contbr. CD-ROM Hostetler's Jazz and Art Life, 2003, CD Hostetler Jazz Band, 2003; featured Hostetler, Four Decades (PBS), 1988, Family of Man, Expo '71, Montreal, Que., Can., Ohio Arts Coun. Honor Exhbn., 1971, Eye on Art (CBS), 1970, (movie) The Group, 1966, featured artist (books) The Artful Home, Furniture, Sculpture and Objects, 2003; featured artist: books Hostetler the Carver, 1992, Masters of the Wood Sculpture, 1980, American Craftsman, 1979, Fine Woodworking-Design Book Two, 1979, Sculpture Casting, 1972, Contemporary Art with Wood, 1968. Served with U.S. Army, 1944—46. Recipient Ohioana Lifetime Achievement award, 1989. Home: PO Box 989 Athens OH 45701 Office: Hostetler Gallery PO Box 2222 Nantucket MA 02584

HOSTETTER, AMOS BARR, JR., cable television executive; b. Jan. 12, 1937; s. Amos Barr and Leola (Conroy) Hostetter; married; 3 children. BA cum laude, Amherst Coll., 1958; MBA, Harvard U., 1961. Asst. to v.p. fin. Am. & Fgn. Power Co., N.Y.C., 1958—59; investment analyst Cambridge (Mass.) Capital Corp., 1961—63; co-founder, exec. v.p. Continental Cablevision, Inc., Boston, 1963—80, pres., CEO, 1980—85, chmn., CEO, 1985—96; CEO MediaOne, Inc., Boston, 1996—2000; chmn. Pilot House Assoc., LLC; chmn., CEO Continental Cablevision, Inc. (name changed to Media One), 1985—96; founder, bd. dirs. Cable Satellite Pub. Affairs Network (C-SPAN), 1979—. Bd. dirs. Commodities Corp., Princeton, NJ; trustee various mut. funds Mass. Fin. Svcs., 1985—; bd. mem. AT&T, 1999—2003. Trustee Children's TV Workshop, N.Y.C., 1980—, New Eng. Med. Ctr. Hosp., Boston, 1982—; bd. overseers Mus. Fine Arts, Boston, 1987—; bd. dirs. Corp. Pub. Broadcasting, Washington, 1975—79, Walter Kaitz Found., 1981—. Named Man of Yr., Cablevision Mag., 1972. Mem.: Internat. Radio and TV Soc., Nat. Cable TV Assn. (nat. chmn. 1973—74, dir. 1968—75, 1982—, Larry Boggs award 1975), Amherst Coll. Soc. Alumni (pres. 1982—84, exec. com. 1982—, chmn. 1987—). Office: The Pilot House Lewis Wharf Boston MA 02110*

HOSTETTER, MARGARET K., pediatrician, medical educator; MD, Baylor U. Diplomate Am. Bd. Pediatrics with subspecialty in pediat. infectious diseases. Resident Children's Hosp., Boston; fellow in pediat. infectious disease Harvard Med. Sch./Beth Israel Hosp., Boston; with U. Minn., Mpls.; prof. pediats., sect. chief pediat. immunology Yale U., New Haven, chmn. dept. pediatrs.; physician-in-chief Yale-New Haven Children's Hosp. Mem.: Inst. of Medicine of NAS. Office: Yale Univ Sch Medicine 333 Cedar St LMP 4085 PO Box 208064 New Haven CT 06520-8064

HOSTETTLER, JOHN N., congressman; b. Evansville, Ind., July 19, 1961; s. Earl Eugene and Esther Aline (Hollingsworth) H.; m. Elizabeth Ann Hamman, Nov. 12, 1983; children: Matthew, Amanda, Jaclyn. BSME, Rose-Hulman Inst. Tech., 1983. Reg. profl. engr. Engr. So. Ind. Gas and Electric, Evansville, 1986-94; mem. U.S. Congress from 8th Ind. Dist., Washington, 1995—; mem. Agriculture and National Security coms.; mem. Judiciary Com. Vice chair House Armed Services Comm. Special Oversight Panel on Terrorism, 2001—. Deacon 12th Avenue Gen. Baptist, 1986-1995. Republican. Baptist. Office: US Ho of Reps 1214 Longworth HOB Washington DC 20515-1408

HOSTLER, CHARLES WARREN, retired ambassador, international affairs consultant; b. Chgo., Dec. 12, 1919; s. Sidney Marvin and Catherine (Marshall) Hostler; m. Chin-Yeh Rose Hostler; 1 child, Charles Warren Jr. BA, U. Calif. at Los Angeles, L.A., 1942; MA, Am. U., Beirut, Lebanon, 1955, Georgetown U., 1950, PhD, 1956. Commd. 2d lt. U.S. Air Force, 1942, advanced through grades to col., 1955; ret., 1963; dir. internat. ops. McDonnell Douglas Corp., Middle East, Beirut, 1965-67, mgr. internat. ops. Paris, 1963-65, mgr. internat. mktg., missiles and space, 1967-69; pres. Hostler Investment Co., Coronado, Calif., 1967—; chmn. bd. Irvine (Calif.) Nat. Bank, 1972-74; dir. Wynn's Internat., Inc., Fullerton, Calif., 1971-74; dep. asst. sec. for internat. commerce, dir. Bur. Internat. Commerce, U.S. Dept. Commerce, Washington, 1974-76; regional v.p. Mid-East and Africa, E-Systems Inc., Cairo, 1976-77; pres. Pacific SW Capital Corp., San Diego, 1977-89; ambassador U.S. Govt., Bahrain, 1989-93. Hon. consul gen. Kingdom of Bahrain, 1993—; adj. prof. polit. sci. San Diego State U., 1999—. Author: Turkism and the Soviets, 1957, The Turks of Central Asia, 1993, Soldier to Ambassador, 2004. Chmn. Calif. Contractors State Lic. Bd., 1973—79, San Diego County Local Agy. Formation Commn., 1979—89, Calif. State Park and Recreation Commn., 1983—89; pres. San Diego Consular Corps, 1996—98; chmn., bd. dirs. People-to-People Internat. Decorated Purple Heart, Legion of Merit, Legion of Honor (France); recipient decorations from 9 nations, Eisenhower Disting. Svc. award, Fgn. Affairs award for Pub. Svc., U.S. State Dept., Pub. Svc. award, U. Calif., L.A., 2005. Mem.: VFW (life), Coun. Am. Ambs., Mid. East Inst. (bd. govs. 1962—80, 1993—), Vets. of Office of Strategic Svcs., Mil. Order Purple Heart (life), Mil. Officers Assn. of Am. (life), Navy League (life). Office: 1101 First St # 302 Coronado CA 92118-1474 Personal E-mail: hostler@san.rr.com.

HOSTON, GERMAINE ANNETTE, political science professor; b. Trenton, NJ; d. Walter Lee and Veretta Louise H. AB in Politics summa cum laude, Princeton U., 1975; MA in Govt., Harvard U., 1978, PhD in Govt., 1981. Rsch. asst. Princeton U., NJ, 1973-75; tchg. asst. Harvard U., Cambridge, Mass., 1977-78; asst. prof. polit. sci. Johns Hopkins U., Balt., 1980-86, assoc. prof. polit. sci., 1986-92; prof. polit. sci. U. Calif., San Diego, 1992—, dir. Ctr. for Democratization and Econ. Devel., 1993-99; founder, pres. Inst. Trans Pacific Studies in Values, Culture and Politics, 1999—. Vis. prof. L'Ecole des Hautes Etudes en Sci. Sociales, Paris, 1986, Osaka City U., Japan, 1990, U. Tokyo, 1991; faculty advisor Chinese lang. program Johns Hopkins U., 1981-92, undergrad. ethics bd., 1980-83, pub. interest investment adv. com., 1982-85, undergrad. admissions com., 1983-84, 86-89, pres.'s human climate task force, 1987, dir. undergrad. program, 1987, 88-89, mem. com. undergrad. studies, 1987-91, organizer comparative politics colloquium, 1987-89, dept. colloquium, 1987-89, 91-92; Japanese studies program com. U. Calif., San Diego, 1992—, Chinese studies program, 1994—, field coord. comparative politics, 1994—95, dir. grad. studies comparative politics, 1997-98; bd. dir. Inst. East-West Security Studies, NYC, 1990-97; Am. adv. com. Japan Found., 1992—; edn. abroad program com. U. Calif., 1996—; adv. com. Calif. Ctr. Asia Soc.; mem. com. tech. comms. Inst. East West Security Studies, 1997—; participant numerous workshops and seminars; lectr. in field. Author: Marxism and the Crisis of Development in Prewar Japan: The Debate on Japanese Capitalism, 1986, The State, Identity, and the National Question in China and Japan, 1994, (with others) The Biographical Dictionary of Neo-Marxism, 1985, The Biographical Dictionary of Marxism, 1986, Culture and Identity: Japanese Intellectuals During the Interwar Years, 1990, The Routledge Dictionary of Twentieth-Century Political Thinkers, 1992; mem. edtl. bd. Jour. Politics, 1997—2001; contbr. articles to profl. jours. Active Md. Food Com., 1983-92, program concepts subcom. CROSS ROADS Com., Diocese of Md., 1987-88, outreach com. St. David's Episcopal Ch., Balt., standing commn. human affairs Gen. Conv. of the Episcopal Ch., 1991-97; chair peace and justice commn. Episcopal Diocese Md., 1984-87, co-chair companion diocese com., 1987-92, chair CROSS ROADS program bd., 1988-92; exec. bd. dir. Balt. Clergy and Laity Concerned, 1985-86; alternate, regular lay del. 69th Gen. Conv. of The Episcopal Ch., Detroit, 1988; trustee Va. Theol. Sem., 1988-2000; lay del. 70th Gen. Conv. of The Episcopal Ch., Phoenix, Ariz., 1991; dep. Nat. Conv. Episcopal Ch., 1988-93. Am. Legion Aux. scholar, 1972, Am. Logistical Assn. scholar, 1972-76; fellow Harvard U., 1975-77, NSF, 1975-77; Lehman fellow Harvard U., 1978-79, Fgn. Lang. and Area Studies fellow, 1978-79; fellow Am. Assn. Univ. Women Ednl. Found., 1979-80; Fgn. Rsch. scholar U. Tokyo, 1979, 82, 84, 85, 86, 91; Travel grantee Assn. Asian Studies, Japan-U.S. Friendship Commn., 1981; Internat. fellow Internat. Fedn. Univ. Women, 1982, 83; Postdoctoral grantee Social Sci. Rsch. Coun., 1983; fellow NEH, 1983; Kenan Endowment grantee Johns Hopkins U., 1984-85; fellow Rockefeller Found. Internat. Rels., 1985-88; Travel grantee Assn. Asian Studies, 1991; grantee Japan-US Friendship Commn., 1997; rsch. grantee Acad. Senate Com. on Rsch., 1996. Mem. Asia Soc. (trustee 1994—2000), Am. Polit. Sci. Assn. (mem. coun. 1991-93, mem. com. on internat. polit. sci. 1997—2003, v.p. 1998—), Assn. Asian Studies (mem. N.E. Asia coun. 1992-95, vice-chair N.E. Asia coun. 1993—94, nominated editor Jour. Asian Studies 1994, mem. coun. on fgn. rels. 1990—), Internat. Platform Assn., Pacific Coun. on Internat. Policy, Women's Fgn. Policy Group. Democrat. Episcopalian. Avocations: reading, cooking, sailing, tennis, working out. Office: 9921 Carmel Mountain Rd Ste 323 San Diego CA 92129 Business E-Mail: ghoston@myesa.com.

HOTALING, ROBERT BACHMAN, urban planner, educator; b. Syracuse, NY, July 19, 1918; s. Elliot Danforth and Florence (Bachman) Hotaling; m. M. Janet Kelley, Nov. 20, 1943 (dec.); children: Marilyn Kelley, Brock Elliot, William Austin, Richard Chapman; m. Jeanne Bryant, July 31, 1971 (dec.); m. Phyllis Hargrave, July 27, 2001. BS in Environ. Sci. and Forestry, Syracuse U., 1942; M of Urban and Regional Planning, Mich. State U., 1952. Staff dir. McFadzean, Everly Rose and Assocs., Chgo., 1946-49; dir. state and local planning R.I. Exec. Dept., Providence, 1952-55; tech. coord. for planning Interstate hwy. systems through New Eng., R.I., Mass. and Conn., 1954-55; city planning dir., urban renewal planner Portland, Maine, 1955-57; acting dir., sec. Greater Portland Regional Planning Commn., 1956-57; prof. urban and regional planning Coll. Social Sci., Mich. State U., East Lansing, 1957-81; prof. lifelong edn. Inst. Cmty. Devel., Mich. State U., East Lansing, 1957-81; prof. emeritus Mich. State U., 1981—; assoc. McKenna and Assocs., Farmington Hills, Mich., 1992—, Freeman, Smith & Assocs., Lansing, Mich., 1992—, Pub. Sector Cons., Lansing, 1992—. Pres. Urban Cons., Inc., 1962-66; pres., owner Robert B. Hotaling and Assoc., 1949—; expert witness to law firms, state and fed. agys., philanthropic orgns.; cons., lectr., seminarian Mich. Twp. Assn., 1963-81, Mich. Mcpl. League, 1978-94; mem. Mich. State Bd. of Registration for Profl. Community Planners, 1967-81, chmn., 1970-72, 76-79; cons. to state agys., polit. orgns. and corps. Author: Michigan Local Planning Commissioners Handbook (3 edits.), Michigan Township Planning and Zoning Handbook (2 edits.); chmn. editorial com. Mich. Laws Relating to Planning (3 edits.); contbr. articles to profl. jours. Mem. twp. planning commn. 1958-70, 87-94, 96-2001, chmn. 1969-70, 1998-2000, Meridian Twp., Ingham County, Mich.; mem. Meridian Twp. charter com., chmn., 1970-73; mem. Meridian Twp. Zoning Bd. of Appeals, 1969-70, 87, chmn. 1969-70; mem. strategic planning com. for planning future of Meridan Twp., Gov.'s State Legis. Zoning Revision Com., 1977-79; bd. dirs. Mich. Parks Assn., 1960-68; charter mem. Am. Inst. Cert. Profl. Cmty. Planners, 1954-81; mem. Mich. State Bd. Registration for Profl. Cmty. Planners State Exam. Com., 1969, 99, Am. Inst. Planners Nat. Exam. Com. for Profl. Planners, 1977-78; pres. Cadgewith Farms Homeowners assn., 2002—. Capt. C.E., U.S. Army, 1942-46. Recipient Meritorious Svc. award Mich. Mcpl. League, 1994. Mem. Mich. Soc. Consulting Planners (bd. dirs. 1979—). Episcopalian. Home and Office: PO Box 304 Haslett MI 48840-0304 Office Phone: 517-702-9615. Personal E-mail: rbhjbh@aol.com.

HOTCHKISS, HENRY WASHINGTON, real estate broker, financial consultant; b. Meshed, Iran, Oct. 31, 1937; s. Henry and Mary Bell (Clark) Hotchkiss. BA, Bowdoin Coll., 1958. French tchr. Choate Sch., Wallingford, Conn., 1959—62; v.p. Chem. Bank, N.Y.C., 1962—80, Chem. Bank Internat., San Francisco, 1973—80; dir. corp. rels., mgr. Credit Suisse, San Francisco, 1980—87; fin. cons., 1989—; with Dan Mello Real Estate, 1994—2003, Mello & Hotchkiss Real Estate, 2003—. Bd. dirs. Calif. Coun. Internat. Trade, 1976—87; dir. Indonesia-U.S. Bus. Seminar, L.A., 1979. Bd. dirs. Gordonstown Am. Found., 1986—2004, pres., 1986—99; chmn. Capt. Joshua Slocum Centennial Com., Fairhaven, Mass., 1995—98; bd. dirs. Joshua Slocum Soc. Internat., Inc., 1998—2001; assoc. bd. regents L.I. Coll. Hosp., 1969—71, pres., 1971, bd. regents, 1971—73. Capt. USAR, 1958—69. Mem.: Soc. of the Cin., SAR, Mayflower Soc., St. Francis Yacht Club (San Francisco), Explorers Club N.Y. (treas. No. Calif. chpt. 1984—86). Home: 80 Fort St Fairhaven MA 02719-2812

HOTCHKISS, JANET MCCANN, secondary school educator; b. White Plains, N.Y., July 11, 1950; d. Albino M. and M. Catherine (Bodette) Grellet; m. Jonathan B. Hotchkiss, May 3, 1980; children: Craig, Kristina, Kevin, Marsha, Robert, Catherine. BS, Northeastern U., 1973; MS, Coll. New Rochelle, 1987. Cert. secondary English tchr., spl. edn. tchr., elem. tchr. Tchr. Greenburgh Eleven UFSD, Dobbs Ferry, NY, 1990—, White Plains (N.Y.) Pub. Schs., 1990—. Mem. Coun. Exceptional Children, 1995—, N.Y. State English Coun., 2003; mem. policy bd. Westchester Tchrs. Ctr., 1994—97; mem. N.Y. Adult and Continuing Cmty. Edn., 1995—. Co-author: Kosovo: Caught in the Middle, 2001. Named Tchr. of Yr. in N.Y. State, N.Y. Adult Continuing Cmty. Edn., 2001; grantee, Westchester Tchr.'s Ctr., 1996, 1999, 2002, Tech. and Literacy Challenge, 2000, The Living History Found., 2002. Mem.: Orton Guillingham Soc., White Plains (N.Y.) Coll. Club (scholarship com. 2003). Office: Greenburgh Eleven UFSD PO Box 501 Dobbs Ferry NY 10522

HOTCHNER, AARON EDWARD, author; b. St. Louis, June 28, 1920; s. Samuel and Sally (Rossman) H.; children: Timothy, Holly, Tracy. AB, LLB, Washington U., St. Louis, 1941, LHD (hon.), 1992. Bar: Mo. 1941. Practiced law in, St. Louis, 1941-42; articles editor Cosmopolitan mag., 1948-50. V.p., treas. Newman's Own, Inc.; v.p. Hole in the Wall Gang Camp. Freelance writer short stories and articles in various mags. including Sat. Eve. Post, Esquire, Readers Digest, 1950—; TV playwright Playhouse 90, 1958-60; adapted major Hemingway works for TV including For Whom The Bell Tolls, 1958, The Killers, 1959; writer screenplay Adventures of a Young Man, 1961; author: The Dangerous American, 1958, Papa Hemingway: A Personal Memoir, 1966, revised, 1999, Treasure, 1970, King of the Hill, 1972, Looking for Miracles, 1974, Doris Day, 1976, Sophia, Living and Loving, 1979, The Man Who Lived at the Ritz, 1981, Choice People, 1984, Hemingway and His World, 1989, Blown Away, 1990, Louisiana Purchase, 1996, After the Storm, 2000, Dreams of Glory, 2001, The Day I Fired Alan Ladd, 2002, (with Paul Newman) Shameless Exploitation, 2003, Everyone Comes to Elaine's, 2004, Dear Papa, Dear Hotch, 2005; playwright: The Short Happy Life, 1961, The White House, 1964, The Hemingway Hero, 1967, Do You Take This Man?,

1970, Sweet Prince, 1980, Let 'Em Rot, 1987, Welcome to the Club, 1989, Courtroom Cantata, 1995, Exactly Like You, 1996, Papa Hemingway (rev.), 1999, Exactly Like You, 1999, After the Storm, 2000, The World of Nick Adams, 2001. Founding dir. Hole in the Wall Gang Fund. Served to maj. USAAF, 1942-46, NATOUS. Recipient Disting. Alumni award Law Sch., Washington U., 1992. Mem. Mo. Bar Assn., Writers Guild Am., Dramatists Guild, PEN, Authors Guild, Authors Guild Found. (bd. dirs.), Century Club. Address: 14 Hillandale Rd Westport CT 06880-5225 Office Phone: 203-222-0136. Business E-Mail: ahotchner@newmansown.com.

HOTCHNER, HOLLY, museum director, curator, conservator; BA in Art History and Studio Art, Trinity Coll., 1973; MA in Art History, diploma conservation, N.Y. Inst. Fine Arts, 1982. Exhbns. cataloguer, collections cataloguer Mus. Modern Art, N.Y.C., 1973-76; chief conservator N.Y. Hist. Soc., N.Y.C., 1984-88, dir. mus., 1984-95; dir. Am. Craft Mus. (now Museum of Arts and Design), N.Y.C., 1996—. Bd. dirs. Art Alliance for Contemporary Glass, 1999—, Friends of Fiber Art; chmn. bd. 235 E. 73rd Owners Corp., 1994-2000; mem. edn. com. Whitney Mus. Am. Art, 1994-98; mem. bd. trustees N.Y. Landmarks Conservancy, 1996—; mem. adv. bd. Friends of Contemporary Ceramics; lectr., panelist, juror in field. Fellow Am. Inst. Conservation, Internat. Inst. Conservation; mem. Am. Assn. Mus., Art Table, Phi Beta Kappa. Office: Museum of Arts and Design 40 W 53rd St New York NY 10019-6106 Office Phone: 212-956-3535.

HOTELLING, HAROLD, law and economics educator; b. N.Y.C., Dec. 26, 1945; s. Harold and Susanna Porter (Edmondson) H.; m. Barbara M. Anthony, May 4, 1974; children: Harold, George, James, Claire, Charles. AB, Columbia U., 1966; JD, U. N.C., 1972; MA, Duke U., 1975, PhD, 1982. Bar: N.C. 1973. Legal advisor U. N.C., Chapel Hill, 1972-73; instr. bus. law U. Ky., Lexington, 1977-79, asst. prof., 1980-84; asst. prof. dept. econs. Oakland U., Rochester, Mich., 1984-89; assoc. prof. econs. Lawrence Technol. U., Southfield, Mich., 1989—, chmn. dept. humanities social scis. and comm., 1994-99. Contbr. articles to profl. jours. Episcopalian. Home: 2112 Bretton Dr S Rochester Hills MI 48309-2952 Office: Lawrence Technol U Dept Humanities Southfield MI 48075 Office Phone: 248-204-3530. Business E-Mail: hotelling@ltu.edu.

HOTEZ, PETER JAY, research scientist, educator; b. Hartford, Conn., May 5, 1958; s. Edward Joseph and Jean (Goldberg) H.; m. Ann Elizabeth Frifield, Sept. 14, 1987; children: Matthew, Emily, Rachel, Daniel. BA magna cum laude, Yale U., 1980; PhD, Rockefeller U., 1986; MD, Cornell U., 1987. Resident Mass. Gen. Hosp., Boston, 1987-89; postdoctoral fellow Yale U., New Haven, 1989-91, instr., 1991-92, asst. prof., 1992-95, assoc. prof., 1995—; prof., chair dept. microbiology, topical med. George Wash. U. Vis. prof. Chinese Acad. Preventive Medicine, Shanghai, 1997; adv. bd. Congas Memorial Inst., Sabin Vaccine Inst. Author: Parasitic Diseases, 1995; patentee in field. Named hon. prof. Chinese Acad. Preventive Medicine, 1997. Mem. Am. Soc. Tropical Medicine and Hygiene, Am. Soc. Parasitologists, Pediatric Infectious Disease Soc. (adv. bd. jour., Young Investigator award 1993), Soc. Pediatric Rsch. Home: 4547 Minuteman Dr Rockville MD 20853-1263 Office: 2300 I St NW Washington DC 20037

HOTH, STEVEN SERGEY, lawyer, educator; b. Jan. 30, 1941; s. Donald Leroy and Ina Dorothy (Barr) H.; m. JoEllen Maly, July 29, 1967; children: Andrew Steven, Peter Lindsey. AB, Grinnell Coll., 1962; JD, U. Iowa, 1966; postgrad., U. Pa., 1968, Oxford (Eng.) U., 1973. Bar: U.S. Ct. Appeals (8th cir.) 1966, U.S. Tax Ct. 1967, U.S. Ct. Claims 1967, U.S. Dist. Ct. Iowa 1968, U.S. Dist. Ct. ND 1968, U.S. Dist. Ct. SD 1968, U.S. Supreme Ct. 1973, U.S. Ct. Appeals (7th cir.) 1982. Law clk. to chief justice U.S. Ct. Appeals (8th cir.), Fargo, ND, 1967-68; assoc. Hirsch, Adams, Hoth & Krekel, Burlington, Iowa, 1968-72, ptnr., 1972-91; pvt. practice Burlington, 1992—. Asst. atty. Des Moines County, Burlington, 1968-72, atty., 1972-83; alt. mcpl. judge, Burlington, 1968-69; lectr. criminal law Southeastern C.C., West Burlington, 1972-82; assoc. prof. polit. sci. Iowa Wesleyan Coll., Mt. Pleasant, 1981-82; Pres. of Amerail, Inc., Iowa Truck Rail, Amerail, Inc.; pres. Burlington Truck Rail, Burlington Short Line R.R. Inc., Iowa Internat. Investments, Burlington Storage and Transfer; sec. Burlington Loading Co. Contbr. numerous articles to profl. jours. Chmn. Des Moines County Civil Svc. Commn.; trustee Charles H. Rand Lecture Trust; mem. Des Moines County Conf. Com., Des Moines County Conf. Bd.; dir. Burlington Med. Ctr. Staff Found.; moderator 1st Congl. Ch., Burlington; bd. dir. UN Assn.; clk. Burlington North Bottoms Levy and Drainage Dist.; bd. mem., pres. Burlington Cmty. Sch. Dist. Bd. Edn., chmn. commn. on ministry, mem. exec. com. Nat. Assn. Congl. Christian Chs., moderator; treas. 1st dist. Dem. Com.; bd. dirs. Legal Aid Soc. Planned Parenthood Des Moines County. Recipient Chmn.'s award ARC, 1980; Reginald Heber Smith fellow in legal aid Cheyenne River Indian Reservation, Eagle Butte, SD, 1967-68; named Lord of Foleshill. Mem. Missionary Soc.-Nat. Assn. Congl. Christian Chs., ABA (internat. sect., tax sect.), Iowa State Bar Assn. (liaison to Iowa Med. Soc.), Des Moines County Bar Assn., Am. Judicature Soc., Agrl. Law Com., Iowa Def. Coun., Iowa Archaeol. Soc., Soc. for German Am. Studies, Manorial Soc. Gt. Britain, Grinnell Coll. Alumni Assn. (bd. dirs.), Malawi Soc., Burlington-West Burlington C. of C. (bd. dirs.), Nat. Assn. Congrl. Christian Ch., Burlington Golf Club, New Crystal Lake Club (pres.), Elks, Eagles, Masons, Rotary. Office: PO Box 982 Hoth Bldg 200 Jefferson St Burlington IA 52601 Office Phone: 319-754-5000. Business E-Mail: hothlaw@mchsi.com.

HOTOKE, SHIGERU, retired music educator; b. Eleele, Hawaii, Jan. 21, 1927; s. Moroichi and Chiyeko Hotoke; m. Grace Sera Hotoke, Apr. 4, 1951; children: Richard, Ryan. BE, U. Hawaii, 1950, 5th Yr. diploma, 1951; postgrad., U. So. Calif. Tchr. Dept. Edn., Honolulu, 1952—86. Singer Robert Shaw Chorale, 1953—54; dir. Sounds of Young Hawaii, 1963—86; assoc. dir. Idyllwild Sch. Music, Calif., 1964—; artistic dir. Hawaii Music Festival; dir. Gleemen Plus of Honolulu, 1984—85. Dir. Aloha Neighbor Program, Hawaii; mem. demonstration team Police Athletic League, Hawaii; choral dir. Honolulu Symphony; singer, actor Cmty. Theatre, Hawaii Opera; choir dir. Ch. of the Crossroads, Honolulu, 1950—53, Ctrl. Union Ch., Honolulu, soloist. With U.S. Army, 1945—47. Named Father of the Yr. in Edn., Honolulu C. of C., 1964, State Tchr. of Yr., NEA, 1972; recipient Spl. Bicentennial award, Valley Forge Tchrs. medal, Freedom Found. Valley Forge, 1972, Freedom award, Sertoma, Disting. Alumnus award, U. Hawaii, 2004. Mem.: Hawaii Edn. Assn. (bd. dirs.), Hawaii Music Edn. Assn. (v.p.), Sigma Alpha Iota. Episcopalian. Achievements include first to educational travel for students and later forming Kailua H.S. Madrigal Singers (Sounds of Young Hawaii); directed concerts in U.S., Europe, Africa, Israel, Istanbul, India, Malaysia, Singapore, Sri Lanka, Australia, Phillipines, Hong Kong, Japan. Avocations: fishing, golf, gardening.

HOTT, KEVIN MICHAEL, electrical engineer; b. Lebanon, Pa., Oct. 20, 1978; s. James Albert Hott and Linda Alice Bechtel. BSEE, Pa. State U., 2005. Elec. technician gas turbine USN, Norfolk, Va., 1997—2001; sys. engr. Lockheed Martin, King of Prussia, Pa., 2005—. Decorated Achievement medal USMC, USN, Armed Forces Svc. medal; named Outstanding Sr., Pa. State U., 2005; recipient Kosovo Campaign medal, USN, Walker award, Pa. State U., 2005, Scholastic Achievement award, 2005. Mem.: IEEE. Avocations: softball, hockey. Home: 66 Oliver Dr Palmyra PA 17078

HOTZ, HENRY PALMER, retired physicist; b. Fayetteville, Ark., Oct. 17, 1925; s. Henry Gustav and Stella (Palmer) H.; m. Marie Brase, Aug. 22, 1952; children: Henry Brase, Mary Palmer, Martha Marie. BS, U. Ark., 1948; PhD, Washington U., St. Louis, 1953. Asst. prof. physics Auburn U., Ala., 1953-58, Okla. State U., Stillwater, 1958-64; assoc. prof. Marietta Coll., Ohio, 1964-66; physicist, scientist-in-residence U.S. Naval Radiol. Def. Lab., San Francisco, 1966-67; assoc. prof. U. Mo., Rolla, 1967-71; physicist Qanta Metrix div. Finnigan Corp., Sunnyvale, Calif., 1971-74; sr. scientist Nuclear Equipment Corp., San Carlos, Calif., 1974-79, Envirotech Measurement Systems, Palo Alto, Calif., 1979-82, Dohrmann div. Xertex Corp., Santa Clara, Calif., 1982-86; sr. scientist Rosemount Analytical Div. Dohrmann, 1983-91; cons. Burlingame, Calif., 1991-2001; ret., 2001. Cons. USAF, 1958-62; mem. lectr. selection com. for Hartman Hotz Lectrs. in law, liberal arts U. Ark. Served with USNR, 1944-46. Mem. Am. Phys. Soc., Am. Assn. Physics Tchrs., AAAS, Phi Beta Kappa, Sigma Xi, Sigma Pi Sigma, Pi Mu Epsilon, Sigma Nu Lodges: Masons. Methodist. Home: 290 Stilt Ct Foster City CA 94404-1323

HOTZ, MARTHA PAULINE, artist; b. Looogootee, Ind., July 11, 1927; d. Francis Orval and Ethel Beatrice (Bradley) Summers; m. Donald Leo Hotz, Nov. 5, 1949; children: Donald Frederick, Daniel Richard, Anthony Francis, Timothy Lee, Jeffery Alan. Student, Art Instrns., Mpls., 1962-65, Art Acad., Ferdinand, Ind., 1965-67. Sec. Schwitzer-Cummins, Indpls., 1946-49; bookkeeper Reliance Mfg. Co., Loogootee, Ind., 1950-53; paste-up artist Loogootee Tribune, 1963-65, 71-86; v.p., buyer Hotz & Sons Corp., Loogootee, 1964-70; free lance artist, instr. Polly's Paintings, Loogootee, 1986—. Illustrator: (bookcover) Echoes from the Mountains, 1990, (book) Around the Clock in Rhyme and Time, 1991, (bookcover) When God Stepped In, 1992; more than 35postcards, 1986-. Pres. Tri County Art Guild, Loogootee, 1965-75, Daviess County Art League, Washington, Ind., 1991-92, adv. bd., 1992-98. Mem. VFW Aux., KC Aux., Legion of Mary. Roman Catholic. Avocations: poet, drawing, flowers and gardening, reading. Home: PO Box 244 Loogootee IN 47553-0244

HOTZ, ROBERT LEE, writer, editor; b. Hartford, Conn., Mar. 7, 1950; s. Robert B. and Joan (Willison) H.; m. Jennifer Hall Arlen, May 21, 1988; children: Michael Arlen, Robert Arlen. BA magna cum laude, MA, Tufts U., 1973. Tech. editor Intermetrics, Inc., Cambridge, Mass., 1973-76; reporter The News-Virginian, Waynesboro, 1976-79, The Pitts. Press, 1979-84; sci. writer The Atlanta Jour.-Constn., 1984-90, projects editor, 1991-93; sci. editor, 1993; sci. writer The L.A. (Calif.) Times, 1993—. Participant NSF Antarctica Expeditions, 1987, 95, 01. Author: Designs on Life: Exploring the New Frontiers of Human Fertility, 1991; contbr. articles to profl. publs. Recipient Sci. Journalism award AAAS, 1977, 88, 97, Ga. Best Reporting award AP, 1986, Metro Staff Pulitzer Prize spot news, 1995, Walter Sullivan award Am. Geophys. Soc., 1995, Journalism award ASCE, 1995, Media award Nat. Mental Health Assn., 1996; nominated Pulitzer prize 1986, 2004. Mem. Nat. Assn. Sci. Writers (bd. dirs.), Soc. Profl. Journalists (Ray Sprigle Meml. award 1982, 84, Nat. Mag. Writing award 2000, Non-Deadline Reporting award 2004), Sigma Xi (hon.), Nat. Press Club. Episcopalian. Home: 237 Thompson St Apt 7B New York NY 10012 Office: The LA Times NY Bur 2 Park Ave 8th Fl New York NY 10016 Office Phone: 212-448-2849. Personal E-mail: leehotz@earthlink.net. Business E-Mail: lee.hotz@latimes.com.

HOTZE, CHARLES WAYNE, publishing executive; b. Moline, Ill., Feb. 19, 1919; s. Charles Edmund and Nellie (Gibbs) H.; m. Hazel Ann Tebbens, Dec. 20, 1956; children: Karen Ann, Carla Ann. BA, U. Ill., 1941. Pres., chmn. bd. Fowle Printing Co., Milw., 1953-55; pres. Pub. Clin. Med., Northfield, Ill., 1954—, Med. Digest, Inc., 1955—, C. W. Hotze Bldg. Corp., 1956—, Pediatrics Digest, Inc., 1962—, Psychiatry Digest, 1962—, Dermatology Digest, 1963—, Ob/Gyn Digest, 1964—, Urology Digest, 1964—, Cardiology Digest, 1966, Med. Comm., Inc., 1968—; chmn. bd. Lake County Press, Inc., Waukegan, Ill., 1971-78; pres. K&C Land Devel. Corp., 1993—. O.R.L. Digest, 1971—, Ophthalmology Digest, 1971—, Orthopedics Digest, 1973—, Pharmacy Digest, 1978—, Veterinary Digest, 1978—, Radiology Digest, 1979, Anesthesiology Digest, 1981—. Served to 1st lt. Infantry, AUS, 1942-44. Mem. Soc. Acad. Achievement, Am. Med. Writers Assn., Pharm. Advt. Club, Midwest Pharm. Advt. Club, Ams. Armorial Ancestry, Mayflower Soc., SAR, Am. Legion, Benevolent and Protective Order of Elks, Psi Upsilon. Clubs: Sunset Ridge (Northfield, Ill.). Home: 1950 Sunset Ridge Rd Northfield IL 60093-1060 Office: PO Box 8021 Northfield IL 60093-8021

HOUARNER, GERARD, rehabilitation services professional; b. N.Y.C., NY, May 24, 1955; s. Joseph and Anne Houarner; m. Linda Addison, Feb. 26, 2004; 1 child, Brian. BA, City Coll. of NY, 1973—77; MA, Columbia U., 1980, MEd, 1981. Cert. rehab. counselor. Counselor Postgraduate Ctr. for Mental Health, N.Y.C., NY, 1981—82, Beth Israel Methodone Program, N.Y.C., 1982—85; clin. supr. Fordham Fremont CMHC, Bronx, NY, 1985—87; dir. rehab. svcs. St. Christopher, Queens, NY, 1987—89; supr. rehab. svcs. Bronx Psychiatric Ctr., Bronx, NY, 1989—. Author: The Bard of Sorcery, 1986; editor: (fiction) Space and Time Mag., 1998—; author: The Road To Hell, 1999, The Beast That Was Max, 2001, Visions Through Shattered Lens, 2002, Black Orchids From Aum, 2001, I Love You and There is Nothing You Can Do About It, 2003, Painfreak, 1996; co-editor: Dead Cat's Traveling Circus of Wonder and Miracle Medicine Show, 2005, Dead Cats Bouncing, 2002; editor: Going Postal, 1998. E-mail: oddist55@aol.com.

HOUBOLT, JOHN CORNELIUS, physicist; b. Altoona, Iowa, Apr. 10, 1919; s. John H. and Hendreika (Van Ingen) H.; m. Mary Morris, June 14, 1949; children: Mary Cornelia, Joanna, Julie. BS, U. Ill., 1940, MS, 1942; PhD, Swiss Fed. Inst. Tech., Zurich, 1958, hon. doctorate, 1975, Clarkson U., 1990. Bridge engr. I.C. R.R., 1940; city engr. Waukegan, Ill., 1941; aero. research scientist NASA, Hampton, Va., 1942-49; assoc. chief dynamic loads div. NACA-NASA, 1949-62; chief theoretical mechanics div. NASA, 1962-63; sr. v.p., dir. Aero Research Asso. Princeton Inc., N.J., 1963-76; chief scientist Langley Research Center, Hampton, Va., 1976-85. Cons. and adviser to govt. agys. and industry, 1985—; instr. grad. extension div. U. Va., 1944—, Va. Poly. Inst., 1958—; exchange scientist Royal Aircraft Establishment, Eng., 1949; dir. Doweave, Inc., Walker-Gordon Labs.; Mem. Air Force Scientific Adv. Bd. Asso. editor: Jour. Spacecraft and Rockets. Recipient Rockefeller Pub. Svc. award, 1956, Exceptional Sci. Achievement award NASA, 1963, Structures, Structural Dynamics and Materials award AIAA, 1967, Disting. Civil Engring. Alumni award U. Ill., 1969, Illini Achievement award U. Ill., 1970, Dryden Rsch. lectr. award, 1972, Space Act award NASA, 1983, Pa. Engr. of Yr. award, 1989, U. Ill. Alumni award, 1997, Spirit of St. Louis medal, 2000. Fellow AIAA (hon. v.p. tech.); mem. Nat. Acad. Engrs., Tau Beta Pi, Chi Epsilon, Phi Kappa Chi, Sigma Xi. Achievements include rsch., numerous reports in aeros., aeroelasticity, structures, atmosphere turbulence, space flight and moon landing. Office: Langley Rsch Ctr NASA Hampton VA 23665

HOUCK, MARK HEDRICH, engineering educator; b. Balt., May 14, 1951; s. Walter Clifton and Ruth Marie (Hedrich) H.; m. Margaret Ann Nolan, Sept. 1, 1972; children: Timothy Daniel, Megan Hillary, Brigid Elyse. B in Engring. Sci., Johns Hopkins U., 1972, PhD, 1976. Registered profl. engr., Ind., Md. Rsch. asst. prof. dept. civil engring. U. Wash., Seattle, 1975—77; asst prof. sch. civil engring. Purdue U., West Lafayette, Ind., 1977—82, assoc. prof. sch. civil engring., 1982-87, prof. sch. civil engring., 1987-92, head hydraulic and systems engring., 1991-92; dr. of univ. Johns Hopkins U., Balt., 1989—90; prof. urban systems, engring., ops. rsch. Sch. Info. Tech. and Engring. George Mason U. Fairfax, Va., 1992—2005, chair CEIE dept., 1998—2002. Pres. Omtek Engring., Inc., West Lafayette, 1983-1991; v.p. Water Resources Mgmt., Inc., Columbia, Md., 1988-89; vis. prof. Heriot-Watt U., Edinburgh, Scottland, 2003. Assoc. editor Water Resources Rsch. Jour., 1981-85; co-editor Jour. Civil Engineering & Environmental Systems, London, 2003-05; contbr. articles to profl. jours. Fellow Johns Hopkins U., 1975-76. Fellow ASCE (chmn. emerging techs. com. 1986-88, chmn. water resources systems com. 1984, Walter L. Huber Rsch. Prize 1988); mem. Nat. Soc. Profl. Engrs., Am. Geophysical Union, Inst. Mgmt. Sci., Ind. Acad. Sci. (chmn. engring. div. 1981), Chi Epsilon, Sigma Xi, Omega Rho. Avocation: running. Office: George Mason U Sci and Tech I Bldg Sci And Tech I Rm 103 Fairfax VA 22030 Business E-Mail: mhouck@gmu.edu.

HOUCK, RUDOLPH S.(ROB), lawyer; b. Scranton, Pa., Nov. 15, 1947; Student, Ludwig-Maximilian Univ., Institut für ausländisches und internationales Wirtschaftsrecht, Goethe University; BA cum laude, Univ. Tex., Austin, 1969; JD, Univ. Chgo., 1972; LLM, Internat.Law Inst., Georgetown Univ., 1981. Bar: Pa. 1972, NY 1982. Ptnr., chmn., internat. group Alston & Bird LLP, NYC. Mem. Atlantik-Brücke; bd. dir. Deutscher Verein; bus. adv. bd. Am. Coun. on Germany. Office: Alston & Bird LLP 90 Park Ave New York NY 10016-1387 Office Phone: 212-210-9418. Office Fax: 212-210-9444. Business E-Mail: rhouck@alston.com.

HOUDE-WALTER, SUSAN, optics scientist, educator; b. NYC; BA, Sarah Lawrence Coll., 1976; MS, U. Rochester, 1983, PhD, 1987. Co-founder LaserMax, Inc., 1989, pres., 2000—02; prof. optics U. Rochester, 2002—. Presenter in field. Chair editl. adv. com. Optics & Photonics News, spl. editorship Jour. Non-Crystalline Solids, MRS Bulletin. Recipient 3M Faculty award for rsch. Fellow: Am. Ceramic Soc., Optical Soc. Am. (search com. 1997—98, nom. com. 1999, pres.-elect 2004—). Achievements include research in optical materials, especially optical glass and the molecular structure of multicomponent glasses. Office: Inst Optics Wilson Blvd Wilmont Bldg Rochester NY 14627-9000 Office Phone: 585-275-7629. Office Fax: 585-244-4936. Business E-Mail: shw@optics.rochester.edu.

HOUGGARD, SANTA CAROL HALL, family nurse practitioner, consultant; b. Ermine, Ky., Nov. 9, 1940; d. Russell L. and Ila (Amburgey) Hall; m. Byron L. Houggard, Apr. 30, 1965; children: Teresa Bramlet, Sutherland, Ronald L. Diploma, Sch. Profl. Nursing, Harlan, Ky., 1961; BSN cum laude, U. San Diego, 1981, MS in Nursing, 1983. Cert. family nurse practitioner. Staff nurse Whitesburg (Ky.) Meml. Hosp., 1961-62; nurse USN, 1962-65; pvt. duty nurse, 1965-77; nurse practitioner North County Health Svcs., San Marcos, Calif.; clin. adminstr., nurse practitioner Mountain Health Project, Campo, Calif., 1977-79; instr. U. San Diego, 1983-85; ind. contractor family nurse practitioner, Santee, Calif., 1985-88; family nurse practitioner NAV-CARE, San Diego, 1988-89, Mountain Health Ctr., Campo, 1989-91, So. Indian Health Coun., 1991-95; prof. nursing Ariz. Western Coll., Yuma, Ariz., 1998—2005; freelance health info. cons. Yuma, Ariz., 2005—. Lt. (j.g.) USN, 1962-65. Mem.: Ariz. Nurses Assn., ANA, Sigma Theta Tau. Home: 12124 S Sandra Ave Yuma AZ 85367-6026 Personal E-mail: houggard@hotmail.com.

HOUGH, AUBREY JOHNSTON, JR., pathologist, physician, educator; b. Little Rock, July 20, 1944; s. Aubrey Johnston and Thelma Willeen (Miller) H.; m. Linda Ann Yaeger, June 10, 1968; children: Charles Prentiss, Robert Page. BA, Hendrix Coll., 1966; MD, Vanderbilt U., 1970. Diplomate Am. Bd. Pathology. From resident Dept. Pathology to prof. Vanderbilt U., Nashville, 1970—2004, prof., 2004—, assoc. dean translational rsch., 2004—; clin. assoc. Nat. Inst. Arthritis & Metabolic Disease, Bethesda, Md., 1972-74. Chief of staff U. Ark. Hosp., Little Rock, 1986-88; pres. Ark. Acad. Pathology, Little Rock, 1982-86, Coun. of Dept. Chmn. U. Ark. Coll. of Medicine, Little Rock, 1987-88; chief of staff U. Hosp. of Ark., 1986-88, 98-2000; mem. pathology test com. Nat. Bd. Med. Examiners, 1989-92, chmn., 1993-95, comp II com., 1992-95; mem. Nat. Bd. Med. Examiners, 1996-99; mem. residency rev. com. for pathology Accreditation Coun. Med. Edn., 1990-96. Author: Tumors of the Adrenal Gland, 1987; contbr. numerous articles on orthopedic diseases to profl. jours, chpts. to books; assoc. editor Human Pathology, 1988-97; editorial bd. Am. Jour. Pathology. Alumni fund rep. Hendrix Coll., Conway, Ark., 1983-86; chmn. Shideler Chemistry Edn. Endowment, 1991-97. Served as surgeon USPHS, 1972-74. Basic Sci. Grantee Nat. Inst. Gen. Med. Studies, 1978, Altheimer Found., 1984, Nat. Inst. Arthritis, 1988; recipient Dirs. Commendation VA, 1980, Disting. Svc. award U. Ark., Little Rock, 1985, Disting. Alumni Hendrix Coll., 1999. Fellow Coll. Am. Pathologists (field inspector 1977-88); mem. AMA, AAUP, U.S.-Can. Acad. Pathology, Am. Soc. Clin. Pathologists, Am. Soc. Investigative Pathology, Assn. Clin. Scientists (Brown Meml. lectr 1986), Arthur Purdy Stout Soc., Assn. Pathology Chmn. (mem. publ. affairs com. 1985—, chmn. 1993-96), Orthopedic Rsch. Soc., History of Medicine Assocs. (bd. dirs. 1986-88), Assn. Am. Med. Colls. (mem. coun. academic soc. Washington 1985-89, statewide advisory com. bioterrorism, 2002—). Clubs: Bapt. Med. Dental (Memphis) (program chair 1983-84). Democrat. Home: 23 Lorine Cir Little Rock AR 72205-2530 Office: U Ark for Med Scis 4301 W Markham St # 517 Little Rock AR 72205-7101 Office Phone: 501-686-5369. Business E-Mail: houghaubreyJ@uams.edu.

HOUGH, LAWRENCE A., former financial organization executive; In engring., Stanford U.; grad., Sloan Sch. of Mgmt., MIT. Fin. analyst Stanford U.; with Student Loan Mktg. Assn., Washington, D.C., 1973-77, 79-96, exec. v.p., mktg. svcs. and systems, pres., chief exec. officer, 1990-96; pres., CEO Albert Lord, 1996—; CEO, co-chmn. Sato Travel, Washington, 1999—. Chmn. bd. Shakespeare Theater, Washington. Office: Sato Travel 511 Shaw Rd Sterling VA 20166-9402

HOUGH, LESLIE SELDON, educational administrator; b. Springfield, Ohio, Oct. 2, 1946; s. Donald Woodrow and Stella Alta (Finney) H.; m. Sharon Ann Cornell, May 31, 1969; children: Amity Melinda, Amanda Michelle, Leslie Elizabeth. BA, Olivet Nazarene U., 1969; MA, U. Va., 1973, PhD, 1977. Co-dir. Ohio labor history project Ohio Hist. Soc., Columbus, 1975-77; dir. archives labor urban affairs Walter P. Reuther Libr. Wayne State U., Detroit, 1992-97; dir. spl. collections Ga. State U., Atlanta, 1977-92, dir. W.J. Usery Jr. Ctr. for the Workpl., 1997—. Cons. Clayton County Water Authority, Riverdale, Ga., 1988-90, Equifax, Inc., Atlanta, 1990-92. Mem. adv. bd. Mich. Hist. Records, Lansing, 1993-97; bd. dirs. Ga. Humanities Coun., Atlanta, 1988-92. With U.S. Army, 1970-71. Democrat. Presbyterian. Avocation: running. Office: Ga State Univ WJ Usery Jr Ctr for Workpl Atlanta GA 30303 Home: 987 Emory Parc Place Decatur GA 30033

HOUGH, MICHAEL BRADY, music educator; s. William Brady and Betty Anne Hough; m. Jennifer Wright Corbell, July 12, 2003. B in Music Edn., Winthrop U., Rock Hill, S.C., 2000, MM in Conducting, 2002. Cert. tchr. K-12 N.C. Dept. of Ed. Sales assoc. Music and Arts, Charlotte, NC, 1996—2002; marching band technician Northwestern H.S., Rock Hill, 1998—2002; adj. faculty Winthrop U., Rock Hill, 2000—02; band dir. Providence H.S., Charlotte, 2003—. Pvt. musical instr., Charlotte, 1997—; marching band instr., Charlotte, 1997—; freelance musician, Charlotte, 1998—; marching band drill writer, Charlotte, 2000—. Dir.: (musical) Grease. Recipient Bruce Thompson Concerto Competition winner, Winthro U. Dept. of Music, 2001. Mem.: Internation Clarinet Assn. (assoc.), Music Educators Nat. Conf. (assoc.), Phi Mu Alpha (assoc.; treas. 1998—2005). Office: Providence H S Bands 1800 Pineville Matthews Rd Charlotte NC 28270 Office Phone: 704-849-0550. Office Fax: 980-343-3956. E-mail: michael.hough@cms.k12.nc.us.

HOUGH, ROBERT ALAN, civil engineer; b. East Orange, N.J., Aug. 6, 1959; s. Robert Elmer and Margaret (Dean) Hough; m. Marianthony Kiernan Hough. AB in Civil Engring., Lafayette Coll., 1981; MBA in Mgmt., Fairleigh Dickinson U., 1995. Registered profl. engr., N.J. Dept. head water/wastewater engring. dept. Van Note-Harvey Assocs., Princeton, NJ, 1981—2002, head dept., 1994—2002; twp. engr. Twp. of Woolwich, NJ, 1993—2002; borough engr. Borough of Pennington, NJ, 2000—02; I/I project engr. Princeton Sewer Oper. Com., 2002—. Bd. engr. Bd. Pennington, Mercer County, 2000—02. Class rep. Pingry Sch. Alumni Assn., 1977—, bd. dirs., 1981—, v.p., 2004—; bd. dirs., pony league dir., mgr., coach Springfield Jr. Baseball League, Inc., 1985—, pres., 1989—90; mem. bd. Union County Regional HS Dist. No. 1, 1997, Springfield Twp. Planning Bd., 2000—04. Mem.: ASCE, NSPE, N.J. Soc. Mcpl. Engrs., N.J. Assn. Environ. Authorities, Water Environ. Fedn., N.J. Soc. Profl. Engrs., Am. Water Works Assn. Roman Catholic. Avocations: softball, golf. Home: 172 Racquet Rd Wall NJ 07719 Office: Princeton Sewer Opers Com c/o Burough of Princeton Monument Dr Princeton NJ 08542-0390 Office Phone: 609-252-2364. Personal E-mail: bmhough15@aol.com. Business E-Mail: rhough@princetonboro.org.

HOUGH, THOMAS HENRY MICHAEL, retired lawyer, educator; b. Midland, Pa., Aug. 4, 1933; s. Bert Patrick and Marguerite (Mullen) H.; m. Jocelyn Peltz, Aug. 20, 1956; children: Jocelyn, Thomas Henry Michael. AB, Dickinson Coll., 1955; JD, Dickinson Sch. Law, 1958. Bar: Pa. 1959, U.S. Ct. Appeals (3d cir.) 1975, U.S. Supreme Ct. 1970. Field atty. NLRB, Pitts., 1959-60; atty. United Steelworkers Am., 1960-68; ptnr. Lucchino, Gaitens & Hough, Pitts., 1968-79, Hough & Gleason, PC, Pitts., 1980-94, Barry Fasulo & Hough, PC, Pitts., 1994—2002, ret., 2002. Adj. assoc. prof. pub. sector arbitration and pub. sector collective bargaining Grad. Sch. Pub. and Internat. Affairs, U. Pitts., 1973-97.

HOUGH, WINSTON, artist; b. Hartford, Mich., July 12, 1928; s. Elbert Vere and Dorris Elizabeth H.; m. Joan Ginns, Oct. 23, 1954 (div. June 1985); m. Alice Christine Daly, Nov. 30, 1985; children: Elliott Vere, Geoffrey Winston, Elise Ingrid, Roderick Garret. BFA, Sch. Art Inst., Chgo., 1955; MA, Northeastern Ill. U., 1971. Asst. prof. art Va. Commonwealth U., Richmond, 1956-62; lectr. art U. Ill., Chgo., 1964-65; tchr. City Colls. Chgo., 1969-90. Guest lectr. art dept. State U. Ill., 1968. *Was staff artist for U.S. Navy from 1946-48 for Jax Air News (station weekly), NAS Jacksonville; did cartoons and photo montages. Since 1952, work has been explorations of invented figures; most of these from imagination. In recent years, has been working more and more from everyday life.* One person shows include South Bend Art Ctr., 1954, Morris Gallery, N.Y.C., 1957, Palmer House Galleries, 1959, I.F.A. Gallery, Washington, 1961, Paul Theobald Book Store Art Gallery, 1978, Concordia U. Ferguson Gallery, 1987, Beverly Arts Ctr., Pillsbury Concourse Gallery, 1988, Art Reach Gallery, Columbus, Ohio, 1990; exhibited in group shows Exhbn. Momentum, 1953, Art Inst. Chgo., 1955, Valentine Mus., 1957-58, 60, Winston-Salem Gallery of Fine Arts, 1958-68, Roko Gallery, N.Y.C., 1964, I.F.A. Gallery, 1961-83, Evanston Art Ctr., 1973, Benjamin Galleries, 1975, Mclean County Art Ctr., Bloomington, 1987-95, 4th Presbyn. Ch., 1989; represented in pub. collections Midwest Stock Exch. Svc. Corp., Champion Fed. Savs. and Loan. Served USN, 1946—48. Recipient Birmingham Ala. Watercolor Soc. award, 1958, Best of Oils, Best of Acrylics, Rockport Pub., 1996, Best of Show, Bucktown Art Fest., 1997, Watercolor Expressions, 1999; Daniell Vandergrift scholar, 1952; Huntington Hartford Found. fellow, 1959. Mem. Chgo. Artists Coalition. Address: 937 Echo Ln Glenview IL 60025-3327

HOUGHAM, NORMAN RUSSELL, diversified financial services company executive; b. Correctionville, Iowa, Sept. 28, 1937; s. Russell Lowell and Geneva Marie (Lafferty) H.; m. Evelyn Joy Foley, Apr. 10, 1960; 1 child, Jill. Ed., Am. Inst. Banking, 1969; diploma, Sch. Bank Adminstrn., 1980. Clk. Earlham (Iowa) Savs. Bank, 1959-60; cashier Capital City State Bank, Des Moines, 1960-76; v.p. Brenton Nat. Bank, Des Moines, 1976-82; sr. v.p. Am. Fed. Savs. and Loan, Des Moines, 1982-90; mng. agt. Resolution Trust Corp., 1990-94; CFO Midwest Fin. Svcs. Ltd., 1995—. Bd. dirs. Earlham Swim Pool Devel. Corp., 1972; mem. bd. edn. Earlham Sch., 1986; bd. dirs., treas. Pioneer Pl. Retirement Homes, Earlham, 1998—; bd. dirs., chmn. fin. com. Earlham Ch. of Christ, 1999; trustee Earlham Pub. Libr., 1990. Recipient Bd. Dirs. award Des Moines chpt. Am. Inst. Banking, 1972, Instr. Appreciation award Inst. for Fin. Edn., 1983, award of merit Earlham Bd. Edn., 1986, Spl. Achievement award FDIC, 1992, Cert. of Appreciation RTC, 1992. Mem. Masons. Republican. Avocations: reading, teaching. Home: 235 NE 3d St PO Box 344 Earlham IA 50072-0344 Office: PO Box 277 Adel IA 50003-0277 Personal E-mail: normnevie@hotmail.com. Business E-Mail: hougham@ncasi.com.

HOUGHTALEN, BRANDON, music educator, director; b. Indpls., Mar. 17, 1979; s. Barry and Jan Houghtalen; m. Lori Marie Norton, May 30, 2004. MusB, U. Tenn., Knoxville, 2002. Cert. edn. State of Ga., 2002. Assoc. dir. of bands McIntosh H.S., Peachtree City, Ga., 2002—. Dir. McIntosh H.S. Marching Band, Peachtree City, Ga., 2002—. Arranger (marching band and chamber music). Named Winner, Collegiate Brass Artist Contest, Tenn. Music Teachers Assn., 1998. Mem.: Ga. Music Educators Assn., Nat. Band Assn., Phi Mu Alpha Sinfonia (chpt. treas., edn. officer 1998—2001, Outstanding Sinfonian Award 2002). Methodist. Achievements include participated in conducting symposia with Donald Hunsberger, James Jordan, Robert Rumbelow, Mallory Thompson, and Jerry Junkin. Avocations: travel, scuba diving. Office: McIntosh HS Bands 201 Walt Banks Road Peachtree City GA 30269 Office Phone: 770-631-3267. Office Fax: 770-631-3278.

HOUGHTALING, MICHAEL KIRK, mental health services professional, director; b. Kingston, N.Y., May 22, 1961; s. John Henry and Mary Ann Houghtaling. BA, Hofstra U., 1983; MA, SUNY, New Paltz, N.Y., 1989. Lic. profl. counselor N.J. Bd. Marriage and Family. From therapist to dir. adult mental health Jersey City (N.J.) Med. Ctr., 1990—99, dir. adult mental health, 1999—2003; dir. outpatient care Smith Cmty. Mental Health, Sunrise, Fla., 2004—. Mem. sys. rev. com. Huson County, Secaucus, NJ, 1992—2003. Mem.: APA (assoc.), Am. Counseling Assn., Broward County Mus. Art. Home: 10321 NE 22 Ave Fort Lauderdale FL 33308 Office: Smith Cmty Mental Health 4265 N Pine Island Rd Sunrise FL 33351

HOUGHTALING, PAMELA ANN, communications professional, writer; b. Catskill, NY, July 8, 1949; d. Stanley Kenneth and Mildred Edythe (Fyfe) H. BA, Princeton U., 1971; M in Internat. Affairs, Russian Inst., Columbia U., 1974, cert., 1976. Internat. rels. analyst Libr. of Congress, Washington, 1974-75, U.S. GAO, Washington, 1976-77; pub. affairs specialist IBM Corp., Washington, 1977-81; sr. external programs analyst IBM World Trade Americas/Far East Corp., North Tarrytown, N.Y., 1981-82; mgr. labor affairs/bus. practices U.S. Coun. Internat. Bus., N.Y.C., 1982-84; comms. specialist-advt. IBM Corp., Boca Raton, Fla., 1984-86, staff comms. specialist White Plains, N.Y., 1986-88, comms. cons., 1988-90; sr. mktg. specialist Wang Labs., Bethesda, Md., 1990-93; pub. rels. dir. STG Mktg. Comm., 1993-94; mgr. mktg. comm. Cable & Wireless, Inc., Vienna, Va., 1994-95; tech. comms. cons. Johns Hopkins U., Laurel, Md., 1995—98, contractor to Applied Physics Lab., 1998-99; mktg. mgr. Info. Tech. Lab. Nat. Inst. Stds. and Tech., Gaithersburg, Md., 2000—03, 2005—; fellow U.S. Dept. Commerce Sci. and Tech., 2003—04; with Office Def. Rsch. and Engring. Dept. Def., 2003—04. Mem. AAAS, Armed Forces Comms. and Electronics Assn., Nat. Assn. Sci. Writers, Toastmasters Internat.

HOUGHTELLING, AYRES, artist, architectural engineer; b. Defiance, Ohio, Feb. 12, 1912; s. Charles Wesley Houghtelling and Elizabeth Overbaugh; m. Lydia Amaddeo, Nov. 22, 1974. Student, San Mateo Coll., Stanford U. Allegorically depicted Shakespeare's works (two of which are permanently exhibited in Civici Mus., Venice, Italy); one man show includes The City of Paris, San Francisco; exhibited in group shows at San Francisco World's Fair, Fountainelle Hotel, Omaha, Jocelyn Mus., Omaha, Plz. Hotel, Hollywood, Calif.; prin. archtl. works include 23 pavillions 1964 World's Fair, Air France, Am. Airlines, Am. Petroleum Inst., Beach-Nut Corp., Coca-Cola, Continental Iins., Christian Sci. Pavilion, Chrysler Corp., De-Beers Consolidated Mines, Ea. Airlines, Edison Electric Inst., Gen. Dynamics Corp., Iberian Airlines, L.I. Asn., Nat. Airlines, New England States Pavilion, N.Y. State Pavilion, Owens Corning Glass, Pharm. Mfrs., Proposed Space and Motion Theme, Travelers Ins., TWA Airlines, United Airlines; illustrator for several art books and Nasa publs.; inventor pull-top can opener. Home: 60 Sutton Pl S New York NY 10022

HOUGHTON, ALAN NOURSE, educational association administrator, consultant; b. Hartford, Conn., Jan. 17, 1924; m. Elizabeth T. Jones, Mar. 30, 1946; children: Alan Nourse, Elizabeth Boardman, John Barnard, Suzanne Tolles. AB cum laude, Harvard U., 1946, AM, 1951; postgrad., Columbia U., 1951, U. Conn., 1961, 62-63. Faculty Groton (Mass.) Sch., 1946-51; chmn. classics dept. Loomis Sch., Windsor, Conn., 1951-55; headmaster Pine Point Sch., Stonington, 1955-67, Renbrook Sch., West Hartford, 1967-73; exec. dir. Conn. Assn. Ind. Schs., 1974-89; ednl. cons. Madison, 1989-94. Mem. Sch. Bldg. Com., Lyme, Conn., 1959, Zoning Bd. Appeals, 1959-61, Zoning and Planning Commn., 1963-65, Bd. Fin., 1971-75, Lyme Dem. Town Com., 1957-63; trustee Blair Acad., Blairstown, N.J., Pine Point Sch., Stonington, Conn., Renbrook Sch., Country Sch., Madison, Conn.; corporator Hartford Hosp. 1st lt. USAAF, 1943-45. Decorated D.F.C., Air medal with three oak leaf clusters; Houghton Wing named for him at Pine Point Sch. Mem. Conn. Assn. Ind. Schs. (tchrs. edn. and profl. stds. rep. 1963-66, v.p., pres.), Classical Assn. New Eng., Mile Creek Beach Club (bd. govs. 1958-73), Harvard Club (N.Y.C.), Madison Winter Club, Phi Delta Kappa, Pi Eta. Home: Evergreen Woods 88 Notch Hill Rd # 124 North Branford CT 06471

HOUGHTON, AMORY, JR., former congressman; b. Corning, N.Y., Aug. 7, 1926; m. Priscilla Dewey Houghton; 4 children. BA, Harvard U., 1950, MA, 1952; PhD (hon.), Alfred U., 1963, Albion Coll., 1964, Cen. Coll., 1966, Clarkson Coll. Tech., 1968, Elmira Coll., 1982, Hartwick Coll., 1983, Houghton Coll., 1983. Exec. officer Corning Glass Works, 1951-86; mem. U.S. Congress from 29st N.Y. dist. (formerly 31st), Washington, 1987—2005; mem. internat. rels. com., ways and means com., chmn. oversight subcom., vice-chmn. subcom. on Africa. Mem. Grace Commn., Bus. Council N.Y. State, Bus. Adv. Commn. for Gov. N.Y., Labor-Industry Coalition for Internat. Trade. Trustee Brookings Instn. With USMC, 1945-46. Mem. Corning C. of C., Rotary. Republican.

HOUGHTON, JAMES, performing company executive; Founding artistic dir. Signature Theatre Co., NYC, 1991—; artistic dir. New Harmony Project, 1996—99, O'Neill Playwrights Conference, 1999—2003; artistic advisor Guthrie Theatre. Mem. lecture com. London Academy of Music and Dramatic Art; guest lecturer Hallmark Creative Leadership Conference, Edward Albee Last Frontier Playwriting Conference, Dramatists Guild, Sewanee Writers Conference, William Inge Theatre Festival; bd. mem. A.R.T./New York. Dir.: (plays) The Last of the Thorntons, The American Clock, Curse of the Starving Class, Heathen Valley, Ambrosio, Mr. Peters' Connections. Mem.: Soc. of Stage Directors and Choreographers. Office: Signature Theatre Co 630 Ninth Ave Ste 1106 New York NY 10036

HOUGHTON, JAMES RICHARDSON, manufacturing executive; b. Corning, NY, Apr. 6, 1936; s. Amory and Laura (Richardson) H.; m. May Tuckerman Kinnicutt, June 30, 1962; children: James DeKay, Nina Bayard. AB, Harvard U., 1958, MBA, 1962. With Goldman, Sachs & Co., N.Y.C., 1959-61; with Corning Glass Works (name changed to Corning Inc. 1989), 1962-96; European area mgr. Corning Glass Works, Zurich, Switzerland, 1964-68, v.p., gen. mgr. consumer products divsn., 1968-71, vice chmn. bd., dir., chmn. exec. com., 1971-83, chmn. bd., CEO, 1983-96, 2002—05, chmn. bd., 2005—. Bd. dirs. Met. Life Ins. Co., Exxon Mobil Corp.; mem. Harvard Corp. Trustee Corning Inc. Found., Corning Mus. Glass, Pierpont Morgan Libr., N.Y.C., Met. Mus. Art, Bus. Coun. With U.S. Army, 1959-60. Mem.: Corning Country; River, Harvard, Univ., Links (N.Y.C.); Brookline (Mass.) Country; Tarratine (Dark Harbor, Maine); Augusta (Ga.) Nat. Golf; Rolling Rock, Laurel Valley Golf (Ligonier, Pa.). Episcopalian. Office: Corning Inc MP HQ E2-6 One Riverfront Plz Corning NY 14831

HOUGHTON, JOHN WILLIAM, literature educator; s. Forrest Floyd Houghton and Leta Felicia Kingery. AB cum laude, Harvard Coll., 1975; AM, Ind. U., 1977; MAR summa cum laude, Yale Div. Sch., 1989; diploma in Anglican studies, Berkeley Div. Sch. Yale, 1989; MMS, U. Notre Dame, 1991, PhD, 1994. Neville-Parry chair in English John Burroughs Sch., Ladue, Mo., 1978—87; instr. English and history Mary Inst. and St. Louis Country Day Sch., Ladue, Mo., 1994—99; chaplain, chair dept. religious studies Episc. Sch. Baton Rouge, 1999—2004; chair, dept. English Canterbury Sch., Fort Wayne, Ind., 2005—. Author: (novel) Rough Magicke; assistant lit. editor (mag.) River Styx; author: Falconry and other poems; contbr. (collected essays) Tolkien the Medievalist; contbr. articles to profl. jours. and encys. Vestry mem., jr. warden, sr. warden Episc. Ch. of Holy Communion, University City, Mo., 1985—99; mem. Consortium for Tchg. of Mid. Ages, Kalamazoo, 1998—2003. Recipient Nelson Burr prize, Hist. Soc. Episc. Ch., 1998; Dorothy A. Given fellow, Episc. Ch. Found., 1990—93. Mem.: Soc. Ind. Pioneers. Episcopalian. Home: 609 Houghton St Culver IN 46511 Office: Canterbury Sch 3210 Smith Rd Fort Wayne IN 46804 Personal E-mail: numenor@aya.yale.edu.

HOUGHTON, KAREN THERESA, reading specialist educator, mathematics educator; d. Ralph Paul and Katherine Theresa Iacobucci; m. Harold Alan Houghton, Jan. 4, 1975; children: Brandon, Theresa. BS in Bus. Edn., Empire State Coll., 1983; MS in Edn., Coll. St. Rose, 1990. Cert. reading tchr. NY, 1997, nursery and kindergarten tchr. grades 1-6 NY, 1997. Sub. tchr. Averill Pk. Sch., NY, East Greenbush Schs., NY, Berlin and Wynantskill Schs., NY, 1988—94; remedial reading and math tchr. East Greenbush Ctrl. Schs., 1994—. Bldg. level specialist sci. D.P. Sutherland Sch., Nassau, NY, 1995—2003, bldg. level specialist math., 1997—99; tchr. CAS reading, CAS adminstr. SUNY, Albany, 2003—; mem., rschr. ednl. com. East Greenbush Sch. Vol. Book Ho. Stuyvesant Plz., Albany, NY, 2003—04; mem. Arthritis Found., Northeastern NY chpt., 2005—, Arbor Day Found., 2003—, Defenders Wildlife, 2004—, Wildlife Guardians, 2004—, Humane Soc. US, 2004—05, World Wildlife Fund, 2004—05, Nature Conservancy, 2004—05; assoc. mem. Nat. Wildlife Fedn., 2004—05. Mem.: ASCD, Internat. Reading Assn., Nat. Wildlife Fedn., Wildlife Land Trust, Nat. Pks. Conservation Assn. Avocations: reading, travel, cooking.

HOUGHTON, KATHARINE, actress; b. Hartford, Conn., Mar. 10, 1945; d. Ellsworth Strong and Marion Houghton (Hepburn) Grant. BA, Sarah Lawrence Coll., Bronxville, N.Y., 1965. Founding mem. Pilgrim Repertory Co. (Shakespeare touring co. sponsored by Ky. Arts Commn.), 1971-72, SC Arts Commn., 1972, Miss. Arts Commn., 1973, Conn. Arts Commn., St. Joseph Coll., 1974; lectr. in field. Debut on Broadway stage in A Very Rich Woman, 1965; appeared in stage plays Charley's Aunt, New Orleans Repertory, 1966, The Front Page, Broadway, 1968, Ten O'Clock Scholar, Royal Poinciana Playhouse, Fla., 1969, The Private Ear/The Public Eye, Sullivan, Ill., 1969, Sabrina Fair, Ivoryton Playhouse, 1968, The Miracle Worker, Sullivan, Ill., A Scent of Flowers (Theatre World award), Off Broadway, 1969, Misalliance, Hartford Stage Co., 1970, The Taming of the Shrew, Actors Theatre, Louisville, 1970, Poor Richard, Tartuffe, 1970, Ring Around the Moon, Hartford Stage Co., 1970, Major Barbara, The Glass Menagerie, Actors Theatre of Louisville, 1971, Play It Again Sam, Actors Theatre of Louisville, 1971, Suddenly Last Summer, Ivanhoe, Chgo., 1973, The Prodigal Daughter, Kennedy Ctr., Washington, 1973, Bell, Book and Candle, Pensacola, Fla., 1974, The Rainmaker, Ind. Repertory Co., 1975, Spiders Web, Atlanta, 1977, Hedda Gabler, Nashville, 1978, Dear Liar, Dayton, Ohio, 1978, 13 Rue de L'Amour, Ind. Repertory Co., 1978, Antigone, Nashville, 1979, Uncle Vanya, Acad. Festival Theatre, Lake Forest, 1979, Forty Carats, Radford U. Theatre, Va., 1979, A Doll's House, St. Edward's U. Theatre, Tex., 1979, The Sea Gull, Pitts. Pub. Theatre, 1979, The Glass Menagerie, Pa. Stage Co., 1980, Taming of the Shrew, Pa. State Festival, 1980, Terra Nova, Actors Theatre of Louisville, 1980, The Merchant of Venice, South Coast Repertory, Costa Mesa, Calif., 1981, A Touch of the Poet, Yale Repertory Theatre, 1983, To Heaven in a Swing, Am. Place Theatre, N.Y.C., tour various theaters, 1983-85, Sally's Gone She's Left Her Name, Am. Festival Theatre, NH, 1984-86, Vivat, Vivat Regina, Mad Woman of Chaillot, The Time of Your Life, Children of the Sun, Mirror Repertory Co., N.Y.C., 1985, A Bill of Divorcement, Westport Country Playhouse, Conn., 1985, One Slight Hitch, Charlotte Repertory Co., 1986, To Heaven in a Swing, Amherst Coll., Bowdoin Coll., 1986, and Bronson Alcott Centennial Celebration, 1988, The Hooded Eye, West Bank Downstairs Theatre Bar, 1987, Ivoryton Playhouse, 1987, Murder in the Cathedral, West Point Cadet Chapel, 1987, The Leaves of Vallombrosa, 1988, Our Town, Broadway, 1988-89, Love Letters, Ivoryton Playhouse, 1989, To Kill A Mockingbird, Paper Mill Playhouse, NJ, 1991, Best Kept Secret, A Dangerous Liaison in the Cold War, 1998, Berkshire Theatre Festival, 2000, NJ Repertory Theatre, 2001, Sch. House Theatre, Croton Falls, NY, 2001, Lettice & Lovage, Ivoryton Playhouse, 2002; motion pictures include Guess Who's Coming to Dinner, 1967, The Gardener, 1972, Eyes of the Amaryllis, 1981, Mr. North, 1987, Billy Bathgate, 1990, Ethan Frome, 1992, The Night We Never Met, 1992, Kalamazoo, 1993, Let It Be You, 1994, The Pursuit of Happiness, 2003, Kinsey, 2003; TV series The Adams Chronicles, 1975; TV mini-series I'll Take Manhattan, 1986; appeared on TV in Legacy of Fear, 1974, The Color of Friendship, 1981, (day-time serials) One Life to Live, 1989, All My Children, 1992; toured in Sabrina Fair, 1975, The Mousetrap, Arms and the Man, Dear Liar, 1976, The Streets of New York, Westport, Conn., Guildford, NH, Dennis, Mass., Denver, 1980; appeared in To True to Be Good, Acad. Festival Theatre, Lake Forest, Ill., 1977, Spingold Theatre, Waltham, Mass., 1977, Annenberg Ctr., Phila., 1977; author: (plays) To Heaven in a Swing, 1982, Merlin, 1984, Buddha, On The Shady Side, The Right Number, 1986, (book) The Marry Month of May, 1988; (stage prodns.) Phone Play, 1988, Good Grief, 1988, Mortal Friends, 1988 (stage prodn. premiere 1988), The Lick Penny Lover, 1988, Only Angels, 1997, (screenplays) The Heart of the Matter, 1989, Journey to Glasnost, 1990, Good Grief, 1991, Motherman, 1993, Acting in Concert, 1994, Spot, 1996; co-author: Two Beastly Tales, 1975; editor: MHG: A Biography, 1989; written, performed in lectr. engagements: The Secret Life of Louisa May Alcott, Small Press Ctr., NYC, 1998, Women of Achievement Series, The Mount, Lenox, Mass., 2002, My Grandmother's House Near the River, Conn. River Mus., 1999, The Wadsworth Atheneum, Conn., 1999, The Hope Club, Providence, 2000, The Cosmopolitan Club, NYC, 2002, Katharine Times Three, Conn. Hist. Soc., 1999, Wadsworth Atheneum, 2000, Denver Town Hall, 2001, Met. Mus. Art., NYC, 2001 (Conn. Womens Hall Fame 2003), How Katharine Hepburn Became A Political Activist Without Actually Being One, 2003; appeared Larry King Live, 2003. Mem. Dramatists Guild.

HOUGHTON, MICHAEL, geneticist; PhD, U. London, 1976. Sr. rsch. investigator human interferon genetics Searle Rsch. Labs., Buckinghamshire, England; with Chiron Corp., Emeryville, Calif., 1982, dir. non-A non-B hepatitis rsch., v.p. hepatitis rsch. Recipient Karl Landsteiner Meml. award, Am. Assn. Blood Banks, 1992, Albert Lasker award Clin. Med. Rsch., 2000. Achievements include first to conduct work leading to the discovery of the virus that causes hepatitis C; development of screening methods that reduce the risk of blood transfusion-associated hepatitis in the U.S. from 30% in 1970 to virtually zero in 2000. Office: Chiron Corp 4560 Horton St Emeryville CA 94608

HOUGHTON, RAYMOND CARL, JR., education educator; b. Greenfield, Mass., May 26, 1947; s. Raymond Carl and Phyllis Irene (Richason) H.; m. Jan Marie Laws, Sept. 22, 1973; children: Raymond James, April Monica, Amy Rose. BS in Math., Norwich U., 1969; MS in Computer Sci., George Washington U., 1975; MSEE, Johns Hopkins U., 1980; PhD in Computer Sci., Duke U., 1991. Computer operator Norwich U., Northfield, Vt., 1967-69; specialist programmer power transformer dept. GE Co., Pittsfield, Mass., 1969-70, mathematician armament dept. Burlington, Vt., 1972-73; mem. tech. staff Computer Scis. Corp., Silver Spring, Md., 1974-75; data systems analyst computer security applications div. Nat. Security Agy., Ft. Meade, Md., 1975-78; computer scientist Inst. Computer Scis. and Tech./Nat. Bur. Standards, Gaithersburg, Md., 1978-83; instrnl. rsch. asst. dept. computer sci. Duke U., Durham, N.C., 1984-91; assoc. prof. dept. math. and computer sci. Augusta (Ga.) State U., 1987—93; lectr. Skidmore (N.Y.) Coll., 1993-95; owner Cyber Haus, Delmar, NY, 1995—99; town historian Bethlehem, NY, 2005—. Bd. advisers, columnist Software Engring: Tools, Techniques, Practice, 1990-94, info. sys. delegate, Peoples Rep. China, 2000; adj. prof. SUNY Sch. Bus., Albany, 1997-2000; mission in understanding del. People to People Amb. Programs, Vietnam, 2002; spkr. in field. Contbr. articles to profl. jours.;, author history-based travel books. 1st lt. U.S. Army, 1971-72, Vietnam. Decorated Purple Heart; recipient Certs. of Recognition, U.S. Dept. Commerce, 1981, 83, cert. appreciation IEEE Computer Soc., 1985. Mem.: IEEE, Assn. Computing Machinery, 101st Airborne Divsn. Assn., People to People Internat. Lutheran. Office: Cyber Haus 159 Delaware Ave #145 Delmar NY 12054-1369 Office Phone: 518-478-9798. Personal E-mail: cyhaus@msn.com.

HOUGHTON, ROBERT CHARLES, secondary school educator; b. Dover, N.H., Apr. 12, 1958; s. Raymond David and Barbara Jean Houghton. Student, USCG Acad., New London, Conn., 1976-77; BA with honors, U. Calif., Riverside, 1987, postgrad., 1987-89; MA in Ednl. Adminstrn., Chapman U., 1999. Cert. tchr., adminstr., Calif. Various teaching positions, 1977-80; pharmacy technician Anaheim (Calif.) Meml./Brea (Calif.) Cmty., 1980-85; teaching asst. U. Calif., Riverside, 1988-90; instr. Mt. San Jacinto (Calif.) Coll., 1989-90; tchr. Desert Sands Unified, Indio, Calif., 1990—, interim asst. prin., 1997-98, creator P.R.I.D.E. curriculum. Counselor Chem. Awareness Network, Indio, Calif., 1990—; computer cons. Desert Sands Unified Sch. Dist., Indio, 1994—; resident tchr. Calif. State U., San Bernardino, 1994—95; asst. tour dir. Lakeland Tours, Washington, 1991—2001; magnet grant coord. Pre-Med. Acad. Mem. NEA, Nat. Coun. Social Studies, Nat. Geographic Soc., Calif. Tchrs. Assn., Nat. Trust Historic Preservation, Civil War Trust. Republican. Avocations: travel, photography, reading, hiking, camping. Home: 79320 Port Royal Ave Indio CA 92201-1262 Office: 81195 Miles Ave Indio CA 92201-2807

HOUK, BENJAMIN NOAH, performing company executive, choreographer; b. Seattle, Apr. 4, 1962; s. Robert Louis Houk and Marilyn Joan (Haugen) Sundin; m. Lauri-Michelle Rohde, July 11, 1991; children: Madeline, Katherine;children from previous marriage: Marissa, Skylar. Studied dance, Amherst Ballet Acad., 1978, Jan Collum Sch. Ballet, 1979, Jo Emery Sch., 1979-80, N.Y. studios, 1980-83, Robert Joffrey Workshop, 1981, Am. Ballet Ctr., 1980-83, Pacific NW Ballet, 1983—; student, U. Wash., 1988—. Prin. dancer Pacific Northwest Ballet, Seattle, 1983—; asst. dir. Bravo Ballet Arts in Edn. Program, Seattle, 1993-96; with Pacific Northwest Ballet, Seattle, 1987-89, soloist, 1987—, prin. dancer, 1989-96; M.C., coord. Joffrey, N.Y.C., 1983; artistic dir., choreographer Nashville Ballet, 1996-99; artistic dir. Fort Worth Dallas Ballet, 1998—2001; dir. Dance Acad., San Marcos, Calif., 2001—. Guest artist guest Orange County Ballet, Ithaca, NY, 1981, Koslovs and Friends, San Francisco, 1985, Ballet Oreg., Portland, 1988, Ballet Chgo., 1989, Nev. Dance Theatre, Las Vegas, 1990, Tacoma Perf. Dance Co., 1980, Nevada Festival Ballet, 1993—94, Maui Ballet Co., 1994; dance instr., lectr., 1984—. Dancer (ballets) Pacific Northwest Ballet include Romeo in The Tragedy of Romeo and Juliet, Sigfried in Swan Lake, Franz in Coppelia, The Prince in The Nutcracker, others include Albrecht in Giselle, Othello in The Moor's Pavane, choreographer Capriole Suite, 1988, By When, 1989, Shard, 1990, First Light, 1992, Schubert 2-4-5, 1994, Bete Noir, 1993, Across and Back, 1994, Nutcracker, 1995, Open Water, 1995, Aida, 1997, Passage, 1998, Swan Lake (after Petipa), 1998; TV appearance Disney Presents Bill Nye the Science Guy, 1994. Artistic dir. Benefit for the Homeless, Everett, Wash., 1990—91. Grantee Tacoma (Wash.) Arts Coun., 1986. Mem.: Am. Guild Mus. Artists. Avocations: reading, windsurfing, pottery, mountain climbing, painting. Office: 1635 Rancho Santa Fe Ste 203 San Marcos CA 92069 Address: Houk 3225 River Lodge Trl N Apt 727 Fort Worth TX 76116-0842

HOUK, JAMES CHARLES, physiologist, educator; b. Northville, Mich., June 3, 1939; s. James Charles and Elowene (Tower) H.; m. Antoinette Iacuzio, Dec. 28, 1963; children: Philip, Nadia, Peter. BSEE, Mich. Tech. U., 1961; MSEE, MIT, 1963; PhD, Harvard U., 1966. Instr. Harvard U. Med. Sch., 1967-69, asst. prof., 1969-73; lectr. MIT, 1971-73; assoc. prof. Johns Hopkins U. Med. Sch., 1973-78; adj. assoc. prof. U. N.C., 1975; prof. physiology Northwestern U. Med. Sch., 1978—, chair dept. physiology, 1978—2001. Co-author: Medical Physiology 14th edit., 1980, Handbook of Physiology--The Nervous System II, 1981, Encyclopedia of Neuroscience, 1987, Models of Information Processing in the Basal Ganglia, 1995; contbr. chpts. to books. Recipient Javits award NIH, 1984-92. Mem. IEEE, AAAS, Soc. for Neurosci., Am. Physiol. Soc., European Neurosci. Assn., Assn. Chmn. Depts. Physiology, Internat. Neural Network Soc. Office: Northwestern U 303 E Chicago Ave Chicago IL 60611-3093 Office Phone: 312-503-8219.

HOUK, KENDALL NEWCOMB, chemistry professor; b. Nashville, Tenn., Feb. 27, 1943; s. Charles H. and Janet Houk; 1 child, Kendall M.; m. Robin L. Garrell. AB, Harvard U., 1964, MS, 1966, PhD, 1968. Asst. prof. chemistry La. State U., Baton Rouge, 1968-72, assoc. prof., 1972-75, prof., 1975-80, U. Pitts., 1980-86, UCLA, 1986-91, chmn. dept. chemistry and biochemistry, 1991-94. Dir. chemistry divsn. NSF, 1988—90. Contbr. articles to profl. jours. Recipient Schrodinger medal World Assn. Theoretically Oriented Chemists, 1998. Fellow AAAS; mem. Internat. Acad. Quantum Molecular Sci., Am. Chem. Soc. (Cope Scholar award 1988, James Flack Norris award 1991, award for computers in chemistry and pharm. sci. 2003). Office: UCLA Dept Chemistry Biochemistry 405 Hilgard Ave Los Angeles CA 90095-9000 E-mail: houk@chem.ucla.edu.

HOULE, JOSEPH E., mathematics professor; b. Hartford, Conn., Oct. 11, 1930; s. Joseph E. and Rena (Cyr) H.; m. Constance Deschamps, June 19, 1954; children— Marie, Joseph, Celia, Elizabeth, Amy, Bernice. AB, Cath. U.

Am., 1952, MA, 1954, PhD, 1959. From instr. to assoc. prof. math. Georgetown U., 1953-62; assoc. prof. Seton Hall U., 1962-63; prof. math. Pace U., N.Y.C., 1963-94, chmn. dept., 1963-70, dean Dyson Coll. Arts and Scis., 1971-90, vice provost, 1987-90. Dir. Ctr. for Applied Ethics, 1982-93, emeritus, 1994—; Internat. Exec. Svc. Corps. vol. exec. Ministry of Edn., Budapest, Hungary, 1991. Fellow N.Y. Acad. Scis. (chmn. sect. math. 1968-69), Phi Beta Kappa Soc.; mem. Math. Assn. Am., Sigma Xi. Roman Catholic. Home: A188 Harrogate 400 Locust St Lakewood NJ 08701-7411

HOULIHAN, CHARLES DANIEL, JR., lawyer; b. Boston, June 15, 1953; s. Charles Daniel and Barbara Ann (Keohane) H.; m. Shelley Savran, May 28, 1978; children: Meghan, Brenna. BA, U. Mass., 1975; JD, Syracuse U., 1978. Bar: Tex. 1979, U.S. Ct. Appeals (5th cir.) 1983, U.S. Dist. Ct. (we. dist.) Tex. 1984, Conn. 1993, U.S. Dist. Ct. Conn. 1993; cert. mediator. Law clk. to chief judge U.S. Dist. Ct. Va., Roanoke, 1978—79; shareholder Matthews & Branscomb, San Antonio, 1979—92; of counsel Hebb & Gitlin, Hartford, Conn., 1992—94; pvt. practice Simsbury, Conn., 1995—. Spkr. in field. Chair Simsbury Econ. Devel. Commn., 1995-98, Simsbury Zoning Commn., 2005—; bd. dirs. Hartford Symphony Orch., 1997-2001; pres. Simsbury Main St. Partnership, 1997-98, dir. 1996—; vice chair Talcott Mountain Music Festival, 1996-98, chair, 1999-00. Mem. ABA (vice chmn. torts and non-profit, charitable and religious orgns. 1990-93), Conn. Bar Assn. (exec. com. constrn. law sect.), Am. Inns of Ct. (San Antonio and Hartford chpts., sec. William Sessions chpt. 1985, pres. 1997-98), Simsbury C. of C. (bd. dirs.), Order of Coif, Phi Beta Kappa. Roman Catholic. Home: 2 Somerset Ln Simsbury CT 06070-1716 Office: 1276 Hopmeadow St PO Box 582 Simsbury CT 06070-0582 E-mail: cdhatty@aol.com.

HOULIHAN, CHRISTINE MURRAY, pediatrician; MD, Georgetown U. Sch. Medicine, Washington, D.C., 1991—95. Asst. prof., pediat. Med. Coll. Va., Richmond, 2002—03; neurodevelopmental pediatrician Carilion Roanoke Cmty. Hosp., Va., 2002—03; hospitalist Cumberland Hosp., New Kent, Va., 2002—03; asst. prof., pediat. U. Va., Charlottesville, 2003—. Office: Univ Va 2270 Ivy Rd Charlottesville VA 22903 Office Phone: 434-924-5411.

HOULIHAN, DAVID PAUL, lawyer; b. Youngstown, Ohio, May 14, 1937; s. Paul V. and Delcie (Norman) H.; m. Marlene K. Betras, Aug. 13, 1960; children: Kevin, Rex, Laura, Brian. BS, Youngstown State U., 1959; postgrad., Purdue U., 1960; LLB, Georgetown U., 1964. Bar: D.C. 1965, U.S. Ct. Appeals (D.C. cir.) 1965, U.S. Supreme Ct. 1968, U.S. Ct. Internat. Trade 1976, U.S. Ct. Customs and Patent Appeals 1976, U.S. Ct. Appeals (Fed. cir.) 1982. Analyst U.S. Internat. Trade Commn., Washington, 1960-64; counsel U.S.-Japan trade council Stitt & Hemmendinger, Washington, 1964-68; ptnr. Daniels, Houlihan & Palmeter P.C., Washington, 1968-84, Mudge, Rose, Guthrie, Alexander & Ferdon, Washington, 1984-95, White & Case, Washington, 1995—. Lectr. Oxford U., Eng., 1972; chmn. Keidanren Seminar: Dumping, Customs and Tax Aspects of Transfer Pricing. Contbr. articles to profl. jours. Mem. ABA, D.C. Bar Assn., British-Am. C. of C. Democrat. Roman Catholic. Avocations: sailing, music. Address: White & Case 701 13th St NW Washington DC 20005-3807 Personal E-mail: dhoulihan@whitecase.com.

HOULIHAN, GAIL LANIER, child advocate, educator; b. Mt. Vernon, N.Y., Sept. 15, 1936; d. Fred K. Cordes and Burniece Ruth Oliver Phillips; m. Raymond D'Arsey Houlihan, Jr., May 16, 1959 (div. July 1997); children: Jeffrey John, Raymond D'Arsey III, Michael William, Pamela Lanier, Sean Patrick. BA in English, Douglass Coll., New Brunswick, N.J., 1958. With exec. mgmt. trainee program Doubledy Pub. Co., N.Y.C., 1958-59; elem. sch. tchr. Pennsauken (N.J.) Sch. Dist., 1959; conf. coord. for nat. conf. Nat. Assn. Foster Care Reviewers, 1991-92. Mem. Gov.'s Com. for Children, Youth and Families, 1978-82; mem. township com. Bordentown (N.J.) Twp. Govt., 1982-88, dep. mayor, 1985, 87, mayor, 1986; mem. Bordentown Twp. Planning Bd., 1986-88; founding mem. Bordentown Sewerage Authority, 1986, vice chmn., 1986, chmn., 1987, 91, bd. dirs., 1986-92; coord. Bordentown Twp. Emergency Mgmt., 1987-91; mem. State Health Planning Bd., 1994—; active N.J. State Adv. Coun., Trenton, 1979—, mem. exec. com., 1979-86; trustee Assn. for Children of N.J., Newark, 1980—, treas., 1989-91, adminstrv. v.p., 1995-97; bd. dirs. Cmty. Concerts of Bordentown, 1980-91, pres., 1986-88; bd. dirs. Prevention Edn., Inc., Lawrence Twp., N.J., 1990-92; vice chmn. Children's Interagy. Coordinating Coun., Mt. Holly, N.J., 1993-97, chmn., 1997—; bd. dirs. Morris Hall St. Lawrence Rehab. Ctr., 1993—; chair cmty. svc. bd. MH/StL, 1998—. Home: 119 Chatsworth Ave Beach Haven NJ 08008-1538

HOULIHAN, GERALD JOHN, lawyer; b. Cortland, N.Y., Aug. 26, 1943; s. Robert Emmett and Helen (Corsi) H.; m. Claudia C. Kitchens; children: Andrea, Gerald Jr., Maureen, Katherine, Colleen. BS, U. Notre Dame, 1965; JD, Syracuse U., 1968. Bar: N.Y. 1968, U.S. Dist. Ct. (we. dist.) N.Y. 1968, U.S. Ct. Appeals (2nd cir.) 1972, U.S. Supreme Ct. 1980, U.S. Ct. Appeals (5th cir.) 1981, U.S. Ct. Appeals (11th cir.) 1981, Fla. 1985, U.S. Dist. Ct. (so. dist.) Fla. 1985, U.S. Dist. Ct. (so. dist.) N.Y. 1986, U.S. Dist. Ct. (no. dist.) Fla. 1986, U.S. Ct. Appeals (4th and D.C. cirs.) 1987, U.S. Dist. Ct. (middle dist.) Fla., 1987. Assoc. Harris, Beach, Keating et al., Rochester, N.Y., 1968-72; asst. U.S. atty. U.S. Atty.'s Office, Rochester, 1972-81; sr. litigation counsel U.S. Dept. Justice, Rochester, 1981-82; chief asst. U.S. atty. U.S. Atty.'s Office, Miami, Fla., 1982-85; ptnr. Steel Hector & Davis, Miami, 1985-91; mem. Greenberg, Traurig, Hoffman, Lipoff, Rosen & Quentel, P.A., Miami, 1991-95; ptnr. Houlihan & Ptnrs., P.A., 1995—. Advocate Am. Bd. Trial Advocates. Belle L. Landry scholar Syracuse Soc. Mem. Fed. Bar Assn. (pres. 1993-94, bd. dirs. Miami chpt. 1988—), Order of Coif. Democrat. Home: 5191 SW 76th St Miami FL 33143-6015 Office: Houlihan & Ptnrs PA 2600 S Douglas Rd Ste 600 Miami FL 33134-6100 E-mail: gjhoulihan@aol.com.

HOUNGUES, DESIRE MENSANH, dean; s. Brigitte Houngues. PhD, Boston U., 1993—97; BA, U. Benin, 1989. Cambridge Certificate Cambridge Internat. Exam., 1990. Dean Savannah Coll. of Art and Design Sch. Lib. Arts, Ga., 2002—. Office: Savannah Coll of Art and Design Charlton Savannah GA 31402 Office Phone: 912-695-5801. Business E-Mail: dhoungue@scad.edu.

HOUNSOU, DJIMON GASTON, actor; b. Benin, West Africa, Apr. 24, 1964; arrived in U.S., 1990; Actor: (films) Without You I'm Nothing, 1990, Unlawful Entry, 1992, Stargate, 1994, Amistad, 1997 (Image award for outstanding lead actor in a motion picture, 1998), Ill Gotten Gains, 1997, The Small Hours, 1997, Deep Rising, 1998, Passage du milieu, 2000, Gladiator, 2000, The Tag, 2001, Le Boulet, 2002, The Four Feathers, 2002, In America, 2002 (award for best supporting actor San Diego Film Critics Soc., 2003, Ind. Spirit award for best supporting male, 2004, Golden Satellite award for best supporting actor in a drama, 2004, Acad. award nomination for best supporting actor, 2004), Heroes, 2003, Biker Boyz, 2003, Lara Croft Tomb Raider: The Cradle of Life, 2003, Blueberry, 2004, Constantine, 2005, Beauty Shop, 2005, The Island, 2005, (guest appearance): (TV series) Beverly Hills, 90210, 1990, ER, 1999, Soul Food, 2001, Alias, 2003, 2004.*

HOUNTRAS, PETER TIMOTHY, psychologist, educator; b. Memphis, Dec. 7, 1927; s. Timothy John and Ethel (Trakas) H.; m. Helen Madias, Nov. 21, 1954; children: John, Dean. BS cum laude, U. Toledo, 1946; MA, U. Mich., 1951, PhD, 1955. Instr. U. Mich., 1954-57; asst. prof. psychology and edn. U. Pitts., 1957-59, assoc. prof., 1959-61; assoc. prof. ednl. psychology, guidance and counseling Northwestern U., Evanston, Ill., 1961-66; prof. counseling and guidance, chmn. dept. U. N.D., Grand Forks, 1966-70; dean of counseling services Eastern Mich. U., Ypsilanti, 1970-76, adj. prof. psychology, 1972-76; cons. psychologist, 1957—. Regional counseling and testing cons. Bur. Employment Security, U.S. Dept. Labor, 1966—; cons. to U.S. Office of Edn., 1967— Author: Mental Hygiene, 1961, Manifest Anxiety and Achievement, 1970; Contbr. articles profl. jours. Supr. psychologist Pine Rest Christian Hosp., 1989—. Recipient Distinguished Service Citation Gov. N.D., 1969 Fellow Am. Psychol. Assn.; mem. Am. Personnel and Guidance Assn., Ill., Midwestern psychol. assns., Assn. Counselor Educators and Suprs., Psychologists Interested in Advancement Psychotherapy, Am. Ednl. Research Assn., A.A.U.P., Mich. Psychol. Assn., Sigma Xi, Psi Chi, Phi Kappa Phi, Phi Delta Kappa, Kappa Delta Pi. Presbyn. (elder). Club: Rotarian. Home: 5911 Marshwood Dr Sylvania OH 43560-1018 Office Phone: 419-824-0626.

HOUP, HELEN A., conservator; b. Los Angeles, Apr. 25, 1946; d. Homer Wendell and Marion Peacock Avey; m. Jonathan Marshall Houp, June 25, 1943; 1 child, Jonathan Gates. BA, U. Calif., 1968. Lab tech. Kimbell Art Mus., Ft. Worth, 1972—74, apprentice conservator, 1976—82; assoc. conservator Perry Hoston & Assoc., 1982—2001; head of conservation Helen A. Houp Fine Art Conservation, Dallas, 2001—. Mem.: Caseta, Tex. Art Collectors Organ., Western Assn. Art Conservators, Am. Inst. Conservators. Office: Helen A Houp 2626 Lombardy Ln 106 Dallas TX 75220 Office Phone: 214-366-4700. Office Fax: 214-366-4740.

HOUPIS, CONSTANTINE HARRY, retired electrical engineering educator; b. Lowell, Mass., June 16, 1922; s. Harry John and Metaxia (Gourokous) H.; m. Mary Stephens, Aug. 28, 1960; children: Harry C., Angella S. Student, Wayne U., 1941-43; BS, U. Ill., 1947, MS, 1948; PhD, U. Wyo., 1971. Spl. rsch. asst. U. Ill., 1947—48; devel. elec. engr. Babcock & Wilcox Co., Alliance, Ohio, 1948—49; instr. elec. engring. Wayne State U., 1949—51; prin. elec. engr. Battelle Meml. Inst., Columbus, Ohio, 1951—52; prof. elec. engring. Air Force Inst. Tech., Wright-Patterson AFB, Ohio, 1952—96, prof. emeritus, 1997—. Guest lectr. Nat. Tech. U. Athens, 1958, 99, U. Patras, 1984, Weizmann Inst. Sci., 1984, U. Strathclyde, 1995, Binghampton U., 1996; sr. rsch. assoc. Air Force Rsch. Lab., 1981-97, sr. rsch. assoc. emeritus, 1997—. Author: (with J.J. D'Azzo) Feedback Control System Analysis and Synthesis, 1960, 2d edit., 1966; Principles of Electrical Engineering: Electric Circuits, Electronics, Energy Conversion, Control Systems Computers, 1968; Linear Control Systems Analysis and Design: Conventional and Modern, 1975, 4th edit., 1995, (with J.J. D'Azzo and Stuart N. Sheldon) Linear Control Systems and Analysis with MATLAB, 2003, 5d edit.; (with J. Lubelfeld) Outline of Pulse Circuits; (with G.B. Lamont) Digital Control Systems: Theory Software, Hardware, 1985, 2d edit., 1992; (with S. Rasmussen) Quantitative Feedback Theory: Fundamentals and Applications, 1999, also articles on automatic controls in profl. jours. in U.S., U.K. and Europe. Served with AUS, 1942-46. Recipient Outstanding Engr. award Dayton Area Nat. Engrs. Week, 1962, Outstanding Civilian Career Svc. award, 1997, Outstanding Engring. Alumnus award U. Wyo., 2002. Fellow IEEE; mem. Am. Soc. Engring. Edn., Am. Hellenic Edn. Progressive Assn., Tau Beta Pi, Eta Kappa Nu. Greek Orthodox. Home: 1125 Brittany Hills Dr Dayton OH 45459-1415 Office: Air Force Inst Tech 2950 Hobson Way WPAFB Dayton OH 45433-7765

HOUPT, JAMES EDWARD, lawyer; b. Calif., 1951; m. Leslie Ann Jones Houpt. BA with distinction, Calif. State U., Chico, 1976; JD cum laude, Harvard U., 1992. Bar: Va. 1992, D.C. 1992, U.S. Ct. Appeals (4th cir.) 1992, Md. 1993, Calif. 1997, U.S. Ct. Appeals (9th cir.) 1997. News dir. Sta. KNVR-FM, Paradise, Calif., 1978-80; anchor, reporter Sta. KHSL-AM-TV, Chico, 1980-85; sr. reporter Sta. KOLO-TV, Reno, 1985-89; assoc. Baker & Hostetler, Washington, 1992-97; assoc. of counsel, ptnr. Orrick, Herrington & Sutcliffe LLP, Sacramento, 1997—. Lectr. journalism Calif. State U., 1981, 85; adj. prof. law sch. U. Calif., Davis, vis. prof., 1999, 2000, reported cases Women's Resource Network v. Gourley, 2004, Thompson vs. Miller, 2003, In re Stone & Webster Inc., 2002, Berkla vs. Corel, 2002, Rosenaur vs. Scherer, 2001. Author: (booklet) Access to Electronic Records, 1990, The Libel Curtain: A Comparison of Canadian & American Libel Law, 1994, Going On-Line: Is the World Wide Web a Web for the Unwary?, 1996, Boarding a Moving Bus: Developing an Internet Risk Management Strategy, 1997, The Courts and the Internet: A Match Made in Hell?, 2000; contbr. articles to legal and gen. interest publs. With USN, 1970—74. Recipient Cert. of Merit, Calif.-Nev. AP TV-Radio Assn., 1983, 84, 86. Mem. ABA, Va. State Bar Assn., D.C. Bar, Calif. Bar Assn., VFW, Am. Legion. Avocations: photography, hiking, canoeing. Office: Orrick, Herrington & Sutcliffe LLP 400 Capitol Mall Ste 3000 Sacramento CA 95814-4497 Office Phone: 916-329-7949.

HOUPT, JEFFREY LYLE, psychiatrist, educator, former dean; b. Phila., Aug. 13, 1941; s. H. Lyle and Elizabeth (McAlpine) Houpt; m. Corinne A. Anderson, Dec. 28, 1964; children: Brian Jeffrey, Eric Robert. BS in Zoology, Wheaton Coll., 1963; MD, Baylor Coll. Medicine, 1967. Diplomate Am. Bd. Psychiatry and Neurology. Intern Boston City Hosp., 1967-68; resident in psychiatry Yale U., New Haven, 1968-71; staff med. officer Oak Knoll Naval Hosp., Oakland, Calif., 1971-73; adj. asst. prof. psychiatry Presbyn. Hosp., San Francisco, 1973-75; asst. prof. to prof. psychiatry Duke Med. Ctr., Durham, NC, 1975-83; prof. psychiatry, chmn. dept. Emory U. Sch. Medicine, Atlanta, 1983-90; dean Sch. Medicine Emory U., Atlanta, 1988-96; dean Sch. Medicine, vice chancellor for med. affairs U. N.C., Chapel Hill, 1997—2004; CEO U. N.C. Health Sys., Chapel Hill, 1998—2004; exec. coach, cons. to acad. health ctrs., 2004—. Author: The Importance of Mental Health Services for General Health Care, 1979; contbr. articles to med. jours. Lt. comdr. USN, 1971-73 Fellow Am. Coll. Psychiatry (pres.), Am. Psychiat. Assn. Home: 51319 Eastchurch Chapel Hill NC 27517-8302 Office: U NC at Chapel Hill CB # 7000 Chapel Hill NC 27599-7000 Office Phone: 919-942-8943. E-mail: jhoupt01@bellsouth.net.

HOURCADE, JACK JOSEPH, special education educator; b. New Orleans, Jan. 12, 1953; s. Joseph Peter and Emelie Marie (Le Blanc) H.; m. Carol Lynn Gentry, May 30, 1977; 1 child, Michael Jay. BA, U. Southwestern La., Lafayette, 1974; MEd, U. Ariz., 1975; PhD, U. Mo., 1979. Behavioral specialist The Children's Ctr., Orlando, Fla., 1975-76; teaching asst. U. Mo., Columbia, 1976-79; prof. Ea. Ky. U., Richmond, 1979-82, La. Tech. U., Ruston, 1982-87, Boise (Idaho) State U., 1987—. Assoc. editor Teaching Exceptional Children, Washington, 1986—. Contbr. articles to profl. jours. Gregory doctoral fellow U. Mo., 1975; named Outstanding Young Man of Am., 1983, Researcher of Yr. La. Tech. U., 1986. Mem. Council for Exceptional Children, Am. Assn. Mental Deficiency, Assn. Persons with Severe Handicaps. Democrat. Avocations: composing music, audio recording. Home: 418 W Mayfair Ct Boise ID 83706-4361 Office: Boise State U Dept Tchr Edn 1910 University Dr Dept Tchr Boise ID 83725-0399

HOUSE, CHARLETTA, librarian; b. Mobile, Ala., July 9, 1937; d. Charlie and Nevada (Travis) H. BS, Ala. State U., 1959; MLS, U.Md., 1973; MEd, Salisbury State U., 1993. Acquisitions asst. libr. Ala. A&M Libr., Normal, Ala., 1963-68; asst. libr. circulation dept. U. Md. Eastern Shore, Princess Anne, 1968-71, head circulation dept., 1972-83; circulation, reference libr. Salisbury (Md.) State U., 1984-86, reference, spl. collection libr., 1986—. Mem. Wicomico County Commn. of Women, Dem. Club of Wicomico County. Mem. AAUW, LWV, NAACP, Md. Libr. Assn., The Links, Inc., Kappa Delta Pi, Delta Sigma Theta Sorority, Inc. Methodist. Avocation: reading. Office: Salisbury Univ Blackwell Libr 1101 Camden Ave Salisbury MD 21801-6860

HOUSE, DAVID C., diversified financial services company executive; BS in Bus. Admin., U. Minn. Sales, mktg. Procter & Gamble, 1972—83; v.p., gen. mgr., client mgmt. Majers Corp., 1983—87; v.p. sales, mktg. PepsiCo U.S.A., 1987—89; sr. v.p., sales, mktg., operations Reebok Internat., Inc., 1989—93; sr. v.p., sales and field mktg. Am. Express, U.S. Establishment Svcs. Group, 1993—95, pres., 1995—2000; group pres. Am. Express Co., Global Network & Establishment Svcs., Travelers Cheque, N.Y.C., NY, 2000—. Co-chmn. Am. Express Diversity Coun. Mem. HS Trask, The Harlem Children's Zone, N.Y.C. Mem.: The World Travel & Tourism Coun. Office: Am Express Co World Fin Ctr 200 Vesey St New York NY 10285

HOUSE, FREDRICK CRISLER, allergist; b. Atlanta, 1941; MD, Med. Coll. Ga., 1968. Diplomate Am. Bd. Allergy & Immunology, Am. Bd. Internal Medicine. Intern Meml. Hosp., Savannah, Ga., 1968-69; resident Med. Coll. Ga., Augusta, 1969-71, asst. clin. prof. medicine; fellow in allergy and immunology Walter Reed Army Med. Ctr., Washington, 1972-74; with U. Hosp., Augusta. Fellow Am. Acad. Allergy and Immunology, Med. Assn. Ga., Southeastern Allergy Assn. Office: 3646 Wheeler Rd Augusta GA 30909-6519

HOUSE, JAMES STEPHEN, sociological social psychologist, educator; b. Phila., Jan. 27, 1944; s. James Jr. and Virginia Miller (Sturgis) H.; m. Wendy Fisher, May 13, 1967; children: Jeff, Erin. BA, Haverford Coll., 1965; PhD, U. Mich., 1972. From. instr. to assoc. prof. sociology Duke U., Durham, NC, 1970-78; assoc. prof. sociology/assoc. rsch. scientist Survey Rsch. U. Mich., Ann Arbor, 1978-82, assoc. chair dept. sociology, 1981-84, prof. sociology, rsch. prof. Survey Rsch. Ctr., 1982—, chair dept. sociology, 1986-90, dir. Survey Rsch. Ctr., Inst. Social Rsch., 1991-2001. Author: Work Stress and Social Support, 1981; co-editor: Sociological Perspectives on Social Psychology, 1995, A Telescope on Society, 2004; assoc. editor Social Psychology Quar., 1988-91, Jour. Health & Social Behavior, 1997-2000, Internat. Ency. of the Social and Behavioral Scis., 2001; contbr. chpts. to books and articles to profl. jours. Guggenheim fellow, 1986-87. Fellow: AAAS, Soc. Behavioral Medicine, Am. Acad. Arts and Scis.; mem.: Soc. for Epidemiol. Rsch., Soc. for Psychol. Study of Social Issues, Acad. Behavioral Medicine Rsch., Am. Sociol. Assn., Inst. Medicine of NAS. Office: Univ Mich Inst Social Rsch PO Box 1248 Ann Arbor MI 48106-1248 Office Phone: 734-764-6526. Business E-Mail: jimhouse@umich.edu.

HOUSE, JENNIFER LYNN, school librarian; b. Lima, Peru, Oct. 18, 1955; d. John Howard and Mary Virginia House. MS in Early Childhood Edn., E. Tex. State U. Cert. Irlen Inst., 2002. Kindergarten ESL tchr. John W. Carpenter Elem., Dallas, 1978—86, Stevens Pk. Elem., Dallas, 1986—2001, lead reading tchr., 2001—03, lead tchr., 2003—04, libr., 2004—. Named Tchr. of Yr., Stevens Pk. Elem., 1992—93, 2001—02; recipient Outstanding Svc. award, 2001—03; grantee, Jr. League, 1992—93. Mem.: Assn. Tex. Profl. Educators, Parent Tchr. Assn., Tex. Sch. Libr. Assn., Dallas Assn. Sch. Libr., Tex. Libr. Assn., Internat. Reading Assn. R-Liberal. Baptist. Avocations: mystery novels, singing. Office: Stevens Park Elem 2615 W Colorado Blvd Dallas TX 75211 Office Phone: 972-794-4206. Personal E-mail: diddle6@academicplanet.com. E-mail: jhouse@dallasisd.org.

HOUSE, JOHN WILLIAM, otolaryngologist; b. L.A., July 12, 1941; s. Howard and Helen House; m. Barbara Breithaupt, Mar. 28, 1993; children: Hans, Chris, Kurt, Steven, Kevin. BS, U. So. Calif., 1964, MD, 1967. Intern L.A. County-U. So. Calif. Med. Ctr., 1967-68; resident Glendale (Calif.) Adventist Hosp., 1971-72, L.A. County Med. Ctr., 1972-74; fellow Otologic Med. Group, L.A., 1974, pvt. practice, 1975—; pres. House Ear Inst., L.A., 1987—. Mem. editorial bd. Am. J. Otology, 1986—; contbr. articles to jours. in field. Admissions com. interviewer, U. So. Calif. Sch. Medicine, Los Angeles, 1976—; mem. Los Angeles County Sheriff's Res. Med. Co. Capt. U.S. Army, 1969-71. Recipient Hocks Meml. award Am. Tinnitus Assn., 1988; named Tchr. of Yr., U. So. Calif. Family Practice Dept., 1987. Fellow Am. Acad. Otolaryngology/Head and Neck Surgery; mem. AMA, Am. Neurotology Soc. (program chmn. 1976—, pres. 1998-99), Am. Otol. Soc. (past pres.), Triologic Soc., Am. Soc. Mil. Otolaryngologists, Pan-Am. Assn. Otorhinolaryngology Broncho Esophagology, Jonathan Club (Los Angeles). Avocations: skiing, computers, running, swimming. Office: House Ear Clinic Inc 2100 W 3rd St Fl 1 Los Angeles CA 90057-1922 Office Phone: 213-483-9530.

HOUSE, JULIA K., secondary school educator, music educator; B of Music in Vocal Performance, U. Montevallo, 1975; MusM in Choral Lit. & Conducting, U. South Fla., 1997. Edn. cert. Fla. State U., 1991. Dir. promotion and devel. WKGC-FM Gulf Coast Coll., Panama City, Fla., 1978—82; dir. promotions WPAP-FM, 1983—84; case worker Dept. Human Resource Svcs., 1984—89; dir. ch. choir Messiah Luth. Ch., 1984—98; tchr. music Bay High Sch., 1989—. Dir., founder Emerald Coast Chorale, Panama City, 1998—. Mem.: Music Educators Nat. Conf., Am. Choral Dirs. Assn., Fla. Vocal Assn., Internat. Soc. Music Edn. Avocations: music, travel, gardening. Office: Bay High Sch 1200 Harrison Ave Panama City FL 32401

HOUSE, KAREN ELLIOTT, publishing executive, editor, journalist; b. Matador, Tex., Dec. 7, 1947; d. Ted and Bailey Elliott; m. Arthur House, Apr. 5, 1975 (div. Sept. 1983); m. Peter Kann, June 4, 1984; children: Hillary, Petra, Jason, Jade. BJ, U. Tex., 1970; postgrad. Inst. Politics, Harvard U. Edn. reporter Dallas Morning News, 1970-71, with Washington bur., 1971-74; regulatory corr. Wall Street Jour., Washington, 1974-75, energy and agr. corr., 1975-78, diplomatic corr., 1978-84, fgn. editor N.Y.C., 1984-89; v.p., Internat. Group Dow Jones & Co., 1989-95, pres. Internat. Group, 1995—, sr. v.p., pub. Wall St. Jour., 2002—. Bd. dirs. Rand Corp.; mem. adv. bd. Ctr. Strategic Internat. Studies; dir. Coun. on Foriegn Rels. Trustee Boston U. Recipient Edward Weintal award for Diplomatic Reporting, Georgetown U., 1980-81, Edwin Hood award for Diplomatic Reporting Nat. Press Club, 1982, Disting. Achievement award U. So. Calif., 1984, Pulitzer prize for Internat. Reporting, 1984, Overseas Press Club Bob Considine award, 1984, 88; Harvard fellow, 1982; named one of most powerful women, Forbes mag., 2005. Fellow Nat. Acad. Arts and Scis. Office: Dow Jones & Co 200 Liberty St Fl 9 New York NY 10281-1003 E-mail: karen.house@dowjones.com.*

HOUSE, ROBERT WILLIAM, music educator; b. Bristow, Okla., Nov. 28, 1920; s. Richard Morton and Elizabeth (Swartz) H.; m. Esther Jean Hawkins, June 5, 1943 (dec. Oct. 1977); children: R. Edmund, Richard M., Russell L., Kathryn M.; m. Mary Elaine Thornton Wallace, Mar. 12, 1979. BFA, Okla. State U., 1941; MusM, Eastman Sch. Music, 1942; EdD, U. Ill., 1954. Asst. prof. band, cello, wind instruments Nebr. State Coll., Kearney, 1946-55; prof. orch., cello and music edn., chmn. music dept. U. Minn., Duluth, 1955-67; dir. Sch. Music, So. Ill. U., Carbondale, 1967-76; head music dept. East Tex. State U., 1976-84, orch. dir., 1984-89. Cons. Ednl. Testing Service, 1962-66 Prin. cellist, Duluth Symphony, 1955-67, Mesquite Symphony, 1987—, N.E. Tex. Symphony Orch., 1989-98; author: (with Charles Leonhard) Foundations and Principles of Music Education, 1959, rev., 1972, Instrumental Music for Today's Schools, 1965, Administration in Music Education, 1973; mem. editorial bd.: Jour. of Research in Music Edn, 1958-70; mng. editor: The Ill. Music Educator, 1975-76. Served with AUS, 1942-46, ETO. Mem. Nat. Assn. Schs. Music (panel evaluators 1966-76, chmn. com. on tchr. edn. in music 1963-67, chmn. com. on ethics 1970-72, com. on research and publs. 1973-75, chmn. com. nominations 1980-81), Music Educators Research Council (nat. chmn. 1958-60), Music Educators Nat. Conf. (mem. publs. planning com. 1972-82, chmn. 1976-82, pres.-elect North Central div. 1974-76, mem. com. for advancement music edn. 1976-80), Am. String Tchrs. Assn. (sec. Tex. unit 1978-80) Home: 3020 Ridge Rd Rockwall TX 75032

HOUSE, STEPHEN EUGENE, information systems consultant; b. Pueblo, Colo., July 18, 1951; s. Floyd Eugene and Jewell (Brame) H.; m. Cheryl Virginia Ashby, Mar. 15, 1975; children: Deborah Lynne, Mark Stephen. BS in Bus. Info. Systems, West Coast U., 1992. Programmer Calif. Sch. Employees Assn., San Jose, 1976-79; programmer/analyst Marysville (Calif.) Joint Unified Sch. Dist., 1979-80; tech. lead Mervyns, Hayward, Calif., 1980-85, Lucky Stores, Inc., Dublin, Calif., 1985-87; project lead Northrop, Pica Rivera, Calif., 1987-92; tech. cons. Computer Profls. Inc., Charlotte, N.C., 1992-97; mem. profl. staff Compuware Corp., Charlotte, 1997—.

HOUSE, W(ILLIAM) MICHAEL, lawyer; b. Birmingham, Ala., Dec. 19, 1945; s. B. William and Kathryn Regina (Cantrell) H.; children: Tanner, Slade, Kate. BS, Auburn U., 1968; JD, U. Ala., 1971. Bar: Ala. 1971, D.C. 1992. Legal asst. to Congressman James M. Collins, Washington, 1971-72; atty. Ala. Supreme Ct., Montgomery, 1972-76; assoc. Odom, Argo, Enslen, Montgomery, 1976-79; chief of staff Sen. Howell Heflin, Washington, 1979-86; of counsel McNair Law Firm, Washington, 1986-88; ptnr. Shaw, Pittman et al, Washington, 1988-91, Hogan & Hartson LLP, Washington, 1991—, chair legis. group. Pres. Ala. Young Lawyers, 1976; chmn. Ala. Citizens Conf., Ala. State Cts., 1974-75; co-chmn. Potomac Group Dem. Nat. Com., 1987-93; mem. bus. adv. coun. Auburn Sch. Bus., 1990-93; mem.

pres.'s cabinet U. Ala., 2000—. Capt. U.S. Army, 1971—80. Named Ala. Outstanding Young Man, Ala. JC's, 1979. Mem. Ala. Bar Assn. (award of merit 1974), Am. Judicature Soc. (bd. dirs.), Soc. Internat. Bus. Fellows (bd. dirs.), Pi Kappa Alpha (bd. dirs. Meml. Found. 1980-86). Avocations: tennis, reading. Office: Hogan & Hartson LLP 555 13th St NW Ste 800E Washington DC 20004-1161 Office Phone: 202-637-5636. Office Fax: 202-637-5910. Business E-Mail: wmhouse@hhlaw.com.

HOUSE-HENDRICK, KAREN SUE, nursing consultant; b. San Francisco, July 16, 1958; d. Mathas Dean and Marilyn Frances (Weigand) House., Casa Loma Coll., 1985; AS in Nursing, SUNY at Albany, 1987. Psychiat. charge nurse Woodview Calabasas (Calif.) Hosp., 1985-87, Treatment Ctrs. Am., Van Nuys, Calif., 1987-88; cons., RN Valley Village Devel. Ctr., Reseda, Calif., 1988; plastic surg. nurse George Sanders, M.D., Encino, Calif., 1986—; nurse New Image Found., 1989—97, Mid Valley Youth Ctr., 1991—2000; dir. nursing Encino Surgicenter (Sanders), 1992—. Dir. nursing Devel. Tng. Svcs. for Devel. Disabled, 1988—95; nurse cons. New Horizons for Developmentally Disabled, 1993, Exceptional Children's Found., 2001—; nurse specialist, collagen and Botox trainer, 1998—. Instr., vol. ARC. Recipient Simi Valley Free Clinic Scholarship. Mem. Encino C. of C. Office: 16633 Ventura Blvd Ste 110 Encino CA 91436-1834 Office Phone: 818-981-3333. Business E-Mail: karen@drsanders.com. E-mail: khouse6783@aol.com.

HOUSEHOLDER, LARRY, state official, small business owner; m. Taundra Householder; children: Derek, Adam, Matthew, Nathan, Luke. Grad. in polit. sci., Ohio U., 1982. Commr. Perry County; Dist. 78 Ohio Ho. Rep., 2001—. Bd. chmn. Tri-County CAA; mem. L.F.C.P. Solid Waste Bd., Perry County Planning Commn. Coach Youth Baseball. Named Hon. State farmer, 1995. Mem.: NFIB, C.of C., Rules and Ref. Com. (chmn.), 33d Degree Scottish Rite, Aladdin Temple Shrine (amb.), Moose, Eagles, Lions, Grange, Farm Bur. Achievements include Speaker Householder running for state representative in 1996 where he has worked diligently to promote economic development, infrastructure, and improved education.

HOUSEKNECHT, STEPHEN, artist, educator; b. Batavia, N.Y., Nov. 15, 1951; s. William K. and Marianne Houseknecht. A. A. Humanities, Genesee C.C., Batavia, NY, 1972; BA in Art, Buffalo State Coll., Buffalo, NY, 1975; MFA in Photography, SUNY at Buffalo, Buffalo, NY, 1980. Vis. rsch. curator and project developer of the houseknecht collection of photography NY State Mus., Albany, NY, 1991—92; instr. of photography and art history Genesee C.C., Batavia, NY, 1988—90; lectr., fine arts photography Buffalo State Coll., Buffalo, 1992—. Photographic history / exhibition, Genesee County History Dept/ Printing Glass Plate Negative Collection, phase 1 (NY State Coun. of the Arts Decentralization Program, 2002), photographic exhibition, Persistence Of Vision: Extended Family Album (NY State Coun. of the Arts Decentralization Program, 1993), rephotographic survey/ photo exhibition, Genesee: Then and Again, A Hundred Year Photographic Perspective (NY State Coun. of the Arts Decentralization Program, 1991), photographic exhibition, Persistence Of Vision: Extended Family Album (The NY State Legislature Local Initative Grant (Natural Heritage Trust), 1990), Persistence Of Vision: Extended Family Album A First Local Exhibition (NY State Coun. of the Arts Decentralization Program, 1989), exhibited in group shows at Schweinfurth Meml. Art Ctr., Auburn, NY, 2003, 80th Ann. Spring Show, Erie Arts Mus., Pa., 2003, Buffalo State Fine Arts and Design Dept. Exhbn., 1998—, 73d Ann. Spring Show, Erie Arts Mus., Pa., 1996, 75th Ann. Spring Show, Erie Arts Mus., Pa., 1998, Buffalo Artists Studio, 1996, 45th Ann. Western NY Exhbn., 1994, NY State Mus., 1994, Burchfield-Penny Regional Arts Ctr., Buffalo, 1993, Fall Mus. Faculty Show, 1992, Spring Mus. Faculty Show, 1992, 1992, Mus. of the Hudson Highlands, Cornwall-on-Hudson, NY, 1989, AAO Gallery, Buffalo, Foto Gallery, NYC, 1983, 39th Ann. Western NY Exhbn, Albright Knox Art Gallery, Buffalo, 1982, Artist's Gallery, 1982, 58th Ann. Spring Show, Erie Arts Mus., Pa., 1981, Keenan Ctr., Lockport, NY, 1980, Artist's Gallery, 1980, Alamo Gallery, SUNY at Buffalo, 1979, AAO Gallery, Buffalo, 1979, Andromeda Gallery Ltd., 1976, Educated Eye, Finerline Gallery, 2004, Made in N.Y., 2004, Schweinfurth Meml. Gallery, Auburn, N.Y., 2004, Arsa Artists Collection Albright Knox Gallery, 2004, The Weeks Gallery's Global Collection of Photography, Jamestown, N.Y., 2005, Represented in permanent collections The Collector's Gallery Albright Knoex Gallery, N.Y.S. Mus., Albany, Weeks Gallery, Jamestown CC. Avocations: working with WWII aircraft, working with chow chows. Home: 10895 Warner Rd Darien Center NY 14040 Office: Upton Hall 114 Buffalo State College 1300 Elmwood Ave Buffalo NY 14222 Office Phone: 716-878-6635. Business E-Mail: houseksj@buffalostate.edu.

HOUSEL, DAVID, athletic director; b. York, Oct. 18, 1946; m. Susan McIntosh. BA, Auburn U., 1969. News editor Huntsville (Ala.) News, 1969-70; from adminstrv. asst. athletic office Auburn (Ala.) U., 1970-72, instr. journalism, advisor newspaper, 1972-80, asst. dir. sports info., dir., asst. athletic dir., 1980-94, athletic dir., 1994—. Author: Saturdays to Remember, From the Desk of David Housel--A Collection of Auburn Stories. Mem. Phi Gamma Delta, Omicron Delta Kappa. Office: Auburn Univ Athletic Dept PO Box 351 Auburn AL 36831-0351

HOUSEMAN, ANN ELIZABETH LORD, educational administrator; b. New Orleans, Mar. 21, 1936; d. Noah Louis and Florence Marguerite (Coyle) Lord; m. Evan Kenny Houseman, June 25, 1960; children: Adrienne Ann, Jeannette Louise, Yvonne Elizabeth. BA, Barnard Coll., 1957; MA, Columbia U., 1962; PhD, U. Del., 1969. State supr. reading Dept. Pub. Instrn., Del., 1977-79; prin. M.L. King Jr. Elem. Sch., Wilmington, Del., 1979-80; adminstr., exec. dir. Del. State Arts Coun., Wilmington, 1980-84; acting dir. Divsn. Hist. and Cultural Affairs State of Del., Wilmington, 1983-84; prin. P.S. du Pont Intermediate Sch., Wilmington, 1984-91; dir. Mid.-Atlantic States Arts Consortium, Balt., 1980-84. Adv. bd. Rockwood Mus., Wilmington, 1981-94; bd. dirs. Opera Del., Inc., Wilmington, 1984-97, pres., 1991-93, dir. devel., 1994-95, coord. adv. bd., 1996; bd. dirs. Del. Theatre Co., Wilmington, 1984-90; bd. dirs. Aux. Alfred I. duPont Hosp. for Children, 1997-2004, pres., 2000-01. Republican. Presbyterian. Business E-Mail: houseman@udel.edu.

HOUSEMAN, GERALD L., political science professor, writer; b. Marshalltown, Iowa, Apr. 12, 1939; s. Lawrence D. and Mary N. (Smith) H.; m. Penelope Lyon, Feb. 11, 1961 (dec. 1994); children: Christopher, Elisabeth, Victoria; m. Juliana Sujata, 1999. BA, Calif. State U., Hayward, 1965, MA, 1967; PhD, U. Ill., 1971. Asst. prof. polit. sci. Ind. U., Ft. Wayne, 1971-76, assoc. prof., 1976-82, prof., 1982-2000; ret., 2000. Vis. prof. New Coll., Durham, Eng., 1975-76, Calif. State Polytech. U., San Luis Obispo, 1983-84, U. Calif., Irvine, 1984-85, St. Mary's Coll. Calif., 1985-86, Ind. U. Coop. Program in Malaysia, 1989-90, 94, 95, Fulbright Program, Indonesia, 1993-94, Malaysia, 2000-01. Author: (with H. Mark Roelofs) The American Political System 1983, G.D.H. Cole, 1979, The Right of Mobility, 1979, City of the Right, Urban Applications of American Political Thought, 1982, State and Local Government: The New Battleground, 1986; (with Michael W. McCann) Judging the Constitution, 1989, Questioning the Law in Corporate Americia: Agenda for Reform, 1993, America and the Pacific Rim: Coming to Terms with New Realities, 1995, Researching Indonesia: A Guide to Political Analysis, 2004. Mem. Transit Authority Bd., Ft. Wayne, 1973-75; city planning commr., 1982-83; Dem. candidate 4th dist. Ind. U.S. Ho. of Reps., 1996. With USMC, 1954-57. Grantee NSF, 1970, Ford Found., 1973, 74, NEH, 1977-78, 87, Ind. U. fellow 1973, 74, 77; recipient Wildavsky award Best Pub. Policy Article of Yr., Policy Studies Orgn., 1994. Mem Am. Polit. Sci. Assn. (seminar grantee 1980, 81), Asian Studies Assn., Ind. Polit. Sci. Assn. (pres. 1979-80). Address: 4706 S Thor St Spokane WA 99223-7115 E-mail: Houseman412@aol.com.

HOUSER, CONSTANCE W., writer, artist; b. Goshen, N.Y., Aug. 16; d. Charles A. and Josephine E. Woodward; m. James C. Houser, Sept. 21, 1972; children: J. Jackson, Katrina J. AA, Palm Beach C.C., Fla., 1970; BFA, Fla. Atlantic U., 1971. News, edit., features Palm Beach Post-Times, Miami Herald, Fla., 1954—62; columnist, book reviewer Palm Beach Times, Lake Worth News, Fla., 1962—69; art reviewer Art Mags., N.Y.C., 1960—70; art features, art profiles Art Voices South, Fla., 1960—70; artist profiles Art News, 1970—79. Owner 4 Points Photo Ctr., West Palm Beach, Fla., 1958—69; art tchr. for srs., computer tutor, judge art and photo competitions. Over 10 one-woman shows, Exhibited in group shows at Gallery Camino, Real, Fla., Peter Rudolph Galleries, N.Y.; contbr. articles to profl. mags. and newspapers. Mem. Hobe Sound Art League, Fla., 1996—2000, Hobe Sound Women's Club, Fla., 1996—2000; v.p. Rep. Club, West Palm Beach, Fla., 1960—80. Recipient awards, Norton Gallery of Art, West Palm Beach, 1967, Soc. of the 4-Arts, 1970—74, Art Competition awards, Hortt Mus., 1974—79. Mem.: AAUW, Nat. Soc. Arts and Letters, Gallery Players (bd. dirs., pres., v.p.), 4-Points Photo Club (pres., Woman of Distinction nominee 2004). Republican. Episcopalian. Home: 8338 SE Coconut St Hobe Sound FL 33455

HOUSER, DONALD RUSSELL, mechanical engineering educator, consultant; b. River Falls, Wis., Sept. 2, 1941; s. Elmont Ellsworth and Helen (Bunker) H.; m. Colleen Marie Collins, Dec. 30, 1967; children: Kelle, Kerri, Joshua. BS, U. Wis., 1964, MS, 1965, PhD, 1969. Registered profl. engr., Ohio. Instr. U. Wis., Madison, 1967-68; from asst. prof. to prof. Ohio State U., Columbus, 1968—2003, emeritus prof., 2003—, dir. Gear Dynamics and Gear Noise Rsch. Lab., 1979—, dir. Ctr. for Automotive Rsch., 1994-99. V.p. Gear Rsch. Inst., State Coll., Pa., 1990-99. Author: Gear Noise, 1991; contbg. editor Sound and Vibration mag., 1988-96; assoc. editor Jour. Mech. Design, 1993-94; mem. adv. bd. JSME Internat. Jour., 1996-2000; contbr. articles to profl. jours. Elder St. Andrews Presbyn. Ch., Columbus, 1972-75. Fellow ASME (legis. liaison Ohio coun. 1976-80, Century II medallion 1980); mem. Am. Gear Mfrs. Assn. (acad.), Soc. Automotive Engrs., Am. Helicopter Soc. Roman Catholic. Achievements include development of technology for measuring gear transmission error under load. Office: Ohio State U 206 W 18th Ave Columbus OH 43210-1189 Office Phone: 614-292-5860. Business E-Mail: houser.4@osu.edu.

HOUSER, DOUGLAS GUY, lawyer; b. Oregon City, Oreg., July 11, 1935; s. Roy B. and Shirley (Knight) H.; m. Lucy Anne Latham, Sept. 1, 1961; children: Brooks Bonham, Bradley Knight, Anne Elizabeth. BA, Willamette U., 1957; JD, Stanford, 1960. Bar: Oreg. 1960. Practice in Portland, 1961—; ptnr. Bullivant, Houser PC, 1965—. Chmn. com. on continuing legal edn. Oreg. State Bar, 1969-70, chmn. com. jud. adminstrn., 1975, bd. bar examiners, 1970-72, mem. bd. bar govs., 1977-80, treas., 1979-80; judge protem Circuit Ct., 1973-77; gen. counsel NIKE, Inc., 1972-84, dir, 1972—; bd. overseers RAND Inst. for Civil Justice; gen. counsel Soc. Registered Profl. Adjusters; former gen. counsel Pacific N.W. Life Ins. Co.; lectr. Contbr. articles to profl. publs. Legal adviser Portland Sch. Dist. 1 Race and Edn. Com., 1963-64; mem. Eagle bd. Columbia-Pacific council Boy Scouts Am., 1962-70; past v.p., treas., bd. dirs. Waverley Children's Home; trustee Willamette U.; bd. visitors Stanford U. Sch. Law, 1978-80, 8991, 96-98, 98-2000, Willamette U. Law Sch., 1986; chmn. Oreg. State Jud. Fitness Commn., 1980—. Fellow Am. Bar Found. (life), Am. Coll. Trial Lawyers, Internat. Acad. Trial Lawyers; mem. ABA (past chmn. tort and ins. practice sect.), Multnomah County Bar Assn. (chmn. com. continuing legal edn. 1977), Oreg. Assn. Def. Counsel (dir. 1972-76, pres. 1976-77), Def. Research Inst. (bd. dirs. 1990-93, sec.-treas. 1993—), Fedn. Def. and Corp. Counsel (chmn. bd. dirs. 1991-92), Am. Judicature Soc. (bd. dirs. 1985-88), Internat. Assn. Def. Counsel, Stanford Law Soc. Oreg., Am. Law Inst., Nat. Jud. Coll. (adv. coun. 1990—), Willamette U. Alumni Assn. (pres. 1972-74, bd. trustees 1971—), Beta Theta Pi, Phi Delta Phi, Omicron Delta Kappa, Pi Gamma Mu. Republican. Episcopalian (trustee Diocese Oreg. 1972-75, sr. warden). Clubs: Waverly Country, Arlington, Multnommah Athletic. Home: 11621 SW Military Ln Portland OR 97219 Office: Bullivant Houser Bailey PC Portland OR 97204-2089 Office Phone: 503-228-6351. E-mail: doug.heuser@bullivant.com.

HOUSER, HAROLD BYRON, epidemiologist; b. North Liberty, Ind., Nov. 22, 1921; s. Edgar Allen and Gladys Chloe (Stillson) H.; m. Clara Jane Goin, Sept. 18, 1944; children: Cristene, Edgar, John, Susan, James. AB, Ind. U., 1942, MD, 1944. Intern U.S. Marine Hosp., New Orleans, 1944-45; resident Crile VA Hosp., Cleve., 1947-49; asst. prof. medicine SUNY, Syracuse, 1952-58; asst. prof. medicine and community health Case Western Res. U., 1958-64, assoc. prof., 1965-74, prof. epidemiology, 1974-92, prof. emeritus, 1992—, chmn. dept. biometry, 1975-85, chmn. dept. epidemiology and biostats., 1985-92; cons. in field. Contbr. numerous articles to profl. jours. Served with U.S. Army, 1945-47, 49-52. Recipient Group Lasker award Am. Pub. Health Assn., 1954, Disting. Civilian award Dept. Def., 1973 Fellow Infectious Diseases Soc.; mem. Am. Epidemiol. Soc. (pres. 1991). Home: #CS 9103 5950 N Fountains Ave Tucson AZ 85704 E-mail: halhous@aol.com.

HOUSER, JIM (JAMES COWING HOUSER JR.), artist; b. Dade City, Fla., Nov. 12, 1928; s. James C. and Martha (Futch) H.; m. Constance Woodward; children: James Jackson, Katrina J. BS, Ringling Sch. Art, 1949; BFA, Fla. So. Coll., 1951; postgrad., Art Inst. Chgo., 1952; MFA, U. Fla., 1953. Represented by Rudolph Galleries, Coral Gables, Fla., 1964—90, Woodstock, NY, 1964-90; exhibited Grand Ctrl. Moderns Gallery, NYC, 1966—; represented by Gallery Camino Real, Boca Raton, Fla., 1972—, David Findlay Galleries, NYC, 1974-84, Sherry French Gallery, 1985. Sr. instr. art Ky. Wesleyan Coll., Owensboro, 1954-60, art chmn., 1964-70, dir. art gallery, 1974-91; art instr. Palm Beach C.C.; artist Notre Dame U., 1970; Cornell U., NYU, 1971: judge local and nat. art competitions; lectr. in field. Exhibited in group shows at Dept. State Spl. Exhbn., Washington, 1967—, one-man shows include Gallery Camino Real, 1972—89, 1999, 2003, Brevard C.C., 1973, Orlando, Fla., 1974, Cocoa, Valencia C.C., David Findlay Galleries, NYC, 1976, 1978, 1981, 1983, Northwood Inst., 1986, Palm Beach C.C., 1988, others, exhibited in group shows at Major Fla. Artist Invitational Exhbn., Sarasota, Fla., 1981—92, No. Miami Mus. Art Ctr., No. Miami, Fla., 1985, So. Fla. Invitational Exhbn., 1991, Ft. Lauderdale Mus. Art, Men's Art Northwood U., West Palm Beach, Fla., 1994, Festival Internat. Peinture, Cagnes-sur-Mer, France, 2001, Represented in permanent collections Boca Raton Mus. Art, Notre Dame U., Cornell U., NYU, Palm Beach Soc. Four Arts, U. Miami, Bethlehem Art Ctr., Pa., Dulin Gallery Art, Tenn., Syracuse U., Owensboro Mus. Art, Ky., Hunt Knight, L.A.; author: (video texts) Color for the Artist, 1975. Selection com. Palm Beach Coun. Arts, 1987; art. rev. bd. scholarship awards Palm Beach Post-Times, 1982-87. Recipient Merit award, Ft. Lauderdale Mus., 1974, Atwater Kent award, 1977, 1989, Akston Found. award, 1977, Philip Hulitar award, 1982, Four Arts award, 1992—93, Soc. Four Arts, West Palm Beach, established Connie and Jim Houser award, Contempary Exhbn. Soc. Four Arts, 1996—2002. Mem.: Soc. of the Four Arts (Cert. of Appreciation 1996). Republican. Methodist. Avocations: music, photography, computer. Home and Office: 8338 SE Coconut St Hobe Sound FL 33455-2911

HOUSER, NATHAN, philosopher, educator; b. Auburn, Ind., May 10, 1944; s. Frank F. and Viola M. (Hose) Houser; m. Aleta Halme, Dec. 12, 1975; children: Jesse, Ezra. PhD, U. Waterloo, 1985. Asst. prof. philosophy Ind. U., Indpls., 1986-91, assoc. prof. philosophy, 1991-97, prof. philosophy, 1997—, prof. Am. studies, 1997—, founding faculty mem. Sch. of Informatics, 2000. Dir. Peirce Edition Project, 1993—; dir. Inst. Am. Thought Charles S. Pierce Soc., 2003, pres. Asst. editor: Writings of Charles S. Peirce, 1983—85, assoc. editor:, 1985—93, gen. editor:, 1993—; co-editor: Essential Peirce, 1992, vol. 2, 1998, Studies in the Logic of Charles Sanders Peirce, 1997; mem. adv. bd. Modern Logic Pub., 1993—. Fulbright-Hays fellow, 1978, Devel. grantee, Prince Charitable Trusts, 1996, Collaborative Rsch. grantee, NEH, 1997, 1999, 2001, 2003. Mem.: Assn. Documentary Editing, Semiotic Soc. Am., History Sci. Soc., Soc. Advancement Am. Philosophy, Am. Philos. Assn., Charles S. Peirce Soc. Office: CA545 IUPUI 425 University Blvd Indianapolis IN 46202-5148 Office Phone: 317-274-2173. E-mail: nhouser@iupui.edu.

HOUSER, RONALD EDWARD, lawyer, arbitrator, mediator; b. Fairbury, Nebr., Aug. 11, 1949; s. Edward Erle and Lois Charlotte (Dux) H.; m. Linda Marie Webber, June 13, 1971 (div. 1985); children: Angela Marie, Brian Edward, Darren James; m. Beatrice Virginia McMullen Bupp, July 24, 1993. DVM, U. Mo., 1974; MS, Ohio State U., 1979; JD, U. Ga., 1990. Bar: Ga. 1990, U.S. Dist. Ct. (mid., no. and so. dist.) Ga. 1990, U.S. Ct. Appeals (11th cir.) 1990, U.S. Ct. Mil. Appeals 1993, U.S. Supreme Ct. 1993. Asst. instr. Univ. Nebr., Lincoln, 1979-83; owner, mgr. Lincoln Animal Health Clinic, 1983-85; atty. Cook, Noell, Tolley, Bates & Michael, Athens, Ga., 1990—. Contbr. articles to profl. jours. Mem. Nebr. State Bd. Health, 1980-84. Mem. Nat. Lawyers Assn., Nebr. Vet. Med. Assn. (dist. pres. 1979-81), Christian Legal Soc., Res. Officers Assn., Am. Legion, Phi Alpha Delta, Sigma Xi. Avocations: sports, reading, gardening. Home: PO Box 502 Athens GA 30603-0502 Office: Cook Noell Tolley Bates & Michael LLP 304 E Washington St Athens GA 30601-2751

HOUSE-SOREMEKUN, BESSIE, political science professor; b. Lanett, Ala. d. William Penn House Sr. and Jo Frances House; m. Maurice Soremekun, July 14, 2001; 1 child, Adrianna Midamba. BA Magna Cum Laude in English, Huntingdon Coll., 1978; MA in internat. studies, U. Denver, 1980, PhD in internat. studies, 1988. Asst. prof. to assoc. prof. Kent State U., Dept of Polit. Sci., Kent, Ohio, 1989—. Exec. dir., founder Ctr. for the Study and Develop. of Minority Bus., Kent, Ohio, 2003. Author: Confronting the Odds: African American Entrepreneurship in Cleveland, Ohio, 2002 (Henry Howe Book Award, 2003); co-editor: African Market Women and Economic Power: The Role of Women in African Economic Development, 1995; author: Class Development and Gender Inequality in Kenya, 1990. Grantee, Cleve. Found., 1999—2002, Ohio Bd. of Regents, 1997—99, Ohio Urban U. Program, 1995, 2000. Mem.: Assn. of Afro Life and Hist., African Studies Assn., Links, Inc., Kent Chpt., Phi Beta Delta, Alpha Beta, Sigma, Sigma, Sigma. Democrat. Methodist. Avocations: reading, writing books, poetry. Home: PO Box 22226 Beachwood OH 44122 Office: Kent State U Kent OH 44242 E-mail: bhouse@kent.edu.

HOUSEWORTH, RICHARD COURT, state agency administrator; b. Harveyville, Kans., Jan. 18, 1928; s. Court Henry and Mabel (Lynch) H.; m. Laura Louise Jennings, Nov. 1, 1952; children: Louise, Lucile, Court. BS, U. Kans., 1950. Mgmt. trainee Lawrence Nat. Bank, Kans., 1951-52; pres. 1st Nat. Bank, Harveyville, 1952-55; exec. v.p. Ariz. Bank, Phoenix, 1955-87, cons., 1987-88; dir. Export-Import Bank of the US, Washington, 1988-91; alt. U.S. exec. dir. The Inter-American Devel. Bank, Washington, 1991-93; supt. of banks, Banking Dept. State of Ariz., 1993—. Past chmn. Conf. of State Bank Suprs., Washington; chmn. Fed. Fin. Instns. Examinations Coun., Washington, 2004. Past pres. Better Bus. Bur., Tucson; past chmn. bd. Pacific Coast Banking Sch. U. Wash.; past pres. Barrow Neurol. Inst. of St. Joseph's Hosp.; past chmn. Valley of the Sun Visitors and Conv. Bur. Served with U.S. Army, 1946-48. Recipient 1st Disting. Service award Scottsdale Jaycees, 1962 Mem. Ariz. C. of C. (1st pres., dir.), Tucson C. of C. (past pres.), Am. Inst. Banking (past pres. Maricopa chpt.), Ariz. Bankers Assn. (past pres.), Urban League of Phoenix (past chmn.), Paradise Valley Club, Met. Club, Phi Delta Theta. Republican. Episcopalian. Home: 5434 E Lincoln Dr # 83 Paradise Valley AZ 85253-4118 Office: Supt of Banks 2910 N 44th St Ste 310 Phoenix AZ 85018-7270 Office Phone: 602-255-4421. Business E-Mail: houseworth@azbanking.com.

HOUSEWRIGHT, DAVID W., writer; b. Minn., Feb. 1955; m. Renee Valois; 2 children. BA in Journalism and English, Coll. of St Thomas, 1977. Reporter, Albert Lea, Minn.; co-owner advt. agy.; instr., novel writing Univ. Minn. Author: Penance, 1995 (Edgar award, Best First Mystery, Mystery Writers of Am., 1996), Practice to Deceive, 1997 (Minn. Book award, 1998), Dearly Departed, 1999, Hard Ticket Home, 2004, Tin City, 2005. Mailing: c/o Alison Picard Agy PO Box 2000 Cotuit MA 02635 E-mail: housewrightvalois@comcast.net.*

HOUSH, E. WILLIAM, manufacturing executive; b. West Orange, N.J., Feb. 15, 1932; m. Margot Housh; 1 child, Donna. BS in Econs., Wharton Sch., U. Pa., 1954. Various positions IBM Corp., 1954—69; dir. info. and data processing systems IBM World Trade Corp., 1965—69; pres. Cybernetics World Trade Corp., 1969—71, Wright Line Inc. subs. Barry Wright Corp., Watertown, Worcester, Mass., 1971—. V.p. United Way, chmn. campaign, 1982; chmn. bd. dirs. Ctrl. New Eng. Coll. Tech.; bd. dirs. New Eng. Coun. Served with USAF, 1955—57. Mem.: Bus. and Instl. Furniture Mfrs. Assn. (dir.,), Ctrl. Mass. Employers Assn. (past chmn.), Worcester. Office: Hon Industries Inc 414 E 3rd St PO Box 1109 Muscatine IL 52761-7109

HOUSHIAR, BOBBIE KAY, language arts educator; b. Fort Smith, Ark., Nov. 28; d. Ernest and Virgil Straham. BA, Saginaw Valley State U., 1973; MA in Elem. Edn. Adminstrn., Cen. Mich. U., 1975, Cert. Gen. Edn. Adminstrn., 1978. Elem. tchr. Saginaw (Mich.) Pub. Schs., 1973-74, jr. high tchr., 1975-76, tchr. middle sch., 1983—; learning ctr. coord. Saginaw Valley State U., University Center, Mich., 1974-75, instr. reading, 1974-75; tchr. ESL Refugee Ctr. of Saginaw, 1982-83. Instr. ind. study Cen. Mich. U., Saginaw, 1988-90; tutor bilingual students Delta Coll., Saginaw, 1987-96; supr./student tchrs. Saginaw Pub. Schs., 1988—; oratorical/writing instr. Saginaw Pub. Schs., 1983—. Editor: Young Writers in Michigan, 1989. Vol. Saginaw County chpt. ARC, 1996-99; mem./vol. League of Cath. Women, Saginaw, 1976—. Recipient Recognition award Saginaw Infant Mortality Coalition award, Saginaw Cooperative Hosp., 1998, Educator of Yr. award, Saginaw Coop. Hosp., 1999, Excellence in Tchg. English Writing Skills award, Saginaw Bd. Edn., 2002, Accent on Achievement award, Saginaw Pub. Sch. Bd. of Edn., 2002, others. Mem. NEA, Saginaw Edn. Assn., Mich. Edn. Assn., Nat. Coun. Tchrs. of English, ASCD, Mich. Mid. Sch. Assn., Delta Sigma Theta. Democrat. Roman Catholic. Avocations: reading, student mentor, tennis, swimming, horses. Office: South Middle Sch 224 N Elm St Saginaw MI 48602-2651 Office Phone: 989-791-4145. Personal E-mail: slamak67@charter.net. Business E-Mail: bhoushiar@spsd.net.

HOUSHMAND, ALI A., academic administrator; BA in Math., U. Essex, 1981, MS in Math. Stats., 1983; PhD in Indsl. and Ops. Engring., U. Mich., 1989. Assoc. prof. indsl. engring. U. Cin., dir. grad. studies, dir. student assessment; assoc. provost Drexel U., 2000—04, dean, 2001—04, interim provost, 2004—. Office: Office of the Provost Drexel Univ 3001 Market St Philadelphia PA 19104 Business E-Mail: pad32@drexel.edu.

HOUSKA-GREEN, KATHLEEN ANN, marketing professional, public relations executive; b. Hinsdale, Ill., May 15, 1974; d. Frank Stanley and Joan Margaret (McCarthy) Houska; m. Patrick E. Green, Aug. 22, 1998; children: Ryan F. Green, Colin D. Green. BA in Orgnl./Corp. Comms. with honors, No. Ill. U., 1996. Intern Marcy Monyek and Assocs., Chgo., summer 1995, asst. mktg. assoc., 1996-97; pub. rels. coord. D.C. Systems, Oakbrook Terrace, Ill., 1997-99; mktg. comms. specialist Comark, Inc., Bloomingdale, Ill., 1999—2000; pres. Green Creative Svcs., Geneva, Ill., 2000—. Contbr. articles to profl. publs. Vol. Students with Disabilities, No. Ill. U., 1995-96. Mem.: Bus. Mktg. Assn. (mem. pub. rels. com.), Women in Comms., Inc. (v.p. programming 1994—95, pres. 1995—96). Avocations: Irish dancing, running, reading, writing, biking. Home: 39W372 W Mallory Dr Geneva IL 60134

HOUSTON, ALLAN WADE, professional basketball player; b. Louisville, Apr. 4, 1971; s. Wade and Alice Houston; m. Tamara Houston; 2 children. BA in African-Am. Studies, U. Tenn., 1993. Guard Detroit Pistons, 1993—96, New York Knicks, 1996—; mem. All-Star Team, 2000, 2001, US Olympic Basketball Team, Sydney, Australia, 2000. Featured sports couple (with Tamara) Swimsuit Issue, Sports Illustrated, 1999; actor: (films) Black and White, 2000; contestant (with Tamara) NBA Week, Wheel of Fortune, 2003. Named one of 99 Good Guys in Sports, The Sporting News, 2000, 2001, 2002, 2003, 2004; recipient Olympic Gold Medal, 2000. Achievements include NBA Draft first round eleventh pick, 1993. Office: New York Knicks Madison Square Garden 2 Penn Plz New York NY 10121-0101

HOUSTON, ALMA FAYE, psychiatrist; b. Chgo., Oct. 4, 1944; d. Harlan Eugene and Ruth Viola (Minster) H. BA, U. Ark., 1966; BS in medicine, MD, U. Ark., Little Rock, 1969, JD, 1980. Diplomate Am. Bd. Psychiatry and

Neurology. Intern Baylor U. Med. Ctr., Dallas, 1969-70; resident in psychiatry U. Utah Univ. Hosp., Salt Lake City, 1970-72; with U. Ark. Med. Ctr., Little Rock, 1972-73; fellow child psychiatry Lafayette Clinic, Detroit, 1973-74; dir. Fullerton Adolescent Ctr. Ark. State Hosp., Little Rock, 1975-78; pvt. practice Little Rock, 1978-81; asst. prof. psychiatry Coll. Medicine Northeast Ohio U., Canton, 1981—2003, dir. psychiatry residency Coll. Medicine Akron, 1983-84; pvt. practice, cons., 1985-86; child psychiatrist Child Guidance and Family Solution, Akron, Ohio, 1983—, med. dir., 1989—93. Republican. Baptist. Avocation: percussionist in a folk music band. Office: Child Guidance and Family Solution 312 Locust St Akron OH 44302

HOUSTON, CAROLINE MARGARET, editor; b. Harrogate, Eng., May 8, 1964; came to U.S., 1975; d. William H. and Sylvia (Fineron) H. BA in Internat. Studies and Mid East Studies, George Mason U., 1989, postgrad., 1990—. Cert. fluency in Farsi and French; cert. diamontologist and gemologist Diamond Coun. Am.; lic. pvt. pilot. Editor Maxim Techs., Vienna, Va., 1988-89; sec. Am. Near East Refugee Aid, Washington and Israel, 1989-90; asst. sec., treas. World Resources Inst., Washington, 1990-91; asst. dir. client svcs. Britches of Georgetowne, McLean, Va., 1991-92; reference copyright sr. clk., preservation technician Libr. Congress, Washington, 1992-95, copyright office automation asst., 1995-2000; prodn. control specialist Dominion Semiconductor LLC, Manassas, Va., 2000—. Devel. cons. Legacy Internat., Jerusalem, 1990-91. Violinist with semi-profl. orchs., 1972-84. Mem. NOW, Amnesty Internat.; chmn., treas. Episcopal Ch. of Va., No. Va. chpt. Holy Land Com.; EMT, Greater Manassas Vol. Rescue Squad, 2000—. Mem. NAFE, Internat. Studies Assn., Mid. East Inst., Libr. Congress Profl. Assn. (chair membership com., co-chair pub. affairs com.), Atlantic Coun. U.S. Avocations: study of languages, piloting, martial arts, computer programs. Home: 8174 Peakwood Ct Apt 6 Manassas VA 20111-2143 Office: Dominion Semicondr LLC 9600 Godwin Dr Manassas VA 20110 E-mail: houstoncaroline@aol.com.

HOUSTON, C(LARENCE) STUART, radiologist, educator; b. Williston, N.D., Sept. 26, 1927; s. Clarence Joseph and Sigridur (Christianson) H.; m. Mary Isabel Belcher, Aug. 12, 1951; children: Stanley, Margaret, David, Donald. MD, U. Man., Winnipeg, Can., 1951; DLitt, U. Sask., Saskatoon, Can., 1987. Demonstrator in anatomy U. Sask., 1960-61, teaching fellow in radiology, 1963-64, lectr., 1964-65, asst. prof., 1965-67, assoc. prof., 1967-69, prof., 1969-95, emeritus prof., 1995—, head dept. med. imaging, 1982-87. Author: To the Arctic by Canoe, 1974, Pioneer of Vision, 1980, Arctic Ordeal, 1984, R.G. Ferguson, Crusader, 1991, Arctic Artist, 1994, Steps on the Road to Medicare, 2002, Eighteenth-Century Naturalists of Hudson Bay, 2003; editor jour. Can. Assn. Radiologists, 1976-81. Recipient Roland Michener Conservation award Can. Wildlife Fedn., 1986, Douglas H. Pimlott Conservation award Can. Nature Fedn., 1988, Ralph D. Bird award Man. Naturalists' Soc., 1989, Doris Huestis Speirs award Soc. Can. Ornithologists, 1989, Eugene Eisenmann medal Linnean Soc. N.Y., 1990, Sask. Order of Merit, 1992, Officer of Order of Can., 1993. Mem. Can. Soc. for History of Medicine (pres. 1987-89), Royal Coll. Physicians and Surgeons (mem. coun. 1984-90, chmn. specialty com. 1984-88), Am. Ornithologists' Union (mem. coun. 1978-80, chmn. memls. com. 1984—, v.p. 1990-91, Marion Jenkinson Svc. award, 2004). Avocation: bird banding. Home: 863 University Dr Saskatoon SK Canada S7N 0J8 E-mail: houstons@duke.usask.ca.

HOUSTON, DOROTHY MIDDLETON, elementary school educator; b. LaGrange, Ga., Oct. 23, 1936; d. Robert Meriwether and Marie Elizabeth (Davis) Middleton; m. Richard Gray Houston Sr., June 3, 1956; children: Jean, Ann, Richard Jr., Thomas Sandy. BS in Edn., U. Ga., 1958, MEd, 1970. Tchr. Auburn (Ga.) Elem. Sch., 1958-59; tchr. phys. edn. DuPont Manual High Sch., Louisville, 1959-62; instr. women's dept. phys. edn. U. Ga., Athens, 1970-71; tchr. phys. edn. Woodstock (Ga.) Elem. Sch., 1971-72, Brumby Elem. Sch., Marietta, Ga., 1972-77, Murdock Elem. Sch., Marietta, Ga., 1977-81; tchr. Teasley Elem. Sch., Smyrna, Ga., 1981-95; ret., 1995. Childcare program adminstr. Internat. Student Conf., Toccoa, Ga., 1986; tchr. tng. Pub. Schs. Ga., 1969-92. Mem.: Ga. Ret. Educators Assn. (area XV dir. 2004—), Cobb-Marietta Ret. Educators (pres. 2001—02), Kappa Delta Pi, Phi Kappa Phi. Baptist. Avocations: exercise, recreational crafts, gardening. Home: 1849 Service Dr NE Marietta GA 30066-1917

HOUSTON, E. JAMES, JR., banker, consultant; b. Highland Park, Mich., Sept. 25, 1939; s. Ernest James and Frieda Mary (Milligan) H.; m. Ann Draper, Dec. 16, 1961; children: James Lee, Jay Douglas, m. M. Aleen Bateman, Sept. 1, 2001, 1 child, Chanda Brae. BS in Finance, Wayne State U., 1964, MBA, 1967. Asst. v.p. Bank of the Commonwealth, Detroit, 1957-69; v.p. Birmingham Bloomfield Bank, Mich., 1969—70, pres., 1970—71; exec. v.p. Fidelity Bank Mich., 1971; pres. Houston & Assos., Inc., Birmingham, Mich., 1971—91; mgr. loan rev. Republic Bancorp Inc., Ann Arbor, 1991—93, mgr. loan control, 1993—94, loan control officer, 1994—95, v.p. loan control, 1995—2003; v.p. strategic asset mgmt. dept. Franklin Bank, N.A., Southfield, 2003—. Lectr. fin. Wayne State U. Sch. Bus. Adminstrn., Detroit, 1971—. Active Bloomfield Hills Hockey Assn.; pres. pro tem Village of Bingham Farms Village Council; chmn. Southfield Twp. Citizens' Com.; v.p. Hickory Hollow Homeowners Assn.; trustee Southeastern Oakland County Water Authority; mem. Community House Assn., Birmingham; bd. dirs. CATV, Birmingham YMCA; mem. parents council Brookside Sch., Cranbrook, Mich.; pres. Brookside Sch. Dads Club; mem. Cranbrook Arena Com. Mem. Birmingham-Bloomfield C. of C., Greater Detroit C. of C. Clubs: Wayne State U. Alumni;. Lodges: Rotary. Republican. Presbyterian. Home: 7140 Round Hill Dr Apt B-1 Waterford MI 48327

HOUSTON, ELIZABETH REECE MANASCO, correctional education consultant; b. Birmingham, Ala., June 19, 1935; d. Reuben Cleveland and Beulah Elizabeth (Reece) Manasco; m. Joseph Brantley Houston; 1 child, Joseph Brantley Houston III. BS, U. Tex., 1956; MEd, Boston Coll., 1969. Cert. elem. tchr., Calif., cert. spl. edn. tchr., Calif., cert. community coll. instr., Calif.; cert. adminstr., Calif. Tchr., elem. Ridgefield (Conn.) Schs., 1962-63; staff, spl. edn. Sudbury (Mass.) Schs., 1965-68; staff intern Wayland (Mass.) High Sch., 1972; tchr., home bound Northampton (Mass.) Schs., 1972-73; program dir. Jack Douglas Ctr., San Jose, Calif., 1974-76; tchr. specialist spl. edn., coord. classroom svcs., dir. alternative schs. Santa Clara County Office Edn., San Jose, Calif., 1976-94. Instr. San Jose State U., 1980—86, U. Calif., Santa Cruz, 1982—85, Santa Clara U., 1991—94; cons. Houston Rsch. Assocs., Saratoga, Calif., 1981—; mem. neighborhood accountability bd. County of Santa Clara Probation Dept., 2002—04. Author: (manual) Behavior Management for School Bus Drivers, 1980, Classroom Management, 1984, Synergistic Learning, 1986, Learning Disabilities in Psychology for Correctional Education, 1992. Recipient President's award Soc. Photo-Optical Instrumentation Engrs., 1979, Classroom Mgmt. Program award Sch. Bds. Assn., 1984, Svc. to Youth award, Juvenile Ct. Sch. Adminstrs. of Calif., 1989-94; grantee Santa Clara County Office Edn. Tchr. Advisor Program U.S. Sec. Edn., 1983-84. Home: 12150 Country Squire Ln Saratoga CA 95070-3444

HOUSTON, FRANK MATT, dermatologist; b. New Orleans, Dec. 15, 1939; s. Matt Francis and Amanda Vallie (Welch) H.; m. Helen Butler, Apr. 24, 1965; children: F. Matt, Catherine E.C., Amanda J.B. BS, La. State U., 1960, MD, 1964. Diplomate Am. Bd. Dermatology. Intern Johns Hopkins U., Balt., resident; physician, dermatologist Greensboro (N.C.) Dermatology Assocs., 1970—. Cons. Moses H. Cone Hosp., Greensboro, N.C., Wesley Long Hosp. Greensboro, 1970—; adj. asst clin. prof. dermatology U. N.C. Sch. of Medicine, Chapel Hill, 1980—. Bd. dirs. Greensboro Hist. Mus., Greensboro Preservation Soc., Greensboro Symphony Soc., Greensboro Opera Co. Capt. U.S. Army, 1965-71. Fellow Am. Acad. Dermatology; mem. AMA, ACP, N.C. Soc. Medicine, Royal Coll. Physicians, Am. Skin Assn. (sci. adv. com. to bd. dirs.), Greensboro City Club (bd. dirs.), Greensboro Country Club, Surf Club (Wrightsville Beach, N.C.). Republican. Episcopalian. Avocations: travel, aerobics, music. Office: Greensboro Dermatology 2704 Saint Jude St Greensboro NC 27405-3670 Personal E-mail: f_houston@bellsouth.net.

HOUSTON, GEORGE R., JR., college president; BSBA, Georgetown U. 1st in class, 1961; MBA, George Washington U., 1967; DHH (hon.), Georgetown U., 1982. CPA, D.C. Acct. Schumaker & Yates CPAs, Washington, 1961-66; asst. prof. acctg. Georgetown U., Washington, 1966-92, disting. prof., 1992-94, treas., 1970-92, v.p. for fin. affairs and treas., 1974-90, sr. v.p. and treas., 1990-92, mng. dir. endowment fund, 1992-94; pres. Mt. St. Mary's Coll., Emmitsburg, Md., 1994—2003. Site visitor Middle States Assn. Acad. Accreditation Svc., 1974-89, fin. cons., 1991-93, fin. reviewer, 1993; mem. bd. cons. Riggs Nat. Bank; sr. exec. adv. coun. Met. Washington Minority Bus. Enterprises; mem. Pres.' Commn. on White House Fellowships Selection Panel. Contbr. articles to profl. jours.; presenter papers to edn. and fin. confs. Mem. Holy Trinity Ch. Adminstrv. Coun., Nat. Com. of Arts for the Handicapped, Woodstock Theol. Ctr.; adj. lectr. in acctg. Georgetown U., 1962-66. Mem. AICPA, D.C. Inst. CPA's (1st place achievment award 1961), Nat. Assn. Coll. and Univ. Officers, Georgetown U. Alumni Assn. (ann. award 1976), C. of C. Frederick County, Beta Gamma Sigma (hon.), Phi Lambda Theta (hon.). Office: Mount St Mary's Coll Office of Pres 16300 Old Emmitsburg Rd Emmitsburg MD 21727-7700

HOUSTON, GERRY ANN, oncologist; b. Baldwyn, Miss., July 16, 1953; d. Jeff Davis and Frances Holland (Agnew) Goodson; m. Terry L. Houston, Dec. 18, 1976 (dec. May 1987); 1 child, Claire Holland; m. Abe John Malouf, July 23, 1988. BA, U. Miss., 1974, MD, 1978. Diplomate Am. Bd. Internal Medicine, Am. Bd. Medical Oncology, Am. Bd. Hospice and Palliative Care. Intern U. Med. Ctr., Jackson, Miss., 1978-79; resident U. Med. Ctr., Jackson, Miss., 1979-81, fellow oncology, 1981-83; ptnr. Jackson (Miss.) Oncology Assocs., 1987—. Staff physician Miss. Bapt. Med. Ctr., Jackson, 1983—, Ctr. Miss. Med. Ctr., Jackson, 1983—, St. Dominic Hosp., Jackson, 1983—, River Oaks Hosp., Jackson, 1983—, Univ. Med. Ctr., Jackson, 1983—; med. dir. Hospice Ministries, Jackson, 1989—; mem. exec. com. Bapt. Med. Ctr., 1994, pres. staff, 2003—04; med. dir. Bapt. Comprehensive Breast Ctr., 1997—. Contbr. articles to profl. jours. Chmn. exec. com. Miss. divsn. Am. Cancer Soc., 1993-95, pres., bd. dirs., 1989-93. Clin. rsch. fellow, Am. Cancer Soc. Fellow ACP; mem. AMA, Nat. Hospice Orgn., Acad. Hospice Physicians, So. Assn. Oncology, Am. Soc. Clin. Oncology, Alpha Omega Alpha. Episcopalian. Avocations: jogging, reading, skiing. Office: Jackson Oncology Assocs 1227 N State St Ste 101 Jackson MS 39202-2413 Office Phone: 601-355-2485. Business E-Mail: ghouston@mbmc.org.

HOUSTON, GLORIA, author, educator, consultant; b. Marion, NC, Nov. 24; d. James Myron and Ruth Houston; children: M. Diane Gainforth, Julie Ann Floen. BS, Appalachian State, 1963; MEd., U. S.Fla., 1983, PhD, 1989. Lit., writing cons. various orgns., 1979—; founding coord. Suncoast Young Authors Conf. Coll. Edn., U. So. Fla., Tampa, 1985-94, adj. instr., 1982—87. Cons. IBM/Goodhousekeeping Tell Me a Story Project, 1989; lectr. in field; presenter workshops nationwide. Author: The Year of the Perfect Christmas Tree, 1988 (Pubs. Weekly best seller list, other commendations), Littlejim, 1990, 2d edit., 2005, My Great Aunt Arizona, 1991, Littlejim's Gift, 1994, Mountain Valor, 1995, Littlejim's Dreams, 1997, Bright Freedom's Song, 1998, How Writing Works, 2003; contbr. articles to profl. jours. and mags. Fla. Endowment for the Humanities scholar, 1988-89; recipient Disting. Alumnae Rododendron Soc.award Appalachian State U., Excellence in Edn. award for Literacy from Partnerships in Edn., 1990. Mem. Authors Guild (Disting. Educator), Soc. Children's Book Writers Avocations: travel, reading, folklore. Office Phone: 704-542-6497. Personal E-mail: gloriahouston@bellsouth.net.

HOUSTON, IVAN JAMES, insurance company executive; b. Los Angeles, June 15, 1925; s. Norman Oliver and Doris Talbot (Young) H.; m. Philippa Elizabeth Jones, July 15, 1946; children: Pamela, Kathleen, Ivan Abbott. BS, U. Calif., Berkeley, 1948; postgrad., U. Man., 1948-49; LLD, U. La Verne, 1993. With Golden State Mut. Life Ins. Co., L.A., 1948—, v.p., actuary, 1962-66, sr. v.p., actuary, 1966-70, pres., CEO, 1970-77, chmn., pres., 1977-80, chmn., CEO, 1980-90, chmn., 1990—. Bd. dirs. First Interstate Bank Calif., Pacific Telesis Corp., Family Savs., Kaiser Aluminum and Chem. Corp., Metro-Media, Broadway Fed. Savs. and Loan. Mem. L.A. World Affairs Coun., 1970—; chmn. ctrl. region United Way, Inc., L.A., 1973-75, mem. corp. bd. dirs., 1973-80, v.p., 1973-75; bd. dirs. M & M Assn., L.A. Urban League, pres., 1977-; bd. fellows Claremont U. Ctr., 1972-80; bd. regents Loyola Marymount U., 1972-75, 79-82; bd. visitors Anderson Grad. Sch. Mgmt., UCLA, 1990-93; pres. City of L.A. Human Rels. Commn., 1993-95, 99-2000; mem. United Way of L.A, Cath. Charities of L.A. With Inf. AUS, 1944-45. Decorated Purple Heart, Bronze Star; knight comdr. Order St. Gregory the Great. Fellow Life Office Mgmt. Inst.; mem. Am. Acad. Actuaries, Am. Internat. Actuarial Assn., L.A. Actuarial Club, Conf. Cons. Actuaries (assoc.), Am. Coun. Life Ins. (dir.), Life Office Mgmt. Assn. (dir., mem. exec. com. 1972-75, chmn. 1979), Mil. Order of Purple Heart, DAV (life), Calif. C. of C. (dir.), L.A. Area C. of C. (dir.), Town Hall, Calif. Club, Cosmos Club, Kappa Alpha Psi, Sigma Pi Phi. Roman Catholic. Home: 5111 S Holt Ave Los Angeles CA 90056-1117 Personal E-mail: ihouston@aol.com.

HOUSTON, JAMES GORMAN, JR., retired state supreme court justice; b. Eufaula, Ala., Mar. 11, 1933; s. James Gorman and Mildred (Vance) H.; m. Martha Martin, Dec. 3, 1955; children: Mildred Vance, J. Gorman III. BS, Auburn U., 1955; LLB, U. Ala., 1956, JD, 1969. Bar: Ala. 1956. Law clk. to chief justice Ala. Supreme Ct., Montgomery, 1956-57; ptnr. Houston & Martin, P.C., Eufaula, 1960-85; assoc. justice Ala. Supreme Ct., Montgomery, 1985—2003, acting chief justice, 2003—04; ret., 2005; of counsel Lightfoot, Franklin & White, LLC, Birmingham, Ala., 2005—. County atty. Barbour County, Clayton, Ala., 1961-79. Contbr. numerous opinions to So. Reporter; contbr. articles to profl. jours. Mayor pro tem, alderman City of Eufaula, 1964-70; pres. Heritage Assn., Eufaula, Ala., 1979-82; mem. Ala. Commn. on Uniform State Laws. 1st lt. JAGC, USAF, 1957-60. Named Citizen of Yr., City of Eufaula, 1979; recipient Alumni Achievement in Humanities award Auburn Univ., 1993. Fellow Am. Bar Found.; mem. ABA, Ala. Bar Assn., Ala. State Bar (examiner 1979-82, disciplinary commn. 1984-85, state bar commr. 1982-85), Barbour County Bar Assn. (pres. 1975), Eufaula C. of C. (pres. 1974). Republican. Methodist. Office: Lightfoot Franklin & White LLC The Clark Bldg 400 20th St N Birmingham AL 35203-3200 Office Phone: 205-581-0700, 334-834-4414. Business E-Mail: ghouston@lfwlaw.com.

HOUSTON, JAMES R., government agency administrator; B in Physics, U. Calif., Berkeley, 1969; M in Physics, U. Chgo., 1970; M in Coastal and Oceanographic Engring., U. Fla., 1974, PhD in Engring. Scis., 1978. Rsch. physicist, Nuclear Weapons Effects Divsn. US Army Engr. R & D Ctr., 1970—72, rsch. hydraulic engr., Hydraulics Lab. (HL), 1972—83, chief of rsch. divsn., Coastal Engring. Rsch. Ctr. (CERC), 1983—86, prog. mgr. for the Shore Protection and Restoration Prog. and Harbor Entrances and Coastal Channels Prog., 1983—86, dir., Coastal Engring. Rsch. Ctr. (CERC), 1986, dir., Coastal and Hydraulics Lab. (CHL) (result of merge of CERC and HL), 1997—2002, dir. Vicksburg, Miss., 2000—. Published over 120 technical reports and papers. Named Eminent Spkr., Institution Engrs. (Australia); recipient Sr. Exec. Svc. (SES) Meritorious Presidential Rank award (awarded two), Dept. of Army R & D Achievement award, Army Commendation medal, Nat. Beach Advocacy award, 1997, Morrough P. O'Brien award, Am. Shore and Beach Preservation Assn., 2003. Mem.: Phi Kappa Phi, Phi Beta Kappa. Office: US Army Engr R & D Ctr 3909 Halls Ferry Rd Vicksburg MS 39180-6199 Fax: 601-634-2361.

HOUSTON, JAMES RUSSELL (RUSS HOUSTON), retired minister; b. Gloversville, N.Y., Oct. 15, 1922; s. Cyril Wyshart and Anna Belle (Wilson) H.; m. Shirley Joan Walters, July 29, 1952; children: Jeffrey, Shawn, Kurt, Kim, Traci. BA, Ky. Christian Coll., 1945, Butler U., 1947; MDiv, Christian Theol. Sem., 1957. Ordained minister Christian Ch. (Disciples of Christ), Aug. 12, 1945. Pastor First Christian Ch., Cayuga, Ind., 1948-54, Park Christian Ch., Dennison, Ohio, 1954-60, Bethany Christian Ch., Evansville, Ind., 1960-64, Ctrl. Christian Ch., Pocatello, Idaho, 1964-86, ret. min. emeritus, 1987—. Morning devotions pastor KSEI Radio, Pocatello, 1966-81; asst. chaplain VA, Pocatello, 1994—; bd. dirs. N.W. Region Christian Ch., Beaverton, Oreg., 1970-75. Chaplain Greater Cleve. BSA Res., Clendening, Ohio, 1957-59; rep. ecumenical ministery Idaho State U., Pocatello, 1964-68; pres. Pocatello Ministerial Assn., 1966-67, 69-70; bd. dirs. Idaho-Oreg. Sight Conservation Found., Boise, 1965, ARC, Pocatello, 1970-77; chaplain, lt. col. Civil Air Patrol, Pocatello, 1968-78; instnl. rev. rep. Bannock Regional Med. Ctr., Pocatello, 1990-95, Pocatello Regional Med. Ctr, 1990-95. Named Lion of Yr., Lions Club Internat., 1963, Lifetime Hon. Tail Twister, Pocatello Lions Club, 1987; recipient Svc. award Bannock Regional Med. Ctr., 1986. Avocations: lyric writing, hunting, fishing, rv travel, spectator sports. Home: 1771 N Honeysuckle Ln Inkom ID 83245-1612

HOUSTON, JOSEPH BRANTLEY, JR., optical instrument company executive; b. Birmingham, Ala., June 15, 1934; s. Joseph Brantley and Inez (Graben) H.; m. Elizabeth Reece Manasco; 1 child, J. Brantley III. AB in Astronomy, U. Tex., 1956; MS, Northeastern U., 1969. Commd. 2d lt. C.E., U.S. Army, 1956, advanced through grades to capt., 1968; optical engr. Perkin-Elmer, Wilton, Conn., 1961-64; mgr. massive optics, chief engr. underwater optical sys. Itek Corp., Lexington, Mass., 1964-71; asst. to pres. Kollmorgen E-O Divsn., Northampton, Mass., 1971-73; v.p. advanced devel. and spl. projects Itek Corp., Sunnyvale, Calif., 1973-81; founder Houston Rsch. Assocs., Saratoga, Calif., 1981—, Houston Tech. Internat., Inc., San Jose, Calif., 1991-97; founder, exec. dir. Forum for Mil. Applications of Directed Energy, Huntsville, Ala., 1989-96. Contbr. articles to profl. jours.; inventor. Recipient Outstanding Civilian Svc. medal U.S. Army, 1987. Fellow Internat. Soc. Optical Engring. (life; pres. 1977-78, advanced tech. advisor 1981—, Goddard award 1982); mem. Optical Soc. Am. (founder, pres. New Eng. sect., chair Fabrication and Testing Tech. Group, editor Optical Workshop Notebook). Office: 12150 Country Squire Ln Saratoga CA 95070-3444

HOUSTON, NIOKA HEATH, elementary school educator; b. Jeffersonville, Vt., Sept. 27, 1949; d. Merrill Benjamen and Marjorie Elaine (West) Heath; m. Gary Houston, Aug. 31, 1971; children: Megan, Joseph, Jesse, Anne. BS in elem. edn., U. Vt., 1971, M in edn., 1989. Cert. mid. childhood generalist 2004. Tchr. Hyde Pk. Elem. Sch., Hyde Pk., Vt., 1971—77; adj. prof. U. Vt., Burlington, Vt., 1994—97; tchr. Wolcott Elem. Sch., Wolcott, Vt., 1984—. Cons. Orleans Soutwest Writing Coun., Hardwick, Vt., 2005; writing network leader Vt. State DOE, Montpelier, Vt., 1990—2003. Vol. Craftsbury Chamber Players Bd., Craftsbury, Vt., 1984—. Mem.: Nat. Coun. Tchrs. of English, Vt. Tchrs. English Lang. Arts, Vt. Coun. on Reading. Independent. Office: Wolcott Elem Sch Sch House Hill Wolcott VT 05680 Office Phone: 802-472-6551, 802-472-6552. Personal E-mail: c5862536@yahoo.com.

HOUSTON, PAUL DAVID, school association administrator; b. Springfield, Ohio, Apr. 10, 1944; s. Paul Doran and Irene Almeda (Sansom) H.; m. Marilyn Kay Bowyer, Aug. 27, 1966 (div. July 1986); children: Lisa Lenore, Suzanne Elizabeth, Caroline Michelle; m. Jovel Kane, June 27, 1988 (div. Aug. 1997). BA, Ohio State U., 1966; MAT, U. N.C., 1968; cert. advanced study, Harvard U., 1971, EdD, 1973; D (hon.), Duquesne U., 1997. Tchr. Chapel Hill (N.C.) City Schs., 1968-70; prin. Summit (N.J.) City Schs., 1972-74; asst. supt. Birmingham (Ala.) City Schs., 1974-77; supt. Princeton (N.J.) Regional Schs., 1977-86, Tucson Unified Sch. Dist., 1986-91, Riverside (Calif.) Unified Schs., 1991-94; exec. dir. Am. Assn. Sch. Adminstrs., Arlington, Va., 1994—. Vis. prof. Brigham Young U., Princeton U.; pres. S.W. Regional Labs. Bd., 1989-90. Author: Articles of Faith and Hope for Public Education, 1997; co-author: Exploding the Myths, 1993, The Board Savvy Superintendent, 2002; contbr. articles to profl. jours. Pres. N.J. Interscholastic Assn.; bd. dirs. Princeton and Tucson Libr., 1977-87, YMCA, 1977-87. Finis E. Engleman scholar, 1972; recipient Richard Green Leadership award Coun. of Great City Schs., 1991; named Exec. Educator of the Month Exec. Educator, 1985, 100 Outstanding Exec. Educators in N.Am., 1984, 93. Mem. Rotary (pres. 1983-84), Phi Delta Kappa. Home: 136 N Union St Alexandria VA 22314-3247 Office: Am Assn Sch Adminstrs 801 N Quincy St Ste 700 Arlington VA 22203-1720

HOUSTON, RON, professional society administrator; b. Austin, Tex, 1948; BA, U. Tex., 1971, BBA, 1984, BS, 1989, M in Libr. and Info. Sci., 1995, postgrad., 1999—. Founder, dir., and trustee Soc. Folk Dance Historians, Austin, Tex., 1987—. Dir. of exhibitions, seminars, retreats and courses, 1970—; cons., rsch. libr. in field, 1989—. Author: (research reports) Folk Dance Problem Solver, 1987—, (demographic study) Folk Dance Phone Book and Group Directory, 1993—, (catalog) Folk Dance Catalogue, 1967. With USMC, 1969—71. Recipient Token of Appreciation, San Antonio Coll. Folk Dance Festival, 2003; scholar Polonia Choreographic Sch., Kosciusko Found., 1981—83; Presdl. scholar, U. Tex., 2000, Continuing Edn. fellow, 2003—04. Mem.: Nat. Folk Orgn. (corr.), Internat. Coun. for Traditional Music, Panna Maria Hist. Soc. (life), Soc. Folk Dance Historians (hon.; trustee 1987—), Royal Scottish Country Dance Soc. (life; cert. tchr., Miss Jean Milligan scholar 1983). Avocations: study of socio-economic and political injustice, study of the fringes of reason. Office: Soc Folk Dance Historians 2100 Rio Grande St Austin TX 78705-5578

HOUSTON, STANLEY DUNSMORE, retired public relations executive; b. Toronto, July 17, 1930; s. Archibald Laing and Mary (Dunsmore) H.; m. Pauline Lennox, Oct. 20, 1955 (div. July 1975; children: Wayne Cameron, Scott Gregory, Kevin Edward; m. Suzanne Fogarty, Sept. 15, 1978 (div. Nov. 1990). Grad. secondary sch., Humberside Collegiate, Toronto, 1948. Journalist editor Toronto Telegram, 1948-59; exec. v.p. Pub. Rels. Svcs. Ltd., Toronto, 1959-72; pres., chief exec. officer The Houston Group Communications Ltd., Toronto, 1972-90; chmn., chief exec. officer Edelman Houston Group, Toronto, 1990-96. Dir. L'Agence des Relationnistes de Montreal, 1974, Toronto Waterfront Coun., 1988-92, Daniel J. Edelman, Inc., Chgo.; mem. editorial adv. bd. The Sponsorship Report, Toronto. Author feature articles Macleans, Mayfair, Saturday Night; organized World Curling Championship, 1959-69; founder Can. Ladies Curling Assn. and Championship, 1960; promoted 1st Can. World Cup Ski Race, 1965; inaugurated Can. Grand Prix auto race, 1967; created duMaurier Classic (LPGA major golf event), 1974. Mem. Can. Ladies Profl. Golf (pres. 1974), Ont. M.S. Soc. (dir. 1984-87), Can. Pub. Rels. Soc., Nat. Club, World Trade Ctr., Credit Valley Golf and Country Club, Variety Club of Ont., Tent 28. Home (Winter): 4508 Nassau Rd Bradenton FL 34210

HOUSTON, WHITNEY, vocalist, recording artist; b. East Orange, N.J., Aug. 9, 1963; d. John R. and Cissy Houston; m. Bobby Brown, July 18, 1992; 1 child, Bobbi Kristina Houston Brown. LHD (hon.), Grambling U., 1988. Mem. New Hope Bapt. Jr. Choir, 1974, background vocalist Chaka Khan, Lou Rawls, Cissy Houston, 1978, appeared in Cissy Houston night club act, fashion model Glamour Mag., Seventeen mag., 1981, record debut (duet with Teddy Pendergrass) Hold Me, 1984; singer: (albums) Whitney Houston, 1985 (Grammy Award Best Pop Vocal Performance, 1985, Favorite Pop/Rock Album and Favorite Soul/R&B Album, Am. Music award, 1986), Whitney, 1987 (Grammy Award Best Pop Vocal Performance, 1987, Album of Yr., Soul Train Music Award, 1988, Best LP R&B/Dance and Best LP Rock/Pop, First Annual Garden State Music Award (NJ), 1988), I'm Your Baby Tonight, 1990 (Best R&B Album, Billboard Music Award, 1991), My Love Is Your Love, 1998 (Grammy Award Best Female R&B Vocal Performance, 2000), The Greatest Hits, 2000, Love, Whitney, 2001, Just Whitney, 2002; singer: (appears on) The Bodyguard soundtrack (song "I Will Always Love You"), 1992 (Grammy Awards: Record Of The Year, Album Of The Year, Best Pop Vocal Performance, 1993, Favorite Pop/Rock Single and Favorite Soul/R&B Single, Am. Music Award, 1994, Favorite Pop/Rock Album and Favorite Adult Contemporary Album, Am. Music Award, 1994, Best R&B Single, Soul Train Music Award, 1993, Best R&B Song of Yr., Soul Train Music Award, 1994, Album of Yr., Billboard Music Award, 1993, Soundtrack Album, Billboard Music Award, 1993, Album Most Weeks at #1, Billboard Music Award, 1993, World Single, Billboard Music Award, 1993, Hot 100 Single, Billboard Music Award, 1993, Single Most Weeks at #1, Billboard Music Award, 1993, R&B Single, Billboard Music Award, 1993, R&B Album, Billboard Music Award, 1993, Outstanding Album, NAACP Image Award, 1994, Outstanding Soundtrack Album, Film, or TV, NAACP Image Award,

1994, Favorite New Music Video, People's Choice Award, 1993, Best Song, MTV Movie Award, 1993), Waiting to Exhale soundtrack, 1995 (Favorite Soundtrack, Am. Music Award, 1997, Outstanding Album, NAACP Image Award, 1996, Outstanding Soundtrack, NAACP Image Award, 1996), The Preacher's Wife, 1996 (Outstanding Album, NAACP Image Award, 1997), Prince of Egypt soundtrack (song "When You Believe" with Mariah Carey), 1998; appeared in HBO TV spl. Welcome Home, Heroes, With Whitney Houston, 1991 (Performance in a Musical Special or Series, Cable Ace Award, 1991); actor: (films) The Bodyguard, 1992, Waiting To Exhale, 1995, The Preacher's Wife, 1996 (Image award Outstanding Lead Actress in a motion picture, 1997, Outstanding Gospel Artist, NAACP Image Award, 1997, Outstanding Actress in a Motion Picture, NAACP Image Award, 1997, Favorite Female-R&B, Blockbuster Entertainment Award, 1997), Scratch the Surface, 1997; (TV series) Being Bobby Brown, 2005; performer: Rainforest Benefit at Carnegie Hall, 1994; actor, exec. prodr.: (TV films) Cinderella, 1997, The Cheetah Girls, 2003; prodr.: (films) The Princess Diaries, 2001. Founder The Whitney Houston Found. for Children, Inc. Named Favorite Pop/Rock Female Vocalist, Am. Music Award, 1986, 1987, 1988, Favorite Soul/R&B Female Vocalist, 1986, 1988, Favorite Pop/Rock Female Artist, 1994, Favorite Soul/R&B Female Artist, 1994, Favorite Adult Contemporary Artist, 1997, Best R&B Singles Artist, Billboard Music Award, 1991, Best R&B Album Artist, 1991, Best R&B Artist, 1991, World Artist, 1993, Hot 100 Singles Artist, 1993, R&B Singles Artist, 1993, Entertainer of Yr., NAACP Image Award, 1994, Outstanding Female Artist, 1994, 2000, Favorite Female Musical Performer, People's Choice Award, 1987, 1988, 1989, 1993, 1998, Best Female Vocalist, Rock/Pop and Best Female Vocalist, R&B/Dance, First Annual Garden State Music Award (NJ), 1988, Best Female Singer, Nickelodeon Kids Choice Award, 1988, Favorite Female Vocalist, People Mag. Reader Poll, 1988, Best Selling Am. Recording Artist of Yr., World's Best Selling: Pop Artist, R&B Artist, Overall Recording Artist, Recording Artist of Era, World Music Award, 1994; named to Hall of Fame Inductee, Nickelodeon Kids Choice Award, 1996; recipient Favorite Soul/R&B Single, "You Give Good Love", Am. Music Award, 1985, Favorite Soul/R&B Video Single, "Saving All My Love", 1985, Favorite Pop/Rock Single, ' I Wanna Dance With Somebody", 1987, Outstanding Music Video, "I'm Every Women", NAACP Image Award, 1994, Outstanding Song, "OExhale (Shoop Shoop)", 1996, Best Female Video of Yr., "How Will I Know", MTV Award, 1986, Best Music Video "I Wanna Dance With Somebody", First Annual Garden State Music Award (NJ), 1988, Best Single Rock/Pop and Best Single R&B/Dance, "So Emotional", 1988, Best R&B/Soul Single, Female, "O Exhale (Shoop Shoop), Soul Train Music Award, 1996, Emmy award, Outstanding Individual Performance in a Variety or Music Program, 1986, Emmy award, Outstanding Musical Performance in a Sports Program, "One Moment In Time", Special Olympics, 1988, Disting. Artist/Humanitarian award, Nat. Urban Coalition, 1988, Outstanding Achievement in Humanitarian award, Govt. Switzerland, 1988, Light Contributing Leadership award, appointed by George Bush Points of Light, 1990, Frederick D. Patterson award, United Negro College Fund Founder award, 1990, Hitmakers award, Songwriters Hall of Fame, 1990, Essence award for Performing Arts, 1990, Am. Cinema Performer of Yr. award, 1991, Music award, Am. Black Achievement award, 1991, Brass Ring award, Children's Diabetes Found., 1992, Award of Merit, Am. Music Award, 1994, Sammy Davis Jr. Entertainer of Yr. award, Soul Train Music Award, 1994, VH-1 Honor for Whitney Houston Found. for Children, 1995, Disting. Achievement in Music and Fil/Video, Second Annual Internat. Achievement in Arts award, 1995, Soul Train 25th Anniversary Hall of Fame award, 1995, Triumphant Spirit award, Essence Mag., 1997, Top Contribution to Gospel by a Mainstream Artist, Gospel Music Assn., 1997, Pop Award " Count On Me", ASCAP, 1997, Quincy Jones Career Achievement award, Soul Train Music Award, 1998, Artist of the Decade, 2000, Internat. Album of Yr., NRJ Award, 2000, BET Lifetime Achievement award, 2002.*

HOUSTON, WILLIAM ROBERT MONTGOMERY, ophthalmologist, surgeon; b. Mansfield, Ohio, Nov. 13, 1922; s. William T. and Frances (Hursh) Houston; m. Marguerite LeBau Browne, Apr. 25, 1968; children: William Erling Tenney, Marguerite Elisabeth LaBau, Selby Cabot Truitt Vanderbilt. BA, Oberlin Coll., 1944; MD, We. Res. U., 1948. Diplomate Am. Bd. Ophthalmology. Intern Meth. Hosp., Bklyn., 1948—49, Ill. Eye and Ear Infirmary, Chgo., 1949—50; resident N.Y. Eye and Ear Infirmary, 1950—52; practice medicine specializing in ophthalmic surgery Mansfield, 1952—. Fellow retinal vascular disease NYU, 1968—69; mem. staff Mansfield Gen. Hosp., NYU Bellevue Med. Ctr.; assoc. prof. clin. ophthalmology NYU Sch. Medicine. Editor: Ohio Records and Pioneer Families, 1970—. Pres. Mansfield Symphony Soc., 1965—68, Mansfield Civic Music Assn., 1965; mem. Mansfield City Sch. Bd., 1962—65, v.p., 1965. Capt. med. corps USAF, 1952—55. Recipient Honor award, Acad. Ophthalmology. Fellow: Internat. Coll. Surgeons; mem.: SR (color guard 1961—71), Ohio Geneal. Soc. (trustee 1955—), Nat. Geneal. Soc. (Merit award), N.Y. Geneal. and Biog. Soc. (life), Ohio Hist. Soc. (life). Address: 456 Park Ave W Mansfield OH 44906-3118

HOUSWORTH, ELIZABETH ANN, mathematics professor; b. Decatur, Ga., Aug. 30, 1965; d. William Jere and Sara Ann Housworth; m. Nets Hawk Katz, Aug. 14, 2002; 1 child, Dagon Dcfn Katz. PhD in Math., U. Va., 1992; BA with hons. in Math., Emory U., 1986. Rsch. asst. prof. Purdue U., West Lafayette, Ind., 1992—94; asst. prof., Dunham Jackson U. of Minn., Mpls., 1995—96; asst. prof. U. of Oreg., Eugene, Oreg., 1994—2002; assoc. prof. Ind. U., Bloomington, Ind., 2002—. Contbr. articles to prof. jours. Recipient G.T. Whyburn fellow, U. Va., 1986-1987; grantee Modeling Recombination, NSF, 2003-2006, (Co-PI) FIBR: Causes and Consequences of Recombination, 2003-2008, IGMS: Probability Stats. in Ecology, Evolution, 2000-2001, Isoperimetric-Type Inequalities Arising from the Study of Brownian Motion in Domains Normalized by Inradius, 1995-1997. Mem.: Phi Beta Kappa. Office: Mathematics Dept Indiana U Bloomington IN 47405 Business E-Mail: ehouswor@indiana.edu.

HOUTMAN, CARL J., chemical engineer, researcher; b. Volga, S.D., Dec. 31, 1960; s. Charles Allen and Karen Ruth Houtman; m. Jacqueline J. Jaeger, Jan. 29, 1960; children: Ethan Jacob, Melinda Rose. BChE, U. Minn., 1983, MS in Chem. Engring., 1985; PhD in Chem. Engring., U. Del., 1990. Chateaubriand fellow Institut du researches sur la catalyse, Lyon, France, 1990—91; rsch. assoc. U. Wis., Madison, Wis., 1991—95, vis. asst. prof., 1995—96, assoc. scientist, 1996—98; rsch. chem. engr. Forest Products Lab. USDA, Madison, 1998—. Grantee, US Postal Svc., 1999—. Mem.: TAPPI (sub com. chair 1998—2005), Local Union (v.p. 1999—). Achievements include development of environmentally benign adhesives for stamps; improved biological pulping methods; patents pending for chemical pulping methods. Office: USDA FS Forest Products Laboratory One Gifford Pinchot Drive Madison WI 53726 Office Phone: 608-231-9445. Office Fax: 608-231-9538. E-mail: choutman@fs.fed.us.

HOUTSMA, PETER C., lawyer; b. Denver, 1951; BA in Polit. Sci. and Econs. magna cum laude, U. Colo., 1973; JD magna cum laude, Cornell U., 1976. Bar: Colo. 1976. Mem. Holland & Hart, Denver, 1976—. Mem. Am. Arbitration Assn. (panel arbitrators), Order of Coif, Phi Beta Kappa. Office: Holland & Hart PO Box 8749 Denver CO 80201-8749 Office Phone: 303-295-8259. Personal E-mail: phoutsma@hollandhart.com.

HOUTZ, DUANE TALBOTT, hospital administrator; b. Kansas City, Mo., Apr. 28, 1933; s. Dudley and Helen (Talbott) H.; m. Margaret McNiel; children: Erik Siegfried, Jamie Houtz Harvey. BS, U. Kans., 1955; MHA, Washington U., St. Louis, 1960. Asst. dir. Shands Teaching Hosp. and Clinics, Gainesville, Fla., 1961-65; asst. prof. Ctr. for Health and Hosp. Adminstrn., U. Fla., Gainesville, 1964-65; adminstr., exec. v.p. Baptist Med. Ctr., Montclair-Birmingham, Ala., 1965-75; hosp. dir. Alton Ochsner Med. Found., New Orleans, 1975-77; pres. Morton F. Plant Hosp., Clearwater, Fla., 1977-92, pres. emeritus, 1992—; nat. advisor to the health care industry Pershing Yoakley & Assocs., P.C., 1995-99; ptnr. Corrigo Health Care Solutions, 2000—. Chmn. Southeastern Hosp. Conf., 1986-87; chmn., pres. SunHealth Care Plans Fla., 1986-87; bd. dirs. SunHealth Enterprises Inc., SunHealth Corp.; advisor Corrigo Health Care Solutions, LLC, 1998—. Contbr. articles to profl. jours. Bd. dirs. Cmty. Svc. Coun., Birmingham, 1972-75, United Way of Pinellas County, 1987-93, campaign chmn. med. divsn., 1992-94; bd. dirs. Fla. League for Nursing, 1989-98, Bay Area Hosp. Coun./Tampa Bay Hosp. Coun., 1990-95, Morton Plant Found., 1990-96; mem. Fla. Geriatric Rsch. Bd., 1993-98; adv. bd. Jr. League Pinellas County, 1993-94; active Vets. Affairs Mgmt. Assistance Coun., 1996—; vice-chmn. Sun Coast Health Coun., 1998-2003; mem. fundraising bd. Magic Found., 2005. Capt. USAF, 1955-58. Recipient Acad. award USAF Basic Flight Sch., 1956, award of merit Fla. Hosp. Rsch. and Edn. Found., 1993, Washington U. Hosp. Adminstrn. Program Alumni of Yr. award, 1996; fellow Birmingham Bapt. Hosp. Found., 1985. Fellow Am. Coll. Healthcare Execs. (Regents award 1992); mem. Nat. League Nursing (bd. dirs.), Am. Hosp. Assn. (vice-chmn. council nursing 1983, rsch. com.), Assn. Voluntary Hosps. Fla. (bd. dirs. 1979-83, pres. 1979-80), Fla. Hosp. Assn. (trustee, bd. dirs. 1979-82), Greater Clearwater C. of C. (Outstanding Citizen selection com. 1982, bd. govs. 1984-87, bd. govs. 1987-88), Pinellas Suncoast C. of C. (adv. coun. 1984-87), Kiwanis (pres. Birmingham chpt. 1970-71), Phi Delta Theta. E-mail: dhoutz1@tampabay.rr.com.

HOUTZAGER, MARIANNE JOHANNA (MARIAN DE BOYEN), writer, artist, photographer; b. The Hague, Aug. 31, 1953; d. Joseph Houtzager and Gisèle Van Boeyen. HAVO, NTI, Rotterdam, Holland, 1972. Author: (booklet) The Winterwren, 1994, The Orca, 1995, (book) Action Skoatter in the Lead, 2000, Flowers for Pim - a year of grief, 2004; one-person shows include (gouaches) Town Hall Krimpen a/d Yssel, 1976, (photographs) Wolvega Racecourse, 1996; exhibited group shows (gouaches) Gallery Los, Krimpen a/d Yssel, 1977. Recipient Am. Medal of Honor. Mem.: Leefbaar Rotterdam, Lijst Pim Fortuyn, Internat. Order of Merit. Avocations: drawing, photographing, private flying, co-owner trotting horse. Home: PO Box 143 2920 AC Krimpen Netherlands E-mail: mdeboyen@wanadoo.nl.

HOUZE, HERBERT GEORGE, writer; b. Brockville, Ont., Can., Apr. 18, 1947; s. McLean and Grace Lynham (Sayce) H.; m. Carolyn Pierce Johnson, July 8, 1972 (div. May 1990); children: Jennifer E., Alexander J. M., Andrew W.; m. Christine Mary Reinhard, Sept. 13, 1996. BA, McMaster U., Hamilton, Ont., 1969; MA, Vanderbilt U., 1971. Curator of mil. history Chgo. Hist. Soc., 1973-76; curator Winchester Mus. Buffalo Bill Hist. Ctr., Cody, Wyo., 1983-91. Advisor Royal Mil. Coll. Can. Mus., Kingston, Ont., 1979—; dir. John McLaren & Sons Distillers Ltd., London and Perth, 1990-; internat. rep. Arms and Armor, Bonhams and Butterfields, San Francisco, 2004-. Author: (books) Knightly Musings, 1988, The Sumptuous Flaske, 1989, To the Dreams of Youth, 1992, Winchester History, 1994, Colt Rifles & Muskets, 1996, Winchester Model 52, 1997, Winchester Bolt Action Rifles, 1998, Winchester Model 1876 Centennial Rifle, 2001, Arming the West, 2001, Colt Presentations, 2002, Colt & Its Collectors, 2003. Mem. Arms and Armour Soc. London, Armor & Arms Club N.Y., Les Amis du Musee de Liege. E-mail: herb.houze@bonhams.com.

HOVAKIMYAN, NAIRA, mathematician, educator; b. Yerevan, Armenia, Sept. 21, 1966; arrived in U.S., 1998; d. Viktor Hovakimyan and Emma Tumanyan. BS, MS in Theoretical Mechanics and Applied Math., Yerevan State U., 1988; PhD in Physics and Math., Russian Acad. Scis., Moscow, 1992. Jr. rsch. scientist Inst. Mechanics, Armenian Acad. Scis., Yerevan, 1992—94, sr. rsch. scientist, 1995—97; postdoctoral scholar INRIA (French Nat. Inst. Computer Sci. and Control), Sophia Antipolis, France, 1997—97; vis. rsch. scientist Sch. Aerospace Engring., Ga. Inst. Tech., Atlanta, 1998—2000, rsch. scientist II, 2001—03; assoc. prof. Va. Poly. Inst. and State U., Blacksburg, 2003—. Presenter in field. Contbr. articles to profl. jours. Recipient Internat. Best Paper award, Soc Instrument and Control Engrs., 1996, Pride@Boeing award, Boeing Co., 2004; grantee, Soros Found., 1993—94; German Acad. Exch. Svc. scholar, Stuttgart U., Inst. for Computer Applications, 1994—95. Mem.: AMS, AIAA, IEEE Control Sys. Soc. (sr.), Internat. Soc. Dynamic Games. Orthodox Christian. Achievements include patents for adaptive control system having direct output feedback and related apparatuses and methods; patents pending for error observer for adaptive output feedback; adaptive state estimation for unknown nonlinear processes; an improved method for adding adaptation to an existing control system applicable to non-minimum phase nonlinear systems; adaptive control with input saturation; a low-pass adaptive control design with improved transient performance. Office: Va Poly Inst and State Univ Dept AOE 215 Randolph Hall Blacksburg VA 24061-0203 Office Phone: 540-231-7989. Business E-Mail: nhovakim@vt.edu.

HOVANESSIAN, SHAHEN ALEXANDER, electrical engineer, educator, consultant; b. Tehran, Iran, Sept. 6, 1931; arrived in US, 1949; s. Alexander and Jenik (Thadeus) H.; m. Mary Mashourian, Sept. 17, 1960; children: Linda Larsen and Christina Tchaparian (twins). BSEE, UCLA, 1954, MSME, 1955, PhDEE, 1958. Registered profl. engr., Calif. Research scientist Chevron Research Corp., La Habra, Calif., 1958-63; sr. scientist Hughes Aircraft Co., El Segundo, Calif., 1963-86; sr. tech. specialist Aerospace Corp., El Segundo, Calif., 1986-96; lectr. UCLA, 1962—; cons. engr. L.A., 1996—. Mem. adv. group for aerospace R & D NATO, 1985-87. Author: (with Louis A. Pipes) Matrix—Computer Methods in Engineering, 1969; Digital—Computer Methods in Engineering, 1969; Radar, Detection and Tracking Systems, 1973; Computational Mathematics in Engineering, 1976; Synthetic Array and Imaging Radars, 1980; Radar System Design and Analysis, 1984; Introduction to Sensor Systems, 1988; (with Khalil Seyrafi) Introduction to Electro-Optical Imaging and Tracking Systems, 1993; editor Computers and Elec. Engring., 1973-76. Inventor radar computer Fellow IEEE (U.S. del. Moscow 1973, disting. lectr.); mem. ASME, Sigma Xi, Tau Beta Pi. Democrat. Roman Catholic. Avocations: investments, real estate. Home: 3039 Greentree Ct Los Angeles CA 90077-2020 Personal E-mail: shovaness@aol.com.

HOVDE, CARL FREDERICK, language professional, educator; b. Meadville, Pa., Oct. 11, 1926; s. Bryn J. and Therese (Arneson) H.; m. Jane Hale Norris, Aug. 27, 1960; children— Katherine Hale, Sarah Theresse, Peter Bryn. BA, Columbia, 1950; MA, Princeton, 1954; PhD, 1956. Instr. English Ohio State U., 1955-58; vis. lectr. U. Muenster, W. Germany, 1958-60; mem. faculty Columbia, N.Y.C., 1960—, asso. prof. English, 1964-69, prof. English, 1969—; emeritus, 1995; dean coll. Columbia, 1968-72. Vis. prof. U. Guanabara, Brazil, 1964, Umea, Sweden, 1989. Served with AUS, 1944-46. Fellow Villa Serbelloni, 1994. Home: 460 Riverside Dr New York NY 10027-6801 Office: Columbia Univ 602 Philosophy Hall Broadway & 116th St New York NY 10027

HOVEL, ESTHER HARRISON, art educator; b. San Antonio, Tex., Jan. 12, 1917; d. Randolph Williamson and Carrie Esther (Clements) Harrison; m. Elliott Logan Hovel, Sept. 30, 1935; children: Richard Elliott, Dorothy Auverne. BA, Incarnate Word Coll., 1935; postgrad., Oxford U., 1979, British Inst. Art, Florence, Italy, 1980. Civil svc. auditor U.S. Govt. Office of Price Adminstrn., San Antonio, 1942-44; interior decorator Parkway Interior Design Studio, El Paso, Tex., 1968-72; instr. stained glass and sculpture El Paso Mus. Art, 1972-78; tchr. sculpture Albuquerque Sr. Ctrs., 1983-85. Docent El Paso Mus. Art, 1972-82. Exhibited sculpture Museo De Artes, Juarez, Mexico, 1981 (1st place 1981). Bd. dirs. YMCA, Albuquerque, 1963-64 (plaque 1964); charter mem. and bd. dirs. Contact Lifeline Internat., Albuquerque, 1982-92 (2 plaques 1986, 90); mem. Com. on Bicentennial of U.S. Constitution, Washington and N.M., 1987-89. Recipient 2 medals Exxon Corp., 1986, 89, Medal of Merit Pres. Ronald Reagan, 1987; grantee Exxon Corp., 1986, 90. Mem. Jr. League Internat. (various offices 1948-97, emeritus mem.), Rotary "Anns" (various offices). Republican. Mem. Christian Ch. Avocations: sculpture, stained glass, painting, travel, volunteerism. Home: 7524 Bear Canyon Rd NE Albuquerque NM 87109-3847

HOVER, JOHN CALVIN, II, banker; b. Orange, N.J., May 13, 1943; s. John Curry and Edith Margaret (Hopkins) H.; m. Jacqueline Whitley, Sept. 4, 1997; 1 child, Margaret Biddle. BA in English Lit., U. Pa., 1965, MBA in Mktg., 1967; postgrad., Aspen Inst., 1988. With Chem. Bank, 1968-76; with corp. banking and personal banking U.S. Trust Co. of N.Y., N.Y.C., 1976-80, sr. v.p., div. mgr., pvt. banking, 1980-91, exec. v.p. asset mgmt., pvt. banking group, 1991-98; retired, 1999. Chmn. U.S. Trust Pvt. Equity Fund; bd. dirs. New Hope & Ivyland R.R., Pa., Tweedy Browne Fund Inc.; chmn. bd. overseers, U. Mus., Phila. Trustee U. Pa., Phila. Mem. St. Nicholas Soc., 1st Troop Phila. City Cav., Soc. Colonial Wars, St. Andrews Soc., Most Venerable Order of Hosp. of St. John of Jerusalem, Knickerbocker Club, Univ. Club, Penn Club NY (pres.), Psi Upsilon. Avocation: railroadiana. Home: PO Box 676 3039 Durham Rd Buckingham PA 18912 E-mail: jhover@erols.com.

HOVING, JOHN HANNES FORESTER, consulting firm executive; b. N.Y.C., July 18, 1923; s. Hannes and Mary Alma (Gilbert) H.; m. Anne Fisher Spiers, Feb. 1, 1958; children: Christopher, Karen Anne, Katherine Jean. BA in History, U. Chgo., 1947. Radio news editor, reporter Milw. Jour., Capital Times, Madison, Wis., 1947-51; asst. to chmn. Democratic Nat. Com., 1952-54; exec. positions Kefauver, Stevenson, Johnson, Humphrey, Sanford presdl. campaigns; asst. to presdl. asst. for trade policy 1962; v.p. exec. action Air Transp. Assn. Am., Washington, 1956-64; propr. cons. firm Washington, 1964-72; sr. v.p. Federated Dept. Stores, Inc., Cin., 1972-82; pres. The Hoving Group (cons. firm), Washington, 1982—. Chmn. Washington Theol. Consortium, 1993-96; mem. adv. bd. Fashion Inst. Design Merchandising; past dep. chmn. planning Dem. Nat. Com. With AUS, 1943-46. Decorated Purple Heart, Bronze Star Mem. Am. Assn. Polit. Cons., Met. Club, Nat. Press Club, Nat. Capital Dem., Queen City Club (Cin.), Lotos Club (N.Y.C.). Home: 415 Dogleg Dr Williamsburg VA 23188 E-mail: hovings@aol.com.

HOVING, THOMAS, museum director, consultant, writer; b. N.Y.C., Jan. 15, 1931; s. Walter and Mary (Osgood Field) H.; m. Nancy Melissa Bell, Oct. 3, 1953; 1 dau., Petrea Bell. BA, Princeton U., 1953, MFA, 1958, PhD, 1959, HHD (hon.), 1968; LHD (hon.), Hofstra U., 1966; LLD (hon.), Pratt Inst., 1967; DFA (hon.), NYU, 1968; LittD (hon.), Middlebury Coll., 1968. Staff Medieval Met. Mus. Art and The Cloisters, 1959-65, curator, 1965-66; commr. parks N.Y.C., 1966-67; adminstr. Dept. Recreation and Cultural Affairs, 1967; dir. Met. Mus. Art, 1967-77; pres. Hoving Assocs., Inc., museum and cultural affairs cons. firm N.Y.C., 1977—; pres. spl. mus. exhibitions The Planning Corp., 1983-91; arts and entertainment corr. ABC-TV show 20/20, 1978-84; editor Connoisseur mag., 1981-91. Author: Guide to the Cloisters, 1964, The Chase, The Capture, 1975, Kuerners and Olsons; exhbn. catalogue, 1976, Two Worlds of Andrew Wyeth: A Conversation with Andrew Wyeth, 1978, Tutankhamun, The Untold Story, 1978, King of the Confessors, 1981, Masterpiece, 1986, Discovery, 1989, Making the Mummies Dance, 1993, Andrew Wyeth: Autobiography, 1995, False Impressions, The Search for Big Time Art Fakes, 1996, Greatest Works of Art of Western Civilization, 1997, Art for Dummies, 1999, The Art of Dan Namingha, 2000, Am. Gothic, 2005, Materpieces, The Curators' Game, 2005; contbr. articles on art, parks and recreation to profl. publs., mags. and newspapers. Past trustee Inst. Fine Arts NYU. Lt. USMC, 1953-55. Decorated knight Legion of Honor France; recipient Bronze medal Citizens Budget Com., 1966, Cue mag. award, 1966, Disting. Achievement award Advt. Club Am., 1966, Disting. Contbn. award Park Assn. N.Y.C., 1967, Elsie de Wolfe award Am. Inst. Interior Designers, 1967, Woodrow Wilson award Princeton U., 1977 Mem. AIA (hon.) Office: Hoving Assocs Inc 150 E 73rd St New York NY 10021-4362 E-mail: tomhoving@earthlink.net.

HOVIS, JOHN, corporate financial executive; married; 3 children. PhD in Econ., U.Wyo. Sales Avnet, Inc., 1992, successive positions as bus. analyst for the bus. process re-engring. group, mgr. of planning and analyst, 1995—97, served as creator and dir. of Avnet's competitive intelligence ctr, the Bus. Intelligence Office (BIO), named v.p. and dir. global stragic planning, overseeing investor rels. efforts, 1999, corp. v.p., 1999, dir. Avnet's expanded investor rels. dept., 2001—. Taught econ., fin.,and stats. U. Md. Mem.: Nat. Electronics Distbr. Assn.(NEDA), Soc. of Competitive Intelligence Prof., Strategic Leadership Forum, Ind. Adv. Com., Nat. Investor Rels. Inst., Phi Beta Kappa, Am. Grad. Sch. of Intern. Mgmt. Beta Gamma Sigma Chpt. Office: Avnet Inc 2211 S 47th St Phoenix AZ 85034

HOVIS, JULIE MIRANDA, elementary school educator; b. Tupelo, Miss., Oct. 30, 1977; d. Guy Lee Hovis, Jr. and Ralna Eve English. BS in Family Studies and Child Devel., Ariz. State U., 2001; Med, U. Phoenix, 2003. Nanny, Scottsdale, Ariz., 1994—2001; intern U.S. Senate, Washington, 1999—99; tchrs. asst. Villa Montessori Sch., Phoenix, 2001—03; tchr. Whittier Elem. Sch., 2003—. Monitoring resource tchr. Whittier Elem. Sch., 2004—. Translator translation for deaf sorority sisters. Mem. First Christian Ch. North Hollywood, Calif., 1989. Mem.: Sigma Kappa (continuing mem. chair, risk mgr. 1997—99). Liberal. Avocations: reading, painting, travel, museums. Home: 13616 N 43rd St # 205 Phoenix AZ 85032 Office: Whittier Elem Sch 2000 N 16th St Phoenix AZ 85006 Office Phone: 602-257-3925. Personal E-mail: juliemhovis@aol.com.

HOVLAND, ERIC JEFFREY, dean, endodontics educator; b. Oct. 9, 1946; married. Student, Lehigh U., 1964-66; BS, U. Md., 1968, DDS, 1972; MS in Adult Edn., Va. Commonwealth U., 1977; MBA in Health Care, Loyola Coll., 1980. Clin. instr. dept endodontics Med. Coll. Va., Sch. Dentistry, 1975-77; asst. prof. endodontics U. Md., Balt. Coll. Dental Surgery, 1977-82, dir. undergrad. clinics, Office Clin. Affairs, 1980—84, acting assoc. dean clin. affairs, 1981, assoc. prof. endodontics, 1982-89, chmn. dept. endodontics, 1985—93, dir. advanced splty. edn. in endodontics, 1986—87, prof. endodontics, 1989-93, acting v.p. for acad. affairs, 1991; prof. dept. endodontics La. State U. Med. Ctr. Sch. Dentistry, New Orleans, 1993—, dean, 1993—. Mem. cons. med. staff VA Hosp., New Orleans, 1994—, Med. Ctr. La., New Orleans, 1994—; cons. Northeast regional Bd. Dental Examiners, 1990-93, VA Hosp., Perry Pt., Md., the Johns Hopkins Hosp., Balt., 1980-85, U. Md. Hosp., 1978-82, others; pvt. practice endodontics, 1977-88. Contbr. articles to profl. jours., chpts. to books; mem. editorial bd. Oral Surgery, Oral Medicine, Oral Pathology, Oral Radiology, endodontics Jour., 1995—; clin. assoc. editor Balt. Coll. Dental Surgery Jour. 1975-79. With USAF, 1973—75. Fellow Internat. Coll. Dentists, Am. Coll. Dentists; mem. ADA (chmn. 1992-93, mem. adv. com. advanced edn. in endodontics 1990-96), Am. Assn. Endodontists (chmn. honors and awards com. 1997-98, nominations com. 1996, internat. rels. com. 1994-95, constitution and bylaws com. 1994-95, Pres.'s Cir. 1994-95, pres. 1993-94, others), Am. Assn. Dental Schs. (legis. adv. com. 1996—, info. tech. adv. com. 1996—, coun. of deans and house of dels. 1993—), coun. of faculties and house of dels. 1983-86), Md. State Dental Assn. (strategic planning com. 1990, fin. com. 1985-87, others), La. State Dental Assn. (house of dels. 1994-95), New Orleans Dental Assn., Internat. Assn. for Dental Rsch., Am. Assn. for Dental Rsch., Internat. Assn. Dental Traumatology, So. Conf. of Deans and Dental Examiners (pres. 1995-96), Endodontic Soc. South Africa (hon.), Alumni Assn. of Balt. Coll. Dental Surgery U. Md. (chmn. class reunion 1982, 87). Alumni Assn. Sch. Bus. Loyola Coll. Office: La State U Sch Dentistry Office of Dean 1100 Florida Ave New Orleans LA 70119-2714

HOVMAND, SVEND, chemical engineer; b. Nakskov, Denmark, Jan. 3, 1939; came to U.S., 1977; s. Eyvind Frederic and Yrsa (Petersen) H.; m. Beverly Ann Cocozella, Dec. 17, 1966; children: Peter, Lars. MSCE, The Tech. U. Copenhagen, 1961; PhD in Chem. Engring., U. Cambridge, 1968. Postdoctoral resident asst. U. Cambridge, England, 1968—69; R&D mgr. Niro Atomizer, Copenhagen, 1970—77; v.p. Niro Atomizer Inc., Columbia, Md., 1977—89; pres. Bowen Engring., Sommerville, NJ, 1982—89, Niro Ceramic Inc., Columbia, 1983—89, Crossville Ceramics, Tenn., 1989—2005, chmn., 2005—. Patents in the field. Named to Ceramic Tile Distbr. Assn. Hall Fame, 2001. Mem.: Nat. Tile Contractors Assn. (bd. dirs. 2000—04, Cornerstone award 2002), Ceramic Tile Edn. Found. (bd. dirs. 1996—98), Tile Coun. of Am. (bd. dirs. 1990—, pres. 1994—95, 2003—05), Ctr. for Profl. Advancement (dir. indsl. drying course 1980—89). Office: Crossville Inc 346 Sweeny Dr Crossville TN 38555-5459 Business E-Mail: shovmand@crossvilleinc.com.

HOVNANIAN, ARA K., real estate developer; b. 1957; MBA, U. Pa., 1979. With Hovnanian Enterprises Inc., Red Bank, NJ, 1979, exec. v.p., 1983—88, pres., 1988—, CEO, 1997—. Adv. coun. PNC Bank, Monmouth Real Estate

Investment Corp., NJ. Mem. Coun. on Affordable Housing, NJ, 1985, 1990, Governor's Econ. Master Plan Commn., NJ, 1994. Office: Hovnanian Enterprises Inc 10 Highway 35 PO Box 5000 Red Bank NJ 07701-5997*

HOVNANIAN, KEVORK S., real estate developer; b. 1923; married. Founder Hovnanian Enterprises Inc., Red Bank, NJ, 1959, CEO, 1967—97, chmn., 1967—. Recipient Harvard Dively Award for Leadership in Corp. Pub. Initiatives, 1992, President's Medal, NJ Inst. Tech., 1996. Office: Hovnanian Enterprises Inc 10 Hwy 35 PO Box 500 Red Bank NJ 07701-5902*

HOVSEPIAN, LEON, artist, designer; b. Bloomsburg, Pa., Nov. 20, 1915; m. Mary Bedeian, Mar. 28, 1941; children: Leon II, Marlene Markarian. Cert., Worcester Art Mus., 1937; BFA, Yale U., 1941. Art instr. Bancroft Sch., Worcester, Mass., 1936-37, N.H. Womens Coll., New Haven, 1940-41, Worcester Art Mus. Sch., 1941-82; pres. TriArt Designers, Worcester, 1941—; art instr. Clark U., Worcester, 1982-83. Designer chapels in Archeveche de Papeete, Tahiti, 1983-84, chapels Oblates of Mary Immaculata, Haiti, 1977-78, stained glass windows Narthex-Ch. of Our Saviour, Worcester, 1988, baptismal font Ch. Our Saviour, Worcester, 1989; painting Baptism of Christ Ch. of Our Saviour, Worcester, 1989; one-man shows include Armenian Libr. and Mus. Am., Inc., 1991, Aurora Gallery, Worcester; represented in permanent collections City Hall, Manchester, England, Town Hall, Worcester, Eng., Mus. Modern Art, Erevan, USSR; represented in numerous pub. and pvt. collections. Scholar St. Wulstan, 1932-40, Alice Kimball English Travel, Yale U., 1941; Ford Found. grantee, 1979. Mem. Bohemian's Club, Pi Alpha. Avocations: travel, sketching, photography. Home: 96 Squantum St Worcester MA 01606-1874 Office: TriArt Designers 96 Squantum St Worcester MA 01606-1838 Office Phone: 508-853-8156.

HOW, HOTON, electrical engineer; b. Taichung, Taiwan, Oct. 10, 1954; s. Pei-Yin How and Su-Yien Kao; m. Qian Zhan, Mar. 29, 1957; 1 child, Joan Chi. DSc, MIT, 1987. Adj. prof. Northeastern U., Boston, 1996—; pres. Hotech, Inc., Belmont, Mass., 2001—. Cons. ElectroMagnetic Applications, Inc., Boston, 1991—. Contbr. articles to profl. jours.; 8 patents in field, 8 patents pending. Grantee, NSF, 1994, 1996, 2002, 2003. Home: 262 Clifton St Belmont MA 02478 Office: Hotech Inc 829 Concord St # C Cambridge MA 02138 Business E-Mail: hotonhow@hotech.com.

HOWALD, JOHN WILLIAM, lawyer; b. St. Louis, Dec. 21, 1935; s. Herbert John and Irene Dorothy (Weber) H.; m. Nina M. Zierenderg, June 15, 1957 (div. 1970); children: Deborah A., Catherine A., Laura A., John William; m. Betty L. Curtis, Feb. 14, 1971 (div. 1999); 1 stepchild, Tracy L.; m. Nancy J. Owens, Mar. 1, 2003. BS, U. Mo., 1957; JD, St. Louis U., 1962. Bar: Mo. 1962, U.S. Dist. Ct. (ea. dist.) Mo. 1962, U.S. Ct. Appeals (8th cir.) 1965, U.S. Supreme Ct. 1985. V.p. sales Eureka Svc. and Equip. Co., Eureka, Mo., 1959-62; ptnr. Sheehan, Furtaw & Howald, Hillsboro, Mo., 1963-64, Thurman, Nixon, Smith & Howald, Hillsboro, 1964-70, Thurman, Nixon, Smith, Howald, Weber & Bowles, Hillsboro, 1970-80, Thurman, Smith, Howald, Weber & Bowles, Hillsboro, 1989-91, Thurman, Howald, Weber, Bowles & Senkel, Hillsboro, 1991-95, Thurman, Howald, Weber, Senkel & Norrick, L.L.C., Hillsboro, 1995—. Bd. dirs. LaBarque Ent. of Jefferson County, Hillsboro, 1965-2002, Rustic Hills Resort Ltd., Hillsboro, 1968—. Mem. Mo. Ethics Commn., 1994-98, vice-chmn., 1995-96, chmn., 1996-98. Lt. (j.g.) USN, 1957-59. Recipient Spl. award, Meramec Basin Assn., 1967, 69. Fellow Am. Bar Found., Am. Coll. Trust and Estate Counsel (Mo. chmn. 1987-92); mem. ABA, Estate Planning Coun. St. Louis (pres. 1990-91), Mo. Bar Assn. (bd. govs. 1975-87, Pres. Spl. award 1979), Jefferson County Bar Assn. (pres. 1963-64). Avocations: travel, golf. Home: 701 Vista Glen Ct Eureka MO 63025 Office: Thurman Howald Weber Senkel & Norrick LLC PO Box 800 One Thurman Ct Hillsboro MO 63050 Office Phone: 636-789-2601. E-mail: howald@thurmanlaw.com.

HOWARD, ALEX T., JR., federal judge; b. 1924; Student, U. Ala., 1942, student, 1946, Auburn U., 1942-44; JD, Vanderbilt U., 1950. U.S. probation officer, Mobile, Ala., 1950-51; ptnr. Johnstone, Adams, Howard, Bailey & Gordon, Mobile, 1951-86; U.S. commr. U.S. Dist. Ct. (so. dist.) Ala., 1956-70, judge Mobile, 1986—, chief judge, 1989-94, sr. judge, 1996—. Assoc. editor Am. Maritime Cases for Port of Mobile. Served to 2d lt. U.S. Army, 1943-46. Mem. ABA, Internat. Soc. Barristers, Internat. Assn. of Ins. Counsel, Maritime Law Assn. of U.S., Southeastern Admiralty Law Inst. (dir. 1978-80), Ala. Bar Assn., Ala. Def. Lawyers Assn. (dir. late 1950's), Mobile Bar Assn. (pres. 1973). Office: 4201 Rochester Rd Mobile AL 36608-2238

HOWARD, ARTHUR ELLSWORTH DICK, law educator; b. Richmond, Va., July 5, 1933; s. Thomas Landon and Marie Antoinette (Dick) H. BA, U. Richmond, 1954; LLB, U. Va., 1961; BA with honors, Oxford U., 1960, MA, 1965; LLD (hon.), James Madison U., 1983, U. Richmond, 1984, Campbell U., 1986, Coll. William and Mary, 1991, Wake Forest U., 2000. Bar: Va., D.C. 1961. Asso. Covington & Burling, Washington, 1961-62; law clk. to Supreme Ct. Justice Hugo L. Black, Washington, 1962-64; assoc. prof. law U. Va., Charlottesville, 1964-67, prof., 1967-76, White Burkett Miller prof. law and public affairs, 1976—, assoc. dean, 1967-69, dir. Ctr. for Pub. Svc., 1988-89, Roy L. and Rosamond Woodruff Morgan rsch. prof., 2001—. Bd. dirs. Am. Ditchley Found.; counsel sessions Gen. Assembly Va., 1969—70. Author: Commentaries on the Constitution of Virginia, 2 vols., 1974 (Phi Beta Kappa prize), The Road from Runnymede: Magna Carta and Constitutionalism in America, 1968, (with Baker and Derr) Church, State and Politics, 1982, Democracy's Dawn, 1991, Constitution-Making in Eastern Europe, 1993, Magna Carta: Text and Commentary, 1998; bd. editors The American Oxonian, 1968—, The Wilson Quar., 1977—. Chmn., exec. dir. Va. Commn. on Constl. Revision, 1968-69; chmn. Va. Commn. on Bicentennial of U.S. Constn., 1985-92; mem. Va. Ind. Bicentennial Commn., 1966-83; vice chmn. Magna Carta Commn. Va., 1965-66; Va. sec. Rhodes Scholarship Trust, 1970—; counselor to Gov. of Va., 1982-86; bd. dirs. James Madison Meml. Found., Jamestown-Yorktown Found., 2003—; hon. mem. High Table Christ Ch., Oxford, 2002. With U.S. Army, 1954-56. Recipient Disting. Prof. award U. Va., 1981, Randa medal Czech Republic, 1996, George C. Marshall award internat. law and diplomacy World Affairs Coun., 2004; fellow Woodrow Wilson Internat. Ctr. for Scholars, Smithsonian Instn., Washington, 1974-75, 76-77; fellow Ctr. Advanced Studies U. Va., 1970-71, 76-77, 82-83; Rhodes scholar Oxford U., 1958-60; Disting. Vis. scholar in residence Rhodes Ho., Oxford U., 2001. Mem. Va. Bar Assn. (v.p. 1970-71), Va. Acad. Laureates (chmn. 1981-92), Cosmos Club (Washington), Oxford and Cambridge Club (London). Episcopalian. Home: 627 Park St Charlottesville VA 22902-4654 Office: U Va Sch Law 580 Massie Rd Charlottesville VA 22903-1738 Office Phone: 434-924-3097. E-mail: adh3m@virginia.edu.

HOWARD, CARL, retired lawyer; b. Chgo., July 23, 1920; m. Kathleen Agnes Costello, May 10, 1953; 1 child, Carl. AB, DePauw U., 1942; JD, U. Calif., San Francisco, 1949. Bar: Calif. 1951. Supervising dep. corps. commr. State of Calif., San Francisco, 1951-69; supervisory asst., asst. house counsel Fed. Home Loan Bank of San Francisco, 1970-75; legal counsel Home Fed. Savs. and Loan Assn., San Francisco, 1976-88, chmn. bd. dirs., 1985-86; assoc. Kerner, Colangelo & Imlay, 1976-86; sole practice San Francisco, 1987—96; ret., 1997. Lt. USNR, 1942-46, PTO. Mem. State Bar Calif., Am. Legion. Republican. Roman Catholic. Avocations: walking, golf, bicycling. Home: 2450 Quintara St San Francisco CA 94116-1139

HOWARD, CAROL HAMANN, artist; b. Cleve., Oct. 3, 1928; d. Carl F. and Constance (Kline) Hamann; div. 1975; children: Constance, Catherine, Virginia. Student, Skidmore Coll., 1946-48; BFA, Pratt Inst., 1951; postgrad., U. Wis., Mex. Art Workshop, Positano Art Workshop. Tchr. of ceramics and sculpture to blind at IHB; mem. women's com. Bklyn. Mus.; treas. Atlantic Gallery, N.Y.C., 1984-87, bd. dirs., 1987-89, 2000-2003. Solo exhbns. include: Salena Gallery, L.I. U., Bklyn., End of Main Gallery, Essex, Conn., Atlantic Gallery, N.Y.C., 1976, 78, 81, 83, 86, 88, 90, 93, 95, 98, 2001, Intown Club Gallery, Cleve., Chester (Conn.) Gallery, Citifin, Milan, 1987, La Galleria 9, Bologne, Italy, Galleria and Colonne, La Citifin, Florence, Italy, 1988, Citibank, Milan, 1989; group shows include: Nat. Acad. Design, World Trade Ctr., Bklyn. Mus., Cleve. Mus., Touchstone Gallery, Washington, Salamagundi Club; represented in corp. collections. Mem. N.Y. Artist Equity (bd. dirs.), Roebling Soc., Conn. Watercolor Soc., Nat. Painters of Casine and Acrylic, Audubon Artists, Essex Art Assn., Clinton Art Assn. Office: Atlantic Gallery 40 Wooster St New York NY 10013

HOWARD, CAROL SPENCER, librarian, journalist; b. Great Bend, Kans., 1944; d. Thomas Glendon and Margaret Merle (Jackson) Spencer; m. William Neal Howard, Dec. 31, 1977 (div. July 1987); 1 child, Morgan William. BA in Journalism, English and Edn., Baylor U., 1967; MLS, U. Tex., 1974. Cert. libr. City desk reporter Waco (Tex.) News-Tribune, 1965-67; guest editor Mademoiselle mag., N.Y.C., 1966; womens' news reporter Houston Post, 1969; libr. Austin Ind. Sch. Dist., 1974—86, 1991—97, San Antonio Ind. Sch. Dist., 1989-90, Del Valle (Tex.) Ind. Sch. Dist., 1990-91; children's book reviewer Austin Am. Statesman, 1984-90. Freelance journalist, children's lit. cons. Contbr. articles to profl. jours. Fellow U. Tex., 1973-74. Home: PO Box 302019 Austin TX 78703-0034

HOWARD, CAROLYN F., elementary school educator; d. Ray Harold and Julia Melba (Reagan) Wooten; 1 child, Ron R. BS, West Tex. A&M U., Canyon, Tex., 1968, MEd, 1984. Cert. mid-mgmt. West Tex. A&M U., supr. Tex. Tech, reading recovery tchr. leader Tex. Women's U. Tchr. fourth grade Amarillo ISD, Amarillo, Tex., 1968—72; tchr. first grade Vernon ISD, Vernon, Tex., 1972—73, Amarillo ISD, Amarillo, Tex., 1973—79, Cartwright #84, Phoenix, 1979—80; reading skills tchr. Amarillo ISD, Amarillo, Tex., 1980—84; title 1 coord., trainer results based monitoring, reading recovery tchr leader Region 16 ESC, Amarillo, Tex., 1984—2002; reading recovery tchr leader Portales Mcpl. Schs., Portales, N.Mex., 2002—, literacy leader, 2002—. Quality N.Mex. examiner N.Mex. Pub. Edn. Dept., Santa Fe, 2003—05. Classroom tchr. grant, Tchr. Orgn. Dumas, 1963. Mem.: Assn. Supervision and Curriculum Devel., Reading Recovery Coun. N.Am., Panhandle Reading Assn. (pres.), Phi Delta Kappa (sec.). Baptist. Avocations: reading, walking. Home: 915 S Main St Portales NM 88130 Office: Portales Mcpl Schs 501 S Abilene Portales NM 88130 Office Phone: 505-356-5347.

HOWARD, CECIL BYRON, pediatrician; b. Wallins, Ky., Apr. 16, 1927; s. William Knott and Maggie (Cawood) H.; m. Rebekah Ann Buckley, Mar. 4, 1931; children: Mark Byron, Sally Ann Howard Truxal, Maggie Elizabeth Howard Ray. BA, Vanderbilt U., 1949, MD, 1953. Intern U. Va. Hosp., Charlottesville, 1953-54; resident U. Tex. Med. Br., Galveston, 1954-56; pediatrician pvt. practice, Maryville, Tenn., 1956—. Dir. Christian Ch. Found. Handicapped, 1983—; elder 1st Christian Ch., Maryville, 1961-2003; scoutmaster Boy Scouts Am., 1964-79, chmn. Tuckaleechee Dist. Great Smoky Mountain Coun., 1973-75; mem. Blount County D.H.S. Child Abuse Rev. Team, 1965-2002. With U.S. Army, 1945-47. Fellow Am. Acad. Pediatrics; mem. Blount County Med. Soc. (pres. 1973), Maryville Optimist Club (pres. 1973). Republican. Avocations: hiking, piano, reading. Office: 1103 E Lamar Alexander Pkwy Maryville TN 37804-5130 Office Phone: 865-982-8473.

HOWARD, CLIFTON MERTON, psychiatrist; b. Quincy, Mass., Aug. 11, 1922; s. Clifton Merton and Ruth Gilkey (Henderson); m. Margaret Carroll, June 16, 1951 (div. Aug. 1964); children: Kristen, Lauren, Siri; m. Susan D. Krex., May 30, 1965; children: Michael Scott, Jonathan, Robert. SB, Harvard U., 1944, AM, 1947; MD, Columbia U., 1963. Diplomate Am. Bd. Med. Examiners. Rsch. physicist divsn. of Atomic Energy Com. Brookhaven Nat. Lab., 1947-48; founder Waveforms, Inc., 1951-53; pres., CEO Electronic Workshop Sales Corp., 1951-59, Sound Workshop, Inc. and E.W. Assocs., Inc., 1953-59; intern Mt. Sinai Hosp., N.Y.C., 1963-64; resident in psychiatry Columbia-Presbyn. Med. Ctr., 1964-65, N.Y. State Psychiat. Inst., N.Y.C., 1965-66; sr. psychiat. resident Drug Rsch. Svc., 1966-67; dir. evening Psychiat. Clinic, Mt. Carmel Guild, Union City, N.J., 1964-67; asst. attending psychiatrist Vanderbilt Clinic, Columbia Presbyn. Med. Ctr., 1969-75; cons. in psychiatry Columbia Presbyn. Med. Ctr., 1969-75, assoc. attending psychiatrist, psychiat. drug rsch. unit, 1971-75; pvt. practice N.Y.C., 1967-98, N.J., 1980—. Instr. engrng. dept., Harvard Coll., 1946; instr. physics dept. CCNY, 1948-50, NYU, 1948-54, instr. psychiatry dept. Columbia Coll. of P&S, 1967-71, assoc. in psychiatry dept., 1971-75. Staff writer APPLE computer mag., 1982-85; founder, pres., CEO S&H Software, Inc.; Apple computer cert. software developer lic. to Reader's Digest, D.C. Heath Co., John T. Wiley & Sons, and others. Lt. USNR, 1943-46, PTO. Mem. APA, Ams. of Armorial Ancestry, Ancient and Hon. Artillery Co. of Mass., Baronial Order of Magna Charta, Flagon and Trencher, Gen. Soc. Mayflower Descs. (surgeon gen. N.J. soc. 1978-84, 99), Jamestowne Soc., New Eng. Hist. and Geneal. Soc., Old Bridgewater Hist. Soc., Order Founders and Patriots of Am., Order of the Crown of Charlemagne, Soc. Descs. of Colonial Clergy, Soc. Ams. Royal Descent, Descs. of Illegitimate Sons and Daus. of Kings and Queens of England (aka Royal Bastard Soc.), Soc. Colonial Wars, Sons of Revolution, SAR. Avocations: genealogy, computers, medieval history, gardening. Home and Office: 105 Lakeview Dr Old Tappan NJ 07675-7071

HOWARD, DAN F., retired art educator, artist; b. Iowa City, Iowa, Aug. 4, 1931; s. Harold M. and Laura A. Howard; m. Barbara J. Glaman, Nov. 1, 1958. BA, Iowa U., Iowa City, 1953; MFA, Iowa U., 1958. From instr. to assoc. prof. Ark. State U., Jonesboro, 1958—71, chmn. divsn. art, 1965—71; chmn. divsn. art, prof., dept. head Kansas State U., Manhattan, 1971—74; prof. and dept. head U. Nebr., Lincoln, 1974—83, prof. art, 1983—96. Creator 750 works of art (painting and drawings), including Nat. Mus. Am. Art, Washington, Chautuqua (NY) Instn., Hallmark Corp., Kansas City, Mo., 3M, Mpls. Contbr. paintings to pub. collections including Mus. Nebr. Art. 1st lt. USAF, 1953—55. Recipient 100 prizes, awards and honors. Achievements include painting Bondage Series/Carrot most honored painting in Nebraska, recipient of four major national painting competition awards. Avocations: art, stamp collecting/philately, music, theater, sports. Home: 2110 Heritage Pines Ct Lincoln NE 68506 Office: U Nebr Dept Art 120 Richards Hall Lincoln NE 68588 Office Phone: 402-472-5119.

HOWARD, DAVID, ballet master and school administrator; b. London, June 14, 1937; came to U.S., 1966; s. Walter and Dorothy (Fell) Edwards. Grad., Arts Ednl. Sch., London, 1955; D (hon.), Oklahoma City U., 1998. Mem. faculty Sch. Ballet, Harkness House for Ballet Arts, N.Y.C., 1966—; prin. tchr. Harkness Ballet Co., N.Y.C., 1967—; dir. Sch. Ballet Harkness House for Ballet Arts, N.Y.C., 1969—; founder David Howard Sch. Ballet, N.Y.C., 1977; co. tchr. Am. Ballet Theatre, 1990—2002, 2002—03. Am. judicator 1st Internat. Ballet Competition, Miss., 1979; co-dir., co-founder Northeastern Ballet Summer Sch., Bard Coll., 1979; assoc. artistic dir. Catskill Ballet Theatre, 1980; founder David Howard Dance Ctr., N.Y.C., 1986—; mem. founding bd. Swiss Profl. Sch., Zurich; guest tchr. Royal Ballet, 1986—87, 1993, 95, San Francisco Ballet, Juilliard Sch., New Sch. U., 2004—; guest tchr., coach Am. Ballet Theatre, 1990—93, 1998—99, 2000—01, tchr. training program; guest tchr., coach Bejart Ballet, 1992—94; guest tchr. Royal Ballet, 1998—2001; artistic advisor Nat. Dance Co. Mex., Mexico City, 1996—97; artistic assoc. Marin Dance Theatre, San Rafael, Calif., 1996—97; tng. David Howard Found., Seattle, Tulsa, Dallas, Erie, Pa., Boston, N.Y.C., 1990—96; tchr. steps Broadway Dance Ballet Acad., East N.Y.C., 1996—2001; tchr. N.Y. On The Rd., 1996—2001, Broadway Dance Steps, 2004—05; tng. program Internat. Ballet Competition, Jackson, Miss., 1998; mem. faculty Joffrey/New Sch. U., N.Y.C., 1998—2002; tng. program Internat. Ballet Competition, 2002; guest tchr., coach Royal Ballet, 2004—05. Prin. dancer London Palladium, 1955—57, soloist Royal Ballet Eng., 1958—63, Nat. Ballet Can., 1963—64, appeared in (musical) Little Me, London, 1964—66; collaborator double album ballet music:; with Royal Ballet Eng., 1957—63, Royal Ballet, 1997—2001, 1991—92; with Royal Ballet, 2003—; with Royal Ballet, 2004, Finnish Nat. Ballet, 1999, Royal Swedish Ballet, 1977—, Finnish Ballet, 2004, Hett Nat. Ballet, Holland, 2004, choreographer Rachmaninoff Suite, 1971—, Divertissement D'Adam, 1971—, Rossini Variations, 1973, Designs in Shades of Baroque, 1974, Fantasy, 1980, David Howard Shoe, Prima Soft, 2004, others; tchg. record albums include David Howard in Class, rec. (DVD) Turns, Leaps and Bounds, A Dancer's Class, Celebration, Royal Danish Ballet, 2005, Royal Balley, 2005—, rec. 25 video tapes, 125 CDs on ballet. Recipient Dance Master of Am. ann. award, 1983. Mem. Regional Dance Am. (dir. pres.), royal Acad. Dancing, London Actors Equity (Adeline Genee Silver medal for male dancers 1954). Business E-Mail: masterteacher@rcn.com. *Have followed with great enthusiasm the growth of dance in the United States and have dedicated myself to the development of ballet training in America and bring it to a higher level. Have devoted time and effort to Regional Dance America, which reflects and contributes to the ever increasing size of ballet audiences across America. With this happening, no longer will the dancers who are developed each year have to seek employment within the long established European system of state-supported ballet houses, which is fast changing in 2005.*

HOWARD, DAVID, retired educational administrator; b. Delaware, Ohio, Sept. 24, 1929; s. Dale David and Clarine (Morehouse) H. BA, Ohio Wesleyan U., 1953; student, Columbia U, 1961—62, student, 1986, NYU, 1985—86. Lic. tchr., attendance coordinator, N.Y. News writer Australian Broadcasting Co., Sydney, 1955; editl. asst. N.Y. Times, 1956—58; tchr. social studies N.Y.C. Bd. of Edn., 1958—82, hotel and shelter ednl. coord., 1982—89; asst. supr. N.Y.C. Truancy Patrol Teams, 1989—2005. Author: Night Lights Went Out, 1966, Casa Alhambra, 1968, Picker of the Kingdom, 1999, Springtime for Kelly, 2001. Reservist FEMA, N.Y.C., 1980—. Lt. col. USAFR, 1953-75. Mem. Mystery Writers of Am., English Speaking Union. Republican. Protestant. N.Y.C. Anchor & Saber. Home: 324 E 61st St Apt 20 New York NY 10021-8709

HOWARD, DAVID ALLYN, history professor; b. Lynn, Mass., Nov. 1, 1942; m. Irmgard Matilda Keeler, Mar. 21, 1969; children: Deborah Keeler, William Keeler. PhD, Duke U., 1972. Prof. history Houghton Coll., NY, 1969—. Author: (book) Conquistador in Chains: Cabeza de Vaca and the American Indians. Independent. Office: Houghton Coll One Willard Ave Houghton NY 14744

HOWARD, DAVID E., artist; b. N.Y.C., Jan. 25, 1952; s. John C. and Florence (Martino) H. Student, Ohio U., 1969-71; MFA, San Francisco Art Inst., 1974. Comml. photographer, Athens, Ohio, 1969-71; tchr. photography San Francisco Ctr. for Visual Studies, 1971-74, visual artist in photography, 1975—, dir., 1975—. Vis. instr. City Coll. San Francisco; grad. isntr. San Francisco Art Inst. Author: Photography for Visual Communicators, (monographs) Realities, 1976, Perspectives, 1978, The Last Filipino Head Hunters, 2001, American Artist, 1990, Objective Reality of Illusionistic Perceptions, 1970, The Hidden World of the Naga, 2003, Sacred Journey: The Ganges to the Himalayas Taschen, 2004, The World of Tattoo, 2005; photography numerous periodicals including Village Voice, N.Y.C., San Francisco Chronicle, Artweek, N.Y. Art Revs., 1990, L.A. Reader, Tribal Arts mag., 1998, 2002, Filipinas, 1998, Patagonia Mag., 2002, TV Documentary series; one-man shows include G. Ray Hawkins Gallery, LA, Calif., Images Gallery N.Y.C., U. Calif. Extension, John Bolles Gallery, San Francisco, Hirshhorn Mus., Smithsonian Instn., Washington, San Francisco Art Inst., Ohio U., Athens, Thomas J. Crowe Gallery, L.A., Madison (Wis.) Art Ctr., Lehigh U., Pa., Fourth Street Gallery, N.Y.C., Intersection Gallery, San Francisco, Third Eye Gallery, N.Y.C., Ctr. for Visual Studies, San Francisco, Hutchinson Community Coll., Kans., Hank Baum Gallery, San Francisco, Martin Webber Gallery, 1986, Marc Richards Gallery, L.A., 1987, E.Z.T.V., L.A., 1987, 88, G. Ray Hawkins Gallery, L.A., 1988, Fine Arts Mus. L.I., 1989, Phila. Mus. Art, 1990, San Jose, Calif., 2000; numerous group shows including Art Commn. Gallery, San Francisco, DeYoung Mus., San Francisco, Oakland (Calif.) Mus., Palace of Fine Arts, San Francisco, Camera Work, L.A., Erie (Pa.) Art Ctr., Vorpal Gallery, 1985, Cal. State U., 1988, San Francisco Pub. Libr., 1987, Video Refuses, 1986, Hadley Martin Gallery, San Francisco, 1987, Fine Art Mus. L.I., 1989, Chandler Gallery, Seattle, 1991; represented in collections Mus. Modern Art, N.Y.C., Oakland (Calif.) Mus., San Francisco Mus. Modern Art, City of San Francisco, De Saisset Art Gallery, Santa Clara, Calif., Whitney Mus. Am. Art, Hirshhorn Mus., Smithsonian Instn., Art Ctr., Waco, Tex., Memphis Brooks Mus., Memphis, Akron (Ohio) Art Mus., Am. Mus. Natural History, N.Y.C. Spl. Collections; pvt. collections; prodr. videotape New York's East Village Art Scene, 1985, California's Art Scene, 1986, others; prodr. exptl. films: Analysis of Realities, 1974, Levels of Consciousness, 1976, Levels of Reality; prodr., dir. Art Seen, TV comml. documentary series on contemporary art televised in N.Y.C., L.A., San Francisco, Miami, Fla., Portland, Oreg., New Orleans, San Francisco, aired PBS, 1994, T.V. show Keith Haring: Artist at Work, selected segments shown Whitney Mus., Hirschhorn-Smithsonian Instn.; internat. exhbns. 10th and 13th Internat. Exhbns. Contemporay Art, Royan, France, 34thand 41st Internat. Salons of Japan, Tokyo, and 5 cities, Mex. Exhbn., Ex Convento de Carman, Guadalajara, 31st Cork Film Festival, 1986, Chgo. Film Festival, 1986, 42nd San Francisco Internatl. Film Fest., 1999, Presidio Earth Days Fest., 1999; other mus., galleries, univs. in U.S. and Europe; produced and directed films New York's East Village Art Scene, 1985, California's Art Scen, Parts 1 & 2, Levels of consciousness, Levels of Reality; presenter weekly cable TV series; Blackstar syndicated photographer, N.Y.C.; video journalist Asia-Pacific Econ. Conf., 1996, (documentary) Bill Clinton Pres. U.S. and 15 other heads of states, Manila, Philippines, 1996. Recipient San Francisco Art Festival award. Home and Office: Visual Studies 49 Rivoli St San Francisco CA 94117-4306 Business E-Mail: info@artexhibitionrentals.com.

HOWARD, DAVID L., conductor, baritone; b. Oklahoma City, Aug. 18, 1973; m. Andrea L. Weirick; children: Stuart, Abigail. MusB Edn., U. of Ctrl. Okla., 1997, MusM with honors, 1999; postgrad., Mich. State U. Cert. tchr. Okla. Choral dir. Monroney Jr. H.S., Midwest City, Okla., 1999—2001, Choctaw H.S., Okla., 2001—04; grad. assst. Mich. State U. Sch. Music, Lansing, 2004—. Artistic dir./conductor Midwest Choral Soc., Midwest City, 2000—04, Steiner Chorale, 2005—. Choral Gabriel Faure's Requiem, 2000, Antonio Vivaldi's Gloria, 2001, John Rutter's Gloria, 2001, George F. Handel's Messiah, 2002—05, Howard Hanson's Song of Democracy, 2003, Leonard Bernstein's Chichester Psalms, 2004; singer: (oratorio) Handel's Messiah, 2002, 2004, Ralph Vaughan Williams' Five Mystical Songs, 2005, (recital) Robert Schumann's Dichterliebe, Op. 48, 1999, 2000, Ralph Vaughan Williams' Songs of Travel and Gerald Finzi's Let Us Garlands Bring, Op. 18, 2003, (Operas) W.A. Mozart's Don Giovanni & Cosi Fan Tutte, 1998, Giuseppe Verdi's La Forza del Destino, 1998, Handel's Samson, 1999, Johann Strauss' Die Fledermaus, 2003. Min. music Howard Meml. Bapt. Ch., Oklahoma City, 1999—2003; choral dir. United Methodist Ch., Grand Ledge, Mich., 2004—. Mem.: Mich. Choral Dirs. Assn., Internat. Fedn. for Choral Music, East Ctrl. Okla. Choral Directors Assn. (v.p. 2002—), Music Educators Nat. Conf., Am. Choral Directors Assn., Alpha Chi, Pi Sigma Alpha. Home: 1627 S Pennsylvania Ave Lansing MI 48910 Personal E-mail: howard72@msu.edu.

HOWARD, DAVID MILES, lawyer; b. New Rochelle, N.Y., May 29, 1959; s. Leon M. and Helen J. (Lepow) H.; m. Dale P. Schomer, Apr. 17, 1988; children: Rachel, Emma. AB cum laude, Princeton (N.J.) U., 1981; JD cum laude, U. Pa., 1984. Bar: Pa. 1984, U.S. Dist. Ct. (ea. dist.) Pa. 1984, U.S. Ct. Appeals (3rd cir.) 1996. Law clk. to Hon. Marvin Katz U.S. Dist. Ct. (ea. dist) Pa., 1984-85; assoc. Dechert Price & Rhoads, Phila., 1985-87, ptnr., 1996—; atty. White House counsel, Washington, 1987; asst. U.S. atty. U.S. Atty.'s Office, Phila., 1987-94. Lectr. U. Pa. Law Sch., Phila., 1995-97. Editor: Univ. Pa. Law Rev., 1982—84. Named 1 of Pa. "Super Lawyers" Phila. Mag. Mem.: ABA (co-chmn., subcom. corp. internal investigations), Order of the Coif. Office: Dechert LLP 4000 Bell Atlantic Tower 1717 Arch St Lbby 3 Philadelphia PA 19103-2713 Office Phone: 215-994-2218. Business E-Mail: david.howard@dechert.com.

HOWARD, DAVIS JONATHAN, lawyer, educator, writer; b. S.I., N.Y., Dec. 8, 1954; s. Royal Marwin and Muriel Lu (Russell) H. BA summa cum laude, Wagner Coll., 1976; JD, Yale U., 1982. Bar: N.Y. 1983, N.J. 1986, U.S. Dist. Ct. (so. and ea. dists.) N.Y. 1983, U.S. Dist. Ct. N.J. 1986, U.S. Ct. Appeals (3d cir.) 1987, U.S. Ct. Appeals (4th cir.) 1988, U.S. Ct. Appeals (2d cir.) 1994. Assoc. Robson & Miller, N.Y.C., 1983-85, Sills Cummis Zuckerman Radin Tischman Epstein & Gross, P.A., Newark, 1985-92; ptnr. Parry &

Howard, P.A., Elizabeth, N.J., 1993-98; pvt. practice Staten Island, NY, 1998—2002. Lectr. law Rutgers U. Sch. Law, Newark, 1987-89; faculty legal seminars, symposiums; adjunct Coll. of Staten Island, CUNY, 1999. Contbr. articles to legal jours.; editor-in-chief, co-founder Shepard's N.J. Ins. Law and Regulation Reporter, 1991. Dir. alumni sch. com. Yale U., 1989-96. Mem.: ABA, ATLA, Am. Soc. Writers on Legal Subjects, Def. Rsch. Inst., N.Y. County Lawyers Assn., N.J. Bar Assn., N.Y. State Bar Assn., Scribes. Home and Office: 46 Longfellow Ave Staten Island NY 10301-4616 Fax: 718-816-4961. E-mail: dajho@aol.com.

HOWARD, DEAN DENTON, electrical engineer, researcher, consultant; BSEE, Purdue U., 1949; MSEE, U. Md., 1951. Elec. engr. Naval Research Lab., Washington, 1949-84; cons. in elec. engring. Kaman Corp., Alexandria, Va., 1984-94; cons. in field, 1994—. Instr. George Washington U., Washington, 1983-94. Author: (with others) Radar Handbook, 1990; co-author: Radar Handbook, 1970, Airborne Radar, 1961; contbr. articles to IEEE jour.; patentee (multiple) in monopulse radar and related fields. Served with USN, 1945-46 Recipient Radar Devel. award U.S. Navy, 1978, Meritorious Civilian Service award, 1980 Fellow IEEE; mem. Research Soc. Am. Avocation: amateur radio.

HOWARD, DESMOND KEVIN, professional football player; b. Cleveland, May 15, 1970; BA Comm. Studies, U. Mich. Wide receiver Washington Redskins, 1992-94; wide receiver, kick returner Jacksonville Jaguars, 1995, Green Bay Packers, 1996-97, Oakland Raiders, 1997-98; wide receiver Detroit Lions, 1999—. Named College Football Player of the Year, The Sporting News, 1991; recipient Heisman Trophy, 1991, Maxwell award, 1991, MVP Super Bowl XXXI, 1997.

HOWARD, DONALD SEARCY, banker; b. Leadville, Colo., Aug. 13, 1928; s. Paul Parker and Amanda Jane (Searcy) H.; m. Phyllis Havey, Oct. 1, 1955; children: Steven, Julie, Rebecca, Martin BSBA, Northwestern U., 1950; MBA, Harvard U., 1955. Rsch. assoc. Bus. Sch., Harvard U., Boston, 1955-57; ofcl. asst. overseas div. Citibank, London, 1957; asst. cashier Citibank, N.A., N.Y.C., 1959-60, asst. v.p., 1960-63, v.p., 1963-69, dep. comptroller, 1969-72; sr. v.p.-fin. Citicorp-Citibank, 1972-79, exec. v.p., chief fin. officer, 1980-88; chief fin. officer Salomon Inc., N.Y.C., 1988-93. Mem. fin. acctg. stds. adv. com. Fin. Acctg. Bd., Stamford, Conn., 1985-88; mem. Internat. Acctg. Stds. Adv. Commn., London, 1986-93; dir. Bank Leumi U.S.A., 1994—, Green Garden, Inc., Bedford, Pa., 1986-2002, Consolidated Purchasing Svcs., Bernardsville, N.J., 1987-99, dir., Howard Vending, Miami, 2001-, Green Garden Products LLC, Bedford, 2002—. Co-Author: Managing The Liability Side of the Balance Sheet, 1976, Evolving Concepts of Bank Capital Management, 1980 Chair emeritus trustees Cornerstone Sch., Jersey City, 1993-2002; trustee Vis. Nurse Assn. Ctrl. N.J., 1995-97. Lt. comdr. USNR, 1950-57, Korea. Mem. Am. Bankers Assn. (chief fin. officer's exec. com. 1984-87). Presbyterian. E-mail: Phyldonhow@aol.com.

HOWARD, ELIZABETH ANN BLANTON, transportation executive; b. Spindale, N.C., Mar. 14, 1934; d. John Lloyd and Monnie Clare (Geer) Blanton; m. Bill O. Howard, Aug. 13, 1950; children: Deborah Monette Howard Gustafson, Michael Ray. Grad. H.S., Rutherfordton, N.C.; real estate student, U. S.C., 1965. Sales rep. Reserve Life Ins. Co., Rutherfordton, N.C., 1956-63; sec., salesperson Johnny Barker Real Estate, Columbia, S.C., 1963-65; sec. A.M. Pullen & Co., Columbia, 1963-65; owner, mgr. Ann's Sample Shop, Columbia, S.C., 1965-81; pres. Modubilt Corp., Columbia, 1965-75, First Comml. Assocs., Inc., Columbia, 1965-75, Ann's Rag Time Van, Columbia, 1979-88; sec., treas. Howard's Courier Svc., Inc., Rutherfordton, N.C., 1990-2000, v.p., 2000—. Bldg. project mgr. Gen. Svc. Adminstrn., 1960's. Contbg. editor: Creative Ways to Raise Funds and Activate Alumni, 1995; contbr. History Book for Spindale United Meth. Ch. Pres. Spindale Elem. PTA, 1959, Belvedere Elem. PTA, Columbia, S.C., 1963-66; bd. dirs. Rutherfordton, N.C. C. of C., 1991-92, 96-99; pres. bd. dirs. Rutherford County Concert Assn., 2000-; bd. dirs. Habitat, 2000-2002. Named Sec. of Yr. WIOS Radio, Columbia S.C., 1967; recipient Charles Z. Flack award, Rutherfordton, N.C., 1992, award for svc. Am. Cancer Soc., 1994-96, Gov.'s award 2000. Mem. Sears Coun. of Career Women (charter), Rutherfordton Hist. Soc., Rutherfordton Ctrl. H.S. Alumni Assn. (pres. 1992—, All Class Reunion award 1992), Nat. Honor Soc.02099712 Democrat. Methodist. Avocations: travel, rehabilitation of older homes, reading. Home: 1198 Oak Springs Rd Rutherfordton NC 28139-8099 Office: PO Box 475 Spindale NC 28160-0475

HOWARD, FLORENCE ROSTRON, home economics educator; b. Chester, Pa., May 11, 1933; d. George Sanderson and Josephine (Dankelman) Rostron. BS, Cedar Crest Coll., Allentown, Pa., 1955; MEd, Western Md. Coll., 1979. Tchr. home econs. Nether Providence High Sch., Wallingford, Pa., 1955-58, Towson (Md.) Town Jr. High., 1958-60; tchr., chmn. dept. home econs. Johnnycake Mid. Sch., Balt., 1960-89; ret., 1989. Part-time travel counselor, 1990—. Active Boy Scouts Am., Balt., 1972-88, sec. local unit, 1976-88. Mem. NEA (life), Am. Home Econs. Assn., Md. State Tchrs. Assn. (life), Md. Retired Tchrs. Assn., Md. Home Econs. Assn. (com. chmn. 1985-87, mem. nominating com. 1987-89), Md. Home Econs. Tchrs. Assn. (v.p. 1968-72), Balt. County Home Econs. Tchrs. Assn. (chmn. social com. 1979-89), Met. Area Assn. Home Economists (v.p. 1984-91). Republican. Presbyterian. E-mail: PRosTrav@aol.com.

HOWARD, GARY SCOTT, communications executive; b. Waukegan, Ill., Feb. 21, 1951; s. Clarence Turner Howard and Jan E. (Reimer) Searcy; m. Jacquelyn Jule Milne, Apr. 22, 1978; children: Gentry, Matthew, Chad. BS in Acctg., Colo. State U., 1973. Audit mgr. Arthur Andersen, Denver, 1973-80; v.p. Castle Pines Land Co., Denver, 1980-82; v.p. fin., treas., sec. The Sienna Co., Boulder, Colo., 1982-84; v.p., treas. United Cable TV, Denver, 1987-89; sr. v.p., treas. United Artists Entertainment Co., 1989, sr. v.p., chief adminstrv. officer, 1990—. Mem. Am. Inst. CPA's, Colo. Soc. CPA's. Roman Catholic. Avocations: hockey, sports.

HOWARD, GENE CLAUDE, lawyer, retired state senator; b. Perry, Okla., Sept. 26, 1926; s. Joe W. and Nell L. (Brown) Howard; m. Belva J. Prestidge, Dec. 28, 1979; children: Jean Ann, Joe Ted, Belinda Janice. JD, U. Okla., 1951. Bar: Okla. 1950, U.S. Ct. Mil. Appeals 1956, U.S. Supreme Ct. 1956. Ptnr. Howard & Widdows & Bufogle PC, and predecessors, Tulsa, 1952—; mem. Okla. Ho. of Reps., 1958-62, Okla. Senate, 1964-82, pres. pro tem, 1974-81. Mem. exec. com. Coun. State Govts., 1974—76; chmn. Okla. State and Edn. employees Group Ins. Bd., 1990—98; bd. dirs. Cubic Energy Corp., Local Okla. Bank, 1992—2004; trustee Phila. Mortgage Trust, Okla. Coll. Savs. Plan, 1998—2002. Mem. So. Growth Policy Bd., 1972—76; pres. Okla. Jr. Dems., 1954; del. Dem. Nat. Conv., 1964. With U.S. Army, 1944—46, PTO, lt. col. USAF, 1961—62. Mem.: Phi Delta Phi, Tulsa County Bar Assn. (Outstanding Young Atty. 1953), Okla. Bar Assn. Democrat. Mem. Disciples Of Christ. Home: 2404 E 29th St Tulsa OK 74114-5619 Office: Howard Widdows & Bufogle PC 1500 Nations Bank Ctr 15W6 Tulsa OK 74119 Office Phone: 918-744-7440. Personal E-mail: howardgc@swbell.net.

HOWARD, GEORGE, JR., federal judge; b. Pine Bluff, Ark., May 13, 1924; Student, Lincoln U., 1951; BS, U. Ark., JD, 1954; LL.D., 1976. Bar: Ark. bar 1953, U.S. Supreme Ct. bar 1959. Pvt. practice law, Pine Bluff, 1953-77; spl. assoc. justice Ark. Supreme Ct., 1976, assoc. justice, 1977; justice U.S. Ct. Appeals, Ark., 1979-80; U.S. dist. judge, Eastern dist. Little Rock, 1980—. Mem. Ark. Claims Commn., 1969-77; chmn. Ark. adv. com. Civil Rights Commn. Recipient citation in recognition of faithful and disting. svc. as mem. Supreme Ct. Com. of Profl. Conduct, 1980, disting. jurist award Jud. Coun. Nat. Bar Assn., 1980, Wiley A. Branton Issues Symposium award, 1990; voted outstanding trial judge 1984-85 Ark. Trial Lawyers Assn.; inducted Ark.'s Black Hall of Fame, 1994; recipient keepers of the spirit award Univ. Ark., Pine Bluff, 1995, quality svc. award Ark. Dem. Black Caucus, 1995, Drum Major award, Ark. Martin Luther King, Jr., Commn., 2003. Mem. ABA, Ark. Bar Assn. (Disting. Svc. Pursuit Justice award 2003), Jefferson County Bar Assn. (pres.) Baptist.

HOWARD, GEORGE TURNER, JR., retired surgeon; b. Harlan, Ky., May 31, 1913; MD, Harvard U., 1937; LLD, Lincoln Meml. U., 1996. Diplomate Am. Bd. Surgery. Intern, then resident in surgery Boston City Hosp., 1937-41; resident in surgery Meml. Hosp. Cancer and Allied Disease, N.Y.C., 1941-42; mem. staff St. Mary's Hosp., Ft. Sanders Hosp., U. Tenn. Meml. Hosp., Children's Hosp., East Tenn. Bapt. Hosp.; ret., 1982. Fellow ACS, Royal Soc. Health, Acad. Internat. Medicine, Southeastern Surg. Congress. Home: 1209 Scenic Dr Knoxville TN 37919-7645

HOWARD, GLEN SCOTT, foundation executive, lawyer; b. Birmingham, Ala., May 28, 1950; s. Jack and Bernice (Koffman) H.; m. Lauren Oldak, Sept. 2, 1978; 1 child, Gregory Alan. AB cum laude, Harvard Coll., 1971; JD, U. Chgo., 1974. Bar: DC 1976. Law clk. to chief judge US Dist. Ct., Atlanta, 1974-76; assoc. Sutherland, Asbill & Brennan, Washington, 1976-81, ptnr., 1981-96; gen. counsel, COO Fannie Mae Found., Washington, 1996-97, sr. advisor, 1997-99, sr. v.p., gen. counsel, 2000—. Performer radio show and record album: Classics Illustrated, 1984; contbr. articles to profl. jours. Bd. dirs. Goodwill of Greater Washington, 1996-, vice-chair, 1999-2004, compliance officer, 2004-; bd. dirs. Greater DC Cares, Washington, 1997-, chair, 2001-03; pres. United Arts Orgn. Greater Washington, 2000—; bd. dirs. Leadership Washington, 1999-2005, Greater Washington Bd. Trade, 2002-03, Ams. for Arts, 2005—; Helen Hayes Awards, 2005; Workforce Orgns. Regional Collaboration, 2005-; chair Greater Washington Bus. Philanthropy Summit, 1999-2002, Sept. 11th Fund Distbn. Com., Greater Washington, 2001-04; cmty. adv. bd. mem. John F. Kennedy Ctr. for Performing Arts, 2004—; tchr. Temple Sinai Religious Sch., 1997—. Mem.: ABA, Choral Arts Soc. Democrat. Jewish. Office: Fannie Mae Found 4000 Wisconsin Ave NW N Tower Ste 1 Washington DC 20016-2800 Office Phone: 202-274-8090. Business E-Mail: ghoward@fanniemaefoundation.org.

HOWARD, H. WILLIAM, information technology executive; BS in sci. and engring., Princeton U.; MBA, Stanford U. Sales and mgmt. positions IBM, Systems Industries, Inc., Memorex; former v.p. info. tech. Bechtel Group; former corp. v.p. info. tech., chief info. officer Inland Steel Industries, Inc., Chgo.; chief info. officer Sun Microsystems, Inc., Santa Clara, Calif., 1998—. Office: Sun Microsystems Inc 4150 Network Cir Santa Clara CA 95054 Office Phone: 650-960-1300, 800-555-9786. Office Fax: 408-276-3804.

HOWARD, HARRY CLAY, lawyer; b. Rockwood, Tenn., May 1, 1929; s. Harry Clay and Julia Roe (Cannon) H.; m. Mary Helen Harrison, June 12, 1951 (dec. Dec. 1997); children: Helen Howard Porter (dec.), Anne Howard Freihofer; m. Telside Matthews Strickland, Dec. 15, 1998. BA, Vanderbilt U., 1951; LLB, Emory U., 1955. Bar: Ga. 1955. Sr. ptnr. King & Spalding, Atlanta, 1956-92, ret. ptnr., 1993—. Bd. dirs. Avondale Mills Inc. Mem. coun. Emory Law Sch., 1975-85, chmn., 1976-77; bd. dirs. Cen. Atlanta Progress Inc., 1981-85, Wesley Woods Geriatric Hosps., 1987-93, chmn., 1988-92; trustee Wesley Homes Inc., 1961-93, chmn., 1981-86; past trustee Oglethorpe U., The Lovett Sch. 1st lt. USMC, 1951-53. Mem. Am. Law Inst., State Bar Ga., Atlanta Bar Assn., Lawyers Club Atlanta, Piedmont Driving Club, Peachtree Golf Club, Highlands Country Club, Phi Beta Kappa, Omicron Delta Kappa. Office: King & Spalding 191 Peachtree St NE Ste 4900 Atlanta GA 30303-1740

HOWARD, HERBERT HOOVER, broadcasting and communications educator; b. Johnson City, Tenn., Nov. 7, 1928; s. Bonnie Robert and Laura Elizabeth (Crumley) H.; m. Alpha Sells Day, Nov. 16, 1956; 1 child, Joseph David. BS, E. Tenn. State U., Johnson City, 1952, MS, 1955; cert., U. N.C., 1959; PhD in Mass Comm., Ohio U., 1973. Announcer, program dir. Sta. WJHL-AM-FM-TV, Johnson City, 1951-58; writer, announcer Sta. WCHL & WUNC-TV, Chapel Hill, N.C., 1958-59; from instr. to radio network mgr. U. Tenn., 1959-70, from asst. to assoc. prof. communications, 1970-80, prof. broadcasting Knoxville, 1980-99, prof. emeritus, 1999—, asst. dean Coll. Communications, 1981-93, acting dean, 1990-91; assoc. dean, 1993-99. Mem. cmty. adv. bd. WSJK-WKOP Pub. TV, 1995—; pres. Tazewell TV Corp., 1996—. Author: Multiple Ownership in Television and Broadcasting, 1979, (textbook) Radio, TV, and Cable Programming, 1984, 94, Broadcast Advertising, 1979, 88, 91; contbr. articles to profl. jours. Mem. Soc. Profl. Journalists, Assn. Edn. in Journalism and Mass. Comms., Broadcast Edn. Assn. (Disting. Edn. Svc. award 2000), Optimists (So. Knoxville v.p. 1972—, pres. 1974, lt. gov. Tenn. dist. internat. chpt. 1976). Republican. Presbyterian. Avocations: travel, stamp collecting/philately. Home: 1724 S Hills Dr Knoxville TN 37920-2937 Office: U Tenn 333 Communications Bldg Knoxville TN 37996-0001 E-mail: herbhoward1@att.net.

HOWARD, J. TIMOTHY, former finance company executive; m. Debra Howard; children: Julia, Lauren. B in Econs. magna cum laude, M in Econs., UCLA. Fin. adv. Chase Econometric Assocs., 1975; v.p., sr. fin. economist Wells Fargo Bank, San Francisco; v.p., chief economist Fannie Mae, 1982, sr. v.p. econs. and planning, exec. v.p. econs., strategic planning and fin. analysis, 1987-88, exec. v.p. asset mgmt., 1988-90, exec. v.p., CFO, 1990—2004, vice chmn., 2003—04. Bd. dirs. CarrAmerica Realty Corp. Trustee, mem. exec. com., officer The Washington Opera; trustee Holton-Arms Sch.; bd. dirs. Wharton Fin. Instns. Ctr.

HOWARD, J. WOODFORD, JR., retired political science professor; b. Ashland, Ky., July 5, 1931; s. J. Woodford and Florence Alberta (Stephens) H.; m. Valerie Hope Barclay, Apr. 10, 1960; 1 child, Elaine Howard Christ. BA summa cum laude, Duke U., 1952; M.P.A., Princeton U., 1954, MA, 1955, PhD, 1959. Instr. Lafayette Coll., Easton, Pa., 1958-59; postdoctoral fellow Harvard Law Sch., 1961-62; asst. prof. Lafayette Coll., 1959-62, Duke U., 1962-66, assoc. prof., 1966-67, Johns Hopkins U., 1967-69, prof. polit. sci. Balt., 1969-75, Thomas P. Stran prof., 1975-96, Thomas P. Stran prof. emeritus, 1996—, chmn. dept., 1973-75; ret., 1996. Author: Mr. Justice Murphy: A Political Biography, 1968, Courts of Appeals in the Federal Judicial System, 1981 (cert. merit ABA 1982); mem. editl. bd. Law and Soc. Rev., 1975-76, 78-82, Am. Polit. Sci. Rev., 1977-81, Jour. Politics, 1979-93, Johns Hopkins U. Press, 1991-93; subject of essay in The Pioneers of Judicial Behavior, edited by Nancy Maveety, 2003; contbr. articles to profl. jours. Mem. history program adv. com. Fed. Jud. Ctr., 1989-95; trustee Balt. Mus. Art; mem. music com. Balt. Symphony Orch.; bd. dirs. Shriver Hall Concert Series; vestryman Ch. of Redeemer, Balt., 1988-90. Lt. USAF, 1955-57. Named to Hall of Fame, Floyd Co., Ky., 1957; recipient Outstanding Tchr. awards and citations, Lafayette Coll., 1960, Duke U., 1966, Johns Hopkins U., 1969, 1970, 1993, Pub. award, Harcourt Coll., 2001. Mem.: Law and Soc. Assn., Am. Judicature Soc., Nat. Capitol Area Polit. Sci. Assn. (coun. 1986—89), So. Polit. Sci. Assn., Am. Polit. Sci. Assn., Filson Hist. Soc., Supreme Ct. Hist. Soc., Princeton Club (N.Y.C.), 14 Hamilton St. Club (Balt.), Phi Beta Kappa, Omicron Delta Kappa. Office: Johns Hopkins U Dept Polit Sci Baltimore MD 21218-2685

HOWARD, JACK, industrial relations specialist, consultant; b. Santa Ana, Calif., Aug. 26, 1924; s. Floyd Willie and Inez (Cooley) H.; m. Margaret Anne McKinnon, Aug. 25, 1950 (dec.); children: Marc, Anne. AB, U. Calif., Berkeley, 1948; MA, UCLA, 1952. Reporter Springfield (Ohio) Daily News, 1949-51; labor editor San Francisco Chronicle, 1952-60; chief investigator govt. information subcom. U.S. Ho. of Reps., 1960-63; spl. asst. to undersec. of Labor, 1963-64; adminstr. Neighborhood Youth Corps, 1964-66, Bur. of Work Programs, 1966-67; exec. asst. to Sec. Labor, 1968; v.p. Ednl. Scis. Programs, Inc., N.Y.C., 1969-71; sec.-treas., cons. William Benton Found., N.Y.C., 1971-80; asst. to pub. Ency. Brit., N.Y.C., 1971-73; asst. dir. Twentieth Century Fund, N.Y.C., 1974-76; asst. to pres. Am. Fedn. State, County and Mcpl. Employees AFL-CIO, 1976-97; ind. cons., 1997—. Internat. v.p. Am. Newspaper Guild-AFL-CIO, 1957-60 With AUS, 1943-46. Congl. fellow Am. Polit. Sci. Assn., 1957-58; Recipient Distinguished Svc. award Dept. Labor, 1965 Mem. ACLU. Home: 219 5th St NE Washington DC 20002-5919 Personal E-mail: howardjack@hotmail.com.

HOWARD, JAMES JOSEPH, III, utility company executive; b. Pitts., July 1, 1935; s. James Joseph Jr. and Flossie (Wenzel) H.; m. Donna J. Fowler; children: James J. IV, Catherine A., Christine A., William F. BBA, U. Pitts., 1957; MS, MIT, 1970. With Bell Telephone of Pa., Pitts., 1957-78, v.p., gen. mgr., 1976-78; v.p. ops. Wis. Telephone Co., Milw., 1978-79, exec. v.p., chief operating officer, 1979-81, pres., chief exec. officer, 1981-83, chmn., chief exec. officer, 1983; pres., chief operating officer Ameritech, Chgo., 1983-87, dir.; pres., chief exec. officer No. States Power Co., Mpls., 1987—, chmn., 1988—, Xcel Energy, 2000-2001, chmn. emeritus. Bd. dirs. Walgreen Co., Deerfield, Ill., No. States Power Co., Mpls., Honeywell, Mpls., Fed. Res. Bank of Mpls., Ecolab, St. Paul, ReliaStar Fin., Mpls., Edison Electric Inst., Electric Power Rsch. Inst., chmn. Nuclear Energy Inst. Trustee U. St. Thomas, St. Paul. Sloan fellow MIT, 1969. Mem. Conf. Bd. N.Y.*

HOWARD, JAMES KENTON, academic administrator, journalist; b. June 30, 1943; s. Arthur R. and Dora G. (Utt) H.; m. Lynn M. Marsh, Sept. 23, 1982; children: Lara L., James M. BA, U. Okla., 1965, MA, 1979; Inst. Ednl. Mgmt., Harvard U., 1991. Asst. dean students U. Okla., Norman, 1965-67, asst. to pres., 1967-68, asst. to v.p. for univ. rels. and devel., 1978; editor Northland Press, Flagstaff, Ariz., 1972-77; cons. Okla. Dept. Public Safety, Oklahoma City, 1977; asst. dean student affairs Northeastern State U., Tahlequah, Okla., 1978-79, dir. univ. svcs., 1979-82, asst. prof. journalism, 1979—2004, v.p. adminstrn., 1982-91, v.p. bus. and devel., 1991—2004, trustee NSU Found., 1981-90, 92—, v.p. emeritus, 2005—. Mem. Coun. Bus. Officers, Okla. State Regents for Higher Edn., 1982-2004; adv. dir. BancFirst, 1995—. Author: Ten Years With the Cowboy Artists of America, 1976. Bd. dirs. Friends of Mus. No. Ariz., 1974-77; chmn. No. Ariz. campaign March of Dimes, 1973-74; founding chmn. Cherokee County Cmty. Sentencing Coun., 1997—; No. Ariz. coord. Babbit for Atty. Gen. Campaign, 1974; trustee Flagstaff-Coconino County Pub. Libr., 1976-77, chmn. bd. trustees, 1976-77; pres. Indian Nations Soccer Coun., 1981-82; bd. dirs. Indian Nations coun. Boy Scouts Am., 1990-94, Okla. Found. for Excellence, 1996—; trustee Tahlequah Pub. Schs. Found., 1990-2000, founding chair, 1990-98; bd. dirs. Leadership Okla., 1990—, mem. exec. com., 1990-98, pres., 1994-95, mem. Class II, 1988-89; bd. dirs. Okla. Assn. of Coll. and Univ. Bus. Officers, 1993-98, pres., 1996-97; bd. dirs. Okla. Acad. for State Goals, 1993—, chair, 1999-2000; founding pres. Boys and Girls Club of Tahlequah, 1996-2000; pres., Coll. Assn. Liability Mgmt., 1996-98, 2002-2004; bd. dirs. Okla. Arts Inst., 1997—, Okla. Music Hall of Fame, 2000-2004, Communities Found. Okla., 2000-02, bd. govs., 2002—; founding pres. Tahlequah Comty. Found., 2003—. With USAF, 1968-72. Recipient Eason Book Collection award, 1965, Book Design award Rounce and Coffin Club of L.A., 1974-75, Citation of Profl. Merit Northeastern State U., 1991, Excellence in Okla. Leadership award, 1995, Disting. leadership award Nat. Assn. Cmty. Leadership, 1995-96; named Outstanding Citizen, Tahlequah Area C. of C. Mem. U. Okla. Assn. (life), Nat. Cowboy Hall of Fame and Western Heritage Ctr. (life), Tahlequah Area C. of C. (bd. dirs. 1985-88), Mensa, Rotary (past pres., Paul Harris fellow), Sigma Delta Chi, Kappa Tau Alpha, Lambda Chi Alpha.

HOWARD, JAMES WEBB, brokerage house executive, engineer, lawyer; b. Evansville, Ind., Sept. 17, 1925; s. Joseph R. and Velma (Cobb) H.; m. Phyllis Jean Brandt, Dec. 27, 1948; children: Sheila Rae, Sharon Kae. BS in Mech. Engring, Purdue U., 1949; postgrad., Akron (Ohio) Law Sch., 1950-51, Cleve. Marshall Law Sch., 1951-52; MBA, Case Western Res. U., 1962; JD, Western State Coll. Law, 1976. Registered profl. engr., Ind., Ohio. Jr. project engr. Firestone Tire & Rubber Co., Akron, 1949-50; gen. foreman Cadillac Motor Car div. GM, 1950-53; mgmt. cons. M.K. Sheppard & Co., Cleve., 1953-56; plant mgr. Lewis Welding & Engring. Corp., Ohio, 1956-58; underwriter The Ohio Co., Columbus, 1959; chmn. Growth Capital, Inc., Chgo., 1960-98; pvt. practice law San Diego, 1979-85. Pres. Meister Brau, Inc., Chgo., 1965-73, The Home Mart, San Diego, 1974-82; mng. agt., fin. instn. specialist FDIC/RTC, 1985-90; specialist in charge Office of FDIC-DOL, Portland, Oreg., 1986-87. Developer of "Lite" beer. Co-chmn. Chgo. com. Ill. Sesquicentennial Com., 1968. Served with AUS, 1943-46. Decorated Bronze Star, Parachutist badge, Combat Inf. badge. Mem. ASME, Nat. Assn. Small Bus. Investment Cos. (past pres.), State Bar Calif., Grad. Bus. Alumni Assn. Western Res. U. (past gov.), Masons, Tau Kappa Epsilon, Pi Tau Sigma, Beta Gamma Sigma. Methodist. Personal E-mail: jhoward46@cox.net.

HOWARD, JEFF DAVID, volunteer, retired military officer; b. Dallas, June 14, 1961; s. M.J. and Mary E. Howard; children: Joshua Michael, Allison Maggie. BS in Geog., U. Ctrl. Ark., 1983. Enlisted U.S. Army, 1979, advanced through grades to maj., 1987, ret., 2003; claims examiner, mgr., clk. VA Regional Office, Little Rock, 1986—93. Artist one man show FT Smith Art Ctr., 2004; other numerous paintings. Vol. Multicultural Ctr. Ft. Smith, Ark., 1998-2003, bd. dirs., 1998-2003; Red Kettle coord., procurement vol., vol. adminstrv. asst. The Salvation Army, Ft. Smith, 1996-2003; missionary Fgn. Mission Bd., So. Bapt. Conv., Moscow, Yalta, Ukraine, 1991; vol. Interfaith Disaster Recovery Ctr., Ft. Smith, 1996-97; vol., bd. dirs. Alzheimer's Assn., Ft. Smith, 1997; vol. Ctrl. Christian Ch., Ft. Smith, 1994—; dep. dir. gen. Internat. Biog. Ctr., Cambridge, Eng., 2003. Named Vol. of Yr., Salvation Army, 1996, 97, 98, 99. Mem. Disabled Am. Vets. (Gold Leader award 1997), Spl. Forces Assn., Am. Biography Soc. Avocations: painting, volunteering, fine automobiles, collecting military and foreign country memorabilia, collecting coins and precious metals. Home: PO Box 2194 Fort Smith AR 72902-2194

HOWARD, JEFFREY HJALMAR, lawyer; b. N.Y.C., Aug. 23, 1944; s. Virgil Edward and Margaretta E. H.; m. Brenda H. Howard, June 19, 1966; children: Taggart Harrison, Brooke Kennedy. BA in Philosophy, Randolph-Macon Coll., 1966; postgrad. (English Speaking Union scholar) U. Edinburgh (Scotland), 1965; LLB, U. Va., 1969. Bar: D.C. 1970, U.S. Sup. Ct. 1978, Va. 1987. Law clk. Circuit Ct., Montgomery County, Md., 1969-70; assoc. Covington & Burling, Washington, 1970-74; assoc. gen. counsel for toxics, pesticides and solid waste U.S. EPA, Washington, 1974-76; ptnr. Crowell & Moring, 1989—; lectr. antitrust and environ. law U. Va. 1976-89; lectr. environ. law Peking U., Peoples Republic of China, 1986. Mem. ABA, D.C. Bar Assn., Va. Soc. Fellows, Order Coif, Alpha Psi Omega, Alpha Epsilon Pi, Delta Sigma Rho-Tau Kappa Alpha, Omicron Delta Kappa. Editorial bd. Va. Law Rev., 1967-69; contbr. chpts. to books and articles to profl. jours. Home: 1021 Duchess St Mc Lean VA 22102-2007 Office: 1001 Pennsylvania Ave NW Washington DC 20004-2505 Office Phone: 202-624-2909. E-mail: jhoward@crowell.com.

HOWARD, JEFFREY R., federal judge; b. Claremont, NH, Nov. 4, 1955; m. Marie Howard; 2 children. BA, Plymouth St Coll-Univ N.H., 1978; JD, Law Ctr-Georgetown U, 1981. Off. of NH atty. gen., 1981—88; dep. atty. gen. State of NH, 1988—89; U.S. atty. Dist. of NH, Concord, 1989—92; atty. gen. State of NH, 1993—97; ptnr. Choate Hall & Stewart, 1997—2001; pvt. practice Jeffrey R. Howard, Esq., 2001—02; judge US Ct. Appeals 1st Cir., 2002—. Mem. atty. gen. adv. com. Attys. Gen. Thornburg & Barr. Named Citizen of Yr., Salisbury, NH, 2000. Office: 1 Warren Rudman US Courthouse 55 Pleasant St Concord NH 03301*

HOWARD, JOHN, federal agency administrator; MD, Loyola U., 1974; M of Occupational Health, Harvard Sch. Pub. Health, 1982; JD, UCLA, 1986; LLM, George Wash. U., 1987. Bd. Certified Occupational Physician. Internist UCLA Sch. Medicine Pulmonary Fellowship Program, Cedars-Sinai Med. Ctr., L.A.; med. dir. and chief clinician Philip Mandelker AIDS Prevention Clinic; asst. counselor to Under Sec. Health and Human Svcs.; asst. prof. environmental and occupational medicine U. Calif. at Irvine; chief Divsn. Occupational Safety and Health, State of Calif. Dept. Indsl. Rels., 1991—; dir. CDC, Nat. Inst. for Occupational Safety and Health (NIOSH), 2002—. Office: Hubert H Humphrey Bldg 200 Independence SW Rm 715H Washington DC 20201

HOWARD, JOHN ADDISON, retired academic administrator; b. Evanston, Ill., Aug. 10, 1921; s. Hubert Elmer and Edith (Sackett) H.; m. Janette Marie Nobis, Aug. 11, 1951; children: Marie Starr, Steven Lamson, Martha Nobis, Katherine Louise. Student, Princeton U., 1939-42; BS, Northwestern U.,

1947, MA, 1949, PhD, 1962; LL.D., Grove City Coll., 1972, Brigham Young U., 1976, Rockford Coll., 1980. Instr. French Palos Verdes Coll., Rolling Hills, Calif., 1947-49, dean students, 1949-51, v.p., 1950-51, pres., 1951-55; exec. vice chmn. Pres.'s Com. on Govt. Contracts, 1956-57; pres. Rockford (Ill.) Coll., 1960-77; dir. Rockford Coll. Inst., 1977-80; pres. The Rockford Inst., 1980-86, counselor, 1986-97; sr. fellow The Howard Ctr. Religion, Family & Soc., 1997—. Author: Detoxifying the Culture, 2001; contbg. author: Dilemmas Facing the Nation, 1979. Mem. U.S. Commn. on Marijuana and Drug Abuse, 1971-73, Pres.'s Task Force on Priorities in Higher Edn., 1969-70; pres. Ingersoll Found., 1983—2003. Served to 1st lt. AUS, 1942-45. Decorated Silver Star with oak leaf cluster, Purple Heart with oak leaf cluster; recipient Horatio Alger award, 1967, Educator of Yr. Religious Heritage Am., 1980. Mem. Am. Assn. Pres. Ind. Colls. and Univs. (pres. 1969-72), Phila. Soc. (pres. 1979-81), Rotary, Phi Beta Kappa. Home: 1802 Birchwood Ln Rockford IL 61107-1878 Office Phone: 815-964-5819.

HOWARD, JOHN LAWRENCE, federal agency lawyer; b. Danville, Ill., May 16, 1957; s. Charles R. and Kathryn (Tormohlen) H.; m. Julia Louise Steinfirst, Oct. 13, 1984. BS, Ind. U., 1979, JD, 1982; LLM, George Washington U., 1989. Bar: Ind., 1982, U.S. Supreme Ct., 1986, Fed. Cir. Ct., 1987, U.S. Ct. Appeals (4th cir.), 1989. Dep. prosecutor 30th Jud. Cir., Rensselaer, Ind., 1982-84; lawyer U.S. Office Pers. Mgmt., Washington, 1984-85; spl. asst. to gen. counsel U.S. Consumer Product Safety Commn., Washington, 1984-85; legal counsel to chmn. U.S. Merit System Protection Bd., Washington, 1986-88; assoc. dep. atty. gen. U.S. Dept. Justice, Washington, 1988-90; dep. counsel to v.p. Office of V.P., Washington, 1990—; counsel to v.p. Dan Quayle, 1991-93; various positions Tenneco, Inc., 1993—95, gen. counsel, 1998—99; sr. v.p. & gen. counsel W.W. Grainger, Inc., 2000—. Contbr. articles to profl. jours. Mem. Fed. Bar Assn., Fed. Cir. Bar Assn., Army & Navy Club Washington. Republican. Office: WW Grainger 100 Grainger Pkwy Lake Forest IL 60045-5201 Business E-Mail: john_howard@grainger.com.

HOWARD, JOHN LINDSAY, lawyer; b. Drumheller, Alta., Can., Nov. 18, 1931; s. Lindsay Lee and Nancy (Martin) H.; m. Jeannette Huguenin, Nov. 21, 1969. B.Comm., U. B.C., 1959, LL.B., 1961; LL.M., Harvard U., 1968; postgrad., McGill U., Montreal, Can., 1967. Bar: B.C. 1962, Que. 1967, Fed. Queen's Counsel 1977. Mem. Brahan, Dickerson & Howard, Vancouver, B.C., 1962-67, Tansey, de Grandpre, Montreal, 1968-71; asst. dep. minister Fed. Dept. Consumer and Corp. Affairs, Ottawa, Ont., 1971-79; sr. v.p. law and corp. affairs MacMillan Bloedel Ltd., Vancouver, 1979-96, cons., corp. dir., comml. law arbitrator, 1996—; dir. Investment Dealers Assn. Can., 1996—. Bus. law arbitrator. Co-author: Proposals for a New Corporation Law for Canada, 1971, Proposals for a Securities Market Law for Canada, 1979. Home: PO Box 831 Sooke BC Canada V0S 1N0 Office Phone: 250-642-4489. E-mail: johnlhoward@shaw.ca.

HOWARD, JOHN VINCENT, JR., lawyer; b. San Tomé, Venezuela, Jan. 27, 1962; s. John Vincent and Diane Shirley (Page) H.; m. Val Marie Schmuhl, Aug. 24, 1991. BA in History, Washington and Lee U., 1984; LLM, U. Colo., 1987. Bar: Colo. Assoc. Brian A. Jeffrey, P.C., Evergreen, Colo., 1987; exec. v.p., gen. counsel Columbine JDS Sys. Inc., Laser Tech Color Inc.; chief intellectual property counsel Andersen Worldwide, S.C., Chgo.; chief counsel Quark Inc., Denver; sr. v.p., gen. counsel Vertis Inc., Balt., 2000—. Book reviewer Trial Talk, 1990-92. Coach Colo. High Sch. Mock Trial Team, Evergreen, 1988—; trustee Hammond-Harwood Assn., Annapolis. Mem. Kiwanis, Phi Eta Sigma, Kappa Sigma (sec. 1983). Episcopalian. Avocations: golf, skiing, creative writing. Office: Vertis Inc 250 W Pratt St Baltimore MD 21201*

HOWARD, JOSEPH HARVEY, retired librarian; b. Olustee, Okla., Jan. 15, 1931; s. William Lester and Letitia Browder (Dickey) H.; m. Patricia Shaughnessy Schiebel, Apr. 10, 1980. B in Mus. Edn., U. Okla., 1952, MLS, 1957. Assoc. dir. pub. svcs. U. Colo. Libr., Boulder, 1960-63; vol. Peace Corps, Kuala Lumpur, Malaysia, 1963-65; head catalog dept. Washington U., St. Louis, 1956-67; asst. chief descriptive cataloging divsn. Libr. of Congress, Washington, 1967-68, chief descriptive cataloging divsn., 1968-72, chief serial record divsn., 1972-75, asst. dir. (cataloging) processing dept., 1975-76, asst. libr. for processing svcs., 1976-83; dir. Nat. Agrl. Libr., Beltsville, Md., 1983-94, ret., 1994. Author: Malay Manuscripts— A Bibliographical Guide, 1966. Served with AUS, 1952-54. Recipient Outstanding Svc. to Librarianship award U. Okla., 1979. Mem. ALA (Melvil Dewey medal 1985) Personal E-mail: jhhoward@comcast.net.

HOWARD, JUDITH LOIS, artist, art gallery owner; b. Chippewa Falls, Wis., Mar. 31, 1936; d. Roland Martin and Dorothy Lois (McCulloch) Hanson; m. William Lee Howard, Mar. 22, 1959 (div. Mar. 1991); children: Christian Scott, Craig Matthew; m. Steven R. Dewey, Apr. 10, 1999. BA, San Jose (Calif.) State U., 1958; MS, So. Oreg. State Coll., 1973. Mem. faculty San Jose State U., 1963; art specialist Medford (Oreg.) Sch. Dist., 1966-78; artist, designer Hanson Howard Gallery, Ashland, Oreg., 1979—. Cons. in field. Commr. Oreg. Arts Commn., Salem, 1983-96; pres. Ashland Gallery Assn., 2001-04. Mem. Oreg. Advs. for the Arts, Arts Coun. So. Oreg., Schneider Mus. of Art. Democrat. Methodist. Office: Hanson Howard Gallery 82 N Main St Ashland OR 97520-2782 Office Phone: 503-488-2562.

HOWARD, JUWAN, professional basketball player; b. Chgo., Feb. 7, 1973; Student, U. Mich., 1994. Profl. basketball player Washington Wizards (formerly Washington Bullets), Landover, Md., 1994—2001, Dallas Mavericks, 2001—02, Denver Nuggets, 2002—03, Orlando Magic, 2003—04, Houston Rockets, 2004—. Vol. From the Heart. Named H.S. player of year Ill., 1991, Rookie of Month, NBA, Feb. 1994. Office: c/o Houston Rockets 1510 Polk St Houston TX 77002

HOWARD, KATHLEEN, computer company executive; b. Norman, Okla., Nov. 3, 1947; d. Robert Adrian and Jane Elizabeth (Morgens) H.; m. Lawrence W. Osgood, Aug. 10, 1968 (div. Sept. 1970); m. Norman Edlo Gibat, Oct. 15, 1971. Student, U. Okla., 1966—68. Typesetter Selenby Press, Norman, 1968—72; owner, pres. Noguska Industries, Fostoria, Ohio, 1973—; co-founder Home Wine Mchts., Chgo., 1976; cons. Bechtel Corp., Ann Arbor, Mich., 1980—, Gaithersburg, Md., 1980—; chairperson Am. Software Project, 1985; ptnr. Popular Topics Pubs., 1993—; cons. Xerox Corp., Rochester, NY, 1998—. Author: All You Need to Know About MSDOS, 1993; co-author, illustrator: Lore of Still Building, 1972; co-author: Making Wine, Beer and Merry, 1973, Computer Comix Mag., 1986; pres. Popular Topics Press, Inc., also jours. and bus. mgmt. software. Treas. United Way of Fostoria, 1986-88, 2d v.p. 1988-90; bd. dirs. Pvt. Industry Coun., 1988-90. Recipient Founders award Home Wine and Beer Trade Assn. Chgo., 1976. Mem. BBB, Nat. Fedn. Ind. Bus., C. of C. (bd. dirs. 1986-92), Employer's Assn. Toledo, Altrusa Internat. Club (sec. Fostoria chpt. 1984-85, pres. 1986-88, editor dist. #5 1988-90, pres. 2001-03). Avocations: painting, printing, travel, reading. Office: Noguska Industries 741 N Countyline St Fostoria OH 44830-1566 Office Phone: 419-435-0404. Personal E-mail: knoguska@yahoo.com. Business E-Mail: khoward@noguska.com.

HOWARD, LEE MILTON, international health consultant; b. India, Nov. 9, 1922; s. John A. and Grace Mary (Lemen) H.; m. Maxwell C. Croft, June 22, 1946; children: Regan Ellis, Christine Baker, Kirk Anderson, Gene Reid. B.Sc., Baylor U., 1945; MD, Johns Hopkins U., 1947, M.P.H., 1958, Dr.P.H., 1959. Diplomate: Am. Bd. Preventive Medicine. Med. and surg. resident Church Home Hosp., Balt., 1947-50; mem. med. staff Clough Meml. Hosp., Ongole, Andhra, India, 1950-53; dir. Victoria Meml. Hosp., Warangal, Andhra, India, 1953-56; physician Med. Care Clinic, Johns Hopkins Hosp., 1957; U.S. adviser on malaria Philippines, 1960-62; U.S. regional malaria adviser Far East AID, 1962-64; chief malaria br. health div. AID, Washington, 1964-66; dep. dir. health svc. Office Tech. Coop. and Rsch., 1966-67, dir., 1967, Office Health, Devel. Support Bur., 1967-80; mem. expert co. on malaria WHO, 1966-79, chmn. com., 1970, adviser parasitic diseases, 1970; mem. U.S. del. World Health Assembly, 1969-79, WHO cons. on resource moblzn., 1979-81. AID devel. fellow, 1979-80; vis. asso. prof. parasitology Inst. Hygiene, U. Philippines, 1960—; vis. lectr. Johns Hopkins U. Sch. Pub. Health, Harvard Sch. Pub. Health, Yale U., Boston U., Tulane U.; lectr. Takemi Sympoisum, U. Tokyo, 1988; vis. fellow Inst. Devel. Studies, U. Sussex, 1979; mem. U.S. del., PAHO directing coun.; chief office resource mblzn. PAHO, 1981-82, office of external affairs, 1982-87; cons. to AID, WHO, World Bank, 1987—; sec., mem. exec. com. Gorgas Meml. Inst., 1972; mem. U.S. Sr. Exec. Svc. Recipient Superior Honor award AID, 1974, Disting. Career Svc. award AID, 1987, Disting. Alumnus award Baylor U., 2001; rsch. fellow U.S. Armed Forces Epidemiol. Bd., 1958-59. Fellow Am. Pub. Health Assn., Royal Soc. Tropical Medicine and Hygiene; mem. Am. Soc. Tropical Medicine and Hygiene, Philippine Pub. Health Assn., Johns Hopkins U. Sch. Pub. Health Soc. Alumni (pres. 1984-85), Soc. Scholars (Johns Hopkins U.), Nat. Coun. Internat. Health (charter mem.), Diplomatic and Consular Officers Ret., Cosmos Club (Washington). Home: 647 Azalea Dr Apt 1 Rockville MD 20850-2012

HOWARD, LELAND WILLIAM, writer; b. Jackson, Tenn., Feb. 3, 1950; s. Leland William and Bernice (Ball) H. Student, U. of the South, Sewanee, Tenn., 1968—71; cert. in French, Sorbonne, Paris, 1987; BA in English Lit. and Creative Writing, Hunter Coll., 2004. Publicist Millbrook Playhouse, Mill Hall, Pa., summer 1990. Contbr. articles to Impact, Gulf South Gay News, 1984, The Advocate, 1985, The Olivetree Rev., 1999; coord. "The Gay Writes" Southeastern Conf. Lesbians and Gay Men, New Orleans, 1985. Author: (poetry) Steps Below, 1983, The Grass Hut, 1993; author: Pirouettes Get No Applause in Goldengrove, 1997, 2d edit., 2002, screenplay, 1999. Mem. New Orleans Gay Mens' Chorus, 1983, First Nat. Gay Choral Festival, N.Y.C., 1983. Mem. La. Gay Polit. Action Caucus, Crescent City Coalition. Democrat. Episcopalian. Avocations: swimming, drawing, pets, singing, theater. Home: 533 W 49th St Apt 2FE New York NY 10019-7121 Personal E-mail: lelandwhoward@aol.com.

HOWARD, LYN JENNIFER, medical educator; b. Buxton, U.K., Jan. 19, 1938; came to U.S., 1965; naturalized, 1971; d. Peter and Bess (Donnelly) Marsh; m. Burtis Howard, Mar. 13, 1965 (div. 1988); children: Peter Howard, Thia Howard; m. Jack Alexander, Sept. 10, 1995. BA, Oxford U., 1960, MA, BM, BCh, 1964. Diplomate Am. Bd. Internal Medicine, Am. Bd. Nutrition. Intern London Hosp., 1964-65, Kans. City Med. Ctr., 1965-66, resident, 1966-70; fellow in clin. nutrition and gastroenterology Vanderbilt Hosp., 1971-73; dir. clin. nutrition program Albany (N.Y.) Med. Coll., 1973-80, asst. prof. medicine, pediat., 1973-76, assoc. prof. medicine, pediat., 1977-84, prof. medicine, 1984—, head divsn. clin. nutrition, 1986—. Asst. dir. Clin. Studies Ctr., Albany Med. Ctr., 1973-78; attending physician Albany Med. Ctr. Hosp., 1973—; attending physician, cons. clin. nutrition Albany VA Hosp., 1973—; cons. pediat. gastroenterology St. Peter's Hosp., Albany, 1974—; med. dir. Albany Home Health Resources, 1991-92; mem. working group Nat. Commn. Digestive Diseases, 1977; mem. NIH Consensus Devel. Conf., 1978, nutrition rsch. directions, 1979, spl. study sect. clin. nutrition rsch. units, 1980, nutrition study sect., 1989-93; cons. AMA Drug Evaluations, 1982, Medicare, Blue Cross/Blue Shield S.C., 1987—; keynote spkr. Australian Soc. Parenteral and Enteral Nutrition, Perth, 1993, 1st Clin. Nutrition Symposium, Kuala Lumpor, Malaysia, 1994. Contbg. editor Nutrition Reviews, 1981-87, 89; mem. editl. bd. Jour. Drug-Nutrient Interactions, 1984, Contemporary Issues in Clin. Nutrition, 1985, Jour. Am. Soc. Parenteral and Enteral Nutrition, 1987-90; contbr. articles, abstracts to profl. jours., chpts. to books. Exec. dir. Oley Found. for Home Parenteral and Enteral Nutrition, 1983-87, pres., 1987-91, med. dir., 1991; pres. Camphill Found., Pa., 1994. Recipient Clifton C. Thorne Cmty. Svc. award, 1990, Physician of Yr. award Albany chpt. Crohn's Colitis Found. Am., 1991; elected 1st woman mem. Great Lakes Interurban Club, 1990; Major County scholar, 1956; grantee Nutrition Found., 1973-79, U.S. Dept. Agriculture, 1978-81, William F. Donner Found., 1983, Oley Found. for Home Parenteral and Enteral Nutrition Patients, 1983—, Home Health Care of Am., 1983-88, Hosp. for Incurables Found., 1987-88, 91, Schaeffer Found. for Faculty Devel., 1988. Fellow Royal Coll. Physicians, Am. Coll. Physicians, Am. Coll. Nutrition (dir. 1985-88); mem. Am. Bd. Nutrition (dir. 1980, pres. 1982-84), Brit. Med. Assn., Am. Soc. Parenteral and Enteral Nutrition (abstract selection com. 1980, nutrition support standards com. 1984, future directions com. 1991, OASIS working group 1991-92, award 1992), Am. Soc. Clin. Nutrition (rsch. com. 1978, edn. com. 1979, councilor 1982-85, chair post grad. clin. nutrition tng. com. 1983-88, clin. practice in health and disease 1991), Am. Inst. Nutrition, Am. Gastroent. Assn. (co-organizer post grad. tng. course 1987, tng. and edn. com. 1988-91, abstract selection com. 1989), N.Am. Soc. Pediat. Gastroenterology, Am. Fedn. Clin. Rsch. (abstract selection com. 1986), Alpha Omega Alpha. Office: Albany Med Coll Albany NY 12208 Office Phone: 518-262-5299.

HOWARD, MARILYN, school system administrator; BA in Edn., U. Idaho, 1960, MSc in Edn., 1965; EdD, Brigham Young U., 1986; postgrad., Idaho State U. adj. faculty Idaho State U., U. Idaho. Prin. Moscow West Park Elementary Sch., 1988—99; supervisor, devel. pre-school Moscow sch. dists., 1996—99; supt. pub. instrn. Idaho State Dept. Edn., Boise, Idaho, 1999—. Past state pres. Internat. Reading Assn., nat. rsch. and studies com; bd. dirs. State Bd. Edn., State Land Bd., Northwest Regional Edn. Lab. Office: Idaho State Dept Edn 650 W State St PO Box 83720 Boise ID 83720-0027 Office Phone: 208-332-6811. E-mail: mlhoward@sde.state.id.us.

HOWARD, MELVIN, financial executive; b. Boston, Jan. 5, 1935; s. John M. and Molly (Sagar) H.; m. Beverly Ruth Kahan, June 9, 1957; children: Brian David, Marjorie Lyn. BA, U. Mass., 1957; MS, Columbia U., 1959. Fin. exec. Ford Motor Co., Dearborn, Mich., 1959-67; v.p. adminstrn. Shoe Corps. of Am., Columbus, Ohio, 1967-70; contr., sr. v.p. fin., chief fin. officer Xerox Corp., 1970-84, exec. v.p., chmn. fin. svcs., 1984-86, vice chmn. of bd., 1986-90, bd. dirs., 1982-90; pres., CEO Ehrlich Bober Fin. Corp., 1990-92; mng. dir. Taurus Adv. Group, 1993-94. Bd. dirs. Gould Pumps, Inc., Sector Mgmt., Inc. Trustee Nursing and Home Care, Commonwealth Coll. 1st lt. AUS, 1957. Mem. Birchwood Country Club, Frenchman's Creek Country Club, Beta Gamma Sigma. Home: 3139 Miro Dr S Palm Beach Gardens FL 33410-1285

HOWARD, MICHAEL ELIOT, historian, educator; b. London, Nov. 29, 1922; s. Geoffrey Eliot and Edith Julia Emma (Edinger) H. MA, U. Oxford, 1948, LittD, 1976, Leeds (Eng.) U.; DLitt, U. London, 1988. Asst. lectr. history Kings Coll. U. London, 1947-53, lectr. war studies, 1953-62; prof. war studies U. London, 1963-68; fellow higher defence studies All Souls Coll., Oxford, 1968-77; prof. history of war U. Oxford, 1977-80, regius prof. modern history, 1980-89; prof. history Yale U., New Haven, 1989-93. Pres. emeritus Internat. Inst. Strategic Studies, London. Author: The Franco Prussian War, 1961 (Duff Cooper Prize, 1962), Grand Strategy, vol. IV, 1971 (Wolfson award for history), War in European History, 1976, The Invention of Peace, 2002, The First World War, 2003, many others. Served to capt. Brit. Army, 1942-45. Decorated Mil. Cross His Majesty King George VI, comdr. Brit. Empire, companion of Honor, Order of Merit; recipient Atlantic award, NATO, 1989; created Knight Bachelor, 1986. Fellow Brit. Acad., U.S. Acad. Arts and Scis., Athenaeum Club, Garrick Club (London). Anglican.

HOWARD, MILDRED, sculptor; b. San Francisco, 1945; AA, cert. in fashion arts, Coll. Alameda, 1977; MFA in Fiberworks, John F. Kennedy U., 1985. One-woman shows include Mill Valley (Calif.) Old Post Office, 1984, Dade County Libr., Miami, Fla., 1985, Calif. State U., Hayward, 1987, Headlands Ctr. for the Arts, Sausalito, Calif., 1991, San Francisco Art Inst., 1991, Gallery Paule Anglim, San Francisco, 1991, 93, INTAR, N.Y.C., 1992, U. Art Gallery, Sonoma State U., Rohnert Park, Calif., 1992, San Jose (Calif.) Mus. Art, 1994, Hammonds House Galleries, Atlanta, 1994, Capp St. Project, San Francisco, 1994; group exhbns. include Security Pacific Gallery, San Francisco, 1992, Lew Allen Gallery, Santa Fe, 1992, Shea & Bornstein Gallery, Santa Monica, 1992, Creative Time, N.Y.C., 1992, Berkeley Art Ctr., 1992, Nina Nielsen Gallery, Boston, 1993, New Mus. Contemporary Art, N.Y.C., 1993, Calif. Crafts Mus., San Francisco, 1994, U. Calif. Berkeley Mus. Art, Sci. and Culture, 1994, Laney Coll., Oakland, Calif., 1994, The Mus. at Blackhawk, Danville, Calif., 1994, Hampton (Va.) U. Mus., 1994, Gallery Resche, Paris, 1994, Yerba Buena Ctr. for the Arts, San Francisco, 1994, Installation Gallery, San Diego, 1994, Jewett Hall Gallery, U. Maine, Augusta, 1994, CCAC, Oakland, 1994, Oakland Mus., 1994, Louis Stern Fine Arts, L.A., 1995, Gallery Concord, 1995, Gallery II, U. Bradford, 1998, City Gallery, Leicester, 1999, LewAllen Contemporary, Santa Fe, 2000, Mus. Glass: Internat. Ctr. for Contemporary Art, Tacoma, 2002, Neuberger Mus. Art Biennial, 2003, Nielsen Gallery, Boston, 2003, others; represented in permanent collections Oakland Mus., Wadsworth Atheneum, Hartford, Conn., Rene and Veronica di Rosa Found., Napa, Calif., Frederick R. Weisman Art Mus., Calif. African Am. Mus., pvt. collections. Recipient Bank of Am. award, San Francisco, 1975, Small Projects award Inter Arts Marin, San Rafael, Calif., 1984, Adaline Kent award San Francisco Art Inst., 1991, Visual Artists award Flintridge Found., 2001-02; fellow in mixed media Calif. Arts Coun., 1990, Lila A. Wallace/Reader's Digest Internat. Traveling fellow, 1992-93; grantee Calif. Arts Coun., 2003. Office: 1925 Adam Clayton Powell Jr Blvd #7L New York NY 10026-2237

HOWARD, M(OSES) WILLIAM, JR., minister; b. Americus, Ga., Mar. 3, 1946; s. M. William and Laura (Turner) H.; m. Barbara Jean Wright, July 11, 1970; children: Matthew Weldon, Adam Turner, Maisha Wright BA, Morehouse Coll., 1968, L.H.D., 1984; M.Div., Princeton Theol. Sem., 1972; D.D., Miles Coll., 1979, Central Coll., 1980; LLD, Bloomfield Coll., 2001. Ordained to ministry Am. Baptist Ch., 1974; exec. dir. Black Council, Ref. Ch. in Am., N.Y.C., 1972-92; pres. N.Y. Theol. Sem., N.Y.C., 1992-00; pastor Bethany Baptist Ch., Newark, 2000—. Bd. dirs. Nat. Conf. Black Churchmen, 1975-80; moderator Commn. of World Council Chs. Program to Combat Racism, 1976-78; bd. dirs. Nat. Media Found.; pres. Nat. Council Chs., 1979-81; condr. Christmas services for hostages Am. embassy, Tehran, Iran, 1979; chmn. UN Seminar on Bank Loans to South Africa, Zurich, 1981; chmn. ecumenical delegation to Syria, 1984, instrumental (with Rev. Jesse Jackson) in obtaining release of Lt. Robert O. Goodman, USN; chair religious com. to welcome Nelson Mandela to U.S.A., 1990. Researcher: Born to Rebel - Autobiography of Benjamin Elijah Mays, 1967; editor: monthly newsletter Black Caucus RCA, 1973-92; pub., producer ann. lectureship, 1975-92. Active YMCA; trustee Trenton State Coll., 1981-82, Nat. Urban League; bd. dirs. Children's Def. Fund, The Independent Sector, United Way of Essex and West Hudson, 2004—; founding mem. People for Am. Way; pres. Am. Com. on Africa, 1987-92; bd. govs. Rutgers U., 2004—. Recipient Disting. Service award as chmn. Commn. on Justice, Liberation and Human Fulfillment, Disting. Alumnus award Princeton Theol. Sem., 1984; decorated comdr. Order Knights of Holy Sepulchre. Mem. NAACP, Assn. Theol. Schs. in U.S. and Can. (sec. 1998-2000), Coun. Fgn. Rels., Sigma Pi Phi. Baptist. Office: Bethany Baptist Ch 275 W Market St Newark NJ 07103 Business E-Mail: mwhoward@bethany-newark.org. *Perhaps the greatest challenge to humanity today is to see that our moral and ethical development catches up, and keeps pace with, our advances in technology.*

HOWARD, NATHAN SOUTHARD, brokerage house executive, lawyer; b. Marysville, Ohio, May 4, 1941; s. Cone Howard Jr. and Catherine (Southard) H.; divorced; children— Ercil Coleman, Lyndsay Christine BA, William and Mary Coll., 1962, JD, 1965. V.p. White Weld & Co., N.Y.C., 1972—75, Prudential-Bache Securities, Inc., N.Y.C., 1975—80, assoc. dir., 1980—82, mng. dir., 1985—89; dir. energy and utilities group Barclays de Zoete Wedd Corp. Fin., N.Y.C., 1990—93; v.p. energy divsn. Bank of New York, N.Y.C., 1993—. Bd. dirs. People Symphony Concerts, N.Y.C., 1982— Mem. ABA, N.Y. State Bar, N.Y. Soc. Securities Analysts, Bond Club N.Y., Univ. Club (N.Y.C.). Home: 19 East 80 St 3C New York NY 10021 Office: Bank of New York 1 Wall St 19th Fl New York NY 10286 E-mail: nhoward@bankofny.com.

HOWARD, PHILIP KING, lawyer; b. Atlanta, Oct. 24, 1948; s. John R. and Charlotte Howard; m. Alexandra Cushing, Nov. 23, 1972; children: Olivia, Charlotte, Lily, Alexander BA, Yale U., 1970; JD, U. Va., 1974. Bar: N.Y. 1975, U.S. Dist. Ct. (so. and ea. dists.) N.Y. 1975, U.S. Ct. Appeals (2d cir.) 1975, U.S. Ct. Appeals (4th cir.) 1997, U.S. Supreme Ct. 1978. Assoc. Sullivan & Cromwell, N.Y.C., 1974-83; ptnr. Howard Smith and Levin, N.Y.C., 1983-99; ptnr., vice-chmn. Covington & Burling, N.Y.C., 1999—. Author: The Death of Common Sense, 1995, The Collapse of The Common good, 2001. Chmn. Mcpl. Art Soc., N.Y.C., 1997-, Common Good, N.Y.C., Wash., 2002-; trustee Am. Acad. in Rome, N.Y.C. and Rome, 1995-99. Home: 24 Gramercy Park S New York NY 10003-1700 Office: Covington & Burling 1330 Ave of Americas New York NY 10019 Office Phone: 212-841-1068.

HOWARD, PIERRE, former state official; m. Nancy Elizabeth (Barnes); children: Christopher, Caroline. Grad., U. Ga., 1965, JD, 1968. Former mem. Ga. Senate, Atlanta, former asst. floor leader, former chmn. human resources com.; lt. gov. State of Ga., Atlanta, 1991-98; ptnr. Spl. Corp. Strategies, Atlanta, 1999—; co-founder Insider Advantage.com, Atlanta. Recipient Nathan Davis Award AMA, 1996. Mem. Phi Beta Kappa. Office: InsiderAdvantage.com 4401 Northside Pkwy Ste 130 Atlanta GA 30327

HOWARD, RICHARD RALSTON, II, medical health advisor, financial consultant; b. Winnfield, Kans., May 26, 1948; s. Richard Ralston and Ione (Mayer) H. BBA, Loyola U., New Orleans, 1970; MPH, Tulane U., 1977, MS, 1984, DrPH, 1988. Researcher Loyola U., 1973; educator Dominican Coll., New Orleans, 1977; educator Sch. Pub. Health Tulane U., New Orleans, 1978-82, researcher Sch. Medicine, 1979-88; med. health advisor Howard Med. Clinic, Slidell, La., 1982-91; founder The Inst. Econ. Tech. Rsch., New Orleans, 1993—. NIH grantee, 1979; VA grantee, 1984. Mem. Internat. Platform Assn., Am. Assn. Individual Investors, Beta Beta Beta. Achievements include research on the impact of the health food industry on nutrition awareness, cocaine testing through quantitative tear analysis, vitamin C and ophthalmic wound healing. Home: 3531 Nashville Ave New Orleans LA 70125-4339 Personal E-mail: rhoward787@aol.com.

HOWARD, ROBERT ELLIOTT, former federal official, consultant, educator; b. Staten Island, N.Y., Feb. 19, 1933; s. David and Helen (Gresser) H.; m. Bulbul Batra, Mar. 24, 1957; children: Nina Howard Regan, Nicholas, Sarah. AB, Columbia U., 1952; DPhil, Oxford U., Eng., 1957. Rsch. fellow in physics Carnegie Inst. Tech., Carnegie-Mellon U., Pitts., 1958-60; rsch. physicist Nat. Bur. Standards, Washington, 1960-67; mem. profl. staff Office Mgmt. and Budget, Washington, 1968-87, dep. assoc. dir. for nat. security, 1987-90, assoc. dir. for nat. security and internat. affairs, 1990-93; vis. prof. Nat. Defense Univ., Washington, 1993-95; pres. Key Assocs., 1995—. Adj. prof. nat. security studies Georgetown U., Washington, 1993—2002; vis. rsch. physicist U.K. Atomic Energy Authority, Harwell, England, 1962. Contbr. numerous articles to profl. jours. Recipient Presdl. Meritorious Exec. award, 1987, Presdl. Disting. Exec. award, 1990; Fulbright fellow Indian Inst. Tech., New Delhi, 1966. Fellow Am. Phys. Soc. Republican. Avocations: walking, reading, arts, tennis. Office Phone: 202-337-7487. Personal E-mail: rhoward9@erols.com.

HOWARD, ROBERT FRANKLIN, observatory administrator, astronomer; b. Delaware, Ohio, Dec. 30, 1932; s. David Dale and Clarine Edna (Morehouse) H.; m. Margaret Teresa Farnon, Oct. 4, 1958; children: Thomas Colin, Alan Robert, Moira Catharine BA, Ohio Wesleyan U., 1954; PhD, Princeton U., 1957. Carnegie fellow Mt. Wilson and Palomar Obs., Pasadena, Calif., 1957-59, staff mem., 1961-81; asst. prof. U. Mass., Amherst, 1959-61; asst. dir. for Mt. Wilson Mt. Wilson & Las Campanas Obs., Pasadena, 1981-84; dir. Nat. Solar Obs., Tucson, 1984-88, astronomer, 1988-98, astronomer emeritus, 1998—. Editor: Solar Magnetic Fields, 1971; editor: (jour.) Solar Physics, 1987-98; contbr. articles to profl. jours. Mem. Am. Astron. Soc. (Hale prize 2003), Internat. Astron. Union.

HOWARD, ROBERT STAPLES, newspaper publisher; b. Wheaton, Minn., Oct. 23, 1924; s. Earl Eaton and Helen Elizabeth (Staples) H.; m. Lillian Irene Crabtree, Sept. 2, 1945; children: Thomas, Andrea, William, David. Student, U. Minn., 1942, student, 1945. Pub. various daily, weekly newspapers,

1946-55; pub. Chester, Pa. Times, 1955-61; Pres. Howard Publs. (18 daily newspapers), 1961—2002. With AUS, 1942-43; 2d lt. USAAF, 1944-45. Home: PO Box 1337 Rancho Santa Fe CA 92067-1337 Office: 2525 Pio Pico Dr Ste 202 Carlsbad CA 92008-0570

HOWARD, RON, film director; b. Duncan, Okla., Mar. 1, 1954; s. Rance and Jean Howard; m. Cheryl Alley, June 7, 1975; 4 children: Bryce, Jocelyn, Paige, Reed. Student, U. So. Calif., Los Angeles Valley Coll. Co-chmn. Imagine Films Entertainment, L.A. Actor: (theatre) The Seven Year Itch, 1956, Hole in the Head, 1963; (TV series) The Andy Griffith Show, 1960-68, The Smith Family, 1971-72, Happy Days, 1974-80, Fonz and the Happy Days Gang (voice), 1980, Mork & Mindy, 1982-83, Laverne & Shirley, 1982-83, The Fonz Hour, 1982-83, Arrested Development (voice), 2003-; (TV films) A Boy Called Nuthin, 1967, Smoke, 1970, The Migrants, 1974, Locusts, 1974, Huckleberry Finn, 1975, I'm a Fool, 1976, Act of Love, 1980, Where Have All the Children Gone, 1980, Bitter Harvest, 1981, Fire on the Mountain, 1981, Return to Mayberry, 1986; (TV appearances) Dennis the Meance, 1959, 60, Johnny Ringo, 1959, The Twilight Zone, 1959, The DuPont Show with June Allyson, 1959, General Electric Theater, 1959, Insight, 1959, The New Breed, 1962, Route 66, 1962, The Eleventh Hour, 1963, The Great Adventure, 1964, Dr. Kildare, 1964, The Fugitive, 1964, The Big Valley, 1965, Gomer Pyle, U.S.M.C., 1966, I Spy, 1966, The Monroes, 1967, Mayberry R.F.D., 1968, The F.B.I., 1968, Lancer, 1968, Land of the Giants, 1969, Daniel Boone, 1969, Gunsmoke, 1969, Lassie, 1970, Love, American Style, 1972, The Bold Ones: The New Doctors, 1972, Bonanza, 1972, M*A*S*H, 1973, The Waltons, 1974, Laverne & Shirley, 1976, 79, Happy Days, 1983, 84, The Simpsons (voice), 1998, Frasier (voice), 1999; (films) The Journey, 1959, Door-to-Door Maniac, 1961, The Music Man, 1962, The Courtship of Eddie's Father, 1963, Village of the Giants, 1965, The Wild Country, 1971, American Graffiti, 1973, Happy Mother's Day, Love George, 1973, The Spikes Gang, 1974, Eat My Dust!, 1976, The Shootist, 1976, Grand Theft Auto, 1977, More American Graffiti, 1979, Osmosis Jones (voice), 2001; dir. (films) Deed of Daring-Do, 1969, Night Shift, 1982, Splash, 1984, Cocoon, 1985, Willow, 1988, Backdraft, 1991, The Paper, 1994, Apollo 13, 1995 (DGA award dir. achievement, 1996), Ransom, 1996; dir., prodr. (films) Edtv, 1999, How the Grinch Stole Christmas, 2000, A Beautiful Mind, 2001 (Academy award best dir., 2002, Broadcast Film Critics Assoc. award best dir., 2002, DGA award dir. achievement, 2002), The Missing, 2003, Cinderella Man, 2005; actor, dir., writer (films) Grand Theft Auto, 1977; dir., prodr., writer (films) Far and Away, 1992; dir., exec. prodr. (films) Gung Ho, 1986; dir., writer (films) Parenthood, 1989; exec. prodr. (films) Leo and Loree, 1980, No Man's Land, 1987, Vibes, 1988, Clean and Sober, 1988, The Burbs, 1989, Closet Land, 1991; prodr. (films) The Chamber, 1996, Inventing the Abbotts, 1997, Beyond the Mat, 1999, The Alamo, 2004, Inside Deep Throat, 2005; dir. (TV films) Through the Magic Pyramid, 1981; dir., writer, (TV films) Cotton Candy, 1978; dir., prodr. (TV films) Skyward, 1980, No Greater Gift, 1985, Take Five, 1987; exec. prodr. (TV films) Skyward Christmas, 1981, When Your Lover Leaves, 1983, Into Thin Air, 1985, Student Affairs, 1999, Boarding School, 2002; prodr. Student Affairs, 1999; exec. prodr. (TV series) Maximum Security, 1984, Parenthood, 1990, Hiller and Diller, 1997, Sports Night, 1998-2000, Felicity, 1998-2002, The PJs, 1999-2001, Wonderland, 2000, The Beast, 2001, 24, 2001-, Arrested Development, 2003-; prodr. (miniseries) From the Earth to the Moon, 1998 (Emmy award outstanding miniseries, 1998) Named one of 50 Most Powerful People in Hollywood, Premiere mag., 2004, 2005. Mem. AFTRA, SAG, Acad. Motion Picture Arts and Scis. Office: Richard Lovett CAA 9830 Wilshire Blvd Beverly Hills CA 90212*

HOWARD, RONALD A., systems engineer, educator; DSc in Elec. Engring., MIT, 1958. Prof. dept. engring.-econ. sys./ops. rsch. Stanford U., 1965—. Founder, dir. Strategic Decisions Group; dir. Decisions and Ethics Ctr. Author: Dynamic Programming and Markov Processes, 1960, Dynamic Probabilistic Systems, 1971, Readings in Decision Analysis, 1977, READINGS on The Principles and Applications of Decision Analysis, 1984, Decision Analysis, 1996; contbr. numerous articles to profl. jours. Fellow IEEE; mem. NAE, TIMS, Operational Rsch. Soc. (U.K., Frank P. Ramsey medal for disting. contbns. in decision analysis 1986). Office: Dept Engring-Econ Sys/Ops Rsch Terman Engring Ctr Rm 324 Stanford U Stanford CA 94305-4023 E-mail: rhoward@leland.stanford.edu.

HOWARD, ROSCOE CONKLIN, JR., lawyer, former prosecutor; b. 1952; m. Deborah Ryan Howard; children: Ryan, Adam. AB, Brown U., 1974; JD, U. Va., 1977. Bar: Va. 1977, D.C. 1978. Summer assoc. Brown, Wood, Ivey, Mitchell & Petty, N.Y.C., 1976; law clk. to Hon. Raymond L. Finch, Territorial Ct. V.I., Christiansted, St. Croix, 1977—78; assoc. Jones, Day, Reavis & Pogue, Washington, 1978—79, Crowell & Moring, Washington, 1979—81; staff atty. FTC, Washington, 1981—84; asst. U.S. atty. Office of U.S. Atty. D.C., 1984—87, Office of U.S. Atty. (ea. dist.) Va., Alexandria divsn., 1987—89, Office of U.S. Atty. (ea. dist.) Va., Richmond divsn., 1989—91; assoc. ind. counsel In Re Samuel R. Pierce, 1991—94; assoc. prof. law U. Kans. Sch. Law, Lawrence, 1994—97, prof. law, 1999—2001; assoc. ind. counsel In Re A. Michael Espy, 1997—98; U.S. atty. DC dist. US Dept. Justice, 2001—04; atty., ptnr. Sheppard, Mullin, Richter & Hampton LLP, 2004—. Faculty advisor Black Am. Law Students Assn., 1994—. The Criminal Procedure Review, 1994—97; assoc. ind. counsel Office of Ind. Counsel, Alexandria, Va., 1997—98. Sec. Lawrence Pub. Libr. Found. Bd., 1997, 1998—; bd. trustees Culver Ednl. Found., Ind., 1989—97; vol. Am. Heart Assn., 1996; v.p. Culver Mil. Acad. Alumni Legion Bd., Ind., 1978—82. Mem.: Assn. Am. Law Schs. (adv. bd. 1996—99, exec. com. 2001—), Kans. Bar Assn. (task force on criminal justice funding 1995—96), D.C. Bar Assn., Va. Bar Assn. Office: Sheppard Mullin Richter & Hampton 11th Fl East 1300 I St NW Washington DC 20005 Home: 4405 Ivory Coast Ct Chantilly VA 20151-2426 Office Phone: 202-218-0008. Business E-Mail: rhoward@sheppardmullin.com.

HOWARD, SAMUEL HOUSTON, communications company executive, health care executive; b. Marietta, Okla., May 8, 1939; s. Houston and Nellie M. (Gaines) H.; m. Karan Anica Wilson, Dec. 29, 1962; children: Anica Lynne, Samuel H. II. BS, Okla. State U., 1961; MA, Stanford U., 1963. Chmn. Phoenix Comm. Inc., Nashville, 1972—; v.p. fin. and bus. Meharry Med. Coll., Nashville, 1973-77; v.p. planning Hosp. Affiliates Internat., Nashville, 1977-80, v.p., treas., 1980-81, Hosp. Corp. Am., Nashville, 1981-85, sr. v.p. pub. affairs, 1985-88; chmn. Phoenix Holdings, Inc., Nashville, 1987—; owner Sta. Sta. WVOL, Nashville, 1976—, Sta. WQQK-FM, Nashville, 1980—; pres., CEO, Phoenix Healthcare, Inc., Nashville. Bd. dirs. Genesis Health Ventures, Pa., Nashville Electric Svc. Trustee Fisk U., Nashville, 1984-96; mem. Tenn. Indsl. and Agrl. Devel. Commn., 1985-88; chmn. Nashville Conv. Ctr. Commn., 1986-87. Recipient Gov.'s Outstanding Tennessean award State of Tenn., 1981, Disting. Businessman of Yr. U. Tenn., 1985, Silver Beaver award Boy Scouts Am., Nashville, 1990, Humanitarian award Nashville Coun. Christians and Jews, 1993; Samuel H. Howard Day named in his honor City of Nashville, 1981; named to Bus. Hall of Fame, Okla. State U., 1983; named Businessman of Yr., Nashville Bus. Jour., 1995. Mem. Fedn. Am. Health Systems (bd. dirs. 1980-94, past pres., Pres.'s Achievement award 1980, 84), Am. Hosp. Assn. (select del.), Fin. Execs. Inst. (so. v.p. 1979-86), Nashville C. of C. (bd. dirs. 1990—, Businessman of Yr. award 1995), Rotary, Alpha Phi Alpha, Sigma Pi Phi. Baptist. Home: 5320 Cherry Blossom Trl Nashville TN 37215-5228 Office: Ste 300 109 Westpark Dr Brentwood TN 37027-5062

HOWARD, SHELLEY, visual arts educator, consultant; b. Toledo, Aug. 29, 1952; d. William Kenneth and Patricia Ann Howard. BFA, Bowling Green State U., 1974; MA in Edn., U. No. Colo., 1993. Cert. K-12 art tchr. Ohio, Colo. Extended studies instr. Adams State Coll., Alamosa, Colo., 1994—96; adj. instr. U. No. Colo., Greeley, 1996—2000; dist. visual arts curriculum coord. Cherry Creek Sch. Dist. #5, Greenwood Village, Colo., 1996—2003; visual arts educator Overland H.S., Aurora, Colo., 1981—, visual arts dept. coord., 1983—. Co-founder, bd. dirs., facilitator, leadership trainer ArtSource Colo., A Ctr. for the Advancement of Art in Edn., Denver, 1995—99; art edn. rep. Colo. Alliance for Arts Edn. Bd., Denver, 1999—2000; visual arts advisor to state commr. of edn. Colo. Dept. of Edn., Denver, 2000—03. Exhibitions include One Woman Retrospective, Colo. and N.Mex. Watermedia and Pastel Landscapes. Singer, soloist Episcopal and Cath. Dioceses, Denver, 1981—99. Mem.: Colo. Art Edn. Assn. (pres.-elect, pres., past pres. 1998—2004, Colo. Marion Quin Dix. Leadership award 2002), Nat. Art Edn. Assn. (corr.; del. 1998—2002, chair host state com. nat. conv. 2004), ArtSource Colo. (life). Avocations: painting, travel. Home: 419 Washington St Denver CO 80203 Office: Overland HS 12400 E Jewell Ave Aurora CO 80012 Office Phone: 303-777-7786. Personal E-mail: showart419@aol.com.

HOWARD, STEVE, mathematician, educator; s. Kenneth and Joanne Howard; m. Laura Mason, June 19, 1993; children: Mason, Parker. BS, Lynchburg Coll., 1982; MA, Wake Forest U., 1985. Math. instr. Ctrl. Va. Gov.'s Sch., Lynchburg, Va., 1990—. Office Phone: 434-582-1104.

HOWARD, TERRENCE DASHON, actor; b. Chicago, Ill., Mar. 11, 1969; BS in Chem. Engring., Pratt Inst. Actor: (TV films) The Jacksons: An American Dream, 1992, The O.J. Simpson Story, 1995, Shadow-Ops, 1995, King of the World, 2000, Boycott, 2001, Lackawanna Blues, 2005, Their Eyes Were Watching God, 2005; (TV series) Tall Hopes, 1993, Sparks, 1996, Mama Flora's Family, 1998, Street Time, 2001; (films) Who's the Man?, 1993, Mr. Holland's Opus, 1995, Lotto Land, 1995, Dead Presidents, 1995, Sunset Park, 1996, Johns, 1996, Double Tap, 1997, Butter, 1998, Spark, 1998, The Players Club, 1998, Valerie Flake, 1999, Best Laid Plans, 1999, The Best Man, 1999 (NAACP Image award for best actor, 2000, Chicago Film Critics award, 2000, Spirit award, 2000), Big Momma's House, 2000, Love Beat the Hell Outta Me, 2000, Investigating Sex, 2001, Angel Eyes, 2001, Glitter, 2001, Hart's War, 2002, Biker Boyz, 2003, Love Chronicles, 2003, Crash, 2004, Ray, 2004, Hustle & Flow, 2005, The Salon, 2005, Four Brothers, 2005, Animal, 2005. Office: ICM 8942 Wilshire Blvd Beverly Hills CA 90211*

HOWARD, TERRY THOMAS, obstetrician, gynecologist; b. Cleve., May 14, 1943; s. Henry and Paula H.; m. Phyllis C. Schaevitz, Aug. 21, 1965; children: Jennifer, Jason, Brian. AB magna cum laude, Columbia U., 1965; MD, Harvard Med. Sch., 1969. Diplomate Am. Bd. Ob-Gyn. Intern, resident gen. surgery Beth Israel Hosp., Boston, 1969-71; resident ob-gyn Boston Hosp. for Women (now named Brigham & Womens Hosp.), 1971-74; physician Chelmsford (Mass.) Med. Assocs., 1974-88, Harvard Cmty. Health Plan, Chelmsford, 1988-97, Harvard Vanguard Med. Assocs. (formerly Harvard Cmty. Health Plan), Chelmsford, 1998-2000; pvt. practice Chelmsford, 2000—. Trustee Lowell (Mass.) Gen. Hosp., 1987-2003, trustee emeritus, 2003—. Bd. dirs. Friends of the Children Concert Band, Chelmsford, 1981—, Lowell Cmty. Health Ctr., 2002–; trustee Congregation Shalom, Chelmsford, 1993-96. Fellow Am. Coll. Obstetrics & Gynecology, Am. Coll. Surgeons; mem. Am. Soc. Reproductive Medicine.

HOWARD, TIMOTHY RAY, elementary school educator, historian; b. Chatsworth, Ga., Apr. 14, 1960; s. James Bradford and Odetta Bramblett Howard. BA, Berry Coll., 1982; MEd, W.Ga. Coll., 1986, EdS, 1994. Cert. mid. & secondary edn. & gifted edn., support specialist. Tchr. Murray County Jr. High & HS, Chatsworth, Ga., 1982—83, Murray County Jr. HS, 1983—86, Murray Mid. Sch., 1986—89, Bagley Mid. Sch., 1989—. Acad. bowl coach Murray Jr. High & Mid. Schs., 1985—89, Bagley Mid. Sch., Chatsworth, 1989—, sponsor nat. jr. Beta Club, 1989—. Author, editor (books) Murray County Heritage, 1987, The Vann House Speaks Again, 1989, Murray County School Days, 1990; contbr. articles to profl. jours. Officer, trustee Whitfield-Murray Historical Soc., Dalton, 1976—; chmn. Chatsworth-Murray County Libr. Bd., 2000—05, Murray County Red Cross, Chatsworth, 1986—96. Recipient Tchr. of Yr. award, Murray County Schs., 1986, 1989, STAR Tchr. award, 1999, 2000, State Am. History Tchr. of Yr. award, 1994. Mem.: NEA, Ga. Humanities Council, Murray & Ga. Assn. Educators. Baptist. Avocations: history, reading, stamp collecting/philately, coin collecting/numismatics, volunteering. Office: Bagley Mid Sch 4600 Hwy 225 N Chatsworth GA 30705

HOWARD, VIVIAN AMICK, music educator; b. Columbia, S.C., Aug. 18, 1955; d. Odis Leroy and Mary Ada (Shealy) Amick; m. Thomas (Andy) Andrew Howard, July 1, 1978; children: Drew, Kathleen. B in Music Edn., Lenoir-Rhyne Coll., 1977; cert. in level I Orff, Westminster Choir Coll.; cert. in AP music theory, Oglethorpe U. Tchr. Glen Alpine (N.C.) Jr. HS, 1977—78, Stanley (N.C.) Jr. HS, 1981—84, Harrisburg (N.C.) Elem. Sch., 1995—2001; tchr., choral dir. Jay M. Robinson HS, Concord, NC, 2001—. Advisor Tri-M Music Honor Soc., Concord, 2004—. Choir mem., substitute dir., organist Calvary Luth. Ch., 1982—. Mem.: Music Educators Nat. Conf. Avocations: singing, piano, reading, calligraphy. Home: 2228 Quail Dr NW Concord NC 28027 Office: Jay M Robinson HS 300 Pitts School Rd SW Concord NC 28027 Office Phone: 704-788-4500. Business E-Mail: vhoward@cabarrus.k12.nc.us.

HOWARD, W. SCOTT, language educator; b. Englewwod, N.J., Nov. 6, 1963; PhD, Univ. Wash., Seattle, Wash., 1998. Asst. prof. Dept. of English, Univ. Denver, Denver, 1998—. Office: Univ Denver 495 Sturm Hall Denver CO 80208 Office Phone: 303-871-2887.

HOWARD, WILLIAM GATES, JR., electronics company executive; b. Boston, Nov. 6, 1941; s. William Gates and Mary Louise (Creager) H.; m. Kathleen Louretta Shipp, June 4, 1983. BEE with distinction, Cornell U., 1964, MS, 1965; PhD, U. Calif.-Berkeley, 1967. Asst. prof. dept. elec. engring. and computer scis. U. Calif.-Berkeley, 1967-69; group ops. mgr. Motorola Semicondr. Group, Mesa, Ariz., 1969-76; v.p., dir. tech. and planning Motorola Semicondr. Sector, Phoenix, 1976-83; v.p., dir. R&D Motorola Inc., Schaumburg, Ill., 1983-87; sr. fellow Nat. Acad. Engring., Washington, 1987-91; chmn. bd. dirs. Thunderbird Technologies, Inc. Dir. BEI Techs., Inc., Ramtron Internat Corp., Credence Sys. Corp., Xilinx, Inc., Sandia Corp.; chmn. semicondr. tech. adv. com. US Dept. Commerce, 1978-83; chmn. adv. group on electron devices Dept. Def., 1982-99, mem. def. sci. bd., 1996—; mem. study com. on tech. and implications of VLSI, NAS, 1980; chmn. vis. com. on advanced tech. Nat. Inst. Stds. and Tech., 1988-92; chmn. Def. Sci. Bd. Task Force on Microelectronics Rsch. Facilities, 1991-92; mem. Sandia Pres. Adv. Coun., 1997-00; chmn. bd. dirs. Credence Sys., Inc. Author: (with D.J. Hamilton) Basic Integrated Circuit Engineering, 1976, (with B. Guile) Profiting from Innovation, 1992; patentee (with J.B. Cecil) improved reference current source, ladder termination circuit, three terminal zener diode. Fellow AAAS, IEEE (vice chmn. circuits and systems soc. 1976-78); mem. Nat. Acad. of Engring., Sigma Xi, Phi Kappa Phi, Eta Kappa Nu, Tau Beta Pi. Office: 10642 E San Salvador Dr Scottsdale AZ 85258-6114

HOWARD, WILLIAM MATTHEW, arbitrator, writer, lawyer; b. Oak Park, Ill., Dec. 16, 1934; s. William and Martha Geraldine (Herlock) H.; children: Matthew William, Stephanie Sue. BSBA, U. Mo., 1956, JD, 1958; postgrad., U. Nice, France, 1976, U. London, 1977; PhD, Ariz. State U., 1995. Bar: Mo. 1958, U.S. Supreme Ct. 1986; cert. mediator and arbitrator, Fla. Supreme Ct. Jr. ptnr. Bryan Cave, St. Louis, 1958-66; gen. counsel, asst. to pres. U.S. Steel Co., Granite City, Ill., 1966—69; pres. Thomson Internat. Co., Thibodaux, La., 1969-70; founder, pres., chmn. bd. The Catalyst Group, Phoenix, 1970-97; dean, ctr. adminstr. The Union Inst., San Diego, 1997-99; pres. Dispute Solutions, Inc., Scottsdale, Ariz., 1999—. Mem. adj. faculty U. Mo., Columbia, 1956-58, St. Louis U., 1958-61, Ariz. State U., 1994-96, Ottawa U., 1994-96, Nova Southeastern U., 1996-97; chmn. unauthorized practice law com. Mo. Bar, St. Louis, 1964-65; chmn. bd. N.V. Vulcaansoord, Terborg, The Netherlands, 1975-78, E. Chalmers Holdings, Ltd., Glasgow, Scotland, 1977-78; exec. com. Chem. Bank, Irvine, Calif., 1985-90; vis. lectr. UCLA, 1987; arbitrator Am. Arbitration Assn., N.Y.C., 1987—, N.Y. Stock Exch., 1987—, Nt. Assn. Securities Dealers, Chgo., 1987—, Nat. Futures Assn., Chgo., 1988—, Am. Stock Exch., N.Y.C., 1988; hearing officer Mo. Dept. Natural Resources, Jefferson City, 1987-89, Internat. Ct. Arbitration, 1993—, Inter-Am. Comml. Arbitration Commn., 1993—; mem. Fla. Automobile Arbitration Bd., 1997-98; bd. dirs. Xeric Corp., Denver, Phoenix. Editor newsletter Extras, 1970—; exec. producer: (motion picture) Twice a Woman, 1979; contbr. numerous articles and revs. to various jours. Bd. dirs. U. Mo. Alumni Assn., 1986, Breckenridge (Colo.) Film Festival, 1989, Actors Theatre Phoenix, 1990; mem. club adv. bd. Phoenix Art Mus., 1990; dir. Scottsdale Cultural Coun., 1991. Mem. Am. Arbitration Assn. (regional adv. com.), Soc. Profls. in Dispute Resolution, Fla. Acad. Mediators, Nat. Inst. Dispute Resolution, Mensa, Order of Coif. Avocations: literature, travel, theater, visual arts, skiing. Office: PO Box 9249 Phoenix AZ 85068-9249 Personal E-mail: howardbill@msn.com.

HOWARD, WILLIAM PERCY, physician; b. Canton, Miss., Dec. 29, 1947; s. John Wesley Griffin and Ann (Wallace) H.; m. Nancy Rose Moyers, May 25, 1980; children: John W.G. II, Ann Skidmore, Ashley Elizabeth. BS in Chem. Engring., Miss. State U., 1970; MD, U. Miss., 1979. Chem. engr. Miss. Chem. Corp., Yazoo City, 1970-75; resident Univ. Med. Ctr., Jackson, Miss., 1979-82; staff physician emergency physician MEA Med. Sys., Jackson, 1982-90, clin. staff physician, 1990—. Chmn. bd. dirs. Miss. Emergency Assn., 1997-99, 1st Intermed Corp., 1997—, CEO, 2003—; mem. physicians adv. com. Blue Cross-Blue Shield, 1993—. Named Madison (Miss.) County Cattleman of Yr., 1991, Madison County Conservation Farmer of Yr., 2001, Miss. Angus Assn. Progressive Breeder of the Yr., 2003. Fellow Am. Acad. Family Practitioners; mem. AMA, Miss. State Med. Assn., Am. Angus Assn., Miss. Angus Assn. (Breeder of Yr. 2003). Republican. Methodist. Avocations: antiques, history, architecture, cattle farming. Office: MEA Med Clinic 5606 Old Canton Rd Jackson MS 39211-4217

HOWARD-JOHNSON, CAROLYN, writer, consultant; b. Salt Lake City, Apr. 4, 1939; d. Roberta and W. Gordon Howard; m. Lance G. Johnson, Feb. 19, 1958; children: Erika A. Lamoureaux, Trenton H. Johnson. BA, U. So. Calif, 1973. Cert. adult instr. UCLA, 2005. Cons., Calif., 1973—. Author: This is the Place (eight awards, 2001), Harkening: A Collection of Stories Remembered (three Awards, 2003), The Frugal Book Promoter: How to Do What Your Publisher Won't (USA Book News' Best Profl. book, 2004), (poetry) Tracings. Spkr., contbr. Small Publishers of N.Am., Colo., 2001—05. Named Woman of Yr. in Arts and Entertainment, Calif. State Legis. Mem.: Nat. Assn. Women's Writers, Delta Gamma. Personal E-mail: hojonews@aol.com.

HOWARD-PEEBLES, PATRICIA N., clinical cytogeneticist; b. Lawton, Okla., Nov. 24, 1941; d. J. Marion and R. Leona (prestidge) Howard; m. Thomas M. Peebles, Aug. 16, 1975. BSEd, U. Ctrl. Okla., 1963; student, Randolph-Macon Coll. Women, 1964; PhD in Zoology (Genetics), U Tex. at Austin, 1969. Diplomate Am. Bd. Med. Genetics; cert. clin. cytogeneticist, med. geneticist. Sci. and history tchr. Piedmont (Okla.) Pub. Schs., 1963-64; biochem. technician biochemistry sect. biology divsn. Oak Ridge (Tenn.) Nat. Lab., 1964-66; instr. rsch. pediatrics dept. pediatrics, instr. cytotech. U. Okla. Health Scis. Ctr., Oklahoma City, 1971-72; asst. prof., dir. Cytogenetics Lab. U. So. Miss., Hattiesburg, 1973-77, assoc. prof., dir. Cytogenetics Lab., 1977-80; assoc. prof. dept. pub. health, staff Lab. Med. Genetics U. Ala., Birmingham, 1980-81; assoc. prof., dir. Cytogenetics Lab. dept. pathology U. Tex. Health Sci. Ctr., Dallas, 1981-85, prof., dir. Cytogenetics Lab., 1985-87; prof. dept. human genetics Med. Coll. Va., Richmond, 1987-2001; clin. cytogeneticist, dir. postnatal lab. Genetics & IVF Inst., Fairfax, Va., 1987-98, co-dir. cytogenetics lab., 1998-2000; genetic, cytogenetic cons., 2000—. Am. Cancer Soc. postdoctoral fellow dept. human genetics U. Mich. Med. Sch., Ann Arbor, 1969-70, dept. human genetics and devel. Coll. Physicians and Surgeons, Columbia U., N.Y.C., 1970-71; genetic cons. Ellisville (Miss.) State Sch., 1973-80; attending staff dept. pathology Parkland Meml. Hosp., Dallas County Hosp. Dist., 1981-87; mem. sci. adv. com. Fragile X Found., 1985-2002; mem. Internat. Standing Com. on Human Cytogenetic Nomenclature, 1991-96. Contbr. articles to profl. jours., chpts. to books; reviewer Am. Jour. Human Genetics, Am. Jour. Med. Genetics, Clin. Genetics, Human Genetics. Fellow Am. Coll. Med. Genetics (founding mem.); mem. Am. Soc. Human Genetics, Assn. Genetic Technologists, Tex. Genetics Soc. (chmn. planning com. ann. meeting 1984), Delta Kappa Gamma, Sigma Xi. Baptist. Office Phone: 214-893-8635. Personal E-mail: phpeebles@yahoo.com.

HOWARDS, STUART S., urologist, educator; b. Milw., Mar. 29, 1937; s. Harvey H. and Anne (Levin) H.; m. Carter N. Howards, Aug. 20, 1966; children: Penelope P., Hugh N. BA, Yale U., 1959; MD, Columbia U., 1963. Intern in surgery Peter Bent Brigham Hosp., Boston, 1963-64, resident in urology, 1968-71; resident in surgery Childrens Hosp., Boston, 1964-65; rsch. assoc. NIH, Bethesda, Md., 1965-68; asst. prof. urology and physiology U. Va., Charlotteville, 1971-74, assoc. prof., 1974-76, prof., 1976—, chief divsn. pediat. urology, 1986—; exec. sec. Am. Bd. Urology, Charlottesville, Va. Chmn. exam com. Am. Bd. Urology, 1985-91, trustee, 1986-92, pres., 1992-93, exec. sec., 1997—; sr. urologic advisor to dir. NIDDK/NIH. Editor: Infertility in the Male, 1991, 3d edit., 1997, Adult and Pediatric Urology, 1991, 3d edit., 1995; editor Jour. Urology, 1983-2000. Maj. USPHS, 1965-68. Recipient Career Investigation award NIH, 1973-78. Fellow Am. Acad. Pediats.; mem. Am. Urol. Assn. (Golden Cystoscope award 1981, Scott award 1990, Hugh Young award 1991, Disting. Svc. award 2001), Clin. Soc. Genitourinary Surgeons, Am. Soc. Reproductive Medicine (bd. dirs. 1994-96, treas. 1996—), Soc. Andrology, Genitourinary Surgeons, Am. Assn. Genito-Urinary Surgeons (sec.-treas. 1992-97), Am. Bd. Urology (trustee 1987-93, pres. 1993, exec. dir. 1997—), NIDDY, NIH (sr. urology advisor to the dir., 2002—), Nat. Bd. Med. Examiners. Office Phone: 434-924-9559. Business E-Mail: ssh4e@virginia.edu.

HOWARD-WYNE, JOSIE, elementary school educator; b. Columbus, Miss., Nov. 6, 1947; d. Frank Earl Howard and Annie Lee Nelson-Howard; m. William James Wyne, Jr.; 1 child, Lisa Shennet Stinson. BS, Western Mich. U., Kalamazoo, 1972, Masters, 1976. Tchr./instructional specialist Kalamazoo Pub. Schs., 1972—. Mem.: NEA, Kairos Dwelling (bd. dirs. 1998—99), Chain Lake Dist. Assn. (treas. 2002—), Kalamazoo Ednl. Assn., Northside Assn. for Ednl. Advancement (sec. 1986—), Dulcet Club (program chmn. 1975—), Delta Sigma Theta (Golden Life mem. 1975—), Alpha Delta Kappa. Baptist. Avocations: singing, travel, sewing, crossword puzzles, mentoring. Home: 4202 Kingsbrook Dr Kalamazoo MI 49006 Office: Kalamazoo Pub Sch 1220 Howard St Kalamazoo MI 49006

HOWARTH, WILLIAM (LOUIS HOWARTH), literature and language professor, writer; b. Mpls., Nov. 26, 1940; s. Nelson Oliver and Mary Watson (Prindiville) H. BA with highest distinction, U. Ill., 1962; MA, U. Va., 1963, PhD, 1967. Instr. Princeton (N.J.) U., 1966-68, asst. prof., 1968-73, assoc. prof., 1973-81, prof. English, 1981—. Mem. exec. com. Princeton Environ. Inst.; advisor Program in Environ. Studies, Program in Am. Studies Princeton (N.J.) U.; cons. Ctr. for Edits. of Am. Authors, 1974, Rockefeller Bros. Fund, 1976, Geraldine W. Dodge Found., 1981, Nat. Geog. Soc., 1984, Corp. for Pub. Broadcasting, 1986, NEH, 1987, Nat. Rural Studies Coun., 1988, Atlantic Ctr. for Arts, 1990, Santa Fe Environ. Coun., 1991, ALA, 1993, Assn. for the Study of Lit. and Environment, 1994, Kellogg Found., 1995, Arthur Vining Davis Found., 1998, AAAS, 2000. Author: Nature in American Life, 1972, The John McPhee Reader, 1976, The Book of Concord, 1982, Thoreau in the Mountains, 1982, Traveling the Trans-Canada, 1987, Mountaineering in the Sierra Nevada, 1989, Walking with Thoreau, 2001; author book chpts.; editor-in-chief: The Writings of Henry D. Thoreau, 1972-80; mem. numerous editl. bds.; editl. adviser numerous jours. and pubs.; contbr. articles to profl. jours. Woodrow Wilson Found. fellow, 1966, Henry E. Huntington Libr. fellow, 1968, NEH fellow, 1977, John E. Annan BiCentennial Preceptor, Princeton, 1973, Pew and Templeton Founds. fellow, 2000, Princeton Environ. Inst., 2004. Mem. MLA, Am. Studies Assn., Thoreau Soc. Am. (pres. 1975-76), Am. Soc. Environ. History, Am. Lit. Assn., Nat. Geographic Soc. (contract writer 1978—), Nat. Rural Studies Coun. (assoc.), Assn. for the Study of Lit. and Environ. (adv. bd.), Am. Soc. Environ. History (adv. bd.), Ctr. for Am. Places (bd. dirs.), Phi Beta Kappa. Office: Princeton U 22 McCosh Hall Princeton NJ 08544-1607

HOWAT, JOHN KEITH, retired museum executive; b. Denver, Apr. 12, 1937; s. James Bowcott and Nancy Selden (Skinker) H.; m. Anne Hadley, June 21, 1958; children: Karen Louise, Laura Anne. Grad., Phillips Exeter

Acad., 1955; BA, Harvard U., 1959, MA, 1962. Curator Hyde Collection, Glens Falls, N.Y., 1962-64; Ford fellow NYU Inst. Fine Arts, 1965—66; Chester Dale fellow Met. Mus. Art, N.Y.C., 1966—67, asst. curator dept. Am. paintings and sculpture, 1967-68, assoc. curator-in-charge, 1968-70, curator, 1970-82, chmn. depts. Am. art, 1982—2001. Mem. adv. com. archives Am. art Smithsonian Instn., 1969—; trustee Archives of Am. Art, 1988—, N.Y. Society Libr., 2002—. Author exhbn. catalogs John Frederick Kensett: An American Master, 1985, An American Paradise: The World of The Hudson River School, 1987, Art and the Empire City: New York, 1825-1861, 2000. Mem. Union Club, Grolier Club, Century Assn. Home: 1100 Park Ave New York NY 10128-1202

HOWDEN, FRANK NEWTON, priest, humanities educator; b. Phila., Mar. 23, 1916; s. John George and Sarah Harvey (McFarlane) H.; m. Cornelia Jane Fenton, Oct. 7, 1943 (dec. Aug. 1981); children: Robert Newton, William John McFarlane, Susan Catherine Victoria Howden Blanchard, Sarah Jane Fenton; m. Mary Valerie Clark, Apr. 23, 1983. AB, U. of the South, 1940; STB, Gen. Theol. Sem., N.Y.C., 1943; MS, Ctrl. Conn. U., 1968; postgrad., McGill U., Montreal, Can., 1953-56. Ordained priest Episcopal Ch.; cert. tchr., Conn. Curate St. Peter's Ch., Auburn, N.Y., 1943-44, All Angels Ch., N.Y.C., 1944-45; priest in charge (vicar) St. John's Ch., Sewaren and Fords, N.J., 1945-48; rector St. Luke's Ch., St. Albans, Vt., 1951-56, Trinity Ch., Waterbury, Conn., 1956-66; history tchr. Woodbury (Conn.) H.S., 1966-69; prof. humanities Waterbury State Tech. Coll., 1970-82; rector Trinity Ch., Lime Rock, Conn., 1969-85, elected rector emeritus, 1985—. Pres. Priests' Fellowship, Conn., 1958-59; archdeacon New Haven County, Diocese of Conn., 1963-66, dean Litchfield Deanery, 1984-85. Author: A Rule of Life, 1954, Life Here and Hereafter, 1992. 1st lt. Chaplain Corps, U.S. Army, 1948-51, chaplain Vt. Nat. Guard, 1952-56. Mem. St. Margaret's Soc. (assoc.), Over-Seas League (London), English-Speaking Union. Democrat. Avocations: photography, audio-visual presentations, preaching and taking services in Anglican churches. Home and Office: 9 Argyle Rd Southborough Tunbridge Wells TN4 0SU England Office Phone: 001 44 1892 58838. E-mail: fnhowden@aol.com.

HOWE, CARROLL VICTOR, construction equipment company executive; b. Kearny, N.J., Dec. 12, 1923; s. Wright and Ada (Hodge) H.; m. Nancy Osborne Stivers, Nov. 24, 1951 (div.); 1 child: Gregory Carroll; m. Priscilla Howland Greene, Mar. 1, 1957 (div.); children: Gregory Carroll, Christopher David; m. Eilene Crawley Pierson, Apr. 14, 1984 (div.). BA, Princeton U., 1947; MFA, Yale U., 1950. Writer, producer Pemeho Prodns., N.Y.C., 1950-51, free lance actor, writer, 1952-54; salesman Atlas Rigging Supply Corp., Newark, 1954-56, office mgr., 1956-57, sales mgr., 1957-58, v.p., 1958-62, pres., 1962-94, ret., 1994; pres. Arsco Industries, Inc., Newark, 1966-2000, ret., 2000. Bd. dirs. Select Ins. Group of North Am., 1987-94. Author: Best One-Act Plays, 1949-1950, 1950, (play) The Long Fall, 1950, 1957, Best Short Plays, 1917-1957, 1957. Bd. dirs., pres. 15 Tenant Shareholders, Inc., N.Y.C., 1978-81, Alumni Coun. Yale U. Grad. Sch. Drama, 1988-94; mem. bd. govs. Newark Acad., Livingston, N.J., 1990-94; mng. ptnr. Crollar Assocs. Newark, 1983-94. Served from pvt. to 2d lt. USMCR, 1942-46, 1st lt. to capt., 1951-52. Recipient Applause award N.J. Theatre Group, 1989. Mem. Wildlife Conservation Soc., USA Track & Field, Boat/US, AAII, Am. Mensa Ltd., Quadrangle Club, Princeton Club Sarasota, Yale Club of Suncoast, Westhampton Yacht Squadron (treas. 1970-72, vice commodore 1972-74, commodore 1974-76, dir. 1976-80), Bradenton Yacht Club, Ivy League Club. Humanist. Home: 2914 River Trace Cir Bradenton FL 34208

HOWE, DANIEL WALKER, historian, educator; b. Ogden, Utah, Jan. 10, 1937; s. Maurice Langdon and Lucie (Walker) H.; m. Sandra Fay Shumway, Sept. 3, 1961; children: Rebecca, Christopher, Stephen. AB magna cum laude, Harvard U., 1959; MA, Oxford (Eng.) U., 1965; PhD, U. Calif., Berkeley, 1966. From instr. to assoc. prof. history Yale U., 1966-73; assoc. prof. history UCLA, 1973-77, prof., 1977-92, chmn. dept., 1983-87. Harmsworth vis. prof. Am. history, Oxford (Eng.) U., 1989-90, Rhodes prof. Am. history, 1992-2002; vis. prof. Yale U., 2001. Author: The Unitarian Conscience, 1970, The American Whigs: An Anthology, 1973, Victorian America, 1976, The Political Culture of the American Whigs, 1979, Making the American Self, 1997. Served to lt. U.S. Army, 1959-60. Kent fellow Danforth Found., 1964-66; Charles Warren Center for Studies in Am. History fellow, 1970-71; NEH fellow, 1975-76; Guggenheim fellow, 1984-85; Huntington Libr. fellow, 1992, 94, 2002-03. Fellow: Royal Hist. Soc.; mem.: Am. Hist. Assn., Soc. Historians Early Am. Rep. (pres. 2000—01), Soc. Am Historians, Oxford and Cambridge Club (London). Episcopalian. Home: 3814 Cody Rd Sherman Oaks CA 91403-5019 E-mail: howe@history.ucla.edu.

HOWE, DRAYTON FORD, JR., lawyer; b. Seattle, Nov. 17, 1931; s. Drayton Ford and Virginia (Wester) H.; m. Joyce Arnold, June 21, 1952; 1 son, James Drayton. AB, U. Calif., Berkeley, 1953; LLB, U. Calif., San Francisco, 1957. Bar: Calif. 1958. CPA Calif. Atty. IRS, 1958-61; tax dept. supr. Ernst & Ernst, San Francisco, 1962-67; ptnr. Bishop, Barry, Howe, Haney & Ryder, San Francisco, 1968—. Lectr. on tax matters U. Calif. extension, 1966-76. Mem. Calif. Bar Assn., San Francisco Bar Assn. (chmn. client relations com. 1977), Calif. Soc. CPA's. Office: Bishop Barry Howe Haney & Ryder 2000 Powell St Ste 1425 Emeryville CA 94608-1861 Office Phone: 510-596-0888. E-mail: dhowe@bbhhr.com.

HOWE, FISHER, management consultant, government agency administrator; b. Winnetka, Ill., May 17, 1914; s. Lawrence and Hester (Davis) H.; m. Deborah Froelicher, June 4, 1945; children: Elizabeth, Shippen. AB, Harvard U., 1935; student, Nat. War Coll., 1948. Salesman Coats & Clarks Thread Co., N.Y.C., 1935-40, Patons & Baldwins, Ltd., Yorkshire, England, 1936-37; mem. staff Office of Dir., OSS, Washington, London, Mediterranean, Far East, 1941-45; fgn. svc. officer Dept. State, 1945-68, spl. asst. under sec. of state, econ. affairs, 1945-46, dep. dir. Bur. Intelligence and Rsch., exec. sec., dir. exec. secretariat, 1956-58; dep. chief of mission and charge Am. Embassy, Oslo, 1958-62, The Hague, Netherlands, 1962-65; mem. policy planning coun., 1965-68; exec. dir., asst. dean Johns Hopkins U. Sch. Advanced Internat. Studies, 1968-72; dep. exec. dir. Commn. on Orgn. of Govt. for Conduct of Fgn. Policy, Washington, 1973-75; sec., gen. adv. com. Energy R & D Adminstrn., 1975-77; dir. instl. rels. Resources for the Future, Inc., 1978-82; ptnr. Lavender/Howe & Assocs., Washington, 1982—. Author: Computer and Foreign Affairs, 1968, Fund Raising and the Nonprofit Board Member, 1988, Board Member's Guide to Fund Raising, 1991, Welcome to the Board, 1995, Board Member's Guide to Strategic Planning, 1997, The Nonprofit Leadership Team: Building the Board-Executive Director Partnership, 2003. Trustee Fountain Valley Sch., Colorado Springs, Colo., Pilgrim Soc., Plymouth, Mass., STRIVE, Washington. Served to lt. USNR, 1943-44, overseas svc. Mem. Metroplitan Club (Washington), Mill Reef (Antigua). Address: Ingleside # 637 3050 Military Rd NW Washington DC 20015

HOWE, FLORENCE, literature educator, writer, publisher; b. NYC, Mar. 17, 1929; d. Samuel and Frances (Stilly) Rosenfeld AB, Hunter Coll., 1950; AM, Smith Coll., 1951; postgrad., U. Wis., 1951—54; DHL (hon.), New Eng. Coll., 1977, Skidmore Coll., 1979, DePauw U., 1987, SUNY Coll., Old Westbury, 1992, Pace U., 2000, Chatham Coll., 2000, U. Wis., 2004. Tchg. asst. U. Wis., Madison, 1951-54; instr. Hofstra Coll., 1954-57; lectr. English Queens Coll., CUNY, 1956-57; asst. prof. English Goucher Coll., 1960-71; prof. humanities and Am. studies SUNY, Old Westbury, 1971-85; prof. English City. Coll. and Grad. Sch., CUNY, 1985-95, Grad. Sch./CUNY, 1995—2001; pres., dir. The Feminist Press at CUNY, 1970—2000. Vis. prof. U. Utah, 1973, 75, U. Wash., 1974, John F. Kennedy Inst. Am. Studies Free U. Berlin, 1978, Oberlin Coll., 1978, Denison U., 1979, MLA Summer Inst. U. Ala., 1979, Coll. of Wooster, 1980; found. edit. Women's Studies Quarterly, 1972-82. Author: The Conspiracy of the Young, 1970, Seven Years Later: Women's Studies Programs in 1976, 1977, Myths of Coeducation: Selected Essays, 1964-1984, 1984; editor: (with Ellen Bass) No More Masks! An Anthology of Poems by Women, 1973, Women and the Power to Change, 1975; (with Nancy Hoffman) Women Working: An Anthology of Stories and Poems, 1979; (with Suzanne Howard, Mary Jo Boehm Strauss) Everywoman's Guide to Colleges and Universities, 1982; (with Marsha Saxton) With Wings: An Anthology of Literature by and About Disabled Women, 1987; (with John Mack Faragher) Women and Higher Education in American History, 1988, Tradition and the Talents of Women, 1991, No More Masks, An Anthology of 20th Century American Women Poets, 1993, The Politics of Women's Studies: Testimony from 30 Founding Mothers, 2000, (with Jean Casella) Almost Touching the Skies: Women's Coming of Age Stories, 2000; mem. editl. bd. Women's Studies: An Interdisciplinary Jour., 1971—, SIGNS: Women in Culture and Society, 1974-80, Jour. Edn., 1976—, The Correspondence of Lydia Marie Child, 1977-81, Research in the Humanities, 1977—; contbr. articles to profl. jours. Recipient Mina Shaughnessy award, Fund for Improvement of Post-Secondary Edn., 1982—83, Rockefeller Found., Bellagio, 2001, 2002, 2003, 2004, 2005; grantee U.S. Dept. State, 1983, 1993; NEH fellow, 1971—73, Ford Found. fellow, 1974—75, Fulbright fellow, India, 1977, Mellon fellow, Wellesley Coll., 1979, Rockefeller Found. fellow, Bellagio, 1997. Office: The Feminist Press at CUNY 365 Fifth Ave New York NY 10016-4309 Office Phone: 212-817-7917. Business E-Mail: fhowe@gc.cuny.edu.

HOWE, G. EDWIN, healthcare executive; m. Suzanne Howe. Degree in bus. adminstrn., U. Wis., 1962; MBA, U. Chgo. From adminstrv. asst. to asst. dir. Ohio State U. Hosps.; pres. St. Luke's Hosp., Milw., 1974—87, Aurora Health Care, Milw., 1987—. Office: Aurora Health Care PO Box 343910 Milwaukee WI 53234-3910

HOWE, JAMES EVERETT, investment company executive; b. N.Y.C., Mar. 30, 1930; s. Ernest Joseph and Gladys Montgomery (Sills) H.; m. Judith DePuy Keating, May 9, 1959; children: James E. Jr., David K. BA, Williams Coll., 1952; MBA, Columbia U., 1954. CFA. Statistician J.P. Morgan & Co., N.Y.C., 1956-59; investment research officer Morgan Guaranty Trust Co., N.Y.C., 1959-65; sr. analyst Tri-Continental Corp., N.Y.C., 1965-80; asst. v.p., voting shareholder J&W Seligman & Co., N.Y.C., 1980-81; chmn. investment com. Charles Edison Fund, Newark, 1981—. Trustee Brook Found., N.Y.C., 1966-72, Charles Edison Fund, 1972—; bd. deacons Brick Presbyn. Ch., N.Y.C., 1963-66. 1st lt. USAF, 1954-56, ETO Recipient Fin. award, Wall Street Jour., 1954. Mem. N.Y. Soc. Security Analysts, CFA Inst., Machinery Analysts N.Y. (charter, pres. 1967-68), Environ. Control Analysts N.Y. (charter, pres. 1975), Jamestowne Soc., Princeton Co. (charter, gov. 1993-94), Genesee Valley Club, Nassau Club, Alpha Kappa Psi. Republican. Presbyterian. Avocation: photography. Home: 33 Keats Rd Short Hills NJ 07078-2913

HOWE, JAMES TARSICIUS, retired insurance company executive; b. Calcutta, India, Nov. 1924; came to U.S., 1975; s. Joseph Ne-Ching and Anna Su-Cheng (Huang) Hou; m. Juliana Wong, Feb. 1948; children: Christopher, Celine, Catherine, Charles, Caroline. Diploma in Bus. Adminstrn., Chinese U. Hong Kong, 1969; postgrad. in Advanced Mgmt., Lingnam Inst. Bus. Adminstrn., Hong Kong. Trainee Bank of China, Calcutta, 1942-45, various managerial positions Calcutta and, Pakistan, 1945-51; mng. ptnr. import and export firm Karachi, Pakistan, 1951-54; various exec. positions Am. Internat. Underwriters (Pakistan) Ltd., 1954-65, Am. Internat. Underwriters (Far East) Inc., 1965-73; pres., mng. dir. Am. Internat. Underwriters, Hong Kong, 1973-75; asst. treas. Am. Internat. Group, Inc., N.Y.C., 1975—76, treas., 1976—81, v.p., 1981—92; ret., 1992. Bd. dirs., mem. audit and conduct coms. A.I.G. Life Ins. Co. Ltd., Can., A.I.G. Assurance Co., Can.; past bd. dirs., vice chmn. AICCO; ret. treas. C.V. Starr & Co., Inc., also numerous other subs.; advisor U.S. Congl. Adv. Bd. Decorated knight Grant Cross Holy Sepulchre of Jerusalem, Roman Cath. Ch.; named hon. Ky. Col., 1979. Mem.: Internat. Platform Assn., Internat. Real Estate Appraisers, Internat. Real Estate Inst., Nat. Assn. U.S. Corp. Treas., Am. Mgmt. Assn., Nat. Assn. Rev. Appraisers and Mortgage Underwriters (sr.), Serra Club (N.Y.C.), Royal Hong Kong Jockey Club, Am. Club Hong Kong (life absent mem.), Royal Hong Kong Golf Club (life absent mem.), Hong Kong Country Club, Chinese Cath. Club (life), KC (grand knight Short Hills coun.), Rotary. Home: Palace Pl Ste 3601 1 Palace Pier Ct Etobicoke ON Canada M8V 3W9

HOWE, JANICE W., lawyer; BA cum laude, Conn. Coll., 1973; JD cum laude, Suffolk U., 1981. Bar: Mass. 1981. Asst. dist. atty. Mass.; ptnr. Bingham McCutchen LLP, Boston, co-chairperson product liability practice group. Appointed by Governor Mass. to Judicial Nominating Com. Ea. Region, 1996—2002; appointed to Spl. Judicial Nominating Com. Juvenile Ct., 1993—95. Office: Bingham McCutchen LLP 150 Federal St Boston MA 02110-1726 Office Phone: 617-951-8504. Office Fax: 617-951-8736. Business E-Mail: janice.howe@bingham.com.

HOWE, JOHN KINGMAN, manufacturing, sales and marketing executive; b. Everett, Wash., Nov. 7, 1945; s. John Cutler and Nancy Carpenter (Kingman_) H.; m. Loretta Kerr, aug. 27, 1966; children: Steven Cutler, Nancy Kingman. Student, Ohio State U., 1963-65. Field technician Data Corp., Dayton, Ohio, 1965-66; letter carrier U.S. Postal Svc., Dayton, 1966; sales rep. E.S. Klosterman Co., Dayton, 1966-71; v.p., 1971-72; v.p. sales, dir. Springfield Binder Corp., Ohio, 1981-84; dir., pres., CEO, 1984-95; dir., pres., The John K. Howe Co., Inc., Dayton, 1972-87, chmn., CEO, 1987—. Dir., pres. The John K. Howe Co., Inc., Dayton, Ohio, 1972-87, chmn., chief exec. officer, dir. 1987—; pres. Cutler-Kingman, Inc. div. Thump Properties, Cin., 1979-86, owner, 1986-2000; gen. ptnr. H&B Enterprises, Dayton, 1977-86, Design Investment Properties, Dayton, 1979-86, BMR Properties, Ltd., Dayton, 1979-82; adminstr. John K. Howe Co./Profit Sharing, Cin., 1973—, John K. Howe Co./Pension Plan, 1976—; owner Androscoggin Designs, Dayton, 1979-86. Pres. South Dixie Bus. Assn., 1989-91, chmn., 1992-94, chmn., 1992-94; pres. woods of Lincoln Park Homeownern's Assn., 1992-94; mem. Fraze Pavilion fund raising com., 1991-92; mem. Confreried de la Chaines de Rotisseurs Bailliage de Cin., 1993-2000; chmn. ops. com. Adams Place Condominium Owners Assn., Inc., 1996-98, v.p., bd. mgrs., 1998-99, pres. bd. mgrs., 1999-2000. Republican. Presbyterian. Office: 644 Linn St Ste 801 Cincinnati OH 45203-1738 E-mail: howe.jk@ehowe.com.

HOWE, JOHN PRENTICE, III, health facility administrator, physician; b. Jackson, Tenn., Mar. 7, 1943; s. John Prentice and Phyllis (MacDonald) H.; m. Tyrrell Flawn; children: Lindsey Warren, Brooke Olmsted, John Prentice IV. BA, Amherst Coll., 1965; MD, Boston U., 1969. Diplomate Am. Bd. Internal Medicine, internal medicine and cardiovascular disease. Research assoc. cellular physiology Amherst Coll., 1963-64; research assoc. cardiovascular physiology Boston U. Sch. of Medicine, 1966-67; lectr. medicine Boston U. Sch. Medicine, 1972-73; intern Boston City Hosp., 1969-70, asst. resident, 1970-71; rsch. fellow in medicine Harvard U., 1971-73, Peter Bent Brigham Hosp., 1971-73; survey physician Framingham Cardiovascular Disease Study, Nat. Heart and Lung Inst., 1971; asst. clin. prof. medicine U. Hawaii, 1973-75; from asst. prof. medicine to assoc. prof. U. Mass., 1975-85, assoc. prof., 1977-85, vice-chmn. dept. medicine, 1975-78, asst. dean continuing edn. for physicians, 1976-78, assoc. dean profl. affairs and continuing edn., 1978-80, acad. dean, 1980-85, vice chancellor, 1980-85, acting chmn. dept. anatomy, 1982-85; pres. U. Tex. Health Scis. Ctr., San Antonio, 1985-2000; pres., CEO Project HOPE, Millwood, Va., 2001—. Prof. medicine, U. Tex. Health Sci. Ctr., San Antonio, 1985—; chief of staff, U. Mass. Hosp., 1978-80. Mem. editl. bd. Archives Internal Medicine, 1991—2004; contbr. articles to profl. jours., chpts. to books. Trustee S.W. Found. for Biomed. Rsch., S.W. Rsch. Inst. Maj. M.C, U.S. Army, 1973-75. Alfred P. Sloan scholar Amherst Coll., 1962-65; recipient Ruth Hunter Johnson award Boston U. Sch. of Medicine, 1969 Fellow: Am. Coll. Chest Physicians, Am. Coll. Cardiology, ACP; mem.: Bexar County Med. Soc. (exec. com. 1985—2000, 1985—2000, pres. 1996), Tex. Soc. Biomed. Rsch. (past pres.), Tex. Med. Soc. (coun. med. edn. 1986—2001, ho. of dels. 1989—2001, pres.-elect 1997—98, pres. 1998—99), Am. Heart Assn. (fellow coun. clin. cardiology), AMA (coun. on sci. affairs 1993—2001, del. ho. dels. 1995—2001), Omicron Kappa Epsilon, Alpha Omega Alpha. Avocations: tennis, skiing. Business E-Mail: jhowe@projecthope.org.

HOWE, JONATHAN THOMAS, lawyer; b. Evanston, Ill., Dec. 16, 1940; s. Frederick King and Rosalie Charlotte (Volz) H.; m. Lois Helene Braun, July 12, 1963; children: Heather C., Jonathan Thomas Jr., Sara E. BA with honors, Northwestern U., 1963; JD with distinction, Duke U., 1966. Bar: Ill. 1966, U.S. Dist. Ct. (no. dist.) Ill. 1966, U.S. Ct. Appeals (7th cir.) 1967, U.S. Tax Ct. 1968, U.S. Supreme Ct. 1970, U.S. Ct. Appeals (D.C. cir.) 1976, U.S. Ct. Appeals (9th cir.) 1980, U.S. Ct. Appeals (4th, 5th, 11th dirs.) 1983, U.S. Claims Ct. 1990. Ptnr. Jenner & Block, Chgo., 1966-85, sr. ptnr. in charge assn. and adminstrv. law dept., 1978-85; founding and sr. ptnr., pres. Howe & Hutton, Chgo., Washington & St. Louis, 1985—. Exec. and adv. coms. to Ill. Sec. of State to revise the Ill. Not for Profit Act, 1983-86; dir. Pacific Mut. Realty Investors, Inc., 1985-86; dir. cable TV options for public Chgo. Access Corp., 1995-97, Bostrom Corp., 2001—. Contbg. editor Ill. Inst. for Continuing Legal Edn., 1973—, Sporting Goods Bus., 1977-91, Meeting News, 1978-88, Meetings Mgr., 1988—, Meetings and Convs., 1991—; contbr. articles to profl. jours.; legal editor Meetings and Convs., 1990—. Mem. Dist. 27 Bd. Edn., Northbrook, Ill., 1969-89, sec., 1969-72, pres., 1973-84; chmn. bd. trustees Sch. Employee Benefit Trust, 1979-85; founding bd. dirs., pres. Sch. Mgmt. Found. Ill., 1976-84; mem. exec. com. Northfield Twp. Rep. Orgn., 1967-71; bd. deacons Village Presbyn. Ch. Northbrook, 1975-78, trustee, 1981-83; mem. Arts and Music Forum, 4th Presbyn. Ch., Chgo., 1990-93; spl. advisor Pres.'s Coun. Phys. Fitness and Sports, 1983-87, Duke Univ. Sch. of Law Bd. of Visitors (life mem.). Named Industry Leader of Yr., Meeting Industry, 1987, Sch. Bd. Mem. Yr. (twice), Ill. State Bd. Edn.; recipient Internat. Found. PaceSetters award Hospitality Sales Mktg. Assn., 1996. Fellow Internat. Forum of Travel and Tourism Advs., Am. Soc. Assn. Execs. (vice-chmn. legal com. 1983-86), Am. Bar Found.; mem. Internat. Assn. Conv. and Hosp. Indsl. Attys. (founder), ABA (antitrust sect. Nat. Inst. com., trade assn. law com. corp. banking and bus. law sect., sect. on litigation, adminstrv. law sect.; internat. law com., continuing edn. com., tort and ins. practice, vice-chmn. com. sports law 1986—, standing com. meetings and travel 1988-93, spl. advisor 1993—), Task Force on Membership Benefits for Disabled Lawyers, Ill. Bar Assn. (antitrust sect., civil practice sect., sch. law sect., adminstrv. law sect.; co-editor Antitrust Newsletter 1968-70), Chgo. Bar Assn. (def. of prisoners com. 1966-83, antitrust law com. 1971—, continuing edn. com. 1977—, chmn. assn. and non-profit soc. law com. 1984-86), Am. Soc. Assn. Execs. (vice-chmn. legal com., founding mem. legal sect.), NY Soc. Assn. Execs., Acad. Hospitality Industry Attys. (founder, bd. dirs. 1994—, pres. 2001—), Nat. Sch. Bds. Assn. (nat. bd. dirs. 1979-89, exec. com. 1981-89, sec.-treas. 1983-85, 2d v.p. 1985-86, chmn. devel. com. 1982-87, pres. 1987-88), DC Bar Assn., Am. Judicature Soc., Ill. Assn. Sch. Bds. (pres. 1977-79, bd. dirs. 1971-88), Chi Bar Found. (life), Assn. Forum Chicagoland (assoc.), Nat. Sch. Bds. Found. (pres./trustee 1995-2002), U.S. C. of C. (legal coun. 1998—), Greater Washington Soc. Assn. Execs., Legal Club, Law Club, Mid-Am. Club, Tower Club, Univ. Club Chgo., Order of Coif, Psi Upsilon. Home: 126 W Delaware Pl Chicago IL 60610-3252 Office: 20 N Wacker Dr Ste 4200 Chicago IL 60606-9833 Office Phone: 312-263-3001. Business E-Mail: jth@howehutton.com.

HOWE, LYMAN HAROLD, III, chemist, researcher; b. Wilkes-Barre, Pa., Nov. 5, 1938; s. Lyman Harold and Esther Madeline (Smith) H.; m. Mary Louise Reinhart, June 16, 1962; 1 child, Jennifer. BS, Duke U., 1960; MS, Emory U., 1961; PhD, U. Tenn., 1966. Rsch. assoc. Emory U., 1960-61; rsch. and teaching assoc. U. Tenn., 1962-66; rsch. chemist water mgmt. TVA, Chattanooga, 1966-97. Co-author publs. in field. Fellow ASTM (water com. results advisor 1976-97, Max Hecht award 1985, Award of Merit 1993); mem. Am. Chem. Soc., Am. Contact Bridge League (Ace of Clubs award, third place Chattanooga Club Master of Yr. award 1989, reviewer environ. sci. and tech. 1989), U.S. Chess Fedn. Clubs: Torch (1st v.p. chpt. 1981, pres. 1982-83, 2d v.p. 1984-88). Presbyterian. Home: 1241 Mountain Brook Cir Signal Mountain TN 37377-2127 Personal E-mail: lymanhoweIII@msn.com.

HOWE, MARTHA MORGAN, microbiologist, educator; b. NYC, Sept. 29, 1945; d. Charles Hermann and Miriam Hudson (Wagner) M.; m. Terrance Gary Cooper. AB, Bryn Mawr Coll., 1966; PhD, MIT, 1972. Postdoctoral fellow Cold Spring Harbor Lab, N.Y., 1972-74; asst. prof. bacteriology U. Wis., Madison, 1975-77, assoc. prof., 1977-81, prof., 1981-84, Vilas prof., 1984-86; Van Vleet prof. virology U. Tenn., Memphis, 1986—. Mem. genetic biology rev. panel NSF, 1980-82, adv. panel prokaryotic biology, 2004—; mem. gen. rsch. support rev. com. NIH, Bethesda, 1982-86, mem. microbial physiology and genetics 2 study sec., 1997-2001; mem. sci. adv. com. instnl. rsch. grants Am. Cancer Soc., 1991-94. Assoc. editor Virology, 1983-92, Genetics, 1994; mem. editorial bd. Jour. Bacteriology, 1985-90; contbr. articles to profl. jours. and books. Recipient Rsch. Career Devel. award NIH, 1978; H.I. Romnes Faculty fellow U. Wis., 1981; Amoco Teaching award U. Wis., 1981. Fellow Am. Acad. Microbiology (bd. govs. 1991-99); mem. Am. Soc. Microbiology (chmn. divsn. H 1983, councillor divsn. H 1989-91, chmn. com. on awards 1990-96, pres.-elect 1999-2000, pres. 2000-2001, past pres. 2001-2002, Eli Lilly award 1985, ASM Founders Disting. Svc. award 1999), Am. Soc. Biochemistry and Molecular Biology, Genetics Soc. Am. (bd. dirs. 1989-91, program com. 1989-90). Office: U Tenn Dept Molecular Scis 858 Madison Ave Memphis TN 38163-0001 Office Phone: 901-448-8215. Business E-Mail: mhowe@utmem.edu.

HOWE, RICHARD RIVES, lawyer; b. Portland, Oreg., Dec. 21, 1942; s. Hubert Shattuck Jr. and Anna Gertrude (Moody) H.; m. Elizabeth Anne Crowell, Aug. 29, 1964; 1 child, Richard Rives Jr. BA, Yale U., 1964; JD, Harvard U., 1967. Bar: N.Y. 1968, U.S. Ct. Appeals (2d cir.) 1973, U.S. Dist. Ct. (so. and ea. dists.) N.Y. 1973, U.S. Supreme Ct. 1973. Assoc. Sullivan & Cromwell, N.Y.C., 1967-74, ptnr., 1974—. Exec. com. Nat. Com. Am. Fgn. Policy, Inc., 2000—. Pres., bd. dirs. Peoples' Symphony Concerts, N.Y.C., 1983—, bd. dirs. Bar Assurance and Reinsurance Ltd., Bermuda, 1994—. Mem.: ABA (com. on corp. practice, fed. regulation securities com., legal opinions com.), Assn. Bar City N.Y., N.Y. State Bar Assn. (chmn. securities regulation com. 1982—86, mem. exec. com. 1982—99, chmn. 1992—93, bus. law sect.), Pi Sigma Alpha, Phi Beta Kappa. Democrat. Home: 86 Woodfield Dr Short Hills NJ 07078-1654 Office: Sullivan & Cromwell Fl 32 125 Broad St Fl 32 New York NY 10004-2498 Office Phone: 212-558-3612. Business E-Mail: hower@sullcrom.com.

HOWE, ROBERT WILSON, education educator; b. Klamath Falls, Oreg., July 9, 1932; s. Fred Phillip and Adelaide Alice H.; m. Alma Ann Felton, Mar. 1955; children: Jeanine Adele, Jeffrey Philip. BA, Willamette U., 1954; MS, Oreg. State U., 1962, EdD, 1964. Tchr., counselor Arlington (Wash.) pub. schs., 1955-60; instr. Oreg. State U., 1961-63; asst. prof. Ohio State U., 1963-66, assoc. prof., 1967-70, prof., 1970-91, prof. emeritus, 1991—, chmn. dept. sci. and math edn., 1969-77. Dir. sci., math. environ. edn. ERIC Clearinghouse, 1968-90, EQ/IRC, 1977-91; spl. chair Nat. Taiwan Normal U., Taipei, 1993, 95-97; cons. fed. agys., schs. state and fgn. govts. Author, co-author books; mem. editl. bd. Jour. Sci. Edn., 1970-93; contbr. articles to profl. jours.; mem. internat. editl. adv. bd. Procs. Nat. Sci. Coun., Republic of China: Math., Sci. and Tech. Edn., 1996—. Trustees Ctr. Sci. and Industry, Columbus, Ohio. NSF fellow, 1959, 60, 61; EPA grantee, 1977-84, 87, 90; vis. scholar Nat. Rsch. Coun. Republic of China, 1989. Fellow Ohio Acad. Sci.; mem. Nat. Assn. Rsch. Sci. Tchg. (hon. life), Nat. Sci. Tchrs. Assn., Assn. Educators Tchg. of Sci.(hon. life), Phi Delta Kappa, Sigma Alpha Epsilon. Methodist. Home and Office: 4099 NW Sierra Dr Camas WA 98607-8518

HOWE, SANDRA JO, library director; b. St. Louis, Sept. 30, 1960; d. Raymond Lee and Elizabeth Ann Griffin; m. Steven Howe, June 24, 1977 (div. Nov. 1978); children: Beth Marie Howe, Ricky A. Rudd. Student, Culver-Stockton Coll., 1997-99. Pharmacy technician Grand Leader Pharmacy, Canton, Mo., 1981-87; mgr., cons. Mo. Pizza Co., Canton, 1993-96; asst. libr. Canton Pub. Libr., 1996-97, dir., 1997—. Mem. ALA, ACLU, Mo. Libr. Assn. Avocations: reading, promoting literacy, nature walks, gardening. Office: Canton Pub Libr 409 Lewis St Canton MO 63435-1529 E-mail: sjhowe@yahoo.com.

HOWE, WARREN BILLINGS, physician; b. Jackson Heights, N.Y., Oct. 25, 1940; s. John Hanna and Francelia (Rose) H.; m. Hedwig Neslanik, Aug. 7, 1971; children: Elizabeth Rose, Sarah Billings. BA, U. Rochester, 1962; MD, Washington U., St. Louis, 1965. Diplomate in family medicine and sports medicine Am. Bd. Family Practice, Nat. Bd. Med. Examiners. Intern Phila. Gen. Hosp., 1965-66; resident physician Highland Hosp./U. Rochester, 1969-71; family physician Family Medicine Clinic of Oak Harbor (Wash.), Inc., PS, 1971-92; student health physician, univ. team physician We. Wash. U., Bellingham, 1992—. Team physician Oak Harbor H.S., 1972-92; head tournament physician Wash. State H.S. Wrestling Championships, Tacoma, 1989—; attending physician Seattle Goodwill Games, 1990; clin. asst. prof. U. Wash. Sch. Medicine, 1975-82; bd. dirs. Nat. Operating Com. on Stds. for Athletic Equipment. Contbr. articles to profl. jours. and chpts. to books; editl. bd. The Physician and Sports Medicine Jour., 1984—. Bd. dirs. Oak Harbor Sch. Dist. #201, 1975-87; chmn. Oak Harbor Citizen's Com. for Sch. Support, 1988-90. Lt. comdr. USN, 1966-69, Vietnam. Recipient Disting. Svc. award City of Oak Harbor, 1984; named to Nat. Wrestling Hall of Fame, 2003; Paul Harris fellowship Oak Harbor Rotary Club. Fellow: Am. Acad. Family Physicians, Am. Coll. Sports Medicine (chair membership com. 1986—95, Citation award 2005); mem.: Am. Coll. Health Assn., Am. Med. Soc. for Sports Medicine (Humanitarian award 2002), Wash. State Med. Assn. Presbyterian. Home: 4222 Northridge Way Bellingham WA 98226-7804 Office: WWU Student Health Ctr 2001 Bill McDonald Pkwy Bellingham WA 98225-9132 Office Phone: 360-650-3400. Business E-Mail: warrenbh@pol.net.

HOWE, WILLIAM HUGH, artist; b. Stockton, Calif., June 18, 1928; s. Edwin Walter and Eugenia (Mercante) H. AB, Ottawa (Kans.) U., 1951. Illustrator Western Auto Supply, Kansas City, Mo., 1952, Kansas City Mdse. Mart, 1953-56; comml. artist U.S. Army C.E., Kansas City, 1958-64, Howard Needles Tammen & Bergendoff Cons. Engrs., Kansas City, 1964-68, Urban & Regional Planning, 1968-70; freelance artist, 1970—. Exhibited paintings of butterflies Philbrook Art Ctr., Tulsa, Ft. Worth Children's Mus., Montserrat Gallery, N.Y.C., Witte Meml. Art Mus., San Antonio, Anthropology Mus., Chapultepec Park, Mexico City, Alice Sabatini Gallery, Topeka Pub. Libr., 2002, Powell Gardens, Kingsville, 2003; represented in permanent collections: Smithsonian Instn., Washington, Franklin Mint (Pa.), Cranbook Inst., Bloomfield Hills, Mich., U. Mich. Exhibits Mus., Ann Arbor, Oak Knoll Mus., Clayton, Mo., Am. Mus. Natural History, N.Y.C., Denver Mus. Natural History, Am. Baptist Assembly, Green Lake, Wis., Mowbray Union, Ottawa U., Kans., Ctrl. Mo. State Coll., Warrensburg, Mich. State U., East Lansing, U. Wyo. Art Mus., Laramie, San Diego Mus. Nat. History, Balboa Park, U. Ariz., Tuscon, Ill. State Mus. Art, Springfield, Mont. Hist. Soc., Helena, Wyo. State Art Mus., Cheyenne, Ariz. State U., Tempe, Milw. Pub. Mus., State Capitol Bldg., Denver, Denver Pub. Libr., Kansas City (Mo.) Mus. History Sci., Presdl. Palace, Tamazunchale, San Luis Potosi, Mexico, Ottawa (Kans.) Jr. H.S., Am. Heritage Wildlife cards Am. Butterflies, 1983, U. Kans., 1994, U. Calif. Berkeley, Allyn Mus. Entomology, Sarasota, U. Colo., Colo. State U., Calif. Acad. Scis., San Francisco, Oakland (Calif.) Mus., James Ford Bell Mus., U. Minn. (Mpls.), Coutts Art Mus., 1997; Author-artist: Our Butterflies and Moths, 1964, The Butterflies of North America, 1975, Butterfly Chart of North America, 1979, Butterfly sect. Readers Digest North American Wildlife, 1980; co-author (with Carlos R. Beutelspacher Baights), U.N.A.M., Mexico City, 1984; one man shows Caroline Kingcade Gallery, North Kansas City, Mo., 1988, Coutts Mus. of Art, El Dorado, 1997, Dallas Mus. Natural History, Fair Park, 1999, George P. Spiva Art Ctr., Joplin, Mo., 1999, Alice Sabatini Art Gallery, Topeka, 2002, Shawnee County Libr., Topeka, 2002, Heard Mus., McKinney, Tex., 2005; TV show Hoy Mismo, 1986. Mem. Ottawa Cmty. Arts Coun., Leavenworth Arts. Coun.; mem. Larry Hatteberg's "Kans. People" KAKE-TV, Wichita. Named Am. Artist Am. References, 1990. Mem. Jour. Lepidopterists Soc., Burroughs Nature Club, Audubon Soc. Mo., Ctrl. States Entomol. Soc., Los Angeles County Mus., Spiva Art Ctr., Dallas Mus. Natural History, Mus. Culture and Natural History, Harvard Bot. Mus., Powell Gardens, Kingsville, Mo., Salina (Kans.) Pub. Libr., Lawrence (Kans.) Pub. Libr., Coffeyville (Kans.) Pub. Libr., Pittsburg (Kans.) Pub. Libr., Hutchinson (Kans.) Pub. Libr. Democrat. Episcopalian. Avocation: collecting butterflies in Mexico and Guatemala. Home: Hidden Meadows 1604 S Hickory St Apt E-5 Ottawa KS 66067

HOWELL, BENJAMIN FRANKLIN, JR., geophysicist, educator; b. Princeton, N.J., June 12, 1917; s. Benjamin Franklin and Claire M. (Mead) H.; m. Constance M. Benson, June 30, 1943 (dec.); children: Barbara Carolyn, Catherine Ann (dec.), Bonnie Andrea, James Benjamin. AB, Princeton U., 1939; MS, Calif. Inst. Tech., 1942, Ph. D., 1949. Research engr. div. war research U. Calif. at San Diego, 1942-45; geophysicist United Geophys. Co., 1946-49; faculty Pa. State U., 1949—, prof. geophysics, 1953—, head dept. geophysics and geochemistry, 1949-63; asst. dean Grad. Sch. Pa. State U., 1968-70, assoc. dean, 1970-82, assoc. dean emeritus, 1982—. Chief cons. seismologist Vibratech Enging. Co., Hazleton, Pa., 1955-69 Author: Introduction to Geophysics, 1959, Earth and Universe, 1972, Introduction to Seismological Research: History and Development, 1990; Editor: Contributions in Geophysics in Honor of Beno Gutenberg, 1958. Fellow Am. Geophys. Union (sec. sect. tectonophysics 1956-59, sect. seismology 1959-63), Geol. Soc. Am.; mem. soc. Exploration Geophysics, Seismol. Soc. Am. (pres. 1963-64), Phi Beta Kappa, Sigma Xi. Baptist. Home: 1143 Smithfield Cir State College PA 16801-6424 Office: 402 Deike Bldg University Park PA 16802-2713 Personal E-mail: howellbf@aol.com.

HOWELL, BERYL A., lawyer; b. 1956; m. Michael Rosenfeld; 3 children, Jared, Alina, Calla. BA with honors, Bryn Mawr Coll., 1978; JD, Columbia Univ. Law clk. to Hon. Dickinson A. Debevoise U.S. Dist. Ct. N.J.; assoc. Schulte Roth & Zabel, N.Y.; asst. U.S. atty. (ea. dist.) N.Y. US Dept. Justice, 1987—93; gen. counsel U.S. Senate Judiciary Com., 1993—2003; exec. v.p., mng. dir. & gen. counsel Stroz Friedberg LLC, Washington, 2003—. Commr. U.S. Sentencing Commn., 2004—. Recipient First Amendment award, Soc. Profl. Journalists, 2004; Harlan Fiske Stone scholar, Columbia Univ. Office: Stroz Friedberg LLC Suite 200 1150 Connecticut Ave NW Washington DC 20036

HOWELL, BRADLEY SUE, librarian; b. McKinney, Tex., July 15, 1933; d. Jessie Leonard and Carrie Pearl (Nickerson) LaFon; m. Richard Dunn Howell, May 18, 1957; children: Mark Richard, Celeste Ella, Jane Elizabeth. BS in Edn., So. Meth. U., 1955; MS in Libr. Sci., East Tex. State U., 1968. Tchr. J.B. Hood Jr. High Sch., Dallas, 1955-56, Mineral Wells (Tex.) Jr. High Sch., 1957-58; libr. Ascher Silberstein Sch., Dallas, 1963, San Jacinto Sch., Dallas, 1960-62, 65-81, Woodrow Wilson High Sch., Dallas, 1981—. Pres. Tex. United Meth. Hist. Soc., 1980—84, v.p., 2000—04; sec. South Ctr. Jurisdiction Archives and history of United Meth. Ch., 1980—88; v.p. local ch. sect. The United Meth. Hist. Soc., 1989—95, chmn., 1995—99; pres. PTA Woodrow Wilson H.S., 1983—84; leader Camp Fire, Inc., 1970—; v.p. South Ctrl. Jurisdiction, Archives and History The United Meth. Ch., 2000—04. Recipient Wakan award Camp Fire, Inc., 1976, Hilteni award, 19782, Sawnequas award, 1988, Gulick Vol. award, 1998, Terrific Tchr. award Tex. PTA, 1984, Jim Collins Outstanding award, 1986, Honor award Nat. Sch. Pub. Relation Assn., 1986, Dallas Positive Parents award, 1987; Golden Flame award, 1990; elected Woodrow Wilson H.S. Hall of Fame, 1999. Mem.: Am. Libr. Svcs. to Children (Newbery com. 1980), Tex. Libr. Assn. (chmn. archives and history roundtable 1990—92), Tex. Assn. Sch. Librs., Dallas Assn. Sch. Librs. (pres. 1975—76), Freedoms Found. and Valley Forge (pres. Dallas chpt. 1997—99, v.p. edn. 2003—05), Pi Lambda Theta (pres. Alpha Sigma chpt. 1997—2002), Delta Psi Kappa, Phi Delta Kappa, Alpha Delta Pi, Delta Kappa Gamma (state achievement award 1988, Golden Gift Leadership Mgmt. award 1985). Democrat. Home: 722 Ridgeway St Dallas TX 75214-4453 Office: Woodrow Wilson High Sch 100 S Glasgow Dr Dallas TX 75214-4598 Office Phone: 972-502-4455. E-mail: brhowell@dallaslsd.org.

HOWELL, CATHERINE JEANINE, retired secondary school educator; b. Benton, Ill, Apr. 15, 1935; d. Lloyd William Reed and Lena Pearl (Armstrong) Goodin; m. Charles Lindy Barnfield, Apr. 13, 1950 (div. Apr. 23, 1973); m. Charles E. Howell, June 28, 1975; children: Alan Reed, Robert, Timothy Michael Barnfield; stepchildren: Crystal Lea, Carla Sue. A in Technol., So. Ill. U., 1962, BA, 1968, MS in Edn., 1976, postgrad. specialist, 1986. Cert. educator and supr., Ill. Clk. Kroger, Benton, Ill., 1957-60; elem. tchr. Benton Elem. Sch. Dist. 47, 1968-70; secondary art tchr. Marion Cmty. Unit Sch. Dist. 2, Ill., 1970-94; ret., 1994. Instr. art John A. Logan C.C., Carterville, Ill., 1975-89, 97-98, instr. vocat. edn., 1992, part-time acad. instr. art, 1997-98, part time asst. literacy coord., 2001—; cons. in field. Prin. work includes Strings of Creation, 1988, Portrait Sketch of Brenda Edgar, 1991; currently, part time asst. Lit. Coord. @ John A. Logan CC, Carterville, Ill. Art judge DuQuoin (Ill.) State Fair, 1990-91; mem. Ill. State Bd. Edn. Leadership Cadre, 1989-98; co-founder Downstate Art Educator's Assn. Recipient Award of Excellence Ill. State Bd. Edn., 1988, Sch. Bell award Williamson Co. ESR, 1988-89, Outstanding Art Educator award Ill. Alliance for Arts Edn., 1988, Ill. Art Educator award, 1989, Nat. Ill. Art Educator award, 1990, Senate Resolution Senator James Rea, 1989, Proclamation Gov. James Thompson, 1990; Ill. Art Ed. (IAEA) art Tchr. of the Yr., State of Ill., 1989. Mem. AAUW, Ill. Art Edn. Assn. (sec. dir. 1990), Little Egypt Arts Assn. on LEAA Bd. of Dir., Ill. Ret. Tchrs. Assn.,So. Ill. U. Alumni Life, Downstate Art Edn. (life), Elk Ladies, Delta Kappa Gamma, Phi Kappa Phi, Beta Sigma Phi. Avocations: graphic art, computer graphics, selling antiques, network marketing. Home: 114 N Chamberlain Dr Marion IL 62959-5503

HOWELL, CHARLES MAITLAND, dermatologist; b. Thomasville, N.C., Apr. 14, 1914; s. Cyrus Maitl and Lilly Mae (Ammons) H.; m. Betty Jane Myers, Feb. 12, 1949; children: Elizabeth Myers, Pamela Jane. BS, Wake Forest U., Winston-Salem, N.C., 1935; MD, U. Pa., 1937. Intern Charity Hosp., New Orleans, 1937-38; resident in medicine Burlington County Hosp., Mt. Holley, N.J., 1938-39; sch. physician Lawrenceville (N.J.) Sch., 1939-42; resident in pathology N.C. Baptist Hosp., Winston-Salem, 1947-48; resident in dermatology Columbia-Presbyn. Med. Ctr., N.Y.C., 1948-50; resident in allergy Roosevelt Hosp., N.Y.C., 1950-51; practice medicine specializing in dermatology Winston-Salem, 1951—. Mem. staff N.C. Bapt., Forsyth Meml. hosps.; mem. faculty Bowman Gray Sch. Medicine, Wake Forest U., 1951-86, head. sect., 1984-86, prof. dermatology, 1967-84, prof. emeritus, 1984, head sect., 1961-86, acting head sect., 1984-86. Served as officer M.C. AUS, 1942-46. Fellow Am. Acad. Dermatology, Am. Acad. Allergy; mem. N. Am. Clin. Dermatol. Soc., N.Y. Acad. Scis. Clubs: Old Town (Winston-Salem); Bermuda Run Country (Clemmons, N.C.). Democrat. Baptist. Home: 1100 E Kent Rd Winston Salem NC 27104-1116 Office: 340 Pershing Ave Winston Salem NC 27103-2513 Office Phone: 336-725-8422. Office Fax: 336-725-8423.

HOWELL, DEBORAH S., career officer; b. Greenville, S.C. BA in Math., MPA; cert., Amphibious Warfare Sch., Naval War Coll., Federal Exec. Inst., Harvard U., Maxwell Sch., MIT. From presidential mgmt. intern to budget program analyst, dep. branch head of manpower policy USMC, Arlington, Va., 1979-94, asst. dep. chief of staff manpower and reserve affairs, 1994—.

HOWELL, DONALD LEE, lawyer; b. Waco, Tex., Jan. 31, 1935; s. Hilton Emory and Louise Howell; m. Gwendolyn Avera, June 13, 1957; children: Daniel Liege, Alison Avera, Anne Turner. BA cum laude, Baylor U., 1956; JD with honors, U. Tex., 1963. Bar: Tex. 1963. Assoc. Vinson & Elkins, Houston, 1963-70, ptnr., 1970—, mem. mgmt. com., 1980-99. Capt. USAFR, 1956—59. Fellow Am. Bar Found., Tex. Bar Found., Houston Bar Found., Am. Law Inst.; mem. ABA, Am. Coll. Bond Counsel, Houston Bar Assn., Nat. Assn. Bond Lawyers (pres. 1981-82, bd. dirs. 1979-83), Attys. Liability Assurance Soc. (Bermuda bd. dirs. 1992-2005, chmn. 2000-02, U.S. bd. dirs. 1992-2005, chmn. 2000-02), Houston Club, Houston Ctr. Club, Order of Coif, Phi Delta Phi. Democrat. Episcopalian. Business E-Mail: dhowell@velaw.com.

HOWELL, EVERETTE IRL, physicist, researcher; b. Shelby, Miss., Jan. 4, 1914; s. Thomas Daniel and Helen Lundy (Eason) H.; m. Beverly Ione McLaurin, June 12, 1943; children— Everette Irl, Marcia Marie, Beverly Jeannine. BA, Miss. Coll., 1936; MS, Vanderbilt U., 1937; PhD, U. N.C., 1940. Prof. phys. sci. Belhaven Coll., 1940-48; head dept. physics Miss. State U., 1948-79, prof., 1948-79, prof. emeritus, 1979—. Summer teaching physics dept. Vanderbilt U., 1946, U. Fla., 1947; summer research participant Oak Ridge Nat. Lab., 1950, 51 Contbr. articles to sci. publs. Mem. Am. Inst. Physics, Am. Phys. Soc., Am. Assn. Physics Tchrs., Miss. Acad. Scis., Sigma Xi, Phi Kappa Phi. Presbyn. (elder). Address: 10100 Hillview Rd Apt 410 Pensacola FL 32514-5457

HOWELL, FRANCIS CLARK, paleo-anthropologist; b. Kansas City, Mo., Nov. 27, 1925; s. Edward Ray and Myrtle Marie (Clark) H.; m. Betty Ann Tomsen, June 17, 1955; children: Brian David, Jennifer Clare. PhB, U. Chgo., 1949, MA, 1951, PhD, 1953. Instr. anatomy Washington U., St. Louis, 1953-55; asst. prof. to prof. anthropology U. Chgo., 1955-70; prof. anthropology U. Calif.-Berkeley, 1970-91, emeritus prof., 1991—. Contbr. numerous articles on human biol. and cultural evolution to profl. jours. Trustee L.S.B. Leakey Found., 1969—. Served with USN, 1944-46 Recipient Franklin L. Burr prize, Nat. Geographic Soc., 1993, Leakey prize L.S.B. Leakey Fedn., 1998, Charles Robert Darwin Lifetime Achievement award Am. Assn. Phys. Anthropologists, 1998. Fellow Am. Acad. Arts and Scis.; mem. Nat. Acad. Scis., Am. Philos. Soc., AAAS, Calif. Acad. Sci. (trustee 1975-1991, Fellows medal 1990), Acad. des Scis., Inst. de France. Home: 1994 San Antonio Ave Berkeley CA 94707-1620 Office: U Calif Mus Vertebrate Zoology Berkeley CA 94720-3160

HOWELL, GEORGE, art critic; Writer, Washington DC and Baltimore area art scene Art Papers, Atlanta, 1994—, documentation production specialist, 2000—. Office: Art Papers PO Box 5748 Atlanta GA 31107 Office Phone: 404-588-1837. Office Fax: 404-588-1836.*

HOWELL, GEORGE BEDELL, investment company executive; b. Schenectady, Sept. 19, 1919; s. Jesse M. and Grace (Gerhaeusser) Howell; m. Mary Barbara Crohurst, July 10, 1944; children: Raymond Gary, Terry Barbara, Janice Patricia, Nancy Jo, George Bedell Jr. BS in Adminstrv. Engring., Cornell U., 1942. With GE, 1946-59; v.p. mfg. Leece Neville Co., Cleve., 1959-61, Royal Electric Co., Pawtucket, R.I., 1961-62; dir. ops. packaging equipment and product devel. Acme Steel Co. (merged with Interlake Steel Corp. 1965), 1962-64; v.p. adminstrv. svc. Interlake Steel Corp., Chgo., 1964-66, v.p. internat. divsn., v.p. Acme Products divsn., 1966-70; CEO Golconda Corp., Chgo., 1970-72; v.p. devel. Internat. Minerals & Chems. Corp., 1972-73, sr. v.p., pres. industry group, 1974-77, exec. v.p., 1977-81; pres., CEO Wurlitzer Co., 1982-86, chmn., pres., CEO, 1986-87, vice chmn., 1987-88; prin. Mid West Ptnrs., Chgo., 1988-89; gen. ptnr. Pfingsten Ptnrs., Chgo., 1989-94, ptnr., 1994—2003, mem. adv. bd., 2002—03; chmn. Hallcrest Holding Corp., 1992-97. Chmn. bd. trustees Village of Oak Brook, Ill., 1965—73, pres., 1973—79; mem. McGraw Wildlife Found.; trustee Christ Ch., Oak Brook, vice chmn., 1992—97, trustee emeritus, 1998; mem. univ. coun. Cornell U., 2001—. N.Y. State and Univ. scholar, Cornell U., 1942. Mem.: Ocean Reef Club (Fla.), Medinah Country Club. Office: 520 Lake Cook Rd Ste 375 Deerfield IL 60015-5632 Office Phone: 847-374-9140. Business E-Mail: ghowell@pfingsten.com. *Trust in God. Balance family, work, church and government service. Live every day of your life.*

HOWELL, HARLEY THOMAS, lawyer; b. Chgo., June 5, 1937; s. Harley W. and Geneva (Engelmann) H.; m. Aliceann A. McLaughlin, Apr. 23, 1983; children by previous marriage: Shelley A. Young, Rebecca L., Emily S. AB, Princeton U., 1959; JD, Yale U., 1962. Bar: Md. 1962, U.S. Supreme Ct. 1966, D.C. 1972. Law clk. to chief judge U.S. Ct. Appeals (4th cir.), 1962-63; assoc. Semmes, Bowen & Semmes, Balt., 1966-72, ptnr., 1972-92, Howell, Gately, Whitney & Carter LLP, Towson, Md., 1992-98, counsel, 1998-99; ptnr. Howell & Gately, Balt., 1999—2002, counsel, 2002—03. Mem. Gov.'s Commn. to Revise Annotated Code Md., 1975-85; mem. standing com. on rules of practice and procedure Ct. Appeals of Md., 1985-2000. Bd. dirs. Balt. Symphony Orch., 1975—, sec., 1986-2003, exec. com., 1986-2005; bd. dirs. Sinai Hosp. of Balt., 2003—, Md. Hist. Soc., 2004—; trustee Sheppard and Enoch Pratt Health Sys., Towson, 1991—. Capt. JAG Corps, U.S. Army, 1963-66. Decorated Army Commendation medal. Fellow Am. Coll. Trial Lawyers, Am. Acad. Appellate Lawyers, Md. Bar Found.; mem. ABA, Md. State Bar Assn., Bar Assn. Balt. City, Balt. County Bar Assn., D.C. Bar Assn., Fed. Bar Assn., Wine and Food Soc., Wranglers Law Club (Balt.), Am. Coll. Barristers. Home: 1012 Chestnut Ridge Dr Lutherville Timonium MD 21093-1716 Office: Howell & Gately One Charles Ctr 19th Fl 100 N Charles St Baltimore MD 21201 E-mail: hthomas37@comcast.net.

HOWELL, HILTON HATCHETT, JR., marketing executive; b. Waco, Tex., Mar. 25, 1962; s. Hilton Hatchett Sr. and Donna (Massingill) H.; m. Robin Mary Robinson, June 15, 1991; children: Hilton Hatchett III, Alston Elizabeth. BA, Baylor U., 1984, JD cum laude, 1988; MBA, U. Tex., 1990. Bar: Ga. 1993, Tex. 1988. Atty. Liddell, Sapp, Zivley, Hill & Laboon, Houston, 1989-91; exec. v.p., dir. Delta Life Ins. Co., Delta Fire and Casualty Ins. Co., Atlanta, 1991—, Atlantic Am. Corp., Atlanta, 1991-95, pres., CEO, 1995—; v.p., sec., dir. Bull Run Corp., Atlanta, 1993—. Dir. Am. So. Ins. Cos., Atlanta, Gray Comm. Sys., Atlanta. Bd. dirs. Ga. Dept. Human Resources, Atlanta, 1993-97; trustee Woodruff Arts Ctr., Inc., 1998—; mem. bd. regents Univ. Sys. of Ga., 1997—. Mem. Piedmont Driving Club, Capital City Club, Diplomats, Benedicts, Hedonia Club, Young Pres.'s Orgn. Baptist. Avocations: golf, hunting. Office: Atlantic Am Corp 4370 Peachtree Rd NE Atlanta GA 30319-3023

HOWELL, IRVIN WENDELL, JR., physician, consultant; b. Nashville, Tenn., Oct. 6, 1944; s. Irvin Wendell and Evelyn Yvonne Howell; m. Susan Elizabeth Seboek, July 20, 1990; children: Jasmine Ameri, Sarah E. Bullard. BS in Biology, Tenn. State U., 1966, M in Biology, 1969; MD, Meharry Med. Coll., 1974. Cert. nurses asst., home health provider. Resident family practice Meharry Med. Coll., Hubbard Hosp., Nashville, 1975—78; commd. ensign USN, 1978, advanced through grades to lt. comdr., family practice physician, Med. Corps, 1978—87, ret., 1987; med. investigator fraud Simpson Orthop. Group, Carson, Calif., 1989—92; quality assurance cons. Morningside Primary Care Ctr., L.A., 1992—94; med. dir. Queen City Med. Group, Long Beach, Calif., 1993—97; med. mktg. cons. Medassis Inst., Long Beach, 1997—, Edn. Commn. for Foreign Med. Grads., Los Angeles. Med. cons. Medasis Inst., Long Beach, 1992—96; quality assurance auditor U. So. Calif. Indep. Physicians Assn., L.A., 1994—96. Author: New Era of Terror, 2002 (Letter of Recognition signed by Pres. Bush, 2002); contbr. articles to newspaper. Mem.: Acad. Mil. Physicians, Am. Acad. Family Physicians. Baptist. Avocations: cooking, reading, running, writing, classical music. Home: 20619 Kenwood Ave Torrance CA 90503

HOWELL, JAMES BURT, III, retired agricultural products company sales consultant; b. Dec. 11, 1933; s. James Burt and Catharine Stanger (Sparks) H.; m. Lorraine Marie Chanatry, Feb. 18, 1995. BS with honors, Rutgers U., 1956; MBA, U. Del., 1980. Agrl. sales rep. Allied Chem. Corp., Phila., 1957-59; sales cons. Asgrow Seed Co. subs. Upjohn Co., Vineland, NJ, 1960—2002; ret., 2002. Bd. dirs. Advance Weight Systems, Inc., LaGrange, Ohio. Mem. ofcl. bd. (session) 1st Presbyn. Ch. of Cedarville, 1960—; admissions liaison officer U.S. Mil. Acad., West Point, N.Y., 1973—; chmn. Lawrence Twp. Zoning Bd. Adjustment. With U.S. Army, 1957, col. USAR. Recipient Burpee Hort. award, Rutgers U., 1955. Mem.: Res. Officers Assn. U.S., N.J. Agri-Bus. Assn. (Heritage award 2003), Vegetable Growers Assn. N.J., Nat. Def. Indsl. Assn., Alpha Zeta (Centennial Honor Roll 1997), Alpha Gamma Rho (Bros. of the Century award), Phi Beta Kappa. Home and Office: 23 Shadow Brooke Dr Bridgeton NJ 08302 Office Phone: 856-453-9765.

HOWELL, JAMES EDWIN, economist, educator; b. Sterling, Colo., Mar. 6, 1928; s. James William, Jr. and Lois (Brown) H.; m. Linda Leinbach, 1965; children: Kenneth E., William J., Jan E., Caitlyn B. BA, Fresno State Coll., 1950; MA, U. Ill., 1951, Yale U., 1953, PhD, 1955. Instr. econs. and stats. Yale U., 1954-56; mem. staff Ford Found., 1956-58, 62, cons., 1958-72; Theodore J. Kreps prof. econs. Stanford U., 1958—, asso. dean Grad. Sch. Bus., 1965-70; vis. prof. econs. London Bus. Sch., 1992. Dir. gen. Internat. Inst. Mgmt. and Adminstrn., Berlin, 1970-72; dir. Stanford-Insead Advanced Mgmt. Program, European Inst. Bus. Adminstrn., France, 1979-81; sometime prof., lectr. U. Hawaii, U. Calif.-Berkeley, Stanford in Vienna, U. Pa., Nat. U. Singapore, London Bus. Sch.; vis. prof. Humboldt U., Berlin, 1995; cons. U.S. and Europe; bd. dirs. Edn. Devel. Corp. Author/co-author: Higher Education for Business, 1959, European Economics-East and West, 1967, Mathematical Analysis for Business Decisions, 1963, 2d edit., 1971, (with G. L. Bach) Economics, 11th edit., 1987. Served with AUS, 1946-47. Ford Found. faculty fellow Harvard U., 1959-60; NSF sr. postdoctoral fellow London Sch. Econs., 1963-64; recipient Davis award for lifetime achievement Stanford U., 1996. Mem.: University Club (N.Y.C.). Office: Stanford U Grad Sch Bus Stanford CA 94305-5015

HOWELL, JAMES TENNYSON, allergist, immunologist, pediatrician; b. Memphis, Jan. 25, 1944; MD, U. Ark., 1970. Diplomate Am. Bd. Allergy & Immunology, Am. Bd. Pediatrics. Intern Tampa Gen. Hosp., 1970-71; resident in pediatrics Children's Med. Ctr., Dallas, 1973-76; fellow in allergy and immunology Tex., Galveston, 1976-78; with St. Edwards Mercy Med. Ctr., Ft. Smith, Ark., 1976-78. Fellow Am. Coll. Allergy, Asthma and Immunology; mem. AMA, Am. Acad. Pediatrics. Office: Cooper Clinic 6801 Rogers Ave Fort Smith AR 72903-3296

HOWELL, JEFFERSON DAVIS, JR., aerospace transportation executive, retired military officer; b. Victoria, Tex., Aug. 10, 1939; m. Janel Crutchfield; children: Jefferson Davis, III, Melissa Jane. BA in Polit. sci., U. Tex., Austin, 1961, MA in Econs., 1970. 2nd. lt. to infantry ofcer USMC, 1961—64, naval aviator, 1964—73; instr. econs. U.S. Naval Acad., 1973—76; exec. officer Marine fighter attack squadron 212, 1977—80, comdr., 1978—80; staff tours include various positions Hdqtrs. Marine Corps and Pentagon; with aviation dept. Hdqtrs. Marine Corps, Washington, 1981—84, 1987—89, comdr. marine aircraft group, 1984—86, chief of staff 1st Marine Brigade Hawaii, 1986—87; asst. chief of staff for Joint Opers./sr. USN officer Hdqtrs. Allied Forces North/NATO, Kolsas, Oslo, Norway, 1989-91, asst. dep. chief of staff for aviation, 1991-92; inspector gen. USMC, 1992, comdr. 2d Marine Aircraft Wing, 1992—94; dep. comdr. Marine Forces Pacific, 1994—95; various command duties to commdr. Marine Forces Pacific/Commanding Gen., Fleet Marine Force, Camp H.M. Smith, Hawaii, 1995—98; ret., 1998; dep. program mgr., Johnson Space Ctr. Safety, Reliability and Quality Assurance Sci. Applications Internat. Corp., Houston, 1999, program mgr., safety contract, 1999—2002, sr. v.p.; dir. Johnson Space Ctr., Austin, Tex., 2002—. Decorated Def. Superior Svc. medal, Disting. Svc. medal, Legion of Merit, Bronze Star medal with Combat "V", Air medal with two individual and 25 strike/flt. awards, Navy Commendation medal with Combat "V"; recipient John Paul Jones award for Inspirational Leadership, Navy League U.S., Outstanding Leadership medal, NASA, 2003, Disting. Svc. medal, 2005. Office: NASA Johnson Space Ctr Mailcode AA 2101 NASA Pky Houston TX 77058 Office Phone: 281-483-5309. Business E-Mail: jefferson.d.howell@nasa.gov.

HOWELL, JOEL DUBOSE, internist, educator; b. Tex., May 11, 1953; s. Wilson and Nora (Levitas) Howell; m. Linda C. Samuelson, June 26, 1976; children: Jonathan Samuelson, Benjamin Samuelson. BS, Mich. State U., 1975; MD, U. Chgo., 1979; PhD in History and Sociology of Sci., U. Pa., 1987. Intern, resident in internal medicine U. Chgo., 1979-82; Robert Wood Johnson clin. scholar U. Pa., Phila., 1982-84; instr. U. Mich., Ann Arbor, 1984-86, asst. prof., 1986-90, assoc. prof., 1990-97, prof., 1997—, Victor Vaughan prof. history medicine, 2001—. Editor: (book) Technology and American Medicine Practice: 1880-1930, 1988, Medical Lives and Scientific Medicine at Michigan; author: Technology in the Hospital, 1995. Scholar Henry J. Kaiser Family Fedn. Faculty, 1989—92, Charles E. Culpeper Found. Med. Humanities, 1992—96. Fellow: ACP, Am. Osler Soc., Am. Assn. History Medicine. Office Phone: 734-647-4844. E-mail: jhowell@umich.edu.

HOWELL, JOEL WALTER, III, lawyer; b. Jackson, Miss., Dec. 25, 1949; s. Joel W. and Elizabeth (Harris) H.; m. Wilhelmina C. Pontus, June 25, 1983. BA, Millsaps Coll., 1971; JD, Columbia U., 1974. Bar: Tex. 1974, U.S. Ct.

Appeals (5th cir.) 1974, Miss. 1975, U.S. Dist. Ct. (no. and so. dists.) Miss. 1975. Ptnr. Daniel, Coker, Horton, Bell & Dukes, Jackson, 1975-80; pvt. practice, Jackson, 1981—. Adj. faculty law sch. Miss. Coll., Jackson, 1988. Contbg. editor, case notes and comments editor Columbia Jour. Transnat. Law, 1973-74. Mem. ABA, ATLA, Tex. Bar Assn., Miss. Bar (chair tech. com. 2003-04, tech. com., exec. com.), Hinds County Bar Assn. (small firm practice com. 1993-94, chair 1995, computer columnist newsletter 1996—, webmaster 1997—), Miss. Trial Lawyers Assn., Miss. Def. Lawyers Assn., Def. Rsch. Inst., Miss. Bankruptcy Conf. Home: 50 St Andrews Dr Jackson MS 39211-2466 Office: PO Box 16772 5446 Executive Pl Jackson MS 39206-4103 E-mail: jwh3@mindspring.com.

HOWELL, JOHN FLOYD, insurance company executive; b. Mt. Juliet, Tenn., Dec. 24, 1932; s. Robert Lee and Rachel Mae (Draper) H.; m. Margaret Ann Herring, Dec. 27, 1955; children: John Floyd, Leigh Ann, Stephen Donelson. Student, Vanderbilt U., 1951-53; BA, U. Iowa, 1955, postgrad., 1955-56. Actuarial asst. Nat. Life & Accident Ins. Co., Nashville, 1963-64, asst. actuary, 1964-65, 2d v.p., 1965-71, v.p., 1971-81, sr. v.p., 1981-83, also dir.; v.p., chief actuary Ind. Life & Accident Ins. Co., 1984-88, sr. v.p., chief actuary, 1989-96, ret., 1996. Bd. dirs. Vol. Jacksonville, 1984-89, Mental Health Resource Ctr., Jacksonville, 1987-90, Fla. Meth. Bd. Pensions, 1988-96, Jacksonville Urban League, 1992-95; mem. adv. bd. Montgomery Bell Acad., 1995—. Fellow Soc. Actuaries; mem. Am. Acad. Actuaries, Richland Country Club (Nashville). Methodist. Home: 2200 Harding Pl #2 Nashville TN 37215-4145

HOWELL, JOHN MCDADE, retired academic administrator, political scientist, educator; b. Five Points, Ala., Jan. 28, 1922; s. John William and Bettie Mae (Lee) H.; m. Gladys Evelyn David, Aug. 9, 1952; children: David Noble, Joseph Lee. AB, U. Ala., 1948, MA, 1949; PhD, Duke U., 1954. Instr. U. Idaho, 1950, Randolph-Macon Woman's Coll., Lynchburg, Va., 1951-52, Duke U., 1952-53; asst. prof. Sweet Briar Coll., Lynchburg, 1953-54, Memphis State U., 1954-57; assoc. prof. East Carolina U., Greenville, NC, 1957-61, prof., 1961-87, chmn. polit. sci. dept., 1963-66, dean Coll. Arts and Scis., 1966-69, dean Grad. Sch., 1969-73, vice chancellor for acad. affairs, 1973-79, chancellor, 1982-87. Author: (with others) Conflict of International Obligations and State Interests, 1972; contbr.: (with others) chpts. to The International Law Standard and Commonwealth Developments, 1966, De Lege Pactorum, 1970; contbr. articles to profl. jours. Served with USAAF, 1942-45. Decorated Bronze Star. Mem. Phi Beta Kappa, Phi Kappa Phi, Pi Sigma Alpha. Home: 1953 Quail Ridge Rd Apt E Greenville NC 27858-5599

HOWELL, JOHN REID, mechanical engineering educator, dean; b. Columbus, Ohio, June 13, 1936; s. Frederick Edward and Hilma Lavilla (Kief) H.; m. Arlene Elizabeth Pollitt, June 20, 1959 (div. 1974); m. Susan Gooch Conway, May 20, 1979; children: John Reid Jr., Keli Dianne, David Lee. BSChemE, Case Inst. Tech., 1958, MSChemE, 1960, PhD, 1962. Registered profl. engr. Aerospace engr. NASA Lewis Rsch. Ctr., Cleve., 1961-68; assoc. prof. U. Houston, 1969-73, prof., 1973-78; dir. Energy Inst. U. Houston, 1975-78; vis. prof. mech. engring. U. Tex., Austin, 1978-79, prof., 1979-82, E.C.H. Bantel prof., 1982-90, Baker-Hughes Centennial prof. dept. mech. engring., 1990—, Ernest Cockrell, Jr. Meml. chair, 2003—, chmn. mech. engring. dept., 1986-90, dir. Ctr. for Energy Studies, 1988-91, assoc. dean for rsch. Coll. Engring., 1996-99, dir. Ctr. for Advanced Mfg., 2004—. Dir. thermal transport and thermal processing program NSF, 1994-95. Co-author: Thermal Radiation Heat Transfer, 1972, 4th edit., 2002, Design of Solar Thermal Systems, 1984, Fundamentals of Engineering Thermodynamics, 1987, 2d edit., 1992, Catalog of Radiation Configuration Factors, 2d edit., 2000; editor: Journal of Heat Transfer, 1995-2000; contbr. articles to profl. jours. Commr. Renewable Energy Resources Comm., Austin, 1980-81. Served to 1st lt. USAF, 1962-65. Recipient Spl. Svc. award NASA, 1965, Ralph Coats Roe award Am. Soc. Engring. Edn., 1987, Max Jakob award AIChE/ASME, 1998; named to Hon. Order Ky. Cols., 1980. Fellow ASME (Heat Transfer Meml. award 1991), AIAA (Thermophysics award 1990); mem. Russian Acad. Scis. (elected fgn. mem. 1999), Nat. Acad. Engrs. (elected mem. 2005). Office: U Tex Dept Mech Engring 1 University Station C2200 Austin TX 78712 Business E-Mail: jhowell@mail.utexas.edu.

HOWELL, JULIUS AMMONS, retired plastic surgeon; b. Thomasville, N.C., Apr. 14, 1914; s. Cyrus Maitland and Lillie Mae (Ammons) H.; m. Octavia Anne Southern, Oct. 20, 1951; children: Anne, Karen, Robin. LLB, Wake Forest U., 1935, BS, 1940; MD, U. Pa., Phila., 1943. Diplomate Am. Bd. Plastic & Reconstructive Surgery, Am. Bd. Otolaryngology. Chief plastic surgery sect. Bowman Gray Sch. Medicine, Winston Salem, N.C., 1959-84, prof. emeritus plastic surgery, 1984-2000; lectr. Sch. Law Wake Forest U., Winston Salem, N.C., 1978-94; pvt. practice Winston Salem, N.C., 1984-99; ret., 1999. Mem. medico-legal com. N.C. Med. Soc., Raleigh, 1960-93, S.E. Soc. Plastic Surgery; mem. adv. com. N.C. Indsl. com., Raleigh, 1976-86; trustee Blue Cross/Blue Shield, Chapel Hill, 1964-68. Co-author: Plastic Surgery, 1979. Julius Ammons Howell Endowed Chair Surgery named in his honor Bowman Gray Sch. Medicine, 1995. Mem. ACS; Am. Soc. Plastic & Reconstructive Surgery (medicolegal com.), Am. Assn. Plastic Surgeons. Baptist.

HOWELL, KAREN JANE, private school educator; b. Mpls., Apr. 24, 1946; d. John and Lorraine (Quale) Borgen; m. John Morris Howell; children: Laura, John. AS in Math. and Sci., Cottey Jr. Coll., Nevada, Mo., 1966; BS in Elem. Edn. Sci. and Math., U. No. Colo., Greeley, 1968; MS Science & Gifted Education, University Of Virginia, Alexandria, Va, 1980—83. Cert. 5/6th Grade Team Tchr. 1968, 6th Grade Gifted Tchr. 1971, K-6th Gifted Program Tchr. 1983. Team tchr. John Adams and Carver Elem. Schs., Colorado Springs, Colo., 1968—73; tchr. gifted 3-6th grade Math. and Sci. Washington Mill and Stratford Landing Elem. Schs., Alexandria, Va., 1973—83; tchr. gifted program Tokeneke Elem. Sch., Darien, Conn., 1983—85; 5-8th science, 1-8 art teacher Hillel Academy, Fairfield, Ct, 1985—. Art / science docent Smithsonian Instn. and Am. Mus. Nat. History, Washington, 1974—82; guide Discovery Mus., Bridgeport, Conn., 1985—. Author: (various workshops, teaching modules) Using Art Properties With Mus. Tours, 1980-1990, 1990, (teacher's guide) Motivational Techniques, Math Manipulatives, 1988,1992, 1994. Chairperson, bd. dirs. Fairfield (Conn.) Internat. Dance Co., 1990—2002; judge Conn. State Invention Conv., Hartford, 1983—87. Recipient Presdl. award for Excellence in Sci. Tchg., State of Conn., 1989, Presdl. award for Excellence in Math. Tchg., 1989, First Sci. Tchr. award, State Sci. Fair Conn., 1996, 1st Place, Middle Schs., Conn. State Sci. Fair, 1995, 1996, 1997, 1998, 1999. Mem.: NEA, Am. Chem. Soc., Nat. Math. Tchrs. Assn., Conn. Earth Tchrs. Assn., Conn. Sci. Tchrs. Assn. (Conn. Sci. Tchr. of Yr. award 2002), Nat. Sci. Tchrs. Assn., Audubon Soc., Am. Mensa, Am. Ballet Theater (assoc.). Methodist. Avocations: ballet, jazz, dance. Office: Hillel Academy 1571 Stratfield Rd Fairfield CT 06432 Personal E-mail: j.howell@comsoc.org.

HOWELL, KIRK DAVID, entrepreneur, consultant; b. Columbus, Nebr., Oct. 12, 1960; s. Keith David and Myrna Dee Howell; m. Loné Astrup Howell, Aug. 21, 1988; 1 child, Meekah Alexander. BS in Forest Resources, U. Ga., 1994, MS in Forest Regeneration, 1996; PhD in Silviculture & Nursery Sci., Clemson U., 2001. Reforestation tech. Evergreen Forestry Svc., Sand Point, Idaho, 1982—89; contract forest worker U. Ga., Athens, Ga., 1992—98; rsch. assistantship Clemson U., Clemson, SC, 1998—2001; owner, CEO Color Wheel Carpet Care, Inc., Auburn, Ga., 1989—; CEO, rsch. cons. Timberwolf Internat., Inc., 1998—. Airman 1st class USAF, Little Rock, Ark. Mem.: Soc. Am. Foresters. Seventh-Day Adventist. Achievements include invention of perforated container; manual hand-sewing press. Avocations: soccer, billiards, writing, landscaping, woodworking. Office: Color Wheel Carpet Care & Timberwolf Internat PO Box 26 Auburn GA 30011 Home: 1539 Oakhill Rd Auburn GA 30011

HOWELL, LAURA CLARK, biologist, educator, small business owner; d. Louie Earl Clark and Laura Elizabeth Stewart; m. Charles Samuel Howell. BS in Biology, Jacksonville State U., 1968; MS in Biology, Samford U., 1970; EdS, Jacksonville State U., 1984; postgrad., U. Ala., Birmingham. Cert. profl. tchr. Ala., profl. guidance counselor Ala., registered psychometrist Ala., cert. profl. tchr. Ga. Microbiologist Ala. Dept. Pub. Health, Anniston, 1968; tchr. biology B.B. Comer Meml. Sch., Sylacauga, Ala., 1970—71; tchr. sci., anatomy, physiology, biology, chmn. sci. dept. Wellborn H.S., Anniston, 1971—94. Adj. instr. biology Jacksonville State U., Ala., 1975, supr. student tchrs., 96; adj. instr. biology, botany, zoology Gadsden State C.C., Anniston, 1983—91. Recipient Medal and Cert. Appreciation, SAR, 2003, Educator award, United Daus. Confederacy, 1980, Martha Washington medal, SAR, 2005. Mem.: DAR (Ala. Soc. scholarship chair 2003—, field genealogist), Order Descs. of Ancient Planters (charter) (Ala. br. historian), Nat. Assn. Biology Tchrs., The Plantagenet Soc., Colonial Dames XVII Century (state historian 2005—), Ala.-Benton Geneal. Soc., Anniston Mus. League, Ala. Geneal. Soc., U.S. Daus. War of 1812, Magna Charta Dames & Barons (herald, state v.p.), The Jamestowne Soc., Athena Study Club, Persephone Garden Club, Ams. Royal Descent, Colonial Order of Crown, Knights of Most Nobel Order Garter, Kappa Delta Pi, Alpha Delta Kappa, Delta Kappa Gamma. Methodist. Office: Anniston Coin and Jewelry 802 Quintard Ave Anniston AL 36201

HOWELL, NEIL, music educator; m. Jill Dacus, June 13, 1998. MusB in Edn., U. SC, 1988, MusM in Edn., 1991; degree in Sch. Adminstrn., Lincoln Meml. U., Harrogate, TN, 2003. Professional Teaching Certificate Ga., 1984. Dir. of bands Heritage H.S., Conyers, Ga., 1993—, Dreher H.S., Columbia, SC, 1993—94. Mem.: Phi Mu Alpha Sinfonia (life; pres., historian 1986—87, Outstanding Mem. 1987). Republican. Bapt. Avocations: markmanship, electrical engineering, travel. E-mail: nhowell@rockdale.k12.ga.us.

HOWELL, RALPH RODNEY, pediatrician, geneticist, educator; b. Concord, N.C., June 10, 1931; s. Fred Lee and Grace Mary (Blackwelder) H.; m. Sarah Vosburg Esselstyn, Nov. 19, 1960 (dec.); children: Grace Meyer, Elizabeth Eriksson, John Esselstyn. BS, Davidson Coll., 1953; MD, Duke U., 1957. Cert. Am. Bd. Pediatrics, Am. Bd. Med. Genetics/Clin. Biochem. Genetics. Intern Duke U., 1957-58, resident in pediatrics, 1958-59, research fellow in pediatrics and medicine, 1959-60; clin. assoc. and staff NIH, Bethesda, Md., 1960-64; assoc. prof. pediatrics Johns Hopkins U., Balt., 1964-72; pediatrician-in-chief Univ. Children's Hosp. at Hermann, Houston, 1972-87, chmn. med. bd., 1972-87; David Park prof. U. Tex. Med. Sch., Houston, 1972-89, chmn. dept. pediatrics, 1972-87; prof., chmn. dept. pediatrics U. Miami Sch. Medicine, 1989—2003, chmn. emeritus, prof., 2003—; sec. med. staff Jackson Meml. Hosp., Miami, 1992-93, v.p. med. staff, 1993-97, pres. med. staff, 1997-99; spl. asst. to dir. NICHD/NIH, Bethesda, Md., 2003—. Cons. pediat. M.D. Anderson Hosp. and Tumor Inst., 1972-89; mem. metabolism study sect. NIH, 1973-77, chmn. maternal and child health adv. com., 1983-86; mem. exec. com. Nat. Practitioner Data Bank, 1995-98; mem. nat. clin. adv. com. Nat. Found. March of Dimes, 1973-79; bd. dirs. Muscular Dystrophy Assn., chmn. sci. adv. bd.; vis. prof. Inst. Molecular Genetics, Baylor Coll. Medicine, Houston, 1988; chief pediat. Holtz Childrens Hosp., U. Miami-Jackson Meml. Med. Ctr., 1989-2003; mem. nat. adv. coun. Nat. Inst. Child Health and Human Devel., 1999-2003; chair HHS Sec.'s Adv. Com. on Genetic Testing in Children and Newborns, 2004—. Author: (with G.H. Thomas) Selected Screening Tests for Genetic Metabolic Diseases, 1973, (with F.H. Morriss, L.K. Pickering) Role of Human Milk in Infant Nutrition, 1986; contbr. articles to profl. jours. Trustee Jackson Lab. Bar Harbor, Maine, 1985-2003; dir. Rip van Winkle Found., Claverack, N.Y., 1987-92, pres., 1992—; bd. dirs. Congl. Ch. Found., Coconut Grove, Fla., Dr. John T. Macdonald Found., Coral Gables, Fla., 2003-. Served to sr. surgeon, 1960—64, USPHS. Recipient Klauber Lectureship, Greenwood Genetic Ctr., 2004. Fellow AAAS, Am. Acad. Pediatrics (com. on genetics); mem. AMA (ho. of dels. 1998—), Am. Pediatric Soc., Soc. Pediatric Rsch., Houston Pediatric Soc. (pres. 1978-79), Tex. Med. Assn., Soc. Inborn Errors of Metabolism (pres. 1981), Miami Pediatric Soc., Fla. Med. Assn., Am. Coll. Med. Genetics (bd. dirs. 1991—, treas. 1995-96, pres.-elect 1997-98, pres. 1999—2000), Am. Coll. Med. Genetics (found. pres. 2003—), Nat. Human Genome Rsch. Inst. (chmn. ethical, social and legal issues rev. group 1996-2003), Pi Kappa Alpha, Cosmos Club (Washington). Congregationalist. Avocations: flying, classic auto collector. Office: U Miami Sch Medicine Dept Pediatrics D-820 PO Box 16820 Miami FL 33101-6820 Business E-Mail: rhowell@miami.edu.

HOWELL, ROBERT EDWARD, hospital administrator; b. Marietta, Ohio, Jan. 19, 1949; married; 3 children. BS, Muskingham Coll., 1971; MS in Hosp. and Health Svcs. Adminstrn., Ohio State U., 1977. Assoc. dir. U. Minn. Hosps. and Clinics, Mpls., 1980-86; exec. dir. Med. Coll. Ga. Hosps. and Clinics, Augusta, 1986-94; dir., CEO, U. Iowa Hosps. and Clinics, Iowa City, 1994—. Mem. exec. com. Accreditation Coun. for Grad. Med. Edn. Mem. Coun. Tchg. Hosps. (past chmn.), Am. Assn. Med. Colls. (exec. com.), Am. Hosp. Assn. (coord. com. med. edn.), Univ. Health System Consortium (exec. com.). Office: U VA Med Ctr 3007 McKim Hall PO Box 800809 Charlottesville VA 22908-0809

HOWELL, R(OBERT) THOMAS, JR., lawyer, former food company executive; b. Racine, Wis., July 18, 1942; s. Robert T. and Margaret Paris (Billings) H.; m. Karen Wallace Corbett, May 11, 1968; children: Clarinda, Margaret, Robert. AB, Williams Coll., 1964; JD, U. Wis., 1967; postgrad., Harvard U., 1981. Bar: Wis. 1968, Ill. 1968, U.S. Dist. Ct. (no. dist.) Ill. 1968, U.S. Tax Ct. Assoc. Hopkins & Sutter, Chgo., 1967-71; atty. The Quaker Oats Co., Chgo., 1971-77, counsel, 1977-80, v.p., assoc. gen. corp. counsel, 1980-84, v.p., gen. corp. counsel, 1984-96, corp. sec., 1994-96; of counsel Seyfarth Shaw, Chgo., 1997—. Bd. dirs. Ill. Inst. of Continuing Legal Edn., Lawyers for Creative Arts. Editor (mags.) Barrister, 1975-77, Compleat Lawyer, 1983-87. Bd. dirs. Metro. Family Svcs.; bd. dirs. Chgo. Bar Found., 1987—, pres., 1991-93; trustee 4th Presbyn. Ch., Chgo., 1989-92, pres., 1994-96; bd. dirs. Chgo. Equity Fund, 1992-96. Capt. USAR, 1966-72. Mem. ABA, Ill. Bar Assn., Wis. Bar Assn., Chgo. Bar Assn. (bd. mgrs. 1977-79, chmn. young lawyers sect. 1974-75), Lawyers Club Chgo. (pres. 2004-05), Econ. Club Chgo., Univ. Club Chgo. (bd. dirs. 1982-85, 87-88, v.p.). Presbyterian. Home: 853 W Chalmers Pl Chicago IL 60614-3233 Office: Seyfarth Shaw 55 E Monroe St Ste 4200 Chicago IL 60603-5863 E-mail: thowell@seyfarth.com.

HOWELL, SCOTT NEWELL, computer company executive, state legislator; b. Provo, Utah, Sept. 28, 1953; s. Varon L. and Kathryn (Tuttle) H.; m. Linda Skanchy, Sept. 8, 1978; children: Bryan, Bradley, Jason, Jeffrey. BA, U. Utah, 1978. With sales IBM Corp., mgr., global policy exec.; chair., Utah State Judicial Conduct Review Comm., 1990—; mem. Utah Senate, Salt Lake City, 1990—, minority leader, 1993—; mem. Nat. Conference State Legislators, 1992—. Mem. Utah info. tech. com. Utah Senate, transportation & environ. quality appropriations subcom., mem. state & local affairs standing com.; chmn. Nat. Acad. Fin., Salt Lake City, 1991-93. Bd. dirs. Utah Chpt. Nat. Children's Protection of Child Abuse, Salt Lake City, 1992-93, visually handicapped divsn. United Way, Salt Lake City, 1992-93; trustee Utah Symphony, 1994—. Mem., Nat. Academy of Finance (chair. 1990-92); Utah Info. Tech. Assoc., Intermountain Healthcare, State Legis. Leaders Found., Dem. Leadership Coun., Harvard Policy Group. Democrat. Mem. Lds Ch. Address: 319 State Capitol Salt Lake City UT 84114 Home: 5630 Lions Cross Cir Granite Bay CA 95746-9027

HOWELL, TERRY ALLEN, agricultural engineer; b. Dallas, Sept. 7, 1947; s. Levi Lowe III and Lila Lee (Allen) H.; m. Mary Sue Parkerson, Feb. 22, 1969; children: Terry A. Jr., Lisa K. Dreibrodt, Michael S. BS, Tex. A&M U., 1969, MS, 1970, PhD, 1974. Rsch. asst. Tex. A&M U., College Station, 1969-70, rsch. assoc., 1971-74; asst. prof. N.Mex. State U., Las Cruces, 1975, Tex. A&M U., College Station, 1976-79; agr. engr. USDA ARS, Fresno, Calif., 1979-83, Bushland, Tex., 1983—. Co-author: Modification of the Aerial Environment Crops, 1979, Design and Operation of Farm Irrigation Systems, 1980, Limitations to Effective Water Use in Crop Production, 1983, Irrigation of Agricultural Crops, 1991, Agricultural System Models, 2002, Encyclopedia of Water Science, 2003; co-editor, co-author: Management of Farm Irrigation Systems, 1991. Tchr. Paramount Bapt. Ch., Amarillo, 1985-94, deacon, 1987—; troop com. chmn. Boy Scouts Am., Amarillo, 1991-93. Recipient Tex. Environ. Excellence award in agr. Tex. Natural Resource Conservation Commn., 1999, Fed. Energy and Water Mgmt. award U.S. Dept. Energy, 199, Tech. Transfer award ARS, 1999, Sr. Scientist Yr. ARS, So. Plaias area, 2000. Fellow ASAE (chmn. soil and water divsn. 1987-88, Paper award 1972, 74, 80, soil and water divsn. editor 1993-97, Hancor award 2000), Am. Soc. Agronomy (A-3 divsn. chair 1999-2000); mem. ASCE (chmn. irrigation water requirements com. 1990-93, Tipton award 1997), Soil Sci. Soc. Am., Irrigation Assn. (life; Person of Yr. award 1995), Coun. for Agrl. Sci. and Tech., Tex. Agrl. Irrigation Assn. Office: USDA ARS PO Box 10 Bushland TX 79012-0010 Business E-Mail: tahowell@cprl.ars.usda.gov.

HOWELL, THOMAS, history professor; b. Houston, Jan. 20, 1944; s. John Thomas and Hazel (Hall) H.; m. Donna Jo Walker, Aug. 14, 1971; children: Catherine Jewel, Judith Hazel. BA, La. Coll., 1964; MA, La. State U., 1966, PhD, 1971. Instr. La. State U., 1967-68, La. Coll., Pineville, 1968-70, asst. prof., 1970-72, assoc. prof., 1972-77, prof., 1977, Crowell prof., 1984—, chmn. dept. history and polit. sci., 1975-95, chmn. divsn. social and behavioral scis., 1995-2000, chmn. divsn. history and polit. sci., 2000—. Lectr. La. Endowment for Humanities, 1983, 86, 87, 1990—96, 2001—, project dir., 1989, 2000, 03. Mem. La. Elections Integrity Commn., 1980—86, vice-chmn., 1981; coord. La. Civitan Youth Citizenship Seminar, 1975—76; commr. Gulf Coast Athletic Conf., 1981—; mem. NAIA Nat. Eligibility Commn., 1983—, chmn., 1994—; mem. hearing com. disciplinary bd. La. Bar Assn., 1995—2001. Mellon summer fellow, 1981; Fulbright lectr. U. Iceland, 1986-87; inductee Nat. Assn. Intercollegiate Athletics Hall of Fame, 1999. Mem. La. Hist. Assn., So. Hist. Assn., SW Assn. Pre-Law Advisers, Orgn. Am. Historians, Alpha Chi, Omicron Delta Kappa. Baptist. Home: 216 Myrtle St Pineville LA 71360-5164 Office: La Coll Dept History Pineville LA 71359-0001 Office Phone: 318-487-7102. E-mail: howell@lacollege.edu.

HOWELL, WILLIAM ASHLEY, III, lawyer; b. Raleigh, N.C., Jan. 2, 1949; s. William Ashley II and Caroline Erskine Greenleaf; m. Esther Holland, Dec. 22, 1973. BS, Troy State U., 1972; postgrad., U. Ala., Birmingham, 1974-75; JD, Birmingham Sch. Law, 1977. Bar: Ala. 1977, U.S. Dist. Ct. (no. dist.) Ala. 1977, U.S. Ct. Appeals (5th cir.) 1977, U.S. Supreme Ct. 1982, U.S. Ct. Appeals (11th cir.) 1983, U.S. Dist. Ct. (mid. dist.) Ala. 1987. Atty. pub. defender divsn. Legal Aid Soc. of Birmingham, 1977—78, civil divsn. Legal Aid Soc. of Birmingham, 1978—81; dist. office atty. SBA, Birmingham, 1980—82, supervising atty. Ala. Dist., 1982—; spl. asst. U.S. Atty. (mid. dist.), Ala., 1988—, U.S. Atty. (so. dist.), Ala., 2002—. Part-time instr. legal and social environ. and human resources mgmt. Jefferson State C.C., Birmingham, 1993. Contbr. articles to profl. jours. Vol. reader Radio Reading Svc. Network for Blind, 1991—93; mem. Shelby County Econ. Devel. Coun., 1993—94, Hispanic Outreach Commn., 2000—01, Highland Crest Homeowners Assn., 2002—; del. state conv. Episc. Ch. of Ala., various yrs.; bd. dirs. Hoover Homeowners Assn., 1977—81, Southside Ministries, Inc., 1990—91, v.p. bd. dirs., 1990—91; bd. dirs. SafeHouse of Shelby County, Inc., 1990—93, vice chmn., 1991—93. Recipient Am. Jurisprudence Criminal Procedure Book award. Mem. ABA (sect. corporation, banking and bus. law), Nat. Parks and Conservation Soc. (life), Fed. Bar Assn. (sec. Birmingham chpt. 1980-81, del. nat. conv. 1993, 94, del. mid yr. meeting, 1994-95), Ala. Bar Assn. (com. on future of the profession 1978-81, 83-84, com. on quality of life 1992-93, sect. bankruptcy and corp. law, sect. bankruptcy and comml. law, sect. corp. counsel, sect. banking and bus. law), Nature Conservancy (life), Birmingham Bar Assn., Birmingham Venture Club, Sierra Club (life), Sigma Delta Kappa (v.p., Outstanding Sr. award 1977). Episcopalian. Office: US Small Bus Adminstrn 801 Tom Martin Dr Ste 201 Birmingham AL 35211-4436 Fax: 205-290-7443. E-mail: william.howell@sba.gov.

HOWELL, WILLIAM PAGE, real estate company executive; b. Carnegie, Okla., July 27, 1952; s. Herman Glen and Muriel Joyce (Raby) H.; 1 child, Blake Alexander Sewell-Howell. BS, Southwestern U., Weatherford, Okla., 1975; MS, U. Okla., 1976. Chief exec. officer, pres. Howell Assocs., Norman, Okla., 1976-84; dir. Saudi Arabian Investment Corp., Dallas, London, 1984-87; dir. acquisitions Mitsui Fudosan (N.Y.) Inc., N.Y.C., 1987-93; prin., ptnr. Peninsula Mgmt. Corp., N.Y.C., 1993—; pres. Howell Assocs. of N.Y., N.Y.C., 1993—; mng. ptnr. Cushman Peninsula Asset Mgmt. Group, N.Y.C., 1993—; chmn., pres. Boutique Hotels and Resorts, N.Y.C., 1998—; chmn., CEO, H.A.I. Investment Advisors, N.Y.C., 1999—. Dir. adv. bd. Comml. Property News, N.Y.C., 1990—. Demographics coord. Dem. Nat. Com., Atlanta, 1976-77. Mem. Urban Land Inst., Assn. Fgn. Investors in U.S. Real Estate, Fedn. Internat. Adminstrs. de Bein Conseils Immobiliers, Japan Soc., N.Y. Real Estate Club, Internat. Devel. Rsch. Coun. Avocations: flying, skiing, skydiving, fishing, golf.

HOWELL, WILLIAM ROBERT, retail company executive; b. Claremore, Okla., Jan. 3, 1936; s. William Roosevelt and Opal Theo (Swan) H.; m. Judy Howell; children: Ann Elizabeth, Teresa Lynn. BBA, U. Okla., 1958. With J.C. Penney Co., Inc., 1958—, store mgr. Tulsa, 1968-69; dist. mgr., dir. Treasury Stores subs., Dallas, 1969-71, div. v.p., dir. domestic devel. N.Y.C., 1973-76, regional v.p., western regional mgr., 1976-79, sr. v.p., dir. merchandising, mktg. and catalog, 1979-81, exec. v.p., 1981-82, vice chmn. bd. dirs, 1982-83, chmn., chief exec. officer, 1983-97; chmn. emeritus J.C. Penney Co., Inc., Plano, Tex., 1997—. Bd. dirs. Exxon-Mobil Corp., Pfizer Corp., Bankers Trust Co., Halliburton Co., The Williams Cos., Am. Electric Power, Viseon. Mem. Bus. Coun., Dirs.' Table, Delta Sigma Pi, Beta Gamma Sigma. Home: PO Box 2800 Carefree AZ 85377-2800

HOWELLS, JEFFREY P., computer company executive; B in Acctg., Stetson U. CPA. Sr. audit mgr. Price Waterhouse; v.p. fin. Tech Data, 1991-92; CFO Tech Data Corp., 1992-93, sr. v.p. fin., CFO, 1993-97, exec. v.p., CFO, 1997—. Mailing: PO Box 6260 Clearwater FL 33758-6260 Office: Tech Data Corp 5350 Tech Data Dr Clearwater FL 33760-3122

HOWELLS, WILLIAM WHITE, anthropology educator; b. N.Y.C., Nov. 27, 1908; s. John Mead and Abby MacDougall (White) H.; m. Muriel Gurdon Seabury, June 15, 1929; children— Gurdon Howells Metz, William Dean SB, Harvard U., 1930, PhD, 1934; DSc (hon.), Beloit Coll., 1975, U. Witwatersrand, 1985. From asst. prof. to prof. anthropology U. Wis., 1939-54, prof. integrated liberal studies, 1948-54; prof. anthropology Harvard U., 1954-74, prof. emeritus, 1974—. Hon. fellow Sch. Am. Research, 1975 Author: Mankind So Far, 1944, The Heathens, 1948, Back of History, 1954, Mankind in the Making, 1959, rev. edit., 1967, The Pacific Islanders, 1973, Cranial Variation in Man, 1973, Evolution of the Genus Homo, 1973, Skull Shapes and The Map, 1989, Getting Here: The Story of Human Evolution, 1993, Who's Who in Skulls, 1995; editor: Early Man in the Far East, 1949, Ideas on Human Evolution, 1962, Paleoanthropology in the People's Republic of China, 1977, Am. Jour. Phys. Anthropology, 1949-54; assoc. editor Human Biology, 1955-74. Served as lt. USNR, 1943-46 Recipient Viking Fund medal in phys. anthropology, 1954 Fellow AAAS, Indian Anthrop. Assn. (fgn.), Am. Acad. Arts and Scis., Am. Anthrop. Assn. (pres. 1951, Disting. Service award 1978), Soc. Antiquaries London; mem. NAS, Austrian Acad. Scis., Mass. Hist. Soc., Am. Assn. of Physical Anthropologists (sec., treas. 1939-41, Charles R. Darwin Lifetime Achievement award 1992); corr. mem. Geog. Soc. Lisbon, Anthrop. Soc. Paris (Broca prix du Centenaire 1980), Anthrop. Soc. Vienna, Royal Soc. South Africa (fgn.), Soc. for Biol. Anthropology Spain (corr.), Harvard Faculty Club Home: 11 Lawrence Ln Kittery Point ME 03905-5104

HOWENSTINE, E. JAY, housing economist; b. Stanford, Ky., Aug. 12, 1914; s. E. Jay and Roberta (O'Bannon) H.; m. Elsie Craig Greenhalgh, Dec. 27, 1958; children: Robert Jay, Richard Allen, Judith Ann, Patricia Ann. BA, Miami U., Oxford, Ohio, 1936; MA, Ohio State U., 1938, PhD, 1942. Instr. in econs. No. Mich. U., Marquette, 1939-41; assoc. prof. Park Coll., Parkville, Mo., 1942-44; agrl. economist USDA, Washington, 1944-46; housing economist Nat. Housing Adminstrn., Washington, 1946-47; economist UN Relief and Rehab. Adminstrn., Washington, 1947-48; housing economist Internat. Labour Office, Geneva, 1948-67; internat. rsch. coord. HUD, Washington,

1967-86; cons. Internat. Cons. Svcs., Arlington, Va., 1986—. Co-covenor Coalition for Housing in Arlington, 1987—. Author: Compensatory Employment Programmes, 1968, Foreign Housing Subsidy Systems, 1974, Attacking Housing Costs, 1983, Housing Vouchers, 1986, The New Housing Shortage, 1993; bd. editors Cities, 1981—. Ohio State U. fellow, 1938-39, scholar, 1936-38. Avocations: tennis, swimming, camping. Home: 2948 26th St N Arlington VA 22207-4959

HOWER, EILEEN M., music educator; b. Suffern, N.Y., Dec. 30, 1960; d. William Joseph and Barbara Walton Murphy; m. William Edwin Hower, Sept. 26, 1998; children: Christopher Ryan Bickford, Robert Patrick Bickford. MusB in Music Edn., SUNY, Potsdam, 1982; MA in Music Edn., Marywood U., Scranton, Pa., 1997. Music educator Ctrl. Columbia Mid. Sch., Bloomsburg, Pa., 1992—. Recipient Tchr. of Yr. award, Wal-Mart, Inc., 1995, Tchr. of Month, WBRE TV, Scranton, Pa., 2002, Citation of Excellence, Pa. Music Educators Nat. Conf. Dist. VIII, 2004-2005. Mem.: Am. Choral Dirs. Assn. (repertoire and stds. chair for mid. sch. choirs 2003—04, pres.-elect 2005—), Music Educators Nat. Conf., Berwick Ramblers, Pi Kappa Lambda. Republican. Roman Catholic. Achievements include Choirs accepted to perform at divisional and national conventions of the American Choral Directors Association and at state and divisional conventions of the Music Educators National Conference; Guest clinician at state, divisional and national conferences of Music Educators National Conference and American Choral Directors Association. Avocations: running, hiking, gardening, cooking. Home: 101 Old Field Dr Bloomsburg PA 17815 Office: Ctrl Columbia Mid Sch 4777 Old Berwick Rd Bloomsburg PA 17815 Office Phone: 570-784-6103. Business E-Mail: ehower@ccsd.cc.

HOWER, FRANK BEARD, JR., retired banker; b. Louisville, Ky., Nov. 26, 1928; s. Frank Beard and Katharine (Coffman) H.; m. Virginia W. Barker, Dec. 30, 1954; children: Frank Beard III, William. AB, Centre Coll., Danville, Ky., 1950. With Liberty Nat. Bank, Louisville, 1950-90, exec. v.p., 1967-71, pres., 1971-90, CEO, chmn. bd. dirs., 1973-90, ret., 1990. Bd. dirs. Falls City Industries, Inc., Louisville, Bank One, Ky., Norton Health Sys., Inc., Am. Life and Accident Ins. Co., Churchill Downs Inc., Anthem Inc.; chmn. Norton Kosair Childrens Hosp., Inc., 1983-84. Trustee J. Graham Brown Found., U. Louisville; chmn. regional adv. bd. Comptr. of Currency, 1976; mem. Ky. Registry of Election Finance, 1966-70, Ky. Econ. Progress Commn., 1964-70; vice chmn. Ky.-Tenn. Export Coun.; gen. chmn. United Appeal, 1969; chmn. Greater Louisville Fund for the Arts, 1976; v.p. Louisville Philharm. Orch., 1974-75; chmn. Regional Airport Authority of Louisville and Jefferson County, Louisville Devel. Com.; bd. dirs., chmn. U. Louisville; trustee, chmn. Ky. Ind. Coll. Found.; trustee Centre Coll.; mem. Actors Theatre Bd. Maj. USMCR, 1951-52, Korea. Mem. Am., Ky. bankers assns., Robert Morris Assos., Assn. Res. City Bankers, Louisville C. of C. (pres. 1973) Republican. Episcopalian.

HOWER, PHILIP LELAND, semiconductor device engineer; b. Reading, Pa., Apr. 9, 1934; s. Frank B. and Gladys (Fox) H.; m. Suzanne Mulvey, Apr. 28, 1962; children: Benjamin L., Suzanne E. BSEE, Lehigh U., 1956; MSEE, U. So. Calif., 1958; PhDEE, Stanford U., 1967. Tech. staff Fairchild R&D, Palo Alto, Calif., 1966-71; adv. engr. Westinghouse R&D, Pitts., 1971-81; prin. scientist Unitrode Corp., Watertown, Mass., 1981-92; prin. engr. Unitrode Integrated Cirs., Merrimack, N.H., 1992-99; disting. mem. tech. staff Tex. Instruments, Manchester, NH, 1999—. Contbr. 40 articles to profl. jours. Fellow IEEE (life); mem. IEEE Power Electronics Soc. (William E. Newell award 1986, disting. lectr., 1999). Achievements include patents for semiconductor device design. Home: 315 Border Rd Concord MA 01742-4625 Office: Tex Instruments 50 Phillippe Cote St Manchester NH 03101 E-mail: phil_hower@ti.com.

HOWES, GEOFFREY CHANDLER, language educator; b. Detroit, Mich., Nov. 6, 1955; s. Geoffrey Chandler and Joan Margaret Coleman Howes; m. Christen Anita Giblin, Sept. 1, 1979; 1 child, James Coleman. B A, Mich. State U., 1973—77; AM, U. of Mich., 1977—78, PhD, 1977—85. Prof. Bowling Green State U., Ohio, 2002—; vis. instr. U. of Minn., 1985—86; asst. prof. Bowling Green State U., 1986—93, assoc. prof., 1993—2002. Dir., academic yr. abroad Bowling Green State U., Salzburg, Austria, 2002—03. Co-editor: (scholarly journal) Modern Austrian Literature. Ctrl. com. mem. Wood County Dem. Party, Bowling Green, Ohio, 2002—. Guest Visits of Fgn. Scholars, Austrian Ministry of Edn., 1987, Fulbright Grad. fellowship, Austrian-American Ednl. Commn., 1982—83. Mem.: Am. Assn. of Teachers of German, MLA, Midwest MLA, Modern Austrian Lit. and Culture Assn. (jour. editor 2000—), Town and Gown. D-Liberal. Roman Catholic. Avocations: travel, local history, music, writing. Office: Bowling Green State Univ German Russian and E Asian Langs Bowling Green OH 43403-0219 Office Phone: 419-372-7139. Office Fax: 419-372-2571. Personal E-mail: howesgeoffrey@hotmail.com. E-mail: ghowes@bgnet.bgsu.edu.

HOWES, JAMES GUERDON, communications company executive; b. Balt. s. James Harold and Edna Esther (Lowman) H. BS, U. Md., 1967, MBA, 1969. Staff asst. U.S. Senate, Washington, 1965-68; regional mktg. adminstrn. Hertz Corp., Balt., 1972-75; commr. aviation Dutchess County, Poughkeepsie, N.Y., 1975-80; airport dir. St. Petersburg-Clearwater (Fla.) Internat. Airport, 1980-2001; pres. Atlas Comm., Tampa, 2001—. Producer radio programs Choral Masterpieces, 1985-95, King of Instruments, 1983-95, Sacred Classics, 1995—, other CD's and concerts. Committeeman Rep. Nat. Com. Campaign, Washington, 1974-84, Riverside Ch., N.Y.C., 1976-80; v.p. Boy Scouts Am., Largo, Fla., 1987-91, nat. coun. rep., 1992-96. Capt. USAF, 1969-72. Recipient So. divsn. Airport of Yr. Safety award, 1998; named Man of Yr., Bermuda Hotel Assn., 2004. Mem. Am. Assn. Airport Execs., Southeastern Airport Mgrs. Assn. (pres. 1993-94), Belleair Country Club. Methodist. Avocations: flying, scuba diving, classical music, photography, white water rafting. Home: 41 Pine Wood Cir Safety Harbor FL 34695-5421 also: 6 Crow's Nest Hill Bailey's Bay CR 04 Bermuda Office: PO Box 5534 Baltimore MD 21285 Office Phone: 727-726-0400. E-mail: jghowes@compuserve.com.

HOWES, LORRAINE DE WET, fashion designer, educator; b. Port Elizabeth, South Africa, Dec. 24, 1933; arrived in U.S., 1957; d. Jacobus Egnatius and Johanna Elizabeth (Lowenburg) de W. Student, Sch. Fashion Design, Boston, 1957-58. Apprentice Jonathan Logan & Adam Leslie, Johannesburg, South Africa, 1953-55; apprentice, wookroom asst., model Norman Hartnell, designer to the Queen, London, 1955-57; model Peter Lumley Agy., London, 1955-57; designer, dept. mgr. Design Rsch. Inc., Cambridge, Mass., 1957-59; model Hart Agy., Boston, 1957-76; designer, mgr. Estabrook & Newell, Boston, 1959-62; designer, owner Lorraine de Wet, Boston, 1962-79; mem. adj. faculty dept. apparel design RISD, Providence, 1972-76, asst. prof., assoc. prof., 1976-82, acting head dept., 1976-79, head dept., 1979-99, prof., 1988-2000, prof. emeritus, 2000—, interim dean arch. and design, 2000-2001. Designer, cons. apparel industry and theatre, 1979—2000; dir. Hamilton Cornell Mass., 1986-2000; design and tech. edn. cons. apparel and textiles Hangzhou Econ. Commn., China, 1986-88; mem. individual grants panel Nat. Endowment for Arts, 1994. Named Faculty Mem. of Yr., RISD Alumni Assn., 1984-85; recipient John R. Frazier Excellence in Tchg. award RISD, 1993, Hon. Alumna award RISD, 1995, Helen Rowe Metcalf award 2003; named champion R.I. Pub. Links, 1983, 84. Mem.: Costume Soc. Am., Fashion Inst. Tech. Design Lab., Fashion Group. Avocation: golf. Office: RISD Dept Apparel Design 2 College St Providence RI 02903-2784

HOWES, SOPHIA DUBOSE, writer; b. Balt., Apr. 20, 1954; d. John Carleton and Marie Josephine (Meeth) Jones; m. Edward Phillip Howes, Jan. 26, 1996; 1 child, Michael Laurence. BFA with honors, NYU, 1982, MFA, 1994; JD, Fordham U., 2002. Legal asst. Skadden, Arps, Slate, Meagher & Flom, NYC, 1984-93; script reader Haft Nassiter Co., NYC, 1994; editl. assoc. Matthew Bender & Co. Inc., NYC, 1994-97. Extern Fordham U. Sch. Law, Surrogate's Ct., NYC, 1999; rsch. asst. Securities Arbitration Clinic, Fordham Law Sch., 2000, Writing Rsch., ECPAT, summer 2001. Playwright: Better Dresses, Rosetta's Eyes, 1988, 1988, Adamov, 1992, two-act play The Poisoned Kiss, 1994; mem. staff Fordham Environ. Law Jour., 1999-2000; sr. notes and comments editor, 2000-01; dir. Who's Afraid of Virginia Woolf, 2004, The Tempest, 2004. Recipient Grad. award in playwriting, NYU-Tisch Sch. Arts, 1994, Seidman award for talent, 1982. Mem. Dramatists Guild. Avocation: mountain climbing. E-mail: edwardhowes@juno.com.

HOWEY, JOHN RICHARD, architect, writer; b. New Haven, Jan. 13, 1933; s. Joseph Herman and Dorothy Pauline (Good) H.; m. Maria Andrea Hatges, Sept. 8, 1968; children: John Michael, Dorothy Anne. Student, Wooster Coll., 1951-52; BS, Ga. Inst. Tech., 1956, BArch, 1957. Registered architect Fla. With various archtl. firms, Fla., 1958—64, 1958—64; pres. John Howey, Architect, AIA, Tampa, Fla., 1964—73, John Howey Assocs., Tampa, Fla., 1973—. Pres. Baypark, Inc., Tampa, 1988—. Prin. works include coll. bldgs. U. So. Fla., 1975, Louis Pappas Restaurant, Tarpon Springs, Fla., 1975 (honor design award AIA 1976), office bldg. 101 S. Franklin St., Tampa, 1980 (Fla. Preservation award 1984), Williers Residence, Tampa, 1980 (honor design award AIA 1981), modular urban transit shelters, 1977 (U.S. patent 1980, honor design award AIA 1985), Tehran, Iran Libr. Project, 1978, Baypark Pl. apt. bldgs., Tampa, 1989 (honor design award AIA 1989, Millenium Award of Honor, 2000), others; author: The Sarasota School of Architecture, 1995; co-author: Florida Architecture, A Celebration, 2000. With U.S. Army Corps of Engrs., 1957-58. Fellow AIA (Fla./Caribbean region Design Excellence Honor award 1985, Fla. chpt. Medal of Honor 1986); mem. Sertoma Club (bd. dirs. 1970-73), Exch. Club. Episcopalian. Achievements include featured in 1000 Architects, 2004; 100 of the World's Best Houses, 2003. Avocations: photography, painting. Home: 2538 W Palm Dr Tampa FL 33629-7314 Address: John Howey Assocs 121 W Whiting St Tampa FL 33602-5136 Personal E-mail: jhoweyarch@tampabay.rr.com.

HOWITT, ARNOLD MARTIN, academic administrator, educator; b. N.Y.C., Jan. 6, 1947; s. Wilfred D. and Mildred (Wolch) H.; m. Maryalice Sloan; children: Matthew, Molly, Alexandra, Mark. BA, Columbia U., 1969; MA, Harvard U., 1971, PhD, 1976. Asst. prof. Brown U., Providence, 1974-76, Harvard U., Cambridge, Mass., 1976-80, assoc. prof., 1980-82, assoc. dir. Taubman Ctr. State and Local Govt., Kennedy Sch. Govt., 1983-93, exec. dir. Taubman Ctr. State and Local Govt., Kennedy Sch. Govt., 1993—. Exec. dir. Coop. Mobility Program, MIT, Cambridge, 1998-2001; cons. in field; part-time lectr. SUNY, Albany, 1984-92, U. Wash., Seattle, 1988—, dir. Exec. Session on Domestic Preparedness for Terrorism, Kennedy Sch. Govt., 1999-2003. Author: Managing Federalism, 1984; co-author, editor: Perspectives on Management Capacity Building, 1986, Countering Terrorism, 2003; contbr. articles to profl. jours. Office: Harvard U Kennedy Sch Govt 79 JF Kennedy St Cambridge MA 02138-5801

HOWITT, JOHN P., lawyer; b. L.A., Calif., Jan. 22, 1953; AB magna cum laude, UCLA, 1975, JD, 1978. Bar: Calif. 1978, N.Y. 1988. Consult fgn. law, law firm of Nagashima & Ohno, Tokyo, 1981—83; ptnr. Paul, Hastings, Janofsky & Walker LLP, N.Y.C., co-chmn. aviation practice group. Mem.: Order Coif. Office: Paul Hastings Janosky & Walker LLP 75 E 55th St First Floor New York NY 10022-3205 Office Phone: 212-318-6005. Office Fax: 212-230-7712. Business E-Mail: johnhowitt@paulhastings.com.

HOWLAND, BETTE, writer; b. Chgo., Jan. 28, 1937; d. Sam and Jessie (Berger) Sotonoff; m. Howard C. Howland (div.); children— Frank, Jacob. BA, U. Chgo., 1955. Assoc. prof. com. social thought U. Chgo., 1993-97. Author: W-3, 1974, Blue in Chicago, 1978 (1st prize Friends of Am. Writers), Things to Come and Go, 1983, Trial, 1998, Calm Sea and Prosperous Voyage, 1999. Fellow Rockefeller Found., 1969, Marsden Found., 1971, Guggenheim Found., 1978, Nat. Endowment for the Arts, 1981, MacArthur Found., 1984. Jewish. Address: PO Box 405 Union Pier MI 49129-0405 E-mail: bettehowland@yahoo.com.

HOWLAND, ELLENMARIE MYERS, retired educator; b. Crescent, Okla., July 13, 1939; d. John Wendell and Velma Marie (Wilson) Myers; m. Ronald L. Howland, June 17, 1961; 1 child, Ann Marie. BS, Oklahoma City U., 1961, MEd, 1976. Cert. elem. tchr., Okla. Tchr. Putnam City Sch. Dist., Oklahoma City, ret., 1998—. Numerous leadership roles local church and community orgns. Mem. Putman City Reading Coun., Okla. Edn. Assn., NEA, Delta Zeta (past pres. Oklahome City chpt.). Address: 5613 NW 107th Terr Oklahoma City OK 73162-7002

HOWLAND, JOAN SIDNEY, law librarian, educator; b. Eureka, Calif., Apr. 9, 1951; d. Robert Sidney and Ruth Mary Howland. BA, U. Calif., Davis, 1971; MA, U. Tex., 1973; MLS, Calif. State U., San Jose, 1975; JD, Santa Clara (Calif.) U., 1983; MBA, U. Minn., 1997. Assoc. librarian for pub. svcs. Stanford (Calif.) U. Law Library, 1975-83, Harvard U. Law Library, Cambridge, Mass., 1983-86; dep. dir. U. Calif. Law Library, Berkeley, 1986-92; dir. law libr., Roger F. Noreen prof. law U. Minn. Sch. of Law, 1992—, assoc. dean info. tech., 2001—. Questions and answers column editor Law Libr. Jour., 1986-91; memt. column editor Trends in Law Libr. Mgmt. & Tech., 1987-94. Mem. ALA, ABA (com. on accreditation 2001—), Am. Assn. Law Librs., Am. Assn. Law Schs., Am. Indian Libr. Assn. (treas. 1992—), Am. Law Inst. Office: U Minn Law Sch 229 19th Ave S Minneapolis MN 55455-0400

HOWLAND, RICHARD HUBBARD, architectural historian; b. Providence, Aug. 23, 1910; S. Carl Badger and Cora Augusta (Hubbard) H. AB, Brown U., 1931, also hon. doctor's degree; A.M., Harvard U., 1933; PhD, Johns Hopkins U., 1946. Fellow Agora excavations, Athens, Greece, 1936-38; instr. Wellesley Coll., 1939-42; chief pictorial records sect. OSS, 1943-44; founder dept. history art Johns Hopkins, 1947, chmn. dept., 1947-56; pres. Nat. Trust for Historic Preservation, 1956-60; chmn. dept. civil history Smithsonian Instn., Washington, 1960-67, spl. asst. to sec., 1968-85. Trustee Am. Sch. Classical Studies, Athens; founding mem. Am. Com. Internat. Commn. Historic Sites and Monuments. Author: (with Eleanor Spencer) Architecture of Baltimore, 1954, Greek Lamps and Their Survivals, 1958. Trustee Irish Georgian Soc., Evergreen Found. Decorated Order Brit. Empire, Order George I (Greece), U.S. Order St. John of Jerusalem. Fellow Royal Soc. of the Arts; mem. Soc. Archtl. Historians (founding mem.), English Speaking Union, Soc. Cincinnati (hon.), Md. Soc. Colonial Wars, Victorian Soc. in Am. (former pres.), Century Assn., Knickerbocker Club, 14 West Hamilton St. Club, Cosmos Club, Arts Club, Dacor-Bacon Club, City Tavern Club, Phi Gamma Delta. Home: 3900 Cathedral Ave NW Apt 712A Washington DC 20016-5299 Fax: 202-338-4384.

HOWLAND, RICHARD MOULTON, retired lawyer; b. Glen Cove, L.I., N.Y., Jan. 2, 1940; s. Richard Moulton and Natalie (Fuller) H.; m. Julie Rose Keschl, Sept. 28, 1974 (div.); children: Kimberly Merrill, Gillian Fuller. BA, Amherst Coll., 1961; JD, Columbia U., 1968. Bar: Mass. 1968. Assoc. firm Nutter, McLennen & Fish, Boston, 1968-69, DiMento & Sullivan, Boston, 1969-70; atty. for students U. Mass., Amherst, 1970-74; practice law Amherst, 1974-2000; Legal Infirmary Amherst, 1997-98; ret., 2001. Adj. prof. U. Mass., 1972-76, Western New Eng. Coll. Sch. Law, 1993-94; vis. lectr. Amherst Coll., 1983, mock trial team coach, 1989-98; mock trial team coach Tufts Coll., 1998, Deerfield Acad., 1999-2000, Southwick H.S., 1999-2000; tchr. constnl. law, history, social studies Springfield H.S. Sci. and Tech., 2001—. Co-editor: Mass. Lawyers Weekly, 1979—94; emeritus:, 1994, statistician: New Eng. Blizzard, 1996—98, Conn. Pride, 1999—2000, Springfield Sirens Pro Soccer, 1999—2000. Asst. moderator Town of Leverett, 1988—93, moderator, 1993—96; mem. Leverett Sch. Bldg. Com., 1988—89; trustee Art Inst. Boston, 1990—92, Greenfield C. C. Found., 1991—97, Amherst Regional H.S. Coun., 1993—95, Amherst Hist. Soc., 1990—95; pres. Leverett PTO, 1981—85; mem. devel. com. Pioneer Valley H.S. of the Performing Arts, 1996—97; pres. Interfaith Housing Corp., Amherst, 1984—93; bd. dirs. Leverett Craftsmen and Artists, Inc., 1986—2001, treas., 1988—89, v.p., 1988—89, pres., 1989—2001; bd. dirs. Cmty. Multisvc. Inc., Northampton, Mass., 1987—93; trustee Wildwood Cemetery Assn., 1987—; bd. dirs., sec. Responsible Hospitality Inst., 1990—95; mem. host com. Russia-Amherst Exchange City of Petrozavadsk, 1988—; del. rep. Town of Amherst to Sister City, Kanegasaki, Japan, 1992—95; chair Amherst-Kanegasaki Sister Com., 1994—95; mem. bd. career com. Hampshire-Franklin Sch., 1995—98; cert. master ofcl. U.S. Assn. Track and Field, 1996—; Western Mass. track and field ofcl., 1995—; Western Mass. football ofcl., 1995—; referee FIFA Soccer, 1997—; active Connecticut Valley Soccer Ofcls. Assn., 1995—; collegiate water polo ofcl., 1997—2000; asst. coach varsity girls soccer Amherst Regional H.S., 1995—99; v.p. Western Mass. track and field, 2002—. Lt. j.g. USNR, 1961—65. Named Hon. Life Citizen, Town of Leverett, Mass., 2002. Mem. ABA (chmn. profl. liability com. Gen. Practice Sect. 1987-90, chmn. certification and specialization com. Gen. Practice Sect. 1992-95, chmn. family law com. 1995-96, chmn. certification, specialization and law sch. curriculum com. 1996-98, mem. coun. 1997-2001), Mass. Bar Assn. (chmn. com. on chem. dependency, Mass. Community Svc. award 1984), Franklin Bar Assn., Hampshire Bar Assn. (del. to Mass. Bar Assn., sec., v.p. 1986), Mass. Acad. Trial Lawyers, Amherst C. of C. (pres. 1985-93, Dakin medallion 1995), Nat. High Sch. Slavic Honor Soc. (hon.), Amherst Alumni Athletic Assn. (bd. dirs. 1995—), Skating Club (past v.p., treas. 1987-96, Amherst). Democrat. Home: 326 N Pleasant St Amherst MA 01002-1706 E-mail: rmh1240@hotmail.com.

HOWLAND, WILLARD J., radiologist, educator; b. Neosho, Mo., Aug. 28, 1927; s. Willard Jay and Grace Darlene (Murphy) H.; m. Kathleen V. Jones, July 28, 1945; children: Wyck, Candice, Charles, Thomas, Heather AB, U. Kans., 1948, MD, 1950; MA, U. Minn., 1958; DSc (hon.), Coll. Med. N.E. Ohio, 1990. Intern U.S. Naval Hosp., Newport, R.I., 1950-51; pvt. practice medicine Kans., 1951-55; resident Mayo Clinic, Rochester, Minn., 1955-58; radiologist Ohio Valley Gen. Hosp., Wheeling, W.Va., 1959-67; prof., dir. diagnostic radiology Med. Units U. Tenn., Memphis, 1967-68; dir., chmn. dept. radiology Aultman Hosp., Canton, Ohio, 1968-87, pres. med. staff, 1978; prof., chmn. radiology coun. Coll. Medicine N.E. Ohio U., Rootstown, 1976-87, program dir. integrated radiology residency, 1976-87. Author, co-author three books and rsch. papers in field. With U.S. Army, 1945-46, USN, 1950-51. Fellow Am. Coll. Radiology; mem. AMA, Radiol. Soc. N.Am., Am. Roentgen Ray Soc., Ohio State Radiol. Soc. (pres. 1980-81), Masons. Republican. Presbyterian. Home and Office: 4521 Bishops Gate Rd NW Canton OH 44708 Office Phone: 330-479-1046. Personal E-mail: whowland1@neo.rr.com.

HOWLETT, BYRON ELLIS, JR., academic administrator; b. San Antonio, June 18, 1967; s. Hazel Rosser Howlett (Stepmother) and Milton Patterson (Stepfather), Willie Don Fuller III (Stepfather), Byron Ellis Howlett Sr. and Henrietta Coleman Fuller; life ptnr. Frank William Stranzl, Apr. 12, 2000. BA in Geography, UCLA, 1990; MA in Edn., Calif. State U., San Bernardino, 1994; postgrad., U. La Verne, 2003—. Residence coord. UCLA, 1990; asst. residential life coord. Calif. State U., San Bernardino, 1990—93; resident dir. semester at sea U. Pitts., 1993; area coord. Calif. State U., Northridge, 1993—95; coord. of multicultural edn. Calif. Poly. Inst., Pomona, 1995—99, assoc. dir. residential life, 1999—2000; asst. dir. residential colls. U. So. Calif., L.A., 2000—02; dir. housing and residential life U. La Verne, Calif., 2002—. Creator (cultural tour) Gay Tour of L.A. Master: Cal Poly Pomona Black Faculty and Staff Assn. (vice chair, adminstrv. affairs 1998—2000); fellow: PACURH (life); mem.: Calif. Coll. Pers. Assn. (co-pres. 2001—02), NASPA (assoc.), ACPA (assoc.), Nat. Assn. of Multicultural Educators (assoc.), CCPA (assoc.), Western Assn. Coll. and Univ. Housing Officers (assoc.; v.p. 1996—97, pres.-elect 2002—03, pres. 2003—04), Order of the Golden Bruin (assoc.). Avocations: travel, trivia. Office: U La Verne 1950 Third St La Verne CA 91750-4401 Office Phone: 909-593-3511.

HOWLETT, CLIFFORD THEODORE, JR., (KIP HOWLETT), chemicals executive; b. Portland, Oreg., Oct. 19, 1945; s. Clifford T. and Lois (Ellis) H.; children: Beth, Ted, Michael; m. Marybeth Rossomando, Nov. 8, 1997. BA, Johns Hopkins U., 1967; JD, Willamette U., 1974. Bar: Oreg. 1974. Counsel, project dir. Western Environ. Trade Assn., Portland, 1973-75; v.p. environment and govt. affairs Ga.-Pacific Corp., Washington, 1988-94; vice-pres. for policy National Policy Forum, Wash., DC, 1994—. Chmn. Inter-Industry Wood Dust com., Washington, 1988—. Author: The Pitfalls and Possibilities of Planning, 1973, The Biomass Potential of Short Rotation Farms, 1977, Forest and Mill Residues as Potential Sources of Biomass, 1977. Mem. Alumni Schs. com. Johns Hopkins U., 1988—; bd. dirs. Boys and Girls Clubs of Greater Washington, 1999. With U.S. Army, 1968-70. Mem. ABA, Oreg. Bar Assn., Am. Paper Inst. (chmn. dioxin potency com. 1988—, chmn. joint occupational health study com. with Nat. Forest Products Assn. 1988—), NAM (chmn. OSHA policy com. 1988—). Home: 6635 Byrns Pl Mc Lean VA 22101-4419 Office: Chlorine Chemistry Council 1300 Wilson Blvd Arlington VA 22209-2307

HOWLETT, PHYLLIS LOU, retired athletics conference administrator; b. Indianola, Iowa, Oct. 23, 1932; d. James Clarence and Mabel L. (Fisher) Hickman; m. Jerry H. Howlett, Jan. 2, 1955 (dec. June 1972); children: Timothy A. (dec. Jan. 2005), Jane A. Field; m. Ronlin Royer, Dec. 30, 1977. BA, Simpson Coll., 1954. Tchr. phys. edn. Oskaloosa (Iowa) H.S., 1954-55; psychometrist Drake U., Des Moines, 1956-57, asst. to men's athletics dir., 1974-79; asst. dir. athletics U. Kans., Lawrence, 1979-82; asst. commr. Big Ten Conf., Inc., Park Ridge, Ill., 1982-97. Mem. football TV com., NCAA, 1980-87, women's golf com., 1983-89, chmn. com. on women's athletics, 1987-94, spl. com. women's basketball TV, 1989-90, chair com. for women's corp. mktg., 1990-94, divsn. I championship com., 1990-95, first woman chair exec. com., 1990-97, chair task force on gender equity, 1992-94, exec. dir. search com., 1993, spl. com. divsn. I football playoff, adminstrv. com., 1995-97, joint policy bd., 1995-97, sec.-treas., 1995-97, coun., 1995-97, fin. com., chair, 1995-97, treas. found. bd., 1995-97; exec. com., NACDA, 1986-90. Editor: (yearbook) Simpson Coll., 1953—54. Chair Iowa Commn. Status of Women, 1976-79; pres. Vol. Bus. of Greater Des Moines, 1969-70; chair Arts and Recreation Coun. of Greater Des Moines, 1975; pres. Iowa Children's and Family Svcs., 1973; nat. pres. Assn. Vol. Bus. Am., Inc., 1972-73. Named to, Simpson Coll. Hall of Fame, 1985, Indianola H.S. Hall of Fame, 1997, NACDA Hall of Fame, 2000; recipient Alumni Achievement award, Simpson Coll., 1988, Adminstrv. Achievement award, NACDA, 1995, Honda award of Merit, 1997, Spl. award, All-Am. Football Found., 1998, Lifetime Achievement award, Ind. Sports Corp., 1997, Svc. award, Assn. Vol. Mem. Nat. Assn. Coll. Women's Athletics Adminstrs. (Lifetime Achievement award 2000), Pi Beta Phi (pres. Iowa Beta chpt. 1953-54). Home: PO Box 1117 Abiquiu NM 87510-1117

HOWLEY, PETER MAXWELL, pathology educator; b. New Brunswick, NJ, Oct. 9, 1946; s. Bartholomew Maxwell and Grace (Size) Howley; m. Ann Margaret McElwee, Aug. 23, 1969; children: Cristin, Megan, Maura. AB, Princeton U., 1968; M Med. Sci., Rutgers U., 1970; MD, Harvard U., 1972. Diplomate Am. Bd. Pathology. Intern Mass. Gen. Hosp., Boston, 1972—73; commd. lt. USPHS, 1973, advanced through grades to capt., 1985; rsch. assoc. NIH, Bethesda, Md., 1973—75; resident in pathology Nat. Cancer Inst., Bethesda, 1975—77, prin. investigator, 1977—84, lab. chief, 1984—93; ret., 1993; George Fabyan prof. comparative pathology, chmn. dept. Harvard Med. Sch., Boston, 1993—2004, Shattuck prof. pathologicalanat, 2004—. Mem. sci. adv. bd. ONYX Pharm. Co., Richmond, Calif., 1992—97, Baxter Internat., Deerfield, Ill., 1995—, Enanta Pharm. Co., Cambridge, Mass., 1999—2003; chair Nat. Cancer Policy Bd., 1997—2000. Editor: The Molecular Basis of Cancer, 1996, 2nd edit., 2001, Fields Virology, 4th edit., 2001; contbr. over 230 articles to med. jours. Recipient Wallace P. Rowe award, Nat. Inst. Allergy and Infectious Diseases, 1986, Meritorious Svc. award, USPHS, 1989, Paul Ehrlich-Ludwig Darmstaedter prize, Govt. of Germany, 1994, Rous-Whipple award, Am. Soc. Investigative Pathology, 2004. Fellow: AAAS, Am. Acad. Microbiology; mem.: NAS, Am. Acad. Arts and Scis., Inst. Medicine. Achievements include patent for Recombinant DNA Process Utilizing Papillomavirus DNA as a Vector. Office: Harvard Med Sch New Rsch Bldg Rm 950 77 Ave Louis Pasteur Boston MA 02115 Business E-Mail: peter_howley@hms.harvard.edu.

HOWLEY, TERESA MOOREHOUSE, artist; b. Canadiagua, N.Y., Aug. 22, 1944; d. William Joel Moorehouse and Ella Olive Haviland Knapp; m. John Leidenfrost, May 19, 1975 (dec. Sept. 1998); 1 child, Isadora Gabrielle Leidenfrost; m. John Joseph Howley, July 1990. Grad., Penn Yan (N.Y.) Acad., 1962. Computer graphics illustrator Cornell U., Ithaca, NY, 1985—2002; sculptor, 1962—. Avocation: community service. Home: 99 Etna Rd Ithaca NY 14850 Office Phone: 607-347-4849. E-mail: tch3@cornell.edu.

HOWORTH, DAVID BISHOP, lawyer; b. Temple, Tex., Feb. 6, 1947; s. Marion Beckett and Mary Hartwell (Bishop) H.; m. Martha Ellen Peacock, Aug. 29, 1970; children: Katherine Somerville, Emily Hartwell. BA, Yale U., 1971; JD, U. Miss., 1975. ar: N.Y. 1976, Oreg. 1990, Wash. 1996, Miss. 2000, U.S. Dist. Ct. (so. and ea. dists.) N.Y. 1977, U.S. Ct. Appeals (2d cir.) 1984, U.S. Dist. Ct. Oreg. 1990, U.S. Ct. Appeals (9th cir.) 1991. Assoc. Dewey Ballantine, N.Y.C., 1975-77, 78-83, ptnr., 1984-90; asst. prof. law U. Miss., University, 1977-78, vis. assoc. prof. law, 2000—. Mem. ABA, N.Y. State Bar Assn., Assn. Bar City of N.Y. Home: 1420 S 10th St Oxford MS 38655 E-mail: dhoworth@olemiss.edu.

HOWREY, EUGENE PHILIP, economics professor, consultant; b. Geneva, Ill., Dec. 1, 1937; s. Eugene Edgar and Ellen Pauline (Boord) H.; children: Patricia Marie, Richard Philip, Margaret Ellen, Mark McCall. AB, Drake U., 1959; PhD, U. N.C., 1964; MA (hon.), U. Pa., 1972. Asst. prof. econs. Princeton U., N.J., 1963-69; assoc. prof. econs. U. Pa., Phila., 1969-73; prof. econs. U. Mich., Ann Arbor, 1973—, prof. stats., 1978—. Cons. Mathematica, Inc., Princeton, 1965-75; guest lectr. Inst. Advanced Studies, Vienna, 1974, 76. Contbr. articles to profl. jours. Research grantee NSF, 1975, 79, 84 Mem. Ann Arbor Velo Club, Ann Arbor Bicycle Touring Club (pres. 1979-80), Phi Beta Kappa. Roman Catholic. Avocation: bicycling. Home: 2152 Overlook Ct Ann Arbor MI 48103-2336 Office: U Mich Dept Econs Ann Arbor MI 48109 Business E-Mail: eph@umich.edu.

HOWRY, JOE R., newspaper editor; B in history and polit. sci., U. Mont. Various positions with newspapers in Mont.; sports writer to city editor Nev. State Jour. and Reno (Nev.) Evening Gazette; mng. editor Salem (Oreg.) Statesman-Jour., Ventura (Calif.) County Star, 1992—2004, v.p., editor, 2004—. Address: Ventura County Star 5250 Ralston St Ventura CA 93003-7318

HOWSE, CATHY L., writer, researcher, entrepreneur; b. Murfreesboro, Tenn., Dec. 16, 1955; d. John Edd Sr. and Elmira Howse; children; Gregory Simpson Jr., Brandon J. BS, Met. State Coll., Denver, 1987. Author: Ultra Black Hair, 1990, 2000, Ultra Black Hair Growth II, 1994. Achievements include development of a method for hair growth and lengthening for black women. Office: UBH Publs Inc PO Box 22678 Denver CO 80222 E-mail: mail@ubhpublications.com.

HOWSE, JENNIFER LOUISE, foundation administrator; b. Glendale, Calif., Jan. 31, 1945; d. Benjamin McCausland and Patricia Louise (Naylor) H. BA, Fla. State U., 1966, MA, 1968, PhD in Child Lang. Devel., 1973; LHD (hon.), SUNY, Bklyn., 1990. Rsch. asst., instr. Inst. Human Devel. Coll. Edn., Fla. State U., Tallahassee, 1967-69; dir. planning and evaluation Wakulla County (Fla.) Sch. System, 1969-72; dir. NARC/HEW Liaison Project Nat. Assn. for Retarded Citizens, Govtl. Affairs Office, Washington, 1972-73; dir. Developmental Disabilities Bur., dir. Bur. Tech. Assistance and Regulation Fla. Dept. Health and Rehab. Svcs., Tallahassee, 1973-75; exec. dir. Willowbrook Rev. Panel, N.Y.C., 1975-78; assoc. commr. N.Y. State Office Mental Retardation and Developmental Disabilities, N.Y.C., 1978-80; state commr. for mental retardation Dept. Pub. Welfare, Harrisburg, Pa., 1980-85; exec. dir. Greater N.Y. chpt. March of Dimes Birth Defects Found., N.Y.C., 1985-89, pres. White Plains, NY, 1990—. Advisor Ctr. for Family Life in Sunset Park, Bklyn., 1992—. Bd. dirs. Salk Inst., La Jolla, Calif.; active Pew Environ. Health Comm. Office: March Dimes Birth Defects Found 1275 Mamaroneck Ave White Plains NY 10605-5298

HOWSE, ROBERT LLOYD, law educator, consultant; b. Toronto, Ontario, Canada, Aug. 21, 1958; s. Hebert Lloyd Howse and Susan Gladys Winsor; m. Denyse Marie Laure Goulet, June 23, 1984. BA with high distinction, U. Toronto, 1980; LLB (hon.), U. Toronto Faculty of Law, 1989; LLM, Harvard Law Sch., 1990. Mem., policy planning secretariat Dept. External Affairs, Govt. of Can., Ottawa, 1983—84; 3rd, 2nd sec., polit. and econ. Embassy of Can., Belgrade, Yugoslavia, 1984—86; asst. prof., assoc. prof. law U. Toronto, 1990—99; Alene and Allan F. Smith Prof. Law U. Mich., Ann Arbor. Reporter law of world trade orgn. Am. Law Inst., Phila., 2002—; mem. editl. adv. bd. European Jour. Internat. Law, Florence, Italy, 2001—, Legal Issues Econ. Integration, Amsterdam, Netherlands, 2001—; mem. group ind. experts European Commn., Global Governance Project, DG Trade, Brussels, 2001—02; assoc. dir. Ctr. Study State and Market, 1995—98; mem. faculty, m.i.l.e. program World Trade Inst., Berne, Switzerland, 2000—; vis. prof. law Harvard Law Sch., Cambridge, Mass., 1989—89. Co-author: The Regulation of International Trade, 2nd edition, Restorative Justice: A Conceptual Framework; co-editor: The Federal Vision; co-translator Alexandre Kojeve Outline of a Phenomenology of Right. Pro bono legal cons. Nat. Wildlife Fedn., Washington, 2000—02; co-founder Can. for All Canadians Referendum NO Com., Ottawa, 1992—92. Fellow, C.D. Howe Inst., 2001—. Avocations: creative writing, weightlifting, dogs. Home: 11980 Bemis Rd Manchester MI 48158 Office: U Mich Law Sch Hutchins Hall #337 625 S State St Ann Arbor MI 48109-1215 E-mail: rhowse@umich.edu.*

HOWSON, TAMAR D., pharmaceutical executive; Sr. v.p., dir. bus. devel., mgr. SR One Ltd. venture capital fund SmithKline Beecham, 2000—01; biotechnology cons. to CEO Bristol-Myers Squibb, 2000—01, sr. v.p. corp. devel., 2001—. Former ind. bus. cons., corp. advisor. Office: Bristol-Myers Squibb Co 345 Park Ave New York NY 10154-0037*

HOXIE, FREDERICK EUGENE, history professor; b. Hoolehua, Hawaii, Apr. 22, 1947; s. John Wadman and Catherine (Agee) H.; m. Elizabeth Anne Schroder, July 11, 1970 (dec. Dec. 1983); children: Silas, Charles; m. Holly Frances Hanscom, Jan. 3, 1986; stepchildren: Stephen Hoskins, Philip Hoskins. BA, Amherst Coll., 1969, PhD in Humane Letters (hon.), 1994; MA, Brandeis U., 1976, PhD, 1977; PhD in Humane Letters (hon.), L.I. U., 2000. Tchr. Phila. Pub. Schs., 1969-70; high sch. tchr. Punahou Sch., Honolulu, 1970-72; asst. prof. Antioch Coll., Yellow Springs, Ohio, 1977-82, assoc. prof., 1982-83; dir. D'Arcy McNickle Ctr. for Am. Indian History, Newberry Libr., Chgo., 1983-94, v.p. rsch. and edn., 1994-98; Swanlund prof. history U. Ill., Urbana, 1998—. Cons. Cheyenne River Sioux Tribe, Eagle Butte, S.D., 1977-78, U.S. Senate Com. on Indian Affairs, Washington, 1989-90, Little Big Horn Coll., Crow Agency, Mt., 1990-98, Nat. Park Svc., Denver Support Ctr., 1997-98, Dept. of Justice, 2000-01, 04—. Author: A Final Promise, 1984, 2d edit., 2001, Parading Through History, 1995; editor: Indians in American History, 1988, 2d edit., 1997, Ency. of North American Indians, 1996, Talking Back to Civilization, 2001, Lewis and Clark and the Indian Country, 2004—. Bd. dirs. Ill. Humanities Coun., Chgo., 1997-2003; trustee Nat. Mus. Am. Indian, Smithsonian, 1990-95, Amherst Coll., 2001—. Humanities fellow Rockefeller Found., 1984-85, fellow NEH, 1990-91, fellow Mellon Found., 2005. Mem. Am. Hist. Assn. (program chmn. 1992), Am. Soc. for Ethnohistory (pres. 1995-96), Orgn. Am. Historians (exec. bd. 1997-2000). Avocations: running, tennis. Office: U Ill Dept History 309 Gregory Hall 810 S Wright St Urbana IL 61801-3644 E-mail: hoxie@uicu.edu.

HOXIE, JOEL P., lawyer; b. Waterloo, Iowa, Dec. 4, 1948; s. Wirt Pierce and Jeanne (Ogle) H.; m. Cynthia Ann Mast, Aug. 12, 1978; children: Robert Lewis, Laura Ann. AB, Princeton U., 1971; JD, U. Iowa, 1978. Atty. Snell & Wilmer, Phoenix, 1978—. Trustee Heard Mus., Phoenix, 1990-2004, pres. 1995-97, pres. bd. trustees, life trustee 2005; pres. Princeton Alumni Assn. No. Ariz., Phoenix, 1990-2003. Lt. USN, 1971-75. Mem. Nat. Bar Assn., Ariz. State Bar Assn., County Bar Assn., Securities Industry Assn. (legal and compliance divsn. 1992—), Phoenix Country Club (bd. dirs. 2001—). Methodist. Avocations: golf, tennis, swimming, hiking. Home: 5301 E Mariposa St Phoenix AZ 85018-3029 Office: Snell & Wilmer 1 Arizona Ctr Phoenix AZ 85004 Office Phone: 602-382-6264. E-mail: jhoxie@swlaw.com.

HOXIE, RALPH GORDON, academic administrator, writer; b. Waterloo, Iowa, Mar. 18, 1919; s. Charles Ray and Ada May (Little) H.; m. Louise Lobitz, Dec. 23, 1953 (dec. 1992); m. Ada B. Edgerton, June 21, 1997. BA, U. No. Iowa, 1940; MA, U. Wis., 1941; PhD, Columbia, 1950; LLD (hon.), Chung-ang U., 1965; LittD (hon.), D'Youville Coll., 1966; grad., Air War Coll., 1971; LHD (hon.), Gannon U., 1988, Wesley Coll., 1989, U. No. Iowa, 1990, Shepherd Coll., 1992, Teikyo Post U., 1994, Long Island U., 1995, Fitchburg State Coll., 1997. Roberts fellow Columbia, 1946-47, Roberts travelling fellow, 1947-48, asst. to provost, 1948-49; asst. prof. history, gen. editor Social Sci. Found.; asst. to chancellor U. Denver, 1950-53; project asso. Columbia Bicentennial History, 1953-54; dean Coll. Liberal Arts and Scis., L.I. U., 1954-55; acting dean C. W. Post Coll., 1954-55, dean, 1955-60, provost, 1960-62, pres., 1962-68; chancellor L.I. U., 1964-68, cons., 1968-69; pres. Center for Study of Presidency, 1969-95; chmn. Ctr. for Study of Presidency, 1995-96, pres., chmn. emeritus, 1997—. Pub. mem. Fgn. Svc. officer selection bd. U.S. Dept. State; vis. lectr. U. Ala., U. Calif., Irvine, Columbia U., U. Colo., Colo. State U., U. Wyo., Chapman Coll., U. No. Colo., Colo. Coll., Gannon U., Gettysburg Coll., Heidelberg Coll., U. Kans., Kans. State U., Muskingum Coll., Post Coll., St. Francis Coll. N.Y., USAF Acad., Naval War Coll., Nat. Archives, Nat. War Coll., Oglethorpe U., U. Genoa, Italy, U. Pitts., U. Tex., El Paso, U Wis., Northwestern U., U. No. Iowa; bd. govs. Banque Continentale br. Franklin Nat. Bank. Author: John W. Burgess, American Scholar, 1950, Command Decision and the Presidency, 1977, (with others) A History of The Faculty of Political Science, Columbia University, 1955, Organizing and Staffing the Presidency, 1980; editor: Frontiers for Freedom, 1952, The White House: Organization and Operations, 1971, The Presidency of the 1970's, 1973, The Presidency and Information Policy, 1981, The Presidency and National Security Policy, 1984; editor Presdl. Studies Quar., 1970-95; contbg. author: (with others) Freedom and Authority in Our Time, 1953, The Coattailless Landslide, 1974, Power and the Presidency, 1976, Classics of the American Presidency, 1980, The Blessings of Liberty, 1987, Popular Images of American Presidents, 1988, Rating Game in American Politics, 1988, Science and Technology Advice to the President, Congress, and Judiciary, 1988, The American Presidency: Historical and Contemporary Perspectives, 1988, Points of View, 1988, The Presidency in Transition, 1989, Dictionary of American History, 1996, Points of View, 1998, Moral Authority of Government, 1999; contbr. articles to profl. jours. and encys. Bd. dirs. United Fund L.I., Bklyn. Inst. Arts and Scis., Tibetan Found., L.I. Coun. Alcoholism, Bklyn. chpt. ARC Greater N.Y.; chmn., pres. bd. dirs. Am. Friends Chung-ang U.; pres. Pub. Mems. Assn. Fgn. Svc.; trustee Air Force Hist. Found., U. No. Iowa Found., Nat. Inst. Social Scis., Kosciuszko Found. N.Y., Mackinac Coll., North Shore chpt. Am. Assn. UN, Downtown Bklyn. Assn., Coun. Higher Ednl. Instns. N.Y.C.; mem. adv. bd. L.I. Air res. Ctr.; co-founder, mem. adv. coun. Robert A. Taft Inst. Govt.; sec. Nassau County Commn. on Govt. Revision; co-chmn. Nassau-Suffolk Conf. Christians and Jews; dir., pres. Great-N.Y. Coun. Fgn. Students; bd. govs. Human Resources Ctr., N.Y. Korean Vets. Meml. Commn. Served to capt. USAAF, 1942-46; brig. gen. USAF ret. Decorated Meritorious Svc. medal, Legion of Merit, Korean Cultural medal, numerous other medals; recipient Disting. Svc. medal City N.Y., 1965, Alumni Achievement award U. No. Iowa, 1965, Alumni Achievement award Columbia U., 1997, Columbia award for Disting. Achievment, 1997; named Man of Yr. Paderewski Found., 1966, Man of Yr. Eloy Alfaro Found., 1966. Fellow Am. Studies Assn. Met. N.Y.; mem. Am. Hist. Assn., Internat. Assn. Univ. Pres., Am. Polit. Sci. Assn., Acad. of Polit. Sci., Navy League, Air Force Assn., Res. Officers Assn. (pres. Mitchel chpt.), V.F.W., Am. Legion, L.I. Assn. (dir.), Am. Polar Soc., Kappa Delta Pi, Pi Gamma Mu, Alpha Sigma Lambda, Delta Sigma Pi, Gamma Theta Upsilon. Clubs: Century Assn., Met., Columbia Univ. Faculty House (N.Y.C.); Met. (Washington); Bklyn., Montauk (Bklyn.); Old Westbury Golf and Country and Mill River (hon.). Episcopalian. Home: PO Box 248 Oyster Bay NY 11771-0248 Office: PO Box 248 Oyster Bay NY 11771-0248 E-mail: rghoxie@aol.com. *Each day I seek to ask how I can better serve others. Assuredly, in so serving, ours will be the richest of dividends and life takes on an ever-fuller meaning.*

HOXIE, ROBERT PRYNNE, retired entomologist; b. St. Louis, Mar. 14, 1936; s. Robert Lee Hoxie and Helen Louise Hughes. BS in Agr., U. Ariz., 1961; MS in Entomology, Mich. State U., 1974. Cryptographer U.S. Dept. Def., Ft. Ord, Calif., 1964-67; biol. rsch. technician USDA, East Lansing, Mich., 1967-75, support scientist in entomology Agrl. Rsch. Svc., 1975-86; entomologist USDA Agrl. Rsch. Svcs., West Lafayette, Ind., 1986-90, weed scientist, safety officer, 1990-98, ret., 1999. Contbr. articles to sci. and profl. jours. Mem. Coleopterist Soc., N.Y. Entomol. Soc., Sigma Xi. Home: 8134 W 400 N West Lafayette IN 47906 E-mail: rph6@mindspring.com.

HOXTER, CURTIS JOSEPH, international economic advisor, public relations executive; b. July 20, 1922; s. Jacob and Hanna (Katzenstein) Hoxter; m. Grace Lewis, Feb. 4, 1945 (dec.); children: Ronald Alan, Victoria Ann, Audrey Theresa(dec.); m. Allegra Branson, Jan. 2, 1981. AB, NYU, 1948, MA, 1950. Staff contbr. AUFBAU-Reconstn., NYC, 1939-40; feature writer, reporter L.I. (NY) Daily Press, 1940-42; editor, writer, analyst Office War Info., NYC, 1943-45; pub. info. officer Dept. State, 1945-47; dir. pub. rels. Internat. C. of C., 1948-53; info. cons. (Marshall Plan) Econ. Cooperation Adminstrn., Washington, 1950-55; exec. v.p. George Peabody and Assocs., Inc., 1953-56; pvt. practice, 1956—. Pub. rels. cons. various cos., fin. instns. and govt. agys.; columnist Scripps-Howard Newspapers; adviser U.S. Com. for UN Day; editl. advisor Internat. Economy mag.; advisor on internat. econ. and fin. problems to global agys., U.S. Del. Disarmament Conf., London; mem. internat. adv. bd. Bus. Week Chief Exec. Roundtable; exec. dir. adv. com. to Chancellor of Austria; mem. adv. com. Grad. Sch. Internat. Rels., U. Calif., San Diego; sr. advisor to pres. European Commn. Contbr. and commentator articles to nat. mags. and newspapers. With AUS, WWII. Decorated Grand Cross of Merit Govt. of Austria, 1991, Grand Cross of Merit Govt. of Germany, 2003. Mem. Met. Club (NYC), Econ. Club NY, Leewood Country Club, Coral Beach and Tennis Club (Bermuda), Univ. Club (Washington). Office: 380 Lexington Ave New York NY 10168-0002 Office Phone: 212-818-0303. Business E-Mail: hoxter.inc@verizon.net.

HOY, CYRUS HENRY, language professional, educator; b. St. Marys, W.Va., Feb. 26, 1926; s. Albert Pierce and Marie Dorothy (West) H. BA, U. Va., 1950, MA, 1951, PhD, 1954. Instr. English U. Va., 1954-56; asst. prof. Vanderbilt U., 1956-60, asso. prof., 1960-64; prof. English U. Rochester, N.Y., 1964-76, John B. Trevor prof. English and comparative lit., 1976-94, John B. Trevor prof. emeritus, 1994—, chmn. dept. English, 1984-88. Author: The Hyacinth Room, An Investigation Into the Nature of Comedy, Tragedy, and Tragicomedy, 1964; author: intro., notes and commentaries to The Dramatic Works of Thomas Dekker, 4 vols., 1980; mem. editl. bd. Shakespeare Quar., 1968-90, Medieval and Renaissance Drama, 1980-92; gen. editor: Regents Renaissance Drama Series, 1964-76; co-editor Dramatic Works in the Beaumont and Fletcher Canon, Vol. 1, 1966, Vol. 2, 1970, Vol. 3, 1976, Vol. 4, 1979, Vol. 5, 1982, Vol. 6, 1984, Vol. 7, 1989, Vol. 8, 1992, Vol. 9, 1994, Vol. 10, 1996; contbr. articles to profl. jours. Fulbright scholar, 1952-53; Guggenheim fellow, 1962-63 Democrat. Presbyterian. Office: U Rochester Dept English Rochester NY 14627 Home: 1570 East Ave Apt 309 Rochester NY 14610-1637

HOY, GEORGE PHILIP, clergyman, county official, state legislator; b. Indpls., Feb. 5, 1937; s. Clarence Augustus Hoy and Margaret Louise (Etter) Wooley; m. Barbara J. Turpen, Aug. 11, 1957 (dec. Feb. 1987); 1 foster child, Richard H. Johnson children: Rene Hoy Riegle, Sherri Hoy Haas, Matthew Philip; m. Sandra L. Knipe, July 30, 1999; stepchildren: Wendy Knipe Bredhold, Benjamin Knipe. BA, Ky. Wesleyan Coll., 1958; MDiv, So. Bapt. Theol. Sem., 1962. Ordained to ministry United Ch. of Christ, 1962, Nat. Bapt. Conv. 1997. Pastor Union United Ch. of Christ, Evansville, Ind., 1962—72, Faith United Ch. of Christ, Ft. Wayne, Ind., 1975—80, St. Matthew's United Ch. of Christ, Evansville, 1981—87; dir. Youth Svc. Bur., Evansville, 1972—75; pastor St. Peter's United Ch. of Christ, Evansville, 1987—94; interim pastor Zion United Ch. of Christ, Henderson, Ky., 2003; mem. Ind. Ho. Reps., 2004—. Mem. faculty Brescia U., Owensboro, Ky., 1970-72; chaplain Evansville State Hosp., 1966-72, Fraternal Order Police, Evansville, 1982-92, chaplain, life mem.; dir. Tri-State Food Bank, Evansville, 1987-2000; del. gen. synod Ind.-Ky. Conf., United Ch. of Christ, 1978-81; bd. dirs. Vanderburgh County Cmty. Corrections.; bd. dirs., fin. chmn. Pigeon Creek Greenway. Religion columnist Evansville Press, 1983-93. Vol. Habitat for Humanity, Americus, Ga., 1980-81; active City-County Human Rels. Commn., Evansville, 1984-93; bd. dirs. Leadership Evansville, 1987-92, Outreach Ministries, Evansville, 1987-93; regional bd. adv. Ch. World Svc., 1987-2002; mem. Bread for the World, Amnesty Internat., Police Athletic League; active Vanderburgh County Coun., 1992—, pres., 1994-95, v.p., 1997; v.p. Vanderburgh County Coun., 1997; mem. property tax adjustment bd. appeals Vanderburgh County Soil and Water Conservation Dist.; chair fin. Pigeon Creek Greenway; chmn. hunger walk CROP; bd. dirs. Sustainable Cmtys. Coalition; pres. Evansville Area Cmty. Chs.; city county data bd., preservation com., Old Liberty Bapt. Ch.; bd. dirs. Matthew 25 AIDS Svcs.; property tax replacement study commn. State of Ind.; chaplain Ctrl. Labor Coun. AFL/CIO. Recipient Doing The Right Thing award, Evansville Psychiat. Children's Ctr., 2002, ecumenical award Evansville Area Coun. of Chs., 1987, Native Am. award Coun. of Bear, Evansville, 1988, Individual Achievement award Leadership Evansville, 1998, Martin Luther King Jr. Cmty. Svc. award Black Leadership Conf., 2000, Starfish award Tri-State Food Bank, 2000, award for outstanding svc. to foster parents, Sagamore of the Wabash award, 2000, others; named Legislator of Yr., Ind. divsn. Isaak Walton League, 2005; named to CROP Honor Roll, 1997, Hon. Order Ky. Cols., Hall of Fame, Ctrl. H.S., 2001. Mem. NAACP, ACLU, Internat. Brotherhood Magicians, Ind. Psychol. Assn., Tri-State Pastors Circle (pres. 1984-85), Northside Ministerial Assn., Interdenominational Ministers Alliance, Downtown Ministerial Assn., Evansville Tri-State Assn. (pres. 1972-75), Greenpeace, Silent Singers (hon.), Henderson Ministerial Assn., Tri-State Alliance Christmas Project Com. Democrat. Avocations: music, art, drama, dance performing, model railroading. Home: 217 Cherry St Evansville IN 47713-1242 Office Phone: 800-382-9842. E-mail: revgph@aol.com, h77@in.gov.

HOY, HAROLD JOSEPH, marketing educator, author, management consultant, retail executive, military officer; b. Pine Grove, Pa. s. Harold Jefferson and Naomi E. H.; m. Z. Jane Brown, July 2, 1960; children: Kathryn Burgess, Elisabeth Wermuth, Suzanne Hoy-Wong, Kristen Shugrue. BS, Pa. State U., 1955; MBA, U. Hartford, 1973; postgrad., U. Conn., 1981, Harvard U., 1986, Pa. State U., 1990, U. London, 2005—. Gen. mgr. Montgomery Ward & Co., Chgo., 1963-67, D & L Stores, New Britain, Conn., 1967-81; prof. mktg. Ctrl. Conn. State U., New Britain, 1974-79; prof. U. Conn., Storrs, 1977-79; prof. mktg. and mgmt., faculty coun., grad. faculty Pa. State U., 1979-91; prof. Elizabethtown (Pa.) Coll., 1992—93; pres. H.J. Hoy Assocs. Mgmt. Cons., Pine Grove, Pa., 1979—2004, Marion, Conn., 1979—2004; mem. Woodrow Wilson Inst. Internat. Scholars, Washington, 1994-95. Founder, dir. Pa. State U. Small Bus. Devel. Ctr.; dir. U.S. Small Bus. Inst., Pa. State U., Harrisburg; dir. internat. rsch. scholars Harvard U., 1997; mem. Pa. State White House Conf. on Small Bus. and Fed. White House Conf. on Small Bus., Washington, 1987, CATO Inst., Washington, 2003. Author, editl. reviewer coll. book pubs. and acad. mgmt. and mktg. jours; contbr. articles to profl. jours. including Columbia U. Jour. of World Business and coll. textbooks. Eagle Scout, Boy Scouts Am.; Capt. 1st co. Gov.'s Foot Guard Ct. Army N.G., Hartford, Conn. 1st lt. Fin. Corps, U.S. Army; capt. Continental Army Command. Named Wisdom Hall of Fame fellow, 1997. Mem. Am. Mktg. Assn., Acad. Mktg. Sci., Acad. Internat. Bus., Internat. Coun. for Small Bus., Nature Conservancy, Natural Resources Def. Coun., Masons (32 deg.), Nat. Sojourners, Royal Arch, Knights Templar, Sierra Club, Smithsonian Inst. Avocations: photography, international business research, stamp collecting/philately.

HOY, MARJORIE ANN, entomology educator; b. Kansas City, Kans., May 19, 1941; d. Dayton J. and Marjorie Jean (Acker) Wolf; m. James B. Hoy; 1 child, Benjamin Lee AB, U. Kans., 1963; MS, U. Calif., Berkeley, 1966, PhD, 1972. Asst. entomologist Conn. Agrl. Expt. Sta., New Haven, 1973-75; rsch. entomologist U.S. Forest Svc., Hamden, Conn., 1975-76; asst. prof. entomology U. Calif., Berkeley, 1976-80, assoc. prof. entomology, 1980-82, prof. entomology, 1982-92, prof. emeritus, 1992—; Fischer, Davies and Eckes prof., dept. entomology and nematology U. Fla., Gainesville, 1992—; chmn. Calif. Gypsy Moth Sci. Adv. Panel, 1982—; mem. genetics resources adv. com. USDA, 1992—, mem. adv. com. agrl. biotech., 2000—02; mem. com. on biol. threats to agrl. plants and animals NRC and NAS, 2001—02. Chmn. Calif. Gypsy Moth Sci. Adv. Panel, 1982—; mem. genetics resources adv. com. USDA, 1992—, mem. adv. com. agrl. biotech., 2000—01; F.E. Guyton disting. lectr. Auburn (Ala.) U., 1997; mem. com. on biol. threats to agrl. plants and animals NRC and NAS, 2001—02; sci. cons. transgenic insects Pew Initiative Food and Biotech. Editor, co-editor: Genetics in Relation to Insect Managment, 1979, Recent Advances in Knowledge of the Phytoseiidae, 1982, Biological Control of Pests by Mites, 1983, Biological Control in Agricultural IPM Systems, 1985, Insect Molecular Genetics, 1994, 2d edit., 2003, The Phytoseiidae as Biological Control Agents of Pest Mites and Insects: A Bibliography, 1996, Managing the Citrus Leafminer, 1996; mem. editorial bd. Exptl. and Applied Acarology, Biol. Control, Biocontrol Sci. and Tech., Environ. Biosafety Rsch.; contbr. articles to profl. jours. Mem. Sec. Agrl.'s adv. com. agrl. biotechnology; cons. Pew Charitable Trust. Recipient citation for outstanding achievments in regulatory entomology Fla. Divsn. Plant Industry, 1995, USDA honor award Sec. of Agr., 1996, award for sci. Nat. Agri-Mktg. Assn., 1998, sr. faculty award U. Fla. chpt. Gamma Sigma Delta, 1998, Biol. Control Scientist of Yr., Internat. Orgn. Biol. Control, 2004. Fellow AAAS, Royal Entomol. Soc. London, Entomol. Soc. Am. (mem. Pacific br. governing bd. 1985, Bussart award 1986, Founder's Meml. award 1992), Coun. Agr. Sci. and Tech. (Charles Black award 2004); mem. Nat. Acad. Scis. (com. on biol. threats to agr. plants and animals), NY Acad. Scis., Am. Genetic Assn., Internat. Orgn. Biol. Control (v.p. 1984-85, Disting. Scientist award 2004), Am. Inst. Biol. Scis. (adv. coun. 1996-98, governing bd. 1999-2001), Acarological Soc. Am. (governing bd. 1980-84, pres. 1992), Soc. for Study of Evolution, Fla. Entomological Soc. (Team Rsch. award 1997, Outstanding Tchg. award 1999), Phi Beta Kappa, Sigma Xi (chpt. sec. 1979-81, Sr. Faculty Rsch. award 1996). Avocations: hiking, gardening, snorkeling. Home: 4320 SW 83rd Way Gainesville FL 32608-4131 Office: U Fla Dept Entomology and Nematology PO Box 110620 Gainesville FL 32611-0620 Office Phone: 352-392-1901. Business E-Mail: mahoy@ifas.ufl.edu.

HOY, RONALD RAYMOND, neurobiology educator; b. Walla Walla, Wash., Jan. 12, 1939; s. Edward and Alice (Howe) H.; m. Margaret Christina Nelson, June 1, 1980; 1 child, Timothy. BS in Zoology, Wash. State U., 1962; PhD in Biology, Stanford U., 1968. Dir. neural systems and behavior course Marine Biol. Lab., Woods Hole, Mass., 1979-84, dir. Grass fellowship program, 1988-90; prof. neurobiology and behavior to David & Dorothy Merksamer Prof. Biology Cornell U., Ithaca, NY, 1986—, chmn. dept., 1988-91. Trustee The Grass Found., 1985-88, 90—. Recipient Jacob Javits Award, Nat. Inst. Neurol. & Communication Diseases and Stroke, 1986; grantee professorship, Howard Hughes Med. Inst., 2002—. Fellow: AAAS; mem.: NIDCD (study sect. 1991—95, Exec. Coun.), Sigma Xi, Phi Beta Kappa. Office: Cornell U Sect Neurobiology and Behavior S G Mudd Hall Ithaca NY 14853 Office Phone: 607-254-4318, 607-254-4317. Office Fax: 607-254-4308. E-mail: rrh3@cornell.edu.

HOY, SUELLEN, historian; b. Chgo., Aug. 14, 1942; d. Christopher J. and Imelda E. Hoy; m. Walter Nugent, Nov. 1, 1986. BA, St. Mary's Coll., Notre Dame, Ind., 1965; MA, Ind. U., 1971, PhD, 1975. Asst. prof. SUNY, Plattsburgh, 1974-75; dir. Pub. Works Hist. Soc., Chgo., 1975-81; assoc. dir. N.C. Div. Archives & History, Raleigh, 1981-87; adj. prof. U. Notre Dame, 1987-91; NEH fellow Granger, Ind., 1992-93. Vis. prof. U. Coll. Dublin, Ireland, 1991-92; vis. assoc. prof. U. Notre Dame, 1995-98, guest prof., 1999—. Author: Chasing Dirt: American Pursuit of Cleanliness, 1995;

co-author: History of Public Works in The United States, 1976, Public Works History in The United States, 1982, From Dublin to New Orleans: The Journey of Nora and Alice, 1994; contbr. articles to Jour. Urban History Bd. dirs. N.C. Humanities Com., Greensboro, 1984-87. Recipient Irish Am. Cultural Inst. award, Dublin, 1991-92; NEH fellow, 1986-87, 92-93; rsch. grantee Spencer Found., 1996-97, Louisville Inst., 1999; Abigail Quigley McCarthy Centennial fellow, 1995-96. Mem. Orgn. Am. Historians (exec. bd. 1986-89), Am. Hist. Assn. (nominating com. 1987-89), Nat. Coun. Pub. History (bd. dirs.), Pub. Works Hist. Soc. (pres. 1986-87). Avocations: walking, reading. Home: 578 Roger Williams 204 Highland Park IL 60035 Business E-Mail: shoy@nd.edu.

HOYE, LINDA LEE, special education educator; d. Hugh Thorton and Hazel Marie Paul; m. Robert Eugene Hoye, Apr. 17, 1971; children: Justin, Ashley, Ryan. Assoc. degree, Pennsylvania Valley C.C., Kansas City, 1970; BS in Dental Hygiene, U. Mo., Kansas City, 1974, MA in Spl. Edn., 1990. Registered dental hygienist Mo.; cert. tchr. Mo. Dental asst. Dr. Les Ottaway, Overland Park, Kans., 1970—74; dental hygienist Dr. Bill Spiller, Kansas City, Mo., 1974—84, Dr. Dan Muehlebach, Kansas City, Mo., 1984—90; tchr. spl. edn. Belton (Md.) Sch. Dist. # 124, 1990—, bldg. coord., 1996—. Coach Spl. Olympics, 2005; choir mem. St. Sabina's Cath. Ch., 2000—. Named Tchr. of Yr., Cambridge Elem., 2000. Mem.: Belton Nat. Educators Assn. (past pres. 2002—04), Lambda Lambda of Beta Sigma Phi (pres., treas. 1989—). Roman Catholic. Home: 8001 E 163d Ter Belton MO 64012

HOYE, MARIA PILAR, lawyer; BS, Calif. State U., Northridge, 1988; JD, UCLA, 1991. Bar: Calif. 1991. With Latham & Watkins, L.A., 1991—, ptnr., 1998—. Former adj. prof. environ. law U. So. Calif. Mem.: Orange County Bar Assn. (mem. exec. com. environ. law sect.), Calif. State Bar. Office: Latham and Watkins LLP 633 W Fifth St Ste 4000 Los Angeles CA 90071

HOYE, ROBERT EARL, systems science educator; b. Warwick, R.I., Jan. 12, 1931; s. S. Earl and Alice (Landry) H.; m. Patricia Buswell, Aug. 20, 1955 (dec. May 22, 2002); children: Robert Earl Jr., Joanne D., Peter M., Kathleen B. BA, Providence Coll., 1953; MS, St. John's U., N.Y.C., 1955; PhD, U. Wis., Madison, 1973. Instr. St. John's U., 1953-55; dir. guidance Middleboro (Mass.) Pub. Schs., 1955-56, Rutland (Vt.) Pub. Schs., 1956-57; dean Champlain (Vt.) Coll., 1957-58; supt. Frontier Regional Sch. Dist., Deerfield, Mass., 1958-60; New Eng. dir. Sci. Rsch. Assocs. subs. IBM, Chgo., 1960-65; nat. dir. Learning Systems div. Xerox Corp., N.Y.C., 1965-66; dir. Instrnl. Media Lab. U. Wis., Milw., 1966-73; asst. v.p. U. Louisville, 1974-81, prof. cmty. health Sch. Medicine, 1981-92, prof. urban policy, coord. grad. program in health systems, 1981-95, prof. edn., 1992-95, prof. emeritus, 1995—. Cons. to mgmt., Louisville, 1966—; mem. faculty health svcs. Walden U., 1988—; vis. prof. exec. leadership U. Sarasota, 1995-2001 Author: Index to Computer Based Learning, 1973; co-author: Home Health, 1996; editor Edn. Jour., 1968-73; also articles. Recipient cert. of merit San Diego State U., 1983, Grad. Teaching Excellence award U. Louisville, 1984, gold medal Project Innovation, 1984, Outstanding Faculty Mem. award Walden U., 2000. Fellow Am. Acad. Med. Adminstrs. (diplomate, chmn. editl. bd. 1986-94), Royal Soc. Health (Statesman in Healthcare Adminstrn. award 1992). Democrat. Roman Catholic. Home: 2238 Wynnewood Cir Louisville KY 40222-6342 E-mail: rhoye@waldenu.edu.

HOYER, STENY HAMILTON, congressman; b. NYC, June 14, 1939; s. Steen T. and Jean Baldwin (Slade) H.; m. Judith Elaine Pickett, June 17, 1961 (dec. Feb. 1997); children: Susan, Stefany, Anne. BS, U. Md., 1963; LLB, Georgetown U., 1966. Bar: Md. 1966. Exec. asst. to U.S. senator, 1962-66; assoc. Haislip & Yewell, Marlow Heights, Md., 1966-69, Hoyer & Fannon, District Heights, Md., 1969-81; pvt. practice, 1981-89; mem. U.S. Ho. of Reps. from 5th Md. dist., 1981—, mem. appropriations com., co-chmn. House Dem. steering com., 1989-94; ranking mem. Commn. on Security and Coop. in Europe; ranking mem. HAC; minority whip, 2002—. Mem. Md. Senate, 1966-78, pres., 1975-78, chmn. Prince George's County del., mem. fin., joint budget and audit coms., 1968, chmn. joint commn. on intergovtl. cooperation, 1971. Mem. Md. Bd. Higher Edn., 1978-81; mem. Balt. Council Fgn. Relations; bd. visitors U. Md. Sch. Pub. Affairs Mem. U. Md. Alumni Assn. (trustee), Phi Sigma Alpha, Omicron Delta Kappa, Delta Theta Phi, Sigma Chi. Democrat. Baptist. Home: 40740 Parlett Morgan Rd Mechanicsville MD 20659-4708 Office: US House of Reps 1705 Longworth Hob Washington DC 20515-0001*

HOYLE, SHETINA YEVETTE, librarian; b. Jackson, Tenn., Sept. 21, 1969; d. Alecia Yevette Brown; 1 child, Brandon. BFA, Lambuth U., 1991. Tchr. aide Lambuth Presch., Jackson, 1988—89; sales assoc. Goldsmith's, Jackson, 1988—89; customer svc. rep. Bancorp South, Jackson, 1991—97; libr. Jackson Madison County Libr., Jackson, 1997—. Ch. musician First Bapt. Ch., Jackson, 1989—. Mem.: Jaycees, Delta Sigma Theta. Baptist. Avocations: reading, crafts, piano, aerobics. Home: 1005 N Royal St Jackson TN 38301 Office: Jackson Madison County Libr 433 E Lafayette St Jackson TN 38301

HOYNES, LOUIS LENOIR, JR., lawyer; b. Indpls., Sept. 23, 1935; s. Louis L. and Catharine (Parker) H.; m. Judith E. Kass, Oct. 12, 1958 (div. 1979); children: Thomas M., William D., Ellen B.; m. Virginia Devin, Dec. 9, 1979. AB, Columbia U., 1957; JD cum laude, Harvard U., 1962. Bar: NY 1963, US Supreme Ct. 1967, US Dist. Ct. (so. dist.) NY, US Ct. Appeals (2d, 7th and 9th cirs.). Assoc. Willkie Farr & Gallagher, N.Y.C., 1962-68, ptnr., 1969-90; counsel Nat. League Profl. Baseball Clubs, 1970-90; sr. v.p., gen. counsel Wyeth (formerly) Am. Home Products Corp., 1990-2000; exec. v.p. gen. counsel Am. Home Products Corp. (now Wyeth), 2000—03. Lectr. law Columbia U., N.Y.C., 1982-91; bd. dirs. Cytec Industries Inc., 1994-, US C. of C. Inst. Legal Reform, 2002-; trustee Food and Drug Law Inst., 1994-02. Served to lt. USNR, 1957-59, PTO. Mem. ABA, N.Y. State Bar Assn., Assn. of City of Bar of N.Y., The Assn. Gen. Counsel. Home: 47 Cornwells Beach Rd Sands Point NY 11050-1305

HOYT, CLARK FREELAND, journalist, editor; b. Providence, Nov. 20, 1942; s. Charles Freeland and Maude Leslie (King) H.; m. Jane Ann Hauser, Sept. 30, 1967 (div. Jan. 1978); m. Linda Kauss, Aug. 22, 1988. AB, Columbia Coll., 1964. Research asst. to U.S. Senator, Washington, 1964-66; reporter Lakeland (Fla.) Ledger, 1966-68; politics writer Detroit Free Press, 1968-70; Washington corr. Miami Herald, 1970-73; nat. corr. Knight Newspapers, Washington, 1973-75, news editor Washington bur., 1975-77; bus. editor Detroit Free Press, 1977-79, conv. editor, 1979-80, asst. to exec. editor, 1980-81; mng. editor Wichita Eagle-Beacon, Kans., 1981-85; news editor Washington Bur., Knight-Ridder Newspapers, 1985-87, bur. chief, 1987-93, v.p. news, 1993-99, Washington editor, 1999—. Recipient Pulitzer prize nat. reporting, 1973. Mem. Nat. Press Club (fin. sec., bd. govs. 1975), Gridiron Club. Home: 655 Mine Ridge Rd Great Falls VA 22066-2704 Office: 700 12th St NW Ste 1000 Washington DC 20005-3994

HOYT, COLEMAN WILLIAMS, postal consultant; b. NYC, Nov. 11, 1925; s. Colgate and Muriel (Williams) H.; m. Cecilia Lucia Guarana, Oct. 21, 1972; children: Coleman Williams, Andrew Erskine, Stephen Tecumseh. B of Naval Sci., Tufts U., 1945; BS, Yale U., 1948. With Reader's Digest Assn., Pleasantville, N.Y., 1948-87, mgr. book prodn., 1950-61, mgr. book subscription svc., 1961-63, mgr. subscription svc. RCA Victor Record Club, 1963-65, mgr. corp. distbn., 1965-76, v.p., dir. distbn., 1976-87; pvt. practice cons. Woodstock, Vt., 1987—. Mem. Postmaster Gen.'s Mailers Tech. Adv. Com., 1968—, chmn., 1971-73. Pub. mem. USIA inspection team, Lebanon, 1971; nat. trustee Outward Bound, Inc., 1972-88; trustee Vt. Land Trust, 1988-93, vice chmn., 1989-92. Ensign USNR, 1943-46. Recipient Disting. Svc. award U.S. Postal Svc., 1973, Donald Mumma award Graphics Comm. Assn., 1987, Miles Kimball award Mail Advt. Svc. Assn., 1987. Mem. Mag. Pubs. Assn. (chmn. postal com. 1974-80), Direct Mktg. Assn. (bd. dirs. 1973-79, chmn. govt. affairs com. 1983-86), Pub. Mems. Assn. of Fgn. Svc., Assn. Postal Commerce (bd. dirs. 1982—), Continuity Shippers Assn. (exec. dir. 1997—), Yale Club of N.Y., Squadron A Club, Lakota Club. Republican. Episcopalian. Home and Office: Saddlebow Farm 2351 N Bridgewater Rd Woodstock VT 05091-9670 Office Phone: 802-672-3634.

HOYT, DAVID A., bank executive; Loan officer Union Bank, Calif.; vice chair real estate, capital markets, internat. Wells Fargo & Co., 1997—98, group exec. v.p. wholesale banking, 1998—. Mem. finl svcs. roundtable, mem. adv. coun. U. So. Calif. Lust Ctr. Real Estate. Mem.: Urban Land Inst. Office: Wells Fargo & Co 420 Montgomery St San Francisco CA 94163

HOYT, EARL EDWARD, JR., industrial designer; b. Binghamton, NY, July 16, 1936; s. Earl Edward and Lea (LaRue) H.; m. Bernice Phillips Maseritz, Aug. 20, 1960; children: Earl Edward III, Justin Phillips. B with honors in Indsl. Design, Pratt Inst., 1960. Designer Donald Deskey Assocs., N.Y.C., 1960-65; pres. The Hoyt Group, 1965—. Instr. Sch. Visual Arts, N.Y.C., Pratt Inst., Rutgers Sch. Package Engring.; lectr. in field. Served with U.S. Army, 1954-56. Recipient awards archtl. design concept Am. Inst. Architects, 1964, Package Yr. Package Design Mag., 1970, Grand/Excellence in Design and Quality Soc. Plastic Industy, 1972, design Am. Inst. Graphic Artists Competition, 1st prize splty. design innovation-1st prize household products-1st prize communication excellence N.J. chpt. Packaging Inst. USA, 1979, package yr. Food and Drug Packaging Mag., 1978, 80, Jupiter Engring. excellence in design Western Plastics Exposition, 1980, package design excellence Clio, 1978, 81, 87, outstanding packaging achievement NJ Packaging Execs. Club, 1982-83, 86 (best of show/package yr.). Mem. Indsl. Designers Soc. Am. Republican. Achievements include patents in field. Avocations: watercolor artist, skiing, fishing, outdoor activities, guitar. Home: 318 Blue Mountain Lake East Stroudsburg PA 18301 Fax: 570-476-4109. Business E-Mail: thehoytgroup@pennswoods.net.

HOYT, HERBERT AUSTIN AIKINS, television producer; b. Buffalo, June 20, 1937; s. John Davidson Hill and Amie Dean (Aikins) Hoyt. BA, Yale Univ., 1959. Reporter Niagara Falls Gazette, NY, 1963-64; prodr., exec. prodr. WGBH Ednl. Found., Boston, 1965—2003; with Austin Hoyt Prodns., 2003—. Prodr. TV programs including The Advocates, 1969-74; Enterprise: The Wildcatter, 1981; Vietnam: A Television History, Tet 1968; L.B.J. Goes to War, 1964-65, (Emmy, Writers Guild of Am. awards); Reagan's New Federalism: Shift or Shaft?, 1983; The Nuclear Age, 1989; exec. prodr. Zoom, 1974-75; In Search of the Real America, 1975-78; Frontline Spl. Report: Crisis in Central America, 1985, Mexico, 1988; Korea: The Unknown War, 1990; Am. Experience: Eisenhower, 1993, The Windsors, 1994, 2002, The Churchills, 1996; American Experience: Carnegie, The Richest Man in the World, 1997, Reagan, 1998 (Peabody award), MacArthur, 1999 (Emmy award), PBS Millennium, 2000, American Experience: Chgo. City of the Century, 2003, Victory in the Pacific, 2005. Mem.: Somerset Club (Boston), Yale Club (N.Y.C.). Home: 11 Wright St #3 Cambridge MA 02138 Office: 90 Windom St #5 Boston MA 02134 Office Phone: 617-787-9990. Personal E-mail: austinhoyt@fastmail.fm.

HOYT, JAMES, educator; b. L.A., Mar. 26, 1923; s. James and Mabel Ruth (Lockard) Hoyt; m. Elizabeth Jean McKeen, July 6, 1952; children: Jeremy, Joshua. AB, U. Mich., 1945; MA, U. Calif., 1951, PhD, 1962; DLitt, Sejong U., 1996. Spl. officer U.S. Embassies, China, 1954—56; dir. Am. Cultural Ctrs., Hiroshima, Japan, Niigata, Japan, 1957—62; cultural affairs officer U.S. Embassy, Bolivia, 1962—64, Mexico City, 1965—67; desk officer for Japan, Korea, Micronesia, Washington, 1967—68; co-chmn. for Latin Am., Mex. and Asia Fgn. Svc. Inst., Arlington, Va., 1968—69; spl. asst. to amb. U.S. Embassy, Tokyo, 1969—72, cultural attache Manila, Philippines, 1972—76, Seoul, 1977—83; prof. Sejong U., 1984—86. Chmn. bd. Fulbright Commn., 1969—83; prof. Western Wash. U., Skagit Valley Coll., U. Hawaii, Acad. of Korean Studies, 1986—. Author: Songs of the Dragons, 1971, History of Classical Korean Literature, 2000. Maj. USAR, 1942—58. Fellow: China Inst.; mem.: Royal Asiatic Soc., Korean Br. (pres. 1981—82). Avocation: Japanese gardening. Home: 102 Channel Hts Way Friday Harbor WA 98250

HOYT, JAMES LAWRENCE, journalism educator, writer; b. Wausau, Wis., July 18, 1943; s. Lawrence Beryl and Eleanor (Kischel) H.; m. Cheryl Johannes, July 23, 1966; children: Randall James, Rebecca Cheryl, Diane Caroline. BS, U. Wis., 1965, MS, 1967, PhD, 1970; postgrad., U. Pa., 1967-68. Reporter Sta. WTMJ-TV, Milw., 1965-67; prof. journalism Ind. U., Bloomington, 1970-73; writer, editor NBC News, Washington, 1972; prof. journalism U. Wis., Madison, 1973—; dir. U. Wis. Sch. Journalism, Madison, 1981-91. Chmn. athletic bd., faculty rep. NACC Big Ten Conf. Western Collegiate Hockey Assn., U. Wis., Madison, 1991-2001. Author: Mass Media in Perspective, 1984, Writing News for Broadcast, 1994; contbr. articles to profl. jours. Recipient Carol Brewer award Wis. Associated Press, 1996. Mem. Assn. for Edn. in Journalism and Mass Comm. (Disting. Broadcast Educator 2002), Radio-TV News Dirs. Assn., Broadcast Edn. Assn., Internat. Radio-TV Soc. (Frank Stanton fellow 2001). Methodist. Avocation: hockey. Home: 4709 Fond Du Lac Trl Madison WI 53705-4812 Office: U Wis Sch Journalism 821 University Ave Madison WI 53706-1412 Business E-Mail: jlhoyt@wisc.edu.

HOYT, JOHN ARTHUR, cultural organization administrator, minister; b. Marietta, Ohio, Mar. 30, 1932; s. Claremont Earl and Margaret Adeline (Hawkins) H.; m. Gertrude Ellen Mohnkern, June 7, 1957; children: Margaret Rose, Karen Elizabeth, Anne Christine, Julie Kay. BA, Rio Grande Coll., 1954, DD, 1968; MDiv, Colgate Rochester Div. Sch., 1958; Dr honoris causa, U. Bucharest, Romania, 1995; LHD (hon.), St. Thomas U., Miami, Fla., 1998, U. St. Petersburg, Russia, 1997. Ordained to ministry Baptist Ch., 1957; pastor Allen Park (Mich.) Bapt. Ch., 1958-60, First Presbyn. Ch., Leroy, N.Y., 1960-64; sr. minister Drayton Ave. Presbyn. Ch., Ferndale, Mich., 1964-68, First Presbyn. Ch., Fort Wayne, Ind., 1968-70; pres. Humane Soc. U.S., Washington, 1970-91, chief exec., 1992-97; pres. emeritus, 1997—; pres. Humane Soc. Internat., Washington, 1991-94; pres., dir. Humane Soc. of Can., Toronto, 1994-98; vice chmn. bd. dirs. EarthKind Internat., Washington, London, 1991-98; pres. Earthkind, U.S., Washington, 1994-97. Author: Animals in Peril: How "Sustainable Use" is Wiping Out the World's Wildlife, 1994. Pres. Nat. Assn. Humane and Environ. Edn., East Haddam, Conn., 1970-94, chmn. bd. dirs. 1973-95; trustee Rio Grande (Ohio) Coll., 1979-86, Lake Erie Coll., Painesville, Ohio, 1986-88; bd. dirs. The Am. Fondouk, Boston, 1986-97, Earth Day 1990, 1989-90, Global Tomorrow Coalition, 1989-94; pres. World Soc. for Protection of Animals, London, 1986-90, v.p., 1990-98; dir. Ctr. Respect Life and Environment, Washington, 1986-; dir. Internat. Ctr. Earth Concerns, Calif., 1994-; mem. Earth Charter Commn.; v.p. Internat. Devel. Conf., Washington, 1997-99, 01-03; dir. Bear Castle Property Owners Assn., Bumpbass, Va., 2001—; hon. v.p. Inst. for Animals and Society, Balt., 2004-. Recipient Disting. Alumnus award Rio Grande Coll., Founders award for Humane Excellence ASPCA, 1991, George T. Angell Humanitarian award Mass. SPCA, 1992, Pres.'s Disting. Ministry award Sch. of Theology at Claremont, Calif., 1995, Reverence for Life Commendation Albert Schwertzer Inst. for the Humanities, 1998. Home: 320 Bear Castle Dr Bumpass VA 23024-4925 Office: Humane Soc US 2100 L St NW Ste 500 Washington DC 20037-1596 Office Phone: 540-894-4479.

HOYT, KENNETH BOYD, social studies educator, writer; b. Cherokee, Iowa, July 13, 1924; s. Paul Fuller and Mary Helen (Tinker) H.; m. Phyllis June Howland, May 25, 1946; children: Andrew Paul, Roger Alan, Elinore Jane. BS, U. Md., 1948; MA, George Washington U., 1950; PhD, U. Minn., 1954; Ed.D. (hon.), Crete Coll., 1981. Tchr., counselor Northeast (Md.) High Sch., 1948-49; dir. guidance Westminster (Md.) High Sch., 1949-50; tchg. asst. U. Minn., 1950-51, instr. ednl. psychology, 1951-54; asst. prof. U. Iowa, Iowa City, 1954-57, assoc. prof., 1957-60, prof. edn., 1961-69; dir. Splty. Oriented Student Research Program, prof. edn. U. Md., Silver Spring, 1969-74; dir. office career edn. U.S. Office Edn., 1974-82; disting. vis. scholar Embry Riddle Aero. U., 1982-84; Univ. Disting. prof. edn. Kans. State U., 1984—2003; dir. counseling high skills vo-tech career options program Kansas State U., 1993-98, prof. emeritus, 2003—. Cons. Ordnance Civilian Personnel Agy., 1954-60, Iowa Dept. Pub. Instrn., 1954-69, U.S. Dept. Labor, 1956-68, 65—, U.S. Office Edn., 1958—, Nat. Inst. Edn., 1973—. Author: (with L.A. Van Dyke) The Drop-Out Problem in Iowa High Schools, 1958, (with C.P. Froehlich) Guidance Testing, 1960, Selecting Employees for Developmental Opportunites and Guidance Services; Suggested Policies for Iowa Schools, 1963, Career Education: Contributions to an Evolving Concept, 1976, Career Education: Where It Is and Where It Is Going, 1981; co-author: Career Education: What It Is and How To Do It, 1972, Career Education and the Elementary School Teacher, 1973, Career Education in the Middle Junior High School, 1973, Career Education for Gifted and Talented Students, 1974, Career Education in the High School, 1977, Counseling for High Skills, 2001; Editor: Counselor Education and Supervision, 1961-65; Mem. editorial bd.: Personnel and Guidance Jour, 1960-63; Contbr. articles to profl. jours. Served with AUS, 1943—46. Fellow APA (divsn. 17); mem. Am. Counseling Assn. (pres. 1966-67, Arthur Hitchcock Outstanding Disting. Profl. Svc. award, 1994), Am. Vocat. Assn. (Outstanding Svc. award 1972), Assn. Counselor Edn. and Supervision (Disting. Svc. award 1965, Outstanding Career award 1990), Nat. Career Devel. Assn. (Eminent Career award 1981, pres. elect 1991-92, pres. 1992-93), Am. Sch. Counselors Assn., Am. Ednl. Rsch. Assn., Nat. Assn. for Industry Edn. Cooperation (vice-chmn. 1992—), Phi Delta Kappa. Home: 149 N Dartmouth Dr Manhattan KS 66503-3021 Office: Kans State U Coll of Edn 369 Bluemont Hall Manhattan KS 66506-5300 Address: 13816 Sheradan Ave Urbandale IA 50323 Office Phone: 785-532-5889. Business E-Mail: khoyt@isu.edu.

HOYT, MARY FINCH, writer, media consultant, retired federal official; b. Calif. 2 children. Free-lance mag. writer, speechwriter, formerly with Ladies' Home Jour. mag.; info. officer Peace Corps; pres. sec. to Mrs. Edmund Muskie, 1968; pres. sec. to Mrs. George McGovern, 1972; former ptnr. McClure, Schultz and Hoyt (pub. rels.).; press sec. to Mrs. Rosalynn Carter and East Wing coord. The White House, Washington, 1977-81; dir. communications Nat. Trust for Hist. Preservation, Washington, 1989-93; author, editor, media cons., 1993—. Author: American Women of the Space Age, 1966; author: (with Eleanor McGovern) Uphill: A Personal Story, 1974; author: East Wing: Politics, the Press and a First Lady, 2001. Mem. Presdl. Commn., 1977. Democrat.

HOYT, MONT POWELL, lawyer; b. Oklahoma City, Apr. 3, 1940; s. Lester Dean and Paula (Powell) H.; m. Alice Nathalie Ryan, June 15, 1974; children: Mont Powell Jr., Kathleen, Michael, Caroline. BA, Northwestern U., 1962; JD, Okla. Law Sch., 1965; M in Comparative Law, U. Chgo., 1968. Bar: Okla. 1965, Tex. 1968. Law clk. U.S. Dist. Ct., Oklahoma City, 1965; stagiaire to French advocat Paris, 1967-68; assoc. Baker & Botts, Houston, 1968-75, ptnr., 1975-92; shareholder Verner, Liipfert, Bernhard, McPherson & Hand, Houston, 1993-94; ptnr. Hughes & Luce, Houston, 1994-2001, Shook, Hardy & Bacon, Houston, 2001—04, Munsch, Hardt, Kopf & Harr P.C., Houston, 2004—. Adj. prof. law U. Houston, 1970—76; sec. Houston Com. Fgn. Rels., 1993—; hon. consul gen. for Malaysia in Tex., 2003—. Contbr. articles to profl. jours. Bd. dirs. French Am. Found., N.Y.C., 1979-85, Mexican Cultural Inst., 1991-95, Fgn. Policy Assn., 1991-93; mem. Latin Am. adv. bd. Americas Soc., 1992—. Mem.: ABA (chmn. sect. internat. law and practice 1984—85), InterAm. C. of C. (bd. dirs. 1991—99, chmn. 1996—98), German Am. C. of C. (bd. dirs. 1978—94), Am. Arbitration Assn., Am. Soc. Internat. Law, Am. Law Inst., Internat. Bar Assn. (coun. sect. of energy and nat. resources law 1983—86), Coun. on Fgn. Rels. (chmn. Houston 1991—92), U. Chgo. Law Sch. Alumni Assn. (v.p. 1990—91), Houston Internat. Arbitration Club, Met. Club (Washington), Houston Country Club. Avocations: spanish language study, running, international affairs, amateur radio. Office: PO Box 131026 Houston TX 77219-1026 E-mail: mhoyt1@houston.rr.com.

HOYT, ROBERT F., lawyer; b. Sept. 8, 1964; BS with honors, Cornell Univ., 1986; MA, JD cum laude, Univ. Pa., 1989. Bar: Pa. 1990, DC 1991. Law clk. Judge Herbert P. Wilkins, Supreme Judicial Ct. Mass., 1989—90; ptnr., vice chmn. Securities dept., mem. mgmt. com. Wilmer Cutler Pickering Hale & Dorr, Washington. Office: Wilmer Cutler Pickering Hale & Dorr 2445 M St NW Washington DC 20037 Office Phone: 202-663-6193. Office Fax: 202-663-6363. Business E-Mail: robert.hoyt@wilmerhale.com.

HOYT, ROGER FRANKLIN, physicist; b. Evergreen Park, Ill., Aug. 16, 1949; s. William Abe and Betty Jane H.; m. Jennifer Ann, June 24, 1978; children: Elizabeth, David. BS, U. Ill., Champaign/Urbana, 1971; MS, U. Calif., San Diego, 1975, PhD, 1978. Rsch. staff IBM, San Jose, 1982-94, mgr./program dir., 1994—. Rev. panel mem Nat. Rsch. Coun., Washington, 1992—98. Mem. editl. bd. Jour. Info. Storage and Processing, 1997—2003, IEEE Transactions on Magnetics, 2003—, contbg. author Magnetic Disk Drive, 1997—; mem. editl. bd.: Micro + Nanosystems and Information Storage + Processing Systems, 2003—. Vestry mem. Episcopal Ch. Almaden, Calif., 1986-89; storage chmn., Nat. Electronics Initiative, 1996-; bd. dirs. Santa Theresa Urban Mission, San Jose, 2003—. Corp. U.S. Army, 1971—78. Decorated Army Commendation medal. Fellow: IEEE (dir. San Francisco coun. 1996—97, editor-in-chief IEEE press 1997—98, 3d Millennium medal 2000); mem.: Magestic Disk Heritage Ctr. (bd. mem.), IBM Acad. of Tech., N.Y. Acad. Scis., Am. Phys. Soc. Republican. Episcopalian. Achievements include patents for inventions in field. Office Phone: 408-997-1826. E-mail: roger.hoyt@sbcglobal.net.

HOZESKI, BRUCE WILLIAM, English language and literature educator; b. Grand Rapids, Mich., Feb. 28, 1941; s. Gerard Thadeus and Dorothy Elizabeth (Platschore) H.; m. Kathleen Antoinette Tuma, Sept. 9, 1967; 1 child, Alison Michelle Dunch. AA, St. Peter's Coll., Balt., 1961; BA, Aquinas Coll., 1964; MA, Mich. State U., 1966, PhD, 1969. Instr. Lansing (Mich.) Community Coll., 1967-69; grad. asst. Mich. State U., East Lansing, 1964-69; from asst. prof. to prof. English Ball State U., Muncie, Ind., 1969—, dir. grad. programs in English, 1998—2001, chair dept. English, 2004—. Author: Hildegard of Bingen's Scivias, 1986, Hildegard of Bingen's Liber Vitae Meritorum, 1993, Hildegard of Bingen: The Book of the Rewards of Life, 1997, Hildegard von Bingen's Mystical Visions, 1998, Hildegard's Healing Plants: From Her Medieval Classic Physica, 2001; bibliographer: (with Lorrayne Y. Baird-Lange and Bege K. Bowers) An Annotated Chaucer Bibliography, 1989-92, Studies in the Age of Chaucer; contbr. An Annotated Chaucer Bibliography, 1993—, Studies in the Age of Chaucer; mem. editl. bd. Classical and Modern Lit., A. Quar., 1988—; editor-in-chief, mng. editor Ball State U. Forum, 1984-90; contbr. chpts. to books, articles to profl. jours. Mem. Medieval Acad. Am., Early English Text Soc., New Chaucer Soc., The Medieval and Renaissance Drama Soc., Medieval Assn. Midwest (editor 1982-85, v.p. 2000-01, pres. 2001-02), Internat. Soc. Hildegard (founder, exec. sec. 1989—, pres. 1984-89, treas. 2001—), Lambda Iota (exec. sec., treas. 1995—), Phi Kappa Phi, Omicron Delta Kappa. Roman Catholic. Avocations: tennis, flower gardening. Home: 7404 W Augusta Blvd Yorktown IN 47396-9353 Office: Ball State U Dept English 2000 W University Ave Muncie IN 47306-0460 Office Phone: 765-285-8584. Business E-Mail: bhozeski@bsu.edu.

HOZUMI, MOTOO, medical educator, researcher; b. Fukushima, Japan, Mar. 12, 1933; s. Akiine and Fumi Hozumi; m. Sakiko Wakabayashi, May 4, 1963; children: Yuko, Masamichi, Ayako. BSc, Tokyo U. Edn., 1956, MSc, 1958, Dsc, 1961. Rsch. mem. Nat. Cancer Ctr. Rsch. Inst., Tokyo, 1962-64, chief ctrl. lab., 1964-75; dir. dept. chemotherapy Saitama (Japan) Cancer Ctr. Rsch. Inst., 1975-93, dir., 1990-93; spl. rsch. Saitama (Japan) Cancer Ctr., 1993-96. Rsch. mem. Roswell Park Meml. Inst., Buffalo, N.Y., 1965-67; vis. prof. Showa U. Med. Sch., Tokyo, 1988-2001; cons. Japan Immunoresearch Inst., Takasaki, Japan, 1993-98. Author: Advances in Cancer Research, 1983, Ciba Foundation Symposium, 1990, Status of Differentiation Therapy, 1991, (rev. jour.) CRC Critical Rev. Oncol./Hematol., 1985, Internat. Jour. Hematology, 1998. Recipient Princess Takamatsu Cancer Rsch. Found. prize, 1974. Mem. AAAS, Japanese Cancer Assn. (councilor 1973-98, emeritus mem. 1999—), Japan Hematol. Soc. (councilor 1992-98, meritorious mem. 1999—), Am. Assn. for Cancer Rsch. Avocation: music. Home: 12-288 Fukasaku Minuma Saitama 337-0003 Japan Personal E-mail: hozumim@olive.ocn.ne.jp.

HRABAL, ANTONIN, physician, educator; b. Prilepy, Kromeriz, Czech Republic, May 21, 1957; s. Bedrich and Stepanka (Von Larisch) H. MD, Charles U., Prague, Czech Republic, 1982, PhD, 1992; DSc, U. San Jose, Costa Rica, 1998. Med. diplomate. Rschr. Charles U., Prague, 1976-88, physician, tchr., 1985-92; physician, rschr. Inst. Hippokrates, 1992-99; tchr. Palacki U., Olomouc, Czech Republic, 1989-97, 99, U. Ctr. Inst. Hippokrates, 1997—. Chmn. Inst. Hippokrates, 1992-99; head physician U. Hosp., 1995-99; founder Found. Nadace Hippokrates, 1997-99; head rsch. Univ. Ctr., 1998-99. Mem. N.Y. Acad. Scis. Achievements include inventor of regeneration of tissues by deep stimulation through interference of electric and magnetic fields; deep brain stimulation; special immunomodulation diagnostic and therapeutic methodology therapy of autoimmune diseases, anti-aging methodology/telomeraza and hormone replacement. Home: 45053 Casa De Mariposa Indian Wells CA 92210 Personal E-mail: professorhrabal@yahoo.com.

HRABUSA, JOHN T., human resources specialist, food products executive; m. Sue Hrabusa; 4 children. BS in Bus. Adminstrn., U. Akron. Various positions in dist. mgmt. and human resource mgmt. Sherwin Williams Co.; v.p. human resources Office Depot, Inc., Publix Super Markets, Inc., Lakeland, Fla., 2004—, sr. v.p. human resources and public affairs, 2005—. Bd. dirs. James Madison Inst. Office: Publix Super Markets Inc 3300 Publix Corp Pkwy Lakeland FL 33811 Office Phone: 863-688-1188. Office Fax: 863-284-5532.*

HRACHOVINA, FREDERICK VINCENT, osteopath, physician, surgeon; b. St. Paul, Minn., Sept. 2, 1926; s. Vincent Frank and Beatrice (Funda) H.; m. Joan Halverson, July 2, 1955 BA in Chemistry, Macalester Coll., St. Paul, 1948; DO, Kirksville Coll. Osteo. Med., Mo., 1956. Chemist Mpls.-St. Paul area, 1948-51; intern Clare Gen. Osteo. Hosp., Mich., 1956-57; pvt. practice Mpls. Minn., 1957-84; asst. prof. osteo. principles and practices Nova Southeastern U. Coll. Osteo. Medicine, Ft. Lauderdale, Fla., 1985-88; founder, pres. Physician Placement Svc., Fla. and Minn., 1973—; med. dir. Associated Bioscience, Inc., Mpls., 1992, Sera-Tec Biologicals Inc., Jacksonville, Fla., 1993-94; staff physician Allegheny Biologicals, Inc., Jacksonville, 1995-96; med. dir. Serologicals, Jacksonville, 1996; med. ins. examiner Hooper Holmes, Inc., St. Petersburg, Ft. Myers, Fla., 1997—; ins. med. examiner Examination Mgmt. Svcs., Inc., Tampa, Ft. Myers, Fla., 1998—. Bd. dirs. Internat. Acad. Osteopathics Medicine; lectr. Internat. Acad. Osteo. Medicine, Brussels, 1984; mem. Northlands Regional Med. Program, Inc., 1971—73, Health Svcs. Devel. Com., Regional Adv. Group; founder, faculty advisor Fla. Acad. Osteopathy Student Assn., Nova Southeastern U. Coll. Osteo. Medicine, Ft. Lauderdale, Fla., 1987; staff physician Centeon Bio-Svcs. Plasma Corp., St. Paul, 1998; v.p. med. rels., mem. adv. bd. Sinofresh Labs., Venice, Fla., 2002. Author: Microscopic Anatomy, 1952; Methods of Development of New Osteopathic Medical Colleges in the Next Millennium, 1977; contbr. articles to profl. jours.; patent pending in field. Mem. Crow Wing County (Minn.) Portage-Crooked Lake Preservation Soc., 1977—, Sr. Citizen Assn., Garrison, Minn., 1991—, Deerwood Civic and Commerce Assn., Deerwood, Minn., 1992—; chmn. street lights program Pinebrook South, Venice, Fla. Grantee Smith Kline & French Labs., 1973, 89, Hill Labs, Gusman Med. Equipment, 1987. Mem. Am. Coll. Osteo. Family Practice (life), Am. Osteo. Assn. (life, coun. fed. health programs, drug enforcement adminstrn. prescribers working com. 1974-75), Am. Acad. Osteopathy (life), Am. Coll. Sr. Osteo. Medicine Physicians and Surgeons, Inc. (pres., treas., bd. dirs., registered agt.), Am. Assn. Sr. Physicians, Am. Osteo. Acad. Sports Medicine (life), Am. Blood Resources Assn., Am. Assn. Blood Banks, Gulf Coast Hibiscus Soc. (presdl. liason to Venice C. of C. 1996), Minn. Osteo. Assn. (life, pres. 1965-66, exec. dir. 1966-74, pub. rels. dir. 1974-75), Assn. Osteo. State Exec. Dirs. (pres. 1970-71, dir. 1971-74, founder nat. legis. sem. 1974), Am. Coll. Osteopathic Family Practice (life) (lectr. Mo. soc.), Fla. Acad. Osteopathy (trustee, chmn. audit and membership com.), Fla. Osteo Found. (v.p.), Ga. Osteo. Med. Assn. (chmn. Olympic com. 1995-96), Fla Osteo. Med. Assn. (Dade county chpt. chmn. osteo. lit. com., conv. chmn. dist. two 1994, dist. #7 Sarasota County, chmn. legis. com. dist. 11, v.p. dist. 7, long range planning com., mem. com., chmn. 175th ann. founder party, dist. v.p. mktg., chmn. mktg. com.), Fla. Osteo. Med. Assn. (dist. 5, 7, 11), Internat. Acad. Osteo. Medicine (trustee), Minn. Gymnastic Assn. (founder Floor Exercise 1962-72), Fla. Acad. Osteopathy Student Assn. at Southeastern Coll. Osteo. Medicine (originator, advisor), Dade-Broward Osteo. Med. County Soc., Duval County Osteo. Soc., Sarasota County Osteo. Soc., Twin-City Model A Ford Club, Pierce Arrow Soc. (sec. Fla. region 1988, news reporter Arrow Driver Midwest region, Mpls., life, founder Midwest region, 1983, dir./treas., 1983-84, gen. chmn. Midwest region swapmeet, Golden Valley, Minn., 1990, nat. dir. 1983-84, contbr. articles to Arrow Jour.), Venice C. of C. (mem. membership com., mem. amb. com.), Cadillac LaSalle Club (founder 1978, treas. North Star region 1978-83), Classic Car Club Am. (life, membership chmn. Minn. upper midwest region 1977, sec. 1978, Gold Coast region-Fla.), Antique Auto Club. Am. (life, news reporter St. Paul chpt., Minn. region, Ft. Lauderdale region, Jacksonville region, Venice chpt., Lemon Bay region, judge at nat. meet Venice, Fla. 1997), Breakfast Club Mpls., Y.E.S. Club 1st Nat. Bank Deerwood (Minn.), Scottish Rite, Valley of St. Paul, Lions (Bay Lake, Minn. del. to internat. conv., Miami, Fla., 1989), Optimist Club (dir. Mpls. 1959-62, 69-72, pres. 1970-71, gen. chmn. fl. exercise Olympic gymnastic program 1959-65), Masons (life, Capitol City #217, St. Paul), Shriners (life mem. Zuhrah Shrine Temple, Mpls., fund raising com.), Phi Sigma Gamma (life, nat. pres. 1987-89, pres. grand coun. and found. 1987-89, grand coun. advisor and chmn. bd.), Arlington Shrine Club (Jacksonville), Cummer Gallery of Art and Gardens (Jacksonville), Arlington Preservation Soc. (Jacksonville), Venice Shrine Club (Fla.), Aadzuhma Shrine Club (Brainerd, Minn.), Manasota Fossil Club, Airstream Fla. Suncoast Club, Wally Byam Caravan Club, Internat. Airstream Inc. Home: 1238 Lucaya Ave Venice FL 34285-6407

HRICAK, HEDVIG, radiologist; came to U.S., 1972; MD, U. Zagreb, 1970; DMS, Karolinska Inst., 1992; Dr. (hon.), Ludwig Maximilion U., 2005. Diplomate Am. Bd. Radiology 1978. Intern in radiology Hosp. M. Stojanovic, Zagreb, 1971—72; resident in radiology St. Joseph Mercy Hosp., Pontiac, Mich., 1974—77; fellow in diagnostic radiology Henry Ford Hosp., Detroit, sr. staff diagnostic radiology, 1978—81; asst. clin. prof. diagnostic radiology U. Mich., Ann Arbor, 1979—81; from asst. prof. to assoc. prof. U. Calif., San Francisco, 1982—86, prof. radiology, urology, radiation oncology, ob-gyn., 1986—99; chief abdominal sect. dept. radiology U. Calif. Med Ctr., San Francisco, 1982—2000; chmn. dept. radiology Meml. Sloan-Kettering Cancer Ctr., NY, 1999—; prof. radiology Weill Med. Coll. Cornell U., NY, 2000—. Hon. prof. U. Zagreb, 1997; vis. prof. ovr 30 instns. Author 20 books in field; assoc. editor, Jour. of Magnetic Resonance Imaging, 2001—, Radiology, 1998—, Jour. of Women's Imaging, 1996—, others; contbr. more than 280 articles to sci. and profl. jours. Recipient Marie Curie award, Soc. Women in Radiology, 2002, Beclere medal, 2005; grantee numerous grants in field, including NIH, Nat. Cancer Inst., Am. Cancer Soc., Dept. of Def.;, numerous hon. lectureships. Fellow Am. Coll. Radiology, Internat. Soc. Magnetic Resonance in Medicine (gold medal 2003), Soc. Uroradiology (corrs. mem., pres. 2001-03); mem. Acad. Radiology Rsch. (bd. dirs. 1997—), Radiol. Soc. N.Am. (chmn. pub. info. adv. bd. 1997-2002, bd. dirs. 2003—), Soc. for the Advancement of Women's Imaging (pres. 1997-99), Calif. Acad. Medicine (pres. 1999), Croation Acad. Sci. and Art (hon.), German, Radiol. Soc. (hon.), German Roentgen Soc. (hon.) Brit. Inst. Radiologists (hon.), Inst. of Medicine. E-mail: hricakh@mskcc.org.

HRINAK, DONNA JEAN, lawyer, former ambassador; b. Sewickley, Pa., Mar. 28, 1951; d. John and Mary (Pukach) H.; m. Gabino (Lou) Flores, July 15, 1977; 1 child, Wyatt A. Flores. Student, George Washington U., 1971; BA, Mich. State U., 1972; Student, U. Notre Dame, 1973—74. Dep. prin. officer Am. Embassy, Mexico City, 1974—76, Warsaw, 1977-79, narcotics affairs officer Bogota, Colombia, 1979-81; regional affairs officer for C.Am. US Dept. State, Washington, 1982-84; dep. prin. officer U.S. Consultate Gen., Sao Paulo, Brazil, 1984-87; political counselor Am. Embassy, Caracas, Venezuela, 1987—89, dep. chief of mission Teguciagalpa, Honduras, 1989-91; dep. asst. sec. for inter-Am. affairs US Dept. State, Washington, 1991-93; coord. for policy Miami Summit of Ams., 1994; amb. to Dominican Republic US Dept. State, Santo Domingo, 1994—98, amb. to Bolivia La Paz, 1998—2000, amb. to Venezuela Caracas, 2000—02, amb. to Brazil Brasilia, 2002—04; sr. counselor, internat. trade & govt. affairs Steel Hector & Davis LLP, Miami, 2004—. Named one of Ams. Ten Outstanding Young Working Women, Glamour mag., 1985. Mem. Am. Fgn. Svc. Assn., Exec. Women in Govt., Inter-Am. Dialogue Fgn. Policy Assn. Avocations: reading mysteries, playing tennis, watching baseball. Office: Steel Hector & Davis LLP 200 S Biscayne Blvd Miami FL 33131-2398 E-mail: dhrinak@steelhector.com.

HRINCZENKO, BORYS WALTER, oncologist, hematologist, medical educator, medical researcher, consultant; s. Walter and Maria Hrinczenko; m. Helena Teresa Marcyniak, Sept. 5, 1992; 1 child, Nicholas. BA magna cum laude, NYU, N.Y.C., 1975; PhD, U. Kans., Lawrence, 1983; MD, SUNY, Bklyn., 1992. Diplomate Nat. Bd. of Med. Examiners, 1993, Am. Bd. of Internal Medicine, 2000, sub speciality of hematology Am. Bd. of Internal Medicine, 2004, subspecialty hematology Am. Bd. Internal Medicine, 2004, lic. physician Minn., 1993, Ala., 2000, Ohio, 2004. Rsch. assoc. U. Chgo., 1983—85; project supr. Nat. Starch & Chem. Co., Bridgewater, NJ, 1985—88; med. intern & resident Mayo Clinic, Rochester, Minn., 1992—95; hematology/oncology fellow NIH, Bethesda, Md., 1995—98, clin. rsch. assoc., 1998—2000; asst. prof. of medicine U. Ala., Birmingham, 2000—04; asst. prof. medicine Case We. Res. U., Cleve., 2005—. Cons. TheraMed, Inc., Rockville, Md., 2000, Network for Oncology Comm. and Rsch., Atlanta, 2003; oncology investigator rsch. adv. bd. Amgen, Inc., Thousand Oaks, Calif., 2003; mem. editl. bd., sci. manuscript reviewer Foxwell Davies & Co., London, 2003; med. adv. bd. Physicians Consulting Network, Mt. Arlington, NJ, 2003; spkr. rep. Millennium Pharms., Inc., Boston, 2003; mem. Clin. Adv. Panel, West Orange, NJ, 2003. Contbr. articles to profl. jours. Named one of America's Top Physicians, Consumer's Rsch. Coun. of Am., 2003; recipient Caducean Soc., NYU, 1973, NYU Coat of Arms Soc., 1974, Founder's Day award, 1975; NY State Regents scholarship, NY Bd. of Edn., 1971, Berger Scholarship in Chemistry, U. Kans., 1978. Mem.: ACP, AMA, Am. Chem. Soc., N.Y. Acad. of Sci., Am. Soc. of Clin. Oncology, Am. Soc. of Hematology, Phi Lambda Upsilon. Achievements include the first to discover anomalous dendritic cell function in sickle cell disease; the first to outline the unusual purine biochemical catabolic process in sickle cell disease and explored potential therpeutic targets; the first to show that platelets from sickle cell disease patients display an atypical response to nitric oxide drugs; research in applied biomedical imaging techniques and discovered abnormal mitochondrial function in the skeletal muscle of sickle cell disease patients; discovered useful biomarkers of oxidative stress in sickle cell disease that assessed disease severity and response to therapy. Avocations: photography, chess, piano, ping pong/table tennis. Home: 160 Herrmann Dr Avon Lake OH 44012-1739

HRISTOVA, KRASSIMIRA RADOYKOVA, microbiologist, researcher; b. Sofia, Bulgaria, Feb. 17, 1964; d. Radoiko Gerov and Iordanka Asenova Hristov; m. Ivaylo Iliev Hristov, Mar. 1, 1987; 1 child, Radostina. MS with great distinction, Sofia U., 1987, PhD, 1993. Microbiologist Inst. Molecular Biology, Bulgarian Acad. Scis., Sofia, 1993-94; rsch. assoc. Nat. Bank for Indsl. Microorganisms and Cell Cultures, Sofia, 1994-98, mem. adv. bd.; postdoctoral rsch. assoc. U. Ill., Urbana-Champaign, 1998-2000, U. Calif., Davis, 2000—. Contbg. author: Bulgarian Antarctic Research, 1996; contbr. articles to sci. jours., including Environ. Microbiology, Applied and Environ. Microbiology, Biotech. and Biotech. Equipment. Postgrad. scholar Russian Fed. Govt., 1991, lab. scholar FEMS, Osnabruck, Germany, 1992; fellow UNESCO, Budapest, Hungary, 1995, Govt. of Que. fellow U. Sherbrooke, 1997. Mem. AAAS, Am. Soc. for Microbiology, Internat. Soc. for Microbial Ecology, Union Scientists in Bulgaria, Bulgarian Soc. for Microbiology. Office: U Calif LAWR Dept One Shields Ave Davis CA 95616 Fax: 530 752-1552. E-mail: krhristova@ucdavis.edu.

HRITZ, GEORGE F., lawyer; b. Hyde Park, NY, Aug. 28, 1948; s. George F. and Margaret M. (Callahan) H.; m. Mary Elizabeth Noonan; 1 child, Amelia C. Hritz. AB, Princeton U., 1969; JD, Columbia U., 1973. Bar: NY 1974, DC 1978, U.S. Supreme Ct. 1979. Law clk. U.S. Dist. Ct. (ea. dist.) NY, NYC, 1973; assoc. Cravath, Swaine & Moore, NYC, 1974-77; counsel U.S. Senate Select Com. Ethics Korean Inquiry, Washington, 1977-78; ptnr. Moore & Foster, Washington, 1978-80, Davis, Weber & Edwards, NYC, 1980-2000; assoc. ind. counsel Washington, 1986-89; ptnr. Hogan & Hartson, LLP, NYC, 2000—. Mem. adv. com. U.S. Dist. Ct. (ea. dist.) NY, 1990—. Trustee Fed. Bar Found., 1998-2004; bd. dirs. exec. com. Internat. Rescue Com., 1982—; chmn. planning bd. Village of Sleepy Hollow, NY, 1993-97; bd. dirs. exec. com. Princeton in Africa, 2000—, pres., 2004—. Mem. Fed. Bar Coun., DC Bar Assn. Office: Hogan & Hartson LLP Ste 2500 875 Third Ave New York NY 10022 Office Phone: 212-918-3517. Business E-Mail: gfhritz@hhlaw.com.

HRITZ, KARIN C., special education educator; b. Richmond Heights, Mo., Mar. 2, 1967; d. Thomas Donald and Sharon Sue Hritz. AA, Saddleback CC, 2000; BA, Chapman U., 2003, MA in Spl. Edn., 2005. Cert. specialist credential mild/moderate Calif., 2004, multiple subject credential Calif., 2004. Spl. edn. tchr. Paramount HS, Calif., 2004—. Roman Catholic. Avocation: travel. Office: Paraount HS Downey Ave Paramount CA 90723

HRITZ, PAMELA LYNNE, accountant; b. Windber, Pa., Apr. 30, 1962; d. John Irvin and Sally Jane (Baldwin) H.; m. Walter Thomas Haven, Sept. 27, 2003. AS, Monroe County (Mich.) C.C., 1983; BS in Acctg., U. N.C., Wilmington, 1992. Teller Monroe (Mich.) Bank and Trust Co., 1983-85; teller, svcs. supr. State Employees Credit Union, Raleigh, N.C., 1985-89, part-time teller, 1989-91, loan officer, 1992, acct. I, 1992-95, gen. ledger supr., acct. II, 1995—2000, sr. fin. analyst, 2002—. Leader Young Adult Ministries, Wilmington, N.C., 1992. Mem. Inst. Mgmt. Accts. (v.p. pub. rels. 1991-92). Republican. Methodist. Office: State Employees Credit Union 1000 Wade Ave Raleigh NC 27605-1157

HRMA, PAVEL, materials scientist, educator; b. Prague, Czech Republic, Oct. 3, 1939; s. Jindrich and Marie Hrma. MS, Inst. Chem. Tech. Prague, 1961, PhD, 1969. Tech. mgr. Flat Glass Industry, Olovi, Czech Republic, 1961—63; rsch. scientist Czechoslovak Acad. Scis., Prague, 1969—81; sr. lectr. U. Sheffield, England, 1981—82; rsch. prof. Case We. Res. U., Cleve., 1982—89; staff scientist Pacific NW Nat. Lab., Richland, Wash., 1989—. Cons. Corning Industry, Corning, NY, 1986—89. Contbr. articles to profl. jours. Fellow: Am. Ceramic Soc.; mem.: Materials Rsch. Soc. Office: Pacific Northwest National Lab K6-24 PO Box 999 Richland WA 99354 Office Phone: 509-376-5092. Business E-Mail: pavel.hrma@pnl.gov.

HRNA, DANIEL JOSEPH, pharmacist, lawyer; b. Taylor, Tex., March 19, 1940; s. Stephan Peter and Anna Ludmilla (Baran) H.; BS, U. Houston, 1963, JD, 1970; m. Velma Isobel Lesson, Sept. 3, 1963 (dec. Jan. 1994); children: Anna Marie, Daniel Steven, Brian Keith. Bar: Tex. 1972. In mgmt., Gunning-Casteel Co., El Paso, Tex., 1963-65; dir. pharmacy svcs. Tex. Inst. Rehab. & Rsch., Houston, 1966-79; dir. pharmacy Alief Gen. Hosp., Belhaven Hosp., Houston, 1979-85, West Houston Med. Ctr., 1985-88; mem. faculty Baylor U. Coll. Medicine, 1977-79, Sharpstown Gen. Hosp., 1988-94; with Owen Healthcare, Inc. at Sharpstown Gen. Hosp., 1990-94; pvt. practice, 1994—; pres. Rx-IBR Corp. Mem. ABA, Am. Pharm. Assn., Tex. Pharmacy Assn., State Bar Tex., Tex. Soc. Hosp. Pharmacists, Am. Soc. Pharmacy Law, Am. Hosp. Assn., Harris County Pharm. Assn., Houston Bar Assn., Galveston-Houston Pharm. Hosp. Assn., Czech Heritage Soc. Tex. (legal adv., trustee), Profl. Photographers Guild Houston (hon.), Delta Theta Phi, Kappa Psi, Phi Delta Chi. Roman Catholic. Office: 11920 Beechnut St Houston TX 77072-4034

HRONES, STEPHEN BAYLIS, lawyer, educator; b. Boston, Jan. 20, 1942; s. John Anthony and Margaret (Baylis) H.; m. Anneliese Zion, Sept. 11, 1970; children: Christopher, Katja. BA cum laude, Harvard U., 1964; postgrad., U. Sorbonne, Paris, 1964-65; JD, U. Mich., 1968. Bar: Iowa 1969, Mass. 1972, U.S. Dist. Ct. Mass. 1973, U.S. Ct. Appeals (1st cir.) 1979, U.S. Supreme Ct. 1991. Pvt. practice, Heidelberg, Germany, 1970-72; pvt. practice Boston, 1973-86; ptnr. Hrones and Harwood, Boston, 1986-90, Hrones and Garrity, Boston, 1990—2004, Hrones, Garrity and Hedges, Boston, 2005—. Clin. assoc. Suffolk U. Law Sch., Boston, 1979-82; faculty adv. Harvard Law Sch., 1988—; instr. Northeastern Law Sch., 1998, Mass. Continuing Legal Edn. Programs, 1988—; commentator CNN, Fox and other local sta. Author: How To Try a Criminal Case, 1982, Criminal Practice Handbook, 1995, 2d edit., 1999, Massachusetts Jury (Criminal) Instructions, 2d edit., 1999; contbr. articles to profl. jours. Trustee Orgn. for Assabet River, 1990-99; schs. and scholarship com. Harvard U.; fundraiser Harvard Coll. Fund, 1985—. Fulbright scholar, 1968-69; recipient Edward J. Duggan Pvt. Counsel award Com. for Pub. Counsel Svcs., 2000; named Super Lawyer, Mass. Lawyers, 2004, 05 Mem. ACLU, Nat. Assn. Criminal Def. Lawyers, Mass. Assn. Criminal Def. Lawyers, Mass. Bar Assn., Boston Bar Assn., Nat. Lawyers Guild, Fulbright Assocs. Democrat. Avocations: squash, skiing, wind-surfing, vegetable gardening, reading. Home: 39 Winslow St Concord MA 01742-3817 Office: Hrones Garrity and Hedges Lewis Wharf Bay 232 Boston MA 02110 Office Phone: 617-227-4019. E-mail: sbhlaw@comcast.net.

HRUBAN, RALPH HARVEY, pathologist, educator; b. Chgo., July 28, 1959; s. Zdenek and Jarmila (Stanek) H.; m. Claire Elizabeth Desaulnier, May 26, 1985; children: Zoe Marie, Emily Anne, Carolyn Anna. BA, U. Chgo., 1981; MD, Johns Hopkins U., 1985. Lic. pathologist, Md. Intern in pathology Johns Hopkins Hosp., Balt., 1985-86, resident in pathology, 1986-88, chief resident in pathology, 1989-90, asst. prof. pathology, 1990-93, assoc. prof. pathology, 1993—99, prof. pathology, 1999—, asst. prof. otolaryngol head and neck surgery, 1993-95, assoc. prof. oncology, 1995—99, prof. oncology, 1999—, dir. divsn. cardiovascular-respiratory pathology, 1993—99, dir. divsn. gastrointestinal-liver pathology, 1998—. Pathologist Johns Hopkins Hosp., Blrt., 1990—. Meml. Sloan-Kettering fellow, 1988-89. Office: Johns Hopkins Hosp Dept Pathology Baltimore MD 21231

HRUBY, GEORGE GEOFFREY, writer, educator; b. Cleve., Nov. 20, 1954; s. John Franklin and Mary Katherine Hruby; m. Alison Heron, Apr. 27, 2003; 1 child, Katherine Hope. BA in English, Syracuse U., N.Y., 1972—76; MEd in Lang. Edn., U. Ga., Athens, 1992—95, PhD in Reading Edn., 1996—2002. Freelance writer, 1980—92; journalist, columnist Swinnett Daily News/Forsyth Daily News, Gainesbille, Ga., 1984—86; owner, mgr. The Point, Atlanta, 1988—92; tchr-in-tng. Meadowcreek High Sch., 1994—95, Barrow County High Sch., 1994—95; investor, operator High-Hat Club, Athens, Ga., 1993—96; grad. asst. U. Ga., 1995—97, grad. asst. dept. reading edn., 1997—2002, adj. prof., 2002—03; asst. prof. Utah State U., Logan, 2003—. Editl. rev. bd. mem. Reading Rsch. Quar., Newark, 2003—; bd. dirs. Am. Reading Forum, Sanibel Island, Fla., 2004—. Contbr. articles to profl. jours. Mem. Cache Chamber Music Soc., Logan, Utah, 2003—05. Fellow, Inst. of Behavioral Rsch., Cognitive Studies Group, U. Ga., 1997; scholar, Am. Reading Forum, 1999. Mem.: APA, Soc. for Neuroscience, Internat. Reading Assn., Am. Ednl. Assn. (spl. interest group chair 1999—2002), Nat. Reading Conf. Independent. Episcopalian. Achievements include research in system dynamics of literacy development. Avocations: oenology, organic gardening, travel. Home: 1655 Sunset Dr Logan UT 84321 Office: Utah State Univ 2815 Old Main Hill Logan UT 84322 Office Phone: 435-797-7145. E-mail: george.hruby@usu.edu.

HRUSKA, ALAN J., lawyer; b. N.Y.C., July 9, 1933; BA, Yale U., 1955, LL.B., 1958. Bar: N.Y. 1959, U.S. Supreme Ct. 1970. Assoc. firm Cravath, Swaine & Moore, N.Y.C., 1958-67, ptnr., 1968—; chmn. planning and program com. 2d Circuit Jud. Conf., 1974-80; co-chmn. 2d Circuit Commn. Reduction of Burdens and Costs in Civil Litigation, 1977-80; commr. N.Y. State Exec. Adv. Commn. on Adminstrn. of Justice, 1981-83; chmn. bd. SoHo Press, Inc., 1986—; CEO The Talking Pictures Co., 2001—. Author: Borrowed Time, 1984; dir.(Writer, Dir.): (films) Nola, 2005. Bd. dirs. Legal Action Ctr., 2000—. Mem.: ABA, Fund for Modern Cts. (bd. dirs. 1994—), Inst. Jud. Adminstrn. (trustee 1978—92, pres. 1982—85, bd. dirs. 1992—2002), Fed. Bar Coun. (trustee 1976—, pres. 1984—86), Assn. Bar City of N.Y. (sec. 1965—66), N.Y. State Bar Assn., Am. Coll. Trial Lawyers, Ctr. for Pub. Resources (exec. com. 1984—2002). Office: Cravath Swaine & Moore 825 8th Ave Fl 38 New York NY 10019-7475

HRUSKA, KEITH ANTHONY, nephrologist, medical educator; b. Sidney, Nebr., Aug. 9, 1944; s. Herbert Louis and Ellen Hruska; m. Pamela Jean Higgins, Dec. 27, 1966; children: Kerstin Clark, Keith Anthony, Kemper Luke. BS, Creighton U., 1965, MD, 1969. Resident Cornel U., N.Y.C., 1969—71; fellow in nephrology Washington U., St. Louis, 1972—74, instr. medicine, 1974—75, asst. prof. medicine, 1975—81, assoc. prof. medicine, 1982—86, prof. medicine, 1986—, prof. pediat., 2001—. Founder, bd. dirs. Isto Technologies, St. Louis, 1995—2003; med. dir. MidAmerica Transplant Svcs., St. Louis, 1980—. Author basic rsch. manuscript in bone kideny disease. Mem.: Am. Soc. Cell Biology, Am. Soc. Bone and Mineral Rsch., Am. Soc. Nephrology. Avocations: gardening, running, snowboarding. Office: Washington U Sch Medicine 5th Fl MPRB 660 S Euclid Avenue Saint Louis MO 63110 Office Phone: 314-286-2772. E-mail: hruska_k@wustl.edu, hruska_k@peds.wustl.edu.

HRUSKA, LAURA CHAPMAN, publisher, lawyer; b. N.Y.C. d. Henry Kruse and Katherine (Bab) Chapman; m. Alan J. Hruska; children: Bronwen, Andrew Chapman, Matthew Ross. AB with honors, Cornell U., 1955; LLB with honors, Yale U., 1958. Bar: N.Y. 1959. Assoc. Rogers & Wells, N.Y.C., 1958-65; writer Dutton, Doubleday, N.Y.C., 1975-78; founder, assoc. pub. Soho Press, Inc., N.Y.C., 1986—. Author: Legal Relations, 1978; editor over 150 books, 1987—. Mem. Order of the Coif, Phi Beta Kappa, Pi Kappa Phi.

HRUTKAY, LIDELLA WILSON, lawyer, state legislator; b. Morgantown, W.Va., Nov. 24, 1960; d. Amos Clark and Bertha Marie (Eloi) W.; m. Mark Oliver Hrutkay, June 14, 1986; 1 child, Gregory James. BS in Bus., W.Va. U., 1983; JD, Ohio No. U., 1987. Bar: W.Va. 1989, D.C. 1990. Sec. Amos C. Wilson, L.C., Logan, W.Va., 1979-89, lawyer, 1989-93; lawyer, pres. Wilson and Hrutkay Law Offices, L.C., Logan, 1993—; mem. W.Va. Ho. of Dels., 2001—. Mem. W.Va. Ho. of Dels., Charleston. Rep. 7th senatorial dist. W.Va. Dem. Platform Com., Charleston, 2000. Mem. ABA, Nat. Orgn. Social Security Claiments Reps. (sustaining), W.Va. Bar Assn., Order Ea. Star. Avocations: bowling, cooking, fishing, camping, car races. Office: Wilson and Hrutkay Law Offices LC PO Box 1760 Logan WV 25601

HRYCAK, PETER, mechanical engineer, educator; b. Przemysl, Poland, July 8, 1923; arrived in U.S., 1949, naturalized, 1956; s. Eugene and Ludmyla (Dobrzanska) Hrycak; m. Rea Meta Limberg, June 13, 1949; children: Maria(dec.), Michael Paul, Orest W. T., Alexandra Martha. Student, U. Tubingen, Germany, 1946-48; BS with honors, U. Minn., 1954, MS, 1955, PhD, 1960. Registered profl. engr., N.J. Adminstrv. asst. French Mil. Govt. in Germany, 1947-49; instr. mech. engring. U. Minn., Mpls., 1955-60; mem. tech. staff Bell Telephone Labs., Murray Hill, N.J., 1960-65; sr. project engr. Curtiss-Wright Corp., Woodridge, N.J., 1965; assoc. prof. mech. engring. N.J. Inst. Tech., 1965-68, prof., 1968-93, prof. emeritus, 1993—, dir. jet rsch. lab., 1966-93. Participant in internat. and nat. conf. on engring. and applied sci. Contbr. articles to profl. jours.; one of original Telstar designers. Bd. dirs. Ukrainian Congress Com. Am., Mpls., 1956—60, Plast Camp, East Chatham, NY, 1963—68; v.p. Ukrainian Music Found., 1977—97; pres. Peremyschyna, 1993—. NASA grantee, 1967—68, NSF grantee, 1982—84. Mem.: ASME, AIAA (sr.), Ukrainian Acad. Arts and Scis. U.S., Shevchenko Sci. Soc., Nat. Ukrainian Acad. Engring. Scis., Am. Geophys. Union, Ukrainian Engrs. Soc. Am. (pres. 1966—67), Inst. Eviron. Scis. (sr.), Tau Beta Pi, Sigma Xi, Pi Tau Sigma. Home: 19 Roselle Ave Cranford NJ 07016-2532 Office: NJ Inst Tech 323 Martin Luther King Jr Blvd Newark NJ 07102-1824 Personal E-mail: mphrycak@aol.com.

HRYNKOW, SHARON HEMOND, federal agency administrator, neuroscientist, researcher; BA in Biology, R.I. Coll., 1983; PhD in Neurosci., U. Conn., 1990; postdoctoral studies, U. Oslo, Norway, 1990-92. Sci. officer U.S. Dept. State, Washington, 1992-95; sci. policy analyst Fogarty Internat. Ctr., NIH, Bethesda, Md., 1995-97, spl. asst. office of dir., 1997-99, dep. dir., 2000—04, acting dir., 2004—. Mem. adv. bd. Nat. Coun. for Internat. Health, Washington, 1997. Contbr. articles to profl., peer-reviewed jours. includng Jour. Neurosci., Developmental Brain Rsch., and others; chief drafter on strategy and policy toward internat. HIV/AIDS, State Dept. U.S. Recipient Lette N. Sangstad award (rsch. stipend) Oslo, Norway, 1990-92. Mem. AAAS (Diplomacy fellowship 1992-94), Coun. on Fgn. Rels., Am. Scandinavian Assn., Norwegian Soc. of Washington, Am. Pub. Health Assn., Soc. for Neurosci., Women in Neurosci. Office: Fogarty Internat Ctr NIH Bldg 31 Rm B2C02 Bethesda MD 20892

HSI, DAVID CHING HENG, plant pathologist, geneticist, educator; b. Shanghai, May 17, 1928; came to US, 1948, naturalized, 1961. s. Yulin and Sue Jean (King) H.; m. Kathy S.W. Chiang, 1952; children: Andrew C., Steven D. BSA, St. John's U., Shanghai, 1948; MS, U. Ga., 1949; PhD, U. Minn., 1951. Grad. teaching asst. U. Minn., St. Paul, 1950; postdoctoral fellow US Cotton Field Sta., Sacaton, Ariz., 1951-52; mem. faculty N.Mex. State U., Las Cruces, 1952—, prof. plant pathology and genetics, 1968-92, prof. emeritus, 1992—. Cons. AID, Pakistan, 1970; coord. external evaluation panel Peanut Collaborative Rsch. Support Program, USA, West Africa, S.E. Asia, 1993-95; acad. exch. People's Republic China, 1978, 84, 85, Republic China, 1979, 81, 82, Brazil and Argentina, 1980, Australia, 1983, South Africa, 1981; judge sr. botany N.Mex. Sci. and Engring. Fair, 1979—; adj. prof. biology U. N.Mex., 1986—. Author rsch. papers in field; co-developer new crop cultivars. Past bd. dir., treas. Carver Pub. Libr., Clovis, N.Mex.; elder 1st Presbyn. Ch., Albuquerque, workship com. chmn., 1981-82, adult edn. com. chmn., 1988-91, pers. com., 1995-98; mem. nat. adv. coun. discipleship and worship Gen. Assembly United Presbyn. Ch. USA, 1978-81, mem. nat. theol. reflections working group, 1980-81, mem. ednl. and congl. nurture unit, 1991-93, N.Mex. Child Abuse Neglect Prevention Implementation Task Force, 1993-97; mem. bd. edn. Albuquerque Pub. Schs., 1982, sec. bd. edn., 1983, v.p., 1984; bd. dir. Mid. Rio Grande Coun. Govts., 1983, 84; chair Albuquerque Sisters Cities Bd., 1986-88; 1st v.p. Albuquerque Sister Cities Found., 1995-96, pres., 1996-98; chair Albuquerque Biopark Adv. Bd., 2003-05; mem. com. higher edn. Gen. Assembly The Presbyn. Ch. (USA), 1991-93, preparation ministry com., Presbytery Santa Fe, 1993-98, chair, 1996-97; co-chair N.Mex. Advocates for Children and Families, 1993-95, vice chair, 1995-98; bd. dir. Greater Albuquerque Vol. Adminstr., 1992-95, 97-99, Project Change, 1994-98, v.p., 1996-98; v.p. Albuquerque Edn. Retirees, 1995-96, pres., 1996-98; v.p. Edn. Success Alliance, 1996-98; trustee All Faiths Receiving Home, 1997-03; trustee, Sandia Prep Sch., 2001-03; bd. dir., v.p. Explora Sci. Ctr. and Children Mus. Albuquerque, 1998—, v.p., 2002-; v.p. The Friendship Force of N.Mex., 2001, pres., 2002. Recipient Disting. Rsch. award Coll. Agr. and Home Econs. N.Mex. State U., 1971, Disting. Svc. award, 1985, Albuquerque Human Rights awad, 1997; inducted into Sr. Citizen's Hall of Fame, 1993. Fellow AAAS (hon., coun. mem. 1998-2004, Southwestern and Rocky Mountain divsn., exec. com. 1993-95, pres.-elect 1995-96, pres. 96-97); mem. Internat. Soc. Plant Pathology, Am. Phytopath. Soc. (judge Internat. Sci. and Engring. Fair 1983), Nat. Sweet Potato Collaborators Group (chmn. sprout prodn. and root piece propagation com. 1982-84), Nat. Geog. Soc., Am. Peanut Rsch. and Edn. Soc. (chmn. site selection com. 1981, award com., pres.-elect 1981, pres. 1982), N.Mex. Acad. Sci. (chmn. com. 1980, pres. 1981, 82, treas. 1984-92, dist. scientist award 1984), Nat. Assn. Acad. Sci. (pres.-elect 1992-93, pres. 1993-94), N.Mex. Chinese Assn. (pres. 1983-84, 92-93, treas. 1985-86, past bd. dir.), Chinese Am. Citizens Alliance (v.p. Albuquerque lodge 1988-92, v.p. 2002-04, pres. 2004—), Albuquerque Coun. for Internat. Visitors (v.p. 1988, pres. 1989-91), Sigma Xi (life, N.Mex. coord. centennial celebration, sr. editor commemorative pub. Frm Sundaggers to Space Exploration), Kiwanis Internat. (past pres. Clovis, past chmn. spl. program com., past bd. dir. Albuquerque). Home and Office: 2504 Griegos Pl NW Albuquerque NM 87107-2874 E-mail: Davidnkathyhsi@aol.com. *In grateful appreciation of my God-given talents and opportunities, my privileged academic trainings in China and U.S.A., and my professional experience and associations with world-wide scientists, I shall continue to contribute to the scientific advancement and practice, and to promote human understanding and international cooperation for the betterment of mankind and for the glorification of my Creator.*

HSI, EDWARD YANG, lawyer, venture capitalist; b. Ann Arbor, Mich., May 30, 1957; s. Peter Hwei-Yang and Priscilla Lai-Fong (Lam) H.; m. Denise Chur-Yee Tso, Aug. 3, 1985; 2 children, Edward Yang II, Clarissa Sian Li-Hwa. BS, U. So. Calif., 1980; MBA, Duke U., 1983; JD, U. Calif., Davis, 1986. Bar: Calif. 1986, U.S. Dist. Ct. (cen. dist.) Calif. 1987, U.S. Ct. Appeals (9th cir.) 1987, U.S. Tax Ct. 1988, U.S. Supreme Court 1991. Tax intern Coca Cola Co., L.A., 1983, Lear Siegler Inc., Santa Monica, Calif., 1984; assoc. Lawler, Felix & Hall, L.A., 1986-87, Morrison & Foerster, L.A., 1987-89, Thelen, Marrin, Johnson & Bridges, L.A., 1989, Baker & McKenzie, Hong Kong, Singapore, 1989-92; of counsel Tilleke & Gibbins/Jones, Day, Reavis & Pogue, Bangkok, 1992—, Tilleke & Gibbins Cons., Ltd., Indochina, 1992—; group gen. counsel Humpuss Group Indonesia, Jakarta, Singapore, 1992-94; pres., CEO Humpuss Arun Aromatics Petrochemicals, Jakarta, Arun, Sumatra, 1994—96; exec. dir. Dharmala Group, Jakarta, 1997; vice chmn., CEO Asean Infrastructure Holdings Ltd., Jakarta, 1997—; chmn., CEO Asean Energy Group Ltd., Jakarta, 1998—. Spl. advisor to the shareholders Gunung Sewu Group and Duta Anggada Group, Jakarta, 1997; founder, prin. Grant Thornton Taira Hsi and Taira & Hsi, Internat. in cooperation with Kaye Scholer LLP, Jakarta, 1998—2000; advisor Govt. of Republic of Indonesia on a Policy Proposal for the Econ. Restoration of Province of Aceh, to chmn. of Indonesian Parliament DPR on a Nat. Econ. Revitalization Policy, 1998—99; mng. dir. Asia-Pacific region Mysmart Solutions, Inc., 2000—01; spl. advisor to chmn. Shingfa Group, Taipei, 2001—02; advisor Golkar Parliamentary Party of The Republic of Indonesia Del. to Taiwan to address Bilateral Internat. Cooperation in the Labor and Energy Sectors, 2002; bd. dirs. DEH Asia Ltd., VBP Ltd., AO Asia Ltd., Asia Beta Capital Ltd.; co-founder, CEO New Template Media Group, LA, 2003—; COO Pacific Republic Capital, a Med. Ventures Group, 2003—. Editor: Income Taxation of Foreign Related Transaction, 5 vols., 1987; contbr. articles on tax to profl. jours. Mem. founding coun. World Peace and Diplomacy Forum, Cambridge, England, 2003—. Mem.: ABA, World Peace and Diplomacy Forum (mem. founding coun., Cambridge 2003—), L.A. County Bar Assn., State Bar Calif., U. Calif. Alumni Assn., Duke Alumni Assn., Hong Kong Stanley Residents' Assn., Tuen Ng Dragon Boat Races Festival (co-chmn., ATT and Baker & McKenzie entry), Indonesian Bus. Soc., Hong Kong Assn., Am. C. of C.-Hong Kong, Punahou Sch. Alumni Assn., Order of Coif, Phi Kappa Tau, Alpha Mu Alpha, Phi Delta Phi. Democrat. Avocations: southeast asian art, jazz drumming, classical music, anthropology, discipleship. Home: 819 S Ridgeside Dr Monterey Park CA 91754-3724 Office: Chase Plaza 21st Fl Jalan Jenderal Sudirman Kav 21 Jakarta 12910 Indonesia Office Phone: 011-62-818-7000-05. E-mail: eyhsi@yahoo.com.

HSI, MORRIS YU, mechanical engineer, educator; b. Taipei, Taiwan, Aug. 23, 1951; s. En Sui and I Hsian (Wang) H.; m. Linda Syau Lin Chang, Aug. 28, 1982. BSME with honors, Nat. Cheng Kung U., Tainan, Taiwan, 1974; MSME, Iowa State U., 1979; PhD in Applied Mechanics, U. Mich., 1987; MBA, U. Detroit, 2001. Registered profl. engr., Mich. Mech. engr. Taiwan Power Co., Keelung, 1976-77; product design engr. Ford Motor Co., Dearborn, Mich., 1987-92, tech. specialist, 1992—2000, Visteon Automotive Sys., Plymouth, Mich., 2000—01; sr. engr. Hutchinson FTS, Troy, Mich., 2001—. Reviewer, evaluator of tech. publs. profl. socs.; adj. faculty U. Detroit Mercy, 2003—. Contbr. articles to profl. jours. 2d lt. Taiwanese Army, 1974-76. Recipient Henry Ford Technol. award Ford Motor Co., 1990, Mich. Outstanding Engr. in Industry Am. Consulting Engrs. Coun. Mich. and Mich. Soc. Profl. Engrs., 1999. Mem.: NSPE, Mich. Soc. Profl. Engrs. (dir. Detroit Metro chpt. 1999—), Soc. Automotive Engrs. (noise and vibration gen. com.), Beta Gamma Sigma. Achievements include pioneering in application of computational aeroacoustics to automotive projects; pioneering in application of computational fluid dynamics to analyze and design vehicle's underhood thermal environment; patents pending on noise control of automotive climate control systems. Home: 46922 Enterprise Dr Northville MI 48167-1034 Office: Hutchinson FTS 1835 Technology Dr Troy MI 48083 E-mail: hsimorris@hotmail.com.

HSIA, MARTIN EDGAR, lawyer; b. London, Eng., Sept. 30, 1957; came to U.S., 1963; s. Yujen Edward and Juliet Wai Mun (Yuen) H.; children: Robert Edward Tien Ming, Kyla Martina Mei Ming. BA with honors, Brown U., 1978; JD cum laude, Georgetown U., 1981. Bar: Hawaii 1981, U.S. Ct. Appeals (fed. cir.) 1990, U.S. Patent and Trademark Office 1986. Paralegal Drug Enforcement Adminstrn., Washington, 1979-80; cons. Office Tech. Assessment U.S. Congress, Washington, 1980-81; assoc. Cades Schutte Fleming & Wright, Honolulu, 1981-88, ptnr., 1988—. Mem. Licensing Execs. Soc., Internat. Trademark Assn., Patent and Trademark Office Soc., Computer Law Assn., Am. Intellectual Property Law Assn., Hawaii Bar Assn. (intellectual property and tech. sect.), Hawaii Venture Capital Assn. (sec. 1988—), Hawaii Tech. Trad. Assn. (asst. sec. 2000-). Avocations: music, ice hockey, science fiction. Office: Cades Schutte LLP 1000 Bishop St Fl 12 Honolulu HI 96813-4212 Office Phone: 808-544-3835. Business E-Mail: mhsia@cades.com.

HSIAO, KUANG-TING, mechanical engineer, educator, researcher; s. Fong-Shen and Wong-Hsiu-Lang Hsiao; m. Juo-Wen Mao, Aug. 17, 2000. BS, Nat. Taiwan U., 1987—91; PhD, U. Del., 1994—2000. Postdoctoral fellow U. Del., Newark, 1999—2000, rsch. assoc., 2000—03; asst. prof. mech. engring. U. South Ala., Mobile, 2003—. Mem.: SAMPE (assoc.), ASME (assoc.). Achievements include modeling transport phenomena in porous media in Liquid Composite Molding processes and developing intelligent, advanced materials processing technology; This technology utilizes computers to automatically design, monitor and control Liquid Composite Molding processes. Office: Mech Engring Dept EGCB 212 U South Ala Mobile AL 36688 Office Phone: 251-460-7889. E-mail: kuangtinghsiao@yahoo.com.

HSIAO, MICHAEL S., electrical engineer, educator; b. Keelung, Taiwan; s. Ming-Yang Hsiao. PhD, U. Ill., 1997. Asst. prof. Rutgers U., Piscataway, N.J., 1997—; now with Va. Tech. NSF grantee, 2001. Mem. IEEE. E-mail: mhsiao@ece.rutgers.edu.

HSIEH, DIN-YU, applied mathematics professor; b. Jiangsu, Peoples Republic of China, Mar. 25, 1933; arrived in the U.S., 1955; s. K.S. and C. (Wei) H.; m. Lily Kwang-Fei Chow, Dec. 26, 1958; children: Paul, Daniel. BS, Nat. Taiwan U., 1954; MS, Brown U., Providence, 1957; PhD, Calif. Inst. Tech., Pasadena, 1960. Rsch. fellow Calif. Inst. Tech., 1960-63, asst. prof., 1963-68; assoc. prof. Brown U., 1968-78, prof., 1978-2000; prof., head dept. math. Hong Kong U. Sci. & Tech., 1990-96, acting dean sci., 1990-91, 92, prof. math., 1996—98; dir. Zhou Pei-Yuan Ctr. for Applied Math., Tsinghua U., Beijing, 2002—. Cons. Jet Propulsion Lab. Pasadena, 1963-67; advisor Ningbo (Peoples Republic of China) U., 1986—. Author: Asymptotic Methods, 1983, Fluid Dynamics, 1987, America, America, 1990, Amid Hills, by the Lake, 1991, Contemplating China, 1991, Wave and Stability in Fluids, 1994, Swallow Flying, 1998. Mem. Am. Phys. Soc., Hong Kong Math. Soc., Edn. and Sci. Soc. (pres. 1987-90), Hong Kong Soc. Theoretical and Applied Mechanics (founding pres. 1996-97). Avocation: swimming. Office: Zhou Pei-Yuan Ctr for Applied Math Tsinghua U Beijing 100084 China E-mail: mahsieh@ust.hk.

HSIEH, MARINA CING, lawyer, educator; b. Waco, Tex., Aug. 30, 1960; d. George S. C. and Rose S. C. (Pu) H. AB, Harvard U., 1982; JD, U. Calif., Berkeley, 1988. Bar: Pa., 1990; U.S. Ct. Appeals (3rd cir.) 1992; U.S. Supreme Ct. 1996. Staff Hon. Leo T. McCarthy, Lt. Gov., Calif., 1983-85; law clk. to Hon. Louis H. Pollak U.S. Dist. Ct., Phila., 1988-89; law clk. to Hon. John Paul Stevens U.S. Supreme Ct., Washington, 1989-90; asst. counsel NAACP Legal Defense and Ednl. Fund, Inc., N.Y.C., 1990-93; acting law prof. U. Calif., Berkeley, 1993-99; asst. prof. law U. Md., Balt., 1999—2005; asst. dean academic and profl. redevel. Santa Clare U. Sch. Law, Calif., 2005—. Lectr. Bar/Bri, 1996—. Author: (with others) Asian American Almanac, 1994. Mem. ACLU (bd. dirs. 1997-), Alumni of Deep Springs and Telluride Assn., Bar Assn. N.Y.C. (fed. legis. com. 1992-94). Office Phone: 408-554-2764. Business E-Mail: mhsieh@scu.edu.

HSIEH, TSUI-HSIA, artist, educator; b. Chia-yi, Taiwan, 1946; arrived in US, 1986; d. Wan-jin and Moo-chin Hsieh. BA, Nat. Taiwan Normal U., Taipei, 1981. Founder Jay Yuan Tong Arts Sch., Flushing, NY, 1986—; prin., owner Jay Yuan Tong Art Gallery, Flushing, 2005—. One-woman shows include Taipei Provincial Mus., 1983, Nat. Mus. History, Taipei, 1984, Princeton U., 1995, St. John's U., 1999, Hsin-Chu Cultural Ctr., Taiwan, 2002; author: Tsui-Hsia Hsieh's Paintings, 1999. Named Disting. Art Educator, Ministry Edn., Taiwan, 1982. Office Phone: 718-591-5227.

HSIEH, WING CHEONG, optometrist, educator; b. Hong Kong, May 2, 1956; s. Chao Joseph and Nancy Kwok Hsieh; m. Sharon Kay Tharp, Sept. 29, 1984; children: Eric, Suzanne, Sierra. BA in Biophysics, U. Calif., Berkeley, 1978; OD, Ind. U., 1982. Pvt. practice, San Francisco, 1982—84; optometrist Kaiser Med. Ctr., Hayward, Calif., 1984—85; pvt. practice Muncie, Ind., 1985—87; resident in ocular disease Vision Ednl. Found., Northeastern State U., Oklahoma City, 1987—88; optometrist, dir. clinic Jones Eye Clinic, Sioux City, Iowa, 1989—. Clin. examiner Nat. Bds. Examiners Optometry, 1990—; adj. clin. faculty U. Montreal, Quebec, Canada, 1995—97, So. Coll. Optometry, Memphis, 2002—. Author: (chpt.) Handbook of Primary Care Optometry, Jones Eye Clinic Optometric Training Manual, Cornea Research Foundation Optometric Educational Manual; author: (editor, publisher) (magazine) CyberVision; contbr. articles. Recipient Presdl. Citation, Nebr. Optometric Assn., 1995. Fellow: Am. Acad. Optometry; mem.: Am. Optometric Assn. Office: Jones Eye Clinic 4405 Hamilton Blvd Sioux City IA 51104 E-mail: wing.hsieh@joneseyeclinic.com.

HSU, CHARLES JUI-CHENG, manufacturing company executive, advertising agent; b. Taipei, Republic of China, Mar. 17, 1930; came to U.S., 1958; s. Neng-Tsai and (Kao-Yung) H. MA, Baylor U., 1965. Owner, mgr. Retaw Co., Flushing, N.Y., 1965—; exec. mgr. Charles Michelson Inc., N.Y.C., 1965-66; pres. Retawmatic Corp., N.Y.C., 1968—99; mgr. Retawmatic Co. Am., N.Y.C., 2002—. Patentee water or oil detecting devices field. Mem. Am. Mus. Natural History. Mem. AAAS, Taiwan Mchts. Assn., Smithsonian Instn., Nat. Audubon Soc., Nat. Geographic Soc. Address: 149-11C 41st Ave Flushing NY 11355 Office Phone: 718-886-0502.

HSU, CHENG, decision sciences and engineering systems educator; b. Taipei, Taiwan, May 11, 1951; came to U.S., 1976; s. Chung-Yu and Te-Zeng (Yeh) H.; m. Susan Hsu; m. Susan; 1 child, Diana. BS in Indsl. Engring., Tunghai U., Taichung, Taiwan, 1973; MS, Ohio State U., 1978, PhD, 1983. Info. engr. China Tech. Cons., Inc., Taipei, 1975-76; grad. rsch. asst. Ohio State U., Columbus, 1977-80, grad. teaching assoc., 1980-82; asst. prof. decision scis. and engring. systems Rensselaer Poly. Inst., Troy, N.Y., 1982-88, assoc. prof., 1988-96, dir. undergrad. programs, 1989-91, dir. doctoral program, 1994—2001, prof., 1996—. Cons. Coopers & Lybrand, Albany, N.Y., 1988, Digital Equipment Corp., Nashua, N.H., 1991, Gen. Electric R&D, Schenectady, N.Y., 1995—; co-founder, bd. dirs. EnterNet, Inc., 2000-04; patentee in field. Author: Enterprise Integration and Modeling: The Metadatabase Approach, 1996, Innovative Planning for Electronic Commerce and Enterprises: A Reference Model, 2000. Grantee GM, 1986—89, DEC, 1986—89, Johnson & Johnson, 1986—89, Aluminum Co. Am., 1992—95, Digital Equipment Corp., 1992—95, GE, 1986—95, GM, 1986—95, IBM, 1986—95, A T & T, 1987, NATO, 1988, State of N.Y., 1988, NSF, 1991—96, Samsung, 1995—98, U.S. Army, 1995—96, N.Y. State Dept. Transp., 1997—99, 2002—04. Mem. IEEE (sr.), ACM, Soc. Mfg. Engrs. (sr.), Prodn. and Ops. Mgmt. Soc., N. Am. Chinese Bus. Educators Assn. (bd. dirs. 1988-90). Republican. Home: 168 Maxwell Rd Newtonville NY 12110-4949 Office: Rensselaer Poly Inst 5219 CII Troy NY 12180-3590

HSU, CHIEH SU, applied mechanics engineering educator, researcher; b. Soochow, Kiangsu, China, May 27, 1922; came to U.S., 1947. s. Chung yu and Yong Feng (Wu) H.; m. Helen Yung-Feng Tse, Mar. 28, 1953; children: Raymond Hwa-Chi, Katherine Hwa-Ling. BS, Nat. Inst. Tech., Chungking, China, 1945; MS, Stanford U., 1948, PhD, 1950. Project engr. IBM Corp., Poughkeepsie, N.Y., 1951-55; assoc. prof. U. Toledo, 1955-58, Univ Calif.-Berkeley, 1958-64, prof., 1964—, chmn. div. applied mechanics, 1969-70. Sci. adv. bd. Alexander von Humboldt Found. Fed. Republic Germany, Bonn, 1985—; US nat. com. theoretical and applied mechanics US Nat. Acad. Scis., 1985-90. Author: Cell-to-Cell Mapping, 1987; contbg. author: Thin-Shell Structures, 1974, Advances in Applied Mechanics, vol. 17, 1977; tech. editor Jour. Applied Mechanics, N.Y.C., 1976-82; assoc. editor profl. jours.; author of over 106 tech. papers. Recipient Alexander von Humboldt award Fed. Republic Germany, 1986; Guggenheim Found. fellow, 1964-65; Miller Rsch. prof., U. Calif., Berkeley, 1973-74. Fellow ASME (Centennial award 1980, N.O. Myklestad award 1995) Am. Acad. Mechanics; mem. Acoustical Soc. Am., Soc. Indsl. and Applied Math., U. S. Nat. Acad. Engring., Acad. Sinica, Sigma Xi. Office: U Calif Dept Mech Engring Berkeley CA 94720-1740

HSU, CHO-YUN, history professor; b. Amoy, China, July 10, 1930; came to U.S., 1970; s. Feng-chao and Ying (Tsang) H.; m. Man-li Sun, Feb. 9, 1969; 1 child, Leo BA, Nat. Taiwan U., 1953, MA, 1956; PhD, U. Chgo., 1962; D of Humanities, U. Khust, 2000. Asst. rsch. fellow, 1956-62; assoc. research fellow Academia Sinica, Taiwan, 1962-67; rsch. fellow Inst. History and Philology, Academia Sinica, Taiwan, 1967-70; assoc. prof. Nat. Taiwan U., 1962-65, prof., 1965-70, chmn., 1963-70; prof. history and sociology U. Pitts., 1970-83, univ. prof., 1983-98, univ. prof. emeritus, 1999—; Weilun chair, prof. hist. Chinese U. of Hong Kong, 1991-98, hon. prof., 1998—. John Burns prof. U. Hawaii, 1996; Semans vis. prof. Duke U., 1999—; disting. chair Academia Sinica, 1999-2000; Y.K. Pao chair, prof. Hong Kong U. Sci. and Tech., 2001. Author: Introduction to Historical Research, 1965, Anthology of Studies in Ancient China, 1967, Ancient China in Transition, 1968, Han Agriculture, 1980, History of Western Chou Period, 1984, Western Chou Civilization, 1988; columnist various newspapers; contbr. articles to profl. jours. Bd. dirs. Chiang Ching-Kuo Found., 1989—, Hwanying Found., 1998—. Recipient Asian Studies Program award UCIS, U. Pitts., 1977; Fulbright-Hays Rsch. fellow, 1978 Mem. Academia Sinica Taiwan (academician), Coun. Academie Sinica, Assn. Asian Studies (Disting. Contbn. award 2004), Am. Assn. Chinese Studies (pres. 1985-87), Phi Beta Kappa. Avocation: reading. Office: U Pitts Dept History 3M36 Forbes Quad Pittsburgh PA 15260

HSU, EMILIE TIEN-JUNG, lawyer; d. Yao-Wen Hsu and Wen-Ching Lin. Baccalaureat, Lycee Gabriel Faure, Paris, 1991; AB, Columbia U., 1994; JD, Columbia Law Sch., 1997. Bar: NY 1999. Assoc. Winthrop Stimson Putnam & Roberts, N.Y.C., 1997—98, Debevoise & Plimpton LLP, N.Y.C., 1998—2001, 2002—, Morgan Stanley, N.Y.C., 2001—02. Mem.: N.Y. State Bar Assn. Business E-Mail: ehsu@debevoise.com.

HSU, HUI-CHIN, psychologist, educator; d. Tsi-Wei and Chin Hou Hsu. PhD, Purdue U., West Lafayette, Ind., 1994. Rsch. assoc. Duke U., Durham, NC, 1992—94, U. of Utah, Salt Lake City, 1994—98; asst. prof. U. of Ga., Athens, Ga., 1998—2004, assoc. prof., 2004—. Contbr. articles to profl. jours. Grantee Devel. Sci. Rsch. grantee, Nat. Inst. of Child Health and Human Devel., 2001—03; scholar Fulbright Rsch. award, Coun. for Internat. Exch. of Scholars, 2005—06. Mem.: Internat. Soc. on Infant Studies, APA, Soc. for Rsch. in Child Devel. (assoc.), Phi Beta Delta (hon.). Office: University of Georgia CFD Stanford St Athens GA 30602 Business E-Mail: hchin@fcs.uga.edu.

HSU, IMMANUEL CHUNG YUEH, history professor; b. Shanghai, May 6, 1923; came to U.S., 1949, naturalized, 1962; s. Thomas K.S. and Mary (Loh) H.; m. Dolores Menstell, Apr. 14, 1962; 1 child, Vadim Menstell. BA, Yenching U., China, 1946; MA, U. Minn., 1950; PhD (Harvard-Yenching fellow), Harvard U., 1954. Postdoctoral research fellow Harvard U., 1955-58; vis. asso. prof. history, vis. prof. Harvard Summer Sch., 1961, 64, 68, 75; asst. prof. history U. Calif. at Santa Barbara, 1959-60, assoc. prof., 1960-65, prof., 1965-91, chmn. history dept., 1970-72. Faculty rsch. lectr., 1971; mem. del. to Chinese Acad. Scis., Beijing, spring 1979, 80; vis. prof. Hamburg U., Germany, spring 1973, Stockholm U., 1990, Leningrad (St. Petersburg) U., 1991; Fulbright lectr., 1973; vis. Wei Lun prof. The Chinese U. Hong Kong, 1998. Author: Intellectual Trends in the Ch'ing Period, 1959, China's Entrance into the Family of Nations, 1960, The Ili Crisis: A Study of Sino-Russian Diplomacy, 1871-1881, 1965, The Rise of Modern China, 1970, 2d edit., 1975, internat. edit., 1975-76, 3d edit., 1983, 4th edit., 1990, 5th edit., 1995 (Commonwealth Lit. priz of Calif. 1971), 6th edit., 2000, Chinese trans., 2001-02; editor: Readings in Modern Chinese History, 1971, Late Ch'ing Foreign Relations, 1866-1905, in The Cambridge History of China, Vol. 11, 1980, China Without Mao, 1983, 2d edit., 1990. Guggenheim fellow, 1962-63; Nat. Acad. Scis. disting. scholar to China, spring 1983 Mem. Am., Pacific hist. assns., Assn. Asian Studies, Assn. Ch'ing Studies. Office: U Calif Dept History Santa Barbara CA 93106 E-mail: dhsu5@cox.net.

HSU, JUDY, newscaster; b. Taipei, Taiwan; U.S. married; 1 child. BA in Broadcast Journalism, U. Ill., Champaign, 1992. With WPGU-FM, Champaign-Urbana, Ill., 1993—94, WCIA-TV, Champaign-Urbana, Ill., 1993—94; reporter KFMB-TV, San Diego, 1994—95, weekend anchor, 1995—96, anchor 4pm news, 1996—2001; anchor afternoon news updates KFMB-AM, San Diego, 1996—2001; co-anchor News This Morning and reporter WLS-TV, Chgo., 2001—, host All About Kids. Named one of San Diego Women Who Mean Bus., San Diego Bus. Jour.; recipient Best One-Hour Newscast Emmy, Outstanding Achievement Splty. Reporting Emmy, Best News Story, San Diego Press Club, Best Series, Best Show. Mem.: NATAS, Asian Am. Journalists Assn. Office: WLS-TV 190 N State St Chicago IL 60601

HSU, LIFANG, statistician, department chairman; b. Kaohsiung, Taiwan, Mar. 10, 1951; arrived in U.S., 1976; d. Yew Ting Hsu and Li Hwa Hwang; m. Pinyuen Chen, May 16, 1976; 1 child, Hannah Chen. BS in Math., Nat. ChengKung U., Tainan, Taiwan, 1973; MS in Math., U. Miami, 1978; MS in Applied Stats., U. Calif. Santa Barbara, Goleta, 1979, PHD in Math. Stats., 1983. Math. tchr. Nat. Panchiao H.S., Taipei, Taiwan, 1973—76; tchg. asst. Bucknell U., Lewisburg, Pa., 1976, U. Miami, Coral Gables, Fla., 1977—78, U. Calif. Santa Barbara, Goleta, 1978—83; asst. prof. SUNY, Oswego, 1983—89, Le Moyne Coll., Syracuse, NY, 1989—93, assoc. prof., 1993—2000, chair, prof., 2000—. Mem. exa.n com. Regent Coll., Albany, NY, 1994—96, on-line facilitator for stats., 2000—01. Contbr. articles to profl. jours.; guest editor: spl. issue Comms. in Stats. jour., 2003—. Summer Rsch. fellow, Air Force Office Sci. Rsch., Rome AFB, 1993, R&D grantee, LeMoyne Coll., Syracuse, 1990—91, 1992—93, 1995—96, 2001. Mem.: Math. Assn. Am., Am. Statis. Assn. (pres.-elect and program chair Syracuse chpt. 1997, pres. Syracuse chpt. 1998, mem. exec. com. Syracuse chpt. 1994—97, 1999—), Inst. Math. Stats. Avocations: drawing, swimming. Office: Le Moyne Coll 1419 Salt Springs Rd Syracuse NY 13214 Business E-Mail: hsu@lemoyne.edu.

HSU, MING-YU, engineering educator; b. Kweiyang, Kweichow, China, Dec. 4, 1925; s. Pei-Kung and Wan-Ju (Hsiao) H.; m. Chih-Ju Yao, Jan. 1, 1952; children: Chi-Hsing, Chi-Yun, Chi-En, Chi-Cheng. BE, Nat. Kweichow U., 1948; Dipl.Engr., Delft Tech. U., The Netherlands, 1959. Registered profl. engr., Ill., Ga., Fla., S.C. Prof. Cheng-Kung U., Tainan, Taiwan, 1960-68; dir. Land Devel. Commn., Taipei, 1960-68; engring. cons. Ministry of Housing & Utilities, Sehba, Libya, 1968-71; sr. engr. Philipp Holzmann Ag., Hamburg, Fed. Republic of Germany, 1971-74, Weber, Griffith & Mellican, Galesburg, Ill., 1974-80; chief engr. Chatham Engring.

Co., Savannah, Ga., 1980-82; sr. cons. Hussey, Gay, Bell & DeYoung, Inc., Savannah, 1982—; prof. Savannah Coll. of Art and Design, 1986—. Designed and constructed numerous indsl. office, apt. and comml. bldgs., marine structures including docks, loading platforms, marinas, shipyards and water and waste water treatment structures. Contbr. articles on structural engring. to profl. jours. Mem. Nat. Soc. Profl. Engrs., ASCE. Home: 1115 Wilmington Island Rd Savannah GA 31410-4508 Office: Hussey Gay Bell & DeYoung 329 Commercial Dr Savannah GA 31406-3630

HSU, S. DANA, biologist; b. Tainan, Taiwan, Apr. 7, 1956; arrived in U.S., 1964; BS, George Washington U., 1978; MS, Hood Coll., 1986; JD, Am. U., 1994. Bar: Md. 1995, D.C. 1996, U.S. Patent and Trademark Office 1998. Biologist NIH, Bethesda, Md., 1977—. Contbr. articles to profl. jours. Mem.: Am. Intellectual Property Law Assn. Avocations: gardening, crafts, reading. Office: NIH 30 Convent Dr MSC 4349 Bldg 30 Rm 303 Bethesda MD 20892

HSU, SHU-DEAN, hematologist, oncologist; b. Chiba, Japan, Feb. 21, 1943; came to U.S., 1972; s. Tetzu and Takako (Koo) Minoyama; m. San-San Hsu, Mar. 3, 1973; children: Deborah Te-Lan, Peter Jie-Te. MD, Taipei (Taiwan) Med. Coll., 1968. Diplomate Am. Bd. Internal Medicine, Am. Bd. Hematology, Am. Bd. Med. Oncology. Asst. in medicine Mt. Sinai Sch. Medicine, N.Y.C., 1975-77; asst. instr. medicine U. Tex., Galveston, 1977-78; lectr. in medicine Tex. A&M U., Temple, 1978-80; asst. prof. medicine U. Ark., Little Rock, 1980-83; practice medicine specializing in hematology-oncology Visalia (Calif.) Med. Clinic, 1983-00, Sequoia Regional Cancer Ctr., Visalia, 2000—. Chief hematology and oncology VA Med. Ctr., Temple, Tex., 1978-80. Contbr. articles to profl. jours. Fellow ACP; mem. N.Y. Acad. Scis., Am. Soc. Clin. Oncology, Am. Soc. Hematology, Calif. Med. Assn., Tulare County Med. Soc. Clubs: Visalia Racquet. Home: 1410 W Main St Visalia CA 93291 Office: Sequoia Regional Cancer Ctr 4945 W Cypress Visalia CA 93277 Office Phone: 559-624-3000, 559-734-3156. Business E-Mail: dhsu@kdhcd.com.

HSU, STEPHEN DE, medical educator; b. Tianjin, China, June 11, 1955; arrived in U.S., 1982; s. Xukai Hsu and YunLian Qian; m. Yan Ping Wang, Dec. 5, 1995; children: Alexander, Andrew. BS, Wuhan U., China, 1982; MA, Montclair State U., 1985; PhD, U. Cinn., 1990. Fellow Sloan-Kettering Inst., N.Y.C., 1991—95; commentor, host ESPN Internat., Bristol, Conn., 1995—98; asst. prof. Nat. U. Singapore, Singapore, 1997—98; rsch. fellow N.Y. U., N.Y.C., 1998—99; asst. prof. Med. Coll. Ga., Augusta, 1999—2004, assoc. prof., 2004—. Contbr. articles to profl. jours. Recipient Ruth L. Kirstein Rsch. Svc. award, Nat. Cancer Inst., 1998; Rsch. grant, 2003. Mem.: Am. Assn. Dental Rsch., Am. Assn. Cancer Rsch. Achievements include invention of mega-t green tea chewing gum; green tea skin care line. Avocations: travel, sports, history. Home: 4476 Woodberry Ct Evans GA 30809 Office: Med Coll Ga AD1443 Sch Dentistry Augusta GA 30912 Office Phone: 706-721-2317.

HSU, STEPHEN MING, materials scientist, chemical engineer; b. Shanghai, Nov. 20, 1943; s. Chu-chen and Man-Yeo Hsu; m. Stella P. Lee, Sept. 8, 1968; children: Stephanie C., Vivian C. BSChemE, Va. Poly. Inst. State U., 1968; MSChemE, Pa. State U., 1972, PhD in Chem. Engring., 1976. Project engr. Dorr Oliver, 1968; rsch. engr. Amoco, 1974-78; group leader Nat. Inst. Stds. and Tech., Gaithersburg, Md., 1978-85, chief ceramics divsn., 1985-92, group leader surface properties ceramics divsn., 1992—2002, leader nanomech. properties group, 2002—, leader nanotribology group, 2002—. Vis. prof. chem. engring. Pa. State U., 1991—92, adj. prof. chem. engring., 1983—97; adj. prof. materials scis. U. Md., 1994—98; Eshbach fellow Ctr. Engring. Tribology Northwestern U., 1992; postdoctoral rsch. advisor Nuc. Regulatory Commn., 1980—; panelist nat. materials adv. bd. NAS, 1985, mem. com. on ceramic tribology, ant. materials adv. bd., 1986—87; chmn. Gordon Rsch. Conf. on Tribology, 1988, lectr., 80, 84, 86, 88, 92; mem. Nat. Steering Com. on Superconductivity Rsch. for Power Transmission, 1987—91; chair numerous confs.; nat. tech. coord. Internat. Energy Agy. Annex III on Advanced Materials, 2003—. Contbr. articles to profl. jours. Recipient Capt. Alfred E. Hunt Meml. medal, 1980, Bronze medal for Superior Fed. Svc., Dept. Commerce, 1983, Silver medal for Meritorious Fed. Svc., 1990; Diamond Shamrock grad. fellow, 1971; fellow Soc. Tribologists and Lubricating Engrs., 2000. Mem.: ASTM (mem. petroluem products 1978—92, mem. recycled oil products 1979—87, mem. automotive products 1979—92, mem. analytical methods 1979—92), TMS ASME (rsch. com. on tribology 1984—92), AIChE, Am. Ceramics Soc. (mem. tribology working group 1985—86, dir. program on phase diagrams 1989—91), Versailles Agreement on Advanced Materials and Stds. (co-chmn. tech. working are on wear test methods 1995—, co-chmn. tech. working area on nanotech. 2001—, chair Internat. Energy Agy. study group on surface tech. 2003—), Orgn. Chinese Am. (founding pres. Chgo. chpt. 1976), Soc. Tribologists and Lubricating Engrs. (chmn. paper solicitation 1983, paper solicitation chmn. com. 1984, analytical com. 1985—86, chmn. ann. meeting program com. 1986, membership com. 1987—90, dir. 1987—94, steering com. mem. Wear Conf. 1995—97, mem. adv. bd. Asian fluid and lubrication conf. 1995—, mem. editl adv. bd. Tribology Letters 1995—, sec., treas. Wear Materials Conf. 1997—99, v.p. 1999—2001, pres. 2001—, chair World Tribology Congress program com. 2003, Al Sonntag award 1991), Soc. Automotive Engrs., Asian Pacific Am. Coun. (award 1987), Phi Lambda Upsilon, Phi Kappa Phi. Avocations: tennis, reading, bridge. Office: Nat Inst Stds and Tech Rm A265 Bldg 223 Mailcode 8520 I-270 & Quince Orch Gaithersburg MD 20899-0001 Business E-Mail: stephen.hsu@nist.gov.

HSU, THEODORE A., chiropractor; b. Akron, Ohio, July 16, 1967; s. Tom and Gloria (Young) Hsu; m. Cynthia A. Swain, Mar. 20, 2004. BA, Coll. William and Mary, Williamsburg, Va., 1990; DO, Palmer Coll. Chiropractic West, San Jose, Calif., 2000. Cert. chiropractor Calif., 2001. Content dir., knowledge Visual Sci., Palo Alto, Calif., 2000—; chiropractor pvt. practice, Los Gatos, Calif., 2001—. Mem.: San Francisco Bay Monster Hooligan Assn. (co-pres. 2001—). Office: Hsu Chiropractic 2516 Samaritan Dr Ste D San Jose CA 95124 Office Phone: 408-656-1576. Business E-Mail: dnft@dr-hsu.com.

HSU, THOMAS TSENG-CHUANG, civil engineer, educator; b. Swatow, China, July 28, 1933; came to U.S., 1958; s. Benjamin D.H. and Lucy S.K. (Ma) Zi; m. Laura H.N. Ling, July 20, 1963; children: Lynne Ling, Mia Ming. BS, Harbin (China) Poly. U., 1957; MS, Cornell U., 1960, PhD, 1962. Engr. structural rsch. lab. Portland Cement Assn., Skokie, Ill., 1962-68; assoc. prof. structural engring. U. Miami, Coral Gables, Fla., 1968-73, prof., 1973-79, dept. chmn., 1974-78; vis. prof. dept. civil engring. Nat. Taiwan U., Taipei, 1979-80; prof. structural engring. U. Houston, 1980—, chmn., 1980-84, Moores univ. prof., 1998—. Eshbach disting. vis. prof. Tech. Inst., Northwestern U., 1991-92; prin. investigator NSF, Washington, 1970—; cons. Kaiser Transit Group, Dade County, Fla.; 1977-79. Author: Torsion of Reinforced Concrete, 1984, Unified Theory of Reinforced Concrete, 1993; contbr. articles to profl. jours. Recipient Rsch. medal Am. Soc. Engring. Edn., 1969, Award of Excellence, Halliburton Found., 1990; named Hon. Disting. Prof., Harbin Inst. Civil and Archtl. Engring., China, 1993. Fellow ASCE (Walter L. Huber Rsch. prize 1974), Am. Concrete Inst. (Leonard C. Wason medal 1965, Arthur R. Anderson award 1990). Home: 5034 Glenmeadow Dr Houston TX 77096-4212 Office: U Houston Dept Civil Environ Engring Houston TX 77204-0001 Office Phone: 713-743-4268. Business E-Mail: thsu@uh.edu.

HSU, TSONG HAN, chemist, researcher; b. Linhai, Zheqiang, China, Oct. 10, 1922; arrived in U.S., 1962; s. pao sun Hsu and Fon wha Ho; m. Qi Wen Zhang Hsu, May 18, 1995; 1 adopted child, Wu Jun; m. Mayaung Tai Hsu, Nov. 6, 1950 (dec. Feb. 11, 1987). BS, Amoy (China) U., 1947; MS, Auburn U., Ala., 1964, PhD, 1968. Sr. scientist U.S. Plywood-Champion Papers, Brewster, NY, 1968—72; sr. rsch. and devel. chemist RSA Corp., Ardsley, NY, 1972—75; project dir. UN Internat. Devel. Orgn., Langoon, Myanmar, 1976—79; rsch. assoc. Jim Walter Rsch. Corp., St. Petersburg, Fla., 1980—82; sr. resin chemist Hillyard Chem. Co., St. Joseph, Mo., 1982—87. Fellow: Am. Inst. of Chemists. Achievements include patents for adhesives, paints and coatings. Home: 1548 81st Ave North Saint Petersburg FL 33704-4055

HSUEH, CHUN-TU, political scientist, educator, foundation administrator, historian; b. Canton, Guangzhou, China, 1922; came to U.S., 1949, naturalized, 1960; m. Cordelia Teh-hua Huang, Dec. 13, 1952 (dec. 2002). Cert., China Sch. Jornalism, Hong Kong, 1939; LLB, Chaoyang U., China, 1946, Raffles Coll., Singapore, 1946-49; MA, Columbia U., 1953, PhD, 1958; hon. doctorate, U. San Martín de Porres, Lima, Peru, 1984, Inst. Far Ea. Studies, Russian Acad. Scis., 1999. Research assoc. polit. sci. Stanford U., 1959-62; lectr. history U. Hong Kong, 1962-64; vis. assoc. prof. SUNY, Plattsburgh, 1964-65; assoc. prof. U. Md., College Park, 1965-68, prof. politics, 1968-92; pres. Huang Hsing Found., Md., 1990—. Prof. Columbia U., summer 1969, 89; sr. assoc. mem. St. Antony's Coll., Oxford U., 1969; vis. prof., acting dir. Free U. Berlin, 1970; prof. Harvard U., summer 1979, 84; vis. scholar Peking U., 1983, Hebrew U., Jerusalem, 1984; disting. vis. prof. Zhongshan U., Guangzhou, China, 1983—, Wuhan U., 1984—, Peking U., 1989—, Zhejiang U., 1992—, Hunan U., 1996—, Shandong U., 1999—; adv. prof. Fudan U., Shanghai, 1985—; vis. fellow Australian Nat. U., Canberra, 1985; rsch. assoc. Ctr. for Chinese Studies U. Calif., Berkeley, 1985-86; chmn. Washington and S.E. Regional Seminar on China, 1974-81; exec. dir. Asian Polit. Scientists Group in U.S.A., 1975-2000; mem. vis. com., dept. internat. rels. Lehigh U., 1979-85; pres., chmn., Huang Hsing Found., Md., 1990—; vis. prof. U. Hong Kong, Trinity term, 1985, hon. prof., 1991-96; hon. prof. People's U., China, 1993—, Fgn. Affairs Coll., Beijing, 1996—, Jianghan U., Wuhan, China, 1987—, Ningxia U., 1992—, Nanjing Normal U., 1996—, Grad. Sch., Chinese Acad. Social Scis., 1998—, The Confucius Acad., Shandong, 1998—; trustee Jinan U., Guangzhou, China, 1989—, Nanjing Normal U., 1997—, Nanjing U., 1998—; advisor Sun Yat-sen Found., Guangzhou, 1992—; bd. dirs. Atlantic Coun. U.S., Washington, 1994-2003, Russian Rsch. Ctr. Chinese Acad. Social Scis., 1996—; hon. pres. Internat. Studies Assn., Shandong Province, 1998—; advisor Churchill Coll., U. Cambridge, 1998—, mem. exec. com. Atlantic Coun. Found., 1999—; hon. dir. Chaoyang Ctr. for Legal Studies, People's U. China, 2000—; hon. fellow Inst. Russian, East European and Ctrl. Asian Studies, Chinese Acad. Social Scis. Author: Huang Hsing and the Chinese Revolution, 1961, Chinese edit., 1980; editor, contbr. Revolutionary Leaders of Modern China, 1971, French edit., 1973, Dimensions of China's Foreign Relations, 1977, Asian Political Scientists in North America: Professional and Ethnic Problems, 1977, China's Foreign Relations: New Perspectives, 1982, Traditional Government in Imperial China: A Critical Analysis, 1982, The Chinese Revolution of 1911: New Perspectives, 1986, author/editor (books in Chinese with English title) People, Places and Politics, 1991, China and Her Neighbors: Prospects for the 21st Century, 1995, New Dimensions of China's Diplomacy, 1997, The New Russia: Politics, Economics and Diplomacy, 1997, Modernization of the Legal System and China's Economic Development, 1997, Confucianism and Modernization of Chinese Culture, 1998, Trade and Economic Relations Between China and Russia, 1999, China and Central Asia, 1999, Sun Tzu's Art of War and Its Value in Modern Times, 1999, Social Change in the Chinese Communities in Southeast Asia after World War II, 1999, Prospects for China's Relations with Europe in the 21st Century, 2000, Japan in Turbulence, 2001, A Strategic Study of Establishing a Maritime Shandong, 2000, Europe and China in the 21st Century, 2000, Social Life and Ideas Change in Modern China, 2001, The Cradle of Modern Chinese Jurisprudence: The History of Chaoyang University, 2001, Russian Siberia and the Far East, 2002, Central and Eastern Europe in Transition, 2002, Confucianism and Modernization, 2004. Mem. Nat. Bicentennial Ethnic-Racial Coun., 1974-76, Nat. Com. on U.S.-China Rels., 1976—; mem. adv. com. Md. Bicentennial Commn., 1975-76; mem. nat. exec. com. Caucus for New Polit. Sci., 1973-75. Named Benefactor, Columbia U., 2004. Mem.: Am. Polit. Sci. Assn., Western Returned Scholars Assn. (hon. chmn. Found. 1994—, Beijing, overseas hon. v.p.), Assn. for Asian Studies (chmn. com. on scholars of Asian descent 1981—84). Achievements include honored benefactor Columbia U., 2004. Office: 14017 Wagon Way Silver Spring MD 20906-2065

HSUEH, EDDY C., surgeon, oncologist; b. Taichung, Taiwan, May 18, 1965; s. Yuan-tu Hsueh and Chai Hsu; m. Hui-ling Lee, Apr. 17, 1965; children: Joanne, Brandon. BA, U. Chgo., 1987, MD, 1991. Resident in gen. surgery SUNY, Bklyn., 1991—96; asst. dir. surg. oncology John Wayne Cancer Inst., Santa Monica, Calif., 1999—, dir. immunotherapy enhancement, 2000—03; assoc. prof. surgery St. Louis U., Mo., 2003—. Recipient Young Oncologist Essay award, Am. Radium Soc., 1997, Mentored Clin. Scientist Devel. award, Nat. Cancer Inst., 2000—; grantee Tech. Transfer program, Calif. Dept. Health Svcs., 2000—02. Fellow: ACS (life); mem.: AMA (licentiate), Assn. for Academic Surgery (licentiate), Soc. Surg. Oncology (licentiate Best Clin. Rsch. award 1998), Am. Assn. for Cancer Rsch. (licentiate), Am. Soc. Clin. Oncology (licentiate Merit award 1997, 1998, 2000, Young Investigator award 1999, Career Devel. award 2001—). Achievements include research in elucidating the specific immunologic response in killing tumor cells; defining the predictive factors associated with cancer patient survival; development of novel strategy for immune mediated killing of cancer cells. Avocations: reading, travel, swimming. Office: St Louis U Dept Surgery 3635 Vista at Grand Blvd Saint Louis MO 63110 Office Phone: 314-577-8566. E-mail: echsueh@msn.com.

HSUEH, WEI, pathologist, educator; b. Inner Mongolia, China, Apr. 21, 1944; d. Hsing-ruh and Yu-ing H.; m. Frank González-Crussi, 1978. MD, Nat. Taiwan U., Taipei, 1968; PhD, Ind. U., 1972. Diplomate Am. Bd. Pathology. Assoc. pathologist Children's Meml. Hosp., Chgo., 1978—; asst. prof. pathology Northwestern U. Med. Sch., Chgo., 1978-83, assoc. prof. pathology with tenure, 1983-90, prof. pathology, 1990—. Mem. GMA-2 study sect. NIH, 1992-96; mem. reversite site visit NIH/NICHD, 1992; spl. reveiwer NSF, March of Dimes, Chgo. Lung Assn., Scleroderma, NIH, 2000, 03, B.C. Health Rsch. Found., Can. Contbr. over 100 articles to profl. jours., 9 chpts. to books. Grantee Nat. Inst. Allergy and Infectious Diseases, 1979-84, NIH/Nat. Inst. Diabetes, Digestive and Kidney Diseases, 1984-2002, Nat. Inst. Child Health and Human Devel., 1994-99. Mem. Am. Assn. Investigative Pathologists, Am. Assn. Immunologists, Internat. Acad. Pathology. Office: Children's Meml Hosp 2300 N Childrens Plz Chicago IL 60614-3394 Business E-Mail: whsueh@childrensmemorial.org.

HSU-LI, MAGDALEN, singer, poet, painter; d. George Tze-Ching Li. BFA in Painting, Rhode Island Sch. of Design; attended, Cornish Coll. of Arts. Founder Chickpop Records, 1997—, Femme Vitale, Seattle Women's Music and Arts Coalition, 1997. Singer: (albums) Muscle and Bone, 1997, Evolution, 1998, Fire, 2001. Office: Chickpop Records 117 E Louisa St PO Box 422 Seattle WA 98102*

HU, CHENMING, electrical engineering educator; b. Beijing, July 12, 1947; came to U.S., 1969; m. Margaret Hu, Feb. 14, 1972; children: Raymond, Jason. BS, Nat. Taiwan U., Taipei, 1968; MS, U. Calif., Berkeley, 1970, PhD, 1973. Asst. prof. MIT, 1973-76; prof. U. Calif., Berkeley, 1976—, Chancellor's prof., 1998-2000, Taiwan Semicondr. Mfg. Corp. Disting. prof. microelectronics, 2000—. Mgr. nonvolatile memory devel. Nat. Semicondr., Santa Clara, 1980-81; hon. prof. Beijing U., 1988, Tsing Hwa U., 1991, Chinese Acad. Sci., 1991; dir. Joint Svcs. Electronics Program, 1989-92, Indsl. Liaison Program, 1992-95; founder, chmn. Celestry Design Tech. Inc., 1995-2003, chief tech. officer Taiwan Semicondr. Mfg. Co., 2001-04. Co-author: Solar Cells, 1983, Advanced MOS Device Physics, 1989, Nonvolatile Semiconductor Memory, 1991, MOSFET Modeling, 1999; patentee solid state devices and tech.; contbr. over 800 articles to profl. jours. Chmn. bd. East Bay Chinese Sch., Oakland, Calif., 1989-91. Recipient Design News Excellence in Design award, 1991, Semiconductor Rsch. Corp. Tech. Excellence award, 1992, Outstanding Inventor award, 1993, R&D 100 award, 1996, Monie Ferst award Sigma Xi, 1998, W.Y. Pang Found. award for rsch. excellence, 1999. Fellow IEEE (editl. bd. Trans. on Electronic Devices 1986-88, Jack Morton award 1997, Solid State Circuits award 2002, Paul Rappaport award 2004), NAE, Inst. Physics. Office: U Calif Dept Elec Engring Computer Sci Berkeley CA 94720-0001 E-mail: hu@eecs.berkeley.edu.

HU, CHI YU, physicist, educator; b. Szchwan, China, Feb. 12, 1933; arrived in U.S., 1957, naturalized, 1974; s. T. C. and P. S. (Yang) Hu; children: Marica, Mark, Albert, Han Chin. BS, Nat. Taiwan U., 1955; PhD, MIT, 1962. Rsch. assoc. St. John's U., Jamaica, NY, 1962-63; asst. prof. physics Calif. State U., Long Beach, 1963-68, assoc. prof., 1968-72, prof., 1972—. NSF vis. prof. UCLA, 1988—90. Contbr. articles to prof. jours. Fellow NSF summer, 1965, 1976; grantee, NSF, 1969—70, 1986—88, 1988—90, 1990—, Calif. State U. Long Beach Found., 1965, 1966, 1970, 1972, Dept. Energy, 1986—88. Mem.: Am. Phys. Soc. Office: Calif State U Dept Physics Long Beach CA 90840-0001 Business E-Mail: chihu@csulb.edu.

HU, HONGDE, mathematics professor; m. Vicky Liu; children: Lisa, Angela. BA, Pingniang Coll., China, 1982; PhD, McGill U., 1993. Asst. prof. York U., Toronto, Canada, 1993—95; postdoctoral fellow U. Que., Montreal, 1995—96; lectr. U. Pa., Phila., 1996—99; asst. prof. Calif. State U.-Monterey Bay, Seaside, 1999—2002, assoc. prof., 2003—. Vis. rschr. Stanford (Calif.) U., 1997, U. Sydney, Australia, 1998, ElectroTech. Lab., Osaka, Japan, 2000; chmn. Mathcom com. Calif. State U.-Monterey Bay, 2000—. Contbr. articles to profl. jours., confs. Grantee Agy. of Indsl. Sci and Tech., Japan, 2000. Mem.: Assn. Symbolic Logic, Am. Math. Soc., Can. Math Soc. Office: Calif State U-Monterey Bay 100 Campus Ctr Seaside CA 93955 Office Phone: 831-582-3851.

HU, HUPING, biophysicist, lawyer; b. Wenshui, Shanxi, China, Sept. 19, 1962; arrived in US, 1987; s. Yongchang Hu and Cuifang Sun; m. Maoxin Wu, Jan. 19, 1986; children: Alice, Allen. BS, Shanxi Agrl. U., China, 1983; MS, Lanzhou U., Gansu, China, 1986; PhD, U. Ill., 1991; JD, NY Law Sch., 1998. Lic.: NY State Appellate Divsn. (2nd Dept.) 1999, bar: 1999. Rsch. asst. U. Ill., Champaign-Urbana; CEO H&W Mgmt. Corp., Champaign, 1991—93; legal asst. Bronx Dist. Atty.s Office, NYC, 1995—96; sci. cons. Stein & Associates, P.C., NYC, 1996—98; prin. Huping Hu Atty. at Law, NYC, 1999—; chief scientist Biophysics Consulting Group, NYC, 2000—. Contbr. articles to profl. jours. Recipient Best Grad. Student award, Lanzhou U., China, 1984—85. Mem.: ABA, NY State Bar Assn. D-Conservative. Achievements include founder of Scientific God Institute; proponent of the spin-mediated consciousness theory that says spins carried by nuclei in neural membranes are the linchpins between mind and brain, that is, spin is the mind-pixel; first to proponent of the oxygen pathway perturbation hypothesis which says that oxygen pathway perturbations by anesthetics play key roles in anesthesia. Office: Biophysics Consulting Group 136-40 39th Avenue Suite 502 Flushing NY 11354 Office Phone: 718-358-2085. Office Fax: 718-358-2086. Personal E-mail: drhu@att.net. E-mail: hupinghu@quantumbrain.org.

HU, JOSEPH YUAN-CHUNG, artist, educator; b. Kans. City, Sept. 12, 1976; s. Teh-Kon and Shiu-Ling Hu. BFA, Art Inst. Chgo., 1998; MFA, Pa. Acad. Fine Arts, 2001. Adj. instr. Camden County Coll., Blackwood, NJ, 2002—04, Cumberland County Coll., Vineland, NJ, 2001—02. Pres. membership Vox Populi, Phila., 2004—. Represented in permanent collections Pa. Acad. Fine Arts, Phila., Pa., Sprint Corporate Art Collection, Overland Park, Kansas. Bd. dirs. Vox Populi, 2004—05. Recipient Judith McGregor Caldwell Purchase prize, Pa. Acad. Fine Arts, Phila., Pa., 2001; fellow, Independence Found., Phila., Pa., 2002, SoPhilArt Altes Spital Begegnungszentrum, Solothurn, Switzerland, 2003. Mem.: Coll. Art Assn. Home: 1162 South Darien Street 2nd Floor Philadelphia PA 19147 Personal E-mail: joseph@josephhu.net.

HU, LI, art educator; b. Shanghai, Sept. 16, 1950; s. Renzhi Hu and Keren He; m. Ping Li, Feb. 22, 1988; children: Yichen Hu, Elina Hu. BFA, Shanghai U., 1986; MFA, U. S.D., 1993. Art designer Xiechang Sewing Machine Co., Shanghai, 1977-83; asst. prof. Shanghai U., 1986-89; assoc. prof. U. Wis., Oshkosh, 1993—. Solo shows include Tusculum Coll., Tenn., Rosewood Arts Ctr., 2004, North Central Coll., Naperville, Ill., 2002, Ripon (Wis.) Coll., 2001, Hopper House Art Ctr., Nyack, N.Y., 2001, So. Oreg. U., Ashland, 2001, Coll. of Siskiyous, Weed, Calif., 2000, 1078 Gallery, Chico, Calif., 2000, Lakeland Coll., Sheboygan, Wis., 2000, Morehead State U., Kent, 1999, U. Wis., Madison, 1999, Reno City Hall Gallery, 1999, Art Inst. and Gallery, Salisbury, Md., 1999, Art Ctr. in Orange, Va., 1999, Colo. State U., Ft. Collins, 1998, Coker Coll., Hartsville, S.C., 1998, Linfield State Coll., McMinnville, Oreg., 1998, McHenry County Coll., Crystal Lake, Ill., 1998, Chadron State Coll., Nebr., 1997, Kansas City Artists Coalition, Kansas City, Mo., 1997, Mont. State U., Billings, 1996, Corvallis Arts Ctr., Oreg., 1996, Minnetonka Ctr. for the Art, Wayzata, Minn., 1995, Bloominton Art Ctr., Minn., 1995, U. SD, Vermillion, St. Louis C.C., others; group shows include U. S.D., Vermillion, St. Louis C.C., Calif. State U., Long Beach, 2003, Ohio State U., Mansfield, 2002, Taipai Fine Art Mus., Taiwan, 2001, Leslie Powell Gallery, Lawton, Okla., 1997, 2000, Smithtown Twp. Arts Coun., St. James, N.Y., 1997, Korean Cultural Ctr., L.A., 1996, Medici Art Ctr., Phila., 1996, San Francisco State U. Student Ctr. Art Gallery, Calif., 1995, Berkeley Art Ctr., Calif., 1995, Royal Garden Gallery, Copenhagen, 1987, Hunte Coll., N.Y., 1986, Kobe (Japan) Agr. Mus., 1986, Shanghai Art Mus., 1986, 87, 89, Coll. Visual Arts, St. Paul, 2001, Taipai Fine Art Mus., Taiwan, 2001 others; work collected at Sioux City Art Ctr., Iowa, U. S.D., Vermillion, Ripon Coll., Wis., Coal and Oil Corp., Ji Lu, Japan, Art Corp. of Japan-China, Kobe, Japan. Recipient Hon. Mention Okla.: Centerfold, Seventh, Leslie Powell Gallery, Lawton and the U. of Sci. and Art, Chickacha, 1997, Faculty Devel. Rsch. grant U. Wis., Oshkosh, 1996, 1995, Juror's award Berkeley Art Ctr. Assn., Calif., 1995, others. Home: 4365 Bellhaven Ln Oshkosh WI 54904 Office Phone: 920-424-7059. Business E-Mail: Hu@uwosh.edu.

HU, PETER CHI, geneticist, educator; s. Ying Chih and Jo Chi Hu; m. Cynthia Yang, Dec. 16, 1990; children: Alexander Bo, Justin Bo. BA, Purdue U., 1991; MS, Lamar U., 1995. Instr. U. Tex. MD Anderson Cancer Ctr., Houston, 2003—04, asst. prof., 2004—. Edn. coord. U. Tex. MD Anderson Cancer Ctr., 2000—04. Mem.: AGT (assoc.), TACLS (assoc.; bd. dirs. 2005, commr. edn. 2005). Office Phone: 713-563-3095.

HU, QI, meteorologist, educator; b. Hancheng, Shaanxi, China, Nov. 4, 1957; US, 1984; s. Ruji and Cuiying Hu; m. Yunyu Xi, Feb. 12, 1983; children: Aillie Y., Karen Y., Christopher Y. BS, Lanzhou (China) U., 1982; MS, Colo. State U., 1986, PhD, 1992. Rsch. scientist SUNY, Albany, NY, 1992—94, Pacific N.W. Nat. Labs., Richland, Wash., 1994—95; dir. Mo. Climate Ctr., Columbia, Mo., 1995—99; assoc. prof. U. Nebr., Lincoln, Nebr., 1999—. Rsch. asst. prof. U. Mo., Columbia, 1995—99. Contbr. articles to profl. jours. Grantee, Nat. Oceanic and Atmospheric Adminstrn., 1997—2004, Dept. Agr., 1997—2004, Dept. Energy, 1997—2004, NSF, 1997—2004, U.S. Geol. Survey, 1997—2004. Fellow: Ctr. Gt. Plains Studies; mem.: Am. Geophys. Union, Am. Assn. State Climatologists (assoc.), Am. Meteorol. Soc., U. Nebr. Student Photographers Club (advisor 2002—04). Independent. Achievements include discovery of low-frequency oscillations in radiative-convective systems; multidecadal alternation of the El Nino effect on summer rainfall in the central United States; multidecadal alternation of the sea surface temperature and land process effect on southwest U.S. monsoon rainfall. Avocations: basketball, painting, climbing. Office: University of Nebraska-Lincoln 237 LW Chase Hall Lincoln NE 68583-0728 Office Phone: 402-472-6642. Office Fax: 402-472-6614. Business E-Mail: qhu2@unl.edu.

HU, QINHONG, geochemist, researcher; s. Jin-Min and Yu-Dei (Zhang) Hu; m. Li Mao, Sept. 30, 1991; children: Simon M., Sonya M. BS, Zhejing U., Hangzhou, China, 1986; MS, Chinese Acad. Scis., Nanjing, 1989; PhD, U. Ariz., 1995. Scientist Lawrence Berkeley Nat. Lab., Berkeley, Calif., 1997—2002; staff scientist Lawrence Livermore Nat. Lab., Calif., 2002—. Contbr. articles to profl. jours. Vol. Chinese Am. Cooperation Coun. Chinese Sch., Pleasanton, Calif., 2004—05. Recipient 3rd award in Natural Sci. Rsch., Chinese Acad. Scis., 1996, Outstanding Performance award, Lawrence Berkeley Nat. Lab., 2000, Spot Recognition award, 2000. Mem.: Geochemical Soc., Groundwater Resources Assn. Calif., Am. Geophys. Union. Achievements include research in international planning team member for long-term diffusion test at Grimsel Test Site, national cooperative for the disposal of radioactive waste (Nagra), Switzerland. Office: Lawrence Livermore Nat Lab 7000 East Ave Livermore CA CA 94 Office Phone: 925-422-6774. E-mail: hu7@llnl.gov.

HU, WEIGANG, software engineer; b. Ji-An, Jiangxi, China, Apr. 4, 1965; s. Yuanyu Hu and Jumei Fu; m. Guangping Grace Wang, Sept. 10, 2001; children: Zhengyi, Zhengjia Jennifer. PhD, Huazhong U. Sci. and Tech., Wuhan, China, 1994. Assoc. prof. Huazhong U. Sci. and Tech., Wuhan, 1994—97; post doctoral rschr. IRIS - Swinburne U. of Tech., Hawthorn, Australia, 1996—97; rsch. assoc. Wayne State U., Detroit, 1997—99; sofware engr. Ford Motor Co., Dearborn, Mich., 1999—2000, sys. analyst, 2003—; sr. project engr. Visteon Corp., Allen Park, Mich., 2000—03. Leader Chinese Soccer Club Windsor, Canada, 2000—04. Achievements include development of knowledge-based design and manufacturing support system; research in theories and methods of knowledge-based engineering; case-based reasoning strategy in knowledge-based engineering design. Office Phone: 313-248-2218. Personal E-mail: ae3091@yahoo.com.

HU, YIPING, metallurgical engineer; b. Honghu, Hubei, China, Jan. 23, 1958; s. Zhaozhi Hu and Dingming Liu; m. Zanping Liu, Dec. 25, 1988; 1 child, Dianna. BS in Metallurgical Engring., Wuhan Inst. Tech., China, 1981; MS in Materials Sci., Mich. State U., 1996, PhD, 2000. Sr. instr. Guangdong Tech. Sch. of Light Industry, Guang Zhou, China, 1982—92; devel. engr. Quantum Laser Corp., Norcross, Ga., 1999—99; sr. engr. Honeywell-Greer Engines, Systems & Services, Greer, SC, 2000—. Mem.: The Minerals, Metals & Materials Soc., ASM Internat. Achievements include pioneer to employ laser cladding technique to make rotary cutting dies, dramatically reduce production costs and greatly prolong service life; methods for repair of single crystal superalloys by laser welding and products thereof; patents pending for Multi-Laser Beam Welding High-Strength Superalloys; a new coaxial nozzle design for laser cladding/welding process; high-strength superalloy joining method for repairing turbine blades; modified MCrAlY coatings on turbine blade tips with improved durability; methods for repairing titanium alloy components. Home: 18 Collier Lane Greer SC 29650 Office: Honeywell International 85 Beeco Road Greer SC 29650 Office Phone: 864-801-2174. Personal E-mail: yipinghu1@yahoo.com. E-mail: yiping.hu@honeywell.com.

HU, ZHIYU, research scientist, educator; b. Kunming, Yunnan Province, China, June 30, 1965; s. Wenguo Hu and Ping Li; m. Hongzhi Li, June 2, 1965; children: Lydia, Liana. BS, Yunnan U., 1986; MA, Fisk U., 1995; PhD, U. Tenn., 2000, EMBA, 2004. Asst. engr. Kunming Inst. Tech., Kunming, 1986—90; team leader and tchr. Yangbi Detachment of Vols. in Ednl. Svc., Yangbi, 1988—89; exchange vis. scholar U. Va., Charlottesville, 1990—93; gradute rsch. asst. Oak Ridge Nat. Lab., Oak Ridge, Tenn., 1995—2000; head Protiveris, Inc., Rockville, Md., 2000—02; staff scientist Oak Ridge Nat. Lab., Tenn., 2002—; rsch. asst. prof. U. Tenn., 2002—. Cons. Protiveris, Inc., Rockville, 2002—. Named Outstanding Vol. Tchr., Dept. of Edn. Yunnan Province, 1989; named to 11th Discover Mag. awards for technol. innovation, Discover Mag., 2000; recipient Southeast FLC award for excellence in tech. transfer, 2003, Excellence award in tech., Nat. Fed. Lab. Consortium, 2004. Mem.: Microscopy Soc. Am., Materials Rsch. Soc., Electrochem. Soc., Am. Physics Soc., Sigma Pi Sigma. Office: Oak Ridge Nat Lab Bethel Valley Rd PO Box 2008 Oak Ridge TN 37831-6123 Office Phone: 865-574-8461. Business E-Mail: huzn@ornl.gov.

HUA, FRED HUIZHONG, materials scientist; s. Dingfang Hua and Cai Zhang; m. Wenlian Zhou. PhD, McMaster U., 1998; B Engring, Hunan U., China, 1981. Rsch. asst. McMaster U., 1992—98; sr. rsch. engr. McDermott Tech. Inc., Alliance, Ohio, 1998—2002; sr. materials engr. Bechtel SAIC Co., LLC, Las Vegas, Nev., 2002—. Rsch. engr. Shanghai Rsch. Inst. Materials, Shanghai, 1982—91. Recipient Nat. award, Chinese Nat. Com. of Sci. & Tech., 1991/1992. Mem.: Nat. Assn. of Corrosion Engineers, Internat. (life). Achievements include research in Yucca Mountain project, which aims to secure the nuclear waste containment 10,000 years. Office: Bechtel SAIC Co LLC 1180 Town Center Dr Las Vegas NV 89144 Office Phone: 702-295-7597. Office Fax: 702-295-4496. Personal E-mail: midway_hua@yahoo.com. E-mail: fred_hua@ymp.gov.

HUA, XIANXIN, cell and cancer biology educator; b. Tongshan, Hubei, China, Aug. 27, 1962; s. Chengda Hua and Donge Jia; m. Wei Gao, June 1988; children: Connie, Michael. MD, Hubei Med. Coll., 1983; PhD, U. Tex. Southwestern Med. Ctr., Dallas, 1995. Postdoc. clin. scientist, Whitehead Inst., MIT, Cambridge, 1996-2000; asst. prof. cell biology, cancer biology, U. Pa., Phila., 2000—. Recipient Howard Temin award Nat. Cancer Inst., 1998, Career Devel. award Burroughs Welcome Fund, 1998, Rita Allen Scholar, 2002, Am. Cancer Soc. Rsch. Scholar, 2003. Em. AAAS. Office: Univ Pa 412 BRB 2/3 421 Curie Blvd Philadelphia PA 19104-6160

HUANG, CHENG-TEH JAMES, linguistics educator; b. Hualien, Taiwan, China, June 4, 1948; s. Ching-Fa Huang and Hsui-O Chen; m. Hsiao-Y Emily Huang, Nov. 30, 1977; children: Yiching Deborah, David J. BA, Nat. Taiwan Normal U., Taipei, China, 1972; MA, Nat. Taiwan Normal U., Taipei, Taiwan, 1974; PhD, MIT, 1982. Asst. prof. U. Hawaii, Honolulu, 1982-83, Nat. Tsing Hua U., Hsinchu, Taiwan, 1983-85; from asst. prof. to assoc. prof. Cornell U., Ithaca, N.Y., 1985-90; prof. U. Calif., Irvine, 1989-2001, Harvard U., Cambridge, Mass., 2001—. Vis. prof. Linguistic Inst., 1986, 91, 97, U. Paris, 1991; dir. Summer Inst. Chinese Linguistics, Santa Cruz, 1991, Cornell, 1997. Co-editor: Squibs and discussions, 1987-89; mem. editl. bd. Lang. Rsch., 1984—, Jour. Japanese Linguistics, 1985—, Linguistic Inquiry, 1987—, Nat. Lang. and Linguistic Theory, 1987-91, Oxford Series Comparative Grammar, 1989—, Nat. Lang. Linguistics, 1991—, Syntax: Theoretical and Exptl. Approaches, 1997—, Jour. Generative Grammar, 1998—; editor-in-chief Contemporary Chinese Linguistics, 1994—, Studies in Contemporary Linguistic Theories, 1996—; contbr. articles to profl. jours. Fulbright fellow, 1978-82, Guggenheim fellow, 1988-89, Sr. Scholar fellow Chiang Ching-Kuo Found., 1996-97, fellow Ctr. Advanced Study Behavioral Scis., 1997-98. Mem. Linguistic Soc. Am. (mem. program com. 1992-95, mem. com. linguistic insts. and fellowships 1997), Internat. Assn. Chinese Linguistics (pres. 2000). Office: Harvard U Dept Linguistics Cambridge MA 02138 Home: 43 Russell St Somerville MA 02144-3023 E-mail: jhuang@uci.edu.

HUANG, EUGENE YUCHING, civil engineer, educator; b. Changsha, China, Nov. 28, 1917; came to U.S., 1948, naturalized, 1962; s. Sam and Yi Yun (Chao) H.; m. Helen M. Woo, Aug. 20, 1955; children: Martha, Pearl, William, Mary, Priscilla, Stephen. *Eugene Huang's daughter, Martha, AB1978 Harvard, PhD 1999 Columbia, is a free-lance writer. His daughter, Pearl, SB 1980 MIT, PhD 1990 Princeton, is employed as vice president, oncology proliferative diseases for Glaxo Smith Kline Co. Eugene's son, William, AB 1981 Harvard, JD 1986 Yale, PhD, 1998 University of California Berkeley, is an attorney in Washington DC. His daughter, Mary, AB 1984 Harvard, MD 1988 Duke, is an oncologist at Massachusetts General Hospital. His daughter, Priscilla, SB1986 MIT, MBA 1990 Pennsylvania, is employed as controller for Merck Vaccines, a unit of Merck Co. His son, Stephen, BS 1990 Yale, MD 1995 Pennsylvania, is an endocrinologist at Boston Children's hospital.* MS, U. Utah, 1950; D.Sc., U. Mich., 1954. Registered profl. engr., Ill., Mich. Asst. engr. Chinese Nat. Hwy. Adminstrn., 1941-45, asso. engr., 1945-48; research asst. Engring. Research Inst., U. Mich., 1953-54; research asst. prof. civil engring. U. Ill., Urbana, 1954-58, asso. prof., 1958-63; prof. transp. engring. Mich. Tech. U., Houghton, 1963-84; acting head dept. civil engring., 1979-80; acting dean of grad. studies Mich. Tech. U., Houghton, 1981-83, prof. emeritus transp. engring., 1984—. Cons. transp. systems design, soil mechanics, 1954— Author: Overview of the American Transportation System, 1976; contbr. numerous articles on transp. design systems and research on materials for pavement to profl. jours. Recipient Faculty Research award Mich. Tech. U., 1967 Fellow ASCE; mem. AAAS, ASTM, NRC (transp. rsch. bd. 1954), Am. Soc. Engring. Edn., Assn. Asphalt Paving Technologists, Inst. for Opns. Rsch. and the Mgmt. Scis., Am. Ry. Engring. Assn., Sigma Xi, Chi Epsilon, Tau Beta Pi, Phi Tau Phi. Episcopalian. Home: 400 Garnet St Houghton MI 49931-1420

HUANG, GUIYOU, English studies educator, writer; b. Xinjiang, China, Dec. 24, 1961; came to U.S., 1989; s. Huang Honglai and Dong Xiuqin; m. Yufeng Qian; 1 child, George Ian. BA in English, Qufu Tchrs. U., 1983; MA in English, Peking U., 1989; PhD in English, Tex. A&M U., 1993. Instr. Qufu Tchrs. U., 1983-86; tchg. asst. Peking U., 1986-89; editl. asst. South Ctrl. Rev. Tex. A&M U., College Station, 1989-93, lectr., 1993-95; asst. prof. Kutztown U., Pa., 1995-2000, assoc. prof., 2000—03, prof., 2003—04, dir. univ. honors program, 2000—04, chair dept. English, 2002—04; prof. English, dir. Honors Coll. Grand Valley State U., 2004—05, dean undergrad. studies and programs, 2005—. Author: Whitmanism, Imagism, and Modernism in China and America, 1997; editor: Asian American Autobiographers, 2001, Asian American Poets, 2002, Asian American Short Story Writers, 2003, Asian American Literary Studies, 2005; contbr. articles to profl. jours. Recipient Profl. Devel. awards State Sys. Higher Edn. Pa., 1997-98, 2003. Mem. MLA, Am. Lit. Assn., Am. Studies Assn., South Cen. MLA, Frederick Douglass Inst., Assn. for Asian Am. Studies, Am. Assn. Univ. Adminstrs. Avocations: swimming, travel, cooking, fishing, conversation. Home: 14178 SW 54th St Miramar FL 33027 Office Phone: 305-474-6865. E-mail: ghuang@stu.edu.

HUANG, H.K. (BERNIE HUANG), radiologist, educator; DSc, George Washington U., 1971. Prof., vice chmn. dept. radiol. scis. UCLA, 1982—92; prof., vice chmn. U. Calif., San Francisco, 1992—2000; prof., dir. U. So. Calif., LA, 2000—; hon. prof. Shanghai Inst. Tech Physics, Chinese Acad. Sci., 2000—; chair prof. Hong Kong Poly. Univ., 2000—. Cons. Hong Kong Hosp. Authority, 2002—03, Princess Margaret Hosp., Hong Kong, 2003—, NIH, Bethesda, Md., 1990—. Named Hon. Pres., Internat. CARS Congress, 2003; grantee, NIH, 1985—2005. Fellow: Am Inst. Med. Biol. Engrs. (founding mem.); mem.: European PACS Soc. (hon.), Royal Coll. Radiologists London (hon.). Office: Dept Radiology Univ SC 4676 Admiralty Way Ste 601 Marina Del Rey CA 90292 Office Phone: 310-448-9435.

HUANG, HSIEN-LU, electrical engineer; b. Hsiang-Hsiang, Hunan, China, Dec. 12, 1923; s. Shao-Ju and Ching (Yu) Huang; m. Hui-Lien Peng Huang, Jan. 1, 1947; children: Su, Na-Ching Chang, Kung, Janet Tu, Chin, Samuel Lin, Hsin, Chris Lu, Sung-Ping, Emanuel Lin, Peter Sung-an, Nina Wang. BSEE, Nat. Hunan U., 1944; MSEE, Va. Polytechnic Inst./State U., 1968, PhD in Elec. Engring., 1969. Cert. mgr. Rockwell Nat. Mgmt. Assn. Maj. Chinese Air Force, 1944-64, prodn. control chief, quality control officer, dep. squadron comdr. Nanking and Taiwan, 1944-64; assoc. prof. in elec. engring. Taipei Inst. Technology, 1960-66; instr. in elec. engring. Va. Polytechnic Inst. and State U., Blacksburg, 1968-69; asst. prof. in elec. engring. W.Va. U., Morgantown, 1970-74; devel. design engr. Barber - Colman Co., Rockford, Ill., 1975-76, Bridgeport Machines Control Co., Horsham, Pa., 1977-79; sr. elec. engr. and reliability engr. specialist Ford Aerospace and Comms. Corp., Houston, 1979-85; lead reliability engr. Rockwell Space Opers. Co., Houston, 1986-96; mem. engring. staff United Space Alliance West, Houston, 1996—. Contbr. articles to profl. publs. Elder, advisor Phila. Chinese Bible Study Fellowship, 1977—79; elder, evangelist Clear Lake Chinese Ch., Houston, 1979—; founder, coord. Space Christians Fellowship & Bible Study, Clear Lake, Houston, 1980—. Recipient Nat. Fidelity/Dilligence medal, Pres. of China, 1955, Group Achievement award, Lyndon B. Johnson Space Ctr., Houston, 1983. Fellow: AIAA (assoc.); mem.: IEEE (life), Nat. Mgmt. Assn. (cert. mgr.). Avocations: Bible study, personal evangelism, Christian fellowship, church visitation, family spiritual retreat. Home: 470 Buoy Rd Webster TX 77598-2505 Office: United Space Alliance-West 600 Gemini St Houston TX 77058-2754 Office Phone: 281-282-4598. Personal E-mail: hlhuang@email.com. Business E-Mail: Hsien.L.Huang@usa-spaceops.com.

HUANG, JEN-HSUN, electronics executive; b. Taiwan; m. Lori Huang; 2 children. BSEE, Oreg.State U., 1984; MSEE, Stanford (Calif.) U. Microprocessor designer Advanced Micro Devices; dir. coreware LSI Logic; cofounder NVIDIA Corp., Santa Clara, Calif., 1993—, pres., 1993—, CEO, 1993—. Office: NVIDIA Corp 2701 San Tomas Expy Santa Clara CA 95050*

HUANG, JINHUA, mechanical engineer, researcher; arrived in U.S., 1996; s. Guizhi Huang and Yiying Wu; m. Ming Chen, Aug. 10, 1995. BEE, Hefei (China) U. Tech.; PhD, Clemson U., 2000. Grad. rsch. asst. Shanghai JiaoTong U., 1986—89; lectr. Hefei (China) U. Tech., 1989—96; tchg. asst. Clemson (SC) U., 1996—97, rsch. asst., 1997—2000; prin. investigator AeroChem Corp., Gainesville, Fla., 2000—, U. Fla., Gainesville, 2000—. Expert reviewer Jour. Mech. Design, N.Y.C., 1998—2003. People's scholar, Hefei U. Tech., 1984. Mem.: AIAA, ASME. Achievements include patents for strong and light structures with holes; discovery of two-phase phenomena for osteonal bones to arrest cracks; design of methodologies for the optimization design of superb products. Home: 902 SW16th Ave Gainesville FL 32601 Office: AeroChem Corp 902 SW 16th Ave Gainesville FL 32601 Personal E-mail: david_jinhuahuang@yahoo.com.

HUANG, JULIAN, pediatrician, consultant; MD, U. Pitts., 1987. Diplomate Am. Bd. Pediatrics. Pediatrician Healthcare S. / Scituate (Mass.) Pediat., 1992—; chmn. dept. pediat. S. Shore Hosp., South Weymouth, Mass., 2000—02; clin. instr. Boston U. Med. Sch., 2002—. Pediatric cons. Glaxo Smith Kline, Research Triangle Park, NC, 2003—; bd. dirs., exec. bd. Integrated Healthware; bd. dirs. Healthcare S., Physician Strategies, LLC. Author: Spinehealth.com. Fellow: Am. Acad. Pediat.; mem.: Ambulatory Pediat. Assn., Am. Med. Informatics Assn., Norfolk South Dist. Med. Soc., Mass. Med. Soc. (exec. com. infotech 2003—05). Office: Healthcare S Scituate Pediat 10 New Driftway Ste 201 Scituate MA 02066 Office Phone: 781-545-9225.

HUANG, LIMIN, chemist, researcher; b. Jiangyin, Jiangsu Province, China, Apr. 17, 1970; s. Mantang and Wenyu (Cai) Huang; m. Lingling Wei, Apr. 28, 1998. PhD in Chemistry, Fudan U., Shanghai, China, 1997. Rsch. asst. Fudan U., Shanghai, 1992—97, lectr., 1997—2000; postdoctoral rschr. U. of Calif., Calif., 2000—02; postdoctoral rsch. scientist Columbia U., N.Y.C., 2002—. Contbr. articles to profl. jours., 2000. Recipient TIAN Award, TIAN Fund, 1997, award, Guanghua Edn. Fund, 1994. Mem.: Am. Chem. Soc., Internat. Zeolite Assn., Material Rsch. Soc. Achievements include patents for Synthesis of composite mesomicroporous materials. Office: Columbia Univ 500 W 120th St New York NY 10027 Personal E-mail: lmhuang70@yahoo.com. Business E-Mail: lh2036@columbia.edu.

HUANG, LINDA CHEN, plastic surgeon; b. Ithaca, N.Y., July 24, 1952; MD, Stanford U., 1979. Chmn. plastic surgery St. Joseph Hosp., Denver. Office: 1601 E 19th Ave Ste 3150 Denver CO 80218-1220 Office Phone: 303-831-8400.

HUANG, MICHAEL BAILOU, librarian; b. Shanghai, May 10, 1956; s. Yulin Huang and Shuru Tang; m. Helen Hui Shi, Sept. 29, 1984; 1 child, Jenny Junyan. BA in English Lit., Shanghai Tchrs. U., China, 1982; MLS, Clarion U., Pa., 1989; MEd, Elmira Coll., N.Y., 1997. Cert. libr. N.Y., 1990. Tchr. English Minhang HS, Shanghai, 1982—88; ref. libr., head interlibrary loan dept. Steele Meml. Libr., Elmira, 1990—97; sr. asst. libr. Oswego State U., 1997—99, SUNY Health Scis. Ctr. Libr., Stony Brook, 1999—. Vis. scholar Capital Normal U. Libr., Beijing, 1998. Contbr. In the Turn of the Centuries: Retrospect and Prospect of Libraries, 1999, The 21st Century Libraries: Development and Transformation, 2000, Global Digital Library Development in the New Millennium, 2001; contbr. articles to profl. jours. Recipient Finest Paper award, China Soc. for Libr. Sci. Ann. Conf., 1999, 2002; grantee Prof. Devel. and Quality of Working Life grant, N.Y. State United Univ. Professions, 1998, Profl. Devel. grant, State U. Librs. Assn., 1998. Mem.: Med. Libr. Assn., State Univ. of N.Y. Librs. Assn., Chinese Aml. Librs. Assn., Med. Libr. Assn. (Outstanding Contbn. by a New Mem. award N.J.-N.Y. chpt. 2000). Home: 15 Lyndon Lne South Setauket NY 11720 Office: Suny Stony Brook Health Sciences Library 8034 Suny,Hsc Level 3 Rm 136 Stony Brook NY 11794-8034 Office Phone: 631-444-3794. Office Fax: 631-444-6649. Business E-Mail: michael.b.huang@sunysb.edu.

HUANG, PAN MING, soil science educator; b. Pu-tse, Taiwan, Sept. 2, 1934; arrived in Can., 1965; s. Rong Yi and Koh (Chiu) H.; m. Yun Yin Lin, Dec. 26, 1964; children: Daniel Chian Yuan, Crystal Ling Hui. BSA, Nat. Chung Hsing U., Taichung, Taiwan, 1957; MSc, U. Man., Winnipeg, Can., 1962; PhD, U. Wis., Madison, 1966. Cert. prof. agrologist. Asst. prof. soil sci. U. Sask., Saskatoon, Canada, 1965-71, assoc. prof., 1971-78, prof., 1978—. Invited rsch. chair Nat. Taiwan U., 1996, 2003, 04; nat. vis. prof., head dept. soil sci. Nat. Chung Hsing U., 1975-76; mem. agr. adv. bd. Lewis Pubs., 1991—; hon. prof. Huazhong Agr. U., 1992—, Guanxi Agrl U., 1993—, Henan Agrl. U., 1996—, Langzhou U., 1999—; acad. advisor Chinese Acad. Scis., 1996—; hon. scientist Rural Adminstrn., Republic of Korea. Author: Soil Chemistry, 1991, Environmental Soil Chemistry and Its Impact on Agriculture and the Ecosystem, 2000; mem. editl. bd.: Chemosphere, 1987—97, Pedosphere, 1990—, Trends in Agr. Sci., 1991—95, Advances in Environ. Sci., 1993, Geodema, 1994—, Soil Sci. Plant Nutrition, 1998—, Water, Air, and Soil Pollution, 1998—2001, Humic Substances in the Environment, 1998—; editor: 14 books; spl. editor, mem. editl. bd.: Water Pollution Rsch. Jour. Can., 1983—89, 1991—93, Agro's Ann. Rev. Crop Ecology, 1995—, mem. editl. adv. bd.: Trends in Soil Sci., 1995—; contbr. over 300 articles to profl. jours., chapters to books. Bd. dirs. Saskatoon Chinese Mandarin Sch., 1977-79, Saskatoon Soc. for Study Chinese Culture, 1983—. 2d lt. Taiwan Mil. Tng. Corps, 1957-59. Grantee UN Environment Programme, Nat. Scis. and Engring. Rsch. Coun. Can., numerous other agys., 1965—. Fellow: AAAS, The World Innovation Found., Am. Soc. Agronomy, Soil Sci. Soc. Am. (rep. Clay Minerals Soc. 1979—83, chmn. divsn. S-9 1983—84, bd. dirs. 1983—84, editor spl. pub. 1986, Internat. Soil Sci. award com. 1986—87, assoc. editor 1987—92, Marion L. and Christie M. Jackson Soil Sci. award com. 1990—92, rep. to Internat. Union Pure and Applied Chemistry 1990—2000, fellow com. 1992—94, chmn.-elect divsn. S-2 1993—94, chmn. 1994—95, past chmn. 1995—96, spl. awards com. 1995—96, chair nominations com. divsn. S-2 1995—96, bd. dirs. 1995—96, editor spl. pub. 1998, Soil Sci. Rsch. award 2000), Can. Soc. Soil Sci.; mem.: Can. Network Toxicology (team on metal speciation 1993—96), Internat. Human Substances Soc. (leader Can. nat. chpt. 1992—), Internat. Union Pure and Applied Chemistry (assoc.; commn. environ. analytical chemistry 1993—95, titular mem. com. fundamental environ. chemistry 1995—97, 1999—2001, assoc. divsn. chemistry and the environment 2001—), Internat. Assn. Study Clays (treas. 1993—2001), NY Acad. Scis., Am. Chem. Soc., Internat. Union Soil Sci. (chmn. working group MO 1990—2004, chmn. coomn. 2.5 soil interfacial reactions 2004—), Sigma Xi. Avocations: music, reading. Home: 130 Mount Allison Cres Saskatoon SK Canada S7H 4A5 Office: U Sask Dept Soil Sci Campus Dr 51 Saskatoon SK Canada S7N 5A8 Office Phone: 306-966-6838. Business E-Mail: Huangp@usask.sask.ca.

HUANG, ROBERT, electronics manufacturing executive; BS elec. engring., Kyushu U., Japan; MS, U. Rochester; MBA, MIT. Sales mgr. Advanced Micro Devices; founder Compac Microelectronics, 1980; founder, pres., CEO Synnex (formerly Compac Microelectronics), Fremont, Calif., 1992—. Office: Synnex Info Tech Inc 3797 Spinnaker Ct Fremont CA 94538*

HUANG, ROBIN K., research scientist; b. Narragansett, R.I., Mar. 5, 1973; s. Nancy and T. C. Huang. BS, MIT, 1995; MS, PhD, Stanford U., 2000. Mem. tech. staff Lincoln Lab. MIT, Lexington, Mass., 2000—. Scholar, Soc. for Exploration Geophysicists, 1993—96; D.J. Lovell Scholarship, Soc. for Photoinstrumental Engrs., 1993. Mem.: IEEE, Lasers and Electro-Optics Soc. (referee 2003—05). Achievements include first to Stimulated emission of exciton-polaritons in a microcavity; development of High power single mode semiconductor lasers. Office: MIT Lincoln Laboratory 244 Wood Street Lexington MA 02420 Office Phone: 781-981-4416. E-mail: huang@ll.mit.edu.

HUANG, SHENG HE, medical educator; b. Lian Yuan, Hunan, China, Oct. 1, 1950; came to U.S., 1985; s. Yu-sheng Huang and Mei-Xiang Zen; m. Chun-Hua Wu, Sept. 8, 1978; children: Min, Wendy. Grad., 1st Mil. Med. U. China, 1973, Peking Union Med. Coll., 1981. Rsch. assoc. Peking Union Med. Coll., 1982-85; vis. asst. prof. Sch. Medicine U. Colo., Denver, 1985-86; postdoctoral fellow Childrens Hosp. L.A., 1986-89, rsch. assoc., 1989-97; asst. prof. rsch. Sch. Medicine U. So. Calif., L.A., 1997—2004, assoc. prof. Rsch. Sch. Medicine, 2004—. Author: (book) Clinical Use of Enzymes, 1984; co-author: Nature Encyclopedia of Human Genome, 2003; mem. rev. bd. Jour. Molecular Biology and Biotech., 1999—. Recipient First award NIH, 1997. Mem. Am. Assn. Cancer Rsch., Am. Soc. Microbiology. Achievements include development of Infectomics: the holistic and integrative study of interplay between microbial pathogens and their hosts and the application of computational and omic approaches in the field of infectious diseases. Office: Childrens Hosp LA Divsn Infectious Disease 4650 W Sunset Blvd Los Angeles CA 90027-6062 Business E-Mail: shhuang@hsc.usc.edu.

HUANG, SHOUHUA, electronics engineer; b. Hubei, China, Nov. 28, 1956; arrived in U.S., 1994; m. Dongmei Huang; children: Davy, Andrew. BS, Nanjing U., 1980; ME, Wuhan (China) Rsch. Inst. Posts and Telecom., 1986; PhD, Beijing U. Posts and Telecom., 1992. Engr. Ministry of Aeronautics and Space China, 1980-83, Wuhan Rsch. Inst. Posts and Telecom., 1986-88; postdoctoral fellow Tsinghua U., Beijing, 1992-94; rsch. assoc. U. So. Calif., L.A., 1994-95; rsch. engr. E-Tek Dynamics, Inc., San Jose, Calif., 1995-97; sr. engr. Osicom Techs., Inc., San Diego, 1997-99, Jet Propulsion Lab., Pasadena, Calif., 1999—. Translator: Guide to Programs/National Natural Science Foundation of China, 1992, 1993; contbr. articles to profl. jours. Mem.: IEEE (sr.), Internat. Soc. Optical Engring., Optical Soc. Am. Achievements include patents in field; research in 6-channel OC-48 (6x2.4 gb/s) 9,000 km WDM optical communications system; 6x2.4 Gbit/s circulating loop with 100 km DSF (Dispersion Shifted Fiber); LD characterization systems; others. Avocation: swimming. Office Phone: 818-354-0451. Business E-Mail: shouhua.huang@jpl.nasa.gov.

HUANG, THOMAS SHI-TAO, electrical engineering educator, researcher; b. Shanghai, June 26, 1936; came to U.S., 1958; s. Chien Liang and Allen (Chien) H.; m. Margaret Y. Nee, Apr. 4, 1959; children: Caroline B., Marjorie A., Thomas T., Gregory T. BS, Nat. Taiwan U., Taipei, 1956; MS, MIT, 1960, ScD, 1963. Asst. prof. MIT, Cambridge, Mass., 1963-67, assoc. prof., 1967-73; prof. Purdue U., West Lafayette, Ind., 1973-80, U. Ill., Urbana, 1980—, 1996—. Vis. prof. Swiss Inst. Tech., Zurich, U. Hannover, Federal Republic of Germany, U. Que., Can., others; cons. IBM, AT&T Bell Labs., MIT Lincoln Lab., Kodak, others. Author 6 books; editor 15 books; contbr. more than 500 articles to tech. jours. Recipient A. V. Humboldt U.S. Sr. Scientist award Alexander V. Humboldt Found., 1976-77, Honda Lifetime Achievement award, 2000; Guggenheim fellow, 1971-72; fellow Japan Assn. for Promotion of Sci., 1986. Fellow IEEE (Signal Processing Soc. Tech. Achievement award 1987, Soc. award 1991, Third Millennium medal 2000, Jack S. Kilby medal 2001), Optical Soc. Am., Internat. Assn. for Pattern Recognition (King-Sun Fu Prize, 2002), Internat. Optical Engring. Soc.; mem. NAE, Chinese Acad. Engring. (fgn.), Chinese Acad. Scis. (fgn.). Office: Univ Ill Beckman Inst 405 N Mathews Ave Urbana IL 61801-2325 Office Phone: 217-244-1638.

HUANG, TING-CHIA, chemical engineering professor, researcher; b. Tainan, Taiwan, June 1, 1932; s. Tzuo and Nai (Yeh) H.; m. Juei-Chin Wan, Jan. 19, 1958; children: Ling-Yuang, Ling-Huei, Ping-Hsien, Chao-Cheng. BS, Nat. Cheng Kung U., Tainan, 1955; D Engring., U. Tokyo, 1979. Tchg. asst. dept. chem. engring. Nat. Cheng Kung U., 1956-60, instr., 1960-65, assoc. prof., 1965-68, prof., 1968—, chmn., dir. dept., 1981-87, v.p., 1995-97, acting pres., 1996-97; nat. chair prof. Ministry of Edn., 1997—2000. IAEA rsch. fellow Japan Atomic Energy Rsch. Inst., Tokai-mura, Ibaraki-Ken, 1962; rsch. assoc. U. Houston, 1969-70; tech. cons. ChiMeng Indsl. Co., Ltd., Hsin-Hua, Taiwan, 1979-99; cons. Ministry Edn., Taipei, Taiwan, 1988-94, Kang Hsiang Lan Pharmaceutice Co., Ltd., Yung-Kan Ind. Park, Tainan Syan,

Taiwan, 1989—, Vedan Enterprise Corp., Shalu Taichung, Taiwan, 1999—2004. Author: Experimental Physical Chemistry, 1963, 20th edit., 1987, Chemical Engineering Thermodynamics, 1971, Physical Chemistry, 1978, 5th edit., 1990, Experiments in Physical Chemistry, 1983, 3d edit., 1988; regional editor Waste Mgmt. jour.; contbr. over 190 articles to profl. jours. Recipient Engring. Sci. award Hsu's Found., 1975, Engring. Acad. award Ministry Edn., 1979, Outstanding Rsch. award Ministry Edn., 1983, 84, Nat. Sci. Coun., 1986-94; named Outstanding Invited Rschr. Nat. Rsch. Coun., 1995-98. Mem. AIChE, Chinese Inst. Engrs. (best paper award 1975, 85, 96, 99, Outstanding Engring. Prof. award 1991), Chinese Inst. Chem. Engrs. (assoc. editor-in-chief jour. 1986-2000, Chin Kai-Ying award 1991, Best Paper award 1994, 95, 99, Chem. Engr. Inst. prize 1997), Chinese Chem. Soc., Soc. Chem. Engrs. Japan, Chinese Inst. Mining Engring. (Best Paper award 1989, 95), Phi Tau Phi. Avocations: reading, inventing, writing, music, ping pong/table tennis. Address: 4th fl 23 Alley 17 Ln 133 Sec 2 Chong Hua E Rd Tainan 70104 Taiwan Office: Nat Cheng Kung U No 1 Ta'-Siue Rd Tainan 70101 Taiwan Office Phone: 06-2757575-62630. Business E-Mail: tchuang@mail.ncku.edu.tw.

HUANG, WENDY WAN-JUOH, lawyer; b. Taipei, Taiwan, Aug. 3, 1966; came to the U.S., 1977; d. Tsung-Che and Sheree (Shen) H.; m. Kermit Marsh, July 6, 1996; two children: Dermot, Connor. BA, Cornell U., 1988; JD, Boston U., 1992. Bar: Calif. 1993, D.C. 1994, N.Y. 1994. Intern UN Com. on U.S.-China Rels., N.Y.C., 1986, Internat. Bus. Cons., Washington, 1987; asst. editor P.C. Mag., N.Y.C., 1988-89; law clk. San Diego (Calif.) City Attys., 1990, U.S. Atty.-So. Dist. N.Y., N.Y.C., 1991, L.A. (Calif.) Dist. Attys., 1991; assoc. Law Firm of Kinkle, Rodiger & Spriggs, L.A., 1992-94, Knapp, Marsh, Jones & Doran, L.A., 1994-97, Burkley, Greenberg, Fields & Whitcombe, 1997—2000; chief gen. counsel Olen Cos., Newport Beach, Calif., 2000—05; exec. v.p., gen. counsel Crown Realty and Devel. Corp., Irvine, Calif., 2005—. Sec., chmn. Pacific Rim bd. govs. Calif. Chinese Bar Assn., L.A., 1993—; judge pro tem, LA Superior Ct.; arbitrator LA County Bar Client Dispute Svcs.; legal cons. Sta. KPFK Radio, Voice of Am. Radio, Chinese Daily News. Writer, actress Words Across Cultures Theatre Co., L.A., 1993; actress, dancer Bethune Theatre Danse, L.A., 1993; editl. bd. L.A. Lawyer mag. Recipient Westinghouse Nat. Sci. Talent Search scholarship NSF, Washington, 1984. Mem. L.A. County Bar Inns of Ct., Orgn. Chinese Ams. (pres.), Screen Actors Guild. Democrat. Avocations: tennis, piano. Home: 8571 Edgemont Cir Westminster CA 92683-7216 Office: Crown Realty and Devel 18201 Von Karmen Ave Ste 950 Irvine CA 92612 Office Phone: 949-567-5861. E-mail: whuang@crowndev.com.

HUANG, WENLIN, research scientist; b. Wuhan, Hubei, China, Oct. 1, 1953; s. Zhudong Huang and Yuzheng Fong; m. Marilyn X. Zhou, Nov. 7, 1993; 1 child, Manli. BS, Three Gonges U., Yicheng, Hubei, China, 1975; PhD, Academia Sinica, Wuhan, China, 1986; postgrad., Princeton (N.J.) U., 1996. Rsch. asst. prof. Wuhan Inst. Vitology, 1986-88; dir., founder pharm. co. Wuhan, 1988-91; vis. fellow Princeton U., 1991-96, with rsch. staff, 1996-97; rsch. scientist Allegheny U., Phila., 1997-98; prof. Sen Yat-Sen Med. U., Guangzhou, China, 1998-2001; sr. rsch. scientist Advanced Vital Rsch. Inst., Yonkers, N.Y., 1998—. Guest prof. Fourth Mil. U., Xi An, China, 1998; v.p. US-China Econ. and Trading Promotion Coun., N.Y.C., 1999—; adv. bd. Microbiology Inst. Acad. Sci., Guangdong, China, 2000— Patentee in field. Recipient award NIH, 1995, 97, Nat. Sci. Found., 1998, Nat. Edn. Minister, China, 1999. Mem. AAAS, Soc. Chinese Am. Professors (bd. dirs. 1995—), Infectious Diseases Soc. Am., Soc. Microbiology Am., Am. Cancer Rsch. Assn., N.Y. Acad. Sci. Avocations: travel, reading. Home: 576 Province Line Rd Allentown NJ 08501 E-mail: wl_huang@hotmail.com.

HUANG, YEN TI, civil engineer; b. Taipei, Taiwan, Feb. 4, 1927; came to U.S., 1957; s. Tan Kun Huang and Mu Lin; m. Toshiko Naomi Saito Imano, July 4, 1958; 1 child, Philip Po-Wen. BSc, Nat. Taiwan U., Taipei, 1950; MASc, U. Toronto, Can., 1957; PhD, Columbia U., 1961. Registered profl. engr., Tex., N.Mex., Ont., Taiwan. Mem. rsch. staff Sperry Rand Rsch. Ctr., Sudbury, Mass., 1961-63; project geophysicist Atlantic Refining Co., Dallas, 1963-65; sr. geophysicist Geotech (subs. Teledyne Co.), Garland, Tex., 1965-68; mem. tech. staff Collins Radio Co., Richardson, Tex., 1968-70; CEO, pres. Y.T. Huang & Assocs., Dallas, 1970—, San Tai Internat. Corp., Dallas, 1973—. Adj. prof. U. Tex., Arlington. Founder of numerical transform theorem used in digital transform; patentee gyroscopic apparatus, modular inflatable dome structures, modular space framed earthquake resistant structures, modular roof structures, semi-submerged, movable, modular offshore platforms, and multipurpose offshore modular platform. Co-chmn. Tex. Asian Rep. Caucus, 1982, Spkr.'s Inner Circle, 2000; mem. Rep. Senatorial Inner Circle, 2000; conv. del. advisor from Tex., Rep. Nat. Conv., 2000. Named Rep. of Yr. representing Tex., 2001, Rep. Businessman of Yr., 2003; named to Presdl. Roundtable, 2004; recipient Outstanding Alumnus award, Nat. Taiwan U. Alumni Assn., 1999, Rep. Senatorial medal of freedom, 2002, Rep. Gold medal, 2002; scholar Econ. Coop. Am. /Joint Commn. on Rural Reconstruction Scholar, Taiwan Dept. Edn., 1951—52. Mem. ASCE (life; com. tower found. design stds. 1989-96), Internat. Soc. Offshore and Polar Engrs. (session chmn. 1991-94), N.Y. Acad. Scis., Tech. Club Dallas (v.p. 1993-95, pres.-elect 1996, pres. 1997), Rotary, Dallas Coun. on World Affairs. Unitarian Universalist. Avocations: photography, music, travel, history. Office: YT Huang & Assocs Inc/Santai Internat Corp Windy Forest Pl 9638 Greenville Ave Dallas TX 75374-4006 E-mail: yen853@aol.com.

HUANG, YING CHIANG DAVID, physicist, educator; s. Hsiu Hsiung Huang and Su Lan Lin; m. Chih Ling Lynn Chen; 1 child, Wei Chih Robbie. BS, Nat. Taiwan Normal U., Taipei, 1969; PhD, Temple U., 1986. Cert. therapeutic med. physics Am. Bd. Radiology, med. physics diagnostic radiology N.Y., med. nuc. physics N.Y., med. health physics N.Y. Med. physicist Meml. Sloan-Kettering Cancer Ctr, N.Y.C., 1989—90; chief med. physics sect. Meml. Sloan-Kettering at Mercy Med. Ctr, Rockville Centre, NY, 2002—; sr. med. physicist LI Jewish Med. Ctr, New Hyde Park, NY, 1990—95; asst. prof. Albert Einstein Med. Coll., 1991—93; chmn. med. physics dept. Sun Yat-Sen Cancer Ctr., Taipei, 1995—2002; assoc. prof. Young-Ming and Chung Gung U., 1995—2002. Vis. prof. Beijing U., 2004—, Taipei Med. U., 2003—. Recipient 1St prize for Rsch. Poster, Atomic Energy Coun., 2002; grantee, 1996—99, Nat. Sci. Coun., 2000, 2001, 2002, Bur. of Health Ins., 2000; scholar Rsch. scholar, Temple U., 1981—86. Mem.: Am. Coll. Radiology, Am. Assn. Physicist Medicine, Chinese Soc. Med. Physics (hon.; pres. 1999—2002, cert. med. physics therapeutic radiology). Avocations: travel, swimming, reading. Personal E-mail: ycdavidh@yahoo.com.

HUBACH, FRANCIS P. (FRANK), JR., lawyer; b. Cleve. BA, John Carroll Univ., 1965; JD magna cum laude, Univ. Mich., 1968. Bar: Tex. 1981. Coord. real estate practice Jones Day, prin.-in-charge Dallas office, 1992—. Bd. dir. Tate Lectr. Series So. Meth. Univ., Dallas; mem., pres. adv. coun. Dallas Ctr. for Performing Arts; bd. trustees Catholic Found., Dallas. Fellow: Dallas Bar Found.; mem.: Dallas Bar Assn., Order of Coif. Office: Jones Day 2727 N Harwood St Dallas TX 75201-1515 Office Phone: 214-969-2915. Office Fax: 214-969-5100. Business E-Mail: fphubach@jonesday.com.

HUBACH, JOSEPH F., electronics executive, lawyer; b. Cleve., Jan. 4, 1958; BA in polit. sci., John Carroll U., 1980; JD, Case Western Res. U., 1983. Bar: Ohio 1983, Tex. 1989. With Tex. Instruments, Dallas, 1984—, v.p., asst. gen. counsel, 1998—2000, sr. v.p., gen. counsel, corp. sec., 2000—. Mem. adv. bd. Inst. for Law and Tech. Ctr. for Am. and Internat. Law. Bd. regents John Carroll U. Mem.: ABA, Ohio Bar Assn., Tex. Bar Assn. (mem. sect. intellectual property, sect. bus. law), Greater Dallas C. of C. (exec. com. bd. dirs.). Office: Tex Instruments Inc 12500 TI Blvd Dallas TX 75266-4136

HUBALEK, SHIRLEY KAY, music educator; s. Arthur Chester and Lois Thelma Hubalek; m. John Alan Lawver (div.). Student, Ft. Hays State U., 1970—72; BS, U. Md., 1976; BFA, Md. Inst., 1982; postgrad., Towson U., 1999. Pvt. piano, voice instr.m, Balt., 1992—; music dir. Rodgers Forge United Meth. Ch., Balt., 1997—2005, Our Lady Victory Ch., Balt., 2005—. Art specialist, Balt., 1987—2000; adj. faculty Anne Arundel C.C., Severna Park, Md., 1986—, Catonsville (Md.) C.C., 1987—, Towson State U., 1993—94, Essex Cmty. Coll., 1994; autism music specialist, Balt., 2003—. Author: I Can't Draw a Straight Line, 1997, Crossroads: The Challenge of Lifelong Learning, 1997; contbr. chapters to books; cover artist: Voices of Women, 1993; exhibitions include Md. Fedn. Art, Annapolis, 1984, one-woman shows include St. John's United Meth. Ch., Balt., 1984, exhibitions include Slayton House Gallery, 1985, City Hall Courtyard Galleries, Balt., 1986, one-woman shows include Village Club, 1986, exhibitions include Park School Gallery, Balt., 1989, Md. Fedn. Art, Annapolis, 1991, exhibited in group shows at Quiet Water State Pk., 1991, exhibitions include Montpelier Cultural Arts Ctr., 1996, 2005, Fells Point Creative Alliance, 1998, Howard County Arts Coun., 2005. Mem.: Howard County Arts Coun., Am. Guild Organists.

HUBAND, FRANK LOUIS, educational association executive; b. Washington, July 12, 1938; m. Carol Singer. BS, Cornell U., 1961, PhD, 1967; JD, Yale U., 1975. Bar: D.C. 1975, U.S. Patent Office, 1977; registered prof. engr., Tex. Asst. prof. elec. engring. and math. scis. Rice U., Houston, 1966-72; owner, pres. Engring. Systems, Houston, 1972-73; atty., advisor FEA, Washington, 1975-76; div. dir. NSF, Washington, 1976-90; exec. dir. Am. Soc. for Engring. Edn., Washington, 1990—; sec. gen. IACEE, 2002—. Cons. Tex. Instrument, 1968-75; lectr. George Mason U., Fairfax, Va., George Washington U. Author: Protection of Computer Systems and Software, 1986. Mem. IEEE, ABA, NSPE, Am. Chem. Soc., Am. Inst. Physics, Internat. Assn. for Continuing Engring. Edn. (sec. gen.). Office: Am Soc for Engring Edn 1818 N St NW Ste 600 Washington DC 20036-2476 E-mail: f.huband@asee.org.

HUBBARD, ALLAN BROOKS, federal official, former chemical company executive; b. Jackson, Tenn., Sept. 8, 1947; s. George and Elizabeth (Beesley) H.; m. Kathryn Fortune, June 9, 1979; 1 child, William Fortune. BA cum laude, Vanderbilt U., 1969; MBA, JD, Harvard U. Pres. World Wide Chems., Inc., Indpls., 1977—, E & A Industries, Inc., Indpls., 1983—; dep. chief of staff to Vice Pres. Dan Quayle The White House, Washington, 1990—92, asst. to the Pres. for econ. policy, 2005—; dir. The Nat. Econ. Coun., Washington, 2005—. Exec. dir. Pres. Coun. on Competitiveness, 1990—92; volunteer chmn. Ind. State Rep. Party, 1993—94. Bd. dirs. Indpls. Entrepreneurship Acad., The Children's Mus., Greater Indpls. Progress Com., U.S. Open Clay Court Championships, Inc.; mem. steering com. Vols. for Youth; fundraiser Vanderbilt U., numerous local art and civic groups; active various local polit. campaigns. Named Small Bus. Person of Yr., SBA, 1983. Mem. Ind. State C. of C. (bd. dirs.), Young Pres.'s Orgn., The Penrod Soc. Republican. Office: The White House 1600 Pennsylvania Ave NW 2nd Fl W Wing Washington DC 20500*

HUBBARD, ARTHUR THORNTON, chemist, educator; b. Alameda, Calif., Sept. 17, 1941; s. John White and Ruth Frances (Gapen) H.; children: David A., Lynne F. BA, Westmont Coll., 1963; PhD, Calif. Inst. Tech., 1967. Prof. chemistry U. Hawaii, Honolulu, 1967-76, U. Calif., Santa Barbara, 1976-86; Ohio eminent scholar and prof. chemistry U. Cin., 1986-99, dir. Surface Ctr., 1986-99; dir. Santa Barbara Sci. Project, 1999—. Chmn. Ohio Sci. and Engring. Roundtable, 1990-95. Co-editor Jour. Colloid and Interface Sci., 1993—; series editor Interface Sci and Tech, 2001—; Surfactant Sci. Series; editor: Encyclopedia of Surface and Colloid Science. Mem. Am. Chem. Soc. (assoc. editor jour. Langmuir 1984-90, vice chair surface and colloid div. 1999, chair-elect 2000, chair 2001, Kendall award 1989), Electrochem. Soc. (David C. Grahame award 1993), Am. Phys. Soc. Office: Santa Barbara Sci Project PO Box 42530 Santa Barbara CA 93140-2530

HUBBARD, DEAN LEON, academic administrator; b. Nyssa, Oreg., June 17, 1939; s. Gaileon and Rhodene (Barton) H.; m. Aleta Ann Thornton, July 12, 1959; children: Melody Ann, Dean Paul John, Joy Marie BA, Andrews U., 1961, MA, 1962; diploma in Korean Lang., Yunsei U., Seoul, Korea, 1968; PhD, Stanford U., 1979. Dir. English Lang. Schs., Seoul, 1966-71; asst. to pres. Loma Linda U., Calif., 1974-76; acad. dean Union Coll., Lincoln, Nebr., 1976-80, pres., 1980-84, NW Mo. State U., Maryville, 1984—. Chair Acad. Quality Consortium, 1993-96; examiner Malcolm Baldridge Nat. Quality Award, 1993-96; judges panel Mo. Quality Award, 1994-96; adv. coun. edn. statistics U.S. Dept. Edn., 1997-99. Mem. ACE Leadership Devel. Coun., 1996-98. Avocation: classical music. Office: NW Mo State U Office of President AD143 800 University Dr Maryville MO 64468-6001

HUBBARD, ELEANOR A., sociologist, educator; b. Grundy County, Iowa, Nov. 2, 1939; d. Ernest and Beatrice Draper; m. Dennis Hubbard, June 13, 1964; children: Kirsten A., Natasha L. MA, PhD, U. Colo., 1993. Sr. instr. U. Colo., Boulder, 1993—. Owner, trainer, cons. DiversityWorks, Boulder, 1995—. Trustee BPW Edn. Found., Boulder, 2002—03. Mem.: Am. Sociol. Assn. Avocations: bicycling, hiking, skiing, travel. Office: U Colo Sociology Dept CB 327 Boulder CO 80309 Office Phone: 303-492-8838. Business E-Mail: hubbarde@colorado.edu.

HUBBARD, ELIZABETH, actress; b. N.Y.C. d. Benjamin Alldritt and Elizabeth (Wright) H.; divorced; 1 son, Jeremy Danby Bennett. AB cum laude, Radcliffe Coll.; postgrad., Royal Acad. Dramatic Art, London. Leading role: CBS daytime TV serial As the World Turns, 1984— (9 Emmy nominations for Best Leading Actress), NBC daytime TV serial The Doctors (Best Leading Actress Emmy), First Ladies' Diary (Best Leading Actress Emmy); appeared on Broadway in Present Laughter, Joe Egg, Time for Singing, Look Back in Anger, I Remember Mama (musical), The Physicists (Clarence Derwent award), others; appeared in off-Broadway prodn. Boys from Syracuse, Threepenny Opera (musicals); movie appearances include I Never Sang for My Father, The Bell Jar, Ordinary People, Center Stage; frequent guest TV talk shows. Former bd. dirs. Found. in Motion, Immigration and Refugee Svcs. Am., U.S. Com. for Refugees. Recipient Silver medal, Royal Acad. Dramatic Art. Mem.: NATAS (bd. govs.), AFTRA (former bd. dirs.).

HUBBARD, GREGORY SCOTT, physicist; b. Lexington, Ky., Dec. 27, 1948; s. Robert Nicholas and Nancy Clay (Brown) Hubbard; m. Susan Artimissa Ruggeri, Aug. 1, 1982. BA, Vanderbilt U., 1970; postgrad., U. Calif., Berkeley, 1975-77; doctorate with honors (hon.), Polytech. U., Madrid, 2005. Lab. engr. physics dept. Vanderbilt U., Nashville, 1970-73; staff scientist Lawrence Berkeley Lab. Dept. Instrument Techs., Berkeley, 1974-80; dir. rsch. & devel. Canberra Industries, Inc., Detector Products Divsn., Novato, Calif., 1980-82; v.p., gen. mgr. Canberra Semiconductor, Novato, 1982-85; cons., owner Hubbard Cons. Svcs., 1978—. Cons. SRI Internat., Menlo Park, Calif., 1979—86, sr. rsch. physicist, 1986—87; divsn. staff scientist space exploration projects office Ames Rsch. Ctr., NASA, Moffett Field, Calif., 1987—90, chief space instrumentation and studies br., 1990—92, dep. chief space projects divsn., 1992—96, assoc. dir. space directorate, 1996—97, dep. dir. space directorate, 1997—99, assoc. ctr. dir., 1999—2001, dep. ctr. dir. rsch., 2001—02, ctr. dir., 2002—; mem. Fed. Sr. Exec. Svc., 1997—; study mgr. Mars Pathfinder Mission, 1990—91, Ames project mgr., 1992—96; mission mgr. Lunar Prospector Mission, 1994—99; interim dir. NASA Astrobiology Inst., 1998—99; Mars program dir. NASA Hdqrs., 2000—01; mem. Columbia Accident Investigation Bd.; lectr in field. Recipient Exceptional Achievement medal, NASA, 1994, 2001, Outstanding Leadership medal, 1998, 1999, 2002, Disting. Svc. medal, 2004, Excеptional Svc. medal, 2005, Laurels for Accomplishments in Space, Aviation Week, 1997, 1998, 2003, Von Karman medal in Astronautics, Am. Inst. Aeronautics and Astronautics, 2004; Founders scholarship, Vanderbilt U., 1966. Fellow: AIAA (Von Karman medal 2004); mem.: IEEE, Calif. Coun. Sci. Tech., Am. Phys. Soc., Internat. Acad. Astronautics (Engring. Sci. award 2004), Nuc. Sci. Soc., Commonwealth Club Calif., Hon. Order Ky. Cols. Home: 103 Fey Dr Burlingame CA 94010

HUBBARD, HAROLD MEAD, energy and environmental scientist, consultant, retired research executive; b. Beloit, Kans., Apr. 16, 1924; s. Clarence Richard and Elizabeth (Mead) H.; m. Doreen J. Wallace, Aug. 13, 1948 (div. 1975); children: Stuart W., David D.; m. Barbara Bell Czarnecki, May 9, 1976 (div. 1987), remarried Sept. 9, 1999. BS, U. Kans., 1948, PhD, 1951; DSc (hon.), Regis U., 1984. Instr. chemistry U. Kans., Lawrence, 1949-51; rsch. chemist, rsch. mgr., lab. mgr. E. I. DuPont de Nemours & Co., Inc., Wilmington, Del., 1951-69; dir. phys. sci. Midwest Rsch. Inst., Kansas City, Mo., 1970-75, v.p. rsch., 1976-78, sr. v.p. ops., 1979-82, exec. v.p., 1983-90; dir. Solar Energy Rsch. Inst., 1982-90; Spark M. Matsunaga disting. fellow in energy and environ. U. Hawaii at Manoa, 1991-96; pres., CEO Pacific Internat. Ctr. for High Tech. Rsch., Honolulu, 1992-95. Vis. sr. fellow Resources for the Future, 1990-91; bd. dirs. Guaranty State Bank; chmn. Nat. Rsch. Coun. bd. on energy and environ. sys., 1991-96. With U.S. Army, 1942-45. Mem. Mo. Acad. Sci. (councillor at large 1977-80), Tech. Transfer Soc. (v.p. 1978-79), Am. Chem. Soc., AAAS, Acad. Sci. (nat. assoc.), Am. Solar Energy Soc., Colo. Renewable Energy Soc. (pres. 1996-97), Sigma Xi, Delta Upsilon, Cosmos Club. Home: 3938 SW Linden Ct Lees Summit MO 64082-4643 Personal E-mail: hubbet@aol.com.

HUBBARD, HARVEY HART, aeroacoustician, noise control engineer, consultant; b. Swanton, Vt., June 17, 1921; s. Horace Waite and Elbie (Hart) H.; m. Sadie Margaret Miller; children: Thomas W., Susan H., Pamela L., Walter R. BSEE, U. Vt., 1942. Engr. Westinghouse Mfg. Co., Pitts., 1942; br. chief NASA, Hampton, Va., 1945-59, asst. div. chief, 1959-80; sr. rsch. assoc. Coll. William and Mary, Williamsburg, Va., 1981-85; cons. Bionetics Inc., Hampton, 1985-87, Planning Rsch. Corp., Hampton, 1987—. Author over 130 book chpts. and tech. reports in aeroacoustics rsch. and noise control engring., 1949-99. Lt. col. USAF, 1942-45, PTO. Recipient Sonic Boom Rsch. award, 1968, Medal for Exceptional Sci. Achievement, 1969, NASA, medal for Disting. Pub. Svc., 1992. Fellow AIAA (assoc., Aeroacoustics medal 1979), Acoustical Soc. Am. (pres. 1989-90, Silver medal in noise 1978); mem. Inst. of Noise Control Engring. (pres. 1979). Presbyterian. Home: 955 Harpersville Rd Apt 2053 Newport News VA 23601

HUBBARD, HERBERT HENDRIX, lawyer; b. Balt., Sept. 20, 1922; s. Amberson Hardy and Louise Virginia (Hendrix) H.; m. Joanne Hileman Nottingham, June 5, 1948 (dec. Sept. 2002); children: Melissa Hubbard O'Donnell, Alison Hubbard. JD, U. Md., Balt., 1950. Bar: Md. 1950, U.S. Dist. Ct. Md. 1950, U.S. Ct. Appeals (4th cir.) 1953, U.S. Supreme Ct. 1963. Clk. to dist. judge U.S. Dist. Ct. Md., Balt., 1950-51; assoc. France, Rouzer & Harris, Balt., 1951-52, 54-59; asst. U.S. atty. Dist. Md., Balt., 1952-53, 1st asst. U.S. atty., 1953-54; atty., ptnr. Weinberg & Green, Balt., 1959—98; gen. counsel Forest Haven Nursing Home, Balt., 2001—; counsel Saul Ewing, Balt., 1998—2001, of counsel, 2001—03. Founding dir. Devel. Credit Fund, Inc., Balt., 1984-96. Chmn., corp. devel. coun. Sheppard & Enoch Pratt Hosp., Balt., 1978-86. Mem. ABA, Md. Bar Assn. (founding, chmn. profl. liability ins. com. 1976-82), Bar Assn. Ins. Trust (trustee 1976-88), Legal Mut. Liability Ins. Soc. Md. (bd. dirs., 1986-2005, sr vp., exec. com. 1986-2004, founding dir.), Order of Coif, U. Md. Law Review. Episcopalian. Avocation: bridge. Home: Blakehurst 1055 W Joppa Rd Towson MD 21204 Office: 701 Edmondson Ave Catonsville MD 21228 Office Phone: 410-747-7425 50. Business E-Mail: forestlaw@viabit.com.

HUBBARD, HOWARD JAMES, bishop; b. Troy, N.Y., Oct. 31, 1938; s. Howard James and Elizabeth D. (Burke) H. BA, St. Joseph's Sem., Yonkers, N.Y., 1960; STL, Gregorian U., Rome, 1964; DD (hon.), Siena Coll., 1977; LHD (hon.), Coll. St. Rose, 1977. Ordained priest Roman Catholic Ch., Rome, 1963; former parish priest St. Joseph's Ch., Schenectady, 1964; parish priest Cathedral Parish, Albany, 1964-65; Ordained bishop, 1977; bishop of Albany Diocese of Albany, NY, 1977—. Asst. dir. Cath. Charities, Schenectady, 1966; chaplain Convent of the Sacred Heart, Kenwood, Albany, 1966; dir. Providence House, Albany, 1966; vicar gen. Diocese of Albany, 1976; dir. Cath. Interracial Coun.; coord. Urban Apostolate, from 1972; dir. Office of Pastoral Planning, Albany, 1974-76; diocesan consultor Diocese of Albany, 1976-77. Pres. Urban League. Office: Bishop of Albany Pastoral Ctr 40 N Main Ave PO Box 6480 Albany NY 12203-1963 Address: 125 Eagle St Albany NY 12202-1718

HUBBARD, JOHN RANDOLPH, retired academic administrator; b. Belton, Tex., Dec. 3, 1918; s. Louis Herman and Bertha (Altizer) H.; m. Lucille Luckett, Jan. 29, 1947 (div. Dec. 1983); children: Elisa, Melisse, Kristin. AB, U. Tex., 1938, A.M., 1939, PhD, 1950; L.H.D., Hebrew Union Coll., Los Angeles, 1971, Westminster Coll., Fulton, Mo., 1977; LL.D., Sch. of Ozarks, 1973, U. So. Calif., 1980. Pvt. sec. to ICC commr., 1939-41; teaching fellow U. Tex., 1946-48; vis. asst. prof. Brit. history La. State U., 1948; asst. prof. European history Tulane U., 1949-52, asso. prof., 1953-58, prof., 1958-65; dean Newcomb Coll., 1953-65; vis. asst. prof. European history Yale, 1952-53; chief edn. adviser U.S. AID, India, 1965-69; v.p. for acad. affairs, provost U. So. Calif., Los Angeles, 1969-70, pres., 1970-80, pres. emeritus, 1980—, John R. Hubbard Chair Brit. history, 1980—; U.S. amb. to India, 1988-89. Co-chmn. Indo-U.S. Subcommn. on Edn. and Culture, 1982—. Contbr.: articles and revs. to Jour. Modern History; other ednl. jours. Mem. bd. Tulane-Lyceum Assn., 1953-65, Isidore Newman Sch., 1953-65; mem. Region 12 selection com. Woodrow Wilson Fellowship Program, also chmn., 1955-65; mem. bd. U.S. Edn. Found., India; mem. Indian adv. bd. Women's Coll. Faculty Exchange program; pres. bd. Am. Internat. Sch., New Delhi; mem. So. Calif. adv. bd. Inst. Internat. Edn.; trustee Scholarships for Children of Am. Mil. Personnel; bd. dirs. Community TV So. Calif., Los Angeles. Served as an aviator in USN, 1941-46; flight instr. and patrol plane comdr. Atlantic and Pacific fleets; lt. comdr. Res. Decorated D.F.C., Air medals (4); chevalier des Palmes Académiques; Stella della Solidarietá Italiana Italy; Order of Taj 3d degree Iran; recipient Disting. Services to Higher Edn. in U.S. award Tulane U., New Orleans, 1976; Air U. award, 1976; Disting. Alumnus award U. Tex., Austin, 1978, Alben W. Barkley medal for disitng. svc., 1989. Mem. Am., Miss. Valley hist. assns., So. Hist. Soc. (exec. council 1954-56), Anglo-Am. Hist. Soc., Assn. Ind. Calif. Colls. and Univs. (trustee), Am. Council Edn. (commn. on fed. relations 1975-77), Assn. Am. Univs. (council on fed. relations 1975-79), Orgn. Am. Historians, Conf. Brit. Studies, Am. Council Learned Socs., Phi Beta Kappa, Phi Delta Kappa, Alpha Kappa Psi, Delta Kappa Epsilon, Omicron Delta Kappa. Clubs: Royal Aero (London), Athenaeum (London); Los Angeles Country; California (Los Angeles); University (N.Y.C.); Cosmos (Washington). Office: U So Calif Dept History Los Angeles CA 90089-0001 *The fear of false knowledge is the beginning of wisdom.*

HUBBARD, LINCOLN BEALS, medical physicist, consultant; b. Hawkesbury, Ontario, Sept. 8, 1940; arrived in U.S., 1957; s. Carroll Chauncey and Mary Lunn (Beals) Hubbard; m. Nancy Ann Krieger, Apr. 3, 1961; children: Jill, Katrina. BS in Physics, U. NH, 1961; PhD, MIT, 1967. Diplomate Am. Bd. Radiology, cert. health physicist Am. Bd. Health Physics. Postdoctoral appointee Argonne Nat. Lab., 1966—68; asst. prof. math. and physics Knoxville (Tenn.) Coll., 1968—70; asst. prof. physics Furman U., Greenville, SC, 1970—74; chief physicist Mt. Sinai Hosp., Chgo., 1974—75, 1979—2002, Cook County Hosp., Chgo., 1975—88; prof. med. physics Rush U., 1986—; ptnr. Fields, Griffith, Hubbard & Assoc., Ltd., 1978—93; pres. Hubbard, Broadbent & Assoc., Ltd., 1993—. Author (with S.S. Stefani): Mathematics for Technologists, 1979; author: (with G.B. Greenfield) Computers in Radiology, 1984. Fellow: Am. Coll. Radiology, Am. Assn. Physicists in Medicine. Home and Office: 4113 W End Rd Downers Grove IL 60515-2307 Office Phone: 630-963-2913.

HUBBARD, MARGUERITE, retired elementary school educator; b. Elmhurst, Ill., Oct. 23, 1948; d. Edward C. and Mary Margaret Hinchley; m. Gary Lowell Hubbard, May 10, 1989; stepchildren: Audrey, Todd. BA, Elmhurst Coll., 1970; MS, U. Ill., 1975. Cert. tchr. music K-12 Ill., elem. tchr. Ill. Music tchr. Bellflower Sch. Dist., Ill., 1971—79, Belvidere Sch. Dist., Ill., 1979—, ret., 2004. Singer Rockford Cmty. Chorale, Ill., 1980—89, 1998—2000. Mem.: NEA, Belvidere Edn. Assn. (bldg. rep. 1996—), Music Educator's Nat. Conf. Avocations: reading, swimming, crafts, walking.

HUBBARD, MARY D., history educator; d. Jess and Mary Donnell; m. Thomas Michael Hubbard, Nov. 21, 1969; 1 child, Lisa Stark. BA, Wash. U., St. Louis, 1965; MA in Gifted Edn., U. Ala., Birmingham, 1983. Cert.

adolescence and young adulthood social studies Nat. Bd. for Profl. Tchg. Standards, 2000. Tchr. gifted and talented English and history Gresham Jr. H.S., Birmingham, Ala., 1983—89; tchr. history and dept. chair Jefferson County Internat. Baccalaureate Sch., 1989—99; tchr. English Mountain Brook H.S., Mountain Brook, 1999—2000; tchr. history Ala. Sch. Fine Arts, Birmingham, 2000—. Tchr. advisor Ency. of Ala., Auburn; presenter at seminars on gifted and talented. Presdl. appointee NEH, Washington, 1999—2000; bd. mem. and sec. Ala. Humanities Found., Birmingham, Ala., 2004—. Fellow summer seminars, NEH, 1985, 1991, 1994, 1999, 2004. Mem.: Nat. Coun. History Edn. (state coord. 2004), Ala. Assn. of Historians (v.p. 2004—, Biennial Tchr. of Merit award 2000). Office: Ala Sch of Fine Arts 1800 8th Ave N Birmingham AL 35203 Office Phone: 205-252-9241. E-mail: mhubbard@asfa.k12.al.us.

HUBBARD, MICHELE MASANEK, secondary school educator, soccer coach; s. Ronald Julian and Stephanie Ann Masanek; m. Rodney Wade Hubbard, July 10, 1999. BE, Bowling Green State U., Ohio, 1992; ME, Wright State U., Dayton, 2004. Tchr. Winston Woods Sch., Forest Pk., Ohio, 1994—95, Fairfield City Schs., 1995—2005. Girl's soccer coach Fairfield HS, 1994—2004, boy's asst. soccer coach, 2004—; coach Odyssey of the Mind, Ohio, 1995—98. Supporter Young Life, Fairfield, 1995—, Athletes in Action, Fairfield, 1999—, Fellowship of Christian Athletes, Fairfield, Ohio, 1999—. Nominee Ashland Tchr. of Yr., 1994, Tchr. of Yr., Walt Disney, 2000, 2004, Fairfield City Schs., 2004, Tchr. of Week, WMOH, 2004; recipient Fairfield Sch. Bell award, Fairfield City Schs., 1999, 2000, 2001, 2002, 2003, 2004, Fairfield Amb. award, 2004. Mem.: Pi Lambda Theta, Phi Kappa Phi. Democrat. Avocations: soccer, running. Office: Fairfield City Schs 255 Donald Dr Fairfield OH 45014

HUBBARD, R. GLENN (ROBERT GLENN HUBBARD), academic administrator, former federal agency administrator; b. Apopka, Fla., Sept. 4, 1958; s. Charles Whistnant and Myrtle Jean (Dabbs) H. BA, BS, U. Cen. Fla., 1979; AM, Harvard U., 1981, PhD, 1983. Prof. econs. Northwestern U., Evanston, Ill., 1983-87; Russell L. Carson prof. econs. and fin. Columbia U., N.Y.C., 1988—, dean Bus. Sch., 2004—; dep. asst. sec. U.S. Dept. Treasury, Washington, 1991-92; chmn. Coun. Econ. Adv., Washington, 2001—03. John M. Olin fellow, Nat. Bur. Econ. Rsch., Cambridge, Mass., 1987-88; cons., U.S. Dept. State, Dept. Energy, Internat. Trade Commn., Social Security Adminstrn., Nat. Petroleum Coun., numerous pvt. corps.; chmn., U.S. Pres. Coun. Econ. Advs., 2001-2003. Editor: Asymmetric Information, Corporate Finance and Investment, 1989; contbr. numerous articles to profl. jours. Grantee, NSF, 1983—. Mem. Am. Econ. Assn., Econometric Soc., Royal Econ. Assn., Am. Fin. Assn. Republican. Presbyterian. Avocations: reading, theater, travel. Office: Columbia U Grad Sch Bus 3022 Broadway 609 Uris Hall New York NY 10027 Business E-Mail: rgh1@columbia.edu.

HUBBARD, RICHARD L., lawyer; b. Dallas, May 27, 1943; BA magna cum laude, Williams Coll., 1964; LLB magna cum laude, Harvard U., 1967. Bar: D.C. 1968. Law clk. to Hon. Arnold Raum U.S. Tax Ct., 1967-69; ptnr., Tax & Estates Practice Group Arnold & Porter, Washington, 1969—. Mem. Phi Beta Kappa. Office: Arnold & Porter Thurman Arnold Bldg 555 12th St NW Washington DC 20004-1206 Office Phone: 202-942-5755. Office Fax: 202-942-5999. Business E-Mail: richard.hubbard@aporter.com.

HUBBARD, RUTH, retired biology professor; b. Vienna, Mar. 3, 1924; arrived in US, 1938; d. Richard and Helene (Ehrlich) Hoffmann; m. Frank Twombly Hubbard, Dec. 26, 1942 (div. 1951); m. George Wald, June 11, 1958; children: Elijah, Deborah Hannah. AB, Radcliffe Coll., 1944, PhD, 1950; DSc (hon.), Macalester Coll., 1991, U. Toronto, Ont., Can., 1991, So. Meth. U., 1997, Clark U., 2003; LHD (hon.), So. Ill. U., Edwardsville, 1991. Lab. technician Tenn. Pub. Health Svc., Chattanooga, 1945-46; fellow U. Coll. Hosp. Med. Sch., London, 1948-49; Guggenheim fellow Carlsberg Lab., Copenhagen, 1952-53; rsch. fellow Harvard U., Cambridge, Mass., 1950-52, 54-58, rsch. assoc., lectr., 1958-74, prof., 1974-90, prof. emerita, 1990—. Vis. prof. MIT, Cambridge, 1972; cons. Boston Women's Healthbook Collective 1982—; Regents lectr. U. Calif, Berkeley, 2002. Author: (with Margaret Randall) The Shape of Red: Insider/Outsider Reflections, 1988; author: The Politics of Women's Biology, 1990, (with Elijah Wald) Exploding the Gene Myth, 1993, 97, 99, Profitable Promises: Essays on Women, Science and Health, 1995; editor: Women Look at Biology Looking at Women, 1979, Genes and Gender II, 1979, Biological Woman--The Convenient Myth, 1982, Woman's Nature: Rationalizations of Inequality, 1983, Reinventing Biology: Respect for Life and the Creation of Knowledge, 1995; contbr. more than 250 articles on sci. and women's issues to profl. and lay books and jours. Adv. coun. mem. Nat. Women's Health Network, Washington, 1980-85; bd. dirs. Coun. Responsible Genetics, Boston, 1982-2002, Boston Women's Health Book Collective, 1998-99; mem. adv. bd. Boston Women's Fund, 1983-85, 2000-02; mem. adv. bd. Civil Liberties Union of Mass., 1990-91, 95—, bd. dirs., 1991-95. Recipient Paul Karrer medal Swiss Chem. Soc., 1967, Peace and Freedom award Women's Internat. League for Peace and Freedom, 1985, Feminist Marathoner award Boston chpt. NOW, 1991, Disting. Svc. award Am. Inst. Biol. Sci., 1992, Luther Knight Macnair award, ACLU, 2005. Fellow AAAS; mem. Marine Biol. Lab. (trustee 1973-78, trustee emerita 1990—), Soc. Biol. Chemists, Nat. Women's Studies Assn., Phi Beta Kappa, Sigma Xi. Avocations: reading, music, yoga, swimming. Home: 21 Lakeview Ave Cambridge MA 02138-3325 Office Phone: 617-495-4909.

HUBBARD, STANLEY STUB, broadcast executive; b. St. Paul, May 28, 1933; s. Stanley Eugene and Didrikke A. (Stub) H.; m. Karen Elizabeth Holmen, June 13, 1959; children: Kathryn Elizabeth Hubbard Rominski, Stanley Eugene II, Virginia Anne Hubbard Morris, Robert Winston, Julia Didrikke Coyte. BA, U. Minn., 1955; PhD (hon.), Hamline U., 1995, U. Minn., 2004. With Hubbard Broadcasting, St. Paul, 1951—, pres., 1967—, chmn., CEO, 1983—; past chmn. US Satellite Broadcasting Co., Inc., 1981—99. Mem. broadcast adv. com. on comm. subcom. Ho. of Reps., 1977—79; mem. adv. com. on advanced TV, FCC, 1988—95; mem. US Nat. Inf. Infastructure Adv. Coun., 1994—96. Contbr. articles to profl. jours. Chmn. St. Croix Valley Youth Ctr., 1968—; trustee Hubbard Broadcasting Found.; mem. bd. dirs. U. Minn. Found., Mpls., Assn. Maximum Svc. TV, U. St. Thomas, Minn. Bus. Partnership, Heart Rhythm Found.; past advisor Gov.'s Crime Commn., Ramsey County Ice Arena Com.; past bd. dirs. The Guthrie Theater, The Psychoanalytic Found. of Minn., Sci. Mus. of Minn., Am. Friends of Jamaica; past mem. Hazelden adv. com. Met. Airports Pub. Found. Adv. Bd.; bd. visitors U. Minn. Med. Sch., 2004; steering com. Salvation Army Twin Citites; chmn. pres. coun. Twin Cities Pub. TV, 2004. Recipient Ellis Island Medal of Honor, 2004, Mitchell Charnley award Northwest Broadcast News Assn., 1991, Internat. Humanitarian award Am. Friends of Jamaica, 1989, Arthur C. Clarke award Satellite Broadcasting and Comm. Assn., 1994, DreamMaker award Children's Cancer Rsch. Fund, 1994, Disting. Svc. award Nat. Assn. Broadcasters, 1995, Spurgeon award Boy Scouts Am., 1985, Avatar award Broadcast Cable and Fin. Mgmt., 1995, Human Rights award Am. Jewish Com., 1995, Cmty. Leadership award Mpls./St. Paul chpt. Alzheimer's Assn., 1995, Most Innovative Product award Minn. High Tech. Coun., 1995, Journalism Innovator award U. Nebr., 1996, Minn. Family Bus. award U. St. Thomas, 1996, Disting. Alumnus award Breck Sch., 1996, Minn. and Dakotas Entrepreneur of Yr. award, 1996, Heritage award US Hockey Hall of Fame, 1996, U. Minn. M Club Hall of Fame Lifetime Achievement award, 1996, Broadcasters' Found. Golden Mike award, 1997, Acad. of Achievement's Golden Plate award, 1997; named to Broadcasting and Cable Hall of Fame, 1991, Soc. Satellite Profl. Internat. Space Hall of Fame, 1992, Acad. Achievement's Golden Plate award, 1997, Broadcast Pioneer award Minn. Broadcasters Assn., 1998, John Hogan Disting. Svc. award Radio & TV News Dir. Assn., 2000, Promax TV Century award, 2003; inductee St. Croix Valley Athletics Hall of Fame, 2000, Pavek Mus. of Broadcasting Hall of Fame, 2001, ProMax TV Cent. Award, 2003; named one of First Fifty Giants of Broadcasting Libr. Am. Broadcasing, 2003. Mem. Nat. Acad. TV Arts and Scis. (past chmn. bd. trustees, found. pres. 2003—, Minn. chpt. Silver Cir. award 2001, Golden Cir. award 2004), Broadcast Pioneers, Internat. Radio and TV Soc. Avocations: sailing and boating, reading, photography. Office: Hubbard Broadcasting Inc 3415 University Ave W Saint Paul MN 55114-2099 Office Phone: 651-642-4200. Business E-Mail: jmahoney@hbi.com.

HUBBARD, THOMAS C., former ambassador; b. Ky., 1943; m. Joan Magnusson; 2 children. Grad., U. Ala., 1965. With U.S. Fgn. Svc., 1965—, polit./econ. officer Santo Domingo, Dominican republic, econ./comml. officer Fukuoka, Japan, mem. polit. section U.S. Embassy Tokyo, 1971-73, 78-81; econ. officer Japan Desk Dept. State, 1973-75; exec. sec. to delegation U.S. Mission to OECD, Paris, 1975, energy advisor; dir. tng. and liaison staff Bur. Pers. Dept. State, Washington, dep. dir. Philippine Desk, 1984-85, country dir. Philippines Desk, 1985-87; dep. chief of mission U.S. Embassy, Kuala Lumpur, Malaysia, 1987-89; minister-counselor Sr. Fgn. Svc., 1989-90; minister, dep. chief of mission U.S. Embassy, Manila, 1990-93; dep. asst. sec. for East Asian and Pacific Affairs Dept. State, Washington, 1993-96; U.S. amb. to Republic of the Philippines and Republic of Palau Manila, 1996—2001; U.S. amb. to Republic of Korea U.S. Dept. State, Seoul, 2001—04. Legis. asst. Congressman Jim Leach, Iowa, 1981; prin. dep. asst. East Asian and Pacific affairs Sec. of State, 2000—01. Mem. Phi Beta Kappa.

HUBBARD, WILLIAM BOGEL, planetary sciences educator; b. Liberty, Tex., Nov. 14, 1940; s. William Bogel and Marie Hubbard; m. Jean North Gilliland, June 8, 1963; children: Lynne Marie, Laurie North. BA, Rice U., Houston, 1962; PhD, U. Calif., Berkeley, 1967. Rsch. fellow Calif. Inst. Tech., Pasadena, 1967-68; asst. prof. astronomy U. Tex., Austin, 1968-72; assoc. prof. planetary scis. U. Ariz., Tucson, 1972-75, dir. Lunar and Planetary Lab., 1977-81, prof., 1975—. Cons. Lawrence Livermore (Calif.) Nat. Lab., 1972-86, NASA, 1994—; prin. investigator NASA, 1974—, NSF, 1970, 79, 83, 86-93; exch. scientist USSR Nat. Acad. Sci., 1973, mem. com. div. for planetary scis., 1985-88; mem. com. on planetary and lunar exploration NRC, 2003—. Contbr. articles to profl. jours.; assoc. editor Icarus, 1980-2003; receiving editor New Astronomy, 2004-. Fellow AAAS, Japan Soc. for Promotion of Sci., Am. Geophys. Union; mem. Am. Astron. Soc., Internat. Astron. Union, Am. Hereford Assn., Nat. Cattlemen's Beef Assn., Sigma Xi. Democrat. Episcopalian. Home: 2618 E Devon St Tucson AZ 85716-5506 Office: U Ariz Lunar & Planetary Lab Tucson AZ 85721-0092

HUBBARD, WILLIAM JAMES, library director; b. Grand Rapids, Mich., July 17, 1941; s. Willard Wright and Sara (Rast) H.; m. Barbara Ockun, Sept. 8, 1962; children: William, Thomas, James, Gregory. AB, Dartmouth Coll., 1963; MLS, SUNY, Geneseo, 1972. Engr., supr. Rochester (N.Y.) Telephone Corp., 1963-71; contract libr. Xerox Corp., Webster, N.Y., 1971-72; libr. circulation SUNY, Fredonia, 1973-75; libr. user svcs. Va. Tech., Blacksburg, 1975-80; dir. libr. svcs., dir.automation-networks, act. state libr. Va. State Libr., Richmond, 1980-88; univ. libr. Jacksonville (Ala.) State U., 1988—. Author: Stack Management, 1981; assoc. editor Ala. Librarian; contbr. articles to profl. jours. Mem. Ala. Libr. Assn., Nat. Assn. Scholars, Am. Soc. Info. Sci. and Tech., Assn. Knowledgework. Office: State U Univ Libr Jacksonville AL 36265 Business E-Mail: bhubbard@jsu.edu. E-mail: williamj@hubbards.org.

HUBBARD, WILLIAM KEITH, former federal agency administrator; b. Rocky Mount, N.C., Jan. 12, 1949; s. Ryan Buckhannon and Maple Eliza (Moore) H.; m. Bobbie Norris Sutton Hubbard, Feb. 5, 1975; children: Helen Elizabeth, Erin Katherine, William Andrew. BA, U. N.C., 1970; MA, Am. U., 1976. Assoc. commr. for policy FDA, Washington, 1991-99, sr. assoc. commr. for policy, planning and legislation, 1999—2005. Recipient Disting. Svc. award (4 times), US Dept. Health & Human Services, Award of Merit (4 times), FDA, Presdl. Meritorious Rank award, 1998.

HUBBARD, WILLIAM NEILL, JR., retired pharmaceutical executive; b. Fairmont, N.C., Oct. 15, 1919; s. William Neill and Mary Emma (Fenegan) H.; m. Elizabeth Terleski, Dec. 28, 1945 (dec. Mar. 1984); children: William Neill III, Michael J. (dec.), Mary E., Elizabeth A., Susan E.; m. Joyce Elaine Wixson, Apr. 3, 1987. AB, Columbia U., 1942; postgrad., U. N.C. Sch. Medicine; MD, NYU, 1944. Mem. house staff 3d med. div. Bellevue Hosp., N.Y.C., 1944-50; instr. medicine N.Y. U., 1950-53, asst. prof., 1953-59; asst. dean, then assoc. dean N.Y. U. Coll. Medicine, 1951-59; dean U. Mich. Med. Sch., 1959-70, assoc. prof. internal medicine, 1959-64, prof., 1964-70; dir. U. Mich. Med. Center, 1969-70; gen. mgr. pharm. div., v.p. Upjohn Co., 1970-72, exec. v.p., 1972-74, pres., 1974-84, dir., 1968-91. Dir. Johnson Controls, Inc., Consumers Power; bd. dirs. Pharm. Mfrs. Assn., 1978-80, 81-84, chmn. bd., 1980-81; chmn. coun. health care tech. Inst. Medicine of NAS, 1986-90; cons. USPHS; trustee N.Y. Acad. of Medicine, 1994-2002; bd. dirs. Pan-Am. Health and Edn. Found., 1996-2001. Mem. Nat. Adv. Commn. on Libraries, 1966-68; med. adv. com. W.K. Kellogg Found., 1959-67, trustee, 1979-92; mem. Gov.'s Adv. Com. on Edn. Health Care, 1965-69; trustee Bronson Meth. Hosp., 1970-84; chmn. Gov.'s Action Com. on Corrections, 1972-73; mem. panel ednl. consultants Commn. on Edn. for Health Adminstrn., 1973-75; mem. com. on med. edn. Brown U., 1974-77; mem. nat. sci. bd. NSF, 1974-80, cons. to bd., 1980-83; bd. dirs. Family Health Internat. (formerly Internat. Fertility Research Program), 1981-90; mem. bd. sci. and tech. for internat. devel. Nat. Acad. Scis., 1978-80, Council on Sci. and Tech. for Devel., 1978-83; bd. visitors in East Asian studies U. Mich., 1976-80; bd. overseers Morehouse Coll. Medicine, 1976-81; bd. dirs. Nat. Med. Fellowships, Inc., 1973-75, Nat. Fund. Med. Edn., 1962-75; trustee Kalamazoo Coll., 1973-78, Columbia U., N.Y.C., 1981-89; mem. bd. regents Nat. Library of Medicine, 1963-67, 72-76, chmn., 1965-67, 74-76, cons., 1976-84; bd. dirs. Am. Near East Refugee Aid, 1977-82; dir. devel. council U. Mich., 1979-87; mem. population adv. panel Office of Technology Assessment, U.S. Congress, 1979-81; chmn. bd. visitors Med. Ctr. U. Mich., 1989-99; bd. visitors U. Mich. Sch. of Nursing, 1995-98, Columbia U. Sch. Nursing, 1990-99. Fellow ACP, Am. Acad. Arts and Scis., Royal Soc. Medicine; mem. AMA, Inst. Medicine of NAS, Harvey Soc., N.Y. Acad. Medicine, Soc. Alumni Bellevue Hosp., Mich. Med. Soc. (coun. 1960-62), Kalamazoo Acad. Medicine, Am. Soc. Clin. Pharmacology and Therapeutics, Assn. Am. Med. Colls. (disting. svc. mem.; pres. 1966-67), Jamestown Soc., Sigma Xi, Alpha Omega Alpha. Home: 3634 Woodcliff Dr Kalamazoo MI 49008-2513 E-mail: W.N.Hubbard@worldnet.att.net.

HUBBE, HENRY ERNEST, financial forecaster, funds manager; b. Hamburg, Germany, Aug. 13, 1932; came to U.S., 1958; s. H.V. and Ingeborg M. (Schroeder) H.; m. Mary E. Wylie, 1961; children: John, Michael. BA, NYU, 1971, MBA, 1974. Area adminstr. Bank of Am. NT&SA, San Francisco, 1958-63; asst. v.p. Citibank N.Am., N.Y.C., 1963-74; sr. v.p. European Am. Bank, N.Y.C., 1974-84; mng. dir. Fintech (UK) Ltd., London, 1985-96, Fintech Asset Mgmt., London, 1985-96; pres. Fintech (USA) Ltd., N.Y.C., N.Y., 1996—. Mem. faculty Am. Inst. Banking, N.Y.C., 1974-83; guest speaker internat. confs., profl. orgns.; panel mem. Bus. Internat., London. Creator proprietary computer software; contbr. articles to profl. jours. Mem. Beta Gamma Sigma (v.p. 1971—). Avocation: golf. E-mail: fintech@concentric.net.

HUBBELL, BILLY JAMES, lawyer; b. Pine Bluff, Ark., May 21, 1949; s. Arley E. and Mary M. (Duke) H.; m. Judy C. Webb, Feb. 21, 1981; children: Jennifer Leigh, William Griffin. BE, U. Cen. Ark., 1971; JD, U. Ark, Little Rock, 1978. Bar: Ark. 1978, U.S. Dist. Ct. (ea. dist.) Ark. 1978, U.S. Ct. Appeals (8th cir.) 1987. Tchr. Grady (Ark.) High Sch., 1971-78; assoc. Smith and Smith, McGehee, Ark., 1978-79; ptnr. Smith, Hubbell and Drake, McGehee, 1979-86, Griffin, Rainwater & Draper, P.A., Crossett, Ark., 1987-90; dep. prosecuting atty. Ashley County, Ark., 1989-90; dist. judge Crossett, 1991—; pvt. practice, 1991—. Candidate Ark. Ho. of Reps., Lincoln County, 1984, 10th Jud. Dist. Cir./Chancery Judge, 1998. Sgt. USAR, 1970-76. Mem. Ark. Bar Assn., S.E. Ark. Legal Inst. (chmn. 1984-85, Ashley County Bar Assn. (past pres.), Ark. Trial Lawyers Assn. Democrat. Seventh Day Adventist. Avocations: jogging, computers. Office: PO Box 574 Crossett AR 71635-0574 Office Phone: 870-364-6114. Business E-Mail: billy@hubbelllaw.net.

HUBBELL, DAVID SMITH, surgeon, educator; b. Dallas, Aug. 29, 1922; s. Jay Broadus and Lucinda (Smith) H.; m. Barbara Baynard, July 3, 1947; children: Katherine, Lawrence, Daniel. AB, Duke U., 1943, MD, 1946. Diplomate Am. Bd. Surgery, Am. Bd. Thoracic Surgery. Pathologist U.S. Army Tripler Hosp., Honolulu, 1947-49; resident and Am. Cancer Soc. fellow in surgery Yale U. Hosp., New Haven, 1949-54; attending surgeon Bayfront and St. Anthony's Hosp., St. Petersburg, Fla., 1955-85; prof. gebs. surgery and anatomy U. So. Fla., Tampa, 1985—, prof. emeritus, 2000—. Capt. M.C., U.S. Army, 1947-49. Recipient award for outstanding rsch. Moffitt Cancer Ctr., Tampa, 1994. Fellow Am. Cancer Soc. (life mem.); mem. ACS (pres. Fla. chpt. 1973-74), Fla. Assn. Thoracic Surgeons (pres. 1980-81), Pinellas County Med. Soc. (pres. 1969-70), Rotary. Republican. Presbyterian. Achievements include research in medical education, control of pain, chest tumors. Office: Moffitt Cancer Ctr 12902 Magnolia Dr Tampa FL 33612-9416

HUBBELL, FLOYD ALLAN, internist, educator; b. Waco, Tex., Nov. 13, 1948; s. F.E. and Margaret (Fraser) H.; m. Nancy Cooper, May 23, 1975; 1 child, Andrew Allan. BA, Baylor U., 1971, MD, 1974; MS in Pub. Health, UCLA, 1983. Diplomate Am. Bd. Internal Medicine. Intern, then resident Long Beach med. program U. Calif., Irvine, 1975-78, asst. prof. medicine, 1981-89, assoc. prof. medicine and social ecology, 1989-97, prof. medicine and social ecology, 1997—, dir. primary care internal medicine residency, 1992-97, chief divsn. gen. internal medicine and primary care, 1992—2002, dir. Ctr. for Health Policy and Rsch., 1993—2003, chair dept. medicine, 2002—. Contbr. articles to profl. jours. Fellow ACP; mem. APHA, Soc. Gen. Internal Medicine, Physicians for Social Responsibility, Assn. Profs. Medicine. Democrat. Avocations: reading, skiing, water sports. Office: Dept Medicine UCI Med Ctr 101 City Dr Bldg 200 720 Orange CA 92868-4076 E-mail: fahubbel@uci.edu.

HUBBELL, FRED SHELTON, insurance company executive; b. Des Moines, Apr. 25, 1951; s. James Windsor Jr. and Helen (Houx) H.; m. Charlotte Beyer, Aug. 28, 1976; children: Lauren, Meredith, Frederick. BA, U. N.C., 1973; JD, U. Iowa, 1976; PMD cert., Harvard Grad. Sch. Bus., 1983. Assoc. Dewey, Ballantine, Bushby, Palmer, N.Y.C., 1976-79, Hughes, Hubbard & Reed, N.Y.C., 1979-81, Mumford, Schrage & Zurek, Des Moines, 1981-83; v.p. Equitable of Iowa Cos., Des Moines, 1983-85; pres., chief exec. officer Younkers, Inc., Des Moines, 1985-87; pres., chief operating officer Equitable of Iowa Cos., Des Moines, from 1987, pres., chief exec. officer, bd. dirs.; chmn. Equitable Life Ins. Co. of Iowa, Des Moines; gen. mgr. ING Fin. Services Internat. N. Am., 1997—99; pres., CEO, Retail Fin. Services ING, 1997—99; chmn. exec. com. ING Fin. Services Internat., 1999—2000, ING Americas, 2000—, ING Asia/Pacific, 2000—03; exec. bd. ING Groep NV, 2000—. Contbr. articles to profl. jours. Bd. dirs. Planned Parenthood of Mid-Iowa, Des Moines, 1982—, Simpson Coll., Indianola, Iowa, 1985; bd. govs. Iowa Coll. Found., Des Moines, 1987; trustee Mercy Hosp. Med. Ctr., Des Moines, 1984. Mem. Young Pres. Orgn., Greater Des Moines C. of C. (bd. dirs. 1985). Clubs: Wakonda, Des Moines (Des Moines). Democrat. Episcopalian. Avocations: running, golf, travel. Office: ING Americas 5780 Powers Ferry Rd NW Atlanta GA 30327

HUBBELL, JOHN HOWARD, radiation physicist; b. Ann Arbor, Mich., Apr. 9, 1925; s. Howard Adams Hubbell and Mildred Jeanetta (Lipe) Hubbell Dyson; m. Jean Garber Norford, June 11, 1955; children: Anne Virginia Hubbell Cooper, Shelton Eric, Wendy Jean Hubbell Carballo. BS in Engring. Physics, U. Mich., 1949, MS in Physics, 1950; dr. honoris causa, U. Cordoba, 1996. Rschr. x-ray crystal diffraction group Nat. Bur. Stds. (name now Nat. Inst. Stds. & Tech.), Washington, 1950-51, rschr. thermodynamics sect., 1951, rschr. radiation theory group, 1951-62, dir. x-ray and ionizing radiation data ctr. Washington & Gaithersburg, Md., 1963-81, rschr. Ctr. for Radiation Rsch. Gaithersburg, 1982-88, rschr., cons. Photon and Charged Particle Data Ctr., 1988—. Mem. cross sect. evaluation working group Brookhaven (N.Y.) Nat. Lab., 1965—; cons. Lawrence Livermore (Calif.) Nat. Lab., 1966—, Lawrence Berkeley (Calif.) Nat. Lab., 1966—, Internat. Atomic Energy Agy., Vienna, 1987—, WHO, Geneva, 1989—; sec. task force on x-ray absorption coefficients Internat. Union Crystallography, 1979—; lectr. USSR Acad. Scis., 1979, People's Republic of China State Bur. Metrology, 1987, 93, India under Indo-U.S. Spl. Fgn. Currency Program, 1972, 74, 90; invited lectr. Japanese Soc. Radiol. Tech., Nagoya Ann. Conf., Kyoto, Osaka, 1995; vis. prof. U. Cordoba, Argentina, 1996. Author: Photon Cross Sections, Attenuation Coefficients and Energy Absorption Coefficients, 1969; editor: Jour. Applied Radiation and Isotopes, 1988—92; editor-in-chief: Radiation Physics and Chemistry, 1992—2001, cons. editor:, 2002—; contbr. articles to profl. jours. and encys., chapters to books. Scoutmaster, Boy Scouts Am., Washington, 1953-60; ch. sch. tchr. Foundry United Methodist Ch., Washington, 1963-78. With U.S. Army, 1943-45, ETO. Decorated Bronze Star; recipient Faculty medal Tech. U. Prague, 1982; named Outstanding Alumnus U. Mich. Nuc. Engring. Dept., 1995. Fellow Am. Nuc. Soc. (Radiation Industry award 1985, Profl. Excellence award 1990), Health Physics Soc. (chmn. gen. radiation protection sect., stds. com. 1984-90, Disting. Sci. Achievement award 2001), Am. Phys. Soc.; mem. Soc. Nuc. Medicine (Paul C. Aebersold award 1985), Internat. Radiation Physics Soc. (pres. 1994-97, sec. to adv. bd. 2000--), Radiation Rsch. Soc., Hubbell Family Hist. Soc., Internat. Higher Edn. Acad. Scis. (Moscow). Achievements include development of computationally tractable solutions for the (now called) Hubbell rectangular source integral and Epstein-Hubbell generalized elliptic-type integral. Avocations: eclipse chasing, playing harmonica. Office: Nat Inst Standards and Tech Mail Stop 8463 Rad Physics Bldg Rm C-314 Gaithersburg MD 20899-8463 Home: 514 Russell Ave Gaithersburg MD 20877-2866 Business E-Mail: john.hubbell@nist.gov. *In this later stage of my life I view my global science connections more and more as an opportunistic tool toward realizing, incrementally at least, Teilhard de Chardin's envisioned "noosphere" (humanity as a caring communicating "thinking skin" of the earth), declaring the pragmatic and compelling authenticity of the option of a friendly cosmos as not only a place in which to live, but also to bravely wear as a suit of clothes, in contrast to the hostile and judgmental cosmos envisioned, dwelt in, and worn by many.*

HUBBELL, KATHERINE JEAN, retired marketing professional; b. Norfolk, Va., Mar. 5, 1951; d. Lester Earle and Katherine Jean (Bush) Hubbell; m. Daryl Paul Domning, July 10, 1987; 1 child, Charlotte Roxanna Domning. BA in English, Clemson U., 1974, BS in Math., 1974; MBA in Mktg., Va. Polytech. Inst. & State U., 1991. Info. sys. engr. MITRE Corp., McLean, Va., 1975-79, tech. staff Bedford, Mass., 1980—81; design engr. GE, Wilmington, Mass., 1979-80; budget assoc. nat. hdqrs. ARC, Washington, 1982-92; mktg. cons. Dominion Group, Vienna, Va., 1993-98; with Nat. Found. Women Bus. Owners, Washington, 1999—2001; ret. Prime Vol Opportunities, 2002. Vol, recreation ARC Bethesda Naval Hosp., 1976—79; vol. Holy Cross Hospice, 1984—87; vol., allocations com. United Way Nat. Capitol Area, 1989—91; vol. Network Nat., Cath. social justice lobby, Washington, 2003—; vol., database mgr. Nat. Christian Life Cmty. U.S., 1993—97; vol., strategic planning com. Christian Life Cmty. Mid-Atlantic Region, 1989—90, vol., co-chair, 1995—2001, vol., devel. officer, 2003—; vol., adv. com. The Arc of Montgomery County, 2000. Home: 9211 Wendell St Silver Spring MD 20901-3533

HUBBELL, ROBERT B., lawyer; BA English, Political Science, magna cum laude, Loyola Marymount Univ., 1978; JD magna cum laude, Loyola Law School, 1981. Bar: Calif., Am. Bar. Assoc. Atty. Heller, Ehrman, White, & McAuliffe, LLP, 1991—, Firmwide Managing Shareholder. Pres. Legal Aid Foundation of Los Angeles, 2000—01. Office: Heller Ehrman White & McAuliffe 333 Bush St San Francisco CA 94104 Office Phone: 213-689-7563. Office Fax: 213-614-1868. E-mail: rhubbell@hewm.com.

HUBBLE, SUSAN LUNSFORD, art educator; d. Hunter Lee Lunsford, Jr. and Margaret Reagan Lunsford; m. Joseph Emory Hubble, Dec. 6, 1986; 1 child, Samuel Glenn. Bachelors of Fine Arts (BFA), Va. Commonwealth U., Richmond, Virginia, 1974—77; M in Liberal Arts and Scis., Hollins U., 1994. Art tchr. King George (Va.) H.S., 1978—88; art tchr., art dept. chairperson Staunton River H.S., Moneta, Va., 1988—. Sec. Sunday Sch., mem.

choir/hospitality/libr. com. Shady Grove Bapt. Ch., Blue Ridge, Va., 1993—2005. Named S.W. Region Secondary Art Tchr. of Yr., S.W. Va. Art Edn. Assn., 2002. Mem.: Va. Art Edn. Assn. (membership chair 2000—03, Secondary Art Tchr. of Yr. for State of Va. 2002, Art Educator of Yr. Va. 2005), Nat. Art Edn. Assn. (assoc.). Avocations: art, travel, reading. Office: Staunton River High School 1095 Golden Eagle Dr Moneta VA 24121 Office Phone: 540-297-7151. Business E-Mail: shubble@bedford.k12.va.us.

HUBBS, CLARK, zoologist, researcher; b. Ann Arbor, Mich., Mar. 15, 1921; s. Carl Leavitt and Laura Cornelia (Clark) H.; m. Catherine Vickery Symons; children: Laura Ellen Hubbs Tait, John Clark, Ann Frances Hubbs Weissman. BA, U. Mich., 1942; PhD, Stanford U., 1951. Instr. zoology U. Tex., Austin, 1949-52, asst. prof., 1952-57, assoc. prof., 1957-63, prof., 1963-88, Regents prof., 1988-91, Regents prof. emeritus, 1991—, chmn. biology dept., 1974-76, chmn. zoology dept., 1978-86, with grad. faculty dept. marine sci., 1987-91; curator ichthyology Tex. Meml. Mus., 1978—. Mem. grad. faculty Tex. A&M U., 1969-83; vis. prof. U. Okla., Kingston, 1970-84; bd. dirs. Hubbs/Sea World Rsch. Inst., San Diego; faculty advisor U. de Nuevo Leon, Monterey, Mex., 1985-87; biology advisor Bd. Higher Edn., Little Rock, 1987, Jackson, Miss., 1983; leader Rio Grande Fishes Recovery Team, U.S. Interior Dept., Albuquerque, 1978—; mem. adv. com. Fish, Wildlife and Parks, U.S. Interior Dept., Washington, 1975-77; mem. sci. adv. com. Bass Anglers Sportsmans Soc., Montgomery, Ala., 1974-92; mem. environ. adv. bd. Tex. Utilities, Dallas, 1971-2001, emeritus, 2001—; chmn. inland task force, power plant sitting com., Office of Gov., Austin, Tex., 1971-72; mem. nuclear power adv. com. Tex. Energy Adv. Council, Austin, 1978-80; U.S. rep. European Ichthyological Congress, 1985-88; bd. dirs. Nature Conservancy of Tex., 1988-94; mem. rev. com. USDI, San Juan. Mng. editor: Copeia, 1971—84; contbr. articles to profl. jours. Mem. NRC Com. on Glen Canyon Releases in to the Colorado River, 1991-96; bd. dirs. Tex. Environ. Def., 1997—. Served with U.S. Army, 1942-46, PTO. Named Educator and Researcher of Yr., Tex. chpt. Am. Fisheries Soc., 1978, Student award named in his honor; recipient Excellence, Golden and Hon. awards Am. Fisheries Soc., 1988; Clark Hubbs Endowed Professorship in Zoology established in his honor, Dept. Zoology, Clark Hubbs Aquarium named in his honor. Mem. Am. Soc. Ichthyologists and Herpetologists (pres. 1987, lifetime achievement award 1992, Robert K. Johnson award 2004), Am. Inst. Fish Rsch. Biol. (pres. 1995-98), Tex. Acad. Scis. (pres. 1972-73, Disting. Scientist of Yr. 1998), S.W. Assn. Naturalists (pres. 1966-67, W.F. Blair Eminent Naturalist 1990, George M. Sutton award 1996, Clark Hubbs Student Poster award named in his honor 2000), Sociedad Iotiológica Mexicana Asociación Cientifica (hon.). Office: U Tex Sect Integrative Biology Austin TX 78712 Office Phone: 512-471-1176. Business E-Mail: hubbs@mail.utexas.edu.

HUBBS, DONALD HARVEY, foundation executive; b. Kingman, Ariz., Jan. 3, 1918; s. Wayne and Grace Lillian (Hoose) H.; m. Flora Vincent, June 14, 1945; children: Donald Jr., Susan Tyner, Diane Schultz, Wayne, David, Adrienne Busk. BA in Edn., Ariz. State U., 1940; JD, Southwestern U., 1956. CPA; bar: Calif. 1956. Acct. Wright and Hubbs, LA, 1945-67; pvt. practice atty. LA, 1956-81; pres., dir. Conrad N. Hilton Found., LA, 1981-98, chmn. bd., CEO, 1998—2005. Bd. dirs. TWA Airline, 1977, Vita Pakt Citrus Products Co.; regent Mt. St. Mary's Coll., 1983-98; bd. councilors U. So. Calif. Law Sch., 1992-99, Donald H. Hubbs Disting. Profs. Chair U. Houston. Hon. chief of the tribes of Kapatinga and Oku, Ghana; spkr. So. Govs. Conf., 1986. 1st lt. (inf.) U.S. Army. Decorated Purple Heart; recipient Anne Sullivan medal Perkins Sch. for the Blind, 1992, Humanitarian award Nat. Coun. Juvenile and Family Ct. Judges, 1994, Humanitarian award Family Violence Prevention Fund, 2000, Spirit of Helen Keller award Helen Keller Internat., 1995. Mem. State Bar of Calif., So. Calif. Assn. for Philanthropy (pres. 1985-86), Riviera Country Club, LA Country Club. Avocations: cattle ranching, hunting, fishing, golf. Home: 1658 San Onofre Dr Pacific Palisades CA 90272-2735

HUBE, RICHARD W., state representative, small business owner; b. Hartford, Conn., Jan. 31, 1947; BA, Colgate U., 1971. Rep. Vt. State Ho. Reps., 1999—, mem. Commerce com., 1999—2000, vice chair Govt. Ops. com., 2000—01, mem. Govt. Ops. com., 2003—04, asst. min. leader, 2003—04, mem. House Rules and Joint Rules com., 2003—. Trustee U. Vt., Chapel of the Snows; dir. Stratton Winhall Edn. Found. Republican. Office: PO Box 93 South Londonderry VT 05155 also: State House 115 State St Montpelier VT 05633 Office Phone: 802-828-2231. E-mail: Huberick@sover.net.*

HUBEL, DAVID HUNTER, physiologist, science educator; b. Windsor, Ont., Can., Feb. 27, 1926; s. Jesse Hervey and Elsie (Hunter) Hubel; m. Shirley Ruth Izzard, June 20, 1953; children: Carl Andrew, Eric David, Paul Matthew. BSc, McGill U., 1947, MD, 1951, DSc (hon.), 1978; AM (hon.), Harvard U., 1962; DSc (hon.), U. Man., 1983; DHL (hon.), Johns Hopkins U., 1990; DSci, U. Western Ont., 1993; DSc, Oxford U., 1994, Gustavus Adolphus Coll., 1994, Ohio State U., 1995; D (hon.), U. Madrid, 1997, Univ. Miguel, 1998; JD (hon.), Dalhousie U., 1998; D (hon.), U. Toronto, 2002; D in optometry (hon.), SUNY, 2004; D (hon.), McMaster, 2005. Intern Montreal Gen. Hosp., 1951—52; asst. resident neurology Montreal Neurol. Inst., 1952—53, fellow clin. neurophysiology, 1953—54; asst. resident neurology Johns Hopkins Hosp., 1954—55; rsch. fellow Walter Reed Army Inst. Rsch., Washington, 1955—58; sr. fellow neurol. scis. group Johns Hopkins U., 1958—59; faculty Harvard U. Med. Sch., 1959—, George Packer Berry prof. physiology, chmn. dept., 1967—68, George Packer Berry prof. neurobiology, 1968—82, John Franklin Enders U. prof., 1982—, rsch. prof. Neurobiology. Lectr. in field; George Eastman prof., Oxford, England, 1991—92; rschr. brain mechanisms in vision; spkr. in field. With AUS, 1955—58. Recipient Trustees award, Rsch. to Prevent Blindness, 1971, Lewis S. Rosentiel award for disting. work in basic med. rsch., 1972, Karl Lashley prize, Am. Philos. Soc., 1977, Louisa Gross Horwitz prize, Columbia U., 1978, Dickson prize in medicine, U. Pitts., 1979, Ledile prize, Harvard U., 1980, Nobel prize in physiology or medicine, 1981, Outstanding Sci. Leadership award, Nat. Assn. for Biomed. Rsch., 1990, City of Medicine award, 1990, Glen A. Fry medal, Coll. Optometry, Ohio State U., 1991, First Ann. George A. Miller lectr., Cognitive Neurosci. Soc., Gerald award, Soc. Neurosci., 1993, Helen Keller award, Helen Keller Eye Rsch. Found., 1995, Wilder Penfield Lecture, Montreal Neurological Inst., 1998, Frontiers in Neuroscience Lecture, Case Western Reserve U., 2000, Disting. Canadians Spkr. Series, Corpus Christi Coll., 2001. Fellow: AAAS, Am. Acad. Arts & Scis.; mem.: NAS, Acadmica Europaea (fgn. mem.), Royal Soc. London, Am. Philos. Soc. (Karl Spencer Lashley prize 1977), Johns Hopkins U. Soc. Scholars, Spanish Soc.Ophthalmology (hon.), Assn. Rsch. in Vision and Ophthalmology (Friedenwald award 1975), Soc. for Neurosci. (Bwditch lectr. 1966), Deutsche Acad. der Naturforscher Leopoldina (Grass lectr. 1976, Gerard award 1993), Am. Physiol. Soc., Sigma Xi. Office: Harvard U Med Sch Dept Neurobiology WAB213 220 Longwood Ave Boston MA 02115-5701

HUBER, SISTER ALBERTA, academic administrator; b. Rock Island, Ill., Feb. 12, 1917; d. Albert and Lydia (Hofer) H. BA, Coll. St. Catherine, St. Paul, 1939; MA, U. Minn., 1945; PhD, U. Notre Dame, 1954. Mem. faculty Coll. St. Catherine, 1940—, prof. English, 1953-97; prof. emerita, 1997; chmn. dept. Coll. St. Catherine, 1960-63, acad. dean, 1962-64, pres., 1964-79, pres. emerita, 2005. Trustee Avila Coll., Kansas City, Mo., 1986-97, St. Joseph's Hosp., St. Paul, 1971-80; pres. UN Assn. Minn., 1980-81; bd. dirs. St. Paul YMCA, 1986-92. Decorated Chevalier, Ordre des Palmes Acad.; recipient Outstanding Achievement award U. Minn. Alumni Assn., 1981. Mem. Phi Beta Kappa, Pi Gamma Mu. Office: Apt 111 1322 Alton St Saint Paul MN 55116 Personal E-mail: mthom17349@aol.com.

HUBER, DAVID G., theater educator, actor; b. Salt Lake City, June 5, 1967; s. Huber Ronald Leo and Karen Rae Huber; children: Allison, Amanda, Alexander. Bachelors, U. Utah, 1996. Cert. Tchr. N.Mex, 1998. Youth track and field coach Salt Lake County, Taylorsville, Utah, 1986—97; theater educator Mt. Vernon Acad., Murray, Utah, 1994—97; cross country coach Farmington HS, 1997—, tchr., 1998—. Workman high sch. theatre educator, Calif. Actor: (plays) Black River Traders; author: (plays) Race, Pane. Youth coord. Salt Lake Valley Drug and alcohol abuse prevention coalition, Salt Lake City; dir./founder Identity Improv Troupe, Salt Lake City, 1990—93; hosp. intervention team/speakers team Salt Lake Rape Crisis Ctr., 1991—93; youth AIDS edn. coord. MCCB, Logan, Utah, 1997—98; hosp. intervention team SJ Rape Crisis Team, Farmington, N.Mex., 2003.

HUBER, DAVID L., prosecutor; b. Louisville, Ky. BA in polit. sci., U. Louisville, JD, 1968. Assoc. with Mr. Fred M. Goldberg, Ky.; legis. asst. to chief legis. asst. US Senator Marlowe Cook; chief adminstrv. officer Jefferson County Govt., 1978—85; 2nd v.p. and dir. govt. rels. and compliance Capital Holding Corp.; v.p., gen. counsel Glenmore Distilleries Co.; gen. counsel to US Senator Mitch McConnell; asst. US atty. (we. dist.) Ky US Dept. Justice, 1991—2003, US atty., 2003—. Recipient Commissioner's Spl. Citation, US Food and Drug Adminstrn. Office: US Atty Western Dist Bank Louisville Bldg 510 W Broadway Louisville KY 40202

HUBER, DON LAWRENCE, publisher; b. Milw., Aug. 17, 1928; s. Wallace Fred and Florence (Bleck) H.; m. Joan Mac Monnies, June 23, 1951. Student, Carthage (Ill.) Coll., 1946-48; BS in English, Northwestern U., 1950. Sales exec. sta. WOR (radio), N.Y.C., 1957-58; owner, gen. mgr. Sta. KALE-Radio, Pasco, Washington, 1958-60; mgr. advt. Standard Rate and Data Service, N.Y.C., 1961-70; v.p., pub. Computer and Communication Decisions, Hayden, N.J., 1970-87, VNU Bus. Press.; pvt. practice specializing in bldg. pvt. homes, 1990—. Painter oil landscape paintings, 1990—. Served with USN, 1946-48. Mem. Sales Execs. N.Y., Navy League, Am. Artists Profl. League, Salamagundi Club, Hudson Valley Art Assn. Clubs: Northwestern University (N.Y.C.). Home and Office: 24 Rolling Dr Glen Head NY 11545-2613 Office Phone: 516-626-3359. Personal E-mail: donlhubr@aol.com.

HUBER, DONALD SIMON, physician; b. Clarendon, Pa., Apr. 18, 1929; s. Walter Casper and Mary Agnes (Earley) H.; m. Mary Hanks, Sept. 6, 1958; children: Donald Scott, Mark Walter, Mary Lisa. BA, Duke U., 1951, MD, 1954. Diplomate Am. Bd. Internal Medicine, Am. Bd. Allergy and Immunology. Intern Charity Hosp., New Orleans, 1954-55; resident internal medicine Tulane U. Hosp., New Orleans, 1955-56, 58-60; pvt. practice Huntsville, Ala., 1960-96 (ret. 1996); clin. assoc. prof. medicine Sch. Primary Med. Care, Huntsville, 1985—. Med. dir. Cmty. Free Clinic., 1998—. Lt. commdr. USN, 1956-58, USNR, 1958-60. Fellow Am. Coll. Allergists; mem. AMA, Am. Acad. Allergy and Immunology, Ala. Soc. Allergy and Immunology (pres. 1985), Huntsville Rotary Club (bd. dirs. 1978). Republican. Methodist. Avocation: travel. Home: 507 Holmes Ave Huntsville AL 35801 E-mail: donhuber@knology.net.

HUBER, H. RONALD, management consultant, educator; b. Ottomwa, Iowa, June 10, 1929; s. Herman and Joy Cecil (Roberts) Huber; m. Charlotte M. Haskell, Aug. 19, 1950; children: Marcia Joyanne, Ronda Lee, Christopher R. BA, Simpson Coll., 1950; MA, Truman State U., 1951; student in Labor Rels., U. So. Calif., 1955—64. Cert. presenter Creative Mgmt. Inst., Mo., 1989. Safety engr. Revere Copper & Brass, Chgo., 1953—55; mgr. employment Columbia Broadcasting Sys., Hollywood, Calif., 1955—56; mgr. human resources John J. Foster MRG Co., Costa Mesa, Calif., 1956—57; mgr. labor rels. Alpha Beta Markets, Inc., La Habra, Calif., 1957—66; sr. v.p. Alfred M. Lewis, Inc., Riverside, Calif., 1966—89; mgmt. cons. HRH Rsch., Riverside, 1989—; prof. bus. mgmt. Chapman U., Orange, Calif., 1992—2003. Pres. Alpha Beta Credit Union; vice chmn. supt. measure 8 monitoring group Citizens U. Com. Author: Human Resource Practices For Managers, 1988; co-author: This Year At Alfred M. Lewis, 1987. 1st v.p. United Way, Riverside, 1980; chmn. personnel bd. County Riverside, 1982—86, Riverside (Calif.) County Housing, 1986—92; chmn. human resources bd. City Riverside, 1994—2003. Cpl. U.S. Army, 1951—53. Mem.: High Twelve, Masons, Rotary (various positions, Paul Harris fellow). Republican. Presbyn. Avocations: fishing, biblical history, cruising. Home: 366C Avenda Castilla Laguna Woods CA 92637 Office: Chapman Univ 333 North Glassell Orange CA 92866

HUBER, J. KENDALL, lawyer; b. Norfolk, Va., Nov. 24, 1954; m. Deborah Huber. BA, Va. Poly. Inst. and State U., 1976; JD, U. Va., 1979. Bar: Va. 1980, Md. 1981, Tenn. 1999. Sr. assoc. Piper Rudnick LLP, Balt., 1983—90; v.p., dep. gen. counsel USF&G Corp., Balt., 1990—98, Legg Mason Inc., 1998—99; exec. v.p., gen. counsel, sec. Promus Hotel Corp., Memphis, 1999—2000; v.p., gen. counsel, asst. sec. Allmerica Fin. Corp., Worcester, Mass., 2000—02, sr. v.p., gen. counsel, 2002—. Lt. JACG USN, 1980—83. Office: Allmerica Fin Corp 440 Lincoln St Worcester MA 01653-0002

HUBER, MARGARET ANN, college president; b. Rochester, Pa., July 27, 1949; d. Francis Xavier and Mary Ann (Socash) H. BS in Chemistry, Duquesne U., 1972; MSA, U. Notre Dame, 1975; PhD, U. Mich., 1979. Joined Sisters of Divine Providence, Roman Cath. Ch., 1967-93. Tchr. jr. high sch. St. Martin Sch., Pitts., 1971-72; asst. to acad. dean LaRoche Coll., Pitts., 1972-75, dir. planning, 1978-80, exec. v.p., 1980-81, pres., 1981-92; rsch. assoc. U. Mich., Ann Arbor, 1978; exec. dir. Archdiocese of Santa Fe Cath. Found., 1993-94; pres. Coll. of Notre Dame, Belmont, Calif., 1994—. Mem. Am. Assn. for Higher Edn. Democrat. Office: Coll of Notre Dame 1500 Ralston Ave Belmont CA 94002-1908

HUBER, MARIANNE JEANNE, art dealer, appraiser; b. Amboy, Ill., June 9, 1936; d. John Francis and Jeannette Marie (Wurth) Faivre; m. Robert L. Huber, Oct. 3, 1959; children: Michael Robert, Stephan Louis, Edward Francis. BA, Cardinal Stritch Coll., Milw., 1958. 6th grade tchr. St. Andrew's Sch., Rock Falls, Ill., 1958-59; jr. high tchr. Garside Sch., Mexico City, 1959-61; art dealer, cons. Huber Primitive Art, N.Y.C. and Dixon, Ill., 1963—; founder, pres. New World Art Svcs., N.Y.C. and Dixon, Ill., 1993—. Lectr., cons. Primitive Art Soc., Chgo., 1987, Freeport (Ill.) Art Mus., 1993, Indpls. Mus. Art, 1994, Nprstk Mus., Prague, Czech Republic, 1995; participant Maya Meetings, Austin, Tex., 1985—. Author: Echoes of a Distant Flute, 1984; co-prodr., author (documentary films) The Cuna, 1980, Nebaj, Cotzal and Chajul, 1987, 2003 Maya Calendar, 2004 Maya Calendar, collector, organizer traveling exhbns. The Cuna, 1980—. Election judge Ogle County, Ill., 1993—; committeewoman Dem. Precinct, 2002—. Mem.: LWV, AAUW, Ethnographic Art Soc., Am. Appraisers Assn., Am. Soc. Appraisers, Am. Assn. Dealers in Ancient Oriental and Primitive Art, Phidian Soc., Ill. Dem. Women, Indpls. Met. Mus. Art, Internat. Platform Assn. (gov. 1993—2001), Delta Epsilon Sigma. Democrat. Avocations: hiking, wilderness camping, painting, piano, travel. Home and Office: 1012 Timber Trail Dr Dixon IL 61021-8934 Office Phone: 815-652-4196. E-mail: tellapple@yahoo.com.

HUBER, MARY SUSAN, music educator; b. Buffalo, Feb. 14, 1946; d. Floyd M. Zaepfel and Thelma Zaeptel; m. David Conrad Huber, Dec. 27, 1971; children: David Conrad Jr., Kevin Michael. BS in Music, Daemen Coll., 1969; MEd in Music, State U. Buffalo, 1971; M in Ednl. Leadership, U. North Fla., 1991. Elem. music tchr. Maryvale Sch. Sys., Buffalo, 1969—74, Lakeland Prep, Orlando, Fla., 1980—81, North Shore Elem., Jacksonville, Fla., 1981—85, Loretto Elem., Jacksonville, 1985—89, Mandarin Oaks Elem., Jacksonville, 1989—90; mid. sch. choral dir. Mandarin Mid. Sch., Jacksonville, 1990—. Contbr. articles to mags. and newsletters. Mem. citizens opinion rsch. forum County of Duval, Jacksonville, 1987; life mem. Duval County PTA, 1987—; mem. choir St. Joseph Cath. Ch., 1999—2002. Named Educator of Yr., Jaycee's, Jacksonville, 1987, Tchr. of Yr., Rotary, Mandarin, 1998. Mem.: Duval County Elem. Tchrs. Assn. (past elem. pres.). Republican. Roman Catholic. Home: 11068 Great Western Ln W Jacksonville FL 32257

HUBER, MELBA STEWART, dance educator, dance studio owner, historian, retailer; b. Tex., Oct. 1, 1927; d. Carl E. and Melba (Holt) Stewart; m. William C. Kinsolving Jr.; children: William Carey, Keith Brian; m. James M. Huber (dec.); 1 child, Melba Laurin. AA, Lamar Coll., 1946; student, U. Tex. Establisher, owner Melba's, Inc., McAllen, Tex., 1958—; founder McAllen (Tex.) Dance Theatre Co., 1970; tchr. Black Cmty. at Huston-Tillotson Coll., 1948—49. Columnist, tap amb. Internat. Tap Assn.; regional rep. Gus Giordano's Jazz Dance World Congress; panelist St. Louis Tap Festival, NY Tradition in Tap, NY Tap Festivals. Columnist Tap Talk, NY Dance Pages, Dance and the Arts mag., 1988-97; columnist Tappin' In, Dancer mag., 1998—; prodr.: (broadway) Jelly's Last Jam. Recipient Plaudit award Nat. Dance Assn. Am. Alliance for Health, Physical Edn. and Recreation, 1970, Flo-Bert award N.Y. Com. to Celebrate Nat. Tap Dance Day, 1996, Savion Glover award St. Louis Tap Festival, 1998, Preservation of Our Heritage in American Dance award, Oklahoma City U., 1999, Women of Distinction award Detroit Tap Festival, 2000; named for Life Achievement in the Art of Dance and Gymnastics, presented Tex. Flag Tex. State Senate, 1997. Mem. Tex. Assn. Tchrs. Dancing (pres. 1973-74, honoree 1997), South Tex. Dance Masters Assn. (Mem. of Yr. 1989). Home: PO Box 3664 Mcallen TX 78502-3664 Office: Melbas Sch Dance 2100 N 10th Mcallen TX 78502 Office Phone: 956-686-1411. Personal E-mail: melhuber@swbell.net.

HUBER, PAUL WILLIAM, biochemistry professor, researcher; b. Medford, Mass., July 23, 1951; s. William Francis and Catherine (Sheridan) H. BS, Boston Coll., 1973; PhD, Purdue U., 1978. NIH postdoctoral fellow U. Chgo., 1979-81, rsch. assoc., 1982-85; asst. prof. U. Notre Dame, Ind., 1985-92, assoc. prof., 1992—2003, assoc. chmn., 1993-97, prof., 2003—. Vis. fellow Yale U., 1997. Contbr. articles to profl. jours. Recipient John A. Kaneb award for undergrad. tchg., U. Notre Dame, 2001. Mem. AAAS, Am. Soc. Biochemistry and Molecular Biology. Home: 1215 E Irvington Ave South Bend IN 46614-1417 Office: U Notre Dame Dept Chemistry/Biochemistry Notre Dame IN 46556 Office Phone: 574-631-6042. Business E-Mail: phuber@nd.edu.

HUBER, RICHARD GREGORY, lawyer, educator; b. Indpls., June 29, 1919; s. Hugh Joseph and Laura Marie (Becker) H.; m. Katherine Elizabeth McDonald, June 21, 1950 (dec.); children: Katherine, Richard, Mary, Elizabeth, Stephen, Mark. BS, U.S. Naval Acad, 1942; JD, U. Iowa, 1950; LLM, Harvard U., 1951; LLD (hon.), New England Sch. Law, 1985, Northeastern U., 1987, Roger Williams U., 1996. Instr. law U. Iowa, 1950; assoc. prof. law U. S.C., 1952-54; assoc. prof. Tulane U., 1954-57, Boston Coll., 1957-59, prof., 1959-90, dean, 1970-85; disting. prof. Roger Williams U., Bristol, R.I., 1993-95; prof. New England Sch. Law, Newton, Mass., 1995-99. Adj. faculty Boston Coll., 1999-2004. Contbr. articles and book revs. to profl. jours. Past chairperson pers. and fin. coms. Mass. chpt. Multiple Sclerosis Soc.; past pres. bd. trustees Beaver Country Day Sch. With USN, 1941-47, 51-52. Mem. ABA (del., mem. coun. legal edn. 1981-85, trustee law sch. admissions coun 1983-85), Soc. Am. Law Tchrs., Assn. Am. Law Schs. (pres. 1988-89), Coun. Legal Edn. Opportunity (pres. 1975-79), Am. Judicature Soc., Mass. Bar Assn., Mass. Bar Found. Democrat. Roman Catholic. Home: 406 Woodward St Waban MA 02468-1523 Office: 885 Centre St Newton MA 02459-1148

HUBER, ROBERT, biochemist, educator; b. Munich, Feb. 20, 1937; s. Sebastian and Helene (Kebinger) H.; m. Christa Huber, 1960; children: Ulrike, Martin, Robert, Julia Diploma, Tech. Universität Munich, 1960, PhD, 1963, Habilitation, 1968; D (hon.), U. Catholic de Louvain, 1987, U. Ljubljana, 1989; D for Medicine and Surgery (hon.), U. 'Tor Vergata', 1991; D (hon.), Univ. Nova de Lisboa, 2000, U. AutÓnoma de Barcelona, 2000, Tsinghua U., 2003. External prof. Tech. U. Munich, 1976; prof., dir. Max-Planck-Inst. for Biochemistry, Martinsried, Germany, 1972—2005, dir. emeritus, 2005—. Hon. prof. Ocean U., Qingdao, 2002, Peking U., 2003, Sichuan U., Chengdu, 2003, Shanghai Second Med. U., 2004. Editor Jour. Molecular Biology. Order for Merit for Sci. and Arts (Germany); Keilin medal Biochem. Soc. London, Richard Kuhn medal Soc. German Chemists, 1987, E.K. Frey-E. Werle meml. medal, 1989, Kone award Assn. Clin. Biochemists, 1990, Sir Hans Krebs medal, 1992, Linus Pauling medal, 1993, 94, Disting. Svc. award Miami Biotech. Winter Symposia, 1995, Max Tishler prize Harvard U., 1997, Max Bergmann medal U. Tübingen, 1997, co-recipient Nobel prize for chemistry, 1988. Fellow Royal Soc. London, Third World Acad. Scis., Am. Acad. Microbiology; mem. NAS (U.S.A.) (fgn. assoc.), European Molecular Biology Orgn. (coun. mem.), Japanese Biochem. Soc. (hon.), Am. Soc. Biol. Chemists (hon.), Swedish Soc. Biophysics (hon.), Croatian Acad. Scis. and Art (corr.), European Molecular Biology Orgn. Office: Max Planck Inst Biochem Am Klopferspitz 18 Martinsried Munich 82152 Germany Business E-Mail: huber@biochem.mpg.de.

HUBER, SCOTT, transportation services executive; b. St. Louis, 1964; BSBA, U. Mo., St. Louis, 1985, BS in Fin., 1986; JD, St. Louis U., 1989. Bar: Mo. 1989, Ill. 1990, US Ct. Appeals 8th Cir. 1990, US Dist. Ct. Ea. Dist. Mo. 1990. Gen. counsel Unigroup, Inc., Fenton, Mo. Office: Unigroup Inc 1 Premier Dr Fenton MO 63026

HUBERMAN, BENJAMIN, technology consultant; b. Havana, Cuba, Jan. 25, 1938; came to U.S., 1946; s. Henry and Marcella (Waisman) H.; m. Gisela Bialik, Oct. 13, 1963; children: Jonathan, Martin. AB, Columbia Coll., 1959; BS, Columbia U., 1960; diploma of Imperial Coll., U. London (Eng.), 1962. Sr. official Arms Control & Disarmament Agy., Washington, 1966-73, Nat. Security Coun., Washington, 1973-75; dir., policy evaluation Nuclear Regulatory Commn., Washington, 1975-77; sr. official Office Sci. and Tech. Policy, Washington, 1977-81; dep. sci. advisor to pres. White House, Washington, 1981; v.p. Cons. Internat. Group, Inc., Washington, 1982-88, pres., 1988-90, Huberman Cons. Group, Washington, 1990—; v.p. GBH Radio Inc., Fisher Island, Fla., 1997—. Chmn. exec. panel Chief Naval Ops. Atlantic Coun., Washington. Lt. USN, 1960-66. Fulbright scholar, London, 1960-61. Mem. Coun. Fgn. Rels., Met. Club, Cosmos Club (Washington). Home: 5012 Fisher Island Dr Fisher Island FL 33109 Office: Huberman Cons Group 1090 Vermont Ave NW Ste 800 Washington DC 20005-4961

HUBERMAN, JEFFREY ALLEN, architect; b. Boston, Jan. 2, 1942; s. Sidney H. and Miriam (Walker) H.; m. Barbara Kemp, May 16, 1964 (div.); children: Amy Beth, Marc Walker. BArch, U. Fla., 1964. Designer Odell Assocs., Charlotte, NC, 1964-67, Wolf-Johnson Assocs., Charlotte, 1967-69; designer, arch. Wolf Assocs., Charlotte, 1970-71; ptnr. Gantt Huberman Archs., Charlotte, 1971—. Mem. N.C. Bd. Architecture, 1995—, sec., 1996-97, treas., 1997—, v.p., 1999—, pres., 2001-03. Chmn. ann. fund drive Charlotte-Mecklenburg Arts and Sci. Coun., 1975-81, v.p., 1977-78, bd. dirs., 1977; bd. dirs. Charlotte Opera Assn., 1966-82, pres., 1979-81; pres. Children's Theatre, 1984-85, bd. dirs., 1981-87; bd. dirs. Temple Beth El, 1968-83, Charlotte-Mecklenburg Cmty. Rels. Com., 1974-84, Planned Parenthood of Greater Charlotte, 1978-80, Charlotte Jr. Soccer Found., 1978-82, Tarradiddle Players, 1986-87; chmn. Charlotte Clean City Com., 1975-77; youth soccer coach, 1975-84; com. mem. Performing Arts Ctr. Adv. Ctr., 1983-85; adv. com. Charlotte/Douglas Internat. Airport, 1987-88, art adv. com., 1992—. Fellow AIA (chmn. honor awards com. 1972, treas. Charlotte, N.C. sect. 1976-77, chmn. audit com. 1987, bd. dirs. 1987-92, long range planning com. 1990, component resources com. 1992, pres. N.C. chpt. 1991, N.C. Archtl. Found. 1994, N.C. Gold medal 2002), Nat. Coun. Archtl. Registration Bd. (juror divsns. B and C archtl. registration exam. 1984-86, chmn. divsn. B graphic 1989, master jurors com. 1986, archtl. registration exam. com. 1996-97, intern devel. program com. 1998-2002, chair, 2000-02, procedures and documents com. 2000-05, chmn. 2004-05, chair reciprocity impediment task force 2002-04, So. region sec. 2003-04, bd. dirs. 2005-). Office: Gantt Huberman Architects 500 N Tryon St Charlotte NC 28202-2232

HUBERMAN, RICHARD LEE, lawyer; b. Lynn, Mass., Dec. 6, 1953; s. Irving Morris and Selma Edythe (Wolk) H. AB, Harvard U., 1975, JD, 1978. Bar: Mass. 1979, D.C. 1979. Atty. Office of Rail Pub. Counsel, Washington, 1978-80; counsel subcom. on commerce, consumer protection and competitiveness (formerly commerce, transp. and tourism) U.S. Ho. of Reps., Washington, 1980-95, mem. prof. staff Com. on Edn. and Workforce, 1995—97; pvt. practice Washington, 1997-98; counsel to commr. and chmn. Occupl. Safety and Health Rev. Commn., Washington, 1998—. Mem. ABA, Mass. Bar Assn., Harvard Law Sch. Assn. Clubs: Harvard (Washington). Democrat. Home: 2141 P St NW Apt 302 Washington DC 20037-1031 Office: Occupl Safety and Health Rev Commn 1120 20th St NW Washington DC 20036 Office Phone: 202-606-5370. Business E-Mail: rhuberman@oshrc.gov.

HUBERT, JEAN-LUC, chemicals executive; b. Metz, Moselle, France, Mar. 13, 1960; s. Andre and Franziska (Schmidt) H. Diplome Ingenieur, Diplome Detudes Approfondies, Ecole Centrale Paris, 1982; MS in Mech. and Nuclear Engrng., Northwestern U., 1985; M in Project Mgmt. with distinction, Keller Grad. Sch., 1996. Simulation engr. Didier Werke, Wiesbaden, Germany, 1981; engr. Iron and Steel Rsch. Inst., Metz, France, 1983; cryogenic applications engr. L'Air Liquide, Paris, 1985—86; R&D mgr. cryogenic refrigeration processes Liquid Air Corp., Countryside, Ill., 1986—89, project mgr. new processes devel. group, 1989—93; concurrent multi project mgr., primary metals and combustion, mktg. and applications group Air Liquide America Corp, Countryside, Ill., 1993—95; applied tech. engrng. dept. mgr. Air Liquide Am. Corp., Countryside, Ill., 1995—99, mgr. ctrl. engrng. dept., bus. devel. group, 1999—2001; mgr. customer equipment and installation design Air Liquide Am. LP, Houston, 2001—. New process devel. cons. Liquid Air Corp./Energy Systems, Lake Charles, La., 1987-90, BIG3/INS, Houston, 1990-91, exceptional ops. mgr., coord. subcontractors, regional svc. and sales coord. applications unit, 1992-93; tech. expert bulk ops. Air liquide Worldwide group, 2003—. Patentee cryogenic food freezing, cryogenic embrittlement processes, pipeline rehab. processes, multi-step combined mech./thermal stripping processes, supercritical chemical extraction processes, ozone based food sanitizing processes. 2d lt. French Navy, 1982—83. Tuition fellow Georges Lurcy Found., 1984, Henri Blanchenay fellow French Inst., 1984, Bieneck/Didier fellow, Fed. Rep. Ger., 1984, Northwestern U. Rsch. assistantship, 1984. Mem. ASME, Inst. Food Technologists (profl.), Internat. Inst. Refrigeration, Iron and Steel Soc. Achievements include 7 US, Canadian and 2 European patents for High Efficiency Linear Freezer, for Method and Apparatus for Enhancing Production Capacity and Flexibility of a Multi-tier Refrigeration Tunnel, for Process and Apparatus for Embrittling and Subsequently Removing an Outer Protective Coating of a Pipe or Pipeline, and for Efficiency Process and Apparatus for same and for a fast efficient, low-cost stripping process of non-metallic layers from steel substrates, for supercritical CO2 pressure swing absorption based cleaning methods and systems and for process and equipment for sanitizing food using ozone. Home: 16402 Willingham Way Houston TX 77095 Office: Air Liquide America LP 2700 Post Oak Houston TX 77056 Business E-Mail: jean-luc.hubert@airliquide.com. E-mail: Dillingen@att.net, jlhdilnal@aol.com.

HUBERT, JUDD DAVID, language educator; b. Toledo, Jan. 17, 1917; s. David Booth and Irma Judd Hubert; m. Renée Isabelle Riese, Feb. 14, 1950; 1 child, Candice June. BA, Middlebury Coll., 1941; MA, Columbia U., 1942, PhD, 1951. Instr. French and history U.S. Merchant Marine Acad., Kings Point, NY, 1946—47; instr. French Rutgers U., New Brunswick, NJ, 1947—51; lectr. French Columbia U., N.Y.C., 1951—53; asst. prof. French Harvard U., Cambridge, Mass., 1953—57; prof. French UCLA, 1957—65, U. Ill., Urbana, 1965—67, U. Calif., Irvine, 1967—87, prof. emeritus, 1987—. Author: L'Esthétique des Fleurs du Mal, 1953, 1972, Essai d'exégèse racinienne, 1956, Essai d'exégès racinienne, 1986, Molière and the Comedy of Intellect, 1962, 1972, 1974, Metatheater: The Example of Shakespeare, 1991, Corneille's Performative Metaphors, 1997; co-author (with R.R. Hubert): The Cutting Edge of Reading: Artist's Books, 1999; contbr. articles to profl. jours. Sgt. U.S. Air Corps, 1942—46. Fulbright Rsch. fellow, France, 1956—57, Guggenheim fellow, 1962—63. Mem.: MLA (editl. com.). Home: 1106 Cambridge Ln Newport Beach CA 92660 Office: Dept French and Italian Univ California-Irvine 1 UCI Humanities 312 Irvine CA 92697 E-mail: jhubert@uci.edu.

HUBLOU, ROSEMARIE See **EDELSTEIN, ROSEMARIE**

HUBSCHMAN, HENRY A., lawyer; b. Newark, N.J., Aug. 12, 1947; s. Morris and Esther (Weissman) H.; m. Joanne L. Goode; children: Lilly, Josie, Ellis, Nathan. BA summa cum laude, Rutgers U., 1969; JD magna cum laude, M Pub. Policy, Harvard U., 1973. Bar: Mass. 1973, N.J. 1974, D.C. 1974, Ohio 1994. Law clk. U.S. Dist. Ct. Mass., Boston, 1973-74; assoc. Fried, Frank, Harris, Shriver & Jacobson, Washington, 1974-77, 79-80, ptnr., 1980-92; v.p., gen. counsel, bus. devel. GE Aircraft Engines, Cin., 1992-97; pres., CEO GE Capital Aviation Svcs., Stamford, Conn., 1997—. Exec. asst. to Sec. HUD, Washington, 1977-79; bd. dir. Fed. Nat. Mortgage Assn., 1979-81. Jewish. Home: 37 Hillside Rd Greenwich CT 06830-4834 Office: GE Commll Aviation Svcs 201 High Ridge Rd Stamford CT 06905-3417

HUCH, RONALD KIND, historian, educator; s. Emory Wallace and Anna Ophelia Huch; m. Margo Lynn Laskowski; children: Diane, Anita, Jocelyn, Elanor. BA, Thiel Coll., 1962; MA, Pa. State U., 1964; PhD, U. Mich., 1971. Asst. prof. Murray (Ky.) State U., 1967—68; from instr. to prof. U. Minn., Duluth, 1968—86; prof. Dickinson (ND) State U., 1986—92; chmn. history U. Papua New Guinea, Port Moresby, 1992—2000; prof., chmn. dept. history Ea. Ky. U., Richmond, 2000—. Cons. Ednl. Testing Svc., Princeton, NJ, 1988—. Author: The Radical Lord Radnor, 1977, Henry, Lord Brougham: Later Years, 1993, From Blacksmith Shop to Modern Hospital, 1985; co-author: Joseph Hume: The People's M.P., 1985; contbr. articles to profl. jours. Founder History Scholarships for Papua New Guineans, Port Moresby, 1996; v.p. NC chpt. AAUP, 1990—91. Recipient Solon Buck award, Minn. Hist. Soc., 1981; fellow, Am. Philos. Soc., 1971, 1975, 1977, 1981, Am. Coun. Learned Socs., 1973; summer fellow, NEH, Washington, 1988. Mem.: Anglo-Am. Historians, N.Am. Conf. Brit. Studies, Am. Hist. Assn. Avocation: horse racing. Office: Ea Ky U Dept History 521 Lancaster Ave Richmond KY 40475 Fax: 859-622-1357. Business E-Mail: ron.huch@eku.edu.

HUCHRA, JOHN PETER, astronomer, educator; b. Jersey City, N.J., Dec. 23, 1948; s. Mieczyslaw Piotr and Helen Ann Huchra; m. Rebecca M. Henderson; 1 child, Harry Matthew. BS, MIT, 1970; PhD, Calif. Inst. Tech., 1976. Ctr. fellow Ctr. for Astrophysics, Cambridge, Mass., 1976-78; astronomer Smithsonian Astrophys. Obs., Cambridge, Mass., 1978-89, sr. astronomer, 1989—; lectr. dept. astronomy Harvard U., Cambridge, Mass., 1979-84, prof. dept. astronomy, 1984—2002, Robert O. and Holly Thomis Doyle prof. cosmology, 2002—; assoc. dir. Ctr. for Astrophysics, Cambridge, Mass., 1989—98; dir. F.L. Whipple Observatory, 1994-98. Mem. coun. Space Telescope Sci. Inst., Balt., 1987-95; chmn. working group on galaxy radial velocities Internat. Astron. Union, Paris, 1988—; chmn. large astron. data base working group NASA/IPAC, Washington, 1988-92; mem. astronomy and astrophysics survey Optical Panel, NAS, NRC, 1989-90; adv. bd. and vis. com. Arecibo Obs., Ithaca, N.Y., 1989-92; users com. Cerro Tololo Inter-Am. Obs., La Serena, Chile, 1989-91; vis. com. ESO, 1993-97; mem. NRC Com. on Astronomy and Astrophysics, 1994-2001, co-chmn. 1997-2001; mem. AURA, bd. dirs., 1995-, chair, 2001-04; mem. NRC bd. on physics and astronomy, 1997-2003, chair, 2000-03; chair NOAO Future Directions Com., 1998-99; vis. prof. Cambridge U., 2003—; mem. math. and phys. sci. adv. com. NSF, 2003—; lectr. in field. Contbr. chapters to books to profl. jours. Rsch. grantee, NASA, 1979—, Smithsonian Inst., 1980, NSF, 1984-89, 99—. Fellow AAAS (Newcomb Cleve. award 1990), Am. Phys. Soc. AIP (pub. policy com. 1988-95); mem. NAS, Am. Acad. Arts and Scis., Am. Astron. Soc. (pub. bd. chmn., 1986-88, councilor 1998-2001, sci. editor Astrophys. Jour. 1998-2003), Royal Astron. Soc., Astron. Soc. of the Pacific, Am. Phys. Soc. Astrophysics Divsn. (exec. com. 1996-97), Nat. Environ. Leadership Coun., Wilderness Soc., Nat. Audubon Soc., Mass. Audubon Soc., Union of Concerned Scientists, Nature Conservancy, Trustees of Reservations, Appalachian Trail Conf., Am. Contract Bridge League, Greenpeace, Green Mtn. Club, Appalachian Mtn. Club, Sierra Club, Sigma Xi, Gamma Nu. Achievements include discovery of Comet Huchra, of nearest gravitational lens; revision of cosmic distance scale; completion of first and second Center for Astrophysics Redshift Survey; measurement of infall of our Milky Way Galaxy into the Virgo Cluster; discovery of Great Wall of Galaxies, 2 Micron All Sky Survey. Office: Harvard-Smithsonian Ctr Astrophysics 60 Garden St Cambridge MA 02138-1516 Office Phone: 617-495-7375.

HUCHTEMAN, RALPH DOUGLAS, lawyer; b. Garland, Tex., Oct. 8, 1946; s. Ray Edwin and Hazel Laverne (Clark) H.; m. Sherry Lynn Horner, Mar. 12, 1994; children: Lara Victoria, Brett Norman, Bryan Randolff. AA, Okla. Mil. Acad., 1966; BA in Polit. Sci., Okla. State U., 1969; JD, Okla. U., 1972. Bar: Okla. 1972, U.S. Dist. Ct. (we. dist.) Okla. 1972. Ptnr. Doak & Huchteman, Oklahoma City, 1972-73, Wolf & Wolf P.C. (formerly Wolf, Wolf, Huchteman & Graven), Norman, Okla., 1982-88; prin. Huchteman Law Offices, Norman, 1989-98; staff atty. Legal Aid Svcs. of Okla., Inc., Bartlesville, 1998-99, mng. atty., 1999—. Assoc. mcpl. judge, Noble, Okla., 1990-98, Blanchard, Okla., 1992-98; vis. asst. prof. Coll. Bus., Okla. U., 1972-73; temporary justice Okla. Ct. Appeals, Oklahoma City, 1982-83. State exec. sec. Student Lobby for Higher Edn., Stillwater, Okla., 1968-69. 1st lt. U.s. Army, 1973. T.A. Shadid scholar Okla. U., 1969; recipient A.C. Hunt Practice award Okla. U., 1972. Mem. ATLA, Okla. Bar Assn., Okla. Trial Lawyers Assn. Democrat. Office: Legal Aid Svcs Okla Inc 217 S Choctaw Ave Bartlesville OK 74003-2837 E-mail: rhuchteman@aol.com, ralph.huchteman@legalaidok.org.

HUCHTON, PAUL JOSEPH, JR., pediatrician; b. El Paso, Tex., Mar. 15, 1934; s. Paul Joseph Sr. and Eugenia Cregor (Kimbrough) H.; m. Sheila Ann Borsian, June 1, 1963; children: Hadley Ann Bernhard, David Morgan, Amy H. Anderson, Karen H. Hammer. BA, U. Tex., 1954; MD, Vanderbilt U., 1958. Diplomate Am. Bd. Pediat. Intern Vanderbilt U. Hosp., Nashville, 1958-59; resident U. Chgo., 1959-60; from resident to chief resident U. Colo., Denver, 1960-61; pvt. practice specializing in pediat., El Paso, 1963—. Mem. staff Providence and Sierra Med. Ctr., El Paso. Mem Tex. Med. Assn. (del., counsellor 1970-93), El Paso County Med. Soc. (pres. 1985), Rotary Club El Paso (pres. 1980, Paul Harris award 1983). Republican. Mem. Vestry St. Francis On The Hill. Avocations: long distance cycling, computers. Office: 1515 N Oregon St El Paso TX 79902-4042 E-mail: phuchton@elp.rr.com.

HUCK, DANIEL N., lawyer, educator; b. Parkersburg, W.Va. m. Deborah McDaniel, Dec. 21, 1991; 1 child, Joseph Frumenti. BA, Bucknell U., 1984; JD, Northeastern U., 1987; MA, Marietta Coll., 2001; D in Edn., W.Va. U., 2001. Dep. atty. gen., atty. gen. City of Charleston, 1987-90; gen. counsel to gov. State of W.Va., Charleston, 1990-94; atty. Huck & Gillooly, Charleston, 1994-95; city atty. City of Charleston, W.Va., 1995-96; dist. mgr. Am. Gen. Fin. Svcs., Charleston, 1995-97; atty. Allen Guthrie & McHugh, Charleston, 1997-99; instr. Marshall U., Huntington, W.Va., 1999-2001; asst. prof. Marietta (Ohio) Coll., 2001—. Chmn. W.Va. Gov.'s Juvenile Justice Com., Charleston, 1995-98, W.Va. Regional Jail Correctional Authority, Charleston, 1996-2001. Contbr. articles to profl. jours. Mem. Charleston Mcpl. Planning Commn., 1995-98. Mem. ABA, ARC, W.Va. Bar Assn., Omicron Delta Kappa, Phi Delta Kappa. Avocations: coin collecting/numismatics, chess, guitar, travel. Home: 8 Sylvan Way Marietta OH 45750-9626

HUCK, JOHN LLOYD, pharmaceutical executive; b. Bklyn., July 17, 1922; s. John Lloyd and Adrienne (Warner) H.; m. Dorothy Bertha Foehr, Nov. 20, 1943; children: Lloyd E., Jeanne Huck Leslie-Hughes, Virginia Huck Stalcup. BS in Chemistry, Pa. State U., 1946. Research chemist Hoffmann-LaRoche, Nutley, N.J., 1946, sales rep., 1948, dir. sales tng., 1951, asst. gen. sales mgr., 1955, dir. product devel., 1958; dir. mktg. Merck Sharp & Dohme Div., West Point, Pa., 1958; v.p. mktg. planning MSD div., 1966, v.p. sales and mktg., 1968, exec. v.p., 1969, exec. v.p., gen. mgr., 1972, pres., 1973; sr. v.p. Merck & Co., Rahway, N.J., 1975, exec. v.p., 1977, dir., 1977-86, pres., chief operating officer, 1978-85, chmn. bd., 1985-86; chmn. bd., chief exec. officer Nova Pharm. Corp., Morristown, N.J., 1986-88, chmn. bd., 1988-91. Patentee in field. Trustee Pa. State U., 1977-92, v.p., 1985-88, pres. bd., 1988-91; trustee Morristown Meml. Health Found., Inc., N.J., 1979-96, chmn. bd., 1986-88; trustee Geraldine R. Dodge Found., 1987-2003. 1st lt. USAAF, 1942-46. Alumni fellow Coll. Medicine Pa. State U., 1980, Coll. of Sci., 1983; named to Nutley Hall of Fame, 2003. Mem. Centre Hills Country Club. Republican. Home: 233 Lion's Hill Rd State College PA 16803

HUCK, L. FRANCIS, lawyer; b. Pittsfield, Mass., May 5, 1947; s. Lewis Francis Joseph and Rosemary (Ahearn) H.; m. Natalie Anne Murphy, June 10, 1978; children: Amelia Emerson, Rosemary Alice, Charles Randolph. AB, Harvard U., 1969; JD, Stanford U., 1972. Assoc. Simpson, Thacher & Bartlett, N.Y.C., 1972-79, ptnr., 1980—, mem. exec. com. Mem. Harvard Club N.Y.C., Wee Burn Club, ABA, Bar Assn. City N.Y. Democrat. Office: Simpson Thacher & Bartlett 425 Lexington Ave Fl 15 New York NY 10017-3954 Office Phone: 212-455-7025. Office Fax: 212-455-2502. Business E-Mail: lfhuck@stblaw.com.

HUCKABEE, HARLOW MAXWELL, lawyer, writer; b. Wichita Falls, Tex., Jan. 22, 1918; s. Edwin Cleveland and Gladys Idella (Bonney) H.; m. Gloria Charlotte Comstock, Jan. 10, 1942; children: Bonney M., David C., Stephen M. BA, Harvard U., 1948; JD, Georgetown U., 1951. Bar: U.S. Dist. Ct. D.C. 1952, U.S. Ct. Appeals (D.C. cir.) 1952. Cashier br. office Columbian Nat. Life Ins. Co., Boston, 1935-40; lawyer Fed. Housing Adminstrn., Washington, 1955-56; trial lawyer, criminal sect., tax divsn. U.S. Justice Dept., Washington, 1956-63; lawyer IRS, Washington, 1963-67; trial lawyer organized crime and racketeering sect. U.S. Justice Dept., Washington, 1967-68, trial lawyer criminal sect., tax divsn., 1968-80. Author: Lawyers, Psychiatrists and Criminal Law, 1980, Mental Disability Issues in the Criminal Justice System: What They Are, Who Evaluates Them, How and When, 2000; contbr. articles to profl. jours. and legal publs. including Diminished Capacity Dilemma in the Federal System, 1991. Maj. U.S. Army, 1940-45, 48-55, ETO, Korea; lt. col. USAR, 1961. Methodist. Home: 5100 Fillmore Ave Apt 913 Alexandria VA 22311-5048

HUCKABEE, JAMES C., music educator; b. Mobile, Ala., Apr. 4, 1972; s. Allaway and Barbara Huckabee; m. Elizabeth Huckabee, Aug. 20, 1994; children: Bethany V., Lucas K. BA, Huntington Coll., 1994; MS in Edn., Troy State U., 1997, EdS, 1998. Cert. computer technician. Ins. agent Alfer Ins., Troy, Ala., 1994—96; band. dir. Montgomery Pub. Schs., Ala., 1996—97, music specialist, 2002—; band. dir. Barbour County Schs., Clayton, 1997—99; pvt. practice Montgomery, 1999—2002. Mem.: Omicron Delta Kappa, Kappa Delta Pi, Phi Kappa Phi. Republican. Baptist. Avocation: water-skiing. Home: 526 Lurene Cir Montgomery AL 36109

HUCKABEE, MICHAEL DALE, governor; b. Hope, Ark., Aug. 24, 1955; m. Janet McCain, May 25, 1974; children: John Mark, David, Sarah. BA in Religion, Ouachita Bapt. U., Arkadelphia, Ark., 1976; postgrad., Southwestern Bapt. Theol. Sem., Ft. Worth, 1976-77; D of Humanities (hon.), John Brown Univ, 1991; D of Laws (hon.), Ouachita Baptist U., Arkadelphia, Ark., 1992. Ordained to ministry So. Bapt. Conv., 1974. Pastor Walnut Street Bapt. Ch., Arkadelphia, 1974-75, Immanuel Bapt. Ch., Pine Bluff, Ark., 1980-85, Beech Street 1st Bapt. Ch., Texarkana, Ark., 1986—96; pres. KBSC-TV, Texarkana, Ark., 1987—92, Cambridge Communications, Texarkana, Ark., 1992—96; lt. gov. State of Ark., 1993-96, gov., 1996—. Founder, past pres. Am. Christian TV Sys., Pine Bluff; pres. Ark. Bapt. Conv., 1989-91; mem. Interstate Oil and Gas Compact Commn. (past chmn.); state chmn., Delta Regional Authority; mem. Nat. Gov. Assn. (vice chmn.). Author: (books) Character is the Issue, 1997, Kids Who Kill, 1998, Living Beyond Your Lifetime, 2000, Quit Digging Your Grave With a Knife and Fork, 2005. So. Technology Coun., So. Internat. Trade Coun. Republican. Baptist. Avocations: hunting, fishing, reading, playing bass guitar in his band, Capitol Offense. Office: Office of the Gov State Capitol Rm 250 Little Rock AR 72201-1088

HUCKABEE, MICHELLE W., parochial school educator; b. Olean, N.Y., July 31, 1959; d. Leroy S. and Bonna B. Williams; m. Mike Huckabee, Oct. 6, 1984; children: Aaron, Peter, John, Faith. With Valley Christian Acad., Roswell, N.Mex. Presdl. scholar, Westminster Coll., 1977. Avocations: reading, music, needlepoint. Office: Valley Christian Acad 505 N Sycamore Roswell NM 88201

HUCKABY, GARY CARLTON, lawyer; b. Lanett, Ala., July 12, 1938; s. Carl Walker and Mary Evelyn (Meriwether) H.; m. Jeanne Davey Huckaby, Feb. 23, 1963; children: Gary Jr., John Stephen, Michael Stewart. BA, U. Ala., 1960, JD, 1962. Bar: U.S. Supreme Ct. 1963, U.S. Ct. of Mil. Appeals 1963, U.S. Ct. Appeals (5th and 11th cirs.) 1963, U.S. Dist. Ct. (no., middle and so. dists) Ala. 1963. Law clk. to chief justice Ala. Supreme Ct., Montgomery, 1962-63; asst. U.S. Sen. Lister Hill, Washington, 1963; ptnr. Smith, Huckaby & Graves, Huntsville, Ala., 1966-85, Bradley, Arant, Rose & White, Huntsville, 1985—; dir. Ala. Ctr. for Law & Civic Edn., 1992—2001. Dir. coun. Internat. Visitors of Huntsville-Madison County, 1983-89, Tenn. Valley Boy Scouts Am., 1975-79, Mental Health Assn. Madison County, 1970-78, Ala. Law Sch. Found., 1981—; pres. Huntsville-Madison County Mental Health Bd., 1977-80, Madison County Heart Assn., 1968; active Citizens Com. on Higher Edn. of Ala. Legis., 1976, judicial sect. of Huntsville-Madison County Local Govt. Study Com., 1969. Capt. USAF, 1963-66. Fellow Am. Bar Found., Am. Coll. Trial Lawyers; mem. ABA (bd. govs. 1990-91, house of delegates, chmn. standing com. on lawyer referral and info. services 1982-85, chmn. spl. com. on delivery of legal services 1976-79, standing com. on lawyers pub. service responsibility 1987-90, consortium on legal services and the pub. 1976-79, task force on pub. edn. 1978, standing com. on lawyers in the armed forces 1971-73), Ala. State Bar (pres., bd. commrs. 1981-87, exec. com. 1982-83, 84-85, 87-88, chmn. governance com. 1986-87, action group on professionalism, disciplinary bd. 1981-87; recipient award of merit 1986), Huntsville-Madison County Bar Assn. (pres. 1977-78, chmn. grievance com. 1976, bench and bar relations 1981, convention host com. 1971, law day com. 1968), Am. Judicature Soc. (former bd. dirs.), Rotary. Democrat. Episcopalian. Home: 701 Greene St SE Huntsville AL 35801-4232 Office: Bradley Arant Rose & White 200 Clinton Ave W Ste 900 Huntsville AL 35801-4900 Office Phone: 256-517-5140. Business E-Mail: ghuckaby@bradleyarant.com.

HUCKEBY, ED D., academic administrator, composer, conductor; b. Ada, Okla., July 9, 1948; s. Cecil S. and Lula F. Huckeby; m. Latricia A. Wilson, June 5, 1970; children: Angela Dawn Corr, Amanda Deanne Davis. BA in Edn., East Ctrl. State Coll., 1970; M in Music Edn., U. Okla., 1974; EdD, Okla. State U., 1989. Cert. tchr., adminstr. State Dept. Edn., Okla. Dir. bands Allen (Okla.) Pub. Schs., 1968—70; dir. instrumental music Poteau (Okla.) Pub. Schs., 1970—76; dept. head, dean grad. sch. Northwestern Okla. State U., Alva, 1976—98; exec. dir. Tulsa (Okla.) Ballet Theatre, Inc., 1998—99; chief academic and oper. officer/assoc. v.p. for academic affairs Northeastern State U., Broken Arrow, Okla., 1999—. Mem. Educators Leadership Acad., Edmond, Okla., 1999—2000, Mayor's Arts Task Force, Tulsa, 2002—03; pres. Higher Edn. Cultural Roundtable, Tulsa, 2002—03; edn. chair Broken Arrow Leadership Acad. Composer: over 140 published works. Co-chair Tulsa Area United Way Campaign, Broken Arrow, 2002—03. Named to Hall of Fame, Okla. Bandmasters Assn., 1996; recipient Serious Music award, ASCAP, 1992—2004. Mem.: Broken Arrow C. of C., Rotary Internat. Avocations: music, golf, travel. Home: 4832 W Dallas St Broken Arrow OK 74012 Office: Northeastern State University 3100 E New Orleans Broken Arrow OK 74014 E-mail: huckeby@nsuok.edu.

HUCKINS, HAROLD AARON, chemical engineer; b. Cambridge, Mass., Nov. 28, 1924; s. Harold Aaron and Julia E. (Nugent) H.; m. Elizabeth L. Kearns, Nov. 15, 1952; children: Richard W., Robert M., Christopher N., Patricia A., Leslie K. BSChemE, Northeastern U., 1945; ASME, Lowell Inst., 1946; postgrad., Boston U., 1947—49, U. Pitts., 1950—52. Chem. process engr., asst. project mgr. Monsanto Chem. Co., Boston-Everett, Mass., 1945—49; sr. process engr., group leader Koppers Co. Chem. Divsn., Pitts., 1949—53; mgr. pilot plants, project mgr. Sci. Design Co., Inc., NYC, 1953—66; v.p. tech. ops. Oxirane Chem. Co., Princeton, NJ, 1966—73; v.p. tech. assessment Halcon SD Group, NYC, 1973—85; pres. Princeton Advanced Tech., Inc., 1985—. Dir. Assn. Cons. Chemists and Chem. Engrs. divsn., NYC, 1990-93, program chair, 1992-93; dir. Materials Tech. Inst., St. Louis, 1976-85; spkr. local groups/TV global energy trends; presenter in field. Co-author: The Chemical Plant, 1966; contbr. articles to profl. jours. Fellow AIChE (chair ctrl. Jersey sect. 1976-77, dir mgmt. divsn. 1981-82, dir. materials engrng. and sci. divsn. 1992-93, chmn. chem. tech. materials com. 1983-84, chmn. John Fritz medal commn. 1989, chmn. entrepreneurial forum 1994—, Chem. Engrng. Practice award 1994); mem. Am. Soc. Materials, Am. Chem. Soc., Am. Ceramic Soc., Nat. Assn. Corrosion Engrs. (conf. chmn. 1984), Am. Inst. Aero. Astronautics, Comml. Devel. Assn., Mensa Internat., Country Club of Hilton Head Island, Port Royal Racquet Club, Hilton Head Ski Club (bd. dirs.). Achievements include patents for chemical process technology. Home and Office: Princeton Advanced Tech Inc 4 Bertram Pl Hilton Head Island SC 29928-3936 Office Phone: 843-689-9211. Office Fax: 843-689-9212. Personal E-mail: hhuckins@hargray.com.

HUCKMAN, MICHAEL SAUL, neuroradiologist, educator; b. Newark, Aug. 20, 1936; s. Louis Fillmore and Mollie (Lehman) H.; m. Beverly Joy Blachman, Aug. 2, 1964; children: Andrew Garfield, Robert Steven. AB, Princeton U., 1958; MD, St. Louis U., 1962. Rotating intern, then resident in radiology Phila. Gen. Hosp., 1962-63, 65-68; fellow in neuroradiology Edward Mallinckrodt Inst. Radiology, Washington U., St. Louis, also univ. instr. radiology, 1968-70; mem. faculty Rush Med. Coll., Chgo., 1970—, prof. radiology, 1978—; dir. sect. neuroradiology Rush U. Med. Ctr., 1970—; mem. faculty Cook County Grad. Sch. Medicine, 1972-91. Cons. Nat. Ctr. for Health Care Tech., 1980-81; sec.-gen. XVI Symposium Neuroradiologicum, 1994-98. Mem. editorial bd. Jour. Computer Assisted Tomography, 1976-94, Radiographics, 1983-87, Applied Radiology, 1987-89; cons. editor Am. Jour. Roentgenology, 1990-91; contbr. articles to med. jours. Served with USNR, 1963-65. Spl. fellow Nat. Inst. Neurol. Diseases and Blindness, 1968-70 Fellow Am. Coll. Radiology; mem. AMA, Am. Soc. Neuroradiology (sec. 1980-83, pres. elect 1986-87, pres. 1987-88, editor-in-chief Am. Jour. Neuroradiology 1989-97, editor emeritus 1998—, archivist 1998—, Gold medal 1999), Radiol. Soc. N.Am. (Gold medal 2002), Am. Soc. Head and Neck Radiology, Am. Roentgen Ray Soc., Assn. Univ. Radiologists, European Soc. Neuroradiology, Am. Soc. Pediatric Neuroradiology, World Fedn. Neuroradiol. Socs. (historian 1993-97, v.p. 1997—, pres.-elect 1998, pres. 2002—), Ill. Med. Soc., Ill. Radiol. Soc., Chgo. Med. Soc., Blockley Radiol. Soc., Soc. for Scholarly Publ., Japanese Soc. Neuroradiology (hon.), Coun. Biology Editors, Soc. Fifth Line, Indian Soc. Neuroradiology (hon. life), Sigma Xi, Phi Delta Epsilon. Clubs: Princeton Alumni of Chgo. (trustee 1982-84), Caxton. Jewish. Home: 175 E Delaware Pl Apt 7401 Chicago IL 60611-1731 Office: 1753 W Congress Pky Chicago IL 60612-3809 E-mail: m.huckman@comcast.net.

HUCLES, ANGELA KHALIA, professional soccer player; b. Va. Beach, Va., July 5, 1978; BA in anthropology, U. Va., 2000. Soccer player, midfielder U.S. Women's Nat. Team, 2001; mem. Boston Breakers, WUSA, 2001—03, San Diego Spirit, 2003—. Columnist women's sports Boston Metro, 2002. Named First Team All-ACC, 1996, 1997, 1998, 1999, Mid Atlantic All-Star, 1996, 1997, 1998, 1999. Office: US Soccer Fedn 1801 S Prairie Ave Chicago IL 60616

HUDACSKO, DENNIS WAYNE, urban planner; b. New Brunswick, NJ, Dec. 13, 1945; s. Dennis and Mary Valerie (Haydu) Hudacsko; m. Mary Joan Tatu, July 29, 1977 (div. Aug. 1993); children: Elyse Cselle, Marc Denes; m. Karen Annette Sagan, Jan. 23, 1995. BA cum laude, Rutgers U., 1972, M in City and Regional Planning, 1975. Planning asst. Planning & Design Assocs., Somerset, N.J., 1972-73; planner Union County Planning Bd., Elizabeth, N.J., 1973-75; sr. planner Union County Mgr., Elizabeth, N.J., 1975-76; dir. planning City of Elizabeth, 1976-86, Piscataway (N.J.), 1986-87, Candeub, Fleissig & Assocs., Springfield, N.J., 1987-89; with T&M Assocs., Middletown, NJ, 1989—97; propr. Dennis W. Hudacsko- Zoning & Planning Consulting, Bedminster, NJ, 1997—. Instr. Rutgers U. Extension, New Brunswick, N.J., 1976-77, Union Coll., Cranford, N.J., 1987—; mem. Union County Econ. Devel. Program Com., 1973-86; bd. advs. Middlesex County Air Quality Program, New Brunswick, 1974-76. Editor: (newsletter) Advanced Planning, 1976-86. Bd. dirs. Citizen's League of Elizabeth, 1986—; commr. Riverside (NJ) Planning Bd., 1971—72; mem. NJAPA Legislative Com., 1992—, Bedminster Township Planning Bd., 1998—; mem. Bedminster Township Environ. Commn., 1999—; mem. Bedmnster Township Landscape Adv. Com., 2000—, Raritan Watershed Mgmt. Plan Tech. Adv. Com., 2001, Habitat for Humanity, site selection com., 1997—. Served to sgt. USAF, 1966—70. Grantee EPA, HUD, Food and Drug Adminstrn., Dept. Transp., 1978. Mem. Am. Planning Assn., Urban Land Inst., Am. Inst. Cert

Planners, N.J. Profl. Planners, Mensa. Mem. Reformed Ch. of Am. Club: Central Jersey Bike (Metuchen). Avocation: bicycle touring. Office: Zoning & Planning Consulting 135-2 Cowperthwaite Rd Bedminster NJ 07921

HUDAK, THOMAS F(RANCIS), finance company executive; b. Donora, Pa., Jan. 29, 1942; s. Thomas Joseph and Ann Marie (Petrus) H.; m. Dorothy Ann Palko, July 27, 1963; children: Diana Lynn, Debra Ann, Thomas David. BS, St. Vincent Coll., 1963; MBA, Ohio State U., 1968. Bar: C.P.A., Ohio. Accountant Coopers & Lybrand, Columbus, Ohio, 1963-65; dept. mgr., data processing Western Electric Corp., Columbus, 1965-66; fin. controls mgr. Indsl. Nucleonics Co., Columbus, 1966-69; sr. v.p. fin., chief fin. officer G.C. Murphy Co., McKeesport, Pa., 1969-85, chmn. bd., 1981-85; pres. Hudak & Assocs. Treas. Mack Realty Co., McKeesport, Murphy Devel. Corp., Court House Village Co., Spotsylvania Realty Co.; bd. dirs., pres. Terry Farris Stores, Inc.; mem. adv. bd. Liberty Mut. Ins. Co.; corp. comptr. PPG Industries, Inc., Pitts., 1986-89; chmn. bd. dirs., pres. Continental Plastics, Inc., 1989-95; bd. dirs. RXI Corp. Bd. dirs., pres. G.C. Murphy Co. Found. Mem. AICPA, U.S. C. of C., Fin. Execs. Inst. (dir. Pitts. chpt. 1982-85), Risk and Ins. Mgmt. Soc., Nat. Retail Mchts. Assn. (dir. fin. div. 1982-85), Nat. Assn. Corp. Dirs., Machinery and Allied Products Inst. (fin. coun.), Assn. Spice Traders, Assn. Dressings and Sauces, Peanut Butter and Nut Processors Assn. Personal E-mail: tfhudak@comcast.net.

HUDDLE, FRANKLIN PIERCE, JR., diplomat; b. Providence, May 9, 1943; s. Franklin Pierce and Clare (Scott) H.; m. Chanya Sawangrot, May 13, 1988; 1 child, Pavarage. BA, Brown U., 1965; postgrad., Columbia U., 1965-66; MA, Harvard U., 1970, PhD, 1978. Coord. Arabic affairs Peace Corps, Bisbee, 1968-69; instr. Harvard U., Cambridge, Mass., 1970-74; with Dept. of State, Washington and abroad, 1975—2003, charge d'affaires Rangoon, Burma, 1990-94; dir. Pacific Island Affairs, 1994-96; consul gen. Bombay, 1996-99, Toronto, 1999—2001; amb. to Tajikistan, 2001—03. Author: Libyan Arabic, 1966; author, editor: Let's Go Europe, 1972; co-author: Nationalities of the USSR, 1975; photography shows in Thailand, Nepal and Washington, 1980, 81, 84; patentee rocket coatings, 1960. Recipient Rivkin award, Presdl. Meritorious award, Sec. of State Lifetime Achievement award; Ford Found. grantee; Wayland scholar. Mem. Phi Beta Kappa. Avocations: piano, chess, ice skating. Office: 211 Arlington Ave Kensington CA 94707

HUDDLESTON, JOSEPH RUSSELL, judge; b. Glasgow, Ky., Feb. 5, 1937; s. Paul Russell and Laura Frances (Martin) H.; m. Heidi Wood, Sept. 12, 1959; children: Johanna, Lisa, Kristina. AB, Princeton U., 1959; JD, U. Va., 1962, LLM, 1997. Bar: Ky. 1962, U.S. Ct. Appeals (6th cir.) 1963, U.S. Supreme Ct. 1970. Ptnr. Huddleston Bros., Bowling Green, Ky., 1962-87; judge Warren Cir. Ct. Divsn. I, Bowling Green, 1987-91, Ky. Ct. Appeals, Bowling Green, 1991—2003, sr. judge, 2003—. Mem. Adv. Com. for Criminal Law Revision, 1969-71; exec. com. Ky. Crime Commn., 1972-77. Named Ky. Outstanding Trial Judge, 1990. Fellow Am. Bar Found.; mem. ABA, Ky. Bar Assn. (ho. of dels. 1971-80), ATLA (state del. 1981-82), Ky. Acad. Trial Attys. (bd. govs. 1975-87, pres. 1978), Bowling Green Bar Assn. (pres. 1972), So. Ky. Estate Planning Coun. (pres. 1983), Rotary Internat. (Paul Harris fellow), Bowling Green-Warren County C. of C. (bd. dirs. 1987-91), Port Oliver Yacht Club (commodore), Commonwealth Yacht Club, Country Club of Hilton Head. Democrat. Episcopalian. Home: 644 Minnie Way Bowling Green KY 42101-9210

HUDDLESTON, ROBERT C., academic administrator; m. Linda Huddleston. AA, Ariz. Western Coll.; BA, MA in Bus. Adminstrn., No. Ariz. U.; PhD Vocational Edn./Higher Edn. Adminstrn., Colo. State U. Div. chmn. bus., dir. of cooperative edn. and Job placement, prof. bus. Arizona Western Coll., Yuma; assoc. dean instrn. San Juan Coll., Farmington, N.Mex.; dean instrn. GateWay CC, Phoenix; pres. Dixie State Coll., St. George, Utah, 1993—. Office: Dixie State Coll 225 S 700 E Saint George UT 84770*

HUDDLESTON, VICKI JEAN, diplomat; b. San Diego, Dec. 13, 1942; d. Howard Stevens and Duane Louise (Dickinson) Latham; m. Robert Webb Huddleston, Jan. 31, 1970; children: Robert Stevens, Alexandra Duane. BA, U. Colo., 1964; MA, Johns Hopkins U., 1975. Chief econ. sect. Am. Embassy, Freetown, Sierra Leone, 1977-80, Bamako, Mali, 1983-86; internat. economist Dept. of State, Washington, 1980-82, econ. officer Office of Mexican Affairs, 1982-83, country officer for Bolivia, 1986-89, dep. dir. Office of Cuban Affairs, 1989-91, dir. Office of Cuban Affairs, 1991-93; charge d'affaires Am. Embassy, Port au Prince, Haiti, 1993, dep. chief of mission, 1993-95; amb. Rep. of Madagascar, 1995-97; dep. asst. secy. for Africa Dept. of State, Washington, 1997—99; prin. officer U.S. Interest Sect., Havana, Cuba, 1999—2002; U.S. amb. to Mali, 2002—. Dep. dir. Am. Inst. for Free Labor Devel., Rio de Janiero, Brazil, 1969-72, program officer, Lima, Peru, 1966-68. Vol. U.S. Peace Corps, 1964-66. Am. Polit. Sci. Congl. fellow, 1988-89; recipient Disting. Honor award, Presdl. Meritorious Svc. award, several Superior Honor awards. Mem. Am. Fgn. Svc. Assn., Alumni Johns Hopkins. Presbyterian. Avocations: skiing, scuba diving (master). Home: 14-16 rue Rainitouo Antsahauola Madagascar

HUDEL, CHESTELLA ALVIS, athletics educator; b. Temple, Okla., Jan. 13, 1931; d. James Chester and Jewel (McCain) Alvis; m. William August Hudel, June 14, 1952 (dec. June 1962); children: Mary Hudel Rinne, Nancy Hudel Parten, Joan Hudel Patrick. BS in Child Devel., Tex. Women's U., 1950. Tchr. Port Arthur (Tex.) Ind. Sch., 1950-53, Ridgewood Park Pre-Sch., Dallas, 1962-86; trainer Red Cross, Dallas, 1975—; adapted aquatics dir. YWCA, Dallas, 1975—. Trainer water safety instrs. Red Cross, Dallas, 1975-96; coach Spl. Olympics, 1993-98; educator Down's Syndrome Guild/Dallas Ind. Sch. Dist., 1994-96; counselor for breast cancer survivors Encore YWCA/Komen Found., Dallas, 1995-98. Elder Northridge Presbyn. Ch., Dallas, 1979-98; com. on adminstrn. YWCA, Dallas, 1980-86; active Northridge Learning Ctr. Bd., Northridge Presbyn. Ch., Dallas, 1987-97, active Bachman Recreation Ctr., Dallas, Park Cities YMCA, Dallas; swim program leader Light House for the Blind, 1986-90, Tom Landry Ctr. Baylor Hosp., 2003—; resource person Parent to Parent, 1993. Named Profl. of Yr. in recognition of oustanding svcs., Red Cross, Dallas, 2004, Vol. of Yr., Helping Agys. Serving Richardson, Tex., 1990; recipient Golden Rule award, J.C. Penney, Dallas, 1983, Extra Step award, Red Cross, Dallas, 1989, Spirit of Red Cross award, 1990, Vol. Spirit award, GM, Dallas, 1992, George Washington medal of honor, Freedom Found. Valley Forge, Dallas, 1997. Mem. Assn. for Retarded Citizens. Avocations: journal and scrapbook making, piano, bridge, bible study. Home: 8719 Coppertowne Ln Dallas TX 75243-8087 Personal E-mail: aquaches@sbcglobal.net.

HUDELSON, DIANE SUSAN, elementary school educator; b. Hibbing, Minn., May 3, 1961; d. Bernard and Viola Brekke McCauley; m. Carl Walter Hudelson, Feb. 14, 1987; children: Carly Elizabeth, Brekke Leo. BAS, U. of Minn. at Duluth, 1983. Tchr. Phoenix Day Sch., 1983—84; title I tchr. Wash. Elem., Hibbing, Minn., 1984—85; tchr. Jefferson Elem., Hibbing, 1985—2003, Greenhaven Elem., Hibbing, 2003—. Sec. Relicensure Com., Hibbing, Minn., 2002—; mem. Hibbing United Educators, 1983—. Office: Greenhaven Elem 323 E 39th St Hibbing MN 55746 Office Phone: 218-263-8332.

HUDES, NANA BRENDA, marketing professional; b. N.Y.C., Nov. 25; d. Harry and Anita Lorraine (Seiken) Richter; m. Barton Hudes, Sept. 2, 1958 (div. Sept. 1972); children: Layne A., Michael F., Meredith A. Student, Skidmore Coll.; BA magna cum laude, Pace U., 1974; MS with honors, Coll. of New Rochelle, 1976. Dir. mail mktg. mgr. Pergamon Press, Elmsford, N.Y., 1979-80, spl. sales mgr., 1980-81; mktg. mgr. Knowledge Industry Publs., White Plains, N.Y., 1981-82, Grolier Electronic Pub., Danbury, Conn., 1982-84, dir. mktg., 1984-86; mktg. mgr. R.R. Bowker, New Providence, N.J., 1986-88, mktg. dir., 1988-91, sr. dir. mktg., 1991-99. Tchr. social studies Rye Neck (N.Y.) Mid. Sch., 1978-79; pres. NH Assocs., Mktg. Cons., 2000-01; dir. libr. mktg. Columbia U. Press, 2001—. Dist. leader, county committeeperson Dem. Party, Matawan Twp., N.J., 1964. Home: 233 E 69th St New York NY 10021-5414 Personal E-mail: nhudes@mindspring.com.

HUDGEL, DAVID WILLIAM, allergist, immunologist, educator; b. Rockford, Ill., 1941; MD, U. Iowa, 1967. Diplomate Am. Bd. Allergy and Immunology. Intern Cin. Gen. Hosp., 1967-68; resident in internal medicine U. Colo., Ft. Collins, 1970-72; fellow in immunology Nat. Jewish Hosp., Denver, 1972-74; prof. allergy and immunology Case We. Res. U., Cleve. Attending physician Cleve. Metrohealth Med. Ctr. Mem. Am. Assn. Anatomists, Am. Coll. Chest Physicians, Am. Psychosomatic Soc., Am. Thoracic Soc. Office: 2500 Metrohealth Dr Cleveland OH 44109-1900

HUDGENS, MICHAEL THOMAS, SR., author, educator; b. Wichita Falls, Tex., July 9, 1938; s. Grady Merwyn and Iris Ann (Hawkins) H.; children: Alexander, Patrick, Michael Jr. BA, Loyola Marymount U., L.A., 1977, MA, 1980; PhD, U. S.D., 1998. Theater and film critic, arts editor The Houston Post, 1967-73; sci. editor various, 1973-80, Hughes Electronics, L.A., 1980-91; assoc. prof. humanities S.D. Sch. Mines and Tech., Rapid City, 1991—. Lectr. in field. Author Donald Barthelme, Postmodern American Writer, 2001; contbr. articles to profl. jours., mags. and newspapers. Avocations: radio operating, astronomy. Home: 12304 Renata Dr Black Hawk SD 57718-7583 Office Phone: 605-394-2686. Personal E-mail: mhudgens@rushmore.com.

HUDGENS, SANDRA LAWLER, retired state official; b. New Orleans, Feb. 15, 1944; d. Avril Lawler and Peggy V. (Crager) Kelly; m. Adolfo DiGennaro, Oct. 20, 1967 (div. 1970); 1 child, Daniel Darryn DiGennaro; m. Stanley Dalton Hudgens, Feb. 17, 1973; children: Stephanie Hudgens Cap, Richard Stanley, Michael Shane. Student, U. Nev., 1962-64, U. Grenoble, France, 1964-65, U. Aix-Marseille, Nice, France, 1965, U. Nev., Las Vegas, 1980-2000. Traffic ct. clk. III Clark County Juvenile Ct. Svcs., Las Vegas, 1965-71; planning commr. City of Las Vegas, 1988-92, chmn. planning commn., 1991-92; br. mgr. registration divsn. Dept. Motor Vehicles and Pub. Safety, State of Nev., Las Vegas, 1971-96. Rep. Weststar FCU, Las Vegas, 1988-96; advocate State of Nev. Employees Assn., Las Vegas, 1971-96; coord. State of Nev. team City of Las Vegas Corp. Challenge, 1987-90; dir. so. chpt. Am. Fedn. State, County and Mcpl. Employees/State Nev. Employees Assn. retirees AFL/CIO. Past treas., sec. Las Vegas Civic Ballet Assn., Las Vegas, 1987-93; treas. Women's Dem. Club Clark County, Las Vegas, 1996-97, pres., 1998; chmn., vice-chmn. United Blood Svcs. Adv. Coun., Las Vegas, 1993-96; chmn. 1st Ann. Flood Awareness Week, mem. adv. coun. Clark County Regional Flood Dist., Las Vegas, 1987-88; treas., sec., badge and advancement counselor Boy Scouts Am., Las Vegas, 1976-90; internat. living stones coord. Episcopal Diocese of Nev., 2002—. Mem.: Am. Bus. Women's Assn. (chmn. souvenir program Western Regional Conf. 1997), Commn. Ministries, Ret. Pub. Employees Nev. (v.p. 1999—2000, pres. 2000—01, 2002—04). Democrat. Episcopalian. Avocations: hunting, knitting, photography, rving, biking. Home: PO Box 2103 Dayton NV 89403-2103

HUDGINS, J. WILLIAM, musician, educator; b. San Antonio, Apr. 5, 1959; s. Jack William and Ermyne Lee Hudgins; m. Nancy Guinn Hudgins, Nov. 7, 1993; 1 child, Jackson Moss. MusB, Johns Hopkins U., 1980; MusM, Temple U., 1982. Musician, percussionist Boston Symphony Orch., 1990—; endorser Zildjian Cymbal Co., Norwell, 1996—; tchr. New Eng. Conservatory, Boston, 2005—. Musician: (jazz performance, rec.) Next Level (critical acclaim), Emotion and Intellect (critical acclaim). Recipient First prize Concours recital competition, Peabody Conservatory Johns Hopkins U., 1980, Concerto Soloist award, Boston Pops, 1996, Boston Symphony Orch., 1998; Joseph E. Maddy scholar Johns Hopkins U., Interlochen Arts Acad., 1976-1980. Mem.: Stockbridge Golf Club (assoc.). Avocations: music, golf, skiing. Office: Boston Symphony Orch 301 Massachusetts Ave Boston MA 02115

HUDGINS, WILLIE L., JR., lawyer; b. LaCrosse, Va., Mar. 5, 1943; BB, Howard U., 1965; JD, Howard U. Law Sch., 1968. Bar: Va. 1968, DC 1971, US Supreme Ct. 1973. Dep. chief Antitrust Divsn., US Dept. Justice; atty. Collier, Shannon, Scott, PLLC, DC. Named one of Am. Top Black Atty., Black Enterprise, 2003. Mem.: ABA, Section Antitrust Law, Va. State Bar, Washington DC Bar, US Supreme Ct. Office: Collier Shannon Scott PLLC 3050 K St NW Ste 400 Washington DC 20007 Office Phone: 202-342-8586. Business E-Mail: whudgins@colliershannon.com.

HUDIAK, DAVID MICHAEL, academic administrator, lawyer; b. Darby, Pa., June 27, 1953; s. Michael Paul and Sophie Marie (Glowaski) Hudiak; m. Veronica Ann Barbone, Aug. 28, 1982; children: David Michael, Christopher Andrew, Jonathan Joseph. BA, Haverford Coll., 1975; JD, U. Pa., 1978. Bar: Pa. 1979, U.S. Dist. Ct. (ea. dist.) Pa. 1979, NJ 1981, U.S. Dist. Ct. NJ 1981. Assoc. Jerome H. Ellis, Phila., 1978-79, Berson, Fineman & Bernstein, Phila., 1979-80; pvt. practice Aldan, Pa., 1980-81; dir. tng. paralegal program PJA Sch., Upper Darby, Pa., 1982—, acting dir., 1983-89, dir., 1989—, v.p., 1989—, also bd. dirs.; v.p., sec.-treas., bd. dirs. 7900 West Chester Pike Corp., 1994—. Mem. staff Nat. Ctr. Ednl. Testing, Phila., 1982—87; instr. Villanova (Pa.) U., 1985. Mem. Havertown Choristers; active U. Pa. Light Opera Co., 1977—84; mem. 10th Synod Archdiocese of Phila., 2002; active mem., parish coun., lector, cantor St. Eugene Parish. Mem.: ABA, Pa. Bar Assn., Founders Club Haverford Coll. Office: PJA Sch 7900 W Chester Pike Upper Darby PA 19082-1917 Office Phone: 610-789-6700. Business E-Mail: pjaschool@dvol.com.

HUDIK, MARTIN FRANCIS, hospital administrator, educator, consultant, writer; b. Chgo., Mar. 27, 1949; s. Joseph and Rose (Ricker) H.; m. Eileen Hudik; 1 child, Theresa Margaret. AAS in Engring., Morton Coll., 1969; BS in Mech. and Aerospace Engring., Ill. Inst. Tech., 1971; BPA, Jackson State U., 1974; MBA, Loyola U., 1975; postgrad., U. Sarasota, 1975-76. Cert. health care safety mgr., hazard control mgr., hazardous materials mgr., OSHA hazardous materials response instr., hazardous materials incident comdr., disaster coord., police instr., Ill., security cert. instr., Ill. With Ill. Masonic Med. Ctr., Chgo., 1969-94, dir. risk mgmt., 1974-79, asst. adminstr., 1979-94; facilities engring. mgr. Bethany/Adv. Hosp., 1997-98; health care cons., 2000—; bus. mgr. St. Bernadine Parish, 2001—. Capt. tng. divsn. Cicero (Ill.) Police Dept., tng. and internal affairs divsn., aux. divsn., 1971-99, U.S. Dept. Commerce, 2000, ind. cons., 2000; instr. Nat. Safety Coun. Safety Tng. Inst., Chgo., 1977-85; cons. Coun. Tech. users Consumer Products, Underwriters Labs., Chgo., 1977-96; instr., lt. U.S. Def. Civil Preparedness Agy. Staff Coll., Battle Creek, Mich., 1977-85; liaison officer to Cook County Emergency Svcs.; asst. dir. Emergency Svcs. and disaster Agy. Town of Cicero, 1988-97; founding pres. Cook County Emergency Mgmt. Coun., 1991-92; exec. bd., pres. U.S. Postal Svc. Postal Customer Adv. Coun., Cicero, 1996-99, sec. exec. bd., 2003—; mem. exec. bd. Chicagoland Postal Adv. Coun., 1994—; exec. bd. advisor Cicero PCAC, 1998—. Co-chmn. Archdiocese of Chicago Deanery IV-C, 1999—2003; active Cath. Edn. Com., 2000—03; pastoral coun. Archdiocese Chgo., 2000—03; pres. sch. bd. Mary Queen of Heaven Sch., Cicero, 1977—79, 1984—86, Mary Queen of Heaven Ch. Coun., 1979—81, 1983—86, St. Leonard Parish Coun., 1998—2001, St. Bernardine Parish Coun., 2001—, I.M.M.C. Employee Club, 1983—86. Recipient Presdl. Sports award, Amateur Athletic Union, 1978, 1980—81, 2000, Meritorious Svc. award, Town of Cicero, 1990, Spl. Svc. award Underwriters Lab., 1992, medal of Merit, 1996, Emergency Svcs. Achievement award, 1997, Police Achievement award, 1998, Spl. Svc. award, Cook County Sheriffs Dept., 1993, Excellence in Svc. award, U.S. Postal Svc., 1997, Outstanding Effort award, 1998, Outstanding Svcs. award, Cicero Postal Coun., 1998, Svc. Recognition award, 1999, Outstanding Performance award, 2001, Volunteerism award, U.S. Postal Svc., 2002, Svc. Recognition award, Archdiocese of Chgo., 2003; scholar state scholar, Ill., 1969—71. Mem. Am. Coll. Healthcare Execs., Am. Soc. Hosp. Risk Mgmt., Nat. Fire Protection Assn., Am. Soc. SafetyEngrs. (profl.), Am. Soc. Law and Medicine, Ill. Hosp. Security and Safety Assn. (co-founder 1976, founding pres. 1976-77, hon. dir. 1977-82), Cath. Alumni Club Chgo. (bd. dirs. 1983-84, 86), Mensa, Masons (3d degree, Berwyn, Ill. chpt.), KC (mem. 4th degree cardinal coun., Svc. award 2002), Pi Tau Sigma, Tau Beta Pi, Alpha Sigma Nu. Republican. Roman Catholic. Home: 7246 W Harrison St Forest Park IL 60130-2345 Office: 6845 Riverside Dr Berwyn IL 60402-2231

HUDKINS, JOHN W., lawyer; b. Inglewood, Calif., Jan. 12, 1946; s. Ralph Emerson and Genevieve Delores H.; m. Diana Byler, Feb. 16, 1969. BA, Calif. State U., Hayward, 1968; MBA, U. Nev., Las Vegas, 1971; JD, U. of Pacific, 1976; LLM, George Washington U., 1983. Bar: Iowa 1976, Calif. 1977, U.S. Ct. Mil. Appeals 1976, Fla. 1995. Commd. 2d lt. USAF, 1968, advanced through grades to lt. col., 1983, ret., 1988; sr. counsel Aerojet-Gen. Corp., Sacramento, 1988-94; dir. bus. mgmt. Olin Ordnance, Downey, Calif., 1994-95, sr. counsel St. Petersburg, Fla., 1995-96, v.p., chief counsel, 1996-97; v.p., dep. gen. counsel Primex Tech., Inc., St. Petersburg, Fla., 1997-2001; dep. gen. counsel Gen. Dynamics Ordnance and Tactical Sys., 2001; legal counsel to bd. mgrs. Am. Ordinance, 2002—03. Bd. dirs. Vandenberg Fed. Credit Union, Lompoc, Calif., 1983-85, Prince William (Va.) County Soccer Assn., 1985-88. Mem. ABA (pub. contract law sect.), Nat. Security Indsl. Assn. (chair legal com.). Home: 7649 E Torrey Point Cir Mesa AZ 85207-1188

HUDNALL, JARRETT, JR., management consultant, educator, marketing professional; b. Rhome, Tex., Oct. 6, 1931; s. Jarrett and Katherine (Wilson) H.; m. Sarah Ruth Warren, Nov. 24, 1955; children: Jarrett Joseph, William Warren, Katherine Lee, Thomas Wilson. Student, Arlington (Tex.) State Coll., 1948-50; BBA, U. Tex., Austin, 1953, MBA, 1956; PhD, U. Ala., 1966. Lectr. U. Tex., 1955-56; asst. prof. Arlington State Coll., 1956-58; instr. U. Ala., 1958-61; asst. prof. La. Tech. U., 1961-62, assoc. prof. mktg., 1962-67, prof., head dept. bus., 1967-77; exec. Superior Supply Co., Inc., 1978-83, P&A div. Ciba-Geigy, 1983-84; v.p. Rohcar, Inc., 1984-90; prof. mgmt. and mktg. Stephen F. Austin State U., Nacogdoches, Tex., 1985-92; dean coll. bus. and commerce U. West Ala., Livingston, 1992-94; prof. mktg. Miss. U. for Women, Columbus, 1994—2002; emeritus; emeritus designee Assn. Collegiate Bus. Schs. & Programs, 2002—. Vice pres. Ctrl. Asian Cons., LLC; bd. dirs. SBI; cons. firms in chem. fertilizer, petroleum, farm equipment mfg., bus.; cons. agrl. and econ. devel. products W. Republic of Uzbekistan, 1995; vis. prof. mktg. Huron U., London, 2000, 02. Author: (with A.L. Seeyle) Compensation of Retail Department Store and Specialty Store Salesman in Major Texas Cities, 1957, Attitudes of Gulf Service Station Dealers Toward Minor Tuneup and Repair Work, 1963, An Economic Analysis of Income and Employment in a Four-State Deep South Region, 1950-60, 1966. Lt. AUS, 1953-55. Gulf Oil Corp. fellow, 1963. Mem. VFW, Am. Mktg. Assn., So. Mktg. Assn., S.W. Fedn. Allied Disciplines, Am. Collegiate Retailing Assn., So. and Southwestern Bus. Dean's Assn., Small Bus. Inst. Dirs.' Assn., Allied Acads., Kiwanis Internat., Sigma Iota Epsilon, Beta Gamma Sigma, Alpha Kappa Psi, Kappa Delta Pi, Delta Mu Delta. Democrat. Baptist. Home: 1003 Lakeview Dr Ruston LA 71270-5233 Personal E-mail: jhud@cox-internet.com.

HUDNER, PHILIP, lawyer, rancher; b. San Jose, Calif., Feb. 24, 1931; s. Paul Joseph and Mary E. (Dooling) H.; m. Carla Raven, Aug. 6, 1966; children: Paul Theodor, Mary Carla. BA with great distinction, Stanford U., 1952, LL.B., 1955. Bar: Calif. 1955. Lawyer Pillsbury, Madison & Sutro, San Francisco, 1958—, ptnr., 1970-99, Botto Law Group, San Francisco, 1999—; rancher San Benito County, Calif., 1970—. Asst. editor: Stanford Law Rev., 1954-55; author articles on estate and trust law. Pres. Soc. Calif. Pioneers, 1976-78, Louise M. Davies Found., 2002—, Charles D. and Frances K. Field Fund, 2003—; sec.-treas. Drum Found., 2003—. Served with U.S. Army, 1956-58. Fellow Am. Bar Found.; mem. Internat. Acad. Estate and Trust Law (steering com. 1974-75, exec. coun. 1980-85), San Benito County Saddle Horse Assn., Order of Malta, Phi Beta Kappa, Pacific Union Club, Lagunitas Country Club, Frontier Boys, Bohemian Club, Rancheros Visitadores. Democrat. Roman Catholic. Office: Botto Law Group 180 Montgomery St Fl 16 San Francisco CA 94104-3104

HUDNUT, ROBERT KILBORNE, clergyman, author; b. Cin., Jan. 7, 1934; s. William Herbert and Elizabeth (Kilborne) H.; m. Mary Lou Lundell; children by previous marriage: Heidi, Robert Kilborne, Heather, Matthew. BA with highest honors, Princeton, 1956; M.Div., Union Theol. Sem., N.Y.C., 1959. Ordained to ministry Presbyn. Ch., 1959; asst. minister Westminster Presbyn. Ch., Albany, N.Y., 1959-62; minister St. Luke Presbyn. Ch., Wayzata, Minn., 1962-73, Winnetka (Ill.) Presbyn. Ch., 1975-94. Exec. dir. Minn. Pub. Interest Research Group, 1973-75; Co-chmn. Minn. Joint Religious Legis. Coalition, 1970-75. Author: Surprised by God, 1967, A Sensitive Man and the Christ, 1971, A Thinking Man and the Christ, 1971, The Sleeping Giant: Arousing Church Power in America, 1971, An Active Man and the Christ, 1972, Arousing the Sleeping Giant: How to Organize Your Church for Action, 1973, Church Growth Is Not the Point, 1975, The Bootstrap Fallacy: What The Self-Help Books Don't Tell You, 1978, This People-This Parish, 1986, Meeting God in the Darkness, 1989, Emerson's Aesthetic, 1996, Call Waiting, 1999. Pres. Greater Met. Fedn. Twin Cities, 1970—72; chmn. Citizens Adv. Com. on Interstate 394, 1971—75; mem. planning commn. City of Cottage Grove, Minn., 2001—05; chmn. Dem. Party 33d Senatorial Dist. Minn., 1970—72, Minnetonka Dem. Party, 1970—72; fusion candidate for mayor City of Albany, 1961; chmn. Philbrook for Gov. Campaign, 2004—; nat. chmn. Presbyns. for Ch. Renewal, 1971; bd. dirs. Minn. Coun. Chs., 1964—70; trustee Princeton U., 1972—76, Asheville (N.C.) Sch., 1979—2003. Rockefeller fellow, 1956; named Outstanding Young Man Minnetonka, 1967; recipient Distinguished Service award Minnetonka Tchrs. Assn., 1969 Mem. Phi Beta Kappa. Home and Office: 7145 65th St S Cottage Grove MN 55016-1130 Office Phone: 651-768-7190.

HUDNUT, STEWART SKINNER, manufacturing executive, lawyer; b. Cin., Apr. 29, 1939; s. William Herbert and Elizabeth Allen (Kilborne) H.; children: Alexander Putnam, Andrew Gerard, Nathaniel Parker. AB summa cum laude, Princeton U., 1961; postgrad., Oxford U., Eng., 1962; JD, Harvard U., 1965; environ. law cert., Pace U., 1991. Bar: NY 1965, US Dist. Ct. So. and Ea. Districts NY 1966, US Ct. Appeals 2nd Cir. 1966, US Supreme Ct. 1972. Assoc. Davis Polk & Wardwell, NYC, 1965-67, 71-73, Paris, 1968-70; v.p., counsel Bankers Trust Co., 1973-77; v.p., gen. counsel, sec. Scovill Mfg. Co., Waterbury, Conn., 1977-87; sr. v.p., gen. counsel, sec. Mcpl. Bond Investors Assurance Corp., White Plains, NY, 1987-89, Ill. Tool Works Inc., Glenview, Ill., 1992—. Bd. dirs. Lyric Opera Guild of Chgo., Chgo. Shakespeare Theater, Assn. for Protection of Adirondacks, Kenilworth Union Ch.; instr. Voyageur Outward Bound Sch., 1989-90. Woodrow Wilson fellow, Keasbey fellow Christ Ch. Oxford U., Eng., 1962. Mem. ABA, Ill. Bar Assn., Phi Beta Kappa. Republican. Presbyterian. Office: Ill Tool Works Inc 3600 W Lake Ave Glenview IL 60025-5811

HUDNUT, WILLIAM HERBERT, III, not-for-profit developer, political scientist; b. Cin., Oct. 17, 1932; s. William Herbert Jr. and Elizabeth (Kilborne) H.; m. Beverly Guidara; children: Michael Conger, Laura Anne (dec.), Timothy Norton, William Herbert IV, Theodore Beecher, George Mattheson (dec.), Christopher Shew. BA magna cum laude, Princeton U., 1954; MDiv summa cum laude, Union Theol. Sem., N.Y.C., 1957; DD (hon.), Hanover Coll., 1967, Wabash Coll., 1969; LLD (hon.), Butler U., 1980, Anderson Coll., 1982, Franklin Coll., 1983, Millikin U., 1987, Ind. U., 1994, Elmhurst Coll., 1996, Youngstown State U., 2002; LittD (hon.), U. Indpls., 1981; DPS (hon.), Blackburn Coll., 1987, Christian Theol. Seminary, 2004. Ordained to ministry Presbyn. Ch., 1957. Asst. min. Westminster Ch., Buffalo, 1957-60; pastor 1st Presbyn. Ch., Annapolis, Md., 1960-63; dir. Westminster Found., Annapolis, 1960-63; sr. min. 2d Presbyn. Ch., Indpls., 1963-72; mem. 93d Congress from Ind., 1973-74; dir. dept. cmty. affairs Ind. Ctrl. U., Indpls., 1975; mayor City of Indpls., 1976-91; fellow Inst. Politics Harvard U., 1992; sr. fellow Hudson Inst., Indpls., 1992-94; pres. Civic Fedn., Chgo., 1994-96; sr. resident fellow The Urban Land Inst., Washington, 1996—. Mem. Presdl. Adv. Com. on Federalism, 1981-84. Author: Minister/Mayor, 1987, The Hudnut Years in Indianapolis, 1976-1991, 1995, Cities on the Rebound, 1998, Half Way to Everywhere, 2003; editor: Union Sem. Quar. Rev., 1956-57; contbr. sermons, articles to profl. publs. Mem. Bd.

Pub. Safety, Indpls., 1970-71, Rep. Nat. Com., 1987; pres. Anne Arundel County Mental Health Assn., 1961-63; pres., bd. dirs. Marion County Mental Health Assn., 1966-68, Westminster Found., Purdue U., 1969-73; bd. dirs. Cmty. Svc. Coun. Met. Indpls., 1964-68, Family Svc. Assn., 1966-72, Flanner House, 1968-72; pres. trustees Darrow Sch., New Lebanon, N.Y., 1968-75; Task Force on Fed. Deficit, 1981; mem. Adv. Commn. on Intergovtl. Rels., 1984-90; bd. dirs. Indpls. Ctr. for Adv. Rsch., 1976-91, Humane Soc., 1983-91; trustee Roosevelt Ctr. Am. Policy Studies, Washington, 1984-87; Pleasant Run Children's Home Found. bd., 1992-94, Children's Home & Aid Soc. Ill., 1994-96; co-vice chmn. Alliance for Redesigning Govt., 1992-2000; mem. Police Found. Bd., 1997—; mem. Nat. Assn. Securities Dealers Regulation Bd., 1996-98, Nat. Adjudicatory Coun., 1998; mem. accreditation bd. Am. Planning Assn., 1998-2001; mem. Town Coun., Chevy Chase, Md., 2000—, mayor, 2004—; active Millenial Housing Com., 2000-01. Recipient William Booth award Salvation Army, 1984, Russell G. Lloyd Disting. Svc. award Ind. Assn. Cities and Towns, 1985, Rosa Parks award Am. Assn. for Affirmative Action, 1992, Woodrow Wilson award Princeton U., 1986, Disting. Urban Mayor award Nat. Urban Coalition, 1987; named All-Pro City Mgmt. Team, City and State mag., 1986, 89, 92; fellow Nat. Acad. Pub. Adminstrn., 1994—. Mem. Columbia Club Indpls. (bd. dir. 1994-96), Cosmos Club, Kiwanis, Masons (33 deg.), Phi Beta Kappa. Office: The Urban Land Inst 1025 Thomas Jefferson St NW Washington DC 20007-5201 Office Phone: 202-624-7000. Business E-Mail: bhudnut@uli.org. *Life is relationships, and whatever we can do to enlighten and strengthen each other, in the family circle, among our friends, in business, in society at large, will help. This requires ardor and self-surrender, faith, hope and humor.*

HUDSON, ALAN C.H., music educator, tropical fruit farmer; s. George Clyde and Lydia Helena Hudson; m. Cathy Lee Horne, Jan. 6, 1973; children: Emma Jean, Amanda Lynn. B in Music Edn., Boston U., 1973. String tchr. Milford (Mass.) Schs., 1973—74; gen. music tchr. Airbase Elem. Sch., Miami, 1974—75, orch. tchr., Redland Mid. Sch., Miami, 1975—98, Coral Reef Sr. H.S., Miami, 1998—. Recipient Fla. Orchestral Tchr. of Yr. award, Am. String Tchrs. Assn., 2002. Mem.: Fla. Orchestral Assn. (v.p. 1998—98). Avocations: lychee farming, violin repair.

HUDSON, BARBARA, writer, actor; b. St. James, Minn., Feb. 2, 1921; d. Lloyd Edwin and Lois (Hardin) H.; m. Jesse Wilbert Powers, Oct. 27, 1946 (div. Apr. 1970); children: Jean Lois, Cathy Colleen; m. Lawrence Kneeland Dudley, Dec. 5, 1971 (div. Apr. 1979). BA, U. Iowa, 1942; MA, U. So. Calif., 1952. Tchr. drama, speech Southgate (Calif.) H.S., 1944-45; youth dir. Hollywood (Calif.) Presbyn. Ch., 1945-47; tech. writer secret publications Litton Industries, Canoga Park, Calif., 1959—61; assoc. prof. Calif. Luth. U., Thousand Oaks, 1961-75; missionary Calvary Cmty. Ch., Westlake Village, Calif., 1980—. Author: Bob Pierce, Going With God, 1956 (Winner Faith on the Rocks, Guideposts Story Contest, 1977), The Henrietta Mears Story, 1958, Where Is God, 1970, The Greatest Play Ever Written, 1970, God's Power in Your Life, 1971, Bridge of Nothing Less, 1975, (videos) Women of the Bible, 1990; writer, prodr., dir. (pageant) Here I Stand, 1967, Bridge of Nothing Less, 1975, Forward in Faith, 1975, God of the Mountain, 1952-57; contbr. articles to profl. jours.; internat. touring in one woman show Women of Glory, 1982—. 2d lt. in 1st officer's class USMCWR, 1943—45, U.S. Mem. DAR, Gamma Phi Beta, Zeta Phi Eta, Pi Kappa Delta (Diamond award 1939). Republican. Office: PO Box 3722 Thousand Oaks CA 91359 Home: 1851 Village Ct Thousand Oaks CA 91362 Office Phone: 805-495-4932. Personal E-mail: barbarahudsonwob@aol.com.

HUDSON, BARRY A., lawyer; b. Greenville, N.C., Nov. 22, 1946; s. Howell Ashley and Lillian Jeannette (Moore) H.; m. Patricia A. Schroeder, Aug. 20, 1968 (div. Feb. 1994); children: Theodore David, Sarah Meredith; m. Christine M. Wolfe, Aug. 16, 1995. BA, U. Colo., 1971, JD, 1974. Pvt. practice, Wheat Ridge, Colo., 1974—. Mem. Centennial Estate Planning Coun., Lakewood, Colo., 1981, 97; gen. counsel Wheat Ridge Sanitation, 1981—, Wheat Ridge Water, 1982—, Wheat Ridge Fire Dist., 1988—. Recipient award for legal svcs. to the poor Thursday Night Bar, 1974—. Mem. Colo. Bar Assn. (Legal Svcs. to the Poor award 1982—), 1st Jud. Bar Assn., Wheat Ridge C. of C. (pres., bd. dirs., Disting. Svc. award 1984), Wheat Ridge Optimists (sec.). Democrat. Methodist. Office: Barry A Hudson 3705 Kipling St Ste 206 Wheat Ridge CO 80033-2896 E-mail: barryh@prodigy.net.

HUDSON, C. B., JR., insurance company executive; b. 1947; BS, Okla. Univ., 1968. With Travelers Life Ins., Hartford, Conn., 1968-74; exec. v.p. Globe Life & Accident Ins. Co., Okla. City, 1974-82; pres., CEO United Am. Ins. Co., 1982—; CEO, chmn. Torchmark Corp. Office: Torchmark Corp America 2001 Third Ave S Birmingham AL 35233

HUDSON, CAROLYN BRAUER, application developer, educator; b. Durham, NC, Dec. 17, 1945; d. Alfred Theodor and Hildegard Franziska (Wolf) Brauer; children: Paul Benjamin, Joel Stephen. BS in Math., U. NC, 1967; MA in Forestry, Duke U., 1969; MS in Geology, U. SC, 1979, PhD in Geology, 1995. Assoc. dir. office rsch. and evaluation, asst. prof. N.C. Ctrl. U., Durham, 1970—72; rsch. assoc. Nat. Lab. for Higher Edn., Durham, 1971—72; tchg. assoc. U. S.C., Columbia, 1973—74, tchg. asst., 1990—92, tchg. assoc., 1993—, applications analyst, 1999—; vis. scientist Geol. Survey of Can., Ottawa, 1979—82; statistician S.C. State Govt., Columbia, 1997—98. Mem. S.C. Gov's Nuc. Adv. Coun., Columbia, 2001—; tech. coord. profl. women on campus U. S.C., Columbia, 2000—. Contbr. articles to profl. jours., photos to books. Vol. area pub. sch., 1978—93; Leader Boy Scouts of Am./Scouts Can., 1979—95; vol. Congaree Nat. Pk., Hopkins, SC, 1999—. Recipient Dist. Merit award, Boy Scouts of Am., 1988, Silver Beaver award, 1991, Shofar award, 1993, Profl. Devel. award, Profl. Women on Campus, 2000. Mem.: U. N.C. Alumni Assn. (life), Friends of Congaree Swamp (edn. com. 1996—2005, bd. dirs. 2005—), Women of Reform Judaism (v.p. 1975—76), Audubon, Sierra Club (nuc. affairs subcom. 2001—, computer chair 2003—05), Hadassah (life; bd. dirs. 1983—84), LWV. Democrat. Jewish. Avocations: hiking, music, travel, reading, photography. Home: 115 Arcadia Springs Cir Columbia SC 29206 Office Phone: 803-777-2358. Business E-Mail: hudson-carolyn@sc.edu.

HUDSON, CELESTE NUTTING, education educator, consultant, reading clinic administrator; b. Nashville, Sept. 18, 1927; d. John Winthrop Chandler and Hilda Bass (Alexander) Nutting; m. Frank Alden Hudson III, Dec. 30, 1948 (dec.); m. Robert Daniel Quartell, June 3, 1989; children: Frank Alden Hudson IV (dec.), Jo Ann Hudson Algermissen, Celeste Jane Hudson Norman, Jack Winthrop N. Hudson. BS, Oreg. Coll. Edn., 1952; MS, So. Ill. U., 1963, PhD, 1973. Cert. tchr., Tenn., Oreg., Mo. Iowa. Tchr. pub. schs., Crossville, Tenn., 1949—51, Salem, Oreg., 1952—53, West Walnut Manor, Mo., 1953—54, Normandy Sch. Dist., St. Louis County, Mo., 1954—66; reading coord. Sikeston Pub. Schs., Mo., 1966—69, Charleston, Mo., 1969—72; traveling cons. Ednl. Devel. Labs., Huntington, NY, 1970—71; mem. clin. staff So. Ill. U. Reading Ctr., 1972; asst. prof. edn. St. Ambrose Coll., 1972—75, U. Tenn., Chattanooga, 1975—76; dir. children's reading clinic St. Ambrose U. (formerly St. Ambrose Coll.), 1973—94; project dir. Learning Skills Ctr. St. Ambrose U., 1976—80, asst. prof. edn., 1976—78, assoc. prof., 1979—86, prof., 1986—94, prof. emeritus, 1995—. Dir. elem. edn. St. Ambrose U., 1972-94, chmn. dept. edn., 1980-84, divsn. chmn., 1984-87, faculty vice-chair, 1989-90, faculty chair, 1990-91; staff cons. Chandler Acad., 2002—, cons. cons. Chandler Acad., 2004—. Author: Handbook for Remedial Reading, 1967, Cognitive Listening and the Reading of Second Grade Children, 1973, The Effect of Visual Fatigue on Reading, 1990, Longitudinal Study of Children in Clinical Reading, 1994. Active Kimberly Village Bd., Davenport, Iowa, 1979-83, Trinity Hosp. Aux., 2001-04; chmn. worship com., Asbury Meth. Ch., 1985-90, choir, 1978-98, bell choir, 1995-97; co-chmn. Sarah Cir., 1996-99. Mem.: AARP, DAR (Hist. Soc.), AAUW (Lit. club), AAUP, Ret. Tchrs. Assn. Garfield Sch., Normandy Ret. Tchrs. Assn., Davenport Area Ret. Tchrs. Assn., Internat. Reading Assn. (Scott County coun. 1976—2003), Iowa Assn. Colls. Tchr. Edn. (exec. bd. 1989—92), Red Hat Soc., UDC (3rd v.p. 1966—70), New Eng. Women (pres.-elect 1994—95, pres. 1996—2003, yearbook chmn. 2004—05), Sun City Computer Club, Real Granddaughter's Club, Original Music Students Club (corr. sec. 1995—96), Ret. Tchrs. Club, Quad City Women's Investment Club (treas. 2001—05), Bettendorf Lionels (treas. 1998—2002), Kappa Delta Pi (sponsor 1974—96), Alpha Delta Kappa (life; past pres.). Address: St Ambrose U Box E 140 518 W Locust St Davenport IA 52803-2829 Personal E-mail: drhcnhq@aol.com.

HUDSON, CHARLES DAUGHERTY, insurance executive; b. La Grange, Ga., Mar. 17, 1927; s. J.D. and Janie (Hill) H.; m. Ida Cason Callaway, May 1, 1955; children: Jane Alice Hudson Craig, Ellen Pinson Hudson Harris, Charles Daugherty, Ida Hudson Russell. Student, Auburn U., 1945-48, LHD (hon.), 1992; LLD, La Grange Coll.; LHD (hon.), Mercer U., 1987. Ptnr. Hudson Hardware Co., La Grange, 1950-57, Hammond-Hudson Ins. Agy., La Grange, 1957-58, owner, 1958-78; pres. Hammond, Hudson & Holder INc., 1978-94, chmn. bd., 1994—. Bd. dirs., mem. exec. com. Citizens & So. Nat. Bank, La Grange, 1964-90; bd. dirs. Citizens & So. Ga. Corp., Citizens & So. Nat. Bank, Atlanta, C&S Investment Advisors, Inc., Atlanta, C&S Ga. Corp.; acting pres. La Grange Coll., 1979-80; v.p., bd. dirs. la Grange Industries, 1956—, Hudson Maddox Enterprises, 1965-95; ptnr. PCH Properties, 1981—; chmn. bd. dirs. First Annuity Corp., La Grange; bd. dirs., chmn. trust com. NationsBank of Ga. Recipient Pres.'s award Colonial Life Ins. Co., 1966, 69-70, 75-80, Disting. Alumni award Ga. Mil. Acad.-Woodward Acad., 1971, Disting. Svc. award Ga. Hosp. Assn., 1980, Respect Law award Optimists Assn., 1977, Van Landingham Commitment to Edn. award, 1996, Pub. Svc. award Ga. Assn. AIA, 1977, Leading Producer award Aetna Life and Casualty, 1979; Paul Harris fellow, 1984. Mem. Am. Legion, Ga. Assn. Ind. Ins. Agts., Ga. Sch. Bd. Assn. (area dir.), SAR, Amicale de Group LaFayette (hon.). Chattahoochee Valley Art Assn., La Grange C. of C. (bd. dirs.), Newcomen Soc. N.Am., Ga. Hosp. Assn. (trustee 1980—), U. Ga. Gridiron Secret Soc., Highland Country Club (chmn. bd. 1999—), Lafayette Club, Commerce Club Atlanta, Aetna Life and Casualty Presidents, Masons, Shriners, Elks, Rotary (pres. 1964-65), Sigma Alpha Epsilon, Beta Gamma Sigma. Home: 407 Country Club Rd Lagrange GA 30240-2031 Office: Hammond Hudson & Holder Inc 200 Broad St Lagrange GA 30240-2722

HUDSON, CHRISTOPHER JOHN, publisher; b. Watford, Eng., June 8, 1948; s. Joseph Edward and Gladys Jenny Patricia (Madgwick) Hudson; m. Lois Jeanne Lyons, June 16, 1979; children: Thomas, Ellen, Ronald, Timothy, Jonas. BA with honors, Cambridge U., Eng., 1969, MA with honors, 1972. Promotion mgr. Prentice-Hall Internat., Eng., 1969-70, area mgr., 1970-71, mktg. mgr. Englewood Cliffs, N.J., 1971-74, dir. mktg., 1974-76, asst. v.p., 1976; group internat. dir. I.T.T. Pub., N.Y.C., 1976-77; pres. Focal Press, Inc., N.Y.C., 1977-82; v.p., pub. Aperture Found. Inc., N.Y.C., 1983-86; head publs. J. Paul Getty Trust, L.A., 1986—2005; pub. Mus. Modern Art, NYC, 2005—. Author: Guide to International Book Fairs, 1976; pub. Aperture, 1983-86, J. Paul Getty Mus. Jour., 1986-2005. Mem. adv. coun. Nat. Heritage Village, Kioni, Greece; mem. trade with eastern Europe com. Assn. Am. Pubs., N.Y., 1976-79, internat. fairs com., 1986-88. Mem.: Internat. Assn. Scholarly Pubs. (sec.-gen. 1994—97, chmn. internat. contracts com.), Internat. Pubs. Assn., U.S. Mus. Publ. Group (chmn. 1989—), Internat. Assn. Mus. Publs. (Frankfurt, Fed. Republic Germany chmn. 1992—95), Hellenic Soc. (London), Travelers' Century Club (bd. dirs., treas.), Oxford & Cambridge Club (London). Avocations: rural preservation projects in england, greece and california. Office: Mus Modern Art 11 W 53rd St New York NY 10019-5497 Office Phone: 212-708-9445. Business E-Mail: christopher_hudson@moma.org.

HUDSON, DARRIL, political scientist, educator; b. Trousdale, Okla., Dec. 18, 1931; s. Frank Wilks Hudson and Emma Lee (Jackson) Van Meter. BA, U. Calif., Berkeley, 1954; MSc in Internat. Rels., London Sch. Econs & Polit. Sci, 1960, PhD, 1965. Lectr. U. Md. Overseas Program, 1959-67; assoc. prof. Md. State Coll., Princess Anne, Md., 1967-68; prof. Calif. State U., Hayward, 1968-93, prof. emeritus, 1993—; vis. prof. Am. U., Paris, 1992-93. Resident dir. German program Calif. State U., Heidelberg, Fed. Republic Germany, 1990-91; Fulbright prof. U. Heidelberg, 1981-82. Author: A Visitor's Guide to American Home Cooking, 1989, The World Council of Churches in International Affairs, 1978, The Ecumenical Movement in World Affairs, 1968. 1st lt. Intelligence Svc., U.S. Army, 1955-58. Rsch. fellow Alexander von Humboldt Found., Bonn, Heidelberg, Fed. Republic Germany, 1966-67, 75, 89; recipient H.C. Richards prize Gray's Inn, London, 1965. Mem. Am. Friends of Paris Opera, Conservatory of Music San Francisco, San Francisco Opera Assn. Democrat. Avocations: cooking, writing, travel. Home: 443 Fair Oaks St San Francisco CA 94110-3618 E-mail: darrilh@yahoo.com.

HUDSON, DAVID M., minister; b. Charleston, W.Va., Sept. 24, 1948; s. Charles R. and Margaret M. (Coleman) H.; m. Brenda J. Roach, Sept. 22, 1967; children: Nathaniel, Derek. Student, W.Va. State Coll., 1966, Apostolic Bible Inst., 1966-67, Tex. Bible Coll., 1968; DTh (hon.), Ind. Bible Coll., 1988. Ordained minister United Pentecostal Ch., 1973. Youth pres. United Pentecostal Ch., Indpls., 1980-85; sr. pastor Riverside Apostoic Ch., 1985—; exec. presbyter United Pentecostal Ch., St. Louis, 1994-96, harvestime radio commr., 1990—, gen. bd. presbyters, 1994-96. Adj. prof. Ind. Bible Coll., Indpls., 1995—; bd. govs. Apostolic Coalition, Washington, 1987-91; mem. adv. bd. Passion-Fire Internat., 1998—; sec. treas. W.Va. dist. United Pentecostal Ch., Charleston, 1994—; internat. spkr. in field. Editor Apostolic Voice, 1987-89. Bd. dirs. Citizens Concerned for Cmty. Values, Morgantown, W.Va., 1990—; co-chmn. Israel prayer breakfast Religious Roundtable, Memphis, 1991. Named Nat. Pres. of Yr. United Pentecostal Ch., 1984, Internat. Pres. of Yr., 1985. Avocations: travel, reading, exercise. Home: PO Box 2069 Morgantown WV 26502-2069

HUDSON, DAWN EMILY, food service executive; b. Worcester, Mass., Nov. 27, 1957; d. Kenneth Dunlap and Nancy (Selin) H.; m. Bruce Kershaw Beach, Aug. 31, 1980. BA, Dartmouth Coll., 1979. Asst. acct. exec., acct. exec. Compton Advt., N.Y.C., 1979-82; product mgr. Clairol, Div. Bristol Myers, N.Y.C., 1982-83; acct. supr., mgmt. supr. ptnr. Tatham-Laird Kudner Inc., Chgo., 1983-86; mgmt. supr. group acct. dir. sr. v.p., mng. ptnr., exec. v.p. DDB Needham, Worldwide, Chgo., 1986-94; exec. v.p., dir. client svcs. DDB Needham Worldwide N.Y., N.Y.C., 1994—; mng. dir. D'Arcy Masius Benton & Bowles, NY; exec. v.p. sales and mktg. Frito-Lay (subsidiary of Pepsi), 1996—98; sr. v.p. strategy and mktg. Pepsi-Cola N.Am., 1998—2002, pres., 2002—. Mem. editorial bd. Dartmouth Coll. Alumni Mag., 1993—. Mem. Dartmouth Coll. Alumni Coun., 1993—, career counsel graduates, 1979-88. Named one of most powerful women, Forbes mag., 2005. Republican. Methodist. Avocations: avid tennis player, golf, skiing. Office: Pepsi Co North America 700 Anderson Hill Rd Purchase NY 10577*

HUDSON, DEAN, tax accountant; married; 4 children. BA in Acctg., U. West Fla.; student, Harvard U. Bus. Sch. CPA, Ga. Tax sr. Arthur Andersen & Co., Atlanta; with So. Co. Svcs. Inc., 1973—, from tax acct. to asst. v.p., v.p., comptroller, CFO; comtroller The So. Co., Atlanta. Mem. Roswell (Ga.) United Meth. Ch. Mem AICPA, Ga. So. CPA. Office: 270 Peachtree St NW Atlanta GA 30303-1247

HUDSON, DENNIS LEE, lawyer, retired arbitrator, federal official; b. St. Louis, Jan. 5, 1936; s. Lewis Jefferson and Helen Mabel (Buchanan) H.; children: Karen Marie, Karla Sue, Mary Ashley. BA, U. Ill., 1958; JD, John Marshall Law Sch., 1972. Bar: Ill. 1972, U.S. Dist. Ct. (so. and no. dists.) Ill. 1972. Ins. IRS, Chgo., 1962-72; spl. agt. GSA, Chgo., 1972-78, spl. agt.-in-charge, 1978-83, regional insp. gen., 1983-87; supervisory spl. agt. Dept. Justice-GSA Task Force, Washington, 1978; arbitrator Circuit Ct. Cook County, Ill., 1987-93; prof. criminal justice Coll. of DuPage, Glen Ellyn, Ill., 1996—. Adv. bd. Suburban Law Enforcement Acad., Glen Ellyn, Ill., 1999—; adv. bd. campus police Coll. DuPage, Glen Ellyn, 1999—; deacon Grace Luth. Ch., La Grange, Ill., 1977—81; lay eucharistic min. All Sts. Episcopal Ch., Western Springs, Ill., 1999—; bd. govs. Theatre Western Springs, Ill., 1978—81, 1991—92, 2005—, acting laureate, 2004—; bd. dirs. Pendulum Theatre Co., Chgo., 2001—. With U.S. Army, 1959—61. John N. Jewett scholar, 1972, Am. Jurisprudence scholar, 1972. Mem. ABA, Ill. Bar Assn. Office: Coll Dupage Health Social and Behavioral Scis Progra 425 Fawell Blvd Glen Ellyn IL 60137

HUDSON, DONALD J., retired brokerage house executive; b. Vancouver, B.C., Can., Sept. 26, 1930; BA in Econs. and Math., U. B.C., 1952; LLD (hon.), Simon Fraser U., 1993. With Shell Oil Co. of Can. Ltd., 1952—53; dir. sales devel. Can. Pacific Airlines, Vancouver, 1953—54; sr. v.p. Pacific div. T. Eaton Co., Ltd., Vancouver, 1954—81; pres. Vancouver Stock Exch., 1982—95. Trustee Endowment Fund YMCA Greater Vancouver; past chmn. bd. govs., Simon Fraser U., 1988-90; past chmn., bd. trustees, St. Paul's Hosp., 1983-85. Mem.: Vancouver Club, Vancouver Lawn Tennis Club.

HUDSON, EDWARD RANDALL, JR., gas and oil industry executive; b. Ft. Worth, Tex., July 24, 1934; s. Edward Randall and Josphine Terrell (Smith) H.; m. Ann Frasher, Sept. 19, 1959; children: Edward Randall III, Frasher Hudson Pergande. BA, U. Tex., 1955; JD, Harvard U., 1958. Owner, oil prodr. Hudson Oil, Ft. Worth. Vice-chmn. cultural property com. U.S. Info. Agy.; bd. dirs. Kimbell Art Found., Aspen Ctr. Physics; sec. bd. dirs. Burnett Found.; past chmn. bd. dirs. Modern Art Mus. Ft. Worth; nat. com., founding co-chmn. bd. dirs. Aspen Art Mus. Mem. Ft. Worth Club, River Crest Country Club, Argyle, Knickerbocker, Steeplechase, Order of the Alamo, Phi Beta Kappa. Avocation: art collecting. Home: 55 Westover Ter Fort Worth TX 76107-3106 also: 750 Castle Creek Dr Aspen CO 81611-1138 Office: Hudson Oil 616 Texas St Fort Worth TX 76102-4696 E-mail: eh34@compuserve.com.

HUDSON, EDWARD VOYLE, apparel executive; b. Seymour, Mo., Apr. 3, 1915; s. Marion A. and Alma (Von Gonten) H.; m. Margaret Carolyn Greely, Dec. 24, 1939; children: Edward G., Carolyn K. Student, Bellingham Normal Coll., 1933-36, U. Wash., 1938. Asst. to mgr. Natural Hard Metal Co., Bellingham, 1935—37; ptnr. Met. Laundry Co., Tacoma, 1938—39; propr., mgr. Peerless Laundry & Linen Supply Co., Tacoma, 1939—. Propr. Ind. Laundry & Everett Linen Supply Co., 1946-74, 99 Cleaners and Launderers Co., Tacoma, 1957-59; chmn. Tacoma Pub. Utilities, 1959-60; trustee United Mut. Savs. Bank; bd. dirs. Tacoma Better Bus. Bur., 1977—; mem. regional bd., SBA, 1965. Pres. Wash. Conf. on Unemployment Compensation, 1975-76; pres. Tacoma Boys' Club, 1970; v.p. Puget Sound USO, 1972-91; elder Emmanuel Presbyn. Ch., 1974—; past campaign mgr., pres. Tacoma-Pierce County United Good Neighbors. Recipient Disting. Citizen's cert. USAF Mil. Airlift Com., 1977; U.S. Dept. Def. medal for outstanding pub. svc., 1978. Mem. Tacoma Sales and Mktg. Execs. (pres. 1957-58), Pacific NW Laundry, Dry Clearning and Linen Supply Assn. (pres. 1959, treas. 1965-75), Internat. Fabricare Inst. (dir. dist. 7, treas. 1979, pres. 1982), Am. Security Coun. Bd., Tacoma C. of C. (pres. 1965), Air Force Assn. (pres. Tacoma chpt. 1976-77, v.p. Wash. state 1983-84, pres. 1985-86), Navy League, Puget Sound Indsl. Devel. Coun. (chmn. 1967), Tacoma-Ft. Lewis Olympia Army Assn. (past pres.), Elks Club (vice chmn. bd. trustees 1984, chmn. 1985-86), Shriners (potentate 1979), Masons, Scottish Rite, Tacoma Club, Tacoma Country and Golf Club, Jesters Club, Rotary (pres. Tacoma chpt. 1967-68), Tacoma Knife and Fork Club (pres. 1964). Republican. Home: 3901 N 37th St Tacoma WA 98407-5636 Office: Peerless Laundry & Linen Supply Co 2902 S 12th St Tacoma WA 98405-2598

HUDSON, ERNIE, actor; b. Benton Harbor, Mich., Dec. 17, 1945; m. Jeannie Moore, 1963 (div. 1976); 2 children; m. Linda Kingsberg, 1985; 2 children. Grad., Wayne State U.; attended, U. Minn. Movies include Joy of Sex, 1984, Ghostbusters, 1984, Love on the Run, 1985, The Dirty Dozen: The Fatal Mission, 1988, Ghostbusters II, 1989, The Hand That Rocks the Cradle, 1992, Wild Palms, 1993, Heart and Souls, 1993, Sugar Hill, 1994, No Escape, 1994, The Crow, 1994, The Cowboy Way, 1994, Airheads, 1994, Speechless, 1994, The Basketball Diaries, 1995, Congo, 1995, The Substitute, 1996, Operation Delta Force, 1997, Mr. Magoo, 1997, Stranger in the Kingdom, 1998, October 22, 1998, Butter, 1998, Best of the Best 4: Without Warning, 1998, Shark Attack, 1999, Lillie, 1999, Everything's Jake, 2000, Red Letters, 2000, The Watcher, 2000, Miss Congeniality, 2000, Halfway Decent, 2003, Anne B. Real, 2003, (voice) Clifford's Really Big Movie, 2004, Sledge: The Untold Story, 2005, Marilyn Hotchkiss' Ballroom Dancing and Charm School, 2005, Miss Congeniality 2: Armed and Fabulous, 2005; TV movies include Tornado!, 1996, The Cherokee Kid, 1996, Clover, 1997, American Hero: The Michael Jordan Story, 1999, Miracle on the 17th Green, 1999, Nowhere to Land, 2000, Walking Shadow, 2001, A Town Without Christmas, 2001, Lackawanna Blues, 2005; TV series include Highcliffe Manor, 1979, The Last Precinct, 1986, Broken Badges, 1990, Oz, 1997-2003, HRT, 2001, 10-8 Officers on Duty, 2003-04; guest appearances include Fantasy Island, 1978, Baa Baa Blacksheep, 1978, The Incredible Hulk, 1979, One Day at a Time, 1979, Too Close for Comfort, 1980, Diff'rent Strokes, 1981, Little House on the Prarie, 1981, Bosom Buddies, 1981, Taxi, 1981, The Dukes of Hazzard, 1982, Flamingo Road, 1982, Webster, 1983, The A-Team, 1983, St. Elsewhere, 1984, Gimme a Break!, 1986, Mike Hammer, 1986, Full House, 1987, Super Mario Bros. Super Show!, 1989, Tales from the Crypt, 1993, Grace Under Fire, 1996, Arli$$, 1998, Touched by an Angel, 2001, Without a Trace, 2003, Everwood, 2004 others. Reserve dep. sheriff San Bernardino County, Calif., 1989—. Office: Gersh Agy 232 N Canon Dr Beverly Hills CA 90210-5302*

HUDSON, FRANKLIN, real estate developer, lawyer; b. N.Y.C., Nov. 1948; s. Alec N. Hudson. BBA., Sam Houston State U., 1971; JD, St. Mary's U., 1974. Bar: Tex. 1975, U.S. Dist. Ct. Tex., U.S. Supreme Ct., Wash., D.C., U.S. Ct. of Appeals, Atlanta, New Orleans and San Francisco, Mem. Nat. Assn. Home Builders, Nat. Multi Family Council, State Bar Assn. Tex. Office: c/o PO Box 460029 Houston TX 77056-8029

HUDSON, FRANKLIN DONALD, manufacturing executive, consultant; b. Asheville, N.C., July 21, 1933; s. Halbert Austin and Lillian Naomi (Cook) H.; m. Rosemary Wheatley, Dec. 1, 1956; children: Lawrence Jamison, Lauren Jean. B.E.E., Yale U., 1955; MBA, NYU, 1962; postgrad., Pace U., 1972-75. Sales rep. RCA, N.Y.C., 1959-62; Latin Am. gen. mgr. Fed. Pacific Electric Co., P.R., 1962-68; dir. mktg. GTE Sylvania, 1968-71; dir. Home Equipment div. Singer Co., N.Y.C., 1971-75; v.p. internat. Corometrics Med. Systems, Inc., Wallingford, Conn., 1975-78; v.p. planning and devel. Norlin Corp., White Plains, N.Y., 1978-81; founder, exec. v.p. Integrated Genetics, Inc., 1981-85; founder, bd. dirs. Organogenesis Inc., 1985-89; founder, pres. TSI Corp., 1987-90, Protarga, Inc., 1990-93; biotech. cons., 1995—; pres., dir. VIMRX Pharms., Inc., Stamford, Conn., 1994-95. Chmn. Bio-Brite, Inc., 1990—; adj. prof. NYU, Boston U., Yale U. Bd. overseers Boston Symphony Orch., 1993—2002; asst. dir. Campaign for Yale, 1978; trustee Quinsigamond Coll., 1989—92. Capt. USAF, 1955—58. Mem.: Assn. Yale U. Alumni (bd. dirs.), Russell Trust Assn., Somerset Club, Hawk's Nest Golf Club, Kittansett Club, Sippican Tennis Club, Tau Beta Pi. Episcopalian.

HUDSON, FREDERICK BERNARD, management consultant; b. Chgo., Oct. 29, 1947; s. Joseph Thomas and Nellie (Parham) H.; m. Yvonne Marjorie Hudson, July 9, 1994. BA, Wayne State U., 1969; postgrad., Yale U., 1969—70; MA, New Sch. Social Rsch., 1975. Registered city planner, Am. Inst. City Planners, 1979. Adminstr. cmty. rels. for N.J. Odyssey Ho., N.Y.C., 1971-73; spl. program asst. Nat. Urban League, N.Y.C., 1973-75; rsch. assoc. Afram Assocs., N.Y.C., 1975; program cons. City Univ. Rsch. Found., N.Y.C., 1975-76; project dir. Elon Michels and Assocs., Detroit, 1977—78; staff analyst Detroit City Coun., 1978-79; vis. asst. prof., coord. So. Ill. U., Edwardsville, 1979-80; dir. pub. rels. Frederick Douglass Creative Arts Ctr., N.Y.C., 1981-82; ednl. officer Am. Bus. Inst., N.Y.C., 1986-89; pres. Centaur Consultants, N.Y.C., 1983—, Spectrum Imports, 1996—. Mem. faculty Coll. New Rochelle, So. Ill. U., Ednl. Found. Dist. Coun. 37 (local of Am. Fedn. State, County and Mcpl. Employees); Am. Bus. Inst. Mgmt. and Comm. cons. to Coro Found., Asia Pacific Found., NuArtist Prodns., Art Mattan Prod., Milw. Ednl. Found., New Future Found., MicroBanking Network, AT & T, Reality Ho., Nat. Drug Prevention Week, Mothers of Harlem Bus. Incubator, Fed. Emergency Mgmt. Adminstrn., Yale Coun. Cmty. Affairs, N.J. Dept.

Correction, candidates for state and nat. polit. offices; expert witness, presenter in field Prodr. (TV program) Take It to the Hill, 1995-99; guest and commentator numerous TV and radio programs, including HBO and ABC News; contbr. opinion columns to mags., poems to lit. jours. and anthology; co-author (jazz oratorio) Let Us Now Praise Righteous Men, 1969; author: What's In a Number? An Evaluation of a Title I Program, 1975, A Business Plan for a Multi-National Entertainment E-Commerce Business, 2000; screenwriter (TV drama) Things We Take, 1992; prodr. (TV series) The Undercover Man, 1993-95 Organizer Nat. Action Network, 1995—, Oct. 22 Movement, 2000—, Internat. Action Ctr., 2000—; hon. chmn. small bus. adv. coun. Nat. Rep. Congl. Com. Recipient Mayor's commendation, City of Newark, 1974, Emerging New Writer award, PEN, 1984, Outstanding Achievement in Poetry Silver award cup Internat. Soc. Poets, 2002, 03; name inscribed on Wall of Tolerance, Montgomery, Ala., 2002. Mem. Am. Mgmt. Assn., Film Video Arts Assn., Mensa. Office: Centaur Consultants 1510 E 172 St Ste 4 Bronx NY 10472 Office Phone: 718-378-7109. E-mail: fhdsn@aol.com.

HUDSON, G. ELIZABETH, musicologist; b. Walnut Creek, Calif., Dec. 31, 1961; d. Keith P. and Arlene D. Hudson; m. Stephan M. Prock, Sept. 1, 1991; children: Kaiulani Rose, Chloe Lynne. BA, Smith Coll., 1986; MA, Cornell U., 1991, PhD, 1993. Assoc. prof. dept. music U. Va., Charlottesville, 1991—. Book rev. editor The Opera Quar., 1992-94; contbr. articles to profl. jours.; editor: Giuseppe Verdi: Il Corsaro, 1997. NEH fellow, 1994, Am. Musicol. Soc. fellow, 1991. Mem. Am. Musicol. Soc. Office: Univ of Virginia Dept Music 112 Old Cabell Hall Charlottesville VA 22903

HUDSON, HAROLD JORDON, JR., retired insurance executive; b. Kansas City, Mo., Mar. 10, 1924; s. Harold Jordan and Fannie (Jenkins) H.; m. Patricia Louise Orr, Oct. 1, 1949. BS, U. Mo., 1945, LL.B., 1948; grad., Advanced Mgmt. Program, Harvard U., 1968. Bar: Mo. 1948. Practiced in, Kansas City, until 1952; atty. Comml. Union Co., Kansas City, 1952-53, Cleve., 1953-56; with Gen. Reins. Corp., N.Y.C., 1956-83, asst. sec., 1958-61, sec., 1961-62, v.p., 1963-68, sr. v.p., 1968-70, pres., 1970-71, 1971-72, chief exec. officer, 1971-83, chmn., 1973-83, also dir. Chmn. Reins. Assn. Am., 1975-76. Mem. Mo. Bar, Phi Delta Phi, Kappa Alpha. Clubs: Brook (N.Y.C.); Indian Harbor Yacht, Greenwich Country (Greenwich, Conn.); Cat Cay Yacht (Bahamas); Card Sound Golf. Office: PO Box 10350 Stamford CT 06904-2350 Personal E-mail: hhudii@aol.com.

HUDSON, JEFFREY REID, lawyer; b. Santa Monica, Calif., Mar. 15, 1952; s. Caswell Hadden and Donna Rita (Mazzulla) H.; children: Joan Louise, Reid Adams. BA, Claremont McKenna Coll., 1974; JD, Harvard U., 1978. Bar: Calif. 1978. Assoc. Gibson, Dunn & Crutcher, L.A., 1978-85, ptnr., 1986—. Office: Gibson Dunn & Crutcher 333 S Grand Ave Ste 4700 Los Angeles CA 90071-3197

HUDSON, JERRY E., foundation administrator; b. Chattanooga, Mar. 3, 1938; s. Clarence E. and Laura (Campbell) H.; m. Myra Ann Jared, June 11, 1957; children: Judith, Laura, Janet, Angela. BA, David Lipscomb Coll., 1959; MA, Tulane U., 1961, PhD, 1965; LL.D. (hon.), Pepperdine U., 1983; D of Comm. (hon.), Tokyo Internat. U., 1997; LHD (hon.), U. Portland, 1997, Willamette U., 1997. Systems engr. IBM, Atlanta, 1961; prof. Coll. Arts and Scis., Pepperdine U., 1962-75; provost, dean Coll. Arts and Scis., Malibu Campus, Pepperdine U., 1971-75; pres. Hamline U., St. Paul, 1975-80, Willamette U., Salem, Oreg., 1980-97; exec. v.p. Collins Found., Portland, Oreg., 1997—. Dir. Portland Gen. Co., E.I.I.A. Bd. dirs. PGE Found. Mem. Nat. Assn. Ind. Colls. (bd. dirs.), Phi Alpha Theta. Office: Collins Found 1618 SW 1st Ave Portland OR 97201-5752 Home: 2020 SW Market Street Dr Apt 402 Portland OR 97201-7719 E-mail: jhudson@collinsfoundation.org.

HUDSON, JOHN BOSWELL, sociologist, educator; b. Decatur, Ill., Dec. 1, 1930; s. George Taylor and Margaret Shirley (Boswell) H.; m. Sandra Lee Cermak, Mar. 16, 1957; children: Scott Martin, Bradford Taylor. Student, Reed Coll., 1948-51; BA, U. Oreg., 1952; MA, U. Wash., 1956; postgrad., Cornell U., 1957-60, PhD, 1963. Asst. prof. sociology Humboldt State U., Arcata, Calif., 1960-61, Cornell U., Ithaca, N.Y., 1961-64, Lehigh U., Bethlehem, Pa., 1964-65, Syracuse (N.Y.) U., 1965-66; rsch. assoc. Harvard U., 1966-67; rsch. sociologist Mass. Dept. Mental Health, Boston, 1967-68; sr. sociologist Abt Assocs., Inc., Cambridge, Mass., 1968-69; prof. sociology Trent U., Peterborough, Ont., Can., 1969-73; asst. adminstr. Brockton (Mass.) Multi-Svc. Ctr., 1973-74; lectr. bus. adminstrn. Northeastern U., Boston, 1974-76; cons. Cambridge, 1976-78; pres., treas. Cambridge Condominium Collaborative, Inc., 1978-86, chmn., treas., 1986-93; dir. edn. and tng. DeWolfe New Eng., 1994, v.p. for organizational devel., 1995-97. Vis. scientist dept. behavioral scis. Harvard Sch. Pub. Health, summers 1971, 72, winter-spring, 1973; lectr. real estate Boston U., 1988-90. Author: Creativity and Innovation, 1966, Functional Analysis as a Strategy for Studying Social Change and Stability, 1967, Policy-Oriented Basic Research, 1969, Social Policy and Theoretical Sociology, 1970, An Empirical Validation of Hypothesis-Generating Strategies, 1970, Social Structure and Culture: A Conceptual Analysis, 1971, Perspectives on Offender Rehabilitation, 1971, The Structure of Innovation, 1971, A Proposal for a Center of Innovation, 1971, Nursing Education in Transition, 1972, Residential Care for the Mentally Retarded, 1972, The Interface Between Theory and Practice, 1979, Theory, Practice, and Paradigm Shifts, 1992. Mem. mgmt. com. Sch. Nursing, Peterborough Civic Hosp., 1970-72; bd. dirs. Brockton Area Assn. for Retarded Citizens, 1974-75; mem. City Mgr.'s Cable TV Adv. Com., Cambridge, 1979-85; chmn. Cambridge Condominium Network, 1979-86; docent U. Iowa Mus. Art, 1998-2002; bd. dirs. Coun. Internat. Visitors to Iowa Cities, 1999-2000, Iowa Arts Coun., 2002--; elected del. Imagine Iowa 2010, 2001. Social Sci. Rsch. Coun. fellow Stanford U., summer 1964; Recipient award of merit Peterborough Assn. for Mentally Retarded, 1972; named Cambridge Realtor of Yr., Greater Boston Real Estate Bd., 1993; Larry Echholt Award for Arts/Culture Advocacy, Johnson County Cultural Alliance, Iowa, 2002. Mem. Nat. Assn. Realtors (cert. real estate brokerage mgr. 1989, cert. internat. property specialist 1994, cert. residential specialist 1994, chair internat. adv. group 1997, mem. internat. ops. com. 1997-98), Cmty. Assns. Inst. (named Colleague of Yr. New Eng. chpt. 1985), New Eng. Sociol. Assn. (treas. 1979-82, v.p. 1987-90, pres.-elect 1990-91, pres. 1991-92, Pioneer award 1991). Home: 782 Westside Dr Iowa City IA 52246-4341 E-mail: John.B.Hudson@att.net.

HUDSON, JOHN IRVIN, retired career officer; b. Louisville, Oct. 12, 1932; s. Irvin Hudson and Elizabeth (Reid) Hudson Hornbeck; m. Zetta Ann Yates, June 27, 1954; children: Reid Irvin, Lori Ann, John Yates, Clark Ray BS in Bus. Mgmt., Murray State U., 1971. Commd. 2nd lt. USMC, 1954, advanced through grades to lt. gen., 1987; comdg. officer Marine Fighter Attack Squadron 115, Vietnam, 1968, Marine Corps Air Sta., Yuma, Ariz., 1977-80; asst. wing comdr. 2nd Marine Air Wing, Cherry Point, N.C., 1980-81; comdg. gen. Landing Force Tng. Command/At.,4th Marine Amphibious Brigade, Norfolk, Va., 1981-83, 3rd Marine Aircraft Wing, El Toro, Calif., 1985-87, First Marine Amphibious Force, Campen, Calif., 1986-87; dep. chief staff for manpower Hdqrs. USMC, Washington, 1987-89; dir. U.S. Marine Corps Edn. Ctr., Quantico, Va., 1983-85; ret. active duty Hdqrs. USMC, Washington, 1989. Apptd. to Ariz. State Transp. Bd., 1994-2000, chmn. 1999; apptd. commr. Ariz. Power Authority, 2000—; apptd. bd. dirs. Greater Yuma Port Authority, chmn., 2000-02; operating bd. dirs. Yuma Regional Med. Ctr., 2001—. Decorated DFC, DSM, Bronze Star, Air medals, Silver Hawk; flew 308 combat missions in Vietnam in F-4 Phantom; inductee Early and Pioneer Naval Aviators' Assn., 1998. Mem. VFW, Golden Eagles, Marine Corps Aviation Assn. (life), Marine Corps Assn., Marine Corps Hist. Soc., Order of Daedalians (life). Avocations: sports, sailing, hunting, fishing. Home: 12439 E Del Rico Yuma AZ 85367-7366 Personal E-mail: johnihudson@aol.com.

HUDSON, JOHN LESTER, chemical engineering professor; b. Chgo., 1937; s. John Jones and Linda Madeline (Panozzo) H.; m. Janette Glenore Caton, June 29, 1963; children: Ann, Barbara, Sarah. BS, U. Ill., 1959; MS in Engring., Princeton U., 1960; PhD, Northwestern U., 1962. Registered profl. engr., Ill. Asst. prof. chm. engring. U. Ill.-Urbana, 1963-69, assoc. prof., 1969-75; prof., chmn. dept. chem. engring. U. Va., Charlottesville, 1975-85, mem. Ctr Advanced Studies, 1985-86, prof., 1986-88, Wills Johnson prof., 1988—. Mgr. Ill. Div. Air Pollution Control, Springfield, 1974-75; cons. to various industires and govt. agys., 1966— Contbr. articles to profl. jours. Recipient sr. Humboldt prize, 1989; NSF fellow, 1962, Fulbright fellow, 1961-63, 82-83. Mem. AIChE (Wilhelm award 1991), Am. Chem. Soc. Home: 1920 Thomson Rd Charlottesville VA 22903-2419 Office: U Va Dept Chem Engring 102 Engineers Wy Box 400741 Charlottesville VA 22904-4741 Business E-Mail: hudson@virginia.edu.

HUDSON, KATE, actress; b. L.A., Calif., Apr. 19, 1979; d. Bill Hudson and Goldie Hawn; m. Chris Robinson, Dec. 31, 2000; 1 child. Co-head (with Kurt Russell, Goldie Hawn, Oliver Hudson) Cosmic Entertainment, 2003. Actor: (films) Desert Blue, 1998, Ricochet River, 1998, 200 Cigarettes, 1999, About Adam, 2000, Gossip, 2000, Almost Famous, 2000 (Golden Globe award for Best Supporting Actress, 2001), Dr. T and the Women, 2000, The Cutting Room, 2001, The Four Feathers, 2002, How to Lose a Guy in 10 Days, 2003, Alex and Emma, 2003, Le Divorce, 2003, Raising Helen, 2004, The Skeleton Key, 2005; (TV series) Party of Five, 1996, EZ Streets, 1997; exec. prodr.: (TV films) 14 Hours, 2005. Named one of Most Powerful People in Hollywood, Premiere mag., 2003.*

HUDSON, KATHERINE MARY, manufacturing executive; b. Rochester, N.Y., Jan. 19, 1947; d. Edward Klock and Helen Mary (Rubacha) Nellis; m. Robert Orneal Hudson, Sept. 13, 1980; 1 child, Robert Klock. Student, Oberlin coll., 1964-66; BS in Mgmt., Ind. U., 1968; postgrad., Cornell U., 1968-69. Various positions in fin., investor rels., communications, gen. mgr. instant photography Eastman Kodak Co., Rochester, 1970-87, chief info. officer, 1988-91, v.p., gen. mgr. printing and pub. imaging, 1991-93; pres., CEO Brady Corp., Milw., 1994—2003, chmn. bd., 2003. Bd. dirs. CNH Global N.V., Charming Shoppes, Inc. Trustee Alverno Coll., 1994—; bd. dirs. Med. Coll. Wis., 1995—. Recipient Chief of the Yr. award Info. Week Mag., 1990, Athena award Rochester C. of C., 1992, WESG Breaking Glass Ceiling award, 1993, Sacajewea award, 1995; Lehman fellow N.Y. State, 1968; named Wis. Bus. Leader of Yr., 1995. Republican. Avocations: golf, fishing, creative writing. E-mail: knh53092@yahoo.com.

HUDSON, LEONARD DEAN, physician; b. Everett, Wash., May 7, 1938; s. Marshall W. and Blanche V. (Morgan) H.; children: Sean Marshall, Margaret Kahle, Sherry Elizabeth, Kevin Arthur. BS, Wash. State U., Pullman, 1960; MD, U. Wash., Seattle, 1964. Diplomate: Am. Bd. Internal Medicine (pulmonary disease). Intern Bellevue Hosp. Ctr., N.Y.C., 1964-65; resident in internal medicine N.Y. Hosp., 1965-66, U. Wash. Hosps., 1968-69; chief resident Harborview Med. Ctr., Seattle; also instr. U. Wash. Med. Sch., 1967-70; Am. Thoracic Soc. fellow in pulmonary diseases U. Colo. Med. Ctr., 1970-71, instr., then asst. prof. medicine, 1971-73; mem. faculty U. Wash. Med. Ctr., 1973—, assoc. prof. medicine, 1976-82, prof., 1982—, head pulmonary critical care medicine divsn., 1985—2003; endowed chair in pulmonary disease rsch. U. Wash. Hosps., 1999—; chief pulmonary critical care medicine divsn., med. dir. MICU, Harborview Med. Ctr., 1976-86. Chmn. Tb adv. com. Wash. Dept. Social and Health Svcs. Author papers, revs. in field. With USPHS, 1966-68. Named Outstanding Resident, Harborview Med. Ctr. Fellow ACP, Am. Coll. Chest Physicians (state gov. 1980-87); mem. Am. Fedn. Clin. Rsch., Am. Thoracic Soc. (sec.-treas. 1983-84, v.p. 1993-94, pres.-elect 1994-95, pres. 1995-96), Western Soc. Clin. Rsch., Assn. Am. Physicians, Wash. Lung. Assn. (dir., Vol. Hall of Fame 1977), Wash. Thoracic Soc., Seattle Flounders Soc., Phi Beta Kappa. Democrat. Office: Harborview Med Ctr Mailbox 359762 325 9th Ave Seattle WA 98104-2420

HUDSON, MANLEY O., JR., lawyer; b. Boston, June 25, 1932; s. Manley O. and Janet (Aldrich) H.; m. Olivia d'Ormesson, July 1, 1971 (dec. May 2000); children: Nicholas Aldrich, Antonia Maria Conchita. AB, Harvard U., 1953, LL.B., 1956. Bar: N.Y. 1964. Law clk. Justice Stanley Reed, U.S. Supreme Ct., Washington, 1956-57; assoc. Cleary, Gottlieb, Steen & Hamilton, 1958-68, ptnr. N.Y.C., London, Paris, 1968—2001. Contbr. articles to profl. jours. Mem. Coun. Fgn. Rels., Century Assn. Office: Cleary Gottlieb Steen & Hamilton City Place House 55 Basinghall St London EC2V 5EH England Business E-Mail: mhudson@cgsh.com.

HUDSON, MARGUERITE W., secondary school educator; b. Pitkin, La., June 10, 1929; BS, Northwestern State U., 1949; MA in Edn., No. Colo. U., 1951; MA in English Arts, Northwestern State U., 1969. Tchr. scis. Ouachita Parish H.S., Monroe, La., 1949—50, Haynesville (La.) High Sch., 1951—61, Bossier High Sch., Bossier City, La., 1961—69; instr. English Bossier Parish C.C., Bossier City, 1970—79, Centenary Coll., Shreveport, La., 1982—83; tchr., supr. Ga. Mil. Acad., Barksdale AFB, 1980—90; sch. bd. mem., pres. Bossier Sch. Bd., Benton, La., 1991—98; ret., 1991. Named one of 100 Outstanding Women of Century. Mem.: NEA, La. Educators Assn. Democrat. Baptist. Avocation: water skiing, dancing, creative writing class, travel, Bridge. Home: 4497 Palmetto Rd Benton LA 71006

HUDSON, MCKINLEY, retired military officer, retired zoological park administrator; b. Cin., May 13, 1941; BS, Ctrl. State U., Wilberforce, Ohio, 1963; MS, So. Ill. U., 1974; MA, Naval War Coll., Newport, R.I., 1986. Commd. 2d lt. U.S. Army, 1963, advanced through grades to col., 1985, retired, 1993, commdr. 548th composite support battalion, 1983-85, commdr. 80th area support group Chevres, Belgium, 1986-88, chief of staff mil. traffic mgmt. command Oakland, Calif., 1988-93; dep. dir. Nat. Zoological Park Smithsonian Instn., Washington, 1994—2002. Decorated Legion of Merit, Bronze Star with Oak Leaf cluster. Mem. Assn. U.S. Army, Assn. Am. Zoos and Aquariums, U.S. Army Transp. Corps. Regiment (Disting. Mem. Regiment 1993), Nat. Defense Transp. Assn. (Nat. award for disting. svc. 1992), Kappa Alpha Psi. Home: 13 Cabin Creek Ct Burtonsville MD 20866

HUDSON, MICHAEL CRAIG, political science professor; b. New Haven, June 2, 1938; s. Robert Bowman and Joan (Loram) H.; m. Vera George Wahbe, June 16, 1963; children: Leila Olga, Aida Joan. BA with honors, Swarthmore Coll., 1959; MA, Yale U., 1960, PhD, 1964; Cert. in Arabic, Princeton U., 1961. History tchr. Am. Community Sch., Beirut, 1962-63; instr. Swarthmore (Pa.) Coll., 1963-64; asst. prof. Bklyn. Coll., CUNY, N.Y.C., 1964-70; assoc. prof. Johns Hopkins U., Sch. Advanced Internat. Studies, Washington, 1970-75; assoc. to prof. Georgetown U., Washington, 1975—; dir. Georgetown U. Ctr. for Contemporary Arab Studies, Washington, 1976—89, 1999—2000, 2003—; Seif Ghobash prof. of Arab studies Sch. Fgn. Svc. Georgetown U., Washington, 1980—. Bd. dirs. Nat. Coun. on U.S./Arab Rels., Washington; cons., lectr. U.S. State Dept.; commentator on Mid. Ea. affairs to U.S. and internat. news media; lectr. at univs. in Mid. East, Europe, Japan, China, Australia. Mem. editl. bd. Internat. Jour. of Mid. East Studies, 1980-86, Cambridge U. Press Mid. East Studies, 1989-98; author: The Precarious Republic (Lebanon), 1968, Arab Politics: The Search for Legitimacy, 1977; co-author: World Handbook of Political and Social Indicators, 1972; editor: The Palestinians: New Directions, 1990, Middle East Dilemma: The Politics and Economics of Arab Integration, 1999; contbr. numerous articles to jours. in field. Bd. dirs Ctr. for Mid. East Studies, Macquarie U., Sydney, Australia; bd. trustees Rene Moawad Found., Lebanon. Robert R. McCormick fellow Yale U., 1959-63, fellow Ford Found., 1970-71, Guggenheim fellow, 1975-76, Fulbright fellow, 1994; grantee Am. Philos. Soc., 1965, 68. Fellow Mid. East Studies Assn. of N.Am. (pres. 1987); mem. The Mid. East Inst., Am. Polit. Sci. Assn., Internat. Studies Assn., Coun. on Fgn. Rels., Am. Inst. Yemeni Studies. Avocations: drawing, painting, book collecting, swimming, running. Office: Georgetown U Ctr for Contemporary Arab Studies Sch Fgn Svc 241 Intercultural Ctr Washington DC 20057-1020 Business E-Mail: hudsonm@georgetown.edu.

HUDSON, MICHEL COLETTE, management consultant; b. Houston; d. Arthur James and Dorothy Ann (Newton) Rutrough; m. Scott V. Hudson; 1 child, David. BA, U. St. Thomas, 1982. Cert. fund raising exec. CFRE Profl. Certification Bd., 2001. Dir. devel. info. sys. U. St. Thomas, Houston, 1983—85; coord. alumni/devel. rsch. and records U. Mo., Columbia, 1987—90, mgr. alumni/devel. rsch. and records, 1990—95; dir. devel. svcs. Seton Healthcare Network, Austin, Tex., 1995—97, v.p. devel. svcs., 1997—2001; campaign mgr. centennial campaigns The Seton Fund, Austin, 2001—01; owner Gnu Gap Consulting, Round Rock, Tex., 2001—. Online instr. FUNDCLASS, 1998, 2003; instr. fund raising mgmt. cert. program U. Tex., Austin, 2000—; instr. Austin C.C. Ctr. for Cmty.-Based and Nonprofit Orgns., 2003; presenter in field. Contbr. articles to profl. jours.; editor (and co-author): Prospect Research Fundamentals, 1997. Membership svcs. coord., hospitality chair Columbia Art League, 1993—95; v.p. Columbia Choral Ensemble, 1994—95. Mem.: DAR, Writers League Tex. (fundraising com. 1998—99), Am. Prospect Rsch. Assn.-Mo. Chpt. (pres., v.p., newsletter editor/pub. 1992—95), Internat. Assn. Theater and Stage Employees (trustee 1994—95), Assn. Profl. Rschrs. for Advancement (pres., conf. chair, membership svcs. dir. 1994—2001, nominations com. 2002, disting. svc. award com. mem. 2004—05, Disting. Svc. award 2003), Cir. of Friends (sec./publ. design 1997—2003). Office: Gnu Gap Consulting 1805 Gnu Gap Round Rock TX 78664 Personal E-mail: gnugap@yahoo.com.

HUDSON, MILES, retired special education educator; b. Brewer, Maine, Aug. 22, 1940; s. Fredrick and Elsie (Bailey) H. BS, U. Maine, Farmington, 1963. Cert. spl. edn. tchr., Maine, Mass. Founder, program coord. spl. edn. program, Millinocket, Maine, 1963-68; founder spl. edn. class MDI H.S., Bar Harbor, Maine, 1968-70; unit leader spl. edn. Methuen (Mass.) Pub. Schs., 1970-74; vocat. spl. edn. tchr. Minuteman Vocat. Tech. H.S., Lexington, Mass., 1974-80; spl. edn. tchr. Dr. Franklin Perkins Schs., Lancaster, Mass., 1980-83; head tchr. for autistic and psychotic children Devereaux Found., Rutland, Mass., 1985-86; vocat. instr. Bangor (Maine) Mental Health Inst., 1986-87; program dir. Capacito Learning Ctr., Ellsworth, Maine, 1986-87; spl. edn. tchr., founder summer program Town of Jonesport (Maine) Schs., 1987-90; ret., 1992. Mem. Countywide Regional Tchr. Support Com. Author: Survey of Special Education Classes in Maine, 1963. Home: 307 S Lubec Rd Lubec ME 04652-9627 E-mail: mlshdn@maineline.net.

HUDSON, PHYLLIS JANECKE, librarian; b. Rock Island, Ill., Aug. 16, 1933; d. Clair Gordon and Helen Marie (Caffery) Janecke; m. Paul Alfred Hudson, Apr. 9, 1955; children: Helen Leora, Nancy Jan, Paula Kay, J. Phillip, Danae Claire. BS, U. Ill., 1964; MLS, 1970. Reference librarian Edn. Library U. Ill., Urbana, 1969-71, asst. librarian, 1971-72; head circulation Library U. Cen. Fla., Orlando, 1972-73, cataloger, 1973-74, reference librarian, 1974—. Editor: (column) Florida Libraries, 1978; contbr. articles to profl. jours. Mem. ALA, Fla. Library Assn., Spl. Library Assn., Fla. Online Users Group, Fla. Assn. Coll. and Research Libraries (pres. 1982-83), United Faculty of Fla. (pres. U. Cen. Fla. chpt. 1981-83, 1987-88, lobbyist 1981-83, v.p. 1984-86, chief negotiator state univ. system 1984-86), Fla. Teaching Profession Assn. of NEA (bd. dirs. 1987-89), NOW (officer Seminole County chpt. 1980-82). Democrat Office: U Central Fla 203 Library Orlando FL 32816-0001 Office Phone: 407-823-2584. Business E-Mail: phudson@mail.ucf.edu.

HUDSON, R. READ, lawyer, food products executive; b. Little Rock, Apr. 11, 1958; BSBA, U. Ark., 1980, JD, 1987; LLM, Boston U., 1988. Bar: Ark. 1988, U.S. Ct. Appeals (8th cir.) 1989, U.S. Dist. Ct. (ea. and we. dists.) Ark. 1991. With Tyson Foods, Inc., 1992—, sec., sr. counsel Springdale, Ark., 1998—. Mem. ABA (mem. sect. on bus. law), Ark. Bar Assn., Washington County Bar Assn. Office: PO Box 2020 2210 W Oaklawn Dr Springdale AR 72762-6900

HUDSON, RALPH P., physicist; b. Wellingborough, Eng., Oct. 14, 1924; came to U.S., 1949, naturalized, 1960. s. Harold and Ada (Jenkinson) H.; m. Nancy Brisby, July 9, 1947; children: Geoffrey R., Wendy E. BA, Merton Coll., Oxford U., 1944, MA, PhD, Oxford U., 1949; DSc (hon.), Purdue U., 2001. Sci. officer U.K. Ministry Supply, Birmingham, Eng., Montreal, Que. and Chalk River, Ont., Can., 1944-46; vis. lectr. Purdue U., 1949-50, asst. prof., 1950-51; with Nat. Bur. Standards, Washington, 1951-80, chief cryogenic physics sect., 1954-61, chief heat div., 1961-78; dep. dir. Center for Absolute Phys. Quantities, 1978-80; dir. publs. Internat. Bur. Weights and Measures, Sèvres, France, 1980-89; program dir. low temperature physics NSF, Washington, 1989-92. Cons. in field, 1993—; guest worker fundamental constants data ctr. Nat. Inst. Stds. & Tech., 1998—. Editor: Metrologia, 1980-89, editl. cons., 1995—. Mem. U.K. Home Guard, 1941-43, U.K. Atomic Energy Program, 1944-46. Recipient Silver and Gold medals Dept. Commerce, 1957; Samuel Wesley Stratton award Nat. Bur. Standards, 1964; Edward U. Condon award, 1976; Guggenheim fellow, 1960-61 Fellow Am. Phys. Soc., Franklin Inst. (John Price Wetherill medal 1962); mem. Cosmos Club (Washington). Achievements include spl. rsch. on behavior of matter near absolute zero temperature; first demonstrated the non-conservation of parity in the weak interactions. Home: 3152 Gracefield Rd Apt G23 Silver Spring MD 20904 E-mail: ralph.hudson@nist.gov.

HUDSON, RICHARD ALBERT, music educator, musicologist, composer; b. Alma, Mich., Mar. 19, 1924; s. Albert and Ruth (Ellis) Hudson. BS, Calif. Inst. Tech., 1944; BMus, Oberlin Conservatory of Music, 1949; MMus, Syracuse U., 1951; PhD, UCLA, 1967. Assoc. prof. organ and music theory Converse Coll., Spartanburg, SC, 1949—50; instr. organ and music theory Oberlin (Ohio) Conservatory of Music, 1953—55; pvt. tchr. organ L.A., Calif., 1955—59; libr. asst. UCLA, 1955—66, assoc. prof. music, music libr., 1967—74, prof. music, 1974—91, emeritus prof. music, 1991—. Author: Passacaglio and Ciaccona, 1981; editor: The Folia, the Saraband, the Passacaglia, and the Chaconne (4 vols.), 1982; author: The Allemande, the Balletto, and the Tanz (2 vols.), 1986, Stolen Time: The History of Tempo Rubato, 1994, paperback edit., 1997; editor: (music) Benedict Schultheiss: The Complete Keyboard Works, 1993; composer: Trios for Organ, 2 vols., 1971—72, reprinted, 1997, Suite of Organ Carols, 1976, Hymn Preludes and Free Accompaniments, 1978, Hymn Trios for the New Organist (4 vols.), 1994—95, The Time of Christmas, 1997; contbr. articles to New Grove Dictionary, 1980, 2d edit., 2001 and to profl. jours. Ensign USN, 1943—46. Grantee, Am. Coun. Learned Socs., 1973—74; Fulbright scholar, The Netherlands, 1952—53. Mem.: Am. Guild Organists, Internat. Musicol. Soc., Am. Musicol. Soc. Home: 7036 Bevis Ave Van Nuys CA 91405-3007 Office: UCLA Dept Musicology 2443 Schoenberg Hall Los Angeles CA 90095-1623 Office Phone: 310-206-3187. Business E-Mail: hudson@ucla.edu.

HUDSON, RICHARD L., retired adult education educator, minister; b. Watertown, NY, Dec. 1, 1920; s. Milo Alfred and Marion (Davidson) Hudson; m. Beatrice Evalin Olson, Apr. 23, 1955; children: Margery Elise, Pamela Kristine. AB, Syracuse U., 1944, PhD, 1970; BD, Yale U., 1947, STM, 1950. Ordained to ministry United Meth. Ch., 1945. Asst. min. Rome (NY) Meth. Ch., 1946-48, Meth. Ch., Parish, NY, 1950-54; commentator Religion Makes News, Sta. WSYR, Syracuse, NY; dir. pub. rels. Syracuse Area United Meth. Ch., 1954-56; min. Meth. Ch., Carthage, NY, 1956-58; Cokesbury fellow, grad. asst. Syracuse U., 1958-61; mem. faculty Wyoming Sem., Kingston, Pa., 1961-64, New Eng. Coll., Henniker, NH, 1964-83, prof., 1971-83, prof. emeritus, 1983—, dean humanities, 1970-71. Adj. prof. history Post Coll., Waterbury, Conn., 1985—91, Quinnipiac Coll., Hamden, Conn., 1987—97. Author: A Burden for Souls, 1950, A Student's Guide to the New Testament, 1963, The Challenge of Dissent, 1970; editor: The ONly Henniker on Earth, 1980. Chmn. Henniker HIst. Soc., 1976—83; docent Canterbury Shaker Village, 1975—83, New Haven Colony Hist. Soc., 1984—93, bd. dirs., 1988—90. Mem.: Nat. Assn. Scholars, Mayflower Soc., Tabard, Tau Theta Upsilon, Theta Chi Beta. Home and Office: 44 Cloudland Rd North Haven CT 06473-4006

HUDSON, ROBERT PAUL, medical educator; b. Kansas City, Feb. 23, 1926; s. Chester Lloyd and Jean (Emerson) H.; m. Olive Jean Grimes, Aug. 1, 1948 (div. 1963); children: Robert E., Donald K., Timothy M.; m. Martha Isabelle Holter, July 10, 1965; children: Stephen, Laurel. BA, U. Kans., 1949, MD, 1952; MA, Johns Hopkins U., 1966. Instr. U. Kans., Kansas City, 1958-59, assoc. in medicine, 1959-63, asst. prof., 1964-69, assoc. prof., 1969—, prof., chmn. history of medicine, 1969-95, ret. Author: Disease and Its Control, 1983; mem. editl. bd. Bull. History of Medicine, Balt., 1981-94;

contbr. articles to profl. jours. 1st lt. U.S. Army, 1953-55. Master ACP; mem. Am. Assn. for History of Medicine (pres. 1984-86), Am. Osler Soc. (bd. govs., pres. 1987-88). Home: 12925 S Frontier Rd Olathe KS 66061-8647 Office: Kans U Med Ctr 39th And Rainbow Blvd Kansas City KS 66160-0001 E-mail: lastroma@earthlink.net.

HUDSON, RONALD MORGAN, aviation planner; b. Anniston, Ala., May 7, 1954; s. James Alphus and Mildred Christine (Morgan) H.; m. Marsha Carol Smith, Dec. 27, 1974 (div. Oct. 1989); children: Jereme Brandon, Sara Elizabeth; m. Connie M. Luckey, Nov. 13, 1993. BS in Aviation Mgmt., Auburn U., 1976. Aviation planner Wainwright Engring. Co., Montgomery, Ala., 1978—81, Ralph Burke Assocs., Park Ridge, Ill., 1981—85; sr. assoc. mgr. aviation Knight Architects, Engrs., Planners, Inc., Chgo., 1985—96; assoc. ptnr. Hanson Profl. Svcs. Inc., Oak Brook, Ill., 1996—. Mem. Am. Planning Assn., Am. Inst. Cert. Planners, Am. Assn. Airport Execs., Ill. Pub. Airports Assn. Avocations: biking, travel. Home: 1710 E Oakton St Arlington Heights IL 60004-5000 E-mail: ronaldhudson@comcast.net.

HUDSON, ROXANNE FRANCES, reading professor, researcher; b. Portand, Jan. 18, 1967; d. Lloyd Ray Hudson and Andrea J. Martin; m. John G. Bellow, June 21, 1991. BA cum laude, Gonzaga U., 1989; MEd in Exceptional Children, Western Wash. U., 1994; PhD in Spl. Edn., U. Fla., 2002. Cert. tchr. various exceptionalities K-12 Fla. With U.S. Peace Corps, Philippines, 1989—90; tchr. Pike Sch., NH, 1990—91, Secret Harbor Sch., Anacortes, Wash., 1991—93; faculty asst. Western Wash. U., 1993—94; spl. edn. tchr. Wash. and Fla., 1994—99; course instr. asst., rsch. asst. dept. spl. edn. U. Fla., 1999—2001; asst. prof. dept. tchg. and learning Wash. State U., Pullman, 2002—04; asst. prof. childhood edn., reading, disability svcs. Fla. State U., Tallahassee, 2004—. Adj. lectr. dept. spl. edn. U. Fla., 2004; presenter in field. Contbr. articles to profl. jours. Recipient Pres.'s award, U. Fla., 2001, Initial Career award, U.S. Dept. Edn., Office Spl. Edn. Programs, 2004; grantee Carnegie Found. for Advancement of Tchg., 2002, Wash. State Office of Supt. Pub. Instrn., 2003, U.S. Dept. Edn., 2000, 2003;, 2004. Mem.: Am. Ednl. Rsch. Assn., Internat. Reading Assn., Soc. for Sci. Study of Reading, Coun. Exceptional Children (Exemplary Poster award 2003), Alpha Sigma Nu. Independent. Office: Fla Ctr Reading Rsch 227 N Bronough St Ste 7250 Tallahassee FL 32301 Office Phone: 850-921-0712.

HUDSON, ROY DAVAGE, retired pharmaceutical executive; b. Chattanooga, June 30, 1930; s. Roy and Everence (Wilkerson) H.; m. Constance Joan Taylor, Aug. 31, 1956; children: Hollye Lynne, David Kendall. BS, Livingstone Coll., 1955; MS, U. Mich., 1957, PhD, 1962; MA, Brown U., 1968; LL.D., Lehigh U., 1974, Princeton, 1975. Asst. prof. pharmacology U. Mich. Sch. Medicine, 1961-66; assoc. prof. med. sci. Brown U. Sch. Medicine, 1966-70, assoc. dean grad. sch., 1966-69; pres. Hampton U., 1970-76; dir. rsch. planning and coordination Parke, Davis Pharm. Co., Ann Arbor, Mich., 1976; v.p. rsch. planning Warner Lambert/Parke-Davis Pharm. Rsch. Divsn., Ann Arbor, 1977-79; mgr. sci. liaison Upjohn Co., Kalamazoo, 1979-81, mgr. CNS diseases rsch., 1981—85, dir. CNS diseases rsch., 1985-87; v.p. pharm. rsch. divsn. Europe Upjohn Co., Brussels, 1987-90; corp. v.p. pub. rels. Upjohn Co., Kalamazoo, 1990-92, ret., 1992. Adj. prof. Black Americana studies Western Mich. U., Kalamazoo, 1993; interim exec. dir., CEO Guidance Clinic, Kalamazoo, 1993; interim pres. Livingstone Coll., Salisbury, N.C., 1995-96; dir. Parke-Davis & Co., United Va. Bank-Citizens and Marine, United Va. Bankshares, Comerica Bank-Mich., Chesapeake and Potomac Telephone Co. of Va. Contbr. articles to profl. jours., chpts. to books. Mem. screening com. Danforth Grad. Fellowships, 1962-78; mem. adv. council Danforth Grad. Fellows program Danforth Found., 1972-79; chmn. Va. Com. on Selection Rhodes Scholars, 1973; mem. Commn. on Fed. Relations, Am. Council on Edn., 1972-76, bd. dirs., 1973-76; mem. adv. council to dir. NIH, 1974—; Mem. R.I. Commn. Econ. Devel., 1967-69, R.I. Urban League scholarship com., 1966-70; mem. inst. policy commn. So. Regional Edn. Bd.; bd. dirs. Afro-Am. Soc. Conn. Coll., Kalamazoo Area Math and Sci. Ctr., Kalamazoo Area Academic Achievement Program, ARC; bd. dirs., v.p. Nat. Assn. Equal Opportunity in Higher Edn.; trustee Brown U., Livingstone Coll., Peninsula United Community Services, Spelman Coll. Served with USAF, 1948-52. Recipient Disting. Alumni award Livingstone Coll.; Outstanding Civilian Service award U.S. Army.; Danforth Grad. fellow, 1955-61 Mem. Am. Soc. Pharmacology and Exptl. Therapeutics, Peninsula C. of C., NAACP (life, 1st v.p., Golden Heritage), AAAS, N.Y. Acad. Scis., Sigma Xi, Phi Kappa Phi, Phi Sigma, Beta Kappa Chi, Kappa Delta Pi, Omega Psi Phi, Gamma Alpha, Alpha Kappa Mu. Home: 7057 Oak Highlands Dr Kalamazoo MI 49009-7508 E-mail: r.d.hudson@worldnet.att.net.

HUDSON, SHEILA DONNETTE, waste management administrator; b. Dayton, Ohio, Feb. 9, 1961; d. James R. Hudson and Shirley Lawson Spangler. BS in Agr., U. Tenn., 1984, MPH in Occupl./Environ. Health & Safety, 1995. Cert. hazardous materials mgr. Rsch. technician Oak Ridge Nat. Lab., 1988-91; environ. technician Lockheed Martin Energy Sys., Oak Ridge, 1991-93, waste disposal coord., 1993-96; waste specialist Pacific We. Techs., Oak Ridge, 1996-97; mgr. transp./waste mgmt. Molten Metal Tech., Oak Ridge, 1997-98; mgr. transp./waste ops. Brit. Nuc. Fuel, Inc., Oak Ridge, 1998—2004, chmn., 2001, cons., 2004—. Democrat. Avocations: horseback riding, hiking, softball, canoeing, travel. Home: RR2 Box 212 Lewisburg WV 24901 Office: 234 Seneca Trail Ronceverte WV 24970 Fax: 423-241-5041. Office Phone: 304-661-1802. E-mail: shudson878@cs.com.

HUDSON, SHERRILL W., energy executive; m. Mary Ann Hudson; 3 children. With Deloitte and Touche, LLP, 1965—2002; mem. bd. TECO Energy, 2003—, CEO and Chmn., 2004—. Chmn. audit com. Standard Register, mem. compensation com.; past chmn. and exec. com. Fla. Internat. Univ. Office: TECO Energy 702 N Franklin St Tampa FL 33602*

HUDSON, STANTON HAROLD, JR., public relations executive, educator, academic administrator; b. Syracuse, NY, Jan. 28, 1951; s. Stanton Harold Sr. and Lucille (Shea) Hudson. Cert. in Lang. and History, U. Caen, France, 1970; BA in History/Polit. Sci., Canisius Coll., 1972; postgrad., SUNY, Buffalo, 1974—76, Syracuse U., 1995—98. Legis. asst., asst. pub. rels. dir. Erie County Rep. Com., Buffalo, 1971-73; dir. pub. rels. and fin. Greater Niagara Frontier Coun. Boy Scouts Am., Buffalo, 1977-79; dir. pub. rels. Ellis Singer & Webb Advt., Buffalo, 1979-80; asst. v.p., mgr. mktg. communications M&T Bank, Buffalo, 1980-85; exec. dir. Shea's Ctr. Performing Arts, Buffalo, 1986; pres. Hudson Mktg. Comm., Buffalo, 1987-88; sr. dir. advt. and pub. rels. Blue Cross Western N.Y., Inc., Buffalo, 1988-91; prin. Fredrickson & Hudson Assocs., Buffalo, 1991-92, Hudson & Assocs. Pub. Rels., Inc., Buffalo, 1992—. Asst. prof. Canisius Coll., 1993—2004, dir. grad. program orgnl. comm. & devel., 1995—2004; pres., CEO Am. Lung Assn. N.Y. State, 2004—. Editor: (newsletter) M&T Bank Observer, 1981—82 (Project PICA Grand award United Way Buffalo and Erie County); mng. editor: newsletter Blue Cross Ink, 1991. Chmn. pub. rels. and mktg. coms. Greater Buffalo chpt. ARC, 1989—92, bd. dirs. Greater Buffalo chpt., 1991—92; bd. dirs. ARC Blood Svcs., N.Y.-Pa. Region, 1993—2003; bd. dirs., exec. com. Greater Buffalo Opera Co., 1991—93; trustee, mktg. com. Theodore Roosevelt Inaugural Nat. Hist. Site Found., 1994—, co-chair 2001 Pan Am. Expo. centennial celebration com.; bd. dirs. Buffalo Coun. on World Affairs, 1994—2002, co-chair mktg. com., 1994—98; Success By 6 awareness com. Buffalo and Erie County United Way, 1997—2004, leadership coun., 1998—2004; bd. dirs. East Hill Found., 2000—; mem. Erie County Cultural Resources Adv. Bd., 2000—04, mem. exec. com., 2003—04; chmn. Erie Niagara Tobacco-Free Coalition, 1999—2000, 2003—04; mem. cap. campaign cabinet Burchfield Penney Art Ctr., 2004; bd. dirs. Ctr. Arts U. Buffalo, 2004. Recipient Gold Star award, Nat. Adv. Agy. Network, 1979, Gold Quill award, Internat. Assn. of Bus. Communicators, 1984, Francis V. Hanavan Meml. award, Am. Lung Assn. We. N.Y., 1997, CEO's award, 2002, Brotherhood/Sisterhood award, Nat. Conf. for Cmty. and Justice, 1999, Pres. award, Theodore Roosevelt Inaugural Nat. Hist. Site Found., 2002. Mem.: Am. Lung Assn. (bd. dirs. We. N.Y. affiliate 1984—2004, bd. dirs. N.Y. state constituent 1986—2004, pres.-elect 1995—98, pres. 1998—2004, nat. bd. dirs. 2000—04, mem. numerous panels and coms.), Western NY Grantmakers Assn. (v.p. 2003—04), Coordinated Care Mgmt. Corp. (mktg. com. 1994—98), Western N.Y. Comms. Steering Com. (chair 1991—92), Am. Mktg. Assn. (v.p. comms. Buffalo/Niagara chpt. 1991—92), Pub. Rels. Soc. Am. (treas. Buffalo/Niagara chpt. 1986—89, accredited 1989, pres.-elect 1989—90, pres. 1990—91, treas. N.E. dist. 1992, chair 1994, nat. nominating com. 1995, nat. assembly del. 1997—2000, universal accreditation bd. 1998—2000, mem. profl. devel. task force 2001—03, nat. assembly del. 2002—04, mem. Coll. Fellows 2002—, mem. ednl. affairs com. 2003—04, mem. ednl. affairs task force 2003—04, Practitioner of the Yr. Buffalo/Niagara chpt. 1993, Excalibur award 1993, 1994, 1995, 1997, Nat. Paul M. Lund Pub. Svc. award 1997, accredited 1989), Pub. Rels. Student Soc. Am. (nat. profl. advisor 1996—2000, nat. faculty advisor 2003—04), Rotary (past dir.). Avocations: theater, jazz, reading, travel. Office Phone: 518-453-0172. Personal E-mail: shud012851@aol.com. Business E-Mail: shudson@alanys.org.

HUDSON, TIMOTHY LEON, nursing educator; b. Macon, Ga., Sept. 30, 1971; s. Leon Radford Hudson and Janice Lynette Bassett; m. Rebecca Lynn McAfee, June 24, 1995; children: Blakely, Jacob. AS in Nursing, Ga. Southwestern U., 1993, BS in Nursing, 1995; MS in Adminstrn., Ctrl. Mich. U., 1999; MEd, Okla. U., 2001; PhD candidate in Bus. Adminstrn., Touro U. Internat., 2001—. Diplomate Am. Coll. Healthcare Execs., cert. healthcare exec. Am. Coll. Healthcare Execs.; CCRN, AACN, nursing adminstr., AACN. Charge nurse gen. surg. unit Sumter Regional Hosp., Americus, Ga., 1993-95; charge nurse surg. intensive care unit Walter Reed Army Med. Ctr., Washington, 1996-99; asst. head nurse emergency med. treatment 212th Mobile Army Surg. Hosp., Miesau, Germany, 1999-2001; chief staff devel. Landstuhl (Germany) Regional Med. Ctr., 1999-2001; nurse presdl. svc. White House Med. Unit, Washington, 2001—. Nuc., biol. and chem. med. officer 212th MASH and Landstuhl Regional Med. Ctr., 1999—2001; chem., biol. and radiological officer White House Med. Unit, 2001—; chief decontamination team Landstuhl Regional Med. Ctr., 1999—2001, mock code coord., 1999—2001, Walter Reed Army Med. Ctr., 1997—99; mem. adj. faculty European divsn. U. Md. Author: Modular Instruction Manual, 1998; med. topics editor: Soldier, Airman, Sailor and Marine Internet Newsletter, 1999—2001; editor (critical care newsletter): Walter Reed Army Med. Ctr., 1997—99; editor: (med. nursing newsletter), 1996—97. Foster parent Kaiserslautern (Germany) Mil. Cmty. Foster Care Program, 1999—2001; cmty. vol. Army Cmty. Svc., Kaiserslautern, Germany, 1999—2001. Capt. U.S. Army, 1995—. Recipient Parachutist badge, U.S. Army, 1993, Air Assault badge, 1997, Army Achievement medal, 1997, 98, Meritorious Svc. medal, 1999, 2001, Army Commendation medal, 2000, Kosovo Campaign medal, 2000, Mil. Outstanding Vol. Svc. award, 2001, award NATO, 2000; named Outstanding Young Man of Am., 1998. Mem. ANA, Am. Assn. Critical Care Nurses, Ga. Nurses Assn. Office: White House Med Unit 1600 Pennsylvania Ave Washington DC 20500 Home: 3305 Placido Pl Fayetteville NC 28306-8083 E-mail: tlhudson@hotmail.com.

HUDSON, WALTER TIREE, artist; b. Lynchburg, Va., Apr. 10, 1943; s. Randolph Ward Hudson and Frances Anderson Tyree. Student, Ctrl. Va. C.C., 1997, Stratford Career Inst., 2001—. Owner Linchberg Folk Arts, Doggywood Lit. Prodns. Exhibitions include Seven Hills Art Club, 1985, The Framery, 1985—2000, Haley's Antiques, 1985—2002, Lynchburg Pub. Housing Authority, 1986—2000, Lynchburg Social Svcs., 1987—99, Lynchburg Pub. Libr., 1987—, Amelia Pride, 1988, Lynchburg Recreation Dept., 1988—2001, Daily Bread, 1989—, Adult Daycare Ctr.-Va. Bapt. Hosp., 1989—94, Lynchburg Art Festival, 1991, Elks Nat. Home, 1992, Robert Hicks Collection, 1992, Ehrich's Opticians, 1992—2003, Va. Episcopal Sch., 1988, 1993—97, G.H. Vander Elst Collection, 1993, U. Tex., Houston, 1993, Lynchburg Fine Arts Ctr., Lynchburg PO, 1994, Lynchburg Voter Registration Office, 1995, Free Clinic of Va., 1995—2003, Irby L. Hudson Collection, 1995, Jacob Hunt Show, 1995—, 101 Quinlan St., 1996, Doggiewood Collection, 1996, Linchbird and Linchberg "1997", De Z Night Jump, 1997, 707 Mansfield Avenue, 1998, Ah Holloween Spring, 1998, Spring Fling, 1998—99, Blue Berg, 1998, Community Market, 1999, Linchbird, Red, White and Blue, 1999, West End Story, 1999, The Mormon Auction, 1999, Crossus "99", WSET TV News, 1999, Cornucopia, 2000, Mental Blocks, 2000, Calif. Poly of San Luis Obispo, 2000, KSU Found. Gift of Manhattan Kans., 2000, Linchberg Berginia, 2000, E.C. Glass HS, 2000, Lynchburg Jour., 2001, Social Svcs., 2001, Facetous Art, 2002, Art Diploma, 2003, High School Diploma, 2003, Melinda's, 2004, McCraws, 2004, Creative Writing Diploma, 2004, Automobile Mechanic Diploma, 2004, Accounting Diploma, 2005, The Best Green House, 2005, Legal Assistant Diploma, 2005. Mem. Rep. Nat. Com., 2003; active mem. Ct. St. United Meth. Ch.; mem. Coll. Hill Bapt. Ch., 2003, Thomas Road Bapt. Ch., 1984. Served Airborne U.S. Army, 1960—63. Recipient Men of Achievement award, 1996. Mem.: 82nd Airborne Div. Assn., The Statue of Liberty Ellis Island Foundation, Inc. (Millennial Certificate for Philanthropic Recognition 2000), 504th ABN Club, Blue Ridge All Airborne Club, Lynchburg Stamp Club. Republican. Mem. Lds Ch. Achievements include hitchhiked all 48 continous U.S. States, 1973-79. Avocations: stamp collecting/philately, reading, walking. Home: 3475 Fort Ave Apt 326 Lynchburg VA 24501-3834

HUDSON, WILLIAM JEFFREY, JR., manufacturing executive; b. Ill., May 20, 1934; s. William J. Sr. and Olga Georgevna (de Tarnowsky) H.; m. Margaret Royal, June 11, 1957; children: William J. III, Scott D., Robert C. BS in Elec. Engring., M. Cert. Elec. Engring., Cornell U., 1957; postgrad., Drexel U., 1959-61. From market rschr. to vice chmn. AMP Inc., Harrisburg, Pa., 1961—98, vice chmn., 1998—99, also bd. dirs. Bd. dirs. Goodyear Tire and Rubber Co., Applied Systems Intelligence, Inc., Cornell U. Coun. Engring. Adv. Coun.; mem. investment com. High Street Capital, 1999—. Contbr. articles to profl. jours.; 12 patents in field. Bd. dirs. Applied Systems Intelligence, Inc., 2002—; mem. bd. advisors Hershey Med. Ctr., 1994-2000; chmn. Pa. Export Trade Com., 1995-96; bd. dirs., exec. com. Team Pa., 1995-2003, work force investment bd. mem., chmn. employment stats. com., 1999—; mem. Pa. Human Resource Investment Coun., 1996—, chmn., 1996-99 Lt. (j.g.) USN, 1957-61. Mem. Nat. Elec. Mfrs. Assn. (exec. com., bd. govs. 1994-99), Nat. Assn. Mfrs. (exec. com., bd. dirs. 1993-98, vice chmn. 1997-98), Elec. Mfrs. Club (bd. dirs. 1993-98), Bus. Roundtable, U.S. Coun. Internat. Bus. (exec. com., chmn. Pa. Export Trade Coun., 1995-96, Team Pa. Human Resource Investment Coun., 1996-99, others).

HUDSON, WILLIAM L., conductor; Studies with Anthony Gigliotti, Max Rudolph, Erich Leindorf; grad., Phila. Mus. Acad., U. Pa., Yale U.; conducting student, Tanglewood Music Festival, Curtis Inst. Music, Phila. Conservatory. Condr., music dir. Fairfax Symphony Orch., Annandale, Va. Prof. music, condr. opera prodns. and symphony orch. U. Md.; faculty mem. Conducting Inst. Am. Symphony Orch. League; music dir. Shenandoah Valley Music Festival, 1979—. Bd. dirs. No. Va. Youth Symphony, Fairfax (Va.) Chorale Soc.; mem. adv. panel Fairfax County Coun. Arts; hon. chmn. Fairfax Spotlight on Arts, 1990. Recipient Outstanding Music Dir./Condr. award Washington Area Music Assn., 1985. Office: Fairfax Symphony Orchestra 1505 Farm Credit Dr Mc Lean VA 22102-5001

HUDSON-ZONN, ELIZA, nurse, psychologist; b. Monrovia, Liberia, Dec. 12, 1956; arrived in U.S., 1978; d. Hartzell Gleh and Joan Eliza (Roberts) Killen; m. Henry Clay Hudson, July 28, 1979 (div. Apr. 1985); 1 child, Kimberly Clayde; m. Mawuli Sonny Zonn, July 31, 1988; 1 child, Jewel Lorraine. BA in Psychology, BSC in Nursing, U. So. Miss., 1984. RN, N.J., Tex. Pvt. duty nurse Maxim Healthcare, Inc., South Orange, NJ, 1990—; critical care nurse Midpoint Profl. Agy., East Orange, NJ, 1988; supervising nurse Interim Healthcare, Inc., Morristown, NJ, 1990—; staff nurse Montclair Gen. Hosp., NJ, 1989—91; pvt. nurse Beth-Israel Med. Ctr., Newark, 1988—92; staff nurse United Children's Hosp., Newark, 1989—92; critical care nurse Nat. Staffing Assn. Inc., East Orange, 1988—2004; DON Med. Day Care Ctr., New Cmty. Extended Care, Newark, 2003—. Charge nurse Cmty. Psychiat. Ctr., Houston, 1993. Rural health vol. Red Cross Liberia, Monrovia, 1973—74; women's refugees health adv. Union Sierra Leone for Liberia, 1990—95; human rights adv. Movement for Justice in Africa, 1975—; coord., health svcs. dir. Liberian Cmty. Assn. N.J., 2001; membership recruiter Student Unification Party, Monrovia, 1975—76; counselor Providence Bapt. Ch., 1975, St. Elmo Bapt. Ch., 1982. Recipient Pub. Svc. award East Miss. Bapt. Women Conv., 1972; So. Bapt. Conv. scholar, 1978-84, Nat. Bapt. Conv. scholar, 1972-84. Mem.: Nat. Staffing Assn. Skilled Home Care Nursing, Suehn Acad. Alumni Assn. (founding mem. 1995). Democrat. Avocations: reading, writing, athletics, decoration, antiques collecting. Home: 64 Hillyer St Orange NJ 07050 Office: Nat Staffing Assocs Inc 134 Evergreen Pl East Orange NJ 07018 Office Phone: 973-675-1163.

HUDSPETH, ALMETRA KAVANAUGH, elementary school educator; b. San Antonio, Jan. 22, 1952; d. Wilbert L.D. Kavanaugh and Kathryn Kavanaugh Gray; m. Vernon Howard Hudspeth Jr., Aug. 17, 1974; children: Crystal LaShell, Almetra Joy. BA, St. Mary's U., San Antonio, 1974; M in Edn., U. Incarnate Word, San Antonio, 1997. Cert. K-8 tchr. Tex. Tchr. Ave. D Elem. Sch. Killeen (Tex.) Ind. Sch. Dist., 1975—80; tchr. Graebner Elem. Sch. San Antonio (Tex.) Ind. Sch. Dist., 1992—. Mem. various coms. Graebner Elem. Sch. San Antonio (Tex.) Ind. Sch. Dist., 1980—. Contbr. articles to profl. jours. Sunday sch. tchr. Reinbow Hills Bapt. Ch., 1988—, choir mem., 1988—. Scholar, St. Mary's U., 1970. Baptist. Avocations: bowling, reading, gardening, computer games. Home: 2702 Oak Mill San Antonio TX 78251 Office: Graebner Elem Sch 530 Hoover Ave San Antonio TX 78225

HUDSPETH, CHALMERS MAC, lawyer, educator; b. Denton, Tex., Oct. 18, 1919; s. Junia Evans and Ethel (Burns) H.; m. Demaris Eleanor De Lange, Jan. 30, 1945; children: Albert James, Thomas Richard, Helen Demaris. BA, Rice U., Houston, 1940; JD, U. Tex., 1946. Bar: Tex. 1946. Pvt. practice, Houston, 1947—; of counsel De Lange Hudspeth McConnell and Tibbets LLP, 1988—; asst. prof. law U. Tex. at Austin, 1946-47; lectr. govt. Rice U., 1947—, bd. govs., 1980-89, trustee, 1982-89, trustee emeritus, 1989—. Bd. dirs. Stewart Title Guaranty Co. Contbr. articles to profl. jours. Mem. bi-racial com. Houston Ind. Sch. Dist., 1955-56; trustee, v.p. Brown Found., 1983-89. Served to lt. USNR, 1942-45. Fellow Am. Bar Found., Tex. Bar Found.; mem. ABA, Tex. Bar Assn., State Bar Tex. (dir. 1966-68, v.p. 1968-69), Houston Philos. Soc. (pres. 1964-65), Petroleum Club of Houston, Chancellors, Order of Coif, Phi Delta Phi. Office: De Lange Hudspeth McConnell & Tibbets LLP Eight Greenway Plz Ste 1300 Houston TX 77046 Office Phone: 713-871-2000.

HUDSPETH, HARRY LEE, federal judge; b. Dallas, Dec. 28, 1935; s. Harry Ellis and Hattilee (Dudney) H.; m. Vicki Kathryn Round, Nov. 27, 1971; children: Melinda, Mary Kathryn. BA, U. Tex., Austin, 1955, JD, 1958. Bar: Tex. 1958. Trial atty. Dept. Justice, Washington, 1959-62; asst. U.S. atty. Western Dist. Tex., El Paso, 1962-69; assoc. Peticolas, Luscombe & Stephens, El Paso, 1969-77; U.S. magistrate El Paso, 1977-79; judge U.S. Dist. Ct. (we. dist.) Tex., El Paso, 1979—2001; chief judge U.S. Dist. Ct. (we. dist) Tex., El Paso, 1992-1999; sr. judge U.S. Dist. Ct., Austin, Tex., 2001—. Bd. dirs. Sun Carnival Assn., 1976, Met. YMCA El Paso, 1980-88. Mem. Travis Cnty Bar Assn., U. Tex. Ex-students Assn. (exec. coun. 1980-86), Chancellors, Order of Coif, Phi Beta Kappa. Democrat. Mem. Christian Ch. (Disciples Of Christ). Office: US Dist Ct We Dist Tex 903 San Jacinto Ste 440 Austin TX 78701 Office Phone: 512-916-5837.

HUDSPETH, HARVEY GRESHAM, history professor; b. Clarksdale, Miss., Oct. 17, 1955; s. Joseph MacDonald Hudspeth and Martha Lou Shelton. BA in History and Polit. Sci., U. Miss., 1978, JD, 1981, PhD in History, 1994. Bar: Miss. 1981, U.S. Dist. Ct. (no. dist.) Miss. 1981, U.S. Dist. Ct. (so. dist.) Miss. 1984, U.S. Ct. Appeals (5th cir.) 1985, Ill. 1989. Staff atty. Miss. Sec. of State, Jackson, 1981-83; pvt. practice Gulfport, Miss., 1983-85; land analyst Shell Oil Co., Houston, 1985-87; title examiner 1st Am. Title, Chgo., 1987-89; credit adminstr. Citicorp, Chgo., 1989-90; tchg. asst. U. Miss., University, 1991-94; history program coord., asst. prof. history Mississippi Valley State U., Itta Bena, Miss., 1994-2000, assoc. prof., 2000—. Presenter in field. Contbr. to books: Tennessee Encyclopedia of History, 1998, Booker T. Washington: Essays, 1998, Encyclopedia of the Supreme Court, 2001, Encyclopedia of the Gilded Age, 2003, Franklin D. Roosevelt and the Transformation of the Supreme Court, 2003, Mississippi Encyclopedia of History, 2005; contbr. articles to profl. jours. Chmn. Com. to Elect Joe Hudspeth Pub. Svc. Commr., Miss., 1983. Recipient Miss. Humanities Coun. Tchr. of Yr. award, 2001, WTHS Marshall Wingfield award, 1998, EBHS Charles J. Kennedy award, 2005. Mem. Am. Hist. Assn., Orgn. Am. Historians, Miss. Hist. Assn., Gulf South Hist. Assn., So. Conf. on Afro-Am. Studies, Inc., Econ. and Bus. Hist. Soc. (trustee 2000-01. pres.-elect 2001-02, pres. 2002-03), Miss. Bar Assn., Ill. Bar Assn. Republican. Presbyterian. Avocations: travel, politics, reading. Home: 14000 Hwy 82 West PO Box 5045 Itta Bena MS 38941 Office: Mississippi Valley State U 14000 Highway 82 W Itta Bena MS 38941-1401

HUDSPETH, STEPHEN MASON, lawyer; b. Pitts., Jan. 22, 1947; s. Harold Mason and Edna Mary (Lawrenson) H.; m. Rebecca Anne Ellis, Apr. 3, 1971; children: David, Catherine. BA, MA magna cum laude, Yale U., 1968, JD, 1971. Bar: N.Y. 1973, Pa. 1973, U.S. Dist. Ct. (so. and ea. dists.) N.Y. 1973, U.S. Ct. Appeals (2d cir. 1973), Mass. 1974, U.S. Dist. Ct. (ea. dist.) Pa. 1975, U.S. Ct. Appeals (1st cir.) 1976, U.S. Ct. Appeals (3d cir.) 1977, U.S. Supreme Ct. 1980, Maine 1987. Assoc. Lord, Day & Lord, N.Y.C., until 1979, ptnr., 1979-86, Coudert Bros., N.Y.C., 1986—, mem. exec. com., 1990-93, also head litigation dept., 1994—. Adj. asst. prof. bus. law Wagner Coll., 1973-83. Co-author: Transfer Pricing under U.S. Law, 1995; contbr. articles to profl. jours., chpts. to books. Vestryman St. Alban's Episcopal Ch., S.I., N.Y., 1979-85, warden, 1985-87; chmn. Stewardship Commn., Diocese of N.Y., 1987-95; vestryman St. Matthew's Episcopal Ch., Wilton, Conn., 1989-92, warden, 1992-95; bd. dirs. Union Theol. Sem., 2000—. Capt. C.E., USAR, 1968-73. Mem. ABA, N.Y. State Bar Assn., Assn. Bar City N.Y., Phi Beta Kappa. Office: Coudert Bros 1114 Ave of Americas 4th Fl New York NY 10036-7710 Office Phone: 212-626-4442. Personal E-mail: hudspeths@comcast.com. Business E-Mail: dahuds@optonline.net.

HUEBL, HUBERT CARL, surgeon; b. Glendive, Mont., Sept. 12, 1932; s. Hubert Carl Huebl and Ida Mae Myers; m. Helen Katherine Sugrue, Feb. 23, 1963; children: John, Michael, Katherine Doyle, Carolyn. BA, U. Chgo., 1952; MD, Washington U., 1956. Bd. cert. gen. and thoracic surgery. Intern gen. and thoracic surgery Bellevue Hosp., N.Y.C., 1959-62, Wayne State U., Detroit, 1962-67; thoracic surgeon Cardiothoracic Assocs., Malden, Mass., 1968-77; gen. surgeon Dearborn (Mich.) Surg. Assocs., 1977-2000; clin. asst. prof. Wayne State U./Oakwood Hosp., 2000—. Lt. USNR, 1957-59. Mem. ACS, AMA, Soc. Thoracic Surgeons, Mich. State Med. Soc., Wayne County Med. Soc. Roman Catholic. Office: 18101 Oakwood Blvd Ste 131 Dearborn MI 48124-5031 Office Phone: 313-593-8660. E-mail: hhuebls@aol.com.

HUEBNER, CHARLES J., toy manufacturing executive; married; 2 children. BA, Hamilton Coll.; MBA, Wharton Sch., U. Pa. With Procter & Gamble, Cin.; co-founder ERS Internat.; with Coca-Cola, Atlanta, Houston, Tokyo; sr. v.p.- strategic planning Hasbro, Inc., 2000—01; CEO Wizards of the Coast, Hasbro, Inc., 2001—. Office: Wizards of the Coast 1027 Newport Ave Pawtucket RI 02862-1059

HUEBNER, DAVID, lawyer; b. Mahanoy City, Pa., May 7, 1960; AB summa cum laude, Princeton Univ., 1982; JD, Yale Univ., 1986. Bar: Calif. 1989, DC 1992, NY 1998, US Dist. Ct. (no., ctrl., ea. & no. Calif.), US Ct. Appeals (9th & Fed. cir.), US Ct. Internat. Trade, US Supreme Ct. Exec. asst. to Hon. Koji Kakizawa, mem. lower house of Diet, Tokyo, 1984—85; ptnr., Global Litigation practice Coudert Bros. LLP, LA, chmn., 2003—05. Adj. prof. Univ. So. Calif. Law Sch.; chmn. & commr. Calif. Law Revision Commn., 2000—04; pres. & commr. LA City Quality & Productivity Commn., 1994—97; counsel Ind. Commn. on LA Police Dept., 1991. Editor (in chief): Yale Jour. on Regulation. Henry Luce scholar. Mem.: LA Com. on Fgn. Rels. (founding mem.), Phi Beta Kappa. Office: Coudert Bros LLP 333 S Hope St Los Angeles CA 90071 Office Phone: 213-229-2900. Office Fax: 213-229-2999. Business E-Mail: huenberd@coudert.com.

HUEBNER, JEFF, art journalist, freelance writer; BA, Western Mich. U., 1982. Contbr. (articles) Chgo. Reader, Ill. Mag., Ill. Times, contbr. (articles and art reviews) ARTnews, Public Art Review, Sculpture, New Art Examiner, Ceramics Monthly, Labor's Heritage, Chicago mag., and Chicago Tribune and others., writer, editor Chicago Public Art Group Magazine; co-author (with Olivia Gude): Urban Art Chicago: A Guide to Community Murals, Mosaics, and Sculptures, 2000; author: Murals: The Great Walls of Joliet, 2001, Chicago Parks Rediscovered (photographs by Frank Dina), 2002; contbr. author Marcos Raya: Fetishizing the Imaginary, 2004. Mem.: Chgo. Art Critics Assn. Address: 1237 N Maplewood Ave Chicago IL 60622-2858 Office Phone: 773-489-2340. Personal E-mail: majawo@earthlink.net.

HUEBNER, JOHN STEPHEN, geologist; b. Bryn Mawr, Pa., 1940; s. John and Elizabeth Huebner; m. Emily Mayer Zug, June 16, 1962; children: Christopher, Jeffrey. AB magna cum laude, Princeton U., 1962; PhD, Johns Hopkins U., 1967. Rsch. geologist U.S. Geol. Survey, 1967-97. Cons. NASA, 1976-78; lectr. George Washington U., 1971; sec.-treas. Am. Geol. Inst., 1974-75. Assoc. editor Jour. Geophys. Rsch., 1977-79; Contbr. articles profl. jours. Pres. Wood Acres Citizens Assn., 1977—78; sec. Cosmos Club Found., 1998—99, treas., 1999—2005. Recipient Meritorious Svc. award U.S. Dept. Interior, 1995. Fellow Mineral. Soc. Am. (bd. dirs. 1985-88, recipient MSA award 1978); mem. AAAS, Geochem. Soc. (treas. 1972-75), Am. Geophys. Union, Geol. Soc. Washington (sec. 1972, v.p. 1991, pres. 1992, bd. dirs. 2000-2001), Cosmos Club Washington (treas. 2003-05), Sigma Xi. Home: 6102 Cromwell Dr Bethesda MD 20816-3410 Personal E-mail: shuebner@radix.net.

HUELSMANN, SISTER JOETTA, religious educator; b. Bresse, Ill., Sept. 23, 1948; d. Edward Anthony and Eleanor Mary (Voss) H. B English, Alverno Coll., 1971; M Social Ministry, St. Mary's Coll., Winona, Minn., 1977; postgrad., Shalem Inst./Washington Theological Union, Washington, 1992. Elem. tchr. various parochial schs., Ill. and Ind., 1971-76; pastoral minister Our Lady of the Holy Spirit Parish, Mt. Zion, Ill., 1977-80, Holy Trinity Parish, Stonington, Ill., 1977-81, St. Stanislaus Parish, Macon, Ill., 1977-81, St. Boniface Parish, Edwardsville, Ill., 1981-82; co-dir. Community Growth Ctr., Richmond, Minn., 1982-85; mem. staff Covenant House of Prayer, Burlington, Iowa, 1985-86; resident asst. Sacred Heart House of Prayer, Rock Island, Ill., 1986-87; dir. religious edn. St. Mary Parish, Quincy, Ill., 1987—. Mem. real Religious Educators Area Leadership, Springfield, Ill., 1987-91; mem. core Coords. Religious Edn., Springfield, 1987—; mem. Rite Christian Initiation of Adults Com., Springfield, 1991—; mem. missions concerns com. Poor Handmaids of Jesus Christ, Donaldson, Ind., 1989-93. Mem. Nat. Cath. Ednl. Assn. (Dir. of Religious Edn. of Month award 1992), Ill. Pastoral Coords. and Dirs. Roman Catholic. Avocations: fishing, singing, guitar, reading, embroidery. Office: St Mary Parish 1119 S 7th St Quincy IL 62301-5369

HUENEFELD, JOHN CARL, management consultant, newsletter editor; b. Memphis, Sept. 25, 1928; s. Arnold Paul and Kittie Rowland Sanderson Huenefeld; m. Georgia Louis Mills, Apr. 3, 1951; children: Carl Frederick II, Jan, Kurt Lofton, Charles Konrad. BS, Kans. State Coll., 1950; MA, U. Ark., 1954. Mktg. mgr. Beacon Press, Boston, 1965-68; pres., founder, sr. cons. The Huenefeld Co., Inc., Bedford, Mass., 1969—. Seminar presenter in field. Author: Community Activist's Handbook, 1970, Huenefeld Guide to Book Publishing, 1993, 2d edit., 2001, (newsletter) Huenefeld Report, 1973—2001. Sgt. 1st class U.S. Army, 1950-52. Recipient Ben Franklin award Publishers Mktg. Assn., 1987. Democrat. Unitarian-Universalist. Avocations: reading, gardening. Office: 15 Putnam RD Bedford MA 01730-1540

HUENEFELD, THOMAS ERNST, financial consultant, retired banker; b. Cin., July 7, 1937; s. Carl Ernst and Catherine Louise (Messer) H.; m. Catherine Ann Cogburn, Feb. 5, 1960; children: Richard Ernst, Amy Cogburn. BS in Bus. Adminstrn., U. Fla., 1961; grad. Nat. Comml. Lending Grad. Sch., U. Okla., 1975. Cert. comml. lender Am. Bankers Assn.; cert. lender-bus. banking Inst. Cert. Bankers. Mgmt. trainee Huenefeld Co., Cin., 1961—62, asst. sec., buyer, 1963—65; credit analyst First Nat. Bank Cin. (now U.S. Bank, N.A.), 1966—68, asst. cashier, 1968—69, asst. v.p., 1969—75, v.p., 1975—83, sr. v.p., 1983—96; ret., 1996. Cons. Star Banc Corp. (now U.S. Bancorp), Cin., 1997-98; dir. Wolf Machine Co., S. Eastern Materials Corp., Archiable Electric Co., Eastern Machinery Co., Ninth St. Garage, Inc., Logan & Kanawha Coal Co., Inc., Safegard Corp. Author: Pittsburgh's Historic East End: In and Around Point Breeze 1914, 2001. Bd. mgrs. Emanuel Cmty. Ctr., Cin., 1965—70, pres., 1968—70; trustee Huenefeld Meml., Inc., Cin., 1965—72, treas., 1965—69; trustee Funds for Self Enterprise, Cin., 1972—76, pres., 1973—76; trustee Cin. Musical Festival Assn., 1976—82, mem. exec. com., 1977—79; trustee Betts Ho. Rsch. Ctr., 1999—2002, mem. adv. bd., investment com., 2002—; trustee Cmty. Ltd. Care Dialysis Ctr., Cin., 1978—85, Mercantile Libr., 1979—2001, v.p., chmn. fin. com., 1983—88, life mem., 2001—; trustee Spring Grove Heritage Found., 2001—, chmn., 2004—; trustee MagnaCare Health Plan, 1988—91, v.p., chmn. fin. com., 1990—91; trustee Ohio Hist. Soc. Found., 2002—04, vice chmn., 2004; dir., treas., investment com. chmn. Pub. Libr. of Cin. and Hamilton County Found., 2004—; mem. adv. bd. Riemenschneider Bach Inst. Baldwin-Wallace Coll., 1988—; mem. history adv. bd. Cin. Mus. Ctr., 1997—; mem. adv. bd. Scarlet Oaks Retirement Com., 1998—, Emery Ctr. Corp., 1999—2002; trustee Bethesda Found., 2004—; mem. investment com. Bethesda Inc., 2004—. Mem. Am. Fin. Assn. (life), Fin. Mgmt. Assn. (life), Risk Mgmt. Assn. (life), Cin. Assn. Credit and Fin. Mgmt. (dir. 1972-76), Am. Inst. Banking, Newcomen Soc. N.Am., Ohio Hist. Soc. (life, trustee 2001-04), Ohioana Libr. Assn. (life), Cin. Hist. Soc. (life, trustee 1979-87, mem. exec. com. 1983-85, v.p. 1985-89), Cin. Preservation Assn. (trustee 1989-95, adv. bd. 1995—), Cincinnatus Assn. (exec. com. 1983-84), Cin. Country Club, Queen City Club, Bankers Club, The Assemblies (chmn. 1972-73), Univ. Club (bd. govs. 1982-89), Univ. Club Cin. Found. (trustee 1989-96), Fanfare (pres. 1979-80), Friends William Howard Taft Birthplace (trustee 1997-03), Sigma Chi (life). Republican. Methodist. Home and Office: 3440 Principio Ave Cincinnati OH 45208-4240

HUENING, WALTER CARL, JR., retired consulting application engineer; b. Boston, Feb. 10, 1923; s. Walter Carl and Gladys (Whittemore) H.; m. Margaret Laurence McGeary, Aug. 5, 1944 (dec. 1986); children: Peter Carl, Susan Laurence Huening Locke; m. Elizabeth Ann Young Wright, Apr. 9, 1988. BSEE magna cum laude, Tufts U., 1944. Registered profl. engr., N.Y., Ohio. Instr. elec. engring. Tufts U., Medford, Mass., 1946-48; distbn. engr. plant engring. dept. GE, Lynn, Mass., 1948-50, application engr. indsl. power engring. Schenectady, N.Y., 1952-56, product planner protective devices dept. Plainville, Conn., 1956-58, design engr. vacuum cleaner dept. Cleve., 1958-59, application engr. comml. and mcpl. dept. Schenectady, 1960-62, application engr. steel mill, 1962-68, cons. application engr. indsl. power engring., 1968-89. Mem. U.S. nat. com. Internat. Electrotech. Commn., tech. advisor on Tech. Com. 73 matters, 1972-89. Contbr. tech. papers to jours. and chpts. to books; patentee vacuum cleaner latch. Lt. comdr. USNR, 1944-46, 50-52, ret. Fellow IEEE (life, R. H. Kaufmann award 1988, Indsl. and Comml. Power Systems Dept. Achievement award 1989, prizes for papers 1970, 82); mem. Tau Beta Pi. Independent. Avocations: photography, collecting recorded traditional jazz music. Address: 1229 Godfrey Ln Niskayuna NY 12309-1241 Personal E-mail: whueningjr@aol.com.

HUERTA, SERGIO, physician, researcher; b. Mexico City, Dec. 21, 1966; s. David Huerta and Edelmira Yepez; m. Hsiao Ching Li, June 19, 1999. MD, UCLA Sch. of Medicine, Los Angeles, Calif., 1994—98; BS, U. of Calif., LA, Los Angeles, Calif., 1990—92; AA, West LA Coll., Culver City, Calif., 1988—90. Doctor of Medicine Med. Bd. of Calif., Calif., 2001. Surg. resident U. of Calif., Irvine, Orange, Calif., 1998—; fellow in nutritional oncology UCLA Ctr. for Human Nutrition, Los Angeles, Calif., 2000—02. Inaugural chmn. of the western student med. forum residents' sect. Western Student Med. Forum and the Am. Fedn. for Med. Rsch., Carmel, Calif., 2001—02, chmn. of the western student med. forum residents' sect., 2002—03; founder and provider of a clinic mng. obesity in an indigent population Venice Family Clinic, Venice, Calif., 2001—02. Author: The Pocket Rev. of Surgery; contbr. articles to profl. jours. Recipient Emil Bogen Rsch. prize, UCLA Sch. Medicine, 1998, Travel award, Am. Fedn. for Med. Rsch., 2002; grantee, UCLA Ctr. for Human Nutrition, 2001; scholar Travel award, Am. Inst. for Cancer Rsch., 2000; Nutritional Oncology fellow, NIH, 2000—02, Outstanding Rsch. fellow, UCLA Ctr. for Human Nutrition, 2002. Mem.: AMA, North Am. Assn. for the Study of Obesity, Am. Assn. for Cancer Rsch. (Minority in Cancer Rsch. award 2001—02, Minority Scholar-in-Tng. award 2002), Am. Gastroent. Assn. Office: UCLA Ctr for Human Nutrition 12-217 Warren Hall 900 Veteran Ave Los Angeles CA 90095 Personal E-mail: shuerta@pol.net.

HUESTIS, CHARLES BENJAMIN, former academic administrator; b. Seattle, Jan. 27, 1920; s. Claude Erwin and Eloise Marie (Pettit) H.; m. Kathryn Alice Porter, Mar. 1, 1942; children: Stephen Porter, Jeffrey Charles, Robin Rebecca. Student, Griffin Murphy Coll., Seattle, 1938-39, U. Calif. Berkeley, 1946. With Seattle First Nat. Bank, 1941; acct. Rheem Mfg. Co., Richmond, Calif., 1946-51, chief acct. aircraft div. Downey, Calif., 1951-54, corp. comptroller, 1954-56; v.p., treas. Hall-Scott Inc., Berkeley, Calif., 1956, exec. v.p., dir., treas., 1956-57; adminstrv. cons. Overseas Nat. Airways, Oakland, Calif., 1957-58; controller El Segundo div. Hughes Aircraft Co., 1958-59, controller Tucson div., 1959, treas., chmn. finance com., 1960-66, v.p., 1962-66; v.p., treas., dir. Am. Mt. Everest Expdn., 1963; v.p. bus. and finance Duke U., Durham, N.C., 1966-83, sr. v.p., 1983-85, sr. v.p. emeritus, 1985—; dir. Technomics, Inc., Falls Church, Va., 1966-76; chmn. bd. Sta. WDBS, 1970-76. Bd. dirs. Santa Barbara (Calif.) Research Ctr., 1959-66; bd. dirs., mem. exec. com. Research Triangle Found., Research Triangle Park, N.C., 1969-85; trustee Research Triangle Inst., Research Triangle Park, 1967-79, Sierra Club Found., 1969-79; commr. N.C. Marine Fisheries, 1985-87; trustee N.C. Nature Conservancy., 1977-86, 87-96, chmn., 1979-83; bd. dirs. N.C. Ednl. Facilities Fin. Agy., 1987-91—; climbing leader Duke-Gettysburg Expdn. to Kurdistan, 1982. Served with U.S Army Signal Corps, 1942-45. Mem. Explorers Club (v.p. research and edn. 1987-88), Am. Alpine Club. Home: 1803 Woodburn Rd Durham NC 27705-5724

HUET, RAUL, psychiatrist; b. Mexico City, Jan. 25, 1953; arrived in US, 1954; s. Raul Huet Sobrado and Yolanda Juan Franco de Huet. *Father, Raul, earned medical degree from University National Autonoma of Mexico. He died in 1974. Mother, Yolanda Juan Franco, earned her master's in romance languages, magna cum laude, from University of Missouri in Kansas City. She also earned a master's in psychology from University of Kansas. She died in 2004. Sister, Yolanda Huet-Vaughn, earned her medical degree from Meharry Medical College. She has a private practice. Sister, Rocio, earned her medical degree from University of Michigan. She also has a private practice. Yvette Huet-Hudson, PhD, earned her degree from the University of Kansas. She is a professor of biology at the University of North Carolina.* MD, Kans. U. Sch. Medicine, 1982. Cert. diplomate Psychiatry Am. Bd. Psychiatry and Neurology. Rschr. asst. Kans. U. Sch. Medicine, Dept. Physiology, Kans. City, 1985—87; psychiatrist Labette Ctr. for Mental Health Svcs., Inc., Parsons, Kans., 1997—2004, Wyandot Ctr. for Cmty. Behavioral Healthcare, Inc., Kans. City, 2004—. Psychiatric cons. Labette County Med. Ctr., Parsons, Kans., 2002—04, Providence Med. Ctr., Kansas City, Kans., 2004—; clin. asst. prof. psychiatry Kans. U. Sch. Medicine, Dept. Psychiatry, 2004—. Author: Ischemic Colitis - Digestive Diseases, 1987. Mem.: AMA, Med. Soc. Johnson and Wyandotte Counties, Kans. Psychiatric Soc., Kans. Med. Soc., Am. Psychiatric Assn., Hispanic C. of C. Republican. Cath. Avocations: tennis, movie videos, spy novels. Home: 3917 W 84th St Apt A Prairie Village KS 66207 Office: Wyandot Ctr for Cmty Behavioral Healthcare Inc 7840 Wash Ave Kansas City KS 66112 Office Phone: 913-328-4600. Office Fax: 913-328-4604. E-mail: rahuet@sbcglobal.net.

HUETSON, NORMA JEAN, retired elementary education educator; b. Adams, Nebr., Mar. 31, 1933; d. Minert Jacob and Olga Meta (Krumm) Behrens; m. Russel Wayne Huetson, June 7, 1953; children: Curtis Lynn, Angela Joy. BS in Edn., U. Nebr., 1973. Elem. tchr. Gage County Schs., Adams, Nebr., 1950-53, Lancaster County Rural Schs., Adams, 1953-56, Crete, Nebr., 1958-62, Saline County Rural Schs., Crete, 1962-64, Lincoln (Nebr.) Pub. Schs., 1973—96, ret., 1996. Recipient scholarship State Tchr.'s Coll., 1950. Mem. NEA, Nebr. State Tchrs. Assn., Lincoln Educators Assn. Lutheran. Avocations: sewing, reading.

HUEY, JOHN WESLEY, JR., editor; b. Atlanta, Apr. 18, 1948; s. John Wesley and Helen (Cahill) Huey; m. Kathryn White (div. 1981); 1 child, John Wesley IV; m. Sue Yeargan (dec. 1986); m. Kate Ellis, 1993; 1 child, Cole. BA in English, U. Ga., 1970. Reporter DeKalb New Era, Decatur, Ga., 1972-74, Atlanta Constn., 1974-75, Wall St. Jour., Dallas, 1975-79, bur. chief Atlanta, 1979-82, mng. editor Brussels, 1982-83, editor, 1983-84, sr. spl. corr. Atlanta, 1984-86; Atlanta bur. chief, 1986—88; contbg. editor Fortune mag., 1988; editor Southpoint mag., Atlanta, 1989—90; sr. editor Fortune mag., 1990—95; mng. editor Fortune, 1995—2001; editorial dir. Time Inc., 2001—. Mem. adv. bd. Grady Coll., U. Ga. Served to lt. (j.g.) USN, 1970-72. Recipient Editor of the Yr., Ad Age mag., 1997. Mem.: ASME, Coun. on Fgn. Rels. Methodist. Office: Time Inc 1271 Avenue Of The Americas New York NY 10020-1300 E-mail: Laura_Whitaker@timeinc.com.

HUEY, WARD L(IGON), JR., retired media executive; b. Dallas, Apr. 26, 1938; s. Ward Ligon and Irene Helen (Freeman) H.; m. Marian Kennedy Powell, Oct. 28, 1961; children: Ward L. III, David Powell. BA, So. Meth. U., 1960. Successively with dept. prodn., sales svc. mgr. local sales, regional sales mgr., gen. sales mgr. Sta. WFAA-TV, Dallas, 1960-67, sta. mgr., 1972-75; v.p., gen. mgr. Belo Broadcasting Corp., Dallas, from 1975; vice chmn. bd. dirs., pres. broadcast div. A. H. Belo Corp., Dallas, 1987—2001. Chmn. affiliate bd. govs. ABC-TV, 1981-82; chmn. bd. TV Operators Caucus, 1989. Mem. exec. com. So. Meth. U. Meadows Sch. Arts, 1986—, Goodwill Industries Dallas, 1978-79, State Fair Tex., 1992—; bd. dirs. Children's Med. Found. Tex., Dallas, 1985-94, Dallas Found., 1993—; trustee So. Meth. U., 1996—. Named Disting. Alumni, Highland Park H.S., 1998, Pioneer of Yr., Tex. Broadcasters, 2000; named to, Broadcasting and Cable Hall of Fame, 1999, Nat. TV Acad. Mgmt. Hall of Fame, 2004; recipient Disting. Alumni award, So. Meth. U., 2000. Mem. Maximum Svc. TV Assn. (vice chmn. 1988-94), TV Bur. Advt. (past bd. dirs., exec. com. 1984-88), Assn. Broadcast Execs. Tex. (bd. dirs. 1977-78), Dallas Advt. League (bd. dirs. 1975-76), Salesmanship Club Dallas (pres. 1992-93), Dallas Country Club. Methodist. Avocations: skiing, boating, swimming, golf, music.

HUF, CAROL ELINOR, tax service company executive; b. Milw., Apr. 21, 1940; d. William Weiss and Florence H. (Melcher) Weiss Lange; m. Walter Franklin Huf, Sept. 9, 1961; children: Mardell Leslie, Walter Albert III. Student, Valparaiso U., 1958-60, Waukesha County Tech. Inst., 1968-69. Tax preparer H&R Block, Milw., 1967-84, instr. tax sch., 1969-83; job svc. interviewer State of Wis., Waukesha, 1984; pres. Personalized Tax Svc., Inc., West Allis, Wis., 1984—. Divsn. mgr. Primerica (formerly A.L. Williams), 1986. Vol. worker Girl Scouts US, Waukesha, 1970-80, Boy Scouts Am., Waukesha, 1975-92; swimming referee Wis. Interscholastic Athletic Assn., Milw., 1972-84. Recipient award Boy Scouts Am. Mem.: Wis. Assn. Accts., Nat. Assn. Tax Practitioners (Wis. bd. dirs. 1989—96), Nat. Soc. Pub. Accts., Met. Swimming Ofcls., U.S. Golf Assn. (regional affairs com. 1991—), Wis. Womens Pub. Links Golf Assn. (state tournament chairperson 1987, 2d v.p. 1988—, state tournament chairperson 1990, 1994, past pres.). Lutheran. Home: 5508 Bauers Dr West Bend WI 53095-8782 Office: Personalized Tax Service Inc PO Box 1123 West Bend WI 53095

HUFANDA, JOSEPH, dentist; DDS, U. Mich. Resident Upper Peninsula Rural Health Svcs.; co-founder Ballantyne Ctr. for Dentistry, Charlotte, NC. Mem.: Am. Acad. Cosmetic Dentistry, Charlotte Dental Soc., NC Dental Soc., Am. Dental Assn. Office: Ballantyne Ctr for Dentistry Ste K 15105 John J Delaney Dr Charlotte NC 28277 Office Phone: 704-540-2255. E-mail: drjoe@ballantynedentistry.com.*

HUFBAUER, GARY CLYDE, economist, lawyer, educator; b. San Diego, Apr. 3, 1939; s. Clarence Clyde and Arabelle Maxwell (McKee) H.; children: Randall Clyde Revelle (dec.), Ellen Arabelle Scripps, Romain Clyde; m. Valerie Parra, 1996. AB, Harvard U., 1960; PhD, King's Coll., Cambridge U., Eng., 1963; JD, Georgetown U., 1980. Bar: D.C. 1980, Md. 1980. Mem. faculty dept. econs. U. N.Mex., Albuquerque, 1963-74, prof., 1970-74; dir. internat. tax staff U.S. Dept. Treasury, Washington, 1974-77; dep. asst. Sec. Treasury, Internat. Trade and Investment Policy, 1977-80; mem. firm Rose, Schmidt, Chapman, Duff & Hasley, Washington, 1980-85; dep. dir. Internat. Law Inst., Georgetown Law Ctr., Washington, 1980-82; Wallenberg prof. fin. Georgetown U., Washington, 1985-92; dir. studies Coun. on Fgn. Rels., N.Y.C., 1997-98; sr. fellow Inst. Internat. Econs., Washington, 1982-85, 92-97, 98—. Mem. Harvard Devel. Adv. Svc., Pakistan, 1967-69; vis. prof. Stockholm Sch. Econs., 1974, Cambridge U., 1973, Georgetown U., 1975. Author: Economic Sanctions Reconsidered, 1990, World Capital Markets, 2001. Ford Found. fellow, 1966-67; Fulbright rsch. scholar, 1973 Mem. Am. Econ. Assn., Nat. Economists Club. Episcopalian. Office: Inst for Internat Econs 1750 Massachusetts Ave NW Washington DC 20036-1903 Office Phone: 202-328-9000.

HUFBAUER, KARL GEORGE, science historian, sculptor; b. San Diego, July 7, 1937; s. Clarence Clyde and Arabelle Maxwell (McKee) H.; m. Sarah Grant Brannon, Aug. 6, 1960; children: Sarah Beth, Benjamin Grant, Ruth Arabelle. BS in Engring. Sci., Stanford U., 1959; diploma in history and philos. sci., Oxford (Eng.) U., 1961; PhD in History of Sci., U. Calif., Berkeley, 1970. From asst. prof. to prof. dept. history U. Calif., Irvine, 1966—99, prof. emeritus, 1999—; contract historian NASA, Washington, 1984-90. Chair dept. history U. Calif., Irvine, 1992-96; dir. UC Scandinavian Study Ctr., Lund, Sweden, 1997-99; affiliate prof. history, U. Wash., 2000—. Author: Formation of German Chemical Community, 1982, Exploring the Sun, 1991 (Emme prize 1993). Co-presiding officer Stop Polluting Our Newport, Newport Beach, Calif., 1987-92. Mem.: Northwest Stone Sculptors Assn. (bd. dirs. 2002—). Mem. Green Party. Home: 3319 37th Ave S Seattle WA 98144-7015 Office Phone: 206-725-2277. E-mail: sallykarl@earthlink.net.

HUFF, C(LARENCE) RONALD, sociologist, criminologist, educator; b. Covington, Ky., Nov. 10, 1945; s. Nathaniel Warren G. and Irene Opal (Mills) H.; m. Patricia Ann Plankenhorn, June 15, 1968; children: Tamara Lynn, Tiffany Dawn. BA, Capital U., 1968; MSW, U. Mich., 1970; PhD, Ohio State U., 1974. Social worker Franklin County Children's Svcs., Columbus, Ohio, 1968; social work intern Pontiac (Mich.) State Hosp. and Family Svc. Met. Detroit, 1969-70; dir. psychiat. social work Lima (Ohio) State Hosp., 1970-71; chief psychiat. social worker N.W. Cmty. Mental Health Ctr., Lima, 1971-72; grad. tchg. assoc. sociology Ohio State U., 1972-74; asst. prof. social ecology U. Calif., Irvine, 1974-76; asst. prof. sociology Purdue U., 1976-79; assoc. prof. pub. policy/mgmt. Ohio State U., Columbus, 1979-87, dir. Criminal Justice Rsch. Ctr., 1979-99, prof., 1987-99, prof. emeritus, 1999—, dir. Sch. Pub. Policy and Mgmt., 1994-99; dean Sch. Social Ecology U. Calif., Irvine, 1999—, prof. criminology, law and society, 1999—, prof. sociology, 2004—. Vis. prof. U. Hawaii, 1995; cons. Bur. Justice Stats., Nat. Inst. Justice, Nat. Inst. Corrections, Nat. Inst. Juvenile Justice and Delinquency Prevention, U.S. Senate Jud. Com., NSF, FBI, others; expert witness fed. and state cts. Author: Youth Violence: Prevention, Intervention, and Social Policy, 1999, Convicted But Innocent: Wrongful Conviction and Public Policy, 1996, (Outstanding Acad. Book award Choice Mag., 1996), The Gang Intervention Handbook, 1993, Gangs in America, 1990, 2d edit., 1996, 3rd edit., 2002, House Arrest and Correctional Policy: Doing Time at Home, 1988, The Mad, The Bad, and The Different: Essays in Honor of Simon Dinitz, 1981, Attorneys as Activists: Evaluating the American Bar Association's BASICS Program, 1979, Contemporary Corrections: Social Control and Conflict, 1977, Planning Correctional Reform, 1975, and others; mem. editl. bd. various jours.; contbr. articles to profl. jours., chpts. to books. Recipient Nat. Security award Mershon Found., 1980, prize New Eng. Sch. Law, 1981, Outstanding Tchg. award, 1985, Donald R. Cressey award Nat. Coun. on Crime and Delinquency, 1992, Paul Tappan award Western Soc. Criminology, 1993, Herbert Bloch award Am. Soc. Criminology, 1994; grantee ABA, 1974-77, Purdue U., 1978, Dept. Justice, 1978-79, 85-88, 91-95, Ohio Dept. Mental Health, 1982-83, 84-85, 85-87, Gov.'s Office Criminal Justice, 1985-88, 92-95, 98, Ohio Dept. Youth Svcs., 1989-90, Ohio State U./Ohio Bd. Regents, 1990-92. Fellow Western Soc. Criminology, Am. Soc. Criminology (exec. bd., pres.-elect 1999-2000, pres. 2000-01, Herbert Bloch award 1994); mem. Acad. Criminal Justice Scis., Nat. Coun. on Crime and Delinquency, Phi Kappa Phi, Phi Beta Delta. Office: U Calif Irvine Sch Social Ecology 300 Social Ecology I Irvine CA 92697-7050 Office Phone: 949-824-6094. Business E-Mail: rhuff@uci.edu.

HUFF, JIMMY LAURENCE, nurse; b. La Junta, Colo., Feb. 16, 1950; s. Russell Loyal Huff and Pauline Ellen (Porter) Kibler; m. Julia Ann Belden, Jan. 20, 1973 (div. Aug. 1982); 1 child, Annessa. AA, North Platte Coll., 1970; student, Nebr. Western Coll., 1970-71; diploma, West Nebr. Gen. Hosp. Sch. Nursing, 1973; AAS, ITT Tech., Nashville, 1989; B in Applied Sci. Electronics Engring., ITT Tech., Indpls., 1990. Charge nurse, surgical/orthopedic unit West Nebr. Gen. Hosp., Scottsbluff, 1973-74, assoc. dir. nursing, 1974-76; assoc. charge nurse med. ward USAF Med. Ctr., Wright-Patterson AFB, Ohio, 1976-78; OIC spl. med. equipment, flight nurse 9th Aeromedical Evacuation Squadron, Clark AB, Philippines, 1978-80; flight clin. coord. 9th Aeromedical Evacuation Sqdn., Clark AB, Philippines, 1980-81; asst. charge nurse-multiservice ward USAF Hosp., Blytheville AFB, Ark., 1981-82, charge nurse, outpatient svcs., 1982-84, OIC emergency svcs., 1984-86; night charge nurse orthopedic unit HCA Donelson Hosp., Inc., Nashville, 1986-89; staff nurse orthopedics St. Vincent Hosp., Indpls., 1989-90, staff devel. cons. orthopedics, 1990-91; applications analyst St. Thomas Health Svcs., Info. Tech. Svcs., Nashville, 1991—. Clin. advisor sch. nursing, West Nebr. Gen. Hosp., 1973-76; cons. Lifeflight, Memphis, 1984-86. Maj. USAFR, mobilized Desert Shield/Storm, 1991, ret., 1996. Mem. IEEE, Am. Legion. Lutheran. Home: 120 Tomarand Rd Antioch TN 37013-3639 E-mail: jim.huff@baptisthospital.com.

HUFF, MONA L., information technology executive; b. NYC, Dec. 24, 1947; d. Joseph and Minnie Levine; m. Charles Joseph Huff, Oct. 13, 1984; 1 child, C. Ryan. BA, Hunter Coll.; MS, Yeshiva U. Cert. sch. dist. adminstr. NY State Edn. Dept, 1984, math. tchr. 7-12 NY State Edn. Dept., 1973. Adj. instr. Pace U., White Plains, NY; dir. tech. Edgemont Union Free Sch. Dist., Scarsdale, NY, tchr. math.; dir. computer edn. Union Free Sch. Dist., Tarrytown, chair math. dept, tchr. math., New Rochelle H.S., Lexington H.S., Mass. Coun. mem. NY State Regents Adv. Coun. Learning Techs., 1987—90. Pres. New Rochelle Coun. PTAs, 1997—99; asst. dir. Westchester Dist. PTA, 1992—95. Grantee, NY State Legis., 1996, Edgemont Sch. Found., 2003, 2004, 2005. Mem.: NY State Assn. Computers and Techs. Edn. (v.p., state conf. chair 1988—89, pres. 1989—90, v.p., state conf. chair 1994—95, dir. 1984—94), St Cecilia Chorus (treas. 1990—2001). Avocation: singing. Office: Edgemont Union Free Sch Dist 200 White Oak Ln Scarsdale NY 10583 Office Phone: 914-725-1500 589.

HUFF, RUSSELL JOSEPH, public relations and publishing executive; b. Chgo., Feb. 24, 1936; s. Russell Winfield and Virgilist Marie (McMahon) H.; m. Beverly Diane Staschke, 1968; 1 child, Michelle Lynn. BA in Philosophy cum laude, U. Notre Dame, 1958; BS in Theology, Cath. U. Santiago (Chile), 1960; MA in Comm. Arts, U. Notre Dame, 1968. Ordained priest Roman Cath. Ch., 1962. Exec. editor Cath. Boy and Miss., Notre Dame, Ind., 1963-68; mng. editor Nation's Schs., McGraw Hill, Chgo., 1968-70; v.p. pub. affairs Homart Devel. Co., Chgo., 1971-76; dir. pub. rels. Sears, Roebuck Co. Internat. Ops., Chgo., 1976-82; dir. pub. affairs Sears Roebuck Found. Internat. Projects, Chgo., 1981-82; sr. v.p., sales and mktg. dir. Mineca Internat., Inc., Chgo., 1982-84; v.p., pub. rels. Lofino Poppa Devel. Corp., Sarasota, Fla., 1984-85; pres., co-owner R.J. Huff & Assocs., Inc., Sarasota, 1985—2001; real estate broker Sarasota, 1985-2001. Author: Come Build My Church, 1966, On Wings of Adventure, 1967, Wings of WWII, 1985 (award 1986), Companion to Wings of World War II, 1987, Winging It, Vols. I and

II, 1992, David McCampbell USN Ace of Aces, 2004; editor, pub. (jour.) Wings and Things of the World, 1987-93, Wings and Things of the World for Sale, 1993-95; cons., editl. contbr. Aviation Treasures, 1995—; sr. editor The Nobody's Fool Fin. Market Analyst Pub., 1996-98. Care min. leader Ch. Incarnation Parish Coun., 1998-2002; future planning and rev. com., stewardship comm. chmn., Internat. Peace and Justice chmn., Recipient Outstanding Mag. award Cath. Press Assn., 1965, 67; named for Best Cover, Nation's Schs., 1968; cert. Gemol. Inst. Am.; cert. jr. coll. tchr., Calif. Mem. Pub. Rels. Soc. Am. (accredited 1976—), Chicagoland Mil. Collectors Soc. (dir. quar. expositions 1981-82), Am. Soc. Mil. Insignia Collectors, Orders and Medals Soc. Am., Nat. Fgn. Trade Coun., Pub. Affairs Coun., Conf. Bd., Internat. Bus. Coun., Internat. Vis. Ctr. Chgo., Ptnrs. of the Ams. (cert. for advancement L.Am. rels. 1980), São Paulo Ptnrs. (cert. for advancement Brazil-U.S. rels. 1979, dir. Ill.), Chgo. Assn. of Commerce and Industry, U.S.-Spanish C. of C. of Middle West (dir.), War Memorabilia Collectors Soc. (exec. dir.). Roman Catholic. Office: 4062 Kingston Ter Sarasota FL 34238-2632 Personal E-mail: russjhuff@comcast.net.

HUFF, WILLIAM BRAID, retired publishing company executive; b. Lynn, Mass., Apr. 18, 1950; s. Harold Butler and Mary Stewart (Braid) Huff; m. Karen Murphy, May 4, 1985; children: Thomas Murphy, Kathryn Braid. BS, Bowdoin Coll., 1972; MBA, Darthmouth Coll., 1974. CPA Mass. Staff acct. Arthur Andersen, Boston, 1974—76; contr. Affiliated Broadcasting, Boston, 1976—82, treas., 1982—86, sr. v.p., 1984—86; contr. Affiliated Publs., Boston, 1982—86, v.p., 1986—89, CFO, 1989—91, exec. v.p., CFO, 1991—97; sr. v.p., CFO Boston Globe Newspaper Co., 1992—97, pres., CFO, 1997—2001. Chmn. Morgan Meml. Goodwill; pres. Wayland Pub. Sch. Found. Mem.: AICPAs, Mass. Soc. CPAs, Weston Golf Club (v.p.). Republican. Episcopalian. Avocations: skiing, soccer, golf. Home: 5 Sherman Bridge Rd Wayland MA 01778-1213 E-mail: wbraidhuff@yahoo.com.

HUFFINE, COY LEE, retired chemical engineer; b. Knoxville, Apr. 2, 1924; s. Coy Mann and Inez Belle (Story) Huffine; m. Virginia Elizabeth Browne, Mar. 31, 1951; children: Jeremy Bennett, Lucinda Jane. BS, U. Tenn., 1945, MS, 1947; PhD, Columbia U., 1953. Prin. engr. aircraft nuc. propulsion program GE, Oak Ridge, Cin., 1951-59; rsch. ceramist GE Research Lab., Schenectady, 1959-60; project mgr. devel. and mfg. Apollo spacecraft Heat Shield, space sys. div. Avco Corp., Lowell, Mass., 1960-67; with IBM, Rochester, Minn., 1968-87, mgr. component tech. info. sys. divsn., 1980-87. Cons., lectr. in field. Lay-lectr. history and philosophy sci. Unitarian-Universalist Ch. With USN, 1945—46. Mem.: AIME, N.Y. Acad. Scis., Am. Ceramic Soc., Nat. Inst. Cermic Engrs., Am. Inst. Chem. Engrs., Sigma Xi. Home: 2247 5th Ave NE Rochester MN 55906-4017 Office Phone: 507-282-0550.

HUFFINES, MARION LOIS, academic administrator, linguist, educator, language educator; BA magna cum laude, Maryville Coll., 1963; MA, Ind. U., 1969, PhD in Germanic Linguistics, 1971; postgrad., U. Ill., 1969, postgrad., 1978, SUNY, Oswego, 1976, Georgetown U., 1985. Asst. prof. German Bucknell U., Lewisburg, Pa., 1971—77, assoc. prof. German and linguistics, 1977—88, prof. German and linguistics, 1988—, dir. linguistics program, 1975—84, dir. German program, 1982—84, chair dept. modern langs., lits. and linguistics, 1984—85, dir. writing program and writing ctr., 1987—98, dir. grad. studies, 1987—, dir. summer sch., 1990—98, affirmative action officer, 1993—2004, assoc. dean for spl. acad. programs, 1996—98, assoc. v.p. for acad. affairs, 1998—. Office: Assoc VP for Acad Affairs Bucknell Univ Lewisburg PA 17837

HUFFINGTON, ANITA, sculptor; b. Balt., Dec. 25, 1934; d. Norris Jackson and Agnes (Hook) H.; m. Manuel Rubin Duque, Sept. 17, 1957 (div. Nov. 1964); 1 child, Lisa Huffington Duque; m. Henry Sutter, Dec. 4, 1964. BA, CCNY, 1973, MFA, 1975. Resident La Napoule (France) Art Found., 1996. One-woman exhbns. include U. Ark., Fayetteville, 1982, Valley House Gallery, Dallas, 1986, Benton Gallery, Southampton, NY, 1989, Ark. Art Ctr., Little Rock, 1990, O'Hara Gallery, NYC, 1994, 96, 99, 2001, 04, U. Ctrl. Ark., Conway, 1997, Triangle Gallery, San Francisco, 1998, Lisa Kurts Gallery, Memphis, 1999, 2003, 05, Morris Mus., Augusta, Ga., 2004, Walton Art Ctr., Fayetteville, Ar., 2004; 2-person show Lisa Kurts Gallery, 1995; 3-person shows Louis Stern Gallery, West Hollywood, Calif., 1996, Triangle Gallery, San Francisco, 1996; group exhbn. include Internat. Women's Art Festival, NYC, 1976, U. Ark., Fayetteville, 1978, 92, Ark. Arts Ctr., Little Rock, 1979-81, Territorial Restoration Gallery, Little Rock, 1981, Harris Gallery, Houston, Tex., 1981-93, Sculptural Arts Mus., Altanta, 1982, Benton Gallery, Southampton, NY, 1988, Kornbluth Gallery, Fair Lawn, NJ, 1989, The Art Show, 7th Regiment Armory, NYC, 1989-2005, Art of the 20th Century 7th Regiment Armory, N.Y.C., 2003, 04, 05, Ft. Smith (Ark.) Art Ctr., 1990, Salon de Mars, Paris, 1992, U. Pa., Phila. US Artists Art Fair, Pa. Acad., 1992-2002, 2003, ARTexas, Dallas, 1993-94, Art Fair Seattle, 1995-97, Art Miami (Fla.), 1996, 98, Triangle Gallery, San Francisco, 1996, 99, 2000, Am. Acad. Arts and Letters, NYC, 1997, Columbus (Ga.) Mus. and Miss. Mus. Art, Jackson, 1997, Am. Acad. Arts and Letters, 1997, Two Sculptors, Inc., NYC, 1998, Valley House Gallery, Dallas, 1998, Art Palm Beach, 1998, 99, 2000, 01, Dallas Internat. Art and Antiques Fair, 2000-02, 50th Anniversary Show, Valley Ho. Gallery, Dallas, Hist. Ark. Mus., Little Rock, 2001; permanent collections include Met. Mus. Art, N.Y.C., 2002, others; featured in various profl. publ., mag., newspapers, and videos. Recipient Jimmy Ernst award Am. Acad. Arts and Letters, 1997, others; Visual arts fellow Ark. Arts Coun.

HUFFINGTON, ARIANNA, writer; b. Athens, Greece, July 15, 1950; came to U.S., 1980; d. Constantine Stassinopoulos and Helen Georgiadis; m. Michael Huffington, Apr. 12, 1986 (div. 1997); children: Christina, Isabella. MA in Econ., Cambridge U., Eng., 1971. Syndicated columnist Tribune Media Svcs., 1995—; co-founder Detroit Project. Bd. mem. A Place Called Home, LA, Archer Sch. for Girls, Reform Inst.; adv. bd. Coun. on Am. Politics, George Washington Univ.; Independent party candidate for gov State of Calif., 2003. Author: The Female Woman, 1974, After Reason, 1978, Maria Callas: The Woman Behind the Legend, 1981, Picasso: Creator and Destroyer, 1988, The Gods of Greece, 1993, The Fourth Instinct, 1994, Greetings From the Lincoln Bedroom, 1998, How to Overthrow the Government, 2000, Pigs at the Trough: How Corporate Greed and Political Corruption are Undermining America, 2003, Fanatics and Fools: The Game Plan for Winning Back America, 2004; guest appearances on Larry King Live, Oprah, Nightline, Inside Politics, Charlie Rose, Crossfire, Hardball, Good Morning America, Today Show, McLaughlin Group, and the O'Reilly Factor, launched a news and opinion web site including blogs written by more than 200 celebrities and leaders, including a feature called The Huffington Post, 2005. First place, Funniest Celebrity in Washington standup comedy contest. Office: Arianna Online 1158 26th St PO Box 428 Santa Monica CA 90403 Business E-Mail: arianna@ariannaonline.com.*

HUFFMAN, CADY, actress; b. Santa Barbara, Calif., Feb. 2, 1965; d. Clifford Roy and Lorayne Dolores (Rote) H.; m. William Healy, 1994. Pvt. studies with Nathan Lam, L.A., 1983-85, Maria Gobetti, 1984-85, Bill Reed, N.Y.C., 1987-90, Fred Kareman, 1988. Actress Broadway plays La Cage Aux Folles, 1983-84, Big Deal, 1985, The Will Rogers Follies, 1991-93, Steel Pier, 1997, The Producers, 2001-03 (Tony award best actress, 2001); (off Broadway) Gemini, 1990, Italian American Reconciliation, 1990, As You Like It, 1989, The Baker's Wife, 1982, They're Playing Our Song, 1983, Jekyll and Hyde, 1989, Dame Edna: The Royal Tour, 1999-2000, Short Talks on the Universe, 2002; TV shows The Guiding Light, 1986, Another World, 1987, Pig Sty, 1995, Mad About You, 1995, Law & Order: Criminal Intent, 2001, Curb Your Enthusiasm, 2004; films Hero, 1992, Space Marines, 1996, Sunday on the Rocks, 2004 (also prodr.); appeared in more than 30 TV commls., 1985-90. Vol. recreational therapist The Lighthouse, N.Y.C., 1986-87 Recipient 3d Place award Pacific REgional Ballet Assn., 1980. Avocations: piano, swimming, dance, singing.

HUFFMAN, D. C., JR., pharmacist, educator, health science association administrator; BS in Pharmacy, U. Ark., 1966; PhD in Pharmacy Administrn., U. Miss., 1971. Pharmacist Crank Drug Co., Inc., Little Rock, 1966-67; asst. prof., dir. divsn. pharmacy adminstrn. U. Tenn. Coll. Pharmacy, Memphis, 1970-73, assoc. prof., chmn. dept. pharmaceutics, 1973; exec. v.p. Am. Coll. Apothecaries, 1971—, prof., chmn. dept. pharmacy, 1974-89, vice chancellor adminstrn., 1984-89; exec. dir. NCPA Mgmt. Inst., Alexandria, Va., 1989-2000; sr. v.p. practice and mgmt. NCPA, Alexandria, Va., 1992-2000. Presenter numerous seminars. Contbr. articles to profl. jours. Archer Drug Co. scholar, 1966; recipient Lederle Faculty award, 1971; fellow NDEA, 1967-70, Am. Found. for Pharm. Edn., 1967-70. Fellow Am. Coll Apothecaries (exec. v.p.); mem. AAAS, Am. Assn. Colls. Pharmacy, Am. Pharm. Assn., Tenn. Pharm. Assn., Okla. Pharm. Assn. (hon.), Ark. Pharm. Assn. (hon. life), Am. Soc. Assn. Execs., Nat. Cmty. Pharmacists Assn., Kappa Psi, Rho Chi. Office: American College of Apothecaries 2830 Summer Oaks Dr Bartlett TN 38134-3811 Office Phone: 901-383-8119. Business E-Mail: dc@acainfo.org.

HUFFMAN, DAVID CURTIS, minister; b. Burlington, N.C., Mar. 28, 1950; s. Donald Tyson and Merle (Walker) H.; m. Elaine Janine Wolf, June 25, 1988; children: Katherine Elizabeth Wolf, Anna Elaine Huffman. BA, U. N.C., 1972; MDiv, Princeton Theol. Sem., 1976. Ordained to ministry Presbyn. Ch. (U.S.A.), 1976. Student asst. min. Franklin Lakes (N.J.) Presbyn. Ch., 1973-76; asst. min. Old South Ch., Boston, 1976-79, assoc. min., 1979-81; pastor Trinity Presbyn. Ch., Raleigh, N.C., 1981—. Chmn. profl. devel. com. Orange Presbytery, Durham, N.C., 1982-84, chmn. peacemaking com., 1982-85, mem. com. on ministry, 1983-87; chmn. com. on ministry New Hope Presbytery, Rocky Mount, N.C., 1988-90, 93, examinations com., 1995-2000, 2005—; pres. Presbyn. Urban Coun., Raleigh, 1988; commr. to gen. assembly Presbyn. Ch., U.S.A., 1995; vice chair bd. Triangle Pastoral Counseling Ctr., 1999-2001; moderator, New Hope Presbytery 2002; class steward Princeton Theol. Seminary, 2003—. Merrill fellow Harvard Div. Sch., 1986. Mem. Sustaining Pastoral Excellence Project (Lilly Grant 2003-05), Soc. Bibl. Lit., The Company of Pastors, Rehoboth Book Study, Presbyn. Mins. Assn. Raleigh, Phi Beta Kappa, Beta Theta Pi. Democrat. Home: 8705 Mansfield Dr Raleigh NC 27613-1337 Office: Trinity Presbyn Ch 3120 New Hope Rd Raleigh NC 27604-4948

HUFFMAN, DAVID LEE, chemistry professor, researcher; b. Bloomington, Ind., Sept. 15, 1960; s. Randall Leland and Juanita June Huffman; m. Ruthann Stewart, May 31, 1983; children: David, Rachel. BS, Bob Jones U., 1983; MS, Ill. State U., 1988; PhD, U. Ill., 1994. Tchg. asst. Ill. State U., Normal, 1986—88, U. Ill., Urbana-Champaign, 1988—90, rsch. asst., 1990—93; NRSA postdoctoral fellow Northwestern U., Evanston, Ill., 1994—97; adj. faculty Trinity Internat. U., Deerfield, Ill., 1997; postdoctoral fellow Northwestern U., 1998, Molecular Toxicology postdoctoral fellow, 1999—2001; vis. scientist U. Florence, Italy, 2000, 2005; vis. scholar Northwestern U., 2001—04; asst. prof. Western Mich. U., Kalamazoo, 2001—. Advisory bd. Internat. Conf. Bioinorganic Chemistry, Ann Arbor, Mich., 2003—05; com. mem. Internat. Conf. Bioinorganic Chemistry 12, Ann Arbor, 2003—05. Adv. mem. Internat. Conf. for Bioinorganic Chemistry-12, Ann Arbor, Mich., 2003—. Recipient Nat. Rsch. Svc. award, Nat. Insts. Health, 1994—97, Molecular Toxicology Postdoctoral, 1999—2001, Gramm Travel fellowship, Robert H. Lurie Cancer Ctr., 1999. Mem.: AAAS (poster award 1992), Am. Soc. Biochemistry and Molecular Biology, Am. Assn. Study of Liver Disease, Am. Chem. Soc. Office: Western Mich Univ 1903 W Michigan Ave Kalamazoo MI 49008 Office Fax: 269-387-2909. Business E-Mail: david.huffman@wmich.edu.

HUFFMAN, DELTON CLEON, JR., pharmacy association executive; b. St. Louis, Feb. 18, 1943; s. Delton Cleon and Kathryn (Saegesser) H.; m. Judy Hill, Aug. 11, 1962; children: Kimberly Lea, Jeffrey Keith. BS in Pharmacy, U. Ark., 1966; PhD, U. Miss., 1971. Pharmacist Crank Drug Co., Inc., Little Rock, 1966—67; asst. prof., dir. divsn. pharmacy adminstrn. U. Tenn. Coll. Pharmacy, Memphis, 1970—73, asso. prof., chmn. dept. pharmaceutics, 1973; exec. v.p. Am. Coll. Apothecaries, 1971—, also prof., chmn. dept. pharmacy, 1974—89, vice chancellor adminstrn., 1984—89; exec. dir. Nat. Cmty. Pharmacists Assn. Mgmt. Inst., Alexandria, Va., 1989—99, sr. v.p. practice and mgmt., 1992—99. Contbr. articles to profl. lit. Recipient Lederle Faculty award, 1971; NDEA fellow, 1967-70; Am. Found. for Pharm. Edn. fellow, 1967-70; Archer Drug Co. scholar, 1966. Fellow Am. Coll. Apothecaries; mem. AAAS, Am. Assn. Colls. Pharmacy, Am. Pharm. Assn., Nat. Cmty. Pharmacists Assn., Tenn. Pharm. Assn., Okla. Pharm. Assn. (hon.), Ark. Pharm. Assn. (hon., life), Am. Soc. Assn. Execs., Kappa Psi, Rho Chi. Home: 6020 Willoughby Oak Ln Bartlett TN 38135-1464 Office: 2830 Summer Oaks Dr Bartlett TN 38134-3811

HUFFMAN, DURWARD ROY, academic administrator, electrical engineer; b. Little Mountain, S.C., Jan. 22, 1939; s. Roy Otho and Mabel Amanda (Huffstettler) H.; m. Lillian Hope Farrell, Apr. 18, 1959; children: Donald Durward, Heatherlyn. BSEE, Heald Engring. Coll., 1963; MSEE, U. Colo., 1966; EdD in Higher Edn., U. Sarasota, 1980. Registered profl. engr., Pa. Asst. design engr. Westinghouse Elec. Corp., Sunnyvale, Calif., 1963-64; instr. elec. engring. U. Colo., Boulder, 1965-67; elec. engr. Corning (N.Y.) Glass Works, 1967-68; sr. process control engr. Corning Glass Works, Wellsboro, Pa., 1968; assoc. prof. elec.-electronic engring. tech. Luzerne County C.C., Wilkes-Barre, Pa., 1968-73, chmn. dept., 1971-73; faculty Midlands Tech. Coll., Columbia, S.C., 1973-75; assoc. dean Nashville State Tech. Inst., 1976-87, acting dean instrn., 1985-86; pres. No. Maine Tech. Coll., Presque Isle, 1987-2001; acad. officer Maine C.C. Sys., Augusta, 1994-2001, chief acad. officer, 2001—04; cons. CC, 2004—. Presenter in field; chair tech. accreditation commn. Accreditation Bd. Engring. and Tech., 1989-90. Editor-in-chief, Jour. Engring. Tech., 1990-92, pub. editor, 1987-89. Mem. steering com. Ctrl. Aroostook County (Maine) Job Opportunity Zone, 1988-91; bd. dirs. Leaders Encouraging Aroostook Devel., 1988-2001, sec., 1988-93; bd. dirs. Maine Rsch. and Productivity Coun., 1988-92; mem. pub. policy com. Maine Alzheimer's Assn., 2001—. Fellow Accreditation Bd. Engring. and Tech. (life); mem. IEEE (sr., life), Am. Soc. Engring. Edn. (divsn. engring. tech. exec. bd. 1981-82, sec. 1982-84), Am. Assn. C.C. (commn. on cmty. and workforce devel. 1995-97, com. on academic, student, cmty. devel. 1998-2001), Engring. Tech. Leadership Inst. (mem. exec. com. 1978-79, 86-87), New Eng. Assn. Schs. and Colls. (chairperson accreditation team 1990, 95, 97, 98, team mem. 1994-96), Rotary (chairperson com. on vocat. svc. 1988-89, dist. 7810 scholarships subcom. 1996-2000), Presque Isle Club, Eta Kappa Nu. Republican. Avocation: volunteer work.

HUFFMAN, FELICITY (FLICKA HUFFMAN), actress; b. Bedford, NY, Dec. 9, 1962; m. H. William Macy, Sept. 6, 1997; children: Sofia Grace, Georgia Grace. BFA in Drama, NYU, Tisch Sch. Arts, 1988. Actress (TV films) A Home Run for Love, 1978, Lip Service, 1988, Golden Years, 1991, Quicksand:No Escape, 1992, The Water Engine, 1992, The Heart of Justice, 1993, Harrison: Cry of the City, 1996, The Underworld, 1997, A Slight Case of Murder, 1999, Snap Decision, 2001, The Heart Department, 2001, Path to War, 2002, Reversible Errors, 2004, (films) Things Change, Reversal of Fortune, 1990, Hackers, 1995, The Spanish Prisoner, 1997, Magnolia, 1999, House Hunting, 2003, Raising Helen, 2004, Christmas with the Kranks, 2004, (TV series) Bedtime, 1996, Sports Night, 1998, Desperate Housewives, 2004— (co-recipient, Outstanding Performance by an Ensemble in a Drama Series, Screen Actors Guild award, 2005), (TV miniseries) Out of Order, 2003; performer: (plays) Speed-the-Plow, The Three Sisters, Boy's Life, Cryptogram (Off Broadway Theater award (OBIE), 1997); guest appearances The Human Factor, 1992, Raven, 1992, Law & Order, 1992, 1997, The X Files, 1993, Early Edition, 1996, Chicago Hope, 1997, The West Wing, 2001, Kim Possible, 2002, 2003, Frazier, 2003, The DA, 2004. Office: Desperate Housewives Touchstone Televison 100 Universal City Plaza Bldg 2128 Ste G Universal City CA 91608*

HUFFMAN, FORDHAM E., lawyer; b. Hilliard, Ohio, 1954; BA, Ohio State Univ., 1977, JD, 1980. Bar: Ga. 1980, Ohio 1984. Law clk. Judge Max Rosenn, US Ct. of Appeals, Third Cir., 1980; now ptnr.-in-charge Columbus office Jones Day, Ohio. Editor-in-chief Law Rev., 1980. Mem.: Columbus (Ohio) Bar Assn., Ohio State Bar Assn., State Bar of Ga. Office: Jones Day 325 John H McConnel Blvd Ste 600 PO Box 165017 Columbus OH 43216-5017 Office Phone: 614-469-3934. Office Fax: 614-461-4198. Business E-Mail: fehuffman@jonesday.com.

HUFFMAN, GERALD P., science administrator, educator; b. Steubenville, Ohio, Sept. 12, 1938; s. Sherwood John and Anne Virginia Huffman; m. Shelby-Jean Walker; children: Scott Bradley, Brad Christopher, Kirsten Ahn Rowland. PhD, W.Va. U., 1965. Rsch. scientist Fundamental Rsch. Lab., U.S. Steel Corp., Monroeville, Pa., 1965—85; pres. MacroAtom, Inc., Monroeville, 1985—86; dir. Consortium for Fossil Fuel Sci. U. Ky., Lexington, 1986—, prof. depts. chem. and materials engring. and physics, 1986—. Editor: (jour.) Fuel Processing Technology, numerous conf. proceedings; contbr. 280 scientific papers to profl. jours., conf. procs., and books. Recipient Henry Marion Howe medal, Am. Soc. for Metals, 1984, Best Fundamental Paper award South Tex. sect., AIChE, 1995, Wall of Honor award, West Liberty State Coll. Alumni Assn., 2004, 44 rsch. grants and contracts, various govt. agys. and industry, 1972—2004. Mem.: Am. Chem. Soc. (chair divsn. fuel chemistry 1997—98, cert. of merit divsn. environ. chemistry 1998). Achievements include 6 patents and patents pending for catalyst development, conversion of hydrocarbons to hydrogen and carbon nanatubes, and coversion of waste plastic to lubricating oil; research in catalysis; coversion of coal, natural gas, and waste plastics into clean liquid fuels and hydrogen; C1 chemistry; XAFS and Mössbauer spectroscopy; electron microscopy; toxic trace metals, and fine airborne particulate matter. Home: 908 Belmere Dr Lexington KY 40509 Office: U Ky 533 S Limestone St Lexington KY 40506-0043 Office Phone: 859-257-4027. Office Fax: 859-257-7215. Personal E-mail: gphuffman@insightbb.com. E-mail: huffman@engr.uky.edu.

HUFFMAN, GREGORY SCOTT COMBEST, lawyer; b. Austin, Tex., Dec. 19, 1946; s. Calvin Combest and Olive Agnes (Weaver) H.; m. Mary L. Murphy, Feb. 1, 1986. Student, Stanford U., France, 1966—67; BA in History with great distinction, Stanford U., 1969; postgrad., London Sch. of Econs., 1971—72; JD, Harvard U., 1973. Bar: Tex. 1973, U.S. Dist. Cts. Tex. 1974, U.S. Ct. Appeals (5th cir.) 1975, U.S. Supreme Ct. 1976. From assoc. to sr. ptnr. Thompson & Knight, Dallas, 1973—, also dir. Chief editor (monographs) Texas Free Enterprise and Antitrust Act, 1984-90, Texas Antitrust and Related Statutes, 1991—. Pres. Northern Hills Neighborhood Assn., 1980; bd. dirs. Common Cause of Tex., 1979-81, Love Field Citizens Action Commn., 1980-83, Appleseed Found., 1996-2001; adminstrv. chmn., bd. dirs. Tex. Appleseed, 1996-2001; active Tex. Supreme Ct. Adv. Com. on Professionalism. Fellow Tex. Bar Found., Dallas Bar Found.; mem. ABA (antitrust and litigation sect.), Tex. Bar Assn. (antitrust and litigation sect., chmn. unlawful practice law com. 1981-83, chmn. lawyer referral svc. com. 1982-83, bd. legal specialization 1974-77, chmn. antitrust and bus. litigation sect. 1991-92, bd. dirs. 1983—, task force on unauthorized practice of law, author of reports, presdl. citation 2000, cert. of merit 2001), Am. Bd. Trial Advocates, Dallas Bar Assn. (antitrust sect., sec.-treas. 1981, chmn. unauthorized practice law com. 1979, chmn. lawyer referral svc. com. 1980-81, chmn. profl. svcs. com. 1986-87, chmn. spkrs. com. 1999-2000, chmn. CLE com. 2001, bd. dirs. antitrust sect. 1981, 89-2002, bd. dirs. litigation sect. 1988), Harvard Law Sch. Assn. Tex. (pres. 1987-88), Tower Club Dallas, Phi Beta Kappa, Sigma Alpha Epsilon. Methodist. Home: 8234 Garland Rd Dallas TX 75218-4417 Office: Thompson & Knight 1700 Pacific Ave Ste 3300 Dallas TX 75201-4693 Office Phone: 214-969-1144. Business E-Mail: huffmang@tklaw.com.

HUFFMAN, JAMES THOMAS WILLIAM, oil industry executive; b. Norman, Okla., Mar. 27, 1947; s. Thomas William and Dorlese M. (Hicks) H.; children: Laura Anne, Christopher James. BBA, Baylor U., 1970. CPA. Mgr. Arthur Andersen & Co., Houston, 1970-76; sr. mgr. Price, Waterhouse & Co., Denver, 1976-79; v.p. Credo Petroleum Corp., 1978-80, pres., 1980-81, chmn., chief exec. officer, 1981—, also dir. Dir. Huffman Heat Exchangers Inc.; dir. XF&R, Inc.; pres., dir. SECO Energy Corp.; pres., dir. United Oil Corp. Mem. AICPA, Tex., Colo. socs. CPAs, Petroleum Landman, Ind. Petroleum Assn. Am., Ind. Petroleum Assn. Mountain State, Petroleum Accts. Soc.

HUFFMAN, JANET FAYE, secondary school educator; b. Liberal, Kans., Feb. 20, 1946; d. Kenneth D. and Ursula Idella Garten; divorced; children: Heidi Ann, Heather Sue. BA, U. Colo., 1968; MS, Ft. Hays (Kans.) State U., 1970. Cert. secondary English tchr., Mo. Tchr. Platte Community Coll., Columbus, Nebr., 1970-71, Arriba (Colo.) High Sch., 1980-82; English tchr. Limon (Colo.) High Sch., 1982—. Author: (poems) Inward Perspective, 1990. Mem. Limon Edn. Assn. (sec. 1990-91), Order of Eastern Star (worth matron 1989-90), First United Meth. Ch., Limon Heritage Soc. Avocations: reading, travel. Home: PO Box 846 Limon CO 80828 Office: Limon Sch PO Box 249 Limon CO 80828-0249

HUFFMAN, JOAN BREWER, history professor; b. Springfield, Ohio, Aug. 18, 1937; d. James Clarence and Berniece (Notter) Brewer; m. James Russell Huffman, Aug. 21, 1959; children: Jill Elizabeth, Jean Elaine. AB, Ohio U., 1959; MA, Ga. State U., 1968, PhD, 1980. Adj. prof. Wesleyan Coll., Macon, Ga., 1981-82; instr. history Macon State Coll., 1968-72, asst. prof., 1972-81, assoc. prof., 1981-86, prof., 1986-2000, prof. emerita, 2000—; owner The Printed Page, Macon, Ga., 1993-97, Picture Perfect, 1995—. Chmn. History adv. com. U. Sys. Ga., 1986—87. Contbr. articles to profl. jours. Mem., bd. dirs. Oklahatchee Pk., Perry, Ga., 1966-68, Macon State Coll. Found., 1985-90, Ga. Humanities Coun., Atlanta, 1983-87. Katharine C. Bleckley scholar English-Speaking Union, 1977; recipient Gov.'s award in the humanities, 1998. Mem. N.Am. Conf. on Brit. Studies, Am. Hist. Assn., Southern Hist. Assn. (membership com. 1988-89), Ga. Assn. Historians (pres. 1982-83), Phi Beta Kappa, Phi Alpha Theta (award 1978). Home: 135 Covington Pl Macon GA 31210-4445 Office Phone: 478-746-6365. E-mail: huffmanj@bellsouth.net.

HUFFMAN, JOHN CURTIS, chemist; b. Kokomo, Ind., Dec. 9, 1941; s. Millard William and Lorene Gladys (Patmore) H.; m. Carolyn Jean Nash, Sept. 4, 1964; children: John Nash, Charles Curtis. BS in Chemistry, Ind. U., 1964, MS in Chemistry, 1968, PhD in Chemistry, 1974. Crystallographer Ind. U., Bloomington, 1968-74, dir. Molecular Structure Ctr., 1974—, sr. scientist in chemistry, 1984—, dir. Informatics Rsch. Inst., 2002—, adj. prof. informatics, 2003—. Pres. Xtelletx Software, Bloomington; cons. various drug and chem. cos. Contbr. over 800 articles to profl. jours. Vol. Boy Scouts Am. Recipient Polyhedron Best Paper award Pergamon Press, 1987. Mem. AAAS, Am. Crystallographic Assn., Am. Chem. Soc., Am. Inst. Physics, Sigma Xi. Avocation: computer programming. Office: Ind U Chemistry Dept Bloomington IN 47405

HUFFMAN, MARY FRANCES, retired secondary school educator; b. Montgomery, Ala., Apr. 30, 1911; d. Mary Huffman; m. Alexander Lee, June 28, 1936 (div. Aug. 1938); 1 child, Patricia Day Smoke. BS, Ala. State U., 1951, MEd, 1961; postgrad., So. U., Baton Rouge, La., 1960, Beloit Coll., 1963, Talladega Coll., 1963—64. Cert. elem. and secondary tchr. Ala. Tchr. Elem. Schs., Troy, Ala., 1929-30, Prattville, Ala., 1930-32, Lowndes County, Ala., 1932-42, Union Springs, Ala., 1943-45, Montgomery, 1945-73, ret., 1973—. Sec. Nat. Caucus & Ctr. Black Aged, Congress Christian Edn., 1955—, Montgomery County Multi-Black Caucus; counselor Montgomery-Antioch Dist., Ala. State Women; me. program com. YMCA, 1969; treas. Alonzo Mitchell OES 636, Montgomery, 1980; Sunday sch. tchr. Holt St. Bapt. Ch., sec. matrons cir.; with Lilly Baptist Ch., 2002. Mem.: AARP, NEA, AAUW, Montgomery County Ret. Tchrs. Assn., Assn. Ret. Tchrs. Am., Twelve Tribes (rec. sec. Montgomery). Avocation: travel.

HUFFMAN, PATRICIA NELL, entrepreneur; b. Springfield, Mo., Sept. 25, 1947; d. Rex Eugene and Helen Marie (Appleby) Riggs; m. Frank Dale Huffman, June 18, 1966 (div. Apr. 2003); children: Chad, Heather, Tyler. Student, Joplin Jr. Coll., 1966. Saleswoman Sta. KTVJ-TV, Joplin, Mo., 1972—77; designer, mktg. ADI-Comml. Interiors, Tulsa, 1983—84; pres., designer Bittersweet, Inc., Joplin, 1984—89; founder, pres. By Invitation

Only, 1986—89. Co-owner, bd. dirs., sec. J-Town Billiards, Sports Bar and Grill, 1999—; cons. in field. Designer country gift items, 1978—. Vol. Mental Health Ctr., Joplin, 1965, Am. Heart Assn., Joplin, 1980, Family Self Help Ctr., Joplin, 1981—, United Way, Joplin, 1982; pres. Women's Support Group, Joplin, 1983-85, Family Violence Coun., 1996-97, bd. dirs., pres. bd.; bd. dirs. Children's Ctr., 1997-2001; co-founder S.A.F.E. Coalition, 1989-97. Recipient Women Helping Women award, 1998, House Resolution No. 785 for volunteerism with children and women State of Mo., 1994. Mem. Exch. Club (Book of Golden Deeds award 1996). Avocations: bridge, creative writing, billiards, painting, illustrating and writing children's books. Office: PO Box 2159 2502 S Main St Joplin MO 64803-2159 Office Phone: 417-659-9777. E-mail: jtownsportsbar@sbcglobal.net, paintinglibra@sbcglobal.net.

HUFFMAN, ROBERT ALLEN, JR., lawyer; b. Tucson, Dec. 30, 1950; s. Robert Allen and Ruth Jane (Hicks) Huffman; m. Marjorie Kavanagh, Dec. 30, 1976; children: Katharine Kavanagh, Elizabeth Rooney, Robert Allen III, Simeon Ross. BBA, U. Okla., 1973, JD, 1976. Bar: Okla. 1977, U.S. Dist. Ct. (no. dist.) Okla. 1977, U.S. Ct. Appeals (10th cir.) 1978, U.S. Supreme Ct. 1982. Assoc. Huffman, Arrington, Kihle, Gaberino & Dunn, Tulsa, Okla., 1977—81, ptnr., 1981—97, Edwards & Huffmann LLP, Tulsa, 1997—. Mem.: ABA, Fed. Energy Bar Assn., Tulsa County Bar Assn., Southern Hills Country Club (Tulsa). Republican. Roman Catholic. Home: 5937 S Columbia Ave Tulsa OK 74105-7319 E-mail: rhuffman@edwardshuffman.com.

HUFFMAN, THOMAS DAVID, church music director, organist; b. Elkins, W.Va., Nov. 11, 1952; s. Elvin D. and Lenore C. Huffman; m. Lucinda E. Croasmun, June 10, 1978; 1 child, Christopher D. MusB, W.Va. U., 1978, MusM, 1981. Dir. of music, organist United Meth. Temple, Beckley, W.Va., 1981—84, 1st United Meth. Ch., Dunedin, Fla., 1984—. Founding dir. Beckley Cmty. Chorus, 1981—84. Mem.: Am. Guild English Handbell Ringers, Choristers Guild, Am. Guild Organists (dean Clearwater (Fla.) chpt. 2003—04), Fellowship of United Methodists in Music and Worship Arts, Am. Choral Dirs. Assn. Methodist. Home: 1261 Royal Oak Dr Dunedin FL 34698 Office: 1st United Meth Ch 421 Main St Dunedin FL 34698 Office Phone: 727-733-4139. Home Fax: 727-733-7813; Office Fax: 727-733-7813. Personal E-mail: hufftom@aol.com.

HUFFMAN, WALTER B., retired army officer, dean, law educator; b. Keesler AFB, Miss., Oct. 8, 1944; m. Anne Robison; children: Burl, Becky, Ross. BS, Tex. Tech U., 1967, MEd, 1968, JD with highest honors, 1977. Commd. 2d lt. U.S. Army, 1968, advanced through grades to maj. gen.; judge adv. in various assignments including Desert Shield/Desert Storm, 1977-97; judge advocate gen. U.S. Army, 1997—2002; ret., 2002; dean, prof. law Sch. Law Tex. Tech. U., Lubbock, 2002—. Editor-in-chief Tex. Tech Law Rev. Decorated Legion of Merit with one oak leaf cluster, Bronze Star medal with 2 oak leaf clusters, Hungarian Disting. Svc. medal. Office: Tex Tech Univ Sch Law 18th and Hartford Lubbock TX 79409

HUFFORD, DAVID J., humanities educator; b. Cortland, N.Y., May 14, 1944; s. Charles Lewellyn and Marjorie Emma (Slawson) H.; m. Mary Ann Bucklin, Sept. 21, 1996; children: Gwyneth Ellin, David Gordon, Annamarie Davida, Moses Mitchell. BA in English, Lycoming Coll., 1966; MA in Folklore, U. Pa., 1968, PhD in Folklore & Folklife, 1974. Pa. state folklorist and dir. Pa. Hist. Mus. Commn., Harrisburg, 1969-70; rschr., asst. prof. Meml. U. of Newfoundland, 1971-74; asst. prof. Coll. of Medicine Pa. State U., Hershey, 1974-80, assoc. prof., 1980-92, prof., 1992—, Univ. prof. and chair, 2003—. Adj. prof. folkore U. Pa., Phila., 1993—; adj. prof. religious studies, 1999—; commr.-at-large Pa. Heritage Affairs, Harrisburg, 1988—. Mem. editl. bd. Alternative Therapies in Health and Medicine, 1994—; mem. editl. adv. bd. Pennsylvania Folklife, 1993—, Folkore in Use, 1992—; author: The Terror That Comes in the Night, 1982, Japanese edit., 1998 (award 1983), The World Was Flooded With Light, 1985; co-editor Jour. Philosophy and Medicine 18, 1993; editor Western Folkore jour., 1995. Bd. dirs. Pa. Spl. Olympics, Harrisburg, 1989—. Mem. NIH (cancer adv. panel Nat. Ctr. Complementary and Alternative Medicine 1998—), Am. Folkore Soc. (sec. 1976-80), Internat. Assn. Folklore Fellows. Byzantine Catholic. Avocations: gardening, music. Office: The Milton S Hershey Med Ctr Dept Humanities PO Box 850 Hershey PA 17033-0850 Office Phone: 717-531-8037. E-mail: dhufford@psu.edu.

HUFFSTETLER, PALMER EUGENE, lawyer; b. Shelby, N.C., Dec. 21, 1937; s. Daniel S. and Ethel (Turner) H.; m. Mary Ann Beam, Aug. 9, 1958; children: Palmer Eugene, Ben Beam, Brian Tad. BA, Wake Forest U., 1959, JD, 1961. Bar: N.C. 1961. Practiced in, Kings Mountain, N.C., 1961-62, Raleigh, N.C., 1962-64; with State Farm Ins. Co., Orlando, Fla., 1962; gen. legal counsel Carolina Freight Corp., Cherryville, N.C., 1964-93, sec., 1969-90, sr. v.p., 1969-89, exec. v.p., 1985-93, pres., 1993-95; ret., 1995; pres., CEO Blue Chip Inc., 1997-99. Author, composer: Senior Man on Carolina Line, Fifty Years Ago. Chmn. Cherryville Zoning Bd. Adjustment, 1967-70; active N.C. Gasoline and Oil Insp. Bd., 1974-76; class chmn. Wake Forest Coll. Fund, 1971-79, decade chmn.Wake Forest Law Sch. Law Adv. Com., 1981-82; governing body, chmn. adminstrv. com. So. Piedmont Health Systems Agy., 1975-77; mem. Cherryville Econ. Devel. Commn., 1982-87, Cherryville Econ. Devel. Com., 1995-97; pres. Cherryville Devel. Corp., 1986—; bd. dirs. C. Grier Beam Truck Mus., 1982-2002, pres. 1982-96; bd. dirs. Schiele Mus., Gastonia, N.C., 1985-88, Gaston Meml. Hosp., 1990-93, vice-chmn. bd.; active N.C. Gov.'s Hwy. Safety Commn., 1985-88, Gov.'s Bus. Com., N.C., 1993-95; v.p. Ctrl. and So. Rate Bur., 1984-89; trustee Brevard Coll., 1987-93. Mem. N.C. State Bar, N.C. Bar Assn. (mem. adminstrv. bd. 1965-69, 71-72, chmn. adminstrv. bd., trustee 1970-73, fin. com. 1994-2002), First United Meth. Ch. (coun. 2002-2004). Methodist. Home: 2141 Fairways Dr Cherryville NC 28021-2115

HUFFSTETLER, VICKIE PLAXICO, elementary school educator; b. Atlanta, Apr. 25, 1956; d. David Livingstone and Helen Ray (Goldsmith) Plaxico; m. J. Jay Huffstetler, Nov. 3, 1979; 1 child, Philip Plaxico. BS in Secondary Edn., U. S.C., Spartanburg, 1977; MEd in Elem. Edn., Converse U., 1982, edn. specialist cert., 1993. Cert. tchr., S.C. Assoc. tchr. Corinth Elem. Sch., Gaffney, S.C., 1978; tchr. Goucher Elem. Sch., Gaffney, 1978—98; tchr. lead tchr. in sci. and social studies Ewing Mid. Sch., 1998—. Lead tchr. Tchrs. Leading Tchrs., 1994; insvc. leader Sci. Methods, 1984—; H.O.M.E. team leader North Point Ch.; mem. mid.-sch. state sci. validation panel, SACS chmn.; presenter in field. Leader Girl Scouts Am., Gaffney, 1978—, counselor, 1988—; instr. ARC, Gaffney, 1980-86; bd. dirs. West End Bapt. Weekday Ministry to Children, Gaffney, 1986-90; Sunday Sch. tchr. Named Outstanding Leader Piedmont Area Girls Scouts, Gaffney, 1986. Mem. Internat. Reading Assn., S.C. Sci. Coun., Palmetto State Tchr. Assn. (bldg. coord.), Nat. Sci. Tchrs. Assn., S.C. Earth Sci. Tchr. Assn., Omicron Delta Kappa, Phi Kappa Phi. Baptist. Avocations: Star Trek, crafting, reading, U.S. space program. Office: John E Ewing Mid Sch 171 E Jr High Rd Gaffney SC 29340

HUFNAGEL, LINDA ANN, biology professor, researcher; b. Teaneck, N.J., Nov. 7, 1939; d. Ernest Albert and Frances Marie (Hrbek) H.; m. Dov Jaron, 1969; children: Shulamit, Tamara; m. Robert Van Zackroff, June 1984. BA, U. Vt., 1961, MS, 1963; PhD, U. Pa., 1967. Lectr. U. Pa., Phila., summer 1967; NSF postdoctoral fellow Yale U., New Haven, 1967-69; rsch. assoc. Columbia U., N.Y.C., 1970; asst. prof. Oakland C.C., Farmington, Mich., 1970; rsch. assoc. Wayne State U., Detroit, 1971-73; lectr. biology U. R.I., Kingston, 1973-75, asst. prof., 1975-79, assoc. prof., 1979-86, prof., 1986—, dir. cen. electron microscope facility, 1973-96. NSF rsch. grantee, U. R.I., 1975, Am. Heart Assn. rsch. grantee, 1979, Steps fellow, Marine Biol. Lab., Woods Hole, Mass., 1978—79. Office: U RI Dept Cell Mol Biol Kingston RI 02881 Office Phone: 401-874-5914. Business E-Mail: lhufnagel@uri.edu.

HUFSTEDLER, SETH MARTIN, lawyer; b. Dewar, Okla., Sept. 20, 1922; s. Seth Martin and Myrtle (Younts) H.; m. Shirley Ann Mount, Aug. 16, 1949; 1 child, Steven. BA magna cum laude, U. So. Calif., 1944; LL.B., Stanford U., 1949. Bar: Calif. 1950. Pvt. practice, L.A.; assoc. Lillick, Geary & McHose, 1950-51; with Charles E. Beardsley, 1951-53; ptnr. Beardsley, Hufstedler & Kemble, 1953-81, Hufstedler, Miller, Carlson & Beardsley, 1981-88, Hufstedler, Kaus & Ettinger, L.A., 1988-94; Hufstedler & Kaus, 1994-95; sr. of counsel Morrison & Foerster LLP, 1995—. Mem. Calif. Jud. Coun., 1977—78. Legis. editor Stanford U. Law Rev., 1948—49. Sec. regional planning coun. United Way, 1971-75; co-chmn. Pub. Commn. County Govt., L.A., 1975-76, 89-92; trustee AEFC Pension Fund, 1978-82; mem. Calif Citizens Commn. on Tort Reform, 1976-77; bd. visitors Stanford Law Sch., chmn., 1972-73. Lt. (j.g.) USNR, 1943-46. Mem. ABA (chmn. action commn. to reduce ct costs and delay 1979-81, mem. coun. sr. bar div. 1986-89, chmn. 1987-88), Los Angeles County Bar Assn. (trustee 1963-65, 66-70, pres. 1969-70, Shattuck Price award 1976), State Bar Calif. (bd. govs. 1971-74, pres. 1973-74, Bernard Witkin medal 2002), Am. Judicature Soc., Am. Law Inst., Am. Coll. Trial Lawyers, Am. Bar Found. (bd. govs. 1975-86, pres. 1982-84), Chancery Club (pres. 1974-75), Order of Coif, Phi Beta Kappa, Phi Kappa Phi, Delta Tau Delta. Democrat. Office: Morrison & Foerster 555 W 5th St Ste 3500 Los Angeles CA 90013-1024 Office Phone: 213-892-5804.

HUFSTEDLER, SHIRLEY MOUNT (MRS. SETH M. HUFSTEDLER), lawyer, former federal judge; b. Denver, Aug. 24, 1925; d. Earl Stanley and Eva (Von Behren) Mount; m. Seth Martin Hufstedler, Aug. 16, 1949; 1 son, Steven Mark. BBA, U. N.Mex., 1945, LLD (hon.), 1972; LLB, Stanford U., 1949; LLD (hon.), U. Wyo., 1970, Gonzaga U., 1970, Occidental Coll., 1971, Tufts U., 1974, U. So. Calif., 1976, Georgetown U., 1976, U. Pa., 1976, Columbia U., 1977, U. Mich., 1979, Yale U., 1981, Rutgers U., 1981, Claremont U. Ctr., 1981, Smith Coll., 1982, Syracuse U., 1983, Mt. Holyoke Coll., 1985; PHH (hon.), Hood Coll., 1981, Hebrew Union Coll., 1986, Tulane U., 1988. Bar: Calif. 1950. Mem. firm Beardsley, Hufstedler & Kemble, L.A., 1951-61; practiced in L.A., 1961; judge Superior Ct., County L.A., 1961-66; justice Ct. Appeals 2d dist., 1966-68; circuit judge U.S. Ct. Appeals 9th cir., 1968-79; sec. U.S. Dept. Edn., 1979-81; ptnr. Hufstedler & Kaus, L.A., 1981-95; sr. of counsel Morrison & Foerster LLP, L.A., 1995—. Emeritus dir. Hewlett Packard Co., US West, Inc.; bd. dirs. Harman Internat. Industries. Mem. staff Stanford Law Rev, 1947-49; articles and book rev. editor, 1948-49. Trustee Calif. Inst. Tech., Occidental Coll., 1972-89, Aspen Inst., Colonial Williamsburg Found., 1976-93, Constl. Rights Found., 1978-80, Nat. Resources Def. Coun., 1983-85, Carnegie Endowment for Internat. Peace, 1983-94; bd. dirs. John T. and Catherine MacArthur Found., 1983—2002; chair U.S. Commn. on Immigration Reform, 1996-97. Named Woman of Yr. Ladies Home Jour., 1976; recipient UCLA medal, 1981. Fellow Am. Acad. Arts and Scis.; mem. ABA (medal 1995), L.A. Bar Assn., Town Hall, Am. Law Inst. (coun. 1974-84), Am. Bar Found., Women Lawyers Assn. (pres. 1957-58), Am. Judicature Soc., Assn. of the Bar of City of N.Y., Coun. on Fgn. Rels. (emeritus), Order of Coif. Office: Morrison & Foerster LLP 555 W 5th St Ste 3500 Los Angeles CA 90013-1024 Office Phone: 213-892-5804. Business E-Mail: shirhufs@mofo.com.

HUG, CARL CASIMIR, JR., anesthesiology educator, pharmacology educator, medical ethics educator; b. Canton, OH, Dec. 20, 1936; s. Carl Casimir and Aimee Cecelia (McArdle) H.; m. Marilyn Ann France, May 12, 1956; children: Patricia Ann DeStephano, Michael Stephen, Joan Marie Daniel, Mary Lynn Higgins, Lori Renee Mauldin. BS in Pharmacy summa cum laude, Duquesne U., 1958; PhD in Pharmacology, U. Mich., 1963, MD with distinction, 1967. Diplomate Am. Bd. Anesthesiology 1975, recert., 1993. From instr. to assoc. prof. pharmacology U. Mich., Ann Arbor, 1963-71; from assoc. prof. anesthesiology and pharmacology to emeritus prof. Emory U. Sch. Medicine, Atlanta, 1972—, dep. chmn. for rsch., 1987-95, dep. chmn. for acad. affairs, 1995—2001; faculty assoc. Emory U. Ctr. for Ethics, 2001—. Vis. rsch. prof. U. Leiden, The Netherlands, 1982, dir. Am. Bd. Anesthesiology, 1984-96, v.p. 1990-92, pres. 1992-93; bd. dirs. Found. Anesthesia Edn. Rsch. 1993-2002, v.p. 1995-98, pres. 1998-2001; councilor-at-large Assn. U. Anesthesiologists 1980-83, pres. 1984-96; vis. prof. in field, lectr. in field, grantee in field. Author: Alfentanil: Pharmacology and Uses in Anesthesia, 1984; New Developments in Drugs Used in Anaesthesia, 1991; editor Pharmacokinetics of Anaesthesia, 1984; editor Anesthesiology, 1979-88; contbr. 94 manuscripts, 129 publs., 128 abstracts in field. Chmn. St. Francis Sch. Bd., Ann Arbor, Mich., 1967—71; coach Little League, Ann Arbor, 1967—71; active Corpus Christi Cath. Ch., Stone Mountain, Ga., 1972—96, St. John Neumann Cath. Ch., Liburn, Ga., 1997—. Recipient Lifetime Achievement award Am. Soc. Critical Care Anesthesiologists, 2002; Ralph M. Waters, MD award Ill. Soc. Anesthesiologists, 2004; named Tchr. of Yr. Emory U. Anesthesiology, 1989, Excellence in Cardiothoracic Anesthesiology award, 1998; hon. lectr. at numerous univs. Fellow Royal Coll. Anaesthetists (Eng.) (hon.), Australian and New Zealand Coll. Anaesthetists (hon.), Am. Coll. Anesthesiologists; mem. Belgian Soc. Anesthesia and Reanimation (hon.), Am. Soc. Anesthesiologists (mem., chmn. various coms. 1976—, named Emery A. Rovenstine lectr. 1999), Assn. Cardiac Anesthesiologists, Soc. Cardiovasc. Anesthesiologists, Am. Soc. Clin. Pharmacology and Therapeutics, Am. Soc. Pharmacology and Expl. Therapeutics. Roman Catholic. Avocations: bicycling, walking, racquetball, piano. Office: Emory Univ Hosp Dept Anesthesiology 1364 Clifton Rd NE Atlanta GA 30322-1104 Office Phone: 404-778-3917. Business E-Mail: chug@emory.edu.

HUG, PROCTER RALPH, JR., federal judge; b. Reno, Mar. 11, 1931; s. Procter Ralph and Margaret (Beverly) H.; m. Barbara Van Meter, Apr. 4, 1954; children: Cheryl Ann English, Procter J., Elyse Marie Pasha. BS, U. Nev., 1953; LLB, JD, Stanford U., 1958. Bar: Nev. 1958. Mem. Springer, McKissick & Hug, 1958—63, Woodburn, Wedge, Blakey, Folsom & Hug, Reno, 1963—77; U.S. judge 9th Cir. Ct. Appeals, Reno, 1977—2002, U.S. chief judge, 1996—2000, sr. judge, 2002—. Dep. atty. gen. State of Nev., 1971—76; v.p. dir. Nev. Tel. & Telegraph Co., 1958—77. Mem. bd. regents U. Nev., 1962—71, chmn., 1969—71; bd. visitors Stanford Law Sch.; mem. Nev. Humanities Commn., 1988—94; vol. civilian aid sect. U.S. Army, 1977. Lt. (j.g.) USNR, 1953—55. Named Alumnus of Yr., U. Nev., 1988; recipient Outstanding Alumnus award, 1967, Disting. Nevadan citation, 1982. Mem.: ABA (bd. govs. 1976—78), Stanford Law Soc. Nev. (past pres.), U. Nev. Alumni Assn. (past pres.), Nat. Assn. Coll. and Univ. Attys. (past mem. exec. bd.), Nat. Jud. Coll. (bd. dirs. 1977—78, 2001—, chmn. 2004—), Am. Judicare Soc. (bd. dirs. 1975—77). Office: US Ct Appeals 9th Cir US Courthouse Fed Bldg 400 S Virginia St Ste 708 Reno NV 89501-2181 Office Phone: 775-686-5949.

HUG, RICHARD ERNEST, small business owner; b. Paterson, N.J., Jan. 11, 1935; s. Gustave T. and Nelly (Rutishauser) H.; m. Lois-Ann Schack, Sept. 1, 1956; children: Donald R., Cynthia A. BS, Duke U., 1956, M in Forestry, 1957; DHL, U. Balt., 1991. Engr. forest products divsn. Koppers Co., Inc., Pitts., 1957-62, tech. rep., 1962-66, tech. sales rep., 1966-68, area sales mgr., 1968-70, mgr. product devel., 1970-72, gen. mgr. laminated products, 1972-73, v.p., gen. mgr. environ. systems divsn., 1973-74, corp. v.p., 1973-83; pres., CEO, owner Environ. Elements Corp., Balt., 1983-88, chmn., CEO, 1988-90, chmn., 1990-95, chmn. emeritus, 1995—; owner, chmn. Deco-Sign Products, Inc., 1991—; owner, CEO, chmn. Hug Enterprises, Inc., 1991—; owner, chmn. The Great Am. Car Wash, etc., Inc., 1992—. Mem. Md. Health Resources Planning Commn., 1984-88; bd. dirs. Nat. Aquarium, Balt., 1981-94, chmn., 1988-91; bd. dirs. Nat. Aquarium Found., 1995— Bd. dirs. Blue Cross-Blue Shield Md., 1973-94, Boy Scouts Am., Balt., 1974-85, Greater Balt. Com., 1978, 84-88, Loyola Coll. Md., 1982—, U. Md. Med. System, 1984-95, U. Md. Med. System Found., 2000—, Jr. Achievement Ctrl. Md., 1985-95, Duke U. Sch. Environ., 1986—, chair, 1988-95, Am. Auto Assn., Md., 1988—, Mid Atlantic Am. Auto Assn., 1990—, Md. Internat. Ctr., 1984-95, Downtown Balt. Ctr., 1991-94, Walters Art Mus., 1992-97, Environ. Forum, 1993-95, Hospice Chesapeake, 1993-98, Diehl Graphsoft, 1996-2000, Marco Group, 1985—2004, Annapolis Ctr., 2001—; campaign chmn. United Way Ctrl. Md., 1979, 80, chmn., 1987-89; chmn. finance Ellen Sauerbrey for Gov., 1994-98, Md. Rep. Party, 1999-2000, Bob Ehrlich for Gov., 2001-, Md. Bush for Pres. Campaign, 1999-2000, 03-04; bd. dirs. Kennedy Krieger Inst., 1981-, chair, 1984-86; bd. dirs. Ind. Coll. Fund Md., 1978-88; bd. dirs. Balt. Symphony Orch., 1989-2004, CEO coun., 1988-90, Leadership Md., 1995—, chmn., 1995-96; mem. chancellor's adv. coun. U. Md., 1990-2002; bd. regents Univ. Sys. Md., 2003-; chmn. Md. U.S. Olympics Commn., 1987-88; mem. Young Pres.'s Orgn., 1974-85, chmn., 1980. Recipient Pres. medal Loyola Coll., 1992, Disting. Svc. award YMCA, 2005; named Md. Rep. Man Yr., 2002; named to Chimes Hall Fame, 2003 Mem. Chesapeake Pres. Orgn. (chmn. 1994-95), Chief Execs. Orgn., Water and Wastewater Equipment Mfrs. Assn. (bd. dirs. 1983-88), Inst. Clear Air Cos. (bd. dirs. 1980-94, pres. 1990-94), Nat. Assn. Mfrs. (bd. dirs. 1983-94), Md. Ctr. Bus. Mgmt. (bd. dirs. 1984-95, chmn. 1987-92), Md. Bus. for Responsible Govt. (bd. dirs. 1995—, chmn. 2000-04), Md. C. of C. (bd. dirs. 1981-95, v.p. 1981-84, chmn. 1985-87), Ctr. Club (bd. govs. 1993—, membership chmn. 1994-2000, v.p. 1997—, Silver Beaver award 1985, Nat. Outstanding Fund Raiser 1992). Home: 992 Stonington Dr Arnold MD 21012-1654 Office: Hug Enterprises Inc 3700 Koppers St Ste 134 Baltimore MD 21227-1020 Office Phone: 410-368-7324.

HUGANIR, RICHARD LEWIS, neuroscientist, educator, researcher; b. Phila., Mar. 25, 1953; s. George H. and Helen R. Huganir; children: Nicole R., Adam S. BS, Vassar Coll., 1975; PhD, Cornell U., 1982. Postdoctoral fellow dept. pharmacology Yale U. Sch. Medicine, New Haven, 1982—83; postdoctoral fellow lab. molecular and cellular neuroscience The Rockefeller U., NYC, 1983—84, asst. prof. lab. molecular and cellular neuroscience, 1984—87; assoc. investigator dept. neuroscience Howard Hughes Med. Inst., Balt., 1988—93, investigator, 1993—; assoc. prof. dept. neuroscience Johns Hopkins U. Sch. Medicine, Balt., 1988—93; prof. Johns Hopkins U., Balt., 1993—. Assoc. editor: Jour. Biol. Chemistry, 1995—2000, Jour. Neurosci., 1996—, mem. editl. bd.: Neuron, 1993—; contbr. chapters to books, articles to profl. jours. Recipient PDZ domains and excitatory synaptic function award, NIH, 1997—2005, Disting. Investigator award, Nat. Alliance for Rsch. on Schizophrenia and Depression, 1999—2000, Role of AMPA receptor modification in ALS award, Johns Hopkins Ctr. for ALS Rsch., 2000-2002, Regulation of the NMDA receptor signaling complex award, NIH, 2001-2006. Fellow: AAAS; mem.: NAS, Am. Soc. Biochemistry and Molecular Biology, Soc. Neurosci. (chmn. program com. 2000—02, treas. 2003—04, Young Investigator award 1991), Am. Acad. Arts and Scis. (Santiago Grisolia award 2004). Office: HHMI/Johns Hopkins Univ 904A PCTB 725 N Wolfe St Baltimore MD 21205 Office Phone: 410-955-4050. Business E-Mail: rhuganir@jhmi.edu.

HUGE, HARRY, lawyer; b. Deshler, Nebr., Sept. 16, 1937; s. Arthur and Dorothy (Vor de Strasse) H.; m. Reba Kinne, July 2, 1960; 1 child, Theodore. AB, Nebr. Wesleyan U., 1959; JD, Georgetown U., 1963. Bar: Ill. 1963, DC 1965, SC 1985. Assoc. Chapman & Cutler, Chgo., 1963-65; from assoc. to ptnr. Arnold & Porter, Washington, 1965-76; sr. ptnr. Donovan, Leisure, Rogovin, Huge & Schiller, Washington, 1976-92, Shea and Gould Internat., Washington, 1992-94; ptnr. Powell Goldstein Frazer & Murphy, Washington, 1995—2002, The Huge Law Firm PLLC, 2002—. Chmn., trustee United Mine Workers Health and Retirement Funds, 1973-78; chmn. bd. dirs. Hollings Cancer Ctr. Med. U. S.C., Charleston; trustee Shook and Fletcher Asbestos Settlement Trust, Washington, 2002—; chmn. Armstrong World Industries Settlement Trust, Wilmington, Del. Contbr. articles to profl. jours. Pres. Voter Edn. Project, Atlanta, 1974-78; mem. Pres.'s Gen. Adv. Com. Arms Control, 1977-81; trustee Nebr. Wesleyan U., 1978—; mem. task force local govt. Greater Washington Rsch. Ctr., 1981-82; spl. master Friends for All Children, Inc., U.S. Dist. Ct. DC; mem. Nat. Tobacco Settlement Arbitration Panel, Durham, NC. With U.S. Army, 1960; officer USNG, 1960-65. Mem.: ABA (co-chmn. legis. com. litig. sect. 1981), Inst. Human Virology (bd. dirs. U. Md., Balt. 1996—2001), DC Bar Assn. (bd. profl. responsibility 1976—81). Home: 25 E Battery St Charleston SC 29401-2740 Office: The Huge Law Firm PLLC Market Square North 401 Ninth St NW Ste 450 Washington DC 20004 Office Phone: 843-722-1628. E-mail: harryhuge@comcast.net.

HUGENBERG, PATRICIA ELLEN PETRIE, product designer; b. N.Y.C., Oct. 17, 1934; d. Milton John Petrie and Miriam Lois Lampke-Rubenstein-Petrie; m. George John Hugenberg, Jan. 18, 1958; 1 child, Kurt John James. Student, Briarcliff Jr. Coll., 1954, U. Calif., Berkeley, 1966. Guidette NBC, N.Y.C., 1956; designer, resch. developer Designs for Prodn., Sausalito, Calif.; inventor games, toys, med. items, Sigi Design, San Francisco; pres. PPH Designs. Mem. pending bd. Milton & Carroll Petrie Found. for New Millenium, N.Y.C. Photographer: (book cover jacket) Baltimore; prin. works include plexiglass knitting needles, plexiglass embedded light space age stardust galaxy hammocks, space age crutch, new saddle design for mobile riding easels, kitchen veg-garnisher punch; patents pending in field. Mem. NRA. Avocations: music, painting, horseback riding, travel, gardens. Home and Office: 10 Leeward Rd Belvedere CA 94920-2321

HUGG, HAROLD J., music educator, director; b. Great Falls, Mont., Sept. 22, 1959; s. Forrest and Catherine Hugg; m. Karen K. Martin, June 15, 2002; 1 child, Jessica. MusB in Edn., Mont. State U., 1981. Cert. tchr. music Office Pub. Instrn., Mont. Dir. bands Augusta (Mont.) H.S., 1981—83; instr. elem. band Gt. Falls (Mont.) Pub. Schs., 1990—92; dir. bands East Mid. Sch., Great Falls, 1992—. Mem.: Mont. Band Masters Assn. (sec. 2002—05, treas. 2002—05), Phi Beta Mu (sec. treasure 2000—02). Home: 121 Riverview Dr E Great Falls MT 59404 Office: East Middle School 4040 Central Ave Great Falls MT 59401 Personal E-mail: jkbxbnd81@yahoo.com.

HUGGETT, MONICA, performing company executive, musician; b. Eng. Studied at, Royal Acad. Music. Co-founder Amsterdam Baroque Orch., 1980, dir., 1980—87; artistic dir. Portland Baroque Orch., Oreg., 1995—. Prof. baroque violin Royal Acad. Music, London. Violinists Mozart: The 5 Violin Concertos, 1999, Vivaldi: The Four Seasons, 2000, Mozart: Violin Concertos 3 & 4, 2000, Mozart: Violin Concertos No.1, 2 & 5, 2000, Vivaldi: The Four Seasons/Four Concertos, 2000. Fellow: Royal Acad. Music. Office: Portland Baroque Orch 1020 SW Taylor St #275 Portland OR 97205-2577*

HUGGINS, AMY BRANUM, music educator; b. Memphis, Dec. 20, 1954; d. Leon and Scharlene Oney Branum; m. R. David Huggins, May 8, 1976; children: Alexander, Stephanie. MusM in Edn. with Kodaly emphasis, Holy Name Coll., Oakland, Calif., 1985; MusB in Edn., Peabody Conservatory of Music, 1976. Pvt. piano instr., Balt., 1973—; early music tng. faculty prep. divsn. Peabody Conservatory of Music, Balt., 1976—83, music theory faculty prep. divsn., 1976—83, curriculum designer prep. divsn., 1976; condr., founder The Pine Grove Madrigals, Balt., 1976—; vocal music specialist Pine Grove Elem. Sch., Balt., 1976—; master tchr., supr. of student tchrs. Peabody Conservatory of Music, Shenandoah Conservatory of Music, Towson State U., U. of Md., Loyola Coll., Balt., 1978—; organizer, dir. choral festivals Balt. County Pub. Schs., Balt., 1980—90; instr. Children's Chorus of Md., Balt., 1983—86; curriculum designer Balt. County Pub. Schs., 1991; pvt. voice instr. Balt., 1997—; cons. Children's Chorus of Md., Balt., 1998—99; dir., co-founder The Am. Kodaly Inst., Balt., 2000—; instr. grad. studies program Loyola Coll. in Md., Balt., 2001—. Kodaly clinician, cons. Orgn. of Am. Kodaly Educators, Moorhead, Minn., 1978—, Md. United Specialists in Kodaly, Balt., 1978—. Author: Elements: A Sight Singing and Rhythm Reading Book for Beginners, 1982, Kodaly, American Style, 2001, Folk Guitar for the Music Educator, 2002, 5-String Banjo for the Music Educator, 2003; columnist: The Kodaly Envoy, 2003—05; contbr. articles to profl. jours. Bd. dirs., sec. Children's Chorus of Md., 1981—83. Scholar, Mu Phi Epsilon Alumni Assn., 1975. Mem.: OAKE (overseer 1997—98, chair nat. conf. planning com. 1997—98, 1983—85, overseer tchr. tng. com. 1983—85, 1997—98), MENC, The VoiceCare Network, Soc. for Rsch. in Music Edn., Soc. for Music Tchr. Edn., Md. Music Educators Assn., Am. Choral Dirs. Assn., Orgn. of Am. Kodaly Educators (v.p. 1983—85, 1997—98), Md. United Specialists in Kodaly (pres. 1996—98, 1982—84, 1998—99, mem. at large 1995—96, sec. 1980—82), Mu Phi Epsilon. Home: 307 Southway Baltimore MD 21218 Office: Pine Grove Sch 2701 Summit Ave Baltimore MD 21234 Office Phone: 410-887-5267. Personal E-mail: amybhuggins@yahoo.com.

HUGGINS, BOB, former college basketball coach; b. Morgantown, W.Va., Sept. 21, 1953; s. Charles Huggins; m. June Ann Fillman; children: Jenna Leigh, Jacqueline. BS magna cum laude, U. W.Va., 1977, MA in Health Adminstrn., 1978. Grad. asst. basketball coach U. W.Va., Morgantown, 1977-78; asst. basketball coach Ohio State U., Columbus, 1978-90; head coach Walsh Coll., Canton, Ohio, 1980-83; asst. basketball coach U. Ctrl. Fla., Orlando, 1983-84; head basketball coach U. Akron, Ohio, 1984-89, U. Cin., 1989—2005. Mem. basketball coaching staff U.S. World Univ. Games team, 1993. Founder Bob Huggins Found., 1997-98. Named Coach of the Yr. dist. 22 NAIA, 1981-82, 1982-83, area 6, 1982-83, Mid-Ohio Conf., 1981-82, 1982-83, Ohio Valley, 1984-85, Metro Conf., 1989-90, Dapper Dan Man of Yr., 1986-87, dist. 4 USBWA, 1991-92, Conf. USA, 1996-98, 98-99, 99-2000, Mideast Coach of Yr. Basketball Times, 1991-92, 95-96, Co-Nat. Coach of Yr., 1991-92 Hoop Scoop mag., finalist for AP Coach of Yr., 1991-92, Ohio Coll. Coach of Yr. Columbus Dispatch, 1991-92, 1995-96, Nat. Coll. Coach of Yr., Playboy Mag., 1992-93, Midseason Coach of Yr. USA Today, 1991-92 season, Mideast Coach of Yr. Basketball Times, 1995-96 season, Nat. Coach. of Yr. Basketball Times, 1997-98 season, The Sporting News, 1999-2000 season, ESPN.com, 2001-02 season; recipient Ray Meyer award Gt. Midwest conf., 1991-92, 92-93, Ray Meyer award Conf. USA Coach of Yr, 1997-98, 1998-99, 1999-2000. Achievements include his 517-184 record (.738) amassed during his 22 seasons as a head coach ranks him sixth in winning percentage and 18th in victories among active Division 1 mentors; his string of 12 consecutive NCAA tournament appearances is the third-longest active streak; his teams have won over 20 games in all but three of his 22 campaigns and he has averaged 23.5 victories a season, 26.3 wins per campaign over the past eight years; he has compiled a 349-112 record (.757) in his 14 years at Cincinatti, making him the most winning coach in terms of victories and percentage in the school's rich basketball history.

HUGGINS, CHARLES EDWARD, obstetrician, gynecologist, educator; b. Hartsville, SC, Nov. 16, 1944; s. Charles Witherspoon Huggins and Frances Sue (Fountain) Evans; m. Mary Ellen Esto, May 29, 1966; children: Chadwick Edward, Laura Ruth, Mary Elizabeth. BS, Wofford Coll., 1965; MD, Med. U. S.C., 1969. Diplomate Am. Bd. Ob-Gyn. Intern Strong Meml. Hosp., Rochester, 1969-70; resident in ob-gyn. Med. U. S.C. Hosp., Charleston, 1970-74; chief of ob-gyn. Roper Hosp., Charleston; chmn. ob-gyn. dept. Bon Secours St. Francis Hosp., Charleston, 1999—. Clin. assoc. prof. Med. U. S.C.; mem. exec. bd. Roper Hosp., Charleston,1992-95, perinatal adv. bd., Charleston, 1992-95. Leader Boy Scouts of Am., Mt. Pleasant, S.C., 1978-88; coach Hungry Neck Internat. Soccer, Mt. Pleasant, 1978-88. Lt. Cmdr. USN, 1974-76. Fellow ACOG, South Atlantic Assn. Ob-Gyn. (chair state com. 1995-98); mem. AMA, Am. Fertility Soc., NYAS, S.C. Med. Assn., Charleston County Med. Soc., Pi Kappa Phi (archon 1962—), Phi Rho Sigma. Presbyterian. Office Phone: 843-820-5300. Fax: 843-577-4193.

HUGGINS, CHARLOTTE SUSAN HARRISON, retired secondary school educator, writer, travel company executive; b. Rockford, Ill., May 13, 1933; d. Lyle Lux and Alta May (Bowers) Harrison; m. Rollin Charles Huggins Jr., Apr. 26, 1952; children: Cynthia Charlotte Peters, Shirley Ann Cooper, John Charles. *On father's side, a direct descendant of Sir Antoine Trabue, a French Huguenot who came to Maniken-Town, Virginia, in 1692, and of Joseph Sallee, also of Maniken-Town, who gave money and supplies to the Revolutionary cause during the American Revolution. On mother's side, direct descendant of Thomas Newbold, who arrived in America in 1678, settling in Lewes, Delaware. Great-great grandfather Francis Marion Newbold married Comfort Rodney, niece of Delaware's best-known patriot, Caesar Augustus Rodney. Francis Marion Newbold moved West in 1820. His son became a large landowner in Moultrie County, Illinois.* Student, Knox Coll., 1951-52; AB magna cum laude, Harvard U., 1958; MA, Northwestern U., 1960, postgrad., 1971-73; cert. in conversation French, Berlitz Lang. Sch. Asst. editor Hollister Publs., Inc., Wilmette, Ill., 1959—65; tchr. advanced placement English New Trier H.S., Winnetka, Ill., 1965—, master tchr., 1979, leader tchr., 1988. With Task Force Commn. on Grading, 1973—74; Sabbatical project 1 yr. world travel History-Lit. Prospectus; cons. Asian Studies New Trier, 1987—88; mem. New Trier Supts. Commn. on Censorship, 1991; critic tchr. Northwestern U.; cons. McDougall-Littel's Young Writer's Manual, 1985—88; asst. sponsor Echoes, 1981—, Trevia, 1982, 83; sponsor New Trier News, 1988—; pres. Harrison Farms, Inc., Lovington, Ill., 1976—; spkr. North Suburban Geneal. Soc., 1990; instr., travel expert New Trier Adult Edn. Keys to the World's Last Mysteries, 1986—; presenter in field. *Currently engaged in a writing project about a friend and prominent Cambodian who was killed in 1979 during the Khmer Rouge revolution in Cambodia. The book will include a personal correspondence, interviews with family and friends, and extensive research based on travel to France and Southeast Asia. A second work-in-progress is a history of Ms. Huggins' family, the Newbolds, describing their immigration from England in 1678, their life in Delaware in the 1700's, and their journey west to settle in Indiana and Illinois.* Author: A Sequential Course in Composition Grades 9-12, 1979, A History of New Trier High School, 1982, Passage to Anaheim: An Historical Biography of Pioneer Families, 1984, Cambodia: A Place in Time, 1987; author: (video tapes) The Glory That was Greece, 1987; author: The World of Charles Dickens, 1987; editor: The Cornog Years, 2002. Women's bd. St. Leonard's House, Chgo., 1965—75; active Ctrl. Sch. PTA Bd., Wilmette, Ill., 1960—64; assocs. bd. Northwestern U. Settlement, Chgo., 1965—, pres., 1999—, fundraising com., 1997—, ctrl. bd. com., 2003—. Recipient Citizenship award, DAR, 1953, award, Phi Beta Kappa, 1957, Am. Legion, 1959, Cert. of Merit Graphic Arts Competition, Printing Industries of Am., 1983, 1st pl. award, Am. Scholastic Press Assn., 1990, Cert. of Merit, Am. Newspaper Pubs. Assn., 1990. Mem.: DAR (historian 1999—2000, regent 2000—02, parliamentarian 2002—), ASCD, MLA, NEA, Ill. Ret. Tchrs. Assn., Ill. Journalism Edn. Assn. (sec. 1997—97, awards chmn., bd. dirs., Life Achievement award 2001), New Trier Edn. Assn. (sec. 1992, pres.-elect 1994, pres. 1995—96, parliamentarian 2003—), Ill. Assn. Tchrs. English, Ill. Edn. Assn., Nat. Scholastic Press Assn. (conv. del. 1991, spring conf. rep. 1991—92, 1992—93, 1993—94, presenter fall and spring conv. 1993—94, spring conf. rep. 1994—95, presenter fall and spring conv. 1994—95, 1994—95, spring conf. rep. 1995—96, presenter fall and spring conv. 1995—96, 1996—, newspaper judge, All-Am. Newspaper award 1990—91, Life Achievement award 2001), Nat. Coun. Tchrs. English, Silent Samaritan Assn., Alliance Français, Harvard U. Alumni Assn. (admissions candidate interviewer), Radcliffe Coll. Alunmae Assn., Lyric Opera (assoc.), New Trier Ret. Tchrs. Assn. (newsletter editor), Women Comm., Inc., Nat. Huguenot Soc., Quill and Scroll (bd. dirs. 1992—93, George Gallup award 1990), Ill. Huguenot Soc., Columbia Scholastic Press Assn. (del. 1990, newspaper judge), Jr. Aux. U. Chgo. Cancer Rsch. Bd., Northwestern U. Alumni Assn., Mary Crane League, Art Inst. Chgo. (life), Chgo. Farmers, Terra Mus. Chgo. (charter), Knox Coll. Alumni Assn. (class donations rep., class rep. 2005, 50 Yr. Club 2005), Wilmette-Kenilworth Club, Univ. Club Chgo., Women's Club Wilmette, Mich. Shores Club, Pi Beta Phi (North Shore Chgo. alumnae bd., publicity chair). Home: 700 Greenwood Ave Wilmette IL 60091-1748 Office: 385 Winnetka Ave Winnetka IL 60093-4238 Personal E-mail: chantezch@aol.com.

HUGGINS, JAMES BERNARD, communications executive; b. Parkersburg, W.Va., June 5, 1950; s. Bernard Alonzo and Evelyn Belle (Wiblin) H.; divorced; 1 Stepchild, Jeremy Hawk; children: Jennifer Ashton, James B.A. III. AA, W.Va. U., Parkersburg, 1970; BA, W.Va. U., Morgantown, 1972; PhD in Internat. Bus., U. Wexford, Switzerland, 2001. Asst. Office of Senate Majority Whip, Washington, 1973-76; office mgr. U.S. Sen. Robert C. Byrd, Washington, 1976-93, state dir., 1985-91; prof. staff mem. U.S. Senate Appropriations Com., Washington, 1991-93; sr. mng. assoc. Linton Mields Reisler & Cottone, Washington, 1992-94; pres. The Cottone & Huggins Group, Washington, 1994—; chmn. Ctr. for Sino-Am. Trade. Co-chmn. Nat. Legis. Liaison Com.; dir. Fed. Liaison. Col. USAF/CAP; maj.- gen. U.S. Svc. Commd. Decorated Disting. Svc. medal with 5 oak leaf clusters, others. Mem. Nat. Conf. State Socs. (treas. 1980), W.Va. Soc. Washington (pres. 1980-82), W.Va. U. Alumni Assn. (nat. capital chpt.). Democrat. Episcopalian. Avocations: sailing, flying, scuba diving. Office: The Cottone and Huggins Group 601 Pennsylvania Ave NW Ste 900 S Washington DC 20004

HUGGINS, LOIS M., human resources specialist, consumer products company executive; BA, Franklin and Marshall Coll. Various positions Sara Lee Corp., Chgo., 1987—97; divisional v.p. human resources Sara Lee Intimate Apparel, 1997—2000; leader orgn. devel. and diversity initiative Sara Lee Corp., 2000—03, v.p. human resources, 2003—04, sr. v.p. global human resources, 2004—. Co-chair global human resources steering com. Sara Lee Corp., Chgo., bd. dirs. Office: Sara Lee Corp 3 First National Plz Chicago IL 60602-4260 Office Phone: 312-726-2600. Office Fax: 312-726-3712.*

HUGHES, A. N., psychotherapist; b. Ft. Meade, Md. d. G.M. and G.T. Nolen; m. E.L. Hughes, Oct. 21, 1961; 1 child, Andrew G. BS in Psychology, Rollins Coll., 1985, MA in Counseling, 1986; student in pub. speaking and human rels., Dale Carnegie Inst., 1981; student, Duke U., 1950-52. Lic. mental health counselor; nat. cert. counselor; nat. cert. gerontol. counselor. Supr. top secret control, audio/visual and small parts supply U.S. Army, Continental U.S. and Tokyo; adminstrv. sec. Sys. Devel. Corp., Rand Corp., Santa Monica, Calif.; adminstrv. asst., editor, exec. sec., adminstrv. sec. Aerospace Corp., El Segundo, Calif.; staff therapist Circles of Care, Melbourne, Fla. Developer program for leading divorce support groups for Brevard Women's Ctr. Various leadership positions PTA, Pittsford, NY, Brookfield, Wis., 1968—81; mem. Brevard Cmty. Chorus, 1991—, adv. bd., 1997; mem. Citizen's Emergency Response Team (CERT), 1999—2001; various vol. positions in several organizations in Brevard County, 1991—. Mem. DAR, Fla. Coun. on Aging, Space Coast PC Users Group, Geneal. Soc. South Brevard, Suntree Country Club, Suntree Master Homeowners Assn. (Twin Lakes rep. 1997—), Brevard County Alumnae Assn. of Kappa Kappa Gamma, Kappa Kappa Gamma. Avocations: photoimaging, exercise, genealogy, choral singing. Office: PO Box 410162 Melbourne FL 32941-0162

HUGHES, ALFRED CLIFTON, archbishop; b. Boston, Dec. 2, 1932; s. Alfred Clifton and Ellen Cecelia (Hennessey) H. AB, St. John's Sem. Coll., 1954; STL, Gregorian U., Rome, 1958, STD, 1961. Ordained priest Roman Cath. Ch., 1957, ordained bishop Roman Cath. Ch., 1981. Asst. pastor St. Stephen's Parish, Framingham, Mass., 1958—59, Our Lady Help of Christians, Newton, Mass., 1961—62; lectr. St. John's Sem., Brighton, 1962—65, spiritual dir., 1965—81, rector, 1981—86; aux. bishop Archdiocese of Boston, 1981—93; regional bishop of Merrimack Region, 1986—90; vicar for adminstrn. Archdiocese of Boston, 1990—93; bishop of Baton Rouge, 1993—2001; coadjutor archbishop of New Orleans Archdiocese of New Orleans, 2001—02, archbishop of New Orleans, 2002—. Chmn. com. on doctrine U.S. Cath. Conf. Bishops, 1991—94, com. on use of catechism, 1995—. Author: Preparing for Church Ministry, 1979, Spiritual Masters, 1999; chmn. editl. bd.: Nat. Dir. for Catechesis; contbr. articles to profl. jours. Recipient Mellon and Davis Founds. grant, 1976. Mem.: Catholic Theol. Soc. Am. Roman Catholic. Office: Archdiocese of New Orleans 7887 Walmsley Avenue New Orleans LA 70125-3496*

HUGHES, ALLEN, music critic; b. Brownsburg, Ind., Dec. 28, 1921; s. Maurice McKinley and Bess (Collyer) H.; m. Marian Nina Berklich, Mar. 28, 1964. Student, George Washington U., 1940-42; BA, U. Mich., 1946, B.Mus., 1947; postgrad., N.Y. U., 1948-50. Lectr. music Toledo Mus. Art, 1946-47; asst. editor, critic Mus. Am., 1950-53; free-lance writer Paris, France, 1953-55; music critic N.Y. Herald Tribune, 1955-60; mem. music faculty Bklyn. Coll., 1958-60; music critic N.Y. Times, 1960-61, asst. dance critic, 1961-62, dance critic, 1962-65, music critic, 1965-86. Served to lt. (j.g.) USNR, 1943-46. Office: 1255 N Gulfstream Ave Sarasota FL 34236

HUGHES, ANN HIGHTOWER, retired economist, trade association administrator; b. Birmingham, Ala., Nov. 24, 1938; d. Brady Alexander and Juanita (Pope) H. BA, George Washington U., 1963, MA, 1969. Asst. U.S. trade rep. Exec. Office of Pres., Washington, 1978-81; dep. asst. sec. trade agreements Dept. Commerce, Washington, 1981-82, dep. asst. sec. Western Hemisphere, 1982-95; dir. C & M Internat., Washington, 1995-97; ret. Recipient meritorious exec. award Pres. of U.S., 1982, 88, disting. exec. award, 1993. Avocation: breeding champion miniature Schnauzers.

HUGHES, ARTHUR HYDE, accountant, energy industry executive, accountant; b. Lansing, Mich., May 15, 1952; s. Francis Aloysius and Alice Catherine (Hyde) H.; m. Ellen Marie Krempa, Feb. 13, 1982; children: Bradley Allan, Allison Marie. BS magna cum laude, Fla. State U., 1974; postgrad., U. Tex., Dallas, 1978. CPA Tex. Treas. Excella Trading Corp., Ft. Worth, 1977-79; revenue analyst gas revenue acctg. ARCO, Dallas, 1975-82, sr. acct. oil revenue acctg., 1982-85, client rep. revenue projects group, 1985-87, supr. gas data svcs., 1987-88, supr. gas sys. redevel., 1988-89, prodn. acctg. cons., 1989-90, sr. revenue compliance auditor, 1990-96; internat. acct. ARCO Algeria, 1996; pvt. practice petroleum auditing, cons., 1996-97; mgr. exploration prodn. and fin. software Allegro Devel., Inc., 1997-98; prin. cons. Oracle Energy Co., 1998-2000; oil & gas subject matter expert Akili Sys. Group, 2000-01; mgr. revenue acctg. and joint interest billing Vernon E. Faulconer, Inc., Tyler, Tex., 2001—03, contr., 2004—. Mem. Petroleum Data Exch. Steering Com., Denver, 1985-87, chmn. Gas Revenue Acctg., Data Exch. Com. (subs Petroleum Data Exch.) Dallas, 1986-87, spl. com. electronic data exch. of Coun. of Petroleum Acctg. Socs., Dallas, 1986—. Contbr. articles to profl. jours.; developer petroleum industry Gas Revenue Acctg. Data Exchange system with Gen. Elec., 1985. Alt. del. Tex. Rep. Conv., 1982; active Nat. Right to Life, Washington; active Citizen's Com. for Right To Keep and Bear Arms, Second Amendment Found. Mem. AICPA, Tex. Soc. CPAs, Petroleum Acctg. Soc., NRA (life), Tex. Rifle Assn., Ducks Unltd., Toastmasters, Gun Owner Am., Mensa, Intertel, Phi Eta Sigma, Phi Kappa Phi, Beta Gamma Sigma. Roman Catholic. Avocations: target shooting, reading, chess. Home: 1404 Woodlands Dr Tyler TX 75703-5718 Office: Vernon E Faulconer Inc Woodgate Centre Ste 160 1001 ESE Loop 323 Tyler TX 75701 Office Phone: 903-581-4382 x227. Personal E-mail: arthughes@cox.net. Business E-Mail: ahughes@vefinc.com.

HUGHES, AUSTIN LELAND, biological sciences educator; b. Washington, Sept. 10, 1949; s. Edward Riley and Josephine (Nicholls) H.; m. Mary Ann Hughes, Apr. 30, 1980; children: Austin Leland, Helen W. AB, Georgetown U., 1969; MS, W.Va. U., 1980; PhD, Ind. U., 1984. Asst. prof. Pa. State U., University Park, 1990-96, assoc. prof., 1996-99; prof. biol. scis. U. S.C., Columbia, 2000—, dir. Biotech. Inst., 2002—. Author: Evolution and Human Kinship, 1988, Adaptive Evolunion of General Genomes, 1999; assoc. editor: Molecular Phylogenetics and Evolution, 2003—; contbr. over 200 articles to profl. jours. Recipient Ryan Philosophy medal Georgetown U., 1969; NIH Rsch. Career Devel. award, 1992-97. Mem. Soc. for Study of Evolution, Soc. for Molecular Biology and Evolution. Roman Catholic. Office: Y SC 700 Sumter St Columbia SC 29208-0001 Office Phone: 803-777-9186.

HUGHES, BARNARD, actor; b. Bedford Hills, N.Y., July 16, 1915; s. Owen and Madge (Kiernan) H.; m. Helen Stenborg, Apr. 19, 1950; 2 children. Student, Manhattan Coll., DHL (hon.), 1989. Stage debut with Shakespeare Fellowship Co. in The Taming of the Shrew, N.Y.C., 1934; actor (plays) including Please, Mrs. Garibaldi, 1939, Herself, Mrs. Patrick Crowley, 1939, The Ivy Green, 1949, Dinosaur Wharf, 1951, The Teahouse of the August Moon, 1956, A Bell for Adano, 1957, Home of the Brave, 1957, The Will and The Way, 1957, Enrico IV, 1958, A Majority of One, 1959, Advise and Consent, 1960, Rosmersholm, 1962, A Doll's House, 1963, The Advocate, 1963, Nobody Loves and Albatross, 1963, Hamlet, 1964, I Was Dancing, 1964, Generation, 1965, Hogan's Goat, 1965, How Now Dow Jones, 1967, The Wrong-Way Light Bulb, 1969, Sheep on the Runway, 1970, Line, 1971, Abelard and Heloise, 1971, Older People, 1972, Hamlet, 1972, Much Ado About Nothing, 1972 (Tony nomination 1973), Uncle Vanya, 1973, The Good Doctor, 1973, The Merry Wives of Windsor, 1974, Pericles, Prince of Tyre, 1974, All Over Town, 1974, The Three Sisters, 1977, The Devil's Disciple, 1977, 78, Da, 1978 (Tony award Best Actor 1978, Outer Critics Circle award 1978), Homeward Bound, 1980, Iceman Cometh, 1981, 85, Translations, 1981, Tartuffe, 1982, Angels Fall, 1982, 83, End of the World, 1984, The Sky is No Limit, 1984, You Can't Take It With You (Abbey Theatre, Dublin, Ireland), 1989, Prelude to A Kiss, 1990, Da, 1999, (Olympia Theatre, Dublin, Ireland) 1993, Waiting in the Wings, 1999, (films) including The Young Doctors, 1961, Hamlet, 1964, Midnight Cowboy, 1969, Where's Poppa?, 1970, Deadhead Miles, 1970, The Pursuit of Happiness, 1971, The Hospital, 1971, Cold Turkey, 1971, Rage, 1972, Sisters, 1973, Oh God!, 1977, First Monday in October, 1981, Tron, 1982, Best Friends, 1982, Maxie, 1985, Where are the Children?, 1986, The Lost Boys, 1987, Da (Olymoia Theatre, Dublin, Ireland), 1988, Doc Hollywood, 1991, Sister Act II: Back in the Habit, 1993, Odd Couple II, 1997, The Cradle Will Rock, 1998, (TV movies) including Guilty or Innocent: The Sam Sheppard Murder Case, 1975, 1975, Tell Me My Name, 1977, See How She Runs, 1978, Homeward Bound, 1980, The Sky's No Limit, 1984, Agatha Cristie's A Carribean Mystery, 1983, Night of Courage, 1986, A Hobo's Christmas, 1987, Day One, 1989, Home Fires Burning, 1989, Guts and Glory: The Rise and Fall of Oliver North, 1989, The Incident, 1990, Miracle Child, 1993; star: (TV series) Doc, 1975-76, Mr. Merlin, 1981-82, The Cavanaughs, 1986-87, Blossom, 1991-93. With U.S. Army, 1943-45, No. Africa, Italy. Recipient St. Clair Bayfield award, 1973; elected to Theatre Hall of Fame, 1991. Office: Withum Smith Brown 331 Newman Springs Rd Ste 125 Red Bank NJ 07701-5654

HUGHES, BERNARD WALLACE, sales executive; b. Dowajaic, Mich., July 31, 1921; s. John Samuel and Myrtle Elise (Wallace) Hughes; m. Wilda Eileen Palmer-Hughes (dec. Feb. 1988); m. Ann Florence Niese, Apr. 29, 1989 (dec. Dec. 1993). BS in bus. adminstrn., Shurtleff Coll., 1947, MA in market rsch., 1949. Core maker Sibley Machine and Foundry, South Bend, Ind., 1939—41; adult program sec. YMCA, Alton, Ill., 1948—50; ptnr. General Lubricant Co., E. St. Louis, Ill., 1951—63; industrial mgr. Richfield Oil, San Francisco, 1963—69; founder Hughes Oil Co., Monterey, Calif., 1969—96. Founder Exchange Club Athletic Banquets, Alton, Ill., 1950—52; bd. mem. Oakland Trade Assn., Oakland, Calif., 1964—65. Author: Covert Bracelet, 2001, Codan's Conflicts, 2002, Playing It Along, 2003. Football coach Children's Home, Alton, Ill., 1952—53; dir., chmn. Ministerial Alliance YMCA, Alton, Ill., 1948—50; official rules keeper Northern Calif. Golf Assn., Monterey, Calif., 1975—88; starter rules keeper U.S. Golf Assn., 1975—88. With U.S. Army, 1942—45, Asiatic-Pacific. Recipient Silver Bronze award, Boy Scouts of Am., 1988, Merit award, Monterey Boys Area Coun., 1978, Cert. Appreciation, 1979. Avocations: golf, saxophone, bridge, classic car restoration. Home: PO Box 5081 Colesburg IA 52035 E-mail: bwhughesyuokon@sbcglobal.com.

HUGHES, BEVERLY, artist; b. Elizabeth City, N.C., Feb. 24; d. Alexander and Rosa (Butts) H.; children: Tiffany, Christopher. Student, Cumberland County Coll., Vineland, N.J., 1967-68, Burlington County Coll., Pemberton, N.J., 1970-72; BFA, Moore Coll. Art, 1976. Adv. com. C.C. Phila., 1995, Paul Robeson House, 1998. Exhbns. include Children's Inaugural Salute for Gov., Harrisburg, 1995, Phila. Flower Show, 2002, 2003, Riverfront Renaissance Gallery, Millville, N.J., 2003, Phila. Cathedral, 2003, Millville Meml. H.S., 2003, Barn Studio of Art, Millville, 2002, Wood Elem. Sch., 2002, Morris Arboretum, 2001, Children's Hosp. Phila., 2001; represented in permanent collection Afro Am. History Mus., Phila., Del Bello Gallery, Toronto, Nat. Conf. Artists, Bklyn., New Eng. Fine Arts Inst., Boston, Martha Stewart, Fran Aulston, Marcy Ufberg. Ednl. cons. West Park Ch., 1993—; vol. art tchr. Lea Sch., 1991-94; vol. Ralston House, Phila. Avocations: singing gospel music, fencing, collecting scale models of fighter jets. Home: 1103 Surrey Ave Millville NJ 08332

HUGHES, BLAKE, retired professional society administrator, retired publishing executive; b. N.Y.C., June 24, 1914; s. Ferdinand Holme and Ines (de Cordova) H.; m. Betty Jean Wolf, Aug. 26, 1951; children: Diane Elizabeth, Brian Blake. Degre de civilisation, Sorbonne U., Paris, 1935; AB summa cum laude, Dartmouth Coll., 1936; postgrad., Columbia U., 1936-37. Salesman Edward B. Smith & Co., Smith, Barney & Co., investment bankers, N.Y.C., 1936-38, N.Y. Life Ins. Co., 1939-40; promotion mgr. Engring. News Record, Constrn. Methods, McGraw-Hill Inc., N.Y.C., 1947-50; promotion mgr., dir. mktg. Archtl. Record F.W. Dodge Corp., N.Y.C., 1951-61; assoc. pub. Archtl. Record McGraw-Hill Inc., N.Y.C., 1961-68, pub. Archtl. Record, 1968-80, pub. House & Home, 1976-77; pres. Internat. Inst. for Architecture, Washington, 1978-81. Author: (novels) A Lifetime's Too Short, 2002, (short stories) Good Job, 2001, Loves and Consequences, 2005, Collected Poems, 2005. Trustee Unity (Maine) Coll., 1965-75; pres. Internat. Archtl. Found., 1973-78; bd. dirs. Nat. Home Improvement Coun., 1976-77. Lt. USNR, 1940-45. Decorated Order of Fatherland War (Russia). Mem. Union Internat. Architects (archtl. critics com. 1978-80), Appalachian Housing Inst. (bd. dirs.), Charleston Artist Guild (pres. 1990-91), English Speaking Union (pres. Charleston chpt. 1995-96), Carolina Yacht Club, Phi Beta Kappa, Delta Sigma Rho. Home: 109 E Bay St Apt 2C Charleston SC 29401-2549

HUGHES, BRADLEY RICHARD, finance company executive; b. Detroit, Oct. 8, 1954; s. John Arthur and Nancy Irene (Middleton) H.; m. Linda McCants, Feb. 14, 1977; children: Bradley Richard Jr., Brian Jeffrey. AA, Oakland Coll., 1974; BS in Journalism, BJ, U. Colo., 1979, MBA in Fin. and Mktg., 1981, MS in Telecommunications, 1990. Cert. office automation profl., cert. systems profl. Buyer Joslins Co., Denver, 1979; mktg. adminstr. Mountain Bell, Denver, 1980-82; ch. cons. AT&T Info. Systems, mktg. exec. AT&T, Denver, 1983-86, acct. exec., 1986-87; mktg. mgr. U.S. West, Denver, 1987-95; dir. U. Colo. Coll. Engring., Denver, 1995—. Exec.-on-loan U. Colo. Coll. Engring. Contbr. articles to bus. publs. Bd. dirs. Brandychase Assn.; state del., committeeman Rep. Party Colo.; dir. Inst. for Govt. Innovation; bd. dirs. Olmsted Pavilion, dir. Colo. Chess Acad. Mem. IEEE, Assn. MBA Execs., U.S. Chess Fedn., Internat. Platform Assn., Mensa, Intertel, Assn. Telecom. Profls., Am. Mgmt. Assn., Am. Mktg. Assn., Info. Industry Assn., Office Automation Soc. Internat., World Future Soc., Triple Nine Soc., Internat. Soc. Philos. Inquiry, Assn. Computing Machinery. Republican. Lutheran (Mo. Synod). Home: 6567 S Richfield St Centennial CO 80016 Office: Qwest Comm 1801 California Ste 1920 Denver CO 80202 Office Phone: 303-896-4099. Personal E-mail: bradleyhughes@comcast.net, brad.hughes@qwest.com.

HUGHES, BRIGID, former editor; d. Patrick and Patricia. BA in English, Northwestern U., 1994. Intern The Paris Rev., N.Y.C., 1995, editor, 1995—2000, mng. editor, 2000—04, exec. editor, 2004—05. Office: The Paris Review 541 E 72nd St New York NY 10021

HUGHES, BYRON WILLIAM, oil industry executive; b. Clarksdale, Miss., Nov. 8, 1945; s. Byron B. and Francis C. (Turner) H.; m. Sarah Eileen Goodwin, June 23, 1973 (div.); children: Jennifer E. Hughes Crosby, Stephanie Ann. BA, U. Miss., 1968; JD, Jackson Sch. Law (now Miss. Coll. Law), 1971. Bar: Miss. 1971, U.S. Supreme Ct. 1975; cert. real estate appraiser. Atty., abstractor Miss. Hwy. Dept., 1971-76; atty., ind. landman Byron Hughes Oil Exploration Co., Jackson, Miss., 1976-92; prosecutor, child support enforcement atty. Miss. Dept. Human Svcs., 1992—. Tchr. high sch.; real estate broker. Spl. sheriffs dep., vol., Bolivar County, Miss. Mem. ABA, Miss. Bar Assn., Hinds County Bar Assn., Bolivar County Bar Assn., Am. Judicature Soc., Nat. Assn. Real Estate Appraisers, Miss. Child Support Assn., Miss. Assn. Petroleum Landmen, Ala. Landmen Assn., Black Warrior Basin Petroleum Landmen Assn., Am. Assn. Petroleum Landmen (cert. profl. landman 1991), Ole Miss. Alumni Assn., Miss. Coll. Alumni Assn., Miss. Art Assn., Cleve. Exch. Club, Sigma Delta Kappa. Methodist. Home and Office: PO Box 1485 Jackson MS 39215-1485

HUGHES, CATHERINE L. (CATHY HUGHES), radio personality, broadcast executive; b. Omaha, Apr. 22, 1947; 1 child. Student, Creighton U., U. Nebr. Lectr., asst. to dean comm. Howard U., Washington, 1971—73; gen. sales mgr. WHUR Radio, 1973—78; v.p., gen. mgr. WYCB Radio, 1978—80; owner, operator WOL-AM Radio, 1980—; now founder, chairperson Radio One. Trustee Lincoln U.; small bus. adv. com. Fed. Res. Bank. Bd. mem. Piney Woods Sch., Balt. Mus. Art. Named Bus. Person of the Yr., Nat. Black C. of C., 1998, Prudential Media Black Woman on Wall St., 1999; recipient Mayor's Bus. award, 1995—99, Thomas A. Dorsey Leadership award, 1996, D.C. Cmty. Svc. award, 1995; scholar, Living Vision Scholarship Fund, 1995.

Achievements include first to to be an African American woman to head a firm publicly traded on a stock exchange in the United States. Office: Radio One Inc 100 St Paul St Baltimore MD 21202

HUGHES, CHARLES E., III, plastic surgeon; b. Chgo., Mar. 19, 1943; s. Charles E. and Jane Wittig (McClintock) H.; m. Ellen Alice Schowe, Nov. 1, 1963; children: Kristian, Chad, Adnrew, Polly. BS, Northwestern U., Chgo., 1966, MD, 1969. Diploamte Am. Bd. Plastic Surgery. Fellow in surg. oncology Am. Cancer Soc., Chgo., 1973-74; resident Northwestern U., 1974-76; asst. prof. plastic surgery Ind. U., Inspls., 1976-82; pvt. practice Geech Grove, Ind., 1983—. Contbr. articles to profl. jours. Fellow ACS (fgn. lang. editor jour. 1974-88); mem. Lipoplasty Soc. (pres. 1995—), Am. Soc. Plastic and Reconstructive Surgeons, Am. Soc. Aesthetic Plastic Surgery, Cleft Palate Soc. Avocations: exercise, sailing, reading, travel. Office: 1500 Albany St Beech Grove IN 46107-1555

HUGHES, CHRISTOPHER ADAM, conductor, educator; s. Ronald Dee and Kathleen Ann Hughes. BA magna cum laude, Western State Coll., 1994; MMus, VanderCook Coll. of Music, Chgo., 1997; postgrad., U. of Colo., Boulder, 2002—. Lic. profl. educator Colo. Dept. of Edn. Dir. of instrumental music Grand Junction Ctrl. H.S., Grand Junction, Colo., 1994—2000; instrumental music condr. Smoky Hill H.S., Aurora, Colo., 2000—02; grad. asst./educator U. of Colo., Boulder, 2002—. 1st v.p. Colo. Band Directors Assn., Denver, 1997—2001; honor ensemble condr., Denver, Craig, Delta, Greeley, Westminster, Arkansas Valley, Colo., 1999—2002; cmty. band condr. Performer Colo. Brass Band, 1991—, Rocky Mountain Brass Works, 2000—. Scholar Grad. Tchg./Rsch. Assistantship, U. of Colo. Mem.: Coll. Band Dirs. Nat. Assn., Colo. Music Educators Assn., Am. Sch. Band Dirs. Assn., Internat. Trumpet Guild, Kappa Delta Pi. Avocations: restoration of 1957 Chevrolets, domestic and international travel, mountain climbing, sight seeing. Home: 3940 S Hannibal Street Aurora CO 80013 E-mail: christopher.hughes@colorado.edu.

HUGHES, CLYDE MATTHEW, religious denomination executive; b. Huntington, W.Va., Dec. 7, 1948; s. Donald Lee and Audrey Arlene (Stevers) H.; m. Linda May Daniels, June 10, 1972; children: Crystal, Dustin, Tina, Wesley, Timothy, Penny, Heidi, Robin. Diploma, Amb. Bible Inst., London, Ohio, 1972; BA, Cedarville (Ohio) Coll., 1974; MA, Meth. Theol. Sch. in Ohio, 1980; DD, Heritage Bible Coll., Dunn, N.C., 1994. Ordained to ministry Internat. Pentecostal Ch. of Christ, 1974. Pastor Internat. Pentecostal Ch. of Christ, Hillsboro, Ohio, 1981-82, nat. dir. Sunday sch. London, 1976-82, dir. ch. ministries, 1982-84, asst. gen. overseer, 1984-90, gen. overseer, chmn. gen. bd., 1990—. Mem. nat. com. Mission Am., 1997—; bd. dirs. Beulah Heights Bible Coll., Atlanta, 1982—, chmn. bd. 1990-96. Editor-in-chief The Pentecostal Leader; contbr. articles to religious publs. Chmn. bd. dirs. Locust Grove Rest Home, 1990-98. Mem. Nat. Assn. Evangs. (bd. dirs. 1990—2001), Madison County Evang. Assn. (bd. dirs. 1990-2001), London Ministerial Assn., Chs. United with Israel (bd. gov. 2002-), Mission Am. (nat. com. 1997-), Pentecostal/Charismatic Chs. N.Am. (bd. dirs. 1994—, exec. com. 2001), Internat. Pentecostal Press Assn. (N.Am. chpt. exec. com., 2001—, second v.p.). Mem. Internat. Pentecostal Ch. Of Christ. Home: 7040 Danville Rd London OH 43140-9766

HUGHES, CRYSTAL DARLENE, elementary school educator; b. Cook Sta., Mo., Aug. 19, 1952; d. Robert Ira and Matred Dorthy Martin; m. Alfred Maynard Hughes, Mar. 28, 2005; children: Benjamin C. White, Phillip J. White. BS in Elem. Edn., S.E. Mo. State U., 1974. Lic. minister United Christian Faith Ministries, 2005; cert. tchr. Mo., lic. realtor Mo., 2002, cert. spl. edn. Tchr. Great-Phelps Sch. Dist., Salem, Mo., 1974—76, 1979—84; tchr., supr. Calvary Christian Acad., Salem, Mo., 1976—77; dir. edn. Muskegan (Mont.) Tem Challenge, 1977—78; tchr. Northwood Schs., Salem, 1985—88, 1995—98, B.W. Robinson State Sch., Rolla, Mo., 2000—. Musician Canaan Cmty. Ch. Home: 202 W 8th St Salem MO 65560

HUGHES, DAVID HENRY, manufacturing executive; b. Orlando, Fla., Dec. 20, 1942; s. Harry C. and Pauline B. Hughes; m. Rebecca Wilkins; 1 child, Kristin E.; m. Linda Cooper, Apr. 26, 1986; children: Patrick, Shelby. BS, U. Fla., 1965, JD, 1967. Mgmt. trainee Hughes Supply Inc., Orlando, 1968-72, COO, 1972—74, pres., 1974—94, CEO, 1975—2003, chmn., 1986—. Bd. dirs. Sun Banks Inc., Orlando, SunTrust Banks Inc., Atlanta, Darden Restaurants Inc., Brown & Brown Inc. Active Orlando Regional Healthcare Sys. Mem. Fla. Bar Assn., Fla. Coun. of 100. Republican. Avocations: golf, fishing. Office: Hughes Supply 501 W Church St Orlando FL 32805*

HUGHES, DEBORAH BRAY, special education educator; b. Dallas, May 29, 1953; d. Von M. Bray and Francis Barton Harris; m. David M. Park; children: Delain Barton, Devon Bray Miller. BS Magna cum laude in interdisciplinary studies, U. No. Tex., 2001. Cert. tchr. Tex., 2002. Tchg. asst. autistic group Garland (Tex.) Coop. Behavioral Ctr., 1977—79; tchr. Lake Highlands Christ. Child Enrichment Ctr., Dallas, 1983—84, Rockwall (Tex.) Pvt. Sch., 1987—88; tchr., dir. ops., v.p. mktg. Mem. Sch. of the Oaks, Houston, 1988—91; legal asst. Brown & Brown, Wetzel, Herron, & Drucker, LLP, Houston, 1991—94; behavioral therapist Pvt. Practice, The Woodlands, 1995—98, U. Houston, Tex. Young Autism Project, 1995—98; spl. edn. tchr. Denton Ind. Sch. Dist., 2002—. Adv. bd. Mem. Sch. Oaks Found., 1988—91. Author: (poem) World of Poetry Anthology, 1988 (Golden Poet award, 1988). Vol. So. Poverty Law Ctr., ACLU, March of Dimes, Habitat for Humanity, The Carter Ctr. Mem.: Families Early Autism Treatment, No. Tex., Nat. Assn. Edn. of Young Children, Golden Key Nat., Kappa Delta Pi, Internat. Honor Soc. in Edn. Avocations: reading, writing, art, music. Office: Denton Ind Sch Dist 3300 Evers Pkwy Denton TX 76201

HUGHES, DONNA JEAN, librarian; b. Alexandria, Va., Mar. 24, 1959; d. John William and Wilma Connie (Beavers) H. BS cum laude, Longwood Coll., Farmville, Va., 1981; MS in Libr. Sci., U. N.C., Chapel Hill, 1985. Lic. tchr., Va. Children's libr. Thomas Hackney Braswell Meml. Libr., Rocky Mount, N.C., 1983-88, Wake County Pub. Librs., Raleigh, N.C., 1988-90; children's svcs. and outreach svcs. libr. Handley Regional Libr., Winchester, Va., 1990—. Adj. prof. childrens lit. George Mason U., spring 2000; storyteller, artreach artist Clarke County Schs., 1996—. Youth svcs. adv. com. Libr. of Va., Richmond, 1991-96; music dir. Broadway (Va.) Bapt. Ch., 1990—, Sunday sch. dir., 1991—; co-founder singles ministry Sunset Avenue Bapt. Ch., Rocky Mount, 1984-90; singer Shenandoah Valley Chorus, 1990-95, Evangelism Missions Panama, 1996-99. Named Employee of Yr., City of Winchester, 1992. Mem. ALA, Va. Libr. Assn. (Jefferson Cup award com. 1995-96), Children and Young Adult Roundtable (chair 1994-95), Lord Fairfax Assn. of Educators of Young Children, Nat. Assn. Educators of Young Children, Nat. Storytelling Assn., Quota Internat. (com. chair, bd. dirs. 1994-96), New Market Garden Club (com. chair 1992—), Phi Kappa Phi. Baptist. Avocations: storytelling, barbershop singing, gardening, swimming, hymn singing. Office: Handley Regional Libr 100 W Piccadilly St Winchester VA 22601-3916

HUGHES, DOROTHY ZULA DILLARD, genealogy researcher, retired educator; b. Altus, Okla., July 21, 1909; d. James Melton and Wilma Katherine (Pelley) Dillard; m. Robert Claire Hughes, Aug. 19, 1934 (dec. Jan. 1968); children: Thomas James, Dorothy Barbara Hughes Buzzell. BA, U. N.Mex., 1929; MA, N.Mex. Highlands U., 1934. Cert. tchr., N.Mex., Tex. Tchr. grades 1 and 2 Eddy County, Cottonwood, N.Mex., 1927-28, tchr. grades 1, 2, 3 Loving, N.Mex., summer 1929; tchr. grade 2 Edison Sch., Carlsbad, N.Mex., 1929-33; tchr. grades 1-5 Eddy County, Otis, N.Mex., summer 1930; tchr. English, Carlsbad H.S., 1933-35; tchr. Coyote Canyon Day Sch., U.S. Indian Svc., Tohatchi, N.Mex., 1935-36; tchr. grade 1 West Sch., Carlsbad, 1937-38; tchr. English, Ysleta (Tex.) H.S., 1947-55, head dept. English, 1953-55; tchr. social studies and history O.L. Staton Jr. H.S., Lubbock, Tex., 1955; tchr. English, Lubbock H.S., 1955-72. Author, pub.: Nancy Anderson Chapter NSDAR, 1983, 84; author, compiler: Our Hughes Ancestors, 1990, Dillard in Culpeper County, Virginia, 1996; author: Teacher of the Navajo 1935-1936, 1985. Vol. geneal. aide Mahon Libr., Lubbock, 1974-2000; tchr. genealogy L.E.A.R.N., Tex. Tech U., Lubbock, 1980-82; lectr. on genealogy to various clubs, Lubbock, 1975-98; compiler Dillard Database, Dillard Family Assn., Dillard, Ga., 1994—. Fellow Tex. State Geneal. Soc. (2d v.p. 1985-87, 1st Place Manuscript award 1985, 96, 98, 2d Place 1993); mem. Nat. Geneal. Soc., Nat. Soc. DAR (regent Nancy Anderson chpt. 1982-86), Nat. Ret. Tchrs. Assn., Tex. Ret. Tchrs. Assn., Lubbock Ret. Tchrs. Assn., So. Plains Geneal. Soc. (Vol. award, pres. 1979-80), Soc. Genealogists London. Republican. Avocations: reading, writing, travel, gardening, research. Home: 4623 Twisting Rd Houston TX 77084-4885

HUGHES, DOUG, theater director; s. Barnard Hughes and Helen Stenborg; m. Lynn Fusco. Grad., Harvard U. Assoc. artistic dir. Seattle Repertory Theatre; resident dir. MCC Theater, NYC. Dir.: (Broadway plays) Frozen, 2004, Doubt, 2005— (Tony Award for best direction of a play, 2005, Outer Critics Circle award, outstanding direction of a play, 2005, Drama Desk award, outstanding director of a play, 2005, Lucille Lortel award, outstanding director, 2005), A Touch of the Poet, 2005—, A Naked Girl on the Appian Way, 2005, (Broadway Shows) Escape: 6 Ways to Get Away (1), 2004, Escape: 6 Ways to Get Away (2), 2005, (off-Broadway) Paris Letter, 2005; (plays) Last Easter, Scattergood, Frozen, The Grey Zone (Obie award), Engaged, Flesh and Blood (Callaway award), The Beard of Avon, A Question of Mercy, John Guare's Lake Hollywood, An Experiment with an Air Pump; co-dir.: Othello; co-prodr.: Wit (MCC award). Recipient Obie award for sustained excellence of direction, Village Voice, 2005. Office: MCC Theater 8th Fl 145 W 28th St New York NY 10001*

HUGHES, EDWARD F. X., finance educator, preventive medicine physician; b. Boston, Jan. 10, 1942; s. Joseph Daniel and Elizabeth (Dempsey) H.; m. Susan Lane Mooney, Feb. 11, 1967; children: Edward, John, Dempsey. BA in Philosophy, Amherst Coll., 1962; MD, Harvard U., 1966; MPH, Columbia U., 1969. Intern, resident surg. Columbia-Presbyn. Med. Ctr., N.Y.C., 1966-68; instr. to assoc. prof. Mt. Sinai Sch. Medicine, N.Y.C., 1969-77; rsch. assoc. Nat. Bur. Economic Research, N.Y.C., 1970-77; prof. prevention medicine Med. Sch., Northwestern U., 1977—; founder, dir. ctr. health svc. policy rsch. Northwestern U. Med. Sch., Chgo., 1977-94; prof. health industry mgmt. and mgmt. & strategy J. L. Kellogg Grad. Sch. Mgmt., Northwestern U., Evanston, Ill., 1977—, dir. health industry mgmt. program, 1980—83, co-dir. biotech. program, 2001—. Cons. Nat. Ctr. Health Services Research, Rockville, Md., 1975-82, AMA, Chgo., 1981-83, Midwest Bus. Group on Health, Chgo., 1983-85; expert witness providers health Plans and pharm. firms, 1993—. Editor: Hospital Cost Containment: A Policy Analysis, 1979, A Perspective on Quality in American health Care, 1988 (Bradley award 1962, Health Career Scientist award 1973-75); mem. editl. bd. Managed Care Interface (Latiolias Honor medal 1999, Beta Gamma Sigma award), Jour. Clin. Outcomes, Group Health News, Counseline; contbr. articles to profl. jours. Health Care Financing Adminstrn. grantee, Washington, 1978-84, Ford Found., 1983-86, Robert Wood Johnson Found, 1978-82, NIH, 1983-95, Pew Charitable Trusts, 1990-92, Baxter Found., 1991-96. Fellow N.Y. Acad. Medicine, Am. Coll. Physician Execs.; mem. APHA, Americas Health Ins. Plans (acad. dir. exec. leadership program), Assn. Health Svcs. Rsch. (co-founder, v.p. 1981-83, bd. dirs. 1981-84), Assn. Tchrs. Preventive Medicine (bd. dirs. 1973-76), Med. Adminstrs. Conf., Nat. Assn. Managed Care Physicians (med. adv. bd.), Boston Latin Sch. Chgo. Club (bd. dirs. 1983-86), Chapoquoit Yacht Club (West Famouth, Mass.) Home: 810 Lincoln St Evanston IL 60201-2405 Office: Kellogg Sch Mgmt 2001 Sheridan Rd Evanston IL 60208-0814 Office Phone: 847-491-8384. E-mail: efx-hughes@kellogg.northwestern.edu.

HUGHES, EDWARD JOHN, artist; b. North Vancouver, B.C., Feb. 17, 1913; s. Edward Samuel Daniell and Katherine Mary (McLean) H.; m. Fern Rosabell Irvine Smith, Feb. 10, 1940 (dec. 1974). Grad., Vancouver Sch. Art, 1933; D Fine Art (hon.), U. Victoria, 1995; DLL (hon.), Emily Carr Inst. Art & Design, Vancouver, B.C., 1997, Malaspina Univ.-Coll., Nanaimo, B.C., 2000. Exhbns. include retrospective, Vancouver Art Gallery, 1967, Surrey Art Gallery, Art Gallery of Greater Victoria, Edmonton Art Gallery, Calgary Glenbow Gallery, 1983-85, Nat. Gallery Can., Beaverbrook Gallery, Fredericton, 1983-85; represented in permanent collections, Nat. Gallery Can., Ottawa, Art Gallery Ont., Toronto, Vancouver Art Gallery, Montreal Mus. Fine Art, Greater Victoria Art Gallery; ofcl. Army war artist, 1942-46. Served with Can. Army, 1939-46. Recipient Can. Council grants, 1958, 63, 67, 70 Mem. Royal Can. Acad. Arts, Order of Can. Presbyterian. Address: 2449 Heather St Duncan BC Canada V9L 2Z6

HUGHES, ELIZABETH R. (BETH), lawyer; b. Easton, Md., Apr. 13, 1956; AB cum laude, Harvard Univ., 1978; JD with honors, Univ. Md., 1981. Bar: Md. 1981, DC 1999, Va. 2001. Joined Venable LLP, 1981, ptnr., chairwoman, corp. fin., mergers, acquisitions group Washington. Bd. dir. Open Door of Baltimore, Inc. Finalist Top Wash. Lawyers in corp. fin., Wash. Bus. Jour., 2004. Mem.: ABA, Va. Bar Assn., DC Bar Assn., Md. State Bar Assn. (chair, com. on corp. law 2000—01), Bar Assn. Baltimore City. Avocations: golf, fishing. Office: Venable LLP 575 7th St NW Washington DC 20004 Office Phone: 202-344-8049. Office Fax: 202-344-8300. Business E-Mail: erhughes@venable.com.

HUGHES, ERIC SCOTT, music educator; b. Troy, NY, Apr. 6, 1974; s. John Robert and Ernestine Julia Hughes. MusB, SUNY, Potsdam, 1992—96; MA, George Mason U., 1996—97. Tchr. instrumental music East Ramapo Ctrl. Sch. Dist., Spring Valley, NY, 1997—2000; tchr. instrumental music . Niskayuna (NY) Ctrl. Sch. Dist., 2000—. Mem.: Music Educators Nat. Conf., NY State Sch. Music Assn., Kappa Delta Pi. Avocation: tennis. Home: 14 James Street Cohoes NY 12047 Office: Niskayuna Central School District 1626 Balltown Road Niskayuna NY 12309 Personal E-mail: ericscotthughes@aol.com.

HUGHES, EUGENE MORGAN, university president; b. Scottsbluff, Nebr., Apr. 3, 1934; s. Ruby Melvin and Hazel Marie (Griffith) H.; m. Margaret Ann Romeo; children: Deborah Kaye, Greg Eugene, Lisa Ann; stepchildren: Jeff, Mark, Christi. Diploma, Neb. Western Coll., 1954; BS in Math. magna cum laude, Chadron State Coll., 1956; MS in Math., Kans. State U., 1958; PhD in Math., George Peabody Coll. for Tchrs., Vanderbilt U., 1968; LHD (hon.), No. Ariz. U., 1997; LHD, Chadron State Coll., 2003. Grad. asst. dept. math. Kans. State U., Manhattan, 1956-57; instr. math. Nebr. State Tchrs. Coll. at Chadron, 1957-58; asst. prof. math., head dept. Chadron State Coll., 1958-66, assoc. prof., 1966-69, prof. math., 1969-70, dir. rsch., 1965-66, asst. to the pres., 1966-68, dean adminstrn., 1968-70; grad. asst. dept. math. George Peabody Coll. for Tchrs., Nashville, 1962-63, 64-65, asst. to undergrad. dean, 1964, asst. to pres., 1964-65; instr. Peabody Demonstration Sch., 1963-64; prof. math. No. Ariz. U., Flagstaff, 1970-93, prof. math. emeritus, 1993—, dean Coll. Arts and Scis., 1970-71, provost univ. arts and sci. edn., 1971-72, acad. v.p., 1972-79, pres., 1979-93, pres. emeritus, 1993—; pres. Wichita State U., 1993-98, pres. emeritus, 1998—; interim pres. Ea. Ky. U., 2001; prs. Mus. No. Ariz., 2002—03. Cons. Nebr. Dept. Edn., 1966-70; mem. adv. bd. United Bank Ariz., 1980-82; mem. nat. adv. bd. Ctr. for Study of Sport in Society, 1990; mem. adv. bd. Bank IV, 1993-97; bd. dirs. NationsBank N.A. (Midwest), mem. adv. bd., 1997-98, bd. dirs. First State Bank, 1999—. Mem. staff bd. trustees Nebr. State Colls., Lincoln, 1969-70; co-dir. workshop tchr. edn. North Cen. Assn. U. Minn., 1968-70; officer fed. ednl. programs, Nebr., Ariz., 1966-93; mem. Ariz. Commn. Postsecondary Edn.; bd. fellows Am. Grad. Sch. Internat. Mgmt., 1980-93; mem. Gov.'s Com. Quality Edn., Chadron Housing Authority, 1968-70, Pres.' Commn. NCAA; mem. Ariz. State Bd. Edn., 1982-87, 90-93, pres., 1992-93; mem. Flagstaff Summer Festival, Ariz. Coun. Humanities and Pub. Policy, Mus. No. Ariz., Grand Canyon coun, Boy Scouts Am.; chair Ariz. Leadership Adv. Coun., 1990-93; mem. Ariz. Town Hall; commr. Western Interstate Commn. for Higher Edn., 1992-93; mem. Gov.'s Strategic Partnership for Econ. Devel., 1992; mem. Christopher Columbus Quincentenary Commn., 1990-91; sec., mem. Wichita/Sedgwick Partnership for Growth, 1993-97, Wichita/Sedgwick County Employment Tng. Bd., 1993-96; bd. dirs. Kids Voting Kans., 1997-98, Mus. North Ariz., 2002-03, emeritus dir., 2003—; trustee Assn. Western Univs. Inc., 1997-98. Ariz. Acad. NSF fellow, 1963, 64; recipient Chief Manuelito award Navajo Tribe, 1976, Disting. Svc. award Chadron State Coll., 1982, Flagstaff Citizen of Yr., 1988, Disting. Math. Grad. award Kans. State U., 1990, Buddy Joe Bojack Humanitarian award, 1992, Cmty. Svc. award, 1994; named Hon. Chmn. black Bd. Dirs., 1989, Outstanding Citizen, Wichita Soc. of Profl. Engrs., 1998, Kans. Soc. Profl. Engrs., 1998. Mem. Am. Assn. State Colls.and Univs. (past chmn. & mem. com. on grad. sties 1979—, bd. dirs., mem. com. on accreditation, 1980—, treas.), Math. Assn. Am. (vis. lectr. secondary schs. Western Nebr. 1962), North Cen. Assn. Colls.nd Secondary Schs. (coord. 1968-72, cons./evaluator 1977—), Nat. Coun. Tchrs. of Math., Wichita Area C. of C., Flagstaff C. of C., Blue Key, Golden Key, Masons, Elks, Rotary (past pres., Paul Harris fellow 1975), Pi Mu Epsilon, Phi Delta Kappa, Kappa Mu Epsilon, Phi Kappa Phi. Personal E-mail: ozinaz@juno.com.

HUGHES, FRANCIS P., medical association administrator; PhD. Exec. v.p. Am. Bd. Anesthesiology, Raleigh, NC. Office: Am Bd Anesthesiology 4101 Lake Boone Trl Ste 510 Raleigh NC 27607-7506

HUGHES, GRACE-FLORES, federal agency administrator; b. Taft, Tex., June 11, 1946; d. Adan Flores and Catalina San Miguel; m. Harley Arnold Hughes, May 25, 1980. BA, U. D.C., 1977; MPA, Harvard U., 1980. Sec. Dept. Air Force Kelly AFB, San Antonio, 1967-70, Pentagon-Office Sec. of Def., Washington, 1970-72; program asst., social sci. analyst HEW, Washington, 1972-78; social sci. analyst, acting dir. Office Hispanic Ams. HHS, Washington, 1978-81; vis. prof. Nebr. Wesleyan U., Lincoln, 1982-83, U. Nebr., Omaha, 1984; spl. asst. SBA, Washington, 1985-88, assoc. adminstr. for minority small bus., 1988; dir. community rels. Dept. Justice, Washington, 1988-92; pres. Grace, Inc., Alexandria, Va.; v.p. for intergovtl. affairs USTAK, LLCcs., Inc. Spl. asst. Reagan/Bush '84 Campaign, Nebr. and Washington, 1984, 50th Presdl. Inaugural, Washington, 1984-85, Office Pub. Liaison, The White House, 1985. Author: The Bureaucrat, Categorized Workforce, 1992; co-author: New Book of Knowledge, 1980; chair adv. bd. Harvard Jour. Hispanic Policy, 1989—; The Use and Abuse of Diversity Mag., 1994, Hispanic Mag., 1996. Adv. mem. U.S. Senate Rep. Task Force, Washington, 1988-91; alumni exec. bd. J.F. Kennedy Sch. Govt., Harvard U., Cambridge, Mass., 1989-93; mem. Rep. Hispanic Assembly, 1984—; apptd. by Gov. Allen of Va. to Bd. for Profl. and Occpl. Regulations, 1994—, Bd. for Agr. and Consumer Svcs., 1997—; bd. dirs. Hispanic Found. for Arts; apptd. by Pres. Bush Fed. Svc. Impasses Panel, 2000. Recipient Excellence award Nev. Econ. Devel. Corp., 1988, Leadership award Am. GI Forum, Omaha, 1989; named one of 100 Most Influential Hispanics in U.S. Hispanic Bus. Mag., 1988. Mem. Assn. Pub. Adminstrs. (Outstanding Pub. Svc. award 1990), Hispanic Bus. Roundtable, Coun. in Excellence in Govt. (prin.), Fedn. Rep. Women, Mex.-Am. Women's Nat. Assn., Univ. Club (Washington). Episcopalian. Avocations: tennis, jogging, aerobics, equestrian. Home and Office: 5208 Bedlington Ter Alexandria VA 22304-3551 Office Phone: 703-395-2863. E-mail: harley45@aol.com.

HUGHES, GREGORY, information technology executive; BS in elec. engring., MS in elec. engring. and computer sci., MIT; MBA, Stanford Grad. Sch. Bus. Founder, CEO Granite Microsystems; ptnr. McKinsey & Co., 1993—2003; exec. v.p. global svcs. VERITAS Software Corp., Mountain View, Calif., 2003—. Office: VERITAS Software Corp 350 Ellis St Mountain View CA 94043

HUGHES, HARRISON G., horticulture educator; BS, Eastern Ill. U.; PhD, Purdue U. Prof., Dept. Horticulture Colo. State U., Fort Collins. Recipient Outstanding Graduate Educator award. Office: Colo State U Dept Horticulture and Landscape Arch 210 Shepardson Bldg 1173 Campus Delivery Fort Collins CO 80523-1173 Office Phone: 970-491-7050. Business E-Mail: harrison.hughes@colostate.edu.

HUGHES, JACQUELINE EMMA, information systems specialist; b. Baltimore, Md., Feb. 10, 1968; d. Hugh Price Hughes Jr. and Reta Theresa Hughes; m. Donald W. Tebo, Jr. BA in Psychology, Coll. Notre Dame Md., Balt., 1990; MBA, U. Phoenix, Columbia, Md., 2001; student, Capella U., 2005—. CPR, First Aid, and AED Instructor ARC, 2002. Armorer USMC Reserves, Savannah, Ga., 1988—99; counselor Mgmt. Tng. Corp., Washington, 1992—99; counseling mgr. Adams and Assocs., Laurel, Md., 1995—96; info. systems specialist TCU Manpower Tng. Dept., Rockville, Md., 1999—. Innovation com. mem. Mgmt. Tng. Corp., Randallstown, Md., 1993; cultural diversity coord. Adams and Assocs., Laure, Md., 1995—96. Author: (poetry) Look, 1999. Chair, Relay for Life Am. Cancer Soc., 2002—03. Mem.: AAUW, NAFE. Avocations: travel, volunteer work. Personal E-mail: jetebo@comcast.net.

HUGHES, JAMES MITCHELL, epidemiologist, educator; b. Pitts., Aug. 11, 1945; s. James Paul and Adelaide (Mitchell) H.; m. Pamela Mary Parsons, June 12, 1971; children: Andrew Saban, Mitchell Parsons. BA, Stanford U., 1966, MD, 1971. Diplomate Am. Bd. Preventive Medicine, Am. Bd. Internal Medicine, Am. Bd. Infectious Diseases. Intern U. Wash., Seattle, 1971-72; epidemic intelligence svc. officer Ctr. for Disease Control, Atlanta, 1973-75; resident internal medicine U. Wash., Seattle, 1972-73, 75-76; fellow infectious diseases U. Va., Charlottesville, 1976-78; chief water-related diseases activity, asst. chief enteric diseases br. Bur. Epidemiology, Ctr. for Disease Control, Atlanta, 1978-81; chief surveillance and prevention br., asst. dir. med. sci., hosp. infections program Ctr. for Infectious Diseases, Ctrs. for Disease Control, Atlanta, 1981-83, dir. hosp. infections program, 1983-88; dep. dir. Nat. Ctr. for Infectious Diseases, Ctr. for Disease Control, Atlanta, 1988-92; dir. Nat. Ctr. for Infectious Diseases, Ctrs. for Disease Control and Prevention, 1992; clin. assoc. prof. Emory U., Atlanta, 1993-2001; clin. prof. dept. medicine Emory U. Sch. Medicine, 2001—. Clin. assoc. prof. divsn. geographic medicine, dept. medicine, U. Va., Charlottesville, 1979-82; clin. asst. prof. divsn. infectious diseases, dept. medicine Emory U., Atlanta, 1981-93; staff physician Atlanta VA Hosp., 1989—; adj. prof. dept. epidemiology Rollins Sch. Pub. Health, Emory U., 1994—. Contbr. articles to profl. jours., chpts. in books. Baseball coach North Decatur (Ga.) Youth Assn., 1981-90; pres. Westchester Sch. PTA, Decatur, 1986-87. Asst. surgeon gen. USPHS, 1973-75, 76—. Recipient Meritorious Svc. medal USPHS, Atlanta, 1986, Outstanding Svc. medal, 1989, Disting. Svc. medal, 1997. Fellow ACP, AAAS, Infectious Diseases Soc. Am.; mem. APHA, Inst. of Medicine, Am. Soc. Microbiology, Am. Soc. Tropical Medicine and Hygiene, Am. Epidemiol. Soc., Royal Soc. Tropical Medicine and Hygiene, Soc. Epidemiol. Rsch., U. So. Calif. Alumni Assn. (bd. govs. 1995-97), Stanford U. Alumni Club Ga. (pres. 1980-82). Avocations: sports, travel. Office: NCID Mail Stop C12 CDC 1600 Clifton Rd NE Atlanta GA 30329-4018 E-mail: jmh2@cdc.gov.

HUGHES, JAMES PAUL, physician; b. Wilkinsburg, Pa., Apr. 9, 1920; s. Paul S. and Sara C. (Coleman) Hughes; m. Adelaide C. Mitchell, June 21, 1944; 1 child, James Mitchell. BS, U. Pitts., 1944, MD, 1945; D in Indsl. Medicine, U. Cin., 1952. Diplomate Am. Bd. Preventive Medicine. Intern St. Francis Hosp., Pitts., 1945—46; resident in pathology Univ. Hosps., Cleve., 1948—49; fellow in indsl. medicine Kettering Lab. U. Cin., 1949—51; physician The Tex. Co., 1951—52, The Ethyl Corp., Cin., 1952—57; chief Bur. Indsl. Health Dept. Health City of Cin., 1952—55; med. dir. Kaiser Aluminum & Chem. Corp., Oakland, Calif., 1957—82; sr. ptnr. Hughes-Lewis Assocs., Oakland, Calif., 1982—88; asst. prof. indsl. medicine U. Cin., 1952—55; assoc. prof. preventive medicine Ohio State U., 1955—57; exec. v.p., dir. Kaiser Found. Internat., 1967—76; project dir. U.S. Peace Corps Health projects, 1966—68, USAID med. relief project, Port Harcourt, Nigeria, 1970—72, Health Svcs. on Bandama River project, Kossou, Côte d'Ivoire, 1970—72; v.p. health svcs. Kaiser Industries Corp., 1972—74; clin. assoc. prof. occupl. medicine U. Calif., San Francisco, 1979—96; med. dir. occupl. health svcs. Merritt Peralta Med. Ctr., Oakland, Calif., 1982—86. Mem. hearing bd. Bay Area Air Quality Mgmt. Dist., Calif., 1989—98; mem. U. Calif. Pres.'s Coun. on Nat. Labs., Lawrence Berkeley, Lawrence Livermore, Los Alamos; mem. panel on environment, safety and health, 1993—98. Author (with N.H. Proctor): Chemical Hazards of the Workplace,

1978, 1996; editor-in-chief Health Hazards of the Workplace Report, 1989—91. Chmn. com. for industry Coun. Tropical Health, Harvard U. Sch. Pub. Health, 1969—76. Served to capt. U.S. Army, 1946—48. Decorated Officier de l'Ordre Nat. Ivoirien Abidjan. Fellow: ACP, Am. Coll. Occupl. and Environ. Medicine (past pres., Health Achievement award 1972, Kehoe award 1982, Knudsen award 1996); mem.: Inst. Medicine NAS. Home: 124 Guilford Rd Piedmont CA 94611-3805

HUGHES, JANET LOUISE, artist; b. Easton, Pa., June 10, 1927; d. William Stewart and Cecilia Louise (Fulmer) H.; divorced; 1 child, David Tod. Student, Baum Art Sch., Allentown, Pa., 1935-45, Moore Inst. Art, Phila., 1945-46, Fashion Acad., N.Y.C., 1946-47, Lehigh U., 1947-49. With Laros Lingerie Co., Bethlehem, Pa., 1950-54; artist R&D lab. Binney and Smith Inc., Easton, Pa., 1955-60. Art instr. in field. One woman shows include Lafayette Coll., Pa., Womens Club of Easton, Pa., Little York Gallery, N.J., Walpack Art Gallery, N.J., Dover (N.J.) Art League, Easton Cmty. Art League, Nazerath (Pa.) Pub. Libr., Washington Libr., N.J., Easton Nat. Bank, Elkton County Bank and Trust, Md.; exhibited in group shows including Walpack Art Gallery; represented in permanent collections. Mem. Tri-State Profl. Artists, Easton Cmty. Art League, Sussex County Art Soc., Parkland Art League Allentown, Kittatinney Art Group, Allentown Art Mus., Nat. Mus. Women in the Arts.

HUGHES, JOAN MOTTOLA, education association representative; b. July 3, 1953; m. Jonathan T. Hughes. BA, Gordon Coll., Wenham, Mass., 1974; MEd, Lesley Coll., 1979, Columbia U., 1996; EdD, Columbia U., 2001; postgrad., Harvard U., 1985. Tchr. English, Georgetown (Mass.) Pub. Schs., 1974-86; field rep. Conn. Edn. Assn., Wilton, 1986—. Field rep. Mass. Tchrs. Assn., Boston, part-time 1983-86. Mem. Indsl. Rels. Rsch. Assn., Phi Delta Kappa, Kappa Delta Pi. Office: 7 Hollyhock Ln Wilton CT 06897-4414 E-mail: joanh@cea.org.

HUGHES, (ROBERT) JOHN, journalist, educator; b. Neath, Wales, Apr. 28, 1930; came to U.S., 1954; s. Evan John and Dellis May (Williams) H.; m. Vera Elizabeth Pockman (div. 1987); children: Wendy Elizabeth, Mark Evan; m. Peggy Janeane Jordan, 1988; 1 child, Evan Jordan. LLD (hon.), Colby Coll., 1978; HHD (hon.), So. Utah U., 1994. Africa corr. Christian Sci. Monitor, 1955-61, Far East corr., 1964-70, editor Boston, 1970-79, columnist, 1985—, dir. radio broadcasting, 1987-89; pres. Hughes Newspapers, Orleans, Mass., 1977-85; assoc. dir. USIA, Washington, 1981-82; dir. Voice of Am., Washington, 1982; asst. sec. of state Dept. State, Washington, 1982-85; asst. sec.-gen. UN, N.Y.C., 1995; editor Deseret News, Salt Lake City, 1997—. Pres., pub., editor Concord Comm., Rockland, Maine, 1989-91; prof., dir. internat. media studies program Brigham Young U., Provo, Utah, 1991-96; chmn. Pres. Bush Commn. on U.S. Govt. Internat. Broadcasting, 1991, Presdl./Congressional Commn. Broadcasting to People's Republic China, 1992. Author: The New Face of Africa, 1961, Indonesian Upheaval, 1967. Nieman fellow, Harvard U., 1961-62; recipient Pulitzer prize, 1967, Yankee = quill Sigma Delta Chi, 1977. Mem. Am. Soc. Newspaper Editors (past pres.), Coun. Fgn. Rels., Overseas Press Club (Best Reporting from Overseas 1970). Office: Deseret Morning News PO Box 1257 Salt Lake City UT 84110-1257

HUGHES, JOHN HAROLD, surgeon, educator; b. New Rochelle, NY, Feb. 17, 1936; s. Harold Tegai and Ida (Erickson) H.; m. Janet Gail Williams, Mar. 7, 1964; children: Stephen A.T., Megan Elizabeth, John E.Q. BA, Yale U., 1957; MD, Cornell U., 1961. Diplomate Am. Bd. Surgery. Intern in surgery St. Luke's Hosp., N.Y.C., 1961-62, resident in surgery, 1962-66; chief of surgery Ft. Benjamin Harrison, Indpls., 1966-67; surgeon Hardin Meml. Hosp., Kenton, Ohio, 1968-74; asst. prof., dir. clinics Med. Coll. Ohio, Toledo, 1974-77; assoc. prof., dir. emergency svcs. U. Ariz., Tucson, 1977-81; surgeon, prof. surgery Naval Hosp. Long Beach, Calif., 1982-85; surgeon Naval Hosp. Oak Knoll, Oakland, Calif., 1990-91; med. dir. Casa Grande (Ariz.) Clinic, 1992-93; pvt. practice Casa Grande, Ariz., 1993—2000. Clin. instr. surgery Columbia U., N.Y.C., 1965-66; lectr. U. Ariz., Tucson, 1981—; clin. prof. surgery USUHS, Bethesda. 1990-96, adj. prof., 1996—; lectr. U. Ariz., 2002-03; cons. Paxis, 2002—. Contbr. over 65 articles to profl. jours.; editor emergency medicine jour. Hosp. Medicine, 1979—90; editorial reviewer jour. Mil. Medicine, 1987—; book reviewer jour. Profl. Safety, 1981—. Commr. health Hardin County, Ohio, 1969-74; pres. Hardin County Med. Soc., Kenton, Ohio, 1973-74. Capt. USNR, 1982—. Grantee, Nat. Cancer Inst., 1976, NIMH, 1979. Fellow ACS; mem. AAAS, Assn. Mil. Surgeons, Soc. Med. Cons. to Armed Forces (assoc.), Pima County Med. Soc., Tucson Surg. Soc., Nanotech. Cluster Ariz., Sigma Xi. Presbyterian. Home: 7712 E Oakwood Cir Tucson AZ 85750-2338

HUGHES, JOHN RUSSELL, neurologist, educator; b. DuBois, Pa., Dec. 19, 1928; s. John Henry and Alice (Cooper) H.; m. Mary Ann Dick, June 14, 1958; children: John Russell Jr. (dec.), Christopher Alan, Thomas Gregory, Cheryl Ann. AB summa cum laude, Franklin and Marshall Coll., 1950; BA with honors, Oxford (Eng.) U., 1952, MA with honors, 1955, DM (hon.), 1976; PhD, Harvard U., 1954; MD, Northwestern U., 1975. Neurophysiologist NIH, 1954-56; dir. electroencephalography dept. Meyer Hosp., SUNY, 1956-63; dir. div. lab. scis., including electroencephalography Northwestern U. Med. Center, 1963-77, prof. neurology, 1968—; dir. EEG and Epilepsy Clinic, U. Ill. Med. Center, 1977—; staff U. Ill. Hosp., Community Hosp., Geneva, Delnor Hosp., St. Charles; dir.neurophysiology Humana-Michael-Reese Med. Ctr., 1992—. Cons. Chgo. VA Westside Hosp., Mercyville and Copley Meml. Hosp., Aurora, Ill., others; participant debate on brain death BBC-TV; bd. dirs. Am. Bd. EEG and Neurophysiology; participant Am. Med. EEG Assn.; rep. Internat. Fedn. EEG and Clin. Neurophysiology lectr. tour of Africa, 1989; keynote speaker Internat. Course of Neurophysiology, Oxford U., 1993, invited speaker, 1996, 99, 02, 05; invited spkr. Damascus Med. Sch., Syria, 1998, Royal Soc. of Medicine, London, 2003; lectr. in field. Author: Functional Organization of the Diencephalon, 1957, Atlas on Cerebral Death and Coma, 1976, Chinese Translation, 1997, Japanese Translation, 1998, EEG in Clinical Practice, 1982, 2d edit., 1994, EEG Evoked Potentials in Psychiatry and Behavioral Neurology, 1983; contbr. articles to profl. jours. Command Surgeon, USAR, 1986-90, with Army Med. R & D Command, 1990—, mobilization replacement for maj. gen., comdr. Recipient Alumni award Franklin and Marshall Coll., 1978, Lifetime Achievement award Am. EEG and Clin. Neurophysiol. Soc., 2000. Mem. Am. Electroencephalography Soc. (treas. 1965-68), Eastern Electroencephalography Soc. (sec.-treas. 1961-64), Ctrl. Electroencephalography Soc., Am. Med. EEG Assn. (bd. dirs.), Am. Bd. EEG and Neurophysiology (bd. dirs.), Internat. EEG and Clin. Neurophysiology (bd. dirs.), Am. Acad. EEG (bd. dirs.), Brit. Soc. of neurophysiology (hon.), Chgo. Acad. Medicine, Am. Epilepsy Soc., Am. Physiol. Soc., Soc. Neuroscis., Am. Acad. Neurology, Phi Beta Kappa, Sigma Xi (lectr. 1960—) Achievements include research on coding in central nervous system, new theory on neural mechanisms in olfaction, electro-clin. correlations in different types of epilepsy, organic aspects in juvenile delinquency. Home: 720 Roslyn Ter Evanston IL 60201-1722 Office: U Ill Consultation Clinic Epilepsy 912 S Wood St Chicago IL 60612-7325 E-mail: JHughes@uic.edu. *Always be ahead of your colleagues in every endeavor by having done it before they do. Do what you must do now to leave time for innovation later.*

HUGHES, JOHN W., film producer, screenwriter, film director; b. Lansing, Mich., Feb. 18, 1950; m. Nancy Ludwig; children: John III, James. With Needham Harper & Steers, Chgo.; copywriter, creative dir. Leo Burnett Co.; editor National Lampoon; founder, pres. Hughes Entertainment, 1985—. Screenwriter: National Lampoon's Class Reunion, 1982, National Lampoon's Vacation, 1983, Mr. Mom, 1983, Nate and Hayes, 1983, National Lampoon's European Vacation, 1985, (as Edmond Dantes), 101 Dalmations, 1996, Maid in Manhattan, 2002, Just Visiting, 2001; screenwriter, prodr.: Pretty in Pink, 1986, Some Kind of Wonderful, 1987, The Great Outdoors, 1988, National Lampoon's Christmas Vacation, 1989, Home Alone, 1990, Career Opportunities, 1990, Dutch, 1991, Home Alone 2: Lost in New York, 1992, Dennis the Menace, 1993, Baby's Day Out, 1994, Miracle on 34th Street, 1994, 101 Dalmations, 1996, Flubber, 1997, Home Alone 3, 1997, Reach the Rock, 1998; screenwriter, dir.: Sixteen Candles, 1984, Weird Science, 1985; screenwriter, dir., prodr.: The Breakfast Club, 1985, Ferris Bueller's Day Off, 1986, Planes, Trains and Automobiles, 1987, She's Having a Baby, 1988, Uncle Buck, 1989, Curly Sue, 1991; prodr.: Only the Lonely, 1991, NewPort South, 2001; TV writer: Home Alone 2, 2002, National Lampoon's American Adventure, 2000. Recipient Commitment to Chgo. award, 1990; named NATO/ShoWest Prodr. of Yr., 1990. also: c/o Michael Wimer Creative Artists Agy 9830 Wilshire Blvd Beverly Hills CA 90212-1804

HUGHES, J(OHNSON) DONALD, history professor, editor; b. Santa Monica, Calif., June 5, 1932; s. Johnson and Vannelia Anna (Blanchfield) H.; m. Pamela Louise Peters, June 8, 1964; children: Peter, Melissa, Joy. AB, UCLA, 1954; S.T.B., Boston U., 1957, PhD, 1960; postgrad., Am. Sch. Classical Studies, Greece, 1966-67. Asst. prof. history U. Denver, 1967-72, assoc. prof. history, 1972-77, prof. history, 1977—, Evans prof., 1994—, chair dept. history, 2000—01. Author: Ecology in Ancient Civilizations, 1975; In The House of Stone And Light, 1978 (Nat. Pk. Service award 1977-78); North American Indian Ecology, 1983, Pan's Travail: Environmental Problems of the Ancient Greeks and Romans, 1994, An Environmental History of the World: Humankind's Changing Role in the Community of Life, 2001, The Mediterranean: An Environmental History, 2005; editor: Ecological Consciousness, 1981, The Face of the Earth: Environment and World History, 2000; editor Environ. Rev., 1983-85, mem. editl. bd., 1986-95, Environ. Ethics, 1981-89, Environ. History, 1995—. Boston U. fellow, 1957; Danforth Found. assoc., 1965—; Lindbergh grantee, 1987. Mem. Am. Inst. Archaeology, Am. Soc. Environ. History (exec. bd. 1983-85, Disting. Svc. award 2000), European Soc. Environ. History, Forest History Soc., Am. Hist. Assn., Phi Beta Kappa. Home: 2580 S University Blvd Apt 1001 Denver CO 80210-6159 Office: U Denver Dept History Denver CO 80208-0001

HUGHES, JOYCE ANNE, law educator; b. Feb. 7, 1940. BA, Carleton U., 1961; JD, U. Minn., 1965. Bar: Minn. 1965, Ill. 1976. Law clk. Earl R. Larson U.S. Dist. Judge Minn., 1965-67; assoc. Howard, LeFevere, Lefler, Mpls., 1967-71; assoc. prof. U. Minn., 1971-75; assoc. prof. Northwestern U., 1975-79, prof., 1979—; gen. counsel Chgo. Transit Authority, 1984-88; dir. Fed. Home Loan Bank of Chgo. 1980-84; mem. Ill. Sup. Ct. Com. on Evidence, 1971-77; mem. U.S. del. to Belgrade Conf. to Review Helsinki Accord, 1977-78. Mem. Chgo. Bd. Edn., 1980-82. Mem. Order of Coif, Phi Beta Kappa. Office: Northwestern U Sch Law 357 E Chicago Ave Chicago IL 60611-3059 Office Phone: 312-503-8373. E-mail: jahughes@law.northwestern.edu.*

HUGHES, JOYCE ANNE, history educator; b. Parma, Mo., Aug. 27, 1939; d. Rutherford Ancil and Syble Delores Corlew; m. John Edward Hughes, Oct. 1, 1955; children: Michael E., Johnny Alan, Kevin W. AA, Three Rivers C.C., 1989; BS cum laude, Southeast Mo. State U., 1991; MEd, Southwest Bapt. U., 2002. Cert. tchg. Mo. Tchr. Malden R-1 Schs., Malden, Mo., 1993—2005. Mem.: MSTA, Alpha Chi, Kappa Delta Pi, Phi Theta Kappa. Home: RT 2 Box 295 Malden MO 63863 Office Phone: 573-276-5718.

HUGHES, KAREN PARFITT, federal agency administrator; b. Paris, Dec. 27, 1956; m. Jerry L. Hughes; 1 child, Robert. BA in English, BFA in journalism, So. Meth. U., 1977. Television reporter KXAS-TV, Dallas/Ft. Worth, Tex., 1977—84; Tex. media coord. Reagan/Bush Campaign, 1984; media cons. Rep. Party of Tex., 1985—91, exec. dir., 1991—94; dir. comm. to Gov. George W. Bush State of Tex., 1994—2001; dir. comm. Bush-Cheney campaign, 2000; counselor to Pres. The White House, Washington, 2001—02; advisor Bush-Cheney campaign, 2004; under sec. for pub. diplomacy & pub. affairs US Dept. State, Washington, 2005—. Author: Ten Minutes From Normal, 2004. Office: US Dept State 2201 C St NW Rm 7261 Washington DC 20520

HUGHES, KAYLENE, historian, educator; b. Modesto, Calif., Aug. 4, 1952; BA, Miami-Dade (Fla.) Jr. Coll., 1972, Fla. Internat. U., 1976; MA, Fla. State U., 1977, PhD, 1985. Intern Fla. State Dept. Archives Records Mgmt., Tallahassee, 1977; Claims Control Supr. Sys. Devel. Corp., Tallahassee, 1978-81; editl. asst. Fla. Hotel and Motel Jour., Tallahassee, 1983-85; dir. edn., rsch. mgr. Fla. Hotel and Motel Assn., Tallahassee, 1985-87; historian U.S. Army Aviation & Missile Command, Redstone Arsenal, Ala., 1987—. Grad. asst. Fla. State U., Tallahassee, 1976-77, tchg. asst., 1981-83; adj. instr. history John C. Calhoun C.C., Huntsville, Ala., 1990—. Author: Florida's Lodging Industry: The First 75 Years, 1987, The Missile's Red Glare, 1992, Redstone Army Airfield: A Tradition of Aviation Support, 1992, Redstone Arsenal's Role in Operation Desert Shield/Desert Storm, 1992; contbr. articles to jours. and newspapers. Grantee Fla. State U., 1983. Mem. Phi Alpha Theta (sec. 1982-85), Phi Theta Kappa. Home: 342 Pawnee Trl SE Huntsville AL 35803-2280 Business E-Mail: kaylene.hughes@redstone.army.mil.

HUGHES, KENT HIGGON, economist; b. Portland, Oreg., Feb. 23, 1941; s. John Kenneth and Gwladys (Higgon) H.; m. Virginia Carrington Sammon; children: John Kenneth, Jeff, Krista. BA, Yale U., 1962; LLB, Harvard U., 1965; PhD, Washington U., 1976. Bar: D.C. 1971. Fellow Internat. Legal Ctr., Sao Paulo, Brazil, 1967-69; atty. Urban Law Inst., Washington, 1970-71; legis. counsel Office of Sen. Vance Hartke, Washington, 1971-72; analyst Congl. Rsch. Svc., Washington, 1973-76; sr. economist Joint Econ. Com., Washington, 1977-82; legis. dir. Office Sen. Gary Hart, Washington, 1983-84; staff dir. trade subcom. Ho. Reps. Fgn. Affairs Com., Washington, 1985-87; chief economist Dem. policy com. U.S. Senate, Washington, 1987-90; pres. Coun. on Competitiveness, 1990-93; assoc. dep. sec. of commerce U.S. Dept. of Commerce, Washington, 1993-99; pub. policy scholar Woodrow Wilson Internat. Ctr., Washington, 1999-2001; dir. Sci., Tech. Am. and Global Economy Program Woodrow Wilson Ctr., 2001—04, dir. Program on Sci., Tech. Am. & Global Economy, 2005—. Author: Trade, Taxes, Transnationals, 1979, Building the Next American Century, 2005; contbr. articles to profl. jours. Mem. ABA, Am. Econ. Assn., D.C. Bar Assn. Avocations: languages, rugby, collecting political memorabilia. Home: 4961 Allan Rd Bethesda MD 20816-2721 Office: Woodrow Wilson Internat Ctr One Woodrow Wilson Plaza 1300 Pennsylvania Ave NW Washington DC 20004-3027 Business E-Mail: Hugheske@wwic.si.edu.

HUGHES, KEVIN MICHAEL, academic administrator; b. Chambersburg, Pa., Feb. 18, 1969; s. Francis Joseph and Ellen Swenson Hughes; m. Amy Beth McDermaid, Apr. 27, 1996; children: Sean Patrick, Erin Colleen. BA, James Madison U., 1991; MEd, U. S.C., 1993; PhD, Coll. William and Mary, 2004. Cert. conflict mediation Pitts. Conflict Mediation Group, 1995. Asst. to dean of students Carnegie Mellon U., Pittsburgh, Pa., 1993—95, coord. student life, 1995—98; dir. campus activities NC Wesleyan Coll., Rocky Mount, NC, 1998—99, assoc. dean students, 1999—2000; coord. jud. affairs Christopher Newport U., Newport News, Va., 2000—04, dir. student life, 2004—. Ropes course facilitator Ligonier Camp and Conf. Ctr., Ligonier, Pa., 1994—98, Jumonville Camp and Conf. Ctr., 1995—98; host town com.-housing and activities Spl. Olympics World Games, Rocky Mount, NC, 1999; ropes course facilitator Coll. William and Mary, Williamsburg, Va., 2000—03. Election ofcl. James City County, Va., 2002—04. Mem.: Assn. Study Higher Edn. (assoc.), Assn. Student Jud. Affairs (assoc.), Order of Omega, Kappa Delta Pi, Omicron Delta Kappa, Phi Alpha Theta. Independent. Roman Catholic. Avocations: sports memorabilia collecting, weightlifting, sports. Office: Christopher Newport U 1 University Pl Newport News VA 23606 Office Phone: 757-594-7260. Office Fax: 757-594-8737. E-mail: kmhughes@cnu.edu.

HUGHES, LAKECIA DENISE, minister; b. Gary, Ind., Nov. 20, 1971; d. Lonnie Hughes and Marie Bolton. AAS info. systems mgmt., CCAF USAF, Tampa, Fla., 1995; BS Psychology, Troy State U., 2000. Ordained minister Life Changing Ministry, Ft. Walton Beach. Command and control specialist USAF, Fayetteville, NC, 1991—93, resource mgr. Kunsan AB, Republic of Korea, 1993—94, tng. and security mgr. Ft. Walton Beach, Fla., 1998—2003, fin. mgr., 2001—; mgr. residential habilitation Ft. Walton Beach, 2003—. Author: (Book) Singled Out for Success, 2003. Family support nurturer Habitat for Humanity, 2002—03, Life Changing Ministry, Ft. Walton Beach, Fla. Staff sgt. USAF. Republican. Avocations: ceramics, bowling, poetry.

HUGHES, LINDA J., newspaper publisher; b. Princeton, B.C., Can., Sept. 27, 1950; d. Edward Rees and Madge Preston (Bryan) H.; m. George Fredrick Ward, Dec. 16, 1978; children: Sean Ward, Kate Ward. BA, U. Victoria (B.C.), 1972; LittD (hon.), Athabasca U., 1997; diploma in journalism (hon.), Grant MacEwan C.C., Edmonton, Alta., Can., 1999; LLD (hon.), U. Alberta, 2003. With Edmonton Jour., Alta., Can., 1976—, from reporter to asst. mng. editor, 1984-87, editor, 1987-92, pub., 1992—. Southam fellow U. Toronto, Ont., Can., 1977-78; recipient Disting. Citizen award Grant MacEwan C.C., 1999, Dist. Alumni award U. Victoria, 2000. Office: Edmonton Journal 10006 101st St PO Box 2421 Edmonton AB Canada T5J 2S6 E-mail: lhughes@thejournalcanwest.com.

HUGHES, LYNN NETTLETON, federal judge; m. Olive (Allen). BA, U. Ala., 1963; JD, U. Tex., 1968; LLM, U. Va., 1992. Bar: Tex., 1966. Pvt. practice, Houston, 1966-79; judge Dist. Ct. Tex., Houston, 1979-85; U.S. dist. judge So. Dist. Tex., Houston, 1985—. Adj. prof. South Tex. Coll. Law, 1973-2003, U. Tex., 1990-91, 2000-01; Tex. del. Nat. Conf. State Trial Judges, 1983-85; cons. Tex. Jud. Budget Bd., 1984; lectr. Tex. Coll. Judiciary, 1983; mem. task force on revision rules of civil procedure Supreme Ct. Tex., 1993-94; cons. on constn. Moldova, 1993, European Community, 1989, Ukraine, 1995, Romania, 1996, Albania, 1997; mem. jud. adv. bd. Law and Econs. Ctr., George Mason U., 1999—. Mem. adv. bd. Houston Jour. Internat. Law, 1981—, chmn., 1989-99. Trustee Rift Valley Rsch. Mission, 1978—; mem. St. Martin's Episcopal Ch.; dir. Houston World Affairs Coun., 1997—, co-chair 1999-2000. Mem.: FBA (bd. dirs. Houston chpt. 1986—89), ABA, Am. Inns of Ct. XV (pres. 1986—92), Houston Philos. Soc. (exec. com. 2000—03), Am. Anthrop. Assn., Am. Soc. Legal History, Am. Judicature Soc., Tex. State Bar (selection, compensation and tenure state judges com. 1981—85, ct. cost, delay and efficiency com. 1981—90, vice chmn. 1982—83, nominations com. jud. sect. 1983, vice chmn. 1984—86, liaison with law schs. com. 1987—92, plain lang. com. 1989—96), Houston Bar Assn., Maritime Law Assn., Am. Law Inst., Coun. on Fgn. Rels., Houston Com. Fgn. Rels. (chmn. 2003—04). Office: US Ct Hse 11122 515 Rusk St Houston TX 77002-2605 Home: PO Box 61565 Houston TX 77208 Office Phone: 713-250-5900. Business E-Mail: lnh@txs.uscourts.gov.

HUGHES, MARIJA MATICH, law librarian; b. Belgrade, Yugoslavia; came to U.S., 1960, naturalized, 1971; d. Zarija and Antonija (Hudowsky) Matich. BA in Music, Mokranjac, Belgrade; BA in English, U. Belgrade and Calif. State U.; MLS, U. Md.; student, McGeorge Sch. Law; MHA in Health Care Adminstrn., George Washington U., 1985, M. in Adminstrv. Scis., 1989. Counselor, gen. mgr. Career Counseling Service, Sacramento, Calif., 1962-64; sec. to mgr. Sacramento State Coll., 1965-66; student librarian High John program U. Md., Fairmont Heights, 1967; reference librarian Calif. State Law Library, Sacramento, 1968; head reference library-faculty liasion librarian Hastings Coll. Law U. Calif., San Francisco, 1969-72; head law librarian AT&T, Washington, 1972-73; chief law librarian Nat. Clearinghouse Library, U.S. Commn. on Civil Rights, Washington, 1973-86; tech. info. specialist U.S. Dept. Labor, OSHA, Tech. Date Ctr., 1988—; owner, pub. Hughes Press. Author (compiler): The Sexual Barrier, Legal and Econ. Aspects of Employment, vols. 1 and 2, 1970—73, The Sexual Barriers: Legal, Medical, Economic and Social Aspects of Sex Discrimination, 1977, Computer Health Hazards, 1990, 1993, Computer Health Hazards, Eng. translation, 1996, Sick From Computers, 1994, Computers, Antennas, Cellular Telephones and Power Lines Health Hazards, 1996, Shadow at the Ball, 2001; contbr. articles to profl. jours. Mem. Am. Assn. Law Librs., Bioelectromagnetics Soc., Consumer Utilities Bd. Home: 2400 Virginia Ave NW Apt C501 Washington DC 20037-2644 Office Phone: 202-293-2686.

HUGHES, MARTIN P., insurance company executive; Chmn. Assurex Internat.; from mem. staff to pres. Mack and Parker, Inc., 1973—90, pres., 1990—99, chmn., 1999—2001, HUB Internat. Ltd., Chgo., 1999—. CEO, 1999—. Bd. dir. Assurex Mktg. Group, Coun. Ins. Agents and Brokers. Office: HUB International Ltd 55 East Jackson Blvd Chicago IL 60604

HUGHES, MARVALENE, academic administrator; Student, Tuskegee U., NYU, Columbia U.; PhD in Counseling and Adminstrn., Fla. State U.; postgrad., Harvard U., U. Calif., San Diego. Dir. counseling and career devel. Eckerd Coll., Fla.; dir. counseling svcs. and placement, prof. and adminstr. San Diego State U.; assoc. v.p. student affairs Ariz. State U.; v.p. student affairs, prof. counseling and human svcs. U. Toledo; v.p. student affairs, vice provost, prof. ednl. psychology U. Minn.; pres. Calif. State U., Stanislaus, 1994—2005, Dillard U., New Orleans, 2005—. Nat., internat. keynote spkr. Contbr. chpts. to books and articles to profl. jours. Keynoter Pres.-to-Pres. Address, Internat. Conf. Pres. and Chancellors, Puerto Rico, 1999; chmn. Women Pres. and Chancellors Am. Assn. State Colls. and Univs., 1999—, prof. devel. com.; adv. bd. 1st Nat. Women's Mus.; mem. divsn. II pres. coun. NCAA, mem. divsn. II budget and fin. com., liason pres. coun. divsn. II student athlete adv. com.; mem. evaluation com. Accrediting Commn. Sr. Colls. and Univs., We. Assn. Schs. and Colls.; mem. Lt. Gov.'s Commn One Calif., 1999. Mem. Leadership Calif. Office: Dillard Univ 2601 Gentilly Blvd New Orleans LA 70122*

HUGHES, MARY KATHERINE, lawyer; b. July 16, 1949; d. John Chamberlain and Marjorie (Anstey) Hughes; m. Andrew H. Eker, July 7, 1982. BBA cum laude, U. Alaska, 1971; JD, Willamette U., 1974; postgrad., Heriot-Watt U., Edinburgh, Scotland, 1971. Bar: Alaska 1975. Ptnr. Hughes, Thorsness, Gantz, Powell & Brundin, Anchorage, 1974—95; mcpl. atty. Municipality of Anchorage, 1995—2000; of counsel Hughes, Thorsness, Powell, Huddleston & Bauman, 2001—05; Alaska state dir. Office US Senator Lisa Markowski, 2005—. Talk show host AM 700 KBYR, 2002—. Trustee Willamette U., 1997—; bd. visitors WUCL, 1978—2001; bd. dirs. Alaska Repertory Theatre, 1986—88, pres., 1987—88; commr. Alaska Code Revision Commn., 1987—94; bd. visitors U. Alaska, Fairbanks, 1994—2002, bd. regents, 2002—; bd. dirs. Anchorage Econ. Devel. Corp., 1989—, chmn., 1994; mem. Providence Anchorage Adv. Coun., 1993—2005, Providence Alaska Found., 1998—2005, chair, 2002—04; lawyer rep. 9th Cir. Jud. Conf., 1995—2000; pres. Alaska Bar Found., 1984—98, trustee, 2001—, Athena Soc., 2003—. Fellow: U. Alaska Found. (trustee 1990—), Am. Bar Found.; mem.: Internat. Mcpl. Lawyers Assn. (state chair 1995—96, regional v.p. 1997—2000), Anchorage Assn. Women Lawyers (pres. 1976—77), Alaska Bar Assn. (bd. govs. 1981—84, pres. 1983—84), Soroptimists (pres. 1986—87), Delta Theta Phi. Republican. Roman Catholic. Home: 1592 Coffey Ln Anchorage AK 99501-4977 Office Phone: 907-274-6290. E-mail: mkhughes@acsalaska.net.

HUGHES, MARY SORROWS, artist; b. Washington, Oct. 28, 1945; d. Howard Earl and Martha Jane (Summerville) Sorrows; m. Frank Broox Hughes, May 22, 1967; 1 child, Broox Bradley. BA in Art, Centenary Coll., 1967, MA in Edn., 1978. Draftsman for civil engring. dept. Texaco, New Orleans, 1967-70; owner, freelance artist Shreveport, La., 1979—. Illustrator Total Tales, 1984; included in The Best of Watercolor, 1995, Best of Watercolor: Painting Color, 1997, Floral Inspirations, 1998, Splash 7: The Qualities of LIght, 2002; represented in permanent collections Southwestern Electric Power Co., Shreveport, Burgess Corp. Collection, Calif.; featured artist Watercolor Mag., 2003; featured artist donor Phila. House Auction and Fund Raiser for AIDS, 2003. Bd. dirs. Child Care Svcs., Inc. of N.W. La., Shreveport, 1987-91, pres., 1991; Artport Airport Exhibit and Fundraiser for AIDS, Shreveport, 1991-2002; worker Habitat for Humanity, Shreveport, 1992, 94; trustee St. Luke's Meth. Ch., Shreveport, 1993-95, chair bldg. com., 1986; bd. dirs. Shreveport Art Guild, Friends of the Meadows Mus., 2000-03. Recipient Gary Field, Landry & Bradford award, La. Women Artists, 1994. Mem.: La. Watercolor Soc. (signature mem. 2004, chosen as one of 10 artists for Hwy. Haiku 2002, Pres. award Internat. Show 2005), Hoover Watercolor Soc. (pres. 1986, treas., publicity chair, others, Jurors Choice award 2001, Transparent Watercolor award 2003), La. Artists (pres. 1994, 1998), Watercolor West (Yarka St. Petersberg Mdse. award 1995, Signature Mem. award 1996, W. Burgess Purchase prize 1998), Southwestern Watercolor Soc. (Signature Mem. award 1991, Edgar A. Whitney award 1992, Ansel Merchandise award 1999, Canson-Talons Inc. award 2000), Med. Aux. Wives Club. Democrat. Avocations: exercise, gardening, travel, reading, playing the flute. Home: 530 Atkins Ave Shreveport LA 71104-4448 Studio: 1700 Creswell Ave Shreveport LA 71101-4726 Office Phone: 318-222-2912. E-mail: maryhughes@marysorrowshughes.com.

HUGHES, MICHAEL RANDOLPH, evangelist; b. Newport News, Va. s. Luke Jr. and Patsy Ruth (Jewell) H.; m. Carolyn Delight Williamson, Mar. 20, 1981; children: Amanda, Patsy. Diploma, Memphis Sch. Preaching, 1976; cert. in theology, Ala. Christian Sch. Religion, 1982, BA, 1984; MS, Troy State U., 1987; MA, So. Christian U., 2001; PhD, Wiltshire U., 2005. Min. Newport News Ch. of Christ, 1977-80, 81-83, Ch. of Christ of Clyattville, Ga., 1980-81, 83-85, City Boulevard Ch. of Christ, Waycross, Ga., 1985-87, Hampton (Va.) Ch. of Christ, 1988-92; instr. Bible Ga. Christian Sch., Dasher, 1985-87; min. Green's Lake Road Ch. of Christ, East Ridge, Tenn., 1992-97; min., elder Marion (Ark.) Ch. of Christ, 1997—; prof. So. Christian U., Montgomery, Ala., 1999—. Dir., instr. Bible, Idlewild Christian Camp, Surry, Va., 1977-80; youth worker Ga. Christian Children's Home, Dasher, 1985-87; missionary Mil. Outreach, Germany, 1988-90, Chs. of Christ, India, Malaysia, Taiwan, 1992—; program analyst HB Software, 1996—; co-founder, co-owner HB Software, 1997—. Author: Tax Record System, 1980; contbr. articles to relgious publs. Cmty. organizer North End Huntington Heights Preservation Assn., Newport News, 1977—80; tax preparer VITA, Valdosta, Ga., 1986—87; mem. Ark. Gov.'s Steering Com. on Abstinence Edn., 2000—01; elected ofcl., chmn. Crittenden County Ark. Rep. Ctrl. Com., 2000—02; chmn. 1st Cong. Dist. Ark./Ea. Region, 2002—03; chmn. ea. region 1st Congl. Dist. Rep. Party of Ark., 2002—. Recipient award of merit Memphis Sch. Preaching, 1977. Mem. Givens Orgn., Memphis Sch. Preaching Alumni Assn. (bd. dirs. 1991-95, 98—). Avocations: coin collecting/numismatics, tennis, bowling. Home: 72 Military Rd PO Box 209 Marion AR 72364-0209 Office: Marion Ch Christ PO Box 209 Marion AR 72364-0209 Office Phone: 870-759-1849. E-mail: borninva@aol.com.

HUGHES, MICHAELA KELLY, actress; b. Morristown, N.J., Mar. 31; d. Joseph Francis and Mary Elizabeth (Coughlin) H. Scholarship student, Houston Ballet Acad., 1970-73; part-time scholarship student, Sch. Am. Ballet, 1971. Founder, owner Classic Stocking Co., 1992—. Child actress with Alley Theatre, Houston, 1969, 71, mem. Houston Ballet, 1974, Eliot Feld Ballet, N.Y.C., 1975—, prin. dancer, 1974-79, mem. Am. Ballet Theatre, 1979-81; Broadway appearances include On Your Toes, 1982, as Gloria Upson in Mame, 1983, Raggedy Ann, 1986, as Cassie in A Chorus Line, 1987, Anything Goes, 1988, (films) Hellfighters, A Chorus Line, Alice, The Human Quality; appeared as Fiona in Another World (serial), Loving, Saturday Night Live, Veronica's Closet (sitcom), numerous television comls. Mem. AFTRA, SAG, AEA, Am. Guild Mus. Artists.

HUGHES, MIKE, advertising executive; b. Washington, May 27, 1948; s. James Richard and Ann Marie (Lucas) H.; m. Ginny Lee Ferguson, Apr. 12, 1975; children: Preston Ferguson, (dec.)Jason Christopher. BA, Washington & Lee U., 1970. Reporter Richmond (Va.) News Leader, 1965-70, copy editor, reporter, 1970; reporter Richmond Times Dispatch, 1967-70; copywriter Clinton E. Frank Advt., 1971-72, Martin & Woltz Advt., Richmond, 1973; creative dir. Lawler & Ballard, Richmond, 1974; founder, ptnr. Hughes Wynne, Richmond, 1975-78; exec.v.p., creative dir. Martin Agy., Richmond, 1978-99, dir., 1983-99, vice chmn., 1986-99, ptnr., 1999—; dir. Alan Newman Rsch., Richmond, 1982—. Contbr. articles to Richmond mag. Mem. adv. bd. N.Y. Art Dirs. awards, 1978—, CA mag. awards, 1978—. Mem. One Club for Copy and Art (One Show awards 1978—), Advt. Club of Richmond (bd. dirs., v.p. scholarship chmn., Addy awards chmn., program chmn., pub. svc. chmn., Addy awards). Home: 7501 Riverside Dr Richmond VA 23225-1244 Office: Martin Agy One Shockoe Plz Richmond VA 23219-4132

HUGHES, PATRICK M., federal agency administrator, retired military officer; b. Great Falls, Mont., Sept. 19, 1942; m. Karlene Kay Nuber, Apr. 1962; 2 children. BS, Mont. State U., 1968; MA in Bus. Mgmt., Ctrl. Mich. U., 1978; Grad., US Army Command & Gen. Staff Coll.; Ph.D (hon.), Mont. State U., Jt. Mil. Intelligence Coll. Commd. officer U.S. Army, 1962, advanced through grades to lt. gen., 1996, ret., 1999; dir. Def. Intelligence Agy., 1996—99; pres. PMH Enterprises LLC; asst. sec. for info. analysis US Dept. Homeland Security, Washington, 2003—. Decorated Def. Disting. Svc. award (3 times), Silver Star, Legion of Merit, Bronze Star (3 times), Purple Heart; recipient Nat. Intelligence Disting. Svc. medal, CIA Dir.'s medal, Dir.'s award for Disting. Svc. from the Exec. Office of the Pres. Office of Nat. Drug Control Policy. Office: US Dept Homeland Security 3801 Nebraska Ave NW Washington DC 20393*

HUGHES, PATTI L., social sciences educator; BS, No. Mich. U., Marquette, 1980; MS in Environ. Studies, Andrew Jackson U., Birmingham, Ala., 2000. Social sci. educator Burt Twp. Schs., Grand Marais, Mich., 1980—97; social sci. educator, dept. chair Munising Pub. Schs., Mich., 1997—. Recipient Kellogg Excellence in Edn., Kellogg Found., 1997. Mem.: NEA, Mich. Edn. Assn., Phi Kappa Theta (life). Conservative. Baptist. Avocations: reading, music, boating. Office: Munising HS 800 W Munising Ave Munising MI 49862 Office Phone: 906-387-2103.

HUGHES, PAUL, elementary school educator; s. Jerald Stacy and Christine Buckner Hughes; m. Cathy Keen, Dec. 20, 1980; children: Stacy, Jonathan. BS, BA, William Carey Coll., Hattiesburg, Miss., 1979, Med, 1983. MCSE A-Physics Miss., 1981; cert. AA-Social Studies Miss., 1983, AA-Biology Miss., 1983, A-Chemisty Miss., 1981, AA-Gen. Sci. Miss., 1983, Social Studies-History/Adolescence and Young Adulthood Nat. Bd. for Profl. Tchg. Standards, 2003. Tchr. Hattiesburg Pub. Schs., Hattiesburg, Miss., 1981—, varsity golf coach, 1996—, secondary social studies dept. chair, 2002—04. Trainer-middle schs. inst. Miss. Dept. of Edn., Long Beach, Miss., 2004—; master tchr. Nat. Coun. for History Edn., Vinita, Okla., 2004; adj. instr., biol. sci. William Carey Coll., Hattiesburg, Miss., 1984—95; adj. instr., biol. scis. U. So. Miss., Hattiesburg, Miss., 1993—95. Mus. acquisition com. Hattiesburg Area Hist. Soc., Hattiesburg, Miss., 1995—98; alumni coun. rep. William Carey Coll., Hattiesburg, Miss., 2000—02. Recipient NASA/NEWMAST-National Space and Technologies Lab., NASA, 1987; Earthwatch-Discovering Alfred the Gt., S. A. Rosenbaum Found., 1998, Earthwatch-Yorkshire's Roman Past, The Phil Hardin Found., 1986. Mem.: Miss. Assn. of Coaches, Nat. Coun. for History Edn. (assoc.), Orgn. of Am. Historians (assoc.). Avocation: music.

HUGHES, PAUL LUCIEN, art gallery owner; b. N.Y.C., Apr. 8, 1938; s. Paul Joseph and Yvonne (DeVoluy) Hughes; m. Nancy Souther, Dec. 16, 1961; children: Danielle, Amy. Attended, Kenyon Coll., 1956—57, Army Lang. Sch., 1958—59; BA, NYU, 1967; postgrad., Sch. Visual Arts, 1968—69. Russian interpreter U.S. Army, Berlin, 1960—61; assoc. buyer J.C. Penney, N.Y.C., 1961—65; sales rep. Knoll Internat., N.Y.C., 1965—71, regional mgr. Denver, 1971—75; prin. Inkfish Gallery, Denver, 1975—. Office: Inkfish Gallery 116 S Broadway Denver CO 80209-1508

HUGHES, RALPH EUGENE, management educator; BA, Lenoir Rhyne Coll., 1964; MBA, U. N.C. Greensboro, 1971; D of Bus. Adminstrn., U. Ky., 1975. Asst. prof. U. Wis. Oshkosh, 1974—76; assoc. prof. Miss. State U., Starkville, 1976—79; prof. W.Va. U., Morgantown, 1979—85, East Carolina U., Greenville, NC, 1985—. Contbr. articles to profl. jours. E-4 USAF, 1958—62. Office: Coll Business East Carolina Univ Greenville NC 27858 E-mail: hughesr@mail.ecu.edu.

HUGHES, RAY HARRISON, minister, church official; b. Calhoun, Ga., Mar. 7, 1924; s. J.H. and Emma Hughes; m. Marian Euverla Tidwell; children: Janice, Ray H., Donald, Anita. AA, Lee Coll.; BA, Tenn. Wesleyan Coll.; MS, EdD, U. Tenn.; LittD, Lee Coll., Cleveland. Ordained to ministry Ch. of God, 1950. Pastor Fairfield Ch. of God (Ill.), 1945-46; pastor North Chattanooga Ch. of God, 1948-52; organized churches in Spain, Md., Ill., Tenn., Ga., North Chattanooga Ch. of God, 1948-52; Nat. Sunday Sch. and youth dir., 1952-56; pres. Lee Coll., Cleveland, Tenn., 1960-66, 82-84; pres. theol. seminary Ch. God Sch. Theology, 1984-86; Md.-Del.-D.C. overseer Ch. of God, 1956-60, 3rd asst. gen. overseer, 1966-68, 92-94, mem. exec. coun., 1956-60, 62-82, 86-90, 92-96, 99-2000, exec. dir. gen. bd. edn., 1970-72, 2d asst. gen. overseer, 1968-70, 1st asst. gen. overseer, 1970-72, 76-78, 86-90, 94-96. Gen. overseer, 1972-74, 78-82, 96, Ga. overseer, 1974-76; spkr. for convs., preaching missions, ministers retreats. Author: Planning for Sunday School Programs, 1960, Order of Future Events, 1962, What is Pentecost?, 1963, The Effect of Lee College on World Missions, 1963, The Transition of Church Related Junior Colleges To Senior Colleges, 1966, Church of God Distinctives, 1968, The Outpouring of the Spirit, Dynamics of Sunday School Growth, 1980, Pentecostal Preaching, 1981, Who is the Holy Ghost, 1992, Lord, Show Us Thy Glory, 1997, The Cross: Love's Necessity, 1999, The Rapture and Revelation, 2000; editor the Pilot; contbr. articles to profl. jours. Chmn. Pentecostal Fellowship of N.Am., Pentecostal World Conf., 1989-98, Hall of Prophets Ch. of God Theol. Sem. Mem. Nat. Assn. Evangelicals (pres.), Pi Delta Omicron, Phi Delta Kappa. Address: PO Box 4815 Cleveland TN 37320-4815

HUGHES, ROBERT G., minister, religious organization administrator; AB cum laude, Lehigh U.; MDiv, Luth. Theol. Sem., 1962; ThM, Princeton Theol. Sem., 1974, PhD cum laude, 1981; DD (hon.), Muhlenberg Coll., 1992. Asst. pastor St. Matthew Luth. Ch., Springfield, 1962—63; pastor Good Shephed Luth. Ch., Ashland, 1963—69, Christ's United Luth. Ch., 1969—71; mem. faculty Luth. Theol. Sem., Phila., 1971—2002, pres., 1990—99, St. John chair practical theology, 1988, emeritus, 2002. Cons. in field. Author: A Trumpet in Darkness: Preaching to Mourners, 1985; author: (with Robert Kysar) Preaching Doctrine for the Twenty-First Century, 1997; author: (with LeRoy Aden) Preaching God's Compassion, 2002. Recipient Disting. Alumni award, Luth. Theol. Sem., 2001. Mem.: Acad. Preachers (editor, author Acad. Accents 1983—95), Acad. Homiletics. Home: 8 Bass Ct Ocean City NJ 08226 Home Fax: 609-398-6928. E-mail: rghdlh@earthlink.net.

HUGHES, ROBERT HARRISON, former agricultural products executive; b. Puunene, Hawaii, Mar. 23, 1917; s. Robert Edwin and Alice Thayer (Walker) H.; m. Nadine Jeannette Hegler, Aug. 24, 1940 (div. 1983); children: Robert Lawrence, Linton Alice, Carole Nadine.; m. Judith R. Gething, Jan. 28, 1983. B.Sc. in Sugar Tech, U. Hawaii, 1938. With Hawaiian Comml. & Sugar Co., 1939—62, sugar mill supt., 1962—65; prodn. mgr., v.p. tech. services C. Brewer & Co., Ltd., Honolulu, 1965-69, sr. v.p. Hawaiian ops., 1969-77, exec. v.p., 1977-80, dir. subs., 1966-80; pres. Hawaiian Sugar Planters Assn., Aiea, 1981-85; dir. Mauna Loa Resources Inc., 1986-95. Mem. bd. regents U. Hawaii, 1961-66; trustee Hawaii Conf. Found., 1966-85, Hawaii Loa Coll., 1980-89, Moloka'i Mus. and Cultural Ctr., 1984-91, Hawaiian Hist. Soc., 1990-94, U. Hawaii Found., 1963-65, 73-78, pres., 1967-68; bd. dirs. Hawaii Multi-Cultural Ctr., 1979-81, Samaritan Counseling Ctr. Hawaii, 1985-91; chmn. adv. bd. Cancer Rsch. Ctr., Hawaii, 1979-81; pres. Hawaii conf. United Ch. of Christ, 1962-63. Mem. Hawaiian Sugar Planters Assn. (dir. 1972-80), Hawaiian Hist. Soc., Orgn. of Am. Historians. Home: 1080 S Beretania #902 Honolulu HI 96814-1445

HUGHES, SANDRA MICHELLE, education administrator, educator; b. Port Arthur, Tex., Oct. 18, 1944; d. Romain Joseph and Bessie Irene (Jones) Prejean; m. Donald Atley Hughes, Sept. 5, 1964; children: Heather Patrice, Matthew Donald. Student, Stephen F. Austin U., 1963-64, Lamar U., 1964-65. Area pres. Womens Aglow Internat., Houston, 1977-80; Ptnrs. in Edn. asst. Alief Ind. Sch. Dist., Houston, 1990-92; Ptnrs. in Edn. specialist Katy (Tex.) Ind. Sch. Dist., 1992—. Cons. Strategic Planning Svcs., Houston, 1997—. Author/editor Partners in Education Ann. Report, 1992-97 (Tex. Sch. Pub. Rels. award 1997); co-author, editor: (workbook) Strategic Planning for Partnerships, 1997. Young adult Sunday sch. tchr. First Bapt. Ch., Katy, 1990—; mktg. com./bd. Jr. Achievement, West Houston, Tex., 1992—. Recipient Exemplary Program award Nat. Assn. Ptnrs. in Edn., 1995, Sci. Edn. Workgroup award Exxon Chem. Ams., 1996. Mem. Nat. Assn. Facilitators, Tex. Sch. Pub. Rels. Assn., Tex. Assn. Ptnrs. in Edn.(area coord. 1995-97), Houston West C. of C. (edn. com. 1995—), Delta Kappa Gamma (hon.). Republican. Baptist. Avocations: gourmet cooking, walking. Home: PO Box 1785 Normangee TX 77871-1785

HUGHES, SARAH, figure skater; b. Great Neck, N.Y., May 2, 1985; Student, Yale U. Mem. U.S. Olympic Team, Salt Lake City, 2002. Competitive history includes: 1st place North Atlantic Novice, 1997, 1st place North Atlantic Novice, 1998, 1st place Eastern Jr., 1998, 1st place U.S. Championships Jr., 1998, 1998, 1st place World Jr. Team Selection Competition, 1st place Vienna Cup, 1999, 4th place Skate America, 1st place Keri Lotion vs. The World (Team USA-1st place), 1999, Gold Medal, Olympic Winter Games, 2002. recipient Sullivan award, 2002, ESPY award for best olympian; names USOC Sports Woman of the Yr., 2002, March of Dimes Sports Woman of the Yr., 2002 Avocations: reading, tennis, violin. Office: USFSA 20 1st St Colorado Springs CO 80906-3624

HUGHES, SHARON MARY, trade association executive; b. Chgo., July 28, 1952; d. George Ingersoll and Rose Myrtle (Reed) H. BA in Polit. Sci. and Comm. cum laude, Am. U., 1980, MS in Bus., Govt. Rels., 1985. Freelance photographer, N.Y.C., 1972-76; advt. account exec. R.L. Newport and Co., N.Y.C., 1976-78; direct mail advt. mgr. John Wanamaker's, Phila., 1981-83; legis. intern U.S. Congressman James Florio, Washington, 1985; asst. dir. legis. affairs Nat. Food Processors Assn., Washington, 1985-87; mgr. govt. affairs Synthetic Organic Chem. Mfrs. Assn., Washington, 1987-89; exec. v.p. Nat. Coun. Agrl. Employers, Washington, 1989—. U.S. employer rep. Internat. Labour Orgn. High-Level Meeting on Achieving Equality in Employment for Migrant Workers, 2000; U.S. employer advisor 88th and 89th Session, Internat. Labor Conf, 2000, 01. Mem., sodalist Holy Rosary Ch. Sodality, Washington, 1989— (sec. 1997-99). Mem.: Greater Wash. Soc. Assn. Execs., Am. Soc. Assn. Execs. (cert. assn. exec.), Am. League Lobbyists (bd. dirs. 2002—, sec. 2003—04), Women in Govt. Rels. (co-chmn. environ. task force 1988—89, mem. agrl. task force 1989—90, co-chmn. congl. rels. com. 1992—93, bd. dirs. 1996—98), Phi Kappa Phi. Roman Catholic. Avocations: photography, skiing, golf, history, travel. Office: Nat Coun Agrl Employers 1112 16th St NW Ste 920 Washington DC 20036-4825 Fax: 202-728-0303. Office Phone: 202-728-0300. E-mail: hughes@NCAEonline.org.

HUGHES, STANLEY JOHN, retired mycologist; b. Llanelli, S. Wales, Sept. 17, 1918; emigrated to Can., 1952, naturalized, 1967; s. John Thomas and Gertrude (Roberts) H.; m. Lyndell Anne Rutherford, Oct. 11, 1958; children— Robert Conway, Glenys Anne, David Stanley. B.Sc. with honors, U. Wales, Aberystwyth, 1941, M.Sc., 1943, D.Sc., 1954. Asst. to adv. mycologist Nat. Agrl. Advisory Ser. U. Wales, 1941-45; asst. mycologist Commonwealth Mycological Inst., Kew, Eng., 1945-52; mycologist Research br. Agr. Can. Central Exptl. Farm, Ottawa, Ont., 1952-58, sr. mycologist, 1958-62; prin. mycologist Rsch. br. Agr. Can. Central Exptl. Farm (Ctr. for Land and Biol. Resources Rsch., 1962-83; hon. rsch. assoc., 1983—. Sr. research fellow New Zealand Dept. Sci. and Indsl. Research, 1963; Exchange scientist Nat. Research Councils of Can. and Brazil, 1974 Contbr. articles in field to profl. jours. Recipient Jakob Eriksson Gold medal, 1969; George Lawson medal, 1981 Fellow Royal Soc. Can., Linnean Soc. London (fgn. mem.); mem. Mycological Soc. Am. (pres. 1975; Disting. mycologist award 1985); British Mycological Soc. (fgn. v.p. and honorary mem. 1987), Internat. Mycological Assn. (v.p. 1977-83, hon. v.p. XVI internat. botanical congress 1999). Home: 360 Hamilton Ave Ottawa ON Canada K1Y 1C5 Office: Ea Cereal/Oilseed Rsch Ctr Agrl and Agri-Food Can Ctrl Exptl Farm Ottawa ON Canada K1A 0C6 Personal E-mail: sjhughes@sympatico.ca.

HUGHES, STEPHEN H., virologist, researcher; PhD, Harvard U. Postdoctoral rsch. with Dr. J. Michael Bishop and Harold Varmus U. Calif., San Francisco; sr. staff investigator Cold Spring Harbor Lab.; established the Gene Expression in Eukaryotes Sect.(subsequently called the Retroviral Replication and Vector Design Sect.) ABL Rsch. Program, 1984—88, dep. dir., 1988—95; dir. Molecular Basis of Carcinogenesis Lab., 1995—99; chief, retroviral replication lab. HIV Drug Resistance Program, Nat. Cancer Inst., 1999—, chief, vector design and replication sect. Researcher Rutgers U., Ctr. of Advanced Biotechnology and Medicine, Piscataway, NJ, 1987—; co-organizer, retroviruses and viral vectors mtgs. Cold Spring Harbor Lab.; co-organizer, annual mtg. on Oncogenes. Named one of Most Frequently Cited AIDS Researchers, Science Watch, 1996. Partnered with Edward Arnold in 1987 at Rutgers University Laboratory, Center of Advanced Biotechnology and Medicine, to work with a 30 member research team to develop a trio of drugs that are believed to destroy HIV, the virus that causes AIDS, tenifovir, or the DAPY (diarylpyrimidine). Office: Nat Cancer Inst HIV Drug Resistance Program NCI-Frederick PO Box B Bldg 539 Frederick MD 21702-1201 Office Phone: 301-846-1619. Office Fax: 301-846-6966. Business E-Mail: hughes@ncifcrf.gov.*

HUGHES, STEVEN JAY, lawyer; b. Fayetteville, Ark., Nov. 7, 1948; s. Howard and Jimmie Louise (Williams) H.; m. Leora Donna Halfhill, July 22, 1972; children: Christopher Blake, Clayton Brent. BS in Edn., U. Ark., Fayetteville, 1970; JD, U. Ark., Little Rock, 1978; LLM, DePaul U., 1993. Bar: Ark. 1978, U.S. Dist. Ct. (ea. dist.) Ark. 1978, U.S. Ct. Appeals (8th cir.) 1978, U.S. Supreme Ct. 1981, Mo. 1993. Sole practice, Jacksonville, Ark., 1978-92; owner Hughes Legal Rsch., 1994-96; assoc. Mickel Law Firm, PA, Little Rock, 1998—99; atty. U.S. Army C.E., Chgo., 1999—. Bd. dirs. Tiara Condominium Property Owners Assn., chmn., 1994-96. Alderman Jacksonville City Coun., 1979-81; commr. Jacksonville Planning Commn., 1982-85; mem. U. Ark. Razorback Letterman's Club, Little Rock, 1985, Ark. Sports Hall of Fame, 1985; bd. dirs. Jacksonville Boys Club, 1979-92, pres., 1982-83. Mem. Assn. Trial Lawyers Am., Ark. Bar Assn., Delta Theta Phi (life, dist. chancellor 1983-93). Clubs: Pres. award 1984). Lodges: Kiwanis (pres. Jacksonville club 1983-84, Kiwanian of Yr. award 1979-80, Disting. Baptist. Avocation: sports. Office: 111 N Canal Ste 600 Chicago IL 60606 Home: 6 E Monroe St #1602 Chicago IL 60603-2736 E-mail: hughessj380@msn.com.

HUGHES, THOMAS J.R., mechanical engineering educator, consultant; b. Bklyn., Aug. 3, 1943; s. Joseph Anthony and Mae (Bland) H.; m. Susan Elizabeth Weh, July 1, 1972; children: Emily Susan, Ian Thomas, Elizabeth Claire. B.M.E., Pratt Inst., Bklyn., 1965; M.M.E., Pratt Inst., 1967; MA in Math., PhD in Engring. Sci., U. Calif.-Berkeley, 1974; Doctorate (hon.), U. Catholique de Louvain, Belgium, 2003. Mech. design engr. Grumman Aerospace, Bethpage, N.Y., 1965-66; R & D Gen. Dynamics, Groton, Conn., 1967—69; lectr., asst. rsch. engr. U. Calif., Berkeley, 1975-76; assoc. prof. structural mechanics Calif. Inst. Tech., Pasadena, 1976-80; assoc. prof. mech. engring. Stanford U., Calif., 1980-82, prof., 1983—, chmn. divsn. applied mechanics, 1984-88, 94—, chmn. dept. mech. engring., 1988-89; founder, chmn. CENTRIC Engring. Sys., Inc., 1990-99. Galileo vis. prof. Scuola Normale Superiore, Pisa, Italy, 1999; Eshbach vis. prof. Northwestern U., 2000; cons. in field. Author: A Short Course in Fluid Mechanics, 1976, Mathematical Foundations of Elasticity, 1983, The Finite Element Method: Linear Static and Dynamic Finite Element Analysis, 1987, Computational Inelasticity, 1998; editor: Nonlinear Finite Element Analysis of Plate and Shells, 1981, Computational Methods in Transient Analysis, 1983; editor Jour. of Computer Methods in Applied Mechanics and Engring., 1980—; contbr. numerous articles to profl. jours. Recipient Computational Mechanics prize Japan Soc. Mech. Engrs., 1993. Fellow AAAS, ASME (Melville medal 1979, Worcester Reed Warner medal 1998), AIAA (assoc.), ASCE (Huber prize 1978), Internat. Assn. Computational Mechanics (pres. 1998-2002, Gauss-Newton medal), Am. Acad. Mechanics, U.S. Assn. Computational Mechanics (pres. 1990-92, von Neumann medal 1997), Nat. Acad. Engring; mem. Sigma Xi, Phi Beta Kappa. Office: U Tex at Austin 1 University Sta C0200 201 E 24th St ACES 6 412 Austin TX 78712-0027 Business E-Mail: hughes@ices.utexas.edu.

HUGHES, THOMAS LOWE, foundation executive; b. Mankato, Minn., Dec. 11, 1925; s. Evan Raymond and Alice (Lowe) H.; m. Jean Hurlburt Reiman, May 7, 1955 (dec. Dec. 1993); children: Thomas Evan, Allan Cameron; m. Jane Dudley Casey Kuczynski, Nov. 25, 1995. BA summa cum laude, Carleton Coll., 1947, LHD (hon.), 1974; BPhil and MA in Politics (Rhodes scholar), Balliol Coll., Oxford (Eng.) U., 1949; LLB, JD, Yale U., 1952; LLD (hon.), Washington Coll., 1973, Denison U., 1980, Fla. Internat. U., 1986; HHD (hon.), Washington and Jefferson Coll., 1979. Bar: Minn. 1952, U.S. Supreme Ct. 1960, U.S. Dist. Ct. D.C. 1968. Profl. staff mem. U.S. Senate Subcom. on Labor and Labor-Mgmt. Relations, Com. on Labor and Pub. Welfare, 1951-52; assoc. prof. polit. sci. and internat. rels. U. So. Calif., 1953; asso. prof. polit. sci. and internat. relations Trinity Coll., Tex., 1954, George Washington U., 1957-58; exec. sec. to gov. of Conn., 1954-55; legis. counsel Sen. Hubert Humphrey, 1955-58; adminstrv. asst. U.S. Rep. Chester Bowles, 1959-60; spl. asst. to under sec. state Dept. State, 1961, dep. dir. intelligence and research, 1961-63, dir. intelligence and research with rank of asst. sec. state, 1963-69; minister, dep. chief mission Am. embassy, London, 1969-70; planning and coordination staff Dept. State, 1970-71; pres., trustee Carnegie Endowment for Internat. Peace, 1971-91, pres. emeritus, hon. trustee, 1991—. Former chmn. nuclear proliferation and safeguards adv. panel Office Tech. Assessment, Congress U.S.; co-chmn. Coun. P.R.-U.S. Affairs; internat. adv. bd. Battelle, Pacific Northwest Nat. Lab.; vis. sr. rsch. fellow German Hist. Inst., Washington. Author: The Hohenzollerns; editor: Indian Chiefs of Southern Minnesota; mem. editorial bd. Fgn. Policy Mag., 1971—, chmn., 1971-91; contbr. articles to profl. jours. Vol. Kibbutz Ein Hashofet, Israel, 1950; trustee, sec. German Marshall Fund U.S., 1972-82; mem. Trilateral Commn., 1973-83; trustee Am. Inst. Contemporary German Studies, Am. Acad., Berlin, Social Sci. Found., U. Denver; past bd. govs. Ditchley Found., Eng.; vis. com. Ctr. for Internat. Studies, Harvard U., 1971-76; bd. visitors Ctr. for German and European Studies, Georgetown U.; bd. dirs. Arms Control Assn.; adv. coun. Woodrow Wilson Sch., Princeton U.; mem. adv. bd. Fundacion Luis Munoz Marin, San Juan, P.R.; chmn. U.S.-U.K. Bicentennial Fellowships Com. on Arts, 1975-78; adv. com. Hubert H. Humphrey Inst. Pub. Affairs U. Minn.; staff dir. platform com. Dem. Nat. Conv., 1960. Maj. JAGC, USAF, 1952-54. Recipient Arthur S. Fleming Outstanding Pub. Svc. award, 1964. Mem. Inst. Internat. de Geopolitique Paris, N.Y. Coun. Fgn. Rels., Inst. Current World Affairs (trustee), Internat. Inst. Strategic Studies London (trustee Am. com.), Am. Acad. Diplomacy, Am. Assn. Rhodes Scholars, Washington Inst. Fgn. Affairs (pres., exec. com.), Atlantic Coun. U.S. (bd. dirs.), Oxford-Cambridge Assn. Washington (former chmn.), Women's Fgn. Policy Group, New England Hist. Geneal. Soc., Scottish Genealogy Soc., Soc. Mayflower Descs., Mid-Atlantic Club (chmn.), Cosmos Club, Century Assn. (N.Y.C.), Oxford (Eng.) Union, Knight of St. John (Johanniterorden, Balley Brandenburg), Phi Beta Kappa, Phi Delta Phi. Episcopalian. Office: German Hist Inst 1607 New Hampshire Ave NW Washington DC 20009-2562 Office Phone: 301-656-1420. Personal E-mail: thoshughes@aol.com.

HUGHES, THOMAS PARKE, history professor; b. Richmond, Va., Sept. 13, 1923; s. Hunter Russell and Mary Bronaugh (Quisenberry) H.; m. Agatha Chipley, Aug. 7, 1948; children: Thomas P. (dec.), Agatha H., Lucian P. BME, U. Va., 1947, PhD, 1953; D (hon.), Royal Inst. Tech., Stockholm, 2000, Northwestern U., 2001. Instr. U. Va., Charlottesville, 1951-54; asst. prof. history Sweet Briar (Va.) Coll., 1954-56; assoc. prof. history Washington and Lee U., Lexington, Va., 1956-63, MIT, Cambridge, 1963-66; prof. history Inst. Tech., So. Meth. U., Dallas, 1969-73; mem. faculty U. Pa., Phila., 1973-94, prof. history and sociology of sci., 1973-94, Andrew W. Mellon prof., 1987-94, prof. emeritus, 1994—. Vis. assoc. prof. history Johns Hopkins U., Balt., 1966-69; Torsten Althin prof. Royal Inst. Tech., Stockholm, 1985-90; founding rsch. prof. Tech. Univ., Darmstadt, Germany, 1986-87; vis. rsch. prof. Wissenschaftszentrum Berlin, 1988-94; vis. prof. MIT, 1991, 93, 94—, E.T.H. Zürich, 1997, Stanford U., 1999—2001. Author: Elmer Sperry: Inventor and Engineer, 1971 (Dexter prize), Networks of Power: Electrification in Western Society 1880-1930, 1983 (Dexter prize), American Genesis: A Century of Invention and Technological Enthusiasm

1870-1970, 1989 (Pulitzer Prize finalist); editor: (with Agatha C. Hughes) Lewis Mumford: Public Intellectual, 1990, Rescuing Prometheus, 1998, Systems, Experts, and Computers, 2000, Human-Built World, 2004. Chmn. NRC com., 1996—99; mem. adv. coun. Smithsonian Inst., 1984—90. Served to lt. (j.g.) USN, 1943—46. Fulbright postdoctoral fellow, Germany, 1958—59, NSF fellow, 1975, Inst. Advanced Study fellow, Berlin, 1983, Guggenheim fellow, 1986. Mem. NAE, Soc. History of Tech. (pres. 1978-80, Leonardo da Vinci medal 1984), Soc. Social Studies Sci. (Bernal prize 1990), History of Sci. Soc. (coun. 1976-79), Am. Acad. Arts and Scis., Johns Hopkins U. Soc. Scholars, Swedish Royal Acad. Engring. Scis., Am. Philos. Soc., Phi Beta Kappa. E-mail: thughes@sas.upenn.edu.

HUGHES, VESTER THOMAS, JR., lawyer; b. San Angelo, Tex., May 24, 1928; s. Vester Thomas and Mary Ellen (Tisdale) H. Student, Baylor U., 1945—46; BA with distinction, Rice U., 1949; LLB cum laude, Harvard U., 1952. Bar: Tex. 1952. Law clk. U.S. Supreme Ct., 1952; assoc. Robertson, Jackson, Payne, Lancaster & Walker, Dallas, 1955-58; ptnr. Jackson, Walker, Winstead, Cantwell & Miller, Dallas, 1958-76, Hughes, Luce, Hennessy, Smith & Castle, Dallas, 1976—, Hughes & Hill, Dallas, 1979-85, Hughes & Luce, Dallas, 1985—. Bd. dirs. Exell Cattle Co., Amarillo, Tex., LX Cattle Co., Amarillo, Sammons Enterprises, Inc.; adv. dir. First Nat. Bank Mertzon; sr. tax counsel Cmtys. Found. of Tex., Inc.; mem. adv. com. Tex. Supreme Ct., 1985-93. Contbr. articles on fed. taxation to profl. jours. Bd. dirs. Juvenile Diabetes Found. Inc., Dallas, 1982—; trustee Dallas Bapt. U., 1967-77; v.p., trustee, exec. com. Tex. Scottish Rite Hosp. for Children, 1967—; bd. overseers vis. com. Harvard Law Sch., 1969-75. 1st lt. JAGC U.S. Army, 1952-55. Named one of Best Lawyers in Dallas, D Mag., 2003, 2005. Mem.: Tex. Bar Found. (Outstanding Fifty-Yr. Lawyer Award 2003), State Bar Tex. (Outstanding Tex. Tax Lawyer Award 2003), Am. Coll. Trust and Estate Counsel, Ctr. Am. & Intern. Law, Am. Coll. Tax Counsel, Am. Law Inst. (coun. 1958—), Dallas Bar Assn., Tex. Bar Assn., ABA (mem. coun. sect. taxation 1969—73), Harvard Club (NYC), Met. Club (Washington), Order Ea. Star, Masons, Sigma Xi, Phi Beta Kappa. Democrat. Baptist. Avocations: travel, community and church activities, reading. Office: Hughes & Luce 1717 Main St Ste 2800 Dallas TX 75201-4685 Office Phone: 214-939-5433. Personal E-mail: vhughes@hughesluce.com.

HUGHES, WALTER THOMPSON, pediatrician, educator; b. Cleve., May 16, 1930; s. Walter Thompson and Millie Hasentine (Collette) H.; m. Frances J. Skinner, Nov. 24, 1957; children: Carla, Gregory, Christopher. MD, U. Tenn., 1954. Diplomate Am. Bd. Pediatrics. Resident in pediatrics U. Tenn. Coll. Medicine, Memphis, 1955-57, prof. pediatrics and microbiology, 1969-77, prof. pediatrics, 1981—; mem. St. Jude Children's Rsch. Hosp., Memphis, 1969-77, mem., chair dept. infectious diseases, 1981-95; mem. staff Walter Reed Army Med. Ctr., Ft. Detrick, Md., 1957-59; pvt. practice pediatrics Cleve., 1959-61; instr. to prof. U. Louisville Sch. Medicine, 1961-69; Eudowood prof. pediatrics, dir. div. infectious diseases Johns Hopkins U. Sch. Medicine, Balt., 1977-81; Arthur Ashe chair in pediat. AIDS rsch. St. Jude Children's Rsch. Hosp., Memphis, 1993-98, emeritus mem., 1998—. Capt. U.S. Army, 1957-59. Fellow Am. Acad. Pediatrics; mem. Am. Pediatric Soc., Infectious Diseases Soc. Am., Soc. Pediatric Rsch., Pediatric Infectious Diseases Soc. (pres. 1983-85). Republican. Methodist. Home: 854 River Park Dr Memphis TN 38103-0804 Office: St Jude Children's Rsch Hosp 332 N Lauderdale St Memphis TN 38105-2729 Office Phone: 901-495-3485. Personal E-mail: FHU577483@aol.com. Business E-Mail: walter.hughes@stjude.org.

HUGHES, WILLIAM ANTHONY, retired bishop; b. Youngstown, Ohio, Sept. 23, 1921; s. James Francis and Anna Marie (Philbin) H. Degree, St. Charles Sem., Balt., St. Mary's Sem., Cleve.; MA in Edn., Notre Dame U., 1956. Ordained priest Roman Cath. Ch., 1946. Pastor chs., Boardman and Massillon, Ohio, 1946—55; prin. Cardinal Mooney H. S., Youngstown, Ohio, 1956—65; supt. schs. Diocese of Youngstown, 1965—72, Episcopal vicar of edn., 1972—73, vicar gen., 1973—74; aux. bishop, 1974—79; bishop of Covington Ky., 1979—; ret., 1995. Office: Cathedral of Assemption 1140 Madison Ave Covington KY 41011-3116*

HUGHES, WILLIAM JOHN, former congressman, diplomat; b. Salem, N.J., Oct. 17, 1932; s. William W. and Pauline H.; m. Nancy L. Gibson; children: Nancy Lynne, Barbara Ann, Tama Beth, William John. AB, Rutgers U., 1955, JD, 1958, LLD (hon.), 1995; LHD (hon.), Mt. Vernon Coll., 1984; LLD (hon.), Richard Stockton State Coll., 1994, Glassboro State Coll., 1992; AA (hon.), Cumberland County Coll., 1994; AS (hon.), Atlantic Cape Cmty. Coll., 2004. Bar: N.J. 1959. Ptnr. Loveland, Hughes & Garrett, Ocean City, N.J., 1968-78; 1st asst. pros. atty. Cape May County, N.J., 1960-70; mem. 94th-103rd Congresses from 2d N.J. dist., Washington, D.C., 1974-95; amb. to Panama U.S. Dept. State, 1995-98; Clifford P. Case prof. pub. affairs Rutgers U., 1997; disting. scholar ethics and pub. policy Richard Stockton Coll. N.J., Pomona, 1999—; prof. Rutgers U., 1999—; of counsel Riker, Danzig, Scherer, Hyland & Perretti, LLP, 2000—. Bd. govs. Shore Meml. Hosp., Somers Point, NJ, 1972—76; bd. trustees Shore Meml. Hosp. Found., 2001—, Ocean City Tabernacle Assn., 2002—; bd. dirs. South Jersey Industries, 2002—. Recipient Ann. Planning award Am. Planning Assn., 1979, Disting. Citizen award Atlantic Area coun. Boy Scouts Am., 1982, Legislator of Yr. award VFW, 1982, Pres.'s award Nat. Dist. Attys. Assn., 1982, Legis. Leadership award Nat. Assn. Chain Drug Stores, 1984, Humanitarian citiation Food Mktg. Chain Drug Stores and N.J. Food Council, 1984, Legis. award Nat. Assn. Police Orgns., 1984, Legis. Achievement award Fed. Law Enforcement Officers Assn., 1984, Man of Yr. award Girl Scouts Am., 1986, Legis. award N.J. Foster Parents Assn., 1986, Leo Fraser Super Achiever award Juvenile Diabetes Found., 1987, Arthur E. Armitage Sr. Disting. Alumni award Rutgers U., 1987, Disting. Info. Processing Pub. Service award Data Processing Mgmt. Assn., 1987, Rutgers U. medal, 1992, Distinction in Pub. Svc. award Am. Rivers, 1993, Congressional Advocacy award, 1994, Spirit of South Jersey award South Jersey Devel. Coun., 1994, Career Achievement award in pub. svc. N.J. Edn. Assn., 1995; named Congressman of Yr., Nat. Assn. Police Orgns., 1986, Hall of Disting. Alumni award Rutgers U., 1997, Jefferson medal award N.J. Intellectual Property Law Assn., 1995, Judge John F. Gerry award for adminstrv. justice, 2000, South Jerseyan of Yr. award Rand Inst.,2003 Pub. Affairs, Rutgers U. Fellow Am. Bar Found.; mem. ABA, N.J. Bar Assn., Ocean City Hist. Soc. (bd. dir. 1972-76), Ocean City C. of C. (bd. dir. 1960—), Exch. of Ocean City Club (pres. 1965-66, Nat. Big E. award 1965), Masons (master lodge, Worshipful Master 1969). Democrat. Episcopalian. Home: 1019 Wesley Rd Ocean City NJ 08226-4754 Office Phone: 609-396-2121. Personal E-mail: ambjack1@aol.com.

HUGHES, WILLIAM JOSEPH, management consultant; b. Kansas City, Mo., Oct. 11, 1953; s. Joseph and Ann H.; m. Mary Alice Knight, Apr. 25, 1981; 3 children. BSME, U. Va., 1975. Various positions Brown & Root, Inc., Houston, 1975-79; sr. cons. Arthur Andersen & Co., S.C., Houston, 1979-81, mgr., 1981-87; ptnr. Accenture, Houston, 1987—2003; ret., 2003. Editor, contbg. author: Natural Gas Trends, 1988; author: Process Centering, 2001. Mem. ASME. Episcopalian. Avocations: sailing, skiing, golf, tennis. Office: 12518 Winding Brook Houston TX 77024 Office Phone: 281-433-4323.

HUGHES, WILLIAM LEWIS, retired dean, electrical engineer; b. Rapid City, S.D., Dec. 2, 1926; s. Clarence William and Newell (Chase) H.; m. Stella Marie Platt, June 9, 1950; children: Elizabeth Helen, James Edward, Judith Lee, Michael George. BS in Elec. Engring, S.D. Sch. Mines and Tech., 1949; MS, Iowa State U., 1950, PhD, 1952; DSc (hon.), S.D. Sch. Mines and Tech., 2000. Broadcast and TV engr., 1946-49; mem. faculty Iowa State U., 1949-60; prof. elec. engring., 1959-60; prof. elec. engring., head Sch. Elec. Engring., Okla. State U., Stillwater, 1960-76, Clark A. Dunn prof. engring., 1976-86, dir. Engring. Energy Lab., 1976-86; pres. InEn Corp, 1972-88; v.p. S.D. Sch. Mines and Tech., Rapid City, 1988-93; pres. Dakota Alpha Inc., 1994—. Chmn. ad hoc com. NAS, 1976, 79, mem. bd. sci. and tech. in devel., 1983; chmn. NAS/Philippine Govt. del. to Philippines, 1978, Indonesia, 1979, India, 1979, 85, 89, Thailand, 1990, 93; cons. industry and govt.; mem. indsl. com. TV frequency allocation studies FCC, 1957-59. Author: Nonlinear electrical Networks, 1960; also articles; co-author: Lines, Waves and Antennas, 1961, 2d edit., 1973; contbr. sects. to 6 engring. handbooks. Served with USNR, World War II. Named S.D. Profl. Engr. of Yr., S.D. Engring. Soc., 1995. Fellow IEEE; mem. NSPE (life, Disting. Svc. award 1997), Sigma Xi, Sigma Tau, Tau Beta pi, Eta Kappa Nu, Pi Mu Epsilon. Achievements include patentee nonlinear systems, color TV systems, direct energy conversions systems. Home: 6118 Greenleaf Ct Rapid City SD 57702-8845 E-mail: bhughesrc@aol.com.

HUGHEY, BILLY, publishing executive; b. Mangum, Oka., Feb. 18, 1952; s. Harold Floyd and Bonnie Mae Hughey; m. Janice Sue Koos, Oct. 11, 1984; children: Noah John, Dylan Luke, Jordan; 1 child, Brooklyn Hope. BBA, U. Okla., 1974. Founder, pres. Rainbow Studies Internat., El Reno, Okla., 1970—. Developer The Rainbow Study Bible, 1986 (Angel award, 1993, Gold Book award, 1993, Gold Star Gallery award, 1995); author: The Rainbow Study Bible-King James Version, 1986, The Living Rainbow Study Bible, 1989, The NIV Rainbow Study Bible, 1992, A Rainbow of Hope, 1994, Biblia de Estudo Em Cores, 1995, Biblia de Estudio Arco Iris, 1995, Biblia de Estudio Em Cores, 1995, Gifts for the Family, 1997, Gifts of Love, 1997, Gifts of Faith, 1997, Gifts for Life's Journeys, 1997, Gifts of Hope Blank Journal, 1998, Gifts of Hope Perpetual Calendar, 1998, Momentos Para Graduados, 1998, Momentos Para Madres, 1998, Momentos Para Padres, 1998, The KJV Rainbow Study Bible-Illustrated Reference Edition, 1998, The Rainbow Study Bible for Windows, 1999, The Catholic Rainbow Study Bible, 2001, The Ultimate Student Bible, 2003, The Ultimate Catholic Student Bible, 2003. Youth coach various teams; founder, pres. A Cross the Heartlands Found., El Reno, 1999—; Sunday sch. tchr. First Bapt. Ch., El Reno; bd. dirs. YMCA, El Reno, 1980, El Reno Pub. Schs. Found., Inc., 1981, Mobile Meals El Reno, 1982. Recipient Key to the City of Birmingham, 1986, Disting. Alumni award, El Reno HS, 2001. Mem.: Nat. Religious Broadcasters, Evangelical Christian Publ. Assn., Fellowship Christian Athletes, Billy Graham Evangelistic Assn. (counselor). Achievements include patents for Bearly Sports Bears. Avocations: reading, writing, sports, travel. Home: 1502 Ridgecrest Dr El Reno OK 73036 Office: Rainbow Studies Internat 1950 S Shepard El Reno OK 73036

HUGHEY, BRENDA JOYCE, supervisor; b. Linton, Ind., Jan. 23, 1951; d. William L. and Mary Margaret Pritchard; m. David Nelson Hughey, July 23, 1977; children: Allison, Brock. BS, Ind. State U., 1973, MS, 1977. Cert. administr. and supr. Middle Tenn. State U., 1994, career ladder III. Tchr. Switz City (Ind.) Elem. Sch., 1973—77, Franklin (Tenn.) Jr. High, 1978—84, Franklin (Tenn.) Mid. Sch., 1984—89; asst. prin. Liberty Elem. Sch., Franklin, Tenn., 1990—96; spl. edn. supr. Franklin (Tenn.) Spl. Sch. Dist., 1996—. Bd. dirs. Ct. Apptd. Spl. Adv., Franklin, Tenn., 2003—. Mem.: Tenn. Assn. Spl. Edn. Suprs., Assn. of Supervision and Curriculum Devel., Coun. for Exceptional Children. Baptist. Avocations: reading, gardening. Office: Franklin Spl Sch Dist 507 New Hwy 96W Franklin TN 37069 Home: 1420 Lewisburg Pike Franklin TN 37064 Office Phone: 615-794-6624. E-mail: Brenda@fssd.org.

HUGHEY, JAMES FLETCHER, JR., lawyer; b. Jacksonville, Fla., Aug. 15, 1945; s. James Fletcher and Geraldine (Hammack) Hughey; m. Janice Johnson Hughey, Aug. 15, 1968; children: James Fletcher III, Elizabeth Bond. AB, U. Ala., 1967, JD, 1970; LLM in Taxation, NYU, 1972. Bar: Ala. 1970. Assoc. Balch & Bingham, Birmingham, Ala., 1972—77, ptnr., 1978—, chair exec. com., mng. ptnr., 1990—. Mem. exec. bd. Greater Ala. coun. Boy Scouts Am.; trustee Daniel Found. Ala., 1996—; bd. dirs. United Way Ctrl. Ala., 1993—, Leadership Birmingham, 1991—, Leadership Ala., 1995—, Lakeshore Found., Lakeshore Hosp., 1978—91, chmn., 1986—87. Fellow Am. Bar Found., Am. Law Found.; mem. ABA, Ala. State Bar (bd. bar examiners 1982-86), Birmingham Bar Assn., Ala. Law Inst., U. Ala. Law Sch. Alumni Assn. (pres. 1992), Rotary Club of Birmingham (pres. 2005), Birmingham C. of C. (bus. coun. Ala.), Birmingham Country Club (pres. 1996). Episcopalian. Office: Balch & Bingham LLP PO Box 306 1710 6th Ave N Birmingham AL 35201-2015 Office Phone: 205-226-3469. Business E-Mail: jhughey@balch.com.

HUGHEY, RICHARD KOHLMAN, writer, lawyer; b. Chgo., July 6, 1934; BA cum laude, Santa Clara (Calif.) U., 1958, JD cum laude, 1963. Bar: Calif. 1964, U.S. Ct. Appeals (9th cir.) 1964, U.S. Supreme Ct. 1972. Atty. Pacific Gas & Elec. Co., San Francisco, 1963-69, Berry, Davis & McInerny, Oakland, Calif., 1969-71; ptnr. Caputo, Liccardo, Rossi & Kohlman, San Jose, Calif., 1971-75; lectr. law, dir. CLE Santa Clara U., 1975-80; mng. editor Bancroft-Whitney Co., San Francisco, 1980-91, Lawyers Coop. Pub. Co., Rochester, NY, 1992-94; history and lit. biography writer, 1995—; columnist Mountain Democrat, Placerville, Calif., 1997—. Author: Jeffers Country Revisited: Beauty Without Price, 1996, Computer Technology in Civil Litigation, 1990, Trial Lawyers Manual, 1978, Jeffers in Antrim, 2003, El Dorado: California's Empire County, 2003, Golden Girl, 2003, Bullion Bead, 2004; co-author: Petroglyphs: Poetry and Fiction, 1994, Hey Lew: Homage to Lew Welch, 1997; editor: Am. Jury Trials, 1980—90, Proof of Facts, 1982—90; bd. editors Calif. State Bar Jour., 1972—75, editor-in-chief Santa Clara Law Rev., 1961—63. Avocation: photography.

HUGHEY SURMAN, STACY LEIGH, education educator; d. Melissa Wiginton Hughey; m. Darren Edward Surman, Mar. 20, 2004. BS in Early Childhood and Elem. Edn., U. Ala., 1999, MA in Elem. Edn., 2001, postgrad. in Ednl. Rsch., 2003—. Cert. tchr. Ala., 1999. Dir. records The Office Cmty. Svc. and Volunteerism, Tuscaloosa, Ala., 1997—2001; grad. rsch. asst. The U. Ala., Tuscaloosa, 1999—2001, grad. tchg. asst., 2003—, grad. asst. for tng. and data collection Project CORE, 2004—; tchr. Carrollton (Ala.) Elem. Sch. Pickens County Sch. Sys., 2001—02; tchr. Woodland Forrest Elem. Sch. Tuscaloosa (Ala.) City Sch. Sys., 2002—03. Mem. standing com. U. Ala., 2000—01, mem. sub-com. undergrad. tchg. and learning, 2000—01; presenter in field. Author: (web site) Math and Reading: A database of picture books for use in mathematics education. Fellow, The U. Ala., 2003—04; scholar, Rotary, Huntsville, AL, 1995—96; Steven V. Mitchell Alumni scholar, The U. Ala. Alumni, 1995—99. Mem.: Ala.-Miss. Sociol. Assn. (conf. planner 2004—05), Internat. Dyslexia Assn., Nat. Coun. Tchrs. English, Internat. Reading Assn., Nat. Reading Conf., Am. Ednl. Rsch. Assn., Alpha Delta Kappa, The Friends of The U. Ala. Arboretum (sec. 2004—), Kappa Delta Epsilon, Kappa Delta Pi, Phi Kappa Phi. Conservative. Baptist. Avocations: travel, antiques, gardening, cooking. Office: The University of Alabama Ed Research Box 870232 Tucaloosa AL 35487-0232 Personal E-mail: s.hugheysurman@gmail.com.

HUGLO, MICHEL VICTOR, musicologist; b. Lille, France, Dec. 14, 1921; arrived in U.S., 1998; m. Marthe Morel, Apr. 1960 (dec. July 1992); m. Barbara Haggh-Huglo, Mar. 4, 1998. PhD (hon.), U. Chgo. Dir. rsch. Nat. Ctr. Scientific Rsch., Paris, dir. emeritus. Author: Les Tonaires; contbr. articles to profl. jours. Mem.: Am. Musicological Soc. (corr.). Office: U Md Sch Music 3110C Clarice Smith Performing Arts Ctr College Park MD 20742

HUGO, NORMAN ELIOT, retired plastic surgeon, retired educator; b. Beverly, Mass., Sept. 23, 1933; s. Victor Joseph and Helen Bernadette (Box) Hugo; m. Geraldine P Tonry, Oct. 10, 1959; children: Helen, William, Geraldine, Norman, Catherine. BA, Williams Coll., 1955, DSc (hon.), 1989; MD, Cornell U. Med. Coll., 1959. Diplomate (dir 1982-88, vice chmn 1987-88, residency rev comt, accreditation coun, grad med educ, 1994-98) Am Bd Plastic Surg. Intern, resident Cornell U. Surg. Svc., Bellevue Hosp., N.Y.C., 1959-63; resident N.Y. Hosp.-Cornell Med. Ctr., 1963-65, univ. instr. surgery, 1966-65; asst. prof. Ind. U.; asst. chief plastic surgeon Walter Reed Army Med. Ctr., 1967-69; assoc. prof. U. Chgo., 1969-71; chief plastic and reconstructive surgery Michael Reese Hosp., Chgo., 1969-71, Passavant Hosp., Chgo., 1971-79; assoc. prof. Northwestern U., Chgo., 1971-82; dir. plastic surgery Lakeside VA Hosp., 1971-77; chief plastic and reconstructive surgery Columbia U.-Presbyn. Med. Ctr., N.Y.C., 1982-95; prof. Columbia U. Coll. Physicians & Surgeons, 1982-98, prof. emeritus, 1998—; ret., 1998. Maj MC AUS, 1967—69. Mem.: AMA (del 1983—88), ACS, Am Burn Soc, NY Acad Sci, Soc Head and Neck Surgeons, Asn Acad Surg, Am Clefts Palate Soc, Plastic Surg Research Coun, Chicago Soc Plastic Surg (secy 1979—81, vpres 1981—82), Am Soc Aesthetic Plastic Surg (secy 1979—82), Am Asn Plastic and Reconstructive Surgeons (trustee 1982—84), Am Soc Plastic and Reconstructive Surgeons (trustee 1981—84, historian 1982—84, vpres 1985—86, pres-elect 1986—87, pres 1987—88, bd dirs educ found), Touchdown Club Am (dir. 2002—), Union Club (New York City) (gov. 2002—), Williams Club. Home: 37 Carriage Ln New Canaan CT 06840-4401 Office: Columbia U Coll Physicians and Surgeons 161 Fort Washington Ave New York NY 10032-3713 Office Phone: 203-966-2434. Personal E-mail: normanehugo@msn.com.

HUHEEY, MARILYN JANE, ophthalmologist, educator; b. Cin., Aug. 31, 1935; d. George Mercer and Mary Jane (Weaver) H. BS in Math., Ohio U., Athens, 1958; MS in Physiology, U. Okla., 1966; MD, U. Ky., 1970. Diplomate Am. Bd. Ophthalmology. Tchr. math. James Ford Rhodes H.S., Cleve., 1956-58; biostatistician Nat. Jewish Hosp., Denver, 1958-60; life sci. engr. Stanley Aviation Corp., Denver, 1960-63, N.Am. Aviation Co., L.A., 1963-67; intern U. Ky. Hosp., 1970-71; emergency room physician Jewish Hosp., Mercy Hosp., Bethesda Hosp., Cin., 1971-72; ship's doctor, 1972; resident in ophthalmology Ohio State U. Hosp., Columbus, 1972-75; practice medicine specializing in ophthalmology Columbus, 1975—. Mem. staff Univ. Hosp., Grant Hosp., St. Anthony Hosp., 1975-79; clin. asst. prof. Ohio State U. Med. Sch., 1976—, dir. course ophthalmologic receptionist/aides, 1976; mem. Peer Rev. Sys. Bd., 1986-92, exec. com., 1988-92; mem. Ohio Optical Dispensers Bd., 1986-91; bd. dirs. Ctrl. Ohio Radio Reading Svc., 1997—2003; mem. Ohio Bd. Cosmetology, 1999—. Dem. candidate for Ohio Senate, 1982; mem. Wicked Investment Club, 1998—, pres. 1999-2004, treas., 2005—. Fellow Am. Acad. Ophthalmology; mem. AAUP, Am. Assn. Ophthalmologists, Ohio Ophthalmol. Soc. (bd. govs. 1984-89, del. to Ohio State Med. Assn. 1984-88), Franklin County Acad. Medicine (profl. rels. com. 1979-82, legis. com. 1981-89, edn. and program com. 1981-88, chmn. 1982-85, chmn. cmty. rels. com. 1987-90, chmn. resolution com. 1987-92, mem. fin. com. 1988-92), Ohio Soc. Prevent Blindness (chmn. med. adv. bd. 1978-80), Ohio State Med. Assn. (dr.-nurse liaison com. 1983-87), Columbus EENT Soc., Am. Coun. of the Blind (bd. dirs. 1995-96), Life Care Alliance (pres. sustaining bd. 1987-88), United Way (planning com. 1992-93), LWV, Columbus Coun. World Affairs, Columbus Bus. and Profl. Women's Club, Columbus C. of C., Grandview Area Bus. Assn., Federated Dem. Women Ohio, Columbus Area Women's Polit. Caucus, Columbus Met. Club (forum com. 1982-85, fundraising com. 1983-84, chmn. 10th anniversary com. 1986), Mercedes Benz Club (dir. 1981-83), Zonta (program com. 1984-86, chmn. internat. com. 1983), Herb Soc., Phi Mu. Home: 2396 Northwest Blvd Columbus OH 43221-3829 Office: 1335 Dublin Rd Ste 25A Columbus OH 43215-1000 Office Phone: 614-488-8836. E-mail: mhuheey.1@yahoo.com.

HUHNKE, RAYMOND LEROY, engineering educator; BS in Agrl. Engring., Purdue U., 1973; MS in Agrl. Engring., U. Ill., 1974; PhD in Agrl. Engring., Iowa State U., 1980. Registered profl. agrl. engr., Iowa. Instr. agrl. engring. dept. Iowa State U., Ames, 1974-76; plan svc. engr. Midwest Plan Svc., Ames, 1976-80; asst. prof. agrl. engring. dept. Okla. State U., Stillwater, 1980-85, assoc. prof. agrl. engring. dept., 1985-90, prof. biosys. and agrl. engring. dept., 1990—, extension agrl. engr., 1980—. Vis. scientist agrl. engring. dept. U. Wis., Madison, 1993. Contbr. numerous articles to profl. jours., chpts. to books; co-creator videos including Cattle Handling Safety, 1998, Livestock Safety for Kids, 2000, others. Fellow Am. Soc. Agrl. Engrs. (Nolan Mitchell Young Extension Worker Engring. Achievement award, Extension Ednl. Aids Blue Ribbon awards (10); mem. Alpha Zeta, Alpha Epsilon, Gamma Sigma Delta, Epsilon Sigma Phi, Sigma Xi. Home: 1814 W Liberty Ave Stillwater OK 74075-2012 Office: Okla State U 214 Agriculture Hall Stillwater OK 74078-6020 E-mail: rhuhnke@okstate.edu.

HUHS, JOHN I., lawyer; b. Galveston, Tex., Sept. 18, 1944; s. Roy E. and Martha Mae (Hansen) H.; m. Vivian C. Swindley, 1970 (div. 1978), Renee J. Stillings, 2005. BA, U. Wash., 1966; MBA with honors, JD with honors, Stanford U., 1970. Bar: NY 1971, DC 1981. Internat. cons. Satra Cons. Corp., NYC, 1970-73; sr. staff White House Office Mgmt. & Budget Nat. Security, Internat. Affairs, Washington, 1973—76; ptnr. Pisar & Huhs, NYC, 1976—85; sr. v.p., gen. counsel Tendler, Beretz Assocs., Ltd., NYC, 1985-87; pvt. practice NYC, 1987-88; sr. ptnr., chmn. internat. practice LeBoeuf, Lamb, Greene & MacRae LLP, NYC, 1989—, co-mng. ptnr., founder Moscow office, founder, mng. ptnr. Almaty office. Prin. Ctr. for Excellence in Govt., 1984—99. Contbr. articles on internat. law, bus. and fin. to profl. jours.; comment editor Stanford Law Rev., 1967-69. Mem. bd. visitors Stanford Law Sch., 1996-98, 2004-. Mem.: ABA (chmn. com. on Soviet and Ea. European law 1982—85, chmn. com. internat. comml. trans. 1985—90, coun. sect. internat. law and practice 1988—92, rep. to Union Internat. Avocats 1991—94), DC Bar Assn., NY State Bar Assn. (chmn. internat. investment devel. com. 1987—91), Assn. of Bar of City of NY (internat. trade com. 1987—89, com. Newly Ind. States of former Soviet Union 1989—2000), 175 E. 74th Corp. (pres.), U. Club NYC, Order of Coif. Office: LeBoeuf Lamb Greene MacRae LLP 125 W 55th St New York NY 10019-5369 Office Phone: 212-424-8182. Office Fax: 212-424-8500. Business E-Mail: jhuhs@llgm.com.

HUHTALA, MARIE THERESE, federal agency administrator, former ambassador; b. L.A., Mar. 26, 1949; d. Joseph E. Sr. and Rosemary E. (Williamson) Mackey; m. Eino A. Huhtala Jr., July 10, 1971; children: Karen Rose, Jorma David. BA in French, Santa Clara U., 1971; diploma, Nat. War Coll., 1988; MA, Laval U., 1995. Joined Fgn. Svc., Dept. State, Washington, 1972; consular officer Am. Embassy, Paris, 1973-75; vice consul U.S. Consulate, Chiang Mai, Thailand, 1976-79; secretariat staff officer Fgn. Svc., Dept. State, Washington, 1979-80, congl. rels. officer, 1980-81, country officer for Chad, 1981-83, polit. officer U.S. Consulate Gen. Hong Kong, 1985-87, chief East Asian assignments, bur. pers. divsn. Washington, 1988-90, dep. dir. Vietnam, Laos and Cambodia affairs, 1990-92, consul gen. U.S. Consulate Gen. Que., Canada, 1992—95; dep. chief mission U.S. Embassy, Bangkok, 1998—2001; U.S. amb. to Malaysia US Dept. State, 2001—04, dep. asst. sec. E. Asian & Pacific affairs Washington, 2004—. Bd. dirs. Orchestre Symphonique de Que., 1992—. Recipient Superior Honor award, Dept. of State, Meritorious Honor award. Mem. Am. Fgn. Svc. Assn., Acad. Polit. Sci., Nat. War Coll. Alumni Assn., Rotary Club of Que. (hon.). Roman Catholic. Achievements include speaks fluent French and Thai. Avocation: choral singing. Office: US Dept State 2201 C St NW Washington DC 20520

HUI, HELEN YUEN HING, lawyer; b. Hong Kong, Jan. 3, 1944; d. Lap Sam and Shuk Han (Cheng) H.; m. Gordon Lew, July 12, 1969; 1 child, Beverly. BA, Smith Coll., 1967; MSW, U. Calif., Berkeley, 1970; JD, U. Calif., San Francisco, 1974. Bar: Calif. 1975. Intern ACLU, San Francisco, 1973; assoc. Hardesty & Lau, 1973-77; ptnr. Law Office Lau & Lee, 1977-79, Law Office Lee & Hui, 1979-88; prin. Law Offices of Helen Y.H. Hui, San Francisco, 1988—. Spkr., panelist in field. Officer, dir. East/West Pub. Co., San Francisco, 1968—; dir., pres. Chinese Newcomers Svc. Ctr., San Francisco, 1977-83, 94-2000; v.p. Childcare Law Ctr., 1987-88; officer, dir., adv. bd. Self-Help for Elderly, San Francisco, 1977—; pres. N.E. Med. Svc., 1982-88, Chinatown Cmty. Childrens Ctr., 1986-88; co-chair Chinese Culture Found., San Francisco, 1994-98; pres. San Francisco Bay chpt. Orgn. Chinese Ams., 1996-97; citizen adv. bd. Chinese for Affirmative Action, World Affairs Coun., 1994—; dir. Angel Island Immigration Sta. Found., 1994-97, Am. Lung Assn., 1995-96; gen. counsel Lions Club, 2002-; pres. Golden Gateway Commons I Assn., 2004-05. Mem. ABA, LWV, Am. Immigration Lawyers Assn. (pres. no. Calif. chpt. 1992-93, editor Key Issues in Immigration Law 1992, writer, spkr. ann. confs. 1995, 96, chair advocacy task force, 2000-02, chair Asian interest group, 2000-04), State Bar Calif. (cert. specialist in immigration and nationality law, commr. immigration law adv. commn. 1991-94, pro bono svc. awards), Asian Am. Bar Assn. Greater Bay Area, Bar Assn. San Francisco, Queens Bench. Avocation: classical music. Office: 456 Montgomery St Ste 700 San Francisco CA 94104-1280

HUI, SAI-HUNG, emergency medical professional; s. Tak-Ming and Au-Chu Hui; m. Rena C. Hui, Feb. 14, 1998; 1 child, Aaron. BS in Neuroscis., BS in Psychobiology, UCLA, 2000, postgrad., 2001—05. Chair UCLA Emergency Medicine Interest Group, 2001—03. Editor-in-chief: UCLA Undergraduate Sci. Jour. (UCLA Vice Provost award, 2001). Mem.: Emergency Medicine Resident Assn. (regional coord. nat. med. student com. 2003—), Soc. Acad. Emergency Medicine, Am. Coll. Emergency Physician, Alpha Gamma Sigma. Achievements include design of UCLA Emergency Medicine Interest Group Official Webpage; development of UCLA Emergency Medicine Interest Group Alcohol Poisoning Educational Project; research in prediction of variation in motor vehicle accident outcome. Personal E-mail: joshhui@ucla.edu.

HUIBERTS, PIETER J., development chemist; b. Woerden, Utrecht, The Netherlands, Nov. 20, 1971; arrived in U.S., 1998; s. Dirk Huiberts and Marianne Huiberts-Klok. BSc in Biochemistry, Hogeschool, West-Brabant, Etten-Leur, The Netherlands, 1998. Cert. safe microbiologic techniques. Intern FMC BioProducts, Rockland, Maine, 1997-98; analytical chemist Biowhittaker Molecular Applications, Rockland, 1999, devel. chemist Walkersville, Md., 2000—02, rsch. chemist, database specialist, 2002, Cambrex Biosci. Walkersville Inc., 2002—. Home: #402 160C Willowdale Dr Frederick MD 21702 Office: Cambrex Biosci Walkersville Inc 8830 Biggs Ford Rd Walkersville MD 21793 Office Fax: 301-845-4868. E-mail: phuiberts@yahoo.com, piet.huiberts@cambrex.com.

HUIE, CAROL P., information science educator; b. Kingston, Jamaica; AAS, Hostos C.C., N.Y.C., 1986; BSc, Lehman Coll., N.Y.C., 1988; MS, CCNY, 1994; postgrad., CUNY, 1994—99; doctoral student in computer info. sys., Nova Southeastern U., 2001—. Patient acct.coord. New Rochelle Med. Ctr., New Rochelle, NY, 1988-91; coll. lab tech. Hostos Community Coll., Bronx, NY, 1991-98, instr., 1994—2000, asst. professor, 2000—. Mem.: IEEE, Assn. Computing Machinery, Schomburg Ctr. Rsch. Black Culture, Consortium for Computing in Small Colls., CUNY Acad. for Humanities and Scis., Delta Pi Epsilon. Office Phone: 718-518-6550. Personal E-mail: tennishuie@aol.com. E-mail: chuie@hostos.cuny.edu.

HUISMAN, RHONDA KAY, school librarian, educator; b. Vermillion, SD, Oct. 19, 1971; d. Thomas Joseph Aldrich and Charmaine Rhonda Steuerwald; m. Shawn Mark Huisman, Dec. 30, 1989; children: Dillon Wade children: Kyle Shawn, Ian Mark, Tanner Jon. BS in Edn. and English, U. SD, 2001; MA in Edn., Briar Cliff U., 2005. Cert. grades 7-12 lang. arts tchr. SD, 2001. Tchr. aide Children's Care Hosp. and Sch., Sioux Falls, SD, 1996—98; lang. arts tchr. Irene Sch. Dist., SD, 2001—02; libr. aide Sioux Ctr. Cmty. Sch., 2002—03; coord. of libr. svcs NW Iowa CC, Sheldon, Iowa, 2003—. Quiz bowl coach Sioux Ctr. Cmty. Sch., Iowa, 2003—; adj. faculty NW Iowa CC, Sheldon, 2004—. Pres. Head Start Policy Coun., Sioux Falls, SD, 1997. Mem.: AAUP, ASCD, ALA, Assn. of Coll. and Rsch. Librs., Iowa Libr. Assn. Home: 131 Third Ave Sioux Center IA 51250 Office: Northwest Iowa CC 603 W Park St Sheldon IA 51201 Office Fax: 712-324-4157.

HUISSA, ALI, librarian; b. Beni Khiar, Nabeul, Tunisia, Aug. 7, 1957; m. Faten Najar, Mar. 19, 2000. M in Libr. and Info. Sci., Ind. U., 1988. Libr., Middle East and Islamic studies bibliographer Ind. U., 1988. Mem. hearing bd. Cornell U., 1992-95, mem. rev. bd., 1995—. Mem. Am. Libr. Assn. (com. mem. 1992-95, mem. Near East and South Asia subocom. internat. rels. com. 1997-99), Middle East Librs.' Assn. N. Am. (webmaster, list owner 1995—). Home: 2250 N Triphammer Rd Ithaca NY 14850 Office: Cornell U 504 Olin Ithaca NY 14851 Fax: (607) 255-6110. E-mail: ah16@cornell.edu.

HUITT, JIMMIE L., rancher, oil and gas industry executive, real estate developer; b. Gurdon, Ark., Aug. 21, 1923; s. John Wesley and Almedia (Hatten) H.; m. Janis C. Mann, Oct. 30, 1945; children— Jimmie L., Jr., Allan Jerome BS in Chem. Engring., La. Tech. U., 1944; MS in Chem. Engring., U. Okla., 1948, PhD, 1951. Research engr. Mobil Oil Corp., Dallas, 1951-56, Gulf Research Co., Pitts., 1956-67; ops. coordinator Kuwait Oil Co., London, 1967-71; gen. mgr. Gulf Oil-Zaire, Kinshasa, 1971-74; mng. dir. Gulf Oil-Nigeria, Lagos, 1974-76; sr. v.p., exec. v.p. Gulf Oil Exploration and Prodn. Co., Houston, 1976-81, pres., 1981-85; rancher Four Jays Ranch, Industry, Tex., 1986—. Contbr. articles to profl. jours.; patentee in field Served to 1st lt. U.S. Army, 1944-47 Mem. Soc. Petroleum Engrs. (chmn. various coms. 1956—), Masons, Shriners. Republican. Office: Four Jays Ranch PO Box 236 Industry TX 78944-0236

HUITT, KEITH DAVID, music educator, history educator; b. Wynnewood, Okla., Nov. 28, 1960; s. Gains Astor and Vera LaHoma Huitt; m. Mary Kay Brenholtz, May 26, 1984; 1 child, Sabrina Nicole. MusB Edn., East Ctrl. Okla. State U., Ada, Okla, 1981; Med, East Ctrl. Okla. State U., Ada, Okla., 1983. Cert. Tchg. Okla. State Dept. of Edn., 1982. Dir.bands Wynnewood Pub. Schs., Wynnewood, Okla., 1983—. Mem.: Music Educators Nat. Conf. R-Consevative. United Meth. Avocation: music. Home: 502 N Taylor Wynnewood OK 73098 Office: Wynnewood Bands 702 E Kerr Wynnewood OK 73098 Office Phone: 405-665-1114. Office Fax: 405-665-5425. Personal E-mail: keithhuitt@yahoo.com.

HUIZENGA, H. WAYNE, entrepreneur, professional sports team executive; b. Evergreen Park, Ill., Dec. 29, 1939; s. G. Harry and Jean (Riddering) Huizenga; m. Martha Jean Pike, Apr. 17, 1972; children: H. Wayne Jr., H. Scott, Ray, Pamela Ann. Student, Calvin Coll., 1957-58. Vice chmn., pres., chief operating officer Waste Mgmt. Inc., Oak Brook, Ill., 1968-84; chmn. Huizenga Holdings, Inc., Ft. Lauderdale, Fla., 1984—; chmn., chief exec. officer Blockbuster Entertainment Corp., Ft. Lauderdale, 1987-94; owner Florida Marlins, Miami, 1992-99, Fla. Panthers, Sunrise, Fla., 1993—2001; chmn. Boca Resorts, Inc., Boca Raton, Fla., 1996—2004, AutoNation Inc., Ft. Lauderdale, 1994—2002. Owner Miami Dolphins and Dolphins Stadium. Mem. Fla. Victory Com., 1988-89, Team Repub. Nat. Com., Washington, 1988-90; organizer Broward Victory 90 PAC, Ft. Lauderdale, 1989-90. Recipient Entrepreneur of Yr. award Wharton Sch. U. Pa., 1989, Excalibur Award Bus. Leader of Yr. News/Sun Sentinel, 1990, Silver Medallion Brotherhood award Broward Region Nat. Conf. Christians and Jews, 1990, Laureates award Jr. Achievement Broward and Palm Beach Counties, 1990, Jim Murphy Humanitarian Award The Emerald Soc., 1990, Entrepreneur of Yr. award Disting. Panel Judges Fla., 1990, Man of Yr. Billboard/Time Mag., 1990, Man of Yr. Juvenile Diabetes Found., 1990, Fla. Free Enterpriser of Yr. award Fla. Coun. on Econ. Edn., 1990, commendation for youth restricted video State of Fla. Office of Gov., 1989, Hon. Mem. Appreciation award Bond Club Ft. Lauderdale, 1989; honored with endowed teaching chair Broward Community Coll., 1990. Mem. Lauderdale Yacht Club, Tournament Players Club, Fisher Island Club, Ocean Reef Club, Cat Cay Yacht Club, Coral ridge Country Club, Linville Ridge Country Club. Avocations: golf, collecting antique cars. Office: Huizenga Holdings 450 E Las Olas Blvd Ste 1500 Fort Lauderdale FL 33301-4212

HUIZENGA, JOHN ROBERT, nuclear chemist, educator; b. Fulton, Ill., Apr. 21, 1921; s. Harry M. and Josie B. (Brands) H.; m. Dorothy J. Koeze, Feb. 1, 1946; children: Linda J., Jann H., Robert J., Joel T. AB, Calvin Coll., 1944; PhD, U. Ill., 1949. Lab. supr. Manhattan Wartime Project, Oak Ridge, 1944-46; instr. Calvin Coll., Grand Rapids, Mich., 1946-47; assoc. scientist Argonne Nat. Lab., Chgo., 1949-57, sr. scientist, 1958-67; professorial lectr. chemistry U. Chgo., 1963-67; prof. chemistry and physics U. Rochester, 1967-78, Tracy H. Harris prof. chemistry and physics, 1978-91, Tracy H. Harris prof. emeritus chemistry and physics, 1991—, chmn. dept. chemistry, 1983-88. Vis. prof. Joliot-Curie Lab., U. Paris, 1964-65, Japan Soc. for Promotion of Sci., 1968; chmn. Nat. Acad. Sci.-NRC Com. on Nuclear Sci., 1974-77; mem. energy rsch. adv. bd. Dept. Energy, 1984-90; numerous adv. vis. coms. to univs., govt. and nat. labs. Author: (with R. Vandenbosch) Nuclear Fission, 1973; (with W.U. Schröder) Damped Nuclear Reactions, 1984; Cold Fusion: The Scientific Fiasco of the Century, 1992; contbr. articles to profl. jours. Fulbright fellow Netherlands, 1954-55; Guggenheim fellow Paris, 1964-65; Guggenheim fellow Berkeley, Calif., 1973; Guggenheim fellow Munich, W.Ger., 1974; Guggenheim fellow Copenhagen, 1974; recipient E.O. Lawrence award AEC, 1966, Leroy Rundle Grumman medal, 1991; named Disting. Alumnus Calvin Coll., 1975 Fellow AAAS, Am. Phys. Soc., Am. Acad. Arts and Scis.; mem. NAS (chmn. NAS-NRC com. on nuclear and radiochemistry 1988-91), Am. Chem. Soc. (award for nuclear applications in chemistry 1975), Phi Beta Kappa, Sigma Xi, Phi Kappa Phi. Home: 43 McMichael Dr Pinehurst NC 28374-6702 E-mail: johnrhuizenga@earthlink.net.

HULBERT, LINDA ANN, academic librarian; b. Racine, Wis., Nov. 10, 1947; d. David and Ruth (Alk) H.; m. A. Kent Rissman, Dec. 1, 1991; m. Shelley B. Plattner, Aug. 24, 1969 (div. 1976). BA, Washington U., St. Louis, 1969; MLS, U. Iowa, Iowa City, 1973; MA in Pub. Adminstrn., St. Louis U., 1993. Sch. librarian Parkway Sch. Dist., St. Louis, 1969-70, Mehlville Sch. Dist., St. Louis, 1970-71; adj. lectr. in libr. science Syracuse U., 1985; med. ref. libr. U. Iowa Health Scis. Ctr., Iowa City, 1973-77; collection devel. librarian SUNY, Health Scis. Ctr., Syracuse, 1977-87; asst. dir. tech. svcs. St. Louis U., 1988-98; dir. tech. and access svcs. So. Ill. U., Edwardsville, 1998—2002; assoc. dir. tech. svc. U. St. Thomas, St. Paul, 2002—. Cons. in field. Mem. ALA, N.Am. Serials Interest Group (co-chmn. conf. planning 2005), Med. Libr. Assn. (membership com. 1980-83), St. Louis Med. Libraries (chair 1984-86). Avocations: downhill skiing, biking, walking, reading. Office: O'Shaugnessy Frey Libr U St Thomas 2115 Summit Ave Saint Paul MN 55105 Home: 6801 Telemark Trail Edina MN 55436 Office Phone: 651-962-5016.

HULBERT, PAUL WILLIAM, JR., paper, lumber company executive; b. Washington, June 21, 1944; s. Paul William and Charlotte Mary (Johnson) Hulbert; m. Katherine Bren, Aug. 10, 1985; children: Paul William III, Jennifer Linda, Brian. BA in History, Denison U., 1966; MBA, U. Mich., 1971. Contr. Wickes Land Devel., Saginaw, Mich., 1969—71; mng. dir. Wickes Europe, The Hague, Netherlands, 1971—75; v.p. corp. devel. Wickes Corp., San Diego, 1975—77; sr. v.p., gen. mgr. Wickes Lumber, Saginaw, 1978—80; sr. v.p., group officer Wickes Cos., Inc., San Diego, 1980—82, Santa Monica, Calif., 1982—85; pres. Sequoia Supply Divsn. Wickes Corp., Irvine, Calif., 1985—86; pres. Sequoia Supply, Inc., Irvine, 1987—89, Prime Source, Inc., Dallas, 1990—. Avocations: sports, coaching youth sports, golf. Office: Prime Source Inc 2115 E Belt Line Rd Carrollton TX 75006-5624

HULBERT, RICHARD WOODWARD, lawyer; b. Cambridge, Mass., Sept. 24, 1929; s. Woodward Dennis and Clifford (Halliday) H.; m. Dorothy Marie Hanni, Apr. 21,1954; children: Jonathan, Ann, Laura, Mary. AB, Harvard U., 1951, LLB, 1955. Bar: N.Y. 1956. Assoc. Cleary, Gottlieb, Steen & Hamilton, N.Y.C., 1955-65, ptnr., 1966-83, 89-96, Paris, 1983-89, mng. ptnr., 1979-84, sr. counsel, 1997—. Lectr. in law U. Calif., Berkeley, 1988; adj. prof. NYU Law Sch., 1990—; vis. prof. law Am. U. Armenia, 2004; vice chmn. internat. ct. arbitration Internat. C. of C., 1994-99. Trustee Bklyn. Mus., 1992-2004, Bklyn. Bot. Garden, 1982-98, 99—; mem. Internat. C. of C. Commn. Internat. Arbitration, 2001—. Sheldon fellow in history Harvard U., 1951-52 Mem. ABA, N.Y. Bar Assn., Assn. of Bar of City of N.Y., Bklyn. Bar Assn., N.Y. County Lawyers Assn., Am. Law Inst., Century Assn., India House, Heights Casino. Democrat. Home: 141 Henry St Brooklyn NY 11201-2501 Office: Cleary Gottlieb STeen & Hamilton LLP 1 Liberty Plz New York NY 10006-1470 Office Phone: 212-225-2050. Business E-Mail: rhulbert@cgsh.com.

HULBERT, STEPHEN THOMPSON, academic administrator; BS in Edn., Worcester (Mass.) State Coll., 1966; MEd, U. Mass., Amherst, 1968; DEd, SUNY, Albany, 1972. Dir. student activities and residence life Western New England Coll., Springfield, Mass., 1968-70; cons. Univ. Assocs. Inc., Washington, 1971-72; exec. asst. to the pres. Mansfield (Pa.) U., 1972-77; v.p. for fin. and adminstrn. Slippery Rock (Pa.) U., 1977-88; v.p. adminstrv. svcs., treas. bd. trustees U. Northern Colo., Greeley, 1988-91, interim pres., 1991, sr. v.p., 1992-94, provost, v.p. for acad. affairs, 1994-96; commr. higher edn., CEO R.I. Bd. of Govs. for Higher Edn., Providence, 1996-99; chancellor U. Mont.-Western, Dillon, 1999—2003; pres. Nicholls (La.) State U., 2003—. Mcpl. coun. Grove City, Pa., 1986-88; adv. bd. Franklin Regional Hosp., Franklin, Pa., 1985-88; mem. exec. bd. Longs Peak coun. Boy Scouts Am., 1991-96, disting. citizen com. chair, 1992, others; mayor's adv. task force City of Greeley, 1992-96, U. No. Colo. Found., Inc., 1991-96, R.I. Children's Crusade for Higher Edn., 1996-99, U. of No. Colo. Rsch. Corp., Inc., 1988-96, chair 1994-96, vice chair 1992-94, corp. treas. 1988-92; steering com. Edn. Comms., 1988—99; bd. govs. Colo. Alliance for Sci., 1995-96. Mem. Am. Assn. for Higher Edn., Nat. Assn. Intercollegiate Athletics (coun. pres.), Frontier Athletic Conf. (chair coun. pres. 2000-03), Phi Delta Kappa. Home: 906 E 1st St Thibodaux LA 70301 Office: Nicholls State U PO Box 2001 Thibodaux LA 70310 Office Phone: 983-448-4000. Business E-Mail: stephen.hulbert@nicholls.edu.

HULBURT, LUCILLE HALL, artist, educator; b. Portland, Oreg., Oct. 31, 1924; d. Allen Bergen and Agnes Edna (Davis) Hall; m. Frank Theodore Hulburt, Nov. 28, 1943; children: Robert, Carol Davalos, Clarke. Grad. h.s., Whitefish, Mont. Asst. milliner, illustrator Hat Co., N.Y.C., 1944; cafe owner, operator San Diego, 1950—52; profl. artist Vancouver, Wash., 1978—; resident artist Artist's Gallery 21, Vancouver, 1988—. Tchr. children and adult art clases, schs. and home studio, Vancouver, 1978—; artist in residence Wash. State Arts Commn., 1987-88; co-founder, coop. Artists Gallery 21, Vancouver, 1988—; cons. nat. Western Art Show and Auction, Trails West, Vancouver; organizer, com. mem. ann. Summer Art at the Ctr., Vancouver, 1986; judge/jurist art exhibits. Founder, pres. Boundary Assn. Retarded Children, Bonners Ferry, Idaho, 1964-65; com. mem. 1st Bldg. Com., Columbia Arts Ctr., Vancouver, 1980-81; bd. mem. Local Arts Promotion, Vancouver, 1992, 93. Recipient Best of Show award Western Art Show and Auction, Chinook, Mont., 1983, 84, Cmty. Svc. award Arts Coun., Clark County, Wash., 1988, Windsor-Newton award Watercolor 91, 1991. Mem. S.W. Wash. Watercolor Soc. (co-founder, pres. 1979, 80, 84), Soc. Washington Artists (Grumbacher Silver medal 1990), Am. Artists Profl. League, Order Ea. Star (life), N.W. Watercolor Soc. Avocations: gardening, sewing, swimming. Office: Hulburt Studio 5515 NE 58th St Vancouver WA 98661-2146

HULET, ERVIN KENNETH, retired nuclear chemist; b. Baker, Oreg., May 7, 1926; s. Frank E. and Marjorie (Suiter) H.; m. Betty Jo Gardner, Sept. 10, 1949 (dec. Jan. 1992); children: Carri, Randall Gardner. BS, Stanford U., 1949; PhD, U. Calif. at Berkeley, 1953. AEC grad. student U. Calif. Radiation Lab., Berkeley, 1949-53; research chemist nuclear chemistry div. Lawrence Livermore Nat. Lab., Livermore, Calif., 1953-66, group leader, 1966-91, ret., active emeritus, 1991—. Achievements include discovery of divalent oxidation state in actinide elements; co-discovery of symmetric fission in actinides. Served with USNR, 1944-46. Fulbright scholar Norway; Welch Found. lectr., 1990; recipient Am. Chem. Soc. award for Nuc. Chemistry, 1994. Fellow AAAS, Am. Inst. Chemists (chmn. Golden Gate chpt. 1992); mem. Am. Chem. Soc. (chmn. divsn. nuclear chemistry and tech. 1987, award in nuclear chemistry 1994), Am. Phys. Soc. Achievements include co-discovery of Element 106; discovery of bimodel fission. E-mail: ekhulet@comcast.net.

HULET, RANDALL GARDNER, physics professor; b. Walnut Creek, Calif., Apr. 27, 1956; s. Ervin Kenneth and Betty Jo (Gardner) H.; m. Lourdes Teresa Hernandez, Aug. 16, 1980; children: Benjamin Hernandez, Gabriella Alison. BS in Physics, Stanford U., 1978; PhD in Physics, MIT, 1984; PhD (hon.), Utrecht Univ., 2002. Rsch. asst. MIT, Cambridge, Mass., 1978-84, rsch. assoc., 1984-85; Nat. Rsch. Coun. postdoctoral fellow Nat. Inst. Standards and Tech., Boulder, Colo., 1985-87; asst. prof. physics Rice U., Houston, 1987-92, assoc. prof. physics, 1992-96, prof., 1996-99, Fayez Sarofim prof. physics, 1999—. Contbr. articles to profl. jours. Alfred P. Sloan fellow, 1988; Nat. Inst. Standards and Tech. grantee, 1988-91; recipient Presdl. Young Investigator's award NSF, 1989. I.I. Rabi Prize, Am. Physical Soc., 1995, NASA Exceptional Sci. Achievement medal, 2004. Fellow: AAAS, Am. Phys. Soc.; mem.: Am. Acad. Arts and Scis. Office: Rice U Dept Physics and Astronomy MS61 Houston TX 77251 E-mail: randy@atomcool.rice.edu.

HULKA, JAROSLAV FABIAN, obstetrician, gynecologist; b. N.Y.C., Sept. 29, 1930; s. Jaroslav Hugo and Milada (Touskova) H.; m. Barbara E. Sorenson, Nov. 13, 1954; children— Carol Ann, Gregory Fabian, Bryan Herbert. BA, Harvard U., 1952; MD, Columbia U., 1956. Diplomate: Am. Bd. Ob-Gyn. Intern Roosevelt Hosp., N.Y.C., 1956-57; resident Sloane Hosp. for Women, Columbia-Presbyn. Med. Center, N.Y.C., 1957-60; Josiah Macy, Jr. fellow Columbia-Presbyn. Med. Center, 1960-61; practice medicine specializing in Ob-Gyn, 1961—; asst. prof. Ob-Gyn U. Pitts. Sch. Medicine, 1961-66, asso. mem. grad. faculty, 1962-66, acting chmn. dept. Ob-Gyn, 1963-64; asso. prof. dept. Ob-Gyn Sch. Medicine, U. N.C., Chapel Hill, 1967-76, prof. dept. Ob-Gyn and dept. maternal and child health, 1976-96. Author: Textbook of Laparoscopy, 1985, 3d edit., 1997; patentee in field. Assoc. dir. Carolina Population Center, 1967-74. Recipient Excel award Soc. of Laparoendoscopic Surgeons, 1994. Fellow ACOG; mem. Soc. for Gynecol. Investigation, Am. Assn. Gynecol. Laparoscopists (pres. 1980), Am. Fertility Soc., Soc. Reproductive Surgeons (founding), N.C. State Bar (bd. legal specialization 1990-96), Planned Parenthood Fed. Am. (chair nat. med. com. 1991-94), Soc. Physicians for Reproductive Choice and Health (founding). Achievements include development of and teaching of worldwide use of clips for female sterilization by laparoscopy; demonstration of local anesthesia for safer procedures. Home: 2317 Honeysuckle Rd Chapel Hill NC 27514-1716 Office: Population Ctr 123 W Franklin St Chapel Hill NC 27516-2524 E-mail: jhulka@unc.edu.

HULKOWER, MARK J., lawyer; BS with honors, Cornell U., 1980; JD magna cum laude, Georgetown U., 1984. Bar: Pa. 1985, DC 1986. Law clerk US Ct. of Appeals, DC Circuit, Washington, 1984—85; asst. US atty. Ea. Dist., Va., 1989—95; ptnr., white collar criminal defense practice Steptoe & Johnson LLP, Washington, 1995—. Lecturer US Dept. Justice, FBI; adjunct prof. George Washington U. Office: Steptoe & Johnson LLP 1330 Connecticut AveNW Washington DC 20036 Office Phone: 202-429-6221. Office Fax: 202-429-3902. Business E-Mail: mhulkower@steptoe.com.

HULL, BRETT A., professional hockey player; b. Belleville, Ont., Can., Aug. 9, 1964; s. Bobby Hull. Student, U. Minn., Duluth, 1984-86. Forward Calgary Flames, 1986—88, St. Louis Blues, 1988—96, Dallas Stars, 1999—2001, Detroit Red Wings, 2001—04, Phoenix Coyotes, 2004—. Player NHL All-Star 1st Team, 1990—92, U.S. Olympic Hockey Team, Nagano, 1998, Salt Lake City, 2002, Team U.S.A., World Cup of Hockey, 1996, 2004. Named NHL Player of Yr., The Sporting News, 1989—90, 1991—92, All-Star Game MVP, 1992; named to NHL All-Star Game, 1989, 1990, 1992—94, 1996, 1997, 2001; recipient Lady Byng Meml. Trophy, 1989, 1990, Hart Meml. Trophy, 1990—91, Dodge Ram Tough award, 1989—90, 1990—91, Lester B. Pearson award, 1990—91. Achievements include led NHL in goals, 1989-92; mem. World Cup Champion Team U.S.A., 1996; mem. Stanley Cup Champions, Dallas Stars, 1999, Detroit Red Wings, 2002. Office: c/o Phoenix Coyotes 9375 E Bell Rd Scottsdale AZ 85260

HULL, CATHY, artist, illustrator; b. N.Y.C., Nov. 4, 1946; d. Max H. and Magda M. (Stern) H.; m. Neil S. Janovic; 1 child, Julie. BA, Conn. Coll., 1968; cert., Sch. Visual Arts, N.Y.C., 1970. Instr. illustration and portfolio Sch. Visual Arts, N.Y.C., 1983-94, Parsons Sch. Design, N.Y.C., 1994—. Juror The 6th World Cartoon Gallery, Skopje, 1974, Soc. Pub. Designers, N.Y.C., 1982, Soc. Illustrators, N.Y.C., 1983, The Biennale of Humor, Fredrikstad, Norway, 1987, The 6th Internat. Simavi Cartoon Competition, Istanbul, Turkey, 1988 Contbr. to anthologies, books, mags. and newspapers including Time, Penthouse, Newsweek, Esquire, Playboy, MSNBC, Fortune, Wall Street Jour., Washington Post, Forbes, Chgo. Tribune, Ency. Brit., Disney, Sports Illustrated, N.Y. Times, Bus. Week, Travel and Leisure, Money, others; group shows include The 17th Nat. Print Exhbn., Bklyn., 1970, AIGA Show, N.Y.C., 1970-71, 74, Printing Industries Am., 1971, Soc. Illustrators, 1973, 80, 85, 94, 2001, World Cartoon Gallery, Skopje, former Yugoslavia, 1972-75, Art Dir.'s Club, 1974, 82, Internat. Cartoon Exhbn., Istanbul, Turkey, 1974, Switzerland, 1974, 78, 80, 82, 90, Athens, Greece, 1975, Soc. Publ. Designers, 1974, 82, Musée de Beaubourg, Paris, 1977, Pacific Design Ctr., L.A., 1980, The Md. Inst., 1981, Scottsdale (Ariz.) Ctr. for Arts, 1981, Soc. Newspaper Design, 1984-85, Butler Inst. Am. Art, Youngstown, Ohio, 1983, Am. Peace Poster Exhibit, 1985, Quebec City Exhbn., Society of Illustrators, 2002; represented in permanent collections including Mus. Caricatures and Cartoons, Basel, Switzerland, Soc. Illustrators Advt. Ann. show, Smithtown Twp. Arts Coun.; designer and pub. playing cards sold at Cooper Hewitt Mus., N.Y., N.Y. Pub. Libr., L.A. County Mus. Art, St. Louis Art Mus., Chgo. Mus. Art, Nat. Mus. Scotland, Seibu, Japan, Contemporary Mus. of Honolulu, Contemporary Mus. San Diego, High Mus. Atlanta, Meml. Exhbn., Mus. Am. Illustration, 2002, Herbert F. Johnson Mus. of Art, 2002, Cornell U., Karikatur and Cartoon Mus., Basel, Switzerland, 2003, Mus. Am. Illustration, 2004, RSVP Portraits Show and N.Y. Times Show, Mus. Am. Illustration, 2004. Exec. bd. Friends of the H.S. Art and Design, 2002—. Office: 180 E 79th St New York NY 10021-0437 Personal E-mail: cmhull@aol.com. Business E-Mail: chull@nyc.rr.com.

HULL, CHARLES WILLIAM, retired special education educator; b. East St. Louis, Ill., Feb. 23, 1936; s. William Semple Hull and Jessie Marie (Brennan) Poole; m. Beverly Kay Julian, Aug. 19, 1967; 1 child, William Kenneth. BA in Econs., Cen. Meth. Coll., 1964; MEd, Olivet Nazarene Coll., 1974; AA (hon.), Joliet Jr. Coll., 1987. Tchr. elem. grades Taft Sch., Lockport, Ill., 1965-67; tchr. spl. edn. S.W. Cook County Coop. Assn. for Spl. Edn., Oak Forest, Ill., 1967-99; ret., 1999. Permanent exhibits include Tchr's Ret. Office Bldg., Springfield, Ill. Past bd. dirs., v.p., chmn. fund raising Easter Seals Will and Grundy Counties; dist. leader Am. Cancer Soc., 1984, residential campaign chmn., 1985; vol., mem. adv. bd. Big Bros.-Big Sisters Will County; Cub Scouts com. chmn. Boy Scouts Am., 1980-81, commr. Rainbow coun., bd. dirs. troop 61; choir, past trustee Faith United Meth. Ch.; Will County walkathon chmn. March of Dimes, 1979; chmn. Canal Days events Will County Hist. Soc., 1987; mem. Nat. Trust for Hist. Preservation, Lockport Area Geneal. Hist. Soc.; bd. dirs. Joliet Project Pride, Will County Project Pride, 2000-03; life mem. Friends of Ill. and Mich. Canal. Cpl. USMC, 1955-58. Recipient Congl. Medal of Merit, 1985, Frederick Bartleson Meml. award Will County Hist. Soc., 1985, Citizen of Week award Sta. WBBM, Chgo., 1985, Leadership award Am. Cancer Soc., 1985, Outstanding Svc. award Big Bros.-Big Sisters Will County, letter of commendation Pres. of U.S., 1986, 89, Disting. Svc. award Joliet Jr. Coll., 1987, Citizen of Month award Southtown Economist, plaque KC; inducted into Joliet/Will County Hall of Pride, 2002. Mem. 1st Marine Divsn. Assn., Coalition for Citizens with Disabilities in Ill. (life), Will County Old-Timers Baseball Assn., Am. Legion, Masons (32 degree), Masonic Lodge (Elwood, Ill., life), Shriners (pres. Joliet club 1983, Shriner of Yr. 1989), KC, Medina Temple, Cumberland Scottish Rite Club, Lions (pres. Manhattan club 1984, chmn. youth and fgn. exch. dist. 1986-87, bd. dirs. Lockport chpt.), Will County Hist. Soc. (pres. 1989), Joliet Area Ret. Tchrs. Assn., Ill. Ret. Tchrs. Assn., Pleasant Hill Hist. Soc., Royal Order Scotland. Republican. Methodist. Home: PO Box 429 Pleasant Hill TN 38578 Personal E-mail: beehul@earthlink.net.

HULL, CORDELL WILLIAM, investor; b. Dayton, Ohio, Sept. 12, 1933; s. Murel George and Julia (Barto) H.; m. Susan G. Ruder, May 10, 1958; children: Bradford W., Pamela H., Andrew R. B of Engring., U. Dayton, 1956; MS, MIT, 1957; JD, Harvard U., 1962; doctorate (hon.), Dominican U. Registered profl. engr., Mass.; bar: Ohio 1962; lic. contractor Calif. Atty. Taft, Stettinius & Hollister, Cin., 1962-64, C & I Girdler, Cin., 1964-66; gen. counsel, treas., pres. C&I Girdler, Internat., Brussels, 1966-70; v.p. Bechtel Overseas Corp., San Francisco, 1970-73; pres., dir. Am. Express Mcht. Bank, London, 1973-75; v.p., treas. Bechtel Corp. and Bechtel Power, San Francisco, 1975-80; pres. Bechtel Fin. Svcs., San Francisco, 1975-82; v.p., CFO Bechtel Group Inc., 1980-85; pres. Bechtel Power Corp., 1987-89, dir.; chmn. Bechtel Enterprises, 1990-95. Bd. dirs. Fremont Group, Inc.; former chmn. audit commn. Gilead Scis., 2001—04; mem. Accenture Energy Adv. Bd.; mgr. HWC LLC; former chmn. adv. com. U.S. Eximbank; former mem. svcs.

policy com. Office of U.S. Trade Rep. Trustee Dominican Coll.; bd. trustees U. Dayton. Mem. Pacific Union Club, Menlo Country Club, Pasadera Country Club. also: HWC LLC 400 Oyster Point Blvd Ste 540 South San Francisco CA 94080

HULL, DAVID GEORGE, aerospace engineering educator, researcher; b. Oak Park, Ill., Mar. 27, 1937; s. John Lawrence Hull and Elizabeth Christine (Carstensen) Meyer; m. Meredith Lynn Kiesel, June 2, 1962 (div. July 1980); children: David, Andrew, Matthew; m. Vicki Jan Poole, June 30, 1983; children: Katherine, Emily. BS, Purdue U., 1959; MS, U. Wash., 1962; PhD, Rice U., 1967. Staff assoc. Boeing Sci. Research Labs., Seattle, 1959-64; research assoc. Rice U., Houston, 1964-66; asst. prof. U. Tex., Austin, 1966-71, assoc. prof., 1971-77, prof., 1977-85, M.J. Thompson Regents prof., 1985—. Cons. several aerospace cos. Assoc. editor 2 jours.; author: Optimal Control Theory for Applications, 2003; reviewer several engring. jours.; contbr. more than 55 articles to profl. jours. Recipient/co-recipient more than 50 grants and contracts; recipient award Best paper, AAS/AIAA Space Flt. Mechanics Conf., Albuquerque, 1995. Mem. AIAA (assoc. fellow, atmospheric flight mechanics tech. com. 1974-77, guidance and control tech. com. 1984-87), AAS (sr. mem.), Delta Tau Delta (treas. Purdue U. 1958-59). Office: U Tex ASE/EM C0600 Austin TX 78712-0235 Office Phone: 512-471-4908. Business E-Mail: dghull@mail.utexas.edu.

HULL, DENNIS JACQUES, retired counselor; b. Orange, NJ, June 8, 1945; s. Jacques Lionel and Ora May (Holdman) H.; m. Elizabeth Ann Martin, Sept. 7, 1969; 1 child, Jonathan. BA in Psychology, Calif. State Univ., Hayward, 1968, MS in Counseling, 1975. Cert. counselor Nat. Bd. Cert. Counselors, Inc. Counselor L.A. Harbor Coll., Wilmington, Calif., 1979-84, Western Nev. C.C., Carson City, 1984-86, coord. counseling svcs., 1987-94, dir. counseling svcs., 1994—2002, interim dean student svcs., 2002—04; ret., 2004. With USAF, 1968-72. Mem. Am. Counseling Assn., Calif. Assn. Counseling Devel., Calif. C.C. Counselors Assn. (bd. dirs., so. conf. chair 1983-84).

HULL, E. PATRICK, lawyer; b. Jefferson City, Tenn., Mar. 17, 1949; s. Erwin and Elizabeth Sue (Shipley) H.; children: Daniel Patrick, Christopher Douglas, Michael Erwin. BSIE, U. Tenn., 1971, JD, 1975. Bar: Tenn. 1976, U.S. Dist. Ct. (ea. dist.) Tenn. 1977, U.S. Ct. Appeals (6th cir.) 1988, U.S. Supreme Ct. 1995. Assoc. Wilson, Worley, Gamble & Ward, Kingsport, Tenn., 1976-79, ptnr., 1980-82, Hull & Hansen, Kingsport, 1982-84; min. Columbia, S.C., 1984-86; pvt. practice Kingsport, 1986—. Adj. faculty East Tenn. State U., Johnson City, 1993—. Author: Portraits of Forgiveness, Conversations with Matthew; editor: Spl. Edn. Newsletter, 1988-92; contbr. articles to profl. jours. Com. mem. ARC, Kingsport, 1994-95; bd. dirs., sec. Youth Athletic Adv. Bd., Kingsport, 1994-95; bd. assocs. Emmanuel Sch. Religion, 1996—. Mem. Tenn. Bar Assn., Tenn. Coun. Sch. Bd. Attys. (pres. 1990-92), Nat. Coun. Sch. Bd. Attys. Avocations: fly fishing, writing, painting, tennis. Office: 229 E New St Kingsport TN 37660-4333 Home: PO Box 1388 Kingsport TN 37662-1388

HULL, EDMUND J., former ambassador; b. Keokuk, Iowa, Dec. 1949; married; 2 children. Diploma with honors, Princeton U.; postgrad. in strategic issues with Sir Michael Howard, Oxford U., 1986—87. Numerous positions including dir. No. Gulf Affairs during the Gulf War; dep. chief of mission and charge d'Affaires U.S. Embassy, Cairo, 1993—96; former dir. Office of Peacekeeing; former acting coord. for counterterroism U.S. Dept. of State, U.S. amb. to Yemen Sana'a, 2001—04. Vol. Peace Corps, Tunisia, 1971—73. Recipient Meritorious Honor award, Superior Honor awards, U.S. Dept. of State, Baker-Wilkins award, 1995.

HULL, ELAINE MANGELSDORF, psychology professor; b. Houston, Aug. 15, 1940; d. Paul August and Mary Eleanor (Stephens) Mangelsdorf; m. Richard Thompson Hull, May 30, 1962; 1 child, Geoffrey Alaric (dec.). BA, Austin Coll., Sherman, Tex., 1963; PhD, Ind. U., 1967. Asst. prof. psychology SUNY, Buffalo, 1967-73, assoc. prof., 1973-86, prof., 1986—2004, dir. biopsychology grad. program, 1996—2004; prof. psychology Fla. State U., Tallahassee, 2004—. Contbr., 75 articles to sci. jours. Recipient Chancellor's award for excellence in teaching SUNY, Buffalo, 1975, Tchg. award, SUNY Students Assn., 1986, N.Y. State Union Univ. Profls. Excellence award 1990, Disting. Alumna award Austin Coll., 2004; grantee NIMH. Mem. APA, AAAS, Am. Psycol. Soc., Internat. Acad. Sex Rsch., Soc. Neurosci., Internat. Soc. Psychoneuroendocrinology, N.Y. Acad. Scis Democrat. Avocations: jogging, classical music. Office: 3241 Heather Hill Ln Tallahassee FL 32309 Office Phone: 850-645-2389. Business E-Mail: hull@psy.fsu.edu.

HULL, FRANK MAYS, federal judge; b. Augusta, Ga., Dec. 9, 1948; d. James M. Hull Jr. and Frank (Mays) Pride; m. Antonin Aeck, Apr. 16, 1977; children: Richard Hull Aeck, Molly Hull Aeck. AB, Randolph-Macon Women's Coll., 1970; JD cum laude, Emory U., 1973. Bar: Ga. 1973, U.S. Ct. Appeals (5th cir.) 1973, U.S. Dist. Ct. (no. dist.) Ga. 1974, U.S. Ct. Appeals (11th cir.) 1982. Law clk. to Hon. Elbert P. Tuttle U.S. Ct. Appeals (5th cir.), Atlanta, 1973—74; assoc. Powell, Goldstein, Frazer & Murphy, Atlanta, 1974—80, ptnr., 1980—84; judge State Ct. Fulton County, Atlanta, 1984—90, Superior Ct. Fulton County, Atlanta, 1990—94, U.S. Dist. Ct. (no. dist.) Ga., 1994—97, U.S. Ct. Appeals (11th cir.), 1997—. Mem. commn. on family violence State of Ga., 1992—94, commn. on gender bias in jud. sys., 1988—90. Mem. Leadership Atlanta, 1986—, program co-chair criminal justice com., 1988—89; Sunday sch. tchr. Cathedral St. Philip, Atlanta, 1983—88, children's com., 1981—82, outreach com., 1989—91; bd. dirs. Met. Atlanta Mediation Ctr., Inc., 1976—79, Atlanta Vol. Lawyers Assn., 1988—91. Fellow, AAUW, 1973—. Mem.: ABA (fin. sec. long range planning com. tort and ins. practice sect. 1979—82, chmn. contract documents divsn., forum com. on constrn. industry 1983—85, editl. staff jour. 1981—85, vice chmn. fidelity and surety law com. 1978—85), Nat. Assn. Women Judges, Ga. Assn. Women Lawyers, Atlanta Bar Assn., Am. Judicature Soc. (bd. dirs. 1990—96), Ga. Bar Assn., Order of Coif. Office: US Ct of Appeals 56 Forsyth St NW Rm 300 Atlanta GA 30303-2289*

HULL, FREDERICK ALBERT, artist, writer; b. Norfolk, Va., July 27, 1931; s. William Barr and Velma Beatrice Hull; m. Joan Arnold, Aug. 4, 1956; children: Frederick William, Christopher John. BA in Art, Calif. State U., Sacramento, 1971, MPA, 1977. Chief of design dept. Reed & Reese Corp., Pasadena, Calif., 1961—63; asst. br. chief graphic br. 323 Flying Tng. Wing, Mather AFB, Calif., 1963—72; art and prodn. editor The Navigator mag. Dept Air Force, Mather AFB, Calif., 1972—87; syndicated cartoonist Adventure Features Syndicate newspapers, Glendale, Calif., 1976—90; instr. journalism Calif. State U., Sacramento, 1981; dir., writer, artist Hull Features Syndicate, Am. Internat. Features, Calif. and Mo., 1991—95; sr. signature artist, master painter No. Calif. Artists Inc., Carmichael, 1995—; also bd. dirs. No. Calif. Artists Inc. NCA, Carmichael. Designer, publ. asst. dir. Calif. State Mil. Mus., Sacramento, 1982-92; mem. art show and promotion bds. Sacramento Fine Art Ctr., Carmichael, 1997—. Maj. U.S. Army, 1954-56, with Calif. State Mil. Reserve, 1982-96. Recipient numerous nat. and internat. juried show awards for oil painting. Mem.: Sigma Delta Chi, Phi Kappa Tau. Avocations: sailing, bike riding, jogging, weightlifting, woodworking. Home: 2512 G St Sacramento CA 95816-3610 E-mail: fredhull@cwnet.com.

HULL, GERALD W., JR., lawyer; b. Newark, 1940; BBA, Univ. Miami, 1962; LLB, Rutgers Univ., 1965. Bar: NJ 1965. Legal sec. to Hon. Arthur Lewis Superior Ct., NJ appellate divsn.; sr. real estate ptnr., co-head, real estate practice group Drinker Biddle & Reath LLP, Florham Park, NJ; mng. ptnr., 2002—; and mem., mgmt. com. Drinker Biddle & Reath LLP. Recipient Lifetime Achievement award in Real Estate, Nat. Assn. Industrial and Office Properties, 1996. Office: Drinker Biddle & Reath LLP 500 Campus Dr Florham Park NJ 07932-1047 Office Phone: 973-549-7000. Office Fax: 973-360-9831. Business E-Mail: gerald.hull@dbr.com.

HULL, GRETCHEN GAEBELEIN, lay worker, writer, lecturer; b. Bklyn., Feb. 5, 1930; d. Frank Ely and Dorothy Laura (Medd) Gaebelein; m. Philip Glasgow Hull, Oct. 24, 1952; children: Jeffrey R., Sanford D., Meredyth Hull Smith. BA magna cum laude, Bryn Mawr Coll., 1950; postgrad., Columbia U., 1950-52; DLitt (hon.), Houghton Coll., 1995. Major presenter Internat. Coun. on Bibl. Inerrancy, Chgo., 1986; guest lectr. London Inst. on Contemporary Christianity, 1988; lectr. at large Christians for Bibl. Equality, St. Paul, 1988-2000; major presenter Presbyn. Ch. (U.S.A.) Nat. Abortion Dialogue, Kansas City, Mo., 1989; disting. scholar lectr. Thomas F. Staley Found., Stony Brook, N.Y., 1991. Elder Presbyn. Ch. (U.S.A.); mem. Madison Ave. Presbyn. Ch., N.Y.C.; vis. prof. Regent Coll., Vancouver, B.C., 1992. Author: Equal to Serve, 1987; (with others) Women, Authority and the Bible, 1986, Applying the Scriptures, 1987, Study Bible for Women (New Testament), 1996, The Global God, 1998, The Gospel with Extra Salt, 2000, The IVP Women's Bible Commentary, 2002; editor Priscilla Papers, 1989-99; contbg. editor Perspectives, 1992—; mem. editl. bd. Prism, 1994—; contbr. articles to religious mags. Trustee Cold Spring Harbor Village Improvement Soc., 1966-69, Soc. of St. Johnland, Kings Park, N.Y., 1972-75. Mem. Woman's Union Missionary Soc. Am. (bd. dirs. 1954-71), Presbyns. United for Bibl. Concerns (bd. dirs. 1973-75), L.I. Presbytery (gen. coun. 1981-83), Christians for Bibl. Equality (bd. dirs. 1987-94), Latin Am. Mission (trustee 1989-95), Evangelicals for Social Action (bd. dirs. 1991-99, 2001—), Network Presbyn. Women in Leadership (steering com. 1994-98), Presbyns. for Renewal (bd. dirs. 1994-2000). Home and Office: 63 Meadow Lakes Hightstown NJ 08520

HULL, HERBERT MITCHELL, botanist, researcher; b. La Jolla, Calif., Aug. 19, 1919; s. Daniel Ray and Emma (Kammeyer) H.; m. Mary Randall Mattison, Mar. 4, 1950; children: Laurinda Lee, Daniel James. AA, Pasadena City Coll., 1939; BS, U. Calif., Berkeley, 1946; PhD, Calif. Inst. Tech., 1951. Research fellow Calif. Inst. Tech., 1949-52; plant physiologist U.S. Dept. Agr., Tucson, 1952-78; prof. renewable natural resources U. Ariz., 1966-85, prof. emeritus, 1985—. Served as meteorologist and pilot USAAF, 1941-46. Fellow AAAS, Ariz.-Nev. Acad. Sci.; mem. Am. Soc. Plant Biologists, Bot. Soc. Am., Sigma Xi, Alpha Zeta. Presbyterian. Home: 4040 W Sweetwater Dr Tucson AZ 85745-9757

HULL, J(AMES) RICHARD, retired lawyer; b. Keokuk, Iowa, Dec. 5, 1933; s. James Robert and Alberta Margaret (Bouseman) H.; m. Patricia M. Kiesner, June 14, 1958; children— Elizabeth Ann Hull Whims, James Robert, David Glen. BA, Ill. Wesleyan U., 1955; JD, Northwestern U., 1958. Bar: Ill. 1958, Fla. 1978. V.p., sec., gen. counsel Honeggers & Co., Inc., Fairbury, Ill., 1959-65, also bd. dirs.; staff atty. Am. Hosp. Supply Corp., Evanston, Ill., 1965-68, chief atty., asst. sec., 1968-70, corp. sec., 1970-71, corp. sec., corp. gen. counsel, 1971-79, gen. counsel, 1979-84; sr. v.p., sec., gen. counsel Household Internat. Inc., Northbrook, Ill., 1984-93, sr. v.p., of counsel, 1993-94; ret. Mem. planning com. Northwestern U. Corp. Counsel Inst., 1992-93, chmn. Northwestern Corp. Counsel Ctr., 1993. Bd. trustees, bd. visitors Ill. Wesleyan U.; pres. Prestancia Cmty. Assn. Fellow Am. Bar Found., Am. Law Inst.; mem. ABA, Ill. Bar Assn., Fla. Bar Assn., Chgo. Bar Assn. (chmn. corp. law dept.), North Shore Gen. Counsels, Northwestern U. Sch. Law Alumni Assn. (pres.), Sigma Chi, Legal Club (Chgo.), Law Club (Chgo.), Skokie Country Club (Glencoe, Ill.), Gator Creek Golf Club (Sarasota, Fla.), T.P.C. Club (Prestancia, Fla.), Prestancia Cmty. Assn. (pres. 1995-96), Champion Hills Golf Club (Hendersonville, N.C.), Hendersonville Country Club. Home (Winter): 4634 Mirada Way #24 Sarasota FL 34238 Home (Summer): 21 LaCoste Dr Hendersonville NC 28739 E-mail: dph4634@aol.com. *Success will come to those who plan and rehearse. Set your goals, define your strategies and implement your tactics. Your goals must always determine and never justify the means toward achievement.*

HULL, JANE DEE, former governor, former state legislator; b. Kansas City, Mo., Aug. 8, 1935; d. Justin D. and Mildred (Swenson) Bowersock; m. Terrance Ward Hull, Feb. 12, 1954; children: Jeannette Shipley, Robin Hillebrand, Jeff, Mike. BS in elem. edn., U. Kans., 1957; postgrad. in polit. sci., Ariz. State U., postgrad. in econs., 1972-78; grad., Josephson Sch. of Ethics, 1993. Former state legislator Ariz. Ho. of Reps., Phoenix, 1979—93, spkr. pro tem, 1993, chmn. ethics com., chmn. econ. devel., 1993, mem. legis. coun., 1993, mem. gov.'s internat. trade and tourism adv. bd., 1993, mem. gov.'s strategic partnership for econ. devel., 1993, mem. gov.'s office of employement implementation task force, 1993, spkr. of house, 1989—93, house majority whip, 1987-88; former sec. of state State of Ariz., Phoenix, 1995—97, former gov., 1997—2003; pub. del. to the UN, 2004—05. Author (edited by Michael S. Josephson and Wes Hanson): The Power of Character; author: Character in Soc.: The Challenge of Pub. Svc.; contbr. opinion pieces to periodicals and newspapers. Mem. dean's coun. Ariz. State U., 1989—92; assoc. mem. Heard Mus. Guild; mem. Maricopa Med. Aux., Ariz. State Med. Aux., Valley Citizens League, Charter 100, Ariz. Women's Forum; hon. chmn. Race for the Cure; hon. bd. mem. Teach for Am.; assoc. mem. Cactus Wren Rep. Women; mem. Freedom Found., North Phoenix Rep. Women, 1970; Trunk 'N Tusk Legis. Liaison Ariz. Rep. Party, 1993; mem. Gov.'s Emergency Coun., Ariz. -Mex. Commn., Phoenix Commn. on Internat. Rels.; Ariz. chmn. George W. Bush for Pres., 2000; mem. Adv. Coun. Hist. Preservation; chmn. Western Gov.'s Assn., 2002, Border Gov.'s Assn., 2002; bd. dir. Morrison Inst. for Pub. Policy, Beatitudes D.O.A.R., 1992, Ariz. Town Hall, Ariz. Econs. Coun. Recipient Econ. Devel. award, Ariz. Innovation Network, 1993, Spl. Achievement award, Nat. Notary Assn., 1997, Appreciation award, No. Ariz. U. Sch. of Forestry students, 2000. Mem. Nat. Orgn. of Women Legislators, Am. Legis. Exch. Coun., Nat. Rep. Legislators Assn. (Nat. Legislator of Yr. award 1989), Soroptimists (hon.). Republican. Roman Catholic.

HULL, JOHN DANIEL, IV, lawyer; b. Washington, Feb. 27, 1953; s. John Daniel III and Arlene (Reemer) Hull. BA cum laude, Duke U., 1975; JD, U. Cin., 1978. Bar: DC 1980, U.S. Dist. Ct. DC 1983, U.S. Ct. Appeals (DC cir.) 1984, U.S. Ct. Appeals (10th cir.) 1986, Md. 1989, Pa. 1989, U.S. Dist. Ct. (we. dist.) Pa. 1989, U.S. Ct. Appeals (3d cir.) 1989, U.S. Supreme Ct. 1989, Calif. 2002, U.S. Dist. Ct. (so. dist.) Calif. 2002, U.S. Dist. Ct. Md. 1992. Legis. asst. 93d & 96th U.S. Congresses, Washington, 1974, 78-81; assoc. Rose, Schmidt & Dixon, Washington, 1981-87, ptnr., 1988-92, Hull McGuire PC, Pitts., Washington, and San Diego, 1992—. Mem.: U. Cin. Law Rev., 1976—77, editor student articles:, 1977—78. Mem. planning bd. Rancho Bernardo Calif., 1998—2004. Fellow Congress of Ctr. for Internat. Legal Studies, Salzburg, Austria. Mem.: ABA, Calif. Bar Assn., Internat. Bar Assn., Pa. Bar Assn., Md. Bar Assn., Bar Assn. DC, Internat. Bus. Law Consortium (Austria and London, mem. bus. devel. group), Tara Club, Duke Club. Office: Hull McGuire PC 32 Fl US Steel Tower 600 Grant St Pittsburgh PA 15219-2702 also: Hull McGuire PC 888 17th St NW Ste 1200 Washington DC 20006 also: Hull McGuire PC Merrill Lynch Bldg 701 B St Fl 10 San Diego CA 92101 Office Phone: 619-239-9400. Business E-Mail: jdhull@hullmcguire.com.

HULL, KATHRYN BLOMQUIST, music educator, composer, consultant; b. Sanders, Idaho, June 14, 1928; d. Willett S. and Ruby V. (Simons) Blomquist; m. Robert M. Hull, Apr. 28, 1957 (div. 1990); children: Laurice, Craig, Eric. BA, Pasadena Coll., 1949. Piano tchr. Ind. music tchr., composer, 1949—; supr. of office svcs. Stanford Rsch. Inst., Palo Alto, L.A., 1951-57; statis. analyst Pacific Fin., L.A., 1957-59; music tchr. Mt. Olive Christian Elem. Sch., La Crescenta, Calif., 1971-73; mng. dir. Guild Opera Co., Hollywood, Calif., 1985-87; exec. dir. Glendale Regional Arts Coun., Calif., 1982-90; pub. Delos Publs., Verdugo City, Calif., 1984—; cons. For the Arts, 1986—; chief devel. officer ArtScope, Palm Desert, Calif., 1987-91; tchr. music theory Coll. Desert, Palm Desert, 1990-92. Bd. dirs. Virginia Waring Internat. Piano Competition. Contbr. articles to profl. jours. Bd. dirs. Pasadena Boys Choir, 1982—92, Glendale Chamber Orch., 1983—89, Glendale Youth Orch., 1989—90, La Quinta Open Air Mus., 1996—2000; mem. fine arts task force Glendale Unified Sch. Dist., 1983; commr. La Quinta Cultural Commn., 1994—2000; founder, pres. Coachella Valley Arts Alliance, 2000—03, 2005—. Recipient Hon. Svc. award, Calif. Congress Parents and Tchrs., 1977, Svc. to the Arts award, Glendale Reg. Arts coun., 1979, dedication of Symphony No. 1, Brooke Halpin, Pasadena, 1982. Mem.: Music Tchrs. of Desert (pres. 2004), Calif. Assn. Profl. Music Tchrs. (bd. dirs. 1968—2002), Music Tchrs. Nat. Assn. (bd. dirs. Cin. 1983—2003, treas. 1993—97, v.p. profl. activities 2001—03), Assocs. Brand Libr. and Art Ctr. (life), Steinway Soc. Riverside County (sec. 2004—05, pres. 2005—), Palm Desert C. of C. (mem. arts com. 1990—93, Svc. to Arts award 1992), Glendale C. of C. (amb. 1978—90). Republican. Presbyterian. Avocations: reading, travel. Home and Office: PO Box 947 La Quinta CA 92247-0947 Personal E-mail: kathyhull@aol.com.

HULL, LEWIS WOODRUFF, manufacturing executive; b. Scranton, Pa., Oct. 16, 1916; s. Robert Alonzo and Clara Lucelia (Woodruff) H.; m. Margaret (Burns) Carson, June 7, 1947; children: Arthur, Martha, Stephen, Rebecca. BS in Chem. Engring., MIT, 1938. Divsn. mgr. F. J. Stokes Co., Phila., 1938—52; pres. Hull Corp., 1952—2002, Hull Vac Pump Corp., Ivyland, Pa., 2003—, Hull Freeze-dry Corp., Ivyland, 2003—. Bd. dir. Hull Internat. Ltd., Girvan, Scotland, Hull-Japan Ltd., Tokyo, Advanced System Design, Evergreen, Colo., Willow Grove Bancorp, Maple Glen, Pa., Pa. Free Enterprise Found., Erie, Pa. (v.p.); dir. Mid-Atlantic Employers Assn., Trooper, Pa. Contbr. articles to profl. jours.; patentee in field. Bd. dir. Heritage Conservancy, Doylestown, Pa. Mem. Plastics Pioneers Assn. (past pres.), Am. Vacuum Soc. (past pres.), Soaring Soc. Am. (former sec.), Rotary. Republican. Avocations: sailplaning, tennis. Home: 277 W Bristol Rd Southampton PA 18966-1070 Office: Hull Vac Pump Corp 73 Steamwhistle Dr Warminster PA 18974-4875 Office Phone: 215-355-3995. Business E-Mail: claire@hullvacpumps.com.

HULL, MCALLISTER HOBART, JR., retired university administrator; b. Birmingham, Ala., Sept. 1, 1923; s. McAllister Hobart and Grace (Johnson) H.; m. Mary Muska, Mar. 23, 1946; children: John McAllister, Wendy Ann. BS with highest honors, Yale U., 1948, PhD in Physics, 1951. Tech. asst. Los Alamos (N.Mex.) Lab., 1944-46; from instr. to assoc. prof. physics Yale U., 1951-66; prof. physics, chmn. dept. Oreg. State U., 1966-69, SUNY, Buffalo, 1969-72, dean Grad. Sch., 1972-74, dean. grad. and profl. edn., 1974-77; provost U. N.Mex., 1977-85, counselor to pres., 1985-88, prof. emeritus physics, 1988—. Adviser to supt. schs., Hamden, Conn., 1958-65. Author papers, books, chpts. in books, articles in encys. Bd. dirs. Western N.Y. Reactor Facility, 1970-72; trustee N.E. Radio Obs. Corp., 1971-77; pres. Western Regional Sci. Labs., 1977; chmn. tech. adv. com. N.Mex. Energy Rsch. Inst., 1981-83, mem., 1983-88; co-chmn. Nat. Task Force on Ednl. Tech., 1984-86. Served with AUS, 1943-46. Faculty fellow Yale U., 1964-65. Fellow Am. Phys. Soc.; mem. Am. Assn. Physics Tchrs. (chmn. Oreg. sect. 1967-68). Business E-Mail: machull@unm.edu. *Experience says that everyone is sometimes wise, no one is always wise. One mustdevelop the willingness to listen for wisdom from whatever source, the judgment to identify it, the skill to use it: only in this way can one's talents, however modest or extensive, be optimally enhanced and the number of wasted efforts minimized.*

HULL, PHILIP GLASGOW, lawyer; b. St. Albans, Vt., Feb. 17, 1925; s. Charles Herman and Gladys Gertrude (Glasgow) H.; m. Gretchen Elizabeth Gaebelein, Oct. 24, 1952; children: Jeffrey R., Sanford D., Meredyth Hull Smith. AB, Middlebury Coll., 1949; LLB, Columbia U., 1952. Bar: N.Y. 1952, Fla. 1977. Staff mem. subcom. on adminstrn. internal revenue laws, com. on ways and means U.S. Ho. of Reps., Washington, 1951; assoc. Winthrop, Stimson, Putnam & Roberts, N.Y.C., 1952-63, ptnr., 1964-97, sr. counsel, 1998-2000, Pillsbury Winthrop, N.Y.C., 2001—05, Pillsbury Winthrop Shaw Pittman, 2005—. Mem. Sch. Revenue Com., Cold Spring Harbor, N.Y., 1963-65; bd. dirs. Eagle Dock Found., Cold Spring Harbor, 1971-74, People's Symphony Concerts, N.Y.C., 1977—, L.I. Philharm., 1979-81; trustee L.Am. Mission, Miami, Fla., 1969-79; elder Ctrl. Presbyn. Ch., Huntington, N.Y., 1956-78; mem. nat. mssions bd. United Presbyn. Ch., U.S.A., 1967-73; trustee Madison Avenue Presbyn. Ch., N.Y.C., 1989-94, pres., 1993-94; mem. Lloyd Harbor Conservation Adv. Coun., 1973-77. With U.S. Army, 1943-46. Ellis fellow, Kent scholar, Stone scholar Columbia U. Mem. Am. Coll. Trust and Estate Counsel, NY State Bar Assn., Christian Legal Soc. (bd. dirs. 1984-97), Fellowship Christians in Univs. and Schs. (trustee 1983-90), Univ. Club NYC (bd. dirs. 1986-90), Cold Spring Harbor Beach Club, Blue Key, Phi Beta Kappa. Office: Pillsbury Winthrop 1540 Broadway New York NY 10036-4039 Office Phone: 212-858-1502.

HULL, RAYMOND WHITFORD, public relations executive; b. Cohoes, N.Y., Oct. 13, 1946; s. Raymond W. and J. Ruth (Barber) H. BS, Syracuse U., 1971. Spl. asst. to Gov. Nelson A. Rockefeller, Albany, N.Y., 1971; conf. asst. to commr. N.Y. State Dept. Environ. Conservation, Albany, 1971-74; exec. dir. Spl. Joint Legis. Commn. on Petroleum Distbn., Albany, 1974-75; asst. headmaster Hoosac Sch., Hoosick, N.Y., 1975-77; area coordinator N.Y. State Assembly, Albany, 1977-79; staff dir. N.Y. State Senate Com. on Energy, Albany, 1979-85; dir. pub. affairs Niagara Mohawk Power Corp., Albany, 1985-89; pub. affairs cons. Albany, 1990-96; assoc. commr. N.Y. State Dept. Motor Vehicles, Albany, 1996—. V.p. Rensselaer City Sch. Bd., N.Y., 1981-86; treas. bd. trustees Hoosac Sch., 1974-81, Rennsselaer City Hist. Soc., 1980—, pres., 1994; trustee Rennselaer county hist. Soc., 1986-94. Mem.: Ft. Orange (Albany); SAR (N.Y.C.). Republican. Episcopalian. Avocations: historical architecture, art. Home: The Patroon Agts House 15 Forbes Ave Rensselaer NY 12144-1622 E-mail: RayHull@aol.com.

HULL, RICHARD FRANKLIN, insurance brokerage executive; b. N.Y.C., Nov. 8, 1931; s. Washington and Emily G. (Stevenson) H.; children: Richard Franklin, David Townsend, Christopher Cornelius. Student, U. Va., 1953. Underwriter Crum & Forster Group, N.Y.C., 1953-56; pres. Hull & Co., Washington, 1956-62, Ft. Lauderdale, Fla., 1962—. Served with USMC, 1950-53. Mem. Am. Assn. Mng. Gen. Agts., Nat. Assn. Profl. Surplus Lines Assn., Ill. Surplus Lines Assn., Nat. Assn. Ins. Agts., Fla. Assn. Ins. Agts., Profl. Ins. Agts. Assn., Ind. Agts. Assn., Balboa Bay Club, Lauderdale Yacht Club, Lago Mar Country Club, Lloyd's Yacht Club, Rod and Reel Club, Ocean Reef Club, Lyford Cay Club, Cat Cay Club, Jockey Club, Royal Nassau Sailing Club, City of London Club. Home: 2401 Del Lago Dr Fort Lauderdale FL 33316-2301 Office: 2150 S Andrews Ave Fort Lauderdale FL 33316-3432 E-mail: rhull@hullco.com.

HULL, ROBERT JOE, lawyer; b. Ft. Monmouth, N.J., Dec. 16, 1944; s. Thurman Beuford and Helen Louise (Bracey) H.; m. Susan Diane Hull, Mar. 12, 1966; 1 child, Robert Steven. BA, U. Tex., 1966, JD, 1969. Bar: Tex. 1969, Calif. 1970, U.S. Dist. Ct. (ctrl. dist.) Calif. 1970, U.S. Ct. Appeals (9th cir.) 1970, U.S. Tax. Ct. 1971, U.S. Supreme Ct. 1992. Assoc. Sheppard, Mullin, Richter & Hampton, L.A., 1969-76, ptnr., 1976-98, Bracewell & Patterson LLP, Houston, 1998—. Co-author: Representing Start-Up Companies, 1992, (annual) ABA Sales & Use Tax Handbook; mem. editorial bd., contbr. Jour. Multistate Taxation, 1991—. Mem. Tex. Bar Found., Brae Burn Country Club, Houstonian Golf Club, Houston Club. Avocation: golf. Home: 2607 Sutton Ct Houston TX 77027-5246 Office: Bracewell & Giuliani LLP S Twr Penzoil Pl 711 Louisiana St Ste 2300 Houston TX 77002-2770 Office Phone: 713-221-1589. Business E-Mail: joe.hull@bracewellgiuliani.com.

HULL, ROGER HAROLD, academic administrator; b. NYC, June 18, 1942; s. Max Harold and Magda Mary (Stern) H.; children: Roberto Franklin, Lincoln Macgregor. AB cum laude, Dartmouth Coll., 1964; LL.B., Yale U., 1967; LL.M., U. Va., 1972, S.JD, 1974; LHD, Rockford Coll., 1988; LLD, Beloit Coll., 1992. Bar: N.Y. 1968. Assoc. firm White & Case, N.Y.C., 1967—71; spl. counsel to gov., Va., 1971—74; spl. asst. to chmn., dep. staff dir. Interag. Task Force Law of Sea, NSC, 1974—76; v.p. devel. Syracuse U., 1976—79, v.p. devel. and planning, 1979—81; pres. Beloit (Wis.) Coll., 1981—90, Union Coll., Schenectady, 1990—; chancellor Union U., 1990—. Mem. U.S. del. Law of Sea Conf., 1974-76; adj. prof. Syracuse Univ. Law Sch., 1976-81; bd. visitors Coll. William and Mary, Williamsburg, Va., 1970-74; mem. pub. instns. task force Assn. Gov. Bds., 1975. Author: The Irish Triangle, 1976; co-author: Law and Vietnam, 1968. Co-founder, vice chair Schenectady 2000. Named Schenectady County Person of Yr., 1998, Patroon, 1999, Schnectady C. of C. Exec. of Yr., 2002; recipient Cmty. Leadership award, 1999. Mem. Am. Soc. Internat. Law, Univ. Club Office: Union Coll Pres Office Schenectady NY 12308 Office Phone: 518-388-6101. E-mail: hullr@union.edu.

HULL, SPRING SASHA, researcher; b. Wichita, Kans., Apr. 21, 1979; d. Dennis Cecil and Eugenia Lynn Richardson; m. Daniel Ely Hull, Aug. 5, 2000; 1 child, Sasha Elle. BA, Wichita State U., 2002, MA, 2004. Grad. tchg. asst. Wichita State U., 2002—; psychol. test adminstr. Ctr. For Human Devel., 2003—. Mem.: Human Factors and Ergonomics Soc. Office: Wichita State U 1845 Fairmount Wichita KS 67260 Office Phone: 316-978-3170. Personal E-mail: sshull@wichita.edu.

HULL, SUZANNE WHITE, writer, retired cultural organization administrator; b. Orange, N.J., Aug. 24, 1921; d. Gordon Stowe and Lillian (Siegling) White; m. George I. Hull, Feb. 20, 1943 (dec. Mar. 1990); children: George Gordon, James Rutledge, Anne Elizabeth Hull Sheldon. BA with honors, Swarthmore Coll., 1943; MSLS, U. So. Calif., 1967. Mem. staff Huntington Libr., Art Gallery and Bot. Gardens, San Marino, Calif., 1969-86, dir. adminstrn. and pub. svcs., 1972-86, also prin. officer. Cons. Women Writers Project, Brown U., 1989-2001. Author: Chaste, Silent and Obedient, English Books for Women, 1475-1640, 1982, 88, Women According to Men: The World of Tudor-Stuart Women, 1996, Japanese edit., 2003; editor: State of the Art in Women's Studies, 1986. Charter pres. Portola Jr. HS PTA, LA, 1960-62; pres. Children's Svc. League, 1963-64, YWCA, LA, 1967-69; alumni coun. Swarthmore Coll., 1959-62, 83-86, mem.-at-large, 1986-89; adv. bd. Hagley Mus. and Libr., Wilmington, Del., 1983-86, Betty Friedan Think Tank, U. So. Calif., 1985-93, Early Modern Englishwoman: A Facsimile Libr. Essential Works, 1995-2001; hon. life mem. Calif. Congress Parents and Tchrs.; bd. dirs. Pasadena Planned Parenthood Assn., 1978-83, adv. com., 1983-2004; founder-chmn. Swarthmore-LA Connection, 1984-85, bd. dirs., 1985-92; founder Huntington Women's Studies Seminar, 1984, steering com., 1984-91, adv. bd., 1991-96; organizing com. Soc. for Study of Early Modern Women, 1993-94; hon. mem. Huntington Women's Com. Mem. Monumental Brass Soc. (U.K.), Renaissance Soc., Brit. Studies Conf., Western Assn. Women Historians, Soc. Study of Early Modern Women, Authors Guild, Beta Phi Mu (chpt. dir. 1981-84).

HULL, THOMAS A., credit union executive; b. Binghamton, N.Y., June 5, 1963; m. Maureen A. Moody; children: Tommy J., Molly F. MS, Syracuse U., 1992. V.p., chief info. officer Welch Allyn, Skaneateles, NY, 2002—04, Visions Fed. Credit Union, Endicott, NY, 2004—. Dir., youth commr. Hillcrest Cmty. Assn., Binghamton, 1999—2004; bd. dirs. Fenton Cmty. Assn., Binghamton, 1999—2004. Home: 1214 Cornell Ave Binghamton NY 13901 Office: Visions Fed Credit Union 3301 Country Club Rd Endicott NY 13760 Office Phone: 605-321-0550. Personal E-mail: thull@visionsfcu.org.

HULL, THOMAS GRAY, federal judge; b. 1926; m. Joan Brandon; children: Leslie, Brandon, Amy. Student, Tusculum Coll.; JD, U. Tenn., 1951. Atty. Easterly and Hull, Greeneville, Tenn., 1951-63; mem. Tenn. Ho. of Reps., 1955-65; atty., prin. Thomas G. Hull, 1951-72; chief clk. Tenn. Ho. of Reps., 1969-70; judge 20th Jud. Cir., Greeneville, Morristown and Rogersville, Tenn., 1972-79; legal counsel to Tenn. Gov. Lamar Alexander, 1979-81; judge U.S. Dist. Ct. (ea. dist.) Tenn., 1983—. Served as cpl. U.S. Army, 1944-46. Mem. Tenn. Bar Assn. (chmn. East dist. com. 1969), Greenville Bar Assn. (pres. 1969-71), Tenn. Jud. Conf. (del. 1972-79, vice chmn. 1974-75, com. to draft uniform charges for trial judges). Republican. Office: Office of US Dist Judge 220 W Depot St Greeneville TN 37743*

HULL, WILLIAM EDWARD, theology educator; b. Birmingham, Ala., May 28, 1930; s. William Edward and Margaret (King) H.; m. Julia Wylodine Hester, July 26, 1952; children: David William, Susan Virginia. BA, Samford U., 1951; MDiv, So. Bapt. Theol. Sem., Louisville, 1954, PhD, 1960; postgrad., U. Gottingen, Germany, 1962—63, Harvard U., 1971. Ordained to ministry Bapt. Ch., 1950. Pastor Beulah Bapt. Ch., Wetumpka, Ala., 1950-51, Cedar Hill Bapt. Ch., Owenton, Ky., 1952-53, 1st Bapt. Ch., New Castle, Ky., 1953-58; from instr. to assoc. prof. So. Bapt. Theol. Sem., Louisville, 1954-67, prof., 1967-75, dean theology and provost, 1969-75; pastor 1st Bapt. Ch., Shreveport, La., 1975-87; provost Samford U., Birmingham, 1987-96, Univ. prof., 1987-2000, rsch. prof., 2000—. Author: Gospel of John, 1964, Broadman Bible Commentary, 1970, Beyond the Barriers, 1981, Love in Four Dimensions, 1982, The Christian Experience of Salvation, 1987, Southern Baptist Higher Education: Retrospect and Prospect, 2001, The Quest for Spiritual Maturity, 2004, The Four-Way Test: Core Values of the Rotary Movement, 2004, (with others): Professor in the Pulpit, 1963, The Truth That Makes Men Free, 1966, Salvation in Our Time, 1978, Set Apart for Service, 1980, Celebrating Christ's Presence Through the Spirit, 1981, The Twentieth Century Pulpit, Vol. II, 1981, Minister's Manual, 1983-87, 2000, 02, 03, 04, Biblical Preaching: An Expositor's Treasury, 1983, Preaching in Today's World, 1984, Heralds to a New Age, 1985, Getting Ready for Sunday: A Practical Guide for Worship Planning, 1989, Best Sermons 2, 1989, The University Through the Eyes of Faith, 1998, Putting Women in Their Place: Moving Beyond Gender Stereotypes in Church and Home, 2003; contbr. articles to profl. publs. Mem. Futureshape Shreveport (La.) Commn., 1985-87. Recipient Denominational Svc. award Samford U., 1974, Liberty Bell award Shreveport Bar Assn., 1984, Brotherhood and Humanitarian award NCCJ, 1987, Charles D. Johnson Outstanding Educator award Assn. So. Bapt. Colls. and Schs., 1999. Mem. Nat. Assn. Bapt. Profs. Religion (pres. 1967-68), Am. Acad. Religion, Soc. Bibl. Lit., The Club (Birmingham), Vestavia Country Club (Birmingham), Rotary, Phi Kappa Phi, Phi Eta Sigma, Omicron Delta Kappa. Baptist. Home: 435 Vesclub Way Birmingham AL 35216-1357 Office Phone: 205-726-4030. Business E-Mail: wehull@samford.edu.

HULLETT, SANDRAL, hospital administrator, health facility administrator; b. Birmingham, Ala. BS in Biology, Ala. A&M U., 1967; MD, Med. Coll. of Pa., 1976; MPH, U. Ala., Birmingham, 1987, LHD (hon.), 1999. Lic. home nursing adminstr., Ala., 1988. Resident in family practice; physician, dir. Family HealthCare of Ala.; exec. dir. West Ala. Health Svcs., Inc., 1976—2001; interim dir. Cooper Green Hosp., Birmingham, 2001, CEO, med. dir., 2001—. Project dir., prin. investigator grants NCI, The Robert Wood Johnson Found., The Kellogg Found., Nat. Heart, Lung and Blood Inst., The Ford Found.; mem. practicing physicians adv. coun. U.S. Dept. HHS, Intercultural Cancer Coun.; mem. steering com. Ala. Partnership for Cancer Control in Underserved Populations; adv. com. Minority Med. Edn. Program; treasurer Nat. Assn. Public Hospitals & Health Sys., 2003—. Contbr. articles to profl. jours. Active numerous civic orgns. including Ala. Women's Hall of Fame, Leadership Am., Family Practice Rural Health Bd.; bd. trustees U. Ala., 1982—2001; trustee U. Ala. System, 1995—2001; bd. dirs. UAB Health System. Named Rural Practitioner of the Yr., Nat. Rural Health Assn.; named one of Top 100 Black Physicians in Am., Black Enterprise Mag., 2001; recipient Clin. Recognition award for edn. and tng., Nat. Assn. Cmty. Health Ctrs., 1993, Disting. Leadership award, Leadership Ala., 1996, Rural Leadership Image award, Nat. Black Chs. Family Coun., 1998, Women in Sci. award, Environmental & Occupational Health Sci. Inst., 2002. Mem.: Inst. of Medicine of NAS (com. on environ. justice, com. on changing mkt., managed care and the future viability of safety). Office: Cooper Green Hosp 1515 6th Ave S Birmingham AL 35462: West Alabama Health Svcs PO Box 599 Eutaw AL 35462

HULLETTE, ROBERT SCOTT, minister; b. Fort Jackson, SC, Mar. 2, 1970; s. Austin Lee and Ilan Gallion Hullette; m. Charity McRae, July 1, 1989. B Christian Ministry cum laude, Lee U., 2004. Ordained bishop Ch. of God, 2001. Assoc. pastor Valdese (NC) Ch. of God, 1995—2002; sr. pastor Cooleemee (NC) Ch. of God, 2002—. State youth and Christian edn. bd. mem. Western NC Ch. of God, Charlotte, 2002—04. Active foster parenting program; mem. Davie County Ministerial Assn., Mocksville, NC, 2003. Mem. Ch. Of God. Avocations: reading, exercise. Office: Cooleemee Ch of God PO Box 357 Cooleemee NC 27014 Business E-Mail: pastor@coolcog.org.

HULLS, JAMES ROBERT, emergency physician; b. Columbus, Ohio, Sept. 5, 1947; s. Charles Robert and Margaret Rose (Chichka) Hulls; m. Suzanne Lynn Evans, Dec. 18, 1971; children: Michelle, Kristin. BA, Ohio State U., 1969, MD, 1973. Diplomate Am. Bd. Emergency Medicine, Am. Bd. Forensic Examiners, 2004. Resident U. South Fla., 1973-74; emergency physician Univ. Cmty. Hosp., Tampa, Fla., 1974—, asst. dir. emergency dept., 1993-96, 98-99; asst. dir. Franklin, Favata Hulls, Md., 1989—; co-dir. emergency dept. Suncoast Hosp., 2005—. Med. advisor City of Tampa Fire Rescue, 1978—96; clin. preceptor emergency medicine Nova U. Coll. Medicine, 1994—99, clin. asst. prof., 1999—; preceptor physician assts. program U. Nebr., 1998—99. V.p. North Hillsborough chpt. Am. Heart Assn., 1996—97, pres., 1997—98. Fellow: Am. Coll. Emergency Physicians; mem.: AMA (life), Hillsborough County Med. Assn. (mem. editl. bd. 1993—, restaurant reviewer Bulletin mag. 1997—99, 2001—). Methodist. Avocations: photography, travel, diving, swimming. Office: Univ Cmty Hosp 3100 E Fletcher Ave Tampa FL 33613-4613

HULME, POLLY ADELE, family practice nurse practitioner, educator; d. William Edward and Lucy Vivian Hulme; 1 child, Alberto Lazo-Hulme. BSN, Pacific Luth. U., 1971—75; MA, U. of Minn., 1976—80; MSN, U. of Tex. at Arlington, 1990—92; PhD, U. of Iowa, 1992—97. RN Nebr., 1975, cert. family nurse practitioner, ANA, 1992. Staff rn Unity Hosp., Fridley, Minn., 1975—78; float rn Med. Pers. Pool, Mpls., 1978—81; nursing instr. Minn. State U.- Mankato, 1979—80, Stella Maris Escuela de Enfermeria, Zacapu, Mexico, 1981—82; english instr. Universidad Autonoma de Benito Juarez de Oaxaca, Mexico, 1982—85; health careers instr. Humbert Humphrey Job Corps Ctr., St. Paul, 1986—87; health services mgr. Laredo Job Corps Ctr., Tex., 1987—90; nurse practitioner Proteus Migrant Health Program, Muscatine, Iowa, 1993—96, Planned Parenthood of Greater Iowa, 1996—97; assoc. prof. U. of Nebr. Med. Ctr., Coll. of Nursing, 1998—. Nurse practitioner SONA Family Health Care Ctr., Omaha, 1998—; out-patient self-management diabetes program adv. com. Nebr. Med. Ctr., 2002—. Author: (research article) Child Abuse & Neglect; contbr. articles to profl. jours. Recipient Rsch. Presentation award, Am. Acad. of Nurse Practitioners, 1993; fellow, U. of Iowa, 1993—94, Nat. Insitutue of Nursing Rsch., 1994—97; grantee, Sigma Theta Tau, Gamma Chpt., 1996—97, U.S. HHS, 1999—2002. Mem.: Nat. Orgn. of Nurse Practitioner Faculties, Midwest Nursing Rsch. Soc., Sigma Theta Tau, ANA, Am. Acad. of Nurse Practitioners (nebr. rep. 2000—04). Lutheran. Avocation: gardening. Office: Univ of Nebr Med Ctr 985330 Nebr Med Ctr Omaha NE 68198-5330 Office Phone: 402-559-6563. Business E-Mail: phulme@unmc.edu.

HULSE, ROBERT DOUGLAS, high technology executive; b. Niagara Falls, N.Y., Aug. 16, 1943; s. Robert Edwin and Helen Louise (Kenny) H.; m. Nancy Louise Musser, Aug. 20, 1966 (div. 1986); children: Anne Warren, Robert Alexander; m. Karen Alice Karlberg, Dec. 31, 1987. AB, Princeton U., 1965; SMChemE, MIT, 1966, SM in Mgmt., 1968. Mgr. bus. analysis Halcon Internat. Inc., N.Y.C., 1968-73, dir. bus. planning, 1973-76; v.p., gen. mgr. Halcon Catalyst Industries, Little Ferry, N.J., 1976-82; v.p. planning & devel. Engelhard Industries, Iselin, N.J., 1982-84; pres., chief exec. officer i-STAT Corp., Princeton, N.J., 1984-86, Sunstone Inc., Dayton, N.J., 1986-87; vice chmn. Princeton Entrepreneurial Resources, 1988-90; pres., chief exec. officer SDTX Technologies, Inc., Princeton, 1989—; v.p. bus. devel. Enzon, Inc., Piscataway, N.J., 1991-94; exec. dir. The Sage Group, Bridgewater, N.J., 1995—, also bd. dirs.; gen. ptnr. SAE Ventures, New Canaan, Conn., 1997-2001; pres., COO Hemispherx Biopharma, Inc., Phila., 1996—97, 2005—. Cons. in field; dir. SDTX Technologies, Inc., Princeton, 1989—; pres., dir. Captiva Technologies, Princeton, 1989—; dir. Carnegie Venture Resources, Inc., Princeton, The Sage Group, Bridgewater; mem. adv. bd. Commercialization Ctr. for Innovative Tech., New Brunswick. Dir. Gotham Light Opera Soc., N.Y.C., 1969-73; treas. Bloomingdale House of Music, N.Y.C., 1979-84. Named Univ. scholar Princeton U., 1961. Mem. The Licensing Execs. Soc., Soc. Competitive Intelligence Profls., Controlled Release Soc., Princeton Club NY, The Union League Club, Doubles, Sigma Xi, Phi Beta Kappa. Republican. Episcopalian. Avocations: chess, tennis. Office: The Sage Group 3322 Rte 22 W Bldg 2 Ste 201 Branchburg NJ 08876 Home: 706 Sayre Drive Princeton NJ 08540 Office Phone: 908-231-9644 21. Personal E-mail: Doughulse@aol.com.

HULSE, RUSSELL ALAN, physicist; b. NYC, Nov. 28, 1950; s. Alan Earle and Betty Joan (Wedemeyer) Hulse. BS, Cooper Union, 1970; MS, U. Mass., 1972, PhD, 1975. Rsch. assoc. Nat. Radio Astronomy Observatory, Charlottesville, Va., 1975—77; mem. tech. staff Princeton U. Plasma Physics Lab., 1977—80, staff rsch. physicist, 1980—84, rsch. physicist, 1984—92, prin. rsch. physicist, 1992—. Vis. prof. physics, math., sci. edn. U. Tex., Dallas, 2003. Contbr. articles to profl. jours. Recipient Nobel prize in physics, 1993. Fellow: Inst. of Physics, Am. Phys. Soc.; mem.: Soc. for Industrial & Applied Math, Am. Astron. Soc. Achievements include discovery of first binary pulsar - a twin star system that provides a rare natural laboratory in which to test Albert Einstein's prediction that moving objects emit gravitational waves. Avocations: clay target shooting, bird watching, cross country skiing, canoeing, hiking. Office: Princeton Plasma Physics Lab MS32 C-Site B 145 A PPL Box 451 Princeton NJ 08543-0451*

HULSEBOSCH, DANIEL JOSEPH, historian, educator; b. Scarsdale, N.Y., Nov. 6, 1965; s. Edward J. and Jane Mangan Hulsebosch. AB, Colgate U., 1987; JD, Columbia U., 1991; AM, Harvard U., 1993, PhD, 1999. Assoc. prof. Sch. of Law St. Louis (Mo.) U., 1999—2005; prof. NYU Sch. Law, N.Y.C., NY, 2005—. Cons. in field. Author: Constituting Empire: New York and the Transformation of Constitutionalism in the Atlantic World, 1664-1830, 2005; contbr. articles to profl. jours. Fellow Samuel I. Golieb fellowship, N.Y. U. Sch. of Law, 1998—99; grantee Whiting fellowship in the Humanities, Harvard U., 1996—97. Mem.: Soc. for Historians of the Early Republic, Am. Soc. for Legal History, Omohundro Inst. for Early Am. History and Culture (assoc.), Phi Beta Kappa. Office: NYU Sch Law 40 Washington Sq S New York NY 10012 E-mail: daniel.hulsebosch@nyu.edu.

HULSEMAN, ROBERT L., manufacturing executive; b. 1932; Pres. Solo Cup Co., Highland Park, Ill., 1953-90, pres., CEO, 1990—, also dir.; pres., CEO SCC Holding Co., Highland Park, Ill., also chmn., dir. Office: Solo Cup Co 1700 Old Deerfield Rd Highland Park IL 60035-3792*

HULSHOF, KENNY C., congressman; b. Sikeston, Mo., May 22, 1958; m. Renee Lynn Howell. BS in Agricultural Economics, U. Mo., 1980; JD, U. Miss., 1983. Public defender Cape Girardeau County, 1983—86, asst. prosecutor, 1986—89; special prosecutor Mo. Atty. Gen. Office, 1989—96; mem. U.S. Congress from Mo. 9th Dist., 1997—, Ways & Means Com., Ho. Budget Com., Ho. Ethics Com., Health Subcom. Rep. candidate for Boone County Prosecutor, 1992, U.S. House, 1994, 96. Mem.: Nat. Rifle Assn., Nat. Dist. Atty. Assoc., Mo. Bar Assn., Miss. Bar Assn. Republican. Roman Catholic. Office: US Ho of Reps 412 Cannon Ho Office Bldg Washington DC 20515-2509*

HULSTRAND, GEORGE EUGENE, lawyer; b. Cannon Falls, Minn., Aug. 3, 1918; s. John George and Alice Elizabeth (Holm) H.; m. Mabel Elizabeth Ericson, Sept. 7, 1946; children: George E. Jr., Brian Douglas, Darlene Lucette, Jeanne Louise. BA, Gustavus Adolphus Coll., 1943; JD, Yale U., 1946. Bar: Minn. 1947, U.S. Dist. Ct. Minn. 1951, U.S. Supreme Ct. 1977, U.S. Ct. Claims 1990. Assoc. Roy A. Hendrickson, Willmar, Minn., 1947-53; ptnr. Hulstrand, Anderson, Larson, Hanson & Saunders, Willmar, 1953-97; pvt. practice Willmar, 1997—. Asst. county atty. Kandiyohi County, Willmar, 1947-50. Contbr. articles to mags. Mem. Willmar City Coun., 1953-56; chmn. Willmar Planning Commn., 1956-67, 74-80, Kandiyohi County Dem.-Farmer-Labor Party, Willmar, 1957-72; bd. dirs. Willmar Cmty. Coll. Found., 1965-94. Mem. ABA, Minn. Bar Assn. (bd. govs. 1977-83, cert. sr. counselor 1997), 12th Dist. Bar Assn., Am. Judicature Soc., Willmar Jaycees (Disting. Service award 1952, Outstanding Citizen award 1979). Lodges: Lions, Elks. Lutheran. Avocations: music, writing, golf, travel. Home: 325 N 7th St Willmar MN 56201 Office: PO Box 1860 Wilmar Bldg 201 4th St SW Willmar MN 56201-1860 Office Phone: 350-235-4307.

HULTGREN, DENNIS EUGENE, farmer, management consultant; b. Union County, S.D., Mar. 19, 1929; s. John Alfred and Esther Marie (Johnson) H.; m. Nelda Ethelyn Olson, Aug. 3, 1957; children: Nancy Hultgren Forsythe, Jean Hultgren Doty, Jahn Dennis, Ruth Dorothy Hultgren Henneman. Grad. high sch. Farmer, Union County, 1953—. Commr., chmn. Union County Planning and Zoning Bd., 1972-83; mem. bd. bylaw revision Union County Electric Co., 1983-85. Pres. bd. Union Creek Cemetry, 1958—; pres. bd. mgrs. Union-Sayles Watershed Dist., 1965-70; exec. bd. S.D. Farm Bur., Union County, 1996—, pres., 1998—; treas. Sioux Valley Twp., Union County, 1980—; treas., bd. dirs. W. Union Sch., 1957-67; chmn. Union County Sch. Bd., 1961-68; pres. Alcester (S.D.) Sch. Bd., 1970-77; chmn. Alcester PTA, 1967-68; mem. tech. bd. rev. Southeastern Coun. Govts., Sioux Falls, 1976-77; bd. dirs. Siouxland Interstate Met. Planning Coun., Sioux City, 1977-83, sec. coun. ofcls., 1978-83; bd. dirs. Old Opera House Cmty. Theater, Akron, Iowa, Akron Area Action Assn., 1983-85, Akron Devel. Corp., 1985-90; Rep. precinct committeeman, 1970, Union County Rep. Ctrl. Com., 1970—; chmn. S.D. State Bd. Equalization, 1987-95, S.D. State Resolutions Com.; mem. synod stewardship bd. Western Iowa Synod Luth. Ch., 1987-90, elected synod assembly bus. and coun. com., 1991-93, synod bus. and coun. com., 1997-99, synod coun. Western Iowa Synod, 1997-2000; S.D. del. Rep. nat. Conv., New Orleans, 1988. Served with AUS, 1951-53, Korea. Decorated Combat Infantry Badge, 3 Bronze Battle Stars; recipient Outstanding Dedication and Svc. award Old Opera House Cmty. Theatre, 1984, Sioux City Siouxland Disting. Citizen award Siouxland Interstate Met. Planning Coun., 1983, Jefferson award Sta. KELO-TV, 1985, Outstanding Cmty. Svc. award Lions Internat., 1985. Mem. NRA, Farm Bur., Farmers Union (exec. bd. Union County 1987-90), S.D. Livestock Feeders Assn., Nat. Cattlemen's Assn., Associated Sch. Bds. S.D. (Merit award 1976), Am. Legion (exec. bd. Akron 1978-92, comdr. Akron 1980-81, 85-86, historian 1981-96, trustee 1983-90, 96—, vice comdr. 9th dist. 1989, chmn. athletics and contest com. Dept. of Iowa Am. Legion, 1991-92, 97-99, 2002-03, judge adv. 9th dist. Iowa 1993—), VFW (Alcester, S.D., vice-comdr. 1995-97, comdr. 2000-02). Lutheran (mem. bd. 1967-70, 82-84, 90-93, 2001—, lay chmn. 1970, 82-93, chmn. centennial com. 1974, chmn. 125th anniversary com. 1999, chmn. ch. bd. 2001-03). Address: Hulteboda Farm 47953 309th St Akron IA 51001-7575 E-mail: dennel@ascnet.com.

HULTGREN, GLENN M., chiropractor; b. Westby, Mont., Dec. 27, 1932; s. Luther E. and Mae Agnes (Englar) H.; m. M. Marylou Johnston, Feb. 26, 1955; children: Bonnie, Robert, Barry, Bethel. Student, Jamestown Coll., 1950-52; DC, Palmer Coll. Chiropractic, Davenport, Iowa, 1955. Cert. Internat. Chiropractors Coun. Imaging. Pvt. practice, Bismarck, ND, 1955—58, Fort Collins, Colo., 1958—. Mem. Bd. Chiropractic Examiners, Colo., 1982-88; mem. Ctr. for Bioethics and Human Dignity, Chgo., 1997—; pres. Christian Bioethics Awareness, Inc. Mem. Am. Back Soc., AAAS, Christian Chiropractors Assn. (exec. sec. 1958—), Colo. Chiropractic Assn. (pres. 1974), Congress Chiropractic State Assns. (pres. 1977-80), Gideons. Home: 1913 Sequoia Fort Collins CO 80525 Office: 4745 Boardwalk Bldg C-1 Fort Collins CO 80525 Office Phone: 970-223-1941. E-mail: gmhultgren@bigplanet.com.

HULTQUIST, TIMOTHY ALLEN, investment banker; b. Faribault, Minn., Apr. 1, 1950; s. Wayne Burdette and Helen Sorg (Armitage) H.; m. Cynthia Marie Mealhouse, May 29, 1972; children: Kirsten Lee, Matthew Anton, Andrew Thomas. BA summa cum laude, Macalester Coll., 1972; MBA, U. Chgo., 1975. Asst. mgr. First Nat. Bank Chgo., London, 1975-76, asst. v.p. N.Y.C., 1976-79, v.p., fgn. exchange mgr. Chgo., 1979-81, sr. v.p. fgn. exchange, 1981-82; prin. Morgan Stanley & Co., Inc., N.Y.C., 1982-84, mng. dir., 1985-95, adv. dir., 1995—, chief London office, 1988-92, mem. mgmt. com., 1988-95; head fgn. exch., commodities Morgan Stanley Svcs., 1992-95. Bd. dirs., Depository Trust Co., 1993-95; mem. Fgn. Exch. Com., 1992-95. Trustee Macalester Coll., St. Paul, 1985—, vice chmn. bd., 1992-94, chair bd. dirs. 1995-2000; pres. Hultquist Found., 1992—; trustee Russell Sage Found., 1995—. Mem. Coun. on Fgn. Rels., Winged Foot Golf Club, Greenwich Country Club, Phi Beta Kappa. Congregationalist. Avocations: golf, music, reading, travel. Office: Morgan Stanley & Co Inc 1221 Avenue Of The Americas New York NY 10020-1008

HULTSTRAND, CHARLES JOHN, architect; b. Mt. Vernon, Ohio, Dec. 26, 1951; s. Donald M. and Marjorie R. (Richter) H.; m. Kathi, Brooke, Andrew, Caroline, Clay, Kristi, Scott. BSE, Princeton U., 1974; MArch, Rice U., 1977. Registered architect, S.C. Assoc., project designer Golemon & Rolfe Architects, Houston, 1977-83; prin., exec. v.p., dir. of design The Boudreaux Group, Inc., Columbia, SC, 1983—2003; ptnr., dir. design Neal-Prince & Ptnrs., Greenville, SC, 2003—. Guest lectr. Clemson (S.C.) U. Coll. Architecture, 1993-2005, Cornerstone Nat. Conf. 2005; mem. steering com. Onions & Orchids Award Program, Columbia, 1988, jury mem., 1989; mem. steering com. Columbia R/UDAT Commn., 1987; v.p. Terrace Lake, Inc.; bd. dirs. Columbia Devel. Corp., Faith and Form, 2005-. Pres. parent tchr. fellowship Ben Lippen Sch., Columbia, 1991-94, mem. bd. mgrs., 1991—, v.p. bd., 1995-2000; mem. fundraising com., 1993-2002; deacon Cornerstone Presbyn. Ch., Columbia, 1988-91, First Presbyn. Ch., Columbia, 1997-99, 2000-03, vice chmn., 2001-02, chmn., 2003; mem. bd. Faith & Form, 2005-; pres. Yokemen Svc. Orgn., 1982-83; vol. ARC Hurricane Hugo Relief, 1990, SCETV Fundraising, Columbia, 1991; mem. sch. com. Princeton Alumni Assn., 2000-05. Named Columbia Small Bus. Person of Yr., Greater Columbia C. of C., 2003; recipient AIA SC Honor Award, Columbia Internat. U. Prayer Towers, 1988, St. Francis of Assisi Episcopal Ch., 1988, Brick Assn. of Carolinas Pres. Award, St. Christopher's Episcopal Ch., 1996, Merit Award Columbia Chpt. AIA, 1996, SC Conservatory, 1996, Clemson U. Student Housing, 1996, Honor Award Brick Assn. of Carolinas, 1998, Honor Award, USC Athletic Practice Faculty, 1999, Historic Columbia Found. Preservation Award, Flinn Hall Classroom Bldg., 2000, Bldg. of Yr. Award for Archtl. Steel, The Berkeley Bldg., Con/Steel Alliance, 2003. Mem. AIA (pres. S.C. chpt. 1996, v.p./pres.-elect S.C. chpt. 1995, sec.-treas. S.C. chpt. 1993-94, chmn. spkrs. bur. 1988-90, dir. Columbia sect. 1988-90, chmn. govt. affairs commn. S.C. chpt. 1990-93, bd. dirs., advisor intern devel. program 1990-94, state engr.'s com. 2002-03, 2005), S.C. Archtl. Soc. (bd. dirs./sec. 1997-99), Columbia Design League (bd. dirs. 1997-98), Columbia Coun. Archs. (pres. 1986-87, bd. dirs. 1984-87), Princeton Alumni Assn. S.C. (treas. 1990-94), Greater Columbia C. of C. Avocations: reading, walking, tennis, golf. Office: Neal-Prince & Ptnrs Ste 300 110 W North St Greenville SC 29601 Office Phone: 864-235-0405. E-mail: chuck@neal-prince.com.

HUM, VANCE YORK, technology consulting executive; b. San Francisco, Apr. 19, 1948; s. Bing Wai and Jean Bik-Tsun (Pong) H.; children: Matthew Ta, Christina Lee, Jonathan Derek-Lee. BSEE, U. Md., 1971, postgrad., 1983—, George Washington U., 1977—83. Engr. Singer-Link Divsn., Silver Spring, Md., 1970; engr., field engr. Bendix Field Engring., Columbia, Md., 1971-72; primary examiner U.S. Patent & Trademark Bd., Arlington, Va., 1972-83; v.p. ops. Cheung Labs., Inc., Lanham-Seabrook, Md., 1983-86; v.p. fin. Cheung Labs. Inc., Lanham-Seabrook, Md., 1985-86; v.p. ops. Century Techs., Inc., Silver Spring, 1988-89; CEO, bd. dirs. Marc's Distbg., Inc., Jessup, Md., 1987-88; CEO, pres. I.M. Systems Group, Inc., Kensington, Md., 1986-87, 89—. Chmn. bd. dirs. I.M. Systems Group, Inc., Md., 1989—; chmn. audit/supervisory com. Lee Fed. Credit Union, Washington, 1977-83; adv. bd. Pacific Savs. and Loan Assn., McLean, Va., 1979-80; chmn. strategic planning com. Nat. Assn. Corp. Dirs., Balt.-Washington, 1989; mem. No. Va. Technology Coun., 2001. Troop treas. Boy Scouts Am., Bethesda/Chevy Chase, Md., 1993—; hon. co-chmn. Bus. Adv. Coun.; active Nat. Rep. Congrl. Com. Mem. Herndon (Va.) C. of C., Monte Jade Sci. and Tech. Assn. Greater Washington D.C. Area (bd. dirs. 1999). Avocations: tennis, golf, Karate, skiing, gardening, jiu-jitsu. Office: IM Sys Group Inc 3401 Bexhill Pl Kensington MD 20895-3105 Business E-Mail: humv@imsg.com.

HUMANN, L. PHILLIP, bank executive; BA Auburn U., 1967, MS Auburn U., 1969. Chmn., CEO Trust Company Bank, Atlanta, 1985—89; exec. v.p. SunTrust Banks, Inc., Atlanta, 1989—90, sr. v.p., 1990—91; pres. SunTrust (formerly SunTrust Banks, Inc.), Atlanta, 1991—, chmn., CEO, 1998—.

Mem. bd. dirs. Coca-Cola Enterprises Inc., Equifax Inc., Haverty Furniture Companies, Inc. Office: SunTrust 303 Peachtree St NE Atlanta GA 30308-3201 also: PO Box 4418 Atlanta GA 30308-4418*

HUMANN, RICHARD, artist; s. Richard Charles Human and Estella Marie Chonko; m. Susan Darmiento, Nov. 6, 1993. AAS, Harriman Coll., 1981. Represented by Lance Fung Gallery, NYC, 1997—. Installation, Psycho Killer, Evidence of My Being, A Childish Fear, exhibitions include Palazzo Zorzi, Venice Biennale, Venice, 2003, Kemi (Finland) Art Mus., Archivio Emily Harvey, Venice, Italy, 2003, Body Lang., Karolyn Sherwood Gallery, Des Moines, 2003, Possessions for Judgment Day, Project Row Houses, Houston, TX, exhibited in group shows at NY Art, S*MOVA (Sonoma Mus. of Visual Arts, Sonoma, CA, 2002, Mapping the Vicinity, Voorkamer Gallery, Lier, Belgium, 2002, Ssamzie Site Specific, Ssamzie Space, Seoul, Korea, 2001, The Last Waltz, Gallery St. Gertrud, Malm, Sweden, 2000, The Planet Art Gallery, Cape Town, South Africa, 1998, 5 from Williamsburg, Leo Kamen Gallery, Toronto, Can., 1998.

HUMAY, PRISCILLA, artist; b. Chgo.; d. Francis Joseph and Helen (Balun) Humay; m. Joseph K. Duffy, 1988; children: Michele, Anton, Priscilla, Demetrios. B.F.A., Sch. of the Art Inst. Chgo., 1969; M.S. in Visual Design, Inst. Design, Ill. Inst. Tech., 1971; postgrad. Charles U., Prague, Czech Republic, 1972, 73. Tchr., Deerpath Art League, Lake Forest, Ill., 1983—, Jewish Cultural Ctrs., Chgo., 1971; lectr. Willowbrook High Sch., 1971, Oakton Community Coll., 1974, Morton Grove, Ill., 1974, Govs. State U., Park Forest, Ill., 1974; gallery co-dir. ARC Gallery and Ednl. Found., Chgo., 1978-79; art festival coordinator, bd. dirs. Alumni Assn. Sch. of Art Inst. Chgo., 1975, 76; med. illustrator, graphic designer, visual designer, illustrator, 1973—; tchr., lectr. Coll. Lake County, Ill., 1997-2001, Peninsula Art Sch., Door County, Wis., 2003-05, Suburban Fine Art, Highland Park, Ill., 2004-05, pub. rels. dir. Nat. Bd. Colored Pencil Soc. Am., 1998-2003; Author: Best of Colored Pencil V, 1996, Best of Colored Pencil III, 1999, Colored Pencil Explorations, 2002, The Artist's Magazine, 2005; solo exhibits include Oak Park, 1967, Gallery at Garrett at Northwestern U., 1975, ARC Gallery, 1974, 76, Illini Union Gallery, U. Ill., Champaign-Urbana, 1978, Elgin Ill. Symphony, 1988, Frizzel Gallery, 2000, Portals Gallery, 2001, Catch 22 Gallery, 2005; participant group exhibits, also juried exhibit Films by Women 1974, Mus. of Art Inst. Chgo., Infusion Gallery, 2005, Eastman Gallery, 2005-, juried open spectrum David Adler Cultural Ctr., Libertyville, Ill, 1989; gallery representations include Main Bank of Chgo., Household Internat. Corp., Citizens Bank of Waukegan, Ill. Bell Telephone Collection, Kemper Group, Bonfoey Gallery, Catch 232 Gallery, Eastman Gallery, Hanson Gallery, Paul 'Ard Gallery, Customs House Gallery, Deerpath Gallery, ARC Gallery; pvt. collections include U.S., W.Ger., Holland, Czechoslovakia; juror for animated film Chgo. Internat. Film Festival, 1978, Chgo. Hist. Soc. Archives, Bauhaus Archieve, Germany, Inst. Design Archive, U. I.C.C. Libr. Pres. Lake Forest-Lake Bluff Jr. Women, 1981-82; founder, dir. Lake Forest-Lake Bluff Concerned Citizens for Peace, 1982, 83; chmn. of events Art for Nuclear Weapons Freeze at Richard Gray Gallery, Chgo., 1983; pres. Lake Bluff-Lake Forest Com. of Arden Shore Assn. Home for Boys, 1982; pres. Arden Shore Assn. Home for Boys & Girls, 1983, 84; treas. bd. Deerpath Art League, 1983, 84. Recipient Cert. of Merit Chgo. Internat. Film Festival, 1971, Jury award Evanston (Ill.) Art Festival, 1971, Purchase awards Citizens Bank of Waukegan, 1982, Household Internat. Corp. Collection, 1982, Kemper Group Collection, 1989, 2d place graphics award Fall Festival Deerpath Art League, Lake Forest, 1982, 1st Place Graphics award, 1983, 1st Place Prairie Ctr. for Arts award, Schaumburg, Ill., 2004. Mem. AAUW. E-mail: humay@comcast.net. Home and Office: 2125 Maplewood Dr Gurnee IL 60031-6313 Mailing: 138 Whistler Rd Highland Park IL 60035-5902

HUMAYUN, MARK S., ophthalmologist, educator; BS, Georgetown U., 1984; MD, Duke U. Med. Sch., 1989; PhD, U. N.C., 1994. Cert. Am. Bd. Ophthalmology, 1995, lic. Calif., 1993, Md., 1994, Fla., 1994. Clin. preceptor Duke Eye Ctr., N.C., 1993—95; asst. prof. Willmer Ophthalmology Inst., Md., 1995—99, assoc. prof., 2000—01; prof., assoc. dir. rsch. Doheny Eye Inst. at U. S.C. Sch. Medicine, L.A., 2001—. Retinal cons. Columbia Med. Plan, 1996—97; vis. prof. Kresge Eye Inst., Detroit, 1998, Oakland Eye Inst., Rochester, Mich., 1998; bd. mem. Springer Serres BMP-BME, Calif., 2001—; invited lectr. numerous univs. and assns. Author: numerous peer- and non-peer-reviewed articles and book chpts. Grantee numerous rsch. grants. Mem. Am. Ophthal. Soc., Am. Acad. Ophthalmology, AMA, Assn. Rsch. in Vision and Ophthalmology, Biomed. Engring. in Medicine and Biology Soc., IEEE Engring. in Medicine and Biology Soc., The Macula Soc., The Retina Soc., Soc. Neuroscience, Am. Soc. Retinal Specialists, Wilmer Resident Assn., Bd. Sci. Counselors for Nat. Space Biomed. Rsch. Inst. Achievements include patents for Visual Prothesis and methods of using same; Retinal Microstimulation; method for prevential outer retinal stimulation.

HUMBERT, DARREN MARK, music educator; b. Mt. Lebanon, Pa., Apr. 23, 1971; s. Harold L. and Beverley M. Humbert; m. Heather L Grimes, May 26, 2001; 1 child, Mark T. BFA, Carnegie Mellon U., 1993; MM, Duquesne U., 1996. Music instr. West Allegheny Sch. Dist., Imperial, Pa., 1997—. Percussion instr. West Allegheny H.S., 1991—. Mem.: Am. Fedn. of Musicians, Percussive Arts Soc., Pa. Music Educators Assn. Avocation: bicycling. Home: 34 South East Dr Oakdale PA 15071

HUMBERT, KIMBERLY RAMSAY, secondary school educator; b. Brookville, Pa., Jan. 20, 1972; d. Carl Frederick Ramsay and Linda Carol Ramsay-Marietta, Jon Robert Marietta (Stepfather); m. Scott A. Humbert, Feb. 1, 1997; 1 child, Matthew Scott. BS in Edn., Slippery Rock (Pa.) U., 1996. Cert. tchr. Commonwealth Pa., 1996. Student tchr. New Brighton (Pa.) Area Sch. Dist., 1996; substitute tchr. Mt. Gallitzin Acad., Baden, Pa., 1997, Connellsville (Pa.) Area Sch. Dist., 1997—98; tchr. english lang. arts Connellsville (Pa.) Area Sr. H.S., 1998—. Med. coord., coach Fayette County Spl. Olympics, Connellsville, Pa., 1998—99, sec., coach, 2003—05; conselor children's recreation United Cerebral Palsy, Butler, Pa., 1993—96, counselor adult recreation, edn., 1993—96; tchr. music, dir. program vacation bible sch. First Bapt. Ch. Fairchance, Pa., 1998—2001; dir. bell choir dir., mem. praise and worship team Ctrl. Fellowship Ch., Connellsville, Pa., 2003—05. Named Educator of Yr., Fayette C. of C., 1999—2004; recipient DisneyHand Tchr. awards, Walt Disney Co., 2005. Mem.: NEA (assoc.), Pa. State Edn. Assn. (assoc.), Phi Sigma Sigma (assoc.). Conservative-R. Baptist. Avocations: rock climbing, singing, cross stitch. Office: Connellsville Area School District 201 Falcon Drive Connellsville PA 15425-5599 Office Phone: 724-628-1350. Office Fax: 724-628-0280. E-mail: khumbert@casdfalcons.org.

HUMBLE, MONTY GARFIELD, lawyer; b. Cameron, Tex., Dec. 20, 1951; s. Don Garfield Humble and Betty Sue (Maedgen) French; m. Donell Lou Moss, Mar. 12, 1976 (div. June 1981); m. Macy A. Melton, Oct. 23, 1993; children: Megan Elizabeth, John Marshall, Nicole Marie, Crawford Melton. BA, U. Tex., 1974, JD, 1976. Assoc. Clark, Thomas, Winters and Shapiro, Austin, Tex., 1972-82, Vinson & Elkins, Houston, 1982-86, ptnr. Dallas, 1986—. Bd. dirs. Ft. Worth Ballet, 1990-94, Dallas Opera, 1987-92, Tex. Gen. Counsel Forum, 2001-2003, Tex. Nanotech. Initiative, 2002—; gen. counsel Superconducting Super Collider Devel. Authority, 1987-94; active Leadership Dallas, 1988, Greater Dallas Planning Coun.; legal adv. Dallas City Charter Revision Com., 1990; adv. coun. U. Tex. Dallas External Rsch., 2002—. Fellow Dallas Bar Found., Tex. Bar Found.; mem. ABA, State Bar Tex., Nat. Assn. Bond Lawyers (steering com. 1985-87, 94-96, bd. dirs. 2001—, treas. 2002-2003, pres.-elect 2003-04, pres. 2004—), Am. Coll. Bond Coun., Dean's Roundtable, U. Tex. Sch. Law, Health Care Fin. Mgrs. Assn. (bd. dirs. 1990-92), Crescent Club, Bent Tree Country Club, Phi Beta Kappa. Republican. Office: Vinson & Elkins LLP 2001 Ross Ave Ste 3700 Dallas TX 75201-2975 Office Phone: 214-220-7746. E-mail: mhumble@velaw.com.

HUME, BRIT (ALEXANDER BRITTON HUME), journalist; b. Washington, June 22, 1943; s. George and Virginia Powell (Minnigerode) H.; m. Clare Stoner, Feb. 10, 1965 (div. 1992); children: Louis, Virginia, Alexander Jr. (dec.); m. Kim Schiller, June 1, 1993. BA, U. Va., 1965. Reporter Hartford Times, Conn., 1965-67, UPI, Hartford, Conn., 1967, Balt. Evening Sun, 1968; fellow Washington Journalism Ctr., 1969; reporter Jack Anderson Column, Washington, 1970-72; freelance journalist Washington, 1973; cons. ABC News, Washington, 1973-76, corr., 1976-97, Capitol Hill corr., White House corr., 1989—96; columnist Washington Post Writers Group, 1987-99; joined FOX News Channel, Washington, 1996, chief Washington corr., mng. editor, 1997—, anchor Special Report with Brit Hume. Contbr. World News Tonight with Peter Jennings, Nightline and This Week ABC News; regular panelist FOX News Sunday; contbr. news analysis FOX News Channel, oversee news content. Author: Death and the Mines, 1971, Inside Story, 1974. Recipient Emmy award, 1991; Sol Taishoff Award for Excellence in Broadcast Journalism, Nat. Press Found., 2003; named Best in Bus. by Am. Journalism Rev., 1992, 94 Mem. Met. Club, Chevy Chase Club, St. Andrews Soc. Episcopal. Office: FOX News Channel 400 N Capitol St NW Ste 550 Washington DC 20001-1502*

HUME, CAMERON R., former ambassador; married; 4 children. Grad., Princeton U.; LLB, Am. U. With U.S. Fgn. Svc., 1970—, vice consul Palermo, advisor on human rights U.S. Mission to UN, mem. Sec. of State's planning staff, desk officer South Africa, polit. counselor Damascus, Beirut, dir. field sch. Tunis, advisor on Middle East, U.S. Mission to UN, 1986-90, sr. advisor, 1990, dep. chief of mission U.S. Embassy to Holy See Rome, 1991-94, minister-counselor for polit. affairs U.S. Mission to UN, 1994-97, U.S. amb. Democratic Republic of Algeria Alger-Gare, 1997—2000, U.S. amb. Republic South Africa, 2001—04. Author: The United Nations, Iran and Iraq, 1994, Ending Mozambique's War, 1994; contbr. articles to profl. jours. Coun. on Fgn. Rels. fellow, 1975-76, Harvard U. Ctr. for Internat. Affairs fellow, 1989-90; U.S. Inst. of Peace guest scholar, 1994.

HUME, ELLEN HUNSBERGER, media analyst, journalist; b. Chevy Chase, Md., Apr. 24, 1947; d. Warren Seabury and Ruth (Pedersen) H.; m. John Shattuck, Feb. 14, 1991; 1 child, Susannah; stepchildren: Jessica, Rebecca, Peter. BA, Harvard U., 1968; PhD (hon.), Daniel Webster Coll., 1990, Kenyon Coll., 2001. Reporter Somerville (Mass.) Jour., 1968-69; feature writer Santa Barbara (Calif.) News Press, 1969-70; pub. service dir., copy writer KTMS Radio, Santa Barbara, 1970-72; edn. reporter Ypsilanti (Mich.) Press, 1972-73; bus. reporter Detroit Free Press, 1973-75; met. reporter L.A. Times, 1975-77, congl. reporter Washington, 1977-83; White House corr., polit. writer Wall St. Jour., Washington, 1983-88; exec. dir. Shorenstein Ctr. on Press and Politics Harvard U., Cambridge, Mass., 1988-93; moderator The Editors TV program, Montreal, Que., 1990-93; adj. lectr. Kennedy Sch. Govt., 1991-93, Medill Sch. Journalism, 1993-94; dir. Ctr. on Media and Soc., U. Mass., Boston. Commentator Washington Week in Rev. PBS-TV, 1973—88, CNN, 1993—97; exec. dir. The Democracy Project PBS, 1996—98; cons. US-AID, 2002, Knight Found.; bd. dirs. Internews, Shorenstein Ctr. Fellow Kennedy Inst. Politics, Harvard U., 1981, Annenberg Washington Program, 1993—95. Mem.: Coun. of Fgn. Rels. Methodist. Address: 121 Hunnewell Ave Newton MA 02458 Business E-Mail: ellen.hume@umb.edu.

HUME, FREDERICK RAYMOND, electronics company executive; b. Los Angeles, Feb. 23, 1943; s. Laurence Frederick and Willetta Fredericka (Balderson) H.; m. Betty Ruth Dudley, Mar. 30, 1963; children: Joy Anne Sprague, Frederick William III. Student, Calif. State U., Long Beach, 1960-61, Biola Coll., 1961-62. Test engr. Autoretics div. Rockwell, Anaheim, Calif., 1964-67, research engr., 1967-72; mgr. new products John Fluke Mfg. Co. Inc., Everett, Wash., 1972-76, div. gen. mgr., 1976-80, v.p., 1980-88; v.p., gen. mgr. Keithley Investments, Cleve., 1988—. Bd. dirs. Artech Corp., Seattle, 1985—. Author: Transactions of IEEE, 1973. Inventor radio frequency power testing equipment, broadband spectral intensity measurement system. Chmn. Wash. High Tech. Coordinating Bd., Seattle, 1983-87; co. chmn. Jr. Achievement, Seattle, 1984. Mem. Higher Edn. Fin. Assn. (bd. dirs. 1987—), Am. Electronics Assn. (bd. dirs. 1982-86), Nat. Acad. Sci. (panel mem. 1986—), Electronics Edn. Found. (bd. dirs. 1985—), Soc. Mfg. Engrs. (sr. mem. 1983—), Precision Measurements Assn. (pres. 1978-79). Avocation: literature. Office Phone: 425-367-6213. Business E-Mail: humef@dataio.com.

HUME, JAMES BORDEN, foundation administrator, director; b. Halifax, N.S., Can., Nov. 6, 1950; s. Thomas White and Elizabeth Mae (Spears) Hume; m. Penelope Ann Morris, June 3, 1972; children: Kathryn Ann, David Stuart. BA, U. Calgary, Alta., Can., 1972. Chartered Acct. V.p. TIW Industries Ltd., Ottawa, Ont., Can., 1978-80; pres. Hume Mgmt. Cons. Ltd., Calgary, 1980-85, Kanesco Holdings Ltd., Calgary, 1985—. Pres. The Kahanoff Found., 1984—; bd. dirs. Can. West Found., Ecotrust Can., Southwestern Resources Group, The Kahanoff Found., Calgary, Hudson's Bay Co. Fellow, Inst. Chartered Accts., 2002. Mem.: Can. Inst. Chartered Accts. Office: Kahanoff Found 101 6th Ave SW Ste 105 Calgary AB Canada T2P 5K7 Office Phone: 403-237-7896. Business E-Mail: info@kahanoff.com.

HUME, SUSAN RACHEL, finance educator; b. Englewood, N.J., Aug. 25, 1952; d. Philip and Anna Ann (Petrowski) Nachtigal; m. John Elliott Hume, Dec. 27, 1975; children: Philip John, Scot Elliott. BA, Douglass Coll., 1974; MBA, Rutgers U. Grad. Sch. Mgmt., 1976; PhD, CUNY, 2003. Bank analyst N.Y. Fed. Res. Bank, 1976-77, sr. credit analyst, 1977-79; sr. comml. loan officer 1st Pa. Bank, Phila., 1979-81; asst. v.p. Mfrs. Hanover Trust Co., N.Y.C., 1982-83, v.p., 1983-84, dept. head, hedge funding and asset liability mgmt., 1984-88; adj. assoc. prof. fin. and econs. Rider Coll., 1988-90; asst. adj. prof. Fairleigh Dickinson, Madison, N.J., 1991-93; adj. prof. dept. fin. and econs. Baruch Coll., N.Y.C., 1993—. Mem. Douglass Alumnae Endowment Fund Fin. Com., 1985—; pres. Douglass Coll. Class of 1974, 1990-; mem. internat. seminar interest rate risk mgmt. N.Y. Inst. Fin., N.Y.C., 1990-92. Mem. choir, Sunday Sch. tchr. Presbyn. Ch., Glendale; mem. investment com. Glendale Presbyn. Ch.; active Boy Scouts Am., PTO Cedar Hill and Ridge H.S.; former chairperson McGinn Elem. Sch. PTA Reading Program. Recipient Heller alumni award Rutgers U., 1976. Mem.: Beta Gamma Sigma.

HUME-DAWSON, RODNEY BABATUNE, education educator; b. Freeteown, Sierra, W Africia, Nov. 18, 1972; arrived in U.S., 1996; s. Patrick B. Hume-Dawson and Christina L.M. Hume-Dwason; m. Audrey Deslina Hume-Dawson, July 5, 2003. BA, U. Sierra Leone, 1995; MA, Calif. State U., Carson, Calif., 2002. Cert. single subject tchg. 2001. Child adv. UNICEF Nat. Coun. of Children, Freetown, adv. polio & youth; founder, nat. sec. SLUDI, Freetown, South Africa; tchr. L.A. Unified Sch. Dist., L.A., impact coord.; Bishops warden St. Georges Episc. Ch., Hawthorne, Calif.; ednl. cons. Rodney Dawson's Cons., Gardena, Calif. Contbr. articles pub. to profl jour., scientific papers. Mem. Nat. Coun. for Children, Freetown, 1991—96; sec. Sierrra Leone Union on Disability, 1991—96. Grantee won various grants to attend conf. worldwide. Fellow: Univ. Calif. Writing Project; mem.: Nat. Tchrs. of English, Calif. Reading Assn., So. Bay Reading Coun. Episc. Avocations: reading, writing, acting, dance, cooking. Office: Rodney Hume-Dawson's Ednl Cons 1594 W 146th St #6 Gardena CA 90247

HUMES, GLORIA JEAN, secondary school educator; b. Vienna, Ga., June 3, 1951; d. Johnnie and Bunesba Green; m. Anthony Eugene Humes, Dec. 19, 1971; 1 child, Charissa Briana. BS in Vocat. Home Econs. Edn., Fla. Internat. U., 1978, MS, 1981. Cert. behavioral consultant Logos Christian Sch.; vocat. home econs. tchr. Fla. Tchr., head dept. Am. Sr. H.S., Hialeah, Fla., 1979—2000, ednl. specialist, 2000—. Author: (book) Divorced! Marriage Over! But God!, 2002, (shorty story) The Christmas Daddy Moved, 2004. Hospitality and family life leader New Way Fellowship Ch., Opa Locka, Fla., 1998—2004. Named Amb. of the Yr., United Way, 2003—04; recipient Am. Values award, 2004. Mem.: Am. Assn. Family and Consumer Scis. (nat. sec. 2003—). Democrat. Avocations: writing, reading, travel, sewing. Home: 18865 NW 54th Ct Opa Locka FL 33055 Office: Miami-Dade County Pub Schs 1450 NE 2nd Ave Rm 826 Miami FL 33132 Office Phone: 305-995-1845. Office Fax: 305-995-1896. Personal E-mail: apteacher1@aol.com. Business E-Mail: ghumes@dadeschools.net.

HUMES, GRAHAM, investment banker; b. Williamsport, Pa., Oct. 8, 1932; s. Samuel and Elenor (Graham) H.; m. Elizabeth Schwartz Hershey, June 17, 1978; children: Margaret, Kathryn, Malcolm, Elizabeth, John Hershey, Lisa Hershey. BA, Williams Coll., 1954; MBA, Harvard U., 1958. Mng. ptnr. Butcher & Singer, Inc., Phila., 1958-74; sr. v.p. Girard Bank-Mellon Bank, Phila., 1974-87; mng. dir. Legg Mason Wood Walker, Inc., Phila., 1987-93; founder, gen. dir. CARESBAC, St. Petersburg, Russia, 1993-95. Bd. dirs. Brunschwig & Fils, North White Plains, NY, Baltic Cranberry Corp., St. Petersburg, Russia, George M. Leader Family Corp., Hershey, Pa.; trustee Fgn. Policy Rsch. Inst., Phila., Presbyn. Children's Village, Rosemont, Pa. Mem. Merion Cricket Club, Phila. Club, Harvard Bus. Sch. Club. Republican. also: PO Box 368 Cherry Valley NY 13320-0368 Office Phone: 610-293-9023.

HUMES, HARVEY DAVID, nephrologist, educator; b. Honolulu, Nov. 20, 1947; s. William and Nancy Humes; m. Dolores Humes; 1 child, Michael David. BA, U. Calif., Berkeley, 1969; MD, U. Calif., San Francisco, 1973. Diplomate Am. Bd. Internal Medicine. Intern Moffit Hosp. and U. Calif. Hosps., San Francisco, 1973—74; resident U. Calif. Hosps., San Francisco, 1974—75; clin. fellow nephrology U. Pa. Hosp., Phila., 1975—76; rsch. fellow lab. kidney & electrolyte physiology Peter Bent Brigham Hosp., Boston, 1976—77; from instr. to asst. prof. medicine Peter Bent Brigham Hosp./Harvard Med. Sch., Boston, 1977—79; from asst. prof. to assoc. prof. internal medicine U. Mich., Ann Arbor, 1979—86, prof. internal medicine, 1986—, John G. Searle prof., chmn. internal medicine, 1996—2000; founder, gen. ptnr., mgr. EpiGenesis, LLC; founder, dir., chief sci. officer Nephros Therapeutics, Inc.; founder, pres. Innovative Biotherapies, Inc.; founder, chief med. officer Interventional Therapeutic Sys., Inc.; founder, mem. med. adv. bd. Sorbent Therapeutics, Inc. Mem. sci. adv. bd. NephRx; cons. Sandoz Pharm., Bristol-Meyers-Squibb, Sterling-Winthrop, AmGen., Dow Chem.; dir., chief Nephrology Rsch. Labs., U. Mich., Ann Arbor, 1980-81; chief med. svc. VA Med. Ctr., Ann Arbor, 1983-96. Editor: Current Opinion in Internal Medicine, 2001—; editor-in-chief: Kelley's Textbook of Internal Medicine, 1997—2001; mem. editl. bd. Am. Jour. Medicine, 1997—; mem. editl. bd.: Seminars in Nephrology, 1993—, Internat. Yearbook of Nephrology, 1989—; contbr. articles to profl. jours. Grantee Nat. Kidney Found., 1981-85, 87-88, PHS, 1987—, VA, 1982—, Am. Heart Assn., 1982-87, 94-95. Fellow: AAAS, ACP; mem.: Am. Soc. Artificial Internal Organs (trustee), Ctrl. Soc. Clin. Rsch. (past pres.), Nat. Kidney Found. Mich., Nat. Kidney Found. (Pres. award), Internat. Soc. Nephrology, Am. Fedn. Clin. Rsch., Am. Soc. Nephrology, Am. Heart Assn., Am. Soc. Clin. Investigation, Assn. Prof. Medicine, Am. Physiol. Soc., Phi Beta Kappa, Alpha Omega Alpha. Achievements include development of bioartificial kidney; research in cellular basis of acute renal failure, biochemical basis of aminoglycoside-induced acute renal failure, cyclosporine nephrotoxicity, lipid alterations in ischemic acute renal failure, free-radical-induced mitochondrial injury, molecular basis of renal repair in acute renal failure, molecular basis of kidney tubulogenesis. Office: U Mich Med Sch Box 0651 4520 MSRB I, 1150 W Medical Ctr Ann Arbor MI 48109 Office Phone: 734-647-8018. Business E-Mail: dhumes@umich.edu.

HUMES, JAMES CALHOUN, lawyer, communications consultant, writer, educator; b. Williamsport, Pa., Oct. 31, 1934; s. Samuel Hamilton and Elenor Kathryn (Graham) H.; m. Dianne Stuart, July 25, 1957; children: Mary Stuart Quillen, Rachel Bailey. Student, Hill Sch., Stowe Sch., Eng., Williams Coll., 1953-55; AB, George Washington U., 1959, JD, 1962. Bar: Pa. 1963. Mem. Pa. Ho. of Reps., Harrisburg, 1962-65; exec. dir. Phila. Bar Assn., 1967-69; presdl. asst. policy planning sect. White House, Washington, 1969-70; dir. Office Policy and Plans, U.S. Dept. State, Washington, 1970-72; presdl. asst. White House Staff, Washington; White House cons. to Pres. Ford, Washington, 1976-77; Woodrow Wilson fellow Smithsonian Instn., Washington, 1982-83; adj. prof. Williams Coll., 1986-87; prof. Colo. State U., Pueblo, 1997—2004; vis. fellow U. Denver. Mem. U.S. Commn. for UNESCO; adj. prof. U. Pa., 1985-99; editl. advisor Pres. Ford's memoirs A Time To Heal. Author: Sweet Dream, 1966, Instant Eloquence, 1973, Podium Humor, 1975, Roles Speakers Play, 1976, How to Get Invited to the White House, 1977, Winston Churchill: Speaker of the Century, 1980, Talk Your Way to the Top, 1980, Standing Ovation, 1988, Sir Winston Method, 1991, The Benjamin Franklin Factor, 1992, My Fellow Americans, 1992, Citizen Shakespeare, 1993, Wit and Wisdom of Churchill, 1994, Wit and Wisdom of Benjamin Franklin, 1995, Wit and Wisdom of Abraham Lincoln, 1996, Confessions of a White House Ghost Writer, 1997, Nixon's Ten Commandments of Statecraft, 1998, Eisenhower and Churchill: The Partnership that Saved the World, 2001, Speak Like Churchill Stand Like Lincoln, 2002, Which President Killed a Man, 2002, Winston Churchill, 2003. Decorated Order of Brit. Empire. Fellow Royal Soc. of Art; mem. SAR, St. Nicholas Soc. NY, Soc. Pilgrims, Soc. Cin., Order of Magna Charta, Union League Club, Phila. Cricket Club, Brook Club (NY). Republican. Presbyterian. Home: 4404 Turnberry Cres Pueblo CO 81001-1162

HUMICK, THOMAS CHARLES CAMPBELL, lawyer; b. NYC, Aug. 7, 1947; s. Anthony and Elizabeth Campbell (Meredith) H.; m. Nancy June Young, June 7, 1969; 1 child, Nicole Elizabeth Campbell. BA, Rutgers U., 1969; JD, Suffolk U., 1972; postgrad., London Sch. Econs.-Polit. Sci., 1977-78. Bar: N.J. 1972, U.S. Ct. Appeals (3d cir.) 1976, U.S. Supreme Ct. 1977, N.Y. 1981. Law clk. Superior Ct. N.J., 1972-73; assoc. Riker, Danzig, Scherer & Debevoise, Newark and Morristown, N.J., 1973-77; ptnr. Francis & Berry, Morristown, 1978-84, Dillon, Bitar & Luther, Morristown, 1985-92, Schenck, Price, Smith & King, Morristown, 1992—. Arbitrator U.S. Dist. Ct. N.J., 1985; del. Jud. Conf. 3d Jud. Cir. U.S., 1975—79; dist. X ethics com. NJ Supreme Ct., 1983—87; jud. selection com. Morris County, NJ, 1995—96. Contbg. author: Valuation for Eminent Domain, 1973; mem. editl. bd. Suffolk U. Law Rev., 1970-71, N.J. Lawyer, 1993-94. Trustee Peck Sch., 1993-98; trustee Richmond Fellowship N.J., 1982-89, pres., 1984. Mem.: ABA, FBA, Am. Bd. of Trial Advocates, Morris County Bar Assn. (trustee 1995—2000), NJ Bar Assn., Bay Head Yacht Club. Presbyterian. Home: PO Box 152 Morristown NJ 07963-0152 Office: Schenck Price Smith & King 10 Washington St Morristown NJ 07963-0905 E-mail: tcch@spsk.com.

HUML, DONALD SCOTT, manufacturing executive; b. Lake Geneva, Wis., May 8, 1946; s. Robert Francis and Shirley (Roberts) H.; m. Joyce Cora Featherstone, Oct. 2, 1965; children: Tiffany Lynn, Alison Michelle, Andrew Scott. BBA, Marquette U., 1969; MBA, Temple U., 1980. Mgr. treasury ops. Allis-Chalmers Corp., West Allis, Wis., 1970-73; dir. fin. services Certain-Teed Corp., Valley Forge, Pa., 1973-75, asst. treas., 1975-78, v.p., treas., 1978-81, v.p., comptroller, 1981-83, v.p., div. pres., 1983-86, v.p., group pres., 1986-89, v.p., chief fin. officer, 1989-90; v.p., CFO Saint-Gobain Corp., Valley Forge, Pa., 1990-94; sr. v.p., CFO Snap-on Inc., Kenosha, Wis., 1994—2002; CFO Greif, Inc., Delaware, Ohio, 2002—. Mem. adv. bd. Marquette U. Sch. Bus. Adminstrn. Mem. Am. Mgmt. Assn., Fin. Execs. Inst., Conf. Bd. CFO Coun., Leading CFOs, Beta Gamma Sigma. Republican. Roman Catholic. Avocations: tennis, running, reading. Home: 1808 Wingate Dr Delaware OH 43015 Office: Greif Inc 425 Winter Rd Delaware OH 43015 Office Phone: 740-549-6137. Business E-Mail: don.huml@greif.com. E-mail: dhuml@columbus.rr.com.

HUMMEL, ANGELA FAYE, principal; b. Winchester, Ky., Sept. 27, 1972; d. Nancy Sewell; m. Angela Faye Sewell, Sept. 27, 1972. Bachelor's and Master's degrees, Ea. Ky. U., 1997, Master's degree, 2005. Tchr. Shearer Elem., Winchester, Ky., 1999—2005; prin. Mem.: ASCD. Republican. Avocations: gardening, livestock, hunting, fishing. Office Phone: 859-737-3042. Personal E-mail: hummelangela@wmconnect.com.

HUMMEL, GREGORY WILLIAM, lawyer; b. Sterling, Ill., Feb. 25, 1949; s. Osborne William and Vivian LaVera (Guess) H.; m. Teresa Lynn Beveroth, June 20, 1970; children: Andrea Lynn, Brandon Gregory. BA, MacMurray Coll., 1971; JD, Northwestern U., 1974. Bar: Ill. 1974, U.S. Dist. Ct. (no. dist.) Ill. 1974. Assoc. Rusnak, Deutsch & Gilbert, Chgo., 1974-78; ptnr. Rudnick & Wolfe, Chgo., 1978-97; mem. Bell, Boyd & Lloyd LLC, Chgo., 1997—. Editor Jour. Criminal Law & Criminology Northwestern U., 1973-

74; co-author: Illinois Real Estate Forms, 1989; contbr. articles to law jours. Mem. gov. coun. Luth. Gen. Hosp. Advocate Health Care Sys.; trustee Mac Murray Coll., Jacksonville, Ill., 1986-2001; trustee, sec.-treas. Homes for Children Found; bd. advisors Chgo. area coun. Boy Scouts Am., ChildServ; trustee Nat. Inst. Constrn. Law and Practice. Mem. Internat. Bar Assn. (past co-chmn. com. internat. constrn. projects), Am. Coll. Constrn. Lawyers (past pres.), Urban Land Inst. (trustee), Urban Land Inst. Found. (gov.), Chgo. Dist. Coun. (past chmn.), Lambda Alpha Internat. (Ely chpt. past pres.), Econ. Club (Chgo.). Office: Bell Boyd & Lloyd LLC 3 1st Nat Plaza 70 W Madison St Ste 3300 Chicago IL 60602-4207 E-mail: ghummel@bellboyd.com.

HUMMEL, JOHN, information technology executive; Head, info. sys. Specialty Labs. Inc., Santa Monica, Calif., Brim, Inc., Portland, Oreg., Health Svc. Pharmacy/Option Care, Vancouver, Wash.; dir., sys. integration Sutter Health, Sacramento, 1997—99, chief info. officer, 1999—2002, sr. v.p., info. tech., 2002—. Commnr. Certification Commn. for Healthcare Info. Tech. Named one of top tech. innovators, Info. Week mag., 2004. Office: SVP Info Tech Sutter Health 2200 River Plz Dr Sacramento CA 95833

HUMMEL, KAY JEAN, physical therapist; b. Cleve., Apr. 24, 1943; d. Lloyd Elmer and Olive Agnes (Latou) Hetherington; m. Charles William Hummel (div. Feb. 1984); children: Patrick H., Robin E. BA, Miami U., Oxford, Ohio, 1965; cert. in phys. therapy, Columbia U., N.Y., 1966. Lic. phys. therapist, La.; cert. ofcl. Games Uniting Mind and Body. Staff phys. therapist St. Joseph's Hosp., Chgo., 1966-68, Wrightwood Extended Care Facility, Chgo., 1967-68, Suburban Hosp., Bethesda, Md., 1969, Holy Cross Hosp., Silver Spring, Md., 1969-70; asst. chief phys. therapist Community Gen. Hosp., Syracuse, N.Y., 1970-76; itinerant phys. therapist Caddo Parish Schs., Shreveport, La., 1976—; pvt. practice Shreveport, 1985—. Games Uniting Mind & Body, Inc. classifer and cert. ofcl. Mem. U.S. Cerebral Palsy Athletic Assn. (regional classifier), Presbyn. Women: Presbytery of the Pines Coord. Team, North La. Scottish Soc., elder, Presbyn. Ch., Kappa Delta Alumni Assn. Office: 3004 Knight St Shreveport LA 71105-2506 Office Phone: 318-219-0191 x 420.

HUMMEL, KEITH R., lawyer; b. Bklyn., June 3, 1965; BA, Univ. Notre Dame, 1987; JD magna cum laude, Georgetown Univ., 1990. Bar: NY 1991. Assoc. Cravath Swaine & Moore LLP, NYC, 1990—98, ptnr., litig., 1998—. Notes and comments sr. editor Georgetown Law Jour. Mem.: Order of Coif. Office: Cravath Swaine & Moore LLP Worldwide Plz 825 Eighth Ave New York NY 10019-7475 Office Phone: 212-474-1772. Office Fax: 212-474-3700. Business E-Mail: khummel@cravath.com.

HUMMEL, MARGARET P., state representative; b. Binghamton, N.Y., Mar. 24, 1940; m. Manfred K. Hummel; four children. BA, Coll. New Rochelle, 1962; MA, Boston Coll., 1968, St. Michaels Coll., 1981. Mem. Vt. Ho. of Reps., 1996—2004. Mem. Underhill Selectboard, 1992—2001; chair Underhill Planning Commn.; mem. Burlington Sch. Gifted and Talented Task Force; trustee U. Vt., 1999—2005. Roman Catholic. Office: 38 Poker Hill Underhill VT 05489-9644

HUMMEL, ROBERT PAUL, retired surgeon, educator; b. Bellevue, Ky., Sept. 17, 1928; s. Robert Paul and Clara (Rechtin) H.; m. Helen Beam, June 26, 1954; children— Claire, Molli, Robert Paul BS, Xavier U., 1947; MD, U. Cin., 1951. Diplomate Am. Bd. Surgery. Intern Duke U. Hosp., Durham, N.C., 1951-52; resident in surgery Cin. Gen. Hosp., 1952-54, 56-59, chief resident in surgery, 1959-60; instr. surgery U. Cin., 1959-63, asst. prof. surgery, 1963-67, assoc. prof. surgery, 1967-76, prof. surgery, 1976-97, vice chmn. dept. surgery, 1984-97; asst. attending surgeon Cin. Gen. Hosp., 1959-64, clinician, surg. out-patient dept., 1960—, attending surgeon, 1965-97, Children's Hosp. Cin., 1964-97; chief of staff Univ. Hosp., 1992-97, emeritus prof. surgery, 1997, ret., 1997. Mem. staff U. Hosp.; bd. dirs. Cin. Bell Inc., U. Hosp., Cin. Art Acad. Served with U.S. Army, 1954-56 Mem. ACS (gov. 1979-85), AMA, Am. Surg. Assn., Am. Assn. Surgery of Trauma, Am. Burn Assn., So. Surg. Halsted Soc., Soc. Surgery Alimentary Tract, Cen. Surg. Assn. (treas. 1978-81), Ohio Med. Assn., Cin. Acad. Medicine (sec. 1977, pres. 1981), Cin. Surg. Soc. (pres. 1977), U. Cin. Grad. Surg. Soc. (pres. 1985-91), Queen City Club, Ocean Reef Club, Cin. Country Club, Commonwealth Club, Sigma Xi, Alpha Omega Alpha. Republican. Roman Catholic. also: 3 South Rd Key Largo FL 33037-3746

HUMMEL, ROLF ERICH, materials scientist, educator; b. Sindelfingen, Germany, July 21, 1934; m. Val Hummel, 1961; children: Barbara, Andrea, Sirka. Diplom physiker, U. Stuttgart, Fed. Republic Germany, 1960, PhD, 1963. came to U.S., 1964. Rsch. assoc. Max-Planck Inst., Stuttgart, 1958-63; asst. prof. U. Fla., Gainesville, 1964-69, assoc. prof., 1969-74, prof. materials sci., 1974—. Vis. prof. Max-Planck Inst., Stuttgart, 1971-72, U. Paris, 1981, Kyoto (Japan) U., 1987-88, NAS, China, 1988, U. Wellington, New Zealand, 1995. Author: Optische Eigenschaften Von Metallen und Legierungen, 1971, Electro and Thermo Transport in Metals and Alloys, 1976, Electronic Properties of Materials, 1985, 3d edit., 2001, Handbook of Optical Properties Vol. I and II, 1995, Understanding Materials Science, 2d edit., 2004; contbr. articles to profl. jours. Mem. Am. Phys. Soc., Materials Rsch. Soc., Metall. Soc. Avocations: cello, cabinet making. Office: U Fla Dept Materials Sci and Engring Gainesville FL 32611

HUMPHREY, CHARLES EDWARD, JR., lawyer; b. Detroit, Jan. 20, 1943; s. Charles Edward and Betty Jane (Bixby) H.; children: Jennifer Jane Castle, Jordan Susan Trigler. BBA, U. Mich., 1964, JD cum laude, MBA, U. Mich., 1968. Bar: Mich. 1968, Tex. 1971, Colo. 1982. Assoc. Evans & Luptak, 1968; atty., fin. adviser SEC, Washington, 1969-71; ptnr. Foreman & Dyess, Houston, 1971-81; pres. Ptnrs. Oil Co., Houston, 1981-82; ptnr. Kirkland & Ellis, Denver, 1982-87; pres. Addoms & Humphrey (a bus. devel. co.), 1986-88; of counsel Cohen, Brame & Smith, 1987—88; pres. Vector Video, Inc., 1987-89, Venture Capital Investments, 1989—. Chmn. Advanced Cable Systems, Inc., 1989-99; mng. ptnr. Signature Stes., 1989-98; founder Tournament of Champions of Poker, 1999, chmn., 1999-2001; founder, mng. ptnr. Team Pegasus, 1998-2001; webmaster www.gambling-law-us.com, 2003—. Bd. dirs. Houston Civil Liberties Union, 1973-77, treas., 1975-77; pres. Tex. Civil Liberties Union, 1978-79, Ctrl. City Opera House Assn., 1982-84. Mailing: 1755 Swadley St Lakewood CO 80215 E-mail: cehjr@umich.edu.

HUMPHREY, CRAIG REED, social studies educator; b. Grand Rapids, Mich., Oct. 14, 1942; s. Roger and Ruth Reed Humphrey; m. Catherine Elaine Clark, Aug. 6, 1966; children: Michelle Ruth, Gwen Allison. BA, Bowling Green State U., 1964; MA, Brown U., 1967, PhD, 1971. Asst. prof. Coll. William and Mary, Williamsburg, Va., 1969—71, Pa. State U., University Park, 1971—77, assoc. prof., 1977—2001, assoc. prof. emeritus of sociology and demography, 2001—. Vis. assoc. prof. rural sociology U. Wis., Madison, 1987; vis. assoc. prof. Yale U., New Haven, 1996—97. Co-author: Environment, Energy and Society, 1982, Environment, Energy and Society: A New Synthesis, 2002, Environment. Energy and Society: Exemplary Works, 2003. Pres. Cmty. Land Trust, State College, Pa., 2002—03, sec., 2004—05; elected coun. mem. State Coll. Borough Coun., 2004—. Mem.: Rural Sociol. Soc. (assoc. editor 2002—04), Am. Sociol. Assn. (mem. sect. on environment and tech. 1986—88, Disting. Contbn. award 2003). Democrat. Episcopalian. Avocations: sailing, gardening, writing, physical fitness. Home: 227 W Prospect Ave State College PA 16801 Office: Pa State Univ Dept Sociology 215 Oswald Tower University Park PA 16802 Office Phone: 814-865-0591. Business E-Mail: ch8@psu.edu.

HUMPHREY, DIANA YOUNG, fundraiser; b. Balt., Feb. 7, 1938; d. Edwin Parson and Elizabeth Miller (Hoskins) Young; m. David Henry Carls, July 27, 1963 (div. Dec. 17, 1997); children: Peter Van Patten Carls, Elizabeth Roy Carls, Susan Montanye Carls; m. George Lee Humphrey, May 22, 1999. AB, Smith Coll., Northampton, Mass., 1960. Lic. real estate broker, Mass., 1978. Fgn. rights sales Little, Brown & Co., Inc., Boston, 1960-63; speech writer DNA Rsch., N.Y.C., 1963-64; vol. fund raiser John V. Lindsay, N.Y.C., 1964-65, Smith Coll., Northampton, Mass., 1970-75, 90-95, Smith Coll. Club, Concord, Mass., 1976-89, Jr. League of Boston, 1967—; bd. mem. devel. Ctr. House, Inc., Boston, 1981-94; fund raiser events Boston Symphony Orch., 1975—; dir. edn. Hawthorne Ptnrs. Inc. Fund raising, events Mass. Soc. for Prevention of Cruelty to Children, Boston, 1997—. Editor: Huntington Hartford Gallery Modern Art, N.Y.C., 1963. Speechwriter, Nelson A. Rockefeller Presdl. campaign, N.Y.C., 1963-64; active John V. Lindsay for Mayor, N.Y.C., 1964-65; mem., chmn. Wayland (Mass.) Planning Bd., 1976-81, Wayland Housing Partnership, 1987—; mem. adv. com. REACH, Waltham, Mass.; mem. Patriots' Trail coun. Girl Scouts U.S. Mem. Jr. League of Boston, Weston Golf Club. Episcopalian. Avocations: golf, travel, gardening, singing, politics. Home: 42 Cutting Cross Way Wayland MA 01778-3845

HUMPHREY, DUDLEY, lawyer; b. Dec. 1933; AB, Duke U., 1955; JD with honors, U. N.C., 1961. Bar: N.C. 1961. With Kilpatrick Stockton LLP, Winston-Salem, NC. Mem.: N.C. State Bar (pres. 2003). Office: Kilpatrick Stockton LLP 1001 W Fourth St Winston Salem NC 27101-2400 Business E-Mail: dhumphrey@kilpatrickstockton.com.

HUMPHREY, GEORGE MAGOFFIN, II, plastic molding company executive; b. Cleve., Mar. 19, 1942; s. Gilbert Watts and Louise (Ireland) H.; m. Marguerite Burton, June 19, 1964 (div. 1989); children: Mary O., Sandra; m. Patience Ryan, June 22, 1991. BA, Yale U., 1964; JD, U. Mich., 1967. Bar: Ohio 1967. Sales rep. Hanna Mining Co., Cleve., 1970-72, European rep., 1972-77, sales rep., 1977-78, mgr. sales, 1978, v.p. sales, 1978-80, sr. v.p. fin., 1980-81, sr. v.p. sales, dir., 1981-84; mng. dir. Russell Reynolds Assocs., Cleve., 1984-87; gen. ptnr. Philips Industries, Ltd., Cleve., 1987-94; pres. Extrudex, Cleve., 1990—. Trustee Cleve. Mus. Art, Cleve. Mus. Natural History, Cleve. Scholarship Programs, Inc., Univ. Hosps. Cleve. Served to capt. USMC, 1967-70. Mem. Union Club (Cleve.). Republican. Episcopalian. Home: 18 W Mather Ln Bratenahl OH 44108-1158 Office: Extrudex 310 Figgie Dr Painesville OH 44077-3028 Office Phone: 216-363-1036.

HUMPHREY, JAMES E., manufacturing executive; Pres. Floor Products Am., Armstrong World Industries, 1968—99; from v.p., gen. mgr. windows and doors to COO Andersen Windows Corp., Bayport, Minn., 1999—2002, pres., 2002—, CEO, 2003—; also bd. dirs. Bd. dirs. Bayport Found., Regions Hosp. Found., Courage Ctr. Office: Andersen Windows Corp 100 Fourth Ave N Bayport MN 55003

HUMPHREY, OWEN EVERETT, retired education administrator; b. Wautoma, Wis., Oct. 25, 1920; s. Marion A. and Flora A. (Helms) H.; m. Billye A. Cox, Apr. 6, 1946 (dec. Dec. 1974); children: Reba, Ivye. BS, U. Wis., Whitewater, 1947; MS, U. Ark., 1949; advanced cert., U. Ill., 1954. Life gen. supervisory cert. grades K-14. Elem. classroom tchr. Four Corners Sch., Plainfield, Wis., 1941-42; jr. high art and sci. tchr. Jefferson Sch., Sheboygan, Wis., 1947-48; elem. classroom tchr. and prin. Holcomb, Mo., 1949-50, Lincoln Sch., Mattoon, Ill., 1950-55; supervising prin. various elem. schs., Peotone, Ill., 1955-57; elem. tchr. Nameoki Sch., Granite City, Ill., 1957-59; elem. prin. Maryville Sch., Granite City, 1959-67; curriculum coord. Sch. Dist. #9, Granite City, 1967-79; adminstrv. asst. Regional Supt. of Schs., Madison County, Ill., 1979-81, 85-87; ret., 1987. Leader parent study groups Ea. Ill. U., Mattoon, 1950-54; PTA field unit organizer Ill. Congress of Parents and Tchrs., Mattoon, 1952-54; coord. local dist. planning Sch. Dist. #9, Granite City, 1973-79; rep. Ill. State Curriculum Coun., Springfield, 1980-81. Co-author: The Greening of Gateway East, 1984; contbr. poetry to Nat. Libr. of Poetry anthologies; contbr. articles to profl. jours. Dir. chorus Area Coun. PTA, Mattoon, 1950-54, Granite City Area Coun. PTA, 1957-59; dir. Granite City Steel Mixed Chorus, 1958-60; actor Creative Arts Theatrical Soc., 1992--. Sgt. U.S. Army Infantry, 1942-45, ETO. Recipient Area Coun. PTA award Granite City, Ill., 1979. Mem. NEA (life), ASCD (life), Ill. ASCD (life, bd. dirs.), Internat. Poets Soc. (life), Creative Arts Theatrical Soc. (bd. govs.), Miners Inst. Found. (bd. dirs. 2002-03), Phi Delta Kappa (Gateway East chpt. sec., historian, v.p., pres., Svc. Key award 1984, George H. Reavis Assoc. award 1991). Avocation: composing music and lyrics. Home: 18 Wilson Park Dr Granite City IL 62040-3550 Personal E-mail: oweneh@aol.com.

HUMPHREY, PATRICK PAUL, pharmacologist; b. Pietersburg, South Africa, Jan. 28, 1946; s. Gordon William and Judith Suzanne (LeRoux) H.; m. Mary Frances Letford, Sept. 14, 1968; children: Patrick Tobias, Damian Paul, Joel Anthony. B Pharmacy with honors, U. London, 1968, PhD in Pharmacology, 1972. Qualified pharmacist. Lectr. physiology dept. St. Mary's Hosp. Med. Sch., London, 1971-72; rsch. leader dept. pharmacology Allen and Hanbury, Ware, Eng., 1972-80; head dept. pharmacology Glaxo Group Rsch. Ltd., Ware, 1980-83, dir. divsn. pharmacology, 1983-92; dir. Glaxo Inst. Applied Pharmacology, U. Cambridge, England, 1992—2001; hon. prof., 1994—2001; dir. Glaxo Wellcom Headache Rsch. Group, 1999—2001; exec. v.p. rsch. Theravance (formerly Advanced Medicine), South San Francisco, Calif., 2001—. Mem. com. for receptor nomenclature and drug classification Internat. Union Pharmacology, 1990-2002, mem. exec. com., 1998-2002; chmn. receptor nomenclature com. Serotonin Club, 1987-93. Co-editor: Serotonin: Actions, Receptors, Pathophysiology, 1989, Receptor Classification, 1997, The Triptans, 2001; editor Brit. Jour. Pharmacology, 1984-90; team leader drug discovery and devel. Anti-Migraine Drug Sumatriptan (trademarks Imitrex and Imigran), 1972-92. Recipient Mullard award Royal Soc., 1997, OBE award, 1999. Fellow Royal Pharm. Soc.; mem. Am. Gastroenterological Assn., Brit. Pharm. Soc., Soc. Neurosci., Internat. Headache Soc. Roman Catholic. Avocations: fishing, playing real (royal) tennis, gardening, ornithology. Office: Theravance Inc 901 Gateway Blvd South San Francisco CA 94080 Office Phone: 650-808-3704. E-mail: phumphrey@theravance.com.

HUMPHREY, ROGER GAVIN, music educator; b. Alma, Mich., Apr. 1, 1948; s. Wallace Otto and Margaret Louise Humphrey; m. Barbara Elaine Mead, Oct. 20, 1979; children: Alexis Sylvon Gorlock, Joshua Jacob Strieff; children: Shawn Aileen Acosta-Arellano, Eric Jay Lovejoy. Guitar instr. Marshalls Sch. of Music, Lansing, Mich., 1981—, Olivet Coll., Mich., 1988—, Alma Coll., Mich., 1992—. Owner/pres. First Music, St. Louis, 1995. Author: (book) Learning the Guitar Vol. I & Vol. II, My 1st Guitar Book, My 2nd Guitar Book, etc. Elder Peace Luth. Ch., Alma, Mich., 1994—98. E-4 USAF, 1967—71, Mich. and Japan. Grant, U. S. Govt., 1976—78. Mem.: Phi Mu Alpha. Independent. Lutheran. Avocation: bicycling. Office: Olivet College Arts/Communications Dept 320 S Main St Olivet MI 49076-9406 Personal E-mail: humphreyroger@netscape.net. E-mail: rhumphrey@olivetcollege.edu.

HUMPHREY, SAMUEL STOCKWELL, town official, physicist; b. Canton Center, Conn., Apr. 25, 1923; s. Harold William and A. Genevieve (Stockwell) H.; m. Mary Elizabeth Mills, Feb. 4, 1945; children: Warren Mills, Kenneth Stockwell, Marianne Ruth. BS, U. Conn., 1948; MA, Wesleyan U., Middletown, Conn., 1950; postgrad., U. Utah, 1961-63. Enlisted USAF, 1942, advanced through grades to lt. col., 1966, ret., 1971; physicist Wesleyan U., 1948-51; cons. physicist Canton, Conn., 1971-74; tchr. physics Canton (Conn.) High Schs., 1973-74, real estate broker, 1975-93; first selectman Town of Canton, 1983-87, selectman, 1989-91, mem. bd. fin., 1997—; mgr. Cherry Brook Farm LLC. Dir. Conn. Conf. Municipalities, Conn. Interlocal Risk Mgmt. Agys. (CIRMA), 1987; bd. dirs. Sundown Ski Patrol, Inc.; mem. policy bd. and exec. com. Capitol Region Coun. of Govts., 1983-87; cons. physicist RCA, Burlington, Mass., 1971-74, Martin Marietta, Orlando, Fla., 1971-72; co-founder Simsbury (Conn.) Bank & Trust Co.; researcher in field. Author, editor numerous studies and reports. Trustee, treas. 1st Congl. Ch., Canton Ctr., 1972-85; chmn. Hist. Dist. Commn., Canton, 1972-80, Mcpl. Bd. Fin., Canton, 1975-83, 97—; justice of peace State of Conn., 1974—. Recipient numerous awards and decorations USAF and Philippines; Wesleyan U. fellow, 1948-50. Mem. Optical Soc. Am. (emeritus), Air Force Assn., Conn. Christmas Tree Growers Assn. (bd. dirs. 1984-90, v.p. 1990, pres. 1992-95), New Eng. Christmas Tree Assn. (dir. 1990—), Hanscom Flying Club (Bedford, Mass., pres. 1955-59), Skiesta Club (pres. 1964-68), Sigma Xi (assoc.), Sigma Pi Sigma. Republican. Mem. United Ch. of Christ. Avocation: ski patrol. Home: Box 150 96 Barbourtown Rd Canton Center CT 06020-0150 Office Phone: 860-693-4066. E-mail: sshumphrey@aol.com.

HUMPHREY, STEPHEN M., paperboard company executive; b. Oct. 10, 1944; BS, Siena Coll., 1967. With GE Co., 1967—81; pres. on-hwy. products bus. Rockwell Internat. Corp., 1981—94; chmn., pres., CEO Nat. Gypsum Co., Charlotte, NC, 1994—96; pres, CEO Riverwood Internat. Corp, Atlanta, 1997—2003; also bd. dirs. Riverwood Internat. Corp., Atlanta; pres., CEO Graphic Packaging Corp. (formerly Riverwood Internat. Corp.), Atlanta, 2003—. Office: Riverwood Intl Corp 814 Livingston Ct SE Marietta GA 30067-8940

HUMPHREY, WATTS SHERMAN, information technology executive, writer; b. Battle Creek, Mich., July 4, 1927; s. Watts Sherman Humphrey and Katharine (Strong) Osborne; m. Barbara Fallon, May 22, 1954; children: Katharine Pickman, Lisa Fish, Sarah DeCamello, Watts Jr., Peter, Erica Jarrett, Christopher. BS in Physics, U. Chgo., 1949, MBA, 1951; MS in Physics, Ill. Inst. Tech., 1950; PhD in Software Engring. (hon.), Embry Riddle Aero. U., 1998. Electronics engr. Fermi Inst. U. Chgo., 1949-51, dir. sci. pers. Chgo. Midway Lab., 1951-53; mgr. computing devel. Sylvania Electric Products, Natick, Mass., 1953-59; instr. computer design Northeastern U., Boston, 1956-59; with IBM, White Plains, N.Y., 1959-86, mgr. teleprocessing systems devel., 1959-64, dir. systems application engring., Armonk, N.Y., 1964-65, dir. time sharing systems, White Plains, 1965-66, dir. programming, 1966-68, v.p. tech. devel., Armonk, 1968-70, dir. Endicott (N.Y.) Labs., 1970-72, dir. policy devel., Armonk, 1972-79, dir. tech. assessment, White Plains, 1979-83, dir. programming quality and process, Poughkeepsie, N.Y., 1983-86; dir. software process program Software Engring. Inst. Carnegie Mellon U., Pitts., 1986-91, fellow, 1991—. Chmn. adv. bd. IBM Systems Rsch. Inst., N.Y.C., 1973-82. Author: Switching Circuits with Computer Applications, 1958, Managing for Innovation, Leading Technical People, 1987, Managing the Software Process, 1989, A Discipline for Software Engineering, 1995, Managing Technical People, Innovation, Teamwork and the Software Process, 1997, Introduction to the Personal Software Process, 1997, Introduction to the Team Software Process, 1999, Winning with Software: an Executive Strategy, 2002, PSP: A Self-Improvement Process for Software Engineers, 2005; contbr. numerous articles to profl. jours.; (mem. editl. bd.) Jour. Sys. and Software, 1988-96, Software Process, Improvement and Practice, 1996-, Empirical Software Engring., 1996-. Bd. examiners Malcolm Baldridge Nat. Quality Award, 1991; sci. adv. com. Std. System Ctr. USAF, 1989-92. With USN, 1944-46. Recipient Aerospace Software Engineering award Am. Inst. of Aeronautics and Astronautics, 1993, Boeing award for leadership and innovation in software process improvement, 2000, Nat. medal of Tech., Pres. U.S., 2003; Watts Humphrey Software Quality Inst. in Chennai, India, named in his honor, 2000. Fellow IEEE (editorial bds. Spectrum 1982-83, The Institute 1982-83, reviewer Software 1984, Computer 1984, IBM System Jour. 1989); mem. Assn. for Computing Machinery, Inst. for Radio Engrs. (chmn. computer sect. 1959). Democrat. Achievements include patents in field. Avocations: running, piano, bridge. Office: Carnegie Mellon U Software Engring Inst 4500 5th Ave Pittsburgh PA 15213-2612

HUMPHREYS, BETSY L., librarian; BA, Smith Coll., 1969; MLS, U. Md., 1972. Joined Nat. Libr. Medicine NIH, 1973, dep. asst. dir. libr. ops., 1984—99, asst. dir. health svcs. rsch. info, 1993—, assoc. dir. libr. ops., 1999—. Pub. and presenter in field including Eileen Roach Cunningham Lectr., Vanderbilt U., 1999, Priscilla Mayden Lectr., U. Utah, 1999, Janet Doe Lectr., Med Libr. Assn., 2001. Contbr. articles to profl. jours. Recipient Alumna of Year, Coll. Info. Studies Alumni Chpt., 2003. Fellow Am. Coll. Med. Informatics (1990-); mem. Inst. Medicine Nat. Acad. Sciences, Acad. Health Info. Profls. (disting. mem.), Am. Med. Informatics Assn., Med. Libr. Assn., Acad. Health Svcs. Rsch. and Health Policy. Office: Nat Libr Medicine NIH 8600 Rockville Pike Bldg 38 Bethesda MD 20894-0001

HUMPHREYS, DANIEL JAMES, elementary school educator; b. Humboldt, Tenn., May 6, 1953; s. James Benjamin and Hermione Humphreys; m. Paula Gay Wuertemberger, June 18, 1981; children: Jennifer Lee, Sarah Elizabeth, John Daniel. B of Music Edn., U. Miss., 1975, M of Music Edn., 1978. Tchr. Neshoba Mid. Sch., Philadelphia, Miss., 1975—76, Risley Mid. Sch., Brunswick, Ga., 1976—77, South Mid. Sch., Edinburg, Tex., 1977—80, William Adams Jr. High Sch., Alice, 1982—88, Owensboro Mid. Sch., Ky., 1988—. Mem. class schedule com. OWensboro Mid. Sch., 1997—; condr., performer Bend in River Brass Band, Newburg, Ind., 1992—. Performer: Premier Brass Quartet, 1997—2000, Owensboro Brass Quartet, 1995—. Mid. sch. band participant Ky. Music Educators Assn., 2003, 2005. Named Mid. Sch. Band Dir. of Yr., Ky. Music Educators Assn., 1997—98, 2001—02; recipient 25 Yr. Svc. award, 2000—01. Mem.: NEA, Music Educators Nat. Conf., Phi Beta Mu. Avocations: woodworking, reading. Home: 3520 Comanche Pl Owensboro KY 42301

HUMPHREYS, JEAN SURRATT, social sciences educator; b. Midland, Tex., Dec. 20, 1957; d. Marshall England and Margaret Nash Surratt; m. John R Humphreys, May 29, 1982; children: Lauren Ann, Jordan Nash, Joshua Neal. MA - Sociology, Baylor U., 1981. Teacher's Certification - Mathematics/Sociology Tex., 1979. Math tchr. Kimball H.S., Dallas, 1980—82; math. tchr. LaVega H.S., Bellmead, Tex., 1982—83; asst. prof. / dept. coord. Dallas Bapt. U., 1992—. Site based decision team Young Jr. High/Ditto Elem., Arlington, Tex., 1996—2000; tournaments Martin Basketball Booster, Arlington, Tex., 2004—05; officer Parent Tchr. Assn./ Martin High/Young Jr./Ditto Elem., Arlington, Tex., 1990—2003; chair Bahama Bash Entertainment, 2004—05. Recipient Alpha Chi, East Tex. Bapt. U., 1976-1978, Faculty of Yr. award, Dallas Bapt. U., 2004; fellow Sociology, Baylor U., 1978-1979. Mem.: Assn. for the Sci. Study of Religion (treas. 1998—2001), Southwestern Sociol. Assn., Soc. for Applied Sociology. Office: Dallas Baptist U 3000 Mountain Creek Parkway Dallas TX 75211 E-mail: jean@dbu.edu.

HUMPHREYS, JERE THOMAS, music educator, consultant; b. Humboldt, Tenn., Mar. 26, 1949; s. James Benjamin and Hermione Shelnutt Humphreys; m. Alexandra Houzouri, July 2, 2002; children: David James, Ioannis Houzouris. MusB in Music Edn., U. Miss., 1971; MusM in Clarinet Performance, Fla. State U., 1976; PhD in Music Edn., U. Mich., 1984. Music tchr., band dir. Quitman (Mass.) Consol. Schs., 1972—75; asst. prof. Huntingdon Coll., Montgomery, Ala., 1977—79; asst. to assoc. prof. music W.Va. U., Morgantown, 1981—87; assoc. to prof. music Ariz. State U., Tempe, 1987—. Cons. Morrison Inst. Pub. Policy, Tempe, Ariz., 1995—96; acad. specialist U.S. Dept. State, U. Kiril and U. Metodij, Skopje, Macedonia, 1996; guest lectr. Uludag U., Bursa, Turkey, 1998, W.Va. U., Morgantown, 2000, U. Reading, England, 2002, Wayne State U., Detroit, 2003; vis. prof. Univ. Coll., Buenos Aires, 2004; guest lectr. U. Kiril and Metodis, 2005, U. Miss., 2005. Author: (book chapter) Popular Music in the American Schools: What the Past Tells Us About the Present and the Future, Precursors of Musical Aptitude Testing: From the Greeks through the Work of Francis Galton, Instrumental Music in American Education: In Service of Many Masters, Research on Music Ensembles; contbr. articles to profl. jours.; mem. editl. com.: UPDATE: Applications of Rsch. in Music Edn., 1988—92, S.E. Jour. Music Edn., 1989—92, Quar. Jour. Music Tchg. and Learning, 1989—97, Bull. Hist. Rsch. in Music Edn., 1989—99, Jour. Band Rsch., 1997—, Bull. Coun. Rsch. in Music Edn., 1998—, Action, Criticism, and Theory for Music Education, 2002—, Jour. Rsch. in Music Edn., 2002—, Jour. Hist. Rsch. in Music Edn., 2003—, Internat. Jour. Music Edn., 2004—, Music Paedagodics, 2004—. Constrn. crew chief Habitat for Humanity Valley of the Sun, Phoenix, 1998—, outreach com. mem., 2003—, means and methods com. mem., 2004—; bd. dirs. Habitat for Humanity Macedonia. With U.S. Army N.G., 1971—77. Recipient MENC Citation of Excellence in Rsch. award, Music Educators Nat. Conf., 1985, Disting. Svc. award, Bull. Hist. Rsch. in Music Edn., 1992; fellow, U. Mich., 1980—81, Fulbright Commn., U.S. Dept. State, 2002; grantee, U.S. Info. Agy., U.S. Dept. State, 1996, Ariz. Arts Edn. Rsch. Inst., 1998—99; European Union/Greek Ministry

Edn. grant, 2005. Mem.: Fulbright Assn. (mem. arts task force and internat. edn. task force 2003, bd. dirs. Ariz. chpt. 2005—), Greek Soc. Music Edn. (sci. adv. bd. 2000), Coll. Music Soc. (adv. com. music edn. mem. 1986—88), Internat. Soc. Music Edn. (nat. adv. bd. 1992—94), Music Educators Nat. Conf. (exec. com. music edn. rsch. coun. 1988—98, exec. com. 1995—2000, hall of fame bd. mem. 2002—, chair history spl. rsch. interest group 2004—). D-Liberal. Avocations: travel, reading. Home: 825 E Redondo Dr Tempe AZ 85282 Office: Ariz State Univ Sch Music Box 852870405 Tempe AZ 85287-0405 Office Phone: 480-965-4997. E-mail: jere.humphreys@asu.edu.

HUMPHREYS, JOSEPHINE, writer; b. Charleston, S.C., Feb. 2, 1945; d. William and Martha Humphreys. AB, Duke U., 1967; MA, Yale U., 1968. Author: Dreams of Sleep, 1984 (Ernest Hemingway Found. award 1985), Rich in Love, 1987, The Fireman's Fair, 1991, Nowhere Else on Earth, 2000 (So. Book award 2001). Recipient Lyndhurst Found. prize, 1985, Hillsdale prize, 1993; Guggenheim fellow, 1984; Woodrow Wilson Found. fellow, 1967, Danforth Found. fellow, 1967. Fellow So. Writers. Home and Office: care Harriet Wasserman Agy 137 E 36th St Ste 190 New York NY 10016-3528

HUMPHREYS, KENNETH KING, engineer, educator, professional society administrator; b. Pitts., Jan. 19, 1938; s. Meredith Harold and Olga (Adamitis) H.; m. Harriet Elizabeth Moss, May 6, 1961; children: Kenneth King, Keith Alan, Kevin James, Karen Elizabeth. BS, Carnegie Inst. Tech., 1959, postgrad., 1961-62, U. Pitts., 1965; MS, W.Va. U., 1967; PhD, Kennedy Western U., 1990. Registered profl. engr., Pa., N.C., W.Va.; cert. cost engr. U.S., Mex., Internat. Tech. asst. Applied Research Lab.-U.S. Steel Corp., 1959-60, tech. assoc. Monroeville, Pa., 1960-62, asst. technologist Universal, Pa., 1962-63, assoc. research engr., 1963-65; cost engr. W. Va. U. Coal Research Bur., Morgantown, 1965-67, sr. staff and cost engr., 1967-71, asst. dir., 1971-81; asst. prof. Coll. Mineral and Energy Resources-W. Va., Morgantown, 1970-73; assoc. prof. Coll. Mineral and Energy Resources-W. Va. U., Morgantown, 1973-76, prof., 1976-82, adj. prof., 1982-92, asst. to dean, 1971-77, chmn. minerals program, 1978-81, asst. dean acad. affairs, 1979-82; exec. dir. Am. Assn. Cost Engrs., 1971-92. Engring. cons. metallurgy and fuel tech., 1963—82; engring. cons. cost engring. and project mgmt., 1993—. Author: Basic Cost Engineering, 1981, 2d edit., 1986, 3d edit., 1996, What Every Engineer Should Know About Ethics, 1999; editor: Control and Management of Capital Projects, 2d edit., 1992, reprint edit., 1998; co-author, co-editor: Basic Mathematics and Computer Applications for Coal Preparation and Mining, 1983; co-author, assoc. editor: Coal Preparation, 4th edit., 1979; co-author, editor: Project and Cost Engineers' Handbook, 4th edit., 2005; co-author, co-editor: Mechanical Estimating Guidebook, 5th edit., 1987, 6th edit., 1995; co-author, editor: Jelen's Cost and Optimization Engineering, 3d edit., 1991; editor: Effective Project Management Through Applied Cost and Schedule Control, 1996; contbr. articles to prof. jours.; patentee in field. Leader Allegheny Trails, Piedmont and Mountaineer area couns. Boy Scouts Am., 1961—, dist. commr. Mountaineer area coun., 1969-72, dist. tng. chmn., 1972-74, 90, chmn. coun. tng., 1975-77, exec. bd., 1987-89, leadership devel. com., area 6 East Cen. region, 1977-79, dist. commr. Piedmont coun., 1996-97, rechartering com., 1997-99, asst. dist. commr., 1999-2002, asst. coun. commr., 2003—, internat. rep., 2001-; deacon 1st Presbyn. Ch., Morgantown, W.Va., 1968-70, ruling elder, 1972-75, 90-92, pres. congregation, 1975-77; deacon Waldensian Presbyn. Ch., Valdese, N.C., 1995-97, treas., 1995-96. Recipient Silver Beaver award Mountaineer Area Coun. Boy Scouts Am., 1973, Disting. Silver Beaver award Boy Scouts Am., 1990; recipient dist. award of merit Mountaineer Area Coun. Boy Scouts Am., 1969, Woodbadge award Mountaineer Area Coun. Boy Scouts Am., 1971, 50-Year Vets. award Boy Scouts Am., 1998, Het Schaap mit vijf Poten award Royal Netherlands Industries Fair, 1977; named Hon. West Virginian Gov. West Virginia, 1974. Fellow NSPE (life mem.), Assn. Cost Engrs. (U.K.), Assn. Advancement Cost Engring. Internat. (nat. chmn. 1969-71, 1998-2004, Mem. of Moment, nat. bd. dirs. 1971, exec. dir. 1971-92, award of merit 1993, award recognition 1979, pub. Cost Engring. mag. 1981-92, co-editor trans. 1982-92, pres. No. W.Va. sect. 1989-91, pres. Catawba Valley, Charlotte, N.C. sect. 1994-96), Profl. Engrs. N.C. (ethics steering com. 1995—, chmn. ethics com. 1999-2001, Engr. of Yr. award 1999), Assn. Italiana di Ingegneria Economica; mem. Soc. Mexicana de Ingenieria Economica Financiera y de Costos (Mex.), Cost Engring. Assn. So. Africa (hon. life), Internat. Cost Engring. Coun. (sec.-treas. 1976—, disting. internat. fellow), W.Va. Soc. Profl. Engrs. (bd. dirs. 1971-76, 83-92, v.p. 1980-81, pres. 1982-83, W.Va. Engr. of Yr. 1986), Morgantown Soc. Profl. Engrs. (pres. 1969-70, bd. dirs. 1970-76), Am. Assn. Engring. Socs. (bd. govs. 1979-83), Coun. Engring. Splty. Bds. (pres.-elect 1990-92, pres. 1992-93), Sigma Xi, Beta Theta Pi (asst. gen. sec. 1987-91), Alpha Phi Omega. Democrat. Home and Office: 1168 Hidden Lake Dr Granite Falls NC 28630-8592

HUMPHREYS, PAUL WILLIAM, philosophy educator, consultant; b. London, Jan. 17, 1950; came to U.S., 1971; s. William Edward and Florence C. (Didcock) H.; m. Diane Gail Snustad, July 14, 1984; children: Emily Victoria, Alexandra Elizabeth. BSc, U. Sussex, U.K., 1971; MA, MS, Stanford U., 1974, PhD, 1976. From asst. to assoc. prof. philosophy U. Va., Charlottesville, 1978-91, prof., 1991—, chmn., 1996—97, 1999—2004; v.p. Assn. for Founds. Sci., 1995-99. Seminar dir. NEH, Va., 1991, 95; cons. EPA, CDC, BCG; vis. prof. CNRS, Paris, France, 2005. Author: Chances of Explanation, 1989, Extending Ourselves, 2004; editor: Synthese, 1991—98, Foundations of Science, 1993—98, Oxford Studies in the Philosophy of Science, 1999—. Recipient Fulbright travel award, 1971, Scholars award NSF, 1984. Mem. Am. Philos. Assn., Philosophy Sci. Assn. (mem. gov. bd. 1997-2000), Keswick Soc. (chmn. 2000—). Home: 323 Kent Rd Charlottesville VA 22903-2409 Office: U Va Dept Philosophy PO Box 400780 Charlottesville VA 22903-4780

HUMPHREYS, ROBERT RUSSELL, lawyer, consultant, arbitrator; b. Eugene, Oreg., May 7, 1938; s. Russell Wallace and Roberta Lois (Bennett) H.; m. Natalia Dimitrievna Lucenko; children: Tatyana Roberta, Grigori Robert. BA, U. Wash., 1959; LLB, George Washington U., 1965. Bar: Va. 1965, D.C. 1966, U.S. Dist. Ct. (D.C.) 1966, U.S. Ct. Appeals (D.C. cir.) 1985, U.S. Ct. Appeals (4th cir.) 2000, Ct. Fed. Claims 2001, U.S. Ct. Appeals (1st cir.) 2003. Law clk. Barco, Cook & Patton, Washington, 1963-64, Keller & Heckman, Washington, 1964; mgr. pub. affairs services Air Transport Assn. Am., Washington, 1965-66; asst. to v.p. fed. affairs, 1966-71; spl. counsel com. on labor and human resources U.S. Senate, Washington, 1971-77; commr. Rehab. Services Adminstrn., HEW, Washington, 1977-80; ptnr. Hoffheimer & Johnson, Washington, 1980-83, Humphreys & Mitchell, Washington, 1983-88; cons. MARC Assocs., Inc., Washington, 1988-94; pvt. practice law, Washington, 1988—; pres. The Humphreys Group, Washington, 1991-95; pres., ceo Jennings Randolph Inst., Washington, 1998—; hearing officer State of N.C., 2002. Spkr. nat., internat. confs. Author: Compliance Manual on Americans with Disabilities Act; contbr. articles to profl. jours. Incorporator, bd. dirs., treas., counsel Nat. Ctr. for Barrier-Free Environ., 1975-77, 81-84; bd. dirs. Va. Spl. Olympics, 1982-84. Mem. D.C. Bar Assn., George Washington U. Law Alumni Assn., Va. State Bar, Phi Delta Phi. Achievements include being the prin. Senate draftsman for Black Lung Benefits Act, 1972, Rehab. Act, 1973, Randolph-Sheppard Act Amendments, 1974, Black Lung Benefits Reform Act, 1977. Office Phone: 202-363-2200. Personal E-mail: humphreyslaw@att.net.

HUMPHREYS TROY, PATRICIA, communications executive; b. Birmingham, June 3, 1946; m. Stephen Richard Troy; 1 child, David. BS in Edn., Auburn U., 1968, MEd, 1969; cert. advanced study in edn., Loyola Coll., 1989; cert., Inst. Orgn. Mgmt., U.S. Chamber at U. Del., 1999. Cert. assn. exec. Grad. tchg. asst. Auburn U., 1968—69; asst. libr. McKendree Coll., 1969—71; adj. instr. Chapman Coll., 1972—75; libr. Wroxeter-on-Severn, 1978—80; adminstrv. dir., media dir. Chesapeake Acad.1, 1980—89; pres., CEO Bay Media Inc., 1989—, Next Wave Group LLC, 2001—; CEO, Facetswoman, Inc., 2004—. Past vice-chair bd. trustees, chair strategic planning com. Anne Arundel Health Sys. and Anne Arundel Med. Ctr.; exec. dir., adminstr. Assn. for Women in Comms., 1996—2004. Unit pres. Am. Cancer Soc., 1986—92; pres. Panhellenic of Annapolis, 1976, Cultural Arts Found. Anne Arundel County, 1995—99, Greater Severna Park Coun., 1990—93; chair Small Area Plan for Severna Park, Anne Arundel County, 1997—2002, Anne Arundel County Cancer Control Task Force, 1994—96; bd. trustees, founding vice chair Chesapeake Acad., 1980—; grad. Leadership Anne Arundel; founding chair Assn. for Severna Park Improvement, Renewal and Enhancement, Inc., 1994—. Named One of Md.'s Top 100 Women, Daily Record, 1997, 1999, 2001, Bus. Leader of Yr., Anne Arundel Trade Coun., 1996, Women in Bus. Advocate, Md. Small Bus. Assn., Independence Day Parade Grand Marshal, Greater Severna Park Chamber, 1993; recipient Exec. citation for cmty. svc., Anne Arundel County, 1999, Disting. Alumni award, Leadership Anne Arundel, 1997, TWIN award, Anne Arundel County YWCA, 1996. Mem.: Am. Soc. Assn. Exec. (cert.), Anne Arundel Trade Coun./Annapolis and Anne Arundel County Chamber (edn. chmn. 1990—), Am. Bus. Women's Assn. (pres. Severn River/Md. Capital chpt. 1980—81, Woman of Yr. Severn River 1991, Bus. Assoc. of Yr., Severn River 1992, named among Top 10 Women in Bus. 2003), Women in Comms. (pres. Md. profl. chpt. 1991—92). Office: Ste S-28 780 Ritchie Hwy Severna Park MD 21146 Office Phone: 410-647-7231. E-mail: pat@facetowoman.com.

HUMPHRIES, ASA ALAN, JR., biologist, educator, dean; b. Anniston, Ala., Sept. 6, 1924; s. Asa Allen and Myree (Adamson) Humphries; m. LaNelle Wright, Sept. 10, 1949 (dec. 1969); children: Susan Myree, David Alan, Ann Wesley; m. Laurie Cecilia Lee, July 22, 1972; 1 child, Laura Catherine. AB, Emory U., 1948, MS, 1949; AM, Princeton U., 1952, PhD, 1953. Instr. biology Emory U., Atlanta, 1949-50, from asst. prof. to assoc prof. dept. biology, 1954-67, prof. biology, 1967-81, chmn. dept. biology, 1974-81; anatomy instr. U. Va. Sch. Medicine, Charlottesville, 1953-54; prof. Transylvania U., Lexington, Ky., 1981-94, prof. emeritus, 1994—, v.p., dean, 1981-83, exec. v.p., dean, 1983-91, dean spl. programs, 1991-94, dean emeritus, 1994—. Mem. editl. bd.: U. Press Ky., 1981—94; contbr. articles to profl. jours. Trustee Lexington Clin. Found., 1986—; bd. dirs. Ky. Inst. Internat. Studies, 1990—94, Operation Read, Lexington, 1993—99, 2001—02. With U.S. Army, 1943—46. Recipient Am. Rsch. award, Assn. S.E. Biologists, 1956, Transylvania medal, 2001; fellow, NATO, NSF, Procter, Princeton U., 1952—53; grantee Rsch., NSF, NIH, Rockefeller Found., 1959—. Mem.: AAAS, Soc. Devel. Biology, Optimist Club Internat., Alpha Tau Omega, Omicron Delta Kappa (leadership hon.), Sigma Xi. Democrat. Home and Office: 2009 Des Cognets Ln Lexington KY 40502-3040 Personal E-mail: asa.humphries@gte.net.

HUMPHRIES, EDWARD FRANCIS, lawyer; b. S.I., NY, May 25, 1957; s. Robert Edward and Joan D. (Mauter) H.; m. Colleen Kennedy, July 21, 1990; 1 child, Stephen Edward. BBA magna cum laude, Bernard M. Baruch Coll., 1981; JD, Fordham U., 1984. Bar: N.J. 1984, U.S. Dist. Ct. N.J. 1984, N.Y. 1985, U.S. Dist. Ct. (ea. and so. dists.) N.Y. 1985, U.S. Dist. Ct. (we. dist.) N.Y. 1987, Pa. 1990, Hawaii 1990, U.S. Supreme Ct. 1990, U.S. Dist. Ct. Hawaii 1991; lic. capt. USCG. Assoc. Amabile & Erman, Bklyn., 1984-86, 87-92, ptnr., 1993—; assoc. Pegalis & Wachsman, Great Neck, N.Y., 1986-87. Trustee Soc. Hill East Condominium Assn., East Brunswick, N.J., 1987-90, pres., 1988-90; co-chmn. Homeowners Assn. Coun. East Brunswick, 1988-90; vice-chmn. East Brunswick Planning Bd., 1989-90; pres. East Brunswick Rep. Club, 1989-91; mem. strategic planning com. Staten Island Acad., 2003-05. Recipient Morton Wollman medal Bernard M. Baruch Coll., 1981. Mem. NY State Bar Assn., Hawaii State Bar Assn., Princess Bay Boatman's Assn. (vice commodore 2002—, bd. dirs. 2002—), Beta Gamma Sigma, Sigma Iota Epsilon. Republican. Roman Catholic. Home: 451 Manor Rd Staten Island NY 10314-2963 Office: Amabile & Erman 1000 South Ave Staten Island NY 10314-3430

HUMPHRIES, FREDERICK S., former university president; b. Apalachicola, Fla., Dec. 26, 1935; m. Antoinette Humphries; children: Frederick S., Robin Tanya, Laurence Anthony. BS magna cum laude, Fla. A&M U., 1957; PhD in Phys. Chemistry (fellow), U. Pitts., 1964. Pvt. tutor sci. and math., 1959-64; asst. prof. chemistry U. Minn., Mpls., 1966-67; asso. prof. chemistry Fla. A&M U., 1964-67, prof. chemistry, 1964-67, dir. 13 coll. curriculum program, 1967-68; dir. summer confs. Inst. for Services to Edn., 1968-74, dir. interdisciplinary program, 1973-74, dir. two-univs. grad. program in sci., 1973-74, v.p., 1970-74; pres. Tenn. State U., Nashville, 1974-85, Fla. A&M U., Tallahassee, 1985—2001, Nat. Assn. for Equal Opportunity in Higher Edn., 2002—04. Cons. to various colls. and univs.; mem. bd. grad. advocates Meharry Med. Coll. 1976, co-chmn. Reston's Black Focus, 1973; bd. dirs. So. Growth, Nat. Merit Scholarship Corp. Bd.; bd. regents 5-Yr. Working Group for Agriculture, chmn. State Univ. System of Fla.; adv. coun. Panhandle Regional Ctr. Excellence in Math., Sci., Computers, Tech.-FAMU & U., West Fla.; Nat. Assn. Ednl. Opportunities sci. and tech. adv. com., vice chmn. bd. dirs.; mem. EIS adv. com. HBCUs. Contbr. articles on higher edn. to profl. publs. Chmn. Fairfax county Anti-Poverty Commn., 1972-74, White House Sci. and Tech. Adv. Com., on Edn. Blacks in Fla.; bd. dirs. YMCA, 1975—, Walmart Corp., Brinker Internat., Barnett Bank Tallahassee; bd. ann. minority bus. Youth Ednl. Svc. Embarkment; commn. Future of South, 1986, com. tech. and innovation commn.; steering com. Apalachicola Bay Area Resource Planning and Mgmt.; subcom. Fed. Student Fin. Assistance-Office for the Advancement of Pub. Black Colls., chmn. adv. com. Recipient Disting. Svc. to Advancement of Edn. for Black Americans award Inst. for Svcs. to Edn., Disting. Edn. and Adminstr.; Meritorious award Fla. A&M U., Human Rels. award Met. Human Rels. Commn., Nashville, 1978, Thurgood Marshall Ednl. Achievement award Johnson Publ. Co., 1990; named an Outstanding Alumnus of Pitts. U., 1986, Floridian of Yr., Orlando Sentinel, 1999. Mem. NIH (nat. adv. com. neurol. and communicative disorders and stroke coun.), AAUP, AAAS, NAACP, Am. Chem. Soc., Am. Assn. Higher Edn., Nat. Assn. State Univs. and Land-Grant Colls. (chmn.), Nat. Assn. Equal Opportunity Bd. Dirs. (chmn.), Assn. Minority Rsch. Univ., Alpha Kappa Mu (pres., award), Alpha Phi Alpha (Meritorious Svc. award). Office: Fla A&M U Office of President Tallahassee FL 32307

HUMPHRIES, JOAN ROPES, psychologist, educator; b. Bklyn., Oct. 17, 1928; d. Lawrence Gardner and Adele Lydia (Zimmermann) Ropes; m. Charles C. Humphries, Apr. 4, 1957; children: Peggy Ann, Charlene Adele. BA, U. Miami, 1950; MS, Fla. State U., 1955; PhD, La. State U., 1963. Registered lobbyist State of Fla. Part-time instr. psychology dept. U. Miami, Coral Gables, Fla., 1964—66; prof. behavioral studies dept. Miami-Dade Coll., 1966—. Presenter, lectr. in field cruise ship Costa Romantica. Editl. staff, maj. author The Application of Scientific Behaviorism to Humanistic Phenomena, 1975, Rev. Edit., 1979, prodr. & host, Sigma Series video, cert. for TV Strategies in Global Modern Academia: Issues and Answers in Higher Education, 1993—94, Strategies in Global Modern Academia: Issues and Answers in Higher Education II, 1995; prodr.: (video series) Strategies in Global Modern Academia: Issues and Answers in Higher Education, III, 1996—97, Strategies in Global Modern Academia: Issues and Answers in Higher Education, IV, 2001—02, W2RN (cert.). Mem. Biofeedback Del., China, 1995; mem. Citizen Amb. Program Psychic Arts Del. to Russia, 1997; mem. Citizen Amb. Program Am. Mus. Natural History; life mem. Pastorius Home Assn., Inc., 2001; mem. Citizen Amb. Program Vizcayans Mus., Aldren Kindred of Am., Inc.; mem. Citizen Amb. Program Nat. Trust Hist. Preservation, The Charles F. Menninger Soc., People to People; mem. ladies aux. Fla. Soc. SAR; mem. Nat. Mus. Women in Arts; mem. women's history month com. Jr. Honor Women Recognition, women's leadership seminar. Recipient award in hon. of women recognition, Women's Hist. Month com. and Women's Leadership Seminar, 2003. Mem.: AAUP (past v.p. Fla. conf. 1986—88, pres. of chpt., Miami-Dade Coll. 1986—, mem. exec. bd. Fla. conf. 1989—90, former v.p., sec. Miami-Dade Coll.), AAAS, AAUW (life; former v.p. Tamiami br. 1983—88, Appreciation award 1977), APA (life), Dade-Monroe Psychol. Assn., Fla. Psychol. Assn., Biofeedback Soc. Am. (pres. 1990—), Noetic Scis., NY Acad. Scis. (life), Assn. Applied Psychophysiology and Biofeedback, Inst. Evaluation, Diagnosis and Treatment (past v.p. 1975—87, pres. 1987—, former bd. dirs.), Internat. Soc. for Study Subtle Energies and Energy Medicine (charter), Physicians for Social Responsibility, Am. Psychol. Soc. (charter), Am. Inst. Parliamentarians, (Biltmore Hotel) Coral Gables, Pilgrim John Howland Soc., Hist. Homeowners Coral Gables, Heredity Order Descs. of Colonial Govs., Regines in Miami, North Campus Spkrs. Bur. (Cmty. Lecture Series award), Internat. Platform Assn. (bd. govs. 1979—, Silver Bowl award 1993), Mexico Beach C. of C. (bus. 1991—95), Colonial Dames 17th Century, Soc. Mayflower Descs. (elder William Brewster colony), Cellar Club, Coral Gables Country Club (life), Jockey Club (life), Phi Lambda Pi, Phi Lambda (Founder's Plaque 1976, Appreciation award 1987). Democrat. Achievements include research in biofeedback and human consciousness. Home: 1311 Alhambra Cir Coral Gables FL 33134-3521 Office Phone: 305-443-8433.

HUMPHRIES, JOHN O'NEAL, cardiologist, educator, dean; b. Columbia, S.C., Oct. 22, 1931; s. Arthur Lee and Helen Elliott (O'Neal) H.; m. Mary Ellen Cregan, Mar. 13, 1954; children: Arthur Thomas, Ellen Cregan, John Elliott. BS, Duke U., 1952; MD, Johns Hopkins U., 1956. Diplomate Am. Bd. Internal Medicine (mem. bd. subsplty. cardiovascular disease 1974-79). Intern Johns Hopkins Hosp., 1957; asst. resident Osler Med. Service, Osler Med. Svc., 1958-60, resident physician pvt. med. svc., 1962-64, staff physician, 1962-79; rsch. fellow in cardiology U. London, St. George's Hosp., 1960-61, Johns Hopkins U. Med. Sch., 1956-57, 61-62, mem. faculty, 1964-79, Robert L. Levy prof. cardiology, 1975-79, prof. medicine, 1976-79; O.B. Mayer Sr. and Jr. prof. medicine U. S.C., Columbia, 1979-86, prof. medicine, 1979-96; disting. prof. medicine, dean emeritus, 1997—; chmn. dept. medicine U. S.C., Columbia, 1979-87, dean Sch. Medicine, 1983-94. Contbr. articles to med. publs.; mem. editl. bd. various jours. Bd. dirs. Md. Ballet, Balt., 1975-78. Master ACP (bd. govs. for S.C. chpt. 1986-90), Am. Coll. Cardiology (bd. govs. for Md. chpt. 1973-76); mem. Am. Fedn. Clin. Rsch., Am. Heart Assn. (fellow coun . clin. cardiology, chmn. postgrad. edn. com., exec. com. 1972-75), Cen. Md. Heart Assn. (pres. 1972-73), Md. Heart Assn. (pres. 1976-77), Assn. Univ. Cardiologists, Am. Clin. and Climatol. Assn., Alpha Omega Alpha. Office: U SC Sch Medicine Columbia SC 29208-0001

HUMPHRIES, JUDY LYNN, lawyer, nurse; b. Charleston, W.Va., Nov. 20, 1946; d. Robert Elmer and Arravelva Virginia (Davis) H.; m. Michael Allen Grant, Dec. 29, 1971; children: Susan Lindley, Christopher Allen, Elizabeth Davis. BSN, W.Va. U., 1968; MS, U. Md., 1970; JD, William & Mary Coll., 1977. Bar: Va. 1977, W.Va. 1978, D.C. 1980. Instr. in psychiatric nursing W.Va. U., Morgantown, 1970-72, asst. prof. upper div. nursing, 1977-78; psychiat. nurse Veterans Hosp., Cin., 1972-73; asst. prosecutor Monongalia County, Morgantown, 1978-81; sole practice Fairmont, W.Va., 1980-90; instr. health law and med. ethics Fairmont State Coll., 1984-86, adj. prof., 1984-87. Cons. J.B. Lippincott Pubs., Phila., 1985; asst. prosecuter Marion County, W.Va., 1986-88; bd. dirs. Fairmont Gen. Hosp. Inc., 1988-90. Bd. dirs. Monongalia County Youth Svcs. Ctr., 1981-83, Hope, Inc., Task Force on Domestic Violence, 1986-89. Mem. ABA, LWV. Democrat. Episcopalian. Home: RR 7 Box 349 Fairmont WV 26554-8932

HUMPHRIES, M. CLAYTON, JR., lawyer; b. Opelika, Alabama, Mar. 8, 1953; BA cum laude, Birmingham-So. Coll., 1975; JD, U. Ala., 1978. Bar: Ala. 1978. Law clk. Ala. Supreme Ct., 1978—79, U.S. Dist. Ct. Ala. (mid. dist.), 1980; v.p., gen. counsel Westpoint Stevens, Inc., West Point, Ga. Mem.: ABA, Ala. State Bar Assn. Office: Westpoint Stevens Inc 507 W 10th St PO Box 71 West Point GA 31833-1232 Office Phone: 706-645-4115. E-mail: humphries.clay@wpstv.com.

HUMPHRY, JAMES, III, retired librarian, publishing executive, educator; b. Springfield, Mass., July 21, 1916; s. James and Elizabeth Lucy (Ames) H.; m. Priscilla Eaton, Dec. 26, 1942; children: Susan H. Zolnier, Elizabeth Ames Schnabel. AB, Harvard U., 1939; MS, Columbia U., 1941. Reference asst. N.Y. Pub. Library, 1939-41, 46, chief map divsn., 1946; librarian, prof. bibliography Colby Coll.; bus. mgr. Colby Coll. Press, 1947-57; chief librarian Met. Mus. Art, 1957-68; v.p. H.W. Wilson Co., Bronx, 1968-82, pres., dir. found., 1995-2000, also bd. dirs., 1968—; prof. Pratt Inst., Bklyn., 1982-98. Lectr. Columbia Sch. Libr. Svc., 1967-68; vis. assoc. prof. Grad. Sch. Libr. Studies, U. Hawaii, 1983; libr. cons. Am. Heritage, 1965-68, John Wiley & Sons, 1966-69, Coun. Advancement Small Colls., 1956, Gossage Regan Assocs., N.Y.C., 1988-96; coord. Maine Libr. Assn. for ALA sponsored Library Services bill, 1948-49, 55-57; nat. bd. Libr. Presdl. Papers, 1967-69; adminstr. grants-in-aid program N.Y. State Council Arts, 1967-68 Compiler, Library of Edwin Arlington Robinson, 1950; Editor: (with Carl J. Weber) Fitzgerald's Rubaiyat, 1959; Contbr. articles to mags. and jours. Trustee, chmn. adv. com. Archives Am. Art, 1967-88; mem. fine arts vis. com. Harvard U., 1967-73; mem. adv. council St. John's U. Congress for Librarians, 1963-67; bd. dirs. Huguenot YMCA; trustee N.Y. Met. Reference and Research Library Agy., 1967-77, Westchester Library System, 1974-83, New Rochelle Pub. Libr., 1977-87, Thomas Paine Nat. Hist. Assn., 1980-96; pres. Westchester Libr. System. 1980-82, New Rochelle Pub. Library 1979-80, 82, New Rochelle Pub. Libr. Found., 1994-96. With AUS, 1942-46, maj. U.S. Army, 1951-54; lt. col. USAR. Mem. ALA (councilor 1959-63, 67-69, chmn. com. on Wilson index reference services div. 1959-65, mem. subscription books com. 1963-66), Met. Mus. Art Employees Assn. (pres. 1961-63, gov. 1958-66), Maine Library Assn. (pres. 1955-56), Am. Assn. Museums (chmn. library group), Archons of Colophon (convener 1963-65), N.Y. Library Assn. (cons.), Spl. Libraries Assn. (chpt. vice chmn., chmn. mus. group 1962-64, N.Y. conf. chmn. 1967), Assn. Coll. and Research Libraries (pres., dir. 1966-69), Internat. Council Museums (corr.) Clubs: Grolier, N.Y. Library (council 1959-67, pres. 1965-66), Harvard (N.Y.C.). Home: 31 Kirkland Village Cir Bethlehem PA 18017-4753

HUND, THOMAS N., rail transportation executive; BA in Bus. Adminstrn., Loyola U.; MBA, U. Chgo., 1988. Acct. Burlington Northern Santa Fe Corp., 1983-89, asst. v.p., contr., 1989-90, v.p., contr., 1990-95, sr. v.p., CFO, 1999-2000, exec. v.p., CFO, 2001—. Mem. Amer. Inst. of CPA's. Office: Berlington Nothern Santa Fa 2650 Lou Menk Dr 2nd Fl Fort Worth TX 76131-2830

HUNDER, GENE GERALD, rheumatologist, educator; b. Lake City, Minn., Feb. 7, 1932; s. Tilman James and Melita Henrietta (Bremer) H.; m. Ingeborg Anne Hanson, May 6, 1990; children: Heidi, Jennifer, Gregory,Grant, Naomi, Stephanie. Student, St. Olaf Coll., 1950—52; BA, U. Minn. (Mpls.), 1954, MD, 1958, MS, 1963. Diplomate Am. Bd. Internal Medicine. Intern. Strong Meml. Hosp., Rochester, N.Y., 1958-59, resident, 1959-61, Mayo Clinic, Rochester, Minn., 1961-64; instr. internal medicine Mayo Grad. Sch., Rochester, Minn., 1966-67, asst. prof. internal medicine, 1968-73, assoc. prof., 1973-78, prof., 1978—, full mem. internal medicine, 1981—, cons. internal medicine and rheumatology; prof. internal medicine Mayo Clinic Mayo found., Rochester, Minn., 1978—; head sect. rheumatology Mayo Clinic, 1976-81. Chmn. rheumatology rsch. com., 1976-81, 87, clin. investigator tng. program Mayo Grad. Sch., 1981-84, chmn. div. rheumatology 1987-96; Philip Showalter Hench lect. Ariz. Med . Soc., Phoenix, 1965; Charles W. Thomas lectr. Med. Coll. Va., Charlottesville, 1979; Carl Pearson lectr. Los Angeles County Med. Assn., 1983; Henry J. Lehrhoff lectr. Clarkson Hosp., Omaha, 1989, Nana Swartz lectr. Swedish Med. Soc., 1994, Gilbert Galens Meml. lectr. William Beaumont Hosp., Detroit, 1995. Co-author: Physical Examination of the Joints, 1978; editor: Rheumatology, 1978, Atlas of Rheumatology, 1998, 2002, Mayo Clinic on Arthritis, 1999, 2002; assoc. editor: Jour. Lab and Clin. Medicine, 1979-81; editor Jour. Current Opinion in Rheumatology, 1992-2000, Jour. Arthritis Care and Rsch., 2000-05; mem. editl. bd. Jour. Rheumatology, 1982—, Jours. Musculoskeletal Medicine, 1983-2001, Annals Internal Medicine, 1998-2001, ISI List of Frequently Cited Clin. Investigators. Mem. ho. dels. Arthritis Found., Atlanta, 1980-83, trustee, 1985; mem. exec. com. Minn. Arthritis Found., Mpls., 1984-90. Nu Sigma Nu scholar, 1955, Minn. Med. Found. acad. scholar, 1955. Fellow ACP; mem. AMA, Am. Bd. Internal Medicine, AAAS. Ctrl. Soc. Clin. Research (mem. program com.), Am. Soc. Clin. Rheumatology (pres.), Am. Coll. Rheumatology (mem. exec. com. 1976-77, v.p. cen. region 1987, pres. cen. region, 1989, bd. dir. 1988-92, Master award 1997, Disting. Rheumatologist 2004), Phi Beta Kappa, Alpha Omega Alpha. Republican. Lutheran. Home: RR 1 Box 132B Zumbro Falls MN 55991-9725 Office: Mayo Clinic 200 1st St SW Rochester MN 55905-0002 Office Phone: 507-284-2511. Business E-Mail: ghunder@mayo.edu.

HUNDERT, EDWARD M., academic administrator; b. Woodbridge, N.J. m. Mary Hundert; 3 children. BS in Math. and History of Sci. and Medicine, summa cum laude, Yale U., 1978; MA in Philosophy, Politics and Econs., first class honors, Oxford U., 1980; MD, Harvard U., 1984. Diplomate Am. Bd. Neurology and Psychiatry. Med. intern Mount Auburn Hosp., Cambridge, Mass., 1984—85; resident in adult psychiatry, rsch. fellow, Labs. for Psychiatric Rsch. McLean Hosp., Belmont, Mass., 1985—88, chief resident, 1987—88; clin. fellow in psychiatry Harvard Med. Sch., Boston, 1984—88, instr. psychiatry, 1988—90, asst. prof. psychiatry, 1990—93, asst. prof. med. ethics, 1990—97, assoc. dean for student affairs, 1990—97, assoc. master, William B. Castle Soc., 1992—97, assoc. prof. psychiatry, 1994—97, faculty fellow, Harvard U. Mind/Brain/Behavior Initiative, 1996—99; prof. psychiatry U. Rochester Sch. Medicine and Dentistry, 1997—2002; prof. med. humanities U. Rochester (N.Y.) Sch. Medicine and Dentistry, 1997—2002, sr. assoc. dean for med. edn., 1997—2000, dean, 2000—02; pres. Case Western Res. U., Cleve., 2002—, prof. biomed. ethics, 2002—. Asst. psychiatrist McLean Hosp., Belmont, 1988—94, hosp. ethicist, 1988—97, assoc. psychiatrist, 1995—97; psychiatrist Strong Meml. Hosp., Rochester, NY, 1997—2002. Author: Philosophy, Psychiatry and Neuroscience: Three Approaches to the Mind, 1989, Lessons from an Optical Illusion: On Nature and Nurture, Knowledge and Values, 1995. Mem.: Phi Beta Kappa. Office: Case Western Res U Adelbert Hall 216 10900 Euclid Ave Cleveland OH 44106-7001*

HUNDLEY, NORRIS CECIL, JR., historian, educator; b. Houston, Oct. 26, 1935; s. Norris Cecil and Helen Marie (Mundine) H.; m. Carol Marie Beckquist, June 8, 1957; children: Wendy Michelle Hundley Harris, Jacqueline Marie Hundley Reid. AA, Mt. San Antonio Coll., 1956; AB, Whittier Coll., 1958; PhD (Univ. fellow), UCLA, 1963. Instr. U. Houston, 1963-64; asst. prof. Am. history UCLA, 1964-69, assoc. prof., 1969-73, prof., 1973-94, prof. emeritus, 1994—, chmn. exec. com. Inst. Am. Cultures, 1976-93, chmn. univ. program on Mex., 1981-94, acting dir. Latin Am. Ctr., 1989-90, dir. Latin Am. Ctr., 1990-94. Exec. com. U. Calif. Consortium on Mex. and the U.S., 1981-86; adv. com. Calif. water atlas project Calif. Office Planning and Research, 1977-79 Author: Dividing the Waters: A Century of Controversy Between the United States and Mexico, 1966, Water and the West: The Colorado River Compact and the Politics of Water in the American West, 1975, The Great Thirst: Californians and Water 1770s-1990s, 1992, Las aguas divididas: Un siglo de controversia entre México y Estados Unidos, 2000, The Great Thirst: Californians and Water-A History, 2001; co-author: The Calif. Water Atlas, 1979, California: History of a Remarkable State, 1982; editor: The American Indian, 1974, The Chicano, 1975, The Asian American, 1976; co-editor: The American West: Frontier and Region, 1969, Golden State Series, 1978-2002; mng. editor Pacific Hist. Rev., 1968-97; mem. editl. bd. Jour. San Diego History, 1970-79, Calif. Hist. Soc., 1980-89; contbr. articles to profl. jours. Bd. dirs. John and LaRee Caughey Found., 1983-2000, Henry J. Bruman Ednl. Found., 1983-2003, Forest History Soc., 1987-93. Recipient award of merit Calif. Hist. Soc., 1979; Am. Philos. Soc. grantee, 1964, 71, Ford Found. grantee, 1968-69, U. Calif. Water Resources Ctr. grantee, 1969-72, 91, 2000, Sourisseau Acad. grantee, 1972, NEH grantee, 1983-89, Hewlett Found. grantee, 1986-89, U. Calif. Regents faculty fellow in humanities, 1975, Guggenheim fellow, 1978-79, Hist. Soc. So. Calif. fellow, 1996—; Whitsett lectr., 2000. Mem. Am. Hist. Assn. (exec. coun. Pacific Coast br. 1968-97, v.p. 1993-94, pres. 1994-95), Western History Assn. (coun. 1985-88, 93-97, pres. 1994-95, Winther award 1973, 79), Orgn. Am. Historians. Office: UCLA Dept History Los Angeles CA 90095-1473 E-mail: hundley@history.ucla.edu.

HUNDLEY, ROBERT WILLIAMS, medical services facility administrator; b. Suffolk, Va., Feb. 20, 1949; s. Leonard Earl and Katherine Elizabeth (Williams) H.; m. Patricia Dale Raiford; July 6, 1979; children: Adrienne, Matthw, Susan. Student, Louisburg Coll., 1967-69; BS, U. Richmond, 1971. Sales mgr. Garnett Oil Co., Suffolk, Va., 1971-74, Supreme Petroleum, Suffolk, 1974-78; exec. dir. Community Physicians, Virginia Beach, Va., 1978-84, Emergency Physicians of Tidewater, Virginia Beach, 1984—, also bd. dirs. Bd. dirs. Tidewater Emergency Med. Services, Norfolk, Va. Mem., officer Nansemond-Suffolk Vol. Rescue Squad, 1963—; vestry mem. St. Paul's Episco. Ch., Suffolk, 1974-78; mem. bd. dirs. Suffolk Hwy. Safety Commn., 1976-79. Named First Citizen, Cosmopolitan Club, 1976, one of Outstanding Young Men of Am., local Jaycees, 1978, nat. Jaycees, 1978-79. Mem. Va. Hosp. Assn., Nat. Registry Emergency Med. Techs. Lodges: Kiwanis (pres. Suffolk club 1979).

HUNDLEY, RONNIE, academic administrator; b. Columbus, Ga., July 18, 1950; s. Jack and Gwendolyn B. (Sasser) Hawthorne; m. Kathy A. Marcure, Apr. 28, 1972; children: Noel, Rhonda, Maria. BSME in Engring., U. Wash., 1974; MSME, Navy Postgrad., 1982, Degree of Engr., 1984. Registered profl. engr., Wash. Dir. engring. tech. Henry Cogswell Coll., Everett, Wash., 1989-91, acad. dean, 1991-93, pres., 1993—. Comdr. USN, 1968-89. Mem. ASME, Am. Assn. Higher Edn. Avocations: hiking, watercolor. Office: Henry Cogswell Coll 3002 Colby Ave Everett WA 98201-4012 E-mail: r.hundley@henrycogswell.edu.

HUNDT, REED ERIC, information industry advisor, lawyer; b. Ann Arbor, Mich., Mar. 3, 1948; s. Neal H. and Viola (Pullan) H.; m. Elizabeth Ann Katz, Oct. 26, 1980; children: Adam Elias, Nathaniel Pullan, Sara. BA, Yale U., 1969, JD, 1974. Bar: U.S. Dist. Ct. Md. 1974, U.S. Ct. Appeals (4th cir.) 1975, U.S. Dist. Ct. (cen. and no. dists.) Calif. 1976, U.S. Ct. Appeals (9th cir.) 1976, U.S. Supreme Ct. 1977, U.S. Tax Ct. 1978, U.S. Ct. Appeals (3d cir.) 1979, U.S. Dist. Ct. D.C. 1980, U.S. Ct. Appeals (D.C. cir.) 1980. Law clk. to presiding justice U.S. Ct. Appeals (4th cir.), Balt., 1974-75; assoc. Latham & Watkins, Washington, 1975-81, ptnr., 1982-94; chmn. FCC, Washington, 1994-97; prin. Charles Ross Ptnrs., LLC, Washington, Md., 1997—; sr. adv. McKinsey & Co. Mem. adv. com. and tchr. Yale Law Sch. and Yale Sch. of Mgmt.; bd. dirs. Allegiance Telecom, Inc., Northpoint Commn. Inc., Novell Inc., 1998—, Phone.com, Inc., Global Connect Partners, Core Express, Inc., Sigma Networks; spl. adv. Madison Dearborn Partners; venture ptnr. Benchmark Capital. Book rev. editor Yale U. Law Rev., 1974-75; author: (chpt. 9) Antitrust Adviser '85; contbr. articles to profl. jours. Mem. Environ. Task Force of Dem. Policy Com., Washington, 1986. Recipient Voice for Children Leadership award, Disting. Svc. award, Nat. Assn. of Elem. Sch. Principals, Nat. Assn. of Sec. Sch. Principals, Helen Keller Outstanding Pub. Svc. award, Am. Found. for the Blind. Mem. ABA. Office: Lawler Metzer & Milkman 2001 K St NW #802 Washington DC 20006-1044

HUNEYCUTT, ALICE RUTH, lawyer; b. New Haven, Jan. 10, 1951; d. C. Jerome and Alberta (Piner) H.; m. Howard Mark Bernstein, Nov. 28, 1981; children: Ashley Laughton, Laura Whitney. BA in History, Duke U., 1972; JD, U. Miami (Fla.), 1979. Bar: Fla. 1980, U.S. Dist. Ct. (so. dist.) Fla. 1980, U.S. Ct. Appeals (5th cir.) 1980, U.S. Dist. Ct. (mid. dist.) Fla. 1982, U.S. Ct. Appeals (11th cir.) 1982. Corp. counsel Burger King Corp., Miami, 1980-82; assoc. Stearns Weaver Miller Weissler Alhadeff & Sitterson, P.A., Tampa, Fla., 1982-84, ptnr., 1984—. Bd. dirs. Am. Heart Assn., Tampa, 1986-91, chmn. elect, 1988-89, chmn. 1990-91. Mem. ABA (corp., banking and bus law sect.), Fla. Bar Assn. (pres.'s Pro Bono Svc. award 1987), Fla. Assn. Women Lawyers. Democrat. Methodist. Home: 1400 72nd Ave NE Saint Petersburg FL 33702-4610 Office: 401 E Jackson St Ste 2200 Tampa FL 33602-5251 Office Phone: 813-222-5031. E-mail: ahuneycutt@swmwas.com.

HUNG, CHAO-SHUN, economics educator, researcher; b. Taiwan, Republic China, Jan. 20, 1942; came to U.S., 1969, naturalized, 1977; s. Chiang-shu and Yu-mei (Chen) H.; m. Jane Anne Chien, May 14, 1984. B.A., Taiwan Normal U., Taipei, Republic China, 1964; M.B.A., St. Louis U., 1972; Ph.D. in Econs., Tex. A&M U., 1982. Asst. prof. econs. Fla. Atlantic U., Boca Raton, 1982-88; assoc. prof. econs., 1988-93, prof. emeritus, 1994—; bd. dir. of Grad. Studies in Econs. Fla. Atlantic U., Boca Raton, 1982-94, chmn. dept. econs., 1992-94. Lt. Chinese Marine Corps., 1964-65, Taiwan. Mem. Am. Econ. Assn. Avocations: fishing, swimming, classical music. Office: Fla Atlantic U U Dept Econs 500 NW 20th St Boca Raton FL 33431-6415

HUNG, CHIH-MING, research scientist; s. Chien-Chen and Shiyin Hung; m. Chia-Chun Yang. BS, Nat. Cen. U., Chung-Li, Taiwan, 1993; MS, U. Fla., 1997, PhD, 2000. Rschr. U. Fla., Gainesville, 1996—2000; rfic design mgr. Tex. Instruments Inc., Dallas, 2000—. Second lt. U.S. Army, 1993—95, Taiwan. Recipient Tex. Instruments Grad. fellowship, 1999—2000, Outstanding Acad. Achievement Honor, 2000, Semiconductor Rsch. Corp. Copper Design Contest Winner, 1999, 2000. Mem.: IEEE (Dallas Engr. of Yr. 2004). Achievements include research in Pioneering research in the RFIC area. Office: Wtbu 12500 Tl Blvd MS8728 Dallas TX 75243 Office Phone: 214-480-4246.

HUNG, CHIN-CHENG, art educator, artist; s. Chao-Ho and Fen Chen Hung; m. Hsiu-Yuan Cheng, Oct. 1, 1992; 1 child, Jared. MFA in Painting, Savannah Coll. of Art and Design, 1999. Cert. technician of screen printing Taiwan Govt., 1997. Commd. 2d lt. Taiwan Army, 1987, advanced through grades to maj., 1996; platoon leader 10th Corps, Taiwan Army, Taichung, 1987—88, co. asst. comdr., 1988—91; retinue (aide) of maj. gen. Penghu Frontier Def. Corps, Taiwan Army, Makung, Penghu County, 1991—93; bn. asst. comdr. 8th Corps, Taiwan Army, Gaoxiong, 1993—95, officer of propaganda dept., 1995—97; prof. of found. studies Savannah Coll. of Art and Design, Savannah, Ga., 1997—. Guest lectr. Chinese calligrapgy, watercolor, and painiting Youth Activity Ctr., China Youth Corps, Makung, Penghu County, Taiwan, 1991—94; art dir. dept. fine arts 8th Corps, Taiwan Army, Gaoxiong, 1995—97; ind. artist, Savannah, Ga. One-man shows include Person, Place, and Thing, 1999, Candid Sight, 2000, Anatomy of Life Drawing, 2002, group exhibition, Thousand People Fine Arts Show (First Pl., 1983), Far from Home 1999 International Student Exhibition (Hon. Mention Award, 1999), Dimensions 1999 (So. Cmty. Bank & Trust Award, 1999), Faculty Show '99, Looking at Color, The Art of Drawing, Pastels U.S.A., Men at Art, Group Show of Fine Arts Department, 7th Annual National Juried Pastel Competition 2001, Prints, Drawings and Pastels, Out of the Classroom, Pastels on High International Exhibition 2001 (Mdse. Award, 2001), Renaissance in Pastel (Strathmore Artists Products Pastel Paper, 2001), 10th Annual National Pastel Painting Exhibition (First Pl., 2001), School of Fine Arts Faculty Exhibition, Atlanta Chinese Artist Association Annual Member's Exhibition, Oh, Baby, Cromaception, 2002, Graduation Show, Atlanta Chinese Artist Association Annual Member's Exhibition, Vision 2002, Chromaception, 2003, Contemporary Focus: Mirroring the Creative Self, 32nd Annual Exhibition for "Pastel Only, The Armed Forces Juried Fine Arts Exhibition, Provincial Juried Fine Arts Exhibition, The Army 8th Corps Fine Arts Exhibition, National Juried Fine Arts Exhibition, Alexander Hall Open Studios, The Commemorative Exhibition of Mr. Jing-Guo (First Pl., Chinese calligraphy and watercolor, 1987), interview (scad tv), Candid Sight; musician: (interview) musical performance (Hansheng Broadcasting Station), musical performance (Central Broadcasting Station), musical performance (Broadcasting Corporation of China); interview (scad tv), Chromaception, 2002, magazine (the pastel journal), Finalists of Pastel 100, Figure category, magazine (pastel artist international), Master Pastel Artists of the World - United States Showcase; musician: (musical performance) Confession (The Best Vocalist and The Best Music, 1987), (performance) musical performance (Chinese Television Service), musical performance (China Television Co. Ltd, musical performance (Taiwan Television Enterprise); contbr. articles to profl. jours. Decorated Medal of Pao Star, Taiwan Army, Medal of Brilliant Star, Medal of Loyalty and Diligence,; recipient 1st pl. in Chinese calligraphy, Keelung City Fine Arts Exhbn., City of Keelung, Taiwan, 1985, Best Vocalist for 2d Ann. Golden Panpipe Prize mus. competition, Dept. of Def., Taiwan, 1995, Cert. of Hon. Citizenship, Taiwan Govt., 1997, Outstanding Achievement Award in Screen Printing, Taipei City Profl. Tng. Ctr., 1997, Purchase award, Internat. Birthday Illustration Competition, Savannah Coll. of Art and Design, 1998, Popular Vote award, 32d Ann. Exhbn. for Pastel Only, Pastel Soc. of Am., 2004. Mem.: Atlanta Chinese Art Assn., Chinese-Am. Acad. and Profl. Assn. in Southea. US, Pastel Soc. Am., Coll. Art Assn. Achievements include selected for Sotheby's International Young Art 2001 Program, The Lovers series of paintings featured in New York, Tel Aviv, Israel, and Artlink online auction in 2000; pastel painting featured in The Pastel Journal as a finalist for 2d Annual Pastel 100 competition in 2001; paintings featured in New American Paintings magazine for its Open Studios 2001 Southern Competition. Avocations: painting and drawing, travel, singing, musical instruments. Home: 14 Steeple Run Way Savannah GA 31405 Office: Savannah Coll of Art and Design 420 E Anderson St Savannah GA 31401 Office Phone: 912-525-6621. Home Fax: 912-232-0748; Office Fax: 912-525-6606. Personal E-mail: chung3@comcast.net. Business E-Mail: chung@scad.edu.

HUNG, DONALD LU-CHENG, electrical engineer, computer engineer, educator; s. Timothy Teh-Ying Hung and Sophia Ren-Fan Wu; m. Judith Yee Hung; 1 child, Leonard. BSEE, Tongji U., 1982; MS, Case Western Res. U., 1986, PhD, 1990. Asst., assoc. full prof. Gannon U., Pa., 1990—95, Wash. State U., 1995—99, San Jose State U., Calif., 1999—. Vis. prof. The Chinese U. Hong Kong, 1998—99; guest prof. Tongji U. Shanghai, 2005—; steering com. mem. 8th Joint Conf. Info. Scis., Salt Lake City, 2005; chair 8th Internat. Conf. Computer Sci. and Informatics, Salt Lake City, 2005. Mem.: IEEE (sr.), Eta Kappa Nu (hon.). Office: San Jose State U One Washington Sq San Jose CA 95192-0180 Business E-Mail: dhung2@email.sjsu.edu.

HUNG, EDWARD, research scientist; s. Hei Chun Hung and Sau Lan Lam. BEng, U. Hong Kong, Hong Kong, 1998, MPhil, 2000; MS, U. Md., Coll. Pk., 2002, PhD, 2005. Grad. rsch. asst. U. Md., Coll. Pk., Md., 2003—05; asst. prof. Hong Kong Poly. U., Hung Hom, Hong Kong. Contbr. articles pub. to profl. jour., scientific papers presentations to conf. Recipient Student Prize, Hong Kong Instn. of Engrs., 1996-1997; grantee Travel Grant, U. Md., 2004, Dr. Lo Kwee Seong Edn. Found. Travel and Conf. Grants, U. Hong Kong, 2000, Conf. Grants, 2000; scholar Postgraduate Scholarship, Hong Kong and China Gas Co. Ltd. and U. Hong Kong, 1998-1999, Stephen Kam-Chuen Cheong Meml. Scholarships, Stephen Kam-Chuen Cheong Meml. Edn. Fund, 1995-1998, Scholarships, Croucher Found., 2000-2003, Hung Hing Ying Scholarship, U. Hong Kong, 1999-2000, Scholarship, Epson Found., 1999-2000, Postgraduate Studentships, U. Hong Kong, 1998-2000, Swire Scholarships, 1998-2000; Fellowships, U. Md., 2000-2002. Mem.: ACM (Assn. for Computing Machinery)., Swire Scholars Assn., Phi Kappa Phi. Office: Hong Kong Poly U Dept Computing Hung Hom Kowloon Hong Kong Office Phone: 301-422-0025. Business E-Mail: ehung@cs.umd.edu.

HUNG, JAMES CHEN, engineering educator, consultant; b. Foochow, Republic of China, Dec. 18, 1929; s. David Shen and Pearl C. (Chao) H.; m. Sufenne Huang, Apr. 3, 1958; children: John Y., Samuel M., Stephen T. BEE, Nat. Taiwan U., 1953; MEE, NYU, 1956, DEng, 1961. Registered profl. engr., Tenn. Instr. NYU, 1956-61; asst. prof. U. Tenn., Knoxville, 1961-62, assoc. prof., 1962-65, prof., 1965-84, disting. service prof., 1984-99, prof. emeritus, 1999—. V.p. Poly-Analytics, Inc., Knoxville; hon. prof. Nanjing U. Aerospace & Astrophysics, 1989, South China U. Tech., 1994, Hunan U., Peoples Republic of China, 1996; cons. prof. Northwestern Poly. U., Chongging U., S.W. China Tchrs. U., 1984—. Contbr. articles to profl. jours. Recipient Technology award NASA, 1969, Cert. NASA, 1970, Brooks Disting. Engring. Prof. award, U. Tenn., 1973. Fellow: IEEE (editor IEEE Trans. on Indsl. Electronics 1991—95, gen. chmn. internat. symposium on indsl. electronics, Xian, China 1992, gen. chmn. internat. conf. indsl. tech. 1994, 1996, tech. activity bd. 1998—99, gen. chmn. internat. symposium on indsl. electronics, L'Aquila, Italy 2002, tech. track chair internat. conf. indsl. elecs. 2003, 2004, gen. chair internat. conf. indsl. tech. 2005, hon. gen. chair internat conf. factory automation and emerging tech. 2005, Anthony J. Hornfeck Svc. award 1995, Eugene Mittelmann Achievement award 2000, Millennium medal 2000), Indsl. Electronics Soc. (v.p. 1996, pres.-elect 1997, pres. 1998—99, chair nomination com. 2003—); mem.: Phi Kappa Phi, Eta Kappa Nu, Tau Beta Pi, Sigma Xi. Methodist.

HUNG, MEI-JONG CHOW, social worker; b. Taipei, Taiwan, Republic China, Oct. 7, 1937; s. Wen-tung Yeh Chow; m. Chao-huang Hung, Mar. 24, 1964; children: Jennifer Ching-yi, John Ching-tsung. BS, Nat. Taiwan U., 1960; MSW, Simmons Coll. Sch. Social Work, 1963. Cert. social worker, hypnotherapist. Mental health counselor Taipei Pub. Health Teaching Demonstration, 1963-66; asst. prof. Taiwan U., 1964-66; social work supr. Johns Hopkins Hosp., Balt., 1969-71; pvt. practice social work Columbia, Md., 1972—. Vol. cmty. recreational social work, 1988—; co-prodr. Opera Internat., Washington, 1999—, prodr., 2002—. Fellow, WHO. Mem. NASW, Acad. Cert. Social Workers. Home and Office: 7255 Meadow Wood Way Clarksville MD 21029-1714 Address: PO Box 140 Fulton MD 20759-0140

HUNGAR, THOMAS G., federal agency administrator; BS, Williamette U., 1984; JD, Yale U., 1987. Law clk. to Hon. Alex Kozinski US Ct. Appeals (9th cir.), 1987—88; law clk. to Justice Anthony M. Kennedy US Supreme Ct., Washington, 1988—89; asst. solicitor gen. US Dept. Justice, Washington, 1989—94, dep. solicitor gen., 2003—; ptnr. Gibson, Dunn & Crutcher LLP, 1994—2003. Office: US Dept Justice 950 Pennsylvania Ave NW Washington DC 20530

HUNGATE, BRUCE ARTHUR, biologist, educator; b. Seattle, Mar. 18, 1967; s. Dan Piper and Connie Cunningham Hungate; m. Jane Claire Marks; children: Dylan, Nona. BA in Music and English, BS in Biol. Scis., Stanford U., 1990; PhD in Integrative Biology, U. Calif., Berkeley, 1995. Rschr. Smithsonian Environ. Rsch. Ctr., Edgewater, Md., 1995—97; asst. prof. No. Ariz. U., Flagstaff, 1998—2001, assoc. prof., 2001—. Contbr. articles to profl. jours. Office: No Ariz Univ Dept Biol Scis Flagstaff AZ 86011

HUNGATE, JOSEPH IRVIN, III, information technology executive; b. San Antonio, Nov. 17, 1956; s. Joseph Irvin Jr. and Betty Lou (Hatzenbuehler) H.; m. Santa Michelle Haines, May 15, 1993; children: Brittany Nicole, Annabel Sue, Charlotte Elizabeth. BS in Computer Sci., U. S.C., 1979, MS in Computer Sci., 1981; postgrad., U. Va., 1982-83. Tchg. asst. U. S.C., Columbia, 1979-81; sr. systems analyst GE, Charlottesville, Va., 1981-85; mgr. software devel. TRW, Fairfax, Va., 1985-88, prin. investigator, 1996-97, mgr. field engring. London, 1988-93; supervisory computer scientist Nat. Inst. Stds. and Tech. U.S. Dept. Commerce, Gaithersburg, Md., 1993-96; supervisory computer scientist Office of Insp. Gen., U.S. Dept. Commerce, 1997-99; assoc. dir. info. resource mgmt. office Ctrs. for Disease Control, Atlanta, 1999-2000; asst. inspector gen. info. technology, chief info. officer Treas. Insp. Gen. Tax Adminstrn., Washington, 2000—, chairperson exec. resource bd., 2001—. Mem. EIA Working Group RS-511, Detroit, 1983-85; recruitment coord. Affirmative Action, Fairfax, 1986-88; spl. liaison European Workshop on Open Sys., Brussels, 1993-96; chmn. Open Sys. Implementator's Workshop, Gaithersburg, 1993-97. Mem. Va. Student Aid Found., Charlottesville, 1985—, UVA Rotunda Soc., 2000-; vol. coord. blood svcs. ARC, Fairfax, 1985-88; vol. Arlington County (Va.) Dem. Com., 1985-88; bd. dirs. Hungate Family Hist. Soc., Inc., Chevy Chase, Md., 1989—. Recipient commendation USN, London, 1990; scholar S.C. Ednl. Found., 1975. Mem. Computer Soc. of IEEE, Assn. for Computing Machinery, Am. Mgmt. Assn., Sr. Execs. Assn., Sigma Phi Epsilon. Methodist. Avocations: collecting wine, golf, sailing, skeet, travel. Home: 5818 N 27th St Arlington VA 22207 Office: 1125 15th St Ste 700A Washington DC 20005 E-mail: joseph.hungate@tigta.treas.gov.

HUNGER, J(OHN) DAVID, business educator; b. May 17, 1941; s. Jackson Steele and Elizabeth (Carey) H.; m. Betty Johnson, Aug. 2, 1969; children: Karen, Susan, Laura, Merry. BA, Bowling Green (Ohio) State U., 1963; MBA, Ohio State U., 1966, PhD, 1973. Selling supr. Lazarus Dept. Store, Columbus, Ohio, 1965-66; brand asst. Procter and Gamble Co., Cin., 1968-69; asst. dir. grad. bus. programs Ohio State U., Columbus, 1970-72; instr. Baldwin-Wallace Coll., Berea, Ohio, 1972-73; prof. U. Va., Charlottesville, 1973-82; strategic mgmt. prof. Iowa State U. Coll. Bus., Ames, 1982—. Prof. bus. George Mason U., Fairfax, Va., 1986-87; past pres. bd. dirs. Iowa State U. Press; cons. to bus., fed. and state agys. Author (with T.L. Wheelen): Strategic Management and Business Policy, 1983, 9th rev. edit., 2004, An Assessment of Undergraduate Business Education in the U.S., 1980, Cases in Strategic Management and Business Policy, 9th rev. edit., 2004, Essentials of Strategic Management, 1997, 3d edit., 2003, Concepts in Strategic Management and Business Policy, 9th rev. edit., 2004; contbr. articles to profl. jours. Capt. Mil. Intelligence, U.S. Army, 1966-68. Decorated Bronze Star. Mem. Acad. Mgmt., N.Am. Case Rsch. Assn. (past pres.), Soc. for Case Rsch. (past pres.), Strategic Mgmt. Soc., US Assn. for Small Bus. and Entrepreneurship (past v.p.). Office: Iowa State U Coll Bus 3212 Gerdin Bus Bldg Ames IA 50011-1350 Office Phone: 515-294-8463. E-mail: jdhunger@iastate.edu.

HUNGERFORD, CONSTANCE CAIN, art educator; b. Chgo., Apr. 26, 1948; d. Craig John and Jocelyn Enid (Mason) Cain. B.A., Wellesley Coll., 1970; M.A., U. Calif.-Berkeley, 1972, Ph.D., 1977. Instr. to prof. history of art Swarthmore (Pa.) Coll., 1975—, chmn. dept. art, 1981-86 . Exhibitions include Ernest Meissonier Musee der Veaux Arts, Lyons, 1993; contbr. articles to profl. jours. Samuel H. Kress nat. fellow, 1973-75; Am. Council Learned Socs. grantee-in-aid, 1978; Am. Philos. Soc. grantee 1980. Mem. Coll. Art Assn. Am., AAUW (award 1983), Phi Beta Kappa. Office: Swarthmore Coll Dept Art 500 College Ave Swarthmore PA 19081-1306

HUNGERFORD, DAVID SAMUEL, orthopedic surgeon, educator; b. Rochester, NY, May 4, 1938; s. Francis Samuel and Marjorie Ellen (Wilson) H.; m. Uta-Heide Jung, July 20, 1962; children: Marc Wilson, Kyle Sasha, Lars Daniel. BA, Colgate U., 1960; MD, U. Rochester, 1964. Diplomate Am. Bd. Orthopaedic Surgery. Asst. prof. orthopaedic surgery Johns Hopkins U., Balt., 1972-78; chief orthopaedic surgery VA Hosp., Balt., 1975-80, Good Samaritan Hosp., Balt., 1972—, chief div. arthritis surgery, 1979—2001; assoc. prof. orthopaedic surgery Johns Hopkins U. Sch. Medicine, Balt., 1978-86, prof. orthopaedic surgery, 1987—. Cons. Balt. City Hosp., 1972-85, Children's Hosp., 1972-80, East Balt. Med. Ctr., 1972-78; co-dir. Johns Hopkins U. Ctr. for Osteonecrosis Rsch. and Edn., 1995—; bd. dirs. Nat. Osteonecrosis Found. Author: Progress in Orthopaedics, 1977, Ischemia and Necroses of Bone, 1980, Total Knee Arthroplasty: A Comprehensive Approach, 1984, Total Hip Arthroplasty: A New Approach, 1984, Bone Circulation, 1984, Disorders of the Patello Femoral Joint, 1990, Videobook of Total Knee Arthroplasty, 1994; founding editor Jour. Arthroplasty, 1985-93. Elder Cen. Presbyn. Ch., Balt., 1974-83; dir. Crippled Children's United Rehab. Effort, 1997—, Christian Orthopaedic Ptrs., 1997—; chmn. bd. Med. Assistance Program Internat., 1998—. Maj. U.S. Army, 1969. Recipient George Hoyt Whipple award, 1965; named Disting. So. Orthopedist, So. Orthopedic Assn., 2002; Colgate U. scholar, 1956-59, GM scholar, 1956-59, U. Rochester scholar, 1959-61, Girdlestone Meml. scholar Oxford U., Eng., 1969-70; fellow USPHS, Paris, 1961-62, Carl Berg traveling fellow, 1973. Mem. Johns Hopkins Med. and Surg. Soc., Md. Orthopaedic Soc., Arthritis Found., Md. Soc. Rheumatic Diseases, Am. Rheumatism Assn., Orthopaedic Rsch. Soc., Hip Soc., Am. Assn. Orthopaedic Surgeons, Am. Assn. Hip Knee Surgeons, Soc. Internat. de Chirurgie Orthopedique et de Traumatologie, Knee Soc. (pres. 1994), Girdlestone Orthopaedic Soc. (chmn. 2005-). Republican. Home: 10715 Pot Spring Rd Cockeysville Hunt Valley MD 21030-3019 Office: Good Samaritan Hosp Profl Office Bldg G-1 5601 Loch Raven Blvd Baltimore MD 21239-2991 also: Johns Hopkins U Sch Medicine Dept Orthopaedic Surgery Baltimore MD 21205 Office Phone: 410-532-4732. Business E-Mail: dhunger1@jhmi.edu.

HUNGERFORD, GARY A., insurance company executive, columnist, writer, editor; b. Bklyn., Apr. 20, 1948; s. Gene and Ann Hungerford; m. Eleanor Haragsim, Oct. 4, 1969. BBA cum laude, Coll. Ins., N.Y.C., 1974; MBA, Coll. Ins., 1978; grad., U.S. Army Svc. Rifle Small Arms Firing Sch., 1992. CPCU, ASLI. With Guardian Life Ins. Co., 1965-67, Providence Washington Ins. Co., 1967-68, The Atlantic Cos., 1968-74, Midland Ins. Co., 1974-76, Drake Ins. Co. of N.Y., 1976-78, Mead Reinsurance Corp., 1978-80, Yorktown Indemnity Co., 1980-82, Tri-County Facilities, Ltd./Tri-County Facilities N.J., Inc., 1982-85; pres., CEO Spl. Risk Facilities, Ltd., Lindenhurst, N.Y., 1985—; chmn., CEO CompuPub. Svcs., Ltd., Lindenhurst, 1987—; chmn. Hungerford Arms Co., Ltd., Lindenhurst, 1988—; v.p., dir. Protective Ins. Agy., Ridgewood, N.Y., 1983—. Past editor, pub. Lindenhurst's Chamber News, 1990—95, former columnist, South Bays' News, Suffolk Alliance Sportmen's Newsletter, The Bullet. Author: NYSRPA's

Education and Training Directory, 1992, History of New York State Rifle and Pistol Association, 1997, Atlantic Mutual's No-Fault Automobile Insurance Manual; contbr. numerous ins.-related articles to profl. jours. Sponsor U.S. Olympic Shooting Team; life mem. N.Y. State Conservation Coun.; mem. Glock Sport Shooting Found.; mem. small bus. adv. com. N.Y. Senate; mem. Rocky Mountain Elk Found. With U.S. Army, 1968—70. Mem.: NRA (life; mem. field support team, polit. preference com. 1992, mem. Inst. Legis. Action, mem. Polit. Victory Fund, cert. firearms instr., Golden Eagles), Rocky Mtn. Elk Found., Nat. Assn. Federally Lic. Firearms Dealers, L.I. Computer Assn., Nat. Assn. Desktop Pubs., Ind. Ins. Agts. N.Y., Profl. Ins. Wholesalers Assn., Profl. Ins. Agts. N.Y., Casualty and Surety Soc. N.Y., Ind. Ins. Agts. Assn., Soc. Ins. Rsch., Soc. CPCU, Law Enforcement Alliance Am. (life), Coastal Conservation Alliance, Izaak Walton League, Lindenhusrt C. of C. (past chmn.), Coll. Ins. Alumni Assn., Citizen's Com. for Right to Keep and Bear Arms (life), Shooter's Com. Polit. Edn. (life), Theodore Roosevelt Conservation Assn. (life), Coll. Ins. MBA Soc., Wildlife Forever, Conservation Alliance N.Y., L.I. Dahlia Soc., L.I. Beach Buggy Assn., N.Y. State Rifle and Pistol Assn. (life; past bd. dirs., past chmn. fin. com., past chmn. range com., past printing com., past hist. com., past omnibus com.), United Gamefish Anglers, Inc. (life), N.Y. Sportfishing Fedn. (life), Varmint Hunters Assn. (life), Gun Owners Am. (life), Free Hunters (life), M-1 Carbine Collectors Assn., Garand Collectors' Assn., Northeastern Arms Collectors Assn., Internat. Game Fish Assn., Suffolk Alliance Sportsmen (del., firearms chmn., past v.p., dir.), Bass Anglers' Sportsman's Soc., Whitetails Unlimited, Nassau County Fish and Game Assn., Old Bethpage Rifle and Pistol Club (trustee), N.Am. Hunting Club (life), Lindenhurst Lions. Republican. Avocations: chess, fishing, hunting, shooting sports, computers, photography. Office: Spl Risk Facilities Ltd 101 N Wellwood Ave Lindenhurst NY 11757-4001

HUNGWE, KEDMON NYASHA, education educator, researcher; b. Harare, Zimbabwe, May 2, 1956; s. Elliott Bera and Chipo Hungwe; m. Chipo Mazimbe, Sept. 4, 1982; children: Ruvimbo Gamuchirai, Tendeukai Ratidzo, Tsitsi Fadzai, Manjere Mwarianesu. BS, U. of Rhodesia, Harare, Zimbabwe, 1978; MS, U. of Wis., Madison, 1987; PhD, Mich. State U., East Lansing, 1999. Lic. secondary tchr. Ministry of Edn., Zimbabwe. Tchr. Harare H.S., Harare, Zimbabwe, 1981—83; lectr. Ministry of Edn. in Zimbabwe, Harare, 1984—85, U. of Zimbabwe, Harare, 1987—2002; asst. prof. Mich. Technol. U., Houghton, Mich., 2002—. Cons. Dept. for Internat. Devel., UK, So. Ctr. for Energy and Environment. Contbr. book; editor: (web site) African cinema: a new series of reviews, criticism and theory; contbr. articles to profl. jours. Mem. Children's Performing Arts Workshop, Zimbabwe; jury mem. Zimbabwe Film Festival, Harare. Fellow, Candice Thoman Found. fellow, 1994—95, Robert Mugabe fellow, Mich. State U., 1992—97; scholar, World U. Svc. scholar, 1976—78, US AID scholar, 1985—87. Mem.: Nat. Coun. of Tchrs. of Math., Am. Ednl. Rsch. Assn. (mem.), Phi Kappa Phi. Methodist. Achievements include research in filmmaking in Southern Africa. Avocations: reading, travel, film critic. Office: Michigan Technological University 1400 Townsend Dr Houghton MI 49931 Personal E-mail: khungwe@mtu.edu.

HUNIA, EDWARD MARK, foundation executive; b. Sharon, Pa., Jan. 8, 1946; s. Edward and Estelle (Maleski) H.; m. Mary Sue Marburger, Sept. 25, 1976; children: Stephen, Adam. BSME, Carnegie Mellon U., 1967, MSME, 1968; MBA, U. Pitts., 1971. CFA. Sr. systems analyst Pitts. Plate Glass Industries, 1968-73; asst. to treas. Carnegie Mellon U., Pitts., 1973-76, dir. internal audit, 1976-78, asst. controller, dir. fin. systems, 1978-81, treas., 1981-90; v.p. for finance, treas. U. Pitts., 1990-92; sr. v.p., treas. The Kresge Found., Troy, Mich., 1992—. Mem. Assn. for Investment Mgmt. and Rsch., Fin. Analysts Soc. Detroit. Avocations: tennis, golf, running, books. Home: 4393 Barchester Dr Bloomfield Hills MI 48302-2116 Office: The Kresge Found PO Box 3151 Troy MI 48007-3151

HUNKE, DAVID L., publisher; b. Houston; Grad., U. Kans., Lawrence. With Kansas City Star; dir. advt. Miami Herald; with Gannett Co. Inc., 1992—, exec. v.p. for mktg. Cin. Enquirer and Cin. Post, 1997-99, pub., pres. digital edits. Rochester Dem. and Chronicle, 1999—2005; pres., pub. Detroit Free Press, Gannett Co. Inc., Mich., 2005—. Recipient Lifetime Humanitarian award, Lifetime Assistance Found., 2004. Office: Detroit Free Press 600 West Fort St Detroit MI 48226*

HUNKELE, LESTER MARTIN, III, retired federal agency administrator; b. Bklyn., Aug. 16, 1947; s. Lester Martin Jr. and Agnes Veronica (Tarpey) H.; m. Diane Kathryn Sotiridy, Mar. 30, 1974. BS, U.S. Mil. Acad., 1969; MS in Constrn. Engring., Purdue U., 1975; diploma, Indsl. Coll. Armed Forces, 1988. Registered profl. engr., Va.; cert. plant engr.; cert. constrn. mgr., LEED acredited profl. Commd. 2d lt. U.S. Army, 1969, advanced through grades to capt., 1979; lt. col. USAR, 1990; ret., 1995; logistics officer 809 Engring. Bn., 1970-71, engr. officer, 1970-71; engr. officer army engring. sch. U.S. Army, Ft. Belvoir, Va., 1971-74, asst. area engr. Balt. dist. C.E., 1975-79, resigned Washington, 1979; civil engr. office chief engrs. Dept. Army, Washington, 1979-81, asst. chief constrn. mgmt. office chief army res., 1981-83; asst. head facilities HQs USMC, Washington, 1983-85; dir. facilities office asst. sec. def. res. affairs Dept. Def., Washington, 1985-88, prin. dir. materiel and facilities, 1988-89; dep. asst. sec. for facilities Dept. Vets. Affairs, Washington, 1989-92, dep. asst. sec. facilities oversight, 1992-93; exec. dir. Pa. Ave. Devel. Corp., Washington, 1993-96; exec. project mgr. Gen. Svcs. Adminstrn., Washington, 1996; project exec. Clark Constrn. Group, 1996-99; assoc. v.p. DMJMH&N, Arlington, Va., 1999-2001, v.p., 2001—02, sr. v.p., 2002—04; pres. Hunkele Cons., Annapolis, Md., 2004—. Mem. ASCE, NSPE (mem. govt. adv. group), CMAA. Assn. Facilities Engrs., Soc. Am. Mil. Engrs. (dir. Washington chpt. 1984-88), Fed. Exec. Inst. Alumni Assn. (membership chmn. 1987), West Point Soc. (co-founder Annapolis chpt. 1986—), Urban Land Inst., Lambda Alpha. Avocations: sailing, skiing, scuba diving. Home: 3259 Chrisland Dr Annapolis MD 21403-4352 Office Phone: 443-995-6897. E-mail: leshunkele@comcast.net.

HUNKER, JEFFREY, dean; B in Engring. and Applied Physics, Harvard Coll.; PhD in Bus. Adminstrn. in Managerial Econs., Harvard Bus. Sch. Cons. Boston Consulting Group; dir. Crit. Infrastructure Assurance Office (CIAO) U.S. Dept. Commerce, dep. asst. to sec., sr. policy advisor sec.; v.p., mergers, and acquisitions Kidder Peabody and Co., NY; sr. dir. crit. infrastructure, nat. security coun. Clinton Adminstrn., 1996—2000; dean Heinz Sch. Carnegie Mellon U., 2001—. With Dept. Commerce Nat. Security Coun. Mem. Photography Coun. Mus. Modern Art (MOMA). Achievements include development of 1st-ever national strategy for cyber-security and protecting critical information, Internet, and computer systems; President's 2000 Cyber-Security Summit with internet leaders; Partnership for Critical Infrastructure Security, a national organization with over 130 Frotune 500 companies as members. Office: H John Heinz III Sch Pub Policy & Mgmt Carnegie Mellon U Pittsburgh PA 15213-3890 Office Phone: 412-268-4897. Business E-Mail: jhunker@andrew.cmu.edu.

HUNKINS, RAYMOND BREEDLOVE, lawyer, rancher; b. Culver City, Calif., Mar. 19, 1939; s. Charles F. and Louise (Breedlove) H.; m. Mary Deborah McBride, Dec. 12, 1967; children: Amanda, Blake, Ashley. BA, U. Wyo., 1966, JD, 1968. Ptnr. Jones, Jones, Vines & Hunkins, Wheatland, Wyo., 1968—. Local rules com. U.S. Dist. Ct., 1990—; spl. counsel U. Wyo., Laramie, State of Wyo., Cheyenne; mem. faculty Western Trial Adv. Inst., 1993—95, Wyo. Supreme Ct. Commn. Jud. Salary and Benefits, 1996—98; owner Thunderhead Ranches, Albany and Platte Counties, Wyo.; gen. ptnr. Split Rock Land & Cattle Co.; spl. asst. atty. gen., Wyo.; founder, pres. Wyo. chpt. Federalist Soc. for Law and Pub. Policy Studies, 2003—04; bd. dirs. Found. for Laramie. Chmn. Platte County Reps., Wheatland, 1972-74, chmn. adv. coun. Coll. Commerce and Industry, U. Wyo., 1978-79; bd. dirs. U. Wyo. Found., 1996-2002, Found. Laramie, 2002—, Laramie Peak Mus., 1989—; bd. advisors Am. Heritage Ctr., 1995-99; mem. Gov.'s Crime Commn., 1970-78; pres. Wyo. U. Alumni Assn., 1973-74, commr. Wyo. Aeronautics Commn., 1987-98; moderator United Ch. Christ, 1997-98; Rep. candidate for Gov. Wyo., 2002, Wyo. del. Rep. Nat. Convention, 2004. With USMCR, 1956-60 Recipient Outstanding Advisor award Phi Delta Theta, 1968, Big Horn Mountain Roundup Pax Irvine award, 1989, Disting. Alumnus award 2005 Fellow Am. Coll. Trial Lawyers (Wyo. state chmn. 1998-2000, nat. ethics com. 2000—), Internat. Soc. Barristers, Am. Bd. Trial Advs.; mem. ABA (aviation com. 1980-86, forum com. on constrn. industry litigation sect.), Wyo. Bar Assn. (chmn. grievance com. 1980-86, mem. com. on civil pattern jury instrns. 1999-2002, state bar-law sch. com., bench-bar rels. com.), Wyo. Trial Lawyers Assn. (past pres.) Office: Jones Jones Vines & Hunkins PO Drawer 189 9th and Maple Wheatland WY 82201

HUNNICUTT, CHARLES ALVIN, lawyer; b. LaGrange, Ga., Dec. 7, 1950; s. William Oliver and Mary Olivia (Leggett) Hunnicutt. BS, Am. U., 1972; JD, U. Ga., 1975; LLM, U. Brussels, Belgium, 1976. Bar: Ga. 1975, D.C. 1978, U.S. Dist. Ct. D.C. 1978, U.S. Ct. Appeals (D.C. cir.) 1978, U.S. Ct. Internat. Trade 1980, U.S. Ct. Appeals (fed. cir.) 1981, U.S. Supreme Ct. 1981. Dep. dir. State of Ga. Office, Brussels, 1975-76; ops. mgr. Presdl. Pers. The White House, Washington, 1976-77; exec. asst. to under sec. internat. trade U.S. Dept. Commerce, Washington, 1977-80; legal advisor to chmn. Internat. Trade Commn., Washington, 1980-87; ptnr. Robins, Kaplan, Miller & Ciresi, Washington, 1987—96, mng. ptnr., 1989—91, ptnr., 1999—2005, mem. exec. bd., 2003—04; advisor to Govt. of Ukraine on accession to Gen. Agreement on Tariffs and Trade World Trade Orgn., Kiev, 1994-95; asst. sec. for aviation and internat. affairs U.S. Dept. Transp., Washington, 1996-99; ptnr. Troutman Sanders LLP, Washington, 2005—. Adj. prof. Am. U. Coll. Law, Washington, 1988—91. Bd. visitors U. Ga. Sch. Law., 2000—04. Mem.: FBA, ABA (internat. trade steering com., air and space law forum), Internat. Bar Assn., Am. Soc. Internat. Law (exec. coun. 1999—2002, chair budget com. 2000—04), Washington Fgn. Law Soc. (pres. 1987—88), Ga. State Bar, Bar Assn. D.C., Internat. Aviation Club (bd. dirs. 2001—, pres. 2004—). Democrat. Presbyterian. Office: Troutman Sanders LLP 401 9th St NW Ste 1000 Washington DC 20004-2134 Office Phone: 202-274-2957. Personal E-mail: hunnca@aol.com. Business E-Mail: charles.hunnicutt@troutmansanders.com.

HUNSAKER, BARRY, JR., lawyer; b. Mesa, Ariz., May 4, 1950; BS, Tex. A&M U., 1972, MS, 1973, PhD, 1976; JD, U. Tex., 1979. Bar: Tex. 1979. Ptnr. Vinson & Elkins, LLP; sr. v.p., gen. counsel EOG Resources, Inc., Houston, 1996—. Bd. dirs. Houston Pub. Libr. Mem.: State Bar Tex., Order of Coif, Tau Beta Pi, Sigma Gamma Tau, Phi Kappa Phi. Office: EOG Resources Inc 333 Clay St PO Box 4362 Houston TX 77002

HUNSBERGER, ALICE CHANDLER, religion educator, human rights activist, scholar; b. Washington, June 25, 1952; d. George Shepherd and Ruth Margaret (Stillman) H.; m. Angelo Gelpi, Aug. 12, 1977 (div. Aug. 1994); 1 child, Adriane. BA cum laude, NYU, 1974; MA, Columbia U., 1977, MPhil, 1979, PhD, 1992. Rsch. asst. Middle East langs. Columbia U., N.Y.C., 1974-77; instr. Queens Coll./CUNY, N.Y.C., 1977, Aryamehr U. Tech., Isfahan, Iran, 1977-78, U. P.R., Rio Piedras, 1978; devel. assoc. Seamen's Ch. Inst., N.Y.C., 1984-88; assoc. dir. devel. Amnesty Internat., N.Y.C., 1988-99; adj. asst. prof. program in religion Hunter Coll./CUNY, N.Y.C., 1992-95; rsch. fellow Inst. Ismaili Studies, London, 1999—. Lectr. in internat. human rights and Islamic philosophy; cons. various orgns., 1993—; seminar lectr. Cambridge (Eng.) U., 1994, Inst. for Ismaili Studies, London, 1997, Sorbonne U., Paris, 2001. Author: Nasir Khusraw, The Ruby of Badakhshan: A Portrait of the Persian Poet, Traveller and Philosopher, 2000; tech. editor Soc. for Islamic Philosophy and Sci., N.Y.C., 1980-91. Recipient 2d prize for Best Dissertation in Iranian Studies, Found. for Iranian Studies, 1992. Mem. Middle East Studies Assn., Soc. for Iranian Studies (treas. 1992-94), Columbia U. Seminar in Iranian Studies (acting chair 1998-99), Am. Acad. Religion, Am. Philos. Soc., Assn. for Study of Persian Speaking Socs. (bd. mem. 2000—). Democrat. Avocation: learning languages. Office: Inst Ismaili Studies 42-44 Grosvenor Gardens London SW1W 0EB England E-mail: ahunsberger@iis.ac.uk.

HUNSCHE, ELKE GRETA IRMA, economist; b. Osnabrueck, Germany, July 27, 1970; arrived in U.S.A., 2001; d. Gerd and Edith Hunsche. Diploma rerum politicum, U. Osnabrueck, Germany, 1991—96. Mgr., global health outcomes Searle, High Wycombe, England, 1999—2000; mgr., health outcomes Ethicon Endo Surgery, Norderstedt, Germany, 2000—00; dir., outcomes rsch. Merck & Co., Inc., Whitehouse Sta., NJ, 2001—. Home: 259 Laurel Ct Whitehouse Station NJ 08889 Personal E-mail: elkehunsche@yahoo.com.

HUNSICKER, GERRY, former professional sports team executive; b. Collegeville, Pa. m. Irene Hunsicker; 1 dau., Kelly. BS, St. Joseph's U., Pa., 1972. Pitching coach, asst. athletic dir. Fla. Internat. U., Miami, 1973-78; staff Houston Astros, 1978-81; v.p. Paine Webber, Houston, 1984-88; dir. minor league ops. N.Y. Mets, 1988-90, dir. baseball ops., 1990-95; gen. mgr. Houston Astros, 1995—2004. Office: Houston Astros PO Box 288 Houston TX 77001-0288

HUNSPERGER, ELIZABETH JANE, art and design consultant, educator; b. Phila., Aug. 30, 1938; d. Francis Charles and Elizabeth Julia Thorpe; m. Robert George Hunsperger, Sept. 13, 1958; 1 child, Lisa Marie. AA in Design, Santa Monica Coll., 1974; student, UCLA, 1975-76; BA in Art History, U. Del., 1978; postgrad., Rutgers U., 1978-81; MA in Edn., Del. State Coll., 1993; postgrad. in ednl. technology, U. Del. Designer Huntingdon Mills, Phila., 1960-63, Rothschild's, Ithaca, N.Y., 1963-65, Cornell U., Ithaca, 1965-67; freelance designer Malibu, Calif., 1967-76; art and design cons., lectr. Art & Sci. Assocs., Newark, Del., 1980—2001, Galena, Md., 2001—. Art tchr. Cath. Diocese of Wilmington, 1988-95, Kent County High Sch., Md., 2002-; art and spl. edn. tchr. Red Clay Consolidated Sch. Dist. A.I. duPont H.S., Greenville, Del., 1995-97, Shorehaven Sch., Chesapeake City, Md., 1997-99, A.I. duPont Inst., Wilmington, Del., 1999—; with Leech Sch., 1994; cons. Arts and Sci. Assocs., Ednl. and Design Svcs., Newark, Del., 1995—; coord. Delmarva Edn. Action Learning Project; educator Kent County (Md.) Pub. Schs., 2002. Exhbns. include Malibu Art Assn. Show, 1973-74, Newark Art Show, 1987-88. Founding mem. bd. dirs., v.p. Newark Housing Ministry, Inc., 1983-94, pres., 1989-91; mem. social concerns com. and drug and alcohol task force Del.; active Coun. Exceptional Children. Recipient Outstanding Svc. award YWCA, Santa Monica, Calif., 1972, award of recognition Missionhurst, 1982, Gov.'s Vol. of the Yr. award State of Del., 1990. Mem. Nat. Art Edn. Assn., Am. Craft Coun., Art Educators of Del. (bd. dirs., pres.), Debutante Assemlby Club (N.Y.C.). Episcopal. Home: 14040 S Mill Rd Galena MD 21635 E-mail: elizabeth_hunsperger@usa.net.

HUNSTEIN, CAROL, state supreme court justice; b. Miami, Fla., Aug. 16, 1944; AA, Miami-Dade Jr. Coll., 1970; BS, Fla. Atlantic U., 1972; JD, Stetson U., 1976, LLD (hon.), 1993. Bar: Ga. 1976; U.S. Dist. Ct. 1978; U.S. Ct. Appeals 1978; U.S. Supreme Ct. 1989. Atty. Hunstein & Hunstein, Atlanta, 1976-84; judge Superior Ct. of Ga. (Stone Mt. cir.), 1984-92; justice Supreme Ct. of Ga., Atlanta, 1992—, presiding justice, 2005—. Chair Ga. Commn. on Gender Bias in the Judicial System 1989—; pres. Coun. of Superior Ct. Judges of Ga., 1990-91; adj. prof. Sch. Law Emory U., 1991—; former chair State Commn. on Child Support; former mem. Chief Justice's Commn. on Professionalism; liaison to Gender Equality Commn. Bd. dirs. Ga. Campaign Adolescent Pregnancy Prevention, 1992—; chair Ga. Child Support Commn., 1993, 98, Supreme Ct. Equality Commn. Recipient Clint Green Trial Advocacy award 1976, Women Who Made A Difference award Dekalb Women's Network 1986, Outstanding Svc. commendation Ga. Legislature, 1993, Cmty. Svc. award Emory U. Legal Assn. for Women Students., 1993, Gender Justice award Ga. Commn. Family Violence, 1999, Margaret Brent award ABA, 1999; inducted to Fla. Atlantic U. Hall of Fame, 1993. Mem. Ga. Assn. of Women Lawyers, Nat. Assn. of Women Judges (dir. 1988-90), Bleckley Inn of Ct., State Bar Ga. Office: Supreme Ct Ga 244 Washington Street Atlanta GA 30334-9007 Office Phone: 404-656-3475. E-mail: hunsteic@supreme.courts.state.ga.us.

HUNSUCKER, ROBERT DUDLEY, physicist, electrical engineer, educator, researcher; b. Portland, Oreg., Mar. 15, 1930; s. Robert Deets and Johnnie Morris (Kuykendal) H.; m. Judith Mary Cotter, Apr. 28, 1956 (dec. Nov. 1980); children: Edith Louise, Jeanne Marie, Cynthia Lee; m. Phyllis Marie Hoover, July 25, 1981. BS in Physics, Oreg. State U., 1954, MS in Physics, 1958; PhD in Elec. Engring., U. Colo., 1969. Asst. prof. Geophysics Inst. U. Alaska, Fairbanks, 1958-64, assoc. prof. Geophysics Inst., 1971-78, prof. Geophysics Inst., 1978-87, prof. emeritus physics and elec. engring., sr. cons., 1988—; physicist Nat. Bur. Stds., Boulder, Colo., 1964-67; sr. project leader ITS Office of Telecom. Sci., Boulder, 1967-71. Radio propagation cons.; adj. prof. Pa. State U., 1993, 1995—96, Oreg. Inst. Tech., 1995—2002. Author 2 Tech. Books; editor (in chief): Radio Sci., 1995—2002; assoc. editor: URSI Radioscience Bull., 1998—; contbr. articles to profl. jours. Served to lt., chief engr., boat group comdr. USNR, 1954—67. Fellow AAAS, IEEE (Alaska Engr. of Yr. Alaska sect. 1988, recipient outstanding achievement award IEEE region 6 1988); mem. Am. Geophys. Union, U.S. Commn. Internat. Union of Radio Sci., Sigma Xi, Sigma Pi Sigma, Eta Kappa Nu, Mensa. Republican. Lutheran. Avocations: fishing, amateur radio operation, writing. Office Phone: 541-885-8786. Business E-Mail: rdhrpc1@charter.net.

HUNSUCKER, WAYNE (CARL WAYNE HUNSUCKER), architectural firm executive, educator; b. Morganton, N.C., Feb. 16, 1945; s. Earnest Howard and Reba (Laughridge) H.; m. Edith Mabel Whittaker Guisto, May 23, 1990; children: Wendy Edith Guisto, Bret Thomas Guisto. Student, Old Dominion Coll.; BFA, Coll. William and Mary, 1968; BArch with Distinction, U. Ariz., 1975. Lic. architect, Calif., Nev., Idaho, Oreg., Wash., Ariz.; cert. Nat. Coun. Archtl. Registration Bds. Archtl. draftsman Woodmoor Corp., Colorado Springs, Colo., 1971-72; architect-in-training James Gresham & Assocs., Tuscon, 1975-76; prin., pres. Hummel Hunsucker Archs., Boise, Idaho, 1976—, prin.-in-charge office ops. Spokane, Wash., 1998—. Part-time draftsperson Forrest Coile & Assocs., Newport News, Va., 1959-63; asst. instr. U. Ariz. Prin. works include U.S. Courthouse and Fed. Office Bldg., Boise, Idaho, Earl F. Chandler Bldg., Boise, Benton County Jud. Facility, San Francisco, Orchard Pl. Office Complex, Boise, 1st Security Bank addition and remodel, Nampa Main Br., Blue Cross Idaho, Idaho N.G. Armory Annex, Boise, various bldgs. Mt. Home AFB (Citation and Design awards Dept. Air Force), Mountain Home Town Jr. High Sch. addition; co-author: (text books) Architectural Drafting, 1976, Neighborhood Planning - Case Study of the Sam Hughes Neighborhood. Bd. dirs. Ada County Hist. Soc., 1989-90, Boise; mem. Lincoln Day Banquet Com., Boise, 1984-86; mem. licensing bd. Idaho Outfitters and Guides, 1996—; bd. mem. Bldg. Owners and Mgrs. Assn., Boise chpt., 1998. 1st lt. U.S. Army, 1969-71, Vietnam. Recipient Citation award USAF, Best Stand Alone Bldg. award TAC Air Force, 1984, Henry Adams Fund for Excellence award. Mem. AIA (state pres. 1990, pres. ctrl. sect. Idaho chpt. 1988, Silver medal 1976), Nat. Coun. Archtl. Registration Bds. Avocations: bird hunting, fishing, boating. Office: Hummel Architects PA 2785 N Bogus Basin Rd Boise ID 83702-0911

HUNT, ALBERT R., editor; b. Charlottesville, Va., Dec. 4, 1942; s. Albert R. and Ann G. (Lillard) H.; m. Judy C. Woodruff, Apr. 5, 1980; children: Jeffrey Woodruff, Benjamin Woodruff, Lauren Ann Lee. BA in Polit. Sci., Wake Forest U., 1965. Reporter Wall St. Jour., N.Y.C., 1965-67, Boston, 1967-69, Washington, 1969-71, polit. reporter, 1972-83, bur. chief, 1983-93, exec. Washington editor, 1993—2005; mng. editor, govt. reporting Bloomberg News, Washington, 2005—. Author: (with others) American Elections of 1980, American Elections of 1982, American Elections of 1984, Elections American Style, 1987; participant in TV program CNN Capital Gang. Bd. visitors Wake Forest U., Winston-Salem, N.C., 1979-85, trustee, 1987; sr. adv. bd. Shorenstein Barone Ctr. for Press, Politics and Pub. Policy, Harvard U., Cambridge, Mass.; pres. Dow Jones Newspaper Fund, 1993-2002. Mem. Am. Polit. Sci. Assn. (congl. fellowship adv. com. 1981—). Office: Bloomberg News 1399 New York Ave NW Washington DC 20005

HUNT, BARNABAS JOHN, priest, religious organization administrator; b. Sayre, Pa., Jan. 6, 1937; s. Clarence Elmer and Margarite Frances (Bennett) H. BS in Edn., Pa. State U., 1958; postgrad., Elmira Coll., 1960-61, Portland State U., 1969-70, Clackamas C.C., 1970-71, Mt. Hood C.C., 1973-74. Joined Soc. St. Paul, 1961, ordained priest Episcopal Ch. 1984, installed and seated as hon. canon of St. Paul's Cathedral, San Diego, 2000; cert. h.s. tchr. H.s. tchr. Pub. Schs., Candor, N.Y., 1958-61; headmaster St. Luke's Sch., Soc. St. Paul, Gresham, Oreg., 1961-64; lic. adminstr. St. Jude's Nursing Home, Inc., Portland and Sandy, Oreg., 1964-73; assoc. rector Soc. St. Paul, Palm Desert, Calif., 1975-89, rector, 1989—; brother in charge St. Paul's Press, Sandy, Oreg., 1969-76. Treas. Desert Samaritans for Elderly, Palm Desert, Calif., 1997-98. Mem. Tri-County Bd., Oreg. Agy. on Aging, 1971-76; pres. Sandy C. of C., 1972; mem. Sandy City Coun., 1975-76, candidate for City Coun., City of Palm Desert, 1986; pres. St. Jude's Home, Inc., Oreg., 1989—; pres. adv. bd. The Carlotta, 1985-92, vice chmn. resource devel. fund bd., 1993-97; bd. dirs. St. Paul's Episcopal Home, Inc., San Diego, 2000—; chpt. mem. St. Paul's Episocal Cathedral, San Diego, 2000—. Fellow Am. Coll. Health Care Adminstrs. (pres. Coll. Found. 1984-87); mem. Nat. Guild Churchmen (pres. 1982—), Conf. on Religious Life in Anglican Communion (v.p. 1992-97, archivist 1982—). Episcopalian. Home and Office: Soc of St Paul Inc PO Box 34548 San Diego CA 92163-4548 Fax: 619-542-8660. Office Phone: 619-542-8660. E-mail: anbssp@earthlink.net.

HUNT, BONNIE, actress; m. John Murphy, 1988. Actor: (films) Rain Man, 1988, Beethoven, 1992, Dave, 1993, Beethoven's 2nd, 1993, Only You, 1994, Now and Then, 1995, Jumanji, 1995 (Saturn award for best actress), Getting Away with Murder, 1996, Jerry Maguire, 1996, Kissing a Fool, 1998, A Bug's Life (voice), 1998, Random Hearts, 1999, The Green Mile, 1999, Monsters, Inc. (voice), 2001, Stolen Summer, 2002, Cheaper By the Dozen, 2003; (TV series) Davis Rules, 1992, The Building, 1993; actor, prodr. The Bonnie Hunt Show, 1995 (Founder's award Viewers for Quality TV awards 1996); actor, dir., writer (films) Return to Me, 1998 (TV series) Life With Bonnie, 2002-04. Office: Creative Artists Agy 9830 Wilshire Blvd Beverly Hills CA 90212-1825

HUNT, BRENDA SUE DAVIS, missionary outreach executive, secondary school educator; d. John Warren Davis, Jr. and Mary Jane Davis; 1 child, Sarah Lynn. BS in Edn., Ill. State U., 1973; postgrad., Western N.Mex. U., 1980—81, Blackhawk Coll., 1991. Owner, originator Hear Ye Him nonprofit missionary outreach, 1976—90; owner As Eye See It Photography, 1980—2000; owner, originator Safe Child Internat., 1990—. Author: Educating the Church on Incest and Other Sex Crimes, 2005, Cry Blood! One Child's Journey Through Incest, 2005, Somebody Touched Me Wrong!, 2005. Founder Hear Ye Him, 1976—90; active Ctrl. Ch. of Christ. Avocations: survival work, quilting, cooking, writing, inventing. Home: 107 N Yates St Alpha IL 61413 Office: Safe Child Internat R2 Box 9J Alpha IL 61413

HUNT, BRIAN BASSETT, music director; b. Owensboro, Ky., Aug. 17, 1956; s. Weldon Hunt Jr. and Laura Jane Bassett; m. Cathy Joan Stevenson, June 9, 1979; children: Sarah Bennett, Whitney Laine. Assoc. in Data Processing, Lexington (Ky.) C.C., 1987; B Music Edn., U. Ky., 1979, M Sacred Music, 2004. Dir. of music, organist Mary Queen of Holy Rosary Parish, Lexington, 2001—04; organist, asst. dir. of music Cathedral of Christ the King, Lexington, 2004—. Instr. sem. choir Lexington Theol. Sem., 2002—03. Pastoral Musician scholar, GIA/Nat. Assn. Pastoral Musicians, 2002. Mem.: Am. Guild Organists (dean 1984—86, yearbook editor Lexington chpt. 2001—), Nat. Assn. Pastoral Musicians (program coord. local chpt. 2002), Royal Sch. Ch. Music (corr.). Democrat. Roman Catholic. Avocation: reading. Home: 1008 Claiborne Way Lexington KY 40517 Office: Cathedral of Christ the King 299 Colony Blvd Lexington KY 40502 Office Phone: 859-335-3695. E-mail: bhunt@cdlex.org.

HUNT, CRAIG A., paper company executive; BA econ., JD, U. Kansas. Atty. Shook, Hardy & Bacon, Kansas City, Mo.; sr. counsel, asst. sec. Jefferson Smurfit, 1993—98; v.p., sec., gen. counsel Smurfit-Stone Container Corp., Chgo., 1998—. Office: Smurfit-Stone Container 150 N Michigan Ave Chicago IL 60601

HUNT, DAVID EVANS, lawyer; b. Wilkes-Barre, Pa., May 10, 1953; s. James Dixon and Twyla (Burkert) H.; m. Denise M. Barbera, Aug. 21, 1976 (div. 1984); 1 child Christopher Evans; m. Elizabeth S. Pearce, Sept. 5, 1987; children: Alexandra Stacy, Thomas Dixon. AB, Dartmouth Coll., 1975; JD, U. Chgo., 1978. Bar: N.Y. 1979, U.S. Dist. Ct. (so. and ea. dists.) N.Y. 1979, Maine 1982, U.S. Dist. Ct. Maine 1982, U.S. Tax Ct. 1982, Fla. 1999. Assoc. Debevoise & Plimpton, N.Y.C., 1978-81; ptnr. Pierce, Atwood, Scribner, Allen, Smith & Lancaster, Portland, Maine, 1981-92, McCandless & Hunt, Portland, Maine, 1992-97; sole practitioner Portland, 1997—. Adj. prof. U. Maine Law Sch., Portland, 1991—92, Portland, 2000—02. Co-author: Maine Will and Trust Forms Annotated, 1994, Maine Estate Administration, 1996. Officer, dir. Maine Estate Planning Coun., Portland, 1986-94. Fellow: Am. Coll. Trust and Estate Counsel (state chair 1997—2001, regent 2001—03); mem.: ABA, Cumberland County Bar Assn., N.Y. State Bar Assn., Maine State Bar Assn., Fla. Bar, Woodlands Club. Episcopalian. Avocations: classical Latin, skiing. Home: 6 Highland St Portland ME 04103-3005 Office: 511 Congress St Portland ME 04101-3411 Office Phone: 207-773-5100. Business E-Mail: dhunt@mainewills.com.

HUNT, DAVID FORD, lawyer; b. Ft. Worth, Apr. 7, 1931; s. John Greffrey and Bernice (Ford) H. BS, North Tex. State U., 1954; JD, Vanderbilt U., 1960. Bar: Tex. 1961, U.S. Dist. Ct. (no. dist.) Tex., U.S. Dist. Ct. (we. dist.) Tex., U.S. Dist. Ct. (ea. dist.) Tex.U.S. Ct. Appeals (5th and 11th cir.), U.S. Supreme Ct. Law clk. to U.S. dist. judge No. Dist. Tex., 1960-62; pvt. practice, Dallas, 1962-94; ptnr. Jenkens & Gilchrist, P.C., Dallas, 1980-92, of counsel, 1993-94; atty. pvt. practice, Denton County, Tex., 1995—. Chmn. com. on admissions Dist. 6 Tex. State Bd. Law Examiners, 1978-87 Contbr. articles to legal jours. Co-chmn. pollwatchers com. Dallas County Republican Com., 1964; Sec. Bootstrap Ranch, 1972-74; pres. So. Methodist U. Lambda Chi Edn. Found., 1972-76, dir. Internat. Lambda Chi Edn. Found., 1966-68. Served with AUS, 1954-56. Mem. Tex. Bar Assn., Tex. Bar Found., Vanderbilt U. Law Sch. Alumni Assn. (pres. Dallas chpt. 1972-75), Lambda Chi (chancellor 1966-68). Home and Office: 1849 Bridle Bit Rd Flower Mound TX 75022-6571

HUNT, DONALD FREDERICK, chemistry educator; b. Hyannis, Mass., Apr. 25, 1941; s. Sheldon Leslie and Vena Elizabeth (Knowles) H.; m. Linda Lee Carson, June 12, 1965; children: Amanda Montgomery, Caroline Moore. BS in Chemistry, U. Mass., 1962, PhD in Chemistry, 1967. Asst. prof. chemistry U. Va., Charlottesville, 1967-73, assoc. prof., 1973-78, prof., 1978-93, Univ. prof. chemistry and pathology, 1993—. Recipient Charles H. Stone award ACS-Piedmont Sect., 1990, Va.'s Outstanding Scientist award Va. Sci. Mus., 1992, Pehr Edman award Methods in Protein Sequence Analysis Conf., 1992, Disting. Contbn. award Am. Soc. for Mass Spectrometry, 1994, The Christian B. Anfinsen award Protein Soc., 1996, Thomson medal award Internat. Soc. Mass Spectrometry, 2000. Mem. Am. Chem. Soc. (Chem. Instrumentation award 1997, Frank H. Field and Joe L. Franklin award 2000). Office: U Va Chemistry Dept McCormick Rd Charlottesville VA 22901 E-mail: dfh@virginia.edu.

HUNT, EARL STEPHEN, federal agency administrator; b. Chattanooga, Nov. 28, 1948; s. Earl Gladstone, Jr. and Mary Anne (Kyker) Hunt; m. Edeltraut Gilgan, Sept. 6, 1986. BA with honors, Emory and Henry Coll., 1971; MA, U. Ariz., 1973; PhD, U. Va., 1979; MLS, CAS, Syracuse U., 2000. Instr. Fla. So. Coll., Lakeland, 1980-81; edn. cons. Nashville, N.Y.C., 1980-82; editor, cons. Washington, 1982-86; sr. rsch. analyst U.S. Dept. Edn., Washington, 1986—94, sr. internat. rels. specialist internat. affairs staff Office Sec., 2002—; planning dir. Nat. Libr. Edn., 1995—2002; mgr. U.S. Network Edn. Info., 1997—. Mem. drug prevention task force U.S. Dept. Edn., Washington, 1986—89; cons. U.S. Dept. Labor, Washington, 1990—, NSF, Washington, 1990—, U.S. Trade Rep., Washington, 1999—, U.S. Dept. Homeland Security, Washington, 2001—. Co-editor: (book) The Apocalyptic Premise: Nuclear Arms Debated, 1982; author: Drug Prevention Curricula, 1993, Mapping the World of Education: The Comparative Database System, 1994, Professional Workers as Learners, 1992, A Guide to the International Interpretation of U.S. Education Program Data, 1993; co-author: Classification of Instructional Programs, 1990, 2d edit., 2000; contbr. articles to profl. jours. Mem. Sangamore-Brooks Ln. Citizens' Assn., Bethesda, Md., 1990—. Grantee, USIA, 1982. Mem.: Acad. Polit. Sci., Am. Assn. Higher Edn., Nat. Contract Mgmt. Assn., Phi Delta Kappa, Blue Key, Phi Gamma Mu, Alpha Phi Omega (life). Methodist. Avocations: reading, travel, gardening, cooking. Home: 5209 Sangamore Rd Bethesda MD 20816-2324 Office: US Dept Edn Internat Affairs Staff OUS Rm 6W242 FB6 400 Maryland Ave SW Washington DC 20202 Business E-Mail: stephen.hunt@ed.gov.

HUNT, EDMUND FRANKLIN, JR., secondary school educator; b. Stamford, Conn., May 1, 1955; s. Edmund F. and Patricia M. (LaCroix) H.; m. Dominique Anne O'Donovan, May 26, 1984; children: Alexandra and Ned. BA in Psychology, Dartmouth Coll., 1977; MA in History, U. Rochester, 1988. Tchr. history Vermont Acad., Saxtons River, 1977-81; asst. varsity men's soccer coach Dartmouth Coll., Hanover, N.H., 1981; tchr. history Hartford High Sch., White River Junction, Vt., 1982; tchr. history, dept. chmn. Allendale Columbia Sch., Rochester, N.Y., 1982—. Recipient Excellence in Tchg. award U. Rochester, 1992, 2002, Carl L. Stevenson tchg. award, 1994, Gleason chair in Tchg. Excellence, 1998 Mem. Nat. Coun. for Social Studies, Orgn. Am. Historians. Avocations: reading, music, soccer. Home: 1 Folkside Ln Fairport NY 14450 Office: Allendale Columbia Sch 519 Allens Creek Rd Rochester NY 14618-3497 E-mail: hunt@allendalecolumbia.org.

HUNT, EFFIE NEVA, retired dean, literature educator; b. Waverly, Ill., June 19, 1922; d. Abraham Luther and Fannie Ethel (Ritter) H. AB, MacMurray Coll. for Women, 1944; MA, U. Ill., 1945, PhD, 1950; postgrad., Columbia U., 1953, Univ. Coll., U. London, 1949-50. Key-punch operator U.S. Treasury, 1945; spl. librarian Harvard U., 1947, U. Pa., 1948; Instr. English U. Ill., 1950-51; librarian Library of Congress, Washington, 1951-52; asst. prof. English Mankato State Coll., 1952-59; prof. Radford Coll., 1959-63, chmn. dept. English, 1961-63; prof. Ind. State U., 1963-86; dean Ind. State U. (Coll. Arts and Scis.), 1974-86, dean and prof. emerita, 1987—. Author articles in field. Fulbright grantee, 1949-50 Mem. AAUP, MLA, Nat. Council Tchrs. English, Am. Assn. Higher Edn., Audubon Soc. Home: 3365 Wabash Ave Apt 4 Terre Haute IN 47803-1655 Office: Ind State U Root Hall Eng Dept Terre Haute IN 47809-0001

HUNT, EVERETT CLAIR, engineering educator, researcher, consultant; b. Stamford, Conn., Dec. 28, 1928; s. Benjamin G. and Dorothy (Griffith) H.; m. Jay Kilby, July 12, 1952; children: Gerilyn, Scott, Erik. BS in Engring., U.S. Mcht. Marine Acad., 1951; MS in Engring., Rensselaer Inst. Tech., 1958; MS, Northeastern U., 1972; DSc, Eurotech., 1988. Registered profl. engr., Mass.; chartered engr., U.K. Engr. GE, Schenectady, NY, 1954-65, project mgr. Lynn, Mass., 1965-66, cons. Schenectady, 1966-67, engring. mgr. Portland, Maine, 1967-69, mgr. quality control Lynn, 1969-75; dir. Sun Shipbuilding, Chester, Pa., 1975-79; prof. U.S. Mcht. Marine Acad., Kings Point, NY, 1979-84; dir. rsch., prof. Webb Inst., Glen Cove, NY, 1984-92; pvt. practice cons., 1992—. Adj. prof. Widner Coll., Chester, Pa., 1978-79; cons. engr. 1993—. Author: Marine Engineering Economics and Cost Analysis, 1994; editor, author: Modern Marine Engineering, Vol. I, 1999, Vol. II, 2002; patentee forced circulation steam generator. Lt. USN, 1951-52, Korea. Recipient Bronze medal U.S. Dept. Transp., 1984. Fellow Inst. Marine Engrs.; mem. Pan-Am. Inst. Naval Engrs. Republican. Anglican. Avocations: hiking, mountain climbing, sailing, canoeing. Home and Office: PO Box 308 Warner NH 03278-0308 E-mail: huntec@tds.net.

HUNT, FRANCIS HOWARD, retired navy laboratory official; b. Emporia, Kans., Apr. 12, 1919; s. Frederick Raymond and Mabel (Holmes) Hunt; m. Kathleen McLean, June 4, 1945 (dec. Sept. 1992); children: Deborah Mary, Laurie Jane, Peter Raymond; m. Mary Alice Fish, July 16, 1993. BA, Wesleyan U., 1941. Supr. records Columbia U. divsn. War Research, New London, Conn., 1941—43, tech. editor, writer, 1943—44; with U.S. Navy Underwater Sound Lab., Fort Trumbull, New London, Conn., 1945—70, successively asst. to asst. tech. dir., 1945—47, staff asst. to tech. dir., head tech. info. divsn., 1947—60, assoc. tech. dir. for administrn., 1960—70; assoc. dir. center operations Naval Underwater Systems Ctr., Newport, RI, 1970—76. Mem. East Lyme Zoning Bd. of Appeals, 1956—, sec., 1960—78, chmn., 1978—97; past charter mem. East Lyme Flood and Erosion Control Bd.; mem. Conn. Fedn. Planning and Zoning Agencies. Bd. dir. E. Lyme Pub. Libr., 1962—83, Child Guidance Clin. So.Eastern Conn., 1959—62; past mem. East Lyme H.S. Planning Com., Niantic (Conn.) Boy Scout Com.; justice of peace, 1985—; past mem. East Lyme Rep. Town Com.; bd. dir. East Lyme Nursing Assn., 1964—66. Served with AUS, 1944—45. Decorated Purple Heart, Bronze Star Medal WWII, Battle of the Bulge; named Melvin Jones Fellow for Dedicated Humanitarian Services, Lions Clubs Internat. Found., 1997; recipient Outstanding mem. Town Commn., East Lyme C. of C., 1972, 1981. Mem.: IEEE (life), Disabled Am. Vets., Nat. Assn. Ret. Fed. Employees, Gov. William Bradford Compact, Soc. of Cin. in Conn., Soc. Colonial Wars in Conn., Conn., Lebanon, Columbia hist. socs., Conn. Huguenot Soc. (pres. 1990—96), Conn. Soc. SAR (mem. bd. mgrs. 1980—87, registrar 1984—87, Patriot medal 1987, Silver good citizenship medal 1992), Nat. Huguenot Soc. (chaplain gen. 1993—95), Soc. Mayflower Descendents in Conn., New Eng. Historic Geneal. Soc., Conn. Soc. Genealogists, R.I. Geneal. Soc., Lions (past pres. Niantic club). Baptist. Home: 2 Strawberry Ln Niantic CT 06357-1936

HUNT, FRANKLIN GRIGGS, lawyer; b. Jenks, Okla., Dec. 21, 1930; s. John Wesley and Alta (Johnson) H.; m. Marilyn Glenn Maxfield, July 12, 1958; children— Laura Suzanne, Molly Frances AB, Harvard U., 1952, LL.B., 1959. Bar: N.Y., 1960. Assoc. Lord, Day and Lord, N.Y.C., 1959-64, ptnr., 1965-93, of counsel, 1993-94; sr. advisor Morgan, Lewis & Bockius, N.Y.C., 1994—. Assoc. editor Am. Maritime Cases, 1982-92; contbr. articles to profl. jours. Mem. adv. bd. Inst. Intercultural Studies, N.Y.C., 1985—; bd. dirs. Friends of Archaeology, Office Archaeol. Studies, Mus. N.Mex. Lt. (j.g.) USN, 1952—55. Mem. ABA, N.Y.C. Bar Assn., Maritime Law Assn. U.S., AAAS, Am. Phys. Soc. Avocations: ballet, archaeology. Home: 43 W 61st St Apt 22M New York NY 10023-7618 E-mail: hunt@cybermesa.com.

HUNT, FREDERICK TALLEY DRUM, JR., association executive; b. Martinique, French West Indies, Sept. 19, 1947; s. Frederick Talley Drum and Eleanor Conly H.; m. Acacia Lynn Graham, Dec. 4, 1976. Ba, Vanderbilt U., 1970. Medal hon. specialist and ceremonies U.S. Army, Washington, 1971—73; dir. program devel. manufactured Housing Inst., Washington, 1973-74; pres. Hunt Assocs., Washington, 1974-75; asst. dir. field svcs. Nat. Assn. Life Underwriters, 1975-77; dir. comm., govt. liaison Am. Acad. Actuaries, Washington, 1977-80; pres. Soc. Profl. Benefit Adminstrs., 1980—. Pres., owner Hunt Mgmt. Sys., 1982—; advisor White House, Congress, others; spkr. in field. Contbr. articles to profl. jours. Mem.: Soc. Cin., Miles River Yacht Club, Met. Club, Aztec Club of 1847. Home: Westmoreland Hills 5308 Blackstone Rd Bethesda MD 20816-1803 also: 228 Riverside Rd Edgewater MD 21037-1505 Office: Hunt Mgmt Systems 2 Wisconsin Cir Ste 670 Chevy Chase MD 20815-7043

HUNT, GEORGE WILLIAM, priest, magazine editor; b. N.Y.C., Jan. 22, 1937; s. George Aloysius and Grace Winifred (Jordan) H. AB, Fordham U., 1961, MA, 1963; PhL, Woodstock Coll., 1961, STL, 1967; STM, Yale U., 1968; PhD, Syracuse U., 1974; DHL (hon.), Spring Hill Coll., 1991, Loyola Coll., Balt., 1993, Fairfield U., 1996. Joined S.J., 1954; ordained priest Roman Cath. Ch., 1967. Asst. prof. St. Peter's Coll., Jersey City, 1968-70; assoc. prof. Le Moyne Coll., Syracuse, N.Y., 1973-81; vis. prof. Georgetown U., Washington, 1983-84; pres., editor in chief Am. mag., N.Y.C., 1984-98; dir. Arch. Hughes Inst. of Religion and Culture Fordham U., Bronx, N.Y., 1999—. Author: (literary criticsm) John Updike and the Three Great Secret Things, 1980 (Christianity lit. award 1981), John Cheever: The Hobgoblin Company of Love, 1983.Y Trustee Boston Coll., 1985—, Carnegie Coun. on Ethics and Internat. Affairs, 1986—, Holy Cross Coll., Worcester, Mass., 1990—, Loyola Coll., Balt., 1994—, Le Moyne Coll., Syracuse, 1995—; trustee emeritus U. Detroit, 1984—. Roman Catholic. Home and Office: Fordham U Arch Hughes Inst Religion and Culture 441 E Fordham Rd Bronx NY 10458-5149

HUNT, GERALD WALLACE, lawyer; b. Portland, Oreg., Oct. 31, 1939; BSBA in Econs., U. Denver, 1961, JD, 1964; LLM in Taxation, Washington U., 1981. Bar: Colo. 1964, Ariz. 1968, Tex. 1996, Alaska 1999, cert.: Ariz. Bd. Legal Specialization (tax specialist). Asst. trust officer The Ariz. Bank, Phoenix, 1967-69; atty. Westover, Keddie, et al, Yuma, Ariz., 1969-73; pvt. practice law Yuma, 1973-74; atty. Hunt & Clark, Yuma, 1974-75, Hunt, Stanley & Hossler, Yuma, 1975-96, Hunt, Tallan & Hossler, Yuma, 1996-97, Hunt, Kenworthy and Hossler, Yuma, 1998—2002, Hunt, Kenworthy, Meerchaum & Hossler, Yuma, 2002—04. Treas. Excel Group, Yuma, 1998—99, chair, 2000—02; bd. dirs. Greater Yuma Port Authority, 2000. Bd. dirs. Saguaro Found., 2004—. Fellow: Am. Coll. Trust and Estate Counsel; mem.: ABA, Tex. Bar, Alaska Bar, Colo. State Bar, Ariz. State Bar, Internat. Mcpl. Lawyers Assn. Office: Hunt Kenworthy & Hossler 330 W 24th St Yuma AZ 85364-6455

HUNT, GORDON, lawyer; b. LA, Oct. 26, 1934; s. Howard Wilson and Esther Nita (Dempsey) H. BA in Polit. Sci, UCLA, 1956; JD, U. So. Calif., 1959. Bar: Calif. 1960. Law clk. Appellate Dept., Superior Ct. L.A. County, 1959-60; mem. firm Behymer & Hoffman, Los Angeles, 1960-65; partner firm Behymer, Hoffman & Hunt, Los Angeles, 1965-68; ptnr. firm Munns, Kofford, Hoffman, Hunt & Throckmorton, Pasadena, 1969-90, Hunt, Ortman, Blasco, Palffy & Rossell, Pasadena, 1990-95; mem. Hunt, Ortman, Blasco, Palffy & Rossell Inc., 1995—. Lectr. UCLA, various yrs.; chmn. legal adv. com. Assoc. Gen. Contractors Calif., 1985; arbitrator L.A. Superior Ct., State of Calif. Author: Construction Surety and Bonding Handbook; co-author: California Construction Law, 16th edit.; contbr. numerous articles to legal jours. Mem. ABA, Calif. Bar Assn. (del. Conv. 1964-69), L.A. County Bar Assn. (real property com. 1965-66, exec. com. 1970-72, sec. 1972-73, vice chmn. 1972-75, chmn. real property sect. 1975-76, co-chmn. continuing edn. bar com. 1969-71, Outstanding Real Estate Lawyer award 2000, Outstanding Achievement in Constrn. Law 2004), Am. Arbitration Assn. (arbitrator, mediator). Office: 301 N Lake Ave Fl 7 Pasadena CA 91101-4108 Office Phone: 626-440-5200. Business E-Mail: goff@hobpr.com.

HUNT, H(AROLD) KEITH, retired business management educator, marketing consultant; b. Apr. 16, 1938; married; 8 children. BS in Mktg. and Mgmt., U. Utah, 1961, MBA, 1962; PhD in Mktg., Northwestern U., 1972. Instr. Imperial Valley Coll., El Centro, Calif., 1962-64; teaching asst. Northwestern U., 1964-66, instr., 1966-67; asst. prof. bus. adminstrn. and journalism U. Iowa, 1967-73; cons., staff mem. Office Policy Planning and Evaluation, FTC, Washington, 1973-74; assoc. prof. bus. adminstrn. U. Wyo., Laramie, 1974-75; assoc. prof. bus. mgmt. Brigham Young U., Provo, Utah, 1975-78, prof., 1978—. Participant, chmn. various workshops, seminars, meetings; research expert, cons., expert witness on consumer research FTC, 1974-81; cons., expert witness div. drug advt. FDA, 1975-82; cons., adv. on consumer research Consumer and Corp. Affairs Can., 1978-82. Editor: Advances in Consumer Research, vol. 5, 1977; co-editor conf. proc. (with Frances Magrabi) Interdisciplinary Consumer Research, 1980, (with Ralph Day) Consumer Satisfaction/Dissatisfaction and Complaining Behavior, 8 vols., 1975-85, Jour. 1988—. Elected to Orem City Coun., Utah, 1986-93. Recipient Maeser Research award Brigham Young U., 1981; scholar-in-residence adv. dept. U. Ill., 1979; vis. research scholar Coll. Home Econs., U. Ala., 1980; vis. research scholar dept. mktg. and transp. U. Tenn., 1981; NSF grantee, 1975-77 Mem. Assn. Consumer Research (pres. 1979, exec. sec. 1983-2000, 1st Disting. Svc. award 1989), Am. Acad. Advt. (pres. 1982-83, exec. sec. 1983-86, elected fellow 1987), Am. Mktg. Assn., Soc. Consumer Psychology, Am. Council on Consumer Interests, Beta Gamma Sigma, Kappa Tau Alpha, Omicron Delta Epsilon, Phi Kappa Phi Home: 835 E High Country Dr Orem UT 84097-2370 Business E-Mail: hkhunt@byu.edu.

HUNT, HAZEL ANALUE STANFIELD, retired accountant; b. Butler, Mo., Apr. 4, 1921; d. Vernon Arthur and Myrrl Millicent (Henderson) Stanfield; m. Marvie Avanell Hunt, July 25, 1942; 1 child, Roger LeRoy. Grad., Sawyer Sch. Bus., L.A., 1939. Supr., bookkeeper, sec. Nethercutt Labs., Santa Monica, Calif., 1940-45; v.p., treas. Dwyer-Curlett, Inc., L.A., 1946-86; ret., 1986. Pres. Nat. Assn. Accts., West Los Angeles, 1970-96, other offices. Mem. DAR, Beta Sigma Phi (pres. 1942, other offices). Presbyterian. Home: 1575 E Washington Blvd Apt 312 Pasadena CA 91104-2663 Personal E-mail: hash@mailstation.com.

HUNT, HELEN, actress; b. L.A., June 15, 1963; d. Gordon and Jane Hunt; 1 child. TV appearances include Amy Prentiss, The Swiss Family Robinson, The Fitzpatricks, It Takes Two, Having Babies, Land of Little Rain, Weekend, Mary Tyler Moore Show, Family, St. Elsewhere; TV movies include Pioneer Woman, All Together Now, Death Scream, The Spell, Transplant, Angel Dusted, Child Bride of Short Creek, The Miracle of Cathy Miller, Desperate Lives, Quarterback Princess, Bill: On His Own, Choices of the Heart, Sweet Revenge, Why Are You Here?, Murder In New Hampshire: The Pamela Smart Story, 1991, In the Comfort of Darkness, 1992; TV series Mad About You, 1992-99 (Emmy nomination, Lead Actress - Comedy, 1993, 94, Golden Globe award for Best Actress, musical or comedy, 1994, 95, Emmy award for Best Leading Actress in a Comedy series, 1996); films include Rollercoaster, 1977, Girls Just Want To Have Fun, 1985, Trancers, 1985, Empire, 1985, Peggy Sue Got Married, 1986, Project X, 1987, Miles From Home, 1988, Next Of Kin, 1989, The Waterdance, 1992, Only You, 1992, Bob Roberts, 1992, Mr. Saturday Night, 1992, Kiss of Death, 1995, Twister, 1996, As Good As It Gets, 1997 (Acad. award Best Actress in a Leading Role 1997), Twister: Ride It Out, 1998, Twelfth Night, 1998, Dr. T and the Women, 2000, Pay It Forward, 2000, Cast Away, 2000, What Women Want, 2000, Curse of the Jade Scorpion, 2001; plays include: Life (X)3, 2003 Address: Connie Tavel Mgmt 9171 Wilshire Blvd Beverly Hills CA 90210-5530

HUNT, J. B. (JOHNNIE BRYAN HUNT), retired transportation executive; m. Johnelle DeBusk, 1952; 2 children. Chmn. (ret.) J.B. Hunt Group, Lowell, Ark., 1969—95, sr. chmn., 1995—. Served Army. Named Transp. Person of Yr., Traffic Club NY, 1995, Ark Person of Yr., Ark. Masonic Lodge, 1995; named to AMCA Hall of Fame, Arkansas Motor Carriers Assoc, 1991, Am. Acad. Achievement, 1993, (with wife) Univ. Ark. Bus. Hall of Fame, 2001; recipient (with wife), Arkansans of Yr., Ark. Easter Seals, 1990, Salzberg Practitioner award, Syracuse U., 1999. Office: JB Hunt Transport Services Inc 615 JB Hunt Corporate Dr Lowell AR 72745

HUNT, JAMES BAXTER, JR., lawyer, former governor; b. Guilford County, N.C., May 16, 1937; s. James Baxter and Elsie (Brame) Hunt; m. Carolyn Joyce Leonard, Aug. 20, 1958; children: Rebecca Hunt Hawley, James Baxter Hunt III, Rachel Nilender, Elizabeth Amigh. BS in Agrl. Edn., N.C. State U., 1959, MS in Agrl. Cons., 1962; JD, U. N.C., 1964. Bar: N.C. 1964. Econ. advisor H.M. Govt. of Nepal for Ford Found., 1964—66; ptnr. Kirby, Webb and Hunt, 1966—72; lt. gov. State of N.C., 1973—77, gov., 1977—85, gov., 1993—2001; ptnr. Poyner and Spruill, Raleigh, NC, 1985—93; mem. Womble Carlyle Sandridge & Rice, Raleigh, 2001—. Originator, bd. dirs. Triangle East; chmn. N.C. State U. Emerging Issues Forum; bd. visitors Wake Forst U.; founding chmn. Nat. Bd. for Profl. Tchg. Stds., 1987, Nat. Ctr. for Pub. Policy and Higher Edn., 1998. Author: Rally Around the Precinct, 1968. Trustee Atlantic Christian Coll.; mem. Carnegie Forum on Edn. and Econ. Task Force on Tchg. as a Profl., 1986; chmn. Nat. Commn. on Tchg. and Am.'s Future, 1994; state pres. Young Dems., 1968; del. Dem. Nat. Conv., 1968. Named Outstanding Young Man of Yr., Wilson Jr. C. of C., 1969, Outstanding Govt. Ofcl. in Cmty. Edn., Nat. Assn. Cmty. Edn., 1977; recipient 1st Harry S. Truman award, Nat. Young Dems., 1975, James Bryant Conant award, Edn. Commn. States, 1984, Nat. 4-H Outstanding Alumnus award, 1984, Soil Conservation Honors award, 1986, Child Health Adv. award, Am. Acad. Pediat., 1994, Friend of Edn. award, Horace Mann League, 1999. Mem.: Nat. Govs. Assn. (chmn. task force on technol. innovation mem. exec. com., chmn. edn. com. states and nat. task force on edn. for econ. growth 1982—83, leadership team on controlling crime and violence 1994, chmn. nat. edn. goals panel 1997—). Presbyterian. Office: Womble Carlyle Sandridge & Rice 150 Fayetteville St Mall Ste 2100 PO Box 831 Raleigh NC 27602

HUNT, JAMES CALVIN, physician, academic administrator; b. Lexington, N.C., Sept. 11, 1925; s. James Lee and Sarah Della (Frank) Hunt; m. Irene Kivett, Sept. 17, 1949; children: James Calvin, Michael S., Cynthia Irene. AB, Catawba Coll., 1949; MD, Bowman Gray Sch. Medicine, 1953; MS, U. Minn., 1958; ScD, Wake Forest U., 1992. Diplomate Am. Bd. Internal Medicine. Intern N.C. Bapt. Hosp., Winston-Salem, 1953-54; resident, fellow Mayo Grad Sch. Medicine, Rochester, Minn., 1954-58; practice medicine, specializing in internal medicine (cardiovasc.-renal diseases) Rochester, 1958-78; cons., instr. to asst. prof. dept. medicine Mayo Clinic and Mayo Med. Sch., 1958-63, assoc. prof., chmn. divsn. nephrology, 1963-72, prof., chmn. dept. medicine, 1973-78; prof., assoc. dean clin. ednl. programs Mayo Med. Sch., 1972-74; prof. medicine U. Tenn., Memphis, 1978—, dean Coll. Medicine, 1978-81, v.p. health affairs, chancellor Univ. Health Scis. Ctr., 1981-93, univ. disting. prof., dir. clin. scholars program, 1993—2001, v.p. health affairs, chancellor emeritus, 2001—. Mem. adv. coun. Nat. Heart, Lung and Blood Inst. NIH, 1976—81. Contbr. articles to profl. jours. Pres. Nat. Kidney Found., 1973—76; mem. Congl. Tech. Adv. Coun., 1987—96; bd. dirs. Memphis Downtown Neighbors Assn., 1995—99, pres., 1997—98; mem. adv. bd. Goals for Memphis, 1987—95; bd. dirs. YMCA, Memphis, Memphis Riverfront Devel. Corp., 1999—, sec., 2000—02; trustee Le Bonheur Children's Med. Ctr., 1981—93, Christian Bros. Coll., 1983—96; mem. cmty. adv. bd. Bapt. Meml. Hosp., 1986—; bd. dirs. Bapt. Meml. Coll. Health Scis., 1995—, chair acad. affairs com., 1998—; mem. adv. bd. Rhodes Coll. With USAAF, 1943—46, ETO. Recipient Disting. Svc. award, Bowman Gray Sch. Medicine, Wake Forest U., 1975, Disting. Alumnus award, Catawba Coll., 1974, Educator of the Yr. award, Memphis State U., 1986, Outstanding Alumnus award, Mayo Found., 1991, Gift of Life award, Nat. Kidney Found., 1991. Fellow: ACP, Am. Heart Assn. (mem. coun. circulation), Am. Coll. Cardiology; mem.: AMA, Am. Soc. Clin. Pharmacology and Therapeutics, Am. Soc. Internal Medicine, Coun. High Blood Pressure Rsch., Soc. Nuc. Medicine, Internat. Soc. Hypertension, Internat. Am. Socs. Nephrology, Sigma Xi, Phi Rho Sigma, Alpha Omega Alpha. Home and Office: 3381 Moss Rose Dr Memphis TN 38115-4263

HUNT, JAMES L., lawyer; b. Chgo., Oct. 20, 1942; BA magna cum laude, DePauw U., 1964; JD, Northwestern U., 1967. Bar: Calif. 1967. Atty. McCutchen, Doyle, Brown & Enersen, San Francisco, 1967, ptnr., chmn. firm, 1988—91, 1999—2001, chmn. litig. dept., 1991—95; ptnr. Bingham McCutchen LLP, San Francisco, 2001—, chmn. litig. practice group. Atty. rep. 9th Cir. Jud. Conf., 1991-94; bd. dirs. The Lurie Co.; trustee The Lurie Found. Assoc. editor: Northwestern U. Law Rev., 1966-67. Bd. dirs. San Francisco Giants; bd. visitors Northwestern U. Law Sch., 1989—. Named a No. Calif. Super Lawyer, Law & Politics & SF Mag., 2004. Mem. Am. Coll. Trial Lawyers, Phi Beta Kappa, Order Coif. Office: Bingham McCutchen LLP 3 Embarcadero Ctr Ste 18000 San Francisco CA 94111-4003 Office Phone: 415-393-2212. Business E-Mail: james.hunt@bingham.com.

HUNT, JOHN DAVID, retired bank executive; b. Worcester, Mass., May 2, 1925; s. John J. and Honorea B. (Tully) H.; m. Claire A. Sullivan, June 25, 1949; children: Barbara A., Kathryn R. AB, Brown U., 1949; postgrad. Advanced Mgmt. Program, Harvard U., 1973; DBA (hon.), Anna Maria Coll., 1982. Accountant Harry W. Wallis & Co., Worcester, 1949-50; with Worcester County Nat. Bank (now Fleet Bank), 1952—; asst. v.p. Worcester County Nat. Bank (now Shawmut Worcester County Bank N.A.), 1959-61, v.p., 1961-69, sr. v.p., 1969-73, exec. v.p., 1973-77, pres., 1977-87, chmn. bd., 1983, chmn. exec. com., 1987-90, ret., 1990. Bd. dirs. Worcester Bus. Devel. Corp., pres., 1981-82, chmn., 1987-99; trustee Allmerica Investment Trust, 1977-95, Allmerica Securities Inc., 1977-95, Mass. Biotech Rsch. Inst., 1985-98; instr. Am. Inst. Banking, 1957-60. Chmn. fund drive Greater Worcester United Appeal, 1972; Bd. dirs. United Cerebral Palsy Assn. Worcester County,

1957-67, bd. dirs. U. Mass. Medical Ctr. Found.; Worcester Better Bus. Bur., 1964-69, Catholic Charities Worcester, 1971-75, United Way Worcester, NCCJ, 1979-86; trustee Hahnemann Hosp., 1966-78, Assumption Coll., 1975-80; corporator St. Vincent Hosp.; mem. Worcester Redevel. Authority, 1983-85; adv. bd. dept. mgmt. Worcester Poly. Inst.; chmn. Civic Ctr. Commn., 1985-90; trustee Fund Edn. in Econs., 1980-85, chmn., 1984-85; bd. dirs. Worcester Mcpl. Research Bur., Inc., 1985-89. Served to lt. USNR, 1943-47, 50-52. Recipient Outstanding Young Man award Worcester County, 1961, Isaiah Thomas award Advt. Club Worcester, 1987, Peace medal State of Israel, 1987. Mem. Am. Inst. Banking, Robert Morris Assocs. (bd. govs. 1966-71, pres. New Eng. chpt. 1969-70), Am. Bankers Assn. (governing council), Mass. Bankers Assn., bd. govs. (1974-79, chmn. 1977), Worcester Area C. of C. (chmn. 1984, bd. dirs. 1980-99), Alpha Delta Phi. Clubs: Worcester County Brown, Worcester, Worcester Country, Oyster Harbors. Republican. Roman Catholic. Home: 770 Salisbury St Worcester MA 01609-1155

HUNT, JOHN MORTIMER, JR., classical studies educator; b. Bryn Mawr, Pa., Sept. 21, 1943; s. John Mortimer and Ruth Pierson (Ott) H. AB, Lafayette Coll., 1965; MA, Bryn Mawr Coll., 1968, PhD, 1970. From asst. prof. to assoc. prof. classical studies Villanova (Pa.) U., 1970-91, prof., 1991—, chmn. dept. classical studies, 1993-99, dir. classical studies, 1999—. Instr. Latin Lafayette Coll., Easton, Pa., 1970; vis. assoc. prof. U. Calif., Santa Barbara, 1978—80. Mem. editl. bd. Classical Philology, 1976—2001; contbr. articles to profl. publs. Grad. fellow, Cornell U., 1965—66. Mem.: Delano Kindred, Roger Williams Family Assn., Colonial Soc. Pa., Soc. Colonial Wars in Pa., Soc. Mayflower Descs. Pa. (state historian 1999—2000, editor The Pa. Mayflower, Most Disting. Pilgrim award 2003), Pa. Soc. S.R., Franklin Inn Club, Ancient and Honorable Artillery Co. Mass. Episcopalian. Avocations: genealogy, early American history, opera. Office: Villanova U Dept Classical and Modern Langs & Lits Villanova PA 19085-1699 Office Phone: 610-519-4678. Business E-Mail: john.hunt@villanova.edu. E-mail: louisaruth@aol.com.

HUNT, J(ULIAN) COURTENAY, artist; b. Jacksonville, Fla., Sept. 17, 1917; s. Julian Schley and Ruth Rosalind (Loftin) Hunt. Student, Ringling Sch. Art, Farnsworth Sch. Art. Tchr. pvt. classes painting. One-man shows include Cummer Gallery, Jacksonville, exhibited in group shows at Palm Beach Art Gallery, Soc. Four Arts, Palm Beach, Audubon Artists Am., N.Y.C., Allied Artists Am., Atlanta High Mus., St. Augustine (Fla.) Art Assn., Sarasota (Fla.) Art Assn., Nortno Art Gallery Palm Beaches, Represented in permanent collections U. Fla., Gainesville, Jacksonville U., City Hall of Jacksonville, Duval County Cir. Ct., Jacksonville Ind. Life Ins Co., P.A.S.T.A. Gallery, St. Augustine, Fla. With USAF, ETO. Home and Office: 2248 Carnes St Orange Park FL 32073

HUNT, KAY NORD, lawyer; b. Carver, Minn., June 26, 1955; d. Edward John and Carol Valentine (Lunde) Nord; m. Gary C. Hunt, June 25, 1977 (div. Dec. 1987). BA summa cum laude, Gustavus Adolphus Coll., 1977; JD, Marquette U., 1981. Bar: Wis. 1981, Minn. 1982, US Dist. Ct. (ea., we. dist. Wis. 1981, Minn. 1982), US Ct. Appeals (7th, 8th cir. 1982), US Supreme Ct. 2000. Law clk. Wis. Ct. Appeals, Milw., 1981-82; atty., appellate litig. Lommen Nelson Cole & Stageberg, Mpls., 1982—. Adj. prof. Univ. St. Thomas Sch. Law, 2003—. Bd. mem. Ramsy County Humane Soc., St. Paul, 1997—. Mem. ABA, Am. Acad. Appellate Lawyers, State Bar Wis., Minn. State Bar Assn., Minn. Def. Lawyers (amicus curia com.), Hennepin County Bar Assn., Amdahl Inn of Ct. Office: Lommen Nelson Cole & Stageberg 2000 IDS Ctr 80 S 8th St Minneapolis MN 55402-2100 Office Phone: 612-336-9341. Office Fax: 612-339-8064. Business E-Mail: kay@lommen.com.

HUNT, KEVIN J., food products executive; With Ralcorp Holdings, Inc., St. Louis, 1985—, corp. v.p., 1995—2003, pres., co-CEO, 2003—, bd. dirs., 2004—05; CEO Bremner, Inc., 1995—, Nutcracker Brands, Inc., 2003—. Office: Ralcorp Holdings Inc ste 2900 800 MarketSt Saint Louis MO 63101 Office Phone: 314-877-7000. Office Fax: 314-877-7666.*

HUNT, L. SUSAN, publishing executive; BA in Acctg., Stetson U., 1982; MBA, Rollins Coll., 1996. Auditor Peat Marwick Mitchell, Jacksonville, Fla., 1982—86, Price Waterhouse, Orlando, Fla.; asst. contr., ops. adminstrn. mgr., prodn. mgr. Orlando Sentinel, 1986—97; v.p. ops. South Fla. Sun-Sentinel, Ft. Lauderdale, 1997—99, v.p., gen. mgr., 1999—2001; pub., pres., CEO Morning Call, Allentown, Pa., 2001—. Office: Morning Call 101 N 6th St PO Box 1260 Allentown PA 18105

HUNT, LAMAR, professional football team executive; b. Aug. 2, 1932; s. H.L. and Lyda (Bunker) H.; m. Norma Hunt; children: Lamar, Sharron, Clark, Daniel. BS, So. Meth. U., 1956. Founder, owner Kansas City Chiefs, NFL, 1959—, pres., 1959-76, chmn., 1977-78; founder, pres. AFL, 1959; (became Am. Football Conf.-NFL 1970); pres. Am. Football Conf., 1970—. Bd. dirs. Profl. Football Hall of Fame, Canton, Ohio. Named Salesman of Yr., Kansas City Advt. and Sales Execs. Club, 1963, Southwesterner of Yr., Tex. Sportswriters Assn., 1959. Office: Kans City Chiefs 1 Arrowhead Dr Kansas City MO 64129-1651*

HUNT, LAWRENCE HALLEY, JR., lawyer; b. July 15, 1943; s. Lawrence Halley Sr. and Mary Hamilton (Johnson) H.; m. Katherine Collins; children: Caroline Smith, Laura Hamilton, Darwin Halley. AB, Dartmouth Coll., 1965; cert., Inst. d'Etudes Politiques, Paris, 1966; JD, U. Chgo., 1969. Bar: N.Y. 1970, Ill. 1971, U.S. Ct. Appeals (9th cir.) 1980, U.S. Ct. Appeals (2d cir.) 1981, U.S. Supreme Ct. 1981. Assoc. Davis Polk & Wardwell, N.Y.C., 1969-70, Sidley & Austin, Chgo., 1970-75; ptnr. Sidley Austin Brown & Wood, Chgo., 1975—, mem. exec. com., 1985—2002. Mem. securities adv. com. Ill. Sec. of State, Springfield, Ill., 1977—87; prof. grad. program fin. svcs. law Ill. Inst. Tech.-Chgo.-Kent Coll. Law, 1987—99. Mng. editor U. Chgo. Law Review, 1968-69. James B. Reynolds scholar Dartmouth Coll., 1965-66. Mem.: ABA (com. on commodity regulation, past chmn. subcom. on futures commn. merchants, past mem. exec. coun.), Internat. Bar Assn. (past chmn. bus. law com. sub-com. futures and options), Indian Hill Club, Chgo. Club, Mid-Day Club. Office: Sidley Austin Brown & Wood Bank One Plz 10 South Dearborn St Chicago IL 60603 Office Phone: 312-853-7000. E-mail: lhunt@sidley.com.

HUNT, LEIGH RAPHAEL, playwright; b. Seattle, Feb. 4, 1941; s. Charles Raphael Hunt and Mary Elizabeth Griffith; m. Janice Leach (div.); m. Roxanne Sonia Cossette, Apr. 21, 1971; children: Kelly, Siegfried Fianna Marat. Stuntman Metro Goldwyn Mayer, Hollywood, Calif., 1962—69; lectr. in playwriting Pierce Coll., Lakewood, Wash., 1998—99. Founder, dir. Pierce County Playwrights Festival, Tacoma, 1991—2001. Author: (plays) Circle the Wagons, 0198—1988 (1st Playwrights Forum awards, 1989), There's No Place Like Home, 1999—2000 (2d New Century Writers award, 2001), Parent of the Even, 2000—01 (5th New Century Writers award, 2003), Borrowed Breath, 2001—02 (2d New Century Writers award, 2003). Home: 4708 Dunbar Dr NW Gig Harbor WA 98335-8066

HUNT, LORRAINE T., lieutenant governor; b. Niagara Falls, N.Y., Mar. 11, 1939; Student, Westlake Coll. Music. Former pres., CEO Perri Inc.; founder, also bd. dirs. Continental Nat. Bank; lt. gov. State of Nev., 1998—, pres. Senate, 1999—. Bd. dirs. First Security Bank Nev.; chmn. bd. trustees Las Vegas Convention and Visitors Authority; former commr. and vice chair Nev. Commn. on Tourism; dir. Nev. Hotel/Motel Assn.; vice chmn. Nev. Motion Picture Found., Nev. Motion Picture Commn. Commr. Clark county Commn., 1995-99; mem. cmty. bd. Wells Fargo Bank Named U.S. Small Bus. Adv. of the Yr., 1989, Nev. Restauranteur of Yr., 1992, Rep. Woman of Yr., 1996, Woman of Yr., Nev. Ballet Theater, 1996; recipient Govs. award for excellence in bus., 1987, Free Enterprise award, 1993, First Lifetime Achievement award, Govs. Conf. on Tourism, 1993. Republican. Office: 101 N Carson St Ste 2 Carson City NV 89701-4786 also: 555 E Washington Ave Ste 5500 Las Vegas NV 89101-1081

HUNT, MARK ALAN, museum director; b. Topeka, May 21, 1949; s. Ira B. and Marjorie May (McConnell) H.; m. Cynthia E. Rush, Feb. 21, 1976; children: Alexander Rush, Alice Claire. BA magna cum laude, Washburn U., 1971; MA, Cooperstown Grad. Programs, N.Y. State U. Coll., Oneonta, 1982; grad., Mus. Mgmt. Inst. U. Calif., Berkeley, 1983. Dir. Plymouth (Mich.) Hist. Mus., 1976; curator exhibits Kans. Hist. Soc., Topeka, 1976, asst. dir. mus., 1976-79, dir. mus., 1979-88, dir. mus. and hist. sites, 1988-90; dir. Nat. Scouting Mus., Murray (Ky.) State U., 1990-96, Ronald Reagan Presdl. Libr. and Mus., Simi Valley, Calif., 1996-2000; dep. dir./curator Franklin D. Roosevelt Libr., Hyde Park, N.Y., 2000—. Cons. Menninger Found., 1980, Nat. Endowment Humanities, 1974, 75, 77, 1978, Mus. Assessment Program; instr. mus. adminstrn., U. Kans., 1987-89; mem. adv. coun. Ea. Ill. U. Hist. Adminstrn. Program, 1992-96. Contbr. articles to profl. jours. Bd. dirs. Mulvane Art Ctr., Washburn U., 1988-89, Land Between the Lakes Assn., 1994-96; mem. master planning com. Ward-Meade Hist. Park, 1986-89; mem. Bus. Coun. for Arts, 1990-96; grad. Leadership Murray, 1994, Murray Tourism Commn., 1995-96; mem. Ventura County (Calif.) Cultural Tourism Collaborative, 1998-2000, Moorpark (Calif.) Coll. Found. Bd., 1999; bd. dirs. World Affairs Coun. Mid-Hudson Valley, 2003-. Recipient award for excellence, Kans. Mus. Assn., 1991; Wiseman scholar, 1967—68, Washburn scholar, 1968—71, Clark fellow, 1973—74, Alumni fellow, Washburn U., 1998. Mem. Am. Assn. State and Local History (chmn. state membership com. 1976-85, cons., mem. program com. ann. meeting 1988, 92, mem. edn. com. 1981-84, mem. local arrangements com. ann. meeting 1985, mem. membership task force 1993-97, mem. nat. governing coun. 1991-95, mem. profl. std. and ethics com. 2001—), Mountain Plains Mus. Assn. (mem. bd. 1977, Kans. rep.), Calif. Assn. Mus. (dist. rep. on CAM bd. 1998-99), Kans. Mus. Assn. (pres. 1978-80, Excellence award 1991), Ky. Assn. Mus. (bd. dirs. 1994-96), Am. Assn. Mus. (mem. accreditation vis. com., mem. mus. studies task force 1988-89), Southeastern Mus. Assn. (bd. dirs. 1995-96), Murray-Calloway County C. of C., Rotary Internat., Kappa Sigma, Phi Kappa Phi. Methodist. Home: 16 Yates Blvd Poughkeepsie NY 12601-5006 Office: Franklin D Roosevelt Libr 4079 Albany Post Rd Hyde Park NY 12538-1917 Office Phone: 845-486-7746. Business E-Mail: mark.hunt@nara.gov.

HUNT, MARY ALICE, library science educator; b. Lima, Ohio, Apr. 14, 1928; d. Blair T. and Grace (Henry) H. BA, Fla. State U., Tallahassee, 1950, MA, 1953; PhD, Ind. U., Bloomington, 1973. Instr., librarian Fla. State U., Tallahassee, 1955-61, asst. prof., 1961-74, assoc. prof., 1974-82, prof., 1982-95, assoc. dean, 1986-95, prof. emerita, 1995—. Author: Transitions: An Informal History of a School Celebrating its 50th Anniversary, 1997; co-author: Multimedia Indexes, Lists, etc., 1975; editor: Multimedia Approach To Children's Literature, 1983, (periodical) FSU/SLIS Alumni Newsletter, 1966-95, Florida Libraries, 1961-67; assoc. editor: (book) Folders of Ideas for Library Excellence, 1991. Mem. Sr. Ctr. Art Coun., 2004—. Recipient Art Vol. of Yr. award, Sr. Ctr. Art Coun., 2004. Mem. ALA (councilor at large 1986-94, 96-2000), Southeastern Library Assn., Fla. Assn. Media in Edn., Delta Kappa Gamma, Pi Lambda Theta (life), Pi Kappa Phi, Beta Phi Mu. Avocations: gardening, reading, photography, pastel drawing and watercolor painting. Home: 1603 Kolopakin Nene Tallahassee FL 32301-4733

HUNT, MARY REILLY, organization executive; b. N.Y.C., Apr. 17, 1921; d. Philip R. and Mary C. (Harten) Reilly; m. Robert R. Hunt, Apr. 10, 1943,; children: Marianne Schram, Philip R., Robert R., Elise Hannah. Student, CCNY, 1939; DHL (hon.), Thomas More Coll., 2005. Tax investigator Ind. Dept. Revenue, 1970-80; pres. Ind. Right to Life, 1973-77; treas. Nat. Right to Life Com., Washington, 1974, 77, 78, mem. exec. com., 1974, 76-81, vice chmn., 1976, exec. dir., 1978, dir. devel., 1979-94, v.p. devel., 1994-97, hon. bd. mem., 1983—; v.p. devel. Nat. Life Ctr., Woodbury, 1997—; pres. Mary Reilly Hunt & Assoc., Inc., South Bend, Ind., 1985—. Bd. dirs., v.p. YWCA, 1968-73, bd. dirs. Mental Health Assn. St. Joseph Co., 1972-78; candidate for state legis., 1988; mem. St. Joseph County Rep. Women precinct com., South Bend, 1964-79, alt. del. to Nat. Rep. Conv., 1976, 84, 88, 92; mem. Souht Bend Symphony Women's Assn. Recipient St. Patrick's medal St. Patrick's Coll. and Sem. (Ireland), 1996. Mem. NAFE, Women Bus. Owners, Am. Soc. Sovereign Mil. Order of Malta. Republican. Roman Catholic. Avocations: gardening, antique collecting. Office: Nat Life Ctr 1102 N Lafayette Blvd South Bend IN 46617-1136

HUNT, MATTHEW DAVID, music educator; b. Flint, Mich., Jan. 27, 1976; s. David Edward and Catherine Lynn Hunt; m. Danielle Lorraine Block, Mar. 30, 2002. BME, U. Mich., 1999; MEd, Armstrong Atlantic State U., Savannah, GA, 2005. Profl. Educator Cert. SC, 2003, Profl Educator Cert. Mich., 1999. Tchr. Lake Fenton Cmty. Schs., Mich., 1999—2002; adj. faculty U. of Michigan Flint, Mich., 2001; guest tchr. Waterford Cmty. Sch. Dist., Mich., 2002—03; gen. music tchr. Beaufort County Sch. Dist., Bluffton, SC, 2003—; o-1 lt. SC. State Guard, Columbia, SC, 2004—. Counselor supr. Waterford Parks and Recreation, Mich., 2003—03. Author: (children's book of poetry) There's A Mouse. Res. dep. sheriff Various Counties, SC, 2005—. Recipient State Guardsman Yr., SC State Guard, 2004, Star Student Award for Academic and Musical Excellence, Music Teacher's Nat. Assn., 1999. Mem.: Am. Assn. for Adult and Continuing Edn., Music Educators Nat. Conf., SC. Music Educators Assn., State Guard Assn. US. Methodist. Avocations: running, travel, cooking, music, outdoors. Office Phone: 843-322-7700.

HUNT, MAURICE ARTHUR, language educator, researcher; b. Lansing, Mich., Oct. 30, 1942; s. Elmore Clare and Irene Elizabeth H.; m. Pamela Helene Coyle, June 24, 1978; children: Alison, Jeffrey, Andrew, Thomas. BA, U. Mich., 1964; MA, U. Calif., Berkeley, 1966, PhD, 1970. Instr. English Coll. Marin, Kentfield, Calif., 1970-73; lectr. English Dominican Coll., San Rafael, Calif., 1974-75; vis. asst. prof. English Ariz. State U., Tempe, 1980-81; from asst. to assoc. prof. English Baylor U., Waco, Tex., 1981-93, prof. English, 1993—2003, rsch. prof., 2003—, chair dept. English, 1996—. Mem. adv. bd. writing ctr. Tex. A&M U., College Station, 1985—; dir. Baylor Advanced Placement Inst., Waco, 1994-95, Baylor Freshman Composition Program, Waco, 1982-98; mem. exec. com. South Ctrl. Renaissance Conf., College Station, 1988-90; pres. Coll. Conf. Tchrs. English, 2005—. Author: Shakespeare's Romance of the Word, 1990, Shakespeare's Labored Art, 1995, Shakespeare's Religious Allusiveness: Its Play and Tolerance, 2004; editor: Approaches to Teaching "The Tempest" and Other Late Romances, 1992, "The Winter's Tale": Critical Essays, 1995, Approaches to Teaching Shakespeare's "Romeo and Juliet", 2000, Approaches to Teaching Shakespeare's "Othello", 2005; assoc. editor Papers on Lang. and Lit., 1996-, The Upstart Crow: A Shakespeare Jour., 1990-; mem. editl. bd. Shakespeare and the Classroom, 1993-; contbr. articles to profl. jours. Fundraiser United Way Bay Area, San Francisco, 1976-80; bd. dirs. Alameda County Tng. and Employment Bd., Oakland, Calif., 1977-78. Rsch. grantee Baylor U., 1986—; named to Greater Lansing Area Sports Hall of Fame, Portland HS Sports Hall of Fame, Mich. Mem. MLA (mem. New Variorum Shakespeare com., 2004-), Fulbright Grants (mem. so. region, mem. nat. screening com.), Shakespeare Assn. Am., S. Ctrl. Renaissance Conf. (mem. exec. com. 1984-), Internat. Assn. Univ. Profs. English, Phi Beta Kappa. Democrat. Episcopalian. Avocations: jogging, sports. Home: 321 Oakwood Ln Hewitt TX 76643-3027 Office: 500 Speight Ave Waco TX 76798-7404 Office Phone: 254-710-1768. E-mail: maurice_hunt@baylor.edu.

HUNT, MICHAEL O'LEARY, wood science educator, engineering educator; b. Louisville, Dec. 9, 1935; s. George Henry and Tressie (Truax) H.; children: Elizabeth H. Schwartz, Lynne T. Lattimer, Michael O. Jr. BS, U. Ky., 1957; M.Forestry, Duke U., 1958; PhD, N.C. State U., 1970. Product engr. Wood Products div. Singer Co., Pickens, S.C., 1959-60; asst. prof. wood sci. Purdue U., West Lafayette, Ind., 1960-70, assoc. prof., 1970-79, prof., 1979—, dir. Wood Rsch. Lab., 1979—2002. Contbr. articles over 80 articles to profl. jours. Chmn. campus preservation com. Wabash Valley Trust for Historic Preservation, Lafayette. Recipient Servaas Meml. award Hist. Landmarks Found. of Ind., 1994, H. Fannon award Lafayette Neighborhood Housing Svcs., 1998, Downie Meml. award Wabash Valley Trust, 2002. Mem. Forest Products Soc. (pres. 1990-91, Fred Gottschalk Meml. award 1984), Soc. of Wood Sci. and Tech., Assn. Preservation Tech., Rotary. Achievements include patent for lightweight, high-performance structural particleboard. Office: Purdue Univ Wood Rsch Lab West Lafayette IN 47907-2033 E-mail: huntm@purdue.edu.

HUNT, NORMA JEAN, elementary school educator; b. St. Louis, May 23, 1945; d. Wilbur George and Neva Marie (Halley) Huebner; m. William Joseph Hunt, June 17, 1978; children: Heather Jan, Richard William. AB, Harris-Stowe Coll., St. Louis, 1967; MAT, Webster U., 1982. Tchr. Lindbergh Sch. Dist., St. Louis, 1967—. Mem. Mo. State Tchrs. Assn. Baptist. Home: 9951 Musick Rd Saint Louis MO 63123-5011 Office: Sappington Sch 11011 Gravois Rd Saint Louis MO 63126-3601

HUNT, RAY L., petroleum company executive; b. 1943; s. H. L. and Ruth (Ray) Hunt; m. Nancy Ann Hunt; 5 children. BBA, So. Meth. U., 1965. With Hunt Oil Co., Dallas, 1958—2004; former chmn. Hunt Oil. Co., Dallas; chmn., pres., CEO Hunt Consolidated Inc., Dallas, 1994—. Exec. com., bd. trustees So. Mich. U.; bd. trustees Ctr. for Strategic & Internat. Studies, Washington; bd. trustees. Southern Methodist Univ., Dallas; bd. mem. Presdl. Fgn. Intelligence Adv. Bd., 2001; bd. dir. Halliburton Co., King Ranch, Inc., Pepsico, Inc., The Cooper Inst., Electronic Data Sys., Dallas; chmn. bd. Fed. Res. Bank, Dallas; exec. com. Southwestern Medical Found., Dallas. Named to Tex. Bus. Hall of Fame, 1992. Mem.: Am. Petroleum Inst. (exec., pub. policy com., chmn. 1991—94). Office: Hunt Consolidated Inc 1445 Ross At Field Dallas TX 75202*

HUNT, RICHARD, sculptor; b. Chgo., Sept. 12, 1935; BA, Sch. of Art Inst. Chgo., 1957. Instr. Sch. Art Inst. Chgo., 1960-61, U. Ill., Chgo., 1960-62. Vis. prof. Chouinard Art Sch., L.A., 1964, Northern Ill. U., De Kalb, summer 1968, Northwestern U., Evanston, Ill., 1968-69; vis. artist Yale U., New Haven, 1964, Purdue U., Ind., 1965, Wis. State U., Oshkosh, 1969, So. Ill. U., Carbondale, 1969, Washington U., 1977-78; artist cons. Hobart Welding Sch., Troy, Ohio, 1969; artist-in-residence, Eastern Mich. U., Ypsilanti, 1988. Prin. works include individual exhibitions: U. Notre Dame, Ind., 1966, Cleve. Mus. Art, 1967, Milw. Art Ctr., 1967, Fisk U., Nashville, 1968, Mus. Modern Art N.Y., 1971, Art Inst. Chgo., 1971, U. Iowa, 1975, Balt. Mus. Art, 1980, Columbia U., N.Y., 1981, Bklyn. Artist Cultural Assn., 1982, Terry Distenfass Gallery, N.Y., 1983, 84, 86, Gwenda Jay Gallery, Chgo., 1991, Louis Newmann Gallery, 1991, Shiduni Gallery, Santa Fe, 1992; group exhibitions: World's Fair, Seattle, 1962, World Festival of Negro Art, Dakar, Senegal, 1966, 100 Artist, 100 Years: Alumni of Sch. Art Inst. Chgo, 1979, also collections at Met. Mus. Art N.Y., Mus. Modern Art, N.Y., Whitney Mus., N.Y., Albright-Knox Art Gallery, Buffalo, Hirshorn Mus. and Sculpture Garden, Washington, Cleve. Mus. Art, Art Inst. Chgo., Milw. Art Ctr., William Nelson Rockhill Gallery Art, Kansas City, Mo., Nat. Mus. Israel, Jerusalem, Dorsky Gallery. Bd. dirs. Coll. Art Assn., 1972-76, Am. Coun. for Arts, 1974—; trustee Mus. Contemporary Art, Chgo., 1975-79; mem. Nat. Coun. Arts, 1968-74, Ill. Arts Coun., 1970-75. Served with U.S. Army, 1958-60. James Nelson Raymond Travel fellowship Art Inst. Chgo., 1957, Guggenheim fellowship, 1962, Tamarind fellowship Artist Ford Found., 1965, Cassandra Found. fellowship, 1970; recipient Logan Prize, 1956, 61, 62, Palmer Prize, 1957; named Outstanding Chicagoan in the Arts Chgo. Jr. C. of C., 1971. Office: 379 W Broadway New York NY 10012-5121 also: Printworks Gallery 311 W Superior St Ste 105 Chicago IL 60610-3548*

HUNT, ROBERT GAYLE, former government official; b. Greeley, Colo., Aug. 2, 1933; s. Ray and Myrtle Marie (Dunham) Hunt; m. Harriet Gertrude McNeel, June 10, 1955 (div. 1978); children: Leslie Lynn Hunt Cowen, Linda Jean, Julia Gail Hunt Walsh, Gregg Bryan, Robert John. BA, U. No. Colo., 1955; MPA, Syracuse U., 1957; student, Fed. Exec. Inst., Charlottesville, Va., 1973, Western Exec. Sem. Ctr., (fed. govt.), 1991. Various positions housing and cmty. devel. programs HUD, Washington, 1957-79; spl. asst. to dep. asst. sec. FHA, 1979-89; dir. mgmt. svcs. divsn., 1989-97; ret., 1997. Pres. Kings Park Civic Assn., Springfield, Va., 1966-67; elder Providence Presbyterian Ch., Fairfax, Va., 1968-71, 79-82, 1986-89; pres. Fairfax County Fedn. Citizens Assn., 1970-71; chmn. Citizens for Sch. Bonds, 1973; mem. Fairfax County Sch. Bd., 1973-77; pres. Social Ctr. for Psychiat. Rehab., Inc., 1983-85; pres. Fairfax Com. of 100, 1986-88; bd. dirs. No. Va. Mental Health Assn., 1988-94, v.p., 1992-93, vice-chmn.; Fairfax County Adv. Task Force on Cultural Facility, 1988-89; spokesperson Clean Water Coalition, 1970; supt. Fairfax County Pub. Sch., cmty. adv. com., 1971-1972, 1997-99; mem. pres.'s cir. Psychiat. Rehab. Svcs., Inc., 1994—, mem. planned giving com., 1996-97; chmn. Cmty. Ministry No. Va., 1984-86, 96-2000. Named Outstanding Citizen, Kings Park Civic Assn., 1975; recipient citations Fairfax County Sch. Bd., 1973, Disting. Svc. award, 1977, Citizen of Yr. award Fairfax County, Va., 1999, Washington Post trophy, 1999. Mem. Chesapeake Harbour Yacht Club (Annapolis, Md.). Avocation: sailing. Home: 8910 Cromwell Dr Springfield VA 22151-1120 E-mail: robhuu@aol.com.

HUNT, RONALD J., dean, dental educator; DDS, U. Iowa, 1973, MS in dental pub. health, 1982. Diplomate Am. Bd. Dental Pub. Health, 1986. Assoc. prof., dental ecology U. NC Sch. Dentistry, 1986—88, prof., dental ecology, 1990—92, asst. dean, 1992—98, assoc. dean academic affairs, 1992—98; dean, Harry Lyons Prof. Va. Commonwealth U. Sch. Dentistry, Richmond, Va., 1999—. Disting. vis. scholar U. Adelaide, Australia, 1990; fellow Am. Assn. Dental Schools, Washington, DC, 1997. Office: PO Box 980566 Richmond VA 23298

HUNT, ROY E., geotechnical and geological engineer, consultant; b. Newark, Oct. 8, 1928; s. Roy Clark and Alma Jockers Hunt; m. Marilia B. Bengaly, June 29, 1946; children: Alex B., Robert R., Nancy Greenwell, Laurie Enoch, Kathy Corcoran. BS, Upsala Coll., 1952; MA in Civil Engring., Columbia U., 1956. Lic. engr., N.J., NY, Pa.; geologist Pa., Del., cert. profl. geologist Am. Inst. Profl. Geologists. Geologist, engr. Greer & McClelland, Upper Montclair, NJ, 1952—56; civil engr. Esso Rsch. & Engring. Corp., Linden, 1956—59; assoc. Woodward, Clyde, Sherard & Assocs., Clifton, 1959—65; ptnr. Joseph S. Ward & Assocs., Caldwell, 1965—74; geotechnical engr. Technosolo, S.A., Rio de Janeiro, 1974—79, Roy E. Hunt, Cons. Engr., 1979—88; assoc. Woodward-Clyde Cons., Plymouth Meeting, Pa., 1988—94; cons. geotech. engr. Roy E. Hunt, Cons. Engr., Bricktown, NJ, 1994—. Lectr. U. Pa., Phila., 2004—; adj. prof. Drexel U., 1989—2000. Author: (text book) Geotechnical Engineering Investigation Manual (Claire P. Holdridge award, 1984, E.B. Burwell Jr. Meml. award, 1984), Geotechnical Engineering Techniques and Practices (Claire P. Holdridge award, 1988), Geotechnical Engineering Investigation Handbook, 2d Ed. With U.S. Army, 1946—48. Fellow: ASCE (life); mem.: Am. Inst. Profl. Geologists, Assn. Engring. Geologists. Home and Office: 149 Richard St Brick NJ 08724 Office Phone: 732-840-6733.

HUNT, SWANEE G., public policy educator, former ambassador; b. Dallas, May 1, 1950; m. Charles Alexander Ansbacher; 3 children. BA, Tex. Christian U., 1972; MA, Ball State U., 1976; MA in Religion, Iliff Sch. of Theology, 1977, PhD (hon.), 1986, Webster U., 1994. Pres. Hunt Alternatives Fund, 1981—; co-founder Karis Community, 1980-83; min. pastoral care Capital Heights Presbyn. Ch., 1983; vice chair Denver Community Mental Health Commn., 1983-87; with Gov. Policy Acad. on Families and Children at Risk, 1989-90; chair Colo. Coord. Coun. Housing and the Homeless, 1989-92; U.S. amb. to Austria, 1993-97; dir. Women and Pub. Policy Program, Kennedy Sch. Govt. Harvard. Composer The Witness Cantata, 1985; author: This Was Not Our War: Bosnian Women Reclaiming the Peace, 2004; syndicated columnist Scripps Howard. Bd. dirs., co-founder Women's Found. Colo.; chair Mayor's Human Capital Agenda Coun., 1992-93; co-chair Denver Initiative Children and Families; mem. UN High Commn. on Refugees; mem. Internat. Crisis Group, Internat. Alert. Recipient Martin Luther King Humanitarian award U. Colo., 1992, NCCJ, 1992, Denver Urban Ministries, 1991, United Meth. Ch., 1989, Internat. Women's Forum, 1989, Sta. KUSA-TV, 1989, Caring Connection, 1989, Nat. Mental Health Assn., 1985, Mental Health Assn. Colo., 1984, 94, Mile High award United Way, 1993, Am. Heritage award Anti-Defamation League, 1995, Cordon Bleu du Saint Esprit Peace award, 1996, Humanitarian Lifetime Svc. award Denver Holocaust Awareness, 1997, Together for Peace award, 1997, 3 decorations Austrian

Govt., 1997, Amb. award The Conflict Ctr., 1997, Inst. for Internat. Edn. award, 1998. Office: 168 Brattle St Cambridge MA 02138-3309 also: Kennedy Sch Govt 79 Jfk St Rm T110A Cambridge MA 02138-5801*

HUNT, T(HOMAS) W(EBB), retired religion educator; b. Mammoth Spring, Ark., Sept. 28, 1929; s. Thomas Hubert and Ethel Clara (Webb) H.; m. M. Laverne Hill, July 22, 1951; children: Melana Claire Hunt Monroe. *Daughter, Melana Hunt Monroe, has become well known as a speaker in many churches and Christian meetings. Her BS was from Texas Christian University in 1976. She co-authored From Heaven's View with T.W. Hunt in 2002. She serves on many civic and church committees and services. Her best known conference is "Christian Womanhood".* MusB, Ouachita Bapt. U., 1950; MusM, N. Tex. State U., 1957, PhD, 1967. Faculty Southwestern Bapt. Theol. Sem., Ft. Worth, 1963-87; life cons. for prayer Lifeway Christian Resources, Nashville, 1987-94; ret. Bapt. Sunday Sch. Bd., Nashville, 1994. Lectr. in field; confs. on the five continents; mem. adv. coun. Life Action Ministries; mem. bd. ref. Union U., Prayer Power Ministries. Author: The Doctrine of Prayer, 1985, Music in Missions, 1986, The Disciple's Prayer Life, 1988, Church Ministry Prayer Manual, 1994, The Mind of Christ, 1995, In God's Presence, 1995, From Heaven's View, 2002, The Life-Changing Power of Prayer, 2002, Prayer and Kingdom Advance, 2004; founder, author: course in music in missions. Home: 3915 Cypress Hill Dr Spring TX 77388-5798 Office Phone: 281-288-7209. E-mail: lhhunt@sbcglobal.net. *In a rapidly changing world, we rely on a God who does not change.*

HUNT, WAYNE ROBERT, SR., non-profit organization executive; b. Mt. Holly, NJ, Feb. 23, 1948; s. Edward Middleton Sr. and Sarah Isabel (Pope) H.; m. Elizabeth Evans Caputi, Oct. 23, 1982; children: Brandi Leigh, Wayne Robert Karr, Joshua David, Jacob Cody. BSBA, William Jewell Coll., 1970; MPA, Rutgers U., 1993; student, Command and Gen. Staff Coll., 1995. Cert. pub. mgr., facilitator. Mgr. Edward M. Hunt & Son Inc., Mt. Holly, 1970—79; spl. staff officer mech. sect., engring. divsn. NJ Dept. Def., Trenton, 1979—82, asst. bur. chief facilities mgmt. bur., 1982—88; contracting officer/bur. chief installations divsn. ops. bur. NJ Dept. Mil. and Vets. Affairs, Lawrenceville, 1986—94, dir. installations divsn., 1994—99, chief info. officer, 1999—2003, chief fin. & info. officer, fiscal and adminstrv. svs. divsn., 2003—04; chief of staff N.G. Assn. U.S., 2005—. Field assoc. orgnl. leadership devel. sec. Nat. Guard Bur., 1986-92. Deacon New Life Christian Ch.; past pres. Union Fire Co. #2. Lt. col. NJ Army Nat. Guard, 1970—; Bn. Comdr.; anti-terrorism- force protection sect. chief; sch. bd. dirs., Morrisville Sch. Bd., 2001-2004, sec., 2004—. Decorated Meritorious Svc. medal, (5) Army Commendation medals; recipient Proclamation for Svc. to State, Gov. James J. Florio, 1993, Cert. of Recognition, Drumthwacket Found., 1992, Letter of Appreciation, NJ Statue of Liberty Svc., NJ Dept. Mil. and Vets. Affairs Group award, 1995, Rancocas Valley Regional H.S. VIP Hall of Fame, 1997, NJ State Teamwork Award, 2002, Gov. McGreevey's Achievement Coin, 2003; letter of appreciation from Gov. McGreevey, 2003; named Man of Yr., 2004. Mem. ASPA (Cert. Achievement 2002), Am. Mgmt. Assn., Pub. Sector Mgr. Assn., NJ Soc. Cert. Pub. Mgr., Am. Acad. Cert. Pub. Mgr. (past pres.), N.G. Exec. Dir. Assn. (1st v.p., 2d v.p., chmn. nominations com., by-laws com.), N.G. Assn. US (Dist. Svc. medal 2003, Man of Yr. 2003), ABI (Medal of Honor 2003), N.G. Assn. NJ (sec. 1987-2004, Pres.'s award 1997), 114th Regtl. Assn., Trenton Arty. Officers Assn., Enlisted Assn. NJ, Masons (32 degree), Nat. Assn. Chief Info. Officers, Nat. Assn. State Mil. Resource Mgrs.; Elks, Pi Alpha Alpha. Avocations: golf, camping, jogging, weight training. Home: 247 N Pennsylvania Ave Morrisville PA 19067-1103 Office: Nat Guard Assn of US One Massachusetts Ave Washington DC 20001 Office Phone: 202-405-5895. Personal E-mail: hu114@aol.com.

HUNT, WILLIAM B., pulmonologist; b. Lexington, N.C., Sept. 27, 1927; s. William B. and Maxine (Cox) H.; married; children: William B., III, Anne, Alex, Sarah. BS, Wake Forest U., 1948; MD, Bowman Gray Sch. Medicine, Winston Salem, N.C., 1953. Diplomate Am. Bd. Internal Medicine, Am. Bd. Allergy and Immunology. Intern, resident U. Va., Charlottesville, 1953-55, resident, fellow, 1957-59, assoc. prof., 1960-75, asst. dean Sch. Medicine, 1972-75; fellow gastroenterology Bowman Gray Sch. Medicine, Winston Salem, 1959-60; instr. internal medicine N.Y. Med. Coll., N.Y.C., 1959-60; from clin. assoc. prof. medicine to clin. prof. medicine East Carolina Sch. Medicine, Greenville, N.C., 1975—; staff physician Craven Regional Med. Ctr., New Bern, N.C., 1975—, med. dir. cardiopulmonary svcs., 1975-95. Cons. N.C. Health Dept., TB Control Br., 1997-2000; TB control physician Craven County Health Dept., 1999—; mem. N.C. TB Peer Rev. Com., 1996—. Pres. Ea. Area Health Edn. Ctr., 1990-95. Recipient Douglas Southhall Freeman award Va. Lung Assn., 1975, Disting. Alumnus award Bowman Gray Sch. Medicine, 1973, Robert Bageant award Va. Soc. Respiratory Care, 1987. Fellow Am. Coll. Chest Physicians, Am. Thoracic Soc., Am. Coll. Physicians; mem. N.C. Med. Soc. (councillor 1978, exec. com. 1981), Va. Thoracic Soc. (pres. 1974), N.C. Thoracic Soc. (pres. 1984), N.C. Lung Assn. (pres. 1986), Craven Pamlico Jones Med. Soc. (pres. 1984). Democrat. Episcopalian. Avocations: skiing, golf, flying, sailing, tennis. Home: 1617 King Mountain Rd Charlottesville VA 22901

HUNT, WILLIAM E., SR., retired state supreme court justice; b. 1923; BA, LLB, U. Mont., JD, 1955. Bar: 1955. Judge State Workers' Compensation Ct., 1975-81; justice Mont. Supreme Ct., Helena, 1984—2001.

HUNTE, MICHAEL D., investment advisor, securities trader; AA in Liberal Arts, CUNY; BusB in Mgmt. and Adminstrn., Molloy Coll., Rockville Ctr., N.Y.; MBA, Adelphi U., Garden City, N.Y. Cert. series 7, 55, 63, 66,31, registered options prin. series 4, lic. NASDAQ, NYSE, CBOE, AMEX, PBW, PCSE. Retail OTC and bond trader Fin. Clearing & Svcs. Corp., N.Y.C., NY, 1983—88; sr. trader AVP/agy. Citicorp Securities Svcs., Inc., 1988—99; lead brokerage trader USAA Investment Mgmt. Co., San Antonio, 2000; equity trader Adamson Bros., Inc., Paramus, NJ, 2000; client support analyst OpenLink Fin., Inc., Uniondale, NY, 2001—02; fgn. exch. trader Global FX Remote Group, LLC, N.Y.C., 2003—04; fin. advisor Morgan Stanley DW, Inc., Melville, 2004—. Recipient Customer Svc. award, Citicorp Securities Svcs., Inc. Address: 380 Second Pl Uniondale NY 11553

HUNTEMAN, DANIEL GILBERT, lawyer, investment advisor; b. Milw., Jan. 20, 1946; BA in Econs., U. Wis., Milw., 1968; JD, Marquette U., 1972. Bar: Wis. 1972; CFP; cert. fund specialist; chartered mut. fund counselor; registered investment advisor. Buyer, atty. Yankee Builders Supply Inc., Milw., 1970-73; owner, lawyer Kelley's Sawmill, Inc., Milw., 1976-94; pvt. practice, Milw., 1973-75, 95—. Mem. Inst. Bus. and Fin., Internat. Assn. Fin. Planners, Fin. Planning Assn., State Bar Wis. Office: 7419 Hennessey Ave Wauwatosa WI 53213-1249

HUNTEN, DONALD MOUNT, planetary scientist, educator; b. Montreal, Mar. 1, 1925; came to U.S., 1963, naturalized, 1979; s. Kenneth William and Winnifred Binnmore (Mount) H.; m. Isobel Ann Rubenstein, Dec. 28, 1949 (div. Apr. 1995); children: Keith Atherton, Mark Ross; m. Ann Louise Sprague, May 21, 1995. B.Sc., U. Western Ont., 1946; PhD, McGill U., 1950. From research asso. to prof. physics U. Sask. (Can.), Saskatoon, 1950-63; physicist Kitt Peak Nat. Obs., Tucson, 1963-77; sci. adv. to asso. adminstr. for space sci. NASA, Washington, 1976-77; prof. planetary scis. U. Ariz., Tucson, 1977-88, Regents prof., 1988—. Cons. NASA, 1964—. Author: Introduction to Electronics, 1964; (with J.W. Chamberlain) Theory of Planetary Atmospheres, 1987; contbr. articles to profl. jours. Recipient Pub. Svc. medal NASA, 1977, 85,96, medal for exceptional sci. achievement, 1980, Space Sci. award Com. on Space Rsch., 2000. Mem.: AAAS, Can. Assn. Physicists (editor 1961—63), Royal Soc. Can., Nat. Acad. Scis., Internat. Assn. Geomagnetism and Aeronomy, Internat. Union Geodesy and Geophysics, Internat. Astron. Union, Am. Astron. Soc. (chmn. divsn. planetary scis. 1977), Am. Geophys. Union (John Adam Fleming medal 1998), Am. Phys. Soc., Cosmos Club (Washington), Explorers Club. Home: 3445 W Foxes Den Dr Tucson AZ 85745-5102 Office: U Ariz Dept Planetary Scis Tucson AZ 85721-0001 Business E-Mail: dhunten@lpl.arizona.edu.

HUNTER, BEVERLY CLAIRE, research scientist, educator; b. Pitts., Apr. 19, 1941; d. Eldon Clare and Ethel Mae (Kamer) Roberts m. Harold G. Hunter, Jan. 7, 1966; children: Cynthia Claire, Gregory Shawn. BA cum laude (Nat. Merit scholar), U. Pitts., 1963. Cert. Geographic Info. Sys. George Mason Univ., 2003. Computer programmer U.S. Navy, 1964-65; systems engr. IBM Corp., 1965-66; dir. instructional programming Human Resources Rsch. Orgn., Alexandria, Va., 1966-68, sr. staff scientist, 1970-87; staff scientist Matrix Rsch., Alexandria, 1969; lead scientist BBN Corp., 1993-98, NSFf, program mgr. rsch. on tchg. and learning, 1989—93; scientist Boston Coll., 1998-99; pres. Piedmont Rsch. Inst., Amissville, Va., 1999—. Cons. U.S. Congress, U.S. Office Edn., Bell Labs., Telenet Comms.: pres. Targeted Learning Corp., 1983-89; adj. prof. U. San Francisco, 1985-86; v.p. Piedmont Rsch. Ctr., 1979-80; peer reviewer. Co-author: Learning Alternatives in U.S. Education: Where Student and Computer Meet, 1975, Computer Literacy, 1982; Author: My Students Use Computers, 1984 Guide to Learning Resources for Users of IBM Personal Computers, Scholastic U.S. History Data Bases, 1985, Scholastic U.S. Government Data Bases, 1985, Scholastic Life Science Data Bases, 1985, Scholastic Physical Sciences Data Bases, 1985, Scholastic World Geography Data Bases, 1986, Scholastic Poetry and Mythology Data Bases, 1986, Scholastic Literature Data Bases, 1986, Scholastic Constitution Then and Now Data Files, 1987, Scholastic Weather and Climate Data Files, 1987, Working with the U.S. Congress, 1988, Online Searching in the Curriculum, 1989; Scientists at Work hypermedia data base; editor Edn. and Computing Internat. Jour.; contbr. articles to publs. Grantee, N.S.F., 1979—2003. Mem.: Internat. Soc. Tech. in Edn., Rappanhannock League Environ. Protection (bd. dirs.), Nature Conservancy, Assn. Computing Machinery. Office: Piedmont Rsch Inst 130 Mossie Ln Amissville VA 20106-4152

HUNTER, BILLY (G. WILLIAM HUNTER), sports association administrator, lawyer; b. Cherry Hill, NJ, Nov. 5, 1942; Grad., Syracuse U.; JD, Howard U., 1969, U. Calif., Berkeley, 1970. US atty. (no. dist.) Calif. US Dept. Justice, 1976—83; pvt. practice defense and entertainment industry litigator; exec. dir. NBA Players Assn., 1996—. Football player Wash. Redskins and Miami Dolphins, 1965—66. Named to Little League Mus. Hall of Excellence, 2000.*

HUNTER, BRENDA ANN, writer, psychologist; b. Statesville, NC, Feb. 2, 1941; d. Ray Cameron and Florence Maureen (Smith) Morrison; m. David Lynn Larson, June 23, 1963; children: Holly Larson, Kristen Blair; m. Don R. Hunter, Feb. 23, 1975. BA in English, Wheaton Coll., 1963; MA in English, SUNY, Buffalo, 1967; PhD in Psychology, Georgetown U., 1990. Psychologist Minirth, Meier and Byrd Clinic, Arlington, Va., 1991—97; pvt. practice, 1980—. Instr. U. NC, Asheville, Georgetown U.; conf., presenter, spkr. in field. Author: Beyond Divorce, 1978, Where Have All the Mothers Gone?, 1984, Home by Choice, 1991, In the Company of Women, 1994, What Every Mother Needs to Know About Babies, 1994, A Wedding is a Family Affair, 1995, In the Company of Friends, 1996, The Power of Mother Love, 1997, My God, Do You Love Me?, 1998, Staying Alive: Life Changing Strategies for Surviving Cancer, 2004; contbr. articles to profl. jours. Home: 95147 Vance Knoll Chapel Hill NC 27517 E-mail: drbrendamhunter@bellsouth.net.

HUNTER, BYNUM MERRITT, lawyer; b. Greensboro, N.C., June 13, 1925; s. Hill McIver and Annie (Merritt) H.; m. Ann Fulenwider, June 22, 1957 (div. 1968); children: Ann Shirley, Mary Parker; m. Mary Lane Yancey, Aug. 7, 1969 (div. 1978); m. Mary Bonneau McElveen, June 13, 1980; 1 son, Bynum Jr. AB, U. N.C., 1945, JD, 1949. Bar: N.C. 1949. Ptnr. Smith & Moore LLP. Served with USNR, 1943-46, 51-53. Fellow Am. Coll. Trial Lawyers, Am. Bar Found. (life mem.); mem. ABA, Internat. Assn. Def. Counsel, Am. Judicature Soc., Greensboro Bar Assn. (pres. 1965-66) 4th Cir. Jud. Conf., N.C. Bar Assn., Zeta Psi, Phi Delta Phi. Clubs: Rotary. Home: 710 Country Club Dr Greensboro NC 27408-5714 Office: Smith Moore LLP Ste 1400 PO Box 21927 300 N Green St Greensboro NC 27420-1927 Office Phone: 336-378-5200. Business E-Mail: bynum.hunter@smithmoorelaw.com.

HUNTER, CHARLES AMOS, music educator, musician; b. Portsmouth, Va., Jan. 24, 1948; s. Amos Charles Hunter and Josephine Ward RIddick; m. Valerie Denise Bowen, Apr. 3, 1976; children: Kelli Beamon, Charles. BS, Norfolk (Va.) State U., 1971, MusM Edn., 1996. Customer svc. Ford Motor Credit, Norfolk, Va., 1973—92; band dir. John F. Kennedy Mid. Sch., Suffolk, Va., 1993—; band leader The Positive Sounds Band, Chesapeake, Va., 1964—. Writer/prodr. Shiptown Records, Norfolk, Va., 1969—78; writer/prodr./ Butterfly Record Co., Portsmouth, Va., 1981—85; band leader Exec. Ste. (band), Portsmouth, Va., 1980—86. Prodr.: (musical recording) I Almost Blew My Mind, 1971, You're The One I Need, 1971, (musical recordng) My Mind Holds On To Yesterday, 1972 (Prodr. of the yr., 1973), (musical recording) He's Still Your Man, 1972, When It Comes To Loving You, 1982 (Mcdonalds' Top Ten, 1983). Mem.: NEA, Suffolk Music Educators Assn., Broadcast Music Internat., Music Educators Nat. Conf., Edn. Assn. Suffolk. Conservative. Methodist. Avocations: politics, crossword puzzles, reading, piano. Office: John F Kennedy Middle Sch 2325 E Washington St Suffolk VA 23434 Office Phone: 757-925-5560.

HUNTER, CHRISTINE, opera executive; Held various positions including pres., chmn. bd., chmn. exec. com. Washington Nat. Opera, 1974—2004; adv. dir. Metropolitan Opera, NYC, mng. dir., 1983—87, exec. com. mem., 1987—2003, chmn. exec. com., 2003—, chmn. bd., 2005—. Mem.: Gramma Fisher Found. (chmn.). Office: Metropolitan Opera Lincoln Center New York NY 10023*

HUNTER, CHRISTOPHER, retired mathematics professor; b. Manchester, England, May 28, 1934; m. Hilda M. Salmon, 1961; children: James, Alison, Rosemary, Andrew. BA, Cambridge U., 1957, PhD in Math., 1960, ScD, 1993. Rsch. assoc. math. MIT, 1960-61, lectr., 1961-62; rsch. fellow Trinity Coll. Cambridge U., 1962-64; dir. appl. math. Fla. State U., 1970-83, 89-95, prof., 1970-91, McKenzie prof. math., 1991—2003, chmn. dept., 1993-99, ret., 2003. Mem.: Royal Astron. Soc. London, Internat. Astron. Union, Soc. Indsl. and Applied Math., Am. Astron. Soc. (Dirk Brouwer award 1995). Office: Fla State U Dept Mathematics Tallahassee FL 32306-4510

HUNTER, DOUGLAS LEE, communications executive; b. Greeley, Colo., May 3, 1948; s. Delmer Eural and Helen Converse (Haines) H.; m. Janet Lee Snook, May 26, 1970; children: Darin Douglas, Joel Christopher, Eric Andrew, Jennifer Lee. BA, U. Sioux Falls, 1979; postgrad., N.Am. Bapt. Sem., 1977—79. Elevator constructor Carter Elevator Co., Inc., Sioux Falls, 1971—72, rep., 1972—74, contr., 1974—78, sec.-treas., 1978—82, v.p., 1982—87, pres., 1987—93; ptnr. Lifters Ltd., Sioux Falls, 1984—90, CEO, 1987—96; v.p. Fellowship or Cos. Christ, Internat., 1994—97; pres. Media Asia, 1997—99; Atlanta regional dir. Christian Leadership Concepts, 1999—2000; exec. ravi Zacharias Internat. Min., 2000—03; pres. Bus. Ptnrs. Internat., Duluth, Ga., 2003—. Bd. dirs. Home Fed. Savs. Bank, HF Fin. Corp.; U.S. del. Forum Bus. in Vietnam, Ho Chi Minh City, 1993; guest lectr. Nat. Econs. U., Hanoi, Vietnam, 1995. Mem. gen. bd. Christian Ch., Indpls., 1984-88; mem. regional bd. Christian Ch. in the Upper Midwest, Des Moines, 1985-87; bd. dirs. Glory House, Sioux Falls, 1983-86; leader Bible Study Fellowship, Sioux Falls, 1981-92; vice chmn. Greater Sioux Empire Billy Graham Crusade, 1986-87; mem. internat. bd. dirs. Fellowship of Cos. for Christ Internat., 1993-95; bd. dirs. Am. Mongolia Found., 1992-99; active S.D. Trade Del. to Mongolia, 1993-99; trustee N.Am. Bapt. Sem., 1989-2001; bd. dirs. Providence Christian Acad., 1998—2002, chmn., 1999—2002. Named Outstanding Young Religious Leader Sioux Falls Jaycees, 1974. Mem. S.D. Family Bus. Coun., Sen. Larry Pressler's Small Bus. Adv. Com., Nat. Assn. Elevator Contrs., Nat. Assn. Elevator Safety Authorities, Constrn. Specifications Inst., Christian Businessmen's Com. U.S., Sioux Falls C. of C. Republican. Avocations: golf, tennis, reading, music. Home: 695 Wyndham Place Cir Lawrenceville GA 30044-3629 Office: 9500 Medlock Bridge Rd Duluth GA 30097 Office Phone: 678-405-2212. E-mail: DougH@perimeter.org.

HUNTER, DUNCAN LEE, congressman; b. Riverside, Calif., May 31, 1948; m. Lynne Layh, 1973; children: Robert Samuel, Duncan Duane. Attended, U. Calif., Santa Barbara, U. Mt., 1966—67; BSL, Western State U., 1976, JD, 1976. Bar: Calif. 1976. Pvt. practice, San Diego; mem. U.S. Congress from 52nd Calif. dist., 1981—, mem., chmn. armed svcs. com. Mem. Congressional Jobs and Fair Trade Caucus; co-chair Congressional Task Force on Bowhunting, Nat. Security Caucus. With U.S. Army, 1969-71, Vietnam. Decorated Air medal, bronze star. Mem. Navy League. Republican. Baptist. Office: US Ho of Reps 2265 Rayburn Ho Office Bldg Washington DC 20515-0001

HUNTER, DURANT ADAMS, executive search company executive; b. North Adams, Mass., Nov. 25, 1948; s. Richard Andrew and Lucy (Adams) H.; m. Sara Hoagland, June 10, 1978; children: John, Abigail. AB, U. NC, 1971; MPA, George Washington U., 1973. Staff asst. to Congressman Silvio O. Conte U.S. Ho. of Reps., Washington, 1971-72; program dir. Internat. Mgmt. and Devel. Inst., Washington, 1973-74; asst. v.p. J.P. Morgan Co., NYC, 1974-81; v.p., COO James Hunter Machine Co., North Adams, 1981-83; exec. v.p. HM Internat., Wellesley, Mass., 1983-85; mng. dir. Boyden Internat., Boston, 1985-89; ptnr. Gardiner Stone Hunter Internat., Boston, 1989-92; pres., CEO Pendleton James Assocs. Inc., Boston, 1992-2000; CEO Whitehead Mann Inc., 2000—03, Ridgeway Advisors, LLC, 2003—. Mem. Wellesley Planning Bd., 1983-86; bd. dirs. Boys and Girls Clubs, Boston, 1988—, Wide Horizons Children's Svcs., Waltham, Mass., 1989—, Mass. Cultural Coun.; trustee The Wang Ctr. Performing Arts, Boston, 1995—, Principia Coll., 2004—; bd. dirs. Mass. Cultural Coun. Mem.: Hole-in-the-Wall Golf Club (Naples, Fla.), Ekwanok Country Club (Manchester, Vt.), Royal Automobile Club (London), The Country Club (Brookline, Mass.), Univ. Club (NYC), Bus. Assoc. Club (pres. 1989). Home: 153 Ridgeway Rd Weston MA 02493-2724 Office: Ten Post Office Sq Ste 960 Boston MA 02109 Business E-Mail: andy.hunter@ridgewaypartners.com.

HUNTER, EARLE LESLIE, III, retired professional association executive; b. Juneau, Alaska, Nov. 23, 1929; s. Earle and Mary Uinta (Kirk) H.; m. Helen Doreen Dawson, Jan. 19, 1954; children: Barbara, James, Robert. BS, Ill. Coll. Optometry, Chgo., 1956, OD, 1957, DOS, 1988, New Eng. Coll. Optometry, 1995. Practice optometry, Juneau, 1957-59, McMinnville, Oreg., 1959-71; dir. clinics Pacific U., Forest Grove, Oreg., 1971-74; dir. primary care Am. Optometric Assn., St. Louis, 1974-78, asst. exec. dir., 1978-84, interim exec. dir., 1984-85, dep. exec. dir., 1985-87, exec. dir., 1987-95; ret., 1995—99; spl. asst. to the dean U. Mo. Sch. Optometry, 1999-2001. Sec. Z.80 com. Am. Nat. Stds. Inst., 1974-95. Contbr. articles to profl. jours. County chmn. various gubernatorial campaigns; vice chmn. Oreg. Health Commn., 1971-74. Named Optometrist of Yr., Oreg. Optometric Assn., 1971, Jr. Citizen of Yr., Jaycees, McMinnville, 1961. Fellow APHA, Am. Acad. Optometry; mem. Optical Soc. Am., Am. Soc. Assn. Execs. (com. 1981-93), St. Louis Soc. Assn. Execs. (pres. 1983-84), U.S. C. of C. (assn. com.), Tomb and Key, Univ. Club (St. Louis), Masons, Elks, Beta Sigma Kappa. Republican. Episcopalian. Avocations: sailing, golf. Home: 213 Orchard Ave Saint Louis MO 63119-2523

HUNTER, EDWINA EARLE, elementary school educator; b. Caswell County, N.C., Dec. 29, 1943; d. Edgar Earl and Bessie C. (Brown) Palmer; m. James W. Hunter, July 2, 1966; children: James W. Jr., Anika Z., Isaac Earl. BA, Spelman Coll., 1964; MA in Teaching, Smith Coll., 1966. Tchr. vocal music El Paso (Tex.) Schs., 1975-77, Prince George's County Schs., Laurel, Md., 1977—. Instr. El Paso C.C., 1975-76; cons. Smithsonian Mus., Washington, 1978. Transcriber, performer rec. Children's Songs for Games from Africa, 1979. Named Outstanding Alumna, Nat. Assn. For Equal Opportunity in Higher Edn., 1989; grantee NEH, Vienna, Austria, 1990. Mem. Nat. Guild Piano Tchrs., Suzuki Assn. Am., Md. Music Educators, Nat. Alumnae Assn. Spelman Coll. (sec. Columbia chpt. 1985-87, pres. 1988-92, sec.-treas. N.E. region 1991-93, named Alumna of Yr. Columbia chpt., 2001). Democrat. Home: 10721 Graeloch Rd Laurel MD 20723-1122 Office: James H Harrison Elem Sch 13200 Larchdale Rd Laurel MD 20708-1744 Office Phone: 301-497-3650. Personal E-mail: edwinahunter@msn.com.

HUNTER, FORREST WALKER, lawyer; b. Arlington, Va., Jan. 25, 1950; s. Dallas Walker and Ann Arsell (Wheat) H.; m. Susan Gladys Zsamer, June 8, 1974; children: Andrew Chastain, Alison Christian. BA, U. Va., 1972; JD, Emory U., 1975. Bar: Ga. 1975, U.S. Dist. Ct. (no. dist.) Ga. 1978, U.S. Ct. Appeals (5th cir.) 1978, U.S. Ct. Appeals (11th cir.) 1981, U.S. Dist. Ct. (mid. dist.) Ga. 1982, U.S. Dist. Ct. (so. dist.) Ga. 1983, U.S. Ct. Appeals (6th cir.) 1988, U.S. Dist. Ct. (we. dist.) Mich. 1994, U.S. Ct. Appeals (7th cir.) 1996, U.S. Dist. Ct. (ea. dist.) Tex. 1999, U.S. Dist. Ct. (no. dist.) Ind. 2002. Atty. Office Chief Counsel IRS, Dept. Treasurey, Washington, 1975-77, sr. atty. Office. Regional Counsel Atlanta, 1977-81; assoc. Jones, Bird & Howell and Alston & Bird, Atlanta, 1981-85; ptnr., labor, employment litig. Alston & Bird LLP, Atlanta, 1985—. Bd. dirs. Boys and Girls Clubs of Metro Atlanta, 1984. Named one of Legal Elite, Ga. Trend, 2004, Super Lawyers, Atlanta Mag., 2005. Mem. Am. Health Lawyers Assn., Ga. Acad. Hosp. Attys., Lawyers Club Atlanta, Atlanta Bar Assn., U. Va. Alumni Assn., Emory U. Alumni Assn. Office: Alston & Bird LLP 1 Atlantic Ctr 1201 W Peachtree St NW Atlanta GA 30309-3424 Office Phone: 404-881-7190.

HUNTER, FRANCES ELLEN CROFT, music educator; b. Greensboro, N.C., Jan. 25, 1941; d. John Wilkins Croft Sr. and Zara Louise Fisher Croft; m. C. Linwood Hunter, Jan. 25, 1964 (dec. Sept. 2, 1996); 1 child, Leticia Collette. BFA, Ohio U., 1962. Cert. tchr. music N.C., Ohio. Tchr. music Hoke County Schs., Raeford, NC, 1962—64, Harnett County Schs., Johnsonville, NC, 1964—65, Fayetteville City Schs., NC, 1965—70, Ft. Bragg Schs., NC, 1971—2001. Singer Cumberland Oratorio Singers, Fayetteville, 2003, bd. dirs., 2004—; singer and accompanist Ft. Bragg Stars and Stripes Singers, Fayetteville, 2003. Composer: Here's Looking At You Yr. 2000, 1987. Vol. Fayetteville Festival of Flight, 2003, Teen Involvement Projects, Inc.; vol. reader svc. for blind Southeastern NC Radio Reading Svc. Inc., 2004. Recipient Svc. award, Music Educators Nat. Conf./N.C. Music Educators Assn., 1999, Cert. of Retirement, Dept. Def. Edn. Activity, 2001. Mem.: Nat. Assn. Ret. Fed. Employees, NC Ret. Govt. Employees' Assn., Music Educators Nat. Conf. Lutheran. Avocations: reading, dance.

HUNTER, FRANCIS E., JR., pharmacologist, educator; b. Alliance, Ohio, June 6, 1916; s. Francis Edmund Hunter and Edith Mae Kayler; m. Alice Schott Hunter, June 15, 1940; children: Nancy Hunter Zvolanek, Linda Hunter Esposito. BS, Mt. Union Coll., Alliance, Ohio, 1938; PhD, U. Rochester, N.Y., 1941. Instr. biochemistry and pharmacology U. Rochester, 1938—41; instr. to prof. pharmacology dept. Washington U. Med. Sch., St. Louis, 1941—84, prof. emeritus, 1984—. Mem.: AAAS, Am. Soc. Biol. Chemists, Am. Soc. Pharmacology and Exptl. Therapeutics, Am. Chem. Soc. Avocations: gardening, travel. Home: 147 Timbercrest Rd Saint Louis MO 63122-1311 Office: Washington U Med Sch 660 S Euclid Ave Saint Louis MO 63110

HUNTER, GARRETT BELL, investment banker; b. N.Y.C., Apr. 11, 1937; s. John W. and Helene (Bond Lipe) H.; m. Lynn M. Cowell, Oct. 6, 1962; children: Lee, Andrew, Sarah. AB in Philosphy, Brown U., 1960; MBA in Fin., NYU, 1965; postgrad., Stonier Grad. Sch. Banking, 1973. V.p. Midlantic Nat. Bank, Newark, 1960-73, Nat. State Bank, Elizabeth, N.J., 1973-77; sr. v.p. R.I. Hosp. Trust Nat. Bank, Providence, 1977-89; pres. Bus. Devel. Co. of R.I., 1989—. Bd. dirs. Lab-Volt, Farmingdale, N.J., Bus. Devel. Co. of R.I., Providence. Home: 150 Tamarack Dr East Greenwich RI 02818-2204 Office Phone: 401-351-3036. Business E-Mail: ghunter@bdcri.com.

HUNTER, GLEN HERBERT, secondary school educator; b. Bremerton, Wash., Oct. 10, 1948; s. Herbert Clarence and Mirth Maining (Burklund) H.; m. Irene Fern Muir, July 25, 1970; 1 child, Eric Richard. BS in Math., Portland (Oreg.) State U., 1973, MS in Teaching in Math., 1990. Cert. tchr., Wash. Tchr. math. Sandy (Oreg.) Elem. Sch. Dist., 1973-74, Centralia (Wash.) Sch. Dist., 1974-80; engring. aide Boeing Co., Everett, Wash., 1980-84; tchr. math., dept. chmn. Chehalis (Wash.) Sch. Dist., 1984—. Mem. NEA, Math. Assn. Am., Am. Math. Soc., Nat. Coun. Tchrs. Math., Wash. State Math. Coun., Oreg. Coun. for Tchrs. Math., Wash. Edn. Assn., Chehalis Edn. Assn.

(v.p. 1975-78). Presbyterian. Home: 7211 Lighthouse Ln NE Olympia WA 98506-9206 Office: WF West High Sch 342 SW 16th St Chehalis WA 98532-3898 Office Phone: 360-807-7235. E-mail: ghunter@chohalis.k12.wa.us.

HUNTER, HANSEN FRENCH, III, political scientist, consultant; b. Detroit, July 13, 1959; s. Hansen French, Jr. and Margaret Louise (Mitchell) Hunter. BS, Ea. Mich. U., 1982; MS, Ctrl. Mich. U., 1995; MA in Polit. Sci., Wayne State U., Detroit Mich., 2005. Cert. peace officer Tex. Commn. Law Enforcement Stds. & Edn. Cert. peace officer Tex. So. U., Houston, 1981—84; contact rep. Dhhs Social Security Adminstrn., Detroit, 1986—95; non cert. substitute instr. Detroit Pub. Schs., 1995—96; conflict resolution trainer Dean Rsch. and Comm. LLC, Detroit, 2001. Mem.: Midwest Polit. Sci. Assn, Acad. Polit. Sci. (assoc.), Nat. Assn Housing and Redevelopment Ofcls. (assoc.), Am. Polit. Sci. Assn (assoc.), Sigma Iota Epsilon (life), Delta Sigma Pi (life; pledge line pres. v.p. profl. activities 1978—81). Democrat. Episcopalian. Avocations: bodybuilding, travel. Home: 250 Harbortown Dr E Apt 102 Detroit MI 48207 Personal E-mail: hansenhunter@hotmail.com.

HUNTER, HARLEN CHARLES, orthopedic surgeon; b. Estherville, Iowa, Sept. 23, 1940; s. Roy Harold and Helen Iola (King) H.; m. JoAnn Wilson, June 30, 1962; children: Harlen Todd, Juliann Kristin. BA, Drake U., 1962; DO, Coll. Osteo. Med. and Surgery, Des Moines, 1967. Diplomate Am. Osteo. Bd. Orthop. Surgery, Am. Osteo. Acad. Sports Medicine. Intern Normandy Osteo. Hosp., St. Louis, 1967-68, resident in orthops., 1968-72, chmn. dept. orthops., 1976-77; founder Orthopedics and Sports Medicine, PC, Bedford, Ind.; chmn. dept. surgery Bedford Regional Med. Ctr., 2002—04. Founder, orthop. surgeon Mid-States Orthop. Sports Medicine Clinics of Am., Ltd. SPORTS Med. Ctrs., Chesterfield, Mo., Fairview Heights, Ill., Jerseyville, Ill., Herman, Mo., 1977-99, Hunter Trauma Team, 1988-92; founder, pres. Life Style Health Systems, 1992; assoc. prof. orthop. Kansas City Coll. Osteopathy, 1993; adj. prof. Lake Erie Coll. Osteo. Medicine, 1995—; mem. staff Normandy Osteopathic, 1972-90, Outpatient Surgery Ctr., St. Louis, 1990-99, Luth. Med. Ctr., 1989-99, St. Joe's of Kirkwood, 1990-99, Bedford Med. Ctr., Dunn Meml.; clin. instr. Kirksville Coll. Osteo. Medicine; orthop. cons., team physician to high schs.; pres. Health Specialists, Inc.; program dir. sports medicine Family Physicians, 1993, 94; sponsor, lectr. sports and occupl. emergency medicine, 1997—; host weekly TV program Raceology Weekly Spl. on Motorsports; mem. med. adv. bd. Mo. Athletic Activities Assn.; cons. sports medicine Sports St. Louis newspaper; founder Ann. Sports Medicine Clinic for Trainers and Coaches, 1 yr. fellowship in sports medicine; nat. lectr. various social, profl. orgns.; adj. clin. assoc. prof. Coll. Osteo. Surgery, Des Moines; orthop. surgeon Iowa State Boys Basketball Tournament, 1966-85; founder Mobile Sports Medicine Semi Truck, 1988, Hunter Sports Medicine Clinic, Belleville, Ill.; sponsor U.S. Biathalon Assn., 1989; staff photographer Ind. Motor Speedway, 1973—, Daytona Internat. Speedway, 1979-96; adv. bd. Motorsport Rsch. Group Human Performance Internat., Daytona Beach, Fla., 1990—; mem. Sports Medicine Commn. Ind. State Med. Assn. Co-author: Motorsports Medicine, 1992; host daily radio program Making a Difference, For Your Health; host weekly nat. radio program Sports Medicine Hour with Dr. Hunter; contbr. articles to profl. jours. Pres. adv. bd. Bedford Salvation Army; candidate Lawrence County Commr., 2004. Recipient Clinic Spkr. award Iowa H.S. Baseball Coaches Assn., 1982, 83, Hall of Fame award Mo. Athletic Trainers Assn., 1987, Sibley Medallion award for outstanding svc. Lindenwood U., Ann. Outstanding Soccer Player of Yr. award Mo. Athletic Club, Hunter 100 Stock Car Race, Peveley, Mo., Bob Scott Photography award Indpls. Motor Speedway, 2002; named Businessman of Yr., Nat. Rep. Congl. Com., 2003; Harlen C. Hunter Sports Complex named in his honor Lindenwood U., St. Charles, Mo., 1988. Fellow Am. Coll. Osteo. Surgeons, Am. Osteo Acad. Orthops. (past chmn. com. on athletic injuries), Am. Osteo. Acad. Sports Medicine; mem. Am. Osteo. Assn., Mo. Assn. Osteo. Physicians and Surgeons (medallion award 1990), Am. Coll. Sports Medicine, Am. Orthop. Soc. Sports Medicine (del. sports medicine exch. program to China 1985), AMA, Am. Coll. Occupl. Medicine, Ind. Med. Assn. (sports medicine com. 1999—), Ind. Osteo. Assn. (bd. trustees 2003-), St. Louis Met. Med. Assn., Sports Car Club Am. (med. dir. pro racing 1989-91), World Congress Motorsport Scis., St. Louis Auto Racing Club (Amb. award 1989, 91), 500 Old Timers Club, The Butler Soc., Elks, Lions, Masons, Shriners. Republican. Methodist. Home: 604 Heltonville Rd E Bedford IN 47421-9250 Office: Ortho & Sports Medicine 2407 16th St Bedford IN 47421-3510 Business E-Mail: drsptmed@insightbb.com.

HUNTER, HENLEY A., federal judge; b. 1944; BA, U. Ark., 1966; JD, La. State U., 1969. Law clk. La. Ct. Appeals (2d cir.), 1969; ptnr. Eatman & Hunter, 1970-87; bankruptcy judge U.S. Dist. Ct. (we. dist.) La., Alexandria, 1987—, chief bankruptcy judge, 1995-2000. Mem. ABA, La. State Bar Assn., Alexandria Bar Assn., Am. Judicature Soc., Nat. Conf. Bankruptcy Judges. Office: US Bankruptcy Ct 300 Jackson St Alexandria LA 71301-8357 Fax: 318-443-8195. Office Phone: 318-443-8083.

HUNTER, HERBERT ERWIN, aerospace engineer; b. Washington, June 11, 1934; s. Herbert C. and A. Paula (Dieterich) H.; m. Helen Louise Shelhorse, June 11, 1956 (div. 1978); children: Erwin, David, Shirley Black, Patricia Copeland, Linda Markiewicz; m. Jeanne Theresa Parent, Nov. 25, 1978; stepchildren: Richard Kinsella, William Kinsella, Katey McMahon, Philip Kinsella. BS in Aerospace Engring., U. Md., 1956; MS in Aerospace Engring., Calif. Inst. Tech., Pasadena, 1957, PhD in Aerospace Engring., 1960. Dept. mgr. AVCO Corp., Wilmington, Mass., 1963-73; pres., founder, chmn. bd. dirs. Adapt Svc. Corp., Reading, Mass., 1973-83; assoc. fellow Nichols Rsch. Corp., Huntsville, Ala., 1983-94; co-founder Applied Data Trends, Inc., Huntsville, 1994, pres., 1994-2000, pres. emeritus, 2000—, dir., 1994—2004. Dir. QPC, Inc., 2000-2004. Contbr. articles to Jour. Aerospace Scis., Jour. Math Physics, Jour. Climate Applied Meteorology, Jour. Atmospheric Ocean Tech. With USAF, 1960-63. Mem. AAAS, AIAA, Am. Meteorol. Soc., Soc. of Photo-Optical Instrumentation Engrs. Baptist. Home: 8912 Hogan Dr SE Huntsville AL 35802-3436 Office: Applied Data Trends Inc 215 Wynn Dr Ste 321 Huntsville AL 35805 Office Phone: 256-881-7270. Personal E-mail: herbhunter@aol.com.

HUNTER, HOLLY, actress; b. Conyers, Ga., Mar. 20, 1958; d. Charles Edwin and Opal Marguerite (Catledge) H; m. Janusz Kaminski, May 20, 1995 (div. 2001). BFA, Carnegie-Mellon U., 1980. Actress: (films) The Burning, 1981, Swing Shift, 1984, Broadcast News, 1987 (Acad. Award nomination for best actress, 1988), Raising Arizona, 1987, End of the Line, 1988, Always, 1989, Miss Firecracker, 1989, Animal Behavior, 1989, Once Around, 1991, The Piano, 1993 (Cannes Film Festival Award for best actress, 1993, Golden Globe for best actress, 1994, Acad. Award for best actress, 1994), The Firm, 1993 (Acad. Award nomination for best supporting actress, 1994), Home for the Holidays, 1995, Copycat, 1995, Crash, 1996, Hurly-burly, 1997, A Life Less Ordinary, 1997, Living Out Loud, 1998, Jesus' Son, 1999, Things You Can Tell Just By Looking at Her, 2000 (Emmy nomination for best supporting actress in a miniseries or movie, 2001), Woman Wanted, 2000, Timecode, 2000, O Brother, Where Art Thou, 2000, Moonlight Mile, 2002, Levity, 2003, Little Black Book, 2004, The Incredibles (voice), 2004; (TV) Svengali, 1983, An Uncommon Love, 1983, With Intent to Kill, 1984, A Gathering of Old Men, 1987, Roe vs. Wade, 1989 (Emmy for best actress in a miniseries or special, 1989), Crazy in Love, 1992, The Positively True Adventures of the Alleged Texas Cheerleader-Murdering Mom, 1993 (Emmy for best actress in a miniseries or special, 1993, CableACE award for best actress in a movie or miniseries, 1994), Harlan County War, 2000 (Emmy nomination for best actress in a miniseries or movie, 2000), When Billie Beat Bobby, 2001 (Emmy nomination for best actress in a miniseries or movie, 2001); (Broadway stage prodns.) Crimes of the Heart, 1982, The Wake of Jamey Foster, 1982, Impossible Marriage, 1998; (regional stage prodns.) Buried Child, A Doll's House, Artichoke; (other stage prodns.) include A Lie of the Mind, L.A., Battery, N.Y.C., Miss Firecracker Contest, 1984, The Person I Once Was, N.Y.C.; Actress, exec. prodr.: (films) Thirteen, 2003 (Acad. Award nomination for best supporting actress, 2004, Golden Globe nomination for best supporting actress, 2004, Screen Actors Guild Award nomination for best supporting actress, 2004). Bd. dirs. Calif. Abortion Rights Action League.

HUNTER, HOWARD OWEN, academic administrator, law educator; b. Brunswick, Ga., Oct. 14, 1946; m. Susan Frankel, Nov. 27, 1971; 1 child, Emily Atwood Plotkin. BA in Russian Studies, Yale U., 1968, JD, 1971. Bar: Ga. 1971. Assoc. atty. Hogan & Hartson, Washington, 1971-72, Hansell, Post, Brandon & Dorsey, Atlanta, 1972-76; asst. prof. Emory U. Sch. Law, Atlanta, 1976-79, assoc. prof., 1979-82, assoc. dean, 1979-80, prof., 1982—, prof. law, dean, 1989-2001, provost, exec. v.p. for acad. affairs, 2001—. Dir. Ga. Vol. Lawyers for the Arts, Inc., 1975-89, sec., 1975-77, treas., 1978-80, v.p., 1980-82, pres., 1984-87; vis. prof. law U. Va. Sch. Law, Charlottesville, 1982-83; hon. prof. law U. Hong Kong, 1986; vis. Mills E. Godwin prof. law Coll. William & Mary, Williamsburg, Va., 1989; mem. Chief Justice Commn. on Professionalism, 1990—, Supreme Ct. Commn. on Indigent Def., 2000—; bd. trustees Fed. Def. Program, 1991-97; lectr. in field. Author: Freedom of Information Handbook: Georgia, 1979, Modern Law of Contracts: Breach and Remedies, 1986, supplements, 1987, 88, 89, 90, 91, 92, 93, Modern Law of Contracts: Formation, Performance, Relationships, 1987, supplements, 1988, 89, 90, 91, 92, 93, Modern Law of Contracts, revised edit., 1993, supplements, 1994, 95, 96, 97, 98, 2d rev. edit., 1999, supplements, 2000, 01, (with Mogens Pedersen) Recent Reforms in Swedish Higher Education, 1980; contbr. articles to profl. jours.; mem. editl. bd. Jour. of Contract Law, 1988—. Fulbright Sr. scholar U. Sydney, 1988. Mem. ABA, Assn. Am. Law Schs., Am. Law Inst. (mem. consultative com. on revisions to article 2 of UCC), State Bar Ga. (mem. editl. bd. Ga. State Bar Jour. 1977-82), Decatur-DeKalb Bar Assn., Atlanta Bar Assn. (vol. lawyer project on illegal Cuban immigrants 1985-87, vol. lawyer in representation of Cuban inmates at fed. prison in Talladega, Ala. 1988, bd. dirs. internat. transaction sect. 1995—), Inst. Continuing Legal Edn. (vice-chmn. bd. trustees 1993-97), Inst. Continuing Judicial Edn. (bd. trustees 1989-2001). Avocations: bicycling, jogging, fishing, travel. Office: 404 Adminstrn Bldg Emory Univ Atlanta GA 30322 E-mail: hunter@emory.edu.

HUNTER, IAN W., engineering educator, researcher; BSc, U. Auckland, 1974, MSc, 1975, DCP, 1976, PhD, 1980. Hatsopoulos prof. mech. engring., prof. biol. engring. Mass. Inst. Tech., Cambridge, dir. BioInstrumentation lab. Achievements include research in nanostructured actuator polymers, optimization of conducting polymer actuators, model-based control of mechanically active materials. Office: Mass Inst Tech BioInstrumentation Lab 77 Massachusetts Ave Rm 3-154 Cambridge MA 02139 Office Phone: 617-253-4763. Office Fax: 617-252-1849. E-mail: ihunter@mit.edu.

HUNTER, JACK DUVAL, retired lawyer; b. Elkhart, Ind., Jan. 14, 1937; s. William Stanley and Marjorie Irene (Upson) H.; m. Marsha Ann Goodsell, Nov. 14, 1958 (dec.); children: Jack, Jon, Justin. BBA, U. Mich., 1959, LLB, 1961. Bar: Mich. 1961, Ind. 1962. Atty. Lincoln Nat. Life Ins. Co., Ft. Wayne, Ind., 1961-64, asst. counsel, 1964-68, v.p., gen. counsel, 1975-79, sr. v.p., gen. counsel, 1979-86, exec. v.p., gen. counsel, 1986-99. Asst. gen. counsel, asst. sec. Lincoln Nat. Corp., Ft. Wayne and Phila., 1968-71, gen. counsel, 1971-2002, v.p., 1972-79, sr. v.p., 1979-86, exec. v.p., 1986-2002. Life trustee Ind. Nature Conservancy, chmn. bd. trustees, 1993-95. Recipient Oak Leaf award Nature Conservancy, 1997. Mem. ABA, Ind. State Bar Assn., Allen County Bar Assn., Assn. Life Ins. Counsel (pres. 1995-96, Anderson Disting. Svc. award 2002), Am. Coun. Life Ins. (chmn. legal sect. 1991). Personal E-mail: jack.hunter2@verizon.net.

HUNTER, JACK DUVAL, II, lawyer; b. Ann Arbor, Mich., July 15, 1959; s. Jack Duval and Marsha Ann (Goodsell) (dec.) H.; m. Denise Marie Hodge, June 27, 1981; children: Adam Duval, Benjamin Robert. BSCE, Purdue U., 1982, MSCE, 1984; JD, St. Mary's U., 1986. Bar: Tex. 1986, U.S. Dist. Ct. (so. dist.) Tex. 1987, U.S. Ct. Appeals (5th cir.) 1987, U.S. Supreme Ct. 1990; engr. in tng., Ind., Tex. Assoc. Johnson & Davis, Harlingen, Tex., 1986-88; asst. dist. atty. Hidalgo County Courthouse, Edinburg, Tex., 1989-91; gen. atty. Immigration and Naturalization Svc., 1991-93; pvt. practice lawyer Harlingen, Tex., 1993-96, Edinburg, 1996-98; atty. Dyer & Assocs., McAllen, Tex., 1999-2000; pvt. practice Harlingen, 2000—. Mem. bd. advs. St. Mary's U., 1985-86; adj. prof. Reynaldo G. Garza Sch. of Law, 1989-91; adj. instr. Tex. State Tech. Coll., Harlingen, 1999-2000, Howard Payne U., Harlingen, 2001; lectr. Lorman Constrn. Lien Law sem., McAllen, Tex., 2000. Assoc. editor St. Mary's Law Jour., 1985-86. Bd. dirs. Harlingen Boys' and Girls' Club, 1987-88. Mem. NRA (endowment), Heritage Soc., Coll. State Bar Tex., State Bar Tex. (adminstrn. of rules and evidence com.), Cameron County Bar Assn., Hidalgo County Bar Assn., Juvenile Ct. Conf. Com. (lectr. 1990), Tex. State Rifle Assn. (endowment 2002), Buckmasters (life), Valley Sportsmans Club of the Lower Rio Grande Valley (life), Order of Barristers, Whittington Ctr. (life), N.Am. Hunting Club (life), Phi Delta Phi (exchequer 1985-86). Democrat. Baptist. E-mail: jason@aol.com.

HUNTER, JACK E., judge; b. Alexandria, La., May 24, 1945; s. William A. and Lucy A. Hunter; m. Marciela Sanchez, Aug. 12, 1989 (div. Dec. 2001). BBA, U. Houston, 1969; JD, South Tex. Coll. Law, Houston, 1974. Bar: Tex., bd. cert. criminal law: Tex. 1st asst. dist. atty., acting dist. atty. Nueces County Dist. Atty.'s Office, Corpus Christi, Tex., 1977—83; chief judge Corpus Christi Mcpl. Ct., Corpus Christi, Tex., 1983—86; state dist. judge 94th Dist. Ct., Corpus Christi, Tex., 1987—. Adv. com. legal asst. program Del Mar Coll., Corpus Christi, 1990—; past adj. prof. arts and humanities Tex. A&M C.C., Corpus Christi. Author: From The Bench, 2005, Osaka Spa Murders, 2005; contbr. articles to legal jours. Past chmn. Nueces County Gang Task Force; past adv. chair Leadership Corpus Christi XXII; adminstrv. judge Nueces County Bd. Judges; past chmn. Nueces County Juvenile Bd.; founder Texans Against Gangs; past dist. chmn. Boy Scouts Am. Sp4 U.S. Army, 1970—72. Recipient Spirit of Benevolence award, Coastal Bend Coun. Alcohol and Drug Abuse, 1998, Citizen of Yr. award, Arthritis Found. Corpus Christi, 2000; fellow, Tex. Bar Found. Mem.: Corpus Christi Bar Assn. (chmn. continued legal edn. 1989—, Cecil Burney Humanitarian award 1990), Teen Ct. Inc. (co-founder, pres. 1990—). Democrat. Roman Catholic. Avocations: reading, exercise, travel. Office: 94th Dist Ct Nueces County Courthouse 901 Leopard St Corpus Christi TX 78401 E-mail: drehler@nueces.esc2.net.

HUNTER, JAMES AUSTEN, JR., lawyer; b. Phoenix, June 19, 1941; s. James Austen and Elizabeth Aileen (Holt) H.; m. Donna Gabriele, Aug. 24, 1973; 1 child, James A. AB, Cath. U. Am., 1963, LL.B., 1966. Bar: N.Y. 1967, Pa. 1975, U.S. Supreme Ct. 1974. Assoc. firm Sullivan & Cromwell, N.Y.C., 1967-74; assoc. firm Morgan, Lewis & Bockius, LLP, Phila., 1974-77, ptnr., 1977—. Home: 1001 Red Rose Ln Villanova PA 19085-2118 Office: Morgan Lewis & Bockius LLP 1701 Market St Philadelphia PA 19103-2903 Office Phone: 215-963-5381. E-mail: jhunter@morganlewis.com.

HUNTER, JAMES EDWARD, chemist, consultant; b. Phila., May 4, 1945; s. James Bruce and Ruth Moyer (Lenker) H.; m. Marilyn Kay Jones, Aug. 24, 1968; children: Melanie Kay, Timothy Edward. BS in Chemistry, Lehigh U., 1967; MS in Biochemistry, U. Wis., 1969, PhD in Biochemistry, 1974. Staff nutritionist Procter & Gamble Co., Cin., 1974-92, staff toxicologist, 1992-95, staff toxicologist regulatory affairs, 1995-96; adj. prof. chemistry Cin. State Tech. and Cmty. Coll., 1997-98, U. Cin., 1998—. Mem. biol. subcom. of tech. com. Inst. of Shortening and Edible Oils, Inc., Washington, 1981-93, chmn. biol. subcom., 1985-93; mem. human nutrition bd. of sci. counselors USDA, Washington, 1990-92; mem. oral health com. and subcom. on fatty acids and health Internat. Life Scis. Inst., Washington, 1985-92. Editor: (booklet) Food Fats and Oils, 5th edit., 1982, 6th edit., 1988, 7th edit., 1994; contbr. numerous articles to profl. jours. including Jour. Am. Oil Chemists Soc., Am. Jour. Clin. Nutrition. V.p., chmn. fundraisers St. Xavier H.S. Music Promoters Bd., Cin., 1992-94; sec., mem. com. mgmt. Powel Crosley Jr. YMCA, Cin., 1980-86, sec., 1982-86; cubmaster Boy Scouts Am., Cin., 1985-87. With U.S. Army, 1969-71. Mem.: Am. Soc. for Nutritional Scis., Am. Chem. Soc. (chair various local coms.), Am. Oil Chemists Soc. (bd. dirs., treas. local chpt. 1990—93), Runners Club Greater Cin. (v.p. 1994—95, sec. 1995—), Tau Beta Pi, Sigma Xi, Phi Beta Kappa. Avocations: ragtime piano, running, swimming, photography, woodworking. Office Phone: 513-556-9215. E-mail: hunterje@email.uc.edu.

HUNTER, J(AMES) PAUL, literature and language professor, literary critic; b. Jamestown, NY, June 29, 1934; s. Paul W. and Florence I. (Walmer) H.; children: Debra, Lisa, Paul III, Anne, Ellen Harris. AB, Ind. Central Coll., 1955; MA, Miami U., Oxford, Ohio, 1957; PhD, Rice U., 1963. Instr., U. Fla., Gainesville, 1957-59, Williams Coll., Williamstown, Mass., 1962-64; asst. prof. U. Calif., Riverside, 1964-66; assoc. prof. English Emory U., Atlanta, 1966-68, prof., 1968-80, chmn. dept., 1973-79; prof. English, dean Coll. Arts and Sci., U. Rochester, N.Y., 1981-86; prof. English U. Chgo., 1987—, Chester D. Tripp prof. humanities, 1990-96, Barbara E. and Richard J. Franke prof. humanities, 1996—2001; dir. Franke Inst. for the Humanities, 1996—2001, Franke prof. emeritus, 2001—; prof. of English U. of Va., 2001—. Gen. editor Bedford Cultural Edits., 1994—. Author: The Reluctant Pilgrim, 1966, Occasional Form, 1975, Norton Introduction to Poetry, 8th edit., 2002, Norton Introduction to Literature, 9th edit., 2005, New Worlds of Literature, 2d edit., 1994, Before Novels, 1990; co-editor: Rhetorics of Order/Ordering Rhetorics, 1989; editor: Norton Critical Edition of Mary Shelley's Frankenstein, 1996. Sr. advisor Andrew W. Mellon Found., 1999—. Guggenheim fellow, 1976-77, NEH fellow, 1985-86, Nat. Humanities Ctr. fellow, 1986, 95-96. Mem. MLA, Am. Soc. 18th Century Studies (Louis Gottschalk prize 1991, 2d v.p. 1994-95, 1st v.p. 1995-96, pres. 1996-97), Southeastern Am. Soc. 18th Century Studies (pres. 1977-78), Soc. Atlantic MLA (pres. 1992-93), N.E. Am. Soc. 18th Century Studies (pres. 1982-83), Ill. Humanities Coun. (chair 2000-04). Office Phone: 312-458-9978. Business E-Mail: jph7f@virginia.edu.

HUNTER, JOHN C., III, chemicals executive; b. LaGrange, Ga., Mar. 1, 1947; BS in Chem. Engring., Ga. Inst. Tech., 1969; MBA, U. Houston, 1977. Joined Monsanto Co., 1969, pres. fibers, 1997; pres., COO, CEO, chmn. Solutia, Inc. Lt. U.S. Army, 1970-72. Address: 575 Maryville Center Dr Saint Louis MO 63141

HUNTER, JOHN GERARD, plastic surgeon; b. N.Y.C., Oct. 6, 1955; s. Vincent Ambrose and Ann Theresa (Milligan) H.; m. Ann Mary DiMaio, Sept. 18, 1982 (div. 1991). BS, Fordham U., 1977; MD magna cum laude, SUNY, Bklyn., 1983. Diplomate Nat. Bd. Med. Examiners, Am. Bd. Plastic Surgery. Intern, resident in surgery Mt. Sinai Med. Ctr., N.Y.C., 1983-86; resident, chief resident in plastic surgery SUNY Health Sci. Ctr., Bklyn., 1986-88, clin. instr. plastic surgery, 1988-91, clin. asst. prof. plastic surgery, 1991-96; asst. attending surgeon St. Luke's-Roosevelt Hosp. Ctr., N.Y.C., 1990—2001, Cabrini Med. Ctr., N.Y.C., 1988-92, Beekman Downtown Hosp., N.Y.C., 1988-93, 1988-93, 94-96; attending and chief plastic surgery N.Y. Meth. Hosp.; clin. asst. prof. plastic surgery Cornell U., 1996—2003, clin. assoc. prof., 2003—; vice chmn. dept. surgery N.Y. Meth. Hosp., 2004—. Plastic surgery cons. N.Y.-N.J. Knights, 1991-93. Contbr. articles to profl. jours. Mosby scholar Mosby Pub. Co., 1983. Fellow ACS, Am. Acad. Pediatrics, N.Y. Acad. Medicine (chmn. sect. Plastic Surgery 1999-2000, 2002-03); mem. AMA, Am. Soc. Plastic and Reconstructive Surgeons, N.Y. Regional Soc. Plastic and Reconstructive Surgery (v.p. 2000, pres. 2002), N.Y. Surg. Soc., Am. Soc. Aesthetic Plastic Surgery, Alpha Omega Alpha. Office: 47 E 63rd St New York NY 10021-7315 Office Phone: 212-751-4444.

HUNTER, JOHN ORR, college president; b. Newfane, N.Y., Mar. 17, 1933; s. Alexander and Jane (Robertson) H.; m. Lyla Beth Brown, Aug. 31, 1957; children: Elaine, John, Susan, Elizabeth. BA, U. Buffalo, 1959, MA, 1964; EdD, SUNY, Buffalo, 1968; postgrad., St. Bonaventure U., Harvard U., 1976. Prof. Niagara C.C., Sanborn, NY, 1963-69, dean, 1969-78; pres. Coll. Lake County, Grayslake, Ill., 1978-86, Alfred (N.Y.) State Coll., 1986-93; founding pres. Cambria County (Pa.) C.C., 1994—; pres. W.Va. No. C.C., 2000—. Spl. cons. FEPADE, El Salvador, 1988-94; mem. Afred Tech. Resources, Inc., 1990—; bd. dirs. Bank of Highland Park, Ill. Author: Values and the Future: Models of Community College Development, 1979; contbr. articles to jours. in field. Trustee Nioga Libr. System, 1973-78; mem. Abbott Scholarship Found., 1979-86, Lake County SBA Corp., 1980-86, Ill. Community Coll. Bd. Planning Adv. Coun., 1980-81, Lake County Econ. Devel. Commn., 1981-86, exec. coun. Steuben Area Boy Scouts Am., 1987-88; chmn. Wellsville adv. bd. Salvation Army, 1988—; bd. dirs. Hornell YMCA, 1989—. 1st lt. arty. U.S. Army, 1954-57. Recipient award Lake County Freedom Found.; N.Y. Jaycees pub. speaking champion, 1964. Mem. U.S. Navy League (hon.), Ill. Coun. Pub. Community Coll. Presidents (curriculum com. chmn. 1981-82, econ. devel. com. chmn. 1983-84, sec., treas., 1984-85, chmn. elect 1985-86), Ill. Bd. Higher Edn. (spl. com. on undergrad. edn. reform 1985-86), Pres. Assn. of Colls. of Tech. Office: SUNY Coll Tech Alfred NY 14802 Home: Apt A6 98 Edgwood St Wheeling WV 26003-5739 E-mail: jhunter@northern.wvnet.edu.

HUNTER, J(OHN) ROBERT, insurance consumer advocate; b. New Orleans, Nov. 20, 1936; s. J. Robert and Alberta M. (Cox) H.; m. Carole A. Means, Mar. 6, 1976; children: Laura Jeanne, James Douglas, John Robert, III. BS, Clarkson U., 1958; grad. Program for Sr. Mgrs., Harvard U., 1976. Dir. of ins. Atlantic Mut. Ins. Co., 1960-61; supervisory actuary Ins. Svcs. Office, N.Y.C., 1961-67; asst. actuary Mut. Ins. Rating Bur., N.Y.C., 1967-71; chief actuary Fed. Ins. Adminstrn., HUD, Washington, 1971-74, acting adminstr., 1974-76, adminstr., 1976-77, dep. fed. ins. adminstr., 1977-80; founder, pres. Nat. Ins. Consumer Orgn., 1980-93; ins. commr. State of Tex., 1993-94; dir. ins. Consumer Fedn. Am., Arlington, Va., 1994—. Author: Taking the Bite Out of Insurance, 1980, Profitability and Investment Income in Property Casualty Insurance, 1983, Insurance in California, 1986, Pay at the Pump Private No Fault Auto Insurance, 1992, Proposition 103 Revisited: A Consumer Triumph, 1993, Auto Insurance, Progress but More to Be Done, 1995, America's Distrous Disaster Insurance System, 1998, Premium Deceit, 1999, Texas Tort Reform's Incredible Shrinking Savings, 1999, Changes in State Insurance Department Resources, 2000, California Auto REgulation The Best in Nation, 2001, Medical Malpractice Insurance: Stable Losses/Unstable Rates, 2002, Home Insurance Rates Rise Sharply, 2003, Insurers Undermine Terrorism Insurance Law, 2003. Pres. Freeport (N.Y.) Cmty. Chorale, 1970-71; pres., founder Rockville (Md.) Musical Theatre, 1974-75; vestryman Christ Ch., Alexandria, 1982-84, 91-93. Recipient award for excellence Sec. HUD, 1977, Ester Peterson award for consumer lifetime achievement Consumer Fedn. Am., 2002. Fellow Casualty Actuarial Soc.; mem. Am. Acad. Actuaries, Internat. Actuarial Assn. Home: 2202 24th St N Arlington VA 22207-4904 Office Phone: 703-528-0062. Personal E-mail: loonlakeme@aol.com.

HUNTER, KENNETH M., business information systems educator; b. Muskegon, Mich., Jan. 11, 1943; s. Merlin Arthur and Dorothy Elaine Hunter. PhD, U. Wis., 1968. Asst. prof. math. La. State U., Baton Rouge, 1968—71; prof. William James Coll., Allendale, Mich., 1971—78; assoc. prof. Sangamon State U., Springfield, Ill., 1978—79; sys. analyst Baxter Travenol Labs., Chgo., 1979—80; assoc. prof. U. Pacific, Stockton, Calif., 1980—83; asst. prof. San Francisco State U., 1983—84, prof. bus. info. sys., 1988—; assoc. prof. Aquinas Coll., Grand Rapids, Mich., 1984—85; sys. analyst W.W. Engring. and Sci., Grand Rapids, Mich., 1985—88. Democrat. Achievements include patents for search engines, fuzzy finite state non-deterministic automata.

HUNTER, KENT ROBERT, minister, religious administrator; b. Detroit, Sept. 23, 1947; s. Robert W. Hunter and Delores L. (Mix) Licorish; m. Janet M. Hasselman, Aug. 16, 1969; children: Laura, Jonathan. BA, Concordia Sr. Coll., Ft. Wayne, Ind., 1969; MDiv, Concordia Sem., St. Louis, 1973; PhD, Lutheran Sch. of Theology, Chgo., 1975; D of Ministry, Fuller Theol. Sem., 1977. Sr. pastor Our Savior Luth. Ch., Detroit, 1974-79; pastor Zion Evang. Luth Ch., Corunna, Ind., 1981-86; pres. N.Am. Soc. for Ch. Growth, 1988, Ch. Growth Ctr., Corunna, 1978—; sr. editor Strategies for Today's Leader Global Ch. Growth Mag., Corunna, 1987—. Radio personality The Ch. Doctor, 1991—; owner, opeator Nimrod Acres Tree Farm. Author: Moving the Church into Action, 1989, Discover your Windows, 2002, The Jesus Enterprise 2004; co-author: Courageous Churches, 1991, The Lord's Harvest and the Rural Church, 1993, Foundations for Church Growth: Biblical Basics for the Local Church, 1994, Your Church Has Personality, 1997, Confessions of a Church Growth Enthusiast, 1997. Mem. Internat. Am. Soc. for Ch. Growth. Office: Ch Growth Ctr 1230 Us Highway 6 Corunna IN 46730-9705

HUNTER, LARRY DEAN, lawyer; b. Leon, Iowa, Apr. 10, 1950; s. Doyle J. and Dorothy B. (Grey) H.; m. Rita K. Barker, Jan. 24, 1971; children: Nathan (dec.), Allison. BS with high distinction, U. Iowa, 1971; AM, JD magna cum laude, U. Mich., 1974, CPhil in Econs., 1975. Bar: Va. 1975, Mich. 1978, Calif. 1992. Assoc. McGuire Woods & Battle, Richmond, Va., 1975-77; asst. counsel, internat. counsel Clark Equipment Co., Buchanan, Mich., 1977-80; ptnr. Honigman, Miller, Schwartz and Cohn, Detroit, 1980-93; asst. gen. counsel Hughes Electronics Corp., L.A., 1993-98, corp. v.p., 1998—2001, sr. v.p., gen. counsel El Segundo, Calif., 2002—03, DIRECTV, Inc., El Segundo, Calif., 1996-98; chmn. pres. DIRECTV Japan Mgmt., Inc., Tokyo, 1998-2000; exec. v.p., gen. counsel, sec. The DIRECTV Group, Inc., El Segundo, Calif., 2004—. Mem. faculty Wayne State U. Law Sch., Detroit, 1987-89. Mem. Order of Coif. Home: 1101 S Catalina Ave Redondo Beach CA 90277 Office: The DIRECTV Group Inc 2250 E Imperial Hwy El Segundo CA 90245 Office Phone: 310-964-0723. Personal E-mail: larry.hunter@directv.com.

HUNTER, LARRY LEE, retired electrical engineer; b. Versailles, Mo., Mar. 5, 1938; s. Donnan Kleber and Molly Opal (Roe) H.; m. Marcella Ann Avey, Feb. 1, 1959; children: Cynthia Lynn Hunter Morency, Stuart Roe. BSEE, U. Mo., 1963; MBA, Fla. Inst. Tech., 1984. Sys. test engr. McDonnell Aircraft Corp., St. Louis, 1963—65; design engr. Magnavox Co., Urbana, Ill., 1965—66, R&D engr., 1966—67; project engr. LTV Electrosystems, Garland, Tex., 1967—68, sys. engr., 1968—70; program mgr. Dorsett Electronics, Tulsa, 1970—73, Harris Corp., Melbourne, Fla., 1973—75, bus. area mgr., 1975—85; v.p. mktg., engring., program mgmt. Teledyne Lewisburg, Tenn., 1985—88; pres. L.H. Assocs., Columbia, Tenn., 1988—90; founder, gen. mgr. Precision Cable divsn. AMP Inc., Harrisburg, Pa. and Greensboro, NC, 1990—96, dir. global cable sys. bus. group, 1996—97; pres. L. Hunter Assocs., Inc., Tampa, Fla., 1997—2001. Contbr. articles to profl. jours. Mem.: IEEE (sr.), EE Scholastic (hon.), Eta Kappa Nu. Republican. Methodist. Achievements include invention of medical thermometer. Avocations: hunting, fishing, golf. Home: 16309 E Course Dr Tampa FL 33624-1127 E-mail: lhunter@tampabay.rr.com.

HUNTER, LELAND CLAIR, JR., management consultant; b. Phila., Feb. 22, 1925; s. Leland Clair and Lillian Mae (Failor) H.; m. Elva Joy Charlton, July 5, 1946; children: Charlton Lee, Steven Kent, Brian Scott, Donna Joy. BS, Villanova U., 1948; postgrad., Columbia U., 1944-45; MBA, Fla. Research Inst., 1971; grad., Advanced Mgmt. Program, Harvard U., 1973. Test engr. Gen. Electric Co., Phila., 1949-50; with Fla. Power & Light Co., 1950-88, v.p. indsl. relations Miami, 1966-72, v.p. transmission and distbn., 1972-73, group v.p., 1973-78, sr. v.p., 1978-88; pres. Leland Hunter Mgmt. Cons., Miami, 1988—; chmn. Hunter, Voehl and Lewis, 1995—; conf. co-chair Nat. Youth Crime Prevention Conf.; editor Charlton Pub. Co., 1998, pres., 2001. Mem. spl. labor com. Sec. of Labor U.S., 1975-76; mem. Labor and Mgmt. Polit. Action Com. for Utility Industry, 1977, Gov.'s Adv. Coun. Productivity, 1981—; pres. Leland Hunter Mgmt. Cons. Vice chmn. adv. com. Dade County (Fla.) Sch. Bd., 1966; bd. govs. Gold Coast AAU, 1967-68; bd. dirs. Crime Commn. of Greater Miami, 1974—; chmn. bd. Victoria Hosp., 1984-88; dir. Pro-Fish of Fla.; Fla. Lawyers Prepaid Legal Services Inc. Crime Commn. of Greater Miami, 1980—; bd. advisors Stetson U.; mem. bus. adv. com. Brookings Instn., Washington; exec. v.p. Atlantic Gamefish Found.; mem. Blue Ribbon Com. to Save Miami's Fin. Future, 1996; mem. County Mgrs. Com. to Stop Corruption in Dade County Politics, 1999. Served with USN, 1943-46. Recipient Key to City Toledo and Coral Gables Fla.). Mem. Am. Soc. Tng. Dirs. (pres. local chpt. 1955-56), Fla. Athletic Club (pres. 1962), Coral Gables Country Club, Univ. Miami Club. Home and Office: 7881 SW 180th St Miami FL 33157-6216

HUNTER, LESLIE GENE, history educator; b. Meadville, Pa., Sept. 26, 1941; s. George Harper and Gladys Laverne (Bowland) H.; m. Cecilia Aros, Aug. 15, 1969; children: Louis, Raquel, Daniel, Joseph. BA in History, U. Ariz., 1964, MA in History, 1966, PhD in History, 1971. Asst. prof. Tex. A&M U., Kingsville, 1969-74, assoc. prof., 1974-81, prof., 1981—, Regents prof., 1998—, chmn. dept. history, 1986-90, 91-96. Mem. faculty exch. Kiev (Ukraine) Policy Inst., 1991. Editor: Historic Kingsville, Texas, 1994; author (computer software) Missions in Spanish Tex., 1987; editor Jour. South Tex., 1997—;mem. editl. bd. Jour. South Tex., 1989—, Social Studies Texan, 1989—; contbr. articles to profl. jours. Chair hist. rev. bd. City of Kingsville, Tex., 1987—; amb. Inst. Texan Culture, 1994—. Mem. AAUP, Tex. Coun. Social Studies, Tex. Computer Edn. Assn., South Tex. Hist. Assn., S.W. Mission Rsch. Ctr., Phi Alpha Theta. Democrat. Episcopalian. Avocation: computer technology. Home: 811 W Alice Ave Kingsville TX 78363-4262 Office: Tex A&M U Dept History Kingsville TX 78363 E-mail: kflgh00@tamuk.edu.

HUNTER, MICHAEL, publishing executive; b. Atlanta, Dec. 11, 1941; s. Joel H. and Eleanor Johnson; m. Katherine Garlick, Aug. 2, 1975. BA cum laude, Harvard U., 1964; postgrad., Columbia U., 1965-67. Dir. Spectrum Books, Prentice-Hall Inc., Englewood Cliffs., N.J., 1974-80; pres. Gen. Pub. div. Prentice-Hall Inc., Englewood Cliffs., N.J., 1980-85; pres. Hunter Pub. Co., N.Y., 1985—. Mem. Am. Assn. Pubs. (exec. council Gen. Pub. div.) Clubs: University (N.Y.C.). Home: 239 S Beach Rd Hobe Sound FL 33455-2511 Office: Hunter Pub Co 130 Campus Plz Edison NJ 08837-3936 Office Phone: 772-546-7986. Business E-Mail: michael@hunterpublishing.com.

HUNTER, MICHAEL JAMES, state government official, lawyer, educator; b. Enid, Okla., July 2, 1956; s. James Chester Hunter and Phyllis Merle Brinker; m. Cheryl Lynn Plaxico, Dec. 26, 1981; children: Barret Michael, Hayden Brock. BA in History, Okla. State U., 1978; JD, U. Okla., 1982. Bar: Okla. Ptnr. Crabtree & Miller, Okla. City, 1981-85, George, Moore, Hammons & Hunter, Okla. City, 1985-87; of counsel Musser & Bunch, Okla. City, 1987-93; gen. counsel Okla. Corp. Commn., 1993-94; chief of staff Congressman J.C. Watts, Jr., 1995-99; sec. of state State of Okla., 1999—2002; COO Am. Coun. Life Insurers, 2002—. Del. Rep. Nat. Conv., Detroit, 1980, New Orleans, 1988; chmn. Rep. Caucus, 1988-90; state rep. Okla. Ho. of Reps., Okla. City, 1984-90, mem. Constitution Revision Study Commn. Named One of Okla.'s Best Legislators, The Daily Oklahoman, Okla. City, 1987; recipient Legis. Appreciation award, Okla. Dist. Atty.'s Assn., Okla. City, 1988. Mem. Okla. Bar Assn., Okla. County Bar Assn. Republican. Presbyterian. Avocations: baseball, books, movies. Office: ACLI 101 Constitution Ave NW Washington DC 20001 Home: 10754 Terkes VW Great Falls VA 22066-1644

HUNTER, MILTON, construction company executive, retired career military officer; b. Houston, May 1, 1943; married; 2 children. BS in Archtl. Engring., Wash. State U., 1967; M in Engring., U. Wash., 1978; grad. Exec. Devel. Program, U. Va., 1988; postgrad., Tex. A&M U., 1990, Harvard U., 1994; DSc (hon.), N.J. Inst. Tech., 1997. Registered profl. engr., D.C. Commd. 2d lt. U.S. Army, 1967, advanced through grades to maj. gen.; instr. Tactical Bridging br., dept. applied engring. U.S. Army Engr. Sch., Ft. Belvoir, Va.; comdr. and dist. engr. Seattle Dist. U.S. Army CE, comdg. gen., divsn. engr. South Pacific, San Francisco, chief of staff Washington, comdg. gen., divsn. engr. North Atlantic divsn. N.Y., condg. gen., divsn. engr. North Atlantic divsn. Washington, 1997-2000, dep. chief of engineers., dep. comdr., 2000—01; sr. v.p. infrastructure and tech. group Parsons Corp., Pasadena, Calif., 2002—. Decorated Legion of Merit (2), Bronze Star medal, DSM, others; recipient Disting. Alumni award Wash. State U., 1991; named to Outstanding Young of Am., 1979. Fellow Soc. Am. Mil. Engrs.; mem. Army Engr. Regtl. Assn., Assn. U.S. Army, Tau Beta Pi. Office: Parsons Corp 100 W Walnut St Pasadena CA 91124

HUNTER, PATRICIA RAE (TRICIA HUNTER), state official; b. Appleton, Minn., June 15, 1952; d. Harlan Ottowa and Clara Elizabeth (Tryhus) H.; m. Clark Waldon Crabbe, May 28, 1978 (div. July 1994); 1 child, Samantha Marcantonio-Hunter. AS in Nursing, Good Samaritan Hosp., Phoenix, 1974; BS in Nursing, U. San Diego, 1981; M in Nursing, UCLA, 1985. RN; cert. oper. rm. nurse. Surg. svcs. educator Stanford (Calif.) Hosp., 1983-85; oper. rm. supr. Alexian Bros., San Jose, Calif., 1985-86; dir. surg. svcs. Cmty. Hosp. Chula Vista, Calif., 1986-89; mem. Calif. State Assembly, San Diego, 1989-92; spl. asst. Gov. Wilson Office Statewide Health Planning and Devel., Sacramento, 1993-94; commr. Calif. Med. Assistance Commn., Sacramento, 1994—98, sr. v.p., mng. dir., 1998—2002, The Flannery Group, San Diego, 1997—2002; prin., owner Govt. Rels. Group, Inc., 2004—. Bd. mem. Premier Home & Health, Phoenix, 1994-95; cons. Summit Schs., Ontario, Calif., 1992-93, hosp., Monterey, Calif., 1984—; mem. adv. bd. Alheimers Assn., San Diego, 1990-92, Arthritis Found., 1990-92. Pres. Calif. Rep. League, 1995-97. Named Rookie Legislator of Yr., Calif. Psychol. Assn., 1990, Legislator of Yr. Calif. Nurse Practitioners Assn., 1992; recipient Alice Pauly award Nat. Women Polit. Caucus, San Diego, 1991. Mem. ANA (v.p. 1982-85), Assn. Oper. Rm. Nurses, NWPC, Bus. and Profl. Orgn., Rotary (bd. mem. 1993-94), Sigma Theta Tau (leadership award 1991). Republican. Lutheran. Home: 3260 E Fox Run Way San Diego CA 92111-7723 Office: Govt Rels Group Inc 1121 L St Ste 409 Sacramento CA 95814 Office Phone: 916-447-7821. Personal E-mail: thunter930@aol.com. Business E-Mail: grg@saclobby.com.

HUNTER, RICHARD EDWARD, retired physician; b. Worcester, Mass., May 30, 1919; s. William and Catherine (Powers) H.; m. M. Minta Shaw, Jan. 30, 1993; children: Todd Wayne, Elayne Cheryl, Jill Elizabeth, Amy Louise. AB, Clark U., 1941; MD, Boston U., 1944. Diplomate Am. Bd. Ob-Gyn. Intern Worcester City Hosp., 1944-45; resident gen. surgery Framingham (Mass.) Union Hosp., 1947; resident ob-gyn Mercy Hosp., Balt., 1947-49; practice medicine specializing ob-gyn Worcester, 1949—; prof. dept. ob-gyn U. Mass., Worcester, 1976—, chmn. dept. ob-gyn, 1976-89, emeritus prof., 1989—; ret., 1999. Contbr. articles to med. jours. Served with US Army, 1945-47. Mem. ACS, ACOG, New Eng. Assn. Gynecologic Oncologists, Soc. Gynecologic Oncology, Boston Obstetric Soc., New Eng. Cancer Soc., Am. Soc. Clin. Oncology, Soc. Gynecologic Surgeons, Royal Soc. Medicine. Republican. Home: 406 Browning Ln Worcester MA 01609 Office: 55 Lake Ave N Worcester MA 01655-0002

HUNTER, ROBERT GRAMS, retired language educator; b. Milbank, S.D., Nov. 12, 1927; s. Donald Raymond and Esther (Grams) H.; m. Anne Ziesmer, Aug. 25, 1956; children: Timothy, Catherine. BA, Harvard, 1949; MA, Columbia, 1957, PhD, 1962. Instr. Robert Coll., Istanbul, Turkey, 1949-52; successively instr., asst. prof., asso. prof. Dartmouth, 1959-70; Kenan prof. English Vanderbilt U., Nashville, 1970-82; Frensley prof. English So. Meth. U., Dallas, 1982-97; ret., 1997. Author: Shakespeare and the Comedy of Forgiveness, 1965, Shakespeare and the Mystery of God's Judgments, 1976. Served with AUS, 1952-54. Home: 5923 Hillcrest Ave Dallas TX 75205-2262

HUNTER, SUSAN GAIL, publishing executive; b. Akron, Ohio, Aug. 3, 1950; d. Robert A. and Genevieve G. (Reneker) H. BA, Wittenberg U., 1972. Prodn. editor Charles E. Merrill Pub., Columbus, Ohio, 1972-75; copy editor W.B. Saunders Co., Phila., 1975-77, assoc. med. editor, 1977-79, mktg. dir., 1979-83; dir. mktg. Am. Chem. Soc., Washington, 1983-85; exec. v.p. Butterworth-Heinemann, Stoneham, Mass., 1985-92; pres. Decker Periodicals, Hamilton, Ont., Can., 1992-93; sr. v.p. Appleton & Lange, Stamford, Conn., 1993-99; owner, ptnr. Andover Pub. Svcs., Harrisburg, Pa., 1999—. Mem. STM Internat. Pubs., Assn. Am. Pubrs. (profl. and scholarly pub. div. exec. coun. 1992), Am. Med. Pub. Assn. (bd. dirs. 1990-92), Soc. Scholarly Pub., Boston Bookbuilders, Literacy Vols. of Am., Mensa, Sigma Kappa (sec. 1987-91). Avocations: bridge, golf. Home: 1717 Mitchell Rd Harrisburg PA 17110-3129 Office: Andover Pub Svcs Harrisburg PA 17110 E-mail: sghunter@andoverpub.com.

HUNTER, TRACY ALEXANDER, priest; b. Fresno, Calif., Apr. 11, 1967; s. Robert Corwin and Gloria June Hunter; m. Katrine Chava Petermon, June 14, 1985 (dec. Aug. 10, 1985); 1 child, Ulises Korbyn. Cert. supreme grandmaster Hakuno-Kai Martial Arts, Calif., 1979, ministerial credentials Universal Life Ch., 1995. Singer, musician Grateful Frog, Fresno, Calif., 1979—85; martial arts instr. Fei Lung Fighting Soc., Fresno, Calif., 1986—93; priest Raven's Troth Kindred, Fresno, Calif., 1993—2000; fight choreographer Raven's Stead Guild, Hanford, Calif., 2000—03; priest Pagan Heart Kindred, Fresno, Calif., 2003—; martial arts instr. Pagan Heart Warriors, Fresno, Calif., 2000—. Profl. fighter NIA, 1973—85; body guard trainer Internat. Acad., Fresno, Calif., 1985—; religious tchr. Ravens Troth / Pagan Heart, Fresno, Calif., 1993—. Mem. activist for pagan rights Temple of the Pagan Heart, Fresno, Calif., 2003—. Mem. Asatru Ch. Avocations: poetry, music, reenacting, foreign languages, history. Home and Office: 5258 E Platt Fresno CA 93727 Office Phone: 559-255-7073.

HUNTER, VICTOR LEE, marketing executive, consultant; b. Garrett, Ind., Mar. 1, 1947; s. John Joseph and Martha May (Brown) H.; m. Linda Ann Loudermilk, Dec. 19, 1969; children: Jed, Andrew, Matthew, Holly. BS, Purdue U., 1969; MBA, Harvard U., 1971. Dir. mktg. Kreuger, Inc., Green Bay, Wis., 1971-75; pres. B&I Furniture, Milw., 1975-81, Hunter Bus. Group, LLC, Milw., 1981—. Bd. dirs. Wm. K. Walthers Co., Milw. Author: Business-to-Business Marketing: Creating a Community of Customers, 1997. Lay leader United Meth. Ch., Whitefish Bay, Wis., 1985; mem. exec. com. Greater Milw. Conv. and Visitors Bur. Mem. Direct Mktg. Assn., Wis. Pres.' Orgn., Bus. to Bus. Direct Mktg. Coun., Strategic Accounts Mgmt. Assn. (bd. dirs.). Office: Hunter Business Group PO Box 12970 Milwaukee WI 53212-0970 Office Phone: 414-203-8066. Business E-Mail: vhunter@hunterbusiness.com.

HUNTER, WILLIAM ANDREW, education educator; b. North Little Rock, Ark., Sept. 6, 1913; s. William James Columbus and Jessie Dorothy (Berry) H.; m. Alma Rose Burgess, June 6, 1938. AA, Dunbar Jr. Coll., Little Rock, 1933; BS, Wilberforce (Ohio) U., 1936; MS, Iowa State U., 1948, PhD, 1952. Cert. tchr., Ark., Ala. Tchr. math. and sci. Dunbar H.S., Little Rock, 1936-42; asst. prof. edn. Tuskegee Inst., Ala., 1950-56, assoc. prof., 1956-63, prof. edn., 1964-73, dean sch. edn., 1957-73; dir. multicultural project Am. Assn. Colls. Tchr. Edn., Washington, 1973-74; dir. rsch. inst. Iowa State U., Ames, 1974-83, prof. edn. emeritus, 1983—. Chief acad. officer Tuskegee Inst.-Liberian Govt.-US AID to establish schs. in Liberia, West Africa, 1960-70; programs adv. bd. Ednl. Testing Svc., Princeton, N.J., 1973-77; adv. com. multicultural requirements Iowa State Dept. Edn., Des Moines, 1975-80; found. rep. CSRA/Phi Delta Kappa, Bloomington, Ind., 1984-86. Author: Leaves of Sand, 2003; co-author: Educational Systems in Southeast Asia in Comparaison with Systems in U.S., 1979, Educational Computing: Needs Assessment, 1983; editor: Multicultural Education Through Competency Based Teacher Education, 1974. Mem. So. Poverty Law Ctr., Montgomery, Ala., 1984, Affirmative Action Com., Iowa State U., Ames, 1978-83; life mem. Tuskegee Civic Assn., 1950—; mem. Commn. on Christian Unity and Interreligious Affairs, 1988, chair, 1994—. With U.S. Army, 1942-46. Recipient Lagomarcino Laureate award for outstanding contbns. tchr. prep Iowa State U. Coll. Edn., 1981, Disting. Achievement award, 1973, Outstanding Svc. to Teaching Profession, Sch. Edn., Tuskegee Inst., 1972. Mem. Am. Assn. Colls. Tchr. Edn. (bd. dirs. 1966-73, pres. 1973-74, Pres.'s award 1974), NEA (life), Phi Delta Kappa, Kappa Delta Pi, Beta Kappa Chi, Kappa Alpha Psi. Methodist. Avocations: creative writing, gardening, painting, creative handiwork. Home: 2202 Country Club Ct Augusta GA 30904-3506

HUNTER, WILLIAM DENNIS, lawyer; b. Boise, Idaho, June 26, 1943; s. William Gregory and Lorene (Persilla) H.; m. Jane Emily Porter, Apr. 30, 1966; children: Keith Alan, Elise Aubrey. BA, Stanford U., 1965; JD, U. Calif., San Francisco, 1973. Bar: Calif. 1973, U.S. Dist. Ct. (no. dist.) Calif. 1974, U.S. Ct. Appeals (9th cir.) 1974, U.S. Supreme Ct. 1996. Assoc. Pettit & Martin, San Francisco, 1973-79, ptnr., 1980-92, counsel, 1993-95, Collette & Erickson LLP, San Francisco, 1995-2000; regional counsel The Nature Conservancy, San Francisco, 2000—. Bd. dirs. City Celebration, Inc., San Francisco, 1984-91, pres., 1989-91. Recipient Service award Calif. Nature Conservancy, 1987. Mem. ABA, Calif. State Bar Assn., San Francisco Bar Assn., Nat. Assn. Installation Devel. (regional dir. 1993-2000), Order of coif. Democrat. Office: The Nature Conservancy 201 Mission St 4th Fl San Francisco CA 94105

HUNTER, WILLIAM JAY, JR., lawyer; b. Champaign, Ill., Sept. 19, 1944; s. William Jay and Joan Edna (Werstler) H.; m. Jennifer Diane Newcomer, Jan. 3, 1970; children: Matthew Jay, Amy Elizabeth, Nathan Andrew. BA in Econs., Northwestern U., 1965; JD, George Washington U., 1974. Bar: D.C. 1975, U.S. Dist. Ct. D.C. 1975, U.S. Ct. Appeals (D.C. and 5th cirs.) 1978, U.S. Supreme Ct. 1978, U.S. Ct. Appeals (9th cir.) 1980, U.S. Ct. Appeals (7th dir.) 1986, Ky. 1988, U.S. Ct. Appeals (6th cir.) 1992. From assoc. to ptnr. Howrey & Simon, Washington, 1974-86; v.p., gen. counsel, sec. Capital Holding Corp. (now Aegon USA), Louisville, 1987-88; dep. gen. counsel I.C.H. Corp., Louisville, 1989-92; ptnr. Middleton Reutlinger, Louisville, 1992—2003, Stoll, Keenon & Park, Louisville, 2003—. Designer of pension products; antitrust lawyer; contbr. numerous articles to profl. jours. Mem. Jefferson County AIDS Task Force, Louisville, 1988. 1st lt. U.S. Army, 1968-70, Korea. Democrat. Christian. Avocations: skiing, running, gardening. Home: 2540 Ransdell Ave Louisville KY 40204-2115 Office: 2650 Aegon Ctr 400 W Market St Louisville KY 40202 Office Phone: 502-568-9100. Business E-Mail: hunter@skp.com.

HUNTER, WILLIAM PAUL, agricultural studies educator; b. Parsons, Kans., Oct. 18, 1952; s. Paul William and Helen (Ruhamah) Hunter. BS in Agr., Kans. State U., 1974; MS in Agrl. Edn., U. Mo., 1981, PhD in Agrl. Edn., 1983. Tchr. Burlingame (Kans.) HS, 1974—75, Westmoreland (Kans.) HS, 1975—77, Salisbury (Mo.) HS, 1977—81; rsch. asst. Instrnl. Materials Lab. U. Mo., Columbia, 1981—83; curriculum specialist vocat. agr. svc. U. Ill., Urbana-Champaign, 1983—90, agrl. comm. specialist, 1991—93; instr. Pratt (Kans.) CC, 1993—. Part-time instr. Parkland Coll., Champaign, 1985—93; computer cons., Champaign, 1987—93; trainer Ill. Computer Corp., Monticello, 1992—93. 2d v.p. Sunflower Resource Conservation and Devel. Area, Harper, Kans., 1996—98, 1st v.p., 1998—; Sunday sch. tchr., choir mem., deacon 1st So. Bapt. Ch., Pratt. Mem.: Assn. Career and Tech. Edn., Kans. Assn. Agrl. Educators, Nat. Assn. Agrl. Educators (asst. v.p. Region II 2001—03, v.p. 2003—). Republican. Avocations: golf, travel, genealogy. Home: 408 S Pine St Pratt KS 67124 Office: Pratt CC 348 NE SR 61 Pratt KS 67124

HUNTER BLAIR, PAULINE CLARKE, author; b. Kirkby-in-Ashfield, Eng., May 19, 1921; d. Charles Leopold and Dorothy Kathleen (Milum) Clarke; m. Peter Hunter Blair, Feb., 1969. BA with honors, Somerville Coll., Oxford U., Eng., 1943. Free-lance writer, 1948—. Lectr. Author (writing as Pauline Clarke): (novels) The Pekinese Princess, 1948, The Great Can, 1952, The White Elephant, 1952, Smith's Hoard, 1955, The Boy with the Erpingham Hood, 1956, Sandy the Sailor, 1956, James, The Policeman, 1957, James and the Robbers, 1959, Torolv The Fatherless, 1959, 2d edit., 1973, The Lord of the Castle, 1960, The Robin Hooders, 1960, James and the Smugglers, 1961, Keep the Pot Boiling, 1961, The Twelve and the Genii, 1962 (Libr. Assn. Carnegie medal, 1962, Lewis Carrol Shelf award, 1963, Deutsche Jugend Buchpreis, 1968), Silver Bells and Cockle Shells, 1962, James and the Black Van, 1963, Crowds of Creatures, 1964, The Bonfire Party, 1966, The Two Faces of Silenus, 1972; author: (under pseudonym Helen Clare) Five Dolls in a House, 1953, Merlin's Magic, 1953, Bel The Giant and Other Stories, 1956, Five Dolls and the Monkey, 1956, Five Dolls in the Snow, 1957, Five Dolls and Their Friends, 1959, Seven White Pebbles, 1960, Five Dolls and the Duke, 1963, The Cat and the Fiddle and Other Stories from Bel, the Giant, 1968; author: (writing as Pauline Hunter Blair) The Nelson Boy, 1999, A Thorough Seaman, 2000, Warscape, 2001, Jacob's Ladder, 2003; book reviewer, contbr.: Times Lit. Supplement. Mem.: Brit. Soc. Authors. Home: Church Farm House Bottisham Cambridge CB5 9BA England Office: care Curtis Brown Ltd Haymarket House 28/29 Haymarket London SW1Y 4SP England also: care John Cushman Assocs Inc 24 E 38th St New York NY 10016-2502 Office Phone: 01223/811223.

HUNTERTON, C. STANLEY, lawyer; BA, Syracuse (N.Y.) U., 1970, JD, 1974. Bar: Nev. Spl. atty. Organized Crine and Racketeering Sect. U.S. Dept. Justice, Detroit, 1975—78, Las Vegas, 1978—84; dep. chief counsel Pres.'s Commn. Organized Crime, 1984—85; atty. Hunterton and Assocs. Law Firm, 1986—2002; sr. v.p. Sierra Pacific Resources, Reno, 2002—, gen counsel, 2002—, corp. sec., 2002—. Spl. counsel Ethics Rev. Bd. City Las Vegas; mem. standing com. jud. ethics State Bar Nev., mem. election practice com. Master: Nev. Am. Inns Ct.; fellow: ACTL; mem.: Clark County Bar Assn. Avocations: tennis, golf. Office: Sierra Pacific Resources 6100 Neil Rd Reno NV 89511

HUNTINGTON, DAVID MACK GOODE, foundation administrator; b. Millsboro, Del., Dec. 18, 1926; s. M. Paul St. Agnan and Lona Marie (Goode) H.; m. Mary Elizabeth Putman, Dec. 3, 1955; children: James Barrett, Sarah Phelps Yannett, Samuel Porter. BA, Harvard U., 1949, EdM, 1954. Adminstrv. asst. customer rels. Irving Trust Co., N.Y.C., 1949-52; supr., speech therapist Martin Hall, Bristol, R.I., 1952-55; asst. dir. office student placement Harvard U., Cambridge, Mass., 1955-59; assoc. dean student dir. placement Grad. Sch. Bus. U. Chgo., 1959-64, assoc. dir. devel., 1965-67, dir. devel., asst, to dean div. biol. scis., exec. dir., sec. Cancer Rsch. Found., 1967-69; exec. dir., sec. Milw. Found., 1970-92, cons., 1993—; sec. Faye McBeath Found., 1970-86; adminstr. Walter & Olive Stiemke Found., 1970-84. Incorporator, hon. dir. Porter-Phelps-Huntington Found., Hadley, Mass.; bd. dirs. Shorewood Civic Improvement Found., 1973-83; chmn. com. on cmty. found. Coun. on Founds., 1980-81, mem. on-site cons. program; cons. new and revitalizing cmty. founds., 1986-89; founder, chmn., bd. dirs. Donor's Forum Wis.; trustee Mich. Cmty. Founds. Youth Project, 1990-93; bd. dirs. St. John's Home of Milw., 1994-2000, chmn. St John's Arts Bd., 1995-2000; bd. dirs. Trustees of Funds and Endowments, Inc., Episcopal Diocese of Mllw., 1997-2002, Sunrise Found., Inc., 1997—. Mem. Univ. Club, Harvard Club of Wis. Episcopalian. Home: 4043 N Lake Dr Milwaukee WI 53211-2145 Office: 1020 N Broadway Milwaukee WI 53202-3157

HUNTINGTON, EARL LLOYD, lawyer, retired gas industry executive; b. Orangeville, Utah, Sept. 2, 1929; s. Lloyd S. and Hannah Annette (Cox) H.; m. Phyllis Ann Reed; children: Jane, Ann, Stephen. BS, U. Utah, 1951, JD, 1956; LL.M., Georgetown U., 1959. Bar: Utah 1956, D.C. 1959, N.Y. 1966, Conn. 1988. Trial atty. Dept. Justice, Washington, 1956-63; counsel Texasgulf Inc., NYC, 1963-74, v.p., gen. counsel, 1974-81, sr. v.p., gen. counsel, 1981-90, also bd. dir., 1981-94; sr. v.p., gen. counsel, dir. Elf Aquitaine Inc., 1982-90, ret., 1990. Case note editor U. Utah Law Rev., 55-56. Served with U.S. Army, 1951-53. Mem. Monarch Country Club, Country Club Darien, Order of Coif, Phi Delta Phi, Beta Gamma Sigma.

HUNTINGTON, HILLARD GRISWOLD, economist; b. Boston, Apr. 10, 1944; s. Hillard Bell and Ruth Smedley (Wheeler) H.; m. Honor Mary Griffin, Sept. 30, 1972; children: Honora Redmond, Emma Anne Hillard. BS, Cornell U., 1967; MA, SUNY, Binghamton, 1972, PhD, 1974. Staff economist Fed. Energy Adminstrn., Washington, 1974-77; dir., sr. economist Data Resources, Inc., Washington, 1977-80; exec. dir. Energy Modeling Forum Stanford (Calif.) U., 1980—. Vol. U.S. Peace Corps., Pub. Utilities Authority, Monrovia, Liberia, 1967-69; vis. rsch. assoc. Inst. Devel. Studies, U. Nairobi, Kenya, 1972-73; mem. joint U.S.-U.S.S.R. Nat. Acad. Sci. Panel on Energy Conservation, 1986-90; peer rev. panel Nat. Acid Precipitation Assessment Program Task Force, Ctrs. for Excellence Govt. Can., Nat. Petroleum Coun., Commn. for Environ. Coop. N.Am.; cons. Argonne Nat. Lab., Electric Power Rsch. Inst., others. Editor Macroeconomic Impacts of Energy Shocks, 1987, N. Am. Natural Gas Markets: selected tech. studies, 1989, Designing Competitive Electricity Markets, 1998. Life fellow Clare Hall, Cambridge (Eng.) U. Sr.fellow U.S. Assn. for Energy Econs. (sr., pres. 1997), Internat. Assn. Energy Econs. (v.p. publs. 1990-92, program chmn. N.Am. conf., program chmn. internat. conf.), Am. Statis. Assn. (com. on energy stats. 1992-94), Am. Econ. Assn. Home: 305 Hermosa Way Menlo Park CA 94025-5821 Office: Stanford U 450 Terman Ctr Stanford CA 94305-4026 E-mail: hillh@stanford.edu.

HUNTINGTON, JAMES CANTINE, JR., retired equipment manufacturing company executive; b. Detroit, Mar. 21, 1928; s. James Cantine and Joanna (Donlon) H.; m. Bettyanne Hopkins, Sept. 21, 1973; children: James, Ann, Patricia, Carol, Judith, Amy. B.E.E., Cornell U., 1950. Mktg. exec. Harnischfeger Corp., Milw., 1953-62; cons. Milw., 1962-64; mgr. Colt Industries, Beloit, Wis., 1964-67; v.p., dir. Clark Equipment Co., Buchanan, Mich., 1967-76; sr. v.p. Am. Standard, Inc., 1976-88; ret., 1988. Served with AUS, 1945-47, 50-53. Mem. Constrn. Industry Mfrs. Assn., Delta Kappa Epsilon, Tau Beta Pi, Eta Kappa Nu. Home: 613 Twin Pine Rd Pittsburgh PA 15215-1568

HUNTINGTON, LAWRENCE SMITH, investment banker; b. NYC, June 13, 1935; s. Prescott B. and Sarah H. (Powell) H.; m. Olivia Hallowell (div.); children: Christopher Bowditch, Charles Stewart Butler, Matthew Hallowell; m. Caroline Ballard BA, Harvard U., 1957; LL.B., New York Law Sch., 1964, LLD (hon.), 1998. With Fiduciary Trust Co. Internat., N.Y.C., 1961-2000, pres., CEO, 1973-99, chmn. bd., CEO, 1983-2000. Dir. Bus. Execs. for Nat. Security, 1993-2000, Woods Hole Rsch. Ctr., 1994—, chmn., 1997—; bd. dirs. Continuum Health Ptnrs., 1996—. Bd. dirs. St. Luke's-Roosevelt Hosp., N.Y.C., 1974, chmn., 1975-81, 96-2001; bd. dirs. World Wildlife Fund, Washington, 1977-96, chmn., 1984-86, mem. nat. coun., 1996-2002; bd. dirs. Trinity Ch., N.Y.C.; bd. dirs. Citizens Budget Com., N.Y.C., 1970—, trustee, 1970—2004, chmn. 1978-84, The Commonwealth Fund, 1989—2004, N.Y. Law Sch., 1984—2004, chmn., 1992-97, Opsail, 1992—; mem. adv. bd. N.Y. State Common Retirement Fund Investment Com., 1981-87; dir. Josiah Macy, Jr. Found., 1981—2004; trustee Santa Fe Inst., 1988-98; trustee South Street Seaport, 1988—, chmn., 1999—, chair, 2004—; mem. adv. bd. NASD Internat. Mkts., 1994-99. Lt. USCG, 1959-61 Mem.: Explorers Club, N.Y. Yacht Club (trustee, commodore 2002—), Am. Alpine Club, Century Assn. Office Phone: 212-717-8633.

HUNTINGTON, ROBERT HOWARD, business management executive; b. Mpls., Mar. 25, 1955; s. Robert Howard and Cecelia (Benchak) H.; m. Susan Mary McCafferty; children: Ashley, Aidan. BA, Middlebury Coll., 1978, MA, 1983; MBA, Dartmouth Coll., 1985; EdD, Harvard U., 1997. Asst. mgr. Gen. Foods Corp., White Plains, NY, 1987—89, mgr., 1989—91, dir., 1991—96; v.p. Allied Domecq Quick Svc. Restaurants, White Plains, NY, 1996—. Tchg. fellow grad. sch. edn. Harvard U., Cambridge, Mass., 1991-92, instr. summer sch., 1991; tchg. asst. Harvard Ext. Sch., 1988-90; bd. trustees Lasell Coll., Newton, Mass., 1998—. Bd. dirs. First Parish Unitarian-Universalist, Medfield. Fellow: Phi Beta Kappa; mem.: Sierra Club. Home: 70 Adams St Medfield MA 02052-1614 Office: Allied Domecq Quick Svc Restaurants 14 Pacella Park Dr Randolph MA 02368-1773

HUNTINGTON, SAMUEL PHILLIPS, political science educator; b. N.Y.C., Apr. 18, 1927; s. Richard T. and Dorothy S. (Phillips) H.; m. Nancy Alice Arkelyan, Sept. 8, 1957; children: Timothy Mayo, Nicholas Phillips. BA, Yale U., 1946; MA, U. Chgo., 1948; PhD, Harvard U., 1951. Instr. govt. Harvard U., Cambridge, Mass., 1950-53, asst. prof. govt., 1953-58, prof., 1962—, Thomson prof. govt., 1967-81, Clarence Dillon prof. internat. affairs, 1981-82, Eaton prof. sci. of govt., 1982—, chmn. dept., 1982-95; Albert J. Weatherhead univ. prof., 1995—. Research assoc. def. policy Brookings Instn., Washington, 1952-53; faculty research fellow Social Sci. Research Council, N.Y.C., 1954-57; asst. dir. Inst. War and Peace Studies, Columbia U., 1958-59, research assoc., 1958-63, assoc. dir., 1959-62, assoc. prof. govt., 1959-62, Ford research prof., 1960-61; research assoc. Ctr. for Internat. Affairs, Harvard U., 1963-64, mem. faculty, 1964—, exec. com., 1966—, assoc. dir., 1973-78, acting dir., 1975-76, dir., 1978-89; dir. John M. Olin Inst. for Strategic Studies, 1989-2000; vis. fellow All Souls Coll., Oxford (Eng.) U., 1973; coordinator security planning Nat. Security Council, 1977-78; trustee Inst. Def. Analysis, 1985-98; cons. numerous govt. agys.; chmn. Harvard Acad. Internat. & Area Studies, 1996—. Author: The Soldier and the State, 1957, The Common Defense, 1961, Political Order in Changing Societies, 1968, American Politics: The Promise of Disharmony, 1981, The Third Wave: Democratization in the Late Twentieth Century, 1991, The Clash of Civilizations and the Remaking of the World Order, 1996; co-author: Political Power: USA-USSR, 1964, The Crisis of Democracy, 1975, No Easy Choice: Political Participation in Developing Countries, 1976; editor: Changing Patterns of Military Politics, 1962, The Strategic Imperative, 1982; co-editor: Foreign Policy (quar.), 1970-77, Authoritarian Politics in Modern Society, The Dynamics of Established One-Party Systems, 1970, Global Dilemmas, 1985, Reorganizing America's Defense, 1985, Understanding Political Development, 1986, Culture Matters: How Values Shape Human Progress, 2000; also articles. Chmn. coun. on Vietnamese studies S.E. Asia Devel. Adv. Group, 1966-69; mem. Presdl. Task Force on Internat. Devel., 1969-70, Commn. on U.S.-Latin Am. Rels., 1974-76, Commn. on Integrated Long-Term Strategy, 1986-88, Commn. on Protecting and Reducing Govt. Secrecy, 1995-97; trustee Internat. Devel. Found., 1969-76. Served with AUS, 1946-47. Recipient Silver Pen award Jour. Fund, 1960, Grawemeyer World Order award, 1992; fellow Ctr. for Advanced Study in Behavioral Scis., Stanford, 1969-70. Fellow Am. Acad. Arts and Scis.; mem. Internat. Polit. Sci. Assn. (coun. 1973-75), Coun. on Fgn. Rels., Interrnat. Inst. Strategic Studies, Am. Polit. Sci. Assn. (coun. 1969-71, v.p. 1984-85, pres.-elect 1985-86, pres. 1986-87). Office: Harvard Acad for Internat and Area Studies 1737 Cambridge St Cambridge MA 02138-3016

HUNTLEY, JAMES ROBERT, government official, international affairs scholar; b. Tacoma, July 27, 1923; s. Wells and Laura H.; m. Colleen Grounds Smith, May 27, 1967; children by previous marriage: Mark, David, Virginia, Jean. BA in Econs., Sociology magna cum laude, U. Wash., 1948, postgrad., 1951; MA in Internat. Rels., Harvard U., 1956. Cons. Wash. Parks Recreation Commn., Olympia, 1949-51; exch. of persons officer U.S. Fgn. Svc., Frankfurt, Nuremberg, Germany, 1952-54; dir. cultural ctr. USIA, Hof/Saale, Germany, 1954-55; USIA postgrad. scholar Harvard U., 1955-56; asst. to Pres.'s coord. for Hungarian relief Washington, 1956; European regional affairs officer USIA, Washington, 1956-58; dep. pub. affairs officer U.S. Mission to European Cmtys., Brussels, 1958-60; mem. U.S. Del. to Atlantic Congress, London, 1959; sec. organizing com. Atlantic Inst., Brussels and Milan, 1960, exec. officer and co-founder Paris, 1960-63; dir. Atlantic Inst. (N.Am. Office), Washington, 1963-65; founder, sec. Com. Atlantic Studies, 1963-65; sec. edn. com. NATO Parliamentarians Conf., Brussels, 1960-64; program assoc., internat. affairs divsn. Ford Found., N.Y.C., 1965-67; sec. gen. Coun. Atlantic Colls., London, 1967-68; ind. writer, cons., lectr., internat. affairs Guildford, England, 1968-74; founder, sec. Assn. Mid-Atlantic Clubs, 1970-74; founder, sec. gen. Standing Conf. Atlantic Orgns., 1972-74; rsch. fellow, sr. advisor to pres. on internat. affairs Battelle Meml. Inst., Seattle, 1974-83; pres., CEO Atlantic Coun. of U.S., Washington, 1983-85; ind. cons., author internat. affairs, 1985—. European corr., environ. affairs Saturday Rev./World, 1972-74; Corrs. World Wide, London, 1970-74; European corr. Non-Profit Report, 1970-74. Author: The NATO Story, 1965, (with W.R. Burgess) Europe and America - The Next Ten Years, 1970, Man's Environment and the Atlantic Alliance, 1972, Uniting the Democracies, 1980, Pax Democratica—A Strategy for the 21st Century, 1998, 2d edit., 2001; contbr. articles to profl. jours. Bd. dirs. Internat. Standing Conf. Phlanthropy, 1969-74, Assn. to Unite Democracies, 1976-94, Seattle Com. Fgn. Rels., 1975-78, World Affairs Coun. Seattle, 1975-83, adv. bd. 1986—, Bainbridge Island Land Trust, 1994-97; founding chmn. Coms. for a Cmty. of Democracies, 1979-92; co-founder 21st Century Found., 1987-91; mem. adv. bd. 21st Century Trust, London, 1988—; co-founder Next Century Initiative, 1992-95, New Century Initiative, 1996-99, pres. 1996-98; co-founder, v.p. Coun. for Cmty. of Democracies, 1999—. Carnegie fellow U. Wash., 1949-51; recipient Disting. Eagle Scout award 1995; named Kappa Sigma Man of Yr., 1999 Mem. Rainier Club (Seattle), DACOR (Washington). Home and Office: 1213 Towne Rd Sequim WA 98382-8849 E-mail: huntleypax@aol.com. *For a full life, embrace a worthy cause. Mine is the unity of the democracies. America's most precious asset is its free political system. It can be successfully defended only if we merge our force, our hearts and our fortune with like-minded peoples. Like-mindedness is not simply a gift of history; it must be cultivated. My life's aim has been to forge consensus among the democracies as a prelude to the creation of a free, just, and durable world order.*

HUNTLEY, ROBERT JOSEPH, management consultant; b. Rochester, N.Y., May 28, 1924; s. Carroll Thomas and Margaret (Mosier) H.; m. Patricia Ann Pss, Aug. 25, 1945; children: Timothy Robert, Debra Ann, Jon Joseph. Student, U. Redlands, 1943-44; BS, U. So. Calif., 1947, MS, 1952, D in Pub. Adminstrn., 1974. Mem. budget bur. City of L.A., 1947-52; asst. adminstrv. officer City of Beverly Hills (Calif.), 1952-56; city adminstr. City os Santa Paula (Calif.), 1957-58, City oa La Habra (Calif.), 1959-64; exec. Alpha Beta Amce Markets, La Habra, 1964-67; city adminstr. City of Westminster (Calif.), 1967-77; exec. asst. County of Orange (Calif.), 1977-80, chief labor rels., 1980-82, chief personnel ops., 1982-84; exec. dir. Hughes Enterprises, Laguna Hills, Calif., 1984-85. Lectr., U. So. Calif., 1953-58, 70-74, Ventura Coll., 1958; asst. prof. Calif. State U., Fullerton, 1964-65; lectr. Golden West Coll., Orange Coast Coll., Calif. State U. at Davis, prof. Calif. State U. at Long Beach, 1971-79. Author: History of Administrative Research, 1952, Public Relations Training, 1954, The American City Manager, 1974. Mem. pres. Mcpl. Water Dist. Orange County, 1989-95, Gov.'s Policy Com. Local Govt. Reform Task Force, 1973; active United Crusade. With USN, 1941-45; PTO. Mem. Am. Acad. Polit. and Social Sci., Am. Soc. Pub. Adminstrn., Western Govtl. Rsch. Assn., Internat. City Mgmt. Assn., League Calif. Cities (exec. com. 1964-72), Blue Key, Pi Sigma Alpha, Phi Kappa Tau. Republican. Roman Catholic. Home: 15172 Vermont St Westminster CA 92683-6136 Office: PO Box 430 Westminster CA 92684-0430

HUNTLEY, ROBERT STEPHEN, newspaper editor; b. Winston-Salem, N.C., Mar. 6, 1943; m. Linda Fabry; children: Kristine Elizabeth, Katherine Vallie. BA in Journalism, U. N.C., 1965. Reporter UPI, various locations, 1965-69, writer, editor broadcast and gen. news depts. Chgo., 1969-77, exec. editor nat. broadcast dept., 1977-78; bur. chief Commodity News Svc., Chgo., 1978-79, U.S. News & World Report, Chgo., 1979-82, assoc. editor Washington, 1982-85, sr. editor, 1985-86; reporter, rewrite specialist Chgo. Sun Times, 1986-90, met. editor, 1990-91, asst. mng. editor/metro, 1991-97; editl. page editor, 1997—. Bd. dirs. City News Bur., Chgo, 1993-97, pres., 1996; media fellow Hoover Instit. Stanford U., 2001 Author (with Truman K. Gibson): Knocking Down Barriers: My fight for Black America. V.p. Ill. Freedom of Info. Coun., 1994. Recipient Stick-O-Type award for feature writing Chgo. Newspaper Guild, 1987, Appreciation cert. for outstanding contbns. to freedom of info. Nat. Ctr. Freedom of Info. Studies at Loyola U.-Chgo., 1993. Office: Chgo Sun-Times 350 N Orleans Chicago IL 60654 Office Phone: 312-321-2535. Business E-Mail: shuntley@suntimes.com.

HUNTLEY, WILLIAM BARNEY, religious studies professor; b. Feb. 19, 1933; AB, Duke U; BD, Yale U; PhD, Duke U. Chaplain Westminster (Mo.) Coll., Mo., 1964-74, chmn. divsn. humanities, 1969-72, dean of students, 1972-74; assoc. dean Waseda U., Tokyo, 1986-87; chair dept. religious studies U. Redlands (Calif.), 1977-82, 84-86, 1997—, dir. Asian studies program, 1991—2002, Crawford prof. of religious studies, 2000—. Author: Experiencing Japan; contbr. articles to profl. jours. Scholar-in-residence Reitaku U., Kashiwa, Japan, 1988-89. Address: 1474 Pacific St Redlands CA 92373-6936 Office: U Redlands 1200 E Colton Ave PO Box 3080 Redlands CA 92373-0999 Office Phone: 909-793-2121. Office Fax: 909-793-2029.

HUNTLEY-WRIGHT, JOAN AUGUSTA (JOAN AUGUSTA HUNTLEY), musician; b. Tulsa, Aug. 17, 1934; d. John Augustus and Edna Ruby (Van Brunt) Murphy; m. Robert Walter Huntley, Sept. 6, 1955 (div. Feb. 14, 1981); children: Robert John, Gene Bush, Dawn Elise, Ben Patrick; m. Wilfred Cleveland Wright, Sept. 13, 1992 (dec. Apr. 2001). Student, New Eng. Conservatory, 1952-53, U. Tulsa, 1953-54, Boston U. & N.E. Conservatory, 1954-55, Roosevelt U., Chgo., 1970-72, Thronton C.C., 1970-72; B in Violin Performance, New Eng. Conservatory Music, 1981; M in Violin Performance, U. Mass., Lowell, 1990. Violinist Tulsa Philharm. Symphony, 1949-52, 53-54; first violinist Tassan Quartet, Chgo., 1962-64, Hucasa Trio, Chgo., 1964-72; concert mistress, leader of various orchestras and chamber ensembles, 1964—; artist in residence Thornton C.C., Harvey, Ill., 1968-72; first violinist Bowforte Ensemble, Boston, 1973-81; assoc. prof. Berklee Coll. of Music, Boston, 1985-91. Designed, tchr. pre-sch. instrumental and ear tng. classes Raygor Day Sch., Matteson, Ill, 1963-65, Humpty-Dumpty and YMCA Nursery Schs., Beverly, Mass., 1976-78; organizer benefit concerts for tornado victims, Ill., 1968. Creator, performer radio program Music Personalities KAKC, Tulsa, 1953; mgr., music dir., founder LaFemme/LaFemme Women Composers Ensemble, 1990-95; soloist Tulsa Philharm., 1952, Park Forest (Ill.) Symphony, 1958, 60, 62, Salem (Mass.) Philharm., 1981, 89; performer with Phila. Piano Quartet, 1997-99, Charlotee (Fla.) Symphony Orch., 2001— Mem. Ill. Constitutional Com.; active in Boy Scouts Am. and Girl Scouts; active in PTA. Recipient Profl. Devel. award Mass. Assn. Women in Edn., 1995. Mem. AAUW, S.W. Fla. Symphony. Avocations: avid reader, walking, working out. Office Phone: 978-973-1860. E-mail: wcompwill@cs.com.

HUNTOON, ABBY ELIZABETH, artist, educator; b. Providence, R.I., Sept. 8, 1951; d. William Huntoon and Marjorie (Aldrich) Bradshaw; m. Phil Kaelin, Sept. 25, 1993. BS, Trinity Coll., 1973; MFA from program in Artisanry, Boston U., 1985. Instr. Boston U., 1983-84; co-owner, adminstr., tchr. Sawyer St. Studios, South Portland, Maine, 1989—. Project coord. Main Coll. of Art, 1988, mem. Maine Arts Commn., Visual Arts Panel, 1988-92; summer instr. Maine Coll. of Art, 1989, 90; workshop conductor Maine Coll. of Art, 1989, 95, U. Southern Maine, 1991. Artist: works exhibited at Makers 86, Bowdoin Mus. of Art, Brunswick, Maine, 1986, Ceramics Now, 27th Ceramic Nat. Exhibition (traveling U.S. for 2 years), 1987, Maine Coast Artists, Portland, Maine, 1988, 46th Ceramics Annual, Lang Art Gallery, Scripps Coll., Claremont, Calif., 1990; Northeastern Splendor (chosen ceramics rep. from Maine) Boston, 1991, Makers 93, Portland Mus. of Art, 1993; one person shows Architectural Ceramics, Frick Gallery, Belfast, Maine, 1990, 93; two person show Lakes Gallery, South Casco, Maine, 1995, Old York Hist. Soc., 1997, Round Top Ctr. for the Arts, 1997, Robert Clements Gallery, Portland, 1997; corp. collections include Putnam Hayes and Bartlett Inc., Cambridge, Mass., Standish Ayer and Wood, Boston, The Index Group Inc., Cambridge. Recipient Merit award Maine Crafts Assn., 1986; grantee: NEA, 1988. Avocations: sailing, skiing, political activities. Office: Sawyer Street Studios 131 Sawyer St South Portland ME 04106-2127

HUNTRESS, WESLEY THEODORE, JR., research scientist; b. Washington, Apr. 11, 1942; s. Wesley Theodore and Elizabeth Agnes (Moran) H.; m. Roseann Albano, June 22, 1973; 1 child, Garret. BS, Brown U., 1964; PhD, Stanford U., 1968. Scientist Jet Propulsion Lab., Pasadena, Calif., 1968-88; dep. dir earth sci. NASA, Washington, 1988-90, dir. solar system exploration, 1990-93, assoc. adminstr. space sci., 1993-98; dir. geophys. lab. Carnegie Instn. Washington, 1998—. Office: Geophys Lab Carnegie Instn Washington 5251 Broad Branch Rd NW Washington DC 20015-1305

HUNTSBERGER, THOMAS ALLEN, lawyer; b. Palo Alto, Calif., Apr. 22, 1949; s. Ralph Francis and Margaret Ruth (Kroener) H.; m. Barbara Doyle, May 12, 1973; children: Briana, Jenna, Alex. AB, Harvard U., 1972; JD, U. Oreg. Law Sch., 1976. Assoc. Ackerman & Dewenter, Springfield, Oreg., 1977-80; ptnr. Ackerman, Dewenter & Huntsberger, Springfield, 1981-96, Thomas A. Huntsberger, PC, Springfield, 1996—. Trustee U.S. Trustees Office, Eugene, Oreg., 1980. Mem. Oreg. State Bar, Lane County Bar (bankruptcy com. 1986). Democrat. Episcopalian. Home: 2212 Agate St Eugene OR 97403-1761 Office: Thomas A Huntsberger PC 870 W Centennial Blvd Springfield OR 97477-2835 Fax: 541-746-3201. E-mail: tahunts@callatg.com.

HUNTSMAN, JON MEADE, JR., governor, former federal agency administrator; b. Palo Alto, Calif., Mar. 26, 1960; s. Jon Meade and Karen (Haight) H.; m. Mary Katherine Cooper, Nov. 18, 1983; children: Mary Anne, Abigail, Elizabeth, Jon III. AB, U. Pa., 1987. Spl. asst. to chmn. Rep. Nat. Com., Washington, 1982; staff asst. The White House, Washington, 1983; state dir. UT Reagan-Bush campaign, Salt Lake City, 1984; v.p., dir. Huntsman Pacific Chem. Corp., Taipei, Taiwan, 1987-88; dep. asst. sec. Internat. Trade Administrn., Washington, 1989-90; dep. asst. sec. commerce for E. Asia and Pacific Affairs US Dept. Commerce, Washington, 1990-91; US amb. to Singapore US Dept. State, 1992—93; dep. US trade rep. & US trade amb. Office U.S. Trade Rep., Washington, 2001—03; chmn., CEO Huntsman Family Holdings Co. LLC, 2003—04; gov. State of UT, Salt Lake City, 2005—. Chmn. U.S.-China Comml. Commn. Groups, Washington, 1990-91, U.S.-Mongolia Trade Facilitation Group, 1990-91; exec. sec. U.S.-Thailand Joint Comml. Commn., 1990-91, U.S. Pacific Islands Joint Comml. Commn., 1990-91; pres., CEO Huntsman Cancer Found., 1995-2001. State dir. Utah Reagan-Bush campaign, Salt Lake City, 1984; chmn. Utah Reagan-Bush Inaugural Com., Salt Lake City, 1985; nat. del. Rep. Conv., 1984, 86. Mem. Internat. Club Washington, Asia Soc. Republican. Mem. Lds Ch. Office: Office of Gov UT E Office Bldg Ste E220 PO Box 142220 Salt Lake City UT 84114

HUNTSMAN, LAWRENCE DARROW, lawyer, director; b. Jan. 21, 1934; s. Orson Lawrence and Vera Maude (Day) H.; m. Lynn Maroe; children by previous marriage: Laura, Kathleen, Marguerite, Holbrook. Bar: Va. 1959, D.C. 1961. Clk. D.C. Superior Ct., 1959-60; asst. corp. counsel D.C., 1960-64, Miller, Brown & Gildenhorn, 1964-69; ptnr. Brown, Gildenhorn & Statland, Washington, 1969-75; pres. Pan Mediterranean Shipping Corp., 1975-82, Assorted Techs. Inc., 1994-97; dir. Ashley Corp.; gen. counsel KeyByte Techs., Inc., 1993-97. Mem. D.C. Bar Assn., Va. Bar Assn. Home: 223 Harpers Ferry Dr Locust Grove VA 22508 Office: 223 Harpers Ferry Dr Locust Grove VA 22508-5149 E-mail: ldhuntsman@earthlink.net.

HUNTSMAN, LEE L., former academic administrator, director; BSc in elec. engring., Stanford U., 1963; PhD in biomedical engring., U. Pa., 1968. Dir, ctr. for bioengineering U. Wash., 1980—96, assoc. dean for sci. affairs, sch. of medicine, 1993—96, provost, v.p. acad. affairs Seattle, 1997—2002, interim pres., 2002—03, pres., 2003—04, pres. emeritus, 2004—. Mem. Whitaker Found. Governing Com., 1994—98; chmn. Working Gorup on Rev. of Bioengineering and Tech. Instrumentation Develop. Rsch. for the Ctro for Sci. Rev of the NIH, 1998. Fellow: Am. Ins. of Med. and Biol. Engring., Am. Assn. for the Advancement of Sci.

HUNTWORK, JAMES RODEN, lawyer; b. Milw., May 6, 1948; s. Daniel Lawrence and Gladys (Roden) H.; m. Patience Tipton Huntwork, July 7, 1972; children: Andrew Stuart, Sarah Noel. BA with distinction, Shimer Coll., 1968; JD, Yale U., 1972, MA Econs., 1973. Bar: Mass. 1972, Ariz. 1977. Atty. Sullivan & Worcester, Boston, 1972-77, Jennings, Strouss & Salmon, Phoenix, 1977-91, Fennemore Craig, Phoenix, 1992-98, Salmon, Lewis & Weldon, Phoenix, Ariz., 1998—. Dir. exec. com. Phoenix Econ. Growth Corp., 1987-91; state ballot security chmn. Ariz. Rep. Party, Phoenix, 1992—; originator The Comml. Law Project for Ukraine, 1991—; mem. Ariz. Ind. Redistricting Commn., 2000—. Co-recipient Judge Learned Hand Human Rels. award Am. Jewish Com., 1992. Mem. ABA, Ariz. Bar Assn., Maricopa County Bar Assn., Phoenix C. of C. (N.Am. Free Trade Task Force 1991-95). Republican. Office: Ste 200 2850 E Camelback Rd Phoenix AZ 85016-4316 Business E-Mail: jrh@slwplc.com. E-mail: jrh@huntwork.net.

HUNWICK, JOHN OWEN, history professor, language educator; b. Chard, England; arrived in U.S., 1981; s. Cyril Owen Hunwick and Doris Louise Miller; m. Uwa Udensi Hunwick, July 2, 1966; children: Yvette, Ann-Claire, David; children: Joseph, Maryam. BA, U. London, 1959, PhD, 1974. Tchr. English Alfred Sch. Boys, Omdurman, Sudan, 1959—60; lectr. U. Ibadan, Nigeria, 1960—67; lectr. Arabic Sch. Oriental and African Studies U. London, 1967—69; prof. history, prof. religion U. Ghana, Accra, Ghana, 1969—77; dir. Arabic Lang. Unit Am. U., Cairo, 1977—81; prof. history Northwestern U., Evanston, Ill., 1981—, interim dir. African Studies Program, 1987—89. Author: Shari'a in Songham, 1984, Arabic Literature of Abia vol. II, 1993, vol. IV, 2003; translator: Timbuktu of the Songhay Empire, 1999; co-author: The Africa Diaspora - The Mediterranean Lands of Islam, 2002. Lt. Somaliland Scouts, 1955—56. Mem.: Inst. Study Islamic Thought in Africa (emeritus dir.), African Studies Assn. (Text prize 2001). Home: 9057 Tamaroa Terrace Skokie IL 60076 Office: Program African Studies 620 Library Place Evanston IL 60208

HUNZICKER, WARREN JOHN, retired cardiologist, medical educator, consultant, health facility administrator; b. Lawrence, Kans., Sept. 26, 1920; s. Carl John and Edith (Glenn) H.; m. Marjorie Jean Owen, Apr. 16, 1946; children— Karen Hunzicker Putnam, Kathleen Ann AB, U. Kans., 1942, MD, 1944; postgrad. in medicine, Harvard U. Hosps., Peter Bent Brigham and Boston City Hosps., 1946-48. Intern St. Luke's Hosp., 1944-45; practice medicine specializing in cardiology Spokane, Wash., 1948-51, 54-58; med. dir. Nat. Life & Accident Co., Nashville, 1958-60; v.p., med. dir. Kansas City Life, Mo., 1960-80; sr. v.p. med. N.Am. Reassurance, N.Y.C., 1980-86. Assoc. clin. prof. medicine U. Mo., Kansas City, 1961-82; dir. M.I.B. Inc., Boston; med. cons. Life Ins. Med. Research Fund, Washington, 1983-97; bd. dirs. Kansas City Life Ins. Co. Contbr. articles to profl. jours. Served to lt. M.C., USNR, 1941-46, 52-53, Korea Levine fellow in cardiology Harvard U. (Peter Bent Brigham Hosp.), 1951-52 Fellow Am. Coll. Cardiology; mem. AMA, Council Life Ins. (chmn. med. sect. 1971-72), Assn. Ins. Med. Dirs. (exec. council 1971-73), Mo. Med. Assn., Union League of N.Y.C. Republican. Methodist. Avocation: fishing.

HUO, BONNIE KWAN, artist; b. China, Nov. 23, 1949; d. Hok Pui and Tai Wah (Wong) Kwan; m. Rex W.C. Huo, Feb. 10, 1972; 1 child, Alina. BA, U. Calif., Berkeley, 1971; postgrad. diploma in edn., U. Hong Kong, 1972. Sole proprietor Anything Aesthetic, Hong Kong, 1987—. One-woman exhibits include Kowloon Shangrila Hotel, Hong Kong, 1989, Shenzhen Art Mus., China, 1993, Letty's Gallery, Vancouver, 1994, Pristine Harmony Art Ctr., Taipei, 1995, Modest Art Gallery, Toronto, Traditional Chinese Cultural Soc., Montreal, 1996, Melbourne Chinese Mus. & Sydney Chinese Culture Ctr., 1998, World Jour. Gallery, San Francisco, 2000, World Jour. Gallery, L.A., U. Indpls., Shenzhen Art Mus., 2003; represented in permanent collections Singapore Nat. Mus., Shenzhen Art Mus., Australia Chinese Mus., U. Indpls., Sotheby's Fine Modern Chinese Painting Auction. Recipient Cert. of Honor Suprs. of City and County of San Francisco and numerous art awards. Mem. Hong Kong Lingnan Art Assn. (vice chair), Fedn. Can. Artists, Hong Kong Lan Ting Soc. (v.p.), Internat. Calligraphy Alliance (Hong Kong chpt.), Hong Kong Arts Develop. Coun. (examiner). Avocations: travel, attending cultural events, reading, poetry. Fax: (852) 2838-9362. E-mail: ufomail@netfront.net.

HUO, YANGCHUNG PAUL, business educator; b. Taichung, Taiwan, July 2, 1955; s. Ya-Fei Huo and Hua-Ying Tang; m. Yulin Alice Jen, Aug. 8, 1981; children: George, Dennis, Andrew. BSEE, Nat. Taiwan U., Taipei, 1977; MBA, Nat. Chengchi U., Taipei, 1979; PhD in Bus. Adminstrn., U. Calif., Berkeley, 1987. Asst. prof. Calif. State U., Chico, 1986—88, Wash. State U., Pullman, 1988—94, assoc. prof., 1994—97; Jewett disting. prof. U. Puget Sound, Tacoma, 1997—2002, dir. Sch. Bus. and Leadership, 2000—02; dean Sch. Bus. U. Bridgeport, Conn., 2003—. Bd. dirs. East Fairfield County United Way, Bridgeport, 2004—; mem. adv. bd. Am. Culture Exch., Seattle, 1999—2004. Recipient Best Paper award, SW Acad. Mgmt. Ann. Conf., 1990, Top Performer award educators' divsn., AT&T Collegiate Investment Challenge, 1991. Mem.: Fedn. Bus. Disciplines, Assn. NE Bus. Deans, Acad. Mgmt. Office: U Bridgeport 230 Park Ave Bridgeport CT 06601

HUPFER, CHARLES J., manufacturing executive; b. Lincolnton, NC; BS in Acctg., U. NC, Chapel Hill; MBA, U. NC, Charlotte. CPA, cert. mgmt. acct. With Sonoco Products Co., Hartsville, SC, 1975—79, from dir. internat. fin. and acctg. to treas., 1980—95, CFO, v.p., corp. sec., 2002—. Office: Sonoco Products Co N 2d St Hartsville SC 29551-0160

HUPP, JAMES R., dean, dental educator; b. Iron Mountain, Mich. m. Carmen Hupp, June 19, 1976; children: Jamie, Justin, Joelle, Jordan. BS in biol. sciences, U. Calif., Irvine, 1973; DMD cum laude, Harvard Sch. Dental Medicine, 1977; MD, U. Conn. Sch. Medicine, 1982; JD, Rutgers U., Newark, 1995; MBA, Loyola U., 2000. Diplomate American Board of Oral and Maxillofacial Surgery, 1982. Resident in oral-maxillofacial surgery U. Conn. Sch. Dental Medicine, 1980; intern in internal medicine UCLA Med. Ctr., 1983; asst. prof. dept. oral-maxillofacial surgery Vanderbilt U. Sch. Medicine, Nashville, 1983—85; chief oral-maxillofacial surg. svc. V.A. Med. Ctr., Nashville, 1983—85; dir. oral-maxillofacial surg. svc. Met. Nashville Gen. Hosp., 1983—85; asst. prof. dept. surgery U. Conn. Sch. Medicine, 1985—89; asst. prof. dept. oral-maxillofacial surgery U. Conn. Sch. Dental Medicine, 1985—89; assoc. chief of staff, J. Dempsey Univ. Hosp. U. Conn. Health Ctr., 1987—89, dir. oral-maxillofacial surgery residency, 1988—89; chair, assoc. prof. oral-maxillofacial surgery U. Medicine and Dentistry N.J., 1989—94, dir. oral-maxillofacial surgery residency program, 1992—93, chair dept. dental medicine, 1994, dir. divsn. oral-maxillofacial surgery, Univ. Hosp., 1994; chair, prof. oral-maxillofacial surgery U. Md. Dental Sch., Baltimore, 1994—2002; chair dept. dentistry U. Md. Med. System, Baltimore, 1994—2002; CEO U. Md. Oral-Maxillofacial Surgical Associates, 1994—2002; dir. oral-maxillofacial surgery residency program U. Md. Med. Ctr., Baltimore, 1996—99, 2001; dean U. Miss. Sch. Dentistry, 2002—, prof. oral-maxillofacial surgery, 2002—. Mem. editl. bd. Oral Surgery, Oral Medicine and Oral Pathology, 1993—; team dentist Baltimore Ravens, NFL, 1996—97; adj. prof. oral surgery/pharmacology U. Pa. Sch. Dental Medicine, 1997—. Fellow: Pierre Fauchard Acad., Am. Assn. Oral and Maxillofacial Surgeons (mem. rsch. sect. 1985—), Am. Coll. Surgeons, Am. Coll. Dentists; mem.: Am. Assn. Dental Rsch., Internat. Assn. Dental Rsch., AMA, ADA, Am. Dental Edn. Assn., Am. Bd. Oral and Maxillofacial Surgeons (dir. 1996—, mem. fin. com. 1999—, mem. exec. com. 2000—, sec.-treas. 2000—01, v.p. 2001—02, pres. 2002—03). Office: 2500 N State St Jackson MS 39216

HUPPE, ALEX, public relations executive; b. Princeton, NJ, June 18, 1947; s. Bernard F. and Mary Lois (McMaster) Huppe. BA with honors, Harpur Coll., 1969; MA, U. Va., 1971. Prof. English Western Piedmont C.C., Morganton, NC, 1971-79, asst. to pres., 1979-80; asst. dean Boston U., 1980-85; dir. news Dartmouth Coll., Hanover, N.H., 1985-95; dir. pub. affairs Harvard U., Cambridge, Mass., 1995—99, v.p., cons., 1999—. Rschr. Smith/Huppe Rsch., Boston, 1980—85; adj. prof. English Maine Maritime Acad., 2002—; adv. bd. Harpur Coll., 1998—. Co-author: (book) Alaska National Communication Program, 1982. Pres. River City Arts, 1993—95; bd. dirs. SUNY Binghamton Alumni, 2003—; chmn. bd. dirs. Celo Health and Edn. Corp., Burnsville, NC, 1973—78; bd. dirs. Assocs. Boston Pub. Libr., 1997—2002, Castine Hist. Soc., 2001—. Mem.: NATAS (New Eng. chpt. gov. 1983—87, dir., Disting. Svc. award 1987), Ivy League News Dirs. (sec. 1988—91), Pub. Rels. Soc. Am. (exec. bd. counselors higher edn. 1998). Avocations: sailing, skiing, auto restoration. Personal E-mail: alexhuppe@aol.com.

HUPPER, JOHN ROSCOE, retired lawyer; b. NYC, June 16, 1925; s. Roscoe Henderson and Dorothy Wallace (Healy) Hupper; m. Joyce Shirley McCoy, June 14, 1952; children: John R. Jr., Gail J., Craig W. AB, Bowdoin Coll., 1949; LLB, Harvard U., 1952. Bar: N.Y. 1954, U.S. Supreme Ct. 1960. Assoc. Cravath, Swaine & Moore LLP, N.Y.C., 1952—60, ptnr., 1961—95; ret., 1996—. Trustee Allen-Stevenson Sch., 1968—96; bd. dirs. Travelers Aid Soc., NY, 1962—79, Legal Aid Soc., N.Y.C., 1971—76; overseer Bowdoin Coll., 1970—82, trustee, 1982—95. With U.S. Army, 1943—46. Fellow: Am. Coll. Trial Lawyers; mem.: ABA, N.Y. Supreme Ct. (mem. com. character and fitness appellate divsn. 1st dept. 1992—, spl. master 1982—), Assn. Bar City of N.Y., N.Y. State Bar Assn., Down Town Assn., Union Club, Univ. Club, Apawamis Club. Republican. Home: 105 E 67th St New York NY 10021-5901 Office: Cravath Swaine and Moore LLP 825 8th Ave New York NY 10019-7475 Office Phone: 212-474-1313.

HUR, STEPHEN PONYI, civil engineer, management consultant, educator; b. Beijing, Hopei, China, Jan. 27, 1947; came to U.S., 1982; s. Mingan and Wenshien (Lu) H.; m. Lian Lihua Chiang, Mar. 8, 1975; children: Harry Yenhung, Cathy Chiayi. BS, Chungyuan U., 1968; MSCE, W. Va. U., 1973; Mgmt. Devel. Program cert., Taiwan U., 1982. Civil engr. Asia Cement Corp., Hsinchu, Taiwan, 1969-71; plant engr. Oriental Chem. Fiber Corp., Hsinchu, 1973-76; assoc. prof., chmn. civil engring. dept. Minghsin Coll. Engring., Hsinchu, 1976-78; gen. mgr. Join Engring. Cons., Taipei, 1978-83; sec., treas. Postech Construction Co., Belmont, Calif., 1983-86; pres. Standard Products, Foster City, Calif., 1984—. Tech. adviser Pacific Camus Corp., Taipei, 1979-82; v.p. Long Bon Development Co., Taiwan, 1992—; mng. dir. Long Jee Holding Co., Malaysia, 1999—; chmn. Ko Hun Construction Co., Taiwan, 2000—; lectr. civil engring. dept. Tankang U., Taipei, 1980-90. Author: Construction Management, 1977, Modern Masonry, 1980, Small R.C. Building Design, 1981, Industrialized Housing, 1981, Small Business in USA, 1988, The English-Speaking Chinese, 1990, The Story of English Language, 1991. Mem. Am. Concrete Inst., Soc. Theoretical and Applied Mechanics, Chinese Inst. Engrs., The Smithsonian Assn., People to People Internat., Internat. Platform Assn. Avocation: chinese classical music and opera. Office: Standard Products 999C Edgewater Blvd # 171 San Mateo CA 94404-3777 also: Long Jee Holding Co 22-01A 165 Jalan Ampang Kuala Lumpur 50450 Malaysia E-mail: pyhur@mstc.kohun.com.tw.

HUR, SU-RYONG, physician, anesthesiologist; b. Korea, Feb. 8, 1942; s. Hyung Keun and JaeKyung (Kim) H.; m. Myung Ja; children: Jennifer, Steven, Michelle. MD, Seoul Nat. U., 1966. Diplomate Am. Bd. Anesthesiology. Intern Union Hosp., Fall River, Mass., 1966-67; resident St. Vincent's Hosp, Worcester, Mass., 1967-68, Mass. Gen. Hosp., Boston, 1968-71; staff anesthesiologist St. Michael's Hosp., 1975—; asst. prof. anesthesiology Med. Coll. Wis., 1971-75, mem. clin. faculty anesthesiology, 1976—, asst. prof. anesthesiology Milw., 2005—; staff anesthesiologist Firoedtert Meml. Luth. Hosp., 2004—. Contbr. articles to profl. jours. Fellow Am. Coll. Anesthesiologists; mem. AMA, Internat. Anesthesia Rsch. Soc., Am. Soc. Anesthesiologists, Korean Am. Med. Assn., Wis. Soc. Anesthesiologists, State Med. Soc. of Wis., Med. Soc. of Milw. County, Milw. Soc. of Anesthesiologists. Office: Anesthesia Dept Froedtert Luth Meml Hosp 9200 W Wisconsin Ave Milwaukee WI 35296-4999 Office Phone: 414-805-6100. Home Fax: 262-241-3415; Office Fax: 414-805-6147.

HURAS, WILLIAM DAVID, retired bishop; b. Kitchener, Ont., Can., Sept. 22, 1932; s. William Adam and Frieda Dorothea (Rose) H.; m. Barbara Elizabeth Lotz, Oct. 5, 1957; children— David, Matthew, Andrea. BA, Waterloo Coll., Ont., 1954; BD, Waterloo Sem., Ont., 1963; MTh, Knox Coll., Toronto, Ont., 1968; MDiv, Waterloo Luth. U., 1973; DD (hon.), Wilfred Laurier U., Waterloo, 1980, Huron Coll., London, Ont., 1989. Ordained to ministry Luth. Ch. in Am., 1957. Pastor St. James Luth. Ch., Refrew, Ont., 1957-62, Advent Luth. Ch., North York, 1962-78; bishop Eastern Can. Synod Luth. Ch. in Am., Kitchener, 1978-85, Eastern Synod Evangel. Luth. Ch. in Can., 1986-98; ret., 1998. Exec. com. Can. sect. of Luth. Ch. in Am., 1969-79, Luth. Merger Commn., Can., 1978-85; pres. Luth. Coun. Can., 1985-88; chmn. Group Svcs. Inc., Evangelical Luth. Ch. in Can., 1993—2001; mem. Anglican-Luth. Jt. Working Group, 1995-2001. Bd. govs. Waterloo Luth. U., 1966-75, Waterloo Luth. Sem., 1973-75, 78-2004. Mem. Order of St. Lazarus of Jerusalem (Ecclesiastical Grand cross 1985). Lutheran. *We are called by God and God covets an affirmative response. To say "yes" to God is to say "yes" to all of life and to all of God's people.*

HURBURGH, CHARLES R., agricultural studies educator; BS in agrl. engring., Iowa State U., 1973, MS in agrl. engring., 1980, PhD in agrl. engring., 1981. Farm worker Hurburgh Family Farm, Iowa, 1972—76; grad. rsch. asst. Iowa State U., Iowa, 1976, instr., 1976—78, instr., tchr., rsch., 1978—82, asst. prof. to assoc. prof. to prof., tchr., rsch., 1982—; prof. in charge Iowa Grain Quality Initiative, Iowa, 1998—. Named Pro Farmer Man of Yr., State of Iowa, 1998; recipient Andersen Rsch. award, 2000, Leader award, Grain Elevator and Processing Soc. Industry, 2002. Mem.: Coun. on Near Infrared Spectroscopy, Internat. Diffuse Relectance Coun., Soc. for Applied Spectroscopy, Am. Oil Chemists Soc. (Outstanding Paper award 1989, Best Article, Protein Divsn. 1991), Grain Elevator and Processing Soc., Iowa Acad. Sci., Am. Soc. Cereal Chemists, Am. Soc. Agrl. Engrs. (Young Engr. of Yr., Mid-Ctrl. Region 1989, Young Engr. of Yr., Iowa Section 1989), Alpha Epsilon, Gamma Sigma Delta. Republican. Presbyn. Home: 2519 Meadow Glen Ames IA 50014 Office Phone: 515-294-8629. Office Fax: 515-294-6383. E-mail: churburghjr@mchsi.com.

HURD, BYRON THOMAS, retired publishing executive; b. Roseville, Mich., 1933; s. Clark Frank and Evelyn (Sybelden) H.; m. Barbara Jean Ekeroth; children: Thomas E., Roger A., J. Douglas, James B. BSBA in Advt. and Mktg., Wayne State U., 1954. Sales mgr. Detroit Free Press, 1954—55, Milne & Jones, Royal Oak, Mich., 1955—56, Detroit Times, 1956—59; account mgr. Milne Circulation Sales, Inc., Bloomfield Hills, Mich., 1959—65; agt. Bankers Life Co., Des Moines, 1965—66; promotion mgr. Chgo. Today, Chgo. Tribune, 1966—74; owner, cons. Circulation Specialists, Homewood, Ill., 1974—77; exec. dir. circulation The Star Newspapers, Chicago Heights, Ill., 1977—95; ret., 1995. Panelist, discussion leader, session master, com. mem. No. Ill. Newspapers Assn., DeKalb. Contbr. Publishers handbook, 1988. Elder, pres. governing bd. Flossmoor (Ill.) Cmty. Ch., 1988. Mem. Ctrl. States Circulation Mgrs. Assn., Suburban Newspapers Am. (conf., sem. com.), Audit Bur. Circulation (voting rep.), Circulation Mgmt. Ill., Rotary (dir. cmty. svc. 1978-79, dir. internat. svc. 1979-80, sec. 1981-82, v.p. 1982-83, pres. 1983-84, dist. dir. pub. rels. 1984-86, dist. govs. aide 1986-87, dist. dir. vocat. svc. 1987-88, host Soviet Emerging Leaders 1988, Finnish 1989, dist. dir. group study exch. with India 1990, dist. conf. com. master ceremonies 1987-88, dist. conf. com. chmn. 1989-90), Flossmoor Country Club (sports and pastimes com. 1988), Marietta Country Club, Internat. Golfing Fellowship of Rotary (life), U.S. Golfing Fellowship of Rotary (life) Avocations: golf, drawing, painting. Personal E-mail: bbhurd@clearsurf.com.

HURD, DAVID GARY, music educator, actor, musician; b. Utica, NY, July 6, 1947; s. Daniel and Helen Hurd; m. Diane Kenney (div.); children: Kristin, Erik; m. Julie Ann Selis; children: Kiera Lutz, Krystal Lutz, Lauren Lutz, Alex Lutz. BS in Music, SUNY, Potsdam, 1970; MA in Music Edn., Tchrs. Coll. Columbia U., 1973. Cert. in tchg. State of NY. Music tchr. New Rochelle Pub. Schs., New Rochelle, 1970; band dir. Nanuet Pub. Schs., NY, 1970—, dir. music, 1980—90. Actor, model River Rats Repertory Co., 1984—90. Actor: (commls.) Ky. Fried Chicken, Chevrolet, Mastercard, (HBO program) Tracey Ullman Show. Life mem. PTO, 1999. Nominee Art Educator of Yr., Rockland County Arts Coun., 2003; recipient Tchr. of Yr., Nanuet Schs., Rockland County, NY, 1975. Mem.: NY State, Rockland County Music Educators Assn. (past pres. 1989—95). Avocations: acting, modelling, trombone, trumpet. Home: 277 Martis Pl Mahwah NJ 07430 Office: Nanuet HS 103 Church St Nanuet NY 10954 Office Phone: 845-627-9827.

HURD, ERIC RAY, rheumatologist, internist, educator; b. Columbus, Kans., July 5, 1936; s. Myron Alexander and Isobel (Moore) H.; m. Beverly Jean Button, June 14, 1962; children: Sherryl Lynn, Susan Rae, Brent Eric. BS, U. Tulsa, 1958; MD, U. Okla., 1962. Intern St. John's Hosp., Tulsa, 1962-63, resident in internal medicine, 1963-65; research fellow U. Tex., Dallas, 1965-67, instr. internal medicine, 1967-68, asst. prof., 1968-73, assoc. prof., 1973-80, prof., 1980—. Cons. rheumatologist, attending physician Parkland, VA Hosps.; dir. John Peter Smith Hosp. Arthritis Clinic, Ft. Worth; chief rheumatology VA Hosp., 1982—, mem. immunology research merit rev. bd.; assoc. Baylor Arthritis Ctr., 1981—; mem. med. and sci. com. North Tex. Arthritis Found., bd. med. dirs., 1988—, chmn. profl. edn. com.; traveling guest lectr. Tex. Med. Assn., Belgium and Fed. Republic Germany, 1990. Contbr. articles to profl. jours. Served to maj. U.S. Army, 1963-74. Recipient Clin. Scholar award Arthritis Found., 1975-77; named Outstanding Cons. Faculty Mem. John Peter Smith Hosp., 1983-84, Outstanding Part-time Clin. Prof. John Peter Smith Hosp., 1989-90. Mem. ACP, Am. Assn. Immunologists, Am. Fedn. Clin. Research, Am. Rheumatism Assn. (cooperating clinics com. 1968-74, Founding Fellow 1986), Tex. Rheumatism Assn. (sec.-treas. 1976-79, 2d v.p. 1979-80), Tex. Med. Soc., Dallas County Med. Soc., Phi Eta Sigma. Democrat. Methodist. Office: Arthritis Ctrs Tex 712 N Washington Ave Ste 200 Dallas TX 75246-1632 Office Phone: 214-823-6503.

HURD, GALE ANNE, film producer; b. L.A., Oct. 25, 1955; d. Frank E. and Lolita (Espiau) H. Degree in econs. and communications, Stanford U., 1977. Dir. mktg. and publicity, co-producer New World Pictures, L.A., 1977-82; pres., producer Pacific Western Prodns., L.A., 1982—. Producer: (films) The Terminator, 1984 (Grand Prix Avoriaz Film Festival award), Aliens 1986 (nominated for 7 Acad. awards, recipient Best Sound Effects Editing award, Best Visual Effects award Acad. Picture Arts & Scis.), Alien Nation (Saturn award for best sci. fiction film), The Abyss, 1989 (nominated for 4 Acad. awards, Best Visual Effects award), The Waterdance, 1991 (2 TFP Spirit awards, 2 Sundance Film Festival awards), Cast a Deadly Spell, 1991 (Emmy award), Raising Cain, 1992, No Escape, 1994, Safe Passage (Beatrice Wood award for Creative Achievement), 1994, The Ghost and the Darkness,(Acad. award) 1996, The Relic, 1996, Going West in America, 1996, Dante's Peak, 1997, Virus, 1997, Dead Man on Campus, 1997, Armageddon, 1998, Dick, 1999, Clockstoppers 2002, The Hulk, 2003 (TV series) Adventure, Inc., 2002, Punisher, 2004, (TV pilot) Coven, 2004; exec. producer: (films) Switchback, 1997, Tremors, 1990, Downtown, 1990, Terminator 2, 1991 (winner 3 Acad. awards), Witch Hunt, 1994, Sugartime, 1995, Terminator 3, 2004, Punisher, 2004; creative cons. (TV program) Alien Nation, 1989-90. Juror Focus Student Film Awards, 1989, 90; chmn. Nicholl Fellowship Acad. Motion Picture Arts & Scis., 1989—; mem. Show Coalition, 1988—; mem. Hollywood (Calif.) Women's Polit. Com., 1987—; mem. U.S. Film Festival Juror; bd. dirs. IFP/West, Artists Rights Found.; trustee Am. Film Inst.; bd. dirs. L.A. Internat. Film Festival, Coral Reef Rsch. Found., Ams. for a Safe Future; mentor Peter Stark Motion Picture Producing Program, Sch. of Cinema-TV, U. of So. Calif., Women in Film Mentor Program. Recipient Spl. Merit award Nat. Assn. Theater Owners, 1986, Stanford-La Entrepreneur of Yr. award Bus. Sch. Alumni L.A., 1990, Fla. Film Festival award, 1994, Women in Film Crystal award, 1998, Ind. Vision award Temucala Film Festival, 2001, Nat. Bd. Rev. Prodr.'s award, 2004, Global Green Millennium award, 2004, Israel Film Festival Visionary award, 2004, Saturn awards, Donald Reed award, 2004; named Prodr. of Yr., Stunt Awards, 2003. Mem. AMPAS (prodr.'s br. exec. com. 1990—, chair festival grants com.), Am. Film Inst. (trustee 1989—), Americans for a Safe Future (bd. dirs. 1993—), Prodr.'s Guild Am. (bd. dirs.), Women in Film (bd. dirs. 1989-90, 2000—03), Inst. for Rsch. on Women and Gender (nat. adv. panel 1997-2000), Feminist Majority, The Ocean Consrvancy (bd. dirs. 2001—, Heal the Bay, Reef Check Internat. Seakeepers Soc., Mulholland Tomorrow, The Trusteeship, Explorers Club (N.Y.C.), Jamestowne Soc., Nat. Soc. DAR, Phi Beta Kappa. Avocations: scuba diving, paso fino horses. Office: Valhalla Motion Pictures 8530 Wilshire Blvd Ste 400 Beverly Hills CA 90211

HURD, HEIDI M., dean, humanities educator, law educator; b. Laramie, Wyo., Oct. 19, 1960; d. Carroll Parsons and Jeanne Marie H.; children: Gillian K.J. and Aidan A. (twins). BA with honors, Queen's U., Kingston, Ont., Can., 1982; MA, Dalhousie U., Halifax, N.S., Can., 1984; JD, U. So. Calif., L.A., 1988, PhD, 1992. Asst. prof. U. Pa. Law Sch., Phila., 1989-94, prof. law and philosophy, 1994—2002, assoc. dean, 1994-96, co-dir. Inst. Law and Philosophy, 1998—2000; Herzog rsch. prof. law U. San Diego, 2000—02; dean, prof. philosophy, David Baum prof. law U. of Ill. Coll. Law, 2002—. Vis. asst. prof. dept. philosophy U. Iowa, Iowa City, 1991-92; vis. prof. law U. Va. Law Sch., Charlottesville, 1997-98. Author: Moral Combat, 1999; contbr. articles to profl. jours. Office: U Illinois College Law Dean Office 504 E Pennsylvania Ave Champaign IL 61820-6909 Office Phone: 217-333-9857. E-mail: hhurd@law.uiuc.edu.

HURD, J. NICHOLAS, executive recruiting consultant, former banker; b. Boston, Dec. 10, 1942; m. Joan Hinton; children: Jennifer H. Auber, Marshall H., P. MacKenzie. BA in Econs., Hobart Coll., 1965; postgrad., Stanford U. Bus. Sch., Grad. Sch. Credit and Fin. Mgmt., summers 1971-73; grad. Advanced Mgmt. Program, Harvard U., 1979. Dist. mgr. Mfrs. Hanover Trust, N.Y.C., 1965, 74-77; sr. v.p. Hartford (Conn.) Nat. Bank, 1977-82; exec. v.p. Old Stone Bank, Old Stone Corp., Providence, 1982-84; mng. dir. Russell Reynolds Assocs., Inc., Boston, 1985—; dir. Emersons Investment Mgmt., Boston. Corporate overseer Ptnrs. Healthcare Sys., Boston, 1990-99. Bd. overseers The Huntington Theatre Co., Boston. Mem. R.I. Country Club (Barrington), Southport Yacht Club (West Southport, Maine), Moorings Club (Vero Bch., Fla.), Harvard Club (Boston). Office: Russell Reynolds Assocs Inc One Federal St 25th Fl Boston MA 02110

HURD, JERRIE, writer; b. Idaho Falls, Idaho, Apr. 3, 1949; d. Jared Wirkus and Colleen Nielsen; m. Jon Hurd, June 30, 1967; children: Devin Jared, Ethan Jon. BA, U. Colo., 1969; MFA, U. Oreg., 1981. Author: Miss Ellie'sPurple Sage Saloon, 1995, Kate Burke Shoots the Old West, 1997, The Lady Pinkerton Gets Her Man, 1997. Bd. trustees Autry Mus. of Western Heritage, 2002—; bd. editors Conf. World Affairs, U. Colo. Boulder Campus, 2000—; bd. dirs. Boulder Media Women, Boulder Media Ctr., 2005—. Mem. Women Writing the West (pres., founder 1996-98), Weste Writers Am. (bd. dirs. 1998-2000), Women of West Mus. (bd. dirs., treas. 1996-2002). Democrat. Office: PO Box 12 Boulder CO 80306-0012 Office Phone: 303-444-3475.

HURD, JOHN R., lawyer; b. San Francisco, May 4, 1942; BA, Harvard U., 1964; student, U. Ctrl. del Ecuador; LLB, U. Tex., 1967. Bar: Tex. 1967. Mem. Vinson & Elkins L.L.P., Houston. Office: Vinson & Elkins 2500 First City Tower 1001 Fannin St Ste 3300 Houston TX 77002-6706 Address: 10 Blenheim San Antonio TX 78209

HURD, JOSEPH KINDALL, JR., obstetrician, gynecologist; b. Hoisington, Kans., Feb. 12, 1938; MD, Harvard U., 1964. Cert. ob.-gyn. Intern Boston City Hosp., 1964-65, resident in surgery, 1965-66; resident in ob.-gyn. Bronx (N.Y.) Mcpl. Hosp. Ctr., 1966-70; with Walson Army Hosp., Ft. Dix, NJ, 1970—72, Lahey Clinic Med. Ctr., Burlington, Mass., 1972—, chair dept. gynecology, 1988—2000. Clin. instr. surgery Harvard U., 1972—; clin. asst. prof. Tufts U. Sch. Medicine, Boston, 1996—. Named one of Top 100 Black Physicians in Am., Black Enterprise Mag., 2001. Fellow Am. Coll. Ob.-Gyn., ACS; mem. AMA, Nat. Med. Assn. Office: Lahey Med Ctr 41 Mall Rd Burlington MA 01805-0001 Office Phone: 781-744-8495. Business E-Mail: jkhurd@massmed.org.

HURD, MARK V., computer company executive; b. NYC; married; 2 children. BBA, Baylor U., Waco, Tex., 1979. With NCR Corp., 1980—2005; sr. v.p. Teradata Solutions Group (divsn. NCR Corp.), 1998—2000; COO Teradata (divsn. NCR Corp.), 2000—02; exec. v.p. NCR Corp., 2000—01, co-pres. Dayton, Ohio, 2001—02, COO, 2002—03, CEO, 2003—05; pres., CEO Hewlett-Packard Co., Palo Alto, Calif., 2005—, also bd. dirs., 2005—. Co-author (with Lars Nyberg): The Value Factor: How Global Leaders Use Information. Bd. visitors Fuqua Sch. Bus. Duke U.; bd. trustees, Dayton Area Chap. Am. Red Cross. Avocation: tennis. Office: Hewlett Packard Co 3000 Hanover St Palo Alto CA 94304-1185 Office Phone: 650-857-1501. Office Fax: 650-857-5518.*

HURD, MARY K., civil engineer, writer; BSCE, Iowa State U., Ames; postgrad, U. Chgo., U. Mich., U. Ill. Assoc. editor spl. tech. publs. Am. Concrete Inst., 1966-67, staff engr. Detroit, 1967-76; engr.-writer, cons., 1976-80, 90—; engring. editor Concrete Constrn. Mag., Addison, Ill., 1983-90, editor, 1981-83; pres. engr. publs. Farmington Hills, Mich. Past chmn. bd. dirs. Concrete Improvement Bd. Author: Formwork for Concrete, 1963, 7th edit., 2005; contbr. articles in field to profl. jours. including Constrn. Specifier, Concrete Internat., Jour. Am. Concrete Inst., Internat. Jour. of Ferrocement, Revista IMCYC Mexico, Pub. Works, Concrete Constrn., Concrete Prodr., PCI Jour., presenter and organizer in field. Recipient Profl. Achievement in Engring. Citation award Iowa State U., 1982, Outstanding Achievement award Concrete Improvement Bd. Detroit, 1990, Anson Marston medal Iowa State U. Coll. Engring., 2004; named one of 125 Top People of Past 125 Years in Constrn. Industry. Mem. ASCE (life), Am. Concrete Inst. (hon. mem., past mem. bd. dirs., organizing chmn. com. 124 concrete aesthetics, com. 347 formwork for concrete, past pres. Mich. chpt., Constrn. Practice award 1982, 88, Delmar L. Bloem Disting. Svc. award 1990, Arthur Y. Moy award Mich. chpt. 1994, Henry C. Turner medal 1995); mem. Am. Soc. Concrete Contractors, Precast/Prestressed Concrete Inst. (profl.), The Concrete Soc. (U.K.), Constrn. Writers Assn., Tau Beta Pi, Phi Kappa Phi. Address: 33742 Lyncroft Rd Farmington Hills MI 48331-3647 Office Phone: 248-474-1369.

HURD, RICHARD NELSON, pharmaceutical company executive; b. Evanston, Ill., Feb. 25, 1926; s. Charles DeWitt and Mary Ormsby (Nelson) H.; m. Jocelyn Fillmore Martin, Dec. 22, 1950; children: Melanie Gray, Suzanne Dewitt. BS, U. Mich., 1946; PhD U. Minn., 1956. Chemist Gen. Electric Co., Schenectady, N.Y., 1948-49; R&D group leader Koppers Co., Pitts., 1956-57; rsch. chemist Mallinckrodt Chem. Works, St. Louis, 1957-63, group leader, 1963-66, Comml. Solvents Corp., Terre Haute, Ind., 1966-68, sect. head, 1968-71; mgr. sci. affairs G. D. Searle Internat. Co., Skokie, Ill., 1972-73, dir. mfg. and tech. affairs, 1973-77; rep. to internat. tech com. Pharm. Mfrs. Assn., Skokie, Ill., 1973-77; v.p. tech. affairs Elder Pharms., Bryan, Ohio, 1977-81; v.p. rsch. & devel. U.S. Proprietary Drugs & Toiletries div. Schering-Plough Corp., Memphis, 1981-83; v.p. sci affairs Moleculon, Inc., Cambridge, Mass., 1984-88; v.p. regulatory affairs Pharmaco-LSR, Inc., Austin, Tex., 1989-94; prin. Hurd & Assocs., Inc., Evanston, ILL., 1994—. Contbr. articles to profl. jours.; patentee in field. Mem. Ferguson-Florissant (Mo.) Sch. Bd., 1964-66; bd. dirs. United Fund of Wabash Valley (Ind.), 1969-71. With USN, 1943-46, 53-55. E.I. DuPont de Nemours & Co., Inc. fellow, 1956. Fellow AAAS; mem. Am. Acad. Dermatology (life), Am. Soc. Photobiology, Am. Chem. Soc., N.Y. Acad. Sci., Am. Pharm. Assn., Am. Assn. Pharm. Scientists, Food and Drug Law Inst., Drug Info. Assn., Sigma XI, Mich. Shores Club (Wilmette, Ill.). Presbyterian. Achievements include codevelopment of Ralgro and Oxsoralen; research in thioamides as a class of organic compounds; development of macrocyclic synthetic routes for natural products; development of psoralens for photochemotherapy of dermatologic disorders. E-mail: hurdreg@earthlink.net.

HURD, SUZANNE SHELDON, retired federal agency health science director; b. Elmira, N.Y., Dec. 17, 1939; d. Victor Sheldon H. BS, Bates Coll., 1961; MS, U. Wash., 1963, PhD, 1967. Post-doctoral fellow U. Calif., Berkeley, 1967-69; grants assoc. NIH, Bethesda, Md., 1969-70; health sci. adminstr. Nat. Heart, Lung and Blood Inst., Bethesda, 1970-78, dep. dir. div. lung diseases, 1979-84, dir. divsn. lung diseases, 1984-99; acting dir. Nat. Inst. Nursing Rsch., Bethesda, 1994-95; acting dir. Women's Health Initiative Nat. Heart, Lung and Blood Inst., Bethesda, 1997-99; sci. dir. global initiative for asthma Med. Comm. Resources, Inc., Gig Harbor, Wash., 2000—, sci. dir. global initiative chronic obstructive lung disease, 2000—. Mem. Am. Thoracic Soc. E-mail: shurd@prodigy.net.

HUREWITZ, FLORENCE, painter, educator; d. Isadore and Deborah Ohringer Kirshenblut; m. Benjamin Hurewitz; children: Steven, Michael. BFA, Cooper Union Sch. Art and Architecture, 1976. Designer stained glass Rambusch & Co., N.Y.C.; asst. curator exhibits Cooper Union Mus.; mem. fine arts faculty Bergen C.C., Paramus, NJ, 1973—85; instr. painting Art Ctr. No. N.J., New Milford, 1985—. Mem. art adv. bd. Fairlawn Pub. Libr., Fairlawn, NJ, 1970—. Exhibitions include NJ State Mus., Painters and

Sculptors Soc. N.J., Jersey City, Nat. Acad., N.Y.C., Monmouth Coll., N.J., Nat. Acad. Galleries, N.Y.C., Peoria Art Mus., Ill., Edward Williams Coll., Jersey City Mus., Norfolk Mus. Art, Va., Marietta Coll., Ohio, Charleston Art Gallery, W.Va., Pallazzo Vecchio, Florence, Italy, Salvator Rosa, Naples, Italy, Larsen Gallery, Brigham Young U., Utah, Jesse Besser Mus., Alpena, Mich, Washington County Mus. Fine Arts, Hagerstown, Md., Am. Embassy, Tel Aviv, numerous others. Mem.: Women's Caucus for Arts, Artists Equity, Nat. Assn. Women Artists (medal honor 1975, 1986), Coll. Art Assn. Home: 0-95 Midland Ave Fair Lawn NJ 07410

HUREWITZ, PHALEN GILBERT, lawyer; b. Fall River, Mass., Nov. 25, 1936; m. Renee Rosengarten, June 18, 1961; children: Deborah, Matthew, Daniel. AB magna cum laude, Dartmouth Coll., 1958; LLB, Stanford U., 1961. Bar: Calif. 1962. Clk. to justice Calif. Dist. Ct. Appeal for 1st Dist., awd, 1961-62; ptnr. Cooper, Epstein & Hurewitz, Beverly Hills, Calif., 1966-93, Manatt, Phelps & Phillips, L.A., 1993-97, Isaacman, Kaufman & Painter P.C., Beverly Hills, 1997—. Prof. Calif. Coll. Law, 1967-70. Co-founder Widows Ctr., Temple Isaiah, 1975, Am. Chamber Symphony, 1982; pres. Temple Isaiah, 1975-76; mem. legal adv. com. Beverly Hills Bd. Edn., 1980-83; pres. Alternative Living for Aging, 1983-86; pres. Met. Region Jewish Fedn., 1986-88; bd. dirs. Jewish Fedn. Coun.; pres. Jewish Family Svc., 1991-94, Bur. Jewish Edn., 1994-97; chair L.A. County Commn. for Children and Families, 1999-2001; mem. L.A. County Children and Families First Proposition 10 Commn; also bd. mem. numerous other orgns.; mem. L.A. County Commn. for Children & Families, 1992-2005. Mem. ABA, State Bar Calif., Los Angeles County Bar Assn., Beverly Hills Bar Assn., Calif. Copyright Conf., L.A. Copyright Soc., Phi Beta Kappa. Office: Isaacman Kaufman & Painter 8484 Wilshire Blvd Ste 850 Beverly Hills CA 90211-3222 E-mail: hurewitz@ikplaw.com.

HURLBERT, ROGER WILLIAM, information technology executive; b. San Francisco, Feb. 18, 1941; s. William G. and Mary (Greene) H.; m. Karen C. Haslag, Nov. 6, 1982; children: Sage, Mica, Chula, Monk, Morris, Cassie. BS in Community Devel., So. Ill. U., 1965. Newspaper editor and reporter various, San Francisco Bay Area, 1958-62; pvt. practice investigation Ill., 1963-65; advisor San Francisco Planning Urban Rsch. Assn., 1969-87; pres. Sage Info. Svcs., Glen Ellen, Calif., 1988—. Compiler U.S. Land Data Base, 1972—. Pres. Haight-Ashbury Neighborhood Coun., San Francisco, 1959-61. With U.S. Army, 1966-68, Vietnam. Recipient Cert. of Merit, San Francisco Coun. Dist. Mchts. Assn., 1972. Mem. Real Estate Info. Profls. Assn. (sec. 1998-03), Direct Mktg. Assn., Mail Advt. Svc. Assn. Internat., League of Men Voters (v.p. 1959—), Internat. Assn. of Assessing Officials. Democrat. Office: Sage Info Svcs 13606 Arnold Dr PO Box 1832 Glen Ellen CA 95442-1832

HURLBURT, HARLEY ERNEST, ocean modeling and prediction scientist; b. Bennington, Vt., Apr. 12, 1943; s. Paul Rhodes and Evelyn Arlene (Lockhart) H.; m. Cheryl Elaine Finch, Jan. 10, 1998. BS in Physics, Union Coll., Schenectady, NY, 1965; MS, Fla. State U., 1971, PhD in Meteorology, 1974. NASA trainee Fla. State U., 1970-72; postdoctoral fellow advanced studies program Nat. Ctr. Atmospheric Rsch., Boulder, Colo., 1974-75; staff scientist JAYCOR, Alexandria, Va., 1975-77; oceanographer Naval Rsch. Lab. and related orgns., Stennis Space Ctr., Miss., 1977—, br. head, 1983-85, sr. scientist ocean modeling and prediction, 2000—. Adj. faculty marine sci. U. So. Miss., Stennis Space Ctr., 1993—; adj. faculty meteorology Fla. State U., Tallahassee, 1995—; nat. adv. panel satellite surface stress working group NASA, 1981-84, minerals mgmt. svc. interagy. adv. group, 1982-89, world ocean circulation experiment working group on numerical modeling, 1984-96, USN space oceanography working group, 1986-89; co-chmn. working group on global prediction sys., ocean prediction workshop, 1986; internat. working group on acoustic monitoring of world ocean Sci. Com. Oceanic Rsch., 1991-98; internat. working group on modelling subarctic North Pacific circulation North Pacific Marine Sci. Orgn., 1994-95; sci. steering team Internat. Global Ocean Data Assimilation Experiment, 1998—; mem. NASA High Resolution Ocean Topography Sci. Working Group, 2001, NASA Wide Swath Ocean Altimeter Sci. Working Group, 2002-03; project leader to develop eddy-resolving global ocean prediction models for USN, 1987—. Contbr. numerous articles to profl. jours. V.p. Burgundy Citizens Assn., 1976-77. Weather officer USAF, 1965-69. Scholar Union Coll., 1965; recipient Disting. Scientist medal 13th Internat. Colloquium, Liege, Belgium, 1981, Publ. award for best basic rsch. paper Naval Ocean R & D Activity, 1980, 90; grantee Office Naval Rsch., 1975-77, 84—, Dept. Energy, 1975-78, Tex. A&M U., 1976, Office of Naval Tech., 1987-93, Space Warfare Sys., 1989-94, Advanced Rsch. Projects Agy., 1993-95, Strategic Environ. Rsch. and Devel. Program, 1994-95, Def. Dept. High Performance Computing Challenge, 1997—, Nat. Ocean Partnership Program, 1997—; case study on Eddy-resolving Global Ocean Modeling and Prediction included in 2000 Computerworld Smithsonian Collection archived in Smithsonian's Nat. Mus. Am. History's permanent rsch. collection. Mem. Am. Meteorol. Soc., Am. Geophys. Union, Oceanography Soc., Phi Sigma Kappa, Sigma Xi (Kaminski Publ. award 1991), Sigma Tau, Chi Epsilon Pi. Methodist. Achievements include research on the oceanic onset of El Nino and the dynamics of loop current eddy shedding in the Gulf of Mexico; discovery of the impact of upper ocean-topographic coupling via flow instabilities on upper ocean current pathways, including the Gulf Stream in the Atlantic and the Kuroshio in the Pacific; transition of the world's first eddy-resolving global ocean prediction system to the Naval Oceanographic Office for operational use. Home: 507 Hermitage Ct Pearl River LA 70452-3903 Office: Naval Rsch Lab Code 7304 Bay Saint Louis MS 39529 Office Phone: 228-688-4626. E-mail: hurlburt@nrlssc.navy.mil.

HURLBUT, ROBERT HAROLD, health care services executive; b. Rochester, N.Y., Mar. 9, 1935; s. Harold Leroy and Martha Irene (Fincher) H.; m. Barbara Cox, June 14, 1958; children: Robert W., Christine A. Hurlbut Bean. Student, Coll. Hotel Adminstrn., Cornell U., 1953-56. Adminstr., dir. Pillars Nursing Home, Rochester, 1956—80, Elmcrest Nursing Home, Churchville, NY, 1960—75, Elm Manor Nursing Home, Canandaigua, N.Y., 1960—, Penfield Nursing Home, Rochester, 1963—, Avon (N.Y.) Nursing Home, 1964—, Newark (N.Y.) Nursing Home, 1965—, Lakeshore Nursing Home, Rochester, 1972—. Bd. dirs. HSBC, Strong Meml. Hosp.; organizer, adminstrv. dir. hdqrs. Rohm Svcs. Corp., Rochester, 1964—; organizer, pres. hdqrs. Vari-Care Inc., Rochester, 1969—93; commr. N.Y. State Ins. Fund; mem. adv. coun. Cornell U. Hotel Sch., 2003—. Trustee U. Rochester; St. John Fisher Coll., 1983—98, trustee emeritus; mem. adv. bd. U. Rochester; trustee Eastman Dental Ctr. Found.; pres. Hurlbut Trust, 1994; mem. bd. govs. Strong Meml. Hosp., 1992—, chmn. bd. dirs., 2005—. Fellow Am. Coll. Health Care Adminstrs.; mem. Greater Met. C. of C. (past chmn. bd. dirs.), Genesee Valley Club, Oak Hill Country Club, Cornell Soc. Hotelmen, Lambda Chi Alpha. Home: 200 Sheldon Rd Honeoye Falls NY 14472-9316 Office: Hurlbut Trust 740 East Ave Rochester NY 14607-2107 Office Phone: 585-271-1650.

HURLBUT, TERRY ALLISON, pathologist; b. Richmond, Va., Nov. 24, 1957; s. Terry A. and Evelyn I. (Randlette) H.; m. Sharon L. Clouston, Oct. 24, 1998. BS, Yale Coll., 1980; MD, Baylor Coll. Medicine, 1985. Pathology residency Vanderbilt U., Nashville, 1986-89; fellowship pathology Dartmouth Med. Sch., Hanover, N.H., 1989-91; pathology residency Monmouth Med. Ctr., Long Branch, N.J., 1991-93; clin. pathologist Kimball Med. Ctr, Lakewood, N.J., 1993-95; dir. informatics Lakewood Pathology Assn., 1993-99; clin. pathologist Meml. Hosp. Burlington County, Mt. Holly, N.J., 1996-99. Co-author: The Laboratory Consultant, 1992; contbr. article to profl. jours. Fellow Coll. Am. Pathologists. Republican. Baptist. Home: 5 Grosvenor Rd Short Hills NJ 07078-1603 E-mail: hurlbutta@comcast.net.

HURLEY, ALFRED FRANCIS, historian, academic administrator emeritus, retired air force officer; b. Bklyn., Oct. 16, 1928; s. Patrick Francis and Margaret Teresa (Coakley) H.; m. Joanna Helen Leahy, Jan. 24, 1953; children: Alfred F., Thomas J., Mark P., Claire T., John K. BA summa cum laude, St. John's U., 1950; MA, Princeton U., 1958, PhD, 1961. Enlisted USAF, 1950, commd. lt., 1952, tng. officer, instr. navigator, 1952—56; from instr. to asst. prof. history USAF Acad., 1958—63, prof., head dept. history, 1966—80; navigator, exec. officer USAF Hdqrs., Germany, War Plans Staff, Joint Chiefs of Staff, 1963—66; bd. mem. Acad. Bd., 1977-80; advanced through grades to brig. gen. USAF, ret., 1980; v.p. adminstrv. affairs U. North Tex. (formerly North Tex. State U.), Denton, 1980-82, pres., 1982-2000, prof. history, 1981—; chancellor U. North Tex. Sys., 2000—02. Mem. adv. com. USAF hist. program sect. USAF, Washington, 1982-86, chmn., 1984-86; mem. bd. visitors Air U., 1993-97. Author: Billy Mitchell, Crusader for Air Power, 1964, (rev. edit.), 1975; contbg. author: Winged Shield, Winged Sword, History of the USAF, 1997; co-editor: Air Power and Warfare, 1979. Decorated Legion of Merit (2); Guggenheim fellow, 1971-72, Eisenhower Inst., Smithsonian fellow, 1976-77; recipient Pres.'s medal St. John's U., 1990. Mem.: Tex. Philos. Soc. (pres. 2003—04, bd. dirs. 2004—), Dallas Citizens Coun. (bd. dirs. 2000—02), North Tex. Commn. (bd. dirs. 1986—2000, chmn. 1995—97, bd. dirs. 2004—), Alliance for Higher Edn. of North Tex. (trustee 1983—89, chmn. coun. of pres. 1989—90), Tex. Coun. Pub. Univ. Pres. and Chancellors (chmn. 1987—89), Coalition Urban and Met. Univs. (co-chair 1993—2002, mem. exec. com. 2002—04), Am. Hist. Assn. (chmn. NASA fellowship com. 1993—94), Am. Coun. Edn. (commn. leadership 1993—96), Am. Assn. State Colls. and Univs. (coun. state reps. 1989—92), Air Force Hist. Found. (trustee 1980—), Am. Mil. Inst. (trustee 1973—78, 1981—85). Roman Catholic. Home: 828 Skylark Dr Denton TX 76205-8012 Office: U North Tex Dept History Denton TX 76203-0650 Office Phone: 940-369-8924. Business E-Mail: hurley@unt.edu.

HURLEY, ALLISON RUTH, mentor coach specialist; b. Escanaba, Mich., Nov. 2, 1961; d. Paula Ann and Donald Faye Marvic (Stepfather). BS in Edn., Marian Coll. of Fond du Lac, Wis., 1986. Site dir. YMCA of Greater Sacramento, 1988—91; practicum/placement coord. Calif. Nanny Coll., Sacramento, 1991—92; resource and referral counselor Child Action, Inc., Sacramento, 1997; early head start program mgr. Calif. Human Devel. Corp. Head Start/Early Head Start for Yolo County, Woodland, 1999—2003; mentor coach specialist Devel. Assocs., Inc., Walnut Creek, Calif., 2003—; exec. dir. First Bapt. Head Start, Pittsburg, Calif., 2003—05; family childcare mgr. E Ctr. Migrant and Seasonal Head Start, Marysville, La., 2005—. Edn. specialist Calif. Human Devel. Corp. Head Start for Yolo County, Woodland, Calif., 1997—99. Mem.: NAFE, AAUW (treas. 1986—87), Calif. Head Start Assn., Infant Devel. Assn. (bd. dirs. 2001), Nat. Head Start (assoc.). Office: Nat Migrant and Seasonal Head Start 1128 Yuba St Marysville CA 95901

HURLEY, ALLYSON KINGSLEY, dentist; b. Buffalo, June 15, 1949; d. Norman and Marion (Legler) Kingsley; m. Lawrence Joseph Hurley, May 28, 1977; children: Michael William, Kathryn Elizabeth. Student, Barat Coll., 1967-68; degree in dental hygiene, Marquette U., 1970, BS, 1971; DDS, Howard U., 1977. Pvt. practice dental hygiene, Washington, 1971-77; resident VA Hosp., Lyons, N.J., 1977-78; gen. practice dentistry Chatham, N.J., 1978—. Attending dentist Overlook Hosp., Summit, NJ, 1979—, dir. resident adminstrn., 1980-85, edn. com., 1981-86; clin. instr. dental hygiene Union County Tech. Inst., Scotch Plains, NJ, 1979-81, selection com. for dental dept., 1987; coord. kindergarten-4th grades dental health program Chatham Boro Sch. Sys., 1978-92; active oral cancer screening program Chatham Boro Jr. Women's Club, 1980-82. Editor, contbg. author newsletter Word of Mouth, 1981—; author Your Child's Teeth, 1984; contbg. author: Love Is the Best Medicine, 2001; exhibited in group shows at Overlook Hosp., Summit, Summit Coll.; field contbr. Nature Photographer. Alumni recruiter Marquette U., Morris County, N.J., 1977-83; bd. dirs. Am. Cancer Soc., Morris County, 1981-83; chair Scholarship Found. of the Chathams, Inc., 1985-95. Master Acad. Gen. Dentistry; fellow Internat. Acad. Dental-Facial Esthetics; mem. ADA, AAUW, Am. Acad. Cosmetic Dentistry (accredited, 2 Gold medals 2004), N.Am. Nature Photography Assn., NJ Acad. Cosmetic Dentistry (pres. 2000-02), Tri-County Dental Soc. (bd. dirs. 1982-83), Internat. Dental Lectr., Internat. Platform Assn., NY Acad. Scis., NJ Assn. Women Bus. Owners, Assn. Media Photographers, Nat. Assn. Photoshop Profls., Drew Art Assn., Chatham Twp. Art League, Columbia U. Dental Study Club, No. NJ Women's Study Club (pres. 1980-82, 86-, sec. 1983-86), Newcomer's Club Chatham Township, Acad. Esthetic and Restorative Dentistry Study Club Republican. Roman Catholic. Office: Allyson Kingsley Hurley DDS 585 Main St Chatham NJ 07928-2104

HURLEY, BRIAN J., insurance company executive; BS in Indsl. Engring., U. Toronto; diploma in Advanced Mgmt. Program, Harvard U. From loss prevention specialist to exec. v.p. FM Global, Johnston, RI, 1970—89, exec. v.p., 1989—. Office: FM Global 1301 Atwood Ave Johnston RI 02919

HURLEY, CHERYL JOYCE, book publishing executive; b. Pitts., Oct. 30, 1947; d. John and Violet der Norsek; m. Kevin Hurley, July 27, 1974. Lang. and lit. cert., Université de Lyon, France, 1968; AB, Ohio U., 1969; MA, U. Mich., 1971. Research assoc. MLA, N.Y.C., 1972-74, dir. spl. programs, 1974-79; pub. The Library of America, N.Y.C., 1979—88, pres., 1988—. Cons. in field. Contbr. articles to profl. jours. Trustee French Inst./Alliance Francaise, 1992—, v.p., exec. com., 1994—, chmn. libr. com., 1996—, Samuel H. Kress Found., 1999—; adv. com. N.Y. 100 Centennial, 1997-98; mem. humanities adv. coun. N.Y. Pub. Libr., 1996—; mem. dean's adv. bd. Rackham Grad. Sch. U. Mich., 2000-; mem. vis. com. printed books Pierpont Morgan Libr., 2005-. Rackham fellow, 1969—70. Mem.: Assn. Internationale de Bibliophilie, Am. Antiquarian Soc. (councillor 1999—), Bridgehampton Club, Colony Club, Grolier Club, Century Assn., Phi Beta Kappa. Home: 1172 Park Ave New York NY 10128-1213 Office: Libr of Am 14 E 60th St New York NY 10022-1006

HURLEY, DAVID ROSS, music educator; b. Rome, Ga. s. Gene Benny and Marceline Hurley. BA, Univ. Mich., Ann Harbor, Mich., 1980; MA, Univ. Chgo., Chgo., Ill., 1990, PhD, 1991. Prof. Pitts, State Univ., Pitts., Kans., 1996—. Author: Handel's Muse, 2001; contbr. articles pub. to profl. jour. Recipient Striped Aston Magna, Nat. Endowment for the Humanities, 1997. Mem.: Am. Handel Soc.

HURLEY, DEAN C., bank executive, lawyer; b. South Weymouth, Mass., Oct. 16, 1954; s. Dean C. and Neva (Richards) H.; m. Laura Ann Beck, Apr. 5, 1997; children: Mackenzie Katherine, Caroline Jeanette, Margaret Neva, Dean C. III. BS, Fairleigh Dickinson U., 1976, MBA, 1978; JD, N.Y. Law Sch., 1985. Bar: N.J. 1985, D.C. 1986. Asst. ops. mgr. Fieldcrest Mills, Inc., N.Y.C., 1976-77; spl. projects mgr. Citicorp Credit Svcs. Inc., N.Y.C., 1978-86; v.p., dir. fin. planning First Jersey Nat. Corp., Jersey City, 1986-88; v.p. asset strategies A/L. Mgmt. Dae Ichi Kangyo Bank div. The CIT Group, 1988-95; v.p. portfolio sales group Meenan, McDevitt & Co., Inc., 1996-98; v.p. debt, currencies, commodities and derivatices comml. mortgage acquisitions group Société Générale, N.Y.C., 1998—2003, dir. debt, currencies, commodities and derivatices comml. mortgage backed securitization group, 2003—. Active Christian Ctr.; trustee, recording sec. Livingston Symphony Orch., 1993-97. Mem.: Nat. Assn. Securities Dealers, Omicron Delta Epsilon, Phi Delta Phi. Republican. Avocations: flying, boating. Home: 23 Cider Mill Ln Port Murray NJ 07865-3202 Office: Société Générale 1221 Avenue Of The Americas New York NY 10020-1001

HURLEY, DENIS R., federal judge; b. 1937; BS, U. Pa., 1959; MBA, Columbia U., 1962; LLB, Fordham U., 1966. Assoc. Bond, Schoenck and King, Syracuse, N.Y., 1966-68; prin. asst. dist. atty. Dist. Attys. Office, Suffolk County, N.Y., 1968-70; assoc., then ptnr. Pike, Behringer & Hurley (and successor firms), Riverhead, N.Y., 1970-82; judge N.Y. State Family Ct., 1983-87; acting justice N.Y. Supreme Ct., Suffolk County, 1987-88; judge N.Y. State County Ct., Suffolk County, 1988-91; fed. judge U.S. Dist. Ct. (ea. dist.) N.Y., Bklyn., 1991—, now sr. judge. Adj. prof. Touro Law Sch., Huntington, NY, 1995—97. Office: US Dist Ct PO Box 9014 Central Islip NY 11722-9014*

HURLEY, ELIZABETH, actress, model, film producer; b. Hampshire, Eng., June 10, 1965; Student, London Studio Ctr. Head devel. Simian Films, London and L.A., 1994—; model, cosmetic rep. Estee Lauder. Actress appearing in TV programs and movies including (films) Die Tote Stadt, 1987, Rowing with the Wind, 1988, Bloody Atlantic, 1991, The Orchid House, 1991, Passenger 57, 1992, El Largo Invierno, 1992, Beyond Bedlam, 1993, Goldeneye, 1995, Mad Dogs and Englishmen, Austin Powers: International Man of Mystery, 1997, (TV movies) The Shamrock Conspiracy, 1995, Samson and Delilah, 1996, Permanent Midnight, 1998, Edtv, 1999, My Favorite Martian, 1999, Austin Powers: The Spy Who Shagged Me, 1999, The Weight of Water, 2000, Bedazzled, 2000, Serving Sarah, 2002, Method, 2004, (TV series) Cristabel, 1989, Rumpole and the Barrow Boy, 1989, Sharpe II, 1995; host (TV spl.) The World of James Bond, 1995; prodr. Mickey Blue Eyes, 1999. Office: Creative Artists Agy 9830 Wilshire Blvd Beverly Hills CA 90212-1804

HURLEY, FRANCIS T., retired archbishop; b. San Francisco, Jan. 12, 1927; Grad., St. Patrick Sem., Menlo Park, Calif., Cath. U. Am. Ordained priest Roman Cath. Ch., 1951, consecrated bishop 1970. With Nat. Cath. Welfare Conf., Washington, asst. sec., 1958—68; assoc. sec. Nat. Cath. Welfare Conf. (now U.S. Cath. Conf.), 1968—70; titular bishop Daimlaig, aux. bishop Diocese of Juneau, Alaska, 1970—71, bishop, 1971—76; archbishop Archdiocese of Anchorage, 1976—2001, archbishop emeritus, 2001—. Roman Catholic.*

HURLEY, FRANK THOMAS, JR., realtor; b. Washington, Oct. 18, 1924; s. Frank Thomas and Lucille (Trent) H.; m. Betty Guisinger, Aug. 9, 1997. AA, St. Petersburg Jr. Coll., 1948; BA, U. Fla., 1950. Reporter St. Petersburg (Fla.) Evening Independent, 1948-53; editor Arcadia (Calif.) Tribune, 1956-57; reporter Los Angeles Herald Express, 1957; v.p. Frank T. Hurley Assocs., Inc. realtors, 1958-64, pres., 1964—. Sec., dir. Beau Monde, Inc., 1977-79. Author: Surf, Sand and Post Card Sunsets, 1977, Pass-a-Grille Vignettes, 1999. Elected St. Petersburg Beach Bd. Commrs., 1965—69; chmn. Pinellas County Traffic Safety Coun., 1968—69; apptd. mem. Pinellas County Hist. Commn., 1993—, chmn., 2003; pres. Pass-A-Grille Cmty. Assn., 1963; mem. St. Petersburg Mus. Fine Arts, St. Pete Beach Aesthetic and Hist. Rev. Bd., chmn., 1994—96; apptd. mem. Pinellas County Sesquicentennial Coord. Com., 1995; pres. Gulf Beach Bd. Realtors, 1969; bd. govs. Palms of Pasadena Hosp., 1979—86. With USAAF, 1943—46. Mem. Fla. Assn. Realtors (dir., dist. v.p. 1971), St. Petersburg Suncoast Assn. Realtors (life, Ambassadors award 1994), St. Petersburg Beach C. of C. (dir., pres. 1975-76, Citizen of Yr. award 1983), Fla. Hist. Soc., Ky. Col., Am. Legion, Pass-A-Grille Yacht Club, Sigma Delta Chi, Sigma Tau Delta. Home: 2808 Sunset Way Saint Petersburg Beach FL 33706-4133 Office: 2506 Pass A Grille Way Saint Petersburg Beach FL 33706-4160 Office Phone: 727-367-1949.

HURLEY, GRADY SCHELL, lawyer; b. New Orleans, Nov. 29, 1954; s. Daniel Patrick and Jocelyn Mary (Schell) H.; children: Joshua, Benjamin, Mary Elizabeth, William, John. BA, Tulane U., 1976, JD, 1979, LLM, 1981. Bar: La. 1979, U.S. Dist. Ct. (ea., mid. and we. dists.) La. 1979, U.S. Ct. Appeals (5th and 11th cirs.) 1980, U.S. Supreme Ct. 1986. Assoc. Jones, Walker, Waechter, Poitevent, Carrere and Denegre, New Orleans, 1979-84, ptnr., 1984—. Mem. nat. bd. Tulane Admiralty Law Inst. Editor: Damages Recoverable in Maritime Matters, 1984, Briefly Speaking, 1993. Mem. ABA (House of Delegates, 2003-05, chmn. subcom. on wrongful death and workers compensation 1990-94), Fed. Bar Assn., La. Bar Assn. (dist. rep. young lawyers sect. 1986, La. Bar examiner 1989—, elected Bar Found.), New Orleans Bar Assn. (chmn. maritime law com. 1990-92, exec. bd. 1994—, pres.-elect 2001, pres. 2002), Am. Inns of Court (chpt. pres.), Maritime Law Assn. (maritime pers. com., proctor, chmn. offshore industires com.), S.E. Admiralty Law Inst. (bd. dirs. 2004-), Tulane U. Alumni Assn. (bd. dirs. 1986-96, pres. 1995, chmn. 35th ann. ednl. conf.), Mariner Club. Republican. Roman Catholic. Avocations: sports, reading, painting, movies. Office: Jones Walker Waechter Poitevent Carrère & Denègre 201 St Charles Ave Ste 5000 New Orleans LA 70170-5100 Office Phone: 504-582-8000.

HURLEY, HILLARY M., music educator; d. Lyle and Patricia Hurley. BS, Abilene Christian U., Tex., 1999. Vocal music dir. Parsons Jr. H.S., Redding, Calif., 2002—. Dir. Riverfront Playhouse, Redding, Calif., 2005. Mem.: Internat. Assn. of Jazz Educators, Calif. Music Educators Assn. Office Phone: 530-224-4190.

HURLEY, JOHN KENNETH, real estate company executive, merchant banking executive; b. Washington, Nov. 28, 1931; s. Frank T. and Lucille (Trent) H.; m. June Carol Morgan, June 19, 1954 (div. 1976); children: Sean Kenneth, Kathleen Patricia; m. Joyce Carol Winemiller, Mar. 30, 1980 (div. 1990). AA, St. Petersburg Jr. Coll., 1952; BS, Fla. State U., 1954; MBA, Suffield U., 1995, PhD, 2005, Canterbury U., 2000. Chmn. of bd. Frank T. Hurley Assocs., Inc., St. Petersburg Beach, Fla., 1954—; pres. Hurley Marine Corp., St. Petersburg Beach, 1980—, Pass-a-Grille Trading Co., St. Petersburg Beach, 1982—, J. Kenneth Hurley Co., St. Petersburg Beach, 1984—. Ptnr. Joyce Hurley Natural Food Products, St. Petersburg Beach, 1982-94; mng. dir. Baytree Investors, St. Petersburg Beach, 1993-97; guest lectr. more than 40 colls. and univs. Pub. Palma Ceia - MacDill News, Tampa, Fla., 1972-76; pub. poet in numerous periodicals and anthologies. Bd. dirs. Orthomolecular Research Ctr., St. Petersburg Beach, 1955-85; chmn. Zoning and Planning Bd., St. Petersburg Beach, 1968-71; pres. Friends St. Petersburg Beach Library, 1976-78. Mem. Am. Philos. Assn., Gulf Beach Seminole Bd. Realtors, Slocum Soc., Ky. Coll., Cauliflower Alley Club. Republican. Mem. United Ch. of Christ. Club: Pass-a-Grille (Fla.) Yacht (sec. 1978-80). Avocations: yachting, passenger vessel certified master. Home: 2122 W Vina Del Mar Blvd Saint Petersburg FL 33706-2842 Office: 2506 Pass A Grille Way Saint Petersburg FL 33706-4160

HURLEY, MORRIS ELMER, JR., management consultant; b. Berkeley, Calif., Mar. 26, 1920; s. Morris Elmer Sr. and Alice Grace (Johnson) H.; m. Jeanne Marie Bassett, Jan. 31, 1943; children: Morris Elmer III, James, Richard, Steven, Robert. AB, Harvard, 1941, MBA, 1943; PhD, Syracuse U., 1956. Asst. dean Coll. Bus. Adminstrn., Syracuse (N.Y.) U., 1946-53, acting dean, 1953-54, dean, 1954-58, instr. mgmt., 1946-48, asst. prof., 1948-53, assoc. prof., 1953-57, prof., 1957-60, Istituto Direzionale ENI, San Donato Milanese, Italy, 1958, IPSOA Istituto Post-Universitairo Torino, Italy, 1959-61; dir. mgmt. edn. programs U. Berkeley, 1961—. Assoc. economist N.Y. Dept. Commerce, 1948; rsch. aide Study for Ford Found., 1949; cons. prof. IBM Exec. Sch. Blaricum, Holland, 1960-61; mem. San Francisco C.C. Faculty, 1974-91, pres. acad. senate, 1979-81; bd. dirs. WIZ Corp., Empire Casting Co. Author: Elements of Business Administration, 1953, Economic Development and Regionalism, 1956, Business Administration, 2d edit., 1960, Managing Human Endeavor, 1975, Supervision and Management, 1980, Business Management, 1991, Supervision, 1992, Presentation of Reports, 1993, Sexual Harassment, 1993, Training the Trainer, 1994. Mem. Syracuse city planning commn., 1957-58; bd. dirs. Portsmouth (Va.) Community Chest, 1944-46, Frank S. Hiscock Legal Aid Soc., Syracuse, 1951-54; mem. Piedmont Charter Rev. Commn., 1981-82. Served from ensign to lt. USNR, 1943-46; mem. Res. Mem. ASTD, Am. Econ. Assn., Acad. Mgmt., Acad. Polit. and Social Sci., George F. Baker Scholars, Phi Beta Kappa, Beta Gamma Sigma, Pi Eta, Sigma Iota Epsilon, Alpha Kappa Psi. Home and Office: 19221 Black Oak Ln Grass Valley CA 95949-8348

HURLEY, R. BRUCE, lawyer; b. Harlingen, Tex. BSS, Southwestern Univ., 1986; JD cum laude, Univ. Houston, 1989. Bar: Tex. 1989. Ptnr., Litigation Practice Group King & Spalding, LLP, Houston. Mem. Greater Houston Partnership; bd. mem. Univ. Houston Law Ctr. Fellow: Houston Bar Found.; mem.: Houston Volunteer Lawyers Assn., Def. Rsch. Inst., ABA, State Bar Tex., Houston Bar Assn., Tex. Accountants & Lawyers for the Arts. Office: King & Spalding LLP 1100 Louisiana Houston TX 77002 Office Phone: 713-276-7383. Office Fax: 713-751-3290. Business E-Mail: bhurley@kslaw.com.

HURLEY, WALTER ALLISON, bishop; b. Fredericton, Can., May 30, 1937; BA, Sacred Heart Sem.; MDiv, St. John's Sem.; grad studies in Edn., U. Detroit; JCL, Cath. U. of Am., 1984. Ordained priest, 1965; assoc. pastor St. Dorothy, Warren, Mich., 1965—69; vicar Warren-Centerline, 1969—72; pastor St. Cyprian, Riverview, 1972—76, Sacred Heart, Roseville, 1976—79,

St. Lucy, St. Clair Shores, 1979—82, Our Lady of Sorrows Parish, Farmington, 1990—2003; judicial vicar Met. Tribune Archdiocese of Detroit, 1984—89, Moderator of the Curia, 1986—90; ordained bishop, 2003; Aux. Bishop of Detroit, 2003—05; Bishop of Grand Rapids, 2005—. Cardinal's del. and project mgr. for construction of Pope John Paul II Cultural Ctr., Washington, 1995—2001; del. of Cardinal Maida for matters relating to issues of sexual abuse by clergy and religious, 1988—95, 2002—. Roman Catholic. Office: Diocese of Grand Rapids 660 Burton St SE Grand Rapids MI 49507*

HURLEY, WILLIAM JOSEPH, retired information technology executive; b. N.Y.C., June 14, 1939; s. William and Anna Rita (Hubschman) Hurley; m. Dorothy Ann Mellett, Sept. 23, 1961 (dec.); children: William, Terrianne, Barbara, Daniel; m. Marianne F. Jordan, Mar. 17, 1990. BBA, Pace U., 1968, MBA, 1973. Dir. info. sys. Gen. Foods Corp., White Plains, NY, 1973—79; dir. sys. devel. Securities Industry Automation Corp., N.Y.C., 1979; dir. mgmt. info. sys. Schering Plough Corp., Kenilworth, NJ, 1979—81, sr. dir. mgmt. info. sys., 1981—83, v.p. mgmt. info. svc., 1983—88; v.p. world wide info. sys. Technicon Corp., Tarrytown, NY, 1988—90; dir. info. sys. Miles Inc., Tarrytown, 1990—95; ret., 1995. Pres. New City (N.Y.) Vol. Fire Engine Co. 1, 1979—81; commr. New City Fire Dist., 1983—94. With USMC, 1956—59. Mem.: Assn. Sys. Mgmt. (v.p. 1981), Soc. Info. Mgmt., Am. Legion. Republican. Roman Catholic. Avocation: financial planning. Home: Unit 504 3150 N A1A Fort Pierce FL 34949-8868 Office Phone: 772-466-5908. Personal E-mail: bhurley317@aol.com.

HURLIN, DAN, actor, theater director; Artistic dir. Andy's Summer Playhouse, Wilton, NH, 1987—93; instr. Bowdoin Coll., Bennington Coll., Barnard Coll., Princeton U., Sarah Lawrence Coll.; dir. Pupet Lab at Arts St. Ann's, Bklyn. Dir.: No(thing so powerful as) Truth, 1995, Constance and Ferdinand, 1991, The Jazz Section, 1989, A Cool Million, 1990, Quintland, 1992, The Day the Ketchup Turned Blue, 1997, The Shoulder, 1998, Everyday Uses for Sight, 2000, Hiroshima Maiden, 2004. Recipient Village Voice OBIE award, 1990, New York Dance and performance Award, A.K.A. Bessie, 2000, Alpert award in the Arts, 2004, Alpert award in the arts, 2004; Guggenheim fellow, 2002. Office: 72-74 E 3rd St #5B New York NY 10003

HURLOCK, JAMES BICKFORD, retired lawyer; b. Chgo., Aug. 7, 1933; s. James Bickford and Elizabeth (Charls) Hurlock; m. Margaret Lyn Holding, July 1, 1961; children: James Bickford III, Burton Charls, Matthew Hunter. AB, Princeton U., 1955; BA, Oxford U., 1957, MA, 1960; JD, Harvard U., 1959. Bar: N.Y. 1960, U.S. Supreme Ct. 1967. Assoc. White & Case, N.Y.C., 1959—66, ptnr., 1967—2000; ret., 2000. Bd. dirs. Orient Express Hotels, Ltd., Stolt-Nielsen S.A., Stolt Offshore S.A. Trustee N.Y. Presbyn. Hosp.; chmn. Parker Sch. Fgn. and Comparative Law; trustee Woods Hole Oceanog. Inst.; chmn. U.S. Assn. for UNHCR. Recipient Rhodes scholarship, 1955. Mem.: ABA, Am. Law Inst., N.Y. State Bar Assn., N.Y. Yacht Club, River Club. Republican. Episcopalian. Home: 46 Byram Dr Greenwich CT 06830-7008 Office: White & Case 1155 Avenue Of The Americas New York NY 10036-2787 Office Phone: 212-819-8282. Personal E-mail: jhurlock46byram@aol.com.

HURNYAK, CHRISTINA KAISER, lawyer; b. Noblesville, Ind., Dec. 22, 1949; d. Albert Michael and Lois Angie (Gatton) Kaiser; m. Cyril Hurnyak, June 24, 1972. BA cum laude, Wittenberg U., 1972; JD, SUNY-Buffalo, 1979. Bar: N.Y. 1980, Pa. 1996, U.S. Dist. Ct. (we. dist.) Pa. 1998, bd. cert. civil trial advocate: Nat. Bd. Trial Advocacy. Mem. support staff McKinsey & Co., Inc., mgmt. cons., Chgo., 1972-75; law clk. Justice Norman J. Wolf, N.Y. Supreme Ct., Buffalo, 1980-81; assoc. Dempsey & Dempsey, Buffalo, 1979-80, 81-90, Grossman, Levine & Civiletto, Niagara Falls, N.Y., 1990-95, Tarasi, Tarasi & Fishman, P.C. (formerly Tarasi Law Firm), Pitts., 1998—. Mem.: ABA, ATLA, Pa. State Bar Assn., Pa. Trial Lawyers Assn., Allegheny County Bar Assn. Democrat. Lutheran. Office: Tarasi Tarasi & Fishman PC 510 3rd Ave Pittsburgh PA 15219-2107 Office Phone: 412-391-7135.

HURON, RODERICK EUGENE, minister, writer; b. Chesapeake, Ohio, Dec. 5, 1934; s. Raymond Clarence and Minnie Opal (Williams) Huron; m. Autumn June Hostetter, July 24, 1956; children: Lila Kay Huron Albinger, Eric Scott, Sara Lynn Huron Myers. BA, Ky. Christian Coll., 1956; MEd, U. Pitts., 1967; postgrad., U. Akron, 1968—70. Ordained to ministry Christian Chs. and Chs. of Christ, 1958; cert. meeting profl. Min. Highlawn Ch. of Christ, Huntington, W.Va., 1956—57; youth min. 1st Christian Ch., Canton, Ohio, 1957—62; min. LaBelle View Ch. of Christ, Steubenville, Ohio, 1962—67, West Akron Ch. of Christ, Ohio, 1968—71; missionary Toronto Christian Mission, 1971—75; sr. min. North Industry Christian Ch., Canton, 1976—84; dir.-elect N.Am. Christian Conv., Cin., 1984—86, conv. dir., 1986—97; pres. Meeting Excellence, 1997—2001; min. of membership devel. Lakeside Christian Ch., Ft. Mitchell, Ky., 1997—, min. involvement Lakeside Park, 1997—; dir. svc. learning Cin. Christian U., 2003—. Guest on various TV and radio programs. Author: Do You Know Who You Are, 1976, Checkpoint, 1979 (Sherwood E. Wirt award Billy Graham Evangelist Assn.), Christian Minister's Manual, 1984 (Gold Medallion award Evang. Christian Pub. Assn.), Say Hello to Life, 1984, Bible Stories for Children, 1995, Love, Laughter, and Leadership: The Ministry of Wayne B Smith, 2004; contbr. articles to religious jours. Republican. Mem. Christian Ch. E-mail: rod.huron@ccuniversity.edu.

HURRELL, JAMES WILSON, environmental scientist; b. Cin., Ohio, Mar. 5, 1962; s. Wilson Albert and Janice Mae Hurrell; m. Catherine Blair Pedigo, Aug. 11, 1990; children: Rachel Caitlin, Sarah Catherine. PhD, Purdue U., 1990. Rsch. scientist to sr. scientist Climate and Global Dynamics Divsn., Nat. Ctr. for Atmospheric Rsch., Boulder, Colo., 1990—. Dir. Climate and Global Dynamics Divsn., Nat. Ctr. for Atmospheric Rsch., Boulder, Colo., 2004—. Contbr. articles to profl. jours. Recipient Outstanding Alumnus, Purdue U., Dept. of Earth and Atmospheric Scis., 2004, U. Indpls., 2001; Esch Scholar, 1983. Mem.: Royal Meteorol. Soc., Am. Geophys. Union, Am. Meteorol. Soc. Achievements include research in on climate and climate change. Office: Nat Ctr for Atmospheric Rsch 1850 Table Mesa Dr Boulder CO 80305 Office Phone: 303-497-1383. Office Fax: 303-497-1333. Personal E-mail: jhurrell@ucar.edu.

HURST, DEBORAH, pediatric hematologist; b. Washington, May 9, 1946; d. Willard and Frances (Wilson) H.; m. Stephen Mershon Senter, June 14, 1970; children: Carlin, Daniel. BA, Harvard U., 1968; MD, Med. Coll. Pa., 1974. Diplomate Nat. Bd. Med. Examiners, Am. Bd. Pediatrics, Am. Bd. Pediatric Hematology-Oncology. Intern Bellevue Hosp., NYU Hosp., N.Y.C., 1974-75, resident in pediatrics, 1975-76; ambulatory pediatric fellow Bellevue Hosp., N.Y.C., 1976-77; hematology, oncology fellow Bellevue Hosp., Columbia U., N.Y.C., 1977-80; assoc. hematologist Childrens Hosp. Oakland, Calif., 1980-92; asst. clin. prof. U. Calif. San Francisco Med. Ctr., 1992—; med. dir. Bayer Corp., Berkeley, Calif., 1992-98; sr. dir. clin. devel. Chiron Corp., Emeryville, Calif., 1998—. Hematology cons. Assn. Asian/Pacific Community Health Orgns., Oakland; dir. Satellite Hematology Clinic/Valley Childrens Hosp., Fresno, Calif., 1984-92; cons. state dept. epidemiology Calif. State Dept. Health, Berkeley, 1992; chelation cons. lead poisoning program Childrens Hosp., Oakland, 1986-92. Contbr. articles to profl. jours. Vol. cons. lead poisoning State Dept. Epidemiology and Toxicology, Berkeley, 1986-92. Fellow Am. Acad. Pediatrics; mem. Am. Soc. Hematology, Am. Soc. Gene Therapy, Am. Soc. Clin. Oncology, Am. Soc. Pediat. Hematology/Oncology, Nat. Hemophilia Found., Internat. Soc. Thrombosis and Hemostasis. Office: Chiron Corp 4560 Horton St MS120 Emeryville CA 94608-2900

HURST, FRANCES See MAYHAR, ARDATH

HURST, GREGORY SQUIRE, investment company executive, theater director, theater producer; b. Oak Park, Ill., Dec. 1, 1947; s. Claude Squire Hurst and Marcia (Tooker) Allen; m. Joyce Barbara Baum, Apr. 4, 1981; children: Alexander Squire, Adam Spencer. BS, Miami U., Oxford, Ohio, 1969; MA, U. Wis., 1973; MFA, U. N.C., 1975; postgrad., U. Pa., 2003. Dir. theater Wayland Acad., Beaver Dam, Wis., 1969-73; instr. acting U. N.C., Chapel Hill, 1973-75; chmn. theater dept. Tarkio (Mo.) Coll., 1975-77; producing artistic dir. Pa. Stage Co., Allentown, 1979-88, George St. Playhouse, New Brunswick, N.J., 1988-97; sr. v.p. investments, fin. advisor UBS, N.Y.C., 1999—, ins. coord. br. office, 2001—. Artistic dir. Mule Barn Theatre, Tarkio, 1975-77; mem. theater panel Mo. Arts Coun., St. Louis, 1975-77, Pa. Coun. Arts, Harrisburg, 1982-85; cons. Found. Devel. Am. Profl. theatre, N.Y.C., 1983; on-site evaluator Nat. Endowment Arts, Washington, 1984-97; mem. mus. theater task force Rockefeller Found., Phila., 1985; founding mem. Playmakers Reperatory Theatre, 1975; vis. prof. Rutgers U., 1989; sr. lectr. Duke U., 1995-96. Librettist (mus. play) Song of Myself, 1981; stage dir. (world premieres) Featherton, Great Expectations, (with Hinton Battle) Shim Sham, (with John Spencer) Walk out of Water, (with Estelle Parsons) Forgiving Typhoid Mary (named One of Best 5 Plays in Am., Time mag. 1991), Greetings, Copperhead, (with Cady Huffman and John Cullum) Jekyll and Hyde, (with Joel Higgins, Christine Andreas) Fields of Ambrosia, West End London Aldwych Theatre, 1996, (with Michael Rupert) Relativity, Sing a Christmas Song, (with Laura Innes and Gabrielle Carteris) Les Liaisons Dangereuse; nat. tour The Acting Co. The Glass Menagerie; prodr. (with Calista Flockhardt) Zara Spook and Other Lures, (with Bebe Neuwirth) Just So, (with Alison Janey) Idioglossia, (With Eli Wallach and Anne Jackson) Spanky & the Fitz; dir. TV shows General Hospital, One Life to Live, Another World, The Guiding Light. Area leader Allentown and Cen. Jersey United Way, 1981-92; exec. v.p., bd. dirs. Stage Dirs. and Choreographers Found., 1989-92, pres., 1992-98, East Coast Dirs. Coun. Recipient Downtown Improvement award City of Allentown, 1987, Outstanding Contbn. award Theatre Assn. Pa., 1988, Vision, dedication, leadership award SDC Found., 1998; Tony nomination for best musical Swinging On A Star; named Best Dir. in N.J. Belmont Avenue Social Club, 1994, Les Liaisons Dangereuse, 1989. Mem. Soc. Stage Dirs., Dramatist Guild, Dirs. Guild Am. (coun. mem. 1997-99), Actors Equity Assn., U. N.C. N.J. Alumni Club (pres. 1999—), Knights of the Vine, Phi Kappa Tau. Democrat. Avocations: golf, antiques, travel, swimming, gourmet cooking, wine collecting. Home: 3 Fernwood Ct East Brunswick NJ 08816-3333 Office Phone: 212-370-7698. E-mail: gsquireh@aol.com, gregory.hurst@ubs.com.

HURST, HEATHER, illustrator; b. Aug. 14, 1975; BA, Skidmore Coll., 1997. Archeological artist and illustrator focusing on creating representations of Mesoamerican structures. Exhibitions include Nat. Gallery Art, Washington, Peabody Mus. Nat. History, illustrations published in National Geographic and Arqueologia Mexicana. Named MacArthur Fellow, John D. and Catherine T. MacArthur Found., 2004. Achievements include the reproduction of the Maya murals of Bonampak.*

HURST, KENNETH THURSTON, publisher; b. London, Apr. 3, 1923; came to U.S., 1947, naturalized, 1953; s. Ralph Thurston and Karen (Tottrup) H.; m. Joan Gee Dec. 10, 1994; children: Lincoln, Brian, Maria Therese. Student pvt. schs. Account exec. Hutzler Advt. Agy., Dayton, Ohio, 1948-53; advt. and promotion mgr. McGraw-Hill Book Co., N.Y.C., 1953-58; advt. and publicity mgr. Hawthorn Books, Inc., N.Y.C., 1958-61; gen. mgr. Prentice-Hall of India Pvt. Ltd., New Delhi, 1961-63; v.p., gen. mgr. Prentice-Hall Internat., Inc., Englewood Cliffs, N.J., 1963-70, exec. v.p., 1970, now pres. Dir. Internat. Book Distbr., Ltd., Prentice-Hall S.E. Asia Ltd., Prentice-Hall India Ltd.; State Dept. adviser to Brazil and Burma; adviser AID Mission to Turkey, 1964, Morocco, 1965; cons. U.S. Info. Agy., U. N.C., U. Scranton, SUNY, MIT, Faculty Folio mag.; lectr. State Dept. Program Bur., NYU, Rockland Community Coll., U. Scranton, Drew U., Wagner Coll., Lake Forest (Ill.) Coll., Olivet (Mich.) Coll., Rosemont Coll., Pa., Oberlin Coll., Ohio, Corning Coll., N.Y., U. Cen. Fla., U. So. Fla., Edison C.C., Pepperdine Coll., Calif., Chestnut Hill (Pa.) Coll., Spearfish Coll., S.D., Rockpoint Colony, Cornell U., Stanford U., Russell Sage Coll., Fla. State U.; faculty ann. pubs. seminar; co-chmn. Internat. Sports Awards, 1982, Pub. Hall of Fame, 1984; mem. policy bd. Ctr. for the Book; chmn. Books Across the Sea. Co-author: Books for National Growth, 1965, Indian Publishing Since Independence, 1980, American Books Abroad, 1986, Spiritual Insights for Daily Living, 1986; author: Live Life First Class, 1985, Paul Brunton: A Personal View, 1988, Living the Good Life, 1989; contbr. articles to profl. jours. Mem. Spiritual Adv. Coun., Elizabeth Kubler-Ross Ctr.; mem. com. to balance budget Ctr. Applied Rsch. in Edn., Internat. Inst. Integral Scis.; trustee Valley Cottage Free Libr.; chmn., mem. nat. exec. coun. Spiritual Frontiers Fellowship; chmn. N.Y. Easter Seal dr., 1983, Paul Brunton Philosophic Found.; bd. dirs. Ctr. for Positive Living; pres., bd. dirs. Collier County Friends of Libr. Assn.; mem. Lee County Libr. Adv. Bd.; v.p. Las Vistas Assn. With Fleet Air Arm Royal Navy, 1942-47. Recipient Presdl. E award and E Star, Pub. Hall of Fame. Mem. Asia Soc., St. John's Old Boys' Assn., Assn. Am. Pubs. (chmn. internat. div., chmn. del. to India 1979, 84, to Thailand 1981), Am. Mgmt. Assn., Inst. Bus. Planning, Mensa, Acad. Religion (trustee), Inst. Near-Death Studies (bd. dirs.), Circumnavigators Club, Forum Club (bd. dirs.), Eng. Speaking Union (bd. dirs.), Internat. Club Fla., Overseas Press Club, Fla. Coun. Humanities, Neapolitan Club, Boston Athletic Club, Publishers Club, Englewood Club (gov.), Rotary (bd. dirs.). Republican. Episcopalian. E-mail: joanhurst@webtv.net.

HURST, LELAND LYLE, natural gas company executive; b. Mooreland, Okla., Oct. 16, 1930; s. Lewis Walter and Ellen Sarah (Riggs) H.; m. Karen Lee Lamkin, Jan. 24, 1969; children: Courtney Anne, Caroline Leigh. BS in Indsl. Engring., Okla. State U., 1952; MS in Petroleum Engring., U. Tulsa, 1958. Registered profl. engr., Okla. With Amoco Prodn. Co., 1958-80; engr. Amoco Prodn. Co. (various locations), 1958-68; staff engr. Amoco Prodn. Co., Calgary, Alta., Can., 1968-70, div. engr. supr. Denver, 1970-73, area supt. Liberal, Kans., 1973-74, asst. div. engr. Denver, 1974-75, gas sales mgr., 1975-80; v.p. Amoco Gas Co., Houston, 1980-81, pres., dir., 1981-86; v.p. mktg. KN Energy Inc., Gasco Inc., 1986-87; v.p. interstate ops., exec. v.p. Gasco Inc., 1987-88, sr. v.p. ops., 1988-95, also bd. dirs., 1992-95; exec. v.p., dir. Indsl. Mechanics Inc., 1987-95, Sunflower Pipeline Co., 1988-95, Rocky Mountain Gas Co., 1992-95, 1992-95, No. Gas Co. Wyo., 1992-95, 1992-95. Bd. dirs., v.p. KN Front Range Oper. Co., KN Wattenberg Co., KN Wattenberg Ltd. Liability Co.; bd. dirs. RMNG Gathering Co., TCP Gathering Co.; v.p. Panola/Rusk Gatherers, Am. Energy Holdings, Inc., Am. Gas Storage, L.P., Am. Gathering, L.P., Am. Processing, L.P., Am. Oil and Gas Corp., Am. Pipeline Co., Am. Webb, Inc., AOG Holdings, Inc., AOG Mgmt., Inc., Caprock Pipeline Co., Red River Gas Pipeline Corp., Red River Pipeline, L.P., RRP Fin. Corp., Webb/Duval Gatherers, Westar Transmission Co., 1995. With Chem. Corps U.S. Army, 1953-55. Served with Chem. Corps U.S. Army, 1953-55. Mem. Rocky Mountain Gas Men's Assn. (bd. dirs. 1977), Soc. Petroleum Engrs. (editl. com. 1953-55), Rocky Mountain Oil and Gas Assn. Colo. (pres. 1995-97, indsl. mechanic chmn. 1995-2004), Natural Gas Men of Houston-New Orleans (v.p.), Houston Club, Denver Petroleum Club. Republican.

HURST, MARGARET CHERYL, elementary school educator, music educator; b. Vancouver, Wash., Oct. 10, 1963; d. Wesley Wayne Poff and Margaret Christine Lubbers; m. Tracy Brian Hurst, Sept. 28, 1985; children: Adrienne Camille, Lauren McKenzie. BA in Edn., Ctrl. Wash. U., 1987. Cert. grades K-12 music and K-8 elem. edn. tchr. Wash. Elem. music specialist Evergreen Sch. Dist., Vancouver, 1988—. Facilitator Marimba Maria Marimba Performing Ensemble, Camas, Wash., 2000—; 3rd horn Yakima (Wash.) Symphony Orch.; pvt. french horn instr. Leader Girl Scouts USA, Vancouver, 1997—99. Mem.: Music Educators Nat. Conf. Avocations: swimming, running, playing french horn and marimbas, bicycling. Office: Fisher's Landing Elementary School 3800 Hiddenbrook Dr Vancouver WA 98683 Office Phone: 360-604-6650.

HURST, PATRICIA ANN, professional golfer; b. San Leandro, Calif., May 23, 1969; m. Jeff Heitt, Oct. 14, 1995; children: Jackson, Reilly. Student, San Jose U. Tchg. pro golfer La Quinta Country Club; golfer Players West mini-tour, winner 5 titles; winner USGA Jr., 1986, USGA Amateur, 1990, Oldsmobile Classic, 1997, Nabisco Dinah Shore, 1998, Electrolux USA, 2000; mem. US Solheim Cup, 1998, 2000, Captain's pick, 2002; mem. U.S. World Amateur team. Avocation: music. Office: care LPGA 100 International Golf Dr Daytona Beach FL 32124-1082

HURST, REBECCA MCNABB, language educator; b. Lynchburg, Va., July 17, 1951; d. Eugene Randolph and Lucy Margurite McNabb; m. Larry Lee Hurst, June 26, 1971; children: Monica Hurst Ferrebee, Meredith Hurst Mabe. MEd in Ednl. Adminstrn., William And Mary, Williamsburg, Va, 1988. Cert. post grad. profl. Va., 1988, nat. bd. cert. tchr., cert. in adolescent/young adult English/lang. arts. Tchr. Menchville HS, Newport News, Va., 1986—99; lead HS tchr. Enterprise Acad., 1999—. Devel. assets coord. Enterprise Acad., Newport News, Va., 2001—, sch. improvement team, 2000—, sch. newspaper founder and sponsor, 2000—. Founding mem. Nat. Campaign For Tolerance, Montgomery, Ala., 2000—03. Recipient Outstanding Youth Adv. award, Greater Peninsula Workplace Devel. Consortium, 2002. Mem.: NEA, Va. Assn. Teachers Of English, Nat. Coun. Tchrs. of English, Newport News Edn. Assn., Va. Edn. Assn., Assn. Supervision and Curriculum Devel. Office: Enterprise Acad Ste 110 813 Diligence Dr Newport News VA 23606 Office Phone: 757-868-3304. Business E-Mail: becky.hurst@nn.k12.va.us.

HURST, RICHARD EDWARD, surgeon; b. Tacoma, Nov. 24, 1942; BS, U. Wash., 1964, MD, 1967. Diplomate Am. Bd. Surgery. Intern Los Angeles County Gen. Hosp., L.A., 1967-68; resident in gen. surgery U. Oreg. Med. Ctr., Portland, 1968-71, 72-73; fellow in Surgery U. Tex.-M.D. Anderson Cancer Inst., Houston, 1971-72; pvt. practice, Vancouver, Wash., 1972—. Mem. staff (S.W. Wash. Hosp., Vancouver, Providence Med. Ctr., Portland; med. edn. dir. hyperbaric unit (Providence Hosp., Portland. Fellow ACS; mem. AMA. Office: 200 NE Mother Joseph Pl Ste 330 Vancouver WA 98664-3288 E-mail: rhurst@thevancouverclinic.com.

HURST, ROBERT JAY, security firm executive; b. NYC, Nov. 5, 1945; s. Kurt and Jeanette (Sachs) Hurst; m. Soledad Deleon Hurst; children from previous marriage: Alexander, Amanda. BA, Clark U., 1966; M in Govt. Adminstrn., U. Pa., 1968, Pub. Fin. fellow, 1969. With investment banking divsn. Merrill Lynch, Pierce, Fenner & Smith, Inc., NYC, 1969-74, v.p., 1974, Goldman, Sachs & Co., NYC, 1974-80, gen. ptnr., 1980—2000, mem. mgmt. com., 1990—2000, co-head investment banking div., 1990—96, head investment banking div., 1996—99, mem. exec. com., 1995—2000, vice chmn., 1999—2000, bd. dir.; CEO 9/11 United Svcs. Group, 2001—. Trustee Whitney Mus. Am. Art, 1998—, pres., 2002—; trustee coun. Nat. Found. for Tchg. Entrepreneurship, bd. dir.; mem. bd. overseers Wharton Sch., U. Pa., coun. on fgn. relations, com. for econ. devel.; trustee Com. Econ. Develop., Ctrl. Pk. Conservancy; bd. trustees Manhattan Inst.; trustee coun. Nat. Gallery Art; bd. dir. Air Clic Inc., NYC 2012, IDB Holding Ltd., Constellation Energy Group, VF Corp; chmn. Jewish Mus., 1997—2002. Recipient Louis Marshall Award, Jewish Theological Soc., 2000. Mem.: Maroon Creek Club (Aspen), Atlantic Golf Club (Bridgehampton), U. Club. Mailing: c/o Whitney Mus Am Art 945 Madison Ave New York NY 10021*

HURT, CHARLES EDWARD, lawyer; b. Charleston, W.Va., Aug. 30, 1930; s. John Franklin and Lillian Grace (McClain) H.; m. Carolyn Hanly, Dec. 18, 1960; children: John Hanly, Sarah Jane. JD, W.Va. U., 1957. Bar: W.Va. 1957, U.S. Dist. Ct. (so. dist.) W.Va. 1957, U.S. Supreme Ct. 1959, S.C. 1988, U.S. Dist. Ct. S.C. 1992. Law clerk U.S. Dist. Ct. W.Va., Charleston, 1957; pvt. practice Charleston, 1958-85; sr. ptnr. Hurt & Carrico, Charleston, 1985-86, Hurt & Barone, Charleston, 1986—90. Prof. Morris Harvey Coll., Charleston, 1961-67; v.p. Elk Nat. Bank, Big Chimney, W.Va., 1977-88; mem. 4th Cir. Jud. Conf. Pres. W.Va. Heart Assn., 1960; mem. jud. com. W.Va. State Bar. With USN, 1948-52, Korea. Mem. Internat. Platform Assn., Am. Arbitration Assn., Tenn. Squire, Hon. Order Ky. Cols., Masons, Phi Alpha Theta, Phi Alpha Delta, Tau Kappa Epsilon. Republican. Lutheran. Home: 1671 Woodvale Dr Charleston WV 25314-2547 Office: PO Box 833 Charleston WV 25323-0833 Office Phone: 304-344-3501.

HURT, JAMES RIGGINS, English language educator; b. Ashland, Ky., May 22, 1934; s. Joe and Martha Clay (Riggins) H.; m. Phyllis Tilton, June 5, 1958; children: Christopher, Ross, Matthew. AB, U. Ky., 1956, MA, 1957; PhD, Ind. U., 1965. Asst. prof. Ind. U., Kokomo, 1963-66; asst. prof. U. Ill., Urbana-Champaign, 1966-69, asso. prof., 1969-73, prof. English, 1973—. Author: Aelfric, 1972, Catiline's Dream, 1972, Film and Theatre, 1974, Writing Illinois, 1992, (play) Abraham Lincoln Walks at Midnight, 1980; co-editor: Literature of the Western World, 1984. Served with U.S. Army, 1957-59. Fellow Ill. Ctr. Advanced Study, 1979-80, 86-87. Mem. MLA, Ill. State Hist. Soc. Home: 1001 W William St Champaign IL 61821-4508 Office: 325 English Bldg 608 S Wright St Urbana IL 61801-3630 E-mail: j-hurt@uiuc.edu.

HURT, JOHN VINCENT, actor; b. Chesterfield, Eng., Jan. 22, 1940; s. Arhould Herbert and Phyllis (Massey) H.; m. Annette Robertson, 1962 (div. 1964); m. Donna Peacock, 1984 (div. 1990); Joan Dalton, 1990 (div. 1996); children: Alexander, Nicholas; m. Ann Rees Meyers, Mar. 2005. Student, Royal Acad. Dramatic Art, 1960-62. Actor: (plays) including Chips with Everything, 1962, Hamp, 1964, Little Malcolm and His Struggle Against the Eunuchs, 1966, Man and Superman, 1969, The Caretaker, 1972, Travesties, 1974, The Shadow of a Gunman, 1978, (films) including (debut) The Wild and the Willing, 1962, A Man for All Seasons, 1966, Before Winter Comes, 1969, Mr. Forbush and the Penguins, 1971, Little Malcolm, 1974, Spectre, 1977, The Disappearance, 1978, The Shout, 1978, Alien, 1978, Midnight Express, 1978, The Elephant Man, 1980, Heaven's Gate, 1981, History of the World Part I, 1981, Night Crossing, 1982, Watership Down, 1982, The Osterman Weekend, 1982, The Hit, 1983, Champions, 1983, '1984', 1985, Rocinonte, 1985, From the Hip, 1986, Jake Speed, 1986, Vincent, 1987, White Mischief, 1987, Aria, 1987, Scandal, 1989, Frankenstein Unbound, 1989, The Field, 1990, Windprints, 1990, King Ralph, 1991, I Dreamt I Woke Up, 1991, Lapse of Memory, 1991, L'Oeil Qui Ment, 1992, Crime and Punishment, 1993, Monolith, 1993, Forraderi, 1994, Second Best, 1994, Even Cowboys Get the Blues, 1994, Rob Roy, 1995, Wild Bill, 1995, Two Nudes Bathing, 1995, Saigon Baby, 1995, Love and Death on Long Island, 1997, Contact, 1997, Bandyta, 1997, The Commissioner, 1998, The Climb, 1998, Night Train, 1998, All the Little Animals, 1998, Le Chateau des singes (voice), 1999, You're Dead, 1999, If.Dog.Rabbit, 1999, New Blood, 1999, The Tigger Movie (voice), 1999, Lost Souls, 2000, Captain Corelli's Mandolin, 2001, Tabloid, 2001, Harry Potter and the Sorcerer's Stone, 2001, Miranda, 2002, Crime and Punishment, 2002, Owning Mahowney, 2003, Dogville (voice), 2003, Hellboy, 2004, Short Order, 2005, Valiant (voice), 2005, Manderlay (voice), 2005, The Skeleton Key, 2005; (TV films) include The Naked Civil Servant, 1974, Caligula in I Claudius, 1974, Crime and Punishment, 1979 (Emmy award 1979), The Storyteller, 1986, Poison Candy, 1987, Scandal, 1988, The Investigation: Inside a Terrorist Bombing, 1990, Who Bombed Birmingham (Granada TV), 1990, Journey to Knock, 1991, Red Fox (BBC), 1991, Dark at Noon, 1991, London Vertigo (play) 1991, Six Characters in Search of an Author, (BBC) 1992, Great Moments In Aviation, 1992, Prisoners in Time, 1995, Krapp's Last Tape, 2000, Bait, 2002, The Alan Clark Diaries, 2004; (TV miniseries) Picture Windows, 1995, Watership Down (voice), 1999. Recipient Brit. Academy award, Brit. Oscar, Golden Globe award, Brit. Emmy. Mem. Brit. Equity, Screen Actors Guild, Am. Acad. of Arts and Scis., AFTRA.*

HURT, WILLIAM, actor; b. Washington, Mar. 20, 1950; s. Henry Luce III (Stepfather) and Claire; m. Mary Beth Supinger (div. 1982); m. Heidi Henderson, Mar. 5, 1989 (div. 1992); children: Sam, William Jr.; children: Alexander Devon, Jeanne. Grad., Tufts U., 1972; student, Juilliard Sch. Joined Oreg. Shakespeare Festival, 1975; performed regularly with Ashland Shakespeare Festival, Oreg.; joined Circle Repertory Theatre, NYC, 1977. Actor: (theatre) including Henry V, 1977, My Life, 1977, Ulysses in Traction, Lulu, 1978, Fifth of July, 1978, Hamlet, 1979, Mary Stuart, 1979, Childe Byron, 1981, The Diviners, 1981, The Great Grandson of Jedediah kohler, 1982, Richard II, 1982, A Midsummer Night's Dream, 1982, Hurlyburly, 1984, Joan of Arc at the Stake, 1985, Love Letters, 1989, Beside Herself, 1989, Ivanov, 1991, (films) Altered States, 1980, Eyewitness, 1981, Body

Heat, 1981, The Big Chill, 1983, Gorky Park, 1983, Kiss of the Spider Woman, 1985 (Best Actor Award, Cannes Film Festival, 1985, Acad. Award for best actor, 1986), Children of a Lesser God, 1986 (Acad. Award nomination for best actor, 1987), Broadcast News, 1987 (Acad. Award nomination for best actor, 1988), A Time of Destiny, 1988, The Accidental Tourist, 1988, I Love You To Death, 1990, Marilyn Hotchkiss' Ballroom Dancing and Charm School (voice), 1990, Alice, 1990, The Doctor, 1991, Until the End of the World, 1991, The Plague, 1992, Mr. Wonderful, 1993, Trial by Jury, 1994, Second Best, 1994, Secrets Shared with a Stranger, 1994, Smoke, 1995, Michael, 1996, Jane Eyre, 1996, A Couch in New York, 1996, Loved, 1997, Dark City, 1998, Lost in Space, 1998, One True Thing, 1998, The Big Brass Ring, 1999, Sunshine, 1999, Do Not Disturb, 1999, The 4th Floor, 1999, The Simian Line, 2000, Artificial Intelligence: AI, 2001, The Contaminated Man, 2001, Rare Birds, 2001, Changing Lanes, 2002, Nearest to Heaven, 2002, Tuck Everlasting, 2002, The Tulse Luper Suitcases: The Moab Story, 2003, The Blue Butterfly, 2004, The Village, 2004, (TV films) Verna: USO Girl, 1978, All the Way Home, 1981, The Miracle Maker (voice), 2000, The Flamingo Rising, 2001, Master Spy: The Robert Hanssen Story, 2002, (TV miniseries)The Best of Families, 1977, Dune 2000, (TV series) Riviere-des-Jeremie, 2001. Recipient 1st Spencer Tracy Award for outstanding screen performances and profl. achievement, UCLA, 1988. Office: c/o Hilda Quille/William Morris 151 S El Camino Dr Beverly Hills CA 90212-2704

HURT, WILLIAM HOLMAN, investment management company executive; b. L.A., Mar. 29, 1927; s. Holman G. and Mary E. (Ortloff) H.; m. Sheridan Ann Stephens, Aug. 10, 1950 (div. May. 1970); children: Kelley Anne Hurt Purnell, Kathleen Constance, Courtney Diana Hurt MacMillan; m. Sarah Sherman, May 28, 1970. BS magna cum laude, U. So. Calif., 1949; MBA, Harvard U., 1951. With Dean Witter & Co., Los Angeles, 1951-71, ptnr., 1959, sr. v.p., 1968-70, exec. v.p., dir., mem. exec. com., dir. mktg. and rsch., 1969-71; chmn. exec. com. Capital Rsch. Co., 1972-77; chief exec. office Capital Group, Inc., L.A., 1978-82; chmn. Capital Strategy Rsch., Inc., 1982—. Adv. com. Coldwell Banker Funds, 1978-99. Mem. bd. councilors Grad. Sch. Bus., U. So. Calif., L.A., 1978-88, vis. com., 1990-96; bd. dirs. L.A. Children's Hosp., 1985— . Served with USNR, 1945-46. Mem. Calif. Club, L.A. Athletic Club, N.Y. Athletic Club, Phi Kappa Phi, Beta Gamma Sigma, Kappa Alpha. Republican. Office: 333 S Hope St Los Angeles CA 90071-1406

HURTADO, ERNEST R., media specialist, educator; b. Pitts., Calif., Aug. 15, 1950; s. Florentino Aviña Hurtado and Micaela Fajardo Ivory; m. Rosario Damiguez (div. May 1994). AA, Diablo Valley Coll.; BA, Mich. State U., 1973; MS, Calif. State U., 1974. L;ibr. Lansing Ind. Sch. Dist., Mich., 1974—77; media specialist Union Sch. Dist., Hayward, Calif., 1977—78; libr. Mich. State U., East Lansing, 1978—79; bilingual tchr. Ft. Worth Ind. Sch. Dist., 1980—83; libr. San Jose Unified Sch. Dist., Calif., 1984—90; tchr. English as 2d lang. East Side Union Sch., 1991—. Instr. traffic sch. Aliane C.C., San Jose, 1995—98; instr. drivers edn. Inst. Traffic Sch., 1991—. Author: Boy with Chocolate Mumps, 2003. Mem. YMCA, 1996—, Mex.-Am. Polit. Assn., San Jose, 1976—. Mem.: Calif. Tchrs. Assn. Democrat. Roman Catholic. Avocations: guitar, chess, basketball, photography. Home: 1663 Kitchener Dr Sunnyvale CA 94087 Office Phone: 408-254-8101.

HURTADO, RODRIGO CLAUDIO, allergist; b. Chile, 1939; MD, U. Chile, Santiago, 1964. Diplomate Am. Bd. Allergy and Immunology, Am. Bd. Pediatrics. Intern U. Chile, 1964, resident, 1968-71; fellow allergy and infectious diseases Georgetown U., Washington, 1972-74; pvt. practice Washington, 1974—; clin. asst. prof. Georgetown U. Med. Sch., Washington, 1974—. Mem. Am. Acad. Pediatrics and Immunology, Am. Acad. Allergy Asthma and Immunology, Am. Acad. Pediatrics, Am. Coll. Allergy. Office: 3450 N Beauregard St Alexandria VA 22302-1200

HURTEAU, GILLES DAVID, retired obstetrician, gynecologist, educator, dean; b. Cornwall, Ont., Can., Nov. 28, 1928; s. Joseph A. and Antoinette (St-Laurent) H.; m. Janine Anita Carriere, June 16, 1956; children: Michele, Jean, Louise, Pierre, Gilles Andre. BA, U. Ottawa, 1951; MD, CM, McGill U., 1955. Licentiate, Med. Council Can., 1956; cert. in ob-gyn. Instr. and clin. asst. Yale U. Med. Sch., New Haven, 1961-62; asst. prof. U. Ottawa Med. Sch., Ont., 1963-66, assoc. prof., 1966, prof. and chmn. dept. ob-gyn, 1967-76, dean Sch. Medicine, 1976-89, dean faculty health scis., 1978-89; exec. dir./registrar Royal Coll. Physicians and Surgeons Can., Ottawa, 1990-95; v.p., bd. governors U. of Ottawa, 2003—, pres., exec. com. of the bd. of governors, 2003—. Bd. govs. U. Ottawa, 1995, chmn. exec. com., vice-chmn. bd. 2003—; bd. dirs. Assoc. Med. Svcs. Inc., Ont. Mem. editl. bd. European Jour. Ob-Gyn and Reproductive Biology, 1970-78; contbr. articles to profl. jours., chpts to books. Mem. coun. Ottawa-Carleton Dist. Health Coun., 1978-84; jt. rsch. rev. task force Ont. Coun. Health, 1977-81; bd. dirs. Ont. Cancer Treatment and Rsch. Found., 1983-92, Physicians Svcs. Inc. Found. Ont., 1984-86, 95-2001. Fellow Royal Coll. Physicians and Surgeons Can. (coun. 1970-78, v.p. 1976-78), Royal Coll. Physicians Ireland (1994—); mem. Coun. Ont. Faculty of Medicine (1976-89), Assn. Can. Med. Colls. (pres. 1981-82). Home: 31 Durham (Priv)-Unit 203 Ottawa ON Canada K1M 2J1 Personal E-mail: gilles.hurteau@sympatico.ca. *Ce que nous connaissons est peu de chose; ce que nous ignorons est immense.*

HURTER, ARTHUR PATRICK, economist, educator; b. Chgo., Jan. 29; s. Arthur P. and Lillian T. (Thums) H.; m. Florence Evalyn Kays; children—Patricia Lyn, Arthur Earl BSChemE, MSChemE, MA in Econs., PhD in Econs., Northwestern U. Chem. engr. Zonlite Rsch. Lab., Evanston, Ill., 1957-58; assoc. dir. Rsch. Transp. Ctr., Northwestern U., Evanston, 1963-65; asst. prof. dept. Indsl. Engring. and Mgmt. Scis. Tech. Inst., Northwestern U., 1962-66, prof., 1970—; prof. of transp., 1992—; chmn. dept. Northwestern U., 1969-89, assoc. prof. fin. Grad. Sch. Mgmt., 1969-70, prof., 1970—. Faculty mem. Newspaper Mgmt. Ctr., Transp. Ctr., 1989—; cons. U. Chgo., ESCOR, Sears Roebuck & Co., Standard Oil of Ind., Ill.; bd. dirs. Ill. Environ. Health Rsch. Ctr., 1972-77; mem. com. Sci. Tech. Adv., Ill. Inst. Natural Resources, 1980-84. Author: The Economics of Private Truck Transportation, 1965, Facility Location and the Theory of Production, 1989; contbr. articles to profl. jours. Pres. Coun. St. Scholastical H.S., 1972-80; elder Granville Ave. Presbyn. Ch., 1976-89; deacon 1st Presbyn. Ch., Evanston, trustee, 2003—. Grantee Resources for the Future, 1964, Office of Naval Research, 1965, NSF, Social Sci. Research Council dissertation fellow Mem. Am. Econ. Assn., Regional Sci. Assn., Ops. Research Soc. Am., Inst. Mgmt. Scis., Inst. Indsl. Engrs., Sigma Xi, Phi Lambda Upsilon, Tau Beta Pi, Alpha Pi Mu (Disting. Engr. award). Home: 1505 W Norwood St Chicago IL 60660-2414 Office: Dept Indsl Engring Mgmt Sci Technological Inst Northwestern U Evanston IL 60208-0001 Office Phone: 847-491-3414. Business E-Mail: hurter@iems.northwestern.edu.

HURTT, FRANCES SCOTT, author; d. Fred Lee and Leona Lee Scott; m. Larry E. Hurtt, June 21, 1974; children: Jason Scott, Jeremy Brandon, Justin Matthew. BA in English and Sec. Edn., Ark. Coll., Batesville, 1974. Cert. sec. tchr., Ark., Mo.; cert. childbirth educator, lactation cons. Tchr. English Salem (Ark.) Sch., 1975-79, Marvel (Ark.) Pub. Sch., 1979-81, Seymour (Mo.) Sch., 1981-83; substitute tchr. Springfield (Mo.) R-12 Schs., 1983-85; mgr. pub. Metropolitan Pub. Co., Springfield, 1985-86; cert. childbirth educator Nat. Assn. Childbirth Educators, 1986-90; med. asst., dir. employee edn. Levi, Harrison, Ark., 1991-95. Cons. in field. Author: EHBE - the First 50 Years, 2000; contbr. articles to profl. jours. Baptist. Avocations: crafts, singing, church.

HURWICZ, LEONID, economist, educator; b. Moscow, 1917; arrived in U.S., 1940; LLM, U. Warsaw, Poland, 1938; DSc (hon.), Northwestern U., 1980; D honoris causa, U. Autónoma de Barcelona, Spain, 1989; D of Econs. honoris causa, Keio U., Tokyo, 1993; LLD (hon.), U. Chgo., 1993; D honoris causa, Warsaw Sch. Econs., Poland, 1994; Dr.rer.pol honoris causa, U. Bielefeld, 2004. Rsch. assoc. Cowles Commn. U. Chgo., 1944—46; from assoc. prof. to prof. Iowa State U., Ames, 1946—49; prof. econ., math. and stats. U. Ill., 1949—51, U. Minn., Mpls., 1951—99, Regents' prof., 1969—88, Regent's prof. emeritus, 1988—, Carlson prof. econs., 1989—92, prof. econs., 1992—. Vis. prof. econs. Stanford U., Calif., 1955—56, 1958—59, Harvard U., Cambridge, Mass., 1969—71, U. Calif., Berkeley, 1976—77, Northwestern U., Evanston, Ill., 1988—89, U. Calif., Santa Barbara, 1998, Calif. Inst. Tech., 1999, U. Mich., Ann Arbor, 2002; Fisher lectr. U. Copenhagen, 1963; hon. prof. Ctrl. China U. Sci. and Tech., Wuhan, 1984; vis. lectr. People's U., Beijing, 1986, Tokyo U., 1982, Hebrew U., Jerusalem, 1993, Australian Econometric Mtgs., Melbourne, 1997; vis. Fulbright lectr. Bangalore U., India, 1965—66; vis. disting. prof. econs. U. Ill., 2001; invited lectr. Chuo U., Keio U., UN U., Inst. Adv. Studies (symposium participation), Tokyo, 1999, Symposium Devel. Western China, Chongqing, 2000, Pub. Econ. Theory Conf. Warwick U., England, 2000; cons. Econ. Design, Istanbul, 2000, Ctr. China U. Sci. and Tech., Wuhan, 2000, Peking U., 2000. Co-author (co-editor (with K.J. Arrow): Studies in Resource Allocation Processes, 1977; co-author: (co-editor (with K.J. Arrow and J. Uzawa) Studies in Linear and Non-Linear Programming, 1958; co-author: (co-editor (with J.S. Chipman) Prefences, Utility and Demand, 1971; co-author: (co-editor (D. Schmeidler and H. Sonnenschein) Social Goals and Social Organization, 1985; editor: Econ. Design, 1993, Review of Econ. Design, 1997, Jour. of pub. Econ. Theory, 1999, Advances in Mathematical Economics, 1999, Econs. Bull., 2001; mem. adv. bd.: Jour. of Math. Econs.; contbr. articles to profl. jours. Recipient Nat. medal Sci., 1990; fellow, Ctr. Advances Studies in Behavioral Scis., 1955—56; scholar Sherman Fairchild Disting. scholar, Calif. Inst. Tech., 1984—85. Fellow: Am. Econ. Assn. (disting., lectr. 1972), Econometric Soc. (pres. 1969); mem.: NAS, Am. Acad. Arts and Scis. Office: Univ Minn Dept Econs 271 19th Ave S Minneapolis MN 55455-0430 Business E-Mail: hurwicz@umn.edu.

HURWITZ, ANDREW D., state supreme court justice; AB in Public & Internat. Affairs, Princeton U., 1968; JD, Yale U., 1972. Bar: Conn. 1973, Ariz. 1974, U.S. Dist. Ct. Ariz. 1975, U.S. Ct. Appeals (9th cir.) 1975, U.S. Supreme Ct. 1976, U.S. Dist. Ct. Conn. 1977, U.S. Ct. Appeals (2d cir.) 1977, U.S. Tax Ct. 1987, U.S. Ct. Appeals (7th cir.) 1987. Law clk. to Hon. Jon O. Newman U.S. Dist. Ct. Conn., 1972; law clk. to Hon. J. Joseph Smith U.S. Ct. Appeals, 1972—73; law clk. to Hon. Potter Stewart U.S. Supreme Ct., 1973—74; with Meyer Hendricks et. al., 1974—80, 1984—95, 1983—95, Osborn Maledon, 1995—2003; assoc. justice Ariz. State Supreme Ct., Phoenix, 2003—. Chief of staff Ariz. Gov. Bruce Babbitt, 1980—83, Ariz. Gov. Rose Mofford, 1988; mem. Ariz. Bd. of Regents, 1988—96, pres., 1992—93; co-chair of transition team Ariz. Gov. Janet Napolitano, 2002; vis. prof. law, civil procedure Ariz. State U., 1994—95, disting. vis. from practice, 2001, adjunct prof. law, ethics, supreme ct. litigation, legislative process, civil procedure, 1977—80, 1988, 2002. Mem. bd. dirs. Ariz. Ctr. for Law in Public Interest, 1986—88, Children's Action Alliance, 1999—2003, sec., 2002—03; chair City of Phoenix Neighborhood Improvement Com., 1986—88, City of Phoenix Street Environment Com., 1989—90. Mem.: State Bar of Ariz. (Com. on Rules of Professional Conduct 1985—90, Examination & Bar Review Com. 1986—87), Phi Beta Kappa. Office: Ariz State Supreme Ct Adminstrv Office Cts 1501 W Washington Phoenix AZ 85007 Office Phone: 602-542-4532.

HURWITZ, ANN, lawyer; b. Portsmouth, Va., Aug. 19, 1953; d. Frederick Dean and Mildred (Wood) Hardy; m. Mitchell Seth Hurwitz, May 30, 1981. BA, U. S.C., 1977; JD, U. N.C., 1980. Bar: Tex. 1983, D.C. 1981, N.C. 1980. Assoc. Thompson, Pikrallidas & Schott, Alexandria, Va., 1980-82, Smith, Underwood, Carmichael & Floyd, Dallas, 1982-84, Evans, Fernandez, Forgerson & Hurwitz, Dallas, 1984-86, Smith, Underwood & Hunter, Dallas, 1987-88; ptnr. Smith & Underwood, Dallas, 1988; mng. ptnr. Dallas off. DLA Piper Rudnick Gray Cary, Dallas. Contbr. articles to profl. jours. Named a Texas Super Lawyer, 2003—04. Mem. ABA (franchising subcom of the small bus. com. of bus. law sect. of corp., banking and bus. law), Tex. State Bar Assn. (franchising com. of intellectual property law sect.), Dallas Bar Assn., N.C. Bar Assn., D.C. Bar Assn. Democrat. Baptist. Office: DLA Piper Rudnick Gray Cary 1717 Main St Dallas TX 75201-4605 Office Phone: 214-743-4521. Office Fax: 214-743-4545. Business E-Mail: ann.hurwitz@dlapiper.com.

HURWITZ, DEENA R., law educator; b. Washington; BA, U. Calif., Santa Cruz, 1980; JD, Northeastern U., 1996. Bar: Mass. 1999. Mem. staff Resource Ctr. for Nonviolence, Calif.; project exec. adminstr. Ctr. Internat. Human Rights Enforcement, Ramallah, 1997; legal counselor UN High Commr. Refugees, Washington, 1997—99; Orgn. for Security and Co-operation in Europe liaison officer to Human Rights Coordination Ctr. of Office High Rep., Bosnia-Herzegovina; dir. Bosnia program Internat. Human Rights Law Group; Robert M. Cover/Allard K. Lowenstein Fellow in Internat. Human Rights Yale Law Sch., 2000—03; dir. human rights program and Internat. Human Rights Law Clinic U. Va. Sch. Law, 2003—. Editor: Walking the Red Line, Israelis in Search of Justice for Palestine, 1992. Office: U Va Sch Law 580 Massie Rd Charlottesville VA 22903-1789 Office Phone: 434-924-4776. E-mail: deena@virginia.edu.

HURWITZ, JOHANNA (JOHANNA FRANK), writer; b. N.Y.C., Oct. 9, 1937; d. Nelson and Tillie (Miller) Frank; m. Uri Hurwitz, Feb. 19, 1962; children: Nomi, Beni. BA, Queens Coll., 1958; MLS, Columbia U., 1959. Libr. children's sect. N.Y. Pub. Libr., 1959-64; lectr. in children's lit. Queen's Coll., N.Y.C., 1965-69; libr. Calhoun Sch., N.Y.C., 1968-75, New Hyde Park (N.Y.) Sch. Dist., 1975-77; libr. children's sect. Great Neck (N.Y.) Pub. Libr., 1978-92. Author: Busybody Nora, 1976, Nora and Mrs. Mind-Your-Own-Business, 1977, The Law of Gravity, 1978, Much Ado About Aldo, 1978, Aldo Applesauce, 1979, New Neighbours for Nora, 1979, Once I Was a Plum Tree, 1980, Superduper Teddy, 1980, Aldo Ice Cream, 1981, Baseball Fever, 1981, The Rabbi's Girls, 1982, Tough-Luck Karen, 1982, Rip-Roaring Russell, 1983, DeDe Takes Charge!, 1984, The Hot and Cold Summer, 1984, The Adventures of Ali Baba Bernstein, 1985, Russell Rides Again, 1985, Hurricane Elaine, 1986, Yellow Blue Jay, 1986, Class Clown, 1987, Russell Sprouts, 1987, The Cold and Hot Winter, 1988, Teacher's Pet, 1988, Anne Frank: Life in Hiding, 1988, Hurray for Ali Baba Bernstein, 1989, Russell and Elisa, 1989, Astrid Lindgren: Storyteller to the World, 1989, Class President, 1990, Aldo Peanut Butter, 1990, School's Out, 1991, E Is for Elisa, 1991, Roz and Ozzie, 1992, Ali Baba Bernstein, Lost and Found, 1992, The Up and Down Spring, 1993, Make Room for Elisa, 1993, Leonard Bernstein: A Passion for Music, 1993, New Shoes for Silvia, 1993, A Word to the Wise, 1994, School Spirit, 1994, A Llama in the Family, 1994, Ozzie on His Own, 1995, Birthday Surprises, 1995, Elisa in the Middle, 1995, Even Stephen, 1996, Down and Up Fall, 1996, Spring Break, 1997, Ever-Clever Elisa, 1997, Helen Keller: Courage in the Dark, 1997, Faraway Summer, 1998, Starting School, 1998, A Dream Come True, 1998, Llama in the Library, 1999, Just Desserts Club, 1999, Summer with Elisa, 2000, Peewee's Tale, 2000, One Small Dog, 2000, Lexi's Tale, 2001, Russell's Secret, 2001, Oh No, Noah!, 2002, PeeWee & Plush, 2002, Dear Emma, 2002, Ethan, Out & About, 2002, Ethan at Home, 2003, Elisa Michaels, Bigger and Better, 2003, Fourth Grade Fuss, 2004. Recipient Bluebonnet award Tex. Libr. Assn., 1987, Wyoming Indian Paintbrush award 1987, W.Va. Children's Book award 1989, Sunshine State award Fla. Libr. Assn., 1990, Miss. Children's Book award Miss. Libr. Assn., 1990, S.C. Children's Book award, 1990, Garden State award N.J. Sch. Libr. Assn., 1991, 94, Weekly Reader Book Club award, 1993, Land of Enchantment award N.Mex., 2004. Mem. PEN, Author's Guild, Soc. Children's Book Writers, Amnesty Internat. Address: 10 Spruce Pl Great Neck NY 11021-1904

HURWITZ, MITCHELL, television producer, writer; b. Nov. 1973; Formerly with Witt,Thomas, Harris Productions. Prodr., writer: (TV series) The Golden Girls, 1990—91; writer The John Larroquette Show, 1993; writer, cons. Less Than Perfect, 2002; writer, exec. prodr. Arrested Development, 2003— (Emmy award for Oustanding Comedy Series, 2003); exec. prodr.: (TV series) Everything's Relative, 1999; exec. prodr., writer: (TV series) The Ellen Show, 2001. Office: c/o Fox Broadcasting Co 10201 West Pico Blvd Los Angeles CA 90035*

HURWITZ, SIDNEY, printmaker; b. Worcester, Mass., 1932; Attended, Sch. of Worcester Art Mus.; BA, Brandeis U.; MFA, Boston U.; attended, Stuttgart Acad. Art, Germany, Skowhegan Sch., Maine. Prof. Wellesley Coll., Brandeis U., Amherst Coll., Boston U., prof. emeritus. Represented in permanent collections Mus. Modern Art, Mus. Fine Arts, Boston, Library of Congress, Victoria & Albert Mus., DeCordova Mus. & Sculpture Pk., Boston Pub. Library, Krakow Nat. Mus. Fulbright Fellowship, Germany. Mailing: Boston U Sch Visual Arts 855 Commonwealth Ave Rm 552 Boston MA 02215*

HURWITZ, SOL, writer, consultant; b. Washington, Aug. 31, 1932; s. Morris Aaron and Rose (Honig) H.; m. Nina Deutch, May 3, 1959; children: Linda, Mark Aaron, Laura. BA, Harvard U., 1953, postgrad., 1955—56, advanced mgmt. program, 1977. Various communication and broadcasting positions, Washington, 1956-60, N.Y.C., 1960-66; assoc. dir. info. Com. for Econ. Devel., N.Y.C., 1966-67, dir. info., 1967-72, v.p., 1972-80, sr. v.p., 1980-90, pres., 1990-97, trustee, 1990—. Bd. dirs. Albert Shanker Inst., Washington. Contbr. articles to N.Y. Times, Washington Post, Christian Sci. Monitor, Barron's, Harvard Mag., others. Trustee Rye (N.Y.) Bd. Edn., 1970-76; overseer Colby Coll., Waterville, Maine, 1980-2001. With USN, 1953-55. Mem. Coun. on Fgn. Rels., Harvard Club N.Y.C., Manursing Island Club (Rye). Avocations: single sculling, hiking, tennis, music, theater. Home and Office: 800 Forest Ave Rye NY 10580-3202

HUSA, KAREL, composer, conductor, educator; b. Prague, Czech Republic, Aug. 7, 1921; came to U.S., 1954, naturalized, 1959; s. Karel and Bozena (Dongresova) H.; m. Simone Perault, Feb. 2, 1952; children: Catherine, Anne-Marie, Elizabeth, Caroline. M summa cum laude, Conservatory and Acad. Music, Prague, 1945, M summa cum laude, 1947; lic. for conducting, Ecole Normale de Paris, 1947; grad., Conservatoire de Paris, 1948; MusD (hon.), Coe Coll., 1976, Cleve. Inst., 1985, Ithaca Coll., 1986, Baldwin-Wallace Conservatory, 1991, Hartwick Coll., 1997, New Eng. Conservatory, 1998; DHL (hon.), Coll. St. Vincent, 1996; ArtsD (hon.), Masaryk U., Czech Republic, 2000, Acad. Musical Arts, 2000. Guest condr. Czechoslovak Radio, Prague, 1945-46; guest condr. orchs. in Hamburg, Germany, Brussels, Paris, Zurich, Switzerland, Suisse Romande, London, Manchester, England, Prague, Stockholm, Hong Kong, Singapore, Japan, Cin., Buffalo, NYC, Boston, Rochester, NY, Balt., San Diego, Syracuse, NY; faculty Cornell U., Ithaca, NY, 1954—, prof. music, 1954—, dir. univ. symphony and chamber orchs., 1972-92, Kappa Alpha prof. music emeritus. Composer: Symphony, 1953, Fantasies for Orchestra, 1957, Divertimento for Brass, 1959, Poem for Viola and Orchestra, 1959, Elegy and Rondeau for Saxophone and Orchestra, 1961, Divertimento for String Orchestra, 1948, String Quartet No. 2, 1952, Portrait for String Orch., 1953, Mosaiques for Orch., 1961, Fresque for Orchestra, rev, 1964, Sonatina for Piano, 1943, Sonatina Violin and Piano, 1945, Sonata for Piano, 1949, Evocations of Slovakia for Clarinet, Viola and Cello, 1951, Eight Duets for Piano, 1955, Twelve Moravian Songs, 1956, Poem for Viola and Orchestra, 1962, Serenade for Woodwind Quintet and Orch., 1963, Concerto for Brass Quintet and Orch., 1965, Two Preludes; flute, clarinet, bassoon, 1966, Music for Percussion, 1966, Concerto for alto saxophone, concert band, 1967, String Quartet No. 3, 1968 (Pulitzer prize 1969), Music for Prague; for Band, 1968, for Orch., 1969, Apotheosis of this Earth for Winds, 1970, Concerto for Percussion and Winds, 1971, Two Sonnets from Michelangelo for Orch., 1971, Concerto for Trumpet and Wind Orch., 1973, Apotheosis of this Earth for Chorus and Orch., 1973, Sonata for Violin and Piano, 1972-73, The Steadfast Tin Soldier; for narrator and orch., 1974, Sonata for Piano, No. 2, 1975, Monodrama, ballet for orch., 1975, An American Te Deum; for mixed chorus, baritone solo, band and organ, 1976, for orch., 1978, Landscapes for Brass Quintet, 1977, Fanfare for Brass Ensemble, 1980, Pastoral for Strings, 1980, Three Moravian Songs, 1981, The Trojan Women, ballet for orch., 1981, Sonata a Tre, 1982, Concerto for Wind Ensemble, 1982 (Sudler award 1983), Cantata, 1983, Smetana Fanfare for Wind Ensemble, 1984, Variations for Violin, Viola, Cello and Piano, 1984 (Friedheim award 1986), Symphonic Suite for Orch., 1984, Intrada for Brass Quintet, 1984, Concerto for Orch., 1986, Concerto for Organ and Orch., 1987, Frammenti for Organ solo, 1987, Concerto for Trumpet and Orch., 1987, Concerto for Violoncello and Orch., 1988 (Grawemeyer award 1993), String Quartet No. 4, 1990, Youth Overture, 1991, Cayuga Lake (Memories), 1992, Concerto for Violin and Orch., 1993, Five Poems for Wood-Wind Quintet, 1994, Les Couleurs Fauves, 1995, Midwest Celebration Fanfare, 1996, Celebration for Orch., 1997, Postcard from Home, 1997, Song, for Mixed Chorus, 2000, others; commns. from, UNESCO, Koussevitsky Found., Nat. Endowment for Arts, Friends of Music at Cornell, Fine Arts Found. Chgo., Ithaca Coll., U. Ga., Chgo. Symphony Orch., Butler U., Washington Music Soc., Coe Coll., NY Philharm., U. So. Calif., Kerze Found., also others.; editor: French Baroque Music: Reconstructions of Old French Baroque works by Lully and Delalande, 1961-68. Recipient prize Prague Acad. Arts, 1948, French Govt. award, 1946-47, L. Boulanger award, 1952, Pulitzer prize in music, 1969, Acad. Inst. Arts and Letters award, 1989, Grawemeyer award U. Louisville, 1993, Serge Koussevitzky Music Found. award, 1993, Czech Republic's medal of merit of 1st degree Pres. V. Havel, 1995, medal of Honor, City of Prague, 1998; Guggenheim fellow, 1964-65. Mem. Internat. Inst. Arts and Letters (life), AAAL, Belgian Royal Acad. Arts and Scis., Am. Music Ctr., Internat. Soc. Contemporary Music, French Soc. Composers, Am. Fedn. Musicians, Kappa Gamma Psi (hon.), Kappa Kappa Psi (hon.), Delta Omicron (hon.), Phi Mu Alpha (hon.). Avocations: painting, sports. Office: Cornell U Dept Music Ithaca NY 14853 also: Karel Husa Archive & Gallery Sch Music Ithaca Coll Ithaca NY 14850 Office Phone: 607-257-7018, 607-274-1367. *As long as there will be museums, concerts, orchestras, libraries, our works will be measured against the masterpieces of the past. For this reason, the search for technical perfection must continue even today, in addition to new ideas and contents. One cannot exist without the other.*

HUSAIN, SHUJAAT, music educator; b. Calcutta, Bengal, India, May 19, 1960; s. Vilayat Khan Husain and Monisha Khan; m. Parveen Khan, Mar. 29, 1984; 1 child, Fiza Khan. Prof. Music U. Wash., Seattle, 1997—. Home: 5238 Whitaker Ave Encino CA 91436

HUSAR, LINDA S., lawyer; b. Chgo., Sept. 12, 1955; BS summa cum laude, Boston U., 1977; JD magna cum laude, Loyola Law Sch., 1980. Bar: Calif. 1980, US Dist. Ct. (No. Dist.) Calif. 1981, US Dist. Ct. (Ea. Dist.) Calif. 1981, US Dist. Ct. (So. Dist.) Calif. 1981, US Dist. Ct. (Ctrl. Dist.) Calif. 1981, US Ct. Appeals (9th Cir.) 1981. Ptnr., labor & employment dept. Thelen Reid & Priest LLP, LA. Mem.: LA County Bar Assn. (Labor Law Sect.), ABA (Labor Law Sect.), Calif. State Bar. Office: Thelen Reid & Priest LLP 333 S Hope St Ste 2900 Los Angeles CA 90071-3048 Office Phone: 213-576-8017. Office Fax: 213-687-1817. Business E-Mail: lshusar@thelenreid.com.

HUSAR, RUDOLF BERTALAN, mechanical engineering educator; b. Martonos, Yugoslavia, Oct. 29, 1941; came to U.S., 1966; s. Ga'bor and Ilona Huszar; m. Janja Djukic, Oct. 8, 1967; children: Maja, Attila. Degree in mech. engring., U. Zagreb, Croatia, 1962; diploma in mech. engring., Tech. U., Germany, 1966; PhDME, U. Minn., 1971. Design technician W. Hofer, Krefeld, Germany, 1962-63; rsch. asst. Tech. U., Berlin, 1963-66; from rsch. asst. to assoc. U. Minn., Mpls., 1966-71; rsch. fellow Calif. Inst. Tech., Pasadena, 1971-73; prof. Washington U., St. Louis, 1973—. Vis. prof. U. Stockholm, 1976; co-chmn. Interagy. Com. Health and Environ. Effects of Advanced Energy Tech., 1978; coop. program mem. Devel. and Appin. Space Tech. Air Pollution, EPA/NASA, 1978; dir. Ctr. for Air Pollution Impact and Trend Analysis (CAPITA), St. Louis, 1979—; mem. com. on atmospheric-biospheric interactions NAS, 1979-81. Editor: Atmospheric Environment, 1980, Indojaras, 1980; mem. adv. bd. Environ. Sci. Tech., 1980; contbr. chpt. to: Air Quality Criteria for Particulate Matter, EPA, 1995. Rsch. fellow U. Glasgow, Scotland, 1965, U. Minn., 1966-71; grantee, EPA, 1973—, NOAA, 1991—, U.S. Dept. Def., 1989-92. Mem. Air & Waste Mgmt. Assoc., Ges. Aerosolforschung. Office: Wash U CAPITA PO Box 1124 Saint Louis MO 63188-1124

HUSAR, WALTER GENE, neurologist, neuroscientist, educator; b. Jersey City, Sept. 24, 1956; s. Walter and Ksenia H. (Dawybida) H. BS in Biology summa cum laude, St. Peter's Coll., Jersey City, 1978; MS in Microbiology,

Rutgers U., 1982; MD, UMDNJ-N.J. Med. Sch., 1988. Diplomate Nat. Bd. Med. Examiners; lic. physician, N.J., N.Y. Adj. instr., then adj. lectr. microbiology St. Peter's Coll., 1979-84; intern in neurology and internal medicine U. Medicine and Dentistry N.J., Newark, 1988-89, resident, then adminstrv. chief resident in neurology, 1989-92, instr. dept. neuroscis. to asst. prof. neuroscis., 1992-99, 99—, attending physician dept. neuroscis. U. Hosp. Newark, 1992—; staff attending physician VA Med. Ctr., East Orange, N.J., 1992—; cons. physician dept. medicine divsn. neurology Holy Name Hosp., Teaneck, NJ, 1992—2003; attending physician St. Clare's Hosp. (formerly N.W. Covenant Med. Ctr.), Denville, N.J., 1997—; pvt. practice Denville, 1997—; regional staff Newton (N.J.) Meml. Hosp., 2001—05; staff Kindred Hosp. Morris County, Dover, NJ, 2004—. Mem. bd. health Twp. of East Hanover, N.J., 1993—, v.p., 1996-97, pres., 1998-2003; mem. stroke coun. Am. Heart Assn., 1992-96. Fellow Acad. Medicine N.J.; mem. AMA, Med. Soc. N.J., Morris County Med. Soc., Am. Acad. Neurology (assoc.), Am. Assn. Electrodiagnostic Medicine (assoc.). Home: 10 Christine Dr East Hanover NJ 07936-3039 Office: Ctrl Morris Neurology 145 Diamond Spring Rd Denville NJ 07834-2744 Office Phone: 973-625-8888. E-mail: dochusar@optonline.net.

HUSARIK, ERNEST ALFRED, educational administrator; b. Gary, Ind., July 2, 1941; m. Elizabeth Ann Bonnette; children: Jennifer, Amy. BA in History, Olivet Nazarene U., 1963; MS in Ednl. Adminstrn., No. Ill. U., 1966; PhD in Ednl. Adminstrn. and Curriculum Devel., Ohio State U., 1973. Supt. Ontario (Ohio) Pub. Schs., 1973—75, Euclid (Ohio) Pub. Schs., 1975—86, Westerville (Ohio) Pub. Schs., 1986—2000, Carmel Clay Sch. Corp., 2000—01; ednl. specialist MS Cons., Inc. Past pres. Sch. Study Coun. Ohio; gd. govs. Westerville Fund; mem. adv. and distbn. com. Martha Holden Jennings Found.; pres. Westerville chpt. Am. Heart Assn.; past chmn. Franklin County Ednl. Coun.; past mem. alumni adv. coun. Ohio State U.; past pres. Euclid C. of C., Ohio. Named Ohio Supr. of Yr., 1994; named one of top 100 Edn. Adminstrs. N.Am., Exec. Educator, 1993. Mem.: ASCD, Hamilton-Boone County Ednl. Svc. Ctr. (chmn.), Franklin County Area Supt.'s Assn. (exec. com.), Ind. Assn. Pub. Sch. Supts., Ohio Assn. Supervision and Curriculum Devel., Ohio State U. Edliners (pres.), Sci. amd Math. Achievement Required for Tomorrow, Ohio Math. and Sci. Coalition (exec. bd.), Buckeye Assn. Sch. Adminstrs. (bd. dirs., pres., Disting. Svc. award 2001), Am. Assn. Sch. Adminstrs., Olivet Nazarene U. Alumni Assn. (past mem. alumni bd. dirs.), Carmel C. of C., Westerville Area C. of C. (bd. dirs.), Rotary (pres. Westerville, Rotarian of Yr.), Sigma Tau Delta, Phi Delta Kappa (past chpt. pres.). Home: 1029 Wood Glen Rd Westerville OH 43081-3240 Office: 1029 Wood Glen Rd Westerville OH 43081-3240 E-mail: edwardH568@aol.com.

HUSARIK, STEPHEN, music educator; b. Chgo., May 23, 1944; s. Stephen Husarik Sr. and Inez Medley. MusB with honors, U. Ill., 1970, MusM, 1972, postgrad., 1972-77; PhD, U. Iowa, 1983. Tchg. asst. U. Ill., Urbana, 1972-74; lectr. Sampson C.C., Clinton, NC, 1976; tchg. asst. U. Iowa, Iowa City, 1977, 79; instr. Lewis U., Lockport, Ill., 1978, Trinity Coll., Palos Hills, Ill., 1980; instr. music and humanities Moraine Valley Coll., Palos Hills, Ill., 1984-89; head carillonneur Westark Coll., Ft. Smith, Ark., 1995—, instr. humanities and music, 1992—2001; prof. humanities and music history U. Ark., Ft. Smith, 2002—. Sr. editor Am. Keyboard Artists, 1987-92; co-author: A History of Westark College, 1999, (online question database) Reality Through the Arts, 2000; editor Who's Who in the Humanities, 1990-92; rec. artist: (piano solos) Pictures at an Exhbn. by Mussorgsky, Scott Joplin and the Ragtime Classics; contbr. numerous articles to profl. jours. and mags Field reader Coun. for Post-Secondary Edn., Washington, 1987; chair tech. com. U. Ark. Ft. Smith, 2004-05 Recipient Nat. Edpress Assn. award, 1987, Master Tchr. award Whirlpool, 2000, Tchr. of Yr. award Ark. Distance Learning Assn., 2002, Excellence in Online Tchg. award Ark. Distance Learning Assn., 2003, European Travel sabbatical, fall 2005; grantee NEH, 1984, 89, 94, Ark. Humanities Coun., 1997. Mem. Am. Musicol. Soc., Am. Liszt Soc., Guild of Carillonneurs of N.Am., Coll. Music Soc., Nat. Assn. Humanities Edn. (newsletter editor 1993-94), Westark Coll. Assn. (chair 1999), Ark. Music Educators Conf. (bd. dirs. 2004). Office Phone: 479-788-7555. Business E-Mail: shusarik@uafortsmith.edu.

HUSBAND, BERTRAM PAUL, lawyer; b. L.A., Aug. 15, 1950; s. Bertram Perry and Ruth (Eatough) H.; m. Beverly Ruth Hyams, May 1, 1987, div. March 6, 2003; children: Joseph Bertram, Daniel James, David Paul. BA, Occidental Coll., 1972; JD, UCLA, 1977. Bar: Calif. 1977, U.S. Dist. Ct. (cen. dist.) Calif. 1978, U.S. Ct. Appeals (9th cir.) 1979, U.S. Dist. Ct. (so. dist.) Calif. 1980, U.S. Dist. Ct. (no. dist.) Calif. 1988, U.S. Tax Ct. 1987. Assoc. Coskey, Coskey & Boxer, L.A., 1978-79, Cooper, Epstein & Hurewitz, Beverly Hills, Calif., 1979-81; pvt. practice L.A., 1981-84; ptnr. Husband & Morris, L.A., 1984-89, Husband & Roberts, L.A. and Encino, Calif., 1989-91; pvt. practice Encino, 1991-94, Valencia, Calif., 1994-97, Burbank, Calif., 1997—2002, Universal City, Calif., 2002—. Adj. prof. law Pepperdine U., Malibu, Calif., 1978—79; lectr. in field. Author equine law column Jour. Agrl. Taxation and Law, 1987-93; writer, producer (ednl. video) Fighting Back: Successfully Representing Your Horse Business to the IRS, 1991; editl. adv. bd. Am. Horse Coun. Tax Bulletin, 1994—. Registered judge Am. Horse Shows Assn., 1975-94; recommended judge Equestrian Trials Inc., 1988-94; dir., gen. counsel Burbank Internat. Children's Film Festival, 2000-03. Fellow, Am. coll. Equine Attys., 2005. Mem. ABA (tax sect., agrl. com., forum com. entertainment and sports industries), L.A. County Bar Assn. (chmn. pro bono oversight com. tax sect. 1987-88, officer entertainment tax com. of tax sect. 1993-96, chair 1995-96), Beverly Hills Bar Assn. (exec. com. entertainment sect. 1992-96), San Fernando Valley Bar Assn. (chair tax sect. 1993-94), Calif. State Bar (tax sect., lectr. 1988 seminar), Internat. Arabian Horse Assn. (vice chair fed. tax study com. 1979-92), Association Internationale du Film d'Animation (Hollywood chpt., dir. 1997-2003, gen. counsel 1997—), World Arabian Horse Orgn. Mem. Ch. of Christ. Avocation: speculative fiction. Office: 10 Universal City Plz Ste 2000 Universal City CA 91608 Office Phone: 888-467-7829. Business E-Mail: Paul.Husband@Husbandlaw.com.

HUSBAND, TERENCE J. (CASEY HUSBAND), editor, writer; s. Joseph Wesley and Mary Margaret (McLaughlin) Husband. BS in Health and Phys. Edn., West Chester U., 1976; BA in Journalism, Temple U., 1978; M in Theol. Studies, Georgetown U., 1996, M in Liberal Studies, 1999; MA in Lit., Am. U., 2004. Cert. in Theol. Studies Georgetown U., Washington, DC. Reporter Daily Local News, West Chester, Pa., 1978—81, columnist, 1982—85, sports editor, 1986—87; mng. editor Snyder Comm., Bethesda, Md., 1984—98; editl. dir. Washington Redskins, Ashburn, Va., 1998—. Office Phone: 703-726-7038.

HUSBY, DONALD EVANS, engineering company executive; b. Mpls., Nov. 30, 1927; s. Olaf and Elsie Louise (Hagen) H.; m. Beverly June Tilbury, Sept. 24, 1949. BS, S.D. State U., 1952. Student engr., jr. asst., sr. engr., mgr. new products Westinghouse Electric Corp., Cleve., 1952-72; engring. mgr., v.p. engring. lighting div. Harvey Hubbell, Inc., Christiansburg, Va., 1972-76; pres. Elliptipar Inc., West Haven, Conn., 1976-78; fellow engr., mgr. engring. sect. Westinghouse Electric Corp., Vicksburg, Miss., 1978-82; engring. mgr. new products devel. Cooper Industries Crouse-Hinds LTG Products div., 1982-84; utility sales mgr. central region Cooper Lighting, Mpls., 1985-89; chief exec. officer Husby & Husby Inc., Madison, Minn., 1990—. Mem. indsl. adv. counsel Underwriters Labs.; provider ednl. seminars in lighting, tech. expert for NVLAP, NIST, U.S. Dept. Commerce. Contbr. articles to profl. jours.; patentee in field. With USN, 1945—47. Fellow Illuminating Engrs. Soc. (chmn., sec., dir., Disting. Service award 1989); mem. Internat. Municipal Signal Assn., Soc. Plastics Engrs., Nat. Elec. Mfrs. Assn., Am. Nat. Standards Inst., Am. Soc. Quality Control, Am. Soc. Engring. Physicists, Miss. Engring. Soc., D.C. Soc. Profl. Engrs., Designers Lighting Forum., Mensa Internat., Toastmasters Internat. Mem. Christian Ch. Home and Office: 705 5th Ave PO Box 66 Madison MN 56256-0066 Office Phone: 320-598-7786.

HUSEBOE, ARTHUR ROBERT, American literature educator; b. Sioux Falls, S.D., Oct. 6, 1931; s. Carl and Lillian Ruth (Auby) H.; m. Doris Louise Eggers, May 27, 1953. BA, Augustana Coll., 1953; MA, U. S.D., 1956; PhD, Ind. U., 1963; LHD (hon.), Dana Coll., 1984. Teaching assoc. Ind. U., Bloomington, 1959-60; instr. U. S.D., Vermillion, 1960-61; prof. Augustana Coll., Sioux Falls, S.D., 1961—. Pres. S.D. Humanities Found., Sioux Falls, 1994-96. Fedn. of State Humanities Couns., Washington, 1988-91; exec. dir. Nordland Heritage Found., Sioux Falls, 1980—. Ctr. Western Studies, Augustana, 1989—; NEH regional heritage chair, 1989—. Author: An Illustrated History of the Arts in South Dakota, 1989, Sir George Etherege, 1987, Herbert Krause, 1985, Sir John Vanbrugh, 1976. Bd. dirs. S.D. Symphony, Sioux Falls, 1966—2005; mem. Nordland Fest Assn., Sioux Falls, 1975—. With U.S. Army, 1953-55. Recipient Gov.'s award in the Arts State of S.D., 1989; NEH grantee, 1975-77, 79-83, 92-94; named to S.D. Hall of Fame, 2001. Mem. MLA, We. Lit. Assn. (pres. 1976-77), Norwegian-Am. Hist. Assn., S.D. Hist. Soc. Lutheran. Avocations: travel, theater, classical music. Home: 813 E 38th St Sioux Falls SD 57105-5939 Office: Ctr for Western Studies Box 727 Augustana Coll Sioux Falls SD 57197-0001 Business E-Mail: arthur_huseboe@augie.edu.

HUSER, GERI D., state official; b. Des Moines, Iowa, July 14, 1963; m. Dan Huser. BA, Briar Cliff Coll., 1985; MBA, Drake U., 2003, JD, 2004. Social worker Polk County Gen. Relief, 1986—90; program mgr. Polk County Family Enrichment Ctr., 1990—96; mem. Met. Planning Orgn., 1990—, Altoona City Coun., 1991—; planning specialist Polk County Social Svcs., 1996—; state rep. Iowa, 1997—. Mem. adminstrv. and rules com.; mem. local govt. com.; mem. transp. com.; mem. ways and means com. Mem. Child Abuse Prevention Coun., 1993—95, Greater Des Moines Housing Partnership, 1995—97; chmn. Met. Planning Orgn., 1996—. Mem.: East Polk Interagy. Assn., Mitchellville C. of C., Pleasant Hill C. of C., S.E. Polk Booster Club. Democrat. Office: State Capitol E 12th and Grand Des Moines IA 50319

HUSER, VOJTECH, medical informatician, researcher; m. Jana Huserova. MD (hon.), Palacky U., Olomouc, Czech Rep., 2003. Rschr. U. Utah, Salt Lake City, 2003—. Office: Univ Utah 30 N 1900 E Salt Lake City UT 84132

HUSHEN, JOHN WALLACE, manufacturing executive; b. Detroit, July 28, 1935; s. J. Wallace and Hilda Carol (Jean) H.; m. Margaret Corinne Aho, Apr. 25, 1959 (div. May 1978); children: Susan Lisa, Jane Louise, Peter Matthew; m. Lane Gay Johnston, Feb. 8, 1985 (div. May 2002); 1 child, John Case. BA, Wayne State U., 1958. Reporter The Detroit News, 1959-66; campaign press sec. Griffin for Senate, Mich., 1966; press sec. U.S. Senator Robert P. Griffin, Washington, 1967-70; dir. pub. info. U.S. Dept. Justice, Washington, 1970-74; dep. press sec. Pres. Gerald R. Ford, Washington, 1974-76; dir. govt. relations Eaton Corp., Washington, 1976-79, dir. pub. affairs Cleve., 1979-81, v.p. govt. rels. Washington, 1981-91, v.p. corp. affairs Cleve., 1991-99. Trustee Citizens League Rsch. Inst., Cleve., pres., 1998-2000; trustee YMCA, Cleve. Mem.: Senate Press Secs. Assn. (pres. 1969—70), Former Senate Aides, St. Andrews South Golf Club, Elkdale Country Club, Capitol Hill Club.

HUSHING, WILLIAM COLLINS, retired manufacturing executive; b. St. Louis, Jan. 22, 1918; s. Sumner Kinney and Anne (Sandner) H.; m. Mary Hardy, Jan. 10, 1946 (dec. 1986); children: Druscilla (dec.), Rebecca Ann. BS in Elec. Engring, U.S. Naval Acad., 1939; MS in Naval Constrn. and Engring, MIT, 1944; student, Harvard Bus. Sch., 1962; DSc (hon.), U. N.H., 1968. Commd. ensign U.S. Navy, 1939, advanced through grades to rear adm., 1967; aide, spl. asst. to chief (Bur. Ships), 1955-57; indsl. engr., comptroller U.S. Naval Shipyard, Mare Island, Calif., 1957-60; supr. shipbldg. U.S. Navy, Electric Boat div. Gen. Dynamics Corp., Groton, Conn., 1960-64; comdr. Naval Shipyard, Portsmouth, N.H., 1964-69; retired, 1969; exec. v.p. Bath Iron Works, 1969-70; pres. Forster Mfg. Co., Inc., 1970-71; mgmt. cons. Kensington Mgmt. Cons., Inc., Stamford, Conn., 1972-78; pres. Maine Multi-Power, Inc., Bath, 1979-91. Decorated Navy Commendation medal, Legion of Merit with Star. Mem. Am. Soc. Naval Engrs. Lutheran. Home: 1640 Twelve Oaks Way Apt 103 North Palm Beach FL 33408-3265

HUSKE, EMILY JEAN, economist; b. Woodruff, Wis., May 5, 1976; d. Howard Leigh and Barbara Jean (McDonald) Huske. BA summa cum laude, BA Bus. Adminstrn., Carthage Coll., 1997. Economist Dept. Commerce, Bur. Econ. Analysis, Washington, 1997—. Singer perform nat. anthem at sports events. Recipient Sr. Econs. award, Carthage Coll., 1997; scholar Lincoln scholar, 1993—97. Mem.: Wis. State Soc., Assn. Evolutionary Econs., Toastmasters Internat., Omicron Delta Epsilon (charter v.p. 1996—97). Democrat. Methodist. Avocations: clarinet, singing, reading. Office: Bur Econs Analysis 1441 L St NW Washington DC 20230

HUSKETH, ALMA ORMOND, retired language educator; b. Dover, N.C., Aug. 17, 1918; d. William Henry and Ella Carrie (White) Ormond; m. Edward Thomas Husketh Jr., June 12, 1943 (dec. May 8, 1986); children: Edward Thomas III, William Ormond, Craig Moss. BA in English, U. N.C., Greensboro, 1939; MS in Libr. Sci., U.N.C., Chapel Hill, 1966. Tchr. Eng. Granville County Bd. Edn., Creedmoor, NC, 1939—44, 1946—60; libr. S. Granville High Sch., Oxford, NC, 1962—80; tchr. Eng. Lenoir Bd. Edn., Kinston, NC, 1944—46; instr. Eng. Vance-Granville C.C., Henderson, NC, 1988—94; ret., 2004. Columnist Butner-Creedmoor News, NC, 1988—2004. Author: (poem) Values, 1999. Tchr., Sunday sch. supt. Banks United Meth. Ch., Franklinton, NC, 1939—2004. Mem.: DAR, N.C. Ret. Sch. Personnel, Frankinton Woman's Club, Saturday Book Club, Alpha Delta Kappa. Democrat. Methodist. Avocations: walking, reading, creative writing. Home: 3577 Brassfield Rd Creedmoor NC 27522 Office Phone: 919-528-0122.

HUSKEY, HARRY DOUGLAS, information and computer science educator; b. Whittier, NC, Jan. 19, 1916; s. Cornelius and Myrtle (Cunningham) H.; m. Velma Elizabeth Roeth, Jan. 2, 1939 (dec. Jan. 1991); children: Carolyn, Roxanne, Harry Douglas, Linda; m. Nancy Grindstaff, Sept. 10, 1994. BS, U. Idaho, 1937; student, Ohio U., 1937—38; MA, Ohio State U., 1940, PhD, 1943. Temp. prin. sci. officer Nat. Phys. Labs., England, 1947; head machine devel. lab. Nat. Bur. Stds., 1948; asst. dir. Inst. Numerical Analysis, 1948-54; assoc. dir. computation lab. Wayne U., Detroit, 1952-53; assoc. prof. U. Calif., Berkeley, 1954-58, prof., 1958-68, vice chmn. elec. engring., 1965-66, prof. info. and computer sci. Santa Cruz, 1968-85, prof. emeritus, 1985—, dir. Computer Ctr., 1968-77, chmn. bd. info. sci., 1976-79, 82-83. Vis. prof. Indian Inst. Tech., Kanpur; (Indo-Am. program), 1963-64, 71, Delhi U., 1971; cons. computer divsn. Bendix, 1954-63; vis. prof. MIT, 1966; mem. computer sci. panel NSF, Naval Rsch. Adv. Com.; cons. on computers for developing countries UN, 1969-71; chmn. com. to advise Brazil on computer sci. edn. NAS, 1970-72; project coord. UNESCO/Burma contract, 1973-79; mem. adv. com. on use microcomputers in developing countries NRC, 1983-85. Co-editor: Computer Handbook, 1962. Recipient Disting. Alumni award Idaho State U., 1978, Pioneer award Nat. Computer Conf., 1978, IEEE Computer Soc., 1982; named U.S. sr.scientist award Fulbright-Alexander von Humboldt Found., Mathematisches Institut der Tech. U. Munich, 1974-75, 25th Ann. medal ENIAC; named to U. Idaho Alumni Hall of Fame, 1989. Fellow AAAS, IEEE (edit. bd., editor-in-chief computer group 1965-71, Centennial award 1984), Brit. Computer Soc.; mem. Am. Math. Soc., Math. Assn. Am., Assn. Computing Machinery (pres. 1960-62), Am. Fedn. Info. Processing Socs. (governing bd. 1961-63), Sigma Xi. Achievements include designing SWAC computer, Bendix G-15 and G-20 computers. Office: U Calif Computer & Info Sci Santa Cruz CA 95064 Home: 518 SummitGlen Ct Spartanburg SC 29307 Personal E-mail: harry_huskey@yahoo.com.

HUSMAN, CATHERINE BIGOT, retired insurance company executive, consultant; b. Des Moines, Feb. 10, 1943; d. Edward George and Ruth Margaret (Cumming) Bigot; m. Charles Erwin Husman, Aug. 5, 1967; 1 child, Matthew Edward. BA with highest distinction, U. Iowa, 1965; MA, Ball State U., 1970. Actuarial asst. Am. United Life Ins. Co., Indpls., 1965—68, assoc. actuary, 1971—74, group actuary, 1974—84, v.p., corp. actuary, 1984—97, v.p., chief actuary, 1997—2002; cons., 2002—04. Mem. group tech. com. Mut. Life Ins. Co., 1986-98; mem. profitability studies com. Life Office Mgmt. Assn. Inc., 1991-99. Mem. women's adv. com. United Way Ctrl. Ind., 1991—93; mem. Exec. Svc. Corps, 2002—, asst. treas., 2005—; docent Pres. Benjamin Harrison Home, 2002—; vol. Ronald McDonald House, Indpls. Mus. Art, Clowes Meml. Hall, 2002—, Indpls. Civic Theater; bd. dirs., mem. fin. com. St. Elizabeth's Home, 1991—99, sec., 1994, mem. exec. com., treas., 1995; bd. dirs., mem. adminstrv. svcs., mem. exec. com. Heritage Place, 1993—99, treas., 1995—99. Fellow Soc. Actuaries; mem. Am. Acad. Actuaries, Actuaries Club Ind., Ky. and Ohio, Actuarial Club Indpls. (pres. 1979-80), Phi Beta Kappa. Republican. Roman Catholic. Avocations: reading, tennis. Home: 1411 N Claridge Way Carmel IN 46032-8333 Personal E-mail: cbhusman@earthlink.net.

HUSSAIN, MOINUDDIN SYED, geologist, engineer, consultant; b. Hyderabad, India, Dec. 28, 1931; s. Karimuddin Syed and Hafeeza Begum (Khan) H.; m. Aziza Moin Quadri, Aug. 20, 1942; children: Qutub, Ayesha, Arju. BS, Osmania U., Hyderabad, 1954; DIC, Imperial Coll., London, 1963; MS, London U., 1964. Registered profl. geologist, Calif. Asst. groundwater geologist Groundwater Devel. Orgn., Lahore, Pakistan, 1955-56; test geologist Std. Vacuum Oil Co. (ESSO), Karachi, Pakistan, 1956-62; superintending geologist Oil and Gas Devel. Corp., Karachi, Pakistan, 1962-69; mgr. exploration/projects Dawood Petroleum Ltd., Karachi, Pakistan, 1969-73; project geologist Hallenbeck McCoy and Assoc., Berkeley, Calif., 1973-75; sr. geologist Dow Chem. Co., USA, Houston, 1975-81; sr. internat. geologist Union Tex. Petroleum Corp., Houston, 1981-85; cons. Hycarbex, Inc., Houston, 1985-93; cons. in petroleum, energy, groundwater Katy, Tex., 1993—. Mem. adv. bd. Petroland Exploration Inc., Houston, 1985—; advisor Dawood Group of Industries, Karachi, 1969-73; del. to Pakistan, U.S. Dept. of Energy; mem. (with Dept. of Energy) Presdl. Mission to Pakistan, 1994-95. Founding mem. Internat. Explorationist Group, Houston, 1984. Mem. Am. Assn. Petroleum Geologists (cert. geologist, alt. del. 1984, Cert. of Recognition award 1987), Bangladesh Geol. Soc. (life), Pak-Am. Petroleum Soc. (founder 1983), Houston Geol. Soc. (Svc. award 1985). Republican. Muslim. Achievements include research on petroleum potential of Pakistan and Bangladesh resulting in several oil and gas discoveries; introduction of API stds. in these countries to replace Soviet technology; establishment of oil producing trend in San Marcos Arch area, Tex. thru Austic Chalk Formation; preparation of feasability studies for establishment of refineries, power plants, fertilizer plants, pig iron plants, LPG projects; design of oil and gas pipelines groundwater resource evaluation and development, basin evaluation, project development and implementation; petroleum exploration and development in the Middle East and Far East; petroleum crude and products market development. Office: Petroland Exploration Inc PO Box 218341 Houston TX 77218-8341 Office Phone: 281-492-2145. Business E-Mail: energyexpln@ev1.com.

HUSSAIN, NAYYER, economics professor; b. Karachi, Sind, Pakistan, Apr. 8, 1954; arrived in U.S., 1981; s. Mazhar and Hussana (Begum) H.; m. Nafisa Vali, July 28, 1984; children: Mustafa, Ali. BA, U. Karachi, 1976, MBA, 1979; MA, Calif. State U., 1983; PhD, U. Pitts., 1988. Sales officer Hussain Sons, Karachi, 1974-76; asst. mktg. mgr. Ummal Quwain Asbestos Ind., United Arab Emirates, 1979-81; tchg. asst. U. Pitts., 1983-84, tchg. fellow, 1984-88; asst. prof. Tougaloo (Miss.) Coll., 1988-91, assoc. prof., 1992—98, chmn. econs. dept., 1989-91, chmn. social sci. divsn., 1991-94, asst. v.p. for acad. affairs, 1994-95, acting v.p. for acad. affairs, 1995—96, v.p. fiscal affairs, 1996—98; fin. advisor Legg Mason Wood Walker, 1999—2001; dir. bus. affairs MedCentral Coll. Nursing, Mansfield, Ohio, 2001—04, v.p. fin. and adminstrn., 2004—. Named Outstanding Tchr., Madison County C. of C., 1991, Higher Edn. Appreciation Day Working for Acad. Excellence award Miss. State Legislature, 1994. Mem. Am. Econ. Assn. (editl. asst. Pitts. 1983-88), Rotary, Omicron Delta Epsilon. Avocations: reading, movies, model building. Office: MedCtrl Coll Nursing 335 Glessner Ave Mansfield OH 44903 Home: 3108 Hemlock Pl Mansfield OH 44903-8416 Office Phone: 419-520-2625. Personal E-mail: teeseeker@yahoo.com.

HUSSAIN, SYED TASEER, biomedical researcher, educator; b. Lahore, Pakistan, Sept. 18, 1943; came to U.S., 1970; s. S. Fayyaz and Riaz (Fatima) H. BS, Punjab U., Pakistan, 1963, BS with honors, 1964, MS, 1965; PhD, U. Utrecht, Netherlands, 1969. Postdoct. fellow Am. Mus. Natural History, N.Y.C., 1970—72; instr. Howard U. Coll. Medicine, Washington, 1972-73, asst. prof., 1973-76, assoc. prof., 1977-85, prof. anatomy, 1985—. Dir. gen. Pakistan Mus. of Natural History, Pakistan Sci. Found., Islamabad, 1985-87; grants reveiwer NSF, 1980—, NATO, 1987—, Nat. Geog. Soc., 1985—; frequent invited spkr. on evolutionary processes, biological changes, climate change and human health. Author, co-author over 60 publs. and several book chpts., contbr. articles to profl. jours. Grantee Smithsonian Instn., 1974-94, NSF, 1977—, Nat. Inst. Environ. Health Scis., 1994. Fellow Pakistan Acad. Geol. Scis.; mem. AAAS, Am. Assn. Anatomy, Soc. Vertebrate Paleontology. Achievements include research in evolution in locomotion and hearing mechanism in mammals; human health and forced climate change; influence of increased temperatures on diseases. Office: Howard Univ Coll Medicine 520 W St NW Washington DC 20001-2337

HUSSEIN, YASSER, research scientist; b. Cairo, Aug. 30, 1972; s. Abdel-Whab Fayez Hussein and Ferial Aly; m. Walaa Abd-Rabouh Ghatati, Jan. 8, 2004. PhD, Ariz. State U., 2003. Rsch., tchg. assoc. Ariz. State U., Tempe, 2000—03; rsch. scientist, engr. Stanford U., Menlo Park, Calif., 2003—. Contbr. articles to profl. jours. Mem.: IEEE. Achievements include research in modeling of high frequency (micro/nano) semiconductor devices.

HUSSEY, JOHN FRANCIS, physician, geriatrician; b. Richmond Hill, N.Y., Jan. 6, 1951; s. John F. Sr. and Jean (Peczyinski) H.; m. Ann Pelley, Sept. 10, 1979; children: Leo, Nicholas. BS in Biology, St. Johns U., 1972; MD, Creighton U., 1976. Cert. ACLS Am. Heart Assn. Intern, resident St. Joseph's Hosp., Omaha; pvt. practice, Augusta, Maine, 1982-90; med. cons. Augusta Mental Health Inst., 1990-95; geriatrician, psychiatry cons. Togus (Maine) VA Hosp., 1995—. Capt. USPHS, 1979-82. Fellow Am. Acad. Family Physicians; mem. Am. Geriat. Soc., Kennebec County Med. Assn. (treas. 1995-96, pres. 1996-97). Office: VA Hosp 1 VA Ctr Sta (171) Tobus ME 04330-6795

HUSSEY, MICHAEL JUDE, obstetrician, educator; b. Boston, Oct. 13, 1959; MD, U. Ill. Bd. cert. ob-gyn., bd. cert. maternal and fetal medicine. Intern internal medicine Louis A. Weiss Meml. Hosp., Chgo.; resident ob-gyn. Loyola U. Med. Ctr., Maywood, Ill., 1991—93; fellow maternal fetal medicine Rush-Presbyn.-St. Lukes Med. Ctr., Chgo., 1993, active staff, Mercy Hosp., Chgo.; cons. Ctrl. DuPage Hosp., Winfield, Ill.; asst. prof. dept. ob-gyn. Rush U. Med. Ctr.; attending physician sect. maternal-fetal medicine Rush Med. Coll.; dir. ob-gyn. med. student edn. program Rush Med. Coll./Rush-Presbyn.-St. Luke's Med. Ctr. Mem.: Intenrat. Soc. for Prenatal Diagnosis, Inst. Ultrasound in Medicine. Achievements include research in central nervous system abnormalities; level II targeted ultrasound and fetal growth abnormalities; ultrasound in diagnosing fetal chromosomal abnormalities. Office: Womens Health Consultants Ste 408 1725 W Harrison Chicago IL 60612

HUSSEY, WILLIAM BERTRAND, retired diplomat; b. Bellingham, Wash., Oct. 23, 1915; s. Bertrand Brokaw and Ruth (Axtell) Hussey; m. Fredricka Boone, Dec. 31, 1940 (div. 1957); children: Crhistina, Pamela, Eva, William Bertrand, Peter; m. Piyachart Bunnag, May 20, 1959. BS, Boston U., 1938; postgrad., UCLA, 1939-40, Naval War Coll., 1953-54. Asst. housing mgmt. supr. U.S. Housing Authority, 1941-42; chmn. London (Eng.) Liaison Group, also State Dept. rep., 1948-52; spl. State Dept. rep., Rome, 1949, Paris, 1950. Chmn. regional conf., Dhahran, Saudi Arabia, 1949; chief civil-mil. rels. sect., Munich, 1952—53; adminstr. officer, Frankfurt, Germany, 1953—55; attache, Rangoon, Burma, 1955—56; consul, Chiengmal, Thailand, 1957—59; acting dep. chief plans and devel. staff Bur. Ednl. and Cultural Affairs, Dept. State, 1959—60, dep. chief cultural presentations divsn., 1960—61; mem. del. regional confs., Beirut, Kampala, Uganda, 1960;

group leader Nat. Strategy Seminar, Asilomar, Calif., 1960; counselor embassy, Lome, Togo, 1961—65, Biantyre, Malawi, 1965—66; chargé d'affaires Am. embassy, Maseru, Lesotho, Tananarive, Madagascar, 1966—67, Port Louis, Mauritius, 1967—68; UN rep. Western Pacific, Apia, Western Samoa, 1969—74; fgn. affairs cons., 1974—; del. UN Law of Sea Conf., 1975—80; assoc. v.p. LA Olympic Organizing Com., 1982—84; dir. govt. rels. Statue of Liberty Centennial, Liberty Weekend, 1986. With U.S. Mcht. Marine, 1930—33, served to lt. comdr. USN, 1942—48, ETO, PTO, capt. USNR. Recipient Superior Svc. award, Sec. of State, 1986. Address: 5563B Via Portora Laguna Woods CA 91637-6960 *We must learn from mistakes. The measure is less the occasional stumble than how quickly and sharply the common cadence of our heritage is restored.*

HUSTAD, THOMAS PEGG, marketing educator; b. Mpls., June 15, 1945; s. Thomas Earl Pegg and John Charles and Dorothy Helen (Anderson) H.; m. Sherry Ann Thomas, Jan. 30, 1971; children: Kathleen, John. BS in Elec. Engring., Purdue U., 1967, MS in Indsl. Mgmt., 1969, PhD in Mktg., 1973. Cert. new product devel. profl. Vis. asst. prof. Purdue U., West Lafayette, Ind., 1971-72; asst. prof. Faculty of Adminstrv. Studies York U., Toronto, Ont., Can., 1972-74, assoc. prof., 1974-76, assoc. prof., mktg. area coord., 1976-77; assoc. prof. mktg. Kelley Sch. Bus. Ind. U., Bloomington-Indpls., 1977-82, prof., 1982—, chmn. MBA program, 1983—85. Chmn. program Ind. U. Ann. Bus. Conf., 1983, 84, co-founder Exec. Forum; adj. prof. philanthropic studies, 1992—96; vis. prof. City U. Hong Kong, 1997, Ljubljana U., Slovenia, 1998, 2000, Steinbeis U., Berlin, 1998—2000, CEU Bus. Sch., Budapest, Hungary, 2003—; exec. dir. Ind. U. Internat. Bus. Forum, 1981—85; cons. N.Am. corps. Govt. of Can.; condr. seminars for U.S., Singapore, Can., European, Asian and Venezuelan industry; mem. selection com. Outstanding Corp. Innovator award, 1978—; interim dir. Johnson Ctr. for Entrepreneurship and Innovation, 2004—05. Author: Approaches to the Teaching of Product Development and Management, 1977, (with others) PDMA Handbook of New Product Development, 1996, 2d edit., 2005; editor: International Competition: The American Challenge, 1986, Managing the Product Development Process, 1989, Product Development: Prospering in a Rapidly Changing World, 1990; founder, editor Jour. Product Innovation Mgmt., 1986-2000; contbr. articles to books and profl. jours. Fulbright fellow, 1987, fellow Ind. U. Ctr. for Entrepreneurship and Innovation, John Kosin Faculty fellow, 1993-2003; Crawford fellow of Product Innovation, 1993—; recipient Eli Lilly MBA Tchg. Excellence award, 1990, Editorship award Elsevier Sci. Pub. Co., 1993, Kelley award for innovative tchg., 1999, Kelley Svc. award 2000, Anbar Emerald Golden prize for practical applications and originality, 2000; named Best Bet Tchr., Bus. Week Mag.; Thomas P. Hustad Best Paper award named in his honor, 1998—. Mem.: PDMA Found. (bd. dirs. 2004—), European Inst. Advanced Studies in Mgmt. (chair ann. conf. 2003), Product Devel. and Mgmt. Assn. (v.p. confs. 1979, pres.-elect 1980, pres. 1981, dir. 1982—83, chmn. publ. com. 1982—84, sec./treas. 1984—96, mgr. assn. office 1984—96, bd. dirs. 1984—2000, 2004—, program. chmn. 3rd ann. conf., Presdl. award 1987), Am. Mktg. Assn. (award 1973), Brown U. Alumni Assn. (Assoc. Alumni award 1963), Internat. Assn. Jazz Record Collectors, Ancient and Hon. Arty. Co., Beta Gamma Sigma, Tau Beta Pi, Phi Eta Sigma. Home: 3101 Daniel St Bloomington IN 47401-2421 Office: Ind U Kelley Sch Bus 1309 E 10th St Bloomington IN 47405-1701 Office Phone: 812-855-1160. Business E-Mail: hustad@indiana.edu.

HUSTED, RUSSELL FOREST, research scientist; b. Lafayette, Ind., Apr. 4, 1950; s. Robert Forest and Miriam Ruth (Jackson) H.; m. Nancy Lee Driscoll, Oct. 25, 1969 (div. Feb. 1986); children: Jacqueline Marie, Randall Forest; m. Ruth Elaine Hurlburt, Nov. 12, 1988. BS in Chemistry with highest distinction, Colo. State U., 1972; PhD in Pharmacology, U. Utah, 1976. Post-doctoral fellow dept. medicine U. Iowa, Iowa City, 1976-79, rsch. scientist dept. medicine, 1979-81, 1982—; asst. prof. U. Conn. Sch. Medicine, Farmington, 1981-82. Contbr. articles to profl. jours. Mem. IA Parks & Recreation Com., North Liberty, 1997—. Mallinckrodt scholar Colo. State U., 1968. Mem. AAAS, Am. Soc. Nephrology, Am. Physiol. Soc., Soc. Gen. Physiology, N.Y. Acad. Sci., Sigma Xi. Democrat. Methodist. Office: Univ Iowa 3180 Medical Labs Iowa City IA 52242 Office Phone: 319-335-7618. Business E-Mail: russell-husted@uiowa.edu.

HUSTED, WILLIAM ARMSTRONG, sales executive; b. London, Feb. 25, 1937; s. John Grinnell Wetmore and Helen Armstrong Husted. *Descendant of the original settlers of Greenwich, CT. On mother's side of family, I am a descendant of John Alden, who came over to the U.S. on the Mayflower.* BS, Hobart Coll., 1959. Jr. analyst group actuarial divsn. Met. Life Ins. Co., N.Y.C., 1959-60, sr. analyst group actuarial divsn. dividend sect., 1961-63, sr. retention analyst group customer rels. and adminstrn. staff, 1964-70; distbr. Amway, Bedford, N.Y., 1976-98; ind. bus. owner Quixtar, Bedford, NY, 1999—. Mem. Rep. Presdl. Legion of Merit, Washington, 1980—; mem. nat. adv. bd. Black America's Polit. Action Com., Hagerstown, Md., 1996—; rep. Congrl. Order of Liberty, 1993, Congl. Order of Freedom, 1995; founding prodr. GOP-TV, 1994—; nat. mem. Libr. of Congress, Washington, 1990— (mem. chmn. adv. bd., 1995); hon. educator St. Joseph's Indian Sch., 1997—; life mem. Rep. Nat. Com., 2002—; mem. scholarship com. Am. Indian Edn. Found., 2004—. Royal Patronage bestowed Principality of Hutt River Province, 1994-95. Mem.: Consumer Reports (life), Kappa Alpha Soc. (mem. exec. coun. 1962—65). Episcopalian. Avocations: collecting stamps, signed first edition books and fine antiques. Home and Office: 46 Greenwich Rd Bedford NY 10506-1509 Office Phone: 914-234-3981.

HUSTING, PETER MARDEN, advertising consultant; b. Bronxville, N.Y., Mar. 28, 1935; s. Charles Ottomar and Jane Alice (Marden) H.; m. Carolyn Riddle, Mar. 26, 1960; children: Jennifer, Gretchen, Charles Ottomar; m. Myrna Diaz, May 11, 1996. BS, U. Wis., 1957; grad., Advanced Mgmt. Program, Harvard U., 1974. Sales rep. Crown Zellerbach Corp., San Francisco, 1958-59; media analyst Leo Burnett Co., Chgo., 1959-61, time buyer, 1961-62, asst. account exec., 1962-63, account exec., 1963-68, v.p., account supr., 1968-72, sr. v.p., account dir., 1972-79, group exec., 1979-86, exec. v.p., 1979-92, dir. human relations internat., 1986-92, also bd. dirs., ret., 1992; pres. Husting Enterprises, Chgo., 1993—. Dir. Columbian Mutual Life Ins. Co., Harley-Davidson Customer Funding Corp. Trustee Shedd Aquarium Soc., Chgo., 1980-94, hon. life trustee, 1995—; bd. dirs. Chgo. Better Govt. Assn., 1976-92, Leadership Coun. Met. Open Cmtys., Chgo., 1980-86, Lyric Opera Guild, 1971-78, Chgo. Forum, 1969-76. Served with AUS, 1958. Mem.: Indian Hill (Winnetka) (bd. govs. 1975-79), The Valley Club (Montecito, Calif.), Coral Casino Club (Santa Barbara). Avocations: flying, swimming, hunting, trekking, golf. Office: Husting Enterprises 150 S Wacker Dr Ste 3100 Chicago IL 60606-4103

HUSTON, ANJELICA, actress; b. Santa Monica, Calif., July 8, 1951; d. John and Enrica Huston; m. Robert Graham, 1992. Student, Loft Studio. Actress appearing in Hamlet, Roundhouse Theatre, London, Tamara, Il Vittorale Theatre, L.A.; appeared in films including A Walk with Love and Death, 1969, Hamlet, 1969, Sinful Davey, 1969, Swashbuckler, 1976, The Last Tycoon, 1976, The Postman Always Rings Twice, 1981, Rose for Emily, 1982, This is Spinal Tap, 1984, The Ice Pirates, 1984, Prizzi's Honor, 1985 (Academy award for best supporting actress 1985, N.Y.Film Critics award 1985, L.A. Film Critics award 1985), Captain Eo, 1986, Gardens of Stone, 1987, The Dead, 1987 (Best Actress award Ind. Filmakers 1987), Mr. North, 1988, A Handfull of Dust, 1988, Witches, 1989, Crimes and Misdemeanors, 1989, Enemies, A Love Story, 1989 (Acad. award nomination 1990), The Grifters, 1990 (Acad. award nomination 1991), The Addams Family, 1991, The Player, 1992, Addams Family Values, 1993, Manhattan Murder Mystery, 1993, The Crossing Guard, 1995, The Perez Family, 1995, Buffalo '66, 1997, Phoenix, 1998, Ever After, 1998, The Golden Bowl, 2000, The Man From Elysian Fields, 2000, The Royal Tenenbaums, 2001, Blood Work, 2002, Barbie as Rapunzel, (voice only), 2002, Daddy Day Care, 2003, Kaena: The Prophecy (voice only), The Life Aquatic with Steve Zissou, 2004; TV films include The Cowboy and the Ballerina, 1984, Family Pictures, 1993, And The Band Played On, 1993, Buffalo Girls, 1995, The Kentucky Derby, 2002, Iron Jawed Angels, 2004 (Golden Globe award for best supporting actress series, miniseries or TV movie, 2005); dir. (films) Bastard Out of Carolina, 1996, (TV films) Riding the Bus with My Sister, 2005; dir, prodr., acted (films) Agnes Browne, 1999; TV mini-series include Lonesome Dove, 1989, The Mists of Aalon, 2001; TV guest appearances Laverne & Shirley, 1976, Inside the Actors Studio, 1994. Office: Internat Creative Mgmt c/o Toni Howard 8942 Wilshire Blvd Beverly Hills CA 90211-1934*

HUSTON, DANIEL CLIFF, geophysicist; b. Anchorage, June 29, 1955; s. Arthur Cliff and Allie Mae (Ogdon) H.; m. Holly Hunter, Oct. 10, 1992; children: Lana Marie, Hayley Allison. BS in Geology and Geophysics, marine option program cert., U. Hawaii, 1980; MA in Geological Scis., U. Tex., 1987. Surveyor Trans Alaska Pipeline, 1975-78; geologist R&M Cons., Anchorage, 1980; geophysicist U.S. Minerals Mgmt. Svc., Anchorage, 1981-83; rsch. asst. Miss. Canyon Project, Austin, 1983-84; project SEER U. Tex. Inst. Geophysics, Austin, 1983-87; geophys. intern Sohio Petroleum Co., San Francisco, summer 1984; geophysicist leader advanced seismic methods group Unocal Sci. and Tech. Divsn., Brea, Calif., 1987-90; sr. geophysicist Unocal Oil and Gas Divsn., Houston, 1991-96; founder, v.p. Hunter 3-D Inc. (geophys. consulting firm), 1996—, Creekside Exploration, Inc. (oil and gas exploration firm), 1999—. Pres. Creekside Exploration, Inc., 1999—; presenter in field. Contbr. articles to profl. jours. Fellow U. Tex. Indsl. Assocs., 1983. Mem. Am. assn. Petroleum Geologists, Soc. Exploration Geophysicists (presenter workshop 1984, ann. conv. 1986, regional conv. 1989). Methodist. Avocations: travel, scuba diving, skiing, weightlifting, reading history. Home: 1635 Creekside Dr Sugar Land TX 77478-4203

HUSTON, GARY WILLIAM, lawyer; b. Velasco, Tex., Aug. 25, 1953; s. Robert Frank and Gloria Esther Marie Huston; m. Mary Ellen Meyer, May 28, 1977; children: Kyle Patrick, Megan Emily. BA, La. State U., 1974; JD, U. Va., 1978; LLM, U. Fla., 1994. Bar: Mo. 1978, U.S. Dist. Ct. (we. dist.) Mo. 1978, Fla. 1995; cert. tax lawyer and wills, trusts and estates, Fla. Bd. Legal Specialization and Edn. Assoc. Smith Gill Fisher Butts, Kansas City, Mo., 1978-79; ptnr. Grier & Swartzman, Kansas City, 1979-89; of counsel Armstrong, Teasdale, Kansas City, 1989-93; atty. Beggs & Lane, Pensacola, Fla., 1994-99; shareholder Clark, Partington, Hart, Larry, Bond & Stackhouse, Pensacola, 1999—. Bd. dirs. Escambia County Sch. Readiness Coalition, 1999—2001, Pensacola Symphony Orch., 2005—; atty. Greater Escambia Cmty. Found., Pensacola, 1995—97; mem. steering com. Leave A Legacy of NW Fla., 2000—02. Top 100 scholar La State U. Alumni Fedn., 1971-74, scholar Sigma Nu Ednl. Found., 1975-76. Mem. Pensacola Estate Planning Coun. (bd. dirs. 1997—), Fla. Bar (com. on rels. with CPAs 2000-02, exec. coun. health law sect. 2004—). Lutheran. Avocations: golf, running, fishing. Office: Clark Partington Hart Larry Bond & Stackhouse 125 W Romana St Ste 800 Pensacola FL 32501-5856 E-mail: ghuston@cphlaw.com.

HUSTON, JOHN CHARLES, law educator; b. Chgo., Mar. 21, 1927; s. Albert Allison and Lillian Helen (Sullivan) H.; m. Joan Frances Mooney, Aug. 1, 1954; children: Mark Allison, Philip John, Paul Francis James; m. Inger Margareta Westerman, May 4, 1979 (dec. 2003). AB, U. Wash., 1950, JD, 1952; LLM, N.Y. U., 1955. Bar: Wash. 1952, N.Y. 1964, U.S. Dist. Ct. (we. dist.) Wash. 1953, U.S. Ct. Appeals (9th cir.) 1953, U.S. Tax Ct. 1977, U.S. Supreme Ct. 1993. Assoc. Kahin, Carmody & Horswill, Seattle, 1952—53; tchg. fellow NYU Law Sch., 1953—54; asst. prof. NYU, 1956—57; asst. co-dir. U. Ankara Legal Rsch. Inst., Turkey, 1954—55; asst. prof. Syracuse (NY) U., 1957—60, assoc. prof., 1960—65, prof., 1965—67; prof., assoc. dean U. Wash., Seattle, 1967—73, prof. law, 1973—96, prof. emeritus, 1996—. Of counsel Carney, Badley, Smith & Spellman, Seattle, 1987—2002, Smith McKenzie Rothwell & Barlow, P.S., Seattle, 2002—; vis. prof. U. Stockholm, 1986, U. Bergen, 1989, Bond U., Australia, 1991. Author: (with Redden) The Mining Law of Turkey, 1956, The Petroleum Law of Turkey, 1956, (with Mucklestone and Cross) Community Property: General Considerations, 1971, (with Price and Treacy) 4th edit., 1994, (with Sullivan and others) Administration of Criminal Justice, 166, 2d edit., 1969, (with Miyatake and Way) Japanese International Taxation, 1983, supplements through 1997, (with Cross and Shields) Community Property Desk Book, 1977, 2d edit., 1989, supplement, 1997, (with Williams) Permanent Establishment, 1993. With USNR, 1945-46; capt. USAFR. Mem.: ABA, Internat. Fiscal Assn. (past regional v.p., past mem. coun.), Japanese Am. Soc. Legal Studies, King County Bar Assn., Wash. State Bar Assn. (chmn. tax sect. 1984—85), Am. Coll. Trust and Estate Coun. Office: 700 Logan Bldg 500 Union St Seattle WA 98101 Personal E-mail: huston@seanet.com.

HUSTON, JOHN DENNIS, English professor; b. N.Y.C., Sept. 21, 1939; s. A. Arthur H. and Jacquelin (Buchenau) Hawkins; m. Priscilla Jane, June 13, 1964 (div. July 1985); children: Katherine, Penn; m. Lisa B. Bryan, Aug. 8, 1988; stepchildren: Rudy Bryan, Kirby Bryan. BA, Wesleyan U., 1961; MA, Yale U., 1964, PhD, 1966. Instr., English Yale U., New Haven, 1966-67, asst. prof., 1967-69; assoc. prof. Rice U., Houston, 1969-80, prof. English, 1980—, Minnie Stevens Piper prof., 2002. Dir. freshman humanities Rice U., 1988-94, 1999-; master Hanszen Coll., 1978-82, 92-98. Author: Shakespeare's Comedies of Play, 1981; co-editor: Classics of the Renaissance Theater, 1969. Named CASE Prof. of Yr., 1989-90, Disting. Alumnus Wesleyan U., 1991; recipient Wilbur Cross medal Yale Grad. Sch., 1992, Meritorious Svc. award Rice Alumni Assn., 2005. Mem. Coll. English Assn. (bd. dirs. 1989-92), Phi Beta Kappa. Democrat. Avocations: running, racquetball, squash, skiing, fishing. Home: 4115 Mcduffie St Houston TX 77098-3419 Office: Rice U Dept English PO Box 1892 Houston TX 77251-1892 E-mail: jdhuston@rice.edu.

HUSTON, JOHN WILSON, military officer, historian; b. Pitts., Mar. 6, 1925; s. James Leslie and Kathryn Rachel (Ray) H.; m. Dorothy Winters Bampton, Aug. 27, 1960; children: Ann, John. BA, Monmouth Coll., 1948; MA, U. Pitts., 1950, PhD, 1957. Served as 1st lt. USAAF, 1943-45; advanced through grades to maj. gen. USAF Res., 1976; recalled to active duty as chief Office of Air Force History, Dept. Air Force, Washington, 1976—; lectr. history U. Pitts., 1949-56; prof. U.S. Naval Acad., Annapolis, 1956-76, chmn. dept. history, 1971-76. Vis. prof. U. Rochester, 1964, Ball State U., 1965, 67, U. Md., 1969; Disting. vis. prof. USAF Acad., 1994-95. Author: American Air Power Comes of Age: General Henry H. "Hap" Arnold's World War II Diaries, 2001. Decorated D.S.M., D.F.C. with oak leaf cluster, Air medal with 3 oak leaf clusters, Joint Service Commendation medal, Air Force Commendation medal. Home: 115 E Lake Dr Annapolis MD 21403-4444 Office: Hdqrs USAF AF/CVAH Bolling Afb Washington DC 20332-0001

HUSTON, MARGO, journalist; b. Waukesha, Wis., Feb. 12, 1943; d. James and Cecile (Timlin) Bremner; m. James Huston, Dec. 9, 1967 (div.); 1 son, Sean Patrick. AB in Journalism, Marquette U., 1965; Certificate in Muslim-Christian Dialogue, 2004. Editl. asst. Marquette U., Milw., 1965-66; feature editor, reporter Waukesha Freeman, 1966-67; feature reporter Milw. Jour., 1967-70, reporter Spectrum, women's and food sects., 1972-79, editl. writer, 1979-84, polit. reporter, 1984—, asst. picture editor, 1985-91, copy editor, 1992-95; reporter Milw. Jour Sentinel (merger Milw. Jour. and The Sentinel), 1995-99; mem. working bd. Cath. Herald, 2000—01; freelance journalist Milw., 2001—. Instr. mass comm. U. Wis., Milw. Mem. Milw. Restorative Justice Task Force, 2004. Recipient Penney-Mo. award for consumer abortion series, 1977, Pulitzer Prize for investigation into plight of elderly, 1977, Clarion award, 1977, Knight of Golden Quill award, Milw. Press club, 1977, Wis. AP writing award, 1977, Spl. award Milw. Soc. Profl. Journalists, 1977, Penney-Mo. Paul Myhre award for excellence, 1978, By-Line award Marquette U. Coll. Journalism, 1980, Wis. UPI Best Editl. award, 1982, Wis. Women's Network award for journalist achievement for women's issues, 1983, Dick Goldensohn Fund award, 1991, 1st place award for investigative reporting Inland Press Assn., 1997, 98, 2d award Enterprise interpretive reporting Wis. Newspaper Assn., 1998; Wis. Arts Bd. Lit. Arts grantee, 1992. Mem. European Project for Interreligious Learning (founding mem., cert. in Muslim-Christian Dialogue 2004), Milw. Press Club (Hall of Fame 2000). E-mail: margo.huston@gmail.com.

HUSTON, SAMUEL RICHARD, health facility executive; b. Newton, Iowa, Apr. 21, 1940; s. Marshall Dwight and Miriam Evelyn (Peake) H.; m. Ann M. Huston; children: Carmen Colleen, Christopher Dwight. BA, U. No. Iowa, 1962; MA, State U. Iowa, 1964. Asst. adminstr. med. ctr. Hosp. of Vt., Burlington, 1964-66; assoc. dir. No. New Eng. Regional Med. Program, Burlington, 1966-68; asst. adminstr. Univ. Hosp. Cleve., 1968-70, from assoc. adminstr. to exec. v.p., COO, 1972—86; assoc. dir. Duke Hosp., Durham, N.C., 1970-72; pres., CEO Lehigh Valley Hosp. Ctr., Allentown, Pa., 1986—87, Allentown Hosp.-Lehigh Valley Hosp. Ctr., Pa., 1987—90; CEO Lehigh Valley Health Network, Lehigh Valley Hosp., Allentown, Pa., 1990—93; pres., CEO St. Luke's Med. Ctr., Cleve., 1994-97, St. Luke's Found. of Cleve., 1997-99; prin. Jay Alix and Assocs., 1999-2000; pres., CEO ViaHealth Sys., Rochester, NY, 2000—. Avocations: reading, music, hunting, golf. Home: 5 Roxbury Ln Pittsford NY 14534 Office: ViaHealth System c/o Rochester Gen Hosp Portland Ave Rochester NY 14621 Office Phone: 585-922-4837. E-mail: sam.huston@viahealth.org.

HUSZAGH, FREDRICK WICKETT, lawyer, educator, information technology executive; b. Evanston, Ill., July 20, 1937; s. Rudolph LeRoy and Dorothea (Wickett) H.; m. Sandra McRae, Apr. 4, 1959; children: Floyd McRae, Fredrick Wickett II, Theodore Wickett II. BA, Northwestern U., 1958; JD, U. Chgo., 1962, LLM, 1963, JSD, 1964. Bar: Ill. 1962, U.S. Dist. Ct. D.C. 1965, U.S. Supreme Ct. 1966. Market rschr. Leo Burnett Co., Chgo., 1958-59; internat. atty. COMSAT, Washington, 1964-67; assoc. Debevoise & Liberman, Washington, 1967-68; asst. prof. law Am. U., Washington, 1968-71; program dir. NSF, Washington, 1971-73; assoc. prof. U. Mont., Missoula, 1973-76, U. Wis., Madison, 1976-77; exec. dir. Dean Rusk Ctr., U. Ga., Athens, 1977-82; prof. U. Ga., 1982—2003, prof. emeritus, 2004—. Chmn. TWH Corp., Athens, 1982—; chmn. Profession Mgmt. Techs., Inc., Athens, 1993-96; cons. TWH Scv. Corp.; cons. Pres. Johnson's Telcommunications Task Force, Washington, 1967-68; co-chmn. Nat. Gov.'s Internat. Trade Staff Commn., Washington, 1979- 81. Author: International Decision-Making Process, 1964, Comparative Facts on Canada, Mexico and U.S., 1979; editor Rusk Ctr. Briefings, 1981-82; contbr. articles to publs. Mem. Econ. Policy Coun., N.Y.C., 1981-89. NSF grantee, 1974-78. Republican. Presbyterian. Office: U Ga Law Sch Athens GA 30602 Office Phone: 706-542-5940. Business E-Mail: huszagh@uga.edu.

HUSZAI, KRISTY RENEE, insurance agent; b. Pensacola, Fla., May 19, 1974; d. Stephen Edward and Mary Ellen Huszai. Grad. H.S., Gaithersburg, Md. Lic. ins. agt. Md. Sales asst. Paul Revere Ins., Rockville, Md., 1993—97; sec. CompDesign, Bethesda, Md., 1997—98; sr. account asst. Mut. Omaha, Washington, 1998—. Republican. Roman Catholic. Avocations: reading, travel, sports.

HUT, A. STEPHEN, lawyer; b. Dec. 6, 1946; BA, Univ. Pa., 1968; JD magna cum laude, Harvard Univ., 1972. Bar: DC 1974. Ptnr., vice chmn. Litigation dept., co-chmn. pro bono & cmty. svc. com. Wilmer Cutler Pickering Hale & Dorr, Washington. Acting spl. asst. to Gen. Counsel U.S. Dept. Def., Washington, 1977; trustee Council for Ct. Excellence, 1991—, mem. exec. com., 1994—98, 2001—. Editor (note): Harvard Law Rev.; contbr. articles to profl. jours. Mem.: Phi Beta Kappa. Office: Wilmer Cutler Pickering Hale & Dorr 1801 Pennsylvania Ave NW Washington DC 20006 Mailing: Wilmer Cutler Pickering Hale & Dorr 2445 M St NW Washington DC 20037 Office Phone: 202-663-6235. Office Fax: 202-663-6363. Business E-Mail: stephen.hut@wilmerhale.com.

HUT, PIET, astrophysics educator; b. Utrecht, Holland, Sept. 26, 1952; came to U.S., 1981. s. Jan Lambertus Hut and Jenneke Johanna Hut-Broekroelofs; m. Eiko Ikegami, July 26, 1991. MS, U. Utrecht, 1977; PhD, U. Amsterdam, Holland, 1981. Asst. prof. astronomy dept. U. Calif., Berkeley, 1984-85; mem. Inst. for Advanced Study, Princeton, N.J., 1981-84, prof., 1985—. Contbr. articles to prof. jours. Mem. Am. Astron. Soc., Dutch Astron. Club, Astron. Soc. Japan. Office: Inst for Advanced Study Olden Ln Princeton NJ 08540 Office Phone: 609-734-8075. E-mail: piet@ias.edu.

HUTCHENS, EUGENE GARLINGTON, academic administrator; b. Birmingham, Ala., Nov. 26, 1929; s. Wallace Luther and Reydonia (Corry) H.; m. Betty Frances Goode, Aug. 26, 1951; children: Dale Eugene, Wayne Goode, Dennis Wade. BA, Samford U., 1952; ThM, New Orleans Bapt. Theol. Sem., 1970; MS in Econs., U. Mo.-Columbia, 1972; D Arts in Theology, Emmanuel Sem., 1999. Ordained to ministry, 1952. Min. North Brewton (Ala.) Bapt. Ch., 1952-56, 1st Bapt. Ch., Ashland, Ala., 1956-63, Highlands Bapt. Ch., Huntsville, Ala., 1963-67; tchr. pub. schs. Huntsville, 1967-71; instr. econs. N.W. Ala. State Jr. Coll., 1972-77, acting pres., 1981, dir. Tuscumbia campus, 1977-89; adminstrv. asst. Shoals C.C., 1989—94, asst. to dean, 1993-95; pastor emeritus Weeden Heights Bapt. Ch., Florence, 1995; prof. Emmanuel Sem., 1995—. Owner radio stas., WKNI AM, Lexington, Ala., WFIX, Rogersville, Ala., 1991-96, mem. Ala. Bapt. State Exec. Bd., 1961-63; v.p. Ala. Bapt. State Pastors Conf., 1966, Ala. Bapt. Hist. Commn., 1992-2000. NSF grantee, 1971-72. Mem. NEA, Ala. Edn. Assn., Ala. Jr. and C.C. Assn. (exec. com. 1981-84), Phi Theta Kappa. Home: 801 E 2nd St Tuscumbia AL 35674-2206

HUTCHENS, GAIL R., chemist; b. Bentonville, Ark., Aug. 22, 1938; d. Sidney Baxter and Mary Dena Maurine (Harral) Rakes; m. Charles Verlin Hutchens, Mar. 4, 1967 (dec. 2002); children: David Charles, Kimberly Gail. Student, Ark. State Tchrs. Coll., 1955—58; grad., U. Tenn., 1961. Exec. v.p. Galbraith Labs., Inc., Knoxville, Tenn., 1959—93; analytical svcs. supr. Materials Engring. & Testing, Oak Ridge, Tenn., 1993—96, Techmer PM, LLC, Clinton, Tenn., 1996—. Emergency first responder instr. Video editor Democrates, Knoxville, TN, 1998. Mem. ASTM, Assn. Offcl. Analytical Chemists, Soc. Plastic Engrs. (local sect. sec. 2002-2004), Am. Chem. Soc., Crestwood Hills Garden Club (pres. 1968-69), Small Chem. Bus. (sec. 1974-75), Beta Club Honor Soc., Alpha Chi. Avocation: diving instruction. Office: Techmer PM LLC 1 Quality Cir Clinton TN 37716-4017 Business E-Mail: ghutchens@Techmerpm.com.

HUTCHENS, JOAN REID, retired elementary school educator, reading specialist, consultant; b. Harrisonburg, Va., May 22, 1947; d. Paul Leslie and Mary (Holsinger) Reid; m. Harry Edward Hutchens, Dec. 27, 1969; children: Stacie Amelia, Kimberly Dawn. BS in Elem. Edn., James Madison U., 1969, MEd, 1994. Cert. tchr., Va.; lic. reading specialist, Va. Tchr. grades 1-7, reading specialist K-12 Rockingham County Pub. Schs., Harrisonburg, Va., 1969—2005; ret. Cons., trainer W.R.I.T. &E. Project/Nat. Diffusion Network, Falls Church, Va. and Glassboro, N.J., 1988-91; writing workshops/assessment workshops Rockingham County Pub. Schs., 1991—, lang. arts curriculum com., 1985—, Blue Ridge Assessment Project Albemarle County Pub. Schs., Charlottesville, Va., 1993-94, Va. State Reading Assn. Presentation, 1995. Recipient grant Rockingham Pub. Sch. Bd., 1992, 93, Blue Ridge Assessment Participant award Va. State Dept. Edn., 1994. Mem. ASCD, Va. Reading Assn., Shenandoah Valley Reading Assn., Phi Beta Kappa. Mem. Brethren Ch. Avocations: boating, fishing, reading professionally, cooking, writing. Home: 14813 Runions Creek Rd Broadway VA 22815-9510 Office: John C Myers Elem Sch Rockingham County Pub Schs Raider Rd Broadway VA 22815

HUTCHENS, TYRA THORNTON, pathologist, educator; b. Newberg, Oreg., Nov. 29, 1921; s. Fred George and Bessie (Adams) H.; m. Betty Lou Gardner, June 7, 1942; children: Tyra Richard, Robert Jay, Rebecca (Mrs. Mark Pearsall). BS, U. Oreg., 1943, MD, 1945. Diplomate: Am. Bd. Pathology, Am. Bd. Nuclear Medicine. Intern Minn. Gen. Hosp., Mpls., 1945—46; AEC postdoctoral research fellow Reed Coll., Med. Sch. U. Oreg., 1948—50; NIH postdoctoral research fellow Med. Sch. U. Oreg., 1951—53; mem. faculty Oreg. Health Scis. U., 1953—, prof., chmn. dept. clin. pathology, 1962—87, prof. emeritus, 1987—, prof. radiotherapy, 1963—71, allied health edn. coord., 1969—77. Vis. lectr. radiobiology Reed Coll., 1955, 56 Mem. adv. bd. Oreg. Regional Med. Program, 1968-75; mem. statuatory radiation adv. com. Oreg. Bd. Health, 1957-69, chmn., 1967-69; founding trustee Am. Bd. Nuc. Medicine, 1971-77, 82-84, sec., 1973-75, 84-85; voting rep. Am. Bd. Med. Specialties, 1973-78, chmn. com. long range planning, 1976-78; mem. sci. adv. bd. Armed Forces Inst. Pathology, 1978-83; chmn. Portland Com. on Fgn. Affairs, 1990-91. Lt. (j.g.) M.C., USNR, 1946-48. Charter mem. Acad. Clin. Lab. Physicians and Scientists, Soc. Nuc. Medicine (de Hevesey Nuc. Medicine Pioneer award 1995), Am. Coll. Nuc. Physicians; mem. AMA, Oreg. Pathologists Assn. (pres. 1968), Pacific N.W. Soc. Nuc. Medicine (pres. 1958), Coll. Am. Pathologists (bd. govs. 1967-74, pres. 1977-79, chmn. commn. on internat. affairs 1979-83, chmn. planning com. 1987 World Congress Pathology), Am. Soc. Clin. Pathologists (bd. registry med. technologists 1967-71), World Assn. of Socs. of Pathology (bur. of pathology 1981-87, 89-93, v.p. 1985-87, pres. 1989-91, chmn. commn. on world stds. 1981-86, Gold Headed Cane award 1995), World Pathology Found. (pres. 1987-89, trustee 1989-91), Assn. Clin. Pathologists (hon.), Italian Soc. Lab. Medicine (hon.), Phi Beta Kappa, Sigma Xi, Alpha Omega Alpha. Achievements include research and publications on radioactive carbon tracer studies of lipid metabolism, clinical radioisotope techniques. Home: 17480 Holy Names Dr 413 Lake Oswego OR 97034 Personal E-mail: tyhutch@comcast.net.

HUTCHEON, LINDA ANN, English language educator; b. Toronto, Aug. 24, 1947; d. Vincent Roy and Elisa (Rossi) Bulfon Bortolotti; m. Michael Alexander Hutcheon, May 30, 1970. BA, U. Toronto, 1969, PhD, 1975; MA, Cornell U., 1971. Prof. McMaster U., Hamilton, Ont., Can., 1976-88, U. Toronto, 1988—95, 1995—. Vis. prof. U. Toronto, 1980-81, 81-82, 84-85, U. Wis., Madison, 1995, U. Ga., 1998, U. Queensland, Australia, 2001, U. Mich. Inst. for the Humanities, 2003. Author: Narcisstic Narrative, 1980 (choice award, 1980), Formalism and the Freudian Aesthetic, 1984, A Theory of Parody, 1985, 2000, A Poetics of Postmodernism, 1988, The Canadian Postmodern, 1988, The Politics of Postmodernism, 1989, 2002, Splitting Images, 1991, Irony's Edge, 1995; author: (with M. Hutcheon) Opera: Desire, Disease, Death, 1996, Bodily Charm: Living Opera, 2000, Opera: The Art of Dying, 2004; assoc. editor: RS/SI, 1982—84, U. Toronto Quar., 1993—; mem. (editl. bd.) Texte, Toronto, 1983—, English Studies in Can., 1984—94, Italian Canadiana, 1984—, Textual Practice, 1987—2003, Can. Rev. Comparative Lit., 1987—, Can. Poetry, 1987—93, PMLA, 1990—92, Essays on Can. Writing, 1992—, Contemporary Lit., 1992—, Modern Fiction Studies, 1993—, CLIO, 1994—, Parallax (U.K.), 1994—. Woodrow Wilson Found. fellow, 1969, Social Scis. and Humanities Rsch. Coun. Can. fellow, 1983, 93-95, 96-99, 2000-03, 04—, co-fellow maj. collaborative rsch. initiatives, 1996-2000; Can. Coun. fellow, 1972-75, Killam Found. fellow, 1978-80, 86-88, Connaught fellow, 1991-92, Guggenheim fellow, 1992-93. Fellow Am. Acad. Arts and Scis.; mem. MLA (del. assembly 1985-88, exec. coun. 1992-96, 2d v.p. 1998, 1st v.p. 1999, pres. 2000), AAAS (elected), Assn. Can. Coll. and Univ. Tchrs. English (exec. mem. 1978-81), Can. Comparative Lit. Assn. (sec.-treas. 1981-83), Internat. Comparative Lit. Assn. (coord. com. lit. history 1992-97).

HUTCHEON, PETER DAVID, lawyer; b. S.I., N.Y., Sept. 11, 1943; s. Peter and Helen Christine (Buckley) H.; m. Elizabeth Ann Demy, June 8, 1969 (div. Jan. 1986); children: Rececca Leigh, Douglas Ian; m. Barbara Mary Silver, Feb. 14, 1986; 1 child, Peter Silver. BA, Williams Coll., 1965; postgrad., Ludwig-Maximilian Universität, Munich, 1965-66; JD, Harvard U., 1969. Bar: N.Y. 1970, N.J. 1975. Assoc. White & Case LLP, N.Y.C., 1968—75, Norris, McLaughlin & Marcus, P.A., Somerville, NJ, 1975—76, mem., 1976—. Chmn. N.J. Corp. and Bus. Law Study Commn., 1989—2001; mem., sec. adv. com. N.J. Bur. Securities, 1993—2001, chmn., 1994—2001. Contbr. articles to profl. jours. Chmn. bd. mgrs. St. Andrews Soc. of N.Y., 1986—87; deacon United Reformed Ch., Somerville, 1977—80; elder Bound Brook Presbyn. Ch., 1996—99. Dankstipendium scholar govt. of the Fed. Republic of Gemany, 1965. Mem. ABA (chmn. sect. of sci. and tech. 1986-87), N.J. State Bar Assn. (chmn. banking law sect. 1982-83, chmn. corp. and bus. sect. 1990-92), N.Y. State Bar Assn., German-Am. Lawyers Assn., Nat. Conf. of Lawyers and Scientists (del. 1988-91), Princeton Area Alumni Assn. of Williams Coll. (pres. 1981-89), Clan Donald (N.Y.). Avocations: wine tasting, singing. Office: Norris McLaughlin & Marcus PA PO Box 1018 721 Rt 202/206 Somerville NJ 08876 Office Phone: 908-722-0700 ext. 216. Business E-Mail: pdhutcheon@nmmlaw.com.

HUTCHEON, WALLACE SCHOONMAKER, historian, educator; b. N.Y.C., June 27, 1933; s. Wallace Schoonmaker and Dorothy Mae (Tate) Hutcheon; m. Margaret Marie Crossen, Sept. 29, 1963; children: Dorothy Lee, Hillary Ann. BS in Agrl. Econs., Pa. State U., 1954; MA in History, George Washington U., 1969, MPhil in History, 1971, PhD in History, 1975. Commd. ensign USNR, 1955, advanced through grades to comdr., 1970; comm. officer Fawtulant Naval Air Sta., Key West, Fla., 1955-59; edn. officer USS Kitty Hawk, 1962-64; air intelligence officer CVW-2, 1964-66, intelligence analyst DIA, 1966-70; released to inactive duty, 1970; lectr. George Mason U., Fairfax, Va., 1970; instr. St. Marys Coll., Md., 1971; from asst. prof. to assoc. prof. history No. Va. CC, Annandale, 1971—80, prof., 1980—, head dept., 1974—, asst. chmn. divsn. social scis. and pub. svcs., 1979—2003, asst. dean Liberal Arts, 2003—. Mgmt. tng. cons. Health Resources Adminstn., HEW, Hyattsville, Md., 1978; cons. mil. evaluations program Am. Coun. Edn., Washington, 1980; cons. coll. history textbooks Houghton-Mifflin Co., Boston, 1992—; pub. spkr. Mariners Mus., DC Historian Luncheon, others. Mem. adv. bd. ann. edits. Dushkin Pub. Co.; author: Robert Fulton: Pioneer of Undersea Warfare, 1981; contbr. manuscripts collection to U.S. Navy History Divsn. Mem. History of City of Fairfax Roundtable, 1995—98; history day judge George Mason U., 1990—2002. Recipient Outstanding Contbns. to Edn. award, Alumni Fedn. No. Va. CC, 1993, 1995, 2003, Golden Apple award, Student Govt., 1999—2000. Mem.: U.S. Capitol Hist. Soc., No. Va. Assn. History (bd. dirs. 1994, v.p. 1994), Orgn. Am. Historians, U.S. Naval Inst., Delta Chi. Democrat. Episcopalian. Avocations: swimming, reading, music, theater. Home: 4425 Village Dr Fairfax VA 22030-5642 Office: No Va CC 8333 Little River Tpke Annandale VA 22003-3743 Business E-Mail: whutcheon@nvcc.edu.

HUTCHESON, J. STERLING, retired allergist, immunologist, physician; b. Richmond, Va., Apr. 17, 1936; s. James P. and Daisy-Clarke (Lorentz) H.; m. Nancy Montgomery Sanders, May 20, 1961; children: Anne Farrar McCausland, Betsy Dulaney. Student, Roanoke Coll., Va., 1953-55; BA, U. Va., 1955-57; MD, The Johns Hopkins U., 1957-61. Diplomate Am. Bd. Allergy and Clin. Immunology. Intern in medicine U. Va., Charlottesville, Va., 1961-62; resident in medicine Med. Coll. Va., Richmond, Va., 1962-64; fellow in allergy and immunology U. Va., Charlottesville, Va., 1964-65; asst. prof. medicine Med. Coll. Va., 1967-68; staff Nalle Clinic, Charlotte, 1968-89; pvt. practice Carolina Asthma and Allergy Ctr., 1990—2005. Founder Allergy Clinic USAF Acad. Hosp., Colo., 1965-67; cons. Blue Cross/Blue Shield of N.C., 1985-2002; adj. assoc. prof. pediats. U. N.C. Sch. Medicine, Carolinas Med. Ctr., Charlotte, 1997-2000. Bd. trustees Charlotte Country Day Sch., 1974-85; bd. dirs. Friends of Music Queens Coll., 1994-96. Capt. USAF M.C. Fellow Am. Acad. Allergy, Asthma and Immunology, Am. Coll. Allergy, Asthma and Immunology; mem. Southeastern Allergy Assn., N.C. Soc. Allergy and Clin. Immunology (former pres.). Episcopalian. Avocations: gardening, hiking, classical music, reading. Home: 339 Green Cove Rd Sugar Mountain Banner Elk NC 28604 Office Phone: 704-372-7900. Personal E-mail: sthutch@skybest.com.

HUTCHESON, JACK ROBERT, hematologist, medical oncologist; b. Rock Hill, S.C., Dec. 26, 1946; s. Jack Robert and Lillian Massey (Dunlap) H.; m. Charlene Marie Dixon, Sept. 14, 1974; children: Gregory Allen, Julia Lynn. BS in Biology, Wake Forest U., 1969; MD, Med. U. S.C., 1973. Diplomate in internal medicine, hematology, oncology Am. Bd. Internal Medicine. Straight med. intern U. Md. Hosp., Balt., 1973-74, resident in medicine, 1974-76; fellow in hematology Med. U. S.C., Charleston, 1976-78; fellow in oncology Emory U., Atlanta, 1978-79; oncologist, hematologist Oncology and Hematology Assocs. of S.W. Va. Inc., Roanoke, 1979—; med. dir. Carilion Health Sys. Oncology Svc. Line, Roanoke, 1996—. Instr., assoc. investigator in hematology Med. U. S.C./VA Hosp., Charleston, 1977-78; assoc. prof. medicine U. Va., Roanoke. Contbr. articles to med. jours. Pres. Scottish Soc. Va. Highlands, Roanoke, 1996, 2000, 01; chair com. on smoking cessation Va. br. Am. Cancer Soc., Roanoke, 1980; mem. Vets. Corps. of Artillary, N.Y. Decorated Most Venerable Order of Hosp. of St. John of Jerusalem, Caballero Grand Cruz Order Don Carlos I (Portugal); recipient Berson Yalow award, Soc. Nuclear Medicine, 1977; grantee for hematology, VA Career Devel., 1977—78. Fellow ACP; mem. Am. Soc. Clin. Oncology, Am. Soc. Hematology, St. Andrews Soc. Presbyterian. Avocations: Jaguar auto restoration, genealogy, Scottish/Celtic activities, bagpipes. Home: 2860 S Jefferson St Roanoke VA 24014-3320 Office: Oncol and Hematol Assocs 2013 S Jefferson St Roanoke VA 24014-2419 Office Phone: 540-982-0237. Personal E-mail: jhut@aol.com. Business E-Mail: jack.hutchesonjr@usoncology.com.

HUTCHESON, JERRY DEE, manufacturing company executive; b. Oct. 31, 1932; s. Radford Andrew and Ethel Mae (Boulware) H.; m. Lynda Lou Weber, Mar. 6, 1953; children: Gerald Dan, Lisa Marie, Vicki Lynn. BS in Physics, Ea. N.Mex. U., 1965; postgrad., Temple U., 1962, U. N.Mex., 1965. Registered profl. engr., Calif. Rsch. engr. RCA, 1959—62; sect. head Motorola, 1962—63; rsch. physicist Dikewood Corp., 1963—66; sr. mem. tech. staff Signetics Corp., 1966—69; engring. mgr. Litton Sys., Sunnyvale, Calif., 1969—70, Fairchild Semiconductor, Mountain View, Calif., 1971; equipment engr., group mgr. Teledyne Semiconductor, Mountain View, 1971—74; dir. engring. DCA Reliability Labs., Sunnyvale, 1974—75; founder, prin. Tech. Ventures, San Jose, Calif., 1975—; CEO VLSI Rsch., Inc., San Jose, 1981—, chmn., 2004—. Contbr. articles to profl. jours. Dem. precinct committeeman, Albuquerque, 1964—66. With USAF, 1951—55. Mem.: NSPE, Am. Soc. Test Engrs., Soc. Photo-Optical Instrumentation Engrs., Semiconductor Equipment and Materials Inst., Calif. Soc. Profl. Engrs., Profl. Engrs. Pvt. Practice, Masons. Presbyterian. Office: VLSI Rsch 2880 Lakeside Dr 350 Santa Clara CA 95054-2822 Office Phone: 408-453-8844.

HUTCHESON, MARK ANDREW, lawyer; b. Phila., Mar. 29, 1942; s. John R. and Mary Helen (Willis) H.; m. Julie A. Olander, June 13, 1964; children: Kirsten Elizabeth, Mark Andrew II, Megan Ann. BA, U. Puget Sound, 1964; LLB, U. Wash., 1967. Bar: Wash. 1967, U.S. Dist. Ct. (we. and ea. dists.) Wash., U.S. Ct. Appeals (9th cir.), U.S. Supreme Ct. Staff counsel Com. on Commerce U.S. Senate, Washington, 1967-68; assoc. Davis Wright Tremaine, Seattle, 1968-72; ptnr. Davis, Wright Tremaine, Seattle, 1973—; mng. ptnr., chief exec. officer Davis Wright Tremaine, Seattle, 1989-94; chmn. Davis, Wright Tremaine, Seattle, 1994—. Mem., co-founder labor law com. Nat. Banking Industry, 1984—. Co-author: Employer's Guide to Strike Planning and Prevention, 1986; contbr. articles to profl. jours. Chmn., trustee Virginia Mason Hosp., Seattle, 1980-2003, Overlake Sch., Redmond, Wash., 1984-89, Epiphany Sch., Seattle, 1982-84, Legal Aid for Wash. Fund, 1991-2003; bd. dirs. Vis. Nurse Svcs., Seattle-King County, 1985-88; trustee Pacific N.W. Ballet, 1991-99, Pacific N.W. Assn. Ind. Schs., 1996-98. Nelson T. Hartson scholar U. Wash., 1966; Deerfield fellow Heritage Found., Deerfield, Mass., 1963. Mem. ABA (health care forum, employment law sect.), Seattle-King County Bar Assn. (employment law sect.), Am. Acad. Hosp. Attys., Am. Hosp. Assn. (labor rels. adv. com. 1978—), Coll. Labor and Employment Lawyers, Greater Seattle C. of C. (bd. dirs. 1991-94), Rainier Club, Seattle Tennis Club, Univ. Club, Order of Coif. Episcopalian. Avocations: sailing, tennis, skiing, reading, travel. Office: Davis Wright Tremaine 2600 Century Sq 1501 4th Ave Seattle WA 98101-1688 Office Phone: 206-628-7678. Business E-Mail: markhutcheson@dwt.com.

HUTCHESON, THOMAS WORTHINGTON, trade association administrator; b. Lake Forest, Ill., July 1, 1958; s. Harold Randolph and Minna Margaret (Adams) Hutcheson. BA, U. Mass., 1980, MEd, 1987, EdD, 1993. Music tchr., 1975—; instr. edn. U. Mass., Amherst, 1987-89, v.p. Grad. Student Senate, 1988-89, rsch. asst. dept. econs., 1989-91; rsch. cons. Nat. Priorities Project, Northampton, Mass., 1991-92; estate cons. Sandwich, Mass., 1996-99; music critic The Recorder, Greenfield, Mass., 1996-99; project coord. Bonnyvale Environ. Edn. Ctr., Brattleboro, Vt., 1996-99, cons., 1992; policy asst. Organic Trade Assn., Greenfield, Mass., 1999-2000, policy coord., 2000—02, assoc. policy dir., 2002—. Musician; arranger choral work: Welcome, Yule!, 1994—; dir.: Shapeshifters Vocal Quartet, 1997—2001, 2004—; contbr. articles to profl. jours. Chmn. Pub. Transp. Com., Amherst, 1989—90, Franklin Regional Planning Bd., Greenfield, 2002—, mem. local emergency planning com., 2002—04; mem. Overall Econ. Devel. Program Policy Com., Greenfield, 1996—99, Greater Franklin Regional Comprehensive Econ. Devel. Strategy Com., 1999—, mem. governing bd., 2004—; chmn. Com. Elec. Industry Regulation, Greenfield, 1996—99. Mem.: Am. Soc. Assn. Execs., Internat. Soc. Ecol. Econs., Am. Planning Assn. Democrat. Mem. Soc. Of Friends. Avocations: Morris dance, family archives, traditional music. Home: 21 Madison Cir Greenfield MA 01301-2723 Office: Organic Trade Assn 60 Wells St Greenfield MA 01301-9654 Personal E-mail: thutcheson@ota.com.

HUTCHINGS, GEORGE HENRY, food company executive; b. Fort Worth, June 23, 1922; s. George H. and Emma (Harder) H.; m. Edith Van Gils, Mar. 23, 1946 (dec.); children: Mark Dennis Lisa Ellen; m. Elizabeth T. Storey, Apr. 10, 1968 (dec.). Student, Tex. A&M, 1940-42. Analyst mktg. research Frito Food Mfg., Dallas, 1946, mgr. mktg. research Los Angeles, 1946-57, div. sales mgr. San Mateo, Calif., 1958-60, div. gen. mgr., 1961, v.p., 1961-62; v.p. for ops. Western zone, 1962—; pres. Nalley's, Inc., Tacoma, 1964, Nalley's div. W.R. Grace & Co., 1966—, ret. Tacoma, 1972-81; pres. Wash. Beverages, Inc., Tacoma, 1972-81. Dir., mem. exec. com. Puget Sound Nat. Bank, Tacoma; cons. 1964-83; dir. mem. examining com. Key Bank of Wash., Tacoma, 1993-94, ret., 1994. Served to capt. USAAF, 1942-46. Decorated D.F.C., Air medal with 7 clusters. Mem. Tacoma Country and Golf Club, Masons. Lutheran. Home: 7419 North St SW Tacoma WA 98498-5213 *A man must know what he stands for before he can logically take a stand against anything.*

HUTCHINGS, JENNIFER KATY, research scientist; b. London, Eng., May 17, 1975; arrived in US, 2001; d. Graham John and Sally Joanna Hutchings; m. Patrick Alan McKeown, Aug. 21, 2004. BSc in Physics, U. Coll. London, 1996, PhD in Remote Sensing, 2001. Rsch. scientist Meteorol. Office UK, Bracknell, England, 2000—01; post doctoral rsch. fellow U. Alaska, Fairbanks, 2001—.

HUTCHINGS, JOHN BARRIE, astronomer, researcher; b. Johannesburg, July 18, 1941; arrived in Can., 1967; BSc, Witwatersrand U., Johannesburg, 1962, MSc, 1964; PhD, U. Cambridge, Eng., 1967. Rsch. scientist Dominion Astrophysics Obs., NRC Can., Victoria, Canada, 1967—. Author numerous rsch. papers and revs., 1964—. Recipient Gold medal Sci. Coun. B.C., 1983, Royal Jubilee medal, 2002. Fellow Royal Soc. Can.; mem. Internat. Astron. Union, Am. Astron. Soc., Can. Astron. Soc. (Beals award 1982). Office: Dominion Astrophysics Obs 5071 W Saanich Rd Victoria BC Canada V9E 2E7 Office Phone: 250-363-0018. E-mail: john.hutchings@nrc.ca.

HUTCHINGS, PETER LOUNSBERY, retired insurance company executive, director; b. N.Y.C., Nov. 1, 1943; s. Robert Spaulding and Kathryn Eleanor (Lounsbery) H.; m. Marsha Kayser, May 27, 1966 (div. 1980); children: Michael, Daniel; m. Martha Deborah Wolfgang, Jan. 16, 1983 BA, Yale U., 1964. CLU, ChFC, FSA. Mem. actuarial program MONY, N.Y.C., 1964-68, dir. group systems, 1969, asst. v.p., 1970-73; v.p., actuary Blue Cross and Blue Shield of Greater N.Y., N.Y.C., 1973-77, sr. v.p., 1977-83; ptnr. Kwasha Lipton, Fort Lee, N.J., 1983-87; exec. v.p., CFO Guardian Life Ins. Co. Am., N.Y.C., 1987—2001. Pres. bd dirs. 300 CPW Corp., 1995-98; pres., bd. dirs. Park Ave. Life (Guardian sub.), 1998-2001, Vis. Nurse Svc. of N.Y., 1999—; bd. dirs. Well Choice. Active 14th St. Bus. Improvement Dist., N.Y.C., 1992-99, pres., 1995-99; bd. dirs. 14th St.-Union Sq. Local Devel. Corp., 1993-99, Children's Orch. Soc., 1999—, Downtown Alliance, 2000-02, Rubin Mus. Art, 2002—; mem. N.Y. Organ Donor Network, 2002—, Friends of Wertheim Nat. Wildlife Refuge, 1999-2002. Fellow Soc. Actuaries; mem. Am. Acad. Actuaries, Actuarial Soc. Greater N.Y. (pres. 1992-93), Med. Health and Rsch. Assn. Avocations: photography, music, travel. Home: 300 Central Park W Apt 14B New York NY 10024-1513 E-mail: mdwplh@mac.com.

HUTCHINS, DIANE ELIZABETH RIDER, librarian; b. Kearny, N.J., June 25, 1951; d. Thomas Lindsay and Dorothy Jane (Sommer) Rider; m. Clifford James Hutchins, Feb. 14, 2002. MusB magna cum laude, Westminster Choir Coll., 1973; MLS, Fla. State U., 1993. Intern preservation dept. U. Fla., Gainesville, 1993; intern free-net libr. Tallahassee (Fla.) Free-Net, 1993; reference libr. Broward County Main Libr., Ft. Lauderdale, Fla., 1994-95; libr., instr. Art Inst. Ft. Lauderdale, 1995-96, dir. Learning Resource Ctr., 1996-98; dean Nevin C. Meinhardt Meml. Libr., 1998-99; collection devel. coord. Washington State Libr., 1999—2002, program mgr. collection mgmt., 2002—. Vice chair, assoc. mem. com. S.E. Fla. Libr. Info. Network, 1996-97, chair assoc. mem. com., 1997-98, ex officio mem. bd. dirs. S.E. Fla. Libr. Info. Network, 1996-99; spl. librs. rep. Fla. Libr. Network Coun., 1998-99. Soloist St. Paul's Chapel, Columbia U., N.Y.C., 1973, Ch. of St. Mary the Virgin, N.Y.C., 1974. Recipient Outstanding Leadership award Wash. State Libr., 2000; Fla. State U. fellow, 1993-94, Coll. Tchg. fellow, 1992-93; Louis Shores scholar, 1992-93. Mem. Spl. Librs. Assn. (dir. Fla. and Caribbean chpt. 1997-99, Fla. rep., steering com. South Atlantic Regional conf. 1997-99), New Eng. Hist. Geneal. Soc., Geneal. Soc. Southwestern Pa., Geneal. Soc. of N.J., Phi Kappa Phi, Beta Phi Mu. Avocations: vegetarian cooking, genealogy, the internet, reading. Office: The Wash State Libr PO Box 42460 Olympia WA 98504-2460 Office Phone: 360-704-7137. E-mail: dhutchins@secstate.wa.gov.

HUTCHINS, JAMES LEIGH, quality assurance professional; b. Bangor, Maine, Aug. 11, 1950; s. Elbridge Leland and Harret Alice (Johnson) H.; m. Dolores Jean Sweezey; children: Sandra Kay, Alice Elizabeth. BS in Electronics Tech., Chapman Coll., Orange, Calif., 1981. Quality assurance engr. McDonnell Douglas Astronautics, Monrovia, Calif., 1983-84; sr. quality assurance engr. Comarco Weapons Sys. Divsn., Ridgecrest, Calif., 1985-86, Endevco, San Juan Capistrano, Calif., 1986; sr. reliability engr. Los Alamos Tech. Assocs., Albuquerque, 1986-88; software product assurance specialist Northrop-Grumman, Palmdale, Calif., 1988-97, cons., 1997-98; mem. tech. staff, S/W quality Boeing, Anaheim, Calif., 1998—. Vice chair L.A. Dem. Ctrl. Com., Region 1, 1994-95; 36th Assembly Dist. coord., Calif. Dem. Party, 1993. Sgt. USMC, 1969-78. Named Man of Yr. 36th Assembly Dist. L.A. County Dem. Ctrl. Com., 1993. Mem. Am. Soc. Quality Control, Elks, Masons, Shriners. Democrat. Avocations: poetry, politics.

HUTCHINS, JOAN MORTHLAND, manufacturing executive, farmer; b. Pasadena, Calif., Aug. 8, 1940; d. Andrew and Constance Amelia (Gordon-Grant) Morthland; children: Andrew E. Bush, Georgia R. Bush, Alan S., Paul M. AB, Radcliffe Coll., 1961; hon. degree, Royal Coll. Music, London, 1979; AAS, SUNY, Farmingdale, 1985. Jr. mathematician Shell Devel. Co. (Shell Oil), Emeryville, Calif., 1961-63; mathematician Corp. for Econ. and Indsl. Rsch., London, England, 1964-65; mgmt. cons. McKinsey & Co., N.Y.C., 1965-67; v.p. devel. Compotite Corp., L.A., 1985-87, pres., 1987-89, pres., CEO, 1989—, MBH Farms, Inc., Elizaville, NY, 1986-2001, chmn., 2001—. Editor McKinsey & Co. Mgmt. Scis. News Bull., 1965-67; contbr. articles to profl. jours. Mem. bd. overseers Harvard U., Cambridge, Mass., 1994—2000, pres., 1999—2000, mem. overseers vis. com. Harvard athletic dept., 1986—91, mem. overseers vis. com. Arnold Arboretum, 1995—2004, chmn., 1997—2004, mem. overseers vis. com. Harvard Grad. Sch. Edn., 1995—, vice chmn., 2003—, mem. overseers vis. com. Harvard music dept., mem. nominating com. for overseers and HAA dirs., 2000—04; mem. adv. bd. Harvard U. Com. on Environment, 2001—04; bd. dirs., v.p. Royal Music Found., N.Y.C., 1978—90; trustee Bowdoin Coll. Summer Music Festival, Brunswick, Maine, 1978—88, L.I. Biol. Assn., Cold Spring Harbor, NY, 1986—88. Recipient Harvard medal, 2004. Mem. Am. Nat. Stds. Inst. (nat. waterproofing stds. com. 1988—), Harvard Alumni Assn. (bd. dirs. 1990-93, nominating com. overseers and dirs., 2000-03), Harvard-Radcliffe Club L.I. (pres. 1988-90). Avocations: skiing, music, sports, ice hockey, travel. Office: Compotite Corp 355 Glendale Blvd Los Angeles CA 90026-5032

HUTCHINS, MARY LOUISE, retired library director; b. Saginaw, Mich., Feb. 8, 1936; d. Herman Martin and Margaret May Janssen; m. Richard Gilbert Hutchins, July 6, 1963; children: Linda Leeanne Hutchins-Knowles, Sharon Suzanne. BA, U. Mich., 1958, MA in Libr. Sci., 1961. Cmty. libr. Willard Libr., Battle Creek, Mich., 1961-63; readers' adv. libr. Flint (Mich.) Pub. Libr., 1964-66; vis. instr. Sch. Libr. Sci. U. Iowa, Iowa City, 1974-75; adminstrv. asst. to libr. dir. U. Miami Sch. Law, Coral Gables, Fla., 1976-80; head reference dept. Verona (N.J.) Pub. Libr., 1981-86; cons. for inter-libr. loan and reference No. Ill. Libr. Sys., Rockford, 1986-88; dir. Bement Pub. Libr., St. Johns, Mich., 1988-94, Branch Dist. Libr., Coldwater, Mich., 1994-2000; ret., 2000. Chair Libr. Adv. Coun., Albion, Mich., 1996—. Active Branch County Econ. Growth Alliance, Coldwater, 1995, 96, Work Group on Teen Suicide, Coldwater, 1998. Recipient Celebrating Literacy award Clinton Reading Coun., Clinton County, Mich., 1990. Mem. ALA, Mich. Libr. Assn. (sec. pub. policy com. 1990-94, Leadership Acad. grad. 1993), Coldwater/Branch County C. of C. Mem. Soc. Of Friends. Avocations: peace and civil rights activities, classical music, swimming.

HUTCHINS, PETER EDWARD, lawyer; b. Nashua, N.H., Jan. 20, 1958; s. Edward Peter and Joyce Martha Hutchins; m. Kathy Hutchins; 1 child, Jamie. BA cum laude, Dartmouth Coll., 1980; JD magna cum laude, Boston Coll., 1983. Bar: N.H. 1983, U.S. Dist. Ct. N.H. 1983. Ptnr. Wiggin & Nourie, P.A., Manchester, N.H., 1983-98, Hall & Hess, PA, Manchester, 1998—2003. Basketball referee, cert. Internat. Assn. Approved Basketball Officials, N.H., 1992—; girls softball umpire, cert. N.H. Softball Umpires Assn., 1994—. Mem. N.H. Bar Assn. (pres. 2001-02). Avocation: officiating high school sports. Office: Wiggin & Nourie PA PO Box 808 Manchester NH 03105-0808

HUTCHINS, ROBERT AYER, architectural consultant; b. NYC, Oct. 19, 1940; s. Robert Senger and Evelyn Reed (Brooks) Hutchins; m. Saran Niel Morgan, Jan. 4, 1964; children: Amey, Elisabeth, Margaret. BA, Harvard U., 1962, MArch, 1965; MDiv, McCormick Theol. Sem., 1992. Cert. Nat. Coun. Archtl. Registration Bds., 1976; lic. architect, Ill. Architect Skidmore, Owings & Merrill, Chgo., 1966—89, ptnr., 1980—89. Pres. Chgo. Architecture Found., 1983—86, v.p., 1986—89. Housing adv. Protestants for the Common Good, 2000—02; bd. dirs. Lincoln Park Zool. Soc., Chgo., 1976—91; bd. govs. Met. Planning Coun., Chgo., 1977—2004; bd. trustees McCormick Theol. Sem., 1990—91. Mem.: AIA (corp.), Chgo. Presbytery Svc. Corps., Chgo. Cultural Affairs Adv. Bd. (vice chmn. 1984—90).

HUTCHINS, TRAVER, publishing executive; Former mgr., corp. sales Lang Commn.; CEO and founder MediZine, Inc., 1997—. Office: Medizine 298 Fifth Ave 2nd Fl New York NY 10001*

HUTCHINSON, ASA (W. ASA HUTCHINSON), lawyer, former federal agency administrator; b. Bentonville, Ark., Dec. 3, 1950; s. John M. and Coral (Mount) Hutchinson; m. Susan Burrell; children: Asa III, Sarah, John, Seth. BS in Acctg., Bob Jones U., 1972; JD, U. Ark., 1975. City atty. City of Bentonville, Ark., 1977—78; US atty. (we. dist.) Ark. US Dept. Justice, 1982-85; ptnr. Karr & Hutchinson, Ft. Smith, Ark., 1986-96; rep. Ark. 3rd dist. U.S. Ho. of Reps., 1996—2001; adminstr. Drug Enforcement Adminstrn. US Dept. Justice, Washington, 2001—03; under sec. for border and transp. security US Dept. Homeland Security, Washington, 2003—05; ptnr., chair, homeland security practice Venable LLP, Washington, 2005—. Judiciary com. U.S. Congress, subcom. crime, subcom. constitution, transp. and infrastructure com., subcom. Water Resources and Environment, subcom. aviation, intelligence com., ethics com., intellectual property subcom.; co-chair Freshmen Bipartisan Campaign Finance Reform Task Force; apptd. to Speakers Task Force for Drug-Free Am.; chmn., Ark. State Rep. Com., 1990-95; past mem. Ark. Jud. Ethics Commn., Ark. Election Commn., Ark. Election Law Revision Commn.; condr. democracy workshops in Russia, 1994; del. White

House Conf. on Aging, 1995; past bd. mem. Western Ark. chpt. Alzheimer's Assn.; mem. bd. dirs. SAFLINK Corp., 2005- Named one of Ten Outstanding Young Leaders in Ark., Ark. Jaycees, 1986. Republican. Office: Venable LLP 575 Seventh St NW Washington DC 20004 Office Phone: 202-344-4000, 501-312-5845. Office Fax: 202-344-8300. Business E-Mail: ahutchinson@venable.com.

HUTCHINSON, DAVID M., management consultant; MS, BS in Engring., U. Calif., Berkeley; MBA in Fin. and Internat. Bus., Santa Clara U. Engring. supr. USN, 1985—92; instr. Diable Valley Coll., 1993—95; rschr. II U. Calif., Berkeley, 1995—99; mgr. info. tech. bus. devel. APL Logistics, 1999—2001; lead sys. analyst Providian Fin., 2001—02; ptnr. Copley Assoc., 2002—. Home: 1339 Belfast Ct Livermore CA 94550

HUTCHINSON, JAMES S. (JAMIE), lawyer; b. Detroit, June 26, 1952; BA, St. Lawrence Univ., 1974; JD, Vanderbilt Univ., 1979. Bar: Ga. 1979, DC 2000. Joined Alston & Bird LLP, 1979, ptnr., leader, employee benefits, exec. compensation group Washington. Staff mem. Vanderbilt Law Rev., 1977—78, exec. articles editor, 1978—79. Exec. bd. Literacy Action, Inc. Fellow: Am. Coll. Employee Benefits Counsel; mem.: ABA, Phi Beta Kappa. Office: Alston & Bird LLP 10th Fl North Bldg 601 Pennsylvania Ave Washington DC 20042-2601 Office Phone: 202-756-3359. Office Fax: 202-756-3333. Business E-Mail: jhutchinson@alston.com.

HUTCHINSON, LYNDA RONETTE (BILLIE HOLLIDAY JR., PRINCESS OF JAZZ, MUNCHIE), vocalist, musician, comedian, actress; b. Queens, N.Y., Dec. 28, 1965; d. Roy Radcliff and Rachel Isabella (Outten) Hutchinson; children: Myisha Daunique Odom, Zaire chase Arzelle. Student, L.I. U., Bklyn., 1991—96. Founder, CEO Diva Soul Records, 2003—. Singer: (performer) Empire Tech. Sch., 1989, L.I. U., 1991, Two Steps Down Jazz Club, 1992—94, Titus Walker's Ujjaama Black Theatre, 1991, St. Nick's Pub, 2000—, Apollo Theatre, 2000, 2001, Lenox Lounge Jazz Club, 2002—, Cotton Club, 2002—, (contestant) Showtime at the Apollo, 1994, Sylvia's 30 Anniversary, 1993; performer: TV show The Cut, 2005, radio; author: (book of poetry) Lend Me Your Ear, 1992. Participant Nat. Action Network Freedom March, 1993. Finalist NYC Housing Authority Talent Search, 1998; recipient Cert. achievement, Internat. Mannequins, Inc., 1995, Certification award, Project Enterprise, 2002, Mel Edwards award, 2003. Mem.: Harlem Arts Alliance, New Amsterdam Musical Assn. Achievements include known as Billie Holiday Jr., Princess of Jazz, and Munchie. Home: Apt 16-G 2370 First Ave New York NY 10035

HUTCHINSON, MARK ROBERT, surgeon; s. Jack E. and Alice Marie Hutchinson; m. Susan Gusich, Apr. 8, 1989; children: Michael, Allison. BS, U. of Ill., 1979, MD, 1987. Cert. Am. Bd. of Orthopaedic Surgeons N.C., 1993. From assoc. prof. to prof. orthop. and sports medicine U. Ill., Chgo., 1993—, dir. sports medicine, 1993. Fellow Ky. Sports Medicine, Lexington, Ky., 1992—93. Author chpts. and profl. pubs. Mem. Am. Coll. of Sports Medicine, Indpls., 2002—; pres. Chgo. Sports Medicine Soc., 1994. Pan Pacific Traveling Fellowship, Am. Orthop. Soc. for Sports Medicine, 2002. Fellow: Am. Acad. Orthop. Surgeons, Am. Coll. Sports Medicine (trustee 2002—); mem.: U.S.A. Gymnastics (head team physician 1995—2000), Ill. Assn. Orthop. Surgeons (treas. 2002—), Chgo. Sports Medicine Soc. (founder 1994, pres., v.p., treas.), Am. Orthop. Soc. Sports Medicine, Arthroscopy Assn. N.Am. (master instr. 1998). Office: 270 MSS M/C 844 839 South Wolcott Chicago IL 60612 Office Phone: 312-996-7161. Business E-Mail: mhutch@uic.edu.

HUTCHINSON, PETER ARTHUR, artist; b. London, Mar. 4, 1930; s. Arthur William Woodhams and Linda Mary Woodhams (West) Hutchinson. BFA, U. Ill., 1960. Author art books; contbr. articles, short stories to profl. publs.; one-man shows include John Gibson Gallery, N.Y.C., 1990, James Mayor Gallery, London, 1996, Galerie Damasquine, Brussels, 1997, Galerie Bugdahn und Kaimer, Düsseldorf, Germany, 1998, 2005, Galerie Helga De Alvear, Madrid, 1998, Kunstverein, Ulm, Germany, 1998, Holly Solomon Gallery, 1998, Biennale De France, Lyon, 1998, Galerie Lucien-Durand, Paris, 1999, Galerie Blancpain/Stepczynski, Geneva, 2001, 04, Lance Fung Gallery, N.Y.C., 2002, Frederieke Taylor Gallery, N.Y.C., 2005; exhibited in group shows including Mus. Modern Art, N.Y.C., 1969, Acad. Art, Berlin, 1988, Herter Gallery, U. Mass. Traveling Exhbn., 1989, Torch Gallery, Amsterdam, 1998, 2005, DNA Gallery, Provincetown, 1994-2003, Fondacion Joan Miro, Barcelona, 2004. Mem. visual arts com. Fine Arts Work Ctr., Provincetown, Mass., 1979-85, 88-89. Fellow Aspen Ctr. for Arts, 1970-71, NEA, 1974, D.A.A.D., Berlin, 1988; grantee Adolph and Esther Gottlieb Found., 1987, Krasner-Pollack Found., 1989. Mem. Am. Rock Garden Club. Avocations: botany, history, biology, horticulture. Home: 10 Holway Ave Provincetown MA 02657-1327 E-mail: hutchinson2@capecod.net.

HUTCHINSON, ROBERT JOSEPH, writer; b. Tacoma, Wash., Nov. 12, 1957; s. A'lan Stanton and Mary Jane Hutchinson; m. Glenn Ellen Duncan, Jan. 6, 1990; children: Robert John, James Timothy, William Kelly, Mary Helen, Jane Anne. BA in Philosophy, Seattle U., 1981; ThM, Fuller Theol. Sem., 2004. Hawaii bur. chief Hollywood Reporter, Calif., 1986—88; mng. editor Hawaii Mag., Irvine, Calif., 1988—90. Author: The Absolute Beginner's Guide to Gambling, 1996, When in Rome: A Journal of Life in Vatican City, 1998; editor: The Book of Vices, 1995. Roman Catholic. Avocations: Aikido, skiing, squash. Personal E-mail: robert@roberthutchinson.com.

HUTCHINSON, THOMAS CUTHBERT, ecology and environmental educator; b. Sunderland, Eng., Feb. 18, 1939; emigrated to Can., 1967; s. Walter and Margaret Amelia (Bell) H.; s. Vivien Coyne, Sept. 8, 1961 (div. 1981); 1 dau., Sally Louise; m. Magda Havas, 1982. BS with honors in Botany, Manchester (Eng.) U., 1960; PhD in Ecology, Sheffield (Eng.) U., 1966. Sir James Knott fellow Newcastle (Eng.) U., 1964-67; asst. prof. dept. botany Toronto U., 1967-71, assoc. prof., 1971-74, prof., 1974-90, chmn. dept., 1976-82; assoc. dir. Inst. Environ. Scis., U. Toronto, 1974-76; prof. faculty of forestry U. Toronto, 1978-90; prof., chair environ. and resource study Trent U., Peterborough, 1991-94, prof. environ. resource studies program, 1994—. Chmn. com. environ. quality criteria NRC Can.; dir. Oliver Ecol. Ctr., Trent U., 1999—. Co-author: Environmental Consequences of Nuclear War, 1986; editor: Heavy Metals in Environment, 1977, Acid Rain Effects on Forests, Crops and Wetlands, 1987; co-editor: Acid Rain Effects on Vegetation, 1980; editor: Environ. Revs., 1990—2004; assoc. editor: Jour. Applied Ecology, —, Ecotoxicology, —, Environ. Pollution, —, Environ. Health, —; contbr. articles to profl. jours. Mem. Royal Agrl. Winter Fair Ont. Com., 1992—. Recipient Faculty Alumni award U. Toronto, 1984, Civic medal City of Toronto, 1991. Fellow Royal Soc. Can. (Miroslaw Romanowski medal 1998), Explorers Club; mem. Am. Agronomy Soc., Coun. of Nat. Scis. and Engring. Rsch. (pres. 1994—2002), Can. Bot. Assn. (George Lawson medal 1982, Trent faculty rsch. award 1998), Am. Ecol. Soc., Brit. Ecol. Soc., Arctic Inst. N.Am., Rare Breeds Can. (bd. dirs. 1992-2003), Can. Cotswold Longwool Assn. (sec.-treas. 1993—). Home: RR # 2 Indian River ON Canada K0L 7B8 Office: Trent U Environ Resource 1600 W Bank Dr Peterborough ON Canada K9J 7B8 Business E-Mail: thutchinson@trentu.ca.

HUTCHISON, ANDREW SANDFORD, archbishop; b. 1938; m. Lois Hutchison; 1 child, David. LTh, Trinity Coll., 1969, DD (hon.), 1994, Montreal Diocesan Theol. Coll., 1993; DCL (hon.), Bishop's U., 2003. Ordained deacon, 1969; asst. curate Christ Ch., Toronto, 1969; ordained priest, 1970; rector Parish of Minden, Haliburton Highlands, 1970-74, St. Francis Ch., Toronto, 1974-81, St. Luke Ch. East York, Toronto, 1981-84; dean Christ Ch. Cathedral, Montreal, 1984-90; consecrated bishop, 1990; Bishop of Montreal, 1990—2004; bishop ordinary Can. Forces, Ottawa, 1997—2004; Archbishop of Ecclesiastical Province of Can., 2002—04; Primate of Can., 2004—. Past pres. Montreal Diocesan Theol. Coll.; vis. Bishop's U., Lennoxville. Bd. governors Lakefield Coll. Sch., 1994—97. Recipient Jerusalem Prize, Can. Zionist Fedn., 1999, Alan Rose Award, Can. Jewish Congress. Office: 80 Hayden St Toronto ON M4Y 3G2 Canada Office Phone: +1 416 924 9199. Office Fax: +1 416 924 0211. Business E-Mail: primate@national.anglican.ca.*

HUTCHISON, BARBARA BAILEY, singer, songwriter; Recipient Grammy award for Best Musical Album for Children "Sleepy Time Lullabyes", 1996. E-mail: barbara@bbhsings.com.

HUTCHISON, CLAUDE B., JR., federal agency administrator; Grad., U. Calif., Berkeley; MBA, Harvard U. Chmn. Smith and Crowley Inc.; mng. dir. strategic mktg. group LEGC, Inc.; dir. Office Asset Enterprise Mgmt. Dept. Vets. Affairs, Washington, 2001—. Served with USNR. Office: US Dept Vets Affairs Mgmt 810 Vermont Ave NW Washington DC 20420 Office Phone: 202-273-7130. E-mail: claude.hutchison@va.gov.

HUTCHISON, DORRIS JEANNETTE, retired microbiologist, educator; b. Carrsville, Ky., Oct. 31, 1918; d. John W. and Maud (Short) H. BS, Western Ky. U., 1940; MS, U. Ky., 1943; PhD, Rutgers U., 1949. Instr. Russell Sage Coll., 1942-44, Vassar Coll., 1944-46; research asst. Rutgers U., 1946-48, research assoc., 1948-49; instr. Wellesley Coll., 1949-51; asst. Sloan-Kettering Inst., N.Y.C., 1951-56, assoc., 1956-60, assoc. mem., 1960-69, mem., 1969-90, mem. emeritus, 1990—, sect. head, 1956-90, acting chief div. exptl. chemotherapy, 1965-66, div. chief drug resistance, 1967-72, co-head lab. exptl. tumor therapy, 1973-74, lab. head drug resistance and cytoregulation, 1973-84, coordinator field edn., 1975-81. Instr. Sloan-Kettering div. Cornell U. Grad. Sch. Med. Sci., N.Y.C., 1952-53, rsch. assoc., 1953-54, asst. prof., 1954-58, assoc. prof., 1958-70, prof. microbiology, 1970-90, prof. emeritus, 1990—, chmn. biology unit, 1968-74, assoc. dir., 1974-87; assoc. dean Cornell U. Grad. Sch. Med. Sci., 1978-87, asst. dean Cornell U., Ithaca, 1978-87; mem. Meml. Sloan-Kettering Cancer Ctr., 1984-90, mem. emeritus, 1990—; del. dir. Am. Cancer Soc., Inc., 1986-90. Bd. dirs. Westchester div. Am. Cancer Soc., 1976-90, exec. com., 1976-91; project chmn. Target 5, 1977-80, v.p., 1979-81, pres., 1981-83, sec., 1983-87, charter mem. So. Westchester Unit, 1984, pres., 1984-86. Named to Order of Ky. Cols., 1988; recipient Disting. Alumna, Western Ky. U., 2003; faculty fellow, Vassar Coll., 1946, USPHS fellow, 1951—53, Phillippe Found. fellow, Paris, 1959, Dorris J. Hutchison fellowship established in her honor, 1999. Fellow N.Y. Acad. Sci., Am. Acad. Microbiology (charter), N.Y. Acad. Medicine (assoc.); mem. AAAS, Am. Assn. for Cancer Edn., Am. Assn. Cancer Research (emeritus), Harvey Soc., Genetics Soc. Am., Am. Inst. Nutrition, Am. Soc. for Microbiology (hon., councilor N.Y.C. br. 1954-58, pres. N.Y.C. br. 1958-60, nat. councilor 1961-63, chmn. nat. meeting 1967, mem. pres.'s fellowship com. 1973-76, chmn. 1975-76), Soc. for Cryobiology (hon. mem.), Am. Genetic Assn., Internat. Soc. Biochem. Pharmacology, N.Y. Soc. Ky. Women (pres. 1988—), N.Y. Found. Ky. Women (pres. 1990-2000), Bronxville Field Club, Elizabeth Hamilton Cullem Svc. Club, 2000—. Achievements include numerous publs. antibiotics and chems. effective in treatment of Tb and leukemia, reports on mechanisms explaining how leukemic cells become resistant to treatment; searches for more effective antileukemia drugs. Home: Stoneridge Unit 4504 186 Jerry Browne Rd Mystic CT 06355 *Achieving goals and providing support and guidance to others, who also wished to become contributors to the well-being of mankind, have been prime concerns to me. The slings and arrows during this time have been totally offset by the personal satisfaction felt as a result of our intangible and tangible achievements.*

HUTCHISON, EDNA RUTH, artist; b. Paoli, Ind., Mar. 7, 1920; d. Charles Floyd and Ora May (Agan) Wright; m. William Ira Hutchison, Mar. 24, 1940; 1 child, Carol Ann Hutchison Wyatt. Student, Ind. U., 1940—46, student, 1957—60. Exhibitions include Brown County Art Gallery, 1960—61, Indiana U., 1961, Morton West Coll., Chgo., 1965, Port St. Lucie Libr., Fla., 1994, others. Teddy Bear lady Treasure Coast Cmty. AIDS Network, Ft. Pierce, Fla., 1997, Christmas Kids St. Lucie County, Ft. Pierce, Fla., 1997—. Recipient 1st pl. oil painting, Nat. League/Am. Penwomen, 1990, 1992, 2nd pl. oil painting, 1991, 1994, 1995, 2nd pl. needlepoint classic, Scripps Aux., 1986. Mem.: Nat. League Am. Pen Women. Avocations: writing, jewelry making, travel, decorating, crafts.

HUTCHISON, JAMES ARTHUR, JR., architectural and engineering company executive; b. Gainesville, Mo., Oct. 25, 1917; s. James Arthur and Dora Ethel (James) H.; m. Imogene Cox, Dec. 5, 1946; children: Judith Lynn, Janet Gayle, James Arthur III. BS in Mech. Engring., Okla. State U., 1940; BS in Aero. Engring., Spartan Sch. Aeronautics, 1942; BS in Acctg., Okla. Sch. Accountancy, 1963. Registered profl. engr. Del., N.J., Md., V.I. Asst. chief engr. Spartan Aircraft Co., Tulsa, Okla., 1943-51; owner H&H Engring. & Constrn. Co., Tulsa, 1951-68; sr. liaison engr. ILC Industries Inc. Appollo Astronaut Program, Dover, Del., 1968-72; v.p. Diamond State Engring., Inc., Dover, 1972-78; founder, chmn. bd. dirs. The JAED Corp., Smyrna, Del., 1978—. Chmn. bd. trustees, chmn. bldg. com. 1st Bapt. Ch., Dover, 1979-90, 97-2000. Mem. Am. Inst. Steel Constrn., Am. Concrete Inst., Ctrl. Del. Pilots Assn. (pres. 1977-78). Republican. Avocation: aircraft flight instruction. Office: The JAED Corp 6 Village Sq Smyrna DE 19977-1852

HUTCHISON, KAY BAILEY, senator; b. Galveston, Tex., July 22, 1943; d. Allan and Kathryn Bailey; m. Ray Hutchison. BA, U. Tex., 1992, LLB, 1967. Bar: Tex. 1967. TV news reporter, Houston, 1969-71; pvt. practice law, 1969-74; press sec. to Anne Armstrong Rep. Nat. Com., 1971; vice-chair Nat. Transp. Safety Bd., 1976-78; asst. prof. U. Tex., Dallas, 1978-79; sr. v.p., gen. counsel Republic Bank Corp., Dallas, 1979-81; pntr. Boyd-Levinson, Ltd., Houston and Dallas, 1981-91; mem. Tex. Ho. of Reps., 1972-76; elected treas. State of Tex., 1990; U.S. senator from Tex. Washington, 1993—; mem. appropriations com., commerce, sci. and transp. com., environment and pub. works com., rules and adminstrn. com. Mem., chmn. Military Constrn. Subcom., commerce, sci. and transp. com. (chmn. Aviation subcom.), environment and pub. works com., rules and adminstrn. com.; chmn., bd. visitors, US Military Acad. at West Point, US Delegate to Commn. on Security and Cooperation in Europe (The Helsinki Commn.); owner McCraw Candies; co-founder Fidelity Nat. Bank. Author: (books) American Heroines: The Spirited Women Who Shaped Our Country, 2004. Recipient Eagle award valued commitment to our nation's Hispanic Cmty., 1993; named Rep. Woman of Yr. Nat. Fedn. Rep. Women, 1995, Outstanding U. Tex. Alumnus, 1995, Texan of Yr. Tex. Legis. Conf., 1997; named to Tex. Women's Hall of Fame, 1997, named one of 100 Most Powerful Women in World, Forbes mag., 2005. Fellow, U. Tex. Law Alumni Assn. (pres. 1985-86). Republican.*

HUTCHISON, MARK STEVENSON, lawyer; b. Syracuse, N.Y., Apr. 28, 1965; s. Edward Ross and Jean Marie (King) H.; m. Robin Jones (dec. 2003); children: James Mark, Anne Catherine, Colton Lee; m. Amanda Wise. BS, Millsaps Coll., 1987; JD, Miss. Coll., 1990. Bar: Miss. 1990, U.S. Dist. Ct. (so. dist.) Miss. 1990. Assoc. Richard Schartz & Assocs., Jackson, Miss., 1990; lawyer Miss. Asbestos Assn., Jackson, 1990-91; pvt. practice Jackson, 1991—. Hall scholar Millsaps Coll., Jackson, 1983, Regents scholar SUNY, Albany, 1983. Mem. ABA, Am. Trial Lawyers Assn., Delta Theta Phi (officer 1988-90). Home: 315 Cox Crossing Madison MS 39110 Office: 5269 Keele St Ste A Jackson MS 39206-4322 Office Phone: 601-366-8911.

HUTCHISON, POLLY ANNA, writer; b. Cheyenne, Wyo., June 3, 1939; d. Marshall Garrett and Anna Louise (Ekstrom) McBee; m. Ronald Irving Pering, June 4, 1962 (div. Apr. 1970); m. Ronald Verene Hutchison, Feb. 14, 1976 (div. Mar. 1992). Student, U. Ga., 1957—59; BS in Edn., Ea. Mont., 1962. Cert. tchr. Mont., Wyo. HS tchr. Red Lodge, Montana & Greybull Wyo. Schs., 1967—70; acting asst. dir. Upward Bound program Ea. Mt. Coll., Billings, 1970—71; instrnl. tech. Courseware, Inc., San Diego, 1977—78; adminstrv. asst. to dir. ministries Christian Retreat, Bradenton, Fla., 1984—85; word processor, transcriber Leonard J. Russo, Honolulu, 1985—89; legal comm. specialist Hawaii Med. Svcs. Assn., Honolulu, 1989—93; med. transcriptionist Wyo. Neurosurgery Assoc., Cheyenne, 1994—2001. Author: Streams of Civilization, 1976, Oh King Live Forever, 1977, Breath of Rapture, 2000. Indexer geneology dept. Laramie County Libr., Cheyenne, 1994—; platform com. Rep. Party, Wyo., 1995—96. Recipient 1st pl., EPA Bicentennial Writing Contest, 1976. Mem.: Hist. Novel Soc., Rocky Mountain Fiction Writers, Wyo. State Hist. Soc., Crow Creek Questers (sec.-treas. 2003—05). Republican. Avocations: making jewelry, embroidery, antique horse collecting.

HUTCHISON, RAY RAY (E. RAY HUTCHISON), lawyer; b. Rockwall, Tex., Sept. 16, 1932; children: Brenda, Julie. BBA with honors, So. Meth. U., 1957, JD cum laude, 1959. Bar: Tex. 1959. Mem. Tex. Ho. Reps., Dallas County, 1972-76, mem. intergovtl. affairs com., chmn. standing subcom. on urban affairs, state affairs, rules com., chmn. full legis. com., Constitutional Revision, intergovtl. affairs com.; mng. ptnr. Hutchison Boyle Brooks & Fisher, Dallas and Austin, Tex., 1969—95; of counsel Vinson & Elkins LLP, Dallas, 1996—. Assoc. editor Southwestern Law Jour. Del. Tex. Constitutional Conv., 1974, mem. local govt. and submission and transition coms.; chmn. Tex. Reps., 1975-78; mem. Rep. Nat. Com., 1975-78, exec. com., 1976-78. Served with USN, 1950-54. Mem. Order of Woolsack, Barristers Fraternity, Delta Theta Phi, Phi Eta Sigma. Office: Trammell Crow Ctr 2001 Ross Avenue Suite 3700 Dallas TX 75201 E-mail: rhutchison@velaw.com.

HUTCHISON, STANLEY PHILIP, retired lawyer; b. Joliet, Ill., Nov. 22, 1923; s. Stuart Philip and Verna (Kinzer) H.; m. Helen Jane Rush, July 25, 1945; children: Norman, Elizabeth. BS, Northwestern U., 1947; LLB, Ill. Inst. Tech., 1951. Bar: Ill. 1951. Legal asst. Washington Nat. Ins. Co., Evanston, 1947-51, asst. counsel, 1951-55, asst. gen. counsel, 1955-58, assoc. gen. counsel, 1958-60, gen. counsel, 1960-63, v.p., gen. counsel, dir., 1963-66, exec. v.p., gen. counsel, dir., 1966-67, exec. v.p., gen. counsel, sec., dir., 1967-70, chmn. exec. com., 1970-73, vice-chmn. bd., 1974-75, chmn. bd., CEO, 1976-88; pres. Wash. Nat. Corp., 1970-83, CEO, 1978-88, chmn. bd., 1983-88; ret., 1988-98. Bd. dirs. Washington Nat. Corp. Pres.'s coun. Nat. Coll. Edn., 1977-88, adv. coun. Kellogg Grad. Sch. Mgmt. Northwestern U., 1981-88; bd. dirs. Evanston Hosp. Corp., 1983-88. Lt. (j.g.) USNR, 1942-46. Mem. Assn. Life Ins. Counsel, Am. Coun. Life Ins. (bd. dir. 1977-81, 84-88), Ill. Life Ins. Coun. (bd. dir. 1978-86, pres. 1983-85), Inc. Econs. Soc. Am. (bd. dir. 1977-85, chmn. 1981-82), Health Ins. Assn. Am. (bd. dirs. 1982-88, chmn. 1987-88). Home: 7501 E Thompson Peak Pky #501 Scottsdale AZ 85255 E-mail: carefreesh@aol.com.

HUTCHISON, VICTOR HOBBS, biologist, educator; b. Blakely, Ga., June 15, 1931; s. Joseph Victor and Veva (Hobbs) H.; m. Theresa Dokos, Dec. 14, 1952; children: Victoria Ann, John Christopher, David Michael, Kenneth Hobbs. BS, N. Ga. Coll., 1952; MA, Duke U., 1956, PhD, 1959; grad., U.S. Army Command and Gen. Staff Coll. Instr. Duke U., 1957-58, faculty fellow, So. Fellowship Fund fellow, 1958-59; mem. faculty U. R.I., 1959-70, prof. biology, 1968-70; dir. Inst. Environ. Biology, 1966—70; prof., chmn. dept. zoology U. Okla., Norman, 1970-80, George Lynn Cross rsch. prof. zoology, 1979-2001, rsch. prof. emeritus, 2001—. Rsch. prof. Universidad de los Andes, Bogotá, Colombia, 1965-66; prin. investigator Nat. Geog. Soc.-U. R.I. herpetological expdn. to Colombia, 1964-65, Nat. Geog. Soc.-U. Okla. expdns. to Lake Titicaca, 1975, Cameroon, 1981. Editor Animal Natural History series, 1991—; rsch. and articles on heat tolerances of lower vertebrates, effects of day-length on metabolism and temperature tolerance of lower vertebrates, physiology of lower vertebrates, physiol. ecology of amphibians and reptiles, respiration in amphibians, behavioral thermoregulation. With U.S. Army, 1952—54, col. med. svc. corp. USAR. Decorated Army Commendation medal, Meritorious Svc. medal; Guggenheim fellow, 1965-66. Fellow AAAS; mem. Am. Inst. Biol. Sci., Am. Soc. Ichthyologists and Herpetologists (pres. 1988), Am. Physiol. Soc., Ecol. Soc. Am., Herpetologists League (exe. com. 1968-71), Soc. Study Amphibians and Reptiles (bd. govs. 1986-88, pres. 1998-99), Explorers Club, Sigma Xi, Phi Sigma, Phi Kappa Phi, Oklahomans for Excellence in Sci. Edn.(founder, 2002). Achievements include demonstration of facultative endothermy in brooding pythons; research on role of skin in amphibian respiration; development of standardized method for determination of critical thermal maximum in animals. Home: 2010 Crestmont Ave Norman OK 73069-6414 Office: U Okla Dept Zoology Norman OK 73019-0001 Office Phone: 405-325-6721.

HUTH, EDWARD JANAVEL, internist, educator, editor; b. Phila., May 15, 1923; s. Edward Gaston and Suzanne Madeleine (Janavel) H.; m. Carol Elizabeth Monnik, Apr. 6, 1957; children: John Edward, James Janavel. BA, Wesleyan U., Middletown, Conn., 1945; MD, U. Pa., 1947. Diplomate Am. Bd. Internal Medicine, Nat. Bd. Med. Examiners. Intern Hosp. of U. Pa., 1947-48, resident medicine, 1949-51, ward physician, 1951-61; mem. Diagnostic Clinic, 1959-61; postdoctoral fellow Life Ins. Med. Research Fund, 1952-53; spl. research fellow USPHS, Univ. Coll. Hosp., London, Eng., 1957-58. Asst. instr. pharmacology U. Pa. Sch. Medicine, Phila., 1948-49, assoc. in medicine, 1951-58, asst. prof. medicine, 1958-61; assoc. prof. comparative medicine Sch. Vet. Medicine, 1963-68; adj. asst. prof. medicine U. Pa. Sch. Medicine, 1966-71, assoc. prof. clin. medicine, 1971-74, adj. clin. prof. medicine, 1974-78, adj. prof. medicine dept. medicine Assoc. Faculty, 1978-91; asst. prof. medicine Woman's Med. Coll., Phila., 1961-62, assoc. prof., 1962-65; chmn. com. on 4th edit. CBE Style Manual Com. Biology Editors, 1971-78, chmn. com. on 6th edit., 1990-95; biomed. comms. study sect. NIH, 1972-76; chmn. subcom. 10 of Com. Z39 Am. Nat. Stds. Inst., 1974-77; mem. UNISIST Working Group on Primary Sources of Info., UNESCO, Paris, 1973-74; bd. regents Nat. Libr. Medicine, 1979-83; office med. applications of rsch. NIH, 2001—; expert com. on info. devel. and dissemination US Pharmacopeia, 2002—. Author: Medical Style and Format, 1987, How to Write and Publish Papers in the Medical Sciences, 1990, Writing and Publishing in Medicine, 1998, SI Units for Clinical Medicine, 1998, Medicine in Quotations, 2000, 2006; asst. editor Annals of Internal Medicine, 1960-63, assoc. editor, 1963-71, editor, 1971-90, editor emeritus, 1990-93, 95—, book rev. editor, 1990-93, 95-96, interim editor, 1994-95; editor Online Jour. Current Clin. Trials, 1991-94, also articles; mem. editl. bd. Nat. Med. Jour. India, 1991—, Transactions and Studies of the Coll. Physicians Phila., 2002—; adv. bd. Croatian Med. Jour., 1998—; rev. editor Pa. Geneal. Mag., 2003. Sec. Harriton Assoc., Bryn Mawr PA, 1991-2005. Served with AUS, 1943—46. Fellow ACP, AAAS (coun. 1968, editor Online Jour. Current Clin. Trials 1991-94), Royal Coll. Physicians (London), Am. Med. Writers Assn. (pres. 1967-68); mem. Coun. Biology Editors (dir. 1970-75, chmn. 1973-74), European Assn. Sci. Editors, Coll. Physicians Phila. (chmn. Wood Inst., Libr. and Mus. com. 2004—, chmn. section on med. history 2005—), Soc. for Scholarly Pub. (dir. 1988-92), Phi Beta Kappa, Sigma Xi, Alpha Omega Alpha, Zeta Phi. Democrat. Home and Office: 1124 Morris Ave Bryn Mawr PA 19010-1712

HUTH, JOHN E., physicist, educator; b. Mar. 1958; AB in Physics, Princeton U., 1979; PhD, U. of Calif.: Berkeley, 1985. Postdoctoral scientist Fermi Nat. Accelerator Lab., 1985—87, Wilson fellow, 1987—90, staff scientist, 1990—93; prof. Harvard U., 1993—, chmn. dept. physics. Office: Harvard U 17 Oxford St Cambridge MA 02138

HUTHNANCE, EDWARD DENNIS, JR., mathematics professor; b. Macon, Ga., Aug. 31, 1942; s. Edwand Dennis and Frances Carolyn (Collins) Huthnance. BS in physics, Ga. Inst. Tech., 1964, MS in math., 1966, PhD in math., 1969. Chair of dept. Newberry Coll., Newberry, SC; math. prof. Midwesters State U., Wichita Falls, Tex., Bloomsburg U., Bloomsburg, Pa. Cons. First Wichita Bk. Contbr. articles various rsch. papers. Mem.: Math. Assn. of Am., Oregon Hist. Soc. Avocations: music, photography. Home: 6131 Peake Rd Macon GA 31220

HUTSON, BENNE COLE, lawyer; b. Southgate, Mich., Aug. 21, 1957; s. Andrew Woodrow Hutson and Hedzeeben Bova; m. Martha Dobie Hennessy, Apr. 30, 1983; children: Michael, Kathleen, Patrick, Colleen. BA summa cum laude, Hillsdale Coll., 1979; JD cum laude, Harvard Law Sch., 1982. Bar: Ohio 1982, N.C. 1986. Assoc. Bricker & Eckler, Columbus, Ohio, 1982-85; ptnr. Helms Mulliss & Wicker, PLLC, Charlotte, 1985—. Mem.: ABA, Mecklenburg County Bar Assn., N.C. Bar Assn., Myers Park Country Club.

Republican. Roman Catholic. Avocations: golf, travel, reading, cooking. Office: Helms Mulliss and Wicker PLLC PO Box 31247 Charlotte NC 28231-1247 Business E-Mail: benne.hutson@hmw.com.

HUTSON, JAMES HOWARD, library director; b. Bridgeport, W.Va., Aug. 8, 1937; s. Howard and Josephine Miller Hutson; m. Kathryn Milner Logee, June 6, 1965; children: Benjamin, Scott. BA, Yale U., 1959, MA, 1960, PhD, 1964. Editor, lectr. history Yale U., New Haven, 1964—69, William and Mary Coll., Williamsburg, Va., 1969—72; from coord. Am. Revolution to chief Manuscript Divsn. Libr. Congress, Washington, 1972—82, chief Manuscript Divsn., 1982—. Mem. Nat. Hist. Pubs. and Records Commn., Washington, 1982—90; adminstrv. officer permanent com. Oliver Wendell Holmes Devise L, Washington, 1976—. Author: John Adams and the Diplomacy of the American Revolution, 1980 (Gilbert Chinard prize, 1981), To Make All Laws: The Congress of the United States, 1989 (prize, 1994), The Sister Republics: Switzerland and the United States, 1776 to the Present, 1992, Religion and the Founding of the American Republic, 1998, Forgotten Features of the Founding: The Recovery of Religious Themes in the Early Republic, 2003. Recipient Intercultural Achievement award, Friends of Switzerland, 1995. Mem.: Mass. Hist. Soc., Cosmos Club, Phi Beta Kappa. Avocations: singing, running, gardening. Home: 1322 Ozkan St Mc Lean VA 22101 Office: Libr Congress Manuscript Divsn James Madison Memorial Washington DC 20540-0001

HUTSON, JEFFREY WOODWARD, lawyer; b. New London, Conn., July 19, 1941; s. John Jenkins and Kathryn Barbara (Himberg) Hutson; m. Susan Office, Nov. 25, 1967; children: Elizabeth Kathryn, Anne Louise. AB, U. Mich., 1963, LLB, 1966. Bar: Ohio 1966, Hawaii 1971. Assoc. Lane, Alton & Horst, Columbus, Ohio, 1966-74, ptnr., 1974—. Arbitrator commercial construction panel Am Arbitration Asn, 1976—. Trustee, vice-chair 6 Pence Sch, 1983—88; mem comt creeds and professionalism Ohio Supreme Ct, 1989—90; chair, bd dirs NW Counseling Servs, 1990—92; regional vpres Def Research Inst, 1991—93. Lt comdr USNR, 1967—71. Fellow: Columbus Bar Found, Ohio State Bar Found, Am Bar Found, Am Col Trials Lawyers, Am Arbit Asn; mem.: Faculty Def Coun Trial Acad, Int Asn Def Counsel, Columbus Bar Asn, Ohio Asn Civil Trial Attys, Ohio Bar Asn, Athletic Club, Scioto Country Club. Avocations: bicycling, reading, music. Office: Lane Alton & Horst 175 S 3rd St Ste 700 Columbus OH 43215-5100 Office Phone: 614-233-4747.

HUTSON, LINDEL G., newspaper editor; Bur. chief AP, Oklahoma City, 1989—. Office: 525 Central Park Dr Ste 202 Oklahoma City OK 73105-1703

HUTSON, MELVIN ROBERT, lawyer; b. Decatur, Ala., Dec. 7, 1947; s. John Robert and Katie Louise (Waddell) H.; children: Melvin, Rachael, Katie, Jamie. BS, U. Ala., 1968, JD, 1971. Bar: Ala. 1971, Ga. 1972, S.C. 1975, D.C. 1978. Atty. NLRB, Atlanta, 1971-73; ptnr. Thompson Mann & Hutson, Greenville, S.C., 1974-98, Melvin Hutson, PA, Greenville, 1998—. Bd. dirs. Primesco, Inc., Mut. Savs. Life Ins. Co., Inc. Chmn. bd. dirs. World Cancer Rsch. Fund, London, 1994—; chmn. AGC Labor Lawyers Coun., 1989-90, Am. Inst. Cancer Rsch., 1982—. Mem. ABA (mem. com. on devel. of law under nat. labor rels. act 1977—, chmn. litigation sect., subcom. on labor mgmt. litigation). Home: 1307 N Main St Greenville SC 29609-4716 Office: PO Box 88 Greenville SC 29602-0088 Office Phone: 864-241-4000. E-mail: mel.hutson@scbar.org.

HUTT, JOHN W., music educator, researcher; Student, Ind. U., 1966—68; MusB, U. Of Wyo., 1970; postgrad., U. of N.Mex., 1970—72; MA, N.Mex. State U. Music tchr. Farmington Mcpl. Schs., Farmington, N.Mex., 1989—2000, Aztec Schs., Aztec, N.Mex., 2000—05. Tubaist. Mem.: N.Mex. Music Educators Assn. Methodist. Avocations: fishing, travel, photography.

HUTT, PETER BARTON, lawyer; b. Buffalo, Nov. 16, 1934; s. Lester Ralph and Louise Rich (Fraser) H.; children: Katherine Zurn, Peter Barton, Sarah Henderson, Everett Fraser. BA magna cum laude, Yale U., 1956; LLB, Harvard U., 1959; LLM, NYU, 1960. Bar: N.Y. 1959, D.C. 1961, U.S. Supreme Ct. 1967. Assoc. Covington & Burling, Washington, 1960-68, ptnr., 1968—71, 1971—2004, sr. counsel, 2004—; chief counsel FDA, Washington, 1971-75. Bd. dir. CV Therapeutics Inc., Palo Alto, Calif., Favrille, Inc., San Diego, Momenta, Inc., Cambridge, Mass., Entegrion, Inc., Chapel Hill, NC, Ista Pharms., Inc., Irvine, Calif., Pervasis Therapeutics, Inc., Boston, Introgen Therapeutics, Inc., Houston, Calif. HealthCare Inst., San Diego; adv. com. to dir. NIH, 1976—81; com. on rsch. tng. NAS, 1976—80; counsel to Alcoholic Beverage Med. Rsch. Found., 1984—85, chmn. bd. dir., 1986—92; mem. Nat. Com. to Rev. Current Proc. for Approval of New Drugs for Cancer and AIDS, Nat. Cancer Inst., 1988—90; mem. nat. bd. Scripps Clinic and Rsch. Found., La Jolla, 1977—85, 1990—95; mem. internat. bd. Scripps Instns. of Medicine and Sci., 1995—2002, Ctr. for Study Drug Devel., Tufts U. Ctr., 1976—99, Ctr. for Advanced Studies, U.Va., 1982—, Inst. for Health Policy Analysis, 1982—, Am. Pharm. Inst., Washington, 1988—92; com. on food laws and regulations Inst. Food Tech.; adv. com. Progress and Freedom Found., 1994—97; adv. bd. Frazier Healthcare Investments, Seattle, 1993—99, Sprout Group, N.Y. and Menlo Park, 1993—, Polaris Venture Ptnrs., Waltham, 1995—, Vanguard Medica Ltd., Guildford, England, 1993—99, Columbia U. Sch. Pub. Health, 1997—2004, Sherbrook Capital Health & Wellness Fund, Lexington, Mass., 1999—, Burrill Neutraceuticals, San Francisco, 2000—; panel mem. U.S. Congl. Office Tech. Assessment; lectr. on food and drug law Harvard U., 1994—, Stanford U., 1998; panel on adminstrv. restructuring NIH, Nat. Acad. Pub. Adminstrn., 2004—. Author: (with Patricia Wald) Dealing with Drug Abuse, 1972, (with Richard Merrill) Food and Drug Law, 1991, (with Bruce Kuhlik) Understanding Export Law, 1998; editor-in-chief U.S. Food Labeling Law, 1991—; contbg. editor: Legal Times of Washington, 1978-86; mem. editl. bd. various jours.; editor: Food and Drug Law: An Electronic Book of Harvard Law School Student Papers. Bd. dirs. Sidwell Friends Sch., Washington, 1976-84; bd. dirs. Legal Action Ctr., N.Y.C., 1976-2003, vice-chmn., 1984-98; bd. dirs. Found. for Biomed. Rsch., 1976-, vice chmn., 1989—; trustee Washington Lawyers Com. for Civil Rights and Urban Affairs, 1976—, Food and Drug Law Inst., 2001-; bd. dirs. Soc. Risk Analysis, 1985-88, 89-92, counsel, 1992—; mem. vis. com. Harvard Sch. Pub. Health, 1980-86. Recipient award of merit FDA, 1972, 75, Disting. Svc. award HEW, 1974, Underwood-Prescott award MIT, 1977, Disting. Alumni award FDA, 2005, Lifetime Achievement award Found. Biomed. Rsch., 2005 Fellow: Soc. Risk Analysis; mem.: Inst. Medicine of NAS (Devel. of Drugs and Vaccines Against AIDS roundtable 1988—94, bd. on health care svcs. 1998—2002). Episcopalian. Home: 124 S Fairfax St Alexandria VA 22314 Office: Covington & Burling 1201 Pennsylvania Ave NW Washington DC 20004-2401 Office Phone: 202-662-5522. E-mail: phutt@cov.com.

HUTTENBACK, ROBERT ARTHUR, academic administrator, educator; b. Frankfurt, Germany, Mar. 8, 1928; s. Otto Henry and Dorothy (Marcuse) H.; m. Freda Braginsky, July 12, 1954; 1 dau., Madeleine Alexandra. BA, U. Calif. at Los Angeles, 1951, PhD, 1959; postgrad., Sch. Oriental and African Studies, U. London, Eng., 1956-57. Mem. faculty Calif. Inst. Tech., Pasadena, 1958-78, asst. prof., 1960-63, assoc. prof., 1963-66, prof. history, 1966-78, master student houses, 1958-69, dean students, 1969-72, chmn. div. humanities and social scis., 1971-77; chancellor U. Calif., Santa Barbara, 1977-86. Cons. Jet Propulsion Lab., Pasadena, 1966-68 Author: British Relations with Sind, 1799-1843, An Anatomy of Imperialism, 1962, (with Leo Rose and Margaret Fisher) Himalayan Battleground-Sino-Indian Rivalry in Ladakh, 1963, The British Imperial Experience, 1966, Gandhi in South Africa, 1971, Racism and Empire, 1976, (with Lance Davis) Mammon and the Pursuit of Empire, 1986, Kashmir and the British Raj, 2004. Served to 1st lt. U.S. Army, 1951-53. Office Phone: 805-388-4693. Personal E-mail: huttenback@earthlink.net.

HUTTER, ADOLPH MATTHEW, JR., cardiologist, educator; b. Fond du Lac, Wis., Feb. 22, 1937; s. Adolph Matthew and Janet (Kay) H.; m. Sylvia H. Murray, June 18, 1960; children: Janice Marie, Adolph Joseph, Elizabeth Kay, Matthew Murray, Jonathan James. BS summa cum laude, Georgetown U., 1959; MD, U. Wis., 1963. Diplomate Am. Bd. Internal Medicine, Am. Bd. Cardiovascular Diseases; lic. physician, Mass. Med. intern Strong Meml. Hosp., Rochester, N.Y., 1963-64; clin. assoc. Nat. Cancer Inst., Bethesda, Md., 1964-66; asst. resident Strong Meml. Hosp., 1966-67, assoc. resident, 1967-68; fellow in medicine (oncology) Georgetown U. Sch. Medicine, Washington, 1965-66; clin. and rsch. fellow in cardiology Mass. Gen. Hosp., Boston, 1968-70; instr. medicine Harvard U. Med. Sch., Boston, 1970-72, asst. prof., 1972-76, assoc. prof., 1976-99, prof., 1999—. Vis. prof. 100 univs. and med. ctrs., 1979-96; asst. in medicine Mass. Gen. Hosp., 1970-72, asst. physician, 1972-76, assoc. physician, 1976-84, physician, 1984—, assoc. dir. CCU, 1970-81, dir., 1981-86, chmn. med. intensive care coord. com., 1986-94; cardiologist Boston Bruins hockey team, 1972—, New Eng. Patriots football team, 1982—. Contbr. over 100 articles to med. jours. Trustee The Roxbury Latin Sch., 1988-90, mem. soc. of fellows, 1995—. Recipient Howard H. Blakeslee award, Am. Heart Assn., 1974; fellow, Roxbury Latin Sch. Fellow: AAAS, ACP, European Soc. Cardiology, Am. Coll. Cardiology (mem. program com. on sci. sessions 1975—76, mem. credentials com. 1976—83, asst. sec. 1981—82, chmn. 1981—83, mem. long-range planning com. 1981—83, trustee 1981—85, mem. ACCEL com. 1982—90, sec. 1984—85, chmn. 1987—90, mem. ACCEL edn. bd. 1987—90, trustee 1987—95, mem. strategic planning com. 1988—92, v.p. 1990—91, mem. exec. com. 1990—94, pres. 1992—93, past pres. 1993—94, mem. chmn. award com. 1993—95, mem. ACCEL edn. bd. 1993—, chmn. govt. rels. com. 1993—, chmn. chpt. rels. com. 1993—, mem. tech. and practice exec. com. 1994—, moderator, convs. expert 2004—, editl. bd. 2004—), CLin Coun. Am. Heart Assn. (mem. com. on postgrad. edn. 1972—75, mem. com. on sci. sessions program 1973—75, mem. sci. sessions com. 1979—81, vice chmn. com. on cardiovasc. disease of elderly 1987—90); mem.: Mass. Med. Soc., Am. Clin. and Climatol. Assn., U. Wis. Med. Alumni Assn., Alpha Omega Alpha. Roman Catholic. Avocations: golf, gardening. Office: Mass Gen Hosp Ambulatory Care Ctr 15 Parkman St Ste 467 Boston MA 02114-3117 Business E-Mail: ahutter@partners.org.

HUTTER, TERESA ANN, art educator; b. Great Bend, Kans., Jan. 25, 1952; d. Harry and Wilma Witterstaetter; children: Trina, Troy. BA in Art Edn., U. Ctrl. Okla., 1987. Nat. bd. cert. tchr. Tchr. art Mustang Pub. Schs., Okla., 1988—; tchr. art camp So. Nazarene U., Bethany, Okla., 1996—2000; host Internat. Children's Art Exhbn., 1995, 2001; tchr. art Jr. Tng. Pks. Assn. Edn. program Okla. C.C., 1994—95. Okla. state judge state reflections program PTA, Oklahoma City, 1996—97. Mem.: NEA, Mustang Area Reading Coun., Nat. Art Edn. Assn., Okla. Edn. Assn., Okla. Art Edn. Assn. (sec. 1992—94, treas. 1994—98, chmn. young talent in Okla. 1998—2000, chmn. wc. region div. 1998—2000, chmn. Okla. elem. div. 2000—04, pres.-elect 2004—, newsletter editor 2004—, newletter editor 2004—, Okla. Elem. Art Educator of Yr. 1995, Okla. Art Educator of Yr. 2000, Youth Arts Month Svc. award 1996, 2000), Delta Kappa Gamma (music chmn. 2000—01). Republican. Methodist. Avocations: reading, pottery, flute, hand bells. Office: Mustang Pub Schs 906 S Heights Dr Mustang OK 73064 Office Phone: 405-376-2409. Personal E-mail: imahoot2@sbcglobal.net. Business E-Mail: huttert@mustangps.org.

HUTTLER, STEPHEN B., lawyer; b. Newport, RI, Sept. 19, 1949; BA cum laude, Syracuse Univ., 1971; JD, Georgetown Univ., 1974; attended, Univ. Munich, Germany. Bar: DC 1975, US Supreme Ct. 1980. Assoc. to ptnr. Shaw Pittman, Washington, 1974—2003, mng. ptnr., 2003—05; vice chmn. & ptnr. Real Estate practice Pillsbury Winthrop Shaw Pittman, Washington, 2005—. Editor: Law & Policy in Internat. Bus. Mem.: ABA, Urban Land Inst. Office: Pillsbury Winthrop Shaw Pittman 2300 N St NW Washington DC 20037-1128 Office Phone: 202-663-8121. Office Fax: 202-663-8007. Business E-Mail: stephen.huttler@pillsburylaw.com.

HUTTNER, CONSTANCE S., lawyer; b. Youngstown, Ohio, 1958; BS in Cellular Immunology, Ohio State U., 1977; JD magna cum laude, Boston Coll., 1980. Bar: NY 1981. Ptnr., patent litigation Skadden, Arps, Slate, Meagher & Flom, LLP, NYC. Co-chmn., Patent Litigation Seminar Practising Law Institute, 2001. Author: Unfit for Jury Determination: Complex Civil Litigation and the Seventh Amendment Right of Trial By Jury, Boston Coll. Law Review, Vol. XX, No. 3, 1979, Markman Practice, Procedures and Tactics, Patent Litigation, Practising Law Inst., 1999, 2000, Markman Practice, Procedures and Tactics, Patent Litigation Strategies Handbook, ABA Sect. of Intellectual Property Law, 2000. Order of the Coif. Mem.: Am. Intellectual Property Law Assn., NY Intellectual Property Law Assn., Phi Beta Kappa. Office: Skadden Arps Slate Meagher & Flom LLP 4 Times Sq New York NY 10036 Office Phone: 212-735-2038. Office Fax: 917-777-2038. Business E-Mail: chutter@skadden.com.

HUTTNER, LOUISE ANN, mathematician, educator; b. Trenton, N.J., June 22, 1946; d. Walter Anthony and Helen Lasek; m. Bruce Alan Huttner, Dec. 4, 1976; children: Walter, Janet. BA in Math., Trenton State Coll., 1968, MA in Math., 1973. Cert. secondary sch. tchr. math., supr. N.J. Math. tchr. Hightstown (N.J.) H.S., 1968—69, Princeton (N.J.) H.S., 1969—72, Haddonfield (N.J.) H.S., 1972—75, Delran (N.J.) H.S., 1975—80; adj. instr. math. Burlington County Coll., Pemberton, NJ, 1980—88, coll. prof. math., 1988—. Author: (workbooks for Calculus I) Mathcad Project I, II, III, IV, 1995, (workbooks for Calculus II) Mathcad Project I, II, 1996; author: (internet course) Calculus I, 2002, Calculus II, 2000. Mem. ch. coun. St. Paul's Luth. Ch., Mt. Holly, NJ, 1998—2000, Sunday sch. tchr., 1980—94. Mem.: NEA, N.J. Edn. Assn., Phi Theta Kappa (advisor Pemberton, N.J. chpt. 2000—). Office: Burlington County Coll 3331 State Rte 38 Mount Laurel NJ 08054 Office Phone: 856-222-9311.

HUTTNER, SIDNEY FREDERICK, librarian; b. Portal, N.D., Feb. 18, 1941; s. Frederick W. and Fern May (Nolting) H.; m. Elizabeth Ann Stege, Oct. 24, 1981; 1 child, Erica Marie. BA in Tutorial Studies, U. Chgo., 1963, MA in Philosophy, 1969. Asst. head spl. collections U. Chgo. Libr., 1970-80; head George Arents Rsch. Libr. Syracuse (N.Y.) Libr., 1980-84; curator spl. collections U. Tulsa Libr., 1984-98; head spl. collections U. Iowa Librs., 1999—. Author: A Register of Artists, Engravers, Booksellers, Bookbinders, Printers and Publishers in New York City, 1821-1842, 1993. Fellow Woodrow Wilson Found., 1963-64. Avocation: bookbinding. Home: 5 Glendale Cir Iowa City IA 52245-3208 Office: Spl Collections U Iowa Librs Iowa City IA 52240-1420 Office Phone: 319-335-5922. Business E-Mail: sid-huttner@uiowa.edu.

HUTTON, CAROLE LEIGH, newspaper editor; b. Framingham, Mass., Aug. 23, 1956; d. James and Norma Inez (Vitali) Hamilton; m. Tom Huff. B Journalism, Mich. State U., 1978. Editor Natick (Mass.) Sun, 1978—79; reporter, city editor, mng. editor Hammond (Ind.) Times, 1979—87; dir. publs. CNA Ins. Cos., Chgo., 1987—88; day city editor, asst editor Detroit News, 1988—90; city editor Detroit Free Press, 1992—95, dep. mng. editor for news, 1995—96, mng. editor, 1996—2002, exec. editor, 2002—03, pub. and editor, 2004—05; with Knight Ridder Co., 2005—. Tutor Detroit Pub. HS, 1994—94. Named one of 100 Most Influential Women in S.W. Mich., Crain's Detroit Bus.; recipient Local News Coverage award, Hoosier State Press Assn., 1982. Mem.: AP Mng. Editors, Mich. AP Editors Assn. (pres., bd. dirs. 2000—), Am. Soc. Newspaper Editors, IAP Mng. Editors.

HUTTON, EDWARD LUKE, medical products executive; b. Bedford, Ind., May 5, 1919; s. Fred and Margaret (Drehobl) H.; m. Kathryn Jane Alexander; children— Edward Alexander, Thomas Charles, Jane Clarke BS with distinction, Ind. U., 1940, MS with distinction, 1941; LLD (hon.), Ind. U., Cumberland Coll., 1992. Dep. dir. Joint Export Import Agy. (USUK), Berlin, 1946-48; v.p. World Commerce Corp., 1948-51; asst. v.p. W.R. Grace & Co., 1951-53, cons., 1960-65, exec. v.p., gen. mgr. Dubois Chems. div., 1965-66, group exec. Specialty Products Group and v.p., 1966-68, exec. v.p., 1968-71; cons. internat. trade and fin., 1953-58; fin. v.p., exec. v.p. Ward Industries, 1958-59; pres., CEO Chemed Corp., Cin., 1971-2001, chmn., dir., 1993—, Omnicare, Inc., Cin., 1993—2003, Roto-Rooter, Inc., 2003—. Chmn. bd. dirs. Nat. San. Supply Co., 1983-97. Co-chmn. Pres.'s Pvt. Sector Survey on Cost Control, exec. com., subcom.; former trustee Millikin U., 1973-84. 1st lt., U.S. Army, 1945-47. Recipient Disting. Alumni Svc. award Ind. U., 1987. Mem. AAUP (governing bd. dirs. 1958—), Econ. Club, Princeton Club, Univ. Club, Queen City Club, Bankers Club. Home: 6680 Miralake Ln Cincinnati OH 45243-2722 Office: Chemed Corp 255 E 5th St Ste 2600 Cincinnati OH 45202-4700 Business E-Mail: chutton@chemed.com.

HUTTON, JOHN EVANS, JR., surgeon, educator, retired military officer; b. N.Y.C., Sept. 9, 1931; s. John Evans and Antoinette (Abbott) H.; m. Barbara Seward Joyce, Apr. 15, 1961; children: John III, Wendy, James, Elizabeth. BA, Wesleyan U., 1953; MD, George Washington U., 1963. Diplomate: Am. Bd. Surgery, Am. Bd. Med. Examiners. Commd. 2d lt. USMC, 1953, advanced through grades to capt., 1962; discharged USMCR; commd. capt. U.S. Army, 1963, advanced through grades to brig. gen., 1989, intern, resident in gen. surgery Walter Reed Army Med. Ctr. Washington, 1963-68, fellow vascular surgery, 1969-70, asst. chief vascular surgery, 1970-71, mem. staff gen. surgery svcs., 1969-71, chief dept. surgery, 1981-84, White House physician, 1984-86, physician to the Pres., 1987-88, chief surgeon 91st Evacuation Hosp., Republic of Vietnam Vietnam, 1968—69, chief vascular surgery, asst. chief gen. surgery Letterman Army Med. Ctr., 1971-74, chief gen. and vascular surgery, program dir., gen. surgery residency Letterman Army Med. Ctr. San Francisco, 1975-81; comdr. 47th Field Hosp., Honduras, 1984; commanding gen. Madigan Army Med. Ctr. U.S. Army, Tacoma, 1989-92; ret., 1992; prof. surgery, chief div. gen. surgery, dept. surg. Uniformed Svcs. U. Sch. Medicine, Bethesda, Md., 1992—, mem. faculty senate, 1996—99, mem. students promotion com., 1993-96, 2002—, mem. instl. rev. bd., 1993-96, mem. com. appointments, promotion and tenure, 1998-99, pres. elect faculty senate, 1997; pres. faculty senate Uniformed Svcs. U. Health Scis., Bethesda, 1998. Assoc. clin. prof. surgery U. Calif., San Francisco, 1978-81, mem. dean's adv. group, 1998-99; assoc. prof. surgery, vice chmn. dept. surgery Uniformed Svcs. U. Health Scis., Bethesda, 1981-84, prof. surgery, 1985—; clin. prof. surgery Tulane U. Sch. Medicine, 1988—, George Washington Sch. Medicine, Washington, 1985—. Contbr. articles, photographs to profl. publs., chpts. to books. Mem. men and boys choir Grace Cathedral, San Francisco, 1971-75. Decorated D.S.M., Bronze Star, Meritorious Svcs. medal with oak leaf cluster, Army Commendation Medal, Navy Commendation Medal, Joint Svc. Commendation Medal, Vietnam Svc. medal with four bronze svc. stars, Nat. DSM with two bronze svc. stars, Naval Occupation medal, WWII, Vietnam Honor medal 1st class, Vietnam Cross of Gallantry; recipient Barron Dominique Larrey award for excellence in surgery, Disting. Svc. medal, Uniformed Svcs. U. Sch. Medicine, 2000. Fellow: ACS; mem.: Soc. Vascular Surgery, Soc. Mil. Cons. Armed Forces (councilor 1988—89, v.p. 2000, pres. 2001), Acad. Medicine Washington D.C., Chesapeake Vascular Soc., Soc. Mil. Vascular Surgery, Am. Assn. Surgery of Trauma, Soc. Clin. Vascular Surgery, Soc. Vascular Surgery, Bay Surg. Soc. (hon.), U.S. Naval Acad. Sailing Squadron, Severn Sailing Assn., St. Francis Yacht Club (membership com. 1978—81). Republican. Episcopalian. Avocations: music, photography, competitive sailing, coaching. Home: 1707 Priscilla Dr Silver Spring MD 20904-1610 Office: Uniformed Svcs U Health Scis Dept Surgery 4301 Jones Bridge Rd Bethesda MD 20814-4712 Office Phone: 301-295-9822.

HUTTON, LAUREN (MARY LAURENCE HUTTON), model, actress; b. Charleston, S.C., Nov. 17, 1943; d. Laurence Hutton. Student, U. Fla., Sophia Newcombe Coll. Fashion model, 1960—. Actress: (feature films) Paper Lion, 1968, Little Fauss and Big Halsey, 1970, Pieces of Dreams, 1970, The Gambler, 1974, Gator, 1976, Welcome to L.A., 1977, Viva Knievel!, 1977, A Wedding, 1978, American Gigolo, 1980, Zorro, the Gay Blade, 1981, Paternity, 1981, Lassiter, 1984, Once Bitten, 1985, A Certain Desire, 1986, Malone, 1987, Guilty As Charged, 1991, My Father, The Hero, 1994; (TV movies) Someone's Watching Me, 1978, Institute for Revenge, 1979, The Cradle Will Rock, 1983, Starflight: The Plane that Couldn't Land, 1983, Scandal Sheet, 1985, Timestalkers, 1987, Perfect People, 1988, Fear, 1990, 54, 1998; (TV series) The Rhinemann Exchange, 1977, Central Park West, 1995-96, (stage prodn.) Extremities.

HUTTON, LORI, music educator; b. Springfield, Mo., Jan. 30, 1965; d. Phillip and Rose Kittrell. B.Mus.Edn., Drury U., Springfield, M., 1988; MS in Secondary Edn., Drury U., 1993. Band dir. Seymour Schs., Seymour, Mo., 1993—94, Lebanon Schs., Lebanon, Mo., 1994—98, Marshfield R-1 Schs., Marshfield, Mo., 1998—. Staff mem. Mo. Ambassadors of Music Europe Tour, Mo., 1990—2004, jazz band dir., Mo., 2006—. Recipient Marshfield Tchr. of the Yr. aard, Marshfield Schs., 2003—04. Mem.: Nat. Assn. for Music Edn., Mo. Unit of Internat. Assn. of Jazz Educators (all state jazz dist. coord. 2002—), Internat. Assn. of Jazz Educators, South Ctrl. Music Educators Assn. (jazz v.p. 2002—), South Ctrl. Mo. Music Educators Assn. (jr. high band v.p. 1998—2002), Mo. Music Educators Assn., Phi Beta Mu. Avocations: travel, bicycling, skiing.

HUTTON, PAUL ANDREW, historian, educator, writer; b. Frankfurt, Germany, Oct. 23, 1949; s. Paul Andrew and Louise Katherine (Johnson) Hutton; m. Vicki Lynne Bauer, 1972 (div. 1985); 1 child, Laura; m. Lynn Terri Brittner, Dec. 31, 1988 (div. 1996); children: Lorena, Paul; m. Tracy Lee Cogdill, Aug. 7, 2001. BA, Ind. U., 1972, MA, 1974, PhD, 1981. Editorial asst. Jour. Am. History, Bloomington, Ind., 1973-77; instr. history Utah State U., Logan, 1977-80, asst. prof., 1980-84, U. N.Mex., Albuquerque, 1984-86, assoc. prof., 1986-96; prof. U. N. Mex., Albuquerque, 1996—. Author: Phil Sheridan and His Army, 1985; editor: Custer and His Times, 1981, Ten Days on the Plains, 1985, Soldiers West, 1987, The Custer Reader, 1992, (series) Eyewitness to the Civil War, 1991-93, Frontier and Region, 1997; writer, co-prodr.: (TV series) Boone & Crockett: The Hunter Heroes, 2001, Carson and Cody: The Hunter Heroes, 2003, Investigating History, 2004-05, (film) Daniel Boone and The Westward Movement, 2002, The Wilderness Road: Spirit of a Nation, 2004; assoc. editor Western Hist. Quar., 1977-84; editor N.Mex. Hist. Rev., 1985-91. Active Little Bighorn Battlefield Indian Meml. Adv. Com., Nat. Park Svc., 1994—2002. Recipient Evans Biography award Brigham Young U., 1986, Paladin award Mont. Hist. Soc., 1991, Western Heritage award Nat. Cowboy Hall of Fame, 1996, 99, 2003, 05; named Mead Disting. Rsch. fellow Huntington Libr., 1988. Mem. Orgn. Am. Historians (Ray A. Billington award 1986), Western Hist. Assn. (exec. dir. 1990—), Soc. for Mil. History, Western Writers Am. (exec. bd. 1997-99, pres. 2002-04, Spur award 1985, 2002, 04, Pres. award 1998, Stirrup award 2000, 04), Writers Guild Am. West. Office: U NMex Dept History Albuquerque NM 87131-0001 Business E-Mail: hutton@unm.edu.

HUTTON, TIMOTHY, actor; b. Malibu, Calif., Aug. 16, 1960; s. Jim and Maryline H.; m. Debra Winger, March 16, 1986 (div.); 1 child, Emmanuel Noah. Appeared in TV movies Zuma Beach, 1978, Best Place to Be, 1979, Baby Makes Six, 1979, Friendly Fire, 1979, Young Love, First Love, 1979, Father Figure, 1980, The Oldest Living Graduate, 1980, Sultan and the Rock Star, 1980, A Long Way Home, 1981, We're Family Again, 1981, Zelda, 1993, The Golden Spiders: A Nero Wolfe Mystery, 2000, Deliberate Intent, 2000, WW3, 2001; films include Ordinary People, 1980 (Best Supporting Actor Acad. award 1981), Taps, 1981, Daniel, 1983, Iceman, 1984, Turk 182, 1985, The Falcon and the Snowman, 1985, Made in Heaven, 1987, A Time of Destiny, 1988, Everybody's All-American, 1988, Betrayed, 1988, Torrents of Spring, 1990, Q & A, 1990, The Temp, 1993, The Dark Half, 1993, French Kiss, 1995, Scenes from Everyday Life, 1995, The Substance of Fire, 1996, Mr. and Mrs. Loving, 1996, Beautiful Girls, 1996, City of Industry, 1997, Playing God, 1997, Deterrence, 1998, The General's Daughter, 1999, Deterrence, 1999, Just One Night, 2000, The Lucky Strike, 2000, Sunshine State, 2002, Secret Window, 2004, Kinsey, 2004; TV series A Nero Wolfe Mystery, 2001, 5ive Days to Midnight, 2004; Broadway includes Prelude to a Kiss, 1990, Babylon Gardens, 1991; dir. video Drive, 1984 (The Cars song); dir. episode Amazing Stories, 1985 (Grandpa's Ghost). Office: Creative Artists Agy 9830 Wilshire Blvd Beverly Hills CA 90212-1804

HUTTON, WILLIAM MICHAEL, manufacturing executive; b. Herrin, Ill., June 15, 1948; s. William T. and Violet (Childress) Hutton; m. Lois A. Piontkowski, Sept. 7, 1968; children: Cynthia L., Pamela. BS in Mgmt. Scis.,

So. Ill. U., 1972; MA in Ops. Mgmt., Norwich U., 1991; PhD in Bus. Adminstrn., Kennedy-Western U., 2003. Cert. foodservice profl., SME mfg. engr. Mgr. machining ops. Ingersoll-Rand, Phillipsburg, NJ, 1973-83; mgr. of mfr. Bendix Aerospace Corp., Eatontown, NJ, 1983-84; v.p. ops. Follett Corp., Easton, Pa., 1984-87, pres., COO, 1988-95; CEO Wilkra Co., Inc., Portland, Pa., 1995, also bd. dirs.; ptnr. Filtration Mfg. Co.; founder, pres. Omega Tools, Inc. Cons. to small mfg. co.; tech. transference orgnl. adaptation consulting Natural Gas Industry; exec. in residence So. Ill. U., 1991—, guest lectr. Coll. Bus.; guest lectr. Moravian Coll.; bd. dirs. Bustin Industries. Author: (book) Competitive Strategy, A Heuristic Model for Linking Manufacturing and Marketing, 1992, Organizational Adaptation Through Strategic Reorientation, A Study of the Gas Distribution Industry; contbr. articles to profl. publs. Chmn. adv. bd. Coll. Bus. and Adminstrn., So. Ill. U., 1989—, Ben Franklin Inst., 1991—; bd. dirs. Forum Lehigh Valley. Named to Hall of Fame Coll. Bus., So. Ill. U., 1994; recipient Alumni Achievement award, 1992, Ben Franklin Innovation award, 2002. Mem.: Acad. Mgmt., Soc. Mfg. Engrs., Ducks Unlimited, Grouse Soc., Young Pres.'s Orgn., So. Ill. U. Alumni Assn. Republican. Roman Catholic. Avocations: computer-aided design, springer spaniel training, fly fishing, upland hunting. Home: 4640 Hillview Dr Nazareth PA 18064-8525 Office: Omega Tools Co Inc PO Box 217 Portland PA 18351 Business E-Mail: hutton@ptd.net.

HUTTON, WINFIELD TRAVIS, management consultant, educator; b. L.A., Aug. 17, 1935; s. Travis Calhoun and Frances (Gardemann) H. BS in Mgmt. summa cum laude, Ohio State U., 1956, MBA, 1957, PhD, 1959. Consumer economist Fed. Res. Bank Atlanta, 1959—62; prof. econs. Hunter Coll., CUNY, 1962—68; prof. European divsn. U. Md., 1968—79, 1993—99; prof. Troy State U.-Europe, Germany, 1979—93. Cons. on mgmt., mktg. and econs. in Europe, 1968—. Author: (mgmt. computer simulations) City Finance, 1994, Simanage, 1998; author computer programs for rsch. stats.; contbr. articles to profl. jours. Lay reader St. Alban's Episcopal Ch., Kaiserslauten, Germany, 1981-88. Mem. AAUP, Am. Mktg. Assn. (manuscript reviewer 1983-94), Am. Econ. Assn., Beta Gamma Sigma. Avocations: opera, folk dancing, walking, bicycling, travel. Address: 15138 Stone Ln N Apt B106 Shoreline WA 98133-6259 also: Goethestr 66 19053 Schwerin Germany Office Phone: 206-417-5681.

HUTZLER, LISA ANN, mental health nurse, psychologist; b. Marietta, Ohio, Oct. 8, 1955; d. Donald Hayes and Winifred Maxine (Clark) Hutzler; m. Ernest Edwin Miller Jr., May 24, 1980; children: Nathan Andrew Miller, Daniel Seth Miller. BA in Psychology, Marietta Coll., 1977; AAS, Parkersburg Community Coll., W.Va., 1980; MA in Psychology, W. Va. Grad. Coll., 1995. RN, W.Va. Nurse adult psychiat. unit Cuyahoga Falls (Ohio) Gen. Hosp., 1982-83; staff nurse adult mental health St. Joseph's Hosp., Parkersburg, 1980-82, 85-91; personal care nurse Braley and Thompson, Vienna, W.Va., 1992-93; staff nurse Health South Western Hills Regional Rehab. Hosp., Vienna, 2002—04; hospice nurse Housecalls Home Health, Hospice and Personal Care, Parkersburg, W.Va., 2004—05. Vol. Boy Scouts Am./standard first aid instr., ARC. Mem. ANA, W.Va. Nurses Assn. Office Phone: 740-568-2232. Personal E-mail: lisahutzler26105@yahoo.com.

HUURMAN, WALTER WILLIAM, pediatric orthopaedic surgeon, educator; b. Rochester, N.Y., Mar. 16, 1936; s. Walter U. and Anna Mae (Lennon) H.; m. Lindsay Ann McGuiness, Dec. 16, 1967; children: Sean Patrick, Anne Lindsay. BS, U. Notre Dame, 1958; MD, Northwestern U., 1962. Diplomate Am. Bd. Orthop. Surgery. Intern Cook County Hosp., Chgo., 1962—63; flight surgeon USS Hornet, San Diego, 1964—66, NAS Miramar, San Diego, 1966—68; resident in orthop. surgery Naval Regional Med. Ctr., Oakland, Calif., 1968—71; dir. pediat. orthop. USN, Oakland, 1973—77; prof. pediat. and orthop. U. Nebr., Omaha, 1977—; dir. pediat. orthop. U. Nebr./Children's Meml. Hosp., Omaha, 1977. Bd. dirs. Nat. Alumni, Northwestern U. Mem. editl. bd. Jour. Pediat. Orthop., 1981-83, Jour. Bone and Joint Surgery, 1983-87, Pediat. in Rev., 1995-2000; reviewer Clin. Orthop. and Related Rsch., 1985—, Jour. Am. Acad. Orthop. Surgeons, 1998—; contbr. articles to sci. and profl. jours Pres., chmn. bd. dirs. Nebr. Arthritis Found., 1984. Capt. USN, 1963-77; res., 1980-95, ret. Fellow ACS, Am. Acad. Orthop. Surgery, Am. Acad. Pediat. (chmn. orthop. sect. 1986-89, mem. exec. com. sect. on sports medicine, 1992-2000); mem. AMA, Am. Orthop. Assn., Omaha Midwest Clin. Soc. (pres. 1994), Nebr. Orthop. Soc. (pres. 2000—), Pediat. Orthop. Soc. N.Am.(bd. dirs. 1994-2000), Acad. Orthop. Soc., Northwestern U. Feinberg Sch. Medicine Alumni Assn. (pres. 2005—) Roman Catholic. Office: U Nebr Med Ctr 600 S 42nd St Omaha NE 68198-1002 Office Phone: 402-492-9767. E-mail: whuurman@ix.netcom.com.

HUVOS, ANDREW, internist, cardiologist, educator; b. Budapest, Hungary, Apr. 23, 1930; came to U.S., 1950; s. Julian Gyula and Magdolna (Matyas) H.; m. Monique Chatriot, June 8, 1959; children: Christine, Anne, Philip. Student, Free U. Brussels, 1948-50, Harvard U., 1951; MD, Boston U., 1955. Diplomate Am. Bd. Internal Medicine, Am. Bd. Cardiovascular Disease. Resident in medicine Yale-New Haven Med. Ctr., 1955-59; fellow in cardiology Mass. Gen. Hosp., Boston, 1961-63; physician-in-charge cardiac catheterization lab. Univ. Hosp., Boston, 1963-70; chief cardiology Faulkner Hosp., Boston, 1970-74, chief medicine, 1974-95; lectr. medicine Harvard Med. Sch., Boston, 1974-86; lectr. medicine and physiology Boston U. Sch. Medicine, 1976—95; prof. medicine Tufts U. Sch. Medicine, Boston, 1985-97, prof. emeritus, 1997—. Dir. Tufts Assoc. Health Plan, 1979-81. Contbr. articles to med. jours., chpts. to books. Chmn. bd. trustees Ecole Bilingue, Inc., Arlington, Mass., 1970-74; trustee Boston Med. Libr., 1981-85. Capt. M.C., U.S. Army, 1959-61. Recipient Excellence in Teaching award Boston U. Sch. Medicine, 1974; USPHS grantee, 1977-83. Fellow: ACP, Mass. Med. Soc. (del., mem. com. on med. edn. 1981—95), Am. Heart Assn., Am. Coll. Chest Physicians (pres. New Eng. States chpt. 1981—83), Am. Coll. Cardiology; mem.: Roxbury Clin. Record Club, Dorchester Med. Club, Alpha Omega Alpha. Presbyterian. Avocations: opera, classical music. Office: Faulkner Hosp Boston MA 02130

HUWAR, ELIZABETH ANNA QUINN, artist, art educator; b. Kittanning, Pa., Dec. 6, 1973; d. Duane LaRoy and Deborah Lynn Quinn. BFA in Fine Arts, Clarion U., 1996; MFA in Fine Arts, Ohio U., 1998, postgrad., 1998—. Cert. tchr. Pa. Program asst. spl. edn. dept. Clarion (Pa.) U., 1992-93, asst. to sec., 1993, asst. to dir. Sandford Gallery, 1994-96; tchg. asst., grad. asst. Ohio U., Athens, 1996-98; art tchr. Blackhawk Area HS, Chipewa, Pa., 2000—03; elem. art tchr. Dubois Area Sch. Dist., 2003—04, Clarion-Limestone Area Sch. Dist., 2004—. Vis. artist Clarion U., Pa., 1996, DuBois Area Schs., 1996; instr. various workshops, seminars Clarion U., 1996—98, Athens, 1996—98; artist educator Andy Warhol Mus., Pitts.; adj. faculty Carlow Coll., Pitts. Author (designer): (ednl. program) Beadworks, 1998; exhibitions include, nationally, locally, internationally. Mem. art edn. grad. com. Ohio U., 1998. Mem.: Clarion County Arts Council, Gov.'s Inst. Arts Educators. Avocations: outdoor activities, collecting antique furniture, creating. E-mail: quinnhuwarliz@hotmail.com.

HUWILER, JOAN P., public relations executive, consultant; b. New Haven, Conn., June 15, 1963; d. Paul F. and Joan E. (Tickey) H. BA in Comm., Southern Conn. State Univ., 1985; MS in Journalism, Boston Univ., 1990. Account coord. Coates Pub. Rels. subs. Mason & Madison Advertising, Bethany, Conn., 1985-86; devel. fund raiser Atty. Gen. Joe Lieberman, Hartford, Conn., 1986; dep. press sec. Office Atty. Gen., State of Conn., Hartford, Conn., 1986-89; media dir. NOW Legal Def. and Edn. Fund, N.Y., 1990-92; cons., 1992-96; exec. dir. Schooner Inc., New Haven, Conn., 1992-93; comms. officer Cmty. Found. for Greater New Haven, New Haven, Conn., 1996-99; mktg. and comm. mgr. S. Ctrl. Regional Water Auth., New Haven, 1999—. Teaching asst. Boston Univ., 1989-90; pub. info. officer Hamden Bd. of Edn., 1984-85; writer, cons. Bank Mart, Bridgeport, Conn., 1985-86. Recipient Vanguard spl. merit award Women in Comm., 1991, Forty Under Forty award Bus. Times New Haven, 1999; named one of 20 Noteworthy Women, Bus. Times New Haven, 2000. Democrat. Avocations: reading, cooking, gardening. Office: S Ctrl Conn Regional Water Auth 90 Sargent Dr New Haven CT 06511-5918

HUXFORD, J. DAVID, retired sales executive; b. Syracuse, NY, Jan. 2, 1925; s. James H. and Marion Louise (McNally) H.; m. Theodora Annette Weeks, Oct. 31, 1946; four children. Student, Le Moyne Coll., 1946—48; BA in Econs., Notre Dame U., 1951. Supply cost mgr. L.A.B. Corp., Skaneateles, NY, 1953-58; contract sales Pitts. Plate Glass Co., Syracuse, 1958-62; archl. rep. PPG Industries, Inc., Skaneateles, 1962-75; contract sales B.R. Johnson & Son, Inc., Syracuse, 1975-77; mfr.'s rep. Roberts-Gordon Inc., Buffalo, Syracuse, 1978-92. Pres. Prodrs. Coun., Syracuse chpt., 1968-69; first industry mem. pres. Constrn. Specifications Inst., Syracuse chpt., 1974-75; trustee Village Bd., Skaneateles, 1963-64, NY State Hunter Instr., 1953-86, chmn. planning bd., 1990-2003, Nat. Rifle Assn. (life mem.). Ret. Capt. USMC Reserve, 1942-63. Home: 52 Fennell St Skaneateles NY 13152-1122 Office: Skaneateles Library Association 49 East Genesee Street Skaneateles NY 13152

HUXLEY, SIR ANDREW (SIR ANDREW FIELDING HUXLEY), physiologist, educator; b. London, Nov. 22, 1917; s. Leonard and Rosalind (Bruce) H.; m. Jocelyn Richenda Gammell Pease, July 5, 1947 (dec. Mar. 2003); children: Janet Rachel, Stewart Leonard, Camilla Rosalind, Eleanor Bruce, Henrietta Catherine, Clare Marjory Pease. BA, Cambridge (Eng.) U., 1938, MA, 1941, ScD (hon.), 1978; MD (hon.), U. Saar, 1964, Marseille U., 1979, Humboldt U., Berlin, 1985, Ulm U., 1993, Charles U., Prague, 1998; DSc (hon.), U. Sheffield, Eng., 1964, U. Leicester, 1967, London U., 1973, U. St. Andrews, Scotland, 1974, U. Aston, Birmingham, Eng., 1977, U. Western Australia, 1982, Oxford U., 1983, U. Pa., 1984, Harvard U., 1984, U. Keele, 1985, East Anglia U., 1985, U. Md., 1987, Brunel U., 1988, U. Hyderabad, 1991, Glasgow U., 1993, Witwatersrand U., 1998; LLD (hon.), U. Birmingham, 1979, Dundee U., 1984; Dr (hon.), York U., 1981, Toyama Med. and Pharm. U., 1995; DHL (hon.), NYU, 1982. Mem. rsch. staff Anti-Aircraft Command, 1940-42, Admiralty, 1942-45; fellow Trinity Coll., Cambridge, 1941-60, 90—, hon. fellow, 1967-90, master, 1984-90, dir. studies, 1952-60. Demonstrator dept. physiology Cambridge U., 1946—50, asst. dir. rsch. dept. physiology, 1951—59, reader exptl. biophysics, 1959—60; Jodrell prof. U. Coll. London, 1960—69, Royal Soc. rsch. prof., 1969—83; emeritus prof. London U., 1983—, hon. fellow, 1980—; fellow Royal Soc. London, 1955—, Croonian lectr., 1967, mem. coun., 1960—62, 1977—79, pres., 1980—85; Herter lectr. Johns Hopkins U., 1959; Jesup lectr. Columbia U., 1964; Forbes lectr., 66; Florey lectr., 82; Blackett Meml. lectr., 84; Fullerian prof. Royal Inst., London, 1967—73; Hans Hecht lectr., Chgo., 1975; Sherrington lectr Liverpool U., 1976—77; Centenary Colloquium lectr. Berlin Inst. Physiology, 1977; Cecil H. and Ida Green vis. prof. U. B.C., 1980; 6th ann. Darwin Lecture, 82; Romanes Lecture Oxford U., 1983; Tarner lectrs. Trinity Coll., Cambridge, 1988; Maulana Abul Kalam Azad Meml. Lecture, New Delhi, 91; C.G. Bernhard lecture Stockholm, 1993; Davson lecture Am. Physiol. Soc., 1998; Wartenweiler lecture Internat. Soc. of Biomechanics, Calgary, 1999. Author: Reflections on Muscle, 1980; editor Jour. Physiology, 1950-57, chmn. bd. Publs. on analysis of nerve conduction (with Hodgkin), physiology of striated muscle, devel. of interference microscope and ultramicrotome. Trustee Brit. Mus. (Natural History), 1981-90, Sci. Mus., 1984-88; mem. Agrl. Rsch. Coun., 1977-80, Nature Conservancy Coun., 1985-88, Animal Procedures Com., 1987-95. Decorated knight bachelor, Order of Merit, Grand Cordon of Sacred Treasure Japan; recipient (with A.L. Hodgkin and J.C. Eccles), Nobel Prize for physiology or medicine, 1963, Swammerdam medal, Soc. for Advancement of Natural Scis., Medicine and Surgery, Amsterdam, 1997, Copley medal, Royal Soc., 1973; fellow, Imperial Coll. Sci., Tech. and Medicine, 1980, Queen Mary and Westfield Coll., 1987, Royal Holloway and Bedford New Coll., 1994. Fellow Royal Acad. Engring. (hon.), Inst. Biology (hon.), Royal Soc. Can. (hon.), Royal Soc. Edinburgh (hon.), Royal Coll. Physicians (hon.), Acad. Med. Sci. (hon.), Indian Nat. Sci. Acad. (fgn.); mem. Physiol. Soc. (hon., rev. lectr. on muscular contraction 1973), Internat. Union Physiol. Scis. (pres. 1986-93), Brit. Biophys. Soc., Found. for Sci. and Tech., Royal Acad. Scis., Letters and Fine Arts Belgium (assoc.), Muscular Dystrophy Campaign (chmn. med. research com. 1974-81, v.p., 1981—), Royal Instn. Gt. Britain (hon.), Anat. Soc. Gt. Britain and Ireland (hon.), Am. Acad. Arts and Scis. (hon.), Am. Philos. Soc. (Penrose lectr. 1986), Brit. Assn. Advancement Sci. (pres. 1976-77), Leopoldina Acad. (hon.), NAS (U.S.) (fgn. assoc.), Royal Acad. Medicine Belgium (assoc.), Dutch Soc. Scis. (fgn.), Royal Danish Acad. Sci. (hon.), Am. Soc. Zoologists (hon.), Royal Irish Acad. (hon.), Japan Acad. (hon.). Home and Office: Manor Field 1 Vicarage Dr Grantchester Cambridge CB3 9NG England Office Phone: +44 (0) 1223 940207.

HUXLEY, MARY ATSUKO, artist; b. Stockton, Calif., Mar. 5, 1930; d. Henry K. and Kiku H. (Kisanuki) Taniguchi; m. Harold Daniels Huxley, 1957. Student, Armstrong Coll., Berkeley, Calif., 1950, San Francisco Art Inst., 1968; pvt. studies with, Thomas C. Leighton, 1970—75. Art show judge regional art clubs, corps., pvt. orgns., and county fairs, 1972-2005. Solo shows include Artists' Coop., San Francisco, 1973, 75, 76, The Univ. Club Invitational, San Francisco, 1976, I. Magnin, San Mateo, 1976, Palo Alto Med. Found., 1992, Galerie Genese, San Mateo, 1993; exhibited in juried group shows at Catharine Lorillard Wolf Art Club, N.Y.C., 1979, Knickerbocker Artists of Am., N.Y.C., 1979, Salmagundi Club Ann., N.Y.C., 1981, Butler Inst. Am. Art, Youngstown, Ohio, 1982, Am. Artists Profl. League, N.Y.C., 1982, 83, 86, 87, 88, Oil Painters of Am. Ann. Nat. Juried Shows, Gallery at Long Grove, Ill., 1993, 94, Taos, N.Mex., 1997, Oil Painters of Am. Ann. Pacific Coast Regional Juried Show, Jones & Terwilliger Gallery, Carmel, Calif., 1997, San Francisco Ann. Art Festival, 1970-74, Renaissance Gallery, Santa Rosa, Calif., 1973, Paramount Theater, Oakland, Calif., 1974, Met. Club Invitational, San Francisco, Marin Soc. Artists Ann., Ross, Calif., 1976, 79, Soc. Western Artists Ann., San Francisco, 1976, 78, 80, Peninsula Art Assn. Ann., Belmont, Calif., 1980, Fresno (Calif.) Fashion Fair Ann., 1981, 84, De Saisset Gallery, U. Santa Clara, Calif., 1979, Lodi (Calif.) Ann. Grape and Art Festival, 1970, 71, 72, 73, 74, 75, 76, 77, 78, 79, 81, San Mateo County Ann. Floral Fiesta, 1975, 76, 77, 78, 79, 81, Charles & Emma Frye Mus. Gallery, Seattle, 1975, Redwood City Women's Club Ann. Flower Show, 1978, Fremont Art Assn. Anns., 1987, 88, 89, John Muir Med. Ctr. invitational, 1999-2000, 3 Com-Synopsis Invitational Traveling Exhibit, 2000-01; numerous others; represented in numerous pvt. and corp. collections in U.S., Europe and Asia. Recipient Marjorie Walter Spl. award San Mateo County Exhbn., 1975, Gold medallion and 1st award San Mateo County Fair Fine Arts Exhbn., 1976, Best of Show award Cultural Arts of Palo Alto and Palo Alto Art Club, 1979, Best of Show and 1st award U. Art Ctr. and Palo Alto Art Club Ann., 1981, Spl. Merit award Oakland Art Assn., John Muir Med. Ctr. Ann., 1989, 1st award Burlingame Art Soc. Anns., 1976, 77, 1st award Redwood City Women's Club Ann. Flower Show, 1978, 1st award Soc. Western Artists Palo Alto Med. Ctr. Ann., 1983, 1st award Soc. Western Artists John Muir Med. Ctr. Ann., 1986, 1st award Fremont Art Assn. Ann., 1989, numerous others. Fellow Am. Artists Profl. League; mem. Soc. Western Artists (signature, trustee 1986-97, bd. dirs. 1972-75, 98, chmn. juried exhbns. 1972-81), Oil Painters Am. (signature), Allied Artists Am., Marin Soc. Artists (signature). Studio: PO Box 5467 San Mateo CA 94402-0467

HUXLIN, KRYSTEL RALUKA, neuroscientist, educator; b. Bucharest, Romania, Apr. 8, 1969; d. Raymond Will and Mary Ellen Huxlin; m. Keith Webster Nehrke, Sept. 13, 1997; 1 child, Jaenelle Marie Nehrke. BSc, U. Sydney, Australia, 1987—91, PhD, 1991—94. Rsch. asst. prof. U. Rochester, NY, 1999—2002, asst. prof., 2002—. Contbr. chapters to books. Bd. mem. Rochester Squash Racquets Assn., NY, 1997—2004. Recipient Beverly Steward Meml. prize, U. Sydney, 1987; fellow, Australian NH&MRC, 1995—97, Australian Med. Found., 1994—95; grantee, McDonnell-Pew Found., 2000—04, Bausch & Lomb Inc., 2001—, CEIS/NYSTAR, 2002—05, Schmitt Program on Integrative Brain Rsch., 2003—05, NIH/NEI, 2004—; scholar, Juvenile Diabetes Found. Internat., 1988, Australian NH&MRC, 1991—94, Brit. Coun., 1992, Australian NH&MRC, 1990; Robert E. McCormick scholar, 2005. Mem.: Faculty for Undergraduate Neurosci., Assn. for Rsch. in Vision and Ophthalmology, Soc. for Neurosci., Vision Sciences Soc., Rsch. to Prevent Blindness (assoc.; ophthal. assoc. 2004—05). Achievements include patents pending for computerized training and evaluation of visual discrimination abilities; research in the neural and molecular substrates of visual recovery after permanent visual cortical damage in adulthood; the optical consequences of corneal wound healing following laser refractive surgery. Avocations: squash, Irish dancing, horseback riding, hiking, violin. Office: Univ Rochester Med Ctr 601 Elmwood Ave Box 314 Rochester NY 14543 Office Phone: 585-275-5495. Office Fax: 585-473-3411. Business E-Mail: huxlin@cvs.rochester.edu.

HUXTABLE, ADA LOUISE, architecture critic; b. N.Y.C. d. Michael Louis and Leah (Rosenthal) Landman; m. L. Garth Huxtable. AB magna cum laude, Hunter Coll.; postgrad., Inst. Fine Arts, NYU; hon. degrees, Harvard U., Yale U., NYU, Washington U., U. Mass., Oberlin Coll., Miami U., R.I. Sch. Design, U. Pa., Radcliffe Coll., Oberlin Coll., Smith Coll., Skidmore Coll., Md. Inst., Mt. Holyoke Coll., Trinity Coll., LaSalle U., Pace Coll., Pratt Inst., Colgate U., Hamilton U., Williams Coll., Rutgers U., Finch Coll., Emerson Coll., C.W. Post Coll. at L.I. U., Cleve. State U., Bard Coll., Fordham U., Parsons Sch. Design, Mass. Coll. Art, Nottingham U., England. Asst. curator architecture and design The Museum of Modern Art, N.Y.C., 1946-50; Fulbright fellow for advanced study in architecture and design Italy, 1950, 52; free-lance writer, contbg. editor to Progressive Architecture and Art in America, 1950-63; architecture critic N.Y. Times, N.Y.C., 1963-82, mem. editorial bd., 1973-82; Cook lectr. in Am. instns. U. Mich., 1977; Hitchcock lect. U. Calif.-Berkeley, 1982. Corp. vis. com. Harvard U. Grad. Sch. Design, Sch. Visual and Environ. Arts; mem. adv. bd. Am. Trust Brit. Libr.; archtl. cons. Nat. Gallery, London, J. Paul Getty Trust, L.A., San Francisco Pub. Libr., Mus. Contemporary Art, Chgo., Kansas City Art Mus.; archtl. critic The Wall Street Jour., 1996—. Author: Pier Luigi Nervi, 1960, Classic New York, 1964, Will They Ever Finish Bruckner Boulevard?, 1970, Kicked a Building Lately?, 1976, The Tall Building Artistically Reconsidered: The Search for a Skyscraper Style, 1985, Goodbye History, Hello Hamburger 1986, Architecture Anyone? 1986, The Unreal America: Architecture and Illusion, 1997, Frank Lloyd Wright, 2004. Recipient 1st Pulitzer prize for disting. criticism, 1970, Spl. award Nat. Trust for Historic Preservation, 1971, Archtl. Criticism medal AIA, 1969, medal for lit. Nat. Arts Club, 1971, Diamond Jubilee medallion City N.Y., 1973, Mayor's Cultural award, 1984, Woman of Yr. award AAUW, 1974, Sec.'s award for conservation U.S. Dept. Interior, 1976, Thomas Jefferson medal U. Va., 1977, Archtl. Criticism medal Acad. d' Architecture Française, 1988; Guggenheim fellow for studies in Am. architecture, 1958, MacArthur fellow, 1981-86, fellow Ctr. for Scholars and Writers, N.Y. Pub. Libr., 1999-00; Henry Allen Moe prize Humanities Am. Philosophical Soc., 1992. Fellow Am. Acad. Arts and Scis., Royal Inst. Brit. Architects (hon.), AAAL; mem. AIA (hon.), Am. Acad. Arts and Letters, Soc. Archtl. Historians. Home: 969 Park Ave New York NY 10028-0322

HUYBRECHTS, AUGUST JOHN, music educator; b. Stabroek, Antwerp, Belgium, Oct. 31, 1920; arrived in U.S., 1952; s. Arthur Ferdinand and Elisa Maria Angelina Huybrechts; m. Louisa Alexandra Janssens, Nov. 11, 1947; children: Dirk Jozef, Frank Felix, Ralph Louis, Paul Arthur, Mary-Elizabeth Miette. BA, Lemmens Inst., 1940, MA, 1942. Organist St. Catherine Ch., Stabroek, 1934—52; organist, choir dir. St. Francis Xavier Ch., Petoskey, Mich., 1952—82, Ch. of Assumption, Albuquerque, 1982—2004. Instr. organ and piano Interlochen (Mich.) Arts Acad., 1972—96. Mem.: Am. Guild Organists (hon. life). Roman Catholic. Home: 1620 Singletary Dr NE Albuquerque NM 87112

HUYBRECHTS, STEVEN MARC, space system technologist; b. Dover, N.H., Dec. 29, 1969; s. Marc Huybrechts and Brigitte Duces, John Strawhorn (Stepfather) and Ellida Yngente (Stepmother); m. Wendy Marie Cubbison, Oct. 11, 2002; children: Rachel Johnson, Caden, Taryn. BSc in Physics and Computer sci., McGill U., Montreal, Can., 1991; MS in Aero. and Astron. Engring., Stanford U., 1992, PhD in Aero. and Astron. Engring., 1995. Rschr. Ctr. for Spacecraft Component Tech., Kirtland AFB, N.Mex., 1992—99, chief, 1999—2002. Recipient Arthur S. Flemming award, Flemming Found. and Georgetown U., 2000, Stellar award, Rotary Nat. Award for Space Achievement, 2000, Sci. and Tech. Achievement award, Air Force Materiel Command, 1997. Fellow: AIAA (sub-com. chair, conf. chair 1999—2002). Achievements include development of many enabling technologies for future space systems. Office: Air Force Rsch Lab 3550 Aberdeen Ave Kirtland Afb NM 87117-5776 Personal E-mail: smhuybrechts@stanfordalumni.org.

HUYCK, CHARLES KRISHNA, geographer, consultant; b. Youngsville, N.C., Dec. 12, 1969; s. Peter Hazelwood Huyck and Jeannie Elizabeth Kellett; m. Melisa Plett, Sept. 9, 1971; children: Mitchel A, Amelia J. BS, U. of Iowa, 1993. GIS programmer analyst EQE, Irvine, 1996—2000; sr. v.p. ImageCat, Long Beach, Calif., 2000—. Contbr. articles to profl. jours. Mem.: EERI, ASPRS, URISA. Roman Catholic. Achievements include invention of Bare-Earth Algorithms for use with SAR and LIDAR Digital Elevation Models. Home: 351 Newport Ave Long Beach CA 90814 Office: ImageCat Inc 400 Oceangate Ste 1050 Long Beach CA 90802 Office Fax: 562-628-1676. Personal E-mail: ckh@imagecatinc.com.

HUYGENS, REMMERT WILLIAM, architect; b. Haarlem, Netherlands, Apr. 19, 1932; came to U.S., 1956, naturalized, 1963; s. Willem and Antoinette (Bruynzeel) H. Diploma dept. architecture, Amsterdam HTS, 1955. With Marcel Breuer, NYC, 1956; pvt. practice Wayland, Mass., 1960—2005, Woodbine, Ga., 2005—. Prin. works include: Campus Rivers Country Day Sch., Weston, Mass., 1960, Longy Concert Hall, Cambridge, Mass., 1966, Interfaith Religious Ctr. Columbia, Md., 1967, campus N.H. Coll., Manchester, 1969-81, The Village of Loon Mountain, Lincoln, N.H., 1973-, Cath. Med. Ctr. Manchester, 1974, Milford (Conn.) Pub. Libr., 1976, Village Green at Stowe, Vt., 1980—, rsch. bldgs. for Biogen Inc., Cambridge and Geneva, 1980, Indian Head Nat. Bank, Nashua, N.H., 1981, Pub. Libr., Framingham, Mass., 1982, Teradyne Circuits Inc., Nashua, 1983, Riverview office tower, Cambridge, 1985, Cochituate Place office bldg., Framingham, 1986 One Memorial Drive office tower, Cambridge, 1986, Constitution Office Complex, Boston, 1987, Water's Edge Resort, Westbrook, Conn., 1987, Franklin Park Zoo, Boston, 1989, Ipswich (Mass.) Country Club, 1989; office parks, residential cmtys. and pvt. residences in U.S., Holland, France, Switzerland, Malaysia, corp. hdqs. and rsch. facilities for Genzyme Corp., Enzytech Inc., BioSurface Technology Inc., ImmunoGen Inc., Digital Equipment Corp., urban planning Guangzhou, China, 100 story office tower, Guangzhou, China, 1990, work exhibited at N.Y. Archtl. League, N.Y. Mus. Modern Art, N.Y., Brockton Art Ctr., Boston Arch. Ctr.; works pub. in numerous books and jours., U.S., Eng., Holland, Italy, Japan, France, Belgium, Germany, China, others, including: Arch. Record, Archtl. Forum, AIA Jour., Am. Home, House and Garden, Progressive Arch., House Beautiful, N.Y. Times, Boston Globe. Recipient Abu-Dhabi Conf. Ctr. award, 1st award Internat. Masonry Inst., Modern Architecture award, Conseil d'Architecture, d'Urbanisme et de l'Environment (CAUE), France, others. Fellow AIA (Progressive Architecture Design awards, Honor awards New Eng. regional coun., award of merit R.I. chpt., Conn. Soc. Archs./AIA Design award). Office: R W Huygens FAIA Arch 140 Lakes Blvd 212 Kingsland GA 31548 Office Phone: 912-729-6548. Business E-Mail: huygensarchitect@tds.com.

HUYNH, QUANG KHAI, biochemist; b. Tuyhoa, Phu Yen, Vietnam, Jan. 10, 1952; s. Dieu H. and Chon Luong; m. Michiko S. Huynh, Aug. 1, 1979; children: Linda, Vicky, Amy. BS, Chiba U., Japan, 1975; MS, U. Osaka Pref., Japan, 1977; PhD, Osaka U., Japan, 1981. Rsch. scientist Monsanto, St. Louis, 1987-90, sr. rsch. specialist, 1990-94, assoc. fellow, 1996-2000; sr. rsch. scientist Monsanto Co./Searle, St. Louis, 1994-96; sci. fellow Pharmacia Corp., St. Louis, 2000—. Sr. rsch. biochemist Monsanto Co., St. Louis, 1985; post doctoral rsch. assoc. U. Tex., Austin, 1981. Contbr. over 40 articles to profl. jours. Grantee NIH, 1981-85; recipient Spl. award Robert A. Welch Found., 1985. Mem. AAAS, Protein Soc., Inflammation Rsch. Soc., Am. Soc. Biochemistry and Molecular Biology. Home: 1905 Powderhorn Pass Ct Wildwood MO 63011 Office: Pharmacia Corp/Monsanto Co 800 W Lindbergh Blvd Saint Louis MO 63167 E-mail: quang.k.huynh@pharmacia.com.

HUYSMAN, ARLENE WEISS, psychologist, educator, writer; b. Phila., 1929; d. Max and Anna (Pearlene) Weiss; m. Pedro Camacho; children: Pamela Claire, James David. BA, Shaw U., 1973; MA, Goddard Coll., 1974;

PhD, Union Inst. Grad., 1980. Diplomate Am. Bd. Psychol. Specialties, Med. Psychology, 1997. Actress, dir. Dramatic Workshop, N.Y.C., 1956—68; music and drama critic and columnist Orlando (Fla.) Sentinel Star, 1966—68; psychodramatist Volusia County Guidance Ctr., Daytona Beach, Fla., 1966—68; free-lance journalist, 1968—70; psychodramatist Psychiat. Inst. Jackson Meml. Hosp., Miami, 1972—77; dir. Adult Day Treatment Ctr., 1974—77, Lithium Clinic, 1976—77; psychodramatist South Fla. State Hosp., Hollywood, 1971—72; psychotherapy supr., Neurosci. program coord. Miami Heart Inst., 1984—; clin. dir. Family Workshop, 1985—, Adult Day Treatment Ctrs., 1987—; founder, dir. Geriatric Adult Day Treatment Ctrs. Adj. asst. prof. Med. Sch. U. Miami, 1976—; adj. prof. Union Inst., 1992—, Antioch U., 1995—; specialist in Bi Polar Disorders, U. Wis., 1980—. Author: A Mother's Tears, 1998, 2002, The Postpartum Effect: Deadly Depression in Mothers, 2003. Mem. adv. panel Fine Arts Coun. Fla., 1976—77. Recipient Best Dirs. award and Best Actress award, Fla. Theatre Festival, 1967. Mem.: APA, Fla. Assn. Practicing Psychologists (bd. dirs., pres.), World Fedn. Mental Health, Am. Assn. Group Psychotherapy and Psychodrama, Am. Soc. Aging, Internat. Assn. Group Psychotherapy, Mental Health Assn. Dade County, Dade County Psychol. Assn. (bd. dirs.), Fla. Psychol. Assn., Am. Coll. Forensic Examiners, Fedn. Partial Hospitalization Study Groups, Moreno Acad., Union Inst. Grad. Alumni Assn. (bd. dirs., southeastern rep., pres.-elect). Office: Ptnrs in Health 3050 Biscayne Blvd Miami FL 33137-4143 Office Phone: 305-571-9996. Personal E-mail: drhuysman@yahoo.com.

HUYSMAN, JAMES DAVID, healthcare executive, consultant; b. N.Y.C., Jan. 27, 1955; s. Michel and Arlene Muriel (Weiss) H.; m. Betsy Catherine Bergner, May 29, 1988. BA in Cmty. Psychology with high honors, U. Fla., 1977; M in Clin. Social Work, Barry U., Miami Shores, Fla., 1987. Diplomate NASW; lic. clin. social worker; cert. addictions profl.; registered lic. real estate broker. Dir. vocat. program Fellowship House, South Miami, Fla., 1984-86; therapist Ctrs. for Psychol. Growth, Miami, Fla., 1986-88; v.p. outreach The Bradford Group, Birmingham, Ala., 1988-92; dir. aftercare The Geraldo Rivera Show, N.Y.C., 1991—; v.p. devel. CareNet Psychol. Mgmt., Nashville, 1993-96; chmn., CEO Ptnrs. in Health Mgmt., Ft. Lauderdale, Fla., 1996—; dir. Aftercare Leeza Show, 1996—. Cons. to Rev. Jesse Jackson, Rainbow Coalition, Washington, 1990-91, largest pub./pvt. treatment grant, Washington, 1989-90, Howell Heflin D.C. Treatment Grant, Bradford Group, Washington, 1989-90, Bennett/Klehr Drug Policy Office, Washington, 1989-90, Geraldo Rivera, Montel Williams, Les Brown, Leeza, other talk shows; founder, dir. 1st Healthcare Network and Aftercare Program for Talk TV; creator nat. talk show; CEO At the End of the Day Prodns. Contbr. over 300 articles to nat. newspapers; appeared on over 70 nat. syndicated talk shows. Bus. devel. OrNdA Healthcorp. Tenet Health Sys.; exec. dir. Leeza Gibbons Memory Found. Recipient Friends Day Founder recognition Cmty. Mental Health Agys., Miami, 1986. Mem. ACLU, Nat. Wildlife Fedn., Nature Conservancy, World Wildlife Fund, Habitat for Humanity, Fla. Alcohol and Drug Abuse Assn. Democrat. Jewish. Avocations: motorcycling, travel, miami ballet, theater, collecting animation and memorabilia. also: Ptnrs in Health Mgmt and Entertainment Mgmt 3050 Biscayne Blvd Ste 908 Miami FL 33137-4143

HUZAR, ELEANOR GOLTZ, historian, educator; b. St. Paul, June 15, 1922; d. Edward Victor and Clare (O'Neill) Goltz; m. Elias Huzar, June 21, 1950 (dec. Dec. 1950); m. Bruce I. Granger, Oct. 11, 1991. BA, U. Minn., 1943; MA, Cornell U., 1945, PhD, 1948. Instr. history Stanford U., Palo Alto, Calif., 1948-50; asst. prof. classics U. Ill., Urbana, 1951-55; assoc. prof. history S.E. Mo. Coll., Cape Girardeau, 1955-59; assoc. prof. classics Carleton Coll., Northfield, Minn., 1959-60; prof. history Mich. State U., East Lansing, 1960-90, chmn. program in classical studies, 1965-90. Mem. selection com. Nat. Endowment for Humanities, Washington, 1979-84, Coun. for Internat. Exchg. Scholars, Washington, 1979-81, Mich. Rhodes Scholars, Ann Arbor, 1981-84, Prix de Rome, Am. Acad., N.Y.C., 1978-80. Author: Mark Antony: A Biography, 1978; contbr. articles and revs. to profl. jours. George Boldt fellow, Cornell U., 1947—48. Mem. Classical Assn. of Mid. West and South (pres. 1984-85), Am. Hist. Assn., Am. Philol. Assn., Archael. Inst. Am. (local pres. 1979-80), Mich. Classical Conf. (pres. 1984-85), Am. Acad. in Rome (adv. coun. 1963-92, exec. com. 1970-73, 88-92), Am. Sch. in Athens (mng. com. 1964-92), Phi Beta Kappa, Phi Kappa Phi. Democrat. Roman Catholic. Avocations: hiking, skiing, travel. Home: 2945 Lincoln Dr Apt 132 Saint Paul MN 55113-1341

HWA, TERENCE TAI-LI, physicist; b. Shanghai, May 30, 1964; came to U.S., 1979; s. Chia-Xu and Rebecca Tsu-Yung (Zhang) H. BS in Physics, Biology, Elec. Engring., Stanford U., 1986; PhD, MIT, 1990. Postdoctoral fellow Harvard U., 1990-93; long-term mem. Inst. for Advanced Study, Princeton, NJ, 1993-94; asst. prof. dept. physics SUNY, Stony Brook, 1994-95; assoc. prof. dept. physics U. Calif., San Diego, 1995—99, prof., 1999—. Recipient Apker award Am. Physics Soc., 1986, Outstanding Young Rschr. award Overseas Chinese Physics Assn., 1983; pre-doctoral fellow IBM, 1989, post-doctoral fellow, 1991, A.P. Sloan Found. fellow, 1994-99, Guggenheim fellow, 1999; recipient Young Investigator award Office Naval Rsch., 1995-98, Young Investigator award Beckman Found., 1997-99, Innovation award Burroughs Wellcome Trust, 2000-04. Mem. Tau Beta Pi. Office: U Calif San Diego Dept Physics M/C 0374 9500 Gilman Dr La Jolla CA 92093-0374 Office Phone: 858-534-7263. E-mail: hwa@ucsd.edu.

HWANG, CORDELIA JONG, chemist; b. NYC, July 14, 1942; d. Goddard and Lilly (Fung) Jong; m. Warren C. Hwang, Mar. 29, 1969; 1 child, Kevin. BA, Barnard Coll., 1964; MS, SUNY, Stony Brook, 1969. Rsch. asst. Columbia U., NYC, 1964-66; analytical chemist Veritron West, Inc., Chatsworth, Calif., 1969-70; asst. lab. dir., chief chemist Pomeroy, Johnston & Bailey Environ. Engrs., Pasadena, Calif., 1970-76; chemist Met. Water Dist. So. Calif., LA, 1976-79, rsch. chemist, 1980-91, sr. chemist, 1992—2000, sr. rsch. chemist, 2001—. Mem. Joint Task Group on Instrumental Identification of Taste and Odor Compounds, 1983-85, Joint Task Group on Nitrosamines, 2004; instr. Citrus Coll., 1974-76; chmn. Joint Task Group on Disinfection by-products: chlorine, 1990. Mem. Am. Chem. Soc., Am. Water Works Assn. (cert. water quality analyst level 3, Calif.-Nev.), Am. Soc. Mass Spectrometry. Office: Met Water Dist So Calif 700 Moreno Ave La Verne CA 91750-3303 E-mail: chwang@mwd.dst.ca.us.

HWANG, DENNIS (DENNIS HWANG-JUNG-MOAK), artist; b. Knoxville, Tenn., Mar. 31; arrived in Korea, 1983, arrived in Am., 1992; Logo designer Google Inc., 2000—, asst. webmaster. Mailing: Google Inc 1600 Amphitheatre Parkway Mountain View CA 94043*

HWANG, HAEJO, toxicologist; b. Chilgok-gun, Kyungpook, Korea (South), Mar. 3, 1966; s. Ki-Ho Hwang and Young-Ja Lee; m. Kyeok Kim, May 24, 1960; 1 child, Hannah Kim. BA, Kyungpook Nat. U., Taegu, Republic of Korea, 1991; PhD, The Ohio State U., Columbus, OH, 2000. Toxicologist Nalco Co., Naperville, Ill., 2001—; post-doctoral fellow U. of Calif., Davis, Davis, Calif., 2000—01. Contbr. articles to profl jours. Cpl. Korean Army, 1985—87, Kyungpook, Korea (South). Fellow Seagrant Indsl. Fellowship, Nat. Seagrant, and Proctor and Gamble, 1997 - 2000. Mem.: Soc. of Environ. Toxicology and Chemistry, Biocide Panel, Am. Chemistry Coun. Achievements include research in Developed a model to be used in predicting ecotoxicity, bioaccumulation, environmental fate and biodegradation of mixtures. Office: Nalco Company 1601 W Diehl Rd Naperville IL 60563 Office Phone: 630-305-1398. Home Fax: 630-305-2986; Office Fax: 630-305-2986. Personal E-mail: hawng42@yahoo.com. E-mail: hhwang@nalco.com.

HWANG, JASON KAO, composer, musician, music educator; b. Lake Forest, Ill., May 12, 1957; s. Kao and Sheila Hwang; m. Gennevieve Lam, Jan. 1986. BFA, NYU, 1979. Lectr. Ctrl. Conservatory, Beijing, 1997; adj. instr. NYU, 2000—; tchg. artist Young Audiences/NY, NYC, 2001—; lectr. Bklyn Coll., 2002. Mem. editl. com. New World Records, NYC; panelist Nat. Endowment for the Arts, Washington, 2002, Fund for U.S. Artists at Internat. Festivals, NYC, 1997. Composer: (chamber opera) The Floating Box, A Story in Chinatown, 2005; violinist, composer (CD) Unfolding Stone, 1990, Flight of Whispers, 1999, Urban Archaeology, 1996, Caverns, 1994, (dance score) Unbroken Thread, (film score) Battery Film, Dance Score, dir., composer (documentary film) Afterbirth, 1983, violinist, arranger M Butterfly, Broadway and nat. tour., 1988—91, composer, violinist du Maurier Ltd. International Jazz Festival, Vancouver, Can., 1993, Jazz Spektakel, Wuppertal, Germany, 1995, Nickelsdorf Konfrontationen Festival, Nickelsdorf, Austria, 1995, Whitney Mus. Contemporary Art at Phillip Morris, NYC, 1996, Inst. Contemporary Art, Boston, 1996, Internat. Festival Musique Actuelle, Victoriaville, Que., Can., 1996, Beijing Internat. Jazz Festival, 1997, Visoin Festival, NYC, 1998, The Freer Gallery, Washington, 1999, violinist with Sin Cha Hong, Pusan, Seoul and Tae Koo, South Korea, 1992, with Reggie Workman Ensemble, Austria, Switzerland, 1993, with Anthony Braxton Quintet, Internat. Akbank Festival, Istanbul, Turkey, 1995, with Henry Threadgill Soc. Situation Dance Band, Verona Jazz Festival, Verona, Italy, 1996, with Vladamir Tarasov Ensemble for New and Improvised Music, Lithuania, Moscow and Arkhengelsk, Russia, 1997. Fellow, NJ. State Coun. on the Arts, 1996, 2002; grantee, Greenwall Found., 1995, Nat. Endowment for Arts, Opera/Musical Theater, 1995, Mary Flagler Cary Charitable Trust, 1995, 1999, Meet the Composer Fund, 1996, Fund for U.S. Artists at Internat. Festivals and Exhbns., 1997, Meet the Composer/New Residencies, 1998—2001, NY Cmty. Trust, 1999, Rockefeller Found. Multi-Arts Prodn. Fund, 2000, Puffin Found., 2001, Nat. Endowment for the Arts, 1999, Margaret Fairbanks Jory Copying Assistance Program of the Am. Music Ctr., 2001. Mem.: Am. Fedn. Musicians (Local 802). Personal E-mail: jkhwang@comcast.net.

HWANG, LI-SAN, technology executive; BSCE, Nat. Taiwan U.; MSCE, Mich. State U.; PhD in Civil Engring., Calif. Inst. Tech. Joined predecessor and held present positions since the acquisition of Water Mgmt. Group of Tetra Tech, Inc., a subsidiary of Honeywell Inc., 1967—88; dir. engring. Tetra Tech, 1972, v.p., 1974, sr. v.p. ops., chmn. bd. dirs., CEO, 1988—. Advisor to numerous gov. and profl. soc. committees. Contbr. articles to profl. publs. in the field of hydrodynamics. Office: Tetra Tech Inc 3475 E Foothill Blvd Pasadena CA 91107 Office Phone: 626-351-4664. Office Fax: 626-351-1188.

HWANG, MICHAEL TIAN-CHUNG, university president; b. Nan Cheng, Jiangxi, China, Mar. 5, 1941; came to U.S., 1964; s. Lu Xian and Hui Quing Wang Hwang; m. Grace Lee Piang, Apr. 4, 1968; children: Joseph, Jean. BA, Tamkang U., Taipei, Taiwan, 1964; MEd, Mercer U., 1967; EdD, Drake U., 1988; DSc, Shenandoah U., 1997. V.p. acad. rsch. programs Oklahoma City U., 1984-88; vis. scholar Harvard U. Grad. Sch. Edn., Cambridge, Mass., 1989; prof., dean internat. studies Tamkang U., 1990-96; pres. Armstrong U., Oakland, Calif., 1997—. Office: Armstrong University 1301 Marina Village Pkwy #340 Alameda CA 94501-1082 E-mail: info@armstrong-u.edu.

HWANG, SHIN JA, linguistics educator; b. Nanam, Ham Kyong, Korea, May 24, 1943; came to U.S., 1966, naturalized, 1979; d. Byung Im and Dong Joo Wol Joo; m. Myung Kyu Hwang, Dec. 16, 1967; children— Harold, Grace, Lisa. B.A., Ewha Women's U., Seoul, Korea, 1961-65; M.L.S., U. Okla., 1968; M.A., U. Tex.-Arlington, 1974, Ph.D., 1981. Librarian, U. So. Calif., Los Angeles, 1968-71; tchr. Summer Inst. Linguistics, Dallas, 1982—; adj. asst. prof. linguistics U. Tex., Arlington, 1984— . Author: Korean Clause Structure, 1975; Discourse Features of Korean Narration, 1986. Contbr. articles to profl. jours. Mem. Linguistic Soc. S.W., Linguistic Soc. Am. Methodist. Home: 210 Genoa Dr Duncanville TX 75116-4320

HWANG, SUN-TAK, chemical engineering educator; b. Choong Buk, Korea, June 24, 1935; came to U.S., 1960, naturalized, 1972; s. Kyu-Yong and Jae-Hung (Song) H.; m. Soon Choi, June 15, 1963; children— Linda, Helen. B.S., Seoul Nat. U., 1958; M.S., U. Iowa, 1962, Ph.D., 1965. Instr. U. Iowa, Iowa City, 1964-65, asst. prof. chem. engring., 1966-69, assoc. prof., 1969-73, prof., 1973-82, dept. chmn., 1982; prof., head dept. chem. engring. U. Cin., 1982—, dir. Ctr. of Excellence in Membrane Tech., 1984—; engr. Mobil Oil Corp., Dallas, 1965-66. Mem. Am. Chem. Soc., Am. Inst. Chem. Engrs., Am. Soc. Engring. Edn., AAAS, AAUP, Sigma Xi, Phi Lambda Upsilon, Tau Beta Pi. Home: 9880 Humphrey Rd Cincinnati OH 45242-5445 Office: U Cin 171 Mill St Cincinnati OH 45221-0012

HWANG, TE-LONG, neurologist, educator; b. Hualien, Taiwan, Republic of China, Nov. 4, 1943; came to U.S., 1976; s. Tien-Fu and Tien (Liu) Hwang; m. Ai-Yu Chau; children: Tang-Hau Jimmy, Tang-Chieh George. MD, Nat. Def. Med. Ctr., Taipei, Taiwan, 1970. Intern New Brunswick (N.J.) Affiliated Hosps., 1976-77; pathology resident North Shore Univ. Hosp., Manhasset, N.Y., 1977-79; neurology resident U. Tex. Med. Sch., Houston, 1979-82; neuro-oncology fellow U. Tex. M.D. Anderson Cancer Ctr., Houston, 1983-85; attending neurologist VA Hosp., Topeka, Kans., 1986-88, Columbia, S.C., 1988—. Assoc. prof. U. S.C. Sch. Medicine, Columbia, 1988-94, prof., 1994—, chief neurology, 2002-. Mem. Am. Acad. Neurology, Am. Stroke Assn., Nat. Stroke Assn., World Fedn. Neurology (neurosonology rsch. group), S.C. Neurol. Assn. Home: 7 Birchbark Ct Columbia SC 29229-9002 Office: 3555 Harden St Ext Columbia SC 29203-6894 Business E-Mail: tlh@gw.mp.sc.edu.

HWANG, WENKE, researcher; b. Taipei, Taiwan, June 1960; s. Tsing-tsu and Dan-hai Hwang; m. Ching-chuan Yang; children: Sandra, Grace, Alan. BA, Nat. Chung-hsing U., Taipei, Taiwan, 1982, MA, 1984; PhD, U. of Md., 1996. Rsch. scientist ctr. for hosp. fin. and mgmt. Johns Hopkins Med. Inst., Balt., 1999—. Cons. in field. Contbr. columns in newspapers Commercial Times Taipei, Taiwan, 1986—88, articles to profl. jours. Fellow, Ctr. for Medicare and Medicaid Svc., 1996; grantee, NIH. Mem.: Am. Pub. Health Assn., Acad. Health Svc. & Rsch. Office: Ctr for Hospital Finance and Management 624 N Broadway Room 307 Baltimore MD 21205 Office Phone: (410)6143199. Office Fax: (410)9552301. Business E-Mail: whwang@comcast.net.

HWU, WEN-JEN, oncologist, educator; b. Taiwan, Republic of China, Nov. 19, 1949; divorced; 2 children: Ai-Jen Poo, Ting Poo. BS in chemistry, Nat. Tsinghua U., Taiwan, 1971; MS in Chemistry, Duquesne U., 1975; PhD in Chemistry, Carnegie-Mellon U., 1976; MD, U. Calif., Irvine, 1982. Diplomate Am. Bd. Internal Medicine, Am. Bd. Med. Oncology; MD, Calif., Conn., N.Y. Rsch. fellow in endocrine biochemistry Purdue U., West Lafayette, Ind., 1976; rsch. fellow in neurophysiology, dept. physiology U. Calif., Irvine, 1976-78; intern and resident in internal medicine U. Calif. Irvine Coll. of Medicine and Med. Ctr., Orange, 1982-85; rsch. fellow in immunology Howard Hughes Med. Inst., Yale U. Sch. Medicine, New Haven, Conn., 1985-86; fellow in med. oncology Yale U. Sch. Medicine, New Haven, 1986-89, fellow in molecular biology, 1987-89, lectr. dept. molecular biophysics and biochemistry, 1987-89, instr. dept. internal medicine, 1989-91, co-dir. GU cancer unit, 1989-92, asst. prof. medicine, 1991-97, assoc. prof., 1997-98, Cornell U., Ithaca, NY, 2001—. Assoc. attending physician melanoma sect. Clin. Immunology Svcs., Meml. Sloan-Kettering Cancer Ctr., N.Y.c., 1999—; lab. instr. gen. chemistry, Duquesne U., Pitts., 1971-73; instr. organic and phys. chemistry labs., Carnegie-Mellon U., Pitts., 1973-75; postdoctoral rsch. fellow dept. physiology, U. Calif., Irvine, 9176-78; acting chief sect. hematology/oncology, VA Med. Ctr., West Haven, Conn., 1994-95, acting dir. cancer ctr., 1994-95; dir. melanoma unit comprehensive cancer ctr., Yale U. Sch. Medicine, New Haven, 1992-98; mem. adv. bd. Am. Cancer Soc., Conn. and South Cen. Middlexex-Meriden-Wallingford Units, 1989-98; chmn. Melanoma Tumor Bd., Yale Cancer, Ctr., 1994-98, Genitourinary Tumor Bd., 1994-98, mem. protocol rev. com., 1995-98. Contbr. numerous articles to sci. and profl. jours. Recipient Clin. Oncology award Am. Cancer Soc., 1986. Mem. ACP, Conn. Oncology Assn., Am. soc. clin. Oncology, Am. Fedn. Med. Rsch., Am. Assn. Cancer Rsch. Office: Meml Sloan-Kettering Cancer Ctr 1275 York Ave New York NY 10021

HYAMS, PETER, film director, producer, cinematographer; b. July 26, 1943; m. George-Ann Spota, Dec. 19, 1964; 3 children. Former news anchor CBS. Dir., writer: (films) Our Time, 1974, Capricorn One, 1978, Hanover Street, 1979, Outland, 1981, The Star Chamber, 1983; dir., cinematographer.: The Presidio, 1988, Stay Tuned, 1992, Timecop, 1994, Sudden Death, 1995, The Relic, 1997, End of Days, 1999, The Musketeer, 2001, A Sound of Thunder, 2005; dir., writer, cinematographer, prodr.: 2010, 1984; exec. prodr.: The Monster Squad, 1987; exec. prodr., dir., cinematographer, Running Scared, 1986. Office: c/o DGA 7920 W Sunset Blvd Los Angeles CA 90046-3300*

HYATT, SUSAN MARIE, theater educator, director, actress; d. Blaine Michael and Marilyn Louise Gay; m. Jeff Hyatt, Sept. 9, 2000; 1 child, Sawyer. BFA in Theatre, Youngstown (Ohio) State U., 1996; MFA in Acting, Fla. Atlantic U., 1999. Artist in residence Ctr. Creative Edn., West Palm Beach, Fla., 1996—2002; dir. edn. Fla. Stage, Manalapan, 2002—. Adj. faculty Fla. Atlantic U., Boca Raton, 2000—02, Lynn U., Boca Raton, 2000—02; bd. dirs. Boynton Beach (Fla.) H.S. Arts Acad., mem. arts adv. bd.; mem. task force arts edn. Palm Beach (Fla.) County Sch. Dist., 2004—; bd. dirs. U.S. Ctr. for Internat. Assn. Theater for Children and Young People. Co-author: (plays) Baby Steps, 2004; actor:. Vol., group leader Transitions, Lantana, Fla., 2004—; dir. Royal Palm Project, 2002—; mem. steering com. Palm Beach (Fla.) County Cultural Coun., 2004—, Ohio Bd. Regents scholar, 1990—94, Youngstown (Ohio) State U. scholar, 1990—94. Mem.: Theatre Comms. Group, Fla. Assn. Theatre Edn., Actors Equity Assn. Avocations: cooking, sewing, travel. Office: Florida Stage 262 S Ocean Blvd Manalapan FL 33462

HYATT, THOMAS KARL, lawyer; b. Warren, Pa., May 2, 1957; s. Anne Louise and Emerson Singen Hyatt; children: Sean, Conor. BA in econs., Boston Coll., 1975—79; JD, U. Pitts. Sch. Law, 1979—82. Bar: DC 1982, Pa. 1989, US Ct. Appeals: (DC cir.), US Dist. Ct.: (DC cir.), US Supreme Ct.: 1988. Atty. Wood, Lucksinger & Epstein, Washington, 1982—83, Schuster & King, Washington, 1983—85, Powers, Pyles, Sutter & Verville, Washington, 1985—96, Ober, Kaler, Grimes & Shriver, Washington, 1997—. Dir. Cath. Network for Vol. Svc., Takoma Park, Md., 2004—. Mem.: ABA, Am. Health Lawyers Assn. (dir. 1992—98, David J. Greenburg Svc. award 2004). Office: Ober Kaler Grimes & Shriver 1401 H St NW Ste 500 Washington DC 20005 Office Phone: 202-326-5039. Office Fax: 202-408-0640. Business E-Mail: tkhyatt@ober.com.

HYATT-WALLACE, KIMBERLY LEANNE, mental health services professional; b. Haverhill, Mass., June 15, 1946; d. John and Elizabeth M. Zila; m. William H. Wallace, May 22, 2004. PhD, Bridgewater Coll., London, 2003. Registered counselor Wash., 2004. Human resources QDC, Hermasossa, Fla., 2001—03; ptnr. Hyatt-Wallace Gender Identity Dysphoria Clinic, Fairview Heights, Ill., 2003—. Author: (screenplays) Outlaw Riders; contbr. articles to profl. jours. Vol. Legal Aid, Clearwater, Fla., 1980. Grantee, Kings Coll., 1991. Mem.: Harry Benjamin Assn. (assoc.). Achievements include research in treatment of gender identity dysphoria and associated conditions. Office Fax: 800-833-4647. Personal E-mail: kimberlyhyatt@hotmail.com.

HYBL, WILLIAM JOSEPH, lawyer, retired foundation administrator; b. Des Moines, July 16, 1942; s. Joseph A. and Geraldine (Evans) H.; m. Kathleen (Horrigan), June 6, 1967; children: William J. Jr., Kyle Horrigan. BA, Colo. Coll., 1964; JD, U. Colo., 1967. Bar: Colo. 1967. Asst. dist. atty. 4th Jud. Dist. El Paso and Teller Counties, 1970—72; pres., dir. Garden City Co., 1973—; dir. Broadmoor Hotel, Inc., 1973—; chmn., CEO, trustee El Pomar Found., Colorado Springs, Colo., 1973—; vice chmn. Broadmoor Hotel, Inc., 1987—; pres. U.S. Olympic Com., 1991—92, 1996—2000; chmn. and CEO U.S. Olympic Found., 2002—; chmn. Internat. Found. for Election Sys., 2003—. Dir. USAA, San Antonio, Kinder Morgan Inc., Houston, First Bank Holding Co., Lakewood, Colo.; mem. Colo. Ho. of Reps., 1972-73; spl. counsel The White House, Washington, 1981; U.S. Rep. to 56th Gen. Assembly of UN, 2001-02. Pres. Air Force Acad. Found.; sec., vice chmn. bd. U.S. Adv. Commn. on Pub. Diplomacy, 1990-97; civilian aide to sec. of army, 1986—. Capt. U.S. Army. 1967-69. Republican. Office Phone: 719-577-5712. Business E-Mail: wjhybl@elpomar.org.

HYDE, ALAN LITCHFIELD, retired lawyer; b. Akron, Ohio, Nov. 4, 1928; s. Howard Linton Hyde and Katharine (Pennington) Litchfield; m. Charlotte Griffin Ross, July 10, 1954; children: Elizabeth Hyde Moore, Pamela. AB magna cum laude, Amherst Coll., 1950; JD, Harvard U., 1953. Bar: Ohio 1953, U.S. Dist. Ct. (no. dist.) Ohio 1955. Assoc. Thompson, Hine and Flory, Cleve., 1953-64, ptnr., 1964-93; ret., 1993. Hon. consul, Mexico, 1969—74. Contbr. articles to profl. jours. Trustee Planned Parenthood Greater Cleve., Inc., 1960-79, 80-81, pres. bd. trustees, 1977-79; sec., gen. counsel Greater Cleve. Growth Assn., 1972-74, 86-88, bd. dirs., 1974-80, 82-86, 88-93; trustee Cleve. World Trade Assn., 1978-81; trustee Cleve. Coun. World Affairs, 1980-93, mem. exec. com., 1980-83. Mem. ABA, Inter-Am. Bar Assn. (coun., com. on Latin Am. Devel.), Greater Cleve. Internat. Lawyers Group, Tavern Club (Cleve.), Chagrin Valley Hunt Club (Gates Mills, Ohio). Republican. Episcopalian.

HYDE, CATHERINE RYAN, short story writer; b. Buffalo, N.Y., Apr. 17, 1955; Instr. writer's conf. Cuesta Coll., San Luis Obispo, Calif.; adminstrv. asst. Santa Barbara (Calif.) Writer's Conf. Author: (novels) Funerals for Horses, 1997, Pay It Forward, 2000, Electric God, 2000, (short story collection) Earthquake Weather, 1998. Recipient Raymond Carver Short Story contest Humboldt State U., 1994, 96, Tobias Wolff award for fiction The Bellingham Rev., 1997; cited in Best American Short Stories, 1999. Office: The Hardy Agy 3020 Bridgeway Ste 204 Sausalito CA 94965-2839 E-mail: info@booklogic.com.

HYDE, CLARENCE BRODIE, II, oil industry executive; b. Ft. Worth, Oct. 22, 1937; s. Clarence Edgar and Frances McCain (Williams) H.; m. Sylvia Flower, June 5, 1960; children: C. Brodie III, Brooke Allison, Brett Kinlock, Blair Elizabeth. BS, Tex. Wesleyan Coll., 1961, LLD (hon.), 1996; MBA, U. Tex., 1963; grad., So. Meth. U., 1973. V.p., asst. mgt. lending group, chmn. loan com. Ft. Worth Nat. Bank, 1964-76; ind. oil prodr. Ft. Worth, 1976-78; pres., chmn. bd. Hyde Oil & Gas Corp., Ft. Worth, 1978—; pres. Hyde Resources Corp., 1997—, Hyde Energy Corp., 1993—. Mem. exec. com., dir. River Plz. Nat. Bank, Ft. Worth, 1983-86; trustee, v.p., treas. The Hyde Found., Ft. Worth, 1981—. Bd. dirs. Tarrant County chpt. Salvation Army, 1969-79, chmn. bd., 1972-74; trustee Trinity Valley Sch., Ft. Worth, 1970; mgmt. com. Camp Amon Cartr, Ft. Worth, 1970-76, adv. mem., 1976—; trustee Tex. Wesleyan Coll., 1971-96, chmn. bd., chmn. exec. com., 1990-94; bd. dirs. Big Bros. Tarrant County, 1971; trustee W.A. Moncrief Radiation Ctr., Ft. Worth, 1971-99, v.p., 1986-99; bd. dirs., mem. exec. Harris Hosp., Ft. Worth, 1971-88, Harris Meth. Health Systems, 1983-87; bd. dirs., treas. Tarrant County chpt. ARC, 1971-73, bd. dirs., 1989-91; bd. dirs., exec. com. Ft. Worth Opera Assn., 1971-99, v.p., treas., 1972-74; bd. dirs., exec. com. Hurst-Euless (Tex.)-Bedford Hosp., 1973-80; bd. dirs. Ft. Worth Arts Coun., 1972-95, pres., 1973-75; chmn. Cmty. Pride Campaign, 1972; bd. dirs. Ann Waggoner Scholarship Fund, 1984—; fin. com. Ft. Worth Country Day Sch., 1985-89; pres. MRC-Trans Co. (subs. Moncrief Radiation Ctr.), 1987-94; bd. dirs. Cancer Care Svcs., 1994-95, adv. bd. dirs., 1995—; dir. Ft. Worth Pub. Libr. Found., 1996-2002. Named Alumnus of Yr., Tex. Wesleyan Coll., 1985. Mem. Ind. Petroleum Assn. Am., Tex. Ind. Prodrs. & Royalty Owners Assn., Tex. & Southwestern Cattle Raisers Assn., Tex. Hosp. Assn., Rivercrest Country Club, Shady Oaks Country Club (Ft. Worth), Steelechase Club (Ridotto), Ft. Worth Petroleum Club, Crescent Club (Dallas). Republican. Methodist. Avocations: hunting, fishing, travel. Home: 8 Westover Rd Fort Worth TX 76107-3103 Office: Hyde Oil & Gas Corp 6300 Ridglea Pl Ste 1018 Fort Worth TX 76116-5778

HYDE, DAVID ROWLEY, lawyer; b. Norwalk, Conn., Aug. 21, 1929; s. Thomas Arthur and Mary Julia (Sass) H.; m. Valerie Rosemary Worrall, Dec. 30, 1961; children: Meredith Ellen, Timothy Worrall. AB, Yale U., 1951, LL.B., 1954. Bar: Conn. 1954, N.Y. 1956, U.S. Supreme Ct. 1969. Assoc. Cahill Gordon & Reindel, N.Y.C., 1954-59, 64-65, ptnr., 1966-90, sr. counsel,

1991—; with U.S. Atty.'s Office, 1959—63, chief civil divsn., 1961—63. Home: 35 W 12th St New York NY 10011-8501 Office: Cahill Gordon & Reindel 80 Pine St New York NY 10005-1702

HYDE, ELLA MAE, small business owner; b. Akron, Ohio, May 9, 1938; d. Wallace Fleming and Mable Alberta (Straub) Burbridge; m. Glenn C. Gurney, Mar. 15, 1957 (div. 1972); children: Lee Allen, Bonnie Sue; m. Allyn J. Hyde, Dec. 20, 1986 (dec. Oct. 1991); children: Debbie Lee, Tina Marie Beadle. Student, Fulton Montgomery Coll., 1984-85. Lic. real estate broker NY. Saleswoman real estate United Farm Agy. Inc., Sprout Brook, N.Y., 1959-69; saleswoman Avon Products Inc., N.Y.C., 1976-84; saleswoman, instr. Artcraft Guild, Balston-Spa, N.Y., 1980-84; sales leader First Apostolic Ch., Amsterdam and Ft. Johnson, N.Y., 1980-90; seamstress, designer Jomas Estelle Fashions, Troy, N.Y., 1986-90, Mohawk Valley Christian Acad., Ft. Johnson, 1986-91; owner Ellie's Creations, Ft. Johnson, 1992—. Designer fashions for pets, wedding fashions. Mem. coms. First Apostolic Ch., 1980, mem. costume dept., 1987-91). Mem. Gloversville Women of the Moose (supper and hosp. com., head fundraiser 1984-86, Acad. of Friendship award 1985). Avocations: sales, sewing, designing, needlecraft, helping others. Office: Ellie's Creations 111 Teller Ave Broadalbin NY 12025-1898 Business E-Mail: coolcat@usadatanet.net.

HYDE, GERALDINE VEOLA, retired secondary school educator; b. Berkeley, Calif., Nov. 26, 1926; d. William Benjamin and Veola (Walker) H.; m. Paul Hyde Graves, Jr., Nov. 12, 1949 (div. Dec. 1960); children: Christine M. Graves Klykken, Catherine A. Graves Okerlund, Geraldine J. Graves Hansen. BA in English, U. Wash., 1948; BA in Edn., Ea. Wash. U., 1960, MA in Edn., 1962. Cert. tchr. K-16, Wash.; life cert. specialist in secondary edn., Calif. English educator Sprague (Wash.) Consol. Schs., 1960-62, Bremerton (Wash.) Sch. Dist., 1962-63, Federal Way (Wash.) Sch. Dist., 1963-66; English, journalism and Polynesian humanities educator Hayward (Calif.) Unified Sch. Dist., 1966-86; ret., 1986. Charter mem. Hist. Hawaii Found., Honolulu, 1977-; founding mem. The Cousteau Soc., Inc., Norfolk, Va., 1973-; life mem. Hawaiian Hist. Soc., Honolulu, 1978-; mem. Molokai Mus. and Cultural Ctr., Kaunakakai, 1986-, Bishop Mus. Assn., Honolulu, 1973-, Mission House Mus., Honolulu, 1994, Bklyn. Hist. Assn., N.Y., 1994, Berkshire Family History Assn., Pittsfield, Mass., 1994-, Richville (N.Y.) Hist. Assn., 1994-, Swanton (Vt.) Hist. Soc., 1998-, N.Y. Geneal. and Biog. Soc., 1999-, New Eng. Hist. Genealogic Soc., 1998-, Gouverneur Hist. Assn., NY, 1998-, New Wing Luke Asian Mus., Seattle, 1994, Upham Family Soc., Inc., Melrose, Mass., 2001-, Calif. Ret. Tchrs Assoc. 2003. Mem. Libr. Congress Assocs. (charter), Nature Conservancy of Hawai'i, Smithsonian Inst. (contbg.), Nat. Geog. Soc., Nat. Trust Historic Preservation, Jr. League Spokane, U. Wash. Alumni Assn. (life), Ea. Wash. U. Alumni Assn. (life). Episcopalian. Avocations: historic and ecologic preservation, genealogy, shell collecting, needlecrafts, crafts. Home: 2050 Springfield Drive 470 Chico CA 95928

HYDE, HENRY JOHN, congressman; b. Chgo., Apr. 18, 1924; s. Henry Clay and Monica (Kelly) Hyde; m. Jeanne Simpson, Nov. 8, 1947 (dec. 1992); children: Henry J., Robert, Laura, Anthony. Student, Duke U., 1943-44; BS, Georgetown U., 1946; JD, Loyola U., Chgo., 1949. Bar: Ill. 1950. Mem. Ill. Gen. Assembly, 1967-74, U.S. Congress from 6th Ill. dist., 1975—; mem. jud. com.; chmn. jud. com., 1995—2001; chmn. internat. rels. com. Author: For Every Idle Silence, 1985, Protecting Our Property Rights. With USN, 1944—46. Mem.: Chgo. Bar Assn. Republican. Roman Catholic. Achievements include appointed by House of Representatives to conduct impeachment proceedings against Harry E. Claiborne, judge of the US Dist. Court for Nevada, 1986; appointed by House of Representatives to conduct impeachment proceedings against Pres. Bill Clinton, 1998. Office: US Ho of Reps 2110 Rayburn Washington DC 20515-1306

HYDE, HERBERT LEE, lawyer; b. Bryson City, N.C., Dec. 12, 1925; s. Ervin M. and Alice (Medlin) H.; m. Kathryn Long, Dec. 25, 1949; children: Deborah, Lynn, Karen, Benjamin, Jane, William. AB, W. Carolina U., 1951; JD, NYU, 1954. Bar: N.C. 1954, U.S. Dist. Ct. (we. dist.) N.C. 1954, U.S. Ct. Appeals (4th cir.) 1957, U.S. Supreme Ct. 1962, U.S. Dist. Ct. (mid. dist.) N.C. 1975, U.S. Dist. Ct. (ea. dist.) N.C. 1980. Ptnr. Van Winkle, Buck, Wall, Starnes & Hyde, Asheville, N.C., 1954-79; sole practice Asheville, 1979—. Sec. N.C. Dept. Crime Control and Pub. Safety, Raleigh, 1979. Author: Genuine Hyde, 1976, My Home is in the Smoky Mountains, 1998, Of Truth and Freedom, 2001, Living and Learning, Just Natural, 2001, Mountain Speaking, 2002; writer (song) The Cold Icy Waters of Swain. Senator N.C. Senate, Raleigh, 1964-66, 1990-94; mem. N.C. Ho. of Reps., Raleigh, 1972-76; chmn. Dem. Exec. Com. of Buncombe County, Asheville, 1988—; chmn. Dem. Congl. Dist. 11, 1988-90, N.C. State Dems., 1990—, chmn., 1993. Named N.C. Bar Assn. Gen. Practice Hall of Fame, 1999. Mem.: Am. Coll. Trial Lawyers. Democrat. Home: 93 Eastview Cir Asheville NC 28806-1150 Office: PO Box 7266 Asheville NC 28802-7266

HYDE, JAMES DUDLEY, lawyer; b. Oklahoma City, May 20, 1944; s. Homer Clark and Winonah Mae Hyde; m. Sue Ann White, Dec. 28, 1966; children: Heatherlyn Corey Hyde Blake, James Devon. BA, U. Okla., 1966; JD, So. Meth. U., 1969; LLM in Taxation, George Washington U., 1974. Bar: Tex. 1969, Okla. 1974. Ptnr., dir. McAfee & Taft, Oklahoma City, 1974—. Pres. S.W. Benefits Assn., Dallas, 2000—01; charter fellow Am. Coll. Employee Benefits Coun., 2002. Chmn. Oklahoma City Pub. Schs. Found., 2002; bd. dirs. Redbud Classic Found., Oklahoma City, 2002. Capt. JAG, 1969—74. Named Outstanding Alumni, U. Okla. Mem.: ABA, Okla. Bar Assn. Office: McAfee & Taft 10th Fl 211 N Robinson Oklahoma City OK 73102

HYDE, JOSEPH R., III, retail auto parts executive; b. Memphis, Dec. 27, 1942; m. Judy Kendall; 2 children; m. Barbara Rosser; 1 child. BS, U. N.C., 1965. With Malone & Hyde, Memphis, 1965—, pres., 1969—88, chmn. bd. dirs., 1972—88; CEO AutoZone, Inc., Memphis, 1986—96, chmn. bd., 1986—; pres. Pittco Inc., 1989—; chmn. GTx Inc., 2000—; gen. ptnr. MB Venture Partners, 2001—. Dir. FedEx Corp. Active Nat. Civil Rights Mus., MIFA, The Blues Found., Ballet Memphis, Goals for Memphis, United Way, Memphis Arts Coun., Jr. Achievement The Memphis Challenge. Mem. Nat. Wholesale Grocers Assn. (dir.), Memphis C. of C. (dir.) Office: Autozone Inc 123 S Front St Memphis TN 38103*

HYDE, LAWRENCE HENRY, JR., manufacturing executive; b. Cambridge, Mass., July 10, 1924; s. Lawrence Henry and Catherine I. (McMahon) H.; m. Lois A. Crehan, May 31, 1947; children— Abigail Ellen, Stephen Lawrence, Lawrence Henry III. AB, Harvard U., 1946, MBA, 1947. With Ford Motor Co., 1947-65, dir. internat. purchasing office, 1960-62; v.p. Philco, 1962-64; with Harris Corp., Cleve., 1965-73; from dir. internat. ops. to group v.p. internat. Am. Motors Corp., Detroit, 1974-83, v.p. internat., 1974-77; group v.p., pres. AM Gen. Corp., 1977-81, exec. v.p., 1982-83; with LTV Corp., 1983-85; divsn. pres. AM Gen., 1983-85; with Harris Graphics Corp., 1985-86, also chmn. bd. dirs.; with Sonex Rsch., Inc., 1986—2003, also chmn. bd. dirs., 1986-93. Chmn. Karnak Investments, Ltd., Bermuda; chmn. U. Investment Fund, Cairo; trustee Am. U., Cairo.

HYDE, M. DEBORAH, neurosurgeon; b. Laurel, Miss., Jan. 18, 1949; d. Sellus Hyde and Ann (Huff) McDonald; m. James Joseph Jackson, June 28, 1986. BS in Biology, Tougaloo Coll, Miss., 1970; MS in Biology, Cleve. State U., 1973; MD, Case Western Reserve U., Cleve., 1977. Diplomate Am. Bd. Neurol. Surgery. Resident Univ. Hosps., Cleve., 1978-82; neurosurgeon Guthrie Med. Ctr., Sayre, Pa., 1982-87; pvt. practice Canoga Pk., Calif., 1987—. Contbg. author: The Courage of Conviction, 1985. Mem. AMA, Congress Neurol. Surgeons, Nat. Med. Assn., Alpha Omega Alpha. Democrat. Office: Deborah Hyde-Jackson MD 7230 Med Ctr Dr #600 West Hills CA 91307

HYDE, MARY ALICE, medical librarian, director; b. Cleve., Feb. 10, 1964; d. Thomas L. and Joanne C. Salem; m. William W. Hyde, May 25, 1991; children: Caroline Elizabeth, Catherine Anne. BA, U. Dayton, 1986; MSc in Libr. Sci., Clarion (Pa.) U., 1990. Med. libr. Winchester (Va.) Med. Ctr., 1991—92; libr. Am. Assn. Med. Colls., Wash., 1992—96; reference libr. ACOG Resource Ctr., Washington, 1996—2002, dir., 2002—. Mem.: Acad. Health Info, Profls., Health Assn. Librs. Sect. (sec., treas. 2001), Mid-Atlantic Med. Libr. Assn., DC Area Health Sci. Libr. (pres. 1999—2001), Med. Libr. Assn. Office: Am Coll Obstetricians & Gynecologists 409 12th St SW Washington DC 20024 E-mail: mhyde@acog.org.

HYDE, THOMAS D., lawyer; b. Kansas City; BA in English, U. Kans., 1970, MBA, 1981; JD, U. Mo., 1975. Atty. Stubbs & Mann, Kansas City, Mo.; with Emerson Electric, St. Louis, Manville Corp., Denver, Stanley Continental; sr. v.p., pres., gen. counsel and CFO MNC Special Assets Bank, Balt.; with Raytheon Co., Lexington, Mass., 1992—2001, v.p., gen. counsel, 1994—98, sr. v.p., gen. counsel, corp. sec., 1998—2001; exec. v.p. for legal and corp. affairs, corp. sec. Wal-Mart Stores, Inc., 2001—. Office: Wal-Mart Stores, Inc 702 SW Eighth St Bentonville AR 72716*

HYERS, THOMAS MORGAN, physician, biomedical researcher; b. Jacksonville, Fla., June 16, 1943; s. John and Joan (Clemens) H.; m. Elizabeth Mclean, June 12, 1965; children: Justin, Adam. BS, Duke U., 1964, MD, 1968. Diplomate Am. Bd. Internal Medicine, Am. Bd. Pulmonary Diseases. Intern in medicine Cleve. Met. Gen. Hosp., 1968-69; asst. chief Nat. Blood Resource Br., Nat. Heart, Lung and Blood Inst., NIH, 1971-72, pulmonary disease adv. com., 1983-86; resident in medicine U. Wash., Seattle, 1972-74; chief resident, instr. medicine, 1974-75; fellow in pulmonary diseases U. Colo. Health Scis. Ctr., Denver, 1975-76, research fellow Cardiovascular Pulmonary Research Lab., 1976-77, asst. prof. medicine, staff physician respiratory care, assoc. investigator, 1977-82; research assoc. Denver VA Med. Ctr., 1979-82; assoc. prof. medicine, dir. div. pulmonary diseases St. Louis U. Med. Ctr., 1982-85, prof. medicine, divsn. dir., 1985-98; dir. NIH Specialized Ctr. Research in Adult Respiratory Failure, 1983-93. Contbr. articles to profl. jours. Served to comdr. USPHS, 1969-71. Named hon. Ky. col. grantee NIH, Nat. Heart, Lung and Blood Inst. Fellow ACP, Am. Coll. Chest Physicians; mem. Am. Heart Assn. (mem. councils on thrombosis and cardiopulmonary disease), Internat. Soc. Thrombosis and Haemostasis, Am. Lung Assn. (Eastern Mo. chpt.), Am. Fedn. Clin. Research, Am. Physiol. Soc., Western Soc. Clin. Investigation, Am. Thoracic Soc., Phi Beta Kappa. Office: CARE Clin Rsch 533 Couch Ave Ste 140 Saint Louis MO 63122-5561 Office Phone: 314-909-9779. E-mail: studies@careinternet.com.

HYLAND, GEOFFREY FYFE, energy executive; b. Montreal; B in Engring., McGill U., Montreal, 1966; MBA, York U., Toronto, Ont., Can., 1972. Pres., COO Shaw Industries Ltd, Toronto, Ont., 1987, pres., CEO, 1994—. Bd. dir. ShawCor Ltd., Enerflex Sys., Ltd., Exco Techs. Ltd., Fortis Inc. Office: ShawCor Ltd 25 Bethridge Rd Toronto ON Canada M9W 1M7 E-mail: ghyland@shawcor.com.

HYLAND, WILLIAM FRANCIS, lawyer; b. Burlington, N.J., July 30, 1923; s. Theodore J. and Margaret M. (Gallagher) H.; m. Joan E. Sharp, Apr. 20, 1946; children: William Francis, Nancy E. Hyland Wiley, Stephen J., Emma L. Hyland McCormack, Margaret M. Hyland Frank, Thomas M. BS in Econs, U. Pa., 1944, LL.B., 1949; D.H.L., Hahnemann Med. Sch. and Hosp., 1976. Bar: N.J. 1949, U.S. Supreme Ct. 1960. Of counsel Riker, Danzig, Scherer, Hyland & Perretti, Morristown, N.J.; atty. gen. N.J., 1974-78. Mem. N.J. Gen. Assembly from Camden County, 1954-61, speaker of house, 1958, acting gov., N.J., 1958; chmn. N.J. Sports and Expn. Authority, 1978-82, commr., 1974-84; pres. N.J. Bd. Pub. Utility Commrs., also mem. cabinet govs. Meyner, Hughes, Byrne, N.J., 1961-68, 74-78; chmn. N.J. Atomic Energy Council, 1968-69, N.J. Commn. Investigation, 1969-71; co-chmn. Reapportionment Commn.; chmn. Brazilian Mission Com., 1962-65; permanent del. Fed. Jud. Conf. 3d Circuit.; del.-at-large Dem. Nat. Conv., 1964, del., 1968; assoc. trustee U. Pa., 1960-74. Served as officer USNR, 1943-46, ETO, PTO. Decorated knight Order of St. Gregory (Pope Paul VI), 1964; recipient Distinguished Service award Camden County Jaycees, 1954, Outstanding Young Man in Govt. N.J. award N.J. Jaycees, 1958, Myrtle Wreath award Camden County So. N.J. region Hadassah, 1977, Pub. Service award Anti-Defamation League of B'nai B'rith, 1982; named Outstanding Citizen of N.J. Advt. Club. N.J., 1979 Mem. ABA (fellow N.J. chpt.), Camden County Bar Assn. (pres. 1959), Nat. Assn. R.R. and Utilities Commrs. (exec. com. 1965-68), Nat. Assn. Attys. Gen. (exec. com. 1975-78, v.p. 1976, pres. elect 1977-78), Phi Kappa Psi. Office: Riker Danzig Scherer Hyland & Perretti Headquarters Plz 1 Speedwell Ave Ste 2 Morristown NJ 07960-6823 Home: 309 Bridgeboro Rd Apt 2345 Moorestown NJ 08057-1427 Office Phone: 973-538-0800.

HYLANDER, WALTER RAYMOND, JR., retired civil engineer; b. July 22, 1924; s. Walter Raymond and Mary Howard (Douglass) H.; m. Marjorie Jean Gunter, Mar. 8, 1951; children: Walter Raymond, Joyce Elizabeth. BS, U.S. Mil. Acad., 1945; MS in Civil Engring., MIT, 1950. Registered profl. engr., N.Y., Miss. Commd. 2d lt. U.S. Army, 1945, advanced through grades to col., 1969, ret., 1973; tng. dir. Bechtel Power Corp., Grand Gulf, Miss., 1974-76; tng. and edn. mgr. Saudi-Arabian Bechtel Co., Jubail, 1976-77; tng. dir. St. Regis Paper Co., Montecello, Miss., 1978-79; chief civil engr. Bechtel Power Corp., Grand Gulf, 1979-86. Chmn. Panel of Experts on Mine Warfare, NATO, London, 1962-65; sr. advisor on engr. tng., Vietnam, 1967-68; mem. U.S. Army Com. on Mil. History, West Point, N.Y., 1972-73; mem. U.S. ACDA, Washington, 1968-69. Contbr. articles to profl. jours. Fellow: ASCE. Methodist. Home: Rosswood Plantation 2513 Red Lick Rd Lorman MS 39096 Personal E-mail: whylander@aol.com.

HYLBERT, PAUL, construction executive; Various field and corp. pos., including mngr. dir. Wickes Europe, and sr. v.p. and gen. mgr. Wickes Lumber, 1966—90; pres. PrimeSource, 1990—2001; pres., CEO Lanoga Corp., Redmond, Wash., 2001—. Mem.: Nat. Bldg. Materials Distbrs. Assn. (pres. 1993). Office: Lanoga Corp 17946 NE 65th St Redmond WA 98052

HYLETT, JONATHON SPENCER, investment company executive; b. Madison Heights, Mich., July 14, 1975; s. John Melvin and Miriam Linda Hulett; m. Kristen Mae House, Nov. 11, 2000. Attended, Calvin Coll., 1995; A in applied sci., Grand Rapids C.C., 1998; B in bus. (hon.), U. San Maritz, England, 1999; M in CIS (hon.), U. San Maritz, 2003. Lic. property casualty insurance Insurance Inst. of Am., 2001, life and health insurance JEL Inst., 2004, cert. notary pub. Colo. Sr. cons. The Thoca roup, Kertwood, Mich., 1993—97; tech. dir. I-2000, Inc, Wyomac, Mich., 1997—99; sr. IT and mktg. cons. Altifore, Inc., Ada, Mich., 1999—2001; sr. tech. engr. eDeploy.Com, Golden, Colo., 2000—01; sr. licensed svc. agent Foremost Ins., Caledonia, Mich., 2001—04; CEO Coipe Investments LLC, Denver, 2004—05. Co-chair Foremost Diversity Coun., Caledonia, Mich., 2001—04; tech. adv. Revision Partners, Kentwood, Mich., 2000—03; svc. projects coord. Grand Rapids Youth Alliance, Grand Rapids, Mich., 1999—2004; fin. peace counselor Pathways Ch., Denver, 2004—. Lobbyist mem. Farmers Legal Action Group, Caledonia, Mich., 2001—04. Recipient Coun. Alumni Appreciation, Foremost Diversity Coun., 2004. Mem.: Colo. Real Estate Network. Independent. Office: PO Box 150955 Lakewood CO 80215-0950 E-mail: sfp@co-ren.com.

HYLLA, LINDA KAY, sister, social worker; b. Granite City, Ill., Mar. 1, 1961; d. Leonard Albert and Loretta Ann Hylla. BA, Fontbonne U., 1987; MSW, Wash. U., St. Louis, 1992. Entrance into Sisters of Divine Providence, 1980; LCSW 1995. Coord. youth and human svc., Granite City, Ill., 1992—95; child care worker St. Elizabeth Med. Ctr., Granite City, 1986—95, outpatient therapist, 1995—2000; vocations dir. Sisters of Divine Providence, Bridgeton, Mo., 2000—. Clin. supr. pvt. practice, Madison, Ill., 1998—; founder Quest Ho., Madison, Ill. Contbr. poetry poetry.com. Bd. dirs. New Opportunities, Madison, 1989—91; chmn. bd. Rm. at the Inn Homeless Shelter, St. Louis County, 2002—03. Named an Internat. Poet of Merit, Internat. Soc. of Poets, 2002; named to, Internat. Soc. Conf., 1999, TREND Hall of Fame, Nat. TREND Conf., St. Louis, 2000; Vocation grant, KC, 2003. Office: Sisters of Divine Providence 3415 Bridgeland Bridgeton MO 63044 E-mail: srlindahylla@hotmail.com.

HYLTON, THOMAS JAMES, author; b. Reading, Pa., Dec. 20, 1948; s. William Harold and Mary Harriet (Kitzmiller) H.; m. Frances Wismer, Aug. 31, 1970. BA, Kutztown U. of Pa., 1970. Reporter The Mercury, Pottstown, Pa., 1970-86, editl. writer, 1986-94. Author: Save Our Land, Save our Towns: A Plan for Pennsylvania, 1995; prodr., host (PBS) Save Our Land, Save Our Towns, 2000. Co-founder Trees Inc., Pottstown, 1983; co-founder Preservation Pottstown, 1984, 10,000 Friends of Pa., 1998. Recipient Am. Planning Assn. award, 1988, 90, 94, Honor award Nat. Trust for Hist. Preservation, 1997, Pulitzer prize for editl. writing, 1990; Pulliam fellow, 1993. Republican. Presbyterian. Home: 222 Chestnut St Pottstown PA 19464-5508 Office Phone: 610-323-6837. Personal E-mail: thomashylton@comcast.net. Business E-Mail: hylton@ptdprolog.net.

HYMAN, ABRAHAM, electrical engineer; b. Bklyn., Mar. 8, 1934; s. Rubin and Regina (Holzman) H.; m. Marianne Daniel, June 19, 1955; children: Debra Hyman Rathauser, Lori Hyman Rones, Karen Hyman Cantor. BEE, Poly. Inst. Bklyn., 1952; MS, Newark Coll. Engring., 1954. Registered profl. engr., N.Y. Chief elec. engr. Med. Equipment R&D Lab., Fort Totten, N.Y., 1955-64; head lab. Office Naval Rsch., Port Washington, N.Y., 1964-66; tech. adminstr. AEC, Upton, N.Y., 1966-71; supr. indsl. hygienist Dept. Labor, Westbury, N.Y., 1971-80, regional indsl. hygienist N.Y.C., 1980-84; mgr. health and safety Unisys Corp., Great Neck, N.Y., 1984-95; safety and health cons. New Hyde Park, N.Y., 1995—. Adj. prof. York Coll., Queens, NY, 1974—78; cons. Poison Control Ctr., Mineola, NY, 1981—; adj. assoc. prof. Staten Island Coll., NY, 1983—95; lectr. Queensboro C.C., Queens, NY, 1994—96. Patentee in field. Bd. dirs. Am. Lung Assn., East Meadow, 1974-99. Mem. IEEE, Am. Acad. Environ. Engrs. (diplomate), NSPE, Am. Conf. Indsl. Hygienists, Sci. Rsch. Soc. Am., Sigma Xi. Avocations: photography, swimming, bicycling. Home and Office: 142 Claudy Ln New Hyde Park NY 11040-1635 Personal E-mail: marab6@aol.com.

HYMAN, ALAN BARRY, lawyer; b. Balt., Apr. 22, 1947; s. Henry and Estelle (Datkyn) H.; m. Sharon Susan Albert, June 22, 1968; children: Cori Ann, Marcie Allison. BA, NYU, 1968, JD, 1971. Bar: N.Y. 1971. Ptnr. Summit Rovins & Feldesman, N.Y.C., 1971-86; ptnr., head bankruptcy & reorganization practice group Proskauer Rose LLP, NYC, 1986—. Lecturer Turnaround Industry Conference, US Trustee Symposium, Am. Bankruptcy Inst., Inst. for Internat. Rsch. Mem. Bar Assn. City N.Y., Bankruptcy Lawyers Bar Assn.; fellow Am. Coll. of Bankruptcy Lawyers. Office: Proskauer Rose LLP 1585 Broadway Fl 27 New York NY 10036-8299

HYMAN, ALBERT LEWIS, cardiologist, educator; b. New Orleans, Nov. 10, 1923; s. David and Mary (Newstadt) Hyman; m. Neil Steiner, Mar. 27, 1964; 1 child, Albert Arthur. BS, La. State U., 1943; MD, 1945; postgrad., U. Cin., U. Paris, U. London, Eng. Diplomate Am. Bd. Internal Medicine. Intern Charity Hosp., 1945-46, resident, 1947-49, sr. vis. physician, 1959-63; resident Cin. Gen. Hosp., 1946-47; instr. medicine La. State U., 1950-56, asst. prof. medicine, 1956-57; asst. prof. Tulane U., 1957-59, assoc. prof., 1959-63, assoc. prof. surgery, 1963-70, prof. rsch. surgery in cardiology, 1970—, prof. clin. medicine Med. Sch., 1983—, adj. prof. pharmacology Med. Sch., 1974—, dir. Cardiac Catheterization Lab., 1957—, Mayerson meml. lectr. in physiology, 2000; prof. medicine in cardiology La. State U. Sch. Medicine. Vis. physician Touro Hosp., Touro Infirmary, electrocardiographer; vis. physician Hotel Dieu Hosp., cons. in cardiology; chief cardiology Sara Mayo Hosp., electrocardiographer; cons. in cardiology USPHS, New Orleans Crippled Children's Hosp., St. Tammany Parish Hosp., VA, Congínton, La., Mercy Hosp., East Jefferson Gen. Hosp., St. Charles Gen. Hosp.; electrocardiographer Metairie Hosp., St. Tammany Hosp.; cons. cardiovasc. disease New Orleans VA Hosp.; cons. cardiology Baton Rouge Gen. Hosp., U.S. Dept. of Justice Fed. Social Security Agy.; Barlow lectr. in medicine U. So. Calif., 1977; mem. internat. sci. com. IV Internat. Symposium Pulmonary Circulation, Charles U., Prague; Mayerson Meml. lectr. dept. physiology Tulane Med. Sch., 1999; Plenary lectr. gene therapy Internat. Congress Pulmonary Circulation, Prague, 1999; vis. prof. SUNY, Stony Brook, 2001, U. S. Ala. Med. Sch., 2001; invited lectr. in field. Mem. editl. bd. Jour. Applied Physiology; contbr. articles to profl. jours. Recipient award for rsch., Hadassah, 1980, Vis. Scientist award, Wellcome Found., U. Coll., London, 1991, Albert Hyman award for excellence in cardiology, Tulane U. Med. Sch., 1997, Disting. Achievement award in sci. and rsch., Orlean Parish Med. Soc., 2001; Tulane Med. Sch. Sect. on Cardiology fellow, 1997. Fellow: ACP, Am. Fedn. Clin. Rsch., Am. Coll. Cardiology, Am. Coll. Chest Physicians; mem.: AAUP, N.Y. Acad. Scis., N.Am. Soc. Pacing and Electrophysiology, Am. Physiol. Soc., New Orleans Surg. Soc. (hon.), So. Med. Soc. (Seale-Harris award 1988), So. Soc. Clin. Investigation (chmn. membership com.), Am. Soc. Pharmacology and Exptl. Therapeutics, La. Heart Assn. (v.p. 1974, Albert L. Hyman Ann. Rsch. award, Wellcome Rsch. Found. Vis. Scientist award U. Coll. London 1992, Disting. Achievement award for outstanding sci. contbns. to cardiopulmonary medicine), Am. Heart Assn. (chmn. sci. com. cardiopulmonary coun. 1981, fellow coun. circulation, fellow coun. clin. cardiology, chmn. cardiopulmonary coun., mem. editl. bd. Circulation Rsch., Jour. Applied Physiology, Am. Jour. Physiology, Heart Disease and Stroke, mem. rsch. com. bd. dirs., mem. coun. cardiopulmonary medicine, regional rep. coun. clin. cardiology, vice-chmn. rsch. com., Dickinson Richards Meml. lectr. 1986, Disting. Sci. Achievement award 1990, Dickinson Richards Meml. lectr. 1992, Disting. Achievement award 1992, Disting. Sci. Achievement award 1993, Disting. Achievement award 1993), Alpha Omega Alpha. Achievements include research in cardiopulmonary circulation. Home: 5467 Marcia Ave New Orleans LA 70124-1052 Office: 3601 Prytania St New Orleans LA 70115-3610 Office Phone: 504-891-6037. Business E-Mail: aahyman@tulane.edu.

HYMAN, BETTY HARPOLE, technology executive; b. Jasper, Tex., Nov. 20, 1938; d. Russell Charles and John Francis (Hilton) Harpole; m. Arthur Siegmar Hyman (dec.); children: Norma Sullivan, Eric, Jonathan, Lee Ann. BA in Psychology, U. Tex., San Antonio, 1979. Spl. project coord. Tex. Stores, San Antonio, 1975-79; communications cons. Southwestern Bell Tel., Midland, Tex. and San Antonio, 1980-82; tech. cons. AT&T/Lucent Technologies, San Antonio, 1983-85;, 1988-2000; ret., 2000; tech. cons. Intelliserve Corp., Dallas, 1987-88; cons. IMS Group, San Antonio, 1985-87; comms. specialist W/IG Comms., 2001—; with IG Comms. Vol., mem. devel. com. San Antonio Spl. Olympics, 1985—; mem. devel. com. San Antonio Conservation Soc., 1975—, San Antonio World Affairs Coun., 1985—92, 1994—; mentor Coaching for Success, 2000—01; mem. Alamo Metro Chorus, 2002—; sec. bd. trustees Unity Ch., 2001—; bd. dirs. South Tex. Children's Habilitation Ctr., San Antonio, 1985—87, bd. trustees, 2003—; mem. Riverfront Task Force in Asheville. Mem. Am. Bus. Women's Assn. (program com. 1987-88), Tex. Tennis Assn. (ranked player 1976-90), Prime Time Tennis Club (v.p. 1985-86), Blue Ridge Dance Club (pres. 1993-94). Republican. Mem. Unity Ch. Avocations: tennis, scuba diving, dance, aerobics. Home: 14223 Savannah Pass San Antonio TX 78216

HYMAN, BRUCE MALCOLM, ophthalmologist; b. N.Y.C., May 22, 1943; s. Malcolm A. and Sylvia S. H.; AB, Columbia U., 1964; MD, NYU, 1968. Intern in surgery Albert Einstein Coll. Medicine/Bronx Mcpl. Hosp., 1968-69; resident in ophthalmology Manhattan Eye, Ear and Throat Hosp., N.Y.C., 1971-74; pvt. practice medicine specializing in ophthalmology, N.Y.C., 1974—; tchr. attending surgeon Manhattan Eye, Ear and Throat Hosp., 1974—; med. cons. U.S. Seaplane Pilots Assn., 1975—, Health Ins. Plan Greater N.Y., 1977—; ophthalmologist to Hotel Trades Coun., Hotel Assn. N.Y.C., 1974—; attending ophthalmologist Roosevelt Hosp., N.Y.C., 1979—, dir. adult outpatient ophthalmology, 1980—; police surgeon N.Y.C., 1977—, dep. chief police surgeon, 1978—; attending ophthalmologist Doctors Hosp., 1979—, Le Roy Hosp., 1979—, St. Luke's Hosp., 1980—; outpatient ophthalmologist N.Y. Hosp., 1975-77; clin. ophthalmologist Columbia Coll. Physicians and Surgeons, 1981—. Served with USPHS, 1969-71. Diplomate

Am. Bd. Ophthalmology. Fellow ACS; mem. N.Y. State, N.Y. County med. socs., Am. Acad. Ophthalmology and Otolaryngology. Contbr. articles to profl. jours. Office: 133 E 64th St New York NY 10021-7045

HYMAN, EARLE, actor, educator; b. Rocky Mount, N.C., Oct. 11, 1926; s. Zachariah and Maria Lilly (Plummer) H. Student, Bklyn. pub. schs. Tchr. Herbert Berghof Sch. Acting, N.Y.C., 1957—, councilor Actors Equity Assn., 1956-71. Roles include Rudolf in Anna Lucasta, N.Y.C., 1943-45, Mister Johnson in Mister Johnson, N.Y.C., 1956, Othello, Am. Shakespeare Festival, Stratford, Conn., 1957, Oscar in The Lady from Dubuque, N.Y.C., 1980, James Tyrone in Long Day's Journey Into Night, N.Y.C., 1981, Russell Huxtable in The Cosby Show, Cherry Orchard, N.Y.C., 2005. Recipient award Theatre World, 1956; recipient Actors Studio, 1980, Gry Statuette Husmodres Teater Forening, Oslo, 1965 Mem. Actors Equity Assn., Screen Actors Guild, AFTRA Clubs: Players (N.Y.C.). Democrat. Episcopalian. Home: 484 W 43rd St Apt 33E New York NY 10036-6331

HYMAN, HAROLD M., history professor, consultant; b. Bklyn., July 24, 1924; s. Abraham and Rebecca (Hermann) H.; m. Ferne Beverly Handelsman, Mar. 11, 1946; children: Lee Rosenthal, Ann Root, William Hyman. BA with honors, U. Calif. L.A., 1948; MA, Columbia U., 1950, PhD, 1952; LHD (hon.), Lincoln Coll., 1984. summer instr. Columbia U., 1953, U. Wash., 1960, Bklyn. Coll., 1962, U. Chgo., 1965; vis. asst. prof. UCLA, 1955-56; sr. Fulbright lectr. in Am. History and Law, grad. faculty polit. sci. U. Tokyo, 1973; faculty of law Keio U., 1973; adj. prof. legal history Bates Coll. Law U. Houston, 1977, of Am. legal history U. Tex. Law Sch., 1986; Meyer vis. disting. prof. legal history NYU Sch. Law, 1982-83; cons. and spkr. in field. Asst. prof. Earlham Coll., 1952-55; assoc. prof. Ariz. State U., 1956-57; prof. UCLA, 1957-63, U. Ill., 1963-68; William P. Hobby Prof. History Rice U., 1968-96, William P. Hobby prof. history emeritus, 1997—. Speaker in field. Author: Era of the Oath: Northern Loyalty Tests During the Civil War and Reconstruction (Albert J. Beveridge award Am. Hist. Assn. 1981), 1954, To Try Men's Souls: Loyalty Tests in American History (Sidney Hillman Found. prize 1960), 1981, Stanton: The Life and Times of Lincoln's Secretary of War, 1962, Soldiers and Spruce: Origins of the Loyal Legion of Loggers and Lumbermen: The Army's Labor Union of World War I, 1963, A More Perfect Union: The Impact of the Civil War and Reconstruction on the Constitution, 1973, Union and Confidence: The 1860s, 1976, (with William Wiecek) Equal Justice Under Law: Constitutional History, 1833-1880, 1982, paperback, 1983, Quiet Past and Stormy Present? War Powers in American History, 1986, American Singularity: The 1787 Northwest Ordinance, the 1862 Homestead-Morrill Acts, and the 1944 GI Bill, 1986, Oleander Odyssey: The Kempners of Galveston, 1870-1980, (Coral H. Tullis Meml. prize Tex. A&M U. Press 1990, T. R. Fehrenbach Book award Tex. Hist. Comsn. 1990, Ottis Lock Endowment award E. Tex. Hist. Assn. 1991), 1990, The Reconstruction Justice of Salmon P. Chase: In re Turner and Texas v. White, 1997, Character and Craftsmanship: A History of Houston's Vinson & Elkins Law Firm, 1917-1990s, 1998; editor (with Ferne B. Hyman) The Circuit Court Opinions of Salmon Portland Chase, 1972; contbr. numerous articles to profl. jours. Elected lay mem. Houston Bar Assn. Grievance Com., 1985-88; mem. numerous U. coms. The Constitution, Law, and Am. Life in the Nineteenth Century: A conf. named in his honor, Rice U. and NYU Sch. Law, 1989; named U.S. Presdl. appointee to permanent com. Oliver Wendell Holmes Trust, 1993-2001. Mem. Am. Hist. Assn. (numerous coms. and offices), Am. Soc. Legal History (pres . 1993-95), Orgn. Am. Historians (various coms. and offices), So. Hist. Assn. Avocation: fishing. Office: Rice University Dept History-MS 42 PO Box 1892 Houston TX 77251-1892

HYMAN, JEROME ELLIOT, lawyer; b. Rosedale, Miss., Dec. 26, 1923; s. Mose and Mary Ann (Sprecher) H.; m. Isabelle Miller, July 1, 1960. AB, Coll. William and Mary, 1944; LL.B. magna cum laude (Fay diploma), Harvard U., 1947. Bar: N.Y. 1949, D.C. 1960. Mem. fgn. funds control staff Dept. Treasury, U.S. Mil. Govt., Frankfurt and Berlin, Germany, 1945-46; law clk. to judge U.S. Ct. Appeals, Boston, 1947-48; assoc. firm Cleary Gottlieb, Steen & Hamilton LLP, N.Y.C., 1948-58, ptnr., 1959-93, sr. counsel, 1994—; trustee, mem. exec. com. Practising Law Inst., N.Y.C., 1972-97, v.p., 1979-86, pres., 1986-96, chmn. bd. trustees, 1996-97, chmn. emeritus, 1997—; sr. v.p., gen. counsel Pan Am World Airways, Inc., 1982-84. Bd. editors: Harvard Law Rev., 1945-47. Pres. Lexington Dem. Club, N.Y.C., 1956-58; counsel N.Y. Com. for Stevenson, 1956; del. various Dem. state and jud. convs.; alumni mem. Harvard Law Sch. Placement Com., 1976-79; nat. chmn. maj. gifts com. Harvard Law Sch. Fund, 1978-80; mem. overseers com. to visit Harvard Law Sch., 1986-92; trustee Lawyers' Com. for Civil Rights Under Law, 1981—; trustee Citizens Budget Commn., N.Y.C., 1991-94, trustee emeritus, 1994—; trustee Endowment Assn. of the Coll. of William and Mary, 1997-03, trustee emeritus, 2003—; mem. dean's adv. bd. Harvard Law Sch., 2000—, exec. com., 2003—. Fellow Am. Bar Found., Phi Beta Kappa Soc.; mem. ABA, Assn. Bar City N.Y. (chmn. com. corp. law 1984-87), Am. Law Inst., Am. Judicature Soc., N.Y. County Lawyers Assn., Tribar Opinion Commn., Harvard Law Sch. Assn. N.Y.C. (trustee 1980-83, v.p. 1984-85, pres. 1985-86), Nat. Harvard Law Sch. Assn. (mem. coun. 1990-93, mem. exec. com. 1991-93), Sky Club. Home: 1125 Park Ave Apt 10B New York NY 10128-1243 Office: Cleary Gottlieb Steen & Hamilton LLP One Liberty Plaza New York NY 10006-1470 Office Phone: 212-225-2010. E-mail: jehyman23@hotmail.com, jhyman@cgsh.com.

HYMAN, LAWRENCE ROBERT, psychiatrist; b. Amsterdam, N.Y., Dec. 7, 1940; s. Morris Arthur and Bertha (Berkman) H.; m. Lois Armstrong Wilson, June 27, 1978; children: Elyse Michelle, Michael Louis, Joshua William. BA, Ohio Wesleyan U., 1963; MD, Chgo. Med. Sch., 1968. Intern then resident U. Wis., Madison, 1968-72; guest worker NIH, Bethesda, Md., 1973-76; asst. prof. Johns Hopkins Sch. Medicine, Balt., 1976-78; resident George Washington U., Washington, 1978-80; asst. clin. prof. U. Md., Balt., 1981-84; pvt. practice Columbia, Md., 1981—; active staff dept. psychiatry Howard County Gen. Hosp., Columbia, Md., 1981—; CEO Orchard Hill Treatment Ctr. for Chem. Dependency, Columbia, 1987-93; CEO, med. dir. Howard Behavioral Health, Inc., 2003—; med. dir. Lawrence R. Hyman MD and Assocs., 1993—, Vis. Speakers Bureau, Lilly, Forest & Wyeth Pharm. Cos., 2003—. Cons. Family Therapy Inst., Rockville, Md., others; bd. dirs. Closecall Am., Inc. Contbg. editor Gould Med. Dictionary, 1979; contbr. articles to profl. jours. Adv. bd. Nat. Kidney Found., Balt., 1971. Maj. M.C., AUS, 1972-76. Recipient USPHS Rsch. Career Devel. award, 1977; NIH fellow, 1972; NIH grantee. Mem. Am. Psychiat. Assn., Md. Psychiat. Soc., Med. and Chirurgical Faculty State of Md., Howard County Med. Soc., Am. Orthopsychiat. Assn. Avocations: sailing, marathons. Home: 3681 Folly Quarter Rd Ellicott City MD 21042-1452 Office: # 201 11055 Little Patuxent Pky Columbia MD 21044

HYMAN, LEONARD STEPHEN, financial consultant, economist, writer; b. N.Y.C., June 5, 1940; s. Milton and Elsie (Reiter) Hyman; m. Judith N. Siegel, July 4, 1965; children: Andrew S., Robert C. BA, N.Y. U., 1961; MA, Cornell U., 1965. Fin. analyst Chase Manhattan Bank, N.Y.C., 1965-72; ptnr. H.C. Wainwright & Co., N.Y.C., 1972-77; v.p. Wainwright Securities, N.Y.C., 1977-78; v.p., head utility rsch. group Merrill Lynch Capital Markets, N.Y.C., 1978-94, 1st v.p., 1987-94; pres. Pvt. Sector Advisors, Inc., Sleepy Hollow, NY, 1994—. Mem. lunar energy enterprise case study task force NASA, 1988—89; mem. bd. advisors Electric Power Rsch. Inst., 1993—99, Enertech Capital, 1999—, Excelergy, 2000—, Internat. Found. Rsch. Exptl. Econ., 2000—; mng. dir. Fulcrum Internat., Ltd., 1995—96; sr. industry advisor Salomon Smith Barney, Inc., 1997—2002; sr. assoc. cons. R. J. Rudden Assocs., 2002—. Author: America's Electric Utilities, 1983; co-author: The New Telecommunications Industry, 1987, The Water Business, 1998, A Blueprint for Transmission, 1999; editor: The Privatization of Public Utilities, 1995; contbr.: Electric Power Strategic Issues, 1983, The Future of Electrical Energy, 1986, Deregulation and Diversification of Utilities, 1988, The Electric Industry in Transition, 1994, The Virtual Utility, 1997, Power Systems Restructuring, 1998, Pricing in Competitive Electricity Markets, 2000; contbr. articles to profl. jours.; mem. editl. bd. Forum for Applied Research and Public Policy, 1993—2002, Cogeneration and Competitive Power Jour., 1999—2002. Mem. adv. com. U.S. Congress-Office Tech. Assessment, Washington, 1983, 1986—87, 1987—88, 1992—93; mem. elec. reliability panel N.Am. Elec. Reliability Coun., 1997; mem. Pa. Task Force Electric Utility Efficiency, Harrisburg, 1982—83. Mem.: AAAS, Inst. Chartered Fin. Analysts, Fin. Analysts Fedn., N.Y. Soc. Security Analysts, Soc. Utility Regulatory Fin. Analysts (bd. dirs.), Phi Beta Kappa. Democrat. Jewish. Avocations: travel, bicycling, music, canoeing. Home and Office: Private Sector Advisors Inc 34 Fremont Rd Tarrytown NY 10591-1118 Office Phone: 631-348-4090 x238. Business E-Mail: lhyman@rjrudden.com.

HYMAN, LESTER SAMUEL, lawyer; b. Providence, July 14, 1931; s. Carl and Alice (Adelman) H.; m. Helen Reeder Sidman, Sept. 19, 1959 (div. 1982); children: David, Andrew, Elizabeth. AB, Brown U., 1952; LLB, Columbia U., 1955. Bar: D.C. 1955, Mass. 1955, U.S. Supreme Ct. 1957. Atty. SEC, Washington, 1955-57; chief asst. to Gov. State of Mass., Boston, 1962-64, sec. commerce, 1964-65; sr. cons. HUD, Washington, 1966-67; ptnr. Leva, Hawes & Symington, Washington, 1969-82; founding ptnr. Swidler & Berlin, Washington, 1982—, sr. of counsel. Lectr. John F. Kennedy Sch. Govt. Harvard U., 1968-69; bd. dirs. CDS Internat., 1988-94. mem. Internat. Oberver Team for nat. election in Haiti, 1990. Author: U.S. Policy Towards Liberia, 1822-2003: Unintended Consequences?, 2003. Bd. dirs. Ctr. Nat. Policy, Washington, 1980—; bd. advisors Close-Up Found.; bd. govs. Am. Jewish Commn., 1980-84; Dem. chmn., Mass., 1967-69, del. Dem. Nat. Conv., 1968, mem. Dem. Charter Reform Commn., 1970, D.C. Cmty. Humanities, 1988-90; bd. dirs. C.C. of Brit. V.I., 1989—, Young Artists, 1989-94; mem. adv. bd. Internat. legal Studies Program, Washington Coll. Law, Am. U., 1990—; apptd. by Pres. Clinton to Franklin Delano Roosevelt Meml. Commn., 1994; trustee Norton Simon Mus. of Art, Pasadena, Calif., 1995-97, U. D.C. Found, 2002; mem. U.S. Presdl. Del. to Guatamalan Peace Accord Signing, 1996; bd. dirs. Brit. V.I. Nat. Park Trust, 1999. Named Outstanding Young Man of Yr., Greater Boston Jr. C. of C., 1964. Mem. Performing Artists Soc. Am. (mng. dir. 1997), Internat. Intellectual Property Inst. (dir. 1998—). Home: 3826 Van Ness St NW Washington DC 20016-2228 Office: Swidler Berlin 3000 K St NW Ste 300 Washington DC 20007-5116 Office Phone: 202-424-7509. E-mail: lshyman@aol.com, lshyman@swidlaw.com.

HYMAN, LEWIS NEIL, investment company executive, investment advisor; b. Johnstown, Pa., Aug. 5, 1949; s. Albert and Helene (Rose) H.; 1 child, Hannah Rose. BA magna cum laude, U. Pitts., 1971, JD, 1974. Bar: Pa. 1974, U.S. Dist. Ct. 1974, U.S. Supreme Ct. 1974; registered investment advisor. Asst. dist. atty. Allegheny County Dist. Atty.'s Office, Pitts., 1974-79; pvt. practice lawyer Pitts., 1979-82, 89-91; investment banker Smith Barney, N.Y.C., Phila., 1982-86; v.p. investment banking and market devel. FGIC, Inc., N.Y.C., 1987-89; pres. The Hartwood Group, Pitts., 1991—, Hartwood Advisors, Inc., Pitts., 1991—; officer Strategic Benefits Group, Inc., Pitts., 1991-95. Lectr. U. Pitts., 1989-91, Allegheny C.C., Pitts., 1989-91, Pa. State U., Pitts., 19890-91, Joseph M. Katz Grad. Sch. Bus./U. Pitts., 1995. Bd. trustees Jewish Chronicle, Ctrl. Scholarship & Loan Referral Svc., Temple Sinai. Univ. scholar U. Pitts., 1971. Mem.: Pa. Bar Assn., Phi Beta Kappa. Avocations: tennis, golf, swimming, photography, sculpture, skiing. Office: The Hartwood Group 5401 Walnut St Pittsburgh PA 15232-2276 Office Phone: 412-687-4800. Personal E-mail: lhyman@att.net.

HYMAN, MARY BLOOM, science education programs coordinator; m. Sigmund M. Hyman, 1947 (dec.); children: Carol Hyman Piccinini, Nancy Louise. BA, Goucher Coll., 1971; MS, Johns Hopkins U., 1977. Asst. dir. Edn. Md. Sci. Ctr., Balt., 1976-81, dir. edn., 1981-90; coord. sci. edn. programs Loyola Coll., Balt., 1990—, coord. Inst. for Child Care Edn., 1992—. Trustee Goucher Coll., Balt. Mus. Art; bd. dirs. Balt. Sch.-Age Child Care Alliance, Johns Hopkins U. Ctr. Talented Youth; mem. Gov.'s Task Force on Compensation of Child Care Providers, 1995-96. Recipient Disting. Women award Gov.'s Office, Annapolis, Md., 1981; Meritorious Svc. award Johns Hopkins U., 1983; Outstanding Svc. to Sci. Edn. award. Assn. Sci. Dept. Chairmen Balt. County Pub. Schs., 1989. Mem. Md. Assn. Sci. Tchrs. (bd. dirs.), Phi Beta Kappa, Phi Delta Kappa. Home: 10815 Longacre Ln Stevenson MD 21153-0665 E-mail: mhyman@loyola.edu.

HYMAN, MICHAEL BRUCE, lawyer; b. Elgin, Ill., July 26, 1952; s. Robert I. and Ruth Hyman; m. Leslie Bland, Aug. 14, 1977; children: Rachel Joy, David Adam. BSJ with honors, Northwestern U., 1974, JD, 1977. Bar: Ill. 1977, U.S. Supreme Ct. 1989. Asst. atty. gen. Antitrust div. State of Ill., Chgo., 1977-79; trial atty. Much Shelist Freed Denenberg Ament & Rubenstein, Chgo., 1979-85, ptnr., 1985—. Chmn. panelist various continuing legal edn. seminars. Columnist Editor's Briefcase, CBA Record, 1988-90, 93—2004, The Red Pencil, 1986-89; contbr. chpt. to book, articles to profl. jours.; host (cable TV program) You and the Law, 1995-2004. Trustee North Shore Congregation Israel, Glencoe, 1980-89, 95-2001, v.p., 1987-89. Mem.: ABA (assoc. editor 1985—89, sect. litig., chmn. antitrust litig. com. 1987—90, mng. editor 1989—90, editor-in-chief Litig. News 1990—92, task force on civil justice reform 1991—93, chmn. monographs and unpub. papers com. 1992—95, editor-in-chief Litig. Docket 1995—2001, Tips From the Trenches 2001—02, jud. divsn. mem. chair 2002—04, chmn. consumer and personal rights litig. com. 2002—, exec. com. lawyer's conf. 2002—, jud. divsn. ann. meeting. co-chair 2004—05), Chgo. Bar Found. (bd. dirs. 2003—), Decalogue Soc. Lawyers (co-chair CLE programs 2001—04, trustee 2001—, fin. sec. 2002—03, rec. sec. 2003—04, pres. 2004—05), Am. Soc. Writers on Legal Subjects (chair book award com. 1997—, bd. dirs. 2004—), Ill. Bar Assn. (antitrust coun. 1981—87, vice chair, sec., co-editor newsletter 1982—85, chmn. coun. 1985—86, rep. on assembly 1986—92, chmn. bench and bar sect. coun. 1990—91, professionalism com. 1992—95, chair 1993—94, rep. on assembly 1994—99, vice chair ARDC com. 1995—96, cable TV com. 1995—, chair ARDC com. 1996—97, chair 1997—99, bench and bar sect. coun. 1998—2003, rep. on assembly 2001—04), Chgo. Bar Assn. (editor-in-chief CBA record 1988—90, 1992—94, CBA News 1994—98, vice-chair class action com. 1999—2000, chair 2000—01, bd. mgrs. 2003—04, 2d v.p. 2003—04, editor-in-chief CBA record 2003—, 1st v.p. 2004—05, pres. 2005—). Jewish. Avocations: writing, Abraham Lincoln. Office: Much Shelist Freed Denenberg Ament & Rubenstein 191 N Wacker Dr Ste 1800 Chicago IL 60606-1615 Office Phone: 312-521-2000. Business E-Mail: mbhyman@muchshelist.com.

HYMAN, MILTON BERNARD, lawyer; b. L.A., Nov. 19, 1941; s. Herbert and Lillian (Rakowitz) Hyman; m. Sheila Goldman, July 4, 1965; children: Lauren Davida, Micah Howard. BA in Econs. with highest honors, UCLA, 1963; JD magna cum laude, Harvard U., 1966. Bar: Calif. 1967. Assoc. Irell & Manella LLP, L.A., 1970-73, ptnr., 1973—. Co-author: Partnerships and Associations: A Policy Critique of the Morrisey Regulations, 1976, Consolidated Returns: Summary of Tax Considerations in Acquisition of Common Parent of Subsidiary Member of Affiliated Group, 1980, Tax Aspects of Corporate Debt Exchanges, Recapitalization and Discharges, 1982, Tax Strategies for Leveraged Buyouts and Other Corporate Acquisitions, 1986, Preservation and Use of Net Operating Losses and Other Tax Attributes in a Consolidated Return Context, rev. edit., 1992, Collier on Bankruptcy Taxation, 1992, Real Estate Workouts and Bankruptcies, 1993, Current Corporate Bankruptcy Tax Issues, 1993, Tax Strategies for Corporate Acquisitions, Dispositions, Financing, Joint Ventures, Reorganizations, and Restructurings, 1995; author: A Transactional Encounter with the Partnership Rules of Subchapter K: The Effects of the Tax Reform Act of 1984, 1984, Net Operating Losses and Other Tax Attributed of Corporate Clients, 1987. Past pres., bd. dirs. Sinai Temple, West Los Angeles, Calif. Capt. JAGC, U.S. Army, 1967-70. Sheldon traveling fellow Harvard U., 1966-67. Mem. ABA (chmn. com. affiliated and related corps. 1981-83, chmn. corp. tax com. 1999-2000), Calif. State Bar Assn., Am. Law Inst. (fed. income tax project tax adv. group 1976—), Masons, Phi Beta Kappa. Jewish. Office: Irell & Manella LLP Ste 900 1800 Avenue Of The Stars Los Angeles CA 90067-4276

HYMAN, MORTON PETER, private equity investment company executive; b. NYC, Jan. 9, 1936; s. Irving S. and Dora (Pfeffer) H.; m. Chris Oliphant Stern, Mar. 18, 1979; children: Sarah Anne, David Jacob. BA, Cornell U., 1956, LLD with distinction, 1959; DHL (hon.), N.Y. Med. Coll. Bar: N.Y. 1960. Assoc. Proskauer Rose Goetz & Mendelsohn, N.Y.C., 1959-63; officer, dir. Overseas Discount Corp., N.Y.C., 1963—2002, Overseas Shipholding Group, Inc., N.Y.C., 1969—2003, CEO, 1999—2003, also chmn., bd. dirs.; CEO MPH Enterprises, LLC, N.Y.C., 2003—. Vice chmn. bd. Discount Bank and Trust Co., 1999-2002. Bd. editors Cornell Law Rev. Vice-chmn. N.Y. State Health Planning Commn., 1977-78; mem. Pub. Health Coun. N.Y., 1971-95, vice chmn., 1975-85, chmn., 1985-95; co-chmn. N.Y. State Health Issues Forum; chmn. N.Y. State Health Care Capital Policy Adv. Com., 1982-94; chmn. bd. trustees Beth Israel Med. Ctr., Continuum Health Ptnrs, Inc.; chmn. bd. trustees St. Luke's-Roosevelt Hosp. Ctr.; vice chmn. N.Y. Eye and Ear Infirmary; vice-chmn. bd. regents L.I. Coll Hosp.; chmn. N.Y. State Joint Exec. and Legis. Task Force on Delivery of Health Care, 1977-80; chmn. N.Y. State Joint Exec. and Legis. Com. on Residential Health Care Facilities, 1977-80; trustee The Brearley Sch., 1993-97; mem. pres. coun. United Hosp. Fund; bd. dirs. United Jewish Appeal Fedn., 1986-91; mem. bd. overseers Albert Einstein Coll. Medicine of Yeshiva U. 2d lt. AUS, 1956-57. Fellow N.Y. Acad. Medicine; mem. N.Y. Bar Assn., Harmonie Club, Order of Coif, Phi Kappa Phi. Republican. Home: 998 5th Ave New York NY 10028-0102 Office: MPH Enterprises LLC 667 Madison Ave New York NY 10021 Office Phone: 212-317-1111.

HYMAN, PAULA E(LLEN), history professor; b. Boston; d. Sydney Max and Ida Frances (Tatelman) H.; m. Stanley Harvey Rosenbaum, June 7, 1969; children: Judith Hyman Rosenbaum, Adina Hyman Rosenbaum. BJED, Hebrew Coll., Brookline, Mass., 1966; BA, Radcliffe Coll., 1968; MA, Columbia U., 1970, PhD, 1975; degree (hon.), Jewish Theol. Sem., 2002. Asst. prof. Columbia U., N.Y.C., 1974-81; assoc. prof. history Jewish Theol. Sem., N.Y.C., 1981-86; dean. Sem., Coll. Jewish Studies, 1981-86; Lady Davis vis. assoc. prof. Hebrew U., Jerusalem, 1986; Lucy Moses prof. history Yale U., New Haven, 1986—. Author: From Dreyfus to Vichy, 1979, The Emancipation of the Jews of Alsace, 1991, Gender and Assimilation in Modern Jewish History, 1995, The Jews of Modern France, 1998; co-author: The Jewish Woman in America, 1976; co-editor: The Jewish Family: Myths and Reality, 1986, Jewish Women in America: An Historical Encyclopedia, 2 vols., 1997; editor: My Life as a Radical Jewish Woman, 2002; series editor Ind. U. Press, Bloomington, 1982—; contbg. editor Sh'ma Mag., N.Y.C., 1977—; contbr. articles to publs. Vice chmn. Zionist Acad. Coun., N.Y.C., 1982-83. NEH summer grantee, 1977; Am. Coun. Learned Socs. fellow, 1978; grantee N.Y. Coun. for Humanities, 1980; NEH fellow, 1986-87. Fellow Am. Acad. Jewish Rsch. (treas. 1995—, v.p. 1999-); mem. Am. Hist. Assn. (com. 1983), Assn. for Jewish Studies (bd. dirs. 1978-81, 83-85, 86—, v.p. for membership 1995-97), Nat. Found. Jewish Culture (chair acad. adv. com. 1996—), Leo Baeck Inst. (bd. dirs. 1979—), Yivo Inst. for Jewish Rsch., Phi Beta Kappa. Jewish. Office: Yale U Dept History New Haven CT 06520

HYMAN, ROGER DAVID, lawyer; b. Oak Ridge, Tenn., Apr. 23, 1957; s. Marshall Leonard and Vera Lorraine (McKinney) H.; m. Elsa Laurencio; children: Cristina Alicia, James Marshall. BA, Vanderbilt U., 1979; JD, U. Tenn., 1984. Clk. Oak Ridge Nat. Lab., 1977-78, 81; air personality, news reporter Stas. WKDA, WKDF, Nashville, 1979; program dir. Sta. WBIR-FM, Knoxville, Tenn., 1979-80; assoc. atty. Hindman & Holt, Attys., Knoxville, Tenn., 1984-85; asst. atty. gen. State of Tenn., Knoxville, 1986-95; with Law Offices of Roger D. Hyman Powell, Tenn., 1995-97; ptnr. Hyman & Carter, PLLC, Powell, Tenn., 1997—. Bd. dirs. Knoxville Christian Sch., 1991-93. Democrat. Mem. Ch. of Christ. Home: 2713 Windemere Ln Powell TN 37849-3782 Office: Hyman & Carter PLLC PO Box 1304 Powell TN 37849-1304 Office Phone: 865-947-0533. Personal E-mail: RDHymanLAW@aol.com.

HYMAN, SEYMOUR C(HARLES), university president; b. N.Y.C., June 3, 1919; s. Jack and Rose (Bernhardt) H.; m. Charlotte Bank, June 26, 1943; children— Carol Joan, Judith Fay. B.Ch.E., CCNY, 1939; M.Sc., Va. Poly. Inst., 1940; PhD, Columbia U., 1950. Registered profl. engr., N.Y., N.J. Engr. Ashland Oil and Refining Co., Ky., 1940-42; prin. engr. Signal Corps Labs., Ft. Monmouth, N.J., 1942-47; dep. chancellor City U. N.Y., 1947-77; pres. William Paterson U. N.J., Wayne, 1977-85. Cons. Atomic Power Reactors, 1950-66 Mem. River Edge Regional Sch. Bd., 1960-61. E-mail: seycha@comcast.net. *I have two guidelines. I have individual and final responsibility for everything I do or not do. I am proud to be identified with my work product.*

HYMAN, STEVEN EDWARD, academic administrator, physiatrist, educator; BA summa cum laude, Yale U., 1974; BA with honors, MA in History and Philosophy of Sci., U. Cambridge, Eng., 1976; MD cum laude, Harvard U., 1980. Diplomate Am. Bd. Psychiatry and Neurology. Intern in medicine Mass. Gen. Hosp., Boston, 1980-81, clin. and rsch. fellow in endocrinology and neurology, 1983-84, rsch. fellow in molecular biology, 1984-88, dir. rsch. dept. psychiatry, 1990-96, dir. divsn. addictions, 1992-95, supr. psychiatric residents, 1984—, dir. neurosci. and biolo. psychiatry curriculum for residents, lectr., 1986—; clin. fellow in medicine Harvard U., Boston, 1980-81, clin. fellow in psychiatry, 1981-84, rsch. fellow in genetics, 1984-87; from instr. in psychiatry to asst. prof. psychiatry Harvard Med. Sch., Boston, 1987-92, assoc. prof. psychiatry, 1993-98, prof. psychiatry, 1998—; dir. NIMH, Rockville, Md., 1996—2001; provost Harvard U., Cambridge, Mass., 2001—. Mem. sci. coun. NARSAD, 1996—; mem. adv. com. Howard Hughes Med. Inst., 1998—, Riken Brain Scis. Inst., Tokyo. Author: (with G.W. Arana) Handbook of Psychiatric Drug Therapy, 1987, 2d edit., 1991, 3d edit. (with G.W. Arana, J.R. Rosenbaum), 1995, (with E. Nestler) The Molecular Foundations of Psychiatry, 1993, Molecular Neuropharmacology: Foundation for Clinical Neuroscience, 2001; editor numerous textbooks; mem. editl. bd. Jour. Geriat. Psychiatry and Neurology, 1987-96, Psychosomatics, 1988-96, Harvard Rev. Psychiatry, 1992—, Am. Jour. Med. Genetics, 1992—, Jour. Neurochemistry, 1994—, Archives Gen. Psychiatry, 1996—, Molecular Psychiatry, 1996—, Neurobiology of Disease, 1996—. Mellon fellow, 1974-76, Dupont-Warren fellow, 1983-84, Langhlin fellow Am. Coll. Psychiatry, 1983; recipient Laughlin award Nat. Psychiatric Endowment Fund, 1984, Physician Scientist award NIDDK, 1985-90, Philip Isenberg award for best tchr. selected by graduating residents McLean Hosp., 1985, Rsch. Scientist Devel. award level 2, 1995-96. Mem. APA, Am. Coll. Neuropsychopharmacology, Soc. Neurosci., Soc. Biolo. Psychiatry; Fellow, Am. Academy Arts & Sciences, 2004. Office: Harvard U Massachusetts Hall Cambridge MA 02138*

HYMAN, URSULA H., lawyer; BA, Immaculate Heart Coll., 1973; MEd, Loyola Marymount Coll., 1977; JD, U. So. Calif., 1983. Bar: Calif. 1983. With Latham & Watkins, L.A., 1983—, ptnr., 1990—. Founding mem. ad hoc com. Chpt. 9 Reform. Bd. dirs. Calif. Philharmonic. Named LA Super Lawyers, LA Mag., 2004, 2005. Mem.: ABA, L.A. Women's Lawyers Assns., Nat. Assn. Bond Lawyers, L.A. County Bar Assn., State Bar Calif., Order of the Coif. Office: Latham and Watkins LLP 633 W Fifth St Ste 4000 Los Angeles CA 90071 Office Phone: 213-485-1234. Business E-Mail: ursula.hyman@lw.com.

HYMEL, L(EZIN) J(OSEPH), lawyer, former prosecutor; b. Baton Rouge, July 2, 1944; s. Lezin Joseph Sr. and Alma K. Hymel; m. Linda N. Hymel, Oct. 6, 1973; children: Traci Lyn, Shea Roach Bonaventure, Kimberly Kaye. BS in Geology, La. State U., 1966, JD, 1969. Bar: La., U.S. Dist. Ct. (ea. dist.) La., U.S. Dist. Ct. (mid. dist.) La., U.S. Dist. Ct. (we. dist.) La., U.S. Ct. Appeals (5th cir.). Pvt. practice, Baton Rouge, 1969—70; staff atty. Office State Atty. Gen., Baton Rouge, 1970—71, asst. atty. gen., 1972—78, dir. criminal divsn., 1992—93; asst. dist. atty. Office 19 Jud. Dist. Atty., Baton Rouge, 1978—79; city judge Baton Rouge City Ct., 1980—83; state dist. ct. judge criminal divsn. 19th Jud. Dist. Ct, Baton Rouge, 1983—90, state dist. ct. judge civil divsn., 1991—92; U.S. atty. Office U.S. Atty., Dept. Justice, Baton Rouge, 1994—2001; ptnr. Sharp Hymel Cerniglia Calvin Weaver & Davis, Baton Rouge, 2001—. Office: Sharp Hymel Cerniglia et al Ste C 15171 So Harrells Ferry Rd Baton Rouge LA 70816 Fax: (225) 755-1065. Office Phone: 225-755-1060. E-mail: ljhymel@sharphenry.com.

HYMES, DELL HATHAWAY, anthropologist, educator; b. Portland, Oreg., June 7, 1927; s. Howard Hathaway and Dorothy (Bowman) H.; m. Virginia Margaret Dosch, Apr. 10, 1954; 1 adopted child, Robert Paul; children: Alison Bowman, Kenneth Dell; 1 stepchild, Vicki (Mrs. David Unruh). BA, Reed Coll., 1950; MA, Ind. U., 1953, PhD, 1955; postgrad., UCLA, 1954-55; degree (hon.), U. Turino, Italy, 2002, U. Mass., Amherst, 2005. From instr. to asst. prof. Harvard U., 1955-60; from assoc. prof. to prof. U. Calif., Berkeley, 1960—65; prof. anthropology U. Pa., 1965-72, prof. folklore and linguistics, 1972-88, prof. sociology, 1974-88, prof. edn., 1975-88, dean Grad. Sch. Edn., 1975-87; prof. anthropology and English U. Va., 1987-90, Commonwealth prof. anthropology, 1990-98, Commonwealth prof. English, 1990-98, emeritus, 1998—. Bd. dirs. Social Sci. Rsch. Coun., 1965-67, 69-70, 71-72. Author: Language in Culture and Society, 1964, The Use of Computers in Anthropology, 1965, Studies in Southwestern Ethnolinguistics, 1967, Pidginization and Creolization of Languages, 1971, Reinventing Anthropology, 1972, Foundations in Sociolinguistics, 1974, Soziolinguistik, 1980, Language in Education, 1980, In Vain I Tried to Tell You, 1981, (with John Fought) American Structuralism, 1981, Essays in the History of Linguistic Anthropology, 1983, Vers la Competence de Communication, 1984, Ethnography, Linguistics, Narrative Inequality, 1996, Now I Know Only So Far, 2003; assoc. editor: Jour. History Behavioral Scis., 1966-93, Am. Jour. Sociology, 1977-80, Jour. Pragmatics, 1977—; contbg. editor: Alcheringa, 1973-80, Theory and Society, 1976-96; editor: Language in Society, 1972-92; poetry editor Anthropology and Humanism, 2003-05. Trustee Ctr. for Applied Linguistics, 1973-78. With AUS, 1945-47. Fellow Ctr. Advanced Study Behavioral Scis., 1957-58, Fellow Clare Hall, Cambridge, Eng., Guggenheim fellow, 1969-70, Nat. Endowment for Humanities sr. fellow, 1972-73. Fellow Am. Acad. Arts and Scis., Am. Folklore Soc. (pres. 1973-74), Brit. Acad.; mem. Am. Anthrop. Assn. (exec. bd. 1968-70, pres. 1983), Am. Assn. Applied Linguistics (pres. 1986), Linguistic Soc. Am. (exec. bd. 1967-69, pres. 1982), Coun. on Anthropology and Edn. (pres. 1978), Consortium Social Sci. Assns. (pres. 1984-85), Folklore Fellows Finland. Home: 205 Montvue Dr Charlottesville VA 22901-2022 Personal E-mail: dhymes@adelphia.net.

HYNES, GARRY, theater director; b. Ballaghadereen, Ireland; Grad., U. Coll. Galway; LLD (hon.), Nat. Coun. for Ednl. Awards, Nat. U. Ireland, 1997. Founder Druid Theatre Co., Galway, Ireland, 1975—, artistic dir., 1975—90, 1994—. The Abbey Theatre, 1990—94. Prodns. include: The Playboy of the Western World, Bailegangaire, Conversations on a Homecoming, Wood of the Whispering, 'Tis a Pity She's a Whore, Lovers' Meeting, The Loves of Cass McGuire, The Beauty Queen of Leenane (Tony award for dir. of a play 1998), The Leenane Trilogy, A Whistle in the Dark, King of the Castle, The Plough and the Stars, The Power of Darkness, Famine, Portia Coughlan, The Man of Mode, The Love of the Nightingale, The Colleen Bawn, The Lonesome West, A Skull in Connemara, Mr. Peter's Connections, Sive, 2002, On Raftery's Hill, 2000; dir. Big Maggie, 2001, Crimes of the Heart, 2001, Sharon's Grave, 2003. Recipient award for best dir. The Irish Times/Electricity Supply Bd. Irish Theatre Awards, 2002. Home: 42 Raymond St Dublin 8 Ireland Office: The Druid Theatre Co Chapel Ln Galway Ireland also: RTE Donnybrook Dublin 4 Ireland E-mail: garryhynes@aol.com.

HYNES, HUGH BERNARD NOEL, biologist, educator; b. Devizes, Eng., Dec. 20, 1917; s. Harry George Claude and Anna Minnie Lucy (Meyer) H.; m. Mary Elizabeth Hinks, Oct. 24, 1942 (dec. Jan. 1999); children: Richard Olding, Elisabeth Anne, Andrew John, Julian David. BSc, U. London, 1938, PhD, 1941, DSc, 1958; DSc (hon.), U. Waterloo, 1983, U. New Brunswick, 2003. With Brit. Ministry Agr., 1941, Brit. Colonial Agrl. Ser., 1942-46; faculty U. Liverpool, Eng., 1947-64; prof. biology U. Waterloo, Ont., Can., 1964-83, Disting. prof. emeritus, 1983—. Cons. in field. Author: The Ecology of Running Water; contbr. numerous articles to profl. jours. Decorated Can. Centennial medal; recipient Naumann/Thienemann medal, Internat. Limnological Assn. Fellow Royal Soc. Can.; mem. Freshwater Biol. Assn., Internat. Assn. Theoretical and Applied Limnology, N.Am. Benthol. Soc. Home: 127 Iroquois Pl Waterloo ON Canada N2L 2S6 Personal E-mail: nhynes@sciborg.uwaterloo.ca.

HYNES, MICHAEL JOSEPH, principal, educator; b. Bay Shore, NY, Jan. 1, 1971; s. Joseph Michael and Linda Marie Hynes; m. Allison Jean Smith, Aug. 29, 1998; children: Lily Kathryn, Theodore Joseph. B in Psychology, Bethany Coll., W.Va., 1994; MS in Edn., Dowling Coll., Oakdale, 1998, postgrad., 2003—. Cert. in ednl. adminstrn. Dowling Coll., 2003. Tchr. Verne Critz Primary Sch., E. Patchogue, NY, 1998—2002; asst. prin. Frank P. Long Intermediate Sch., Bellport, NY, 2002—03, Bellport Mid. Sch., NY, 2003—04, prin., 2004—. Mem.: Dowling Coll. Principals Acad., Am. Ednl. Rsch. Assn., Assn. of Supervision and Curriculum Devel. (assoc.), Principals' Ctr. at Harvard Grad. Sch. (assoc.; cert. in urban edn. 2004), Phi Delta Kappa (assoc.). Independent. Roman Catholic. Avocations: golf, tennis, astronomy, research. Office: Bellport Middle School 35 Kreamer Sayville NY 11716 Office Phone: 631-730-1648.

HYNES, PATRICIA MARY, lawyer; b. N.Y.C., Jan. 26, 1942; BA, CUNY, 1963; LLB, Fordham U., 1966. Bar: N.Y. 1966, U.S. Dist. Ct. (so. and ea. dists.) N.Y. 1969, U.S. Ct. Appeals (2d cir.) 1982. Law clk. to Hon. Joseph C. Zavatt U.S. Dist. Ct. (ea. dist.) N.Y., 1966-67; mem. civil divsn. U.S. Dist. Ct. (so. dist.) N.Y., 1967-71, asst. U.S. atty., 1967-82, chief consumer fraud unit, 1971-78, chief ofcl. corruption and spl. pros. unit, 1978-80, exec. asst. U.S. atty., 1980-82; ptnr. Milberg Weiss Bershad Hynes & Lerach LLP, N.Y.C., 1983-99; of counsel Milberg Weiss Bershad & Schulman LLP, N.Y.C., 2000—. Adj. prof. law Fordham U., 1978—83; lectr. trial advocacy Harvard U. Law Sch., 1983; lectr. Practising Law Inst.; chmn. merit selection panel for N.Y. magistrate judges U.S. Dist. Ct. (so. dist.) N.Y., 2002—; mem. dept. disciplinary com. of appellate divsn. supreme ct. First Jud. Dept., 2005—. Mem. editl. bd. N.Y. Law Jour., 1994—. Mem. NYC Charter Revision Commn., 2002, Gov.'s Exec. Adv. Com. on Adminstrn. Criminal Justice, 1981—82, N.Y. Gov.'s Commn. on Govt. Integrity, 1987—90, Mayor's Adv. Com. on Jud., 1994—2001; chairperson N.Y. Regional Consumer Protection Coun., 1971—72. Named one of 50 Top Women Lawyers, Nat. Law Jour., 1998, 2001. Fellow: Am. Coll. Trial Lawyers; mem.: ABA (chair govt. litig. com. litig. sect. 1984—87, chair securities litig. com. 1987—89, coun. litig. sect. 1989—92, chair pre-trial practice and discovery com. 1992—94, standing com. on fed. jud. 1995—2000, chair 2000—01, criminal justice sect.), Legal Aid Soc. (bd. dirs. 1998—2003, chair bd. dirs. 2004—), Fed. Bar Coun. (trustee 1983—91, treas. 1987—90, v.p. 1990, 1996—), N.Y. State Bar Assn., Assn. of the Bar of the City of N.Y. (exec. com. 1984—88, second century com. 1988—92, del. to ABA, ho. dels. 1990—94, chair fed. cts. com. 1992—95, del., consumer affairs com. 1974—78, criminal law com. 1980—84, police law and policy com. 1981—83, sec. 1982—84, ho. dels. 1983—84), Am. Law Inst. (spl. advisor 1995—2001), Fordham Law Alumni Assn., Fordham U. Law Rev. Office: Milberg Weiss Bershad & Schulman LLP One Penn Plz New York NY 10119

HYNES, RICHARD OLDING, biology researcher, educator; b. Nairobi, Kenya, Nov. 29, 1944; s. Hugh Bernard Noel and Mary Elizabeth (Hinks) H.; m. Fleur Marshall, July 29, 1966; children: Hugh Jonathan, Colin Anthony. BA with honors, U. Cambridge, Eng., 1966, MA, 1970; PhD, MIT, 1971. Asst. prof. biology MIT, Cambridge, 1975-78, assoc. prof., 1978-83, prof. dept. biology, 1983—, assoc. head dept. biology, 1985-89, head, 1989-91, dir. Ctr. for Cancer Rsch., 1991-2001, Daniel K. Ludwig prof. cancer rsch., 1999—; investigator Howard Hughes Med. Inst., Chevy Chase, Md., 1988—. Author: Fibronectins, 1990; editor Tumor Cell Surfaces and Malignancy, 1979, Surfaces of Normal and Malignant Cells, 1979; contbr. articles to profl. jours. Guggenheim Found. fellow, 1982; recipient internat. award Gairdner Found., 1997. Fellow AAAS, Am. Acad. Arts and Scis., Royal Soc. London; mem. Inst. Medicine NAS, Nat. Acad. Scis. Office: MIT Ctr Cancer Rsch EI7-227 77 Massachusetts Ave Cambridge MA 02139-4307 Office Phone: 617-253-6422. Business E-Mail: rohynes@mit.edu.

HYNES, SAMUEL, language educator, writer; b. Chgo., Aug. 29, 1924; s. Samuel Lynn and Margaret (Turner) H.; m. Elizabeth Igleheart, July 28, 1944; children: Miranda, Joanna. BA, U. Minn., 1947; MA, Columbia U., 1948, PhD, 1956. Mem. faculty Swarthmore Coll., 1949-68, prof. English lit., 1965-68; prof. English Northwestern U., Evanston, Ill., 1968-76, Princeton U., 1976-90, Woodrow Wilson prof. lit., 1978-90, Woodrow Wilson prof. lit. emeritus, 1990—. Author: The Pattern of Hardy's Poetry, 1961 (Explicator award, 1962), William Golding, 1964, The Edwardian Turn of Mind, 1968, Edwardian Occasions, 1972, The Auden Generation, 1976, Flights of Passage, 1988, A War Imagined, 1990, The Soldiers' Tale, 1997 (Robert F. Kennedy Book award, 1998), The Growing Seasons, 2003; editor: Further Speculations by T.E. Hulme, 1955, The Author's Craft and Other Critical WRitings of Arnold Bennett, 1968, Romance and Realism, 1970, Complete Poetical Works Thomas Hardy, Vol. I, 1982, Vol. II, 1984, Vol. III, 1985, Vols. IV and V, 1995, Thomas Hardy, 1984, Complete Short Fiction of Joseph Conrad, vols. I-III, 1992, vol. IV, 1993. Served to maj. USMCR, 1943-46, 52-53. Decorated Air medal, DFC; recipient award in lit. Am. Acad. Arts and Letters, 2004; Fulbright fellow, 1953-54, Guggenheim fellow, 1959-60, 81-82, Bollingen fellow, 1964-65, Am. Coun. Learned Socs. fellow, 1969, 85-86; NEH sr. fellow, 1973-74, 77-78, 89-91. Fellow Royal Soc. Lit.; mem. Phi Beta Kappa. Home: 130 Moore St Princeton NJ 08540-3359

HYNES, TERENCE MICHAEL, lawyer; b. Jersey City, Mar. 26, 1954; s. Robert Francis and Eleanor (McGuirk) H.; m. Kathryn Wilson, Jan. 25, 1986; children: Shaylyn Michelle, Meaghan Elizabeth, Patrick Francis. BA in Politic. Sci. with highest distinction, Rutgers Coll., 1976; JD, Duke U., 1979. Bar: D.C. 1979, Interstate Commerce Commn. 1979, U.S. Dist. Ct. (D.C. dist.) 1979, U.S. Ct. Appeals (D.C. cir.) 1979, U.S. Ct. Appeals (7th cir.) 1981, U.S. Ct. Appeals (1st and 2d cirs.) 1997. Assoc. Sidley & Austin, Washington, 1979-86, ptnr., 1986—. With comml. practice clinic Duke U. Law Sch., 1983-89; mem. nat. coun. law sch. fund Duke U., 1986-91; mem. Duke Law Sch. Alumni Coun., 1997—. Mem. ABA (pub. utility law sect. 1979—, antitrust law sect. 1979—), Assn. Transp. Law, Logistics and Policy, Duke U. Gen. Alumni Assn. (bd. dirs. 1984-86). Roman Catholic. Office: Sidley & Austin 1501 K Street NW Ste 900 Washington DC 20006-3705 E-mail: thynes@sidley.com.

HYNES, THOMAS JOHN, academic administrator; b. Brighton, Mass., Nov. 19, 1949; 1 child, Thomas Patrick. BS in Math., U. Mass., 1971; MA, U. N.C., 1972; PhD, U. Mass., 1976. Asst. prof. Baylor U., Waco, Tex., 1975—78; from asst. prof. to assoc. prof. to dean U. Louisville, 1978—90, dean Coll. Arts and Scis., 1990—96; v.p. acad affairs U. West Ga., Carrollton, Ga., 1996—, acting pres., 1999—2000. Chmn. bd. trustees Nat. Debate Tournament, Del., 1987—2002. Author: Counterplan: Theory and Practice, 1987, The Last Frontier, 1990, Aging in America, 1988; editor: Comm. Edn., 2002—04, on-line Jour. Distance Learning Administrn., 1998—. Mem. Ga. Commn. Holocaust, 2000—04; bd. dirs. Carroll Tomorrow, Carrollton, 1999—2000, Ga. Humanities Coun., 2004—. Mem.: Nat. Comm. Assn. (mem. internat. discussion and debate 1985—88, chmn. bd. finance 2002—04, mem. exec. com. 2002—), Woodcock Soc., Rotary (mem. internat. svcs. coun. 1996—). Avocations: running, cooking, travel. Office: Office Academic Affairs Maple St Carrollton GA 30117 Office Phone: 678-839-6445. Business E-Mail: thynes@westga.edu.

HYNSON, RICHARD WASHBURN, conductor, composer; b. Washington, June 6, 1953; s. Richard Washburn and Sandra Stekl Hynson; m. Michelle Hayes Williams; children: James Michael Williams, Jacqueline Jean Williams, Jeffrey Lyle Williams, Jonathan Barnhart Williams, Lydia Dawes. MusB, DePauw U., 1975; MusM, Westminster Choir Coll., 1977; D Mus. Arts, U. Cin., 1986. Music dir., condr. Cin. Choral Soc., 1979—89, Hamilton (Ohio)-Fairfield Symphony Orch., 1979—89, Waukegan (Ill.) Symphony Orch., 1990—98. Adj. prof. U. of Wis., Milw., 1991—97. Composer: (cantata) Evensong, (Christmas cantata) Hymn to the Nativity, various motets, anthems, choral works. Vol. YMCA, Milw., 2000—04. Mem.: Conductors Guild, Chorus Am., Am. Symphony Orch. League. Avocations: gourmet cooking, tennis. Home: 713 Grand Ave Thiensville WI 53092-1437 Office: Bel Canto Chorus and Orch 3195 South Superior Milwaukee WI 53207 Office Phone: 414-481-8801. Home Fax: 262-242-4110; Office Fax: 414-481-8807. Personal E-mail: richardhynson@wi.rr.com. E-mail: info@belcanto.org.

HYNUS, ANITA EILEEN, music educator; b. Huntington, W.Va., Oct. 3, 1959; d. Richard Lee and MaryAnn Campbell; m. James R. Hynus, June 7, 1986; children: Cassandra Ann, Zachary Robert. BA in Music Edn., Marshall U., 1981, MA in Music Edn., 1983. Tchr. music K-12, gen. sci. 7-12 W.Va. Music tchr. Gallia County Local Schs., Gallipolis, Ohio, 1982—90; music edn. Robeson County Pub. Schs., Lumberton, NC, 1990—96; tchr. gen. music, orch. Orange County Schs., Hillsborough, NC, 1996—98; tchr. orch. Wake County Pub. Schs., Raleigh, NC, 1998—. Performer Huntington Pops Orch., 1985—90; elem. strings chmn. Wake County Pub. Schs., 2000—03. Leader Girl Scouts Am., Apex, NC, 2000—03, Cub Scouts Am., Apex, 2000—03. Scholar, Bd. Regents W.Va., 1978—91. Mem.: Profl. Educators N.C. (assoc.), Music Educators Nat. Conf. (assoc.), Delta Omicron (life). Republican. Lutheran. Avocation: travel. Home: 1114 Lexington Farm Rd Apex NC 27502 Office: Martin Mid Sch 1701 Ridge Rd Raleigh NC 27607 Personal E-mail: ahynus@aol.com.

HYODO, HARUO, radiologist, educator; b. Honai-chou, Japan, Mar. 3, 1928; B of Medicine, Tokushuma U., 1959, MD, 1966. Chief clinic of radiology Nat. Kochi Hosp., 1963-65; chief divsn. of radiology Ehime Prefectural Ctrl. Hosp., 1970-77; prof. dept. radiology Dokkyo U. Sch. Medicine, Mibu, Tochigi, Japan, 1977-90; dir. emeritus Ikeda Meml. Hosp., Sukagawa, Fukushima, Japan, 1990—; asst. dir. Fukuda Meml. Hosp., Mooka, Tochigi, 1993—. Guest prof. Dokkyo U. Sch. Medicine, 1994—, Tenjin (China) 2d Med. Coll., 1986—. With Japanese Navy, 1944—45. Mem. German Radiol. Soc., Japanese Radiol. Soc. (cert. radiologist), Japanese Soc. Med. Imaging Tech. (pres. ann. gen. mtg. 1989-90), Japan Biliary Assn. (hon.; pres. ann. congress 1987-88), Japanese Med. Imaging Tech. Assn. (councilor 1980-95), Japanese Soc. Angiography and Interventional Radiology (hon.). Achievements include patents in field. Avocations: photography, motoring, bowling, fishing. Home: 1-9-3 Saiwai-chou Mib-machi Shimotsuga-gun Tochigi 321-0203 Japan Office: Fukuda Meml Hosp 3-10 Namiki-chou Mooka Tochigi 321-43 Japan E-mail: hyodo283@green.ocn.ne.jp.

HYSLOP, DAVID JOHNSON, retired arts administrator; b. Schenectady, June 27, 1942; s. Moses McDickens Hyslop; m. Sally Fefercorn, Aug. 12, 1995; 1 child, Alexander. BS in Music Edn., Ithaca Coll., 1965. Elem. sch. vocal music supr., Elmira Heights, N.Y., 1965-66; mgr. Elmira Symphony Choral Soc., 1966; asst. mng. dir. Minn. Orch., Mpls., 1969-72; gen. mgr. Oreg. Symphony Orch., Portland, 1972-78; exec. dir. St. Louis Symphony Soc., 1978-89, pres., 1989-91, Minn. Orch., 1991—; ret. Bd. dirs. Am. Symphony Orch. League, 1988-96, chmn., 1994, mem. exec. and nominating coms., 1990-93; bd. dirs. Minn. Citizens for Arts, Mpls. Downtown Coun., 1992-97, Mpls. Visitors and Conf. Bur., 1996-98; mem., co-chmn. arts edn. task for Mo. Arts Coun., 1989-90; mem. rec. panel Nat Endowment for Arts, 1986-88, mem. challenge grant panel, 1987-88, mem. music overview panel, 1987-88, mem. music creation and presentation panel, 1999; chmn. music and performing arts com. Regional Commerce and Growth Assn., St. Louis, 1987-89; bd. dirs. Minn. State Fair Found., 2002--. Martha Baird Rockefeller grantee, 1966. Mem. Am. Symphony Orch. League (chmn. major mgrs. and policy com. 1985-87, orch. mgmt. fellowship program 1979-88, orch. assessment program 1988), Regional Orch. Mgrs. Assn. (founder), Minn. Orchestral Assn., Mpls. Club, Arena Club. Avocations: basketball, travel, reading, study of German. Home: 2019 Irving Ave S Minneapolis MN 55405-2521 Office: Minn Orch 1111 Nicollet Mall Minneapolis MN 55403-2477 E-mail: dhyslop@mnorch.org.

HYSLOP, GARY LEE, retired librarian; b. Oakland City, Ind., June 8, 1944; s. H. Boyd and Berniece (McKinney) H. BA, Oakland City U., 1966; MS, Ind. State U., 1974; MLS, Ind. U., 1987. Tchr. Ind. and Ohio Pub. Schs., 1967—77; mgr., officer F & M Fed. Savs. & Loan, Bloomington, Ind., 1977-81; broker, realtor Bloomington, Ind., 1981-82; tchr. Howe Mil. Sch., Ind., 1982-84, Madison Schs., Ind., 1984-86; asst. libr. Calif. State U., Bakersfield, 1988-91; dir. admissions and placement Sch. Libr. and Info. Sci. Ind. U., Bloomington, 1991-93; dir. Curriculum Materials Ctr. U. Ctrl. Fla., 1993-2000. Vol. Kern County Beethoven Festival, Bakersfield, 1988; bd. dirs. Bakersfield Community Theatre, 1989-91, nominating com., 1990-91; bd. regents/united faculty of Fla. task force on libr. issues Fla. State U. System, 1997-98. Recipient Meritorious Performance and Profl. Promise award Calif. State U., 1989, Excellence in Librarianship award U. Ctrl. Fla., 1999. Mem. ALA, SELA, Fla. Faculty Assn., UCF Librs. (personnel adv. com.), Fla. Assn. Coll. Rsch. Librs. (bd. dirs. 1994-97), 15th Ann. Task Force of the Libr. Instrn. Round Table, United Faculty of Fla. (senator 1997-99, chpt. sec.). Avocations: keyboard instruments, volunteerism, travel, writing fiction. Personal E-mail: garyhyslop@hotmail.com. Business E-Mail: ghyslop@mail.ucf.edu.

HYSLOP, NEWTON EVERETT, JR., epidemiologist; b. Newton, Mass., 1935; AB, Harvard U., 1957, MD, 1961. Diplomate Am. Bd. Allergy and Immunology, Am. Bd. Internal Medicine, Am. Bd. Infectious Disease. Intern Mass. Gen. Hosp., Boston, 1961-62, resident in medicine, 1962—63, fellow in infectious disease, 1966—68; rsch. assoc. lab. immunology Nat. Inst. Allergy and Immunology, Bethesda, Md., 1963—65; resident in medicine Peter Bent Brigham Hosp., Boston, 1965—66; with Tulane U. Med. Ctr., New Orleans, 1984—; prof. medicine Tulane U. Instr. to asst. prof. Harvard Med. Sch., 1965—85; asst. to assoc. physician Mass. Gen. Hosp., 1965—85; chief infectious disease sect. Tulane Sch. Medicine; founder and prin. investigator Tulane-La. State U. AIDS Clin. Trials unit, 1987—96, co-PI, 1996—; med. dir. HIV/AIDS/TB In-Patient unit, Charity Hosp., 1991—; Moseley tchg. fellow, vis. scientist dept. biochemistry U. Oxford, 1968—69; clin. head HIV disease mgmt. initiative, health care svcs. divsn. La. State U. Health Scis. Ctr., 1999—. Fellow ACP, Infectious Dis. Soc.; mem. Am. Assn. Immunologists, Am. Soc. Microbiology, Assn. Subspecialty Professors. Office: Tulane U Sch Medicine Infectious Diseases Sect SL87 1430 Tulane Ave New Orleans LA 70112-2699

HYTIER, ADRIENNE DORIS, French language educator; d. Jean and Katharine (Hytier) Matson. BA summa cum laude, Barnard Coll., 1952; MA, Columbia U., 1953, PhD, 1958. Instr. French Vassar Coll., 1959-61, asst. prof., 1961-66, assoc. prof., 1966-70, prof. French Poughkeepsie, N.Y., 1970-96, Lichtenstein Dale prof. French, 1974-96. Vis. assoc. prof. Columbia U., 1966, U. Calif., 1968—69. Editor for French lit.: The 18th Century: A Current Bibliography Since 1970, 25 vols., Two Years of French Foreign Policy: Vichy 1940-42, 1958, 2d edit., 1974, Les Dépêches diplomatiques du Comte de Gobineau en Perse, 1959, La Guerre, 1975, 4th edit., 1991; contbr. articles to profl. jours. Decorated chevalier des Palmes Académiques; fellow, Guggenheim Found., 1967—68. Mem. MLA, Am. Soc. 18th Century Studies, Internat. Soc. 18th Century Studies, Phi Beta Kappa. Home: 71 Raymond Ave Poughkeepsie NY 12603-0372 Office: Vassar Coll Box 372 Poughkeepsie NY 12604-0001

IACOBONI, MARCO, neurologist, neuroscientist; b. Rome, Mar. 13, 1960; came to U.S., 1992; s. Antonio and Rita (Arduini) I.; m. Mirella Dapretto, Sept. 17, 1994; 1 child, Caterina. MD, U. La Sapienza, Rome, 1985, PhD in Neurosci., 1994. Cert. Neurology Bd., Rome. Resident in neurology Med. Sch. La Sapienza, 1987-89, clin. instr., 1989-92; vis. scholar dept. psychology UCLA, 1992-93, postdoctoral fellow human brain mapping divsn., dept. psychology and neurology, 1995—97, asst. rschr. brain mapping divsn., dept. psychology, 1997—99, asst. prof., psychiatry and biobehavioral scis., assoc. prof. psychiatry and biobehaviorial scis., Neuropsychiatric Inst., dir., Transcranial Magnetic Stimulation Lab, Ahmanson Lovelace Brain Mapping Ctr., David Geffen Sch. Medicine. Reviewer: Jour. Neurophysiology, 1995-96, Brain—A Jour. of Neurology, 1994-97, NeurReport, 1997, Brain and Cognition, 1994-95; contbr. rsch. articles to profl. jours. including New Eng. Jour. Medicine, Jour. Neurophysiology. Med. officer Italian Air Force, 1986-87. Recipient Valigia Dell'Inteluetto, Arin, 1992, Advanced Study Inst. award NATO, 1996; fellow Human Frontier Sci. Program, 1993. Office: Ahmanson-Lovelace Brain Mapping Ctr Rm 265 UCLA 660 Charles E Young Dr S Los Angeles CA 90095-7085 Address: Ahmanson-Lovelace Brain Mapping Ctr Rm 159 (lab) UCLA 660 Charles E Young Drive S Los Angeles CA 90095-7085 Office Phone: 310-206-3992. Office Fax: 310-794-7406. Business E-Mail: iacoboni@loni.ucla.edu.

IACOBUCCI, EDWARD E., air transportation executive, former software company executive; BS, Ga. Inst. Tech. Co-founder, v.p., chief tech. officer Citrix Systems Inc., 1989—91, chmn., 1991—2000, WingedFoot Svcs., West Palm Beach, Fla., DayJet. Bd. dir. SCO Group, 2000—. Office: WingedFoot Services 1517 Perimeter Rd West Palm Beach FL 33406*

IACOBUCCI, FRANK, academic administrator, judge; b. Vancouver, BC, Can., June 29, 1937; s. Gabriel and Rosina (Pirillo) I.; m. Nancy Elizabeth Eastham, Oct. 31, 1964; children: Andrew Eastham, Edward Michael, Catherine Elizabeth. B of Commerce, U. BC, Vancouver, 1959, LLB, 1962; LLM, Cambridge U., Eng., 1964, Diploma in Internat. Law, 1966; LLD (hon.), U. BC, 1989, U. Toronto, 1989, U. Ottawa, 1995, U. Victoria, 1996, Law Soc. Upper Can., 2000, McGill U., 2003, U. Waterloo, 2003, U. Calabria, Italy, 2003. Bar: Ont. 1970, Queen's Counsel, 1986. Assoc. Dewey Ballantine et al, NYC, 1964-67; assoc. prof. law U. Toronto, 1967-71, prof. law, 1971-85, assoc. dean faculty of law, 1973-75, v.p. internal affairs, 1975-78, dean faculty of law, 1979-83, v.p., provost, 1983-85; vis. fellow Wolfson Coll., Cambridge, England, 1978; dep. min. of justice and dep. atty. gen. Govt. of Can., Ottawa, 1985-88; chief justice Fed. Ct. of Can., Ottawa, 1988-90; justice Supreme Ct. Can., Ottawa, 1991—2004; interim pres. U. Toronto, 2004—. Mem. Permanent Ct. of Arbitration, 1997-2004; former cons. Ont., Alta., Can. govts.; mem. Ont. Securities Commn., Toronto, 1982-85; dir. Cambridge Can. Trust, 1984-91; mem. Can. Jud. Coun., 1988-91, exec. com., edn. com.; gov. Can. Jud. Ctr., 1989-91; gov. Nat. Jud. Inst., 1992-2004; mem. adv. coun. Internat. Ctr. Criminal Law Reform and Criminal Justice Policy, 1991-93, dir. 1993-2004; bd. dirs. Torstar Corp., 2004-. Co-author: Canadian Business Corporations, 1977, Cases and Materials on Partnerships and Canadian Business Corporations, 1983; co-editor: Materials on Canadian Income Tax, 6th edit., 1985; contbr. chpts. to books, articles to profl. jours. Mem. Islington Residents and Ratepayers Assn., 1971-85; dir. Multicultural History Soc., Ont., 1976-88; v.p. Nat. Congress Italian Cans., 1980-83, dir. Toronto dist., 1979-83; v.p. Can. Inst. Advanced Legal Studies, 1981-85, bd. govs., 1981-85, 91-98; mem. adv. com. Faculty of Law, McGill U., 1996-2004; mem. adv. bd. Inst. Can. Studies, U. Ottawa, 1998-2004. Decorated Commendatore dell'Ordine Al Merito della Repubblica Italiana; named hon. citizen, Mangone, Italy, 1996, Cepagatti, Italy, 2001, Grimaldi, Italy, 2003; recipient Law Soc. medal, Law Soc. Upper Can., 1987, Ordine al merito, Nat. Congress Italian Canadians, Toronto Dist., 1989, 125th Anniversary of Confedn. Can. medal, 1992, Lion d'Or award, Ordre des Fils d'Italie au Can., Montreal, 1995, Cosentino dell'Anno award, Fedn. of Clubs Cosentini of Ont., 1995, Man of the Yr. award, Can. Italian Bus. and Profl. Assn. Toronto, 1985, Italo-Can. of the Yr. award, Confratellanza Italo-Canadese, Vancouver, 1985, Man of Yr. award, Brotherhood Interfaith Soc., Vancouver, Can., 1999, Medaglia d'Argento del Pres. della Repubblica Italiana, 2000, Can.-Italian Nat. award, 2000, Premio Italia nel mondo, Italy in the World award, 2001, Valigia d'Oro award, 2002, award for disting. svc., Ont. Bar Assn., 2003, Anthony P. Pantages medal, Justice Inst. BC, 2004, Italiani nel Mondo award, Rome, Italy, 2004; Newton Rowell fellow, Can. Inst. Internat. Affairs, 1962, McKenzie-King traveling fellow, U. BC, 1963, hon. fellow, St. John's Coll., Cambridge U. Fellow Am. Coll. Trial Lawyers (hon.); mem. Can. Bar Assn., Univ. Club of Toronto, Sigma Tau Chi, Phi Gamma Delta (Disting. Fiji award 1987). Avocations: tennis, golf. Mailing: 17 Wilgar Rd Etobicoke ON Canada M8X 1J3 Office: Office of Pres Simcoe Hall Ste 206 U Toronto Toronto ON Canada M5S 1A1 Office Phone: 416-978-2121.

IACOBUCCI, GUILLERMO ARTURO, chemist; b. Buenos Aires, May 11, 1927; came to U.S., 1962, naturalized 1972. s. Guillermo Cesar and Blanca Nieves (Brana) I.; m. Constanina Maria Gullich, Mar. 28, 1952; children: Eduardo Ernesto, William George. MSc, U. Buenos Aires, 1949, PhD in Organic Chemistry, 1952. Rsch. chemist E.R. Squibb Rsch. Labs., Buenos Aires, 1952-57; rsch. fellow in chemistry Harvard U., Cambridge, Mass., 1958-59; prof. phytochemistry U. Buenos Aires, 1960-61; sr. rsch. chemist Squibb Inst. Med. Rsch., New Brunswick, N.J., 1962-66; head bio-organic chemistry labs. Coca-Cola Co., Atlanta, 1967-74, asst. dir. corp. R&D, 1974-87, mgr. biochemistry and basic organic chemistry group, 1988-93, ret., 1993. Adj. prof. chemistry Emory U., 1975—. Contbr. articles on organic chemistry to sci. jours.; patentee in field. John Simon Guggenheim Meml. Found. fellow, 1958. Fellow Am. Inst. Chemists; mem. AAAS, Assn. Harvard Chemists, Am. Chem. Soc., N.Y. Acad. Scis., Am. Soc. Pharmacognosy, Phytochem. Soc. N.Am., Smithsonian Instn., Planetary Soc., Sigma Xi. Achievements include structure/activity correlations and molecular design of sweeteners; use of enzymes in asymmetric organic synthesis; natural products chemistry. Home: 2660 Peachtree Rd NW Apt 28E Atlanta GA 30305-3680 Office: Emory U Dept of Chemistry 1515 Pierce Dr NE Atlanta GA 30322-1003

IACOCCA, LEE (LIDO ANTHONY IACOCCA), former automotive manufacturing executive, venture capitalist; b. Allentown, Pa., Oct. 15, 1924; s. Nicola and Antoinette (Perrotto) I.; m. Mary McCleary, Sept. 29, 1956 (dec.); m. Darrien Earle, March 30, 1991; children— Kathryn Lisa Hentz, Lia Antoinette Nagy. BS, Lehigh U., 1945; ME, Princeton U., 1946. With Ford Motor Co., Dearborn, Mich., 1946-78, successively mem. field sales staff, various merchandising and tng. activities, asst. dirs. sales mgr. Phila., dist. sales mgr. Washington, 1946-56, truck mktg. mgr. div. office, 1956-57, car mktg. mgr., 1957-60, vehicle market mgr., 1960, v.p.; gen. mgr. Ford Motor Co. (Ford div.), 1960-65, v.p. car and truck group, 1965-69, exec. v.p. of co., 1967-69, pres., 1970-78, Ford N.Am. automobile ops.; pres., chief operating officer Chrysler Corp., Highland Park, Mich., 1978-79, chmn. bd., chief exec. officer, 1979-93; prin. Iacocca Ptnrs., 1994—; pres. Iacoccca Assocs., L.A.; founder EV Global Motors. Bd. dirs. Chrysler Fin. Corp. Author: Iacocca: An Autobiography, 1984, Talking Straight, 1988. Past chmn. Statue of Liberty-Ellis Island Centennial Commn. Wallace Meml. fellow Princeton U. Mem. NAE, Tau Beta Pi. Clubs: Detroit Athletic. Office: 16201 Stagg St Van Nuys CA 91406-1716

IACONO, BRUCE R., painter; b. NYC, Oct. 6, 1955; s. Carmelo J. and Josephine A. Iacono; m. Maureen C. Splain, Aug. 23, 1986. Student, Allgemeine Gewerbeschule, Basel, Switzerland, 1975; BFA, U. of the Arts, Phila., Pa, 1978; student, SUNY, Purchase, N.Y., 1993, Art Students League, N.Y., 1996. Graphic designer Self Employed, Dobbs Ferry, NY, 1979—82; salesman Canon MCS, N.Y., 1982—84; salesman, fin. svcs. Vendor Funding Co., Inc, New Hyde Park, NY, 1984—87, Signal Capital, Fleet Credit Corp., Clifton, NJ, 1987—89; fine artist, painter Self Employed, White Plains, NY, 1989—97; exec. recruiting The Foster McKay Group, N.Y., 1997—98; fine artist, painter Self Employed, White Plains, NY, 1998—. Represented in numerous exhbns. and pvt. collections. Personal E-mail: bruce@bruceiacono.com.

IACONO, JAMES MICHAEL, research and development company executive, nutrition educator; b. Chgo., Dec. 11, 1925; s. Joseph and Angelina (Cutaia) I.; children: Lynn, Joseph, Michael, Rosemary. BS, Loyola U., Chgo., 1950; MS, U. Ill., 1952, PhD, 1954. With U.S. Army Nutrition Ctr., Letterman Army Hosp., Denver, 1954—58; assoc. prof. biochemistry and exptl. medicine U. Cin. Sch. Medicine, 1958—70; chief Lipid Nutrition Lab. Nutrition Inst. Agrl. Rsch. Svc. USDA, Beltsville, Md., 1970-75, dep. asst. adminstrv. nat. program staff Washington, 1975-77, assoc. adminstr. office human nutrition, 1978-82, dir. Western Human Nutrition Rsch. Ctr. San Francisco, 1982-94. Prof. nutrition Sch. Pub. Health UCLA, 1987—. Author over 100 rsch./tech. publs. and chpts. in books relating to nutrition and biochemistry and lipids. With U.S. Army, 1944—46. Recipient Rsch. Career Devel. award NIH, 1964-70. Fellow Am Heart Assn. (coun. on arteriosclerosis and thrombosis), Am. Inst. Chemists; mem. Am. Inst. Nutrition, Am. Soc. Clin. Nutrition, Am. Oil Chemists Soc. Personal E-mail: jiacono25@aol.com.

IACOVELLI, RENALD, writer, critic; Author: The Polity of Beasts, 1994, Lily Snow, 2001, The Adventures of Corker Larue, 2003.

IACUONE, LEANN F., science educator; b. Columbia, S.C., May 28, 1974; d. Nancy and Harold Rabert; m. James Iacuone, July 7, 2001. BS, U. S.C.; MEd, Furman U., Greenville, S.C. Cert. athletic trainer Nat. Athletic Trainers Assn., 1997. Sci. tchr /athletic trainer Laurens Dist. 55 H.S., SC. Pace instr. SC. Dept. of Tchr. Quality, Columbia, 2003—05. Recipient Dist. Tchr. of Yr., Laurens Sch. Dist. 55, 2003. Mem.: ASCD, NATA, NSTA, Phi Delta Kappa (pres.). Office: Laurens District 55 HS 5058 Hwy 76 West Laurens SC 29360 Office Phone: 864-682-3151. E-mail: lrabert@yahoo.com.

IAMELE, RICHARD THOMAS, retired law librarian; b. Newark, NJT, Jan. 29, 1942; BA, Loyola U., L.A., 1963; MSLS, U. So. Calif., 1967; JD, Southwestern U., L.A., 1976. Bar: Calif. 1977. Cataloger U. So. Calif., L.A., 1967-71; asst. cataloger L.A. County Law Libr., 1971-77, asst. ref. libr., 1977-78, asst. libr., 1978-80, libr. dir., 1980—2005; ret., 2005. Mem. ABA, Am. Assn. Law Librs., Calif. Libr. Assn., So. Calif. Assn. Law Librs., Coun. Calif. County Law Librs. (pres. 1981-82, 88-90). Office Phone: 213-629-3531.

IAMMARTINO, NICHOLAS R., corporate communications executive; m. Eileen Iammartino. B in Chem. Engring., Cooper Union; M in Chem. Engring., NYU; MBA in Fin., Adelphi U. Process engr. Esso Rsch. and Engring. Co., 1969-71; bus. and tech. news writer Chem. Engring. mag. McGraw-Hill, 1971-76; chem. industry securities analyst Merrill Lynch, 1976-78; from sr. writer to bus. pubs. mgr. dept. corp. comm. Celanese Corp., 1979-85; corp. mgr. fin. comm. and adminstrn. Philip Morris, Inc., 1985; dir. fin. comm. Borden, Inc., N.Y., 1986-89, dir. external comm., 1989, dir. pub. affairs, 1994-95, v.p. pub. affairs Columbus, Ohio, 1995—. Bd. dirs. Borden Found., Inc.; mem. assn. bd. Columbus Zool. Pk. Assn. Office: Borden Inc 180 E Broad St Columbus OH 43215-3799

IAMS, DENISE ZUCKER, mathematics educator; b. Columbus, Ohio, Sept. 8, 1951; d. Joseph Stanley Zucker and Joan (White) Milner; m. Charles Gary Iams, June 14, 1975. BA, Ohio No. U., 1973; MA, Ashland U., 1983. Math tchr. Baker Mid. Sch., Marion, Ohio, 1973—2003; ret., 2003. Presenter Ohio Vocat. Edn., Columbus, 1989—; math.-sci. tchr. leader Regional Profl. Devel. Ctr., 1995-2000. Presenter Ohio Coun. of Tchrs. of Math., Cleve., 1991. Treas., v.p. Jr. Svc. Guild, Marion, 1976-84; pres. Marion Panhellenic Assn., 1973-79; trustee Marion Edn. Found., 2003—, Marion Gen. Hosp., 2003—, vol. gift shop 2003—. Named Tchr. of Yr. Ohio Coun. on Economic Edn., 1979-80; recipient Teaching of Economics award Internat. Paper Co. Found., 1980; Jennings scholar Martha Holden Jennings Found., Cleve., 1989-90. Mem. ASCD, Nat. Coun. Tchrs. Math., Ohio Coun. Tchrs. Math., (presenter 1991-98, Cen. Ohio Math Tchr. award 1987), Mortar Bd., Phi Delta Kappa (treas. 1990—), Delta Kappa Gamma (pres. 1996-98). Avocations: walking, bicycling, reading, counted cross-stitch. Home: 521 Hane Ave Marion OH 43302-5315

IANNICELLI, JOSEPH, chemical company executive, consultant; b. N.Y.C., Aug. 5, 1929; s. Peter and Catherine (Gugliotti) I.; m. Betty Peterson, June 28, 1978; children: Mark, Rex, Gina. SB, MIT, 1951, PhD, 1955. Rsch. chemist Textile Fibers, E.I. DuPont, Wilmington, Del., 1955-60; tech. dir. Clay Div. J.M. Huber, Macon, Ga., 1960-70; founder, chief exec. officer Aquafine Corp., Brunswick, Ga., 1970—, Aero-Instant Corp., Brunswick, Ga., 1988—; co-founder IMPEX Corp., Brunswick, Ga., 1988—. Cons. Consol. Goldfields Australia, Sydney, 1976-78, Rio Tinto, Madrid, 1980-82, Hoganes, Malmo, Sweden, 1984. Author: Evaluation and Comparison of Crossfield and Solenoid Field Magnetic Filters, 1981; co-author: A Survey-Benneficiation of Industrial Minerals, 1980; contbr. over 30 articles to profl. jours. Pres. Ga. Tidewater Conservation Assn., Brunswick, 1991—92; govt. appointment as mem. Jekyll Island (Ga.) Citizens Resource Coun., 1995—97; foreman Glynn County Grand Jury, Brunswick, 1989; chmn. Glynn County Bd. Edn., 2002; bd. dirs. Jekyll Island (Ga.) Citizens Assn., 1992—96, pres., 1993—95. Recipient Rsch. grant NSF, 1980, 84, Elec. Power Rsch. Inst., 1980, Resolution of Commendation, Ga. Ho. of Reps., 1995. Fellow Am. Inst. Chemists; mem. Tech. Assn. of Pulp and Paper Industry (chmn. pigments com. 1971-72). Achievements include over 100 patents including paramagnetic separator and process, silane modified organo clays, mercaptan scrubber; performed first high temperature superconducting magnetic separation of minerals as part of a team consisting of Aquafine, DuPont and Sumitomo, 1996. Home: 28 Saint Andrews Dr Jekyll Island GA 31527-0901 Office: Aquafine Corp 3963 Darien Hwy Brunswick GA 31525-2423 Office Phone: 912-265-2000.

IANNONE, DOROTHY, visual artist, writer; b. Boston, Aug. 9, 1933; arrived in Germany, 1967; d. William Iannone and Sarah (Nicoletti) Pucci; m. James Phineas Upham, Dec. 17, 1958 (div. Aug. 1967). BA, Boston U., 1957; postgrad., Brandeis U., 1957-58. Trans. agent U.S. Army Base, Boston, 1951—53; co-dir. Stryke Gallery, N.Y.C., 1963—67. Instr. open workshop, Coll. Art, West Berlin, 1977 and 1979; guest artist Rijks Academie, Amsterdam, 1982, 84, Jan Van Eyck Academie, Maastricht, Holland, 1982, 83, Enschede Academie, 1983. Author: Story of Bern, 1970, The Berlin Beauties, 1978, The Whip, 1980, Censorship and the Irrepressible Drive Toward Love and Divinity, 1983, 3d edit., 2002, Courting Ajaxander, 1993; (with Dieter Roth) Dieter and Dorothy: Their Correspondence in Words and Works 1967-1998, 2001; one woman-shows include Stryke Gallery, N.Y.C., 1964-67, Galerie Hansjörg Mayer, Stuttgart, 1967, Galerie Handschin, Basel, 1969, Galerie Wilbrand, Cologne, 1971, Eat Art Galerie, Düsseldorf, 1971, Galerie Jule Hammer, West Berlin, 1971, Galerie Steinmetz, Bonn, 1973, Galerie Edith Wahlandt, Schwäbisch-Gmund, West Germany, 1973, Galerie Sum, Reykjavik, 1974, Galerie Ben Vautier, Nice, France, 1975, Galerie 38, Copenhagen, 1975, Galerie Bama, Paris, 1976, Studio Galerie, Mike Steiner, Berlin, 1977, M. Würthle and O. Wiener Galerie, Berlin, 1977, Haus am Lutzow Platz, Berlin, 1978, Basel Art Fair, Galerie Mike Steiner, Switzerland, 1979, Neue Galerie Stadt Aachen, Ludwig Collection, Germany, 1980, Galerie Wallner, Malmö, Sweden, 1981, Nikolaj, Copenhagen, 1982, Galerie Ars Viva, Berlin, 1982, Galerie Rosenberg, Zürich, 1984, Boekie Woekie, Amsterdam, 1986, Petersen Galerie, Berlin, 1989, Galerie Bernhard Steinmetz, Bonn, Germany, 1990, Kunstfonds, Kunstraum, Bonn, 1990, Kunst-Werke, Berlin, 1992, Galerie Armin Hundertmark, Cologne, Germany, 1994, Galerie Roche, Bremen, Germany, 1995, Basel Art Fair, Galerie Stähli, Zürich, Switzerland, 1995, Galerie Holtmann, Cologne, 1996, New Soc. Fine Arts, Berlin, 1997, Mus. Modern Art, Arnhem, Holland, 1998, Boekie Woekie, Amsterdam, 1998, Galerie Andy Jllien, Zürich, 2001, Galerie Barbara Wien, Berlin, 2001-02, Laura Mars Group, Berlin, 2002, Sprengel Mus., Hanover, Germany, 2005; selected group exhbns. include Galerie Zwirner, Cologne, 1967, Kunsthalle, Bern, Switzerland, 1969, Kunsthalle, Düsseldorf, Germany, 1969, Edinburgh (Scotland) Festival of Arts, 1970, San Antonio Show, Galerie Bama, Paris, 1975, Mus. Modern Art, Paris. 1976, 80, Fondation Maeght, St. Paul-de-Vence, France, 1976, Studio du Passage 44, Brussels, 1976, Neue Galerie Stadt Aachen, Germany, 1976, Maison de la Culture, Rennes, France, 1977, Galerie Camomille, Brussels, 1984, Centre Georges Pompidou, Paris, 1985, Kunst-und Museumsverein, Wuppertal Germany, 1987, The Concealed Mus., Akademie der Kunste, Berlin, 1987-88, Galerie Petersen, Berlin, 1988, Galerie Marlene Frei, Zürich, 1988, Fondation Danae, Pouilly, Valdampierre, France, 1988, Fondazione Mudima, Milan, 1990, Mus. Modern and Contemporary Art, Nice, 1991, Kunsthalle, Düsseldorf, 1992, Mus. Modern Art, Saint-Etienne, France, 1993, Haus am Lutzow Platz, Berlin, 1993, The Books of Artists, Inst. for Fgn. Rels., Berlin, 1995, Goethe Inst., Tel Aviv, 1995, Mus. Contemporary Art, Marseille, France, 1997, Kunsthalle, Steyr, Austria, 1998-99, Hommage à Dieter Roth, Galerie Heinz Holtmann, Cologne, 1998, NORD/LB Galerie, Braunschweig, Germany, 1999, Dieter Roth Acad., Basel, Switzerland, 2000, Pécs, Hungary, 2001, Reykjavik, Iceland, 2002, Lubeck, Germany, 2004, Springhornhof Kunstverein, Neuenkirchen, Germany, 2001, Coninx Mus., Zürich, 2002-03, Soc. Friends of Young Art, Baden-Baden, 2003; permanent collections include Mus. Drawings and Prints, Berlin, Nat. Mus. Women in the Arts, Washington, Ludwig Collection, Neue Galerie Stadt Aachen, Germany, Mus. Modern Art, St. Etienne, France, Bibliotheque Nationale, Paris, Kunst Mus., Basel, Berlinische Galerie, Berlin. Grantee Berlin Artists' Program, 1976, Art Found. Bonn, 1988, Women Artists' Program, Berlin Senate, 1994. Mem. Phi Beta Kappa. Home: Olivaer Platz 16 10707 Berlin Germany

IANNOTTI, JOSEPH PATRICK, orthopedic surgeon; b. NYC, Dec. 16, 1954; s. Frank Thomas and Victoria (Artuso) I.; m. Cindy Baskind, July 12, 1975; 1 child, Matthew; m. Karen Bloomberg, July 26, 2003. BS, Fordham U., 1975; MD, Northwestern U., 1979; PhD in Cell Biology, U. Pa., 1987. Diplomate Am. Bd. Orthopaedic Surgery. Resident in orthopedic surgery U. Pa., Phila., 1979-83, chief resident, 1983-84, asst. prof. orthopedic surgery, 1984-93, assoc. prof., 1993-97, prof., 1997-2000; chief of shoulder svc. Hosp. of U. Pa., Phila., 1988-2000; chmn. dept. orthopaedic surgery Cleve. Clinic Found., 2000—; prof. Cleve. Clinic Lerner Sch. Medicine. Author, editor: Rotator Cuff Disorders, 1992; editor: Basic Science Orthopaedics, 1994, The Shoulder Evaluation and Management, 1999; contbr. over 160 articles to profl. jours. NIH postdoctoral fellow U. Pa., 1980-81; recipient career devel. award NIH, 1984-89, DeForest Willard award U. Pa., 1984; N.Am. travel fellow Am. Orthopaedic Assn., 1985, Am. Brit. Can. fellow, 1993. Fellow Am. Acad. Orthopaedic Surgeons; mem. Orthopaedic Rsch. Soc., Am. Shoulder and Elbow Surgeons, Acad. Orthopaedic Soc., Pa. Orthopaedic Sco. Office: Cleve Clinic Found 9500 Euclid Ave # A-41 Cleveland OH 44195-0001 Office Phone: 216-445-5151. Business E-Mail: iannotj@ccf.org.

IANNUCCI, DOUGLAS EDWARD, mathematics professor; b. Providence, Sept. 22, 1956; s. Albert Hugo and Antonette (DiOrio) Iannucci. PhD in Math., Temple U., 1995. Prof. math. U. VI, St. Thomas, 1994—. Contbr. articles to profl. jours. With USN, 1977—81. Mem.: Math. Assn. Am., Am. Math. Soc., Fibonacci Assn. Home: Nisky Mail PO Box 588 St Thomas VI 00802 Office: Univ VI 2 John Brewers Bay St Thomas VI 00802

IANNUZZI, SALVATORE, information technology executive; married; 3 children. BS in Acctg., St. Francis Coll. With KPMG, Bear Sterns; various sr. leadership positions, including chief adminstrv. officer, COO Europe, COO Global Investment Bank Bankers Trust/ Deutsche Bank; chief adminstrv. officer CIBC World Markets, 2000—04; former non-exec chmn. Symbol Technologies, Holtsville, NY, sr. v.p., chief adminstrv. and fin. officer, 2005—, interim pres., CEO, 2005—. Office: Symbol Technologies One Symbol Plz Holtsville NY 11742-1300 Office Phone: 631-738-2400. Office Fax: 631-738-5990.*

IAPALUCCI, SAMUEL H., financial executive; b. Cresson, Pa., July 19, 1952; s. Anthony F. and Dorthy (Quartz) I.; m. Berniece Reichert, June 5, 1976; children: Amanda Berniece, Cara Elizabeth. BS, St. Francis Coll., Loretto, Pa., 1974; MBA, Duquesne U., 1980. CPA, Pa. Audit sr. Coopers & Lybrand, Pitts., 1974-76; asst. v.p. Equibank, N.A., Pitts., 1976-78; with Allegheny Internat., Inc., Pitts., 1978-91, v.p., treas., 1987-90, v.p., CFO, 1990, cons., 1990-91; v.p., CFO OHM Corp., Findlay, Ohio, 1991—; CFO CH2M Hill Companies, Greenwood Village, CO, sr. v.p., CFO, sec. Mem. AICPA, Pa. Inst. CPAs, Fin. Execs. Inst., Findlay Country Club. Avocations: golf, tennis, reading.

IAQUINTA, LEONARD PHILLIP, retired academic administrator, writer, consultant, not-for-profit fundraiser; b. Kenosha, Wis., Aug. 1, 1944; s. Anthony Sam and Mary Natalie (Gallo) I. *The Gallo and Iaquinta ancestors migrated to the USA from Calabria, the beautiful mountainous southernmost province of mainland Italy. Mr. Iaquinta's maternal grandparents are from the Torcaso and DiCello, and Perri families. They lived near the western coast of Calabria in Platania. His paternal grandparents lived near the eastern coast. Grandmother Arabia from Santa Severina lived in view of the ancient hilltop castle, now stunningly renewed as a learning center and museum. Grandfather Iaquinta lived nearby in smaller Roccabernarda.* BJ, Northwestern U., 1966; M in Journalism, Columbia U., 1967. Dir., cons. World Studies Data Bank Acad. for Ednl. Devel., N.Y.C., 1969-76; dir. field svcs. for alumni rels. Northwestern U., Evanston, Ill., 1977-81; dir. nat. alumni program Columbia U., N.Y.C., 1981-82; devel. officer, alumni dir. Bklyn. Coll. (CUNY), 1982-86; dir. devel. and alumni affairs Ind.-Purdue Univs., Ft. Wayne, 1986-95, Northeastern Ill. U., Chgo., 1995-2001; asst. dean, dir. devel. and alumni rels. Coll. Engring. and Applied Scis. U. Wis., Milw., 2001—03, devel. officer, 2003—04; comm. and fund raising consultant Self-Employed, 2005—; prin. Excellence in Comm., Inc., 2004—. Spkr. various profl. confs. *Mr. Iaquinta specializes in institution building, writing, and program development. At Northeastern Illinois University, he led reinvention of the offices of development and alumni affairs. Additionally, he led the 1998-99 marketing and communications planning team which conducted extensive market research and wrote a marketing and communications plan which included specific goals and action steps. At U. Wis., he creted the first profl. devel. and alumni program for engring. and computer sci., increasing philanthropic funds and performance. Mr. Iaquinta's article, "Selection Savvy, Seven Steps to Hiring A Campaign Consultant was in CASE Currents, May 1999.* Assoc. editor: Notes on Negotiating, 1974; contbr. articles to profl. jours.; chpts to books; author various devel. manuals. Exec. dir. Kenosha United Way, 1976-77, mem. campaign cabinet, 2003; mem. fund adv. com. Greater Milw. Found., 2003—. Recipient 4 nat. alumni programming and fundraising awards Council for Advancement and Support of Edn., 1981, 84, 88, 98; 15 Who Care awards, Vol. Connection of Switchboard of Ft. Wayne, 1990. Mem. Assn. Fundraising Profls., Alliance for Nonprofit Mgmt., Assn. Consultants for Nonprofits, East Wis. Planned Giving Coun., Rotary, Soc. Profl. Journalists, United Way Cmty. Investment Com. Kenosha County. Mem. Congregational Ch. Avocations: gardening, reading, enjoying the arts, travel. Home: 9507 74th St Kenosha WI 53142-8194 Office: Len Laquinta's Excellence in Comm Inc Aurora Health Care 9507 74th St Kenosha WI 53142 Office Phone: 262-716-6605. E-mail: LPIaquinta@cs.com.

IARUSSI, DON, publishing executive; b. N.Y.C., Apr. 9, 1954; s. Ralph and Concetta I. AA, Suffolk Coll., 1975; BS in Mgmt., Old Westbury, 1977; MBA in Mktg., Nat. U., San Diego, 1982; MA in Telecommunicaitons, San Diego State U., 1983; postgrad., Bklyn. Coll., 1988—. Producer San Diego Perspective KYXY, 1979-80, Sta. KPRC Radio, Houston, 1984-85; host, talk show Bug Baytown, Houston, 1985-86; producer KTRH PIT, Houston, 1985-86; publicist Nat. U., San Diego, 1980-83, Jarussi Communications, Houston, 1983—. Pub. rels. dir. Houston Ctr. Attitudinal Healing, 1987-88, Artcetra, 1986-88, publicist Houston AREA Womens Ctr., 1985-86; producer WMCA, N.Y.C., 1983-84; talk show host, "Date Rape", WNYE-NY B.C. Presents. Contbr. articles to profl. jours. Del. Dem. Pasaneva, 1984; pub. rels. for Judge Monny Kugler, San Diego, 1981; mem. People Ethical Treatment Animals. Mem. Am. Women Radio TV, Pub. Rels. Soc. Am., Nat. Orgn. Women, Asson. Bus. Communications, Broadcast Edn. Assn., Nat. Television Acad. Avocations: making futons, photography, bicycling. Home: PO Box 37 New York NY 10037-0037 also: PO Box 100383 Brooklyn NY 11210-0383 Office: 2480 Times Blvd Houston TX 77005-3233

IATROPOULOS, MICHAEL JOHN, health research executive, pathology educator; b. Athens, Greece, Nov. 8, 1938; came to U.S. 1966; s. John Michael and Marina (Yancoglu) I.; m. Barbara Jeanne McNeil, Aug. 27, 1966; children: John Michael, Mary Ellen. AB, Athens Coll., Greece, 1958; MD, U. Tuebingen, Ger., 1964; Dr.Med.Sc., U. Tuebingen, 1965. Research assoc./resident Div. Biomed. Sci., Brown U., Providence, 1966-67; resident dept. internal medicine U. Cologne, Ger., 1967-68; instr. pathology div. biomed. sci. Brown U., 1968-70; resident dept. pathology U. Mo., Columbia, 1970-71; spl. fellow toxicology CEPT Albany (N.Y.) Med. Coll., 1972-74; asst. prof. ICES Albany Med. Coll., Albany, N.Mex., 1974-77, assoc. prof., dep. dir., 1977-78; dept. head MRD Am. Cyanamid Co., Pearl River, N.Y., 1978-89; head regulatory pathology and histopathology Am. Health Found., Valhalla, N.Y., 1989-99; pres. Labpath Mgmt., Inc., Suffern, N.Y., 1989-99. Prof. pathology N.Y. Med. Coll., N.Y., 1989—. Author: New Anticancer Drugs, 1983, Gastrointestinal Toxicology, 1986, Carcinogenicity, 1988, Toxicokinetics and New Drug Development, 1989, Toxicokinetics, 1993; assoc. editor Jour. Toxicologic Pathology, 1999—. Fellow Acad. Toxicol. Scis.; mem. Soc. Toxicology, Soc. Toxicologic Pathologists (councillor 1981-86), Internat. Fedn. Soc. Toxicologic Pathologists (sec.-gen. 1989-95), Japanese Soc. Toxicologic Pathology (hon. mem.), Internat. Acad. Toxicologic Pathology (bd. dirs. 2000—). Home: 6 Bruce Ct Suffern NY 10901-3310 Office: NY Med Coll Dept Pathology Grasslands Rd Valhalla NY 10595

IAVICOLI, MARIO ANTHONY, lawyer; b. Camden, N.J., Aug. 11, 1939; s. Vito Anthony and Angelina Jessie (Marchionese) I.; m. Arlene V. LeDonne, July 6, 1963; children— Michelle, Denise, Laura. BME, Drexel U., 1962; JD, U. Pa., 1965. Bar: NJ 1965. Assoc. Samuel P. Orlando, Camden, 1965-66, Ballen & Batoff, Camden, 1966-68; ptnr. Maressa, Console & Iavicoli, Berlin, N.J., 1968-72; first asst. prosecutor Camden County, 1972-74; pvt. practice Pennsauken, N.J., 1974-79, Haddenfield, 1980—; counsel to spkr. N.J. Gen. Assembly, 1970-72, N.J. Automobile Ins. Study Commn., 1970-74, Camden County Charter Study Commn., 1974, Camden County Republican party, 1974-76, N.J. Rep. party, 1976—; solicitor Haddenfield Borough, 1980—. Author: No Fault and Comparative Negligence in New Jersey, 1973; Drafter: N.J.'s No Fault Law and other companion legislation, 1970-73. Chmn. Camden County Rep. Com., 1978—; Rep. state committeeman, 1976—; mem. Electoral Coll. from, N.J., 1976; solicitor Pennsauken Twp., 1975—; Vice pres. Haddonfield Home Sch. Assn., 1972-73; Bd. dirs. Drexel U. Class Endowment Fund; trustee Haddonfield Civic Assn. Named One of N.J.'s 5 Outstanding Young Men, 1974; recipient Ocean County Bar Assn. award, 1975 Mem. Camden County Jr. C. of C. (counsel 1967-68), ABA (ho. of dels., 2004—, pres. 2003-04), N.J. Bar Assn., Camden County Bar Assn (trustee 1996-98, sec. 1998-99, treas. 1999-2000, 2d v.p. 2000-01, 1st v.p. 2001-02, pres.-elect 2002-03, pres. 2005—, del. to ABA Ho. Dels. 2004—), Sons of Italy, Drexel U. Alumni Assn. (v.p. 1991—), Rotary. Roman Catholic. Home: 340 Marquis Rd Haddonfield NJ 08033-4011 Office: 43 Kings Hwy W Haddonfield NJ 08033-2128 Office Phone: 856-429-0201. E-mail: miavicoli@comcast.net.

IBACH, KIM L., secondary school educator; d. Fred and Margaret Sullivan; m. Patrick Ibach, July 23, 1994. BA in Secondary Scoial sci., U. No. Colo., 1991; MA in Tchg. Am. History, U. Wyo., 1999. Cert. tchr. Wyo. Social studies tchr. Campbell County H.S., Gillette, Wyo., 1992—93, Kelly Walsh H.S., Casper, Wyo., 1993—2004; dir. Am. History Coalition Curriculum and Instruction Ctrl. Svcs. Natrona County Sch. Dist., Casper, Wyo., 2004—. Presenter in field; interviewed on civil rights and hist. method C-SPAN, 2003; reader U.S. history Ednl. Testing Svcs. Advanced Placement, San Antonio, 2003—; mem. adj. faculty Adams State Coll. Extended Studies, 2005—, Casper Coll., 2003—04; adj. faculty mem. extended studies Adams State Coll., 2005—. Pres. Wyo. Coun. for Soc. Studies, 2005—. Finalist Tchr. of Merit award, Nat. History Day, 2003; recipient Outstanding Wyo. Tchr. award, Wyo. Hist. Soc., 2004, Mary K. Bonsteel Tachau Tchg. award, Orgn. Am. Historians, 2003. Office: Natrona County Sch Dist 970 N Glenn Rd Casper WY 82601 Office Phone: 307-577-0354. Business E-Mail: kim_ibach@ncsd.k12.wy.us.

IBACH, ROBERT DANIEL, JR., library director; b. Lynch, Nebr., Dec. 31, 1940; s. Robert Daniel Sr. and Mabel Bertine (Selstad) I.; m. Paula Joanne Hubbling, June 11, 1977. B.R.E., Detroit Bible Coll., 1963; BD, Grace Theol. Sem., Winona Lake, Ind., 1966, ThM, 1969; MLS, Ind. U., 1975. Ordained minister, 1989. Libr. Grace Coll. and Sem., Winona Lake, 1969-86; library dir. Dallas Theol. Sem., 1986—. Archaeologist Heshbon (Jordan) Expedition, 1971-76; library cons. Inst. of Holy Land Studies, Jerusalem, 1989, Seteca, Guatemala City, 2001, 04; peer evaluator So. Assn. Colls. and Schs., 1990-2003. Author: Archaeological Survey of the Hesban Region, 1987; contbg. author: Hesban After 25 Years, 1994, Dictionary of Biblical Imagery,

1998; periodical revs. editor: Bibliotheca Sacra, 1988—; contbr. articles to profl. jours., 1972—. Mem. Soc. Bibl. Lit., Am. Theol. Libr. Assn., Am. Libr. Assn., Tex. Libr. Assn. Home: 3229 Colby Cir Mesquite TX 75149-1875 Office: Dallas Theol Sem 3909 Swiss Ave Dallas TX 75204-6496

IBAÑEZ, ALVARO, patent design company executive, artist; b. Bucaramanga, Santander, Colombia, Jan. 18, 1951; came to U.S., 1981; s. Epimenio and Maria Delia (Muñoz) I.; m. Marta Cecilia Arias, Dec. 30, 1971 (div. Dec. 1991); children: Carlos Humberto, Alvaro Antonio, Diana Saray, Sandra; m. Denise DeVries, Sept. 6, 1997; children: Elena, Austin, Paul, Delia Denise. Fine arts, David Manzur Acad., Bogotá, Colombia, 1972; structural draftman, ACADITEC, Bogotá, Colombia, 1974. Elem. tchr. German Pena Sch., Bogotá, Colombia, 1971; with sales dept. Grolier Internat., Bogotá, Colombia, 1973-74; civil engring. draftsman Adminstrv. Dept. Cmty. Action, Bogotá, Colombia, 1974-76; gen. ins. mgr. Gilabert & CIA, Santa Marta, Colombia, 1976-77; farmer El Roble Ranch, Santa Marta, Colombia, 1976-77; sales mgr. Onix Ltda., Bucaramanga, Colombia, 1977-78; owner, mgr. Distrisiba Ltda., Bucaramanga, Colombia, 1977-80; sales mgr. Coramex Andina Ltda., Bogotá, Colombia, 1980-81; with Radian, Inc., Alexandria, Va., 1984—, Birch, Stewart, Kolasch & Birch, Falls Church, Va., 1985—, Diversified Technologies, Alexandria, Va., 1986—; pres., founder A-Ibañez Art Design, Inc., Falls Church, Va., 1985—; founder Sunrise Studio Gallery, Kilmarnock, Va., 1996—, Pennie & Edmonds, L.L.P., Washington, 1998—. Freelance Pub. Health Ctr., Bogotá, Colombia, 1971-74, Guillermo Victorino SA, Bogotá, 1973-74, Felix A. Clavijo Co., Bogotá, 1973-75, Metron Publicity, Bucaramanga, Colombia, 1977-80, Tulio Ramirez, 1980-81, Fabio Hernandez Salazar, Bogotá, 1980-81; with Lascaris Design Group Internat., Washington, 1984 One-man shows include Georgetown Streets, Washington, 1981, Sovran Bank CC, Springfield, Va., 1985; exhibited in group shows at David Manzur Acad., Bogotá, Colombia, 1974, Dicas Fine Arts Ctr., Bogotá, Colombia, 1979, Santander Indsl. U., Bucaramanga, Colombia, 1979, Arlington Ctr., Va., 1982, Falls Church Recreation Park, Va., 1982, Latin Am. Art League, Alexandria, Va., 1991, Desfile de las Americas, Washington, 1993, Martin Luther King Meml. Libr., Washington, 1994, 96, Art Mus. Ams.-Orgn. Am. States, Washington, 1994, Strathmore Hall Arts Ctr., North Bethesda, Md., 1994, AT&T, Oakton, Va., 1994, Washington, 1994, Cultural Mexican Inst., Washington, 1994, Montgomery County Exec. Office Bldg., Rockville, Md., 1994, Bell Atlantic, Arlington, Va., 1994, Silver Spring, Md., 1994, Torpedo Factory Art League, Alexandria, Va., 1994, Moscoso Gallery, Washington, 1995, Fla. Mus. Hispanic and Latin Am. Art, Miami, 1995, Montgomery County Exec. Office Bldg., Rockville, Md., 1995, NASA Hdqs., Washington, 1995, Pan Am. Health Orgn., Washington, 1995, SED Ctr., Washington, 1996, (retrospective) Falls Church (Va.) Recreation Ctr., 1997, Bell Atlantic Hdqrs., Arlington, Va., 1997, D.C. Arts in the Alley/Georgetown U., Washington, 1998, Moca Gallery, Washington, 1998, Del Ray Artisans, Alexandria, 1998, Barnes & Noble Seven Corners, Falls Church, 1998, Rappahannock Westminster Canterbury, Kilmarnock, Va., 2002, Museo Regional Queretaro Mexico, 2005 Sponsor World Vision, Tacoma, Wash., 1987—, Child Devel. Ctr., Falls Church, Va., 1989—, Crystal Cathedral, Glandale, Calif., 1992—, Beverley Hills United Meth. Ch., Alexandria, Va., 1997, Arts in the Alley Georgetown, D.C., 1998. Recipient 1st prize drawing Prismacolor Contest, 1958. Mem. Worldwide Fine Art Promotions, Hispanic Museo Art, Art League, Torpedo Factory. Republican. Avocations: paint, gardening, music, travel. Home: A Ibañez Art Design Inc PO Box 1060 197 Whittaker Line Kilmarnock VA 22482-3123 Office Phone: 804-435-2880. E-mail: aibanez@rivnet.net.

IBANEZ, MANUEL LUIS, academic administrator, biologist, educator; b. Worcester, Mass., Sept. 23, 1935; s. Ovidio Pedro and Esperanza Fe (Perez) I.; m. Jane Marie Bourquard, Oct. 16, 1970; children: Juana Lia Cristina, Vincent Ovidio, William Dayan, Marc Albert BS cum laude, Wilmington Coll., 1957; MS, Pa. State U., 1959, PhD, 1961. Asst. prof. Bucknell U., Lewisburg, Pa., 1961-62; postdoctoral fellow UCLA, 1962; sr. biochemist IICA de la OEA, Turrialba, Costa Rica, 1962-65; assoc. prof., chmn. dept. U. New Orleans, 1965-70, prof., 1977-90, assoc. dean grad. sch., 1978-82, assoc. vice chancellor acad. affairs, 1982-83, acting vice chancellor, 1983-85, vice chancellor acad. affairs, provost, 1985-89, prof. emeritus, 1990—; pres. Tex. A&M U., Kingsville, 1989-98, named disting. prof. biology, 1998, pres., prof. emeritus; ret., 2000. Bd. regents Smithsonian Instn.; adj. prof. biology Delmar CC, 2000—. Author: Basic Biology of Microorganisms, 1972; contbr. articles to profl. jours. Regent Smithsonian Inst., 1994—; mem. Alliance for Good Govt., New Orleans, 1980. NSF coop. fellow, 1958-61 Mem. Am. Assn. State Colls. and Univs., Kingsville C. of C. (pres. 1991), Rotary, KC, Sigma Xi Democrat. Roman Catholic. Avocations: chess, tennis, bicycling, collections.

IBANEZ, SILVIA SAFILLE, lawyer; b. Havana, Cuba, Nov. 3, 1952; came to U.S., 1961; d. Eduardo and Alicia (Martin) Safille; m. Juan Antonio Ibanez, July 5, 1974; children: Juan-Carlos and Cristina (twins). BBA, U. Miami, Fla., 1973; MS in Acctg., U. Miami, 1974; JD, U. P.R., 1981. Bar: Fla. 1983; CPA, Fla. Auditor Coopers & Lybrand, Miami, Fla., 1974-75, tax specialist, 1977-81; prof. U. Cath. Madre y Maestra, Santiago, Dominican Republic, 1975-76; tax mgr. Main Hurdman CPAs, St. Petersburg, Fla., 1981-84; fin. planner Interstate Securities Co., Fort Myers, Fla., 1985, fin. cons., 1985-87; pvt. practice law Winter Haven, Fla., 1988-93, Orlando, Fla., 1994—. Inst. U. Ctrlo. Fla., 1993-97. Vol. guardian ad-litem representing abused/neglected children 20th and 10th Jud. Cir. Ct. Lee, Polk and Orange Counties, 1986—; active Orange County League of Women Voters; former mem. coun. bd. Polk County Children's Svcs. Vol. guardian ad-litem representing abused/neglected children 20th and 10th Jud. Cir. Ct. Lee, Polk and Orange Counties, 1986—; former mem. coun. bd. Polk County Children's Svcs.; founding mem. Kids Voting Ctrl. Fla. Inc., 2001--. Mem. ABA, AICPA, Fla. Bar Assn., Am. Assn. Attys.-CPAs, Orlando Opera Chorus. Methodist. Office: 7380 Sand Lake Rd Ste 500 Orlando FL 32819-5257 also: 622 Verona St Kissimmee FL 34741 Office Phone: 407-856-9449. E-mail: sibanez@cfl.rr.com.

IBARGUEN, ALBERTO, newspaper executive; b. Rio Piedras, P.R., Feb. 29, 1944; s. Albert E. and Angelica (Bigas) I.; m. Susana E. Lopez, Jan. 8, 1969; 1 child, Diego. BA in History, Wesleyan U., Middletown, Ct., 1966; JD, U. Pa., 1974. Bar: Conn. 1974. Atty. Legal Aid Soc., Hartford, Conn., 1974-76; dir., counsel Conn. Election Commn., Hartford, 1976-77; ptnr. Cloud & Ibarguen, Hartford, 1977-78; atty. Updike, Kelly & Spellacy, Hartford, 1978-79; dep. gen. coun., v.p. public affairs, v.p. pvt banking Conn. Nat. Bank, Hartford, 1979-84; sr. v.p. Hartford Courant, 1984-86; exec. v.p. ops. Newsday/N.Y. Newsday, N.Y.C., 1986-95; pub. El Nuevo Herald, Miami, Fla., 1995-98; v.p. The Miami Herald, 1995-98, pub., 1998—; chmn. Miami Publishing Co., 1998—; pres., CEO John S. & James L. Knight Found., Miami, 2005—. Bd. dirs. Lincoln Ctr. for Performing Arts, N.Y.C., 1990-96, Dade County Found., Com. to Protect Journalists, Fla. Philharm., Pub. Broadcasting Sys., 1997—; trustee Wesleyan U., 1992-95, Smith Coll., 1995-97; mem. bus. commn. Met. Mus. Art, 1990-95. Mem. N.Y. Athletic Club. Office: The Miami Herald One Herald Plaza Miami FL 33132-1693

IBBOTSON, ROGER G., financial educator; b. Chgo., May 27, 1943; s. Arthur E. and Margaret B. I.; m. Jody L. Sindelar, 1983. BS, Purdue U., 1965; MBA, Ind. U., 1967; PhD, U. Chgo., 1974. Economist Bank of Japan, 1969; bond portfolio mgr., treas.'s office U. Chgo., 1971-75, asst. prof. fin. Grad. Sch. Bus., 1975-79, sr. lectr. fin. and exec. dir. Ctr. for Research in Security Prices, 1979-84; prof. Yale U. Sch. Mgmt, 1984—; chmn. Ibbotson Assocs., Inc., Chgo., 1979—; ptnr. Zebra Capital Mgmt., 2001—. Recipient Graham and Dodd award, 1980, 82, 84, 2001, 2003, James Vertin award AIMR, 2002. Mem. Am. Fin. Assn., Am. Econ. Assn., Fin. Mgmt. Assn. Author: (with Rex Sinquefield) Stocks, Bonds, Bills, and Inflation, 3d edit., 1982, (with Gary Brinson) Global Investments, 1993, (with J.C. Francis) Investments, 2002. Home: 75 Old Hartford Tpke Hamden CT 06517-3524 Office: 8 S Michigan Ave Ste 707 Chicago IL 60603-3357

IBDAH, JAMAL A., medical educator; b. Jenin, Jordan, Nov. 18, 1956; s. Ahmad Ibrahim and Arifa Abdul-Rahman Ibdah; m. Mary R. Cantwell, Sept. 23, 1958; children: Khalid Jamal, Malik, Zain. MD, Jordan U. Sch Med, Amman, Jordan, 1975—82; PhD, Med. Coll. of Pa., 1984—87. Cert. Am. Bd. of Internal Medicine, 1994, Am. Bd. of Gastroenterology, 1998. Postdoctoral fellow in biochemistry Med. Coll. of Pa., 1987—88; asst. prof. in biochemistry U. of Jordan, 1988—91; resident, Internal Medicine Wake Forest U. Sch. of Medicine, 1991—94; fellow, Gastroent. Washington U. Sch. of Medicine, 1994—97; asst. prof., Internal Medicine, Gastroent. Wake Forest U. Sch. of Medicine, 1997—2001, assoc. prof., Internal Medicine, Gastroent., 2001—. Contbr. articles to var. profl. jours. Recipient North Am. Conf. for Gastroent. Fellows Award for an Outstanding Program Presentation, Am. Coll. of Gastroenterology, 1997; grantee Career Devel. Award (KO8), NIH, 1997-2002, Innovative Seed Grant in Clin. Rsch. in Liver Diseases, Am. Digestive Health Found., 1998-1999, Rsch. Grant in SIDS, Mar. of Dimes, 1999-2002, Investigator Award (RO1), NIH, 2001-2006. Mem.: Am. Soc. of Biochemistry and Molecular Biology, Am. Soc. of Human Genetics, Am. Assn. for the Study of Liver Diseases, Am. Gastroent. Assn. Achievements include development of an animal mouse model for an inherited disease in children that cause inability to breakdown fat. This model provided for the first time a genetic link to sudden infant death syndrome; published studies that, for the first time, provided an explanation for a serious liver disease in pregnant women and its assn. with an inherited disease in the fetus; published evidence that screening certain infants for a genetic mutation can be life saving. Home: 5224 Huntscroft Ct Winston Salem NC 27106 Office: Wake Forest U Sch Medicine Medical Center Blvd Winston Salem NC 27157 E-mail: jibdah@wfubmc.edu.

IBEKWE, ABASIOFIOK MARK, soil microbiology educator, researcher; b. Ukanafun, Nigeria, Nov. 5, 1956; came to U.S., 1979, naturalized, 1994; s. Mark Rueben and Nko (Essien) I.; m. Mary Brown, May 11, 1985; m. Anieno Amos Ideh, Jan. 6, 1996; children: Uwakmfon, Emem, Idara BS, N.C. Agr. and Tech. State U., 1983, MS, 1984, 90; PhD, U. Md., 1995. Rsch. asst. N.C. Agr. and Tech. State U., Greensboro, 1984-90; rsch. technologist Roche Biomed. Lab., Burlington, Vt., 1989-90; supr. Mid State Farms, Siler City, N.C., 1985-88; rsch. asst. U. Md., College Park, 1990-93, tchg. asst., 1993—. Rsch. microbiologist USDA-ARS, Riverside, Calif.; assoc. rsch. scientist Wash. State U., Pullman. Contbr. articles to profl. jours. including Jour. Environ. Quality, Jour. Applied Microbiology, Applied Microbiol. and Biotech., others. Gen. sec. Nigerian Profls., Washington, 1992—. Mem. Am. Soc. Agronomy, Soil Sci. Soc. Am., Am. Soc. for Microbiology, Environ. S.C. Tech., Soil S.C. Soc., Soil S.C. Soc. Am., Jour. Environ. Quality, Phi Sigma Eta. Avocations: photography, soccer, volleyball, dance. Home: 6983 Harvest Ln Riverside CA 92506-3744 Office: USDA 215 Johnson Rd Pullman WA 99163-8831 Office Phone: 951-369-4828. Business E-Mail: aibekwe@ussl.ang.usda.gov.

IBEN, ICKO, JR., astrophysicist, educator; b. Champaign, Ill., June 27, 1931; s. Icko and Kathryn (Tomlin) I.; m. Miriam Genevieve Fett, Jan. 28, 1956; children: Christine, Timothy, Benjamin, Thomas. BA, Harvard U., 1953; MS, U. Ill., 1954, PhD, 1958. Asst. prof. physics Williams Coll., 1958-61; sr. rsch. fellow in physics Calif. Inst. Tech., Pasadena, 1961—64; assoc. prof. physics MIT, Cambridge, 1964-68, prof., 1968-72; prof. astronomy and physics, head dept. astronomy U. Ill., Champaign-Urbana, 1972-84, prof. astronomy and physics, 1972-89, disting. prof. astronomy and physics Urbana, 1989—99, disting. prof. emeritus, 2000; holder of Eberly family chair in astronomy Pa. State U., 1989-90. Vis. prof. astronomy Harvard U., 1966, 68, 70; vis. fellow Joint Inst. for Lab. Astrophysics U. Colo., 1971—72; vis. prof. astronomy and astrophysics U. Calif., Santa Cruz, 1972; vis. prof. physics and astronomy Inst. for Astronomy U. Hawaii, 1977; adv. panel astronomy sect. NSF, 1972—75; vis. com. Aura Observatories, 1979—82; vis. scientist astronomical coun. Union Soviet Socialist Rep. Acad. Sci., 1985; sr. vis. fellow Australian Nat. U., 1986; vis. prof. U. Bologna, Italy, 1986, Hokkaido U. Grad. Sch. Sci., 2001; sr. rsch. fellow U. Sussex, England, 1986; George Darwin lectr. Royal Astronomical Soc., London, 1984; McMillin lectr. Ohio State U., 1987; vis. eminent scholar U. Ctr. Ga., 1988; guest prof. Christian Albrechts U. Kiel, 1990; sr. fellow Nicolaus Copernicus Astron. Ctr., Warsaw, 2002. Contbr. articles to profl. jours. John Simon Guggenheim Meml. fellow, 1985—86, Japan Soc. for Promotion of Sci. fellow, U. Tokyo, 1985, Niigata U., 1990, vis. Japan Soc. for Promotion of Sci. Eminent Scientist, Hokkaido U., 2003—04. Fellow Royal Astron. Soc. (Eddington medal 1990); mem. Am. Astron. Soc. (councilor 1974-77, Henry Norris Russell lectr. 1989), U.S. Nat. Acad. of Scis., Internat. Astronom. Union. Home: 3910 Clubhouse Dr Champaign IL 61822-9280 Office: U Ill Dept of Astronomy 1002 W Green St Urbana IL 61801-3074

IBERS, JAMES ARTHUR, chemist, educator; b. Los Angeles, June 9, 1930; s. Max Charles and Esther (Imerman) I.; m. Joyce Audrey Henderson, June 10, 1951; children: Jill Tina, Arthur Alan. BS, Calif. Inst. Tech., 1951, PhD, 1954. NSF post-doctoral fellow, Melbourne, Australia, 1954-55; chemist Shell Devel. Co., 1955-61, Brookhaven Nat. Lab., 1961-64; mem. faculty Northwestern U., 1964—, prof. chemistry, 1964-85, Charles E. and Emma H. Morrison prof. chemistry, 1986—. Recipient Disting. alumni award Calif. Inst. Tech., 1997. Mem. NAS, Am. Acad. Arts and Sci., Am. Chem. Soc. (inorganic chemistry award 1979, Disting. Svc. in the Advancement of Inorganic Chemistry award 1992, Linus Pauling award 1994), Am. Crystallographic Assn. (Buerger award 2002). Home: 2657 Orrington Ave Evanston IL 60201-1760 Office: Northwestern U Dept Chemistry Evanston IL 60208-3113 Business E-Mail: ibers@chem.northwestern.edu.

IBLER, GEROLD, finance company executive, consultant; b. Graz, Austria, Nov. 11, 1968; s. Gerold and Elisabeth Ibler; m. Theresa Ibler; children: Mia Cecile Scarbrough, Whitney Michelle Scarbrough, Nicolette Brooke. M. jur, Karl-Franzens-U.Graz, Austria, 1992, Dr iur, 1996; MBA, U. Miami, 1993. Mgr. PricewaterhouseCoopers, Miami, Fla., 1995—2000; European counsel Ferrell Schultz, Miami, Fla., 2000—; pres. Ferrell Schultz Cons., Miami, Fla., 2000—. Mem.: ABA, Miami City Club. Office: Ferrell Schultz 201 S Biscayne Blvd 34th Floor Miami FL 33131 E-mail: gibler@ferrellschultz.com.

IBRAHIM, GEORGE W., physician, health facility administrator; b. Lebanon, Nov. 17, 1936; m. Jean; 1 child, Alastair. Diplomate Am. Bd. Family Practice. Pres. Highland Med. & Diagnostic Clinic, Sebring, Fla., 1980—. Pres., bd. dirs. Health Ctr. Office: Highlands Med & Diagnostic Clinic 6721 US 27 S Sebring FL 33876

IBRAHIM, IBRAHIM N., bishop; b. Telkaif, Mosul, Iraq, Oct. 1, 1937; came to U.S., 1978; s. Namo Ibrahim and Rammo Yono. Grad., Mosul Sem., Iraq, 1951, St. Sulpice Sem., Paris, 1962; STD, Rome, 1975. Dir. sem., Baghdad, Iraq, 1964-68; assoc. pastor St. Joseph Ch., Baghdad, 1975-78; pastor Chaldean Ch., Los Angeles, 1979-82; bishop Chaldean Church of U.S.A., Southfield, Mich., 1982—; first Bishop Eparch Eparchy of St. Thomas the Apostle/Chaldean Cath. Diocese Am., Detroit, 1985—. Chaldean Catholic. Home: Chaldean Diocese USA 25603 Berg Rd Southfield MI 48034-2556 Office Phone: 248-351-0440.

IBRAHIM, JEREMY H. GONZALEZ, lawyer; b. 1963; married; 4 children. BA, Fordham U.; JD, Cath. U. Asst. dist. atty. City of Phila., 1988—91, commr. Commn. Human Rels., 1996—2000; atty. pvt. practice. Mem. US Senate Rep. Task Force on Hispanic Affairs, 1997; mem. jud. commn. Phila. County, 1998—; commr. fgn. claims settlement commn. US Dept. Justice, 2003—; gen. counsel Spanish Am. Law Enforcement Assn. Mem. bd. dirs. Nueva Esperanza Charter HS, Coun. Spanish Speaking Orgn. (El Concilio), Assn. Musicos Latino Am. (AMLA); nat. com. mem. Good Neighbor Partnership Fund, Phila. Found. I, 2000. Office: 1700 Race St 1st Fl Philadelphia PA 19103

IBRAHIM, TAMER SELIM, engineering educator; b. Alexandria, Egypt, Nov. 24, 1972; s. Selim Ibrahim and Sania Ayoub; m. Nevine Demian, Sept. 23, 1971; 1 child, Daniel. BS, Ohio State U., 1996, MS, 1999, PhD, 2003. Grad. rsch. assoc. Ohio State U., Columbus, Ohio, 1996—99, rsch. assoc. engr., 2000—02; asst. prof. U. Okla., Norman, Okla., 2003—. Contbr. chapters to books, articles various profl. jours. Tech. com. program Internat. Soc. of Magnetic Resonance In Medicine, 2003, IEEE: Antenna and Propagation Soc.; expert reviewer Magnetic Resonance in Medicine, IEEE Trans. Biomedical Eng., IEEE Trans. Antenna&Propagation, X-Ray Sci., Medical&Biological Engineering&Computations, IEEE Trans. Microwave Theory&Techniques, MAGMA, Applied Magnetic Resonance; rev. bd. of spl. issue on bioelectromagnetics The Applied Computational Electromagnetics Jour., 2001—01; book reviewer OXFORD U. Press, Wiley Interscience: John Wiley and Sons, Inc, 2004; proposal and grant reviewer The U.S. Civilian Rsch. & Devel. Found., The US Internat. Sci. and Tech. Ctr., 2002—04; session chmn. The IEEE Antenna and Propagation Soc. Ann. Internat. Symposium, Internat. Soc. of Magnetic Resonance In Medicine Ann. Meeting, Columbus, Ohio and Kyoto, Japan, 2003—04; chmn. of the IEEE student chpt. Inst. of Elec. and Computer Engr., Norman, Okla., 2004. Recipient Outstanding Jour. Paper award, ElectroScieince Lab., The Ohio State U., 2000, Outstanding Master Thesis award, The Electro Sci. Lab., The Ohio State U., 1999, Hon. Mention: Internat. Conf. Paper, IEEE Internat. Symposium on Antennas and Propagation, 2000, Internat. Soc. of Magnetic Resonance in Medicine Hardware Meeting, 2001, NSF Student Travel award, IEEE Internat. Symposium on Antennas and Propagation, 2000. Mem.: URSI Commn. K— Electromagnetics in Biology and Medicine, The Internat. Soc. of Magnetic Resonance in Medicine, Inst. of Elec. and Electronics Engr., The Internat. Union of Radio Sci. in the USA (corr.), Tau Beta Pi, Eta Kappa Nu, Phi Kapp Phi. Achievements include patents pending for wireless brain machine interface; development of the electromagnetic prediction code for magnetic reseonance imaging coil design; research in achieving homogneous radio frequency magnetic fields at ultra high field magnetic resonance in imaging; new theories regarding Dielctric Resonance and Power Requirements in Magnetic Resonace Imaging; development of The 18-Tissue Anatomically Detailed Head Model; design of radio frequency coils for the world's first 8 Tesla Whole Body Human Magetic Resonance Imaging System. Office: U Okla 202 W Boyd St Norman OK 73019 Office Phone: 405-325-6475. Office Fax: 405-325-7066. Business E-Mail: ibrahim@ou.edu.

IBSSA, SEIFU, accountant; b. Addis Abeba, Shoa, Ethiopia, Nov. 19, 1958; came to U.S., 1982; s. Ibssa Ido and Gudetu Ilala; m. Mulu Berhane, May 1, 1963; children: Girum S., Aklil S., Nobell S., Simon s. AA in Acctg., Comml. Coll., Addis Ababa, 1980; ASBA, Santa Monica Coll., Calif., 1986; BS in Internat. Bus., San Jose State U., 1992. Supr. acctg. GenPharm Internat., Mountain View, Calif., 1990-94; sr. acct. NEC Electronics, Roseville, Calif., 1994-99; fin. sys. analyst McClatchy Corp., Sacramento, 1999—. Bd. chmn. Ethiopian Cmty. Ctr., Sacramento, 1997-98. Mem. Inst. Mgmt. Accts. Avocations: photography, playing accordion. Office: 2001 P St Sacramento CA 95814-5232

ICAHN, CARL CELIAN, investor; b. Queens, NY, 1936; m. Lila Icahn (div. 1999); children: Brett, Michelle; m. Gail Golden, 1999. BA in philosophy, Princeton U., 1957; postgrad., NYU Sch. Medicine. Apprentice broker Dreyfus Corp., NYC, 1960-63; options mgr. Tessel, Patrick & Co., NYC, 1963-64, Gruntal & Co., 1964-68; chmn., pres. Icahn & Co., NYC, 1968—; chmn., dir. Starfire Holding Corp. (formerly Icahn Holding), 1984—; chmn. ACF Industries Inc., St. Charles, Mo., 1984—, also bd. dirs.; chmn. bd. dirs., pres., CEO Trans World Airlines Inc., NYC, 1985—93; chmn. bd. Am. Real Estate Ptnrs., 1990—, Am. Property Investors Inc., 1990—, Am. Railcar Industries, 1994—; pres., dir. Stratosphere Corp., 1998—2004; chmn. bd. GB Holdings, 2000—, XO Comm., 2003—. Dir. Cadus Pharm. Corp., 1993—. Founder Icahn House, NYC, Carl C. Icahn Charter Sch., NYC. Named one of Top 200 Collectors, ARTnews mag., 2004. Avocation: Collector Old Masters and Impressionist art. Office: Icahn & Co Inc 100 S Bedford Rd Mount Kisco NY 10549-3425 Address: ACF Industries 620 N 2nd St Saint Charles MO 63301-2081*

ICE, DIANA CAROLYN, librarian, writer; BA, U. Calif., Berkeley, 1968; MALS, U. Mich., 1969. Cert. pub. libr. Writer, Burlingham, NY, 1989—; assoc. editor Am. Life Pub. Co., Hurley, NY, 1989—96; libr. SUNY Coll., Oneonta, NY, 1975—88, Orange County CC, Middletown, NY, 1972—75, Creighton U. Alumni Meml. Libr., Omaha, 1969—72. Author: A Bird in Hand and Other Stories, Easy Herb Cooking for Busy People. Mem.: Nat. Writers Assn. (v.p. Hudson Valley chpt. 1989—96), Sci. Fiction and Fantasy Workshop (chmn. welcome com. 1990—). Episcopalian. Avocations: reading, needlecrafts, gardening.

ICE, RICHARD EUGENE, retired minister, retirement housing company executive; b. Ft. Lewis, Wash., Sept. 25, 1930; s. Shirley and Nellie Rebecca (Pedersen) I.; m. Pearl Lucille Daniels, July 17, 1955 (dec. June 1992); children: Lorinda Susan, Diana Laurene, Julianne Adele. AA, Centralia Coll., 1950; BA, Linfield Coll., 1952, LHD (hon.), 1978; MA, Berkeley Bapt. Div. Sch., 1959, DD (hon.), 1995; grad. advanced mgmt. program, Harvard U., 1971. Ordained to ministry, Am. Bapt. Ch., 1954. Pastor Ridgecrest Cmty. Bapt. Ch., Seattle, 1955-59; dir. ch. extension Wash. Bapt. Conv., 1959-61; dir. loans Am. Bapt. Extension Corp., Valley Forge, Pa., 1961-64; assoc. exec. min. Am. Bapt. Chs. West, Oakland, Calif., 1964-67; dep. exec. sec., treas. Am. Bapt. Home Mission Socs., Valley Forge, 1967-72; pres. Am. Bapt. Homes of the West, Oakland, 1972-95, pres. emeritus, 1995—. Dir. Min.'s Life Ins. Co., Mpls., 1975-87, chmn. bd. dirs., 1986-87; bd. dirs. Bapt. Life Assn., Buffalo; pres. Am. Bapt. Homes and Hosps. Assn., 1978-81; v.p. Am. Bapt. Chs. U.S.A., 1990-91; mem. Mins. & Missionaries Benefit Bd., 1982-89; mem. Bapt. Joint Com. Pub. Affairs; trustee Linfield Coll., 1972—, chmn. bd. trustees, 1994—; trustee Calif./Nev. Methodist Homes, 1975-, Bacone Coll., 1968-77, Grad. Theol. Union, Berkeley, Calif., 1982—; trustee Am. Bapt. Sem. of West, Berkeley, 1975—, chmn. bd. trustees, 1987-95, exec. bd. adv. Sch. Econ. and Bus., St. Mary's Coll., Calif. Recipient Disting. Baconian award Bacone Coll., 1977, Disting. Alumnus award Centralia Coll., 1981, Meritorious Svc. award Am. Assn. Homes Aging, 1982, Merit citation Am. Bapt. Homes and Hosps. Assn., 1985, award of Honor Calif. Assn. Homes Aging, 1988. Mem. U.S. Assn. UN, Am. Assn. Homes and Svcs. Aging (Award of Honor 1994), Calif. Assn. Homes Aging, The Oakland 100, Harvard Club San Francisco, Pi Gamma Mu. Democrat. Office: Am Baptist Homes of West 6120 Stoneridge Mall Rd Pleasanton CA 94588-3296

ICE CUBE, (O'SHEA JACKSON), rap artist, actor; b. L.A., June 15, 1969; s. Hosea and "Moms" Doris Jackson.; m. Kim Jackson, 1992; 4 children. Albums: (with NWA) Straight Outta Compton, 1989, (solo) Amerikkka's Most Wanted,1990, Kill At Will, Death Certificate, 1991, The Predator, 1992; actor: (films) Boyz in the Hood, 1991, Trespass, 1992, Higher Learning, 1995, Anaconda, 1997, I Got the Hook Up, 1998, Three Kings, 1999, Ghosts of Mars, 2001, Barbershop, 2002, Torque, 2004, xXx: State of the Union, 2005; actor, screenwriter: The Glass Shield, 1995; actor, prodr: All About the Benjamins, 2002, Friday After Next, 2002, Barbershop 2: Back in Business, 2004, Are We There Yet?, 2005; actor, exec. prodr.: Friday, 1995, Dangerous Ground, 1997, The Players Club, 1998, Next Friday, 2000, Barbershop 2: Back in Business, 2005; exec. prodr., Beauty Shop, 2005. Office: Priority Records 6430 W Sunset Blvd Los Angeles CA 90028-7901

ICENHOWER, DELLA MAUDE, retired school librarian; b. Dalby Springs, Tex., July 18, 1929; d. Clarence Winston and Sarah Della (Young) Dalby; m. James Robert Icenhower, June 3, 1951; 1 child, John Dalby. BS, U. North Tex., 1950; MEd, Tex. A&M U., Commerce, 1955. Tchr. Pewitt Ind. Sch. Dist., Naples, Tex., 1950, Lufkin (Tex.) Ind. Sch. Dist., 1951, Falls County Schs., Rosebud, Tex., 1952-56, Borger (Tex.) Ind. Sch. Dist., 1956-64, Fritch (Tex.) Ind. Sch. Dist., 1964-68; sch. libr. Childress (Tex.) Ind. Sch. Dist., 1967-70, Mansfield (Tex.) Ind. Sch. Dist., 1970-90. Steering com. Mansfield Ind. Sch. Dist., 1994—, technology com., 1997—, supt. search com., 1980-81, election ofcl., 1991—, vol., 1990—; mem. adv. bd. Mansfield Pub. Libr., 1976—. Mem. Delta Kappa Gamma, Phi Delta Kappa, Alpha Delta Kappa, Model A Ford Club. Republican. Baptist. Home: 1044 Church St 108 Sulphur Springs TX 75482 E-mail: jimdelicen@aol.com.

ICE-T, (TRACY MARROW), rap artist, actor; b. Newark, Feb. 16, 1958; m. Nicole Austin, 2004; children: Tracy Marrow Jr., Letesha Marrow. Album: Rhyme Pays, 1987, O.G. Original Gangster, 1991, (with King Tee) Havin' a T Party, 1991, Body Count, 1992, Home Invasion, 1993, The Classic Collection, 1993, (with Body Count) Born Dead, 1994, 7th Deadly Sin, 1999, Greatest Hits: The Evidence, 2001; actor: Breakin', 1984, Breakin' 2, 1984, New Jack City, 1991, Ricochet, 1991, Trespass, 1992, Why Colors?, 1992, Surviving the Game, 1994, Tank Girl, 1995, Johnny Mnemonic, 1995, Mean Guns, 1997, The Deli, 1997, Beyond Utopia, 1997, Crazy Six, 1998, Final Voyage, 1999, Corrupt, 1999, The Wrecking Crew, 1999, Sonic Impact, 1999, The Heist, 1999, Frezno Smooth, 1999, Urban Menace, 1999, Stealth Fighter, 1999, Corrupt, 1999, Guardian, 2000, Gangland, 2000, Luck of the Draw, 2000, The Alternates, 2000, Stranded, 2001, Kept, 2001, Crime Partners, 2001, 3000 miles to Graceland, 2001, Point Doom, 2001, Deadly Rhapsody, 2001, 'R Xmas, 2001, Ticker, 2001, Out Kold, 2001, Ablaze, 2001, On the Edge, 2002, Tracks, 2002; TV Movies: Exiled, 1998, The Disciples, 2000; TV Series: Players, 1997-98, Law and Order: Special Victims Unit, 2000-; author: The Iceberg/Freedom of Speech, Just Watch What You Say, 1989, The Ice Opinion, 1994. Office: Priority Records 6430 W Sunset Blvd Los Angeles CA 90028-7901*

ICHEL, DAVID W., lawyer; b. Newark, May 14, 1953; s. Albert L. and Sylvia (Dreskin) I. BA, Duke U., 1975, JD, 1978. Bar: N.Y. 1979, N.J. 1978, U.S. Supreme Ct. 1983, U.S. Ct. Appeals (2nd cir.) 1984, U.S. Ct. Appeals (9th cir.) 1985, U.S. Dist. Ct. (so. dist.) N.Y. 1979, U.S. Dist. Ct. (ea. dist.) N.Y. 1980, U.S. Dist. Ct. N.J. 1978. With Simpson, Thacher & Bartlett, NYC, 1978-84, ptnr., 1985—. Chmn. bd. MFY Legal Svcs., Inc., products liability com. NY City Bar. Mem. exec. com. divsn. lawyers United Jewish Appeal; mem. bd. visitors Duke Law Sch. Mem. Am. Law Inst., Phi Beta Kappa. Office: Simpson Thacher & Bartlett 425 Lexington Ave Fl 15 New York NY 10017-3954 Office Phone: 212-455-2563. E-mail: dichel@stblaw.com.

ICHIISHI, TATSURO, economics and mathematics educator; b. Seoul, Dec. 16, 1943; came to U.S., 1970; s. Jitsuro and Tomiko Ichiishi; m. Barbara Ann Franklin, Sept. 7, 1973 BA in Econs., Keio U., Tokyo, 1966, MA in Econs., 1968; MA in Math., U. Calif., Berkeley, 1973, PhD in Econs., 1974. Rsch. assoc. Keio U., Tokyo, 1968-73; vis. rsch. fellow Cath. U. Louvain, Heverlee, Belgium, 1974-75; lectr., rsch. assoc. Northwestern U., Evanston, Ill., 1975-76; asst. prof. Carnegie-Mellon U., Pitts., 1976-80; assoc. prof. U. Iowa, Iowa City, 1980-83, prof., 1983-86, Ohio State U., Columbus, 1987—2003, Hitotsubashi U., Tokyo, 2001—02; prof. emeritus Ohio State U., 2004—. Vis. prof. Bilkent U., Ankara, Turkey, 1997; guest prof. Keio U., Tokyo, 1999; dir. Rsch. Ctr. for Math. Econ., 2004—. Author: Game Theory for Economic Analysis, 1983, The Cooperative Nature of the Firm, 1993, Microeconomic Theory, 1997; editor (with Abraham Neyman and Yair Tauman): Game Theory and Applications, 1990; editor: (with Thomas Marschak) Markets, Games and Organizations: Essays in Honor of Roy Radner, 2002; series editor Math. Econs. and Game Theory, 2000—, assoc. editor Rev. Econ. Design, 1997—, mem. editl. bd. Internat. Jour. Game Theory, 1997—, Advances in Mathematical Economics, 1998—, Games and Economic Behavior, 1998—; contbr. articles. Recipient Nikkei-Tosho Bunka Sho award Nihon Keizai Shinbun and Japan Ctr. for Econ. Rsch., 1994; CORE fellow, 1974-75; NSF grantee, 1978-82, 82-85, 92-96. Mem.: Game Theory Soc.

ICHILOV, NEHEMIA, principal, consultant; m. Lisa Ichilov; 2 children. BA, Rutgers U.; M, Jewish Theol. Sem. of Am., N.Y.C. Professoriate cert. U. Ctrl. Fla., 2003, lic. prin. Nat. Bd. of Lic. Spiritual leader Congregation Shalom of Williamsburg, Orlando, Fla., 2002—05; head of sch. Jerome Lippman Jewish Cmty. Day Sch., Akron, Ohio, 2003—. Mem. curriculum adv. com. JSkyway, Boston; adj. asst. prof. Siegal Coll., Cleve. Fellow Steinberg Leadership Inst., Anti-Defamation League; merit fellow, Whizin Inst. for Jewish Family Edn. Mem.: ASCD, Network for Rsch. in Jewish Edn., Am. Edn. Rsch. Assn., Assn. Dirs. of Ctrl. Agys., Kappa Delta Pi. Office: Lippman Day Sch 750 White Pond Dr Akron OH 44320 Office Phone: 330-836-0419. Office Fax: 330-869-2514. E-mail: nammie_ichilov@jewishakron.org.

ICHINO, YOKO, ballet dancer; b. Los Angeles, Cali. Studied with Mia Slavenska, L.A. Mem. Joffrey II, N.Y.C., Joffrey Ballet, N.Y.C., Stuttgart Ballet, Fed. Republic Germany; tchr. ballet, 1976; soloist Am. Ballet Theatre, 1977-81; guest appearances, 1981-82; prin. Nat. Ballet Can., Toronto, Ont., 1982-90. Various guest appearances including World Ballet Festival, Tokyo, 1979, 85, Tokyo Ballet, 1980, with Alexander Godunov and Stars, summer, 1982, Sydney Ballet, Australia, N.Z. Ballet, summer 1984, Ballet de Marseille, 1985-87, Deutsche Opera Ballet Berlin, 1985-90, Munich Opera Ballet, 1987-90, Australian Ballet, 1987, 89, Staatsoper Berlin, 1989, 90, Komische Opera, Berlin, 1991-93, David Nixon's Dance Theater, Berlin, 1990, 91, Birmingham Royal Ballet, 1990-93, Deutsche Opera Ballet, Berlin, 1994-95; tchr. Australian Ballet, 1989, Birmingham Royal Ballet, 1991, 93, Nat. Ballet of Can., 1993, Cullberg Ballet, Sweden, 1994, Nat. Ballet Sch., 1994, 95, Ballet de Monte-Carlo, 1994, Geneva Ballet, 1995-98, Nederlands Dance Theater, 1995, Rambert Dance, 1995, Royal Winnipeg Ballet, 1999; tchr. numerous ballet workshops; dir. profl. program Ballet Met, 1995-2003; guest master tchr., coach No. Ballet Theatre, 2002--. First Am. women recipient medal Third Internat. Ballet Competition, Moscow, 1977. Office: No Ballet Theatre West Park Centre Spen Ln Leeds LS16 5BE England

ICHIYAMA, DENNIS YOSHIHIDE, art educator, educational association administrator; b. Aiea, Hawaii, May 28, 1944; s. Edwin Kiyotada and Florence Fusae (Inoshita) I. BFA, U. Hawaii, 1966; MFA, Yale U., 1968; postgrad., Allgemeine Gewerbeschule, Basel, Switzerland, 1975-77. Instr. U. Bridgeport, Conn., 1968-70; sr. graphic designer Graphic Communications Ltd., Hong Kong, 1970-71; instr. Carnegie-Mellon U., Pitts., 1971-74; asst. prof. Cornell U., Ithaca, N.Y., 1974-75; assoc. prof. Ind. U., Bloomington, 1977-78; asst. prof. U. Ill., Chgo., 1978-79; assoc. prof. Wichita (Kans.) State U., 1979-81; prof., chmn. divsn. art and design Purdue U., West Lafayette, Ind., 1985-92, head dept. visual and performing arts, 1993—. Design cons. U.S. Postal Svc., Washington, 1986, Purdue U. Press, West Lafayette, 1989—, Interior Design Educators Coun., Ithaca, 1985-87; vis. scholar U. Iowa Ctr. for the Book, 1990; fellow to Ctr. for Artistic endeavor Purdue U. Sch. Liberal Arts, 1992; artist-in-residence Hamilton Wood Type & Printing Mus., Wis., 1999-2000, Ctr. for Book and Paper Arts, Columbia Coll., Chgo., 2005; bd. dir. Coll. Art Assn., 2002- Design work exhbns. in Can., U.S., Germany, Finland, France, Czechoslovakia; exhibited in shows at Centre Georges Pompidou, 1985, Poster Biennale, Warsaw, 1982, Biennale of Graphic Design, Brno, Czechoslovakia, 1982, 92, Columbia U. Rare Book and Manuscript Libr.; represented in collection of the Plakatsammlung of the Kunstgewerbemuseum, Zurich, Rochester Inst. of Tech. Libr., N.Y., Lahti Art Mus., Finland, Stern Book Arts and Spl. Collections Ctr., San Francisco Pub. Libr., Purdue U. Librs., The Ruth and Marvin Sackner Archive of Concrete and Visual Poetry; author essays in Contemporary Designers, 1985, T Y P O G R A M S, Pure Type Forms, 2000, The Hamilton Type Specimen Sheets Portfolio, 2001, book revs.; book reviewer Choice (ALA, Assn. Coll./Rsch. Librs.). Grantee Nat. Endowment for Humanities, 1984; IAC master fellow Ind. Arts Commn., 1985, 2001, Nat. Endowment for Arts, 1989, Individual Artist program grantee, 2001-03; Ctr. for Creative Endeavors fellow Purdue U., 1992, 2003—. Mem. Am. Ctr. for Design, Am. Inst. Graphic Arts, Graphic Design Educators Assn., Alliance Typographique Internat., Internat. Soc. Typograhic Designers, Soc. Typographic Arts, Nat. Coun. Art Adminstrs. (nat. bd. dirs. 1998—), Internat. Coun. Fine Arts Deans, Coll. Art Assn. Am. (nat. bd. dirs. 2002—), Arts Ind. (state coun. 1993-99), Hui na opio o Hawaii (advisor 1986-93), Greater Lafayette Mus. Art. Buddhist. Avocations: swiss posters, artists books, Chinese and Japanese seals, printing history, hand bookbinding and letterpress printing. Office: Purdue U Dept Visual/Performing Arts Bldg 552 W Wood St West Lafayette IN 47907 Office Phone: 765-494-3071. E-mail: diad@purdue.edu.

IDASZAK, JEROME JOSEPH, economic journalist; b. Chgo., Dec. 28, 1945; s. Joseph Edward and Estelle Charlotte (Grelecki) I.; m. Geraldine Rae Fehst, Sept. 4, 1976; children: Alexander Jerome, Joshua Adam. B.Journalism, Northwestern U., Evanston, Ill., 1967, M.Journalism, 1968. Reporter Rockford Morning Star, Ill., 1968-70; reporter Chgo. Tribune, Deerfield, Ill., 1974-76; fin. reporter Chgo. Sun Times, 1976-82, fin. columnist, 1982-90, Washington corr., 1985-90; freelance writer and editor, 1991; assoc. editor Kiplinger Washington Editors, 1992—. Fin. commentator Sta. WBBM-AM, Chgo., 1984-85; contbr. Sta. WBEZ-FM, Chgo., 1987-93; grad. journalism instr. Northwestern U., 1984; instr. Inst. for Exptl. Learning, 2002-04. Author: (newspaper series) Farm problems, 1983 (Peter Lisagor award 1984); Asian economy & growth, 1979 (Peter Lisagor award 1980). Vol., U.S. Peace Corps, 1970-72. Brookings Instn. fellow, 1979. Mem. Soc. Profl. Journalists, Nat. Returned Peace Corps. Vols., Chgo. Headline Club (bd. dirs. 1980-85, pres. 1984-85).

IDDINGS, KATHLEEN, poet, editor, publisher, consultant; b. Ohio, June 25, 1945; d. Ralph Myers and Ruth Amelia Wolfe. BS in Edn., Miami U., Oxford, Ohio, 1968. Tchr. various Ohio schs., 1962-74; freelance photojournalist La Jolla, Calif., 1976-80; freelance pub. rels. mgr. San Diego, 1980-81; cons., 1981—; editor, pub. La Jolla Poet's Press, 1981—. Poetry cons. San Diego City Schs., 1990; resident Djerassi Artists' Colony, 1990. Author: (poetry) Sticks, Friction & Fire, 2001, 5 other books of poetry. Named Poet of Millenium, Internat. Poets Acad., 2000; fellow, NEA, 1989; grantee, PEN, 1988, 1990, Calif. Arts Coun., 1994, Carnegie Authors; scholar, Napa Poetry Conf. Mem.: PEN, San Diego Ind. Scholars, Associated Writers Program, Acad. Am. Poets, Univ. Club, Calif. San Diego Faculty Club (Chancellor's Assoc. 1999—2004). Democrat. Avocations: poetry readings, photography, college lectures, poetry contest judge. Office: La Jolla Poets Press PO Box 8638 La Jolla CA 92038-8638 E-mail: KathleenIddings@aol.com.

IDE, ROY WILLIAM, III, lawyer; b. Geneva, Ill., Apr. 23, 1940; s. Roy William and Jenny (Coleman) Ide; m. Gayle Marie Oliver, Jan. 21, 1967; children: Logan, Jennifer, Lucienne. BA cum laude, Washington and Lee U., 1962; LLD, U. Va., 1965; MBA, Ga. State U., 1972. Bar: Ga. 1967, D.C. 1994, U.S. Ct. Appeals (5th and 11th cirs.) 1967, U.S. Supreme Ct. 1969. Law clk. Judge Griffin Bell U.S. Ct. Appeals (5th cir.), 1965—66; assoc. King & Spalding, Atlanta, 1966—71; ptnr. Huie, Sterne & Ide, Atlanta, 1971—77, Kutak Rock (and predecessor firm), Atlanta, 1978—92, mng. ptnr., Atlanta office; ptnr. Long, Aldridge & Norman; sr. v.p., spl. counsel E.F. Hutton and Co., Inc., 1985—87; spl. counsel, mng. dir. Prescott, Ball & Turben, 1988—89; gen. counsel, sec., sr. v.p. Monsanto Co., 1996—2001. Former bd. dirs., mem. exec. com. Atlanta Com. for Olympic Games; counselor U.S. Olympic Com., 1996—2002; bd. dirs. AFC Enterprises. Named one of Atlanta's Five Outstanding Men of Yr., 1976; recipient Arthur Van Briesen award, Nat. Legal Aid and Defender Assn., 1977. Mem.: ABA (ho. of dels., chair young lawyer's divsn. 1976, chair gen. practice sect. 1983—84, chair spl. com. on drug crisis 1991—92, 1992—93, pres. 1993—94), Ga. Bar Assn. (bd. govs.). Office: McKenna Long & Aldridge LLP 303 Peachtree St NE Ste 5300 Atlanta GA 30308 E-mail: bide@mckennalong.com.

IDEN, BRUCE FRANKLIN, lawyer; b. Detroit, Oct. 17, 1955; s. Jacob and Shirlee (Rose) I.; m. Lee Padnick, Sept. 24, 1983; 1 child, Daniel James. BA with honors, U. Mich., 1977; JD, George Washington U., 1981; LLM in Taxation, U. Miami, Fla., 1982. Bar: Fla. 1981, U.S. Dist. Ct. (so. dist.) Fla. 1981, U.S. Tax Ct. 1984, U.S. Ct. Appeals (9th and 11th cirs.) 1984. Adminstrv. asst. U.S. EPA, Washington, 1980; assoc. Milledge & Hermelee, Miami, 1982-85, ptnr., 1985, Milledge, Iden & Snyder, Miami, 1985—. Mem. ABA, Fla. Bar Assn., Dade County Bar Assn. Democrat. Jewish. Avocations: pottery, scuba diving, sailing, photography. Home: 13820 Chathan Pl Fort Lauderdale FL 33325-1227 Office: 3240 Corporate Way Miramar FL 33025-3910 Office Phone: 954-885-0085.

IDING, ALLAN EARL, lawyer; b. Milw., Apr. 29, 1939; s. Earl Herman and Erna Adeline (Albrecht) I.; m. Anne Louise Chaconas, July 9, 1961; children: Kent Earl, Krista Anne Templeman, Bradford A., Andrea Beth Brozynski. BS, Marquette U., 1961, LLB, 1963; DHL (hon.), Nashotah House, 1990. Bar: Wis. 1963, U.S. Dist. Ct. (ea. dist.) Wis. 1963, U.S. Ct. Appeals (7th cir.) 1963. Law clk. U.S. Ct. Appeals (7th cir.), Chgo., 1963—64; assoc. Whyte Hirschboeck Dudek, S.C., Milw., 1964—71, mem., 1971—. Trustee Nashotah House, 1976—; pres., bd. dirs. Wis. DeMolay Found., Milw., 1985—, Wis. Health and Ednl. Facilities Authority, 1978-85, pres., bd. dirs. Todd Wehr Found., Inc., Nashotah House Found., Inc.; chmn. bd. trustees Wis. Scottish Rite Bodies; mem. Wauwatosa (Wis.) Police and Fire Commn., 1978-83. Mem. Blue Mound Golf and Country Club, Masons (grand master Wis. 1981-82). Republican. Episcopalian. Avocation: golf. Home: 9212 Wilson Blvd Milwaukee WI 53226-1729 Office: Whyte Hirschboeck Dudek Ste 1900 555 E Wells St Milwaukee WI 53202 Office Phone: 414-978-5427. Business E-Mail: aiding@whdlaw.com.

IDLE, ERIC, actor, scriptwriter, film producer, lyricist; b. South Shields, Eng., Mar. 29, 1943; Pres. The Cambridge Footlights, 1964-65. TV shows include The Frost Report, Monty Python's Flying Circus, 1969-74, Rutland Weekend TV, 1975, Suddenly Susan, 1999-2000; films include And Now For Something Completely Different, 1971, Monty Python and the Holy Grail, 1975, The Rutles, 1978, Monty Python's Life of Brian, 1979, Monty Python Live at the Hollywood Bowl, 1982, Monty Python's The Meaning of Life, 1983, Yellowbeard, 1983, National Lampoon's European Vacation, 1985, Transformers: The Movie, 1986, The Adventures of Baron Munchausen, 1988, Nuns on the Run, 1990, Too Much Sun, 1991, Mom and Dad Save the World, 1993, Splitting Heirs, 1993, Casper, 1995, The Wind in the Willows, 1996, Burn Hollywood Burn, 1998, Dudley Do-Right, 1999, South Park: Bigger, Longer and Uncut (voice), 1999; writer (broadway plays): Spamalot, 2005 (Drama Desk award, outstanding lyrics, 2005); author The Greedy Bastard Diary: A Comic Tour of America, 2005. Office: Grant & Tani Inc 9100 Wilshire Blvd Ste 1000 Beverly Hills CA 90212-3415 also: William Morris 151 S El Camino Dr Beverly Hills CA 90212-2704

IDOL, ANNA CATHERINE, magazine editor; b. Chgo., July 8, 1941; d. Melvin Oliver and Louise Hildegard (Bullington) Lokensgard; m. William Ross Idol, Oct. 25, 1959 (div. Mar. 1962); 1 child, Laura Jeanne; m. Michael Wataru Sugano, Jan. 28, 1990. BS, Lake Forest (Ill.) Coll., 1980; MBA, Northwestern U., Evanston, Ill., 1982. treas. Chgo. Women in Pub., Chgo., 1970-71. Editor Rand McNally Co., Chgo., 1968-78, product mgr. adult reference, 1983-84; founder, pres. Bullington Laird, Inc., Chgo., 1986—; mng. editor Elks Mag., Chgo., 1997—. Pub.: Center Within, 1988 (award Heartsong Rev. 1989); writer, concept advt. alert, 1990 (Harvey Comm. award). Pres. Am. Buddhist Assn., 1985-93; mem. bd. Buddhist Temple Chgo., 1985-93; v.p. Buddhist Coun. Midwest, 1985-89. Democrat. Buddhist. Avocations: wilderness adventure, travel, reading. Office: Elks Mag 425 W Diversey Pkwy Chicago IL 60614-6196 Office Phone: 773-755-4894. Business E-Mail: annai@elks.org.

IDOL, JAMES DANIEL, JR., chemist, educator, inventor, consultant; b. Harrisonville, Mo., Aug. 7, 1928; s. James Daniel and Gladys Rosita (Lile) I.; m. Marilyn Thorn Randall, 1977. AB, William Jewell Coll., 1949; MS, Purdue U., 1952, PhD, 1955, D.Sc. (hon.), 1980. With Standard Oil Co., Ohio, 1955-77, rsch. supr., 1965-68, rsch. mgr., 1968-77; mgr. venture rsch. Ashland Chem. Co., Columbus, Ohio, 1977-79, v.p., dir. corp. R & D, 1979—88; disting. prof. materials sci. and ceramics sch. engring. Rutgers U., New Brunswick, NJ, 1988—2002, dir. polymer sci. ctr. for advanced materials via immiscible polymer processing, 2002—. Adv. bd. NSF Presdl. Young Investigators Awards, Nat. Inst. Sci. and Tech., 1997—; cons. in field; lectr. chem. engring. dept. Northwestern U., 1978, Stanford U., 1982-83, U. Calif., Berkeley, 1986, Yale U., 1988 U. Chgo., 1998; lectr. Lawrence Berkeley Lab., 1985-86; v.p., program coord. 1st N.Am. Chem. Congress, 1975; program coord. 1st Pacific Rim Chem. Cong., 1979; indsl. rep. U.S. Coun. for Chem. Rsch., 1983—, governing bd., 1985—; panel on frontiers in fossil fuel energy rsch. NRC, 1986, com. on tracking toxic wastes, 1989-93, panel on polymers in the environ. Internat. Union of Pure and Applied Chemistry, 1996, com. on energy conservation in processing of indsl. materials; adv. bd. U. Tex., Tex. A&M, Ohio State U., Purdue U., Okla. State U., Ariz. State U., U. Mass., Case Western Reserve U., 1965-75; com. polymers recycling Internat. Union Pure and Applied Chem., 1993—; mem. U.S. Coun. Chem. Rsch., 1981-89, gov. bd. 1985-88. Chmn. editl. adv. bd.: Indsl. & Engring. Chemistry Jour., 1976—84, mem. editl. adv. bd.: Chem. and Engring. News, 1977—81, Am. Chem. Soc. Symposium Series, 1978—84, Advances in Chemistry Series, 1979—84, Chem. Week Mag., 1980—82, Sci., 1986—91, Jour. Applied Polymer Sci., 1988—; contbr. chapters to books, articles to profl. jours., handbooks and encys. Active Cleve. Welfare Fedn. Recipient Modern Pioneer award NAM, 1965, Disting. Alumnus citation William Jewell Coll., 1971 Fellow AAAS, Am. Inst. Chemists (life; bd. dirs. 1981—, vice-chmn. 1986, chmn. 1987, Chem. Pioneer award 1968, Mems. and Fellows lectr. 1980); mem. Nat. Acad. Engring., Soc. Plastics Industry, Soc. Mfg. Engrs.-Composite Group, Am. Chem. Soc. (indsl. and engring. chemistry divsn., chmn. 1971, chem. innovator designation Chem. and Engring. News mag. 1971, adv. bd. Petroleum Rsch. Fund, 1974-76, Joseph P. Stewart Disting. Svc. award 1975, Creative Invention award 1975), Am. Mgmt. Assn. (R&D coun. 1985-88, Coun. award for Disting. Svc. pkg. coun. 1989-97, mfg. and tech. coun. 1997—), Dirs. of Indsl. Rsch., Am. Inst. Chem. Engrs., Licensing Execs. Soc., Soc. Plastics engrs., Indsl. Rsch. Inst. (rep., chmn. bd. editors 1983-86), Plastics Pioneers Assn., Soc. Chem. Industry (Perkin medal 1979), Ind. Acad. Sci., Catalysis Soc. (Ciapetti award/lectureship 1988), Cleve. Athletic Club, Cosmos Club (Washington), Worthington Hills Country Club, Masons, Shriners, Sigma Xi, Alpha Chi Sigma, Theta Chi Delta, Kappa Mu Epsilon, Alpha Phi Omega, Phi Gamma Delta. Mem. Christian Ch. (Disciples Of Christ). Achievements include invention of process for manufacture acrylonitrile (over 80 plants in 30 countries). This ammoxidation process was designated as Nat. Hist. Chem. Landmark 1996 by Am. Chem. Soc; patents in field. Office: Dept Ceramic & Materials Eng 607 Taylor Rd Rutgers Univ Piscataway NJ 08854-8065 Office Phone: 732-445-5750. E-mail: jdidol@rci.rutgers.edu.

IDRIS, AHAMED H., emergency medicine physician; b. N.Y.C., 1947; MD, Rush Med. Coll., 1979. Diplomate Am. Bd. Internal Medicine, Am. Bd. Emergency Medicine. Resident in internal medicine Cook County Hosp., Chgo., 1979-83; dir. emergency medicine rsch. Shands Tchg. Hosp., Gainesville, Fla., 1994—2003; prof. Surgery and emergency medicine U. Tex., Southwestern Med. Ctr., Dallas, 2003—; dir. Parkland Meml. Hosp., Dallas Ctr. for Resuscitation Rsch., 2003—. Chair nat. basic life support sub-com. Am. Heart Assn., 1999—2002; med. liaison, dir human space flight rescue team NASA, 1994—2003; cons. NIH. With M.C. U.S. Army, 1967—71. Decorated Bronze Star medal. Mem.: US Army Rsch. Team for Advanced Capabilities for Combat Medics, NIH Consortium for Resuscitation Rsch., Steering Com. Office: U Tex Southwestern Med Ctr 5323 Harry Hines Blvd Dallas TX 75390-8579 Office Phone: 214-648-4812.

IDZIK, DANIEL RONALD, retired lawyer; b. Depew, N.Y., Jan. 20, 1935; s. Daniel Henry and Ann Mary (Kolakowski) I.; m. Kathleen Osborne, Oct. 6 1989; children by previous marriage: Christopher, Rebecca, Laura, Susan. BS, SUNY, Buffalo, 1956; LLB, Harvard U., 1963. Bar: N.Y. 1964. Exec. v.p. U.S. Nat. Student Assn., Phila., 1956-57; assoc. sec. World Univ. Svc., Geneva, 1957-60; chief counsel N.Y. State Senate Com. on Labor and Industry, Albany, 1965; from assoc. counsel to gen. counsel Booz, Allen & Hamilton, Inc., N.Y.C., 1967-98; ret., 1998. Chmn. Philharmonia Virtuosi, Westchester County, N.Y., 1988-90, pres. 1987-88, bd. dirs. 1985-91; pres. Coun. for Arts in Westchester, 1983-85, bd. dirs., 1980-85; chmn., Friends of Neuberger Mus., Purchase, N.Y., 1991-93, pres., 1990, bd. dirs., 1987-97; bd. dirs. Buffalo State Coll. Found., 1985—, Jacob's Pillow, 1996—, LongBoat Key Ctr. Arts, 2000—, pres., 2002-04. Recipient Disting. Alumni award SUNY Buffalo, 1986, Arts award Coun,. for the Arts in Westchester, 1990. Mem. Harvard Club of N.Y. (mem. bd. mgrs. 1997-2000). Business E-Mail: daniel_idzik@post.harvard.edu.

IDZIK, MARTIN FRANCIS, lawyer; b. Depew, N.Y., Apr. 2, 1942; s. Daniel Henry and Ann Mary (Kolakowski) I.; m. Patricia Ann O'Brien, Aug. 7, 1965; children: Andrew, Amy. BS, Canisius Coll., 1963; JD, U. Notre Dame, 1966. Bar: N.Y. 1966. Assoc. Phillips, Lytle et al., Buffalo, 1971-76, ptnr., 1977-78, Jamestown, N.Y., 1979—. Bd. trustees Randolph Children's Home, 1993—99. Acting village justice, East Aurora, N.Y.,1972-79; bd. dirs. Chautauqua County Humane Soc., 1989-93, Downtown Jamestown Devel. Task Force, 1988-92, Jamestown YMCA, 1985-87, N.Y. State affiliate of Am. Heart Assn., 1983-85, Southwestern chpt. Am. Heart Assn., 1981-85, Jamestown Cmty. Learning Coun., 1995-2001, Roger Tory Peterson Inst., 2000—; chmn. fund for the Arts in Chautauqua County, 1984-88; pres. Arts Coun. Chautauqua County, 1982-84, United Way South Chautauqua County, 2000-01; mem. Jamestown Civic Ctr. Task Force, 1982-86, N.Y. State Mgmt. Atty.'s Conf., 1978—. Capt. JACG, U.S. Army, 1967-71. Mem. ABA, N.Y. State Bar Assn., Erie County Bar Assn., Jamestown Bar Assn. (pres. 1991-92), No. Chautauqua County Bar Assn., Sportsmen's Club (Stow, N.Y.). Office: Phillips Lytle LLP 8 E 3rd St PO Box 1279 Jamestown NY 14702-1279 Office Phone: 716-483-3903. Business E-Mail: midzik@phillipslytle.com.

IENNER, DON, music company executive; Co-founder,exec. v.p. Millennium Records, 1977—83; v.p. promotion, later exec. v.p., gen. mgr. Arista Records, 1983—89; pres. Columbia Records, N.Y.C., 1989; chmn. Columbia Records Group, N.Y.C., 1994—2004; pres., CEO Sony Music Label Group, U.S., 2004—. Office: Columbia Records 550 Madison Ave New York NY 10022-3211

IERARDI, ERIC JOSEPH, school system administrator; b. Bklyn., May 11, 1950; s. Joseph and Angelina (Vitale) Ierardi. BA, St. Francis Coll., 1973; MEd, Fordham U., 1987. Asst. dir. James A. Kelly Local Hist. Studies Inst., 1973; St. Francis Coll. tchr. St. Bartholomew's Sch., 1974-78; tchr. Our Lady of Grace Sch., Bklyn., 1978-86, St. Mary Star of Sea Sch., 1986-87, asst. on edn. to Bklyn. borough pres., 1979; dist. rep., mgr. Congressman Stephen J. Solarz, 1981-82; prin. St. Francis Xavier Sch., Vicksburg, Miss., 1987-89, St. Francis Paola Sch., Bklyn., 1989-91, St. Pius V, Jamaica, Queens, N.Y., 1991-96; adminstr. David A. Boody Intermediate Sch. 228, Bklyn. Instr. Hinds CC, Bklyn.; U.S. del. Gruppo Savoia, 2000. Author: Gravesend: The Home of Coney Island, 1975, Gravesend: Brooklyn, Coney Island & Sheepshead Bay, 1996, Brooklyn in the 1920s, 1998; contbg. editor: Bklyn. Mag., 1978—79. Past mem. Cmty. Planning Bd. 11, Bklyn.; commr. deeds City of N.Y.; past pres. Gravesend Dem. Club. Decorated knight His Royal Higness Prince Victor Emmanuel IV of Savoy; named Hon. Mayor, Gravesend, Eng., 1977, Knight Officier, Order of Merit Savoy, 2002, Honor Guard, Royal Tombs at Pantheon Rome, 2003; recipient Calabrian of the Yr. award, Brutium Cultural Club, 1979. Mem.: Gravesend Hist. Soc. (pres.), Columbia Tchrs. Assn., Assn. Tchrs. Social Studies, U. S. Fla. Club, Circolog Culturale Club, Order Sons of Italy. Democrat. Roman Catholic. Home: PO Box 5 Upper Black Eddy PA 18972-0005 Office: IS 228 228 Avenue S Brooklyn NY 11223-2746 Office Phone: 718-375-7635 228. Personal E-mail: ericierardi@aol.com.

IEYOUB, RICHARD PHILLIP, lawyer, former state attorney general; b. Lake Charles, La., Aug. 11, 1944; s. Phillip Assad and Virginia Khoury Ieyoub; m. Caprice Brown, Feb. 3, 1995; children: Amy Claire, Nicole Anne, Brennan Jude, Richard Phillip Jr., Khoury Myhand, Christian Brown, Anna Michael. BA in history, McNeese State U., 1968; JD, La. State U., 1972. Bar: La. 1972, U.S. Supreme Ct. Spl. prosecutor to atty. gen. State of La., Baton Rouge, 1972—74; assoc. Camp, Carmouche, Lake Charles, 1974—76; mem. Stockwell, Sievert, Lake Charles, 1976—78, Baggett, McCall, Singleton, Ranier, Ieyoub, Lake Charles, 1978—; pvt. practice Lake Charles; dist. atty. Calcasieu Parish, 1985—92; atty. gen. State of La., 1992—2004; ptnr. Couhig Partners, Baton Rouge, 2004—. Instr. criminal law McNeese State U.; chmn. La. Drug Policy Bd. Active La. Commn. on Law Enforcement; apptd. by gov. to adv. bd. D.A.R.E., La.; chmn. New Orleans Met. Crime Task Force, Gov.'s Military Adv. Commn.; active President's Commn. on Model State Drug Laws, 1992—; parish coun. Immaculate Conception Cathedral Parish, Lake Charles; bd. dirs. S.W. La. Health Counseling Svcs., Crime Stoppers of Lake Charles, St. Jude Children's Rsch. Hosp., 1998—99; vice-chmn. La. coord. Coun. on the Prevention of Drug Abuse and Treatment of Drug Use; bd. dirs.

La. State U. Alumni Assn. Named Outstanding Pub. Ofcl. for Diocese Lake Charles, 1990; recipient Disting. Alumnus award, McNeese State U., 1994, Legis. Leadership award, Nat. Coun. Against Drinking and Driving, 1996, Ochsner Humanitarian award, 1998. Mem.: ABA (vice-chmn. prosecution function com.), So. Attys. Gen. Assn. (elected chmn.), S.W. La. Bar Assn. (exec. com. 1979), Nat. Coll. Dist. Attys. (bd. regents 1991), La. Dist. Attys. Assn. (pres., bd. dirs. 1989—90), Nat. Assn. Attys. Gen. (exec. working group on prosecutorial rels.), Nat. Dist. Attys. Assn. (pres., bd. dirs. 1990—91), La. Bar Assn. (lectr. criminal law), Nat. Assn. Criminal Def. Lawyers, Assn. Trial Lawyers Am., Sierra Club. Democrat. Roman Catholic. Office Phone: 225-612-4670. Business E-Mail: rieyoub@couhigpartners.com.

IEZZA, ANITA KAY, physician assistant; b. Austin, Tex., Oct. 11, 1956; d. Bobby Ray and Elizabeth Frances (McDowell) Hazen; m. Joseph Thomas Iezza, Jan. 5, 1982 (div. Sept. 1993); children: Joseph Thomas, Jr. (dec.), Anita Elizabeth. BS, Physician Assoc., Trevecca Nazarene Coll., Nashville, 1979; MS, L.I. U., 1998. Physician asst. Montefiore Med. Ctr., Bronx, N.Y., 1979—, sr. physician asst., 1992—, HIV primary care trainer, 1991-92. Programs and edn. region v.p. Chpt. 21 Parents Without Ptnrs., Westchester County, N.Y., 1995-96. V.p. Parents Club, St. Catharine Acad., 2001-2002, pres., 2002-03. Mem.: NY State Physician Asst. Assn., Am. Acad. Physician Assts. Roman Catholic. Avocations: art, music, jazz, sports, reading books. Office: Montefiore Med Ctr 111 E 210th St Bronx NY 10467-2401 Business E-Mail: aiezza@montefiore.org.

IFFT, LEWIS GEORGE, III, foundation administrator; b. Uniontown, Pa., July 21, 1951; s. Lewis George Jr. and Miriam Katherine Wilson; m. Kathleen Marie Andersen, Mar. 26, 1983; children: Christopher Andrew, Jonathan Lewis. BS in Bus. Adminstrn., Bowling Green (Ohio) State U., 1973; MBA, Rensselaer Polytechnic Inst., Troy, N.Y., 1979. Ops. mgr. Battery Products Divsn. Union Carbide Corp., 1973-80; asst. reg. mgr. Eastern Region TransAmerica Corp., Elizabeth, NJ, 1980-82, reg. mgr. Eastern Region, 1982, regional mgr. Central Region Chgo., 1982-89; v.p. The Fred Barbara Co., Chgo., 1989-90; v.p., gen. mgr. Global Intermodal Systems, 1990—2004; regional v.p., mem. exec. com. Con Global Industries, San Ramon, Calif., 2004—. Mem. bd. dirs. Global Intermodal Systems, Inc., San Ramon, Calif. Presbyterian. Office: Con Global Industries 11700 Wallisville Rd Houston TX 77013-3421 Personal E-mail: lgifft@cgini.com.

IFFY, LESLIE, medical educator; b. Budapest, Hungary, May 17, 1925; came to U.S., 1969; s. Zoltan and Rozsa (Lantos) I.; m. Margaret Lesniak. MD, U. Budapest, Hungary, 1949; MD (hon.), U. Budapest, 1993. Diplomate Am. Bd. Ob-Gyn. Resident, fellow Országos Testnevelési és Sportegészségügyi Intézet Hosp. Ministry of Health, Budapest, 1951-56; fellow U. Wash., Seattle, 1964; asst. prof. Temple U., Phila., 1969-70; assoc. prof. U. Ill., Chgo., 1971-72, Jefferson Med. Coll., Phila., 1972-73; prof. U. Medicine and Dentistry of N.J., Newark, 1974—; dir. obstetrics U. Hosp., Newark, 1974—. Contbr. over 190 articles to profl. jours. and chpts. to books; editor: Perinatology Case Studies, 1978, 85, Obstetrics and Perinatology, 1981 (in English and Spanish), Operative Perinatology, 1984 (in English, Spanish and Japanese), Operative Obstetrics, 2d edit., 1992. Recipient Dr. Robert Jardine Rsch. prize, U. Glasgow, 1963, award for Disting. Svc., U. Medicine and Dentistry N.J., 2005, Semmelweis Meml. award, U. Budapest, 1993; rsch. fellow, Ford Found., Seattle, 1964, hon. fellow, Hungarian Obstet. Soc., 1986. Fellow Royal Coll. Surgeons (Can.); mem. Cen. Assn. Ob-Gyn. (life), Chgo. Gynecol. Soc., Am. Coll. Legal Medicine (bd. dirs. 1989-95), Royal Coll. Physicians (Edinburgh, Scotland, licentiate), Royal Faculty Physicians and Surgeons (Glasgow, Scotland, licentiate), Romanian Soc. Obstetricians and Gynecologists (hon.). Avocations: music, chess, literature, art. Home: PO Box 550 5 Robin Hood Rd Summit NJ 07901 Office: NJ Med Sch UMDNJ 150 Bergen St Newark NJ 07103 Office Phone: 973-972-5838. E-mail: liffy@comcast.net.

IGALI, BARALADEI DANIEL, Olympic athlete; b. Eniwari, Bayeisa, Nigeria, Feb. 3, 1974; arrived in Can., 1994; s. Maureen Matheny. Student in Mass Comm., Nigeria; student, Simon Fraser U.; BA in Criminology, Simon Fraser U., Burnaby, B.C., Can., 2001, postgrad., 2002—. Named Nat. Wrestling Champion, Nigeria, 1990, African Wrestling Champion, Cairo, 1993, World Champion Wrestler, Ankara, Turkey, 1998, Athlete of Yr., Can., 1999, 2000, 6 Time Can. Nat. Wrestling Champion, 1998—, 4 Time Nigerian Nat. Champion, 1991—94, 2 Time African Champion, 1992—94; recipient Wrestling Gold medal, Olympics, 2000. Avocations: Kabaddi, watching wrestling movies, soccer, surfing the Internet. Office: 8876-140 St PO Box 16531 Surrey BC Canada V3W 2P5 Home: 128-8655 King George Hwy Surrey BC Canada V3W 5C4 Personal E-mail: dynamiteigali@hotmail.com. E-mail: danieligali@aol.com.

IGBINEWEKA, ANDREW OSABUOHIEN, public administration, political science educator; b. Benin City, Edo State, Nigeria, Nov. 30, 1947; came to U.S., 1973, naturalized; s. Igbineweka Moses Iditua and Victoria Ilekhue (Idahor) Igbineweka; m. Pauline Omono Airen, June 24, 1980; children: Ofumwegbe, Oyemwen, Osagie, Osasu, Osaruyi. BA, U. Mary Hardin-Baylor, 1976; MA, U. North Tex., 1979, PhD, 1982. Libr. Immaculate Conception Coll., Benin City, 1968-69; clerical officer High Ct. of Justice Jud. Dept., Benin City, 1969-73; tchg. asst. U. North Tex., Denton, 1976-79; lectr. II, asst. prof. U. Benin, Benin City, 1983-85, lectr. I, 1985-89, sr. lectr., 1989-92, head dept., 1990-91; Disting. vis. prof. U. Calgary, Alta., Can., 1992; vis. prof. Indiana U. Pa., 1992-94; ind. rsch. cons. Pitts., 1994—. Mem., cons. U. Benin Consulting Svcs., 1984-92; therapist Suzanne and Assocs. and Western Bell, Pitts., 1997—; casemanager Shuman Juvenile Detention Ctr., Pitts., 1998—; therapeutic staff support, therapist Sharp Visions Inc., Pitts., 1999—, therapeutic staff support and mobile therapist, Pressly Ridge Schs, Pitts., 1999—. Contbr. chpts. to books and articles to profl. jours. Chmn. Getty's Dormitory, U. Mary Hardin-Baylor, Belton, Tex., 1974-75, v.p. Internat. Club, 1974-75, chmn. Bapt. Students Union Internat., 1974-76, pres., founder chess club, 1975-76; chmn. constn. revision com. Nigerian Students Assn., U. North Tex., 1977, pres., 1981-82; senate mem. U. Benin, 1990-91; chmn. Aduwa Club constn. revision com., Benin City, 1992; vol. Lay Reader's Assn., St. Albert's Cath. Ch., U. Benin, 1984-92, Parish Laity Coun., 1984-92, Group Svcs. to Aged Patients of Beacon Manor, Inc., spring 1994; active St. Paul Cathedral, 1999—. Recipient Internat. Student Scholarship award Southwestern U., Georgetown, Tex., 1973-74, U. Mary Hardin-Baylor, Belton, 1974-76, 75-76, Hon. Scholarship award, 1975-76; grantee U. Benin, Benin City, 1984-85, 87-88, Indiana U. Pa., 1992-93, 93-94. Mem. ASPA, Am. Polit. Sci. Assn., Policy Studies Orgn., Internat. Polit. Sci. Assn. (rsch. com.), Nigerian Inst. Mgmt. Cons. (pub. rels. officer 1986-97), U.S. Chess Fedn. (U. Pitts. chess club chpt.), Pitts. Chess Club, Pi Sigma Alpha, Phi Alpha Theta. Avocations: chess, billiards, soccer coaching, religious activities, cruising the internet.

IGER, ROBERT A., film company executive; b. N.Y.C., Feb. 10, 1951; m. Willow Bay, Oct. 1995; children: Kate, Amanda, Max, William. BA magna cum laude, Ithaca Coll., 1973. Studio supr. ABC-TV, 1974—76; various pos. ABC-TV Sports, 1976—85; former v.p. program planning, development ABC Sports, 1985—87, v.p. program planning and acquisition, 1987—88; exec. v.p. ABC TV Network Group, 1988—89, pres., 1992—94, ABC Entertainment, 1989—92; exec. v.p. Capital Cities/ABC Inc., N.Y.C., 1993—94, pres., COO, 1994—96; pres. ABC, Inc., N.Y.C., 1996—99; chmn. ABC Group, 1999—; pres., COO The Walt Disney Co., Burbank, Calif., 2000—. Trustee Ithaca Coll. Office: The Walt Disney Co 500 S Buena Vista St Burbank CA 91521-0001

IGGERS, GEORG GERSON, history professor; b. Hamburg, Germany, Dec. 7, 1926; came to U.S., 1938, naturalized, 1949; s. Alfred G. and Lizzie (Minden) I.; m. Wilma Abeles, Dec. 23, 1948; children: Jeremy, Daniel, Karl Jonathan. BA, U. Richmond, 1944, DHL, 2001; AM, U. Chgo., 1945, PhD, 1951; postgrad., New Sch. Social Rsch., 1945-46; doctorate (hon.), Philander Smith Coll., 2002. Instr. U. Akron, Ohio, 1948-50; assoc. prof. Philander Smith Coll., Little Rock, 1950-57; from assoc. prof. to prof. Dillard U., New Orleans, 1957-63; assoc. prof. Roosevelt U., Chgo., 1963-65; prof. history SUNY, Buffalo, 1965—, disting. prof., 1978-97, chmn., 1981-84, disting. prof. emeritus, 1997—. Mem. Conf. Group Ctrl. European History, vice chmn., 1989-90, chmn., 1990-91; vis. prof. U. Ark., Fayetteville, 1956-57, 64, U. Rochester, 1970-71, U. Leipzig, Germany, 1992; vis. assoc. prof. Tulane U., New Orleans, 1958-60, 63; vis. scholar Technische Hochschule Darmstadt, Germany, 1991, Forschungsschwerpunkt zeithistorische Studien, Potsdam, Germany, 1993; fellow Woodrow Wilson Ctr. Internat. Scholars, Washington, 1993-94; vis. prof. Aarhus (Denmark) U., 1998, Zentrum für Zeithistorische Forschung, Potsdam, Germany, 1998, U. New Eng. (Australia), 1999, Internat. Forschungszentrum Kulturwissenschaften, Vienna, 2000, U. Vienna, 2002. Author: The Cult of Authority, 1958, The German Conception of History, 1968, New Directions in European Historiography, 1975, Geschichtswissenschaft im 20 Jahrhundert, 1993, Historiography in the Twentieth Century, 1997; co-author (with Wilma Iggers): Zwei Seiten der Geschichte, 2002; editor (with Harold T. Parker): International Handbook of Historical Studies, 1979, The Social History of Politics, 1986; editor: (with James Powell) Leopold von Ranke and the Shaping of the Historical Discipline, 1990, Ein anderer historischer Blick Beispiele ostdeutscher Sozialgeschichte, 1991, Marxist Historiography in Transformation, 1991; co-editor: Storia della Storiografia jour., Geschichtswissenschaft der DDR als Forschungsproblem, Historische Zeitschrift, Sonderband 27, 1998; mem. editl. bd. Zeitschrift für Geschichtswissenschaft, History and Theory. Bd. dirs., counselor Draft and Mil. Counseling Ctr., Buffalo, 1967-89; bd. dirs.Citizens Coun. Human Rels., Buffalo, 1965—; chmn. edn., exec. coms. NAACP, Little Rock, 1951-56, chmn. edn. com., New Orleans, 1957-63, bd. dirs, Buffalo, 1965—, chmn. edn. com., 1965-75, co-chmn. health com., 1979-85. Fellow Guggenheim Found., 1960-61, Rockefeller Found., 1961-62, NEH, 1971-72, 78-79, 85-86, Ctr. Interdisciplinary Rsch., Bielefeld, Fed. Republic Germany, 1986-87; hon. fellow Fulbright Commn. 1978-79, 85-86, 87; recipient Kittler award Technische Hochschule Darmstadt, 1988, Alexander von Humboldt Rsch. prize 1993. Mem. Internat. Commn. Historiography (v.p. 1980-95, pres. 1995-2000, exec. com. 1980-2005), Am. Hist. Assn., German Studies Assn., Acad. Scis. of German Dem. Republic (fgn. mem. 1990-92). Office: Dept History Park Hall SUNY Buffalo NY 14260-4130 Home (Summer): Schillerstrasse 50 D 37083 Göttingen Germany Business E-Mail: iggers@buffalo.edu.

IGLEHART, PATRICIA ANN, business development and communications executive; b. Waco, Tex., Jan. 2, 1944; d. Stephen Austin and Susie Odell (White) I.; m. Lance Dunn Shaw, June 11, 1965 (div. Dec. 1970). Student, Tex. A&M U., 1962-65; BS, N.Mex. State U., 1966; M in Natural Scis., Ariz. State U., 1971; MS in Applied Math. & Statistics, SUNY, Stony Brook, 1975; MS in Math., NYU, 1978; PhD in Math., Stevens Inst. Tech., 1996. Math. tchr. Gadsden H.S., Anthony, N.Mex., 1966-67, Glendale (Ariz.) Union H.S. Dist., 1968-69; math. dept. chmn. Phoenix H.S. Dist., 1969-73; sys. engr. IBM U.S. Eastern Area, Springfield, N.J., 1977-79, Piscataway, N.J., 1979-84; product adminstr. IBM ISG U.S., White Plains, N.Y., 1984-86; sys. engrng. mgr. IBM NA Eastern Area, Harrison, N.Y., 1986-89; sr. program mgr. market rsch. studies and IT opportunity analysis IBM NA S&D Market Analyses, White Plains, N.Y., 1989-98; e-bus. market intelligence Internet divsn. IBM, Somers, N.Y., 1998-99; IBM/Lotus knowledge mgmt. project office IBM Software Group, Somers, N.Y., 1999-2000; with storage svcs. divsn. IBM Global Svcs., Somers, 2001—03; founder and pres. Just As I Am Ministries, Waco, Tex., 2004—. Mem. IBM NA Sr. Fin. Mgmt. Group, 1998; CEO, owner Dry-Glo Mktg., Carmel, N.Y., 1987-90. Bd. dirs. Carmel Civic Assn., 1997-99; bd. mgrs. Woodland Trail, 1998-99; mem. Mission Ch. Assembly of God, Holmes, N.Y. Mem. Am. Math. Soc., Math. Assn. Am., Phi Kappa Phi. Democrat. Avocation: playing piano. Home: 1415 Chapel Hill Dr Waco TX 76712 Personal E-mail: iglehartpa1@aol.com.

IGLESIAS, DAVID CLAUDIO, prosecutor; b. Jan. 1958; B, Wheaton Coll.; JD, U. N.Mex. Asst. atty. gen. N.Mex Atty. Gen. Office; asst. city atty. City of Albuquerque, 1991—94; spl. asst. to sec. transp. White Ho. Fellowship, 1995; chief counsel N.Mex Risk Mgmt. Legal Office, 1995—98; gen. counsel N.Mex Taxation and Revenue Dept., 1998—2001; assoc. Walz and Assoc., Albuquerque; U.S. atty. dist. N.Mex US Dept. Justice, 2001—. Comdr. JAGC USNR. Office: US Atty PO Box 607 Albuquerque NM 87103

IGLESIAS, MARIA ESTRELLA, language educator, writer; b. Granada, Spain, Jan. 11, 1952; arrived in U.S.A., 1977; d. Severiano Iglesias-Galindo and Dolores Tortosa-Orihuela; m. Christopher H. Maurer, Mar. 2, 1977; children: Daniel, Pablo. BA in Journalism, Temple U., 1978; MA in Spanish Lit., U. Pa., 1980. Tchr., Spanish U. Sch. Nashville, 1990—2000; assoc. dir., edn. tchr., U. Ill., 2000—. Co-author: Temas: Invitacion a la Literature Hispanica, 1994, Dreaming in Clay on the Coast of Miss.: Love and Art at Shearwater, 2000. Democrat. Avocation: jewelry making.

IGLEWICZ, BORIS, statistician, educator; b. Omsk, USSR, Oct. 11, 1939; arrived in US, 1952, naturalized, 1959; s. Solomon and Faiga (Brucker) Iglewicz; m. Raja Brody, May 24, 1973; children: David, Alana. BS, Wayne State U., 1962; MA, 1963; PhD, Va. Poly. Inst., 1967. Instr. math. Mich. Tech. U., 1963-64; asst. prof. stats. Case Western Res. U., 1967-69; asso. prof. stats. Temple U., 1969-74, prof., 1974—, dir. Ph.D. program in stats., 1970-76, chmn. dept., 1978-82, dir. biostats. group, 1992-93, dir. biostats. rsch. ctr., 1993—. V.p., dir. Meco Metals Corp., 1974; vis. prof. Harvard U., 1984—85. Author: (with J. Stoyle) An Introduction to Mathematical Reasoning, 1973, (with D.C. Hoaglin) How to Detect and Handle Outliers, 1993; contbr. articles to profl. jours., chpts. to books. NIH fellow, 1964-67; advanced rsch. fellow Harvard U., 1978; recipient Musser Leadership award, 2001, Don Owen award 2003. Fellow: Am. Statis Assn. (pres. Phila. chpt. 1981—83, W.J. Youden award 2001), Royal Statis. Soc.; mem.: Internat. Stats. Inst., Am. Soc. Quality (sr.), Inst. Math. Stats., Biometric Soc., Beta Gamma Sigma, Pi Mu Epsilon, Sigma Xi. Home: 1912 Rolling Ln Cherry Hill NJ 08003-3328 Office: Temple U 1810 N 13th St Dept Stats Philadelphia PA 19122 Office Phone: 215-204-8637. Business E-Mail: borisi@temple.edu.

IGNACIO, REINERE JOHN DY, research scientist; b. Manila, May 26, 1972; s. Reynaldo Mendoza and Lorna Dy I. BS, U. Ill., 1998. Instr. Naval Med. Ctr., Oakland, Calif., 1994-95; sr. rsch. assoc. Pierce Milw., 1998—. Mem. Nat. Sci. Adv. Coun. Alverno Coll., Milw., 2000—. Vol. tchr. Cath. East Elem. Sch., Milw., 2000. With USN, 1991-95. Mem. AAAS, Protein Soc., Soc. Biomolecular Screening. Home: 1533 E Royall Pl 10 Milwaukee WI 53202 Office: Pierce Milw 2202 N Bartlett Ave Milwaukee WI 53202 Fax: 414-227-3759. E-mail: ray.ignacio@perbio.com.

IGNAGNI, KAREN, healthcare association executive; Degree, Providence Coll.; MBA, Loyola U. Formerly with Com. for Nat. Health Ins., HHS; former profl. staff mem. U.S. Senate Labor and Human Resources Com.; dir. Dept. Employee Benefits AFL-CIO, 1990—93; pres., CEO Group Health Assn. Am., 1993—95, Am. Assn. Health Plans, 1995—. Office: Am Assn Health Plans 1129 20th St NW Ste 600 Washington DC 20036

IGNARRO, LOUIS J., pharmacology educator; b. Bklyn., May 31, 1941; m. Sharon Elizabeth Williams, July 1997; 1 child from previous marriage. BA in Pharmacy, Columbia U., 1962; PhD in Pharmacology, U. Minn., 1966; degrees (hon.), U. Madrid, Lund U., U. Gent, U. NC. Postdoctoral rsch., Lab. Chem. Pharmacology Nat. Heart, Lung and Blood Inst., NIH; head, biochem, anti-inflammatory program Geigy Pharmaceuticals, 1968—73; asst. prof., pharmacology Tulane Univ. Sch. Medicine, New Orleans, 1973—79, prof., pharmacology, 1979—85; prof. dept. molecular and med. pharmacology UCLA Sch. Medicine, 1985—. Contbr. articles to profl. jours. Recipient Edward G. Schlieder Found. award, 1973, Merck Rsch. award, 1974, Rsch. Career Devel. award, USPHS, 1975—80, Nobel prize in physiology or medicine, 1998; fellow postdoctoral, NIH, 1966—68. Mem.: NAS, Alpha Omega Alpha (hon.). Achievements include research in biochemical, physiological, and pathophysioilogical roles of nitric oxide and cyclic GMP in mammalian cell function; the transcriptional, translational and catalytic regulation of constitutive and inducible nitric oxide synthases; the role of other biochemical pathways in the regulation of biosynthesis and metabolism of nitric oxide; the biochemical and chemical mechanisms by which nitric oxide elicits cytotoxic effects on invading target cells and microorganisms; the role of nitric oxide as a neurotransmitter in non-adrenergic non-cholinergic neurons innervating various issues. Office: UCLA Sch Medicine Dept Molecular & Med Pharmacology 23-315 Chs 10833 Leconte Ave Los Angeles CA 90095-1735*

IGNATIEV, ALEX, physics researcher; b. Wehingen, Germany, Feb. 14, 1945; U.S. citizen; married; two children. BS, U. Wis., 1966; PhD in Material Sci., Cornell U., 1972. Postdoctoral fellow material sci. SUNY, Stony Brook, 1971—73; from asst. prof. to assoc. prof. physics and chemistry U. Houston, 1974—83, prof. physics and chemistry, 1983—2003, disting. prof., physics, chemistry & elec. and computer engring., 2003—; assoc. dir. Magnetic Info Rsch. Lab., 1984-89. Mem. energy lab. U. Houston, 1975—; lectr. physics Aarhus U., Denmark, 1977-78; Fulbright sr. scholar, 1983; assoc. dir. Space Vacuum Epitaxy Ctr., 1986-88, dir. 1988—; task leader Tex. Ctr. for Superconductivity, 1987—; dir. Tex. Ctr. superconductivity and advanced materials, 2002-. Assoc. editor Vacuum, Space Forum, Research Trends; contbr. numerous articles to profl. jours. Mem. AIAA, AAAS, ASME, IEEE, SPIE, Internat. Acad. Astronautics, Am. Phys. Soc., Am. Vacuum Soc., Am. Chem. Soc., Internat. Solar Energy Soc, The Materials Rsch. Soc., Sigma Xi. Business E-Mail: ignatiev@uh.edu.

IGNATONIS, SANDRA CAROLE AUTRY, special education educator; b. Dixon Mills, Ala., June 6, 1942; d. Charles Franklin Autry; m. Algis Jerome Ignatonis, June 15, 1968; children: Audra Carole, David Jerome. BA, Samford U., 1964; cert. in Gifted Edn., Kennesaw State U., 1989. Cert. tchr., Ga. Tchr. Jefferson County Bd. Edn., Birmingham, Ala., 1964, Huntsville (Ala.) Bd. Edn., 1964-71, Epiphany Cath. Sch., Miami, Fla., 1981, Cobb County Bd. Edn., Marietta, Ga., 1982, Bartow County Bd. Edn., Cartersville, Ga., 1990-92, Sequoria Group, Inc., Roswell, Ga., 1996; with Atlanta real estate divsn. Regions Bank, Atlanta, 1997—. Mem. Sch. Self-Governance Com., Emerson, Ga., 1990-91, Soccer Adv. Bd., Marietta, 1985-89; judge, mem. Social Sci. Fair Competitions, Huntsville, 1964-71. Team mom Metro N. Youth Soccer Assn., Marietta, 1991-92; block parent Somerset Subdivision, Marietta, 1982-86, block capt., 1998-99; polit. chmn. Student Nat. Edn. Assn., Samford U., Birmingham, Ala., 1963-64; bd. dirs. Somerset Home-owners Assn., 1998-99. Recipient grant Samford U. Faculty, 1963. Mem. Ga. Supporters of Gifted, Profl. Assn. Ga. Educators. Republican. Roman Catholic. Avocations: tennis, bowling, gardening, needle work, reading. Office: Regions Bank 400 Embassy Row 6600 Peachtree Dunwoody Rd NE Atlanta GA 30328-1649

IGNOZZI, BRYAN K., management consultant; b. Pitts., Feb. 3, 1971; s. Gus Kenneth and Edith Jan (Andring) I. BS, Allegheny Coll., 1993; MBA, Rollins Coll., 1997. Real estate assoc. J&K Realty, Lower Burrell, Pa., 1991-94; cons. PNC Bank Corp., Pitts., 1994-96; prof. So. Coll., Orlando, 1998—; mgmt. cons. Dreifus Assocs. Ltd., Orlando, 1997-99; sr. cons. KPMG, LLP, Charlotte, N.C., 1998—. Vol. Habitat for Humanity. Mem. Nat. Assn. Campus Card Users, Smart Card Industry Assn., Am. Mktg. Assn. Roman Catholic. Home: 3283 Leechburg Rd Lower Burrell PA 15068-2846 Office: KPMG LLP 2800 Two First Union Ctr Charlotte NC 28282

IGO, GEORGE JEROME, physics professor; b. Greeley, Colo., Sept. 2, 1925; s. Henry J. and Ida J. (Danielsen) I.; m. Nancy Tebow, May 12, 1953; children: Saffron, Peter Alexander. AB, Harvard Coll., 1949; MS, U. Calif., Berkeley, 1951, Phd, 1953. Postdoctoral Yale Univ., 1954, Brook Haven Nat. Lab., Upton, N.Y., 1955-57; instr. Stanford Univ., Palo Alto, Calif., 1957-59; guest prof. Univ. Heidelberg, Germany, 1960; staff mem. Lawrence Berkeley (Calif.) Lab., 1961-66, Los Alamos (N.Mex.) Nat. Lab., 1966-68; prof. UCLA, 1969—. With U.S. Army, 1944-46. Recipient Fulbright Travel award, 1960, Saclay, France, 1970, Sr. Scientist award Alexander von Humboldt Found., 1991, 95. Fellow: Am. Phys. Soc. Office: UCLA Dept Physics 405 Hilgard Ave Los Angeles CA 90095-9000 Office Phone: 213-825-1306. Business E-Mail: igo@physics.ucla.edu.

IGOE, THOMAS J., JR., lawyer; b. St. Louis, Apr. 20, 1947; BA, Yale U., 1969; JD, U. Va., 1972. Bar: NY 1973, lic.: US Dist. Ct. (So. Dist.) NY 1974, US Supreme Ct. 1991, US Ct. Appeals (DC Cir.) 1994, registered: Law Soc. Eng. & Wales (fng. lawyer). Ptnr. Thelen Reid & Priest LLP, NYC, mem. governing bd., partnership coun., head, corp. governance team. Mem.: Assn. Bar City NY, NY Bar, ABA (Bus. Law Sect., Pub. Utility, Comm. & Transp. Law Sect.). Office: Thelen Reid & Priest LLP 975 Third Ave New York NY 10022-6225 Office Phone: 212-603-2110. Office Fax: 212-603-2001. Business E-Mail: tigoe@thelenreid.com.

IGUSA, JUN-ICHI, mathematician, educator; b. Japan, Jan. 30, 1924; arrived in U.S., 1953; s. Shiro and Rui (Fukushima) I.; m. Yoshie Yamamoto, Oct. 7, 1948; children: Kiyoshi, Takeru, Mitsuru. MA, Tokyo Imperial U., 1945; PhD, Kyoto (Japan) U., 1953. Assoc. prof. Kyoto U., 1949—55; rsch. assoc. Harvard U., 1953-55; mem. faculty Johns Hopkins U., 1955—, prof. math., 1961-93, prof. emeritus, 1993—, J.J. Sylvester chair, 1986-93. Chmn. bd. dirs. Japan-U.S. Math. Inst. Johns Hopkins U., 1987-93. Author: Theta Functions, 1972, Forms of Higher Degree, 1978, Local Zeta Functions, 2000; editor-in-chief: Am. Jour. Math., 1978-93. Recipient Order of Sacred Treasure medal, Emperor of Japan, 2004. Mem. Math. Soc. Japan, Am. Math. Soc., Phi Beta Kappa. Home: 14209 Greencroft Ln Hunt Valley MD 21030-1111

IHARA, MICHIO, sculptor; b. Paris, Nov. 17, 1928; naturalized, U.S., 2001; s. Usaburo and Shigeko (Shinkai) I.; m. Doreen Joyce Kaplan, July 7, 1966; 1 child, Akeo. BFA, Tokyo U. Fine Arts, 1953. Fulbright fellow MIT, 1961-62, rsch. assoc., 1962-64; instr. Musashino U. Fine Arts, Tokyo, 1966-69. One-man shows Kanegis Gallery, Boston, 1964, Tokyo Gallery, 1970, Staempfli Gallery, N.Y.C., 1977, 80, 84; numerous group shows in Japan and U.S., 1957-74; important works include marble mural Chuo-koron Pub. Co, Tokyo, 1957; copper relief 275 Wyman St. Office Bldg, Waltham, Mass., 1963; altar canopy Josenji Temple, Tokyo, 1965; metal screen Imperial Theatre, Tokyo, 1966; relief Internat. Christian U, Tokyo, 1967, Fuji Film Co. Bldg, Tokyo, 1969; sculpture Internat. Sculptors Symposium, Osaka, 1970, Wellesley (Mass.) Office Park, 1973, Fitchburg (Mass.) Pub. Library; civic sculpture, Auckland, N.Z., 1977, Constellation Place, Balt., 1978; metal screen Rockefeller Center, N.Y.C., 1978, Neiman-Marcus, Beverly Hills, Calif., New World Hotel, Hong Kong, Pavilion Hotel, Singapore; wall sculpture S.E. Bank, Miami, 1983; suspended sculptures Marriott Marquis Hotel, N.Y.C., 1985, wall sculpture Harvard U., 1985, 89, wind sculpture, Tallahassee City Hall, 1989, tower sculpture Tokyo City Hall, 1991, suspended sculptures AT&T Plaza, Chgo., 1991, Colorado Springs Airport, 1994, Wall Sculpture Ikenoue Ch., Tokyo, 1995, suspended sculpture Lorillard Headquarters, N.C., 1997, interactive sculpture Cyclelight, Boston 1st Night, 1993, suspended sculpture New Eng. Med. Ctr. Hosp., Boston, 2000, sculptures Yokohama Crematorium, Japan, 2002, suspended sculpture Crowne Plz. Hotel, N.Y., 2002, Suspended Sculpture 101 Constitution Ave. Bldg., Washington, D.C., 2003, suspended sculpture Riverside Meth. Hosp., Columbus, Ohio, 2004. Trustee The Artists Found. Mass. JDR 3d Fund grantee, 1970-71; recipient award Mass. Council Arts and Humanities, 1974, Nat. Inst. Arts and Letters/Am. Acad. Arts and Letters award in art, 1973, award Fgn. Min. of Japanese Govt., 1999; Graham Found. fellow, 1963-64; MIT Center for Advanced Visual Studies fellow, 1970-73 Mem. Japan Artists Assn. Address: 63 Wood St Concord MA 01742-2225 Office Phone: 978-369-3731. Personal E-mail: michio.ihara@sprintmail.com.

IHDE, DON, philosopher, educator, dean; b. Hope, Kans., Jan. 14, 1934; s. Melvin Millard and Nell Pearl (Reikeman) I.; m. Carolyn W. Ihde (div.); children: Leslie Ann, Lisa Ihde-Costa, Eric Martin; m. Linda Einhorn, Apr. 4, 1985; 1 child, Mark Hillel. BA, U. Kans., 1956; MDiv, Andover Newton Theol. Sem., 1959; PhD, Boston U., 1964; prof. honoraria, El Rosario U., Bogota, Columbia, 1982. Asst. prof. So. Ill. U., Carbondale, 1964-67, assoc. prof., 1968-69, SUNY, Stony Brook, 1969-70, prof., 1971-86, dean humanities and fine arts, 1985-90, leading prof., 1986—, disting. prof., 1997—. Author: Hermeneutic Phenomenology, 1971, Sense and Significance, 1973,

Listening and Voice, 1976, Experimental Phenomenology, 1977, Technics and Praxis: A Philosophy of Technology, 1979, Existential Technics, 1983, Conequences of Phenomenology, 1986, Technology and the Life World, 1990, Instrumental Realism, 1991, Philosophy of Technology, 1993, Postphenomenology, 1993, Expanding Hermeneutics, 1998, Bodies in Technology, 2001; editor: The Conflict of Interpretations (Paul Ricouer); (with Richard M. Zaner) Phenomenology and Existentialism, 1973, Selected Studies in Phenomenology and Existential Philosophy, vol. IV, 1974, Interdisciplinary Phenomenology, vol. VI, 1977; (with Hugh J. Silverman) Selected Studies in Phenomenology and Existential Philosophy, vols. IX, XI, 1985, (with Evan Selinger) Chasing Technoscience, 2003; mem. editorial bd. Ind. U. Press, Northwestern U. Press. Recipient Jr. award So. Soc. for Philosophy and Psychology, 1966; summer rsch. fellow So. Ill. U., 1966, 67, 68, 69; Fulbright rsch. fellow U. Paris, 1967-68, sr. fellow NEH, 1972, vis. rsch. fellow Australian Nat. U., 1985, vis. scholar U. Sydney, 1991; grantee SUNY, Stony Brook, 1970, NSF, 1981. Mem. AAAS, Am. Philos. Assn. (mem. program com. 1976, 88, nominating com. 1981-83), Am. Psychol. Assn. (mem. sect. D), Heidegger Conf., Husserl Circle, Merleau-Ponty Circle, Nat. Assn. Sci., Tech. and Soc., Soc. Phenomenology and Existential Philosophy (exec. co-dir. 1972-75, 81-84), Soc. Philosophy and Tech. (bd. dirs. 1983-86, editor Ind. series), Phi Beta Kappa. Office: SUNY Dept Philosophy Stony Brook NY 11794-0001 Office Phone: 631-632-7575. Business E-Mail: dihde@sunysb.edu.

IHDE, MARY KATHERINE, retired mathematics educator; b. St. Louis, Jan. 19, 1942; d. Harold Orville and Katharine Marie Nanninga; m. Daniel Carlyle Ihde, Dec. 22, 1968; children: Steven Carlyle, Douglas Harold. BA in Math., Northwestern U., 1964; MS in Math. Edn., Stanford U., 1968. Cert. tchr., N.Y., Calif., Md. Tchr. math. Shawnee Mission (Kans.) H.S. Dist., 1964-67; math. specialist Columbia Grammar and Prep. Sch., N.Y.C., 1969-72; tchr. math. Georgetown Visitation Prep. Sch., Washington, 1981-84; lectr. math. Mt. Vernon Coll., Washington, 1984-85; tchr. math. Nat. Cathedral Sch. for Girls, Washington, 1985-93, chmn. dept., 1989-92; instr. math. Maryville U., St. Louis, 1994-95, Webster U., St. Louis, 1994-95; tchr. math., curriculum coord. Whitfield Sch., St. Louis, 1995-96; math. curriculum cons., 1996—2002; ret., 2002. Recipient 2nd place state level competition award Mathcounts, 1992, 4th place, 1993; fellow Shell Oil Corp., 1967-68. Mem. Nat. Coun. Tchrs. Math., Pi Lambda Theta. Address: 10805 Chicobush Dr NW Albuquerque NM 87114-5550

IHENACHO, DAVID ASONYE, campus chaplain; s. Simeon Ihenacho Onuoha and Grace Manumgbede Osumpere. BA in Philosophy, Bigard Meml. Sem., 1982, BA in Theology, 1987; MA in Religious Studies, Fordham U., 1995; PhD in Religious Studies, Marquette U., 1999. Asst. editor The Leader Newspaper, Owerri, Nigeria, 1982—83; assoc. editor The Guide Newspaper, Ahiara, 1988—94; pastor St. Paul's Parish, Amuzu, 1990—92; rector Mother Ch. Cathedral, Ahiara, 1992—94; chaplain, tchr. Edgewood H.S., Madison, Wis., 1997—98; chaplain Beloit Cath. H.S., 1998—99; resident parochial vicar St. Patrick and St. Joseph Parish, Doylestown And Rio, 1999—2000; chaplain, adj. instr. Sacred Heart U., Fairfield, Conn., 2000—01; chaplain L.I. U., Bklyn., 2001—. Author: The Community Of Eternal Life, African Christianity Rises, 2 Volumes. Instr. Bible Study Group, Bklyn., 2001—05. Scholar, Marquette U., 1997—99. Mem.: Cath. Bibl. Assn., Soc. Bibl. Lit. Independent. Christianity. Avocations: writing, sports, music, travel. Office Phone: 718-488-3359. E-mail: davidihenacho@hotmail.com.

IHNE, EDWARD ALAN, railroad official, city official; b. Seaford, N.Y., Nov. 9, 1951; s. Edward J. and Monica Ann (Selfridge) I.; m. Judith Palmer, June 9, 1973; children: Lisa, Shaun. BS in Mgmt., SUNY, Empire State, 1994. Transp. mgr. L.I. R.R.; dep. mayor Village of Patchogue, N.Y., commr. pub. safety, 1996-99. Vice chmn. Brookhaven Town Conservative Com., 1990-99; mem. exec. com. Suffolk County Conservative Party, 1992-99; N.Y. State Conservative del., 1992-99. Recipient Am. Eagle award Brookhaven Town Conservative Com., 1991. Mem. NRA, Suffolk County Dep. Sheriff Benevolent Assn. (assoc.), Patchogue Fire Dept. Benovelent and Exempt Assn., Elks. Roman Catholic. Home: 26 E 4th St Patchogue NY 11772-2312 Office: 14 Baker St Patchogue NY 11772-3815

IHRIE, ROBERT, oil, gas and real estate company executive; b. Phila., Jan. 4, 1925; s. Theodore Richard and Ella Martha (Anderson) I.; m. Dorothy Myrtle Waltz, July 8, 1944 (div. 1983); children: Robert Jr., Richard William, David Wayne, Nancy Ellen; m. Nancy Jean Joseph, June 8, 1984 BS, valedictorian, Ursinus Coll., 1943; MBA with high distinction, Harvard U., 1947. Process engr., econ. analyst, foreman, head tng. dept. head bus. analysis dept. Esso Std. Oil Co., Baton Rouge, 1947—59; head demand supply coord. planning dept. Exxon Corp., NYC, 1959—62; asst. dep. adminstr. AID, asst. sec. state Dept. State, Washington, 1962—64; v.p. Lippincott and Margulies, Inc., NYC, 1965—68; sr. v.p. Am. Trading and Prodn. Corp., Balt., 1968—, bd. dirs. Bd. dirs. Am. Trading Real Estate Properties, Balt. With U.S. Army, 1943-46. Baker scholar Harvard Grad. Sch. Bus., 1947; recipient Presdl. Citation. Mem. Am. Contract Bridge League (life master 1977). Presbyterian. Avocations: roller dance skating, coaching softball, theater, travel. Home: 212 E Ridgely Rd Lutherville Timonium MD 21093-5239 Office: Am Trading & Prodn Corp PO Box 238 Baltimore MD 21203-0238

IHRIG, JUDSON LA MOURE, chemist; b. Santa Maria, Calif., Nov. 5, 1925; s. Harry Karl and Luella (LaMoure) I.; m. Gwendolyn Adele Montz, July 22, 1950; children: Kristin, Neil Marshall. BS, Haverford Coll., 1949; MA, Princeton U., 1951, PhD, 1952. Asst. prof. chemistry U. Hawaii, 1952-58, assoc. prof., 1958-72, prof., 1972-94, dir. honors program, 1958-64, 87-95, dir. liberal studies program, 1973-79, chmn. chemistry dept., 1981-86, prof. emeritus, 1994—. Cons. chemistry local firms. Author publs. in field. Served with AUS, 1945-46. Mem. Am. Chem. Soc., Phi Beta Kappa, Sigma Xi. Home: 386 Wailupe Cir Honolulu HI 96821-1525 Office: U Hawaii 2545 The Mall Honolulu HI 96822-2233 Office Phone: 808-956-4590.

IIDA, SHUICHI, physicist, educator; b. Kobe, Hyogo-Ken, Japan, Jan. 30, 1926; s. Shunzoh and Sono (Ueda) Iida; m. Kyoko Matsuoka, Apr. 29, 1955; children: Mariko Takahara, Junko Kose. BS in Physics, U. Tokyo, 1947, PhD in Physics, 1958. Asst. prof. U. Tokyo, 1952-58, assoc. prof., 1958-68, prof., 1968-86, prof. emeritus, 1986; prof. Teikyo U., Sagamiko, Kanagawa, Japan, 1988-89, Utsunomiya, Japan, 1989-96. Vis. prof. AT&T Bell Labs., Murray Hill, NJ, 1961—63. Contbr. articles to profl. jours. Mem.: Japan Inst. Metals, Magnetics Soc. Japan, N.Y. Acad. Scis., Japan Soc. Powder and Powder Metallurgy, Physics Soc. Japan, Magnetics Soc. of IEEE, Am. Physics Soc. Achievements include research in ferrites; grand unifying frame for physics; electromagnetism; joint-use of MKSP and SI unit systems; correct representation for electromagnetic momenta; solution of Poincaré paradox; transient energy principle; proof for perfect diamagnetism of perfect conductors; essential q-number theory in biophysics; frontier notion principle; wave particle dualism; EPR problem; cold fusion; livelex f3 structure or filamentary current loops for c-number structure of lepton and hadron particles; electromagnetic origin of particle masses; trefoiled knot structure for proton; electromagnetic origin of weak and strong interactions; contra-particles for neutrinos and pions; Iida diagram for parity violation problems; chipped photon mechanism for redshifts and denial of big-bang cosmology; finding of Iida metric with denial of black hole having surpassed Schwarzschild metric with Einstein equation; Iida structure for electronic order of magnetite; symmetric location of proton for hydrogen bond of ice; proposal for ECTJ mechanism for flagellar motor and strict proof for unified unrestricted Larmor diamagnetism and cyclotron motion; research in solely protons and Iida pions in nuclei; discovery of third fire or explosive proton-electron annihilation in type II supernovae: via-Iida pion spin aligned protons for neutron stars and magnetic flux quantization for all elementary particles; idea of fourth fire or colossal Iida pion-proton annihilation explosion for transmigrating universe with galaxies. Home and Office: 4-23-11 Funabashi Setagaya-ku Tokyo 156-0055 Japan Business E-Mail: s.iida.prof.em.tokyo@proof.ocn.ne.jp.

IINUMA, HIROICHI, finance educator; b. Nakano, Tokyo, Japan, July 8, 1931; s. Yoshimitsu and Haru (Honda) I.; m. Chizuko Yoneda, Apr. 4, 1975. BA, Meiji U., Tokyo, 1954, MA, 1958, postgrad., 1961—64, Dr. in Comml. Sci., 2000. Tchr. Waseda Bus. High Sch., Tokyo, 1958-66; lectr. Wako U., Tokyo, 1966-69, assoc. prof., 1969-74, prof., 1974—2000, head dir. guidance counseling for students, 1977—80, 1991—94, dean faculty of econs., 1980—82, dir., trustee, 1980—82, prof. emeritus, 2000—. Lectr. Tokyo Fuji U., 1965—, Meiji U., Tokyo, 1971—2002, Josai U., 2002—, Takasaki City U. Econs., Gunma, 1973—98; chmn. JETRO Internat. Trade Advisers steering com., 1995—2001; vice chmn. Asian Market Econs. Rsch. Assn., 1997—. Author: Foreign Trade Principles and Practices, 1973, The Change and Future Perspective in International Trade, 1999, The Change and Future Perspective in International Economics and Trade, 2002; co-author: Business Administration, 1977. Mem.: Sci. Coun. Japan (liaison commr. field of internat. econs. study), Japan Soc. Internat. Econs., Japan Soc. for Study Bus. Adminstrn., Union Nat. Econ. Assns. in Japan (trustee 1990—), Japan Acad. Fgn. Trade and Bus. (chief sec. 1967—70, bd. dirs. 1970—, pres. 1995—99, spl. adviser 1999—, dir. 2001—), Soc. Mktg. and Distbn., All Kanto Rsch. Group Assn. for Fgn. Trade (chmn. 1980—83, 1985—89, 1992—98, sr. adviser 1998—). Home and Office: 1-58-10 Hirao Tokyo 206-0823 Japan

IIZUKA, TOSHIAKI, management educator; PhD in Econs., UCLA, 2001. Asst. prof. Vanderbilt U., Owen Grad. Sch. of Mgmt., Nashville, 2001—. Mem.: Am. Econ. Assn. Office: Vanderbilt Univ 401 21st Ave S Nashville TN 37203 Office Phone: 615-343-7747.

IJAZ, MANSOOR, news correspondent; b. 1961; s. Mujaddid Ahmed Ijaz. BS in Physics (magna cum laude), Univ. Va., 1983; MS in Mech. Engring., MIT, 1985. Founder, chmn. The Crescent Partnerships, 1991—; foreign affairs and terrorism analyst FOX News Channel, 2001—. Mem. Coun. on Fgn. Rels. Contbr. to editl. pages of Financial Times, Wall Street Journal, NY Times, LA Times, Washington Post, Newsweek and International Herald Tribune. Office: FOX News Channel 400 N Capitol St NW Ste 550 Washington DC 20001*

IJIRI, YUJI, finance educator; b. Kobe, Japan, Feb. 24, 1935; came to U.S., 1959; s. Takejiro and Hiroko (Hanno) I.; m. Tomoko Nishimura, June 17, 1962; children: Lisa, Yumi. LLB, Ritsumeikan U., Kyoto, Japan, 1956; MS, U. Minn., 1960; PhD, Carnegie Mellon U., 1963; LLD (hon.), DePaul U., 1990; DSc in Bus. Adminstrn. (hon.), Bryant Coll., 1991. CPA, Japan. Staff mem. Price Waterhouse & Co., Tokyo, 1957-59; asst. prof. grad. sch. bus. Stanford (Calif.) U., 1963-65, assoc. prof. grad. sch. bus., 1965-67; prof. grad. sch. indsl. adminstrn. Carnegie Mellon U., Pitts., 1967-75, Robert M. Trueblood prof. acctg. and econs. Tepper Sch. Bus., 1975-87, 1987—. Cons. Gulf Oil Corp., Pitts., 1968-85. Co-author: Skew Distributions and the Sizes of Business Firms, 1977, Kohlers Dictionary for Accountants, 6th edit., 1983, New Directions in Creative and Innovative Management, 1988; author: Momentum Accounting and Triple-Entry Bookkeeping, 1989; editor: Creative and Innovative Approaches to the Science of Management, 1993. Named inductee Acctg. Hall of Fame, Ohio State U., 1989. Fellow Acctg. Researchers Internat. Assn. (pres. 1979-81); mem. Am. Acctg. Assn. (pres. 1982-83, Outstanding Educator 1987), Fin. Execs. Inst. (chpt. bd. dirs. 1977-81), Beta Alpha Psi. Home: 5 Bayard Rd Apt 118 Pittsburgh PA 15213-1904 Office: Tepper Sch Bus Carnegie Mellon U Pittsburgh PA 15213 Business E-Mail: ijiri@cmu.edu.

IKARD, FRANK NEVILLE, JR., lawyer; b. Wichita Falls, Tex., June 26, 1942; s. Frank Neville and Jean (Hunter) I.; children: Frank III, Jean, Charles; m. Kathleen P. Ikard, Feb. 14, 1998. BA, U. Tex., 1965, JD, 1968. Bar: Tex. 1968; cert. Tex. Estate Planning and Probate Law Bd. of Legal Specialization. Assoc. then ptnr. Clark, Thomas, Winters, & Shapiro, Austin, Tex., 1968-84; mng. ptnr. Jenkens & Gilchrist, Austin, 1985-88; ptnr. Johnson & Gibbs, Austin, 1988-92, Ikard & Golden, Austin, 1992—. Bd. dirs. Paramount Theatre, Austin, 1988-89, pres. bd. dirs., 1991-92; mem. Greater Austin Crime Commn. Fellow Am. Coll. Probate Counsel, Tex. Bar Found.; mem. Am. Coll. Trust and Estate Coun. (fiduciary litigation com. 1991-2001), Tex. Acad. Real Estate (pres. probate and trust law coun. 1988-89), State Bar Tex. (chmn., sec.-treas. legis. com. real estate, probate trust law sect. 1983-84, coun. chmn.), Travis County Bar Assn., Tarry House, Headliners, U. Tex. Club. Avocations: fly fishing, photography. Home: 1107 Gaston Ave Austin TX 78703-2507 Office: Ikard and Golden 400 W 15th St 975 Austin TX 78701-1600 E-mail: fni@ikardgolden.com.

IKAWA-SMITH, FUMIKO, anthropologist, educator; b. Kobe, Japan, Sept. 10, 1930; arrived in Canada, 1960; d. Jokei and Sachi (Nakano) Ikawa; m. Takao Sofue, Jan. 1955 (div. 1958); m. Philip Edward Lake Smith, Nov. 1959; 1 child, Douglas Philip Edward. BA, Tsuda Coll., Tokyo, 1953; student Tokyo Met. U., 1954-55; AM in Anthropology, Radcliffe Coll., 1959; PhD in Anthropology, Harvard U., 1974. Asst. prof. McGill U., Montreal, 1968—74, assoc. prof., 1974—79, chmn. dept. anthropology, 1975—80, prof., 1979—2003, dir. Ctr. East Asian Studies, 1983—88, chmn. dept. East Asian langs. and lits., 1983—88, assoc. acad. vice prin., 1991—96. Vis. prof. Canadian studies Kwansei Gakuin U., Japan, 1996-97. Editor: Early Palaeolithic in South and East Asia, 1978, Proc. of First Meeting of The Social Scis. Assn. Can., 1989; mem. editl. bd. Anthrop. Sci., 1998-2002. Decorated Order Sacred Treasure, Gold Rays with Rosette Japan. Fellow Am. Anthrop. Assn. (exec. at-large archeology divsn. 1988-90), Current Anthropology (assoc.); mem. Pacific Sci. Assn. (life), Soc. Am. Archeology, Soc. for East Asian Archaeology (pres. 2004—), Japan Studies Assn. Can. (acting pres. 1988-90, pres. elect 1998-99, pres. 1999-2000, 04—), Indo-Pacific Prehistory Assn. (exec. com. 1990-98), Can. Asian Studies Assn. (chair Japan com. 1991-94), Quebec-Japan Bus. Forum (bd. 1998-2000). Avocations: horticulture, piano. Home: 3955 Ramezay Ave Montreal PQ Canada H3Y 3K3 Office: McGill U Dept Anthropology 855 Sherbrooke St W Montreal PQ Canada H3A 2T7 Office Phone: 514-398-4300. E-mail: fumiko.ikawa-smith@mcgill.ca.

IKEDA, CLYDE JUNICHI, plastic and reconstructive surgeon; b. Kobe, Japan, 1951; s. Paul Tamotsu and Kazu Ikeda. BA, SUNY, Binghamton, 1973; MD, N.Y. Med. Coll., Valhalla, 1979. Resident St. Vincent Hosp., N.Y.C., 1979-83, Francis Meml. Hosp., San Francisco, 1983-86; med. dir. Burn Ctr. St. Francis Meml. Hosp., San Francisco, 1992—2001, med. examiner, 1993—, med. dir. Wound Healing Ctr., 1994—2001; dir. Hosp. de la Familie, 2000—. Asst. clin. prof. plastic surgery U. Calif., San Francisco, 1998-2003, assoc. clin. prof. plastic surgery, 2003—; adj. clin. prof. surgery Stanford Sch. Medicine, 2004—. Recipient Edward Weisband Disting. Alumni award, Binghamton U., 2003, medal of honor, Alumni Assn. N.Y. Med. Coll., 2004. Fellow ACS. Office: 1199 Bush St Ste 640 San Francisco CA 94109-5977

IKEDA, KAZUYOSI, physicist, poet; b. Fukuoka, Japan, July 15, 1928; s. Yosikatu and Misao (Misumi) I.; m. Mieko Akiyama, Nov. 20, 1956; children: Hiroko Ikeda Yamaguti, Yosihumi. 1st degree Rigakusi, Kyushu U., Fukuoka, Japan, 1951, DSc, 1957; D Environ. Sci. (hon.), Internat. Earth Environment U., 1993; DLitt (hon.), London Inst. Applied Rsch., 1995; diploma of honor, Inst. Affaires Internat., 1995, European Acad. Arts, 1999, Internat. Assn. Educators World Peace, 1999, Internat. Rels., 1999, Inst. Intercultural Studies Ala., 1999; DSc (hon.), World Acad., 1995; DHum honoris causa, Intl Acad. Culture/Polit. Sci., 1999. Asst. dept. physics Kyushu U. Faculty Sci., Fukuoka, 1956-60, assoc. prof. dept. physics, 1960-65; assoc. prof. dept. applied physics Osaka (Japan) U. Faculty Engring., 1965-68, prof. theoretical physics dept. applied physics, 1968-89, prof. theoretical and math. physics dept. math. scis., 1989-92, prof. emeritus, 1992—. Pres. Internat. Earth Environment U., Japan, 1995—, prof. theoretical physics, 1992—; bd. adv. coun. Ansted U., 1999—; prof. Internat. Assn. Educators for World Peace, 1999—. Author: ter Haar's Thermostatistics, 1960, Modern Developments in Thermodynamics, 1974, Statistical Thermodynamics, 1975, Mechanics Without Use of Mathematical Formulae--From a Moving Stone to Halley's Comet, 1980, Invitation to Mechanics--From the Fundamentals of Calculus to the Motion of a Comet, with Appendix on a comet in ancient times, 1985, (collection of poems) Bansyoo Hyakusi, 1986, Basic Mechanics, 1987, Basic Thermodynamics--From Entropy to Osmotic Pressure, 1991, The World of God, Creation and Poetry, 1991, Poems on the Hearts of Creation, 1993, Mountains, 1995, North South East and West, 1996, Graphical Theory of Relativity, 1998, Hearts of Myriad Things in the Universe, 1998, Kazuyosi's Poetry on the Animate and the Inanimate, 1998, Poems on Love and Peace, 1998, Songs of the Soul, 1999, Hearts of Innumerous Things in Heaven and Earth, 2000, Kazuyosi's Poems on Myriad Things-For Global Brotherhood and World Peace, 2001, The World of Hearts, 2002, Peace Offerings, 2003, Men and Nature, 2003, Spring Rain, 2003, Universal Songs, 2004, Paeans to Spirit, 2004, Journeys of Heart, 2005, Rainbows to Flowers, 2005; editor Modern Poetry, 1996—; contbr. more than 100 articles to sci. profl. jours.; author serialized poems of seven and five syllable metre, more than 30 lit. books, more than 60 lit. articles, reviews, and essays on poetry; haiku, tanka, Chinese classical fixed-form poetry; translations of Shakespeare's Sonnets into Japanese poems in seven and five syllale metre. Hon. founder, Japan rep. Olympoetry Movement, 1992—. Recipient Yukawa Commemorative Scholarship award Yukawa Found., 1954, World Biographical Hall of Fame award Hist. Preservations Am., 1990, prize Catania e il suo Vulcano, Accademia Ferdinandea Sci. Lettere Arti, 1994, Order of Good Neighbors, Olympoetry Movement Fund, 1996, Albert Einstein Acad. Cert. award for outstanding achievement Albert Einstein Internat. Acad. Found., 1998, Internat. Artistic-Literary prize of Primavera Catanase, Accademia Ferdinandea, Sci. Lettere Arte, 1997, Pandit prize Indian Coun. Natural Medicine Rsch., 1999, Diplome de Reconnaissance Edn. Ecologique, Assn. Internat. des Educateus pour la Paix Mondiole, 1999, Diplome ad Honores, Acad. Europeene des Arts, 1999, Diploma of Honor, Internat. Assn. Educators for World Peace, 1999, Diploma in Internat. Rels. Inst. for Internat. Rels. and Intercultural Studies of Ala. U., 1999, Prize Oscar 2000, Accademia Ferdinandea Sci. Lettere Arte, 2000, Gran Premio d'Autore, Edizioni U., 2000, New Millennium Michael Madhusuden award for best poetry Michael Madhusuden Acad., 2000, Oscar prize, 2000, Accademia Ferdinandea Sci. Lettere Arte, 2000, New Millenium Michael Madhusudan award Best Poetry Michael Madhusudan Acad., 2000, Netaj Subbash Chandra Bose Nat. award for Excellence in field of poetry and environ. sci. Jagruthi Kiran Found., 2001, Internat. Lit. prize Libro d'Oro Edizioni U., 2001; named Knight of Yr., Internat. Writers and Artists Assn., 1995, Knight Templar Order, Lofsensic Ursinius Order, Holy Grail Order, Universal Knights Order, San Ciriaco Order, 1995, Order of Pegasus Highest Degree, Olympoetry Movement Fund, 1996, Pandit prize, Indian Coun. of Natural Medicine and Rsch., 1999, Cultural Doctorate in Poetical Lit., World U. Roundtable, 1999, Best World Poet of Yr. award Poets Internat., 1999, Poet of Millennium award Internat. Poets Acad., 2000, Grand prize author Edizioni Universum, 2000, Netaji Subbash Chandra Bose Nat. award excellence in poetry and environ. sci. Jigruthi Kiran Found., 2001, Premio Letterario Internat., Global Peace and Friendship award India-European Union Friendship Soc., 2001, Knight Commander of Sovereign Order of Ambrosini's, 2001, Ivory Eagle award Home of Letters, 2001, Sphatika (India) Internat. Poet award Supreme Governing Body of Sphatika Prakashana, 2001, Internat. Peace prize United Cultural Conv. USA, 2002, Mandakini Lit. award Internat. Poetry Soc. Bareilly, 2002, Excellence in World Poetry award Internat. Poets Acad., 2002, Voice of Kolkata award Kolkata Lit. Soc., 2003; decorated Knight comdr. Sovereign Order of Ambrosini's, 2001. Libro d'Oro Edizioni Universum, 2001, Golden Book Internat. prize for Sto Mikrokosmo, Edizioni U., 2003, Star of Asia award Poets Internat., 2003, Master Diploma Special Honours in Science and Poetry, World Acad. Letters, 2004, Einstein Chair of Science award, World Acad. Letters, 2004, Silver Book Prize for Universal Songs, Edizioni Universum, 2004, Author of the Year award, Edizioni Universum, 2004, Golden Pen prize, Edizioni Universum, 2004, Omaggio a Dennis Kann Internat. Poetry Prize, Edizioni Universum, 2004, Award of Homage to Dante Alighieri for the Poetical Work Rainbows, 2004, Award of Alessandra Manzoni for Poetical Work Buddhist Images, Edizioni Universum, 2005, Region of Honor award, United Cultural Convention, 2005. Fellow United Writers' Assn. (life), World Lit. Acad. (life), Internat. Poets Acad. (life, Internat. Eminent Poet award 1993); mem. NY Acad. Scis., Am. Biog. Inst. Rsch. Assn. (dep. gov. 1989—, continental gov. 1998—), World Inst. Achievement (life), Lifetime Achievement Acad. (life, Golden Acad. award 1991), Phys. Soc. Japan (com. mem. 1970—, exec. com. centenary 1976-77, chmn. Osaka br. 1976-77, 83-84, editor jour. 1976-78), Internat. Biog. Assn. (life patron 1990-, bd. govs. 2004-), Internat. Biog. Ctr. (dep. dir. gen. 1989—, vice consul 2002—), World Acad. Arts and Culture (life), World Congress of Poets (life), Confedn. Chivalry (mem. grand coun. 1991—, Chevalier Grand Cross 1991), Accademia Ferdinandea Scienze Lettere Arti (academician of honor 1994—), Order Internat. Fellowship (charter 1994—), World Parnassians Guild Internat. (hon. dir. 1995—), Acad. M.I.D.I. (senator 1995—), Coun. of States for Protection of Life (senator 1995—, minister plenipotentiary for Asian States 1999—), Academia Argentina (academician 1995—), Internat. Parliament for Safety and Peace (Medalla al Merito 1995, senator 1999—, Minister plenipotentiary for Japan 1999—), Modern Poets Soc. (bd. dir. 1996—), Modern Poetry (editor 1996-), Rock Pebbles (editor, 2004—), Titas (editl. advisor 2005—), Accademia Internazionale Trinacria Lettere-Arte-Scienze (academician of merit 1997—), Leading Intellectuals of the World (founding charter mem. 1998—), Sci. Fac. Cambridge (founder mem. 2000-), Metverse Muse (lit. life chief patron, 2000-), Internat. Govs. Club, London Diplomatic Acad. (founder 2000—), Planet Soc., Profs.-Students Coalition Unification North East West South (chmn. Osaka U. br. 1987—), Profs. World Peace Acad. (dir. Osaka br. 1988—), Nat. Coalition Unification North East West South (chmn. Osaka br. 1988—), World Peace Acad. (academician 1999—), Academie Scientifique Internat. Vie Univers (sci. academician environ. scis. 1999—), Academia Ecologia (hon. 1999—), Internat. Poetry for Peace Assn. (regional coord. Japan and Asia Pacific 2000—), Jagruthi Kiran Found. (hon. life 2000—), Am. Order of Excellence (founding mem. 2000—), Michael Madhusdan Acad. (chief exec. 2001—), Karuna India Soc. (patron-in-chief 2001—), Chetana Lit. Group (patron-in-chief 2001—), Katha Kshetre (patron 2001—), Inst. der Affaires Internationales (corr. mem., rep. Japan 2002—), Internat. Honour Soc. (founding mem. 2002—), Home of Letters (chief patron 2002-), Voice of Kolkata (patron-in-chief 2003-), Acad. Indo-Asian Lit. (hon. fellow mem 2003-), Brain Wave English Lit-Q (patron 2002-), Creative Writing Criticism Acad.(adv. bd. 2003-), Titiksha (editl. bd. 2003-), Rsch. Soc. Communication in English (hon. adv. bd 2003-), Internat. Writers and Artists Assn. (dir. 2004-), Comissione di Lettera Internat. (exec. mem. 2004-), OMEGA Welfare Organization (patron-in-chief 2004-), Cyberwit Net. Home: Nisi-7-7-11 Aomadani Minoo-si Osaka 562-0023 Japan Office: Osaka U Fac Engring Dept Math Scis 2-1 Yamadaoka Suita-si Osaka 565-0871 Japan

IKEDA, TSUGUO (IKE IKEDA), retired social services administrator; b. Portland, Oreg., Aug. 15, 1924; s. Tom Minoru and Tomoe Ikeda; m. Sumiko Hara, Sept. 2, 1951; children: Wanda Amy, Helen Mari, Julie Ann, Patricia Kiyo. BA, Lewis & Clark Coll., 1949; MSW, U. Wash., 1951. Social group worker Neighborhood House, Seattle, 1951-53; exec. dir. Atlantic St. Ctr., Seattle, 1953-86; pres. Urban Partnerships, Seattle, 1986-88, Tsuguo "Ike" Ikeda and Assoc., Seattle, 1988—2004; ret., 2004. Cons. Commn. on Religion and Race, Washington, 1973, North Northeast Mental Health Ctr., Portland, 1985, others; affirmative action cons. NASW, Washington, 1977; conf. coord. Beyond the Mask of Denial Wash. State Conf. on Drug/Alcohol/Substance Abuse in the Asian/Pacific Islander Cmtys., 1993; coord. Minority Mental Health Colloquium in Wash., 1994-95; coord. Asian Pacific Islander Coming Home Together Summit-95, Tacoma, Asian Pacific Bi-Ann. Leadership Conf., 1995-96, craftsmanship trainer, 1996-98; Tsuguo "Ike" Ikeda, Pub. Svc. ann. award established in 1987; trainer region II Dept. Children and Family Svcs., Yakima, Wash., 1997, API Cons. and Tng. Project, 1998. Mem. Nat. Task Force to develop standards and goals for juv. delinquency, 1976; mem. Gov.'s Select Panel for social and health svcs., Olympia, Wash., 1977; chmn. Asian Am. Task Force, Community Coll., Seattle dist., 1982, King County Coordinated Health Care Initiative Client Edn., Mktg. Subcom., 1993; div. chmn. social agys. Seattle United Way campaign, 1985; vice-chmn. Wash. State Com. on Vocat. Edn., Olympia, 1985-86, chmn. 1986-87; chmn. regional adv. com. Dept. Social and Health Svcs., 1990-91; mem. Gov. Mike Lawry's Commn. on Ethics Govt., Campaign Practices, 1993—; mem. exec. task force King County Dept. Youth Svcs., 1996-97. With Mil. Intelligence Lang. Sch., 1945-46. Named Cmty. Treasure, United Way of King County, 1996; recipient cert. appreciation, U.S. Dept. Justice, Washington, 1975—76,

Am. Dream award, Cmty. Coll. Dist., Seattle, 1984, Asian Counseling & Referral Svc., 1991, 1995, Wing Lake Mus., 1991—92, Atlantic St. Ctr., 1992, Seattle Chinese Post, 1992, Bishop's award, U. Meth. Ch., Tacoma, Wash., 1984, Cmty. Svc. award, Seattle Rotary Club, 1985, Outstanding Citizen award, Mcpl. League, Seattle and King County, 1986, Outstanding Leadership award, Dept. Social and Health Svcs., 1993, Cmty. award, South Pacific Islander Program Seattle Pub. Schs., 1993, Pasasalmat award, Filipino Youth Activities, 1993, Brass Ring award, Asian Am. Polit. Alliance, 1993, Comm. Svc. award, Asian Counseling and Referral Svc., 1994, Disting. Alumnus award, Multicultural Alumni Partnership U. Wash. Alumni Assn., 1996, award, Gen. Bd. Global Ministries, United Meth. Ch., 1995, Alvirita Little Svc. award, Therapeutic Health Svc., 1999, Nordsstrom Cmty. award, 1999, U.S. Presdl. Unit citation for meritorious svcs., Mil. Intelligence Svc., 2001, Local Hero award, Bill and Melinda Gates Found., United Way Campaign, 2001, Disting. Alumni award, U. Washington Sch. Soc. Work, 2005. Mem. NASW (chpt. pres., Social Worker of Yr. 1971, Social Work Pioneer 1995), Vol. Agy. Exec. Coalition (pres., Outstanding Cmty. Svc. award 1979), Ethnic Minority Mental Health Consortium (chmn., Outstanding Leader 1992, David E. "Ned" Skinner Cmty. Svc. award 1990), Minority Exec. Dirs. Coalition (organizer, mem. chmn. 1980-86). Democrat. Methodist. Avocations: stamp collecting/philately, World War II memorabilia.

IKENBERRY, HENRY CEPHAS, JR., lawyer; b. Cloverdale, Va., Mar. 23, 1920; s. Henry Cephas and Bessie (Peters) I.; m. Margaret Sangster Henry, July 3, 1943; children: Anna Catherine Ikenberry Fawell, Mary Margaret Ikenberry Rauck. BA, Bridgewater Coll., 1947; JD, U. Va., 1947. Bar: Va. 1947, W.Va. 1948, D.C. 1948, U.S. Supreme Ct. 1954, U.S. Ct. Claims 1972, U.S. Ct. Appeals (fed. cir.) 1982. Asso. firm Steptoe & Johnson, Washington, 1947-49, 50-53, partner, former chmn. exec. com., 1953-85, of counsel, 1986-92; asst. counsel Gen. Aniline & Film Co., N.Y.C., 1949-50. Mem. com. on unauthorized practice D.C. Ct. Appeals, 1972-76. Ruling elder Chevy Chase Presbyn. Ch., Washington, 1970-72; trustee Mary Baldwin Coll., Staunton, Va., 1979-92, mem. exec. com., 1987-92; life mem., dean's counsel U. Va. Sch. Law; hon. trustee Bridgewater Coll., 2000—. Lt. comdr. USNR, 1941-46, ETO, PTO, Okinawa, The Philippines. Recipient Alumni citation Bridgewater Coll., 1960; named Ky. col., 1973 Mem. Bar Assn. D.C. (chmn. com. on corp. law 1960-61, com. comml. bus. law 1969-72), Raven Soc., Am. Legion, Metropolitan Club, Chesapeake Bay Yacht Club, Chevy Chase Club, Talbot Country Club (Easton, Md.), Order of Coif, Phi Delta Phi, Tau Kappa Alpha. Home: Pine Lodge 26783 Miles River Rd Easton MD 21601-5013 also: PO Box 1518 Easton MD 21601-8929 also: Box N-308 8101 Connecticut Ave Chevy Chase MD 20815

IKENBERRY, STANLEY OLIVER, education educator, director, former university president; b. Lamar, Colo., Mar. 3, 1935; s. Oliver Samuel and Margaret (Moulton) Ikenberry; m. Judith Ellen Life, Aug. 24, 1958; children: David Lawrence, Steven Oliver, John Paul. BA, Shepherd Coll., 1956; MA, Mich. State U., 1957, PhD, 1960, LHD (hon.); LLD (hon.), Millikin U.; LHD (hon.), Millikin U., Ill. Coll., Rush U., W.Va. U., Towson State U., U. Nebr., Bridgewater (Va.) Coll., Bradley U., Shepherd Coll., Roosevelt U., Juniatta Coll., Pa., 2003, Northeastern U. Instr. office evaluation svc. Mich. State U., 1958—60, instr. instl. rsch. office, 1960—62; asst. to provost for instl. rsch., asst. prof. edn. W.Va. U., 1962—65, dean coll. human resources and edn., assoc. prof. edn., 1965—69; prof., assoc. dir. ctr. study higher edn. Pa. State U., 1969—71, sr. v.p., 1971—79; pres. U. Ill., Urbana, 1979—95, pres. emeritus, Regent prof., 1995—; pres. Am. Coun. on Edn., Washington, 1996—2001. Bd. dirs. Pfizer, Inc., N.Y.C., Aquila Inc., Kans. City; pres. bd. overseers Tchrs. Ins. and Annutiy Assn./Coll. Retirement Equities Fund. Named hon. alumnus, Pa. State U. Fellow: Am. Acad. Arts and Scis., Assn. Governing Bds. (sr.); mem.: Assn. Am. Univs. (past chmn.), Wash. Adv. Group (assoc.), Tavern Club (Chgo.), Cosmos Club (Washington), Mid-Am. Club, Comml. Club Chgo. Office: U Ill 347 Education 1310 S 6th St Champaign IL 61820

IKLÉ, FRED CHARLES, former federal agency administrator, policy advisor, defense expert; b. Fex, Switzerland, Aug. 21, 1924; s. Fritz A. and Hedwig M. (Huber) I.; m. Doris Eisemann, Dec. 23, 1959; children: Judith, Miriam. MA in Social Sci, U. Chgo., 1948, PhD in Sociology, 1950. Research assoc. Columbia Bur. Applied Social Research, 1950-54; mem. social sci. dept. Rand Corp., Santa Monica, Calif., 1955—61, head social sci. dept., 1968—73; research assoc. Ctr. for Internat. Affairs Harvard U., 1962-63; prof. polit. sci. Mass. Inst. Tech., 1964-67; dir. U.S. ACDA, Washington, 1973-77; chmn. Conservation Mgmt. Corp., 1978-81, 88—; under-sec. for policy Dept. Def., Washington, 1981-88; Disting. scholar Ctr. for Internat. and Strategic Studies, 1988—. Mem. Dept. Def. Policy Bd.; bd. dirs. Telos Corp.; mem. Nat. Com. on Terrorism, 1999-00, Gov. Smith Richardson Found., 1996—; dir. U.S. Com. for Human Rights in North Korea. Author: The Social Impact of Bomb Destruction, 1958, How Nations Negotiate, 1964, Every War Must End, 1971. Mem. Internat. Inst. Strategic Studies, Coun. Fgn. Rels., Met. Club. Republican. Home: 7010 Glenbrook Rd Bethesda MD 20814-1223 Office: Ctr Strategic & Internat Studies 1800 K St NW Washington DC 20006-2202

IKLÉ, RICHARD ADOLPH, lawyer; b. Mineola, N.Y., Mar. 25, 1930; s. Adolph M. and Ruth Clark; children: Roger Scott, Lisa Kristina, Richard Keith. BA, Amherst Coll., 1953; JD, Columbia U., 1960. Bar: N.Y. 1961, Fla. 1975. Ptnr. Thacher, Proffitt & Wood, NYC., 1960—90; supervisory counsel FDIC, NYC, NJ, Washington, 1990—. Deacon Cmty. Ref. Ch., Manhasset, NY, 1975—80, elder, 1980—82. Lt. USNR, 1953—56. Mem.: ABA, Fla. Bar Assn., N.Y. State Bar Assn., Manhasset Bay Yacht Club (Port Washington, N.Y.), Phi Delta Phi. Avocations: sailing, mountain climbing.

IKOSSI, KIKI, electrical and computer engineer; b. Nicosia, Cyprus, Dec. 23, 1954; came to U.S., 1978; d. George J. and Margarita K. (Vavlitis) Ikossi; children: Georgia-Charithea, Michael-George. BSEE, Nat. Tech. U., Athens, Greece, 1977; MS, U. Cin., 1982, PhD, 1986. Rsch./tchg. asst. U. Cin., 1980-86; sr. rsch. scientist Universal Energy Sys., Dayton, Ohio, 1986-90; asst. prof. elec. and computer engring. La. State U., Baton Rouge, 1990-96, tenured assoc. prof., 1996-99; rsch. elec. engr. Naval Rsch. Lab., Washington, 1999—2003; pres. I-Cube, 2003—. Reviewer NSF, NASA, IEEE, ASEE, LEQSF, Washington, 1993—; summer faculty rsch. fellow Navy-Am. Soc. Engring. Edn. Naval Rsch. Lab., Washington, 1991, sr. summer faculty rsch. fellow, 1992—98; evaluator ABET; adj. prof. Gaorge Mason U., Fairfax, Va., 2004—. Contbr. articles to profl. publs. Recipient 7 awards for contbns., Am. Soc. Engring. Edn./Navy, 1991—98, DON Contbn. award, 1999, 2000, Tech. Transfer award, 2000, 2001, Alan Berman Outstanding Rsch. Publs. award, US Navy, 1998, Indovidual Invention award, 2003; fellow U. Cin. coun. rsch., 1982, 1983, 1979—85; grantee rsch., NSF, USN, La. Quality Support Edn., 1991—. Mem.: AAUW, AAIP, AAAS, IEEE (sr.; mem. tech. program com. 1996—, co-chmn. 1999—2002, sec. dir. program MTTS Wash., N.Va. chpt. 1999—2002, chair 2003—04, sect. sec. 2004, treas. 2005, chmn. subcom. high power devices MTT, chair IMS TPC high power), Women in Engring. (Washington area affinity group vice chair 2002—03, chmn. 2004), Electrochem. Soc. Metall., N.Y. Acad. Sci., Washington Acad. Sci. (founding mem.), Am. Soc. Engring. Edn., Assn. Women in Sci., Soc. Women Engrs. Achievements include refinement of method of moments for deep level transient spectroscopy studies in Semiconductors Devices on exploridory materials; one of the first scientists to incorporate antimonides in III-V compound microelectronic devices; two patents in process; patentee indium phosphide microelectronic device processing. Office: 6275 Gentle Ln Alexandria VA 22310-2260 Office Phone: 703-960-0261. E-mail: ikossi@ieee.org.

ILARDI, VINCENT, historian, educator; b. Newark, N.J., May 15, 1925; s. Vincent and Filippa (Giannazzo) I.; m. Antoinette Ficarra, Dec. 26, 1952; 1 child, Vincent Michael. AB, Rutgers U., 1952; AM, Harvard U., 1953, PhD, 1958. Instr. Carnegie Inst. Tech., Pitts., 1956-57, U. Mass., Amherst, 1957-59, asst. prof. History, 1960-61, assoc. prof. History, 1961-68, prof. History, 1969-95. Vis. rsch. scholar Yale U., New Haven, 1990-93, vis. prof. history, 1993-2000 Author: (with P.M. Kendall) Dispatches With Related Documents of Milanese Ambassadors in France and Burgundy, 1450-1461, 2 vols., 1970-71, Vol. 3, 1466, 1981, Studies in Italian Renaissance Diplomatic History, 1986. Bayard Cutting fellow, 1953, Emerton fellow, 1954, 55-56, Faculty of Arts and Scis. fellow, 1954, Fulbright Rsch. scholar, 1959-60, Am. Philos. Soc. Rsch. grantee, 1960-63, Rockefeller Found. Rsch. grantee, 1961-63, Rockefeller Found. Internat. Rels. Rsch. grantee, 1963-64, Guggenheim fellow, 1970-71, NEH grantee, 1976-85, Nat. Italian Am. Foun. grantee, 1985. Home: 238 N Main St Sunderland MA 01375-9569

ILCHMAN, ALICE STONE, foundation administrator, retired academic administrator, retired government agency administrator; b. Cin., Apr. 18, 1935; d. Donald Crawford and Alice Kathryn (Biermann) Stone; m. Warren Frederick Ilchman, June 11, 1960; children: Frederick Andrew Crawford, Alice Sarah. BA, Mt. Holyoke Coll., 1957; MPA, Maxwell Sch. Citizenship, Syracuse U., 1958; PhD, London Sch. Econs., 1965; LHD, Mt. Holyoke Coll., 1982, Franklin and Marshall Coll., 1983. Asst. to pres., mem. faculty Berkshire C.C., 1961-64; lectr. Ctr. for South and S.E. Asia Studies U. Calif., Berkeley, 1965-73; prof. econs. and edn., dean Wellesley (Mass.) Coll., 1973-78; asst. sec. edn. and cultural affairs Dept. State, 1978; assoc. dir. ednl. and cultural affairs Internat. Comm. Agy., 1978—81; advisor to sec. Smithsonian Instn., 1981; pres. Sarah Lawrence Coll., Bronxville, NY, 1981-98; chmn. bd. Rockefeller Found., N.Y.C., NY, 1995—2000. Dir. Jeannette K. Watson Fellowship, 1999—; intern, asst. to Sen. John F. Kennedy, 1957; dir. Peace Corps Tng. Program for India, 1965-66; chmn. com. on women's employment NAS; sr. advisor Thomas Watson Found., 1999—; bd. dirs. NYNEX, Seligman Group of Investment Cos. Author: The New Men of Knowledge and the New States, 1968, (with W.F. Ilchman) Education and Employment in India, The Policy Nexus, 1976, The Lucky Few and the Worthy Many: Scholarship Competitions and The Future Leaders, 2004. Trustee Mt. Holyoke Coll., 1970-80, Mass. Found. for Humanities and Pub. Policy, 1974-77, East-West Ctr., Honolulu, 1978-81, Expt. in Internat. Living, The Markle Found., The Rockefeller Found., chmn. bd. dirs., acting pres., 1998; former trustee The U. of Cape Town, South Africa, Corp. Adv. Bd., Hotchkiss Sch.; mem. Smithsonian Coun., Yonkers Emergency Fin. Control Bd., 1982-88, Am. Ditchley Found. Program Com., Internat. Rsch. and Exch. Bd., Com. for Econ. Devel., The Masters Sch., Save The Children, Chamber Music Soc. Lincoln Ctr.; bd. dirs. Pub. Broadcasting Corp., 2000—. Hon. fellow Wadham Coll., Oxford U. Mem. NOW Legal Def. Edn. Fund, Coun. Fgn. Rels., Century Assn. (N.Y.C.), Bronxville Field Club. Home: 18 Highland Cir Bronxville NY 10708-5908 Office: Jeannette K Watson Fellowships 31st Fl 810 Seventh Ave New York NY 10019 Office Phone: 212-655-0201. Business E-Mail: ailchman@jkwatson.org.

ILCHMAN, WARREN FREDERICK, academic administrator, foundation administrator, educator; b. Denver, Sept. 6, 1933; s. Frederick Warren and Imogene (Trovinger) I.; m. Alice Crawford Stone, June 11, 1960; children: Frederick Andrew Crawford, Alice Sarah Crawford. BA, Brown U., 1955; PhD, Cambridge (Eng.) U., 1959. Asst. prof. Ctr. Devel. Econs. Williams Coll., Williamstown, Mass., 1960-64; from asst. prof. to prof. polit. sci. U. Calif., Berkeley, 1965-73, dir. Ctr. South and Southeast Asian Studies, 1970-73; vis. prof., rsch. assoc. Ctr. Population Studies, Harvard U., Cambridge, Mass., 1973-74; prof. polit. sci. and econs., dean arts and scis. Grad. Sch., Boston U., 1974-76; program adviser internat. divsn. Ford Found., N.Y.C., 1976-80; v.p. for rsch. and grad. studies SUNY, Albany, 1980-83, provost Nelson A. Rockefeller Coll. Pub. Affairs and Policy, 1983-87, dir. Rockefeller Inst. Govt., 1983-87, exec. v.p., 1987-90; pres. Pratt Inst., Bklyn., 1990-93; exec. dir. ctr. Philanthropy Ind. Univ., Indpls., 1993-97; dir. Paul and Daisy Soros Found., N.Y.C., 1998—. Author: Professional Diplomacy in the U.S, 1961, New Men of Knowledge and the Developing Nations, 1966, Professionals as Agents of Change, 1968, The Political Economy of Change, 1969, rev. edit., 1998 (translated into French, Spanish, Japanese, Hindi and Arabic), Political Economy of Development, 1972, Comparative Public Administration and The Conventional Wisdom, 1973, Policy Sciences and Population, 1975, Education and Employment: The Policy Nexus, 1976, New York in the Year 2000, 1986, Caring and Coping, 1986, Capacity to Change, 1997, Philanthropy and the World's Tradition, 1998, The Lucky Few and the Worthy Many: Selecting the World's Future Leaders, 2004. Bd. dirs. The Masters Sch., The Gen. Theol. Sem., Westchester Cmty. Found.; mem. Am. Friends of the Anglican Ctr. in Rome. Marshall scholar U.K.; recipient Harbison prize Danforth Found., 1969 Mem. Am. Soc. Pub. Adminstrn. (Burchfield award 1965), Asia Soc., Am. Polit. Sci. Assn., N.Y. Acad. Pub. Adminstrn. (Al Smith award), Assn. Asian Studies, Nat. Acad. Pub. Adminstrn., Univ. Club, Bronxville Field Club, Phi Beta Kappa. Episcopalian. Home: 18 Highland Cir Bronxville NY 10708-5908 Office: Paul and Daisy Soros Fellowship Program 400 W 59th St New York NY 10019-1105 Office Phone: 212-547-6926. Business E-Mail: wilchman@sorosny.org.

ILER, ROBERT, actor; b. N.Y.C., Mar. 22, 1985; Actor: (films) The Tic Code, 1999, Tadpole, 2002, Daredevil, 2003; (TV series) The Soprano's, 1999—, (TV appearances include) Oz, 2001, Law and Order: Special Victims Unit, 2004, Late Show with David Letterman, 2004. Office: 1100 Avenue of the Americas New York NY 10036

ILER, WILLIAM A., tobacco company executive; b. Rochester, N.Y., Mar. 27, 1953; s. William C. and Eleanor D. (Phillips) I.; m. Iris J. Lipman, Aug. 15, 1976; 1 child, Sarah M. BA in Psychology, U. Rochester, 1976; postgrad. in bus., Syracuse U., 1979-83. Sales rep. Philip Morris, Inc., Rochester, N.Y., 1976-79, key account mgr. Syracuse, N.Y., 1979-83, mktg. analyst N.Y.C., 1983-84, nat. supermkt. acctg. mgr., 1984-87, nat. programs mgr., 1987-89, sales dir., 1989-95, dir. sales promotions, 1995—2001, dir. CRM promotions merchandising, 2001—03, sr. dir. sales merchandising, 2003—05; ret., 2005; cons., 2005—. Assoc. adv. bd. N.Y. Assn. Conn. Stores, Albany, 1993-95. Mem. Am. Mgmt. Assn., Ardsley Country Club. Avocations: golf, tennis, computer hacking, gardening. Home: 839 Pleasantville Rd Briarcliff NY 10510-2313 Office: 839 Pleasantville Rd Briarcliff Manor NY 10510-2313

ILERI, OMER, electrical engineer, researcher; b. Istanbul, Turkey, Jan. 18, 1979; s. Cahit and Basak Ileri. BSEE, Bogazici U., 2001; MS in Elec. and Comp. Engring., student, Rutgers U., 2003—. Rsch. asst. Winlab Rutgers U., Piscataway, NJ, 2001—. Contbr. articles to profl. jours. Recipient Golden Youth award, 1997. Personal E-mail: omerileri@yahoo.com.

ILES, GREG, writer; b. Germany; Grad., U. Miss., 1983. Author: Spandau Phoenix, 1992, Black Cross, 1995, Mortal Fear, 1997, The Quiet Game, 1999, 24 Hours, 2000, Dead Sleep, 2001, Sleep No More, 2003, The Footprints of God, 2003, Blood Memory, 2005.*

ILES, ROGER DEAN, business educator; b. Detroit, June 11, 1950; s. Virgil Llewellyn and Mary Elizabeth (Lynn) I.; m. Gail Ann Swatzell, Jan. 10, 1971; 1 child, Gwendolyn Christine. AA, Regents Coll., 1990; BS magna cum laude, Crichton Coll., 1992; MBA, U. Memphis, 1997. Enlisted USN, 1969, advanced through grades to chief electronics technician, 1969-89; ret., 1989; switchman Mich. Bell Telephone Co., Dearborn, 1968-69; controller, alumni advisor Crichton Coll., Memphis, 1989-99. Adj. faculty Crichton Coll., Memphis, 1998—2003, U. Memphis, 1998—; chmn., mgr. Shade Tree Engring., Inc., Munford, Tenn., 1992—; online faculty U. Phoenix, 2003—. Memphis campus faculty, 2003—. Bd. dirs. U. Memphis Alumni Assn., 2004—. Mem.: Gideons Internat. (area dir., pres. Tipton County South Camp). Republican. Baptist. Avocations: auto racing, target shooting. Home: 59 Jennifer Cv Brighton TN 38011-6056 Office: PO Box 1248 Munford TN 38058-1248 Office Phone: 901-857-5202. E-mail: etcsw@email.uophx.edu.

ILETT, FRANK, JR., trucking executive; b. Ontario, Oreg., June 21, 1940; s. Frank Kent and Lela Alice (Siver) I.; m. Donna L. Andlovec, Apr. 3, 1971; children: James Frank, Jordan Lee. BA, U. Wash., 1962; MBA, U. Chgo., 1969. CPA Idaho, Ill., Wash. Acct. Ernst & Young, Boise, Cleve., Spokane, 1962-69, mgr. Boise, 1970-72, regional mgr. San Francisco, 1972-73; treas. Interstate Mack, Inc., Boise, 1973-81, pres., CEO, 1981-82; pres. Interstate NationLease, Inc., Boise, 1975-81, Contract Carriers, Inc., Boise, 1983-89, Ilett Transp. Co., Boise, 1985-90; chmn. Carriers/West, Inc., Salem, Oreg., 1986-89; CFO, White GMC Trucks, 1988-92; v.p., CFO, May Trucking Co., Payette, Idaho, 1992-94; acct., mng. ptnr. Frank Ilett, Jr., CPA, Boise, 1994—. Spl. lectr. Boise State U., 1964-67, 94—, St. Mary's Grad. Sch., Moraga, Calif., 1989-92; v.p. I.D.E.A.L., Inc., Nampa, Idaho, 1997-2002; cons. Calif. Hosp. Commn., 1973, Idaho Hosp. Assn., 1974; chmn. Mack Truck Western Region Distbr. Coun., 1979-82; nat. distbr. adv. com. Mack Trucks, Inc., 1980-82; dir. stds. enforcement Idaho State Bd. Accountancy, 1983-84; contr. Idaho Stampede, 2002—. Contbr. articles to profl. jours. Recipient Outstanding Prof. award KPMG, 2003, 05; named Arthur Andersen Outstanding Acctg. Prof., 1996, 2001 Mem.: Inst. Mgmt. Accts., SAR, Gen. Soc. Mayflower Descs., Crane Creek Country Club, Shriners, Masons, Alpha Kappa Psi (Outstanding Bus. Prof. award 1997, named Disting. Faculty Mem., Coll. Bus. 2002). Episcopalian. Home: 1701 Harrison Blvd Boise ID 83702-1015 Office: 1910 University Dr Boise ID 83725 Office Phone: 208-426-2568. Business E-Mail: filett@boisestate.edu.

ILEY, MARTHA STRAWN, music educator; b. Marshville, NC, June 1, 1925; d. Stephen Hasty and Lila Faircloth Strawn; m. Bryce Baxter Iley, Aug. 7, 1948; children: Deborah Iley Hodde, Sheila Iley McLean, Cheryl Iley Lindstrom, Stephanie Iley Salb. BA, East Carolina Tchrs. Coll., 1946; MA, Western Ky. State Coll., 1947; MusM, Winthrop Coll., 1973; EdM, U. NC, Charlotte, 1974; EdD, Nova U., 1979; M Theol. Studies, Gordon-Conwell Theol. Sem., 1998. Cert. Music Tchrs. Nat. Assn. Music tchr. Lincolnton City Sch., 1947—48, Alexander Graham Jr. HS, Charlotte, NC, 1948—52, Charlotte Country Day Sch., 1955—59; min. music Providence Bapt. Ch., Charlotte, 1954—57, Carmel Bapt. Ch., Charlotte, 1968—70, 1975—76; project dir. music edn. Ctrl. Piedmont C.C., Charlotte, 1974—83; founder, chmn. bd. dirs. Met. Music Ministries, Charlotte, 1984—. Editor: (newsletter) ARTY-FACTS, 1983. Bd. dirs., sec. Charlotte Cmty. Concert Assn., 1980—93; dir. recital series Shepherd Ctr., Charlotte, 1980—83; adjudicator piano and voice various orgns., NC, 1980—. Recipient Disting. Music Alumni award, East Carolina U., 2002. Mem.: Charlotte Piano Tchrs. Forum (bd. dirs., pres. 1979—81), Charlotte Clergy Assn., NC Music Tchrs. Assn. (cert. chmn., v.p. 1981—83), Charlotte Music Club (bd. dirs.). Republican. Baptist. Avocations: writing, painting. Home: 10151 Robinson Church Rd Harrisburg NC 28075-6607 Office: Met Music Ministries Inc 1311 Paddock Cir Charlotte NC 28209-2443

ILGAUSKAS, ZYDRUNAS, professional basketball player; b. Kaunas, Lithuania, June 5, 1975; Ctr. Cleve. Cavaliers, 1997—. Selected Schick All-Rookie 1st Team, 1997—98. Office: Cleve Cavaliers Gund Arena One Center Ct Cleveland OH 44115

ILGEN, DOROTHY L., arts foundation executive; Asst. dir. Mo. Arts Coun.; exec. dir. Kans. Arts Commn., Ind. Arts Commn., Indpls., 1995—. Active numerous coms. and commns. various local, state, regional, and nat. orgns.; bd. dirs. Mid-Am. Arts Alliance, Arts Midwest, mem. program planning com.; bd. dirs., mem. planning and budget com., nominating com. Nat. Assembly of State Arts Agys.; panelist arts design panel NEA, Nat. Access Task Force. Office: Indiana Arts Commission 150 W Market St Ste 618 Indianapolis IN 46204

ILITCH, MARIAN, professional hockey team executive, food service executive; m. Michael Ilitch; children: Denise Ilitch Lites, Ron, Mike Jr., Lisa Ilitch Murray, Atanas, Christopher, Carole. Co-owner, sec.-treas. Little Caesar Internat., 1959—, Detroit Red Wings, 1982—; sec.-treas. Olympia Arenas, Inc. (Olympia Entertainment Inc.), 1982—; co-owner, sec.-treas. Fox Theatre, 1987—, Detroit Tigers, 1992—, Little Foxes Fine Gifts, 1992—, The Second City, 1993—, Olympia Devel. LLC, 1996—, Hockeytown Cafe, 1999—, Blue Line Distributing, Uptown Entertainment, Champion Foods; co-founder, vice-chmn. Ilitch Holdings, Inc., 1999—. Recipient Pacesetter Award, Roundtable for Women in Foodservice, 1988, Nat. Preservation Honor Award, 1990. Office: Ilitch Holdings Inc Fox Office Ctr 2211 Woodward Ave Detroit MI 48201-3400

ILITCH, MICHAEL, professional hockey team executive, food products executive; m. Marian Ilitch; children: Denise Ilitch Lites, Ron, Mike Jr., Lisa, Atanas, Christopher, Carole. Founder, owner Little Caesars Restaurant, 1959—; owner, pres. Detroit Red Wings Hockey Team, 1982—; founder Blue Line Distbg., Am.'s Pizza Cafe; owner Olympia Arenas, Inc. (formerly Olympia Stadium Corp.), 1983—, Adirondack Red Wings Hockey Team, Detroit Dr. of Arena Football League; owner, chmn., former pres. Detroit Tigers Baseball Team; chmn. Ilitch Holdings, Inc. Little Caesars Love Kitchen program, 1985—. With USMC, 4 yrs. Named one of 400 Richest Americans, Forbes mag.; named to Hockey Hall of Fame, 2003; recipient Lester Patrick trophy, 1991, Bus. Statesman award, Harvard Bus. Sch. Club Detroit, 1990, Joe Louis award, Sports Illustrated Mag. and Detroit Inst. Arts, Humanitarian of Yr. award, March of Dimes. Office: Detroit Red Wings 600 Civic Center Dr Detroit MI 48226-4419 also: Detroit Tigers Tiger Stadium 2100 Woodward Ave Detroit MI 48201-3470 also: Little Caesars Enterprizes 2211 Woodward Ave Detroit MI 48201-3467*

ILKIN, BAKI, diplomat, Turkish government official; Turkish amb. to Copenhagen; spl. advisor to fgn. min. Govt. of Turkey; Turkish amb. to The Hague; Turkish amb. to USA Washington, 1998—; now acting undersecretary Ministry of Foreign Affairs, Ministry of Foreign Affairs Acting Undersecretary, Ankara, Turkey. Office: 821 United Nations Plaza 10t Fl New York NY 10017 Fax: 202-659-0744.

ILL, CHARLES, III, information technology executive; BS in mech. engring., MBA in fin., Lehigh U.; exec. tng., Wharton and Harvard Bus. Sch. Sales and mktg. IBM, 1978—2003, former v.p. worldwide software geo. sales, mktg. and tech. team; exec. v.p. worldwide sales BEA Systems, Inc., San Jose, Calif., 2003—. Office: BEA Systems Inc 2315 N First St San Jose CA 95131

ILLE, BERNARD GLENN, insurance company executive, director; b. Ponca City, Okla., Feb. 8, 1927; s. Frank Louis and Marie (Cornwell) Ille; m. Mary Lou Allen, Aug. 23, 1952; children: Meredith, Les, Frank. BBA in Fin., U. Okla., 1950. CLU. Agt. Phoenix Mutual Life, Hartford, Conn., 1950-54; gen. agt. Farmers and Bankers Life, Wichita, Kans., 1954-56; asst. v.p. agy. United Founders Life, Oklahoma City, 1956-58, agt. v.p., 1958-60, exec. v.p., dir. agy., 1960-66, pres., 1966-88, pres., CEO, 1988-94, First Life Assurance Co., Oklahoma City, 1994—; pres. BML Cons., Oklahoma City, 1994—; apptd. receiver Mid-Continent Life Ins. Co., Oklahoma City, 1999-2000. Bd. dirs., chmn. audit com. LSB Industries; bd. dirs. Quail Creek Bank, Landmark Nat. Organizer Big Bros., Oklahoma City, 1960; past pres., organizer Nat. Football Found., Oklahoma City, 1969. Recipient Young Pres. Orgn. award, 1966, Kappa Alpha Man of Half Century award, U. Okla. Mem.: Exec. Svc. Corps. Okla. (chmn.), Okla. Assn. Life Ins. Cos. (past pres.), Okla. Life Ins. Guaranty Assn. (chmn. 1984—94), Kiawah Country Club (Kiawah Island, S.C.), Palm Beach Golf and Polo Club (West Palm Beach), Carmel (Calif.) Valley Golf and Country Club, La Quinta Golf and Country Club (Palm Springs), Petroleum Club, Oak Tree Golf and Country Club, Quail Creek Golf and Country Club (Okla. City, Okla.) (organizer), Order Knights of Holy Sepulchre. Democrat. Roman Catholic. Home: 11004 Magnolia Park Oklahoma City OK 73120-5210 Office: BML Cons PO Box 21080 Oklahoma City OK 73156-1080 Office Phone: 405-755-8404. Office Fax: 405-755-8404.

ILLIANO, ANTONIO, language educator, researcher; b. Monte di Procida, Naples, Italy, Apr. 21, 1934; arrived in U.S., 1960; s. Fausto Illiano and Luigina Scotto; m. Elfriede R. Illiano, June 4, 1962; 1 child, Vincent A. DLitt, Univ. Naples, Naples, Italy, 1958; PhD, Univ. Calif., Berkeley, Calif., 1966. Instr. Univ Calif., Santa Barbara, Calif., 1963—66; asst. prof. Univ. Oregon, Eugene, Oreg., 1967—68, Univ. N.C., Chapel Hill, NC, 1969—73, assoc. prof., 1973—81, prof., 1982—. Assoc. editor Forum Italicum, SUNY at Stonibrook; series editor Dictionary of Literary Biography, Detroit. Author: Introduzione alla critica pirandelliana, 1976, Metapsichica e letteratura in Pirandello, 1982, Per l'esegesi del Corbaccio, 1991, Morfologia della narrazione mazoniana, 1993, Sulle sponde del Prepurgatorio, 1997, Da Boccaccio a Pirandello, 1997, Dalla Vita Nuova a Palomar, 1999, Invito al romanzo d'autrice, 2001; co-editor (translator): The Italian Madrigal, 1971, On humor, 1974; co-translator Poeti e filsofi medievali, 1975, (filmscript) Forum Italicum, 1982; co-editor: 20th Century Italian Poets, 1992, Italian Culture, 1993. Mem.: Montesi d'America, Am. Assn. of Tchrs. of Italian. Home: 400 Ridgecrest Dr Chapel Hill NC 27514 Office: Univ NC Chapel Hill NC 27599

ILLNER, MICHAEL DOUGLAS, lawyer; b. Hamilton, Ohio, Nov. 17, 1948; s. Arthur George and Grace Louise Illner; 1 child, Andrew Taylor. BS in Edn., Bowling Green State U., 1972; MA in Edn., Baldwin-Wallace Coll., 1978; JD, U. Akron, 1985. Bar: Ohio 1985. Tchr. Midview Local Schs., Grafton, Ohio, 1972-85; asst. prosecutor Lorain County, Elyria, Ohio, 1985-97; atty. Spike, Meckler, Brill, Illner & Couch, Elyria, 1997—. Roman Catholic. Office: Spike Meckler Brill Illner & Couch 1551 W River Rd N Elyria OH 44035-2729 Office Phone: 440-324-5353. E-mail: millner@spikemeckler.com.

ILLNER-CANIZARO, HANA, physician, oral surgeon, researcher; b. Prague, Czechoslovakia, Nov. 2, 1939; came to U.S., 1968; d. Evzen Pospisil and Emilie (Chrastna) Pospisilova; m. Pavel Illner, June 14, 1963 (div. 1981); children: Martin Illner, Anna Illner; m. Peter Corte Canizaro, Nov. 1, 1982. MD, Charles U., Prague, 1961. Diplomate Am. Bd. Oral Surgery. Resident in oral surgery Inst. of Health, Pribram, Czechoslovakia, 1961-63; attending physician Oral Surgery Clinic, Prague, 1963-68; rsch. assoc. dept. surgery U. Tex. Southwestern Med. Sch., Dallas, 1969-72, instr. surgery, 1972-74, U. Wash. Sch. Medicine, Seattle, 1974-77; asst. prof. surgery Cornell U. Med. Coll., N.Y.C., 1977-81, assoc. prof. surgery, 1981-83, Tex. Tech U. Health Scis. Ctr., Lubbock, 1984-88, prof. surgery, 1988—. Site visitor NIGMS Postdoctoral Tng. Grant, Bethesda, Md., 1987. Mem. editorial bd. Circulatory Shock, N.Y.C., 1981—; manuscript reviewer Surgery, Gynecology and Obstetrics, Chgo., 1985—; contbr. chpts. to books, articles to profl. jours. Grantee NIH, 1979-83, 87-92, Tex. Tech U. Health Scis. Ctr., 1985-86, U.S. dept. Army, 1988-90; Fogarty Sr. Internat. fellow, 1991-92. Mem. Shock Soc. Avocations: remodeling of historical homes, gardening, skiing, pottery. Home: 4622 8th St Lubbock TX 79416-4722 Office: Tex Tech U Health Scis Ctr 3601 4th St Lubbock TX 79430-0001

ILLSON, JAMES ELIAS, management consultant; b. Pitts., Mar. 25, 1953; s. Erwin J. and Esther (Laufe) I.; m. Mary Ann Miller, Oct. 23, 1977 (div. 1983); m. Janis Fortune, Nov. 11, 1984; children: Rebecca, Stuart. BSBA, Drexel U., 1976; MS in Indsl. Adminstrn., Purdue U., 1979. Account mgr. ADP Network Svcs., Hartford, Conn., 1976-78; mgmt. cons. Deloitte & Touche, Detroit, 1979—; pres. and chief operating officer Merisel. Mem. Turnaround Mgmt. Assn., Detroit Athletic Club. Avocations: music, sports cars.

ILLSTON, SUSAN Y., federal judge; b. 1948; BA, Duke U., 1970; JD, Stanford U., 1973. Ptnr. Cotchett, Illston & Pitre, San Francisco, 1973-95; judge U.S. Dist. Ct. (no. dist.) Calif., San Francisco, 1995—. Author: Insurance Coverage in a Toxic Tort Case, A Guide to Toxic Torts, 1987, California Complex Litigation Manual, 1990. Active Legal Aid Soc. San Mateo County, Svc. League San Mateo County. Recipient Appreciation for Vol. Svcs. cert. No. Dist. Calif. Fed. Practice Program, 1989, Svc. and Appreciation cert. 1992. Mem. ABA, ATLA, Assn. Bus. Trial Lawyers, San Mateo County Bar Assn. (Eleanor Falvey award 1994), State Bar Calif. (mem. jud. coun., mem. ethics com. 1975-79, mem. com. on women in law 1985-87, mem. jud. nominees evaluation commn. 1988, mem. exec. com. on litigation 1990-93), Calif. Women Lawyers, Calif. Trial Lawyers Assn., Trial Lawyers for Pub. Justice. Office: US Dist Ct No Dist Calif PO Box 36060 450 Golden Gate Ave San Francisco CA 94102-3661

ILOGIENBOH, CAROLINE O., protective services official, publishing executive; b. Ubiaja, Edo, Nigeria, July 31, 1957; arrived in U.S., 1987; d. Augustine Asa and Esther Oniha Omoifo; m. Ephraim Eghehi Ilogienboh, Feb. 26, 1988; children: Ebinehita, Ofure, Nemedia. BA, U. Alta., Edmonton, Alta., Can., 1982. Cert. criminal justice counselor Addiction Profls. Cert. Bd NJ. Adminstrv. officer Nigerian Telecom., Lagos, 1983—87; social worker Cmty. Svc. N.J., East Orange, 1988—89; probation officer Superior Ct. N.J., East Orange, 1989—; pub. Sun Rose Pubs., East Orange, 2001—. Mem. adv. bd. Minority Concerns Com., Newark, 1999—, Essex County Coalition-Teen Pregnancy, East Orange, NJ, 2000—, Sch. Based Com., Orange, NJ, 2003. Author: Jayda's Story-Lost at Crossroads, 2001, The Return of Tyreek, 2002, poetry. Recipient Appreciation award, Probation Assn. N.J., Atlantic City, 2001. Mem.: Watchung Heights Neighborhood Assn. (program chair 1999—). Avocations: reading, travel, swimming, writing, sewing. Address: PO Box 2314 East Orange NJ 07019 Office: Essex Vicinage Probation Svcs 7th Fl 60 Evergreen Pl East Orange NJ 07018

ILSE-NEUMAN, URSULA, curator; d. Hermann Ilse and Charlotte Troeltsch; m. Lawrence Donald Neuman; 1 child, Andreas Neuman. BA, Hunter College (CUNY), 1977; MA, The New Sch., N.Y.C., 1992; postgrad., Bard Graduate Ctr. Studies Decorative Arts, N.Y.C., 1998—2002. Curator Mus. Arts and Design, N.Y.C., 1992—. Exhbn. juror various nat. and internat. orgns.; curator Corporal Identity - Body Lang., 2003, essayist, 03. Curator, essayist, editor (book) Made in Oakland: The Furniture of Garry Knox Bennett, 2001, (exhbn. catalog) None That Glitters: Perspectives on Jewelry in the Donna Schneier Collection, 2002, Radiant Geometries: Fifteen International Jewelers, 2001; author: (exhbn. catalog) Cabinets of Curiosities: Cabinets of Wonder and Delight; curator, essayist, editor (exhbn. catalog) Corporal Identity-Body Language, 9th Triennial for Form and Content, USA and Germany, 2003; author: (exhbn. catalog) Treasures from the Vault: Contemporary Jewelry, Operas, (Essay) Worthy of the Muses: The Furniture of John Eric Byers, 2001; contbr. essays and articles to publs., selections to exhbn. catalogs; curator, essayist, editor Six Continents of Quilts: The Museum of Arts & Design Collection, 2003. Fellow, Bard Grad. Ctr., 1999—2002, 20th Century Visual Arts fellow, Grad. Ctr., CUNY, 1992. Mem.: Glass Art Soc., Coll. Art Assn., Am. Mus.Assn., Internat. Curators Assn., Art Table, Furniture Soc. (mem. adv. bd. 1999—2002), Phi Beta Kappa. Office: Mus Arts and Design 40 W 53d St New York NY 10019 Office Phone: 212-956-3535 119. Personal E-mail: ursula.neuman@madmuseum.org. E-mail: uneuman@nyc.rr.com.

ILSON, BERNARD, public relations executive; b. NYC; s. Abraham and Goldie Itzkowitz; m. Carol Ruth Geller; children: David, James. BA, Bklyn. Coll.; MA, Columbia U.; PhD, NYU, 1998. Writer NBC TV, NYC, 1955-57, David Alber Assocs., NYC, 1957-58; v.p. Rogers, Cowan and Brenner, NYC, 1958-63; pres. Bernie Ilson, Inc., NYC, 1963—. Founder Hall Fame Am. Humor; past/present clients include Ed Sullivan Show, Beatles Shea Stadium, All in the Family, Monkees, Patridge Family, Grammy Awards, Entertainer Yr. Awards, Motown Records, Tony Bennett, Liberty Mut. Ins. Co., Control Data Corp., Am. Soc. Hypertension, Missoula Children's Theater, Silver Dollar City, Branson, Mo., Mack Ave. Records, Stax Records, Bell Records, Grand Ole Opry, Hee Haw, Negotiation Inst., Liberty Mut. Legends Golf, NBC TV Network, Simon and Schuster, City Mobile Tricentennial, Sister to Sister Found., Games Workshop, Marketplace series on pub. radio, Soupy Sales, Ken Burns Statue Liberty TV spl, Boston Pops 4th July TV spl., Ticketron, Candid Camera, Proctor & Gamble Corp., World Almanac, M.T.H. Electric Trains, Senior Bowl, Art of Negotiation (book). Watercolor artist: Bklyn. Mus. Biennial Watercolor Show, 1954; one-man shows: Keulik Gallery, NYC, Nemisis Galley, NYC; pub., founder Ilson's Inside Information, 1991—; guest appearances (Beatles expert) CBS-TV, ABC Radio Network, Westwood One Radio Network, CNN TV Network. Mem. Writers Guild Am., Acad. TV Arts and Scis., Country Music Assn., Mobile C. of C., Kappa Delta Pi. Clubs: Explorers. Avocations: painting, fishing. Office: 65 W 55th St New York NY 10019-4913 Office Phone: 212-245-7950. Personal E-mail: ilson@aol.com.

ILTIS, HUGH HELLMUT, botanist, educator, advocate; b. Brno, Czechoslovakia, Apr. 7, 1925; arrived in US, 1939, naturalized, 1944; s. Hugo and Anne (Liebscher) I.; m. Grace Schaffel, Dec. 20, 1951 (div. Mar. 1958); children: Frank S., Michael George; m. Carolyn Merchant, Aug. 4, 1961 (div. June 1970); children: David Hugh, John Paul. BA, U. Tenn., 1948; MA, Washington U., St. Louis and Mo. Bot. Garden, 1950, PhD, 1952. Rsch. asst. Mo. Bot. Garden, 1948-52; asst. prof. botany U. Ark., 1952-55; asst. prof. U. Wis.-Madison, 1955-60, assoc. prof., 1960-67, prof., 1967-93, prof. emeritus, 1993—, curator herbarium, 1955-67, dir. univ. herbarium, 1967-93, dir. emeritus, 1993—. Vis. prof. U. Va., Biol. Sta., 1959; world-wide lectr. in field; expdns. to Costa Rica, 1949, 89, Peru, 1962-63, Mex., 1960, 71, 72, 77, 78, 79, 81, 82, 84, 87, 88, 90, 93, 94, 95, 96, Guatemala, 1976, Ecuador, 1977, St. Eustatius, P.R., 1989, USSR, 1975, 79, Nicaragua-Honduras, 1991, Venezuela, 1991, Hawaii, 1967; mem. adv. bd. Flora N.Am., 1970-73, Gov. Wis. Commn. State Forests, 1972-73; rsch. assoc. Mo. Bot. Gardens, Bot. Rsch. Inst. Tex.; co-instigator Reserva Biosfera Sierra de Manantlán, Jalisco, Mex. Author: articles flora of Wis. and Mex., Capparaceae, Cleomaceae, biogeography, evolution of maize and New World agrl., human ecology, especially innate responses to, needs for, natural beauty, diversity, wild nature, and biophilia.; co-author: Flora de Manantlan, 1995, Atlas of the Wisconsin Prairie and Savana Flora, 2000, Checklist of the Vascular Plants of Wis., 2001; editor: Extinction or Preservation: What Biological Future for the South American Tropics?, 1978. With U.S. Army, 1944—46, ETO. Recipient Biologia award, U. Tenn., 1948, Feinstone Environ. award, SUNY, Syracuse, N.Y., 1990, Conservation award, Conservation Coun. Hawaii, 1990, Nat. Wildlife Fedn. Spl. Achievement award, 1992, Puga medal, U. de Guadalajara, Mex., 1994, Disting. Alumnus award, Mo. Bot. Garden, 1999. Fellow AAAS, Linnean Soc. (London); mem. Am. Inst. Biol. Scis., Bot. Soc. Am. (Merit award 1996), Soc. Econ. Botany (Econ. Botanist of Yr. award 1998), Am. Soc. Plant Taxonomists (Asa Gray award 1994), Internat. Assn. Plant Taxonomy, Soc. Bot. Mex., Soc. Study Evolution, Ecol. Soc. Am., Wis. Acad. Arts, Sci. and Letters, Forum for Corr.-Internat. Ctr. Integrative Studies, Nature Conservancy (co-founder and trustee emeritus Wis. chpt., Nat. Oakleaf award 1963), Wilderness Soc., Sierra Club, Nat. Parks Assn., Citizens Natural Resources Assn. Wis., Natural Resource Def. Coun., Environ. Def. Fund, Friends of Earth, Population Connection, Negative Population Growth, Soc. Conservation Biology (Disting. Achievement award 1994), Natural Areas Assn., Sigma Xi, Phi Kappa Phi. Achievements include co-discovery of Zea diploperennis, Z. nicaraguensis (wild species of the maize genus) and Lycopersicon chmielewskii (high sugar-content wild tomatoes). Home: 2784 Marshall Pky Madison WI 53713-1023 Office: U Wis Dept Botany 430 Lincoln Dr Madison WI 53706-1313 Office Phone: 608-262-2792. Office Fax: 608-262-7509. Business E-Mail: tscochra@wisc.edu. E-mail: saw@chorus.net. *If we are to remain healthy and sane, we must concern ourselves with the concept of an Optimum Human Environment, one which must include large portions of the wild and natural environment that shaped our bodies and minds through natural selection over the past millions of years. Hence, only in the preservation of nature, of the world's wild ecosystems and their species, and in a clear comprehension of evolution and the consequent urgent need to reduce both the world's human population and its unsustainable trashing of the environment, can we find the foundations for a meaningful new ethic that will insure a livable world for our children. For their sake, we have to become good ancestors and learn to live within limits.*

ILYAS, MOHAMMAD, nephrologist, physician; b. Karachi, Pakistan, Dec. 25, 1964; MBBS, Dow med. sch., Pakistan, 1990. Clin. asst. prof. U. Fla., Jacksonville, Fla., 1997—2005. South east Islamic Cir. of N.Am. Home: 11054 Daimler Ct Jacksonville FL 32246 Office: Univ Fla 820 Prudential Dr Jacksonville FL 32207 Office Phone: 904-355-1005. Personal E-mail: milyasmd@yahoo.com. Business E-Mail: mohammad.ilyas@jax.ufl.edu.

IM, EASTWOOD, research engineer, information technology manager; s. Chi-Keung and Cheung (Tang) Im; m. Elizabeth Kay, June 3, 1995; children: Alexandria, Aaron. BSEE, U. Ill., 1981, MSEE, 1982, PhD, 1985. Sr. engr. Jet Propulsion Lab., Pasadena, Calif., 1986—96, group supr., 1997—, project mgr., 1999—. Recipient Tech. Excellence award, Jet Propulsion Lab., 2002, Group Achievement award, NASA, 2002, Exceptional Tech. award, 2003. Mem.: IEEE (sr.), Am. Meteorological Soc. Avocations: tennis, golf. Office: Jet Propulsion Lab MS 300-243 4800 Oak Grove Dr Pasadena CA 91109

IM, HYEPIN CHRISTINE, religious organization administrator; BS, U. Calif., Berkeley; MBA, U. So. Calif.; attending, Wesley Theological Seminary. Sponsorship mgr. Calif. Sci. Ctr., community gifts mgr.; venture capitalist Renaissance Capital Partners; founder & pres. Korean Churches for Community Develop., 2001—. Lecturer & speaker Christian Community Develop. Assn., Nat. Council of Korean So. Baptist Churches, US Dept. of Housing and Urban Develop., Asian Am. for Equality, So. Calif. Conference of AME Churches; Am. Memorial Marshall fellow German Marshall Fund, 2001. Pres. Korean Am. Coalition, 1995—96; mem. Pacific Council, 2001—. Office: Korean Churches for Community Develop PO Box 76146 Los Angeles CA 90076-0146*

IM, JAEMO, research scientist; permanent resident, US. s. Jong Tae Lim and Gae Ja Chun; m. Su Young Cho, Jan. 19, 1973; children: Julia Jeongwon children: Joanna Juwon. MS, Stanford U., 1991; PhD, Northwestern U., 1998. Process engr. Applied Materials, Santa Clara, Calif., 1991—93; rsch. assoc. Argonne Nat. Lab., Ill., 1998—2000; device scientist Agere Systems, Alhambra, Calif., 2000—04, Emcore, Alhambra, 2004—. Author: (book) Ferroelectric Thin Films, 1997, In Situ Real-Time Characterization of Thin Films, 2000; contbr. articles to profl. jours. Mem. Light of Love Mission Ch., Pasadena, Calif., 2001—. Fellow, Seiwha Found., 1988; scholar, Northwestern U., 1994. Mem.: Materials Rsch. Soc. (Grad. Student award 1998), Sigma Xi (assoc.). Achievements include patents pending for elimination of destructive processes in capacitors for non-volatile ferroelectric random access memories; design of 10 Gb/s Avalnche Photo Detector; 40 Gb/s PIN Photo Detector; research in designed and constructed a novel in-situ real time surface characterization system (ToF-ISARS); microwave frequency electric-field tunable devices. Home: 3571 Emanuel Dr Glendale CA 91208 Office: Emcore 2015 West Chestnut St Alhambra CA 91803 Office Phone: 626-293-3632. Personal E-mail: jaemue@hotmail.com, imjaemue@yahoo.com. Business E-Mail: jaemo@emcore.com. E-mail: jacmo@emcore.com.

IMADE, LUCKY OSAGIE, political scientist, educator; b. Kano, Nigeria, Dec. 18, 1957; arrived in U.S., 1983; s. Gabriel Agho and Jant Agho Imade; m. Ayowie H. Imade, Dec. 31, 1991; children: Olivia, Lucky Imade, Jr. BA, Shaw U., 1987; MA, Clark U., Atlanta, 1993, PhD, 1995. Instr. polit. sci. Ga. Perimeter Coll., Atlanta, 1995—97; coord. internat. programs Shaw U., Raleigh, NC, 1997—. Fulbright scholar, 1999—2000. Mem.: Edo Soc. Rsch. (pres. 1999—). Avocations: soccer, reading, tennis, travel, basketball. Office: Shaw U 118 E South St Raleigh NC 27601 E-mail: limade@shawu.edu.

IMAGAWA, DAVID KEVIN, surgeon; b. Long Beach, Calif., Aug. 24, 1958; s. David Taoashi Imagawa and Aiko A. Asaki. AB in German Translation, Stanford U., 1979, BS in Biology, 1980; MD, PhD in Pharmacology, Johns Hopkins U., 1986. Clin. instr. UCLA, L.A., 1993—95; asst. prof. U. Calif., Irvine, 1995—99, assoc. prof., 1999—2004, prof. clin. surgery, 2005—. Mem. adv. bd. One Legacy, L.A., 1996—; chief staff U. Calif., 2005—. Fellow: Am. Coll. Surgeons; mem.: Am. Soc. Transplant Surgeons, Pacific Coast Surg. Assn. Office: U Calif Irvine Med Ctr 101 The City Dr Orange CA 92868

IMAI, KOSUKE, education educator; arrived in US, 1999; AM in Stats, Harvard U., Cambridge, Mass., 2002; BA in Liberal Arts, U. Tokyo, Tokyo, Japan, 1998; PhD in Polit. Sci., Harvard U., Cambridge, Mass., 2003. Instr. Princeton U., Princeton, NJ, 2003—04, asst. prof., 2004—. Mem.: Am. Statis. Assn., Am. Polit. Sci. Assn. Office: Princeton Univ Dept of Polit Corwin Hall Princeton NJ 08544 Office Phone: 609-258-6601. Office Fax: 609-258-1110. Business E-Mail: kimai@princeton.edu.

IMANA, JORGE GARRON, artist; b. Sept. 20, 1930; came to U.S., 1964, naturalized, 1974. s. Juan S. and Lola (Garron) I.; m. Cristina Imana; children: George, Ivan. Grad. fine arts acad., U. San Francisco Xavier, 1950. cert. Nat. Sch. for Tchrs., Bolivia, 1952. Prof. art. Nat. Sch. Tchrs., Sucre, 1954-56; prof. biology Padilla Coll., Sucre, 1956-60; head dept. art Inst. Normal Simon Bolivar, La Paz, Bolivia, 1961-62; propr., mgr. The Artists Showroom, San Diego, 1973—. Over 100 one-man shows of paintings in U.S., S. Am., and Europe, 1952—, including: Gallery Banet, La Paz, 1965, Artists Showroom, San Diego, 1964, 66, 68, 74, 76, 77, San Diego Art Inst., 1966, 68, 72, 73, Constrast Gallery, Chula Vista, Calif., 1966, Univ. de Zulia, Maracaibo, Venezuela, 1969, Spanish Village Art Ctr., San Diego, 1974, 75, 76, La Jolla Art Assn. Gallery, 1969, 72-93, Internat. Gallery, Washington, 1976, Galeria de Arte L'Atelier, La Paz, 1977, Mus. Nat., La Paz, 1987, 88, Casa del Arte, La Jolla, Calif., 1987, Simon Patino Found., Bolivia, 1994; numerous group shows including: Fine Arts Gallery, San Diego, 1964, Mus. Modern Art, Paris, 1973; exhibits in galleries of Budapest, Hungary, 1975, Moscow, 1975, Warsaw, Poland, 1976; represented in permanent collections: Mus. Nat., La Paz, Mus. de la Univ. de Potosi, Bolivia, Mus. Nat. de Bogota, Colombia, S. Am. Ministerio de Edn., Managua, Nicaragua, Bolivian Embassy, Moscow and Washington, also pbt. collections in U.S., Europe and Latin Am.; executed many murals including; Colegio Padilla, Sucre, Bolivia, 1958, Colegio Junin, Sucre, Bolivia, 1959, Sindicato de Construccion Civil, Lima, Peru, 1960. Hon. consul of Bolivia, So. Calif., 1969-73. Served to lt. Bolivian Army, 1953. Recipient Mcpl. award Sucre, Bolivia, 1985, Gold Medal, Bolivian Govt., 2003. Mem. San Diego Art Inst., San Diego Watercolor Soc., Internat. Fine Arts Guild, La Jolla Art Assn. Home: Apt 212 2510 Torrey Pines Rd La Jolla CA 92037-3424

IMAYEVA, OLGA BORISOVNA, artist; b. Moscow, Feb. 22, 1945; d. Boris Nicolaevich Gribanov and Klara Borisvna Smith. Exhibitions include N.Y. Internat. Ind. Film, Video & Arts Festival, 1998. Home: 3533 83d St Apt C4 Jackson Heights NY 11372

IMBARUS, AURA, language educator, consultant; b. Sibiu, Romania, July 2, 1971; arrived in US, 1997; d. Stefan Ioan and Aurelia Imbarus; m. Mihai Chiorean, Sept. 2, 1996. BA, Lucian Blaga U., Sibiu, 1995, MA, 1996, PhD, 2002. Cert. tchr. Calif. Asst. prof. English State U. Lucian Blaga, Sibiu, 1995—97; English tchr. Le Conte Humanities Magnet, LA, 1998—2000; English instr. LA City Coll., 1999—2000; English tchr. West H.S., Torrance, Calif., 2000—. English instr. Sylvan Learning Ctr., LA, 1998—99, LA Harbor Coll., Wilmington, Calif., 2000—, Long Beach (Calif.) City Coll., 2002—; ESL instr. El Camino Coll., Torrance, 2001—; interview operator Gallup Pool, Sibiu, 1993—97; head news dept. Radio Contact, Sibiu, 1993—97; mem. editl. bd. Jour. Hosp. Librarianship. Author: Research of Language & Literature, 2000; contbr. articles to profl. jours. Named Outstanding H.S. Tchr., U. Calif., 2001—02. Mem.: AAUW, MLA, Nat. Coun. Tchrs. English, Calif. Tchrs. Assn. Avocations: reading, swimming, ice skating, painting. Home: # 463 384 S Miraleste Dr San Pedro CA 90732-6068 Office: West HS 20401 Victor St Torrance CA 90503 Personal E-mail: auraimbarus@hotmail.com.

IMBEAU, STEPHEN ALAN, allergist; b. Portland, Oreg., Nov. 25, 1947; s. David A. and Marjory Anne (Jacobsen) I.; m. Shirley Ruth Burke, Aug. 18, 1979; children: Stephanie Frances, Andrew Paul, Charles Burke. BA, U. Calif., Berkeley, 1969; MD, U. Calif., San Francisco, 1973. Diplomate Am. Bd. Internal Medicine, Am. Bd. Allergy. Intern U. Wis., Madison, S.C., 1973-74, resident in internal medicine, 1974-75, resident in allergy, 1976-78, resident in infectious diseases, 1978-79; pvt. practice Florence, S.C., 1980—. Budget and control bd. S.C. Data Oversight Coun., 1993—98; founder Coastal Growth Ptnrs. (a Venture Capital Co.), 1997; bd. dirs. Joint Coun. Allergy and Immunology; gen. ptnr. Venture Fund, 2001—, Coastal Growth Ptnrs., 1997—, Trelys Investments, Venture Capital Co., 1997—; co-owner profl. hockey team Columbia Infernos; mem. practicing physicans adv. coun. U.S. HHS Health Care Financing Adminstrn., 2000—03; commr. S.C. Dept. Mental Health, 2003—. Contbr. articles to profl. jours. Chmn. Florence Symphony Orch., 1985-91; bd. dirs. Big Bros., 1989-92, Am. Lung Assn., 1982-86, Florence County Progress, chmn. 1993-95; mem. S.C. Mental Health Commn., 2003—. Fellow ACP; mem. AMA (S.C. alt. del. 1992-98), Am. Acad. Allergists, S.C. Med. Soc. (trustee 1988-90, sec. bd. 1990-94, treas. 1995-97, S.C. Ambassador of the Yr. 1995, pres.-elect 1997, pres. 1998-99, del. to AMA 2004-), Am. Acad. Allergy, Asthma and Immunology (alt. del. to AMA 1999—2004), Joint Coun. Allergy Immunology (bd. mem., sec. 2002-04, treas. 2004—), Florence County Med. Soc. (pres. 1984-85), Lions (pres. 1987-88). Avocations: reading, hunting, stamp collecting/philately. Home: 950 Park Ave Florence SC 29501-5734 Office: 8W E Cheves St Ste 420 Florence SC 29506-2769 Office Phone: 843-679-9335. Personal E-mail: saimbeau@earthlink.net.

IMBER, ANNABELLE CLINTON, state supreme court justice; b. Heber Springs, Ark., July 15, 1950; m. Ariel Barak Imber (dec. 2001); 1 child, William Pierce Clinton. BA magna cum laude, Smith Coll., 1971; postgrad., Inst. for Paralegal Tng., 1971, U. Houston, 1973-75; JD, U. Ark., 1977. Atty. Wright, Lindsey & Jennings Law Firm, Little Rock, Ark., 1977-88; apptd. cir. judge (5th divsn.) Pulaski and Perry Counties, Ark., 1984, elected chancery and probate judge (6th divsn.), 1989-96; elected assoc. justice Ark. Supreme Ct., 1997—. Bd. dirs. Ark. Advs. for Children and Families, 1985-90, pres. 1986-88; bd. dirs Pulaski County Hist. Soc., 1992-95, Congregation B'Nai Israel, 1988-92, 2001-05, Kiwanis Club 1995-98, YMCA of Greater Little Rock and Pulaski County, Our House-A Shelter for Homeless, 1992—, St. Vincent Devel. Found., 1989-93, UAMS Med. Ctr. Dept. Pastoral Care and Edn., 1996—. Mem. ABA, AAUW, Nat. Assn. Women Judges, Ark. Bar Assn., Ark. Women Exec., Assn. of Ark. Women Lawyers (pres. 1980-81, Judge of the Year award 1994), Pulaski County Bar Assn. (bd. dirs. 1982-84). Office: Ark Supreme Ct Justice Bldg 625 Marshall St Little Rock AR 72201-1054 Office Phone: 501-682-6867. Business E-Mail: annabelle.clinton-imber@arkansas.gov.

IMBER, GERALD, plastic surgeon; b. NYC, Jan. 9, 1941; s. George Howard and Rose (Weiss) I.; children: Peter, Jason, Gregory. MD, SUNY, 1966. Diplomate Am. Bd. Plastic Surgery. Intern LI Jewish Med. Ctr., 1966-67; resident Kaiser Hosp., LA, 1970-72, USAF Griffiss AFB Hosp., Rome, NY, 1970-72, NY Presbyn. Hosp.-Cornell Med. Ctr., NYC, 1972-74, attending surgeon, 1974—, clin. asst., prof. of surgery; dir. Imber Clinic, NYC, 1982—. Author: Youth Corridor, 1997, For Men Only, 1998. Trustee Inwood House, NYC, 1998—. Capt. USAF, 1968—70. Mem. Am. Soc. Plastic Surgeons, NE Soc. Plastic Surgeons, NY State Med. Soc., NY County Med. Soc. Avocations: polo, sailing. Office: Imber Clinic 1009 5th Ave New York NY 10028-0155 Office Phone: 212-472-1800. E-mail: drimber@drimber.com.

IMBER, RICHARD JOSEPH, physician, dermatologist; b. Darby, Pa., Apr. 9, 1944; s. Joseph and Geraldine (Frances) I.; m. Helen Lee Stick, Nov. 18, 1971. BS, U. Dayton, 1966; MD, Temple U., 1970. Diplomate Am. Bd. Dermatology. Intern Denver Presbyn. Med. Ctr., 1970-71; resident dept. dermatology U. Colo. Health Sci. Ctr., 1971-74; chief of dermatology USAF Acad., Colorado Springs, 1974-76; sr. staff dermatologist Colo. Permanente Med. Group, Denver, 1976-83; dermatologist Denver Skin Clinic, 1983—. Asst. clin. prof. dermatology U. Colo. Med. Sch., Denver, 1974—. Contbr. articles to profl. jours. Maj. USAF, 1974-76. Fellow Am. Acad. Dermatology; mem. Pacific Dermatologic Assn., Colo. Med. Soc., Denver Med. Soc., Colo. Dermatologic Soc. (sec.-treas. 1980, v.p. 1981, pres. 1982). Avocation: scuba diving. Home: 4020 S Bellaire St Englewood CO 80110-5028 Office: Denver Skin Clinic 2200 E 18th Ave Denver CO 80206-1205

IMBRIE, ANDREW WELSH, composer, educator; b. N.Y.C., Apr. 6, 1921; s. Andrew C. and Dorothy (Welsh) I.; m. Barbara Cushing, Jan. 31, 1953; children: Andrew, John (dec.). AB, Princeton U., 1942; MA, U. Calif.-Berkeley, 1947; DMusic (hon.), San Francisco Conservatory of Music, 2004. Instr. music U. Calif., Berkeley, 1947, 49-51, asst. prof., 1951, assoc. prof., 1957-60, prof., 1960-91, Jerry and Evelyn Hemmings Chambers chair dept.

music, 1989-92. Composer-in-residence Tanglewood Music Ctr., Lenox, Mass., summer 1991; guest prof. Brandeis U., 1982, U. Ala., 1992, U. Chgo., 1994, 96-97, Northwestern U., 1994, NYU, 1995, Fromm prof., Harvard U., fall, 1997. Compositions include 3 symphonies, 5 string quartets, trios, sonatas, songs, orchestral and choral works, works for various chamber ensembles, Angle of Repose (opera), 3 piano concerti, concerti for violin, cello and flute, Dance-cantata Prometheus Bound, Requiem in memoriam John Imbrie (Grammy award nomination 2000), Adam (cantata), From Time to Time (for woodwinds, percussion and string quartet). Bd. dirs. Koussevitzky Found.; bd. govs. San Francisco Symphony, 1982-91. Recipient Circle award N.Y. Music Critics, 1943-44; Alice M. Ditson fellow Columbia U., 1946-47; fellow Am. Acad. in Rome, 1947-49; grantee Nat. Inst. Arts and Letters, 1950; Guggenheim fellow, 1953-54, 60-61; merit award Boston Symphony Orch., 1955; creative arts award Brandeis U., 1958; Naumburg award, 1960; grantee Nat. Found. on Arts and Humanities; composer in residence Am. Acad. Rome, 1967-68; recipient Walter Hinrichsen award Columbia U., 1971 Mem. Am. Acad. Arts and Letters, Am. Acad. Arts and Scis., Phi Beta Kappa. Clubs: Bohemian (San Francisco). Home: 2625 Rose St Berkeley CA 94708-1920

IMBRIGIOTTA, ROBERT A., information technology manager, writer; b. Cleve., June 26, 1958; s. Robert P. and Marlene Ann Imbrigiotta; m. Carol L. Imbrigiotta, Sept. 14, 1991; children: Amy Jo, Chelsea Renee, Alec Anthony. BS in Chem. Engring., U. Fla., 1981. Cert. engring. in tng., Fla., 1990; Project Mgmt. Inst., Fla., 2002. Sr. project mgr. Motorola, Inc, Plantation, Fla., 1983—2003; sr. product devel. mgr. Tyco Safety Products, Boca Raton, 2004—. Author: The Journey to a Bulletproof Lawn - A guide to St. Augustinegrass. Pres. Imperial Point Homeowners Assn., Fort Lauderdale, Fla., 1996—98; dir. Sch. Adv. Coun., St. Coleman Cath. Sch., Pompano Beach, 2004. Mem.: AIChE (assoc.), Project Mgmt. Inst. (assoc.). Conservative. Roman Catholic. Achievements include patent for greens maintenance system. Home: 2010 NE 65th St Fort Lauderdale FL 33308 Personal E-mail: imbo@comcast.net.

IMBROGNO, CYNTHIA, judge; b. 1948; BA, Indiana U. Pa., 1970; JD cum laude, Gonzaga U., 1979. Law clk. to Hon. Justin L. Quackenbush U.S. Dist. Ct. (Wash. ea. dist.), 9th circuit, 1980-83; law clk. Wash. State Ct. of Appeals, 1984; civil rights staff atty. Ea. Dist. of Wash., 1984-85, complex litigation staff atty., 1986-88; with Preston, Thorgrimson, Shidler, Gates & Ellis, 1988-90, Perkins Coie, 1990-91; magistrate judge U.S. Dist. Ct. (Wash. ea. dist.), 9th circuit, Spokane, 1991—. Office: 740 US Courthouse 920 W Riverside Ave Spokane WA 99201-1010

IMEL, JOHN MICHAEL, lawyer; b. Cushing, Okla., Aug. 4, 1932; s. Arthur Blaine and Hazel Monnet (Kelly) I.; m. Patricia Ann Carney, July 31, 1954; children: Blythe Michele, Kathryn Ann, Dixie Lynn, Sally Louise. BS, U. Okla., 1954, JD, 1959. Bar: Okla. 1959, U.S. Dist. Ct. (no. dist.) Okla. 1961, U.S. Ct. Appeals (10th cir.) 1961, U.S. Supreme Ct. 1962, U.S. Dist. Ct. (we. dist.) Okla. 1967, U.S. Dist. Ct. (ea. dist.) Okla. 1971. Asst. atty. County of Tulsa, 1959—60; mcpl. judge City of Tulsa, 1960—61; U.S. atty. U.S. Dept. Justice, Tulsa, 1961—67; ptnr. Moyers, Martin, Santee Imel & Tetrick, Tulsa, 1967—. Regent U. Okla., Norman, 1981-88, chmn., 1987-88; trustee Children's Med. Ctr., Tulsa, 1979-84. Capt. USNR, 1954-77. Fellow Am. Bar Found., Am. Coll. Trial Lawyers (state chmn. 1987-88); mem. Am. Inns of Ct. (program chmn. 1989-90, Exemplary Leadership award 1996), So. Hills Country Club (bd. govs. 1993-99), Tulsa Club (pres. 1990), Rotary (pres. 1968-69). Democrat. Methodist. Avocations: golf, swimming, tennis, reading. Home: 3920 E 58th Pl Tulsa OK 74135-7823 Office: Moyers Martin Santee Imel & Tetrick 401 S Boston Ste 1100 Tulsa OK 74103 Office Phone: 918-582-5281. Business E-Mail: imel@moyersmartin.com.

IMESCH, JOSEPH LEOPOLD, bishop; b. Grosse Pointe Farms, Mich., June 21, 1931; s. Dionys and Margaret (Margelisch) I. BS, Sacred Heart Sem., 1953; student, N.Am. Coll., Rome, 1953-57; STL, Gregorian U., Rome, 1957. Ordained priest Roman Cath. Ch., 1956. Sec. to Cardinal Dearden, 1959—71; pastor Our Lady of Sorrows Ch., Farmington, Mich., 1971—77; titular bishop of Pomaria, aux. bishop of Detroit, 1973—79; asst. bishop N.W. region, 1977—79; bishop of Joliet Ill., 1979—. Office: Chancery Office 425 Summit St Joliet IL 60435-7155*

IMHOF, DAVID CHARLES, music educator; b. Glen Ridge, N.J., Sept. 29, 1960; s. Charles Valentine and Verna Imhof; m. Jill Carol Alderton, Dec. 14, 1985; children: Ryan, Andrew, Jessica. BS, William Paterson Coll., 1982; MusM, Ithaca Coll., 1988. Cert. tchr. music N.J., N.Y. Tchr. Seaford (N.Y.) Jr. HS, 1983—85, Hunterdon Ctrl. HS, Flemington, NJ, 1990—93, Hackettstown (N.J.) Sch. Dist., 1993—; band dir. Hackensack (N.J.) HS, 1985—88, Hillsborough HS, Belle Mead, NJ, 1988—90. Coach Hackettstown In-Line Hockey, 1997—2001, Knowlton (N.J.) Athletic Assn., 1998—; condr. Warren County Sixth Grade Band. Mem.: ASCD, Music Educators Nat. Conf., Phi Delta Kappa. Presbyterian. Avocations: hiking, camping, music. Home: 19 Oak Lane Rd Columbia NJ 07832 Office: Hackettstown Mid Sch 500 Washington St Hackettstown NJ 07840 Office Phone: 908-852-8554.

IMHOFF, WALTER FRANCIS, investment banker; b. Denver, Aug. 7, 1931; s. Walter Peter and Frances Marie (Barkhausen) I.; m. Georgia Ruth Stewart, June 16, 1973; children: Stacy, Randy, Theresa, Michael, Robert. BSBA, Regis U., Denver, 1955; D Pub. Svc. (hon.), Regis U., 1991. Asst. v.p. Coughlin & Co., Denver, 1955-60; pres., chief exec. officer Hanifen, Imhoff Inc., Denver, 1960-2000; mng. dir. Stifel, Nicolaus & Co., 2000—; dir. Republic Fin. Corp., 2001—. Guest lectr. U. Colo., 1976 Trustee Regis Coll., 1975—95, treas., 1976—79, vice chmn., 1981, chmn., 1982—89, life trustee, 1998—; bd. dirs. NCCJ, 1980—89, chmn., 1986—89, life trustee, 1998—; bd. dirs. Arapahoe Libr. Found., 1990—94, Channel 6 Ednl. TV, treas., 1996—97, vice chmn., 1997—98, chmn., 1998—99; bd. dirs. Highland Hills Found., 1993—, Denver Area coun. Boy Scouts Am., 1986—, v.p., 1989—; bd. dirs. St. Joseph's Hosp., mem. exec. com., 1991, vice chmn., 1994, chmn., 1995—98; bd. dirs. Kempe Children's Found., 1992, chmn., 1994—97; bd. dirs. 9 Who Cares, 1998—, Caring for Colo., 2001—; chmn. Colo. Concern, 1988—, St. Joseph Hosp. Found., 2004—; chmn. exec. com. 2% Club, 2000—; trustee Irish Cmty. Ctr., 2001. Named Outstanding Alumnus Regis Coll., 1970 Mem. Bond Club Denver (pres. 1965), Colo. Mcpl. Bond Dealers Assn. (pres. 1973), Mid-Continent Securities Industry Assn. (dir. 1972-75), Securities Industry Assn. (chmn. S.W. region 1991-95, dir. 1993-96), Nat. Assn. Security Dealers, Pub. Securities Assn. (dir. 1972-75), Denver C. of C. (bd. dirs. 1986-91, treas. 1989-91), Rose Hosp. Found., Centennial C. of C. (vice chmn.), NCCJ, Alpha Kappa Psi, Alpha Sigma Nu. Clubs: Denver (pres. 1981-82). Republican. Roman Catholic. Home: 10432 E Ida Pl Greenwood Village CO 80111-3753 Office: 1125 17th St Ste 1600 Denver CO 80202-2024

IMIG, WILLIAM GRAFF, lawyer, lobbyist; b. Omaha, Aug. 13, 1941; s. Jacob H. and Gretchen I.; m. Joyce, Dec. 18, 1976; children: Scott, Kari, Steven BA, Cornell U., 1963, LLB, 1965. Bar: Colo. 1965, U.S. Ct. Appeals (10th cir.) 1965, U.S. Supreme Ct. 1969. Assoc. Sherman & Howard, Denver, 1965-66; v.p., shareholder Ireland, Stapleton, Pryor & Pascoe, Denver, 1970-92; pvt. practice, Denver, 1992—. Colo. counsel Property Casualty Ins. Assn. Am., Des Plaines, Ill., 1971—; Colo. legis. counsel Allstate Ins. Cos., 1982—. Bd. editors Cornell Law rev., 1964-65. Chmn. Colo. Gov.'s Auto Insurance Task Force, 2002; trustee Colo. chpt. Nat. Multiple Sclerosis Soc., 1995-2000. Capt. JAGC, U.S. Army, 1966-70. Mem. Colo. Bar Assn. (bd. govs. 1974-77), Colo. Assn. Commerce and Industry (chmn. tort reform coun., chmn. auto ins. roundtable), City Club of Denver, Denver Law Club, Phi Kappa Phi. Republican. Episcopalian. Home and Office: 1011 S Valentia St #40 Denver CO 80247 Office Phone: 303-337-4822.

IMIRIE, MITCHELL, cultural organization administrator; b. Bethesda, Md., Aug. 5, 1963; s. Vincent John Imirie and Guelda Campbell Imire; life ptnr. Douglas Eugene Noble, Feb. 1, 2003. BFA, Lynchburg (Va.) Coll., 1986; MFA in Theatre Scene Design, Va. Commonwealth U., 1999. Theatre tchr. The Steward Sch., Richmond, Va., 1986—95; facility mgr. Cultural Arts Ctr., Glen Allen, Va., 1999—. Freelance scene designer Henrico Theatre Co., Glen Allen, Va., 1987—. Avocations: theater, music, gardening, renovation of old houses. Office: Cultural Arts Center at Glen Allen 2880 Mountain Road Glen Allen VA 23060 Office Phone: 804-261-6200.

IMMANUEL, LAURA AMELIA, dentist; b. Jakarta, Java, Indonesia, May 11, 1971; d. Gamaliel and Dewi Immanuel. BS, Union Coll., Schenectady, N.Y., 1993; postgrad., Columbia U., N.Y.C., 1993—94; DMD, Tufts U., 1999. Resident in AEGD program SUNY-Stony Brook Dental Sch., 1999—2000; assoc. dentist Total Dental Care, Middle Island, NY, 2000, Dr. Norman Rich, Wantagh, NY, 2000—02, Gentle Dental, Arlington, Mass., 2002—. Recipient award, Internat. Congress of Oral Implantologists, 1999. Mem.: ADA, Mass. Dental Soc., Sigma Xi. Presbyterian. Avocations: photography, painting, music, travel. Office: Gentle Dental 725 Massachusetts Ave Arlington MA 02476

IMMEL, BARBARA K., management consultant; b. Bakersfield, Calif., July 31, 1956; m. Joseph Herbert Immel, Jr., Aug. 31, 1979; children: Joseph Herbert Immel, III, Elizabeth Logan. BA in English, U. Calif., Santa Barbara, 1978, single subject tchg. credential, 1979; grad., Stanford Profl. Pub. Course, 1981, Stanford U. Exec. Pub. Course, 1982, grad., 2002, Buckley Sch. Pub. Speaking, 2000, grad., 2001. Asst. to pres. Vet. Practice Pub. Co., Santa Barbara, 1980—81; tech. editor I-III Syva Co., Palo Alto, Calif., 1982—86; adminstr. Syntex Corp., Palo Alto, 1986—92; compliance mgr. Chiron Corp., Emeryville, Calif., 1993—95; cons. pres. Immel Resources, LLC, Petaluma, Calif., 1995—. Vol. libr. Career Action Ctr., Palo Alto, Calif., 1982—86; instr. U. Calif. Berkeley Ext., 1995—2000, co-dir. drug devel. course, 1998—2000; guest lectr. undergrad. pharmacology course U. Calif., Berkeley, 1999—; cons. in field. Columnist: Biopharm mag., 1996—; contbr. articles to profl. jours., Dekker's Ency. of Pharm. Tech.; editor-in-chief Immel Report, 2004—. Scholar Pres. scholar, U. Calif. Santa Barbara, 1974—78. Mem.: Drug Info. Assn., Am. Soc. for Quality, Regulatory Affairs Profl. Soc., Pharm. Rschrs. and Mfrs. Am. (tng. com. 1988—92), Parenteral Drug Assn. Avocations: reading, travel, crocheting. Office: Immel Resources LLC Ste B 616 Petaluma Blvd North Petaluma CA 94952 Office Phone: 707-778-7222. E-mail: immel@immel.com.

IMMEL, RALPH CONRAD, JR., voice educator, singer; b. Wichita Falls, Tex., July 25, 1936; s. Ralph Conrad and Harriet Faye Immel; m. Nancy Claire Chester, Sept. 7, 1963; 1 child, Christopher Conrad. BA, U. of Tex., Austin, 1959, MusB, 1963, MusM, 1966; Performance Cert., Akademie fuer Musik und Darstellende Kunst, Vienna, Austria, 1965. Programming Certification Computer Learning Ctr., 1985. Lyric baritone Theater der Stadt Bonn, Bonn, Germany, 1966—70; dramatic baritone Landestheater Linz, Linz, Austria, 1970—72. Italian baritone Grazer Oper, Graz, Steyer, Austria, 1972—74; sr. tng. rep. Northrop Grumman Corp., Hawthorne, Calif., 1985—94; class and pvt. voice instr. Cerritos Coll., Norwalk, Calif., 1999—; asst. prof. of vocal arts U. of So. Calif., LA, 1974—78. Singer: (opera) Forty operas - six hundred performances. Fulbright scholar, Fulbright Com., 1963-1964. Mem.: Am. Guild of Musicial Artists. Avocations: antique automobiles, rare books, motorcycling, art, aquariums. Home: 1114 12th St No 203 Santa Monica CA 90403-5418 Home Fax: 310-395-9896. Personal E-mail: cimmelinsm@aol.com.

IMMELT, JEFFREY R., diversified technology and services company executive; b. Cincinnati, Ohio, Feb. 19, 1956; s. Joseph and Donna Immelt; m. Andrea Immelt; 1 child. BA in Applied Math., Dartmouth Coll., 1978; MBA, Harvard U., 1982. With GE Corp. Mktg., 1982; various positions GE Plastics, 1982-89; v.p. consumer svc. GE Appliances, 1989-91, v.p. worldwide mktg. and product mgmt.; v.p., gen. mgr. GE Plastics Am., 1992-96; pres., CEO GE Med. Sys., 1997—2000; pres., chmn. elect GE Co., 2000—01, chmn., CEO, 2001—. Bd. dirs. Catalyst, Robin Hood, N.Y.C. Recipient Man of the Year, Fin. Times, 2003. Office: GE 3135 Easton Tpke Fairfield CT 06431-0002*

IMMELT, STEPHEN J., lawyer; b. Columbus, Ohio, Dec. 27, 1951; s. Joseph Francis and Donna (Wallace) I.; m. Susann Randolph Carroll, June 7, 1976; children: Catherine Carroll, Molly Maccubbin. BA, Yale U., 1974; JD, U. Md., 1977. Bar: Md. 1977, D.C. 1995, U.S. Dist. Ct. Md. 1978, U.S. Dist. Ct. D.C. 1988, U.S. Ct. Appeals (4th cir.) 1978, U.S. Ct. Appeals (D.C. Cir.) 1988, U.S. Ct. Appeals (6th and 9th cirs.) 1992. Law clk. to Hon. Harrison L. Winter U.S. Ct. Appeals (4th cir.), Balt., 1977-78; asst. U.S. atty. U.S. Dept. Justice, Balt., 1979-83; assoc. Piper & Marbury, Balt., 1978-79, 85-86, ptnr., 1986-89; mng. ptnr.-Balt. office Hogan & Hartson, Balt., 1989—, dir. litig. practice group. Mem. adv. bd. Johns Hopkins U. Sch. Nursing, Balt., 1990-98. Bd. dirs. Md. chpt. The Nature Conservancy, Chevy Chase, 1985-96, Valleys Planning Coun., Towson, Md., 1991-97, Balt. Zoo, 1994-2000, Balt. Choral Arts Soc., 1994-2000. Democrat. Avocations: golf, skiing, gardening, outdoors. Office: Hogan & Hartson LLP 111 S Calvert St Ste 1600 Baltimore MD 21202-6191 Office Fax: 410-659-2757, 410-639-6981. Business E-Mail: sjimmelt@hhlaw.com.

IMMERGUT, KARIN J., prosecutor; b. Bklyn. BA, Amherst Coll., 1982; JD, U. Calif., Berkeley, 1987. Bar: Calif. 1987, Vt. 1995, Oreg. 1996. Asst. US atty. Central. Dist., Calif., 1988—94; atty. Gravel & Shea, Burlington, Vt., 1994—96, Covington & Burling, Washington, 1987—89; assoc. independent counsel Office Independent Counsel, Washington, 1998; dep. dist. atty. Portland, Oreg., 1996—98; asst. US atty. dist. Oreg. US Dept. Justice, 1998—2001, US atty., 2003—. Office: US Atty Mark O Hatfield US Courthouse 1000 SW Third Ave Ste 600 Portland OR 97204-2902 Office Phone: 503-727-1000.

IMMERGUT, MEL M., lawyer; b. Bklyn., 1947; BA, U. Pa., 1968; JD, Columbia U., 1971, MBA, 1972. Bar: N.Y. 1972. Ptnr., Global Corp. Dept. Milbank, Tweed, Hadley & McCloy, N.Y.C., 1980—, chmn., 1995—. Bd. dir. Legal Aid Soc.; trustee & past pres. Am. Col. Investment Counsel; trustee Eye Bank for Sight Restoration; past pres. Billfish Found.; bd. vis. Columbia Univ. Law Sch. Mem. Council on Fgn. Rels., ABA, N.Y. State Bar Assn., Assn. Bar City N.Y. Office: Milbank Tweed Hadley & McCloy 1 Chase Manhattan Plz Fl 47 New York NY 10005-1413 Office Phone: 212-530-5730. Office Fax: 212-530-5219. Business E-Mail: mimmergut@milbank.com.*

IMMERMAN, NEIL, academic administrator, computer science educator; BS, MS, Yale U., 1974; PhD, Cornell U., 1980. Grad. program dir., prof. computer sci. U. Mass., Amherst. Author: (book) Descriptive Complexity, 1999. Co-recipient Gödel prize in theoretical computer sci., 1995; recipient Guggenheim fellowship, 2003—04. Fellow: Assn. for Computing Machinery. Office: U Mass Dept Computer Sci Rm 374 140 Governor's Dr Amherst MA 01003-9264

IMMERMAN, STEVEN CURTIS, surgeon, oncologist; b. New Rochelle, N.Y., May 2, 1953; BS in Medicine, Northwestern U., 1975, MD, 1976. Diplomate Am. Bd. Surgery. Intern in gen. surgery Northwestern U., Chgo., 1977, resident in gen. surgery, 1978-81; clin. surg. fellowship in surg. oncology Evanston (Ill.) Hosp., 1980-81; hosp. staff Sacred Heart Hosp., Eau Claire, Wis., 1982—, Luther Hosp., Eau Claire, Wis., 1982—, Oakleaf Surgery Hosp., 1997—; gen., thoracic surgeon Eau Claire, 1994—; clin. asst. prof. family medicine U. Wis. Med. Sch., 1991—. CEO Oakleaf Med. Mgmt., LLP; fellow Am. Coll. Surgeons, 1985—. Contbr. articles to Annals of Thoracic Surgery, Archives of Surgery, and Cancer. Mem. Eau Claire City/County Bd. Health, 1984-88; chmn. Sacred Heart Hosp. Dept. Surgery Morbidity & Mortality Com., 1987-92, St. Joseph's Hosp. Dept. Surgery Morbidity & Mortality Com., 1986-88; med. ethics com. Sacred Heart Hosp., 1992-98. Recipient Northwestern Meml. Hosp. Surg. award, 1980. Fellow ACS; mem. AMA (Physician's Recognition award 1982-83, 90-91, 94—), Wis. Med. Assn., Dunn County Med. Soc., Pepin County Med. Soc., Am. Soc. Gen. Surgeons. Home: 120 Marston Ave Eau Claire WI 54701-3910 Office: Evergreen Surg Inc 719 W Hamilton Ave Eau Claire WI 54701-6938

IMMERSO, JOHN JOSEPH, music educator; b. Plainview, N.Y., July 31, 1963; s. Raymond Edward and Clara F Immerso; m. Tracey Ann Conway, July 25, 1998; children: Nicole, Raymond, Tracey. B in music edn., State U. of NY Coll. at Potsdam, 1985, M in music performance, 1987. Music educator/band dir. Patchogue Medford Sch. Dist., NY, 1987—97; music educator/asst. marching band Hauppauge Sch. Dist., NY, 1992—2004; music dept. coord./band dir. Sag Harbor Sch. Dist., NY, 1997—. Exec. bd. mem. Suffolk County Music Educators Assn., 1988—97; cert. adjudicator NY State Sch. Music Assn., Westbury, 1990—; guest condr. Suffolk County Music Educators Assn., 2000, Nassau County Music Educators Assn., 1996; v.p. NY State Chpt. of the Percussive Arts Soc., 1997—98. Composer: Tranquility No. 1, 1987, Serenity, 1990, South Bay Sonata, 1991. Recipient NYS Educator of the Week, WLNY-TV-55, 1998. Mem.: Suffolk County Music Educators Assn., NY State Sch. Music Assn. Democrat. Roman Cath. Avocations: gardening, carpentry, bicycling. Home: 115 12th Ave Holtsville NY 11742 Office: Sag Harbor Pub Schools 200 Jermain Ave Sag Harbor NY 11963 Office Phone: 631-725-5326 ext. 125. Business E-Mail: jimmerso@sagharbor.k12.ny.us.

IMPARA, JAMES CLEMENT, security firm executive; b. Atlanta, Dec. 4, 1940; s. Gus Thomas and Martha Murial Impara; m. Barbara Sterrett Plake, Nov. 21, 1992; m. Beverly Haggquist Haggquist, Aug. 25, 1960; children: Sean Thomas, Sheryl Impara Sutton. BS, Fla. State U., 1962, MS, 1966, PhD, 1972. Rsch. asst. to adminstr. for ednl. accountability Fla. Dept. of Edn., Tallahassee, 1966—73; dir., state assessment Oreg. Dept. of Edn., Salem, 1973—76; assoc. prof. Va. Poly. Inst. and State U., Blacksburg, 1976—92; prof., dir. Buros Ctr. for Testing, Inst. for Assessment Consultation and Outreach U. Nebr.-Lincoln, 1992—2003, profl. assoc. Buros Ctr. for Testing, Inst. for Assessment Consultation and Outreach, 2003—; sr. dir. test security Caveon LLC, Midvale, Utah, 2003—. Author: (reference book) Mental Measurements Yearbook Series; contbr. articles to profl. jours. Bd. mem., v.p., pres. Nat. Coun. on Measurement in Edn., Washington. With U.S. Army, 1959—62. Recipient Charles Clear award, Va. Ednl. Rsch. Assn., 1983. Mem.: Am. Ednl. Rsch. Assn. (program com.). Office: Caveon LLC 6905 South 1300 E #468 Midvale UT 84047 Office Phone: 801-208-0103. E-mail: jim.impara@caveon.com.

IMPELLIZERI, JOHN C. (JACK IMPELLIZERI), mathematics educator; s. Jack W. and Catherine Impellizeri; m. Mary T. Blaney, Aug. 28, 1982; children: Traci A., Jack P., Jeremy J. BA, SUNY, New Paltz, 1973, MS in edn., 1978. Cert. tchr. NY State Edn. Dept. Math. tchr. Uniondale Pub. Schools, NY, 1985—. Founder/pres. JMI Computer Svcs., Freeport, NY, 1985—; adj. asst. prof. math/computer/stats. dept. Nassau Cmty. Coll., Garden City, NY, 1999—. Author: Basic Mathematics Workbook, (newspaper column) Hyde Pk. Townsman, Anderson Sch.; author, editor, publisher Archbishop Molloy Coun. Yearbook, editor, author, publisher (monthly newsletter) The Molloy Monitor (3rd Pl. Nassau County Bull. Contest, Nassau/Suffolk Chpt. KC, 1998), dir., prodr. (video presentation) RST Presents Lawrence Road JHS; contbr. articles to newspapers. Former first aid instr. ARC, Mineola, NY; founder Yesterday, Today & Tomorrow Entertainment Group, Freeport, NY, 1978—2005, dir., 1978—2005, performer, 1978—2005; former emt/crew chief Port Jefferson Ambulance Corps, NY; former firefighter Freeport Fire Dept. Emergency Co. #9, Freeport; former choral mem. masterwork chorus Masterwork Chorus & Orch., Morristown, NJ; former emt instr. Franklin Gen. Hosp., Lynbrook, NY; former choral mem. St. Cecilia Chorus, NYC; former chief timer, scorer NY Region Sports Car Club Am.; former v.p. sch. bd. Our Holy Redeemer, Freeport, former leader folk group, former co-leader Antioch Weekends, former choir mem. adult choir. Mem.: Nassau Reading Coun., Nat. PTA, Adj. Faculty Assn. (assoc.), Uniondale Teachers Assn. (assoc.), Cardinal Mercier 4th Degree Assembly (assoc.), Friends for LI Heritage (life), KC (webmaster, publr. www.knightsite.com, former mem. supreme coun. internet steering com., former coord. internet workshop, #1 KC Website in World 1997, Website of Yr. 2003, listed #15 in Top 40 Cath. Websites in World 1997), Archbishop Molloy KC Coun. (assoc.; grand knight 1998—2000). Roman Catholic. Personal E-mail: knightsite@aol.com.

IMPELLIZZERI, ANNE ELMENDORF, insurance company executive, non-profit executive; b. Chgo., Jan. 26, 1933; d. Armin and Laura (Gundlach) Elmendorf; m. Julius Simon Impellizzeri, Oct. 12, 1961 (dec.); children: Laura, Theodore (dec.). BA, Smith Coll., 1955; MA, Yale U., 1957. CLU; ChFC. With Met. Life Ins. Co., NYC, 1959—79, from asst. v.p., corp. social responsibility to v.p. group ins., 1979—88; v.p. N.Y.C. Partnership, 1988-90; pres., CEO Blanton-Peale Inst., N.Y.C., 1990-98; exec. dir. Russel Wright's Manitoga, Garrison, NY, 1998—2001. Bd. dirs., v.p. Women's City Club of N.Y.; treas. Bard Music Festival, 1999—2002, sec., 2004—; bd. dirs. Scenic Hudson; v.p. Women's City Club of N.Y., 2004—; treas. Scenic Hudson, 1999—2002, sec., 2004—; trustee Smith Coll., 1991—96; bus. urban issues coun. The Conf. Bd., 1981—85, chair bus. urban issues coun., 1983—85. Trustee Lakeland Bd. Edn., Westchester County, NY, 1967-71, pres., 1970-71; bd. dirs. Nat. Safety Coun., 1974-80; pres. Am. Assn. Gifted Children, 1975-85, chair, 1985-90; trustee Nuveen Mutual Funds Named to Acad. of Women Achievers, YWCA N.Y., 1978; Fulbright grantee, 1955-56. Mem. Yale Club of NYC, Yale Alumni Assn. (bd. govs. 1985-88), Phi Beta Kappa.

IMPERATO, JOSEPH EDWARD, otolaryngologist; b. N.Y.C., Aug. 13, 1936; s. Salvatore James and Rose Ausilia (Leggio) I.; children: Rose, Joseph. BS, St. Peter's Coll., 1969; MD, U. Parma, Italy, 1971. Bd. eligible Am. Bd. Otolaryngology, Am. Bd. Disability Evaluating Physicians; lic. N.Y., N.J., Maine; cert. Ednl. Coun. Fgn. Med. Grads. Intern N.Y. Med. Coll., Flower 5th Ave Hosp., Met. Hosp. Ctr., N.Y.C., 1972-73, resident gen. surgery, 1973-74; resident ear-nose-throat N.Y. Eye and Ear Infirmary, N.Y.C.; fellow Montefiore Hosp ear nose throat, N.Y.C., 1977-78, Lenox Hill Hosp. ear nose throat, N.Y.C., 1978-79; pvt. practice ear, nose and throat N.Y.C., 1980-91; examining physician I N.Y. State Worker's Compensation Bd., N.Y.C., 1992-96; disability physician pvt. practice, 1996—. Cons. ear, nose and throat, Internat. Ctr. for the Disabled, N.Y.C., 1981-84; ear, nose, throat specialist Nassau Queens Med. Group, (part time), 1984-89. Vol. physician Cath. Med. Mission to Honduras, 1984. Mem. AMA, AAAS, N.Y. State Med. Soc., N.Y. County Med. Soc., Surgical Soc. N.Y. Med. Coll., N.Y. Acad. Scis., 99+. Roman Catholic. Home: Ste 2AF 28 Greenwich Ave New York NY 10011-8362

IMPERATO, JOSEPH JOHN, lawyer, composer; b. Jersey City, N.J., Mar. 14, 1956; s. Joseph Francis Imperato and Edith Roslyn (Dubin) Schwimmer. Student, Oberlin Coll., 1974-76; BA, Fla. State U., 1978, JD, 1981. Bar: Fla. 1983; court-cert. forensic audio expert, 2003. Trial atty., tng. instr. Office of Pub. Defender, Miami, Fla., 1982—. Lectr., mock trial coach Dade County sec. schs. and univs., Miami, 1993—; owner ImperaTunes Music, 1997—. Composer musical scores Fox TV Network, 1992-94; composer comml. jingles, 1975— (Addy award 1976), original songs, 1974— (Billboard Mag. Songwriting award 1995); composer, producer original childrens' musicals, 1997—. Mem. ASCAP, Audio Engring. Soc. Office: Office of Pub Defender 1320 NW 14th St Miami FL 33125-1609

IMPERIAL, HENRY L., internist; b. Irosin, Philippines, Apr. 24, 1963; s. Joaquin Sr. and Avelina (Li) I. BS in Med. Tech., Far Ea. U., 1984, MD, 1988. Diplomate Am. Bd. Internal Medicine. Med. resident in primary care internal medicine U. Medicine and Dentistry N.J. Robert Wood Johnson Med. Sch., New Brunswick, 1991-94; primary care/internal medicine physician Brownsville (Tex.) Cmty. Health Ctr., 1994—, asst. med. dir., 1996, med. dir., 1996—. Cmty. faculty East Tex. Area Health Edn. Ctr., 1995—; performance improvement program chmn. Brownsville Cmty Health Ctr., 1996—; clin. asst. prof. cmty. faculty U. Tex. Med. Br., Galveston, 1997—; clin. asst. prof. U. Tex. Health Sci. Ctr., San Antonio, 2000—. Pres. student coun. Far Ea. U. Sch. of Med. Tech., 1983-84. Mem. AMA (Physicians Recognition award

1997), ACP, Tex. Med. Assn./Cameron Willacy Med. Soc., Migrant Clinicians Network. Roman Catholic. Avocations: wine, chess. Office: Brownsville Cmty Health Ctr 2137 E 22nd St Brownsville TX 78521-2908 Office Phone: 956-548-7400. Office Fax: (956) 546-2056. E-mail: hlimperial@hotmail.com.

IMPERIOLI, MICHAEL, actor; b. Mt. Vernon, N.Y., Jan. 1, 1966; m. Victoria Imperioli; 3 children. Actor: (films) Alexa, 1988, Lean on Me, 1989, Goodfella's, 1990, Jungle Fever, 1991, Malcolm X, 1992, Fathers & Sons, 1992, Night We Never Met, 1993, Household Saints, 1993, Joey Breaker, 1993, Men Lie, 1994, Amateur, 1994, Postcards from America, 1994, Scenes From a New World, 1994, Hand Gun, 1994, Bad Boys, 1995, The Basketball Diaries, 1995, Clockers, 1995, Flirt, 1995, Dead Presidents, 1995, The Addiction, 1995, Trouble, 1995, I Shot Andy Warhol, 1996, Girls Town, 1996, Girl 6, 1996, Sweet Nothing, 1996, Tree's Lounge, 1996, Last Man Standing, 1996, Blixa Bargeld Stole My Cowboy Boots, 1996, Under the Bridge, 1997, Office Killer, 1997, The Deli, 1997, A River Made to Drown In, 1997, On the Run, 1999, Summer of Sam, 1999, Auto Motives, 2000, Love in the Time of Money, 2002, Stuey, 2003, My Baby's Daddy, 2004, (voice) Shark Tale, 2004; actor, guest writer (TV series) The Sopranos, 1999— (Emmy award Outstanding Supporting Actor in a Drama Series, 2004); actor: (TV films) Firehouse, 1997, Witness to the Mob, 1998, Disappearing Act, 2000, Hamlet, 2000, The Five People You Meet in Heaven, 2004; writer: films Summer of Sam, 1999. Office: c/o The Endeavor Agy 10th Fl 9601 Wilshire Blvd Beverly Hills CA 90212

IMRAY, THOMAS JOHN, radiologist, educator; b. Milw., Nov. 11, 1939; s. George William and Genevieve (Bresnehan) I.; m. Carla Marie Rake, Aug. 17, 1963; children: John Scott, Jean Ann, Jeff William. BA, Marquette U., 1961, MD, 1965. Diplomate Nat. Bd. Med. Examiners, Am. Bd. Radiology (guest examiner 1975-76, 79, 85-2002). Intern St. Mary's Hosp., San Francisco, 1965-66; resident in radiology U. Minn., Mpls., 1966-70, instr., 1969-70; asst. prof. Med. Coll. of Wis., Milw., 1973-77, assoc. prof., 1977-80, U. Calif., Irvine, 1980-82; prof. and chmn. dept. radiology U. Nebr. Med. Ctr., Omaha, 1982-96, prof. dept. radiology, 1996—. Vis. prof. Vanderbilt U., Nashville, 1976, 82, U. Wis., Madison, 1978, SUNY Downstate Med. Ctr., Bklyn., 1978, Harvard Med. Sch., Boston, 1980, Loyola U. Sch. Medicine, Maywood, Ill., 1980, UCLA-Wadsworth VA Hosp., 1981, UCLA, 1982 Northwestern U. Sch. Medicine, Chgo., 1984, Meth. Hosp., Indpls., 1984, U. Mo., Kans. City, 1985, U. Iowa, Iowa City, 1986, U. Ark., Little Rock, 1987, Keio U. Sch. Medicine, Tokyo, 1989, Mich. State U., 1993. Contbr. articles to profl. jours. Mem. Tech. Task Force on Diagnostic Radiology Nebr. Dept. Health, 1983-84; Major U.S. Army M.C., 1970-73. Co-recipient Magna Cum Laude in Sci. Exhibits award Am. Soc. Neuroradiology, 1987; GE grantee, 1985-87. Fellow Am. Coll. Radiology; mem. AMA (rep. to radiology residency rev. com., 1987), Radiol. Soc. N. Am. (award 1981, 82), Am. Coll. Radiology (com. on satellite communications 1981-83), Am. Roentgen Ray Soc. (award 1986), Assn. Univ. Radiologists, Soc. Chmn. Acad. Radiology Depts., Am. Soc. Uroradiology, Nebr. State Radiol. Soc., Nebr. State Med. Assn., Omaha Metro Med. Soc., Omaha Mid-West Clin. Soc. (hosp. and svc. exhibits com. 1984, award 1986), Omaha C. of C. (task force on edn. 1983-85, edn. coun. steering com. 1984, edn. coun. 1985), Rotary Internat. (program com. 1986), Marquette U. Club (bd. dirs. Omaha chpt., 1987), Alpha Omega Alpha (alumni and faculty mems. com., 1986). Roman Catholic. Avocation: swimming. Office: Nebr Health Sys Dept Radiology 981045 Nebr Med Ctr Omaha NE 68198-1045 Office Phone: 402-559-1010.

IMRE, CHRISTINA JOANNE, lawyer; b. Gary, Ind., Oct. 25, 1950; d. Joseph and Ruth Leone I.; m. Richard Long, Dec. 31, 1991. BA, Mt. St. Mary's Coll., L.A., 1972; MA, U. Notre Dame, 1974; JD, Loyola Law Sch., L.A., 1980. Bar: Calif. 1980, U.S. Ct. Appeals (ninth cir.) 1982, U.S. Dist. Ct. (ctrl. dist.) Calif. 1983, U.S. Dist. Ct. (no. dist.) Calif. 1988,U.S. Dist. Ct. (so. dist.) Calif. 1995, U.S. Supreme Ct., 2000. Assoc. Lascher & Lascher, Ventura, Calif., 1980-83, Law Office of Errol Berk, Ventura, Calif., 1983-84, Pachter, Gold & Schaffer, L.A., 1984-87; sr. atty. Kornblum & McBride, L.A., 1987-89; ptnr. Horvitz & Levy LLP, Encino, Calif., 1989—2000, Crosby, Heafey, Roach & May, Los Angeles, 2000—02, Sedgwick, Detert, Moran & Arnold, LLP, Los Angeles, 2002—. Bd. govs. Calif. Continuing Edn. of Bar, Berkeley, Calif., 1996-2000; chair Calif. Continuing Edn. of Bar Joint Adv. Com., Berkeley, 1995; editorial bd. L.A. Lawyer Mag., L.A., 1996-99; cons. Handling Civil Appeals, Berkeley, 1996, Calif. Trial Practice, Berkeley, 1995; lectr. in field. Editor-in-chief: Loyola of Los Angeles International & Comparative Law Journal, 1979-80; monthly columnist CEB Civil Litigation Reporter; contbr. articles to profl. jours. and chpts. to books. Named one of 50 Most Powerful Women in L.A. Law, L.A. Business Journal, 1998; Loyola Law Sch. fellow, 1979-80, U. Notre Dame fellow, 1972-74. Mem. L.A. County Bar Assn., Defense Rsch. Inst., So. Calif. Defense Counsel Assn. Avocations: music, shakespeare, history, philosophy. Office: Sedgwick Detert Moran & Arnold LLP 801 S Figueroa St 18th Fl Los Angeles CA 90017 E-mail: christina.imre@sdma.com.

IMUS, DON (JOHN DONALD IMUS JR.), radio personality; b. Riverside, Calif., July 23, 1940; m. Deirdre Imus; 1 child, Wyatt; children: Nadine, Toni, Elizabeth, Ashleigh. Radio host WNBC, 1971-88, WFAN, 1988—; TV host MS/NBC, 1996—. Founder, dir. Imus Ranch for Children, Ribera, N. Mex. Author: God's Other Son; co-author: (with Fred Imus) Two Guy's Four Corners, 1997; appeared on Prime Time Live, 20/20, Larry King, David Letterman, CBSs 48 Hours, 60 Minutes, The Today Show. Host radiothon CJ Found. for Sudden Infant Death Syndrome, the Tomorrow's Children's Fund, and the Imus Ranch, 1990—. Served with USMC, 1957—59. Recipient Marconi award, 1990, 1992, 1994, 1997; named Major Market Personality of the Year, Syndicated Personality of the Year; Named Emerson Radio Hall Fame, Nat. Assn. Broadcasters Broadcasting Hall of Fame, Time Mags. Most Influential Ams., 1997. Office: Westwood One Entertainment 1675 Broadway New York NY 10019-5820 also: care WFAN-AM 34-12 36th St Astoria NY 11106

IMWINKELRIED, EDWARD JOHN, law educator; b. San Francisco, Sept. 19, 1946; s. John Joseph and Enes Rose (Gianelli) I.; m. Cynthia Marie Clark, Dec. 30, 1978; children— Marie Elise, Kenneth West BA, U. San Francisco, 1967, JD, 1969. Bar: Calif. 1970, Mo. 1984, U.S. Supreme Ct. 1974. Prof. law U. San Diego, 1974-79; prof. law Washington U., St. Louis, 1979-85, Edward L. Barrett sr. prof. law, 2004; prof. law U. Calif.-Davis, 1985—. Disting. faculty mem. Nat. Coll. Dist. Attys., Houston, 1978— Author: Evidentiary Foundations, 1980, 6th rev. edit., 2005, Uncharged Misconduct Evidence, 1984, rev. edit., 1999, The New Wigmore: Evidentiary Privileges, 2002; co-author: McCormick, Evidence, 5th edit., 1999, Materials for Study of Evidence, 1983, 5th edit., 2002, Scientific Evidence, 1986, 3d edit., 1999, Pretrial Discovery: Strategy and Tactics, 1986, rev. edit., 2004, Courtroom Criminal Evidence, 1987, 3d edit., 1998, California Evidentiary Foundations, 1988, 3d edit., 2000, Dynamics of Trial Practice, 1989, 3d edit., 2002, Exculpatory Evidence, 1990, 3d edit., 2004, Florida Evidentiary Foundations, 1991, 2d edit., 1997, Illinois Evidentiary Foundations, 1991, 2d edit., 1997, Texas Evidentiary Foundations, 1992, 3d edit., 2005, New York Evidentiary Foundations, 1993, 2d edit., 1997, Evidentiary Distinctions, 1993, Colorado Evidentiary Foundations, 1997; contbg. editor Champion pub. Assn. Criminal Def. Lawyers, 1983, Criminal Law Bull. Mem. Am. Acad. Forensic Sci., ABA (continuing edn. com. 1983-84), Am. Assn. Law Schs. (chmn. evidence sect. 1983) Democrat. Roman Catholic. Avocation: jogging. Home: 2204 Shenandoah Pl Davis CA 95616-6603 Office: U Calif Law Sch Davis CA 95616 Office Phone: 530-752-0727. Business E-Mail: ejimwinkelried@ucdavis.edu.

INABINET, GEORGE WALKER, JR., retired state agency administrator; b. Cameron, S.C., Sept. 24, 1927; s. George Walker and Elizabeth (Wolfe) I.; m. Helen Ruth Davis, Sept. 27, 1947; children: Pamela Ruth, Jeffrey Walker. Cert. EE, S.C. Area Trade Sch., Columbia, 1949; Bus. Mgmt. degree, U. S.C., 1951; electronics engr. cert., Nat. Radio Inst., Washington, 1967. Asst. dir. S.C. Dept. Hwys., Columbia, 1951-53; adminstr. transp. S.C. Dept. Edn., Columbia, 1953-90. Chmn. Boy Scouts Am., Sandy Run, S.C., 1965-70; pres. Sandy Run Cmty. Club, 1966-70, S.C. Football Ofcls. Assn., Columbia, 1971-72; mem. White House Coun. on Youth, Washington, 1972-76; chmn. Calhoun County Tri-Centennial Commn., 1970; chmn. adminstrn. bd. Mt. Zion United Meth. Ch., Sandy Run, 1952-75; mem. Gov.'s Com. on Comm.; vice chmn. Calhoun County Planning Commn., 1996—, Calhoun County Facilities Com.; pres. ch. coun. Sandy Run Luth. Ch. Named to S.C. Football Ofcls. Hall of Fame, 2000. Mem. Assn. Pub. Safety Communications Officers (pres. 1979-81), Assn. Pub. Communications Officers (v.p. 1979-80, pres. 1980-81), S.C. Assn. Pupil Transp. (v.p. 1981-82, pres. 1982-83), Am. Legion (chmn. state oratorical com. 1989-97, mem. nat. commn. on Americanism), Masons, Shriners. Avocations: golf, fishing, swimming, all spectator sports. Home: Windy Hill 2496 Old State Rd Swansea SC 29160-9350

INABINET, LAWRENCE ELLIOTT, retired pharmacist; b. Orangeburg, S.C., June 15, 1933; s. Boysie Benjamin and Alrona Minerva (Robinson) I.; m. Velma Vincent Ferguson (div.); children: Rhett Elliott, Bonny Susan Murphy. BS in Pharmacy, U. S.C., 1963. Registered pharmacist, S.C. Retail pharmacist chain and ind. drug stores, 1963-69; staff hosp. pharmacist S.C. State Hosp., Columbia, S.C., 1969-71; staff pharmacist Hawthorne Pharmacy, Columbia, S.C., 1971-72, Hemingway (S.C.) Pharmacy, 1990-93, Revco Drug Stores, Marion, S.C., 1993-95; pharmacy supr. S.C. Dept. Corrections, Columbia, 1972-79; retail pharmacist Ind. Drug Stores, 1979-84; hosp. pharmacist Baker Hosp., North Charleston, S.C., 1984-86; asst. dir. pharmacy Marion (S.C.) Meml. Hosp., 1986-90. Author: (text) Civilian-Military Time Converter; patentee medicating device for animals, timepiece for converting mil. to civilian time and vice versa, 1997; contbr. poems to pubs. Deacon Bapt. ch. With USN, 1954-58. Mem. Am. Legion, Masons (past master, masonic knight templar), Kappa Psi. Avocations: guitar, song writing, sports cards, music. Home: 1704-A Greenwood Park Marion SC 29571-9406

INABINETT, CURTIS BANJAMIN, JR., medical technologist; b. Charleston, SC, Feb. 5, 1959; s. Curtis Benjamin Sr. and Ethel Mae Joy Inabinett. Cert. echocardiographer, Ariz. Heart Inst., 1989; BS in Health Adminstrn., Kennedy Western U., 2005. Owner Mobile Cardiac Ultrasound Svc., Ravenel, SC, 1991—. Cardiac outreach tech. Med. U. SC, Charleston, 1991—. Author: Curtis' Poems, 1985; jazz saxophonist with appearances on BET and PBS-TV. Bd. dirs. Clemson Extension, Charleston, 2002—; mem. Dem. Club, Charleston, 1977—; councilman Town of Ravenel, 2001—. Recipient Honor award, SC Vision Bus. Mag., 1996, Trailblazer award, Charleston Br. NAACP, 1998; grantee, Charleston County Arts Commn., 2002. Mem.: Med. U. SC Stroke Belt Initiative Leadership Team, Soc. Cardiac Sonographers, Am. Soc. Echocardiography, Am. Inst. Ultrasound. Democrat. Achievements include Three patents pending. Avocations: fishing, saxophone, poetry. Home: PO Box 188 Ravenel SC 29470 Office: Cardiac Imaging and Sound PO Box 188 Ravenel SC 29470 Office Phone: 843-729-2985. E-mail: inabinetti@aol.com.

INAGAMI, TADASHI, biochemistry professor; b. Kobe, Japan, Feb. 20, 1931; m. Masako Araki, Nov. 12, 1961 BS, Kyoto U., Japan, 1953, D.Sc., 1963; MS, Yale U., 1955, PhD, 1958. Rsch. staff Yale U., New Haven, 1958-59, rsch. assoc., 1962-66; rsch. staff Kyoto U., Japan, 1959-62; instr. biochemistry Nagoya City U., Japan, 1962; asst. prof. biochemistry Vanderbilt U., Nashville, 1966-69, assoc. prof., 1969-74, prof. biochemistry, 1975-91, dir. hypertension rsch. ctr., 1979-95, Stanford Moore prof. biochemistry, 1991—, prof. medicine, 1992—. Contbr. numerous articles to profl. jours. Fulbright fellow, 1954-55; recipient Roche Vis. Prof. award, 1980, Humboldt Found. award, 1981, Ciba award Am. Heart Assn., 1985, Spa award Belgium Nat. Funds Sci. Rsch., 1986, Sutherland prize Vanderbilt U., 1990, Okamoto Internat. award Japan Vascular Disease Rsch. Found., 1995, award for excellence in cardiovascular rsch. Bristol Meyers Squibb, 1996, award Japan Acad., 1996, Jokichi Takamine award Japan Cardiovasc. Endocrine-Metabolism Soc., 1998, Merit awrad NHLBI, 2000, Charles Park award for excellence inrsch. Vanderbilt U., 2002. Fellow: High Blood Pressure Rsch. Coun.; mem.: Japan Soc. Cardiovascular Endocrinol. Metabolism, Japan Soc. Biochemistry, Japan Soc. Hypertension, Internat. Soc. Hypertension, Am. Soc. Hypertension, Soc. Neurosci., Am. Soc. Cell Biology, Japan Endocrine Soc. (hon.), Japan Soc. Agrl. Chemistry (hon.), Am. Heart Assn. (Rsch. Achievement award 1994), Am. Soc. Pharmacology and Therapeutics, Am. Chem. Soc., Endocrine Soc., Am. Physiol. Soc., Am. Soc. Biol. Chemists and Molecular Biologists. Office: Vanderbilt U Sch Medicine Dept Biochemistry 23D Ave S And Pierce Ave Nashville TN 37232-0146 Office Phone: 615-322-4347. Business E-Mail: tadashi.inagami@vanderbilt.edu.

INAMDAR, SHREERAM P., research scientist, researcher; PhD, Va. Tech, 1996. Asst. prof. SUNY, Buffalo, 2001—. Grantee New Investigator award, USDA-NRI, 2002. Mem.: AGU. Office: SUNY Coll 1300 Elmwood Ave Buffalo NY 14222 Office Phone: 716-878-6229.

INAN, ZABRIN, psychiatrist; d. Sabit and Czatdana Inan. BS magna cum laude, Loyola U., 1989; MD, U. Ill., 1994. Am. Bd. Psychiatry and Neurology. Child, adolescent and adult psychiatrist Linden Oaks Hosp., Naperville, Ill., 2001—02; child and adolescent psychiatrist Helen Ross McNabb Ctr., Knoxville, Tenn., 2002; pvt. practice Chicago, 2002—, Northbrook, Ill., 2002—. Contbr. med. jours. including Psychiatry & Psychopharmacology. Inst. Juvenile Rsch., Child and Adolescent Psychiatry fellow, U. Ill., Chgo., 2001. Mem.: Ill. State Psychiat. Inst., Ill. Med. Soc. (licentiate), Am. Psychiatry Assn. (licentiate), Am. Acad. Child & Adolescent Psychiatry (licentiate). Avocations: tennis, ballet. Home: 1000 North Lake Shore Dr #308 Chicago IL 60611-1312 Office: 680 N Lake Shore Dr Ste 917B Chicago IL 60611 Office Phone: 312-286-1785.

INCANDELA, GERALD JEAN-MARIE, artist; b. Tunis, Tunisia, Feb. 19, 1952; came to U.S., 1977; s. Laurent and Gilda (Solina) I. BA, Janson De Sailly, Paris, 1970; postgrad., U. of Nanterre, Paris, 1971-73. One man shows include Felicity Samuel Gallery, London, 1978, Gallery Jean Chauvelin, Paris, 1978, Charles Cowles Gallery, N.Y., 1981, Robert Fraser Gallery, London, 1984, Mus. Modern Art, Oxford, Eng., 1986, Paul Kasmin, N.Y., 1988, SEBU, Japan, 1990; exhbns. in group shows at Hal Bromm Gallery, 1975, Grey Art Gallery, 1977, Corcoran Gallery, 1978, Jacksonville (Fla.) Mus., 1981, The Drawing Ctr., N.Y.C., 1982, Met. Mus. of N.Y.C., 1982, Mus. of Modern Art, 1983, Walker Art Ctr., 1986, J. Paul Getty Mus., Santa Monica, 1998, Galerie Beyeler, Basel, 2002. Home and Office: 88 Lexington Ave New York NY 10016-8943 Office Phone: 212-679-7568.

INCAPRERA, FRANK PHILIP, internist; b. New Orleans, Aug. 24, 1928; s. Charles and Mamie (Bellipanni) I.; m. Ruth Mary Duhon, Sept. 13, 1952; children: Charles, Cynthia, James, Christopher, Catherine. BS, Loyola U. of South, 1946; MD, La. State U. Med. Sch., 1950. Diplomate Am. Bd. Internal Medicine. Intern Charity Hosp., New Orleans, 1950-51, resident, 1951-52, VA Hosp., New Orleans, 1952-54; practice medicine specializing in internal medicine New Orleans, 1957-97; med. dir. Internal Medicine Group, 1973-97, chief med. officer, 1997-99. Med. dir. Owens-Ill. Glass Co., New Orleans, 1961-85, Kaiser Aluminum Co., Chalmette, La., 1975-84, Tenneco Oil Co., Chalmette, 1978-84, Luth. Nursing Home, 1990-99; assoc. med. dir. Cigna Health Plan of La., 1991-99; co-founder Med. Ctr. E. New Orleans, 1975; clin. assoc. prof. medicine Tulane U. Sch. Medicine, 1971-87, clin. prof. medicine, 1987-99, clin. prof. medicine La. State U., 1994-; adv. bd. Healthcare New Orleans, 1991-96; mem. New Orleans Bd. Health, 1966-70. Bd. dirs. Meth. Hosp., 1971-97, sec. 1992-96, Chateau de Notre Dame, 1977-92, New Orleans Opera Assn., 1975—; mem. New Orleans Human Rels. Com., 1968-70; bd. dirs. Emergency Med. Svcs. Coun., 1977-86, pres. La. southeastern region, 1979-81; bd. dirs. New Orleans East Bus. Assn., 1980-99, v.p. 1981-83; bd. dirs. Luth. Towers, 1988-89, Peace Lake Towers, 1988-89, La. State U. Med. Ctr. Found. Bd., 1989-91, Cristo Sana, 1997—; mem. pastoral care adv. com. So. Bapt. Hosp., 1982-83; mem. pres.'s adv. bd. coun. Loyola U. of South, 1989-96; mem. Mayor's Mil. Adv. Com., New Orleans, 2001—. Capt. USAF, 1955-57. Named Man of Yr., St. Gabriel Holy Name Soc., 1964; recipient Lifetime award Outstanding Svc., Cefalutana Soc., La., 1998, Pres.'s award, New Orleans East Bus. Assn., 2000, Andrew Jackson Higgins award, Mayor's Mil. Adv. Com., 2002, Founders award, Italian-Am. Fedn. of the S.E., 2003, Spirit Charity award, Med. Ctr. La. Found., 2005. Master: ACP (gov. 1995—99, Laureate award 1993); mem.: AMA, La. Soc. Internal Medicine (exec. com. 1975—98, pres. 1983—85), La. State Med. Soc. (v.p. 1975—76, Continuing Med. Edn. award for Outstanding Contributions to advancement of continuing med. edn. in La. 2001), La. Occupl. Medicine Assn. (pres. 1971—72), New Orleans Acad. Internal Medicine (pres. 1969), Orleans Parish Med. Soc. (sec. 1972—74, Outstanding Physician award 2000), La. Med. Soc. (v.p. 1975—76), Am. Coll. Physicians Execs., Am. Geriatrics Soc., La. State U. Med. Sch. Alumni Assn. (pres. 1989—90, Alumnus of Yr. 1996), New Orleans East C. of C. (dir. 1979—85), Optimists Club (bd. dirs. New Orleans 1964—69), Blue Key, Order of St. Louis, Alpha Omega Alpha (Beta chpt., Vol. Clin. Faculty award 2003), Delta Epsilon Sigma. Home: 2218 Lake Oaks Pky New Orleans LA 70122-4345 Personal E-mail: fincaprera@aol.com.

INCO, ELIZABETH MARY, nurse, consultant; b. Troy, N.Y., Jan. 23, 1960; d. Theresa Mary and Andrew Albert Inco. AS in Med. Asst., Becker Jr. Coll., Worcester, Mass., 1978—80; BSN, Russell Sage Coll., Troy, N.Y., 1980—83; Cert. for Legal Nurse Cons., Northeastern U., Boston, 2000—01. RN Mass., 1984, N.H., 1995. Primary nurse Faulkner Hosp., Boston, 1983—84, Lahey Clinic, Burlington, Mass., 1984—85; mktg. mgr., liaison nurse and cmty. health nurse VNA of Middlesex East, Stoneham, Mass., 1985—95; case mgr. Tufts Health Plan, Waltham, Mass., 1995—96; hosp. liaison nurse Sommerville Hosp. Home Care, Mass., 1996—2000; cmty. liaison mgr. VNA of Greater Lowell, Mass., 2000—. Past pres., pres., bd. mem. and v.p. N. Reading Cmty. Chorale, Mass., 1985—; bd. mem. The Cmty. Family, Mass., 2002—. Mem.: Am. Assn. of Legal Nurse Consultants (hon.; legal nurse cons. 2001), Sigma Theta Tau Internat. (hon.; pub. rels. 2001). Office: VNA of Greater Lowell 336 Central St Lowell MA 01853 Office Phone: 978-459-9343. Personal E-mail: bettyinco@earthlink.net.

INCROPERA, FRANK PAUL, mechanical engineering educator; b. Lawrence, Mass., May 12, 1939; s. James Frank and Ann Laura (Leone) I.; m. Andrea Jeanne Eastman, Sept. 2, 1960; children: Terri Ann, Donna Renee, Shaunna Jeanne. BSME, MIT, 1961; MS, Stanford U., 1962, PhD, 1966. Jr. engr. Barry Controls Corp., Watertown, Mass., 1959; thermodynamics engr. Aerojet Gen. Corp., Azusa, Calif., 1961; heat transfer specialist Lockheed Missiles and Space Co., Sunnyvale, Calif., 1962-64; mem. faculty Purdue U., 1966-98, prof. mech. engring., 1973-98, head dept., 1989-98; dean of engring. U. Notre Dame, Ind., 1998—. Cons. in field. Author: Introduction to Molecular Structure and Thermodynamics, 1974, Fundamentals of Heat Transfer, 1985, 90, 96, 2001; Fundamentals of Heat and Mass Transfer, 1981, 85, 90, 96, 2001, Liquid Cooling of Electronic Devices by Single-Phase Convection, 1999; also articles. Recipient Solberg Teaching award Purdue U., 1973, 77, 86, Potter Teaching award, 1973, Von Humboldt sr. scientist award Fed. Republic Germany, 1988; named One of the 100 most frequently cited engrs. in the world Inst. for Sci. Info., 2000. Fellow ASME (Melville medal 1988, Heat Transfer Meml. award 1988, Worcester Reed Warner award 1995); mem. Am. Soc. Engring. Edn. (Ralph C. Roe award 1982, George Westinghouse award 1983), Nat. Acad. Engring. Achievements include invention of bloodless surg. scalpel. Office: U Notre Dame Coll Engring 257 Fitzpatrick Hall Notre Dame IN 46556 Business E-Mail: fpi@nd.edu.

INCULET, ION I., electrical engineer, educator, science association director, consultant; b. Iasi, Moldova, Romania, Feb. 11, 1921; arrived in Can., 1948; s. Ion C. and Ruxanda (Basota) I.; m. Marion Elsie Smith, Aug. 25, 1951; children: Richard, Catherine, Diana. Diploma in engring., Politechnica, Bucuresti, Romania, 1944; M in Engring. Sci., Laval U., Que., 1962; DTechSc (hon.), Bucuresti U., Romania, 1993; DSc (hon.), We. Ont. Can. U., 1996. Advance devel. engr. Can. GE, Peterborough, Ont., 1948-56, mgr. engring., Que., 1956-64; prof. elec. engring. U. Western Ont., London, 1964—, dir. environ. engring., 1966-68, dir. Applied Electrostatics Rsch. Ctr., 1986—. Pres. Elstat, Ltd., London, 1972—; cons. in field. Author: 1 book; contbr. over 110 articles to profl. jours., book chpts.; holder 27 patents. Recipient T.C. Keefer medal Can. Soc. Civil Engring., 1994-95. Fellow IEEE (Centennial medal 1984), Can. Acad. Engring., Inst. Electrostatics of Japan; mem. NSPE (engring. medal 1984), Industry Applications Soc. IEEE (Outstanding Achievement award 1983), Romanian Acad. (hon.). Avocation: skiing. Home: 81 Lloyd Manor Crescent London ON Canada N6H 3Z4 Office: U Western Ont Engring Bldg Electrostatics Rsch Ctr London ON Canada N6A 5B9 Office Phone: 519-661-2002. Business E-Mail: iinculet@uwo.ca.

INDIEK, VICTOR HENRY, finance corporation executive; b. Spearville, Kans., Nov. 15, 1937; s. Ben W. and Helen Ann (Schreck) I.; m. Marlene Gould, June 2, 1962; children: Kathy, Kevin. Student, U. Nebr., 1955-57; BS in Bus., U. Kans., 1959. CPA, Kans. Audit mgr. Arthur Andersen & Co., Kansas City, Mo., 1961-70; pres., chief exec. officer Fed. Home Loan Mortgage Corp., Washington, 1970-77; pres., dir. Builders Capital Corp., Los Angeles, 1977-84; chief fin. officer, exec. v.p. Fin. Corp. of Am., Irvine, Calif., 1984-88; pres., chief exec. officer FarWest Savs. and Loan Assn., Newport Beach, Calif., 1988—; with Kennedy Wilson, 1989-98; pvt. practice in real estate, 1998—. V.p. and pres. regional Assn. Small Businesses Investment Cos., 1979-81, bd. govs. nat. assn., 1982. Mem. Selective Service Bd., Santa Monica, Calif., 1978; capt. United Fund, Kansas City, 1968. Served with USN, 1959-61. Republican. Roman Catholic. Avocations: boating, skiing. Office: 3508 Surfview Ln Corona Del Mar CA 92625-1632 E-mail: vindiek@cox.net.

INDIVIGLIA, SALVATORE JOSEPH, artist, retired military officer; b. N.Y.C., Nov. 16, 1919; s. Joseph and Alfonsina Barbara (Gaeta) I.; widower Jan. 1986; children: Barbara Ann (dec.), Joseph, Lawrence, Dianne. BA, Pratt Inst., 1948; AS, U.S. Naval Acad., 1976. Mural painter asst. Crimi Studio, N.Y.C., 1939-42; art dir. Advt. Printin Co., N.Y.C., 1946-63; art tchr. Mechanics Inst., N.Y.C., 1962-66; v.p. Vogue Wright Studios, N.Y.C., 1963-80; dir. art Electrographic Corp., N.Y.C., Chgo., 1968-70; artist, account exec. Chelsea Photo/Graphics, Inc., N.Y.C., 1981-84. Ofcl. USN combat artist, Washington, 1960-89. Exhibited in group shows at Smithsonian Inst. Operations Palette, 1965, Joe and Emily Lowe Found., 1955, 1963 (Liquitex award, 1997); painter Am. Artist Mag., 1971; McLean Libr. Collection Hofstra U. WWII Posters, 2004; painter watercolors USN Combat Art Collection, N.Y. State Naval Militia, 1962, 1991, 1994, 1996—, featured USN combat artist, Channel 12 TV, N.Y., 2001. Comdr. USNR, 1962-79. Decorated U.S. Navy Commendation medal, Croce Al Merito Di Guerra (Italy), Vietnamese Cross of Gallantry with palm; recipient U.S. Naval Acad. Supt.'s award, 1983. Roman Catholic. Avocations: playing guitar, singing country & western music. Home: 974 Lorraine Dr Franklin Square NY 11010-1813

INEZ, DONNA LEE, hospital administrator; b. Flushing, N.Y. d. Walter and Ruth (Pringle) Jackowski; m. Virgil Inez, May 30, 1968. BS, So. Conn. State U., New Haven, 1965; EdM, Rutgers U., New Brunswick, N.J., 1988. RN, Conn.; cert. BLS instr. Asst. supr. med.-surg. Morristown (N.J.) Meml. Hosp., 1969-72; LPN instr. Morristown Sch. Practical Nursing, 1972-78, nursing edn. instr., 1973-90; nursing edn. instr., clin. info. system coord. Morristown Meml. Hosp., 1984-90; asst. dir., clinical coord. patient care sys. Gen. Hosp. Ctr. Passaic, N.J., 1990-99; ret., 1999. Mem. ANA, Am. Med. Informatics Assn., N.J. State Nurses Assn. (com.), Sigma Theta Tau. Home: 63 Grove Ave Morris Plains NJ 07950-2025

INFANTE, ETTORE FERRARI, mathematician, educator, university administrator; b. Modena, Italy, Aug. 20, 1938; came to U.S., 1954; s. Ferdinando Bassani and Cecilia (Ferrari) I.; m. Trudi C. Miller; children: Cecilia Ann, Michael Gregory. BA, U. Tex., 1958, BS, 1959, PhD, 1962; MA (hon.), Brown U., 1968. Asst. prof. U. Tex., Austin, 1962-65, Brown U., Providence, 1964-68, assoc. prof., 1968-72, prof., 1972-84; div. dir. math. and computer sci. NSF, Washington, 1981-84; prof. math., dean Inst. Tech. U. Minn., Mpls., 1984-91, sr. v.p. for acad. affairs, provost, 1991-96; prof. math., dean Coll. Arts and Scis. Vanderbilt U., Nashville, 1997—. Cons. Humble Oil & Refining Co., Houston, 1962-64, NSF, 1980-81, various research organizations and univs., 1964— Contbr. numerous articles to profl. jours.; patentee in field. Grantee NSF, 1967-84, Office Naval Rsch., 1968-79, Army Rsch. Office, 1967-82, Ctr. Nat. Recherche Scientifique, France, 1972-73; Ford Found. fellow, 1964-65. Fellow Am. Acad. Mechanics; mem. IEEE (sr.), ASME, Soc. for Indsl. and Applied Math. (coun. 1980-82, trustee 1985-91, disting. speaker 1966-68), Am. Math. Soc. Roman Catholic. Office: Vanderbilt U 301 Kirkland Hl Nashville TN 37240-0001

INFANTE, ISA MARIA, political scientist, educator; b. Santo Domingo, Dominican Republic, Sept. 8, 1942; d. Rafael Infante and Dolores Nieves; 1 child, Nina Maria. BA, U. Calif., Santa Cruz, 1973; MA in Comparative Polit. Sys., Yale U., 1975; PhD in Polit. sci., U. Calif., Riverside, 1977; JD, Northeastern U., 2005. Mgmt. trainee Calif. Savs. and Loan Assn., L.A., 1960—61; asst. fgn. corr. L.A. Times, Mexico City, 1961—62; bus. enterprise officer L.A., 1962—64; regional mgr. Strout Realty, Pasadena, Calif., 1964—66; entrepreneur retail stores L.A., Lake Elsinore, Anaheim, Calif., 1966—70; exec. dir. coll. adult rehab. program U. Calif., Riverside, 1970—71; dir. nat. immigration bd. Nat. Lawyers Guild, L.A., 1977; acad. adv. to provost Antioch Coll. West, Antioch U., San Francisco, 1977—78; sr. devel. officer U.S. Human Resources Corp., San Francisco, 1978; spl. asst. to Sarah Weddington, Ewq. Interdepartmental Task Force on Women, White House, Washington, 1978—79; policy fellow and program officer Inst. for Ednl. Leadership/Fund for Improvement of Postsecondary Edn., HEW, Washington, 1978—79; assoc. dean Labor Coll. Empire State Coll., SUNY, N.Y.C., 1979—81; pres. I. Infante Assocs, internat. cons., 1980—. Prof. polit. sci., dir. L.Am. studies dept. Jersey City State Coll., Jersey City, 1983—86; pres. Nat. Hispanic Coalition, Washington, 1978—80; notary pub., 1980—82; mem. Am. Coun. on Edn., 1980—82, Cmty. Bd. 12, Borough of Manhattan, NY, 1980—82; pres. Free, Inc., 2005—. Author (with others): Field Preparation Manual, 1973; contbg. author: Voices From the Ghetto, 1968, The Politics of Teaching Political Science, 1978, Labor Studies Jour., 1981, Political Affairs, 1984. Bd. dirs. Nagle House Co-op, N.Y.C., 1980—82, Solidaridad Humana, Inc., N.Y.C., 1980—82; trustee Ctr. for Integrative Devel., N.Y.C., 1979—82. Pease Barker scholar, 1972—73, Marius de Brabant scholar, 1970—71, Rsch. scholar, NEH, Washington, 1984. Fellow: Am. Polit. Sci. Assn.; mem.: ABA, NAFE, Women's Bar Found. of Mass., Nat. Women's Health Networn, Nat. Women's Polit. Caucus, Univ. and Coll. Labor Assn., L.Am. Studies Assn., Am. Ednl. Rsch. Assn., Internat. Polit. Sci. Assn., Soc.Internat. Devel., Yale Club of Boston, Yale Club of N.Y.C. Mailing: 335 Huntington Ave Apt 52 Boston MA 02115-4409 Office Phone: 617-377-1885. Business E-Mail: isa@aya.yale.edu.

INFUSINO, ACHILLE FRANCIS, financial and administrative support executive; b. Kenosha, Wis, Feb. 8, 1953; s. Frank and Irene (Rende) I.; m. Joyce Marie, Nov. 22, 1975; children: Daniel, Nicholas, Jaclyn, Timothy. BA, Carthage Coll., 1982; MBA, Marquette U., 1987. Pres. Infusino Bros. Constrn. Co., Inc., Kenosha, 1987—, Cellular City Comm., Kenosha, 1987—; founder, sr. project mgr. Project Mgmt. Cons., Kenosha, 1994-2000; v.p. procurement and operational asset mgmt. ATC Leasing Co., Kenosha, 2000—02, sr. UP & gen. mgr., 2002—. Instr. Carthage Coll., 1990; adj. prof. advanced fin. mgmt. U. Wis., Parkside, 2000—; bd. dirs. Bank of Kenosha. Bd. dirs. Kenosha Area Devel. Corp., 1981-87, Salvation Army Adv. Bd., Kenosha, 1983-85; pres. St. Joseph's Interparish Jr. High Sch., Kenosha, 1986-91; chmn. Bd. Building Appeals, City of Kenosha, 1986-88. Mem. Italian Am. Soc., MBA Execs., Assn. Constrn. Insps., Environ. Assessment Assn. Avocations: youth athletic programs, little league baseball. Office: Bd of Trustees St Josephs HS 3614 16th Pl Kenosha WI 53144-3376 also: ATC Leasing 4316 39th Ave Kenosha WI 53144-1962

INGAGLIO, DIEGO AUGUSTUS, dentist; b. Phila., Dec. 4, 1922; s. Salvatore and Maria Concetta (Giordano) I.; m. Geraldine Jean Capizzi, July 11, 1948; children: Marie, Francene. DDS, U. Pa., 1947. With Phila. Mouth Hygiene Dept., 1947-50; asst. clin. dir. Emerson R. Sausser Med. Dental Clinic, Jefferson Hosp., Phila., 1950-51; pvt. practice dentistry Drexel Hill, Pa., 1953—. Staff Suburban Gen. Hosp., Norristown; mem. Congressional Adv Bd. Editor-in-chief U. Pa. Dental Jour., 1945-47. Intergenerational com., Upper Twp. Elem. Sch.; past pres. mature adults, Resurrection Ch., Marmora, N.J., lector for mass readings, mem. Friends for Life com.; mem. Resurrection Ch. Liturgy Group; mem. vocations com. Diocese of Camden. With AUS, 1943-45, 51-53. Fellow Acad. Gen. Dentistry, Acad. Dentistry Internat., Royal Soc. Health; mem. ADA, AAAS, Pa. Dental Assn., Chester-Delaware County Dental Assn., Am. Internat., Philadelphia County Soc. Clin. Hypnosis, Nat. Space Inst., Phila. Physhodontontic Soc. (past pres.), Royal Soc. Hygiene, Nat. Ass.n Fed. Lic. Firearms Dealers, NRA, Cape May County Serra Group (pres. 2002—, trustee, v.p. in charge of membership), Heritage Found., Am. Legion, Omicron Kappa Upsilon, Psi Omega. Address: 670 Breckley Rd Marmora NJ 08223-1158 Personal E-mail: daimarmora@aol.com.

INGALLS, MARIE CECELIE, former state legislator, retail executive; b. Faith, S.D., Mar. 31, 1936; d. Jens P. and Ida B. (Hegre) Jensen; m. Dale D. Ingalls, June 20, 1955; children: Duane (dec.), Delane. BS, Black Hills State Coll., 1973, MS, 1978. Elem. tchr. Meade County Schs., Sturgis, S.D., 1957-72, Faith Sch. Dist. 46-2, 1973-76; elem. prin. Meade Sch. Dist. 46-1, Sturgis, 1976-81; owner, operator Ingalls, Sturgis, 1978-99; mem., asst. majority whip S.D. House Reps., Pierre, 1986-92; lobbyist S.D. Legislature. Bd. dirs. S.D. Retailers Assn., 1990—98, treas., 1992—93. Former sec. S.D. Rep. Orgn; Rep. nominee S.D. Commr. Sch. and Pub. Lands, 1998. Recipient Woman of Achievement award City of Sturgis, 1986, Retail Bus. of Yr. 1998. Mem. S.D. Cattlewomen, S.D. Stockgrowers (edn. chair), S.D. Farm Bur. (bd. dirs. dist. V 1993-2001, 03—, dist. dir. women's com. 2003—), Meade County Farm Bur., Faith C. of C. (pres. 1989), Sturgis C. of C. (past bd. dirs.), Key City Investment Club. Republican. Lutheran. Avocations: knitting, crocheting, piano, reading, golf. Home: 17054 Opal Rd Mud Butte SD 57758 Personal E-mail: mcingalls@gwtc.net.

INGALLS, ROBERT LYNN, retired physicist; b. Spokane, Wash., June 15, 1934; s. Keith Irving and Ruth Louise (Strauss) I.; m. Liisa Vasama, Jan. 28, 1961 (div. Apr. 1993); children: Karen Liisa, Johanna Louise, David Robert. BS, U. Wash., 1956; MS, Carnegie Inst. Tech., 1960, PhD, 1962. Instr. physics Carnegie Inst. Tech., 1961-63; research asso. U. Ill., 1963-65, research asso. prof., 1965-66; asst. prof. U. Wash., Seattle, 1966-69, asso. prof., 1969-74, prof. physics, 1974-2000, prof. emeritus, 2001—. Vis. scholar State U. Groningen, Netherlands, 1972-73 Bassoonist, Seattle Symphony Orch., 1952-57; contbr. articles to profl. jours., books and encys. AEC contract, 1967-77; NSF grantee, 1976-83; Dept. Energy grantee, 1983—. Mem. Am. Phys. Soc., Fedn. Am. Scientists, Sigma Xi, Sigma Phi Epsilon, Zeta Mu Tau. Achievements include first to measure and explain electric quadrupole splitting theory in ferrous compounds; carry out X-ray absorption fine structure studies of matrials at high pressure; discovery of original guaslcrystal tilings. Office: U Wash Dept Physics Seattle WA 98195-0001 Business E-Mail: ingalls@phys.washington.edu.

INGARI, FRANK A., communications executive; Pres., CEO, dir. Shiva Corp., Bedford, Mass., 1993-98; CEO Growth Ally, Winchester, Mass., 1998-99; founder, CEO Wheelhouse Corp., Burlington, Mass., 1999—. Bd. dirs. Sybase, Inc.; bd. govs. Mass. Telecomm. Coun., chmn. programs com.

INGATO, ROBERT JOSEPH, lawyer; b. July 3, 1960; m. Anna B. Ingato. BS, Bucknell U.; JD, Cornell U. Evec. v.p., gen. counsel, sec. CIT Group Inc., Livingston, NJ, 1998—. Office: CIT Group Inc 1 CIT Dr Livingston NJ 07039 Home: 11 Sweetwood Dr Randolph NJ 07869 Office Phone: 973-740-5000. Office Fax: 973-886-5527.

INGBAR, DAVID H., physician, researcher; b. Boston, Aug. 1, 1953; s. Sidney H. and Mary Lee Ingbar; m. Mary E. Meighan, Oct. 14, 1991. BA, Reed Coll., 1974; MD, Harvard Med. Coll., 1978. Diplomate Am. Bd. Internal Medicine. Intern then resident U. Wash., Seattle, chief resident; pulmonary fellow Yale U., New Haven, 1982-85, asst. prof. medicine, 1985-91; assoc. prof. medicine U. Minn., Mpls., 1991-98, prof. medicine, physiology and pediat., 1998—, dir. pulmonary, allergy and critical care divsn., 2001—. Dir. med. ICU and respiratory care Yale New Haven Hosp., 1986-91, U. Minn., 1991—. Office: U MN Pulmonary & Critical Care Dept Medicine Box 276 UMHC 420 Delaware St SE Minneapolis MN 55455-0374 Office Phone: 612-624-0999.

INGBER, LARRY H., lawyer; b. NYC, Apr. 2, 1959; BS, SUNY, Albany, 1979; JD, Rutgers U., 1983. Bar: NY 1984, NJ 1984, Fla. 1984, US Tax Ct., US Dist. Ct. Ea. Dist. NY, US Dist. Ct. So. Dist. NY. Ptnr. Wilson, Elser, Moskowitz, Edelman & Dicker LLP, Garden City, NY. Mem.: Nassau County Bar Assn., NY State Bar Assn. Office: Wilson Elser Moskowitz Edelman & Dicker LLP Ste 510 666 Old Country Rd Garden City NY 11530 Office Phone: 516-228-8900. Office Fax: 516-228-0200. Business E-Mail: ingberl@wemed.com.

INGE, MILTON THOMAS, American literature and culture educator, author; b. Newport News, Va., Mar. 18, 1936; s. Clyde Elmo and Bernice Lucille (Jackson) I.; m. Betty Jean Meredith, 1958 (div. 1977); 1 child, Scott Thomas; m. Tonette Long Bond, 1982 (div. 1991); 1 stepchild, Michael Gordon Bond; m. Donaria Romeiro Carvalho, 1998. BA, Randolph-Macon Coll., 1959; MA, Vanderbilt U., 1960, PhD, 1964. Instr. English Vanderbilt U., 1962-64; asst. prof. Am. thought and lang. Mich. State U., 1964-68, assoc. prof., 1968-69; assoc. prof. English Va. Commonwealth U., Richmond, 1969-73, prof., 1973-80, chmn. dept. English, 1974-80; prof., chmn. dept. English, Clemson U., S.C., 1980-84; resident scholar in Am. studies USIA, Washington, 1982-84; prof. humanities Randolph-Macon Coll., Ashland, Va., 1984—. Reader English Composition Test Coll. Entrance Exam Bd., 1967, 69, 77, 80; Va. Cultural Laureate, 92; dir. USIA Summer Inst. in Am. Studies, 1993—95; liberal studies disting. scholar-in-residence U. Louisville, 2003. Author: Donald Davidson: Essay and Bibliography, 1965, (with T.D. Young) Donald Davidson, 1971, The American Comic Book, 1985, Comics in the Classroom, 1989, Great American Comics: 100 Years of Cartoon Art, 1990, Comics as Culture, 1990, Faulkner, Sut, and Other Southerners, 1992, Perspectives on American Culture: Essays on Humor, Literature, and the Popular Arts, 1994, Anything Can Happen in a Comic Strip: Centennial Reflections on an American Art Form, 1995, William Faulkner: Overlook Illustrated Lives, 2005; editor: (books) Sut Lovingood's Yarns, 1966, 2d edit. 1987, High Times and Hard Times, 1967, Agrarianism in American Literature, 1969, A.B. Longstreet, 1969, Faulkner: A Rose for Emily, 1970, Wm. Byrd of Westover, 1970, Studies in Light in August, 1971, Frontier Humorists: Critical Views, 1975, Ellen Glasgow: Centennial Essays, 1976,(with J. Bryer and M. Duke) Black American Writers: Bibliographic Essays, 2 vols., 1978, Handbook of American Popular Culture, Vol. I, 1978, Vol. II, 1980, Vol. III, 1981, 3 vols. rev. and expanded edits., 1989, Concise Histories of American Popular Culture, 1982, (with E.E. MacDonald) James Branch Cabell: Centennial Essays, 1983, (with J. Bryer and M. Duke) American Women Writers: Bibliographical Essays, 1983, Huck Finn Among the Critics: A Centennial Selection, 1984, rev. edit., 1985, Truman Capote: Conversations, 1987, Naming the Rose: Essays on Umberto Eco's "The Name of the Rose", 1988, Handbook of American Popular Literature, 1988, A Nineteenth Century American Reader, 1988, The Comics, 1991, (with Sergei Chakovsky) Russian Eyes on American Literature, 1992, Dark Laughter: The Satiric Art of Oliver W. Harrington, 1993, Why I Left America and Other Essays of Oliver W. Harrington, 1993, William Faulkner: The Contemporary Reviews, 1994, (with James E. Caron) Sut Lovingood's Nat'ral Born Yarnspinner: Essays on George Washington Harris, 1996, Mark Twain's A Connecticut Yankee in King Arthur's Court, 1997, The Achievement of William Faulkner: A Centennial Tribute, 1998; Conversations with William Faulkner, 1999, "Co. Aytch," or a Side Show of the Big Show and Other Sketches by Samuel R. Watkins, 1999, Charles M. Schulz: Conversations, 2000, (with Ed Piacentino) The Humor of the Old South, 2001, (with Dennis Hall) Greenwood Guide to American Popular Culture, 4 vols., 2002; editor jours. Resources for American Literary Study, 1971-79, American Humor: An Interdisciplinary Newsletter, 1974-79, Studies in American Humor, 2004—; gen. editor Greenwood Press Bio-Bibliographies and Reference Guides in Popular Culture, Cambridge U. Press Am. Critical Archives, U. Press Miss. Studies in Popular Culture; book reviewer: Nashville Tenneseean, Richmond Times-Dispatch. Bd. dirs. Friends of Richmond Pub. Libary; bd. dirs. San Francisco Acad. Comic Art, James Br. Cabell Libr. Assocs., Va. Commonwealth U., Edgar Allen Poe Mus. Recipient Bd. Govs. award Am. Cultural Assn., 1999; fellow So. Fellowship Fund, 1959-62, Newberry Libr., 1987, Va. Found. Humanities, 1987, 93; grantee Fulbright-Hays, 1967-68, 71, 79, 88, 94, Mich. State U., 1965, 66, 68, Am. Philos. Soc., 1970, Clemson U., 1981, NEH, 1986, 91, 92; recipient Disting. Alumnus award Randolph-Macon Coll., 1995. Mem. MLA (hon. life, del. assembly 1976-78, 2001-03, chmn. elections com. 1980), South Atlantic MLA (program com. 1982-85, chmn. 1986, v.p. 1987, pres. 1988-89), Am. Studies Assn., Popular Culture Assn., Am. Humor Studies Assn. (pres. 1978, 88, Charlie award 1996), Soc. Study So. Lit. (exec. coun. 1971-73, 78-80, 86-88), Melville Soc., Ellen Glasgow Soc. (exec. coun. 1974-84, pres. 1987-88), Mus. Cartoon Art (nominating com. Hall of Fame 1975-95), European Assn. Am. Studies, So. Studies Forum (founder, exec. coun. 1988—), Popular Culture Assn. in South (v.p. 1987-88, pres. 1988-89), Mark Twain Cir. (chmn. nominating com. 1987-88), Mark Twain Cir. Am. (hon.), Cosmos Club, Phi Beta Kappa, Omicron Delta Kappa, Pi Delta Epsilon, Lambda Chi Alpha. Home: PO Box 129 Ashland VA 23005-0129 Office Phone: 804-752-7282. Business E-Mail: tinge@rmc.edu.

INGEBRITSEN, CHRISTINE, Scandinavian studies educator; b. Boston, Apr. 2, 1962; d. Karl John and Shirley (Phillips) I.; m. Jame sEdwin Rogers, July 28, 1996; 1 child, Christian Jonathan Ingebritsen Rogers. BA, William Smith Coll., 1984; MA, Columbia U., 1986; PhD, Cornell U., 1993. Lectr. U. Wash., Seattle, 1992-93, asst. prof. Scandinavian studies, 1993-2000, assoc. prof. Scandinavian studies, 2000—, chair, European Studies program, 1998—. Author: The Nordic States and European Unity, 1998; co-author: Globalization, 2000; mem. edit. bd., Cooperation and Conflict, Oslo, 1998—. Fulbright scholar, N.Y.C., 1986-87. Mem. NACC (bd. mem.), Swedish Club. Office: U Washington Dept Scandinavian Studies Seattle WA 98195

INGELS, JACK EDWARD, horticulture educator; b. Indpls., Mar. 28, 1942; s. Carl Eugene and Mary Louise (Fultz) I. BS, Purdue U., 1964; MS, Rutgers U., 1966; postgrad., Ball State U., 1968-70. Rsch. asst. Rutgers U., New Brunswick, N.J., 1964-66; prof. SUNY, Cobleskill, 1966-89, disting. teaching prof., 1990—. Hort. cons. J.C. Penney Corp., N.Y.C., 1966-69; landscape designer, 1966—; hort. and/or landscape cons. numerous small cos., 1970—; pres. J. Ingels Assoc., 1991—. Author: Landscaping: Principles and Practices, 6th edit., 2003, Ornamental Horticulture: Science, Operations, and Management, 3d edit., 2000. Chmn. Cobleskill Restoration and Devel., Inc., 1991—, bd. dirs., 1988—; pres. Timothy Murphy Gourmet Soc., 1989—; mem. Schoharie County Coun. on Arts, Cobleskill, Albany Inst. of History and Art; bd. dirs. Cobleskill Partnership, 1996—. Named one of Top Ten Landscape Educators in Am., Landscape Mgmt. mag., 1995. Mem. Associated Landscape Contractors Am., Northeastern N.Y. Nursery Assn., Genesee-Finger Lakes Nursery Assn., Univ. Club (Albany, N.Y.), Moose, Elks. Avocations: gourmet cooking, landscape garden history, travel. Home: 139 Jay St Cobleskill NY 12043 Office: SUNY Horticulture Dept Cobleskill NY 12043 Business E-Mail: ingelsje@cobleskill.edu. *To teach is a privilege that permits me to touch lives. To teach well is my obligation.*

INGELS, MARTY, agent, broadcast executive; b. Bklyn., Mar. 9, 1936; s. Jacob and Minnie (Crown) Ingerman; m. Jean Maire Frassinelli, Aug. 3, 1960 (div. 1969); m. Shirley Jones, 1977. Ed., Erasmus High Sch., 1951-53, Forest Hills High Sch., 1953-55. Founder Ingels Inc., 1975—; formed Stoneypoint Prodns., 1981; TV and motion picture producer U.S. and Abroad; mgr. of Shirley Jones. Star: Dickens and Fenster series, ABC-TV, 1964; co-star: Pruitts of Southampton, 1968-69; films include Armored Command, 1962, Horizontal Lieutenant, 1965, Busy Body, 1967, Ladies Man, 1966, If It's Tuesday This Must Be Belgium, 1970, Wild and Wonderful, 1965, Guide for a Married Man, 1968; numerous TV appearances. Active various charity drives. Achievements include Owning the world's largest celebrity brokerage service, 1974; widely noted as the Henry Kissinger of Madison Avenue. Office: Network Prodns 4531 Noeline Way Encino CA 91436

INGELSON, BRIAN CHARLES, music educator, director; s. Ed and Jean Gladys Dora Ingelson; m. Beverley Faye Iles, Aug. 4, 1990; children: Sean Talbot Anderson, Matthew Ernest, William Brian. BA, U. of Calgary, 1984; MEd, U. of Mo., 1990. Cert. tchr. State of Calif., 2001, Province of Alta., 1985. Band dir. Calgary (Can.) Bd. of Edn., 1985—89, 1990—94; supr. student tchrs. U. of Nev., Las Vegas, 1994—95; prof. of music C.C. of So. Nev., Las Vegas, 1994—95; dir. of bands Palm Springs (Calif.) HS., 1995—. Condr. Sydney (Australia) Music Festival, 1997, Brianzza (Italy) Bandistico Internat., 1998, Disneyland Paris, Paris, 1998; prof. music Coll. of the Desert, Palm Desert, Calif., 1996—99. Condr.: Spirit of The Sands. Edn. liason Palm Springs (Calif.) Cmty. Concerts, 2001. Named Oustanding Music Dir.-Westside Story, Desert Theater League, 2001; recipient Alta. Achievement award in Arts, Province of Alta., 1988, Tchr. of the Yr. award, Soroptomist Internat., 1997, Congl. Cert. of Recognition award, US Congress, 1998, Wal-Mart Tchr. of the Yr. award, Cathedral City Wal-Mart, 2000, Congl. Cert. of Recognition, US Congress, 2000; scholar, U. of Mo., Columbia, 1989—90. Mem.: Music Educators Nat. Conf. Office: Palm Springs High School 2401 East Baristo Rd Palm Springs CA 92262 Personal E-mail: bband@gte.net. E-mail: bcingelson@psusd.k12.ca.us.

INGERSOLL, PAUL MILLS, banker; b. Phila., Apr. 13, 1928; s. John H.W. and Frances Paul (Mills) I.; m. Eleanor S. Koehler, Oct. 6, 1951; children: Eleanor Ingersoll Sylvestro, Rita W., Frances M. BA, Princeton U., 1950. With Provident Nat. Bank, Phila., 1963-78, v.p. adminstrn. and exec. mgmt., 1969, sr. v.p. retail banking divsn., 1969-73, pres., chief adminstrv. officer, 1973-78. Pres., bd. dirs. Beaver Mgmt. Corp.; bd. dirs. Haverford Trust Co.; cons. Christie, Manson & Woods Internat., Inc. Trustee Emeritus Drexel U., Bryn Mawr (Pa.) Hosp. 1st lt. AUS, 1950-52. Recipient Human Rights award Am. Jewish Com., 1973. Mem. Merion Cricket Club, State in Schuylkill, The Cts., The Rabbit. Democrat. Episcopalian.

INGERSOLL, WILLIAM BOLEY, lawyer, real estate developer; b. Washington, Sept. 21, 1938; s. William Brown and Loraine (Boley) I.; m. Carolyn Grace Potter, Sept. 8, 1963; children: William Brett, Courtney Lynn, Wayne Brandon, Dana Lee. BS, Brigham Young U., 1964; JD, Cath. U. Am., 1968. Bar: Va. 1968, D.C. 1969. Atty. Office of Corp. Counsel D.C., 1967-69, Office Gen. Counsel HUD, 1969-70; ptnr. Fried, Klewans, Ingersoll & Bloch, Washington, 1970-72; pres. Ingersoll and Bloch Corp., Washington, 1972—; of counsel Holland & Knight, Washington, 1998—. Mng. ptnr. JC Assocs. Real Estate Devel., Washington, 1973—; gen. counsel Am. Resort Devel. Assn.; chmn. Trust Communities Inc., Washington, 1999—, Power Corp., Washington, 2000—; lectr. in field. Co-editor-in-chief Land Devel. Law Reporter, Land Trends, 1973—, The Digest of State Land Sales, 1976—, Time Sharing Law Reporter, 1980—, D.C. Real Estate Reporter, 1982—, Real Estate Opportunity Report, 1986; contbr. in field. Bd. dirs. Nat. Timesharing Coun., 1981—; mem. Garrison Presdl. Commn., 1984; mem. bd. adv. J. Ruben Clark Law Sch., 1987-93, chmn., 1991-93; bishop McLean (Va.) Ward, LDS Ch.; mem. nat. adv. com. Inside Real Estate, 1985—. Mem. ABA, FBA, D.C. Bar Assn., Va. Bar Assn., Va. Assn. Trial Lawyers, Land Devel. Inst. (vice chmn.), Brigham Young U. Alumni Assn. (bd. dirs. 1984-92), Order of Coif, Univ. Club Washington, Boca Raton (Fla.) Resort and Club. Home: 713 Potomac Knolls Dr Mc Lean VA 22102-1421 also: Holland & Knight Ste 100 2099 Pennsylvania Ave NW Washington DC 20006-1816 Office Phone: 202-955-3000. E-mail: wingersoll@hklaw.com.

INGHAM, NORMAN WILLIAM, literature educator, educator, genealogist; b. Holyoke, Mass., Dec. 31, 1934; s. Earl Morris and Gladys May (Rust) I. AB, Middlebury Coll. in German and Russian cum laude, 1957; postgrad. Slavic philology, Free U. Berlin, 1957-58; MA in Russian lang. and lit., U. Mich., 1959; postgrad. in Russian lang. and lit., Leningrad (USSR) State U., 1961-62; PhD in Slavic langs. and lit., Harvard U., 1963. Cert. genealogist. Postdoctoral researcher Czechoslovak Acad. Scis., Prague, Czechoslovakia, 1963-64; asst. prof. dept Slavic langs. and lits. Ind. U., Bloomington, 1964-65; asst. prof. Harvard U., Cambridge, Mass., 1965-70, lectr., 1970-71; assoc. prof. U. Chgo., 1971-82, prof., 1982—, chmn. dept., 1977-83, dir. Eastern Europe and USSR lang. and area ctr., 1978-91. Mem. Am. Com. Slavists, 1977-83; mem. com. Slavic and Ea. European studies U. Chgo., 1979-91, chmn., 1982-91, also other coms.; dir. Ctr. for East European and Russian/Eurasian Studies, 1991-96; cert. genealogist, 1994—. Author: E.T.A. Hoffman's Reception in Russia, 1974; editor: Church and Culture in Old Russia, 1991; co-editor: (with Joachim T. Baer) Mnemozina: Studia litteraria russica in honorem Vsevolod Setchkarev; mem. editorial bd. Slavic and East European Jour., 1978-87, adv. bd., 1987-89; assoc. editor Byzantine Studies, 1973-81; contbg. editor The Am. Genealogist, 1995—; contbr. and translator articles and book revs. Fulbright fellow, 1957-58, vis. fellow Dumbarton Oaks Ctr. for Byzantine Studies, 1972-73. Mem. Am. Assn. Advancement Slavic Studies (rep. coun. on mem. instns. 1985-96, area rep. nat. adv. com. for Ea. European lang. programs 1985-96), Am. Assn. Tchrs. Slavic and East European Langs., Early Slavic Studies Assn. (v.p. 1993-95, pres. 1995-97), Chgo. Consortium for Slavic and East European Studies (v.p. 1982-84, 98, pres. 1984-86, 98-2000, exec. coun. 1992-94), Phi Beta Kappa. Office: U Chgo Slavic Dept 1130 E 59th St Chicago IL 60637-1539 Office Phone: 773-702-8931. Business E-Mail: ningham@uchicago.edu.

INGIS, GAIL, interior designer, educator, photographer, artist, writer; b. Nov. 1, 1935; d. Bernard and Claire Gerber; m. Thomas H. Claus; children: Linda Sklar, Richard, Paul. Student, CUNY, 1953; grad. in interior architecture-design, N.Y. Sch. Interior Design, 1973, BFA, 1980; postgrad., Pratt Inst., N.J. Ins. Tech., Parsons Sch. Design. Prin. Ingis Design Assocs., Woodcliff Lake, N.J., Fairfield, Conn., 1970—. Adj. prof. U. Bridgeport, Conn., 2001—02, U. New Haven, 2002—, Fairfield U., Conn., 2003—. Exhibitions include Agora Gallery SOHO, NYC, U. New Haven, Represented in permanent collections. Troop leader U.S. Girl Scouts, N.Y.C. and Woodcliff Lake, 1964—69; bd. trustees The Lockwood Mathews Mansion Mus., Norwalk, Conn. Recipient Watercolor Painting award, Wall St. Gallery, 1997, Cooper Lighting award, 23d Ann. Nat. Lighting Competition, 1999. Mem.: AIA (profl. affiliate), Westport Arts Ctr., Wilton Arts Coun. (Watercolor award 2003), Rowayton Art Assn., Milford Arts Coun., Lyme Art Assn., New Haven Arts League, Shoreline Alliance for Arts, Guilford Art League, Madison Art Soc., Interior Design Educators Coun., Illuminating Engring. Soc. N.Am., Am. Soc. Interior Designers (admissions com. N.J. chpt. 1978, edn. chmn. 1978—86, co-chmn. pro-licensing com. 1984—86, bd. dirs. 1985—97, com. legis. for interior designers 1988—90, edn. chmn. 1994—95, bd. dirs. Conn. chpt. 1996—97, editor newsletter 1996—2004, Svc. award 1978, 1982—87, 2003, 2004), U.S. Profl. Tennis Assn. (cert. instr.), Westport Arts League. Home and Office: 200 Old Black Rock Tpke Fairfield CT 06825-

INGLE, M(ORTON) BLAKEMAN, chemicals executive; b. Carlsbad, N.Mex., Apr. 25, 1942; s. Morton Blakeman and Bette Ruth Ingle; m. Connie Sue Cochran; children: David, Glenn. BS in Biology and Chemistry, Ft. Lewis Coll., 1964; MS in Microbiology and Biochemistry, Colo. State U., 1966, PhD in Microbiology and Biochemistry, 1968. Corp. staff v.p. R&D Internat. Minerals & Chem., Northbrook, Ill., 1980, v.p. R&D, 1980-85, v.p., chief tech. officer, 1985-87, sr. v.p., chief adminstrv. and tech. officer, 1987-88; sr. v.p., pres. Pitman-Moore, Inc., Lake Forest, Ill., 1988-89, exec. v.p., pres., 1989-90; pres., chief oper. officer IMCERA Group Inc., Northbrook, 1990-91, pres., chief exec. officer, 1991-92. Editor sci. jour., 1974-79; contbr. numerous articles to profl. jours., book chpts. Bd. dirs. United Way Lake County, Glen Oaks, Ill., 1992. Recipient Disting. Achievement award Coll. Vet. Medicine and Biomed. Sci., Colo. State U. Fellow Am. Acad. Microbiology; mem. Am. Soc. for Microbiology, Japan Am. Soc., Brit. N.Am. Com., Northwestern U. Assocs. Address: 7733 Forsyth Blvd Saint Louis MO 63105-1817

INGLE, ROBERT P., retail executive; b. 1933; married. Grad., U. Miami, 1958. Sales rep. Kraft Foods, Miami, Fla., 1958-61; produce mgr. Colonial Stores, Asheville, N.C., 1961-63; chmn., dir. Ingles Markets Inc., Black Mountain, NC, 1963—2004, CEO, 1963—. Office: Ingles Markets Inc 2913 US Hwy 70 E Black Mountain NC 28711*

INGLEFIELD, JOSEPH T., JR., allergist, immunologist, pediatrician; b. Duquesne, Pa., Apr. 29, 1930; MD, U. Rochester, 1957. Diplomate Am. Bd. Allergy & Immunology, Am. Bd. Pediatrics. Intern William Beaumont Army Hosp., El Paso, Tex., 1957-58; resident Tripler Army Hosp., Honolulu, 1958-60; fellow in pediatrics and allergies Children's Hosp., Washington, 1969-72; with Fairfax Hosp., Falls Church, Va. Mem. AMA, MSV, Am. Acad. Pediatrics, Assn. Am. Physicians, North Va. Pediatric Soc. Office: 107 N Virginia Ave Falls Church VA 22046-3324 Fax: (703) 532-1984. E-mail: dratopyst@aol.com.

INGLEHART, MARITA ROHR, psychologist, educator, researcher; b. Ludwigshafen, Germany, Aug. 23, 1951; came to U.S., 1984; d. Karl Julius and Rita (Schreck) Rohr; m. Ekkehard Rosch, Aug. 13, 1973 (div. May 1978); m. Ronald Franklin Inglehart, Apr. 5, 1986; children: Ronald Charles, Marita Helen; stepchildren: Elizabeth, Rachel. Diploma in psychology, U. Mannheim, Germany, 1975, PhD, 1978, Habilitation, 1983. Asst. prof. U. Mannheim, 1975-78; rsch. scientist Ctr. for Decision Making, U. Mannheim, 1978-83; pvt. dozent U. Mannheim, 1983-90; vis. prof. U. Mich., Ann Arbor, 1984-86; rsch. assoc. Ctr. for Rsch. on Learning and Teaching, U. Mich., Ann Arbor, 1986-93; assoc. prof. Dental Sch., adj. assoc. prof. dept. psychology U. Mich., Ann Arbor, 1993—. Vis. prof. U. Mich., Ann Arbor, 1984-86, adj. asst. prof., 1986-93. Author: Critical Life Events, 1988, Reactions to Critical Life Events, 1991; editor: Integration of Immigrants, 1979, Oral Health-Related Quality of Life, 2002. Mem. APA, Am. Psychol. Soc., Am. Dental Edn. Assn., Am. ASsn. Dental Rsch., German Soc. Psychology, European Assn. Exptl. Social Psychology. Roman Catholic. Home: 2626 Geddes Ave Ann Arbor MI 48104-2715 Office: U Mich Dental Sch Dept PPG Ann Arbor MI 48109 Business E-Mail: mri@umich.edu.

INGLES, JOSEPH LEGRAND, social services administrator, political science professor; b. June 15, 1939; s. Vernal Willard and Helen Josephine (Graziano) Ingles; m. Hazel Jeanette Palmer, Aug. 18, 1962; children: Sally Van Dyke, Christine Walker, Joette Smith, Robert, Michael. BS, Brigham Young U., 1964; PhD, U. Mo., 1968. Rsch. asst. U. Mo., Columbia, 1967-68; grant policy specialist HEW, Washington, 1970-72; asst. prof. govt. and politics U. Md., College Park, 1968-75; dir. human resources Wasatch Front Regional Coun., Bountiful, Utah, 1975-77; utility consumer adv. Com. on Consumer Svc., Utah, 1977-93; medicaid mgr., third party liability and health Utah Dept. Human Svcs., Salt Lake City, 1993-94; child support mgr. Intake,Locate and Orders Office Recovery Svcs., Dept. Human Svcs., Salt Lake City, 1994-96, computer software trainer, 1996—. Spec faculty mem family and consumer studies Univ Utah, 1995; consult Ellingson Kilpack Assocs, Salt Lake City, 1972, Bonneville Research Corp, Santa Monica, Calif., 1971, US Dept Commerce, 1970; spec faculty mem Salt Lake Ctr Brigham Young Univ, 1988—94. Mem W Bountiful City Coun, 1982—88. Fellow, NDEA, 1964—67; grantee, Univ Md, 1969. Fellow: Am Soc Pub Admin (fellowship 1970—71); mem.: Nat Asn State Utility Consumer Advs (mem gas comt 1983—93), Nat Asn Regulatory Utility Comnrs (staff subcom on consumer affairs 1982—93), Snowbird Iron Blosam Lodge (chmn budget and fin comt 1987—96). Mem. Lds Ch. Home: 1485 N 1100 W Woods Cross UT 84087-1828 E-mail: Jingles@HS.State.UT.US.

INGLIS, ROBERT D. (BOB INGLIS), congressman; b. Savannah, Ga, Oct. 11, 1959; m. Mary Anne Williams, Aug. 7, 1982; children: Robert D. Jr., Mary Ashton, Anne McCullough, Mabel Andrews, Sara Meade. AB summa cum laude in Polit. Sci., Duke U., 1981; JD, U. Va. Sch. Law, 1984. Atty. Leatherwood, Walker, Todd & Mann P.C., Greenville, SC, 1986—92, 1999—2004; mem. U.S. Ho. Reps., 103d-105th Congresses, 4th Dist. SC, 1993—98, U.S. Ho. Reps., 109th Congress, 4th Dist. SC, 2005—; mem. Budget/Judiciary com. Chmn. 4th Congl. Dist. South Carolinians to Limit Congl. Terms; mem. Leadership Greenville Class XVI; loaned exec. Greenville County United Way, 1987; mem. exec. com. Greenville County Rep. Party; mem. exec. com. First Monday in Greenville. Mem. S.C. Bar Assn., Greenville County Bar Assn., Phi Beta Kappa. Republican. Office: US House of Repr 330 Cannon House Office Bldg Washington DC 20515 Office Phone: 202-225-2701.*

INGOLD, CATHERINE WHITE, academic administrator; b. Columbia, S.C., Mar. 15, 1949; d. Hiram Hutchison and Annelle (Stover) White; m. Wesley Thomas Ingold, June 13, 1970; 1 child, Thomas Bradford Hutchison. Student, U. Paris-Sorbonne, 1969; BS in French with honors, Hollins Coll., 1970; MA in Romance Langs., U. Va., 1972, PhD in French, 1979; DHum honoris causa, Francis Marion U., Florence, S.C., 1992. Assoc. prof. romance langs. Gallaudet U., Washington, 1973-88, dir. hons. program, 1980-85, dean arts and scis., 1985-86, provost, v.p. acad. affairs, 1986-88; pres. Am. U. of Paris, 1988-92, Curry Coll., Milton, Mass., 1992-96. Acting dir. Nat. Fgn. Lang. Ctr. Johns Hopkins U., 1996—2000, U. Md., 2000—. Recipient Prix Morot-Sir de Langue et Littérature françaises (Hollins). Mem. MLA, Nat. Collegiate Honors Coun., Lychnos Soc. (U.Va.), Phi Beta Kappa. Episcopalian. Home: 2015 N Brandywine St Arlington VA 22207-2200 Office: Nat Fgn Lang Ctr Patapsco Bldg Ste 2132 5201 Paint Branch Pkwy College Park MD 20742 Office Phone: 301-405-9828. Business E-Mail: cwingold@nflc.org.

INGOLD, KEITH USHERWOOD, chemist, educator; b. Leeds, Eng., May 31, 1929; s. Christopher Kelk and Edith (Usherwood) I.; m. Carmen Cairine Hodgkin, Apr. 7, 1956; children: Christopher Frank (dec.), John Hilary, Diana Hilda. BSc with honors in Chemistry, Univ. Coll., London, 1949; DPhil, Oxford (Eng.) U., 1951; DSc (hon.), U. Guelph, 1985; LLD (hon.), Mt. Allison U., 1987; DSc (hon.), St. Andrews U., Scotland, 1989, Carleton U., 1992, McMaster U., 1995; LLD (hon.), Dalhousie U., 1996; Laurea Honoris Causa in Biology, U. Ancona, Italy, 1999. Postdoctoral fellow NRC Can., Ottawa, 1951-53, rsch. officer, 1955-77, assoc. dir. chemistry, 1977-90, disting. rsch. scientist, 1990—. Adj. prof. U. Guelph, Ont., Can., 1985-87, Brunel U., U.K., 1983-94, Carleton U. Ottawa, Can., 1991—, St. Andrews U., U.K., 1997—; postdoctoral fellow U. B.C., 1953-55; vis. scientist Chevron Rsch. Co., Richmond, Calif., 1966, Univ. Coll., London, 1969, 72, Ford Motor Co., 1971, Esso Rsch. and Engring. Co., Linden, N.J., 1973, U. Western Ont., 1975, 1993, Iowa State U., 1975, U. Bologna, Italy, 1975, 93, U. Adelaide, Australia, 1979, U. Grenoble, France, 1983, Australian Nat. U., 1987, 99, U. Freiburg, Germany, 1990, 91, U. Essen, Germany, 1990, U. Dusseldorf, Germany, 1991, U. Leiden, The Netherlands, 1992, 93, U. St. Andrews, Scotland, 1998. Decorated Order of Can., 1995; recipient Can. Silver Jubilee medal, 1977, Queen Elizbeth II Golden Jubilee medal, 2002, Humboldt Sr. Rsch. Fellowship award, Germany, 1989, Veris award, 1989, Lansdown Visitor award U. Victoria, B.C., 1990, Mangini prize U. Bologna, 1990, Izaak Walton Killam Meml. prize Can. Coun., 1992, Gold medal for sci. and engring. Natural Scis. and Engring. Coun. Can., 1998; Carnegie fellow U. St. Andrews, Scotland, 1977; vis. fellow Japan Soc. for Promotion of Sci., 1982, Italian Nat. Rsch. Coun., 1983; Nat. Sci. Coun. Republic China lectr., 1992. Fellow Royal Soc. Can. (treas. 1979-81, Centennial medal 1982, Henry Marshall Tory medal 1985), Royal Soc. (London, Davy medal 1990, Royal medal 2000), Chem. Inst. Can. (medal 1981, Syntex award for phys. organic chemistry 1983), Univ. Coll. (London), Royal Soc. Edinburgh (hon.); mem. Am. Chem. Soc. (award petroleum chemistry 1968, Pauling award 1988, Arthur C. Cope scholar 1992, James Flack Norris award phys. organic chemistry 1993), Chem. Soc. (award kinetics and mechanism 1978), Can. Soc. Chem. (v.p. 1985-87, pres. 1987-88, Alfred Bader award in organic chemistry 1989), Royal Soc. Chemistry (Ingold lectr. 1990), World Innovation Fund (hon.). Achievements include research papers on free radical chemistry. Home: 72 Ryeburn Dr Ottawa ON Canada K1V 1H5 Office: Nat Rsch Coun of Can Ottawa ON Canada K1A 0R6 Office Phone: 613-990-0938. E-mail: keith.ingold@nrc.ca.

INGOLFSLAND, DENNIS ELDON, school librarian, religious studies educator; b. Minot, ND, June 19, 1954; s. Eldon Fred and Donna Ingolfsland; married, July 6, 1974. MA in Libr. sci., U. Mo., 1984; MA in Theol. studies, Fuller Theol. Sem., 90; DPhil, Oxford Grad. Sch., Tenn., 1999. Dir. libr. svcs., dean students Ariz. Coll. Bible, Phoenix, 1984—91; reference libr. George Fox Coll., Newberg, Oreg., 1991—92; dir. libr. svcs. Bryan Coll., Dayton, Tenn., 1992—2001; dir. libr. and media svcs. Crown Coll., St. Bonifacius, Minn., 2001—. Contbr. articles to profl. jours. With USAF, 1975—81. Named to, Oxford Round Table, 2005; travel grantee, Appalachian Coll. Assn., 2001, faculty scholar, Crown Coll., 2002. Mem.: Assn. Christian Librarians, Evang. Theol. Soc. Office: Crown Coll 8700 College View Dr Saint Bonifacius MN 55375

INGOLFSSON-FASSBIND, URSULA G., music educator; b. Zurich, Switzerland, Dec. 22, 1943; arrived in U.S., 1980; d. Franz Bernardin Fassbind and Gertrud M. Schmucki; m. Ketill Ingolfsson; children: Katla Soffia, Judith, Mirjam, Bera Bjorg. Nat. tchrs. diploma, Conservatory Zurich, 1965, soloist diploma, 1968; postgrad., U. Ariz., 1969—70. Tchg. asst. Conservatory Zurich, 1966—68; with Reykjavik (Iceland) Music Coll., 1970—79, Settlement Music Sch., Phila., 1987—2000; founder, dir., tchr., performer Leopold Mozart Acad. and Franz Fassbind Found., Phila., 2001—. Founder, dir. Leopold Mozart Chamber Music Concerts, 2002—. Grantee Excellency in Tchg. grant, Wilmington (Del.) Piano Co., 2003. Mem.: Am. Composers Guild, Music Tchr. Nat. Assn. Democrat. Avocations: painting, gardening. Home and Office: Leopold Mozart Acad 4833 Pulaski Ave Philadelphia PA 19144 Office Phone: 215-848-1370. Personal E-mail: lmozartacademy@aol.com.

INGRAHAM, CHERIE ANN, apparel designer, environmentalist, writer, educator; b. Niagara Falls, N.Y. d. Richard Lewis and Jeanette (Treichler) Ingraham; m. Richard Bruce Feuerman, Mar. 18, 1989. A in bus. adminstr., Niagara County C.C., 1973; A in fashion design, Fashion Inst. of Tech., 1976. Asst. designer Kayser Roth, N.Y., 1976—78, Craftex Inc., N.Y., 1978—79; designer Say-Lu Inc, N.Y., 1979—89; designer, merchandiser Hampton Industries, N.Y., 1989—99, Kellwood, N.Y., 1999—2001; v.p. merchandiser & design Jaclyn Inc., N.Y., 2001—. Author: (childrens book) Chuckie Goodnight A Bedtime Story, 2004. Founder, pres. The Chuckie Goodnight Found. for the Environ., 2001—04; mem. Town of Southeast Open Space Com., Brewster, NY, 2004. Mem.: The Putnam County Land Trust, Concerned Residents of Southeast, Riverkeeper Inc., Trust for Pub. Land, Friends of the Great Swamp. Avocations: gardening, canoeing, writing, reading, art.

INGRAHAM, EDWARD CLARKE, JR., retired foreign service officer; b. Mineola, N.Y., Feb. 2, 1922; s. Edward Clarke and Dorothy Hathaway (Sutton) I.; m. Susan Hartman, Jan. 25, 1947; children: John Edward, James William, Elizabeth Ann Ingraham Reed. BA, Dartmouth Coll., 1943; postgrad., Cornell U., 1957-58. Editorial asst. Moody's Investors Service, N.Y.C., 1946-47; joined U.S. Fgn. Service, 1947; vice consul Cochabamba, Bolivia, 1947-48; 3d sec. embassy La Paz, Bolivia, 1948-50; vice consul Hong Kong, 1950-51, Perth, Australia, 1951-54; consul Madras, India, 1954-56; 2d sec. embassy Djakarta, Indonesia, 1958-60; officer charge Australia-New Zealand affairs State Dept., 1961-62, officer charge Indonesian affairs, 1962-65; assigned Nat. War Coll., 1965-66; chief of embassy polit. sect. Rangoon, Burma, 1966-69; dep. dir. research and analysis for East Asia, State Dept., 1969-71; polit. counselor embassy Islamabad, Pakistan, 1971-74; dir. Office of Indonesian, Malaysian and Singapore Affairs, State Dept., Washington, 1974-77; dep. chief mission Am. embassy, Singapore, 1977-79; diplomat in residence Lake Forest (Ill.) Coll., 1979-80; ret., 1980; freedom of info. advisor U.S. Dept. State, 1980-95. Mem. U.S. del. ANZUS council meeting, Canberra, Australia, 1962, Intergovtl. Group on Indonesia, Amsterdam, Netherlands, 1975, 77 Served with USAAF, 1943-45, ETO. Mem. Am. Fgn. Service Assn. Address: 7711 Tomlinson Ave Cabin John MD 20818-1304 E-mail: edingrdham@aol.com.

INGRAHAM, JAMES H., diversified financial services company executive; BBA, JD, U. Kans. Atty. Breyfogle, Gardner, Davis & Kreamer, Olathe, Kans.; legal dept. H&R Block, 1980, sec., 1990—2002; asst. v.p., corp. counsel sec. H&R Block Tax Svcs., 1993—96; v.p. legal sec. H&R Block, 1996—99, v.p., gen. counsel, 1999—2001; sr. v.p., gen. counsel sec. H&R Block Inc., Kans. City, Mo., 2001—. Office: H&R Block Inc 4400 Main St Kansas City MO 64111

INGRAHAM, LAURA, lawyer, political commentator; b. Glastonbury, Conn. BA in Russian and English lit., Dartmouth Coll.; JD, U. Va. Sch. of Law, 1991. Speechwriter White House and Dept. Edn. and Transp., 1986—88; law clerk to Supreme Ct. Justice Clarence Thomas and Ralph K. Winter, US Ct. Appeals Second Cir., 1992—93; criminal def. lawyer Skadden, Arps, Slate, Meagher & Flom, Wash., DC, 1993—96; host Watch It! with Laura Ingraham, MSNBC, 1996—2000, nat. syndicated radio program, The Laura Ingraham Show, 2001—. Co-founder The Dark Ages Weekend. Author: The Hillary Trap: Looking for Power in All the Wrong Places, 2000, Shut Up & Sing: How the Elites in Hollywood, Politics...and the UN are Subverting America, 2003; contbr. NY Times, Wash. Post, LA Times, San Francisco Chronicle. Office: Talk Radio Network PO Box 3755 Central Point OR 97502

INGRAM, BARBARA AVERETT, minister; b. Decatur, Ga., May 8, 1960; d. Charles Cole and Avarilla Gleen (Caldwell) Averett; m. George Conley Ingram IV, Nov. 7, 1987; children: Martha-Conley Elizabeth, Rebekah-Ann Elizabeth. AS, Montreat-Anderson Coll., 1981; BA, Pfeiffer Coll., 1983; MDiv, Emory U., 1986; D of Ministry, Columbia Theol. Sem., 2003. Ordained to ministry United Meth. Ch. as deacon, 1986, as elder, 1988. Assoc. min. 1st United Meth. Ch., Lenoir, N.C., 1986-87, Cen. United Meth. Ch., Mt. Airy, N.C., 1987-88; sr. min. Ogburn Meml. United Meth. Ch., Winston-Salem, NC, 1988—91, Ann St.-Bogers Chapel UMC, Concord, NC, 1991—, Shiloh UMC, Concord, 1997, Lebanon-Fairfield United Meth. Ch., Denver, NC, 2000—05; assoc. pastor Midway United Meth. Ch., Alpharetta, Ga., 2004—05; sr. pastor Woodstock (Ga.) United Meth. Ch., Big Springs, Ga., 2005. Del. conf. Rule Ch. Ministry, 2004. Republican. E-mail: circleofprayers@comcast.net.

INGRAM, CHARLES CLARK, JR., energy executive; b. Dec. 10, 1916; s. Charles Clark and Winnie (Edwards) I.; m. Maxine Waterbury, Jan. 29, 1939; children: James C., Jack R. BS, U. Okla., 1940; LLD, Oral Roberts U., 1983. Registered profl. engr., Okla. With Oneok Inc., Tulsa, 1940—, pres., 1966-71, CEO, 1966-81, chmn., 1966-87, chmn. emeritus, 1987—. Former chmn. bd. trustees Frontiers of Sci. Found. of Okla., Inc., 1973-74; former adv. bd. Downtown Tulsa Unlimited; former bd. govs. Am. Citizenship Ctr., Oklahoma City; mem. pres.'s bd. visitors, chmn. Tulsa Engring. Coun., U. Okla. Maj. AUS, WWII, 1941-46. Named to Okla. Hall of fame, 1982. Mem. AIME, Am. Assn. Petroleum Geologists, Am. Gas Assn. (chmn. 1979-80), So. Gas Assn. (past pres.), Engrs. Soc. Tulsa, Okla. State C. of C. (pres. 1981), Oklahoma City C. of C., Tulsa C. of C., Nat. Alliance Businessmen (chmn. Ea. Okla. and Tulsa 1973-74), Propeller Club U.S., Summit Club, So. Hills Country Club (gov., past pres.), Cedar Ridge Country Club (Tulsa), Masons, Sigma Tau, Sigma Gamma Epsilon. Baptist. Office: Oneok Inc 100 W 5th St PO Box 871 Tulsa OK 74102-0871

INGRAM, DAVID B., entertainment company executive; b. Dec. 13, 1962; m. Sarah LeBrun; 1 child, Henry LeBrun. BA in History cum laude, Duke U., 1985; MBA in Mktg., Vanderbilt U., 1989. Dir. rsch. Duke U. Capital Campaign Office, Durham, N.C., 1985-87, dir., found. Young Alumni for The Capital Campaign, 1986-87; asst. to treas. Ingram Industries, Inc., Nashville, 1989-91; dir. sales Ingram Entertainment Inc., La Vergne, Tenn., 1991-92, asst. v.p. sales, 1992-93, v.p. major accounts, 1993-94, pres., COO, 1994—96. Chmn. bd. visitors The Duke Primate Ctr., 1987—; bd. dirs. Montgomery Bell Acad. Mem. Video Software Dealers Assn. (nat. bd. dirs.), Belle Meade Country Club, Golf Club Tenn., Caves Valley Golf Club, Green Spring Valley Hunt Club, Delta Tau Delta. Avocations: golf, bicycling, running, tennis, hunting, reading, investments. Office: Ingram Entertainment Inc Two Ingram Blvd La Vergne TN 37089

INGRAM, DENNY OUZTS, JR., lawyer, law educator; b. Kirbyville, Tex., Mar. 23, 1929; s. Denny Ouzts and Grace Bertha (Smith) I.; m. Ann Elizabeth Rees, July 11, 1952; children: Scott Rees, Stuart Tillman. BA, U. Tex., 1955, JD with honors, 1957. Bar: Tex. 1956, N.Mex. 1967, Utah 1968. Editor Kirbyville Banner, 1949-50; mem. Tex. Ho. of Reps., 1951-52; assoc. Graves, Dougherty, Gee and Hearon (and predecessors), Austin, Tex., 1957, 59-60, partner, 1961-66; asst. prof. law U. Tex., 1957-59, U. N.Mex., 1966-67; prof. U. Utah, 1968-77; ptnr. McGinnis, Lochridge, and Kilgore, Austin, 1977-90, of counsel, 1991—; prof. law Tex. Wesleyan U. Sch. Law, 1991—. Vis. prof. U. Calif., Davis, 1973-74, U. Tex., summers 1968, 75, U. San Diego, 1993; research fellow Southwestern Legal Found., lectr. in field Contbr. numerous articles to law revs., chpts. to books; assoc. note editor: Tex. Law Rev., 1956-57. Research dir. Utah Constn. Revision Com., 1969-71, 73-74. Served with U.S. Army, 1951-54. Fellow Am. Coll. Trust and Estate Counsel, Am. Coll. Tax Counsel, Tex. Bar Found.; mem. ABA, Am. Law Inst. (life), Tex. Bar Assn., Utah Bar Assn., N.Mex. Bar Assn., Chancellors, Order of Coif, Phi Delta Phi. Democrat. Episcopalian. Home: 4055 Hildring Dr E Fort Worth TX 76109-4712 Office: Tex Wesleyan U Sch Law 1515 Commerce St Fort Worth TX 76102-6572

INGRAM, DOUGLAS STEPHEN, lawyer; b. Aug. 31, 1962; BS magna cum laude, Ariz. State U., 1985; JD summa cum laude, U. Ariz., 1988. Bar: Calif. 1988. Atty. Gibson, Dunn & Crutcher, 1988—96; assoc. gen. counsel, asst. sec. Allergen, Inc., Irvine, Calif., 1998—2000, exec. v.p., gen. counsel, sec., 2000—. Mem.: ABA, Am. Soc. Corp. Secretaries, Am. Corp. Counsel Assn., State Bar Calif., Orange County Bar Assn., Order of Coif. Office: Allergan Inc 2525 Dupont Dr PO Box 19534 Irvine CA 92623-9534 Office Phone: 714-246-4535. Office Fax: 714-246-4971. E-mail: ingram_doug@allergan.com.

INGRAM, GEORGE, manufacturing executive; b. Montclair, N.J., Dec. 10, 1920; s. George and Frances Elizabeth (Watts) I.; m. Olive May Holtz, Feb. 15, 1947 (dec. Dec. 1999); children: Patricia (Mrs. S. K. Bone), George III (dec.), Sara, John. BS, Yale U., 1942; MS, Stevens Inst. Tech., 1948. Registered profl. indsl. engr., Pa. Indsl. engr. RCA, 1942-45; cons. mgmt. engr. Stevenson, Jordan & Harrison, Inc., N.Y.C., 1945-51; controller Riegel Paper Corp., 1951-57, Raytheon Co., Lexington, Mass., 1957-60, v.p., 1960-61, v.p. fin., 1961-63, sr. v.p., dir., 1963-68; sr. v.p. Champion Internat., Inc., N.Y.C., 1968-69, exec. v.p., 1969-72, dir., 1968-72; pres., CEO. dir. Reed-Ingram Corp., N.Y.C., 1972-77, cons., 1977-83. Pres. Dionis Corp., Nantucket, Mass., 1977-87; chmn. bd., dir. Deerfield Splty. Papers, Inc., 1973-77, Oneida Packaging Products, Inc., 1973-77, Canadian Glassine Co., Ltd., 1973-77; chmn., sec., dir. Arctos Corp., Quaker Hill, Conn., 1980-86; pres., treas., dir. Fitchburg Engring. Corp., Mass., 1980-86; dir. M/A Com, Inc., Burlington. Mass., 1968-91. Trustee Coll. of Wooster, Ohio, 1970-88. Mem.: ASME, Fin. Execs. Inst. (past pres. Boston chpt., past chmn. nat. com. securites and exchanges regulation), Mary's Assn., Phi Gamma Delta. Republican. Episcopalian. Home and Office: 88 Notch Hill Rd Apt 324 North Branford CT 06471 Office Phone: 203-481-5956. E-mail: geoingram@comcast.net.

INGRAM, HELEN MOYER, political science professor; b. Denver, July 12, 1937; d. Oliver Weldon and Hazel Margaret (Wickard) Hill; m. W. David Laird; children from by previous marriage: Mrill, Maia, Seth. BA, Oberlin Coll., 1959; PhD, Columbia U., 1967. Lectr., asst. prof. polit. sci. U. N.Mex., 1962-69; with Nat. Water Commn., Washington, 1969-72; assoc. prof. polit. sci. U. Ariz., Tucson, 1972-77, prof. polit. sci., 1979-96; dir. Udall Ctr. Studies Pub. Policy, 1988-96; Warmington chair Sch. Social Ecology U. Calif., Irvine, 1995—. Author: (with Dean Mann) Why Policies Succeed of Fail, 1980, (with Nancy Laney and John McCain) A Policy Approach to Representation: Lessons from the Four Corners States, 1980, (with Martin, Laney and Griffin) Saving Water in a Desert City, 1984, (with Brown) Water and Poverty in the Southwest, 1987, Water Politics: Continuity and Change, 1990, (with Nancy Laney and David Gillilan) Divided Waters: Divided Waters: Bridging the U.S.-Mexico Border, 1995, (with Ann Schneider) Policy Design for Democracy, 1997; editor: (with Rathgeb Smith) Public Policy for Democracy, 1993, (with Joachim Blatter) Reflections on Water, 2001 (with Anne Schneider) Deserving and Entitled: Social Constructions and Public Policy, 2005; book rev. editor Am. Polit. Sci. Rev., 1987-92. Mem. ind. sci. bd. Calif. Bay Delta Authority, 2002—05. Sr. fellow, Resources for Future, Washington, 1977—79. Mem. Policy Studies Orgn. (pres. 1985), Am. Polit. Sci. Assn. (coun., treas. 1985-87), Western Polit. Sci. Assn. (past pres., v.p.). Home: 4749 E San Francisco Blvd Tucson AZ 85712-1238 E-mail: hingram@uci.edu.

INGRAM, JAMES MICHAEL, lawyer; b. Memphis, Tenn., May 23, 1960; s. James Milton Ingram III and Janet Kay (Parker) Ingram Girnius. BS in Psychology, Santa Clara U., Calif., 1982; JD, Pepperdine U., Malibu, Calif., 1985. Bar: (Calif.) 1985, U.S. Dist. Ct., Ctrl. Dist. Calif. 1986, U.S. Ct. of Appeals (9th cir.) 1986, U.S. Dist. Ct., No. Dist. Calif. 1988, US Dist. Ct., Ea. Dist. Calif. 1988, U.S. Ct. of Appeals, Fed. Cir. 1990, U.S. Dist. Ct., So. Dist. Tex. 1997. Law clk. Evanns & Walsh, Beverly Hills, Calif., 1983—85, assoc., 1985—87, Law Offices of Mark I. Rosenberg, Century City, Calif., 1987—88, Mount & Stoelker, San Jose, Calif., 1988—96, Law Offices Lester G. Sachs, San Jose, Calif., 1996—2001; mem. Law Offices of James M. Ingram, Irvine, Calif., 2001—. Sec., bd. dirs. Let Them Play Found., Inc., Santa Clara, Calif., 1994—; advisor to bd. dirs., v.p., sec. The Robert Brownlee Found., Mountain View, Calif., 2001—. Mem. St. Thomas More Soc. of Santa Clara County, Santa Clara, Calif., 1998—. Recipient Am. Jurisprudence Award in Torts, Bancroft Whitney - Lawyers Coop. Pub. Co., 1983. Mem.: ATLA, Orange County Bar Assn., Santa Clara County Bar Assn. Conservative. Roman Catholic. Avocations: intercollegiate athletics, equestrian sports, travel, cooking, sport horse breeding. Office: Law Offices James M Ingram 5405 Alton Parkway Ste 5A-739 Irvine CA 92604 E-mail: jmingram@sprynet.com.

INGRAM, JEFFREY CHARLES, lawyer, educator; b. Santa Barbara, Calif., Apr. 8, 1953; s. John Samis and Jeanne Lorraine (McLaughlin) I.; m. Mary Jane Fenner, Mar. 9, 2002; children: Jeffrey C. II, Michael K., Kara Jeanne. Student, Miami U., Oxford, Ohio, 1971-72; BS, Suffolk U., 1974; JD cum laude, So. Calif. Inst. Law, 1979. Bar: Calif. 1979, U.S. Ct. Appeals 1979, U.S. Dist. Ct. (cen. dist.) Calif. 1982, U.S. Dist. Ct. (ea. dist.) Calif. 1990. Assoc. McGahan & Engle, Ventura, Calif., 1979-82, Henderson & Smith, Ventura, 1982-87; mng. atty. Borton, Petrini and Conron, Santa Barbara, Calif., 1987-88; ptnr. Ingram & Assocs., Penn Valley, Calif., 1988—. Prof. Oxnard (Calif.) Coll., 1981-88, U. Calif., Santa Barbara, 1983-88; commr. Nevada County Airport, 1999—; dir. Penn Valley Fire Protection Dist., 2000—. Author: (photography book) Come and Get It, 1972; dir., producer of movie Come and Get It, 1972. Mem. Rep. Party Central Com., 1998—2000. Mem. ABA, Assn. Trial Lawyers Am., Barrister's Club (bd. dirs. 1981-83). Avocations: flying, golf. Office: Ingram & Assocs 10520 Spenceville Rd Penn Valley CA 95946-9413 Office Phone: 530-432-1996.

INGRAM, KENNETH FRANK, retired state supreme court justice; b. Ashland, Ala., July 7, 1929; s. Earnest Frank and Alta Mary (Allen) I.; m. Judith Louise Brown, Sept. 3, 1954; children: Jennifer Lynn Ingram, Kenneth Frank Jr. BS, Auburn U., 1951; LLB, Jones Law Sch., 1963. Bar: Ala. 1963, U.S. Dist. Ct. (no. dist.) Ala. 1965, U.S. Dist. Ct. (mid. dist.) Ala. 1966. City councilman City of Ashland, Ala., 1956-58; mem. Ho. of Reps., Ala., 1958-66; presiding judge 18th Jud. Cir. Ct., Ala., 1968-87; judge Ala. Ct. Civil Appeals, Montgomery, 1987-89, presiding judge, 1989-91; assoc. justice Ala. Supreme Ct., Montgomery, 1991-97. Mem., chmn. Ala. Jud. Inquiry Commn., 1979-87. Contbr. articles on jud. ethics to profl. pubs. With USMC, 1952-54. Mem. Ala. Bar Assn., Masons. Democrat. Meth. Avocations: woodworking, metalcrafting, tennis, swimming. Home: 264 1st St N PO Box 729 Ashland AL 36251-0729

INGRAM, LORI RUTH, performing arts association administrator; b. Cleve., July 25, 1959; d. Howard Gilbert and Jean M. Ruth; children: Adell Alexander III, Katrina Ida Ruth. Degree, Kent State U., 1980, Cleve. State U., 1996. Staff asst. Playhouse Square Ctr., Cleve., 1999—2004. Cons. Arlee M., Cleve., 1996—99, various fashion designers, Dallas, 1996—99, L.A., 1996—99, Batavia, Ill., 1996—99. Asst. editor (magazine) Kitabu Newsletter, 1979, feature writer (newsletter) Vindicator, 1996. Mem. NASA Project, Cleve., 2003—04. Mem.: Urban League Guild (v.p. 1986), Socrates Club. Avocations: poetry, acting, modeling, writing, holistic medicine. Home: 2330 Ashurst Rd University Heights OH 44118 Office: Playhouse Square Ctr 1519 Euclid Ave Cleveland OH 44115

INGRAM, ORRIN HENRY, II, transportation executive; s. Martha Rivers and E. Bronson Ingram. Grad., Vanderbilt U., 1982. With Ingram Industries Inc., Nashville, 1982—, co-pres., 1995—99, pres., CEO, 1999—, bd. dirs., 1999—; chmn. Ingram Barge Co., Nashville. Adv. bd. SunCom; Bd. dirs. eSkye.com, Boys and Girls Club Mid. Tenn., Friends of Warner Pks., Vanderbilt Cancer Ctr. (chmn. 1998-), Bapt. Hosp. Corp.; bd. govs., chmn. U.S. Polo Assn Office: Ingram Industries Inc 1 Belle Mead Pl 4400 Harding Rd Nashville TN 37205-2244

INGRAM, PEGGY JOYCE, secondary school educator; b. Wichita Falls, Tex., Feb. 15, 1943; d. Albert Cronjie and Esther (Wiist) Weiss; m. Darwin Keith Ingram, Aug. 19, 1972; 1 child, Lindsey Michelle. Student, Midwestern U., 1961-62; BS, West Tex. State U., 1966; MNS, U. Okla., 1972; postgrad., Ea. N.Mex. U., 1975. Cert. secondary sci. tchr. Tchr. Palo Duro High Sch., Amarillo, Tex., 1966-72, Texico (N.Mex.) High Sch., 1972-73; tchr., chair sci. dept. Clovis High Sch., 1973—; tchr. Ea. N.Mex. U., Clovis, 1981-82. Participant NASA Honors Workshop, Jet Propulsion Lab., 1990; part-time instr. Clovis C.C., 1991—. Recipient Excellence award Clovis C.C., 2001; named Clovis Educator of Yr., NEA/N.Mex. Clovis Assn., 1997 Mem. NEA, Clovis Edn. Assn., Nat. Sci. Tchrs. Assn., Delta Kappa Gamma. Democrat. Methodist. Avocations: flying, reading. Home: 2501 Williams Ave Clovis NM 88101-3330 Office: Clovis High Sch 1900 N Thornton St Clovis NM 88101-4555

INGRAM, RICHARD THOMAS, educational association executive, consultant; b. McKeesport, Pa., Sept. 29, 1941; s. Henry Stephen and Jean Catherine (Lis) I.; m. Mollie Mangan Brown, Apr. 6, 1968; children: Kirsten Collins, David Thomas. BS, Indiana U. Pa., 1963; MEd, U. Pitts., 1964; EdD, U. Md., 1969. Tchr. h.s. Monroeville Sch. Dist., Monroeville, 1963—64; dir. psychometric svcs. U. Md., College Park, 1965—69; adj. instr. U. So. Calif., 1976, U. Va., 1971—79; program assoc. Assn. Governing Bds. of Univs. and Colls., Washington, 1971—74, exec. dir., 1974—79, exec. v.p., 1978—92, pres., 1992—2005; ret., 2005. Dir. United Educators Ins. Risk Retention Group, Inc., Washington, 1988-99, Am. Coun. on Edn., 1995-96; adv. commr. Edn. Commn. of States, Denver, 1985-95; trustee Dickinson Coll., Pa., 1995-2002. Editor, author: Governing Public Colleges and Universities, 1993, Governing Independent Colleges and Universities, 1993. Trustee U. Charleston, W.Va., 1980—89, Connelly Sch. Holy Child, Potomac, Md., 1987—93, Dickinson Coll., Pa., 1996—2002. Capt. U.S. Army, 1969—71, Vietnam. Recipient Disting. Alumni award Ind. U. Pa., 1992, Outstanding Alumnus Citation, Pa. Coll. Alumni Assn., 1994, Coll. Edn. Alumni Assn. award U. Md., 1996. Mem.: Am. Assn. Higher Edn., Cosmos Club. Avocations: skiing, camping, fly fishing. Home: 12017 Gregerscroft Rd Potomac MD 20854-2148 Office: Assn Governing Bds Univ and Colls 1 Dupont Cir NW Ste 400 Washington DC 20036-1136

INGRAM, ROBERT A., pharmaceutical executive; b. 1942; BSBA, Ea. Ill. U., 1965. Sales rep. Merrell Dow Pharms., sales mgr., v.p. pub. affairs; v.p. govt. affairs Merck & Co., 1985, pres. Merck Frosst Can. Inc., 1988-90; exec. v.p. adminstrv. and regulatory affairs Glaxo Inc., 1990, exec. v.p., 1993, pres., COO, 1993, pres., CEO, 1994, chmn., 1999; CEO Glaxo Wellcome plc., England, 1997; pres., COO Pharm. Ops. GlaxoSmithKline, England, 2001—03, vice chmn. pharms Research Triangle Park, NC, 2003—. Bd. dirs. Wachovia Corp. Office: Divsn Pharms 5 Moore Dr Research Triangle Park NC 27709

INGRAM, ROBERT BRUCE, lawyer; b. Des Moines, July 19, 1940; s. Earl J. and Frances F.; divorced; children: Stephanie, Ashley, Robert. Student, U. Iowa, 1958-61; BA, Drake U., 1962, postgrad., 1962-63; JD, Coll. William and Mary, 1970. Bar: Calif. 1971, Hawaii 1982; mediation tng. Harvard Law Sch. Mediation Workshop, 2002, Ctr. for Dispute Settlement, 2003. With Law Offices of Melvin M. Belli, San Francisco, 1971-78; pvt. practice San Rafael, Calif., 1978—; ptnr. Stearns & Ingram, Honolulu, 1982-92; jud. arbitrator Superior Ct. San Francisco and Marin County, 1980—; judge pro tem Superior Ct. Marin County, 1984—, Superior Ct., San Francisco, 1992—. Keynote spkr. ann. meeting Ga. State Bar, 1979; guest spkr. Iowa Acad. Trial Lawyers Seminar, 1987; lead counsel Pacifica Mud Slide Litigation Class Action, 1985-90; of counsel Price Okamoto, Mimeno & Lum, Honolulu; mediator Early Settlement Program, San Francisco Bar Assn. Contbr. articles to legal jours. Capt. USAF, 1964-68. Mem. ATLA, Am. Bd. Trial Advs., Consumer Attys. Calif., San Francisco Trial Lawyers Assn., Marin County Trial Lawyers Assn. (past pres.). Presbyterian. Office: 4340 Redwood Hwy Ste 352 San Rafael CA 94903-2127 Office Phone: 415-499-0800. E-mail: rbilaw@ingramlawoffices.com.

INGRAM, ROBERT D., lawyer; b. Cobb County, Ga. m. Kelly Ingram; 2 children. B, Kennesaw Coll., Ga.; JD, Emory Univ. Sch. of Law, Atlanta. Ptnr. Moore, Ingram, Johnson & Steele LLP, Marietta, Ga. Named a Spl. Master for disciplinary proceedings, Ga. Supreme Ct. Mem.: Cobb County Bar Assn. (past pres.), State Bar of Ga. (bd. of gov. 1993, exec. com. 1999, pres.-elect 2004, chair, bench and bar com.). Office: Moore Ingram Johnson & Steele 192 Anderson St PO Box 3305 Marietta GA 30061-3305 Office Phone: 770-429-1499.

INGRAM, SAMUEL WILLIAM, JR., lawyer; b. Utica, N.Y., Mar. 20, 1933; s. Samuel William and Mary Elizabeth (Rosen) I.; m. Jane Austin Stokes, Sept. 30, 1961; children: Victoria, William BS, Vanderbilt U., 1954; LLB, Columbia U., 1960. Bar: NY 1960. Assoc. Sullivan & Cromwell, N.Y.C., 1960-67; assoc. Shea Gallop Climenko & Gould, N.Y.C., 1967-68; ptnr. Shea & Gould and predecessors, N.Y.C., 1968-89, Ingram, Yuzek, Gainen, Carroll & Bertolotti LLP, N.Y.C., 1989—. Bd. dirs. Legal Aid Soc., N.Y.C., 1974-86, sec., 1978-86; trustee Green Mountain Valley Sch., Waitsfield, Vt., 1984-87. Served to 1st lt. USMC, 1954-57 Mem. ABA, N.Y. State Bar Assn., Assn. of Bar of City of N.Y. Avocation: athletic and outdoor activities. Home: 332 Long Ridge Rd Pound Ridge NY 10576-2005 Office: Ingram Yuzek Gainen Carroll & Bertolotti LLP 250 Park Ave Ste 600 New York NY 10177-0699 Office Phone: 212-907-9696. E-mail: singram@ingramllp.com.

INGRAM, SHIRLEY JEAN, social worker; b. Louisville, Oct. 22, 1946; BA in Social Sci., U. Hawaii, Pearl City, 1979; MSW, Fla. State U., 1982. Diplomate AM. bd. Social Work; lic. social worker, Ala.; qualified clin. social worker, Md. Case mgr. Geriatric Residential Treatment Ctr., Crestview, Fla., 1982-84; case mgmt. supr. Okaloosa Guidance Ctr., Fort Walton Beach, Fla., 1984-86; family counselor Harbor Oaks Hosp., Fort Walton Beach, 1986-87; pvt. practice Fort Walton Beach, 1987-95; social worker USAF Family Advocacy Office, Hurlburt Field, Fla., 1995—2001; exec. dir. ct.-apptd. juvenile advocates program Madison County Courthouse, Huntsville, Ala., 2001—. Quality assurance bd. dirs. State Dept. Human Svcs., Madison County, Ala. Mem. Mental Health Assn. Okaloosa County (sec. bd. dirs. 1988—, mem. adv. bd. dirs. Area Agy. on Aging, chmn. adv. bd. dirs., Okaloosa County Area Agy. on Aging, pres.), NASW, Long Term Care Ombudsman Coun., AAUW, Sertoma. Home: 312 Mossy Oak Dr Huntsville AL 35806 Office: Madison County Courthouse 100 Northside Sq Huntsville AL 35801 Business E-Mail: cajaoir@co.madison.al.us.

INGRAM, THEODORE FRANCIS, transportation executive; b. St. Louis, Mo., Sept. 9, 1950; s. Melvin Theodore and Laverna Ruth Ingram; m. Christine Clare Loechl; children: Theodore, Jr Francis, Jason Allen. MS in mgmt., Lindenwood U., 1979—83. Mgr. train ops. Union Pacific RR, Shreveport, La., 1984—88, mgr. terminal ops. Little Rock, 1988—90, dir. of safety, health, environment, 1992—95, dir. quality and transp., 1995—96, merger cons., 1996—2000, dir. transp. ops. Los Angeles, 2000—. Human resource cons. Union Pacific RR, Omaha, 1990—92. Recipient Alpha Sigma Tau Honor Soc., Lindenwood U., 1983. Mem.: Sigma Chi Frat. Achievements include development of behavior based safety system for UPRR. Avocation: baseball historian. Home: 4815 Linaro Dr Cypress CA 90630 Office: Union Pacific Railroad 4145 Washington Blvd Los Angeles CA E-mail: tingram2@up.com.

INGRAM, WILLIAM THOMAS, III, mathematics professor; b. McKenzie, Tenn., Nov. 26, 1937; s. William Thomas and Virginia (Howell) I.; m. Barbara Lee Gordon, June 6, 1958; children: William Robert, Kathie Ann, Mark Thomas. BA, Bethel Coll., 1959; MS, La. State U., 1961; PhD, Auburn U., 1964. Instr. Auburn U., Ala., 1961-63; instr. math. U. Houston, 1964-65, asst. prof., 1965-68, assoc. prof., 1968-75, prof., 1975-89, U. Mo., Rolla, 1989—2003, prof. emeritus, 2003—, chmn., 1989-98. Contbr. articles to profl. jours. Mem. Am. Math. Soc., Math. Assn. Am. (Disting. Tchg. award 2003). Presbyterian. Avocation: photography. Home: 284 Windmill Mountain Rd Spring Branch TX 78070 Office: Univ Mo Rolla Dept Math and Statistics Rolla MO 65409-0020

INGRASSIA, ANTHONY FRANK, human resource specialist; b. Middletown, NY, Sept. 22, 1926; s. Joseph and Mary (Dina) I.; m. Eleanor Mae Birkholz, Aug. 9, 1952; children: Michael, Mary, Steve, Laura, Anne, Jane, Lisa, Timothy. BA, U.Wis., 1948. Sports writer Milw. Sentinel, 1948-62; exec. v.p. Milw. Newspaper Guild, 1952-62; asst. dir. Dist. Coun. 48 Am. Fedn. State, County, Mcpl. Employees, AFL-CIO, Milw., 1962-64; labor rels. specialist, labor rels. dir. US P.O. Dept., Washington, 1964-69; dir. office labor-mgmt. rels. US CSC, Washington, 1970-78; asst. dir. labor-mgmt. rels. US Office Pers. Mgmt., Washington, 1979-82, asst. dir. agy. compliance and evaluation, 1982-86, dep. assoc. dir. pers. sys. and oversight, 1986-90, chmn. fed. prevailing rate adv. com., 1990-96; vice chmn., acting chmn. Fed. Salary Coun., Washington, 1992-95, vice chmn., 1995-2000. US del. ILO Pub. Employee Conf., Geneva, 1975-77, 86; spkr. seminar on collective bargaining U. Tel Aviv, 1979; cons. civil svc. reform Govt. Hungary and Poland, Budapest and Warsaw, 1991; cons. civil svc. Govt. of Saudi Arabia, Riyahd, 1986. Vol. Arlington (Va.) Food Assistance Ctr., 1992-97, Hospice, 1996-2002; ombudsman No. Va. Long Term Care Program, 1999-2003. Recipient presdl. rank awards Disting. Govt. Exec., 1980, Meritorious Govt. Exec., 1988. Mem. Soc. Fed. Labor Rels. Profl. (outstanding contbn. to fed. labor rels. award 1983-87), KC. Roman Catholic. Avocations: gardening, golf. Home: 12206 Cathedral Dr Lake Ridge VA 22192

INGRASSIA, LAWRENCE, editor; BA in Journalism, U. Ill., 1974. Reporter Chgo. Sun-Times, 1974—78; reporter Chgo. Bur. The Wall St. Jour., 1978—79, reporter Mpls. Bur., 1979—83, dep. bur. chief London Bur., 1983—86, bur. chief London Bur., 1993—98, bur. chief Boston Bur., 1986—93, spl. project editor, editor, money and investing group, 1999—2003, asst. mng. editor money and investing group, 2003—04; bus. and fin. editor The N.Y. Times, N.Y.C., 2004—. Office: The New York Times 229 W 43rd St New York NY 10036

INGWERSEN, MARTIN LEWIS, water transportation executive; b. Sandusky, Ohio, Nov. 5, 1919; s. John Christian and Irene Catherine (Hinkey) Ingwersen; m. Blanche Robinson, Apr. 26, 1947; children: Brenda, Richard Charles, Martin Lewis. BS, U. Notre Dame, 1941; postgrad., Western Res. U., 1941, Princeton U., 1943. Asst. to hull supt. Gt. Lakes Engring. Works, Ashtabula, Ohio, 1941-43, asst. supt., 1946-49; supt. plant Am. Ship Bldg. Co., Buffalo, 1948-50; mgr. plant Toledo, 1950-52, Lorain, Ohio, 1952-53; v.p. ops., 1954-58; v.p., works mgr. Ingalls Shipbldg. Corp., Pascagoula, Miss., 1958-65, v.p. ops., 1965-67; pres. Md. Shipbldg. and Drydock Co., Balt., 1967-68; exec. v.p. Lockheed Shipbldg. Co., Seattle, 1968-73; pres. Lockheed Shipbldg. and Constrn. Co., Seattle, 1973-76, exec. v.p. office of pres., 1976-86, trustee, 1973-86; cons. shipbldg. and ship repair, 1986—. Bd. dirs. Puget Sound Bridge and Dry Dock Co., Colby Crane & Mfg. Inc. Served to lt. USNR, 1943—46. Mem.: Am. Soc. Naval Engrs., Soc. Naval Archs. and Marine Engrs., Am. Bur. Shipping, Navy League, Notre Dame Club Vero Beach, Propeller Club U.S. Roman Catholic. Home and Office: 940 Turtle Cove Ln #304 Vero Beach FL 32963 Office Phone: 772-492-5075. Personal E-mail: mingwersen@aol.com.

INHOFE, JAMES M., senator; b. Des Moines, Nov. 17, 1934; m. Kay Kirkpatrik; children: Jim, Perry, Molly, Katy. BA, U. Tulsa, 1973. Pres. Quaker Life Ins. Co.; mem. Okla. Ho. Reps., 1967—69, Okla. State Senate, 1969—77; mayor City of Tulsa, 1978-84; mem. 1st Dist. Okla. Ho. of Reps., 1987-94; U.S. senator from Okla., 1994—; mem. armed svcs. com., intelligence com.; mem. environment and pub. works com. Served with U.S. Army, 1955-56. Republican. Office: 453 Russell Senate Bldg Washington DC 20510-0001 E-mail: jim_inhofe@inhofe.senate.gov.*

INIGO, RAFAEL MADRIGAL, retired electrical engineering educator; b. Madrid, June 18, 1932; arrived in U.S., 1963; s. Rafael G. and Francisca V. (Madrigal) I.; m. Eliana Soto, Apr. 29, 1961; children: C. Paulina, Alvaro A. Ing. El., U.T.F. Santa Maria, Val Chile, 1957; MSEE, U. Va., 1965, DSc in EE, 1966. Registered profl. engr., Va. Elec. engr. Braden Coppe Co., Coya, Chile, 1957-61; asst. prof. elec. engring. U.T.F. Santa Maria, Valparaiso, Chile, 1961-66; prof. elec. engring. UT Santa Maria, Valparaiso, 1966-68; assoc. prof. elec. engring. Va. Mil. Inst., Lexington, 1968-74, prof. elec. engring., 1974-78; assoc. prof. elec. engring U. Va., Charlottesville, 1978-85, prof. elec. engring., 1986-97, prof. emeritus, 1997—. Invited prof. U. Deusto, Spain, 1981, 83, 93, U. Seville, Spain, 1988, Rovira Virgili U., Tarragona, Spain, 2000. Author: Teoria de Circuitos, 1977, Vision por Computador, 1986, Robots Industriales Manipuladores, 2002; contbr. articles to profl. jours. Helen Wessel fellow U. Va., 1959, AID fellow U.S. Govt., 1963; Fulbright scholar U. Tech. Nat. Faculty Cordoba, Argentina, 1997. Avocations: photography, canoeing. Office: U Va Thornton Hall Dept Elec Engring Charlottesville VA 22903-6073 E-mail: rafainigo@earthlink.net.

INK, DWIGHT A., government agency administrator; b. Des Moines, Sept. 9, 1922; s. Dwight P. and Edna (Craun) I.; m. Margaret Child, Aug. 31, 1948; children: Stephen, Bruce, Lawrence, Barbara, Lauri; m. Dona A. Wolf, Feb. 14, 1981. BS, Iowa State U., 1947; MA, U. Minn., 1951. Budget and personnel officer City of Fargo (N.D.), 1948-50; chief mcpl. water sect. Bur. Reclamation Dept. Interior, Bismark, N.D., 1950-51; chief reports and statistics br. Savannah River Ops. Office AEC, Oak Ridge, 1952-55, exec. asst. to chmn. Washington, 1958-59, asst. gen. mgr., 1959-66; 1st asst. sec. for adminstrn. HUD, Washington, 1966-69; asst. dir. for exec. mgmt. Office of Mgmt. and Budget, Washington, 1969-73; dep. adminstr., acting adminstr. GSA, Washington, 1973-76, acting adminstr., Mar.-July 1985; exec. dir., pres. personnel project mgmt. CSC, Washington, May-Nov. 1977; v.p. Nat. Consumer Coop. Bank, Washington, 1980-81, U.S. Synthetic Fuels Corp., Washington, 1982-84; ind. cons. McManis and Assocs., Washington, 1984-85; asst. adminstr. USAID, Washington, 1985-88; pres. Inst. of Pub. Adminstrn., N.Y.C., 1988-93, pres. emeritus, 1994—. Exec. dir. Alaska Reconstrn. Commn.; pres. Am. Consortium Internat. Pub. Adminstrn., 1980-83; adminstr. Cmty. Svcs. Adminstrn., Washington, 1981; chmn. White House Task Force on Edn., 1965; bd. dirs. N.Am. Mgmt. Coun., 1989-93; vice chair nat. adv. bd. Ctr. Study of Presidency. Chmn. Charter Commn. S.C., 1955; mem. exec. com. Ga.- Carolina Council Boy Scouts Am., 1954-55. Served to capt. USAR, 1942-58. Recipient Arthur Fleming award as one of the 10 Outstanding Young Men in Govt. U.S. C. of C., 1961, Disting. Svc. award AEC, 1966, Outstanding Achievement awards U. Minn., 1969, Iowa State U., 1986, Disting. Svc. award GSA, 1975, Outstanding Leadership award Assn. Govt. Accts., 1976, Commrs. award for Disting. Svc., CSC, Pub. Adminstr. of Yr. award Brigham Young U., 1978. Mem. Am. Pub. Works Assn. (bd. dirs.), Am. Soc. Pub. Adminstrn. (pres. 1978-79), Nat. Civil Service League (bd. dirs., career service award 1966), Pub. Adminstrn. Service (bd. dirs.), Nat. Acad. Pub. Adminstrn. (trustee), Internat. Inst. Adminstrv. Sci. (v.p. 1980-86), Coun. on Fgn. Rels., Delta Sigma Rho, Phi Kappa Phi. Home: 43725 Collett Mill Ct Leesburg VA 20176-1626

INKELES, ALEX, sociology educator; b. Bklyn., Mar. 4, 1920; s. Meyer and Ray (Gewer) K.; m. Bernadette Mary Kane, Jan. 31, 1942; 1 child, Ann Elizabeth BA, Cornell U., 1941, MA, 1946; postgrad., Washington Sch. Psychiatry, 1943-46; PhD, Columbia U., 1949; student, Boston Psychoanalytic Inst., 1957-59; A.M. (hon.), Harvard U., 1957; prof. honoris causa, Faculdade Candido Mendez, Rio de Janerio, 1969, Faculdade Candido Mendez, 2002. Social sci. research analyst Dept. State and OSS, 1942-46; cons. program evaluation br., internat. broadcasting div. Dept. State, 1949-51; instr. social relations Harvard U., Cambridge, Mass., 1948, lectr., 1948-57, prof. sociology, 1957-71, dir. studies social relations Russian Research Ctr., dir. studies social aspects econ. devel. Ctr. Internat. Affairs, 1963-71, research assoc., 1971-79; Margaret Jacks prof. edn., prof. sociology Stanford U., Calif., 1971-78, prof. sociology, 1978-90; sr. fellow Hoover Inst., 1978—; prof. emeritus, 1990—. Mem. exec. com. behavioral sci. div. NRC, 1968-75; lectr. Nihon U., Japan, 1985. Author: Public Opinion in Soviet Russia, 1950 (Kappa Tau Alpha award 1950, Grant Squires prize Columbia 1955); with R. Bauer, C. Kluckhohn) How the Soviet System Works, 1956, (with R. Bauer) The Soviet Citizen, 1959, Soviet Society (edited with H.K. Geiger), 1961, What is Sociology?, 1964, Readings on Modern Sociology, 1965, Social Change in Soviet Russia, 1968, (with D.H. Smith) Becoming Modern, 1974 (Hadley Cantril award 1974), Exploring Individual Modernity, 1983; editor: (with Masamichi Sasaki) Comparing Nations and Cultures, 1996, National Character: A Psychosocial Perspective, 1997, One World Emerging? Convergence and Divergence in Industrial Societies, 1998; editor-in-chief Ann. Rev. Sociology, 1971-79; editl. cons. Internat. Rev. Cross Cultural Studies; editl. bd. Ethos, Jour. Soc. Psychol. Anthropology, 1978; editor Founds. Modern Sociology Series; adv. editor in sociology to Little, Brown & Co.; contbr. articles to profl. jours. Recipient Cooley Mead award for Disting. Contbn. in Social Psychology, 1982; fellow Ctr. Advanced Study Behavioral Sci., 1955, Founds. Fund Research Psychiatry, 1957-60, Social Scis. Research Council, 1959, Russell Sage Found., 1966, 85, Fulbright Found., 1977, Guggenheim Found., 1978, Bernard van Leer Jerusalem Found., 1979, Rockefeller Found., 1982, Eisenhower Assn., Taiwan, 1984; NAS Disting. Scholar Exchange, China, 1983; grantee Internat. Rsch. and Exchs. Bd., 1989, NSF, 1989. Fellow AAAS (co-chmn. western ctr. 1984-87, chmn. Talcott Parsons award com. 1988-93), Am. Philos. Soc., APA; mem. NIMH, Nat. Inst. Aging (monitoring com. health retirement survey 1990—), Nat. Acad. Scis. (corr. human rights com. 1986-88, mem. com. on scholarly comms. with People's Republic of China, chmn. panel on social sci. and humanities, NRC panel on issues in democratization 1991-92), Am. Sociol. Soc. (coun. 1961-664, v.p. 1975-76), Ea. Sociol. Soc. (pres. 1961-62), World Assn. Pub. Opinion Rsch., Am. Assn. Pub. Opinion Rsch., Inter-Am. Soc. Psychology, Sociol. Rsch. Assn. (exec. com. 1975-79, pres. 1979), Soc. for Study Social Problems. Home: 1001 Hamilton Ave Palo Alto CA 94301-2215 Office: Stanford U Hoover Instn Stanford CA 94305 Office Phone: 650-723-4856. Business E-Mail: inkeles@hoover.stanford.edu.

INKLEY, JOHN JAMES, JR., lawyer; b. St. Louis, Nov. 7, 1945; s. John James Sr. and Morjorie Jane (Kenna) I.; m. Catherine Ann Mattingly, Apr. 13, 1971; children: Caroline Marie, John James III. BSIE, St. Louis U., 1967, JD, 1970; LLM in Taxation, Washington U., St. Louis, 1976. Bar: Mo. 1970, U.S. Dist. Ct. (we. dist.) Mo. 1970, U.S. Dist. Ct. (ea. dist.) Mo. 1975, U.S. Tax Ct. 1975, U.S. Supreme Ct. 1975. Assoc. Padberg, Raack, McSweeney & Slater, St. Louis, 1970-73; ptnr. Summer, Hanlon, Summer, MacDonald & Nouss, St. Louis, 1973-81; city atty. City of Town and Country, Mo., 1979-84, spl. counsel, 1984-88; ptnr. Hanlon, Nouss, Inkley & Coughlin, St. Louis, 1981-83; ptnr., chmn. banking and real estate dept. Suelthaus & Kaplan, St. Louis, 1983-91; ptnr. Armstrong Teasdale LLP (and predecessor firm), St. Louis, 1991—; co-chmn. bus. svcs. group, 1993-2000; exec. com. St. Louis, 1994—. Mem. ABA, Mo. Bar Assn., Bar Assn. Met. St. Louis. Roman Catholic. Home: 35 Muirfield Ln Saint Louis MO 63141-7382 Office: Armstrong Teasdale LLP 1 Metropolitan Sq Ste 2600 Saint Louis MO 63102-2740

INKLEY, SCOTT RUSSELL, JR., state agency administrator; b. Cleve., Mar. 22, 1952; s. Scott Russell Sr. and Josephine (Newcomer) I.; m. Roxanne Munn, Aug. 21, 1982; children: Scott Russell III, Jonathan Welsh, Katherine Chisholm. Certificat d'assiduete, U. Grenoble, France, 1969; BA, Coll. of Wooster, 1974; cert. completion drug studies inst., Ohio State U., 1975; MA, George Washington U., 1979; postgrad., U. S.C., 1979. Specialist edn. Solon (Ohio) Mental Health Ctr., 1974-76; analyst research S.C. Ho. of Reps., Columbia, 1979-82, analyst research and dir. research, Joint Bond Rev. Com., 1981-91, dir. research Ways and Means Com., 1982-91, dir. Policy Devel. and Evaluation Com., 1992, dep. dir. state budget and control bd., 1992-95; dir. S.C. Bus. Gateway, 1995—97, dir. gen. svcs. divsn., 1997—. Mem. higher edn. funding adv. com., Columbia, 1984-91; advisor State Exec. Mgmt. Tng., Columbia, 1986-91. Lectr., facilitator S.C. Youth Leadership, 1984-91. Named one of Outstanding Young Men Am., 1985. Mem. Nat. Assn. State Budget Officers (exec. com. 1983-91), Fiscal Affairs and Govt. Ops. Assn., So. Legis. Conf., Nat. Conf. State Legislators, Internat. Platform Assn., Order of Palmetto. Home: 1025 Lawhorn Rd Blythewood SC 29016-8982 Office: 1201 Main St Ste 420 Columbia SC 29201-3230 Business E-Mail: sinkley@gs.state.us.gov. E-mail: inkley@infoave.net.

INKSTER, JULI, professional golfer; b. Santa Cruz, Calif., June 24, 1960; m. Brian Inkster, July, 1980; 2 daughters. Student, San Jose State U. Professional golfer LPGA, 1983—. Mem. U.S. Solheim Cup teams, 1992, 98, 2000, 2002, 2003; mem. U.S. World Cup Team, 1980, 82. Named a Collegiate All-American, 1979, 1981—82; recipient Rookie of the Year, Golf Digest, 1983, Espy, Outstanding Woman Golfer, ESPN, 2000. Achievements include winning 30 career LPGA victories including the Du Maurier Classic in 1984, and the Kraft Nabisco Championships in 1984 and 1989; winning the the McDonald's LPGA Championship in 1999 and 2000, and the U.S. Women's Open in 1999 and 2002; won U.S. Women's Amateur Title from 1980-1982. Office: care LPGA 100 International Golf Dr Daytona Beach FL 32124-1082

INLOW, RUSH OSBORNE, chemist; b. Seattle, July 10, 1944; s. Edgar Burke and Marigale (Osborne) I.; m. Gloria Elisa Duran, June 7, 1980. BS, U. Wash., 1966; PhD, Vanderbilt U., 1975. Chemist, sect. chief U.S. Dept. Energy, Argonne, Ill., 1975-78, chief nuclear safeguards br. Cruise missile sys. Ops. Office Albuquerque, 1983-84; program mgr. Navy strategic sys., 1984-85; dir. weapon programs divsn., 1985-88; dir. prodn. ops. divsn., 1988-90; asst. mgr. safeguards and security, 1990-94; asst. mgr. nat. def. programs, 1994-96; dep. mgr., 1996-2000; prin. mem. tech. staff Sandia Nat. Labs., 2000—. Apptd. Fed. Sr. Exec. Svc., 1985. Served with USN, 1966-71. Tenn. Eastman fellow, 1974-75; recipient Pres. Meritorious Exec. awrd The White House, Pres. Clinton, 1994. Mem. Am. Chem. Soc., Sigma Xi. Republican. Episcopalian. E-mail: roinlow@sandia.gov.

INMAN, BILLIE JO (ANDREW), writer, retired English educator; b. May 16, 1929; BA, Midwestern State U., 1950; MA, Tulane U., 1951; PhD, U. Tex., 1961. Prof. English U. Ariz., Tucson, 1962-94, ret., 1994. Home: 5531 E North Wilshire Dr Tucson AZ 85711-4569 E-mail: bjainman@aol.com.

INMAN, BOBBY RAY, retired electronics executive; b. Rhonesboro, Tex., Apr. 4, 1931; s. Herman H. and Mertie F. (Hinson) I.; m. Nancy Carolyn Russo, June 14, 1958; children: Thomas, William. BA, U. Tex., 1950; grad., Nat. War Coll., 1972. Commd. ensign U.S. Navy, 1952, advanced through grades to adm., 1981; asst. naval attache Stockholm, 1965-67; exec. asst., sr. aide to vice chief naval ops. Washington, 1972-73; asst. chief staff intelligence on staff comdr. in chief U.S. Pacific Fleet, 1973-74; dir. Naval intelligence Dept. Navy, Washington, 1974-76; vice dir. Def. Intelligence Agy., 1976-77; dir. Nat. Security Agy., Ft. Meade, Md., 1977-81; dep. dir. CIA, 1981-82; chmn., pres., chief exec. officer Microelectronics and Computer Tech. Corp., Austin, Tex., 1983-86; chmn. bd., chief exec. officer Westmark Systems, Inc., Austin, 1986-89; pvt. investor Austin, 1990—; prof., Lyndon B. Johnson Centennial chair in nat. policy U. Tex. Decorated Def. D.S.M., Navy D.S.M., Legion of Merit, Def. Superior Service medal, Meritorious Service medal, Nat. Security medal, Joint Services Commendation medal. Office: 301 Congress Ave Ste 1350 Austin TX 78701

INMAN, JAMES RUSSELL, claims consultant; b. Tucson, May 24, 1936; s. Claude Colbert and Myra Eugenia (Langdon) Inman; m. Charleen M. Bowman Inman, Feb. 22, 1964 (div. 1977); m. Margaret Williams Kendrick, Apr. 26, 1996 (dec. Feb. 2002). Student, Pomona Coll., Claremont, Calif., 1954-60. Supr. res. dept. Honnold Libr. Claremont Coll., 1959-60; supr. casualty claims CNA Ins., L.A., 1961-70; asst. mgr., asbestos specialist, head entertainment claims Firemen's Fund, L.A., Beverly Hills, 1970—83; pres. Wilnor Corp., L.A., 1982—. Claims auditor dirs. and officers claims Harbor/Continental Ins., L.A., 1984-86; claims mgr. Advent Mgmt., L.A., 1987, Completion Bond Co., Century City, Calif., 1988; asst. to pres., claims specialist Am. Multiline Corp., L.A., 1988-92; sr. claims specialist Reliance Ins. Co., Glendale, Calif., 1992-94; expert witness in entertainment claims field. Mem. First Century Families: Calif.; mem. com. Baldwin Hills Dam Disaster, 1968-72; pres. Alcohol Info. Ctr., L.A., 1983-85; pres.'s exec. coun. Woodbury U. Mem. LA Athletic Club, Wilshire Country Club, Sloane Club (London), Mercedes Benz Club Am., Classic Car Club Am., RROC, Rotary Internat. Avocations: classic cars, American and English silver. Home: 623 S Arden Blvd Los Angeles CA 90005-3814

INMAN, LARRY JOE, basketball coach; b. Summer County, Tenn., Jan. 3, 1948; m. Bobby Gene Follis; children: Jody, Latrice, Tiffany. BS, Austin Peay State U., Clarksville, Tenn., 1970; M, Tenn. State U., 1977. Head coach basketball Gallatin (Tenn.) H.S., 1970-73, Mt. Juliet (Tenn.) H.S., 1973-78; head coach women's basketball Mid. Tenn. State U., Murfreesboro, 1978-86, Ea. Ky. U., Richmond, 1987—. Named Coach of Yr., Ohio Valley Conf., 1979—80, 1982—83, 1984—85, 1990—91, 1994—95, 1996—97, 2001, Man of Yr., 2001; recipient Coach of Yr., Ohio Valley Conf., 2005. Mem.: Womans Basketball Coaches Assn. Office: Eastern Ky U Womens Athletic Dept Lancaster Ave Richmond KY 40475 Business E-Mail: larry.inman@eku.edu.

INMAN, MARIANNE ELIZABETH, academic administrator; b. Berwyn, Ill., Jan. 9, 1943; d. Miles V. and Bessee M. (Hejtmanek), Plzak; m. David P. Inman; Aug 1, 1964. BA, Purdue U., 1964; AM, Ind. U., 1967; PhD, U. Tex., 1978. Dir. Comml. Div. World Instruction and Translation, Inc., Arlington, Va., 1969-71; program staff mem. Ctr. for Applied Linguistics, Arlington, 1972-73; lectr. in French No. Va. Community Coll., Bailey's Crossroads, 1973; faculty mem., linguistic researcher Tehran (Iran) U., 1973-75; intern mgmt. edn. rsch. & devel. S.W Ednl. Devel. Lab., Austin, Tex., 1977-78; asst. prof., program dir. Southwestern U., Georgetown, Tex., 1978; dir. English lang. inst. Alaska Pacific U., Anchorage, 1980-87, chairperson all-U. requirements, 1984-88, assoc. dean acad. affairs, 1988-90; v.p. dean of coll. Northland Coll., Ashland, Wis., 1990-95; pres. Ctrl. Meth. Univ., Fayette, Mo., 1995—. Contbr. Pres. Commn. Foreign Lang. and Internat. Studies, Washington, 1978-79; manuscript evaluator The Modern Lang. Jour., Columbus, Ohio, 1979-84; cons. Anchorage Sch. Dist., 1984-90; cons., evaluator The Higher Learning Commn. of N. Cen. Assn. Colls. and Schs., Chgo., 1990—; mem. dean's task force Coun. on Ind. Colls., 1993-95; pres. Ind. Colls. and Univs. Mo., 1996-00. Co-author: English for Medical Students, 1976; co-author and editor: English for Science and Engineering Students, 1977; contbr. articles to profl. jours. Treas. Alaska Humanities Forum, Anchorage, 1982-87; mem. Anchorage Matanuska-Susitna Borough Pvt. Industry Coun., 1983-86; mem. Sister Cities Commn., Anchorage, 1984-90; mem. Multicultural Edn. Adv. Bd., Anchorage, 1987-90; with speakers bur. Wis. Humanities Com., 1992-95, Mcpl. Libr. Bd., 1993-95; active Mo. Humanities Coun., 1997-03, 04—; bd. dirs. Mo. Colls. Fund, Ind. Colls. and Univs. of Mo., Nat. Assn. of Ind. Colleges and Universities, 2005-; mem. bd. Great Rivers Coun. Boy Scouts Am., 1996—; mem. presdl. adv. com. Mo. Coordinating Bd. for Higher Edn. Named Fellow of Grad. Sch., U. Tex. Austin, 1977-78, Nat. Teaching Fellow, Alaska Pacific U., Anchorage, 1980-81; recipient Pub. Svc. award Sister Cities Commn., Anchorage, 1987, Kellogg Found. Nat. fellowship, Battle Creek, Mich., 1988-91. Mem. LWV, Nat. Assn. Women Edn., Nat. Assn. Ind. Colls. and Univs. (bd. dirs.), Am. Assn. Higher Edn., Am. Coun Tchg. Fgn. Langs., Tchrs. English to Speakers Other Langs., Nat. Coun. Tchrs. English, Nat. Assn. Ind. Colls and Univs. (bd. dirs.), Gold Peppers, Mortar Board, Alpha Chi, Alpha Lambda Delta, Delta Rho Kappa, Kappa Delta Pi (mortar bd.), Omicron Delta Kappa, Phi Kappa Phi, Pi Delta Phi, Pi Lambda Theta, Sigma Delta Pi, Sigma Epsilon Pi, Sigma Kappa. Avocations: community theater, hiking, camping, fishing. Office: Central Methodist Univ 411 Central Methodist Sq Fayette MO 65248-1198 Business E-Mail: minman@centralmethodist.edu.

INMAN, STEPHEN EUGENE, finance officer; b. Lawrence, Kans., Oct. 1, 1943; s. Arthur Eugene and Eunice Margaret (Hults) I.; m. Deborah Renée Southern, Dec. 18, 1987; 1 child, Alexandra Renée. BA in Polit. Sci., U. Del., 1965; MA in Polit. Sci., U. Kans., 1975. Commd. 2d lt. U.S. Army, 1965; advanced through grades to col., 1985; ret., 1992; sr. v.p. bus. ops., CFO, MPRI, Inc., Alexandria, 1992—, CFO Govt. Svcs. Group L-3 Comm., 2005—. Bd. dirs. Helping Angels, Inc. Mem. Assn. U.S. Army, U.S. Army War Coll. Assn. Office: MPRI Inc 1201 E Abingdon Dr Ste 425 Alexandria VA 22314-1493 Office Phone: 703-254-0040. E-mail: steveinman@aol.com.

INMAN, WILLIAM PETER, lawyer; b. Cleve., June 29, 1936; s. James B. and Lillian (Frances) I.; m. Judith A. Clay, Feb. 5, 1994; children: William Peter, Elizabeth, David. Student, Miami U., 1954-55; BA, Ohio State U., 1958; JD, Case Western Res. U., 1960, MBA, 1966. Bar: Ohio 1960, Tex. 1985. Tax accountant U.S. Steel Corp., Cleve., 1960-63; asso. trust counsel Central Nat. Bank of Cleve., 1963-66; atty. Sherwin-Williams Co., Cleve., 1966-67, tax counsel, 1967, mgr. tax dept., 1967-68, corporate dir. taxes, 1968-69, asst. sec., dir. taxes, 1969-71, sec., dir. taxes, 1971-75, v.p., sec., asst. treas., 1975-78, v.p., treas., chief fin. officer, 1978-80; v.p. fin., chief fin. officer RTE Corp., Waukesha, Wis., 1980-83; fin. cons. Houston, 1983-85; corp. sec., gen. counsel Mera Bank, Phoenix, 1985-88; gen. counsel CAD-TEL Sys. Inc., Phoenix, 1988-95, Ariz. Bus. Assocs., L.L.C., Phoenix, 1995—. Mem. Greater Cleve. Growth Assn., 1969-80; Trustee Ohio Pub. Expenditure Council, 1969-80, v.p., 1970-73, pres., 1973-75, chmn. bd., 1975-77. Mem. Am. Soc. Corp. Secs., Fin. Execs. Inst., Cleve. Treasurers Club, N.A.M., Ohio Mfrs. Assn., Am., Ohio, Greater Cleve., Tex., Maricopa County, Ariz. bar assns., Estate Planning Council of Cleve., Tax Execs. Inst., Phi Delta Phi, Beta Gamma Sigma, Beta Alpha Psi. Office: 1600 W Monroe 9th Fl Phoenix AZ 85007 Home: 5702 E Sylvia St Scottsdale AZ 85254-4364

INNES, ROB, product designer; Co-founder Innespace Fiberglass, Shasta Lake, Calif., 1997—. Co-developer (with Thomas "Doc" Rowe) of a new marine leisure craft concept that looks like and simulates the movement of a dolphin ("bionic dolphin-Sweet Virgin Angel"-100 horsepower, prop-driven mammal is piloted from a cockpit encased by an F16 canopy and can be driven at speeds exceeding 50 kmh and made to perform like a dolphin. Completed 2001); famous bionic dolphin appeared in Austin Powers Goldmember; pilots "bionic dolphin" in Auckland Harbor, New Zealand in November, 2004; company Innespace Fiberglass designed Jonah, ocean rescue vessel (TARCO Design), Bionic Shark, electric dry ambient submersible, Submersible Deployment Vehicle, dry diesel/ electric with flooding diver deployment chamber, Boxer, electric wet submersible with box wing configuration, Slicky, ultralight 50 hp gas powered semi submersible, Streaker, dry 5 seater recreational semi submersibleel, Angel Electric, wet dmbient submersible. Office: Innespace Fiberglass 13666 Lake Blvd Shasta Lake CA 96019-8942 Office Phone: 530-275-1134, 530-917-4316. Business E-Mail: innespace@jett.net.*

INNES-BROWN, GEORGETTE MEYER, real estate broker, insurance broker; b. Wilmington, Del., Mar. 20, 1918; d. George and Flora Sue (Saunders) Meyer; m. Andrew T. Innes, Jr., Nov. 26, 1947 (dec.); m. Roy Glen Brown, Jr., Mar. 6, 1991. Grad. Real Estate Law, theory, Conveyancing and Practice, Phila. Bd. Realtors Sch., 1945; grad. Fire, Marine, Casualty Ins., North Phila. Realty Bd. Sch., 1946; cert. appraiser, Villanova Coll., 1974. Lic. realtor, Pa., ins. broker and appraiser, Phila. Ins. broker, realtor, Phila., 1945—; ins. broker, 1946—; also appraiser. Residential and single family home builder, Bucks County, Pa., Princeton, N.J., 1955-61. Mem., spkr. Juniata Pk. Civic Assn., Phila., 1984. Recipient Knights Legion award Italian-Am. Press, 1971. Mem. Nat. Assn. Realtors (sec.-treas. and v.p. chpt. 1975-80), Am. Bus. Women's Assn. (chpt. v.p. 1971, Businesswoman of Yr. 1971), Phila. Women's Realty Assn. (pres. bd. govs. 1949-85, pres. 1949-51, Woman of Yr. 1972-73), Phila. Bd. Realtors (v.p. residential divsn. 1975), North Phila. Realty Bd. (v.p. 1975, 76, pres. 1977, Gustav A. Wick award 1979), Del. Coun. Realty Bds. (sec. 1974), Real Estate Multiple Listing Burs. (treas. 1972-76), Sigma Lambda Soc. (chpt. pres. 1948). Avocations: golf, dance, gardening, cooking, embroidery. Home: 1162 SW Walnut Ter Boca Raton FL 33486-5565

INNIS, PAULINE, writer, publishing company executive; b. Devon, England; came to U.S., 1954; m. Walter Deane Innis, Aug. 1, 1959. Attended, U. Manchester, U. London. Author: Hurricane Fighters, 1962, Ernestine or the Pig in the Potting Shed, 1963 (paperback 1992), The Wild Swans Fly, 1964, The Ice Bird, 1965, Wind of the Pampas, 1967, Fire from the Fountains, 1968, Astronumerology, 1971, Gold in the Blue Ridge, 1973, 2d edit., 1980, reprinted 1995, My Trails (transl. from French), 1975, Prayer and Power in the Capital, 1982, The Secret Gardens of Watergate, 1987, Attention: A Quick Guide to Armed Services, 1988, Desert Storm Dairy, 1991, The Nursing Home Companion, 1993, Bridge Across the Seas, 1995, The Gospel of Joseph, 1998, I've Smashed the Devil's Window, 1999; co-author: Protocol, 1977. Bd. dirs. Washington Goodwill Industries Guild, 1962-66; membership chmn. Welcome to Washington Club, 1961-64; co-chmn. Internat. Workshop Capital Spkr.'s Club, 1961-64; pres. Children's Book Guild, 1967-68; dir. Ednl. Commn., bd. dirs. Internat. Conf. Women Writers and Journalists, Nat. Arboretum, 1992-96; criminal justice com. D.C. Commn. on Status of Women; founder vol. program D.C. Women's Detention Ctr.; chmn. women's com. Washington Opera, 1977-79; mem. Liaison Com. Med. Edn., 1979-85; nat. trustee Med. Coll. Pa., 1980—; mem. Edn. Commn. for Fgn. Med. Grads., 1986-97. Named Hoosier Woman of Yr., 1966. Mem. Soc. Women Geographers, Authors League, Smithsonian Assocs. (women's bd.), English-Speaking Union, Spanish-Portuguese Group D.C. (pres. 1965-66), Br. Inst. U.S., Am. Newspaper Women's Club (pres. 1971-73), Internat. Soc. Poets (disting.), Sulgrave Club, Internat. Clubs (co-chair 1997), Venerable Order St. John Jerusalem (comdr.), Internat. Neighbors Club. Home: 2700 Virginia Ave NW Washington DC 20037-1908

INNIS, ROY EMILE ALFREDO, foundation executive; b. St. Croix, V.I., June 6, 1934; s. Alexander and Georgianna (Thomas) I.; m. Doris Valdena Funnye, Feb. 13, 1965; children: Roy Jr. (dec.), Alexander (dec.), Cedric, Patricia, Corinne, Kwame, Niger, Kimathi Mugabe. Student, CCNY, 1953-58. Chem. technician Vick Chem. Co., 1961-63; research asst. cardiovascular research labs. Montefiore Hosp., 1963-67; mem. CORE, 1963—, edn. chmn. Harlem group, 1964-68, chmn., 1965-68, 2d nat. vice chmn., 1967-68, asso. nat. dir., 1968, nat. dir., 1968-70, nat. chmn., nat. dir., 1970-82, nat. chmn., 1982—; founder and chmn. CORE Cmty. Sch., Bronx, N.Y., 1977. Exec. dir. Harlem Commonwealth Council, 1967-68; 1st ofcl. N.Am. del. Orgn. African Unity, Ethiopia, 1973, Uganda, 1975 Contbr.: chpt. to The Endless Crisis, 1973, Black Economic Development, 1970; pub.: chpt. to Profiles in Black, 1976. Served with AUS, 1950-52. Research fellow Met. Applied Research Center, 1967 Office: 817 Broadway New York NY 10003-4709 Office Phone: 212-598-4000. Personal E-mail: corenyc@aol.com.

INOKUTI, MITIO, physicist, educator; b. Tokyo, July 6, 1933; came to U.S., 1962; s. Haruhisa and Takako (Kure) I.; m. Makiko Omori, Mar. 12, 1960; 1 child, Mika. BS, U. Tokyo, 1956, MS, 1958, PhD, 1962. Instr. U. Tokyo, 1961-64; rsch. assoc. Northwestern U., Evanston, Ill., 1962-63, Argonne Nat. Lab., Ill., 1963-65, physicist, 1965-73, sr. physicist, 1973—. Vis. fellow U. Colo., 1970; vis. prof. U. Tokyo, 1978, Odense U., Denmark, 1980; mem. Internat. Commn. on Radiation Units and Measurements, 1985—. Assoc. editor Jour. Applied Physics, 1996—; contbr. articles to profl. jours. Fellow Am. Phys. Soc., Inst. Physics (London); mem. Radiation Research Soc. (assoc. editor 1975-77, councilor 1978-80), Phys. Soc. Japan. Club: Internat. House of Japan (Tokyo). Avocation: reading. Home: 6481 Blackhawk Trl La Grange IL 60525-4317 Office: Argonne Nat Lab 9700 Cass Ave Lemont IL 60439-4803 Office Phone: 630-252-4186. Business E-Mail: inokuti@anl.gov.

INOS, RITA HOCOG, school system administrator; MA in Sch. Adminstrn. and Supervision, San Jose State U., 1983; EdD in Ednl. Planning, Policy and Adminstrn, USC, 1993. Commr. No. Mariana Islands Pub. Sch. System, Saipan, 2002—. Office: No Mariana Islands Pub Sch System 3rd Fl Retirement Fund Bldg Capitol Hill Saipan MP 96950

INOUE, ATSUSHI, computer science and engineering educator, researcher; s. Keikichi and Ritsuko Aki Inoue; m. York Fang Chou, July 24, 2002; 1 child, Haruka. PhD in Comp. Sci. and Engring., U. Cin., 1999. Software engr. Motorola Inc., Austin, Tex., 1989, E-Volv/Shipjack IC, Cin., 1999; rschr. Hitachi Rsch. Lab, Japan, 1990—96; sr. rschr. Lab Internat. Fuzzy Engring., Yokohama, 1993—95; vis. scholar, grad asst. U. Cin., 1996—99; asst. prof. So. Ill. U., Carbondale, 1999—2001, Eastern Wash. U., Cheney, 2002—. Dir. inland NW security systems initiative Eastern Wash. U., Cheney, 2002—, coord. cyber security; mem. program com. FUZZ-IEEE, 2004—05. Editor: Jour. Advanced Computational Intelligence and Intelligent Informatics, 2004—. Recipient Best Pub. award, Japan Soc. Fuzzy Tech. Mem.: AAAI, N. Am. Fuzzy Info. Processing Soc. (Best Student Paper award 1999). Office: Eastern Wash U CSB 202 Cheney WA 99004

INOUE, MICHAEL SHIGERU, industrial engineer, electrical engineer; b. Tokyo, June 27, 1936; came to U.S., 1956; s. Takajiro and Kazu (Morimoto) I.; m. Mary Louise Shuhart, Sept. 23, 1965; children: Stephen M., Rosanne E., Marcus S., Joanne K., Suzanne T. BSEE magna cum laude, U. Dayton, 1959; MSE, Johns Hopkins U., 1963; MSIE, Oreg. State U., 1964, PhD, 1967. Registered profl. engr., Oreg., Calif.; cert. data processor. Sr. rsch. engr. Black and Decker Mfg. Co., Towson, Md., 1960-62; prof. Oreg. State U., Corvallis, 1966-82; mgr. Kyocera Internat., Inc., San Diego, 1982—84, v.p., 1982—2002, sr. advisor, 2002—. Exec. com. corp. assocs. U. San Diego; adv. bd. Ahlers Ctr for Internat. Bus. Co-author: Introduction to Operation Research & Management Science, 1975, Circulo de Qualidad, 1982, Pacific Saury, 1971. Recipient Grad. Rsch. award IBM, 1965. Mem. Inst. Indsl. Engrs. (Oreg. Indsl. Engr. of Yr. award 1976), Japan Soc. of San Diego and Tijuana (pres. 2001-03, pres. emeritus 2003—). Republican. Roman Catholic. Home: 5154 Via Playa Los Santos San Diego CA 92124-1555 Office: Kyocera International Inc 8611 Balboa Ave San Diego CA 92123-1580 Business E-Mail: mike.inoue@kyocera.com.

INOUYE, DANIEL KEN, senator; b. Honolulu, Sept. 7, 1924; s. Hyotaro and Kame Imananga; m. Margaret Shinobu Awamura, June 12, 1949; 1 child, Daniel Ken. AB, U. Hawaii, 1950; JD, George Washington U., 1952. Bar: Hawaii 1953. Dep. pub. prosecutor, Honolulu, 1953-54; pvt. practice, 1954—; mem. Hawaii Territorial Ho. of Reps., 1954-58, Hawaii Territorial Senate, 1958-59, U.S. House of Reps., 1959—62; senator from Hawaii U.S. Senate (now 106th Congress), 1962—; mem. Senate Armed Svcs. Com., 1963—71; sec. Senate Dem. Conf., 1978-88; chmn. Dem. Steering Com., Senate Appropriations Com., 1971—; chmn. subcom. def., mem. Commerce Com., 1969—77; chmn. Senate Select Com. on Intelligence, 1976—79; ranking mem. subcom. budget authorizations Select Com. on Intelligence, 1979-84; chmn. Select Com. Indian Affairs, 1989—94, vice-chmn., 1990—; mem. Select Com. on Presdl. Campaign Activities, 1973-74; chmn. Sen. select com. Secret Mil. Assistance to Iran and Nicaraguan Opposition, 1987. Ranking minority mem. Appropriations subcom. on Def., Commerce, Sci., & Transp. subcom. on surface transp. & merchant marine; mem. Indian Affairs Com., Rules & Adminstrn. Com. Joint Com. on the Libr. & Congl. Intern Program, Dem. Steering & Coordination Com., Joint Com. on Printing; mem. Senate Watergate Com., 1973-74; sr. counselor Kissinger Commn., 1984; chmn. Senate Dem. Ctrl. Am. Study Group, 1984. Author: Journey to Washington. Active YMCA, Boy Scouts Am. Keynoter; temporary chmn. Dem. Nat. Conv., 1968, rules com. chmn., 1980, co-chmn. conv., 1984. Pvt. to capt. AUS, 1943-47. Decorated Medal of Honor, D.S.C., Bronze Star, Purple Heart with cluster; decorated Grand Cordon of the Order of the Rising Sun, Govt. Japan, 2000; named 1 of 10 Outstanding Young Men of Yr. U.S. Jr. C. of C., 1960; recipient Splendid Am. award Thomas A. Dooley Found., 1967 Golden Plate award Am. Acad. Achievement, 1968, Spirit of Hope award USO, 1999, Advocacy Conf. Congl. award Nat. Breast Cancer Coalition, 2002, Friend of Coast award Am. Coastal Coalition, 2002, Doughboy award U.S. Army, 2002, Sonny Montgomery award Nat. Guard Bur., 2003; Daniel K. Inouye Bldg. of Walter Reed Army Inst. Rsch., Naval Med. Rsch. Ctr., Bethesda, Md. dedicated in his honor, 2001; Hart-Dole-Inouye Fed. Ctr., Battle Creek, Mich. named in his honor, 2003. Mem. DAV (past comdr. Hawaii), Honolulu C. of C., Am. Legion (Nat. Comdr.'s award 1973) Clubs: Lion. (Hawaii), 442d Veterans (Hawaii). Democrat. Methodist. Home: 469 Ena Rd Honolulu HI 96815-1749 Office: US Senate 722 Hart Senate Bldg Washington DC 20510-0001*

INOUYE, WAYNE RYO, computer company executive; b. Yuba City, Calif., Aug. 25, 1952; m. Shannon Inouye; children: Lauren, Josh. Student in Biology, U. Calif., Berkeley, Calif., 1971—72. Founder No. Calif. Mktg., 1978; with Good Guys, 1986—95, head audio merchandising, 1986; mgr. Computer-Retailing Divsn. Best Buy, 1995—2001; pres., CEO eMachines, Inc., Irvine, Calif., 2001—04, Gateway Inc., Poway, Calif., 2004—. Avocations: guitar, golf. Office: Gateway Inc 7565 Irvine Ctr Dr Irvine CA 92618 Office Phone: 800-846-2000.*

INSALACO-DE NIGRIS, ANNA MARIA THERESA, middle school educator; b. N.Y.C., Oct. 18, 1947; d. Salvatore and Rosaria (Colletti) Insalaco; m. Michael Peter De Nigris, July 12, 1969; children: Jenniffer Ann, Tamara Alicia. BA in English and Langs., CCNY, 1969; MA in English Linguistics, George Mason U., 1988; postgrad., U. Va. Cert. endorsement in Adminstrn. and Supervision U. Va., 2002, English secondary tchr. Va. Tchr. Spanish and core subjects St. John's, Rubidoux, Calif., 1969-70; ESL specialist Sunset Hills Elem. Sch., San Diego, 1980; tchr. Sunrise Acres Elem. Sch., Las Vegas, Nev., 1984-85; tchr. 1st grade Talent House Pvt. Elem. Sch., Fairfax, Va., 1987-88; tchr. ESL Hammond Jr. High Sch., Alexandria, Va., 1988-90; tchr. Fairfax County Pub. Mid. Schs., 1995—; summer mid. sch. vol. asst. prin. Longfellow Mid. Sch., 2002. Tchr. adult ESL George Mason H.S., Falls Church, Va., 1988—89; chmn. for multicultural forum Coun. for Applied R&D George Mason U., 1990—94; mem. steering com., faculty adv. com. Herndon Mid. Sch., 1995—, program sponsor Reach for Tomorrow, sch.-based lead mentor, 1998—, mentor tchr. for new tchrs., 1999—; coach for Krasnow Inst. George Mason U., 2000—, mem. curriculum adv. com. for social studies with county; mem. sch. adoption com. Va. Dept. Transp., 1991, human rels. com., 1990—96, ESL Portfolio Assessment com., 1993—98; sch.-based mem. for minority achievement in prin.'s cabinet F.C. Hammond Jr. H.S., Alexandria, 1989—90; mem. Continuing Edn. Bd. Fairfax County, 1998—; co-chair WATESOL Secondary Interest Group, 1998—99, chair, 1999—2001; presenter in field; mem. World English Spkrs. Team, 2002—03. Vol. Family Svcs., Wright Patterson AFB, Ohio, 1971-72, ARC, Ohio and S.C., 1971-73; leader Girl Scouts U.S., 1980-87; Fairfax Edn. Assn. scholarship chairperson. Mem. Va. Edn. Assn. (del. 1990—), Nat. Assn. Bilingual Edn., ESL Multi-Cultural Conv. (presenter, facilitator 1989-2004, socio-polit. concerns immigrant rights advocate 1995—), Tchrs. ESL, Washington Tchrs. ESL, Calif. Tchrs. ESL, Va. Assn. Tchrs. English, Fairfax Edn. Assn. (sch. rep., scholarship chmn., del. Va. Edn. Assn. and NEA), Italian-Am. Caucus (v.p. 1997-2000, pres. 2000—). Roman Catholic. Avocations: writing, reading, politics, helping others. Office Phone: 703-904-4801. E-mail: anamaria1@verizon.net, AnnaMaria.DeNigris@fcps.edu.

INSANA, ARTHUR GERARD, writer, director; s. Arthur Joseph and Adelia Insana. Mng. editor On Location Mag., Hollywood, Calif., 1982—83, Shape Mag., Woodland Hills, Calif., 1986; pres./creative dir. CopyWrite Comm., Northridge, Calif., 1986—; writer/prodr. HilanaVision Prodns., Northridge, 1984—86. Dir.(prodr.): (audiodrama) Star Wars: Dark Empire; prodr.(dir.): (business audio) The Message of the Markets, (spiritual audio) Maximize the Moment, (audiobook) Gump & Co., (audiodrama) A Dragon Lover's Treasury of the Fantastic, (audio documentary) Mysteries of the Unknown: The Powers of Healing, Mysteries of the Unknown: Mystic Places; dir.(prodr.): (audiodrama) Star Wars: Dark Empire II; prodr.(dir.): Star Wars: Dark Lords of the Sith, Johnny Mnemonic, (audiobook) The Celestine Vision, (audiodrama) Star Wars: Dark Empire - The Collectors' Edition, The Midnight Club, (audiobook) Rich Kid, Smart Kid (Audie award, 2002, 2003), (business audio) Jack: Straight from the Gut; contbr. articles to profl. jours. Mem.: Audio Publishers Assn. (assoc.). Personal E-mail: art.insana@verizon.net.

INSANA, RONALD GERARD, newscaster; b. Buffalo, N.Y., Mar. 31, 1961; s. Arthur Joseph and Adelia (Pilato) I. BA, Calif. State U., Northridge, 1984. Prodn. asst. Fin. News Network, L.A., 1984, prodr., 1985, news anchor, 1985—91, mng. editor, 1990—91; news anchor Cable News Bus. Channel-TV, Ft. Lee, NJ, 1991—, news anchor, Street Signs. Regular contbr. NBC's Today, Nightly News with Tom Brokaw, Imus in the Morning, others. Author: Traders' Tales, 1999, The Message of the Markets, 2000, Trend Watching: How to Avoid Wall Street's Next Fads, Manias and Bubbles, 2002; prodr., writer: instrnl. videotape Winning Entrepreneurial Style, 1986, columnist: Money Mag., USA Today, 2003—. Bd. dirs. N.Y.C. chpt. Jr. Achievement, 1994. Named one of top 100 business news journalists of the century, TJFR Group, 1999; recipient Emmy nom. for 9/11 coverage, 2001. Roman Catholic. Home: 26 Stonehurst Dr Tenafly NJ 07670-2915 Office: CNBC-TV 2200 Fletcher Ave Fort Lee NJ 07024-5005

INSCHO, EDWARD WILLIAM, physiology educator; b. Owego, N.Y., July 25, 1954; BA in Biology, Mercyhurst Coll., 1976; MS in Biology and Exptl. Medicine, St. Thomas Rsch. Inst., 1978; PhD in Physiology, U. Cin., 1987. Rsch. asst. Biology and Cancer Rsch. Lab. Mercyhurst Coll., Erie, Pa., 1972-76; grad. rsch. asst. dept. biology St. Thomas Rsch. Inst., Cin., 1976-78; lab. asst. dept. neurophysiology Inst. Devel. Rsch., Cin., 1978-80; grad. rsch. asst. dept. physiology and biophysics U. Cin. Coll. Medicine, 1980-87, lab. instr. dept. physiology, 1983-86, med. tutor dept. physiology, 1984-85; physiology lectr. U. Ala., Birmingham, 1988; rsch. instr. dept. physiology Tulane U. Sch. Medicine, New Orleans, 1989-91, rsch. asst. prof. dept. physiology, 1991-92, asst. prof. dept. physiology, 1992-97, assoc. prof. dept. physiology, 1997—. Reviewer Am. Jour. Physiology: Renal, Heart, Regulatory, Hyptersion, Jour. Clin, Investigation, Mineral and Electrolyte Metabolism, Jour. Hypertension, Jour. Am. soc. Nephrology, Clin. Sci., Kidney Internat., Jour. Cardiovasc. Pharmacology, Circulation Rsch., Brit. Jour. Pharmacology, Pflugers Archives; contbr. articles to profl. jours. Recipient Rsch. fellowship NIH, 1984-87, 87, 88, Univ. Rsch. Coun. Travel award U. Cin., 1984, 85, Eckstein Meml. Fund Travel award, U. Cin., 1984, Amgen Young Investigator award Nat. Kidney Found., 1992, 93, Harry Goldblatt award 1998. Mem. Am. Physiol. Soc. (travel award 1993), Am. Heart Assn. (coun. kidney and cardiovasc. disease, travel award 1989, Established Investigator award 1995—, fellow of coun. high blood pressure rsch. 1996). Office: Med Coll Ga Dept Physiology CL #3140 1120 15th St Augusta GA 30912 Office Phone: 706-721-5615. Business E-Mail: einscho@mail.mcg.edu.

INSCHO, JEAN ANDERSON, retired social worker, landscape artist; b. Camden, NJ, Oct. 31, 1936; d. George Myrick and Alfrida Elizabeth (Anderson) Hewitt; m. James Ronald Inscho, June 4, 1955 (div. Mar. 1982); children: James Ronald Jr., Cynthia Ann, Michael Merrick. BA, Fla. Atlantic U., 1971; MA in Coll. Teaching, Auburn U., 1974, postgrad., 1998-99. Instr. So. Union State Jr. Coll., Wadley, Ala., 1973-75; social worker Jefferson County Dept. Human Resources, Birmingham, Ala., 1976-77, Shelby County Dept. Human Resources, Columbiana, Ala., 1977-78, Houston County Dept. Human Resources, Dothan, Ala., 1978-98. Adj. instr. Troy State U., Dothan,

1984-97. Bd. dir., v.p. Adolescent Resource Ctr., 1992-93, sec., 1993-95; mem. Alzheimer's Assn. EPDA fellow Auburn U., 1973, 74. Mem.: Am. Horticultural Therapy Assn. (Ga.-Ala. chpt.), Wiregrass Master Gardeners (pres. 1994—95), Ala. Master Gardeners Assn. (bd. dir., sec. 2003—, sec. 2003, recipient award 2004, Outstanding Svc. and Dedication award 2004), Dist. 7 State Employees Assn. (polit. action com. rep. 1994—98), Ala. State Employees Assn. (bd. dir.), Am. Daffodil Soc. Episcopalian. Avocations: gardening, needlecrafts, church activities.

INSEL, MICHAEL S., lawyer; b. NYC, Apr. 19, 1947; s. Ralph David and Lillian Ruth (Solomon) I.; married; 1 child, Louis Leo. BA, Duke U., 1969; JD, NYU, 1973. Bar: N.Y. 1974, Fla. 1984. Assoc. Kelley Drye & Warren, N.Y.C., 1973-82, ptnr., 1982—; pres. French Am. Vintners LLC. Bd. dirs. Kobrand Corp., N.Y.C., Maison Louis Jadot, S.A., Beaune, France, L & L, S.A., Boe, France, Western Wine Svcs., Inc., North Bergen, N.J., Taittinger C.C.U.C., Reims, France, Kobrand Found., N.Y.C., The Kopf Family Found., Inc., St. Francis Vineyards, Sonoma, Calif., Domaine Carneros, Napa, Calif.; chmn. Goodwill Industries, Astoria, N.Y.; trustee Elsie del Fierro Charitable Trust, N.Y.C., 1985—, Barbara Bell Cumming Found., N.Y.C., 1991—. Mem.: ABA, Fla. Bar Assn., NY State Bar Assn. Avocations: sailing, golf, opera. Office: Kelley Drye & Warren 101 Park Ave Fl 30 New York NY 10178-0062 Office Phone: 212-808-7933. Business E-Mail: minsel@kelleydrye.com.

INSEL, THOMAS R., federal agency administrator, psychiatrist; BA, Boston U., 1971, MD, 1974. Intern Berkshire Med. Ctr., Pittsfield, Mass.; resident Langley Porter Neuropsychiatric Inst., U. Calif., San Francisco; several sci. rsch. positions Nat. Inst. of Mental Health, 1979—94; prof. psychiatry, dir. Yerkes Regional Primate Rsch. Ctr. Emory U., Atlanta, 1994—2002; dir. Nat. Inst. of Mental Health, 2002—. Fellow: Am. Coll. Neuropsychopharmacology; mem.: Inst. Medicine, 2004, Soc. for Biological Psychiatry (A.E. Bennett award 1986). Office: Nat Inst of Mental Health 6001 Executive Blvd Rm 8235 Bethesda MD 20892

INSINGA, RICHARD CHARLES, manufacturing company executive, marketing educator; b. N.Y.C., Apr. 23, 1949; s. Ralph and Lena (Terrano) I.; m. Judith Joy Schnitman, June 7, 1970; children: Ralph Peter, Marc Charles, Lee James. BS, Columbia U., 1970, MS, 1971; MBA, Stanford U., 1973; D of Profl. Studies, Pace U., 1986; PhD (hon.) Siberian Aerospace Acad., 2001. Econ. analyst EPA, Washington, 1973-74; chief econ. analysis sect. EPA, Washington, 1974-76; sr. cons. Booz, Allen & Hamilton Inc., Florham Park, N.J., 1976-77; dir. technology devel. Avco Corp., Greenwich, Conn., 1977-82; rsch. mktg. mgr. United Technologies Rsch. Ctr., East Hartford, Conn., 1982-86; sr. rsch. planner and divsn. coord., 1986-91; instr. mktg. Pace U., 1982, Post Coll., 1984-91; cons. Insinga Assocs., 1991-; instr. mgmt. Cazenovia Coll., 1991-93; lectr. SUNY, Oneonta, 1993-99, asst. prof. mgmt., 1999-2001, assoc. prof. mgmt., 2001-, coord. bus. econs. program, 2002-. Mem. fin. Ridgefield (Conn.) Rep. Town Com., 1988—, vice chmn., 1980-82; mem. Recreation Commn., Glastonbury, Conn., 1987—; justice of the peace, Ridgefield, 1980-82; coach local little league teams; bd. dirs. Capitol Park Condominium Assn., Washington, 1974-76. Recipient Bronze medal EPA, 1976, Silver medal, 1975, Chancellor's award Pace U., 1986; NSF traineeship, 1970-71. Mem. ASME, Acad. Mgmt. Roman Catholic. Avocations: baseball coach, cub master. Home: 13 Tilton Ave Oneonta NY 13820-2619 Office Phone: 607-436-3709. Business E-Mail: insingrc@oneonta.edu.

INSKEEP, RICHARD GLENN, publishing executive; b. Aug. 25, 1924; BS, Ind. U., 1950. Pub. Fort Wayne (Ind.) Jour. Gazette, 1973-97; pres. Jour. Gazette Co., Fort Wayne, 1973—. Pres. Jour. Gazette Found., 1987—. Recipient Sagamore of Wabash award, 1962, 69, Ind. U. Disting. Alumni award, 1992, Hoosier Press Freedom Found. award 1996; inducted into Ind. Journalism Hall of Fame, 1991, Greater Fort Wayne Bus. Hall of Fame, 1998. Home: 11023 Carnoustie Ln Fort Wayne IN 46814-9320 Office: 701 S Clinton St Fort Wayne IN 46802-1806

INSLEE, JAY R., congressman; b. Seattle, Feb. 9, 1951; s. Frank and Adele Inslee; m. Trudi Anne Inslee, Aug. 27, 1972; children: Jack, Connor, Joe. BA in Econs., U. Wash., 1973; JD magna cum laude, Willamette U., 1976. Atty. Peters, Fowler & Inslee, Selah, Wash., 1976-92; mem. from 14th dist. Wash. State Ho. of Reps., 1988-92; mem. from the 4th Dist. State of Wash. U.S. Congress, 1993-95; atty. Gordon, Thomas, Honeywell, Malanca, Peterson and Daheim, Seattle, 1995-96; regional dir., region 10 U.S. Dept. Health & Human Svcs., Seattle, 1997-98; mem. U.S. Congress from 1st Wash. dist., 1999—; resources com., fin. svcs. com.; banking and fin. svcs. com. U.S. Ho. Reps., 1999—. Charter mem. Hoopaholics, 1988—. Democrat. Office: US Ho Reps 308 Cannon Ho Office Bldg Washington DC 20515-4701*

INSLER, STANLEY, philologist, educator; b. N.Y.C., June 23, 1937; AB, Columbia Coll., 1957; postgrad., U. Tubingen, 1960-62; PhD, Yale U., 1963. Mem. faculty Grad. Sch., Yale U., 1963—, now prof. Sanskrit and comparative philology. Cons. NEH Contbr. numerous articles on ancient langs. and lits. of India and Iran to profl. pubIs; translator Songs of Zarathustra. Recipient fellowships Ford Found., fellowships Woodrow Wilson Found., fellowships Yale U. Mem.: Societe Asiatique, Assn. Française des Sanskritists, Royal Asiatic Soc. Gt. Brit. and Ireland, Philological Soc., Cambridge, Eng., Deutsche Morgenlandische Gesellschaft, Am. Oriental Soc. (pres., fin. dir.), Am. Acad. Arts and Scis. Office: Yale U Dept Linguistics Box 208236 New Haven CT 06520-8236 Office Phone: 203-432-2455. E-mail: insler-stanley@yale.edu.

INSOGNA, ANTHONY M., lawyer; b. Bklyn., Sept. 5, 1967; BS in Organic Chemistry, NYU, 1989, MS in Bio-organic Chemistry, 1990; JD, Fordham Univ., 1994. Admitted to practice: US Patent and Trademark Office 1991, bar: NY 1995, DC 1996. Researcher, chemistry departments Columbia Univ. and NYU; law clk., biotechnology group Pennie & Edmonds LLP; now ptnr.-in-charge San Diego office Jones Day. Mem.: ABA, NY Intellectual Property Law Assn., NY State Bar Assn., Am. Chem. Soc., Sigma Xi. Office: Jones Day Ste 300 12750 High Bluff Dr San Diego CA 92130-2083 Office Phone: 858-314-1130. Office Fax: 858-314-1150. Business E-Mail: aminsogna@jonesday.com.

INSPRUCKER, NANCY RHOADES, career officer; b. Fort Campbell, Ky., June 16, 1959; d. Glen Lee and Mary Josephine Rhoades; m. John L. Inspruker III, July 20, 1991 BS in Aero Engring., U.S. Air Force Acad., 1981; MS in Aero. and Astronaut. Engring., Stanford U., 1985. Commd. 2d lt. U.S. Air Force, 1981, advanced through grades to col., 2003; satellite test engr. space divsn. LA, 1981—84; instr. dept. astronautics USAF Acad., Colorado Springs, Colo., 1985-88; chief payload devel. and integration divsn. Office Sec. Air Force, L.A. AFB, 1988-90, chief mission processing divsn., 1990-92; chief sys. engr. Office Def. Landsat Pentagon, Washington, 1992-94; chief sys. engr. divsn. Office of Space Sys. Office Asst. Sec. Air Force, 1994-95, dir. advanced spacecraft acquisition Office Space & Tech., 1995-97; Gen. Moorman space chair Joint Mil. Intelligence Coll., 1997-99; program mgr. medium launch vehicles Space and Missile Ctr., L.A. AFB, Calif., 1999—2002, dep. dir. launch programs, 2002—. Recipient Medal of Merit, Nat. Air Force Assn., 1985; named Colorado Springs Mil. Woman of Yr., Gazette Telegraph newspaper, 1987. Mem. Air Force Assn., Am. Astronautical Soc., Soc. Women Engrs. Avocations: aerobics, long distance running, reading. Home: 2207B Voorhees Ave Redondo Beach CA 90278-2423 Office: SMC/CL 2420 Vela Way Ste 1467 El Segundo CA 90245-4659 Personal E-mail: inspruck@earthlink.net.

INSULZA, JOSÉ MIGUEL, international organization official, former Chilean government official; b. 1943; m. Georgina Nuñez V.; 3 children. Student, St. George' Coll., U. Chile, Facultad Latinoamericana de Ciencias Sociales, U. Mich. Prof. polit. theory U. Chile, 1973; prof. polit. scis. Pontificia U. Católica de Chile, 1973; pol. adviser Ministry Fgn. Rels., Santiago, Chile, 1973, head multilateral econ. affairs dept., 1990-94, undersec. fgn. affairs, 1994; dir. Diplomatic Acad., 1973; rschr., then dir. Instituto de Estudios de Estados Unidos, Centro de Investigación y Docencia Económicas, Mex., 1981-88; prof. U. Autónoma de Mex., 1990-94; dep. chair Internat. Cooperation Agy., 1990-94; min. sec. of the pres. Govt. of Chile, Santiago, 1994-99, min. interior, 1999-2000, 2000—05; sec. gen. OAS, Washington, 2005—. Mem. Consejo Chileno de Relaciones Internacionales, Consejo de Redacción, Nexos Mag. Office: OAS 17th St & Constitution Ave NW Washington DC 20006

INTEMANN, ROBERT LOUIS, physics professor, researcher; b. North Bergen, N.J., Feb. 23, 1938; s. Joseph Louis and Mildred Henrietta (Wood) I.; m. Marguerite Carmela DiNonno, Aug. 22, 1964; 1 child, Peter Michael. BE, Stevens Inst. Tech., 1959, MS, 1961, PhD, 1964. Asst. prof. physics Temple U., Phila., 1964-73, assoc. prof. physics, 1973-84, prof., 1984—, chmn. dept., 1985-90, asst. dean Coll. Arts and Scis., 1971-81, assoc. dean Coll. Sci. and Tech., 2001—05. Vis. scientist Atomic Energy Research Establishment, Harwell, Eng., 1970. Contbr. articles on rsch in theoretical atomic physics. Mem. AAUP, Am. Phys. Soc., Am. Assn. Physics Tchrs., AAAS, Sigma Xi. Avocations: skiing, tennis, photography, travel. Home: 209 Roberts Ave Glenside PA 19038-4108 Office: Temple U Dept Physics Philadelphia PA 19122

INTILLI, SHARON MARIE, television director, small business owner; b. Amsterdam, N.Y., Aug. 11, 1950; d. Francisco Joseph Intilli and Virginia Eleanor (Tallman) Monaco. Cert., Paralegal Inst., 1973; BA in Psychology, Fordham U., 1995. Group assoc. editor Matthew Bender & Co., N.Y.C., 1974-77; prodn. sec. 20/20 program, ABC, N.Y.C., 1977-78, prodn. assoc., 1979-80, program prodn. asst., 1980-82; legal contract adminstr. ABC Sports, N.Y.C., 1978-79, dir., assoc. dir. for freelance projects, 1984-87; staff assoc. dir. ABC Television Network, N.Y.C., 1982-98; freelance assoc. dir., 1998—. Owner GreenBeing, Inc. Contbg. editor Bender's Forms of Discovery, Vols. 15 & 16, 1975. Active Bd. Health, Hillsdale, N.J., 1989-95. Recipient Outstanding Individual Achievement cert. Nat. Acad. TV Arts & Scis., 1980-81. Mem. Dirs. Guild of Am. Avocations: writing, photography, cooking, baking, singing. E-mail: greenbe@att.net. *I believe that, if we are to "make a difference" in our lives and in the lives of others, it is of utmost importance to push past our fears and insecurities and self-centeredness and envision what speaking up or reaching out might actually accomplish. Then visualize doing nothing and think about what that might mean. Your course will be clear.*

INTRILIGATOR, DEVRIE SHAPIRO, physicist; b. N.Y.C. d. Carl and Lillian Shapiro; m. Michael Intriligator; children: Kenneth, James, William, Robert. BS in Physics, MIT, 1962, MS, 1964; PhD in Planetary and Space Physics, UCLA, 1967. NRC-NASA rsch. assoc. NASA, Ames, Calif., 1967-69; rsch. fellow in physics Calif. Inst. Tech., Pasadena, 1969-72, vis. assoc., 1972-73; asst. prof. U. So. Calif., 1972-80; mem. Space Scis. Ctr., 1978-83; sr. rsch. physicist Carmel Rsch. Ctr., Santa Monica, Calif., 1979—; dir. Space Plasma Lab., 1980—. Cons. NASA, NOAA, Jet Propulsion Lab.; chmn. NAS-NRC com. on solar-terrestrial rsch., 1983-86, exec. com. bd. atmospheric sci. and climate, 1983-86, geophysics study com., 1983-86; U.S. nat. rep. Sci. Com. on Solar-Terrestrial Physics, 1983-86; mem. adv. com. NSF Divsn. Atmospheric Sci. Co-editor: Exploration of the Outer Solar System, 1976; contbr. articles to profl. jours. Recipient 3 Achievement awards NASA, Calif. Resolution of Commendation, 1982. Mem. AAAS, Am. Phys. Soc., Am. Geophys. Union, Cosmos Club. Achievements include being a participant Pioneer 10/11 missions to outer planets; Pioneer Venus Orbiter, Pioneers 6, 7, 8 and 9 heliocentric missions. Home: 140 Foxtail Dr Santa Monica CA 90402-2048 Office: Carmel Rsch Ctr PO Box 1732 Santa Monica CA 90406-1732

INTRILIGATOR, MARC STEVEN, lawyer; b. Oceanside, NY, July 14, 1952; s. Alan and Sally (Jacobs) I.; m. Roxann Kathleen Hoff, Aug. 28, 1977; children: Seth Adam, Joshua Ross, Daniel Benjamin. BA, SUNY, Binghamton, 1974; JD, Boston U., 1977. Bar: N.Y. 1978. Assoc. Dreyer and Traub, N.Y.C., 1977-83, assoc. ptnr., 1984-85, sr. ptnr., 1985-96; of counsel Fischbein Badillo Wagner Harding, N.Y.C., 1996—2005; sr. mem. Cozen O'Connor, N.Y.C., 2005—. Projects editor: Boston U. law rev., 1976-77. Past pres. Croton Jewish Ctr., Highlands Country Club. Mem. ABA, Assn. Bar City N.Y., Hollow Brook Golf Club (founding mem.), Tau Epsilon Phi. Office: Cozen O'Connor 909 3rd Ave New York NY 10022-4731 Office Phone: 212-453-3801.

INTRILIGATOR, MICHAEL DAVID, economist, educator; b. N.Y.C., Feb. 5, 1938; s. Allan and Sally Intriligator; m. Devrie Shapiro; children: Kenneth, James, William, Robert. SB in Econs., MIT, 1959; MA, Yale U., 1960; PhD, MIT, 1963. Asst. prof. econs. UCLA, 1963—66, assoc. prof., 1968—72, prof., 1972—, prof. dept. polit. sci., 1981—, prof. dept. policy studies, 1994—, dir. Ctr. Internat. and Strategic Affairs, 1982—92, 2000—02; dir. Jacob Marschak Interdisciplinary Coll., 1977—; dir. Burkle Ctr. Internat. Rels., 2000—02. Cons. Inst. Def. Analysis, 1974—77, ACDA, 1968, Rand Corp., 1962—65; sr. fellow Milken Inst., 1998—. Author: Mathematical Optimization and Economic Theory, 1971; author: (with Ronald Bodkin and Cheng Hsiao) Econometric Models, Techniques, and Applications, 1996; author: (with others) A Forecasting and Policy Simulation Model of the Health Care Sector, 1979; mem. adv. editl. bd.: Math. Social Scis., 1983—; editor (assoc. editor): Jour. Optimization Theory and Applications, 1979—91, Conflict Mgmt. and Peace Sci., 1980—; co-editor: (series) Handbook sin Economics, 1980—, Advanced Textbooks in Economics, 1972—; editor (with Kenneth J. Arrow): (book) Handbook of Mathematical Economics, 3 vols., 1981—85; editor: (with Zvi Griliches) Handbook of Econometrics, 3 vols., 1983—86; editor: (with B. Brodie and R. Kolkowicz) National Security and International Stability, 1983; editor (with H. A. Jacobsen) East-West Conflict: Elite Perceptions and Political Opinions, 1988; editor: numerous others; contbr. articles to profl. jours. Recipient Disting. Tchg. award, UCLA, 1966, Warren C. Scoville Disting. Tchg. award, 1976, 1979, 1982, 1984; fellow Woodrow Wilson, 1959—60, MIT, 1960—61, Ford, 1967—68. Fellow: AAAS, Econometric Soc.; mem.: Russian Acad. Sci., Coun. Fgn. Rels., Internat. Inst. Strategic Studies. Office: UCLA Dept Econs Los Angeles CA 90095-0001 Office Phone: 310-825-4144. Business E-Mail: intriligator@econ.ucla.edu.

INUI, THOMAS SPENCER, physician, educator; b. Balt., July 10, 1943; s. Frank Kazuo and Beulah Mae (Sheetz) Inui; m. Nancy Stowe, June 14, 1969; 1 child, Tazo Stowe. BA, Haverford Coll., 1965; MD, Johns Hopkins U., 1969, ScM, 1973. Diplomate Am. Bd. Internal Medicine. Intern Johns Hopkins Hosp., Balt., 1969—70, resident in internal medicine, 1970—73; clin. scholar Johns Hopkins U., Balt., 1971—73, chief resident, instr., 1973—74; chief of medicine USPHS Indian Hosp., Albuquerque, 1974—76; chief gen. medicine, dir. health svc. rsch. Seattle VA Med. Ctr., 1976—86; dir. Robert Wood Johnson clin. scholars program U. Wash., Seattle, 1977—92, prof. dept. medicine and health svcs., 1985—92, head div. gen. internal medicine, 1986—92; prof., chmn. of dept. ambulatory care and prevention Harvard Med. Sch. and Harvard Pilgrim Health Care, Boston, 1992—2000; pres., CEO Fetzer Inst., 2000—01, Regenstrief Inst., Indianapolis, 2002—. Scholar-in-residence Assn. Am. Med. Coll., 2002. Contbr. articles to profl. publs. Surgeon USPHS, 1974—76. Fellow: ACP; mem.: APHA (mem. coun. 1988—90), Inst. Medicine, Soc. Tchrs. Family Medicine, Assn. Health Svcs. Rsch., Am. Fedn. Med. Rsch., Soc. Gen. Internal Medicine (pres. 1988—89, mem. coun. 1983—89), Alpha Omega Alpha, Phi Beta Kappa. Office: Regenstrief Institute 1050 Wishard Blvd RG-6 Indianapolis IN 46202 E-mail: tinui@iupui.edu.

INVIOLATA, SISTER MARIA, sister, educator; d. Goro Gregory Honma and Elena Mediavilla Planta. BA, City U., Bellevue, Wash., 2000. Mit Gonzaga U., 2002. Tchr. St. Michael's Acad., Spokane, Wash., 1985—. Tchr. cons. N.W. Inland Writing Project, Spokane, Wash., 1997—. Gen. coun. Congregation of Mary Immaculate Queen, Spokane, Wash., 1998—2004. Mem.: N.W. Inland Writing Project (adv. bd. 1997—). Office: St Michael's Acad 8500 N St Michael Rd Spokane WA 99217 Office Phone: 509-467-0986. Office Fax: 509-462-4326.

INWOOD, DAVID GERALD, psychiatrist; b. Bklyn., Mar. 15, 1946; s. Louis Robert and Evelyn (Glasser) I.; m. Linda Rae Avayou, June 22, 1969; children: Shoshanah, Benjamin, Jonathan. BA, Temple U., 1969; MD, U. Autonoma de Guadalajara, Mexico, 1975. Diplomate Am. Bd. Psychiatry and Neurology, Am. Bd. Child and Adolescent Psychiatry. Resident in psychiatry Downstate Med. Ctr., Bklyn., 1977-79, fellowship in child psychiatry, 1979-81; dir. tng. child and adolescent psychiatry SUNY, Health Sci. Ctr., Bklyn., 1984-92; attending psychiatrist Maimonides Med. Ctr., Bklyn., 1981—; pvt. practice, Bklyn. Clin. assoc. prof. psychiatry NYU Med. Ctr., N.Y.C. Editor: Spectrum Post-Partum Disorders, 1985; contbr. chpts. to books. CEO Parents Assn.ofo Child Sch., 1989-92. Mem. Am. Psychiat. Assn., Am. Acad. Child and Adolescent Psychiatry (coord. Bklyn. br. Disaster-Terrorism Response Unit), N.Y. Coun. Child and Adolescent Psychiatry (pres. 1992-93), N.Y. Postgrad. Psychotherapy Inst. for Child and Adolescent Psychiatrists (treas. 1993-96). Jewish. Office: 95 Pierrepont St Brooklyn NY 11201-2704 Office Phone: 718-625-5362.

INZANO, KAREN LEE, advertising agency executive; b. Cleve., July 27, 1946; d. William and Edith (Fisher) Phipps; children: Thomas, Laura, Sharon. Student, Litschert Sch. of Comml. Art, Cleve., 1970-72. Pres., founder AK Graphics Inc., Lakewood, Colo., 1973—2001; exec. dir. Rocky Mt. Coal Mining Inst., 2000—. Instr. advt. and small bus. Red Rocks C.C., 1983-90, mem. mktg. adv. bd., 1986-88. Chmn. Ch. Adminstrv. Bd., audio, visual adv. bd., 1995-97, Red Rocks, C.C.; active caucus Colo. Rep. Com., 1980, Green Mountain Homeowners, Lakewood, 1980-84; sr. v.p. Lakewood on Parade, 1985-86; bd. dirs. Lakewood Sister Cities Internat., 1980-89, Lakewood Civic Found., 1986-94; vol. Children's Advocacy Ctr., 1994-97vol. tchr. Children's Ct. Sch., Jefferson County; mem. D.A.'s Adv. Bd., 1992-94. Named State Champion of Free Enterprise Salesman With A Purpose, 1985; recipient Disting. Svc. award Sister Cities Internat., 1984. Mem. Jefferson County C. of C. (bd. dirs. 1980-90, chmn. bd. 1988-89, Small Bus. Person of Yr. 1982), Denver Advt. Fedn. Typographers Internat. Assn., Mac Users Group # 2, Edn. 2000 #3, Woman Bus. Owners, Colo. Soc. Assn. Execs., Colo. Mining Assn. Avocations: tennis, travel, golf. Home and Office: 8057 S Yukon Way Littleton CO 80128-5510 Office: 8057 S Yukon Way Littleton CO 80128-5510 Office Phone: 303-948-3300. Business E-Mail: mail@rmcmi.org.

IOFFE, VLADIMIR, radiation oncologist; b. St. Petersburg, Russia, Nov. 6, 1974; s. Anna and Mark Ioffe; m. Kecia Dawn Potter, June 21, 2003; m. Kecia Dawn Potter, May 1, 1993 (div. Jan. 1, 2002); children: Shannon Michaela, Erin Jade Bunker, Carson Michael, Jesse James Bunker. MD, U. Md., 2001, grad. magna cum laude, 1997. Intern U. Md. Hosp., Balt., 2001—02; resident in radiation oncology Ea. Va. Med. Sch., Norfolk, 2002—. Contbr. articles to profl. jours. Vol. Summer Camp, Balt., 1992; vol. dept. anesthesiology U. Md. Med. Ctr., Balt., 1995; pres. St. George's Cancer Soc., Balt., 1998—2001; vol. VNA Hospice, Balt., 1998—2000, Prostate Cancer Screening, Norfolk, Va., 2004—04; student rep. bd. dirs. Balt. City Med. Soc., 1998—2002; student rep. MedChi Membership Com., Balt., 1998—2002; Md. state chair AMA-Med.Student's Sect., Balt., 1999—2000; v.p. students' sect. Md. Med. Soc., Balt., 2000—01. Recipient Scholar Athlete award for acad. excellence, U. Md., 1993-1997, Outstanding Student for dept. biochemistry award, U. Md. Alumni, 1997, Student Internship, Roswell Pk. Cancer Inst., 1998, 2d pl. poster award, Am. Coll. Physicians, 2002; scholarships, Md. State Govt., 1997-2001. Mem.: AMA (assoc. Found. Leadership award 2000), Am. Coll. of Radiation Oncology (assoc.), Am. Soc. of Clin. Oncology (assoc.), Radiologic Soc. of N.Am. (assoc. Rsch. award 2004), Am. Soc. for Therapeutic Radiation Oncology (assoc.). Achievements include Authored resolution on prevention of smoking among young adults (2000); The resolution was passed by the MedChi House of Delegates creating a new state medical policy (1/2001); Wrote an amendment to a State Senate bill and defended the amendment with testimony in the Economic and Environmental Affairs Committee (State Senate) on behalf of MedChi and Smoke-Free MD (3/2001); Provided testimony to the Governor's Taskforce on Smoking Cessation; Lobbied Maryland Congressional Representatives and State General Assembly Representatives to support public health and patient advocacy bills. Office: Eastern Va Med Sch 600 Gresham Dr Norfolk VA 23507 Office Phone: 757-668-2075. Office Fax: 757-627-0334. Personal E-mail: vioff001@yahoo.com.

IOFFREDA, MICHAEL DAVID, dermatologist, educator; b. Fürth, Germany, Mar. 27, 1963; s. Pasqualino F. and Lois J. Ioffreda; m. Suzanne M. Narcum, Feb. 24, 1990; children: Paul E., Patrick M., Daniel P., Dylan L. BS, Haverford (Pa.) Coll., 1985; MD, Jefferson Med. Coll., Phila., 1990. Cert. Am. Bd. Dermatology, dermatopathologist Am. Bd. Dermatology and Pathology. Instr. Hosp. of U. Pa., Phila., 1997—98, asst. prof., 1998—99, Pa. State Coll. Medicine-Hershey Med. Ctr., 1999—2005, assoc. prof., 2005—. Author: (textbooks) Atlas of Lever's Histopathology of the Skin; co-author: Lever's Histopathology of the Skin, Facial Plastic Surgery Clinics of North America, Adhesion Molecules in Allergic Disease, Lever's Histopathology of the Skin; med. illustrations, 5 textbooks. Recipient Trainee Investigator award, Soc. Investigative Dermatology, 1993, Resident Scholar Competition award, Dept. Medicine, 1994; grantee, Dept. Pathology, Hershey Med. Ctr., 2001, NIH, 2002—05. Fellow: Am. Acad. Dermatology; mem.: Phila. Dermatol. Soc., Pa. Regional Assn. Dermatopathologists (pres. 2002—03), Am. Soc. Dermatopathology. Roman Catholic. Achievements include development of hand-held two-photon optical biopsy probe. Avocations: art, cooking, making ice cream, stained glass. Office: Milton S Hershey Med Ctr 500 University Dr Hershey PA 17033

IONA, MARIO, retired physicist; b. Berlin, June 17, 1917; came to U.S., 1941, naturalized, 1948; s. Mario G.V. and Dorothee (Berendes) I.; m. Nancy Mossman, Aug. 31, 1949; children: Steven, Ann. PhD, U. Vienna, Austria, 1939; postgrad., U. Uppsala, Sweden, 1939-41. Research asst., instr. U. Chgo., 1941-46; from asst. prof. to prof. physics U. Denver, 1946-85, prof. emeritus, 1985—; coord. High Altitude Labs., Mt. Evans and Echo Lake, Colo., 1946-82; cons. pvt. practice Denver, 1985—. Cons. Denver Schs., 1962-65, 84, Jefferson County Schs., Golden, Colo., 1973, Adams County Sch. Dist. 12, Northglenn, Colo., 1985, Internat. Orgn. for Standardization, tech. adv. group TC 12, 1990—; vis. prof. U. No. Colo., 1971; specialist U. Saugar, India, 1966; cons. in field. Assoc. editor: Physics Tchr., 1962-65, column editor, 1970-2000. Treas., sec., pres. Group Health Assn., Denver, 1952-66. Fellow AAAS; mem. Am. Phys. Soc., Am. Assn. Physics Tchrs. (chmn. com. on SI units and metric edn. 1987-91, Disting. Svc. citation 1971, Millikan Lecture award 1986), Colo.-Wyo. Acad. Sci. (pres. 1974-75), Nat. Sci. Tchrs. Assn., AAUP. Home: 2333 S Columbine St Denver CO 80210-5421 Office: U Denver Dept Physics & Astronomy Denver CO 80208-2238

IONESCU TULCEA, CASSIUS, research mathematician, educator; b. Bucharest, Rumania, Oct. 14, 1923; naturalized, 1967; s. Ioan and Ana (Caselli) Ionescu Tulcea. MS, U. Bucarest, 1946; PhD, Yale, 1959. Mem. faculty U. Bucarest, 1946-57, assoc. prof., 1952-57; research assoc. Yale U., 1957-59, vis. lectr., 1959-61; assoc. prof. U. Pa., 1961-64; prof. U. Ill., Urbana, 1964-66, Northwestern U., Evanston, Ill., 1966-90, prof. emeritus, 1990—. Author: Hilbert Spaces (in Rumanian), 1956, A Book on Casino Craps, 1980, A Book on Casino Blackjack, 1982; co-author: Probability Calculus (in Rumanian), 1956, Calculus, 1968, An Introduction to Calculus, 1969, Honors Calculus, 1970, Topics in the Theory of Liftings, 1969, Sets, 1971, Topology, 1971, A Book on Casino Gambling, 1976; contbr. articles to profl. jours. Recipient Asachi prize Rumanian Acad., 1957. Office: Northwestern U 2033 Sheridan Rd Evanston IL 60208-0830

IORIO, PAM, county official; b. Waterville, Maine, Apr. 27, 1959; d. John J. and Dorothy (Lockett) I.; m. Mark S. Woodard, May 30, 1987; children: Caitlin, Graham. BS in Polit. Sci., The Am. U., 1981; MA in History, U. South Fla., 2001. County commr. Hillsborough County, Tampa, Fla., 1985—92, supr. elections, 1993—2003; mayor Tampa, 2003—. Recipient Disting. Alumnus award, Leadership Fla., 2002. Mem.: Fla. State Assn. Suprs. Elections (pres. 2000). Office: City of Tampa Mayor's Office 306 East Jackson St Tampa FL 33602

IOVEL, ALLA, music educator, writer; arrived in U.S., 1999; d. Michael Shteinberg and Klara Gerlorina; m. Lev Iovel, Dec. 30, 1969; 1 child, Aleksandr. MusB in music theory, Music Coll., Leningrad, Russia, 1969; M in Music Edn., Leningrad State Conservatory, Russia, 1975. Cert. music edn. Pedagogical Inst., Ukraine, 1970. Tchr. piano Bloomfield (N.J.) Coll., 2000—04; pvt. piano tchr., 2005—. Pvt. piano tchr., 2005—, 2005—. Author: (textbook) Instrnl. Points and Methods on Theory of Harmony for Musical Educators, 1993, Lugansk State Coll. of Music, 1999; contbr. chapters to books, articles to profl. jours. Named to Golden Cir. of Tchrs., A.G. De Grado Found., 2001, 2002. Mem.: Music Tchrs. Nat. Assn., Piano Tchr. Soc. of Am. (High Honor Tchrs. award 2001, 2002), The Leschetizky Assn. Achievements include research in technical analysis of musical styles. Avocation: gardening. Home: 4 Lyons Place East Hanover NJ 07936 E-mail: laiovel@yahoo.com.

IOVINE, JIMMY, recording industry executive; b. Bklyn., Mar. 11, 1953; s. Jimmy Iovine Sr.; m. Vicki Iovine. Former engr. The Record Plant, NYC, 1973; ind. prodr., co-head Interscope Records, 1991—. Prodr.: (albums) Patti Smith's Easter, Tom Petty's Damn the Torpedoes, 1979, Tom Petty's Hard Promises, 1981, Tom Petty's Long After Dark, 1982, Stevie Nicks' Bella Donna, 1981, Stevie Nicks' The Wild Heart, 1983, Stevie Nicks' Rock A Little, 1985, Pretenders' Get Close, 1986, U2's Rattle & Hum, 1989. Office: c/o Interscope Comm 10900 Wilshire Blvd Ste 1230 Los Angeles CA 90024-6532*

IOVINO, PAMELA M., federal agency administrator; B in Polit. Sci., Gettysburg Coll. Advanced through grades to capt. USN, 1980—2003, manpower tng. officer Naval Reserve Readiness Command Region Six, 1987, commdg. officer Naval and Marine Corps Reserve Ctr., head legis. liaison br., commdr. Naval and Marine Corps Reserve centers Pitts., Ebensburg, Pa., Moundsville, W.Va., 1998—2001; ret., 2003; acting asst. sec. congl. & legis. affairs US Dept. Veterans Affairs, Washington, 2004, asst. sec. congl. & legis. affairs, 2004—. Decorated Legion of Merit Medal, Meritorious Svc. Medal (two gold stars), Navy Commendation Medal, Navy Achievement Medal, Nat. Def. Medal (two awards), Armed Forces Reserve Medal. Office: US Dept Veterans Affairs 810 Vermont Ave NW Rm 500 Washington DC 20420 Office Phone: 202-273-5611. Office Fax: 202-273-6792.*

IPPEN, ERICH PETER, electrical engineer, educator, physicist; b. Fountain Hill, Pa., Mar. 29, 1940; s. Arthur Thomas and Elisabeth Anne (Wagenplatz) I.; m. Dorothea Ellen Swansen, Sept. 24, 1966; children: Erich Peter, Jason Timothy. S.B., MIT, 1962; MS, U. Calif.-Berkeley, 1965, PhD, 1968. Mem. tech. staff Bell Labs., Holmdel, N.J., 1968-80; vis. prof. MIT, Cambridge, 1977-78, prof. elec. engring., 1980—, Elihu Thomson prof. elec. engring., 1987—, prof. physics, 1996—. Cons. Bell Labs., 1981-2000, Allied Corp., Mt. Bethel, N.J., 1982-90, MIT Lincoln Lab., 1999—. Contbr. articles to profl. jours.; patentee in field. Recipient Edward Longstreth medal Franklin Inst., 1982, Harold E. Edgerton award Soc. Photo-Optical Instrumentation Engrs., 1989, John Scott award City of Phila., 1991, Disting. Engring. Alumnus award U. Calif., Berkeley, 2000, MIT Killian award, 2001. Fellow Am. Acad. Arts and Scis., Optical Soc. Am. (former pres., R.W. Wood prize 1981, C.H. Townes award 2004), IEEE (Morris E. Leeds award 1983, Quantum Elecs. award 1997), Am. Phys. Soc. (Arthur L. Schawlow prize 1997); mem. NAS, NAE, Sigma Xi. Home: 156 School St Belmont MA 02478-3516 Office: MIT 77 Massachusetts Ave Cambridge MA 02139-4307 Office Phone: 617-253-8504. Business E-Mail: ippen@mit.edu.

IPPOLITO, MARIA F., psychologist, educator; b. Chgo., June 29, 1950; d. Robert Phillip and Florence Marie Ippolito; m. James Zarembski, Apr. 1993 (div. 1994). BA in English Lit., Knox Coll., 1972; postgrad., Northwestern U., 1985—88; MA in Psychology, Bowling Green State U., 1993, PhD in Psychology, 1998. Vis. prof. Bowling Green (Ohio) State U., 1999—2000; asst. prof. U. Alaska, Anchorage, 2000—04, assoc. prof., 2005—. Presenter in field. Contbr. articles to profl. jours. and books. Bd. dirs. Child Care Connection, Inc., Anchorage, 2000—, sec. bd. dirs., 2001—05; bd. dirs. 21st Century Early Learning Ctrs., 2003—, sec., 2005—; bd. dirs. Tanaina Child Devel. Ctr., 2004—. Recipient Selkregg Cmty. Svc. and Learning award, U. Alaska, 2005. Mem.: APA (divsn. 2 tchg. of psychology, divsn. 10 psychology and the arts), Nat. Assn. for the Edn. Young Children, Soc. for the Social Studies of Sci., Soc. for Lit. and Sci., Internat. Soc. for the History of Behavioral and Social Scis., Am. Psychol. Soc. Office: Univ Alaska Anchorage 3211 Providence Dr Anchorage AK 99508 Business E-Mail: afmfi@uaa.alaska.edu.

IPSEN, CAROL ANNE, psychiatrist, educator; b. Schenectady, N.Y., Jan. 9, 1951; d. Peter Grover and Joan Stevens (Wilson) I.; m. James Donald Alpert, Aug. 14, 1976; 1 child, Kathryn Ipsen Alpert. BS, U. Mich., 1972; MD, U. Rochester, N.Y., 1978. Diplomate Am. Bd. Psychiatry and Neurology. Intern U. Colo. Med. Ctr., Denver, 1978-79, resident in psychiatry, 1979-82; staff psychiatrist Ft. Logan Mental Health Ctr., Denver, 1982-84; pvt. practice, Denver, 1982-85, Albany, N.Y., 1985—; clin. asst. prof. Albany Med. Coll., 1986—. Mem. Am. Psychiat. Assn. (ethics com. Albany chpt. 1988—). Office: 1240 New Scotland Rd # 204 Slingerlands NY 12159 Office Phone: 518-439-5624.

IPSEN, GRANT RUEL, state legislator, insurance and investments professional; b. Malad, Idaho, Nov. 6, 1932; s. Nephi Ruel and Ada (Hughes) I.; m. Edna Wayne Hughes, July 27, 1956; children: Edna Gaye, LeAnn, Garin Grant, Shawna Lee, Wayne Ruel. BA, Brigham Young U., 1961. CPA, CLU, ChFC. Acct. Ernst & Ernst, Boise, Idaho, 1961-64; sales dept. Mut. of N.Y., Boise, 1964—93; mem. Idaho Senate, Dist. 17, Boise, 1992—2002; ret. Mut. of N.Y. Active Boy Scouts Am., 1945—; co-convener Boise Religious Freedom Com., 1991-94. With U.S. Army, 1956-58. Named Agt. of Yr., Boise Assn. Life Underwriters, 1978, Man of Yr., Mut. of N.Y., 1982. Mem. Million Dollar Round Table (life), Brigham Young Univ. Alumni (bd. dirs. 1987-93). Republican. Mem. Lds Ch. Avocations: reading, outdoor recreation, hiking, travel.

IPYANA, AMINATA FULANI N., law educator; b. Groton, Mass., Feb. 14, 1962; d. James H. and Justine R. Greene. BA, Howard U. Coll. of Liberal Arts, 1980—84; JD, Wash. U. Sch. of Law, 1986—89. Bar: D.C. 1991. Rsch. asst. Wash. U. Sch. of Law, 1987—87; staff atty. Pub. Defender Svc., Washington, 1989—2001; assoc. prof. of law Howard U. Sch. of Law, 2001—. Bd. mem. D.C. Law Students In Ct., 2001—; chair, edn. com. Bd. of Directors, D.C. Law Students In Ct., 2002—; sect. co-chair Assn. of Am. Law Schools - Clinicians of Color, Washington, 2004—. Mem.: D.C. Bar Assn. (sect. ct., lawyers &adminstrn. justice, criminal law and indiv. right), Clin. Sect. - Assn. of Am. Law Schools, Clin. Legal Edn. Assn. (sect. bar admission, legal edn.), ABA. Office: Howard University School of Law 2900 Van Ness St NW Washington DC 20008 E-mail: aipyana@law.howard.edu.

IQBAL, JAHANGIR, molecular biologist, cell biologist; b. Baramulla, India, Apr. 1, 1971; s. Ghulam Hassan Zargar and Hafeeza Begum; m. Nahida Wani, Sept. 20, 2001; 1 child, Zainab Jahangir. PhD, AM U., Aligarh, India, 2000. Gate U. Grants Commn., New Delhi, 1996. Rsch. scientist SUNY Downstate Med. Ctr., Bklyn., 2000—03, rsch. instr., 2003—. Cons. Chylos, Inc., Bklyn., 2002—. Fellow Postdoctoral Rsch. Fellowship Supplement, SUNY Downstate Med. Ctr., 2004-2005. Mem.: Lipid and Vascular Biology Club (assoc.). Achievements include patents for Devel.of MTP assay Kit. Office: SUNY Downstate Med Ctr 450 Clarkson Ave Brooklyn NY 11203 Office Phone: 718-270-1443. Personal E-mail: jiqbal30@hotmail.com.

IQBAL, ZAFAR, neuroscientist, biochemist, educator; b. Lucknow, India, July 12, 1946; came to U.S., 1972, naturalized, 1979; s. Shujaat Ali and Saleha (Begum) Siddiqui. Cert. proficiency in French, Lucknow U., 1965; PhD, All India Inst. Med. Scis., New Delhi, 1971. Jr. research fellow Council Sci. and Indsl. Research, India, 1963-66, research fellow, 1967-68; research scholar Directorate Gen. Health Services, India, 1966-67; asst. research officer Indian Council Med. Research, 1968-71; research assoc. in physiology, investigator Ind. U. Sch. Medicine, Indpls., 1972-82, asst. prof. med. biophysics, 1977-82, asst. prof. biochemistry, 1979-82; asst. prof. neurology and neurosci. Northwestern U. Sch. Medicine, Chgo., 1982-85; assoc. prof. pharmacology Chgo. Med. Sch., 1985-88; assoc. prof. neurology Northwestern U. Inst. for Neuroscience, Chgo., 1989-95; adj. prof. neurology and neurosci. Northwestern U. Med. Sch., 1995—; mem. Northwestern U. Ctr. Devel. Biology, Chgo., 1989—; health sci. specialist VA Cen. Office Med. Rsch. Svc., Washington, 1995—. Contbg. author: Macromolecules in Storage and Transfer of Biological Information, 1969, Macromolecules and Behavior, 1972, Growth and Development of the Brain, 1975, Mechanism, Regulation and Special Function of Protein Synthesis in the Brain, 1977, Peripheral Neuropathies, 1978, Neurochemistry and Clinical Neurology, 1980, Calcium-Binding Proteins, 1980, Axoplasmic Transport, 1981, Calcium and Cell Function, 1982; editor: Axoplasmic Transport, 1986, Recent Progress in Polyamine Research, 1986, The Physiology of Polyamines, 1987; mem. editorial bd. Neurochem. Rsch.; contbr. articles to profl. jours. Bd. dirs. India Cultural Coord. Cmty. Rsch. grantee NIH, 1973-77, Muscular Dystrophy Assn. Am., 1975-77, 94-97, Am. Cancer Soc., 1979-80, NSF, 1981, 84, Juvenile Diabetes Found., 1981, Am. Diabetes Assn., 1980; recipient internat. travel award NSF, 1984, Fidia Rsch. Found. award, 1987, UN Devel. Program Internat. Expert award, 1987, 93, award Am. Soc. for Biochemistry and Molecular Biology, 1994. Mem. AAAS, Am. Physiol. Soc., Indian Acad. Neuroscis., Soc. Biol. Chemists (India), Internat. Brain Rsch. Orgn., Internat. Soc. Neurochemistry (award 1994), Soc. Neurosci., Am. Soc. Neurochemistry, Ind. Acad. Sci. (chmn. cell biology 1982-83), N.Y. Acad. Scis., Biophys. Soc., Soc. Exptl. Biology and Medicine, Assn. Scientists of Indian Origin Am. (counselor 1986—), Ameer Khusro Soc. Am. (v.p.), Lucknow U. Alumni Assn., Lucknow Rschrs. Assn. in Am., All-Indian Inst. of Med. Scis. Assn., Assn. of Communal Harmony in Asia, Orgn. of Univ. Communal Harmony. Home: 19105 Warrior Brook Dr Germantown MD 20874 Personal E-mail: raabta_india@yahoo.com. Business E-Mail: zgbzaf@mail.lm.gov.

IQBAL, ZAFAR MOHD, biochemist, molecular biologist, toxicologist, consultant, cancer researcher, pharmacologist; b. Hyderabad, India, Dec. 12, 1938; came to U.S., 1965, naturalized, 1973; s. M.A. and Haleemunissa (Begum) Rahim. BSc, Osmania U., 1958, MSc, 1962; PhD, U. Md., 1970. Diplomate Am. Bd. Forensic Medicine, Am. Bd. Forensic Examiners. Fellow in molecular pharmacology Nat. Cancer Inst./NIH, Bethesda, Md., 1971-74; asst. prof. pharmacology Case Western Res. U., Cleve., 1974-76; assoc. dir. ERC programs in occupational toxicology U. Ill. Med. Ctr., Chgo., 1980-81, assoc. prof. microbiology, 1977-80, assoc. prof. occupational medicine and environ. health, 1976-93, assoc. prof. preventive medicine, 1982-93; faculty grad. coll. U. Ill., Chgo., 1977-93, dir. Carcinogenesis Labs., 1983-93, chair recombinant DNA instnl. com., 1982-93; chair HIV hazards in rsch. com. U. Ill. Grad. Coll. Faculty, Chgo., 1976-93; dir. Toxicology-Cancer, Chgo., 1987—; affiliate Lurie Cancer Ctr. Northwestern U., Chgo., 1996—. Cons. in field to OSHA, 1980-81, Clements Assocs., 1976-79, Expert Resources, 1982—, Ill. Cancer Coun., 1981-82, Toxicology Cancer, 1987—; lectr. continuing edn.; grant reviewer study sects. NIH; program project reviewer Nat. Cancer Inst., 2000; merit grant reviewer VA, 1981-82; mem. tech. bd. panel Gt. Lakes Protection Fund, 1989—; participant profl. confs.; NSF-Coun. Sci. and Indsl. Rsch. exch. scientist, 1981; sponsor, trainer India-U.S. exch. scientists NSF, 1985-86; peer reviewer: (jours.) Sci., Cancer Rsch., Jour. Biochem., Toxicology, Carcinogenesis, others, also books and films; spl. advisor RRL (India) Dirs., 1980-86; mem. U.S. AID's-Asia Environ. Partnership and Environ Tech. Network Asia, 1994—, Environ. and Tech. Network Asia-Latin Am. Program, 1996—; chair recombinant DNA com. U. Ill., Chgo., 1983-93; contbr. WHO Internat. Agy. for Rsch. Cancer, Tallinn, 1975, Budapest, 1979, Tokyo, 1981, Banff, 1983; mem. exec. bd. sci. and tech. advs. Am. Bd. Forensic Exams., 1997—. Author, editor: Molecular Mechanisms of Toxic Response; Pancreatic Carcinogenesis Mechanisms; editor Jour. Molecular Toxicology and Carcinogenesis; mem. editorial adv. bd. Forensic Examiner, 1995—; exec. bd. sci. and tech. advisors Am. Bd. Forensic Examiners, 1996—; contbr. more than 60 articles to profl. jours. NSF-CSIR exch. scientist, 1981; sponsor, trainer India-U.S. Exch. Scientists, NSF, 1985-86; spl. advisor RRL (India) Dirs., 1980—; pres. Rahim Meml. Found., 1995—. Fellow Coun. Sci. and Indsl. Rsch., India, 1963-65; Fogarty Internat. fellow Nat. Cancer Inst., NIH, 1970-71, staff fellow, 1971-74; grantee Nat. Cancer Inst./NIH, Nat. Inst. Occupational Safety and Health, EPA, State of Ill., 1974-93. Fellow Am. Coll. Forensic Examiners (life, diplomate, bd. cert. forensic medicine, editl. bd. advisors 1995—); mem. AAAS, Am. Assn. Cancer Rsch., Am. Pancreatic Assn., N.Y. Acad. Scis., Am. Chem. Soc., Soc. Toxicology, Am. Coll. Toxicology, Nat. Registry of Forensic Examiners, B.E.S.T. N.Am., Registry Global World Leaders, Soc. Toxicology (molecular biology, carcinogenesis and mechanism splty. sects.), NIHAA, Sigma Xi. Office: Toxicology-Cancer PO Box 60267 Chicago IL 60660-0267 E-mail: toxicancer@yahoo.com.

IRANI, RAY R., oil, gas and chemical company executive; b. Beirut, Jan. 15, 1935; came to U.S., 1953, naturalized, 1956; s. Rida and Naz I.; children: Glenn R., Lillian M., Martin R. BS in Chemistry, Am. U. Beirut, 1953; PhD in Phys. Chemistry, U. So. Calif., 1957. Rsch. scientist, then sr. rsch. scientist Monsanto Co., 1957-67; assoc. dir. new products, then dir. research Diamond Shamrock Corp., 1967-73; with Olin Corp., 1973-83, pres. chems. group, 1978-80, corp. pres., dir. Stamford, Conn., 1980-83, COO, 1981-83; chmn. Occidental Petroleum Corp. subs. Occidental Chem. Corp., Dallas, 1983-94; CEO Occidental Petroleum Corp., subs. Occidental Chem. Corp., Dallas, 1983-91; chmn. Can. Occidental Petroleum Corp. Ltd., Calgary, 1987-99; exec. v.p. Occidental Petroleum Corp., L.A., 1983-84, pres., COO, 1984-91, pres., 1991—96, chmn., CEO, 1991—, also bd. dirs., pres., 2005—. Bd. dirs. Am. Petroleum Inst., Oxy Oil and Gas USA Inc., Occidental Oil and Gas Corp., Occidental Petroleum Investment Corp., Cedars Bank, Kaufman and Broad Home Corp., Jonsson Cancer Ctr. Found./UCLA. Author: Particle Size; also author papers in field; numerous patents in field. Vice chmn. Am. U. Beirut; trustee U. So. Calif., St. John's Hosp. and Health Ctr. Found., Natural History Mus. Los Angeles County; bd. govs. Los Angeles Town Hall, Los Angeles World Affairs Coun. Mem. Nat. Petroleum Coun., Am. Inst. Chemists, Am. Chem. Soc., Sci. Rsch. Soc. Am., Indsl. Rsch. Inst., The Conf. Bd., The CEO Roundtable, Nat. Assn. Mfrs. (bd. dirs.), Am. Petroleum Inst. (bd. dirs.), U.S.-Russia Bus. Coun. Office: Occidental Petroleum 10889 Wilshire Blvd Los Angeles CA 90024-4201*

IRANI, RAYMOND REZA, manufacturing executive; b. Hamadan, Iran, Apr. 27, 1928; came to U.S., 1956, naturalized, 1959; s. Mohammad Taghi and Saheb Sultan I.; m. Nayer Ghadessi, oct. 19, 1962; children: Sheila, Glen. BS in Aviation, Air Acad., Tehran, 1952; grad. in aerotech., Northrop U., 1958; BSEE, Calif. State U., 1965. Engr. Am. Electronics, L.A., 1959-61; chief engr. IMC Magnetics, Maywood, Calif., 1961-69; co-founder, v.p. Computer Devices, Santa Fe Springs, Calif., 1969-77; pres. Rapidsyn Co. div. Dana Corp., Santa Fe Springs, 1977-79. Founder, chmn. Digilog Devices Inc., Los Angeles, 1979; pres., dir. Shinano Kenshi Corp., Culver City, Calif., 1982-2004., mgmt. cons., 2004-; pres. Astrosyn America Inc., Chatsworth Chlif. Editor tech. papers, 1975; patentee. Capt. Iranian Air Force, 1948-56. Iranian Air Force grantee. Business E-Mail: rayirani@sbcglobal.net.

IRBE, ARTURS, professional hockey player; b. Riga, Latvia, Feb. 2, 1967; Goaltender Sharks, 1991-96, Stars, 1996-97, Canucks, 1997-98, Carolina Hurricanes, 1998—2004, Columbus Blue Jackets, 2004—. Goaltender Latvia Nat. Team, World Championships, 1996—2002. Named to NHL All-Star Game, 1994, 1999. Office: Carolina Hurricanes 1400 Edwards Mill Rd Raleigh NC 27607-3624

IREDALE, NANCY L., lawyer; BSFS summa cum laude, Georgetown U., 1969; JD, Yale U., 1972. Bar: D.C. 1973, Calif. 1977. Tax counsel to Senator William Brock Senate Finance Committee, 1976; ptnr. Paul Hastings, Janofsky & Walker, L.A., chmn. cmty. & bar com. Named one of top 100 L.A. County Super Lawyers, Law & Politics Media, 2004, Top 50 Female Super Lawyers, 2005, Super Lawyers/2004, Tax, L.A. Mag. Fellow: Am. Coll. Tax Counsel; mem. Yale Law Sch. Assn. (exec. com. 1982-85), Phi Beta Kappa, Phi Beta Kappa Alumni (councilor alpha assoc.). Achievements include graduating first in class from Sch. Fgn. Svc., Georgetown U; elected first woman pres. 100-years Jonathan Club. Office: Paul Hastings Janofsky & Walker LLP 515 S Flower St Fl 25 Los Angeles CA 90071-2228 Office Phone: 213-683-6232. Office Fax: 213-627-0705. Business E-Mail: nancyiredale@paulhastings.com.

IRELAN, ROBERT WITHERS, retired metal products executive; b. Takoma Park, Md., Mar. 10, 1937; s. Charles Morris and Julia Mae (McKenzie) I.; m. Barbara Lucille Mitchell, Mar. 21, 1959; children: Robert Withers Jr., Jonathan M. BS, U. Md., 1960. Copy reader, copy editor Wall St. Jour., Washington, 1960—66; assoc. editor Nation's Bus. Mag., Washington, 1966—68; rep. pub. rels. Kaiser Industries Corp., Oakland, Calif., 1968—70; exec. asst. to chmn. Kaiser Affiliated Cos., Oakland, 1970—79; mgr. corp. rels. Kaiser Aluminum & Chem. Corp., Oakland, 1979—82, regional v.p. pub. affairs midwest Ravenswood, W.Va., 1982—85, corp. v.p. pub. rels. Oakland, 1985—97, Maxxam Inc., Houston, 1990—99; ret., 1999. Vis. lectr. dept. comm. U. of the Pacific, Stockton, Calif., 2001-02; instr. U. Calif., Davis Ext., 2003—. Co-author, co-editor: Lessons of Leadership, 1967. Mem. U. Md. Alumni Assn., Rancho Murieta Country Club. Democrat. Lutheran. Avocations: golf, travel, theater, sports, reading. Home: 6798 Terreno Dr Rancho Murieta CA 95683 Personal E-mail: golfbob@calweb.com.

IRELAND, BETTY, state official; b. Charleston, W. Va. m. Sam Haddad; children: Chuck, Andy, Alex, Janie. Former teacher W. Va. Pub. Sch. Sys.; former mover Retirement Sys. & Svc.; former v.p. & head pension div. Trust Dept. Nat. Bank of Commerce, Charleston; pres. & CEO Jackson & Kelly Solutions LLC, 2002—; sec. state State of W. Va., Charleston, 2005—. Mem. City of Charleston Bd. of Zoning Appeals, W.Va., 1985—86; rep.-at-large Charleston City Coun., W.Va., 1987—91; citizen expert Pub. Safety Retirement Task Force of Joint Legis. Com. on Pensions & Retirement, W.Va., 1991—92; exec. dir. W. Va. Consolidated Pub. Retirement Bd., 1998—2001. Republican. Office: Office of Sec of State Bldg 1 Suite 157 K 1900 Kanawha Blvd East Charleston WV 25303-0770 Office Phone: 304-558-6000. Office Fax: 304-558-0900. Business E-Mail: wvsos@wvsos.com.

IRELAND, EMORY, lawyer; b. San Diego, Oct. 15, 1944; BA, Yale U., 1966; JD, Stanford U., 1969. Bar: Wis. 1969. Ptnr. Foley & Lardner LLP, Milw., chmn. fin. practice group. Recipient Pres. Award, State Bar Wis. Mem: State Bar Wis., State Bar Ill. Office: Foley & Lardner LLP Firstar Ctr 777 E Wisconsin Ave Ste 3800 Milwaukee WI 53202-5367 Office Phone: 414-297-5624. Office Fax: 414-297-4900. Business E-Mail: eireland@foley.com.

IRELAND, HERBERT ORIN, retired engineering educator; b. Buckley, Ill., June 12, 1919; s. Harvey Glenn and Anna Estella (Perkinson) I.; m. Mary Leota Austin, Mar. 1, 1941; children: Orin Lee, Marin Fae, Jeanne Lu. BS, U. Ill., 1941, MS, 1947, PhD, 1955. From research asst. to prof. civil engring. U. Ill., Urbana, 1946-79, emeritus, 1979—. Cons. soil mechanics and found. engring., 1946—. Contbr.: sect. to Structural Engineering Handbook, 1968; also articles profl. jours. Served from 2d lt. to maj., C.E. AUS, 1941-46. Fellow Am. Soc. C.E., Geol. Soc. Am.; mem. Am. Ry. Engring. Assn., Sigma Xi, Tau Beta Pi, Chi Epsilon. Methodist. Home: 1132 E Township Road 209 Gilman IL 60938-6114 E-mail: oireland@netzero.net.

IRELAND, JAY, broadcast executive; m. Valerie Ireland; 2 children. BA, St. Lawrence Univ., 1977. Fin. mgmt. prog. GE, Lynchburg, Va., 1980—82, corp. audit staff, 1982—88; various fin. and prod. mgmt. positions GE Plastics, Pittsfield, Mass., 1988—90; mng. dir. Polymerland-Europe, Holland, 1990—93; mgr., corp. investor com. GE, Fairfield, 1993—95, v.p., corp. staff, 1995—97; CFO GE Plastics, 1997—99; pres. NBC TV stations, 1999—2004, NBC Universal TV stations, NYC, 2004—. Exec. com. The Quills; bd. dir. ValueVision Media, TV Bur. of Advert., Maximum Svc. TV. Trustee St. Lawrence Univ; trustee, treas. Norman Rockwell Mus., Stockbridge, Mass. With U.S. Army. Office: NBC Universal TV 30 Rockefeller Plz New York NY 10112*

IRELAND, KATHY, actress, apparel designer; b. Glendale, Calif., 1962; d. John and Barbara Ireland; m. Greg Olsen, 1988; children: Erik, Lily, Chloe. CEO, chief designer Kathy Ireland Worldwide. Designer Kathy Ireland Brand began 2000, appearances in Sports Illustrated's Ann. Swimsuit Issues, 25th Anniversary Show Swimsuit Edit., Kathy Ireland LPGA Championship, ESPN, 2001; films include: Alien from L.A., 1988, Necessary Roughness, 1991, Mom and Dad Save the World, 1992, National Lampoon's Loaded Weapon I, 1993, The Player, Mr. Destiny, Amore, Backfire; TV films include Beauty and the Bandit, 1994, Danger Island, 1994, Miami Hustle, 1995, Gridlock, 1996, Once Upon A Christmas, 2000, Twice Upon A Christmas, 2001; TV appearances include: Down the Shore, The Edge, Tales from the Crypt, Without a Clue, Grand, Charles in Charge, Perry Mason, Boy Meets World, Melrose Place, The Watcher, Deadly Games, Sabrina the Teenage Witch, Suddenly Susan, Gun, Cosby, Touched by an Angel, Pensacola, For Your Love, Strong Medicine. Recipient Entrepreneur of Yr., 2001, Mother of Yr., 2004, Received Good Housekeeping Seal, 2004, Bus. Owner of Yr., 2004, Entrepreneural Champian award, 2005. Office: Kathy Ireland Worldwide 15th Fl 10900 Wilshire Blvd Los Angeles CA 90024-4341 Office Phone: 310-557-2700.

IRELAND, OLIVER, lawyer; BA, Yale Univ., 1970; JD, Univ. Tex., 1974. Assoc. gen. counsel bd. mems. office FRS, Washington, 1985-2000; vice-pres., assoc. gen. coun. Fed. Res. Bank Chgo.; ptnr. Morrison Foerster, Washington, 2000—; atty. Fed. Res. Bank Boston. Office: Morrison Foerster Ste 5500 2000 Pennsylvania Ave NW Washington DC 20006-1888 Office Phone: 202-887-1500. Office Fax: 202-887-0763.*

IRELAND, PATRICIA, equal employment consultant; b. Oak Park, Ill., Oct. 19, 1945; d. James Ireland and Joan Filipek; m. James Humble, 1968. BA, U. Tennessee, 1966; JD, U. Miami Law Sch., 1975; hon. degree (hon.), U. R.I., U. Mass. Coll. Law, U. Ind., Sweetbriar Coll. Flight attendant Pan Am. World Airlines, 1967-75; ptnr. Stearns, Weaver, Miller, Weissler, Alhadeff & Sitterson, Miami; nat. pres. NOW, 1991—2001; of counsel Katz, Kutter, Alderman, Bryant & Yon, 2001—03; campaign mgr. Carol Moseley Braun for pres., 2004; pres. Ireland and Assocs., 2004—. Author: What Women Want, 1996; contbr. law rev. Miami Law Sch. Mailing: PO Box 1569 Homestead FL 33090-1569 E-mail: patriciaireland@adelphia.net.

IRELAND, PATRICK, artist; b. Ireland, 1935; came to U.S., 1957; One-man shows include Betty Parsons Gallery, 1970, 1974, Corcoran Gallery Art, Washington, 1974, Los Angeles County Mus. Art, 1974, Seattle Art Mus., 1977, Fogg Art Mus., 1981, Everson Mus., 1987, Orpheus Gallery, Belfast, 1989, Butler Inst. Am. Art, 1994, Brigham Young U., 1995, numerous others, exhibited in group shows at Inst. Contemporary Art, London, 1967, Hirshhorn Mus., 1976, Documenta 6, 1977, Bienale, Venice, 1980, Yale U. Art Gallery, 1982, Bklyn. Mus., 1983, Detroit Inst. Arts, 1987, Museo Tamayo, Mexico City, 1991, Language of Pouvoir, Paris, 1996, Artists of the Millenium, UN, N.Y.C, 1999, Joyce in Art, Royal Hibernian Acad., Dublin, 2004, others, Represented in permanent collections Centre George Pompidou, Paris, Met. Mus. Art, N.Y.C., Nat. Gallery Art, Washington, Nat. Gallery, Australia, Irish Mus. Modern Art, Dublin, Nat. Gallery of Ireland, Hugh Lane Gallery Modern Art, Detroit Inst. Art, Smithsonian Am. Art Mus., Washington, Hirshhorn Mus., others. Mem.: Nat. Coll. Art & Design (assoc.). Studio: 15 W 67th St New York NY 10023-6226

IRELAND, RODERICK L., state supreme court justice; b. Springfield, Mass. m. Alice Alexander. BA, Lincoln U., 1966; JD, Columbia U., 1969; LLM, Harvard U., 1975; PhD, Northeastern U., 1998. Atty. Neighborhood Legal Service, NYC, 1969; staff atty. Harvard Ctr. for Law & Education, Mass., 1970; chief atty. then dep. exec. dir. Roxbury Defenders Com., 1971—73; hearing officer Mass. Civil Service Commn., 1973—75; legal counsel Roxbury Dist. Ct. Clinic, 1974—77; assoc. Burnham, Stern and Shapiro, 1975; asst. sec., chief legal counsel Mass. Exec. Office of Adminstrn. & Fin., 1975—77; chmn. State Bd. of Appeal on Motor Vehicle Liability Policies & Bonds, 1977; assoc. justice Boston Juvenile Ct., 1977—90, Mass.

Appeals Ct., 1990—97, Mass. Supreme Jud. Ct., 1997—. Judge Boston Juvenile Ct., 1977, 90, Mass. Appeals Ct., 1990-97. Author: Massachusetts Juvenile Law, 1993. Mem. Eliot Congregational Ch. Recipient Boston Covenant Peace prize, 1982, Jud. Excellence award, Mass. Judges Conference, 1996, Lawyers Weekly, 2001. Mem.: Boston Bar Assn. (Haskell Cohn Disting. Jud. Service award 1990), Mass. Bar Assn. (Jud. Excellence award 2001). Office: Supreme Jud Ct John Adams Courthouse One Pemberton Sq Boston MA 02108-1735

IRELAND, SHASTA LYNNE, curator, interior designer; b. Mesa, Ariz., Mar. 27, 1976; d. Ronald and Cheryl Ireland. BA in Interior Design, Lubbock Christian U., 1998; MA in Art History, MFA in Art History, Savannah Coll. Art and Design, 2001. Cert. collections mgmt. Campbell Ctr. for Hist. Preservation Studies, 2004. Curator Mighty Eighth Air Force Mus., Savannah, Ga., 2001—, registrar. Forum coord. Am. Soc. Aviation Artists, Savannah, 2002; silent auction coord. All Things Old and Beautiful Art Auction Sr. Citizens Inc., Savannah, 2002—. Mem.: Am. Assn. Museums (curators com.), Southeastern Museums Conf., Am. Assn. for State and Local History, Jr. League Savannah. Office: Mighty Eighth Air Force Museum PO Box 1992 Savannah GA 31402 Office Phone: 912-748-8888. Home Fax: 912-748-0209; Office Fax: 912-748-0209. Business E-Mail: exhibits@mightyeighth.org.

IRENAS, JOSEPH ERON, judge, director; b. Newark, July 13, 1940; s. Zachary and Bessie (Shain) Irenas; m. Nancy Harriet Jacknow, Jan. 1, 1962; children: Amy Ruth, Edward Eron. AB, Princeton U., 1962; JD cum laude, Harvard U., 1965; postgrad., NYU Sch. Law, 1967-70. Bar: N.J. 1965, N.Y. 1982. Law sec. to justice N.J. Supreme Ct., 1965-66; assoc. McCarter & English, Newark, 1966-71, ptnr., 1972-92; judge U.S. Dist. Ct. N.J., 1992—. Trustee Hamilton Investment Trust, Elizabeth, NJ, 1980—83; mem. N.J. Supreme Ct. Dist. Ethics Com., 1984—86, vice chmn., 1986; adj. prof. law Rutgers Sch. Law, Camden, 1985—86, Camden, 1988—97, Camden, 1999—2002, N.J. Bd. Bar Examiners, 1986—88. Contbr. Chmn. bd. trustees United Hosps. of Newark, 1982—83; trustee United Hosps. Found., 1985—92, United Way Essex County, 1988—92, treas., 1990—92. Fellow: Am. Bar Found., Royal Chartered Inst. Arbitrators (London); mem.: ABA, Camden County Bar Assn., N.J. Bar Assn., Am. Law Inst., Union League Club, Nassau Club. Republican. Jewish. Office: Mitchell H Cohen US Courthouse One John F Gerry Plaza PO Box 2097 Camden NJ 08101-2097 Office Phone: 856-757-5223.

IRIBARNE, JOSE, engineering educator; b. Santiago, Chile, July 30, 1962; arrived in U.S., 1992; s. Pedro and Sonja (Friedmann) Iribarne; m. Eugenia Brieva, Oct. 11, 1986; children: Constanza, Elisa. BS Mech. Engring., U.Chile, Santiago, 1985; Diploma Mech. Engring., U. Chile, Santiago, 1986; MS Paper Sci. and Engring., SUNY, Syracuse, 1995, PhD Paper Sci. and Engring., 1999. Registered prof. engr., Colegio de Ingenieros, Chile, 1986. Project engr. Gamma Ingenieros Ltda., Santiago, Chile, 1986—89, Arze, Recine y Asociados, S.A., Santiago, Chile, 1990—92; process engr. Solvay Paperboard LLC, Syracuse, NY, 1999—2000, engring. and tech. mgr., 2000—. Adj. prof. SUNY, Syracuse, NY, 2001—. Contbr. articles and sci. papers to TAPPI Jour. Fulbright Scholar, Fulbright Commn., 1992. Mem.: TAPPI. Achievements include research in Two-stage oxygen delignification, leading to Oxy-Trac process. Office: Solvay Paperboard LLC 53 Industrial Dr Syracuse NY 13204 Office Phone: 315-484-9050 363.

IRICK, LARRY D., lawyer, energy executive; b. 1956; BS, Emporia State U.; JD, Duke U. Bar: 1982. With Westar Energy, Inc., Topeka, 1999—, v.p., gen. counsel, corp. sec. Office: Westar Energy Inc 818 S Kansas Ave PO Box 889 Topeka KS 66601-0889 Office Phone: 785-575-1625.

IRIMIA, ANDREI, physicist; b. Falticeni, Romania, May 29, 1981; s. Alexandru Irimia and Amalia Ioan. BA in Computer Sci. summa cum laude, Lipscomb U., Nashville, 2002; MS in Computer Sci., Vanderbilt U., Nashville, 2004; MS in Physics, Vanderbilt U., 2005. Rsch. physicist Vanderbilt U., Nashville, 2002—. Translator: selected poems by Mihai Eminescu translated from the Romanian language; contbr. articles to profl. jours. Recipient Academic performance award, A.T. Laurian Nat. Coll., Botosani, Romania, 1998, Prize 1, Botosani olympiad of Romanian lang. and lit., Romanian Ministery of Edn., 1996, Prize 1, Botosani olympiad of French lang. and lit., 1998, Prize 1, Botosani olympiad of English lang. and lit., 1998, Spl. acad. achievement award, Nashville Christian Acad., 1999, Poetry performance prize, Botosani ann. francophony festival, 1993, US Pres.'s award for ednl. excellence (Bill Clinton), US Pres.'s office, 1999, Prize 1, Botosani olympiad of Romanian history, Romanian Ministery of Edn., 1996; fellow Rsch. assistantship in atomic structure theory, Vanderbilt U., 2003, Rsch. assistantship in med. image processing, 2003—04, Rsch. assistantship in biophysics, 2004—; scholar Acad. Performance scholar, Gen. Sch. No. 12, Botosani, Romania, 1992—96, Acad. Exch. scholarship to the USA, Soros Found., 1998, Internat. student scholar, Nashville Christian Acad., 1998, Meml. and trustee scholar, Lipscomb U., 1999—2002, Johnston-Foster scholar, 1999—2002, Dean's scholar, 1999—2002, Computer sci. dept. scholar, 2001—02, Izvorul Muresului UNESCO sci. camp scholar, Romanian Ministery of Edn., 1996. Mem.: Alpha Chi. Liberal. Office: Vanderbilt University 2301 Vanderbilt Pl Nashville TN 37235 Office Phone: 615-343-8170.

IRIS, BONNIE (BONNIE IRIS SILVERSTEIN), artist, writer; b. N.Y.C., Aug. 15, 1941; d. Bernard and Hannah Kramer; m. Richard Harold Silverstein, May 27, 1967 (div. Oct. 1987). BA, Queens Coll., 1962; MA, NYU, 1963; postgrad., Art Students League of N.Y., 1970—92, Sch. Visual Arts, 1979—85, New Sch. for Social Rsch., 1979—87, Cooper Union, 1986. Asst. editor IEEE, N.Y.C., 1963—68; prodn. mgr. AIAA, N.Y.C., 1973—75; assoc. editor Watson-Guptill Publs., N.Y.C., 1975—79, devel. editor, 1979—82, sr. editor, 1982—88; acquisitions editor North Light Books, Cin., 1988—90; contbg. writer Watercolor mag. and Am. Artist, N.Y.C., 1977—99, Step-by-Step Graphics, Peoria, Ill., 1995—96. Juror art shows, 1996—; painting demonstrations, critiques for art assns., Boulder-Denver area, 1994—, Waldorf H.S., 2000-04, Arvada Ctr. for Arts, 2000-05 Exhibited at Art Students League of N.Y. Gallery, 1970-92, Nat. Arts Club, N.Y.C, 1990, 91, Salmagundi Club, N.Y.C., 1992, Creede Repertory Theatre, 1993-95, Boulder Art Assn., 1993-98, Glenwood Springs Ann. Fall Festival, 1994, Foothills Art Ctr., 1994, Hildebrandt Gallery, Littleton, Colo., 1994, Longmont Artists Guild, 1995, Louisville Arts Festival, 1995, 96, Faces of Women Show, Las Vegas, N.Mex., 1995, Near Gallery, Boulder, 1996, NCAR Gallery, Boulder, Colo., 1996, This is Colo. Exhbn., Littleton, 1996, 97, 2003 (2d pl. hon. mention), Eight Plein Air Painters Invitational, Boulder, 1998, Open Studios, 1995—, No. Colo. Ann. Art Exhbn., Ft. Collins, 1998, 2001, 03, Parkview Congl. Ch., Aurora, 2000 (Best of Show award 2002, First Pl. Pastel award 2003, Third Pl. Pastel award 2005); art featured in Artists Mag., 1991, Best of Oil Painting, 1997; co-author: Painting and Drawing Animals, Watson-Guptill, 1998; slide lecture Monet and Me, Dairy Ctr. for Arts, Boulder, 1998; participant Richard Schmid Ann. Art Auction, 1997-2003, estes Park Main Air Even, 2003 Mem. Art Students League N.Y. (life), Pastel Soc. Colo., Foothills Art Ctr., Boulder Art Assn. (program dir. 1994-97), Louisville Art Assn., Heritage Fine Arts Guild, Park Hill Art Club. Home: 4500 19th St Lot 124 Boulder CO 80304-0615

IRISH, CAROLYN TANNER, bishop; d. Obert Clark and Grace Adams Tanner; m. Lee Irish (div. 1988); children: Stephen, Jessica, Thomas, Emily; m. Frederick Quinn, 2001. Student, Stanford U.; B in Philosophy with high honors, U. Mich., 1962; MLitt in Moral Philosophy, Oxford U., 1968; MDiv cum laude, Va. Theol. Sem., 1983, doctoral degree (hon.), Westminster Coll., Salt Lake City, U. Utah, Ch. Div. Sch. of the Pacific, Berkeley, Calif., Salt Lake Cmty. Coll., Utah State U. Taught ethics, history, lit. Edmund Burke Sch., Washington; ordained deacon, 1983, priest, 1984; served congregations in Washington, DC, Va, and Mich.; named archdeacon Episcopal Diocese of Mich., 1986; mem. staff Shalem Inst. Spiritual Found., Washington Nat. Cathedral; bishop Episcopal Diocese of Utah, 1996—. Chmn. bd. O.C. Tanner Co., Salt Lake City. Mem. adv. bd. Shalem Inst. Spiritual Formation. Episcopalian. Office: Episcopal Diocese of Utah PO Box 3090 Salt Lake City UT 84110-3090 Office Phone: 801-322-4131.*

IRISH, DIANA MARIA, wildlife rehabilitation agent; b. Grand Rapids, Mich., May 24, 1950; d. Robert Leroy and June Lorraine (Centilli) Newman; m. Harvey Alan Irish, Nov. 22, 1968; children: Timothy, Jamy, Corey, Windy, Robert, Wayne, Shellie. Grad. h.s., Grand Rapids, Mich. Author: My Talking Heart, 1992, Pictures of My Mind, 1994, Wings of Thought; recordings include A Rose for My Daddy and Forest Lane in (tape) Hilltop Country, 1998, Hight Country, Light of the World, Roll Gordon Roll, 1999, Freedom in the Meadow and Prayer of Our Ancesters in (CD) High Country, 1998, Rainbows End, Little Windy and Please Don't Worry in (CD) Light of the World, 1998. Bd. dirs. Coalition Rep. for Govt., Grand Rapids, 1997-99. Recipient Golden Poet award World of Poetry, 1988-99, Homer Honor Soc., 1990, Poet of Merit Internat. Soc. of Poets; named to Internat. Poets Hall of Fame, 1997-99. Mem. Weaving Ethnisity (sec. 1992-2002), C.R.G. (bd. dirs. 1998-2002), Grand Valley Am. Indian Lodge (bd. dirs., sec. 1992-2002), Inter Tribal (mem.-at-large). Avocations: writing, fishing, hunting, native american dancing, doll designer. Home: 5909 Ramsdell Dr NE Rockford MI 49341-9067

IRISH, GEORGE BUTLER, media company executive; b. Decatur, Ill., Feb. 27, 1944; s. Thomas Bone and Carolyn Elizabeth (Gilman) I.; m. Mary Rettig (dec. 2005), Jan. 29, 1966; children: Sandra Lynn, Christine Marie. BA, Millikin U., 1968, PhD (hon.). With dept. advt. sales Decatur Herald & Rev., 1966-67; asst. mgr. personnel Lindsay-Schaub Newspapers, Decatur, 1967-72, mgr. personnel, 1972-76; bus. mgr. Midland (Mich.) Daily Newspapers, 1976-79, gen. mgr., 1979-80, pub., 1980-82, Midland (Tex.) Reporter-Telegram, 1982-84, Beaumont (Tex.) Enterprise, 1984-88, San Antonio Light, 1988-93; group pub. The Hearst Corp., Beaumont, 1985-88, v.p., 1993—98, sr. v.p., 1998—; pres. Hearst Newspapers, 1998—. Pres. Midland Newspapers, Inc., 1982-84; com. chmn. Inland Daily Press Assn., Chgo., 1983—. Mem. bd. counselors St. Elizabeth Hosp., Beaumont, 1987, task force Job Creation and Econ. Devel., Austin, Tex., 1986-87; bd. dirs. San Antonio Econ. Devel. Found., 1988—, San Antonio Med. Found., 1990—, San Antonio Symphony (bd. dirs. 1988-93), Jr. Achievement S. Tex. 1988-93 (exec. com. 1990-93; trustee Southwest Rsch. Inst.; mem. governing coun. San Antonio Edn. Partnership; trustee Millikin U., Decatur, Ill., Incarnate Word Coll.; mem. devel. bd. U. Tex., San Antonio; mem. bd. visitors Trinity U.; mem. devel. bd. U. Tex. Health Sci. Ctr. at San Antonio; mem. exec. com. United Way of San Antonio, 1989—, vice chmn. ann. campaign, 1992, chmn. comm. com., 1989—; mem. exec. bd. Alamo Area Coun. Boy Scouts Am. Named Paul Harris fellow Rotary Internat., 1984 Citizen of the Yr. Sales and Mktg. Exec., 1987; recipient Disting. Service award Jaycees, 1976, Jr. Achievement Silver Leadership award, 1992, Community Svcs. award Brooks Heritage Found., 1992, Golden Rule award J.C. Penney, Merit Loyalty award Millikin U., 1993; honoree People of Vision Soc. To Prevent Blindness, 1992; named Newspaper Leader of Yr. Tex. Daily Newspaper Assn., 1992. Mem. Tex. Daily Newspaper Assn. (pres. 1987-88), Am. Press Assn. (adv. bd.), So. Newspaper Pub. Assn., Am. Newspaper Pub. Assn., San Antonio C. of C. (bd. dirs. 1989-91), Tex. C. of C. (bd. dirs. 1991—, Rotary (various coms.). Clubs: Dominion Country (San Antonio, chmn. bd. 1992—). Roman Catholic. Office: The Hearst Corp 959 8th Ave New York NY 10019-3795*

IRISH, JOEL DAVID, anthropologist; b. Mpls., Sept. 6, 1957; s. Lloyd Donald and Violet Esther (Heller) I.; m. Carol Diann McCracken, July 23, 1994. BS, Mankato State U., 1980; MS, Ariz. State U., 1984, PhD, 1993. Faculty assoc. Mankato (Minn.) State U., 1983-84; teaching assoc. Ariz. State U., Tempe, 1985-88, faculty assoc., 1989-92; archeologist USDA Forest Svcs., Sitka, Alaska, 1990-91; project archaeologist Lobdell and Assocs., Anchorage, 1992; physical anthropologist Office Cultural Resource Mgmt., Tempe, 1989-94; asst. prin. investigator Louis Berger & Assocs., Inc., Phoenix, 1993-94, prin. investigator, 1994-95; asst. prof. U. N.Mex., Albuquerque, 1995-98; assoc. prof., curator phys. anthropology U. Alaska Fairbanks, 1998—. Adj. prof. Ariz. State U., Tempe, 1993-96. Contbr. articles to profl. jours. Grantee, NSF, Washington, 1991, 2001. Mem. Am. Assn. Physical Anthropology, Am. Anthrop. Assn., Soc. Am. Archaeology, Dental Anthropology Assn. (sec.-treas. 1992-95, co-editor newsletter 1990-95, pres. 2002-04), Sigma Xi, Phi Kappa Phi. Achievements include co-originator of the hypoplastic area method for analyzing dental enamel hypoplasia; determined biological affinity estimates of 50 late-pleistocene through modern African samples based on dental discrete traits; study on late Paleolithic Nubian-recent West African affinity. Office: U Alaska Fairbanks Dept Anthropology PO Box 757720 Fairbanks AK 99775-7720 Office Phone: 907-474-6755. E-mail: ffjdi@uaf.edu.

IRISH, LEON EUGENE, lawyer, educator, social services administrator, non-profit organization administrator; b. Superior, Wis., June 19, 1938; s. Edward Eugene and Phyllis Ione (Johnson) I.; m. Karla W. Simon; children: Stephen T., Jessica L., Thomas A., Emily A. BA in History, Stanford U., 1960; JD, U. Mich., 1964; D.Phil in Law, Oxford (Eng.) U., 1973. Law clk. to Assoc. Justice U.S. Supreme Ct. Byron R. White, 1967; cons. Office Fgn. Direct Investments, Dept. Commerce, 1967-68; spl. rep. sec. def. 7th session 3d UN Conf. Law of Sea; mem. Caplin & Drysdale, chartered, Washington, 1968-85; prof. law U. Mich. Law Sch., Ann Arbor, 1985-88; ptnr. Jones, Day, Reavis & Pogue, Washington, 1988-93; v.p., sr. counsel Aetna Life and Casualty Co., Hartford, Conn., 1993-95; pres., chmn. Internat. Ctr. Not-for-Profit Law, Washington, 1992—2002; pres., CEO United Way Internat., Alexandria, Va., 1996; sr. legal cons. World Bank, 1997—2001. Adj. prof. Georgetown U. Law Ctr., 1975-85, Cath. U. Am. Sch. Law, 2003—; regent Am. Coll. Tax Counsel, 1986-89; mem. IRS Commr.'s Adv. Group, 1987; bd. dirs., sec. Vols. Tech. Assistance, 1978-, Found. for Devel. of Polish Agr. 1988-; vis. fellow World Bank, 1995-96; vis. prof. law Ctrl. European U., Budapest, 1998—, Temple U., 2002-2003, pres. Internat. Ctr. for Civil Soc., 2002—. Contbr. articles to legal jours. Mem. ABA, D.C. Bar Assn., Am. Law Inst., Am. Coll. Tax Counsel, Coun. on Fgn. Rels., Am. Coll. Employee Benefits Coun. Democrat. Home: 304 Kyle Rd Crownsville MD 21032-1843 Office Phone: 202-262-7154. Business E-Mail: irish@law.edu.

IRISH, THOMAS JUDSON, retired plastic surgeon; b. Forest City, Iowa, May 23, 1936; m. Sandra Rudolph. BS, Iowa State Coll., 1958; MD, State U. of Iowa, 1962. Intern King County Hosp. (now Harborview Hosp.), Seattle, 1962-63; pvt. practice Forest City, Iowa, 1963-66; resident in gen. surgery U. Colo. Med. Ctr., Denver, 1966-70; resident in plastic surgery Norfolk Gen. Hosp. & Kings Daughters Children's Hosp., Va., 1970-72; pvt. practice Plastic Surgeons NW, Tacoma, 1972—2003; med. dir. Franciscan Wound Care Ctr.; ret., 2003. Fellow in plastic surgery Canniesburn Hosp., Glasgow, Scotland, 1971. Fellow ACS; mem. Am. Soc. Plastic and Reconstructive Surgery, Alpha Omega Alpha. Office Phone: 253-383-1641.

IRIYE, AKIRA, historian, educator; b. Tokyo, Oct. 20, 1934; s. Keishiro and Naoko (Tsukamoto) I.; m. Mitsuko Maeda, May 14, 1960; children: Keiko, Masumi. BA, Haverford Coll., 1957; PhD, Harvard U., 1961. Instr. in history Harvard U., Cambridge, Mass., 1961-64, lectr. in history, 1964-66; asst. prof. history U. Calif., Santa Cruz, 1966-68; assoc. prof. U. Rochester, 1968-69, U. Chgo., 1969-71, prof., 1971-89, disting. service prof., 1983-89, chmn. dept. history, 1979-85; prof. history Harvard U., 1989—91, Charles Warren prof. history, 1991—, chmn. dept. history, 2002—04. Vis. prof. Ecole des Hautes Etudes en Sciences Sociales, Paris, 1986-87, London Sch. Econs., 1992. Author: books, including After Imperialism, 1965, Across the Pacific, 1967, Pacific Estrangement, 1972, The Cold War in Asia, 1974, Power and Culture, 1981, The Origins of the Second World War in Asia and the Pacific, 1987, China and Japan, 1992, The Globalizing of America, 1993, Cultural Internationalism and World Order, 1997, Japan and the Wider World, 1997, Global Community, 2002; editor: The Chinese and the Japanese, 1980, other books. John Simon Guggenheim fellow, 1974-75 Mem. Am. Hist. Assn. (pres. 1988), Am. Acad. Arts and Scis., Orgn. Am. Historians, Soc. Historians Am. Fgn. Relations (pres. 1978) Office: Harvard U Dept History Cambridge MA 02138

IRIZARRY, DORA L., federal judge; b. San Sebastian, Puerto Rico, Jan. 26, 1955; 1 child. BA, Yale U., 1976; JD, Columbia U., 1979. Bar: NY 1981. Asst. D.A., Appeals Bureau Office of the Bronx, 1979—87; with Bronx County Office Special Narcotics Prosecutor, 1981—87; with NY County Office Special Narcotics Prosecutor, 1987—95; asst. D.A. NY County, 1987—95; judge Criminal Ct. NYC, 1995—97, NY State Ct. Claims, 1997—2002; of counsel Hoguet Newman & Regal LLP, 2002—04; judge US Dist. Ct. (Eastern Dist. NY), 2004—. Mem.: Bar Puerto Rican Bar Assn., Com. on the Bench, Assn. Judges Hispanic Heritage (pres. 1997—2002), Fed. Bar Eastern Dist. NY, Fed. Bar Southern Dist. NY, NY State Bar. Office: 225 Cadman Plaza E Brooklyn NY 11201 Business E-Mail: Dora_L_Irizarry@nyed.uscourts.gov.*

IRMAK, SUAT, engineering educator, researcher; b. Adana, Turkey, July 16, 1970; PhD, U. Fla., 2002. Asst. prof. U. Nebr.-Lincoln, 2003—; rsch. engr. U. Fla., Gainesville, 2002—. Rschr. (applied engring. rsch.) Water Resources Engrng. (Young Rschr. Award, 2002). Mem.: ASCE. Achievements include research in Efficient use of natural resources. Office: University of Nebraska-Lincoln 234 LW Chase Hall-E Campus Lincoln NE 68583 Office Phone: 402-472-4865. Office Fax: 402-472-6338. Personal E-mail: sirmak2@unl.edu.

IRMAS, AUDREY MENEIN, philanthropist; m. Sydney Milton Irmas Jr., June 26, 1949 (dec.); children: Deborah, Robert, Matthew. Co-founding trustee Audrey & Sydney Irmas Charitable Found., 1983—, projects include Audrey & Sydney Irmas Campus of the Wilshire Blvd. Temple, Audrey & Sydney Irmas LA Youth Ctr., many others; bd. trustees Mus. Contemporary Art, LA, 1992—, past pres., chmn.; trustee Hirshhorn Mus. and Sculpture Garden, Washington; bd. govs. ctr curator studies Bard Coll., NY. Named one of Top 200 Collectors, ARTnews mag., 2004. Avocation: Collector contemporary art, photography. Office: Audrey & Sydney Irmas Charitable Found Ste 364 16830 Ventura Blvd Encino CA 91436-2797 Office Phone: 818-382-3313. Office Fax: 818-382-3315.

IRMSCHER, CHRISTOPH, literature and language professor, literary critic, editor; b. Tuebingen, Germany, Nov. 25, 1962; s. Hans Dietrich and Elisabeth Irmscher; m. Lauren Bernofsky, Nov. 15, 1999; children: Nicholas, Julia. DPhil, U. Bonn, 1991, Dr.phil.habil., 1998. Lectr. U. Bonn, Germany, 1994—96; lectr. English, history and lit. Harvard U., Cambridge, Mass., 1998—2000; asst. prof. English U. Md., Balt., 2000—03, prof. English, 2003—. Chair, English dept. U. Md., 2005—; vis. asst. prof. English U. Tenn., Knoxville, 1993—94. Author: (book) Longfellow Redux, The Poetics of Natural History (Am. Studies Network Prize; Lit. and Lang. Award, Assn. of Am. Publishers, 2000), Masken der Moderne (Dissertation Prize of the German Assn. for English Studies, 1993); editor: John James Audubon, Writings and Drawings. Recipient CUE award, Harvard U., 2000; fellow, German Rsch. Coun., 1996—98, U. Md., 2001, 2003, NEH, 2005; grantee, Fulbright Commn., 1992, NEH, 2002; scholar, Harvard U., Cambridge, 1996—98; Rodney G. Dennis fellow, Harvard U., Houghton Libr., 2004. Mem.: MLA Am. Lutheran. Avocations: book-collecting, cats. Home: 353 Greenlow Rd Baltimore MD 21228 Office: U Md Eng Dept 1000 Hilltop Cir Baltimore MD 21250 Office Phone: 410-455-2055. Home Fax: 443-612-9160; Office Fax: 410-455-1030. Personal E-mail: irmscher@umbc.edu.

IRONS, ELLEN JANE, educational leadership educator; b. Lewiston, Idaho; m. Ernest M. Irons Jr.; children: Jo Ann Ponder, Teresa Carmack, Elaine Irons, Dan Pavlica. BS in Edn., U. Fla., 1971; MEd, Trinity U., 1975; EdD, Northeastern U., 1984. Tchr. math. San Antonio Ind. Sch. Dist., 1971—74; edn. diagnostician Ft. Sam Houston Ind. Sch. dist., San Antonio, 1975—78; ednl. rschr. Behavior Rsch. Lab., Aberdeen Proving Ground, Md., 1978; sch. psychologist Cecil County Ind. Sch. Dist., Rising Sun, Md., 1978—80; lectr. math. Northeastern U., Boston, 1981—83; spl. edn. specialist Tex. Edn. Agy., Austin, 1984; dir. instrn. Am. Prep. Inst., Killeen, Tex., 1985; elem. prin. La Pryor (Tex.) Ind. Sch. Dist., 1986; ednl. program dir. Tex. Edn. Agy., Austin, 1987—90; dir. curriculum and instrn. Tex. Youth Commn., Austin, 1990—2003; prof. tchr. edn. Tex. Woman's U., Denton, 1993—2004; prof. ednl. leadership Lamar U., Beaumont, Tex., 2004—. Contbr. articles to profl. jours. Mem.: NASP, Assn. Tchr. Educators, Nat. Coun. Profs. Ednl. Adminstrn., Tex. Coun. Adminstrs. Spl. Edn., Phi Delta Kappa, Kappa Delta Pi. Office: Lamar Univ Dept Edn Leadership and Counseling PO Box 10034 Beaumont TX 77710 Office Phone: 409-880-7954. E-mail: jane.irons@lamar.edu.

IRONS, JEREMY JOHN, actor; b. Cowes, Eng., Sept. 19, 1948; s. Paul Dugan and Barbara Anne (Sharpe) Irons; m. Sinead Moira Cusack, Mar. 28, 1978; children: Samuel James, Maximilian Paul. Performer: (plays) John the Baptist in Godspell, 1973, Mick in The Caretaker, 1974, Petruchio in The Taming of the Shrew, 1975, Harry Thunder in Wild Oats, 1976—77, James Jameson in Rear Column, 1978, The Real Thing, 1984 (Tony award, 1984), Harry Thunder in Wild Oats, 1986, Richard II, Leontes in Winter's Tale, The Rover, (films) Nijinsky, 1979, The French Lieutenant's Woman, 1981, Betrayal, 1982, Moonlighting, 1982, The Wild Duck, 1983, Swann in Love, 1983, The Mission, 1985, Chorus of Disapproval, 1988, Australia, 1988, Dead Ringers, 1988 (Best Actor N.Y. Film Critics' Circle, 1988), Danny, the Champion of the World, 1989, Reversal of Fortune, 1990 (Acad. award for Best Actor, 1991, Golden Globe for Best Actor, 1991), Kafka, 1991, Waterland, 1992, Damage, 1992, M. Butterfly, 1993, The House of the Spirits, 1994; performer: (voice) The Lion King, 1994; performer: Die Hard with a Vengeance, 1995, Stealing Beauty, 1996, Lolita, 1997, The Chinese Box, 1997, Man in the Iron Mask, 1998, Dungeons and Dragons, 2000, Fourth Angel, 2000, And Now Ladies and Gentlemen, 2001, Callas Forever, 2001, Mathilde, 2003, Being Julia, 2003, Merchant of Venice, 2004, Kingdom of Heaven, 2004, Casanova, 2004, (TV films) Charles Ryder in Brideshead Revisited, 1980—81, Alex Hepburn in The Captain's Doll, 1982, Tales from Hollywood, 1992, Longitude, 1999, Last Call, 2001. Decorated officier des Artes et Lettres (France). Address: Hutton Mgmt 4 Old Manor Close Askett Bucks HP27 9NA England

IRONS, PAULETTE RILEY, state legislator, lawyer; b. New Orleans, May 19, 1953; d. Florida Wilson; m. Alvin L. Irons; children: Marseah Irons Delatte, Paul-Alvin. BBA, Loyola U., New Orleans, 1975; JD, Tulane U., 1991. Bar: La. 1991. Sr. cons. Small Bus. Devel. and Mgmt. Inst., New Orleans, 1992-93; mem. La. Ho. of Reps., Baton Rouge, 1992-94, La. Senate, Baton Rouge, 1994—. Vice-chmn. transp., hwys. and pub. works com., mem. health and welfare com., formr mem. fin. com., pres. women's caucus,1998, sgt.-at-arms legis. black caucus, 1993-95; sr. cons. Small Bus. Devel. and Mgmt. Inst., New Orleans, 1992-93; adj. prof. Tulane U. Law Clinic, New Orleans, fall 1995; atty. 1st City Ct., New Orleans, 1996-98; atty. Recorder of Mortgages Office, New Orleans, 1997—; adv. bd. women's network Nat. Conf. State Legislators, Denver, 1996—. Pres. bd. dirs. La. Initiative on Teen Pregnancy Prevention, 1995-2001; bd. dirs. New Orleans Area Literacy Coalition. Recipient Woman of Excellence award 2d Bapt. Ch., 1994, Outstanding African Am. Woman, Tulane Black Law Students, 1996, Good Housekeeping award, 2001; named Legislator of Yr., New Orleans Alliance for Good Govt., 1995. Fellow Japan Soc.; mem. LWV, AAUW, Nat. Order Women Legislators, Nat. Order Black Elected Legislators, Women for a Better La., Ind. Women's Orgn., La. League Good Govt. Democrat. Avocations: reading, travel. Address: La Senate Ofc PO Box 94183 Baton Rouge LA 70804-9183 Office: Jud Civil Dist Ct 421 Loyola Ave Room 200B New Orleans LA 70112 Office Phone: 504-592-9250.

IRONS, WILLIAM GEORGE, anthropology educator; b. Garrett, Ind., Dec. 25, 1933; s. George Randall and Eva Aileen (Veazey) I.; m. Marjorie Sue Rogasner, Nov. 4, 1972; children: Julia Rogasner, Marybeth Rogasner. BA, U. Mich., 1960, MA, 1963, PhD, 1969; postgrad., London Sch. Econs., 1964—65. With Army C.E., 1956-58; asst. prof. social rels. Johns Hopkins U., 1969-74; asst. prof. anthropology Pa. State U., 1974-78; assoc. prof. anthropology Northwestern U., Evanston, Ill., 1978-83, prof., 1983—. Cons. Nat. Geog. Soc., NSF, AAAS, Social Sci. Rsch. Coun., Time-Life Books, U. Wash. Press, Random House, Worth Pubs., Rutgers U. Press, U. Tex. Press,

Pelenum Press, Oxford U. Press, Cornell U. Press. Author: Perspectives on Nomadism, 1972, The Yomut Turkmen, 1975, Evolutionary Biology and Human Social Behavior, 1979, Adaptation and Human Behavior, 2000; mem. bd. editors Evolution and Human Behavior. With AUS, 1954-56. Recipient Lifetime Achievement award Commn. on Nomadic Peoples, Internat. Union Anthrop. and Ethnol. Scis.; grantee NSF, 1973, 76, 83, 85, 86, Ford Found., 1974, Harry Frank Guggenheim Found., 1976. Fellow AAAS, Am. Anthrop. Assn.; mem. Assocs. in Current Anthropology, Human Behavior and Evolution Soc. (pres. 2001-03), Internat. Soc. Human Ethology, Internat. Soc. for Behavioral Ecology, Ctr. for Advanced Studies in Religion and Sci., Inst. for Religion in an Age of Sci., Evolutionary Anthropology Soc. (pres. 2004—), Phi Kappa Phi. Achievements include research on Turkmen of Iran, human behavioral ecology, evolutionary ethics. Home: 2604 Payne St Evanston IL 60201-2133 Office: Northwestern U Dept Anthropology 1810 Hinman Ave Evanston IL 60208-0809 Business E-Mail: w-irons@northwestern.edu.

IRONS, WILLIAM LEE, lawyer; b. Birmingham, Ala., June 9, 1941; s. George Vernon and Velma (Wright) Irons. BA, U. Va., 1963; JD, Samford U., 1966. Bar: Ala. 1966, U.S. Dist Ct. (no. dist.) Ala. 1966, U.S. Ct. Appeals (5th cir.) 1966. Dir. mil. justice Maxwell AFB, Ala., 1963—69; law clk. Speir, Robertson & Jackson, Birmingham, 1964—66; asst. judge adv. Whiteman AFB, Mo., 1966, Gunter AFB, 1967—68; ptnr. Speir, Robertson, Jackson & Irons, 1970—71, Speir & Irons, 1971—72, William L. Irons & Assoc., 1972—. U.S. trustee, 1964—86; instr. sr. officers Judge Adv. Gen.'s Sch. Air War coll. Air U. Maxwell AFB; chief inspector city, state and fed. elections Jefferson County, Ala., 2002—. Author: (magazine articles on Am. Revolution era) Colonial Navy, 1992 (U.S. Senate commendation), Chronicles of the Am. Revolutionary War, 1995 (N.Y. State Senate commendation). Candidate Ala. Ho. Reps., 1966; exec. com. Jefferson County Rep. Party; mem. steering com. Jefferson City Rep. Party, 2004; deacon Mountain Brook Bapt. Ch., Sunday sch. supt. Capt. Strategic Air Command USAF. Decorated Commendation medal and citation USAF, Congl. medal of honor project Freedom's Found., Valley Forge, Pa.; named Outstanding Jr. Officer Vietnam War, USAF, 1969; DuPont Regional scholar, U.Va. Mem.: SAR (pres. Ala. chpt., Taylor award 1990), ABA, Nat. Res. Officer Assn., Fed. Bar Assn., Nat. Assn. Cert. Judge Advs., Assn. Trial Lawyers Am., Birmingham Bar Assn., Descendants of Washington's Army at Valley Forge (capt. of the guard, adm. state of Md. 1995), Birmingham Exec. Club (pres. 1978—79), Nat. Lawyers Club, St. Andrews Soc., Newcomen Soc., Sigma Delta Kappa. Republican. Baptist. Home: 3855 Cove Dr Birmingham AL 35213-3801 Office: 1227 City Federal Building Birmingham AL 35203-3714

IRSAY, JAMES STEVEN, professional football team owner; b. Lincolnwood, Ill., June 13, 1959; s. Robert Irsay and Harriet Pogerzelski; m. Margaret Mary Coyle, Aug. 2, 1980; children: Carlie Margaret, Casey Coyle, Kalen. B in Broadcast Journalism, So. Meth. U., 1982. With Balt. Colts., from early 1970's; owner, CEO Indpls. Colts, 1997—. Bd. dirs. Noble Ind. Composer, performer single Hoosier Heartland, 1985, single and video Go Colts, 1985, Colors, 1990. Bd. dirs. United Way Ctrl. Ind.; dir. Greater Indpls. Progress Com. Achievements include purchased in auction Jack Kerouac's orignial scroll of On the Road, 2001. Avocations: weightlifting, guitar, songwriting. Office: Indpls Colts 7001 W 56th St Indianapolis IN 46254-9725 also: Indianapolis Colts PO Box 535000 Indianapolis IN 46253*

IRSFELD, JOHN HENRY, English language educator, novelist; b. Bemidji, Minn., Dec. 2, 1937; s. Hubert Louis and Mary Lillian (McKee) I.; m. Margaret Elizabeth Drushel, Aug. 29, 1965 (div. Feb. 1978); 1 child, Hannah Christine; m. Janet Elizabeth Jones, May 5, 1984. BA, U. Tex., 1959, MA, 1966, PhD, 1969. Tchr. Spanish and English, Calallen, Tex., 1959-60; teaching asst. U. Texas, Austin, 1960-61, 64-68, teaching assoc., 1968-69; from asst. prof. to assoc. prof. English U. Nev., Las Vegas, 1969-73, prof., 1977—, exec. asst. to v.p. acad. affairs, 1984—87, dep. to pres., 1987, v.p., dep. to pres., 1990-94. Author: (novels) Coming Through, 1975, Little Kingdoms, 1976, 89, Rats Alley, 1987, Radio Elvis and Other Stories, 2002. Sgt. inf. U.S. Army, 1961-64. Democrat. Office: U Nev 4505 S Maryland Pkwy Las Vegas NV 89154-9900

IRVIN, HELEN ADCOCK, interior designer; b. Oxford, N.C., Mar. 31, 1939; d. Joseph Solomon and Virginia Daniel Adcock; m. John Lafayette Irvin, Aug. 30, 1959 (div. June 1974); children: Dorothy Anne, John Lafayette Jr., Helen A. Student, U. N.C., Greensboro, 1957. Owner, pres. Helen Irvin Interior Design, Greensboro, N.C., 1985—. Pres. Greensboro Opera Co., Greensboro. Mem. Greensboro Preservation Soc., Greensboro Symphony Guild, Capital City Club, High Hopes Garden Club, Kirkwood Garden Club, Symposium Book Club, Greensboro City Club. Republican. Presbyterian. Avocations: bridge, gardening. Home and Office: 1901 Pembroke Rd Greensboro NC 27408

IRVIN, MICHAEL JEROME, professional football player; b. Ft. Lauderdale, Fla., Mar. 5, 1966; BA in Bus. Mgmt., U. Miami, 1988. Wide receiver Dallas Cowboys, 1988—2000. Player Pro Bowl, 1991—95, Super Bowl XXVII, 1992, Super Bowl XXVIII, 1993, Super Bowl XXX, 1995. Actor: (films) The Longest Yard, 2005. Played in Pro Bowl, 1991-95; named wide receiver The Sporting News NFL All-Pro team, 1991; named outstanding Player of Pro Bowl, 1991. Led league in receiving yards, 1991. Office: Dallas Cowboys One Cowboys Pky Irving TX 75063

IRVIN, MICHAEL P., lawyer; b. Ft. Worth, Apr. 29, 1950; BA, U. Tex., 1972; JD, U. Houston, 1975. Bar: Tex. 1975. Atty. Fulbright & Jaworski L.L.P., Houston, 1975—83, ptnr., 1983—, and head, energy and real property dept. Mem. ABA, Houston Bar Assn., State Bar Tex., Phi Delta Phi, Order of the Barons. Office: Fulbright & Jaworski LLP 1301 McKinney St Ste 5100 Houston TX 77010-3031 Office Phone: 713-651-3705. Office Fax: 713-651-5246. Business E-Mail: mirvin@fulbright.com.

IRVINE, JOHN ALEXANDER, lawyer; b. Sault Ste. Marie, Ont., Can., Mar. 10, 1947; s. Alexander and Ruth Catherine (Woolrich) I.; children from previous marriage: John Alexander, Allison Brooks; m. Lynda Kaye Myska Jenkins, May 24, 1981; children: James Woolrich, William Myska. BS, Auburn U., 1969; JD, Memphis State U., 1972. Bar: Tenn. 1972, Ohio 1982, Tex. 1985. Law clk. U.S. Dist. Ct. (we. dist.) Tenn., 1972-73; asst. dist. atty. gen. 15th Jud. Cir. Tenn., 1973-78; assoc. Glankler, Brown, Gilliland, Chase, Robinson and Raines, Memphis, 1978-81; asst. gen. counsel Mead Corp., Dayton, Ohio, 1981-84; ptnr. Porter & Clements, Houston, 1984-87; prin. Boyer, Norton & Blair, 1987-89; ptnr. Thelen, Marrin, Johnson & Bridges, 1989-94, mng. ptnr. Houston office, mem. mgmt. com., 1991-94; ptnr. Porter & Hedges, L.L.P., 1995—, chmn. litig. practice group, 2002—04, mem. mgmt. com., 2000—02. Bd. dirs. Make-A-Wish Found. Tex. Gulf Coast, 1985-86. Fellow Tex. Bar Found. (sustaining life; chair Region 4 nominating com. 2000), Houston Bar Found. (sustaining life; named Tex. Super Lawyer 2003, 2004); mem. ABA (vice chmn. com. corp. counsel, litig. sect. 1989-91, co-chmn. intellectual properties litig. com. 1996-99, co-chmn. trial practice com. 2000-2003, mem. task force judiciary 2003-, co-chmn. cle programs & evaluations), Internat. Assn. Def. Counsel, Am. Arbitration Assn. (bd. arbitrators), Nat. Assn. Securities Dealers (bd. arbitrators), Tex. Bar Assn., Tenn. Bar Assn., Fed. Bar Assn. (treas. 1997-98, v.p. 1998-99, pres.-elect 1999-2000, pres. 2000—), Memphis Bar Assn. (YLS, bd. dirs. 1976, treas. 1977), Ohio Bar Assn., Houston Bar Assn., Coll. State Bar Tex., Memphis State U. Law Sch. Alumnae Assn. (pres. 1975-76, 77-78), 5th Cir. Ct. Appeals Bar Assn., U.S. C. of C. (coun. on antitrust policy 1983—), Phoenix Club of Memphis (bd. dirs. 1977-79), Def. Rsch. Inst., Champions Golf Club, Houston Met. Racquet Club, Briar Club. Republican. Presbyterian. Avocations: sports, travel, reading. Office Phone: 713-226-6605. Personal E-mail: jirvine@porterhedges.com.

IRVINE, PETER BENNINGTON, clergyman; b. Chattanooga, June 8, 1951; s. James Bennington and Susan (Chambliss) I.; m. Angela Cowan, Mar. 5, 1983; stepchildren: John Clark Rumble, Laura Rumble O'Connell. BA, U. Tenn., 1974, JD, 1979; postgrad., Bread Loaf Sch. of English, 1981—82; MDiv, Gen. Theol. Sem., 2002. Bar: Tenn. 1979, Pa. 1983. Assoc. Chambliss, Bahner, Crutchfield, Gaston & Irvine, Chattanooga, 1979—81; copy editor Chattanooga Times, 1981—82; grant writer, rschr. Seton Hill Coll., Greensburg, Pa., 1983—86, dir. devel., 1986—89; assoc. dir. planned giving U. Pitts., 1989—92, dir. planned giving, 1992—95; dir. devel. and univ. rels. Pa. State U., McKeesport, 1996—99; oblate Order of Julian of Norwich, 2000—; resident chaplain St. Vincent Charity Hosp., 2002—03; chaplain, min. music Maryview State Hosp., Bridgeville, Pa., 2003—; pastoral assoc. Episcopal Ch. of Redeemer, 2003—. Episcopalian. Avocations: reading, canoeing, cross country skiing, music, theater. Office: Maryview Hosp 1601 Mayview Rd Bridgeville PA 15017 Home: 4036 Murray Ave Pittsburgh PA 15217-2702 Personal E-mail: pbirvine@comcast.net.

IRVINE, WILLIAM BURRISS, management consultant; b. Wheeling, W.Va., July 20, 1925; s. Russell Drake and Elizabeth (Carney) I.; m. Allen Claywell; children: William, Mary, Edward. BA in Econs., Cornell U., 1949. V.p. Basil L. Smith Sys., Phila., 1949-66; pres. Pa. Graphic Arts, Inc., Phila., 1966-78, Classified Devel. Corp., Bryn Mawr, Pa., 1978—, Nat. Media Svcs., Wilmington, NC, 2003—. Pres. Victor O'Neil Studios divsn. Herff Jones, Inc., N.Y.C., 1972-75; trustee Cornell Delta Phi Ednl. Found., N.Y., 1985; bd. dirs. Main Line Sch. Night, 1998. Author: Treasury of College Humor, 1947. Mem. St. Elmo Club of Phila., St. Elmo Club of N.Y., Lake White Club, Delta Phi (sec. 1960-62). Republican. Roman Catholic. Personal E-mail: classdev@zoomnet.net.

IRVING, GEORGE STEVEN, actor; b. Springfield, Mass., Nov. 1, 1922; s. Abraham and Rebecca (Sack) Shelasky; m. Maria Karnilova, Oct. 17, 1948; children: Alexander, Katherine. Student, Leland Powers Sch. of Theatre, Boston, 1941. Actor (on Broadway) play, Oklahoma, 1943, Lady in the Dark, 1943, Call Me Mister, 1946, Along Fifth Avenue, 1949, Gentlemen Prefer Blondes, 1949, Two's Company, 1952, Me and Juliet, 1953, Can-Can, 1954, Bells Are Ringing, 1957, The Beggar's Opera, 1957, The Good Soup, 1957, Irma La Douce, 1960, Romulus, 1962, Bravo Giovanni, 1962, Seidman and Son, 1962, Tovarich, 1963, A Murderer Among Us, 1964, Alfie, 1964, Anya, 1965, Galileo, 1967, The Happy Time, 1968, Promenade, 1969, An Evening With Richard Nixon, 1972 (Drama Desk award), Irene, 1973 (Tony award for best supporting actor 1973), On Your Toes, 1983, Me and My Girl, 1986, Cinderella, The Merry Widow, N.Y. City Opera, 1994, The Chocolate Soldier, 2005; stock and touring prodns. E-mail: gsirving@earthlink.net.

IRVING, GEORGE WASHINGTON, III, veterinarian, researcher, small business executive; b. N.Y.C., Apr. 25, 1940; s. George Washington Jr. and Frances (Connell) I.; m. Alice Marie Graves, Dec. 21, 1968; 1 child, George Washington IV. BS, U. Md., 1962; DVM, Purdue U., 1965; MS, Tex. A&M U., 1970. Diplomate Am. Coll. Lab. Animal Medicine, Am. Coll. Vet. Preventive Medicine. Commd. 1st lt. USAF, 1966, advanced through ranks to col., 1984; base veterinarian Niagara Falls Internat. Airport, NY, 1966, 388th Tactical Fighter Wing, Korat, Thailand, 1966-67; base veterinarian Wilford Hall USAF Med. Ctr., Lackland AFB, Tex., 1968; asst. chief vet. edn. br. USAF Sch. Aerospace Medicine, San Antonio, 1970-75; chief divsn. lab. animal medicine Armed Forces Inst. Pathology, Washington, 1976-79; grad. Armed Forces Staff Coll., 1975-76, Air War Coll., 1977; program mgr. Air Force Office Sci. Rsch., Bolling AFB, DC, 1979-82, dir. life sci., 1982-83; USAF liaison U.S. Army Med. R & D Command, Ft. Detrick, Md., 1983-84, dir. med. chem. def. rsch. program, 1984-87; cons. to surgeon gen. USAF, Washington, 1983-95; dir. Armed Forces Radiobiology Rsch. Inst., Bethesda, Md., 1987-91; staff dir. Human Systems Ctr., Brooks AFB, Tex., 1991-94, vice comdr., 1994-95, dir. re-engring., 1995-96; ret. USAF, 1996; v.p. Conceptual MindWorks, Inc., 1996—, v.p. sci. and tech. support svcs. Instr. grad. rsch. program NIH, Bethesda, 1976-85; merit rev. VA, Washington, 1978-84; cons. Stunkard, Miller Assocs., Bowie, Md., 1976-79. Editor: Selected Topics in Laboratory Animal Medicine, 15 vols., 1971-75; contbr. articles to jours. and chpts. to books; editor: Contemporary Topics in Laboratory Animal Sciences, 1995-97. Vice-min. Secular Franciscan Order, Holy Name Province, 1989-91; min. Tex. Dist., Sacred Heart Province, 1992-94, Los Tres Compañeros/The 3 Companions Region, 1994-98; co-chair capital campaign com., St. Joseph Honey Creek Cath. Ch., 2001-, mem. pastoral coun., 2002-, chmn. pastoral coun., 2005—. Decorated Legion of Merit with oak leaf cluster, Def. Superior Svc. medal, Air Force Commendation medal, Army Commendation medal, Meritorious Svc. medal, Joint Svc. Commendation medal, Vietnam Svc. medal. Fellow Aerospace Med. Assn.; mem. AVMA, Assn. Mil. Surgeons of U.S. (McCallam award 1988), D.C. Vet. Med. Assn. (pres. 1982), Am. Assn. for Lab. Animal Sci. (pres. nat. capital area br. 1981-82, v.p. 1998, pres. 1999), San Antonio-Austin Life Scis. Assn. (sec.), Brooks Aerospace Found. (treas.), Brooks Heritage Found., Brooks AFB Rod and Gun Club (pres. 1973-74), San Antonio Greater C. of C. (mem. Mil. Missions Task Force 2003-). Republican. Roman Catholic. Office: Conceptual MindWorks Inc 4318 Woodcock Dr Ste 210 San Antonio TX 78228-1316 Office Phone: 210-737-0777. Business E-Mail: girving@teamcmi.com.

IRVING, GREGORY PRINCE, manufacturing executive; b. Beverly, Mass., Feb. 13, 1946; s. Charles Henry and Margaret May Irving; m. Linda Bromley, Aug. 30, 1980; stepchildren: James R. Shoemaker, Catherine L. Shoemaker. BBA, Nichols Coll., 1969. Pres. Pella Windows & Door Co., San Francisco, 1983—91, Bisley Products, Gaseap, Tenn., 2000—02; v.p. nat. sales Dayton Techs., Chelsea Industries, Extrusion Industry, 1992—2000; v.p. Simonton Windows, Parkersburg, W.Va., 2002—. Republican. Presbyterian. Home: 522 4th St Marietta OH 45750 Office: Simontom Window Co 5300 Briscoe Rd Parkersburg WV 26102

IRVING, JEFFREY ALAN, management consultant, educator, lawyer; b. N.Y.C., May 20, 1947; s. Herbert and Florence (Rapoport) I.; m. Maureen Pickett, July 20, 1988; children: Tara, Michael. BSBA cum laude, U. Denver, 1969; JD, U. Okla., 1973; MBA with honors, Harvard U., 1980. Bar: N.Y. 1974, U.S. Dist. Ct. (ea. and so. dists.) N.Y. 1975, U.S. Ct. Appeals (2d cir.) 1975, U.S. Supreme Ct. 1978. Legal intern Legal Aid Soc., Norman, Okla., 1972-73; assoc. Pincus, Hutner, Seeman & Hasen, N.Y.C., 1973-74; exec. v.p., gen. counsel Global Sysco divsn. Sysco Corp., Garden City, N.Y., 1974-91; pres. food svcs. divsn. Seabrook Bros. and Sons. Inc., 1991-92. Founder, mng. dir. cons. firm, Great Neck N.Y.; mem. faculty Hofstra U. Coll. Bus. Administrn. Editor Human Rights Rsch. Coun. Jour., 1972-73; contbr. articles to Inc. mag., Food Svc. Distbr. mag. Bd. dirs. L.I. chpt. March of Dimes, 1975-91. Mem. Bar N.Y., Nassau County Bar Assn. (ethics com. 1974-80), Freight Users Assn. N.Y. (pres. 1978, bd. dirs. 1975-92). Republican. Avocations: tennis, sailing. Home: 195 Laurel Lane Syosset NY 11791 E-mail: icgnewyork@att.net.

IRVING, JOHN WINSLOW, writer; b. Exeter, N.H., Mar. 2, 1942; s. Colin F.N. and Frances (Winslow) I.; m. Shyla Leary, Aug. 20, 1964 (div. 1981); children: Colin, Brendan; m. Janet Turnbull, June 6, 1987; 1 child, Everett. Student, U. Pitts., 1961-62, U. Vienna, 1963-64; BA, U. N.H., 1965; M.F.A., U. Iowa, 1967. Asst. wrestling coach Phillips Exeter Acad., 1964-65; asst. prof. English Windham Coll., 1967-69, 70-72, Mt. Holyoke Coll., 1975-78; writer-in-residence U. Iowa, 1972-75; with Bread Loaf Writer's Conf., 1976, Brandeis U., 1978-79; asst. wrestling coach Northfield Mt. Hermon Sch., 1981-83, Fessenden Sch., 1984-86; head wrestling coach Vermont Acad., 1987-89. Author: (novels) Setting Free the Bears, 1969, The Water-Method Man, 1972, The 158-Pound Marriage, 1974, The World According to Garp, 1978, The Hotel New Hampshire, 1981, The Cider House Rules, 1985 (Academy award for best adapted screenplay 2000), A Prayer for Owen Meany, 1989, A Son of the Circus, 1994, A Widow for One Year, 1998, The Fourth Hand, 2001, Until I Find You, 2005, others, (collection of short stories and essays) Trying to Save Piggy Sneed, 1996, My Movie Business (a memoir), 1999; contbr. short stories and revs. to other publs. Rockefeller Found. grantee, 1971-72; Nat. Endowment for Arts fellow, 1974-75, Guggenheim fellow, 1976-77; inducted into Nat. Wrestling Hall of Fame, 1992, Am. Acad. of Arts and Letters, 2001.

IRVING, SUSAN JEAN, government executive; b. Washington, Apr. 25, 1949; d. Frederick and Dorothy Jean Irving; m. Joseph Alexander Rieser Jr., Feb. 28, 1976; 1 child, Alexander Hoon Irving Rieser. BA, Wellesley Coll., 1971; MAT, Harvard Grad. Sch. Edn., 1972; M in Pub. Policy, Harvard U., 1974, PhD, 1976. Cert. Govt. Fin. Mgr., Assn. Govt. Accts. Legis. asst. to U.S. Sen. Abe Ribicoff, Washington, 1976-79; staff dir. Exec. Office of the Pres. Pres.'s Coun. of Econ. Advisers, Washington, 1979-81; external rels. officer Internat. Monetary Fund, Washington, 1981-82; v.p. Com. for a Responsible Fed. Budget, Washington, 1982-84; sr. econ. advisor Mondale for Pres., 1984; legis. dir. for U.S. Sen. Max Baucus Washington, 1985; lectr. pub. policy John F. Kennedy Sch. Govt. Harvard U., Cambridge, Mass., 1986-89; faculty Tng. Inst. U.S. Govt. Accountability Office, Washington, 1989—92, assoc. dir. for fed. budget issues, 1992-2000, dir. fed. budget analysis, 2000—; fellow Inst. Politics Harvard U., 1986. Bd. dirs. Am. Assn. Budget and Program Analysis. Co-pres. Stoddert PTA, Washington, 1997-98. Recipient Cert. of Appreciation Am. Assn. for Budget and Program Analysis, 1997, Outstanding Svc. award, 1993. Fellow Nat. Assn. for Pub. Adminstrn.; mem. Assn. Pub. Policy and Mgmt. Avocations: walking, needlepoint on plastic. Office: US GAO 441 G St NW Washington DC 20548-0001 Office Phone: 202-512-9142. Business E-Mail: irvings@gao.gov.

IRVING, THOMAS L., lawyer; b. Salt Lake City, Apr. 29, 1951; BA in Chem. magna cum laude, U. Utah, 1974; JD, Duke U., 1977. Bar: D.C. 1977; U.S. Ct. Appeals (fed. cir.); U.S. Patent Office. Mem. Finnegan, Henderson, Farabow, Garrett & Dunner, Washington. Author: Selected Legal Papers; contbr. to profl. jours. Recipient Am. Jurisprudence Book award Duke U. Sch. Law 1976; named one of best lawyers in intellectual property law, Best Lawyers in Am., 2005. Mem. ABA, Am. Intellectual Property Law Assn. (chmn. CAFC dist. ct. subcommittee 1985-87, chmn. CLE subcommittee 1988-89, chmn. 1989-1991, bd. dirs. 1991—), Am. Chem. Soc., Phi Beta Kappa, Phi Kappa Phi. Office: Finnegan Henderson Farabow Garrett & Dunner LLP 901 New York Ave NW Washington DC 20001-3315 Office Phone: 202-408-4000. Office Fax: 202-408-4400. Business E-Mail: tom.irving@finnegan.com.

IRWIN, ANNA MAE, English language educator; b. Petrolia, Kans., Aug. 19; d. Clarence Newton and Elsie Mildred (Stump) Williams; m. Everett Irwin, Sept. 1, 1938; children: Stanley, Pamela, Steven. BS, Northeastern State U., Tahlequah, Okla., 1940; postgrad., Denver U. and Colo. U., 1960-80. Bookkeeper, typist Fed. Bur. Pub. Rds., Denver, 1942-45; tchr. Denver Pub. Schs., 1945-46; typist State Dept. Employment, Denver, 1958-60; tchr. Aurora (Colo.) Pub. Schs., 1960-84; tutor ESL for refugees State Dept. Edn., Denver, 1988-91. Mem. adv. bd., bd. dirs. Unity Ch., Denver, 1986—; mem. and pres. aux. Goodwill Industries, Denver, 1996—, 2d v.p., 1st v.p. 1992-96, pres. 1993-96; state del., county del., congl. del., precinct com. woman Rep. Party, Denver, 1970-84. Recipient Mary Venable Svc. award for vol. work Goodwill Industries, 1996. Mem. Book Review Club (v.p., program chmn. 1990-93), Cherry Creek Womens Club. Avocations: bridge, travel, book review, ceramics.

IRWIN, BILL, actor, clown; b. Santa Monica, Calif., Apr. 11, 1950; s. Horace and Elizabeth Irwin; m. Martha Roth. BA in Theatre Arts, Oberlin Coll.; grad., Ringling Brothers and Barnum & Bailey's Clown Coll. Actor & writer (plays) The Regard of Flight, 1987, Largely New York, 1989; actor: (plays) The Accidental Death of an Anarchist, Fool Moon (Spl. Tony Award for Live Theatrical Presentation), The Goat, or Who is Sylvia?, 2002, Who's Afraid of Virginia Woolf?, 2005 (Tony Award for best performance by a leading actor in a play, 2005); (films) Manhattan by Numbers, 1993, Stanley's Gig, 2000, How the Grinch Stole Christmas, 2000, The Laramie Project, 2002, Igby Goes Down, 2002, The Truth About Miranda, 2004, The Manchurian Candidate, 2004. Named to Internat. Clown Hall of Fame, 1999.

IRWIN, DIANNE E., psychology educator; b. July 22, 1946; d. Donald J. and Dorothy R. (Shaw) I. AA, Valley Coll., 1970; BA, Calif. State U., San Bernardino, 1972; MA, Calif. State U., Fullerton, 1974; PhD, U.S. Internat. U., 1979. Lectr., instr. Calif. State U.-San Bernardino, 1973, psychometrist, 1974-78, dir. learning ctr., 1974-84; prof. psychology Glendale (Calif.) Community Coll., 1985—, chmn. of psychology, 1992—; asst. chair of soc. science, 2002—; lectr. Valley Coll., San Bernardino, 1973, Calif. State U., Fullerton, 1974; cons. nat. tests, psychol. corp., Harcourt Brace Jovanovich, Inc., 1985-86; mem. Calif. Statewide Legal Compliance com. instructionally related material review, 1979-84; speaker in field. Editor, author (with Sherman) Writing Tutor's Training Manual, 1985; co-author: (with L. Sherman) Writers Tutor Training, 1986; contbr. numerous articles to profl. jours. Mem. APA, Student Pers. Assn., Western Coll. Reading Assn., Western Psychol. Assn., Am. Pers. and Guidance Assn. Home: 918 W Edgemont Dr San Bernardino CA 92405-2023 Office: Glendale Coll 1500 N Verdugo Rd Glendale CA 91208-2809 Office Phone: 818-240-1000 x5460. Business E-Mail: dirwin@glendale.edu.

IRWIN, DONALD PAULDING, lawyer; b. N.Y.C., Oct. 15, 1944; s. Donald McDonald and Sarah Paulding (Ray) Irwin; m. Stoner Winslett; children: Louise Porcher Gray, Elizabeth Sinclair, Alex W. Pankoff, Caroline Winslett. AB, Princeton U., 1965; JD, MA in Polit. sci., Yale U., 1971. Bar: Va. 71, DC 77. Assoc. Hunton & Williams, Richmond, Va., 1971—78, ptnr., 1978—. Mem.: Commonwealth Club (Richmond), Country Club of Va., Met. Club (Washington). Republican. Episcopalian. Avocation: golf. Home: 403 Harlan Cir Richmond VA 23226-1634 Office: Hunton & Williams Riverfront Plz E 951 E Byrd St Richmond VA 23219-1535 Office Phone: 804-788-8357. E-mail: dirwin@hunton.com.

IRWIN, DONNA RICE, music educator; b. Union City, Tenn., Apr. 30, 1970; d. Fred L. and Linda F. Rice; m. David C. Tinnell Jr., June 5, 1993 (div. Dec. 15, 1997); children: Mitchell, Cory; m. Michael D. Irwin, May 27, 2000. MusB in Music Edn., Campbellsville Coll., 1992; MusM in Music Edn., Campbellsville U., 1999; postgrad., U. Ky., 2001—. Cert. tchr. Ky. Admissions asst. Campbellsville (Ky.) Coll., 1992; substitute tchr. Taylor County Mid. Sch., 1992—93; choral dir. Marion County Schs., Lebanon, Ky., 1993—2001; adj. prof. Sch. Music Campbellsville (Ky.) U., 2001—04, asst. prof. edn. Sch. Edn., 2004—. Composer, arranger: choral works. Music dir. Asbury United Meth. Ch., 2003—. Recipient 1st place mixed choir, Festivals of Music, St. Louis, 2001. Mem.: 4th Dist. Choral Dirs.' Assn. (pres. 1999—2001), Ky. Music Educators Assn. (mem. state choral coun. 1999—2001, festival commn. 1999—2001, adjudictor 2001—, named Fourth Dist. U. Music Tchr. of Yr. 2004). Avocations: reading, birdwatching, fishing, boating, camping. Home: 444 Dowell St Campbellsville KY 42718 Office: Campbellsville U 100 University Dr Campbellsville KY 42718 Business E-Mail: drirwin@capmbellsville.edu.

IRWIN, GERALD PORT, physician; b. Muncie, Ind., July 11, 1945; s. Francis Inlow and Helen Marcella (Morgan) I.; m. Martha Sue Vincent, Mar. 10, 1946; 1 child, Tamara Suzette. AB in Biol. Sci., Ind. U., 1968; MD, Ind. U., Indpls., 1972. Diplomate Am. Bd. Family Physicians. Intern and resident Ball Meml. Hosp., Muncie, Ind., 1972-73; pvt. practice Alexandria, Ind., 1973—. Med. dir. Richland Twp. Fire Dept., Anderson. Mem. AMA (Physician Recognition award 1992-95, 98-2001), Am. Acad. Family Physicians,Ind. State Med. Assn., Ind. Assn. Family Physicians, Lions, Elks. Methodist. Avocations: computers, backpacking. Office: PO Box 124 Alexandria IN 46001-0124 Office Phone: 765-724-7711.

IRWIN, GLENN WARD, JR., medical educator, physician, academic administrator; b. Roachdale, Ind., July 18, 1920; s. Glenn Ward and Elsie (Browning) I.; m. Marianna Ashby; children: Ann Graybill Irwin Warden, William Browning, Elizabeth Ashby Irwin Schiffli. BS, Ind. U., Bloomington, 1942; MD, Ind. U., Indpls., 1944; LLD (hon.), Ind. U., 1986, Marian Coll., 1987. Diplomate: Am. Bd. Internal Medicine. Intern Meth. Hosp., Indpls., 1944-45; resident in internal medicine Ind. U. Med. Ctr., Indpls., 1945-46, 48-50; mem. faculty Ind. U., Indpls., 1950—, instr., asst. prof. then assoc. prof., 1950-61, prof. medicine, 1961-86, prof. emeritus, 1986, dean Sch.

Medicine, 1965-73, dean emeritus, 1986, v.p., 1974-86; chancellor Ind. U.-Purdue U., Indpls., 1973-74, chancellor emeritus, 1989. Sr. assoc. Ind. U. Found. Bd. dirs. Goodwill Industries of Ctrl. Ind., Indpls., Greater Indpls. Progress Com., Greater Indpls. YMCA, Walther Med. Rsch. Inst., Walther Oncology Ctr., Indpls. Health Inst., Eiteljorg Mus. Western Art and the Am. Indian; elder 2d Presbyn. Ch. Served to capt. M.C. U.S. Army, 1946-48. Recipient Disting. Alumnus award Ind. U. Sch. Medicine, 1972, Otis R. Bowen Physician County Service award, Benjamin Harrison award, Ind. Acad. award; named Sagamore of the Wabash, Gov. of Ind., 1961, 79, 86. Fellow ACP (gov. for Ind. 1964-70); mem. AMA, Ind. State Med. Assn., Marion County Med. Soc., Ind. Soc. of Chgo., 500 Festival Assn., James Whitcomb Riley Meml. Assn. (bd. govs. 1986—), Newcomen Soc., Sigma Xi, Alpha Omega Alpha, Beta Gamma Sigma, Sigma Theta Tau. Clubs: Columbia (Indpls.), Contemporary (Indpls.), Meridian Hills Country, Skyline (bd. dirs.). Lodges: Masons (33 degree), Rotary. Home: 8025 N Illinois St Indianapolis IN 46260-2938 Office: Ind U-Purdue U at Indpls 1120 South Dr Indianapolis IN 46202-5135 Office Phone: 317-274-5160. E-mail: drglenni@aol.com.

IRWIN, HEATHER MAY, writer, interior designer; b. Troy, N.Y., Feb. 19, 1949; d. Richard Jay and Helen Irma I. Student, SUNY, 1969, New Sch. Contemporary Radio, 1979, Interior Design Sch., 1984. Ordained pastor Dave Robinson Ministries, Family Prayer Ctr., Tulsa, Okla., 2002. Reporter Capital Newspaper Group, Albany, N.Y., 1969-73; freelance writer Insight Mag., Latham, N.Y., 1973-76; owner, pub. The Daily Woman, Watervliet, N.Y., 1976-79; interior designer Mayfair Home Furnishings, Albany, 1980-85; owner, pres. Wingate House of Design, Albany, 1985—91; owner Creations Interior Design Firm, 1992—. Pres. Woman's Counseling Collective, Albany, 1977, Mission Vision Assn., Inc., 1997—; mem. New Hope for Life Ch., Nassau, NY, 1999—2003. Mem. Interior Design Soc. (pres. ea. N.Y. chpt. 1986-88). Clubs: Ecology (Mechecsville, N.Y.) (v.p. 1971). Avocations: swimming, tennis, reading, painting. Home: 49 Hillcrest Rd Latham NY 12110-4135

IRWIN, JOHN DAVID, electrical engineering educator; b. Mpls., Aug. 9, 1939; s. Arthur Fowle and Virginia I.; m. Patricia Edith Watson, Aug. 26, 1961; children: Geri Marie, John David, Laura Lynne. BEE, Auburn U., Ala., 1961; MS, U. Tenn., 1962, PhD, 1967. Mem. tech. staff Bell Labs., Holmdel, NJ, 1967—68; supr. Bell Labs, Holmdel, 1968—69; asst. prof. elec. engring. Auburn U., 1969—72, assoc. prof., 1972—73, assoc. prof., head dept., 1973—76, prof., head dept., 1976—, Earle C. Williams Eminent Scholar and dept. head, 1993—; pres. Southeastern Ctr. for Elec. Engring. Edn., Orlando, Fla., 1983—84. Hon. prof. Chinese Acad. Sci., Inst. for Semiconductors, Beijing, 2004. Author: (with Nelson and Carroll) Introduction to Computer Logic, 1975, (with E.R. Graf) Industrial Noise and Vibration Control, 1979, Basic Engineering Circuit Analysis, 1984, 8th edit. (with R.M. Nelms), 2005, (with V.P. Nelson, H.T. Nagle, B.D. Carroll, J.D. Irwin) Digital Logic Circuit Analysis and Design, 1995, (with D.V. Kerns) Introduction to Electrical Engineering, 1995, On Becoming An Engineer, 1997; editor-in-chief The Industrial Electronics Handbook, 1997, Emerging Multimedia Computer Communication Technologies. Fellow IEEE (editor jour. Indsl. Electronics 1982-83, Centennial medal 1984, IEEE-Indsl. Electronics Soc. A.H. Hornfeck Svc. award 1986, IEEE Region III Outstanding Educator award 1989), Am. Soc. Engring. Edn. (Elec. and Computer Engring. Disting. Educator award 2001); mem. IEEE Edn. Soc. (pres. 1989-90, IEEE-Indsl. Electronics Soc. Achievement award 1991, IEEE Edn. Soc. award 1991, IEEE Edn. Soc./Soc. McGraw Hill Jacob Millman award 1993, Undergrad. Tchg. award 1998, Third Millennium medal 2000, Richard M. Emberson award, 2000). Roman Catholic. Home: PO Box 2740 Auburn AL 36831-2740 Office: Auburn U Dept Engring Auburn AL 36849 Business E-Mail: jdirwin@eng.auburn.edu.

IRWIN, JOHN ROBERT, oil industry executive; b. Melbourne, Australia, July 24, 1945; came to U.S., 1969; s. Robert L. and Daisy O. I.; m. Margo E. Mayon, 1979; children: Joshua R., Elizabeth J. BE with honors, Melbourne U., M Engring. Sci., 1969; MS in Indsl. Adminstrn., Purdue U., 1970; AMP, Harvard Bus. Sch., 1990. Registered profl. engr., Australia. With Kerr-McGee Corp., 1970-72; ops. and mgmt. positions Transworld Drilling Co. (sub. Kerr-McGee Corp.), 1972-75; mgr. ops. Transworld Drilling Co., Sharjah, Nigeria and La., 1975-79, Atwood Oceanics, Inc., Houston, 1979-80, gen. mgr., 1980, v.p., 1980-88, exec. v.p., 1988-92; pres., CEO, 1992—. Bd. dirs. Atwood Oceanics, Inc., Offshore Tech. Conf.; chmn. Internat. Assn. Drilling Contractors, 2000. Fellow: Inst. Engrs. Australia. Avocations: reading, history, Australian Rules football. Office: Atwood Oceanics Inc PO Box 218350 Houston TX 77218-8350 Office Phone: 281-749-7800.

IRWIN, JOHN THOMAS, humanities educator; b. Houston, Apr. 24, 1940; s. William Henry and Marguerite Harriet (Hunsaker) I.; m. Laura Elizabeth Scott, Sept. 23, 1978 (div. 1991); m. Meme Amosso, May 29, 1993. BA, U. St. Thomas, 1962; MA, Rice U., PhD, 1970. Supr. public affairs library NASA Manned Spacecraft Center, Houston, 1966-7; asst. prof. English, Johns Hopkins U., 1970-74, prof. writing seminars, 1977—, Decker prof. in humanities, 1984—, chmn., 1977-96; editor Ga. Rev., U. Ga., 1974-77. Author: Doubling and Incest/Repetition and Revenge, 1975, expanded edit., 1995, The Heisenberg Variations, 1976, American Hieroglyphics, 1980, The Mystery to a Solution, 1994, Just Let Me Say This About That, 1998, As Long As It's Big, 2005; editor: Johns Hopkins Press Fiction and Poetry series, 1978—, Words Brushed by Music, 2004, So the Story Goes, 2005; mem. edtl. bd. Poe Studies, Ariz. Quar.; contbr. articles to profl. jours. Served with USNR, 1963-66. Recipient John Gardner medal Rice U., 1970, Christian Gauss prize, 1994, Scaglione prize for comparative lit., 1994; Danforth fellow, 1962, Guggenheim fellow, 1991. Mem.: Am. Acad. Arts and Scis., Tudor and Stuart Club, F. Scott Fitzgerald Soc., Faulkner Soc., Poe Studies Assn. (v.p. 1995—97), Assn. Lit. Scholars and Critics. Home: 5313 Springlake Way Baltimore MD 21212-3413 Office: Johns Hopkins U Writing Seminars Gilman 135 Baltimore MD 21218 Office Phone: 410-516-6287. Business E-Mail: jirwin@jhu.edu.

IRWIN, JOHN WESLEY, publisher; b. Toronto, Ont., Can., July 11, 1937; s. John Coverdale Watson and Annie Elizabeth (Hiltz) I.; m. Marjorie Eleanor Gray, Dec. 16, 1961; children— John Joseph, Marjorie Elizabeth, Peter David Gordon, Andrew James Gray. BA with honours, U. Toronto, 1959; LLD honoris causa, McMaster U., 1999. Tchr., 1959-60; pres. Book Soc. Can. Ltd. (ednl. books), Agincourt, Ont., 1960-83, Irwin Pub. Inc., 1983-89, Ednl. Project Resources Can. Ltd., Willowdale, Canada, 1994—96, Scripture Union-Can., 1997—2005. Chmn. bd. trustees McMaster Div. Coll., Hamilton, Ont., 1988-99. Recipient Canadian Confedn. medal, 1967 Mem. Assn. Canadian Pubs. (treas. 1977), Canadian Edn. Assn., Can. Copyright Inst. (gov. 1970-77, 81-99), Inter-Varsity Christian Fellowship Can. (life, dir. 1973-2003, chmn. 1979-91), Canadian Feed the Children (chmn. 1992-95), Peiromai Club (Toronto), Empire Club. Anglican. Home: 81 Bayview Ridge Willowdale ON Canada M2L 1E3 Office: 1885 Clements Rd Unit 226 Pickering ON Canada L1W 3U4 E-mail: jirwinc617@rogers.com.

IRWIN, JUDITH WESTPHAL, language educator; b. Kenosha, Wis., Jan. 25, 1949; d. Carl Wells and Beulah (Kessler) Westphal; 1 child, Christina. BA, Ill.Wesleyan U., 1970; MS, PhD, U. Wis. Tchr. 7th grade Dundee (Ill.) Pub. Schs., 1973-75; asst. prof. edn. Purdue U., West Lafayette, Ind., 1978-82; assoc. prof. Loyola U., Chgo., 1982-87; prof. U. Conn., Storrs, 1987—. Conductor numerous lang./writing/comprehension workshops. Author: Teaching Reading Comprehension Processes, 1986, 2d revised edit., 1991; co-author: Promoting Active Reading Comprehension Strategies, 1989; editor: Understanding and Teaching Cohesion Comprehension, 1986; co-editor: Reading/Writing Connections: Learning from Research; contbr. articles to profl. jours. Mem. Instructional Reading Assn., Nat. Coun. Rsch. in English. Office: U Conn Dept Edn Storrs Mansfield CT 06268 also: 47 Whitney Dr Woodstock NY 12498-1947

IRWIN, KENNY, professional race car driver; b. Indpls., Aug. 5, 1969; Named Raybestos Rookie of Yr. award, 1998, NASCAR Craftsman Truck Series Rookie of Yr., 1996, USAC Stoops Freightliner Sprint Car Series Rookie of Yr., 1993. Achievements include 7 wins USAC Stoops Freightliner Sprint Car Series, 1993; finished 2d in points USAC Silver Crown Series, 1996; 5 full seasons USAC Skoal Nat. Midget Series, including 8 wins, 20 2d-place, 59 top-5, 87 top-10, 1996 championship; NASCAR Craftsman Truck Series, 1997—, including 2 wins Metro Dade-Homestead Motorsports Complex, Tex. Motor Speedway, 10th-place finish in series point standings. Avocations: golf, pool.

IRWIN, KERRI LYNNE, pharmacist, writer, small business owner; b. Salinas, Calif., Nov. 10, 1959; d. Leslie Morris Rosenblatt and Marilyn Phyllis Kent; m. George William Irwin, Jan. 14, 1983 (div. July 26, 2003); children: Jennifer Jae, Race Christopher. BS, Oreg. State, Corvallis, 1984. Registered pharmacist Oreg. Pharmacist Patrick's Pharmacy, Bend, Oreg., 1984—87, Ctrl. Oreg. Dist. Hosp., Redmond, 1987—89, Rite Aid, Bend, 1989—92, St. Charles Med. Ctr., Bend, 1992—2003; home care I.V. and Sisters Drug Store, 2003—. Owner Mountain View Bed and Breakfast. Author: (book) What's for Dinner? No Problem!, 2001. Avocations: painting, mountain biking, water-skiing, hiking, gardening. Home: 65705 W Hwy 20 Bend OR 97701

IRWIN, LINDA BELMORE, public relations/marketing consultant; b. Portland, Oreg., Apr. 29, 1950; d. Calvin C. and Dorothy B. (Belmore) Harper; m. Michael Hugh Irwin, June 24, 1989. Student, Portland State U., 1968—72. With Hyatt Regency, New Orleans, 1975-78; catering Hyatt Regency-Capitol Hill, Washington, 1978-80; dir. catering Hyatt, Anaheim, Calif., 1978-80; mgr. Dockside Yacht Sales, Annapolis, Md., 1981-85; dir. sales and mktg. Loew's Hotel, 1985-86; dir. mktg. Annapolis Marriott, 1986-88; ind. mktg. cons. Washington, Dallas, Cin. and Loudoun County, Va., 1988—. Amb. State of Md., Annapolis, 1986-88; mktg. chair Tourism Coun. Annapolis and Anne Arundel County; curricula advisor Anne Arundel C.C.; mem. fund raising com. Ch. Circle Beautification Trust; chair comm., 2002-04, chair fellowship, 2002-03; officer St. Peters Episc. Ch., 2001-04, stewardship com., 2003, mem. vestry bd., 2001-04; sec. Mt. Calvary Guild, 2003-04; vol. Nat. Day Prayer, 2001-2004, Passion Play, Arts in the Alley, 2004, VSA Arts for the Disabled; media/pub. rels. rep. Loudoun County; mem. steering com. Passion Play; chair com. Loudoun Ch. Alliance, 2004; mem. media steering com. Arts in the Alley; bd. dirs. Main St. Loudoun, 2005— Mem. Nat. Banquet mgrs. Guild (founder L.A. chpt.), Nat. Assn. Female Execs. (area dir. 1985—), Annapolis C. of C. (ambassador 1985-88), Greater Washington Soc. of Assn. Execs., Anne Arundel Trade Coun., Md. Tourism Coun. (adv. bd.), Internat. Platform Assn. Republican. Episcopalian. Avocations: sailing, travel, literature, ballet, reading. E-mail: lindairwin@adelphia.net.

IRWIN, MARY JANE, engineering educator; b. Cairo, Ill., July 14, 1949; BS in Math., Memphis State U., 1971; MS in Computer sci., U. Ill., 1975, PhD in Computer sci., 1977; Doctorate (hon.), Chalmers U., Sweden, 1997. Grad. rsch. and grad. tchg. asst. computer sci. U. Ill., Champaign-Urbana, 1972—77; asst. prof. computer sci. Pa. State U., University Park, 1977—83; rsch. staff Supercomputing Rsch. Ctr. Inst. for Def. Analysis, Bowie, Md., 1986; assoc. prof. computer sci. Pa. State U., University Park, Pa., 1983—89, dept. head computer sci., 1991—93, prof. computer sci. and engring., 1989—99, disting. prof. computer sci. and engring., 1999—. Fellow: IEEE (Cert. of Appreciation 1993—95), Assn. Computing Machinery (Leadership award 1993); mem.: Nat. Acad. Engring. Office: Pa State Univ Dept Computer Sci and Engring 227 Pond Lab University Park PA 16802 Home: 108 Yost Dr Spring Mills PA 16875

IRWIN, MATT, physician; b. Sacramento, Calif. s. Richard and Lovinia Burke Irwin; m. Helena Cristina daSilva, Feb. 9, 1993. BSc, U. Va., 1983—88; MSW, Cath. U. of Am., 1995—97; MD, George Wash. U., 1997—2000. Counselor Adventure Bound Sch., Charlottesville, Va., 1988—90; tchr. Lisbon Am. Sch., Portugal, 1991—93, Escuela Am., El Salvador, 1993—95, Woodson Adult H.S., Fairfax, Va., 1995—98; pvt. practice physician Alexandria, Va., 2004—; med. dir. Capital Hospice, Alexandria, Va., 2004—. Donor Tibetan Children's Project, San Francisco, 1977—. Full Merit scholarship, Cath. U. of Am., 1995. Mem.: AMA, Am. Acad. Family Practice. Home: 2226 Willam and Mary Dr Alexandria VA 22308 Office: 517 Wythe St Alexandria VA 22308 Office Phone: 703-780-1261. Personal E-mail: drmattirwin@yahoo.com.

IRWIN, MILDRED LORINE WARRICK, library consultant, volunteer; b. Kellerton, Iowa, June 21, 1917; d. Webie Arthur and Bonnie Lorine (Hyatt) DeVries; m. Carl Wesley Warrick, Feb. 11, 1937 (dec. June 1983); children: Carl Dwayne, Arthur Will; m. John B. Irwin, Feb. 1, 1994 (dec. Apr. 10, 1997). BS in Edn., Drake U., 1959; M of Librarianship, Kans. State Tchrs. Coll., 1970. Cert. tchr., libr., Iowa. Elem. tchr. Monroe Ctr. Rural Sch., Kellerton, Iowa, 1935-37, Denham Rural Sch., Grand River, Iowa, 1945-48, Grand River Ind. Sch., 1948-52, Woodmansee Rural Sch., Decatur, Iowa, 1952-55, Centennial Rural Sch., Decatur, 1955-56; elem. tchr., acting libr. Cen. Decatur Sch., Leon, Iowa, 1956-71, media libr. jr. and sr. high sch., 1971-79; libr. Northminster Presbyn. Ch., Tucson, 1984-93, advisor, 1994—. Media resource instr. Graceland Coll., Lamoni, Iowa, 1971-72; lit. dir. S.W. Iowa Assn. Classroom Tchrs., 1965-69; instr. workshop Tucson Mall, Ariz., 2002, 03. Editor (media packet) Mini History and Quilt Blocks, 1976, Grandma Lori's Nourishing Nuggets for Body and Soul, 1985, As I Recall (Loren Drake), 1989, Foland Family Supplement III, 1983; author: (with Quentin Oiler) Van Der Vlugt Family Record, 1976; compiler, editor Abigail Specials, 1991, Abigail Assemblage, 1996; compiler Tribute to Ferm Mills 1911-1992, 1992; co-editor: (with Dorothy Heitlinger) Milestones and Touchstones, 1993, Musings From the Heart, 1999; compiler Musical Ministry, 2002; contbr. articles to publs. Leader Grand River 4-H Club for Girls, 1954-58; sec. South Ctrl. Iowa Quarter Horse Assn., Chariton, 1967-68; chmn. Decatur County Dems., 1981-83, del., 1970-83; pianist Salvation Army Amphi League of Mercy Rhythm Noters, 1984-90; pianist, dir. Joymakers, 1990—; Sunday Sch. tchr. Decatur United Meth. Ch., 1945-54, 80-83, lay speaker, 1981-83, dir. vacation Bible sch., 1982, 83. Named Classroom Tchr. of Iowa Classrom Tchrs. Assn., 1962, Woman of Yr., Leon Bus. and Profl. Women, 1978, Northminster Presbyn. Ch. Women, 1990; named to Internat. Profl. and Bus. Women Hall of Fame for outstanding achievements in field of edn. and libr. sci., 1995; English and reading grantee Nat. Dept. Edn., 1966. Mem. NEA (life), AAUW (chmn. Tucson creative writing/cultural interests 1986-87, 89-93, historian, 1994—, Honoree award for ednl. found. programs Tucson br., Svc. award 1991), Internat. Reading Assn. (pres. Clarke-Ringgold-Decatur chpts. 1967-68), Cen. Cmty. Tchrs. Assn. (pres. 1961-62), Pima County Ret. Tchrs. Assn. (pres. 1989-90), Decatur County Assn. (pres. 1961-63), Decatur County Ret. Tchrs. Assn. (historian 1980-83), Iowa Edn. Assn. (life), Presbyn. Women (hon. life 1990—), Luth. Ch. Libr. Assn. (historian Tucson area chpt. 1991-92, v.p. 1993-94, pres. 1994-95), Delta Kappa Gamma (pres. Iowa Beta XI chpt. 1974-76, sec. 1984-85, historian Ariz. Alpha Gamma chpt. 1986-89). Democrat. Presbyterian. Avocations: walking, computing, horseback riding, reading, writing.

IRWIN, PHILIP DONNAN, lawyer; b. Madison, Wis., Sept. 6, 1933; s. Constant Louis and Isabel Dorothy (Elfving) I.; m. Sandra L. McMahan, Sept. 14, 1985; children: Jane Donnan, James Haycraft, Victoria Wisnom, Philip Donnan Jr. BA, U. Wyo., 1954; LLB, Stanford U., 1957. Bar: Wyo. 1957, Calif. 1958. Assoc. O'Melveny & Myers, L.A., 1957-65, ptnr., 1965-2000, of counsel, 2000—. Mem. planning com. Inst. Fed. Taxation of U. So. Calif. Law Ctr., 1976—, chairperson, 1995-98; spkr. legal seminars. Contbr. articles legal jours. Trustee Mackenzie Found., Los Angeles, 1969— . Recipient Dana Latham Meml. Lifetime Achievement award, LA County Bar Assn. (Taxation Sect.), 2002. Mem.: Calif. Club (L.A.). Republican. Episcopalian. Office: O'Melveny & Myers 400 S Hope St Rm 1835 Los Angeles CA 90071-2899 Office Phone: 213-430-6467. Business E-Mail: pirwin@omm.com.

IRWIN, R. ROBERT, lawyer; b. Denver, July 27, 1933; s. Royal Robert and Mildred Mary (Wilson) Irwin; m. Sue Ann Scott, Dec. 16, 1956; children: Lori, Stacy, Kristi, Amy. Student, U. Colo., 1951-54; BS in Law, U. Denver, 1955, LLB, 1957. Bar: Colo. 1957, Wyo. 1967. Asst. atty. gen. State of Colo., 1958-66; asst. divsn. atty. Mobil Oil Corp., Casper, Wyo., 1966-70; prin. atty. No. Natural Gas Co., Omaha, 1970-72; sr. atty., asst. sec. Coastal Oil & Gas Corp., Denver, 1972-83; ptnr. Baker & Hostetler, 1983-87; pvt. practice Denver, 1987—. Mem.: Rocky Mountain Oil and Gas Assn., Colo. Bar Assn., Denver Law Club. Republican. Office: 650 S Alton Way Apt 4D Denver CO 80247-1669 Office Phone: 303-344-8074. Business E-Mail: rrisas@msn.com.

IRWIN, RAYMOND D., library science educator, researcher; b. Marysville, Ohio, Dec. 7, 1966; s. Glenn and Celia Irwin. BA, Ohio State U., Columbus, Ohio, 1988; MLIS, Kent State U., Kent, Ohio, 2002; PhD, Ohio State U., Columbus, Ohio, 1996. Fellow John Nicholas Brown Ctr., Brown U., Providence, 1994—94; presdl. fellow Ohio State U. Grad. Sch., Columbus, Ohio, 1994—95; program dir. Just Inst., Columbus, Ohio, 1996—; instr. Kent State U., Kent, Ohio, 2004—. Mem. Irwin Farms, Ltd., Marysville, Ohio, 2000—. Author: (series) Books on Early American History and Culture, 2000— (Best Bibliographies in History, 2003). Recipient Eugene Rosenboom Prize, Ohio State U., 1994, Alumni Rsch. Award, Ohio State U. Grad. Sch., 1993, Robert G. Torbet Prize, Am. Bapt. Hist. Soc., 1993. Mem.: Beta Phi Mu, Phi Kappa Phi. Office: Just Inst 5295 Olentangy River Rd Columbus OH 43235 Office Phone: 614-457-5018.

IRWIN, RICHARD DENNIS, electrical engineering educator; b. Albany, Ga., Mar. 27, 1958; s. Vernon Hugh and Martha Lucille (Carson) I.; children: Katherine Virginia, Thomas Ralph, Elizabeth Martha. BSEE, Miss. State U., Starkville, 1980; MS, Miss. State U., 1983; PhD, Miss. State U., Starkville, 1986. Registered profl. engr., Ohio. Instr. Miss. State U., 1983-86; assoc. sr. staff engr. Control Dynamics Co., Huntsville, Ala., 1986-87; asst. prof. Ohio U., Athens, 1987-90, assoc. prof., 1990-96, prof., 1996—, chair Sch. EECS, 1997—2002, Grad. chair, 1993—97, Thomas prof. engring., 2001—02; dean and moss prof. of engring. tech. Russ Coll. of Engring. and Tech., Athens, 2002—. Cons. Control Dynamics Co., Huntsville, 1988, Systran, Dayton, Ohio, 1991, Wright State U., Dayton, 1990-92, Nichols Rsch., Huntsville, 1992; mem. steering com. Southeastern Symposium on Sys. Theory, 1988—, gen. chmn., 1994; chair-elect Ohio Engring. Deans Coun. Contbr. articles to Jour. Guidance, Control, Dynamics, Jour., Astron. Sci., Jour. Materials Engring. and Performance, Jour. Optimal Control and Applications, others. Recipient Outstanding Achievement award Ohio Soc. Profl. Engrs., 1989, Russ Rsch. award, 1993, Outstanding Mgmt. award NASA, 2001, Outstanding Project Mgmt. award NASA, 2002; NASA faculty fellow, 1988, 89, 90; grantee NASA, 1988-95, Dept. Edn., 1999-2002 Fellow AIAA (assoc.); mem. IEEE (sr.), Am. Astron. Soc., Am. Soc. Engring. Edn., Internat. Fedn. for Automatic Control (aerospace tech. com. 2000—, vice chair 2002-2005, chair, 2005—), Sigma Xi, Phi Kappa Phi, Tau Beta Pi, Eta Kappa Nu. Achievements include development of frequency domain system identification techniques for flexible systems; demonstration of control system design using experimental data models, first Internet accessible flexible structures control lab. Office: Ohio U Stocker 151 Athens OH 45701 Office Phone: 740-593-1479. Business E-Mail: irwind@ohio.edu.

IRWIN, ROBERT JAMES ARMSTRONG, investment company executive; b. Buffalo, June 27, 1927; s. Robert J.A. and Dorothy (McLean) I.; m. Donna Henwood, Sept. 10, 1966; children: William Baird, Elaine Mitchell, Elizabeth Flora, Robert J.A. IV, Ronald Henwood, Derrick Millet. BA, Colgate U., 1949; postgrad., U. Buffalo, 1949-50, Babson Inst. Finance, Wellesley, Mass., 1952-53. With Marine Trust Co. Western N.Y., Buffalo, 1958-66; v.p. Marine Midland Banks, Inc., N.Y.C., 1966-69, sr. v.p., 1969-71; exec. v.p. Dreyfus-Marine Midland Mgmt. Corp., 1970-72; sr. exec. v.p. Niagara Share Corp., Buffalo, 1972-74, pres., 1974-92, CEO, 1988-92, also bd. dirs.; chmn. bd., CEO, treas. ASA Ltd., 1993—2004; chmn., pres., treas. ASA (Bermuda) Ltd., 2004—. Bd. dirs. Boys Club of Western N.Y., 1953; adv. bd. Hauptman Woodward Med. Rsch. Inst., 1975—; trustee Baird Found., 1965—, Old Ft. Niagara Assn., 1986—, Ridley Coll. Scholarship Fund, Inc., James H. Cummings Found., 1978—, N.Y. State Hist. Assn.; pres. Shaw Festival Found. Mem. Saturn Club, Buffalo Canoe, Royal Canadian Yacht (Toronto), Univ. (N.Y.C.). Office: 11 Summer St Buffalo NY 14209-1210 Office Phone: 716-883-2428.

ISAAC, BINA SUSAN, data processing executive; b. Nainital, India, Jan. 9, 1958; arrived in U.S., 1980; d. Rajan Kurian and Susan (Thomas) George; m. Mathew Isaac, July 14, 1980; children: Sonya Susan, Shawn George. BA, Sarah Tucker Coll., Tirunelvelli, India, 1978; MA, Madurai U., India, 1980; MEd, U. Toledo, 1981, MBA, 1984. Coord. computer svcs. and computer ctr. Lourdes Coll., Sylvania, Ohio, 1984-85, dir. computer svcs. and computer ctr., 1985-95, dir. info. tech. dept. svcs., 1995-97, part time instr. math. and phys. sci., 1985-97; from info. sys. dir. to chief tech. Coll. of the Desert, Palm Desert, Calif., 1997—2002, chief tech. officer, dean info. sys. and ednl. tech., 2002—. Instr. Continuing Edn. Dept., Sylvania, 1985-97. Mem. Assn. C.C. Adminstrs. Avocations: playing the piano, reading, outdoor activities. Business E-Mail: bisaac@collegeofthedesert.edu.

ISAAC, STEVEN RICHARD, communications executive; b. Utica, NY, Dec. 19, 1947; s. Anthony Richard and Camille Cecilia (Potaro) I.; m. Martha Cash, Oct. 9, 1982; children: Charles Wesley, Spencer Anthony. BA in English, U. Buffalo, 1969; MS in Edn./Comm., Syracuse U., 1973; postgrad. in bus. adminstrn. program, Fordham U., 1978. Prin. Media Design Assocs., N.Y.C., 1973-75; dir. multimedia products The Am. Mgmt. Assn., N.Y.C., 1975-78; ptnr. Tng. by Design, Inc., N.Y.C., 1978-79; founder, chmn. and CEO Martin Direct, Inc. (formerly The Stenrich Group Inc.), N.Y.C., 1979-96; founder, CEO Martin Interactive, 1995-96; bd. dirs., exec. v.p., COO, The Martin Agy., 1996; pres. mktg. group Cadmus Comm. Corp., Richmond, Va., 1996-97, exec. v.p., 1997-99; CEO DMW Worldwide, 2000—02; exec. v.p. DIMAC Holdings, 2000—02; mng. dir. Interactive Mktg. Inst., Grad. Sch. Bus. Va. Commonwealth U., Richmond, 2002—; prin., owner Isaac Enterprises, LLC, 2003—. Bd. dirs. Charlottesville (Va.) Venture Group; mem. adv. bd. DMW Direct; chmn. bd. Learning website, 2005—; v.p. mktg. Job website, 2004—. Author: Words for Phone: Writing Winning Telephone Scripts; contbr. articles to profl. jours. Mem. cmty. adv. bd. 1st Capital Bank; bd. dirs. Shady Grove YMCA. Mem. Direct Mktg. Assn., Commonwealth Club. Methodist. Office Phone: 804-828-1998. Business E-Mail: srisaac@vcu.edu.

ISAAC, TERESA ANN, mayor, lawyer; b. Lynch, Ky., July 3, 1955; d. Samuel Thomas Sr. and Barbara Ann (Thomas) I.; children: Jacob, Alicyn. BA, Transylvania U., 1976; JD, U. Ky., 1979. Bar: Ky. 1979, U.S. Dist. Ct. (ea. dist.) Ky. 1979, U.S. Ct. Appeals (6th cir.) 1980, U.S. Supreme Ct. 1981, U.S. Ct. Appeals (D.C. cir.) 1984. Pvt. practice, Lexington, Ky., 1979—; vice mayor City of Lexington, 1993-99, mayor, 2002—. Asst. atty. Fayette County Prosecutors Office, Lexington, 1986-88; judge U. Ky. Trial Adv. Competition, Lexington, 1981; assoc. prof. dept. govt. and law Eastern Ky. U., 1983-88; acting dir. Eastern Ky. U. Paralegal Program, Richmond, 1985; legal counsel Ky. Women's Heritage Mus., Inc., 1986, v.p., 1987; selected as one of six Arab-Am. elected ofcls. to monitor the first Palestinian elections, 1996; econs. and govt. prof. Lexington C.C., 1996-97; mem. bldg. com. Fayette County Justice Ctr., 1997. Editor newsletter At Issue, Lexington Forum, 1983-85; pub. The Full Ct. Press, 1986—; author: Sex Equity in Sports Leadership: Implementing the Game Plan in Your Community, 1987. Mem. Lexington Human Resources Adv. Bd., 1982-85, Ky. Displaced Homemaker Adv. Bd., Lexington, 1982-84, NCAA Final Four Host Com., Lexington, 1985; chmn. Ky. Women's Suffrage Day Celebration, 1986—; project dir. Sports Equity Program-Model for South, Ky., 1986—; mem. Philmarm. Guild, 1986—; chmn. Ky. Nat. Women in Sports Day Celebration, 1988; mem.-at-large Lexington-Fayette Urban County Coun., 1990—; bd. dirs. Ky. World Trade Ctr., 1993-97, Housing Found., 1993-97; bd. control Ky. H.S. Athletic Assn., 1993-97; mem. adv. bd. LPGA Jr. Girls Golf Club, 1993-97; mem. Criminal Justice Commn., 1993-97; mem. nat. adv. bd. Dems. 2000, 1993-97; mem. Mil. Support Com., 1997; exec. dir. Lexington Fair Housing Coun., 1999—. Recipient Outstanding Svc. award Lexington Forum, 1985, Woman of Achievement award Miss Ky. Pageant, 1996, Pub. Advocacy award Nat. Assn. Women Bus. Owners, 1998, Sports Equity Leadership award, 1999; named Top 16 Women in Bus., 1995, Best Elected Ofcl. in the Bluegrass,

1994, 50 Most Powerful People in Sports, 1992. Mem. ABA (exec. com. delivery of legal svcs. to women, chair 1987-88, spl. com. on housing and urban devel. law, recipient Silver Key award 1979), AAUW (sec. 1986, state bd. dirs. 1987-88) Fed. Bar Assn., Ky. Bar Assn. (bd. of editors 1983-85, mem. Task Force on Gender Bias in Cts. 1987—), Ky. Acad. Trial Lawyers Assn., Am. Soc. for Pub. Adminstrn., Am. Assn. for Paralegal Edn., Nat. Assn. Women Lawyers (brief bank coord. 1985—), ACLU (chairperson legal panel 1983—), League of Women Voters (voter svc. com. 1985—), Ky. Women Advs. (treas. 1987—, v.p. 1988), Leadership Am., Ky. Women's Polit. Caucus (pres. 1992-93), Lexington C. of C., Phi Mi (legal advisor 1985—). Democrat. Roman Catholic. Avocation: running marathons. Office: Lexington-Fayette Govt Ctr 200 E Main St Lexington KY 40507 Office Phone: 859-258-3100. Business E-Mail: mayor@lfucg.com.

ISAAC, WILLIAM MICHAEL, brokerage house executive, retired government agency administrator; b. Bryan, Ohio, Dec. 21, 1943; s. Charles R. and Ruth L. (Hallberg) I.; m. Carma Sue Dunbar, Aug. 15, 1965 (div. 1993); m. Christine Verney, Nov. 16, 1997; children: David M., Stephanie A., Lennon G., Quinn V. BS, Miami U. Oxford, Ohio, 1966, LLD (hon.), 1984; JD summa cum laude, Ohio State U., 1969. Bar: Wis. 1969, Ky. 1974, D.C. 1986. Mem. firm. Foley & Lardner, Milw., 1969-74; v.p., gen. counsel, sec. First Ky. Nat. Corp., Louisville, 1974-78; chmn. FDIC, Washington, 1978-85; ptnr. Arnold & Porter, Washington, 1985-93; chmn. The Secura Group, Washington, 1985—, Secura Burnett Co. LLC, San Francisco, 1992—; mem. Depository Instns. Deregulation Com., 1981-85, Bush Task Group, 1982-85; chmn. Fed. Fin. Instns. Exam. Coun., 1983-85. Bd. dirs. MPS Group, Inc., Jacksonville, Fla., TransUnion Corp., Chgo. Co-author: Bank Holding Companies: A Practical Guide to Bank Acquisitions and Mergers, 1972; contbr. articles on banking to profl. jours. Mem. nat. coun. Coll. Law, Ohio State U., Columbus, 1980—; mem. bus. adv. coun. Miami U., Oxford, Ohio, 1982—; trustee Miami U. Found., 1988-96; bd. dirs. Ohio State U. Found., The Cmty. Found. of Sarasato County; chmn.-elect Goodwill Ind.; chmn. Isaac Properties Group. Mem. ABA, Wis. Bar Assn., Ky. Bar Assn., Fed. Nat. Mortgage Assn. (adv. bd. 1989-90). Republican. Office: The Secura Group 7799 Leesburg Pike Ste 800N Falls Church VA 22043-2413 Office Phone: 703-749-1560. E-mail: billisaac@comcast.net.

ISAAC-EMMONS, MERLYN HULDA, academic administrator, educator; b. Mt. St. George, Trinidad and Tobago, July 13, 1954; arrived in U.S., 1991, naturalized; d. Vonley and Carona Abigail Isaac; m. Kelvin Strickland Emmons, Nov. 24, 1994; children: Kezreel Emmons, Uzziel Emmons, Kemuel Emmons. AA, Caribbean Union Coll., Maracas, Trinidad, 1977; BS in Edn., Lang. Arts, Andrews Univ., Berrien Springs, Mich., 1989; MEd in Spl. Edn., Atlantic Union Coll., South Lancaster, Mass., 1996; PhD in Ednl. Adminstrn. and Supervision, Trinity Internat. Univ., Springfield, Mo., 1999. Cert. reading U. West Indies, Trinidad, 1984. Clk. I Ministry for Tobago Affairs, Tobago, Trinidad and Tobago, 1972—73; tchr. South Caribbean Conf. Seventh Day Adventists, Trinidad, Trinidad and Tobago, 1973—84, prin., 1984—91; tchr. Northeastern Conf. Seventh Day Adventist, Jamaica, NY, 1993—2004; instr. Medgar Evers Coll., Bklyn., 2001—; v.p., prof. Jehova Jireh Non-Denominational Biblical Inst. Trinity Internat. U., Bklyn., 2002—; instr. Ctr. for Career Pathways Initiatives, 2005—. Instr. GED CUNY, 2003—. Author: Brighten Your Corner: Stories Are Fun, 2001, He Will Not Depart from It, 2003; contbr. articles. Foster parent Jewish Childcare Agy., Miracle Makers Agy., 1996—, Mercy First Guardian Angel Foster Boarding Home, Bklyn., 2005—. Democrat. Seventh Day Adventist. Avocations: reading, travel, writing children's stories, soap operas, storytelling. Home: 573 Van Siclen Ave Brooklyn NY 11207 Office: Medgar Evers Coll CUNY Ctr for Career Pathways Initiatives CP 21 1150 Carroll St Brooklyn NY 11225 Office Phone: 718-270-6468. E-mail: merlynemmons@juno.com, memmons@mec.cuny.edu.

ISAACMAN, ALAN L., lawyer; b. Harrisburg, Pa., July 12, 1942; BS, Pa. State U., 1964; JD, Harvard U., 1967. Bar: Calif. 1968, U.S. Ct. Appeals (1st, 2nd, 4th, 9th and 10th cirs.) 1968, U.S. Supreme Ct. 1968. Law clk. to Hon. Harry Pregerson US Dist. Ct. (ctrl. dist.) Calif., 1969—70; sr. ptnr. Isaacman, Kaufman & Painter, Beverly Hills, Calif. Lectr. in field; mem. bd. dirs. New Frontier Media, Inc., 1999—. Fellow: Am. Coll. Trial Lawyers. Office: Isaacman Kaufman & Painter Ste 850 8484 Wilshire Blvd Beverly Hills CA 90211

ISAACMAN, CARRIE EDEL, actress, educator; d. Max David Isaacman and Joyce Glick (Stepmother), Joanne Isaacman; m. Roger Dale Stude, Mar. 7, 2004. BA, San Francisco State U., 1993; MA, Antioch U., Yellow Springs, Ohio, 2000. Cert. substitute tchr. N.Y. Bd. Edn., 1999. Substitute tchr. N.Y. Bd. Edn., N.Y.C., 1999—2001; contract fin. adminstr. Bear Sterns, N.Y.C., 2001—. Tchg. artist Black Moon Theatre Co., Bklyn., San Francisco Shakespeare Festival, 1996—97. Actor: Calif. Shakespeare Co., N.J. Shakespeare Co., Workshop Theater Co., Kings County Shakespear Co. Recipient Critic's Choice award, Off-Off Broadway Reveiw, 2000. Home: 2 Adrian Avenue #6A Bronx NY 10463 Office Phone: 917-202-1135. Personal E-mail: carrieedel@earthlink.net.

ISAAC NASH, EVA MAE, secondary school educator; b. Natchitoches Parish, La., July 24, 1936; d. Earfus Will Nash and Dollie Mae (Edward) Johnson; m. Will Isaac Jr., July 1, 1961 (dec. May 1970). BA, San Francisco State U., 1974, MS in Edn., MS in Counseling, San Francisco State U., 1979; PhD, Walden U., 1985; diploma (hon.), St. Labre Indian Sch., 1990. Nurse's aide Protestant Episcopal Home, San Francisco, 1957-61; desk clk. Fort Ord (Calif.) Post Exchange, 1961-63; practical nurse Monterey (Calif.) Hosp., 1963-64; tchr. San Francisco Unified Schs., 1974; counselor, instr. City Coll. San Francisco, 1978-79; tchr. Oakland (Calif.) Unified Sch. Dist., 1974—. Pres. sch. adv. coun., Oakland, 1977-78, faculty adv. coun., 1992-93; advt. writer City Coll., San Francisco, 1978; instr. vocat. skill tng., Garfield Sch., Oakland, 1980-81; pub. speaker various ednl. insts. and chs., Oakland, San Francisco, 1982—; lectr. San Jose State U., 1993; creator Language Arts-Step By Step program E. Morris Cox Elem. Sch., Oakland, 1995, 96; author, presenter material in field. Author video tape Hunger: An Assassin in the Classroom, 1993-94. Recipient Community Svc. award Black Caucus of Calif. Assn. Counseling and Devel., 1988, Cert. of Recognition, 1990; named Citizen of the Day, Sta. KABL, 1988. Mem. ASCD, Internat. Reading Assn., Nat. Assn. Female Execs., Am. Personnel and Guidance Assn., Calif. Personnel and Guidance Assn., Internat. Platform Assn. (Hall Fame 1989, Profl. Speaking cert. 1993), Phi Delta Kappa. Democrat. Avocations: travel, hiking, tennis, music, dance. Office: Oakland Unified Sch Dist 1025 2nd Ave Oakland CA 94606-2296

ISAACS, AMY FAY, political organization executive; b. Phoenix, Nov. 11, 1946; d. Richard and Bessie (Wagner) Hamburger; m. John David Isaacs, Oct. 6, 1974; children: Rachel Elizabeth, Stanley Richard. Student, U. Cologne, Germany, 1967-68; BA, Am. U., 1969; MA, Sch. for Internat. Tng., Brattleboro, Vt., 1970. With AID, Washington, 1965-66; tchr. English, Turkish Am. Univs. Assn., Istanbul, 1969; direct mail and fundraising cons., Washington, 1986-87; sr. coord. communications Planned Parenthood Fedn. Am., Washington, 1987-89; various positions Ams. for Dem. Action, Washington, 1969-86, nat. dir., 1989—. Observer del. Liberal Internat., Stockholm, 1984; del. Am. Coun. on Germany, Berlin, Dallas, 1985-87; mem. fin. com. Dukasis for Pres., Washington, 1987-88; mem. quality of care com. Group Health Assn., Washington, 1987-93. Democrat. Jewish. Home: 2018 Pierce Mill Rd NW Washington DC 20010-1023 Office: Ams for Dem Action 1625 K St NW Ste 210 Washington DC 20006-1611

ISAACS, GERALD WILLIAM, retired agricultural engineering educator, consultant; b. Crawfordsville, Ind., Sept. 3, 1927; s. William Paul and Verna Ethel (Johnson) I.; m. Phyllis Joyce Seaton, Aug. 22, 1948; children: Joyce Irene (dec.), David Gerald, Donald Phillip, Joseph Lee (dec.), Susan Verna, Linda Kay. BSEE, Purdue U., 1947, MSEE, 1949; PhD in Agrl. Engring., Mich. State U., 1954. Registered profl. engr., Fla. Grad. asst. agrl. engring. dept. agrl. engring. Mich. State U., E. Lansing, 1952-54; instr. agrl. engring. Dept. Argl. Engring, Purdue U., W. Lafayette, Ind., 1948-52, from asst. prof. agrl. engring to prof. agrl. engring., 1954-1964, prof., head dept. argl. engring., 1964-81; prof., chmn. dept. agrl. engring. U. Fla., Gainesville, 1981-91, prof. emeritus, 1991—. Cons. engr. various mfg. and legal firms, 1958—. Contbr. articles to profl. jours. Recipient Massey Ferguson Gold medal Am. Soc. Agrl. Engrs., 1991, Silver medal Max Eyth Gesselschaft, Germany, 1979. Mem. Polish Acad. Sci., Rotary Internat. (dir. 1976-78, Paul Harris fellow 1993), Am. Soc. Agrl. Engrs. (nat. pres. 1982-83), Soc. German Engrs. (hon. corr. mem.); Verien Deuthes Ingeneurs (corr.). Lutheran. Avocations: photography, travel, music. Office: U Fla Dept Agrl and Biol Engring Frazier Rogers Hall Gainesville FL 32611 Business E-Mail: isaacs@ufl.edu.

ISAACS, GODFREY LEONARD, retired mathematician; b. Cape Town, Republic of South Africa, Feb. 9, 1924; BS, U. Cape Town, 1944, MS, 1945; PhD, U. London, 1950. Lectr. Natal U., Durban, Republic South Africa, 1945-47; lectr. Brikbeck Coll. Birkbeck Coll. U. London, 1948-49; sr. lectr. Witwatersrand U., Johannesburg, Republic South Africa, 1951-60, prof., 1960-67; assoc. prof. Lehman Coll. CUNY, N.Y.C., 1968-70, prof. Lehman Coll., 1970-86, prof. emeritus Lehman Coll., 1986—. Vis. prof. SUNY, Stony Brook, 1966-67. Author: Real Numbers, 1968; contbr. rsch. articles to math. jours. Nuffield fellow Nuffield Found., London, 1960, rsch. fellow CUNY, 1970; Canegie Travel grantee Carnegie Corp., 1966. Mem. AAUP, Am. Math. Soc., Math. Assn. Am., London Math. Soc., N.Y. Acad. Scis. Avocations: music, swimming. Home: 3111 N Ocean Dr Hollywood FL 33019-3725

ISAACS, HAROLD, history professor; b. Newark, Dec. 19, 1936; s. Albert Lewis and Bertha (Wohl) I.; m. Doris Carol Mack, Apr. 25, 1974. BS in History, U. Ala., University, 1958, MA in History, 1960, PhD in History, 1968. Grad. tchg. fellow in history U. Ala., University, 1959-62; instr. in history Memphis State U., 1962-65; asst. prof. history Ga. Southwestern State U., Americus, 1965-70, assoc. prof. history, 1970-79, prof. history, 1979—. Bd. dirs. World Communities Theater, Ctr. Third World Studies, 2005—; bd. advs. Ency. Developing World; scholar cons. Jimmy Carter Residency Program, Author: Jimmy Carter's Peanut Brigade, 1977; founder, editor Jour. of Third World Studies, 1984—. Advisor Young Dems., Ga. Southwestern State U., 1965-80, chmn. faculty capital campaign, 2003; founder, coord. Third World in Perspective Program Seminar Series, 1981—; coord. Black Leaders Lecture Series, 1981. Recipient Tchr. of Yr. award Alpha Phi Alpha, 1982, Outstanding Svc. award Americus Early Bird Civitan Club, 1983, Outstanding Historian and Humanitarian award SABU, 1994, Presdl. Citation for Disting. Svc., 1995, Outstanding Svc. to African Am. and Third World Studies SABU 1996-97, 1997, All-Africa award African Studies and Rsch. Forum, 2001, Internat. Lincoln Ctr. Disting. Leadership and Scholarship award, 2003, faculty award Univ. Sys. Ga. Regents' Hall of Fame, 2004, spl. award for svc. as grand marshal Ga. Southwestern State U., 1994-2005. Mem. Assn. Third World Studies, Inc. (founder, pres., exec. dir., 1983-91, treas. 1983-97, proceedings editor 2002—, Presdl. award 1992, Harold Isaacs award). Democrat. Jewish. Home: 180 Lakeshore Dr Americus GA 31719-8233 Office: Ga Southwestern State U Dept History & Polit Sci 800 Wheatley St Americus GA 31709 Office Phone: 229-931-2078. Business E-Mail: hissacs@canes.gsw.edu.

ISAACS, HART, JR., pathologist, educator; b. L.A., Mar. 7, 1932; s. Hart and Josephine Isaacs; m. Patricia Ann Levi, Aug. 26, 1955; children: Dorothy, Charles, Diana, Donna, Craig. BS, Stanford U., Calif., 1954, MD, 1958. Cert. Ca. Med. Lic. Bd., 1959, Am. Bd. Pathology, 1965. Intern U. Ill. Hosp., Chgo., 1959—60; fellow, biophys. chemistry Johnson Found. Hosp., U. Pa., Phila., 1960—61; resident, pathology Hosp. U. Pa., Phila., 1961—64; resident, pediat. pathology St. Christopher's Hosp. for Children, Phila., 1964—65, Children's Hosp. L.A., 1965—66, assoc. pathologist, 1966—92, Children's Hosp. San Diego, 1992—; assoc. prof., pathology U. Calif. Sch. Medicine, La Jolla, 1992—. Author: Tumors of the Fetus and Newborn, 1997, Tumors of the Fetus & Infant: An Atlas, 2002. Mem.: San Diego County Med. Soc., Coll. Am. Pathologists, Am. Soc. Clin. Pathologists, Soc. for Pediat. Pathology. Avocations: sailing, bonsai, music. Office: Childrens Hosp San Diego 3020 Childrens Way MC 5007 San Diego CA 92123 Office Phone: 858-966-5944.

ISAACS, JEREMY M., finance company executive; b. London, Eng., 1964; Trader Smith New Court, 1972—87, Kleinwert Benson, 1987—89; exec. dir. Goldman Sachs, 1989—96; co-COO, European Equities Lehman Brothers Holdings Inc., 1996, head, global equity derivative bus., 1996—99, head, overall equities bus. in Europe, 1997—99, COO, European bus., 1999—2000, CEO, European bus., 1999—, CEO, Asian opers., 2000—. Mem. exec. com. Lehman Brothers Holdings Inc.; mem. adv. bd. Elec. Data Sys. Corp. Non-exec. dir. St. Mary's NHS Trust, 2003—. Office: Lehman Brother Holdings Inc 745 Seventh Ave New York NY 10019

ISAACS, KENNETH SIDNEY, psychoanalyst, educator; b. Mpls., Apr. 7, 1920; s. Mark William and Sophia (Rai) I.; m. Ruth Elizabeth Johnson, Feb. 21, 1951 (dec. 1967); m. Adele Rella Bodroghy, May 17, 1969; children: Jonathan, James; stepchildren: John, Curtis, Peter and Edward Meissner. BA, U. Minn., 1944; PhD, U. Chgo., 1956; postgrad., Inst. Psychoanalysis, 1957-63. Intern Worcester State Hosp., Mass., 1947-48; trainee VA Mental Hygiene Clinic, Chgo., 1948-50; chief psychologist outpatient clinic system Ill. Dept. Pub. Welfare, 1949-56; research assoc., assoc. prof. U. Ill. Med. Sch., Chgo., 1956-63; practice psychoanalysis Evanston, Ill., 1960—. Supr. psychiat. residency program Evanston Hosp., Northwestern U., 1972-81, Northwestern Meml. Hosp.; pres. Chgo. Ctr. Psychoanalytic Psychology, 1984-87; cons. to schs., hosps., clinics, pvt. practitioners and industry; sr. cons. Beta Consulting Ltd.; pres. Kenisa Drilling Co., 1982-93, Kenisa Securities Co., 1982-93, Kenisa Oil Co., 1982-95. Author: Again with Feeling, 1989, Uses of Emotion, 1998, (syndicated newspaper column) A Psychologist's Notebook; contbr. articles to profl. publs. Served with AUS, 1943-45, ETO. Mem.: Chgo. Psychoanalytic Soc., Am. Bd. Profl. Psychology (bd. trustees 1994—2001), Am. Bd. Psychoanalysis (chair bd. dirs.), APA (bd. dirs. divsn. pschoanalysis), AAAS, Sigma Xi.

ISAACS, RICHARD B., investigative and protective services professional; b. Evanston, Ill., Nov. 12, 1942; s. Harry Columbus and Natalie I.; m. Catherine Anne Nicodemo, Oct. 25, 1980 (div. 1994). BA, NYU, 1964; MA, Columbia U., 1975. Cert. CPP. V.p. Blackstone & West, Inc., Phila., 1967-69; indsl. photographer N.Y.C., 1970-76; programmer STSC, Inc., N.Y.C., 1976-81; pres. Blackstone & West, Inc., N.Y.C., 1981-89; prin., sr. v.p. The Lubrinco Group, Inc., N.Y.C., 1989-2001. Dir. ASR Instrs. Coun., Arlington, Tex., 1983-2001. Author: (book) The Seven Steps to Personal Safety, 1993, rev. 1998; editor: The Bus. Security e-Jour., 1998-2001; others. Vol. Peace Corps, Colombia, 1964-66. Mem. Am. Soc. Law Enforcement Trainers (mem. security com. 1999-2001), Tactical Response Assn., Soc. Competitive Intelligence Profls., Internat. Assn. Counterterroism and Security Profls. Avocations: poetry, translating, flying, 50-meter free pistol, Aikido. Office: The Lubrinco Group Inc 215 Park Ave S Ste 711 New York NY 10003-1603 E-mail: rbisaacs@lubrinco.com.

ISAACS, ROBERT CHARLES, retired lawyer; b. July 16, 1919; s. David and Elsie (Weiss) I.; m. Doris Frances Shapiro, Nov. 20, 1943 (dec. 1982); 1 child, Leigh Richard; m. Mary Lou Anderson, Dec. 12, 1986. BA cum laude, NYU, 1941, JD, 1943. Bar: N.Y. 1943. Dep. asst. atty. gen. N.Y. State Dept. Law, Albany, 1943, spl. asst. atty. gen., 1946; ptnr. Nordlinger Riegelman Benetar, N.Y.C., 1946-71, Aranow Brodsky Bohlinger Benetar & Einhorn, N.Y.C., 1972-79, Benetar Isaacs Bernstein & Schair, N.Y.C., 1979-88. Mem. Lebanon (N.H.) Zoning Bd. Adjustment, 1988-2004; adj. prof. law St. John's U. Sch. Law, N.Y.C., 1961-72; mem. panel mediators and fact finders N.Y. State Pub. Employment Rels. Bd., 1968-88. Contbr. articles to profl. publs. Capt. U.S. Army, 1943-45, 51. Mem. ABA, ASCAP, Am. Arbitration Assn. (mem. panel arbitrators 1988), N.Y.C. Bar Assn., NYU Law Review Alumni Assn. Home: 5 Village Green West Lebanon NH 03784-1506

ISAACS, ROGER DAVID, public relations executive; b. Boston, Oct. 23, 1925; s. Raphael and Agnes (Wolfstein) I.; m. Joyce R. Wexler, Oct. 23, 1949; children: Gillian, Jan. Student, U. Wis., 1943; AB, Bard Coll., 1949. With Pub. Rels. Bd., Inc., Chgo., 1948—, account supr., 1948-51, ptnr., 1951-60, exec. v.p., 1960-66, pres., 1966-75, chmn., pres., 1975-86; chmn. PRB, a Needham Porter Novelli Co., Chgo.; exec. v.p., gen. mgr. Doremus Porter Novelli, Chgo., 1986-89; sr. counselor Porter/Novelli, Chgo., 1989-91, The Fin. Rels. Bd., Inc., Chgo., 1991—. Bd. dirs. North Bank, Chgo. Past bd. dirs. Anti-Defamation League Chgo., Jewish Family and Cmty. Svc., Sr. ctrs. Met. Chgo., Highland Park Hosp., Met. Crusade of Mercy, Suburban Fine Arts Ctr., Asthma and Allergy Found., Spertus Coll.; cmty. adv. bd. Sta. WBEZ; bd. dirs. Chgo. Crime Commn.; libr. vis. com. Spertus Inst.; life bd. dirs. Evanston Northwestern Healthcare Found. With AUS, 1943-45. Decorated Purple Heart. Mem. Pub. Rels. Soc. Am. (accredited), Met. Club, Publicity Club Chgo. Home: 1045 Hillcrest Rd Glencoe IL 60022-1215 Personal E-mail: joroisaacs@aol.com.

ISAACS, SUSAN, writer, scriptwriter; b. Bklyn., Dec. 7, 1943; d. Morton and Helen (Asher) I.; m. Elkan Abramowitz, Aug. 11, 1968; children: Andrew, Elizabeth. Student, Queens Coll., 1965, DHL (hon.), 1996; LittD (hon.), Dowling Coll., 1988. From editorial asst. to sr. editor Seventeen mag., N.Y.C., 1965-70; freelance writer, 1970-76. Author: Compromising Positions, 1978, Close Relations, 1980, Almost Paradise, 1984, Shining Through, 1988, Magic Hour, 1991, After All These Years, 1993, Lily White, 1996, Red, White and Blue, 1998, Brave Dames and Wimpettes: What Women Are Really Doing on Page and Screen, 1999, Long Time No See, 2001, Any Place I Hang My Hat, 2004; screenwriter Compromising Positions, 1985; screenwriter, co-producer Hello Again, 1987. Trustee Queens Coll. Found.; bd. dirs. North Shore Child and Family Guidance Assn; adv. bd. Nassau County Coalition Against Domestic Violence; bd. trustees Walt Whitman Birthplace Assn. Recipient Writers for Writers award Poets and Writers, 1996, The John Steinbeck award, 1999. Mem. PEN, Mystery Writers Am. (pres. 2001-02), Nat. Book Critic Circle, Poets and Writers (bd. dirs. 1994—, chmn. 1998—), Authors Guild, Internat. Assn. Crime Writers, Feminists for Free Expression, Creative Coalition, Am. Soc. Journalists and Authors. Jewish.

ISAACS-BRIGHT, SUSAN VIRGINIA KIRKPATRICK, librarian, consultant, advocate; b. West Point, Miss., Oct. 28, 1949; d. William Robert and Sara Rebecca I.; m. Wayne Milford Roberts, 1970 (div. 1979); children: David Wayne, Julie Andrea; m. Stephen Dewitt Bright, 1989. BS, U. S.C., 1971, MLS, 1974, EdD, 1997. Libr. tech. asst. U. S.C., Aiken, S.C., 1972-73, assoc. prof. libr. sci, asst. libr. pub. svcs., 1974-86; libr. Aiken Tech. Coll., 1986-90; mgr. tech. info. ctr. Westinghouse Savannah River Co, Aiken, 1990-96, sr. libr., libr. supr., 1996—. Mem. Aiken County Pub. Libr. Adv. Bd., 1996—; facilitator ALA learning disabilities workshop at Aiken County Pub. Libr., 1997. Author: (play) This Promise Is Unto You, 1997; (dissertation) Learning Disabilities: An Adult Discovery, 1997; editor (newsletter) The Libr. Connection, 1990-96. Mem. Pres. Regan's Project Serve, 1982; chairperson MIdland Valley Libr. Fund Dr., Langley, S.C., 1989-90; bd. trustees Aiken County Pub. Libr., 1997—. Cert. trainer Dept. Energy's Tng. Accreditation Tng. Bd., 1993, 95. Mem. AAUW (nominee young scholars U. S.C. 1979), Spl. Libr. Assn., S.C. Libr. Assn. (many offices including pres. 1981-84, Presidential Gavel award 1984), Ctrl. Savannah River Area Libr Assn. (chair mem. com. 1980-81, mem. grants-in-aid com., scholarship winner 1972), Learning Disabilities Assn. S.C. (bd. dirs. 2002—). Avocations: piano, singing, writing, fishing. Home: 1824 Lundee Dr Aiken SC 29803-5706 Office: Westinghouse Savannah River Co Libr Bldg 773-A Aiken SC 19808 Office Phone: 803-725-7752. E-mail: svisaacs@aol.com.

ISAACSON, ALLEN IRA, lawyer; s. Bernard and Sylvia Isaacson; m. Dena Mishkoff, Mar. 8, 1970; 1 child, David Andrew. AB, Princeton U., 1960; LLB, Yale U., 1963; postgrad., U. Melbourne, Australia, 1963-64; LLM in Taxation, NYU, 1973. Bar: NY 1966. Assoc. Fried, Frank, Harris, Shriver & Jacobson, N.Y.C., 1966-70, ptnr., 1970—2004, of counsel, 2004—. Fulbright fellow, 1963—64. Mem. ABA, N.Y. State Bar Assn., Assn. of Bar of City of N.Y. Home: 15 W 81st St New York NY 10024-6022 Office: Fried Frank Harris Shriver & Jacobson 1 New York Plz Fl 22 New York NY 10004-1980 Office Phone: 212-859-8180. E-mail: allen.isaacson@ffhsj.com.

ISAACSON, BOND R., finance company executive; BA in Econs. Various positions IBM Corp.; with mgmt. staff Visa USA; payments exec. Bank of Am. Corp.; from exec. v.p. to co-CEO Concord EFS, Inc., Memphis, 2002—03, co-CEO, 2003—. Office: Concord EFS Inc 2525 Horizon Lake Dr Ste 120 Memphis TN 38133

ISAACSON, EDITH L., civic leader; b. N.Y.C., Jan. 18, 1920; d. I.A. and Bertha (Evans) Lipsig; m. Selian Hebald; children: Anne Mandelbaum, Selian Jr.; m. William J. Isaacson. Student, Radcliffe Coll., 1936-39, 41; LLB, St. Lawrence U., 1943. Pres. Forest Knolls Corp., N.Y.C., 1960-95, Norman Homes Corp., N.Y.C., 1968-95. Bd. govs. Medford Leas Residents Assn., 1990-92, v.p., 1991-92. Author biographies Am. artists; writer club handbooks. Fellow Pierpont Morgan Libr., N.Y.C.; mem. Carnegie Coun. Ethics Internat. Affairs, founders com. Am. Symphony Orch., N.Y., 1962; nat. sec. Women's Am. Orgn. Rehab. through Tng., 1950; trustee Allergy Found. Am.; bd. govs. Medford Leas Residents Assn., 1991; mem. Res. Fund Com., 1992-2000. Mem. Radcliffe Coll. Alumnae Assn. (chmn. clubs 1966), Harvard Clyb (N.Y.C.), Cosmopolitan Club (N.Y.C.) (bd. govs. 1987-2000), Radcliffe Club (pres. Washington 1969, N.Y.C. 1959, 63, bd. sponsors 1974-2000). Home and Office: 499 Medford Leas Medford NJ 08055-2215

ISAACSON, MELISSA MAE, music educator; MusM, Brigham Young U., 2004. Cert. Kodaly Utah. Tchr. Brigham Young U., Provo, 2001—04, The Waterford Sch., Sandy, Utah, 2004—. Dir. Utah Youth Singers, Centerville, 2005—. Mem.: Am. Choral Dir.'s Assn.

ISAACSON, MILTON STANLEY (JIM ISAACSON), research and development company executive, engineer; b. Dayton, Ohio, Apr. 23, 1932; s. Max and Sylvia Mariam (Kirsin) I.; m. Joan Sue Koor, Sept. 4, 1955; children: Julie Fay, Jill Ellen, Jan Lynn. BSEE, Ohio State U., 1955. Registered profl. engr., Ohio. Successively design engr., mgr. quality control, div. mgr., dir. R & D Globe Industries, Dayton, 1957-70; pres. Nu-Tech Industries, Inc., Trotwood, Ohio, 1970—. Officer, bd. dirs. Food Svcs., Dayton, 1970-95. Patentee brushless DC motors and medical devices. Bd. dirs. Grace House Sexual Abuse Resource Ctr., Dayton, 1985—, pres., 1985-89; bd. dirs. Temple Israel Found., 1987-90, pres., 1990; v.p. Jewish Fedn. Greater Dayton, 1984—; bd. dirs. Big Bros./Big Sisters of Greater Dayton, 1965-95, pres., 1978-79; bd. dirs. Old Time Newsies, 1969—, pres., 1991-92. 1st lt. USAF, 1955-57. Recipient Dr. Alan F. Wasserman Leadership award Jewish Fedn. Dayton, 1972, Boss of the Yr. award Nat. First Vall chpt. Am. Bus. Womens Assn., 1975, Outstanding Pub. Svc. award Sta. WKEF, Dayton, 1979, Outstanding Svc. award Big Bros./Big Sisters of Greater Dayton, 1977, 88, 304 Cmty. svc. award, 2002, Hon. Judge Carl D. Kessler Meml. award The Grace House, 1991. Mem. IEEE, Rotary (pres. Trotwood club 1989, sec. 1993—), Eta Kappa Nu. Avocations: fishing, travel. Office: Nu-Tech Industries Inc 5905 Wolf Creek Pike Dayton OH 45426-2439

ISAACSON, ROBERT LEE, psychologist, educator; b. Detroit, Sept. 26, 1928; s. Emil Alfred and Evelyn (Johnson) I.; m. Susan Doherty, Dec. 16, 1956 (div. 1972); children: Gunnar, Lars, Mary Ingrid, Mary Christina; m. Ann W. Braden, Dec. 31, 1974; stepchildren: Richard, Milly Braden AB in Psychology, U. Mich., 1950, MS in Psychology, 1954, PhD in Psychology, 1958. Co-dir. U. Fla. Ctr. for Neurobiol. Sci., Gainesville, 1970-78; grad. research prof. U. Fla., Gainesville, 1977-78; disting. prof. psychology SUNY, Binghamton, 1978—, dir. Ctr. for Neurobehavioral Sci., 1978-88, Bartle prof., 1998—; prof. U. Cordoba, 2002; hon. prof. Nat. Univ. Cordoba, Argentina, 2000. Author: Limbic System, 2d edit., 1982; editor: (with others) Expression of Knowledge, 1982, The Hippocampus, vols. 3-4, 1986, The Vulnerable Brain and Environmental Risks, vols. 1-2, 1992, vol. 3, 1994. Pres. Alachua County Assn. for Retarded Children, Gainesville, 1973-75;

chmn. dist. III Human Rights Advocacy Com., Gainesville, 1975-77. Served with USN, 1950-53, Korea Holloway fellow U.S. Navy, 1946-50; grantee NSF, NIH, U.S. Army Surgeon Gen., NIMH. Fellow APA, AAAS; mem. Internat. Behavioral Neurosci. Soc. (councilor 1991-95, pres. 1999, Myers Lifetime Achievement award 2002), Soc. for Neurosci. (pres. cen. N.Y. chpt. 1982-84), Assn. Neurosci. Depts. Programs, Am. Physiol. Soc., Sec. Health Rehab. Svcs. State of Fla. (mem. Blue Ribbon com. 1976), Nat. Rsch. Coun. (mem. subcom. on fluoride in drinking water, 2003-05). Office: Binghamton Univ Dept Psychology Binghamton NY 13902-6000 Office Phone: 607-777-6764. Business E-Mail: isaacson@binghamton.edu.

ISAACSON, ROBERT LOUIS, investment company executive; b. Chgo., Apr. 21, 1944; s. Abe B. and Laverne (Skolka) I. BS, Mich. State U., 1966. Mktg. mgr. Florasynth, Inc., San Francisco, 1966-69, br. mgr. Lincolnwood and Palo Alto, Calif., 1969-72; br. office mgr. Geldermann, Palo Alto, 1972-76; founder, pres. Commodity Investment Cons., Los Altos, Calif., 1976—, Future Funding Cons., Menlo Park, Calif., 1976—. Co-founder, co-chmn. Nat. Assn. Futures Trading Advisors; bd. dirs. Futures Industry Assn. Edn. and Tng., Williams & Clarissa, Inc.; bd. dirs., exec. com., membership com. Nat. Futures Assn.; membership Nat. Futures Assn. Regional Bus. Conduct Com.; v.p. Lind-Waldock Co., Chgo.; pres. Interalliance U.S.A. Contbr. articles to mags and profl. jours. Founder Fun for Lunch Bunch. With U.S. Mil., 1966-72. Recipient Doncheon award Managed Accounts Report, 1984. Mem. San Francisco Futures Soc., Managed Futures Assn. (past co-chmn., bd. dirs.), Asian Pacific Managed Futures Assn. (bd. dirs., founding mem.), World Trading Day CARE (exec. com.), Peninsula Commodities Club, Elks, Kiwanis. Avocations: jogging, biking, horseback riding, flying, sailing. Office: Commodity Investment Cons Future Funding Cons 380 La Questa Way Woodside CA 94062-2428 Office Phone: 650-851-8507. E-mail: isaacson@worldnet.att.net.

ISAACSON, SAMUEL B., lawyer; b. Johnstown, Pa., June 28, 1957; BA magna cum laude, Dickinson Coll., 1979; JD, Pa. State Univ., 1982. Bar: Pa. 1982, Ill. 1983, DC 1985. Ptnr., head of Chgo. Litigation group DLA Piper Rudnick Gray Cary, Chgo. Mem.: ABA, Ill. State Bar Assn., Chgo. Bar Assn., Def. Rsch. Inst., Lawyers Club Chgo., Fedn. of Insurance & Corp. Counsel, Phi Beta Kappa. Office: DLA Piper Rudnick Gray Cary Suite 1900 203 N LaSalle St Chicago IL 60601-1293 Office Phone: 312-368-2163. Office Fax: 312-251-5827. Business E-Mail: samuel.isaacson@dlapiper.com.

ISAACSON, STEVEN ROBERT, surgeon; b. Bronx, N.Y., 1947; BS, Pa. State U., 1969; MD, Thomas Jefferson U., 1973. Bd. cert. radiation oncology Am. Bd. Radiology, bd. cert. otolaryngology Am. Bd. Otolaryngology. Attending physician Columbia Presbyn. Med. Ctr., 1988—; intern surgery Abington Meml. Hosp., 1973—74, resident surgery, 1974—75; resident otolaryngology U. Pa., 1975—78; resident radiation oncology SUNY Health Sci. Ctr., Bklyn., 1985—88; co-dir. Ctr. for Radiosurgery Columbia Presbyn. Med. Ctr., 1998—. Asst. prof. radiation oncology and otolaryngology Columbia Coll. Physicians and Surgeons, Columbia U., N.Y.C., 1990—94, assoc. prof. clin. radiation oncology and clin. otolaryngology, 1994—98, assoc. prof. clin. radiation oncology and clin. otolaryngology/head and neck surgery in dentistry, 1998—. Office: Columbia Presbyn Med Ctr BHN-Bll Dept Rad Oncol 622 W 168th St New York NY 10032-3720

ISAACSON, WALTER SEFF, think-tank executive; b. New Orleans, May 20, 1952; s. Irwin and Betsy (Seff) I.; m. Cathy Wright, Sept. 15, 1984; 1 child, Elizabeth Carter. BA, Harvard U., 1974; MA, Oxford (Eng.) U., 1976. Reporter Sunday Times London, 1976-77; reporter, columnist States-Item, New Orleans, 1977-78; staff writer Time mag., NYC, 1978-79, polit. corr. Washington, 1979-81, assoc. editor NYC, 1981-84, sr. editor, 1985-91, asst. mng. editor, 1991-93; editor New Media Time Inc., NYC, 1993—95; mng. editor Time mag., NYC, 1995—2000; editl. dir. Time Inc., NYC, 2000—01; chmn., CEO CNN News Group, 2001—03; pres., CEO The Aspen Inst., Washington, 2003—. Bd. dirs. Reader's Digest Assn., Tulane U., Nat. Constn. Ctr., Shakespeare Theatre of Washington. Author: Pro and Con, 1983, Kissinger: A Biography, 1992, Benjamin Franklin: An American Life, 2003; co-author: The Wise Men, 1986 (Harry Truman Book prize 1987). Chmn. bd. Teach for Am. Rhodes scholar, 1974; recipient Overseas Press Club award, N.Y.C., 1981, 84, 87. Mem. Coun. Fgn. Rels., Century Assn., Met. Club of Washington. Office: Aspen Institute One Dupont Cir Ste 700 Washington DC 20036 Office Phone: 202-736-5840.

ISABLE, ALISHA, elementary school educator; d. Anthony and Antoinette I. BS in Elem. Edn., Morgan State U., Balt., 1999; MS in Ednl. Leadership, Towson U., 2004. Std. Profl. Cert. Md. State Dept. of Edn., 1999. Tchr. 3rd grade math. Balt. City Pub. Schs., Balt., 1999—2002, tchr. grade 4, 2002—. Master tchr. Future Tchrs. of Am., Balt., 2003—; founder pvt. tutoring svc.; creator website for students, 2000—01. Home: 2305 Tarelton Ln Parkville MD 21234 Office: Midtown Acad Baltimore MD 21217 Personal E-mail: abisable@yahoo.com.

ISAF, FRED THOMAS, lawyer; b. Jacksonville, NC, Nov. 18, 1950; s. Thomas Fred and Rowanda (Maloof) Isaf; m. June J. Jeffcoat, Aug. 18, 1973; children: Julie, Thomas, Christa. BA, Duke U., 1972; JD, Emory U., 1975, LLM in Taxation, 1978. Bar: Ga. 1975, US Tax Ct. 1978. Shareholder Roberts and Isaf, PC, Atlanta, 1986-94, Roberts, Isaf & Summers, PC, Atlanta, 1994-99; ptnr. McGuire Woods LLP, Atlanta, 1999—2003, Atlanta mng. ptnr., 2003—. Dir. Pinecrest Acad., Atlanta, 1995—2002. Named a Ga. Super Lawyer, Law and Politics and Atlanta Mag., 2004, 2005; named Ga. Super Lawyers, Law and Politics, Atlanta Mags., 2004, 2005. Mem.: State Bar Ga., Cherokee Town and Country Club (sec. 1993, bd. dirs. 1994—2000, v.p. 1997, pres. 1998—99), Order of Barristers, Order of the Coif. Office: McGuire Woods Ste 2100 1170 Peachtree St Atlanta GA 30309 Office Phone: 404-443-5712. Business E-Mail: fisaf@mcguirewoods.com.

ISAKI, LUCY POWER SLYNGSTAD, lawyer; b. Jersey City, Oct. 21, 1945; d. Charles Edward and Ann Mary (Power) Slyngstad; m. Paul S. Isaki, Aug. 26, 1967. BA summa cum laude, Seattle U., 1973; JD cum laude, U. Puget Sound, 1977. Bar: Wash. 1977. Case worker San Joaquin County Welfare, Stockton, Calif., 1968-70, Alameda County Welfare, Oakland, Calif., 1971-73; legal intern King County Prosecutor's Office, 1976-77; law clk. to hon. Justice Hamilton Wash. Supreme Ct., 1977-78; ptnr. Bogle & Gates, Seattle, 1978—99; sr. asst. atty. gen. State of Wash., 1999—; mem. exec. team for Atty. Gen. Gregoire, Seattle, 2001—04. Cons. Region X, HHS, 1975; chair task force on alternative dispute resolution Atty. Gen. Gregoire, 1993-94. Bd. dirs. King County Family Svcs., Seattle, 1982-84, Wash. State Coun. Crime and Delinquency, 1981, Northwest Kidney Ctr., 2001—, vice chair, 2003-05, chair, 2005—; treas. Mother's Against Violence in Am., 1994; trustee emeritus U. Puget Sound, 1985—, Seattle Youth Symphony, 1995, Ea. Wash. U., 1998-99; chmn. law sch. bd. visitors Seattle U., 1984-96; trustee Legal Found., Wash., 1992-95, sec. bd. dirs. 1993, v.p. bd. dirs. 1994, pres. 1995; pres. Kinnear Vistas Homeowners' Assn., 2003-2005. Dean's scholar U. Puget Sound, 1976-77; recipient Disting. Law Grad. award U. Puget Sound, 1984, Majis award Seattle U., 1997. Mem. Wash. Women Lawyers (pres. Seattle-King County chpt. 1982, v.p. 1984), ABA (ho. of dels. 1995-97), Wash. State Bar Assn. (bd. govs. 2000-03), King County Bar Assn. (sec. 1986-87, trustee 1987-90, treas. 1995-97, 1st v.p. 1998, pres. 1999-2000, chair govt. lawyers sect. 2004—), U. Puget Sound Law Alumni Soc. (pres. 1979). Democrat. Office: Atty Gens Office 900 4th Ave Ste 2000 Seattle WA 98164-1076 Office Phone: 206-389-2598. E-mail: lucyi@atg.wa.gov.

ISAKOFF, SHELDON ERWIN, chemical engineer; b. Bklyn., May 25, 1925; s. Harry and Rebecca I.; m. Anita Ginsburg, Aug. 18, 1946; 1 son, Peter D. BS, Columbia U., 1945, MS, 1947, PhD, 1952. Guest fellow Brookhaven Nat. Lab., Upton, N.Y., 1949-50; with E.I. duPont de Nemours & Co., Inc., Wilmington, Del., 1951-90, dir. engring. research and devel., 1975-90, ret., 1990. Mem. Nat. Materials Adv. Bd., 1980-82; adj. prof. Columbia U., 1990—; trustee, United Engring. Trust, 1992-98, pres., 1995-97. Vice chair bd. Chem. Heritage Found., 1992-94, chair, 1995-98. With USNR, 1943-46. Recipient Egleston medal Columbia U., 1994, Alumni medal, 1996. Fellow AIChE (past dir., Founders award 1980, Inst. lectr. 1984, materials divsn. award 1986, v.p., pres.-elect 1989, pres. 1990, Thomas H. Chilton award, Wilmington sect. 1994, Mgmt. Divsn. award 1997, Van Antwerpen award 1997), AAAS; mem. NAE, Am. Chem. Soc., Sigma Xi, Tau Beta Phi, Phi Lambda Upsilon. Home: 102 Center Mill Rd Chadds Ford PA 19317-9212 E-mail: isakoffshe@aol.com.

ISAKOVIC, ABDEL, physicist, researcher; b. Stolac, Herzegovina, Bosnia-Herzegovina, Dec. 4, 1971; arrived in U.S., 1998; s. Smajo Isakovic and Fadila Culic. BSc, U. Sarajevo, Bosnia-Herzegovina, 1996; MSc, U. Minn., 2000, PhD in Physics, 2003. Rsch. asst. U. Minn., Mpls., 1999—2002; postdoctoral rschr. Cornell U., 2003—. Tchg. asst. U. Sarajevo, 1996—98, U. Minn., 1998—99. Fellow SpinTechI fellow, Strategic Analysis Inc., 2001, 3M Sci. and Engring. fellow, U. Minn., 2002—03. Mem.: AAAS, Bosnian Phys. Soc. (v.p. 1997—98), Soc. Indsl. Applied Math., Materials Rsch. Soc., Am. Phys. Soc. Achievements include research in magnetic anisotropy in ferromagnet/semiconductor hetersostructures; feasibility of transport of spin polarized carriers from semiconductors into ferromagnet; injection of spin polarized electrons from ferromagnet into semiconductor; collective transport phenomena, electronic crystals. Avocations: travel, archaeology, history. Office: Lab Atomic and Solid State Physics Physics Dept Clark Hall B3/A16 Cornell Univ Ithaca NY 14853 E-mail: isakovic@ccmn.cornell.edu.

ISAKSEN, ROBERT L., retired bishop; b. Bklyn. m. Beverly Sievertsen; children: Elisabeth, Lois. BA, Concordia Coll., Moorhead, Minn., 1957; MDiv, Luther Sem., St. Paul, 1961; STM, N.Y. Theol. Sem., 1971; DD (hon.), Upsala Coll., 1990. Ordained to ministry Am. Luth. Ch., 1961. Vicar St. Timothy Luth. Ch., Chgo., 1960; pastor Bethlehem, Bronx, N.Y., 1961-62, St. Peters, Bronx, 1962-68, Bethlehem, Baldwin, N.Y., 1972-81; Bronx Luth. coord. Planning Assn. of Bronx Luth. Chs., 1968-72; mission dir. Am. Luth. Ch., 1981-87; bishop New Eng. Synod Evang. Luth. Ch. in Am., Worcester, Mass., 1987-2000; ret.; interim pastor Stavanger Internat. Ch., Stavanger, Norway, 2003; transition pastor Trinity Luth. Ch., Great Barrington, Mass., 2003—04. Vis. prof. Yale Divinity Sch., 2001; adv. bishop to Bd. for Outreach, Evang. Luth. Ch. in Am., 1988-91, adv. bishop to Ch. Coun., 1992-97; chair Boston Ch. Leaders Covenant, 1995-96; pres. New Eng. Conf. Ch. Leaders, 1993. Bd. dirs. Luth. Immigration and Refugee Svcs., N.Y.C., 1983-87. Mem., Hendrick Hudson Male Chorus, 2002-. Lutheran. Home: 175 Ashley Hill Rd Brainard NY 12024 E-mail: bpisak1@yahoo.com.

ISAKSON, JOHNNY (JOHN HARDY ISAKSON), senator, former congressman; b. Atlanta, Ga., Dec. 28, 1944; m. Dianne Isakson; children John, Kevin, Julie BBA, U. Ga., 1966. Businessman, Atlanta; mem. Ga. Ho. Reps., 1976—90, Ga. St. Senate, 1993—96, U.S. Congress from 6th Ga. dist., 1999—2005; vice chmn. 21st century competitiveness subcom.; US senator from Ga., 2005—. Mem. Edn. and the Workforce, Transp. and Infrastructure coms.; chmn., Ga. St. Bd. Edn., 1996-99 Winner spl. election to succeed Rep. Newt Gingrich, who resigned, 1999; represented Cobb County in the Ga. legislature 17 yrs.; Rep. candidate for gov. of Ga., 1990, Rep. primary candidate for U.S. Senate, 1996; Sunday sch. tchr. Mt. Zion Meth. Ch., 1978—. Republican. Methodist. Office: US Senate 416 Russel Senate Office Bldg Washington DC 20510*

ISAYEV, AVRAAM ISAYEVICH, polymer engineer, educator; b. Privolnoe, Azerbaijan, Russia, Oct. 17, 1942; s. Isai S. and Basia Isayev; m. Lubov M. Dadasheva, July 26, 1969; 1 child, Daniela. MSChemE, Azerbaijan Inst. Oil & Chem., Baku, 1964; PhD in Polymer Engring., USSR Acad. Scis., Moscow, 1970; MS in Applied Math., Inst. Electronic Machine Bldg., Moscow, 1975. Rsch. assoc. State Rsch. Inst. Nitrogen Industries, Severodonetsk, Russia, 1965—66; predoctoral Inst. of Petrochem. Synthesis Russia Acad. Sci., Moscow, 1967—69, rsch. assoc., 1970—76; sr. rsch. fellow Israel Inst. Tech., Haifa, 1977—78; sr. rsch. assoc. Cornell U., Ithaca, NY, 1979—83; assoc. prof. Inst. Polymer Engring., U. Akron, Ohio, 1983—87, prof., 1987—2001, dir. mold tech., 1987—, disting. prof., 2001—. Guest prof. U. Aachen, Germany, 1986, U. Linz, Austria, 1993, Kyoto Inst. Tech., Japan, 1996, Inst. Polymer Rsch., Dresden, Germany, 1997, U. Sao Carlos, Brazil, 1997; expert on plastics processing technologies, Malaysia, 1995. Editor: Injection Compression Molding Fund, 1987, Modelling of Polymer Processing, 1991, Liquid Crystalline Polymer Systems Technological Advances, 1996, Rubber Recycling, 2005; contbr. articles Internat. Ency. of Composites, Ency. of Polymer Sci. and Engring., Ency. of Matter, Sci. and Tech. and others. Expert witness U.S. Ho. of Reps., Washington, 1988; expert U.S. Army Rsch. Office, 1991; rev. panel NSF, Washington, 1991, 94, 2000-04. NASA fellow, 1985; recipient Laureate of Young Scientists USSR Acad. Scis., 1970, Cert. of Appreciation, U. Akron Bd. Trustees, 1988, 93, Outstanding Rschr. award U. Akron Alumni Assn., 1996, Silver medal The Inst. Materials, London, 1997, Vinogradov prize G. V. Vinogradov Soc. Rheology, Moscow, 2000, Omnova Solutions Signature Univ. award, Akron, 2000, 02, Cert. Recognition for Exemplary Svc., Mortar Bd. and Omicron Delta Kappa, 2003; named Disting. Corp. Inventor, Am. Soc. Patent Holders, 1995. Mem. Am. Chem. Soc. (Melvin Mooney Disting. Tech. award rubber divsn. 1999), NY Acad. Scis., Soc. Plastics Engrs. (Cert. of Recognition 1994), Polymer Processing Soc. (treas. 1989-91), Soc. Rheology. Jewish. Achievements include 23 patents for Self-Reinforced Composites, Devulcanization of Rubbers and Decrosslinking of Crosslinked Plastics; in-situ copolymerization in polymer blends, multi-layer conductive and nonconductive polymers; fundamental research in polymer and composite processing. Office: U Akron Inst Polymer Engring 230 S Forge St Akron OH 44325-0301 Business E-Mail: aisayev@uakron.edu.

ISBELL, DAVID BRADFORD, lawyer, educator; b. New Haven, Feb. 18, 1929; s. Percy Ernest and Dorothy Mae (Crabb) I.; m. Florence Bachrach, July 21, 1971; children: Christopher Pascal, Virginia Anne, Nicholas Bradford. BA, Yale U., 1949, LLB, 1956. Bar: Conn., 1956, DC 1957. Assoc. Covington & Burling, Washington, 1957-59, 61-65, ptnr., 1965-98, sr. counsel, 1998—; asst. staff dir. U.S. Commn. on Civil Rights, Washington, 1959-61. Lectr. Sch. Law U. Va., 1962—, Georgetown U. Law Ctr., 1996—. Bd. dirs. ACLU, 1965-92; chmn. exec. bd. Vets. Consortium Pro Bono Program, 1992-05. 2nd lt. US Army, 1951-53. Mem.: ABA (mem. ho. dels. 1986—96, chmn. com. on ethics & profl. responsibility 1991—94), D.C. Bar (gov. 1978—82, pres. 1983—84), Cosmos Club. Home: 3709 Bradley Ln Bethesda MD 20815-4256 Office: Covington & Burling 1201 Pennsylvania Ave NW Washington DC 20004 Office Phone: 202-662-5518. Personal E-mail: disbell@cov.com.

ISBELL, HAROLD MAX, writer, investor; b. Maquoketa, Iowa, Sept. 20, 1936; s. H. Max and Marcella E. Isbell; m. Mary Carolyn Cosgriff, June 15, 1963; children: Walter Harold, Susan Elizabeth, David Harold, Alice Kathleen. BA cum laude, Loras Coll., 1959; MA, U. Notre Dame, 1962; grad., U. Mich. Grad Sch. Bank Mgmt., 1982. Instr. U. Notre Dame, South Bend, Ind., 1963-64; asst. prof. San Francisco Coll. for Women, 1964-69; assoc. prof. St. Mary's Coll., 1969-72; with Continental Bank & Trust Co., Salt Lake City, 1972-83, v.p., 1977-83, comml. credit officer, 1978-83, also bd. dirs. Editor, translator: The Last Poets of Imperial Rome, 1971, Ovid: Heroides, 1990; contbr. to publs. in field of classical Latin lit. and contemporary Am. lit. Trustee Judge Meml. Cath. H.S., Salt Lake City, 1977-84; mem. Utah Coun. for Handicapped and Developmentally Disabled Persons, 1980-81; bd. dirs. Ballet West, 1983-90, emeritus, 1990—, Story Line Press, 1994-99, Smuin Ballets, San Francisco, 1994-99; founder Cath. Found. Utah, pres., 1984-86, trustee, 1984-89. Mem. AAAS, MLA, Medieval Acad. Am., Alta Club. Democrat. Roman Catholic.

ISBISTER, JENEFIR DIANE WILKINSON, microbiologist, researcher, educator, consultant; b. Rahway, N.J., June 4, 1936; d. Edwin Guy and Alvira Marie (Andrews) Wilkinson; m. James David Isbister, July 23, 1960; children: Wendy Jill Isbister Kalavritinos, Kirstin Ann Isbister Hammond. BS, Newberry (S.C.) Coll., 1957; MS in Med. Tech., Jefferson Med. Sch., Phila., 1958; PhD in Microbiology, U. Md., 1977. Med. technologist Princeton (N.J.) Hosp., 1958-60; instr. med. tech. sch. George Washington U., Washington, 1960-62, rsch. asst., 1976-77; rsch. microbiologist Environ. Biospherics, Inc., Rockville, 1978-80; group leader environ. microbiology dept. Atlantic Rsch. Corp., Alexandria, Va., 1980-89; pvt. practice cons. microbiologist Potomac, Md., 1989—; sr. tech. advisor ARCTECH, Inc., Chantilly, Va., 1989-92. Adj. prof. George Mason U., 1988-92, rsch. prof., 1992—; cons. Orkand Corp., Silver Spring, Md., 1979-80, U.S. DOE, Pitts., 1988-89, Advancis Pharm., Gaithersburg, Md., 2001—. Contbr. to book, articles to profl. jours. Sci. fair judge Montgomery and Fairfax County Schs., Md. and Va., 1975—; bd. dirs. Bedford (Pa.) Springs Music Festival, 1984-89. Va.-Carolina Chem. Corp. scholar, 1953; recipient Congl. High Tech. award Congl. Caucus for Sci. and Tech., 1985. Mem. ASTM (vice chair 1983-92, 99-2002), Am. Soc. for Microbiology, Am. Soc. for Clin. Pathologists, Cosmos Club, Phi Kappa Phi, Phi Sigma, Chi Beta Phi. Episcopalian. Avocations: reading, music, tennis, restoring old houses and furniture. Home: 9521 Accord Dr Rockville MD 20854-4302 Office: George Mason U Rm 303E Prince William II 10900 University Blvd Manassas VA 20110 E-mail: jisbiste@gmu.edu.

ISBURGH, ANNE MARIE, engineering manager; b. Ft. Dix, N.J., July 29, 1957; d. Ernest Francis and Virginia Marion Condina; m. Robert Karl Isburgh, Oct. 17, 1981; 1 child, Dane Karl. BSME, Rensselaer Poly. Inst., 1979, MSME, 1980. Registered profl. engr., Ohio. Engr. Buckeye Cellulose, Memphis and Perry, Tenn./Fla., 1980-84; engr. turbine aero & cooling design GE Aircraft Engines, Cin., 1984-88, lead engr. turbine aero & cooling design, 1988-94, staff engr. Turbine Airfoils Ctr. of Excellence, 1994-97, engring. black belt, 1997-99, subsect. mgr. Turbine Airfoils Ctr. of Excellence, 1999—. Patentee in field. Recipient Clarence E. Davies award ASME, 1980. Mem. Elfuns. Home: 11637 Windy Hill Ct Loveland OH 45140-1969 Office: GE Aircraft Engines MD A406 1 Neumann Way Cincinnati OH 45215-1915 Fax: 513-243-3621. Office Phone: 513-243-3697. E-mail: anne.isburgh@ae.ge.com.

ISCHINGER, WOLFGANG, ambassador, diplomat; b. Stuttgart, Germany, Apr. 6, 1946; married; 3 children. Student, U. Bonn, Germany, U. Geneva, Switzerland; law degree, 1972; MA in Internat. Law, Internat. Rels. and Econ., Fletcher Sch. of Law and Diplomacy, 1972—73; postgrad., Harvard U. Asst. to cabinet UN sec. gen., NYC, 1973; with German Fgn. Svc., 1975—, mem. policy planning staff, 1977—79, diplomat German Embassy Washington, 1979—82; mem. cabinet Fgn. Min., Bonn, Germany, 1982—90, pvt. sec., 1985—87; dir. Cabinet and Parliamentary Affairs; min. counselor, head polit. sect. German Embassy, Paris, 1990—93; dir. policy planning staff German Fgn. Office, Bonn, 1993—95, dir. gen. polit. affairs, 1995—98, state sec., 1998—2001, mem. high level German-Russian Strategy Group, 2000—01; ambassador to U.S. Embassy of Germany, Washington, 2001—. Bd. dirs. East-West Inst., NY, Am. Field Svc.; chmn. ambassadors adv. bd. Exec. Coun. on Diplomacy, Washington; bd. dirs. Fletcher Sch. Law and Diplomacy. Avocations: skiing, mountain climbing. Office: Embassy of Germany 4645 Reservoir Rd NW Washington DC 20007

ISCHIROPOULOS, HARRY, medical researcher, educator; b. May 26, 1961; m. Patricia Nikitin; 1 child, Constantinos. BS in Chemistry, Wagner Coll., 1984; MS in Pathology, N.Y. Med. Coll., 1987, PhD in Pathology, 1989. Rsch. fellow dept. anesthesiology U. Ala. Sch. Medicine, Birmingham, 1990-92; rsch. assoc. Inst. Environ. Medicine U. Pa. Sch. Medicine, 1992-94, sr. investigator Inst. Environ. Medicine, rsch. asst. prof. biochemistry and biophysics, 1995—; asst. prof. peds. & biochem./biophysics Stokes Investigator. Contbr. articles to profl. jours., chpts. to books; ad hoc reviewer Am. Jour. Physiology, Jour. Applied Physiology, Circulation, Jour. Leukocyte Biology, Chem. Rsch. in Toxicology, Neurosci. Letters, Biochem. Pharmacology, Respiratory Physiology; mem. editl. bd. Free Radical Biology and Medicine, 1996—; presenter in field. Recipient Am. Inst. Chemists award, 1984, Established Investigator award Am. Heart Assn., 1996—; Parker B. Francis fellowship in Pulmonary Rsch., 1993-96; Dr. Frederic Valergakis Grad. grantee, 1988-89. Mem. AAAS, Internat. Soc. for Free Radical Rsch. (young investigator award 1994), Oxygen Soc. (young investigator award 1995). Office: Childrens Hosp of Phila Abramson Ctr Div Neonatology 3516 Civic Ctr Blvd Philadelphia PA 19104-4318

ISDALE, CHARLES EDWIN, chemical engineer; b. DeQuincy, La., Mar. 10, 1942; s. Vester Edwin and Katherine Gwendolyn (Wincey) I.; m. Lucille Brown, Aug. 26, 1962; children: Charles Edwin Jr., Jennifer Denise Hunt, Amberly Lauren. BSChemE, La. State U., 1965; MBA, So. Ill. U., 1978. Registered profl. engr., Ill., La. Chem. engr. Firestone Synthetic Rubber, Lake Charles, La., 1965-69, A.E. Staley Mfg. Co., Decatur, Ill., 1969-72; dir. engring. and maintenance VIOBIN Corp., Monticello, Ill., 1972-80; pres. Control Enterprises, Inc., Savoy, Ill., 1980-95, College Station, Tex., 1995-97; sr. lectr. dept. chem. engring. Tex. A&M U., College Station, 1998—. Cons. Nabisco Brands, East Hanover, N.J., 1984—, Clorox, Jackson, Miss., 1987—, Alpharma, Chicago Heights, Ill., 1987—, Chinook Group, Sombra, Ont., Can., 1987—. Active Cornerstone Ch., College Station, Tex. Mem. AIChE (sect. chmn. 1972-73), Instrument Soc. of Am. (Man of Yr. 1986). Achievements include design of a configurable multivariate control method, a method for removal of solvent to low ppm levels from enzymes, design of a batch wheat germ oil extraction plant, design of an animal gland extraction plant; patents on processing beef lung for production of heparin. Home: 715 Canterbury Dr College Station TX 77845 Office: Tex A&M U Chem Engring Dept MS3122 College Station TX 77843-3122 E-mail: charles@isdale.com, c-isdale@tamu.edu.

ISDELL, EDWARD NEVILLE, beverage company executive; b. Downpatrick, County Down, Ireland, June 8, 1943; came to U.S., 1989; s. Edward Neville and Margaret (Smith) I.; m. Pamela Anne Gill, Jan. 10, 1970; 1 child, Cara Anne. BA in Social Sci., Cape Town U., Republic of South Africa, 1965; PMD, Harvard Bus. Sch. Mgmt. trainee Edgars Stores Ltd., Johannesburg, 1966, Copperbelt Bottling Co., Kitwe, Zambia, 1966-68; various positions The Coca-Cola Co., Atlanta, Zambia, South Africa, 1968—80, regional mgr. Sydney, Australia, 1980—81; pres. Coca-Cola Bottlers Philippines, Inc., Manila, 1981—84; pres., Central European div. The Coca-Cola Co., Essen, West Germany, 1984—89, sr. v.p., pres. Northeast Europe and Africa group Atlanta, 1989-92, sr. v.p., pres. Northeast Europe and Middle East group, 1993—95, pres., Greater Europe Group, 1995—98; chmn., CEO Coca-Cola Beverages plc, England, 2000—01; CEO Coca-Cola Hellenic Bottling Co. S.A., 2000—01, vice chmn, 2001; sr. internat. cons. to CEO Doug Daft The Coca-Cola Co., 2001—04, chmn., CEO, 2004—. Bd. dirs. Coca-Cola Amatil, Ltd., Australia, Coca-Cola Enterprises, U.S., Coca-Cola FEMSA, S.A. de C.V., Mex., Amalgamated Beverages Gt. Britain. Mem. Ch. of Ireland. Office: The Coca-Cola Co PO Box 1734 Atlanta GA 30301

ISELIN, DONALD GROTE, civil engineer, management consultant; b. Racine, Wis., Sept. 5, 1922; s. Harry Paul and Rose Ellen I.; m. Jacqueline Myers, June 9, 1945; children— Donna Iselin Broom, Michael D., Madeline M. BS, U.S. Naval Acad., Annapolis, 1945; M.C.E., Rensselaer Poly. Inst., 1948; cert. in advanced mgmt. program, Harvard U., 1971. Registered profl. engr., D.C. Commd. ensign U.S. Navy, 1945, advanced through grades to rear adm., 1971, dep. chief civil engrs. Washington, 1973-76, chief civil engrs., 1977-81; ret., 1981; group v.p. Kaiser Engrs., Oakland, Calif., 1981-85. Decorated Legion of Merit (4); recipient Stephen Decatur award Navy League, 1968, Alumnus Engr. award Marquette U., 1980, Disting. Svc. Medal Pres. U.S., 1981. Fellow Soc. Am. Mil. Engrs. (pres. 1978-79); mem. NAE, ASCE, NSPE, AIA (hon.). Republican. Roman Catholic. Home: 2695 Sycamore Canyon Rd Santa Barbara CA 93108-1913

ISELIN, JOHN JAY, foundation president; b. Greenville, S.C., Dec. 8, 1933; s. William Jay and Fannie Harrington (Humphreys) I.; m. Josephine Lea Barnes, Sept. 8, 1956; children: William Jay II, Benjamin Barnes, Josephine Lea, Fannie I. Minot, Alison Jay Russell. AB, Harvard U., 1956, PhD, 1965; BA, Corpus Christi Coll., U. Cambridge, Eng., 1958, MA, 1963; hon. degree, Adelphi U., L.I. U., Lander Coll. Rsch. fellow Brookings Inst., Washington, 1960-61; sr. writer Congl. Quar., Washington, 1961; corr.-editor Newsweek mag., 1962-65, sr. editor nat. affairs, 1965-69; v.p., pub. Harper & Row Publs. Inc., N.Y.C., 1969-71; pres., trustee Ednl. Broadcasting Corp., Channel 13, sta. WNET, N.Y.C., 1971-87; pres. The Cooper Union for the Advancement of Sci. and Art, N.Y.C., 1988-2000; pres. and dir. Marconi Internat. Fellowship Found., 2000—. Adj. prof. Columbia U., 2000—. Mem. bd. overseers Harvard U., 1970-76; mem. Acad. Polit. Sci., mem. Nat. Geog. Soc., Josiah Macy Jr. Found., Ventures in Edn.; Waterford Inst.; mem. Cathedral of St. John the Divine, N.Y. State Archives Inst. Recipient Disting. Citizen award trustees SUNY. Mem. Coun. on Fgn. Rels., Century Club, Harvard Club of N.Y.C. Office: Marconi Foundation 500 Mudd Hall Columbia Univ New York NY 10027 Home: Apt C606 200 E 66th St New York NY 10021-9185 E-mail: jji9@columbia.edu.

ISELY, HENRY PHILIP, association executive, integrative engineer, writer, educator; b. Montezuma, Kans., Oct. 16, 1915; s. James Walter and Jessie M. (Owen) I; m. Margaret Ann Sheesley, June 12, 1948 (dec. 1997); children: Zephyr, LaRock, Lark, Robin, Kemper, Heather Capri; m. Jelica Kungulovska, 2001. Student, South Oreg. Jr. Coll., Ashland, 1934-35, Antioch Coll., Yellow Springs, Ohio, 1935-37. Organizer Action for World Fedn., 1946-50, N.Am. Coun. for People's World Conv., 1954-58, World Com. for World Constl. Conv., 1958, sec. gen., 1959-66, World Constn. and Parliment Assn., Lakewood, Colo., 1966—; organizer worldwide prep. confs. World Constnl. Convention, 1963, 66, 67, 1st session People's World Parliament and World Constl. Conv., Switzerland, 1968; editor assn. jour. Across Frontiers, 1959—; co-organizer Emergency Coun. World Trustees, 1971, World Constituent Assembly, Innsbruck, Austria, 1977, Colombo, Sri Lanka, 1978-79, Troia, Portugal, 1991; organizer Provisional World Parliament 1st session, Brighton, Eng., 1982, 2nd Session, New Delhi, India, 1985, 3d Session, Miami Beach, Fla., 1987; mem. parliament, 1982—. Sec. Working Commn. to Draft World Constn., 1971-77, pres. World Svc. Trust, 1972-78; co-founder Builder Found., Vitamin Cottages, 1955—, (chmn. bd. dir s., 1985—), pres. Earth Rescue Corps., 1984-90, sec.-treas. Grad. Sch. World Problems, 1984-99, pres., 1999—, cabinet mem. Provisional World Govt., 1987—, pres. World Govt. Funding Corp., 1986—, Emergency Earth Rescue Adminstrn., 1995—, co-organizer Global Ratification and Elections Network, 1991— (sec. 1992—), prin. organizer 4th session Provisional World Parliament, Barcelona, Spain, 1996, 5th session, Malta, 2000, organizer first More Oxygen for the World conf., San Antonio, 1998; prof. world problems Grad. Sch. World Problems, 1990—; organizer Com. Five Global Expositions, 2001—. Author: The People Must Write the Peace, 1950, A Call to All Peoples and All National Governments of the Earth, 1961, Outline for the Debate and Drafting of a World Constitution, 1967, Strategy for Reclaiming Earth for Humanity, 1969, Call to a World Constituent Assembly, 1974, Proposal for Immediate Action by an Emergency Council of World Trustees, 1971, Call to A Provisional World Parliament, 1981, People Who Want Peace Must Take Charge of World Affairs, 1982, Plan for Emergency Earth Rescue Administration, 1985, Plan for Earth Finance Credit Corporation, 1987, Climate Crisis, 1989, Technological Breakthroughs for A Global Energy Network, 1991, Bill of Particulars: Why the U.N. Must Be Replaced, 1994, Manifesto for the Inauguration of World Government, 1994, Call to the Fourth Session of the Provisional World Parliament, 1995, Fifth Session, 1997, Critique of the Report of the Commission on Global Governance, 1995, Using Crtedit Careds and Electronic Accountin to Initiate New Global Accounting, Credit and Finance System, 1996, Double Jeopardy and the Phytoplankton Project, 1997, The Fallacy of Treating Labor as a Commodity, 2000, The Immediate Economic Benefits of World Government, 2000, The First Fifteen Global Ministries of World Government, 2002; co-author, editor: A Constitution for the Federation of Earth, 1974, rev. edit., 1991, also author several other world legis. measures adopted at Provisional World Parliament, 1968-96; co-author: Plan for Collaboration in World Constituent Assembly, 1991, Creator treatment for screen drama History Hangs by a Thread, 1993; designer: prefab modular panel sys. constrn., master plan Guacamaya project, Costa Rica; planner five world fairs, five sessions World Parliament, 2000. Candidate for U.S. Congress, 1958. Recipient hon. rsch. doctorate in edn., 1989, Honor award Internat Assn. Educators for World Peace, 1975, Ghandi medal, 1977, Honor award Internat Soc. Universalism, 1993. Mem. ACLU, Am. Acad. Polit. Sci., Fellowship of Reconciliation, World Union, World Federalist Assn., World Future Soc., Earth Island Inst., Populatin Reference Bur., Earth Action, People's Congress, Life Ext. Found., Interfaith Alliance, Internat. Assn. for Hydrogen Energy, Friends of Earth, Wilderness Soc., Solar Energy Soc., Sierra Club, Amnesty Internat., World Resources Inst., Human Rights Watch, Nat. Nutritional Foods Assn., Environ. Def. Fund, Greenpeace, Ctr. for Study of Democratic Instns., War Resistors League, Audubon Soc., Worldwatch Inst., Internat. Assn. Constl. Law, Earth Regeneration Soc., Zero Population Growth, Cancr Control Soc., Mt. Vernon Country Club, Lakewood Country Club. Socialist. Home: Lookout Mountain 241 Zephyr Ave Golden CO 80401-9589 Office: 8800 W 14th Ave Lakewood CO 80215-4817 Fax: 303-237-7685, 303-526-7933. E-mail: wcparliament@uswest.net.

ISEMAN, JOSEPH SEEMAN, lawyer; b. N.Y.C., May 29, 1916; s. Percy Reginald and Edith Helene (Seeman) I.; m. June Lorraine Bang, Dec. 10, 1966; children: Peter A., Frederick J., Ellen M.; stepchildren: Anne Hamilton, Susan E. Hamilton, William C. Hamilton. BA magna cum laude, Harvard U., 1937; LLB, Yale U., 1941; LHD (hon.), Am. U. of Paris, 1997. Bar: N.Y. 1941, D.C. 1970, France, 1986. Investigator, clk. Comml. Factors Corp., 1937-38; atty. WPB, 1941-42; mng. dir. Iranian Airways Corp., 1946; assoc. Chadbourne, Wallace, Parke & Whiteside, N.Y.C., 1946-50, Paul, Weiss, Rifkind, Wharton & Garrison, N.Y.C., 1950-53, ptnr., 1954-86, counsel, 1987—. Counsel Charles F. Kettering Found., 1965-84. *When I die, various taxing authorities will take most of what I've been able to accumulate. Therefore, as I have aged, I have found it painless to give as generously as I can to the persons I love and the causes I respect, and have tried to develop, regardless of cost, a stimulating, far-flung and useful retirement existence. In addition to being a lawyer, I have had a number of secondary careers, including: serving as managing director of the Iranian Airways Corporation in 1946, contributing to the introduction of public television in the New York area, and serving as acting president of Bennington College in Vermont.* Author: A Perfect Sympathy, 1937; contbr. articles to profl. jours. Trustee Bennington Coll., 1969—81, acting pres., 1976; bd. dirs. Acad. for Ednl. Devel., Safe Horizon, 1980—, also chmn.; bd. dirs. The Hastings Ctr., 1999—, Am. U., Paris, 1987—2000, also vice chmn. Capt. USAF, 1942—46. Woodrow Wilson vis. fellow Coll. William and Mary, 1977, Ripon Coll., 1979, Rollins Coll., 1980, De Pauw U., 1980, Fisk U., 1981, Albright Coll., 1982, Hood Coll., 1983, Southwestern U., 1984. Mem. ABA, N.Y. State Bar Assn., Assn. of Bar of City of N.Y., Century Assn., Coveleigh Club, Phi Beta Kappa. Democrat. Office: 1285 6th Ave Rm 2828 New York NY 10019-6064 Office Phone: 212-373-3167. Personal E-mail: jiseman@optonline.net. Business E-Mail: jiseman@paulweiss.com.

ISEMAN, MICHAEL DEE, medical educator; b. St. Paul, Mar. 3, 1939; s. Manuel Wessel and Eileen Catherine (Croghan) I.; m. Joan Marie Christensen, Aug. 31, 1963; children: Thomas Michael, Matthew Charles. BA in History, Princeton U., 1961; MD, Columbia U., 1965. Intern, jr. resident in medicine Columbia Svc., Bellevue Hosp., N.Y.C., 1965-67; sr. resident in medicine Columbia Svc., Harlem Hosp., N.Y.C., 1969-70; fellow pulmonary medicine Harlem Hosp., N.Y.C., 1970-72; assoc. dir. pulmonary svc. Denver Gen. Hosp., 1972-82; chief clin. mycobacteriology svc. Nat. Jewish Med. and Rsch. Ctr., Denver, 1982—2004. Asst. prof. medicine U. Colo. Sch. Medicine, Denver, 1973-79, assoc. prof. medicine, 1979-89, prof., 1989—. Author: A Clinician's Guide to Tuberculosis, 1999; assoc. editor Am. Rev. Respiratory Diseases, N.Y., 1984-89; editor-in-chief Internat. Jour. Tuberculosis and Lung Disease, 1997-2003. Pres. Am. Lung Assn. Colo., Denver, 1982-83; alumni trustee Princeton U., 1981-85. Lt. comdr. USN, 1967-69. Prin. investigator devel. and evaluation of drugs for treatment of mycobacterium avium in AIDS, NIH, 1984-1992. Fellow ACP, Am. Coll. Chest Physicians; mem. Am. Thoracic Soc. (v.p. 1983-84). Presbyterian. Avocations: rowing, skiing, tennis, photography, history. Office: Nat Jewish Med and Rsch Ctr 1400 Jackson St Denver CO 80206-2762 Business E-Mail: isemanm@njc.org.

ISEMINGER, GARY HUDSON, philosophy educator; b. Middleboro, Mass., Mar. 3, 1937; s. Boyd Austin and Harriet Herring (Hudson); m. Andrea Louise Grove, Dec. 18, 1965; children: Andrew, Ellen. BA, Wesleyan U., 1958; MA, Yale U., 1960, PhD, 1961. Instr. philosophy Yale U., 1961-62, Carleton Coll., Northfield, Minn., 1962-63, asst. prof., 1963-68, assoc. prof., 1968-73, prof., 1973-94, William H. Laird prof. philosophy and liberal arts, 1994—2002, Stephen R. Lewis, Jr. prof. philosophy and liberal learning, 2002—04, emeritus, 2004—. Vis. fellow Kings Coll., London, 1966, U. Lancaster, 1991; chair student-faculty adminstrn. com. Carleton Coll., 1970-71, dept. philosophy, 1972-75, 86-89, 98—, ednl. policy com., 1973-74, English dept. rev. com., 1973-74, com. Lucas Lectrs. in Arts, 1977-81, presdl. inauguration, 1987, edn. dept. rev. task force, 1988, Am. studies program rev. com., 1992, mem. tenure and devel. rev. com., 1985-87, Coll. Coun., 1987, Coll. Marshall, 2001—; acad. vis. London Sch. Econs., 1971; vis. prof. philosophy U. Minn., 1979, Mayo Med. Sch., 1986, 87, U. Lancaster, 1994, Trinity Coll. Dublin, 2000, Lingnan U., Hong Kong, 2003; Belgum meml. lectr. St. Olaf Coll., 1997; panelist divsn. fellowships NEH, 1980, 91; commentator Minn. Pub. Radio, 1981; dir. London arts program Associated Colls. Midwest, 1982; cons. Harvard U. Press, Univ. Calif. Press, Prentice-Hall, Cornell U. Press, Holt, Rinehart and Winston, Vanderbilt U. Press, Jour. Aesthetics and Art Criticism, Dialogue, Notre Dame Jour. Formal Logic, Jour. of Philosophy and Phenomenological Rsch., Inquiry; external reviewer, evaluator various philosophy depts.; presenter in field. Author: An Introduction to Deductive Logic, 1968, Logic and Philosophy: Selected Readings, 1968, 2d edit., 1980, Knowledge and Argument, 1984, Intention and Interpretation, 1992, The Aesthetic Function of Art, 2004; mem. editl. bd. Am. Philos. Quar., 1989-92, Jour. of Aesthetics and Art Criticism, 1993—; contbr. articles, revs. to profl. jours. Mem. Minn. Humanities Commn., 1984-90, chair 1988-89 Grantee NSF Coun. Philos. Studies, 1968, Bush Found., 1983, Sloan Found. 1984, Faculty Devel. Endowment, 1989, 94, 2000, NEH, 1990, 91; recipient summer stipend NEH, 1971, 78, Disting. Alumnus award Wesleyan U., 1993; Woodrow Wilson fellow, 1958, fellow Univ. Coll., London, 1975, 78, Inst. Adv. Studies in the Humanities, U. Edinburgh, 1985; vis. scholar Cambridge U., 1996, York U., 2002. Mem. AAUP (pres. Carleton chpt. 1967-68), Am. Philos. Assn. (program com. western divsn. 1982, task force on the philosophy major 1989-90, program com. ctrl. divsn. 1991, chmn. com. on tchg. philosophy 1993-96, com. to award Matchette prize in philosophy 1993-95, bd. officers 1993-96), Am. Soc. Aesthetics (trustee 1996-99), Minn. Philos. Soc. (pres. 1978-79), Phi Beta Kappa (pres. Carleton chpt. 1968-69). Avocations: classical percussion, jazz vibraphone, choral singing. Office: Carleton College One North College St Northfield MN 55057-4002 E-mail: giseming@carleton.edu.

ISENBERG, ABRAHAM CHARLES, shoe manufacturing company executive; b. Lynn, Mass., Feb. 24, 1914; s. Louis and Alice (Lown) I.; m. Thelma F. Sisenwine, Oct. 30, 1938; children: Gerald, Lee Carol, Edward. BS, Wharton Sch., U. Pa., 1935. Cert. paralegal vol., county ct. mediator, lic. mediator, Fla. With Consol. Nat. Shoe Corp., Norwood, Mass., 1935—, exec. v.p., 1967-68, pres., CEO, 1968-72, chmn. bd., treas., 1972-74. Vice chmn. shoe divsn. Greater Boston area Combined Jewish Philanthropies, 1968—. Bd. dirs. New Eng. Anti-Defamation League of B'nai B'rith. Mem. Two Ten Assocs. (bd. dirs. 1956—, v.p. 1969—), Am. Footwear Assn. (bd. dirs. 1968, regional v.p. 1970—), Am. Footwear Inst. (trustee 1970-74), Boston Boot and Shoe Club (exec. com. 1967—, v.p. 1969, pres. 1973), Brandeis U. Men's Assocs. (bd. dirs. 1966—), Beta Sigma Rho. Clubs: Hebrew Rehab. Ctr. Men's (bd. dirs. 1970-72), B'nai B'rith (bd. dirs. 1979—). Home: 2480 N Park Rd Apt 314 Hollywood FL 33021 Personal E-mail: abethelma@webtv.net. *I have found that being honest and ethical with those I associated with in business or community affairs was the most rewarding behavior I could follow. I realize that some who act entirely contrary to these principles appear to be very successful, but I would not want success on those terms.*

ISENBERG, HENRY DAVID, microbiology educator; b. Giessen, Germany, Mar. 9, 1922; came to U.S., 1937, naturalized, 1943; s. Gerson and Flora (Gruenebaum) I.; m. Lila S. Grossman, Feb. 15, 1948; children: Ina Pepi Isenberg Stein, Gerald Alan. BS, CCNY, 1947; MA, Bklyn. Coll., 1951; PhD, St. Johns U., 1959. Diplomate Am. Bd. Med. Microbiology (chmn. 1976-79, Disting. Svc. award 1994). Asst. dir. Angrist Labs., 1947-54; chief microbiology L.I. Jewish Med. Ctr., New Hyde Park, NY, 1954-97, chief emeritus, cons., 1997—2002, chief emeritus microbiology (pathology), dir. infection control (medicine), 2002—05, chief emeritus, 2005—; cons. clin. microbiology Mt. Sinai Med. Ctr., 1997—2001; cons. Univs. Space Rsch. Assn., 1998—; asst. clin. prof. orthopedic surgery SUNY Downstate Med. Ctr., Bklyn., 1963-68, assoc. clin. prof. orthopedic surgery, 1968-71, professorial lectr. orthopedic surgery, 1971-89. Prof. clin. pathology SUNY Health Sci. Ctr., Stony Brook, 1970-89; clin. prof. microbiology and immunology U. South Fla. Sch. Medicine, 1982-87; prof. lab. medicine Albert Einstein Coll. Medicine, 1989-96, prof. pathology, 1996-05, prof. emeritus, 2005—; cons. in microbiology NASA, 1990—; lectr. pathology Mt. Sinai Sch. Medicine, 1998-2001 Editor Jour. Clin. Microbiology, 1974-79, editor-in-chief, 1979-89; editor CRC Critical Revs. in Microbiology, 1978-81; editor in chief: CRC Forum in Bacteriology; sect. editor Manual of Clin. Microbiology, 4th edit.; editor: Manual of Clinical Microbiology, 5th edit.; editor-in-chief Clinical Microbiology Procedures Handbook, 1991-2002, 2d edit. 2002-04, Essential Procedures in Clinical Microbiology, 1997-2002; mem. editl. bd. Applied Microbiology, 1969-74; contbr. numerous articles to profl. jours. and books; patentee in field. Served with U.S. Army, 1943-45. Named Microbiologist of Yr. Lab World Mag., 1978; recipient Kimble awrd, 1980; Profl. Recognition award Am. Bd. Microbiology/Am. Acad. Microbiology, 1994. Fellow Am. Acad. Microbiology (bd. govs.), N.Y. Acad. Scis., Am. Inst. Chemists, Infectious Disease Soc. Am., N.Y. Acad. Medicine; mem AAAS, Am. Soc. Microbiology (Becton-Dickinson award 1979, Alexander C. Sonnenwirth Meml. Lectr. award 1989, Disting. Svc. award N.Y. br. 1991, nat. 1996, hon. mem. 1999), Harvey Soc., Sigma Xi. Jewish. Home: 26922D Grand Ctrl Pky Floral Park NY 11005-1022 E-mail: hisenberg@myc.rr.com.

ISENBERG, HOWARD LEE, manufacturing executive; b. Chgo., Dec. 21, 1936; children: Suzanne, Marc, Alan. BS, U. Pa., 1958. CPA, Ill. V.p. Conley Electronics, Chgo., 1960-63, Barr Co. div. Pittway Corp., Niles, Ill., 1963-68, pres. Barr Co. div., 1969-92; v.p. Pittway Corp., Niles, Ill., 1970-92, CCL Custom Mfg. (acquired Barr Co. in 1992), 1992—. Vice chmn., trustee Lake Forest (Ill.) Acad., 1986-98; trustee Providence-St. Mel H.S., Chgo., 1994—, Nat. Def. U. Found., 2003—; chmn. The Barr Fund, 1993—. Office: CCL Custom Mfg 6133 N River Rd Ste 800 Rosemont IL 60018-5175 Office Phone: 847-825-0060 x 102. Business E-Mail: hisenberg@cclcustom.com.

ISENBERG, JANE FRANCES, language educator, writer; b. Paterson, N.J., Aug. 27, 1940; d. Hymen and Marian Alma (Spitz) Siegendorf; m. Donald Windham Isenberg, Aug. 19, 1962 (dec. June 1985); children: Rachel, Daniel; m. Philip J. Tompkins, Dec. 20, 1997. BA in English, Vassar Coll., Poughkeepsie, N.Y., 1962; MA in English, Southern Conn. State Coll., 1971; PhD in Applied Linguistics, N.Y.U., 1993. English tchr. Richard C. Lee, James Hillhouse H.S., New Haven, Conn., 1962-69; tchr. South Central C.C., New Haven, Conn., 1969-77; dir. Outreach Program Human Resources Adminstrn., New Haven, Conn., 1976-77; tchr. Goddard Coll., Plainfield, Vt., 1975-77; prof. English Hudson County C.C., Jersey City, N.J., 1979—. Tchr. Yale U., New Haven, summers 1977-78, Stevens Inst. Tech., Hoboken, NJ, summer 1982; bd. trustees Jewish Family and Counseling Svcs., Bayonne, NJ, 1994—, The Hudson Sch., Hoboken, NJ, 1979-89, Stevens Coop. Sch., Hoboken, 1978-84; presenter in field. Author: Going by the Book: The Role of Popular Classroom Chronicles in the Professional Development of Teachers, 1994 (James N. Britton award Nat. Coun. Tchrs. English 1994); (novels) The 'M' Word, 1999, Death in a Hot Flash, 2000, Mood Swings to Murder, 2000, Midlife Can Be Murder, 2001, Out of Hormone's Way, 2002, The Proof is in The Patch, 2003, Hot and Bothered, 2003, Hot on the Trail, 2004, co-editor Award Winning Papers, 1993—. Grantee Am. Studies, Yale U., New Haven, Conn., 1965, NDEA, Wesleyan U., Middleton, Conn., 1966; recipient Mid-Career fellowship Princeton (NJ) U., 1991-92. Mem. MLA, Hudson County Country Club Profl. Assn., Hudson Reading Coun., Lang. Educators Appying Reflection Now, Nat. Coun. Tchrs. English, NJ Edn. Assn., NJ Reading Assn., NY Metro. Assn. for Developmental Edn., NY State TESOL. Office: Hudson County CC 25 Path Plz Jersey City NJ 07306-2905

ISENBERG, JEROLD, education educator; BSc, Roosevelt U., 1974; Rabbinic Ordination, B in Hebrew Lit., Hebrew Theol. Coll., 1977; MSc, Northeastern Ill. U., 1978; M in Hebrew Lit., Jewish U. of Am., 1983; MBA, Roosevelt U., 1984; D, Jewish U. of Am., 1988. Asst. to the dean Hebrew Theol. Coll., Skokie, Ill., 1977—81, asst. dean of students, assoc. dean and registrar, 1983—85, v.p. for academic affairs, 1985—94, chancellor - ceo, 1994—. Cons. evaluator North Ctrl. Assn., Chgo., 2004—. Mem.: Rabbinical Coun. of Am., Chgo. Rabbinical Coun. (v.p. 1985—), Assn. for Computing Machinery. Jewish. Office: Hebrew Theological Coll 7135 N Carpenter Rd Skokie IL 60077 Office Phone: 847-982-2500 127. E-mail: isenberg@htcnet.edu.

ISENBERG, STEVEN LAWRENCE, retired publishing executive; b. Detroit, Oct. 19, 1940; s. A.G. Jerry and Lucille (Potaschnik) Isenberg; m. Barbara Lee Levy, Nov. 26, 1967; 1 child, Christopher Michael. BA in English, U. Calif., Berkeley, 1962; BA in English Lang. and Lit., Oxford (Eng.) U., 1964, MA, 1966; JD, Yale U., 1976; DHL (hon.), Adelphi U., 2000. Bar: N.Y. 1976. Asst. to dir. Bur. Budget, N.Y.C., 1967—68; chief staff, asst. to mayor Office of Mayor, N.Y.C., 1969—73; litigator Breed, Abbott and Morgan, N.Y.C., 1976—82; asst. to pub. Newsday, L.I., NY, 1982—83; pub., CEO So. Conn. Newspapers, Stamford, 1983—86; assoc. pub. Newsday, N.Y. Newsday, N.Y.C., 1986—90; pub. Sports, Inc., N.Y.C., 1987—88; exec. v.p. mktg. L.A. Times, 1991—92; deputy pub. Newsday/N.Y. Newsday, Melville, 1992—95; pub. N.Y. Newsday, 1994—95. Reuters fellow Green Coll., Oxford, 1997; vis. prof. U. Calif., Berkeley, 1996; chmn. bd. trustees Adelphi U., Garden City, NY, 1997—2001, pres. ad interim, 1999—2000, chmn. emeritus, 2001—; lectr. Yale Coll., 1999; vis. scholar, lectr. The New Sch., 1999; vis. prof. humanities Polytechnic U., Bklyn., 2000; Batten prof. pub. policy Davidson (N.C.) Coll., 2001; vis. prof. humanities U. Tex., Austin, 2002—. Pres. adv. bd. U. Calif. Coll. Letters and Scis., Berkeley; emeritus chmn. bd. trustees Adelphi U., L.I.; bd. dirs. Franklin & Eleanor Roosevelt Inst.; mem. presdl. campaign staff Robert F. Kennedy, 1968, John V. Lindsay, 1972; bd. dirs. Mcpl. Arts Soc., Com. to Protect Journalists. Mem.: Coun. Fgn. Affairs, Century Assn., Yale Club. Democrat. Jewish. Home: Apt 3N 151 Central Park W New York NY 10023-1514

ISENBERGH, JOSEPH, law educator; b. 1945; BA, Columbia U., 1966; AM, U. Rochester, 1967; JD, Yale U., 1970. Bar: DC 1976. Assoc. Caplin & Drysdale, Washington, 1976-80; asst. prof. U. Chgo., 1980-84, prof., 1984—. Author: (book) International Taxation, 1990, 1995, 2001. Office: U Chgo Law Sch 1111 E 60th St Chicago IL 60637-2776*

ISENHOWER, NELSON NOLAN, anesthesiologist; b. Newton, N.C., Feb. 9, 1948; s. Homer Hallard and Genevieve Elizabeth (Caldwell) I.; m. Rebecca Sue Wilson, Sept. 18, 1976; children: Lori Suzanne, Matthew Wilson. BS cum laude, Wake Forest U., 1970; MD, Bowman Gray Sch. Medicine, 1974. Diplomate Am. Bd. Anesthesiology. Commd. 2d lt. M.C., U.S. Army, 1970, advanced through grades to lt. col., 1983; intern Walter Reed Army Med. Ctr., Washington, 1974-75, resident in anesthesiology, 1975-78; mem. anesthesiology tchg. staff Brooke Army Med. Ctr., Fort Sam Houston, Tex., 1978-79, asst. chief anesthesiology, 1979-80, chief anesthesiology and operative svcs., dir. anesthesiology residency tng., 1980-83; cons. in anesthesiology U.S. Army Health Svcs. Command, 1980-83. Staff anesthesiologist Winchester Med. Ctr. (Va.), 1983—, chmn. dept. anesthesiology, 1987-89, 2nd v.p. med. staff, 1995, 1st v.p., 1996, pres., 1997; med. dir. Surgi-Ctr. Winchester, 1998—. Contbr. articles to profl. jours. Fellow Am. Coll. Anesthesiology; mem. AMA, Med. Soc. Va., No. Va. Med. soc., Am. Soc. Anesthesiology, So. Soc. Anesthesia, Internat. Anesthesia Rsch. Soc., Am. Soc. Reg. Anesthesia, Va. Anesthesiology Soc., Soc. Ambulatory Anesthesia. Republican. Baptist. Office: Winchester Anesthesiologists Inc 878 Fox Dr Winchester VA 22603-2807 Office Phone: 540-662-8336. E-mail: Nisenho@winanes.com.

ISER, WOLFGANG, literature educator, writer; b. Marienberg, Germany, July 22, 1926; s. Paul and Else (Steinbach) I.; m. Lore Reichert, May 24, 1952. Student, U. Leipzig, Germany, 1946, U. Tuebingen, 1946-47, U. Heidelberg, 1947—50; PhD, U. Heidelberg, Germany, 1950. Instr. in English U. Heidelberg, Germany, 1951-52, asst. prof., 1955-57, assoc. prof. English, 1957-60; asst. lectr. in German U. Glasgow, Scotland, 1952-55; prof. English and comparative lit. U. Wuerzburg, Germany, 1960-63, U. Cologne, Germany, 1963-67, U. Constance, Germany, 1967-91, U. Calif., Irvine, 1978—2005. Writings include: (lit. criticism) Die Weltanschauung Henry Fieldings, 1952, Walter Pater: Die Autonomie des Aesthetischen, 1960, English transl., 1987, Die Appelstruktur der Texte, 1970, English transl., 1972, Spensers Arkadien: Fiktion und Geschichte, 1970, English translation, 1981, Der Implizite Leser, 1972, English transl., 1974, Der Akt des Lesens, 1976, English transl., 1976, The Act of Reading: A Theory of Aesthetic Response, 1979, Sterne: Tristram Shandy, 1988, Prospecting: From Reader Response to Literary Anthropology, 1989, Staging Politics: The Lasting Impact of Shakespeare's Historical Plays, 1993, The Fictive and the Imaginary: Charting Literary Anthropology, 1993, The Range of Interpretation, 2000, How to do Theory, 2005; editor: Dargestellte Geschichte in der europaeischen Literatur des 19 Jhdts., 1970, Theorien der Kunst, 1982, Languages of the Unsayable: The Play of Negativity in Literature and Literary Theory, 1989, Translatability of Cultures-Figurations of the Space Between, 1996. Office: U Calif Irvine Dept English Irvine CA 92697-0001

ISERBYT, CHARLOTTE THOMSON, researcher, consultant, writer, educator; b. Bklyn., Oct. 26, 1930; d. Clifton Samuel and Charlotte Deyer Thomson; m. Johan Louis Iserbyt, Sept. 26, 1964; children: Robert Louis, Samuel Thomson. Attended, Katharine Gibbs Sch., 1948—49. Social worker ARC, Anderson Air Force Base, Japan, 1953—55; sec. to amb. US Dept. State, Pretoria, South Africa, 1959—60, Brussels, 1961—63; pres., cofounder Guardians Edn. Maine, Camden, 1978—2000; sr. policy advisor US Dept. Edn., DC, 1980—82; pres. 3D Rsch. Co., Bath, Maine, 1999—. Contbr. articles various profl. jours. Social worker Am. Red Cross, Japan, 1953—55; elected sch. bd. mem. Camden-Rockport Sch. Dist., 1976—79. Mem.: Daughters of Am. Revolution. Independent. Roman Catholic. Office: 3D Rsch Co 1062 Washington St Bath ME 04530 Office Phone: 207-442-0543. Office Fax: 207-442-0551. Personal E-mail: dumbdown@blazenetme.net.

ISH, DANIEL RUSSELL, law educator, academic administrator; b. Loon Lake, Sask., Can., Aug. 28, 1946; s. Leme Jay and Obeline Delia (Sicotte) I.; m. Diane Maureen Cote, Sept. 2, 1967 (div. 1970); m. Bonnie Jeanne Bolger, Dec. 22, 1970; children: Jason Bolger, Rachel Bolger. LLB, BA, U. Sask., 1970; LLM, Osgoode Hall Law Sch., Toronto, Ont., Can., 1974. Bar: Alta. 1971, Sask. 1979; called to Queen's Counsel, 1991. Lawyer H. Lloyd MacKay, Banff, Canada, 1970-71; asst. prof. law McGill U., Montreal, Canada, 1972-75; assoc. prof. U. Sask., Saskatoon, 1975-80, prof. law, 1980—, asst. dean law, 1977-78, dean, 1982—88, 1996—97, 2002—04; dir. Ctr. for Study of Coops., 1989-95. Author: The Taxation of Canadian Co-operatives, 1975, The Law of Canadian Co-operatives, 1981, Co-operatives in Principle and Practice, 1992, Legal Responsibilities of Directors and Officers in Canadian Cooperation, 1996. Pres. Univ. Credit Union, Saskatoon, 1979-80. Fulbright fellow, Stanford U., 1995—96. Mem. Law Found. Sask. (trustee 1982-88, 2002—), Law Soc. Sask. (bencher 1982-88, 2002—). Avocations: skiing, running. Office: U Sask Coll Law Saskatoon SK Canada S7N 5A6

ISHAK, WAGUIH WILLIAM, psychiatrist; b. Port Said, Egypt, Oct. 16, 1964; s. William Makram IsHak and Nawara Yacoub Dawoud; m. Asbasia A Mikhail-IsHak, M.D.; children: William Waguih, Michael Waguih. MD, Cairo U., 1987. Dir., psychiatry residency tng. program Cedars-Sinai Med. Ctr., L.A., 2001—, med. dir., adult outpatient psychiatry, 2003—. Assoc. dir., psychiatry residency program NYU Sch. of Medicine, N.Y.C., 1998—2001. Editor: Outcome Measurement in Psychiatry: A Critical Review (Reviews in the Am. Jour. of Psychiatry and Psychiat. Services, 2003). Fellow: Am. Psychiat. Assn. Achievements include development of Online screening tests for psychiatric disorders. Office: Cedars-Sinai Medical Center 8730 Alden Dr Thalians W-157 Los Angeles CA 90048 Office Phone: 310-423-3481. Office Fax: 310-423-3497.

ISHAQ, ASHFAQ, foundation administrator, economist, educator; BA, Govt. Coll., Lahore, Pakistan; MPA, U. Punjab; PhD in Econs., George Washington U. Economist World Bank; faculty mem. George Washington U.; founder, exec. dir. Internat. Child Art Found., Washington, DC, 1997—. Guest lectr. US Foreign Svcs. Inst. Author: Success in Small & Medium Scale Enterprises, 1987; founder, editor ChildArt mag., 1998—. Grantee Hesselbein Cmty. Fellowship, Peter Drucker Found., 2001. Mem.: Internat. Acad. Digital Arts and Scis. (adv. bd. mem.), World Psychiatry Assn. Office: Internat Child Art Found Ste 1225 1350 Connecticut Ave NW Washington DC 20036 Office Phone: 202-530-1000.*

ISHERWOOD, ROBIN WILLIAMS, music educator; b. Lincoln, Ill., Sept. 18, 1971; d. David C. and Janet L. Williams; m. Joseph M. Isherwood, Dec. 25, 2001. BS in Music Edn., U. North Ala., 1995, MA in Music Edn., 1996. Band dir. Vina (Ala.) HS, 1996—97; asst. band dir., percussion instr. Baldwin County HS, Bay Minette, Ala., 1997—; band dir. Perdido (Ala.) Mid. Sch., 1997—. Musician: Baldwin Pope Band, 1997—; musician: (prin. percussionist) Muscle Shoals Symphony, Riveria Symphony; composer: PF 2001, 2001, Cycle of Life, 2002, Percussion Swing Show, 2004. Mem.: NEA, Music Educators Nat. Conf., Ala. Educators Assn. Baptist. Avocations: gardening, horseback riding, walking, bicycling, travel.

ISHII, AKIRA, parasitologist, allergist; b. Kochi, Japan, July 11, 1937; s. Katsuhiko and Fusae Ishii; m. Fuyuko Ishii, Mar. 20, 1968; children: Ken, Shin. MD, U. Tokyo, 1964, D Med. Sci., 1969; MSc, U. London, 1970. Cert. malaria advanced epidemiology. Rsch. assoc. Inst. Infectious Disease, U. Tokyo, 1969-74; asst. prof. Toyko Med. and Dental U., 1974-78, Inst. Med. Sci., U. Tokyo, 1978-79; prof. Miyazaki (Japan) Med. Coll., 1979-84, Okayama (Japan) U. Med. Sch., 1984-90; dir. dept. parasitology NIH, Tokyo, 1990-95; prof. Jichi Med. Sch., 1995—2003, prof. emeritus, 2003—; prof. Jissen Women's U., 2005—. Com. mem. Japanese Internat. Coop. Agy., Tokyo, 1978—89; panel mem. U.S.-Japan Coop. Med. Program Parasitic Diseases, 1991—95, China-Japan Parasitology Seminar. Mem. editl. bd.: Protozool. Rsch., Allergology Internat. Fellow: Royal Soc. Tropical Medicine and Hygiene, Am. Soc. Tropical Medicine and Hygiene; mem.: German-Japan Assn. for Protozoan Diseases (coun.), Japanese Soc. Pub. Health, Japan Assn. Internat. Health (pres., councilor, mem. exec. bd.), Japanese Soc. Infectious Disease (councilor), Japanese Soc. Allergologists (councilor), Japanese Soc. Med. Ent. Zoology (councilor, Soc. prize), Japanese Soc. Tropical Medicine (councilor), Japanese Soc. Parasitologyy (councilor, Koizumi prize, Katsurado prize). Avocations: mountain trips, golf, tennis. Home: 1-14-11 Matsubara Setagayaku Tokyo 156-0043 Japan E-mail: ishiiaki@jichi.ac.jp.

ISHII, ANTHONY W., judge; b. Santa Ana, Calif., 1946; AS, Reedley Jr. Coll., 1966; PharmD, U. Pacific, 1970; JD, U. Calif., Berkeley, 1973. Dep. city atty. City Atty.'s Office, Sacramento, 1975; dep. pub. defender County of Fresno, 1979; pvt. practice Fresno, 1979—83; justice ct. judge Parlier-Selma Judicial Dist., Fresno, Calif., 1983—93; mcpl. ct. judge Central Valley Mcpl. Ct., Fresno, Calif., 1994—97; judge U.S. Dist. Ct. (ea. dist.) Calif., 1997—. Office: Fed Bldg, Rm 3654 US Courthouse 1130 O St Fresno CA 93721-2201*

ISHII, YOSHINORI, environmental science educator; b. Tokyo, Mar. 14, 1933; s. Kichijiro and Kei Ishii; m. Hiroko Hisamune, Nov. 24, 1963; children: Yutaka, Makoto, Akira. BS, U. Tokyo, 1955, ED, 1977. Exploration geophysicist Teikoku Oil Co., Tokyo, 1955; rsch. geophysicist Japan Petroleum Exploration Co., Tokyo, 1955-67, sr. geophysicist, 1970-71, Japan Nat. Oil Corp., Tokyo, 1967-70; assoc. prof. geophysics U. Tokyo, 1971-78, prof. geophysics, 1978-93, prof. emeritus, 1993—; dep. dir. gen. Nat. Inst. Environ. Studies, Ibaraki, Japan, 1994-96, dir. gen., 1996-98; prof. Toyama U. Internat. Studies, 2000—. Mem. Sci. Coun. of Japan, Tokyo, 1988-91. Author: Introduction to Remote Sensing, 1981, Geophysical Engineering, 1988, Energy and Global Environmental Problems, 1995, Environmental Studies for Citizens, 2001, co-author several books; contbr. numerous articles to profl. jours. Mem. Engring. Acad. Japan, Soc. Exploration Geophysicists of Japan (pres. 1984-85, 1988-89, Best Paper award, Tokyo, 1976), Remote Sensing Soc. Japan, (v.p. 1981-88, pres. 1990-92), Japanese Assn. for Petroleum Tech. (v.p. 1982-86). Avocations: golf, computers. Home: 8-2-14 Hisagi, Zushi Kanagawa 249-0001 Japan Office: Toyama U Internat Studies Oyama-cho Kami-Niikawa-Gun Toyama 930-1292 Japan Office Phone: 076-483-8000. E-mail: tikyuu@qa2.so-net.ne.jp.

ISHIKAWA-FULLMER, JANET SATOMI, psychologist, educator; b. Hilo, Hawaii, Oct. 17, 1925; d. Shinichi and Onao (Kurisu) Saito; m. Calvin Y. Ishikawa, Aug. 15, 1950; 1 child, James A.; m. Daniel W. Fullmer, June 11, 1980. B of Edn., U. Hawaii, 1950, MEd, 1967, MEd, 1969, PhD, 1976; postgrad., Queen's Med. Ctr., 1980—82. Diplomate Am. Acad. Pain Mgmt. Postdoctoral trainee Queen's Med. Ctr., intern pain diagnosis tng., biofeedback/self-hypnosis tng.; prof. Honolulu Bus. Coll., 1953-59; prof., counselor Kapiolani C.C., Honolulu, 1959-73; prof., dir. counseling Honolulu C.C., 1973-74, dean of students, 1974-77; psychologist, pres., treas. Human Resources Devel. Ctr., Inc., Honolulu, 1977—. Cons. United Specialties Co., Tokyo, 1979, Grambling (La.) State U., 1980, 81, Filipino Immigrants in Kalihi, Honolulu, 1979-84, Legis. Ref. Bur., Honolulu, 1984-85, Honolulu Police Dept., 1985; co-founder Waianae (Hawaii) Child and Family Ctr., 1979-92. Co-author: Family Therapy Dictionary, 1991, Manabu: The Diagnosis and Treatment of a Japanese Boy with a Visual Anomaly, 1991; contbr. articles to profl. jours. Commr. Bd. Psychology, Honolulu, 1979-85; co-founder Kilohana United Meth. Ch. and Family Ctr., 1993—. Recipient Outstanding Educator award, Grambling State U., 1977, Pres.'s award, 1984, Disting. Benefactor award, U. Hawaii Coll. Edn., 2004, Disting. Alumna award, 2005. Mem. APA, ACA, Hawaii Psychol. Assn., Pi Lambda Theta (sec. 1967-68, v.p. 1968-69, pres. 1969-70, 96-98), Delta Kappa Gamma (sec., v.p. scholarship 1975, Outstanding Educator award 1975, Thomas Jefferson award 1993, Francis E. Clark award 1993). Avocations: jogging, tennis, dance. Home: 154 Maono Pl Honolulu HI 96821-2529 Office: Human Resources Devel Ctr 1750 Kalakaua Ave Apt 809 Honolulu HI 96826-3725 Office Phone: 808-942-2072.

ISHIMARU, AKIRA, electrical engineering educator; b. Fukuoka, Japan, Mar. 16, 1928; came to U.S., 1952; s. Shigezo and Yumi I.; m. Yuko Kaneda, Nov. 21, 1956; children: John, Jane, James, Joyce. BSEE, U. Tokyo, 1951; PhD, U. Wash., 1958. Registered profl. engr., Wash. Engr. Electro-Tech. Lab, Tokyo, 1951-52; tech. staff Bell Telephone Lab, Holmdel, N.J., 1956; asst. prof. U. Wash., Seattle, 1958-61, assoc. prof., 1961-65, prof. elec. engring., 1965-98, prof. emeritus, 1998—. Vis. assoc. prof. U. Calif., Berkeley, 1963-64; cons. Jet Propulsion Lab., Pasadena, Calif., 1964—, The Boeing Co., Seattle, 1984—. Author: Wave Propagation & Scattering in Random Media, 1978, Electromagnetic Wave Propagation, Radiation and Scattering, 1991; editor: Radio Science, 1982; founding editor Waves in Random Media, U.K., 1990. Recipient Faculty Achievement award Burlington Resources, 1990; Boeing Martin professorship, 1993. Fellow IEEE (editl. bd., Region VI Achievement award 1968, Centennial medal 1984, Antennas and Propagation Disting. Achievement award 1995, Heinrich Hertz medal 1999), IEEE Geosci. and Remote Sensing (Disting. Achievement award 1998, Third Millennium medal 2000), Acoustical Soc. Am., Optical Soc. Am. (assoc. editor jour. 1983), Inst. Physics U.K. (chartered physicist); mem. NAE, Internat. Union Radio Sci. (chmn. commn. B, John Howard Dellinger Gold medal 1999). Home: 2913 165th Pl NE Bellevue WA 98008-2137 Office: U Wash Dept Elec Engring PO Box 352500 Seattle WA 98195-2500 Office Phone: 206-543-2169. Business E-Mail: ishimaru@ee.washington.edu.

ISHLER, HAROLD LEROY, JR., family medicine physician; b. Lock Haven, Pa., Mar. 16, 1941; s. Harold and Marqueta (Guiser) I.; m. Suzanne McNeilly, July 17, 1965; children: Stephanie, Stephen. BS, Pa. State U., 1963; MD, Jefferson Med. Coll., 1967. Diplomate Am. Bd. Family Practice. Office: Ochsner Clinic Baton Rouge 9001 Summa Ave Baton Rouge LA 70809-3726 Office Phone: 225-761-5200.

ISKANDER, JOHN K., epidemiologist, pediatrician; b. Amman, Jordan, Aug. 7, 1964; s. Michel and Betty Iskander; m. Susan K. Duderstadt, May 17, 1997; children: Eleanor, Jonas. BA in Biol. Scis., U. Chgo., 1986; MD, MPH, Tulane U., 1992. Diplomate Am. Bd. Pediat. Resident in pediat. Children's Meml. Hosp., Chgo., 1992—95; pediatrician Albany (Ga.) Area Primary Health Care, 1995—98; med. epidemiologist S.C. Dept. Health, Columbia, 1998—2000, Ctrs. for Disease Control & Prevention, Atlanta, 2000—. Vis. lectr. U. S.C. Sch. Pub. Health, Columbia, 1999—2000; vol. instr. Emory U. Sch. Pub. Health, Atlanta, 2002—; pediatrician Ga. Higlands Med. Svcs., Cumming, 2002—. Vol. presch., Decatur, Ga. Lt. comdr. USPHS, 2001—. Decorated Crisis Response Svc. award USPHS; recipient Commendation medal, Pub. Health Svc., 2005; scholar, Nat. Health Svc. Corps, 1991—92. Fellow: Am. Acad. Pediat.; mem.: Commd. Officers Assn., Delta Omega. Achievements include research in monitoring the safety of vaccines and immunizations. Avocations: reading, travel. Office: Ctrs for Disease Control & Prevention 1600 Clifton Rd MS E-61 Atlanta GA 30333 Office Phone: 404-639-8889. E-mail: jxi0@cdc.gov.

ISKANDER, MAGUED, engineering educator, consultant; arrived in U.S., 1988; s. Gamal and Nadia Iskander; m. Sherine K. Daniel, May 27, 2001; 1 child, Lauren Christie. BSc, Alexandria (Egypt) U., 1985; PhD, U. Tex., 1995. Registered profl. engr., N.Y., Wis., N.J. Engr. Consultative Bur. for Civil Constrn., Alexandria, 1986—88; rsch. asst. U. Tex., Austin, 1988—95; asst. prof. Poly. U., N.Y.C., 1995—2001, assoc. prof., 2001—. Pres. met. sect. geotechnical group ASCE, N.Y.C., 1997—98. Contbr. articles to profl. jours. With Egyptian Air Force, 1985—86. Recipient Career award, NSF, 1999—2003, Excellent Tchg. award, Chi Epsilon Met. Dist., 2000. Mem.: Egyptian-Am. Profls. Soc. (v.p.). Achievements include research in geotechnical engineering. Office: Polytechnic Univ 6 Metrotech Ctr Brooklyn NY 11207 Office Phone: 718-760-3016. Fax: 718-260-3433.

ISKANDER, SYLVIA WIESE, English literature educator; b. Boston, June 27, 1940; d. Herbert Edward and Mary Elizabeth (Cavin) Wiese; m. William H. Patterson Jr., June 2, 1962 (div. Apr. 1977); 1 child, Deborah Ann; m. Awad A. Iskander, May 22, 1982; 1 child, Alexandra Lucia. BS, La. State U., 1961; MA, U. Southwestern La., 1965; PhD, Fla. State U., 1969. Lectr. English, U. Houston, 1965—66; from asst. prof. to prof. U. La., Lafayette, 1969—2001, prof. emeritus, 2002—. Author: Rousseau's Emile and Early Children's Literature, 1971; contbr. articles to profl. jours.; editor (book) The Image of the Child, 1991. Founder Lafayette Greenbelt, 1975. Grantee AAUW, 1975. Mem. MLA, Children's Lit. Assn. (treas. 1994-97, v.p./pres.-elect 1997-98, pres. 1998-99), Internat. Rsch. Soc. Children's Lit., Nat. Coun. Tchrs. English, Phi Kappa Phi. Avocations: reading, travel, gardening.

ISLA, EXU REIDEMER QUERO, protective services official, lawyer, writer; b. Villasis, Pangasinan, The Philippines, May 30, 1941; camd to U.S., 1990; s. Francisco Lopez and Rosenda (Quero) I.; m. Carmen Rosales Isla, June 7, 1970; children: Mary, Christian, John, Imelda, Theresa, Francis. AA, U. Pangasinan, 1960, edn. degree, 1965, postgrad., 1970-72, 80-81, JD, 1985; BA, U. of East, Manila, 1963; bus. adminstrn. degree, Arellano U., The Philippines, 1969; legal asst. diploma, Internat. Corr. Schs., 1969. Instr. social studies U. Pangasinan, 1964-68, 69-72; cmty. devel. worker Presdl. Arms Cmty. Devel., The Philippines, 1968-69; tchr. social studies Manila Pub. Schs., 1968-69; tng. officer Capital Planning Corp., The Philippines, 1971-74; regional tng. officer Bur. Lands, The Philippines, 1974-79; provincial manpower devel. officer Nat. Manpower, Philippines, 1979-87; election registrar Commn. on Elections, The Philippines, 1987-89; legal asst. Nat. Bur. Investigation, The Philippines, 1989-90; probation officer Gary (Ind.) City Ct., 1991—; journalist Gary and N.W. Ind. INFO, 2001—. Rural devel. cons. Presdl. Office for Devel., The Philippines, 1978-81; youth devel. cons. Youth Movement in Barrios, The Philippines, 1978-86; quizzer for cert. exam., 2000. Columnist North Tribune and Ilocos Times, The Philippines, 1974-87, Weekly Express, The Philippines, 1987-89. Presdl. asst. for Province of Abra, Presdl. Regional Office for Devel. Regional Mgmt. Staff, 1978-81; regional sec. Rural Adv. Bd., The Philippines, 1978-81. Recipient provincial award Pangasinan-Dagupan City YMCA, nat. award Nat. YMCA, The Philippines, 1965, Found. for Youth Devel. in The Philippines, award of recognition Ministry Pub. Info., Ilocos Region, 1980, Pangasinan State U., 1981, Provincial Agr. Office Pangasinan, 1984, Mcpl. Coun. Urdaneta, Pangasinan, 1989, Outstanding Adminstr. award KC, The Philippines, 1982, Outstanding Parent award U. Pangasinan H.S., Dagupan City, 1989, Lew Wallace H.S., Gary, 1994. Mem. Am. Probation and Parole Assn., Am. Correctional Assn., Ind. Correctional Assn., Philippine Profl. Assn. (officer 1991—), Internat. Inst. N.W. Ind. (officer 1991—). Home: 5066 Pennsylvania St Gary IN 46409-2738 Office: Gary City Ct 1301 Broadway Gary IN 46407-1326

ISLAM, MUHAMMAD AZADUL, physicist, educator, researcher; b. Bogra, Bangladesh, Dec. 23, 1951; came to U.S., 1975; s. Muhammad Mohsin Ali and Amena Khatun; m. Aziza Gole Afroz, July 24, 1987; children: Crescent Mamnun, Cosmo Hasibul. BSc with honors, Dhaka U., Bangladesh, 1974; MS, U. Ala., 1977; MPhil, Columbia U., 1979, PhD, 1981. Tchg. asst. U. Ala., Tuscaloosa, 1975-77; faculty fellow, then head tchg. asst. Columbia U., N.Y.C., 1977-79; grad. rsch. asst. Columbia Radiation Labs., N.Y.C., 1979-81; postdoctoral fellow Joint Inst. Lab. Astrophysics, U. Colo., Boulder, 1981-83; asst. prof. San Diego State U., 1983-85; asst. prof. physics SUNY, Potsdam, 1985-89, assoc. prof., 1989-97, prof., 1997—, chmn. dept., 1999—2002. NEH vis. scholar Columbia U., N.Y.C., 1993; vis. scholar MIT Cambridge, 1993, Ctr. for Astrophysics Harvard U., 1995. Author: Test Yourself Physics, 1999, Beyond Ordinary Light, 2003; contbr. articles to profl. publs. Talent and merit scholar Comilla Bd. Edn. Mem. AAAS, United Univ. Profs., N.Y. State United Tchrs., Am. Fedn. Tchrs., Islamic Soc. N.Am. (trustee Potsdam chpt. 1990—), N.Y. Acad. Scis., Am. Phys. Soc., Sigma Xi, Sigma Pi Sigma. Avocations: reading, travel, intellectual history of islamic civilisation. Home: 6 Poplar St Potsdam NY 13676-2113 Office: SUNY Dept Physics Potsdam NY 13676 Office Phone: 315-267-2284. Business E-Mail: islamma@potsdam.edu.

ISLAM, NAUSHAD S., pharmacist, government agency administrator; b. Dhaka, Bangladesh, Dec. 21, 1961; arrived in U.S., 1989; s. A.H.M. Rafiqul and Hosne Ara Islam; m. Hasina Islam, July 9, 1990; children: Shadman, Nafisa, Safwan. BS pharmacy, Dhaka Univ., Dhaka, Bangladesh, 1986, MS pharmacy, 1988, Long Island Univ., Brooklyn, N.Y., 1992, MS pharmacy, 1999. Formulation scientist Dupont Pharm., Garden City, NY, 1994—97; sr. assoc. regulatory Schein Pharm., Cherry Hill, NJ, 1997—99; sr. scientist regulatory Solvay Pharm., Atlanta, 1999—2000; mgr. regulatory Schering-Plough Pharm., kenilworth, NJ, 2000—02; assoc. dir. regulatory Sankyo Pharm., Edison, NJ, 2002—. Adj. asst. prof. Long Island Univ. Sch. of Pharmacy, Brooklyn, NY, 2003—. Mem.: Am. Assn. of Pharm. Scientist, Bangladesh-Am. Pharm. (exec. bd. 1994—). Avocations: music, gardening, soccer. Home: 24 Spaniel Ct Kendall Park NJ 08824 Office: Sankyo Pharm 399 Thornall St Edison NJ 08837

ISLER, RAYMOND EARL, engineer; s. Walter Coy and Christine Isler; m. Leonia Annette Denning, Sept. 11, 1999. AAS, Durham Tech. C.C., 2004; BS, NC Ctrl. U., 1981—87. Professional Server Expert IBM Corp./NC, 1997, PSG Entry Level Education IBM Personal Systems Group/NC, 1993, Netfinity Server Support Specialist IBM PC Inst./NC, 1997, IBM Professional Server Specialist IBM PC Inst./NC, 1998, Project Management Fundamentals I IBM Global Campus/NC, 1999, Web Page Design Durham Tech. Cmty. Coll./NC, 2003, Certificate of Achievement: IBM Advanced FAStT/Fibre Storage Workshop IBM PC Inst., 2004, A+, Network+, MCP-(Microsoft Certified Professional), Security+, and CC NC State U., 2005. Dietary svc. aide sr. Duke U. Med. Ctr., Durham, NC, 1978—84; vol. math and computer asst./tutor NCCU Dept of Math & Computer Sci., 1984—88; math tutor and computer lab asst. NCCU-Summer Ventures In Sci. & Math., Durham, NC, 1988—88; mfg. support test IBM Corp., Rtp, NC, 1988—93; math tutor, computer lab asst. NC Ctrl. U., 1989; customer support tech. specialist IBM Corp., Rsch. Triangle Pk., NC, 1993—97, us lead server tech. specialist, 1997—99, ww svc. & support devel. engr./staff scientist, 1999—2001, ww xseries svc. planner, 2001—03, profl. field engr., 2004—05, tech. project mgr., 2005—. Mem. NCCU Alumni Assn., 1988. Recipient IBM Personal Sys. Group Tech. Acheivement, IBM Corp., 1999, IBM Tech. Achievement, 1996, IBM Tech. Server Achievement, 1997. Mem.: NC Acad. of Sci. (assoc.), Math. Programming Soc. (assoc.), Am. Math. Soc. (assoc.), Math. Assn. of Am. (assoc.), NCCU Math & Computer Sci. Club (assoc.; treas. 1985—86, pres. 1986—87). Home: Po Box 1680 Durham NC 27702-1680 Office: IBM Corp 3039 Cornwallis Rd Research Triangle Park NC 27709 Office Phone: 919-254-5419. Personal E-mail: ncman7@netzero.com. E-mail: reisler@us.ibm.com.

ISMACH, ARNOLD HARVEY, retired journalism educator; b. N.Y.C., Dec. 28, 1930; s. Louis and Augusta (Lacher) I.; m. Judy Daniels, June 20, 1959 (div. 1975); children: Richard, Theresa. BA, U. Okla., 1951; MA, UCLA, 1970; PhD, U. Wash., 1975. News editor Union-Bulletin, Walla Walla, Wash., 1954-56; reporter, editor Sun-Telegram, San Bernardino, Calif., 1956-69; prof. journalism U. Minn., Mpls., 1973-85; dean journalism U. Oreg., Eugene, 1985-94, prof. journalism, 1994-97. Cons. Pub. Rels. Ctr., L.A., 1970-75; pres. Comm. Rsch. Ctr., Mpls., 1973-85. Co-author: New Strategies, 1976, Enduring Issues, 1978, Reporting Processes, 1981. Pres. Planned Parenthood S.W. Oreg., 1998-99; dir. ACLU Oreg., 1994-2001. Sgt. U.S. Army, 1951-54. Mem. Soc. Profl. Journalists, Assn. for Edn. in Journalism. Democrat. Avocation: photography. Business E-Mail: aismach@uoregon.edu.

ISMAIL, ABU ZAFAR MOHAMED, physics professor, researcher; b. Keymore, India, Oct. 9, 1930; arrived in U.S., 1982; s. Abulkhair Mohamed and Zakiya Yusuf; children: Atif Zafar, Khurram Zafar, Faiza N. Zafar, Mona S. Zafar. MSc, Panjab U., Lahore, Pakistan, 1952, MA, 1954; BA with Honours, Cambridge (Eng.) U., 1958; DPhil in Elem. Particle Physics, Oxford (Eng.) U., 1964. Tchr. St. Mary's High Sch., Sukkur, Pakistan, 1952-53; instr. Mumtaz Coll., Khairpur Mirs, Pakistan, 1954-56; lectr., sr. lectr. Sind U., Hyderabad, Pakistan, 1958-65, assoc. prof., 1965-71, prof., 1971-72, Tripoli (Libya) U., 1972-82; prof. physics Daemen Coll., Amherst, N.Y., 1983—. Cons. Sci. First Inc., Buffalo, 1991-2004. Contbr. articles on high energy nuclear physics to profl. jours. Scholar Pakistan Ministry Edn., 1953; fellow Colombo PLan, 1960. Mem. Am. Assn. Physics Tchrs., Inst. Physics U.K. Republican. Avocations: photography, writing fiction, stamp and book collecting. Home: 130 Breezewood Common East Amherst NY 14051-1425 Office: Daemen Coll 4380 Main St Amherst NY 14226-3592 Office Phone: 716-839-8374. Business E-Mail: zismail@daemen.edu.

ISMAIL, MOURAD EL-HOUSSIENY, mathematician, educator, researcher; b. Cairo, Apr. 27, 1944; came to U.S., 1974; s. El-Houssieny Mahmoud Ismail and Aisha Mourad El-Shourbagy; m. Thanaa Mohamad Rashed, July 17, 1969. BS, Cairo U., 1964; MS, U. Alberta, Edmonton, 1969, PhD, 1974. Instr. Cairo U., Giza, Egypt, 1964-74; tchg. asst. U. Alberta, 1968-74; asst. scientist U. Wis., Madison, 1974-75; rschr., lectr. U. Toronto, Ont., Can., 1975-76; asst. prof. McMaster U., Hamilton, Ont., Can., 1976-81; asst. to assoc. prof. Ariz. State U., Tempe, 1979-89; prof. math. U. South Fla., Tampa, 1988—2003. Editor: Mathmatical Analysis, 1995, Special Sunctions, q-series, 1997, q-series from a Contemporary Perspective, 2000, Special Functions, 2000; editl. bd. Jour. of Approximation Theory, 2000—, Constructive Approximation, 1988—, The Ramanujan Jour., 1986—; editor (series) Cambridge U. Press, 1993-2000. Rsch. grant Rsch. Coun. of Can., 1977-82, NSF, 1978—, Nat. Security Agy., 1997—, Collaborative and Conf. grant NSF, 1990—. Mem. Am. Math. Soc., Math. Assn. of Am., Can. Math. Soc., Soc. for Indsl. and Applied Math. Avocations: reading, swimming. Office: U Ctrl Fla Dept Math Orlando FL 32816 Office Phone: 407-823-2694. E-mail: ismail@math.ucf.edu.

ISMAIL, SALEEM M, psychiatrist; b. Karachi, Pakistan; arrived in U.S., 1992; s. Muhammad and Hajra Ismail. MBBS, U. Karachi, 1989, MA, 1990. Diplomate Am. Bd. of Psychiatry and Neurology. Staff psychiatrist Marinette County, Wis., 1998—2000; fellow in geriatric psychiatry U. Rochester, 2000—01, asst. prof. psychiatry, 2004—; dir., psychiatric cons. svc. Monroe Cmty. Hosp., 2004—. Cons. psychiatrist Buffalo Psychiatric Ctr., 2003—. Contbr. articles to profl. jours. Mem.: Am. Assn. of Geriatric Psychiatry, Am. Psychiat. Assn. Avocation: travel. Office: Monroe Cmty Hosp 435 E Henrietta Rd Rochester NY 14620

ISMAIL, YAHIA HASSAN, dentist, educator; b. Egypt, Jan. 20, 1938; came to U.S., 1961; s. Hassan Kareem and Horia (Soloman) I.; m. Launa Lutz, Sept. 5, 1968; children: Alan Kareem, Zane Ziad. DDS, Cairo U., 1959; MS, U. Pitts., 1965, DMD, PhD, U. Pitts., 1973. Instr. Dental Sch. Cairo U., 1959-62; asst. prof. prosthodontics U. Pitts., 1962-68, assoc. prof., 1968-70, prof., 1970—, dir. prosthodontic grad. program, 1970—, chmn. dept. prosthodontics, 1973—; dir. acad. affaris, internat. affairs and grad. edn. Dental Medicine, U. Pitts., 1995—2001, Vis. prof., Paris and Marseille, France, Cairo and Alexandria, Egypt, European U., Brussels; mem. staff VA Hosp., Montefiore Hosp., Univ. Med. Ctr. Hosp., St. Margaret's Hosp. Contbr. articles to profl. jours., textbooks. Bd. dirs. Ridgewood Civic Assn., 1969-73; cubmaster Allegheny Trails council Boy Scouts Am.; coach Youth Soccer League Allegheny County. Recipient Chancellor's Pub. Svc. award, 1995. Fellow Internat. Coll. Dentists, Am. Coll. Dentists, Am. Coll. Prosthodontics, Royal Soc. Medicine, Am. Coll. Oral Implantologists, Internat. Congress Oral Implantologists, Am. Acad. Implant Prosthodontics (pres. elect 1989-90, pres. 1990-92); mem. ADA, Internat. Assn. Dentofacial Abnormalities (bd. dirs., sec., treas. 1973-77), Internat. Congress Oral Implantologists (v.p. 1985-86, pres. 1988-89), Am. Prosthodontic Soc. (internat. circuite courses humanities citation), Pa. Prosthodontic Assn. (past pres.), Prosthodontic Soc. Western Pa. (past pres.), Dental Soc. Western Pa. (bd. dirs.), Am. Coll. Oral Implantologists (pres. 1984-86), Am. Coll. Prosthodontists, Am. Assn. Dental Schs., Internat. Assn. Dental Rsch., Royal Coll. Physicians, Univ. Club, Omicron Kappa Upsilon. Republican. Office: U Pittsburgh Sch Dental Med Pittsburgh PA 15261-0001 *Talk about ideas and philosophies rather than other people.*

ISOGAI, MASAHARU, international corporate strategist, retired apparel executive; b. 1939; AMP, Harvard U., 1985. With Ogiya, 1958-76, Jusco Co. Ltd., 1976-88; exec. v.p., gen. mgr. Jusco USA, Inc., 1988-96, sr. advisor, 1996-99; dir. Talbots, 1993-99; chmn. Revman, 1994-99; ret., 1999. Mem. Japanese Youth Goodwill Mission to U.S., 1964. Mem. Japanese Am. Assn. N.Y. (bd. dirs.), Assn. for Better N.Y. (hon. mem. exec. com., spl. amb. from Japan). Office: 401 E 34th St Apt S5J New York NY 10016-6611 Business E-Mail: misogainy@earthlink.net.

ISOM, KEVIN, writer; s. David L. and Tommie F. Isom. BA, Vanderbilt U., 1987; JD, Emory U., 1991. Bar: Ga. 1991. Author: Tongue in Cheek and Other Places, 2000, It Only Hurts When I Polka, 2001, short stories. Harold Stirling Vanderbilt scholar, Vanderbilt U. Mem.: GAPAC (mem. polit. com. 1994—95), Out of Emory (chair 1995—96), Human Rights Campaign.

ISONG, ENO, public health service officer; d. Clement Nyong and Nne C. Isong; m. O. Felix Obi; 1 child, Felix Nyong Obi. BA, U. of Calabar, Calabar, Cross River State, Nigeria, 1987; MA, Howard U., Washington, 1993. News editor/reporter AKBC-TV, Uyo, Nigeria, 1988—90; assoc. editor/columnist TRA Pubs., Albany, Ga., 1990—91; cons. Internat. Ctr. The Smithsonian Instn., Washington, 1993—94; program officer Creative Assoc. Internat. Inc., Washington, 1995—98; sr. program officer The Henry J. Kaiser Family Found., Washington, 1998—. Recipient USAA award, The US Achievement Acad., 1993. Mem.: APHA.

ISQUITH, FRED TAYLOR, lawyer; b. N.Y.C., June 6, 1947; s. Stanley and Rita (Hoskwith) Isquith; m. Susan Nora Goldberg, May 23, 1976; children: Fred, Rebecca. BA, CUNY, 1968; JD, Columbia U., 1971. Bar: N.Y. 1972, U.S. Dist. Ct. (so. and ea. dists.) N.Y. 1975, U.S. Ct. Appeals (2d cir.) 1975, DC 1976, U.S. Supreme Ct. 1983, U.S. Ct. Appeals (8th cir.) 1985, U.S. Ct. Appeals (3d cir.) 1986, U.S. Dist. Ct. (no. dist.) N.Y. 1988, U.S. Ct. Appeals (4th cir.) 1990, U.S. Dist. Ct. (we. dist.) Mich. 1992, U.S. Dist. Ct. Ariz. 1994, U.S. Dist. Ct. (ctrl. dist.) Ill. 1996, U.S. Dist. Ct. Colo. 1999, U.S. Dist. Ct.

Nebr. 2000, U.S. Ct. Appeals (1st cir.) 2000. Assoc. Fulbright & Jaworski, N.Y.C., 1971-75, Kaye Scholer et al, N.Y.C., 1975-80; ptnr. Wolf Haldenstein Adler Freeman & Herz, N.Y.C., 1980—. Lectr. Am. Conf. inst., N.Y. State Bar Assn., N.Y. County Bar Assn., others; mediator Supreme Ct. State of N.Y.; arbitrator Am. Arbitrator Assn.; lectr. in field; bd. dirs. 103 E. 84th St. Corp., Sheinkopf, Ltd. Author: An Introduction to Securities Arbitration, 1994, Real Estate Exit Strategies, 1994, Fundamental Strategies in Securities Litigation, 2000, Federal Civil Practice, 2000, A Scalpel in Your Hand Litigation as a Tool for Forcing Responsible Corporate Guidance, 2002, Anatomy of a Deposition: Preparation for a Deposition in a Complex Financial Case, 2002, The Seven Year Itch: A Survey of Experience Under the 1995 Amendments to the Security Laws, 2003, Wolf in Sheeps Clothing: Tort Reforms, 2004; author: (with Thomas Burr) Ethics: Going Astray By Small Steps, 2004; editor, columnist: Class Act. Mem. devel. com. Friends Sem., N.Y.C., 1992—2004; clk., mem. vestry St. Thomas Ch. Fifth Ave., N.Y.C., 2002—. Mem.: NASCAT (pres.), ABA (mem. internet com. anti-trust law sect.), Bklyn. Bar Assn. (mem. civil practice law and rules com., mem. legis. com., mem. fed. cts. com.), Assn. Bar City of N.Y. (mem. fed. cts. com.), DC Bar Assn., N.Y. County Lawyers Assn. (chmn. bus. torts), N.Y. State Bar Assn. (mem. com. securities, mem. com. legis., arbitrator securities industry deisputes sect.), Columbia Club. Office: Wolf Haldenstein Adler Freeman & Herz 270 Madison Ave New York NY 10016-0601 Office Phone: 212-545-4600. Business E-Mail: isquith@whafh.com.

ISRAEL, ALLEN D., lawyer; b. Seattle, Nov. 28, 1946; m. Nettie Israel. BSME, U. Wash., 1968, MBA, 1971, JD, 1978. Bar: Wash. 1978. Ptnr. Foster Pepper & Shefelman PLLC, Seattle, 1978—. Office: Foster Pepper & Shefelman PLLC 1111 3rd Ave Ste 3400 Seattle WA 98101-3299

ISRAEL, BARRY JOHN, lawyer; b. Rockford, Ill., Mar. 14, 1946; s. Robert John and Bettie Jane (Erickson) I.; childn: Alison, Ashley, Brenna. BA, U. So. Calif., L.A., 1968; JD, George Washington U., 1974. Bar: Calif. 1975, D.C. 1976, U.S. Supreme Ct. 1978, U.S. Dist. Ct. Mariana Islands 1985. Assoc. Clifford & Warnke, Washington, 1975-83; ptnr. Stovall, Spradlin, Armstrong & Israel, Washington, 1983-86, Dorsey & Whitney, Washington, 1988-92, Stroock, Stroock & Lavan, Washington, 1992-95. Spl. counsel, pres. Federated States of Micronesia, 1982-84; spl. asst. atty. gen. Territory Guam, 1990-95; chmn. bd., CEO Danao Internt. Holdings Co., Ltd.; bd. dirs. Jadora Ltd., Millenium Inst. of Lang. Author: (guides) Advance Adjusting Assoc. Investment Guides to the Federated States of Micronesia and the Republic of the Marshall Islands, 1989. 1st lt. U.S. Army, 1969-72. Democrat. Avocations: travel, tennis. Home: 150 Cedar Ln Santa Barbara CA 93108 Address: 24/7 Dinh Tien Hoang Dist 1 Ho Chi Minh City Vietnam Personal E-mail: barryjon@aol.com.

ISRAEL, DAVID, journalist, scriptwriter, film producer; b. NYC, Mar. 17, 1951; s. Hyman and Edith Oringer I.; m. Lindy De Koven, Aug. 8, 1987. BS in Journalism, Northwestern U., 1973. Reporter Chgo. Daily News, 1973-75; columnist Washington Star, 1975-78, Chgo. Tribune, 1978-81, L.A. Herald Examiner, 1981-84; chmn., pres. Big Prodn., Inc., L.A.; prod., writer OCC Prodn., L.A., 1985-88; exec. prodr., writer Lorimar TV, L.A., 1988-92, Paramount Pictures, Hollywood, Calif., 1992-93; writer, exec. prodr. Stephen J. Cannell Prod., Inc., Hollywood, 1993-95. Dir. office of Pres., Los Angeles Olympic Organizing Com., 1984; exec. prodr. House of Frankenstein, NBC, Universal, 1997, exec. prodr. Mutiny, NBC, 1999, Y2K, NBC, 1999, Tremors, SciFi, 2002-03. Supervising prodr., writer: A Comedy Salute to Baseball, NBC, 1985; supervising prodr., writer: Fast Copy, NBC, 1985-86; co-creator, supervising prodr.: Crimes of the Century, 1987-88; co-exec. prodr., writer: Midnight Caller, NBC, Lorimar TV, 1988-91, The Untouchables, Paramount TV, 1992-93; exec. prodr., writer: Jake Lassiter: Justice on the Bayou, NBC, Stephen J. Cannell Prodn., 1995; exec. prodr., writer: Pandora's Clock, NBC, Citadel Entertainment, 1996; consulting prodr., writer, Turks, CBS Studios, USA, 1998-99; coord. prodr. Monday Night Football, ABC Sports, 2000-01. Commr. L.A. (Calif.) Meml. Gliseum Commn., 2005—; bd. dirs. Calif. Sci. Ctr., 2004—, Calif. State Alliance, 2004—, exec. com., 2004—. Mem. AFTRA, Writers Guild Am., Chgo. Athletic Assn., Beverly Hills Tennis Club. Office: care Bob Broder The BWCS Agy 9242 Beverly Blvd Beverly Hills CA 90210

ISRAEL, JEROLD HARVEY, law educator; b. Cleve., June 14, 1934; s. Harry and Florence S. (Schoenfeld) I.; m. Tanya M. Boyarsky, Sept. 28, 1959; children: Lewis, Laurie, Daniel BBA, Western Res. U., 1956; LLB, Yale U., 1959. Bar: Ohio 1959, Mich. 1967. Law clk. to Justice Potter Stewart U.S. Supreme Ct., Washington, 1959-61; asst. prof. Law Sch. U. Mich., Ann Arbor, 1961-64, assoc. prof., 1964-67, prof., 1967-96, Alene and Allan F. Smith prof., 1983-96, prof. emeritus, 1996—; Ed Rood Eminent Scholar in trial advocacy and procedure U. Fla. Coll. Law, Gainesville, 1993—. Exec. sec. Mich. Law Revision Commn., 1972-92; co-reporter Uniform Rules of Criminal Procedure, Nat. Conf. Commrs. Uniform State Laws; Alene and Allen F. Smith prof. emeritus U. Mich., Ann Arbor, 1996—. Co-author: Criminal Procedure Treatise, 1999, White Collar Crime, 2003, Criminal Procedure Hornbook, 2004, Principles of Criminal Procedures: Investigation, 2004, Principles of Criminal Procedure: Post-Investigation, 2004, Criminal Procedure and the Constitution, 2005, Modern Criminal Procedure, 2005. Office: U Fla Law Sch Gainesville FL 32611-2038 Office Phone: 352-273-0966. Business E-Mail: israel@law.ufl.edu.

ISRAEL, JOHN MARTIN, music educator, musician; b. Princeton, Ill., Mar. 14, 1981; s. Gregory Martin and Kara Sue Israel. BA in Music Edn., Lindenwood U., 2004. Educator vocal music New Haven Sch. Dist., Mo., 2004—. Musician St. Louis Brass Band, 2003—05, Original Knights Swing Big Band, 2002—; vocal interm Kirk of Hills Presbyn. Ch., Ladue, 2002—04; musician Alton Mcpl. Band, Alton, Ill., 2002—. Mem.: Music Educators Nat. Conf., Am. Fedn. Musicians, Am. Choral Dirs. Assn., Phi Mu Alpha (province gov. Mo. 2004—05). Home: 442 Parkshire Pl O Fallon MO 63366 Office: New Haven Sch Dist 100 Park Dr New Haven MO 63068 Office Phone: 573-237-2629 143. Home Fax: 626-240-6419. Personal E-mail: jisrael@shamrocks.k12.mo.us.

ISRAEL, KIMBERLY HELD, lawyer; b. Jacksonville, Fla., Aug. 7, 1969; d. Edwin W. and Leslie (Edwards) Held; m. Jonathan Bruce Israel, Apr. 2, 1995; children: Eliza, Allie, Ayden. BA, Vanderbilt U., 1991; JD, U. Fla., 1994. Assoc. Moseley, Warren, Prichard & Parrish, Jacksonville, 1995—99, ptnr., 2000—04, Held & Israel, 2004—. Mem. editl. bd. SEALI, Ga., 2002—04; treas. Fed. Bar Assn., Jacksonville, 2003—04, sec., 2004—. Bd. dirs. Jewish Cmty. Alliance, 2002—04; chmn. editl. bd. Jacksonville Jewish News; bd. dirs. Jacksonville Jewish Fedn. Recipient Young Leadership Award, Jax Jewish Fedn., 2000. Mem.: ABA, Women Bus. Owners of North Fla., Comml. Law League Am., Am. Bankruptcy Inst., Fed. Bar Assn., Maritime Law Assn., Jacksonville Women Lawyer's Assn., Jacksonville Bar Assn., Fla. Bar. Jewish. Office: Held & Israel 1301 Riverplace Blvd #1916 Jacksonville FL 32207 Office Phone: 904-398-7038. Office Fax: 904-398-4283. Business E-Mail: khisrael@hilawfirm.com.

ISRAEL, MARTIN HENRY, astrophysicist, educator, academic administrator; b. Chgo., Jan. 12, 1941; s. Herman and Anna Catherine I.; m. Margaret Ellen Mitouer, June 20, 1965; children: Elisa, Samuel. SB, U. Chgo., 1962; PhD, Calif. Inst. Tech., 1969. Asst. prof. physics Washington U., St. Louis, 1968-72, assoc. prof., 1972-75, prof., 1975—, assoc. dir. McDonnell Ctr. for Space Scis., 1982-87, acting dean faculty arts and scis., 1987-88, dean faculty, 1988-94, vice chancellor, 1994-95, vice chancellor acad. planning, 1995-97. Com. on space astronomy and astrophysics NRC, 1976-79; high energy astrophysics mgmt. ops. working group NASA, 1976-84, co-chair Cosmic Ray Program Working Group, 1980-87, space and earth scis. adv. com., 1985-88, chair Particle Astrophysics Magnet Facility Definition Team, 1985-87, astrophysics coun., 1986-87, prin. investigator Heavy Nuclei Expt. High Energy Astronomy Obs., 1971-89, structure and evolution of the universe subcom., 1996-99, chair ACCESS steering com., 1998-2000, mem. Space Sta. Utilization adv. subcom., 1998-2002, mem. GSFC Space Sci. vis. com., 1997-2001, chair, 2000-01, chair sci. ballooning roadmap team, 2004-05; mem. GSFC Ctr. Dir.'s Vis. Com., 2000-01; chair Space Sci. Working Group, Assn. Am. Univs., 1983-85; chair nat. organizing com. 19th Internat. Cosmic Ray Conf., 1985, 1982-85. Contbr. articles on cosmic ray astrophysics and observation of elemental and isotopic composition of cosmic rays to profl. jours. Sloan Found. fellow, 1970; recipient Exceptional Sci. Achievement award NASA, 1980. Fellow Am. Phys. Soc. (chair astrophysics divsn. 1980-81); mem. Am. Astron. Soc. (mem. exec. com. high energy astrophysics divsn. 1982-84), AAUP, AAAS. Home: 2 Valley View Pl Saint Louis MO 63124-1810 Office: Washington U Campus Box 1105 1 Brookings Dr Saint Louis MO 63130-4899 Office Phone: 314-935-6263. E-mail: mhi@wuphys.wustl.edu.

ISRAEL, RICHARD STANLEY, investment banker; b. Oakland, Calif., Sept. 27, 1931; s. Sybil Noble, July 29, 1962; children: Richard Lee, Lynne, Lawrence. BA, MA, U. Calif., Berkeley, 1953. Copy editor San Francisco Chronicle, 1953-59; publicist CBS TV Network, L.A., 1959-62; sr. v.p. Rogers & Cowan, Beverly Hills, Calif., 1962-69; v.p. Cantor, Fitzgerald, Beverly Hills, 1969-73; pres. Sponsored Cons. Svcs., L.A., 1973—. Bd. dirs. Hurst Labeling Systems. Pres. North Beverly Dr. Homeowners Assn., Beverly Hills, 1986-88; v.p. Temple Emanuel, Beverly Hills, 1988-93, L.A. chpt. Juvenile Diabetes Found. Internat, 1987—. With U.S. Army, 1956-58. Recipient Alumni citation U. Calif. Alumni Assn., Berkeley, 1984. Mem. L.A. Venture Assn. (pres. 1987), Assn. for Corp. Growth (pres. bd. dirs. L.A. chpt.). Democrat. Avocations: volleyball, travel. Office: Dick Israel & Ptnrs 8929 Wilshire Blvd Ste 214 Beverly Hills CA 90211-1951 Office Phone: 310-208-1234. E-mail: rilnay@aol.com.

ISRAEL, ROBERT ALLAN, statistician; b. N.Y.C., Mar. 30, 1933; s. John J. and Ray (Sladkus) I.; m. Barbara Diane Johnston, Jan. 26, 1953; children: John, Richard, Deborah, Pamela, James, Michael. BA, Hofstra Coll., 1954; MS, Columbia U., 1957. Med. analyst Md. State Health Dept., Balt., 1959-63, chief div. statis. rsch., 1963-66; chief mortality stats. br. Nat. Ctr. for Health Stats., Washington, 1966-68, dir. div. vital stats., 1968-72, assoc. dir. for ops., 1972-75, dep. dir., 1975-92, assoc. dir. for internat. stats., 1992-95, ret., 1995. Head WHO collaborating ctr. for disease classification for North Am., 1975-95, ret., 1995; dep. exec. dir. Internat. Inst. for Vital Registration and Statistics, 1997—2005. Co-author: The Methods and Materials of Demography, 1973; co-editor: Encyclopedia of Biostatistics, 1997. Recipient Superior Svc. award U.S. Pub. Health Svc., 1972, 79, scholarship N.Y. State Bd. Regents, 1950-54, fellowship U.S. Public Health Svc., 1956-58, Special Recognition award Asst. Sec. for Health. Fellow APHA (stats. sect. award 1986), Am. Statis. Assn.; mem. Internat. Statis. Inst., Internat. Assn. Ofcl. Stats. Home: 16910 E Laney Ct Fountain Hills AZ 85268 E-mail: risrael@ix.netcom.com.

ISRAEL, STEVE J., congressman; b. Brooklyn, N.Y., May 30, 1958; s. Howard and Madeline Israel; m. Randi Elkins, June 5, 1983; children: Carly, Elana. BA, George Washington U., 1982. Congl. aide U.S. Congress, Washington, 1979-83; consultant Steve Israel Assoc., Huntington, N.Y., 1985—; asst. county exec. County of Suffolk, Hauppauge, N.Y., 1988-92; town councilman Town of Huntington, 1993-2000; exec. dir. Inst. on the Holocaust and Law, Huntington, 1998-2000; mem. U.S. Congress from 2d N.Y. dist., Washington, 2001—; mem. fin. svcs. com., sci. com. Author/editor: Great Jewish Speeches, 1994. Founder Ctr. for Prejudice Reduction, Great Neck, N.Y., 1990; dir. Pederson-Krag Ctr., Huntington, 1996; founder, dir. L.I. Fgn. Affirs Forum, Mingola, N.Y., 1998. Life mem. NAACP; assoc. mem. Sons of Italy. Democrat. Jewish. Avocations: writing, historical rsch. Office: US Ho of Reps 18 W Carver St Huntington NY 11743-3322 also: US Ho of Reps 429 Cannon HOB Washington DC 20515 E-mail: israel@li.net.*

ISRAEL, WERNER, physicist, educator; b. Berlin, Oct. 4, 1931; s. Arthur and Marie (Kappauf) I.; m. Inge Margulies, Jan. 26, 1958; children: Mark Abraham, Pia Lee. BSc, U. Cape Town, 1951, MSc, 1954; PhD, Trinity Coll., Dublin, 1960; DSc (hon.), Queen's U., Kingston, Ont., 1987; Docteur honoris causa, U. Francois Rabelais, France, 1994; DSc (hon.), U. Victoria, B.C., Can., 1999. Asst. prof. physics U. Alta., Canada, 1958-68, prof., 1968-85, Univ. prof., 1985-96; adj. prof. dept. physics and astronomy U. Victoria, Canada, 1996—; hon. prof. dept. physics and astronomy U. B.C., Canada. Sherman Fairchild disting. scholar Calif. Inst. Tech., 1974-75; vis. prof. Dublin Inst. Advanced Studies, 1966-68, U. Cambridge, 1975-76, Institut Henri Poincare, 1976-77, U. Berne, 1980, Kyoto U., 1986, 98; vis. fellow Gonville and Caius Coll., Cambridge, 1985; fellow Can. Inst. for Advanced Rsch., 1986—. Editor: Relativity, Astrophysics and Cosmology, 1973; co-editor: General Relativity, An Einstein Centenary Survey, 1979, 300 Years of Gravitation, 1987. Decorated officer Order of Can.; recipient Izaak Walton Killiam Meml. prize, 1984, Medal in Math. Physics, Ctr. de Recherche Math./Can. Assn. Physicists, 1995, Tomalla Found. for Gravitational Rsch. prize, 1996. Fellow Royal Soc. Can., Royal Soc. (London); mem. Can. Assn. Physicists (medal of Achievement in Physics 1981), Internat. Soc. Gen. Relativity and Gravitation (pres. 1997-2001). Jewish. Office: U Victoria Dept Physics Astronomy Victoria BC Canada V8W 3P6 Business E-Mail: israel@uvic.ca.

ISRAELACHVILI, JACOB NISSIM, chemical engineer; b. Tel Aviv, Aug. 19, 1944; came to U.S., 1986; s. Haim Israelachvili and Hela (Noma) Galili; m. Karina Haglund, Sept. 14, 1971; children: Josefin, Daniela. BA, U. Cambridge, 1968, MA & PhD, 1972. Prof. U. Calif., Santa Barbara, 1986—. V.p. Internat. Assn. Colloid & Interface Scientists, 1986-89. Author: Intermolecular and Surface Forces, 1985, 2d edit., 1991; contbr. articles to profl. jours. Fellow Australian Nat. U., Canberra, 1974-86, Rsch. fellow U. Stockholm, Sweden, 1972-74; recipient Matthew Flinders medal, 1986. Fellow Royal Soc. London, Australian Acad. Sci.; mem. AIChE (Alpha Chi Sigma award 1991), NAS, Nat. Acad. Engring. (fgn. assoc.). Office Phone: 805-893-8407. Business E-Mail: jacob@engineering.ucsb.edu.

ISRAELOFF, SIM, lawyer, mayor; b. San Antonio, July 19, 1958; s. Ozzelle and Joseph Israeloff; m. Teg Hemphill, May 22, 1983; children: Amy Hemphill, Katherine Ann. BBA, U. Tex., 1980, JD, 1983. Bar: Tex. 1983, US Dist. Ct. No. Dist. Tex. 1990, US Dist. Ct. Ea. Dist. Tex. 1990, US Dist. Ct. So. Dist. Tex. 1992, US Dist. Ct. We. Dist. Tex. 1990, US Ct. Appeals Fifth Circuit 1987, US Ct. Fed. Claims 1996, Bd. Cert., Civil Trial Law Tex. Bd. of Legal Specialization 1991. Assoc. Carrington, Coleman, Sloman & Blumenthal, L.L.P., Dallas, 1983—91, ptnr., 1991—95; shareholder, chair of bus. litig. sect. Cowles & Thompson, P.C., 1995—; mayor Town of Fairview, Tex., 2002—. Recipient Tex. Super Lawyer, Tex. Monthly and Law & Politics Mag., 2003, 2004, 2005. Fellow: Dallas Bar Found.; mem.: ABA, Patrick E. Higginbotham Am. Inn of Ct. (barrister 2000—03), Dallas Bar Assn. Avocations: running, gardening. Office: Cowles & Thompson PC 901 Main St Ste 4000 Dallas TX 75202 Office Phone: 214-672-2000. E-mail: sisraeloff@cowlesthompson.com.

ISRAILI, ZAFAR HASAN, pharmacologist, educator; b. Moradabad, India, July 2, 1934; came to U.S., 1961, naturalized, 1977; s. Siddiq Hasan and Zahida Khatun I.; m. Sally Jean Smith, Oct. 24, 1970; children: Shahnaz Joy, Taj Hasan, Rana Shereen. BSc, Aligarh M. U., 1951, MSc, 1953; PhD, U. Kans., 1968. Lectr. chemistry Aligarh M. U., 1953-54, sr. rsch. scholar, 1954-57; rsch. asst., jr. sci. officer AEC India, 1957-61; rsch. assoc. U. Kans., 1968-69; sr. rsch. chemist Alza Corp., Lawrence, Kans., 1969-70; asst. prof. medicine and chemistry Emory U., Atlanta, 1970-75, assoc. prof. chemistry, 1975-78, assoc. prof. medicine, 1975—, prof. chemistry, 1978—. Rsch. pharmacologist Atlanta VA Med. Ctr., Decatur, 1979-87; mem. sci. staff Grady Hosp., Atlanta, 1974—; adj. prof. chemistry Ga. Perimeter Coll., 2004—. Editor Ethnicity and Disease, 1997—; assoc. editor Drug Metabolism Revs., 1974—; mem. editl. bd. Drug Devel. Rsch., 1979—; mem. editl. com. Archives Venezuelan Pharm. Ter., 1983—, Am. Jour. Ther., 2003-; contbr. numerous articles to profl. jours., chpts. to books. Recipient Asia Found. award, 1962; Merit scholar Aligarh M. U., 1953; Merck Sharpe & Dohm grantee, 1977, 85, 87, NIH grantee, 1978-83, VA grantee, 1979-87, Am. Heart Assn. grantee, 1989-91. Mem. Am. Soc. Clin. Pharmacology and Therapeutics, Am. Soc. Pharmacology and Exptl. Therapeutics, Soc. Exptl. Biology and Medicine, Am. Assn. Cancer Rsch., Am. Aging Assn., Am. Chem. Soc., Am. Soc. Hypertension, Chem. Soc. London, Internat. Soc. for Study Xenobiotics, Interam. Soc. Clin. Pharm. Therapeutics (pres.-elect 1997-2000, pres. 2000—), Internat. Soc. on Hypertension in Blacks, Am. Heart Assn., Sigma Xi, Rho Chi, Phi Lambda Upsilon. Moslem. Home: 3567 Cloudland Dr Stone Mountain GA 30083-4005 Office: Emory Univ Sch Medicine Dept Medicine 69 Jesse Hill Jr Dr Atlanta GA 30303-2607 Office Phone: 404-616-5176. Business E-Mail: zisrail@emory.edu.

ISSA, DARRELL E., congressman; b. Cleveland, Ohio, Nov. 1, 1953; m. Kathy; 1 child: William. BA, Siena Heights U., 1976. Founder, pres-CEO Directed Electronics, Vista, Calif., 1982—99; mem. Congress, Calif., 48th dist., 2001—. Mem. House com. on Internat. Rels., House Judiciary com., House com. on Small Bus. Co-chair Calif. Civic Rights Initiative, 1996. Capt. U.S. Army, 1970—80. Recipient Inc. Magazine's Entreprenuer Yr. award, 1994, Ellis Island Medal of Honor. Past chmn. Consumer Electronics Assn., former govr. Electronic Indus. Alliance; dir. Bus.-Industry Political Action com., San Diego Econ. Devel. Assn., Greater San Diego County Chamber of Commerce; past pres. Am. Task Force for Lebanon; served bd. trustees Siena Heights U. Republican. Office: 211 Cannon House Office Bldg Washington DC 20515-0549

ISSA, MARIAM, volunteer, cultural organization administrator; b. Bombay; Founder Pakistani-Am. Volunteers Assn. Bd. mem. & former pres. Asian/Pacific Am. Heritage Assn.; bd. mem. & pres.-elect S. Pacific Chamber of Commerce; mem. Mayoral Adv. Bd. for Internat. Affairs & Develop.-Asia and Asian Am. Voters Coalition; bd. dirs. Asia Soc., Express Theatre, Blaffer Gallery, Pakistani Assn. of Greater Houston, Ancestral Films Festival, Asia World Expo. Home: 18 C E Shady Ln Houston TX 77063*

ISSACHAROFF, SAMUEL, law educator; b. 1954; BA, Binghamton U., 1975; JD, Yale U., 1983. Law clk. to Judge Arlin M. Adams US Ct. Appeals 3rd Cir.; practiced law Washington; joined law faculty U. Tex., 1989, Joseph D. Jamail Centennial Chair in Law; joined law faculty Columbia U., NYC, 1999, Harold R. Medina Prof. Procedural Jurisprudence. Fellow: Am. Acad. Arts and Sciences. Office: Columbia Law Sch 435 W 116th St New York NY 10027 Office Phone: 212-854-2527. Office Fax: 212-854-7946. Business E-Mail: sissac@law.columbia.edu.

ISSARI, MOHAMMAD ALI, film producer, writer, consultant; b. Esfahan, Iran; s. Abbas Bek and Qamar (Soltan) I.; m. Joan Gura Aamodt, 1958; children: Scheherezade, Katayoun, Roxana. BA, U. Tehran, Iran, 1963; MA, U. So. Calif., 1968; PhD, 1979. Films officer Brit. Embassy, Brit. Council Joint Film Div., Tehran, 1944-50; asst. motion picture officer USIS, Tehran, 1950-65; cons. to various Iranian Govt. ministries on film and TV devels., 1950-77; liaison officer Am. and Iranian govt. ofcls., 1950-65; prof. cinema Coll. Communication Arts and Scis. Mich. State U., East Lansing, 1969-81, also dir. instructional film and multimedia prodn., 1969-78; mass media cons., 1981—; pres. Multimedia Prodn. Svcs., Thousand Oaks, Calif., 1989—. Film, public relations adviser to Iranian Oil Operating Cos. in, Iran, 1963-65; spl. cons. on edn. and instructional TV Saudi Arabian Ministry of Info., 1972; tchr. Persian lang. Iran-Am. Soc., Tehran, 1949-59; introduced audio-visual edn. in Iran, 1951; established first film festivals in Iran, 1949. Producer, dir. over 1000 instructional and documentary films, 1956-78; freelance film reporter: Telenews, UPI, CBS Iran, 1959-61; project dir., exec. producer: Ancient Iran Film Series, 1974-78; dir. film prodn. workshops, Cranbrook Inst., Detroit, 1973-74; author: A Picture of Persia, 1977, (with Doris A. Paul) What is Cinema Vérité?, 1979, Cinema in Iran, 1900-1979, 1989; contbr. articles on ednl. comm. and audio-visual instrn. to periodicals and profl. jours. Founder, exec. sec. Youth Orgn. of Iran, 1951-52; v.p. Rugby Football Fedn., Iran, 1952-53, pres., 1954-55. Decorated Order of Magnum Cap Ord: S.F. Danaie M. Sigillum (Denmark), Order of Cavalieres (Italy), Order of Oranje Nassau (The Netherlands), Orders of Kooshesh and Pas (Iran), Order of Esteghlal (Jordan), Order of Ordinis Sancti Silvestri Papae (Pope John 23d); recipient Meritorious Honor award USIA, 1965, Golden Eagle award Couns. for Internat. Non-Theatrical Events, 1975. Mem. Anglo-Iranian Dramatic Soc. (bd. dirs. 1943-50), Mich. Film Assn. (co-founder 1972, bd. dirs. 1972-73), Mid. East Studies Assn., N.Am. Soc. Motion Picture and TV Engrs. (life), Ancient Studies Inst. Inc. (co-founder, pres. 1991, 97-98), House of Iran, Inc. (co-founder, pres. 1990—), Delta Kappa Alpha (v.p. 1967). Fax: 805-498-0550. Office Phone: 805-498-5907. E-mail: issariaj@adelphia.net. *Man will achieve his goals through honesty, hard work and perseverence. The goals worth pursuing are in the service of mankind.*

ISSELBACHER, KURT JULIUS, internist, educator; b. Wirges, Germany, Sept. 12, 1925; arrived in U.S., 1936, naturalized, 1945; s. Albert and Flori (Strauss) Isselbacher; m. Rhoda Solin, June 22, 1955; children: Lisa, Karen, Jody, Eric. AB, Harvard U., 1946, MD cum laude, 1950; ScD (hon.), Northwestern U., 2001. Intern, then resident Mass. Gen. Hosp., Boston, 1950—53, chief gastrointestinal unit, 1957—89, chmn. com. rsch., 1967, dir. Cancer Ctr., 1987—2003, dir. emeritus, 2003—; investigator NIH, 1953—56; prof. medicine Harvard Med. Sch., 1966—, chmn. exec. com. depts. medicine, 1968—97, Mallinckrodt prof. medicine, 1972—97, disting. Mallinckrodt prof. medicine, 1998—, chmn. univ. cancer com., 1972—87. Mem. governing bd. NRC, 1987—90; mem. sci. bd. FDA, 1993; acad. liaison Novartis Biomed. Rsch. Inst., 2002—; trustee Marine Biol. Labs., 2004—; editor Harrison's-on-line, 1999—. Editor-in-chief (Harrison): Principles of Internal Medicine, 1976, 1991—99. Recipient award for disting. achievement in nutrition, Bristol-Myers Squibb, 1991, Sci. Bd. FDA, 1993—97, Tree of Life award, Jewish Nat. Fund, 2001. Fellow: ACP (John Phillips award for disting. achievement in clin. medicine 1989); mem.: NAS (chmn. food and nutrition bd. 1983—88, mem. exec. com., mem. coun. 1987—90, chmn. com. on risk assessment of hazardous air pollutants 1991—94), Inst. Medicine of NAS, Assn. Am. Physicians (pres. 1977—78, Kober medal 2001), Am. Gastroenterology Assn. (pres. 1974—75, Julius Friedenwald medal for outstanding achievement in gastroenterology 1985), Am. Acad. Arts and Scis. Achievements include research in molecular and genetic changes in malignant cells, metastasis in breast and colon cancer. Home: 20 Nobscot Rd Newton MA 02459-1323 Office: Cancer Ctr Mass Gen Hosp 139 13th St Charlestown MA 02129-2023 Office Phone: 617-726-5610. E-mail: Isselbacher@partners.org.

ISSHIKI, MASAYUKI, sociologist, educator, dean; b. Suzuka, Japan, Oct. 21, 1950; s. Mikio Isshiki and Michiko Isshiki-Fujii; m. Miwa Terada, Dec. 28, 1988. BA in Sociology, Sussex Coll., 1980, D in Sociology, 1986. V.p. Sanas Corp., Yokkaichi, Japan, 1980-83; rsch. scientist Triad PCL, Hong Kong, 1986-91; ptnr. Triad Cons., Suzuka, Japan, 1991-93; prof. Suzuka Internat. U., 1994—, dean grad. sch., 2002—. Author: Economic Development in Southeast Asia, 1991, Development of Bamboo, 1992, U.S. Watch, 1995—. Avocations: skiing, farming. Home and Office: Rm C-101 15-11 Minami-Ejima Suzuka Mie 510-0235 Japan E-mail: misshiki@mecha.ne.jp.

ISSLER, HARRY, lawyer; b. Cologne, Germany, Nov. 14, 1935; came to U.S., 1937; s. Max and Fanny (Grunbaum) I.; m. Doris Helen Lukow, June 1, 1958; children: Adriane P. Schorr, M. Valerie Priestley, Stephanie L. Beck. BS, U. Wis., 1955; JD, Cornell U., 1958. Bar: N.Y. 1958, U.S. Supreme Ct. 1962, U.S. Ct. Mil. Appeals 1967, U.S. Dist. Ct. (so. and ea. dists.) N.Y. 1960, U.S. Customs Ct. 1964, U.S. Tax Ct. 1964; cert. specialist in civil trial advocacy Nat. Bo. Trial Advocacy. Assoc. Wing & Wing, N.Y.C., 1958-60; assoc. Fuchsberg & Fuchsberg, N.Y.C., 1960-62; ptnr. Issler & Fein, N.Y.C., 1963-68, Shaw, Issler & Rosenberg, N.Y.C., 1968-70; pvt. practice N.Y.C., 1970-79; ptnr. Issler & Scrage, P.C., N.Y.C., 1980-99; sr. ptnr. The Law Firm of Harry Issler PLLC, N.Y.C., 1999—. Arbitrator Civil Ct., NY County, 1979-91; hearing officer NY State Tax Appeals, 1975-77, Supreme Ct. NY, NY County Med. Malpractice Panel, 1980-91; judge advocate NY State; neutral evaluator mediation panel Supreme Ct., NY County, 1997—; charter mem. Trial Lawyers Care, Inc. Book reviewer: NY Law Jour., 2001—. Trustee N.Y. State Mil. Edl. Found., 1997-2000; exec. v.p. Sutton Area Cmty., Inc., 2000—; v.p. 50 Sutton Pl. South Owners, Inc., 2002-03; pres. 50 Sutton Pl. South Owners Corp., 2003-05. With U.S. Army, 1958-59, N.Y.

Army N.G., 1963-88, ret. brig. gen., 1988. Ford Found. scholar, 1951-55. Mem. ABA, N.Y. State Bar Assn., Assn. of Bar of City of N.Y., Am. Trial Lawyers Assn., N.Y. State Trial Lawyers Assn., 42d Infantry Divsn. Officers Club (N.Y.C.pres. 1979-80), Officers Club (U.S. Mcht. Marine Acad.), 42d Infantry Rainbow Divsn. Assn. (pres. 1989), Phi Alpha Delta, Pi Lambda Phi (Omega chpt. pres. 1953-54). Home: 50 Sutton Pl S New York NY 10022-4167 Office: 110 E 59th St 29th Fl New York NY 10022 Office Phone: 212-371-0200. Business E-Mail: harryissler@lawyer.com.

ISTEL, JACQUES ANDRE, mayor; b. Paris, Jan. 28, 1929; came to U.S., 1940, naturalized, 1951; s. Andre and Yvonne Mathilde Cremieux I.; m. Felicia Juliana Lee, June 14, 1973; 1 dau. by previous marriage, Claudia Yvonne. AB, Princeton, 1949. Stock analyst Andre Istel & Co., N.Y.C., 1950, 55; pres. Parachutes Inc., Orange, Mass., 1957-87, Intramgmt. Inc., N.Y.C., 1962-80; chmn. Pilot Knob Corp., 1982—; mayor Town of Felicity, Calif., 1986—; curator Ctrl. Point for Memories, Calif., 1992—. Pres. VI World Parachuting Championships, 1962; capt. U.S. Parachuting team, 1956, master of sports, USSR, 1956, capt., team leader, 1958; chmn. Mass. Parachuting Commn., 1961-62; life hon. pres. Internat. Parachuting Commn., Fedn. Aero. Internat., 1965-; chmn. Hall of Fame of Parachuting, 1973—, Imp. Co. water commn. 1997—; founder Nat. Collegiate Parachuting League, 1957, World Commemorative Ctr., 1993; co-leader Nat. Geog. Soc. Vilcabamba Expdn., 1964. Author: Coe the Good Dragon at the Center of the World, 1985, Coe le Bon Dragon au Centre du Monde, 1985; editor in granite Museum Walls, 2001—; contbr. articles to encys., profl. jours.; patentee in field. Trustee Inst. for Man and Sci., 1975-82; bd. dirs. Marine Corps Scholarship Found., 1975-85. Served with USMC, 1952-54; lt. col. Res. Recipient Leo Stevens award, 1958, Diplome Paul Tissandier, 1969, Air and Space medal, 2003; decorated chevalier de la Legion D'Honneur; world record holder for parachuting, 1961. Mem. Nat. Aero. Assn. (bd. dirs. 1965-68), Fedn. Internat. des Centres (pres. 1990—), Cercle de l'Union Interalliée (Paris), Marine Corps Res. Officers Assn., DAV (life), Racquet and Tennis Club (N.Y.C.), Princeton Club (N.Y.C.). Home: Northview Felicity CA 92283 also: 10 rue Galilée 75116 Paris France Office: 1 Center Of The World Plz Felicity CA 92283-7777 Office Phone: 760-572-0100. E-mail: ctrworld@aol.com.

ISTOCK, VERNE GEORGE, retired bank executive; b. Sept. 20, 1940; BA in Econs., U. Mich., 1962, MBA in Fin., 1963. Credit analyst trainee NBD Bancorp, Inc., Detroit, 1963—66, group head, 1971-77, head U.S. divsn., 1977-82, sr. v.p., 1979-82, exec. v.p., 1982-85, vice chmn., dir., 1985-93, chmn., CEO, 1994-95, also bd. dirs.; chmn. NBD Bank; pres., CEO First Chgo. NBD Corp., Chgo., 1995-98, chmn., 1996-98; chmn. bd. Bank One Corp., Chgo., 1999—2000, pres., 2000; ret., 2000. Bd. dirs. Kelly Svcs. Inc., Masco Corp., Rockwell Automation, Inc. Bd. dirs. Chgo. Coun. Fgn. Rels., Chgo. Crime Commn. Mem. U. Mich. Alumni Assn. (past pres., lifetime dir.), Bankers Roundtable (past dir.), Econ. Club Chgo. (past dir.), Mich. Bus. Roundtable (past bd. dirs.), Comml. Club of Chgo., Econ. Club Detroit (past dir.), Ill. Bus. Roundtable (past dir.). Office: Bank One Corp 1 Bank One Plz Chicago IL 60670-0001 E-mail: verne_istock@bankone.com.

ISTOMIN, MARTA CASALS, academic administrator, performing company executive; b. PR, Nov. 2, 1936; d. Aquiles and Angelica M. (Martinez) Montanez; m. Pablo Casals, Aug. 3, 1957 (dec. 1973); m. Eugene Istomin, Feb. 15, 1975. Student, Mannes Coll. Music, N.Y.C., 1950-54; Mus.D. (hon.), World U., P.R., 1972; L.H.D. (hon.), Marymount Coll., 1975; Doctorate (hon.), U. P.R., 1984, Dickinson Coll., Carlisle, Pa., 1986; D (hon.), Shenandoah Coll., 1986, Interam. U., P.R., 1989. Prof. cello Conservatory Music, San Juan, P.R., 1961-64; vis. prof. cello Curtis Inst., Phila., 1974-75; co-chmn. bd., music dir. Casals Festival, 1974-77; artistic dir. John F. Kennedy Center for Performing Arts, Washington, 1980-90; dir. gen. Evian Music Festival, France, 1990—; pres. Manhattan Sch. Music, NYC, 1992—. Mem. Nat. Coun. on Arts, 1990; cons. Latin Am. ednl. projects. Trustee Marlboro Sch. Music and Festival; trustee Marymount Sch., NYC, World U. Recipient Puerto Rican Fedn. Women's Clubs award, 1967; award for cultural achievements City of San Juan, 1975; Nat. Conf. Puerto Rican Women award, 1975; Casita Maria medal for outstanding contbns. to culture N.Y.C., 1978; Outstanding Contbns. Performing Arts in Nation's Capitol award, 1983; Family Place Outstanding Community Service award, 1986; Mayor's Excellence in Service Arts award, Washington, 1986; Nat. Fedn. Music Clubs citation, 1987; named Outstanding Woman of Yr. P.R., 1975; Woman of Achievement Sta. WETA-TV, Washington, 1981; Order of Isabella the Cath. govt. Spain, 1986; Officer, Order Arts and Letters govt. France, 1986; Officer's Cross Order Merit govt. Fed. Republic Germany, 1987. Mem. Nat. Coun. on the Arts. Roman Catholic. Office: Manhattan School Music 120 Claremont Ave New York NY 10027-4698*

ISTOOK, ERNEST JAMES, JR., (JIM ISTOOK), congressman, lawyer; b. Fort Worth, Tex., Feb. 11, 1950; s. Ernest James and Dessie Cordelia Lyne I.; m. Judy Lee Bills, 1973; children: Amy, Butch, Chad, Diana, Emily. BA, Baylor U., 1971; JD, Oklahoma City U. Sch. Law, 1976. Reporter, State Capitol Stas. KOMA-TV, Oklahoma City, 1972—73, WKY-Radio, Oklahoma City, 1973—76; dir. Okla. Alcoholic Beverage Control Bd., 1977-78; legal counsel Okla. Gov. David Boren, 1978; dir. Warr Acres/Putnati City C. of C., 1982-86; councilman City of Warr Acres, Okla., 1982-86; atty. Istook & Assocs., 1983-93; mem. Okla. Ho. of Reps., 1986—92, U.S. Congress from 5th Okla. dist., Washington, 1993—; mem. appropriations com. Bd. dirs. Met. Libr. System, 1982-86, chmn., 1985-86 Named Taxpayer Friend of Yr., 1991, One of Ten best Legislators, 1992. Mem.: Kappa Nu. Republican. Mem. Lds Ch. Office: US Ho Reps 2404 Rayburn HOB Office House Members Washington DC 20515-3605*

ITABASHI, HIDEO HENRY, neurologist; b. Los Angeles, July 7, 1926; s. Masakichi and Mitsuko (Kobayashi) I.; m. Yoko Osawa, Feb. 3, 1952; children: Mark Masa, Helen Yoko. AB, Boston U., 1949, MD, 1954; postgrad., Yale U., 1949—50. Diplomate in neuropathology Am. Bd. Pathology. Intern U. Mich. Hosp., Ann Arbor, 1954-55, resident in neurology, 1955-58; assoc. rsch. neurologist U. Calif., San Francisco, 1958-60, asst. clin. prof., 1964-65; asst. neuropathologist Langley Porter Neuropsychiat. Inst., San Francisco, 1960-65; cons. Neuropathologist San Francisco Gen. Hosp., 1964-65; assoc. prof. neurology, pathology U. Mich. Med. Sch., Ann Arbor, 1968-71; prof.-in-residence pathology and neurology UCLA, 1975-93, prof. emeritus, 1993—, acting vice chair dept. pathology Sch. Medicine; acting chair pathology Harbor-UCLA Med. Ctr., 1990-91; cons. neuropathology dept., chief med. examiner-coroner Los Angeles County, 1977—. Cons. VA Hosp., Sepulveda, Calif., 1977-92; spl. fellow in neuropathology Nat. Inst. Neurol. Diseases and Blindness, 1958-60. Contbr. numerous articles on neurol. disorders to med jours. Fellow Am Acad. Forensic Scis.; mem. Am. Assn. Neuropathologists (sr.), Am. Acad. Neurology (sr.). Office: County LA Dept Coroner 1104 N Mission Rd Los Angeles CA 90033

ITAKETO, UMANA THOMPSON, systems and control engineer; b. Edem Aya, Ikot Abasi Akwa Ibom State, Nigeria, Oct. 30, 1959; s. Thompson Itaketo Umana and Dina Thompson Itaketo; m. Ima Umana Essiet, Dec. 26, 1995. Diploma with distinction, Petroleum Tng. Inst., Warri, Nigeria, 1979; B Engring. with honors, U. Tech., Enugu, Nigeria, 1985; M Engring., U. Nigeria, Nsukka, Nigeria, 1989; PhD, Fed. U. Tech., Owerri, Nigeria, 1999. Indsl. attachee Nigerian Agip Oil Co., Pt. Harcourt, Nigeria, 1978, Mobil Oil Co., Eket, Nigeria, 1983; univ. lectr. U. Nigeria, Nsukka, 1986—87; facilities engr. Qua Iboe terminal Mobil Producing Nigeria, Lagos, 1987—96, maintenance engr./supr., 1997—99, ops./maintenance supr. Ubit field, 1999—2000, sr. engr., 2001—02; staff engr. ExxonMobil Prodn. Co., Houston, 2002—. Author: The Design and Implementation of Interface Level Controller, 1985, Investigation into Various Controller Types/Tuning Methods for Improved Systems Response, 1988, State-Space/Matrix System Approaches in the Analysis and Control of Time Delays in Control Loops, 1995 (Coren Regd. 1992), The Development of Optimal Control Strategy for the Control of Non-Linear Systems Under Dynamic States, 1998, The Development of Performance Criterion for Optimal Control Studies on Non-Linear Systems, 1998, The Method of Isoclines In Determining the Stability of Non-Linear Systems Under Dynamic States, 1999, Application of Lyapunov's Second Method in the Stability Analysis of Oil/Gas Separation Process, 1998, Application of Isocline Plots of Non-Linear Systems for Aircraft Stability Under Dynamic States, 1999, The Stability of Non-Linear Systems Under Dynamic States, 1999, The Control of 2nd Order Non-linear Systems by a Proportional-plus-Integral-plus Derivative (PID) Controller, 1999, The Design and Installation of a Dissipation Array System for Lightning Prevention, 1999; contbr. articles to profl. jours.; reviewer AMSE Jours. Active Nat. Youth Svc. Corp., 1985-86. Acad. scholar Cross River State Govt., 1980, Mobil Producing Nigeria, 1980, Fed. Govt. Nigeria, 1986, award Nigerian U. Engring. Students Assn., 2000; recipient Merit Award Internat. Biographical Ctr., 1998, Golden Medal of Honour Am. Biographical Inst., 2000. Fellow Nigerian Soc. Engrs.; mem. IEEE, Instrument Soc. Am., Internat. Fedn. Automatic Control, Coun. Registered Engrs. Nigeria (registered profl. engr.), Internat. Fedn. Automatic Control (affil.), Instrumentation, Sys. and Automation Soc. Methodist. Avocations: football, chess, art, running, high-jumping. Office: ExxonMobil Prodn Co Kellog Tower Ste 854 601 Jefferson St Houston TX 77002

ITANO, HARVEY AKIO, biochemistry educator; b. Sacramento, Nov. 3, 1920; s. Masao and Sumako (Nakahara) I.; m. Rose Nakako Sakemi, Nov. 5, 1949; children: Wayne Masao, Glenn Harvey, David George. BS, U. Calif., Berkeley, 1942; MD, St. Louis U., 1945; PhD, Calif. Inst. Tech., 1950; DSc (hon.), St. Louis U., 1987. Intern City of Detroit Receiving Hosp., 1945-46; commd. officer USPHS, Bethesda, Md., 1950-70, advanced through grades to chief, sect. on chem. genetics, Nat. Inst. Arthritis and Metabolic Diseases, NIH, 1962-70, mem. hematology study sect., NIH, 1959-63, research fellow then sr. research fellow, Calif. Inst. Tech. Pasadena, 1950-54; prof. Dept. Pathology U. Calif. San Diego, La Jolla, 1970-88, prof. emeritus, 1988—. Vis. prof. Osaka (Japan) U., 1961-62, U. Chgo., 1965, U. Calif., San Francsico, 1967; cons. sickle cell anemia, mem. hematology study sect. 1953-63, various sickle cell anemia rev. coms., 1970-81, NIH, Bethesda. Editor: (with Linus Pauling) Molecular Structure and Biological Specificity, 1957; contbr. articles to profl. jours. George Minot lectr., AMA, 1955; Japan Soc. for Promotion of Sci. fellow, Okayama U., 1983-84. Mem. NAS, Am. Acad. Arts and Scis., Am. Chem. Soc. (Eli Lilly award in Biol. Chemistry 1954), Am. Soc. Biochemistry and Molecular Biology, Am. Soc. Hematology, Internat. Soc. Hematology, Phi Beta Kappa, Sigma Xi, Alpha Omega Alpha. Office: U Calif Dept Pathology 9500 Gilman Dr La Jolla CA 92093-0612

ITKIN, IVAN, nuclear scientist, mathematician; b. N.Y.C., Mar. 29, 1936; s. Abraham Aaron and Eda (Kreger) I.; m. Judith Ann Weiss, Aug. 19, 1962 (div. 1975); children: Marc Eric, Laurie Rachel; m. Joyce Lee Hudak, July 12, 1975; 1 child, Max Eugene. BSChemE, Poly. Inst., Bklyn., 1956; M in Nuclear Engring., NYU, 1957; PhD in Math., U. Pitts., 1964; D of Pub. Svc. (hon.), Chatham Coll., 1994. Assoc. scientist Bettis Atomic Power Lab. Westinghouse Electric Corp., Pitts., 1957-59, scientist, 1959-64, sr. scientist, 1964-71, fellow scientist, 1971-73; mem. Pa. Ho. of Reps., Harrisburg, 1973-98; dir. Office Civilian Radioactive Waste Mgmt. U.S. Dept. Energy, Washington, 1999-2001. Majority caucus chmn. Pa. Ho. of Reps., 1982-90, majority whip, 1990-92, majority leader, 1993-94, Democratic whip, 1995-98; Dem. nominee for Pa. gov., 1998; chmn. sci., tech., and resource planning com. Nat. Conf. State Legislators, Denver, 1988; del. Dem. Nat. Conv., 1984, 96; U.S. presdl. elector, 1992, 96. Election judge 19th Dist., 14th Ward, Pa., 1966-68; chmn. 14th Ward Dem. Com., Pitts., 1970-72. Recipient Keystone award Alcoholism and Addiction Assn., 1983, Award of Appreciation, Nat. Fedn. Blind, 1983, Disting. Svc. award Pa. Coll. Optometry, 1986; named House Mem. of Yr., Pa. Jewish Coalition, 1983. Mem. ACLU, Am. Nuclear Soc., Am. Jewish Congress, B'nai B'rith. Home: 3200 N Ocean Blvd Unit 606 Fort Lauderdale FL 33308-7155 Personal E-mail: iitkin@msn.com.

ITKIN, LISA ROBYN, music educator, director; b. Yonkers, N.Y., Aug. 15, 1968; d. Itkin Marvin and Lucienne G. Itkin; m. Judah B. Flum, Oct. 22, 1963. BA, Binghamton (N.Y.) U., 1989; MEd, Pa. State U., 1992. Dir. choral Westlake H.S., Waldorf, Md., 1992—96; dir. choral and drama Gaithersburg (Md.) H.S., 1996—98; dir. choral Watkins Mill H.S., Gaithersburg, 1998—. Asst. dir. Zemer Chai, Rockville, Md., 1997—. Choir dir.: White Ho., 2000—03, Wash. Chorus, 2004. Recipient Side By Side Choir award, Wash. Chorus, 2004. Mem.: Music Choir Educators Assn., Md. Music Educators Assn., Music Educators Nat. Conf., Am. Choral Dirs. Assn. Office: Watkins Mill High School 10301 Apple Ridge Road Gaithersburg MD 20879 Office Phone: 301-840-3984. Office Fax: 301-840-3980. E-mail: lisa_itkin@fc.mcps.k12.md.us.

ITO, CARL SUSUMU, computer engineer; b. Merced, Calfi., Dec. 12, 1959; s. Frank Fumi and Machiko Ito; m. Andrea Rene Spector, Nov. 1, 1985; children: Kevin, Lauren. BA, Pomona Coll., 1982; MS, Calif. State U., 1989. Computer programmer Unisys, San Diego, 1982-89; tchr. San Diego City C.C., 1991-94; sr. computer systems engr. DRS Techs., San Diego, 1989—. Nation chief YMCA Indian Guides, San Diego, 1991—94. Democrat. Avocations: piano, gardening. Home: 5864 Carnegie St San Diego CA 92122 Office: 2535 Camino Del Rio S Ste 300 San Diego CA 92108-3757 Fax: 858-587-0013. E-mail: itocs@icstf.navy.mil.

ITO, NOBORU, electric power industry executive; b. Qindao, Santon, China, Dec. 17, 1921; s. Eisho and Raiko (Watanabe) I.; m. Sachiko Tsuchiya (dec. Nov. 1978); children: Junko, Kyoko. B degree, Tohoku U., Sendai, 1946, D degree, 1973. Engr. Toyo Comm. Co., Kawasaki, 1946-50, Oi Electric Co., Tokyo, 1950-57, chief rschr. Yokohama, 1964-69, dir., 1970-83, cons., 1984-91; pres. Leo-B Corp., Yokohama, 1992—. Scientist Tokyo U., 1960-63, 89-91; lectr. Yamagata U., 1982-83; scientist U. So. Calif., L.A., 1985-86. Recipient invention prize Japan Inst. Invention, 1982, dir. prize Sci. and Tech. Agy. of Japan, 1982, yellow ribbon prize Japan Govt., 1984. Mem. IEEE (sr.), N.Y. Acad. Scis., Japan Phys. Soc., Japan Merits Club. Avocations: learning foreign languages, car trips. Office: Leo-B Corp R1012 6-13-53 Kikuna Kohokuku Yokohama 222 Japan

ITO, YOICHIRO, pathologist, researcher; b. Osaka, Japan, Dec. 22, 1928; came to U.S., 1968, naturalized, 1978; s. Taichi and Ai (Kubota) I.; m. Ryoko Tanioka, Dec. 23, 1963; children: Koichi, Shin. MD, Osaka (Japan) City U., 1958. Intern U.S. Yokosuka (Japan) Naval Hosp., Yokosuka, Japan, 1958—59; resident in pathology Cleve. (Ohio) Met. Gen. Hosp., 1959—61, Michael Reese Hosp., Chgo., 1961—63; instr. physiology Osaka (Japan) City U. Med. Sch., 1963—68; vis. scientist Nat. Heart, Lung and Blood Inst. NIH, Bethesda, Md., 1968—78, med. officer Nat. Heart, Lung and Blood Inst., 1978—. Recipient 1st pl. award ann. sci. rsch. presentation at Cleve. Met. Gen. Hosp., 1960, Tech. Excellence award for devel. blood cell separator, 1979; Fulbright exch. scholar, 1959-63; WHO rsch. travel fund grantee Nat. Inst. Med. Rsch., London, 1968. Mem. N.Y. Acad. Scis., Kenshinkai. Achievements include research on innovation in separation sci., including continuous development of countercurrent chromatography, cell separation methods; initiated and developed countercurrent chromatography; patentee coil planet centrifuge, rotating-seal-free flow-through centrifuge, pH-zone-refining countercurrent chromatography, centrifugal precipitation chromatography. Office: NIH Bldg 50 Rm 3334 9000 Rockville Pike Bethesda MD 20892-8014 Home and Office: 6003 Melvern Drive Bethesda MD 20817 Office Phone: 301-496-1210. Business E-Mail: itoy2@mail.nih.gov.

ITOH, TATSUO, engineering educator; b. Tokyo, May 5, 1940; BS, Yokohama Nat. U., Japan, 1964, MS, 1966; PhD, U. Ill., 1969. Registered profl. engr., Tex. Rsch. assoc. U. Ill., Urbana, 1969-71, rsch. asst. prof., 1971-76; sr. rsch. engr. Stanford Rsch. Inst., Menlo Park, Calif., 1976-77; assoc. prof. U. Ky., Lexington, 1977-78, U. Tex., Austin, 1978-81, prof., 1981-90, Hayden Head prof., 1983-90; prof.and TRW endowed chair UCLA, 1991—. Guest rschr. AEG-Telefunken, Ulm, Fed. Republic of Germany, 1979; vis. prof. Def. Acad. Japan, 1991, U. Leeds, Eng., 1994—; hon. vis. prof. Nanjing Inst. Tech., China; hon. prof. Beijing Aeronautical and Astron. U., China, 1995—; adj. rsch. officer Comms. Rsch. Lab., Ministry of Post and Telecom., Japan, 1994; cons. Tex. Instruments, Dallas, 1979, Hughes Aircraft. Editor (guest): Transactions, 1991. Recipient Engring. Found. faculty awards, 1980-81, Billy and Claude Hocott Disting. Rsch. award, 1988, Disting. Alumnus award U. Ill., 1990, Shida award Min. of Post and Telecom., Japan, 1998, Japan Microwave prize Asia-Pacific Microwave Conf., 1998. Fellow IEEE (Millennium medal 2000, MTT Disting. Microwave Educator award 2000), Nat. Acad. Engring.; mem. Microwave Theory and Techniques Soc. (hon. life; editor 1983-85, pres. 1990, jour. editor Microwave and Guided Wave Letters 1991-94), Internat. Sci. Radio Union (chmn. USNC commn. D 1988-90, chmn. commn. D 1993-96, long range planning com. 1996—), Inst. Electronics and Comm. Engrs., Nat. Acad. Engring. Achievements include invention of millimeter-wave line, 1975; quasi-optical mixer, 1982; non-contact ID, 1995; high power photo detector, 1995. Office: UCLA Dept Elec Engring Los Angeles CA 90095-0001 Home: 12 Eastfield Dr Rolling Hills CA 90274-5226 Office Phone: 310-206-4820. Business E-Mail: itoh@ee.ucla.edu.

ITOH, WILLIAM H., former ambassador; b. Tokyo, May 30, 1943; m. Melinda White; children: Charlotte, Caroline. BA in Social Sci., MA in History, Anthropology, U. N.Mex., 1971. Sec. tchr. Albuquerque Pub. Schs., 1967-68; asst. prof. history Calif. State U., Humboldt, 1972-73; U.S. Dept. State staff asst. and exec. officer Bur. Congl. Rels., 1975-76, congl. rels. office, 1980-83; country officer for Japan Bur. East Asian and Pacific Affairs, 1978-80, spl. asst., 1983-84, Office of Under Sec. for Polit. Affairs, 1984-86; consular and polit. officer U.S. Embassy, London, 1976-78; U.S. consul gen. Western Australia, Perth, 1986-90; dep. exec. sec. and acting exec. sec. Dept. State, 1991-93; exec. sec. NSC White House, Washington, 1993-95; amb. to Kingdom of Thailand U.S. Dept. of State, 1995-98. Prof. internat. studies, dir. Washington Internat. programs, U. N.C., Chapel Hill. Logistics officer USAF, 1967-69.

ITTELSON, LANE, foundation administrator; b. Princeton, N.J., June 2, 1950; s. William H. and Martha (Lane) Ittelson; m. Ellen Threinen, Oct. 17, 1981; 1 child, Margaret Fuller. BA, Columbia Coll., 1972. Dep. state historic preservation officer N.Mex Hist. Preservation Bur., Santa Fe, 1976—82; pres. Hist. Denver, Inc., 1983—86; dep. state historic preservation officer Colo. Hist. Soc., 1989—99; exec. dir. Colo. Hist. Found., 1999—. Office: Colo Hist Found 1300 Broadway Denver CO 80203 Office Phone: 303-894-2503.

ITTLESON, H(ENRY) ANTHONY, foundation executive; b. June 23, 1937; s. Henry and Nancy (Strauss) I.; m. Marianne Sundby, Feb. 6, 1961 (dec.); children: Henry Philip, Christina Bee, Stephanie; m. Chandler Cox Mashek, Apr.17, 2004. BA, Brown U., 1960. Credit adminstr. The CIT Group Inc., N.Y.C., 1961-68, v.p. Equipment Financing subs., 1968-70, asst. to pres., 1970-71, v.p. mktg., 1971-78, v.p. financing div., 1978-81, exec. v.p., 1981-92, exec. spl. projects, 1988-92; chmn. Travent Ltd., 1987-97; chmn., pres. Ittleson Found., 1973—. Trustee Brown U.; trustee S.C. Aquarium. Mem. Brown U. Club, Regency Whist Club, Deepdale Golf Club, Meadow Club, Nat. Golf. Links of Am., L.I. Wyandanch Club, Shinnecock Hills Golf Club, Atlantic Golf Club, Everglades Club, Cordillera Golf Club (Colo.), Loch Lomond Golf Club, Phi Gamma Delta. Home: Poco Sabo Plantation 1185 Poco Sabo Ln Green Pond SC 29446

ITURBIDE, GRACIELA, photographer; b. Mexico City, May 16; married, 1962; children: Manuel, Claudia, Mauricio. Student, U. Nat. Autanoma Mexico, 1969—72. Asst. Manuel Breva. Exhibitions include Galeria José Clemence Orosco, Mexico City, 1975, Midtown Y Gallery, N.Y.C., 1976, Centre Georges Pompldeu, Paris, 1982. Recipient prize, UN Internat. Labor Orgn., 1986, W. Eugene Smith award, 1987; Consejo Mexicano de Fotografia grantee, 1983, Guggenheim Found. grantee, 1987. Mem.: Mexican Coun. Photography (founding mem.). Office: c/o Robert Miller Gallery 524 W 26th St New York NY 10001*

ITZKOFF, NORMAN JAY, lawyer, arbitrator, mediator; b. N.Y.C., Oct. 9, 1940; s. Louis and Rose Itzkoff; divorced; 1 child, Francesca Sandra. BS with distinction, U. Buffalo, 1961; LLB cum laude, Columbia U., 1965. Bar: N.Y. 1965, U.S. Dist. Ct. (so. and ea. dists.) N.Y. 1967, U.S. Ct. Appeals (2d cir.) 1967, U.S. Supreme Ct. 1971. Law clk. to judge U.S. Dist. Ct. (so. dist.) N.Y., N.Y.C., 1965-66; assoc. Cravath, Swaine & Moore, N.Y.C., 1966-74, Roseman & Colin, N.Y.C., 1974-76, ptnr., 1976-86; sr. litigation counsel Siemens Corp., N.Y.C., 1988-93; cons., arbitrator and mediator, 1994—. Gen. counsel Assn. Internat. Photography Art Dealers Inc., N.Y.C., 1981—91. Editor: Dealing with Damages, 1983, Columbia U. Law Rev., 1963-65. Mem. adv. bd. Catskill Ctr. for Photography, Woodstock, N.Y., 1982-87; chmn. adv. bd. Ctr. for Photography at Woodstock, 1987-88. Harlan Fiske Stone scholar, Columbia Law Sch. Mem. ABA (jud. adminstrn. div. lawyers conf., com. on jud. qualification and selection, com. jud.compensation, sect. of litigation, com. corp. counsel), Fed. Bar Coun., N.Y. State Bar Assn. (alt. dispute resolution com., antitrust law sect., mem. coms. on court adminstrn. and practice and procedure, comml. and fed. litigation sect., com. on corp. counsel, entertainment arts and sports law sect., com. on fine arts, internat. law and practice sect. coms. internat. dispute resolution and subcom. arbitration, mcpl. law sect., profl. discipline com., trial lawyers sect., com. on fed. cts., com. on litigation mgmt. and econs.), Assn. Bar City N.Y. (alternative dispute resolution com., profl. discipline com., adv. bd. demonstration observation com., com. on nuclear tech. and law, com. on art law, liaison art law com., chmn. subcom. on state legislation 1983-84, Am. Arbitration Assn. (panel), Ctr. Pub. Resources (com. on disputes with distbrs., dealers and franchisees), NY State Supreme Ct., NY County Comml. Divsn. ADR Advisory Com., US Dist. Ct., EDNY, Arbitration & Mediation Panel, Complaint Mediation Panel, Departmental Disciplinary Com., NY State Appellate Divsn., First Dept., online mediator expert mediators panel, Columbia Club, Westchester Rugby Club (N.Y.C.), Beta Gamma Sigma. Avocations: fine art photography, running. Office: 2600 Netherland Ave New York NY 10463-4801 Office Phone: 718-543-9703. E-mail: normanitzkoff@juno.com.

ITZOE, LINDA VERONICA, language educator; b. York, Pa., Mar. 6, 1940; d. Maurice Edwin and Bertha Mae (Hershey) I. BA in French, Elizabethtown (Pa.) Coll., 1962; MA in English, U. Wyo., 1965; PhD in English, U. Del., 1979. Cert. English, French, social studies tchr., Pa. Tchr. English Warwick Union Sch. Dist., Lititz, Pa., 1962-65; head English dept., 1965-69; instr. English Pa. State U., York, 1969-73; asst. prof. English, 1973-89; assoc. prof. English, 1989—. Editor: Arthur Wilson's The Inconstant Lady: A Critical Edition, 1980, The Swisser, 1984. Named Woman of Yr. St. Peter's Coun. Cath. Women, 1997. Mem. NCTE, MLA, Assembly for Tchr. English Grammar, Assn. bus. Comm., Elizabethtown Bus. and Profl. Women's Club (2nd v.p. 1986-87, pres. 1989-91, Woman of Yr. 1995). Avocations: music, container gardening, church history. Home: 435 N Holly St Elizabethtown PA 17022 Office: Pa State U 1031 Edgecomb Ave York PA 17403 Office Phone: 717-771-4153. E-mail: lvi@psu.edu.

IVANCHENKO, LAUREN MARGARET DOWD, pharmaceutical executive; b. West Orange, NJ, Mar. 20, 1958; d. Bernard Peter and Virginia (Morsell) Dowd; m. John Ivanchenko, Aug. 12, 1990; 1 child, Liana Katherine. BS in Psycho.-Biology, Albright Coll., 1980; postgrad., Rutger's U., 1991—92; MBA, St. Joseph's U., 2002. Sales Bourroughs Wellcome Co., Rsch. Triangle Pk., NC, 1981—84, acct. mgr. med. ctr., 1984—96; therapeutic area specialist Glaxo Wellcome, Inc., 1996—2000; sr. exec. clin. specialist Glaxo Smith Kline, Inc., 2000—. Mem.: Am. Epilepsy Soc., N.J. Epilepsy Soc. (mem. profl. adv. bd. 2001—), Nat. Exch. Club, Beta Gamma Sigma, Phi Delta Sigma. Avocations: piano, reading.

IVANHOE, ROBERT J., lawyer; b. NYC, 1953; BA, Johns Hopkins U., 1975; JD, Am. U., 1978. Bar: N.Y. 1979. Ptnr. Dreyer and Traub, NYC; now shareholder, mem. exec. com., chair nat. real estate practice Greenberg Traurig, LLP, NYC. Sr. editor Am. U. Law Review, 1977-78. Mem. Omicron Delta Kappa, Pi Sigma Alpha. Office: Greenberg Traurig LLP MetLife Bldg 200 Park Ave New York NY 10166 Office Phone: 212-801-9333. Office Fax: 212-801-6400. Business E-Mail: ivanhoer@gtlaw.com.

IVANICK, CAROL W. TRENCHER, lawyer; b. Springfield, Mass., Mar. 6, 1939; d. Joseph George and Daisy Wolf; m. Michael Ira Trencher, July 30, 1960 (div. Feb. 1984); children: Christopher, Daniel, Deborah; m. Peter Alan Ivanick (div. 1998). BA, Wellesley Coll., 1959; JD, Yale U., 1962. Bar: N.Y. 1963. Assoc. Cleary, Gottlieb et al, N.Y.C., 1962-67; ptnr. Dewey, Ballantine LLP, N.Y.C., 1976—2004, of counsel, 2004—. Chmn. adv. com. Pension Benefit Guaranty Corp., Washington, 1978-80; visiting lectr. Yale Law Sch., New Haven, Conn., 1978-79, 82-83. Avocations: ceramics, bowling, tennis. Home: 110 Riverside Dr New York NY 10024-3715 Office: Dewey Ballantine 1301 Avenue Of The Americas New York NY 10019-6022 Office Phone: 212-259-7800. E-mail: civanick@dbllp.com.

IVANKOVA, NATALIYA V., social and health sciences educator, researcher; b. Izmail, Ukraine, Oct. 29, 1959; arrived in U.S., 1997; d. Vladimir M. Ivankov and Tamara M. Ivankova; m. Ivan I. Herbey, Oct. 26, 1990; 1 child, Igor I. Herbey. Specialist, Izmail State Pedagogical Inst., 1981; PhD, Odessa (Ukraine) State U., 1988; MS, U. Nebr., Omaha, 1998; MA, U. Nebr., Lincoln, 2002, PhD, 2004. Lectr., sr. lectr. Izmail State Pedagogical Inst., 1981—92, assoc. prof., 1992—99, dean admissions, 1995—97; rsch. assoc., projects coord., instr. U. Nebr., Lincoln, 2002—04; asst. prof. U. Ala., Birmingham, 2004—. Contbr. articles to profl. jours.; mem. editl. bd.: Online Jour. Distance Learning Adminstrn., 2004. Recipient Academic Status of Dosent, Ministry Edn., Ukraine, 1993, Outstanding Doctoral Dissertation award, Phi Delta Kappa, 2004; E. Muskie/Freedom Support Act fellow, U. S. Info. Agy./Open Soc. Inst., 1997—99, Presdl. Grad. fellow, U. Nebr. Sys., 2002—03. Mem.: Internat. Sloan Consortium on Asynchronous Learning Networks, Am. Assn. for Higher Edn., Assn. for the Study Higher Edn., Am. Ednl. Rsch. Assn. Avocations: reading, music, travel. Home: 2545 - D Mountain Lodge Circle Birmingham AL 35216 Office: Univ Ala at Birmingham EB 202 1530 3rd Ave S Birmingham AL 35294-1250 Office Phone: 205-996-7909.

IVANKOVICH, ANTHONY D., anesthesiologist, educator; b. Debeljaca, Yugoslavia, Mar. 25, 1939; came to U.S., 1965; m. Olga Ivankovich. MD, U. Zagreb, Croatia, 1963. Lic. physician, Ill.; diplomate Am. Bd. Anesthesiology. Resident in internal medicine County Hosp. Nunberg, Fed. Republic Germany, 1963-65; rotating intern Edgewater Hosp., Chgo., 1966; resident in anesthesiology U. of Chgo. Hosps., 1967-68; asst. prof. anesthesiology Stritch Sch. Medicine Loyola U., Maywood, Ill., 1970-71; instr. anesthesiology Pritzker Sch. Medicine U. Chgo., 1969, assoc. prof. anesthesiology, 1972-74; faculy Sch. Medicine Cook County Postgrad., Chgo., 1975—; prof. anesthesiology Rush Med. Coll. Rush Univ. Med. Ctr., 1980; dir. Rush Pain Ctr., chmn. anesthesiology Rush U. Med. Ctr., Chgo., 1980—. Attending anesthesiologist Stritch Sch. Medicine, Loyola U., Chgo., 1970-71, lectr. in anesthesiology, 1971-81; cons. anesthesiology Suburban TB Sanatorium, Hinsdale, Ill., 1970-71, Shriner's Hosp. for Crippled Children, Chgo., 1977-82; attending anesthesiology Michael Reese Med. Ctr., Chgo., 1971-74; chief oper. rm. svcs. 801st Gen. Hosp., USAR, Lincolnwood, Ill., 1971-73, chief surgery, 1973-74, assoc. chief profl. svcs., 1974-76; dir. anesthesia rsch. Michael Reese Med. Ctr., Chgo., 1971-74; chmn. anesthesiology Ill. Masonic Med. Ctr., Chgo., 1974-80, Rush Univ. Med. Ctr., Chgo., 1980—, chmn. coun. surg. chmn. divsn. surg. scis. and svcs., 1992-94, dir. Surg. Hosp., assoc. v.p., 1993—, dir. Women & Children's Hosp., assoc. v.p., 1994—; assoc. examiner Am. Bd. Anesthesiology, 1978; pres. med. staff Rush U. Med. Ctr. (bd. trustees 2005-); presenter in field. Author: (books) Nitroprusside and Other Short-Acting Hypotensive Agents, 1978, (book chpts. with others) Perspective in High Frequency Ventilation, 1983, Current Controversies in Thoracic Surgery, 1986, Anesthesia and ENT Surgery, 1987, Liposomes as Drug Carriers, 1987, Effective Hemostasis in Cardiac Surgery, 1988, Adjuncts to Cancer Therapy, 1989, Advances in Anesthesia, 1990, Cardiothoracic and Vascular Anesthesia Update, 1991, Cardiothoracic and Vascular Anesthesia Update, 1991, Clinical Anesthesia, 1992, Clinical Anesthesia Updates, 1992, Liposomes in Drug Delivery, 1992; contbr. articles and abstracts to profl. jours. Fellow Am. Coll. Anesthesiologists; mem. AMA, Internat. Assn. for Study of Pain, Internat. Anesthesia Rsch. Soc., Am. Soc. Anesthesiologists, Am. Heart Assn., Am. Coll. Chest Physicians, Am. Pain Soc., Pan Am. Med. Assn., Soc. for Intravenous Anesthesia, Ill. Med. Soc., Ill. Soc. Anesthesiologists, Soc. Neurosurg. Anesthesia and Neurologic Supporting Care, Midwest Pain Soc., Chgo. Med. Soc., Chgo. Soc. Anesthesiologists, Inst. of Medicine of Chgo., Chgo. Heart Assn., Sigma Xi. Office: Rush Univ Med Ctr Dept Anesthesiology 1653 W Congress Pkwy Chicago IL 60612-3833 Office Phone: 312-942-3137. E-mail: aivankov@rush.edu.

IVANOV, ALEXANDER V., biochemist, researcher; b. Grodno, Belarus, Nov. 1, 1970; came to U.S., 1995; s. Valerii V. and Elena M. Ivanov; m. Asya V. Grinberg. MS, Grodno State U., 1992; PhD, Med. Coll. Ohio, 2000. Substitute tchr. chemistry, biology Secondary Sch. # 10, Grodno, 1989-91; rsch. asst. Belozersky Inst. Physico-Chem. Biology Moscow State U., 1992-95; fellow Med. Coll. Ohio, Toledo, 2000—02, asst. prof. pharmacology, 2003—; instr. Harvard Med. Sch., Mass. Gen. Hosp., 2004—. Contbr. articles to profl. jours. Winner Belarus round All-USSR Student Biology Olympiad, Ministry of Edn., 1991. Mem. AAAS, Am. Biophys. Soc. Avocations: classical music, piano, tennis, travel. Office: MGH 55 Fruit St Wellman 415 Boston MA 02114 E-mail: aivanov@mco.edu.

IVANOV, ANATOLI F., education educator, researcher; s. Odarka A. Ivanova and Fedir Y. Ivanov; m. Elena G. Galkina, June 24, 1984; children: Irina A. Ivanova, Sergey A. PhD, Inst. of Math., Kiev, Ukraine, 1983. With U. R.I., 1992—94, Inst. Math., NAS, Kiev, Ukraine, 1983—91; rsch. assoc. U. of Ballarat, Australia, 1998—2002; prof. Pa. State U., Wilkes-Barre, 1994—. Author around 100 rsch. articles, papers and pubs. Fellow, Fulbright Found., Chile, 2003, Alexander von Humboldt, Germany, 2004; Rsch. Scholarships, AvH Stiftung (Germany), JSPS (Japan), Fulbright (USA), 1985, 1990, 1997, 1998, 2001, Rch. Scholarships, 2003, 2004. Office: Pa State Univ PO Box PSU Lehman PA 18627 E-mail: afi1@psu.edu.

IVANOV, LYUBEN DIMITROV, naval architecture researcher, educator; b. Varna, Bulgaria, Apr. 14, 1941; came to U.S., 1991; s. Dimitar Dimov and Petra Christova (Grozdeva) I.; m. Svetlana Zekova, Aug. 14, 1965 (div. July 1977); children: Ognyan, Iskra; m. Irina Radeva, Aug. 18, 1977; stepchildren: Ivelin, Michaela. Diploma for Naval Architecture, Higher Naval Sch., Varna, Bulgaria, 0164; PhD, Leningrad Shipbuilding Inst., USSR, 1970. Chartered engr., U.K. Designer Inst. for Shipbuilding, Varna, 1964-66; asst. Tech. Univ., Varna, 1966, reader, head of dept., 1970-74, vice-dean for rsch., 1975-76, vice-dean for continuing edn., 1985-86, dean of faculty of shipbuilding, 1987-89, reader on ship structures, 1989-91; sr. engr. Am. Bur. Shipping, N.Y.C., 1991—. Vis. researcher Univ. Newcastle upon Tyne, U.K., 1974-75; dep. dirs. Inst. for Shipbuilding, Varna, 1986-87, mng. dir. 1987-89; v.p. Bulgarian Shipbuilding Corp., Varna, 1987-88. Mem. editorial bd. Marine Structures Jour., 1988-93. Founder, sec. Union of Bulgarian Scientists in Shipbuilding, Varna, 1982. Recipient badge of Honor, Presidium of the Union of Bulgarian Scientists, Sofia, 1984. Mem. Royal Instn. Naval Architects/U.K. (mem. internat. standing com. practical design of ships and mobile units symposium 1987-93), Soc. Naval Architects and Marine Engrs. Achievements include research in application of probabilistic methods in ship structures design and analysis. Home: 12 Brentwood Oaks Ct The Woodlands TX 77381-2525 Office: Am Bur Shipping ABS Plaza 16855 Northchase Dr Houston TX 77060-6006 Fax: 281-877-5820. Business E-Mail: livanov@eagle.org.

IVANOV, VLADIMIR N., molecular biologist, cancer biologist; b. Baku, Russia, Nov. 17, 1946; s. Tatiana N. Ivanova and Nickolay E. Ivanov; children: Tatiana Ivanova, Daria Ivanova. MS, U. Novosibirsk, Russia, 1970; PhD, Russian Acad. Scis., 1977, DSc, 1990. Rsch. assoc. Meml. Sloan-Kettering Inst., NYC, 1995—97; rsch. asst. prof. Mt. Sinai Med. Sch., 1997—2003; rsch. assoc. scientist Columbia U., 2003—. Assoc. editor Am. Assn. of Immunologists, 2002—. Mem.: Am. Assn. of Immunologists (life). Office: Columbia Univ CRR 630 West 168 St New York NY 10032 Office Phone: 212-305-9967. Office Fax: 212-305-3229. E-mail: vni3@columbia.edu.

IVANOVITCH, MICHAEL S., economist; b. Cetinje, Yugoslavia, Sept. 9, 1939; children: Alexandra, Nicholas, Alexander. Diploma in Law, U. Belgrade, Yugoslavia, 1961; MBA, Columbia U., 1972, M of Philosophy, 1976, PhD, 1977. Rsch. assoc. Columbia U. Inst. on Western Europe, N.Y.C., 1977-78; prof. Columbia U. Grad. Sch. Bus., N.Y.C., 1978-88; internat. economist Fed. Res. Bank of N.Y., N.Y.C., 1978-79; prin. adminstr., sr. economist Orgn. for Econ. Cooperation and Devel., Paris, 1979-89; pres. MSI Global, Inc., N.Y.C. and Paris, 1989—. Advisor Groupe Arnault, Paris, 2000—, The Yasuda Meiji Ins. Co., 1990—, Merrill Lynch, 1996—, ANZ Bank, 1997—. Democrat. Russian Orthodox. Avocation: music. Office: MSI Global Inc 340 W 57th St New York NY 10019-3706 E-mail: mail@msiglobal.com.

IVE, JONATHAN, information technology executive, computer designer; b. London, 1967; Studies design and art, Newcastle Polytechnic (now Northumbria U.), 1985; BA, Doctorate, Newcastle Polytechnic. Ptnr. Tangerine, London, 1989—92; joins design team Apple Computer, Inc., Cupertino, Calif., 1992—, v.p. indsl. design apple computers, 1998—. Work widely exhibited in Europe, N.Am. and Asia, forming permanent collections at many museums. Named as having the greatest impact on popular culture, BBC poll, 2002, New Media Hero, British Interactive Media Assn., 2003, Most Admired in the Creative Industries, Creative Review Peer Poll, 2003, No. 1 on the list. "British Culture's Top 50 Movers and Shakers", BBC 3, 2004; named one of "Best and Brightest", Esquire, 2002, Details, 2002; recipient first Designer of Yr. prize, Design Mus., 2003, Product Designer of Yr. award, BluePrint Magazine, 2004. Fellow: Royal Soc. Arts (Inaugural medal for Design Achievement 1999, awarded title of Royal Designer for Industry 2003). Lead designer of the following launches: iMac, 1998; Apple iBook, the 22" Cinema Display, PowerMac G4 Tower and iSub, 1999; Apple G4 Cube, 2000; Titanium PowerBook G4 and iPod portable MP3 Player, 2001; sunflower-inspired iMac with 15" and 17" floating screens, 2002; eMac, 2002; Apple 12" PowerBook and 17" Powerbook, 1" thick and 6.8 lbs, world's slimmest and lightest 17" notebook computer, 2003. Office: Apple Computer Inc 1 Infinite Loop Cupertino CA 95014 Office Phone: 408-996-1010. Office Fax: 408-974-2113.

IVENS, MARY SUE, microbiologist, medical mycologist; b. Maryville, Tenn., Aug. 23, 1929; d. McPherson Joseph and Sarah Lillie (Hensley) Ivens. BS, East Tenn. State U., 1949; MS NIH rsch. trainee, Tulane U. Sch. Medicine, 1963; PhD, La. State U. Sch. Medicine, 1966; postgrad., Emory U. Sch. Medicine, 1960. Diplomate Am. Bd. Microbiology. Dir. microbiol. and mycol. labs. Lewis-Gate Hosp., Roanoke, Va., 1953—56; rsch. mycologist Ctrs. Disease Control, Atlanta, 1957—60; rsch. assoc. La. State U. Sch. Medicine, New Orleans, 1963—66; instr. medicine La. State U., 1966—72, instr. microbiology, 1966—72, clin. prof., 1972—. Dir. micology lab. La. State U. Sch. Medicine, 1963—72, lectr. sch. dentistry, 1968—70; assoc. prof. natural scis. Dillard U., New Orleans, 1972—; assoc. Marine Biol. Lab., Woods Hole, Mass., 1978—; cons. in field. Contbr. articles to profl. jours. Commr. conf. on ctr. Mycotic sera WHO, 1969; mem. La. assn. def. counsel expert witness bank, 1985—; bd. dirs. La. coun. Girl Scouts US, Cmty Relationships Greater New Orleans, Zoning Bd. River Ridge, La.; mem. exec. bd. River Ridge Civic Assn., 1982—98, sec., 1982—84; chmn. pers. bd. Riverside Bapt. Ch., River Ridge; dir. outreach First Bapt. Ch., New Orleans, 1989—97; chmn. gold medal award com. Sigma Xi, 1978. Recipient Rosicrucian Humanitarian award, 1981; fellow Macy, MBL, 1978—79; grantee NSF, NIH. Mem.: Nat. Inst. Sci., AAAS, Am. Soc. Microbiology (Nat. com. on membership 1983—87), Med. Mycological Soc. Am., Internat. Soc. Human and Animal Mycology, Sigma Xi. Office: Dillard U Div Natural Sci New Orleans LA 70122 Home: 809 Prestwick Dr Maryville TN 37803-6757

IVENS, ROSALIND, artist; b. Phila., Sept. 30, 1955; d. Louis Ivens and Geraldine Bernice Watnick; m. Francis Andrew Adams, Mar. 15, 2002; 1 child, Evan Fishman. BFA, Phila. Coll. Art, 1977. Illustrator freelance, N.Y.C., 1975—; prin., owner Ros the Gardener, Bklyn. Garden cons., garden design, topiary Ros the Gardener, 2000—. Exhibitions include Eye Flower, illustrations in over 40 mags., books, newspapers. Recycle Christmas trees, prune city trees Trees N.Y., Bklyn. Achievements include development of Gardens in city yards utilizing homemade compost and organic methods. Home: 478 12th St Brooklyn NY 11215-7013 Office: Ros the Gardener 478 12th St Brooklyn NY 11215-7013 Office Phone: 718-499-8285. Personal E-mail: rosalindivens@msn.com.

IVER, ROBERT DREW, dentist; b. Miami, Fla., Feb. 6, 1947; s. William Henry and Jeanette (Minden) I.; m. Lisa Marie Stettner-Iver, May 5, 1974. Student, Ohio State U., 1965-66, U. Miami, 1966-68; DDS, Georgetown U., 1972. Pvt. practice dentistry, Miami Beach, Fla., 1974—. Lt. USNR, 1968-81. Fellow ADA; mem. Fla. Dental Assn., East Coast Dist. Dental Soc., Acad. Gen. Dentistry, Miami Beach Dental Soc., Gold Coast Acad. Gen. Dentistry, Am. Radio Relay League, N.Am. Fishing Club, Dade Radio Club Miami, Everglades Amateur Radio Club. Avocations: sports fishing, ham radio operating. Office: 1205 Lincoln Rd Ste 203 Miami FL 33139-2365 Office Phone: 305-672-8894.

IVERS, DONALD LOUIS, federal judge; b. San Diego, May 6, 1941; s. Grant Perrin and Margaret (Ware) I. BA, U. N.Mex., 1963; JD, Am. U., 1971. Bar: U.S. Dist. Ct. (D.C. 1972), U.S. Ct. Appeals (D.C. cir.) 1972, U.S. Ct. Mil. Appeals 1972, U.S. Supreme Ct. 1975. Assoc. Brault, Graham, Scott, Brault, Washington, 1972-78; chief counsel Republican Nat. Com., Washington, 1978-81; gen. counsel 1980 Rep. Nat. Conv. Site Selection Com., 1979-80; chief counsel Fed. Hwy. Adminstrn., U.S. Dept. Transp., 1981-85; counselor to sec., chmn. sec.'s safety rev. task force U.S. Dept. Transp., 1984-85; gen. counsel VA, 1985-89; acting gen. counsel U.S. Dept. Vet. Affairs, 1989-90, asst. to the sec., 1990; judge U.S. Ct. Appeals Vet. Claims, 1990—2004, chief judge, 2004—. Capt. U.S. Army, 1963-68, Vietnam, lt. col. Res., ret. Office: US Ct Appeals Vet Claims 625 Indiana Ave NW Washington DC 20004-2923 Office Phone: 202-501-5878.

IVERSEN, DAVID STEWART, librarian; b. Ames, Iowa, Sept. 5, 1963; s. James Delano and Margery Lynne (Peters) Iversen. BA in English, Dana Coll., 1986; MLS, U. Iowa, 1987; MA in Scandinavian Studies, U. Wis., 1990. Multisvc. libr. Concordia Coll., Moorhead, Minn., 1990—91; libr. catalogue serials Rider U., Lawrenceville, NJ, 1991—95; head cataloging Cowles Libr., Drake U., Des Moines, 1995—96; libr. cataloging Olson Libr. Minot State U., ND, 1996—. Translator: (book chpt.) 1986: A Danish-American Family Saga, 1986, (short story) Old Hans Nielsen's Last Christmas, 1987; compiler (bibliography) Danish Utopias in America, 1988; reviewer: (by Niels Peter Stilling and Anne Lisbeth Olsen) A New Life: Danish Emigration to North America as Described by the Emigrants Themselves in Letters, 1842-1946, 1997; translations of article and short stories by Carl Hansen from Danish to English Travel grantee U. Wis., 1989. Mem. ALA, Danish Am. Heritage Soc., Danish Immigrant Mus., Red River Danes, Alpha Mu Gamma. Lutheran. Avocations: reading, singing, theater. Office: Minot State U Gordon B Olson Libr 500 University Ave W Minot ND 58707-0002 Office Phone: 701-858-3859. Business E-Mail: david.iversen@minotstateu.edu.

IVERSEN, LESLIE LARS, pharmaceutical executive; BA, U. Cambridge, 1961, PhD, 1964. V.p. neurosci. rsch. ctr. Merck, Sharpe & Dohme, 1983—95; founder Panos Therapeutics; chmn. ACADIA Pharmaceuticals Inc., San Diego, 1998—. Vis. prof. dept. pharmacology U. Oxford, Oxford, England; dir. Med. Rsch. Coun. Neuropharmacology Unit, Cambridge, England, 1970—83. Contbr. articles over 350 to profl. jours. Fellow: Royal Soc. London; mem.: Nat. Acad. Sci. (assoc.). Office: ACADIA Pharmaceuticals 3911 Sorrento Valley Blvd San Diego CA 92121

IVERSON, ALLEN EZAIL, professional basketball player; b. Hampton, Va., June 7, 1975; s. Ann Iverson; m. Tawana Turner, Aug. 31, 2001; children: Allen II, Tiaura, Isaiah Rahsaan. Student, Georgetown U., 1994—96. Basketball player Phila. 76ers, 1996—. Mem. U.S. Olympic Basketball Team, Athens, 2004. Founder Cross Over Foundation. Named AP First Team All-Am., 1994, NBA Rookie of Month, Apr., Nov., 1997, MVP Schick Rookie game, 1997, Schick Rookie of Yr., 1997, All-Star game MVP, 2001, NBA MVP, 2001; named to first All-NBA Team, 1999, 2001, second All-NBA Team, 2000, 2002, 2003, Eastern Conference All-Star Team, 2000—05. Achievements include 1st player selected in 1996 NBA draft. Avocations: drawing, reading. Office: Philadelphia 76ers First Union Ctr 3601 S Broad St Ste 4 Philadelphia PA 19148-5287

IVERSON, KRISTINE ANN, federal agency administrator; b. Elgin, Ill, Aug. 15, 1953; d. Theodore and Vivian (Schumaker) I. BA, DePauw U., Greencastle, Ind., 1975; MA, George Mason U., 1985; postgrad., Va. Poly. Inst. and State U., 1978. Legis. aide Rep. John B. Conlan, Washington, 1975-76; legis. asst. Sen. Orrin G. Hatch, Washington, 1977-81, sr. policy advisor, 1993-94, legis. dir., 1995—2001; employment policy dir. Senate Labor and Human Resources Com., Washington, 1981-88, minority staff dir., 1988-92; asst. sec. Congl. intergov. affairs US Dept. Labor, Washington, 2001—. Cons. Reagan-Bush Transition, 1980 Pres. The Ron Freeman Chorale, Arlington, Va., 1987-2000; steering com. George Mason U. Tech. Forum, 1983; del. 11th Dist. Rep. Conv., Fairfax, Va., 1992; mem. DePauw U. Alumni Bd., Greencastle, Ind., 1993-99; mem. Bd. of Visitors 2000-03. Recipient Young Alumni award DePauw U., Greencastle, 1993, John C. Stennis Congrl. fellow, 1999-2000. Mem. Alpha Omicron Pi;mem. The Falls Ch. (Episcopal). Avocations: music, sports. Office: US Dept Labor Congressional Intergovt Affairs 200 Constitution Ave NW Washington DC 20210

IVERSON, ONA LEE, retired elementary school educator; b. Kiester, Minn., Jan. 31, 1930; d. George Conrad and Elsie Esther (Bartz) Wittman; m. Roger Duane Iverson, Feb. 10, 1951; children: Joan, Richard, Neal. Student, Gustavus Adolphus Coll., 1948-51; BA, Briar Cliff Coll., 1971. Tchr. Sioux City Community Schs., Iowa, 1971-90. Author plays for upper elem. students. Activist Dem. Party, 1986—; supts. adv. bd. Sioux City Community Schs., 1987-90. Mem. AAUW, NEA (conv. del. 1977, 1986), Iowa State Edn. Assn. (conv. del. 1986, 1987, Sioux City League Women Voters (bd. dirs. 1983-86), Sioux City Edn. Assn. (pres. 1986-87), Interprofl. Inst. Sioux City (pres.), Sierra Club. Lutheran. Avocations: camping, hiking, travel, reading, playing piano. Home: 33354 Grouse Ave Sioux City IA 51108-9780

IVERSON, PETER JAMES, historian, educator; b. Whittier, Calif, Apr. 4, 1944; s. William James and Adelaide Veronica (Schmitt) I.; m. Kaaren Teresa Gonsoulin, Mar. 7, 1983; children: Erika, Jens, Tim, Scott. BA in History, Carleton Coll., 1967; MA in History, U. Wis., 1969, PhD in History, 1975. Vis. asst. prof. Ariz. State U., Tempe, Ariz., 1975-76; from asst. prof to prof. U. Wyo., Laramie, Wyo., 1976-86; coord. divsn. social and behavioral scis. Ariz. State U., Phoenix, 1986-88, prof. history Tempe, Ariz., 1988—, regents prof. history, 2000—. Panelist, reviewer Nat. Endowment Humanities, Washington, 1986—; vis. prof. Carleton Coll., 1991. Author: The Navajos: A Critical Bibliography, 1976, The Navajo Nation, 1981, Carlos Montezuma, 1982, The Navajos, 1990, When Indians Became Cowboys: Native Peoples and Cattle Ranching in the American West, 1994, Barry Goldwater: Native Arizonan, 1997, We Are Still Here: American Indians in the 20th Century, 1998, Riders of the West: Portraits From Indian Rodeo, 1999, Diné: A History of the Navajos, 2002; co-editor: Indians in American History, 1998; editor: The Plains Indians of the 20th Century, 1985, For Our Navajo People: Din+248 Letters, Speeches, and Petitions, 1900-1960, 2002; co-editor: Major Problems in American Indian History, 1994, 2d edit., 2001; assoc. editor The Historian, 1990-95; editl. bd. Pacific Hist. Rev., 1986-88, Jour. Ariz. History, 1987-89, Social Sci. Jour., 1988-96, Montana: The Magazine of Western History, 1993—, Western Historical Quarterly, 2000-02. Acting dir. McNickle Ctr. for History of Am. Indian, Newberry Libr., 1994-95, mem. adv. bd., 1993-2003; bd. dir. Ariz. Humanities Coun., 1993-99; chmn. Wyo. Coun. Humanities, 1981-82; mem. Heard Mus., Phoenix, 1986—, Desert Bot. Garden, Phoenix, 1986—. Recipient Chief Manuelito Appreciation award Navajo Nation, 1984, Disting. Achievement award Carleton Coll. Alumni Assn., 1992, Lifetime Achievement award Am. Indian Hist. Assn., 1999, Him-Dak Eco-Mus. Svc. award Ak-Chin Indian Cmty., 2001, We. Writers Am. Spur award, 2002, Outstanding Doctoral Mentor award ASU Grad. Coll., 2002, Outstanding rsch. award ASU Alumni Assn., 2005; fellow Newberry Libr., Chgo., 1973-74, NEH, 1982-83, 99-2000, Kellogg Found., Battle Creek, Mich., 1982-85, Guggenheim Found., 1999-2000; Disting. Pub. scholar, Ariz. Humanities Coun., 1999. Mem.: Am. Soc. Ethnohistory (coun. 1991—93, chmn. program com. 1994, chmn. prize com. 1987), We. Social Sci. Assn. (pres. 1988—89), Orgn. Am. Historians, We. History Assn. (chmn. prize com. 1991, co-chmn. program com. 1995, coun. 1995—98, pres. elect 2003—04, pres. 2004—05). Office: Ariz State U Dept History Tempe AZ 85287-4302 E-mail: peter.iverson@asu.edu.

IVERSON, ROBERT LOUIS, JR., internist, physician; b. Borden, Ind., Sept. 3, 1944; s. Robert L. and Agnes Maxine (Knight) I.; m. Elsa Maschmeyer, Sept. 3, 1967 (div. 1982); children: Nathan, Kirsten; m. Deborah A. Budd, June 16, 1984 (dec. May 1996); children: Richard, Colin; m. Amy M. Neidert, May 9, 1998. Student, Wabash Coll., 1962-64; BA, Ind. U., 1970, MD, 1974, Intern, 1974-75. Diplomate Am. Bd. Internal Med., diplomate in critical care medicine, Am. Bd. Internal Med. Intern Ind. U., Indpls., 1974-75; resident (internal med.) Methodist Hosp., Indpls, 1975-77; co-dir. critical care, mem. tchg. staff dept. medicine Meth. Hosp., Indpls., 1977-84; fellow in critical care med. U. So. Calif. Shock Rsch. Unit, Ctr. for Critically Ill, L.A., 1977; vis. lectr. U. So. Calif., L.A., 1977; co-dir. critical care, teaching staff, Dept. of Med. Methodist Hosp., Indpls, 1977-84; asst. prof. medicine Wayne State U., Detroit, 1984-96, assoc. prof. clin. medicine, 1996-2000; dir. med. affairs Hutzel Hosp., Detroit, 1996-97, vice chief med. staff, 1995-97, dir. ICU, 1986-2000, chief critical care medicine, 1988-2000; chief critical care svcs. Vassar Bros. Hosp., Poughkeepsie, NY, 2000—02. Mem. bd. Rudgate Neighborhood Assocs., Bloomfield Hills, Mich. 1996-98; mem. physician leadership coun. Detroit Med. Ctr., 1996-2000; participant Ind. Malpractice Rev. Panels, 1981-85; chief med. officer Oakland County (Mich.) Sheriff's Dept., 1997-2000, tactical med. officer Spl. Response Team (SWAT), 1997-2000. Author: (with others) Respiratory Care of the Neurosurgical Patient, 1983, Septic Shock in Critical Care Clinics, 1988; established adminstrv. core curriculum for intensivists Critical Care Clinics, 1993; contbr. abstracts and articles to profl. jours. Med. advisor to Ind. Coun. Emergency Response Teams, 1980—85; mem. Ind. Symphonic Choir, 1970—84, trustee, 1983—84; hon. dep. sheriff Marion County Sheriff's Dept., 1982—84; bd. dirs. City of Bloomfield Hills, Mich., Rudgate Neighborhood Assn., 1996—98; pres. Ashley Homeowners Assn., Inc., 2004—. With U.S. Army, 1964—67, Vietnam. Fellow: ACP, Am. Coll. Chest Physicians; mem.: AMA (Physicians Recognition award 2002—05), Sarasota County Med. Soc., Fla. State Med. Soc., Wayne County Med. Soc. (elected del. 1990—91), Am. Coll. Physician Execs., Soc. Critical Care Medicine, Fla. Sheriffs Assn., Phi Beta Kappa. Avocations: music, shortwave radio communications, sailing, astronomy, astrophotography. Home: 5421 Ashley Pkwy Sarasota FL 34241 Personal E-mail: robertive@msn.com.

IVES, COLTA FELLER, museum curator, educator; b. San Diego, Apr. 5, 1943; m. E. Garrison Ives, June 14, 1966; 1 child, Lucy Barrett. BA, Mills Coll., 1964; MA, Columbia U., 1966. Staff Met. Mus. Art, N.Y.C., 1966—, curator in charge prints and photographs, 1975-93, curator dept. drawings and prints, 1993—; guest scholar J. Paul Getty Mus., 2002. Adj. prof. Columbia U., 1970-87, NYU Inst. Fine Arts, 2001—. Author: The Great Wave, 1974, Art Libraries Assn. award, 1975, The Flight Into Egypt, 1972, R. Rauschenberg Photos In and Out City Limits: New York, 1981, French Prints in the Era of Impressionism and Symbolism, 1988, Toulouse-Lautrec in the Metropolitan Museum of Art, 1996; co-author: The Painterly Print, 1980, Pierre Bonnard: The Graphic Art, 1989, Daumier Drawings, 1992, Goya in the Metropolitan Museum of Art, 1995, The Private Collection of Edgar Degas, 1997 (Best Show of 1997-98 N.Y.C. Mus. Internat. Assn. Art Critics), Romanticism and the School of Nature, 2000, The Lure of the Exotic: Gauguin in New York Collections, 2002, A Private Passion: Winthrop Collection, Harvard University, 2003 (Best Mus. Catalog of 2003 Assn. Art

Mus. Curators). Chmn. grants com. Met. Mus. Art, 1986-87; bd. dirs. Bidwell House, Mass. J. Paul Getty guest scholar, 2002. Mem. Print Coun. Am. (exec. bd. 1975-77, 84-87, v.p. 1989-93), Assn. Art Mus. Curators (exec. bd. 2002-04, bd. dirs. 2003-04), Grolier Club. Office: Met Mus Art Fifth Ave New York NY 10028-0198

IVES, EDWARD DAWSON, folklore educator; b. White Plains, N.Y., Sept. 4, 1925; s. Warren Livingston and Millicent Clarissa (Dawson) I.; m. Barbara Ann Herrel, Sept. 8, 1951; children— Stephen John, Nathaniel Edward, Sarah Ruth AB, Hamilton Coll., 1948; MA, Columbia U., 1950; PhD, Ind. U., 1962; LLD, U. P.E.I., 1986; DLitt, Meml. U., Newfoundland, 1996. Instr. English Ill. Coll., Jacksonville, 1950-53; lectr. CCNY, 1953-54; instr. English U. Maine, Orono, 1955-62, asst. prof., 1962-64, assoc. prof., 1964-69, prof. folklore, 1969-99, chmn. anthropology dept., 1983-89; dir. Northeast Archives Folklore and Oral History, 1971-99, Maine Folklife Ctr., 1992-99, emeritus, 1999—. Author: Larry Gorman: The Man Who Made the Songs, 1964, reprinted 1993, Lawrence Doyle: The Farmer-Poet of Prince Edward Island, 1971, Joe Scott: The Woodsman-Songmaker, 1978, The Tape Recorded Interview, 1980, reprinted 1995, George Magoon and the Down East Game War, 1988, reprinted 1993, Folksongs of New Brunswick, 1989; (with Bruce Jackson) The World Observed, 1996, The Bonny Earl of Murray, 1997, Drive Dull Care Away, 1999. Served with USMC, 1943-46 Guggenheim fellow, 1965—66. Fellow Am. Folklore Soc.; mem. Oral History Assn. Home: 1392 River Rd Bucksport ME 04416-9708 Office Phone: 207-825-3079. E-mail: sandy_ives@umit.maine.edu.

IVES, H. BRYAN, III, lawyer; b. Charlotte, NC, Sept. 13, 1955; BS in Acctg. with honors, Univ. NC, Chapel Hill, 1977, JD with high honors, 1980. Bar: NC 1980. Ptnr., group leader, capital mkts. practice Alston & Bird LLP, Charlotte, NC. Articles editor NC Law Rev. Mem.: Am. Coll. Tax Counsel, Order of Coif. Office: Alston & Bird LLP Ste 4000 Bank of Am Plz 101 S Tryon St Charlotte NC 28280-4000 Office Phone: 704-444-1002. Office Fax: 704-444-1111. Business E-Mail: bives@alston.com.

IVES, J. ATWOOD, financial executive; b. Atlanta, May 1, 1936; s. Stephen Bradshaw and Ellen (Atwood) I.; m. Elizabeth Saalfield; children: Ian, Anna, Benjamin. BA in Econs., Yale U., 1959; MBA, Stanford U., 1961; AMP, Harvard U., 1975. CPA, Calif. Acct. Price, Waterhouse & Co., San Francisco, 1961-64; fin. analyst Textron, Inc., Providence, 1964-66; ptnr., v.p. Paine Webber Jackson & Curtis, 1966-74; dir. Gen. Cinema Corp., Chestnut Hill, Mass., 1970-92, sr. v.p. fin., CFO, 1974-83, exec. v.p., CFO, 1983-84, vice-chmn., CFO, 1985-91, mem. office of chmn., 1983-91; vice-chmn., CFO The Neiman Marcus Group, Inc., 1987-91, also bd. dirs.; chmn., CEO Eastern Enterprises, 1991-2000; dir. Keyspan Corp., 2000—04. Trustee Ea. Enterprises, Weston, Mass., 1989-2000; ind. chmn. trustees 97 mut. funds advised by Mass. Fin. Svcs. Co., 1992-, trustee, 2004-; corp. adv. bd. Carroll Sch. of Mgmt., Boston Coll. Trustee Mus. Fine Arts, Boston; mem. bd. overseers WGBH Edn. Found.; vice chmn. Becon Hill Village. With U.S. Army, 1961-62. Recipient award Haskins and Sells Found., 1961 Home: 17 W Cedar St Boston MA 02108-1211 Office Phone: 617-723-7069.

IVES, RICHARD DEAN, music educator; b. Hays, Kans., Oct. 3, 1953; s. Max Elmer and LeVonne Lee Ives; m. Janet Elaine Huff, Aug. 2, 1975; children: Tyler Dean, Amber Elaine. BA in Music Edn., FHSU, Hays, 1982, MA in Music Edn., 1988. Instrumental music instr. Fort Larned USD 495, Larned, Kans., 1982—2004. Pres. SW Dist. Kans. Music Educator's Assn., Dodge City, 1998—2000, pres., Wichita, 2003—05. Elder 1st Christian Ch., Larned, 1990—2003. Served USMC, 1975—78, Okinawa. Mem.: NEA, KLAJE (exec. sec.), MENC (state pres.), Phi Beta Mu. Avocations: jazz, reading, golf, sports. Home: 431 S Second St Clearwater KS 67026 E-mail: rdives1@yahoo.com.

IVES, SAMUEL CLIFTON, minister; b. Farmington, Maine, Nov. 13, 1937; s. Alfred H. and Alice (Smith) I.; m. Jane Petherbridge, June 6, 1959; children: Bonnie, Stephen, Jonathan. BA, U. Maine, 1960; MDiv, Boston U., 1963, D in Ministry, 1983. Pastor Cape Elizabeth (Maine) United Meth. Ch., 1962-68, First United Meth. Ch., Bangor, Maine, 1968-73; dir. Maine Conf. Coun. on Ministries, Winthrop, Maine, 1973-77; sr. pastor Waterville (Maine) United Meth. Ch., 1977-86; dist. supt. So. Dist. United Meth. Ch., Portland, Maine, 1986-92; elected bishop United Meth. Ch., assigned to W.Va., Charleston, 1992—2004; ret., 2004. Del. Gen. Conf. United Meth. Ch., 1972, 76, 80, 84, 88, 92; exec. com. Maine Coun. Chs., 1981-92; pres. Appalachian Devel. com., 1996-2000; v.p. W.Va. Coun. of Chs., 1996-2000. Mem. Gen. Bd. Discipleship United Meth. Ch., 1984-92, pres. Gen. Commn. on Religion and Race, 1996-2000, mem. coun. bishops; pres. Gen. Bd. Ch. and Soc., 2000-04. Mem. Assn. Couples for Marriage Enrichment (cert. leader and trainer 1979—). Home: 10 Quaker Lane Portland ME 04103

IVESTER, M. DOUGLAS (MELVIN DOUGLAS IVESTER), retired beverage company executive; b. New Holland, Ga., Mar. 26, 1947; s. Howard Edward and Ada Mae (Pass) Ivester; m. Victoria Kay Grindle, Mar. 20, 1969. BBA cum laude, U. Ga., 1969. Acct. Ernst & Ernst, Altanta, 1969—75; mgr. Ernst & Whinney, Atlanta, 1975—79; asst. contr., dir. corp. auditing The Coca-Cola Co., Atlanta, 1979—91, v.p., contr., 1981—83, sr. v.p. fin., 1983—84, sr. v.p., CFO, 1985—89; pres. European Cmty. Group, 1980—90, Coca-Cola USA, 1990—91, Coca-Cola N.Am. Group, 1991—93, prin. oper. officer, 1993—94, pres., COO, 1994—97, also bd. dirs., chmn., CEO, 1997—2000, ret., 2000; pres. Deer Run Investments LLC, 2001—. Bd. dirs. Georgia Pacific Corp., Sun Trust, Inc., S One Corp.; trustee, dir. U. Ga. Found.; bd. trustees Emory U., 1998—.

IVEY, ANDI, special education educator; d. Costas and Antoinette Zacharoudis; m. R. Mike Ivey, Sept. 29, 1973; children: Tonya Michelle, Brett Jason. BS in Elem. and Spl. Edn., No. Ariz. U., 1973. Ednl. profl. developer. cons. Ivey League, Kailua, Hawaii, 1996—; spl. educator Scottsdale Unified Schs., Ariz., 1983—99. Acad. dean, dept. chairperson Desert Mountain H.S., Scottsdale, 1995—99; dist. profl. developer Scottsdale Unified Schs., 1996—99; team leader, spl. edn. rep. Mohave Mid. Sch., Scottsdale, 1990—95; trainer of trainers - Project Adapt Dept. Edn. State of Ariz., Phoenix, 1994—98, mem. creating equity and access com. Dept. Edn., 1995—95. Named Tchr. of the Yr., Phi Delta Kappa Scottsdale Chpt., 1997, Tchr. of the Yr. - State of Ariz., Learning Disabilities Assn. of Ariz., 1993. Mem.: ASCD, Coun. for Exceptional Children, Phi Delta Kappa (Scottsdale Chpt. Tchr. of the Yr. 1997). Avocations: scuba diving, walking on the beach, swimming, golf, travel. Home and Office: 41 Palione Pl Kailua HI 96734 Personal E-mail: iveyleague@hawaii.rr.com.

IVEY, ARTIS See COOLIO

IVEY, ELIZABETH S., retired physicist, educator; b. Schenectady, NY, Apr. 21, 1935; married, 1957 (div.), remarried, 1982; 5 children. BS in Physics, Simmons Coll., 1957; MA in Tchg., Harvard U., 1959; PhD in Mech. Engring. Acoustics, U. Mass., 1976. Prof. physics Simmons Coll., 1958-59, Bucknell U., 1960-63, Colo. State U., Ft. Collins, 1964-68, assoc. dean faculty, 1982-85, Louise Wolff Kahn prof., from 1985; prof. physics Smith Coll., 1969-90, chmn. dept. physics, 1983-90; provost Macalester Coll., St. Paul, 1990-95, U. Hartford, West Hartford, Conn., 1995-2000, provost emerita, 2000—. Vis. prof. Yale U., 1982. Bd. dirs. Minn. Inst. Talented Youth, 1990-95, World Press Inst., 1990-93, St. Paul Area United Way, 1990-95, Assn. Women Sci., 2001—; bd. trustees Hartford Coll. Women, 1995—, Mitchell Coll. 2003-; corporator Simmons Coll., 2000—. Recipient Woman Engr. award Soc. Women Engrs., 1988. Fellow AAAS; mem. Acoustical Soc. Am., Am. Assn. Physics Tchrs., Assn. Women in Sci. (pres.-elect 2003-04, pres. 2004-06). E-mail: ivey@hartford.edu.

IVEY, JAMES FREDERICK, JR., health facility administrator, physician; b. Orlando, Florida, Apr. 30, 1939; s. James Frederick and Naomi Nell (Milner) I.; m. Nancy Joan Martin, Aug. 5, 1961 (dec. July 2004); children: Mary Nell, James Thomas, John Mark, Samuel Svc., Daniel Dominic; m. Pamela Jean Monroe, Aug. 6, 2005. BS in Biology, Duke U., U. Fla., 1960; MD, Emory Univ., 1964. Diplomate Am. Bd. Family Practice with cert. of added qualifications in geriatrics; FAA sr. aero. med. examiner. Intern Duval Med. Ctr., Jacksonville, Fla., 1964-65; resident Emory U./VA Hosp., Atlanta, 1965-66; physician Clermont, Fla., 1968-69; pvt. practice Palmer, Alaska, 1969-74; owner, physician Valley Med. Ctr., Inc., Palmer, Ala., 1974-91; staff physician Lakeside Med. Ctr. and Family Care, Lakeland, Fla., 1991-92; pvt. practice Lakeland, Fla., 1992-95; staff physician Polk Gen. Hosp., Bartow, Fla., 1995-96, Family First Med. Ctr., Gainesville, Fla., 1996; med. dir. Trenton Med. Ctr., Fla., 1996—2001; physician for jails Gilchrist, Levy, and Dixie counties, Fla., 2001—; physician Alachua Regional Juvenile Detention Ctr., Fla., 2001—, Marion Regional Juvenile Detention Ctr., Fla., 2001—05; med. authority First Step Adolescent Care, Gainesville, Fla., 2003—; med. staff Trenton Med. Ctr., Fla., 2005—, Urgent Care Ctr. of Gainesville, Fla., 2005—. Med. dir. Palmer Pioneer Home, Ala., 1979—91, Nugens Ranch, Wasilla, Ala., 1983—91, Starting Point, Inc., Wasilla, Ala., 1989—91, Arbors at Lakeland Nursing Home, Lakeland, Fla., 1992—96; courtesy clin. asst. prof. dept. cmty. health and family medicine U. Fla. Sch. Medicine. Former med. dir., co-founder Mat-Su Coun. Prevention of Alcoholism and Drug Abuse, Wasilla, Alaska, past chmn. bd. dirs.; elder and lay pastor United Presbyn. Ch., USA. Capt. USAF, 1966—68. Mem. Am. Acad. Family Physicians (pres. Alaska chpt. 1976); Christian Med. and Dental Soc.; Alpha Tau Omega, Phi Kappa Phi, Phi Chi; mem. Trinty United Meth. Ch. Republican. Avocations: golf, music, cosmology, history, philosophy. Home: 6711 NW 38th Ter Gainesville FL 32653 Office: Trenton Med Ctr Inc PO Box 640 911 S Main St Trenton FL 32693-3239 Office Phone: 352-463-2374. Personal E-mail: jivey1@cox.net.

IVEY, KAY ELLEN, state official; b. Repton, Ala., Oct. 15, 1944; d. Boardman Nettles and Barbara Elizabeth Ivey. BS, Auburn U., 1967; cert. in mktg., U. Colo., 1975; cert. in banking, U. South Ala.; cert. in Strategic Leadership for State Execs., Duke U., 1989. Tchr., coach forensics Rio Linda (Calif.) High Sch., 1968-69; asst. v.p. Mchts. Nat. Bank, Mobile, Ala., 1970-79; cabinet officer Office of the Gov., State of Ala., Montgomery, 1979-81; reading clk. Ala. Ho. Reps., 1981-82; exec. v.p. St. Margaret's Hosp. Found., 1982-85; dir. govt. affairs Ala. Commn. Higher Edn., 1985—98; treas. State of Ala., 2003—. Owner, cons. Ivey Enterprises, Montgomery, 1982—; speaker in field. Editor (audio-visual presentation) What Price Freedom (award of Excellence), 1976, St. Margaret's Hosp. Heart tabloid, 1983. Mem. adv. bd. Sch. Bus. Auburn U., 1980-83; candidate Ala. State Auditor, 1982; sec. Ala. div. Am. Cancer Soc., 1985—; bd. dirs. Ala. Girl's State Sch., 1983-85, Stetson Hoedown Rodeo Queen's Pageant, Montgomery, 1986—; bd. trustees Sheriff's Boys and Girls Ranches. Mem. Indsl. Developers Ala., Young Men's Bus. Orgn., Pub. Relations Council Ala. (bd. dirs. 1976-82), DAR (state chmn. 1985-86), Alpha Gamma Delta (disting. citizen award 1986). Republican. Presbyterian. Avocations: horseback riding, public speaking. Office: State Treasurers Office Rm S-106 State Capitol Bldg Montgomery AL 36130

IVEY, MONA KAY, secondary school educator, educational association administrator, consultant; b. Cullman, Ala., Aug. 2, 1949; d. James Monroe and Onvia Alvatine (Rodgers) Caldwell; m. Ronnie Gene Higdon (div.); children: Kevin Paul, Tanya Ramona. BS, U. Ala., Tuscaloosa, Ala., 1971; MA, U. Ala., Birmingham, Ala., 1975, EdD, 1979. Cert. tchr. State Dept. Edn., Ala. Tchr. reading Cold Springs Elem. Sch., Cullman, Ala., 1972—73; tchr. Good Hope Elem. Sch., Cullman, 1973—77, West Point Elem. Sch., Cullman, 1977—97, West Point H.S., Cullman, 1997—; prin., owner Creative Thinking, Cullman. Pronouncer Cullman (Ala.) County Spelling Bee, 1983—2003; ednl. adv. Congl. Youth Leadership Coun., 2001—05. Cover illustrator: Called To Live, 2002. Vol. Hospice, Cullman, 1991—94; missionary Seventh St. Bapt. Ch., Cullman, 2000—04, St. Johns Evang. Ch., Cullman, 2005. Nominee Ret. Tchr. of Yr. award, Cullman (Ala.) County C. of C., 2002; named Elem. Tchr. of Yr., West Point Elem. Sch., 1995; recipient Outstanding Profl. Achievement Commendation award, Sen. Ala., 2002. Mem.: NEA, Ala. Edn. Assn., Cullman (Ala.) County Edn. Assn. (sec. bd. dirs. 1977—87). Republican. Bapt. Avocations: art, travel, gardening. Home: 1605 Co Rd 1246 Cullman AL 35057 Office: West Point High Sch 4314 Co Rd 1141 Cullman AL 35057

IVEY, SUSAN M., tobacco company executive; b. Schenectady, NY, Oct. 31, 1958; m. Trevor Ivey, 1997. BS, U. Fla., Gainesville, 1980; MBA, Bellarmine U., 1987. Trade mktg. repr. Brown & Williamson Tobacco Corp., 1981—83, dist. sales mgr., 1983, dir. mktg. Far East, head internat. brands U.K. London, 1990—94, dir. mktg. British Am. Tobacco Hong Kong, 1994—96, mgr. internat. brands London, 1996—99, sr. v.p. mktg. Louisville, 1999—2000, pres., CEO, 2000—04, Reynolds American Inc., Winston-Salem, NC, 2004—. Office: Reynolds American Inc 401 N Main St Winston Salem NC 27101*

IVEY, THOMAS J., lawyer; b. Leeds, Yorkshire, United Kingdom, 1967; BA cum laude, UCLA, 1989; JD, U. Calif. Boalt Hall Sch. Law, 1992. Bar: Calif. 1993. Ptnr. Skadden, Arps, Slate, Meagher & Flom LLP. Co-chair PLI's seminar on Vulture Capital and Corporate Restructuring, 2002, PLI's seminar on Current Trends in Convertible Debt, 2003. Office: Skadden 525 University Avenue Suite 1100 Palo Alto CA 94301

IVEY, TOM DEXTER, cardiac surgeon; b. Dodgeville, Wis., May 22, 1945; m. Marianne Ivey; children: Bert, Brook. BS, U. Wis., 1967, postgrad., 1967-68, MD with honors, 1970. Acting instr. surgery U. Wash. Sch. Medicine, Seattle, 1975-77, asst. prof. divsn. cardiothoracic surgery, 1977-81, assoc. prof. dept. surgery, 1982-87, chief divsn. cardiothoracic surgery, 1982-88, prof. divsn. cardiothoracic surgery, 1987; prof. surgery U. Cin., 1988—. Attending in cardiac surgery Univ. Hosp.-Harborview and Children's Hosp., Seattle, 1977-88; chief divsn. thoracic and cardiovasc. surgery U. Cin. Hosp., 1988—; trustee Assoc. Univ Physicians, Seattle, 1985. Contbr. chpts. to books. Served with USPHS, 1971-75. Mem. Alpha Omega Alpha, Phi Eta Sigma, Phi Kappa Phi. Office: 2123 Auburn Ave Ste 238 Cincinnati OH 45219-2906

IVEZAJ, VIKTOR N., auditor, consultant; b. Weissenburg, Germany, Jan. 24, 1972; came to U.S., 1973; s. Nikolla and Pashka Ivezaj. BA, Oakland U., 1994; MA, U. Detroit-Mercy, 1998; postgrad., Wayne State U., 1999—. Jud. clk. Wayne County Cir. Ct., Detroit, 1993; dir. cmty. svc. Oakland County Cir. Ct., Pontiac, Mich., 1993-94; law clk. Driggers Schultz & Herbst, P.C., Troy, Mich., 1994-97, Kupelian Ormond & Magy, P.C., Southfield, Mich., 1997-99; recruiter U.S. Dept. Commerce, Sterling Heights, Mich., 1998-99; cons., auditor Perry Johnson, Inc., Southfield, 1999—2002; adj. prof. polit. sci. Baker Coll., Clinton Twp., Mich., 2003—. Lectr., mem. Inter-Univ. Ctr., Dubrovnik, Croatia, 2000-01. Mem. internat. editl. bd. Internat. Jour. Albanian Studies, 1998. Mem.: Am. Polit. Sci. Assn., Acad. Polit. Sci., Automotive Industry Action Group, Phi Beta Delta. Democrat. Roman Catholic. Avocations: collecting literature novels, wine collecting, physical fitness, tutoring in civic literacy. E-mail: vivezaj@vniglobal.com.

IVEZIC, ZELJKO, physicist, researcher; b. Sarajevo, Bosnia, Croatia, Apr. 18, 1965; came to U.S., 1991; s. Dragan and Marija (Jurican) I.; m. Pamela Elizabeth Thies, Dec. 13, 1993. BS in Mech. Engring., U. Zagreb, Croatia, 1990, BS in Physics, 1991; PhD in Physics, U. Ky., 1995. Rschr. U. Zagreb, Croatia, 1990; rsch. asst. U. Ky., Lexington, 1991—; rschr. dept. astrophys. sci. Princeton (N.J.) U., 1996—. Contbr. articles to Astronomy and Astrophysics, The Astrophys. Jour., Internat. Jour. of Heat and Mass Transfer, Jour. of Quantitative Spectroscopy and Heat Transfer. Mem. Am. Phys. Soc., Am. Astron. Soc., Croatian Astron. Soc. Roman Catholic. Home: 3357 Commodore Dr Apt 450 Lexington KY 40502-3639 Office: U Ky Dept Physics & Astronomy Dept Astrophys Sci 177 Cp Bldg Lexington KY 40506-0001

IVIE, EVAN LEON, computer science educator; b. American Fork, UT, May 15, 1931; s. Horace Leon and Ruth (Ashby) Ivie; m. Betty Jo Beck, Mar. 29, 1957; children: Dynette, Mark, Joseph, Robert, Ann, Rebecca, John, James, Mette, Emily, Peter. BS, BES, Brigham Young U., 1956; MS, Stanford U., 1957; PhD, MIT, 1966. Instr. MIT, Cambridge, 1960—66; mem. tech. staff Bell Labs., Murray Hill, NJ, 1966—79; prof. computer sci. Brigham Young U., Provo, Utah, 1979—; pres. Ivie Computer Corp., Provo, 1979—. Expert witness on computers for 12 lawsuits, 1983—; instr., dir. Joseph Smith Acad., Ill., 2002—. Leader Boy Scouts Am., 1954—83; mem. Warren Sch. Bd., NJ, 1975—78; developer Pioneer Ancestral Past, Utah Sesquicentennial, 1997. 1st lt. USAF, 1957—60. Recipient Fulbright scholarship, Kiev Poly. Inst., Ukraine, 1992—93; fellow, Stanford U., 1956—57. Mem.: IEEE (sr.), Assn. Computing Machinery. Republican. Mem. Lds Ch. Achievements include invention of Data Base Computers, 1972; Programmer's Workbench, 1975; Electronic Yellow pages, 1978; Reader's Workbench, 1984. Office: Joseph Smith Acad 165 Wells St Box 215 Nauvoo IL 62354 Office Phone: 217-453-2860 x 400. Business E-Mail: evan@cs.byu.edu, evan@ivies.org.

IVINS, MOLLY, columnist, writer; b. Texas, 1944; d. Jim and Margo I. BA, Smith Coll., 1966; postgrad., Inst. Polit. Sci., 1966; MA in Journalism, Columbia U., Paris, 1967. Former reporter The Houston Chronicle, The Mpls. Star Tribune, 1964-1976; reporter The Texas Observer, Austin, 1970-76, The New York Times, 1976-82, Rocky Mountain bur. chief Denver, 1976-82; former columnist The Dallas Times Herald, 1982-91; columnist Fort Worth Star-Telegram, 1992—2001; syndicated columnist Creators Syndicate, LA, 2001—. Author: Molly Ivins Can't Say That, Can She?, 1991, Nothin' But Good Times Ahead, 1993, You Got to Dance with Them What Brung You, 1998, Shrub, 2000, Bushwhacked, 2003, Who Let the Dogs In?, 2004; contbr. to periodicals including The Nation, N.Y. Times Book Rev., Mother Jones, Ms., Progressive, others. Office: Creators Syndicate 5777 W Century Blvd Los Angeles CA 90045

IVORY, JAMES FRANCIS, film director; b. Berkeley, Calif., June 7, 1928; s. Edward Patrick and Hallie Millicent (DeLoney) Ivory. BFA, U. Oreg., 1951; MA in Cinema, U. So. Calif., 1957. Ptnr. Merchant Ivory Prodns., N.Y.C., 1963—. Dir.: (films) Venice: Theme and Variations, 1957, The Sword and the Flute, 1959, The Householder, 1963, The Delhi Way, 1964, Shakespeare Wallah, 1965, The Guru, 1969, Bombay Talkie, 1970, Adventures of a Brown Man in Search of Civilization, 1971, Savages, 1972, Autobiography of a Princess, 1975, The Wild Party, 1975, Roseland, 1977, Hullabaloo over Georgie and Bonnie's Pictures, 1978, The Five Forty Eight, 1979, The Europeans, 1979, Jane Austen in Manhattan, 1980, Quartet, 1981, Heat and Dust, 1983, The Bostonians, 1984, A Room with a View, 1986 (Acad. Award nominee for best dir.), Maurice, 1987 (Silver Lion shared award with Ermanno Olmi for best dir. Venice Film Festival, 1987), Slaves of New York, 1989, Mr. and Mrs. Bridge, 1990, Howards End, 1992 (Acad. Award nominee for best dir., Cannes Internat. Film Festival 45th Anniversary Prize), The Remains of the Day, 1993 (Academy award nominee, Best dir., 1993), Jefferson in Paris, 1995, Surviving Picasso, 1996; (sets and costumes) Handel's Apollo e Dafne Maggio Musicale, Florence, 1997; dir.: (films) A Soldier's Daughter Never Cries, 1998, The Golden Bowl, 2000, Le Divorce, 2003; contbr. articles to profl. jours.; dir.: (films) The White Countess, 2005. Cpl. U.S. Army, 1953—55. Recipient Comdr. des Arts et Lettres (France), 1996, 1996; Guggenheim fellow, 1973. Mem.: Dirs. Guild Am. (D.W. Griffith award 1995). Democrat. Roman Catholic. Office: Merchant Ivory Prodns 250 W 57th St Ste 1824/5 New York NY 10107-1913 E-mail: contact@merchantivory.com.

IVORY, SHIRLEY CLARK, information scientist, educator; b. Memphis, Nov. 18, 1948; 1 child from previous marriage, Carlton Clark. AS, Sinclair C.C., Dayton, Ohio, 1987; BS in Edn., U. Dayton, 1992; EdM, Wright State U., Dayton, Ohio, 1995; post grad., U. Cin. Cert. profl. Microsoft Corp.; lic. marriage officiant State of Ohio. Edn. analyst NCR Corp., Dayton, Ohio; prof. Sinclair C.C. Recipient Outstanding Svc. award, Black Data Processing Profls., 2002, 10 Yr. Svc. award, Sinclair C.C., 2002. Mem.: Delta Kappa Gamma (2d v.p., scholarship grantee 2004—). Avocations: movies, reading, travel. Home: PO Box 2721 Dayton OH 45401-2721 Office: Sinclair CC 444 W Third St Dayton OH 45402

IVRA, AUGUSTINE LAFRANCHINIAX, pre-school educator; b. Memphis, Tenn., July 24, 1948; s. A J Stuckey and Rosie Elizabeth Weston; children: Terris, Thomas, Arvell. BA, Calif. State Dominguez Hills, 1978. Tchr. Los Angeles Unified Sch. Dist., 1970—. Head tchr. Parent Adv. Com., Los Angeles, 1993—. Mem. Block Club, 1982—. Mem.: United Teachers Los Angeles. Avocations: travel, gardening, antiques.

IVRY, ALFRED LYON, philosophy educator, historian; b. Bklyn., Jan. 14, 1935; s. Morris and Belle (Malamud) I.; m. Joann Saltzman, June 15, 1958; children: Rebecca, Jonathan, Sara Beth, Jessica. BA, Bklyn. Coll., 1957; MA, Brandeis U., 1958, PhD, 1963; D.Phil., Oxford (Eng.) U., 1971. From asst. prof. to assoc. prof. Cornell U., Ithaca, N.Y., 1967-74; prof. Ohio State U., Columbus, 1974-76; prof. Sch. Near Eastern and Judaic Studies Brandeis U., Waltham, Mass., 1976-89, Walter S. Hilborn prof. Mid. Eastern Studies, 1977-89; Skirball prof. Hebrew and Judaic studies NYU, N.Y.C., 1989—, prof. Mid. East studies, 1989—. Co-chmn. Colloquium in Medieval Philosophy, Boston, 1977-81, 84-89; chmn. Colloquium in Medieval Philosophy NYU, 1990-2000; dir. NYU Medieval and Renaissance Ctr., 2002-04. Mem. editl. bd. Univ. Press of New Eng., 1982, 84, 86; editor: (translator) Al-Kindi's Metaphysics, 1974, Moses of Narbonne: Perfection of the Soul, 1977, Alexander Altmann: The Meaning of Jewish Existence, 1991, Averroes' Middle Commentary on Aristotles De anima, 1994, English-Arabic edit., 2002, medieval Hebrew edit., 2003. Trustee Boston Hebrew Coll., 1981-87, adj. prof., 1983-90. Fulbright fellow, 1963-65, 72, 1982-83; grantee NEH, 1978-79, 80-81 Fellow Am. Oriental Soc., Am. Philos. Assn., Assn. for Jewish Studies (bd. dirs. 1971-74), Medieval Acad. Am., Soc. Medieval and Renaissance Philosophy (bd. dirs. 1985-90, v.p. 1993-94, pres. 1995-96), Am. Acad. for Jewish Rsch. (bd. dirs. 1989-2000). Jewish.

IVY, BENJAMIN FRANKLIN, III, financial and real estate investment advisor; b. Bremerton, Wash., May 18, 1936; s. Edward Byron Ivy and Ada Josephine (Anderson) Steele; m. Karen Yvonne Thompson, July 14, 1961 (div. June 1979); children: Britt Annemarie Ivy, Zenah Blair; m. Emily Cecile Rawlins, Apr. 18, 1982 (div. June 1992); m. Catherine Elaine Bracken, May 23, 2000. BME, Cornell U., 1959; MBA, Stanford U., 1961. CFP. Purchasing agent U. Calif., Berkeley, 1960-62; contract adminstr. Lockheed Missiles and Space div., Sunnyvale, Calif., 1962-64; asst. to pres. Tridea subsidiary McDonnell Douglas, Pasadena, Calif., 1964-68; v.p. Mitchum, Jones & Templeton, Inc., Palo Alto, Calif., 1968-74, Paine Webber, Palo Alto, 1974; pres. Morgan Investment Svcs., Inc., Palo Alto, 1974-84; v.p. Morgan, Olmstead, Kennedy & Gardner, Inc., 1974-84; pres., chmn. Ivy Fin. Enterprises, Inc., Palo Alto, 1984—, Ivy Fin. Svcs., Palo Alto. V.p. and registered prin. Assoc. Group, Inc. subs. Pacific Life, L.A., 1984—, dir., 1994-98, Cert. Fin. Planner, 1989—. Founder, former dir. Found. to Eliminate the Nat. Debt, Palo Alto, 1992. Mem. Internat. Assn. Fin. Planners (charter, bd. dirs. 1972-73), Pacific Exch. (assoc.), Cornell U. Alumni Assn., Stanford Alumni Assn. (life), Stanford Bus. Sch. Alumni Assn. (life), Sharon Heights Golf and Country Club, Masons, Elks, Kappa Sigma. Avocations: golf, tennis, poetry, opera, international travel, running. Office: Ivy Fin Enterprises Inc 525 University Ave Fl 6 Palo Alto CA 94301-1903 Office Phone: 650-328-3800.

IVY, CONWAY GAYLE, paint company executive; b. Houston, July 8, 1941; s. John Smith and Caro (Gayle) I.; m. Diane Ellen Cole, May 25, 1973; children: Brice McPherson, Elizabeth Cole. Student, U. Chgo., 1959-62, MBA, 1968; MA in Econs., 1972, postgrad., 1973-74; BS in Natural Scis., Shimer Coll., 1964; postgrad., U. Tex., 1964-65. Geol. asst. John S. Ivy, Houston, 1965-72; securities analyst Halsey Stuart & Co. and successor Bache & Co., Chgo., 1974-75; dir. corp. planning Gould Inc., Rolling Meadows, Ill., 1975-79; v.p. corp. planning and devel. Sherwin-Williams Co., Cleve., 1979-88; v.p., treas., 1989-92; v.p. corp. planning and devel., 1992—. Pres. Ivy Minerals Inc., Boise, Idaho, 1978—. Author numerous analytincal reports on brokerage industry. Trustee Michelson-Morley Centennial Celebration, 1987, Cleve. Inst. Music, 1983-94, treas., 1987-90, vice chmn., 1990-94.

Mem. Am. Econs. Assn., Soc. Mining and Metallurgy and Exploration, am. Inst. Mining Engrs., Houston Club, Phi Gamma Delta. Republican. Office: 101 Prospect Ave NW Cleveland OH 44115-1093

IVY, JOHN L., medical educator, researcher; b. Portsmouth, Va., Dec. 26, 1946; BS in Phys. Edn., Old Dominion U., 1970; MA in Exercise Physiology, U. Md., 1974, PhD in Exercise Physiology, 1976. Tchr. phys. edn. and sci. Thomas Eaton Jr. H.S., Hampton, Va., 1970; biology and physiology tchr., asst. football coach, head golf coach Kecoughtan H.S., Hampton, Va., 1971—73; asst. prof. biokinetics rsch. lab. dept. phys. edn. Temple U., Phila., 1976—77; rsch. assoc. Human Performance Lab., Ball State U., Muncie, Ind., 1976—77; postdoctoral fellow dept. preventive medicine Washington U. Sch. Medicine, St. Louis, 1978—80; asst. prof. dept. phys. edn. Coll. Health and Sch. Medicine dept. pharmacology U. S.C., Columbia, 1980—82; asst. prof. dept. kinesiology and health edn. Coll. Edn. U. Tex., Austin, 1982—84, assoc. prof. dept. kinesiology and health edn. Coll. Edn., 1984—89, prof., dir. exercise scis. labs. dept. kinesiology and health edn. Coll. Edn. and divsn. pharmacology Coll. Pharmacy, 1989—, Margie Gurley Seay Centennial prof., 1998—, chmn. dept. kinesiology and health edn., 1999—. Cons. clin. diabetes and nutrition sect. NIH, Phoenix, 1985—87; cons. com. mil. nutrition rsch. U.S. Army, 1987—88; mem. adv. bd. performance team Women's Athletic Dept. U. Tex., 1988—94; cons. Sports and Cardiovasc. Nutritionists, 1989—92, outside mem. long range planning com., 1989—90; cons. Shaklee U.S., Inc., 1988—93; mem. adv. bd. Q Health Club, 1994—96; cons. U.S. Olympic Com. Sports Medicine com. nutrition, 1992—94; mem. com. mil. nutrition and rsch. rev. panel NAS, 1995—99. Contbr. articles to profl. jours., chapters to books; jour. reviewer Am. Jour. Physiology, Endocrinology and Metabolism, 1993—2001, Jour. Optimal Nutrition, 1993—96, Diabetes, 1987—88, Internat. Jour. Sports Nutrition, 1995—, sect. editor physiology Rsch. Quar. for Exercise and Sport, 1988—91, mem. editl. bd. Medicine and Sci. in Sports and Exercise, 1987—2001, Am. Jour. Physiology, 1995—2001, Internat. Jour. Sport Nutrition, 1997—, reviewer Jour. Applied Physiology, Am. Jour. Physiology, Medicine and Sci. in Sports and Exercise, Internat. Jour. of Sports Medicine, Rsch. Quar., Am. Jour. Clin. Nutrition, Diabetes, Jour. Clin. Investiagation, Internat. Jour. Sports Nutrition, presenter in field. Recipient Nat. Rsch. Svc. award, NIH, 1978—80; grantee, Tex. Heart Assn., Ross Products, Pfizer, Inc., Shaklee U.S., Inc., U.S. Olympic Rsch. Com. Fellow: Am. Acad. Kinesiology Phys. Edn., Am. Coll. Sports Medicine (midwest chpt. 1977—79, southeast chpt. 1980—82, Tex. chpt. bd. trustees 1985—86, bd. trustees rep. for basic and applied sci. 1986—89, ambassador 1986—90, Tex. chpt. exec. dir. 1986—91, organizer, chair symosium diabetes and exercise I regulation of muscle 1988, organizer, chair symposium diabetes and exercise I regulation of muscl 1988, mem. rsch. rev. com. 1991—95, Tex. chpt. bd. trustees 1992—95); mem.: Am. Soc. Clin. Nutrition, Inc., Am. Inst. Nutrition, Am. Diabetes Assn. (mem. nutrition scis. and metabolism coun. 1991—93, mem. exercise coun. 1991—93, sec. exercise coun. 1991—93, program chair exercise coun. 1993, organizer, chair symposium role of exercise and phys. activity in the 1992, organizer, chair symposium exercise through the ages 1994, grantee 1996, rsch. award 1996), Am. Physiol. Soc., Sigma Xi, Phi Epsilon Kappa. Office: U Tex Dept Kinesiology 822 E BEL Austin TX 78712 E-mail: johnivy@mail.utexas.edu.

IVY, ROBERT ADAMS, JR., architect, editor-in-chief; b. Columbus, Miss. m. Holly Ivy; children: Virginia Edmunds, Robert Adams, Benjamin Ledyard. BA cum laude, U. South, 1969; MArch, Tulane U., 1976. Consulting arch., Columbus, 1981-96; editor-in-chief Archtl. Record Mag., N.Y.C., 1996—; editl. dir., v.p. McGraw-Hill Constrn. Publs. Author: Fay Jones: Architect, 1991; editor Architecture South mag., 1993-96; prodr., screenwriter (documentary film) 1,000 Homes. Pres. Greater Columbus, 1987-89; co-founder Greater Columbus Learning Ctr., Inc.; trustee Columbus-Lowndes Libr., 1984—, chmn., 1987, 91; vestry mem. St. Paul's Episcopal Ch., Columbus, 1985-87; adv. bd. The Dwelling Pl., Ctr. for So. Culture, 1993—; commr. U.S. Pavilion Biennale di Venezia, 2002, 04. Lt. USNR, 1970-73. Fellow AIA (bd. dirs. 1993-96), Philippine Inst. Archs.; mem. Am. Architecture Found. (bd. regents 1993-96), Miss. Inst. of Arts and Letters (bd. dirs. 1993—), Inst. Urban Design, Rembrandt Club, Century Assn. Office: Archtl Record 2 Penn Plz New York NY 10121-0101

IWAI, WILFRED KIYOSHI, lawyer; b. Honolulu, Aug. 21, 1941; s. Charles Kazuo and Michiko (Sakimoto) I.; m. Judy Tomiko Yoshimoto, Mar. 1, 1963; children: Kyle K., Tiffany Seiko. BS in Bus., U. Colo., 1963, JD, 1966. Bar: Hawaii 1966, Colo. 1966, U.S. Dist. Ct. Hawaii 1966, U.S. Ct. Appeals (9th cir.) 1966. Dep. corp. counsel State of Hawaii, Honolulu, 1966-71; assoc. Kashiwa & Kanazawa, Honolulu, 1971-75; ptnr. Kashiwa, Iwai, Motooka & Goto, Honolulu, 1975-82, Iwai & Morris, Honolulu, 1982—2001; pvt. practice Wilfred K. Iwai Atty. at Law, A Law Corp., Honolulu, 2002—. Mem. ABA, Hawaii Bar Assn Office: PO Box 61392 Honolulu HI 96839 Office Phone: 808-988-2889.

IWASAKI, TETSUYA, engineering educator; b. Shibukawa, Gumma, Japan, Sept. 29, 1964; d. Tadashi and Mitsue Iwasaki; m. Junko Ito, June 8, 1991; children: Yota, Momo. BS, Tokyo Inst. Tech., 1987, MS, 1990; PhD, Purdue U., 1993. Postdoctoral rschr. Purdue U., West Lafayette, Ind., 1994-95; rsch. assoc. Tokyo Inst. Tech., 1995-96, asst. prof., 1996-97, assoc. prof., 1997-2000; asst. prof. U. Va., Charlottesville, 2000—02, assoc. prof., 2002—04, prof., 2004—. Author: LMI and Control, 1997, A Unified Algebraic Approach to Linear Control Design, 1998. Recipient SICE Pioneer Prize, 2002, NSF Career Award, 2003; grantee, Ministry of Edn., 1995—99, NSF, 2002—, NIH, 2002—. Mem.: ASME, IEEE (sr.), Soc. Instrument and Control Engrs. Avocations: camping, skiing, boomerang. Office: Univ Va Mech & Aero Engring PO Box 400746 Charlottesville VA 22904-4746 E-mail: tediwasaki@hotmail.com.

IWASAWA, ISOO (FRANCIS IWASAWA), accountant, management consultant; b. Yokohama, Kanagawa, Japan, Jan. 9, 1936; d. Matasaku (Joseph) Ninomiya and Haruno (Ann); m. Kinuko (Kay) Sato, Mar. 15, 1963; children: Isoaki, Lisa, Chiharu, Leo. BSc, St. Martin's Coll., Olympia, Wash., 1960; postgrad., U. Wash., 1960-61, Georgetown U., 1961. CPA, Wash. Prin. Ernst & Whinney, Hong Kong, 1984-86; ptnr. Arthur Young, Hong Kong, 1986-89; mng. dir. Asahi Iwasawa & Assocs. Mgmt. Cons. Ltd., Hong Kong, 1989—. Bd. trustees St. Martin's Coll., Olympia, Wash., 2001—. Avocations: gardening, sailing, golf. Office: China Resources Bldg FL 43 No 26 Harbour Rd Rm 4303 Wanchai Hong Kong Office Phone: 852 2511 1230. E-mail: aiamc@netvigator.com.

IX, ROBERT EDWARD, food company executive; b. Woodcliffe, N.J., Oct. 15, 1929; s. William Edward and Helen Elizabeth (Gorman) I.; m. Mildred Gilmore, June 27, 1959; children: Helen Adele, Alesia Gilmore, Robert Owens Gilmore, Julia Ryan, Christopher Prouty. AB, Princeton U., 1951; MBA, Wharton Grad. Sch., U. Pa., 1956; LL.D. (hon.), Marymount Coll., 1978, Sacred Heart U., Conn., 1984. Mgmt. cons. Arthur D. Little Inc., Cambridge, Mass., 1956-64; mktg. dir. Browne-Vintners Co., Distillers Corp.-Seagrams Ltd., N.Y.C., 1964-66; v.p. mktg. Schweppes (USA) Ltd., N.Y.C., 1966-68, pres., 1968; pres., chief exec. officer Cadbury Schweppes Inc., Stamford, Conn., 1970-78; chmn., chief exec. officer Am. region Cadbury Schweppes P.L.C., 1976-86. Bd. dirs. Cadbury Schweppes P.L.C., London, N.E. Bancorp Inc., Union Trust Co., New Eng. Frozen Foods, Inc., Am. Thread Co., Binney & Smith Inc., Royal Doulton Co. Inc., Loctite Corp., Health Waters Inc., Chase Packaging Corp., O'Shaughnessy Funds, Inc. Trustee Marymount Coll., also chmn.; trustee Greenwich (Conn.) Acad., Trinity Pawling Sch. (N.Y.); mem. adv. council N.Y. Med. Coll., Valhalla, N.Y. Served to lt. comdr. USNR, 1951-55. Decorated Knight Sovereign Mil. Order Malta. Mem. Young President's Orgn., World Bus. Coun., Chief Execs. Forum, SW Area Commerce and Industry Assn. Conn. (dir. 1970-80, chmn. bd. 1976-77), Def. Orientation Conf. Assn. (dir.), Grocery Mfrs. Am. (dir. 1981-85), U.S. Navy League (dir. Conn.), Univ. Club (N.Y.C.), Belle Haven Club (Greenwich), Greenwich Country Club, Landmark Club (Stamford, chmn. bd. govs.). Roman Catholic. Personal E-mail: cbix@verizon.net.

IYENGAR, ARUN K., computer scientist; s. Raja M. and Chung Wha L. Iyengar; m. Louise O. Knapp, Jan. 18, 1992; 1 child, Roger A. BA in Chemistry summa cum laude, U. Pa., 1985; MS in Computer Sci., MIT, 1988, PhD in Computer Sci., 1992. Software design engr. Hewlett-Packard Co., Chelmsford, Mass., 1992—95; rsch. staff mem. IBM Rsch., Yorktown Heights, NY, 1995—, master inventor, 2001—. Contbr. scientific papers to profl. jours. Recipient Scholastic Achievement award, Am. Chem. Soc., 1985, Best Paper award, Internat. World Wide Web Confs., 2001, 2003—04;, NSF fellow, 1985—90. Mem.: IEEE (sr.; treas. 1998—2000, vice chair 2000—03, chair tech. com. on internet 2003—), Assn. Computing Machinery, Internat. Fedn. Info. Processing (U.S. nat. del. 1999—, chair working group 6.4 on Internet applications engring. 2000—), Sigma Xi. Achievements include invention of and implementation of widely used methods for improving computer performance; patents for determining how changes to underlying data affect cached objects; systems and methods for persistent and robust memory management; preserving state information in a continuing conversation between a client and server networked via a stateless protocol; new method for debugging optimized computer programs; other national and international patents in field. Office: IBM TJ Watson Rsch Ctr PO Box 704 Yorktown Heights NY 10598 E-mail: aruni@us.ibm.com.

IZARD, JOHN, lawyer; b. Hartford, Conn., Mar. 4, 1923; s. John and Elizabeth (Andrews) I.; m. Mary Bailey, apr. 16, 1955; children: Sarah Izard Pariseau, John Jr., David Bailey. BS, Yale U., 1945; LLB, U. Va., 1949. Bar: Ga. 1950. Assoc. King & Spalding, Atlanta, 1949-52, ptnr., 1952-90. Mem. Adminstrv. Conf. U.S., Washington, 1978—82. Author, pub.: A Traveler's Table, 2002; editor-in-chief Va. Law Rev., 1948; contbr. articles to legal periodicals. Mem. Nat. Com. To Study Antitrust Laws and Procedures, Washington, 1978; trustee Episcopal Media Ctr., Atlanta, 1988—, chmn., 1992-96; trustee U. Va. Law Sch. Found., Charlottesville, 1974-97. Lt. (j.g.) USNR, 1944-46, PTO. Mem. ABA (chmn. antitrust sect. 1974-75), Ga. Bar Assn. (chmn. antitrust sect. 1969-71), Atlanta Legal Aid Soc. (pres. 1960), Lawyers Club Atlanta, Capital City Club (bd. dirs. 1976-79), Peachtree Golf Club, Piedmont Driving Club. Democrat. Episcopalian. Home: 4061 Glen Devon Dr NW Atlanta GA 30327-3613 Office: King & Spalding 191 Peachtree St NE Ste 3900 Atlanta GA 30303-1740 Office Phone: 404-572-4752.

IZATT, REED M., chemistry researcher; b. Logan, Utah, Oct. 10, 1926; s. Alexander Spowart Jr. and Marian (McNeil) I.; m. Helen Felix, Aug. 10, 1949 (dec. July 1998); children: Susan Marie Foster, Linda Jean, Neil Ernest, Ted Alexander, Steven Reed, Anne Marie; m. Virginia Bills Christensen, Oct. 24, 1998; step-children: Mark, Larry, Blake, Scott, Holly. BS, Utah State U., 1951; PhD, Pa. State U., 1954; postgrad., Carnegie Mellon U., 1954-56. Dir. grad. and undergrad. student rsch. Brigham Young U., Provo, Utah, 1956—. Vis. prof. U. Utah, Salt Lake City, 1972, U. Calif., San Diego, 1977. Contbr. articles to profl. jours. and books. Recipient Karl G. Maeser Rsch. and Creative Arts award, 1967, NIH Career Devel. award, 1967-72, Huffman award, 1983, Utah Gov.'s medal for Sci., 1990, Alumni Achievement award, Utah State U., 2001. Fellow: AAAS; mem.: Internat. Symposium on Macrocyclic Chemistry (mem. internat. adv. com.), Calorimetry Conf. (bd. dirs. 1973—76), Utah Acad. Scis., Arts and Letters (Gardner prize 1983), Am. Chem. Soc. (chmn. Salt Lake sect. 1965, councilor Salt Lake and ctrl. Utah sects. 1966—72, mem. local sect. activities com. 1966—72, Separations Sci. and Tech. award 1996, Utah award 1971), Phi Kappa Phi, Sigma Xi (pres. Brigham Young U chpt. 1980—82). Office: Brigham Young U Dept Chem & Biochem C100 Benson Sci Bldg Provo UT 84602-5700

IZAURRALDE, ROBERTO CÉSAR, science educator, researcher; b. Paraná, Argentina, Nov. 5, 1948; s. Hermenegildo Roberto Izaurralde and Elida Nahir Pelayo; m. María Cristina Quiroga Jakas, Oct. 11, 1972; children: Octavio Rafael, María Renée, Bernarda María, Arthur Benjamin. Agronomist Engr., Nat. U. of Córdoba, 1967—72; MS, Kans. State U., 1980—81, PhD, 1982—84. Asst. prof. Nat. U. of Córdoba, Argentina, 1976—86; grad. rsch. asst. Kans. State U., Manhattan, 1982—84; rsch. assoc. U. Alta., Edmonton, Canada, 1986—90, from asst. to assoc. prof., 1990—97; staff scientist Pacific NW Nat. Lab., Washington, 1997—2001; staff scientist, lab. fellow Joint Global Change Rsch. Inst., College Park, Md., 2004; adj. prof. U. Md., College Park, 2002—. Exec. sec. Córdoba U. Exptl. Farm, 1978—80; faculty coun. mem. Nat. U. of Córdoba, 1986—86; cons. Greenhouse Gas Emissions Consortium, Edmonton, Canada, 1995; exec. com. mem. Consortium for Agrl. Soils Mitigation of Greenhouse Gases, Coll. Pk., Md., 2001—; rsch. leader Carbon Sequestration in Terrestrial Ecosystems Rsch. Ctr., Coll. Pk., Md., 2002—. Fellowship, Fulbright Program, 1980—81. Mem.: AAAS, Am. Geophysical Union, Soil Sci. Soc. Am., Am. Soc. Agronomy. Achievements include research in sustainable agricultural production; simulation modeling of anhydrous ammonia retention in soil; simulation modeling of biogeochemical cycles; simulation modeling of climate change impacts on agriculture, water resources and ecosystems; leadership in developing soil carbon sequestration as a tool to mitigate global warming. Avocations: classical music, bicycling. Office: Joint Global Change Rsch Inst 8400 Baltimore Ave Ste 201 College Park MD 20740-2496 E-mail: cesar.izaurralde@pnl.gov.

IZBEKOV, PAVEL, researcher; Diploma, Novosibirsk State U., Russia, 1996; PhD, U. Alaska, 2002. Post doctoral fellow Alaska Volcano Obs., Fairbanks, 2002—. Mem.: Am. Geophys. Union. Office: Geophys Inst 903 Koyukuk Dr Fairbanks AK 99775 Office Phone: 907-474-5269.

IZENBERG, JERRY, sportswriter, columnist, author; b. 1930; Sportswriter & columnist Newark Star-Ledger, 1963—; columnist Newhouse Syndicate. Author: At Large, with Jerry Izenberg, 1968, The Rivals, 1968, How Many Miles to Camelot?: the All-American Sports Myth, 1972, Championship: the NFL Title Games plus Super Bowl, 1973, Great Latin Sports Figures: Proud People, 1976, The Greatest Game Ever Played, 1988, The Jerry Izenberg Collection (The Sportswriters Eye), 1989, No Medals for Trying: A Week in the Life of a Pro Football Team, 1990, New York Giants: Seventy Five Years, 1999; prodr.(or director, writer, narrator): of over 30 TV specials (Emmy award for writing & directing "A Man Named Lombardi"). Founder & pres. Project Pride, NJ. Nominee Pulitzer Prize (15 nominations); named NJ Sportswriter of the Year (5 awards); named to Nat. Sportscasters & Sportswriters Hall of Fame, 2000, NJ Literary Hall of Fame, Athletic Hall of Fame, Rutgers Univ.-Newark; recipient Red Smith award, Assoc. Press Sports Editors, 2000. Office: The Star-Ledger 1 Star-Ledger Plz Newark NJ 07102*

IZENSTARK, JOSEPH LOUIS, retired radiologist, physician, educator; b. Chgo., Mar. 29, 1919; s. Paul and Flora (Berger) I.; m. Elizabeth Kaplan, June 25, 1944; 1 child, Susan Rebecca. BA, U. Calif., Berkeley, 1948; MD, U. Calif., San Francisco, 1951. Diplomate Am. Bd. Radiology, Am. Bd. Nuc. Medicine. Intern USPHS, Chgo., 1951-52; resident Kern Gen. Hosp., Bakersfield, Calif., 1952-53; resident in radiology Cedars of Lebanon Hosp., L.A., 1955-56; chief radiology resident Los Angeles County Harbor Gen. Hosp., Torrance, Calif., 1957-58; practice medicine Inglewood, Calif., 1953-55; practice radiology Bakersfield, 1971-99; dir. radiology Imperial Hosp., Inglewood, 1959-60; asst. prof. radiology Tulane U., 1960-62, assoc. prof., 1963; assoc. prof. radiology Emory U., 1963-67, dir. nuc. medicine, 1963-67; prof. radiology U. So. Calif., 1969-72; prof. health scis. Bakersfield State Coll., 1973-83; ret., 1999. Chief nuc. medicine Cedars of Lebanon Hosp., 1968-71; med. dir. edn. Bakersfield Meml. Hosp., 1983-87; spl. cons. radiol. health USPHS, Calif. Bur. Radiol. Health, U.S. Army; mem. La. Atomic Energy Adv. Coun.; dir. nuc. medicine Crawford W. Long Meml. Hosp.; mem. USPHS Commn. on Radiation Exposure Evaluation, Med. Bd. Calif., 1982-91. Author: Anatomy and Physiology for X-ray Technicians, 1961; contbr. articles to profl. jours. With AUS, 1941-45. Recipient Cert. of Merit, City of New Orleans, 1962, Physician of Yr. award Bakersfield Meml. Hosp., 1988, Outstanding Physician Contbns. to Medicine award Calif. State Assembly, 1992. Fellow Am. Cancer Soc., Am. Coll. Radiology; mem. Soc. Nuclear Medicine (pres. So. Calif. chpt. 1976), So. Valley Radiol. Soc. (pres. 1975), Kern County Med. Soc. (pres. 1978). *Set your goal in a definite clear outline taking each step one at a time, as if climbing a ladder. Think about your goals; don't talk about them. Concentrate your abilities, your studies, your friends while denying yourself luxuries. Make your own decisions; stick by them. Don't have regrets. Be honest, sincere, and dedicated without regard to time. Finally, don't give up the fight— stick to your goal.*

IZEVBIGIE, ERNEST B., biomedical researcher; b. Benin, Nigeria; arrived in US, 1982; s. Benjamin I. and Esther E. (Obasohan) Izevbigie; m. Karen M. Izevbigie; 1 child, Ernest O. Jr. BSc, Tenn. State U., 1986; MSc, U. Tenn., 1988; PhD, Mich. State U., 1996. Dir. quality control Four Stars Products, Inc., Bridgeton, NJ, 1988—89; pvt. practice Sewell, NJ, 1989—91; rsch. asst. Mich. State U., East Lansing, 1992—96; fellow NIH, Bethesda, Md., 1996—98; asst. prof. biology Jackson (Miss.) State U., 1999—2004, assoc. prof. biology, 2004—. Mem. editl. bd.: Med. Sci. Monitor Internat., Cellular and Molecular Biology; contbr. chapters to books. Scholar, Nat. Ctr. for Minority Health and Disparity/NIH, 2004. Mem.: Am. Soc. for Nutritional Sci., Soc. for Exptl. Biology and Medicine, Am. Soc. for Biochemistry and Molecular Biology, Sigma Xi, Gamma Sigma Delta. Achievements include patents for phytochemotherapy for cancer. Avocations: reading, jogging, swimming. Office: Ctr for Environ Health Jackson State Univ 1400 Jr Lynch St Jackson MS 39217 Office Phone: 601-979-3464. Business E-Mail: ernest.b.izevbigie@jsums.edu.

IZMAILOV, ALEXANDER F., physicist, researcher, mathematician; b. Zelenodolsk, USSR, May 17, 1959; came to US, 1990; s. Farid Sh. and Kira M.; m. Lina S. Zeldovich, Sept. 17, 1989 (div. Jan. 1995). BS,MS in Theoret. Physics with honors, Kazan (USSR) U., 1981; PhD in Theoret. and Mathemat. Physics, USSR Acad. Scis., Moscow, 1986. Sr. rsch. scientist USSR Supreme Attestation Bd., 1987. Head Lab. Math. Simulation of Enhanced Oil Recovery, Ministry of Oil and Gas Industry, Moscow, 1981-90; rsch. scientist Lebedev Phys. Inst. USSR Acad. Scis., Moscow, 1986-89; rsch. prof. Poly. U., Bklyn., 1991-2001; v.p. Spear, Leeds & Kellogg, 2000—. Contbr. 45 articles to profl. jours. Grantee NASA, 1995, 97, 98, NSF, 1998, 2000; recipient 2nd prize USSR Competition in Theoret. Physics among undergrads., 1978. Mem. Am. Crystallographic Assn., Sigma Xi. Democrat. Avocations: stamp collecting/philately, surrealistic art, rare history books and documents on ussr. Home: 735 Avenue W Apt 5N Brooklyn NY 11223-5555 E-mail: alexizm@yahoo.com.

IZUCHUKWU, JOHN IFEANYICHUKWU, industrial engineer, mechanical engineer; b. Uke, Nigeria, May 6, 1955; arrived in US, 1976; s. Michael Chike and Cecilia Obiageli (Ikeakor) I.; m. Michele Anthea Palmer, July 22, 1989; children: Michael, John, Joseph. BS in Indsl. Engring., U. Portland, 1980, MS in Mech. Engring., 1984; PhD in Indsl. Engring., Northeastern U., 1994; MBA, Northwestern U., 2002. Base mgr. OEM Mfg., Digital Equipment Corp., Portland, Oreg., 1980-85; computer-aided software engring. mgr. Digital Equipment Corp., Marlboro, Mass., 1985-87, mgr. mech. design automation, 1987, mgr. concurrent engring. and application ctr. for tech. Rochester, N.Y., 1989-91, group mgr. aerospace product strategy Marlboro, 1991-93, worldwide strategy mgr., integrated product devel., 1993-95; team leader, R & D Ethicon Endo-Surgery, Inc., Cin., 1995-98; sr. dir. global rsch., devel. and engring. Mallinckrodt, Inc., St. Charles, Mo., 1998-2001; pres., CEO VITALTECH, Inc., 2001—; CEO Core Devices, Inc., 2001—. Adj. prof. decision scis. Babson Coll., Wellesley, Mass., 1994—95, St. Louis U., 2001—, U. Mo., Rolla. Contbr. articles to engring. jours., including Jour. Mfg. Sci. and Engring.; patentee in field. Mem. ASME, Inst. Indsl. Engring. (sr. mem.). Home: 18002 Pine Canyon Ct Wildwood MO 63005-4938 Office: Mallinckrodt Inc PO Box 5840 Saint Louis MO 63134-0840 Office Phone: 638-519-4805. Personal E-mail: jizuchukwu@aol.com.

IZZI, JOHN, mathematics educator, writer; b. Providence, Dec. 31, 1931; s. Joseph and Elizabeth (Kinney) I.; m. Barbara Ann Freethy, Dec. 18, 1954; children: Kathleen, Donna, James; m. Patricia Margaret Crowley, Aug. 27, 1979; children: John, Matthew, Jessica. BA, Providence Coll., 1953; MEd, RI Coll., 1965; postgrad., U. Vt., 1959, postgrad., 1960, postgrad., 1963, Seton Hall U., 1961, Yale U., 1966, Boston U., 1968—70. Tchr. LaSalle Acad., Providence, 1955-58, Warren (RI) HS, 1958-60, Warwick (RI) Vets. HS, 1960-62, 2003—04, Pilgrim HS, Warwick, 1962—66, 1999—2001, head math. dept., 1968-72, 1968—72, Seekonk (Mass.) HS, 1966-67; state supr. math. Mass. Dept. Edn., 1967-68; head math. dept. Toll Gate HS, Warwick, 1972—88, 2001—02; coord. secondary sch. RI Hosp., 1988-89; tchr. math., sci. Westport (Mass.) HS, 1989-91, math. adviser, biology, sci. tchr.; adj. faculty Bristol (Mass.) C.C., 1992-94. Pres. Smallstate Co., Warwick, 1975—; prin. Warwick Adult Edn., 1987-88; ext. lectr. U. RI, 1976—: math. coach Toll Gate Acad. Decathlon State Champions, 1985, New Eng. Math. League Divsn. Champions, 1989-90; dir. Prep. Inst., Warwick, Math. Edn. Svc., Providence, 1965-66, Toll Gate Metrication Project, Warwick, 1972-73; creator 1st federally funded sch. metrication project in US, 1972, Izzi Metric Slide Chart, 1974, Izzi Decimal Notation, 1974; dir. Smallstate Math. Inst., Warwick, 1989-90, Smallstate Scholarship Svc., Warwick, 1991-93; pres. Smallstate Pub., 1994-96; advisor Am. Security Coun., 1973-79; pres. P & J Izzi Assocs., Warwick, 1997-99; metrication cons. Nat. Coun. Tchrs. Math., 1973—, computer software reviewer, textbook reviewer, 1981-88; adj. faculty C.C. RI, 1981-85, Bristol (Mass.) C.C., 1992-94; metrication cons. State Depts. Edn., New Eng., Pa. and NY, 1977-80. Textbook reviewer AAAS, 1968-74; book reviewer Phi Delta Kappan, 1974-76; author: Metrication, American Style, 1974, Looking at the Metric System, 1977, Adult Metric Guide, 1977, Basic Metric Competency Test, 1977, My Irish, Voices of America, 1991; editl. adviser New England Mathematic Jour., 1982-85; contbr. articles to various publs. Mem. Mass. Gov.'s Hwy. Safety Act Com., 1967-68. With US Army, 1953-55. NSF grantee 1959-61, 63, 66, 68-70; recipient Disting. Achievement award Ednl. Press Assn. Am., 1974; named Best Math. Tchr. Am., Ky. Ednl. TV, 1990. Mem. ASCD, NEA, Am. Fedn. Tchrs., Nat. Coun. Tchrs. Math., Am. Assn. Sch. Adminstrs. Metric Assn., Assn. Tchrs. Math. New Eng., New Eng. Regional Metric Assn. (edn. commr. 1976-80), Mass. Dept. Edn. Assn. (v.p. 1967-68). Home: 243 Greenwood Ave Warwick RI 02886-2015 Personal E-mail: johnizzi@aol.com.

IZZO, HERBERT JOHN, language and linguistics educator, researcher; b. Saginaw, Mich., July 17, 1928; s. Joseph Anthony and Eleanor Bertha (Karau) I.; m. Barbara Suzanne McLaughlin, Sept. 22, 1958 (div); children: Victoria Sue Gutierrez, Alexander John, Sylvia Rachel Hunter, Daniel Stanley; m. Olga Frances Koutna, Dec. 30, 1989. *The family's pedagogical vocation began in 1913 when 19-year-old Eleanor, daughter of German immigrant farmers, taught her first class in a one-room school in Elkton, Michigan. Her son and two of her grandchildren followed in her footsteps: Alex is a professor of mathematics and Vicky an elementary teacher like her grandmother. When (Prof.) Olga Koutna became Mrs. Izzo, the Izzo teaching tradition merged with an even older one; for Olga's grandfather Jan was a teacher in Moravia when Eleanor was a child, and Olga's father Otakar was a professor at the University of Brno.* BA in Spanish, U. Mich., 1950, MA in Spanish and Italian, 1951, BS in Chemistry, 1953, PhD in Linguistics, 1965. Chargé de cours Huê (Vietnam) U., 1958-59; instr. Spanish U. Ariz., Tucson, 1960-61; instr. Spanish and linguistics Stanford (Calif.) U., 1961-64; asst. prof. Spanish San Jose (Calif.) State U., 1964-68; from assoc. to prof. linguistics U. Calgary, Alberta, Can., 1968-88, prof. emeritus, 1988—. Vis. asst. prof. fgn. langs. Mansfield (Pa.) State Coll., 1957; vis. prof. Romance linguistics U. Mich., Ann Arbor, 1977-78, 93-94; vis. prof. linguistics U. Bucharest, Romania, 1975-76; vis. prof. Italian, Stanford U., 1990-91; vis. scholar romance lang. U. Mich., 1996-99, classics 2004-, adv. bd. Quaderni d'Italianistica, Can., 1979—. Author: Tuscan and Etruscan, 1972; editor: The Sixth LACUS Forum, 1980, Italic and Romance, 1985; editor for linguistics Am. Jour. Italian Studies, 1988-2002; translator Lost Papers of Ludwig von Mises, 1998-2001, 05—. Italian Dialect Studies of Carl L. Fernow, 2003. Bd. dirs. Fathers Alberta, Calgary, 1986-87. Grad. fellow U. N.Mex., 1953, Award for Advanced Study, Am. Coun. Learned Socs., 1963, Fulbright-Hays award U.S. Dept. State, 1966, 75. Mem. Am. Assn. Italian Studies, Linguistic Assn. Can. and U.S. (conf. organizer 1978), N.Am. Assn. for History of Lang. Scis. (v.p. 1977-80), Am. Assn. Tchrs. Italian (life), Linguistic Soc. Am. (life), Am. Classical League, Am. Assn. Tchrs. of Spanish and Portuguese (life), Can. Soc. Italian Studies (nominating com. 1977-78, adv. bd. 1974-80), Internat.

Soc. Phonetic Scis., Nat. Assn. Scholars, Phi Beta Kappa, Phi Kappa Phi, Sigma Delta Pi. Avocations: music, history. Home: 2515 Deake Ave Ann Arbor MI 48108-1330 Business E-Mail: hizzo@umich.edu.

IZZO, IRVING VICTOR, III, music educator; b. Poughkeepsie, NY, Nov. 21, 1972; s. Irving Victor Jr. and Jeri Ann Izzo; m. Janine Renee Chan-Izzo, Dec. 8, 2001. BMusEd, Ithaca Coll., N.Y., 1994; M in Music Pedagogy, Hartt Sch. Music U. Hartford, Conn., 2001. Tchr. vocal music New Paltz H.S., NY, 1994—95, Minisink Valley H.S., Slate Hill, 1995—. Festival chairperson N.Y. State Sch. Music Assn., Slate Hill, 1997, 99, 2000, 04; honors chorus chair Orange County Music Educators, 1998, 2000; honors chorus chair zone 9 N.Y. State Sch. Music Assn., Hudson Valley, 1997, Hudson Valley, 99. Mem.: N.Y. State Sch. Music Assn. (Gold award 1996, 1998—99, 2002—05), Orange County Music Educators (publicity chair 1999—2000), Alpha Sinfonia, Phi Mu. Achievements include 2005 Disney Honors Festival participation. Home: Apt 4L 4 Fortune Rd W Middletown NY 10941-1688 Office: Minisink Valley Ctrl Sch Dist Rt 6 Box 217 Slate Hill NY 10973 Office Phone: 845-355-5150 ext 1219. E-mail: vizzo@minisink.com.

IZZO, THOMAS, college basketball coach; b. Iron Mountain, Mich., Jan. 30, 1955; m. Lupe Izzo; 1 child, Raquel. Grad., No. Mich. U., 1977. Head coach Ishpeming (Mich.) H.S., 1977-79; asst. coach No. Mich. U., 1979-83; with Mich. State U., East Lansing, 1983—, head coach, 1995—. Asst. coach Goodwill Games, 2001; head coach USA Pan Am. Games, 2003. Named to No. Mich. U. Hall of Fame, 1990, Upper Peninsula Hall of Fame, 1998; Divn. I Nat. Coach of Year by Nat. Assn of Basketball Coaches, 2001. Office: Mich State U Athletic Dept 222 Breslin Ctr Jensen Fieldhouse East Lansing MI 48824

JAAR, BERNARD GEORGES, nephrologist, researcher; b. Port-au-Prince, Haiti, Oct. 2, 1961; came to France, 1988; s. Georges Saïd and Denise Marie (Dabdoub) J.; m. Addolorata Nocera, Oct. 31, 1987; 2 children: Stephanie, Gabriel Georges. MD (valedictorian), State U. Haiti, 1987; specialist in nephrology (valedictorian), Necker Sch. Medicine, Paris, 1992; diploma in AIDS, St.-Antoine Sch. of Medicine, Paris, 1993. Intern Gen. Hosp. State U. Haiti, Port-au-Prince, 1986-87; comty. medicine resident Ministry of Pub. Health, Arcahaie, Haiti, 1987-88; vol. dr. Ctrs. for Devel. and Health, Port-au-Prince; intern Dialysis Svc. Tenon Hosp., Paris, 1988-89; researcher Hematopoiesis Lab. St.-Antoine Hosp., Paris, 1989-90; resident ICU St. Louis Hosp., Paris, 1990-91, nephrology svc. Tenon Hosp., Paris, 1991-92, clin. asst., 1992-94; rsch. fellow Johns Hopkins Med. Instn., Balt., 1995—. Contbr. articles to profl. jours. Valedictorian State U. of Haiti, 1987, Necker Sch. of Medicine, 1992; recipient Boehringer Mannheim prize, France, 1992. Mem. AAAS, Am. Soc. Nephrology, N.Y. Acad. Scis., French Soc. Nephrology, Am. Heart Assn., Internat. Soc. Nephrology. Roman Catholic. Avocations: jogging, travel, history books, soccer. Office: 2024 E Monument St Ste 2-500 Baltimore MD 21287-0007

JABARA, MICHAEL DEAN, technology and business development entrepreneur; b. Sioux Falls, S.D., Oct. 26, 1952; s. James M. and Jean Marie (Swiden) J.; m. Gundula Beate Dietz, Aug. 26, 1984; children: James Michael, Jenna Mariel. Student, Mich. Tech. U., 1970-72; BSBA, U. Calif., Berkeley, 1974; MBA, Pepperdine U., 1979. Mgr. original Sprint project team So. Pacific Communications Corp., 1976-78; network product mgr. ROLM Corp., 1978-81; cons. McGraw Hill Co., Hamburg (Fed. Republic of Germany) and London, 1982-83; founder, CEO Friend Techs. Inc. (merger VoiceCom Systems, Inc., acquired by Premiere Techs., Inc. 1997), San Francisco, 1984-88; pres. VoiceCom Ventures, San Francisco, 1988-93; mng. dir. Telecom, EMS Group Ltd., London, 1993-95; owner Red Rock Ptnrs., Ltd., Las Vegas, Nev., 1993—; chmn. bd., COO Bingo Card Minder Corp., Stateline, Nev., 1996; owner TOIR LLC, Glenbrook, 1998-99, NewHoldings, Ltd., Las Vegas, 2000—; CEO, chmn. bd. iTruckers, Inc., 2000—; dir. Bus. Devel. Kummer Kaempfer Bonner & Renshaw, Las Vegas, 2002—05; co-owner Highrise Ptnrs. Ltd., 2004—; prin., owner Profile Realty, 2005—. Registered rep., sr. advisor Silver Pacific Advisors, LLC, 2004—; trustee Nev. Devel. Authority, 2002—. Patentee in field. Bd. dirs. Tahoe-Douglas C. of C.; chmn. Tahoe Citizens Com., 1995-2000. Mem.: Mich. Tech Alumni Assn., U. Calif. Berkeley Bus. Alumni, Pepperdine Bus. Alumni, Las Vegas Jaguar Club. Avocations: classic cars, flying. Office: Red Rock Partners Ltd 7th Flr 3800 Howard Hughes Pkwy Las Vegas NV 89109 Office Phone: 702-735-7600. Business E-Mail: mjabara@redrockpartners.com.

JABBAR, ABDUL, physician, educator, gastroenterologist; b. Multan, Punjab, Pakistan, Oct. 14, 1968; s. Muhammad Sharif and Hajira Bibi; m. Nosheen Jabbar, Nov. 12, 2000; 1 child, Ayyan. MD, Nishtar Med. Coll., Pakistan, 1992. Clin. instr. U. Louisville, 2002—03, asst. prof., 2003—. Consulting gastroenterologist Gastroenterologist Group U. Louisville, 2002—; staff attendant VA Hosp. Contbr. rsch. and med. lit. revs. Gastroenterology/Hepatology fellow, Am. Bd. Internal Medicine, 2002. Mem.: Am. Coll. Gastroenterology. Achievements include research in guidelines for intagastric versus intrajejunal feeding. Home: 9911 Fringe Tree Ct Louisville KY 40241 Office: 530 S Jackson St Louisville KS 40202 Office Phone: 502-852-6991. Office Fax: 502-852-0846. Personal E-mail: ajh5@hotmail.com.

JABBOUR, NABIL MILAD, ophthalmologist; b. Beirut, Nov. 11, 1955; came to U.S., 1979; s. Milad S. and Rose J. (Hatem) J.; m. Nina R. Khalifé, Aug. 19, 1979; children: Noel, Jad. BSc, Am. U. Beirut, 1976, MD, 1980. Lic. physician W.Va. Intern in internal medicine Am. U. Beirut, 1979-80, resident dept. ophthalmology, 1980-83; fellow Retina Assocs./Mass. Eye & Ear Infirmary Eye Rsch. Inst. Harvard Med. Sch., Boston, 1983-85, chief fellow, 1984-85; asst. prof. ophthalmology W.Va. U., Morgantown, 1985-89, assoc. prof. ophthalmology, 1989-91; founder, owner Mid-Atlantic Retina Consultations, Morgantown, 1991—. Dir. retina and vitreous svc. W.Va. U., Morgantown, 1987-91, chmn. med. student edn. com., 1989-91, mem. biomed. rsch. support com., 1988-91; pres. ForSight Found., 1991—; chmn. med. records com. W.Va. U. Hosp., 1990-91, mem. patient care rev. com., 1990-91; educator, lectr., presenter in field. Contbr. numerous articles to profl. jours.; creator videotape Jabbour-Nutter Diathermy System Transconjunctival and Transscleral Diathermy; inventor in field. Pres. Parents' Assn. Alliance Christian Sch., 1988-89, bd. dirs., 1989—, pres. bd. dirs., 1991-93; pres. Homeowners' Assn. Willow Wick, 1989-90; chmn. W.Va. Diabetes Eye Coun., 1990-9; mem. W.Va. Diabetes Control Coun., 1990—; pres., trustee Trinity H.S., Morgantown, 1995—; v.p., trustee H.O.M.E., Houston, 1994—. Fellow ACS; mem. Am. Acad. Ophthalmology (honor award 2001), W.Va. Acad. Ophthalmology, Schepens Internat. Soc. (founding), Vitreous Soc., Sigma Xi. Achievements include development of Iris Speculum for open sky vitrectomy, vitreoretinal dissection set, high viscosity contact lens for vitreous surgery, transscleral diathermy electrode, diathermy return path, illuminated dissection spatula for vitrectomy, suction tip with soft guard, irrigation/aspiration manual set, illuminated wide angle contact lens for vitrectomy, right-angled infusion cannula. Office: Mid-Atlantic Retina Consultations Inc 3120 Collins Ferry Rd Morgantown WV 26505-3305

JABLONSKY, ATARAH, retired music educator; b. Jerusalem, Nov. 25, 1927; came to U.S., 1929; d. Abraham Itzak and Sarah (Haack) Wishengrad; m. Marvin Jablonsky, Nov. 30, 1947; children: Karen, Andrew, Eugene, Elliott, Benjamin. MusB, Manhattan Sch. Music, 1948; MS in Edn., Xavier U., 1969. Tchr. piano Neighborhood Music Sch., N.Y.C., 1947-52, U. Cin., 1958-70; lectr. Edgecliff Coll., Cin., 1972-74; tchr. piano Teodtman Sch. Music, Cin., 1986—2002; ret., 2002. Adj. asst. prof. music Coll. Mt. St. Joseph, Cin., 1970—; adjudicator U. Cin., 1970—2001. Contbr. articles to profl. jours. Named Nat. Cert. Tchr. of Yr., Ohio Music Tchrs. Assn., 2000; recipient Found. Fellow, Music Tchrs. Nat. Assn., 2005. Mem. Nat. Guild Piano Tchrs., Ohio Tchrs. Music Assn. (4th v.p.; Tchr. of Yr. award 2000), Tri-County Piano Tchrs. Assn., Keyboard Club Cin. (pres. 1990—). Avocations: reading, swimming, travel. Home: 21 W Charlotte Ave Wyoming OH 45215-2063

JABLONSKY, STEPHEN, music educator, composer, artist, writer; b. N.Y.C., Dec. 5, 1941; s. Benjamin and Adelaide (Robinson) J.; m. Roberta Nusim, Aug. 29, 1965 (div. Jan. 1999); m. Tina Sophia Ostrander, May 23, 2003. BA, CCNY, 1962; postgrad., Harvard U., 1962-63; MA, NYU, 1964, PhD, 1973; postgrad., Bridgeport U., 1982-83; composition studies with Mark Brunswick, Leon Kirchner, Paul Turok, Pierre Boulez. Cert. music tchr., N.Y. Music tchr. N.Y.C. Bd. Edn., 1965—68; asst. dir. Lake Bryn Mawr Camp, Honesdale, Pa., 1968—70; assoc. prof. music theory & composition, humanities CCNY, N.Y.C., 1964—, chmn. music dept., 2002—. Cons. Lifetime Learning Systems, Fairfield, Conn., 1978-90; editor-in-chief The Work and Family Pub. Group, 1993-94; chief fin. officer, dir. computer svcs. Youth Mktg. Internat., 1994-98; v.p. The Weiner Nusim Found., 1997-2004; conducting fellow Nat. Orchestral Assn., N.Y.C., 1973-76; bd. dirs. Musigraphics, Inc., Easton, Conn., 1975-80; profl. artist/graphic designer, 1968—; cons. Youth Mktg. Internat., 1999—, CBS Camera III, 1975-76, Exxon/Affiliate Artists Conducting Program, 1976. Finalist All-Conn. Art Show, the Stamford Mus., 1990-91, All-Conn. Art Show, The Discovery Mus., 1991; author: Tonal Facts and Tonal Theories, 2004, All-Star Rhythm & Pitch Book, 2005; contbg. editor Youth Media Internat., 1999-2001; contbr. articles to profl. jours. NEA fellow, 1975, N.Y. State Regents Teaching fellow, 1962; recipient Founders Day award NYU, 1974. Mem. AAUP, ASCAP, Internat. Trumpet Guild, Stamford Art Assn., New Canaan Soc. for the Arts, Profl. Staff Congress, Coll. Music Soc., Soc. Music Theory, Phi Mu Alpha Sinfonia, Alpha Epsilon Pi. Avocations: tennis, reading, art collector, philanthropy. Home: 1255 Westover Rd Stamford CT 06902-1037 Office: CCNY 138th St And Convent Ave New York NY 10031 Office Phone: 212-650-7663. Personal E-mail: jabo555@optonline.net.

JACCACI, AUGUST THAYER, JR., social architect, educator; b. N.Y.C., Mar. 9, 1937; s. August Thayer and Helen Jenkins Jaccaci; m. Robin Charboneau Middleton, June 28, 1963 (div. June 1982); children: Anthony, Alexander; m. Joanne Karen Hobbs, Oct. 28, 1999. BA, Harvard Coll., 1960, MA in Tchg., 1964; MFA, R.I. Sch. Design, 1965. Tchr., coach Rutland (Vt.) H.S., 1960—61; admissions officer, coach Harvard Coll., Cambridge, Mass., 1961—63; admissions officer, tchr. R.I. Sch. Design, Providence, 1963—65; tchr., coach Phillips Acad. Andover, Mass., 1965—68; arts adminstr., lectr. Boston Coll., Newton, 1968—75; adminstr., coach Lawrence Acad., Groton, Mass., 1976—78; tchr. Burke Mountain Acad., East Burke, Vt., 1983—85; social arch. Unity Scholars, New Gloucester, Maine, 1998—2003. Pres. Metamatrix Assoc., Thetford, Vt., 1978; founder Nature Planning Network, New Gloucester, 2003; ski coach, team capt. FIS World Ski Championships, Vail, Colo., 1989; guest lectr. Stanford Bus. Sch.; cons. Motorola, Fannie Mae, Pillsbury, AT&T, P.W. Minor, Micromentor, Chase Manhattan Bank, J.C. Penney, Polaroid, Vt. Agy. Human Svcs., Arthur Anderson, Xerox, Vol. Hosp. Assn. Am., Toronto Dominion Bank, No. Telecom, Canada, IMD, Europe, Credit Suisse, Europe, Brit. Petroleum, Europe; spkr. in field nat. and internat. Represented in permanent collections, Addison Gallery Am. Art; author: CEO: Chief Evolutionary Officer, 1999, General Periodicity, 2000. Candidate for gov., Vt., 1992, 1994. Recipient Svc. to Humanity Award, PW Minor Co., 2000, Earl award, Religious Futurist, 2002. Mem.: World Future Soc. (pres. Boston chpt. 1975), Creative Edn. Found. (tchr. 1972—2005, Leadership, Svc. and Commitment award 1990). Avocations: skiing, rowing, hiking. Home: 626 Penney Rd New Gloucester ME 04260 E-mail: unityscholars@earthlink.net.

JACELDO-SIEGL, KAREN, chemistry professor; b. Carigara, Leyte, Philippines, July 30, 1960; d. Teddorico Hilario and Carmen Baylon Jaceldo; m. Bernard Christian Siegl, June 24, 2000; 1 child, Cecilia Theresa Jaceldo Siego. BS, U. Tex. at San Antonio, 1984; MS, U. Incarnate Word, 1990; PhD, Loma Linda U., 2003. Rsch. asst. sci. ctr. U. Tex., San Antonio, 1990—93, Houston, 1993; rsch. asst. Loma Linda U., Calif., 1997—2001, tchg. asst., 1998—2001, guest lectr., 2001—03, rsch. assoc., 2002—04, asst. rsch. prof., 2004—. Contbr. articles to profl. jours., Almond Bd. Calif., 2002. Mem.: Delta Omega Soc. Roman Catholic. Avocations: piano, choral music, performing arts. Office: Loma Linda U Sch Pub Health Evans Hall 203 24785 Stewart St Loma Linda CA 92350 Office Fax: 909-558-0419. Business E-Mail: kjaceldo@llu.edu.

JACHE, ALBERT WILLIAM, retired chemistry professor, academic administrator, research scientist; b. Manchester, N.H., Nov. 5, 1924; s. William Frederick and Esther (Ruemely) J.; m. Lucy Ellen Hauslein, June 14, 1948; children: Ann Gail, Ellen Ruth, Philip William, Heidi Verena. BS, U. N.H., 1948, MS, 1950; PhD, U. Wash., 1952. Sr. chemist Air Reduction Co., Murray Hill, N.J., 1952-53; rsch. assoc. dept. physics Duke U., 1953-55; asst. prof. dept. chemistry Tex. A&M U., College Station, 1955-58, assoc. prof., 1958-61; cons. Ozark Mahoning Co., Tulsa, 1960-61, assoc. rsch. dir., 1961-64; sr. rsch. assoc. Olin Mathieson Chem. Corp. (now Olin Corp.), New Haven, 1964-67, sect. mgr., 1965-67, cons., 1967-75; prof. chemistry Marquette U., Milw., 1967-90, prof. emeritus, 1990—, chmn. chem. dept., 1967-72, dean Grad. Sch., 1972-77, assoc. acad. v.p. for health scis., 1974-77, assoc. v.p.-acad. affairs, 1977-85; scientist-in-residence Argonne (Ill.) Nat. Lab., 1985-86, scientist, 1991-96, temporary appointment, 1991-96; with ChemLab, 2000—. Program coordination com. Med. Center S.E. Wis.; lectr. U. Tulsa, 1963-64, New Haven Coll., 1967; cons. Allied Chem. Corp., 1977-78, 2000-; salt panel com. remediation buried and tank wastes NAS/NRC, 1996-97. Trustee Milw. Sci. Ednl. Found.; pres. Milw. Sci. Ednl. Trust, 1973—; trustee Argonne Univs. Assn., 1977-80; chmn. Assn. Grad. Schs. in Cath. Univs., 1973-75; mem. AUA nuclear engring. edn. com. U. Chgo, 1977-89, chmn., 1984, sec., 1989; double bass player River Cities Symphony Orch., 1997-2001, Evergreen Comty. Orch., 1994—, Evergreen String Ensemble, 1994-2000, Marietta Chamber Orch., 1994-97. With AUS, 1942-46. Fellow AAAS (Sr. Scientists and Engrs. Am.), Am. Inst. Chemists; mem. Am. Chem. Soc. (chmn.-elect, program chmn. div. fluorine chemistry 1981, chmn. div. fluorine chemistry 1982), Sigma Xi, Omicron Kappa Upsilon, Alpha Sigma Nu. Achievements include research and numerous patents in the area of inorganic fluorine chemistry with emphasis on anhydrous hydrogen fluoride as a solvent or reaction medium and Hypofluorite chemistry. Home and Office: 301 Ohio St Marietta OH 45750-3139 Personal E-mail: albert@jache.com.

JACHNA, JOSEPH DAVID, photographer, educator; b. Chgo., Sept. 12, 1935; m. Virginia Kemper, 1962; children: Timothy, Heidi, Jody. BS in Art Edn., Inst. Design, Ill. Inst. Tech., 1958, MS in Photography, 1961. Part-time photographic asst. Derwin Studio Darkroom, Chgo., 1953-54; photo-technician Eastman Kodak Labs., Chgo., 1954; photographer's asst. DeSort Studio, Chgo., 1956-58; free-lance photographer Chgo., 1961—; instr. photography Inst. Design, Ill. Inst. Tech., Chgo., 1961—69; assoc. prof. U. Ill., Chgo., 1969—75, prof., 1976—2001, prof. emeritus, 2001—. One-man shows include Art Inst. Chgo., 1961, St. Mary's Coll., Notre Dame, Ind., 1963, U. Ill., Chgo., 1965, 77, Lightfall Gallery Art Ctr., Evanston, Ill., 1970, U. Wis., Milw., 1970, Ctr. for Photog. Studies, Louisville, 1974, Nikon Photog. Salon, Tokyo, 1974, Afterimage Gallery, Dallas, 1975, Visual Studies Workshop Gallery, Rochester, N.Y., 1979, Chgo. Ctr. for Contemporary Photography, 1980, Focus Gallery, San Francisco, 1981, Photogenesis, Albuquerque, 1983, Andover (Mass.) Gallery, 1984, Chgo. State U., 1985, Tweed Mus. Art, Duluth, Minn., 1986, Gallery 954, Chgo., 1993, State of Ill. Galleries, Chgo., Lockport and Springfield, 1994, Fermilab, Batavia, Ill., 1995, Stephen Daiter Gallery, Chgo., 2000, Bruce Silverstein Gallery, N.Y.C., 2003; exhibited in group shows at Art Inst. Chgo, 1963, 83, MIT, Cambridge, 1968, Walker Art Ctr., Mpls., 1973, 89, Renaissance Soc. Gallery U. Chgo., 1975, Mus. Contemporary Art, Chgo., 1977, 96—, Mus. Art RISD, Providence, 1978, Carpenter Ctr. Visual Arts, Harvard U., Cambridge, 1981, Nexus, Atlanta, 1983, Nat. Mus. Art., Washington, 1984, San Francisco Mus. Modern Art, 1985, Internat. Ctr. Photography, Tucson, 1992, Gallery 312, Chgo., 1996, Stockholm Subway, Sweden, 1999, Hyde Park Art Ctr., Chgo., 2001, Stephen Daiter Gallery, Chgo., 2002, 2003, Taken by Design: Photography at the Inst. of Design, 1937-1971, Art Inst. Chgo., 2002; represented in permanent collections, Mus. Modern Art, N.Y.C., Internat. Mus. Photography, George Eastman House, Rochester, N.Y., MIT, San Francisco Mus. Modern Art, Mpls. Inst. Arts, Art Inst. Chgo., Ctr. Photog. Studies, Louisville, Ctr. for Creative Photography, U. Ariz., Tucson. Ferguson Found. grantee, 1973, Nat. Endowment for Arts grantee, 1976, Ill. Arts Council, 1979; Guggenheim fellow, 1980. Home: 5707 W 89 Pl Oak Lawn IL 60453-1225 Business E-Mail: iceman@uic.edu.

JACIR, EMILY, photographer, conceptual artist; b. Palestine, 1970; BA in Art, U. Dallas, 1992; MFA, Memphis Coll. Art, 1994; attended, Whitney Ind. Study Program, NYC, 1998—99. One-woman shows include, Anderson Ranch Arts Ctr., Snowmass Village, Colo., 1997, Eastfield Coll. Gallery, Mesquite, Tex., 1997, Everywhere/Nowhere, SPACES, Cleve., 1999, From Paris to Riyadh (Drawings for my mother), U. Gallery, U South, Sewanee, Tenn., 2000, New Photographs: Bethlehem to Ramallah, Debs & Co. Project Room, NY, 2002, Where We Come From, 2003, Belongings, O-K Ctr. Contemporary Art, Linz, Austria, 2003, Mus. Modern Art, Arnhem, The Netherlands, 2003, LA Internat. Art Biennial, Frumkin Duval Gallery, Santa Monica, Calif., 2003, Artspace Annex II, New Haven, CT, 2003, Woher wir kommen, Künstlerhaus, Bremen, 2004, Den I: a på Moderna: Emily Jacir: Where We Come From, Moderna Museet, Stockholm, 2004, The Khalil Sakakini Cultural Ctr., Ramallah, 2004, Nuova Icona, Venice, 2004, Kunstraum Innsbruck, Innsbruck, 2004, Accumulations, Alexander & Bonin, NY, 2005, exhibited in group shows at 7th Ann. McNeese Nat. Works on Paper, McNeese State, Lake Charles, La., 1994, Women in Art: 12 Tex. Women, Contemporary Art Ctr., Houston, 1997, Xmas, Kent Gallery, NY, 1999, Free for All, Temporary Art Svcs., Chgo., 2000, Carnival in the Eye of the Storm; War/Art/New Technologies, Pacific Northwest Coll. Art, Portland, Oreg., 2000, Greater New York, PS I Contemporary Art Ctr., LI City, 2000, Strangers/Estrangers, PS I Clocktower Gallery, NY, 2001, Lecture Lounge, 2001, Uncommon Threads, Herbert F. Johnson Mus., Cornell U., NY, 2001, Made in Transit, Vacancy Gallery, NY, 2001, Unjustified, Apex Art, NY, 2002, Submerged, Nuremberg, 2002, Right2Fight, Sarah Lawrence Coll., Bronxville, NY, 2002, Queens Internat., Queens Mus. Art, 2002, Settlement, Gallery 400, Chgo., 2002, Global Priority, Hester Art Gallery, U. Mass., 2003, Shatat, Colo. U. Art Galleries, Boulder, 2003, Made in Palestine, Art Car Mus., Houston, 2003, VEIL, Inst. Internat. Arts, London, 2003, 8th Istanbul Biennial, 2003, 100 Cuts, Gallery 312, Chgo., 2004, Empire: Videos for a New World, Md. Inst. Coll. Art, Balt., 2004, Whitney Biennial, Whitney Mus. Am. Art, 2004, Cover Girl: the Female Body & Islam in Contemporary Art, Ise Cultural Found., NY, 2004, Neither Here Nor There: Video Artists Navigate Cultural Displacement, Cheekwood Mus. Art, Nashville, 2004, Election, Am. Fine Arts, NY, 2004, Sometime: Six Works for Film & Video, Anthony Reynolds Gallery, London, 2004, Desenhos: A-Z, Porta 33, Funchal, Ilha da Madeira, 2005. Mailing: c/o Debs & Co 525 West 26th St New York NY 10001*

JACISIN, JOHN JAMES, psychiatrist; b. Ironwood, Mich., June 30, 1942; s. Frank Anthony and Amelia Lucy J.; m. Hoa Thi Hyunh, Feb. 27, 1971; children: Ann, Tina, Kim. Student, Mich. Tech. U., 1960-61; BS in Psychology, U. Mich., 1964, MD, 1968. Intern Mt. Carmel Hosp., Columbus, Ohio, 1968-69; resident in psychiatry U. Mich., Ann Arbor, 1971-74; dir. inpatient psychiatry Riverwood Cmty. Mental Health Ctr., St. Joseph, Mich., 1974-75; dir. psychiat. inpatient svcs. Henry Ford Hosp., Detroit, 1975-81, acting dept. chmn., 1976-77, dir. psychiat. residency tng. program, 1977-87, dept. vice chmn., 1984-87; dir. psychiat. svcs. Fairlane Ctr., 1981-84. Clin. instr. U. Mich. Med. Sch., 1977-87; dir. inpatient svc., Modesto Psychiat. Ctr., Calif., 1987-91, assoc. med. dir., 1991-93; Psychiat. Med. Group, Modesto, 1987—; mem. adj. faculty U. Pacific, 1991-94. Capt. USAF, 1969-71. Decorated Bronze star. Fellow Am. Psychiat. Assn. (disting.); mem. Am. Bd. Psychiatry and Neurology (cert. in psychiatry 1977, geriat. psychiatry 1996), Am. Coll. Clin. Psychiatrists, Anxiety Disorder Assn. Am., Ctrl. Calif. Psychiat. Soc. (pres. Yosemite chpt. 1995-96, 2003—), Obsessive Compulsive Disorder Found. Office: Psychiat Med Group 3425 Coffee Rd Ste 2A Modesto CA 95355-1582 Office Phone: 209-524-9401. E-mail: drjjj42@inreach.com.

JACK, BRADLEY H., investment banker; BA, U. Calif., Berkeley. Assoc., fixed income divsn. Lehman Brothers Holdings Inc., 1984, sector head, investment banking, 1993—96, head, investment banking divsn., 1996—2002, co-COO, 2002—04, office of the chmn., responsible for investment banking, 2004—. Mem. exec. com. Lehman Brothers Holdings Inc. Mem. bd. trustees Juilliard Sch.; bd. dirs. Dorothy Rodbell Cohen Found. Office: Lehman Brothers Holdings Inc 745 Seventh Ave New York NY 10019

JACK, JANIS GRAHAM, judge; b. 1946; RN, St. Thomas Sch. Nursing, 1969; BA, U. Balt., 1974; JD summa cum laude, South Tex. Coll., 1981. Pvt. practice, Corpus Christi, Tex., 1981-94; judge U.S. Dist. Ct. (so. dist.) Tex., Corpus Christi, 1994—. Jud. mem. The Maritime Law Assn. U.S. Mem. ABA, Fed. Judges Assn., Fifth Cir. Dist. Judges Assn., Nat. Assn. Women Judges (jud. conf. com. info. tech.), Tex. Bar Found., State Bar Tex., The Philos. Soc. Tex., Order of Lytae, Phi Alpha Delta. Office: US Dist Ct 1133 N Shoreline Blvd Corpus Christi TX 78401

JACK, MORGANN TAYLLOR, writer, artist; d. William H. and Emma Lee (Williams) Blanks; m. Charles D. Jack, July 21, 1957 (dec. Sept. 20, 1979). AA in Fine Arts, Allan Hancock Coll., 1975. Editl. asst. The Cycler Champlin Oil Co. house organ, Ft. Worth, 1957; columnist, reporter, corr. Santa Barbara News-Press, Lompoc, Calif., 1961—64; freelance journalist AP, Springfield (Mass.) Rep., 1966—68; staff reporter features, 1st editor weekend entertainment supplement, Lompoc Record, 1968—71; feature writer Lompoc Valley News, 1980—84; feature writer, cover artist Cen. Coast Mag., Santa Maria, Calif., 1989—90. Guest artist Binnenheide Art Exhbn., Kevelaer, Germany, 1994. Creator, editor, artist (monthly mag.) Space 'n Lace, VAFB, Calif., 1961—63, (weekly newsletter) Reeflector, Recife, Brazil, 1964—65; commd. garden sculpture, for Lompoc Mayor (reception benefitting Lompoc Mus.), 1978; illustrator (book) A Word About Birds in Rhyme Time, 1984; commd. art, Office Idaho State Treas., 1988—93. Mem. Santa Barbara County Commn. for Women, 1999—2000. Recipient regional awards, juried art shows and competitions, 1951—86, Plaque in Appreciation of Outstanding Comty. Svcs., City of Lompoc, 1968—71. Mem.: Santa Barbara Mus. Art, Nat. Mus. Women in the Arts (charter mem.). Avocations: travel, adventure, reading, paleosciences. Home: PO Box 598 Lompoc CA 93438

JACK, NANCY RAYFORD, retired supplemental resource company executive, consultant; b. Hughes Springs, Tex., June 23, 1939; d. Vernon Lacy and Virginia Ernestine (Turner) Rayford; m. Kermit E. Hundley, Dec. 19, 1979; 1 child by previous marriage, James Bradford Jack, III. Cert. in bus. adminstrn., Keller Grad. Sch. Mgmt., 1980; cert. in acctg., Harper Coll., 1972, cert. in corp. law and tax law, paralegal, 1973. Sr. sec. Gould, Inc., Rolling Meadows, Ill., 1971-73, staff asst., 1973-74, asst. sec., 1974-77, corp. sec., 1977-89, v.p., 1985-89; pres. The Corp. Ofcl. Sec., Wheaton, Ill., 1989-92, Corp. Minutes and More, Wheaton, 1992-99; assoc. dir. The Bus. Owners' Trustee, The Woodlands, Tex., 1999—2005, ret., 2005. Recipient cert. of leadership YWCA Met. Chgo., 1975 Mem.: Kingwood Country Club, Beta Sigma Phi. Home and Office: 162 Linton Downs Pl The Woodlands TX 77382-1692

JACK, PATRICIA ANN, assistant principal; b. Little Rock, Ark. d. Levi and Leanna Johnson; m. Sherwin Jack, June 29, 1980; 1 child, Alese. Master's Adminstrn., Mercy Coll., Manhattan, NY, 2000; Master's Reading, Syracuse U., Syracuse, NY, 1996; BS, Oakwood Coll., Huntsville, AL, 1979. Asst. prin. Bd. of Edn., Brooklyn, NY, 2000—, dist. staff developer, 1999—2000, math/reading staff developer, 1996—99, mentor educator, 1994—96, spl. edn. educator, 1992—94, pre-kindergarten educator Syracuse, NY, 1988—92, grade 4 educator Benton Harbor, Mich., 1983—88. John hopkin's liason Bd. of Edn., Brooklyn, NY, 1996—99, cons. educator, 1994—96, co-chair school-wide program, 1992—94. Recipient Tchr. of the Yr., State of NY and State of Mich., Tchr. of the Yr., Spl. Edn. PS 306, Bklyn., and Benton Harbor, Mich. Avocations: reading, travel, history, antiques, doll collecting.

JACKAMEIT, KEVIN CHARLES, statistician; b. Harrisonburg, Va., Aug. 25, 1973; s. Bonnie Scott Thompson. BS in Stats., Va. Tech., 1996, MBA in Info. and Decision Support Systems, 2000. Data processing technician (mos

251a) Va. Army N.G., Manassas, Va., 1990—; cost analyst / tech. mgr. Tecolote Rsch., Inc., Lexington Park, Md., 1996—. Mem.: Nat. Guard Assn. of US, Va. Nat. Guard Assn., Mil. Officers Assn. Am., Am. Statis. Assn., Soc. of Cost Estimation and Analysis. Home: 6939 Aidan Way King George VA 22485 Office: Tecolote Research Inc 22299 Exploration Dr Lexington Park MD 20653 E-mail: kjackameit@tecolote.com.

JACKEL, LAWRENCE, publishing company executive; b. NYC, July 25; s. Solomon and Sylvia (Fisher) J.; m. Ellen Jane Koons, Sept. 29, 1985; children: Kenneth Isaac, Molly Laurie, Sarah Kate. BBA, CCNY, 1961, MBA, 1966. Acct. Aviquipo, Inc., N.Y.C., 1961-62; fin. exec. Litton Industries, N.Y.C., 1962-68; group controller Alloys Unltd., Inc., N.Y.C., 1968-69; v.p. fin. Litton Ednl. Pub., Inc., N.Y.C., 1969-72, 1969-72, pres. Delmar Pubs. div. Albany, N.Y., 1973-80, 1973-80, exec. v.p., pres. N.Y.C., 1976-80; owner, pres. Tab Books Inc., 1980-90, 1980-90; group v.p. McGraw Hill, Blue Ridge Summit, Pa., 1990-92; pres. Jackel Group Inc.-Cons. and Pubs., Venice, Fla., 1992-93; vice chmn., CEO, owner Lectorum Publs., Inc., N.Y.C., 1993-96; chmn. Promotional Sales Books LLC, N.Y.C., 1996—. Mem.: Univ. Club. Democrat. Jewish. Home: 7702 Cherry Laurel Ct Sarasota FL 34241 E-mail: jackelpub@verizon.net.

JACKELS, BENJAMIN L., restauranteur, educator; b. Wheaton, Ill., Oct. 16, 1975; s. Leroy F and Bonita J Jackels; m. Jodie L. Jackels; children: Garrett Andrew, Austin Phillip. BS in music edn., U. Ill. Urbana-Champaign, 1997. Education Endorsement Ill., 1997. Band dir. Granite City HS, Ill., 1997—2002; owner, operator Culver's of O'Fallon, Ill., 2003—. Instr. Smith Walbridge Clinics, Champaign, Ill., 1997—2003. Recipient Guy M. Duker Instrumental Music Edn. award, U. of Ill. at Urbana-Champaign Sch. of Music, 1997. Mem.: Zeta Psi Frat. of N.Am. (life). Office: Culver's of O'Fallon IL 1702 W Hwy 50 O Fallon IL 62269 Office Phone: 618-624-8430.

JACKELS, MICHAEL OWEN, bishop; b. Rapid City, SD, Apr. 13, 1954; Student, U. Nebr., 1972—74; BA in philosophy, St. Pius X Sem., Erlanger, Ky., 1977; MA in theology (scripture), Mt. St. Mary Sem., Emmitsburg, Md., 1981; STD in spiritual theology, Angelicum U., Rome, 1989. Ordained deacon Diocese of Lincoln, Nebr., 1980, ordained priest, 1981, asst. pastor Cathedral Risen Christ, 1981—82, religion tchr. Pius X HS, 1981—85, asst. pastor St. Thomas Aquinas Ch., U. Nebr., 1982—85, diocesan dir. religious edn., diocesan master of ceremonies, named chaplain Sch. Sisters of Christ the King, 1992, named co-vicar for religious, 1994; named monsignor, 1994; served Congregation for the Doctrine of the Faith, Vatican, 1997—2005; bishop Diocese of Wichita, Kans., 2005. Office: Diocese Wichita 424 N Broadway Wichita KS 67202*

JACKENDOFF, RAY SAUL, linguistics educator; b. Chgo., Jan. 23, 1945; s. Nathaniel and Elaine Muriel (Flanders) J.; m. Hildy Dvorak; children: Amy Sarah, Beth Liana, Daniel Nathan. BA, Swarthmore Coll., 1965; PhD, MIT, 1969. Instr. UCLA, 1969-70; asst. prof. linguistics Brandeis U., Waltham, Mass., 1971-73, assoc. prof., 1973-79, prof., 1979—2005, chmn. linguistics and cognitive sci., 1979-92, 2002—05; prof. philosophy Tufts U., Medford, Mass., 2005—, co-dir. Ctr. for Cognitive Studies, 2005—. Author: Semantic Interpretation in Generative Grammar, 1972 (Arts Humanities award Coun. Grad. Schs. in U.S. 1974), X-Bar Syntax: A Study of Phrase Structure, 1977, Semantics and Cognition, 1983, (with F. Lerdahl) A Generative Theory of Tonal Music, 1983, Consciousness and the Computational Mind, 1987, Semantic Structures, 1990, Languages of the Mind, 1992, Patterns in the Mind, 1993, The Architecture of the Language Faculty, 1997, Foundations of Language, 2002, (with P. Culicover) Simpler Syntax, 2005; mem. editl. bd. Music Perception, Cognitive Sci., Studia Linguistica, Natural Lang. and Linguistic Theory, Trends in Cognitive Scis. Soloist Boston Pops Orch., 1980 Recipient Jean Nicod prize in cognitive philosophy, 2003; Guggenheim fellow, 1993-94, fellow Wissenschaftskolleg zu Berlin, 1999-2000. Mem. Linguistic Soc. Am. (exec. com. 1996-99, 2002-05 pres 2003), Soc. for Philosophy and Psychology (pres. 1990-91), Am. Acad. Arts and Scis. Jewish. Home: 79 Goden St Belmont MA 02478-2934 Office: Tufts U Ctr Cognitive Studies Medford MA 02155

JACKER, CORINNE LITVIN, playwright, writer; b. Chgo., June 29, 1933; d. Thomas Henry and Theresa (Bellak) Litvin. Student, Stanford U., 1950-52; BS, Northwestern U., 1954, MA, 1955, postgrad., 1955-56. Editor Liberal Arts Press, 1959-60, Macmillan Co., 1960-63, Scribner's, 1963-65; story editor Sta. WNET-TV, N.Y.C., 1969-71, CBS-TV, N.Y.C., 1972-74; instr. playwrighting NYU, 1976-78; vis. prof. playwriting Yale U., 1979-81. Adj. prof. Princeton U., 1986, 88, Columbia U., 1988-99, Breadloaf Sch. of English, 1988, NYU, 1990-91, U. Ga., 1995—2003; sci. cons. Benton Project for Broadcasting, U. Chgo., 1988-90. Exec. story editor, head writer (TV series) Best of Families, PBS, N.Y.C., 1975-77; head writer (TV series) Another World, 1981-82; author: Man, Memory, and Machines, 1964 (N.Y. Pub. Library 50 Best Books of Yr. 1964), Window on the Unknown, 1966 (AAAS 50 Best Books of Yr. 1966), A Little History of Cocoa, 1966, The Black Flag of Anarchy, 1968 (Pubs. Weekly 25 Best Books of Yr. 1968), The Biological Revolution, 1971, The Chocolate Bar Bust, 1994; playwright: The Scientific Method, 1970, Seditious Acts, 1970, Travellers, 1973, Breakfast, Lunch, & Dinner, 1975, Bits and Pieces, 1975 (Obie award 1975), Harry Outside, 1975 (Obie award 1975), Night Thoughts & Terminal, 1976, Other People's Tables, 1976, My Life, 1977, After the Season, 1978, Later, 1979, Domestic Issues, 1981, In Place, 1982, Songs from Distant Lands, 1985, (adaptation) Hedda Gabbler, 1989, The Island, 1991, (adaptation) Three Sisters, 1992, In the Dark, 1993, Light, 1993, Getting Home, 1994, A New Life, 1995, The Promised Land, 1995, The Machine Age, 1996, Parties, 2000; TV writer, including: 3 episodes Actors' Choice, NET, 1970 (Emmy citation 1970), Virginia Woolf: The Moment Whole, NET, 1972 (CINE Golden Eagle award 1972); story editor: 4 episode series Benjamin Franklin, CBS, 1974 (Emmy citation 1974); The Adams Chronicles, 1975 (Peabody award 1975); Bicentennial Minutes, 1975, Loose Change, 1978, 3 episode series, NBC, 1978, 3 episodes of Best of Families, NET, 1978, The Jilting of Granny Weatherall, NET, 1980, Night Thoughts and Terminal BBC, 1978, Overdrawn at the Memory Bank, NET, 1983 (Rotterdam Film Festival, Am. Film Inst. Video Feature Film Festival). Rockefeller Found. grantee, 1979-80; residency Villa Serbelloni, Bellagio, Italy, 1987. Mem. Dramatists Guild, Writers Guild Am. East, PEN Home and Office: 110 W 86th St New York NY 10024-4049 Office Phone: 212-496-9698. E-mail: jacaranda@verizon.net.

JACKIEWICZ, FREDERICK WACLAW, priest; b. Kampala, Uganda, Nov. 5, 1944; arrived in U.S., 1956; s. Waclaw Jackiewicz and Maria Szumski. BA, St. Marys Coll., 1967; MDiv, St. Christ Meth. Svc., 1971; MA, U. Detroit, 1971. Ordained 1971. Asst. pastpr St. Hedwig Ch., Trenton, NJ, St. Joan of Arc Ch., Marlton, NJ; adminstr. St. Joseph, Beverly, NJ; pastor St. Jerome Ch., West Long Branch, NJ. Chaplain West Long Branch Rescue Squad, Monmouth Ch., Monmouth U., 1999—2000. Mem.: KC (chaplain). Roman Catholic. Avocations: hiking, travel, historical reading, woodcarving. Home: 19 Pettit Ave South River NJ 08882-1055

JACKIW, ROMAN, physicist, researcher; b. Lublinec, Poland, Nov. 8, 1939; came to U.S., 1949; s. Nicholas and Zenobia (Kostyk) J.; m. So-Young Pi, Sept. 4, 1981; children: Simone Ahlborn, Nicholas, Stefan Pi. BA, Swarthmore Coll., 1961; PhD, Cornell U., 1966; Doctorate (hon.), U. Uppsala, Sweden, 2000, U. Torino, Italy, 2000; Doctorate, Bogolyubov Inst., Kyiv, Ukraine, 2003. Jr. fellow Harvard Soc. of Fellows, Cambridge, Mass., 1966-69; from asst. prof. to Jerrold Zacharias prof. physics MIT, Cambridge, 1969—. Vis. prof. Rockefeller U., N.Y.C., 1977-78, U. Calif., L.A., Santa Barbara, 1980, Columbia U., N.Y.C., 1989-90. Contbr. over 150 articles to profl. jours. Alfred P. Sloan fellow Sloan Found., 1969-71, J.S. Guggenheim fellow Guggenheim Found., 1977-78; recipient Dannie Heineman prize in math. physics Am. Phys. Soc., 1995, Dirac medal and prize Internat. Ctr. for Theoretical Physics, Trieste, Italy, 1998. Fellow Am. Acad. of Arts and Scis., Am. Phys. Soc.; mem. NAS, Nat. Acad. Scis. Ukraine (fgn. mem.). Achievements include research on fundamental processes in nature. Office: MIT NE 24 4085 5 Cambridge Ctr Cambridge MA 02142 Office Phone: 617-253-4830. Business E-Mail: jackiw@lns.mit.edu.

JACKLIN, WILLIAM THOMAS, retired county official, educator; b. Chgo., Dec. 26, 1940; s. Robert and Florence Carrie (Dombrow) J.; m. Bonnie Joy Winquist; 1 child, Laura Carrie. BS, Roosevelt U., 1967; MS in Bus. Edn., Ind. U., 1968. Cert. fraud examiner, govt. fin. mgr. Assoc. instr. Ind. U., 1967-69; V.p. DuPage Corp., Lombard, Ill., 1970-73; inst. bus. Coll. DuPage, Glen Ellyn, Ill., 1969-77; chief dep. auditor DuPage County, 1973, county auditor, 1973-2000. V.p. DuPage County Employees Credit Union, 1978-79, pres., 1979-80; fiscal officer DuPage Met. Enforcement Group, 1987-94; exec. bd. Midwestern Intergovtl. Audit Forum, 1991-2000; bd. dirs. Franciscan Ministries, Inc., 1992-97, DuPage Heritage Gallery, Lombard Historical Commn., 1995-2000; pres. DuPage Heritage Gallery, 1997—. Announcer CRIS Radio for the Blind. Sec. York Twp. Rep. Orgn., 1978-80; treas. Highland Hills Assn., 1975-78; chmn. DuPage County com. Gerald R. Ford presdl. campaign, 1976; alt. del. 1992 Rep. Nat. Conv.; mem. fin. mgmt. project com. Ill. Dept. Commerce and Cmty. Affairs, 1980-82, bd. dirs. Lombard Hist. Soc., v.p., 1983-87, pres., 1987-91. Mem. Assn. Cert. Fraud Examiners, Nat. Assn. Local Govt. Auditors, Inst. Internal Auditors (govt. and pub. affairs com. 1976-82), Ill. Assn. County Auditors (sec.-treas. 1976-78, v.p. 1978-80, pres. 1980-84, treas. 1986-2000), Assn. Govt. Accts., Ind. Soc. of Chgo., Masons (sec. 1979-80), The Montana Club, Phi Delta Kappa. Christian Scientist. Home: 4908 Linscott Downers Grove IL 60515-3537 E-mail: billjacklin@earthlink.net.

JACKMAN, HUGH, actor; b. Sydney, NSW, Australia, Oct. 12, 1968; s. Chris Jackman; m. Deborra-Lee Furness, Feb. 1996; children: Oscar Maximilian, Ava Eliot. BA in Journalism, U. of Technology, Sydney; student, Actor's Ctr., Sydney; grad., Western Australian Acad. Performing Arts, Perth, 1994. Actor: (TV series) Correlli, 1995, Snowy River: The McGregor Saga, 1993, Halifax f.p: Afraid of the Dark, 1998, Oklahoma!, 1999; (films) Hey Mr. Producer, 1998, Paperback Hero, 1999, Erskineville Kings, 1999, X-Men, 2000, Someone Like You, 2001, Swordfish, 2001, Kate & Leopold, 2001, Standing Room Only, 2002, X2, 2003, Van Helsing, 2004, The Fountain, 2005, (Broadway debut) The Boy from Oz, 2003— (Tony award best actor in a musical, 2004, Drama Desk award best actor in a musical, 2004), (other stage appearances) Beauty and the Beast, Oklahoma!, Carousel, 2002; host Tony Awards, 2003, 2004, 2005.*

JACKMAN, JAMES DAVID, lawyer; b. Stubenville, Ohio, Aug. 13, 1960; s. Merle M. and Sarah L. Jackman; m. Lorraine P. Jackman, Apr. 30, 1988; children: Joshua A., Jeremy S. BS in Acctg., U. Akron, 1982; JD, Nova Southeastern U., 1985. Bar: Fla. 1985, Ohio 1990; cert. Am. Bd. Certification Consumer Bankruptcy. Pvt. practice law, pres., Bradenton, Fla., 1986—. Coach YMCA Youth Sports, Bradenton, 1994—. Mem. Kiwanis (com. chmn. 1990—), Masonic Lodge, Shriners. Avocations: football, basketball, youth sports coaching, movies, family activities.

JACKMAN, LLOYD MILES, chemistry professor; b. Goolwa, Australia, Apr. 1, 1926; came to U.S., 1967; s. Charles Stuart and Florence Olive (Green) J.; m. Marie Alma Sandow, 1950; children— Richard Miles, Donald Charles, Andrew Thorpe. BSc, U. Adelaide, Australia, 1945, BSc with honors, 1946, MSc, 1948, PhD, 1951. Asst. lectr. organic chemistry Imperial Coll., London, 1952, lectr., 1953; reader U. London, 1961—62; prof., head dept. organic chemistry U. Melbourne, Australia, 1962—67; prof. chemistry Pa. State U., University Park, 1967—91, prof. emeritus, 1992—. Author: Applications of NMR in Organic Chemistry. Beit fellow U. London, 1951-52; NSF sr. fgn. fellow, 1965; Guggenheim fellow, 1973-74; Wilsmore fellow chemistry, Melbourne, Australia; recipient Humboldt award, Fed. Republic Germany, 1977, 89. Fellow AAAS, Chem. Soc. London, Am. Chem. Soc., Royal Australian Chem. Inst. Home: 710 Glenn Rd State College PA 16803-3414 Office: 152 Davey Lab University Park PA 16802-6300 Office Phone: 814-865-2269. E-mail: lmj@psu.edu.

JACKMAN, ROBERT ALAN, retail executive; b. NYC, Mar. 22, 1939; s. Joseph and Kate Queenie (Silverman) J.; m. Lois Wiederschall, June 10, 1962; children: Jennifer Sharon, Deborah Lynn. BS, U. Bridgeport, 1961. Dir. sales Mattel Inc., Hawthorne, Calif., 1963-75; sr. v.p. mktg. and sales Tyco Industries Inc., Moorestown, NJ, 1975-78; gen. mgr. Aurora Products Inc., Stamford, Conn., 1978-80; ptnr. Scott Lancaster Jackman Mills Atha, Westport, Conn., 1980-83; pres., CEO Leisure Dynamics Inc. divsn. Coleco Industries, Westport, 1983-86; with Oak Tree Publs., San Diego, 1983-87; exec. v.p. Coleco Industries Inc., West Hartford, Conn., 1986-88; gen. mgr. Tomy Am., Inc., Southport, Conn., 1988-90, also bd. dirs.; owner Yes I Can, 1990—. Cons. Harvard U. Bus. Sch. Club, N.Y.C., 1984. Patentee in field. With USAR, 1961—62. Recipient Disting. Alumni award U. Bridgeport (Conn.), 1986. Mem. U. Bridgeport Mktg. Coun., Mission Hills Country Club (Rancho Mirage, Calif.). Avocations: tennis, music, reading. Home: 8 Via Elegante Rancho Mirage CA 92270-1969 Office: 35 325 Date Palm Dr Ste 131 Cathedral City CA 92234-7031 Office Phone: 760-321-1717. E-mail: bob@yesican.com.

JACKMAN, RODERICK VICTOR, distance learning educator; b. Salt Lake City, Dec. 30, 1949; m. Linda Jackman; children: Candace Linda, Roderick Dustin, Sean Larsen. AS in Gen. Edn., Brigham Young U., Provo, 1974; BS in Med. Sociology, U. Utah, 1976, MS in Health Sci., 1979, postgrad. in pub. adminstrn., 1979—81; BS in Biochemistry, Westminister Coll., Salt Lake City, 1997. Chemistry Utah State Office of Edn., 1981, Sociology Utah State Office of Edn., 1981, Medical Anatomy and Physiology Utah State Office of Edn., 1981, Health Occupations Utah State Office of Edn., 1981, Health Science/Health Technology Utah State Office of Edn., 1981, Health Education Utah State Office of Edn., 1981, Advanced Health Science Utah State Office of Edn., 1981. Distance edn. instr. Alpine Sch. Dist., American Fork, Utah, 1981—, Utah Valley State Coll., Orem, 1985—2003, Salt Lake C.C., 2003—. Surg. asst.; advisor Health Occupation Students Am., 1986—; bd. dirs. Utah Health Students Am., 1986—88; pres. health divsn. Utah Vocat. Assn., 1986—87, pres., 1988—89; so. rep. health dept. bd. Edn. Health Divsn. Utah Assn. for Career and Tech., 2005—; head soccer coach Pleasant Grove (Utah) HS, 1982. Recipient Vocat. Excellence award, Utah Health Occupation Students Am., Outstanding Svc. award, Health Occupation Students Am., 1986—2005, Extra Mile Tchg. award, Alpine Sch. Dist., 1989, 2005, Outstanding Tchr. award, Utah Vocat. Assn., 1990, Outstanding Svc. to Edn. award, Utah State Bd. Edn., 1997, Golden Apple Tchr. award, Alpine Sch. Dist., 1997, Outstanding Instr. award, Utah Vocat. Assn., 1998, Students Choice award, Utah Valley State Coll., 1999, Outstanding Interactive Course award, 2002. Home: 748 S Sunny Ln Orem UT 84058 Office: Alpine Sch Dist /Mountain View 665 W Center Orem UT 84057 Personal E-mail: rjackman@alpine.k12.ut.us.

JACK-MOORE, PHYLLIS, strategist, educational consultant; b. Charlotte, N.C., Aug. 23, 1934; d. William Thomas and Connie LaVerne (Childers) Harris; children: Michael Harris, Julie Dawn Jack Rodgers. BA, U. N.C., 1965, MEd, 1969; postgrad., North Tex. State U., 1982-83. Cert. tchr., N.C., Tex. Elem. tchr. Chapel Hill (N.C.) Pub. Schs., 1965-68; staff devel. coordinator Learning Inst. N.C., Durham, 1969-72; child devel. specialist Tex. Dept. Human Resources, Ft. Worth, 1975-77; child care tng. coordinator North Tex. State Univ., Denton, 1978-81; dir., owner Resources for Children, Inc., Ft. Worth, 1984-88; pvt. practice work family strategy, ednl. cons. Ft. Worth, 1988—; assoc. exec. Tex. Assn. of Child Care Resources and Referral Orn., 2005—. Instr. Tarrant County Jr. Coll., Ft. Worth, North Tex. State U., 1982—; frequent guest speaker; appearances on TV; coord. for tng. in establishment of pub. sch. kindergarten program in State of N.C., 1972-73; cons. for family support svcs. State Dept. Pub. Instrn., Raleigh. Contbg. author: Room to Grow; mem. editorial rev. bd. Child Care Quar., Austin, 1984—. Trustee Tarrant County Youth Collaboration, 1982—86; mem. adv. bd. Ft. Worth's A Better Childhood Com., 1990—, Office of Early Childhood Coordination of Tex., 2002—, Healthy Child Care Tex., 2002—; coord. Tex. State Parent Action, 1989—; mem. gov.'s task force Head Start Collaboration, 1991—; bd. dirs. Tarrant County Med. Aus., 1983—84, City of Austin Fund for Child Care Excellence, 2000—; state bd. dirs. Mental Health Assn. in Tex., 2001—. Recipient Brous Outstanding Advocate award, 1984, All State Good Hands award, 1996, Excellence in Child Abuse Prevention award, 2001, Jeannette Watson Advocacy award, Austin, 2002, award Tex. Parents As Tchrs., 2005. Mem. Nat. Assn. for the Edn. of Young Children (gov. bd. nominee 1988—, nat. field rep. 1983—), Tex. Assn. for the Edn. of Young Children (state pres. 1982-83, Adminstr. of the Yr. award 1993), Ft. Worth Assn. for the Edn. of Young Children (pres. 1976-78), So. Assn. for Children Under Six (com. chair 1978-80, conf. co-chair 1987), Rotary, Phi Beta Kappa, Phi Delta Kappa. Clubs: Ft. Worth Woman's (v.p. and auditor 1983-86). Lodges: Rotary. E-mail: pjmoore@flash.net.

JACKNOWITZ, ARTHUR I., pharmacist, educator; b. Bklyn., Dec. 13, 1943; s. Samuel and Miriam Jacknowitz; m. Linda Kroll Jacknowitz. BS in pharmacy, Long Island U., 1967; MS in biochemical pharm., SUNY, 1972; PharmD, U. of the Scis., Phila., 1974. Registered pharmacist WV, Pa., ME. Asst. to assoc. prof. to prof. to chmn. clin. pharm dept. to dist. chair W. Va. U., Morgantown, 1974—. Edit. bd. Drug Info. Jour., Horsham, Pa., 1986—; rev. com. Nat. Pharm. Lic. Exam, Mt. Prospect, Ill., 1991—; Lady Davis vis. prof. Hebrew U., Jerusalem, 1996; mem. adv. panel Internat. Pharm. Abstracts, Washington; bd. dirs. Gerson Lehrman Group Healthcare Coun., Pharmacy Coun. on Hepatitis and Liver Diseases, U.S. Pharm. Conv. Com. on Tellers. Contbr. articles various profl. jours. and chapter books; contbg. editor: US Pharmacist, 1985—88. Pres. Tree of Life Congregation, Morgantown, W.Va., 1988—90; bd. dirs. W.Va. chpt. Alzheimer's Assn., 2002—05. Mem.: Pharmacy Coun. Hepatitis and Liver Diseases, Am. Pharm. Assn., Am. Soc. Health Sys. Pharm., Am. Assn. Colls. Pharmacy, Drug Info. Assn. Achievements include development of Hepatitis C - a series of CE lectures to cmty. and instl. pharmacists nationwide, 2002-2003. Office Phone: 304-293-1468. E-mail: ajacknowitz@hsc.wvu.edu.

JACKOBOICE, SANDRA KAY, artist; b. Detroit, July 22, 1936; d. Virgil Ellsworth and Lucille Elizabeth LeSeur; m. Edward James Jackoboice, Jan. 11, 1958; children: E. Michael, Timothy Jon. BA, Aquinas Coll., Grand Rapids, Mich., 1989. Co-owner Fashion Plate, Grand Rapids, 1975-79; wardrobe cons. Steketees, Grand Rapids, 1980-82; owner Color Plus, Grand Rapids, 1983—. Instr. pastel Von Heibig Ctr. Arts, Naples, Fla., 2001—, Art League, Marcos Island, 2003, 05, Art League Ft. Myers, 2005. One-woman shows include FMB, Lowell, 1993, 1995, City Hall, Bielsko-Biala, Poland, 1995, Terryberry Gallery, Grand Rapids, 1997, Frederick Meijer Gardens, 1998, exhibited in group shows at Bot. Images Exhbn., Lansing, Mich., Artist Alliance Group Shows, represented by, Grand Gallery, Grand Rapids, Tamarack Gallery, Naples, Fla., Freeline Gallery, Suttors Bay, Mich.; featured in Artists' Photo Reference Book, Pastel Artist Internat. mag., Pastel Jour., others. Mem. Jr. League, Grand Rapids, 1962—96, Downtown Mgmt. Bd., Grand Rapids, 1993—96, Grand Rapids Parking Commn., 1993—96; bd. dirs. Arts Coun. Greater Grand Rapids, 1997—2000. Recipient awards for art work. Mem.: League Club, S.W. Fla. Pastel Soc. (founder and advisor bd. dir. 2002—), Internat. Assn. Pastel Socs. (publicity chair and membership chair 2001—, bd. dir. 2003—, v.p. 2005—), Grand Valley Artists, Artists Alliance, Great Lakes Pastel Soc. (pres. 1997—2001, advisor bd. dir. 2002—04, co-founder), Pastel Soc. Am. (assoc.; sig. 2004—). Republican. Avocations: travel, art, tennis, golf. Office: Color Plus PO Box 6775 Grand Rapids MI 49516-6775 Home (Winter): 81 11 Bay Colony Dr Naples FL 34108

JACKSON, ALAN, country songwriter, singer; b. Newnan, Ga. s. Eugene and Ruth Jackson; m. Denise Jackson; children: Mattie, Ali. Student, W. Ga. Coll. Albums include Here in the Real World, 1990, Don't Rock the Jukebox, 1991 (Album of Yr. 1992 Song of Yr. 1992), A Lot About Livin' (and a Little 'Bout Love), 1992 (2 Grammy nominations, Best Country Male Vocal and Song for Chattahoochee), Honky Tonk Christmas, 1993, Who I Am, 1994, The Greatest Hits Collection, 1995, Everything I Love, 1996, High Mileage, 1998, Under the Influence, 1999, When Somebody Loves You, 2000, Drive, 2002, What I Do, 2004. Office: Alan Jackson Fan Club PO Box 121945 Nashville TN 37212-1945 also: Arista Records 7 Music Cir Nashville TN 37203

JACKSON, ALLEN KEITH, retired museum administrator; b. Rocky Ford, Colo., July 22, 1932; s. Monford L. and Leliah Jean (Hipp) Jackson; m. Barbara May Hollard, June 13, 1954; children: Cary Vincent, Deborah Kay, Edward Keith, Fredrick James. BA, U. Denver, 1954; postgrad., Cambridge (Eng.) U., 1955; Th.M. (Elizabeth Iliff Warren fellow), Iliff Sch. Theology, 1958; PhD, Emory U., 1960. Instr. sociology Emory U., 1958-60; chaplain, asst. prof. religion and sociology Morningside Coll., Sioux City, Iowa, 1960-62, dean coll., 1962-67; pres. Huntingdon Coll., Montgomery, Ala., 1968-93; dir. Idaho Mus. Natural History, Idaho State U., Pocatello, 1993—98; exec. dir. Nat. Heritage Ctr., 1998—2002; ret., 2002—. Past pres. Montgomery Area United Appeal. Fulbright scholar, Cambridge U., 1955, honor fellow, Emory U., 1960. Mem.: Ala. Coun. Advancement Pvt. Colls. (pres. 1975—81), Ala. Assn. Ind. Colls. and Univs. (pres. 1969—71), Rotary, Phi Kappa Phi, Beta Theta Pi, Omicron Delta Kappa, Phi Beta Kappa. Home: 633 W Mcnabb Rd Inkom ID 83245-1502 *A worthy aim it seems to me, is to seek the Truth and to share the truths you find.*

JACKSON, ALPHONSO ROY, secretary of housing and urban development; b. Marshall, Tex., Sept. 9, 1946; s. Arthur Todd and Henriette (Green) Jackson; m. Marcia A. Jackson, June 18, 1988; children: Annette Watkins, Lesley Jackson. BS, Truman State U.(formerly N.E. Mo. State), 1968, MA, 1969; JD, Washington U., St. Louis, 1973. Asst. prof. criminal justice and polit. sci. U. Mo., St. Louis, 1973—77; dir. pub. safety City of St. Louis, 1977—81, dep. exec. dir., Housing Authority, 1981—82; dir., cons. svcs. Laventhol & Horwath, St. Louis, 1982-87; CEO Dept. of Pub. and Assisted Housing, Washington, 1987-89; pres. and CEO Housing Authority/City of Dallas, 1989-96; dep. sec. US Dept H.U.D., Washington, 2001—04; acting sec. US Dept. H.U.D., Washington, 2003—04, sec., 2004—. Cons. other city govts.; adj. prof. U. Mo., St. Louis; mem. bd. commrs. Planned Indsl. Expansion City of St. Louis, 1978—; bd. dirs. St. Louis Local devel. Co., 1978—. Contbr. Bd. dirs. Zale-Lipshy Hosp., Dallas, 1992, Truman State U., 1995, Tex. So. U., 1998, Children's Med. Ctr., Dallas, 1996; chmn. Gen. Svcs. Commn. State of Tex., Austin, 1998; mem. task foce edn. Mo. Gov., 1975-76, Sister Cities Internat., 1976-81. Recipient Chmn.'s award Nat. Boys and Girls Clubs of Am., 1997; fellow Kellogg fellow Ctr. Biology nat. Sys., Washington U., 1970-71, U. Oxford, 1977, Danforth Found., 1981, The Aspen Inst. Fellow: Kappa Alpha Psi; mem.: Nat. Bar. Assn., Anniversary Club. Democrat. Roman Catholic. Avocations: jogging, golf, reading. Office: US Dept HUD Robert C Weaver Federal Bldg 451 7th St SW Rm 10000 Washington DC 20410-1047*

JACKSON, AMBROSE CYPRIAN, music educator; b. Washington, June 26, 1940; s. Ambrose Cyprian and Helen Brown Jackson. MusB, Cath. U. Am., 1962, MusM, 1965; D, Ecole des Hautes Etudes en Sciences Sociales, 1979. Asst. prof. Coll. SI, NY, 1987—98, Queensborough Cmty. Coll., NY, 1988—99; tchr. Ellenville Ctrl. Schs., NY, 1999—. Trumpeter/bd. dirs. Woodstock Chamber Orch., 2000—; trumpeter U.S. Army Bd., Wash., DC, 1962—65. Composer music. Specialist, 5th class U.S. Army, 1962—65, Ft. Myers, Arlington, Va. Recipient Ambassadors award, Herbert Spiro, ambassador, 1976. Avocations: farming, fishing. Office: Ellenville Ctrl Schools 28 Maple Ave Ellenville NY 12428 Business E-Mail: ajax@ulster.net.

JACKSON, ANDREW PRESTON, library director; b. Bklyn., Jan. 28, 1947; s. Walter Luther Sr. and Bessie (Lindsey) J. BS, CUNY, 1990, MLS, 1996; pub. librs. profl. cert., SUNY. Asst. supr. pers. processing unit Human Resources Adminstrn. Agy. Child Devel. Pers. Dept., N.Y.C., 1968-70, coord. pers. svcs., 1970-76; customer rels. mgr., contracts mgr. Robinson Chevrolet, Novato, Calif., 1976-79; office mgr. Sesame Press, Inc., N.Y.C., 1979-80; exec. dir. Langston Hughes Cmty. Libr. and Cultural Ctr., Corona, N.Y., 1980—. Lectr. Black history, N.Y.C., 1986—; cons. evaluating Black heritage collections; adj. lectr. York Coll., CUNY, 2001—. Author: Queens Notes: A Work In Progress, Facts About the Forgotten Borough of Queens New York, (foreword) African American Almanac, 9th edit., 2003; contbg. author: Handbook of Black Librarianship; contbr. articles to profl. jours. Chmn. social svcs. adv. coun. Cmty. Planning Bd. Areas 3 and 5, 1984—87; treas. No. Blvd. Mchts. Assn., Corona, 1985—99; cmty. adv. coun. York Coll., 1997—;

active NY State Freedom Trails Commn., Queens Underground RR Com., 1997—; bd. trustees The Renaissance Charter Sch., 1999—; convenor Churchman's fellowship Corona Congl. Ch., 1987—89; nat. adv. bd. CDF Langston Hughes Libr., 2001—03; cmty. adv. bd. Elmhurst (NY) Hosp. Ctr., 1983—97; bd. dirs. York Coll. Alumni Inc., Jamaica, NY, 1990—93, 1996—99, Queens Pub. TV, 1986—; vice chair cmty. adv. bd. Otis Bantum Correctional Ctr., N.Y.C. Dept. Corrections, Rikers Island, NY, 1990—95. Staff sgt. (E-5) USAF, 1964—68, Vietnam. Decorated Bronze Star; named Man of Yr., Nat. Assn. Negro Bus. & Profl. Women's Club, Inc., 1991, Ombudsman award, 1982, East Elmhurst Alumni Inc. Hall of Fame, 1998; recipient Cmty. Svc. award East Elmhurst Track Club, 1986, Tabernacle Cmty. C.M.E. Ch., Nat. Assn. Univ. Women (north shore br.), Cmty. award East Elmhurst-Corona Civic Assn., 1989, Outstanding Leadership in Queens award Queens Fedn. of Churches, 1988, Cert. of Appreciation Kiwanis, 1991, Cmty. Svc. award Minority Mgmt. Assn., NYC, 1992, Cert. of Recognition August Martin HS, 1992, Gov.'s award African-Americans of Distinction, NY State Gov., 1994, Disting. Grad. award Nat. Assn. Equal Opportunity in Higher Edn., 1994, Cert. of Honor, Queens Borough Pres., 1994, Giving It Back, award W.C. Bryant H.S., 1995, Youth Devel. award 115th Police Precinct Coun., 1994, Recognition award NY State Atty. Gen., 2002; Disting. Alumni award York Coll. Alumni Assn., Inc., 1996, Fufilling The Dream award CBS-TV, 1996, Scroll of Honor, 4W Circle of Arts and Enterprise, 1996, Cmty. Svc. award Nat. Coun. Negro Women, 1997, Cmty. Svc. award Elmcor Alumni Assn., 1998, Cmty. Svc. award Concerned African-Am. of Flushing, 1998, Lamplighter award Queens Borough Pub. Libr., 1999, Cmty. Svc. award NY Fire Dept. African Heritage Soc., 2000, Outstanding Contbns. award Combined Treasury Dept., 2001, Appreciation award Grace Episc. Ch., 2001, Cmty. Person of Yr. award Delta Beta Zeta, 2001, Cmty. Activist award United for Progress Dem. Club, Cmty. Svc. award Corona Congl. Ch., 2002, Cultural award Key Women of Am., 2002, Cmty. Leader of Yr. award Alpha Kappa Alpha, 2003, Pinnacle award Jack and Jill of Am., Inc., 2005. Mem. NAACP (life), ALA, ALA Black Libr. Caucus (v.p. 2002-04, pres. 2004—, Libr. Advocacy award 1999, Libr. Outreach award 1999), Pub. Librs. Assn., Libr. Adminstrn. and Mgmt. Assn., N.Y. Black Librs. Caucus, Reforma, N.Y. Libr. Assn. Avocations: speaking with youth, reading, writing. Home: 25-14 97th St East Elmhurst NY 11369-1923 Office: Queens Borough Pub Libr Langston Hughes Comm Libr 100-01 Northern Blvd Corona NY 11368-1038 Office Phone: 718-651-1100. Business E-Mail: andrew.p.jackson@queenslibrary.org.

JACKSON, ANNE (ANNE JACKSON WALLACH), actress; b. Allegheny, Pa., Sept. 3, 1926; d. John Ivan and Stella Germaine (Murray) J.; m. Eli Wallach, Mar. 5, 1948; children: Peter, Roberta, Katherine. Studied with Sanford Meisner and Herbert Berghof at Neighborhood Playhouse, with Lee Strassberg at Actor's Studio; DFA, South Hampton Coll. Tchr. Herbert Berghoff Sch. Profl. debut: Cherry Orchard; mem. Am. Repertory Co.; Broadway plays include: Summer and Smoke, Oh, Men! Oh, Women!, Middle of the Night, Major Barbara, Rhinoceros, Luv, Waltz of the Toreadors, Diary of Anne Frank, 1978, Twice Around the Park, 1982-83, Nest of the Woodgrouse, 1984, Café Crown, 1989, Love Letters, 1991-92, Lost in Yonkers, 1992, In Person, 1993, The Flowering Peach, 1994, off-Broadway plays: Tennessee Williams Remembered, 1999, Mr. Peter's Connection, 1998, Down the Garden Path; London stage performances of The Typists, The Tiger, 1966; film appearances include: So Young, So Bad, 1950, Secret Life of an American Wife, 1968, Dirty Dingus McGee, 1970, Lovers and Other Strangers, 1970, The Shining, 1980, Sam's Son, 1985, Funny About Love, 1992, Folks, 1992, Johnnie Twenties, 1998, Something Sweet, 2000; TV appearances include: 84 Charing Cross Road, Private Battle, Everything's Relative, 1987, Law & Order, 1997, Education of Max Bickford, 2002; TV films: Family Man, Golda I and II, Out on a Limb, Baby M, 1988, The Rescuers: The Lady on the Bicycle, 1997; author: (autobiography) Early Stages, 1979. Recipient Obie award. Mem.: Actor's Studio (life). Office: care Paradigm 200 W 57th St Ste 900 New York NY 10019-3211

JACKSON, BARBARA ANN GARVEY, music educator; b. Normal, Ill., Sept. 27, 1929; d. Neil Ford and Eva Burkhart Garvey; m. Robert Seagrave, 1953 (div. 1958); m. Kern C. Jackson, Mar. 29, 1970; stepchildren: Kern, Ross, Bruce, Paul. MusB, U. Ill., 1950; MusM, Eastman Sch. Music, 1952; PhD in Musicology, Stanford U., 1959. prof. music U. Ark., Fayetteville, 1954-56, 1961-91; prof. emeritus, 1991—. spl. music tchr. Los Angeles Pub. Schs., 1956-57; asst. prof. music Ark. Poly. Coll., Russellville, 1957-61. Author: (with others) Practical Beginning Theory, 1962, 8th edit., 2000, Am. String Tchrs. Assn. Dictionary of Bowing Terms for String Instruments, 1968, 87 (3d edition). Editor, pub., ClarNan Editions, 1984—; editor, pub. music by women composers of the past. Mem. Sigma Alpha Iota (hon.), Pi Kappa Lambda, Phi Kappa Phi,. Democrat. Episcopalian. Avocations: gardening, wildflower photography. Office: ClarNan Editions 235 Baxter Ln Fayetteville AR 72701-2104 E-mail: clarman@ipa.net.

JACKSON, BETTY L. DEASON, real estate developer; b. Wichita, Kans., Mar. 31, 1927; d. Orville John and Ida Mabel (Wolfe) Deason; m. James L. Jackson, July 2, 1966 (dec. Feb. 1983); children: Rebecca Lou, Jennifer Mae. AA, SW Baptist U., Bolivar, Mo., 1946; BA, Cen. Mo. State U., 1963; MA, U. Mo., 1964. Lic. realtor, Kans. Salesperson Sears, Kansas City, Mo., 1943-44; bookkeeping clk. Hallmark Cards, Kansas City, Mo., 1945-46; civil service Camp Pendleton, Oceanside, Calif., 1947; sec. Ford Motor Co., Kansas City, Mo., Jim Taylor Olds Co., Independence, Mo., 1952-54; tchr. Consol. Sch. Dist. #2, Mo., 1954-55, tchr. adminstr. Raytown, Mo., 1963-78; owner mgr. B.J.'s Florist Car Wash Laundramat, Stockton, Mo., 1979-82; owner, ptnr. J and S Realty, Stockton, Mo., 1983—. Officer J-S Corp., Stockton, 1986-94. Mem. Nat. Assn. Realtors, Mo. C. of C., AARP, Greater Ozark Bd. Realtors. Democrat. Baptist. Avocations: play organ, piano, church clubs. Office: Coldwell Banker J-S Realty PO Box 159 Stockton MO 65785-0159 Home: 1600 Garfield St Apt 10 Enumclaw WA 98022-2278

JACKSON, BEVERLEY JOY JACOBSON, columnist, educator; b. L.A., Nov. 20, 1928; d. Phillip and Dorothy Jacobson; m. Robert David Jackson (div. Aug. 1964); 1 child, Tracey Dee. Student, U. So. Calif., UCLA. Daily columnist Santa Barbara News Press, 1968-92, Santa Barbara Ind., 1992—94; internat. lectr., 2003. Nat. lectr. Santa Barbara History, History of China Recreated, Chinese Footbinding, Shoes for Bound Feet, China Today; freelance writer, fgn. corr. Author: Dolls and Doll Houses of Spain, 1970; (with others) I'm Just Wild About Harry, 1979, Spendid Slippers: A Thousand Years of an Erotic Tradition, 1997, Ladder to the Clouds-Intrigues and Traditions of Chinese Rank, 1999, King Fisher Blue, 2002, Shanghai Girl Gets All Dressed Up, 2005 Bd. dirs. Santa Barbara br. Am. Cancer Soc., 1963-92; art mus. coun. LA Mus. Art, 1959-96, docent, 1962-64, costume coun., 1983-92; exec. bd. Channel City Club, 1969-2004; adv. bd. Storyteller Sch. Homeless Children, Santa Barbara Hist. Soc. Mus., Coun. Christmas Cheer, Women's Shelter Bldg., Direct Relief Internat., Nat. Coun. Drug and Alcohol Abuse, Santa Barbara Choral Soc., Am. Oceans Campaign, Hospice Santa Barbara, 1981-92, Stop AIDS Coun., Arthritis Found.; bd. dirs. So. Calif. Com. for Shakespear's Globe Theatre, Friends U. Calif. Libr., Santa Barbara; chmn. Santa Barbara Com. for Visit Queen Elizabeth II, 1982—; founder costume guild Santa Barbara Hist. Soc.; curator Chinese collections Santa Barbara Hist. Mus.; hon. bd. Santa Barbara Salvation Army, Ensemble Theatre Santa Barbara. Mem.: PEN, Commanderie Bordeaux San Francisco. Home: PO Box 5118 Santa Barbara CA 93150-5118 Personal E-mail: bevjack@silcom.com.

JACKSON, BEVERLY ROBERSON, state agency administrator, consultant; b. Kansas City, Mo., Mar. 9, 1950; d. Augustus William and Ora Cooper Roberson; m. David James Jackson, July 5, 1975; children: David Jr., Timothy. BA, Colo. Woman's Coll., 1971; MEd, Columbia U., 1975, EdD, 1978. Cert. tchr. nursery, K-12, trainer. Dir. pub. policy Zero to Three-Nat. Ctr., Washington, 1991—96; head start state collaboration dir. D.C. Govt., 1997—. Ind. edn1. cons. various univs., 1977—. Contbr. Putting Children First, 1996. Fellow, Nat. Govs.' Assn., 2001—02. Mem.: Delta Sigma Theta. Office: Office of Early Childhood Devel 717 14th St NW Ste 450 Washington DC 20005

JACKSON, BILLY MORROW, artist, retired art educator; b. Kansas City, Mo., Feb. 23, 1926; s. Alonzo David and Opal May (Morrow) Jackson; m. Blanche Mary Trice, June 12, 1949 (div. Jan. 1988); children: Lon Allan, Robin Jackson Todd, Aron Drew, Sylvia Marie; m. Siti Mariah Mansor, Feb. 1988. BFA, Washington U., St. Louis, 1949; MFA, U. Ill., 1954. Prof. art U. Ill., Champaign, 1954-87; ret., 1987. One-man shows include Jane Haslem Gallery, Washington, 1990, Popoff Art Gallery, Paris, 2002, Represented in permanent collections Smithsonian Inst., Washington, Nat. Art Gallery, NASA Archives, Union League Club Chgo., Boston Pub. Libr., Met. Mus. Art, N.Y.C., Mus. Legion of Honor, San Francisco, Libr. of Congress, Washington, Springfield (Mo.) Art Mus., Conn. Acad. Fine Arts, Hartford, Artist's Guild, St. Louis, Phila., Free Libr., Evansville (Ind.) Mus. Arts & Scis., Joslyn Art Mus., Omaha, Norfolk Mus., Reading (Pa.) Pub. Libr. and Art Gallery, Lakeview Ctr. Art, Peoria, Ill., Butler Inst. Am. Art, Youngstown, Ohio, Civic Ctr. Art Collection, Springfield, Ill., N.Y. Hilton, N.Y.C., Ill. State Mus., Springfield, World Book Ency., Chgo., Rockefeller Ctr., Dulin Gallery Art, Knoxville, Tenn., Swope Mus., Terre Haute, Ind., Bur. of Peclamation, Washington, EPA, Krannert Art Mus., U. Ill., Champaign, Wichita (Kans.) Art Mus., Gov.'s State Coll., Park Forest South, Ill., Sheldon Meml. Gallery Art, U. Nebr., Lincoln, Busey First Nat. Bank, Champaign, 1st Nat. Bank, Swanlund Bldg., Bechmann Inst., U. Ill., Kedan (Malaysia) State Art Gallery, Nelson-Atkins Mus. Art, Kansas City, Mo., R.I. Sch. Art and Design, Providence, commd. mural, state Capital Bldg., Springfield, Ill., Mara Inst. Tech., Malaysia, Ill. Sch. Deaf, Jacksonville, Quincy (Ill.) Vet. Hosp. and Home, Carle Hosp. Edn. Bldg., Urbana, Ill., Mural Agr. Libr., U. Ill., Champaign, Ill. State Police, 2002, Project 500, U. Ill., 2003; subject of book Billy Morrow Jackson: Interpretation of Time and Light (Howard E. Wooden), 1990, In Our Time (retrospective), 1997, Krannert Art Mus., Champaign; author (with Siti Mariah Jackson): On This Island: Artistic View of Martha's Vineyard, 2004. With USMC, 1944—46, PTO. Democrat. Home: 706 W White St Champaign IL 61820-4706 Office Phone: 217-356-5796. Personal E-mail: jacksonstudios@soltec.net.

JACKSON, BOBBY RAND, minister; b. Wilson, NC, Dec. 14, 1931; s. Joel John and Bessie Francis (Mayo) J.; m. Martha Jane Ketteman, May 30, 1953; children: Stephen Rand, Philip Wayne. BA, Free Will Bapt. Bible Coll., Nashville, 1954; MA, Bob Jones U., Greenville, SC, 1955. Ordained to ministry Free Will Baptists Ch., 1951. Evangelist Free Will Baptists Ch., Nashville, 1955—; asst. moderator Nat. Assn. Free Will Baptists, Nashville, 1972-77, moderator, 1978-87, mem. exec. com., 1972-87, chmn. exec. com., 1978-87, presiding officer of gen. bd., 1978-87. Author: Messages That Matter, 1960, Six Steps to Successful Living, 1962, Awakening in the Wilderness, 1965, Beyond the Stars, 1966; soloist: record albums Softly and Tenderly, 1968, Then Sings My Soul, 1969, Fill My Cup, Lord, 1970, My God and I, 1978, Songs from Two Generations, 1985. Mem. Free Will Bapt. Bible Coll. Alumni Assn., Bob Jones U. Alumni Assn. Home: 1412 E 14th St Greenville NC 27858-4734 E-mail: bjea@greenvillenc.com.

JACKSON, BRIAN MATTHEW, musician, educator; b. Detroit, May 31, 1972; s. Susan D and Elliot J Jackson. BS in Sociology & Philosophy, Western Mich. U., 1994; MA, Calif. Inst. Integral Studies, San Francisco, 1999. Musician Infinite Volume, Memory Systems, I Am Spoonbender, 1996—; sr. quality assurance engr. Rocket Network, San Francisco, 1999—2001; instr. Touro Coll., New York City, 2002—. Music event promoter Form8 /Synth, San Francisco, 2001—03. Vol. Drug Policy Alliance, NYC, 2004. Recipient Academic Achievement award, Sociology Dept., Western Mich. U., 1993, Best Club to Hear the Future, San Francisco Bay Guardian, 2001, Best Pickup Spot for HAL 9000, San Francisco Weekly, 2002; scholar, Western Mich. U., 1990—94. Mem.: Alpha Kappa Delta, Golden Key. Liberal. Achievements include first to develop independent, digital record producing techniques. Avocations: consciousness studies, computers, audio technology, chess, electronic music. E-mail: info@form8.com.

JACKSON, CALVIN CARL, music educator; b. Braddock, Pa., July 11, 1956; s. Sue Elouise Lockette; m. Gale Jean Harpster, Aug. 25, 1997. BFA, Carnegie Mellon U., 1974—78. Music dir. Rick Sheppard and the Drifters, NYC, 1979—81; bass trombone Maracaibo Symphony Orch., Venezuela, 1981, River City Brass Band, 1983—85, prin. trombone Pitts., 1985—; artist lectr. in trombone Carnegie Mellon U., Pitts., 1991—; lectr. in brass and jazz Pitts. H.S. for the Creative and Performing Arts, 1994—; lectr. in lower brass U. of Pitts., 1995—; coord. Pitts. Pub. Schools Ctr. for the Musically Talented, 2004—. Composer (arranger): (songs) For My Lady. Avocations: photography, cooking. Home: 5714 Ellsworth Ave Pittsburgh PA 15232-1744 Office: River City Brass Band PO Box 6436 Pittsburgh PA 15212 Office Phone: 412-322-7222. Personal E-mail: caljac@andrew.cmu.edu.

JACKSON, CAROL E., federal judge; BA, Wellesley Coll., 1973; JD, U. Mich., 1976. With Thompson & Mitchell, St. Louis, 1976-83; counsel Mallinckrodt, Inc., St. Louis, 1983-85; magistrate US Dist. Ct., Ea. Dist. Mo., 1986-92, dist. judge, 1992—, now chief judge. Adj. prof. law Washington U., St. Louis, 1989-92. Trustee St. Louis Art Mus., 1987-91; dir. bi-state chpt. ARC, 1989-91, Mo. Bot. Garden. Mem. Nat. Assn. Women Judges, Fed. Magistrate Judges Assn., Mo. Bar, St. Louis County Bar Assn., Bar Assn. Metro. St. Louis, Mound City Bar Assn., Lawyers Assn. St. Louis. Office: US Dist Ct Eagleton US Courthous Ste 14-148 111 S 10th St Saint Louis MO 63102*

JACKSON, CAROLYN M., school librarian; d. Mary Bertram; children: John Davidson, Scott Davidson, Amanda Davidson. BS in Edn., Ea. Ill. U., 1972, MSLS, 1973. Cert. K-8 tchr. Ill., spl. tchg., libr. Ill., adminstr. Ill. Libr. Decatur (Ill.) Pub. Schools, 1973—94, Franklin Elem. Sch., Decatur, 2000—01, Eisenhower H.S., Decatur, 2001—03; prin. Enterprise Elem. Sch., Decatur, 1994—2000; head libr. Wheeling (Ill.) H.S., 2003—. Bd. dirs. Theatre 7 Cmty. Theater, Decatur, 1984—2000. Nat. Merit scholar, 1968—72. Mem.: ASCD, Ill. Sch. Libr. Media Assn., Kappa Delta Pi, Phi Delta Kappa. Avocations: reading, travel. Office: Wheeling HS 900 S Elmhurst Wheeling IL 60090 Office Phone: 847-718-7086. E-mail: cjackson@d214.org.

JACKSON, CHARLES IAN, writer, consultant; b. Keighley, Yorkshire, Eng., Feb. 11, 1935; s. Harry Sydney and Nellie (Crabtree) J.; m. Margaret Cochrane Storrie, July 10, 1963 (div. 1987); 1 child, Janet Clare Louise; m. Merlyn Hayward Farina (Martin), Aug. 16, 2001. BA, London U., 1956; MS, McGill U., 1959, PhD, 1961. Lectr. in geography London Sch. Econ., 1959-69; head econ. geography sect. Can. Dept. Energy, Mines and Resources, Ottawa, Ont., 1969-71; dir. planning and priorities Ministry of State for Urban Affairs, Ottawa, Ont., Can., 1972-78; sr. econ. affairs officer UN Econ. Commn. Europe, Geneva, Switzerland, 1978-81; exec. dir. Sigma Xi, New Haven, Ct., 1981-87. Cons. water resources UN Econ. Commn. Europe, 1966-67; cons. German Marshall Fund U.S., 1975-77, Ford Found., 1977, Environment Can., 1994-95; rsch. dir. Can. Ho. of Commons Standing Com. on Environment, 1991-92; dir. Chreod Ltd., 1993-97; assoc. fellow Timothy Dwight Coll., Yale U. Translator tech. lit. from French; editor Letters from the 49th Parallel 1857-73, 2000, The Arctic Journals of William Scoresby the Younger 1811-1813, 2003, and other books in field; author: Does Anyone Read Lake Hazen?, 2002, articles on history, resource mgmt. and geography; co-author Great Lakes: Great Legacy?, 1990; columnist (monthly mag.) Notes from Ptolemy, 1969-99. Dir. Found. Preservation of Capt. Cook's Ships, 1999—. Recipient Darton prize Royal Meteorol. Soc., 1962; recipient Evan Durbin prize Inst. Econ. Affairs, 1964. Mem. Hakluyt Soc. (coun. 1967-69), Champlain Soc., Soc. History of Discoveries, Can. Nautical Rsch. Soc. Business E-Mail: ian.j@cshore.com.

JACKSON, CLORA ELLIS, counselor, psychologist, educator; d. Scott and Ethel J. (Peeler) Ellis; m. Harold Coyage Jackson, Jr.; children: Sheriel, Lauren (dec.), Adrienne, Duaine. AA in Secretarial Sci., L.A. S.W. Coll., L.A., 1971; BS in Psychology, U. So. Calif., 1975, MS in Higher Edn., 1977; MS in Counseling, Calif. State U., Long Beach, 1979. Bus. edn. instr. Orange Coast Coll., Costa Mesa, Calif., 1979-80; tchr., counselor L.A. Unified Sch. Dist., 1977-81, sch. psychologist, 1981-83; tchr. bus. edn./math. Long Beach Unified Sch. Dist., 1983-90, counselor, 1990—99. Vol. Habitat for Humanity, 1990—. Mem. AAUW, Women in Arts, Pi Lambda Theta. Mem. Baha'i Faith.

JACKSON, CURTIS (50 CENT), rap artist; b. Queens, N.Y., July 6, 1976; Performer: (songs) How to Rob, 1999, Wanksta, 2002, In Da Club, 2003 (Top R&B/Hip-Hop Song, ASCAP, 2004, Top Rap Song, ASCAP, 2004, Pop Songwriter of Yr., ASCAP, 2004), (albums) Power of the Dollar, 2000, Guess Who's Back, 2001, 50 Cent is the Future, 2001, Get Rich or Die Tryin', 2003; performer: (with G-Unit) Beg for Mercy, 2003; author (with Kris Ex): (autobiography) From Pieces to Weight, 2005. Office: Aftermath/Shady 2221 Peachtree Rd NE Ste D329 Atlanta GA 30309

JACKSON, CYNTHIA ANN, property manager; b. Orange, Tex., Mar. 9, 1950; d. Hazel Lee and Kenneth Reedom (Stepfather); children: William Christopher Green, Roy Edward Elliott Jr. Supr. Weiner's Dept. Store #68, Orange, Tex., 1970—80; receptionist/sec. George B Barron, Atty. at Law, Orange, Tex., 1982—84; receptionist/econ. devel. Greater Orange Area C. of C., Tex., 1987—99; supplement ins. specialist Prin. Fin. Group, Dallas, 1999—2001; profl. imager Orange Savs. Bank, Tex.; mgr. Automnal Back Apartments, 2005—. Pres./owner Heel-2-Toe Boutique, Orange, Tex., 1998—, H.O.P.E. Project Vehicles, Orange, Tex., 2002—, Last Minute Things, Orange, Tex., 2003—; mgr. Autumn Park Apts., Orange, 2004—. City council mem. City of Orange, 2004; bd. dirs. Orange Econ. Devel. com.; pres., CEO Citizens Action to Rehab. East-Town, Orange, 2005; ptnr. Pineywoods Home Team, Lufkin, 2005; pres., CEO Citizens Action to Rehab. East-Town, 2005; ptnr. Pineywoods Home Team, Lufkin, Tex.; minister New Landmark Ministries, Port Arthur, Tex.; former chmn. bd. Planning and Zoning Com. for City of Orange, Tex., 1998—2004; former mem. adv. bd. Conv. and Visitors Bur. for City of Orange, Tex., 2002—04; bd. dirs. Planned Living Assistance Network, Orange, Tex., 2003; former mem. Citizens Adv. Com. for City of Orange, Tex., 2004. Avocations: singing, reading, building decorator screens, computer printshop creations. Personal E-mail: cynja@acninc.net.

JACKSON, CYNTHIA L., lawyer; b. Houston, May 6, 1954; BA, Stanford U., 1976; JD, U. Tex., 1979. Bar: Tex. 1979, Calif. 1980. Mem. Heller, Ehrman, White & McAuliffe, Palo Alto, Calif., 1983—99, Baker & McKenzie, Palo Alto, 1999—. Mem. ABA. Office: Baker & McKenzie 660 Hansen Way Palo Alto CA 94304-1044 Office Phone: 650-856-5572.

JACKSON, DAN ADRIAN, language educator; b. Clarksdale, Miss., Feb. 3, 1938; s. Richard Adrian Jackson and Lucille Brewer; m. Lillian Thibault, Nov. 16, 1968 (div. Jan. 1983). BA, Ottawa (Kans.) U., 1989. Cert. in English and comms., Kans. Tchr. Eureka (Kans.) H.S., 1989-92, Butler County C.C., El Dorado, Kans., 1989-92, Maur Hill Prep. Sch., Atchison, Kans., 1993—2002, chmn. dept. English, 1997—2002; tchr. Atchison H.S., 2002—. Drama coach, debate coach, forensics coach Maur Hill Prep. Sch., 1993-2002. Named Tchr. of Yr., U. Chgo., 1996-97, Tchr. of the Yr. Wal-Mart, Inc., 1998-99. Mem. Lions. Baptist. Home: 221 N 3d # 8 Atchison KS 66002-1740 Office: Atchison HS 1510 W Riley Atchison KS 66002 Office Phone: 913-367-3925. Business E-Mail: djackson@atchison.ks.us.k12.

JACKSON, DARREN RICHARD, retail company executive; b. Detroit, Nov. 13, 1964; s. Richard Dennis and Connie May (Ellis) J.; m. Terry Ann Hall, May 28, 1988; children: Ryan David, Bridget Caffrey. BS in Acctg., Marquette U., 1986. CPA, Wis. Supr. KPMG Peat Marwick, Milw., 1985-89; dir. fin. reporting Carson, Pirie, Scott & Co., Milw., 1989-90, dir. treasury svcs., 1990-91, v.p., treas., CFO, 1992-1998; CFO, Full-line Store Div. Nordstrom, Inc.; sen. v.p. fin. & treas. Best Buy Co., Inc., Mpls., 2000-2001, CFO, 2001—. Office: Best Buy Co 7075 Flying Cloud Dr Eden Prairie MN 55344*

JACKSON, DAVID HUNTSMAN, retired cardiologist; b. Tuscaloosa, Ala., July 17, 1937; s. Ashel Linc and Merle (Baxter) J.; m. Sara Wyatt, June 12, 1960; children: Susan Elizabeth, Sara Lynne. BS, U. Ala., 1959; MD, Med. Coll. Ala., 1963. Diplomate Am. Bd. Internal Medicine, Am. Bd. Cardiovasc. Disease; lic. MD, Ala. Intern Med. Coll. Ala., 1964; resident and tchg. fellow internal medicine Harvard U. Md. Svcs.-Boston City Hosp., 1967—69; fellow cardiovasc. disease U. Ala., Birmingham, 1969—71; asst. prof. cardiology U. Ala. Sch. Medicine, Birmingham, 1971—74; practice medicine specializing in cardiology Birmingham; ret., 2001. Staff U. Ala. Hosps. and Clinics, 1971-74, Bessemer Caraway Hosp., 1974-76, 83-2001, Brookwood Med. Ctr., 1974—, Healthsouth Med. Ctr., 1976—, Shelby Med. Ctr., 1984-2001, Montclair Bapt. Med. Ctr., 1985-2001, Princeton Bapt. Med. Ctr., 1985-2001, St. Vincent's Hosp., 1986—; chief cardiology Brookwood Med. Ctr., 1981-84, vice chmn. dept. medicine, 1984-85. Contbr. articles to profl. jours. Lt. USN, 1964-67. Fellow: ACP, Am. Heart Assn. (coun. clin. cardiology), Coun. on Clin. Cardiology, Am. Coll. Cardiology, Am. Coll. Chest Physicians; mem.: AMA, Am. Soc. Nuclear Cardiology (founding), Am. Soc. Echocardiography, Birmingham Acad. Medicine, Birmingham Soc. Internists, Med. Assn. of State of Ala., Jefferson County Med. Soc., So. Med. Assn., Laennec Soc., Ballistocardiography Rsch. Soc. (editor procs. 1971), Ala. Heart Assn. (bd. dirs. 1975). Avocations: reading, fishing, exercise.

JACKSON, DIONNE BROXTON, chemist; d. Leon and Joan Broxton; m. Brian Jackson, 1998. BS in Chemistry, Spelman Coll., 1991; MA in Indsl. Engring., U. Ctrl. Fla., 1994. Chemist materials sci. lab. NASA Kennedy Space Ctr., 1991—. Mem. environ. monitoring lab. Bionetics Corp., 1988—89, mem. microchem. analysis lab., 1990. Scholar, Spelman Coll. . Avocations: reading, singing, travel. Office: NASA Kennedy Space Ctr Bldg M-7 0355 Rm 1268 Kennedy Space Center FL 32899

JACKSON, DONALD FRANK, organizational development consultant; b. Dallas, Aug. 2, 1941; s. Carter Vaden and Eliose Lovelady Jackson; children: Donald Frank II, Taylor, Shawna, Eric. BS, Ariz. State U., 1969. Rsch. mgr. Phoenix Newspapers, Inc., 1959-70; exec. dir. Cmty. Orgn. for Drug Abuse Control, Phoenix, 1970-72; pres. Don Jackson & Assocs., Phoenix, 1972-77, Don Jackson Co., Phoenix, 1977-95; mng. dir. Don Jackson Co. Ltd., Peterborough, Eng., 1995; pres. Leadership Edge Internat., 1995—. Total Quality Mgmt. cons. ST Microelectronics, Geneva, 1980—; quality leadership, teambldg. cons. USPHS, Indian Health Svcs., Rockville, Md., 1985—; cons., trainer Helenic Mgmt. Assn., Athens, 1988—; team bldg. cons. Ariz. Dept. Pub. Safety, Phoenix, 1979—; human resource mgmt. cons. S-T U., Roussett, France, 1995- Author: Self-Management System, 1985, Performance Appraisal Implementation, 1988, People Power, 1990, (transl. 8 langs.), Total Quality Management, A Latch-Cascade Initiative, 1992, (transl. 8 langs.), Advanced Leadership for Total Quality Management, 1993, Advanced Problem Solving, 1994 (transl. 8 langs.), Responsibility Charting-Improving Communications in Lateral Organizations, 1994, (transl. 8 langs.) Trustee Phoenix Union H.S. Dist., 1969-74, Verde Valley (Ariz.) Pvt. Sch., 1974-75; bd. dirs. Phoenix Execs. Club, 1977; mem. Ariz. State Bd. for Pvt. Post-Secondary Edn., 1995-97. Recipient Liberty Bell award Maricopa County Bar Assn., Phoenix, 1969, Disting. Svc. award Maricopa County Med. Soc., Phoenix, 1970; named Outstanding Young Man of Ariz. Phoenix Jaycees, 1971. Mem.: Am. Soc. Quality Control, Phoenix C. of C., Masons. Avocations: golf, bicycling. Office: PO Box 15202 Scottsdale AZ 85267-5202 Office Phone: 480-367-0101. E-mail: leadershipedge@cox.net.

JACKSON, DONALD WILSON, political science professor, lawyer; b. Houston, Tex., May 15, 1938; s. Enoch Wilson and Ozella Rae J.; m. Joanne Shea, Apr. 20, 1985; children: Daniel Wilson, Michael Oden. BA, So. Meth. U., Dallas, 1959; JD, So. Meth. U., 1962; PhD in Polit. Sci., U. Wis., Madison, 1972. Bar: Tex. 1962, Supreme Ct. 75. Assoc. Storey, Armstrong & Steger, Dallas, 1962—67; instr. polit. sci. So. Meth. U., 1967—68; asst. prof. polit. sci. Idaho State U., Pocatello, Idaho, 1970—74; jud. fellow Supreme Ct. U.S., Washington, 1974—75; Herman Brown prof. polit. sci. Tex. Christian U., Ft. Worth, 1975—. Author: An Introduction to Political Analysis: The Theory and Practice of Allocation, 1978, Even the Children of Strangers:

Equality Under the U.S. Constitution, 1992 (Oustanding Book on Human Rights, Gustavus Myers Center for Human Rights, 1993), The United Kingdom Confronts the European Convention on Human Rights, 1997; editor: Presidential Leadership and Civil Rights Policy, 1995; co-editor: Comparative Judicial Review and Public Policy, 1992. Bd. dirs. ACLU, N.Y.C., 2000—01, Quaker United Nat. Com., N.Y.C., 1997—2000; mem. adv. bd. Am. United for Separation of Ch. and State, Washington, 1995—2001, bd. trustees, 2005—; bd. dirs. Tex. affil. ACLU, Austin, 1992—2001. Named Outstanding Prof. in North Tex., N. Tex. Assn. Phi Beta Kappa, 1984, Tex. Piper Prof., Minnie Stevens Piper Found., 2003; recipient Citizenship Participation: Bill of Rights award, Tarrant County LWV, 1995, Silver Spur award, Planned Parenthood of North Tex., 1997. Mem.: We. Polit. Sci. Assn., Internat. Polit. Sci. Assn. (sec.-treas. 1997—2000, mem. rsch. com. comparative jud. studies), Am. Polit. Sci. Assn. (sec. treas. law and cts. sect. 1996—99), Phi Beta Kappa. Avocations: backpacking, golf. Office: Tex Christian U TCU Box 297021 Fort Worth TX 76129-0001 Office Phone: 817-257-7468. Home Fax: 817-377-4368; Office Fax: 817-257-7397.

JACKSON, DONNA ANN, musician, piano teacher; b. Houston, Sept. 25, 1951; d. Gerald Averitt and Mary Patricia (Helton) Brewer. Student, Baylor U., 1969-71, U. Tex., 1971-72; BMus, Mont. State U., 1978; M Liberal Arts, Houston Bapt. U., 1990. Pianist, vocal coach Intermountain Opera Co., Bozeman, Mont., 1978-79; staff pianist Mont. State U., Bozeman, 1977-79; owner, operator Starnote Music, Brenham & Houston, 1981—; instr. piano Blinn Coll., Brenham, Tex., 1987-90; adminstr. devel. dept. Houston Grand Opera, Houston, 1991-93; organist Reid Meml. Meth. Ch., 1993-95. Creator, producer radio program Radio Central Artsguide, weekly, 1981-88. Organist, Brenham Presbyn. Ch., 1984-87; bd. dirs. Brenham Fine Arts League, 1984-87, Arts Coun. Washington County, Brenham, 1984-89; entertainment dir. Brenham Downtown Assn., 1987-88. Recipient Bronze medal Internat. Piano Recording Competition, 1985; Arts Achievement award Arts Coun. Washington County, 1989. Mem. Music Tchrs. Nat. Assn., Tex. Music Tchrs. Assn., Brenham Area Music Tchrs. Assn. (bd. dirs. 1984-90), Mensa. Democrat. Presbyterian. Avocations: baseball, opera, musical theater. Mailing: 1143 Peachford Ln Houston TX 77062 Office Phone: 281-486-7827. E-mail: starnote@houston.rr.com.

JACKSON, EDWIN ATLEE, physicist, educator; b. Lyons, N.Y., Apr. 18, 1931; s. Frederick Wolcott and Helen Jean (Carroll) J.; m. Cynthia Ann Gregg; children: Eric Hugh, Mark Wolcott. BS in Physics, Syracuse U., 1953, MS in Physics, 1955, PhD in Physics, 1958. Asst. lectr. Brandeis U., Waltham, Mass., 1957—58; postdoctoral Airforce Cambridge Rsch. Ctr., Bedford, Mass., 1958—59; rsch. staff Princeton (N.J.) U., 1959—61; asst. prof. U. Ill., Urbana, 1961—64, assoc. prof., 1964—77, physics prof., 1977—98, prof. emeritus, 1998—. Dir. ctr. for complex systems rsch. Beckman Inst. U. Ill., Urbana, 1989-98; vis. faculty FOM-Inst. Voor Plasma Fysica, Jutphaas, The Netherlands, 1967-68; vis. staff Los Alamos (N.Mex.) Sci. Lab., 1971; vis. prof. Chalmers U., Göteberg, Sweden, 1984; JIFT prof. Nagoya (Japan) U., 1984; core rschr. Santa Fe Inst., 1992-98. Author: Equilibrium Statistical Mechanics, 1968, Perspectives of Nonlinear Dynamics, vol. 1, 1989, vol. 2, 1990, Japanese transl., 1991, Exploring Nature's Dynamics, 2001; contbr. more than 80 articles to profl. jours Fellow Am. Phys. Soc. Office: U Ill Dept Physics 1110 W Green St Dept Physics Urbana IL 61801

JACKSON, ELIJAH, JR., communications executive; m. Delesia Renee, 1995; children: Mercedes Alexis, Elijah Elias. AA in Gen. Studies and Broadcasting, Brigham Young U., Rexburg, Idaho, 1982; AA in Arts and Humanities, Speech, Theatre, and Dance, AA in Speech Comm., Brigham Young U., Hawaii, 1984; BA in Social Sci. Comm., U. Hawaii, Manoa, 1987; postgrad., U. Southwestern La., Lafayette, Polk C.C., Winter Haven, Fla.; LLM in Taxation, U. Hawaii, Manoa, 1988; D of Juridicial Sci. in Taxation, Washington Sch. Law, Sandy, Utah, 1999; DSc in Taxation, Washington Inst. Grad. Studies. Tng. Prog. by Federal Mogul Corp., 1998; entrepreneurship tng., Hawaii C. of C., Honolulu, 1987; Bus. Etiquette and Protocol, U. of Hawaii Manoa, 1986; Fin. Mgmt. for Closely held Bus., Bank of Hawaii, 1985; Eng. Tech., Tampa Tech. Inst., 1981. Editor Oceanic Cablevision, Am. TV Corp., Time Warner Inc., Honolulu TV Com. Corp.; pvt. practice radio and TV project budget mgr., prodr., dir, videographer; legal rschr., legis. aide Com. on Consumer Protection and Commerce State of Hawaii Legislature, Ednl. Incentive Program Inc., Fictitious Names; CEO Jackson Program, 10 years, Jackson Pacific Joint Venture, 10 years, Jackson Instructional TV Sys., 10 years; trustee, fiduciary, promoter JBS Inc. Parent Corp., Hawaii, Fla.; CEO, pres., promoter Jackson Family Limited Partnership, Ltd., 13 years, Jackson Family Limited Trust, 13 years, JBS Inc. Parent Corp., 13 years, Elijah Jackson, Jr., Inc., 13 years; CEO, pres., chmn., promoter Delesia Renee Jackson Inc., 13 years; legal rschr., legislative aide State of Hawaii, 13th Legislature Com. on Consumer Protection and Commerce, Hawaii, 1 year; intern field prod., videographer, ABC affiliate, KITV channel 4, 1 year; graphic design, photography, cons. video system design Sony and CMX videos, 2 years; with Washington Inst. Grad. Studies Grad. Tax Program, Sandy, Utah; owner, founder numerous cos. including Jackson Enterprises Inc. of Lakeland, Jackson Associated Cos. of U.S. of Am., Ltd., Jackson Limousine Svc., Ltd., Paul A. Diggs Cmty. Devel. Corp., JBA Land and Mgmt. Trust Corp., Cashland Inc., Jackson Entertainment and Info. Svcs. Inc., Bangkok, JBS Inc. Parent Corp., Jackson Associated Cos. of Ctrl. Am., Ltd., Jackson Associated Cos. of Pan-Am., Ltd., Jackson Assoc. Cos. of Spanish-Am., Ltd., Jackson Associated Providences of Can., Ltd., Jackson Ten-Perceniers, Ltd., Jacksonvilles Cos. of Ark., Fla., Ill., NC and Tex., Ltd., Jackson Bangkok Thailand Ops., Ltd., Jackson Hague Netherlands Ops., Ltd., Jackson Mexico City Mex. Ops., Ltd., Jackson Dublin Ireland Ops. Ltd., Jackson Valleta Malta, Sicily and Italy Ops., Ltd., Sheol-Hades Compariment Co., Ltd., Jackson Purchase and Exch. Co., Ltd., Pelenike Sask. Legal Co. of Fla., Ltd., Jackson Assoc. Cos. of UK, Ltd., Jackson Associated Cos. of Brazil, Ltd., Jackson Associated Cos. of West Indies, Ltd., Jackson Associated Cos. of East Indies, Ltd., Jackson Booking Agy., Ltd., Jackson Exec. Entertainment Svcs. Trustee, pres. Jackson Internat. Mgmt. Limited, Nassau, Bahamas; assoc. mgr. trainee Discount Auto Parts, Inc.; sales assoc. Anderson News Co., Lakeland, Fla., Tampa, Fla., Knoxville, Tenn; legal rschr., real estate rschr., paralegal JBS Mgmt. and Properties, JBS Land and Water Entertainment and Sports; pres., CEO, trustee, financer, ptnr., tax matter person, nominee, residual interest holder, promoter Jackson Family Limited Partnership, Ltd., Jackson Family Limited Trust, JBS Inc. Parent Corp., Jackson Broadcasting Sys., Inc., JBC Inc. Lead Corp. of Fla. Divsn., Jackson Broadcasting Co., Inc., Elijah Jackson, Inc., Jr., Inc., Jackson Enterprises, Inc., Jackson Commodity Credit Corp., Cashland Inc., Jackson Internat. Telecom. Corp., Jackson, Inc., Jackson Internat. Fin. Corp., others; chmn. bd. Elias, Elisha and Elisabeth Jackson Inc., JBS Mgmt. Corp., Jackson Entertainment Svcs., Inc., EJJ Productions Inc.; pres., CEO JBS Inc., 1986—. Radio/TV project budget mgr., prod., dir., videographer; editor for Oceanic Cablevision a/k/a Amer. TV Corp. a/k/a Time Warner Inc. d/b/a Honolulu TV Comm. Corp. Corp. sec., trustee, mem. Paul A. Diggs Cmty. Devel. Corp., et al; pres., CEO Jackson Merit Nat. and Internat. Scholarship Fund and Found., 1986—. Recipient cert. of appreciation VFW, 1998, 99. Mem. ABA, Amer. Payroll Assn., U. Hawaii Alumni Assn., U. Hawaii Found. also: Wash Inst Grad Studies 2268 Newcastle Dr Sandy UT 84093-1743 Home: 2390 Bob Phillips Rd Bartow FL 33830-6727 Office: 691 WWII Veterans Ln WCI 108 Unit B22/05 Defuniak Springs FL 32433 Fax: 863-686-4659. Office Phone: 800-953-7830. E-mail: elijahpromotions@aol.com.

JACKSON, ERIC ALLEN, philatelist; b. Long Beach, Calif., Jan. 3, 1955; s. Allen Joseph and Janice Meredith (Lyen) J.; m. Theresa Kathleen Strauss Jackson, Mar. 21, 1975 (div. Jan. 1997); children: Amy Marie, Jared Brady, Luke Allen; m. Tamara Jane Kaufman, July 18, 2002. Student, Chapman Coll., Orange, Calif., 1973-75. Owner pvt. practice, Anaheim, Calif., 1973-81; cons. William C. Tatham Stamp Co., Whittier, Calif., 1979-81; owner Whittier (Calif.) Philatelic Svcs., 1981-87; pvt. practice Herndon, Va., 1987-88, Leesport, Pa., 1988—. Expert com. The Philatelic Found., N.Y.C., 1979—, Am. Philatelic Soc., State College, Pa., 1979—, Profl. Stamp Expertising, Newport Beach, Calif., 1987—; bd. dirs., v.p. Am. Revenue Assn., Rockford, Iowa, 1980—, pres., 2001—; cons. Scott Pub. Co., Sidney, Ohio, 1980—. Contbr. articles to profl. jours. Mem. Am. Stamp Dealers Assn. (bd. dirs. 1998—, pres. 2005—), Am. Philatelic Soc., Am. Revenue Assn., Collectors Club of N.Y., Revenue Soc. Great Britain, Berks County C. of C., Berks County Hist. Soc., Nat. Trust for Historic Preservation. Republican. Avocations: antiques, baseball, fishing. Home: 230 Eagleview Dr Mohrsville PA 19541 Office: Eric Jackson Co PO Box 728 Schoolside Pla Ste A-1 Leesport PA 19533-0728 Office Phone: 610-926-6200. E-mail: eric@revenuer.com.

JACKSON, ERIC MICHAEL, marketing executive, writer, media specialist; s. Ronald and Teresa Jackson; m. Beatrice De Luca Jackson. BA in Econs. with honors, Stanford U., 1998. Bus. cons. Arthur Andersen LLP, San Francisco, 1998—99; dir. of mktg. PayPal Inc., Mountain View, Calif., 1999—2002; v.p. of mktg. (interim) PayPal, an eBay Co., Mountain View, Calif., 2003—03; founder, pres. World Ahead Media, Gardena, Calif., 2003—. Adv. bd. The Stanford Rev. Nonprofit Corp., Palo Alto, Calif., 1996—2004; bd. of dirs. World Ahead Media, Gardena, Calif., 2003—; adv. bd. Vanguard PAC, Little Rock, 2004—; spkr. in field. Author: (book) The PayPal Wars: Battles with eBay, the Media, the Mafia, and the Rest of Planet Earth (USA Book News Best Books 2004, 2004, Writers Notes Book award-Best Bus. Book, 2005); contbr. (anthology) Thank You, President Bush: Reflections on the War on Terror, Defense of the Family, and Revival of the Economy, 2004; editor: (newspaper) The Stanford Review, 1996. Mem. Coun. for Nat. Policy, 2004, Nat. Fedn. of Rep. Assemblies, 2004. Recipient Jeff Skoll Cmty. award, eBay Inc., 2002; grantee Acad. Rsch. Grant, Stanford U., 1998. Mem.: Publishers Mktg. Assn. Christian. Achievements include Media commentator - frequent guest on numerous television and talk radio programs; quoted in articles by Reuters, Forbes, US News & World Report, and other publications. Office Phone: 310-217-4165.

JACKSON, FELICITY ANNE, performing arts organization administrator; b. Hitchin, Hertfordshire, Eng., Apr. 16, 1949; d. Brian John and Jacqueline Anne (Barnes) J. BA with honors, Cambridge U., Eng., 1970; B Philosophy, Exeter U., Eng., 1972. Planning coord. Glyndebourne Festival, Sussex, Eng., 1979-82; head artistic planning Nat. Opera, Brussels, 1982-84; casting mgr. Glyndebourne Festival, Sussex, Eng., 1988-90; casting cons. Leipzig Opera, Germany, 1990-92, Netherlands Opera, Amsterdam, Holland, 1990-92; artistic adminstr. Can. Opera Co., Toronto, Can., 1992-94; dir. artistic adminstrn. Glimmerglass Opera, N.Y., 1994-97; gen. mgr. European Union Opera, London, 1997-98. Casting cons. Fla. Grand Opera, 2000-01, ensemble dir., casting mgr., 2001—; artistic cons. Chgo. Opera Theater, 2000-01. Avocations: canoeing, travel. E-mail: fjackson@fgo.org.

JACKSON, FLODONNA A., elementary school educator; b. Wichita Falls, Tex., Aug. 3, 1973; d. Donald and Florence Jackson. MA, Clark Atlanta U., 1997. Cert. ednl. leadership Ga., 1997. Educator Dekalb County Schs., Decatur, Ga., 1997—2001; instrnl. support specialist Ga. Dept. Edn., Atlanta, 2001—03; literacy coach Clayton County Schools, Jonesboro, Ga., 2003—. Recipient Marie Curie: Exceptional Sci. Tchr. award, Flat Shoals Elem. Sch., Dekalb County Schools, 1999. Mem.: Americacan Ednl. Rsch. Assn. (assoc.), Fielding Grad. U. Cluster Leader (assoc.; co-cluster leader 2004—05), Delta Sigma Theta. Avocations: yoga, kickboxing. Office: PO Box 311844 Atlanta GA 31131 Office Phone: 404-675-8026. Office Fax: 404-675-8047. Personal E-mail: zetaup93@bellsouth.net. E-mail: fjackson@clayton.k12.ga.us.

JACKSON, FRANCIS JOSEPH, research and development company executive; b. Providence, May 23, 1932; s. Francis Joseph and Mary Elizabeth (Ryan) J.; m. Mary Veronica Brennan, Sept. 1, 1956 (div. Mar. 1983); children: Mary Cecilia, Paul Francis, Thomas Edward.; m. Nancy M. McMahon, May 21, 1983. BS magna cum laude, Providence Coll., 1954; Sc.M., Brown U., 1957, PhD, 1960. Rsch. assoc. Brown U., 1959-60; sr. scientist Bolt Beranek & Newman Inc., Cambridge, Mass., 1960-68, divsn. v.p., 1968-77, v.p., 1977-79, sr. v.p., 1979-98, cons., 1998-99. Adj. prof. Cath. U., 1973-77. Contbr. articles to profl. jours. Recipient Personal Achievement award Providence Coll., 1989, 75th Diamond Jubilee award Providence Coll., 1992. Fellow Acoustical Soc. Am.; mem. IEEE (sr.), Am. Inst. Physics, Cosmos, Winchester Country Club (bd. dirs. 1992-94), Delta Epsilon Sigma. Home and Office: 14A Plato Ter Winchester MA 01890-2229

JACKSON, FREDERICK HENRY, foreign language educator, linguist; b. Melrose, Mass., Dec. 30, 1943; s. Henry Smith and Constance (Newton) J.; m. Panida Ratanaprasert, Oct. 10, 1969; 1 child, Christopher Newton Jackson. BA in English, U. Calif., Berkeley, 1966; MA in ESL, U. Hawaii, 1973, PhD in Linguistics, 1983. Jr. rschr. U. Hawaii, Honolulu, 1975-81; program coord. Bilingual Edn. Program Micronesia, Honolulu, 1981-82; vis. prof. Chiang-Mai (Thailand) U., 1982-84; asst. prof. Pa. State U., State College, 1984-85; lang. tng. supr. Fgn. Svc. Inst., Arlington, Va., 1985-91, coord. tchr. devel., 1991-98, lang. tng. supr., 1999—. Coord. Fed. Interagy. Lang. Roundtable, Washington, 1999—. Co-compiler (dictionary) Carolinian-English Dictionary, 1991; contbr. articles to profl. jours. Recipient Heroes of Reinvention award Nat. Performance Rev., Washington, 1994. Mem. TESOL, ACTFL, Nat. Coun. Less Commonly Taught Langs. (at-large rep. 1995-97, pres. 2000-2002), Coun. Tchrs. S.E. Asian Langs. (pres. 1990-93), Am. Assn. Applied Linguistics. Home: 2317 N Richmond St Arlington VA 22207-3946 Office Phone: 703-302-7018.

JACKSON, FREDERICK HERBERT, educational administrator; b. New Haven, May 16, 1919; s. Fred and Mary (Butler) J.; m. Eleanor Stearns Whittemore, May 2, 1942; children: Isabel S. Jackson Freeman, David L. AB, Brown U., 1941, LL.D., 1968; A.M., U. Pa., 1948, PhD, 1950. Instr. Marietta Coll., 1948-49, asst. prof., 1949-50; instr. U. Ill., 1950-52, asst. prof., 1952-55; exec. asst. Carnegie Corp. N.Y., N.Y.C., 1955-57, exec. assoc., 1957-64; asst. exec. v.p. N.Y.U., 1964-66, v.p. humanities and social scis., 1966-67; pres. Clark U., Worcester, Mass., 1967-7O; dir. Com. on Instl. Cooperation Big Ten Univs. and U. Chgo., 1970-84. Bd. dirs. Paul Revere Variable Annuity Ins. Co., 1968-91. Author: Simeon Eben Baldwin, American Social Scientist, 1955. Active Rep. Town Meeting, Westport, Conn., 1957-59, 61-67; trustee U. Bridgeport, 1961-71, life trustee, 1971-90; bd. dirs. Worcester Art Mus., 1968-70, Paul Revere Courier Fund, 1971-77, New Trier Citizen's League, 1983-84; acad. adv. com. Ctr. for Study Democratic Instns., 1975-78; commr. Mass. Hist. Commn., 1985-97; bd. dirs. Salisbury Singers, 1985-93; v.p., 1987-88, pres., 1988-91, 92-93, hon. dir. 1993—; trustee Worcester Hist. Mus., 1985-88, v.p., 1986-87; trustee Performing Arts Sch. Worcester, 1996-2001, chmn. 1998-2001; tutor Literacy Vols. of Am., 1996-2000; pres. Willows of Westborough Retirement Cmty. Residents Assn., 2004-05. Mem. Am. Antiquarian Soc., Common Cause (vice chmn. Ill. 1975-77, 82-83), Worcester Club, Phi Beta Kappa. Home: 1 Lyman St Westborough MA 01581-1437 *"I must be useful else wherefore born" has been a guiding principle of my life. During my working years I worked steadily; during my retirement years I have been involved in several volunteer activities. Besides the above, my family has been my greatest source of happiness - my wonderful wife, my children and grandchildren.*

JACKSON, GARY LEE, military analyst; b. Houston, Tex., Sept. 15, 1947; s. Charles Andrew and Ruth Willma (Tew) Jackson; m. Meridel May Pettyjohn, Apr. 3, 1973; children: Gary Lee II, Thomas Jonathan. BA cum laude in polit. sci., Trinity U., 1965—69; PhD in govt., Georgetown U., 1969—85. Cert. Information Systems Security Professional (CISSP) Internat. Info. Systems Security Certification Consortium, 2002. Sr. info. security systems engr. Sci. Applications Internat. Corp., Herndon, Va., 1997—2002; homeland security cons. Northrop Grumman Corp., Alexandria, Va., 2002—. Fellow in polit.-mil. studies Ctr. for Strategic and Internat. Studies, Washington, 1995—96. Asst. troop scoutmaster Boy Scouts of Am., Derwood, Md., 1989—91. Maj. U.S. Army, 1974—94, Ariz., Germany, Tex., Md., Va. Decorated Legion of Merit U.S. Army, Army Commendation medal. Mem.: World Future Soc., Armed Forces Comm. and Electronics Assn. (assoc.), Mil. Officers Assn. of Am. (assoc.), Assn. of the U.S. Army (assoc.), Am. Polit. Sci. Assn. (assoc.), Inst. for Ops. Rsch. and Mgmt. Sciences (assoc.), NRA (assoc.), The Am. Legion (assoc.), VFW (assoc.). Conservative. Christian. Achievements include U.S. Army project director to develop air and land combat-intelligence communications theater-strategic level; theater exploitation study system computer model. Avocations: football, camping, watch collecting, book collecting. Home: 17336 Founders Mill Dr Derwood MD 20855 Office: Northrop Grumman Corp 6940 South Kings Hwy Ste 210 Alexandria VA 22310 Office Phone: 703-971-3108 161. Personal E-mail: jacksondoc@yahoo.com. E-mail: gary.jackson@ngc.com.

JACKSON, GEORGE LYMAN, retired nuclear medicine physician; b. Arlington, Mass., Dec. 17, 1923; s. William and Alice (Tenney) J.; m. Alyce Verne Yeager, Sept. 7, 1946; children: Scott Douglas, Carole Elizabeth, Diane Priscilla, Richard Lee. BS cum laude, Franklin and Marshall Coll., 1944; MD, U. Pa., 1948. Diplomate: Am. Bd. Internal Medicine, Am. Bd. Nuclear Medicine. Intern Hosp. U. Pa., 1948-49, resident, 1949-52; practice medicine specializing in internal medicine Harrisburg, Pa., 1952-63; dir. med. edn., acting med. dir. Harrisburg Hosp., 1963-68, dir. undergrad. fellowships, 1968-69, head sect. nuclear medicine, 1965-75, med. dir. dept. nuclear medicine, 1975-89. Asst. prof. medicine Hahnemann Med. Coll., 1963-68, assoc. prof., 1968-70; clin. assoc. prof. M.S. Hershey Med. Centre, Pa. State U., 1970-76, clin. prof., 1976-90; dir. Harrisburg Hosp. Sch. Nuclear Medicine Tech.; adj. faculty Harrisburg Area Community Coll., Millersville State Coll.; cons., chmn. med. adv. com. Lebanon (Pa.) VA Hosp., 1968-75; nuclear medicine adv. Pa. Dept. Edn., Pa. Med. Soc., Pa. Blue Shield. Author, pub.: Of Thee I Sing, 1993, The Eclectic Club of Harrisburg, 1997, 150th Anniversary of St. Paul's Lutheran Church, 2005; contbr. articles to profl. jours. Mem. Cen. Dauphin Sch. Bd., 1971-73; bd. dirs. Bethesda Mission, Harrisburg Hosp. Med. Edn. and Rsch. Found.; bd. dirs. New Hope Ministries, 1987-93, pres. 1988-93; chmn. archives and collections com. No. York County Hist. and Preservation Soc., 1998-2000. With USNR, 1942-45. Fellow ACP (govs. com. for coll. affairs 1969-76, gov. 1976-80, laureate 1985), Soc. Nuclear Medicine, Am. Coll. Nuclear Physicians (bd. regents), Am. Coll. Nuclear Medicine; mem. Am. Thyroid Assn., Pa. Soc. Internal Medicine (past pres.; chmn. liaison com.), Pa. Coll. Nuclear Medicine (pres.), Joint Rev. Com. Nuclear Medicine Tech., Phi Beta Kappa, Alpha Omega Alpha. Lutheran. Home: 22 N Baltimore St Dillsburg PA 17019-1210 *The efforts of my adult life have been directed primarily at three priorities—family, profession, church. Success in achieving any of these is a consequence of a combination of providence, help from others and personal attributes. Help from others involves, principally, my family (in its largest sense) and of these my wife is most important. She is a source of understanding, wise counsel, inspiration, support and balance. My associates help significantly by their dedication, industry and responsibility. Personal attributes are hard work, absolute honesty, religious belief, and a conviction that the only justification for my professional life is to help the sick patients whom I am privileged to serve.*

JACKSON, GUIDA MYRL, writer, magazine editor, book editor, publisher; b. Clarendon, Tex., Aug. 30; d. James Hurley and Ina (Benson) Miller; m. Prentice Lamar Jackson (div. Jan. 1986); children: Jeffrey Allen, William Andrew, James Tucker, Annabeth Broomall Davis; m. William Hervey Laufer, Feb. 14, 1986. BA, Tex. Tech U.; MA, Calif. State U., 1986; PhD, Greenwich U., 1990. Tchr. secondary sch. English, Houston Ind. Sch. Dist., 1951—53, Ft. Worth Ind. Sch. Dist., 1953—54; pvt. tchr. music, freelance writer, Houston, 1956—71; editor newsletter Tex. Soc. Anesthesiologists, Austin, 1972—80; editor-in-chief Tex. Country Mag., Houston, 1976—78; mng. editor lit. mag. Touchstone, Houston, 1976—. Contbg. editor Houston Town and Country mag., 1975—76; book editor Arte Publico, 1987—88; editor, pub. Panther Creek Press, 1999—; lectr. English U. Houston, 1986—95; instr. Montgomery Coll., 1996—; freelance writer, Houston, The Woodlands, Tex., 1978—. Author: (novels) Passing Through, 1979, A Common Valor, 1980; (play) The Lamentable Affair of the Vicar's Wife, 1989, Showdown at Nosegay Cottage, 1997, The Man From Tegucigalpa, 1998, Julia is Peculiar; (biog. reference) Women Who Ruled, 1990 (best reference lists award Libr. Jour. and Sch. Libr. Jour. 1990), (nonfiction) Virginia Diaspora, 1992, Virginia Diaspora CD-ROM, 2001, (lit. reference) Encyclopedia of Traditional Epic, 1994 (best reference list award ALA), (lit. reference) Traditional Epics: A Literary Companion, 1995, Encyclopedia of Literary Epics, 1996; (reference) Women Rulers Throughout the Ages, 1999; (fiction) The Other Texas, 2005; editor: Heart to Hearth, 1989, African Women Write, 1990, Fall From Innocence, Memoirs of the Great Depression, 1998; (nonfiction) Legacy of the Texas Plains, 1994, Through the Cumberland Gap, 1995. Mem.: Houston Writers Consortium, Writers' Forum, Montgomery Lit. Arts Coun., Dramatists Guild, Woodland Writers Guild, Houston Writers Guild, PEN Ctr. West, Women in Comm. Avocations: music, gardening, poetry. Office: Panther Creek Press PO Box 130233 Spring TX 77393-0233 Personal E-mail: panthercreek3@hotmail.com.

JACKSON, HAROLD, journalist; b. Birmingham, AL, Aug. 14, 1953; s. Lewis and Janye (Wilson) J.; m. Denice Estell Pledger, Apr. 30, 1977; children: Annette Michelle, Dennis Jerome. BS in Journalism and Polit. Sci., Baker U., 1975. Reporter Birmingham Post-Herald, Ala., 1975-80, UPI, Birmingham, Ala., 1980-83, state news editor, 1983-85; asst. nat. editor Phila. Inquirer, 1985-86; asst. city editor Birmingham News, Ala., 1986-87, editorial writer, 1987-94; editl. page writer The Balt. Sun, 1994-99; commentary editor Phila. Inquirer, 1999—2004, dep. editl. page editor, 2004—. Journalist-in-residence Loyola Coll., Balt., 1997-98; Freedom Forum vis. prof. U. Ala., 1993-94. Trustee Baker U., 1997—. Recipient Pulitzer Prize for editorial writing, 1991. Mem. Nat. Assn. Black Journalists (Journalist of Yr. award 1991), Birmingham Assn. Black Journalists (pres. 1987-90), Soc. Profl. Journalists (Green Eyeshade award 1989), Phila. Assn. Black Journalists. Presbyterian. Avocations: reading, aerobic exercise. Home: 57 Fox Hollow Ln Sewell NJ 08080-3139 Office: 400 N Broad St Philadelphia PA 19130-4015 Office Phone: 215-854-5555.

JACKSON, HARRY ANDREW, artist; b. Chgo., Apr. 18, 1924; s. Harry Shapiro and Ellen Grace Jackson; m. Theodora Rehard DuBois, 1946 (div.); m. Grace Hartigan, 1948 (div.); m. Claire Rodgers, 1950 (dec.); m. Joan Hunt, 1951 (div.); m. Sarah Mason, Sept. 10, 1962 (div.); children: Matthew, Molly; m. Tina Lear, Aug. 11, 1973 (div.); children: Jesse, Luke, Chloe. Diploma, H.S., 1945; LLD (hon.), U. Wyo., 1986. Founder fine art foundry, Camaiore, Italy, 1964—, Harry Jackson Studios, Italy, 1965—; CEO Harry Jackson Studios (formerly Wyo. Foundry Studios, Inc.), Cody, Wyo., 1971—; founder Western Arts Found., 1974—; foundry ptnr. Jackson-Mariani Fine Art Foundry, Camaiore, Italy, 1985-98; founder Harry Jackson Art Mus., Cody, Wyo., 1994. Author: Lost Wax Bronze Casting, 1972, New York School Abstract Expressionists, 2000; one man exhbns. include Ninth St. Show, N.Y.C., 1951, Tibor de Nagy Gallery, N.Y.C., 1952, 53, Martha Jackson Gallery, N.Y.C., 1956, M. Knoedler & Co., N.Y.C., 1960, Amon Carter Mus., Fort Worth, 1961, 68, Kennedy Galleries, N.Y.C., 1964, 68, Smithsonian Instn., Washington, 1964, Whitney Gallery Western Art, Cody, 1964, 81, Mont. Hist. Soc., 1964, NAD, 1965, 68, Nat. Cowboy Hall of Fame, Oklahoma City, 1966, XVII Mostra Internazionale d'Arte, Premio del Fiorino, Florence, Italy, 1966, Pennational Artists Ann., Pa., 1967, Mostra de Arte Moderna, Convento di S. Lazzaro, Camaiore, 1968, Am. Artists Profl. League, N.Y., 1968, Cowboy Artists Am., 1971-76, S.W. Mus., L.A., 1979, Smith Gallery, N.Y.C., 1981, 85; major retrospective exhbns. include Buffalo Bill Hist. Ctr., 1981, Palm Springs Desert Mus., 1981, Mpls. Inst. Art, 1982, Camaiore, Italy, 1985, Met. Mus. Art, N.Y.C., 1987; represented in permanent collections Met. Mus. Art, NAD, Nat. Mus. Am. Art, Nat. Portrait Gallery, Washington, Her Majesty Queen Elizabeth II, Sandringam Castle, Eng., Am. Mus. of Gt. Britain, Bath, Eng., U.S. State Dept., Washington, Lyndon Baines Johnson Meml. Libr., Austin, Tex., Ronald Reagan Meml. Libr., Santa Barbara, Calif., Whitney Gallery Western Art, Plains Indian Mus., Buffalo Bill Hist. Ctr., Cody, Wyo., Wadsworth Atheneum, Hartford, Conn., Alberta Glenbow Mus., Calgary, Can., Univ. So. Calif., Stanford (Calif.) Univ., Love Libr. Univ. Nebr., Lincoln, Portsmouth (R.I.) Abbey, S.W. Mus., Gene Autrey Mus., L.A., Nat. Cowboy Hall of Fame, Oklahoma City, Gilcrease Mus., Tulsa, Fort Pitts Mus., Pitts., Amon Carter Mus., Pro Rodeo Cowboy Hall of Fame, Colorado Springs, Colo., Eiteljorg Mus., Indpls., Shelburne (Vt.) Mus., Columbus (Ga.) Mus. Arts & Scis., Oreg. Hist. Soc., Portland, Salt Lake City

Art Ctr., Norfolk (Nebr.) Arts Ctr., Aspen (Colo.) Art Mus., Woolaroc Mus., Bartlesville, Okla., U. Wyo. Art Mus., Laramie, Mont. Hist. Soc., Helena, Norton Mus., Shreveport, La., Columbia U., N.Y.C., Trout Gallery Dickinson Coll., Carlisle, Pa., Ctrl. Wyo. Coll., Riverton, N.W. C.C., Powell, Wyo., Baylor Sch., Chattanooga, Orme Sch., Mayer, Ariz., others; commd. works include (sculpture) William R. Coe Commn., 1959, 60, Fort Pitt Mus., 1964, 73, Plains Indian Mus., Cody, Wyo., Ctrl. Wyo. Coll., Riverton, 1978, 81, Piazza della Chiesa, Capezzano, Pianore, Italy, 1985, Great Western Savs. & Loan, Santa Barbara, Calif., 1985, John Wayne monumental sculpture Beverly Hills, Calif, 1981, 84, (portrait busts) Met. Mus. Trustees, C. Douglas Dillon, 1985, 87, (portrait) "John Wayne" TIME cover, Aug. 8, 1969 (Nat. Best Cover Art award Am. Inst. Graphic Arts 1969), (paintings) Whitney Gallery Western Art, Cody, 1960, 66, (mural) R.K. Mellon. Served with USMC, 1942-45. Decorated Purple Heart with gold star; recipient Gold medal NAD, 1968; grantee Fulbright, 1954, Italian Govt., 1956, 57. Fellow NAD (academician), RISD, Nat. Acad. Western Art, Nat. Sculpture Soc., Am. Artists League; mem. Bohemian Club (San Francisco). Office: PO Box 2836 Cody WY 82414-2836 also: Via Monteggiori 55040 Camaiore Lucca Italy Office Phone: 307-587-5508. Office Fax: 307-587-6362. Personal E-mail: harry@harryjacksonmuseum.org. Business E-Mail: lora@harryjackson.org.

JACKSON, HERB, artist, educator; b. Raleigh, NC, Aug. 16, 1945; s. Walter H. and Virginia (Rogers) Jackson; m. Laura Dudley Grosch, June 9, 1967; children: Leif, Ulysses. BA, Davidson Coll., 1967; postgrad., Philips Universität; MFA, U. N.C., 1970. William H. Williamson prof. art Davidson Coll., NC, 1969—, chmn. dept. art, 1977-94; dir. Art Gallery, 1974-95; mem. artist adv. bd. Mint Mus. Art, Charlotte, NC, 1979-85. Bd. adv. Light Factory, Charlotte, 1990—, NC Dance Theater, NC, 1998. One-man shows include: Mint Mus. Art, Charlotte, 1973, U. Nev., Reno, 1973, Rahr Mus., Manitowoc, Wis., 1973, Jane Haslem Gallery, Washington, 1974, Nielsen Gallery, Boston, 1974, Impressions Gallery, Boston, 1975, 81, Hahn Gallery, Phila., 1976, Dryden Gallery, Charlotte, 1976, Van Straaten Gallery, Chgo., 1977, Frances Aronson Gallery, Atlanta, 1978, NC Mus. Art, Raleigh, 1979, Rowe Gallery, U. NC, Charlotte, 1979, Southeastern Ctr. for Contemporary Art, Winston-Salem, NC, 1981, Phyllis Weil Gallery, NYC, 1981, 83, 85, 87, 88, 90, Princeton Gallery Fine Art, 1982, 83, Oxford (Eng.) Gallery, 1982, DBR Gallery, Cleve., 1983, 84, Mint Mus. Art, Charlotte, 1983, Springfield Mus. Art (Mo.), 1983, Asheville (NC) Mus. Art, 1983, NAS, Washington, 1983, Cheekwood Art Ctr., Nashville, 1983, Reading (Pa.) Art Mus., 1984, Gulbenkian Found., Lisbon, Portugal, 1984, Huntsville (Ala.) Mus. Art, 1984, Jerald Melberg Gallery, Charlotte, 1984, 85, 87, 88, 90, 92, 93, 94, 96, 97, 98, 99, Fay Gold Gallery, Atlanta, 1986, 88, 92, Cumberland Gallery, Nashville, 1987, 96, Judy Youens Gallery, Houston, 1988, Peden Gallery, Raleigh, 1988, 92, 93, Asheville Mus. Art, 1988, Allene Lapides Gallery, Santa Fe, 1989-90, Maurine Littleton Gallery, Washington, 1990, Hickory (NC) Mus. Art, 1993, St. Johns Mus. Art, Wilmington, NC, 1993, Bi-Nat. Cultural Ctr., Arequipa, Peru, 1994, parchman Stremmel Gallery, San Antonio, 1995-2001, Somerhill Gallery, Chapel Hill, NC, 1995, 98, Christa Faut Gallery, Cornelius, NC, 1996, 97, 99, 2000, 02, 03, 05, La. Tech. U., Ruston, 1999, Lmar Dodd Art Ctr., La Grange, Ga., 1999, Greenville (NC) Mus. Art, 2000, Les Yeux du Monde, Charlottesville, Va., 2001, 04, GSI Fine Art, Cleve., 2001, Fayetteville (NC) Mus. Art, 2002, The Art Preserve, Charlotte, 2004; numerous group shows, 1962—, latest being Internat. Print Biennale, Bradford, Eng., 1979, Mint Mus., Charlotte, 1979, 81, Southeastern Ctr. Contemporary Art, Winston-Salem, 1979, Internat. São Paulo (Brazil) Bienal, 1979, Spring Mills Ann. Competition, Lancaster, SC, 1980, Weatherspoon Gallery, Greensboro, NC, 1980, Impressions Gallery, Boston, 1980, Associated Am. Artists, Phila., 1980, Am. Acad. and Inst. Arts and Letters, NYC, 1981, 1987, Bklyn. Mus. Art, 1981, World's Fair, Knoxville, Tenn., 1982, Davos, Switzerland, 1983, Palazzo Venezia, Rome, 1984, Miss. Mus. Art, 1984, U. Denver, 1984, Albuequerque Mus. Art, 1985, Fla. State U., 1985, St. John's Mus. Art, Wilmington, 1986, U. Tex., San Antonio, 1987, Contemporary Arts Ctr. New Orleans, 1988, Kunstsammlungen der Veste Coburg, Fed. Republic Germany, 1988, Lorenzelli Fine Art, Milan, 1989, Exhbn. Hall of Union of Moscow Artists, Moscow, 1989, Samuel P. Harn Mus., Gainesville, Fla., 1990, New Orleans Mus. Art, 1995, Shanxia Govt. Art Gallery, Xian, China, 1996, Morris Mus. Art, Augusta, Ga., 1997, Mus. Del Vidrio, Monterey, Mex., 1999, Vanessa Suchar Fine Arts, London, 2000, Thomas McCormick Gallery, Chgo., 2002; represented in permanent collections: Balt. Mus. Art, Phila. Mus. Art, Victoria and Albert Mus., London, Whitney Mus. Art, NYC, Mpls. Inst. Arts, Nat. Acad. Sci., Washington, Indpls. Mus. Art, Bklyn. Mus., USIA, Japan, U. Wis., Sheboygan, Yale U., New Haven, Mus. Fine Arts, Boston, NY Pub. Libr., Libr. of Congress, Washington, Mint Mus., Charlotte, So. Ill. U., Edwardsville, Kalamazoo Inst. Arts, Mus. Fine Arts, Springfield, Mass., Utah Mus., Salt Lake City, U. Nebr., Lincoln, U. Calif., Riverside, Minn. Mus. Art, St. Paul, Brit. Mus., London, others. Fellow Southeastern Ctr. for Contemporary Art Southeastern Seven, 1981, N.C. Visual Arts, 1984, Nat. Endowment for Arts and So. Arts Fedn., 1986; recipient N.C. award, 1999, Hunter-Hamilton Love of Tchg. award, 2003. Mem. Coll. Art Assn., So. Graphics Coun., Charlotte Artists Coalition (dir. 1980-81), Mecklenberg-Charlotte Arts and Sci. Coun. (dir. 1977-79), Southeastern Coll. Art Conf. Home: PO Box 10 Davidson NC 28036-0010 Office: PO Box 7117 Davidson NC 28035-7117 Office Phone: 704-894-2358. Office Fax: 704-894-2691. E-mail: hejackson@davidson.edu. *The artist's integrity is all he truly has, after all the trends, fads, and movements have faded into history. I try to make art which will stand as a personal statement.*

JACKSON, HOLLYE MCCRUM, art educator, artist; b. Clarendon, Ark., May 16, 1961; d. Samuel Eugene McCrum and Marjorie Lea Grady; 1 child, Brice Corder. BFA, Ark. State U., 1986; postgrad., Harding U., 2003—. Art instr. DeWitt (Ark.) Pub. Schs., 1990—. Adj. instr. Phillips C.C. of U. Ark., DeWitt, 2004—. Leader Girl Scouts U.S., DeWitt, 1991—97, Awana Youth, DeWitt, 1999—2001; Cub scout leader Boy Scouts Am., DeWitt, 2003—05, 2004—05. Named top 100 finalist, Ark. Quar. Challenge, 2003. Mem.: Ark. Art Educators Assn. (ea. regional dir. 2003—). Avocations: painting, drawing, gardening, reading. Home: 4 Crescent Park Dr De Witt AR 72042 Office: DeWitt HS 1614 S Grandview De Witt AR 72042 Office Phone: 870-946-4661.

JACKSON, HOWELL E., law educator; b. NYC, Jan. 4, 1954; BA magna cum laude, Brown U., 1976; JD, MBA magna cum laude, Harvard U., 1982. Bar: DC 1984. Law clk. to Justice Thurgood Marshall US Supreme Ct.; assoc. Arnold & Porter, Washington; asst. prof. law Harvard Law Sch., Cambridge, Mass., 1989—94, prof., 1994—, Finn M.W. Caspersen and Household Internat. Prof. Law, 1999—2004, assoc. dean rsch. and spl. programs, 2001—03, vice dean adminstrn. and budget, 2003—, James S. Reid, Jr. Prof. Law., 2004—. Office: Harvard Law Sch 1563 Massachusetts Ave Cambridge MA 02138 Office Phone: 617-495-5466. Office Fax: 617-496-5156. Business E-Mail: hjackson@law.harvard.edu.

JACKSON, HUNTER, health products executive; PhD in Psychobiology, Yale U., New Haven; postgrad. dept. neurosurgery, U. Va. Assoc. prof. dept. anatomy U. Utah, Salt Lake City; CEO, chmn. bd., founder NPS Pharms., Inc., Salt Lake City, 1986—, pres., 1994—. Office: NPS Pharmaceuticals Inc 420 Chipeta Way Salt Lake City UT 84108-1256*

JACKSON, J. DAVID, lawyer; b. York, Pa., 1949; BA magna cum laude, St. Olaf Coll., 1971; JD summa cum laude, Washington U., 1974. Bar: Minn. 1974. Law clerk 8th cir. U.S. Ct. Appeals, 1974-75; ptnr., trial practice group Dorsey & Whitney, Mpls. Mem. Order of Coif. Office: Dorsey & Whitney Ste 1500 50 S 6th St Minneapolis MN 55402-1498 Office Phone: 612-340-2760. Office Fax: 612-340-2807. Business E-Mail: jackson.j@dorsey.com.

JACKSON, J. GARRETT (GARY JACKSON), airport terminal executive; b. Victoria, Tex. Grad., Marion (Ala.) Mil. Inst., So. Ark. U. Mgmt. trainee Louisville-Jefferson County Air Bd., Standiford Field, 1965—69; airport mgr. Texarkana Mcpl. Airport, Ark., 1969—78, Columbus Met. Airport, Ga., 1978—86; dep. dir. Greenville-Spartanburg (S.C.) Internat. Airport, Greer, SC, 1986—90, exec. dir., 1990—. Office: Greenville-Spartanburg Internat Airport 2000 Gsp Dr Ste 1 Greer SC 29651-6633 E-mail: gjackson@gspairport.com.

JACKSON, JACK LEE, II, mathematics professor, musician; b. Jonesboro, Ark., Mar. 23, 1963; s. Jack Lee and Joy Jackson; m. Dianna Lynn Riley, July 11, 1987; children: Heather Cherie, Ashley Amanda. BS in Math. Edn./Music, Ark. State U., 1984, MS in Math., 1986; PhD in Math., U. Ariz., 1999. Instr. Ark. State U., Jonesboro, 1987—89, U. Ariz., Tucson, 1989—95; assoc. prof. U. Ark., Ft. Smith, 1995—. Musician (3d horn): Ft. Smith Symphony Orch., 1996—. Pres. Ramsey Band Parents Assn., Ft. Smith, 2002—; deacon, musician 1st Christian Ch., Ft. Smith, 1995—. Mem.: Math. Assn. Am., Internat. Horn Soc., Kappa Kappa Psi (life; chpt. sponsor). Home: 3514 Brooken Hill Dr Fort Smith AR 72908 Office: U Ark 5210 Grand Ave Fort Smith AR 72913

JACKSON, JACK P., lawyer; b. NYC, Aug. 4, 1958; BA cum laude, Fordham U., 1979; MBA, Columbia U., 1983; JD, Columbia U. Sch. Law, 1983. Bar: NY 1984. Ptnr., corp. dept. Proskauer Rose LLP, NYC. Named Harlan Fiske Stone Scholar; named one of Top 100 Minority Bus. Leaders NYC, Crain's NY, 2003, Am. Top Black Atty., Black Enterprise, 2003; recipient Whitney M. Young award, Greater NY Coun. Boy Scouts Am., 1999. Mem.: Assn. Bar City NY (mem. task force on minorities, mem. banking law com. 1997—). Office: Proskauer Rose LLP 1585 Broadway New York NY 10036-8299 Office Phone: 212-969-3140. Office Fax: 212-969-2900. Business E-Mail: jjackson@proskauer.com.

JACKSON, JACQUELINE DOUGAN, literature educator, writer; b. Beloit, Wis., May 3, 1928; d. Ronald Arthur and Vera Arlouine (Wardner) Dougan; m. Robert Sumner Jackson, June 17, 1950 (div. 1973); children—Damaris Lee, Megan Trever, Gillian Patricia, Jacqueline Elspeth. BA, Beloit Coll., 1950, H.H.D., 1977; MA, U. Mich., 1951; D.Litt., MacMurray Coll., 1976. Instr. English Kent (Ohio) State U., 1964-68; prof. lit. U. Ill. (formerly Sangamon State U.), Springfield, 1970—. Writer, presenter: radio shows The Author is You, U. Wis. WHA Sch. of Air, 1969-78, Reading and Writing and Radio, WSSU, Springfield, Ill., 1975-94; author: Julie's Secret Sloth, 1953, The Taste of Spruce Gum (Notable Book award 1966), 1966 (Dorothy Canfield Fisher award 1967), Missing Melinda, 1967, Chicken Ten Thousand, 1968, Spring Song, 1969, The Orchestra Mice, 1970, The Endless Pavement, (with William Perlmutter), 1973, Turn Not Pale, Beloved Snail, 1974, Stories from the Round Barn, 1997, More Stories from the Round Barn, 2002; author-illustrator: The Paleface Redskins, 1958, The Ghost Boat, 1969; illustrator: (Chad Walsh) Knock and Enter, 1953. Mem. Phi Beta Kappa. Episcopalian. Home: 816 N 5th St Springfield IL 62702-5215 Business E-Mail: jackson.jacqueline@uis.edu.

JACKSON, JAMES BRUCE, lawyer; b. Kansas City, Mo., Oct. 22, 1951; s. Claude James and Evalyn Nadine (Smith) J.; m. Merrily Teresa Thomson, Oct. 23, 1982. BA, U. Ariz., 1973; JD, U. Mo., Kansas City, 1977. Bar: Mo. 1977, U.S. Dist. Ct. (we. dist.) Mo. 1977, Ariz. 1985, Kans. 1990, U.S. Dist. Ct. Kans. 1990, U.S. Ct. Appeals (8th cir.) 1991. Assoc. counsel Mo. State Hwy. Dept., Kansas City, 1977-85; pvt. practice law Kansas City, 1985—. Adj. prof. Avila Coll. Paralegal Program, Kansas City, 1989-93. Officer Sierra Club Sect., Kansas City, 1985-90. Mem. Ariz. Bar Assn., Mo. Bar Assn., Kans. Bar Assn., Greater Kansas City Bar Assn., Wyandotte County Bar Assn., Alliance Francaise (sec.), Univ. Club (chair Cincinnatus com. 1996—), Phi Delta Theta. Republican. Methodist. Avocations: scuba, private pilot, amateur radio technician. Home: 4417 Harrison St Kansas City MO 64110-1627 Office: # 200 3675 S Noland Rd Independence MO 64055-6505 Office Phone: 816-461-4262.

JACKSON, JAMES F., nuclear engineer, educator; b. Ogden, Utah, Aug. 15, 1939; s. Allyn Boyd and Virginia (Dixon) J.; m. Joan Borger, Aug. 25, 1960; children: James D., Bret A., Tracy L., Wendy L. BS, U. Utah, 1961; MS, MIT, 1962; PhD, UCLA, 1969. Rsch. engr. Atomics Internat., L.A., 1962066; nuclear engr. Argonne Nat. Lab., Idaho Falls, Idaho, 1969-72, group leader Argonne, Ill., 1972-74; assoc. prof. Brigham Young U., Provo, Utah, 1974-76, adj. prof., 1998—; cons. Los Alamos (N.Mex.) Nat. Lab., 1974-76, group/div. leader, 1976-82, dep. assoc. dir., 1979-81, div. leader, 1983-84, assoc. dir., 1984-86, dep. dir., 1986-98, staff mem., 1998-99, cons., 1999—. Contbr. articles to jours. in field. Mem. exec. bd. Community Devel. Com., Los Alamos, 1989-93; bd. dirs. Los Alamos Citizens Against Substance Abuse, 1989-93. Recipient E.O. Lawrence award Dept. Energy, Washington, 1983. Mem. NAE, Am. Nuclear Soc. (safety div. 1967—, exec. com. 1977-80), Tau Beta Pi. Republican. Mem. Lds Ch. Avocations: history, motorsports, photography. Home: 536 Sheffield Dr Provo UT 84604-5666 Office: Los Alamos Nat Lab Ofc Dir Los Alamos NM 87545-0001 Business E-Mail: jackson-james-f@lanl.gov. E-mail: jackson538@comcast.net.

JACKSON, JAMES LEWIS PERDUE, II, entertainment company executive; b. Chattanooga, May 29, 1946; s. James Oliver and Nellie Mae (Perdue) J.; 1 foster child, Abner Isaias Quinones. AA, Long Beach (Calif.) City Coll., 1972, Riverside (Calif.) City Coll., 1974; cert., Am. Bus. Inst., 1989. Cert. tax audit rep. IRS. Head designer, owner Jai et' Cie Haute Couture, L.A., 1983—; head artist and image devel. Platinum Gold Prodns., L.A., 1990-94; CEO, owner TOJA Entertainment Group, N.Y.C., L.A., 1990—; exec. v.p. Leg Records, L.A., 1995-96; food and beverage mgr. Gershwin Hotel, N.Y.C., 1997-98; ptnr. The LeBlanc Group, N.Y.C., 1997-98. West Coast mng. editor Twin Cities Exec. Mag., L.A., 1991-93; prodr. Three Points of Light Prodns., N.Y.C., 1996-99; costume designer Zipper Films, N.Y.C., 1997; author (screenplay) The Mary Wells Story, 1998; exec. prodr. The Tennis Shoe Cowboy, 1999, The Pink Triangle, 1999. Sustaining mem. Rep. Nat. Com., L.A., 1983; active N.Y. Black Rep. Coun., N.Y.C., 1999. With USN, 1964-69. Mem. Motown Alumni Assn. (exec. dir. N.Y.C. chpt.). Republican. Avocations: horse back riding, skiing, modern dance, opera, ballet. Fax: 212-368-0485. E-mail: Jai2cool@aol.com, TOJAEntGrp@aol.com.

JACKSON, JAMES SIDNEY, psychologist, educator; b. Detroit, July 30, 1944; s. Pete James and Johnnie Mae (Wilson) J. BS, Mich. State U., 1966; MA, U. Toledo, 1970; PhD, Wayne State U., 1972. Probation counselor Lucas County Juvenile Ct., Toledo, 1967-68; tchg. and rsch. asst. Wayne State U., Detroit, 1968-71; from asst. prof. to prof. psychology U. Mich., Ann Arbor, 1971—, faculty assoc. Rsch. Ctr. Group Dynamics, 1971—, dir. Rsch. Ctr. Group Dynamics, 1996—2005, faculty assoc. Inst. Gerontology, 1976—, dir. program for rsch. on Black Ams., 1976—, faculty assoc. Ctr. Afro-Am. and African Studies, 1982—, rsch. scientist, 1986—, assoc. dean Rackham Sch. Grad. Studies, 1987-92, prof. pub. health, 1990—, Daniel Katz Collegiate prof., 1994-95, Daniel Katz Disting. Univ. prof. psychology, 1995—; Hill Disting. vis. prof. U. Minn., Ann Arbor, 1995; dir. Ctr. Afro-Am. and African Studies U. Mich., Ann Arbor, 1998—2005, dir. Inst. for Social Rsch., 2005—. Chair sociol. psychology tng. program U. Mich., 1980-86, 93-96; cons. Emergency Sch. Aid Project, 1973-74, Commn. on Equal Opportunity in Psychology, 1970, Project to Provide Psychol. Svcs. to Head Start Programs, 1973-74, European Econ. Commn. Project on Racism, Xenophobia and Immigration, 1989—; mem. com. on aging and com. on status of Black Ams., panel on race, ethnicity and health in later life, Nat. Acad. of Scis., NAS; mem. com. on African Am. Population Year 2000 and 2010 U.S. Census Bur.; mem. nat. adv. com. Boston Mus. Sci., 1998—; mem. Nat. Adv. Coun. on Aging, NIH, 1996-99; mem. bd. sci. counselors, Nat. Inst. Aging; invited rschr. Ecole des Hautes Etudes en Scis. Sociales, Paris, 1992—; disting. lectr. gerontology UCLA, 1992; mem. steering com. Nat. Acad. Aging Soc., 1995—. Author: The Black American Elderly: Research on Physical and Psychosocial Health, 1988, African American Elderly, 2d edit., 1997, (with Gurin P., Hatchett S.) Hope and Independence: Blacks Response to Electoral and Party Politics, 1989, Life in Black America, 1991, (with Chatters L., Taylor R.) Aging in Black America, 1993, (with H. Neighbors) Mental Health in Black America, 1996, (with R. Taylor and L. Clatters) Family Life in Black America, 1997; editor: New Directions: African Americans in a Diversifying Nation, 2000; editl. cons. Jour. Behavioral and Social Scientists; editl. bd. Jour. Gerontology, Applied Social Psychology Ann., Psychol. Bull., Jour. Social Issues; cons. editor Psychology and Aging; contbr. articles to profl. jours. Bd. dirs. Pub. Commn. on Mental Health, Ronald McDonald House, Ann Arbor, 1993—; bd. trustees Greenhills Sch., Ann Arbor, 1997-2003, v.p., 2002-03. Recipient Disting. Faculty Svc. award U. Mich., 1976, Harold R. Johnson Diversity Svc. award U. Mich., 2000; Urban Studies fellow Wayne State U., 1969-70; NSF fellow, 1969; Sr. Postdoctoral fellow Groupe d'Études et de Recherches sur la Science, École des Hautes Études en Sciences Sociales, 1986-87; Sr. Ford Found. Minority Postdoctoral fellow, 1986-87; Fogarty Sr. Internat. fellow, 1993-94; Robert W. Kleemeier award for rsch., Gerontol. Soc. Am. Fellow APA (divs. 9-20, policy and planning bd., fin. com. 1984-86, award for early contbns. 1983, Tenth Anniversary Peace and Social Justice award Soc. for the Study of Peace, Conflict and Violence, Peace Psychology divsn. 2000, com. on internat. rels., 1999-02, chair 2001-02, Disting. Career Contbns. to Rsch. award Divsn. 45, 2001), Am. Psychol. Soc., Gerontol. Soc. Am. (task force on minority issues in gerontology, chmn. 1988-92, ann. sci. conv. program com.); mem. AAAS (past chair sect. social, econ. and polit. scis.), Assn. Advancement of Psychology (trustee 1973-89, chmn. 1978-80), Inst. of Medicine, Nat. Acad. Scis., Black Students Psychol. Assn. (nat. chmn. 1970-71), Assn. Black Psychologists (nat. chmn. 1972-73), Soc. Psychol. Study of Social Issues, World Future Soc., Assn. Behavioral and Social Scientists, Gerontol. Soc. Am. (chair behavioral and social scis. sect. 1997-98), Internat. Platform Assn., NIMH (nat. mental health coun. 1989-93, panel on equal access com. on instl. cooperation 1989-92), Psi Chi, Alpha Phi Alpha. Home: 340 Orchard Hills Dr Ann Arbor MI 48104-1832 Office: U Mich 5110 Inst Social Rsch 426 Thompson St Ann Arbor MI 48104-2321

JACKSON, JANET DAMITA JO, vocalist, dancer; b. Gary, Ind., May 16, 1966; d. Joseph and Katherine J.; m. James DeBarge, 1984 (div. 1985), m. René Elizondo, 1991 (div. 2000). Albums include Janet Jackson, 1982, Dream Street, 1984, Control, 1986, Rhythm Nation 1814, 1991, janet, 1993, Design of a Decade: 1986-1996, 1995, The Velvet Rope, 1997, All For You, 2001 (Grammy award, Best Dance Recording, 2002), Damita Jo, 2004; actress (TV series) Good Times, 1977-1979, A New Kind of Family, 1979, Diff'rent Strokes, 1981-1982, 1984, Fame, 1984-1985; (films) Poetic Justice, 1993 (Academy award nomination Best Original Song 1993), Nutty Professor II: The Klumps, 2000. Recipient 6 Am. Music awards, 1987, 1988, 1991, 5 Grammy nominations, MTV Video Vanguard award, 1990, Grammy award, Best R&B song 1994 for "That's the Way Love Goes" with Terry Lewis and James Harris III; MTV Best Female Video for "If", named one of 50 Most Influential African-Americans, Ebony Mag. 2004. Office: Creative Artists Agency 9830 Wilshire Blvd Beverly Hills CA 90212-1825

JACKSON, JEANNE PELLEGREN, apparel executive; b. Denver, Aug. 10, 1951; d. John James and Barbara (Grove) Pellegren; m. Douglas Emmett Jackson, Nov. 23, 1984; children: Lindsay, Craig. BS in Fin., U. Colo., 1974; MBA, Harvard Bus. Sch., 1978. Buyer, mgr. Bullocks Dept. Stores, L.A., 1978-85; v.p. merchandise mgr. to sr. v.p. direct mail pvt. brands Saks Fifth Ave., N.Y.C., 1985-89; sr. v.p. merchandising Walt Disney Attractions, Orlando, 1989-92; exec. v.p. merchandising Victoria's Secret, Columbus, Ohio, 1992-95; CEO Banana Republic, 1996-2000, Wal-Mart.com, 2000—. Instr. mktg. U. So. Calif., L.A., 1979-81; adv. bd. Navy Exch., Norfolk, Va., 1991—. Bd. dirs. Orlando Mus. Art, 1990-92. Republican. Avocations: skiing, tennis. Office: Walmartcom 135 Constitution Dr Menlo Park CA 94025 Home: 5 Sunset Vis Newport Coast CA 92657-1702

JACKSON, JEFFERY M., information technology executive; BS Econ., Govt., Dartmouth Coll.; MS Mgmt., Northwestern U. From sr. fin. analyst to v.p., controller Am. Airlines, 1984—88; from sr. v.p., CFO Sabre Inc., Southlake, Tex., 1998, exec. v.p., CFO, 2002—. Mem. bd. dirs. Travelocity-.com, 2002—. Office: 3150 Sabre Dr Southlake TX 76092

JACKSON, JEFFREY L., academic administrator; b. Joplin, Mo., Sept. 29, 1958; s. Layton McRay Jackson and Barbara Ann Bryan; m. Jane Wagnon; children: Wilkins, Ellen. BS, U. Kans., 1983; MPH, Uniformed Svcs. U., 1996; MD, Washington U., St. Louis, 1988. Diplomate Am. Bd. Internal Medicine. Dir. gen. medicine fellowship Uniformed Svcs. U., Bethesda, Md., 1996—. Dir. gen. medicine divsn. Uniformed Svcs. U., Bethesda, 1998—, assoc. prof. medicine, 2000—. Contbr. med. rsch. articles to profl. jours. Lt. col. U.S. Army, 1988—2002. Recipient Hamolsky award, SGIM, 1997. Fellow: ACP. Personal E-mail: jejackson@usuhs.mil.

JACKSON, JESSE LOUIS, political organization worker, clergyman; b. Greenville, S.C., Oct. 8, 1941; s. Noah Robinson, Charles Henry (Stepfather) and Helen Burns Jackson; m. Jacqueline Lavinia Brown, 1963; children: Santita, Jesse Louis Jr., Jonathan Luther, Yusef DuBois, Jacqueline Lavinia. Student, U. Ill., 1959-60; BA in Sociology and Economics, NC A&T State U., 1964; student, Chgo. Theol. Sem., 1964—66, MDiv, 2000; hon. degrees, NC A&T State U., Pepperdine U., Oberlin U., Oral Roberts U., U. RI, Howard U., Georgetown U. Ordained to ministry Baptist Ch., 1968; Chgo. dir. Operation Breadbasket project, So. Christian Leadership Conf., Chgo., 1966—67, nat. dir., 1967-71; founder, exec. dir. Operation PUSH (People United to Serve Humanity), Chgo., 1971—96; founder PUSH-Excel and PUSH for Econ. Justice, 1977—96; founder, nat. pres. Nat. Rainbow Coalition Inc., Chgo., 1984—96; shadow senator from DC US Senate, Washington, 1991—96; founder, nat. pres. Rainbow/Push Coalition, Inc., Chgo., 1996—; spl. envoy of the President & Sec. State for the Promotion of Democracy in Africa US Dept. State, Washington, 1997; founder The Wall St. Project, 1997—. Candidate for Dem. nomination US Presdl. Election, 1983—84, 1987—88; lectr. for high schs., colls., prof. audiences in Am., Europe. Host, Both Sides with Jesse Jackson, CNN, 1992-2000; Author: Straight From the Heart, 1987, Keep Hope Alive, 1989; co-author: (with Jesse L. Jackson, Jr.) Legal Lynching: Racism, Injustice, and the Death Penalty, 1996, It's About the Money: How You Can Get Out of Debt, Build Wealth, and Achieve Your Financial Dreams!, 1999. Active Black Coalition for United Cmty. Action, 1969. Recipient Presdl. Award Nat. Med. Assn., 1969, Humanitarian Father of Year Award Nat. Father's Day Com., 1971, Presdl. Medal of Freedom, 2000; named Third Most Admired Man in Am. Gallup Poll, 1985, one of six new leaders on the rise US News World Report. Address: Rainbow PUSH Coalition 930 E 50th St Chicago IL 60615-2702*

JACKSON, JESSE LOUIS, JR., congressman; b. Greenville, S.C., Mar. 11, 1965; m. Sandra Jackson; children: Jessica Donatella, Jesse L. III. BS in Bus. Mgmt., NC A&T U., 1987; MA in Theology, Chgo. Theol. Sem., 1990; JD, U. Ill., 1993. Natl. field dir. The Rainbow Coalition, 1993—95; mem. U.S. Congress from 2d Ill. dist., Washington, 1995—, mem. house appropriations com., 1997—. Co-chair, comm. group Dem. Policy Com.; mem. Congressional Black Caucus, Congressional Steel Caucus. Author: Legal Lynching: Racism, Injustice and the Death Penalty, 1996, It's About the Money, 1999, A More Perfect Union: Advancing New American Rights, 2001. Democrat. Baptist. Office: US Ho of Reps 2419 Rayburn Ho Office Bldg Washington DC 20515-1302*

JACKSON, JEWEL, retired state agency administrator; b. June 3, 1942; d. Willie Burghardt and Bernice Jewel (Mayberry) Norton; children: Steven, June Kelly, Michael, Anthony. With Calif. Youth Authority, 1965-91, group supr. San Andreas & Santa Rosa, 1965-67, youth counselor Ventura, 1967-78, sr. youth counselor Stockton, 1978-81, parole agt., 1986, treatment team supr., program mgr. Whittier & Ione, 1981-91; ret., 1991. Owner Access Legal Document Assistance. Past bd. dirs. Samuel Hancock Christian Sch.; past pres. San Joaquin Valley Girls Horsewomen's Assn. Mem. Internat. Egg Art Guild. Avocations: reading, horseback riding, decorative egg art, decoupage. Home and Office: PO Box 8267 Stockton CA 95208-0267 Office Phone: 209-466-3570. Personal E-mail: accesslda@sbcglobal.net.

JACKSON, JILL ANN KREMER, church administrator, musician; b. Evansville, Ind., Apr. 16, 1957; d. Jerome Walter and Joan Marie (Kunkel) Kremer; m. Bill D. Jackson, June 22, 1991. BSBA, U. Evansville, 1979;

MusB, Ky. Wesleyan Coll., 1994. Office mgr. Newburgh Health Care and Residential Ctr., Ind., 1979—85; adminstrv. asst. Southwestern Ind. Easter Seal Soc., Evansville, 1986—88; pers. asst. Keller-Crescent Co., Evansville, Ind., 1988—89; sec. Cynthia Heights Elem. Sch., Evansville, Ind., 1989—92; dir. of music Simpson United Meth. Ch., Evansville, Ind., 1994—96, Holy Rosary Cath. Ch., Evansville, Ind., 1996—. Composer: (vocal music) I Thank My God, Angels Sing Gloria. Recipient Paul W. Hagan Outstanding Music prize, Ky. Wesleyan Coll., 1994, Dept. of Music award for outstanding sr., 1994. Mem.: Nat. Assn. of Pastoral Musicians (dir. music ministries divsn.). Roman Catholic. Avocations: singing, exercise, stitchery, travel, following St. Louis Cardinals baseball. Office: Holy Rosary Cath Ch 1301 S Green River Rd Evansville IN 47715 Office Phone: 812-477-8923. Business E-Mail: jillj@hrparish.org.

JACKSON, JIMMIE L., retired music educator, retired organist; b. Lakeland, Fla., Mar. 22, 1935; s. Amos Jackson and Essie M. Jackson (Hollie); m. Mary L. Wolfe, June 24, 1961. MusB, Boston U., 1973, MusM, postgrad., Boston U., 1976—. Cert. tchr. Mass. Dept. Edn., 1973. Choir dir., organist First Bapt. Instl. Ch., Lakeland, Fla., 1948—53, St. Michael's & All Angels Episcopal Ch., Tallahassee, 1954—56, Phila. Bapt. Ch., 1955—56, Grace Ch. (Van Vorst), Jersey City, 1956—57, Temple Menorah, Bloomfield, 1956—57, Peoples Bapt. Ch., Boston, 1957—59; office mgr. Samuel Hurwitz Co., 1961—70; choir dir., organist St. James African Orthodox Ch., Oston, 1962—63, Grant A M E Ch., Boston, 1963—69, St. Cyprian's Episcopal Ch., 1969—83; dir. adminstrn. & fin. The Ecumenical Ctr. Roxbury Inc, 1970—72, interim exec. dir., 1972; choral dir. Weston H.S., 1973—74; instr. k-12 music Wellesley Pub. Schs., 1974—88; clinician Mass. Music Educators All-State Conf., Lowell, 1979; choir dir., organist 195th Conv., Episcopal Diocese, Boston, 1980—80, St. Bartholomew's Episcopal Ch., Cambridge, 1984—85; min. music Peoples Bapt. Ch., Boston, 1986—93; program dir., dept. head, music and art Boston Latin Sch., 1988—99; music dir., organist Union United Meth. Ch., 1994—99. Adj. clin. instr. Boston U., 1979—80; adjudicator Boston Pops Auditions, Ayer, 1975, New Eng. Music Festival Assn., Rutland, Vt., 1976—79. Mem. Garrison-Trotter Neighborhood Assn. Inc., Boston; pres. The Couples Club Peoples Bapt. Ch., 1976—93. With U.S. Army, 1959—60. Recipient award, Union United Meth. Ch., 1996. Mem.: Mass. Music Educators Assn. (assoc.), Music Educators Nat. Conf. (assoc.), Am. Guild Organists (assoc.), Am. Choral Dirs. Assn. (life). Home: 76 Cheney St Dorchester MA 02121-2511

JACKSON, JIMMY LEE, state legislator; b. Floydada, Tex., Mar. 20, 1939; s. Vernon Lester and Vivian (Inez) J.; m. Sue Ellen Jackson, June 6, 1959; children: Stephen Bradley, Deborah LeAnne. BA, U. N. Tex., Denton, 1962. Orgnl. dir. Dallas County Rep. Party, 1965-69; ptnr. Jackson-Terry Ins. Agy., Dallas, 1970-73; exec. dir. Dallas County Rep. Party, 1972-74; county commr. Dallas County, 1974—2004. Chmn., vice-chmn. Nat. Assn. Counties Large Urban County Caucus, Washington, 1995-96; chmn. Nat. Assn. Counties Deferred Compensation Adv. Com., Washington, 2002; vice-chmn. Nat. Assn. Counties Transp. and Telecomms. Policy Steering Com., Washington, 1995-2000. Exec. bd. North Ctrl. Tex. Coun. of Govts., Arlington, 1992-99, 2002, chmn. regional transp. coun., 1983-86; bd. dirs., chmn. Dallas Ctrl. Appraisal Dist., 1988-95; bd. dirs. Tex. Assn. Regional Couns., 1996-99; chmn. Tex. Conf. of Urban Counties, 1981; mem. Congressional Dist. Rep. Nat. Delegate Selection Com., 1992, 96; del. Rep. Nat. Conv., 1992; arrangements chmn., 1986, congressional and senatorial dist. caucus chmn., 1990, 92, 94, 96, Rep. State Conv.; pres. Irving Rep. Club, 1979, Rep. Assembly, 1986-87, Metrocrest Rep. Club, 1991-92. Republican. Avocations: fishing, travel. Office: Dallas County Rd and Bridge Dist 1 2311 Joe Field Rd Dallas TX 75229-3328 E-mail: jjackson@dallascounty.org.

JACKSON, J(OHN) DAVID, physicist, researcher; b. London, Ont., Can., Jan. 19, 1925; came to U.S., 1957, naturalized, 1988; s. Walter David and Lillian Margaret Jackson; m. Barbara Cook, June 26, 1949; children: Ian, Nan, Maureen, Mark. BS in Physics and Math., U. Western Ont., 1946, DSc (hon.), 1989; PhD in Physics, MIT, 1949. Rsch. assoc. dept. physics MIT, Cambridge, 1949; from asst. prof. to assoc. prof. math. McGill U., Montreal, Que., Can., 1950-57; from assoc. prof. to prof. physics U. Ill., Urbana, 1957-67; prof. U. Calif., Berkeley, 1967-92, dept. chair, 1978-81, prof. emeritus, 1993—. Vis. fellow Cambridge (Eng.) U., 1970; acting head theory group Fermilab, Batavia, Ill., 1972-73; head physics divsn. Lawrence Berkeley Lab., 1982-84; dep. dir. SSC Cen. Design Group, Berkeley, 1985-87; vis. sr. rsch. fellow Oxford (Eng.) U., 1988-89; mem. vis. com. Argonne Nat. Lab., CERN, SSC Lab., Stanford Linear Accelerator Ctr., others. Author: Physics of Elementary Particles, 1958, Classical Electrodynamics, 1962, rev. edit., 1975, 3d edit., 1998, Mathematics for Quantum Mechanics, 1962; also numerous articles; editor Ann. Rev. Nuclear and Particle Sci., 1977-93. J. S. Guggenheim Found. fellow, 1956-57, Ford Found. fellow, 1963-64. Fellow Am. Phys. Soc.; mem. NAS (elected 1990), Am. Acad. Arts and Scis. (elected 1989), ACLU (life). Avocations: mountain hiking, swimming, scientific bibliophily. Address: Lawrence Berkeley Nat Lab 50A5104 Berkeley CA 94720 Office Phone: 510-486-4490.

JACKSON, JOHN EDWARD, adult education educator, retired military officer; b. Rapid City, S.D., Feb. 11, 1949; s. William Edward Joseph and Bettye Davis (Williams) J.; m. Valerie Lee McGilton, June 5, 1971; children: Gina Marie, Brian Howard. BA in Univ. Studies, U. N.Mex., 1971; MEd, Providence Coll., 1976; MS in Mgmt., Salve Regina U., 1983, cert. of advanced grad. studies, 1998; grad. mgmt. devel. program, Harvard U., 1997. Commd. USN, 1971, advanced through grades to capt., ret., 1998; disbursing officer USS Hunley AS-31, Charleston, S.C., 1972-74; food svc. officer Naval Edn. and Tng. Ctr., Newport, R.I., 1974-76; supply officer USS Joseph Strauss DDG-16, Pearl Harbor, Hawaii, 1976-78; data processing dept. dir. Nava. Supply Ctr., Pearl Harbor, 1978-80; prof. Ctr. Continuing Edn. U.S. Naval War Coll., Newport, 1980-83, prof. dept. nat. security decision-making, 1994-96, dean Coll. Continuing Edn., 1996—, assoc. dean for Distance Education, 2000—, dir. devel. and long range planning, 2002—; divsn. dir. Navy Fleet Material Support Office, Mechanicsburg, Pa., 1983-86; curricular officer U.S. Naval Postgrad. Sch., Monterey, Calif., 1986-90; supply officer USS Sierra AD-18, Charleston, 1990-92; exec. officer Naval Supply Ctr., Charleston, 1992-94; mil. chair logistics Naval War Coll., Newport, RI, 1994—. Speechwriter USN, 1978—. Former editor-in-chief newsletter The Oakleaf; editor: Logistics Leadership Series; contbr. articles to profl. jours. Mem. Soc. Logistics Engrs., Navy Supply Corps Assn. (bd. dirs. 1983-96, pres. 1994-96), Naval War Coll. Found., U.S. Naval Inst. (liaison officer). Home: 7 Mast Ct Middletown RI 02842-7212

JACKSON, JOHN HOLLIS, JR., lawyer; b. Mongomery, Ala., Aug. 21, 1941; s. John Hollis and Erma (Edgeworth) J.; m. Rebecca Mullins, May 27, 1967; 1 child, John Hollis III. AB, U. Ala., 1963, JD, 1966. Bar: Ala. 1966, U.S. Dist. Ct. (no. dist.) Ala. 1969, U.S. Ct. Appeals (11th cir.) 1993. Pvt. practice, Clanton, Ala., 1967—. County atty. Chilton County Commn., Clanton, 1969-; mcpl. judge Clanton, 1971-99, city atty., 1999—; dir. First Nat. Bank, Clanton, 1974-83; mem. adv. bd. Colonial Bank, Clanton, 1983-2003; mcpl. judge, Jemison, Ala., 1984—. Bd. dirs. Chilton-Shelby Mental Health Bd., Calera, Ala., 1974-83, pres., 1974-79; mem. State Dem. Exec. Com., Birmingham, Ala., 1974-98, County Dem. Exec. Com., Chilton County, 1982-94; del. Dem. Nat. Conv., N.Y.C., 1976. 1st lt. U.S. Army, 1966-67. Mem. Ala. Young Lawyers Sect. (exec. com. 1969-70), Chilton County Bar Assn. (pres. 1969, 74), Ala. State Bar Assn. (bd. bar commrs. 1984-87, 93-99, chmn. adv. com. to bd. bar examiners 1986-87, 19th cir. indigent def. commn. 1983—, chmn. disciplinary panel II 1997-99), Kiwanis, Phi Alpha Delta. Democrat. Methodist. Home: Samaria Rd Clanton AL 35045 Office: PO Box 1818 500 2nd Ave S Clanton AL 35046-1818 Office Phone: 205-755-2004. Personal E-mail: jhjatty@bellsouth.net.

JACKSON, JOHN HOWARD, lawyer, educator; b. Kansas City, Mo., Apr. 6, 1932; s. Howard Clifford and Lucile (Deischer) J.; m. Joan Leland, Dec. 16, 1962; children: Jeannette, Lee Ann, Michelle. AB, Princeton U., 1954; JD, U. Mich., 1959. Bar: Wis. 1959, Mo. 1959, Calif. 1964, Mich. 1970. Pvt. practice law, Milw., 1959-61; assoc. prof., prof. law U. Calif., 1961-66; prof. law U. Mich., 1966-97; univ. prof. law Georgetown U., Washington, 1998—, dir. Inst. of Internat. Econ. Law. On leave gen. counsel U.S. Office Spl. Trade Rep., 1973-74, acting deputy spl. rep. for trade, 1974; vis. prof. U. Brussels, 1975-76; vis. fellow Inst. for Internat. Econs., Washington, 1983; Hessel E. Yntema prof. law U. Mich., 1983-97, assoc. v.p. acad. affairs, 1988-89; disting. vis. prof. law Georgetown Law Ctr., Washington, 1986-87, 93; Ford Found. cons. legal edn., vis. prof. U. Delhi, India, 1968-69; Hersch Lauterpacht Meml. lectr. Cambridge (Eng.) U., 2002. Author: World Trade and the Law of GATT, 1969, Contract Law in Modern Society, 1973, 2d edit., 1980, Legal Problems of International Economic Relations, 1977, 4th edit. (with William Davey and Alan Sykes), 2002; (with Jean-Victor Louis and Mitsuo Matsushita) Implementing the Tokyo Round, 1984; (with Edwin Vermulst) Anti-Dumping Law & Practice: Comparative Study, 1989; The World Trading System, 1989, 2d edit., 1997, Restructuring the GATT System, 1990; (with Alan Sykes) Implementing the Urugauy Round, 1997, World Trade Organization, 1998, The Jurisprudence of GATT and the WTO, 2000; editor-in-chief Jour. Internat. Econ. Law; bd. editors: Am. Jour. Internat. Law, Jour. Law and Policy in Internat. Bus., others; contbr. articles to profl. jours. With M.I. U.S. Army, 1954-56. Recipient Wolfgang Friedman Memorial award Columbia U., 1992; Rockefeller Found. fellow for study European community law Brussels, 1975-76 Mem. ABA, Am. Soc. Internat. Law (v.p. 1990-92), Am. Law Inst., Council Fgn. Relations, Phi Beta Kappa, Order of Coif. Office: Georgetown U Law Ctr 600 New Jersey Ave NW Washington DC 20001-2022

JACKSON, JOHN WYANT, medical products executive; b. Corpus Christi, May 25, 1944; s. Donald LeGarde and Marion (McNulty) J; m. Susan Gager, Sept. 6, 1969; children: Alexandra C., Kimberly F., Donald M., Jennifer L. BA, Yale U., 1967; MBA, INSEAD, Fontainbleau, France, 1971; diploma, Inst. Political Sci., Paris, 1966. With Merck & Co., Rahway, NJ, 1971-78; pres. Gemini Med., Warren, NJ, 1991-96; chmn., CEO Celgene Corp., Warren, 1996—. Chmn. Biotech. Coun. N.J Mem. Yale Devel. Bd.; bd. dirs. Gordonstoun Am. Found., U.S. Insead Council. 1st lt. USMC, 1967—70. Decorated Navy Commendation medal; decorated Purple Heart Mem. Soc. Paper Money Collectors. Republican. Episcopalian. Office: Celgene Corp Summit NJ 07901

JACKSON, JON, medical educator, consultant; s. Dale and Marlys Alice Jackson; m. Margaret Ellen Moore, May 1, 1999; 1 child, Maia. BA, Luther Coll., 1983; PhD, U. ND, 1989. Post-doctoral fellow Vanderbilt U., Nashville, 1990—93; asst. prof. Vanderbilt U. Sch. Medicine, 1993—96, U. ND, Grand Forks, 1998—; prin. med. tech. writer Daedalus Consulting, Oakland, Calif., 1996—98; prin., account exec. Jensen, Ramsey and Jackson, San Ramon, 1996—97; cons. Inst. Natural Resources, Berkeley, 1998—2000, Pearson Christensen, Grand Forks, 2002—04. Med. tech. writer Daedalus Consulting, Grand Forks, 1998—; med. writer MedCo Comm., Evergreen, Colo., 1998—2004; investigator Office of Naval Rsch. Author: Corpus: A User's Guide to the Human Body; musician: (musical performance, acappella quartet) 4 Blow Zervo. Vol. ND Mus. Art, 1999—2005; vol. educator Dakota Sci. Ctr., 2003—05; pres. Grand Forks Master Chorale, 1998—2004; mem. North Valley Arts Coun., 2000—05. Recipient In Awe award, Med. Mktg. Assn.; Bush Found. scholar, Archibald Bush Found., 2001—02. Mem.: ND Acad. Sci. (sec., treas. 1999—2005), ND Funeral Dir.'s Assn., Am. Med. Writers Assn., AAAS, Human Anatomy and Physiology Soc., Am. Assn. Anatomists, Grand Forks C. of C., Sigma Xi. Democrat-Npl. Avocations: music, rugby, travel, running. Office: U ND Dept Anatomy and Cell Biology Grand Forks ND 58202-9037 Office Phone: 701-777-2101. Office Fax: 701-777-2477. Personal E-mail: jackson@gra.midco.net. Business E-Mail: jackson@medicine.nodak.edu.

JACKSON, JONATHAN MICHAEL, computer company executive, writer; b. Columbus, Ohio; s. Ben F. and N. Jean Jackson; m. Mary M. Fellows, Feb. 26, 1994; children: Jonathan Jr., Jennifer, Jody, Justin, Jeremy. BA, Capital U., 1976, JD, 1980. Atty., 1981—93; gen. mgr., owner PC Doctors, Inc., Summerville, SC, 1999—. Author: The Return to Brickenden Manor, 2003, I Rode with Morgan, 2004, Terror Times Thirteen, 2004. Mem.: KC, Morgan's Men Assn. (assoc.). Republican. Roman Catholic. Avocations: travel, historical research. Home: 1005 Trotters Blvd Summerville SC 29483 Office: PC Doctors Inc PO Box 13174 Charleston SC 29422 Office Phone: 843-873-1186. E-mail: alexius@sc.rr.com.

JACKSON, JOSEPH ESSARD, religious organization administrator; b. Negril, Jamaica, May 22, 1951; came to the U.S., 1968; s. Redverse and Edna Artilla (Gordon) J.; m. Elaine Marie Jacintho, July 1, 1978; children: Joseph E. II, Jonathan N. BS, Westfield State Coll., 1975; MAR, Yale U. Divinity Sch., 1981; CAS, Harvard U., 1983; DMin, Wesley Theol. Sem., 1993. Ordained to ministry, 1983. Counselor urban edn. program Westfield (Mass.) State Coll., 1972-74, 80; teaching fellow Harvard U., 1982-83; math. tchr. Springfield (Mass.) Pub. Schs., 1983-84; v.p. external rels. Charge, Inc., Glen Ellyn, Ill., 1984; history tchr. Tech. High Sch., Springfield, 1984-86; adj. prof. Ch. of God Sch. Theology, Cleveland, Tenn., 1986-89; sr. pastor Harvest Temple Ch. of God, Forestville, Md., 1989-92; exec. dir. Black ministries Ch. of God Internat. Offices, 1992-98; sr. pastor New Testament Ch. God, Hartford, Conn., 1998—. Asst. prof. religion dept. Bible and Christian Ministries Lee Coll., Cleveland, 1986-89; assoc. min. Ch. of God, Hartford, Conn., 1980-86; keynote speaker many confs. and convs. Author: Reclaiming Our Heritage, 1993; contbr. articles to profl. jours. Active alumni com. Tech. High Sch., 1984-85, Blue Hills Child Care Ctr., Hartford, 1981-86, State Bd. Edn., So. New England, 1984-89, Music Bd., So. New England, 1979-84, State Youth and Christian Edn. Bd. Ch. of God, So. New England; mem. ministerial devel. bd. State of Tenn., 1987-89. Mem. NAACP (bd. dirs. 1984-85), Nat. Assn. Evangelicals (bd. adminstrs. 1993—, mem. exec. com. 1994—, treas. 1995—, World Relief Corp. bd. mem. 1997—). Democrat. Avocations: fishing, writing. Home: 59 Greenlawn St East Hartford CT 06108-2952

JACKSON, JUDY FAYE, academic administrator; b. Robersonville, N.C. d. S. T. and Estella Jackson. BA in French Lang. and Lit., U. N.C., Greensboro; M in Francophone African Lit., Geography and Fgn. Policy, Bucknell U.; PhD in Adminstn., Planning and Social Policy, Harvard U. Mem. faculty English dept. Susquehanna U., 1981—85; various positions Cornell U. Coll. Engring., 1985—89, asst. dir. for advising and counseling, asst. dean for minority programs, asst. dean for advising counseling and minority programs; various positions MIT, 1989—2000, assoc. dean undergrad. edn. and student affairs, dir. minority edn., ombudsman Pres. Office, staff mem. Provost Office, spl. adviser to provost on faculty diversity; exec. asst. to pres., clk. of the corp. Babson Coll., Babson Park, Mass.; assoc. provost for instnl. engagement NYU, NY, 2002—04; dean Vassar Coll., Poughkeepsie, NY, 2004—. Office: Vassar Coll 124 Raymond Ave Poughkeepsie NY 12604

JACKSON, JULIAN ELLIS, food company executive; b. Perry, Fla., Oct. 24, 1913; s. Eddie H. and Eva M. (Reid) J.; m. Laurana H. Filson, Oct. 6, 1956; children: Julian Ellis, Eddie King, Robert Allen, Victor Pharis, Julian Ellis IV, Lester Mitchell. Grad., Andrew Jackson High Sch., Jacksonville, Fla., 1931; DSc (hon.), Jones Coll., 1982. With Great Atlantic & Pacific Stores, 1931—43; pres. Jax Meat Co., 1943—58, Jackson's Minit Markets, Inc., 1958—69, Julian Jackson Investment Co., 1955—, Lil' Champ Food Stores, Inc., 1971—98. Co-owner Jackson-Cowart Realty Co., 1955-97; dir. Fla. Nat. Bank, Jacksonville, Arlington. Past pres. United Cerebral Palsy, Jacksonville; chmn. Jacksonville Boxing Commn., 1952-71; pres. Gator Bowl Assn., 1957, Fla. Baseball League, 1958-60; Bd. dirs. Palmdale Med. Center, Police Athletic League, Jacksonville, Jacksonville Marine Inst., Jones Coll., Jacksonville. Recipient Top Mgmt. award Sales and Mktg. Execs. Jacksonville, 1968; named Super Market Man of Yr., 1960, One of Top 100 Athletes of Jacksonville in Past 100 Yrs., 1999; elected to Fla. Food Inst. Hall of Fame, 1994. Mem. Fla. Super Market Assn. (pres. 1950-59, elected to Fla. Sports Hall of Fame 1994), Fraternal Order of Police, Sportsman Club, Univ. Club (Jacksonville), Univ. Country Club, River Club, Ponte Vedra Club, Masons, Shriners. Home: 7987 Hollyridge Rd Jacksonville FL 32256-7110 Office: Julian Jackson Investment Co 8535 Baymeadows Rd Ste 25 Jacksonville FL 32256-7445

JACKSON, KATE, actress; b. Birmingham, Ala., Oct. 29, 1949; d. Hogan and Ruth Jackson; m. Andrew Stevens, Aug. 23, 1978 (div. 1981); m. David Greenwald, 1982 (div. 1984). Student, U. Miss.; student, Birmingham U.; grad., Am. Acad. Dramatic Arts, 1971. Worked as model. Appeared in TV series Dark Shadows, 1966-71, The Rookies, 1972-76, Charlie's Angels, 1976-79, The Scarecrow and Mrs. King, 1983-87, Baby Boom, 1988-89; TV appearances include Movin' On, The Jimmy Stewart Show; TV movies include: Satan's School for Girls, 1973, Death Cruise, 1974, Killer Bees, 1974, Death Scream, 1975, Charlie's Angels, 1976, Death at Love House, 1976, James at 15, 1977, Topper, 1979, Inmates: A Love Story, 1981, Thin Ice, 1981, Listen to Your Heart, 1983, The Stranger Within, 1990, Quiet Killer, 1992, Homewrecker, 1992, Adrift, 1993, Empty Cradle, 1993, The Shrine of Lorna Love, 1993, Arly Hanks, 1993, Armed and Innocent, 1994, Justice in a Small Town, 1994, The Silence of Adultery, 1995, The Cold Heart of a Killer, 1996, A Kidnapping in a Family, 1996, New Passages, 1996, Panic In the Skies, 1996, What Happened to Bobby Earl, 1997, Sweet Deceptions, 1998, Satan's School for Girls, 2000, A Mother's Testimony, 2001, Miracle Dogs, 2003, Larceny, 2004, No Regrets, 2004; motion picture appearances include: Dirty Tricks, 1981, Making Love, 1982, Loverboy, 1989, Error in Judgement, 1998, Larceny, 2004; dir. numerous episodes The Scarecrow and Mrs. King. Recipient 3 Emmy award nominations Nat. Acad. TV Arts and Scis. Mem. AFTRA, Screen Actors Guild, Actors Equity Assn., Dirs. Guild Am.

JACKSON, KATHERINE CHURCH, retired elementary school educator, literature educator; b. Phila., Apr. 26, 1925; d. John Edward and Katherine Darlington (Short) C.; m. James Kermit Jackson, Dec. 20, 1953; children: James Kermit, Quentin Winfield, Karen J. White. BS in Edn., Cheyney (Pa.) State Tchrs. Coll., 1946; MEd, Temple U., 1951; DEdin Adminstrn., Nova U., 1981. Cert. elem. sch. tchr., supr., prin., Pa. Elem. tchr. Pub. Schs., Oxford, N. Glenside, Pa., 1946-54, collaborator lang. arts, t.v. tchr. Phila., 1956-67, asst. dir., tng. specialist office of sch. vols., 1967-70, dist. supr., dir. reading, 1970-77, elem. prin., 1971-82; asst. prof. Lincoln U., Pa., 1986-87, reading and writing specialist, 1986-2000, ret., 2000. Prodr., photographer: (slide presentation) Parents Help With Reading, 1965; writer, prodr. (t.v. series, script) Reading Inservice for Teachers, 1965; creator, prodr., photographer (slide presentation) PL-142 Works for the Handicapped, 1980. Pres. bd. YWCA, West Chester, Pa., 1984-89; bd. dirs. Cmty. Ctr., West Chester, 1984-91. Recipient Profl. award Bus. and Profl. Women, 1966, Cmty. and Club Svc. award Keystone Federated Women's Club, 1989, Spirit of YWCA, YWCA of Greater West Chester, 1990, Cmty. Svc. award West Chester Black Student Union, 1994 Mem. AAUW, Fanny J. Coppin Federated Women's Club (chpt. pres. 1984—), Bus. Profl. Women (pres. Phila. chpt. 1965-69). Democrat. Episcopalian. Avocations: reading, singing, opera. Home: PO Box 663 Westtown PA 19395-0663

JACKSON, KENNETH ARTHUR, physicist, researcher; b. Connaught, Ont., Can., Oct. 23, 1930; s. Arthur and Susanna (Vatcher) J.; m. Jacqueline Della Olyan, June 20, 1952 (div.); children: Stacy Margaret, Meredith Suzanne, Stuart Keith; m. Camilla M. Maruszewski, June 21, 1980 (div.). BS, U. Toronto, 1952, MS, 1953; PhD, Harvard U., 1956. Postdoctoral fellow Harvard U., Cambridge, Mass., 1956-58, asst. prof. metallurgy, 1958-62; mem. tech. staff Bell Labs., Murray Hill, N.J., 1962-67, head material physics research dept., 1967-81, head optical materials research dept., 1981-89; prof. materials sci. and engring. U. Ariz., 1989—. Lectr. Welch. Found., 1970, 85; mem. research adv. panel Air Force Office Sci. Research, 1976-82, space application bd. Nat. Acad. Sci., 1974-82. Editor-in-chief Optical Materials, 1999—; contbr. articles to profl. jours.; patentee in field. Recipient Mathewson Gold medal AIME, 1966, Crystal growth award AACG, 1993, Frank prize IOCG, 1998, TMS Chalmers award, 2003. Fellow AAAS, The Metall. Soc.-AIME, Am. Phys. Soc.; mem. Internat. Orgn. Crystal Growth (treas. 1978-86, Frank prize 1998), Am. Assn. Crystal Growth (pres. 1968-75, coun., award 1993), Materials Rsch. Soc. (v.p. 1975-77, pres. 1977-78, coun.), Am. Soc. Metals, Engring. Coun. for Profl. Devel. (mem. coun.), Fedn. Materials Soc. (trustee). Office: U Ariz 4715 E Ft Lowell Rd Tucson AZ 85712-1201 E-mail: kaj@aml.arizona.edu.

JACKSON, KENNETH MONROE, lawyer, mediator, actor; b. Kenedy, Tex., Sept. 9, 1936; s. Harry Monroe and Harriette Gould (Hughes) J.; m. Judith Ann Foster J.; 1 child, Kenneth Davis J. BA, So. Meth. U., 1960, JD, 1962; postgrad., Vanderbilt U. Bar: Tex. 1962, Tenn. 1991, U.S. Supreme Ct. 1996, U.S. Dist. Ct. (mid. dist.) Tenn. 1996; cert. civil and family law mediator, Tenn. V.p. contracts, gen. counsel Recon/Optical Inc., Barrington, Ill., 1985-90; v.p., gen. counsel Textron Aerostructures, Nashville, 1990-95; of counsel Neal & Harwell, Nashville, 1995—. Arbitrator, mediator Am. Arbitration Assn., NASD; mem. Fed. Ct. ADR panel. Contbr. articles to profl. publs. Bd. dirs. Nashville Shakespeare Festival, 1996. Recipient Disting. Svc. award Soc. Am. Value Engrs., 1971. Fellow Nat. Contract Mgmt. Assn. (hon. life, cert profl. contract mgr., nat. pres. 1983-84, Charles J. Delaney Meml. writing award 1984); mem. Am. Corp. Counsel Assn. (pres. Tenn. chpt. 1992-93), Nashville Bar Assn. (chairperson ethics and professionalism com. 1994, ADR com. 1998, Pres.'s award 1994, 2001), Coll. of the State Bar Tex., Tenn. Bar Assn. (editor newsletter). Avocation: tennis.

JACKSON, KENNETH TERRY, historian, academic administrator; b. Memphis, July 27, 1939; s. Kenneth Gordon and Elizabeth Owen (Willins) J.; m. Barbara Ann Bruce, Aug. 25, 1962; children: Kevan Parish, Kenneth Gordon (dec.). BA magna cum laude, U. Memphis, 1961; MA, U. Chgo., 1963, PhD, 1966. Asst. prof. history Columbia U., N.Y.C., 1968-71, assoc. prof., 1971-76, prof., 1976-87, Mellon prof., 1987-90, Barzun prof., 1990—, chmn. dept. history, 1994-97. Vis. prof. Princeton (N.J.) U., 1973-74, George Washington U., 1982-83, UCLA, 1986-87; chair Bradley Commn. on History in Schs., 1987-90; chair Nat. Coun. for History Edn., Inc., 1990-92; dir. Lehman Ctr. for Am. History, 2005—. Author: The Ku Klux Klan in the City, 1967, Crabgrass Frontier, 1985 (Bancroft prize 1986, Francis Parkman prize 1986), Silent Cities: The Evolution of the American Cemetery, 1989; co-editor: cities in American History, 1972; editor-in-chief Dictionary of American Biography, 1991-95, Scribner's Encyclopedia of American Lives, 1996—; editor Encyclopedia of New York City, 1995; gen. editor Columbia History of Urban Life, 30 vols., 1980—; co-editor American Vistas, 1971, 7th edit., 1995, Empire City: New York Through the Centuries, 2002. Trustee Nat. Coun. Hist. Edn., 1990—, South St. Seaport Mus., 1989—2001, Transp. Alternatives, 1995—97, Skyscraper Mus., 1996—2001, N.Y. Hist. Soc., 1996—, vice chmn., 1998—2001, pres., CEO, 2001—04; trustee N.Y. State Hist. Assn., 1996—, Henry Luce Found., 2002—, Regional Plan Assn., 2003—; vestryman Trinity Ch. Wall St., 1997—2004. Capt. USAF, 1965—68. Recipient Mark Van Doren Tchg. award Columbia U., 1989, Outstanding Alumni award U. Memphis, 1989, Great Tchr. award Soc. Columbia Grads. 1999; fellow Woodrow Wilson Found., 1961-62, Guggenheim Found., 1983-84; sr. fellow NEH, 1979-80. Mem. Soc. Am. Historians (pres. 1998-2000), Orgn. Am. Historians (pres. 2000-2001), Am. Hist. Assn., Urban Hist. Assn. (pres. 1994-95), Century Assn. Episcopalian. Avocations: skiing, tennis, basketball. Home: 44 Kitchel Rd Mount Kisco NY 10549-4516 Office: Columbia U Dept History 603 Fayerweather Hall New York NY 10027 Office Phone: 212-854-2555.

JACKSON, KINGSBURY TEMPLE, educational consultant, financial consultant; b. Newton, Mass., May 15, 1917; s. Ralph Temple and Elizabeth Mesarole (Rhodes) J.; m. June Stewart Cooper, July 29, 1950 (dec. Feb. 1976). BS, MIT, 1940; postgrad., NYU, 1949—51; MS, U. Ala., 1964, U. So. Calif., 1969, Pepperdine U., 1975. Registered profl. engr., Calif., Ala.; lic. and bonded tax preparer, IRS and Calif. Commd. 2d lt. U.S. Army, 1940, advanced through grades to lt. col., 1961, ret., 1965; comdr. U.S. Army Depot, also Camp Mercer, Republic of Korea, 1957-58; project officer, indsl. project dir. U.S. Army Saturn Space Vehicle Program and Pershing Missile Sys.,

1959-61; dir. U.S. Army Missile Command Engring. Documentation Ctr., Redstone Arsenal, Ala., 1962-63; program coordinator NATO-Hawk Missile System, 1963-65; prin. contracting officer, chief European procurement U.S. Army Ordnance, 1964-65; lectr. mgmt. and engring. Grad. Sch., U. So. Calif., L.A., 1965-69; contractual rels. supr. L.A. Bd. Edn., 1969-82; pres. Contract Consultants, L.A., 1982—, K.T. Jackson, Gen. Contractors, L.A., 1991—. Author: Engineering Documentation Systems Development: Department of Defense and NASA, 1963, Aerospace Propellants and Chemicals: The Manager's Approach, 1968. V.p., mem. bd. dirs. Kingsbury Properties Ltd.; corp. sec., bd. dirs. The Concert Singers, Inc. Mem.: Am. Soc. Automotive Engrs. (rep. to Aerospace gen. stds. divsn. 1962—65), Am. Ordinance Assn. (mem. exec. bd. prodn. technique divsn.,Army rep.to engring. doc. sect. 1962—65), Am. Soc. Mil. Comptrs., Am. Soc. Indsl. Engrs., Nat. Space Soc., Aircraft Owners and Pilots Assn., Calif. Assn. Bus. Ofcls., Ret. Officers Assn. (life), Internat. Assn. Sch. Bus. Ofcls. (emeritus), The Concert Singers Inc., The Planetary Soc., A&E Flying Club, MIT Club (So. and No. Calif.). Home: Ste C302 3400 Paul Sweet Rd Santa Cruz CA 95065-1541 Office: Contract Cons PO Box 402 Capitola CA 95010-0402 Office Phone: 831-464-1547. E-mail: kingtemp@aol.com.

JACKSON, KRISTIN, choreographer, educator; b. Manila, Sept. 14, 1952; arrived in U.S., 1975; d. Lowell Monroe Jackson and Mary Vita Beltran; m. Eric Kevin Achacoso, Dec. 6, 1986. BFA in Editl. Design, U. Philippines, Manila, 1974; MFA in Dance, NYU, 1985. Prin. dancer)(Broadway and nat.) The King and I, N.Y.C., 1978—81; prin. dancer, rehearsal dir. Laura Dean Dancers and Musicians, N.Y.C., 1983—87; adminstrv. asst. N.Y. State Coun. on the Arts, N.Y.C., 1988—89; artistic dir. Kristin Jackson Dance, N.Y.C., 1990—. Adj. assoc. prof. dept. dance Queens Coll., Flushing, NY, 1990—2002, NYU, N.Y.C., 1991—92; panelist Nat. Endowment for the Arts, Washington, 1991—93, Asian Am. Arts Alliance, N.Y.C., 1999; guest spkr. Nat. Fedn. Filipino Ams. Assn., N.Y.C., 1999. Choreographer Still Waters and Gallaun, 1990 (N.Y. State Coun. on the Arts award, 1989), In Their Shoes, 1998 (Ford Found. award, 1997), Wind, 2002 (Jerome Found. award, 2002). Travel grant, Nat. Endowment for the Arts, Arts Internat. Philippines, 1993, Fulbright scholar, U.S. Dept. State, 2002. Mem.: Dance Critics Assn., Actor Equity Assn. Democrat. Episcopalian. Avocations: cooking, painting, writing, music. Home and Office: 37 King St #4A New York NY 10014 E-mail: kristin.jackson@att.net.

JACKSON, LAIRD GRAY, geneticist, internist, educator; b. Seattle, Oct. 10, 1930; married. BA, Pomona Coll., 1951; MD, U. Cin., 1955. Diplomate Am. Bd. Internal Medicine, Am. Bd. Med. Genetics (bd. dirs.). Rotating gen. intern Sacramento County (Calif.) Hosp., 1955-56; resident in internal medicine Jefferson Med. Coll., Phila., 1959-61, NIH postdoctoral fellow med. oncology, 1961-62, instr. medicine, 1962-64, asst. prof. medicine, 1964-66, assoc. prof., 1966-69, assoc. prof. medicine, pediatrics and ob-gyn, 1969-78, prof., 1978—, dir. div. med. genetics, 1969-98. Founder, bd. dirs., treas. Am. Coll. Med. Genetics, 1991-95. Mem. editorial bd. Am. Jour. Med. Genetics, Prenatal Diagnosis, Repository of Human Chromosomal Variants. Capt. USAF, 1956—59. Leukemia Soc. fellow, 1963-65, Leukemia Soc. scholar 1965-70. Fellow ACP; mem. Am. Soc. Human Genetics (social issues com. 1976-80, bd. dirs.), Soc. Pediatric Rsch. Republican. Home and Office: 245 N 15th St Philadelphia PA 19102-1192 Office Phone: 215-762-3155. Business E-Mail: ljackson@drexelmed.edu.

JACKSON, LARRY ARTOPE, retired college president; b. Florence, S.C., Feb. 7, 1925; s. Arthur Edward and Rosa (Gilbert) J.; m. Barbara Atwood, June 27, 1953; children: Elizabeth Jackson Eble, Arthur Edward, Barbara Jackson Allen, Charles Rhett. AB, Wofford Coll., 1947, DLitt (hon.), 1976; MDiv, Union Theol. Sem., 1953; MA, U. Pacific, 1973, DD (hon.), 1961; D in Humanities (hon.), Clemson U., 1991. Ordained to ministry United Meth. Ch., 1953; minister chs., 1953-59; prin. Santiago (Chile) Coll., 1959-64; provost Callison Coll. of U. Pacific, Stockton, Calif., 1964-70; v.p. for adminstrn. U. Evansville, 1970-73; pres. Lander Univ. (formerly Lander Coll.), Greenwood, S.C., 1973-92, ret., 1992. Vis. fellow Wolfson Coll., Cambridge U., 1985; appointed by Gov. to serve as mem. S.C. Commn. on Higher Edn., 2000-2003. Mem. Fulbright Commn. for Chile, 1961-64; mem. Commn. on Black Colls. Related to the Meth. Ch., 1973-76. With USAAF, 1943-45; with Am. Friends Svc. Com., 1948-49. Decorated Air medal with 2 oak leaf clusters. Mem. Rotary. Democrat. Home: 604 Cambridge Ave W Greenwood SC 29649-1967 Office: Lander Univ 301 Stanley Ave Greenwood SC 29649-2045 *Love is the law of life and it is by striving to live under the rule of this law that we find authenticity.*

JACKSON, LARRY C., publishing executive; b. Austin, Tex., Apr. 14, 1944; s. Laurence C. and Mary Ruth (McAngus) J.; m. Susan Blackburn, Dec. 15, 1966; children: Laurence III, Deborah Jackson McClure, Edward. BA in Journalism, U. Tex., 1968. City editor Arlington (Tex.) Daily News, 1967-69; City editor Laredo (Tex.) Times, 1969-71; mng. editor Henderson (Tex.) Daily News, 1971-72; gen. mgr. Austin Citizen, 1972-73; publ. Round Rock (Tex.) Leader, 1973-84, Pecos (Tex.) Enterprise, 1984-87, Corona (Calif.)-Norco Independent, 1987-91; editor, gen. mgr. Wharton (Tex.) Journal-Spectator, 1991—; v.p. River Pubs., Inc., 1994—. Charter pres. YMCA, Round Rock, Tex., 1981; mem. City Charter Commn., Round Rock, 1977; chmn. U.S. Bicentennial Commn., Round Rock, 1975-76; pres. Round Rock C. of C., 1975; bd. dirs. Tex. Newspaper Found., 1994—; mem. City Beautification Commn., Wharton, Tex., 1999-2004; bd. dirs. Wharton County His. Mus., 2000— Paul Harris fellow Rotary Internat. Found., 1995; named Citizen of Yr. Round Rock C. of C., 1984. Mem. Nat. Newspaper Assn. (Tex. state chair 2001--), Tex. Press Assn. (pres. 1998-99), South Tex. Press Assn. (pres. 1996), Rotary (pres. Wharton 1994-95, asst. gov. dist. 5890 2004—), Wharton C. of C. (chmn. bd. 2001-02, Citizen of Yr. 2003), Disciples of Christ Hist. Soc. (life). Republican. Mem. Ch. of Christ. Avocations: teaching bible classes, oboe, travel. Home: 1203 N Fulton St Wharton TX 77488-3129 Office: Wharton Journal-Spectator 115 W Burleson St Wharton TX 77488-5003

JACKSON, LAUREN, professional basketball player; b. Australia, May 11, 1981; Profl. basketball player Seattle Storm, 2001—. Mem. Gems team Jr. World Championships, 1997; mem. WNBL Championship team, 2000. Named WNBA MVP, 2003; named to WNBA All-Star Team, 2001—03, First Team All-WNBA, 2003; recipient Olympics Silver medalist, 2000, Espy Award for Best WNBA Player, 2004, 2005. Achievements include #1 overall pick in WNBA draft, 2001. Office: Seattle Sonics and Storm 351 Elliott Ave W Ste 500 Seattle WA 98119 E-mail: StormFans@sonics-storm.com.*

JACKSON, LAURIE JEAN, artist, art educator; b. Phila., Mar. 20, 1965; d. Arnold Dixon and Jean West (Smith) J.; m. Mark A. Darby, Apr. 10, 1992; children: Deena Alexis, Myah Lynne. BFA in Illustration, BA in History, Carnegie Mellon U., 1987; MFA in Painting, Temple U., 1992. Prof. painting Savannah (Ga.) Coll. Art and Design, 1992—. Resident Skowhegan (Maine) Sch. Painting and Sculpture, 1993. Artist mixed media works, 1996, 97; exhibited works in show at Nat. Mus. Women in the Arts, 1998. Grantee Ga. Coun. Arts, Atlanta, 1995, Individual Artist Grant, Savannah, 1997; recipient fellowship Pollock-Krasner Found., N.Y.C., 1995. Mem. Nat. Mus. Women in Arts. Democrat. Home: 1406 E 53rd St Savannah GA 31404-4608

JACKSON, LAWRENCE V., food service executive; B in Economics, M in Bus. Adminstrn., Harvard U. With Bank of Boston, 1975—79, McKinsey & Co., 1979—80, PepsiCo., 1980—97; sr. v.p. supply ops. Safeway Inc., Pleasanton, Calif., 1997—2003; pres., COO Dollar Gen. Corp., 2003—04; exec. v.p., people divsn. Wal-Mart Stores, Inc., 2004—. Bd. dirs. RadioShack, 2000—, Parsons Corp., Allied Waste. Named one of 50 Most Powerful Black Execs., Fortune mag., 2002. Office: Wal Mart Stores Inc 702 SW 8th St Bentonville AR 72716 Office Phone: 479-273-4000. Office Fax: 479-273-4053.*

JACKSON, LEE, artist; b. N.Y.C. s. Harry and Charlotte (Tallis) J.; m. Adele Grapes, Apr. 11, 1950. Student, Art Students League; with, John Sloan, George Luks. Faculty Sch. for Art Studies, 1947-48, CCNY, 1948-54. One man show Babcock Galleries, 1941, 43, 58, Midtown Gallery, 1989, Midtown Payson Gallery, 1993; exhbns. include Met. Mus. Art, Whitney Mus. Am. Art, Art Inst. Chgo., U. Ill., Corcoran Galleries Art, Va. Mus. Fine Art, Pa. Acad. Art, N.A.D., Mus. City N.Y., Butler Art Inst., Audubon Artists, Nat. Art Mus. Sport, Madison Sq. Garden, 1968, American Drawings 1910-60 Midtown Galleries, 1990, Midtown Payson Galleries, N.Y.C., 1993, others; represented in permanent collections Met. Mus. Art, N.Y.C., Corcoran Galleries Art, Washington, L.A. County Mus. Art, Athens (Ga.) Mus., Walker Art Ctr., Mpls., Art Students League, N.Y.C., Hirchorn Mus. Art, Washington, Malcolm Forbes Mus., N.Y., Lizan-Tapps Gallery, East Hampton, N.Y., 2000. Guggenheim fellow in painting, 1941; recipient ann. purchase prize Nebr. Art Assn., 1946; spl. invitation prize Salmagundi Club, 1950; Thomas G. Clarke prize NAD, 1951; Grumbacher Prize, 1956, 64; prize for painting in oil NAD, 1961, Grumbacher Purchase prize Audubon Artists, 1964. Mem. Art Student's League, Audubon Artists Am., Artists Equity Assn., Am. Water Color Soc., Nat. Soc. Painters in Casein. Home: PO Box 80 Lumber Ln Bridgehampton NY 11932

JACKSON, LISA KEISHA, educational consultant; b. Bklyn, NY, Dec. 16, 1975; d. Keith Joseph and Ida Berneice Jackson. MBA, Nova Southeastern Universtiy, 2001—03. Sales Joan and David Helpern Inc., NYC, 1994—98; asst. product mgr. Frederick Atkins, NYC, 1998—2000; academic advisor Nova Southeastern U., Fort Lauderdale, Fla., 2000, coord. grad. program. Office: Nova Southeastern University 6100 Griffin Rd Davie FL 33314 Office Phone: 954-262-2003. E-mail: lisajack@nova.edu.

JACKSON, MARGARET ELIZABETH, science educator; b. Richmond, Va., Mar. 15, 1930; d. Joseph and Bertha Annette Jackson. BS, Va. Union U.; MA in Sci. Edn., Trinity Coll.; postgrad., Oxford U., 1976—78, George Washington U., 1981, Roehampton Inst. Higher Learning, England, 1985. Resource tchr. sci. Garrison Elem. Sch., Washington, 1968—. Tchr. Howard U., Washington, 1984; devel. sci. materials U.S. Dept. Agr., 1970; tchr. English Elem. Schs., Campo De Criptana, Spain, 1987; writer curriculum Elem. Pub. Schs., Washington, 1980—93; mentor Carnegie Acad. Sci. Edn. Carnegie Instn., Washington, 1995—96. Co-author: Sci. Textbook, 1988. Named Internat. Educator of Yr., 2003. Mem.: ASCD, Smithsonian Instn., N.Y. Acad. Scis., D.C. Sci. Tchrs. Assn., Nat. Sci. Tchrs. Assn. Home: 2505 -13th St NW Apt 501 Washington DC 20009

JACKSON, MARGUERITE FAYE THURSTON, rhetoric and intercultural communications and language educator; d. Claude Lee Carson, Sr. and Myrtle Faye Carson; m. Ronald Lee Jackson, Sept. 6, 1986; 1 child, Garrick V.W. Cooper. AA in Journalism, L.A. City Coll., 1976; BA in Mass. Comm., Calif. State U., San Bernardino, 1999, MA in Tchg. ESL, 2000; PhD in Rhetoric and Intercultural Comm., Howard U., 2003. Cert. Am. Registry Radiologic Techs.; lic. practical nurse, Mo.; broadcaster FCC. Lic. nurse orthopedics Kansas City (Mo.) Gen. Hosp. Sch. Nursing, 1963—65; registered radiologic tech. St. Joseph Hosp. Sch. Rdiologic Tech., Kansas City, Mo., 1965—67; asst. prof., lectr. U. Calif., Riverside; asst. prof. SMART program Dept. Def., Monterey, Calif. Cross-cultural lang. cons. Berlitz Lang. Ctr., Washington. Cert. lang. tutor, vol. Norman Feldhyme Libr. Lit. Program, San Bernardino, Calif., 1999, San Bernardino Unified Sch. Dist. Adult Sch., 1999; chaplain Alpha Kappa Alpha Sorority, San Bernardino, 2000. Recipient Cert. Appreciation for Svc., Berlitz Lang. Ctr., 2002; Sally Casanova Rsch. scholar, Calif. State U., Long Beach, 2000, Ronald E. McNair scholar, 1997—2000, Summer 2000 Pre-doctorate internship scholar, U. Nev., Las Vegas. Mem.: TESOL, Calif. Tchrs. English to Speakers of Other Langs., Nat. Comm. Assn. Avocations: reading, horseback riding, golf. Office: Univ Calif Riverside Dept English 900 University Ave Riverside CA 92521 Personal E-mail: marjackspeaks@yahoo.com.

JACKSON, MARK JAMES, engineering educator; b. Widnes, Lancashire, Eng., Feb. 14, 1967; arrived in U.S., 2001; s. George and Monica Mary Jackson; m. Joanne Lesly Pinnington, July 20, 1990. MA, U. of Cambridge, 1998; MS in Engring., Liverpool (Eng.) U., 1991, PhD, 1995. Chartered engr., Engring. Coun., UK, 1998. Mech. plant engr. I.C.I. Pharmaceuticals, Macclesfield, England, 1988—89, Anglo Blackwells, Widnes, England, 1990—91; tech. mgr. St. Gobain Abrasives Group Unicorn Internat., Gloucester, England, 1992—97; rsch. fellow U. of Cambridge, England, 1997—98; lectr. U. of Liverpool, 1998—2002; prof. of engring. Tenn. Technol. U., Cookeville, Tenn., 2002—04; prof. engring Purdue U., West Lafeyette, Ind., 2004—. V.p., chief tech. officer Vitrified Technologies Inc., Kans.City, 2002—; cons. tech. mgr. St. Gobain Abrasives Group Unicorn Internat., Gloucester, 1997—99; cons. engr. MIJA Ltd., Cambridge, 1997—2000. Contbr. chapters to books, articles to profl. jours. Councillor Halton Borough Coun., Widnes, 2001—02. Recipient prize, Imperial Chem. Industries, 1986; fellow, U. of Cambridge, 1997—98; scholar, Royal Acad. of Engring., 2000, Royal Soc. of London, 2000, Engring. and Phys. Scis. Rsch. Coun., 1992—95. Fellow: Liverpool (Eng.) and North Wales Materials Soc. (hon. sec. 1998—2002), Cambridge (Eng.) Philos. Soc. (life), Liverpool (Eng.) Athenaeum; mem.: ASME, Soc. Mfg. Engrs., Am. Soc. of Materials, Inst. of Materials, Minerals, and Mining, Instn. of Mech. Engrs. (scholar 1990). Labor. Roman Catholic. Achievements include design of manufacturing processes at the micro and nanoscale; invention of piezoelectric nanogrinding process and pulsed water drop micro machining center. Avocations: running, reading, travel, history, debating. Office: Purdue Univ Dept Mech Engring Tech Knoy Hall Tech West Lafayette IN 47907-2021 Office Phone: 765-494-0365. Business E-Mail: jacksomj@purdue.edu.

JACKSON, MARSHA LOUISE, French language educator; b. Macon, Ga. BA, Emory U., 1969; MA, Ga. State U., 1976. French tchr. Clarkston (Ga.) H.S., 1971-76, Tucker (Ga.) H.S., 1976-77, Berkmar H.S., Lilburn, Ga., 1979-82, Parkview H.S., Lilburn, 1987—. Mem. Am. Assn. of Tchrs. of French, Fgn. Lang. Assn. of Ga. Office: Parkview High Sch 998 Cole Rd SW Lilburn GA 30047-5499

JACKSON, MARVIN DENNIS, journalism educator, writer; b. Jackson, Miss., June 30, 1945; s. Roy Dennis and Margie Emma (Cade) Jackson; m. Anna Jean Ferrell, Aug. 26, 1997 (dec. Mar. 8, 2005). BA, Belhaven Coll., Jackson, Miss., 1967; MA, U. Ark., 1970, PhD in English, 1978. From asst. to assoc. prof. English U. Del., Newark, 1978—92, prof. English, 1992—, dir. journalism program, 1995—2003. Seminar dir. Bulgarian Mass Media Devel. Program, U.S. Info. Agy., Sofia, Bulgaria, 1994—95; mem. seminar faculty Nat. Writers Workshop, 1991—. Author: (book) A Programmed Study of Accelerated Reading Skills, 1975; mng. editor (jour.) Irish Renaissance Ann., 1980—83; editor: (jour.) The D.H. Lawrence Review, 1984—94; assoc. editor (book) D.H. Lawrence: An Annotated Bibliography of Writings About Him, Vol. I, 1982, D.H. Lawrence: An Annotated Bibliography of Writings About Him, Vol. II, 1985; co-editor: (book) D.H. Lawrence's Lady, 1985, Critical Essays on D.H. Lawrence, 1988, D.H. Lawrence's Literary Inheritors, 1991, Editing D.H. Lawrence: New Versions of a Modern Author, 1995, The Journalist's Craft, 2002. Recipient Nat. Teaching Award, Poynter Inst. Media Studies, 1982, Harry T. Moore Disting. Scholar Award for Lifetime Achievement in D.H. Lawrence Studies, D.H. Lawrence Soc. N.Am., 1999, College of Arts and Science Outstanding Advisement Award, U. Del., 2000; fellow Gannett Teaching Fellowship, Assn. Edn. Journalism, 1981; sr. fellow, Nat. Endowment for the Humanities, 1999. Mem.: Modern Language Assn., D.H. Lawrence Soc. N.Am. (sec.-treas. 1979—82, pres. 1985—86), Conf. of Editors of Learned Jours., Nat. Assn. Black Journalists (assoc.), Phi Beta Kappa. Democrat. Home: 814 Bradford Ln Newark DE 19711 Office: U Del Dept English 212 Memorial Newark DE 19716 Office Phone: 302-454-1480, 302-831-2361. Business E-Mail: djackson@udel.edu.

JACKSON, MAURICE, history professor; b. Oct. 10, 1950; s. Zeola Ballard; m. Laura Ginsburg; children: Lena, Miles. BA, Antioch Coll., Yellow Springs, Ohio, 1974; MA, Georgetown U., Washington, D.C., 1995, PhD, 2001. Asst. prof., history Georgetown U., Washington, 2001—. Office: Georgetown Univ Dept History 35th L "O" Ave Washington DC 20011

JACKSON, MICHAEL J., automotive retail company executive; Technician Mercedes-Benz dealership, Cherry Hill, N.J.; mng. ptnr. Euro Motorcars, Bethesda, Md.; dist. mgr. Mercedes-Benz N.Am.; sr. mktg. exec. Mercedes-Benz USA, Inc., pres., CEO, responsible for N.Am. bus., until 1999; chmn. AutoNation, Inc., Ft. Lauderdale, Fla., 1999—, CEO, 1999—. Former chmn. Mercedes-Benz Nat. Dealer Coun. Recipient All-Star Dealer award Sports Illustrated, 1990; mem. automotive execs. Dream Team, Automotive News, 2 times; recognized mem. of Mktg. 100, Advt. Age, 4 times; named to Automobile Hall of Fame, 2003; named Automotive Industry Leader of Yr., 2003. Office: AutoNation Inc 110 SE 6th St Fort Lauderdale FL 33301-5000*

JACKSON, MICHAEL JOSEPH, musician; b. Gary, Ind., Aug. 29, 1958; s. Joseph Walter and Katherine Esther (Scruse) Jackson; m. Lisa Marie Presley, May 18, 1994 (div. Jan. 18, 1996); m. Debbie Rowe, Nov. 15, 1996 (div. Oct. 8, 1999); children: Prince Michael, Paris Michael Katherine, Prince Michael II. Student pvt. sch.; LHD (hon.), Fisk U., 1988. Lead singer Jackson-Five (later called The Jacksons), from 1969, recs. for Epic Records, performed at Queen Elizabeth's Silver Jubilee, May 1977; actor: (films) The Wiz, 1978, Moonwalker, 1988, Dangerous the short film, 1993, Men in Black II, 2002; (TV series) The Jacksons, 1976—77; albums with Jackson-Five include Diana Ross Presents the Jackson Five, 1969, ABC, Jackson Five Christmas Album, Third Album, 1970, Goin' Back to Indiana, Greatest Hits, Maybe Tomorrow, 1971, Looking Through the Windows, 1972, Farewell My Summer, Get it Together, Skywriter, 1973, Dancing Machine, 1974, Moving Violation, 1975, Joyful Jukebox Music, 1976, Boogie, 1980, albums with The Jacksons include The Jacksons, 1976, Goin' Places, 1977, Destiny, 1978, Triumph, 1980, The Jacksons Live, 1981, Victory, 1984; musician: (albums) Got To Be There, Ben, 1972, Music and Me, 1973, Forever Michael, The Best of Michael Jackson, 1975, Off the Wall, 1979, Thriller, 1982 (Grammy Award for Best Male Pop Vocal Performance, 1983, Grammy Award for Album of the Yr., 1983, Grammy Award for Best Video Album, 1984), Bad, 1987, Dangerous, 1991, Anthology, 1995, HIStory: Past, Present and Future, Book 1, 1995, Blood on the Dance Floor: HIStory in the Mix, 1997, The Best of Michael Jackson, 2000, HIStory: Greatest Hits, Vol. 1, 2001, Invincible, 2001, Michael Jackson: The Ultimate Collection, 2004; narrator E.T.: The Extra Terrestrial storybook, 1982; author: (autobiography) Moonwalk, 1988, Dancing the Dream Poems and Reflections, 1992; performer: (Sporting Event) Super Bowl XXVII Halftime show, 1993, (TV Special) Michael Jackson: 30th Anniversary TV Special, 2001. Founder Heal the World Found., 1992—2002. Recipient Grammy Award for Best R&B Vocal Performance (Don't Stop 'til You Get Enough), 1979, w/ Quincy Jones, Grammy Award for Producer of the Yr. (Non-Classical), 1983, Grammy Award for Best Recording for Children (E.T. The Extra-Terrestrial), 1983, Grammy Award for Best Rhythm & Blues Song (Billie Jean), 1983, Grammy Award for Best Male R&B Vocal Performance (Billie Jean), 1983, Grammy Award for Best Male Rock Vocal Performance (Beat It), 1983, Grammy Award for Record of the Yr. (Beat It), 1983, w/ Lionel Richie, Grammy Award for Song of the Yr. (We Are The World), 1985, Grammy Award for Best Music Video (Leave Me Alone), 1989, w/ Janet Jackson, Grammy Award for Best Music Video (Scream), 1995, w/ Janet Jackson, MTV Video Music Award for Best Dance Video (Scream), 1995, w/ Janet Jackson, MTV Video Music Award for Best Art Direction (Scream), 1995, w/ Janet Jackson, MTV Video Music Award for Best Choreography (Scream), 1995, Star on Hollywood Walk of Fame, 1984, MTV Vanguard Award, 1988, MTV Movie Award for Best Movie Song (Will You Be There), 1994, Best Selling Male Pop Artist of the Millennium award, World Music Awards, 2000, numerous other awards. Achievements include record for most Grammys won in one year with 8, 1983; inducted into the Rock and Roll Hall of Fame, mem. Jackson 5, 1997, solo artist, 2001; record for best selling album of all-time (Thriller); record for the three best selling albums of all-time, (Thriller, Dangerous, Bad); brother of Janet, LaToya, Randy, Jermaine, Tito, Marlon, and Jackie; owner 2700-acre Neverland Ranch, Calif.*

JACKSON, MICHAEL P., federal agency administrator, former engineering company executive; married; 1 child. BA, U. Houston; PhD in Govt. with distinction, Georgetown U., 1985. Reported to sec. edn. Pres. Reagan adminstrn.; spl. asst. to Pres. George H.W. Bush for cabinet liaison; COO IMS transp. sys. and svcs. Lockheed Martin; sr. v.p., counselor to pres. Am. Trucking Assn., 1993—97; chief of staff to sec. U.S. Dept. Transp., Washington, 1992—93, dep. sec., 2001—03; sr. v.p. AECOM Tech. Corp., Fairfax, Va., 2004—05; dep. sec. US Dept. Homeland Security, 2005—. Rschr. Am. Enterprise Inst.; instr. polit. sci. U. Ga., Georgetown U. Republican. Office: US Dept Homeland Security 3801 Nebraska Ave Washington DC 20528

JACKSON, MICHAEL WAYNE, academic administrator, researcher; s. Levi B. and Carol J. Jackson. BS, Northeastern State U., 1988, MS, 1989. Dir., instl. rsch. assessment Okla. City U., Oklahoma City, 2003—; coord., assessment studies Northeastern State U., Tahlequah, Okla., 1998—2003, staff asst., v.p. academic affairs, 1991—98, lectr./rsch. assoc., 1990—91, coord., student tutoring and career, 1989—90. Rschr. US Navy, Point Loma, Calif., 2004. Fellow Scholars Program, So. Region Edn. Bd., 1998. Mem.: Okla. Acad. Advising Assn. (assoc.; chair, profl. standards and devel. com. 1998—99), Okla. Acad. Advising Assn. (assoc.; pres. 1999—2000), Nat. Acad. Advising Assn. (assoc.; regional conf. co-chair 1998—99). Avocation: travel. Office: Oklahoma City U 2501 North Blackwelder Oklahoma City OK 73106 Office Phone: 405-208-5088. Office Fax: 405-521-5451. E-mail: mjackson@okcu.edu.

JACKSON, MIKE, newscaster; m. Dawn Jackson; children: Nicole, Courtney. AA in Mass Comm., W.Va. State Coll. Ops. mgr., announcer Sta. WBES-FM, Charleston, W.Va.; news dir., anchor, prodr. Sta. WOAY-TV, Oak Hill; anchor Sta. WJLA-TV, Springfield, Va., WWHO-TV, Columbus, Ohio, Sta. WCMH-TV, 1994—. Nominee Emmy awards (2), 1985, 2002; recipient 1st pl. Reporting award, Nat. Assn. Black Journalists, Washington, 1993. Office: WCMH-TV 3165 Plentangy River Rd PO Box 4 Columbus OH 43202

JACKSON, MILES MERRILL, retired university dean; b. Richmond, Va., Apr. 28, 1929; s. Miles Merrill and Thelma Eugertha (Manning) J.; m. Bernice Olivia Roane, Jan. 7, 1954; children: Miles Merrill III, Marsha, Muriel, Melia. BA in English, Va. Union U., 1955; MS, Drexel U., 1956; postgrad., Ind. U., 1961, 64; PhD, Syracuse U., 1974. Br. libr. Free Libr., 1955-58; acting libr. C.P. Huntington Meml. Libr., Hampton (Va.) U., 1958-59, libr., 1959-62, asst. prof. libr. sci., 1958-62; territorial libr. Am. Samoa, 1962-64; chief libr. Trevor Arnett Libr., Atlanta U., 1964-69; also lectr. Sch. Libr. Sci.; assoc. prof. State U. N.Y., Geneseo, 1969-75; prof. U. Hawaii, 1975—, dean, 1983-95, chmn. interdisciplinary program in communication and info. scis., 1985-89; cons. in field, 1995—. Fulbright lectr. U. Tehran, Iran, 1968-69; libr., cons. Fiji, Samoa, Papua New Guinea, Micronesia, USIA India, 1993, Pakistan, 1985, Nat. Libr. Edn., 1996, Govt. Am. Samoa, 1997, Hawaii Pub. Libr. Found., 1986-2000; chmn. bd. Hawaii Lit., Inc., 1985-88; commr. Hawaii Libr. Commn., 1996-97. Editor: A Bibliography of Materials on Negro History and Culture for Young People, 1968, Comparative and International Librarianship, 1971, International Handbook of Contemporary Developments in Librarianship, 1981, Pacific Island Studies: Review of the Literature, 1986, Linkages Over Space and Time, 1993, And They Came: A Brief History of Blacks in Hawaii, 2001, They Followed the Trade Winds: African Americans in Hawaii, 2005; mem. editl. bd. Internat. Jour. Info. Mgmt., Internat. Libr. Rev., 1982-87; founder, editor Pacific Info. and Libr. Svcs. Newsletter; contbr. articles to profl. jours.; book reviewer. Bd. dirs. Cen. YMCA, 1986-94, Hawaii Gov.'s Coun. on Literacy, 1986-96, Hawaii ACLU, 1990-94, office holder in Dem. party of Hawaii, 1992—. With USNR, 1946-48. Recipient Outstanding Alumnus award Va. Union U., 1987; Rsch. grantee Am. Philos. Soc., 1966; Coun. on Libr.

Resources fellow, 1970, vis. fellow Republic of China, 1986; Harold Lancour fgn. travel awardee Beta Phi Mu, 1976 Mem. ALA (chmn. Internat. Rels. Roundtable 1988-89), Assn. for Libr. and Info. Sci. Edn. (pres. 1989-90), Coll. Lang. Assn. (hon. mention poetry 1954, 2d prize award short story 1955) Democrat.

JACKSON, NAGLE, stage director, playwright; b. Seattle, Apr. 28, 1936; s. Paul Joseph and Gertrude (Dunn) J.; m. Sandra L. Suter, Sept. 15, 1963; children: Rebecca J., Hillary J. BA, Whitman Coll., 1958, LittD (hon.), 1995. Resident dir. Am. Conservatory Theatre, San Francisco, 1967-70; artistic dir. Milw. Repertory Theatre, 1970-76, McCarter Theatre, Princeton, NJ, 1979-90; stage dir. N.J. Opera Festival, Lawrenceville, 1985-91; currently assoc. artist Denver Center Theatre Co., Denver; prin. dir. Santa Fe Shakespeare Co. Guest dir. Gorky Theatre, Leningrad, 1988, Trøndelag Teatre, Trondheim, Norway, 1990. Playwright: At This Evening's Performance, 1985, Opera Comique, 1988, They Shoot Horses, Don't They?-The Musical (book and lyrics), 1992, This Day and Age, 1994, The Quick-Change Room, 1995, Moliere Plays Paris, 1996, A Hotel on Marvin Gardens, 2002, Taking Leave, 2002. Fulbright fellow, Paris, 1958; recipient Prize Onassis Found. Internat. Playwrights Competition for "The Elevation of Thieves", 1997. Mem. Soc. Stage Dirs. & Choreographers, The Dramatists Guild. Personal E-mail: naglejackson@att.net.

JACKSON, NANCY MORRISON, architect; b. Pitts., Aug. 15, 1922; d. Robert Kirk and Marcella Genevieve (Pfendler) Morrison; m. George Clark Jackson, Aug. 25, 1945; children: Ellen Jackson Rudy, Robert Clark, Mary Jackson Porter. BArch, Carnegie Mellon U., 1946. Arch. Prack & Prack, Pitts., 1942, Kaiser, Neal & Reid, Pitts., 1943—44, Marks & Simboli, Pitts., 1947, Edward C. Roock, Syracuse, NY, 1958, Austin-Mead, Hartford, Conn., 1967—70, Kane Farrel White, 1970—72; pvt. practice Farmington, Conn., 1972—78; gen. svcs. adminstrn. Washington, 1978—2005. Mem. Nat. Archtl. Accrediting Bd.; citations U.S. State Dept. Mem. admissions coun. Carnegie Mellon U.; mem. Cath. Family Svcs., Commn. for Ecumenical Affairs, Conn. Mem.: AIA (Masterspec rev. com.), Am. Arbitration Assn. (constrn. industry arbitrator), Conn. Soc. Arch. Bd., Arts Club of Washington, Kappa Alpha Theta. Roman Catholic.

JACKSON, O'SHEA See ICE CUBE

JACKSON, OLIVIA A., academic administrator; d. Willie and Jane E. Jackson. BS in Journalism and Comm., U. Fla., 1980; MPA, Ohio State U., Columbus, 1985; PhD in Internat. studies, U. Miami, 1995. Budget analyst Ohio Office of Budget and Mgmt., Columbus, 1984—87; coord. U. Miami's North-South Ctr., Fla., 1989—93, dir., 1993—95; dir., bus. devel. Keith and Schnars, P.A., Pompano, Fla., 1996—98; full-time faculty Fla. Meml. Coll., Miami, 1998—99, dept. chair, 1999—. Pub. rels. for continuing edn. divsn. Fla. Meml. U., Miami, 1999—, enrollment mgmt. for continuing edn. divsn., strategic planner for continuing edn. divsn., 1999—. Univ. rep. C. of C., Broward County, Fla., 2003—; juror Silver Knight, Miami, Fla., 1999; facilitator Wingate Toxic Site Task Force, Fort Lauderdale, Fla., 1997—2000. Recipient Image Committee's Cmty. Svc. Award, Jackson Meml. Hosp., 1999, Outstanding Svc., Profl. Black Fire Fighters' Assn., 1999, Award of Honor, Cuban Doctors in Edn. Assn. Exiled, 2001, Woman of Courage and Vision, Women's History Month, Future Educators of Am., 2001. Mem.: Am. Soc. Pub. Adminstrs., Am. Polit. Sci. Assn. (coll. rep. 1989—), Assn. for Continuing Edn. (coll. rep. 1999—), Nat. Black MBA Assn. Avocations: running, reading, martial arts, travel. Office: Fla Meml U 15800 NW 42nd Ave Miami FL 33054 Office Phone: 305-626-3157. Office Fax: 305-626-3681.

JACKSON, PATRICK JOSEPH, real estate company officer; b. Minn., Mar. 31, 1942; s. Paul Arthur and Lucille Margaret (Cummings) J.; m. Barbara Ann Simpson, July 19, 1964 (div. Apr. 1980); children: Laura Kathleen, Katherine Lucille; m. Shirley Ann Wellman, Sept. 12, 1982 (div. Oct. 1998); m. Kath Jo Holm, Sept. 9, 2001; 1 child, Liza Ann Holm. BS, Portland State U., 1968. Bank loan officer First Nat. Bank of Oreg., Portland, 1964-68; credit mgr. Meier & Frank Corp., Portland, 1968-70; agt., mgr. Aetna Life, San Jose, Calif., 1970-75; dist. mgr. Calif. Casualty, San Jose, 1975-78; gen. agt. Great So. Life, San Jose, 1978-82; account agt., agy. owner Allstate Ins., San Jose, 1982—2001; assoc. Home Realty, 2001—04; pres. Delta Direct Enterprises, Sequim, Wash., 2001—04, Windermere Real Estate, 2004—05, Diversified Realty Group, 2005—. Instr. Santa Clara (Calif.) U., 1974-76. Author: (monograph) The Affairs of, 1978; newspaper columnist, 1978-04. Mem. ins. subcom. Calif. State Senate, 1978; officer Los Gatos (Calif.) Police Res., 1970-78, treas., 1974-78; mem. Sch. Site Coun., Saratoga, Calif., 1978-80; mem. City Coun., Discovery Bay, Calif., 1991-95, mayor, 1993-94. Named Man of Yr., Los Gatos Youth Unltd., 1978. Mem. San Jose Life Underwriters (bd. dirs. 1974-76), No. Calif. Tollycraft Assn. (sec. 1995-97), Sequim Bay Yacht Club, Puget Sound Anglers, Jefferson County Sportsman Club. Republican. Lutheran. Avocations: boating, fishing, shooting, reading. Office: Delta Direct Enterprises 325 E Washington St #106 Sequim WA 98382 E-mail: pjackson@olypen.com.

JACKSON, PAUL HOWARD, minister; b. Topeka, Nov. 10, 1952; s. Dwight Stover and Janice Ilona (Woeltje) J.; m. Elizabeth Ann McGhghy, July 23, 1977; children: Christopher, Jeremy, Catherine, Johanna, Caleb. BA, Washburn U., 1973; MLS, Emporia State U., 1974; MDiv, Concordia Sem., Clayton, Mo., 1979; postgrad., Ind. U., 1993-96; STM, Concordia Theol. Sem., Ft. Wayne, Ind., 1995. Ordained to ministry Luth. Ch.-Mo. Synod, 1979. Pastor St. Paul's Luth. Ch., Wakefield, Nebr., 1979-81, 1st Trinity Luth. Ch., Wayne, Nebr., 1979-81; libr., tchr. Luth. High. Sch. Indpls., 1981-82; libr., prof. St. John's Coll., Winfield, Kans., 1982-85; libr. Winfield (Kans.) Pub. Library, 1985-88; pastor 1st Luth. Ch., Pond Creek, Okla., 1986-88; libr. Concordia Theol. Sem., Ft. Wayne, Ind., 1988-96; multimedia prodr. Concordia Publ. House, St. Louis, 1996-2000; pastor St. Paul Luth. Ch., Texhoma, Okla., 2000—04; instrn/pub. svc. libr. Aims C.C., 2004—. Adj. prof. Concordia U. Wis., Mequon, 1995-00; facilitator Post-Seminary Applied Learning and Support, LCMS Com. on Ministerial Growth and Support, 2002-04. Prodr. W3 Word Witness Worship, 1998-2000, Concordia Self-Study CD-ROM, Concordia Electronic Theological Libr., Luther's Works on CD-ROM; content editor Christian Cyclopedia, Internet Version; contbr. articles to religious jours. Bd. dirs. Trinity Ch. S.E. Asian Mission, Winfield, 1984-86, Wash. Luth. Sch. Assn., 1997-98, v.p. 1997-98; co-chair Winfield Com. for Commemorating the Bicentennial of the Constn., Winfield, 1987-88; chmn. Coalition for Purchase and Renovation, St. John's Coll., Winfield, 1988; sec., treas. exec. com. Area 3 Libr. Svc. Authority, Ft. Wayne, 1990-93; v.p., pres. Chgo. Area Theol. Libr. Assn., 1992-94; organizer Texhoma Christmas Effort, 2000-02. Mem. Rotary Internat. (treas. Texhoma chpt. 2002-03), Phi Kappa Phi, Mu Alpha Pi. Republican. Office: Aims Cmty Coll PO Box 69 Greeley CO 80632 Office Phone: 970-339-6518. Business E-Mail: paul.jackson@aims.edu. *All that I am I owe to my Lord and Savior Jesus Christ. What he has done through his life, death, and resurrection far exceeds anything we will ever accomplish.*

JACKSON, PETER, film director; b. Pukerua Bay, New Zealand, Oct. 31, 1961; s. Bill and Joan Jackson; m. Frances Walsh, 1987; 2 children. Grad. (hon.), Massey U., 2001. Owner WingNut Films, Weta Ltd., Three Foot Six, Nat. Film Unit, New Zealand, 1998—. Dir.(and actor): (films) The Valley, 1976, (and prodr., actor, writer) Bad Taste, 1987, (and prodr., actor, writer) Meet the Feebles, 1989, (and actor, writer) Braindead, 1992, (and screenplay, co-prodr.) Heavenly Creatures, 1994, (and writer, actor, prodr.) The Frighteners, 1996, (and writer, exec. prodr.): Forgotten Silver, 1995, (and screenplay, actor, prodr.): (films) Lord of the Rings: The Fellowship of the Ring, 2001 (Nat. Bd. Rev. award for spl. achievement, 2001, Southea. Film Critics Assn. award best dir., best adapted screenplay, 2001, Las Vegas Film Critics Soc. award best dir., 2001, Fla. Film Critics Cir. award best dir., 2001, Am. Film Inst. award movie of yr., 2001, Golden Satellite award best motion picture, 2001, BAFTA award best film, David Lean award best achievement in direction, 2002), Lord of the Rings: The Two Towers, 2002 (Las Vegas Film Critics award best dir., 2002, Online Film Critics Soc. award best dir., 2002, Dallas-Ft. Worth Film Critics award best dir., 2002), Lord of the Rings: The Return of the King, 2003 (Glden Globe for best dramatic film, 2004, Golden Globe for best dir., 2004, best dir. for 2003, Dir.'s Guild of Am., 2004, Academy Award for best director, 2004, Academy Award for best adapted screenplay, 2004, Academy Award for best picture, 2004); prodr.(and writer): Jack Brown Genius, 1994; co-prodr.: Valley of the Stereos, 1992; co-exec. prodr. (TV series) Ship to Shore, 1993—94; exec. prodr.(and actor): (films) The Long and Short of It, 2003. Named Man of Yr., Australian Empire mag., 2003; named one of 50 Most Powerful People in Hollywood, Premiere mag., 2003, 2004, 2005. Mem.: New Zealand Order of Merit. Office: WingNut Films Ltd PO Box 15 208 Miramar Wellington New Zealand also: Nat Film Unit 23 Frederick St Wellington New Zealand*

JACKSON, PHILIP DOUGLAS, professional basketball coach; b. Deer Lodge, Mont., Sept. 17, 1945; m. June; 5 children. Grad., North Dakota, 1967. Basketball player N.Y. Knicks, 1967-78, N.J. Nets, 1978-80, asst. coach, 1980-82; head coach Albany Patrons (Cen. Basketball Assn.), 1982-87; asst. coach Chicago Bulls, 1987-89, head coach, 1989-98, Los Angeles Lakers, 1999—2004, 2005—. Co-author (with Hugh Delehanty): Sacred Hoops: Spiritual Lessons of a Hardwood Warrior, 1996; co-author: (with Charley Rosen) More Than A Game, 2002; author: The Last Season: A Team in Search of Its Soul, 2004. Mem. NBA Championship Team, 1970, 73; coach NBA championship team, 1991, 92, 93, 96, 97, 98, 2000, 2001, 2002; named Coach of Yr., NBA, 1996. Office: L A Laker Great Western Foru 555 N Nash St El Segundo CA 90245-2818

JACKSON, RANDY, music producer, television personality, musician; b. Baton Rouge, Feb. 29, 1956; s. Herman and Julia Jackson; m. Elizabeth Jackson (div. 1990); 1 child, Taylor; m. Erika Riker, 1995; children: Zoe, Jordan. BA in Music, So. U., 1979. Bass player Journey, 1983—87; v.p. A&R Columbia Records; sr. v.p. A&R MCA Records. Talent judge (TV series) American Idol, 2002—; prodr.: (albums) Truth About Cats & Dogs soundtrack, 1996, First Wives Club soundtrack, 1996, (various artists) Eddie Money, Trisha Covington, Richard Marx, Rahsaan Patterson, Gladys Knight, Jesse Powell, many others; musician (bass player): (instrn. video) Randy Jackson: Mastering the Groove, 1992, albums, Journey, Patti LaBelle, Michael Bolton, Bon Jovi, Mariah Carey, Tracy Chapman, Cher, Kelly Clarkson, Celine Deon, Bob Dylan, Aretha Franklin, Keeny G, Herbie Hancock, Whitney Houston, Billy Idol, Elton John, Madonna, others; co-writer: songs My Saving Grace (from Mariah Carey album "Charmbracelet", 2003, Irresistible (from Mariah Carey album "Charmbracelet", 2003. Office: c/o Brit Reece PMK/HBH 8500 Wilshire Blvd Ste 700 Los Angeles CA 90211

JACKSON, RAYMOND A., federal judge; b. 1949; BA, Norfolk State U., 1970; JD, U. Va., 1973. Capt. U.S. Army JAGC, 1973-77; asst. U.S. atty. Ea. Dist. Va., Norfolk, 1977-93, chief criminal divsn., civil divsn., exec. asst.; judge U.S. Dist. Ct. (ea. dist.) Va., Norfolk, 1993—. Mem. jud. conf. U.S. Ct. Appeals (4th cir.); adj. faculty Marshall Wythe Sch. of Law, Coll. of William and Mary, 1978—93; mem. com. on adminstrn. Magistrate Judges Sys., 1998—2004. Active Day Care and Child Devel. Ctr., Tidewater, 1980—86; mem. exec. com. Va. State Bar, 1991—93; bd. dirs. Peninsula Legal Aid Ctr., 1977. Col. Res. USAR, ret. 1998. Mem.: Va. Law Found., Am. Inn Ct. (Hoffman-l'Anson chpt. pres. 2000—02), South Hampton Rds. Bar Assn., Norfolk-Portsmouth Bar Assn., Old Dominion Bar Assn. (pres. 1984—86), U.S. Dist. Judges Assn. Office: 600 Granby St Norfolk VA 23510-1915

JACKSON, RAYMOND CARL, cytogeneticist; b. Medora, Ind., May 7, 1928; s. Thornton Comadore and Flossie Oliva (Booker) J.; m. T. June Snyder, Oct. 24, 1947; children: Jeffrey Wayne, Rebecca June. AB, Ind. U., 1952, AM, 1953; PhD, Purdue U., 1955. Instr. to asst. prof. U. N.Mex., Albuquerque, 1955-58; asst. prof. of Botany U. Kans., Lawrence, 1958-60, assoc. prof. of Botany, 1961-64, prof. of Botany, 1964-71, prof. and chmn. Botany, 1969-71; prof. and chmn. biol. scis. Tex. Tech U., Lubbock, 1971-78, Horn prof. of Biol. Scis., 1990—. Chmn. interdepartmental PhD Program in Genetics, U. Kans., chmn. dept. Botany, U. Kans., 1969-71; speaker and presenter in field. Contbr. numerous articles to profl. jours. Staff sgt. USAF, 1946-49. Mem. Genetics Soc. Am., Genetics Soc. of Can., Soc. for the Study of Evolution, Botanical Soc. of Am. (BSA Merit award 1992), Am. Soc. Plant Taxonomists, Internat. Orgn. of Plant Biosystematists, Delta Phi Alpha, Sigma Xi, Phi Sigma. Republican. Achievements include research in pairing control genes and their comparative effects at the diploid and polyploid levels; genetics, cytogenetics, and gametic selection in Haplopappus gracilis, cytogenetics of diploid Triticum species. Home: 7922A Aberdeen Ave Lubbock TX 79424-2808 Office: Dept Biol Scis Tex Tech Univ Lubbock TX 79409 Fax: 806-742-2963.

JACKSON, RAYMOND SIDNEY, JR., lawyer; b. Bklyn., Sept. 17, 1938; s. Raymond Sidney and Mary Frost (McInerney) Van Vranken. BA, William Coll., 1960; JD, Harvard U., 1966. Bar: N.Y. 1967, U.S. Dist. Ct. (so. and ea. dists.) N.Y. 1969, U.S. Ct. Appeals (2d cir.) 1969. Assoc. Thacher, Proffitt & Wood, N.Y.C., 1966-76, ptnr., 1976-94, of counsel, 1994—. Mem. South St. Seaport Mus., N.Y.C., 1974—, Gramercy Neighborhood Assocs., N.Y.C., 1974—, Nat. Assn. Coll. and Univ. Attys., 1972. Mem. ABA (vice chmn. admiralty and maritime law com. sect. of tort and ins. practice 1990-92), N.Y. State Bar Assn. (admiralty and maritime com. internat. law and practice sect. 1989-94), Assn. Bar City N.Y. (admiralty com. 1984-85, 88-91), Maritime Law Assn. U.S. (com. on practice and procedure 1976-91). E-mail: rsjacksonj@aol.com.

JACKSON, REGGIE (REGINALD MARTINEZ JACKSON, MR. OCTOBER), former professional baseball player; b. Wyncote, Pa., May 18, 1946; s. Martinez Jackson; m. Juanita Campos (div.). Student, Ariz. State U. Outfielder Kansas City, then Oakland Athletics, 1967-75, Balt. Orioles, 1976, N.Y. Yankees, 1977-81; outfielder, designated hitter Calif. Angels, 1982-86, Oakland Athletics, 1987, advisor, 1988-93, N.Y. Yankees, 1993—. Mem. Am. League All-Star Team, 1969, 71-75, 77-82, 84; former commentator ABC Sports Author: (with Bill Libby) Reggie, 1975, (with Joel Cohen) Inside Hitting, 1975; appearances include (film), The Naked Gun, 1988, Richie Rich, 1994, Bad Day on the Block, 1997, BASEketball, 1998, Summer of Sam, 1999. Inductee Baseball Hall of Fame, 1993; named Most Valuable Player Am. League, 1973, The Sporting News Major League Player of Year, 1973, World Series Most Valuable Player, 1973, 1977; Named to The Sporting News Am. League All-Star Team, 1969, 73, 75, 76, 80. The only non-pitcher to win World Series Most Valuable Player honors twice; hit 3 homeruns in game 6 of 1977 World Series (most homeruns ever by one player in one game); 563 career homeruns. Office: care Matt Merola 185 E 85th St Apt 18G New York NY 10028-2146 also: care NY Yankees Yankee Stadium 161st St and River Ave Bronx NY 10451

JACKSON, REGINALD SHERMAN, JR., lawyer, educator; b. Oct. 8, 1946; s. Reginald Sherman and Frances (Holland) J.; m. Joanne Marie Warren, Aug. 31, 1968; children: Reginald Sherman III, Michael W., Adam H. BA, Ohio State U., 1968, JD, 1971. Bar: Ohio 1971, U.S. Supreme Ct. 1976; cert. civil trial advocate Nat. Bd. Trial Advocacy. Mem. Fuller, Henry, Hodge Snyder, Toledo, 1971-76; asst. U.S. atty. no. dist. Ohio U.S. Dept. Justice, 1976-78; ptnr. Connelly, Jackson & Collier, Toledo, 1978—. Adj. prof. trial practice U. Toledo Coll. Law, 1976-89. Fellow Am. Bar Found., Ohio State Bar Found. (trustee 1998—), Toledo Bar Found. (pres. 1993-98); mem. ABA (ho. of dels. 1996-99, 2001—, exec. com. nat. caucus state bars, litig. sect.), Am. Bd. Trial Advocates, Ohio State Bar Assn. (pres. 2000-01), Toledo Bar Assn. (pres. 1989-90), Toledo Golf Hall of Fame (founder), Toledo Country Club (trustee 1981-93, pres. 1991-93), Rotary (trustee 1994-96, 1st v.p.). Home: 2907 River Rd Maumee OH 43537-3740 Office: Connelly Jackson & Collier 405 Madison Ave Ste 1600 Toledo OH 43604-1226 Office Phone: 419-243-2100. Business E-Mail: rjackson@cjc-law.com.

JACKSON, RENÉE BERNADETTE, English language educator; b. York, Pa., July 20, 1954; d. William Brice and Helen Elizabeth (Webb) J.; 1 child, Karla Janine. BA in Comm., Pa. State Harrisburg, Middletown, 1995, MA in Humanities, 1997; postgrad., Temple U., 1997—. Newsroom intern, journalist Harrisburg Patriot News, 1995; newsroom intern, corr. York (Pa.) Daily Record, 1995-96; rsch. asst. for coord. Master's Humanities Program Pa. State Harrisburg, Middletown, 1995-97; adj. prof. Harrisburg Area C.C., 1997; tchg. asst. African-Am. studies Temple U., Phila., 1997, rsch. asst. broadcasting, telecom. and mass media dept., 1998; adj. English prof. C.C. of Phila., 1999—; GMAT essay evaluator Educl. Testing Svc., Princeton, N.J., 1998—. Mem. AAUW, Assn. for Edn. in Journalism and Mass Comm., Am. Journalism Historians Assn., Nat. Assn. Black Journalists, Assn. for the Study of Afro-Am. Life and History, Assn. Black Women Historians, Soc. Profl. Journalists, Middle-Atlantic Popular Culture Conf. (exec. bd. mem., mem. planning com.). Avocations: historical writing projects, composing piano music, travel. Home: 107 Shelbourne Dr York PA 17403-3821

JACKSON, RHONDA, telecommunications industry executive, poet; b. NYC; d. William Aaron and Emmeline Jackson; m. Ronald Anthony Nurse. AAS, Berkeley Coll., 1995; BA, N.Y. U., 1998; PhD, Berkeley U., 2002, Cosmopolitan U., 2003. Telecom. tech. assoc. Bell Atlantic, N.Y.C., 1980—; pres. Poetress Music, Fresh Meadows, N.Y., 1997—. Exec. dir. Excelsior Multicultural Inst., St. Albans, N.Y., 1997—; amb. People to People, Spokane, Wash., 2000—. Author: The Best Poems of 1997, 1997 (Editors Choice award 1997), Daybreak on the Land, 1997 (Editors Choice award 1997), The Line, 1998, Quiet Moments, 1999. Big sister Big Bros., Big Sisters, NYC, 1997; bd. dirs. Internat. Ambs., Raleigh, N.C., 1999; events coord. City Harvest, NYC, 1999; tutor English and math. Literacy Ptnrs., NYC, 2000; sec.-gen. United Cultural Conv., 2001; pres. Ophelia DeVore Alumni Performing Co., 2001; del. Nat. Writers Assn., 2001; senator World Nations Congress, 2003. Recipient Outstanding Achievement in Poetry, Famous Poets Soc., Ashland, Oreg., 1999, Pres. award for lit. excellence Nat. Authors Registry, Ohio, 2000, Diamond Homer trophy, 1999, Internat. Peace prize United Cultural Conv., 2002; named Poet of Yr., Famous Poets Soc., Ashland, 2000; inductee Internat. Poetry Hall of Fame, Internat. Soc. Poets, Owings Mills, Md., 1998, Profl. Bus. Women's Hall of Fame, 2003, Internat. Honor Soc., Lifetime Achievement award World Congress of Arts, Sci. and Comm., 2005others; honored as one of 500 Living Legends in the World, 2002. Mem. NARAS, Nat. Writers Union, Assn. for Telecom. Execs., Songwriters Guild Am., Nat. Acad. Am. Poets, Assn. Women in Radio and TV. Home: PO Box 650136 Fresh Meadows NY 11365 Office Phone: 212-636-9873. Business E-Mail: contactus@witww.org.

JACKSON, RHONDA GAIL, secondary teacher; b. Albuquerque, Oct. 12, 1954; d. Jack Harold and Glenna Janelle (Welborn) Furr; m. Robert Evans Jackson, June 20, 1975; children: Richard Paul, Lindsey Beth. B in Social Work, Tex. Woman's U., 1977. English secondary edn. Adminstrv. asst. Tex. Women's U., 1977-84; secondary tchr. English and sociology Frisco H.S., Tex., 1990—, English dept. chair, 1998—. Mem. Nat. Coun. Tchrs. English. Home: 11507 Prestige Dr PO Box 2231 Frisco TX 75034-8231 Office: 6401 Parkwood Dr Frisco TX 75034-7239 E-mail: jacksonr@friscoisd.org.

JACKSON, RICHARD JOSEPH, epidemiologist, educator, pediatrician, preventive medicine physician; b. Newark, Oct. 23, 1945; s. Robert Joseph Jackson and Dorothy C. (Devine) Connolly; m. Joan M. Guilford, June 21, 1975; children: Brendan, Devin, Galen. AB in Biology, St. Peter's Coll., Jersey City, 1969; M in Med. Sci., Rutgers Med. Sch., 1971; MD, U. Calif. San Francisco, San Francisco, 1973; MPH in Epidemiology, U. Calif. Berkeley, Berkeley, 1979. Diplomate Am. Bd. Pediatrics, Am. Bd. Preventive Medicine; lic. physician, Calif. Intern, resident U. Calif., San Francisco, 1973-74, 77-78, resident San Francisco Gen. Hosp., 1974-75; officer Epidemic Intelligence Svc. U.S. Pub. Health Svc., Albany, N.Y., 1975-77; spl. epidemiologist World Health Orgn., Bihar State, India, 1976; med. officer Epidemiol. Studies Sect. Calif. State Dept. Health Svcs., Berkeley, 1979-88, acting chief Office Environ. Health Hazard Aassessment Sacramento, 1988-90, chief hazard identification and risk assessment br. Berkeley, 1990-91; chief hazard identification and risk assessment br. office environ. health hazard assessment Calif. EPA, Berkeley, 1991-92; chief divsn. communicable disease control Calif. State Dept. Health Svcs., 1992-94; dir. Nat. Ctr. Environ. Health, Ctrs. Disease Control and Prevention, Atlanta, 1994—2003; sr. advisor to dir. Ctr. Disease Control, Atlanta, 2003—04; state pub. health officer State of Calif., Sacremento, 2004—. Adj. lectr. U. Calif. San Francisco, 1980—, asst. clin. prof., 1986—; adj. prof. Emory U. Rollins Sch. Pub. Health, 1998—. Lt. comdr. USPHS, 1975-77. Office: Calif Dept Health Svcs Dirs Office 1501 Capital Ave Ste 6001 MS 0000 Sacramento CA 95814-5005 E-mail: RJJackson@cdc.gov, rjackso6@dhs.ca.gov.

JACKSON, RICHARD MONTGOMERY, air transportation executive; b. Jacksonville, Fla., Dec. 9, 1920; s. William Kenneth and Katharine (Mitchell) J.; m. Martha Eustis Turner, Sept. 12, 1942; children: Richard Montgomery, Susanne (Mrs. Jeffrey Miller), William Mitchell. B.Sc., Harvard, 1942. With Am. Airlines, Inc., 1945-58; asso. L.S. Rockefeller, 1958-60; with Seaboard World Airlines, Inc., Jamaica, N.Y., 1960-80, pres., chmn. bd., 1960-80; chmn. exec. com. Flying Tiger Line, Jamaica, N.Y., 1980-81. Bd. govs., chmn. The Internat. Air Cargo Assn. Trustee Village of Lloyd Harbor, N.Y., 1960-68; pres. Lloyd Harbor Sch. Bd., 1957-58; trustee, pres. African Wildlife Found.; bd. govs. Huntington (N.Y.) Hosp., 1960-74. Lt. cmmdr. USNR, WWII. Mem.: Piping Rock (Locust Valley, N.Y.); Jupiter Island (Hobe Sound, Fla.); Wings (N.Y.C.); Cold Spring Harbor Beach Club (N.Y.). Home: 84 Mallard Ln Greenport NY 11944-3106

JACKSON, ROBBI JO, agricultural products executive, lawyer; b. Nampa, Idaho, Apr. 12, 1959; d. William R. Jackson and Marilyn K. Samp Jackson Nunez. BS in Fin., U. Colo., Boulder and Denver, 1981; JD, U. Denver, 1987, LLM in Taxation, 1990. Bar: Colo. 1988. Asst. office mgr. Jerome Karsh & Co., Denver, 1982; office mgr. Almirall & Assocs., Englewood, Colo., 1983-84; assoc. Moye, Giles, O'Keefe, Vermeire & Gorrell, Denver, 1989-90, Holme Roberts & Owen, Denver, 1990-92; in-house gen. counsel Cmty. Corrections Svcs., Denver, 1992-96; CEO Enviro Cons. Svc., LLC, Lakewood, Colo., 1996—; of counsel Grund & Nelson, P.C., 2004—. Presenter in field. Mem. staff Adminstrv. Law Rev., Denver, 1985, editor, 1985, mng. editor, 1986-87; co-author course of study materials. Fin. com. Mile-High chpt. ARC, Denver, 1990-92; food delivery person Vols. of Am., Meals-on-Wheels, Denver, 1990-92. Recipient scholarships. Mem.: ABA, Colo. Bar Assn. (chmn. ethics com. 2003—04). Republican. Avocations: running marathons and other races, biking, hiking, swimming, piano and organ playing.

JACKSON, ROBERT ROSCOE, education educator; b. Mather A.F.B., Rancho Cordova, Calif., Nov. 24, 1970; s. Jimmy Joe Jackson and Susan Florence Robertson; m. Carin Bernice Myers, Jan. 3, 1998; 1 child, William Robert. MEd, Tex. Christian U., 2001; MACE, MABS, Dallas Theol. Sem., 1997; BA in acctg., Cedarville U., 1993. Standard Tchr. Elemen. Self Contained Grades 1-6 State Bd. for Educator Tex., 2001, Standard Prin. Cert. Grades EC-12 State Bd. for Educator Tex., 2003, Temp. Prin. Cert. Grades EC-12 State Bd. for Educator Tex., 2003, cert. Ednl. Adminstrn. Certification Tex. Christian U., 2003. Children's pastor intern Trinity Bapt. Ch., Dallas, 1994—94; instr. Dallas Theol. Sem. Ctr. for Bibl. Studies, Dallas, 1995—95; lead sales assoc., adminstrv. asst. Lifeway Christian Stores, Dallas and Richardson, Tex., 1996—98; adminstrv. asst. Holmes Murphy, Dallas, 1998—99, Internat. Solutions, Arlington, Tex., 1999—2000; self contained tchr., dist. class a.c.t. tchr. DeSoto ISD-Cockrell Hill Elem. Sch., DeSoto, Tex., 2000—03; adminstrv. intern DeSoto ISD-Amber Ter. Intermed. Sch., DeSoto, Tex., 2003—; math tchr., dept. head, dist. class a.c.t. tchr. DeSoto ISD Amber Ter. Intermed. Sch., DeSoto, Tex., 2003—; ednl. mentor Tex. A&M U., Commerce, Tex., 2004—. Scope and sequence ednl. cons. Spl. Edn. Dept. DeSoto ISD, DeSoto, Tex., 2004—; ednl. cons. Edn. Svc. Ctr. Region 10, Richardson, Tex., 2004. Author: (hist. essay) Homeward Bound: My Journey; contbr. articles to profl. jours. Bd. mem. Zula B. Wylie Libr., Cedar Hill, Tex., 1999—2001. Grantee Undoing Checkmate, DeSoto ISD Ednl.

Found., 2004-2005, Royal Measurement with the Pharaohs, DeSoto ISD Edn. Found., 2004-2005, Jazzing Up Math Through Reading, 2004-2005, Flying High with Geometric Kites, 2004-2005, DeSoto We Have Lift off from Space Sta. Ctrl., 2004-2005, Sen. Royce West's One Community-One Child Parental Involvement Project Grant for PAT, Edn. Svc. Ctr. Region 10, 2003-2004, Exemplary Exemplars, DeSoto ISD Edn. Found., 2002-2003, Math Manipulatives, 2000-2001; UNT Grad. Sch. Doctoral fellowship, U. North Tex., 2004-2005, Best SW scholarship, Bank of Am., 2004. Mem.: Assn. for Childhood Edn. Internat., Alpha Iota Chpt. of Kappa Delta, Internat. Honor Soc. in Edn., Pi Lambda Theta, Internat. Honor Soc. and PA in Edn., Nat. Assn. of Elem. Principals, Tex. Assn. of Elem. Principals, Assn. of Tex. Profl. Educators, Nat. Coun. of Tchrs. of Math., North Ctrl. Regional Tex. ASCD, Nat. Coun. of Tchrs. of English, Nat. Coun. for the Social Studies, Nat. and Tex. Assn. for Supervision and Curriculum Devel., Clan Donnachaidh Soc. of Scotland (life), Soc. of the Descendants of the Schwenkfeldian Exiles (life). Conservative. Achievements include research to secure a 5-year $750,000 grant from the Dept. of Edn. for Hispanic Administrators for the U. North Tex. Avocations: model railroading, water gardens, digital photography, ham radios. Home: 301 Teakwood Ln Cedar Hill TX 75104 Home Fax: 972-291-5475; Office Fax: 972-274-8247. Personal E-mail: carrock1998@aol.com. E-mail: rjackson@desotoisd.org.

JACKSON, ROBERT WILLIAM, retired utilities executive; b. Beaumont, Tex., June 22, 1930; s. Robert and Elizabeth (Watler) J.; m. Theta Ann Watt, Aug. 14, 1959; 1 child, Robert W. Jr. BBA, U. Tex.; MBA, U. Ill. With Gulf States Utilities Co., Beaumont, Tex., 1955-79, sec., chief fin. officer, 1972-74, sec., treas., chief fin. officer, 1974-75, v.p. fin., chief fin. officer, sec., 1975-79, Cen. Ill. Pub. Svc. Co., Springfield, 1979-80, sr. v.p. fin., chief fin. officer, corp. sec., 1980-95, also bd. dirs.; pres., chief exec. officer CIPSCO Investment Co., Springfield, 1990-95, also bd. dirs.; sr. v.p. CIPSCO Inc., Springfield, 1990, also bd. dirs.; ret., 1995. Bd. dirs. 1st Bank of Ill. Co., Springfield, 1st Nat. Bank Springfield, Sangamon State U. Found.; bd. govs. Econs. Am. Mem. bus. adv. coun. U. Ill.; bd. dirs. Springfield Symphony Orch., United Way of Sangamon County; adv. bd. St. John's Hosp., Springfield. Served with U.S. Army, 1953-55. Mem. Am. Soc. Corp. Secs., Fin. Execs. Inst., Edison Electric Inst. (fin. exec. com.). Methodist.

JACKSON, ROBERTA Q., music educator; d. Donald Robert and Frances Montana McLeod; BA in Music Edn., MacPhail Coll. Music, Mpls., 1964; MA in Music Edn., U. Colo., 1970. Elem. music tchr. Red Wing (Minn.) Pub. Schs., 1964—66; elem. music resource tchr. Mpls. Pub. Schs., 1966—68; choral dir. South H.S., Mpls., 1968—70; music tchr. grades 3-8 Robert Gray Elem., Portland, Oreg., 1972—78, Franklin HS, Portland, Oreg., 1978—80; choral dir. Cedar Park Mid. Sch., Beaverton, Oreg., 1980—85, Five Oaks Mid. Sch., Beaverton, Oreg., 1985—97; founding artistic dir. Portland Symphonic Girlchoir, 1989—. Presenter Internat. Soc. Music Educators Conf., Innsbruck, Austria, 1985. Contbr. articles to profl. jours. Recipient award for adventurous programming, ASCAP/Chorus Am., 2003; Commemorative scholar, Delta Kappa Gamma Internat., 1986, 1990. Mem.: Assn. Choral Music Experience (recording sec. 2000—04, master tchr. diploma 1999, artist tchr. diploma 1997), Internat. Fedn. Choral Music, Am. Choral Dirs. Assn. (pres. Oreg. state 1983—85, repertoire and stds. elem. chair N.W. divsn. 1997—2004, organizing chair children's honor choir N.W. divsn. 1998, 2000, 2002, 2004, presenter nat. conventions 1999, 2001, 03, 05, cert. adjudicator Oreg. 1994—). Avocations: travel, movies, reading, concerts. Office: Portland Symphonic Girlchoir 1436 Montgomery Ave Portland OR 97201 Office Phone: 503-226-6162. E-mail: rjackson@girlchoir.com.

JACKSON, ROGER A., human resources specialist, automotive executive; Various positions Rockwell Internat., 1977—95; v.p. human resources Allen Bradley (subsidiary of Rockwell Internat.), 1991—95; sr. v.p. human resources Lear Corp., Southfield, Mich., 1995—. Office: Lear Corp 21557 Telegraph Rd Southfield MI 48086-5008 Office Phone: 248-447-1500.*

JACKSON, RYNO MARSHALL, forensic psychologist, consultant; b. Reading, Pa., Oct. 12, 1934; s. Jesse and Helen Adelia (Taylor) J.; m. Jacqueline Estelle Coleman, Aug. 10, 1963; children: Michael, David, Tracy. BA in English Edn., Glassboro State U., 1961; MA, Newark State U., 1972; PsyD, Rutgers U., 1985. Cert. sch. psychologist, N.J.; diplomate Am. Coll. Forensic Examiners, Am. Coll. Psychol. Treating Addictions. English tchr. Scotch Plains-Fanwood, N.J., 1961-70; sch. psychologist Plainfield (N.J.) Bd. Edn., 1970-89; forensic psychologist Assocs. in Forensic Psychology, Flemington, NJ, 1989—. Cons. Union County Juvenile and Domestic Rels. Ct., Elizabeth, N.J., 1972-82, Middlesex County Coll., Woodbridge, N.J., 1988-92, Greenbrook Acad., Boundbrook, N.J., 1990—; adj. prof. Newark State Coll., Union, N.J., 1992-96. Juvenile conf. com. advisor, Plainfield, 1986-87; search and rescue pilot CAP, Linden, N.J., 1975-85; coach Little League Baseball, Plainfield, 1972-78, Pee Wee Football, 1975-78. Mem. APA, N.J. Psychol. Assn., N.J. Assn. Black Psychologists, Internat. Soc. Police Surgeons, Am. Mensa, Am. Coll. Forensic Psychology. Home: 1208 Salem Rd Plainfield NJ 07060-3323 Office: Assocs in Forensic Psychology 260 Rt 202-31 N Flemington NJ 08822

JACKSON, SAMUEL L., actor; b. Washington, Dec. 21, 1948; m. LaTanya Richardson; 1 child, Zoe. Actor: (TV series) Happily Ever After: Fairy Tales for Every Child, 1995-99; (TV movies) The Trial of the Moke, 1978, Uncle Tom's Cabin, 1987, Common Ground, 1990, Dead and Alive: The Race for Gus Farace, 1991, Simple Justice, 1993, Assault at West Point, 1994, Against the Wall, 1994; (films) Together for Days, 1972, Ragtime, 1981, Eddie Murphy Raw, 1987, Coming to America, 1988, School Daze, 1988, (voiceover) Mystery Train, 1989, Do The Right Thing, 1989, Sea of Love, 1989, A Shock to the System, 1990, Def by Temptation, 1990, Betsy's Wedding, 1990, Mo' Better Blues, 1990, The Exorcist III, 1990, Goodfellas, 1990, Return of Superfly, 1990, Jungle Fever, 1991 (Best Actor award Cannes International Film Festival), Strictly Business, 1991, Juice, 1992, White Sands, 1992, Patriot Games, 1992, Johnny Suede, 1992, Jumpin' at the Boneyard, 1992, Fathers and Sons, 1992, National Lampoon's Loaded Weapon 1, 1993, Amos & Andrew, 1993, Menace II Society, 1993, Jurassic Park, 1993, True Romance, 1993, Hail Caesar, 1994, Fresh, 1994, Hail Caesar, 1994, The New Age, 1994, Pulp Fiction, 1994, Losing Isiah, 1995, Kiss of Death, 1995, Fluke, 1995, Die Hard With a Vengeance, 1995, The Great White Hype, 1996, Trees Lounge, 1996, The Search for One Eye Jimmy, 1996, A Time to Kill, 1996, The Long Kiss Goodnight, 1996, 187, 1997, Jackie Brown, 1997, Hard Eight, 1997, Eve's Bayou, 1997, Sphere, 1998, Out of Sight, 1998, The Negotiator, 1998, Rules of Engagement, 1999, Mefisto in Onyx, 1999, Star Wars Episode I: The Phantom Menace, 1999, Deep Blue Sea, 1999, Shaft, 2000, Unbreakable, 2000, Changing Lanes, 2002, Star Wars: Episode II - Attack of the Clones, 2002, XXX, 2002, Basic, 2003, S.W.A.T., 2003, In My Country, 2004, Twisted, 2004, Kill Bill: Vol. 2, 2004, The Incredibles (voice), 2004, Coach Carter, 2005, xXx: State of the Union, 2005, Star Wars: Episode III Revenge of the Sith, 2005, The Man, 2005.*

JACKSON, SHIRLEY ANN, academic administrator, physicist; b. Wash., D.C., Aug. 5, 1946; d. George Hiter and Beatrice (Cosby) Jackson; m. Morris A. Washington; 1 child, Alan. BS in Physics, MIT, 1968, PhD in Theoretical Physics, 1973; DSc (hon.), Bloomfield Coll., 1991, Fairleigh Dickinson U., 1993; LLD (hon.), Villanova, 1996. Rsch. assoc. Fermi Nat. Accelerator Lab, Batavia, Ill., 1973—76; mem. tech. staff AT&T Bell Labs, Murray Hill, NJ, 1976—91; prof. physics Rutgers U., Piscataway, NJ, 1991—95; chairperson Nuclear Reg. Commn., 1995—99; U.S. Rep. to Gen. Conf. Internat. Atomic Energy Agy., 1995—99; pres. Rensselaer Poly. Inst., Troy, NY, 1999—. Vis. scientist European Orgn. Nuclear Rsch., Geneva, 1974—75; visitor Stanford Linear Accelerator Ctr., 1976, Aspen Ctr. Physics, 1976—77; mem. com. edn. and employment women in sci. and engring. Nat. Rsch. Coun., 1980—95, cons., 1977—91, NSF, 1977; mem. ednl. coun. MIT, 1976—80; chmn. Internat. Nuclear Regulators Assn., 1997—99; bd. trustees Lincoln U., Pa., 1980—92, exec. com., 1985—92; bd. trustees Rutgers U., 1986—91, bd. gov., mem. ednl. planning and policy com., 1990; bd. trustees Associated U., Inc., 1993, Brookings Instn., 2000—; trustee Georgetown U., Rockefeller U., Emma Willard Sch., Troy, NY, Troy; mem. bd. dirs. NY Stock Exchange, 2003—; mem. Coun. Fgn. Rels.; mem. exec. com. Coun. Competitveness; coun. mem. Govt.-U.-Industry Rsch. Roundtable; dir. FedEx Corp., AT&T Corp., Marathon Oil Corp., Medtronic, Inc., U.S. Steel Corp.; life mem. bd. trustees MIT Corp.; mem. Nat. Adv. Coun. Biomedical Imaging and Bioengineering, Nat. Inst. Health (NIH); US Comptroller-Gen. adv. com. Govt. Acctg. Office (GAO). Editl. adv. bd. (jour.) Jour. Sci. Tech. and Human Values, 1982; contbr. articles to physics jours. Mem. NJ Commn. Sci. and Tech., Com. Status Women in Physics, 1986—88. Named one of 50 Most Important Women in Sci., Discover mag., 2002, 50 Most Inspiring African Am., pub. book, ESSENCE, 2002, 50 R&D Stars to Watch, Industry Week mag., 2002; named to Nat. Women's Hall Fame, 1998, Women Tech. Internat. Found. Hall Fame (WITI), 2000; recipient Candace award, Nat. Coalition 100 Black Women, Salute to Policy Makers award, Exec. Women NJ, 1986, Black Achievers in Industry award, Harlem YMCA, 1986, Thomas Alva Edison award (NJ Gov.'s award), 1993, 100 Women Excellence award, Albany-Colonie Regional C. of C. and Women's Bus. Coun., 2000, eLeadership award, Ctrl. NY Tech. Devel. Orgn. and CASE Ctr., Syracuse U., 2000, Golden Torch award for Lifetime Acheivement in Academia, Nat. Soc. Black Engrs., 2000, Richtmyer Meml. Lecture award, Am. Assn. Physics Tchrs., 2001, Immortal award, 15th Annual Black History Makers award, Associated Black Charities, 2001, Black Engr. Yr. award, US Black Engr. and Info. Tech. mag., 2001; fellow, Ford Found., 1971—73; grantee, 1974—75; trainee, NSF, 1968—71. Fellow: Am. Acad. Arts and Scis., Am. Phys. Soc. (mem. com. status of women in physics 1986); mem.: AAAS Am. Assn. Advancement Sci. (com. sci., freedom and responsibility, pres. 2004), Nat. Acad. Engring., Nat. Soc. Black Physicists (pres. 1980—82), Nat. Inst. Sci., NY Acad. Scis., MIT Alumni Assn. (v.p. 1986), Delta Sigma Theta, Sigma Xi. Office: Rensselaer Polytechnic, Pres Office 3031 Troy Bldg, 3rd Fl 110 8th St Troy NY 12180-3590*

JACKSON, STANLEY EDWARD, retired special education educator; b. Washington, Sept. 3, 1918; s. Eugene Edward and Inez Christine (Booth) Jackson. BS, Miner Tchrs. Coll., Washington, 1939; MA, Columbia U., 1947, diploma, 1948, EdD, 1958; postgrad., Johns Hopkins U., Peabody Inst. Elem. tchr. DC Pub. Schs., 1940-58, elem. sch. prin., 1958-66, dir. spl. edn., 1966-72; gov.-at-large Coun. Exceptional Children, Reston, Va., 1971-72, asst. exec. dir., membership, 1972-82; ret., 1982. Lectr. Cath. U., Washington, 1965—66, asst. prof. edn., 1967; instr. DC Tchrs. Coll., 1971—72, initiator Tchr. Aide Program Spl. Edn. Classes, 1968; founder Juvenile Decency Corps Uplift House, 1964; co-planner Mamie D. Lee Sch. Mentally Retarded, 1968. Author: School Organization for the Mentally Retarded, 1973, Educational Strategies and Services for Exceptional Children, 1976. Pres. Area K Bd. Commrs. Youth Coun., Washington, 1959—65; founder UPLIFT Cmty. House, Washington, 1963, pres. Chpt. 49, 1962—64, 1st pres. Fedn. 524, 1965—66; bd. dirs. Found. Exceptional Children, 1978. With U.S. Army, 1941—45, WWII. Decorated 4 Battle Stars; named Stanley E. Jackson Scholarship in his honor, Peabody Prep., Johns Hopkins U., 1988, Stanley E. Jackson Scholarship award established in his honor, Found. for Exceptional Children, 1980, Philanthropic Honor Roll, George Washington U., 1949—2001; recipient Yes I Care award, Found. for Exceptional Children, 1992, Plaque for Outstanding Svc., Commr. Coun., Washington, 1963, Outstanding Ret. Tchr. award, Jr. Citizens Corps, 1979, Stanley E. Jackson Spl. Edn. award established in his honor, Bd. Edn. D.C. Pub. Schs., 1973, Cert. of Appreciation, Nat. Fedn. Blind, 2001. Mem.: NAACP, AAUP, NEA, Dept. Elem. Sch. Prins., Coun. Exceptional Children, DC Congress Parents and Tchrs., Johns Hopkins Assoc. Program, Urban League, AMVETS, Phi Delta Kappa, Kappa Delta Pi. Avocations: music, coin collecting/numismatics, writing, philanthropy. Home: Apt 703 One E University Pky Baltimore MD 21218

JACKSON, STEPHANIE LEE, artist, massage therapist; b. Ft. Worth, Sept. 6, 1967; d. Sherman Keith Jr. and Pamela Alice Jackson. BA with honors, U. Tex., 1989; BFA, San Francisco Art Inst., 1993. Cert. massage therapist Nat. Holistic Inst., Calif. Founder, dir. Healing Arts, Bklyn., 2003—. Co-founder Three Muses Artspace, San Francisco, 1992. Alpine Art Gallery, GenArt San Francisco; author: (web site) www.stephart.com. Recipient Intriguing Person award, Sandra and Pat Hayashi, Berkeley, Calif., 2002. Mem.: Am. Massage Therapist Assn. (assoc.). Mystic. Avocations: writing, bicycling, travel. Office: Healing Arts 135 Wythe Brooklyn NY 11211 Personal E-mail: stephanieleejackson@yahoo.com.

JACKSON, STEPHEN ERIC, public speaker, life strategist; b. Seymour, Ind., July 9, 1946; s. Ralph Marshall Jackson and Dolly Katherine (Britt) Tudor; m. Cheryl Jane Hallman, June 23, 1967 (div. 1985); children: Kirstina Leigh, Brandi Annette; m. Margaret Ann Skelton, Oct. 17, 1986 (div. 1989); m. Candy Sandler Clinard, Sept. 30, 1995. BA in Sociology, N. Tex. State U., 1976; grad., Tex. Law Enforcement Inst., 1991; MPA, U. North Tex., 1993. Lic. mediator, 1996. Police officer, sgt. Denton (Tex.) Police Dept., 1970-81; customer svc. mgr. Amerace Corp., Denton, 1981-83; dir. police and traffic svcs. U. North Tex., Denton, 1983-98; ptnr. Pathways Ednl. Corp., Irving, Tex., 1998—2001; pres. Pathways Life Mgmt. Seminars, Irving, 1999-2001; founder, pres. Life Strategies Inst. Tex., Ft. Worth, 2001—. Adj. faculty applied econs. U. North Tex., 2000—; public speaker, life mgmt. coord, v.p. Denton County Chiefs of Police, 1986-94. Contbr. articles to profl. jours. Precinct chmn. Denton County Rep. Party, 1982-85; mem. Pub. Transp. Task Force, Denton, 1989; chmn. steering com. Leadership Denton, 1990-95, 95-97, Leadership Denton Alumni Assn., 1991—; mem. parking com. Main St. Denton, Inter-Assn. Task Force on Alcohol and Other Substance Abuse Issues, 1995-97, local assoc. Nat. Coalition Bldg. Inst., 1990—; del./panelist White House Conf. on Hate Crimes, 1997. Mem. Internat. Assn. Campus Law Enforcement Adminstrs. (v.p. 1995-96, pres. elect 1996-97, pres. 1997-98), Tex.-N.Mex. Assn. Coll. and Univ. Police Depts. (Pres.'s award 1985, treas. 1993-96, Adminstr. of Yr. 1993), Internat. Assn. Chiefs of Police. Avocations: golf, tennis. Office: Life Strategies Inst Tex Ste 283 6387B Camp Bowie Fort Worth TX 76116

JACKSON, THAD MARSHALL, health services administrator, medical educator; b. Dallas, May 21, 1933; d. Thad M. and Opal P. (Miller) J.; m. Linda Susan Pfeiffer. BA, San Francisco State U., 1951; MS, U. San Francisco, 1968; PhD, U. Calif., Berkeley, 1974. Lectr. med. microbiology U. Calif., Berkeley, 1971; assoc. prof. dept. pathology Johns Hopkins U. Sch. Hygiene and Pub. Health; v.p. Nestle Coordination Ctr. for Nutrition, 1981—85; owner, dir. Geriatric Retirement Ctr., Norwich, England, 1985—86; dir. issues mgmt. Nestle USA, 1986—96; exec. v.p. Internat. Med. Svcs. for Health, 1996—. Dir. Johns Hopkins U. Internat. Ctr. Med. Rsch. and Tng., Nepal, India, Bangladesh, 1972—79, dir. children's nutrition rsch. unit, Bangladesh, 1972—79; condr. tng. programs in nutrition and primary health care; developer village outreach programs for mothers and children; owner, dir. two nursing homes, 1977—80; cons. Clintec (joint venture Nestle/Baxter Travenol), 1985—86, Save the Children Fedn., 1973—78; adj. prof. dept. pediats. Georgetown U. Sch. Medicine, 1981—; del. Internat. Women's Forum, Beijing, 1995; organizer, dir. Woemn's Forum, Washington; organizer various confs. on nutrition and the elderly; researcher on nutrition; mem. adv. bd. League of Women Voters, 1991—93, Bus. and Profl. Women's Assn., 1991—95; advisor to rsch. protocol com. Cholera Rsch. Labs., Dhaka, 1974—76; advisor Netherlands Embassy, 1976; ad hoc advisor UNICEF, 1972—77. Contbr. articles. Mem. bd. regents Cath. U. Am., 1992—. Fellow U.S. Pub. Health fellowship, 1968—72; grantee, NIH, 1972—74, UN Devel. Programme, 1977, USAID, 1976—77. Mem.: Royal Soc. Tropical Medicine, Am. Soc. Tropical Medicine and Hygiene. Home: PO Box 413 Upperville VA 20185

JACKSON, THEODORE MARSHALL, retired oil industry executive; b. Beaumont, Tex., Oct. 18, 1928; s. Robert and Mary Louise (Watler) J.; m. Maria Pierracou-Dobrowolska Countess de Wernicki de Vladis la Goda, June 19, 1954; 1 child, Mark Andrew. BBA in Engring, U. Tex., Austin, 1951. V.p., sec.-treas. Purvin & Gertz, Inc., Dallas, 1955-71; v.p. treasury and strategic planning New Eng. Petroleum Corp., N.Y.C., 1971-75; v.p. fin. Crown Central Petroleum Corp., Balt., 1975-83, sr. v.p., chief fin. officer, 1984-91, also bd. dirs. Bd. dirs., treas. Bd. of Child Care; emeriti gov. Wesley Theol. Sem. Lt. USNR, 1952-55. Mem. Beta Gamma Sigma, Delta Tau Delta. Republican. Methodist. Home: 8 Wythe Ct Glen Arm MD 21057-9134 E-mail: tmjack8@comcast.net.

JACKSON, THOMAS FRANCIS, III, lawyer; b. Memphis, Oct. 21, 1940; s. Thomas Francis and Sarah Elizabeth (Farris) J.; children: Thomas Francis, Wythe Macrae Bogy. Grad., The Taft Sch.; BA, Rhodes Coll., 1962; LLB, George Washington U., 1967. Bar: Tenn. 1967, U.S. Supreme Ct. 1974. Law clk. to chief judge U.S. Dist. Ct. Western Dist. Tenn., 1967-68; with Armstrong, Allen PLLC, Memphis, 1968-72, Lawler, Humphreys PLLC, Memphis, 1972-83; pvt. practice Memphis, 1983—. Lt. USNR, 1962-67. Mem. ABA, Tenn. Bar Assn., Memphis Bar Assn. Episcopalian. Home: 232 S Highland St Memphis TN 38111-4540 Office: PO Box 111221 Memphis TN 38111-1221 Office Phone: 901-324-1100. Office Fax: 901-324-6997. Business E-Mail: tfj@lawtn.com.

JACKSON, THOMAS GENE, lawyer; b. N.Y.C., Mar. 9, 1949; s. Alan Clark and Clare Seena (Werther) J.; m. Beatrice Lafrance Korab, June 11, 1972; children: Sarah Ann, Alan Edward. AB magna cum laude in English, Dartmouth Coll., 1971; JD, U. Va., 1974. Bar: N.Y. 1975, U.S. Dist. Ct. (so. and ea. dists.) N.Y. 1975, U.S. Ct. Appeals (2d cir.) 1975, U.S. Ct. Appeals (5th cir.) 1978, U.S. Supreme Ct. 1978, U.S. Ct. Appeals (D.C. cir.) 1986. Editor The Rsch. Group, Charlottesville, Va., 1973-74; assoc. Phillips Nizer Benjamin Krim & Ballon LLP, N.Y.C., 1974-82; ptnr. Phillips Nizer LLP, N.Y.C., 1982—. Mem. fed. bar coun. com. 2d Cir. Cts., 1997-2000, chmn. subcom. on tech. in the cts., 1997-2000. Contbr. chapters to books. Mem. Village of Irvington Cable TV Adv. Com., N.Y., 1979-91, 95—, chmn. franchise renewal com., 1991-95; sec. Village of Irvington Environ. Conservation Bd., 1983-87, chmn., 1987—; mem. Dartmouth Coll. Alumni Coun., 1986-89. Mem.: ABA (sect. antitrust law, mem. Clayton Act com., computer industry and internet com., intellectual property com., mem. sect. intellectual property, mem. antitrust matters com., computer programs com., mem. litig. sect., mem. antitrust litig., computer and internet litig. sect.), Assn. Bar City N.Y. (antitrust and trade regulation com. 1988—92, mergers acquisitions and joint ventures subcom. 1991—92), Am. Arbitration Assn. (comml. tribunal 1986—, panel of arbitrators), Dartmouth Coll. Class Secs. Assn. (v.p. 1984—85, pres. 1985—86), Dartmouth Club Westchester (sec. 1984—87, pres. 1987—90), Dartmouth Coll. Club Officers Assn. (exec. com. 1988—91). Home: 32 Hamilton Rd Irvington NY 10533-2311 Office: Phillips Nizer LLP 666 5th Ave New York NY 10103-0084 Office Phone: 212-977-9700. Business E-Mail: tjackson@phillipsnizer.com.

JACKSON, THOMAS HUMPHREY, former academic administrator; b. Kalamazoo, June 20, 1950; s. William Humphrey and Louise Longstreth (Cone) Jackson; m. Bonnie Eileen Gelb; children: Richard, Steven. BA, Williams Coll., 1972; JD, Yale U., 1975. Bar: N.Y. 1976, Calif. 1979. Law clk. to judge U.S. Dist. Ct. N.Y., 1975—76; law clk. to justice U.S. Supreme Ct., Washington, 1976—77; asst. prof., assoc. prof. to prof. Stanford U. Law Sch., Calif., 1977—86; prof. Harvard U. Law Sch., Cambridge, Mass., 1986—88; dean Sch. Law, U. Va., Charlottesville, 1988—91, v.p., provost, 1991—93; pres. U. Rochester, NY, 1994—2005, Disting. U. prof., 2005—. Assoc. Heller, Ehrman, White & McAliffe, San Francisco, 1979—81, spl. counsel, 1981—86. Co-author: Secured Transactions, 1982, Secured Transactions, 3d edit., 2000, Bankruptcy, 1985, Bankruptcy, 3d edit., 2000; author: Logic and Limits of Bankruptcy Law, 1986; mem. editl. bd.: The Found. Press, Inc. Trustee George Eastman House. Office: U Rochester 3-110N Carol Simon Hall Rochester NY 14627

JACKSON, THOMAS O., real estate appraiser, urban planner; BA in Polit. Sci. with honors, U. South Fla., 1975; MA in Polit. Sci., Ohio State U., 1979; M in Regional Planning, U. N.C., 1984; PhD in Urban and Regional Sci., Tex. A&M U., 2000. Cert. gen. real estate appraiser, Tex., Fla. Planning dir. City of West Melbourne, Fla., 1978-80; cmty. assistance cons. Fla. Dept. Cmty. Affairs, Tallahassee, 1983-84; sr. rsch. assoc. Econ. Rsch. Svcs., Inc., Tallahassee, 1984-86; project mgr. BHR Planning Group, Inc., Jacksonville, Fla., 1986-87; sr. cons., devel. econ. group Reynolds, Smith and Hills, Inc., Jacksonville, 1987-92; sr. project mgr. Harland Bartholomew & Assocs., Inc., Jacksonville, 1992-93; pres. Planning Rsch. Svcs., Inc., Jacksonville, 1993-94; dir. fin. adv. svcs. Coopers & Lybrand LLP, Houston, 1994-98; sr. cons. Entrix, Inc., Houston, 1998-99; pres. Real Property Analytics, Inc., College Station, Tex., 2000—. Lectr. Coll. Architecture Tex. A&M U., College Station, 1998-99, lectr. Coll. Bus., 2002-2004, exec. prof. Coll. Bus., 2004-; expert witness, presenter in field. Contbr. articles to profl. jours. Dissertation Rsch. grantee NSF, 1999; Dissertation fellow Lincoln Inst. Land Policy, 1999. Mem. Am. Planning Assn. (bd. dirs. 1993-94, chair legis. com. 1993-94), Am. Real Estate Urban Econ. Assn., Am. Real Estate Soc., Counselors Real Estate (membership devel. com. 1997, edn. com. 1997, pub. policy com. 1997-99, ethics profl. practice com. 1998-2000), Appraisal Inst. (ethics counseling com. 1995-97, mem. task group 1999-2000), Appraisal Found. (mem. appraisal stds. bd. 2001-02), Am. Inst. Cert. Planners, Urban Land Inst. (assoc., reviewer 1993), Houston Assn. Realtors, Omicron Delta Kappa, Phi Kappa Phi, Pi Sigma Alpha, Themis. Office: Real Property Analytics Inc 4805 Spearman Dr College Station TX 77845-4412 E-mail: tomjackson@real-analytics.com.

JACKSON, THOMAS PENFIELD, federal judge; b. Washington, Jan. 10, 1937; s. Thomas Searing and May Elizabeth (Jacobs) J. AB in Govt., Dartmouth Coll., 1958; LLB, Harvard U., 1964. Bar: D.C., Md., U.S. Supreme Ct. 1970. Assoc., ptnr. Jackson & Campbell, P.C., Washington, 1964-82; U.S. dist. judge U.S. Dist. Ct. D.C., Washington, 1982—. Vestryman All Saints' Episcopal Ch., Washington, 1969-75; trustee Gallaudet U., Washington, 1985-99, St. Marys Coll., MD, 2001—. Lt. (j.g.) USN, 1958-61. Fellow Am. Coll. Trial Lawyers; mem. ABA, Bar Assn. D.C. (pres. 1982-83), Rotary. Clubs: Chevy Chase, Metropolitan, Lawyers', Barristers. Republican. Office: US Dist Ct US Courthouse 3rd & Constitution Ave NW Washington DC 20001

JACKSON, TIMOTHY, systems analyst, consultant; b. Chgo., Dec. 16, 1966; s. Laudell and Phyllis Jackson; m. Edna C. Jackson, Jan. 3, 1998; children: Joelle Alise, Laudell Timothy. BS, So. Ill. U., 1990. Programmer CNA Ins. Co., Chgo., 1991—94, tech. analyst, 1996—98; application developer Info. Resources, Chgo., 1994—96; sr. cons. Ascent Consulting Group, New Orleans, 1998—99; system analyst CNG/Donino, New Orleans, 1999—2001; sr. GIS cons. Tobin Internat., Ltd., Houston, 2001—. Pres. T. Jackson & Assocs., Chgo., 1994—; instr. La. C.C., Gretna, 2000—01. Scoutmaster Boy Scouts Am., Kenner, La., 2001. Mem.: Alpha Phi Alpha (historian 1987—88, chaplain 1994—95). Baptist. Avocations: tennis, martial arts, bicycling. Office: Tobin Internat Ltd 9800 Richmond Ave Ste 750 Stafford TX 77477 Business E-Mail: tim-jackson@hotmail.com.

JACKSON, TRACEY L, music educator; b. Greer, SC, June 15, 1972; d. Harold Dean and Linda Tune Leatherman; m. Robert Ray Jackson, June 13, 1992; 1 child, Robert Ray III. BA in music edn. and math., Columbia Coll., 1994; MEd, U. SC, 2002. Nationally Board Certified in Early and Middle Childhood Music. Music tchr. Johnston Elem., SC, 1994—. Chorus tchr. JES Chorus, Johnston, SC, 1998—. Mem.: Palmetto State Teachers Assn. Avocations: piano, photography, scrapbooks, gardening. Home: 5836 Augusta Hwy Leesville SC 29070 Office: Johnston Elem Sch 514 Lee St Johnston SC 29832 Office Phone: 803-275-1755. Personal E-mail: tjackson6@bellsouth.net.

JACKSON, VALERIE PASCUZZI, radiologist, educator; b. Oakland, Calif., Aug. 25, 1952; d. Chris A. Pascuzzi and Janice (Mayne) Pascuzzi; 1 child, Price Arthur III. AB, Ind. U., 1974, MD, 1978. Diplomate Am. Bd. Radiology. Intern, resident in diagnostic radiology Ind. U. Med. Ctr., 1978-82; from asst. prof. radiology to prof. radiology Ind. U. Sch. Medicine, Indpls., 1982-94, John A. Campbell prof. radiology, 1994—. Dir. residency program in radiology Ind. U. Sch. Medicine, 1994—2003, chair dept. radiology, 2004—; trustee Am. Bd. Radiology. Contbr. over 80 articles to profl. jours., chapters to books. Fellow: Soc. Breast Imaging (pres. 1990—92), Am. Coll. Radiology (bd. chancellors, chair 3 coms., pres. 2002—03); mem.: AMA, Radiol. Soc. N.Am., Am. Roentgen Ray Soc., Am. Inst. Ultrasound in Medicine, Alpha Omega Alpha. Office: Indiana U Sch Med Dept Rad 550 N Univ Blvd Rm 0663 Indianapolis IN 46202-2859

JACKSON, VICTORIA LYNN, actress, comedienne; b. Miami, Fla., Aug. 2, 1959; d. James McCaslin and Marlene Esther (Blackstad) J.; m. Nisan Mark Eventoff, Aug. 5, 1984; 1 child, Scarlet Elizabeth. Student, Fla. Bible Coll., 1976-77, Furman U., 1977-79, Auburn U., 1979-80. Actress Summerfest/Town & Gown, Birmingham, Ala., 1980; stand-up comedienne Variety Arts Ctr., L.A., 1982-83, Tonight Show with Jonny Carson, NBC, L.A., 1983—; actress-comedienne The Half Hour Comedy Hour, Dick Clark, L.A., 1983; comedienne Bizarre/John Beiner, Toronto, Can., 1983; actress commls. L.A., 1983—; comedienne Bob Munkhouse Show, London, 1983; actress-comedienne Saturday Night Live, NBC, N.Y.C., 1986—. Actress series Half Nelson, NBC, L.A., pilot Walter Fox, L.A. Actress (films) Stoogemania, Double Exposure, The Pick Up Artist, 1986, Baby Boom, 1987, Couch Trip, 1987, Dream a Lil Dream, 1988, Casual Sex, 1988, UHF with Weird Al, 1989, Family Business, 1990, I Love You to Death, 1990. Mem. ASCAP, SAF, AFTRA. Baptist. Avocations: motherhood, photography, gymnastics.

JACKSON, WANDA BRITTON, elementary school educator; b. Marshall, Tex., Jan. 21, 1954; d. Arthur Britton, Sr. and Nuthel (Sparks) Britton; children: Giles Lee, Henry Olden Jr. BS in Social Sci. Composite, Wiley Coll., 1975; MS in Edn., Tex. So. U., 1981. Cert. social sci. composite Tex. Edn. Agy., mid-mgmt. supt. Tex. Edn. Agy. Tchr. Houston Ind. Sch. Dist., 1975—. Instr. South Dist. Houston Ind. Sch. Dist., 1992—94, yearbook sponsor Evan E. Worthing H.S., 1995—, instr. Crispus Attucks Mid. Sch., 1991—92, instr. Albert L. Thomas Mid. Sch., 1975—91, 1994—95. Active MacGregor Place Civic Club; active voter registration Harris County. Recipient Outstanding Texan award in the field edn., Tex. Black Legis. Caucus, 1991. Mem.: NEA, Houston Tchrs. Assn., Tex. State Tchrs. Assn., Iota Phi Lambda (pres. Beta Pi chpt. 1991—95, 2nd v.p. Beta Pi chpt.). Baptist. Avocations: cooking, swimming, travel. Home: 5119 Stuyvesant Ln Houston TX 77021 E-mail: wjackso6@houston.org.

JACKSON, WILFRIED, banker; b. Lima, Peru, Feb. 15, 1955; came to U.S., 1970; s. Jack and Beni (Rivera) J.; m. Lina Belkis Leon, June 18, 1981 (div. June 1984); m. Linda Sue Matheney, Aug. 31, 1985; children: Nichole Brooke, Blake Wilfried. AS, Miami Dade C.C., 1977; BSEE, Fla. Internat. U., South Miami, 1980, BSIE, 1981. Prodn. ops. ACR Electronics, Hollywood, Fla., 1979-80; mgr. field svcs. ops. Modems Plus, Miami Lakes, Fla., 1980-82; mgr. complex sys. integration Timeplex-Unisys, Tampa, Fla., 1982-84; mgr. advanced Telecomm. sys. Bank of Am.-Internat., Miami, 1984-86; mgr. C.I.O. consumer bank Citibank N.A., Ft. Lauderdale, Fla., 1986-95; pres., CEO Citibank Nev., The Lakes, 1995—. Bd. dirs. Nev. Devel. Authority, Las Vegas; mem. adv. bd. Nev. Capital Devel. Corp., Las Vegas, 1995—. Contbr. articles to profl. jours. Mem. Nev. Bankers Assn. (bd. dirs. 1996—). Republican. Presbyterian. Avocation: flying. Home: 5312 NW 109th Way Coral Springs FL 33076-2750 Office: Heidrick & Struggles 5301 Blue Lagoon Dr Ste 590 Miami FL 33126

JACKSON, WILLIAM DAVID, research and development company executive; b. Edinburgh, Scotland, May 20, 1927; came to U.S., 1955, naturalized, 1968; s. Joseph and Margaret (Johnston) Jackson; m. Eleanor Burdeshaw; children from previous marriage: Margaret Eleanor, David Foster. B.Sc., U. Glasgow, Scotland, 1947, PhD, 1960; postgrad., U. Strathclyde, Glasgow, 1948. Apprentice English Electric Co., Stafford, 1945-47; research asst. elec. engring. dept. U. Strathclyde, Glasgow, 1948-51; lectr. elec. engring. U. Manchester, Eng., 1951-55, 57-58; vis. lectr. dept. elec. engring. MIT, 1955-57, asst. prof., 1958-62, assoc. prof., 1962-66, lectr. elec. engring., 1968-73; vis. prof. Tech. U., Berlin, 1966; prof. elec. engring., dept. energy engring. U. Ill., Chgo., 1966-67; prin. rsch. scientist, dir. tech. edn. Avco-Everett Rsch. Lab., Everett, Mass., 1967-72; prof. elec. engring. U. Tenn. Space Inst., Tullahoma, 1972-73; mgr. Electric Power Research Inst., Palo Alto, Calif., 1973-74; mgr. office coal research Interior Dept., Washington, 1974-75; dir. magnetohydrodynamic div. ERDA, Washington, 1975-77; dir. tech. analysis div. Office Energy Research, Dept. Energy, Washington, 1977-79; pres. Energy Cons., Inc., 1979-84, HMJ Corp., 1982—. Professorial lectr. George Washington U., 1979—91, vis. prof., 1986—87, adj. prof., 1991—; cons. numerous indsl. firms and govt. agencies, 1948—; bd. dirs. Hexogon Inc., prodn. v.p., 1999—2001; bd. dirs. Clean Energy Combustion, Inc., 2001—03; mem. Internat. Magnetohydrodynamic Liaison Group, 1966—, chmn., 1969—74, sec., 1986—2002; coord. coop. program magnetohydrodynamic power generation U.S.-USSR, 1974—79; mem. numerous govt. and internat. coms. and panels. Editor: Electricity From MHD, 1968; editorial bd.: Internat. Jour. Elec. Engring. Edn, 1962-70; editor-in-chief Magnetohydrodynamics: An Internat. Jour., 1987-92. U.K. Fulbright scholar, 1955-57; recipient ILG award Internat. Magnetogydrodynamic Liaison Group, 2005 Fellow Instn. Elec. Engrs. (past com. sec., chmn.), IEEE (sec.-treas. prof. group biomed. electronics Boston sect. 1962-63, energy devel. subcom. 1973—, chmn. 1988-98, energy devel. and power gen. com. 1986-99, mem. steering com. intersoc. energy conversion engring. conf. 1988—2002, conf. program chair 1989, conf. gen. chair 1996, 2002), ASME (past chmn. adv. energy systems divn., energy com. 1986-90), AIAA (assoc.; Energy Sys. award 1995); mem. AAUP, AAAS, Am. Phys. Soc., Am. Soc. Engring. Edn., Sigma Xi. Office: 2814 Jutland Rd Kensington MD 20895-2840 Office Phone: 301-946-1586. E-mail: hmjcorpwdjackson@aol.com.

JACKSON, WILLIAM ELMER, JR., retired packaging company administrator; b. Washington, Pa., Oct. 25, 1935; s. William Elmer and Hazel Celestine (Moore) Jackson; m. Suzanne P. Jackson; children: Randall Lee, Barry Howard. BS in Indsl. Engring., Okla. U., 1966; MBA in Fin., U. Mo., Kansas City, 1970. With Sealright Co. Inc., Overland Pk., Kans., 1966—98, corp. econ. evaluation engr., 1966—69, process engr. central div, 1969—72, profit evaluation specialist, cen. div., 1972—74, corp. mgr. econ. evaluation, 1974—75, corp. ops. analysis mgr., 1975—78, adminstrv. mgr. cent. div., 1978—81, mfg. and control mgr. cen. div., 1981—83, corp. planning and devel., 1983—91, chmn. eastern div. operational study project, 1976, chmn. corp. mfg. info. requirements study project, 1978, chmn. western div. operational study project, 1984, Kansas City plant relocation project, 1987, mem. bus. profile study team, ea. div. plant rearrangement project, 1989—90, plastics plant operational study, 1990, mfg. mgr. ctrl. divsn., 1991—94; mgr. mfg. tech. transfer sealright flexible packaging group, 1994—98. Mng. dir. Sealright of Australia, Brisbane, 1996—98; sec., treas., dir. Agrl. Tech. Internat. Mktg., Inc., Louisburg, Kans., 1984—85. Com. chmn., merit badge counselor Troop 278 Heart of Am. coun. Boy Scouts Am., 1972—74; adv. Jr. Achievement of Greater Kansas City, 1974—75; mem. Brisbane Christian Cmty. Choir, 1996—97, Johnson County Assn. Retarded Citizens, Queensland C. of C., 1996—97; caravan dir. Overland Park Nazarene Ch., 1968—74, mem. choir, 1968—81, 1989—95, 1998—, ch. bd., 1976—79, 1988—95, 1998—, ch. treas., 1977—78, fin. com., 1976—78, mem. house com., 1978—79, 1990—92, vice chmn. fin. com., 1990—91, chmn. youth ministries bd., 1990—93, mem. pers. com., 1992—95, mem. fin. com., 1993—95, 2000—02, chmn. facility comm., 2002—04; chmn. adv. bd. mid-mgmt. program Penn Valley C.C., Kansas City, Mo., 1980—84, 1987—93. With USAF, 1955—59. Mem.: Inst. Indsl. Engrs. (sr.), Fishing Club Am. Republican. Personal E-mail: jackj@attglobal.net.

JACKSON, WILLIAM GENE, computer company executive; b. Opelika, Ala., Nov. 22, 1946; s. John Willis and Lucy (Jackson) J.; m. Rosalyn Miller, June 17, 1989; children: Verzelia Yvett, Gena Nichole, William Gene, Alisa, Claire Bennett. BS in Mgmt. and Mktg., Syracuse U., 1979, AAS in Mgmt., 1976; postgrad., Pace U. With IBM, 1966—, customer engr. Huntsville, Ala., 1966-72, sr. customer engr. Atlanta, 1972-73, field mgr. Miami, Fla., 1973-75, eastern region ops. analyst Harrison, N.Y., 1975-76; br. mgr. N.Y.C., 1976; region ops. mgr. region 3 Montvale, N.J., 1977-78; employee rels. program mgr. pers., office products divsn. hdqrs. Franklin Lakes, N.J., 1979; adminstrv. asst. to dir. ops. west, office products divsn. hdqs., 1980; IBM corp. svc. staff Armonk, N.Y., 1981-82; adminstrv. asst. to pres. customer svc. divsn. Franklin Lakes, 1983; region mgr. customer svc. divsn., region 7 Southfield, Mich., 1983-84; dir. svc. support Nat. Svc. divsn. Area 4, 1984-87; regional mgr., 1987-92; dir. quality U.S. Great Lakes area 4, 1992-95; corp. dir. teleops., 1995-98; dir. copr. mktg. global call ctrs., 1998—. Mem. Corp. Telecomm. Coun., IBM, Worldwide Call Ctr. Ops. Bd., Steering Bd., Internat. Quality and Productivity Bd.; dir., CIO global I/T Teleweb Integraion Corp. Bd. dirs. spl. affairs Jaycees, Wanaque, N.J., 1978-79; mem. Black exec. exch. program Nat. Urban League. Mem. Am. Mgmt. Assn., Am. Exec. Mgmt. Excellence, Am. Execs. for Mgmt. Excellence, Am. Soc. for Quality Control. Office: IBM Corp 18000 W 9 Mile Rd Southfield MI 48075-4009

JACKSON, WILLIAM PAUL, JR., lawyer; b. Bexar, Ala., July 7, 1938; s. William Paul and Evelyn Mabel (Goggans) J.; m. Barbara Anne Seignious, Sept. 30, 1966; children: Jennifer Anne, Susan Barrett, William Paul III. BS in Physics, U. Ala., 1960, JD, 1963. Bar: Ala. 1963, D.C. 1969, Va. 1975. Law clk. to judge Ala. Ct. Appeals, Montgomery, 1965; assoc. Bishop and Carlton, Birmingham, Ala., 1965-68, Todd, Dillon and Sullivan, Washington, 1968-70; founding ptnr. Jackson & Jessup, Washington, 1970-75, Arlington, Va., 1975—76; pres., sr. atty. Jackson & Jessup, PC, Arlington, 1976—2001, McLean, Va., 2002—. Advisor Oren Harris chair of transp. U. Ark., 1974-91. Comments editor U. Ala. Law Rev., 1962, leading articles editor, 1963; conbtr. articles to profl. jours. V.p. McLean Hunt Homeowners Assn., Va., 1974, pres., 1975-76; bd. dirs. McLean Citizens' Assn., 1976-78; pres. McLean Legal Action Fund, Inc., 1977-81; session mem. Lewinsville Presbyn. Ch., 1981-84; v.p. The Marjoribanks Family, 1994-96, pres., 1996-98; active The Alexandria Chorale, 1985-94. 1st lt. Signal Corps, U.S. Army, 1963-65. Recipient Pub. Service awards Am. Radio Relay League, 1958, Merit award Armed Forces Comm. and Electronics Assn., 1963; Sigma Delta Kappa scholar, 1963. Mem. ABA, Ala. State Bar, Va. State Bar, DC Bar, Bar Assn. DC (chmn. computer tech. com. 1998-2000, chmn. mem. com. 2000-01, treas. 2001-02, bd. dirs. 2002-03, chmn. website com. 2004, Presdl. award 2000), Transp. Lawyers Assn. (chmn. legis. com. 1989-90), Bar Assn. D.C. Found. (bd. dirs. 1999-2001), Assn. for Transp. Law, Logistics and Policy (nat. pres. 1991-92, chmn. nominating com. 1992-93, chmn. membership com. 1993-99, chmn. DC chpt. 1989-90, com. govtl. rels. 1975-90, motor editor Assn. Highlights 1992-98, Presdl. award 1994, 99), So. Transp. Logistics Assn. (exec. dir. 1970-99), Ea. Indsl. Traffic League (exec. dir. 1978-88), Bench and Bar Legal Honor Soc. (pres. 1963), Farrah Law Soc. (trustee 2000—), Nat. Soc. DAR (bd. advisors to pres. gen. 2004—), Omicron Delta Kappa Presbyterian (elder). Avocation: amateur radio operator. Home: 1003 Spring Hill Rd Mc Lean VA 22102-1331 Office: Jackson & Jessup PC PO Box 4030 Mc Lean VA 22103 E-mail: wpj@translaw.com.

JACKSON, WILLIAM RICHARD, entrepreneur; b. Nampa, Idaho, Aug. 23, 1936; s. Richard W. and Josie P. (Mulder) J.; m. Marilyn Kay Samp, June 10, 1956 (div. 1975); children: James Lee, Robbi Jo, Jolynn Kay. BA in Secondary Edn., N.W. Nazarene Coll., Nampa, 1957; MA in Secondary Edn. Adminstrn., U. No. Colo., 1961; EdM, U. Denver, 1964, PhD in Higher Edn. Adminstrn. and Rsch., 1991; PhD in, Stanford U., 1991. Owner, operator Janitorial Svc., Walla Walla, Wash., 1950-54; account mgr., collection contractor Montgomery Ward, Walla Walla, Wash., 1953-57; exec. ins. dir. edn. svcs. Idaho Sch. Employment, Boise, 1957-58; sch. tchr., football coach Humanities, Speech & Art, Caldwell, Idaho, 1958-60; tchr. psychology and econs. Englewood (Colo.) Sch. Dist., 1961-64; dir. student coun. Brook Forest Leadership Inst., Evergreen, Colo., 1961-64; co-owner, operator Jackson Bros. Investments, Englewood, 1970-84; co-owner, pres. Internat. Bell Mus., Inc., Evergreen, 1978-86; pres. Jackson Bros. Industries, Evergreen, 1984—, Jackson Internat., Inc., Evergreen, 1984—. Chmn. bd. Petro Silver, Inc., Denver, 1979-83; rsch. cons. in agr., toxic waste remediation and hyperbaric oxygenation medicine; sr. cons. Envrion. Health Found., San Francisco; mem. staff Southwest Rsch. Inst., San Antonio, Tex. Co-author: Brook Forest Leadership Curriculum, 1964, Disciplining Curriculum, 1978; author: Hyperbaric Oxygenation Effects on the Cognitive Function of Memory, Barter, The History, Mystery and Mastery of Mutual Exchange, Humic, Fulvic and Micorbial Balance: Organic Soil Conditioning, Environmental Care & Share, 1995, The Arthritis, Osteoporosis and Silica Link, The Calcium Deception, Fabulous Fulvic Electrolyte, 1995. Co-founder Benevolent Brotherhood Found., Denver, 1971—; bd. dirs. Ch. of the Nazarene, past chmn. bd. edn. Grantee Denver Presbyn. Med. Ctr., 1991, Hyperbaric Oxygen Therapy System, San Diego, 1991, Denver, 1991; recipient 1st Pl. Nat. Self-Publishing award Writer's Digest, 1993. Mem. Internat. Found. Hyperbaric Medicine, Undersea and Hyperbaric Med. Soc. (rsch. cons. 1990—), Stanford U. Alumni Assn., Phi Delta Kappa. Republican. Avocation: bartering. Office: Jackson Internat Rsch Ctr PO Box 1749 Evergreen CO 80437-1749 Personal E-mail: wirjak@jps.net.

JACKSON, WILLIAM VERNON, Latin American studies educator, library science educator; b. Chgo., May 26, 1926; s. William Olof and Lillian (Scharenberg) J. BA summa cum laude, Northwestern U., 1945; MA, Harvard U., 1948, PhD, 1952; MS in L.S., U. Ill., 1951; Diploma honoris causa, U. Central Venezuela, 1968. Tchr. York Community High Sch., Elmhurst, Ill., 1946-47; teaching fellow Harvard U., 1948-50; spl. recruit Libr. of Congress, 1951-52; libr., asst. prof. libr. sci. U. Ill., Urbana, 1952-58, assoc. prof., 1958-62, U. Wis., Madison, 1963-65, faculty rsch. fellow, summers, 1963, 64; prof. libr. sci., dir. internat. libr. info. ctr. U. Pitts., 1966-70; prof. libr. sci. George Peabody Coll. for Tchrs., 1970-76; prof. Spanish and Portuguese Vanderbilt U., Nashville, 1970-76; prof. libr. sci. U. Tex. at Austin, 1976-86, prof. emeritus, 1986—, assoc. Inst. Latin Am. Studies, 1976—. Vis. lectr. U. Minn. Library Sch., summers 1954-56, Columbia U. Sch. Library Service, summers 1960, 90, Syracuse U. Sch. Libr. Sci., summer 1962, Simmons Coll. Sch. Libr. Sci., summer, 1974, 75, Coll. Librarianship, Aberystwyth, Wales, summer 1977, U. Zulia, Maracaibo, Venezuela, summer 1980, Dominican U. Libr. Sci., summers 1981-84, 86, 89-98, 2000, 02-05, Pratt Inst. Sch. Info. & Libr. Sci., summers 1995-98, Coll. of St. Catherine, summer 1999, 2001, L.I. U. Palmer Sch. Libr. and Info. Sci., summer 2001, U. South Fla. 2005; vis. prof. Inter-Am. Libr. Sch., U. Antioquia, Medellín, Colombia, 1960, 68, adviser internat. exec. coun., 1961-63; cons. State Dept., 1956, 59, 61, 62, 67, 77, 2002, 03, 04; Regional AID Office for Ctrl.Am. and Panama, 1965-66, AID Mission to Brazil, 1967-72, AID Mission to Colombia, 1970-71, USIA, 1979-80, 85, 87, 89-92, 94-2000, OAS, 1970-71; Coun. Rectors Brazilian Univs., 1972; cons. rsch. librs. N.Y. Pub. Libr., 1965-70, Hispanic Found., Library Congress, Washington, 1964-65; Fulbright research scholar, France, 1956-57; Fulbright lectr. U. Córdoba (Argentina), 1958, adviser, 1970; adviser U. San Marcos, Peru, 1962, 75; external examiner U. West Indies, Jamaica, 1974-78; cons. Bibliothèque Nationale, France, 1979, 81-87; official rep. 350th anniversary Harvard U., 1986, Libr. of Congress Bicentennial, 2000; sr. fellow Dominican U., 1989—; vis. prof. faculty philosophy and letters U. Buenos Aires, 1991; dir. various activities on the Quin centennial and librs. in Latin Am., 1992; adv. U. Francisco Marroquín, Guatemala, 1992—; U. del Norte, Barranquilla, Colombia, 1993, various univs. and librs. in El Salvador, 1994—, Nat. Libr. and Archives Sch., Mexico City, 1995; advisor Francisco Marroquin Found., 2002--; pres. Coun. Books and Librs. in L.Am., 1993—; lectr. in field *Jackson has long specialized in library development in Latin America, as well as in Latin American collections in the United States. He has made over 90 trips to all parts of the region as consultant to the U.S. government and to many institutions and associations, lecturer, visiting professor and participant in professional meetings. He has written many books, reports, articles, and reviews. In addition, Jackson has studied and written on important American and foreign research libraries. He continues to lecture on philanthropy, higher education, Latin America, libraries and cultural affairs and to give seminars on international librarianship and great libraries and their collections.* Author: Basic Library Techniques, 1955, A Handbook of American Library Resources, 1955, 2d edit., 1962, Studies in Library Resources, 1958, The Foundation Grants Program, 1959, The Libraries of the Associated Colleges of the Midwest, 1960, Aspects of Librarianship in Latin America, 1962, second series, 1992, Library Guide for Brazilian Studies, 1964, The National Textbook Program and Libraries in Brazil, 1967, Resources of Research Libraries, 1969, Steps Toward the Future Development of a National Plan for Library Services in Colombia, 1971, Catalog of Brazilian Acquisitions of Library of Congress, 1964-74, 1977, Resources for Brazilian Studies at the Bibliothèque Nationale, 1980, Library Resources of Harvard University, 1986, Las Megabibliotecas, una Bibliografía Comentada, 1993, Resources of Research Libraries: A Bibliographical Guide to Printed Material, 1998, Nueve Bibliotecarios Distinguidos, 2004; editor: U. Ill. Library Sch. Assn. News Letter, 1954-56, Assn. Coll. Research Libraries Monographs, 1961-66, Latin Am. Collections, 1974, Reference Publications in Latin American Studies, 1977-92, Library and Information Science Education in the Americas: Present and Future, 1981, Library and Information Science in France: A 1983 Overview, 1984, Doce Bibliotecarios Latinoamericanos, 1992; mem. editorial staff Libr. Trends, 1958-62, Ency. Libr. and Info. Sci., 1971-90, Jour. Libr. History, 1976-88, Internat. Jour. Revs. in Libr. and Info. Sci., 1985-88; assoc. editor World Librs., 1990-99, consulting editor, 2000-; contbr. articles to profl. jours. and encys. Mem. ALA (chmn. internat. relations round table 1965-66, trustee endowment funds 1977-86), Ill. Library Assn., Assn. Library and Info. Sci. Edn., Bibliog. Soc. Am., Assn. Coll. and Research Libraries, MLA, Am. Assn. Tchrs. Spanish and Portuguese, Theatre Library Assn., Conf. on Latin Am. History, Latin Am. Studies Assn., Sem. on Acquisition Latin Am. Library Materials (pres. 1977-78), Assn. Caribbean Univ. and Research Libraries, Asociación Paceña de Bibliotecarios (hon.; La Paz, Bolivia), Henry Wade Rogers Soc., Phi Beta Kappa, Beta Phi Mu (pres. 1955-56), Phi Sigma Iota, Sigma Delta Pi (hon.), Phi Lambda Beta (hon.) Clubs: Harvard (Chgo.), Caxton (Chgo.). Home: 196 W Kathleen Dr Park Ridge IL 60068-2618 Office: U Tex Sch Info 1 University Station D 7000 Austin TX 78712-0390

JACKSON, YOCONTALIE ANN, entertainment company executive; b. Camden, N.J., Nov. 8, 1957; d. James Washington and Rosalie Jackson; m. Stanley Leo Jackson; children: Amanda, Kirby. BA, Rutgers U., 1982; MA, So. N.H. U., 1997. Cert.: (paralegal). Paralegal Penn Mutual Life Ins., Phila., 1980—86; divsn. dir. developmental planning City of Camden, NJ, 1988—; CEO East Coast Entertainment Group, Camden, 1991—, Jackson & Assocs., Lindenwold, NJ, 1993—. Bd. dirs. Eleon Dance Co., Phila., 1989—. Prodr.(writer): (recording) Church Folk, 2001; performer (recording) He's Everything to Me, 1993, Anyway You Bless Me, 1995; exec. prodr.(writer): (live recording) An Evening of Elegance with Connie Jackson. Bd. dirs. Friends of Creative Arts, Camden, 2001—, Camden Bd. Edn., 1996, v.p., 1997. Named to Hall of Fame, Woodrow Wilson H.S., Camden, 1998; recipient Image award, Found. 2000, 1996. Mem.: Nat. Alliance of Mkt. Developers. Baptist. Avocations: tennis, basketball, jogging, ping pong/table tennis, chess. Home: 28 Wright Ave Lindenwold NJ 08021

JACKSON, YVONNE, pharmaceutical executive; m. Fred Jackson. BA, Spelmen Coll.; MA, Harvard U. Various mgmt. positions Sears, Roebuck & Co., Torrance, Calif., N.Y.C.; sr. human resources positions Avon Products, Inc., 1980—93; sr. v.p. worldwide human resources Burger King Corp., 1993—99; sr. v.p. human resources Compaq Computer Corp., Houston, 1999—2002, Pfizer, Inc., 2003—. Apptd. Pfizer Leadership Team; chmn. bd. trustees Spelman Coll.; bd. dirs. Inst. Women's Policy Rsch., Girls, Inc.; mem. adv. bd. Catalyst. Office: Pfizer Inc 235 E 42d St New York NY 10017 Office Phone: 212-733-2323.*

JACKSON-CALLANDRET, SHIRLEY LORRAINE, music educator; b. New York city, NY, Aug. 4, 1964; d. Grover and Bert Jackson; m. Shirley Lorraine Jackson, Feb. 24, 1990. BA, Bennett Coll., 1982—86; MA, Fla. Atlantic U., 2000—02. Music tchr. Roward County Pub. Schools, Fort Lauderdale, Fla., 1988—. Adjudicator Broward County NAACP ACTSO Talent Competition, Ft. Lauderdale, Fla., 1991—93; treas. Broward County Music Educator Conf., Ft. Lauderdale, Fla., 1994—95; coord. Broward County Area Music In Our Schools Month, Ft. Lauderdale, Fla., 1995; adjudicator Omega Psi Pfi Frat. Talent Hunt, Ft. Lauderdale, Fla., 1995—2000; coord. Broward County Elem. Honor Choir, Ft. Lauderdale, Fla., 1995, Broward County North Area Music In our Sch. Month Concert, Ft. Lauderdale, Fla., 1995—96; adjudicator South Fla. Regional Showtime At The Apollo Auditions, Ft. Lauderdale, 1995; membership Music Educators Nat. Conf., Ft. Lauderdale, Fla., 1988—; grade chairperson N. Andrews Gardens Elem. Sch. Performing Arts Dept., Ft. Lauderdale, Fla., 2000—01, magnet coord., 2001—. Music director: performance Fla. Citrus Bowl, Disney Magic Music Days; music teacher (performance) Miami Heat Halftime Show, Music Usa Festival (first pl. in elem. show choir category, 2000), Annie Jr; Fiddler On The Roof, Jr; Oklahoma; Into The Woods, Jr. Music dir. Rising Stars Summer Theatre Camp, Ft. Lauderdale, Fla., 1999—2001. Mem.: Nat. Aspiring Educators Sch. Pers., Fed. Educators Assn., Broward County Teachers Union, Fla. Music Educator Assn. (corr.), Nat. Dance Alliance (assoc.). Avocations: singing, dance, travel. Home: 11440 NW 41 St Sunrise FL 33323 Office: Broward County Schools/ North Andrews Ga 345 NE 56 St Fort Lauderdale FL 33334 E-mail: shirlnotes@aol.com.

JACKSON LEE, SHEILA, congresswoman; b. Queens, N.Y., Jan. 12, 1950; d. Erica Shelwyn and Jason Cornelius Bennett; m. Elwyn C. Lee; 2 children. BA, Yale U., 1972; JD, U. Va., 1975. Sr. counsel select com. on assassinations U.S. Ho. of Reps., 1977; trial atty. Fulbright and Jaworski, 1978-80; sr. atty. United Energy Resources, Inc., 1980; assoc. judge Houston Mcpl. Ct., 1987-89; mem. Houston City Coun., 1990-94, U.S. Congress from 18th Tex. dist., 1995—, Homeland Security Com.; mem. judiciary com., sci. com.; ranking dem. subcom. immigration and claims, mem. crime subcom. Mem. Select Com. Homeland Security; 1st vice chmn. Congl. Black Caucus; founder bipartisan Congl. Children's Caucus. Mem.: Tex. State Bar, Tex. Mcpl. Judges Assn., State Bar Assn. Justice Com. Democrat. Office: US House Reps 2435 Rayburn Ho Office Bldg Washington DC 20515-4318 Office Phone: 202-225-3816.*

JACKSON MCCABE, JEWELL, not-for-profit developer; b. Wash., DC, Aug. 2, 1945; d. Hal Jackson; m. Frederick Ward (div.); m. Eugene L. McCabe, Jr. (div.). Attended, Bard Coll., 1963—66; doctorates (hon.), Iona, Tugaloo Coll. Dir. pub. affairs NY Urban Coalition, 1970—73; pub. rels. officer Special Svc. Children NYC, 1973—75; assoc. dir. pub. info. Women's Divsn. Office Gov., NY State, 1975—77; dir. gov. comm. affairs WNET-TV/Thirteen, 1977—82; pres. Nat. Coalition 100 Black Women, 1977—91, chair, 1981—; pres. Jewell Jackson McCabe Assoc. Bd. mem. Reliance Group Holdings, Inc., Alight.com, NYC Investment Fund, Wharton Sch. Bus., Bard Coll., Nat. Alliance Bus., NYC Partnership, Rsch. Am., NYC Commn. Status Women, Children's Advocacy Ctr. Manhattan; chair NY State Job Training Partnership Coun. Mem. US Holocaust Meml. Coun., NY State Coun. on Fiscal and Econ. Priorities. Recipient Guild award, Urban League, 1979, Civic award, Seagrams, 1980, 1980, Cmty. Leadership award, Malcolm/King Coll., 1980. Office: Nat Coalition 100 Black Women Inc 38 W 32nd St Ste 1610 New York NY 10001-3816 Office Phone: 212-947-2196.

JACKSON-MENALDI, MARIA CRISTINA, speech pathology/audiology services professional, educator; d. Eleazar Acisclo Ametrano-Jackson and María Magdalena Ametrano Jackson; m. José Luis Menaldi; 1 child, Veronica Estela Menaldi. PhD in Speech Lang. Pathologist and Audiologist, U. Museo Social Argentino. Dir. Lakeshore Profl. Voice Ctr., Lakeshore Ear, Nose and Throat Ctr., St. Clair Shores, Mich., 1990—2005. Adj. prof. dept. otolaryngology Wayne State U., Sch. of Medicine, St. John Hosp., DMC and Harper Hosp., Detroit, 1996—2005; prof. Sch. Medicine, Buenos Aires, Córdoba, Rosario; spkr. in field. Musician (choir dir. and voice specialist); contbr. articles to profl. jours., chapters to books. Scholar Rotary Internat., U. Sorbonne, 1978. Mem.: Internat. Assn. Logopedics and Phoniatrics (assoc.), Nat. Voice Found. (assoc.). Roman Catholic. Achievements include research in the speaking, singing voice and allergy related to voice problems. Avocations: piano, languages, travel. Office: Lakeshore Profl Voice Center 21000 E Twelve Mile Rds Ste 111 Saint Clair Shores MI 48081 Office Phone: 586-779-7610. Personal E-mail: jmenaldi@wayne.edu.

JACKSON-TKAC, STEPHANIE ANN, nurse; b. Thomasville, NC, Jan. 2, 1960; d. Ellis Wade and Nancy (Myers) Jackson. BSN, East Carolina U., 1982. RN, cert. case mgr., infusion nurse. Staff nurse Pitt County Meml. Hosp., Greenville, N.C., 1981-83, N.C. Bapt. Hosp., Winston-Salem, N.C., 1983-87, Duke U. Med. Ctr., Durham, N.C., 1987-91, Rex Hosp., Raleigh, 1991—92; nurse clinician Health Infusion, Morrisville, 1992—95, Coram Health Care (formerly Health Infusion), Morrisville, 1992—94, infusion care mgr. Goldsboro and Kinston brs., 1995-96; with Chartwell S.E., 1996-97; per diem case mgr. Columbia Home Care, Raleigh, N.C.; home health per diem clin. nurse U. N.C., Chapel Hill; collections spec. Am. Red Cross; case mgr. Killette and Assocs., Inc., 1999—2004; nurse cons. PPD Med. Comm., Durham, NC, 2004; med. case mgr. Crawford & Co., Raleigh, NC, 2005—. Mem.: Infusion Nurses Soc., Case Mgr. Soc. Am. Republican.

JACO, WILLIAM H., mathematics professor, researcher; b. Grafton, W.Va., July 14, 1940; s. William Howard Sr. and Catherine Virginia (White) J.; children: William, Brent; m. Linda Kanewske, May 6, 1978; children: John, Andrew. BA magna cum laude, Fairmont (W.Va.) State Coll., 1962; MA, Pa. State U., 1964; PhD, U. Wis., 1968. Project mathematician Ordinance Rsch. Lab., University Park, Pa., 1962-64; asst. prof. U. Mich., Ann Arbor, 1968-73, Rice U., Houston, 1970-73, assoc. prof., 1973-78, prof., 1978-82; head dept. math. Okla. State U., Stillwater, 1982-87, prof. math., 1982-93; exec. dir. Am. Math. Soc., Providence, R.I., 1988-95; Grayce B. Kerr prof. math. Okla. State U., Stillwater, 1993—. Mem. Joint Policy Bd. for Math., Washington, 1988-95, Bd. Math. Scis., Washington, 1987-90, Inst. for Advanced Study, 1971-72, 78-79, 86; vice chmn. R.I. Math. Scis. Edn. Coalition, Providence, 1990; sr. rsch. fellow Math. Scis. Rsch. Inst., 1984-85, Am. Inst. Math., 2000, bd. dirs. 1997-; professorial rsch. fellow U. Melbourne, Australia, 1987-88, 95-96; Gehring vis. chair. U. Mich., 2005-. Author: Lectures on Three-Manifolds, 1977; co-author: Seifert Fibered Manifolds, 1979; editor: Contemporary Math., 1985-88; contbr. articles to profl. jours. Active Bd. Edn. Devel. Fund, Providence, 1991-95; mem. adv. bd. Roger Williams Coll. Sch. Sci. and Math., Bristol, R.I., 1990-95. Graduate fellow NSF, 1964-67, Postdoctoral fellow NSF, 1971-72; Rsch. grantee, NSF, 1968-88, 96—. Fellow AAAS. Office: Okla State Univ Math Dept 401 Math Scis Stillwater OK 74078-0001 Office Phone: 405-744-5688. Business E-Mail: jaco@math.okstate.edu.

JACOB, ANDREW C, banker; b. Detroit, Mich., Sept. 12, 1960; s. Jacob S Robert and Mavis Jacob, Jerome N Lubin (Stepfather); m. Kristin Austin, Apr. 26, 2002. BS in health, physical edn., Oreg. State U., 0200. Tchg. State of Ariz., 1983. Dir. health and phys. edn. YM YWHA Wash. Heights and Inwood, N.Y.C., NY, 1983—85; CEO Superfit Inc., Clearwater, Fla., 1985—99; pres. World Wide Fin. Services, Inc., Southfield, Mich., 1999—2002; CEO Blue Fin., Phoneix, Ariz., 2002—, Eleabs123.com, 2002—. Author: Secrets Rich People Don't Want You To Know (Ernst and Young Entepenuer of the yr. Finaist, 1998), Secrets Mortgage Companies Don't Want You To Know; contbr. articles to mags.; featured (mortgage expert) CBS, ABC, FOX, NBC. Office Phone: 602-682-BLUE. Personal E-mail: jacob@cashfastfinance.com.

JACOB, BERNARD MICHEL, architect; b. Paris; arrived in U.S., 1950, naturalized; s. Paul and Therese (Abase) J.; m. Rosamond Gale Tryon; children: Clara, Paul. Diploma in architecture, Cooper Union; BArch, U. Minn. Registered architect, Minn. Sr. designer Ellerbe Assocs., St. Paul; head design Grover Dimond & Assocs., St. Paul; co-founder Team 70 Architects, St. Paul, 1970—, pres., 1977—83, Bernard Jacob Architects Ltd., Mpls., 1983—. Mem. constrn. panel Am. Arbitration Assn., 1973—; lectr. Sch. Architecture, U. Minn., Mpls., 1982— Editor: Architecture Minn. Mag., Minn. Soc. Architects, 1970-80; archtl. criticism columnist: Mpls. Star and Tribune, 1980-83, Corp. Report Mag., 1983; reviewer: (archtl. books) Choice Mag.; co-author: Skyway Typology/Mpls., Pocket Architecture/A Walking Guide to the Architecture Downtown Mpls. and St. Paul, 2d. rev. edit., 1988, Letters to Palladio, 1999. Founding chmn. Heritage Preservation Commn., St. Paul; past mem. St. Paul Planning Bd.; apptd. mem. Minn. State Designer Selection Bd., 1987-90; bd. dirs. Winslow House, 1995-97; chmn. archtl. subcom. Minn. Gov.'s Residence Coun., 1996-99. Fellow: AIA. Office: Bernard Jacob Architects Ltd 412 Foshay Tower 821 Marquette Ave Minneapolis MN 55402-2915 Office Phone: 612-332-5517. Business E-Mail: palladio@skypoint.com.

JACOB, BRUCE ROBERT, law educator; b. Chgo., Mar. 26, 1935; s. Edward Carl and Elsie Berthe (Hartmann) J.; m. Ann Wear, Sept. 8, 1962; children: Bruce Ledley, Lee Ann, Brian Edward. BA, Fla. State U., 1957; JD, Stetson U., 1959; LLM, Northwestern U., 1965; SJD, Harvard U., 1980; LLM in Taxation, U. Fla., 1995. Bar: Fla. 1959, Ill. 1965, Mass. 1970, Ohio 1972. Asst. atty. gen. State of Fla., 1960-62; assoc. Holland, Bevis & Smith, Bartow, Fla., 1962-64; asst. to assoc. prof. Emory U. Sch. Law, 1965-69; rsch. assoc. Ctr. for Criminal Justice, Harvard Law Sch., 1969-70; staff atty. Cmty. Legal Assistance Office, Cambridge, Mass., 1970-71; assoc. prof. Coll. Law, Ohio State U., 1971-73, prof., dir. clin. programs, 1973-78; dean, prof. Mercer U. Law Sch., Macon, Ga., 1978-81; v.p., dean, prof. Stetson U. Coll. Law, St. Petersburg, Fla., 1981-94, dean emeritus, prof., 1994—. Contbr. articles to profl. jours. Mem. Fla. Bar, Sigma Chi. Democrat. Home: 1946 Coffee Pot Blvd NE Saint Petersburg FL 33704-4632 Office: Stetson U Coll Law 1401 61st St S Saint Petersburg FL 33707-3246 Office Phone: 727-562-7866. Business E-Mail: jacob@law.stetson.edu.

JACOB, DEIRDRE ANN BRADBURY, manufacturing executive, business educator, consultant; b. Providence, Mar. 7, 1952; d. John Joseph and Marion Damon (Shute) Bradbury; m. Thomas Keenan, Nov. 15, 1975 (div. Dec. 1980); 1 child: Victoria Irene; m. Robert A. Jacob, June 22, 1996; 1 child, Meggin Rosemary. BA in Govt. and Law, Lafayette Coll., 1973. Supr. Procter & Gamble Mfg. Co., S.I., N.Y., 1973-76, mgr. warehouse dept., 1976-79, mgr. shortening and oils, 1979-81, fin. mgr. food plant, 1981-82, mgr. personnel, 1982-86, mgr. total quality and pub. affairs, 1986-91; ptnr. Avraham Y. Goldratt Inst., New Haven, 1991—2005, exec. v.p., 2005—. Cons. Procter & Gamble, S.I., 1987—89, Cin., 1989—91. Trustee Lafayette Coll., 1985-90. Mem. Lafayette Coll. Alumni Assn. (pres. 1992-94, Clifton P. Mayfield award), Maroon Club (Easton, Pa., pres. 1987-89). Roman Catholic. Avocation: singing. Office: Avraham Y Goldratt Inst 442 Orange St New Haven CT 06511-6201 E-mail: dee.jacob@goldratt.com.

JACOB, EDWIN J., lawyer; b. Detroit, Aug. 25, 1927; s. A. Aubrey and Estelle R. (Vesell) J.; m. Constance Dorfman, June 15, 1948; children—Louise B., Beth D., Ellen P. AB cum laude, Harvard U., 1948, JD cum laude, 1951. Bar: N.Y. 1951, U.S. Dist. Ct. (so. dist.) N.Y. 1953, U.S. Dist. Ct. (ea. dist.) N.Y. 1953, U.S. Ct. Appeals (2d cir.) 1954, U.S. Supreme Ct. 1963, U.S. Ct. Appeals (8th cir.) 1981, U.S. Ct. Appeals (10th cir.) 1987. Assoc. Davis Polk Wardwell Sunderland & Kiendl, N.Y.C., 1951-62; ptnr. Cabell, Medinger, Forsyth & Decker, N.Y.C., 1962-69, Lauterstein & Lauterstein, N.Y.C., 1969-72, Jacob, Medinger & Finnegan, LLP, N.Y.C., 1973—. Bd. advisors Inst. for Health Policy Analysis, Georgetown U., 1987-90. Contbr. articles to profl. jours. Mem. nat. bd. Assn. Ref. Zionists Am., 1991-97; trustee Stephen Wise Free Synagogue, 1991—, pres., 1994-96. With USN, 1945-46 Mem. Am. Law Inst., Am. Judicature Soc., Assn. Bar City N.Y. Clubs: Harvard of N.Y.C. Office: Jacob Medinger Finnegan LLP 1270 Ave of Americas New York NY 10020

JACOB, FRANÇOIS, biologist, educator; b. Nancy, France, June 17, 1920; s. Simon and Therese (Franck) Jacob; m. Lysiane Bloch, Nov. 27, 1947 (dec. 1984); children: Pierre, Laurent, Odile, Henri; m. Geneviève Barrier, 1999. MD, Faculty of Medicine, Paris, 1947; D.Sc., Faculty of Scis., Paris, 1954; D.Sc. (hon.), U. Chgo., 1965; Dr honoris causa, various univs. Asst. Pasteur Inst., 1950—56, head dept. cellular genetics, 1960—92, pres., 1982—88; prof. cellular genetics Coll. of France, 1964—92; prof. emeritus Coll. of France and Inst. Pasteur, 1992—. Author: (books) The Logic of Life, 1970, The Possible and the Actual, 1981, The Statue Within, 1987, Of Flies, Mice and Men, 1997. Recipient Charles Leopold Mayer prize, 1962, Nobel prize in physiology and medicine (with A. Lwoff and J. Monod), 1965. Mem.: Royal Acad. Scis. Madrid, Acad. Scis. Hungary, Royal Acad. Medicine Belgique, Royal Soc. (London), Am. Philos Soc., Nat. Acad. Scis., Am. Acad. Arts and Scis. (fgn.), Royal Danish Acad. Scis. and Letters (fgn.), Acad. Française Paris, Acad. Sci. (Paris). Achievements include research in on genetics bacterial cells and viruses; contbr. to mechanisms of information transfer (messenger RNA) and genetic basis of regulatory circuits, early stages of the mouse embryo. Office: Pasteur Inst 25 Rue du Dr Roux 75724 Paris Cedex 15 France Office Phone: 01-45-68-84-87. Business E-Mail: fjacob@pasteur.fr.

JACOB, MARVIN EUGENE, lawyer; b. N.Y.C., Feb. 4, 1935; s. Sam Jacob and Ann (Garfinkel) Law; m. Atara Binnun, Mar. 27, 1960; children: Shalom J., Aviva, Asher. BA, Bklyn. Coll., 1961; JD cum laude, N.Y. Law Sch., 1964. Bar: N.Y. 1964, U.S. Supreme Ct. 1967. Assoc. regional adminstr. SEC, N.Y.C., 1964-79; ptnr. Weil, Gotshal & Manges, N.Y.C., 1979—. Adj. prof. law N.Y. Law Sch., 1972-97. Editor: Restructurings, 1993, Reorganizing Failing Businesses, 1999. Mem. ABA, N.Y. State Bar Assn. Office: Weil Gotshal & Manges 767 5th Ave Fl 29 New York NY 10153-0023 Business E-Mail: marvin.jacob@weil.com.

JACOB, PAUL BERNARD, JR., electrical engineering educator; b. Columbus, Miss., June 9, 1922; s. Paul Bernard and Sarah Dorsey (Jamison) J.; m. Mildred Evelyn Hammack, Aug. 20, 1946; children: William Boswell, Paul Bernard, III. BS in Elec. Engring., Miss. State U., 1944; MS, Northwestern U., 1948. Registered profl. engr., Miss. Engr., Tenn. Eastman Corp., Oak Ridge, 1944-46; mem. faculty Miss. State U., 1946-88, prof. elec. engring., 1956-88, prof. emeritus, 1988—, assoc. head dept., 1962-88, Paul B. Jacob high voltage lab. and Paul B. Jacob endowed prof. chair elec. and computer engring. dept. Cons. in field; mem. steering com. Internat. Symposium on High Voltage Engring., 1987—. Author articles on high voltage engring. Recipient Alumnus of Yr. award Miss. State U., 1987, UOP Tech. award Instrument Soc. Am., 1988 Mem. IEEE (life), Power Engring. Soc. (chmn. com., Com. Disting. Svc. award), Am. Soc. Engring. Edn., Sigma Xi, Tau Beta Pi, Eta Kappa Nu (dir. 1962-63, nat. v.p. 1982-83, nat. pres. 1983-84), Phi Kappa Phi, Sigma Alpha Epsilon (bd. dirs. 1961-69, nat. pres. 1969-71, Disting. Svc. award 1975, Highest Effort award for profl. accomplishments 1986, Merit Key award, Order of the True Gentleman 1994), Omicron Delta Kappa. Clubs: Rotary (past pres. Starkville, Miss.). Baptist. Home and Office: 102 Kenswick Ct Starkville MS 39759-9493 E-mail: pbj@ece.msstate.edu.

JACOB, ROBERT JOSEPH KASSEL, computer scientist, educator; b. Nov. 11, 1950; s. Ezekiel Joseph and Ethel Charlotte (Behr) Jacob; m. Kathryn Ann Allamong, June 9, 1973; children: Charlotte Allamong, Anne Elizabeth. BA, Johns Hopkins U., 1973, MSE, 1974, PhD, 1976. Tchg. asst., rsch. asst. Johns Hopkins U., Balt., 1972—76; computer scientist Naval Rsch. Lab., Washington, 1977—94; assoc. prof., lectr. George Washington U., Washington, 1978—94; assoc. prof. Tufts U., Medford, Mass., 1994—. Vis. prof. media lab. MIT, Cambridge, Mass., 2000—01. Assoc. editor: ACM Trans on Computer-Human Interaction, 1992—; contbr. chpts. to books, articles to profl. publs. Fellow, Johns Hopkins U., 1973—75. Mem.: IEEE, Human Factors Soc., Assn. Computing Machinery (vice pres. Spl. Interest Group Computer-Human Interaction 2001—, Recognition of Svc. award 1994, 1999, 2004). Jewish. Avocations: sailing, piano, designing electronic organs. Home: 30 Valleyfield St Lexington MA 02421-7908 Office: Tufts U Dept Computer Sci Medford MA 02155

JACOB, ROSAMOND TRYON, librarian; b. Mpls., May 20, 1928; d. Philip Dorn and Rachel Chase (Denison) Tryon; m. Bernard Michel Jacob, Feb. 17, 1951; children: Clara, Paul. BA summa cum laude, Smith Coll., 1949; MA in Libr. Sci., U. Minn., 1974. Sec. Thames & Hudson Pubs., N.Y.C., 1950-51, Columbia Law Sch., N.Y.C., 1952-54, U. Minn., Mpls., 1955-59; libr. St. Paul Pub. Libr., 1976—98, ret. Coun. mem. Depository Libr. Coun. to Pub. Printer, Washington, 1985-88. Co-author: Minnesota State Documents: A Guide for Depository Libraries, 1984; author: (newsletter) Documents/Classified, 1980-96; editor: (newsletter) DOCSOUP, 1980-90. Mem. St. Paul LWV, 1965—. Mem. ALA (Bernadine Abbott Hoduski Founder award govt. documents roundtable divsn. 1994), Minn. Libr. Assn. (Disting. Achievement award 1990).

JACOB, STANLEY WALLACE, surgeon, educator; b. Phila., 1924; s. Abraham and Belle (Shulman) J.; m. Marilyn Peters; 1 son, Stephen; m. Beverly Swarts; children: Jeffrey, Darren, Robert; m. Gail Brandis; 1 dau., Elyse. MD cum laude, Ohio State U., 1948. Diplomate Am. Bd. Surgery. Intern Beth Israel Hosp., Boston, 1948-49, resident surgery, 1949-52, 54-56; chief resident surg. svc. Harvard Med. Sch., 1956-57, instr., 1958-59; assoc. vis. surgeon Boston City Hosp., 1958-59; Kemper Found. rsch. scholar ACS, 1957-60; asst. prof. surgery U. Oreg. Med. Sch., Portland, 1959-66, assoc. prof., 1966—; Gerlinger prof. surgery Oreg. Health Scis. U., 1981—. Author: Structure and Function in Man, 5th edit, 1982, Laboratory Guide for Structure and Function in Man, 1982, Dimethyl Sulfoxide Basic Concepts, 1971, Biological Actions of DMSO, 1975, Elements of Anatomy and Physiology, 1989; contbr.: Ency. Britanica. Served to capt. M.C. AUS, 1952-54; col. Res. ret. Recipient Gov.'s award Outstanding N.W. Scientist, 1965; 1st pl. German Sci. award, 1960; Markle scholar med. scis., 1960. Mem. Phi Beta Kappa, Sigma Xi, Alpha Omega Alpha. Achievements include co-discovery of therapeutic usefulness of dimethyl sulfoxide and MSM. Home: 1055 SW Westwood Ct Portland OR 97239-2708 Office: Oreg Health Scis U Dept Surgery 3181 SW Sam Jackson Park Rd Portland OR 97239 Office Phone: 503-494-8474. Business E-Mail: jacobs@ohsu.edu.

JACOB, WALTER CHARLES, lawyer; b. Rockville Centre, N.Y., May 18, 1945; s. Andrew Geza Jacob and Julia Rose Davidis; m. Jennie Ann, Aug. 5, 1972 (div. mar. 1983); children: Wendy Ann, Todd Andrew; m. Avelina Sharpless Jacob, Apr. 16, 1983; 1 child, Allison Elizabeth. BA, Roanoke Coll., 1968; JD, Washington & Lee U., 1971. Assoc. Hall, Monahan, Engle, Mahan & Mitchell, Leesburg, Va., 1971-76, ptnr., 1976-81; prin. Walter C.Jacob, P.C., Leesburg, Va., 1981—. Mem. Rep. Senatorial Inner Cir., Washington, 2000. Mem. Am. Trial Lawyers Assn., Va. Trial Lawyers Assn., Loudoun County Bar Assn. Roman Catholic. Avocations: boating, travel, physical fitness. Home: 4 Thorton Ct Sterling VA 20165 Office: Walter C Jacob PC PO Box 66 Leesburg VA 20178 E-mail: walterc jacobpc@aol.com.

JACOB, WENDY, artist, art educator; BA, Williams Coll., 1980; MFA, Sch. of Art Inst. Chgo., 1989. Instr. performance dept. The Sch. of the Art Inst. of Chgo., 1993; asst. prof. dept. sculpture Coll. Fine Arts Ill. State U.; asst. prof. visual arts MIT, Cambridge, 1999—. Mem. HaHa artists collaborative, 1989—. Work has appeared at, Whitney Mus. Art, NYC, Galerie Walcheturm, Zurich, The Sch. of the Art Inst. of Chgo., Emmanuel Perrotin, Paris, Galerie Karin Schorm, Vienna, Milw. Inst. Art & Design, Schipper and Krome, Cologne, Germany, Centre Nat. d'Art Contemporain, Grenoble, France, Temple Gallery, Tyler Sch. Art, Phila., Krannert Art Mus., U. Ill., Champaign, Cranbrook Art Mus., Cranbrook Acad. Art, Bloomfield Hills, Mich., MIT List Visual Arts Ctr., Cambridge, Chgo. Project Rm., Kemper Mus. Contemporary Art, Kansas City, Madison Art Ctr., Wis., Centre Georges-Pompidou, Paris, Forum for Contemporary Art, St. Louis, Mass. Mus. Contemporary Art, Kunsthaus Graz, Austria. Recipient Bicentennial Medal for disting. achievement, Williams Coll., 1996; New Forms Regional Initiative Grant (with HaHa), Nat. Endowment for the Arts/Rockefeller Found., 1988, Ill. Arts Coun. Artist's Fellowship Award, 1989, Cmty. Arts Assistance Program Grant (with HaHa), City of Chgo., 1990, Louis Comfort Tiffany Found. Artist Fellowship (with HaHa), 1993, Arts Internat. Travel Grant (with HaHa), 1993, U. Rsch. Grant, Ill. State U., 1996, 1998, Creative Capital Found. Grant, 1999, Ill. Arts Coun. Artist's Fellowship Award, 1999, HASS Rsch. Award, MIT, 2001, Class of 1947 Career Devel. Professorship, 2001—04, Mary I. Bunting Inst. Fellow, Radcliffe Inst. Advanced Study, Harvard U., 2004—05. Office: MIT Visual Arts Program 265 Massachusetts Ave N51-317 Cambridge MA 02139*

JACOBI, BONNIE SCHAFFHAUSER, music teacher, pianist; b. Edison, N.J., Dec. 21, 1969; d. Robert Edward and Kathleen Janice Schaffhauser; m. Kenneth William Jacobi, June 14, 1997. BA in Music cum laude, Mt. Holyoke Coll., 1991; MMusic in Piano Performance, U. Tex., 1995; DMA in Music Edn., U. Houston, 2001. Co. mem. Austin Contemporary Ballet, Austin, 1994-95; dance instr. Dancers Workshop, Austin, 1995-96; piano instr. Houston Music Inst., 1996-98; choir dir., organist Christ United Ch. of Christ, Cypress, Tex., 1997-99; music instr. U. Houston Moore Sch. Music, 1996—; music dir., instr., choreographer Banff Pvt. Sch., Houston, 1996—. Music instr., composer Middlesex Sch. Summer Arts, Concord, Mass., 1989, Concord, 90; founder, dir. Austin Sacred Dance Ensemble, 1995—96; mem. Roger Sessions Soc., Wilmington, NC, 1999—. Composer original children's musical Every Kid, 1990; musical dir./composer, adapted 3 children's musicals. Mem. The Humane Soc., Houston, 1998—, Soc. for Prevention of Cruelty to Animals, Houston, 1998—. Recipient 3d prize Internat. Bartok Piano Competition, 1994; Van Cliburn Summer Piano Inst. scholar, 1995. Mem.: Soc. for Am. Music (clinician), Houston Music Tchrs. Assn., Tex. Music Educators Assn. (clinician), Music Tchrs. Nat. Assn., Coll. Music Soc. (clinician), Music Educators Nat. Conf., Pi Kappa Lambda. Methodist. Avocations: ballet, gardening, photography, cinema.

JACOBI, FREDRICK THOMAS, newspaper publisher; b. Neenah, Wis., July 10, 1953; s. H. Paul and Patricia Mary (Steele) J.; m. Kim Lee Muenchow, Aug. 23, 1980; children: James Paul, Steven Thomas. AA in Bus., U. South Fla., 1973; BBA in Fin., Mktg., U. Wis., 1976; MBA in Mktg., U. Wis., Whitewater, 1980. Cert. newspaper circulation. City dist. mgr. Madison (Wis.) Newspapers Inc., 1977-79, city circulation mgr., 1979-80, circulation mgr., 1980-81, mktg. mgr., 1981-82, circulation dir., 1982-85, Gannett Co., Inc., Reno, Nev., 1985-88, regional circulation dir. Arlington, Va., 1988-90; pub., pres. Wausau (Wis.) Daily Herald, Gannett Co., Inc., 1990-92, Springfield (Mo.) News-Leader, 1993-96; v.p. Midwest region Gannett Co., Inc., 1993-96; pub., pres. Ft. Myers (Fla.) News-Press, 1996-2000, Rockford (Ill.) Register-Star, 2000—. Bd. dir. Coun. of 100, Rockford Coll., Inland Press Found.; com. chmn. Sales and Mktg. Exec., Madison, Ill., 1985. Editor Circulation-Central States, 1985. Program chmn. Jr. Achievement of Nev., Reno, 1987—88; pres. Springfield Bus. and Devel. Corp., 1996; bd. dir. Ozarks Press Assn., Make A Wish Mo., Horizon Econ. Devel., 1997—2000, Lee County Pub. Schs. Found., 1997—2000. Mem.: Newspaper Assn. Am., Inland Press Assn., Ill. Press Assn., Young Pres.'s Orgn., The Exec. Com., Rotary. Republican. Roman Catholic. Avocations: micro-computers, running, gardening. Office: Rockford Register Star 99 E State St Rockford IL 61104 Office Phone: 815-987-1451. E-mail: fjacobi1@rockford.gannett.com.

JACOBI, PETER PAUL, journalism educator, writer; b. Berlin, Mar. 15, 1930; came to U.S., 1938, naturalized, 1944; s. Paul A. and Liesbeth (Kron) J.; m. Harriet Ackley, Dec. 8, 1956 (div. 1979); children: Keith Peter, John Wyn. BS in Journalism, Northwestern U., 1952, MS, 1953. Mem. journalism faculty Northwestern U., Evanston, Ill., 1955-81, profl. lectr., 1955-63, asst. prof., 1963-66, assoc. prof., 1966-69, prof. journalism, 1969-81, assoc. dean, 1966-74; communications cons. N.Y.C., 1980-84, Bloomington, Ind., 1985—; prof. journalism Ind. U., Bloomington, 1985-99, prof. emeritus, 1999—. News assignment editor, newscaster, theatre and music reporter NBC, Chgo., 1955-61; news editor ABC, Chgo., 1951-53; radio commentator on music and opera, 1958-65; theatre and film critic Sta. WTTW, Chgo., 1964-74, arts critic, 1975-77; theatre and film critic Hollister Newspapers Suburban Chgo., 1963-70; music columnist Chicagoan mag., 1973-74; script cons. Goodman Theater, Chgo., 1973-75; syndicated commentator on arts and media N.Am. Radio Alliance, 1978-80; arts corr. Christian Sci. Monitor, 1956-81; music critic, columnist Bloomington (Ind.) Herald-Times, 1985—; columnist Arts Indiana, 1987-2001, Editors Only, 1994—, Editor's Workshop, 1995-98. Author: Writing with Style, The News Story and the Feature, 1982, The Messiah Book-The Life and Times of G.F. Handel's Greatest Hit, 1982, (with Jack Hilton) Straight Talk about Videoconferencing, 1986, The Magazine Article: How to Think It, Plan It, Write It, 1991, (with others) From Budapest to Bloomington, Janos Starker and the Hungarian Cello Tradition, 1999; contbg. essayist Lyric Opera Companion, 1991; editor Chgo. Lyric Opera News, 1958-61, Music Mag./Musical Courier, Chgo., 1961-62; contbr. articles on writing to Folio, Ragan Report, other mags., articles on arts to Sat. Rev., Chgo. Daily News, N.Y. Times, Highlights for Children, World Book, others. Mem. AAUP, NATAS, Assn. Edn. in Journalism, Soc. Profl. Journalists, Ind. Arts Commn. (chmn. 1990-93), Arts Midwest, Bloomington Cmty. Arts Commn. Home: 3003 N Browncliff Ln Bloomington IN 47408-1317 Office: Ind U Sch Journalism Bloomington IN 47405 Office Phone: 812-334-0063.

JACOBOWITZ, ELLEN SUE, curator; b. Detroit, Feb. 21, 1948; d. Theodore Mark and Lois Clairesse (Levy) Jacobowitz. BA, U. Mich., 1969, MA, 1970; postgrad. in art history, Bryn Mawr Coll., 1976-83; postgrad., Wharton Sch., 1997. Curator Phila. Mus. Art, 1972-90; adminstr. Cranbrook Inst. Sci., Bloomfield Hills, Mich., 1991-94; adminstr. Temple Emanu-El, Oak Park, Mich., 1995-96. Cons. ArtServe Mich., 1997; primary caregiver, 1998—2004. Author: The Prints of Lucas Van Leyden, 1983, American Graphics, 1860-1940, 1982. Treas. Sat. Luncheon Club, 1995—96, pres., 1999—2000; active Leadership Oakland, Detroit Inst. Arts; bd. dirs. Nat. Coun. Jewish Women, Detroit, 1990—91, Print Coun. Am., Balt., Netherlands Am. Amity Trust, Washington, 1982—84, Mich. Mus. Assn., 1993—94. Mem.: Detroit Inst. Arts, U. Mich. Alumni Assn., Am. Jewish Com. Avocations: cooking, gardening, reading, the arts, sports.

JACOBOWITZ, HAROLD SAUL, lawyer; b. N.Y.C., Aug. 26, 1950; s. William and Miriam (Spector) J.; m. Estrella B. Rivera, Oct. 26, 1972. BA, CUNY, 1972; JD, Rutgers U., 1977. Bar: N.Y. 1977, U.S. Dist. Ct. (so. dist.) N.Y. 1978, U.S. Dist. Ct. (ea. dist.) N.Y. 1978. Assoc. Goldman & Heffernan, N.Y.C., 1977-78; assoc. Zola & Zola, N.Y.C., 1978-79, Goldberg & Lysaght, N.Y.C., 1979-82; from atty. of record to cons. Am. Internat. Group (Jacobowitz, Spessard, Garfinkel & Lesman), N.Y.C., 1982—2001, cons., 2002—04, FOJP Svc. Corp., N.Y.C. Arbitration panel U.S. Dist. Ct. (ea. dist.) N.Y. Mem. ABA, N.Y. State Bar Assn., Assn. Bar City N.Y., N.Y. County Lawyers Assn., Assn. Trial Lawyers N.Y.C. (bd. dirs.).

JACOBS, ALAN MARTIN, physicist, researcher; b. N.Y.C., Nov. 14, 1932; s. Samuel J. and Amelia M. (Ziegler) J.; m. Evelyn Lee Banner, Aug. 7, 1955 (dec. Jan. 1977); children: Frederick Ethen, Heidi Joelle; m. Sharon Lynn Auerbach, Oct. 14, 1978; children: Aaron Michael, Seth Joseph. B.Engring. Physics (John McMullen scholar, LeVerne Noyes scholar, Clevite scholar), Cornell U., Ithaca, N.Y., 1955; postgrad., Oak Ridge Sch. Reactor Tech., 1955-56; MS, in Physics, Pa. State U., 1958, PhD, 1963. Research asso. nuclear reactor facility Pa. State U., 1956-63, mem. faculty, 1963—, prof. nuclear engring., 1968-80; prof. U. Fla., Gainesville, 1980—, chmn. dept. nuclear engring. scis., 1980-82; chief scientist Future Tech, Inc., Gainesville, 1986-87. Cons. to industry. Co-author: Basic Principles of Nuclear Science and Reactors, 1960; patentee dynamic radiography, control of radiation beams by vibrating media, multichannel radiograph, digital x-ray imaging system, snapshot backscatter x-ray imaging system, radiography by selection detection scatter field components. NSF sci. faculty fellow, 1960-61; recipient Glenn Murphy award for nuclear sci. edn. ASEE, 1994. Mem.: Tau Beta Pi, Sigma Xi, Pi Mu Epsilon. Home: 3718 SW 80th Dr Gainesville FL 32608-3662 Office: Dept Nuclear & Radiol Engring U Fla Gainesville FL 32611-8300 E-mail: jacobs@ufl.edu.

JACOBS, ALBERT LIONEL, JR., lawyer; b. Pitts., May 6, 1939; s. Albert Lionel and Sarah Edith (Burns) J.; m. Laurel Elizabeth Moore, Dec. 20, 1960 (div. 1982); children: Laura Jean, Patricia Anne, Albert Lionel III, Robert Charles, Michael Peter; m. Carol S. Fisher, Feb. 6, 1983; children: Daniel Stephen, David Andrew. BA, Harvard U., 1961; JD, Columbia U., 1964. Bar: N.Y. 1964, D.C. 1966, U.S. Dist. Ct. (so., ea., no.), N.Y. 1969, U.S. Dist. Ct. (we. dist.), N.Y. 1978, U.S. Ct. Appeals (D.C. cir., 2d cir.), U.S. Ct. Appeals (1st cir.), 1968, U.S. Ct. Appeals (9th cir.)1982, U.S. Ct. Appeals (10th cir.), U.S. Ct. Appeals (fed. cir.), U.S. Ct. Claims, U.S. Supreme Ct. Ptnr. Jacobs & Jacobs, NYC, 1965-70, pres., chmn. bd. dirs., 1970; pres., ptnr., chmn.

intellectual property dept. Rosenman & Colin, NYC, 1991; now shareholder, nat. chair, intellectual property dept. Greenberg Traurig, LLP, NYC. Bd. dirs. A.L.E. Industries, Inc., N.Y.C., Meditech Ltd., Chappaqua, N.Y., Internat. Bioimmune Systems, Inc. Bd. dirs. Chappaqua (N.Y.) Children's Workshop, 1990-93. Mem. ABA, Harvard Club (N.Y.C., mem. bd. ho. com., chmn. athletic com., chmn. food and wine com.), Univ. Club, N.Y. Athletic Club, Met. Squash Rackets Assn. Avocations: food and wine, squash, skiing, tennis. Office: Greenberg Traurig LLP MetLife Bldg 200 Park Ave New York NY 10166 Office Phone: 212-801-9200. Office Fax: 212-801-6400. Business E-Mail: jacobsa@gtlaw.com.

JACOBS, ANDREW ROBERT, lawyer; b. Newark, Sept. 18, 1946; s. Seymour B. and Pearle (Flaschen) J.; m. Yardana Steinberg, July 10, 1976; 1 child, Suzanne Michal. BA with high honors, Rutgers U., 1968; JD, Columbia U., 1971. Bar: N.J. 1971, D.C. 1976, U.S. Dist. Ct. N.J. 1971, U.S. Ct. of Appeals (3rd cir.) 1974, U.S. Supreme Ct. 1979, U.S. Dist. Ct. (ea. and so. Dists.) N.Y. 1980, N.Y. 1980, Pa. 1981, U.S. Ct. Appeals (2nd cir.) 1984, U.S. Claims Ct. 1986. Law clk. to chief judge U.S. Dist. Ct., Newark, 1971-72; asst. U.S. atty. U.S. Atty.'s Office, Newark, 1972-76; assoc. Cole Berman & Belsky, Rochelle Park, N.J., 1976, Lanigan O'Connell Jacobs & Chazin, Basking Ridge, N.J. and N.Y.C., 1977-78, ptnr., 1979-82; asst. U.S. atty., chief spl. pros., dep. chief criminal div. U.S. Atty.'s Office (ea. dist.), N.Y., 1983-85; ptnr. Horowitz & Jacobs, Hackensack, N.J. and N.Y.C., 1985-89, Gern, Dunetz, Davison & Weinstein, Roseland, N.J. and N.Y.C., 1990-93, Fitzsimmons Ringle & Jacobs, Newark, N.J., Hackensack, N.J. and N.Y.C., 1993-2000, Epstein, Fitzsimmons, Brown, Gioia, Jacobs and Sprouls, P.C., Chatham, Newark, Hackensack, N.Y.C., 2000—. Faculty Practicing Law Inst., N.Y.C., 1980—82; legal writing instr. N.Y. Law Sch., 1981—82; master Justice William J. Brennan, Jr. Inn of Ct., 1995—. Trustee N.J. YM-YWHA Camps, Fairfield, NJ, Milford, Pa., 1985—, pres., 2001—04; trustee Congregation Shomrei Emunah, Montclair, NJ, 1985—96; pres. Rutgers Coll. Alumni Class 1968. Capt. U.S. Army, 1997. Harlan Fiske Stone scholar; recipient U.S. Dept. Justice Spl. commendation award, 1973, 75, U.S. Dept. Treasury ATF cert. of Appreciation, 1976, Jerome Michael prize for Excellence in Trial Advocacy Columbia U. Mem.: ATLA, ABA, Million Dollar Advs. Forum, Assn. Fed. Bar N.J., Essex County Bar Assn., Bergen County Bar Assn., Morris County Bar Assn., Assn. Criminal Def. Lawyers N.J., N.Y. State Trial Lawyers Assn., N.Y. County Lawyers Assn. (fed. cts. com.), N.J. State Bar Assn., Soc. Loyal Sons and Daus. of Rutgers Coll. (elected), Phi Beta Kappa. Home: 47 Haller Dr Cedar Grove NJ 07009 Office: Epstein Fitzsimmons Brown Gioia Jacobs & Sprouls PC Box 901 245 Green Village Rd Chatham NJ 07928 also: 83 Maiden Ln 13th Fl New York NY 10038 also: 2 University Plz Ste 18 Hackensack NJ 07601-6202 also: 50 Park Pl Ste 903 Newark NJ 07102 Office Phone: 973-593-4900. E-mail: ajacobs@epsteinfitz.com.

JACOBS, ARNOLD STEPHEN, lawyer; b. NYC, Feb. 26, 1940; s. Charles Edwin and Harriet (Flug) Jacobs; m. Ellen Margaret Kheel, June 10, 1962; children: Beryl Kheel, Arnold Stephen Jr. BME, Cornell U., 1961, MBA, 1963, LLB with distinction, 1964. Bar: NY 1964. Assoc. Hughes, Hubbard & Reed, NYC, 1964-65, 1967-71; ptnr. Shea & Gould, NYC, 1971-94, Proskauer Rose LLP, NYC, 1994—. Adj. prof. NYU Law Sch., NYC, 1977—91. Author: The Impact of Rule 10b-5, 3 vols., 1974, Litig. and Practice Under Rule 10b-5, 6 vols., 1981—2001, Manual of Corp. Forms for Securities Practice, 4 vols., 1981—, Opinion Letters in Securities Matters: Text-Clause-Law, 3 vols., 1980—, Section 16 of the Securities Exchange Act, 2 vols., 1989—, Disclosure and Remedies Under the Securities Laws, 6 vols., 2002—, The Williams Act: Tender Offers and Stock Accumulations, 1vol., 2005; contbr. articles to profl. jours. Capt. U.S. Army, 1965—67, Korea. Mem.: Assn. Bar City NY (chmn. securities regulation com. 1982—86), NY State Bar Assn., Harmonie Club (NYC). Home: 108 E 82nd St Apt 7A New York NY 10028-1136 Office: Proskauer Rose LLP 1585 Broadway New York NY 10036-8299 Office Phone: 212-969-3210. E-mail: ajacobs@proskauer.com.

JACOBS, ARNOLD STEPHEN, writer, commentator; b. NYC, Mar. 20, 1968; s. Arnold Stephen Jacobs Sr. and Ellen Kheel Jacobs; m. Julie Schoenberg Jacobs, Sept. 9, 2000; 1 child, Jasper Kheel. BA, Brown U., 1990. Commentator NPR, N.Y.C; sr. editor Entertainment Weekly, N.Y.C., 1995—2000; editor at large Esquire, N.Y.C., 2003—; columnist Life Mag., N.Y.C., 2004—, Mental Floss Mag., N.Y.C., 2004—. Editor: What It Feels Like; author: The Know-It-All, America Off-Line, Fractured Fairy Tales, The Two Kings: Jesus and Elvis. Avocations: travel, reading. Office: Esquire 1790 Broadway New York NY 10019 Office Phone: 212-649-4256.

JACOBS, BRADLEY S., rental company executive; CEO Amerex Oil Assocs., Inc., 1979-83; chmn., COO Hamilton Resources Ltd., 1984-89; founder, chmn., CEO United Waste Sys., Inc., 1989-97; co-founder, chmn., CEO United Rentals, Greenwich, 1997—. Office: 4 Greenwich Office Park Greenwich CT 06831-5153

JACOBS, BRUCE EDWARD, management consultant; b. St. Louis, Mar. 27, 1952; s. Robert A. and Sara Lee (Brown) J.; m. Linda C. Schneider, May 26, 1973; children— Robert R., Nicholas C., Luke E., B.S., Washington U., 1976. Indsl. engr. Granite City Steel Co. (Ill.), 1974-75; project engr. Emerson Electric Co., St. Louis, 1976-77, sr. project engr., 1977-78; dir. mfg. Schlueter Mfg. Co., St. Louis, 1978-79; prin. White Haven Cons. Group, St. Louis, 1979-83; supr. cons. Fox & Co., St. Louis, 1983—; pres, CEO Grede Foundries, Milw., 1987—; cons. St. Louis Zoo, 1975-76, Mo. Goodwill Industries, 1976-79; lectr. in field. Patentee in field. Mem. Inst. Mgmt. Cons., Am. Inst. Indsl. Engrs. (Region XI dir., pres. 1980, 1st place award in community affairs 1980, chpt. award of excellence 1980). Republican. Roman Catholic. Home: 6909 Dartmouth Ave Saint Louis MO 63130-3133 Office: Grede Foundries 9898 W Bluemound Rd Milwaukee WI 53226-4365 E-mail: bjacobs@grede.com.*

JACOBS, CARYN LESLIE, lawyer, former prosecutor; b. Chgo., Mar. 3, 1958; d. Edward Jesse and Ann Marie (Paun) J.; m. Daniel Goldman Cedarbaum, Sept. 6, 1987; children: Jacob Jesse, Samuel Goldman. AB with distinction, Stanford U., 1980; JD cum laude, Harvard U., 1983. Bar: Ill., U.S. Dist. Ct. (no. dist.) Ill. 1984, U.S. Ct. Appeals (8th cir.) 1986, U.S. Ct. Appeals (7th cir.) 1987. Law clk. U.S. Dist. Ct. (no. dist.) Ill., Chgo., 1983-85; assoc. Mayer Brown & Platt, Chgo., 1985-88; asst. U.S. atty. Chgo., 1988-93; ptnr. Mayer Brown Rowe & Maw, Chgo., 1993—. Mem. ABA. Mem. Phi Beta Kappa. Office: Mayer Brown Rowe & Maw 190 S LaSalle St Chicago IL 60603-3441

JACOBS, CHARLES NATHAN, editor, writer; b. Paterson, NJ, July 11, 1930; s. Samuel I. and Beatrice J. (Levine) J.; m. Joan Stearns Weiss, May 30, 1953 (div. 1979); children: Julie Gail, JoDee Winger; m. Rosalind H. Eigenfeld, Feb. 21, 1987. BA in Humanities, Columbia Coll., 1952; MS in Journalism, Columbia U., 1953. Reporter N.Y. Jour. Am., N.Y.C., 1950-53; owner Jacobs Dept. Store, Paterson, 1955-80; pub. Alameda Newspaper Group, San Francisco, 1985-87, Garden State Newspapers, Passaic, NJ, 1985—87; pvt. practice editl. cons. Woodcliff Lake, NJ, 1988—90; editor FOCUS Mag., Totowa, N.J., 1990-92; pres., pvt. practice editl. cons. CJ Enterprises, Woodcliff Lake, 1992—; editor Travel World Internat., 2000—02; travel editor That's Life Mag., 2002. Author: The Business of Writing, 1996, (novel) Blood Bond, 2002. Dep. mayor Paterson, 1966-70; campaign mgr. Kramer for Mayor, Paterson, 1966, 70, 74, 78. Sgt. U.S. Army, 1953-55. Recipient Disting. Svc. award Jaycees, Paterson, 1966, Nat. Vol. award Lane Bryant/U.S. Govt., Washington, 1969, various awards Soc. Profl. Journalists, N.Am. Travel Journalists Assn. Mem. N.Am. Travel Journalists Assn. (award winner), N.J. Press Club (award winner), Working Press Assn. (award winner), East West News Bur. (award winner). Jewish. Avocations: skiing, golf, reading, gardening. Home and Office: CJ Enterprises 16 Pinecrest Dr Woodcliff Lake NJ 07677-8220 Office Phone: 201-391-4539. Personal E-mail: jac391@aol.com.

JACOBS, CHARLOTTE DE CROES, medical educator, oncologist; b. Oak Ridge, Tenn., Jan. 27, 1946; BA, U. Rochester, 1968; MD, Washington U., St. Louis, 1972. Diplomate Am. Bd. Internal Medicine, Am. Bd. Med. Oncology, Nat. Bd. Med. Examiners. Intern, jr. resident dept. medicine Washington U. Sch. Medicine, St. Louis, 1972—74; sr. resident dept. medicine U. Calif., San Francisco, 1974—75; postdoctoral fellow divsn. oncology Stanford (Calif.) U. Med. Sch., 1975—77, acting asst. prof. oncology, 1977-80, asst. prof. medicine and oncology, 1980-86, assoc. prof. clin. medicine, 1986-92, assoc. prof. medicine and oncology, 1992-96, prof., 1996—, sr. assoc. dean. edn. and student affairs, 1990-97, acting dir. Clin. Cancer Ctr., 1994-97; dir. Oncology Day Care Ctr. Stanford Med. Ctr., 1977-90, dir. Clin. Cancer Ctr., 1997—2001. Bd. dirs. Nat. Comprehensive Cancer Network, Rockledge, Pa., 1994-2001. Recipient presdl. citation Am. Soc. for Head and Neck Surgery, 1990, Aphrodite Hofsomner award Washington U., 1993. Mem. AMA, Am. Soc. Clin. Oncology (bd. dirs. 1992-95), Am. Assn. for Cancer Rsch. Office: Clin Cancer Ctr Rm 2233 875 Blake Wilbur Dr Stanford CA 94305-5826 Office Phone: 650-725-8738. E-mail: cjacobs@stanford.edu.

JACOBS, CHRISTOPHER B., patent lawyer; b. Ohio, Jan. 18, 1969; BSME, Ohio State U., 1992, JD, 1995. Bar: Ohio 1995, U.S. Dist. Ct. (no. dist.) Ohio 1996, U.S. Ct. Appeals (fed. cir.) 1997, U.S. Patent and Trademark Office 1994. Patent atty., ptnr. Renner, Otto, Boisselle & Sklar, Cleve., 1995—. Mem. Am. Intellectual Property Law Assn., Cleve. Intellectual Property Law Assn. Office: Renner Otto Boisselle & Sklar 1621 Euclid Ave Fl 19 Cleveland OH 44115-2107

JACOBS, DAVID ERNEST, federal agency administrator; married; 2 children. BA in Polit. Sci., Antioch Coll., 1973; BS in Environ. Health, Oakland U., 1983; MS in Tech. and Sci. Policy, Ga. Inst. Tech., 1988; PhD in Environ. Engring., Kennedy Western U., 1998. Cert. indsl. hygienist. Tchg. asst. quantitative analytical chemistry Oakland U., 1982, lectr., coord. qualitative analytical chemistry, 1983; chemist Nat. Stds. Tech. Inc., 1983; environ. rsch. scientist Ga. Inst. Tech., 1983-87, dir. Ga. State Employee Hazardous Chems. Tng. Program, 1987-88, dir. So. Lead-Based Paint Tng. Consortium, 1989-92; dep. dir. Nat. Ctr. for Lead-Safe Housing, Washington, 1992—95, contr., 1995—. Bd. dirs. Nat. Lead Abatement Coun., 1993-95. Author: (Pres.'s task force report) Childhood Lead Poisoning Prevention; contbr. articles to profl. jours. Recipient Spl. Commendation, Dept. Justice, 1999. Mem. APHA, Am. Indsl. Hygiene Assn. (chmn. social concerns com. 1991, nat. nominating com. 1990-92, Ga. sect. sec. 1988, pres. 1989), Am. Acad. Indsl. Hygiene. Office: US Dept HUD 451 7th St SW Rm 7208 Washington DC 20410-0001 Office Phone: 202-607-0938. Personal E-mail: dejacobs@starpower.net. Business E-Mail: david_e._jacobs@hud.gov.

JACOBS, DENNIS, federal judge; b. NYC, Feb. 28, 1944; s. Harry N. and Rose J.; m. Judith Weissman. BA, Queens Coll., 1964; MA, NYU, 1965, JD, 1973. Assoc. Simpson Thacher & Bartlett, NYC, 1973—80, ptnr., 1980—92; judge US Ct. Appeals (2d cir.), NYC, 1992—. Lectr. Queens Coll., 1967—69; mem. Com. on Judicial Resources, Judicial Conf. of US, 1997—, chmn., 1999—. Mem.: Federalist Soc., NYC Bar Assn. Office: US Ct Appeals US Courthouse 40 Foley Sq Rm 1904 New York NY 10007-1502*

JACOBS, DONALD P., retired dean, banking and finance educator; b. Chgo., June 22, 1927; s. David and Bertha (Nevod) J.; children: Elizabeth, Ann, David; m. Dinah Nemeroff, May 28, 1978. BA, Roosevelt Coll., 1949; MA, Columbia U., 1951, PhD, 1956. Mem. research staff Nat. Bur. Econ. Research, 1952-57; instr. Coll. City N.Y., 1955-57; mem. faculty to Morrison prof. fin. Northwestern U. Grad. Sch. Mgmt., 1970-78, chmn. dept., 1969-75, dean, 1975—, Gaylord Freeman Disting. prof. banking, 1978—. Chmn. bd. AMTRAK, 1975-79; bd. dirs. CDW Corp., Prologis Corp., Terex Corp., Conf. Savs. and Residential Financing; co-dir. fin. studies Presdl. Commn. Fin. Structure and Regulation, 1970-71; sr. economist banking and currency com. U.S. Ho. of Reps., 1963-64. Editor proc.: Conf. Savs. and Residential Financing, 1967, 68, 69; contbr. articles to profl. jours. Served with USNR, 1945-46. Ford Found. fellow, 1959-60, 63-64 Mem. Am. Econ. Assn., Am. Statis. Assn., Am. Fin. Assn., Econometrics Soc., Inst. Mgmt. Sci. Office: Northwestern Univ J L Kellogg Grad Sch Mgmt 2001 Sheridan Rd Evanston IL 60208-0814 Office Phone: 847-491-2838.

JACOBS, DONALD PAUL, architect; b. Cleve., Aug. 8, 1942; s. Joseph W. and Minnie Mae (Grieger) J.; m. Sharon Daugherty, Apr. 14, 1963 (dec. Feb. 1992); m. Julie Brinkerhoff, Apr. 24, 1993. BS, U. Cin., 1967. Registered architect, Calif., Tex., Ariz., Nev., Ga., Fla., Colo., Hawaii, N.C., Ill. Draftsman, intern Skidmore, Owings & Merrill, San Francisco, 1967-70; pvt. practice architecture Sea Ranch, 1970-86, chmn. design com., 1975-79; prin. Dorius Archs., Corona del Mar, Calif., 1986-94; pres. JZMK Ptnrs., Irvine, Calif., 1994—. Bd. dirs. Homeaid Am. Prin. works represented to numerous newspapers and magazines. Co-chair Project Playhouse, Homeaid, 1993-95. Mem. AIA (chmn. nat. housing com. 1996, awards 1973-74, 77-78, Bay Area Honor Design Excellence award 1974, Homes for Better Living Merit award 1976, Housing Merit award 1978), Sr. Housing Coun. (bd. dirs. Orange County chpt. 1993-94). Democrat. Avocations: tennis, skiing, hiking. Home: 309 Poppy Ave Corona Del Mar CA 92625-3024

JACOBS, FRANCIS ALBIN, biochemist, educator; b. Mpls., Feb. 23, 1918; s. Anthony and Agnes Ann (Stejskal) J.; m. Dorothy Caldwell, June 5, 1953; children: Christopher, Gregory, Paula, Margaret, John. BS, Regis Coll., Denver, 1939; postgrad, U. Denver, 1939-41; Fellow in Biochemistry, St. Louis U., 1941-49, PhD, 1949. Postdoctoral fellow Nat. Cancer Inst., Bethesda, Md., 1949-51; instr. physiol. chemistry U. Pitts. Sch. Medicine, 1951-52, asst. prof., 1952-54; asst. prof. biochemistry U. N.D. Sch. Medicine, Grand Forks, 1954-56, asso. prof., 1956-64, prof., 1964-87, prof. emeritus, 1987—. Dir., research supr. Nat. Sci. Research Participation Program in Biochemistry, 1959-63; advisor directorate for sci. edn. NSF. Contbr. articles to profl. jours. Mem. bishop's pastoral council Diocese of Fargo, N.D., 1979-86. Fellow AAAS, N.D. Acad. Sci. (editor 1967, 68); mem. Am. Soc. for Biochemistry and Molecular Biology, Am. Soc. for Nutritional Scis., Soc. Exptl. Biology and Medicine, Am. Chem. Soc. (chmn. Red River valley sect. 1971), AAAS, AMA, Sigma Xi (pres. chpt. 1965-66, Faculty award for Outstanding Sci. Resch. U. N.D. chpt. 1982, cert. of recognition 1987), Alpha Sigma Nu, Phi Lambda Upsilon, Phi Rho Sigma. Home: 1525 Robertson Ct Grand Forks ND 58201-7303 E-mail: fjacobs@medicine.nodak.edu. *In teaching and research I find that it is indeed a way of life. Have faith in yourself and your creator. Do what is right, and seek what is true.*

JACOBS, FRANK CHARLES, performing company executive; b. Inpdls., Apr. 9, 1949; s. Ralph Reed and Evelyn Edwina Jacobs; m. Arlene Diane Jacobs, June 6, 1967; children: Brian Douglas, Eric Matthew. BA, DePauw U., 1966, MusB, 1967; MusM, Occidental Coll., 1969; D of Musical Arts, U. Ill., 1973. Prof. music DePauw U., Greencastle, Ind., 1970—75, U. Akron, Ohio, 1975—80; min. music First United Meth. Ch., Cuyahoga Falls, 1980—90; founder., artistic dir. Summit Choral Soc., Akron, 1990—. Home: 2444 Shaddow Ridge Ln Akron OH 44333 Office: Summit Choral Soc 715 E Buchtel Ave Akron OH 44305

JACOBS, GARY N., hotel executive, lawyer; b. NYC, July 12, 1945; m. Robin Jacobs; children: Melissa, Matthew. BA summa cum laude, Brandeis U., 1966; student, London Sch. Economics; LLB, Yale U., 1969. Bar: NY 1970, Calif. 1972. Law clk. Hon. Wilfred Feinberg US Ct. Appeals 2nd cir., 1969—70; from assoc. to ptnr. Wyman, Bautzer, Christensen, Kuchel & Silbert, LA, 1971—88; sr. ptnr. Christensen, Miller, Fink, Jacobs, Glaser, Weil & Shapiro, LLP, LA, 1988—2000, of counsel, 2000—; exec. v.p., gen. counsel MGM Mirage, Las Vegas, 2000—, sec., 2002—. Vis. lectr. UCLA Law Sch., 1982; dir., mem. exec. com. The InterGroup Corp., LA. Bd. governors Am. Jewish Com.; bd. overseers Brandeis U. Grad. Sch. Internat. Economics and Fin.; bd. dirs. Nev. Ballet Theatre; mem. exec. com. Las Vegas Performing Arts Ctr.; bd. dirs. Nev. Cancer Inst. Mem.: Order of Coif, Phi Beta Kappa. Office: MGM Mirage 3600 Las Vegas Blvd South Las Vegas NV 89109 also: Christensen Miller Fink Jacobs Glaser Weil & Shapiro LLP 10250 Constellation Blvd 19th Fl Los Angeles CA 90067*

JACOBS, GARY P., banker; AA in Bus. Mgmt., Crowder Coll.; BS in Bus. Adminstrn., C.W. Post Coll., Greenvale, N.Y. Regional v.p. and sales mgr. Fotomat Corp., Las Vegas, Nev., 1974—82; v.p. and bus. devel. officer Valley Bank of Nev., 1982—90; regional v.p. and bus. devel. officer Primerit Bank, 1990—96; v.p. and br. mgr. Nevada State Bank, 1996—2001, Cal Fed Bank, 2001; asst. v.p. br. mgr. and corp. banker Wells Fargo Bank, 2001—02; v.p. and br. mgr. Valley Bank, 2002—03; area sales mgr. Centex Home Equity, 2003—04; market store mgr. Swaroski Gallery, 2004—05; br. mgr. and loan officer Washington Fed. Savings, 2005—. Address: 4491 Buena Vista Dr Las Vegas NV 89102

JACOBS, GEORGE, broadcast engineering consulting company executive; b. N.Y.C., July 16, 1924; s. Benjamin and Henrietta (Myerson) J.; m. Beatrice Gregerman, May 27, 1947; children: Michele Jacobs Gordon, Joy Jacobs. BEE, Pratt Inst., 1949; MSEE, U. Md., 1960. Registered profl. engr., Md., DC. Govt. exec. Voice of America, USIA, 1949-76; bd. Internat. Broadcasting, Washington, 1976-80; pres. George Jacobs & Assocs., Inc., Silver Spring, Md., 1980—. Commr. Commn. Broadcasting to Cuba, 1983; mem. U.S. Del. major ITU Comm. Confs., 1949-92; sr. advisor to chmn. U.S. Del. ITU Conf. on High Frequency Broadcasting, 1984, 87. Co-author: The Shortwave Propagation Handbook, 1976, 80, rev. edit., 1995; also articles. 2d lt. USAF, 1943-46. Decorated Air medal, 1945; recipient Marconi Gold medal engring. achievement Radio Club of Am., 1977, Superior Honor award U.S. Govt., 1976, Outstanding Performance award 1980; Presdl. Commn. Pres. U.S., 1983; Jack Poppele Broadcast Honor award, 1992, Radio Engring. Achievement award Nat. Assn. Broadcasters, 1997; named to CQ Radio Hall of Fame, 2001. Fellow IEEE, Radio Club of Am.; mem. Assn. Fed. Comms. Cons. Engrs. Avocations: amateur radio, stamp collecting/philately, travel. Office: PO Box 12298 Silver Spring MD 20908-0298 Office Phone: 301-598-1283. E-mail: george@gjainc.com.

JACOBS, GEORGE BRAUN, neurosurgeon; b. Poland, Jan. 9, 1934; naturalized U.S. citizen, 1954; s. Maurice and Lena J.; m. Rosanne Wille, 1980; children: Leigh, Steven, Alec. Jeffrey. Student, NYU, 1952-54; MD, SUNY, Syracuse, 1958; postgrad. in general surgery, Bronx Mcpl. Hosp., 1958-59; postgrad. in neurological surgery, Albert Einstein Coll. of Medicine, 1959-64. Cert. airline transport pilot, flight instr., sr. aviation med. examiner, FAA accident counselor. Attending neurosurgeon Hackensack (N.J.) Med. Ctr., 1965-86, sr. attending neurosurgeon, 1986—, chief neurosurgery sect., 1981-86; attending surgeon Holy Name Hosp., Teaneck, N.J., 1965, chief neurosurgery, 1976-81, 90-94; chief sect. neurosurgery Hackensack (N.J.) U. Med. Ctr., 1970-86; chief spine surgery Hackensack U. Med. Ctr., 1986—; chmn. dept. neurosurgery, chief spine surgery Hackensack (N.J.) U. Med. Ctr., 1986—; dir. spine svcs. Montefiore Med. Ctr. Albert Einstein Coll. Medicine, Bronx, 1992-93; prof. neurological surgery U. Pitts. Sch. Medicine, 1993-94; dir. spine ctr., spine surgery U. Pitts., 1993-94; prof. neurosurgery U. Medicine and Dentistry of N.J., Newark, 1994—. Vis. prof. neurosurgery, U. Saigon, Vietnam, 1965-66; clin. asst. prof. neurosurgery, N.J. Coll. Medicine, Newark, 1970-73; asst. prof. clin. neurosurgery, Albert Einstein Coll. Medicine, 1973-75; assoc. prof. clin. neurosurgery, 1975-89; prof. clin. neurosurgery, 1989-92, prof. neurosurgery, 1992-93; prof. neurosurgery, 1993-1994, prof. surgery N.J. Med. Sch., UMDNJ, 1994-; spkr. numerous convs./cons. in field. Author: (novel) A Simple Twist of Fate, (textbooks) Medical Malpractice: A Guide to Medical Issues, 1986, Textbook of Operatives Spine Surgery, 1999; contbr. numerous articles to profl. jours. and publs. Fellow U.S. Public Health Svc., 1959-60; bd. trustees Lehman Coll. Art Gallery, 1986-87; bd. dirs. Hackensack U. Med. Ctr. Found., 1997—, gov. bd. govs., 1979—; mem. Hillcrest Found. Bd., 1980—; bd. dirs. Lehman Coll. Art Gallery, 1986-87; hon. surgeon Police Dept. City of N.Y. Decorated Army Commendation medal for Vietnam Svc., 1966; Disting. Svc. cert. of Merit Bd. of Chosen Freeholders of Bergen County, 1971. Fellow USPHS, Am. Coll. Surgeons, Am. Coll. Angiology, Internat. Coll. Angiology, Internat. Coll. Surgeons, Scoliosis Rsch. Soc., Cervical Spine Rsch. Soc., N.Am. Spine Soc.; mem. AMA, Internat. Soc. Pediatric Neurosurgery, Internat. Health Policy and Mgmt. Inst., Am. Pain Soc., Am. Assn. Neurol. Surgeons (chmn. liaison com. 1976-78), Bergen County Med. Soc. (trustee 1976, mem. judicial com. 1977-82, chmn. legis. com. 1980), Congress of Neurol. Surgeons, Assn. of Mil. Surgeons of U.S., N.Y. Soc. Neurosurgery, Acad. Medicine N.J., N.J. Neurosurg. Soc. (mem. exec. com. 1973, chmn. peer review com., 1974, pres. 1989-90), Fla. Med. Assn., Fla. Physicians Assn., Soc. Surgeons of N.J., Med. Soc. N.J., San Francisco Neurosurg. Soc. (corr.), others. Avocations: golf, aviation, boating, cooking gourmet.: PO Box 4148 South Hackensack NJ 07606 Address: PO Box 4148 South Hackensack NJ 07606

JACOBS, GRETCHEN HUNTLEY, psychiatrist; b. NYC, July 20, 1941; d. L. Gordon and Gertrude Mary (Eberz) La Pointe; m. Michael Edward Jacobs, Dec. 26, 1965 (div.); children: Dylan Huntley, Danielle La Pointe. BS, Fordham U., N.Y.C., 1963; MD, SUNY, Bklyn., 1968. Diplomate Am. Bd. Psychiatry and Neurology, Am. Bd. Child and Adolescent Psychiatry. Pediatric intern St. Luke's Hosp., N.Y.C., 1968—69; psychiatry resident George Washington U. Hosp., Washington, 1969—71; child psychiatry resident Beth Israel Hosp., Boston, 1972—73, McLean Hosp. Children's Ctr., Waltham, 1973—74; coord. health and human devel. Martha's Vineyard Sch. Sys., 1974—80; pvt. practice adult and adolescent/child psychiatry, 1974—; asst. clin. prof. child psychiatry Tufts U. Med. Sch., Boston, 1974—. Contbr. articles to profl. jours. Cons. Mass. Dept. Pub. Health Svcs. to Multi-Handicapped Children, 1974-75; bd. dirs. Mass. Dept. Social Svcs., 1979-83; founding mem., clin. dir. Vineyard Child Assault Prevention Project, 1986, Com. on Rural Child Psychiatry, 1988-92; mem. Coun. for Young Children. Mem. AMA, NAACP, LWV, Am. Psychiat. Assn., Am. Acad. Child and Adolescent Psychiatry, Mass. Med. Soc. Avocations: music, dance, travel, sailing, theater, basketball. Home and Office: Tashmoo Farm RR 1 Box 600 Vineyard Haven MA 02568-9733

JACOBS, HAROLD ROBERT, mechanical engineer, educator; b. Portland, Oreg., Nov. 19, 1936; s. Harold Henry and Catherine Mae (Gill) Jacobs; m. Georgene Kirkpatrick, Aug. 26, 1961; children: Sara Catherine, Harold Robert, Kenneth Patrick. BS cum laude, U. Portland, 1958; MS in Mech. Engring., Wash. State U., 1961; PhD in Mech. Engring., Ohio State U., 1965. Registered profl. engr., Utah, Wash. Engr. GE, San Jose, Calif., Hanford, Wash., 1958-59, 60; instr. dept. mech. engring. Wash. State U., Pullman, 1959-61; rsch. engr. aerospace divsn. Boeing Co., Seattle, 1961-62, 63; instr. mech engring. Ohio State U., Columbus, 1963-64; mem. tech. staff Aerospace Corp., San Bernadino, Calif., 1964-67; prof. dept. mech. engring. U. Utah, Salt Lake City, 1967-69, from asst. prof. to assoc prof., 1969-74, prof. mech. engring., 1974-84, chmn. fluid mechanics divsn. Coll. Engring., 1974-79, chmn. applied mechanics divsn., 1977-84, chmn. dept. civil engring., 1978-79, assoc. dean rsch., 1981-84; prof., head dept. Pa. State U., University Park, 1984-94, prof. emeritus, 1994—; dean Coll. Engring., prof. Colo. State U., Ft. Collins, 1994—99; chief engr. CEEMS, Bothell, Wash., 1999—. Mem. summer faculty Sandia Nat. Labs., Livermore, Calif., 1981; vis. prof. U. Strathclyde, Glasgow, Scotland, 1976—77, Imperial Coll., U. London, 1992; affiliate prof. U. Wash., Seattle, 1999—; cons. various corps. Mem. internat. adv. bd. Russian Jour. Engring. Thermophysics, 1991—; reviewer: numerous jours.; contbr. articles to profl. jours. Fellow, Ohio State U., 1962—63. Fellow: ASME (chmn. gen. papers, mem. coordinating com. heat transfer divsn., chmn. com. heat transfer mfg. and material processing 1991—94, tech. editor Jour. Heat Transfer 1986—92, mem. numerous coms.), AIAA (assoc.; assoc. adv. coun. Utah sect. 1971—77, treas. 1972—73, chmn. 1974—75, mem. numerous coms., Engr. of the Yr. award 1973); mem.: AIChE (dir. thermal sys. divsn. 1994—96, dir. 1994—96, 2d vice chair 1998—99, 1st vice chair 1999—2000, chair 2000—01, past chair 2001—02), ASEE, Sigma Xi (Ohio State Outstanding Engring. Alumnus 1991). Achievements include patents in field. Office: CEEMS 8045 Toma Ln Clinton WA 98236 Office Phone: 360-579-4207. Business E-Mail: geokir2@whidbey.com.

JACOBS, HARRY MILBURN, JR., advertising executive; b. July 23, 1928; s. Harry Milburn and Nina (Gibbs) J.; m. Barbara Ann Mills; children: Kathryn, Christopher, Letitia. Student, East Carolina U., 1947-49; BFA, Corcoran Coll. Design, 1951. Art dir. The Hecht Co., Washington, 1951-53, Bradham & Co., Greensboro, N.C., 1953-54, sr. art dir., 1956-59; assoc. art dir. Cargill, Wilson & Acree, Richmond, Va., 1959-61, creative dir. Charlotte, N.C., 1961-68, corp. creative dir. Atlanta, 1969-74, pres., 1970-74, Martin Agy., Richmond, Va., 1977-83, 1983-86, chmn. bd., 1993—97, CEO, 1993, chmn. emeritus, 1997. Scoutmaster Boy Scouts Am., 1956—58, mem. exec. coun. Robert E. Lee coun., 1987—89; bd. visitors Sch. Journalism U. N.C., Chapel Hill, Va. Commonwealth U. Found.; bd. visitors East Carolina U., 2001—; bd. overseers Corcoran Coll. Design, Washington; bd. dirs., exec. com. Richmond Renaissance, Tryon Palace Comm.; trustee Woodberry Forest Sch., 1986—2001, St. Mary's Coll., 1986—2001; bd. dirs. Meml. Guidance Clinic, Richmond Children's Mus., Marymount Park, Goodwill Industries, Richmond Sch. Ballet, Virginians in Support of Guard and REs., Downtown Presents. With U.S. Army, 1954—56. Named Advt. Man of Yr. Silver medal, Am. Advt. Fedn., 1972; named to Va. Comm. Hall of Fame, 1986, N.C. Advt. Hall of Fame, 1991, One Club Creative Hall of Fame, N.Y., 2001, Am. Advt. Fedn. Hall of Fame, 2004; recipient numerous advt. awards, Disting. Eagle Scout award, Boy Scouts Am., 1988. Mem. One Club Art & Copy N.Y., Art Dirs. Club of N.Y., Commonwealth Club, Capital Club. Republican. Office: Martin Agy One Shockoe Plaza Richmond VA 23219-4132 E-mail: hjacobs2@cox.net.

JACOBS, HELEN NICHOLS, artist; b. Kent, Conn., Feb. 16, 1924; d. Spencer Baird and Helen (Mather) Nichols; m. Steven M. Jacobs, Jan. 20, 1950; children: Richard, Barbara. Student, Marot Jr. Coll., Thompson, Conn., 1940-42. Instr. oil painting Ridgewood (N.J.) Art Inst., 1970-96. Fellow Am. Artist Profl. League; mem. Hudson Valley Art Assn., Kent Art Assn., Catharine Lorillard Wolfe Art Club. Democrat. Home: 684 Terrace Dr Paramus NJ 07652-4926 E-mail: sj684t@aol.com.

JACOBS, HENRY MADISON, JR., researcher, writer; b. Hornsby, Tenn., Mar. 6, 1935; s. Henry Madison Jacobs, Sr. and Georgia B. Chandler Jacobs; m. Verla Clair Scruggs, Dec. 2, 1955 (div. 1980); children: Michael Lynn, Susan Janet, Elizabeth Ann, Timothy Allen. BA with honors, Memphis State U., 1958; MA, U. Miss, Oxford, 1964; ABD, U. Miss., Oxford, 1970. Lic. real esate broker Miss., Tenn. Commodities broker, Batesville, Miss., 1960—70; chmn. MBA program East N.Mex. U., Portales, 1970—75; real estate, rschr., writer Miss., 1975—99; rschr., writer, 2000—. Founder Multidisciplinary Inst. Environ. Studies East N.Mex. U., Portales, 1971—. Author: (book) The Seven Thunders of the Soul, a Unified General Theory of Behavior, 1995, Los Portales, 1996, The Quantum Physics Version of Jacobs Ladder, 2000, Lawyers as Predators, Clients as Prey, 2002. 1st lt. USAF, 1958—60. Grantee, NEA, 1970—89. Achievements include discovery of a hierarchy of seven universal attitude-motive-combinations that synthesizes the Harvard Thematic Apperception Test, Lüscher Color Psychology from Switzerland, and the physics of Aura Photography. Home and Office: 980 Gin Pond Dr Saulsbury TN 38067 E-mail: jacobs@jacobsladder.com.

JACOBS, IRWIN LAWRENCE, diversified corporate executive; b. Mpls., July 15, 1941; s. Samuel and Rose H. Jacobs; m. Alexandra Light, Aug. 26, 1962; children: Mark, Sheila, Melinda, Randi, Trisha. Student pub. schs. Chmn. Watkins Inc., Winona, Minn., 1978—; pres., CEO Minstar, 1982—94; chmn. Genmar Holdings, Inc., Mpls., 1982—; chmn. bd. Genmar Industries, Inc., Mpls.; chmn. Jacobs Trading Co., Mpls.; pres., CEO Jacobs Investors, Inc., Mpls.; pres. Jacobs Realty II, Inc., Mpls., 1993—, Jacobs Mgmt. Corp., 1983—, Gateway S/B, Inc., 1993—; chmn. Operation Bass, Inc. (now FLW Outdoors), Gilbersville, Ky., 1996—. Mem.: Mpls., Lafayette Country, Oakridge Country. Office: Genmar Holdings Inc 2900 IDS Ctr 80 S 8th St Minneapolis MN 55402-2100

JACOBS, IRWIN MARK, communications executive; b. New Bedford, Mass., Oct. 18, 1933; B in Elec. Engring., Cornell U., 1956; MS, MIT, 1957, ScD, 1959; doctorate (hon.), Technion U., 2000, U. Penn., 2002. Rsch. asst. in elec. engring. MIT, Cambridge, Mass., 1958-59, from asst. to assoc. prof., 1959-66; from assoc. to prof. info. and computer sci. U. Calif., San Diego, 1966-72; co-founder, pres., chmn., CEO Linkabit Corp., 1969—85; chmn. & former CEO Qualcomm Inc., San Diego, 1985—. Cons. Applied Rsch. Lab. Sylvania Elect. Products, Inc., 1959—, Lincoln Lab. MIT, 1961—62, Indsl. Tchg. Mpls. Honeywell, Inc., 1963, Bolt Beranek & Newman, Inc., 1965; NASA resident rsch. fellow Jet Propulsion Lab., 1964—65; chmn. sci. adv. group Def. Comm. Agy. and Engring. Adv. Coun. U. Calif.; mem. Coun. on Competitveness; mem. pub. awareness engring. com. Nat. Acad. Engring.; bd. dirs. Bldg. Engring. and Sci. Talent; vis. com. MIT Lab. for Info. and Decision Sys., Calif. Coun. on Sci. and Tech.; past chmn. U. Calif. Pres. Engring. Adv. Coun. Author: Principles of Communication Engineering, 1965. Named Cornell's Entrepreneur, 1994, Entrepreneur Yr., Master Entrepreneur category, RCR, 1996, inductee for significant contbn. to advancement of wireless, Radio Comm. Report (RCR) Wireless Hall Fame, 2000; recipient Biannual award for outstanding contbn. to aerospace comm., Am. Inst. Aeronautics and Astronautics (AIAA), 1980, elected to, Nat. Acad. Engring., 1982, Disting. Cmty. Svc. award, Anti-Defamation League of B'nai B'rith, 1984, Excel award, Am. Electronics Assn., 1989, Entrepreneur Yr. award, Inst. Am. Entrepreneurs, 1992, San Diego Bus. Leader Yr. award, San Diego Venture Group, 1993, Inventing America's Future award, AEA, 1993, Internat. Citizens award, World Affairs Coun. of San Diego, 1993, Nat. Tech. medal, U.S. Dept. Commerce Tech. Adminstrn., 1994, Albert Einstein award, Am. Soc. Technion, 1996, Person Yr. award, RCR, 1996, Medal Achievement award, Am. Electronics Assn. (AEA), 1998, Ernst & Young Leadership award for Global Integration, Computerworld Smithsonian Award Program, 1999, Golden State award, Bd. Dirs. Calif. Coun. for Internat. Trade, 2000, Dir. Yr. award for Enhancement of Econ. Values, Corp. Dir. Forum, 2000, Scientist Yr. award, Achievement Rewards for Coll. Scientists (ARCS), 2000, Bower award in Bus. Leadership, Franklin Inst., 2001, Innovation award in Comm., The Economist, 2002, Internat. Engring. Consortium Fellow award, 2002, Dr. Morris Chang Exemplary Leadership award, The Fabless Semiconductor Assn. (FSA), 2003; fellow, Am. Acad. Arts and Sci., 2001. Fellow: IEEE (IEEE Alexander Graham Bell Medal 1995); mem.: NAE, Assn. Computing Machinery, Tau Beta Pi (Disting. Alumnus award 2003), Eta Kappa Nu (Eminent Mem. award 2003), Phi Kappa Phi, Sigma Xi. Achievements include patents for several CDMA patents. Office: Qualcomm Inc 5775 Morehouse Dr San Diego CA 92121-1714 also: 10185 Mckellar Ct San Diego CA 92121-4233

JACOBS, JACK BERNARD, state supreme court justice; b. July 23, 1942; s. Louis K. and Phoebe J.; m. Marion Antiles, Apr. 2, 1967; 1 child, Andrew Seth. AB, U. Chgo., 1964; LLB, Harvard U., 1967. Bar: Del. 1968, U.S. Dist. Ct. Del. 1968, U.S. Ct. Appeals (3d cir.) 1968, U.S. Supreme Ct. 1975. Law clk. Del. Chancery and Superior Cts., 1967-68; assoc. Young, Conaway, Stargatt & Taylor, Wilmington, Del., 1968-71, ptnr., 1971-85; vice chancellor Ct. of Chancery State of Del., 1985—2003; justice Del. Supreme Ct, 2003—. Adj. prof. Widener U. Sch. Law, 1986—; chmn. Bar-Bench-Media Conf. Del., 1992-93; faculty continuing legal edn. programs. Contbr. articles to profl. jours. Vice chmn. Nat. Jewish Cmty. Rels. Adv. Coun., 1985-89; bd. dirs. Jewish Fedn. Del., 1981-87, Del. Symphony Assn., 1991-95, Del. Cmty. Found., 1994-2000, chair grants com., 1998-2000, 02-, chmn. governance com., 2002-2004; pres. Milton & Hattie Kutz Home, 1990-92. Fellow: Am. Bar Found.; mem.: ABA (litigation sect., bus. law sect., mem. com. corp. laws 1999—), Harvard Law Sch. Del. (pres. 1986—87), Del. Bar Assn., Am. Judicature Soc. (bd. dirs. 1999—2004), Am. Law Inst. (advisor Restatement (3d) Restitution), Phi Beta Kappa. Democrat. Jewish. Home: 28 Beethoven Dr Wilmington DE 19807-1923 Office: Supreme Ct of Del Carvel State Office Bldg 820 N French St PO Box 1997 Wilmington DE 19899 Business E-Mail: jack.jacobs@state.de.us.

JACOBS, JAMES PAUL, retired insurance executive; b. Augusta, Ark., May 14, 1930; s. James Leonard and Ida Lee (Taylor) J.; m. Joan Gillum, Aug. 18, 1956; 2 children: LeAnn J. Alvarez, Caryl Lynn Watson. Student, Louis A. Allen Mgmt., 1970; Assoc. in mgmt., Ins. Inst. of Am., 1971. Underwriter trainee Ins. Co. of N. Am., Phila., 1954-55, underwriter Richmond, Va., 1955-58, supervising underwriter, 1958-64, underwriting mgr., 1964-68, Detroit, 1968-71; casualty mgr. Montgomery & Collins, Inc., L.A., 1971-73; ptnr. Tabb Brockenbrough & Ragland, Richmond, Va., 1973-1995, ret., 1995. Mem. agts. adv. coun. Comml. Union Ins. Co., Boston, Gt. Am. Ins. Co. Cin., Cigna Cos. Phila., Pa. Mfrs. Assn. Ins. Co., Phila., ITT Hartford, Conn., Jonathan Trumbell Assocs., Md. Ins. Group Agts. Forum, U.S. Fidelity and Guaranty Co.; bd. dirs. "All Industry" Va. "I" Day Corp., Richmond; instr. U. Richmond, 1965-78. Contbr. articles to profl. jours. Active in Colonial Williamsburg Assocs., Friends of Kennedy Ctr., Smithsonian Assocs.; bd. dirs. Daily Planet, Richmond (non-profit orgn. for aiding the homeless), pres., 1995-97. Capt. USMC, 1951-54. Mem. CPCU (bd. dirs. 1979-82, regional v.p. 1981, chpt. officer 1976-79). Republican. Methodist. Avocation: sports fan. E-mail: jake4u@sbcglobal.net. *Strive to exceed expectations in your every endeavor.*

JACOBS, JANIS ELIZABETH, academic administrator; b. Lincoln, Nebr., Mar. 26, 1954; d. Norvel L. and Helen J. (Livingston) J.; m. Kenneth Jackson, Jan. 8, 1976 (div. July 1978); m. Donald Wayne Osgood, May 24, 1980; 1 child, Logan Jean. BS, Colo. State U., 1977; MA, U. Mich., 1983, PhD, 1987. Asst. prof. U. Nebr., Lincoln, 1986-96; prof. Pa. State U., University Park, 1996—, v.p. for adminstrn., 1999—. Adv. com. mem. AD Coun., N.Y.C., 1998—. Investigator Rsch. Grants, 1989—; contbr. chpts. in books and articles to profl. jours. Bd. dirs. Pa. Coll. Tech., Village at Penn State. Mem. APA (mem. exec. com. divsn. 7). Office: Pa State Univ 201 Old Main University Park PA 16802 E-mail: jej6@psu.edu.

JACOBS, JEREMY M., diversified financial services company executive, professional sports team executive; b. Jan. 21, 1940; m. Margaret Jane Davis; 6 children. DHL (hon.), Canisius Coll.; BA, SUNY, Buffalo; grad. advancement mgmt. program, Harvard U. Chmn., CEO Del. North Cos., Buffalo, 1968—; former owner Cin. Royals Basketball team; owner, gov. Boston Bruins, NHL, 1975—; owner, gov. Boston Garden, now Fleet Ctr., 1975—. Active United Way, NCCJ, Joint Ctr. for Polit. and Econ. Studies, Internat. Tennis Hall of Fame. Mem, U.S. Travel & Tourism Promotion adv. bd., 2003-. Office: Del North Company Inc 40 Fountain Plz Buffalo NY 14202-2229 also: 1 Fleetcenter Pl Ste 250 Boston MA 02114-1390

JACOBS, JIM, actor, composer, librettist, playwright; b. Chgo., Oct. 7, 1942; m. Diane Rita Gomez, June 5, 1965 (div. 1974); 1 child, Kristine; m. Denise Nettleton, Apr. 29, 1978 (div. 2003). Student, Chgo. City Coll., 1962-63. Appeared in over 50 cmty. and profl. theatre prodns. including Until the Monkey Comes, 1966, Take Me Along, 1967, Flora, The Red Menace, 1968, Entertaining Mr. Sloane, 1969, The Serpent, 1969, Don't Drink the Water, 1970, Jimmy Shine, 1970, all Chgo., No Place to Be Somebody, nat. touring co., 1971, on Broadway, 1971, The Magnolia Club, Chgo., 1975, The Local Stigmatic, Chgo., 1976; dir. The Ruffian on the Stair, Chgo., 1975; actor: (films) Medium Cool, 1969, Love in a Taxi, 1976, (TV series) Open All Night, 1982; author, lyricist, composer: (with Warren Casey) Grease, Broadway, 1972-80, (Tony award nomination 1972, Grammy award nomination 1972), London-West End, 1973, 77, motion picture, 1979, (revival) Grease, London, 1993— (Olivier award nomination), (revival) Broadway, 1994-98 (Tony award nomination), Grease On Ice (Am. Ice Show Tour), 1998—; author: (with Warren Casey) Island of Lost Coeds, 1979; (with Jim Weston) Bats in the Belfry, 1982; (with Jim Weston) Remember the Night, 1988. Recipient Humanitarian of Yr. award Young Adult Inst., N.Y.C., 1992. Mem. Dramatists Guild, Authors League Am., ASCAP, Actors Equity Assn., Screen Actors Guild., AFTRA. Office: care Ronald Taft PC 18 W 55th St New York NY 10019-5315

JACOBS, JOHN E., lawyer; b. Detroit, Feb. 13, 1947; s. Morton and Gilberta (Jewell) J.; m. Gilda Gail Zalenko, June 6, 1971; children: Rachel H., Jessica E. BA, Mich. State U., 1968; JD, U. Mich., 1971. Bar: Mich. 1971, U.S. Dist. Ct. (ea. dist.) Mich. 1971, U.S. Ct. Appeals (6th cir.) 1984, U.S. Dist. Ct. (we. dist.) Mich. 1997. Assoc. Butzel, Levin, Winston & Quint, Detroit, 1971-76, ptnr., 1976-81; shareholder Mason, Steinhardt, Jacobs, Perlman & Pesick, P.C., Southfield, Mich., 1981-2000, DKW Law Group, P.C., Southfield, 2000—02, Maddin, Hauser, Wartell, Roth & Heller, P.C., 2002—. Contbr. articles to profl. jours. Pres. Jewish Family Svc., Southfield, 1991-93, Temple Emanu-El, Oak Park, Mich., 1995-97. Mem. ABA (mem. consumer fin. svcs. com. 1978—), Jewish Fedn. Met. Detroit (bd. govs. 1997—, mem. exec. com. 1998-99, 2002—). Democrat. Avocations: golf, bicycling. Home: 8353 Hendrie Blvd Huntington Woods MI 48070-1613 Office: Maddin Hauser Wartell Roth & Heller PC Third Fl Essex Ctr 28400 Northwestern Hwy Southfield MI 48034 Office Phone: 248-827-1866. Business E-Mail: jej@maddinhauser.com.

JACOBS, JOHN PATRICK, lawyer; b. Chgo., Ill., Oct. 27, 1945; s. Anthony N. and Bessie (Montgomery) J.; m. Linda I. Grams, Oct. 6, 1973; 1 child, Christine Margaret. BA cum laude, U. Detroit, 1967, JD magna cum laude, 1970. Bar: Mich. 1970, U.S. Dist. Ct. (ea. dist.) Mich. 1970, U.S. Dist. Ct. (we. dist.) Mich. 2004, U.S. Ct. Appeals (6th cir.) 1974, U.S. Ct. Appeals (D.C. cir.) 1988, U.S. Ct. Appeals (4th cir.) 2001, U.S. Supreme Ct. 1978. Law clk. to chief judge Mich. Ct. Appeals, Detroit, 1970-71; assoc., then ptnr. Plunkett & Cooney P.C., Detroit, 1972-92, also bd. dirs.; founding ptnr., prin. mem. O'Leary, O'Leary, Jacobs, Mattson, Perry & Mason P.C., Southfield, Mich., 1992-99; prin., owner John P. Jacobs, P.C., 1999—. Investigator Atty. Grievance Com., Detroit, 1975-84; mem. hearing panel Atty. Discipline Bd., Detroit, 1984-87, 94—; adj. prof. law Sch. Law, U. Detroit, 1983-84, faculty advisor, 1984-89, Pres.'s Cabinet, 1982—; elected rep. State Bar Rep. Assembly, Lansing, Mich., 1980-82, 91-92, 93-96; fellow Mich. State Bar Found., 1990-2005; treas., mem. steering com. Mich. Bench-Bar Appellate Conf. Com., 1994—; apptd. mem. Mich. Supreme Ct. Com. on Appellate Fees, 1990, on Delay Docket Reduction, 2003-05; spl. mediator appellate negotiation program Mich. Ct. Appeals, 1995—; mem. exec. com. Mich. Appellate Bench-Bar Conf. Found., 1996—; appellate counsel to State Bar of Mich., mem. profl. ethics com., 1998, mem. multi-disciplinary practice com., 1999. Bd. editors Mich. Lawyers Weekly. Bd. dirs. Christian Childrens Svcs. Mich., Clinton, 1988-95, 99—, chmn. pub. policy com., 1993-95, pub. policy liaison, 1999—; apptd. mem. State Bar Mich. Blue Ribbon Com. Improving Def. Counsel-Insurer Rels., 1998-99, Appellate Delay Reduction Task Force, 2003-05, Supreme Ct. Com. Regarding Case Mgmt., 2003-05; mem. Detroit Athletic Club. Named Lawyer of Yr., Mich. Lawyers Weekly, 2004, Mgsr. Malloy Cath. Lawyer of Yr., Archdiocese of Detroit, 2001, Lawyer of Yr. Excellence in Def. award, Mich. Def. Trial Counsel, 2004; recipient Robert E. Dice Med. Malpractice Def. Atty. award, Mich. Physicians, 1986, Lawyer of Yr. and Lifetime Achievement award, Mich. Def. Trial Counsel, 2004, Lawyer of Yr.; fellow Reginald Heber Smith fellow, 1971—72. Fellow Am. Acad. Appellate Lawyers, Mich. Std. Jury Instn. (subcom. employment law 1984-87); mem. ABA (litigation sect., appellate subcom., torts and ins. practice), Internat. Assn. Def. Counsel (v.p., amicus curiae com., med. and legal malpractice coms., product liability com.), Fedn. Ins. and Corp. Counsel, Mich. Def. Trial Counsel (chmn. amicus curiae com. 1986-88, chmn. future planning com., bd. dirs. 1989—, treas. 1993-94, sec. 1994-95, v.p. 1995-96, program chair 1990, 94, 95, pres., 1996-97), Def. Rsch. Inst. (state rep. 1997-98, Outstanding Performance Citation 1997, nat. appellate com. steering com. 1997—), Cath. Lawyers Soc. (bd. dirs. 1988-98, emeritus dir. 1998—, pres. 1994-95), Supreme Ct. U.S. Hist. Soc., Supreme Ct. Mich. Hist. Soc., Am. Constitutional Soc. (bd. dirs. 2005), Detroit Athletic Club. Democrat. Roman Catholic. Avocations: collecting antique law books, film.

JACOBS, JON ROBERT, general and vascular surgeon; b. Biloxi, Miss., Jan. 20, 1950; s. Edmond Milliard and Wilda Ruth (McLeod) J.; m. Catherine Monts Harkey, June 22, 1974; children: Carrie Ruth, Christopher Robert, Gregory Stephen, Jeffrey Harkey. Student, Davidson (N.C.) Coll., 1972; D in Medicine, U. S.C., 1977. Rsch. analyst W.S. Hall Psychiat. Inst., Columbia, S.C., 1972-73; min. youth guidance Trinity Episcopal Ch., Columbia, 1973; surgeon Allegheny and Mercy Hosps., Pitts., 1982; physician emergency room Sewickley (Pa.) Hosp., 1982-83; practice medicine specializing in gen. and vascular surgery and surg. and laser dermatology Charleston, SC, 1983—. Named hon. S.C. constable, 1989—. Mem. Fellow ACS. Avocations: pilot, computer programmer, guitarist, electrician, magician. Office: 9213 University Blvd Ste D Charleston SC 29406-9145 Office Phone: 843-797-6564.

JACOBS, JUDITH, county legislator; b. N.Y.C., Jan. 13, 1939; d. George and Dorothy Bodkin; m. Sidney N. Jacobs, June 7, 1959; children: Jacqueline, Leonard, Linda. BA, Hunter Coll., 1960. Cert. in early childhood edn., N.Y. Mem. Nassau County Legislature, Mineola, N.Y., 1996—, minority leader, 1999—, presiding officer, majority leader, 2000—. Committeeperson, zone leader, asst. dist. leader, Town of Oyster Bay leader Dem. Party Nassau County, 1970—. Democrat. Jewish. Avocation: reading.

JACOBS, JULIAN I., federal judge; b. Balt., Aug. 13, 1937; s. Sidney and Bernice (Kellman) J.; m. Donna Buffenstein; children: Richard S., Jennifer K. BA, U. Md., 1958, JD, 1960; LLM, Georgetown U., 1965. Bar: Md., 1960. Atty. chief counsel's office IRS, Washington, 1961-65, trial atty. regional counsel's office Buffalo, 1965-67; assoc. Weinberg & Green, Balt., 1967-69, Hoffberger & Hollander, Balt., 1969-72, Gordon Feinblatt Rothman Hoffberger & Hollander, Balt., 1972-74, ptnr., 1974-84; judge U.S. Tax Ct., Washington, 1984—99, sr. judge, 1999—. Chmn. study commn. Md. Tax Ct., 1978-79, mem. rules com., 1980; mem. spl. study group Md. Gen. Assembly, 1980; adj. prof. grad. tax program U. Balt., 1991-93; adj. prof. law, U. San Diego, 2001; adj. prof. grad. tax program, U. Denver, 2001—. Mem.: U Md. Law Rev. Bd. Mem. Md. State Bar Assn. (past chmn. taxation sect.), Balt. City Bar Assn. (past chmn. tax legis. subcom.). Office: US Tax Ct 400 Second St NW Washington DC 20217-0002 Office Phone: 202-606-8811.

JACOBS, KIMBERLY ANN, elementary school educator; b. Jeanette, Pa., June 10, 1974; d. William Donald and Pamela Dean George; m. Jimmy Jacobs (div.); 1 child, Rachel Gail. BA, Grove City Coll., 1992; MA, U. N.C., 2004. Tchr. kindergarten Pembroke Elem. Sch., NC, 1996—97; tchr. grade 1 Peterson Elem. Sch., Red Springs, NC, 1997—. Mem. grant com. Pub. Schs. Robeson County, Red Springs, NC, 2002—04; mem. literary team Peterson Elem. Sch., 2005—; presenter N.C. Reading Assn. Conf., 2004. Grantee, U.S. Dept. Edn., 2002; Bright Ideas grantee, Lumber River Elect. Co-Op, 2002. Mem.: N.C. Reading Assn., Robeson County Assn. Educators, N.C. Assn. Educators. Methodist. Avocations: reading, camping. Office: Peterson Elem Sch 102 Phillips Ave Red Springs NC 28377-1899 Home: 501 E 2d Ave Apt B Red Springs NC 28377 Office Phone: 910-843-4125.

JACOBS, LAWRENCE A., lawyer, media company executive; b. Phila., May 4, 1955; married; 2 children. BA summa cum laude, Temple U., 1978; JD cum laude, Bklyn. Law Sch., 1981. Bar: NY 1982, Pa. 1984. Ptnr. Squadron, Ellenoff, Plesant & Lehrer, 1991—96; sr. v.p., dep. gen. counsel News Corp., Ltd., NYC, 1996—2001, exec. v.p., 2001—, group gen. counsel, 2005—. Dir. satellite pay-TV Sky Mex., Sky Brasil. Bd. dirs. Cookie Ctr. Learning and Devel., NYC. Mem.: NY State Bar Assn., Assn. Bar City of NY. Office: News Corp Ltd 1211 Avenue of the Americas New York NY 10036 Office Phone: 212-852-7000. Office Fax: 212-768-2029.*

JACOBS, LAWRENCE H., lawyer; b. Paterson, N.J., Feb. 8, 1955; s. Bernard Jacobs and Hortense (Grossman) Roemer; m. Sue Ann Luckman, May 27, 1990; 1 child, Alanna Brooke. BA summa cum laude, Fairleigh Dickinson U., 1977; JD cum laude, Seton Hall U., 1980. Bar: N.J. 1980, U.S. Dist. Ct. N.J. 1980, Fla. 1982. Assoc. Pitney, Hardin, Kipp & Szuch, Morristown, NJ, 1980—83, Francis & Berry, Morristown, 1983—87, ptnr., 1987—88; assoc. Hein, Smith, Berezin, Maloof & Spinella, Hackensack, NJ, 1988—91; ptnr. Hein, Smith, Berezin, Maloof, Spinella & Rogers, Hackensack, 1991—96, Hein, Smith, Berezin, Maloof, Davidson & Jacobs, Hackensack, 1996—98, Hein Smith Berezin Maloof & Jacobs, Hackensack, 1999—. Mem. ABA, N.J. State Bar Assn., Fla. Bar Assn., Bergen County Bar Assn. Avocations: tennis, racquetball, golf. Office: Hein Smith Berezin Maloof & Jacobs 19 Main St Hackensack NJ 07601-7043 E-mail: ljacobs@Heinsmith.com.

JACOBS, LESLIE WILLIAM, lawyer; b. Akron, Ohio, Dec. 5, 1944; s. Leslie Wilson and Louise Francis (Walker) J.; m. Laurie Hutchinson, July 12, 1962; children— Leslie James, Andrew Wilson, Walker Fulton. Student, Denison U., 1962-63; BS, Northwestern U., 1965; JD, Harvard U., 1968. Bar: Ohio 1968, D.C. 1980, U.S. Supreme Ct. 1971, Brussels 1996. Law clk. to Chief Justice Kingsley A. Taft Ohio Supreme Ct., 1968-69; assoc. Thompson, Hine and Flory, Cleve., 1969-76, ptnr., 1976—, chmn. antitrust, internat. and regulatory area, 1988-99; chmn. bus. regulation and trade dept. Thompson Hine LLP and predecessor, Cleve., 1999—. Lectr. conf. bd. Ohio Legal Ctr. Insts., Ohio State Bar Assn. Antitrust and Corp. Counsel Insts., Fed. Bar Assn., ABA, Canadian Inst., Internat. Assn. Young Lawyers, others; mem. Ohio Bd. Bar Examiners, 1990-94. Contbr. articles to profl. jours. Chmn. EconomicsAmerica, 1990-93; mem. vis. com. Case Western Res. U. Sch. Law, 1985-91; trustee, mem. exec. com., chair audit com. The Holden Arboretum; mem. Leadership Cleve., 1988. Lt. comdr. USNR, 1967-79. Fellow Am. Bar Found. (life), Ohio State Bar Found. (life, trustee 1985-87, Ritter award 1997); mem. ABA (ho. dels. 1986—, antitrust law sect. coun. 1985-88, officer 1991-97, state del. 1995-2001, nominating com. 1995-2001, bd. gov. 2001-2004, task force on corp. responsibility), Ohio State Bar Assn. (pres. 1987, Ohio Bar medal 1990), Cleve. Bar Assn. (chmn. jud. selection com. 1982, trustee 1983-85), Am. Law Inst., 6th Cir. Jud. Conf. (life), Nat. Conf. Bar Pres., Harvard Club (N.Y.C.), Chagrin Valley Hunt Club, Union Club (Cleve.), Castalia Trout Club. Republican. Presbyterian. Office: Thompson Hine LLP 3900 Key Ctr 127 Public Sq Cleveland OH 44114-1291 Office Phone: 216-566-5500. Business E-Mail: les.jacobs@thompsonhine.com.

JACOBS, LIBBY SWANSON, state official; b. Lincoln, Nebr., Oct. 1, 1956; m. Steven G. Jacobs. BA, U. Nebr.; MPA, Drake U. Dir. pub. rels. Am. Lung Assn., 1983—86; dir. comms. IA Bankers Assn., 1986—88; mgr., ops. mgr. disability income svcs. Prin. Fin. Group, 1989—96, asst dir., 1996—2002, dir. cmty. rels., 2002—; mem. Iowa Ho. of Reps., Iowa, 1994—, majority whip. Mem. adminstrn. and rules com.; mem. appropriations com.; mem. commerce and regulation com.; mem. state govt. com. Bd. mem. Drake Univ., Blank Children's Hosp.; co-chair Downtown Cmty. Alliance; past chair Midwestern Legis. Conf. Mem.: PEO, LWV, Jr. League Des Moines, Variety Club Iowa. Republican. Office: State Capitol E 12th and Grand Des Moines IA 50319

JACOBS, LINDA JOAN, secondary school educator; b. Balt., Mar. 25, 1941; d. Bernard and Freda (Statter) White; m. Martin H. Jacobs, Aug. 3, 1963. BA, U. Md., 1962, MA, 1965, EdD, 1971. Tchr. Baltimore County Pub. Schs., Towson, Md., 1962-64, resource supr., 1967-68; research teaching asst. U. Md., College Park, 1964-67, asst. prof. spl. edn., 1968-71, undergrad. program coordinator, 1971-73; dir. spl. edn. Anne Arundel County Bd. Edn., Annapolis, Md., 1974-77; asst. supt. Md. State Dept. Edn., Balt., 1977-79; dir. Harbour Sch.-Am Innovative Learning Ctr., Annapolis, 1979-89, The Harbour Sch., Annapolis, 1990—. Sec. bd. dirs. Bernard White & Co., Pikesville, Md., 1979-89, Harbour Sch., Balt.; cons. to over 125 sch. dists. throughout U.S., 1971—; presenter Internat. Coun. for Exceptional Children Conf., 1989, 90, 91. Author: (books) Every Child an Individual, 1987, The Fourth R - Behavin' Right, 1991, 1998, 1999, 2001, 2003. Mem. Gov.'s Commn. on Funding for Spl. Edn., Annapolis, 1975, Gov.'s Adv. Com. on Handicapped, Annapolis, 1977, Com. to Re-elect Lamb, Anne Arundel, Md., 1986. Recipient Gov.'s Citation for 25 Yrs. Service to the Handicapped, 1987. Mem. Assn. Retarded Citizens, Council for Exceptional Children (Md. state pres. 1970-72), Assn. for Children with Learning Disabilities (advisor 1979—), Kappa Delta Pi. Democrat. Jewish. Avocation: photography. Home: 8808 Sonya Rd Randallstown MD 21133-4016 Office: Harbour Sch 1277 Green Holly Dr Annapolis MD 21401-4676

JACOBS, LLOYD A., vascular surgeon; b. Holland, Mich., 1940; MD, Johns Hopkins U., 1968. Diplomate Am. Bd. Surgery. Intern Johns Hopkins Hosp., Balt., 1969-70, resident, 1970-71, U. Calif., San Diego, 1971-72,

Wayne State U., Detroit, 1972-74; prof. surgery U. Mich. Sch. Medicine, Ann Arbor, 1974—2003, sr. assoc. dean, 1996—2003; COO U. Mich. Health Sys., Ann Arbor, 1997—; pres. Med. Coll. Ohio, 2003—. Hosp. appts.: VA Hosp., Ann Arbor, Mich., U. Mich. Hosp., Ann Arbor, chief of staff, VAH Med. Ctr., 1989-96. Fellow ACS; mem. AMA, Internat. Soc. Cardio Vascular Surgeons, Midwest Surgeons Assn. Office: 3045 Arlington Ave ML-213 Toledo OH 43614

JACOBS, MADELEINE, professional society administrator; b. Washington; m. Joseph Jacobs. BS in Chem., George Washington U., 1968, DSc (hon.), 2003; M course work in Organic Chem. completed, U. Md. With Nat. Bur. of Standards (now Nat. Inst. of Standards & Tech.); head, Smithsonian News Svc. and publications mgr. Smithsonian Inst., 1979—86, dir., public affairs, 1986—93; reporter Chem. and Engring. News, 1969—72, mng. editor, 1993—95, editor-in-chief, 1995—2004; exec. dir. and CEO Am. Chem. Soc., 2004—, bd. dirs. Mem.: Coun. for Advancement Sci. Writing (bd. dirs.), Nat. Assn. Sci. Writers. Office: Am Chem Soc 1155 16th St NW Washington DC 20036

JACOBS, MARC, fashion designer; b. NYC, 1963; Student, Parsons Sch. Design, 1981-84. Stock boy Charivari, NYC; designer Ruben Thomas Inc. (under Sketchbook label), NYC, Kashiyama, NYC; debuted his Marc Jacobs label, 1986; v.p., women's Perry Ellis, head designer NYC, 1989—92; creative designer Louis Vuitton, 1997, developed first ready-to-wear line., 1997; designer Mark Jacobs, NYC, 1988—; developed the Marc by Marc Jacobs line, 2001. Recipient Perry Ellis Golden Thimble award, 1984, Women's Designer of the Year award, Council of Fashion Designers Am., 1992; named The Guru of Grunge, Women's Wear Daily. Mem. Coun. of Fashion Designers of Am. (Young Designer 1987, Women's Wear Designer of the Yr. 1992). Democrat. Avocations: films, exercise, music. Office: Marc Jacobs Internat LLC 72 Spring St Fl 9 New York NY 10012-4019 Address: Marc Jacobs 163 Mercer St New York NY 10012 Office Phone: 212-343-0222, 212-343-1490.

JACOBS, MARIAN, advertising agency owner; b. Stockton, Calif., Sept. 11, 1927; d. Paul and Rose (Sallah) J. AA, Stockton Coll. With Bottarini Advt., Stockton, 1948-50; pvt. practice Stockton, 1950-64; with Olympius Advt., Stockton, 1964-78; pvt. practice Stockton, 1978—. Pres. Stockton Advt. Club, 1954, Venture Club, Stockton, 1955; founder Stockton Advt. and Mktg. Club, 1981. Founder Stockton Arts Comms., 1976; co-founder Sunflower Entertainment for Institutionalized, 1976, Women Execs., Stockton, 1978; founding dir. Pixie Woods, Stockton; bd. dir. Goodwill Industries, St. Mary's Dining Room, Alan Short Gallery; mem. Calif. Coun. for the Humanities, 1994-95. Named Stocktonian of Yr., Stockton Bd. Realtors, 1978, Outstanding Citizen, Calif. State Senate and Assembly, 1978, Woman of Yr., State of Calif. Assembly, 2002, Woman of Achievement, Kaiser-Permanente Women's Wellness Conf., 2002, Disting. Alumni Vol., U. of the Pacific, 2003, Marian Jacobs Lit. Forum Stockton Arts Commn. established in her honor; recipient Woman of Achievement award, San Joaquin County Women's Coun., Stockton, 1976, Achievement award, San Joaquin Delta Coll., Stockton, 1978, Friend of Edn. award, Calif. Tchrs. Assn., Stockton, 1988, Stanley McCaffrey Disting. Svc. award, U. of the Pacific, Stockton, 1988, Athena award for businesswoman of Yr., Greater Stockton C. of C., 1989, Role Model award, Tierra del Oro Girl Scouts U.S., 1989, Heart of Gold award, Dameron Hosp. Found., 2000, Bravo award, Stockton Orvii Theater; Paul Harris fellow, Rotary Club, 1994. Republican. Roman Catholic. Avocations: art, photography. Home and Office: 4350 Mallard Creek Cir Stockton CA 95207-5205

JACOBS, MARK, biology professor, dean; b. Princeton, May 19, 1950; s. William Paul and Jane Shaw Jacobs; m. Candace Margaret Clarke, Dec. 29, 1973 (div. June 1998); children: Jeffrey William, Robinson Clarke, Patrick Shaw; m. Ellen Ruth Abelman, Oct. 14, 2000; 1 child, Madeleine Jane. BA, Harvard Coll., 1971; PhD, Stanford U., 1975. Post doctoral fellow NATO, Freiburg, Germany, 1976—77; asst. prof. Swarthmore (Pa.) Coll., 1975—81, assoc. prof., 1981—89, prof., 1989—2003, assoc. provost, 1993—96; prof. Sch. Life Scis., Ariz. State U., Tempe, 2003—, dean Barrett Honors Coll., 2003—. Panel mem. metabolic biology program NSF, Washington, 1984—88; commr., vice chair Mid. States Assn. Commn. Higher Edn., Phila., 1997—2003; mem. com. arts and scis. Franklin Inst., Phila., 1996—2003. Contbr. 23 articles to profl. jours.; editor: Molecular Biology of Plant Growth Control, 1987; assoc. editor-in-chief (sci. jour.) Plant Physiology and Biochemistry, mem. editl. bd. The New Biologist. Named Endowed Chair, Centennial prof. biology, Swarthmore Coll., 1990—2003; fellow, German Acad. Exch. Svc. (DAAD), 1979, Guggenheim Found., 1986—87; grantee, NSF, NIH, USDA, 1976—99. Mem.: Am. Soc. Plant Biologists (nat. treas. 1991—97), Nature Conservancy, Sigma Xi. Office: Barrett Honors Coll Ariz State Univ PO Box 871612 Tempe AZ 85287-1612 Office Phone: 480-965-2354. E-mail: mark.jacobs@asu.edu.

JACOBS, MARK M., energy executive, corporate financial executive; BBA, So. Methodist U.; MBA, Northwestern U. Mng. dir. Goldman, Sachs and Co., with mergers and acquisitions, 1989, energy and power group, 1997, Houston, 1998; exec. v.p., CFO Reliant Resources, 2002—. Mem. bd. dirs. Theatre Under the Stars. Office: Reliant Resources Inc 1000 Main St Houston TX 77002 Mailing: PO Box 148 Houston TX 77001-0148

JACOBS, MARK RANDOLPH, lawyer; b. Columbus, Ohio, June 7, 1953; s. Lee Randolph and Sally Ann (Cummins) J.; m. Linda Beth Rogozinski, Oct. 29, 1983; children: Philip Randolph, Gregory Cummins. BA cum laude with distinction, Yale U., 1979, JD, 1982. Bar: N.Y. 1983, U.S. Dist. Ct. (so. dist.) N.Y. 1983, Conn. 1993. Law clerk Hon. S.W. Kram U.S. Dist. Judge, N.Y., 1983-84; ptnr. Pryor, Cashman, Sherman & Flynn, N.Y., 1988-90, Cadwalader, Wickersham & Taft, N.Y., 1990-92; of counsel Gregory & Adams, Wilton, Conn., 1992-96; ptnr. Jacobs Goldman LLC, Norwalk, Conn., 1997—. Office: Jacobs Goldman LLC Merritt View 383 Main Ave Norwalk CT 06851-1543

JACOBS, MICHAEL ROY, microbiologist, researcher; arrived in U.S., 1979; s. Philip and Ruth Joan Jacobs; m. Gretta Hazel Jacobs; children: Erica Yvonne, Kevin Bryan, Paul Daniel, David Andrew. MB, BChir, U. Witwatersrand, Johannesburg, 1971, Diploma in Tropical Medicine and Hygiene, 1974, Diploma in Pub. Health, 1976, PhD, 1978. Fellow faculty pathology Coll. Medicine South Africa, 1977, diplomate in Pub. Health and Med. Microbiology Am. Bd. Med. Microbiology, 1980. Microbiologist South African Inst. for Med. Rsch., Johannesburg, 1977—79; dir. clin. microbiology U. Hosps. Cleve., 1979—; asst. prof. dept. pathology Case Western Res. U., Cleve., 1979—86, assoc. prof. dept. pathology, 1986—93, prof. dept. pathology, 1993—. Com. mem. Drug Resistant Streptococcus Pneumoniae Therapeutic Working Group, Atlanta, 1977—2000; com. mem. sinusitis guidelines com. Sinus and Allergy Health Partnership, Washington, 1998—2004. Contbr. chapters to books, articles to profl. jours. Mem.: Am. Soc. for Microbiology, Infectious Disease Soc. Am., Royal Coll. Pathologists. Achievements include discovery of first strains of Streptococcus pneumoniae resistant to multiple groups of antimicrobial agents in South Africa in 1978; development of treatment guidelines for acute otitis media; treatment guidelines for community acquired pneumonia; treatment guidelines for acute bacterial rhinosinusitis; research in antimicrobial susceptibility of respiratory tract pathogens. Office: Case Western Reserve Univ/Univ Hospitals 11100 Euclid Ave Cleveland OH 44106

JACOBS, NANCY CAROLYN BAKER, writer; b. Milw., Dec. 9, 1944; d. Alvin Donald and Wilma Carolyn (Robertson) Moll; m. James Ross Baker, Aug. 28, 1965 (div. 1979); 1 child, Bradley; m. Jerome Martin Jacobs, June 20, 1981. BA, U. Minn., 1965, MA, 1973; MFA, U. So. Calif., 1977. Reporter St. Paul Dispatch, 1965-66; pub. rels. writer U. Minn., Mpls., 1966-67, Northwest Airlines, St. Paul, 1967-69; TV scriptwriter Control Data Corp., Mpls., 1971-73; dir. news and pub. Met. State U., St. Paul, 1973-75; author, free lance journalist, 1975—; pvt. investigator Spl. Reports, L.A., 1986-90; journalism lectr. Calif. State U., Northridge, 1977-92. Author: Deadly Companion, 1986, The Turquoise Tattoo, 1991, A Slash of Scarlet, 1992, See Mommy Run, 1992, The Silver Scalpel, 1993, Cradle and All, 1995, Daddy's Gone A-Hunting, 1995, Rocking the Cradle, 1996, Double or Nothing, 2001, Star Struck, 2002, Flash Point, 2002, Ricochet, 2003 (nominated Mary Higgins Clark award Mystery Writers Am.), Desperate Journeys, 2004; (as Nancy C. Baker) Babyselling: The Scandal of Black Market Adoption, 1978, Act II: The Mid-Career Job Change and How to Make It, 1980, New Lives for Former Wives: Displaced Homemakers, 1980, Cashing in on Cooking, 1982, The Beauty Trap: Exploring Woman's Greatest Obsession, 1984, Relative Risk: Living with a Family History of Breast Cancer, 1991 (Am. Med. Writers Assn. Rose Kushner award). Mem. Mystery Writers Am., Pvt. Eye Writers Am., Authors Guild, Sisters in Crime, Internat. Thriller Writers. Personal E-mail: Nancy@NancyBakerJacobs.com.

JACOBS, NORMAN JOSEPH, publishing company executive; b. Chgo., Oct. 28, 1932; s. Herman and Tillie (Chapman) J.; m. Jeri Kolber Rose, Jan. 2, 1977; 1 son, Barry Herman; children by previous marriage: Carey, Murray, Dale. BS in Mktg, U. Ill., 1954. Display salesman Chgo. Daily News, 1954-57; dist. mgr. Davidson Pub. Co., Chgo., 1957-62; v.p. Press-Tech, Inc., Evanston, Ill., 1962-69; pres. Century Pub. Co., Evanston, 1969—. Bd. dirs. Chgo. Bulls. With USNR, 1951—59. Mem. B'nai B'rith, Birchwood Tennis Club, Alpha Delta Sigma, Tau Epsilon Phi. Jewish. Office: Century Pub Co 990 Grove St 4th Fl Evanston IL 60201-6510 Office Phone: 847-491-6440. Business E-Mail: njacobs@centurysports.net.

JACOBS, PAUL, lawyer; b. NYC, Sept. 29, 1946; s. William R. and Sylvia (Wanshel) J.; m. Lisette Simon, Oct. 10, 1979; children: Alexia, Caroline. BA, Colgate U., 1967; JD, Columbia U., 1971. Bar: N.Y. 1971, U.S. Dist. Ct. (so. dist.) N.Y. 1971. Assoc. Reavis & McGrath, N.Y.C., 1971-78, ptnr., 1978-89, Fulbright & Jaworski, N.Y.C., 1989-96, sr. ptnr., 1996—; co-head corp. bus. and banking sect. Fulbright & Jaworski LLP, 2000—. Mem. adv. com. Grace Ventures Corp., Cupertino, Calif., 1988-98, Euro-Am.-I C.V., San Bruno, Calif., 1988-98; sec. Zygo Corp., Middlefield, Conn., 1992—. Mem. N.Y. Bar Assn., N.Y.C. Bar Assn., Phi Beta Kappa, The University Club. Office: Fulbright & Jaworski LLP 666 5th Ave Fl 31 New York NY 10103-3198 Office Phone: 212-318-3000. Office Fax: 212-318-3400. Business E-Mail: pjacobs@fulbright.com.

JACOBS, PAUL A., music educator; b. Washington, Pa., Feb. 1, 1977; s. Mary Jeanne Maggi. MusB, Curtis Inst. Music, 2000; MusM, Yale Sch. Music, 2002. Prin. organist Immaculate Conception Ch., Washington, Pa., 1992—95; organist Wash. Meml. Chapel, Valley Forge, 1995—2000; chair organ dept. The Juilliard Sch., NYC, 2003—; organist and choirmaster Christ and St. Stephen's Ch., 2003—. Recipient Horatio Parker Meml. award, Yale Sch. Music, 2002, Arthur W. Foote award, Harvard Musical Assn., 2003, Disting. Alumni award, Yale Sch. Music, 2005; scholar, Curtis Inst. Music, 1995—2000, Yale Inst. Sacred Music, 2000—03. Mem.: Am. Guild Organists. Conservative. Roman Catholic. Achievements include Performances across North America, South America, Europe, and Australia. Avocations: hiking, travel. Office: The Juilliard Sch 60 Lincoln Ctr Plz New York NY 10023 Office Phone: 212-799-5000. Personal E-mail: pjacobs@juilliard.edu.

JACOBS, PAUL ALAN, lawyer; b. Boston, June 5, 1940; s. Samuel and Sarah (Rodman) J.; m. Carole Ruth Greenstein, Aug. 28, 1962; children: Steven N., Cheryl R., David F., Craig A. BA in Econs. magna cum laude, Tufts U., 1960; JD magna cum laude, U. Denver, 1968. Bar: Colo. 1968, U.S. Dist. Ct. Colo. 1968. Pers. officer First Nat. Bank Denver, 1964-68; assoc. Holme Roberts & Owen, Denver, 1968-73, sr. ptnr., 1973-93; exec. v.p., gen. counsel Colo. Rockies profl. baseball orgn., Denver, 1991-95; ptnr. Jacobs Chase Frick Kleinkopf & Kelley, Denver, 1995—. Bd. dirs. Anti-Defamation League B'nai B'rith, Denver, 1987-95, Colo. Sports Hall of Fame, 2000—, Am. Jewish Com., 2002-. Served to 1st lt. USAF, 1960-63. Recipient Outstanding Alumni award, U. Denver Sturm Coll. Law, 2004. Mem. ABA, Denver Bar Assn., Colo. Bar Assn. Jewish. Avocations: skiing, golf. Home: 4041 S Narcissus Way Denver CO 80237-2025 Office: Independence Plz 1050 17th St Ste 1500 Denver CO 80265-2078 Office Phone: 303-892-4420. Business E-Mail: pjacobs@jcfkk.com.

JACOBS, PAUL E., communications executive; s. Irwin Mark and Joan Jacobs; m. Stacy Jacobs; 3 children. BS, U. Calif., Berkeley, 1984, MS, 1986, PhD in Elec. Engring, 1989. Engring. positions Qualcomm, 1990—95, v.p. & gen. mgr. handset & integrated circuit div., 1995, sr. v.p., 1996, pres. QCP, 1997, exec. v.p., 2000—05, group pres. QWI, 2001, CEO, 2005, mem. exec. com., 1992—. Bd. mem. Mus. Contemporary Art, San Diego, Salk Inst. Biological Studies; mem. adv. bd. U. Calif., Berkeley, Coll. Engring.; chmn. adv. bd. U. Calif., San Diego, Jacobs Sch. Engring. Mem.: Phi Beta Kappa, Eta Kappa Nu, Tau Beta Pi. Office: Corp Hdqs Qualcomm Inc 5775 Morehouse Dr San Diego CA 92121

JACOBS, RALPH, JR., artist; b. El Centro, Calif., May 22, 1940; s. Ralph and Julia Vahe (Kirkorian) J. Paintings appeared in: Prize Winning Art (3 awards), 1964, 65, 66, and New Woman Mag., 1975; one man shows and exhbns. Villa Montalvo, Calif., Stanford Rsch. Inst., Calif., Fresno Art Ctr., Calif., de Young Meml. Mus., Calif., Rosicrucian Mus., Calif., Cunningham Meml. Gallery, Calif., 40th Ann. Nat. Art Exhibit, Utah, Nat. Exhbn. Coun. of Am. Artists Socs., N.Y.C., Am. Artists Profl. League Show, Armenian Allied Arts, Calif., Monterey Peninsula Mus. Art, Calif. Recipient 1st place award Statewide Ann. Santa Cruz Art League Gallery, 1963, 64; 2nd place award Soc. Western Artists Ann. M.H. de Young Mus., 1964; A.E. Klumpkey Meml. award, 1965. Address: PO Box 5906 Carmel CA 93921-5906

JACOBS, RHODA S., state legislator; b. Bklyn. 3 children. BA, Bklyn. Coll. Co-founder, formerly co-dir. Bklyn. Coll. Day Care Ctr.; mem. N.Y. State Assembly, 1978—, asst. spkr., co-chair task force on homeless, task force New Americans, chair majority program com., mem. banks com., higher edn. com., ins. com., health com., womne's caucus. Mem. Bklyn. Women's Polit. Caucus, Nat. Assn. Jewish Legislators (sec., treas.). Office: NY State Assembly LOB Rm 736 Albany NY 12248-0001 Office Phone: 718-434-0446. Business E-Mail: jacobsr@assembly.state.ny.us.

JACOBS, RICHARD E., real estate company executive, sports team owner; 3 children from previous marriage. Ptnr. Jacobs, Visconsi & Jacobs; former chmn., chief exec. officer Cleve. Indians. Office: Richard E Jacobs Group 25425 Center Ridge Rd Cleveland OH 44145-4122

JACOBS, RICHARD JAMES, banker, educator; b. Jamaica, N.Y., Sept. 27, 1941; s. John Beck and Doris Marie (Lewin) J.; m. Jean Anita McIntosh, Aug. 29, 1964; children: Kristine Anne, John McIntosh. BA, Muhlenberg Coll., 1963; MBA, U. Pa., 1965. With Gulf Oil, 1965-72, fin. mgr. Balt., 1970-71, mktg. advisor Pitts., 1971-72; v.p. mktg. and ops. Finnegans, Inc., Chevy Chase, Md., 1972-73; dir. planning Geico Ins. Co., Chevy Chase, 1973-76; v.p., gen. mgr. G.H. Realty, Annapolis, Md., 1976-78; asst. v.p. mktg. Md. Nat. Bank, Balt., 1978-80, v.p. mktg., 1980-86, sr. v.p. mktg., 1986-88, sr. v.p. wholesale support, 1988-90; chmn., CEO Bottom Line Co., Balt., Md., 1990—. Instr. mktg. Md. Banking Sch., Annapolis, 1988-2001; exec. dir. Wholesale Traders Group, 1981-83; prof. mktg. Johns Hopkins U., Balt., 1990-92. Coord. United Way, Balt., 1979; pres. Amberley Community Assn., Annapolis, 1980; off season job coord. Balt. Colts., 1982. Mem. Bank Mktg. Assn. (adv. coun. 1988-89), Mktg. Info. Group, Mchts. Club, Center Club, Fleet Reserve Club. Roman Catholic. Avocations: boating, fishing, cooking, travel. Home: 59 Fox Dr Ocean View DE 19970 Office: Bottom Line Co 1 E Lexington St Baltimore MD 21202-1701 Office Phone: 410-332-4430. Personal E-mail: blcjake@aol.com.

JACOBS, ROBERT ALAN, lawyer; b. Waco, Tex., June 23, 1937; s. Abe and Ruth (Englander) J.; m. Sue C. Braunstein, Aug. 22, 1961; children: Jacqueline Anne, Michelle Keri. BBA, U. Tex., 1957; LLB cum laude, NYU, 1960, LLM in Taxation, 1963. Bar: N.Y. 1961. Assoc. Greenbaum, Wolff & Ernst, N.Y.C., 1961-63; asst. br. chief, chief counsel IRS, Washington, 1963-67; assoc. Paul, Weiss, Rifkind, Wharton & Garrison, N.Y.C., 1967-69; sr. tax mem. Milgrim Thomajan Jacobs & Lee PC, N.Y.C., 1969-87; tax ptnr. Milbank, Tweed, Hadley & McCloy, LLP, N.Y.C., 1987—2002, cons. ptnr., 2002—03, ret. ptnr., 2003—; head low income tax clinic Benjamin A. Cardozo Sch. Law, 2002; underwriting dir. Gulf Ins. Group, 2002. Adj. prof. law NYU, 1976-85; adj. prof. bus. planning Pace Law Sch., 2005—; vis. sr. lectr. taxation, U. Calif. Davis, 1977; spl. counsel to sec. treas., Washington, 1965-67. Note and comment editor NYU Law Rev.; contbr. articles to profl. jours. Mem. adv. group Senate Fin. Com. Staff on Subchpt. C. Revision, 1983-85; arbitrator Civil Ct. City of N.Y., 1972—; bd. dirs. Community Action Legal Svcs., 1978-82, MFY Legal Svcs., 1991-98, N.Y. County Lawyers, 1990-93, 2004—. With U.S. Army, 1960-61, 61-62. Root-Tilden scholar; recipient commendation medal U.S. Army. Mem. ABA (tax sect., asst. sec. 1987-88, chmn. corp. stockholder relationships 1983-85, chmn. task force on pass-through entities 1986-88), Am. Law Inst., Tax Forum (chmn. 1989-2001), Am. Coll. Tax Counsel, N.Y. State Bar Assn. (tax sect., exec. com. 1980—, chair 2001), Tax Club (chmn. 1987-88). Office: 61 Broadway Ste 1601 New York NY 10006 Office Phone: 212-267-2600. Personal E-mail: rajacobs23@aol.com, rjacobs@gfrglawfirm.com.

JACOBS, ROLLY WARREN, judge; b. Nashville, Aug. 26, 1946; s. William Clinton Jr. and Eleanor Olive (Warren) J.; m. Karen Lee Ponist, Sept. 16, 1972; children: Collin Wayne, Tyler Warren. BA in Econs., Washington & Lee U., 1968; JD, U. S.C., 1974. Bar: SC 1975, US Dist. Ct. SC 1975. Assoc. Carl R. Reasonover, Camden, S.C., 1975-77; ptnr. Reasonover & Jacobs, Camden, S.C., 1977-80; pvt. practice law Camden, S.C., 1980-99; judge family ct. 5th Jud. Cir., S.C., 1999—. Asst. city judge Mcpl. Ct., Camden, 1976-77; master in equity S.C. Jud. Sys., Camden, 1978-99; mem. Jud. Coun. for S.C., Columbia, 1989-2000; mem. fee dispute panel S.C. Bar Assn., 1986-93. Bd. dirs. ARC, Camden, 1976-78, Am. Cancer Soc., Camden, 1976-78, United Way, Camden, 1978-82; active Boy Scouts Am., Camden, 1984-96. Capt. U.S. Army, 1968-72. Recipient Dist. Award of Merit Indian Waters Coun. Boy Scouts Am., 1991; named Scouting Family of Yr., 1990. Mem. ABA, VFW, S.C. Bar Assn., Am. Legion, Res. Officers Assn., Elks. Methodist. Home: 418 Lafayette Way Camden SC 29020-1642 Office: Kershaw County Courthouse PO Box 664 Camden SC 29020-0664 Office Phone: 803-425-1500 ext. 5390.

JACOBS, RUTH HARRIET, poet, playwright, sociologist, gerontologist; b. Boston, Nov. 15, 1924; d. Samuel J. Miller and Jane G. (Miller); m. Neal Jacobs, Aug. 1948 (div.); children: Eli, Edith. BS, Boston U, 1964; PhD, Brandeis U., 1969. Reporter, feature writer Herald-Traveler, Boston, 1943-49; tchr. Mass. Bay Community Coll., Northeastern U., 1961-69; prof. sociology Boston U., 1969-82; prof., chmn. dept. sociology Clark U., Worcester, Mass., 1982-87; rsch. scholar women's ctr. Wellesley Coll., Mass., 1985—; prof. human svcs. Springfield Coll., Manchester, N.H., 1988—; lectr. Regis Coll., Weston, Mass., 1989—2002, tchr. lifetime learning, 2005; tchr. Brandeis U., 2000—. Vis. prof. Coll. William and Mary, 1990; vis. rsch. scholar Five Colls. Women's Rsch. Ctr., Mount Holyoke Coll., 1992; spkr. in field. Author: Life After Youth: Female, Forty, What Next, 1979, Button, Button, Who Has the Button, 1983, rev. edit., 1996, (manual) Older Women Surviving and Thriving, 1987, Out of Their Mouths, 1988, Be an Outrageous Older Woman: A.R.A.S.P., 1991, rev. edit., 1993, 2d rev. edit., 1997, We Speak for Peace: An Anthology, 1993, Women Who Touched My Life: A Memoir, 1996, The ABC's of Aging: Mother Ruth Rhymes for Ageing, Sageing and Rageing, 2000, rev. edit., 2005, The ABC's of Aging: Advice from an Outrageous Gerontologist, 2005; co-author: Re-Engagement in Late Life: Re-Employment and Re-Marriage, 1979, (play) Happy Birthday, 2003; contbr. articles to profl. jours., chpts. to books, poetry to anthologies and mags. NIMH grantee, 1972-75; Faculty fellow NSF, 1977-78; recipient Dewing Peace award, Pendle Hill, Walingford, Pa., 1993 Mem.: New Eng. Sociol. Assn. (v.p. 1976, Pioneer award 1993, Athena award for mentoring 1998). Mem. Soc. Of Friends. Home and Office: 75 High Ledge Ave Wellesley MA 02482-1042 Office Phone: 781-237-1793.

JACOBS, SELBY C., medical educator, health facility administrator; BA, Yale U., 1961, MPH, 1972; MD, Case Western U., 1965. Prof. Yale U., New Haven, dir. Conn. Mental Health Ctr. Contbr. articles to profl. jours. Mem.: Am. Psychiatric Assn. Office: Conn Mental Health Ctr 34 Park St New Haven CT 06519-1187 Office Fax: 203-974-7099. E-mail: selby.jacobs@yale.edu.*

JACOBS, SHARON O., lawyer; b. Oklahoma City, Okla., Jan. 26, 1962; 2 children. BA, U. Ga., 1984; JD, U. Mo. Columbia, 1990. Bar: Tenn. 1991, Mo. 1992. Asst. gen. counsel Tenn. Dept. Environment and Conservation, Nashville, 1991—92; asst. atty. gen. Tenn. Atty. Gen. and Reporter, Nashville, 1992—95; assoc., ptnr. Wyatt, Tarrant and Combs, Nashville, 1995—2003; mem. Bone McAllester Norton PLLC, Nashville, 2003—. Co-author: West's Medical Waste Handbook, 1999, West's Medical Waste Handbook, 2d edit., 2000. Pres. Akiva Sch. Bd. Dirs., 2000—02. Mem.: Nashville Bar Assn. (chair Environ. law sect.), Tenn. Bar Assn. (chair, vice chair, sec. 1997—2002, chair Environ. sect. 2001—02, Outstanding Sect. Chair award 2001—02). Avocations: hiking, reading, camping, skiing. Office: Bone McAllester Norton PLLC 511 Union St Ste 1600 Nashville TN 37219 Office Phone: 615-328-6300.

JACOBS, STEPHEN JAY, musician, composer, writer; b. San Francisco, Oct. 7, 1947; s. Martin Phillip and Madeline Louise (Burnley) J. AA in Music, Monterey Peninsula Coll., 1973; postgrad., Calif. State U., Northridge, 1974. Lic. fed. police officer Fed. Law Enforcement Tng. Ctr. Musician, composer Local 47 Am. Fedn. Musicians, L.A., 1973—; writer, poet L.A., 1982—; tchr. life sci. Fauna Edn. Ctr., L.A., 1982; CEO Chui Prodns., L.A., 1982—; police officer U.S. Postal Inspection Svc., L.A., 1995—. Ptnr. Jacobs & Jacobs Concepts, L.A., 1996—. Musician, composer, arranger, writer, narrator, prodr.: (music and text on cassette and CD) This World, 1992; rec. artist Chui Records; contbr. poetry to anthologies (Editors award 1995-96). With U.S. Army, 1965-69, ETO, Vietnam. Mem. NARAS (voting mem.), Internat. Soc. Poets, Am. Fedn. Musicians, Songwriting Guild Am., Fraternal Order Police. Avocations: reading, research, skydiving. Home and Office: Chui Prodns 1259 N Hoover St Los Angeles CA 90029-2009

JACOBS, THOMAS LEROY, author; b. N.Y.C., July 18, 1936; s. Laurence Leroy and Margaret Mary (Heffener) J.; m. Linda Lee Printy, June 16, 1962; children: Belinda, Timothy. BSEE, U.S. Naval Acad., 1958. Commd. ensign USN, 1958, advanced through grades to capt., ret., 1986, asst. to CINCPAC Fleet; program mgr. Boeing Co., Huntington Beach, Calif., 1986-97, cons., 1997-98. Author: King's Pawn, 1998, The Bimini Boys, 2000; contbr. numerous articles to profl. jours. Decorated Legion of Merit (2). Mem. Christian Coalition, U.S. Naval Inst. Republican. Avocations: surfing, swimming, beach volleyball. Home: 61-749 Papailoa Rd Haleiwa HI 96712 Office: 27 Canyon Island Dr Newport Beach CA 92660 E-mail: tom.jacobs@prodigy.net.

JACOBS, TIMOTHY ANDREW, epidemiologist, international health consultant, medical missionary; b. St. Petersburg, Fla., Nov. 5, 1944; s. W. Andrew and Virginia (Ott) J.; m. Carolyn Martin, Nov. 4, 1972; 1 child, Jenny Thuy Ha. BSN, U. Fla., 1970; MS, PNP, U. Utah, 1976; PhD, Internat. Inst. Advanced Studies, 1979; C.T.M., Liverpool (Eng.) Sch. Tropical Medicine, 1982; cert. hosp. epidemiology, U. Iowa, 1985; MPH, Yale U., 1991. Nat. design and media cons. Nat. Assn. Pediatric Nurse Assocs. and Practitioners, Cherry Hill, N.J., 1977-83; asst. prof., co-coord. community health nursing U. N.D., Grand Forks, 1980; vol. epidemiologist, pub. health specialist Vinh Children's Hosp., Vinh City, Vietnam, 1989; pediatric staff nurse I U. Fla. Pediatric Svc., Shands Teaching Hosp., Gainesville, 1970; instr. pediatric nursing U. Utah Coll. Nursing, Salt Lake City, 1976-77; pvt. cons. Internat. Cmty. Health and Epidemiology, New Haven, 1990-94; med. supr., health svcs. mgr. Brown & Root Logcap Med. Clinic, Port-au-Prince, Haiti, 1994-95; med. tech. proposal cons. UN, Rwanda, Angola, 1995; specialist Home Health Care, Tampa, Fla., 1996—. Vol. pub. health scientist, cons. Hanoi (Vietnam) Sch. Pub. Health; cons. epidemiologist Vinh and Huong

Son, Vietnam, 1993; internat. edn. cons. U. Am., New Orleans, 1994; cons. infectious disease epidemiology, consulate of Nicaragua, Miami, Health for Health Svcs. Hurricane Mitch, 1998; cons. Christian Haitian Outreach Clinics and Orphanages, Jeremie and Mariani, Haiti, 1998—; pediatric clin. planner and designer, Carrafour, Haiti, 2002; prin. designer Ambulatory Primary Care Clinic, Mariani, Haiti, 2002; trustee Burnett Internat. U. Sch. Medicine and Health Scis., Port-au-Prince, 2004. Contbg. editor Episource, 1991, 97, Resources in Epidemiology; contbr. articles to profl. jours.; contbr. to poetry jours.; anthologies Daybreak on the Land, 1997, Audiotape Sounds of Poetry, 1997, Archive of the Vietnam Conflict, Personal Papers Collection, 1999. Donor, contbr. Asian Family and Comty. Empowerment Ctr., St. Petersburg, Fla., Caribbean Mercy, Mercy Ships, Garden Valley, Tex., 2001, Love a Child Orphanage and Med. Clinic, Fond Parisien, Haiti, 2001-02. Capt. Nurse Corps, U.S. Army, 1968-73, Vietnam. Recipient Cert. of Achievement in HIV-AIDS Edn., AIDS Project, New Haven, Conn., 1994, Editor's Choice award for outstanding achievement in poetry Nat. Libr. Poetry, 1997. Fellow Royal Soc. Tropical Medicine and Hygiene (London), Am. Biog. Inst. (advisor, rsch. adv. bd.); mem. AMA, VFW, Am. Legion, Vietnam Vets. Am., Nat. Assn. Pediatric Nurse Assocs. and Practitioners (com. dir. graphics & logos mil. chpt., former chmn. nat. art and exhibits subcom., former mem. pub. rels. com., Cert. Recognition 1983), Am. Pub. Health Assn. (epidemiology sect., internat. healthsect., mem. caucus pub. health and faith cmty.), Internat. Assn. Med. Assistance to Travellers, Fla. Pub. Health Assn., Nat. Adolescent Health Promotion Network, Assn. Mil. Surgeons U.S., Ret. Army Nurse Corps Assn., Liverpool Tropical Sch. Assn. (Eng.), Assn. Yale Alumni in Pub. Health, Consortium for Internat. Nursing Edn., Rsch. & Practice, U.S.-Vietnam Friendship Assn., Doctorate Assn. N.Y. Educators, Fleet Marine Force Corpsman Assn. (former Conn. rep., charter mem.), U.S. Navy Corpsmen United Assn., Am. Assn. Navy Hosp. Corpsmen, U.S. Army (Vietnam) 24th Evacuation Hosp. Assn. (com. asv. reunion 1993), Vets. Vietnam Restoration Project, U.S. Com. Scientific Cooperation with Vietnam, N.Y. Acad. of Sci., Walter Reed Army Med. Ctr. Soc. (charter), Spl. Ops. Med. Assn., Soaring Soc. Am., Tampa Bay Soaring Soc. (student pvt. pilot), Sigma Xi, Sigma Theta Tau (charter mem. Gamma Rho chpt.), Phi Kappa Phi. Avocations: racewalking, fishing, travel. Home: 11333 Calgary Cir Tampa FL 33624-4804 Office Phone: 813-269-9094. Personal E-mail: epidoc91@tampabay.rr.com.

JACOBS, TRAVIS BEAL, historian, educator; b. N.Y.C., N.Y., Apr. 22, 1936; s. Albert Charles and Loretta Field (Beal) J.; m. Eleanor Morison (div. 1982); children: Travis Beal, Holmes Morison. AB, Princeton U., 1958; MA, Columbia U., 1960, PhD, 1971. Mem. faculty Middlebury Coll. (Vt.), 1965—, prof. history, 1978-92, Fletcher D. Proctor prof. Am. history, 1992—, chmn. dept. history, 1976-88, 91-95. Editor: Middlebury College General Catalogue: Bicentennial Edition, 2000; co-editor: Navigating The Rapids, 1918-1971, From the Papers of Adolf A. Berle, 1973, Eisenhower at Columbia, 2001, America and the Winter War, 1939-1941, 1981, Dwight D. Eisenhower and the Founding of The American Assembly, 2004. Cons. 20th Century Fund, 1972-73; bd. dirs. Psi Upsilon Found., 1971-98, hon., 1998—; trustee Sheldon Mus., 1984-90, 95-01, pres., 1987-90, hon. trustee, 2003-; pres. Chappaquiddick Island Assn., 1983-86; participant Eisenhower Centennial Programs, 1990. Earhart fellow, 1989-90, 95-96; Fulbright sr. specialists grant, Tunisia, 2004. Mem. Am. Hist. Assn., Ctr. for Study of Presidency, Orgn. Am. Historians, Soc. Historians Fgn. Rels., Vt. Hist. Soc., Princeton Club (N.Y.C.). Episcopalian. Home: 1104 Vt Route 125 Bridport VT 05734-9756 Office: Dept Hist Middlebury Coll Middlebury VT 05753 Office Phone: 802-443-5315. E-mail: tjacobs@middlebury.edu.

JACOBS, VICKI ANN, education educator; b. Cleve., June 17, 1951; d. Donald K. and Frances A. Jacobs; m. Steven L. Canter, 1982; 1 child, Alexander J. Canter. BA in English and Edn., Mich. State U., 1973; MA in English, U. Mass., Boston, 1977; cert. advanced study in reading, language and learning disabilities, Harvard U., 1980, EdD in Reading, Language and Learning Disabilities, 1986. Cert. tchr. English and reading cert. supr. Mass. Tchr. secondary English Holbrook (Mass.) Pub. Schs., 1973-79; mem. adj. faculty in English and edn. Various colls., Boston, 1980-83, St. Michael's Coll., Winooski, Vt., 1980, 83; assoc. faculty mem. Bard Coll. Inst. for Writing and Thinking, Annandale-on Hudson, N.Y., 1983—; coord. writing group Harvard Prins.' Ctr., Cambridge, Mass., 1983-93; instr. reading Harvard U. Grad. Sch. Edn., Cambridge, 1981-90, lectr. edn., 1990—, asst. dir. of tchr. edn. programs, 1986-94, assoc. dir. tchr. edn. programs, 1995—. Cons., lectr. Various orgns., 1981—. Manuscript editor: Harvard Ednl. Rev., 1981—83; co-author: English Grammar and Composition, 1981, 1986, The Reading Crisis: Why Poor Children Fall Behind, 1990; mem. editl. bd. newsletter Mass. Ctr. Tchg. and Learning, 1988—2001, mem. editl. bd. Rsch. in Tchg. English, 1991—96; contbr. articles to profl. jours. Com. mem. attracting sci. and math. PhDs to K-12 edn. NAS/Nat. Rsch. Coun. Fellow, NEH, 1978—79. Recipient EdPress award, 1982; fellow, NEH, 1978—79. Mem.: Am. Edn. Rsch. Assn., Mass. Assn. Tchrs. Edn. (at-large exec. com. 1986—96, pres. 1991—92), Mass. Assn. Coll. and Univ. Reading Educators, Internat. Reading Assn., Nat. Coun. Tchrs. English, Am. Assn. Colls. Tchr. Edn. (Mass. br.). Office: Harvard Grad Sch Edn 311-312 Longfellow Hall Appian Way Cambridge MA 02138

JACOBS, WENDY, editor; b. Conn. d. Gerald and Eileen Jacobs. BA, U. Conn., 1974; postgrad., The Russian Sch., Northfield, Vt., 1974, Ind. U., 1975, U. Toronto, 1978—79. With Jours. divsn. Plenum Pub., N.Y.C., 1974—76, 1976—77; with HIAS, Vienna, 1976, Yorkville Press, Toronto, 1977, Macmillan Can., 1977—78, U. Toronto, 1979—80, Harlequin Books/Torstar Enterprises, 1980—81; cons. and editor, 1981—. Office: 5645 Lakeview Mews Dr Boynton Beach FL 33437

JACOBS, WILLIAM PAUL, botanist, educator; b. Boston, May 25, 1919; s. Vincent H. and Elizabeth (Kennedy) J.; m. Jane Shaw, Mar. 12, 1949; children: Mark, Anne. AB magna cum laude, Harvard U., 1942, PhD, 1946. Research assoc. biology Harvard U., 1946-47; jr. prize fellow Harvard Soc. Fellows, 1947-48; faculty Princeton, 1948—, prof. biology, 1962-89, prof. emeritus, 1989—, W.L. Schultz prof. biology, 1969. Mem. com. innovation lab. study Biol. Scis. Curriculum Study, 1959-64; vis. prof. U. Calif.-Berkeley, 1953, U. Oxford, 1962, U. Lausanne, 1967, U. Colo., 1972, U. Bristol (Eng.), 1980 Author: (with C.E. LaMotte) Regulation in Plants by Hormones, 1964, Plant Hormones and Plant Development, 1979; contbr. articles to sci. publs. Served with M.C. AUS, 1942-44. Recipient Morrison prize, N.Y. Acad. Scis., 1951, Medal, Brno Agrl. U., 1994; fellow Sheldon Travelling fellow, 1944, Lalor fellow, 1950—51, Sr. Postdoctoral fellow, NSF, 1957, Faculty fellow, 1962, Guggenheim fellow, 1967. Mem. Soc. Study Devel. and Growth (pres. 1960-61), Bot. Soc. Am. (Dimond prize 1974), Am. Soc. Plant Physiologists (editorial bd. 1968-72, Barnes award for lifetime achievement 1998), Phycological Soc. Am., Internat. Soc. Plant Morphologists, Internat. Phycological Soc., Internat. Plant Growth Substances Assn. Home: 64 Maclean Cir Princeton NJ 08540-5621 Office: Princeton U Dept Molecular Biology Princeton NJ 08544-0001 E-mail: wpjacobs@princeton.edu.

JACOBS-CAREY, SHEILA L., retired immunologist; b. N.Y.C., Oct. 10, 1939; d. Max and Rosalind Lehrhaupt; m. Richard D. Jacobs, 1961 (div. 1980); children: Marcy G. Little, Sharon L. Jacobs; m. Robert R. Carey, Apr. 21, 1985. BS, Carnegie Inst. Tech., Pitts., 1961; MS, L.I. U., Bklyn., 1964; PhD, Columbia U., N.Y.C., 1968. Instr. SUNY-Downstate Med. Ctr., Bklyn., 1968—71; rsch. asst. CUNY/Lehman Coll., Bronx, 1972—76; rsch. assoc. prof. N.Y. Med. Coll., Valhalla, NY, 1976—81; assoc. prof. Wagner Coll., S.I., NY, 1981—82; sr./prin. scientist Schering-Plough Corp., Bloomfield, NJ, 1982—85; sect. leader Schering-Plough Rsch. Inst., Kenilworth, NJ, 1985—2003; ret., 2004. Lectr. in field. Contbr. articles to profl. jours. Mem. Planned Parenthood. Mem.: AAAS, Internat. Soc. for Interferon and Cytokine Rsch., Am. Chem. Soc., Ocean Conservancy, Nature Conservancy, Audobon Soc., Sierra Club, Phi Sigma, Phi Kappa Phi, Sigma Xi. Avocations: reading, snorkeling, cooking. Home: 52 Ivy Pl Wayne NJ 07470 E-mail: drsjacobs@optonline.net.

JACOBSEN, BETTY, artist, art educator; b. S.I., N.Y., Oct. 12, 1954; d. Kurt R. and Borghild (Tvede) J. BA, Montclair State Coll., 1980; MA, NYU, 1992. Artist, 1954—; tchr. art Bound Brook (N.J.) Sch. Dist., 1980-82, Warren (N.J.) Sch. Dist., 1980-82, Union Cath. Regional High Sch., Scotch Plains, N.J., 1982-85, Summit (N.J.) Sr. High Sch., 1985-86, Hunterdon Central Regional High Sch., Flemington, N.J., 1986—. Resident artist Skidmore Coll., Saratoga Springs, 1989, Va. Ctr. Creative Arts, Sweet Briar, 1989, Millay Colony for Arts, Austerlitz, N.Y., 1991, Dorland Mountain Arts Colony, Temecula, Calif., 1993. Editorial artist the Home News Daily Newspaper, 1985-86; artist: Kalliope: A Journal of Women's Art: The Spiritual Quest, 1989. Mem. N.J. Edn. Assn. Avocations: the arts, outdoor activities. Home: 3897 Gayman Rd Doylestown PA 18901-9032 Office: Hunterdon Central Regional High Sch 84 State Route 31 Flemington NJ 08822-1251

JACOBSEN, DIANE DEMELL, finance company executive, foreign policy specialist; b. N.Y.C., Sept. 21, 1944; d. A. Leonard and Lizette DeMell; m. Thomas H. Jacobsen, June 15, 1985 (dec. July 20, 2002). Bachelors Degree, CUNY, 1965; M in Liberal Arts, Washington U., 1995, M in Internat. Affairs, 2000, PhD in Internat. Affairs, 2003. Sr. exec. Internat. Bus. Machine, Armonk, N.Y., 1965-86; sr. v.p. Bapt. Health Inc., Jacksonville, Fla., 1987-88; pres., CEO Dependable Ins. Group, Jacksonville, 1988-91; pres. DeMell Group, Ponte Vedra Beach, Fla., 1991—2001. Conflict resolution specialist Ctr. for Internat. Understanding, St. Louis; adv. dir. internat. leadership program Washington U., St. Louis, 1998—; adv. group, Coun. Fgn. Rels., 2002-. Commr., trustee St. Louis Art Mus., 1992—; trustee Children's Hosp., St. Louis, 1992—94, Repertory Theater, Webster Grove, Mo., 1992—95; bd. dirs. World Affairs Coun. of Jax. Named Disting. Alumna of Yr., Washington U., 2005; recipient Allison Allas award, Nat. Marrow Donor Program, 2005. Mem.: Women's Fgn. Policy Group. Avocations: woodworking, swimming, bicycling.

JACOBSEN, ERIC N., chemistry professor; BS in Chemistry, NYU, 1982; PhD, U. Calif., Berkeley, 1986. Postdoctoral fellow MIT, 1986—88; asst. prof. U. Illinois, 1988—91, assoc. prof., 1991—93; prof. dept. chemistry Harvard U., Cambridge, Mass., 1993—2001, Sheldon Emery prof. dept. chemistry, 2001—. Consultant Sepracor, Mass., 1990—, Merck, NJ, 1994—, Rhodia ChiRex, Mass., 1994—, Versicor, Calif., 1995—; mem. editorial bds. Advanced Synthesis and Catalysis, Sci. of Synthesis, Jour. Organic Chemistry, Organic Letters, Jour of Combinatorial Chemistry, Jour. Molecular Catalysis, Current Opinion in Drug Discovery & Devel. Co-author: (books) Comprehensive Asymmetric Catalysis: Comprehensive Overviews in Chemistry, 1999, Comprehensive Asymmetric Catalysis: Supplement 1, 2003. Recipient George Granger Brown award, 1981, NIH Postdoctoral Fellowship, 1986-88, NSF Presidential Young Investigator award, 1990, Packard Fellowship Sci. & Engring., 1991, Eli Lilly Grant, 1991, Merck Faculty Devel. award, 1991, Union Carbide Innovation award, 1992, Alfred P. Sloan Found. Fellowship, 1992, Zeneca Chemistry award, 1993, Fluka prize, 1994, Vant Hoff prize, 1998, Piero Pino prize, 1999, Baekeland award, 1999, NIH Merit award, 2002. Fellow: Am. Acad. Arts & Sci., AAAS; mem.: Am. Chemical Soc. (Creative Work in Organic Synthesis award 2001, Chemical Pioneer award 2004). Office: Harvard U Dept Chemistry 12 Oxford St Cambridge MA 02138

JACOBSEN, HARRY R., hospital administrator, physician; MD, U. Ill., 1972. Resident, internal medicine Johns Hopkins U.; resident, nephrology U. Tex. Health Sci. Ctr., Dallas; chief, nephrology U.S. Army Surg. Rsch. Ctr., Brooke Army Med. Ctr., 1976—78; faculty mem. U. Tex. Southwestern Med. Sch., Dallas, 1978—81; prof., medicine, dir., divsn. nephrology Vanderbilt Med. Sch., Nashville, 1981—97, vice chancellor, health affairs, 1997—; CEO Vanderbilt Med. Ctr., Nashville, 1997—. Chair Nat. Com. on Fgn. Med. Edn. and Accreditation; bd. dirs. Assn. Acad. Health Ctrs., Nashville Health Care Coun., Mid. Tenn. Coun., Boy Scouts Am., Evidence-Based Medicine Solutions; bd. dirs., vice chmn. Renal Care Group; chmn., bd. dirs. IMED; dir. Kinetic Concepts, Inc. Contbr. articles to profl. jours.; co-editor: The Principles and Practice of Nephrology. Mem.: Inst. Medicine, Soc. Med. Adminstrs., Assn. of Am. Physicians, Am. Soc. Clin. Investigation. Office: Vanderbilt Univ Med Ctr 21st Ave S and Garland Ave Nashville TN 37232-0001

JACOBSEN, HUGH NEWELL, architect; b. Grand Rapids, Mich., Mar. 11, 1929; s. John Edwall and Lucy Ellen (Newell) J.; m. Robin Kearney, Dec. 27, 1952; children: John Edwall, Matthew Christian, Simon Townsend. BA, U. Md., 1951; B.Arch., M.Arch., Yale, 1955; cert., Archtl. Asso. Sch. Architecture, London, Eng., 1954; L.H.D. (hon.), Gettysburg Coll., 1974, Bradford Coll., 1990; DFA (hon.), U. Md., 1993. Architect with Philip Johnson, New Canaan, Conn., 1955, Keyes, Lethbridge & Condon, Washington, 1957-58; prin. Hugh Newell Jacobsen, FAIA, Washington, 1958—. Lectr. univs.; vis. prof. U. Cairo, Egypt, 1970 Editor: A Guide to the Architecture of Washington, D.C., 1965; prin. works include U.S. Embassy, Paris, addition to U.S. Capital, two Smithsonian Mus. (renovations), So. Vt. Art Ctr. Mem. adv. bd. Internat. Hassan Fathy Inst.; trustee Corcoran Gallery Art, 1973-81, Washington Gallery Modern Art, 1965-69, Washington Theater Club, 1965-72. Served with USAF, 1955-57. John Fitzgerald Kennedy Meml. fellow New Zealand Govt., 1971, Silver medal for distinction in design Tau Sigma Delta, 1981; named to Hall of Fame U. Md., 2000. Fellow AIA (Centennial award 1996, nat. AIA honor awards 1969, 74, 78, 80, 85, 88, numerous AIA chpt. awards, 20 Archtl. Record awards, Outstanding Learning Disabled Achiever award 1990, others); mem. NAD (elected), Cosmos Club (Washington), Century Assn., Yale Club (N.Y.C.). Office: 2529 P St NW Washington DC 20007-3024 Office Phone: 202-337-5200.

JACOBSEN, JEFFREY RICHARD, music educator; b. Dickinson, ND, July 30, 1952; s. Richard Lee and Hope Melba Jacobsen; m. Michele R. Barta, Aug. 16, 1974; 1 child, Nicolai Lee. BS in Music Edn., Mayville State U., 1974; M in Mus. Edn., U. ND, 1982; PhD in Music Edn., U. No. Colo., 1986; Postdoc. in Conducting, Northwestern U., 2001, U. SC., 1996—97; post Doctoral study in Conducting, U. of Iowa, Iowa City, IA, 1996—2002, Cleve. Inst. of Music, Cleveland, OH, 1998—98, Am. Symphony Orchestra League, 2004. Asst. dir. chamber orch., jazz ensemble U. ND, 1981—82; condr. orch., dir. jazz ensemble, jazz combo, assoc. dir. jazz studies program U. No. Colo., 1982—84; dir. orch. and jazz ensemble Boulder Valley Pub. Schs., 1984—94; orch. dir. Blue Valley Sch. Dist., 1994—2001; artistic dir., condr. youth symphony Kansas City Philharm. East Orch., 1995—2001; artistic dir., founding condr. Blue Valley Chamber Orch., Overland Park, Kans., 1996—2001; artistic dir., condr. Orch. of the Pines, Nacogdoches, Tex., 2001—; dir. orch. activities Stephen F. Austin State U., Nacogdoches, Tex., 2001—. Artistic dir. Youth Symphony Kansas City, 1995—2001; prin. bassist Liberty (Mo.) Symphony Orch., Liberty, 1996—2001; bassist Mahler Fest. Orch., Boulder, Colo., 1999—; prin. bassist Puccini Fest., Kansas City, 1999—, Rapides Symphony, Alexandria, La., 2001. Musician (bassist): (rec.) Hot IV, 1985 (Nomination for Grammy in Jazz Category, 1985). Mem. Boulder Musician's Union, Boulder, Colo., 1988—94. Recipient Outstanding Orch. Dir., Kans. Orch. Directors Assn., 2000-2001, Mary Taylor Award for Excellence in Classroom Tchg., Boulder Valley Schools, 1991-1992, Guest Condr., ND All State Orch. Festival, 2001, Region 21/4 Tex. Music Educators Assn., 2001, Region 7 Tex. Music Educators Assn., 2002, Region 17 Tex. Mus. Edn., 2002, Region 7 Tex. Mus. Edn., 2003, Region 20 Tex. Mus. Edn., 2004, Region 19 Tex. Mus. Edn., 2005. Mem.: Tex. Music Educators Assn., Tex. Orch. Dirs Assn., Nat. Sch. Orch. Assn. (divsn. chmn. 1986—88), Am. String Tchrs. Assn., Music Educators Nat. Conf., Internat. Soc. of Bassists, Am. Symphony Orch. League, Conductor's Guild. Avocations: racquetball, bicycling, fly fishing, chess. Office: Stephen F Austin State University Department of Music Nacogdoches TX 75962-3043 Office Phone: 936-468-3885. Personal E-mail: jef@jjacobsen.com. E-mail: jjacobsen@sfasu.edu.

JACOBSEN, JEFFREY SCOTT, environmental scientist; BS in Soil Sci., Calif. Polytech. State U., San Luis Obispo, 1979; MS in Agronomy, Colo. State U., 1982; PhD in Soil Sci. Fertility and Plant Nutrition, Okla. State U., 1985. Rsch asst. dept. agronomy Colo. State U., Fort Collins, 1979-82, technician dept. agronomy, 1982; tchg. asst. dept. agronomy Okla. State U., Stillwater, 1982-86; from asst. prof. to assoc. prof, soil scientist Mont. State U., Bozeman, 1986—, interim head dept. plant, soil and environ. scis., 1994-98, dept. head land resources environ. sci., 1998—. Recipient CIBA-GEIGY award in Agronomy Am. Soc. of Agronomy, 1994. Fellow Am. Soc. Agronomy. Office: Montana State U Dept of Agriculture 202 Linfield Hall PO Box 172860 Bozeman MT 59717-0001

JACOBSEN, JON ANTHONY, banker, lawyer; b. Omaha, Mar. 20, 1961; s. Robert Stanley and Joyce Ann (Hingtgen) Jacobsen; m. Debra Jean Slavin, Feb. 6, 1988; children: Gerard Christopher, Peter James, Jamie Marie. BSBA, Creighton U., 1983; JD, U. Iowa, 1988. Bar: Nebr. 1989, US Dist. Ct. Nebr., US Ct. Appeals (8th cir.) 2004. Mgmt. info. cons. Arthur Andersen & Co., Omaha, 1983—85; pres. Prosthetic Designs, Inc., Davenport, Iowa, 1988—89; assoc. Sherrets & Smith, Omaha, 1989—90; campaign coord. Staskiewicz for Congress, Omaha, 1990; state coord. Assn. Nebr. Cmnty. Action Agencies, Lincoln, Nebr., 1990—91; exec. v.p., finance devel. Sportsworld Complex Co., Omaha, 1990—91; asst. alumni rels. dir. Creighton U., Omaha, 1991—95; mgr. South Pacific Tranquility IcePlex, LLC, Omaha, 1995—2000; v.p., gen. counsel South Pacific Tranquility Inc., Omaha, 1995—2000; sr. mgmt. rep. First Nat. Bank of Omaha, Omaha, 2000—01, trust officer, 2001—04; trust and compliance officer Treynor State Bank, Iowa, 2004—. Instr. Hamilton Coll. (formerly Nebr. Coll. Bus.), Omaha, 1999—. Author: The Win-Win Scenario for Public-Private Partnerships...The Tim Moylan Paradigm for Constitutional Heritage Institute, 1999; assoc. mng. editor Jour. Corp. Law, 1987—88; contbr. articles various pubs. With Nebr. Fed. Cath. Sch. Parents; co-chair Creighton U. Class 1983 20-Yr. Reunion, 2003; Cub/Boy Scout parent Treynor Boy Scouts, Troop/Pack 729, Omaha, 2003—; former den leader, cubmaster Boy Scouts Pack 100, Omaha; vol. George W. Bush President Campaign, 2000; co-chair Bush-Cheney 2004, Pottawattamie County, Iowa, 2003—04; elected Pottawattamie County G.O.P. Ctrl. Com., 2003—; mem. St. Cecilia Cathedral Planned Giving Sub-com., Omaha, 2000—03, St. Cecilia Cathedral Stewardship Devel. Com., 2000—03, chair, 2002—03; with St. Cecilia Cathedral Spiritual Life and Worship Com., 2003—05; mem. St. Cecilia Cathedral Corp. Adv. Bd., Omaha, 2005—, Cath. League Religious and Civil Rights; past fin. sec. Family of Yr. KC, Holy Cross Coun., 1985, charter mem., 1994—; mem. Vision Treynor Com., 2003—04, Coun. Bluffs Estate Planning Coun., 2004—, St. Cecilia Cathedral Corp. Adv. Bd., Omaha, 2005—. Named to Regis HS Hall of Fame, Cedar Rapids, Iowa, 1979; recipient Nat. Forensic League Degree of Distinction award. Mem.: Progressive Bankers Assn. S.W. Iowa (bd. mem. designate 2005), Iowa State Bar Assn., Pottawattamie County Bar Assn., Devel. Stewardship Ctr., Omaha Bar Assn., Nebr. State Bar Assn., Nebr. Fed. Cath. Sch. Parents, KC (charter mem. Holy Cross Coun. 1994—, past fin. sec., Family of Yr. 1985), Miracle Hills Optimist Club, Optimist Club, Beta Gamma Sigma, Alpha Sigma Nu (Creighton Alumni chpt. bd. 2002—, sec. 2003—05). Republican. Roman Catholic. Avocations: golf, swimming, Reagan and modern US pres., John Ford-John Wayne film study, Ellis Peters' Brother Cadfael mystery series. Office: Treynor State Bank 15 E Main St PO Box A Treynor IA 51575 Office Phone: 712-487-3000. Business E-Mail: jon@treynorstatebank.com.

JACOBSEN, LAREN, retired programmer, systems analyst; b. Salt Lake City, June 15, 1937; s. Joseph Smith and Marian (Thomas) J.; m. Audrey Bartlett, July 29, 1970 (div.); children: Andrea, Cecily, Julian. BS, U. Utah, 1963. Programmer IBM, 1963-70; sys. programmer Xerox Computer Svcs., 1970-79; pres. Prescient Investment Co., 1975-82; sr. sys. analyst Quotron Sys., L.A., 1979-86; programmer, analyst Gt. Western Bank, 1987-92; word processing adminstr. Intex Svcs, Inc., Montebello, Calif., 1993-99; data processing specialist ACC Info. Svcs., L.A., 2000—02; ret., 2002. Cons. in field. With USAR, 1961. Mem.: Am. Guild Organists (dean San Jose chpt. 1966—67), Mensa. Home: PO Box 71505 Cottonwood UT 84171 Personal E-mail: larenj@yahoo.com.

JACOBSEN, RAYMOND ALFRED, JR., lawyer; b. Wilmington, Del., Dec. 14, 1949; s. Raymond Alfred and Margaret (Walters) J.; m. Marilyn Perry, Aug. 4, 1973; 1 child, Hunter Perry. BA, U. Del., 1971; JD, Georgetown U., 1975. Bar: D.C. 1975, U.S. Supreme Ct. 1982. From assoc. to ptnr. Howrey & Simon, Washington, 1975-97; dir. antitrust/trade regulation group McDermott, Will & Emery, Washington, 1997—, ptnr., 1997—, chmn. regulatory and govt. affairs dept. and mem. mgmt. com. Adj. prof. internat. anti-trust law Am. U. Law Sch. Spl. projects editor Law & Policy in International Business, 1974-75. Served to capt. U.S. Army, 1975. Mem. ABA (antitrust law sect, litigation sect., internat. law sect., pub. contract law sect.), D.C. Bar Assn., U.S. Supreme Ct. Bar Assn., City Club (Washington), Army and Navy Country Club. Republican. Home: 4205 Maple Tree Ct Alexandria VA 22304-1035 Office: McDermott Will & Emery 600 13th St NW Fl 12 Washington DC 20005-3096 Office Phone: 202-756-8028. Business E-Mail: rayjacobsen@mwe.com.

JACOBSEN, REBECCA HANSON, psychologist; b. Dallas, Oreg., Mar. 1, 1949; d. Earl Willard and Virginia (Van Mourik) H.; m. Michael Anthony Jacobsen, Sept. 25, 1970; 1 child, Leif Peter. BA, CCNY, 1972, MS, 1974; MS, U. Ga., 1980, PhD, 1982. LCewrt. in clin. neuropsychology; bd. cert. clin. neuropsychology, Am. Bd. Profl. Psychology, 1997; lic. psychologist, Calif. Asst. rsch. scientist N.Y. State Psychiat. Inst., 1974-77; grad. teaching asst. U. Oreg., Eugene, 1978-79; psychology intern. VA Med. Ctr., Durham, N.C., 1980-81; asst. prof. Med. Coll. Ga., Augusta, 1983-86; clin. psychologist VA Med. Ctr., Augusta, 1982-86, V.A. Med. Ctr., Sepulveda, Calif., 1986—; clin. asst. prof. Fuller Theol. Sem., Pasadena, Calif., 1987—, Neuropsychiat. Inst. UCLA, 1991—; postdoctoral fellow tng. program neuropsychology, 1988-90; tng. fellow Ind. Consultation Ctr., Bronx, 1974-77. Contbr. articles to profl. jours. U. Ga. fellow, 1981-82. Mem. APA, Internat. Neuropsychol. Soc., Psychologists in Pub. Svc. Avocations: gourmet food, jewelry making. E-mail: rebecca.jacobsen@med.va.gov.

JACOBSEN, RICHARD T., mechanical engineering educator; b. Pocatello, Idaho, Nov. 12, 1941; s. Thorleif (dec.), and Edith Emily (Gladwin) J. dec.); m. Vicki Belle Hopkins, July 16, 1959 (div. Mar. 1973); children: Pamela Sue, Richard T, Eric Ernest; m. Bonnie Lee Stewart, Oct. 19, 1973; 1 child, Jay Michael; stepchild: Erik David Lustig. BSME, U. Idaho, 1963, MSME, 1965; PhD in Engring. Sci., Wash. State U., 1972. Registered profl. engr., Idaho. From instr. to prof. U. Idaho, 1964—77, prof., 1977—, chmn. dept. mech. engring., 1980-85, assoc. dean engring., 1985-90, assoc. dir. Ctr. for Applied Thermodynamic Studies, 1975-86, dir., 1986-99, 2005—, dean engring., 1990-99; chief scientist Idaho Nat. Engring. Environ. Lab. Bechtel BWXT Idaho LLC, 1999—2005, from dep. lab. dir. to assoc. lab. dir. Idaho Nat. Engring. Environ. Lab., 1999—2003, assoc. lab. dir. energy and environ. sci. Idaho Nat. Engring. Environ. Lab., 2003—05. Guest rschr. Nat. Inst. Standards Tech., 1979, 86, 99; mem. annex 18 thermophys. properties environ. acceptable refrigerants com. Internat. Energy Agy., 1991-98; mem. adv. coun. Fed. Lab. Consortium for Tech. Transfer, 2002—, Nat. Environ. Justice, 2003-05; mem. adv. coun Idaho State U. Coll. Engring., 2000-05; instl. rev. bd. protection human subjects in rsch. Idah Nat. Engring. Environ. Lab., 2000-05, chmn., 2001-05 Author: International Union of Pure and Applied Chemistry, Nitrogen-International Thermodynamic Tables of the Fluid State-6, 1979; Oxygen-International Thermodynamic Tables of the Fluid State-9, 1987, Ethylene-International Thermodynamic Tables of the Fluid State-10, 1988, ASHRAE Thermodynamic Properties of Refrigerants (2 vols.), 1986, (monograph series) Thermodynamic Properties of Cryogenic Fluids, 1997; numerous reports on thermodynamic properties of fluids, 1971-; contbr. articles to profl. jours. Recipient Outstanding Engr. award Idaho State U., 2002; NSF sci. faculty fellow, 1968-69; NSF rsch. and travel grantee, 1976-83; Nat. Inst. Standards and Tech. grantee, 1974-91, 95-98, Gas Rsch. Inst. grantee, 1986-91, 1992-98, Dept. Energy grantee, 1991-95. Fellow ASME (faculty advisor 1972-75, 78-84, chmn. region VIII dept. heads com. 1983-85, honors and awards chmn. 1985-91, K-7 tech. com. thermophys. properties 1985—, chmn. 1986-89, 92-95, 2001-04, rsch. tech. com. on water and steam in thermal power systems, 1988—, gen. awards com. 1985-91, chmn. 1988-91, com. on honors 1988-99, vice chmn. 1995-99, mem. bd. on profl. practice and ethics, 1991-2004, v.p. profl. practice 1998-2001, v.p. rsch. 2004-05, v.p. fin. ops. 2005—, Inland Empire Sect. Engr. of Yr. award 1999, Dedicated Svc. award 2003); mem. N.W. Coll. and Univ. Assn. for Sci. (bd. dirs. 1990-93), NSPE, Am. Soc. Engring. Edn., Am. Nuc. Soc., Idaho Rsch. Found. (bd. dirs. 1991-99, 2000—), Soc. Automotive Engrs. (Ralph R. Teetor Edn. award, Detroit 1968), Bonneville County Hist. Soc. (trustee 2001—), ASHRAE (co-recipient Best Tech. Paper award 1984), Federalist Soc. (chmn. environ. and property rights practice group 2003-05), Sigma Xi, Tau Beta Pi, Phi Kappa Phi (Disting. Faculty award 1989). Office: Univ Idaho in Idaho Falls ste 306 1776 Science Ctr Dr Idaho Falls ID 83402 Office Phone: 208-282-7937. Business E-Mail: rtj@if.uidaho.edu.

JACOBSEN, THEODORE H. (TED H. JACOBSEN), labor union administrator, secondary school educator; BS, Fordham U., 1955; postgrad., Hunter Coll., 1957—80, NYU, 1957—80, Columbia U., 1957—80. Cert. HS English tchr. N.Y.C. Tchr. (on leave) N.Y.C. Bd. Edn., 1957—86; editor Labor News and Trade Union Handbook N.Y.C. Ctrl. Labor Coun. AFL-CIO, 1986—. Mem. exec. bd. Jewish Labor Com., N.Y.C., 1977—, Workers Def. League, 1986—, Am. Labor ORT, 1986—; regional v.p. Union Label and Svc. Trades Dept., NY, 1980—96; mem. adv. bd. Harry Van Arsdale Jr. Coll. Labor Studies, Empire State Coll., N.Y.C., 1986—; mem. adv. coun. occupation edn. N.Y.C. Bd. Edn., 1986—2000, vice chmn., 1989—2000; bd. dirs. Nat. Ethnic Coalition Orgns., Inc.; mem. bd. govs. Forum; sec. N.Y.C. Ctrl. Labor Coun. AFL-CIO. Mem. Cmty. Bd. 8, N.Y.C., 1987—93; mem. N.Y.C. Sch. to Work regional coun. Regional Planning Assn.; mem. exec. bd. Friends A. Philip Randolph Campus H.S. City Coll., 1990—; bd. dirs. Cath. Interracial Coun., United Way N.Y., 1988—95, Coun. Environ., N.Y.C., 1988—95, Italian Acad. Found., Nat. Ethnic Coalition Orgns., Inc., Italic Studies Inst.; trustee ARC Greater N.Y., 1989—2001, Italian Hosp. Soc.; mem. exec. bd. Workman's Cir. Home-Geriatric Ctr., 1986—89, treas., 1989—2003; sec. Robert F. Wagner Labor Archives NYU, 1986—; mem. bd. advisors Transition Ctr., N.Y.C. Bd. Edn., Svc. Area Planning Group; mem. Naval War Coll. Found.; mem. N.Y. State coastal mgmt. adv. com. N.Y. Harbor Maritime Industry; charter mem. Battle Normandy Found., 1988—; chmn. N.Y. Trade Union Coun. Histadrut; mem. Asian Pacific Am. Labor Alliance; life mem. Workmen's Cir. Arbeter Ring; patron N.Y.C. Met. Opera. Decorated knight Order of Merit (Italy), comdr. Order Sts. Maurice and Lazarus (Savoy), knight Royal Order Francis I of Bourbon and Two Sicilies; named Man of the Yr., Jewish Heritage Com. and Educators chpt., 1990, June 23, 1993 Theodore 'Ted' Jacobsen Day, Queens Borough Pres., Educator of the Yr., Assn. Tchrs. N.Y., 1986; recipient Cope awards, N.Y. State United Tchrs., 1975, 1978, Best Newsletter award, 1974, 1975, 1979, 1980, 1981, Spl. award educators chpt., Jewish Labor Com., 1986, Roberto Clemente award, Nat. Assn. P.R. Civil Rights, 1988, 75th Anniversary Cert. of Appreciation, U.S. Dept. Labor, 1988, Hurricane Hugo Disaster Relief citation, ARC, 1991, Good Scout award, Greater N.Y. Couns. Boy Scouts Am., 1992, Spl. Recognition award, Hispanic Labor Com., 1992, Leadership Svc. Recognition award, United Way N.Y.C., 1992, Consumer Merit award, N.Y. Consumer Assembly, 1992, Torch of Hope award, Pride Judea, 1993, Congl. Ellis Island medal Honor, 1993, N.Y.C. Coun. citation, 1993, Coalition Labor Union Women award, 1994, John LaFarge award interracial justice, Cath. Interracial Coun. N.Y., 1995, N.Y.C. Nova Ancora Job Tng. Program award of appreciation, N.Y.C. Dept. Probation, 1995, Disting. Svc. award, Internat. Brotherhood Elec. Workers, Local 3, J divsn., 1996, Robert Briscoe award, Emerald Isle Immigration Ctr., 1996, George Meany award, Greater N.Y. Couns. Boy Scouts Am., 1999, Chieftaincy conferment, His Majesty Udumeze of Ohafia, Nigeria. Mem.: NAACP (80th Anniversary Exempler award 1991, golden life heritage), NATAS (bd. govs. N.Y. chpt.), AFTRA, Nat. Italian-Am. Found., TV and Radio Working Press Assn., Internat. Platform Assn., Jewish Heritage Com., Black Trade Unionists Leadership Com., Coalition Labor Union Women, Internat. Labor Comm. Assn., Cath. Tchrs. Assn., Jewish Tchrs. Assn., United Fedn. Tchrs. (P.M. staff 1973—, editor newsletter, chpt. chmn. 1974—86, Eli Trachtenberg award 1966, 1974, 1977, 1981, Albert Lee Smallheiser citation 1976), Actor's Fund (life), Citizens Commn. African Union, United African Congress (coun. elders, adv. bd.), Asia Soc., Lower East Side Tenement (hon. commr. Celebrate Africa Found. 1992—), U.S. Naval Inst., Irish-Am. Studies Com., Irish-Am. Heritage Mus., U.S. Holocaust Meml. Mus. (charter), Masons, Elks, B'nai B'rith (trustee 1989—96, bd. dirs. Adelstein Family Project HOPE Found. Housing Elderly 1992—), Order Sons Italy Am., Loyal League Yiddish Sons Erin (hon.). Avocations: theater, opera, travel. Office: NYC Cen Labor Coun AFL-CIO 31 W 15th St New York NY 10011 E-mail: thjnycusa@aol.com.

JACOBSEN, THOMAS WARREN, retired archaeologist, educator, freelance/self-employed journalist; b. Mankato, Minn., Mar. 18, 1935; s. Maurice and Effie (Jensen) J.; m. Kathryn Jane Anderson, Aug. 18, 1956 (dec. June 1978); children: Mark Thomas, Kirsten; m. Susan K. Lehr, Aug. 1, 1981 (div. Dec. 1991); m. Sharyn Anne Elmquist, Jan. 18, 1997. BA, St. Olaf Coll., 1957; MA, U. Minn., 1960; postgrad., Am. Sch. Classical Studies, Athens, Greece, 1962-63; PhD, U. Pa., 1964. Asst. prof. classics, classical archeology Vanderbilt U., 1964-66; asst. prof. Ind. U., 1966-68, assoc. prof., 1968-75, prof., 1975-92; prof. emeritus, 1992—; chmn. dept. classical studies Ind. U., 1975-78, dir. program in classical archaeology, 1970-85. Staff mem. excavations, Porto Cheli, Greece, 1962, 65, 66, field dir., 1967, dir. excavations at Franchthi Cave, Greece, 1967-96, staff excavations, Kea, Greece, 1963; du Pont spl. rsch. fellow Am. Sch. Classical Studies Athens, 1980-81; vis. scholar Tulane U., 1992—. Gen. editor Excavations at Franchthi Cave, Greece, 1985-96; mem. editorial bd. Archaeology, 1988-92. Served with AUS, 1957. Fulbright scholar Greece, 1962-63; Olivia James fellow Archeol. Inst. Am., Greece, 1968-69; Am. Council Learned Socs. fellow, 1973-74; NSF postdoctoral fellow, 1973-74; Am. Philos. Soc. grantee, 1973-74 Mem. Internat. Clarinet Assn., Modern Greek Studies Assn., Archaeol. Inst. Am. (Charles Eliot Norton Meml. lectr. spring 1988), Am. Sch. Classical Studies (mng. com., emeritus), Hellenic Numismatic Soc. Lutheran. Home: 3970 Laurel St New Orleans LA 70115-1364 Business E-Mail: twj@tulane.edu.

JACOBSON, ALLEN HOWARD, economist; b. NYC, July 5, 1939; s. Jack Joseph and Mary (Laxman) J.; m. Gladys Cecile Safier, Sept. 20, 1970; children: Gennifer Ann, Allison Lindsay. BA, NYU, 1962, postgrad., 1965. Lic. acct. exec. in securities bus., real estate agt., gen. securities prin.; lic. broker/dealer in securities bus. Economist Lional D. Edie & Inc., N.Y.C., 1966-69; sr. economist U.S. Trust Co., N.Y.C., 1969-79; ptnr. Washington Analysis Corp., 1979-87; v.p. NatWest Markets, Washington, 1988-95; sr. v.p. HSBC Securities, Inc., 1995-99; ptnr. Washington Analysis Corp., 1999—. Mem. Nat. Economists Club (v.p. 1982-83, 91-92, bd. govs. 1992-93), Nat. Assn. Bus. Economists (coun. nat. chpt. 1985-86), Washington Assn. Money Mgrs., Montgomery County Assn. Realtors, Lakewood Club, Norbeck Club (bd. dirs. 1981-82). Avocations: tennis, aerobics, real estate, golf, dance. Home: 210 Jersey Ln Rockville MD 20850 Office: Washington Analysis Corp 1120 Connecticut Ave NW Ste 400 Washington DC 20036-3939 Office Phone: 202-756-7710. Business E-Mail: ajacobson@washingtonanalysis.com.

JACOBSON, ANNA SUE, finance company executive; b. Ft. Smith, Ark., Aug. 13, 1940; d. Ray Bradely and Joy Anna (Person) McAlister; m. Lyle Norman Jacobson, Nov. 23, 1958; children: Lyle Michael, Daniel Ray, Julie Ann, Eric Joseph. Cert., Coll. Fin. Planning, 1985. Cert. fin. planner, coll. fin. planning 1985, registered paraplanner. Office mgr. Twin Cities Lithographic Inst., St. Paul, 1963-66, sec., 1971-78; asst. to pres., office mgr. Planners Fin. Svcs., Mpls., 1978-85, asst. corp. treas., 1987-88; fin. paraplanner McAlmont Investment Co., Mpls., 1985-96, office mgr., 1988-96; registered rep. USR Fin. Svc. Inc., 1996-98; nat. retail mktg. coord. Carlson Leisure Group, Minnetonka, Minn., 1998—, nat. retail op. coord. Mpls., 1996; v.p., CFO J&J Splty. Co., 1993—; sr. v.p. AdPro Internat., Inc., Wayzata, Minn., 1996—; acctg. coord. Carlson Wagonlit Travel, 2000—; acctg. specialist Carlson Cos., Inc., Minnetonka, Minn., 2001—. Ind. fin. cons.; co-creator Paraplanning Profession Advisor; bd. dirs. Planners Fin. Svcs.; mem. bd. advisors Coll. Fin. Planning, Denver, 1982—; mem. Fin. Alternatives Mpls., Wayzata, 1996—, Mpls., 1985—; v.p. J & J Splty. Co., St. Paul, 1995—; spkr. in field. Del. Dem. Farmer Labor Com., St. Paul, 1980, campaign chmn. mayoral election, Roseville, Minn., 1983, county commr. city coun. election Roseville, 1980, 84; local chmn. passage of ERA Minn., mem. Am. Lung Assn., St. Paul, Ramsey Found. Minn., Como Cons. Hist. Soc.; past pres. PTA, Minn.; mem. exec. coun. Boy Scouts An., 1977-81; mem. adv. bd. Sch. Dist. 623, Roseville, 1978-81; fund raising com. mem. Twin Cities Pub. TV. Sta., 1975—; mem. ch. coun. deacons St. Michael's Luth. Ch., St. Paul, 1996—, pres. congregation and coun., Roseville, 1998-99. Recipient volunteerism award State Minn., 1981, Cert. Appreciation Minn. Bicentennial Com., 1976; named 1st Fin. Paraplanner in History of Industry. Mem. Internat. Assn. Fin. Planning, Twin Cities Assn. Fin. Planners, Internat. Assn. Bus. and Profl. Women (bd. dirs. 1977-86, pres. 1980-82, Woman Yr. 1982), Minn. Women's Consortium Como Conservatory Hist. Soc., Concordia Acad. Booster Club, Beta Sigma Phi (Nu Phi Mu chpt.). Lutheran. Avocations: tennis, riding, reading, piano, harp. Home: 2171 Dellwood Ave Saint Paul MN 55113-4329 Office: Carlson Leisure Group 701 Lakeshore Pkwy Minnetonka MN 55305-5240 Office Phone: 763-212-6203. E-mail: lnsjacob@aol.com.

JACOBSON, ANTONE GARDNER, retired zoology educator; b. nr. Salt Lake City, May 22, 1929; s. Rufus Ingman and Marvell (Gardner) J.; m. Jacqueline James, July 26, 1962; children: Lauren, Eric. AB, Harvard U., 1951; PhD, Stanford U., 1955. Mem. faculty dept. zoology U. Tex., Austin, 1957—, assoc. prof., 1961-68, prof., 1968-97, prof. emeritus, 1997—; instr. Marine Biol. Lab., Woods Hole, Mass., 1969-70; ret., 1997. Contbr. articles to profl. jours. Harvard Nat. scholar, 1947-51, Henry Newell Honors scholar, 1951-55. Mem. Soc. Devel. Biology, Soc. Integrative & Comparative Biology, Am. Assn. Anatomists, Sigma Xi. Home: 201 Skyline Dr Austin TX 78746-3610 Office: Univ Tex MCDB Pat Labs 1 University Sta CO930 Austin TX 78712-0253 Office Phone: 512-471-5403. Business E-Mail: antone@mail.utexas.edu.

JACOBSON, ARLAND DEAN, religion educator; b. Mitchell, S.D., Sept. 25, 1941; s. Olaf Johannes and Ruth Amelia (Gjesdal) J. m. Wilhelmine Treadwell, Aug. 15, 1964; children: Erik Eugene, Karin Inga. BA, Augustana Coll., 1963; student, Div. Sch., U. Chgo., 1964-65; BD, Luther Theol. Sem., St. Paul, 1967; PhD, Claremont Grad. Sch., 1978. Ordained to ministry Evang. Luth. Ch. Am., 1967. Pastor Scranton (N.D.) Luth. Parish, 1967-71, St. Paul Luth. Ch., Humboldt, S.D., 1974-76; vis. prof. Loyola Marymount U., L.A., 1978-79; asst. prof. Concordia Coll., Moorhead, Minn., 1979-83; exec. dir. CHARIS Ecumenical Ctr. and Fargo-Moorhead Communiversity, Moorhead, 1983—. Chair bd. Great Plains Inst. Theology, Bismarck, N.D., 1969-71; mem. Faith and Order Commn., Minn. Coun. Chs., Mpls., 1985-92. Author: Wisdom Christology in Q, 1978, The First Gospel, 1991, Ecumenical Shared Ministry in the United Methodist Church, 1995, A Journey into our Christian Past, 1999; also numerous articles and revs. Chair conf. planning com. Internat. Coalition for Land-Water Stewardship in the Red River Basin, Moorhead, 1983-85, chair edn. com., 1985-87. Scholar Luth. Theol. Sem., 1966, scholar in residence Inst. for Ecumenical and Cultural Rsch., 1990, Harvard Inst. Mgmt. Lifelong Learning, 1992, Tantur Ecumenical Inst., Jerusalem, 1997; Bush fellow, 1992. Mem. Soc. Bibl. Lit., Cath. Bibl. Assn., Soc. for Advancement Continuing Edn. for Ministry (sec. 1996—), The Jesus Seminar, Westar Inst., Archaeol. Inst. Am., Jazz Arts Group (bd. mem.). Home: PO Box 6 Moorhead MN 56561-0006 Office: Concordia Coll Charis Ecumenical Ctr Moorhead MN 56562-0001 E-mail: jacobson@cord.edu.

JACOBSON, ARTHUR JOHN, law educator; b. N.Y.C., Mar. 22, 1948; s. Harold Gordon and Ruth Fern (Enenstein) J.; m. Joan Ava Lipton, Apr. 25, 1976 (div. 1986); 1 child, Samuel Iser; m. Peninah Ruth Yehudit Petruck, Nov. 22, 1987; 1 child, Benjamin Rafael. BA, Harvard Coll., 1969, JD, 1974, Phd, 1978. Bar: N.Y. 1975, Mass. 1975. Assoc. Cleary Gottlieb Steen & Hamitton, N.Y.C., 1975-77; prof. Cardozo Sch. Law, N.Y.C., 1977—, Max Freund prof. litigation and adv., 1988—. Counsel Sive Paget & Riesel, P.C., N.Y.C., 1989—; Jean Monet prof. of comparative law U. Trento, Italy, Spring 1998. Author: (with Anthony D'Amato) Justice and the Legal System, 1992; editor (with Michael Bamberger) State Limited Liability Company Law, (with Bernhard Schlink) Weimar: A Jurisprudence of Crisis, 2000, (with Michel Rosenfeld) The Longest Night: Polemics and Perspectives on Election 2000, 2002; contbr. articles to profl. jours. Office: Cardozo Sch Law 55 5th Ave Fl 10 New York NY 10003-4391 Business E-Mail: ajacobsn@yu.edu.

JACOBSON, BERNARD, lawyer; b. Hartford, Conn., Feb. 27, 1930; s. Samuel Barnard and Lillian Jacobson; m. Florence Ellen Greenberg, Oct. 7, 1956; children: Daniel John, Alice Lash, Nancy Jacobson-Penn. AB, Amherst Coll., 1951; LLB, Columbia U., 1954. Bar: Conn. 1955, Fla. 1957, U.S. Dist. Ct. (so. dist.) Fla. 1957, U.S. Ct. Appeals (11th cir.) 1961. Pvt. practice, Miami, Fla., 1957-68; ptnr. Fine, Jacobson, Miami, Fla., 1968-94, Holland & Knight LLP, Miami, Fla., 1994—2002, Akerman Senterfitt, Miami, 2002—. Pres., CEO Rep. Mortgage Investors, Miami, 1973-81; presenter in field. Contbr. articles to profl. jours. Chmn. Fla. Congl. Partnership, Miami, 1987; vice chmn. Greater Miami C. of C., 1988-92. With U.S. Army Counter Intelligence Corps, 1955-57. Mem. ABA, Fla. Bar Assn. Avocations: tennis, boating, skiing. Office: Akerman Senterfitt One SE 3d Ave Ste 2800 Miami FL 33131 Office Phone: 305-982-5655. Business E-Mail: bernard.jacobson@akerman.com.

JACOBSON, CHARLES ALLEN, aerospace company executive; b. Cresco, Iowa, June 2, 1925; s. Julius and Beulah Rosella (Peterson) J.; m. Marjorie Helen Minear, June 18, 1947; children: Janelle Paige, Charles Allen Jr., Robert Roger, Julian Kent, Joan Leigh. BS in Aerospace Engring., Iowa State U., 1952; postgrad., St. Louis U., 1956-57. Engr. McDonnell Aircraft Corp., St. Louis, 1952-59, group engr., 1959-64, project dynamics engr., 1964-68; dir. Houston ops. McDonnell Douglas Astronautics Co., 1968-84; v.p., gen. mgr. McDonnell Douglas Tech. Svcs. Co., Huntsville, Ala., 1984-85, McDonnell Douglas Space Systems Co., Houston, 1985-90; pres. GB Tech., Inc., Houston, 1990—. Bd. dirs. M Bank, Clear Lake, Houston; mem. NASA Johnson Space Ctr. Team Excellence Forum; mem. devel. and adv. coun. U. Houston at Clear Lake, 1987-90; mem. Engring Found. adv. coun., U. Tex., Austin, 1989—; pres. Clear Lake Transp. Partnership, Houston, 1990-95, chmn. bd. dirs., 1995—. Dir. Rotary Nat. Award for Space Achievement, Houston, 1984—; dir. Clear Lake Area Econ. Devel. Found., Houston, 1983-84, 86-89, Clear Lake Symphony, Houston, 1987-89; chmn. Bay Area YMCA, Houston, 1981-82; mem. hon. bd. March of Dimes Walk Am., Houston, 1980; vice chmn. fin. Boy Scouts Am. Baysmore dist., 1987-89; adv. dir. Clear Lake Coun. Tech. Socs., 1989—; vice chmn. aerospace Houston area US Savs. Bonds Campaign, 1988. Lt. cmmdr. USNR, 1943-67. Recipient NASA Pub. Svc. medal, 1981, Profl. Achievement Citation for Engring., Iowa State U., Ames, 1988; named Tech. Adminstr. of Yr., Clear Lake Coun. Tech. Socs., 1984; Rotary Internat. Paul Harris fellow, 1983. Fellow AIAA (assoc., Gemini Achievement award 1966); mem. Armed Forces Comms. and Electronics Assn. (bd. dirs. 1987-89), Nat. Contract Mgmt. Assn., Navy League, South Shore Harbor Country Club (bd. dirs. 1987-89), Space Ctr. Rotary (pres. 1982-83). Republican. Avocations: golf, travel. Home: 2908 Doral Ct League City TX 77573-4412 Office: GB Tech Inc 2200 Space Park Dr Ste 400 Houston TX 77058-3680

JACOBSON, CHRISTOPHER JON, music educator; b. Montevideo, Minn., Sept. 17, 1978; s. Robert Allen and Jennifer Mary Jacobson. BA, St. John's U., 2001. Cert. tchr. Minn. Substitute choral dir. Tartan HS, Oakdale, Minn., 2002; dir. choirs Brooklyn Ctr. (Minn.) HS, 2002—04, Chatfield (Minn.) Valley HS, 2004—. Head counselor Nat. Cath. Youth Choir, Collegeville, Minn., 2000—02; music arranger Chosea Valley Carols, 2005. Regents scholar, St. John's U., 1997. Mem.: Music Educators Nat. Conf., Minn. Music Educators Assn., Am. Choral Dirs. Assn. Roman Catholic. Avocations: hiking, swimming. Office: Chosea Valley High Sch 205 Chalon St NE Chatfield MN 55923

JACOBSON, DAVID EDWARD, lawyer; b. Port Chester, NY, May 17, 1949; s. Robert Herzel and Ruth Doris (Rosenzweig) J.; m. Debra Ann Denkensohn, Aug. 10, 1975; 1 child, Andrew. BA in Econs., U. Rochester, 1971; JD, SUNY, Buffalo, 1974; LLM in Taxation, Georgetown U., 1977. Bar: NY 1975, DC 1976, US Tax Ct. 1982, US Ct. Appeals (fed. cir.) 1983. Atty.-advisor Office Chief Counsel, IRS, Washington, 1974-79; tax counsel com. fin. US Senate, Washington, 1979-81; assoc. firm Thelen Reid & Priest LLP, Washington, 1981-86, ptnr., 1986—. Mem. Partnership Coun., 2001-03. Vol. Income Tax Assistance, Arlington, Va., 1977-81; treas. Overlook Townhouse Homeowners Assn., Arlington. Mem. ABA (mem. tax sect. 1982—, vice chmn. regulated utilities com. 1988-90, chmn. 1990-92), NY State Bar Assn. Office: Thelen Reid & Priest LLP 701 Eighth St NW Washington DC 20001-3712 Office Phone: 202-508-4300. Business E-Mail: djacobson@thelenreid.com.

JACOBSON, EUGENE DONALD, medical educator, administrator, researcher; b. Bridgeport, Conn., Feb. 19, 1930; s. Morris and Mary (Mendelsohn) J.; m. Laura Kathryn Osborn, June 9, 1973; children from previous marriage: Laura Ellen, Susan Ruth, Morris David, Daniel Frederick, Miriam Louise. BA, Wesleyan U., 1951; MD, U. Vt., 1955; MS, SUNY, Syracuse, 1960; DM (hon.), Jagiellonian U., 1996. Assoc. prof. UCLA Sch. Medicine, 1965-66; prof., chmn. U. Okla. Sch. Medicine, Oklahoma City, 1966-71, U. Tex. Med. Sch., Houston, 1971-77; vice dean Coll. Medicine U. Cin., 1977-85; dean Sch. Medicine, U. Kans., Kansas City, 1985-88; dean Sch. Medicine U. Colo., Denver, 1988-90, prof., 1990-99, prof. emeritus, 1999—, acting head divsn. gastroenterology, 1994. Cons. NIH, Bethesda, Md., 1968-72, mem. nat. digestive adv. bd., 1985-87; chmn. Nat. Commn., U.S. Congress, Washington, 1977-79; cons. Upjohn Co., Kalamazoo, 1970-87, G. D. Searle and Co., Chgo., 1984-85. Contbr. 320 articles to profl. jours. Served to maj. U.S. Army, 1956-64. NIH Rsch. grantee, 1967-97. Fellow ACP; mem. AMA (ho. of dels. 1991—), Am. Soc. Clin. Investigation, Assn. Am. Physicians, Am. Physiol. Soc., Am. Gastroenterol. Assn. (pres. 1989-90, Friedenwald medal 1998), Am. Digestive Health Found. (bd. dirs., vice chair 1995-98). Office Phone: 415-242-1564.

JACOBSON, FRANK JOEL, cultural organization administrator; b. Phila., Sept. 14, 1948; s. Leonard and June Anette (Groff) J.; m. Stephanie Lou Savage, July 5, 1970; children: Aaron Jeffery, Adam Michael, Ashley Celeste. BA, U. Wis., 1970; MFA, Boston U., 1973. Mng. dir. Mont. Repertory Theater, Missoula, Mo., 1973-75; asst. prof. drama U. Mont., Missoula, 1973-75; program dir. Western States Arts Found., Denver, 1975-77, dir. programs, 1977-78, gen. mgr. budget/planning, 1978-79; exec. dir. Arvada (Colo.) Ctr. for the Arts & Humanities, 1979-85; dir. theatres and arenas City & County of Denver, 1985-87; pres., CEO Scottsdale (Ariz.) Cultural Coun., 1987—. Bd. dirs. Met. Denver Arts Alliance, pres., 1979-85, Rocky Mountain Arts Consortium, pres., 1979-80. Contbr. articles to profl. jours. Mem. panel theater program Nat. Endowment for the Arts, Washington, 1990-92; bd. dirs. Scottsdale Focus, 1988-93, 93-97, Arizonans for Cultural Devel., 1992-97; bd. dirs. Scottsdale Edn. Found., 1994-99, chmn., 1994-96; bd. dirs. Scottsdale Convention and Visitors Bur., 2001—. Mem.: Assn. for Performing Arts Presenters (bd. dirs. 1984—87), Rocky Mountain Theatre Assn. (bd. dirs., pres. 1976—78), Mont. State Theatre Assn. (bd. dirs., pres. 1974—75), Am. Theatre Assn. (bd. dirs. 1976—78), Scottsdale C. of C. (bd. dirs. 2001—). Office: Scottsdale Cultural Council 7380 E 2nd St Scottsdale AZ 85251-5604

JACOBSON, GARY CHARLES, political science professor; b. Orange, Calif., July 7, 1944; s. Charles William and Ruth Hope (Brown) J.; m. Martha Ellen Blake, June 2, 1979. AB in Polit. Sci., Stanford U., 1966; MPhil, Yale U., 1969, PhD in Polit. Sci., 1972. From instr. to assoc. prof. Trinity Coll., Hartford, Conn., 1970-79; from assoc. prof. to prof. polit. sci. U. Calif., San Diego, 1979—; Woodrow Wilson fellow, 1969. Author: Money in Congressional Elections, 1980, (with Samuel Kernell) Strategy and Choice in Congressional Elections, 1981, The Politics of Congressional Elections, 1983, 87, 91, 97, 2000, 2004, The Electoral Origins of Divided Governments, 1990, The Logic of American Politics (with Samuel Kernell), 2000, 2003. Grantee NSF, 1980-82. Mem. Am. Acad. Arts and Scis., Am. Polit. Sci. Assn. (Gladys E. Kammerer award 1981), Western Polit. Sci. Assn., Midwest Polit. Sci. Assn., So. Polit. Sci. Assn. Office: U Calif San Diego Dept Polit Sci # 0521 La Jolla CA 92093

JACOBSON, GARY STEVEN, lawyer; b. Holyoke, Mass., Sept. 4, 1951; s. Rudolph Milton and Frederika Helena (Vanderryn) J.; m. Sharon W. Turkish, June 16, 1974; children: Lowell Daniel, Lee Stuart. BA cum laude, Wesleyan U., Middletown, Conn., 1973; JD, Northwestern U., 1976. Bar: Conn. 1976, N.Y. 1977, N.J. 1977, U.S. Ct. Appeals (3d cir.) 1981, U.S. Ct. Appeals (2d cir.) 1996. Investigative atty. N.Y. State Commn. on Jud. Conduct, N.Y.C., 1976-77; spl. asst. atty. gen. Office Spl. State Prosecutor, N.Y.C., 1977-79; assoc. Hofheimer, Gartlir, Gottlieb & Gross, N.Y.C., 1979-80, Kleinberg, Moroney, Masterson & Schachter, Millburn, N.J., 1980-85, ptnr., 1986-90; of counsel Kelley Drye & Warren, N.Y.C., 1990-91, ptnr., 1992-96, Farer Siegal Fersko, Westfield, NJ, 1996-98; bankruptcy trustee Panel Chpt. 7, 1997—; mem. Gary S. Jacobson, LLC, Mountainside, Springfield, 1998—2002; of counsel Herold and Haines, Warren, NJ, 2002—04, shareholder, 2004—. Co-author: Commercial Litigation in New York State Courts, 1995; editor: Judicial Discipline Reporter, 1976. Republican. Jewish. Home: 99 Susan Dr Chatham NJ 07928-1055 Office: Herold and Haines PA 25 Independence Blvd Warren NJ 07059-6747 Office Phone: 908-647-1022. E-mail: gjacobson@heroldhaines.com.

JACOBSON, GERALDINE MEERBOTT, radiation oncologist; b. Ft. Dix, N.J., July 11, 1950; d. Joseph Otto and Jeanne Adele (Bonnabeau) Meerbott; m. Marcus Jacobson, Mar. 25, 1975 (div. Jan. 1987); 1 child, Justin; m. Patrick R.M. Thomas, Mar. 2, 1996. BS with high honors, Mich. State U., 1972; postgrad., U. South Fla., 1975-76, U. Miami, 1976-77; MD, U. Utah, 1981. Diplomat Am. Bd. Radiology, Nat. Med. Examiners. Intern in pathology U. Utah Med. Sch., Salt Lake City, 1981-82; resident Radiation Therapy Ctr., LDS Hosp., Salt Lake City, 1982-85; vis. resident in radiation therapy Princess Margaret Hosp., Toronto, Can., 1984; instr. Divsn. Radiation Oncology, Dept. Radiology U. Utah Med. Ctr., Toronto, 1985-87; dir. radiation therapy RTOC, Brooksville, Fla., 1987-89; asst. prof., asst. dir. clin. rsch. dept. radiation therapy U. Tex. Med. Br., Galveston, 1989-90; radiation oncologist Lykes Ctr. for Radiation Therapy, Morton Plant Hosp., Clearwater, Fla., 1990-92; med. dir. Bayfront Cancer Care Ctr., St. Petersburg, Fla., 1992—. Oncology com. Bayfront Med. Ctr., 1992—, radiation safet com., 1992—, rsch. and rev. com., 1994—; radiation therapy tech. adv. com. HCC, 1993—; mediation com. Pinellas County Med. Soc., 1990—; presenter in field. Contbr. articles to profl. jours. Bd. dirs. WMNF Community Radio, Tampa, Fal., 1993—. Clin. fellowship Am. Cancer Soc., 1984-85. Mem. AMA, Am. Soc. Therapeutic Radiology and Oncology, Radiol. Soc. N.Am., Am. Soc. Clin. Oncology, Am. Coll. Radiology, Am. Assn. Women Radiologists, Gyn Oncology Group, Radiation Therapy Oncology Group. Office: Bayfront Cancer Care Ctr 701 6th St S Saint Petersburg FL 33701-4814

JACOBSON, GILBERT H., lawyer, director; b. Memphis, Feb. 6, 1956; s. Irvin and Edith (Shainberg) J.; m. Shauna Brown, Aug. 23, 1983; children: Yisroel, Esther, Nechama, Mordechai, Avrohom, Doniel. BBA, Memphis State U., 1980; JD, Touro Coll. Sch. Law, Huntington, N.Y., 1983. Bar: N.Y. 1984, Tenn. 1985, Colo. 1986. Tax cons. Rooney, Pace, Inc., N.Y.C., 1983-84; chief fin. officer Denton Mills, Inc., New Albany, Miss., 1984-85; endowment cons. Coun. of Jewish Fedns., N.Y.C., 1986-90, assoc. dir. endowment devel., 1990-92, assoc. dir. planned giving and found. rels., 1992-95; dir. Endowment Found. UJA Fedn. Bergen County, River Edge, N.J., 1995-99; assoc. exec. dir. planned giving and endowments UJA-Fedn. N.Y., N.Y.C., 1999—2002; mng. dir. Stellar Fin., 2002—. Contbr. articles to profl. jours. Founding pres. Torah Comty. Project, Denver, 1985-86; officer Congregation Adas Israel, Passaic, N.J., 1987-99. Carmi Schwartz fellow Coun. Jewish Fedns., 1993. Mem. N.Y. State Bar Assn. Avocation: talmudic study. Office: Stellar Fin Inc Ste 100 600 Main St Stroudsburg PA 18360 Office Phone: 570-517-3500. Business E-Mail: gjacobson@stellarfinancial.com.

JACOBSON, HERBERT LEONARD, electronics executive; b. N.Y.C., Mar. 22, 1940; BS in E.E., U. R.I., 1961; LL.B., Bklyn. Law Sch., 1965; LL.M., NYU, 1970. Bar: N.Y. 1965, N.J. 1972. Planning engr. Am. Electric Power, 1961-66; patent atty. RCA Corp., 1966-74, counsel, 1974-79, dir.

licensing, 1979-83, staff v.p., 1983-86; exec. v.p. GE and RCA Licensing Mgmt. Operation, Inc., 1986-98, GE Licensing, 1999-2000. Home: 7322 Floranada Way Delray Beach FL 33446-2371

JACOBSON, ISHIER, retired utilities executive; b. Worcester, Mass., June 21, 1922; s. Aaron and Mollie (Mallor) J.; m. Maria Bohm, Dec. 18, 1948; children: Joanna M., Jonathan B., Paula R. BA, Clark U., 1946; MSME, Harvard U., 1947, LLB, 1951. Bar: Conn. 1951. Asst. to pres., gen. counsel Connor Engring. Corp., Danbury, Conn., 1951-53; with Citizens Utilities Co., Stamford, Conn., 1954-90, exec. v.p., 1970, pres., chief oper. officer, 1970-81, pres., chief exec. officer, 1981-90, also dir. Chmn. emeritus bd. dirs. Silver Hill Hosp., New Canaan, Conn. Served to lt. USNR, 1942-46. Home: 326 Four Brooks Rd Stamford CT 06903-4605

JACOBSON, JAMES BASSETT, insurance executive; b. San Francisco, Nov. 16, 1922; s. James Peter and Bertha (Bassett) J.; m. Janice Isabel Meilstrup, Aug. 29, 1949 (dec. Dec. 13, 2001); children: Steven Blair, Karen Christine, Richard Barlow; m. Lesley Evans, Apr. 12, 2004. BS, UCLA, 1947; postgrad., U. Pa., 1947-48; MBA, U. So. Calif., 1954. CLU. With Prudential Ins. Co. Am., various cities, 1948-83, v.p. group pension mktg. Newark, 1967-70, sr. v.p. in charge group ins., 1970-73, pres., western ops. L.A., 1973-83; exec. v.p. CalFed Inc. and Calif. Fed. Savs. & Loan Assn., L.A., 1983-87; chmn., chief exec. officer Beneficial Standard Life Ins. Co., L.A., 1987-88, chmn. bd. dirs., 1984-88; ret., 1988. Chmn. bd. dirs. Bonneville Internat. Corp., Salt Lake City; bd. dirs. Galorath, Inc., El Segundo, Calif. Author: An Analysis of Group Creditors Insurance, 1954. V.p. L.A. Philharm. Assn., 1977-83, bd. dirs., 1975-83; vice chmn. Community TV So. Calif. L.A., 1983, bd. dirs., 1979-83; chmn. bd. dirs. Orthopaedic Hosp., L.A., 1981-84, trustee, 1980-84; chmn. bd. L.A. Ballet, 1974-79, bd. dirs., 1974-83; mem. Calif. Round Table, 1981-83; bd. dirs. Dance Gallery, L.A., 1988-92, NCCJ L.A. Region, 1987-95, co-chair, 1994-96; chmn. bd. trustees Criminal Justice Legal Found., 1993-95, trustee 1990—2004, Sacramento; bd. dirs. v.p. L.A. Area coun. Boy Scouts Am., 1980-85, others. With U.S. Army, 1943-46, 2d lt. res., 1951. Recipient Silver Beaver award Boy Scouts Am., 1984, Cmty. Svc. award UCLA Alumni Assn., 1985. Mem. Am. Coll. CLUs, Calif. C. of C. (bd. dirs. 1974-83), L.A. C. of C. (bd. dirs. 1981-83), Calif. Club, Lochinvars Club (pres. 1981-84).

JACOBSON, JAMES EDMUND, retired newspaper editor; b. Mobile, Ala., Sept. 19, 1934; s. George Frederick and Annie Virginia (Taggart) J.; m. Diana Sue Tremer, Dec. 22, 1956; children— James Edmund, Jr., Jennifer Jo, Jay Alan, Jayna Diane BA, U. Ala., 1958, MA, 1959. Editorial writer The Birmingham News, 1959-66, editorial page editor, 1966-72, asst. mng. editor, 1972-75, mng. editor, 1975-78, editor, 1978-97, contbg. editor, 1997-2000. Mem. steering com. Leadership Birmingham, 1984-94; adv. bd. Salvation Army, 1986-2001; bd. dirs. United Way-Community Chest of Central Ala., 1986-98, chmn., 1997. Served with USAF, 1952-56 Recipient Disting. Alumnus award U. Ala. Journalism Dept., 1968, Sesquicentennial Hon. Prof. award U. Ala., 1981, Presdl. citation U. Ala., 1982. Mem. Am. Soc. Newspaper Editors, Ala. Press Assn. (pres. 1989), Soc. Profl. Journalists (pres. U. Ala. student chpt. 1957-58, pres. Ala. profl. chpt. 1965, 78, 84), Kiwanis. Roman Catholic. Home: 5728 Meadowview Dr Trussville AL 35173-2276 E-mail: jejdsj@aol.com.

JACOBSON, JAMES LAMMA, JR., data processing company executive; b. Washington, May 19, 1946; s. James Lamma Jacobson Sr. and Hazel Virginia (Howard) Jacobson Tatelman; m. Dayle Barbara Jackson, Dec. 30, 1972; children: Julie, Christie, Jennie. BBA, Drexel U., 1969. Systems engr. IBM Corp., Arlington, Va., 1969-70, mktg. rep., 1970-74, mktg. instr. Atlanta, 1975-76, mktg. mgr. Akron, Ohio, 1977-79; founder, pres. Jacore Techs., Inc., Atlanta, 1979-84, chmn., 1985—; exec. cons. Mainline Info. Systems, Tallahassee, 1991-92; pres. Jacobson & Horne, Inc., Tallahassee, 1992—; chmn. JSS Enterprises, 1996—. Chmn. JSS Enterprises, 1996—. Chmn. Vida Nueva of North Fla.; pres. Faith Chapel. Mem. Ch. of God. Avocations: tennis, hunting, fishing. Home and Office: 8 Farnum St Augusta ME 04330-7234

JACOBSON, JEANNE MCKEE, humanities educator, writer; b. New Brunswick, NJ, Oct. 26, 1931; d. Edward Price and Jean Sheppard McKee; m. John H. Jacobson; children: John E., Jean K. Pokrzywka, Jennie, James G. BA, Swarthmore Coll., 1953; MS, SUNY, Brockport, 1973; PhD, SUNY, Albany, 1981. Gen. studies prin. Hebrew Acad. Capital Dist., Albany, N.Y., 1980-87; adj. faculty SUNY-Albany, Coll. St. Rose, 1983-87; from asst. to assoc. prof. Western Mich. U., Kalamazoo, 1987-95, interim dept. chair, 1993-95; adj. prof. Hope Coll., Holland, Mich., 1995-99; rsch. fellow A.C. Van Raalte Inst., Holland, 1995—2003, rsch. fellow emeritus, 2003—. Author (with others): Albertus C. Van Raalte: Dutch Leader & American Patriot, 1996, A Dream Fulfilled, 1997; author: (textbook) Content Area Reading: Integration with the Language Arts, 1998, Detecta-Crostics: Puzzles of Mystery, 2003; editor: Reading Horizons, 1988—95; assoc. editor: Drood Rev. of Mystery, 1989—. Active majority coun. EMILY's List. Democrat. Presbyterian. Avocations: reading, creating puzzles. Home and Office: 1521 S Lakeshore Dr Sarasota FL 34231-3405 E-mail: jacobsonj@hope.edu.

JACOBSON, JEROLD DENNIS, lawyer; b. N.Y.C., Oct. 12, 1940; s. Sidney and Lillian D. (Fink) J.; m. Gertraude M.J. Holle-Suppa, May 4, 1998; children: Diana, Lisa, Pamela. AB, U. Vt., 1962; JD, Cornell U., 1965; LLM in Labor Law, NYU, 1966. Bar: N.Y. 1966, U.S. Dist. Ct. (so. and ea. dists.) N.Y. 1968, U.S. Dist. Ct. (no. dist.) N.Y. 1981, U.S. Ct. Appeals (2d cir.) 1979, U.S. Ct. Appeals (5th cir.), 1980, U.S. Ct. Appeals (11th cir.) 1981, U.S. Supreme Ct. 1982. Assoc. to gen. counsel ILGWU, AFL-CIO, NYC, 1966-69; assoc. Rains, Pogrebin and Scher, NYC, Mineola, NY, 1969—70, Guggenheimer & Untermyer, NYC, 1970-74, ptnr., 1975-85, Summit, Rovins & Feldsman, NYC, 1986-89, Patterson, Belknap, Webb & Tyler, NYC, 1989-91, Proskauer Rose LLP, NYC, 1991—. Lectr. in labor and employment relations law Practising Law Inst., Am. Soc. Law and Medicine, Profl. Edn. Systems, Inc. Contbr. articles to profl. jours. Mem. adv. bd. Nassau County chpt. N.Y. State Civil Liberties Union; mem. adv. bd. U. Vt. Holocaust Study Ctr., U. Vt. Coll. Arts and Scis.; bd. dirs. Harlem Day Charter Sch. Mem. ABA, Legal Aid Soc., Am. Arbitration Assn., NY State Bar Assn. (lectr.). Office: Proskauer Rose LLP 1585 Broadway Fl 20 New York NY 10036-8299 Office Phone: 212-969-3885. Business E-Mail: jjacobson@proskauer.com.

JACOBSON, JERRY IRVING, biophysicist, theoretical physicist, medical researcher; b. Bklyn., Jan. 25, 1946; s. Saul Lane and Miriam (Cassin) J.; children: Solomon, Jacqueline, Faith, Maria, Shere. BA, Bklyn. Coll., 1963-66; DDS, DMD, Temple U., 1970; PhD, CUNY, 1983; PhD in Medicine, Bundel Khand U., 2002. Oral surgeon Tremont Med. Group, Bronx, N.Y., 1972-73, University Ave. Med. Group, Bronx, N.Y., 1973-77; pvt. practice Westchester and New City, N.Y., 1972—; pres. Perspectivism Found., Jupiter, Fla., 1980—, Inst. Theoretical Physics & Advanced Studies for Biophys., Jupiter, 1985—, Alzheimers Rsch. Found., Jupiter, 1990—, Jacobson Resonance Inc., Jupiter, 1991—; Magneto Therapeutics Mfg., Inc., 1994—, Jacobson Resonance Machines Inc., 1995—; prof. rsch., founding dir. microgravity and electromagnetics Inst. Molecular Medicine, U. Calif., Irvine, 1996; CEO, pres. Pioneer Svcs. Internat., Ltd., Deerfield Beach, Fla., 1996—; chmn. dept. applied med. physics and neuromagnetics Nat. Med. and Rsch. Inst., Boca Raton, Fla., 1997—; pres. Pioneer Svcs. Internat. Ltd., Juno Beach, Fla., 1996; chmn. bd., CEO Jacobson Resonance Enterprises, Inc., Juno Beach, Fla., 1998—, chmn. bd., pres., CEO Boco Raton, Fla., 1998—2000, also dir. R&D, dir. sci. and tech., chmn. bd., pres., CEO Boynton Beach, 2000—; pres., chief magnetics therapist Magnetic Resoncnee Therapy Ltd., Bahamas, 2003—04. Spkr. in field. Contbr. articles to profl. jours.; holder med. and plasma physics and agricultural patents and dental patents in U.S. and 80 other countries. Served to capt. Army Dental Corps, 1970-72. Mem. Am. Phys. Soc., Bioelectromagnetics Soc., European Bio-electromagnetics Soc., Italian Assn. Biomed. Physics, Internat. Assn. Biologically Closed Electric Circuits (mem. internat. adv. bd.). Avocations: painting, musical composition, fiction writing, philosophy. Home and Office: 2006 Mainsail Cir Jupiter FL 33477-1418 Office Phone: 561-208-1782. E-mail: drjijacobson@yahoo.com.

JACOBSON, JON L., law educator; BA, Univ. Iowa, 1961, JD, 1963. Bar: Calif. 1964. Atty. Bronson Bronson & McKinnon, San Francisco; Bigelow Fellow Univ. Chgo.; Bernard B. Kliks prof. emeritus Univ. Oreg. Sch. Law; co-dir. Ocean & Coastal Law Ctr., Univ. Oreg. Stockton chair internat. law U.S. Naval War Coll., Newport, RI, 1982—83; Fulbright scholar Scandinavian Inst. Maritime Law, Univ. Oslo. Editor (in chief): Ocean Development & Internat. Law, 1990—99. Office: University of Oregon School of Law 1515 Agate St Eugene OR 97403

JACOBSON, JULIUS H., II, microsurgeon, writer; m. Joan Jacobson. AS, U. Toledo, 1947; MS in Cell Physiology, U. Pa.; MD, John Hopkins Sch. Medicine, 1952. Resident, general and thoracic surgery Columbia-Presbyterian Hosp., NY; dir. surgical rsch. U. Vermont; dir. emeritus, vascular surgery Mt. Sinai Med. Ctr., NY, Distinguished Svc. Prof. Surgery. Author: (Book) The Classical Music Experience, 2002. Named in his honor, Julius H. Jacobson, II award, Vascular Disease Found., 2004. Fellow: Am. Coll. Surgeons. Preeminent pioneer in microsurgery; first surgeon to bring a microscope into the operating room for the entire range of surgery beyond the eye and ear; developed the first microscope "dipliscope" that allowed the surgeon and first assistant to view the operative field simutaneously (now in a collection at the Smithsonian Institution); widely renowned as the inventor of microsurgery, the technique that accounts for half of all neurosurgeries performed in the US; established professorships in vascular surgery(with wife) at John Hopkins University, Hadassah-Hebrew University School of Medicine, Jerusalem, Mount Sinai Medical Center, NY, and (endowed professorship in Biomedical Research) University of Toledo. Address: c/o Mount Sinai Med Ctr 1 Gustave L Levy Pl New York NY 10029*

JACOBSON, KAREN, retired elementary school educator; b. N.Y.C. d. Lawrence and Doris (Case) J. BA in Elem. Edn., SUNY, Potsdam, 1966; MS in Elem. Edn., SUNY, Cortland, 1975; AAS in Advt. Design and Prodn., Mohawk Valley C.C., 1997. Cert. tchr., N.Y. Kindergarten tchr. Mohawk (N.Y.) Sch., summers 1966-72; primary grades tchr. Oriskany (N.Y.) Ctrl. Sch., 1966—; curator Oriskany Mus., 1998—. Mem. Oriskany PTA; bd. trustees Oriskany Pub. Libr., 1995-2000; mem. Battle of Oriskany Hist. Soc., Friends of Oriskany Battlefield. Mem. Oriskany Tchrs. Assn., N.Y. State United Tchrs. Avocations: church, golf, watercolor painting. Home: 310 Ridge Rd Oriskany NY 13424-4723 E-mail: kjake152@aol.com.

JACOBSON, KATHERINE LOUISE, musician, music educator; b. Mpls., Feb. 16, 1948; d. Donald Robert Jacobson and Clarice Adeline Graff; m. Leon Fleisher, Oct. 6, 1982. MusB, St. Olaf Coll., 1970; MusM, Cleve. Inst. Music, 1974. Piano instr. Cleve. Inst. Music, 1970—76, Peabody Inst. Preparatory, Balt., 1976—86; asst. prof. Goucher Coll., Towson, Md., 1980—2005. Piano ensemble coach Peabody Conservatory Music, Balt., 2000—; performer NPR Performance Today, Aspen Summer Music Festival, 2001, 02, 03. Performer: Chgo. Symphony, Balt. Symphony, Balt. Chamber Symphony, Gulbenkian Orch. Portugal, Royal Conservatory Orch., Carnegie Hall. Pres. Fleisher-Jacobson Internat. Children's Edn. Found., Balt., 1990—2001; bd. mem. Young Audiences Md., Balt., 1988—90. Recipient 1st prize, Nat. Piano Ensemble Competition, 1977; grantee, Mayor's Adv. Com. on Art and Culture, Balt., 1990. Mem.: Daus. of Norway. Democrat. Avocations: ballet, yoga, swimming. Office: Peabody Conservatory Music 1 E Mt Vernon Pl Baltimore MD 21202 Office Phone: 410-659-8100 1135.

JACOBSON, KENNETH ALAN, chemist, researcher; b. Euclid, Ohio, July 18, 1953; s. Norman Charles and Gail Ruth (Newberger) J.; children: Gabriel A., Dorit S., Mihal R.; m. Cheryl V. Dare, Nov. 3, 2002. BA in Chemistry, Reed Coll., Portland, Oreg., 1976; MS in Chemistry, U. Calif., San Diego, 1978, PhD in Chemistry, 1981. Chemist Nalco Chem. Co., Anaheim, Calif., 1976; grad. rsch. asst. U. Calif., 1976-81; rsch. fellow Weizmann Inst. Sci., Rehovot, Israel, 1981-83; staff fellow Nat. Inst. Diabetes Digestive, Kidney Diseases NIH, Bethesda, Md., 1983-88, rsch. chemist, 1988—2003, chief molecular recognition, 1993—, sect. chief, 1993—2003, sr. investigator, 2003—, dir. chem. biology, 2003—. Sci. adv. bd. Rsch. Biochems., Internat., Natick, Mass., 1990-2000; adj. prof. Uniformed Svcs. U., 1997—; lectr. in field. Mem. editl. bd. Drug Devel. Rsch., Med. Chem. Rsch., Bioconjugate Chem, Jour. Med. Chem.; contbr. over 400 articles to profl. jours.; patentee in field. Recipient Fassina award 1996; Kroll scholar, 1974, Hillebrand prize, Chem. Soc. of Wash., 2003; Bantrell fellow, 1981-83. Mem. Internat. Soc. Nucleosides, Nucleotides, and Nucleic Acids, Am. Chem. Soc. (chair 2004), Am. Soc. Pharmacology and Exptl. Therapeutics (co-chair symposium 1989), Soc. Neurosci. Avocations: hiking, travel. Office: NIH Bldg 8 Rm B1A-19 Bethesda MD 20892-0810 Business E-Mail: kajacobs@helix.nih.gov.

JACOBSON, LOUIS, art critic; Staff reporter Washington City Paper, Washington, photography art critic. Contbr. articles to ARTNews and Art on Paper mags. Office: Washington City Paper 2390 Champlain St NW Washington DC 20009 Office Phone: 202-332-2100. Office Fax: 202-332-8500.*

JACOBSON, LOUIS ALAN, journalist; s. Raymond Marvin and Eileen Marion Jacobson; m. Elisabeth Layton, June 23, 2001. BA in Pub. and Internat. Affairs, cert. in African-Am. studies, Princeton U., 1992. Virginian-pilot, ledger-star, Virginia Beach, Va., 1991; reporting intern Wall St. Jour., N.Y.C., 1992, Nat. Jour., Washington, 1993, Economist, London, 1993—94; assoc. editor Nat. Jour., Washington, 1994—97, staff corr., lobbying, 1997—2004; dep. editor, columnist Roll Call, 2004—. Contbg. writer Wash. City Paper, Washington, 1992—; contbg. editor Congress Daily, Washington, 1994—2004, Govt. Exec., Washington, 1993—2004; freelance contbr. Economist, 1994—, Wash. Post, Washington, 1996—, Planning, Chgo., 1994—, Foresight, Tokyo, 2001—, Princeton Alumni Weekly, 1995—; columnist breakaway sect. Wall St. Jour., N.Y.C., 2000—01; state legis. handicapper The Cook Polit. Report, 2002; state legis., ballot initiative handicapper The Rothenberg Polit. Report, 2004—. Contbtg. writer (book) The Almanac of American Politics 2000, prin. contbg. writer The Almanac of American Politics 2004. Recipient Wash. Dateline award in arts criticism, Soc. Profl. Journalists, Washington chpt., 2002. Mem.: Assn. Capitol Reporters and Editors, Nat. Book Critics' Cir., Soc. Am. Baseball Rsch. Office: Roll Call 50 F St NW 700 Washington DC 20001 Office Phone: 202-824-6800. E-mail: ljacobson@rollcall.com.

JACOBSON, MARC STEPHEN, pediatrician, educator; b. June 25, 1947; BA, U. Kans., 1969, MD, 1973. Diplomate Am. Bd. Pediatrics; lic. physician, Kans., Mo., Md., N.Y. Resident in pediatrics U. Kans., Kansas City, 1973-77; fellow in adolescent medicine U. Md., Balt., 1977-79, asst. prof. pediatrics, 1979-85, dir. adolescent ambulatory clinic, 1980-85, asst. dir. adolescent medicine div., 1981-85, dir. nutrition lab., 1981-85; attending physician Schneider Children's Hosp., New Hyde Park, N.Y., 1985—, dir. atherosclerosis prevention ctr., 1986—. Asst. prof. pediat. SUNY, Stony Brook, 1985-89; asst. prof. Albert Einstein Coll. Medicine, Bronx, N.Y., 1989, assoc. prof., 1991—; lectr., cons. in field. Ad hoc reviewer Annals of Internal Medicine, 1992—; contbr. abstracts and articles to profl. jours. Mem. women's, infants and children nutrition adv. bd. Md. Dept. Mental Health and Hygiene, Balt., 1982-84; bd. dirs. L.I. Heart Coun., 1986, mem. exec. com., 1989-92, pres., 1993—. Grantee Bressler Fund, 1983-85, HHS Materna and Child Health, 1984-87, L.I. Jewish Med. Ctr., 1986, 88-92, Am. Heart Asn. Nassau County, 1986-87, S.L.E. Found., 1986-88, Merck Sharpe and Dohme, 1990-91. Fellow Am. Acad. Pediatrics (nutrition com. 1985—, chmn. 1987—); mem. AAAC, Am. Heart Assn., Queens Pediatric Soc., N.Y. Acad. Sci., Soc. Adolescent Medicine (jour. adv. com. 1993—), Nassau County Pediatric Soc., Soc. Pediatric Rsch. Home: 7 Woodleft Ave Port Washington NY 11050-2736 Office: Schneider Childrens Hosp Atherosclerosis Prevention New Hyde Park NY 11042

JACOBSON, MARCUS J., retired mechanical engineer; b. Houston, May 2, 1930; s. Max and Bessie Jacobson; m. Judith Sandra Tearle, Sept. 15, 1965; children: Mitzi Schwarz, Barry. BA, Rice U., Houston, 1951; BSME, Rice U., 1952, MS in Mech. Engring., 1954; PhD in Engring., UCLA, 1965. Design engr. Douglas Missiles and Space Divsn., Culver City, Calif., 1952; instr., asst. prof. Rice U., Houston, 1952—62; dynamics engr. Lockheed Calif. Co., Burbank, 1963—64; prin. engr. Northrop Grumman Corp., Hawthorne, Calif., 1964—95; ret., 1995. Contbr. articles to profl. jours. V.p., then pres. bd. dirs. Inglewood Unified Sch. Dist., Inglewood, Calif., 1973—77. Fellow: AIAA (assoc.); mem.: Marina del Rey-Ketubah B'nai B'rith (pres. 2003—05), Tau Beta Pi. Avocation: bridge. Home: 5337 Holt Ave Los Angeles CA 90056

JACOBSON, MARIAN SLUTZ, lawyer; b. Cin., Nov. 10, 1945; d. Leonard Doering and Emily Dana (Wells) Slutz; m. Fruman Jacobson, Sept. 21, 1975; 1 child, Lisa Wells. BA cum laude, Ohio Wesleyan U., 1967; JD, U. Chgo., 1972. Bar: Ill. 1972, U.S. Dist. Ct. (no. dist.) Ill. 1972, U.S. Ct. Appeals (7th cir.) 1973. Assoc. Sonnenschein Nath & Rosenthal, Chgo., 1972-79, ptnr., 1979—. Mem. vis. com. U. Chgo. Law Sch., 1992-94, 05-. Mem. ABA, Chgo. Coun. Lawyers, Met. Club Chgo. (bd. govs. 1998—), Hyde Park Neighborhood Club (bd. dirs. 2003-). Office: Sonnenschein Nath & Rosenthal 233 S Wacker Dr Ste 8000 Chicago IL 60606-6491 Office Phone: 312-876-8167. Business E-Mail: mjacobson@sonnenschein.com.

JACOBSON, MELVIN JOSEPH, applied mathematician, acoustician, educator; b. Providence, Nov. 25, 1928; s. Charles and Rose (Chusmir) J.; m. Dorothy Troup, June 8, 1952 (div. Aug. 1985); children: Deborah Lynn, Donald Bruce; m. Gertrude R. Ackerman, Jan. 27, 2002. AB, Brown U., 1950; MS, Carnegie Inst. Tech., Pitts., 1952, PhD, 1954. Instr. Carnegie Inst. Tech., 1953-54; mem. tech. staff Bell Tel. Labs., Whippany, NJ, 1954-56; asst. prof. math. Rensselaer Poly. Inst., Troy, NY, 1956-58, assoc. prof., 1958-63, prof., 1963-90, prof. emeritus, rsch. cons., 1991—; prin. investigator and cons. Office Naval Rsch. Contracts, 1957-96; contract Unisys. Corp., 1985-88; prin. investigator NSF grant, 1962-67; contract Inst. for Naval Oceanography, 1987-91, NASA, 1988-91, U.S. Mil. Acad. (for U.S. Army Atmospheric Sci. Lab.), West Point, NY, 1989-91. Vis. prof. Rosenstiel Sch. Marine and Atmospheric Sci., U. Miami, Fla., 1963-64, adj. prof., 1969-72; cons. to industry, NRC. Contbr. articles to numerous publs. Fellow Acoustical Soc. Am.; mem. AAUP, Soc. for Indsl. and Applied Math., Sigma Xi, Phi Kappa Phi, Pi Mu Epsilon. Home: 4705 Chandlers Forde Sarasota FL 34235-7120 Personal E-mail: melgeet@aol.com.

JACOBSON, MICHAEL FARADAY, consumer advocate, writer; b. Chgo., July 29, 1943; s. Larry and Janet (Siegel) J.; m. Donna Ruth Lenhoff; 1 child, Sonya. BA, U. Chgo., 1965; postgrad., U. Calif., San Diego, 1965-67; PhD, MIT, 1969. Research assoc. Salk Inst. for Biol. Studies, 1970-71; cons. Ctr. for Study of Responsive Law, 1970-71; co-founder, exec. dir. Ctr. for Sci. in the Pub. Interest, Washington, 1971—. Founder Ctr. for Study Commercialism, 1990. Author: Nutrition Scoreboard, 1975, Eater's Digest, 1972, The Complete Eater's Digest and Nutrition Scoreboard, 1986; (with others) The Booze Merchants, 1983, Salt: The Brand Name Guide to Sodium, 1983, The Changing American Diet, 1983, The Fast Food Guide, 1986, 2d edit., 1991, Marketing Booze to Blacks, 1987, Tainted Booze, 1987, Marketing Disease to Hispanics, 1989, Kitchen Fun for Kids, 1991, Safe Food, 1991; co-editor: Food for People Not for Profit, 1975, Cooking With the Stars, 1992, What Are We Feeding Our Kids?, 1994, Marketing Madness: A Survival Guide for a Consumer Society, 1995, Restaurant Confidential 2002. Originator, nat. coord. Food Day, 1975-77. Office: Ctr for Sci in the Pub Interest 1875 Connecticut Ave NW Ste 300 Washington DC 20009-5736

JACOBSON, MICHAEL R., lawyer, Internet company executive; b. 1954; BA magna cum laude in Econs., Harvard U., 1975; JD, Stanford U., 1981. Bar: Calif. 1981. Ptnr. Cooley Godward LLP; v.p. legal affairs, gen. counsel, sec. eBay Inc., San Jose, Calif., 1998—, now sr. v.p. legal affairs, gen. counsel, sec. Mem.: Phi Beta Kappa. Office: eBay Inc 2145 Hamilton Ave San Jose CA 95125-5905*

JACOBSON, NINA, film company executive; Grad., Brown Univ., 1987. Doc. rschr. Arnold Shapiro Prodns.; story analyst Disney Sunday Movie, 1987; dir. develop. Silver Pictures; head develop. McDonald/Parkes Prodn.; sr. v.p. prodn. Universal Pictures, 1994—95; sr. film exec. DreamWorks SKG, 1995—98; exec. v.p. prodn. Walt Disney Pictures/Hollywood Pictures, 1998; co-pres. Buena Vista Motion Pictures Group (divsn. of Disney), Burbank, Calif., 1999—2000, pres., 2000—. Named one of 100 Most Powerful Women in Entertainment, Hollywood Reporter, 2004, 100 Most Powerful Women in World, Forbes mag., 2005, 50 Most Powerful People in Hollywood, Premiere mag., 2004—05; recipient Crystal award, Women in Film, 2003. Office: Buena Vista Motion Pictures Group 500 S Buena Vista St Burbank CA 91521-9722*

JACOBSON, NORMAN L., retired agricultural educator, researcher; b. Eau Claire, Wis., Sept. 11, 1918; s. Frank R. and Elma E. (Baker) J.; m. Gertrude A. Neff, Aug. 24, 1943; children: Gary, Judy. BS, U. Wis., 1940; MS, Iowa State U., 1941, PhD, 1947. Asst. prof. animal sci. Iowa State U., Ames, 1947-49, assoc. prof., 1949-53, prof., 1953, Disting. prof. agr., 1963-89, assoc. dean Grad. Coll., 1973-88, assoc. v.p. rsch., 1979-88, assoc. provost, 1988-89, dean Grad. Coll. Ames, 1988-89, emeritus disting. prof. agr., 1989—, interim chair dept. food sci. and human nutrition, 1990-92. Contbr. articles to profl. jours., chpts. to books. Served to lt. USN, 1942-46, ETO, PTO. Fellow AAAS, Am. Soc. for Nutritional Scis., Am. Soc. Animal Sci. (Morrison award 1970), Am. Dairy Sci. Assn. (pres. 1972-73, Am. Feed Mfrs. Assn. award 1955, Borden award 1960, award of honor 1978, Disting. Svc. award 1989). Presbyterian. Home: 2200 Hamilton Drive Apt 302 Ames IA 50014-8274 Office: Iowa State U 313 Kildee Hl Ames IA 50011-3150 E-mail: nljacob@iastate.edu.

JACOBSON, PHILLIP LEE, architect, educator; b. Santa Monica, Calif., Aug. 27, 1928; s. Allen Wilhelm and Greta Percy (Rohde) J.; m. Effie Laurel Galbraith, Nov. 6, 1954; children: Rolf Wilhelm, Christina Lee, Erik Mackenzie. B. Archtl. Engring. with honors, Wash. State U., 1952; postgrad. (Fulbright scholar), U. Liverpool, Eng., 1952-53; M.Arch., Finnish Inst. Tech., Helsinki, 1969. Field supr. Gerald C. Field Architect, 1950; designer, draftsman John Maloney Architect, 1951, 53-55; designer, project mgr. Young, Richardson, Carleton & Detlie Architects, 1955-56; designer, project architect John Carl Warnecke Architect, San Francisco, 1956-58; ptnr., design dir. TRA, Seattle, 1958-92; prof. architecture and urban design and planning Coll. Architecture and Urban Planning, U. Wash., Seattle, 1962—2000. Author: Housing and Industrialization in Finland, 1969, The Evolving Architectural Design Process, 1969; contbr. articles to profl. jours.; major archtl. works include Aerospace Research Lab., U. Wash., Seattle, 1969, McCarty Residence Hall, 1960, Highway Adminstrn. Bldg., Olympia, Wash., 1970, Sea-Tac Internat. Airport, 1972, Issaquah (Wash.) High Sch., 1962, State Office Bldg. 2, Olympia, 1976, Sealaska Corporate Hdqrs. Bldg., Juneau, Alaska, 1977, Group Health Hosp., Seattle, 1973, Metro Shelter Program, Seattle, 1977, N.W. Trek Wildlife Preserve, 1976, Rocky Reach/Rock Island Recreation Plan, 1974, master plan mouth of Columbia River, 1976, U. Wash. Biol. Sci. Bldg., 1981, Wegner Hall, Wash. State U., 1982, Wash. Conv. Ctr., 1988, King County Aquatics Ctr., 1990, Albuquerque Airport, 1989, U. Wash. Health Scis. H Wing, 1993. Mem. Seattle Planning and Redevel. Council, 1959-69, v.p., 1966-67; mem. Seattle Landmark Preservation Bd., 1976-81; trustee Pilchuck Sch., 1982-2001, Northwest Trek Found., 1987-94, AIA/Seattle Archtl. Found., 1986-92. With U.S. Army, 1946-47. Fulbright-Hays Sr. Rsch. fellow Finland, 1968-69; named to Order of White Rose Govt. of Finland, 1985; recipient Silver plaque Finnish Soc. Architects, 1992; recipient numerous design awards. Fellow AIA (pres. Wash. state Council 1965, dir. Seattle chpt. 1970-73, sr. council 1970—, Seattle chpt. medal 1994); mem. Am. Inst. Cert. Planners, Phi Kappa Phi, Tau Beta Pi, Tau Sigma Delta, Scarab, Sigma Tau (outstanding alumnus 1967). Office: U Wash PO Box 355720 Seattle WA 98195-5720 E-mail: plj54@msn.com.

JACOBSON, RAYMOND EARL, electronics company entrepreneur and executive; b. St. Paul, May 25, 1922; s. Albert H. and Gertrude W. (Anderson) J.; m. div. 1986; children: Michael David, Karl Raymond, Christopher Eric. BE with high honors, prize for excellence in mech. engring., Yale U., 1944; MBA with distinction, Harvard U., 1948; BA in Econ. and Politics (Rhodes Scholar), Oxford U., 1950, MA, 1954. Asst. to gen. mgr. Polytech Rsch and Devel. Co., Inc., Bklyn., 1951-55; sales mgr. Curtiss-Wright Electronics Divsn., Carlstadt, N.J., 1955-57; dir. mktg. TRW Computers Co., L.A., 1957—60; v.p. ops. Electro-Sci. Investors, Dallas, 1960-63; pres. Whitehall Electronics, Inc., Dallas, 1961-63; chmn. bd. Gen. Electronic Control, Inc., Mpls., 1961-63, Staco, Inc., Dayton, Ohio, 1961-63; pres. Maxson Electronics Corp., Gt. River, N.Y., 1963-64, Jacobson Assocs., San Jose, Calif., 1964-67; co-founder, pres., chmn., CEO Anderson Jacobson, Inc., San Jose, Calif., 1967-88. Chmn. Anderson Jacobson, SA, Paris, 1974-88, Anderson Jacobson, Ltd., London, 1975-88, Anderson Jacobson Can., Ltd./Ltée, Toronto, 1975-85, Anderson Jacobson, GmbH, Cologne, 1978-83, CXR Corp., San Jose, 1988-94; bd. dirs. Tamar Electronics, Inc., L.A., Rawco Instruments, Inc., Dallas, 1960-63, Micro Radionics, Inc., L.A., 1964-67, ComputerMan USA, Inc., Reno, 1997—; lectr. engring., UCLA, 1958-60, lectr. bus. adminstrn. U. Calif. Berkeley, 1965-66; mem. underwriting Lloyd's London, 1975-96. Eagle Scout Boy Scouts Am., 1935, committeeman, 1968-80. Lt. (j.g.) USNR, 1943-46. Mem. Assn. Am. Rhodes Scholars, Oxford Soc., Brasenose Soc., Yale Club, Yale Class of 1944 (exec. com.), Harvard Bus. Sch. Assn., Sigma Xi, Tau Beta Pi.Courtside Tennis Club, Seascape Swim and Racquet Club. Republican. Lutheran. Home: 543 Elk River Ct Reno NV 89511 Office Phone: 775-851-3796.

JACOBSON, RICHARD JOSEPH, lawyer; b. Ft. Benning, Ga., July 12, 1943; s. Harold Gordon and Ruth Fern (Enenstein) J.; m. Judy Josephine Dunbar, Sept. 17, 1966; 1 child, David Dunbar. AB, Harvard U., 1965, PhD, 1970; JD, U. Va., 1977. Bar: Ill. 1977, Va. 1977, D.C. 1979, U.S. Dist. Ct. (no. dist.) 1977, U.S. Ct. Appeals (7th cir.) 1991. Asst. prof. English U. Va., Charlottesville, 1970-74; assoc. Keck, Mahin & Cate, Chgo., 1977-83, ptnr., 1984-96; prin. Flaherty, Jacobson & Youngerman, P.C., Chgo., 1996—. Adj. prof. Sch. Law Northwestern U., Chgo., 1999—. Author: Hawthorne's Conception of the Creative Process, 1965; contbr. articles to profl. jours. Pres. North Park Condominium assn., Chgo., 1978-80. Woodrow Wilson Nat. fellow, 1965. Mem. Va. State Bar Assn., D.C. Bar Assn., Chgo. Bar Assn. (chmn. com. preventing atty. malpractice 2000-2001), Assn. Profl. Responsibility Lawyers, Cliff Dwellers Club, Lawyers Club Chgo., Chgo. Literary Club. Home: 850 W Adams St Apt 3D Chicago IL 60607-3088 Office: Flaherty Jacobson & Youngerman PC 134 N Lasalle St Ste 1600 Chicago IL 60602-1108 Personal E-mail: rjacobson@fjylaw.com.

JACOBSON, RICHARD LEE, lawyer, educator; b. Los Angeles, Nov. 2, 1942; s. Joseph and Betty (Koenig) J.; children: David, Peter, Michael. S.B., U. Chgo., 1964; JD, U. So. Calif., 1970. Bar: Calif. 1971, U.S. Ct. Appeals (9th cir.) 1971, D.C. 1980, U.S. Ct. Appeals (4th cir.) 1980, U.S. Ct. Appeals (D.C. cir.) 1980, U.S. Supreme Ct. 1980, U.S. Ct. Appeals (6th cir.) 1983. Law clk. U.S. Ct. Appeals (9th cir.), 1970-71; law clk. to Assoc. Justice William O. Douglas U.S. Supreme Ct., Washington, 1971-72; assoc. Irell & Manella, Los Angeles, 1973-76; mem. trial unit SEC, Washington, 1977-78, spl. counsel to chmn., 1978-79; ptnr. Mayer, Brown & Platt, Washington, 1980-85; spl. counsel Heller, Ehrman, White & McAuliffe, Palo Alto, 1986-88; of counsel Fulbright & Jaworski, Washington, 1988-89, ptnr., 1990—. Adj. prof. law Georgetown U. Law Ctr., Washington, 1979-86; mem. bd. advisors, sec. Reform Act Litig. Reporter, 1998—. Exec. editor So. Calif. Law Rev., 1969-70; contbr. articles to profl. jours. Bd. dirs. Washington Lawyers Com. for Civil Rights and Urban Affairs, 1983—. Mem. ABA (chmn. subcom. uniformity of local discovery rules 1983-85, chmn. subcom. securities class actions 1995—, fed. regulation securities com., securities litigation com.), Am. Law Inst., Washington Coun. Lawyers (bd. dirs. 1982-86, 88-99, pres. 1985-86), D.C. Bar Assn. (nominations com. 1984-85, steering com. computer law divsn. 1985-86), Assn. SEC Alumni (pres. 1995-97, dir. 1998—), Order of Coif. Office: Fulbright & Jaworski LLP 801 Pennsylvania Ave NW Washington DC 20004-2615

JACOBSON, RICHARD PHILIP, lawyer; b. Livingston, N.J., May 15, 1962; s. Allen Sander and Carol Jacobson; m. Susan B. J., July 22, 1989; children: Rachel Amanda, William Rutter. BA, U. Conn., 1984; JD, Georgetown U., 1987. Bar: N.J. 1987, N.Y. 1996, D.C. 1996, U.S. Ct. Appeals (2d cir.), U.S. Ct. Appeals (3d Cir.). Lawyer Wilentz, Goldman & Spitzer, Woodbridge, N.J., 1987-92, Dunn, Pashman, Hackensack, N.J., 1992-95, Colucci & Umans, N.Y.C., 1995—. Office: Colucci & Umans 101 E 52d St New York NY 10022

JACOBSON, ROBERT ANDREW, chemistry professor; b. Waterbury, Conn., Feb. 16, 1932; s. Carl Andrew and Mary Catherine (O'Donnell) J.; m. Margaret Ann McMahan, May 26, 1962; children: Robert Edward, Cheryl Ann BA, U. Conn., 1954; PhD, U. Minn., 1959. Instr. Princeton U., N.J., 1959-62, asst. prof., 1962-64; assoc. prof. Iowa State U., Ames, 1964-69, full prof., 1969-99, asst. dean Scis. and Humanities, 1982-85, prof. emeritus, 1999—. Chemist Ames Lab, Iowa, 1964-69, sr. chemist, 1969-99. Contbr. articles to profl. jours. Recipient Wilkinson Teaching award Iowa State U., Ames, 1974, 91. Mem. Am. Chem. Soc., Am. Crystallographic Assn. (chmn. apparatus and standards com. 1982-83) Avocations: gardening, painting. Home: 2732 Thompson Dr Ames IA 50010-4759 Office: Iowa State U 1271 Gilman Ames IA 50011-3111 Office Phone: 515-294-1144. E-mail: raj@ameslab.gov.

JACOBSON, SANDRA W., lawyer; b. Bklyn., Feb. 1, 1930; d. Elias and Anna (Goldstein) Weinstein; m. Irving Jacobson, July 31, 1955; 1 child, Bonnie Nancy. BA, Vassar Coll., 1951; LLB, Yale U., 1954. Bar: N.Y. 1955, U.S. Supreme Ct. 1960, U.S. Dist. Ct. (so., ea. dists.) N.Y. 1972, U.S. Ct. Appeals (2nd cir.) 1975. Ptnr. Mulligan, Jacobson & Langenus, N.Y.C., 1964-88, Hall, McNicol, Hamilton & Clark, N.Y.C., 1988-92; sole practitioner N.Y.C., 1992—2003; atty. NY Sisters Place Legal Counsel Ctr., 2003—. Lectr. in family law. Contbr. articles to profl. jours. and chpts. to books. Mem.: ABA (family law sect.), Internat. Acad. Matrimonial Lawyers, Westchester Women's Bar Assn., Ind. Jud. Screening Panel, Com. to Improve Availability of Legal Svcs., Am. Acad. Matrimonial Lawyers (bd. mgrs. N.Y. chpt. 1987—89, 1991—93, chair lawyer specialization com. 1999—2000, bd. mgrs. N.Y. chpt., 1995-98, 2000-2002, v.p., 1998-2000, 2002-), Westchester County Bar Assn., Assn. of Bar of City of N.Y. (com. women in the cts. 1986—96, sec. 1987—90, state cts. of superior juridiction 1987—90, women in the profession 1989—92, chair 1990—93, chmn. 1990—93, judiciary 1995—99, family law 1999—2000, com. matrimonial law, 1984-87, 2001-, chmn. 1990-98), Women's Bar Assn. of State of N.Y. (chair cts. com. 1987—88, CLE com. 1998—99, by-laws 1999—2001, co-chair amicus com. 2002—, matrimonial com., co-chmn. 1987-89, co-chair task force on ct. reogrn.), N.Y. Women's Bar Assn. (matrimonial and family law com. 1984—2000, chmn. 1986—88, jud. screening com. 1987—88, pres. 1989—90, ethics commn. 1990—), N.Y. State Bar Assn. (co-chair lawyer specialization 1999—, family law sect., legis. and exec. com.), Phi Beta Kappa. Office: NY Sisters Place 2 Lyon Pl Ste 300 White Plains NY 10601

JACOBSON, SHELDON HOWARD, engineering educator; b. Montreal, Sept. 9, 1960; BSc, McGill U., 1981, MSc, 1983; PhD, Cornell U., 1988. Asst. prof. Case Western Res. U., Cleve., 1988—93; assoc. prof. Va. Tech., Blacksburg, 1993—99, U. Ill., Urbana, 1999—2002, prof., 2002—, assoc. Ctr. for Advanced Study, 2002—03. Mem. sci. adv. bd. BioPop Inc., Charlotte, NC, 2000—02. Recipient Best Application award, Inst. Indsl. Engring. Ops. Rsch. Divsn., 1998, Aviation Security Rsch. award, Aviation Security Internat., 2002; Willett Faculty scholar, U. Ill., 2002—05, Guggenheim fellow, 2003. Office: Univ Ill 1206 West Green St MC-244 Urbana IL 61801-9505

JACOBSON, SIDNEY, editor; b. N.Y.C., Oct. 20, 1929; s. Reuben and Beatrice (Edelman) J.; m. Ruth Allison, July 4, 1957 (div. Feb. 1975); children: Seth, Kathy Battat; m. Maggi Silverstein, Feb. 26, 1975. BA, NYU, 1950. Exec. editor Harvey Comics, N.Y.C., 1952-83, Marvel Comics, N.Y.C., 1983-89; v.p., editor-in-chief Harvey Comics Entertainment, L.A., 1989—. Author: Streets of Gold, 1985, Another Time, 1989, Pistol: The Story of Pete Reiser, 2004, The 9/11 Commission Report (The Graphic Novel, 2005; writer (comic books) Captain Israel, 1972, The Black Comic Book, 1973, (TV animation series) Johnny Cypher in Dimension Zero, 1975, (TV series) Felix the Cat, 1982, (monthly) You Can't Do That in Comics, 1986; lyricist various popular songs. Mem. Am. Soc. Composers, Authors and Pubs., Am. Guild Authors and Composers, Authors Guild. Home: 11740 Wilshire Blvd Los Angeles CA 90025 Office: Sunland Studios 11835 W Olympic Blvd Los Angeles CA 90064-5001 Office Phone: 310-444-4138. Business E-Mail: sjacobson@sunlandstudios.com.

JACOBSON, THOMAS ELTON, urban planner, county official; b. Mpls., July 2, 1946; s. Elton John and Elizabeth Lou Jacobson; m. Andrea Christine Rask, Nov. 29, 1969; children: Arin, Jared, Timothy. BSCE, U. Minn., 1968, MS in Environ. Planning, 1971. Registered profl. engr., N.D.; lic. Am. Inst. Cert. Planners. Water resource engr. U.S. Army C.E., St. Paul, 1968-70; city planner City of Grand Forks, N.D., 1972-75; vis. asst. prof. U. N.D., Grand Forks, 1975-76; sr. planner City of Sioux Falls, S.D., 1976-78, asst. dir. for planning, 1978-86; dir. planning Chesterfield County, Chesterfield, Va., 1986—2004, dir. revitalization, 2004—. Contbr. articles and photographs to profl. publs. Com. chmn. Richmond (Va.) First Club, 1988-94; mem. Downtown Adv. Com., Richmond, 1996-97; bd. dirs. Better Housing Coalition, Richmond, 1994—, United Way, Sioux Falls, 1983-86; lectr. St. Tammany C. of C., New Orleans, 1998. Mem. Am. Planning Assn. (com. chmn.), Va. Planning Assn. (bd. dirs. 1991-92), Va. Planning Dirs. (pres. 1989-90), Am. Inst. Cert. Planners, Urban Land Inst. (bd. dirs.). Avocations: photography, cosmology, bicycling. Office: Chesterfield County Box 40 Chesterfield VA 23832 Office Phone: 804-748-1040. E-mail: jacobsont@co.chesterfield.va.us.

JACOBSON-WOLF, JOAN ELIZABETH, minister; b. Flint, Mich., July 15, 1949; d. William and Helen Wolf; m. Don M. Jacobson, May 27, 1978; children: Lara Heather, Heidi Kirsten, Joan Noel, Jason Luke. AA, Concordia Coll., 1969; BA in Theology, Valparaiso U., 1972; postgrad., Luth. Sem., Mexico City, Phila. and Columbus, Ohio, 1974-76; M in Div., Luth. Sch. Theology, Chgo., 1978; D in Ministry, McCormick Theol. Seminary, 1986. Ordained minister Luth. Ch., 1979; cert. psychiatric chaplain. Community organizer Cleve. Hispanic Murals, Centro Juvenil de Puertoriqueña; deaconess, missionary Hispanic ministry Trinity Luth., Cleve., 1972-75; intern. asst. minister Berwyn (Ill.) United Luth. Ch., 1977-78; chaplain Tenn. Women's Prison, Nashville, 1978-79, Spencer Youth Ctr., Nashville, 1979-81; minister St. Paul's Luth. Ch., Nashville, 1979-81; chaplain Edison Park Home, Park Ridge, Ill., 1982; pvt. practice as pastoral psychotherapist Owosso, 1988-93; pastor Messiah Luth. Ch., Racine, Wis., 1993—. Author: When to Counsel, When to Refer, 1989; violinist Flint Summer Theater Orch., 1965-67, Ann Arbor (Mich.) Symphony, 1967-69, Valparaiso (Ind.) U. Orch., 1969-72, Cherokee String Quartet, Iowa, 1971, Cleve. Women's Symphony, 1973-75, Oak Park (Ill.) Symphony, 1977, Nashville Symphony, 1978-80. Chaplain Mt. Pleasant Police Dept., 1993—; founder, organizer Little Blessings Childcare Ctr., 1996. Home: 3727 Canada Goose Xing Racine WI 53403-4506 Office: Messiah Luth Ch 3015 Pritchard Dr Racine WI 53406-5401

JACOBS-QUAM, VIVIEN MARIE, retired music educator; b. Dover, N.J., Apr. 8, 1943; d. Charles Jacobs and Elizabeth Toth; m. Leonard Egil Quam, Jan. 6, 1964; 1 child, Leonard Charles Quam. B in Music Edn., Westminster Choir Coll., 1965; MA, Montclair State U., 1972. Cert. music tchr. K-12 NJ. State Dept. Edn., 1965, elem. sch. tchr. NJ. State Dept. Edn., 1986. Tchr. vocal music Morris Hills Regional Bd. Edn., Rockaway, NJ, 1986—2002; organist, choir dir. Sparta United Meth. Ch., Sparta, 1989—2001; tchr. vocal music Lafayette Twp. Sch., Augusta, NJ, 1982—85; organist, choir dir. Union Hill Prebyterian Ch., Denville, NJ, 1982—85; tchr. vocal music Frelinghuysen Twp. Sch., Newton, 1981—85, Sparta Alpine Sch., 1965—66; catering mgr., owner Viking Ho. Delicatessen, Denville, 1972—91. Consulting tchr. fine and performing arts Morris Hills Regional Bd. Edn., Rockaway, NJ, 1998—2002. Singer (soprano soloist): (high holy days) Northwestern U. Orch, Lakeland Youth Symphony, Westminster Choir Coll. Alumni; dir.(Morris Hills H.S. vocal students): (performance of music with orchestra) Carnegie, Avery Fisher, and Alice Tully Halls (included 25th Ann. Bklyn. Philharm., 1990). Chair choral procedures NJ Music Edn. Assn., 1998—2002; chair region I choral performance Region I Sch. Music Assn., 1988—91. Recipient Honor award, Morris Hills Bd. Edn., 1992, Superior Ratings, Madrigal Choir, Music Performance Festivals, 1998—2002, Northwestern N.J. Music Tchr. of Yr., William Paterson U., 2001; fellow, Northwestern U. Sch. Music, 1986. Mem.: N.J. Ret. Educator's Assn. Achievements include original design and a refit for new hardware and software used in the teaching of music theory and graphic arts in computer labs at Morris Hills Regional District schools; development of general music course in the curriculum at Morris Hills Regional District schools for the non-performance student; an accepted (model) proposal for NJ All- State Women's Chorus which allows many additional talented young NJ women to perform in an honor's choir; teaching of music theory, ear traingin and graphic arts in computer labs at Morris Hills Regional District Schools. Avocations: piano, cross stitch, beading. Home: 41 Rogers Ln Sparta NJ 07871 Personal E-mail: vmjq53le@earthlink.net.

JACOBSTEIN, DAVID M., real estate company executive; Grad., Colgate U., George Washington U. Legal asst. Congressman Samuel S. Stratton, U.S. Ho. Reps., 1970; assoc. Thompson Hine & Flory, Cleve.; ptnr. Harris Beach & Wilcox, Rochester, NY; v.p. fin., gen. counsel Sci. Calculations, Inc., Fishers, NY; vice chmn., COO Wilmorite, Inc., Rochester, NY; pres., COO Developers Diversified Realty, Beachwood, Ohio, 1999—, also bd. dirs. Mem.: Internat. Coun. Shopping Ctrs., Urban Land Inst. Office: Developers Diversified Realty 3300 Enterprise Pkwy Beachwood OH 44122

JACOBUS, CHARLES JOSEPH, lawyer, title company executive, writer; b. Ponca City, Okla., Aug. 21, 1947; s. David William and Louise Graham (Johnson) J.; m. Heather Jeanne Jones, June 6, 1970; children: Mary Helen, Charles J. Jr. BS, U. Houston, 1970, JD, 1973. Bar: Tex. 1973; cert. specialist residential and commerical real estate law Tex. Bd. Legal Specialization. Pvt. practice, Houston, 1973-75; staff counsel Tenneco Realty, Inc., Houston, 1975-78, v.p., gen. counsel, 1979—83; chief legal counsel Speedy Muffler King, Deerfield, 1978-79; v.p. Commerce Title Co., Houston, 1983-85; sr. v.p. Charter Title Co., Houston, 1986—; ptnr. Jacobus & Melamed PC, Houston, 1988-97; shareholder Jenkens & Gilchrist, Houston, 1998-99; pvt. practice Bellaire, Tex., 1999—. Adv. dir. Prosperity Bank, Houston; adj. faculty Tex. A&M U., 1986-90; adj. prof. U. Houston Law Ctr., Houston C.C., Champions Sch. Real Estate; course dir. State Bar Tex., 1990; chmn. Tex. Land Title Inst., 2001; mem. broker-lawyer com. Tex. Real Estate Commn. Author: Real Estate Law, 2d edit., 1996, Texas Real Estate Law, 9th edit., 2004; co-author: Mastering Real Estate Titles and Title Insurance in Texas, 1996, Georgia Real Estate, 1995, Ohio Real Estate, 2d edit., 1990, Calif. Real Estate, 1989, Keeping Current with Texas Real Estate, updated annually, Real Estate Principles, 9th edit., 2005, Real Estate, An Introduction to the Profession, 9th edit., 2005, Texas Title Insurance, updated annually, Texas Real Estate Brokerage and the Law of Agency, 2004; co-author: Real Estate Brokerage Law and Practice; editor: Building Blocks of a Commercial Transaction, 1992, Building Blocks of a Residential Real Estate Transaction, 1994, Texas Real Estate Law Deskbook, 1995; editor-in-chief Tex. Forms Manual. Chmn. Planning and Zoning Commn., Bellaire, Tex., 1976-77; bd. dirs. Tax Increment Fin. Dist., Bellaire, 1984-91; chmn. task force on edn. Tex. Real Estate Commn.; chmn. profl. adv. com. dept. urban and regional planning Tex. A&M U., 1988-89; 1st asst. scoutmaster Boy Scout World Jamboree, Holland, 1995, scoutmaster, Chile, 1999; scoutmaster Nat. Boy Scout Jamboree, 1997, 1st asst. scoutmaster, 2001; mayor City of Bellaire, 1998-2000; sec.-treas. Harris County Mayors and Coun. Assn. 1999. Recipient Peggy Hayes Tchg. Excellence award TLTA, 1993, Don Roose award of excellence in real estate edn., 2001. Mem. ABA (acquisitions editor books and pubs. com. 1994-2001, chmn. brokers and brokerage com. 1986-93), Internat. Wine Food Soc. (host Houston chpt. 1993-94), Am. Coll. Real Estate Lawyers, Nat. Assn. Corp. Real Estate Execs. (chpt. v.p.), Tex. Land Title Assn. (chmn. forms manual com., TREC earnest money contract task force), State Bar Tex. (mem. coun. of real estate, probate and trust law sect. 2002—, chmn. title ins. com.), Tex. Real Estate Tchrs. Assn. (Outstanding Real Estate Educator 1986), Houston Real Estate Lawyers Coun., Real Estate Educator's Assn. (pres. 1987-88, Real Estate Educator of Yr. 1986, 2000, Disting. Career award 2004), Houston Bar Assn. (chmn. real estate sect. 1987-88), Internat. Wine and Food Soc. (bd. dirs.), Bellaire/S.W. Houston C. of C. (Outstanding Businessman of Yr. 1990, chmn. Tex. Real Estate Commns. Edn. Task Force, 1999-2000), U. Tex. Mortgage Lending Inst. (faculty), U. Houston Law Alumni Assn. (bd. dirs.), Les Amis Escoffier. Republican. Roman Catholic. Home: 5223 Pine St Bellaire TX 77401-4820 Office: Ste 615 6750 West Loop S Bellaire TX 77401-4525 Office Phone: 713-839-8800. E-mail: jacobusbellaire@aol.com.

JACOBY, BEVERLY SCHREIBER, art consultant; b. Cin., Mar. 25, 1950; d. Ben and Sylvia Schreiber; m. John Eric Jacoby, Aug. 3, 1975; children: Elizabeth, Charles. BA magna cum laude, Barnard Coll., 1972; PhD in Fine Arts, Harvard U., 1983. Expert dept. old master drawings Sotheby's, N.Y.C., 1979-82; fine art cons. Nordstern Ins. Co. Am., N.Y.C., 1985-87; from head dept. old master drawings to sr. tech. expert Christie's, N.Y.C., 1989-92; founder and pres. specializing in approvals, art adv. svcs. and collections mgmt. Beverly Schreiber Jacoby Fine Arts & Appraisal Svcs., Ltd., N.Y.C., 1992—. Art adv. Weininger Found., Inc., 1999-; cons. Naval War Coll. Ctr. Naval Wargaming Studies (CNWS), Newport, R.I., 2000-01; adj. faculty N.Y.U., Programs in Art Adminstrn., Sch. Continuing and Profl. Studies, 2002-; conf. co-dir., Art in an Age of Uncertainty, 2002; lectr. in field of old master drawings, 18th century French art and the life and career of Francois Boucher Contbg. author, N.Y. Law Jour.; contbr. articles to profl. jours and mus. exhbn. catalogs. Chair arts & culture adv. com. 14th Congl. Dist., N.Y.C., 1992—; active Sec. Navy's Adv. Subcom. on Naval History, Washington, 1995-2004; juror 14th Congl. Dist. N.Y. Congl. Arts Caucus Art Competition, 2003-. Guest scholar J. Paul Getty Art Mus., Malibu, 1986; Smithsonian fellow, 1978-79, Agnes Mongan Travelling fellow Harvard U., 1977. Fellow The Pierpont Morgan Libr.; mem. Am. Assn. Mus., Appraisers Assn. Am., N.Y. Hist. Soc. (collections com. 1994-2003, juror scholastic art & writing awards 1995), Soc. History Art Francais, Harvard Club N.Y.; mem. ArtTable, Inc.

JACOBY, COLEMAN, scriptwriter; b. Pitts. s. Harry and Etla (Bernstein) J.; m. Gaby Monet, June 17, 1955; children: Catherine, Antoinette. Grad. high sch., Pitts. Ind. TV scriptwriter, 1950—. Original writer Jackie Gleason Show, creator The Poor Soul, Reggie Van Gleason, Joe the Bartender characters; scriptwriter: (TV series) The Phil Silvers Show (Sgt. Bilko), The Garry Moore Show, Kraft Music Hall, numerous HBO spls., (teleplays) The Wonderful Worls of Burlesque (Emmy award nomination), The Bachelor (Sylvania award). Recipient 4 Emmy awards Nat. Acad. TV Arts and Scis., Christopher award, Sylvania award. Mem. Writers Guild Am. East (life). Clubs: Friars (N.Y.C.). Democrat. Home and Office: 350 E 84th St New York NY 10028-4405

JACOBY, HENRY DONNAN, economist, educator; b. Dallas, June 25, 1935; s. Henry Harris and Margaret Cameron (Miller) J.; m. Martha Hughes Jacoby, Apr. 4, 1959; children— Daniel Donnan, Caroline Hughes. BS in Mech. Engring, U. Tex., Austin, 1957; PhD in Econ, Harvard U., 1967. Systems analyst Tudor Engring. Co., San Francisco, 1959-61; economist Harvard Devel. Adv. Service, Argentina Project, 1963-65; asst. prof. dept. econs. Harvard U., Cambridge, Mass., 1965-69; assoc. prof. polit. economy John F. Kennedy Sch. Govt., 1969-73; prof. mgmt. MIT, Cambridge, 1973—, William. F. Pounds prof. mgmt., 1991—2001, chmn. faculty, 1988-91; dir. global change program, 1991—; dir. Center for Energy Policy Research, 1978-83; vis. scholar London Bus. Sch., 1983-84. Chmn. Mass. Gov.'s Emergy Energy Tech. Adv. Com., 1973-74; mem. Nat. Petroleum Coun., 1975-83. Author: (with F.S. Brooman) Macroeconomics, 1970, (with R. Dorfman and H.A. Thomas, Jr.) Models for Managing Regional Water Quality, 1973, (with J.D. Steinbruner) Clearing The Air, 1973, Analysis of Investment in Electric Power, 1979, (with R. deLucia) Energy Planning for Developing Countries, 1982, (with R.L. Gordon and M.B. Zimmerman) Energy: Markets and Regulation, 1987. Served with USN, 1957-59. Mem. Am. Econ. Assn., Tau Beta Pi. Democrat. Episcopalian. Office: MIT Sloan Sch of Mgmt E40-439 50 Memorial Dr Cambridge MA 02142-1347 Business E-Mail: hjacoby@mit.edu.

JACOBY, IRVING, physician; b. N.Y.C., Sept. 30, 1947; s. Philip Aaron and Sylvia Jacoby; m. Sara Kay Vartanian; children: James Tyler, Kathryn Aaryn. BS magna cum laude, U. Miami, Coral Gables, Fla., 1969; MD, Johns Hopkins U., 1973. Diplomate Am. Bd. Internal Medicine, Am. Bd. Infectious Diseases, Am. Bd. Emergency Medicine, Am. Bd. Preventive Medicine (undersea and hyperbaric medicine). Intern Boston City Hosp., 1973-74, resident in medicine, 1974-75, chief resident, 1978-79; resident in medicine Peter Bent Brigham Hosp., Boston, 1975-76, fellow in infectious diseases, 1976-78; asst. dir. emergency med. svcs. U. Mass. Med. Ctr., Worcester, 1979-84; asst. dir. dept. emergency med. San Diego (Calif.) Med. Ctr. U. Calif., 1984—, assoc. prof. med. surgery San Diego (Calif.) Med. Ctr., 1988-94, hosp. dir. for emergency preparedness and response San Diego (Calif.) Med. Ctr., 2003—, prof. med. surgery San Diego (Calif.) Med. Ctr., 1994—, disaster control officer San Diego (Calif.) Med. Ctr., 1985—. Assoc. dir. Hyperbaric Med. Ctr., 1985—; vis. physician, cons. infectious diseases Soroka Med. Ctr., Ben Gurion U., Beer-Sheva, Israel, 1980; flight physician New Eng. Life Flight, Worcester, 1982-84, Life Flight Aeromed. Program U. Calif., 1984-87. Sect. editor for disaster medicine Jour. Emergency Medicine, 1996—; assoc. editor Undersea and Hyperbaric Medicine, 1996-2002. Comdr. Disaster Med. Assistance Team CA-4, 1991—. Fellow ACP, Am. Coll. Emergency Physicians; mem. Am. Soc. Microbiology, Infectious Diseases Soc. Am., Nat. Assn. Disaster Med. Assistance Teams (vice chair 1999, chmn. 2000-01), Soc. Acad. Emergency Medicine, Undersea and Hyperbaric Med. Soc., World Assn. for Disaster and Emergency Medicine, Disaster Emergency Response Assn., Johns Hopkins Med. and Surg. Assn., Iron Arrow Leadership Soc., Omicron Delta Kappa, Phi Kappa Phi, Alpha Epsilon Delta, Phi Eta Sigma. Office: U Calif Med Ctr 200 W Arbor Dr San Diego CA 92103-8676 Office Phone: 619-543-6216.

JACOBY, JACOB, consumer psychology educator; b. Bklyn., Feb. 17, 1940; s. David and Frances (Berman) Jacoby; m. Francine Crystal Jacoby (div.); children: Robin Ann, Jonathan Scott; m. Renée Berkowitz; 1 child, Dana Eve. BA, Bklyn. Coll., 1961, MS, 1963; PhD, Mich. State U., 1966. Prof. consumer behavior Purdue U., West Lafayette, Ind., 1968-81, NYU, 1981—. Cons. DuPont, Gen. Electric Co., Gen. Motors. Co., Am. Assn. Adv. Agys., Procter and Gamble, Standard Oil, U.S. Senate, FTC, FDA, others Author: Brand Loyalty, 1978, Miscomprehension of Televised Communication, 1980, The Comprehension and Miscomprehension of Print Communications, 1987. Served to 1st lt. USAF, 1965-68 Recipient Outstanding Contbn. to Advt. award Am. Acad. Advt., 1991, Disting. Sci. Contbn. award Soc. for Consumer Psychology, 1996. Fellow APA (pres. divsn. 23 1973-74, Disting. Sci. Rsch. award 1995), Assn. for Consumer Rsch. (pres. 1975); mem. Am. Mktg. Assn. (H.H. Maynard award 1978), Am. Assn. Pub. Opinion Rsch., Advt. Ednl. Found. (bd. dirs.). Jewish. Office: NYU 44 W 4th St New York NY 10012-1106 Personal E-mail: jjacoby@stern.nyu.edu.

JACOBY, JEFF, journalist, commentator; b. Cleve., Feb. 10, 1959; s. Mark and Arlene Fay (Winograd) J. Student, Hebrew U., Jerusalem, 1977; BA with distinction, George Washington U., 1979; JD cum laude, Boston U., 1983. Bar: Ohio 1983. Atty. Baker and Hostetler, Cleve., 1983-84; exec. dir. Mass. Civic Interest Coun., Boston, 1984-85; asst. to pres. Boston U., 1985-87; chief editorial writer Boston Herald, 1987-94; op-ed columnist Boston Globe, 1994—. Columnist Lowell (Mass.) Sun, 1985-86; polit. analyst Sta. WBUR-FM Nat. Pub. Radio, Boston, 1987—; talk show host Sta. WBZ, Boston, 1990-93; commentator Opinion Page, Monitor Channel, Boston, 1991-92; program host Talk of New Eng., New Eng. Cable News, 1992-96. Exec. com. Cuyahoga County Rep. Party, Cleve., 1983-84; dep. campaign mgr. Ray Shamie for U.S. Senate, Boston, 1984. Recipient Breindel award for Excellence in Opinion Journalism, 1999. Jewish. Office: Boston Globe 135 Morrissey Blvd Boston MA 02125-3338*

JACOBY, JOHN PATRICK, lawyer; b. Chgo., Dec. 29, 1957; s. James William and Rose Elizabeth Jacoby; m. Diane G. Gilbert, Oct. 29, 1994; children: Renee Grace, Kyra Jade. BS cum laude, Northwest Mo. State U., 1982; JD, Wash. U. Sch. Law, 1987. Bar: Mo. 1987, Ill. 1988, U.S. Dist. Ct., east. dist., Mo. 1987, U.S. Dist. Ct., so. dist., Ill. 1988, U.S. Dist. Ct., no. dist., Ill. 1994. Atty. Sandberg, Phoenix & Von Gontard, St. Louis, 1987—92; ptnr. Pappas, Jacoby & Marcus, Chgo., 1993—. Lectr. How to Negotiate a Case in Civil Litigation Ill. Inst. on Continuing Legal Edn., 2002—. Chmn. fin. com., mem. sch. bd. South Loop Sch., Chgo., 2002—; pres. Bicycle Homeowner's Assn., Chgo., 1998—2002; treas. Prairie Dist. Owner's Assn., Chgo., 2003—. Recipient Am. Jurisprudence award, Am. Jurisprudence Soc., 1986. Mem.: ATLA, ABA, Def. Rsch. Inst., Chgo. Bar Assn. Avocation: golf. Office: Pappas Jacoby & Marcus 30 W Monroe Ste 800 Chicago IL 60603 Office Phone: 312-382-5363. Office Fax: 312-782-9590. Business E-Mail: jpj@pjmlaw.net.

JACOBY, LOWELL EDWIN, federal agency administrator, career military officer; b. Aug. 28, 1945; m. Celia L. Williams, Dec. 9, 1975. Grad., Aviation Officer Cand. Sch., 1969; student, Navy Postgrad. Sch., 1975; BS in Econs., U. Md.; M in Nat. Security Affairs, Naval Postgrad. Sch. Commd. ensign USN, 1969; advanced through grades to rear admiral, 1994; with fighter sq. 24 USS Hancock (CV-19); intelligence officer seventh fleet detachment Charlie RVN Saigon; current intelligence watchstander, briefing officer, 1973-75; intelligence placement officer, jr. officer assignment officer Naval Mil. Personnel Cmd., 1979-81; head naval ops. br. Navy Field Operational Intelligence Office, dir. Naval Surveillance Info. Ctr.; adminstrv. asst. to dir. naval intelligence, 1983; head, chief naval ops. intelligence plot, 1983; asst. chief of staff, intelligence carrier group eight USS South Carolina, North Atlantic, 1985, USS Nimitz Battle Group, Mediterranean; N2 NATO striking fleet Atlantic, J2 CJTF 120, CJTF 140; head intelligence assignments, placement br. Washington, 1989-90; asst. chief of staff intelligence for comdr. in chief U.S. Pacific fleet, 1990-92; commdg. officer Joint Intelligence Ctr. Pacific, 1992-94; dir. intelligence U.S. Pacific Command, 1994-97; dir. Naval Intelligence; comdr. Office Naval Intelligence, 1997-99; dir. Joint Staff J-2 Pentagon, Washington, 1999—2002; acting dir. Def. Intelligence Agy., Washington, 2002, dir., 2002—. Decorated Def. Disting. Svc. medal, Navy Disting. Svc. medal, Def. Superior Svc. medal, 3 Meritorious Svc. medals, 2 Legion of Merit medals, 2 Navy Commendation medals, Navy Achievement medal, Nat. Intelligence Medal for Achievement Dir. Ctr. Intelligence, Australian Chief of Def. Commendation. Office: Def Intelligence Agy 7400 Def Pentagon Washington DC 20301-7400

JACOBY, NEIL HERMAN, JR., astronautical scientist, engineer, consultant; b. Chgo., Oct. 20, 1940; s. Neil Herman and Clair (Gruhn) J. BA in Astronomy, UCLA, 1965, MS in Engring., 1969. Sci. guide Griffith Obs., L.A., summer 1962; comuter program cons. UCLA Western Data Processing Ctr., 1966-67; tchg. asst. in astrodynamics UCLA Sch. Engring. and Applied Sci., summer 1968; staff scientist Computer Scis. Corp., L.A., 1972-76; sys. analyst Sys. Devel. corp., Santa Monica, Calif., 1977-81; cons. in astrodynamics, astronautics L.A., 1981—. Ind. property mgr., L.A., 1979—. Contbr. articles to sci. and profl. jours. Bd. dirs. Westwood Homeowners Assn., L.A., 1981—. Recipient Internat. Diploma of Honor Am. Order of Excellence, 500 founders of the 21st Century. Mem. AIAA, AAAS, Am. Astronautical Soc. (sr.), N.Y. Acad. Sci., Planetary Soc., Alpha Gamma Sigma. Achievements include development of time series for rapid and accurate missile trajectory deterimination and an orbit determination method using 5 observations; a novel method of non-co-planer orbital transfer for a geocentric satellite; determined that 3 observations of right ascension and declination of a comet are substantially better than 5 observations in determining a comet's orbit because of very high eccentricity of its orbit; development of an original solution to determine preductions of closest approaches of near earth objects; an accurate, rapid and novel numerical integration method for predicting orbits of potentially hazardous asteroids, including perturbations of all planets in our solar system; novel, accurate methods for interplanetary space travel; novel method of determining close earth approaches of potentially hazardous asteroids. Home and Office: 1434 Midvale Ave Los Angeles CA 90024-5406 E-mail: neiljacoby@yahoo.com.

JACOBY, RICHARD ALLEN, pathologist, dermatologist; b. Rochester, N.Y., June 27, 1950; s. Marvin and Florence J.; m. Christine Marie Jacoby, Mar. 25, 1984; children: Benjamin, Joanna. BA, NYU, 1972; MD, Jefferson Med. Coll., 1976. Diplomate Am. Bd. Pathology, Am. Bd. Dermatology, Am. Bd. Dermatopathology. Intern and resident in pathology Lankenau Hosp., Phila., 1976-79; resident and tchg. asst. in pathology NYU, N.Y.C., 1979-80; fellow in dermatopathology NYU Med. Ctr., N.Y.C., 1980-81; resident in dermatology Skin and Cancer Hosp.-Temple U. Health Scis., Phila., 1981-84; dir. dermatopathology Hahneman U., Phila., 1984-88, interim chmn. dermatology, 1986-88; dir. dermatopathology Jefferson Med. Coll., Phila., 1988-97; pres. Inst. for Dermatopathology, Phila., 1997-2000; chief med. officer PathSOURCE, N.Y.C., 1998-2000, Inform Dx, Nashville, 2000-2001; regional mng. dir. Ameripath Phila., Conshohocken, Pa., 2001—. Cons., dermatopathologist Melanoma Program-Jefferson Med. Coll., Phila., 1988-93. Asst. editor Dermatopathology-Practical and Conceptual, 1995-99. Mem. AMA, Am. Acad. Dermatology, Am. Soc. Dermatopathology, Internat. Soc. Dermatopathology, Phila. Dermatologic Soc. Avocation: golf. Home: 118 Muirfield Ct Moorestown NJ 08057 Office: Ameripath Phila 20 Ash St Conshohocken PA 19428

JACOBY, ROBERT HAROLD, management consulting executive; b. N.Y.C., June 9, 1942; s. Harold and Ruth (Johnson) J. BA in Econs., Dartmouth Coll., 1964; MA in Polit. Philosophy, Columbia U., 1998, MPhil, 2001. Cert. mgmt. cons. Prin. Albert Ramond & Assocs. Inc., Chgo., 1968-75; pres. Systemetrics Internat. Inc., Indpls., 1975-77; v.p. Theodore Barry & Assocs., London, 1977-82; ptnr. Deloitte & Touche, N.Y.C., 1982—85; pres. R.H. Jacoby & Assocs. Inc., N.Y.C., 1985—. Contbr. articles to profl. jours. Mem. Acad. Mgmt., Am. Econ. Assn., Nat. Assn. Corp. Dirs., Am. Gas Assn., Strategic Mgmt. Soc., Am. Arbitration Assn. (comml. arbitrator 1982—), The Strategic Leadership Forum. Office: RH Jacoby & Assoc Inc 355 South End Ave New York NY 10280-1005

JACOBY, WILLIAM JEROME, JR., internist, retired military officer; b. Mt. Carmel, Pa., Aug. 9, 1925; s. William Jerome and Florence Marie (White) J.; m. Joeann J. Powroznick, May 5, 1956; children: William Jerome, Teresa Marie. AB, Emory U., 1946; MD, Jefferson Med. Coll., 1950. Diplomate Am. Bd. Internal Medicine. Commd. lt. (j.g.) M.C., USN, 1950, advanced through grades to rear adm., 1972; intern Jefferson Med. Coll. Hosp., Phila., 1950-51, resident in internal medicine, 1951-52, 55-56; Am. Heart Assn. fellow, 1956-57; chmn. dept. medicine U.S. Naval Hosps. Gt. Lakes, Ill., 1964-69, Phila., 1969-72; chmn. dept. medicine, dir. edn. and rsch. Nat. Naval Med. Ctr., Bethesda, Md., 1972-75; comdg. officer Naval Regional Med. Ctr., Portsmouth, Va., 1975-78; dir. med. svcs. VA Cen. Office, Washington, 1978-80, dep. chief med. dir., 1980-83. Assoc. clin. prof. Jefferson Med. Coll., 1969—; prof. medicine George Washington U. Med. Sch., 1972, Eastern Va. Sch. Medicine, Norfolk, 1976-78; mem. adv. coun. Nat. Heart, Lung and Blood Inst., NIH, 1972-75. Contbr. articles to profl. jours. Decorated Legion of Merit, Meritorious Svc. medal. Fellow ACP (Laureate award 1996); mem. Assn. Mil. Surgeons (Founders medal 1974), Alpha Omega Alpha, Phi Beta Pi. Roman Catholic. Home: 737 E Tazewells Way Williamsburg VA 23185-6521

JACOFF, RACHEL, Italian language and literature educator; b. N.Y.C., Apr. 5, 1938; d. Richard and Natalie (Wiener) J. BA, Cornell U., 1959; MA, Harvard U., 1960, MPhil, 1963; PhD, Yale U., 1977. Acting asst. prof. U. Va., Charlottesville, 1974-78; asst. prof. Italian, Wellesley (Mass.) U., 1978-83, assoc. prof., 1983-85, prof., 1985—, Carlson prof. comparative lit., 2001—. Vis. prof. Cornell U., Ithaca, N.Y., 1984; vis. prof. Stanford (Calif.) U., 1989, dir. NEH Stanford Dante Inst., 1988. Co-author: Inferno II: Lectura Dantis Americana, 1989; editor: (essays) Dante: The Poetics of Conversion, 1986 (hon. mention Marraro prize 1987), The Poetry of Allusion, 1991, The Cambridge Companion to Dante, 1993, The Poets' Dante, 2001. Fellow NEH, 1981-82, 91-92, Bunting Inst., 1981, Villa I Tatti, 1982, Stanford Humanities Ctr., 1986-87, Rockefeller Found. Bellagio, 1993, 99, Bogliasco Found., 1999. Mem. MLA, Dante Soc. Am. (coun. 1989-92), Medieval Acad. (asst. editor Speculum 1986-99), Save Venice Charter. Office: Wellesley Coll Dept Italian 106 Central St Wellesley MA 02481-8268

JACONETTY, THOMAS ANTHONY, lawyer; b. Chgo., May 21, 1953; s. George Bernard and Mary Jane (Sgarioto) J.; m. Judith Hamill; 1 child, Nicole Alicia. AB in History and Polit. Sci. summa cum laude with honors, Loyola U., Chgo., 1975; JD, Northwestern U., 1978. Bar: Ill. 1978, U.S. Dist. Ct. (no. dist.) Ill. 1978, U.S. Ct. Appeals (7th cir.) 1979; cert. rev. appraiser. Adminstrv. asst. Chgo. Dept. Aviation, 1979; asst. corp. counsel Chgo. Dept. Law, 1980; asst. to commr. Cook County Bd. Tax Appeals, Chgo., 1981-83, dep. commr., 1983-87, commr., 1988-89, chief dep. commr., 1989—; sole practice Chgo. Lectr. Ill. Inst. for Continuing Legal Edn.; lectr. and presenter Lorman Edn. Svcs., Lincoln Inst. Land Policy, Internat. Assn. of Assessing Officers, Chgo. Chpt. of Appraisal Inst., Commerce Clearing House Ill. State Tax Reports Nat. Bus. Inst., Nat. Assn. of State and Local Equity Funds, NAHB Multi-Family Housing Credit Group, Inst. of Profl. in Taxation. Asst. editor, indexer: Corwin on the Constitution, 1981; author book chpts.; editor: Issues Confronting Properties Affected by Contamination or Environmental Problems, 2002, Valuation of Subsidized Housing, 2003, Illinois Institute Continuing Legal Education, State and Local Taxation, 2004; contbr. articles to profl. jours., property tax policies and adminstr. practices, Can., U.S., 2000. Mem. Cook County Dem. Orgn.; pres., bd. dirs. Polish and Am. Citizens Club, 1981—; pres. Italian Am. Cath. Assn., Chgo., 1981—; mem. Old Timers' Baseball Assn., Art Inst. Chgo., Channel 11-PBS, Mus. Sci. and Industry, Ill. Spl. Olympics, Nat. Trust Hist. Preservation, Libr. of Congress, Ill. Alzheimer's Assn., Civic Fedn. Tax Com.; mem. planning com. Nat. Conf. State Tax Judges, 1999—, chair 2002-04. Mem. ABA, Ill. Bar Assn. (mem. assembly 1988-91, 92-94, state and local taxation sect. coun. and several subcoms., chmn. 1994-95, vice chmn. 1993-94, ad hoc and 4 separate civic fedn. and mayoral coms. on property tax reform, 1994-96, 2000-2001), Chgo. Bar Assn. (chmn. election law com., Ill. gov. transition com. 2002), Internat. Assn. Assessing Officers (arbitrator cir. ct. Cook County, 1990-97, various sects., legal coms., chmn. nat. legal com. 1995-2002, 04-05, Donohoo Essay award, 1996, presdl. citations and spl. svc. award, 2002, twice-nominated Barnard award), Justinian Soc. Italian Lawyers, Northwestern Law Sch. Alumni Assn., Loyola U. Alumni Assn., Pi Sigma Alpha, Alpha Sigma Nu. Avocations: travel, reading. Office: Cook County Bd of Review 118 N Clark St Ste 601 Chicago IL 60602-1311 Office Phone: 312-603-5562.

JACOVER, JEROLD ALAN, lawyer; b. Chgo., Mar. 20, 1945; s. David Louis and Beverly (Funk) J.; m. Judith Lee Greenwald, June 28, 1970; children: Aric Seth, Evan Michael, Brian Ethan. BSEE, U. Wis., 1967; JD, Georgetown U., 1972. Bar: Ohio 1972, Ill. 1973, U.S. Ct. Appeals (7th cir.) 1974, U.S. Ct. Appeals (fed. cir.) 1983. Atty. Ralph Nader, Columbus, Ohio, 1972-73, Brinks Hofer, Gilson and Lione, Chgo., 1973—, pres., 2000—. Mem. ABA, Am. Intellectual Property Law Assn. (bd. dirs. 1994-98), Decalogue Soc. Lawyers, Intellectual Property Law Assn. Chgo. (bd. dirs. 1993-94, 98-99, pres. 2000), Intellectual Property Law Assn. Chgo. Ednl. Found. (pres. 1990-93), Am. Techion Soc. (pres. 1994-97). Office: Brinks Hofer Gilson & Lione Ste 3600 455 N Cityfront Plaza Dr Chicago IL 60611-5599 E-mail: jjacover@brinkshofer.com.

JACOX, MARILYN ESTHER, chemist; b. Utica, NY, Apr. 26, 1929; d. Grant Burlingame and Mary Elizabeth (Dunn) J. BA, Syracuse U., 1951; PhD, Cornell U., 1956; ScD (hon.), Syracuse U., 1993. Postdoctoral rsch. assoc. U. NC, Chapel Hill, NC, 1956-58; fellow in fundamental rsch. Mellon Inst., Pitts., 1958-62; rsch. chemist Nat. Bur. Std., Washington, 1962—; fellow Nat. Bur. Std. (now Nat. Inst. Std. and Tech.), Gaithersburg, Md., 1986-95, sci. emeritus, 1996—. Mem. editl. bd. Revs. Chem. Intermediates, 1984-89, Jour. Chem. Physics, 1989-91; contbr. numerous articles to profl. jours. Recipient gold medal U.S. Dept. Commerce, 1970, Fed. Women's award, 1973, Lippincott award, 1989, Hillebrand prize Chem. Soc. Washington, 1990, WISE lifetime achievement award, 1991, E. Bright Wilson award in Spectroscopy, Am. Chem. Soc., 2003. Fellow AAAS, Am. Phys. Soc., Washington Acad. Scis. (Phys. Sci. award 1968); mem. Am. Chem. Soc. (bd. mgrs. Chem. Soc. Wash. Sect. 2005), Exec. Women in Govt. (sec. 1981, vice-chmn. 1982), Inter-Am. Photochem. Soc. (exec. com. 1978-79), Sigma Xi (pres. NBS chpt. 1988-89). Office: Nat Inst Standards & Tech Optical Technology Division Gaithersburg MD 20899-8441 Office Phone: 301-975-2547. E-mail: marilyn.jacox@nist.gov.

JACQUES, SHARON ANNE, artist, consultant; b. New Orleans, June 14, 1956; d. Charles Gustave and Melrose Josephine (Payne) J.; m. Luis Cruz Azaceta, May 15, 1982; 1 child, Dylan Jacques Cruz Azaceta. BFA, La. State U., 1977, MFA, 1982. Artist educator, program dir. The Mus. Modern Art, N.Y.C., 1983-91; artist educator, lectr. The New Mus. Contemporary Art, N.Y.C., 1988-91; artist, cons. The Contemporary Arts Ctr., 1993—. Lectr. in field. Exhbns. include New Orleans Performing Arts Ctr., 1979, Hansen Gallery, New Orleans, 1980, Broussard Gallery, Baton Rouge, 1980, Foster Hall Gallery, 1981, Panhellenic Gallery, Baton Rouge, 1982, Area X Gallery, 1986, Le Musee Francais, Miami, Fla., 1987, Limelight Club, N.Y.C., 1987-88, Candy Store Gallery, Folsom, Calif., 1987, Sensory Evolution Gallery, N.Y.C., 1988, New Mus. Contemporary Art, N.Y.C., 1988, Mus. Modern Art, 1988-89, Schneider Mus. Art, Ashland, Oreg., 1989, Miami-Dade C.C., 1990-91, Alternative Mus., N.Y.C., 1990, 97, Clocktower, N.Y.C., 1991, John Michael Kohler Arts Ctr., Sheboygan, Wis., 1993, J. Maddux Parker Gallery, Sacramento, 1993, Sylvia Schmidt Gallery, New Orleans, 1994-95, Zeitgeist Alternative Art Ctr., New Orleans, 1998, The Contemporary Arts Ctr., New Orleans, 1999. Mem. N.Y. Roundtable Art Edn. Democrat. Roman Catholic. Home: 4100 Prytania St New Orleans LA 70115-3839 Studio: 3831 Tchoupitoulas St New Orleans LA 70115-1340

JACQUESSON, ALAIN L., librarian; b. Geneva, Nov. 3, 1946; s. Guy and Elisabeth (Giddey) J.; m. Marie-Jose Chanez, Feb. 8, 1975; children: Severine, Mathieu. Responsable Ecole de bibliothecaires, Geneva, 1978—81; project chief U. Geneva, 1981—88; dir. Bibliothèques Municipales, Geneva, 1988—93, Bibliothèque Publique et Universitaire, Geneva, 1993—. Mem. ALA, Assn. of Swiss Librs., Assn. French Librs., Am. Soc. Info. Sci. Office: Bibliotheque Publique Univ Parc des Bastions 1211 Geneva 4 Switzerland Fax: (022) 418-28-01. Office Phone: (022) 418-2800. E-mail: alain.jacquesson@bpu.ville-ge.ch.

JACQUETTE, YVONNE HELENE, artist; b. Pitts., Dec. 15, 1934; Student, R.I. Sch. Design, 1952-56; studies with John Frazier, Robert Hamilton, Herman Cherry, Robert Roche. Instr. Moore Coll. Art, Phila., 1972; instr. painting, vis. artist U. Pa., 1972-76, 79-82, instr. Grad. Sch. Fine Arts, 1979-84; instr. Parsons Sch. Design, 1975-78; instr. painting Pa. Acad. Fine Arts Grad. Sch., 1991—. Vis. artist Nova Scotia Coll. Art, 1974; artist in residence Harvard U., 1995; represented by DC Moore Gallery, N.Y.C., Mary Ryan Gallery (Prints) N.Y.C.; instr. in field. One-woman shows include St. Louis Art Mus., 1983-84, Berggruen Gallery, San Francisco, 1984, Yuracho Seibu-Takanawa Art, Tokyo, 1985, Brooke Alexander Inc., 10 shows 1974-88, 90, 92, 95, N.Y. Mus. Art, Bowdoin Coll. Mus. Art, Maine, 1986, D.C. Moore Gallery, 1997, 2000, 2003, Mary Ryan Gallery, 1997, Huntington (W.Va.) Mus., 1997, Mention: Retrospective, Cantor Arts Ctr., Stanford (Calif.) U., 2002, Colby Coll. Mus., Waterville, Maine, 2002, Utah Mus., Salt Lake City, 2002, Hudson River Mus., Yonkers, NY, 2003; 2-person show Mary Ryan Gallery, 1997; exhibited at Rutgers U. Art Gallery, 1972, Whitney Mus. Art, 1972, N.Y. Cultural Ctr. and U.S. Travelling Show, 1972-73, Internat. Biennial, Tokyo, 1974, Art Inst. Chgo., 1975, Mus. Modern Art, N.Y., 1981-82, Weatherspoon Gallery, N.C., Met. Mus. Art, Mus. Modern Art, Whitney Mus. Am. Art, N.Y., Colby Coll. Mus., Library Congress, Washington, Staatliche Mus., Berlin, Carnegie Inst. Mus. Art, Pitts., Am. Acad. Inst. Arts and Letters, N.Y.; prin. works include painting in oil N. Cen. Bronx Hosp., 1973, five color lithograph Horace Mann Sch., Riverdale, N.Y., 1974, mural for Fed. Bldg. and Post Office, Bangor Maine, 1979-82; prints commissioned by Provincetown Fine Arts Workcenter, 1992, Zimmerli Mus. Rutgers, 1993, Bus. Com. for the Arts, 1994; illustrator Country Rush, Adventures in Poetry, 1982, Aerial, Eyelight Press, 1981, Fast Lanes, 1984; film (with Rudy Burckhardt) Night Fantasies, 1992; set designer Sch. Hardknocks, Dance Theatre Workshop, N.Y.C. and nat. tour, 1989; print commd. by Cleve. Print Club, 1999. Recipient Nat. Acad. Painters award, 1998; Guggenheim Meml. Found. grantee, 1997-98. Mem.: Am. Acad. Arts and Letters (Painting award 1990), Artists Equity Assn., Nat. Acad. (Painting award 1998, Print award 1999). Office: 50 W 29th St New York NY 10001-4227 Personal E-mail: yvonnejb@mymailstation.com.

JADLOW, JANICE WICKSTEAD, finance educator; b. Glen Ridge, N.J., Dec. 4, 1945; d. John Carson and Lucille (Forman) Wickstead; m. Joseph M. Jadlow, Aug. 30, 1969; children: Joanna Christine, Jennifer Lynn. BA, Miami U., 1967; MA, U. Va., 1969; PhD, Okla. State U., 1977. Econ., bd. govs. Fed. Res. Sys., Washington, 1968—69; instr., asst. prof. Okla. State U., Stillwater, 1970—89, assoc, prof., head fin. dept., 1990—. Mem.: Am. Econ. Assn., Fin. Mgmt. Assn., Am. Fin. Assn. Republican. Methodist. Home: 2111 S Walking Trail Dr Stillwater OK 74074-1359

JADOT, JEAN LAMBERT OCTAVE, clergyman; b. Brussels, Nov. 23, 1909; s. Lambert Paul and Gabrielle Marie (Flanneau) J. D.Philosophie Thomiste, U. Catholique Louvain, Belgium, 1930. Ordained priest Roman Catholic Ch., 1934, consecrated bishop, 1968; parish asst., 1934-39; nat. chaplain Jeunesse Etudiante Catholique, 1939-45; chaplain Ecole Royale Militaire, 1945-52; chief chaplain Force Publique Belgian Congo, 1952-60; nat. dir. Propagation of Faith for Belgium, 1960-68; apostolic pro nuncio Thailand; also apostolic del., 1968-71; apostolic pro nuncio in Cameroun and Gabon, also apostolic del. Laos, Malaysia, Singapore, 1971-73; apostolic del. to U.S.A., 1973-80; permanent observer of Holy See to OAS, 1978-80. Pro pres. Secretariat for Non Christians at Vatican, 1980-84; titular arch-bishop of, Zuri, 1968 Served as chaplain Belgian Army, 1945-52. Decorated Order Leopold. Roman Catholic. Address: Val des Seigneurs 32-82 1150 Brussels Belgium Personal E-mail: jjadot@tiscali.be.

JAE, (JAE FRENCH), sculptor; b. Bklyn., Jan. 9, 1947; d. Benjamin and Shirley Shareff; m. John H. French II, May 30, 2001. BA, Pace U.; Sculpture study with, Bruno Lucchesi, N.Y.C., Jacques Lipschitz, Italy, Evangelous Moustakis, Crete, Greece. Sculptress of cast bronze sculptures mantle size to monumental size The World of JAE, N.Y.C., 1972—; designer of jewelry and wearable art Wearable Art, N.Y.C., 2001—. Lectr. in field. Exhibitions include Met. Mus. Art, N.Y.C., Bklyn. Mus. Art, Am. Hellenic Soc., Athens, Greece, Annapolis Naval Acad., Washington, Internat. Art Show, Pietra Santa, Italy, Swarz House, Capetown, South Africa, Chastelleux, Newport, RI; prodr.: (theatre) Broadway League, 1990—; (plays) Say Goodnight Gracie, 2003; Represented in permanent collections. Coord. Boys and Girls Clubs, Newport, RI, 2001—; founder JAE's Arc. Mem.: Preservation Soc. Newport, R.I., ATL Art Club. Avocations: dance, tennis, exploring, travel, cultural activities. Home: The Happy Sculptress PO Box 368 Newport RI 02840 Personal E-mail: jaesculptress@juno.com.

JAEGER, ALVIN A. (AL JAEGER), state official; b. Beulah, N.D., 1943; m. Naomi Berg, 1969 (dec. 1979), m. Kathy Grangaard Anderson, 1986; children: Todd, Stacy, Heidi. Grad., Bismarck State Coll., 1963, Dickinson State U., 1966; postgrad., U. N.D., 1968, Mont. State U., 1970. Tchr. Killdeer High Sch., 1966-69, Kenmare High Sch., 1969-71; with Mobil Oil Corp., 1971-73; real estate broker, 1973-93; sec. of state State of N.D., 1993—. Active Charity Luth. Ch., 1966-72. With N.D. Army N.G., 1980. Named Realtor of Yr. Mem. Nat. Assn. Secs. State (exec. com., com. chmn.), Fargo-Moorhead Area Assn. Realtors (mem. coms. edn., profl. stds., bylaws, multiple listing svc.), N.D. Assn. Realtors (past chairperson state bylaws), Bismarck Kiwanis Club. Office: Sec of State Dept 108 600 E Boulevard Ave Bismarck ND 58505-0500 Office Phone: 701-328-2900.

JAEGER, DAVID ALLEN, economics educator; b. East Orange, N.J., Mar. 30, 1964; s. Philip Edward and Jean Edna (Van De Mark) J.; m. Alison Isdale Beach, June 30, 1990; children: Andrew, Eliza. BA, Williams Coll., 1986; MA, U. Mich., 1990, 93, PhD, 1995. Rsch. asst. MDRC, N.Y.C., 1986-88; rsch. economist U.S. Bur. Labor Stats., Washington, 1995-97; assoc. prof. Hunter Coll. and CUNY Grad. Sch., N.Y.C., 1997-2001, Coll. William and Mary, Williamsburg, Va., 2001—. Vis. assoc. prof. Princeton U., 1999-2000; rsch. fellow nst. for the Study of Labor, Bonn, Germany, 1998—; vis. scholar Fed. Res. Bank of N.Y., 2000-01. Contbr. articles to profl. jours. Alexander von Humboldt rsch. fellow, 2003—04. Mem. Am. Econ. Assn., Am. Statis. Assn., Population Assn. Am., Soc. Labor Economists. Office: Coll William and Mary PO Box 8795 Dept Econs Williamsburg VA 23187-8795 Office Phone: 757-221-2375. Business E-Mail: djaeger@wm.edu.

JAEGER, JAMES A., lawyer; b. Eau Claire, Wis., May 18, 1948; s. Lorn C. and Katherine M. Jaeger; m. Karen L. Petersen, June 20, 1970; children: Jesse W., Andrew L. BA, Luther Coll., Decorah, Iowa, 1970; JD, Georgetown U., Washington, DC, 1975; LLM in Taxation, Temple U., Phila., 1980. Cert. Elder Law Atty.: Nat. Acad. Elderlaw Found., Tucson, Ariz. 2004. Staff attorney IRS Office of Chief Counsel, Washington, DC, Phila., PA, Springfield, Ill., 1975—81; assoc., shareholder Melli Walker Pease & Ruhly SC, Madison, Wis., 1981—90; pvt. practice Jaeger Law Office, Madison, Wis., 1990—91; ptnr. Hill, Glowacki, Jaeger & Hughes LLP, Madison, Wis., 1991—. Chair Elder Law Sect. State Bar, Madison, Wis., 1995—96; mem. bd. govs. State Bar Wis., Madison, 1997—2001. Pres., bd. mem. First Unitarian Soc. Madison, Wis., 2000—; bd. mem. Elder Care Wis., Madison, 1999—, bd. chair, 2003—. Mem.: Nat. Acad. Elderlaw Attys. Unitarian Universalist. Office: Hill Glowacki Jaeger & Hughes LLP 2010 Eastwood Dr 301 Madison WI 53704

JAEGER, JAMES GORDON, retired minister, librarian; b. Morrison, Ill., June 26, 1941; s. Leonard Alfred Otto Jaeger and Margaret Irene Bayles; m. Karen Francis Rowley, June 26, 1971; children: Joy Kathleen, Kenneth James. BA in History, Blackburn Coll., 1963; MLS, Ind. U., 1964; MDiv, Concordia Theol. Sem., 2001. Cataloger, ref. libr. Enoch Pratt Free Libr., Balt., 1964—68; head libr. Mitchell Pub. Libr., Hillsdale, Mich., 1970—77, Kankakee (Ill.) Pub. Libr., 1977—78; head info. svc. Joliet (Ill.) Pub. Libr., 1979—96, coord. coll. develop., 0996—1997; vicar Immanuel Luth. Ch., Saginaw, Mich., 2000—01; chaplain Falls City Zone Luth. Women's Missionary League, 2003—04; pastor Immanuel Luth. Ch., Sterling, Nebr., 2001—04. Lit. tutor Joliet Jr. Coll.1, 1993—94. Mem. Sterling Sr. Citizens Ctr., 2001—04; chaplain Falls City Zone Luth. Women's Missionary League, 2003—04; mem. Sterling Sr. Ctr., 2001—04, Sterling Cmty. Assn., 2003—04, Nat. Pro-Life Alliance, Environ. Def., Amnesty Internat., Feed the Children. Mem.: NWF, Luth. Soc. Svcs. (advancement coun. mem.), Ind. Univ. Alumni Assn., Christian Srs. Assn., Sterling Rock Falls Hist. Soc., Smithsonian Nat. Mus. of the American Indian, Wilderness Soc., Whiteside Cnty Geneal. Soc., Sterling Rock Falls Toastmasters (pres. 2003—06), Sierra Club. Lutheran. Avocations: music, book collecting, stamp collecting/philately, nature study, environmental activities, genealogy, history.

JAEGER, KATHLEEN GRACE, French educator; b. Pitts., May 11, 1944; d. Samuel A. and Grace W. McMullan; m. Erwin G. Jaeger, Aug. 7, 1965; 1 child, Erich B. BA in French and Spanish, U. Northern Iowa, 1965, MA in Spanish, 1969, MA in French, 1974; PhD in French, U. Iowa, 1991. Cert. tchr. French, Spanish and English, Iowa. French, Spanish, English tchr. Clinton (Iowa) H.S., 1965-68; French, Spanish tchr. Cedar Falls (Iowa) H.S., 1969-73; French tchr. Ctrl., East, West H.S., Waterloo, Iowa, 1976-86; French instr. Wartburg Coll., Waverly, Iowa, 1988, Cornell Coll., Mount Vernon, Iowa, 1991; French prof. Graceland Coll., Lamoni, Iowa, 1992—. Com. mem. Intercultural Affairs, Graceland Coll., Lamoni, 1993-99, com. mem. gen. edn., 1995-98, faculty sponsor Alpha Mu Gamma, 1992—; translator

John Deere Corp., Waterloo, Iowa, 1970-72. Author: Male and Female Roles in the 18th Century, 1994; contbr. articles to profl. jours. Scholarship U. Iowa, 1987, Merchant scholarship U. Northern Iowa, 1987-88. Mem. MLA, Am. Assn. of Tchrs. of French, Iowa Fgn. Lang. Assn. Avocations: reading, travel, interior decorating. Home: 110 Four Seasons Dr Waterloo IA 50701-1016 E-mail: kjaeget@graceland.edu.

JAEGER, LESLIE GORDON, university administrator; b. Southport, Eng., Jan. 28, 1926; s. Henry M. and Beatrice A. (Highton) J.; m. Annie Sylvia Dyson, Apr. 3, 1948; children: Valerie Ann, Hilary Frances.; m. Kathleen Grant, July 24, 1981. BA, Cambridge U., 1946, MA, 1950; PhD, London U., 1955, DSc, 1986; DEng (hon), Carlton U., 1991, Meml. U., 1994, Tech. U. of N.S., 1995; LLD (hon.), Dalhousie U., 2005. With W.P. Thompson & Co., Liverpool, Eng., 1948-50, Renold Ltd., Manchester, Eng., 1950-52; mem. faculty Univ. Coll. of Khartoum, 1952-56; Univ. lectr. Cambridge (Eng.) U., 1956-62; prof. civil engring. and applied mechanics McGill U., Montreal, Que., Can., 1962-64, 66-70; Regius prof. engring. U. Edinburgh, Scotland, 1964-66; dean Coll. Engring., U. N.B., Fredericton, 1970-75, acting v.p., 1972-73; acad. v.p. Acadia U., Wolfville, N.S., Can., 1975-80; spl. asst. to pres. Tech. U. N.S., Halifax, 1980-85, v.p. rsch., 1986-93; emeritus rsch. prof. tech. U. N.S., 1993—. Cons. structural engring. Expo '67, Rolls Royce Ltd., Adjeleian & Assocs., Ottawa, and others. Author: (with A.W. Hendry) The Analysis of Grid Frameworks and Related Structures, 2nd edit, 1968, Elementary Theory of Elastic Plates, 1962, Cartesian Tensors in Engineering Science, 1964, (with B. Bakht) Bridge Analysis Simplified, 1985, (with B Bakht) Bridge Analysis by Micro Computing, 1988, (with A.A. Mufti and B. Bakht) Bridge Superstructures, New Developments, 1996; contbr. numerous rsch. papers to profl. jours. Mem. Cambridge City Coun., 1961-62; mem. Nat. Coun. Liberal Party U.K., 1960-62; fellow, mem. bd. govs. Magdalene Coll., Cambridge, 1959-62. With Royal Navy, 1945-48. Decorated Order of Can., 2002; recipient Telford premium Instn. Civil Engrs., 1959, Nat. Rsch. Coun. Can. rsch. grantee, 1962-92, A.B. Sanderson award Can. Soc. Civil Engring., 1983; Gzowski medal Engring. Inst. Can., 1985, cert. of merit Indian Insts. of Engrs., 1989, Assoc. Profl. Engrs. N.S. Engring. award, 1992, P.L. Pratley award, 1993, Julian C. Smith medal Engring. Insts. Can., 1996, Nova award Constrn. Innovation Forum, Mich., 2000. Fellow Royal Soc. Edinburgh, Can. Acad. Engring., Engring. Inst. Can., Can. Soc. for Civil Engring. (pres. 1992-93); mem. Mason Club (N.S.). Office: Dalhousie U 1340 Barrington St Halifax NS Canada B3J 1Y9 Office Phone: 902-494-6029. Office Fax: 902-423-1801. E-mail: leslie.jaeger@ns.sympatico.ca.

JAEGER, MARC JULIUS, physiology educator, researcher; b. Berne, Switzerland, Apr. 4, 1929; came to U.S., 1970; s. Francis K. and Jeanne (Perrin) J.; m. Frances Dick, Dec. 1960 (div. 1972); children: Dominic, Olivia; m. Ina Claire Burlingham-Forbes, June 23, 1973. BA, Gymnasium, Berne, 1948; MD, U. Berne, 1954. Diplomate Swiss Bd. Pulmonary Diseases. Resident, fellow U. Hosp. of Berne, 1954-63; asst. prof. U. Fribourg, Switzerland, 1963-69; assoc. prof. U. Fla. Coll. Medicine, Gainesville, 1970-76, prof. physiology, 1976—2000, prof. emeritus, 2000—. Contbr. over 50 articles to profl. jours., including papers on the separation of gases and isotopes such as U235 and deuterium. Democrat. Achievements include 6 patents for a Method of Separating Solutes and Gases, for a method to Transport Large Amounts of Heat without Coolant and on ventilation of spaces, filled with granules, which have only one opening; research in mechanics of breathing, deep sea diving, air pollution and its effects on the lungs, smoking and its effects on the lungs. Home: 5915 SW 36th Way Gainesville FL 32608-5150 Office: U Fla Coll Medicine Gainesville FL 32610 Business E-Mail: mjaeger@phys.med.ufl.edu.

JAEGER, PATSY ELAINE, retired secondary school educator, artist; b. Douglas, Ariz., Mar. 18, 1936; d. Thomas Conrad and Cora Maxine Forbes; m. John Walter Jaeger, Aug. 26, 1956 (div. Feb. 1984); children: Sherilee Jaeger Zigan, John Everett. BA in Fine Arts, Chapman U., 1961; MA in Art History, Calif. State U., L.A., 1970; MA in Edn. Adminstrn., San Francisco State U., 1988. Life gen. secondary credential life gen. jr. h.s. spl. secondry credential, spl. secondary art credential, preliminary adminstrv. credential, Calif. Tchr. adult edn. oil painting Novato Unified Sch. Dis., 1973—78; tchr. art, chmn. fine arts dept. Torrance (Calif.) H.S., 1962-71; tchr. art and math., chmn. art dept. San Jose Jr. H.S., Novato, Calif., 1974—79; tchr. art and English, chmn. site coun. Hill Jr. H.S., Novato, 1979-83; tchr. English, San Marin H.S., Novato, 1983-95, leadership tchr., 1995-96, tchr. art, 1996-98; semi-ret., 1998; specialist tobacco use edn. Marin County Office Edn., 2000—03, ret., 2003—. Chmn. site rev. team Novato Unified Sch. Dist., 1981; specialist tobacco use edn. Marin County Office Edn., 2000-03. Set designer Cavalleria Rusticana, 1981; cover designer Dimensions III, 1987; contbr. articles to profl. jours. Coord. cmty. vol. program Hill Jr. H.S., 1981-83; chair worship Novato United Meth. Ch., 2005—; chmn. worship com. Novato United Meth. Ch., 2005—, co-v.p. Novato United Meth. Women, 2005—. Recipient Pub. Svc. award U.S. Postal Svc., Torrance, 1968, Tchr. of Yr. award Parent-Tchr.-Student Assn. Hill Jr. H.S., 1983, Extra Step award Marin Spl. Edn. Adv. Com., 1996. Mem. Nat. Mus. Women in Arts (charter), Fine Arts Mus. San Francisco, Novato United Meth. Women (co-v.p. 2005—). Republican. Avocations: book illustration, painting, gardening, singing. Home: 40 Brown Dr Novato CA 94947-7404 Personal E-mail: pjarty@aol.com.

JAEGER, RICHARD CHARLES, electrical engineer, educator, science association director; b. N.Y.C., Sept. 2, 1944; s. O. Fred and Mary Jane (Shatzer) J.; m. Joan Carol Hill, Dec. 28, 1964; children: Peter, Stephanie. BSEE with high honors, M in Elec. Engring., U. Fla., 1966, PhD in Elec. Engring., 1969. Staff engr. IBM Corp., Boca Raton, Fla., 1969—72, adv. engr., 1972-74, 77-79, rsch. staff Yorktown Heights, NY, 1974—76; assoc. prof. Auburn (Ala.) U., 1979—82, prof. elec. engring. dept., 1982—90, alumni prof., 1983—88, disting. prof., 1990—; dir. Ala. Microelectronics Ctr., Auburn, 1984—2000, interim dir. wireless engring., 2001—03. Program com. Internat. Solid State Circuits Conf., San Francisco and N.Y.C., 1978-93, program vice-chmn., 1992, program chmn., 1993; program co-chmn. Internat. VLSI Cirs. Symposium, Kyoto, Japan, 1989, conf. chmn., Honolulu, 1990, exec. comm. chair, 2000—. Author: Introduction to Microelectronic Fabrication, 1988, 2d edit., 2002, Microelectronic Circuit Design, 1997, 2d edit., 2004, Computerized Circuit Analysis Using SPICE Programs, 1997 (IEEE Edn. Soc. McGraw Hill/Jacob Millman award 1998); editor: IEEE Jour. Solid State Cirs., 1995-98; contbr. over 200 articles to profl. jours.; patentee in field. Grantee NSF, Semicondr. Rsch. Corp., Dept. Def., Ala. Rsch. Inst. Fellow IEEE (pres. solid state cirs. coun. 1990-91, v.p. 1988-89, sec. 1984-87, Undergraduate Tchg. award 2004); mem. Computer Soc. IEEE (bd. govs. 1985-86, Outstanding Contbn. award 1984, Golden Core award 1996), IEEE Solid-State Cirs. Soc. (adcom mem. 1996—, v.p. 2004-05, Outstanding Contbn. award 1998, Millenium medal 2000, Outstanding Svc. award, 2004) Home: 2160 Estate Dr Auburn AL 36830 Office: Auburn U Elec and Computer Engring 200 Broun Hall Auburn AL 36849-5201 Office Phone: 334-844-1871. Business E-Mail: jaeger@eng.auburn.edu.

JAEGER, TODD D., music educator; b. Oconomowoc, Wis., Feb. 17, 1961; s. Dennis G. and Barbara A. Jaeger; m. Kim M. Haines, Oct. 5, 1996; children: Lukas, Drew. MusB, Ripon Coll., 1983; M in Music Edn., U. Wis., 1986. Vocal music dir. Platteville (Wis.) HS, 1986—89, Kettle Moraine HS, Wales, Wis., 1989—; dist. music coord. Sch. Dist. Kettle Moraine, Wales, 1995—. Pvt. music tchr., Hartland, Wis., Ashippun, Wis., 1989—. Mem.: Wis. Music Educators Assn. (choral clinician, adjudicator 1986—, mem. state honors choir staff 1994—96), Music Educators Nat. Conf. Avocations: hiking, fishing, reading, antiques. Office: Kettle Moraine HS 349 Oak Crest Dr Wales WI 53183

JAENEN, CORNELIUS JOHN, history professor, consultant; b. Cannington Manor, Can., Feb. 21, 1927; m. Ina May Turner Jaenen. MA, U. Manitoba, Winnipeg, Can., 1950; BEd, U. Manitoba, Can., 1958; PhD, U. Ottawa, Can., 1963; LLD, U. Winnipeg, Can., 1981. Diplome de fin d'etudes, Bordeaux, France. Housemaster Ravenscourt Sch., Winnipeg, Can., 1949-52; instr. Imperial Ethiopian Govt., Addis Ababa, 1952-55; tchr. City if Winnipeg Schs., 1955-58; asst. prof. Meml. U., St. John's, Can., 1958-59; asst. full prof. United Coll., Winnipeg, Can., 1959-67; prof. U. Ottawa, Can., 1967-92, emeritus prof., 1992—. Founding pres. Canadian Ethnic Studies Assn., 1971-73; pres. French Colonial Hist. Soc., 1986-88, Canadian Hist. Assn., 1988-89; chmn. Ethnic Histories Panel, Sec. of State, Can., 1971-86. Author: Friend and Foe, 1976 (Sainte-Marie prize, 1974), The Role of the Church in New France, 1976, The French Regime in the Upper Country of Canada, 1996' author, editor: Les Franco-Ontariens, 1993 (Legault prize, 1993), The Apostles' Doctrine and Fellowship: A Documentary History, 2003; contbr. chpts. to books and essays to jours. Mem. Manitoba Adv. Com. on Bilingualism, Winnipeg, 1963-65, Canadian Consultative Com. on Multiculturalism, Ottawa, 1973-76, Ontario Coun. on Grad. Studies, Toronto, 1973-76; cons. Canadian Mus. Civilization, Ottawa, 1991-2001, Coun. Hist. Found., 2000—. Decorated officer Order of Leopold II; recipient Ronsard medal Govt. France, 1947, Gold medal in Edn., U. Man., 1958. Fellow Royal Soc. Can. (sec. 1999-2004, J.B. Tyrrell medal 1994), Order of Leopold II (officer 2000); mem. Estates-Gen. of French Can Home: 9 Elma St Gloucester ON Canada K1T 3W8 Office: Dept History University of Ottawa Ottawa ON Canada K1N 6N5 Fax: (613) 562-5995. E-mail: history@uottawa.ca.

JAFEK, BRUCE WILLIAM, otolaryngologist, educator; b. Berwyn, Ill., Mar. 4, 1941; s. Robert William and Viola Mabel (Newstrom) J.; m. Mary Bell Kirkpatrick, Sept. 1, 1962; children: Lynette A., Robert K., Timothy B., Britta C., Kayla E., Kristen M. BS, Coe Coll., 1962; postgrad., U. Omaha, 1962; MD, UCLA, 1966; postgrad., Oxford U., 2002—03. Instr. dept. otology/laryngology Johns Hopkins Sch. Medicine, Balt., 1971-73; asst. prof. dept. otolaryngology U. Pa. Med. Sch., Phila., 1973-76; prof., dept. chmn. dept. otolaryngology/head and neck surgery U. Colo. Med. Sch., Denver, 1976-98, prof., 1998—. Served with USPHS, 1971—73. Recipient Fowler award Triologic Soc., 1983, Cottle award Am. Rhinol. Soc., 1991. Mem. Triologic Soc. (west region v.p. 1999), Am. Acad. Otolaryngology/Head and Neck Surgery. Republican. Mem. Lds Ch. Office: U Colo Health Sci Ctr 4200 E 9th Ave # B-205 Denver CO 80220-3706 Office Phone: 303-315-7988. Business E-Mail: bruce.jafek@uchsc.edu.

JAFFA, AYAD A., medical educator, medical researcher; Student, Brunel Tech. Coll., Bristol, Eng., 1975—77; BSc in Biol. Chemistry with honors, U. Essex, Colchester, Eng., 1980, PhD in Biol. Chemistry, 1984. Postdoctoral fellow dept. medicine Med. U. S.C., Charleston, 1984—86, rsch. assoc. dept. medicine, 1986—89, asst. prof. medicine dept. medicine, endocrinology-diabetes-metabolism divsn., 1989—96, asst. prof. pharmacology dept. cell and molecular pharmacology and exptl. therapeutics, 1990—96, mem. grad. faculty, 1991—, assoc. prof. to prof., medicine dept. medicine, divsn. endocrinology-diabetes-med. genetics, 1996—, assoc. prof. to prof., pharmacology dept. cell and molecular pharmacology and exptl. therapeutics, 1996—. Mem. rsch. com. endocrinology-diabetes-med. genetics divsn. Med. U. S.C., Charleston, 1986—; grant reviewer Med. U. Rsch. Com. VA; vis. prof. Cath. U. of Chile, Santiago, 1996; lectr. in field. Manuscript reviewer: Am. Jour. Physiology, Kidney Internat., Life Scis., Jour. Pharmacology and Exptl. Therapeutics, Diabetes; contbr. articles to profl. jours. Recipient FIRST award, 1995; grantee, Med. U. S.C., 1991—92, 1992—93, 1995—96, VA, 1993—, NIH, 1995—. Mem.: Am. Fedn. Clin. Rsch. (Henry Christian award 1995), Am. Diabetes Assn. (exec. mem. fund raising com. S.C. affiliate 1992—96, bd. dirs. 1995—, Rsch. and Devel. award 1990, John A. Colwell award 1992, Rsch. award 1996). Achievements include research in pathogenesis of diabetic nephropathy, mechanisms of progressive renal disease, renal kallikrein-kinin system, kallikrein and renin gene regulation and expression, growth factors and signal transductio. Office: Med U SC Dept Medicine Divsn Endocrinology 171 Ashley Ave Charleston SC 29425-0001*

JAFFA, HARRY VICTOR, political philosophy educator emeritus; b. N.Y.C., Oct. 7, 1918; s. Arthur Sol and Frances (Landau) J.; m. Marjorie Etta Butler, Apr. 25, 1942; children: Donald Alan, Philip Bertran, Karen Louise Jaffa McGoldrick. BA, Yale U., 1939; PhD summa cum laude, New Sch. for Social Rsch., 1951; LLD (hon.), Marietta Coll., 1979, Ripon Coll., 1987. Instr. Queens Coll., CCNY, New Sch. for Social Rsch., 1945-49, U. Chgo., 1949-51, Ohio State U., 1951-64; faculty Claremont (Calif.) McKenna Coll. and Claremont Grad. Sch., 1964-89, Henry Salvatori Rsch. prof. polit. philosophy, 1971-89, prof. emeritus, 1989—; disting. fellow The Claremont Inst., 1989—. Author: Thomism and Aristotelianism: A Study of the Commentary by Thomas Aquinas on the Nicomachean Ethics, 1952, Crisis of the House Divided: An Interpretation of the Issues in the Lincoln-Douglas Debates, 1959, Equality and Liberty, 1965, The Conditions of Freedom, 1975, How to Think About the American Revolution, 1978, American Conservatism and the American Founding, 1984, Original Intent and the Framers of the Constitution: A Disputed Question, 1994, Storm Over the Constitution, 1999, A New Birth of Freedom: Abraham Lincoln and the Coming of the Civil War, 2000; (with Allan Bloom) Shakespeare's Politics, 1964; contbg. author: Shakespeare As Political Thinker, 1981; editor, contbg. author: Statesmanship: Essays in Honor of Sir Winston Churchill, 1982; general editor: Studies in Statesmanship; co-editor: (with Robert Johannsen) In the Name of the People: Speeches and Writings of Lincoln and Douglas in the Ohio Campaign of 1859, 1959. Organizer/dir. Bicycle Racing Program at Claremont Coll., 1976—. Fellow Ford, Rockefeller, Guggenheim, and Earhart founds. Fellow The Claremont Inst. Study of Statesmanship & Political Philosophy (disting.); mem. Am. Polit. Sci. Assn., Winston S. Churchill Assn. (founding pres. 1969—). Republican. Jewish. Avocation: bicycling. Home: 549 W Baughman Ave Claremont CA 91711-3733 Office: Claremont Inst 937 W Foothill Blvd Claremont CA 91711 Office Phone: 709-621-6825.

JAFFE, ALAN STEVEN, lawyer; b. Portland, Maine, Nov. 11, 1939; s. Herman and Rose (Simon) J.; m. Elizabeth L. Reiss, Nov. 3, 1943; children: David, Robert, Richard. BS cum laude, Cornell U. Sch. Industrial & Labor Relations, 1961; LLB cum laude, Columbia U. Sch. of Law, 1964. Bar: NY 1964. Assoc. Poletti, Freiden, Prashker and Gartner, N.Y.C., 1964-65; asst. chief counsel NYC Anti-Poverty Program, 1965-66; assoc. Proskauer Rose LLP, NYC, 1966—73, ptnr., labor & employment law dept., 1973—, chmn., 1999—2005, chmn. policy com., 2005. Bd. dirs. Lincoln Savs. Bank, NYC, 1984-92. Editor Columbia Law Rev., 1962-64. Bd. dirs., v.p. Coun. Jewish Fedns. N.Am., NYC, 1992-99, Jewish Cmty. Rels. Coun., NY, 1987-91; bd. dirs., mem. exec. com. Beth Israel Med. Ctr., 1995-04, Am. Jewish Joint Distbn. Com., 1991—; bd. govs. Jewish Agy. for Israel, 1999-01; pres. Altro Health and Rehab. Svcs., Inc., NYC, 1983-86, pres. UJA Fedn. of NY, 1992-95, bd. dirs. 1980—, chmn. bd. domestic affairs, 1988-91; bd. dirs. NYC Coalition for Homeless, 1995-98; mem. NYC Sports Devel. Corp., 1995-98; bd. dirs., exec. com. Am. Jewish Com., 2002—, chmn. Domestic Policy Commn., 2005-; vice chmn. NY Legal Assistance Group (NYLAG), 2005-; pres. Ednl. Alliance, 2006-. Office: Proskauer Rose LLP 1585 Broadway Fl 27 New York NY 10036-8299

JAFFE, ALBERTO P., musician, educator; b. Rio de Janeiro, May 5, 1935; s. Nathan and Paia (Coslovsky) Jaffe; m. Daisy de Luca, Dec. 5, 1960; children: Claudio, Marcelo, Renata. BCE, Escola Fluminense de Engenharia, Niteroi, Brazil, 1958; MA in violin, Faculdade de Artes da U. Uberlandia, Minas Gerais, Brazil, 1969; post grad. free violin course, Superior School of Music, Cologne, Germany, 1959—61. CEDO, BBC, 1971; musician Ordem dos Musicos do Brasil, 1957. Concert master Orquestra de Camera de Sao Paulo, Brazil, 1961—63; mem. Rio de Janeiro String Quartet, 1964—71, Trio Pro Arte, Rio de Janeiro, 1968—73; prof. U. Ill., Urbana, 1983—85; prin. viola Sinfonia da Camera, Urbana, 1984—85; prof. U. Minas Gerais, Belo Horizonte, Brazil, 1986—92, Pensacola Christian Coll., Fla., 1992—. Artistic dir. Internat. Pro Arte Festival, Teresopolis, Brazil, 1969—88; dir. Summer Music Acad., Pensacola, Fla., 1976—; chamber music and violin tchr. Festival de Inverno, Campos de Jordao, Brazil, 1981—82; dir., music divsn. Nat. Acad. of Arts, Urbana, Ill., 1982—85, artistic dir., 1984. Creator: group instruction method strings Jaffe Method (Best Program Panamerican TV Festival, 1971); performer (with Villa-Lobos String Quartet): (recordings) Bach Sonatas; with Villa-Lobos String Quartet #2: recordings. Pres. music com. Sao Paulo State Sec. Culture, Brazil. Recipient First prize, Villa Lobos Internat. Contest, 1966, Ministerio da Educacao, 1956, Carlos Gomes medal, Rio de Janeiro Govt., 1966. Mem.: Music Tchrs. Nat. Assn. Home: 9179 Woodrun Pl Pensacola FL 32514 Office: Pensacola Christian Coll 250 Brent ln Pensacola FL 32514 Home Fax: 850-478-6573. Personal E-mail: nosad@cox.net.

JAFFE, ANDREW WILLIAM, music educator, composer; b. Washington, Nov. 16, 1951; s. Howard William and Elizabeth (Boudreau) Jaffe; m. Gisele A. Litalien, Aug. 26, 1990; children: Ceora, Sophia, Martin. BA, St. Lawrence U., Canton, N.Y., 1973; postgrad., Berklee Coll. Music, 1974; MusM in Theory Composition, U. Mass., 1977. Dir. jazz ensemble Berklee Coll. Music, Boston, 1977—81; dir. jazz studies Amherst (Mass.) Coll., 1987—99; lectr. music Tufts U., Medford, Mass., 1991—93; lectr. jazz composition U. Mass., Amherst, 1995—98; dir. jazz activities, Lyell B. Cllay artist-in-residence Williams Coll., Williamstown, Mass., 1993—. Mem. cmty. adv. com. U. Mass Fine Arts Ctr., Amherst, 1997—; artistic dir. Williamstown Jazz Festival, 1999—; lectr. in field. Prin. arranger, music dir.: Bill Lowe-Andy Jaffe Repertory Big Band, 1986—93, composer, arranger: albums Manhattan Projections, Double Helix, An Imperfect Storm, 2004, arranger: Kitty Kathryn, Semenya McCord, The Coltrane Big Band, Majid Greenlee, Oh What a Wonder Jesus has Done (Walter Robinson); author: Jazz Harmony, Advance Music, 1996; mem. editl. bd. Jazz Perspectives, 2001; contbr. articles to profl. jours.; mem. editl. bd.: U. Mich. Press. Com. mem. Festival of Hills, Conway, Mass., 1996—. Fellow, Artists Found. Mem.: Internat. Assn. Jazz Educators (Outstanding Svc. to Jazz Edn. 2001), Soc. Am. Music, Coll. Music Soc., Am. Fedn. Music. Avocation: running. Home: PO Box 382 Conway MA 01341 Office: Williams Coll Music Dept 54 Chapin Dr Williamstown MA 01267 Office Phone: 413-597-4049. E-mail: ajaffe@crocker.com.

JAFFE, ARTHUR MICHAEL, physicist, educator; b. N.Y.C., Dec. 22, 1937; s. Henry and Clarisse Jaffe; m. Nora Frances Crow, July 24, 1971; 1 child, Margaret Collins; m. Sarah Robbins Warren, Sept. 12, 1992. AB, Princeton U., 1959; BA, Cambridge U., 1961; PhD, Princeton U., 1966; MA, Harvard U., 1970. Acting asst. prof. math. Stanford U., 1966-67; asst. prof. physics Harvard U., Cambridge, Mass., 1967-69, assoc. prof., 1969-70, prof. physics, 1970-77, prof. math. physics, 1977-85, Landon T. Clay prof. math. and theoretical sci., 1985—, chmn. dept. math., 1987-90. Rsch. fellow Princeton U., 1965—66, vis. prof. math. physics, 1971; rsch. fellow Stanford Linear Accelerator Ctr., 1966—67; mem. Inst. for Advanced Study, 1967; vis. prof. Eidgenössische Technische Hochschule, Zurich, 1968, Rockefeller U., 1977, U. Rome, 1993, Boston U., 2001; mem. pres.'s com. Nat. Medal of Sci., 1997—2002, acting chair, 2001—02; mem. sci. bd. Santa Fe Inst., 1998—; founding mem., dir., pres. Clay Math. Inst., 1998—2002; bd. dirs. Internat. Math. Olympiad, Inst. Schs. of the Future, Project Euclid; bd. dirs. Ctr. Math. Physics U. Hamburg, Germany; bd. dirs. Found. Internat. U., Bremen; mem. Math. Scis. Edn. Bd. of NRC, 2000—, mem. exec. com., 2002—; chmn. bd. Sch. Theoretical Physics Dublin (Ireland) Inst. Advanced Study, 2005—; lectr. in field. Author: Vortices and Monopoles, 1980, Quantum Physics, 1981, 87, Quantum Field Theory and Statistical Mechanics, Expositions, 1985, Constructive Quantum Field Theory, 1985; assoc. editor Jour. Math. Physics, 1970-72; mem. editl. coun. Annals of Physics, 1975-77, asst. editor, 1977-2002; editor Communications Math. Physics, 1976-2000, chief editor, 1979-2000; mem. adv. bd. Letters in Math. Physics, 1975—; editor Progress in Physics, 1979-86, Selecta Mathematica Sovetica, 1980—. Revs. in Mathematical Physics, 1990; contbr. articles to profl. jours. Alfred P. Sloan Found. fellow, 1968-70; Guggenheim Found. fellow, 1977-78, 92; award Math. and Phys. Scis., N.Y. Acad. Sci., 1979; Dannie Heineman prize for Math. Physics, 1980; NSF fellow, 1961-64; NAS Air Force Office Sci. Rsch. fellow, 1965-67. Fellow AAAS (chair math. sect. 2001), Am. Phys. Soc., Am. Acad. Arts and Scis.; mem. U.S. Nat. Acad. Scis., Am. Math. Soc. (exec. com. of coun. 1991-95, pres. 1997-98), Internat. Assn. Math. Physics (pres. 1991-96), Coun. of Sci. Soc. Presidents (chmn. 2000), Joint Policy Bd. for Math. (chair 1998). Home: 27 Lancaster St Cambridge MA 02140-2837 Office Phone: 617-495-4320. Business E-Mail: jaffe@math.harvard.edu.

JAFFE, BERNARD MICHAEL, surgeon; b. NYC; s. Abner I. and Sylvia (Rothman) J.; m. Marlene Lambert, June 4, 1961; children: Mark Allen, Debra Lynn. BA, U. Rochester, 1961; MD, NYU, 1964. Diplomate Am. Bd. Surgery (dir. 1982-88, sr. dir. 1988—, exec. com. 1987-88, rep. to Am. Bd. Med. Specialists 1986-89). Asst. prof. surgery Washington U., St. Louis, 1971-75, assoc. prof., 1975—77, prof., 1977—79; prof., chmn. dept. surgery SUNY Health Sci. Ctr., Bklyn., 1979-92, vice-chmn. dept. surgery, chief divsn. surg. rsch., 1992-2000; prof. surgery Tulane U., New Orleans, 2000—. Author: (with Behrman) Methods of Hormone Radioimmunoassay, 1980; editor-in-chief: Surgical Rounds, 1989—. Served to lt. col. USAF, 1972-74. James IV traveling surg. fellow. Mem. ACS, Assn. Acad. Surgery (pres. 1978-79), Soc. Univ. Surgeons (sec. 1979-82, pres. 1983-84), Am. Surg. Assn., Soc. Clin. Surgery, Surg. Biol. Club I (sec. 1982-85), Am. Soc. Clin. Investigation, Soc. for Surgery Alimentary Tract (pres. 1987-88), So. Surg. Assn., Halsted Soc., Transplant Soc., Soc. for Surg. Oncology, Soc. Exptl. Biology Medicine (councillor 2002-), Phi Beta Kappa, Alpha Omega Alpha. Office: Tulane Univ Med Ctr 1430 Tulane Ave New Orleans LA 70112-2699 Office Phone: 504-988-7123. Business E-Mail: bjaffe@tulane.edu.

JAFFE, CHARLES J., allergist; b. Phila., Feb. 3, 1946; MD, Duke U., 1971, PhD, 1972. Allergist Scripps Meml. Hosp., Encinitas, Calif. Prof. allergy and immunology U. Calif., San Diego. Mem. Am. Coll. Allergy Asthma and Immunology (chair computer sect.), Am. Acad. Allergy Asthma and Immunology (chair med. informatics), Am. Med. Informatics Assn. (chmn. clin. info. syss.).

JAFFÉ, ERNST RICHARD, medical educator, dean; b. Chgo., Jan. 4, 1925; s. Richard Hermann and Berta (Kohn) J.; m. Anne Jane Sylvestre, Aug. 5, 1950; children: Stephanie Anne Green, Richard Sheridan Jaffé. BS, U. Chgo., 1945, MD, MS in Pathology, U. Chgo., 1948; DHL (hon.), Yeshiva U., 1987. Diplomate Am. Bd. Internal Medicine, Hematology, Nat. Bd. Med. Examiners; lic. physician, N.Y. Intern Med. Presbyn. Hosp., N.Y.C., 1948—50, resident, 1953-55; postdoctoral fellow Albert Einstein Coll. of Medicine, Bronx, NY, 1955-57, instr., asst. prof., 1957-62, assoc. prof., 1962-69, prof. medicine, 1969-84, acting dean, 1972-74, 83-84, sr. assoc. dean, 1974-83, 84-91, disting. univ. prof. medicine, 1984-92, disting. univ. prof. medicine emeritus, 1992—. Mem. hematology study sect. Nat. Inst. Health, Bethesda, Md., 1972-82, Hirschl Sci. Adv. Com. I.T. Hirschl Trust, NYC, 1974-92, NY Cmty. Trust Blood Disease Panel, NYC, 1978-97; dir. Belfer Inst. for Advanced Biomed. Studies, 1978-92. Co-editor Seminars in Hematology, 1968-2000, co-editor emeritus, 2000—; editor-in-chief Blood, 1975-77; contbr. articles to profl. jours. Nat. bd. govs. ARC, Washington, 1984-90, chmn. blood svcs. com., 1988-90; bd. dirs. Nat. Marrow Donor Program, 1987-2000; bd. dirs. Henry M. and Lillian Stratton Found., 1985-96, pres., 1989-96; trustee Bergen Cmty. Regional Blood Ctr., 1997-2000 . With U.S. Army, 1944-46; capt. USAF, 1951-53. Named Career Scientist, Health Rsch. Coun.; recipient Charles R. Drew award ARC, 1990. Fellow Internat. Soc. Hematology (counselor 1980-88, v.p. 1984-88, historian 1990—); mem. Am. Soc. Hematology (pres. 1983, historian 1993—, Outstanding Achievement award 1998), Assn. Am. Physicians, Am. Fedn. Clin. Rsch., Am. Soc. Clin. Investigation, Am. Physiol. Soc., Assn. Am. Med. Colls. (emeritus), Coun. Acad. Socs. (adminstrv. bd. 1985-90, chmn. 1989), N.Y. Soc. Study Blood (pres. 1978-80), Soc. for Exptl. Biology and Medicine (pres. 1993-95, past pres. 1995-97), U. Chgo. Alumni Assn. (Profl. Achievement citation 1992), U. Chgo. Med. Alumni Assn. (Disting. Svc. award 1981), Phi Beta Kappa, Sigma Xi, Alpha Omega Alpha. Lutheran. Avocations: photography, reading. Office: Albert Einstein Coll Medicine 1300 Morris Park Ave Bronx NY 10461-1926 Office Phone: 516-944-0232. E-mail: ejaffe@pol.net. *Nothing is more satisfying than to have done a good job and to have earned the affection of your colleagues. However, wife and children are paramount!!.*

JAFFE, F. FILMORE, lawyer, retired judge; b. Chgo., May 4, 1918; s. Jacob Isadore and Goldie (Rabinowitz) J.; m. Mary Main, Nov. 7, 1942; children: Jo Anne, Jay. Student, Southwestern U., 1936-39; JD, Pacific Coast U., 1940. Bar: Calif. 1945, U.S. Supreme Ct. 1964. Practiced law, Los Angeles,

1945-91; ptnr. Bernard & Jaffe, Los Angeles, 1947-74, Jaffe & Jaffe, Los Angeles, 1975-91; apptd. referee Superior Ct. of Los Angeles County, 1991-97, apptd. judge pro tem, 1991-97; ret., 1997; atty. in pvt. practice L.A., 1997—. Mem. L.A. Traffic Commn., 1947-48; arbitrator Am. Arbitration Assn., 1968-91; chmn. pro bono com. Superior Ct. Calif., County of Los Angeles, 1980-86; lectr. on paternity; chair family law indigent paternity panel L.A. County Supr. Ct., 2001—. Served to capt. inf. AUS, 1942-45. Decorated Purple Heart, Croix de Guerre with Silver Star, Bronze Star with oak leaf cluster; honored Human Rights Commn. Los Angeles, Los Angeles County Bd. Suprs.; recipient Pro Bono award State Bar Calif., commendation State Bar Calif., 1983. Mem. ABA, Los Angeles County Bar (honored by family law sect. 1983), Los Angeles Criminal Ct. Bar Assn. (charter mem.), U.S. Supreme Ct. Bar Assn., Masons, Shriners Office: 433 N Camden Dr Ste 400 Beverly Hills CA 90210-4408 Office Phone: 310-859-8921. E-mail: filmorejaffe@sbcglobal.net.

JAFFE, GWEN DANER, museum educator; b. NYC, July 8, 1937; d. Izzy and Selma (Hess) Daner; m. Anthony R. Jaffe; children: Thomas, Elizabeth. BA in Art History, Skidmore Coll., 1957; cert. in elem. tchg., Hofstra U., 1960; postgrad., N.Y. Sch. Interior Design, 1964, Columbia U., 1973. Spl. edn. tchr. Payne Whitney Hosp., 1958-65, Bd. Coop. Ednl. Svcs., Westchester, N.Y., 1958-65; designer Jaffe-Halperin Design Firm, N.Y.C., 1965-86; tour guide Walker Art Ctr., Mpls., 1987-89; tchr. Art Express Sch. mus. program Carnegie Mus. of Art, Pitts., 1989—; mem. staff Peace Arts Exch. program Pitts. Children's Mus., 1992-93; interior designer pvt. practice, 1998—. Designer briefcases and handbags Gwynne Collection, 1993-95, fabric design, 2003. Mem. Fiber Arts Guild. Home: 1056 Lyndhurst Dr Pittsburgh PA 15206

JAFFE, HAROLD W., federal agency administrator; b. Newton, Mass. AB, U. Calif., Berkeley; MD, UCLA. Clin. rsch. investigator, venereal disease control program CDC, Atlanta, epidemic intelligence svc. officer, chief, AIDS epidemiology program, deputy dir. for sci., HIV/AIDS program, dir. AIDS/HIV program, 1992—95, head, HIV, STD and TB lab., acting dir., Nat. Ctr. for HIV, STD and TB prevention, 2001—02, dir., Nat. Ctr. for HIV, STD and TB prevention, 2002—. Office: 1600 Clifton Rd NE E07 Atlanta GA 30333

JAFFE, HELENE D., lawyer; BA magna cum laude, Barnard Coll., 1976; JD, Columbia U. Sch. Law, 1976; Harlan Fiske Stone Scholar. Bar: NY 1977, US Dist. Ct. (So. and Ea. Districts, NY) 1980, US Ct. Appeals (2nd, 3rd, and 8th Districts) 1982, US Supreme Ct. 1982, US Ct. Internat. Trade 1982. Co-head antitrust/competition practice, trade practices and regualtory law dept. Weil, Gotshal & Manges LLP, NYC. Assoc. asst. prof. to adj. assoc. prof. NY U. Sch. Law, 1983—; faculty mem. Ohio Legal Ctr., 1980—; chair Consumer Protection Com.; lectr. in field. Contbr. articles on antitrust, merger, advertising, and marketing issues to profl. publs. Mem.: Assn. Bar City NY (mem. trade regulation com.), NY County Lawyer Assn. (chair, com. on trade regulation), ABA (mem. council antitrust sect., vice-chair Clayton Act Com., antitrust sect.). Office: Weil Gotshal & Manges LLP 767 Fifth Ave New York NY 10153 Office Phone: 212-310-8572. Office Fax: 212-310-8007. Business E-Mail: helene.jaffe@weil.com.

JAFFE, JEFF HUGH, retired food products executive; b. Washington, Dec. 25, 1920; s. Henry A. Jaffe and Mildred (Loewenberg) Auslander; m. Natalie Rubin, Dec. 31, 1945; children: Bonita Jaffe Berens, Holly Anne. BS in Archtl. Engring., Va. Poly. Inst. and State U., 1943. Chmn. bd. dirs., pres. The Chunky Corp. (now Ward Candy, Inc.), 1950-69; pres., CEO candy, chocolate and biscuit group Ward Foods Inc., 1969-71, pres., COO, 1971-72; also bd. dirs. Ward Foods, Inc., 1972-74; chmn. bd. dirs., pres. Schutter Candy Co., 1958-67, Klotz Confection Co., 1960-67; pres., CEO The Schrafft Candy Co., 1974-78; v.p. consumer products group Gulf and Western Industries, 1974-78; pres., CEO Bernan Foods, Inc., 1980-85, ret., 1985. Bd. dirs. Cmty. Nat. Bank of S.I., N.Y., Ward Foods, Inc., Ward Candy Co., Oxford Energy Co.; guest lectr. Harvard Bus. Sch., 1970-84. Bd. dirs., nat. treas. Young Pres.'s Orgn., Woodmere Acad., Martin County (Fla.) Libr. Found.; bd. dirs. Village Hewlett Bay Park; sponsor and patron Fla. Laws of Life Essay Contest for H.S. Students, Martin County, 1999- . Mem. Assn. Mfrs. of Confectionery and Chocolate (past chmn.), Candy Execs. Club, Property Owners Assn. (Sailfish Point, Fla., pres., chmn. transition com., chmn. emeritus, CEO). Home: 6500 SE Harbor Cir Stuart FL 34996-1952

JAFFE, LOUISE, literature and language professor, writer; b. Bronx, NY, May 17, 1936; d. Joseph and Anna (Movitz) Neuwirth; m. Steven Jaffe, Aug. 26, 1962 (div. 1975); 1 child, Aaron Lawrence; m. Leo Gerber, 1993. BA, Queens Coll., 1956; MA, Hunter Coll., 1959; PhD, U. Nebr., 1965; MFA, Bklyn. Coll., 1991. From instr. to prof. English Kingsborough C.C., Bklyn., 1965-95, prof. emerita, 1995—. Author: Hyacinths and Biscuits, 1985, Wisdom Revisited, 1987, Light Breaks, 1995, The Great Horned Owl's Proclamation and Other Hoots, 1997; author numerous poems and fiction stories; mem. editl. bd. Cmty. Review CUNY, 1984—. Recipient First prize N.Y. Poetry Forum, 1980, First prize, First honorable mention Shelley Soc. N.Y., 1983-84, others. Mem.: Am. Mensa. Democrat. Jewish. Avocations: writing, poetry. Home: 2411 E 3rd St Brooklyn NY 11223-5357 Office: Kingsborough Cmty Coll Oriental Blvd Brooklyn NY 11235-4906 E-mail: athena9x@aol.com.

JAFFE, MARK M., lawyer; b. Paterson, N.J., Sept. 18, 1941; s. Irving and Bertha (Margolis) J.; m. June A. Fisher, June 19, 1977. BS in Econs., U. Pa., 1962; JD, Columbia U., 1985. Bar: N.J. 1965, La. 1968, N.Y. 1970, U.S. Dist. Ct. (ea. dist.) N.Y., U.S. Ct. Mil. Appeals, U.S. Ct. Appeals (2d and 5th cirs.), U.S. Dist. Ct. N.J., U.S. Supreme Ct. Assoc. Hill, Betts & Nash, LLP, N.Y.C., 1969-72; ptnr. Hill, Betts & Nash, N.Y.C., 1972—. Lt. USCGR, 1965-68. Mem. ABA, N.J. Bar Assn., La. Bar Assn., Assn. Bar City N.Y., Maritime Law Assn. Home: 377 Rector Pl New York NY 10280-1432 Office: Hill Betts & Nash LLP One World Fin Ctr 200 Liberty St New York NY 10281

JAFFE, MELVIN, security firm executive; b. N.Y.C., May 20, 1919; s. Benjamin and Zelda (Karp) J.; m. Muriel Hamptman, June 9, 1941 (dec. Mar. 1984); children: Marcy, Meredith; m. Suzanne MacMillan, Jan. 20, 1985; children: Cynthia Johnson, Katie Marsico. BS in Edn., Bucknell U., 1940. Pres. Benjamin Jaffe & Son Inc., Bklyn., 1946-68; sr. v.p. investments Morgan Stanley Dean Witter Reynolds, Garden City, NY, 1969—. Pres. Lions Internat., Blkyn., 1965. Staff sgt. U.S. Army, 1942-45, ETO. Mem. Am. Legion (Post 304), Masons. Jewish. Home: 374 Golfview Rd Ste 505C North Palm Beach FL 33408 Home (Summer): Apt 505 374 Golfview Rd North Palm Beach FL 33408-3566 Office Phone: 800-752-2474. Business E-Mail: melvin-jaffe@morganstanley.com.

JAFFE, MURRAY SHERWOOD, retired surgeon; b. Sept. 29, 1926; s. Lester A. and Rosa (Shor) J.; m. Margery Blum, Mar. 26, 1951; children—Emily, Margaret, Dan BS, MD, U. Cin., 1948. Diplomate Am. Bd. Surgery. Intern Barnes Hosp., St. Louis, 1948-49; resident Cin. Gen. Hosp., 1949-50, 52-56, Cin. VA Hosp., 1949-50, 52-56, Dayton VA Hosp., Ohio, 1949-50, 52-56; practice medicine specializing in surgery Cin., 1958-98; asst. chief surgery VA Hosp., Cin., 1958-82; pres. med. staff Jewish Hosp., Cin., 1978-80; pres. Medco Peer Rev., 1981-84; retired surgeon, 1996; assoc. clin. prof. surgery emeritus U. Cin. Pres. Ohio div. Am. Cancer Soc., 1970-71. Served with USN, 1945, 50-52 Mem. ACS, Cin. Surg. Soc., U. Cin. Grad. Surg. Soc., Shriners, Phi Beta Kappa, Alpha Omega Alpha Republican. Jewish. Home: 56 Tradd St Charleston SC 29401-2540 Personal E-mail: jaffems@email.uc.edu.

JAFFE, RICHARD LOUIS, psychiatrist; b. Phila., Feb. 27, 1952; s. William and Annette (Freilich) J.; m. Terry Dee Glass, May 19, 1974; children: Evan, Brian. BS, Pa. State U., 1972; MD, Thomas Jefferson U., 1974. Diplomate Am. Bd. Psychiatry and Neurology. Intern St. Elizabeth's Hosp., Washington, 1974-75; resident Temple U. Hosp., Phila., 1977; teaching unit asst. dir. Temple Hosp., Phila., 1977-82; teaching unit dir. Belmont Ctr., 1982—; clin. assoc. prof. Jefferson Med. Coll., Phila., 2000—. Fellow Am. Psychiat. Assn., Phila. Psychiat. Assn., Assn. for Convulsive Therapy, Coll. Physicians Phila. Office: Belmont Ctr 4200 Monument Rd Philadelphia PA 19131-1625

JAFFE, RICHARD S., lawyer; b. N.Y.C., Apr. 14, 1968; s. Stanley Robert and Myra Jacqueline Jaffe; m. Lainie Joy Jaffe, Aug. 4, 2002. BA, SUNY, Binghamton, 1990; JD, Touro Coll., 1994. Bar: N.Y. 1995, N.J. 1995, D.C. 1995, U.S. Dist. Ct. (so. dist.) NY 1995, U.S. Dist. Ct. (ea. dist.) NY 1995. Assoc. Law Office of Stephen M. Cohen, Lake Success, NY, 1995—98, ptnr., 1998—2004, Cohen & Jaffe, Esquire, 2003—, Law Office of Cohen and Jaffe LLP, Lake Success, 2004—. Mediator Supreme Ct. State of N.Y. Arbitrator Small Claims Ct., Bronx, 2000—. Mem.: ATLA, Nassau County Bar Assn., N.Y. State Trial Lawyers Assn., N.Y. State Bar Assn., Trial Lawyers Care, Inns Of Ct., West Birchwood Civic Assn., Million Dollar Advocates Forum (life). Office: Law Office of Cohen & Jaffe LLP 2001 Marcus Ave Lake Success NY 11042 Office Phone: 516-358-6900.

JAFFE, ROBERT STANLEY, lawyer; b. Walla Walla, Wash., May 16, 1946; BA, U. Wash., 1968, JD, 1972. Bar: Wash. 1972. Ptnr. Preston Gates & Ellis, L.L.P., Seattle, 1986—. Mem. ABA (mem. corp., banking and bus. law sect., mem. small bus. com. 1982-92), Order of Coif. Office: Preston Gates & Ellis 925 4th Ave Ste 2900 Seattle WA 98104-1158 Office Phone: 206-623-7580.

JAFFE, SETH ROTH, lawyer, retail executive; b. N.Y.C., Mar. 8, 1957; s. Harold and Ruth Jaffe; m. Merrie Fanshel, Oct. 20, 1991. AB, Brown U., 1977; JD, U. Mich., 1980. Bar: Calif. 1980, U.S. Dist. Ct. (no. dist.) Calif., U.S. Ct. Appeals (9th cir.). Assoc. McCutchen, Doyle, Brown & Enersen, San Francisco, 1980-84; chief gen. counsel Levi Strauss & Co., San Francisco, 1984—99; sr. v.p., gen. counsel CareThere, Inc., 2000—01; v.p., dep. gen. counsel Williams-Sonoma, Inc., San Francisco, 2002—03, sr. v.p., gen. counsel, sec., 2003—. Office: Williams Sonoma Inc 3250 Van Ness Ave San Francisco CA 94109

JAFFE, SUSAN, ballerina; b. Washington, 1962; Student, Md. Sch. Ballet; student, Sch. Am. Ballet, Am. Ballet Theatre Sch. With Am. Ballet Theatre II, 1978-80; with Am. Ballet Theatre, 1980—, soloist, 1981-83, prin., 1983—2002, tchr., advisor. Repertoire includes: Le Corsaire, The Merry Widow (by Ronald Hynd), Apollo, Eugene Onegin (by John Cranko), La Bayadere, Bouree Fantastique, Carmen, Cinderella, Concerto, Duets, Giselle, The Guards of Amager, Push Comes to Shove, Symphonie Concertante, Ballet Imperial, Coppelia, Etudes, Giselle, Jardin auxLilas, Romeo and Juliet, The Sleeping Beauty, Other Dances, Theme and Variations, Swan Lake, La Sylphide, Undertow, Voluntaries, Dim Lustre, Manon, Gala Performance, Don Quioxte, Cruel World, Sextet, The Snow Maiden, Fall River Legend, Grande Pas Classic, Stepping Stones, Without Words (by Nacho Duato), Anastasia, others; created role Lynne Taylor-Corbett's Great Galloping Gottschalk, Bruch Violin Concerto No. 1, Serious Pleasures; appeared Spoleto in An Evening of Jerome Robbins Ballets, 1982, Known by Heart (Twyla Tharp); appeared with Kirov Ballet, 1988; guest appearances with The Royal Swedish Ballet, The Royal Danish Ballet, The English Nat. Ballet, La Scala Ballet, Milan, 1997, 98, The Royal Ballet, 1998, 2000, Stuttgart Ballet, 1998, 2000, The Munich Opera Ballet, The Vienna State Opera Ballet; dir. (movie) Angie, by Martha Koolidge. Recipient N.Y. Woman-Lancome Paris Woman of Yr. award, 1989, Dance Mag. award, 2003 Office: Am Ballet Theatre 890 Broadway 3d Fl New York NY 10003-1211*

JAFFEE, ANNETTE WILLIAMS, novelist; b. Abilene, Tex., Jan. 10, 1945; d. Jules Henry and Evelyn June (Witensky) Williams; m. Dwight M. Jaffee, Aug. 16, 1964 (div. May 1991); children: Jonathan, Elizabeth. BS, Boston U., 1966. Author: Adult Education, 1981, Recent History, 1988, The Dangerous Age, 1998. N.J. Arts Coun. grantee State of N.J., 1985-86, Geraldine Dodge fellow Yaddo, 1991. Mem. PEN.

JAFFER, STEPHEN C., marketing executive, consultant; b. Asheville, Nc, Sept. 21, 1942; s. Charles Martin Jaffer and Emily Elizabeth Dooley. BA, U. Pitts., 1963. Mktg. cons. Ind., 1993—2004; dir. Boca Raton, 1998—2003. Corp. trainer, Boca Raton, Fla., 1998—2003. Author: (novels) Shrinks, Snake Eyes, Pineapple Blues (Poetry Anthology, 2001), (100 songs) R & B Songbooks (Poetry anthology (3) pub. selections, 2001). Organizer TTC, Inc., Boca Raton, Fla., 2002—04. Conservative. Achievements include invention of Micro tool application. Avocations: conservation, fishing. Home: PO Box 273722 Boca Raton FL 33427

JAFFIN, CHARLES LEONARD, lawyer; b. N.Y.C., Feb. 27, 1928; s. Joseph M. and Rhoda (Abeloff) J.; m. Rosanna Gordon Webster, June 12, 1952; children: David W., Jonathan H., Rhoda E. Murphy, Lora W. Peters, Katherine G. Gibson. AB, Princeton U., 1948; JD, Columbia U., 1951. Bar: N.Y. 1951. Assoc. Carter, Ledyard & Milburn, N.Y.C., 1951-55, Lewis & MacDonald, N.Y.C., 1955-59, ptnr., 1959-60, Battle Fowler and predecessor firms, N.Y.C., 1960-93, of counsel, 1994-2000.

JAGASICH, PAUL ANTHONY, language educator, translator; b. Budapest, Hungary, Mar. 30, 1934; came to U.S., 1965, naturalized 1971; s. Peter Kalman and Etelka (Tar) J.; m. Ea Jane Nagy, oct. 15, 1960; children: Diana, Yvonne. MA, U. N.C., 1970, 71, PhD, 1973; MA, Middlebury Coll., 1983. Med. librarian Med. U., Budapest, 1958-61; major domo, sec. Motel Assn., Budapest, 1961-64; tchr. French and Russian, St. Bernard's Sch., Gladstone, N.J., 1966-68; grad. tchg. asst. U. N.C., Chapel Hill, 1968-73; chmn. prof. fgn. langs. Hampden-Sydney Coll., Va., 1973—. Language educator, translator; b. Budapest, Hungary, Mar. 30, 1934; came to U.S., 1965, naturalized, 1971; s. Peter Kalman and Etelka (Tar) J.; m. Ea Jane Nagy, Oct. 15, 1960; children— Diana, Yvonne. M.A., U. N.C., 1970, 71, Ph.D., 1973; M.A., Middlebury Coll., 1983. Med. librarian Med. U., Budapest, 1958-61; major domo, sec. Motel Assn., Budapest, 1961-64; tchr. French and Russian, St. Bernard's Sch., Gladstone, N.J., 1966-68; grad. teaching asst. U. N.C., Chapel Hill, 1968-73; chmn. prof. fgn. langs. Hampden-Sydney Coll., Va., 1973—. Translator: The Casting of Bells, 1983 (Metthauer award 1985) Mozart in Prague, 1985; Eight Days, 1985, Halley's Comet, 1987, My Cobwebbed Appletree, 1990, Dressed in Light, 1990, Short Love Song About Ctirad and Sarka, 1991, Song About Viktorka, 1991, Maminka, 1991, To Be a Poet, 1992, Starving Artist So Sees the World, 1992, Bozena Nemcova's Fan, 1992, Honeymoon Ride, 1992, The Nightingale Sings Out of Tune, 1992, Over the Waves of TSF, 1992, Only Love, 1994; author Dictionary of Oriental Lexical Elements in Hungarian, 1985, (essay) Heinar Kipphardt, 1986, (essay) All the Beauty of the World, 1991; also short stories and poems, Two Faces of the English Channel, 1991, A Course in Russian Conversation through Videotapes, 1993. Recipient O'Clee Jub. trophy; Named to Internat. Swimming Hall of Fame, 1991; Men. Am. Assn. Tchrs. German, Am. Translators Assn., Am. Literary Translators Assn., Am. Assn. Tchrs. Slavic and East European Langs., Phi Sigma Iota. Republican. Roman Catholic. Translator: The Casting of Bells, 1983 (Metthauer award 1985), Mozart in Prague, 1985, Fight Days, 1985, Halley's Comet, 1987, My Cobwebbed Appletree, 1990, Dressed in Light, 1990, Short Love Song About Ctirad and Sarka, 1991, Song about Viktorka, 1991, Maminka, 1991, To Be a Poet, 1992, Starving Artist So Sees the World, 1992, Bozena Nemcova's Fan, 1992, Honeymoon Ride, 1992, The Nightingale Sings Out of Tune, 1992, Over the Waves of TSF, 1992, Only Love, 1994; author Dictionary of Oriental Lexical Elements in Hungarian, 1985 (essay) Heinar Kipphardt, 1986 (essay) All the Beauty of the World, 1991; also short stories and poems, Two Faces of the English Channel, 1991, A Course in Russian Conversation through Videotapes, 1994. Recipient O'Clee Jub. trophy; named to Internat Swimmin Hall of Fame, 1991. Mem. Am. Assn. Tchrs. German, Am. Translators Assn., Am. Literacry Translators Assn., Am. Assn. Tchrs. Slavic and Eart European Langs., Phi Sigma Iota. Republican. Roman Catholic. Office: Hampden-Sydney Coll College Rd Hampden Sydney VA 23943

JAGDMANN, JUDITH W., state attorney general; d. Glen and Jane Williams; m. Joe Jagdmann; children: Emily, Daniel. Grad., U. Va; JD, U. Richmond. Staff atty. Va State Corp. Commn., 1985—91, asst. gen. counsel, 1991—95, assoc. gen. counsel, 1995—98; dep. atty. gen. State of Va., Richmond, 1998—2005, atty. gen., 2005—. Office: Atty Gen 900 E Main St Richmond VA 23219

JAGENDORF, ANDRÉ TRIDON, physiologist; b. N.Y.C., Oct. 21, 1926; s. Moritz Adolph and Sophie Sheba (Sokolsky) J.; m. Jean Elizabeth Whitenack, June 12, 1952; children: Suzanne E., Judith C., Daniel Z.S. BA, Cornell U., 1948; PhD, Yale U., 1951. Merck postdoctoral fellow UCLA, 1951-53; from asst. prof. to prof. Johns Hopkins U., 1953-66; prof. plant physiology Cornell U., Ithaca, N.Y., 1966—, Liberty H. Bailey prof. plant physiology, 1981-96, Liberty H. Bailey prof. emeritus, 1997—. Author papers, revs. in field. Recipient Outstanding Young Scientist award Md. Acad. Sci., 1961, Kettering Rsch. award, 1963; Weizmann fellow, 1962 Fellow Am. Acad. Arts and Scis., AAAS; mem. NAS, Am. Soc. Plant Physiologists (hon., life, pres. 1967, C.F. Kettering award in photosynthesis, 1978, Charles Reid Barnes award 1989), Am. Soc Biol. Chemists, Am. Soc. Photobiology (councilor 1980), Soc. Gen. Physiologists, Am. Soc. Cell Biology, Japanese Soc. Plant Physiologists. Jewish. Office: Cornell U Plant Biology Dept Plant Sci Bldg Ithaca NY 14853 Office Phone: 607-255-8940. Business E-Mail: atj1@cornell.edu.

JAGER, MELVIN FRANCIS, lawyer; b. Joliet, Ill., Mar. 23, 1937; s. Melvin Van Zandt and Lucille Marie (Callahan) J.; m. Virginia Sue Maitland, Aug. 15, 1959; children: Lori, Jennifer, Scott, Christy. BSME, JD, U. Ill., 1962. Bar: Ill. 1962, D.C. 1962. Assoc. Iron, Birch, Swindler & McKie, Washington, 1962-65; ptnr. Hume, Clement, Brinks, Willian & Olds Ltd., Chgo., 1965-80, Lee, Smith & Jager, Chgo., 1981-83, Niro, Jager & Scavone, Chgo., 1984-85, Brinks, Hofer, Gilson & Lione Ltd., Chgo., 1985—. Adj. prof. law No. Ill. U. Sch. Law, 1979-80, John Marshall Law Sch., 1992, U. Ill. Coll. Law, Champaign, 1992—; chmn. Practicing Law Inst. Trade Secret Protection Symposium, 1986, 89. Author: Trade Secrets Law, 1984; editor U. Ill. Law Rev., 1961-62; contbg. author monograph: Sorting Out the Ownership Rights in Intellectual Property: A Practical Guide to Practical Counseling and Legal Representation, 1980. Mem. bd. edn. Glen Ellyn, Ill., 1974-80; chmn. Civic Betterment Party Nominating Com., Glen Ellyn, 1982-88; chmn. Glen Ellyn Environ. Protection Com., 1971-72; chmn. budget rev. com. Glen Ellyn United Fund, 1972, Glen Ellyn Ednl. Loan Fund trust, 1973. Mem. ABA (chmn. litigation sect. intellectual properties and patents com. 1984-88), Ill. State Bar Assn. (chmn. patent, trademark and copyright, coun. 1982-83, editor newsletter 1979-82), Chgo. Bar Assn., Am. Patent Law Assn., Intellectual Property Law Assn. of Chgo. (pres. 1997), Lic. Execs. Soc. (pres. U.S.A./Can. 1993-94), Am. Law Inst., Glen Ellyn Jaycees (life mem., pres. 1972, trustee), Chgo. Law Club, Union League Club, Phi Gamma Delta, Phi Delta Phi. Republican. Roman Catholic. Office: Brinks Hofer Gilson & Lione Ltd Ste 3600 455 N Cityfront Plaza Dr Chicago IL 60611-5599 Home: 435 E North Water St Chicago IL 60611-5538

JAGERMAN, DAVID LEWIS, mathematician; b. N.Y.C., Ny., Aug. 27; s. Morris and Helen (Bader) J.; m. Adrienne Israel, Sept. 8; children: Diane Tharp, Barbara Magic, Laurie Sutter. BEE, Cooper Union, N.Y.C., 1949; MS in Math., NYU, N.Y.C., 1954, PhD in Math., 1962. Jr. engr. Reeves Instrument Corp., N.Y.C., 1951-55; staff scientist Stavid Engring., Plainfield, N.J., 1955-59; design specialist Convair, San Diego, 1957-59; sr. math. staff cons. System Devel. Corp., Santa Monica, Calif., 1959-63; math. cons. disting. mem. technical staff AT&T Bell Labs., Holmdel, N.J., 1963-89; math. cons. NEC USA, Princeton, N.J., 1989—. Tchr. indsl. math. St. Peters Coll., 1968-73; prof. math. Stevens Inst. Tech., 1967-75, prof. elec. engring. and computer sci., 1984-90; prof. math. Fairleigh Dickinson U., Rutherford, N.J., 1958-67. Cpl. AC U.S. Army, 1942-45. Mem. IEEE (sr.). Achievements include research in stochastic models, queueing systems and teletraffic analysis. Office: RUTCOR Rutgers Ctr Ops Rsch PO Box 5062 New Brunswick NJ 08903-5062

JAGGER, SIR MICK (MICHAEL PHILIP JAGGER), singer, musician; b. Dartford, Kent, Eng., July 26, 1943; s. Joe and Eva Jagger; m. Bianca Perez Morena de Macias, May 12, 1971 (div. Nov. 1979); children: Jade, Karis; m. Jerry Hall, Nov. 21, 1990 (annulled Aug. 13, 1999); children: Elizabeth Scarlett, James Leroy Augustine, Georgia May Ayeesha, Gabriel Luke Beauregard. Student, London Sch. Econs., 1962-64. Mem., lead singer occasional guitarist Rolling Stones, 1962—, tours (of Europe) 1970, 73, 76, 82, 90, 95, 98, 2002, (of U.S.) 1966, 69, 72, 75, 78, 81, 89, 94, 97, 99, 2002, (of Australia), 1973, Europe and Japan, 1990, film appearances include Performance, 1969, Ned Kelly, Gimme Shelter, Sympathy for the Devil, 1970, Ladies and Gentlemen, The Rolling Stones, 1974, Let's Spend the Night Together, 1983, Freejack, 1992, Bent, 1997, The Man From Elysian Fields, 2001; composer (with Keith Richards): (I Can't Get No) Satisfaction, Brown Sugar, Honky Tonk Woman, Jumpin' Jack Flash, Sympathy for the Devil, Get Off My Cloud, Paint it Black, 2000 Light Years from Home, Star Star, Have You Seen Your Mother, Baby (Standing in the Shadows), Mother's Little Helper, Ruby Tuesday, Lady Jane, The Citadel, You Can't Always Get What You Want, Fool to Cry, Start Me Up, She's So Cold, As Tears Go By, Wild Horses; albums with Rolling Stones include England's Newest Hitmakers: The Rolling Stones, 12 x 5, 1964, The Rolling Stones, Now!, December's Children (And Everybody's), Out of Our Heads, 1965, Aftermath, Big Hits, High Tide, & Green Grass, 1966, Between the Buttons, Flowers, Got Live If You Want It, Their Satanic Majesties Request, 1967, Beggars Banquet, 1968, Let it Bleed, Through the Past, Darkly, 1969, Get Yer Ya Yas Out, 1970, Stone Age, Gimme Shelter, Hot Rocks 1964-1971, Jamming with Edward, Milestones, Sticky Fingers, 1971, Exile on Main Street, 1972, No Stone Unturned, More Hot Rocks (Big Hits and Fazed Cookies), Goat's Head Soup, 1973, It's Only Rock and Roll, 1974, Metamorphosis, Rolled Gold, Made in the Shade, 1975, Black and Blue, 1976, Love You Live, 1977, Some Girls, 1978, Emotional Rescue, 1980, Sucking in the Seventies, Tatoo You, 1981, Still Life, 1982, Under Cover, 1983, Rewind (1971-1984), 1984, Dirty Work, 1986, Singles Collection: The London Years, 1989, Steel Wheels (also co-producer), 1989, Flashpoint, 1990, Voodoo Lounge, 1994 (Grammy award Best Rock Album, 1994), Stripped, 1995, The Rolling Stone's Rock and Roll Circus, 1996, Bridges to Babylon, 1997, No Security, 1999, Forty Licks, 2002, Singles: 1965-1967, 2004, Jump Back: The Best of the Rolling Stones, 2004, Live Licks, 2004, A Bigger Bang, 2005, solo albums She's The Boss, 1985, Primitive Cool, 1987, Wandering Spirit, 1993, Goddess In the Doorway, 2001, soundtracks Alfie, 2004 (with David A. Stewart) Golden Globe award for best original song "Old Habits Die Hard", 2005), solo singles include Just Another Night, Let's Work, (with David Bowie) Dancin' in the Streets; prodr.: (films) Enigma, 2001. Named to Rock and Roll Hall of Fame, 1989. Office: Virgin Records 5750 Wilshire Blvd Ste 300 Los Angeles CA 90036-3640

JAGGERS-GRADY, ANNIELAURA, humanities educator; b. Cypert, Ark., Dec. 22, 1918; d. Frederick Franklin Mixon and Laura Odella Walker; m. C.P. Leslie Grady, July 24, 2001; m. Carl Jasper Jaggers (dec.); children: Carl Frederick Jaggers, Christiana Jaggers. BA, Ark. Tech. U., 1962; MA in Humanities, U. Ark., 1965, MA in Philosophy, 1975. Instr. Ark. Tech. U., Russellville, 1965—67, asst. prof., 1967—75, assoc. prof., 1975—91; ret., 1991. Mem. faculty senate Ark. Tech. U., faculty advisor student groups. Democrat. Presbyterian. Avocations: reading, piano. Home: 212 N Sand St Ozone AR 72854

JAGO, RUSSELL PETER, medical educator; b. Torquay, Devon, Great Britain and Northern Ireland, May 11, 1977; m. Alicia Walton Walton, Feb. 21, 2004. PhD, U. Reading, England, 2002. Post doctorate Baylor Coll. of Medicine, Houston, 2002—03, faculty, 2003—. Office: CNRC Baylor Coll Medicine 1100 Bates St Houston TX TX 77 Office Phone: 713-798-6787.

JAGODA, BARRY LIONEL, communications executive, writer; b. Youngstown, Ohio, Feb. 5, 1944; s. Saul S. and Anne (Fradin) Jagoda; m. Karen Bernhardt, 1980. BA, U. Tex., 1966; MS, Columbia U., 1967. Writer, editor NBC News, Washington, 1967-69, NYC; prodr. CBS News, NYC, 1969-75;

ptnr. Houston, Ritz, Cohen, Jagoda, NYC, 1975; TV advisor Jimmy Carter presdl. campaign, 1976; spl. asst. Pres., Washington, 1977-79, cons., 1979-80; pres. Am. Info. Exch., 1980—; dir. news and pub. affairs George Washington U., 1983-87; v.p. Stackig, Sanderson and White Advt. and Pub. Rels., 1988-93, Shandwick Pub. Affairs, Washington, 1993-97, IMPAC Corp., 1997-2001; writer Washington Times, 2001—03; dir. comms. U. Calif., San Diego, 2003—. Recipient Emmy award as producer CBS news special, Watergate 1974. Chmn. bd. dirs. Friends of Raoul Wallenberg Found., 1989-96. Ford Found. fellow, 1967 Mem. Nat. Bus. Travel Assn., Sigma Delta Chi. Home: 9302 La Jolla Farms Rd La Jolla CA 92037-2901 Office: Univ Calif 9500 Gilman Drive San Diego CA 92093 Business E-Mail: bjagoda@ucsd.edu.

JAGR, JAROMIR, professional hockey player; b. Kladno, Czechoslavakia, Feb. 15, 1972; Profl. hockey player Poldi Kladno, 1988—90, Pitts. Penguins, 1990—2001, Washington Capitals, 2001—04, New York Rangers, 2004—; player Czech Republic Olympic Team, 1998, 2002. Player NHL All-star game, 1992, 93, 96, 1998—2004. Named to Czechoslavakian League All-Star Team, 1989—90; recipient Art Ross Trophy, 1995, 1998—2001, Hart Mem. Trophy, 1999, Lester B. Pearson Award, 1999, 2000, Stanley Cup Champion, 1991, 1992, Olympic Gold Medal, 1998. Office: c/o New York Rangers 2 Pennsylvania Plaza New York NY 10121

JAGTIANI, ANIL R., consumer products company executive; b. Pune, Maharashtra, India, Sept. 5, 1960; s. Ram N. and Savitri R. Jagtiani; m. Julapa A. Jagtiani; 1 child, Kiran A. B in Engring., Pune U., 1981; MBA, NYU, 1984. Dir. strategic planning Brunswick Corp., Lake Forest, Ill., 1997—2001; exec. v.p. corp. strategy, devel. and ventures Hallmark Cards, Inc., Kansas City, Mo., 2001—. Bd. dirs. Crown Media, Studio City, Calif.; v.p. Mgmt. Dynamics, White Plains, NY, 1984—90; ptnr. Mktg. Corp. Am., Westport, Conn., 1990—97; bd. dirs. Hallmark Entertainment Holdings, Kansas City, Mo. Scholar, Inlaks Found., London, 1982—84. Avocations: tennis, travel. Home: 1000 Westover Rd Kansas City MO 64113 Office: Hallmark Cards Inc PO Box 419580 MD 201 2501 McGee Kansas City MO 64141-6580 Office Phone: 816-545-2064. Personal E-mail: ajagtiani@hotmail.com. E-mail: ajagti2@hallmark.com.

JAHANGIR, NAUMAN, surgeon; b. Lahore, Pakistan, Aug. 24, 1972; s. Khawaja Salim and Khaulah Jahangir; m. Nudrat Rizvi Hasan Rizvi, Jan. 1, 1996; children: Rafae Nauman, Ehmed Nauman. SSC, Islamabad Coll. For Boys, Pakistan, 1988; HSSC, Cadet Coll., Hassan Abdal, Pakistan, 1990; MB, BS, Aga Khan U., Karachi, Pakistan, 1995. Cert. Instr., Advanced Trauma and Life Support ACS. Resident gen. surgery SUNY, Upstate Med. U., Syracuse, NY, 1997—2002, fellow cardiothoracic surgery, 2002—04. Contbr. scientific papers, articles pub. to profl. jour. Founding mem./treas. FALAH - Students orgn. for patient welfare, Karachi, Pakistan, 1993—95. Recipient Bronze Medal, Pakistan Assn. of Psychiatrists, 1994, President's Gold Medal for the Best Boy Scout of 1997, Pakistan Boy Scouts Assn., 1997; scholar Begum Shafiqa Zia-ul-Haq Scholarship for academic excellence, Aga Khan U., 1994-95, Quaid-e-Azam Merit Scholarship for academic excellence, Fed. Bd. of Edn., Pakistan, 1988, Quaid-e-Azam Merit Scholarship for Academic Excellence, Rawalpindi Bd. of Edn., 1990. Mem.: ACS (candidate group), Cts Net, Soc. of Thoracic Surgeons (candidate group), Alpine Club of Pakistan. Home: 6273 Gulfstream Path Cicero NY 13039 Personal E-mail: jahangirdoc@yahoo.com.

JAHANMIR, SAID, materials scientist, mechanical engineer; b. Mar. 18, 1950; married; 2 children. BSME, U. Wash., 1971; MSME, MIT, 1973, PhD in Mech. Engring., 1976. Instr. mech. engring. MIT, 1975-76; lectr. mech. engring. U. Calif., 1976-77; asst. prof. Sibley Sch. Mech. & Aerospace Engring. Cornell U., 1977-80; sr. staff engr. Exxon Rsch. and Engring. Co., 1980-85; program dir. tribology program NSF, 1985-87; group leader Nat. Inst. Stds. & Tech., 1987—2002; pres., CEO Miti Heart Corp., Gaithersburg, Md., 2002—. Adj. prof. mech. engring. U. Md., 1987-96; adj. prof. U. Del., 1997—; presenter in field. Author: Tribology in Manufacturing Processes, 1994, Friction and Wear of Ceramics, 1994, Machining of Ceramics and Composites, 1999; exec. editor Machining Sci. and Tech. Jour.; contbr. articles to profl. jours., chpts. to books; patentee in field. Mem.: ASME (v.p. rsch. 2001—, chair tribology divsn. 1997—99, bd. rsch. and tech. devel. 1995—98, assoc. editor 1990—93, tribology divsn. exec. com. 1988—90, others, Disting. Svc. award, Mayo D. Hersey award 2001), Am. Soc. for Artificial Internal Organs, Soc. Tribologists and Lubrication Engrs. (fellows com. 1993—99, edn. com. 1987—95, ceramics and composites com. founding chmn. 1987—89, ann. meeting program com. 1987—91, lubrication fundamentals com. 1986—87, Internat. award). Office: Miti Heart Corp PO Box 83610 Gaithersburg MD 20883 Office Phone: 301-869-9720. Business E-Mail: sjahanmir@mitiheart.com.

JAHIEL, RENE INO, physician; b. Boulogne, Seine, France, Mar. 29, 1928; s. Richard and Cecile (Lwovsky) J.; m. Deborah Berg, May 8, 1955; children: Abigail, Richard, Beth. BA, NYU, 1946; MD, SUNY (Downstate Med. Coll.), Bklyn., 1950; PhD, Columbia U., 1957. Intern Montefiore Hosp., N.Y.C., 1950-51; resident Mt. Sinai Hosp., N.Y.C., 1951—52, fellow in virology, 1952-55; exptl. immunologist Nat. Jewish Hosp., Denver, 1957-59; asst. attending pathologist, exptl. pathology Mt. Sinai Hosp., 1959-61; asst. prof. pub. health Cornell U. Med. Coll., N.Y.C., 1961-66; rsch. assoc. prof. preventive medicine NYU, N.Y.C., 1967-70, rsch. prof., 1970-76, rsch. prof. medicine, Sch. Medicine, 1976-88. Cons. health svcs. rsch., policy and planning, 1989—; adj. prof. health svcs., rsch. and policy New Sch. for Social Rsch., 1991-96; dean faculty of sci. and pub. health, Ecole Libre des Hautes Etudes of N.Y., 1991-94, v.p. scis., 1994—, acting pres., 2003-; vis. prof. dept. cmty. medicine and healthcare U. Conn. Health Ctr., 1995-98, lectr., 1999—; pres. Internat. Health Policy Rsch. Corp., Hartford, Conn., 1995—; med. dir. Southbury (Conn.) Tng. Sch., 1993-95; med. cons. State of Conn. Dept. Mental Retardation, 1996-97; tchr. met. leadership program, U. Coll., NYU, 1969-73; physician Assn. for Help for Retarded Children, 1982-88, Young Adult Inst., 1984-89, Assn. for Children with Retarded Mental Devel., 1988-93; cons. Nat. Ctr. for Health Svcs. Rsch., 1983-85; bd. dirs. N.Y. Scientists Com. Pub. Info., 1974-79, Physicians Forum, 1975-84; cons. Yale U Primary Care Tng. Program at Waterbury (Conn.) Hosp., 2000-04. Author sci. rsch. articles on tissue culture, virology, interferon, preventive medicine, health policy, health svcs. rsch., disability, homelessness, sociology of knowledge; editor: Homelessness: A Prevention-Oriented Approach, 1992. Mem. interferon adv. com. Am. Cancer Soc., 1984-93; mem. nat. bd. Com. for Nat. Health Svc., 1976-79, coalition, 1980-85. Lt. USNR, 1955-57. Recipient Daring to Dream award, U. Maine, 2005; grantee, USPHS, 1966—79. Mem. APHA (chmn. com. health svcs. rsch. 1980-87, Med. Care sect. award 1985, governing coun. 1983-85, 99—, chmn. homelessness study group 1984-90, chmn. policy com. caucus on disablement 1989-92, founding chmn. caucus on homelessness 1990-91, chmn. membership com. spl. interest group on disability 1993-97, chair 1998-99, edn. bd. 2000-01), Internat. Assn. Health Policy (bd. dirs. 1998-2000), Physicians for Social Responsibility, Internat. Soc. Sys. Sci. Health Care, Assn. Health Svcs. Rsch. (Spl. Recognition award 1986), World Assn. for Psychosocial Rehab. (chmn. com. on mental handicaps 1992-94), Internat. Soc. for Equity in Health (founding), Acad. Health, Am. Assn. Psychol. Rehab. Office: 250 Main St Unit 732 Hartford CT 06106-1875 Office Phone: 860-547-1202. Business E-Mail: jahiel@nso2.uchc.edu.

JAHNKE, JUDITH MARIE, music educator; b. Chgo., Apr. 22, 1964; d. Paul and Marie J. BM, BS, Elmhurst Coll., 1986; MusM, Northwestern U., 2002. Cert. music tchr., Ill. Tchr. comprehensive music grades K-6 Thomas Jefferson Sch. Cmty. Consolidated Sch. Dist. 15, Palatine, Ill., 1987—. Mem. Ill. Grade Sch. Music Assn. MENC. Avocations: music, art, gardening, crafts, travel. Home: 1413 Columbine Dr Schaumburg IL 60173-2270 Office: Cmty Consolidated Sch Dist 15 Thomas Jefferson Sch 3805 Winston Hoffman Estates IL 60195 Office Phone: 847-963-5442.

JAHNS, JEFFREY, lawyer; b. Chgo., July 6, 1946; s. Maxim G. and Josephine Barbara (Czernek) J.; m. Jill Metcoff, Sept. 8, 1973; children: Anna Hope, Claire Martine, Elizabeth Grace. AB, Villanova U., 1968; JD, U. Chgo., 1971. Bar: Ill. 1971, U.S. Dist. Ct. (no. dist.) Ill. 1971, U.S. Ct. Appeals (7th cir.) 1973, U.S. Supreme Ct. 1974. Assoc. Roan & Grossman, Chgo., 1971-77, ptnr., 1977-81, Seyfarth Shaw LLP, Chgo., 1981—. Mem. tax mgmt. adv. bd. Bur. Nat. Affairs, Washington, 1981--. Co-author: Corporate Acquisition Debt Interest Deduction, 1973; contbr. numerous articles to legal publs., chpts. to books. Trustee, chmn. Chgo. Architecture Found., 1982—; bd. dirs. Prairie Ave. House Mus., 1995-98; trustee, treas. Graham Found., 1998—. Ctr. for Urban Studies fellow U. Chgo., 1969-71. Mem. ABA, Chgo. Bar Assn. (chmn. various coms.), Internat. Coun. Shopping Ctrs., Mid-Day Club, Econ. Club Chgo., Lambda Alpha. Office: Seyfarth Shaw LLP 55 E Monroe St Ste 4200 Chicago IL 60603-5863 Office Phone: 312-269-8819. E-mail: jjahns@seyfarth.com.

JAHRAUS, CHRISTOPHER DEAN, oncologist, educator; b. Linton, N.D., Oct. 18, 1972; s. Cecil Doleroy and Darleen Loetta Jahraus; m. Jennifer Dawn Moyers, June 21, 1997; 1 child, Tyler Ethan. BS, Bethel U., St. Paul, 1995; MD, U. Ala., Birmingham, 2000. Intern in pediat. St. Louis Children's Hosp. Wash. U., 2001; resident in radiation oncology U. Ky. Med. Ctr., 2005; asst. prof. radiation oncology U. Ala., Birmingham, 2005—. Clin. rschr., adv. bd. mem. Salix Pharms., Morrisville, NC, 2002—. Contbr. articles to profl. jours. Recipient Irby award for Rsch. in Immunology, U. Ala. Sch. Medicine, 1995, Roentgen Rsch. award, Radiologic Soc. N.Am., 2004; Selected scholar, Berlex Oncology Found., 2002. Mem.: Radiation Therapy Oncology Group, North Ctrl. Cancer Treatment Group, Am. Coll. Radiology, So. Med. Assn., European Assn. Clin. Rsch., Am. Soc. Pediatric Hematology/Oncology, Am. Coll. Radiation Oncology (Howard H. Wong fellow 2003), Eastern Coop. Oncology Group, Am. Soc. Therapeutic Radiology and Oncology (Resident Clin. Rsch. award 2004), Am. Soc. Clin. Oncology (assoc.). Republican. Southern Baptist. Achievements include patents pending for use of Balsalazide in the amelioration of radiation-induced proctosigmoiditis; research in proper radiotherapy fractionation for pediatric Langerhan's Cell Histiocytosis. Avocations: travel, swimming, fishing, woodworking, fountain pen collecting. Office: U Ala Birmingham 619 19th St S WTI102 Birmingham AL 35249 Office Phone: 205-975-0222. Office Fax: 205-975-0784. Personal E-mail: cdjahraus@msn.com. Business E-Mail: cjahraus@uabmc.edu.

JAIMES, HÉCTOR ALFREDO, Latin American literature educator, researcher, culture educator; b. Barcelona, Venezuela, Dec. 1, 1964; s. Hector Jaimes and Ana Matilde Suarez; m. Sheila M. Healey, Dec. 1, 1988 (div. Nov. 1996). BA, Ctrl. U. Caracas, Venezuela, 1989; MA, NYU, 1992; PhD, U. Pa., Phila., 1998. Asst. prof. L.Am. lit. and culture N.C. State U., Raleigh, 1998—. Author: Abril, 1991, Salvoconducto, 1996, Modernismo y Estética, 1999, La reescritura de la Historia en el ensayo hispanoamericano, 2001; contbr. articles to profl. jours. Mem MLA. Avocations: travel, dance, chess, exercise, reading. Office: NC State U Box 8106 Raleigh NC 27695 Home: Apt 103 1201 Trinity Crest Rd Raleigh NC 27607-4233 E-mail: hajaimes@hotmail.com.

JAIN, DIPAK CHAND, dean, marketing educator, consultant; b. Tezpur, India, June 9, 1957; came to U.S., 1983; s. Jagdish C. and Sumitra (Jain) J.; m. Sushant Jain, Dec. 12, 1989; children: Dhwani, Kalash, Muskaan. BS in math. and stats., Gauhati U., Assam, India, 1976, MS in math. stats., 1978; MS in mgmt. sci., U. Tex., Dallas, 1986, PhD in mktg., 1987. Asst. prof. Gauhati U., 1979-83; teaching and rsch. asst. U. Tex., Dallas, 1983-86; asst. prof. mktg. Kellogg Sch. Mgmt., Northwestern U., Evanston, Ill., 1986-89, assoc. prof., 1990-93, prof. mktg., 1993—94, Sandy and Morton Goldman prof. entrepreneurial studies, 1994—, assoc. dean for acad. affairs, 1996—2001, dean, 2001—. Vis. prof. mktg., Sasin Grad. Inst. Bus. Adminstrn., Chulalongkorn U., Bangkok, 1989-; mktg. dept. editor, Management Science; bd. dirs. Deere & Co., Hartmarx Corp., Peoples Energy Corp., UAL Corp., No. Trust Corp., 2004-; cons. to pharm. and telecom. firms, consumer goods co. Recipient Outstanding Educator Award, State of Assam, India, 1982, Sidney Levy Award for Excellence in Tchg., Kellogg Sch. Mgmt., 1994—95, Alumni Prof. of Yr. Award, 2002, Pravasi Bharatiya Samman Award, govt. India, 2004. Office: Northwestern U 2001 Sheridan Rd Evanston IL 60208-0814

JAIN, JINESH CHAND, chemistry researcher; b. Karahi, Raj, India, Feb. 5, 1952; came to U.S., 1995; s. Pooran Chand and Anguri Devi Jain; m. Kumud Jain, July 3, 1979; children: Mahim, Meha. BSc, U. Rajasthan, Bharatpur, India, 1972, MSc, 1974; PhD, U. Jodhpur, 1978. Rsch. asst. TEA Rsch. Assn., Jorhat, India, 1977-79; postdoctoral fellow U. Alta., Edmonton, Can., 1979-80; rsch. assoc. U. Regina, Can., 1980-82, U. Saskatchewan, Sask., Can., 1982-87, Nat. Rsch. Coun., Sask., Can., 1987-90; rsch. officer U. Saskatchewan, Sask., Can., 1990-95; mem. rsch. faculty U. Notre Dame, Ind., 1995—. Contbr. more than 100 articles to profl. jours. Office: U Notre Dame Dept CE/GEOS Notre Dame IN 46556 E-mail: jain.1@nd.edu.

JAIN, PIYARE LAL, physics professor; b. Punjab, India, Dec. 11, 1921; came to U.S., 1949; naturalized, 1961; s. Labh Ch and Maya (Devi) J.; m. Sulakshana Dhawan, Feb. 15, 1966. BA, Punjab U., 1944, MA, 1948; PhD, Mich. State U., 1954. Research asso. chemistry dept. U. Minn., 1953-54; instr. physics dept. State U. N.Y., Buffalo, 1954-59, asst. prof., 1959-61, assoc. prof., 1961-67, prof., 1967—. Research asso. U. Chgo., 1959-60, Lawrence Radiation Lab., Berkeley, Calif.; vis. prof., Bristol, Eng., 1961-62, U. Wash., Seattle, summer 1960; Fulbright vis. prof. Rajasthan U., India, 1965-66; Sci. adviser Am. embassy AID, New Delhi, India, summer 1966 Recipient Excellence award State of N.Y. and United Univ. Professions, Hind Ratten award Govt. of India, 1994. Fellow Am. Phys. Soc. Achievements include rsch. in sold state physics, electron and nulcear magnetic resonance, cosmic radiation and high energy physics, relativistic heavy ion physics. Home: 223 Surrey Run Buffalo NY 14221-3363 Office: Suny At Buffalo Buffalo NY 14260-0001

JAIN, RAJ, engineering educator; b. Satna, India, Aug. 17, 1951; came to U.S., 1974; s. Shanti Lal and Sulochana Devi Jain; m. Neelu Hathishah; children: Sameer, Amit. B of Engring., A.P.S. U., Rewa, India, 1972; M of Engring., Indian Inst. of Sci., 1974; PhD, Harvard U., 1978. Sr. engr. Digital Equipment Corp., Maynard, Mass., 1978-80, prin. engr. Hudson, Mass., 1980-82, cons. engr. Littleton, Mass., 1983-90, sr. cons. engr., 1991-94; prof. Ohio State U., Columbus, 1994-2000; chief tech. officer, co-founder Nayna Networks, Milpitas, Calif., 2000—05; prof. Washington U., St. Louis, 2005—. Bd. tech. adv. Teradiant Networks, San Jose, Calif.; spkr. in field. Author: Control Theoretic Formulation of Operating Systems Resource Management, 1979, The Art of Computer Systems Performance Analysis, 1991 (award 1992), FDDI Handbook: High-Speed Networking with Fiber and Other Media, 1994, High Performance TCP/IP Networking, 2003; patentee in field. Sec. Jain Ctr. of Greater Boston, Wellesley, Mass., 1978-84. Fellow IEEE, Assn. Computing Machinery. Home: 131 Frontenac Forest Saint Louis MO 63131 Office: CSE Campus Box 1045 Washington U One Brooking Dr Saint Louis MO 63130 Business E-Mail: jain@acm.org.

JAIN, RAKESH K., chemical engineer, tumor biology educator; b. Lalitpur, India, Dec. 18, 1950; came to U.S., 1972; s. Sanat Kumar and Kailash W. Jain; m. Janet Carrick. BTech in Chem. Engring., Indian Inst. Tech., Kanpur, 1972; MS in Chem. Engring., U. Del., 1974, PhD in Chem. Engring., 1975. Asst. prof. chem. and biomed. engring. Columbia U., N.Y.C., 1976-78; from asst. to assoc. prof. chem. and biomed. engring. Carnegie Mellon U., Pitts., 1978-83, prof., 1983-91; Andrew Werk Cook prof. tumor biology dept. radiation oncology Harvard Med. Sch., Boston, 1991—; dir. Edwin L. Steele Lab. for Tumor Biology MGH Cancer Ctr. Mass. Gen. Hosp., Boston, 1991—; prof. Harvard-MIT divsn. health scis. and tech. MIT, Cambridge, Mass., 1991—. Vis. prof. chem. engring. MIT, 1983; vis. prof. bioengring. U. Calif., San Diego, LaJolla, 1984; vis. prof. radiology Stanford (Calif.) U. Med. Sch., 1984; vis. prof. pathophysiology, U. Mainz, Germany, 1990-91; vis. prof. surg. rsch. U. Munich, 1991; vice chmn. Gordon Conf. Microcirculation, 1993; cons. Lab. Pathophysiology, NCI, 1976-84, DuPont Merck Pharm., Wilmington, Del., 1988-90, Hybritech-Lily, San Diego, 1988-93; mem. adv. bd. Pitts. Biomed. Devel. Corp., 1989-91; mem. radiation study sect. NIH, 1991-94; bd. dirs. Am. Cancer Soc.; B.F. Ruth lectr. Iowa State U., Ames, 1983; Allan P. Colburn lectr. U. Del., Newark, 1983; Hugh C. Muldoon lectr. Duquesne U., Pitts., 1986; Kurt Wohl lectr. U. Del., 1992. Mem. edit. bd. Biotech. Progress, 1985—, Microvascular Rsch., 1985—, CRC Crit. Revs. in Biomed. Engring., 1986-95, Cancer Rsch., 1987—, Drug Targeting and Delivery, 1991—, Microcirculation, 1994-2001, Angiogenesis, 1997-, British Journal of Cancer, 1997-, Internat. Journal of Oncology, 1997-, Journal of Theoretical Medicine, 1997, Molecular Imaging, 2002, Clinical Cancer Rsch., 2003, Nature Reviews Cancer (Highlights Section), 2004-. Recipient Rsch. Career Devel. award Nat. Cancer Inst., 1980-85, Abbott Microcirculation award European Soc. Microcirculation, 1990, Sr. Scientist award Alexander von Humboldt Found., 1990-91, Instrumentation for Physiology and Medicine award Am. Microcirculation Soc., 1993, 94, Disting. Alumnus award Indian Inst. Tech., 1994; Outstanding Investigator grantee Nat. Cancer Inst., 1993—; John Simon Guggenheim Meml. Found. fellow, 1983-84. Fellow Am. Inst. Biol. and Med. Engrs. (founder); mem. AIChE (chmn. nat. planning com. area 15e-engring. fundamentals in life scis. 1981-84, chmn. tech. sects. life scis. area 1976-82, 84-86, co-editor AIChE Symposium Series 1983, 86), AAAS, Am. Assn. Cancer Rsch., N.Am. Soc. Biorheology (chmn. membership com. 1988-90), N.Am. Hyperthermia Soc., N.Y. Acad. Scis. (chmn. thermal characteristics of tumors conf. 1979, guest editor Annals N.Y. Acad. Scis. 1980), Internat. Inst. Microcirculation (bd. dirs. 1987-91, co-chmn. cancer cells and tumor microcirculation conf. 1989, Rsch. award 1984), Microcirculation Soc. (chmn. membership com. 1986-88, nomination com. 1993—), Biomed. Engring. Soc. (conf. chmn. ann. meeting 1987, chmn. meeting programming com. 1987-90), Radiation Rsch. Soc., Sigma Xi, Inst. Medicine, 2004. Avocations: swimming, classical music, jazz. Office: Mass Gen Hosp Dept Radiation Oncolog Boston MA 02114

JAIRAM, KHELANAND VISHVAYKANAND, lawyer; b. Queenstown, Essequibo, Guyana, Nov. 29, 1946; came to U.S., 1988; s. Kaiser and Narainee Jairam; m. Joyce B. Gafur, Dec. 2, 1967; children: Shashi, Nishall, Ashwini. Barrister at Law, Inns Ct. Sch., London, 1974; LLB with honors, U. London, 1988; LLM, U. N.Y., N.Y.C., 1990. Bar: Eng. 1974, Wales 1974, Guyana 1974, N.Y. 1991, U.S. Dist. Ct. (so. and ea. dists.) 1991, Trinidad and Tobago, 1997. Pvt. practice, Georgetown, Guyana, 1974-88; tax counsel N.Y.C. Dept. Fin., 1991-94; pvt. practice Law Office K.V. Jairam, N.Y.C., 1994—. Mem. parliament, Govt. of Guyana, 1980-85. Mem. ABA, Am. Trial Lawyers Assn., N.Y. State Bar Assn., Queens County Bar Assn. Democrat. Hindu. Avocations: tennis, cricket. Home: 230 Main St East Rockaway NY 11518-1715 Office: 18915 Jamaica Ave Hollis NY 11423 Office Phone: 718-740-8019. E-mail: kvjairam@aol.com.

JAKAB, IRENE, psychiatrist; b. Oradea, Rumania; came to U.S., 1961, naturalized, 1966; d. Odon and Rosa A. (Riedl) J. MD, Ferencz József U., Kolozsvar, Hungary, 1944; lic. in psychology, pedagogy, philosophy cum laude, Hungarian U., Cluj, Rumania, 1947; PhD summa cum laude, Pazmany Peter U., Budapest, 1948; Dr honoris causa, U. Besançon, France, 1982, U. Pécs, Hungary, 1999. Diplomate Am. Bd. Psychiatry, Am. Bd. Pediatric Neuropsychology. Rotating intern Ferencz József U., 1943-44; resident in psychiatry Univ. Hosp., Kolozsvar, 1944-47, resident in neurology, 1947-50; resident internal medicine Univ. Hosp. for Internal Medicine, Pécs, Hungary, 1950-51; chief physician Univ. Hosp. for Neurology and Psychiatry, Pécs, 1951-59; staff neuropathol. rsch. lab. Neurol. Univ. Clinic, Zurich, 1959-61; sect. chief Kans. Neurol. Inst., Topeka, 1961-63; dir. rsch. and edn., 1966; resident psychiatry Topeka State Hosp., 1963-66; asst. psychiatrist McLean Hosp., Belmont, Mass., 1966-67, assoc. psychiatrist, 1967-74; prof. psychiatry U. Pitts. Med. Sch., 1974-89, prof. emerita, 1989—, co-dir. med. student edn. in psychiatry, 1981-89. Dir. John Merck Program, 1974-81; mem. faculty dept. psychiatry Med. Sch., Pecs, 1951-59; asst. Univ. Hosp. Neurology, Zurich, 1959-61; assoc. psychiatry Harvard U., Boston, 1966-69, asst. prof. psychiatry, 1969-74, program dir. grad course mental retardation, 1970-87; lectr. psychiatry, 1974—; mem. Am. Bd. Pediatric Neuropsychiatry, editor in chief newsletter. Author: Dessins et Peintures des Aliénés, 1956, Zeichnungen und Gemälde der Geisteskranken, 1956, Pictorial Expression in Psychiatry, 1998; editor: Psychiatry and Art, 1968, Art Interpretation and Art Therapy, 1969, Conscious and Unconscious Expressive Art, 1971, Transcultural Aspects of Psychiatric Art, 1975; co-editor: Dynamische Psychiatrie, 1974; mem. editl. bd. Confinia Psychiatrica, 1975-99; contbr. articles to profl. jours. Recipient 1st prize Benjamin Rush Gold medal award for sci. exhibit, 1980, Bronze Chris plaque Columbus Film Festival, 1980, Leadership award Am. Assn. on Mental Deficiency, 1980; Menninger Sch. Psychiatry fellow, Topeka, 1963-66. Mem. AMA, Am. Psychol. Assn., Am. Psychiat. Assn., Société Medico Psychologique de Paris, Internat. Rorschach Soc., N.Y. Acad. Scis., Internat. Soc. Psychopathology of Expression (v.p. 1959—), Am. Soc. Psychopathology of Expression (chmn. 1965—, Ernst Kris Gold Medal award 1988), Royal Soc. of Medicine (overseas fellow), Internat. Soc. Child Psychiatry and Allied Professions, Internat. Assn. Knowledge Engrs. (v.p. for medicine 1988-95), Deutschsprachige Gesellschaft für Psychopathologie des Ausdruckes (hon. Prinzhorn prize 1967), Hungarian Psychiat. Assn. (hon. 1992), World Psychiat. Assn. (co-chmn. sect. on mass and media and mental health, co-chmn. sect. on psychopathology of expression). Home and Office: 74 Lawton St Brookline MA 02446-5801 Office Phone: 617-738-9821.

JAKACKI, DIANE KATHERINE, multimedia entertainment company executive; b. Englewood, N.J., July 27, 1964; d. Bernard and Barbara (Logie) J. BA, Lafayette Coll., 1986. From asst. to mktg. mgr. to website v.p. Home Box Office, N.Y.C., 1987—2001; co-founder, ptnr. Headgear Prodns., New Canaan, Conn., 2001—. Author: (plays) Beowulf: A 20th Century Evening in a 10th Century Mead Hall, 1992, Blocked, 1994, Rubbing Brass, 1996. Youth group leader Congl. Ch., New Canaan, Conn., 1994-96. Avocations: theater, computers, british history, golf, bicycling. Office: Headgear Prodns 30 Crystal St New Canaan CT 06840

JAKES, JOHN, author; b. Chgo., Mar. 31, 1932; s. John Adrian and Bertha (Retz) J.; m. Rachel Ann Payne, June 15, 1951; children: Andrea, Ellen, John Michael, Victoria. AB, DePauw U., 1953, LittD (hon.), 1977; MA, Ohio State U., 1954; LLD (hon.), Wright State U., 1976; LHD (hon.), Winthrop Coll., 1985, U. S.C., 1993, Ohio State U., 1996. With advt. dept. Abbott Labs., 1954-60; with creative dept. various advt. agencies, 1960-69; creative dir. Dancer Fitzgerald Sample Co., Dayton, Ohio, 1969-70. Rsch. fellow dept. history U. S.C., 1989. Author: The Texans Ride North, 1952, A Night for Treason, 1956, Murder He Says, 1958, When the Star Kings Die, 1967, Master of the Dark Gate, 1970, The Kent Family Chronicles: The Bastard, 1974, The Rebels, 1975, The Seekers, 1975, The Furies, 1976, The Titans, 1976, The Warriors, 1977, The Lawless, 1978, The Americans, 1980, North and South Trilogy: North and South, 1982, Love and War, 1984, Heaven and Hell, 1987, California Gold, 1989, Homeland, 1993, In the Big Country, 1993, American Dreams, 1998, On Secret Service, 2000, Charleston, 2002, Savannah (Or) A Gift for Mr. Lincoln, 2004, (juvenile) Susanna of the Alamo, 1986, (musical) Great Expectations - The Musical, 1999; co-editor anthology: New Trails, 1994; editor: (anthology) A Century of Great Western Stories, 2000. Trustee DePauw U. Recipient Ohio Gov.'s award, 1977, ann. lit. award Friends of Rochester Pub. Libr., 1983, Citizen-Celebrity award for libr. advocacy White House Conf. on Libr., 1995, Disting. Alumni award Ohio State U. Coll. Humanities, 1995, Western Heritage Lit. award Nat. Cowboy Hall of Fame, 1995, Profl. Achievement award Ohio State U. Alumni Assn., 1997, Career Achievement award S.C. Humanities Coun., 1998, Cooper medal Thomas Cooper Libr., U. S.C., 2002. Mem. S.C. Acad. Authors, Western Writers Am., Dramatists Guild, Authors Guild, PEN, Writers Guild of Am. (East), Century Assn. Office: care Rembar & Curtis Attys 19 W 44th St New York NY 10036-5902 E-mail: jjfiction@aol.com.

JAKES, T.D., bishop; b. So. Charleston, WV, June 9, 1957; s. Ernest Jakes, Odith Jakes; m. Serita Jakes. CEO Potter's House of Dallas, Inc.; founder Clay School. Host numerous conferences and speaking tours. Recipient Grammy Award, 2004. Office: The Potter's House PO Box 5390 Dallas TX 75208*

JAKES, WILLIAM CHESTER, electrical engineer; b. Milw., May 15, 1922; s. William Chester and Eleanor (Knight) J.; m. Mary Elizabeth Bristle, Sept. 3, 1948; children: Robert, Elizabeth. BS in Elec. Engring., Northwestern U., 1944, MS in Elec. Engring, 1947, PhD, 1949. With Bell Tel. Labs., Inc. (various locations), 1949-87, head radio transmission research dept. Holmdel, N.J., 1963-71; dir. Radio Transmission Lab., North Andover, Mass., 1971-87. Mem. sci. adv. bd. Voice of Am., 1957-58 Contbr. articles to profl. jours.; patentee antennas and comm. systems. With USN, 1944-46. Ph.D. (hon.) Iowa Wesleyan U., 1961; recipient Alumni Merit award Northwestern U., 1962 Fellow IEEE (Paper award 1971, co-recipient Alexander Graham Bell medal 1987); mem. Eta Kappa Nu, Pi Mu Epsilon. Home: 58 Wild Rose Dr Andover MA 01810-4620 *Intense dedication to physics and engineering with constant desire for understanding and intellectual honesty, plus the enjoyment of working with others, have been my guiding principles.*

JAKIELA, KAREN Y., theology studies educator; b. New Orleans; d. Emmett Frank Yuratich and Theresa Amy Barry; children: Allison J. Webb, Gregory A. B in Music Therapy, Loyola U., New Orleans, 1969; MMus, U. N.Mex., 1975. Registered music therapist, cert. catechist Archdiocese of New Orleans. Spl. edn. tchr. Deckbar Elem. Sch., Jefferson, La., 1970; dir. music St. Thomas Cath. Ch., Ruston, La., 1975—89; patient activity coord. Alpine Nursing Home, Ruston, 1980—81; dir. social svcs. Longleaf Nursing Home, Ruston, 1981—90; theology educator Ursuline Acad., New Orleans, 1990—. Accompanist Ursuline H.S. Choir, New Orleans, 1990—; coord. Bach regional piano competition Ursuline Acad., 1995—; asst. music dir. Symphony Chorus of New Orleans, 1998—. Dir. children's choir (CD) A Creole Mass by Wardell Quezergue, 2000; composer: Cantico Del Fratello Solo, 2003. Roman Catholic. Avocations: flying, Tae Kwon Do, painting. Office: Ursuline Acad 2635 State St New Orleans LA 70118

JAKLE, KENNETH RICHARD, broadcast executive; b. Effingham, Ill., Aug. 7, 1942; s. Kenneth Dean and Kaythryn Joan (Loy) J.; m. Sharon S. James, Jan. 12, 1980; children by previous marriage: Ann Elizabeth, Joellen Kaythryn, Richard Edward. BS in Comm., U. Ill., 1964. Sales mgr. Sta. WKEI, Kewanee, Ill., 1964-65; gen. mgr. Sta. WCRA, Effingham, 1965-66; mng. owner Sta. WRMN-AM-FM, Elgin, Ill., 1966-74, pres., 1974—, Sta. WJKL, Elgin, 1974—, Sta. WBIG, Aurora, Ill., 1994—, Radio Shopping Show, Inc.; pres., chmn. Elgin Broadcasting Co., Inc., BIG Broadcasting Co., Inc., Las Vegas Radio Co., Inc., Radio Shopping Show. V.p., dir. Clinton (Ill.) Daily Jour. and Pub., 1979—81; pres. Sta. KSHP, Las Vegas, 1996—; chmn. bd., pres. Elgin Broadcasting Co., Inc., Las Vegas Radio Land Co., Inc.; bd. dirs. First Ill. Valley Bank & Trust Co., First Cmty. Bank. Bd. mgrs., Sherman Hosp., Elgin, chmn. 1993-2001; chmn. Sherman Health Sys., 2001—, chmn. Elgin Econ. Devel. Commn., 1975-77; pres. Elgin YMCA, 1972-73; bd. dirs. Elgin Symphony Orch., Elgin Downtowner, Easter Seal Assn., Upper Kane County Heart Assn., Larkin Home for Children, Salvation Army; bd. dirs. Elgin Devel. Corp., treas.; chmn. bd., pres. Sherman West Ct. Nusing Home; savs. bond chmn. Kane County, 1982-83; founding mem. Elgin Ctr. City Redevel. Corp., bd. dirs., 1991—; mem. Dennis Hastert Fin. Com., 1989—. With USNG, 1964-66. Recipient Disting. Svc. award Jaycees, 1969, Disting. Svc. award Cosmopolitan Club, 1993, Disting. Svc. award Greater Elgin YMCA, 2000. Mem. Nat. Assn. Broadcasters, Nat. Radio Broadcasters Assn., Ill. Broadcasters Assn., Elgin Hist. Soc. (dir.), Greater Elgin C. of C. (1st v.p., exec. com. 1985—, pres. 1988—), Nat. Spkrs. Assn. (bd. dirs. exec. com. 1999—, pres. 2005—), Profl. Spkrs. of Ill. (bd. dirs., pres. 1995-96, recipient Chicagoland Comms. and Leadership award 1995, cert. speaking profl. designation 1999), Rotary (pres. Elgin club 1976-77), Masons, Shriners. Avocation: commercial pilot with multi engine and instrument rating. Home: 9N874 Koshare Cir Elgin IL 60123-8422 Office: Stas WRMN/WJKL 14 Douglas Ave Elgin IL 60120-5546 E-mail: rickjakle@jakle.com.

JAKOBSON, MARK JOHN, retired physics professor; b. Carlyle, Mont., May 4, 1923; s. Hans M. and Bessie Mae (Fessenden) J.; m. Marguerite Elizabeth Thomsen, Aug. 17, 1945; children— Kristin Marie, Sandra Lynne. BA, U. Mont., 1944, MA, 1947; PhD (Whiting fellow), U. Calif. at Berkeley, 1951. Physicist Lawrence Radiation Lab., 1951-52; instr. U. Wash., 1952-53; prof. U. Mont., Missoula, 1953-93, chmn. physics and astronomy dept., 1969-73. Mem. vis. staff Los Alamos Sci. Lab., 1963-96. Served to lt. (j.g.) USNR, 1944-46. Fellow Am. Phys. Soc.; mem. Sigma Xi, Phi Beta Kappa, Pi Mu Epsilon. Democrat. Lutheran. Home: 3000 Queen St Missoula MT 59801-8651 *A dominant force in my life has been a commitment to the work ethic, a commitment that was nurtured by the Depression. As part of that work ethic I have tried to focus my entire being at any given time on a particular problem. I believe that characteristic, when present in a delineated effort, is what identifies the true professional.*

JAKOPEC, CARL THOMAS, pharmaceutical executive; b. Chgo., May 31, 1945; s. Charles George and Lillian (Seps) Jakopec; m. Elizabeth Todd Dunlap, Aug. 23, 1969 (div. Sept. 1976); m. Carol Coon, Jan. 7, 1977; children: Kimberly Jo, Jeffery Allyn. BS in Pharmacy, Drake U., 1969. Registered pharmacist Iowa. Chief pharmacy Walgreen Drug Co., Des Moines, 1969-77; owner Greeley (Colo.) Pharmacy Corp., 1977-81; mgr. govt. sales Marion Labs., Inc., Kansas City, Mo., 1981-95; dir. govt. sales Forest Labs., Inc., N.Y.C., 1996—. Mem. nat. commn. future Drake U., 1988, mem. nat. adv. bd. Coll. Pharmacy, 1997—. Bd. dirs. Little League Baseball, Greeley, Colo., 1977—84. Recipient Distinguished Service award, Marine Corps League, 1992. Mem.: Am. Soc. Health Sys. Pharmacists, Am. Pharm. Assn., Am. Soc. Cons. Pharmacists, Nat. Hot Rod Assn., Ferrari Club Am., Sports Car Club Am. (bd. dirs. 1991—92). Avocations: auto racing, travel, golf. Home and Office: Forest Labs Inc 4033 Highland Castle Ct Las Vegas NV 89129-3664 Office Phone: 702-364-8162.

JAKUB, JAMES W., physician, surgical oncologist; b. Elizabeth, NJ, May 14, 1969; s. Louis E. and Mary B. Jakub; m. Patricia A. Jakub, Jan. 2, 1993; children: James W. Jr., Kyle M., Jack T. BA in Biology (hon.), Western Md. Coll., Westminster, 1991; MD, Med. Coll. Pa., 1995. Lic. Fla., S.C., Med. Lic. Examine U.S., 1995, diplomate Am. Bd. of Surgery, 2001; lic. Fed. DEA, 1995. Gen. surg. intern U. S.C. Med. Sch., Columbia, 1995—96, resident in gen. surgery, 1996—2000; surgeon Carolina Surg. Specialist, Spartenburg, SC, 2000—01; dir. GI oncology program Lakeland Regional Cancer Ctr., Fla., 2002—. Dir. of clin. trials Lakeland Regional Cancer Ctr., Fla., 2003—; presenter in field. Author: The Pathophysiology of Pneumoperitoneum, 1998; contbr. numerous articlees to profl. jours. Breast Surg. Oncology fellow, H. Lee Moffit Cancer Ctr. and Rsch. Inst., U. South Fla., 2001—02. Fellow: ACS, Soc. Surg. Oncology; mem.: Soc. Am. Gastrointestinal Endoscopic Surgeons, Soc. Carolina Surgeons, Am. Soc. Breast Surgeons (Outstanding Sci. Presentation award 2002), Phi Beta Kappa. Office: Lakeland Regional Cancer Ctr 3525 Lakeland Hills Blvd Lakeland FL 33805 E-mail: jim.jakub@lrmc.com.

JAKUBAUSKAS, EDWARD BENEDICT, college president; b. Waterbury, Conn., Apr. 14, 1930; s. Constantine and Barbara (Narstis) J.; m. Ruth Friz, Aug. 29, 1959; children— Carol, Marilyn, Mark, Eric. BA, U. Conn., 1952, MA, 1954; PhD, U. Wis., 1961. Economist FPC, 1956, Dept. Labor, 1956-58; instr. U. Wis., 1961-62, asst. prof. econs., 1962-63; asst. prof. Iowa State U., 1963-65, assoc. prof., 1965-66, prof., 1966-71; dean U. Wyo., 1971-76, prof. econs., 1971-79, v.p. acad. affairs, 1976-79; pres. SUNY, Geneseo, 1979-88, Cen. Mich. U., Mt. Pleasant, 1988-92; cons. in higher edn., 1992—. Author: Manpower Economics, 1971. Served with U.S. Army, 1954-56. Mem. Am. Assn. State Univs. and Colls. Mem. United Chs. of Christ.

JAKUBCZYK, JOHN JOSEPH, lawyer; b. New Britain, Conn., Dec. 21, 1953; s. Stanley Walter and Madeline Regina (Hinchliffe) J.; m. Petra Kunigunda Mead, Jan. 8, 1983; children; Kristan Marie, John Joseph II, Jamie Nicole, Joseph Michael, Michael Thomas, Stanley Walter, Peter Anthony, Samuel Francis, Justin Peter, Anthony Edward, William James. BA in Bus. Adminstrn. and Polit. Sci., U. San Diego, 1976; JD, U. Ariz., 1979. Bar: Ariz. 1979, U.S. Dist. Ct. Ariz. 1979, U.S. Ct. Appeals (9th cir.) 1992, U.S. Supreme Ct. 1989. Atty. pvt. practice, Phoenix, 1979—. Gen. counsel, Ariz. Right to Life, 1990-99, pres. 1999—; spkr. in field. Actor in cmty. theater prodns.; author pro-life articles; radio commentator and host Catechist St. Paul's Cath. Ch., 1982-92. Bd. dirs., cons. Ariz. Youth for Life, Phoenix, 1979-82; trustee Ville de Marie Acad., 1991—, pres., 1995-99, v.p., 1999-2001, treas. 2002—; chmn. polit. action com. Arizonans for Life, 1980-891; pres. Ariz. Right to Life, Phoenix, 1983-85, 99—, bd. dirs. 1983-92, v.p., 1988-89; bd. dirs. Life Ednl. Corp., 1984-90, sec.; founder, pres. S.W. Life and Law Ctr.; bd. advisors Free Speech Advs.; precinct committeeman Rep. Com., Phoenix, 1982-96. Recipient Pro-Life Action League Protector award, 1987, Wallace McWhirter award, 1989, Honor Guard award Alliance Defense Fund. Mem. ATLA, Ariz. State Bar Assn., Nat. Lawyers Assn. (bd. dirs. 1994—), Maricopa County Bar Assn., St. Thomas More Soc., Christian Legal Soc., Cardinal Newman Soc., KC (pro-life chmn. 1982-83), Phi Delta Phi. Office: 2711 N 24th St Ste 200 Phoenix AZ 85008-1052 Office Phone: 602-468-0030. E-mail: jakeslaw@lonet.net.

JAKUBOWSKY, FRANK RAYMOND, religious writer; b. Belfield, N.D., Oct. 11, 1931; s. William and Catherine (O'bach) J. Student, U. N.D., 1950—52. Chemist Sherwin-Williams Paint Co., Emeryville, Calif., 1958—85; pres. Bold Books, Oakland, Calif., 1978—. Editor Spiritfest, Berkeley, Calif., 1997—. Author: Creation, 1978, Jesus Was a Leo, 1979, The Psychological Patterns of Jesus Christ, 1982, The Creative Theory of the Universe, 1983, Caldecott, 1985, Frank on a Farm, 1988, Lake Merritt, 1988, Thank God, I Am Alive, 1989, Whitman Revisted, 1989, Spiritual Symbols for the Astrology of the Soul, 1990, This New World; Birth: Sept. 8, 1958, 1990, Perceptive Types, 1993, Father Figure Frank's Stories, 1996, Inspiration Stories, 1998, Universal Mind, 1998, Big Bang Goes Puff, 1999, My Inspirational Stories, 2004, Oakland's Lake Merritt, 2004. Pfc. U.S. Army, 1952-54. Mem. Urantia Fellowship, Inst. Noetic Scis., Nat. Coun. Geocosmic Rsch. Roman Catholic. Avocation: writing songs for children on fraimba. Home: 1565 Madison St Apt 308 Oakland CA 94612-4511 Office Phone: 510-763-4324. Business E-Mail: boldbooks@sbcglobal.net.

JAKUBS, DEBORAH, university librarian; BA, U. Wis. Madison; MLIS, U. Calif. Berkeley; PhD in Latin Am. history, Stanford U., 1986. With Duke U., Durham, NC, 1983—, previously libr. for Latin Am. & Iberia, head Internat. and Area Studies Dept., dir. Collections Svc., now Rita DiGiallonardo Holloway U. Libr. and Vice Provost for Libr. Affairs, 2005—. Assoc. dir. U. NC-Duke U. Consortium in Latin Am. Studies, 1995—97, 2000—02, dir., 1997—99; chair Area Studies Coun. of Ctr. for Rsch. Libr.; mem. steering com. Program for Latin Am. Libr. & Archival Collections Harvard U.; adj. prof. history Duke U. Mem.: Assn. Rsch. Libraries (vis. program officer 1996—2002). Office: 220 Perkins Libr Duke U Durham NC 27708 Office Phone: 919-660-5800. E-mail: deborah.jakubs@duke.edu.

JAKUC, MONICA, music educator, pianist, fortepianist; b. Newark, Nov. 20, 1943; d. William Vincent and Helen Ann (Dziuban) J. BS, Juilliard Sch. Music, 1964, MS, 1966; student of Leon Fleisher, Peabody Conservatory Music, 1967-69; student of Russell Sherman, New Eng. Conservatory, Boston, 1970-73; postgrad., Amherst Coll., 1982, Georgy Sebok Ernen (Switzerland) Musikdorf, 1983, Alexandra and Roger Pierce Movement for Musicians, 1984, Cornell U., 1987, Columbia U., 1993. Grad. teaching fellow in lit. and materials of music Juilliard Sch. Music, N.Y.C., 1964-66; grad. teaching fellow in piano Peabody Conservatory, Balt., 1967-69; piano instr. Vassar Coll., Poughkeepsie, N.Y., 1966-67; mem. faculty Smith Coll., Northampton, Mass., 1969—, prof. music, 1988—2003, Elsie Irwin Sweeney prof. music, 2003—. Radio appearances include Nat. Pub. Radio, 1990, 91, 92, Interview with Tim Morton, Sta. WHRO-FM, Norfolk, Va., 1992, Interview with Kit Pfeiffer, Maine Pub. Broadcasting Network, 1992, The Listening Room with Bob Sherman, Sta. WQXR, N.Y.C., 1986, Morning Pro Musica with Robert J. Lurtsema, Ea. Pub. Radio Network, 1985, Smith Coll. solo and chamber music recitals, Sta. WFCR-FM, Amherst, Mass., 1971-92; lectr., fortepiano recital Tidewater Music Tchrs. Forum and Old Dominion U., Norfolk, Va., 1992; (video) recital with Margaret Irwin-Brandon in Arcadia Players: A Baroque Celebration. Solo debut recital, London, 1988, N.Y., 1986; ensemble debut recital with two pianos, N.Y., 1980; concerts of music by women composers on modern piano include U. Dayton, Goucher Coll., Skidmore Coll., U. Redlands, Calif., Blue Hill, Maine, 1992; guest fortepiano soloist in all-Mozart program, Arcadia Players, 1991; coord. and fortepiano performer HaydnFest Internat. Conf. and Festival of Recitals, Smith Coll., 1990; guest artist Hist. Piano Concerts, Ashburnham, Mass., 1986-91; solo recitals in Japan, 1987; recorded compact disc Sonatas for Fortepiano by Marianne vonMartinez, Marianna von Auenbrugger and Joseph Haydn, Francesca LE Brun Six Sonatas for Fortepiano and Violin Op. 1. Mem. coun., pres. Broad Brook Coalition, Florence, Mass., 1992-95; mem. Westfield Ctr. for Early Keyboard Studies Jerene Appleby Harnish Fund grantee Smith Coll., 1986, 88, 92. Mem. Early Music Am., Internat. Alliance for Women in Music. Avocations: birding, bicycling, hiking, canoeing. Office: Smith Coll Dept Music Northampton MA 01063-0001 E-mail: mjakuc@smith.edu.

JALALI, BEHNAZ, psychiatrist, educator; b. Mashad, Iran, Jan. 26, 1944; came to U.S., 1968; d. Badiolah and Bahieh (Shahidi) Samimy; m. Mehrdad Jalali, Sept. 18, 1968. MD, Tehran (Iran) U., 1968. Rotating intern Burlington County Meml. Hosp., Mt. Holly, N.J., 1968-69; resident in psychiatry U. Md. Hosp., Balt., 1970-73; asst. prof. psychiatry dept. psychiatry Sch. Medicine Rutgers U., Piscataway, N.J., 1973-76, Yale U., New Haven, Conn., 1976-81, assoc. clin. prof. psychiatry, 1981-85; assoc. clin. prof. psychiatry dept. psychiatry UCLA, 1985-94, clin. prof. psychiatry dept. psychiatry Sch. Medicine, 1994—. Dir. psychotherapy Sch. Medicine Rutgers U., Piscataway, 1973-76; dir. family therapy unit dept. psychiatry Yale U., New Haven, 1976-85; chief clin. med. svcs. Mental Health Clinic, 1987-96; coord. med. student edn. in psychiatry West L.A. VA Hosp., 1985—2000; dir. family therapy clinic W.Va. VA Hosp., 1991—, co-leader Schozophrenia Clinic, Mental Health Clinic, West Los Angeles VA Med. Ctr., 1996—; med. dir. Mental Health Clinic, West La.A. VA Med. Ctr., 2004-. Author: (with others) Ethnicity and Family Therapy, 1982, Clinical Guidlines in Cross-Cultural Mental Health, 1988; contbr. articles to profl. jours. Fellow Am. Psychiatric Assn., Am. Orthopsychiatry Assn., Am. Assn. Social Psychiatry; mem. Am. Family Therapy Assn., So. Calif. Psychiatric Assn. (chair com. for women 1992), World Fedn. Mental Health. Avocations: photography, hiking, cinema, painting. Home: 1203 Roberto Ln Los Angeles CA 90077-2304 Office: UCLA Dept Psychiatry West LA VA Med Ctr B116aa Los Angeles CA 90073-1003 Office Phone: 310-268-4651. Business E-Mail: behnaz.jalali@med.va.gov.

JALALI, ZIBA, epidemiologist; d. Habibollah Jalali and Sedigheh Rahbar. MD, PhD, U. Cologne. Diplomate. Fellow infectious diseases Albert Einstein Coll. Medicine, Bronx, NY, 2003—. Mem.: IDSA. Office Phone: 718-549-0929. Personal E-mail: zibajalali@yahoo.com.

JALBA, MIHAI SERGIU, epidemiologist, pulmonologist, physician, researcher; b. Tecuci, Moldova, Romania, May 28, 1953; arrived in US, 1995; s. Teodor and Olimpia Jalba; m. Lucia Moisa, Apr. 11, 1981 (div. Sept. 11, 2000); children: Theodor Lucian, Heliodor Ioan. MD, Carol Davila U. Medicine, 1980, PhD in Clin. Med. Scis., 2001. Cert. pulmonologist Ministry of Health, Romania, 1994. Intern Nat. Inst. Endocrinology, Bucharest, 1980—83; gen. practitioner Barlad City Hosp., Perieni, Romania, 1984—87, Ialomitza County Hosp., Milosesti, Romania, 1987—91; sci. rschr. Nat. Inst. Pulmonology, Bucharest, 1991—95; assoc. sci. rschr. Bklyn. Hosp., 1996—2001; epidemiologist Dept. of Health, N.Y.C., 2002—03; postdoctoral rsch. fellow Robert Wood Johnson Med. Sch., New Brunswick, NJ, 2004—. Contbr. articles to profl. jours. Mem.: Romanian Soc. Pulmonology (sec. (exec. bd. nat. com.) 1992—95), So. Med. Assn. Achievements include breakthroughs in tuberculosis epidemiology, adult respiratory distress syndrome and asthma research. Avocations: chess, opera, violin. E-mail: drmjalba@netzero.net.

JALBERT, JANELLE JENNIFER, executive recruiter, secondary school educator; d. Gerald Edward and Linda S. Jalbert. AA, Pasadena City Coll., 1995; BA (cum laude), Calif. State U, Northridge, 1998; MEd, Nat. U., 2004. Character edn. cert. U. San Diego Ext., 2004, online tchg. program cert. UCLA Ext., 2005. Tchr. Sun Valley (Calif.) Mid. Sch., 1999—2000, New Ave. Ednl. Ctr., Monterey Park, Calif., 2000—02; owner, educator Solteria Acad., Monrovia, Calif., 2001—; prin., owner Jalbert-Thomason Photography, Arcadia, Calif., 2003—04; tchr. English, activities dir. Monrovia (Calif.) HS, 2004—. Bd. dirs., pres., assoc. Delta Dimensions, 2003—; cons. Hondiat Inc., Arcadia, Calif., 1994—; co-founder, cons. YouCanDo-Travel.com, 2004—; presenter in field. *Over 10 years of non-profit work and twenty years of experience in elementary through university environments led Janelle Jennifer Jalbert to create the Solteria Academy, servicing students struggling in traditional educational settings. The focus is on preparing students for academic experiences as well as successful living working in conjunction with families and communities to develop the support networks critical for student success. Currently, the program is focused on the Los Angeles area and online. Her goal is to go national with a site in California's Central Coast by 2009.* Author: Success Skills, 2001, Character First!, 2004, Get Gatsby and Other Greats in Five Minutes a Day, 2005. Fundraiser, mem. crew Calif. AIDS Ride 4 &5, LA, 1997—98; ptnr. Life in the Word, Fenton, Mo., 2001—, World Changers Ministries, College Park, Ga., 2001—, Jesse Duplants Ministries, New Orleans, 2002—; ptnr. Aaron's Army TD Jakes Ministries, Dallas, 2003—04. Grantee Ednl. award, Sunshine Brooks Found., 1994, Sushine Brooks Found., 1995, John Glyes Ednl. Fund, 1997; scholar Collegiate Honor scholar, Nat. U., 2002. Mem.: Jr. C. of C. (com. Kasukabe, Japan Visitation 1999), Soroptimist Internat. (mem.Arcadia/Monrovia chpt. 2003—04, Youth Citizenship award 1991), Pi Lambda Theta (presenter internat. convention 2005), Blue Key (bd. dirs. 1996—98, Cmty. Svc. award 1996), Foothill Panhellenic, Omicron Delta Kappa (pres. 1997—98), Alpha Gamma Sigma (chair fundraising 1994—95), Sigma Kappa Alumnae (1st v.p. membership 2003—05, advisor Zeta Upsilon chpt.). Avocations: travel, languages, wine, marine activities, photography. Office: Monrovia HS 845 W Colorado Monrovia CA 91016 also: Delta Dimensions Group 19545 Sherman Way #32 Reseda CA 91335 Office Phone: 626-471-2880 ext. 7245, 818-701-9486. E-mail: jalbert@delta-dimensions-group.com, booksnmore4u@gmail.com.

JALENAK, PEGGY EICHENBAUM, volunteer; b. Little Rock, Oct. 14, 1935; d. E. Charles and Helen Lockwood Eichenbaum; m. Leo Richard Jalenak, Jr., Aug. 28, 1955; children: Laurie J. Williamson, Terri J. Mendelson, Jan J. Ordway, E. Charles. Commr., vice chair Tenn. Art Commn., Nashville, 1975—80; bd. dirs., exec. com. Tennesseans for Arts, Nashville, 1981—85; bd. dirs. Tenn. State Mus. Found., Nashville, 1994—2003. Bd. dirs. Nat. Found. Jewish Culture, N.Y.C., 1999—; former bd. dirs. Ballet Memphis, Theatre Memphis, Memphis Arts Coun.; former bd. dirs., sec., treas. Opera Memphis; bd. dirs. Memphis Jewish Fedn., 1997—; bd. dirs., past pres., sec. Memphis Jewish Hist. Soc. Memphis & Mid-South, 1998—; bd. dirs. Temple Israel Mus., 2001—, Bornblum Solomon Schechter Sch., 2002—; adv. bd. Judaic studies program U. Memphis, 2000—. Named Tenn. Arts Amb., Tenn. Arts Commn., 1985. Home: 6025 River Oaks Rd Memphis TN 38120

JALILI, NADER, mechanical engineer, educator; b. Tehran, Iran, Oct. 26, 1970; came to U.S., 1995; s. Ahmad and Delnaz (Doulat Abadi) J.; m. Jaleh Esmailzadeh, Dec. 5, 1993; children: Paneed Fatemeh, Pouya Mohammad. BSc with 1st class honors, Sharif U. tech., Tehran, 1992, MSc with 1st class honors, 1995; PhD, U. Conn., 1998. Design cons. Iranian truck Mfg., Tehran, 1992-93; tchg. asst. Sharif U. Tech., Tehran, 1993-95; design engr. Iranian Crane Mfg., Tehran, 1993-95; lectr. Azad U. Karaj, Iran, 1994-95; design cons. Indsl. Mixers Mfg. Co., Esfehan, Iran, 1994-95; rsch. asst. U. Conn., Storrs, 1995-98; vis. asst. prof. dept. mech. engring. No. Ill. U., DeKalb, 1999-2000; asst. prof. mech. engring. Clemson (S.C.) U., 2000—. Computer cons. Sharif U. Tech., 1993-94, U. Conn., 1997-98. Contbr. articles to profl. jours. Recipient Ralph E. Powe Jr. award, Oak Ridge Associated Univs. Dept. Energy, 2002, Career award, NSF, 2003; U. Conn. scholar fellow, 1995—98. Mem. ASME, IEEE. Moslem. Avocations: volleyball, running, soccer. Home: 108 Shaftsbury Rd Clemson SC 29631 Office Phone: 864-656-5642. Business E-Mail: jalili@clemson.edu.

JALLINS, RICHARD DAVID, lawyer; b. L.A., Mar. 21, 1957; s. Walter Joshua and Elaine Beatrice (Youngerman) J.; m. Katherine Sue Pfeiffer, June 12, 1982; children: Stephen David, Rachel Marie. BA, U. Calif., Santa Barbara, 1978; JD, Calif. Western Sch. Law, 1981. Bar: Calif. 1988, U.S. Dist. Ct. (so. dist.) Calif. 1988. Panel atty. Bd. Prison Terms, Sacramento, 1989-96, Appellate Defenders, Inc., San Diego, 1989-91, Calif. Dept. Corrections, Parole Hearings Divsn., Sacramento, 1992-94; dep. commr. Bd. Prison Terms, 1996—2001, assoc. chief dep. commr., 2001—. Mem. ABA, Orange County Bar Assn., Phi Alpha Delta.

JALOVEC, JOHN S., information technology executive; BS in Bus. Econ. magna cum laude, John Carroll U.; MBA, Cleve. State U.; grad. exec. program, Stanford Grad. Sch. Bus. Cert. sys. profl.; green belt and design Six Sigma. Mgr. new sys. devel. Specialty Chemical Group B.F. Goodrich, Inc., Cleve., 1977—87; dir. bus. automation Avery Denison, Inc., 1987—94; sr. mgr. mgmt. consulting Deloitte Consulting, LLP, 1994—95; v.p. and CIO Pirelli Inc. N.Am., Columbia, SC, 1995—97; mng. dir. enterprise solutions Compuware Inc., Cleve., 1997—98; global IT dir. enterprise programs Delphi, Inc., Detroit, 1998—2001; sr. v.p. and CIO Into Great Co., Cleve., 2001—03; v.p. and CIO global apps. ACS Group Honeywell Internat., Inc., Mpls., 2003—. Mem. Info. Sys. Conf. Bd. Mem.: Soc. Info. Mgrs. Address: 11860 Germaine Terr Eden Prairie MN 55347

JALURIA, YOGESH, mechanical engineering educator; b. Nabha, Punjab, India, Sept. 8, 1949; came to U.S., 1970; s. Jagdishwar and Maya J.; m. Anuradha Malhotra, Sept. 9, 1975; children: Pratik, Aseem, Ankur. BS, Indian Inst. Tech., Delhi, 1970; MS, Cornell U., 1972, PhD, 1974. Mem. tech. staff Bell Labs., Princeton, NJ, 1974-76; asst. prof. Indian Inst. Tech., Kanpur, 1976-80, Rutgers U., New Brunswick, NJ, 1980-82, assoc. prof., 1982-85, prof. of mech. engring., 1985-91, prof. II, disting. prof., 1991—2001, Bd. Govs. prof., 2001—. Cons. David Sarnoff Lab., SRI, Princeton, 1989-90, Steel Authority, Ranchi, India, 1977-80, others; mem. NSF grants rev. panel, other panels, 1996-98; NSF vis. scientist Indian Inst. Tech., 1988-89; lectr. in field; participant workshop on natural convection NSF, Colo., 1982, Indo-Australian Solar Energy Workshop, New Delhi, 1978, others; assoc. tech. editor J. Heat Transfer, 1993-99; mng. editor Computational Mechanics, 1994-99, co-editor, 2000—; spkr. in field Author: Natural Convection Heat and Mass Transfer, 1980; co-author: Computational Heat Transfer, 1986, 2d edit., 2003, Buoyancy Induced Flows, 1988, Computer Methods for Engineering, 1988, Design and Optimization of Thermal Systems, 1998; contbr. chpts. to books: Natural Convection, 1985, Handbook of Single-Phase Convective Heat Transfer, 1987, Energy Storage Systems, 1989, Handbook of Fire Protection, 1995, numerous others; contbr. more than 300 articles and papers to profl. jours. and confs. including Rev. Sci. Instrum., Jour. Heat Transfer, Jour. Thermophysics Heat Transfer, Numerical Heat Transfer, Jour. Fluid Mech., Jour. Numerical Meth. Engring.; mem. editl. adv. bd. Numerical Heat Transfer, 1987—, Internat. Jour. Heat Mass Transfer; mem. editl. bd. Internat. Jour. Numerical Meth. Heat and Flow, 1990—2004, numerous others; reviewer including Applied Mechanics Rev., Jour. Fluid Mechanics, Jour. Heat Transfer, Jour. Solar Energy Engring.; referee numerous articles. NATO Disting. lectr., 1984, 88; recipient cert. of recognition Dept. of Commerce, 1982, Disting. Alumni award IIT, 1994, Max Jakob Meml. award ASME/AIChE, 2002, Thurston lecture award, 2003. Fellow ASME (chmn. nat. heat transfer conf., coord. com. 1991-92, exec. com. heat transfer divsn. 1998-2003, editor Jour. Heat Transfer 2005—, Heat Transfer Mem. award 1995, Worcester Reed Warner medal 1999, Freeman scholar 2000), Am. Phys. Soc., Combustion Inst., India Assn. of East Brunswick (pres. 1985, 91, 94-96), Cornell India Assn. (v.p. 1972-73). Democrat. Hindu. Achievements include patents for Methods and apparatus for heating articles, for Methods and apparatus for avoiding undesirable deposits in crystal growing operations; copyrighted computer software in materials processing and electronics cooling; research in thermal processing of materials, fires, computational heat transfer, natural convection, cooling of electronic equipment and environmental flows, flows rising above finite heated bodies, interaction of buoyant flows with surfaces, buoyant jet flows, mixed convection in enclosures, heat removal from heated elements on a vertical surface, thermal stratification and heat rejection problems, solar energy storage in salt-gradient solar ponds, numerical and experimental simulation of thermal processes in manufacturing systems, computer aided design of thermal systems, knowledge based design methodology, and enclosure fire growth processes. Office: chair Rutgers U Mech Engring Dept New Brunswick NJ 08903 Business E-Mail: jaluria@jove.rutgers.edu.

JAMAR, STEVEN DWIGHT, law educator; b. Ishpeming, Mich., May 11, 1953; s. Dwight W. and Lorraine (Persgard) J.; m. Shelley June Von Hagen-Jamar, May 19, 1979; children: Alexander S., Eric D. BA, Carleton Coll., 1975; JD, Hamline U., 1979; LLM, Georgetown U., 1994. Bar: Minn. 1979, D.C. 1993, U.S. Supreme Ct. 1985. Jud. clk. Minn. Supreme Ct., St. Paul, 1979-80; pvt. practice law Minn., 1980—89; prof. law U. Balt., 1989-90; prof. Sch. Law, Howard U., Washington, 1991—, dir. legal rsch. and writing program, 1990—2002; co-founder, assoc. dir. Inst. Intellectual Property and Social Justice Howard U. Sch. Law, 2002—. Cons. on Environ. Legal Info. Sys. project NASA, 1998-2002; cons. on Global Legal Info. Network to Law Libr. of Congress, 1999—. Rsch. fellow Law Libr. Congress, 2000-01. Mem. ABA, ACLU, Legal Writing Inst. (pres. 1997-98), Am. Soc. Internat. Law, Amnesty Internat., Assn. Legal Writing Dirs. Avocations: canoe camping, soccer, go, photography, guitar. Office: Howard U Sch Law 2900 Van Ness St NW Washington DC 20008-1106

JAMBOR, ROBERT VERNON, lawyer; b. Chgo., Aug. 29, 1936; s. Vernon C. and Anne M. Jambor; m. Arlene M. Gale, Nov. 9, 1957 (dec. Aug. 1993); children: Robyn, Cheryl, Steven; m. Terri J. Skyrme, Jan. 11, 1995. BME, Kettering U., 1958; JD, John Marshall Law Sch., Chgo., 1963. Bar: Ill. 1963, U.S. Dist. Ct. Ill. 1963, U.S. Ct. Appeals (7th cir.) 1974, U.S. Ct. Appeals (fed. cir.) 1982, U.S. Supreme Ct. 1983. Product engr. product devel. Electro-Motive div. Gen. Motors Corp., La Grange, Ill., 1958-63; asso. firm Marks & Clerk, Chgo., 1961-63; patent atty. Borg-Warner Corp., Chgo., 1964-69; ptnr. Haight, Hofeldt, Davis & Jambor, Chgo., 1970-87, Dorn, McEachran, Jambor & Keating, Chgo., 1987—2000; of counsel Jenner & Block, Chgo., 2001. Mem. ABA, Ill. Bar Assn., 7th Cir. Bar Assn., Fed. Cir. Bar Assn., Am. Intellectual Property Law Assn., Intellectual Property Law Assn. Chgo., Internat. Property Owners. Home: 1173 Terrace Ct Lake Geneva WI 53147-5027 Office: Jenner & Block 330 N Wabash Chicago IL 60611 Office Phone: 712-723-2814. Business E-Mail: rjambor@jenner.com.

JAMES, ALLIX BLEDSOE, retired university president; b. Marshall, Tex., Dec. 17, 1922; s. Samuel Horace and Tannie Etta (Judkins) James; m. Sue Nickens, Feb. 14, 1945; children: Alvan Bosworth, Portia Veann. AB, Va. Union U., 1944, MDiv, 1946; ThM, Union Theol. Sem. Va., 1949, ThD, 1957; postgrad., Boston U., summer 1951, Pa. State U., summer 1957; LLD, U. Richmond, 1970; DD, St. Paul's Coll., 1980. Ordained to ministry Bapt. Ch., 1942. Moderator No. Neck Bapt. Assn., 1950-52; minister Union Zion Bapt. Ch., Gloucester, Va., 1944-53, Mt. Zion Bapt. Ch., Downings, Va., 1945-57, 3d Union Bapt. Ch., King William, Va., 1953-70; dean students Va. Union U., Richmond, Va., 1950-57, dean Sch. Theology, 1957-70, Henderson-Griffith prof. pastoral theology, v.p., 1960-70, pres., 1970-79, ret., pres. emeritus, 1979-85, 93—, chancellor, 1985-93. Author: Calling a Pastor in a Baptist Church, Threescore and Ten Plus-the Pilgrimage of an African-American Educator, 1922-, 1997; contbg. editor: The Continuing Quest, 1970. Chmn. Richmond City Planning Commn., 1969—75; dir. Va. Electric and Power Co., Dominion Resources, Inc., Consol bank and Trust Co.; mem. Commn. on Ch. Family Fin. Planning; mem. scholarship selection com. Philip Morris, Inc.; mem. Mayor's Commn. on Human Rels., 1963—65; pres. Norrell Sch. PTA, 1963—65; mem. exec. com. Ctrl. Va. Ednl. TV; mem. Richmond Independence Bicentennial Commn., Richmond Downtown econ. and Devel. Commn.; co-chmn. Northside Cmty. assn., 1964—68; chmn. Univ. Ctr. in Va.; mem. State Bd. Edn. Va., 1975—85, pres., 1980—82; bd. dirs. NCCJ, Va. Inst. Pastoral Care, Task Force for Renewal Urban Strategy and Tng., Richmond chpt. ARC, 1974—75, Better Richmond, Inc., Richmond Downtown Devel. Unltd., Am. Coun. on Edn., 1970—72, Richmond renaissance, Inc., Met. Richmond Leadership; mem. adv. bd. Inst. for Bus. and Cmty. Devel. U. Richmond; bd. fellows Interpreters House, Lake Janaluska, NC; trustee Richmond Meml. Hosp., Nat. Assn. for Equal Opportunity in Edn., v.p.; pres. Richmond Gold Bowl Sponsors, Inc., Nat. Conf. Richmond and Jews, Inc., 1987—90; nat. co-chair Nat. Conf. Christians and Jews, Inc., 1994; chmn. bd. dirs. Cosol. Bank and Trust Co., chmn./bd. dirs., 2001—. Named Citizen of Yr., Astoria Beneficial Club, 1971, Omega Psi Phi, 1972, Univ. chapel named Allix B. James Chapel in his honor, 1992; recipient Disting. Svc. award, Links, Inc., 1971, Ednl. Achievement award, 1985, Good Govt. award, Richmond First Club, 1985, Brotherhood award, NCCJ, 1975, Mozelle E. Manuel Outstanding Svc. award, Met. Bus. League, 1991, Exemplary Vision award, Fullwood Foods, Inc., 1992, Flame Bearers Edn. award, United Negro Coll. Fund, 1997, Excellence in Leadership award, Dominion Va. Power, 2000, Disting. Cmty. Svc. award, Sigma Pi Phi, 2003. Mem.: Clergy Assn. Richmond Area (pres.), Bapt. Gen. Conv. Va. (exec. bd.), Soc. for Advancement Continuing Edn. for Mins. (exec. bd.), Am. Bapt. Conv. (pres. coun. on theol. edn. 1969—72), Am. Assn. Theol. Schs. (pres. 1970—72), Greater Richmond C. of C. (bd. dirs.), Kiwanis (honoree Richmond area Appreciation Dinner 1993), Alpha Phi Alpha (Achievement award 1981, 1985), Alpha Kappa Mu. Office: Va Union U 1500 N Lombardy St Richmond VA 23220-1784

JAMES, ALTON EVERETTE, JR., radiologist; b. Oxford, N.C., Aug. 22, 1938; s. Pattie Royster; children: Everette III, Jeannette, Elizabeth. AB, U. N.C., 1959; MD, Duke U., 1963; MSc, Johns Hopkins Sch. Pub. Health, 1971. Diplomate Am. Bd. Radiology, Am. Bd. Nuc. Medicine. Fellow Harvard Med. Sch., Boston, 1966—69; from asst. to prof. radiology Johns Hopkins Med. Sch., Balt., 1969—74; dir. rsch. radiology Johns Hopkins Hosp., Balt., 1969—74; fellow Royal Soc. Medicine, London, 1974—75; chmn. dept. radiology and radiol. sciences Vanderbilt U. Sch. Medicine, Nashville, 1975—92; founder Vanderbilt Ctr. Med. Imaging Rsch., 1978—; pres. N.C. State U. Sch. Vet. Medicine Found., Raleigh, NC, 1996—98. Vis. scientist Nat. Cancer Inst., 1992—93, NIH, 1992—93; sr. program officer NAS Inst. of Medicine, 1993—94; clin. prof. Georgetown U., 1994—, U. N.C., 1996—; adj. prof., chair emeritus Vanderbilt U. Sch. Medicine, Nashville, 1994—; lectr. Johns Hopkins Med. Sch., Balt., 1993—; bd. visitors U. N.C., 1980; deans coun. Johns Hopkins Bloomberg Sch. Pub. Health, 2002—; founder Russell Morgan Fund, Johns Hopkins, 2002. Author 24 books, 14 monographs; contbr. over 600 articles to profl. jours., 140 chpts. to books. Spl. advisor sci. tech. Office Gov. NC, Raleigh, 1994—96; bd. dirs. Duke U. Med. Sch., 1986—94, N.C. Sch. Vet. Medicine, pres., 1997—98, 2000—01. Capt. U.S. Army, 1964—66. NRC/NAS Picker fellow, 1969-71, Royal Soc. Medicine Hon. fellow, 1974-75. Mem.: Am. Roentgen Ray Soc. (pres. 1992, Gold medal 2003), Assn. Univ. Radiologists (bd. dirs. 1989, pres. 1985, Gold medal 2003), Nat. Coun. Radiation Protection, Can. Radiol. Soc. (hon.), Pres.'s Club (John Hopkins U.), Chancellors Club (U. N.C.), Davison Club, Alpha Omega Alpha. Avocations: writing, collecting N.C. pottery and African American quilts, folk art, collecting 19th and 20th century American art. Home: 205 New Castle Pl Chapel Hill NC 27517 Office: St James Place 205 New Castle Place Chapel Hill NC 27514 Personal E-mail: everette@nc.rr.com.

JAMES, BRUCE ALLAN, radio station owner, general manager; b. St. Johnsbury, Vt., Sept. 20, 1949; s. Horace Darius and Pauline (Fitch) J.; m. Nancy Leigh Roberts, May 17, 1968; children: Suzanne, Aaren. Student, Lyndon State Coll., 1968-71. Mgr. Music Unltd., Lyndonville, Vt., 1969-74; sr. exec. E.M.A. Agy., Claremont, N.H., 1974-79; pres. Bruce James Co., Lyndonville, Vt., 1979-88; mgr. Lyndonville Printing, 1988-90; owner, mgr. WGMT-FM, Lyndonville, Vt., 1990—, WKXH-FM, St. Johnsbury, Vt., 1998—, WSTJ-AM, St. Johnsbury, 1998—, WMTK-FM, Littleton, N.H., 2000—. Adv. bd. Vt. State Mountain Tops Com., Dept. Forest and Parks, Waterbury, 1992-94, mem. planning commn. Town of Lyndon, 1981-83; mem. Town of Lyndon Selectmen, 1986—, chmn., 1989, 91, 92, 94, 97, 2000, 2003; pres. Stars and Stripes Festival, 1993-2004; commr. N.E. Vt. Baseball, 1999—. Named Commr. of Yr., Babe Ruth Baseball, Vt., 1986, Championship Umpire, Vt. Headmasters, 1990, 92, 93, 94, 95, 96, 97, 98, 99, 2000, 01, 02, 04. Mem. Lyndonville Rotary Club (pres. 1989-90), No. Vt. Baseball Umpires (interpretor 1992-95, pres. 1996-98), World Series Umpire Babe Ruth League (16-19 Series 2004), Vt. Assn. Broadcasters (sec. 1995-97, pres. 1997-99), Vt. Baseball Umpires Assn. (pres. 1999—), Internat. Assn. Approved Basketball Officials, Lyndon C. of C. (pres. 1985-90, hon. lifetime dir. 1992). Avocations: baseball and basketball sports official, photography. Home: PO Box 1387 Lyndonville VT 05851-1387 Office: Vt Broadcast Assocs Inc PO Box 97 Lyndonville VT 05851-0097

JAMES, BRUCE RICHARD, publishing executive; b. Cleve., Oct. 19, 1942; s. George R. and Dorothy B. (Watson) J.; m. Jo Ann Osborn, Feb. 5, 1966 (div. Feb. 1982); children: Michael, Jeffrey, Stephen; m. Nora Ellen Thomas, May 11, 1985. BS, Rochester (N.Y.) Inst. Tech., 1964. V.p. Keller-Crescent Co., Evansville, Ind., 1964-70; v.p. Cardinal Co., San Francisco, 1970-73; pres., CEO Uniplan Corp., San Francisco, 1973-83, Electrographic Corp., San Francisco, 1983-93; chmn., CEO Barclays Law Pubs., San Francisco, 1986-94; pres., CEO Nev. New-Tech, Inc., Incline Village, Nev., 1993—; pub. printer of the U.S., 2002—. Mem. dean's adv. coun. U. Nev. Las Vegas Boyd Sch. of Law, 1999-2002; bd. dirs. BIPAC, Washington, 1999-2002; chmn. bd. dirs. Polish-Am. Print Co., Warsaw, 1990-93; pres. Printing Industries of Calif., 1989-91; mem. dean's adv. bd. U. Nev.-Las Vegas Boyd Sch. of Law, 1999-2002; pub. printer, CEO U.S. Govt. Printing Office, 2002—; mem. Nat. Digital Strategy Adv. Bd., 2004-. Candidate U.S. Senate, 1997-98; chmn. bd. trustees Rochester Inst. Tech., 1993—; chair emeritus bd. trustees Sierra Nev. Coll., Incline Village, 1997-2005; mem. Bd. of Equalization, Reno, 1995-97; trustee U. Nev. Desert Rsch. Inst., 1999-2002; dir. Nev. Test Site Devel. Corp., 1999-2002, Western Folklife Ctr., Elko, Nev., 1999-2002; bd. dirs. Cmty. Found. Western Nev., 1999-2002; fin. chmn. Nev. Rep. Party, 2000-02. Commencement spkr. Rochester Inst. Tech., 1998, Alumnus of Yr., 1997; recipient Silver Beaver award Boys Scouts Am., 1992. Mem.: Internat. Wine and Food Soc., Cosmos Club (Washington), Met. Club (Washington), Genesee Valley Club (Rochester N.Y.). Republican. Episcopalian. Office: Office of Pub Printer US Govt Printing Office Washington DC 20401 Office Phone: 202-512-1000. E-mail: publicprinter@gpo.gov.

JAMES, CHARLES ALBERT, lawyer; b. Newark, May 2, 1954; s. Charles Albert and Mary Letitia (Baskerville) J.; 1 child, Kathryn E. BA, Wesleyan U., Middletown, Conn., 1976; JD, George Washington U., Washington, 1979. Bar: D.C. 1979. Atty. FTC, Washington, 1979—85; assoc./ptnr. Jones, Day, Reavis & Pogue, Washington, 1986—91; acting asst. atty. gen. U.S. Dept. Justice, Washington, 1991—93, dep. asst. atty. gen., 1991, asst. atty. gen. Antitrust Divsn., 2001—02; ptnr. Jones, Day, Reavis & Pogue, Washington, 1993—2001; v.p. & gen. coun. ChevronTexaco Corp., San Ramon, Calif., 2002—. Recipient Chmn.'s award FTC, 1985, Edmund Randolph award Dept. Justice, 1992. Mem. ABA (sect. of bus. law chmn. com. 1999), Fed. Bar Assn. (chmn. antitrust com. 1990), U.S. C. of C. (mem. antitrust coun. 1993—), Psi Upsilon. Republican. Office: Office Gen Coun Chevron Texaco Corp 6001 Bollinger Canyon Rd San Ramon CA 94583 Office Phone: 925-842-3232.

JAMES, CHARLES E., JR., lawyer; b. Pontiac, Mich., Sept. 19, 1948; BA, Occidental Coll., 1970; JD with high distinction, U. Ariz. Bar: Ariz. 1973. Ptnr. Gust Rosenfeld, Phoenix, 1979—86, Chapman and Cutler, Phoenix, 1986—92, Snell & Wilmer, Phoenix, 1992—99, Squire, Sanders and Dempsey, Phoenix, 2000—. Mem. ABA, Nat. Assn. Bond Lawyers. Office: Squire Sanders & Dempsey 40 N Central Ave Ste 2700 Phoenix AZ 85004-4498 Office Phone: 602-528-4000. E-mail: cjames@ssd.com.

JAMES, CHARLES (CHUCK) EDWARD, small business owner, writer; b. Chanute, Kans., May 15, 1953; s. Charles Oscar and Margarette Dean James; m. Betty Jean Wilson; m. Karen Ann Voth (div.); 1 child, Jeremiah Lee. Owner Jesse James Mus., Wichita, Kans., 2001—03, Chuck's Custom Body & Paint, Neodesha, Kans., 1989—. Co-author: (book) Jesse James Faked His Death, 2002, Jesse James Faked His Death #2 The Evidence and Science, 2003. Avocations: street rod builder, painting, restoring, motorcycling, car shows. Home: Rt 1 Box 161 Neodesha KS 66757 Office Phone: 620-330-0366. E-mail: dingus@terraworld.net.

JAMES, CHARLES FRANKLIN, JR., retired engineering educator; b. Des Arc, Mo., July 16, 1931; s. Charles Franklin and Beulah Frances (Kyte) J.; m. Mollie Keeler, May 18, 1974; children: Thomas Elisha, Matthew Jeremiah. BS, Purdue U., 1958, MS, 1960, PhD, 1963. Registered profl. engr., Wis. Sr. indsl. engr. McDonnel Aircraft Co., 1963; asst. prof. U. RI, 1963-66, prof., chmn. dept. indsl. engring., 1967-82, co-founder, mem Robotics Rsch. Ctr., 1980-83; C. Paul Stocker prof. engring. Ohio U., Athens, 1982-83; dean Coll. Engring. and Applied Sci., U. Wis.-Milw., 1984-95; academic v.p. Milw. Sch. of Engring., 1995-2000; ret., 2000. Cons. Asian Productivity Orgn.; arbitrator Fed. Mediation and Conciliation Svc., Am. Arbitration Assn.; bd. dirs. Badger Meter Co., Milw. Contbr. articles to profl. jours. Bd. dirs. Clay County (Mo.) Water Dist. No. 7, 2004-; mem. corp. bd. Milw. Sch. Engring. With USAF, 1951-55. Recipient Silver medal Tech. U. Budapest, Hungary, 1989. Mem. NSPE, ASME, Wis. Soc. Profl. Engrs. (pres. Milw. chpt. 1993-94, Outstanding Profl. Engr. in Edn. 1993, state-wide treas. 1994-96), Inst. Indsl. Engrs., Am. Soc. Engring. Edn., Soc. Mfg. Engrs., Am. Foundrymen's Soc., Engrs. and Scis. of Milw. (bd. dirs. 1988-95, v.p. 1991-93, pres.-elect 1993-94, pres. 1994-95). Office Phone: 816-750-4615. Personal E-mail: cfjames@bluebuzz.net.

JAMES, CHRISTOPHER LEWIS, composer; b. Huntington, N.Y., July 20, 1951; s. Roland Giles and Joan Cushman (Levin) James; m. Joanne Elaine Scott (div.); 1 child, Evan. BA, SUNY, Stony Brook, N.Y., 1975; MusM, The Julliard Sch., 1985, MusD, 1987. With performance dept. G. Schirmer, Inc., N.Y., 1980, mgr. Copyright Divsn., 1981—84; tchg. fellow The Julliard Sch., N.Y., 1985—86; mgr. copyright Bourne Internat. Mus. Pub., N.Y., 1986—87; organist, dir. choir N.Y.C. Metro Chs., 1988—94; freelance composer N.Y., 1995—. Composer: numerous songs including most recently, (songs) String Trio, 2003, Sinfonia Concertante, 2004, Woodwind Quintet, 2004, Nocturne-Ballade, 2005, (albums) Carnaval/Carnival, 2002, Strings Attached, 2005. Grantee, Meet the Composer, Inc., 1981; Charles Ives scholarship, AAAL, 1987. Mem.: ASCAP (Standard award), Am. Music Ctr. (grantee 1985). Home: 338 East 15th St New York NY 10003

JAMES, CLARITY (CAROLYNE FAYE JAMES), mezzo soprano; b. Wheatland, Wyo., Apr. 27, 1945; d. Ralph Everett and Gladys Charlotte (Johnson) J. Mus.B., U. Wyo., 1964; Mus.M., Ind. U., 1967. Cert. instr. Radiance Technique. Prof. voice Radford (Va.) U., 1990—. Asst. prof. voice U. Iowa, Iowa City, 1968-72 Debut in opera as Madame Flora in: The Medium, St. Paul Opera, 1971; also sang role with Houston Grand Opera, 1972, Opera Theatre St. Louis, 1976, Augusta (Ga.) Opera Co., 1976; N.Y.C. Opera debut as Baroness in: The Young Lord, 1973; N.Y.C. Opera debut as Widow Begbick in Mahogonny, Opera Co. of Boston, 1973; created role Mother Rainey in: The Sweet Bye and Bye, 1973; Mrs. G. in: Captain Jinks, 1976; Mrs. Cratchit in A Christmas Carol (Musgrave), 1979; created Mrs. Doc in world premiere of A Quiet Place (Leonard Bernstein), Houston, 1983; debut Chgo. Lyric Opera, 1983, Vienna Staatsoper, 1986, National Symphony, 1986, Phila. Orch., 1986; numerous appearances with opera cos. throughout U.S. and fgn. countries including, Dallas Civic Opera, Cin. Opera Co., Netherlands Opera, Amsterdam, Florentine Opera. Rec. artist. Martha Baird Rockefeller grantee, Corbett Found. grantee, 1968; Met. Opera Assn. grantee; recipient Lillian Garabedian award Santa Fe Opera, 1967, Exemplary Alumni award U. Wyo., 1994; named Young Artist Nat. Fedn. Music Clubs, 1972. Office: Radford U Dept Music Radford VA 24142 Office Phone: 540-831-5296. Business E-Mail: cjames@radford.edu.

JAMES, DANIEL, III, career military officer; BA in Psychology, U. Ariz., Tucson, 1968; grad., Air Commd. Staff Coll., 1981. Commd. 2d lt. Air Nat. Guard, 1968, advanced through grades to lt. gen., 2002, dir. Arlington, Va., 2002—. Chmn. Greater Austin Quality Coun., 1998—99. Decorated Legion of Merit, Dissing. Flying Cross with oak leaf cluster, Air medal with six oak leaf clusters, Air Force Commendation medal, Air Force Achievement medal, Vietnam Gallantry Cross with palm; recipient Garvey-Woodson award, Black United Fund Tex., 1995, Outstanding Svc. award, Tex. STARBASE, 1995—96, Benjamin D. Foulois First Flight award, Air Force Assn. Tex., 1997, Cmty. Svc. award, Ctrl. Tex. Combined Fed. Campaign, 1997—98, Honored Patriot award, Selective Svc. Sys., 1998—99, Mil. Svc. commendation, Joint Session Tex. Legis., 1999, Palmetto Patriot award, SC, 1999. Office: Nat Guard Bur 1411 Jeff Davis Hwy Arlington VA 22202

JAMES, DAVID LEE, lawyer, writer, international advisor; b. Chgo., Aug. 23, 1933; s. Roy L. and Ethel (Wells) J.; m. Sheila Feagley, May 26, 1962; children: Pamela, James, Winifred, Paul, Brian, Adam. AB, Harvard U., 1955; JD, U. Chgo., 1960; grad. exec. program, Stanford U., 1979. Bar: NY 1961, NJ 1967, Hawaii 1976, Ill. 1987. With various law firms, N.Y.C., 1960-67; counsel and asst. gen. counsel, asst. sec. Texasgulf Inc., 1967-75; gen. counsel, sec. Dillingham Corp., Honolulu, 1975-77, v.p., gen. counsel, sec., 1977-84, v.p. legal affairs, sec. San Francisco, 1984-85; asst. gen. counsel, asst. sec. Crown Zellerbach Corp., San Francisco, 1985-86; sr. ptnr., sr. corp. atty. Arnstein & Lehr, Chgo., 1987-90, of counsel, 1990-96; chmn. bus. programs East-West Ctr., Honolulu, 1990-92; chief of party and sr. law devel. advisor USAID and Govt. of Indonesia, Jakarta, Indonesia, 1992-93; pres. Bus. Strategies Internat., San Francisco, Calif., 1993—, www.bsicorp.net, San Francisco, 1993—. Hon. consul of Malaysia, Hawaii, 1977-84; adv. bd. Internat. and Comparative Law Ctr., Southwestern Legal Found., Dallas, 1976-91; adv. com. Law of Sea Inst., Honolulu, 1977-84; lectr. in law Stanford U. Sch. Law, 1996-98. Author: Doing Business in Asia, 1993, The Executive Guide to Asia-Pacific Communications, 1995; contbg. editor TheFeature.com; contbr. various articles on bus. and legal subjects. Bd. dirs. Chgo. Chamber Orch., 1988-90, pres. 1989-90, Jr. Achievement Hawaii, 1976-84, Hawaii Opera Theatre, 1981-84, Friends of East-West Ctr., 1982-84; mem. Morristown (N.J.) Bd. Edn., 1967-68. Served to lt. (j.g.) USNR, 1955-57. Mem. Outrigger Canoe Club (Honolulu), Harvard Club (N.Y.C.). Office: Bus Strategies Internat 425 Market St Ste 2200 San Francisco CA 94105-2434 E-mail: djames@bsicorp.net.

JAMES, DONALD M., construction materials executive; b. 1949; Pres. so. divsn. Vulcan Materials, 1994-96, sr. v.p. south constrn. materials group, 1995-96, pres., COO, 1996-97, pres., CEO, 1997, chmn., CEO, 1997—; also bd. dirs. Bd. dirs. Protective Life Corp., So. Co., SouthTrust Corp. Office: Vulcan Materials 1200 Urban Center Dr Birmingham AL 35242

JAMES, DOROTHY LOUISE KING, special education educator; b. Columbus, Miss., Jan. 1, 1952; d. T.B. and Dorothy (Lee) King; m. Willie Earl James, July 7, 1979, children: Ebun, Shantana, Leah, Trinita, Caleb. BS magna cum laude, Harris Stowe Coll., 1979; M in Spl. Edn., U. Mo., 1988; EdD in Guidance Counseling, Lael Coll. and Grad. Sch., 1998. Itinerant resource instr. Northwest High Sch., St. Louis, 1978-80; instr. learning disabilities Cleveland High Sch., St. Louis, 1980-84, Clinton Mid. Sch., St. Louis, 1984-91; resource tchr., unit leader A-team for alternative edn. Stevens Mid. Sch., St. Louis, 1992—2002; resource tchr. Vashon H.S., 2003—. Team leader, resource tchr., The New Vashon HS, 2003—; "A" team unit leader alternative edn. Stevens Mid. Sch. 1988-2000, Drug Free Schs. and Communities Program, 1993; counselor King-James Enterprises, St. Louis, 1988—; team leader, resource tchr., founder Student Response Team, St. Louis, 1988—. Editor (speech) Internat. Yr. of the Child, 1979 (Bravo award Youth Adv. Comsn. St. Louis County Youth Programs), Clinton Middle School Student Handbook, 1989, team leader Drug Free Schools Community Program. Youth adv. mem. Conflict Mediation, 1992-96; mem. support coun. Stevens Mid. Sch., 1992-96; active New Ebenezer Bapt. Ch. Recipient Excellence in Drug Prevention award U.S. Dept. Edn., 1994, cert. of commendatio, 1994; grantee Power X, The Positive Peer Coalition; winner KPLR-TV Promoting Pers. and Comty Health, 1997. Mem. Coun. for Exceptional Children, Alpha Kappa Alpha. Avocations: reading, walking, stamp collecting/philately, cooking. Home and Office: 2431 Strawberry Fields Ct Florissant MO 63033-1765

JAMES, EDGERRIN, professional football player; b. Aug. 1, 1978; Student, Univ. of Miami. Football player Indpls. Colts, 1999—. Guest spkr. DARE prog. various schools; founder Edgerrin James Found. Named NFL Rookie of the Yr., 1999; named to NFL Pro-Bowl, 1999, 2000. Achievements include NFL rushing title, 1999, 2000. Office: Indpls Colts PO Box 535000 Indianapolis IN 46253 also: 7001 West 56th Street Indianapolis IN 46254

JAMES, ELAINE MCLEAN, librarian; b. Boston, June 10, 1948; d. Kelly Edward and LaVonne B. (Todd) McL.; m. Arthur Franklyn James, May 13, 1989. BA, U. Mass., 1970; MS in Libr. Sci., Simmons Coll., 1978; MRE, Gordon-Cornewll Theol. Sem., Hamilton, Mass., 1988. Libr. asst. Boston Pub. Libr., Boston, 1974-76; asst. libr. Cambridge (Mass.) Sch. Dept., 1976-78; libr. Boston Pub. Libr., 1978-88, br. mgr. Uphams Corner Br., 1988—. Chair Black Is...Booklist Com., 1991-92, Social Law Libr. Program Planning Com., Boston, 1993. Bd. dirs. Project Hope Family Shelter, Boston, 1993-94; co-chair Uphams Corner Healthy Boston Coalition, Boston, 1993-94; neighborhood organizer Child Evangelism fellowship, Boston, 1993. Recipient Martin Luther King Jr. Community Svc. award Ctr. for Urban Ministerial Edn., 1988. Mem. ALA, Phi Alpha Chi. Democrat. Baptist. Home: 4 Colonial Ave Dorchester MA 02124-3408 Office: Uphams Corner Br Boston Pub Libr 500 Columbia Rd Dorchester MA 02125-2322

JAMES, ELIZABETH JOAN PLOGSTED, pediatrician, educator; b. Jefferson City, Mo., Jan. 15, 1939; d. Joseph Matthew Plogsted and Maxie Pearl (Manford) Plogsted Acuff; m. Ronald Carney James, Aug. 25, 1962; children: Susan Elizabeth, Jason Michael. BS in Chemistry, Lincoln U., 1960; MD, U. Mo., 1965. Diplomate Am. Bd. Pediat., Am. Bd. Neonatal-Perinatal Medicine. Resident in pediat. U. Mo. Hosps. & Clinics, Columbia, 1965-68, fellow in neonatology, 1968-69, dir. neonatal-perinatal medicine Children's Hosp., 1971—; fellow in neonatal-perinatal medicine U. Colo. Hosps., Denver, 1969-71; from asst. to assoc. prof. pediatrics and obstetrics sch. medicine U. Mo., 1971-83, prof. child health and obstetrics, 1983—. Dir. pediatric edn. program dept. child health sch. medicine U. Mo., Columbia, 1989-98. Mem. editl. bd. Mo. Medicine, 1983—; contbr. chpts. to books and articles to profl. jours. Fellow Am. Acad. Pediat. (sect. neonatal-perinatal medicine); mem. Mo. State Med. Assn., Boone County Med. Soc., Alpha Omega Alpha. Roman Catholic. Avocations: classical music, bicycling, herb gardening. Office: U Mo Hosps & Clinics Childrens Hosp 1 Hospital Dr Columbia MO 65201-5276 Office Phone: 573-882-7919. Business E-Mail: jamese@health.missouri.edu.

JAMES, ELIZABETH R., bank executive; b. Columbus, Ga., June 11, 1961; m. David M. (Sandy) James Jr.; children: David, Parker. BA in polit. sci., Auburn U., 1983; grad., Cannon Fin. Inst. Trust Sch., 1988; grad, Duke U. Exec. Fin., 1990. Mem. staff Trust Dept. Columbus Bank and Trust Co. Synovus Fin. Corp., Columbus, Ga., 1986—89, dir. training TSYS, 1989—90, v.p., human resources dir. TSYS, 1990—94, sr. v.p., human resources dir. TSYS, 1994—95, sr. v.p., human resources divsn. officer Synovus Svc. Corp., 1995—96, pres. Synovus Svc. Corp., 1996—2000, chief people officer, 1996—2003, vice chmn., chief info. officer, 2000—, dir., 2001—. Mem. tech. secretariat adv. group Banking Industry. Chmn. staff parish St. Paul United Meth. Ch., mem. adminstrv. bd.; chmn. The Alexis de Tocqueville Soc. of United Way; bd. dir. Columbus (Ga.) Symphony, Ronald McDonald House; mem. YMCA Task Force Com.; chmn. Leadership Devel. Task Force Gov.'s Comm. for a New Ga. Named Woman of Yr. in Tech., Tech. Assn. of Ga.; named one of The 25 Most Powerful Women in Banking, US Banker mag., 2003. Office: Synovus Financial Corp PO Box 120 Columbus GA 31902

JAMES, ESTELLE, economist, educator; b. Bronx, NY, Dec. 1, 1935; d. Abraham and Lee (Zeichner) Dinerstein; m. Ralph James (div. 1971); children: Deborah, David; m. Harry Lazer, June 27, 1971 (dec. 1994). BS, Cornell U., 1956; PhD, MIT, 1961. Lectr., econs. dept. U. Calif., Berkeley, 1964—65; acting asst. prof. Stanford U., 1965—67; assoc. prof. SUNY, Stony Brook, 1967—72, prof., 1972—94, provost, div. Social and Behavioral Sci., 1975—79, chmn. dept., 1982—86. Vis. scholar Yale U., Australian Nat. U., Tel Aviv U., Brookings Inst., others; cons. World Bank, Washington, 1986—91, sr. economist, 1991—94, lead economist, 1994—2000, cons., 2000—; vis. fellow Urban Inst., Washington, 2002—04; mem. governing bd. Kosovo Pension Saving Trust, 2001—. Author: (book) Hoffa and the Teamsters, 1964, The Nonprofit Sector in Market Economies, 1986, Pub. Policy and Pvt. Ed. in Japan, 1988, The Nonprofit Sector in Internat. Perspective, 1989, Averting the Old Age Crisis, 1994; contbr. articles to profl. jour. Fellow, Woodrow Wilson Internat. Ctr., Washington, 1981—82, Netherlands Inst. Advanced Study, 1986—87, U.S. Dept. Edn., 1988, Sec. of Navy, 1990, AAUW, Soc. Sci. Rsch. Coun.; grantee, Spencer Found., USAID, NEH, Exxon Edn. Found., Mich. Retirement Rsch. Consortium, Smith Richardson Found.; Fulbright awardee, 1979. Mem.: Am. Econs. Assn. Office Phone: 202-338-1451. Business E-Mail: ejames@estellejames.com.

JAMES, ETTA (JAMESETTA HAWKINS), recording artist; b. L.A., Jan. 25, 1938; d. Dorothy Leatherwood Hawkins; m. Artis Dee Mills, May 20, 1969; children: Donto, Sametto. Blues singer Johnny Otis, L.A., 1954, Bihari Bros. Record Co., L.A., 1954, Leonard Chess Record Co., L.A., 1960, Warner Bros., L.A., 1978, Fantasy Record, L.A., 1985, Island Record, L.A., 1988. Record Albums include Respect Yourself, 1997, Love's Been Rough on Me, 1997, Come A Little Closer. The Essential Etta, 1993, Etta James Rocks the House, Etta, Red Hot'n Live, Her Greatest Sides, Vol. 1, Live, 1994, Mystery Lady: Songs of Billie Holliday, 1994 (Grammy award 1994), R&B Dynamite, 1987, reissue, 1991, The Right Time, 1992, Rocks the House, 1992, The Second Time Around, 1989, Seven Year Itch, 1988, Sticking to My Guns, 1990, The Sweetest Peaches, 1989, The Sweetest Peaches: Part One, 1989, The Sweetest Peaches: Part Two, 1989, Tell Mama, 1988, These Foolish Things: The Classic Balladry of Etta James, 1995, Time After Time, (with Eddie Cleanhead Vinson) Blues in the Night, Lane Supper Club, 1986, Blues in the Night, Vol. 2, 1987, Twelve Songs of X-mas, 1988, Life, Love & the Blues, 1988, Heart of a Woman, 1999, 20th Century Master: The Best of Etta James, 1999, Platinum Series, 2000, The Chess Box, 2000, Matriarch of the Blues, 2000, Etta James, 2001, Love Songs, 2001, Blue Gardenia, 2001, Blowin' in the Wind, 2002, Live and Ready, 2002, Burnin' Down the House, 2002, Let's Roll, 2003, Rock Me Baby, 2004, Live in New York, 2005. Recipient Lifetime Achievement award Rigby & Blues Assn., 1989, Living Legends award KJLH, 1989, Image award NAACP, 1990 W.C. Handy award, 1989, Blue Soc. Hall of Fame award, 1991; 5th Handy Blues award, 1993, 94, Soul of Am. Music award, 1992; 8 Grammy nominations, Beyond War award, Best Song, 1984; inducted into Rock & Roll Hall of Fame, 1993; sang opening ceremony of 1984 Olympics. Office: Etta James Enterprises 16409 Sally Ln Riverside CA 92504-5629*

JAMES, FRANCIS EDWARD, JR., investment advisor; b. Woodville, Miss., Jan. 5, 1931; s. Francis Edwin and Ruth (Phillips) J.; m. Iris Senn, Nov. 3, 1952; children: Francis III, Barry, David. BS, La. State U., 1951; MS, Rensselaer Poly. Inst., 1966, PhD, 1967. Commd. 2d lt. USAF, 1950, advanced through grades to col., 1972; prof. mgmt. and statistics, chmn. dept quantitative studies Air Force Inst. Tech., Wright Patterson AFB, 1967-71, dir. grad. edn. div. mgmt. programs, 1972-74; ret. USAF, 1974; pres. James Investment Rsch., Inc., Alpha, Ohio, 1972—. Cons. math. modeling. Author: A Matrix Solution for the General Linear Regression Model; contbr. articles to profl. jours. Bd. dirs. James Capital Alliance, Inc. Decorated Legion of Merit, D.F.C., Air medal, Joint Services Commendation medal, Meritorious Service medal; recipient Outstanding Acad. Achievement award Rensselaer Poly. Inst., 1965, first Alumni Fellow appointment Rensselaer Poly. Inst. Mem. Am. Statis. Assn., Mil. Ops. Research Soc., Am. Fin. Assn., Investment Counsel Assn. Am., Mktg. Technicians Assn., Soc. Logistics Engring. (Eckles award 1973, tech. chmn.), Sigma Iota Epsilon, Epsilon Delta Sigma. Lodges: Masons; Rotary. Home: 2604 Lantz Rd Dayton OH 45434-6627 Office: James Investment Rsch Inc PO Box 8 Alpha OH 45301-0008 *To come up with an outstanding idea is brilliance. To put that idea into action is real genius.*

JAMES, FRANCIS MARSHALL, III, anesthesiologist; b. Phila., Dec. 22, 1935; MD, Hahnemann U., 1961. Intern Phila. Gen. Hosp., 1961—62; resident Hosp. U. Pa., Phila., 1964—67, attending anesthesiologist, 1967—68, NC Bapt. Hosp., Winston-Salem, 1968—2000; assoc. dean grad. med. edn. Wake Forest U., NC, 1999-2000, faculty Sch. Medicine, 1968—2000, chair dept. anesthesiology, 1983—98, prof. emeritus, 2001—. Dir. Am. Bd. Anesthesiology, 1988-2000, pres., 1999-2000. Office: Wake Forest U Sch Medicine Dept Anesthesiology Medical Ctr Blvd Winston Salem NC 27157-1009 Personal E-mail: fmj111@bellsouth.net.

JAMES, GARY DOUGLAS, biological anthropologist, educator, researcher; b. Norwich, Conn., Dec. 6, 1954; s. Godfrey Merchant and Joan (McIlwaine) J.; m. Kathleen Louise Wilson, July 28, 1979. BA, Wake Forest U., 1976; MA, Pa. State U., 1980, PhD, 1984. Part-time instr. Pa. State U., University Park, 1982-84; postdoctoral assoc. Cornell U. Med. Coll., NYC, 1984-86; asst. prof., assoc. rsch. prof. physiology medicine biophysics Med. Coll. Cornell U., NYC, 1991—98; rsch. prof. Decker Sch. Nursing SUNY, Binghamton, 1998—2003, dir. Inst. Primary Preventive Health Care, 1998—, adj. prof. anthropology, 1999—2003, prof. anthropology, 2003—, prof. nursing, 2003—. Adj. prof. dept. psychology SUNY, Binghampton, NY, 2000—. Contbr. chapters to books, articles to profl. jours. Recipient New Investigator Rsch. award NIH, 1986, Internat. Man of Yr. award Internat. Biog. Ctr., 1993; NIH postdoctoral trainee, 1984. Fellow Human Biol. Assn. (sec.-treas. 1992-96, exec. com. 1996-2000), Soc. Behavioral Medicine; mem. AAAS, Am. Assn. Phys. Anthropologists, Internat. Platform Assn., Soc. Study Social Biology, Am. Soc. Hypertension, Am. Anthrop. Assn., Am. Dermatoglyphics Assn. (exec. com. 1996-98, sec. 1998-99, editor newsletter 2001—, pres.-elect, pres. 2002-05), Harvey Soc. Lutheran. Office: Decker Sch of Nursing Binghamton Univ SUNY Box 6000 Binghamton NY 13902-6000 E-mail: gdjames@binghamton.edu.

JAMES, GAY, physical education educator; m. Johnny James. PhD, U. Tex., 1992. Prof. Tex. State U., San Marcos, Tex., 1988—. Presenter in field. Contbr. articles to profl. jours.; co-author: 4 Books. Named Health Tchr. of Yr., Tex. Assn. Health, Phys. Edn., Recreation and Dance, 1999; recipient TAHPERD Honor award, 2003, Scholar award, 2004, Honor Award, So. Dist. Tex. Assn. Health, Phys. Edn., Recreation and Dance, 2004. Office: Texas State University-San Marcos 601 University Drive San Marcos TX 78666 Office Phone: 512-245-2942.

JAMES, GEORGE BARKER, II, investment company executive; b. Haverhill, Mass., May 25, 1937; s. Paul Withington and Ruth (Burns) J.; m. Beverly A. Burch, Sept. 22, 1962; children: Alexander, Christopher, Geoffrey, Matthew. AB, Harvard U., 1959; MBA, Stanford U., 1962. Fiscal dir. E.G. & G. Inc., Bedford, Mass., 1963-67; fin. exec. Am. Brands Inc., N.Y.C., 1967-69; v.p. Pepsico, Inc., N.Y.C., 1969-72; sr. v.p., chief fin. officer Arcata Corp., Menlo Park, Calif., 1972-82; exec. v.p. Crown Zellerbach Corp., San Francisco, 1982-85; sr. v.p., chief fin. officer Levi Strauss & Co., San Francisco, 1985-98. Bd. dirs. Pacific States Industries, Inc., Clayton Group Inc., Crown Vantage Corp (chmn.), Dresdner RCM Capital Corp, Sharper Image, Inc., Callious Software Inc., Canned Foods Inc.; dir. Il Fornaio Restaurants. Author: Industrial Development in the Ohio Valley, 1962. Mem. Andover (Mass.) Town Com., 1965-67; mem. Select Congl. Com. on World Hunger; mem. adv. coun. Calif. State Employees Pension Fund; chmn. bd. dirs. Towle Trust Fund; trustee Nat. Corp. Fund for the Dance, Cate Sch., chairman, Cate Sch., Levi Strauss Found., Stern Grove Festival Assn., Zellerbach Family Fund, San Francisco Ballet Assn., Com. for Econ. Devel.; bd. dirs. Stanford U. Hosp., Calif. Pacific Med. Ctr. KQED; chmn. World Affairs Coun.; mem. San Francisco Com. on Fgn. Rels.; overseer Hoover Instn., Standford U. With AUS, 1960-61. Mem. Pacific Union Club, Bohemian Club, Menlo Circus Club, Harvard Club, N.Y. Athletic Club. Home: 207 Walnut St San Francisco CA 94118-2012

JAMES, GUS JOHN, II, lawyer; b. Koma Yiolou, Cyprus, Dec. 29, 1938; s. John and Salome James; m. Helen Alexion, July 25, 1964; children: Mary Margaret, Nicole. BS in Bus., U. Richmond, 1962; JD, Coll. William and Mary, 1966, LLM in Taxation, 1967. Bar: Va. 1966. Assoc. Kaufman and Oberndorfer, Norfolk, Va., 1966—72, ptnr., 1972—76, mng. ptnr., 1976—81, 1994—; mem. Kaufman & Canoles, Norfolk, 1982—, chmn. exec. com., 1982—84. Editor-in-chief William and Mary Law Rev., 1965—66. Bd. dirs. Med. Ctr. Hosps., Norfolk Symphony, 1978—79, Va. Orch. Group, 1979—81, Old Dominion U. Intercollegiate Found., 1984—88, Old Dominion U. Ednl. Found., Bon Secours DePaul Health Found., 1998—; chmn. Old. Dominion U. Soccer Com.; bd. commrs. Norfolk Airport Authority, 2002—; bd. dirs. Annunciation Greek Orthodox Ch., Norfolk, 1972—80, 1981—84, 1989—92, pres. parish coun., 1973—74, 1984, 1989—92, chmn. Neptune Festival com., 1977—84, 1990—91, chmn. Azalea Festival com., 1976—84, Greek Festival, 1986—2004. With USAR, 1963—68. Mem.: ABA, Norfolk-Portsmouth Bar Assn., Va. Bar Assn., Order Ahepa Club (pres. 1972, 1989), Harbor Club (bd. dirs. 1993—2004, pres. 1995—96), Town Point Club (bd. dirs. 2002—). Home: 1521 Chandon Cres Virginia Beach VA 23454-1367 Office: 150 W Main St Norfolk VA 23510

JAMES, HAMILTON EVANS (TONY JAMES), private equity executive; b. Wyandotte, Mich., Feb. 3, 1951; s. Hamilton Renson and Waleska Bacon (Evans) J.; m. Amabel George Boyce, Aug. 25, 1973; children: Meredith Evans, Rebecca Lee, Hamilton Boyce. BA, Harvard U., 1973, MBA, 1975. Registered rep. N.Y. Stock Exch. From assoc. to sr. v.p. Donaldson, Lufkin & Jenrette, N.Y.C., 1975-87, prin., 1982—, mng. dir., 1987-95, chmn. banking group, 1995—2000, also bd. dirs.; chmn., global investment banking & pvt. equity Credit Suisse First Boston, N.Y.C., 2001—02; pres. Blackstone Group, N.Y.C., 2002—. Bd. dirs. Costo Wholesale, Inc., Kirkland, Wash. Trustee Second Stage Theatre, Choate Rosemary Hall, Trout Unltd. John Harvard scholar, 1973; Baker scholar, 1975 Mem. River Club, Tokeneke Club, Links Club, Wee Burn Country Club, Club Ltd., Little Harbor Club. Republican. Episcopalian. Avocations: fly fishing, paddle tennis. Office: The Blackstone Group 345 Park Ave New York NY 10154 Business E-Mail: james@blackstone.com.

JAMES, HENRY THOMAS, former foundation executive, educator; b. Ferryville, Wis., May 19, 1915; s. Harry T. and Alice (Morgan) J.; . Vienna Lewis, June 6, 1939; children: Angelyn Alice (Mrs. Richard J. Grillo), Henry Thomas, Jennifer Lewis (Mrs. Timothy J. Regan), Mary Ellen (Mrs. Robert S. Lewis), Elizabeth Elinor (Mrs. Betty Folliard), Arthur Earl. BS, Wis. State U., 1938; Ph.M., U. Wis., 1939; PhD, U. Chgo., 1958. High sch. tchr., Barron, Wis., 1939-42; supervising prin. Woodville, Wis., 1942-43; counselor U. Wis., Madison, 1946; supt. schs. Augusta, Wis., 1946-49, Whitewater, Wis., 1949-50; asst. supt. pub. instrn. Wis., 1950-54; lectr. U. Mich., 1954; asso. dir. Midwest Adminstrn. Center, asst. prof., asso. prof., dir. field services U. Chgo. Sch. Edn., 1954-58; prof. Stanford Sch. Edn., 1958-70, dean, 1966-70; pres. Spencer Found., Chgo., 1970-85, pres. emeritus, 1985—. Cons. in field, 1954—, dir. studies sch. bds. and state sch. finance systems, 1954—; mem. N.Y. Fleischmann Commn., 1969-72, Presdl. Task Force on Edn., 1968, 80; adviser subcom. efficiency and innovation in edn. Com. Econ. Devel.; study dir. The Nation's Report Card, 1986-87; series editor various pub. cos.; chmn. vis. com. Ednl. Testing Svc., 1989-90. Sr. author: School Revenue Systems in Five States, 1961, Wealth, Expenditures and Decision-Making for Education, 1963, Determinants of Educational Expenditures in Large Cities of the United States, 1966, The New Cult of Efficiency and Education, 1969; Editor: Boardmanship, 1961; Editorial adv. bd.: Edn. and Urban Society, 1968—, Contemporary Edn. Rev., 1982—; Contbr. articles to profl. jours. Served to lt. USNR, 1943-46. Recipient Distinguished Service award Nat. Assn. State Bds. Edn., 1973, Viterbo Coll. award for service to higher edn., 1975, Outstanding Service award Am. Edn. Fin. Assn., 1988. Mem. Am. Ednl. Research Assn. (chmn. nominating com. 1964-65, cons. editor jour. 1964-70, program chmn. 1968), Am. Assn. Sch. Adminstrs., AAAS, Nat. Acad. Edn., Univ. Council Ednl. Adminstrn., Chgo. Com., Council on Fgn. Relations, Phi Delta Kappa (bd. editorial cons. 1974-85). Presbyterian. Home: Knollwood Village 1047 Village Sq Altoona WI 54720-2558

JAMES, JAMES FRANKLIN, psychiatrist, educator, dean; b. Greenville, N.C., Sept. 2, 1937; married; 7 children. AB in Comparative Lit., U. N.C., 1959; MD, U. Tenn., 1963. Diplomate Am. Bd. Psychiatry and Neurology. Intern Med. Coll. Va., Richmond, 1964—65; resident aerospace medicine U.S. Navy Aerospace Med. Inst., Pensacola, Fla., 1965—66; dir. Lithium project Dorothea Dix Hosp., Raleigh, 1967—69; resident psychiatry U. N.C.-Dorothea Dix Hosp. and Duke U., Raleigh/Durham, 1969; assoc. dep. commr. Ea. Region-N.C., 1969—71; supt. Cherry Hosp., N.C. State Mental Hosp., Goldsboro, 1969—71; part-time pvt. practice gen. and forensic psychiatry, 1969—78; mental health program chief Fresno (Calif.) County Dept. Health, 1971—78, dep. head dir., adult svcs. and mental health program chief, 1974—78; clin. prof. dept. psychiatry U. Okla. Sch. Medicine, 1978—89; chief consultation-liaison psychiatry VA Hosp., Oklahoma City, 1978—89; commr. Okla. Dept. Mental Health, Oklahoma City, 1978—89; attending staff Pitt County Meml. Hosp., 1989—; dir. residency tng. East Carolina U. Sch. Medicine, Greenville, NC, 1989—90, prof., chmn., 1990—2001, asst. dean, dir. personal counseling ctr., prof. dept. psychiat. medicine, 2001—. Founding bd. mem. East Carolina Counseling Ctr., 1998—2001; psychiat. edn. grant rev. cons. Nat. Inst. Mental Health, 1979—85, mem. internal rev. com., 1979—90, state manpower devel. grant rev. cons., 1979—90; examiner Am. Bd. Psychiatry and Neurology, 1985—96; mem. profl. adv. com. Joint Commn. on Accreditation Healthcare Orgns., 1988—89; presenter in field. Mem. editl. bd.: Current Surgery, 1991—, article reviewer: Hosp. and Cmty. Psychiatry, 1978—95, Jour. Medicine and Philosophy, 1991, Psychiat. Svcs., 1995—; contbr. articles to profl. jours. Lt. comdr. USN, 1965—66. Decorated Combat Air medal USN, S.E. Asia Expedition medal, Vietnam Svc. medal, Unit Commendation medal, Comdg. Officers' commendation; recipient Bd. Govs. Excellence in Tchg. award, U. NC, 2005. Fellow: Am. Coll. Mental Health Adminstrs., Am. Coll. Psychiatrists (mem. budget com. 1990—91, mem. nomination com. 1995—96, 2002—03), Am. Psychiat. Assn. (rep. to the assembly 1978, chmn. com. on state svcs. 1982—86, mem. coun. on psychiat. svcs. 1986—90, chmn. coun. on psychiat. svcs. 1988—90, mem. com. to develope a nat. data base for psychiatry 1988—90, mem. joint reference com. 1988—90, mem. budget com. 1990—94, chmn. consortium of chairs of pub. psychiatry components 1990—95, mem. com. on reorganization of fed. agys. 1991—92, mem. search com. for dep. dir. 1993); mem.: AMA, APHA, Pitt County Med. Soc., N.C. Med. Soc., Am. Assn. Mental Health Adminstrs., World Psychiat. Assn., N.C. Psychiat. Assn. (mem. cmty. mental health com. 1989—93, mem. program com. 1991, chmn. program com. 1998). Office: East Carolina Univ Sch Medicine Personal Counseling Ctr Lakeside Annex #3 Greenville NC 27858-2500

JAMES, JEANNETTE ADELINE, state legislator, accountant, small business owner; b. Maquoketa, Iowa, Nov. 19, 1929; d. Forest Claude and Winona Adeline (Meyers) Nims; m. James Arthur James, Feb. 16, 1948; children: James Arthur Jr., Jeannette, Alice Marie. Student, Merritt Davis Sch. Commerce, Salem, Oreg., 1956-57, U. Alaska, 1976—77. Payroll supr. Gen. Foods Corp., Woodburn, Oreg., 1956-66; cost acctg., inventory control clk. Pacific Fence & Wire Co., Portland, Oreg., 1966-67, office mgr., 1968-69; substitute rural carrier U.S. Post Office, Woodburn, 1967-68; owner, mgr., acct. and tax preparer James Bus. Svc., Goldendale, Wash., 1969-75, Anchorage, 1975-77, Fairbanks, Alaska, 1977—83, North Pole, Alaska, 1983—; co-owner, mgr. Jolly Acres Motel, North Pole, 1987—; mem. Alaska Ho. of Reps., Juneau, 1993—2003; chmn. House State Affairs, 1995-2000, jud. com., 1998—2002; vice chmn. Legis. Coun., 1995-96; chmn. joint com. Adminstrv. Regulation Rev., 1997-98, ho. majority leader, 2001—02. Instr. workshop Comm. Dynamics, 1988; railroad advisor to Gov. Morkowski, 2003-. Vice chmn. Klickitat County Dems., Goldendale, 1970-74; bd. dirs. Mus. and Art Inst., Anchorage, 1976-80; pres. Anchorage Internat. Art Inst., 1976-78; chmn. platting bd. Fairbanks North Star Borough, 1980-84, mem. Planning Commn., 1984-87; treas., vice chmn. 18th Dist. Reps., North Pole, Alaska, 1984-92; mem. City of North Pole Econ. Devel. Com., 1992-93; mem. Rep. State Ctrl. Com., 2004—. Named Legislator of Yr., Alaska Farm Bur., 1994, Alaska Outdoor Coun., 2000, Juneau Empire, 2002, Guardian of Small Bus., Nat. Fedn. Ind. Bus., 1998, Friend of Psycology, 2001; recipient Defender of Freedom award, NRA, 1994, Friend of Municipalities award, Alaska Mcpl. League, 1996, Courage in Preserving Equal Access award, Alaska chpt. Safari Club Internat., 2000, Cmty. Svc. award, Arctic Alliance for People, 2001. Mem. Internat. Tng. in Comm. (Alaska State winner speech contest 1981, 86), North Pole C. of C., Emblem Club, Rotary (treas. North Pole 1990, v.p. membership 2004-05, pres.-elect 2005-), Eagles, Women of Moose Presbyterian. Avocations: bowling, dolls, children. Home: 3068 Badger Rd North Pole AK 99705-6117 Office Phone: 907-488-9339. Personal E-mail: jamesjeannette@gci.net.

JAMES, JOHN WHITAKER, SR., finance company executive; b. Summit, N.J., Aug. 19, 1942; s. Nathan Whitaker and Dorothy Jane (Laffey) J.; m. Loretta Marie Porter, Dec. 7, 1968; children: John Whitaker Jr., Laurissa Marie, Corinne Helena, Randolph Whitaker. BA in Econs., Princeton U., 1964; MBA in Fin. and Investment cum laude, NYU, 1970. From ofcl. asst., asst. treas. to asst. v.p. Bankers Trust Co., N.Y.C., 1964-72, v.p. equipment leasing, 1972-76; pres., dir. Bankers Trust of Binghamton, N.Y., 1976-80; v.p., divsn. head Bankers Trust Co., N.Y.C., 1980-82; new bus. strategist E.F. Hutton Credit Corp., Greenwich, Conn., 1983-85; sr. ops. mgr. corp. fin. and equipment leasing Chrysler Capital Corp. (formerly E.F. Hutton Credit Corp.), Greenwich, 1985-91; v.p. Chrysler Capital Corp., Stamford, Conn., 1991-97; pres. MicroGenesis LLC, 1997—; cons. Daimler Chrysler Global Capital Svcs., 1999—. Contbr. articles to profl. jours.; inventor baseball game Diamond Challenge. Campaign chmn. Broome County United Way, Binghamton, 1978; dir., pres. New Canaan chpt. United Way, 1985-90; dir., asst. treas. Family and Children's Svcs., Stamford, 1990-96; dir. New Canaan Cmty. Found., 1991-98, pres., 1998, Family Ctrs. Inc., Greenwich, 1996-97; dir. Christian Cmty. Action, New Haven, Conn., 2000-. With USAR, 1966-70. Mem. Societal Inst. Math. Scis. (bd. dirs., v.p., sec., treas. 1993—2004), David Ackerman Decs. (v.p. 1997-98, pres. 1998—2002), Assn. Blauvelt Desc., Princeton Club New Canaan (treas. 1985—2004). Republican. Presbyterian. Avocations: tennis, genealogy. Home and Office: MicroGenesis LLC 18 Waterbury Ave Madison CT 06443-3205 Office Phone: 203-245-1290. E-mail: jwjsr@aol.com.

JAMES, KATHRYN A., secondary school educator; b. Springfield, Mo., Aug. 1, 1925; d. Joseph Fred and Sybil Mae (Rogers) Giboney; m. Charles Elwyn James, Jan. 24, 1948 (wid. May 1999); children: Kathryne Janette, Jacquelyn Annette, Charles Roger. BSEd, S.W. Mo. State Tchrs. Coll., Springfield, 1945; MA, U. Mo., 1955; postgrad., U. Va., 1968. Life-term tchg. cert. in art, design, and home econs.; tchg. certs. in 6 states. Art supr. Mountain Grove (Mo.) Pub. Schs., 1945-47; art instr. Moberly (Mo.) Jr. Coll., 1947-49, Exptl. Sch., Springfield, Mo., 1949-54; art and home econs. instr. Ashland (Ky.) Pub. Schs., 1954-59; itinerant art tchr. Boyd County (Ky.) Pub. Schs., 1960-63; tchr. U. Ky., Lexington, 1963-65; art inst. Fairfax Pub. Schs., Va., 1965-68; art tchr. Terre Haute (Ind.) Pub. Schs., 1968-73, Springfield (Mo.) Pub. Schs., 1973-87. Judge sewing contests Singer Sewing Machine Co., Ashland, 1957-59, tchr. sewing classes pub. schs., adult evening and pub. sch. art classes, Ashland, 1956-58, Springfield, 1982-83. Author curriculum/art dept. Ashland and Terre Haute schs., 1955, 67-68; designer/banner constructor: Richard Ghephardt, Springfield, 1987. Campaigner Mo. State Legislators, Springfield, 1980-81, others. Recipient Gov.'s award Hon. Order of Ky. Cols., Lexington, 1965. Mem. Ky. Cols., Nat. DAR (flag chmn. 1991—2004, art awards 1995-97). Methodist. Avocations: china painting, interior decorating, freelance art work. Home: 1019 Joanne Dr Webb City MO 64870-1778 Office Phone: 417-673-1642. Personal E-mail: jameswood@joplin.com.

JAMES, KATHY LYNN, art educator; b. Somers Point, NJ, Oct. 7, 1980; d. Paul Raymond and Jean Scott; m. Michael Allinson James, Feb. 8, 1970. BA in Visual Arts and Art History, Rutgers U., 2002; MA in Art Edn., U. Ariz., Tucson, 2004. Tchg. asst. U. Ariz., Tucson, 2002—04, Pa. State U., University Park, 2004—. Fellow, U. Ariz., Grad. Coll., 2003. Mem.: Nat. Art Edn. Assn. (lifelong learning com., presenter convention 2004, 2005). Democrat. Avocations: photography, reading, travel. Home: 1014 Lexington Ave Altoona PA 16601

JAMES, KAY COLES, former federal agency administrator; b. Portsmouth, Va., June 1, 1949; d. Susie Armistead Coles; m. Charles Everett James; children: Charles Jr., Elizabeth, Robert III. BS, Hampton (Va.) Inst., 1971. Traffic svc. advisor C&P Telephone, Roanoke, Va., 1971-72, group supr., 1973, force mgr., 1974; conf. coord. devel. disabilities project State of Va., Richmond, 1978-79; asst. to housing coord. Housing Opportunities Made Equal, Richmond, 1980-81, dir. community edn. and devel., 1981-83; personnel dir. Cir. City Stores, Beltsville, Md., 1983-85; dir. pub. affairs Nat. Right to Life Com., Washington, 1985-88; asst. sec. pub. affairs US Dept. Health and Human Services., Washington, 1989—90; assoc. dir. Office of Nat. Drug Control Policy, 1991—93; sr. v.p. Family Rsch. Coun., 1993—94; sec. Health and Human Resources Dept., Richmond, Va., 1994—96; dean Sch. of Govt. Regent U., 1996—99; sr. fellow of the Citizenship Project Heritage Found., 1999—2001; dir. Office of Personnel Mgmt., Washington, 2001—05. Pres. Black Ams. for Life, Washington, D.C., 1985-88; asst. sec. pub. affairs HHS Office of the Sec., Washington, D.C., 1989—; mem. White House Com. on Children, Washington, D.C., 1988, White House Task Force on Blacks, Washington, D.C., 1988, Nat. Coalition on Pro-Family Issues, Washington, D.C., 1988; co-founder Nat. Family Inst., Washington, D.C., 1987; chair, Nat. Gambling Impact Study Com., 1999-2001. Contbr. numerous articles to jours. and newspapers. Republican. Presbyterian. Avocations: reading, walking, cooking.

JAMES, KESHA MALLORY, computer and business educator; b. Birmingham, Ala., Aug. 26, 1971; m. Lionel James, July 9, 1999; children: Lionel II, Kasey Nicole. BS, Ala. State U., 1994; MEd, Auburn U., 1998, EdS, 2005. A+, IC3, Microsoft Office Specialist Comptia, Certiport, Microsoft. Tchr. bus. edn. Birmingham Bd. of Edn., 1994—2001; instr. bus./computer info. sys. Lawson State C.C., Birmingham, 2001—. Mem.: Internat. Assn. of Adminstrv. Professionals (pres. 2002—05), Alpha Theta Chi, Phi Theta Kappa, Kappa Beta Delta, Alpha Kappa Alpha (life). Home: 199 Woodbury Dr Sterrett AL 35147 Office: Lawson State C C 3060 Wilson Rd Birmingham AL 35221 Office Phone: 205-929-6450. Personal E-mail: keshamjames@msn.com. E-mail: kjames@lawsonstate.edu.

JAMES, KEVIN, III, actor; b. Stony Brook, NY, Apr. 26, 1965; m. Steffiana de la Cruz, June 19, 2004. Attended, Cortland U. Actor: (TV series) Candid Camera, 1991, King of Queens, 1998—; prodr., writer: (TV series) King of Queens, 1999; exec. prodr.:, 2000—; host: Funny Flubs & Screw-Ups, 2000; exec. prodr.: (comedy spl.) Kevin James: Sweat the Small Stuff, 2001; actor: (films) 50 First Dates, 2004, Grilled, 2005, Hitch, 2005; TV appearances include: Everybody Loves Raymond, 1996—99; Cosby, 1998; Martial Law, 1999; Becker, 1999. Named one of 100 Most Creative People, Entertainment Weekly mag., 2001. Office: Sony Pictures TV 10202 W Washington Blvd Culver City CA 90232*

JAMES, LEBRON, professional basketball player; b. Akron, Ohio, Dec. 30, 1984; s. Gloria James; 1 child. Forward Cleve. Cavaliers, 2003—. Mem. U.S. Olympic Basketball team, Athens, 2004. Named Nat. HS Player of Yr., USA Today, 2003, NBA Rookie of the Year, 2004; named one of 100 Most Influential People, Time Mag., 2005; named to NBA All-Star team, 2005; recipient Espy Award for Best Breakthrough, ESPN, 2004. Achievements include picked number 1 in the 2003 NBA Draft; member of the Bronze Medal-winning 2004 United States Olympic Team; youngest player in NBA history to record a triple-double, Jan. 19, 2005; youngest player in NBA history to score fifty points, March 20, 2005. Office: Cleveland Cavaliers 1 Center Ct Cleveland OH 44115-4001*

JAMES, LOUIS MEREDITH, personnel executive; b. St. Augustine, Fla., June 12, 1941; s. Claire Meredith and Katherine Louise (Colson) J.; m. Karen Lee Libby, Nov. 25, 1966 (div. Mar. 1974); children: Michelle Lee, Kevin Meredith; m. Antoinette Frances Guerrero, Dec. 23, 1978; 1 child, Aaron Teague. BA, U. Minn., 1964. Personnel mgr. Army & Air Force Exch. Svc., worldwide, 1967-77; salary and wage specialist Dept. Def. Wage Staff, Rosslyn, Va., 1977-82; dep. chief Dept. Def. Wage Divsn. NAF Br., Arlington, Va., 1982-98, ret., 1998. Commr. Transp. Safety Commn., Vienna, Va., 1986-98, vice chair, 1992-93, chair, 1993-96; mem. Bd. Zoning Appeals, Vienna, 1998-99; mem. Fairfax/Falls Ch. Cmty. Svcs. Bd.; pres. nonprofit corp. Families United for Non-Profit Residences Fund, Housing for Developmentally Disadvantaged. With U.S. Army, 1965, Vietnam. Decorated Purple Heart. Mem. DAV (life), VFW (life), Vietnam Vets. Am. (life mem., local chpt. state coun. and nat. com., bd. dirs., v.p., pres. 1987—, Nat. Mem. of Yr. 1995), Mil. Order of Purple Heart (life), U.S. Army Officer Candidate Sch. Assn. (life), Lions (v.p., bd. dirs., chmn. membership com. Vienna chpt.), Ruritans, Masons. Republican. Presbyterian. Avocations: fishing, sports, classical music, reading. Office Phone: 703-501-6327. Personal E-mail: bigred1vet@yahoo.com.

JAMES, MARC STEPHEN, brokerage house executive; b. Phila., Apr. 17, 1961; s. Charles and Thelma Janet (Graves) J.; m. Melissa Elizbeth Mask, July 15, 1989. BS in Mech. Engring., Carnegie-Mellon U., 1983; MBA in Fin., U. Chgo., 1988. Engr. IBM, Dayton, Ohio, 1983-84, mktg. rep. Bethesda, Md., 1984-85, regional staff rep., 1985-86; index arbitageur Paine Webber, NYC, 1986-90; derivative products originator Chase Securities, Inc., NYC, 1990—94; mng. dir. fixed-income derivatives Bear Stearns & Co., 1994—2001; head corp. derivative sales (Am.) Commerzbank Securities, NYC, 2001—. Author: (with others) Recent Advances in Interest Rates and Currency Slips, 1992. Vol. counselor N.Y. Cares, 1991—. Avocations: tennis, bicycling, basketball. Home: 120 Prospect Park W Brooklyn NY 11215-4207 Office: Commerzbank Securities 1251 Avenue of the Americas New York NY 10020-1104

JAMES, MARION RAY, magazine founder, editor; b. Bellmont, Ill., Dec. 6, 1940; s. Francis Miller and Lorraine A. (Wylie) J.; m. Janet Sue Tennis, June 16, 1960; children: Jeffrey Glenn, David Ray, Daniel Scott, Cheryl Lynne. BS, Oakland City Coll., Ind., 1964; MS, St. Francis Coll., Fort Wayne, Ind., 1978. Sports and city editor Daily Clarion, Princeton, Ind., 1963-65; English tchr. Jac-Cen-Del H.S., Osgood, Ind., 1965-66; indsl. editor Whirlpool Corp., Evansville and LaPorte, Ind., 1966-68, Magnavox Govt. and Indsl. Electronics Co., Fort Wayne, 1968-79; editor, pub., founder Bowhunter mag., Fort Wayne, Ind., 1971-88, editor-in-chief Kalispell, Mont., 1989-2001, editor emeritus, 2001—. Instr. Purdue U., Ft. Wayne, Ind., 1980-88. Author: Bowhunting for Whitetail and Mule Deer, 1975, Successful Bowhunting, 1985, My Place, 1991, The Bowhunter's Handbook, 1997, Of Blind Pigs and Big Bucks, 2002; editor: Pope and Young Book of Bowhunting Records, 1975, 93, 99, Bowhunting Adventures, 1977. Recipient Best Editorial award United Community Svc. Publs., 1970-72; named Alumnus of Yr., Oakland City Coll., 1982; named to Hall of Fame, Mt. Carmel High Sch., Ill., 1983, Archery Hall of Fame, 2003. Mem. Outdoor Writers Assn. Am. (Excellence in Craft Lifetime Achievement award 1999), Ft. Wayne Assn. Bus. Editors (pres. 1975-76, Ft. Wayne Bus. Editor of Yr. award 1969), Toastmasters (Able Toastmaster award), Alpha Phi Gamma, Alpha Psi Omega, Mu Tau Kappa Home: PO Box 1509 Inglefield IN 47618 also: 11631 Blue Grass Rd Evansville IN 47725 Office Phone: 406-862-9340. Personal E-mail: mrjames@cyberport.net. *Read! Being a good reader is the key to good thinking. Develop and expand your mind through active use of the printed word and you will discover a wide world of unlimited possibilities - and ultimate success that comes with self-discovery.*

JAMES, MARK A., lawyer, former state legislator; b. Eugene, Oreg., Oct. 9, 1959; m. Lori M. James; children: Anne A., John S. BS, Lewis and Clark Coll., 1982; JD, U. Ariz., 1985. Bar: U.S. Dist. Ct. Nev., U.S. Dist. Ct. (so. dist.) Tex., U.S. Ct. Appeals (9th and 5th cirs.). Senate judiciary intern Senator Paul Laxalt, Nev., 1981; former mem. Nev. Senate, Dist. 8, Carson City; former Las Vegas County commr.; founder James, Driggs, & Walch; pvt. practice, 2000; of counsel Bullivant Houser Bailey PC. Apptd. Nat. Conf. Commissioners Uniform State Law, Nat. Conf. State Legislators law and justice sect., criminal justice sect., Coun. State Govts. West Trade and Transp. Com., We. Water Policy Com. Articles editor Ariz. Law Rev. Active Clark County Pub. Edn. Found., Boys and Girls Clubs; mem. statewide adv. coun. Water Resources Rsch. of the Desert; bd. dirs. Aquavision, chair water law forum, 1992; bd. dirs. Las Vegas Valley Water Dist., So. Nev. Water Authority, So. Nev. Regional Planning Coalition, Met. Police Dept. Fiscal Affairs Com., Nat. Multiple Sclerosis Soc., Clark County Pub. Edn. Found., statewide adv. coun. water resources rsch. Desert Rsch. Inst., Nev. Earthquake Safety Coun., Family and Child Treatment SW Nev. Named one of Top 40 Lawyers Under 40, Las Vegas Bus. Press, 1994. Mem. ABA, State Bar Nev., State Bar Tex., Nev. Water Resources Assn. Republican. also: Nev State Legis Bldg 401 S Carson St Rm 240 Carson City NV 89701-4747 Office: Bullivant Houser Bailey PC 3980 Howard Hughes Pwy Ste 550 Las Vegas NV 89109 Office Phone: 702-650-6565 708. Office Fax: 702-650-2995. E-mail: mark.james@bullivant.com.

JAMES, MARK EDWARD, psychiatrist; b. Nebraska City, Nebr., Oct. 29, 1955; s. Mark Edward and Norma Jean James; m. Catherine Dianne Moseman, June 30, 1979; 1 child, Catherine Elizabeth. BS, U. Nebr., Lincoln, 1978; MD, U. Nebr. Coll. Medicine, Omaha, 1982. Cert. Am. Bd. Psychiatry and Neurology, 1988. Resident, psychiatry Emory U. Sch. Medicine, Atlanta, 1986, asst. prof., psychiatry, 1986—95, clin. asst. prof., psychiatry, 1996—; dir., inpatient psychiatry Grady Meml. Hosp., Atlanta, 1989—95; pvt. practice Lawrenceville, Ga., 1995—; psychoanalytic tng. Emory U. Psychoanalytic Inst., Atlanta, 1999, asst. tchg. analyst, 2000—02, assoc. tchg. analyst, 2002—. Contbr. chapters to books, articles to profl. jours. Grantee, Am. Psychiatric Assn., 1991. Fellow: Am. Psychol. Assn.; mem.: Am. Psychoanalytic Assn. Office: Mark E James MD 290 Constitution Blvd Ste A Lawrenceville GA 30045

JAMES, MURIEL MARSHALL, writer, lecturer, psychotherapist; b. Berkeley, Calif., Feb. 14, 1917; d. John Albert and Hazel (Knowles) Marshall; m. Paul Wesley James (div.); children: Ann, Duncan, John. BA with honors, U. Calif., Berkeley, 1956; MDiv, Ch. Divinity Sch. Pacific, 1957; EdD, U. Calif., 1964; DMin, U. Calif., Berkeley, 2000. Lic. family psycho therapist, Calif. Instr., coord. ARC, San Francisco, 1941-43; safety inspector Kaiser Shipyards, Richmond, Calif., 1943-44; tchr. Oakland (Calif.) Pub. Schs., 1948-52; min. Orinda (Calif.) Cmty. Ch., 1957-59; dean Laymen's Sch. Religion, Berkeley, Calif., 1959-68; instr. U. Calif. Ext., Berkeley, 1966-69; dir., therapist Oasis Edn. & Treatment Ctr., Lafayette, Calif., 1968-73; psychotherapist pvt. practice, Lafayette, Calif., 1969—. Lectr. James Inst., Lafayette, 1969—. Author, co-author: Born to Win: Transactional Analysis with Gestalt Experiments, 1971, Winning with People: Group Exercises in Transactional Analysis, 1973, Born to Love: Transactional Analysis in the Church, 1973, Transactional Analysis for Moms and Dads: What Do You Do With Them Now That You've Got Them?, 1974, The Power at the Bottom of the Well, 1974, The OK Boss, 1975, The People Book: Transcational Analysis for Students, 1975, The Heart of Friendship, 1976, Techniques for Psychotherapists and Counselors, 1977, A New Self: Self Therapy with Transactional Analysis, 1977, Marriage is for Loving, 1979, Breaking Free: Self-Reparenting for a New Self, 1981, Winning Ways in Health Care, 1981, It's Never Too Late to Be Happy, 1985, expanded edit. 2002, The Better Boss in Multicultural Organizations, 1991, Hearts on Fire: Romance and Achievement in the Lives of Great Women, 1991, Passion for Life: Psychology and the Human Spirit, 1991, Religious Liberty on Trial: Hanserd Knollys, Early Baptist Hero, 1997, Perspectives in Transactional Analysis, 1998; contbr. chpts. to books, articles to profl. jours. Named to Internat. Educators Hall of Fame, 2000. Mem. Interat. Transactional Analysis Assn. (pres. 1980-82). Avocations: friends, family, travel, teaching, creating new books.

JAMES, PATRICK, political science educator; b. Toronto, Ont., Can., Mar. 27, 1957; s. Margaret Elnor; m. Carolyn Cramer, July 6, 1996; 1 child, Ben. BA with honors, U. We. Ont., 1978; PhD, U. Md., 1984. Asst. prof. U. Manitoba, Winnipeg, Can., 1983-84, McGill U., Montreal, 1984-88, assoc. prof., 1988-91; prof. Fla. State U., Tallahassee, 1991-94; prof., chair Iowa State U., Ames, 1994-98, prof., 1999—. Minority advisor Carver Acad., Ames, 1997—; Louise Dyer Peace fellow Hoover Instn., Stanford, Calif., 1991-92; Milton R. Merrill chair Utah State U., Logan, 1997; Lady Davis prof. Hebrew U., Jerusalem, 1999; Thomas O. Enders prof. Canadian studies U. Calgary, 2001. Author, editor: Politics and Rationality, 1993, Wars in the Midst of Peace, 1997, Peace in the Midst of War, 1998, others; editor Internat. Studies Quarterly, 1999—; mem. editl. bd. Internat. Studies Rev., 1999—, Internat. Studies Perspectives, 1999—; contbr. articles to profl. jours. Mem. Internat. Studies Assn., Internat. Polit. Sci. Assn., Internat. Studies Assn. Midwest (pres. 1999-2000), Am. Polit. Sci. Assn., Iowa Conf. Polit. Scientists (pres. 1998-99), Peace Sci. Soc. Avocations: chess, golf. Office: Iowa State U Dept Polit Sci Ames IA 50011-0001 E-mail: pjames@instate.edu.

JAMES, PAUL M., lawyer; b. Providence, Aug. 16, 1963; s. Anita James; m. Rita S. Speziale, Nov. 4, 1988; children: Andrea Katherine, Meghan Elizabeth. BA, Providence Coll.; JD, Boston U., 1988. Bar: Mass. 1988, U.S. Dist. Ct. Mass. 1988. Ptnr. Holland & Knight LLP, Boston, 1988—. Mem.: ABA (Forum on the Constrn. Industry), Boston Bar Assn. (co-chmn. constrn. law com. of real estate sect. 2002—). Office: Holland & Knight LLP 10 St James Ave Boston MA 02116 E-mail: pjames@hklaw.com.

JAMES, PHILIP J., agricultural products executive; b. 1938; With Monsanto Co., St. Louis, 1959-62, Midwest Agrl. Co., Fremont, Nebr., 1962-79, Platte Chem. Co., Fremont, Nebr., 1979-87; pres. United Agrl. Products Co., Greeley, Colo., 1987; sr. v.p. environment, health and safety ConAgra Inc. Dir. Fremont Nat. Bank, 1973—87, Nebraska Wildlife Fed., 1983—86; bd. mem. Nat. Agricultural Chem. Assoc., 1982—84, Fontanelle Forest Assoc., 1983—87, Colorado Nature Conservancy, 1983—, Nebraska Environmental Control Council, 1983—87, Agricultural Council of Am., 1991. Mem.: Colorado Wildlife Comm. Office: United Agrl Products Co 7251 W 4th St Greeley CO 80634-9763

JAMES, P(HYLLIS) D(OROTHY) (BARONESS JAMES OF HOLLAND PARK OF SOUTHWOLD IN COUNTY OF SUFFOLK), author; b. Oxford, Eng., Aug. 3, 1920; d. Sidney Victor and Dorothy May Amelia (Hone) J.; m. Connor Bantry White, 1941 (dec. 1964); children: Clare Bantry, Jane Bantry. Student Brit. schs.; LittD (hons.), U. Buckingham (Eng.), 1992, U. Hertfordshire (Eng.), 1994, U. Glasgow (Scotland), 1995, Durham U., 1998, Portsmouth U., 1999; DLitt, U. London, 1993; D. U. Essex, Eng., 1996. Adminstr. Nat. Health Service, 1949-68; apptd. prin. Civil Svc. Home Office, 1968; prin. Police Dept., 1968-72, Criminal Policy Dept., 1972-79. Author: Cover Her Face, 1962, A Mind to Murder, 1963, Unnatural Causes, 1967, Shroud for a Nightingale, 1971; (with T.A. Critchley) The Maul and the Pear Tree, 1971; An Unsuitable Job for a Woman, 1972, The Black Tower, 1975, Death of an Expert Witness, 1977, Innocent Blood, 1980, The Skull Beneath the Skin, 1982, (play) A Private Treason, 1985, A Taste for Death, 1986, Devices and Desires, 1989, The Children of Men, 1992, Original Sin, 1994, A Certain Justice, 1997, Time to be in Earnest, 1999, Death in Holy Orders, 2001, The Murder Room, 2003, The Lighthouse, 2005. Gov. BBC, 1988-93; bd. dirs. Brit. Coun., 1988-93; bd. dirs., chair lit. adv. panel Arts Coun. Gt. Britain, 1988-92. Decorated Order Brit. Empire, 1983; created life peer (Baroness) of U.K., 1991; assoc. fellow Downing Coll., Cambridge, 1986, hon. fellow, 2000; hon. fellow St. Hilda's Coll., Oxford, 1996, Girton Coll., Cambridge, 2000; recipient Grandmaster award Mystery Writers of Am., 1999. Fellow Royal Soc. Lit., Royal Soc. Arts; mem. Soc. of Authors (chmn. 1984-86, pres. 1997—), Detection Club. Office: Greene & Heaton Ltd 37 Goldhawk Rd London W12 8QQ England

JAMES, RANDALL S., state banking department commissioner; m. Kathy James; children: Allison Dredia, Amanda Johnson. BA in Economics and Gov., U. Tex., 1969; grad. degree, Southern Methodist U. Grad. Sch. Banking, 1982; grad., Tex. Gov.'s Exec. Devel. Prog., 1994. Bank examr. Fed. Deposit Ins. Corp., 1970—80, reg. office review examr. Dallas, 1980—82; credit review mgr. Interfirst Bank (now First Rep. Bank), Austin, Tex., 1982—88; credit examr. Bracewell & Patterson, 1988—89; pvt. practice, 1990—91; banking commr. Tex. Banking Dept., Austin, 1991—. Adv. bd. mem. Sch. Cmty. Bank Mgmt. Tex. Tech. U., Lubbock, Bank Ops. Inst. Tex. A&M U.; adv. bd. mem. Dept. Finance Economics S.W. Tex. St. U., San Marcos; chmn., sec., CSBS Dist. IV; bd. mem. Money Transmitter Regulators' Assn. Office: Tex Banking Dept 2601 N Lamar Blvd Austin TX 78705

JAMES, REESE JOSEPH, physician; b. Detroit, July 20, 1953; s. Robert W. and Agnes C. (Gootee) J.; children: Ashley, Kendall, Graham. BS, Western Mich. U., Kalamazoo, 1975, MA, 1976; DO, Univ. Health Scis., Kansas City, Mo., 1981. Diplomate in diagnostic radiology and neuroradiology Am. Osteo. Bd. Radiology. Intern Okla. Osteo. Hosp., Tulsa, 1981-82; resident U. Health Scis., Kansas City, Mo., 1982-85; fellow Meth. Hosp./Baylor Coll. Medicine, Houston, 1985-87; neuroradiologist Pontiac (Mich.) Osteo. Hosp., 1991—, Lapeer (Mich.) Regional Hosp., 1991—; med. dir. Mich. Resonance Imaging, Rochester Hills, 1992—; clin. prof. Mich. State U., Pontiac, 1992—. Lectr. and presenter in field. Contbr. articles to profl. jours. Mem. AMA, Am. Soc. Neuroradiology (sr. mem.), Am. Soc. Head and Neck Radiology, Soc. Magnetic Resonance Imaging, Soc. Magnetic Resonance in Medicine, Southeastern Neuroradiol. Soc., Radiol. Soc. N.Am., Am. Osteo. Coll. Radiology, Am. Coll. Radiology, Am. Osteo. Assn., Mich. Radiol. Soc., Mich. Med. Soc., Mich. Assn. Osteo. Physicians and Surgeons, Oakland County Osteo. Assn., Lapeer County Osteo. Assn., Lapeer County Med. Soc., Clin. Magnetic Resonance Soc., Soc. Nuclear Medicine. Republican. Office: Pontiac Osteo Hosp 50 N Perry St Pontiac MI 48342-2217

JAMES, ROBERT LEO, advertising agency executive; b. N.Y.C., Sept. 23, 1936; s. Leo Francis and Mildred Virginia (Schaffa) J.; m. Anne Krapp, Feb. 2, 1968; children: Robert Leo, Victoria, Jeffrey. AB, Colgate U., 1958; MBA, Columbia U., 1961. Field researcher Farm Jour., Inc., Cleve., 1956-57; salesman Procter and Gamble Co., Schenectady, 1958-59, office head sales mgr. Syracuse, N.Y., 1959—; new product devel. Colgate Palmolive Co., N.Y.C., 1961-64; sr. v.p., mgmt. svc. dir. Ogilvy and Mather, Inc., N.Y.C., 1964-68; sr. v.p., mgmt. service dir. Marschalk Co., Inc., N.Y.C., 1968, dir., 1968-80, exec. v.p., 1970, gen. mgr., 1971, pres., 1974, chmn. bd., chief exec. officer, 1975-80; vice chmn. Interpub. Group of Cos., Inc., 1980-81, also dir.; vice chmn. McCann-Erickson Worldwide, 1981-85, chmn. bd., pres., 1985-95; chmn. emeritus McCann-Erickson, 1995—. Adj. assoc. prof. mktg. Fordham U., 1968-69. Trustee Fordham Prep. Sch., 1977-83, South Street Seaport Mus., 1990-2002, N.Y. Presbyn. Hosp., N.Y.C.; bd. dirs. March of Dimes, N.Y.C., 1981-88; mem. Corp. Woodshole Oceanographic, 1996, trustee exec. com., 1997—; trustee, v.p. Worldship Trust, 2002—. Mem. NAS (chmn. pres. circle), Am. Assn. Advt. Agys. (chmn. 1992-93), Young Pres. Orgn., Nat. Captioning Inst. (chmn. corp. adv. coun. 1990-94), Internat. Exec. Svc. Corp. (mem. coun. 1988-92, adv. coun. 2000—), The Advt. Coun. (dir. 1992), Smithsonian Inst. (nat. bd. dirs. 1994—), Op Sail (trustee, exec. com. 1994—), N.Y. Yacht Club (trustee, commodore N.Y. Yacht Club 1997-99), Clove Valley Rod and Gun Club (bd. dirs., v.p. 1998-2002), Indian Harbor Yacht Club (bd. dirs. 1986-89), Nat. Air and Space Mus. (chmn. bd. dirs. 1999-2002, bd. dirs.). Home: 68 W Brother Dr Greenwich CT 06830-6751 Office: McCann-Erickson Worldwide New York NY 10017-2798

JAMES, RODNEY ARTHUR, systems administrator, application developer, minister; b. Bklyn., Dec. 1, 1964; s. Arthur Green and Helena Footman; m. Lisa Denise Butler, June 18, 1988; children: Chelsea, Brian. Cert. records specialist, U.S. Army, 1984; BS in Computer sci. and Math., Claflin U., 1988; M in Theology, Internat. Apostolic Coll. Grace and Truth. Data mgr. rsch. analyst S.C. State U., Orangeburg, 1988—2001, computer programmer, 2002—03, network adminstr. PC support, 2003—04. Founder, exec. dir. Lighthouse Learning Ctr., Orangeburg, 2000—03; pastor Lighthouse Apostolic Temple, Orangebuirg, 1998—2004. Served with USAR, 1984—91. Office: SC State U 1890 Program 300 College St Orangeburg SC 29116 Office Phone: 803-536-8461. Personal E-mail: rjames@scsu.edu.

JAMES, ROSE VICTORIA, sculptor, poet; b. East Amherst, N.Y., Feb. 11, 1922; d. Joseph and Mary (Plewniak) Glichowska; m. Clarence William James, Aug. 28, 1943 (dec. Dec. 1995); children: Robert, Sandra Lee, David, Mary, Kevin. Attended, Atlanta Coll. Art, 1960-64; B in Visual Arts in Sculpture, Ga. State U., 1973, postgrad., 1977-78. Legal sec. Law Office, Buffalo, 1941-42; sec. to comdr. Air Stas. Navy Dept., Washington, 1942-43; with pers. dept. Naval Air Station, Alameda, Calif., 1943-44; radio programmer, announcer ARC, Vets. Hosp., Buffalo, 1950-54, Atlanta, 1956-62; tchr., owner Studio 7 North Art Gallery, Roswell, Ga., 1974-76. Freelance artist, studio art instr. regional adult programs, 1960-72; competitive exhibiting artist, 1976-2003; chairperson 1st profl. women artist show Cushman Corp. Colony Sq., Atlanta, 1976; chairperson Atlanta Women in Arts Coop. Gallery, 1979-83; spkr. in field. Exhibited in group shows including Galleria Complex, Marietta, Ga., Colony Sq., Atlanta, Atlanta Hilton Ctr., Peachtree Ctr. Complex, Atlanta, Peachtree Summit, Atlanta, Atlanta Coll. Art Gallery, Woodruff Art Ctr., Atlanta, Bklyn. Coll. Student Ctr., N.Y.C., Alt. Space, N.Y.C., La Grange Coll., Ga., Ga. State U., Atlanta, Southeastern Colls. and Univs. 1-Yr. Traveling Exhibit, Auburn U., Ga. Inst. of Tech., Atlanta, DeKalb Coll., Atlanta, Hanson Gallery, New Orleans, AWIA Gallery, Atlanta, M. Baird Gallery, Atlanta, Handshake Gallery, Atlanta, Marietta Fine Arts Ctr., Ga., High Mus. of Art Regional Juried Art Shows, others. Visual arts panel Fulton County Commrs., Atlanta, 1980-81; panel moderator Ga. State U. So. Scholars on Women, 1981, Atlanta-Fulton County Libr., 1984. Grantee Bur. Cultural Affairs and Atlanta Arts Festival, 1978, Corp. Funding, 1980-81; recipient Mortar Bd. Honor Soc. Outstanding Leadership award, 1973. Mem. Internat. Sculpture Ctr. Republican. Roman Catholic. Avocations: golf, travel, reading, poetry, photography. Home: 6240 Weatherly Dr NW Atlanta GA 30328-3630

JAMES, SHARPE, mayor, state legislator; b. Jacksonville, Fla., Feb. 20, 1936; m. Mary Mattison; children John, Elliott, Kevin. Grad., Montclair State Coll.; M, Springfield Coll.; student, Washington State U., Columbia U., Rutgers U.; LLD (hon.), Montclair State U., 1988; PhD (hon.), Drew U., 1991. Tchr. Newark Pub. Sch. Dist.; former mem. faculty Essex County Coll., Newark, from 1968, prof., dept. chair, athletic dir.; councilman, South Ward City of Newark, 1970—82, councilman-at-large, 1982, mayor, 1986—; mem. NJ Senate, Dist. 29, Trenton, 1999—; comm. NJ State Redevelopment Authority, 1995—. Bd. trustees US Conf. Mayors, v.p. NJ chpt. Served with AUS.; v.p. then pres., Garden State Athletic Conf.; past pres. Nat. League of Cities. Named Mayor of Yr., N.J. Conf. Mayors, 2001, The Most Valuable Pub. Ofcl., City and State Mag.; named to N.J. Elected Officials Hall of Fame, 1999; recipient Arts Leadership award, U.S. Conf. Mayors and Ams. for the Arts, 2002. Democrat. Avocation: tennis. Office: City Hall 920 Broad St Ste 200 Newark NJ 07102-2609 also: 50 Park Place Suite 1535 Newark NJ 07102*

JAMES, SHERMAN ATHONIA, epidemiologist, educator; b. Hartsville, SC, Oct. 25, 1943; s. Jerome and Helen Genese (Bachus) J.; m. Vera Lucia Moura; children: Sherman Alexander, Scott Anthony. AB, Talladega Coll., 1964; PhD, Washington U., 1973. Prof. epidemiology U. N.C., Chapel Hill, 1973-89, U. Mich., Ann Arbor, 1989—2003, assoc. dean acad. affairs Sch. Pub. Health; prof. pub. policy Duke U., Durham, NC, 2003—. Cons. NIMH, NIH, Bethesda, Md., 1979-83, Nat. Heart, Lung and Blood Inst., 1985—, Nat. Inst. Environ. Health Sci., 1990—; cons. NAS, Washington, 1994—. Contbr. articles to profl. jours. Capt. USAF, 1964-69. Fellow Soc. of Fellows, U. Mich., 1993—. Fellow Am. Heart Assn., Acad. Behavioral Medicine Rsch., Soc. Behavioral Medicine, Am. Coll. Epidemiology; mem. Am. Men and Women of Sci. Inst. Medicine. Avocations: travel, photography, tennis, nature walks. Office: Duke Univ 136 Sanford Inst 90245 Durham NC 27708

JAMES, STEFAN KRAIG, marketing professional; b. Kingston, Jamaica, July 11, 1978; s. B. Monte and Karen James. BA in Pub. Rels., Fla. A&M U., 2001; M in Internat. Bus. Adminstrn., Nova Southeastern U., 2004. Mktg. exec. IBM, Atlanta, 1998—98; pub. rels. coord. TelePlaza Website, Hollywood, Fla., 1999—99; account exec. United Way of Broward County, Ft. Lauderdale, Fla., 2002—02; debate tchr./coach Marjory Stoneman Douglas H.S., Parkland, Fla., 2003—04; assoc. mgr., consumer market and knowledge Procter and Gamble, Cin., 2005—. Mktg. cons. various local orgns., Ft. Lauderdale, 2001. Mem.: Nat. Black MBA Assn. (assoc.), Am. Mktg. Assn. (assoc.), Kappa Alpha Psi (assoc.). Democrat. Avocations: fictional writing, soccer, politics, musical history.

JAMES, T. KENNETH, school system administrator; BA, Ark. State U.; MA in Ednl. Adminstrn., PhD in Ednl. Adminstrn. and Supervision, No. Ariz. U., US Internat. U., 1992. Asst. supt. for ednl. svcs. Escondido Union HS Dist., Calif.; supt. schs. Fayette County Pub. Schs., Lexington, Ky., Little Rock, Ark., Van Buren, Ark., Batesville, Ark.; commr. Ark. Dept. Edn., 2004—. Mem. U. Ark. Ednl. Adminstrn. Steering Com., State Adv. Bd. on Reforming Edn., AASA Bd. of Dirs. Mem.: Ark. Assn. of Ednl. Adminstrs. Office: Ark Dept Edn 4 Capitol Mall Little Rock AR 72201 Office Phone: 501-682-4475.*

JAMES, THOMAS A., investment company executive; With Raymond James & Assoc., Raymond James Fin. Inc., St. Petersburg, Fla., 1966—; chmn. Raymond James & Assocs., Raymond James Fin. Inc., St. Petersburg, Fla., 1987—; CEO Raymond James Fin., Inc., St. Petersburg, Fla., 1969—. Office: Raymond James Fin Inc 880 Carillon Pkwy Saint Petersburg FL 33716-1100*

JAMES, THOMAS LARRY, chemistry professor; b. North Platte, Nebr., Sept. 8, 1944; s. James Jennings and Guinevere (Richards) J.; m. Olga Schmidlin; children: Marc, Tristan. BS, U. N.M., 1965; PhD, U. Wis., 1969. Research chemist Celanese Chem. Co., Corpus Christi, Tex., 1969-71; NIH post-doctorate fellow U. Pa., Phila., 1971-73; prof. chem., pharmaceutical chemistry and radiology U. Calif., San Francisco, 1973—, chair dept. pharm. chemistry, 1995—, dir. Magnetic Resonance Lab., 1975. Author: NMR in Biochemistry, 1975; editor: Biomedical NMR, 1984, Methods in Enzymology, 1989, 5th edit., 2005; mem. editl. bd. Jour. Magnetic Resonance, Jour. Biomolecular NMR, Magnetic Resonance Imaging; editor FEBS Letters; contbr. articles to profl. jours. Mem. Internat. Soc. Magnetic Resonance, Am. Biophys. Soc., Am. Chem. Soc., Am. Biochem. Soc., Soc. Magnetic Resonance in Medicine, Phi Beta Kappa, Phi Kappa Phi, Kappa Mu Epsilon. Mem. Cmty. Of Christ. Avocations: skiing, kayaking, travel, photography. Office: U Calif Genentech Hall San Francisco CA 94143-2280 Business E-Mail: james@pollack.ucsf.edu.

JAMES, THOMAS NAUM, cardiologist, educator; b. Amory, Miss., Oct. 24, 1925; s. Naum and Kata J.; m. Gleaves Elizabeth Tynes, June 22, 1948; children: Thomas Mark, Terrence Fenner, Peter Naum. BS, Tulane U., 1946, MD, 1949. Diplomate Am. Bd. Internal Medicine (mem. bd. govs. 1982-88), Bd. Cardiovasc. Diseases (bd. dirs. 1972-78). Intern Henry Ford Hosp., Detroit, 1949-50, resident in internal medicine and cardiology, 1950-53, staff, 1959-68; instr. medicine Tulane U., New Orleans, 1955-58, asst. prof., 1959; prof. medicine U. Ala. Med. Ctr., Birmingham, 1968-87, prof. pathology, 1968-73, assoc. prof. physiology and biophysics, 1969-73, dir. Cardiovasc. Rsch. and Tng. Ctr., 1970-77, chmn. dept. medicine, dir. divsn. cardiovasc. disease, 1973-81, Mary Gertrude Waters prof. cardiology, 1976-87, Disting. prof., 1981-87; prof. medicine, prof. pathology U. Tex. Med. Br., Galveston, 1987—, pres., 1987-97, dir. WHO Cardiovasc. Ctr., 1988-98, Thomas N. and Gleaves T. James disting. chair cardiol. scis., 1997—. U. Tex. Med. Br., Galveston, 1997—; physician-in-chief U. Ala. Hosps., 1973-81; mem. adv.

coun. Nat. Heart Lung and Blood Inst., 1975-79; pres. 10th World Congress Cardiology, 1986; mem. cardiology del. invited by Chinese Med. Assn. to China, 1978; Campbell orator Queens U., Belfast, No. Ireland, 1982; Mikamo lectr. Japan Circulation Soc., 1982; Sir Thomas Lewis lectr. Brit. Cardiac Soc., 1983, Einthoven lectr. U. Leiden, The Netherlands, 1993, Bailey K. Ashford lectr. U. P.R., 1995; hon. lectr. U. Padua, 1998. Author: Anatomy of the Coronary Arteries, 1961, The Etiology of Myocardial Infarction, 1963; Mem. editl. bd. Circulation, 1966-83, Am. Jour. Cardiology, 1968-82, Am. Heart Jour, 1976-79; contbr. articles to profl. jours. Capt. M.C. U.S. Army, 1953-55. Recipient Sesquicentennial Medal of Honor Paul Tulane Coll. Tulane U., 1997, 50-year Lifetime Achievement award Tulane Med. Alumni Assn., 1999, James B. Herrick award Am. Heart Assn., 1999, Disting. Achievement award Soc. Cardiovasc. Pathology, 2005. Fellow ACP (gov. Ala. 1975-79, master 1983); mem. AMA, Am. Clin. and Climatological Assn. (v.p. 1992-93, councillor 1992-93), Assn. Am. Physicians, Am. Soc. Clin. Investigation, Assn. Univ. Cardiologists (pres. 1978-79), Am. Heart Assn. (pres. 1979-80, Herrick award Coun. on Clin. Cardiology 1999), Am. Coll. Cardiology (v.p. 1970-71, trustee 1970-71, 76-81, First Disting. Scientist award 1982, chmn. publs. com. 1994-97), Am. Soc. Pharmacology and Exptl. Therapeutics, Soc. Exptl. Biology of Medicine, Am. Coll. Chest Physicians, Ctrl. Soc. Clin. Rsch., Internat. Soc. and Fedn. Cardiology (pres. 1983-84), WHO (expert adv. panel on cardiovasc. diseases 1988-97), So. Soc. Clin. Investigation, Am. Fedn. Clin. Rsch., Ala. Acad. Honor. Philos. Soc. Tex., Cosmos Club, Mountain Brook Club, Galveston Arty. Club, Phi Beta Kappa, Sigma Xi, Omicron Delta Kappa, Alpha Omega Alpha, Alpha Tau Omega, Phi Chi. Presbyterian. Office: U Tex Med Br 301 University Blvd Galveston TX 77555-0175 Office Phone: 409-747-9645. Business E-Mail: pbbevil@utmb.edu. E-mail: tnj@oakmountain.net.

JAMES, WARREN A., architect; b. Arecibo, P.R., Sept. 22, 1959; s. Warren Alger James and Magdalena Bernat; m. Helen A. Salichs, Nov. 30, 1990 (div. Aug. 1998); 1 child, Alexandra E. BArch, Cornell U., 1982; MS in Bldg. Design, Columbia U., 1984. Lic. N.Y., N.J. Jr. designer Robert A.M. Stern Architects, N.Y.C., 1984—88, Ricardo Bofill/Taller de Arquitectura, Barcelona, 1985—86; prin. pvt. practice, N.Y.C., 1988—. Bd. trustees Museo del Barrio, N.Y.C., 1994—96, mem. adv. bd., 1996—2003, chair adv. bd., 2003—. Author: Ricardo Bofill/Taller de Arquitectura 1960-1986, 1986; editor: Kohn Pedersen Fox: Architecture & Urbanism 1986-1992, 1992. Mem. Nat. Hispanic Bus. Group, N.Y.C., 1996—98. Grantee, Graham Found., Chgo., 1996. Fellow: Inst. Urban Design. Office: 251 W 19th St New York NY 10011-4043 Office Phone: 212-691-0980.

JAMES, WILLIAM HALL, former state official, educator; b. North Providence, R.I., July 20, 1910; s. John William and May (Hall) J.; m. Virginia Stowell, June 24, 1950, 1 child, Hillery Stowell. Student, U. Lausanne, 1928-29; BPhil, Brown U., 1933; MA, Yale U., 1946, PhD, 1955; LLD, U. New Haven, 1976. Tchr. New Canaan (Conn.) Bd. Edn., 1933-36; teaching prin. Easton (Conn.) Bd. Edn., 1936-42, 46-47, supervising prin., 1947-53, supt. schs., 1953-58, Branford (Conn.) Bd. Edn., 1958-66; staff Commn. Higher Edn., Hartford, Conn., 1966-77, dir. accreditation and scholarships, 1966-77; ret., 1977. Cons. Greater New Haven State Tech. Coll., 1977-78, Conn. Commn. Higher Edn., 1980-81; adj. prof. history So. Conn. State Coll., New Haven, 1947-49, adj. prof. econs. and labor-mgmt. rels., 1981-92, adj. prof. labor-mgmt. rels.; adj. prof. internat. rels., Eurasian affairs and history Western Conn. State Coll., Danbury, 1949-58; adj. prof. ednl. adminstrn. U. Bridgeport, Conn., 1958; adj. prof. econs. and indsl. rels. U. New Haven, West Haven, Conn., 1979-90, adj. prof. indls. rels.; adj. prof. labor-mgmt. rels., mgmt. Teikyo Post U., Waterbury, Conn., 1988-93; lectr. in field. Author: The Monetarists and the Current Crisis, 1975. Mem. North Branford (Conn.) Commn. Econ. Devel., 1980-95, chmn., 1981-95; mem. PTA. Maj. USAAF, 1942-46. Recipient Disting. Friend of Greater New Haven State Tech. Coll. award, 1984, Paul Harris Fellow, Rotary Found; named Bradford's Edn. Hall of Fame. Mem. SAR, NEA, Conn. Edn. Assn., Conn. Assn. Pub. Sch. Supts., Conn. Assn. Advancement Sch. Adminstrn., Am. Assn. Sch. Adminstrs., Yale Post-Doctoral Seminar Group (pres. 1968-69), Conn. State Employees Assn., Conn. Coun. Higher Edn. (treas. 1971-77), Am. Assn. Higher Edn., Royal Can. Geog. Soc., Numerical Control Soc., Rotary, Schoolmasters Rotary U.S. (sec.-treas. 1965-69), Am. Legion (post comdr. Easton 1948-49), China-Burma-India Vets. Assn., Exchange Club. Home: 373 Reeds Gap Rd Northford CT 06472-1106

JAMES, WILLIAM LANGFORD, aerospace engineer; b. Southampton, Va., Jan. 13, 1939; s. Leroy and Worthie (Murphy) J.; m. Elaine Cecilia Reed; children: William Jr., Terri Lynne. Student, Va. State Coll., 1956, Hampton Inst., 1958; BS, Calif. State U., Los Angeles, 1962, MS, 1964; postgrad., U. Nev., Reno, 1984; spl. engring. studies, UCLA, 1970-82. Rsch. engr. non-metallic materials lab. N.Am. Aviation, L.A., 1960-67; rsch. analyst tech. staff The Aerospace Corp., El Segundo, 1967-75, materials engr., 1975-85, project engr. program mgmt. office space launch ops., 1985-96, cons. to space ops., 1996—. Contbr. numerous articles and reports to profl. publs.; patentee in field. Recipient numerous awards for USAF space contributions. Mem. AAAS, Soc. Advancement Material and Process Engring. (vice-chmn. 1987-89). Avocations: travel, water sports, big game fishing. Home: PO Box 19735 Los Angeles CA 90019-0735 Office: Aerospace Corp M5 712 Los Angeles CA 90009

JAMES, WILLIAM MILES, instrumental music teacher; b. Panama Canal Zone, Panama, Oct. 3, 1975; s. Michael Lee and Vilma Ester James. MusB Edn., Nicholls State Univesity, Thibodaux, La., 2000; MusM Edn., U. So. Miss., Hattiesburg, 2001. La. Tchg. Cert., Type B La., Instrumental K-12, 429115, 2001. Instrumental music tchr. Patterson HS, La., 2001—02, New Iberia Sr. HS, La., 2002—04, South Terrebonne HS, Bourg, La., 2004—. Grad. assistantship U. So. Miss., Hattiesburg, La., 2000—01; student tchr. Acadiana HS, Lafayette, La., 2001. Recipient Outstanding Instrumental Music Maj., Dept. Performing Arts, Nicholls State U., 1997-1998, Nicholls Honor Student, NSU Alumni Fedn., 1999, 2000, 1998, 1997, Tchr. of Month, New Iberia Sr. HS, 2003; scholar Thad and Gerry Waites Scholarship, Coll. of Arts, U. So. Miss., 2000-2001; James and Eileen Simrall Scholarship, USM Found., 2000-2001. Mem.: La. Music Educators Assn., Dist. VII Band Directors Assn., Nat. Band Assn., Music Educators Nat. Conf., Phi Mu Alpha Sinfonia Frat. Am. Office Phone: 985-868-7828.

JAMES, WILLIAM OWEN, lawyer; b. Great Falls, Mont., Jan. 29, 1965; s. William Owen and Ina Rae James; m. Patricia Ann James, Aug. 19, 1989; children: William, Trevor, Blair. BSBA in Fin. and Banking, U. Ark., 1991; JD, U. Ark., Little Rock, 1994. Bar: Ark., U.S. Dist. Ct. (ea. and we. dists.) Ark., U.S. Ct. Appeals (8th cir.). Prin. James Law Firm, Little Rock, 1994—. Author: (weekly column) View from the Cheap Seats, 2002—. Chmn. cmty. housing adv. bd. City of Little Rock, 2003—. Named Outstanding New Lawyer, Ark. Trial Lawyers Assn., 1996; named one of Best Lawyers in Ark., Ark. Times, 2000, 2002, 40 Under 40, Ark. Bus., 2004; recipient Pres.'s award, Pulaski County Bar Assn., 1996, 2003. Mem.: Ark. Assn. Criminal Def. Lawyers (charter mem., pres.'s award 1999), Nat. Assn. Criminal Def. Lawyers (life). Avocation: golf. Office: James Law Firm 221 W 2d #800 Little Rock AR 72201 Office Phone: 501-375-0900. Office Fax: 501-375-1356. Business E-Mail: wmjamesjr@aol.com.

JAMES, WILLIAM RAMSAY, broadcast executive; b. South Bend, Ind., Oct. 6, 1933; s. William Stubbs and Rose (Ramsay) James; m. Jane Mehrer, Dec. 29, 1955; children: William Harold, Martha Courtney Quay. BS in Mech. Engring., Princeton U., 1955; MBA, Harvard U., 1960. CPA Mich. Plant mgr. N. A. Woodworth Co., Ferndale, Mich., 1960-62; ptnr. Touche Ross & Co., Detroit, 1962-69; v.p., gen. mgr. Sta. WJR, Detroit, 1969-80; exec. v.p. Capital Cities Comm., N.Y.C., 1980-86, pres. Cable TV div. Bloomfield Hills, Mich., 1980-86; pres. James Comm. Inc., 1986-87; mng. ptnr. James Comm. Ptnrs., Bloomfield Hills, 1988—. Trustee, treas. William Beaumont Hosp., Royal Oak, Mich. 1st lt. USAF, 1956—58. Mem.: AICPA, Mich. Assn. CPAs, Everglades Club (Palm Beach, Fla.), Orchard Lake (Mich.) Country Club, Country Club (Bloomfield Hills). Republican. Episcopalian. Office: James Communications Ptnrs 6150 Highland Rd Waterford MI 48327 Office Phone: 248-647-1080. Personal E-mail: wrjames@netcommander.com.

JAMES, WILLIAM W., financial consultant; b. Oct. 12, 1931; s. Will and Clyde (Cowdrey) James; m. Carol Ann Muenter, June 17, 1967; children: Sarah James Banks, David William. AB, Harvard U., 1953. Cert. trust and fin. advisor. Asst. to dir. overseas divsn. Becton Dickinson & Co., Rutherford, NJ, 1956-59; stockbroker Merrill Lynch, Pierce, Fenner & Smith, Inc., St. Louis, 1959-62; with trust divsn. Boatmen's Nat. Bank, St. Louis, 1962-90, v.p. in charge estate planning, sr. v.p., 1972-90; sr. v.p. Boatmen's Trust Co., St. Louis, 1989-96, fin., trust mktg. cons., 1996—. Mem. gift and bequest coun. Barnes Hosp., St. Louis, 1963—67, St. Louis U., 1972—78; dir. Mark Twain Summer Inst., St. Louis, 1987—92. With U.S. Army, 1953—55. Mem.: Am. Inst. Banking, Mo. Bankers Assn., Estate Planning Coun. St. Louis, Harvard Alumni Assn. (bd. dirs. 1987—90), Noonday Club (St. Louis), Mo. Athletic Club, Harvard Faculty Club (Cambridge, Mass.), Harvard Club St. Louis (pres. 1972—73). Republican. Home: 1415 Michele Dr Saint Louis MO 63122-1404

JAMES-DUNSTON, JANET RENÉE, orchestral music teacher, composer, flutist; b. NYC, Mar. 8, 1954; d. John Wesley and Dorothy Alma (Dorrell) James. BA in Music Edn., Bklyn. Coll., 1976; MA in Music Edn., NYU, 1979; profl. diploma in Ednl. Adminstrn., L.I. U., 1995. Cert. sch. dist. adminstr., N.Y., cert. in orchestral music, N.Y.C., cert. tchr. elem. and secondary schs., N.Y.C. Orchestral music tchr. N.Y.C. Pub. Schs., Bklyn., 1979—. Grantee for jazz composition B.M.I. Jazz Composer's Workshop, N.Y.C., 1995-97. Mem. Duke Ellington Soc., Music Educators Nat. Conf., Internat. Assn. Jazz Educators, Phi Delta Kappa, Kappa Delta Phi. Avocation: travel. Home: 301 Cathedral Pkwy Apt 12D New York NY 10026-4064 Office: 111 Bristol St PS 327 Brooklyn NY 11212

JAMESON, GENE LANIER, lawyer; b. Dallas, Jan. 18, 1936; s. Joseph Andrew and Minnie (Kittrell) J.; m. Lois Marie Shanahan, July 19, 1958; children: Holly, Scott. BA in Econs., Tex. A&M, 1958; LLB, U. Tex., 1966. Bar: Tex. 1966, U.S. Supreme Ct. 1975, U.S. Ct. Appeals (5th and 11th cirs.) 1981. Assoc. Stubbeman, et al, Midland, Tex., 1966-69; staff atty. 1st Nat. Bank Dallas/1st Internat. Bankshares, 1969-77; assoc. Coke & Coke, Dallas, 1977-79, ptnr., 1979-84, Jones, Day, Reavis & Pogue, Dallas, 1984-91; dir. Donohoe, Jameson & Carroll, P.C., Dallas, 1991—2001; of counsel Winstead Sechrest & Minick, PC, 2001—. Served to capt. U.S. Army, 1958-63. Home: 10433 Strait Ln Dallas TX 75229-6537 Office: Winstead Sechrest & Minick PC Ste 5400 1201 Elm St Dallas TX 75270 E-mail: gjameson@winstead.com .

JAMESON, J(AMES) LARRY, chemical company executive; b. Elizabethtown, Ky., 1937; s. William Kendrick and Ruth Helen (Krause) J.; m. Mary Louise Wojcik, June 26, 1965; children: Renee, Jennifer, Julie. BA in Math., Bellarmine Coll., 1959; BS in Chem. Engring., U. Detroit, 1963, MBA, 1970. Tech. mgr. automotive products Rinshed Mason et Cie, Paris, 1965-69; ops. mgr. vinyl coated fabrics Inmont Corp., Toledo, 1969-75, v.p., gen. mgr. European ops. London, 1975-79, v.p., gen. mgr. automotive finishes products Detroit, 1979-83, sr. v.p. worldwide automotive, 1983-86; pres. Coatings & Colorants div. BASF, Clifton, N.J., 1986-93; pres., CEO Pirelli Cable Corp., Florham Park, N.J., 1993-96; v.p. Ferro Chem. Corp., Cleve., 1996—. Mem. Soc. Automotive Engrs., Orchard Lake Country Club, The Country Club. Avocations: golf, tennis, skiing, hunting. Office: Ferro Corp 1000 Lakeside Ave E Cleveland OH 44114-1147

JAMESON, JAMES LARRY, medical educator, endocrinologist, internist; b. Fort Benning, Georgia, June 21, 1954; MD, U. North Carolina, Chapel Hill, 1981. Cert. NBME, 1982, Am. Bd. Internal Medicine, 1985, Endocrinology & Metabolism, 1987. Intern Mass. Gen. Hospital, Boston, 1981—82, resident, 1982—83, fellow, 1983—85; rsch. assoc. Howard Hughes Medical Inst., Boston, 1985—87; asst. physician Mass. Gen. Hospital, Boston, 1987—92, chief thyroid unit, 1987—93; asst. prof. Harvard Medical Sch., Boston, 1987—92, assoc. prof., 1992—93; dir. molecular biology Mass. Gen. Hospital, Boston, 1991—93, assoc. physician, 1992—93; dir. endocrinology & metabolism Northwestern U., 1993, Irving S. Cutter prof. medicine div. endocrinology, metabolism, & molecular medicine, 1993—, chmn. medicine, 1993—. Fellow: Am. Acad. Arts & Sciences. Office: Northwestern U Galter Pavilion Ste 3-150 251 E Huron St Chicago IL 60611

JAMESON, PATRICIA MARIAN, government agency administrator; b. Pitts., Mar. 17, 1945; d. Vernon L. and Dorothy Leam (Wilson) J. BA, Northwestern U., 1967; MA, Ohio State U., 1969. With HUD, 1970-2000, project mgr. Detroit, 1976-77, acting dir. housing mgmt., 1978, dep. area mgr. Milw. Area Office, 1978-85, acting area mgr., 1979-80, 82, regional dir. adminstrn. Chgo. Regional Office, 1985-95, dir. adminstrv. svc. ctr. Denver, 1995-2000, ret., 2000. Vol. ARC, Sierra Club; active Denver World Affairs Coun., Internat. Inst. for Edn.; vol. Habitat for Humanity; vol. tax aide program AARP; vol. Project C.U.R.E. Recipient Quality Performance award HUD, 1973, 75, 80, Outstanding Performance award, 1980, 85, 87, 88, 90, 91, 92, 94, 96, 97, 98, 99, 2000, Disting. Svc. award 1992, 2000, Secs. award for Supervisory Excellence, 1998. Mem. NAFE, Fed. Execs. Inst. Alumni Assn., Phi Beta Kappa, Pi Sigma Alpha.

JAMESON, PAUL WRIGHT, lawyer, consultant; b. Evanston, Ill., July 13, 1951; s. John Hulbert Jameson and Barbara Broadhurst Adler; m. Carol Graham Graham, May 5, 1984; children: Nora Elizabeth, Morgan Wright. BA, U. Pitts., 1973, MA, 1976; JD, Georgetown U., 1979. Bar: D.C. 1979. Assoc. Stewart & Stewart, Washington, 1979—84; atty. Schagrin Assocs., Washington, 1985—2001, Hale and Dorr, LLP, Washington, 1991—2002; pres. Jameson Internat., Vienna, Va., 2002—. Mem.: No. Va. Tech. Coun. (biomedtech com., internat. com. 2000). Democrat. Avocations: rock climbing, wine tasting. Home Fax: n/a. Personal E-mail: paul@jameson-international.com.

JAMESON, PAULA ANN, retired lawyer; b. New Orleans, Feb. 19, 1945; d. Paul Henry and Virginia Lee (Powell) Bailey; children: Paul Andrew, Peter Carver. BA, La. State U., 1966; JD, U. Tex., 1969. Bar: Tex. 1969, D.C. 1970, U.S. Dist. Ct. D.C. 1970, U.S. Ct. Appeals (D.C. cir.) 1972, Va. 1973, U.S. Supreme Ct. 1973, U.S. Dist. Ct. (ea. dist.) Va. 1976, U.S. Ct. Appeals (4th cir.) 1976, N.Y. 1978, U.S. Ct. Appeals (5th cir.) 1978, U.S. Ct. Appeals (2d cir.) 1985. Asst. corp. counsel D.C. Corp. Counsel's Office, 1970-73; sr. asst. county atty. Fairfax County Atty.'s Office, Fairfax, Va., 1973-77; atty. Dow Jones & Co., Inc., N.Y.C., 1977-79, ho. counsel, 1979-81, asst. to chmn. bd., 1981-83, ho. counsel, dir. legal dept., 1983-86; sr. v.p., gen. counsel, corp. sec. PBS, Alexandria, Va., 1986-98; ptnr. Arter & Hadden, Washington, 1998-2000; v.p., gen. counsel Gibson Guitar Corp., Nashville, 2000-01; pres. Jameson Legal & Cons. Svcs., McLean, Va., 2000—03; exec. v.p., COO Children's Def. Fund., Washington, 2003—04; ret., 2004. Mem.: D.C. Bar Assn., Fed. Comms. Bar Assn. Democrat. Roman Catholic. Personal E-mail: paulajameson@att.net.

JAMGOCHIAN, VICTORIA, interior designer; b. Richmond, Va., Apr. 18, 1922; d. John A. and Azniv (Marsevonian) Jamgochian. BS in Psychology, Coll. William and Mary, 1946; cert. interior design and architecture, Parsons Sch. Design, N.Y.C., France, Italy, 1955. Cert. comml., residential and office interior designer. Asst. interior designer McMillen, Inc., N.Y.C., 1955-56, Lord and Taylor, N.Y.C., 1956-57; interior designer J. Frank Jones Interiors, Richmond, 1957-61, Miller & Rhoads, Richmond, 1961-67, Thalhimer's Indsl. Design, Richmond, 1967-79; exec. dir. design Chasen's Bus. Interiors, Richmond, 1979—2001. Projects pub. in Hospitality Mag., 1967, Interiors Mag., 1968, 69, Va. Record, 1971. Interior designer (prin. works) Country Club of Va., The Woman's Club, Richmond, Va., Busch Gardens Hospitality Ctr., Williamsburg, Va., Pres.'s House, U. Richmond, Richmond Meml. Hosp., Va. Bapt. Hosp., Lynchburg, Engineer's Club, Richmond, Rotunda Club, Hilton Hotel, Wilmington, NC, Wachovia, Richmond, Chemtreat, Inc., Cascades Restaurant and Meeting Ctr., Woodlands, Colonial Williamsburg, Inc. Mem.: William and Mary Alumni Soc., Kappa Delta. Avocations: tennis, travel, horseback riding, piano. Home: 211 Sleepy Hollow Rd Richmond VA 23229-7153

JAMIESON, GRAHAM A., biochemist, researcher, retired organization official; b. Wellington, New Zealand, Aug. 14, 1929; came to U.S., 1956; s. Andrew Wilson and Nan (Graham) J.; m. Barbara MacLachlan, Feb. 20, 1960; 1 child, Brian. BSc, U. Otago, 1949; MSc with first class honors in Organic Chemistry, U. New Zealand, 1951; PhD Lister Inst. Preventive Medicine, U. London, 1954, DSc, 1972. Research fellow dept. biochemistry Cornell U., N.Y.C., 1956; research biochemist Am. Nat. Red Cross, Bethesda, Md., 1961-64, asst. dir. research, 1964-69, dir. research, 1969-78, assoc. dir. blood services, 1978-84, sr. scientist, 1984—. Vis. scientist NIH, 1957-61, mem. exptl. hematology study sect., 1978-84; lectr. biochemistry Georgetown U., Washington, 1961, professorial lectr., 1966-74, adj. prof., 1974-96; Winzler Meml. lectr. U. Fla., 1975; mem. adv. com. on blood preservation and substitutes U.S. Army Med. Rsch. and Devel. Command, 1980-92, chmn., 1981-92; vis. prof. U. Sao Paulo, Brazil, 1992, U. Barcelona, Spain, 1993. Editor: (with T.J. Greenwalt) Red Cell Membrane-Structure and Function, 1969, Formation and Destruction of Blood Cells, 1970, Glycoproteins of Blood Cells and Plasma, 1971, The Human Red Cell In Vitro, 1974, Transmissible Disease and Blood Transfusion, 1975, Trace Components of Plasma-Isolation and Clinical Significance, 1976, The Granulocyte: Function and Clinical Utilization, 1977, The Blood Platelet in Transfusion Therapy, 1978, (with D.M. Robinson) Mammalian Cell Membranes, Vol. I, 1978—, Generalizations and Methodology, Vol. II, 1978—, The Diversity of Membranes, Vol. III, 1978—, Surface Membranes of Specific Cell Types, Vol. IV, 1978—, Membranes and Cellular Functions, Vol. V, 1978—, Responses of Plasma Membranes; Interaction of Platelets and Tumor Cells, 1982, Platelet Membrane Receptors: Molecular Biology Immunology, Biochemistry and Pathology, 1988; mem. editorial bds. Thrombosis Rsch., 1978-81, Thrombosis Haemostas, 1989—, Internat. Jour. Hematology, 1989—, Blood, 1996—; contbr. articles to profl. jours. Sir George Grey scholar U. New Zealand., 1951, U. Otago 50; John Edmond fellow. Fellow AAAS; mem. Am. Soc. Biol. Chemists, Am. Chem. Soc., Biochem. Soc. (London), Internat. Soc. Thrombosis and Hemostasis (Shirley Johnson award 1997), N.Y. Acad. Scis., Am. Heart Assn. (exec. com., council on thrombosis), Am. Soc. Hematology, Soc. Exptl. Biology and Medicine, Soc. for Complex Carbohydrates (exec. com.) Home: 5622 Johnson Ave Bethesda MD 20817-3504 E-mail: Jamieson_Graham@msn.com.

JAMIESON, JAMES M., manufacturing executive; b. Billings; m. Marie Jamieson; 3 children. BS in Humanities, MIT, 1970, MSCE, 1978. Dir. aircraft interiors Boeing, v.p., gen. mgr. 737-757 programs; exec. v.p. single aisle airplane programs Boeing Comml. Airplanes, sr. v.p. airplane programs; chief project engr. 757 Boeing, 1994—95; sr. v.p., chief tech. officer The Boeing Co., Chgo., 2003—. Boeing exec. focal MIT; chmn. Historically Black Colls. and Univs.; bd. dirs. Pacific Sci. Ctr. Mem.: AIAA. Office: Boeing 100 N Riverside Chicago IL 60606

JAMIESON, JOHN EDWARD, JR., social services administrator, minister; b. Philadelphia, Pa., Mar. 5, 1945; s. John Edward and Frances (Hayes) J.; m. Marilyn T. Haws, June 8, 1968; children: Douglas Stuart, Heather Lynn, Mark Stuart. BA, U. Pa., 1967; MDiv, Ref. Episcopal Sem., Phila., 1970; PhD, Christian Bible Coll., Rocky Mount, N.C., 1990. Ordained to ministry Ref. Episcopal Ch., 1970, Bapt. Ch., 1978. Pastor Trinity Ref. Episcopal Ch., Phila., 1970-73, St. Mark's Ref. Episcopal Ch., Miami, Fla., 1973-75, Hammonton (N.J.) Bapt. Ch., 1978-81; supr. Nepaug Christian Acad., New Hartford, Conn., 1976-78; coord. ops. emergency med. svcs. div. AID Ambulance Svc., Atlantic City, 1982-83; paramedic mobile ICU, West Jersey Health, Camden, N.J., 1983-88; dir. pastoral care Atlantic City Med. Ctr., 1988—2003, dir. patient support, 2003—. Pastor Grace Bible Chapel, Ocean City, N.J., 1988-95; min. pastoral care Cornerstone Ministries, Ocean City, 2000-02; vice chmn. instnl. med. ethics com. Atlantic City Med. Ctr., 1988-96, co-chair, 1996—. Editor Bibl. Bioethics, 1990. Chaplain Somers Point (N.J.) Vol. Rescue Squad, 1987-96, Ocean City Fire Dept., 1995—; bd. dirs. Atlantic County unit Am. Cancer Soc., Absecon, N.J., 1988-90, program coord. Cansurmount support program, 1988-90; bd. trustees Ctrl. Ocean City Union Chapel; exec. v.p. Reformed Bible Inst. Delaware Valley, 2000-01. Mem. Am. Assn. Christian Counselors, So. Jersey Ethics Alliance, Internat. Critical Incident Stress Found., Am. Acad. Experts in Traumatic Stress (bd. cert. expert), Fedn. Fire Chaplains. Republican. Avocations: travel, photography, reading. Office: Atlantic City Med Ctr 1925 Pacific Ave Atlantic City NJ 08401-6713 *When we concentrate our thoughts on that which is true, noble, right, pure, lovely, admirable and excellent we are lifted above the drudgery of life and open ourselves to the possibility of true greatness.*

JAMIESON, MICHAEL LAWRENCE, lawyer; b. Coral Gables, Fla., Mar. 2, 1940; s. Warren Thomas and Ruth Amelia (Gallman) J.; children: Ann Layton, Thomas Howard; m. Elizabeth Marie Peeples, Dec. 31, 1992. BA in English, U. Fla., 1961, JD with honors, 1964. Bar: Fla. 1964, U.S. Dist. Ct. (mid. dist.) Fla. 1964, D.C. 1998, N.Y. 1999. Teaching asst. U. Fla., 1964; law clk. U.S. Ct. Appeals (5th cir.), 1964-65; assoc. Holland & Knight LLP and predecessor firms, Tampa, Fla., 1965-69; ptnr. Holland & Knight and predecessor firms, Tampa, Fla., 1969—2005, chmn. bus. law dept., 1991—2003; of counsel Foley & Lardner, Tampa, 2005—. Editor-in-chief U. Fla. Law Rev., 1963; author: The Corporate Lawyer, 2004, My Life With Chesterfield Smith: America's Lawyer, 2005 Trustee Law Ctr. U. Fla., chmn. bd. dirs., 1986-88; bd. dirs., chmn. Bus. Com. for the Arts Inc., 1989-90; trustee Tampa Bay Performing Arts Ctr. Inc., 1989—, chmn. devel. coun., 1990-91; trustee Cmty. Found. Greater Tampa, 1990-97; chmn. devel. com. Fla. C. of C. Found., 1992-95; mem. Tampa Leadership Conf., Golden Triangle Civic Assn. Recipient Gertrude Brick Law Rev. award, 1963 Fellow Am. Bar Found.; mem. ABA (mem. com on corp. laws, mem. com. on fed. regulation of securities), Am. Law Inst., Hillsborough County Bar Assn., Greater Tampa C. of C. (mem. bd. govs. 1988-91), Com. 100 (mem. policy bd. 1989-92, trustee 1998—), Univ. Club, Tampa Club (bd. dirs. 1985-89, pres. 1987-88), The Down Town Assn., Order of Coif, Phi Kappa Phi. Office: Foley and Lardner 100 N Tampa St Ste 2700 Tampa FL 33602-3644 Office Phone: 813-225-4114. Business E-Mail: mjamieson@foley.com.

JAMIESON, STUART WILLIAM, surgeon, educator; b. Bulawayo, Rhodesia, July 30, 1947; came to U.S., 1977; MB, BS, U. London, 1971. Intern St. Mary's Hosp., London, 1971; resident St. Mary's Hosp., Northwick Park Hosp., Brompton Hosp., London, 1972-77; asst. prof. Stanford U., Calif., 1980-83, assoc. prof., 1983-86; prof., head cardiac surgery U. Minn., Mpls., 1986-89, U. Calif., San Diego, 1989—. Dir. Minn. Heart and Lung Inst., Mpls., 1986-89; pres. Calif. Heart and Lung Inst., San Diego, 1991-95. Co-author: Heart and Heart-Lung Transplantation, 1989; editor: Heart Surgery, 1987; contbr. over 600 papers to med. jours. Recipient Brit. Heart Found. Fellowship award, 1978, Irvine H. Page award Am. Heart Found., 1979, Silver medal Danish Surg. Soc., 1986. Fellow ACS, Royal Coll. Surgeons, Royal Soc. Medicine, Am. Coll. Chest Physicians, Am. Coll. Cardiology; mem. Royal Coll. Physicians (licentiate), Internat. Soc. for Heart Transplantation (pres. 1986-88), Calif. Heart and Lung Inst. (pres. 1991—), Internat. Soc. Cardiothoracic Surgery (pres. 2003-). Office: U Calif Divsn Cardiothoracic Surgery 200 W Arbor Dr San Diego CA 92103-8892

JAMIL, HIKMET J., medical educator, researcher; s. Jamil Raouf Jamil and Bidour Hanna Jwaideh; m. Raja G. Yaldo, Feb. 16, 1968; children: Laith Hikmet, Sada Hikmet Yaldo, Mada Hikmet, Nada Hikmet. MD, U. of Baghdad, Iraq, 1962; Diploma Indsl. Health, The Royal Coll. of Physicans of London, 1975; MSc. in Occupl. Medicine, U. of London, 1975; PhD, U. of Manchester, Eng., 1978. Lic. physician Iraq, 1962, Jordan, 1995. Prof. of occupl. and environ. medicine, Coll. of Medicine, U. of Baghdad, 1978—96; program dir. / cmty. medicine residency program Coll. of Medicine, U. of Baghdad, 1979—96; prof., assoc. dir. occupl. and environmental medicine residency program Dept. of Family Medicine, Wayne State U., Detroit,

2002—, dir. OEM rotation course, 1999—; health cons. ACCESS / Arab Cmty. Health & Rsch. Ctr., Dearborn, Mich., 1997—2005; with Arab Am. and Chaldean Coun., Southfield, Mich., 2005—. Adj. faculty Dept. Occupl. and Environ. Health Sciences, Coll. of Pharmacy and Allied Health Professions Wayne State U., Detroit, 1998—; lectr. and presenter internat. confs. Author: Occupational Health, 1981, Occupational Safety, 1985, Occupational Health and Safety, 1990, 18 others; contbr. more than 108 articles to profl. jours. Officer Med. Corps, 1962—63, Iraq Mil. Recipient Priniciipal Investigator / Rsch. Project award, Ctr. for Victims of Torture, Minn., 2002; grantee Principal Investigator / Rsch. Project grantee, Pfizer Corp., 2004. Fellow: Royal Coll. Physicians Ireland; mem.: Internat. Soc. Iraqi Scientists (pres. 2002—05), Chaldean Am. Assn. for Health Profls. (assoc.; mich. usa 2001—05). Home: 6530 Post Oak Dr West Bloomfield MI 48322 Office: Wayne State University 15400 W McNichols Detroit MI 48235 Office Phone: 313-340-4341. Office Fax: 313-493-9387. Personal E-mail: hjamil@med.wayne.edu.

JAMIN, MATTHEW DANIEL, lawyer, judge; b. New Brunswick, N.J., Nov. 29, 1947; s. Matthew Bernard and Frances Marie (Newburg) J.; m. Christine Frances Bjorkman, June 28, 1969; children: Rebecca, Erica. BA, Colgate U., 1969; JD, Harvard U., 1974. Bar: Alaska 1974, U.S. Dist. Ct. Alaska 1974, U.S. Ct. Appeals (9th cir.) 1980. Staff atty. Alaska Legal Svcs., Anchorage, 1974-75, supervising atty. Kodiak, Alaska, 1975-81; contract atty. Pub. Defender's Office State of Alaska, Kodiak, 1976-82; prin. Matthew D. Jamin, Atty., Kodiak, 1982; ptnr. Jamin & Bolger, Kodiak, 1982-85, Jamin, Ebell, Bolger & Gentry, Kodiak, 1985-97; part-time magistrate judge U.S. Cts., Kodiak, 1984—; shareholder Jamin, Ebell, Schmitt & Mason, Kodiak, 1998—. Part-time instr. U. Alaska Kodiak Coll., 1975—; active Theshold Svcs., Inc., Kodiak, 1985—, pres., 1985-92, 95-96, 99-2000. Mem. Alaska Bar Assn. (Professionalism award 1988), Kodiak Bar Assn. Office: US Dist Ct 323 Carolyn Ave Kodiak AK 99615-6348 Business E-Mail: matt@jesmkod.com.

JAMINI, DEBORAH, singer, music educator, writer, pianist; d. Denise and Marco Aaron Jamini. MusB, Mannes Coll. Music, 1984; MFA, CUNY, 1993. Tchr. piano and music theory Mannes Coll. of Music, N.Y.C., 1985—; music dir., children's choir Trevor Day Sch., 1986—90, Lucy Moses Sch., 1991—95; alto Park Ave. Synagogue Choir, 1998—2002, William Appling Singers and Orch., Poughkeepsie, 1995—2005, Cathedral of St. Patrick Schola, 2005—. Author: Harmony and Composition. Recipient First prize, BACA Bklyn. Arts Coun. Piano Competition, 1982, Prix d'excellence, Ecoles d'arts américaines, Fontainebleau, France, 1983; fellow, 1983; grantee, Mannes Coll. Music, 2003; Project grantee, New Sch. U. Faculty Fund, 2004, writing grantee, 2005. Mem.: Nat. Resource Def. Coun., Coll. Music Soc., Music Theory Soc. N.Y. State, Nat. Trust for Historic Preservation. Avocations: foreign languages, photography, video editing, dance, health/fitness. E-mail: djamini@deborahjamini.com.

JAMISON, DANIEL OLIVER, lawyer; b. Fresno, Calif., Nov. 28, 1952; s. Oliver Morton and Margaret (Ratcliffe) J.; m. Debra Suzanne Parent, May 23, 1981; 1 child, Holly Elizabeth. Student, Claremont Men's Coll., 1970—72; BA in Philosophy, U. Calif., Berkeley, 1974; JD, U. Calif., Davis, 1977. Bar: Calif. 1977, U.S. Dist. Ct. (ea. dist.) Calif. 1977, U.S. Dist. Ct. (no. dist.) Calif. 1982, U.S. Ct. Appeals (9th cir.) 1987. Law clk. to judge M.D. Crocker U.S. Dist. Ct. (ea. dist.) Calif., Fresno, 1977-78; assoc. Stammer, McKnight, Barnum & Bailey, Fresno, 1978-83, ptnr., 1983-95; shareholder Sagaser, Franson, Jamison & Jones (formerly Sagaser, Hansen, Franson & Jamison), 1995—99; pvt. practice Law Offices of Daniel O. Jamison, P.C., Fresno, 1999—. Vol. atty. Calif. H.S., Fresno, 1983-87, 89-94; mem. Assocs. of Valley Children's Hosp., Fresno, 1980-81; co-chmn. Fresno County Law Day, 1995-96; panelist for CEB Selected Issues in Employment Discrimination and Wrongful Discharge Litigation; panelist on indigent care Calif. Soc. for Healthcare Attys.; panelist Lorman Edn. Svcs. on Health Care Corp. and Physician Compliance Programs in Calif., Pres' Circle, Bulldog Found., Calif. State U., Fresno; sustaining mem. Fresno Met. Mus., corp. mem. Comty. Med. Found.; mem. Fresno Hist. Soc. Mem. ABA, Fed. Bar Assn., Fresno County Bar Assn. (spkr.), Calif. C. of C., East Dist. Hist. Soc. (charter mem.), 9th Jud. Cir. Hist. Soc., Calif. Soc. for Healthcare Attys., Am. Health Lawyers Assn. Republican. Avocations: golf, aerobics. Office: 2445 Capitol St Ste 150 Fresno CA 93721-2224 Office Phone: 559-237-0291. Business E-Mail: info@jamisonpc.com.

JAMISON, DEAN TECUMSEH, economist; b. Springfield, Mo., Oct. 10, 1943; s. Marshall Verdine and Mary Dell (Temple) J.; m. Joanne Leslie, Sept. 14, 1971 (div. 1995); children: Julian C., Eliot A., Leslie S.; m. Kin Bing Wu, Jan. 19, 1997. AB in Philosophy, Stanford U., 1966, MS in Engring. Sci., 1967; PhD in Econs., Harvard U., 1970. Asst. prof. grad. sch. bus. Stanford U., Palo Alto, Calif., 1970-73; economist World Bank, Washington, 1976-88, dir., 1992-93, advisor, 1993-98; dir. Ctr. for Pacific Rim Studies UCLA, 1993-2000, prof. Sch. Pub. Health, Grad. Sch. Edn. and Info. Studies, 1988—; dir. econs. adv. svc. WHO, Geneva, 1998-2000; fellow Fogarty Internat. Ctr., NIH, 2001—. Chmn. ad hoc com. on health R&D for developing countries WHO, Geneva, 1996-97; bd. trustees Drug Strategies, 1994—; chmn. bd. on global health Inst. Medicine NAS, 2000-2005; mem. adv. bd. Inst. Human Virology, 2001—. Author (with L. J. Lau): Farmer Education and Farm Efficiency, 1982, Disease Control Priorities in Developing Countries, 1993, World Bank World Development Report 1993: Investing in Health, 1993, WHO World Health Report 1999: Making a Difference, 1999; cons. editor AERA Ency. Rsch., 6th edit., 1992. Fellow Woodrow Wilson Found., 1967, NSF, 1968, Bill and Melinda Gates Found. fellow, 2001. Mem. Inst. Medicine Nat. Acad. Scis. Avocation: tennis. Office: Fogarty Internat Ctr NIH 16 Center Dr MSC 6705 Bethesda MD 20892-6705 Fax: (310) 206-4018. E-mail: jamisond@mail.nih.gov.

JAMISON, DOUGLAS W., venture capitalist; b. 1970; BA, Dartmouth Coll., 1992; MS, U. Utah, 1999. Sr. tech. mgr. tech. transfer office U. Utah, 1997—2002; v.p. Harris and Harris Group, Inc., NY, 2002—, mng. dir., 2004—, pres., COO, CFO, 2005—. Mem. sci. adv. bd. Chlorogen, Inc., St. Louis; mem. adv. bd. Mass. tech. Collaborative Nanotech. Venture Forum. Mem. adv. bd. Nanotechnology Law & Bus. (Jour. Attys., Entrepreneurs, and Investors small scale techs.). Mem.: IEEE, AAAS, Assn. U. Tech. Mgrs. (mem. survey stats. and metrics com.). Office: Harris & Harris Group Inc 111 W 57th St Ste 1100 New York NY 10019 also: Harris & Harris Group Inc 11150 Santa Monica Blvd Ste 1200 Los Angeles CA 90025 Business E-Mail: admin@tinytechvc.com.

JAMISON, HARRISON CLYDE, retired oil company executive; b. St. Louis, Jan. 15, 1925; s. William Clyde and Katherine Maurice (Fitzgerald) J.; m. Beverly Joy Johnson, June 26, 1946; children: Susan, David, Leslie, Daniel, Dale, Nancy, Sara BA cum laude, UCLA. Geologist Richfield Oil Corp., Bakersfield, Calif., 1950-52, Olympia, Wash., 1952-55, L.A., 1955-60, regional exploration supr., 1961-65; Alaska dist. mgr. Atlantic Richfield Co., Anchorage, 1966-69, Alaska coord. Dallas, 1969-70; mgr. govt. rels. Alyeska Pipeline Svc. Co., 1971-72; chief geologist ARCO Oil & Gas Co., Dallas, 1973-80, v.p. dist. mgr. Denver, 1981; pres. ARCO Exploration Co., Dallas, 1981-85; sr. v.p. Atlantic Richfield Co., L.A., 1981-85. Contbr. articles to profl. jours. Former bd. dirs. Tex. Rsch. League, Austin, Dallas Citizens Coun., Mex. Am. Legal Def. and Edn. Fund, Resolution Seismic Svcs. Inc., Wilmington, Del., ARCO Alaska Inc., Thomas Wilson Dibblee Jr. Geol. Found., Hospice of Bend. Fellow Geol. Soc. Am. (former chmn. bd. dirs., trustees GSA Found. 1986-88); mem. Am. Assn. Petroleum Geologists, N.W. Energy Assn. Home and Office: 37615 S Stoney Cliff Ct Tucson AZ 85739-1412

JAMISON, JAYNE, publishing executive; Grad., Penn. St. U., 1978. Advertising dir. American Health, pub.; group pub., parenthood group Gruner & Jahr USA Pub., N.Y.C., 1994—97; pub. v.p. Redbook, 1997—2003; pub., v.p. Seventeen, 2003—. Office: Seventeen Mag 1440 Broadway 13th Fl New York NY 10018 Office Phone: 212-204-4300, 917-934-6601. Office Fax: 917-934-6650.

JAMISON, JOHN CALLISON, business educator, investment banker; b. Lafayette, Ind., July 12, 1934; s. John Ruger and Sara (Callison) J.; m. Carol Ann Sansone, July 7, 1979; children: Kelly Elizabeth Supplee, Deborah Louise Jamison. BS in Indsl. Econs., Purdue U., 1956; MBA, Harvard U., 1961. Assoc. Goldman, Sachs & Co., N.Y.C., 1961-69, ptnr., 1969-82, ltd. ptnr., 1983—99; dean Sch. Bus. Adminstrn., John N. Dalton prof. bus. adminstrn. Coll. William and Mary, Williamsburg, Va., 1983-90; pres. bd., CEO The Mariners' Mus., Newport News, Va., 1991-93, trustee, 1991—2003; pres. Williamsburg Cmty. Trust, 2001—04, chmn., 2005—. Bd. govs. Purdue Found., West Lafayette, Ind., 1979-83; bd. dirs. Theatre Devel. Fund, N.Y.C., 1979-83; mem. corp. Hurricane Island Outward Bound Sch., Rockland, Maine, 1983-95; mem. vis. com. Harvard Grad. Sch. Edn., 1983-89. Lt. USN, 1956-59, PTO. Recipient Old Master award Purdue U., 1977; recipient Sagamore of Wabash award Gov. of Ind., 1982 Mem. Rotary, Beta Gamma Sigma Episcopalian. E-mail: mallardee@aol.com.

JAMISON, JUDITH, dancer; b. Phila., May 10, 1943; d. John Jamison. Student, Fisk U., Phila., Phila. Dance Acad. (now U. of Arts); studied with, Anthony Tudor, John Hines, Delores Brown, John Jones, Joan Kerr, Madame Swaboda. Dancer Alvin Alley's Am. Dance Theatre, N.Y.C., 1965-80; artistic dir. Alvin Ailey's Am. Dance Theatre, N.Y.C., 1990—; dancer, choreographer touring U.S., Europe, Asia, S.Am., Africa, 1980—; formerly with Maurice Hines Dance Sch., N.Y.C.; founder Jamison Project, 1988-91. Vis. disting. prof. U. Arts; guest assoc. artistic dir. 30th ann. tour Alvin Ailey's Am. Dance Theatre, 1990—; guest appearances Harkness Ballet, Am. Ballet Theatre, San Francisco Ballet, Dallas Ballet. Dancer debut Agnes DeMille's The Four Marys, 1965, (Broadway plays) Joseph's Legend, Vienna Opera, Le Spectre de la Rose, Brussels, Paris, N.Y.C., Maskela Language, 1969, Cry, 1971, Choral Dance, 1971, Mary Lou's Mass, 1971, The Lark Ascending, 1972, The Mooche, 1975, Passage, 1978, (Broadway plays) Sophisticated Ladies, 1980, choreographer Divining Hymn for Alvin Ailey Am. Dance Theatre, works for Maurice Bejart, Dancers Unltd., Dallas, Washington Ballet, Jennifer Muller/The Works, Alvin Ailey Repertory Ensemble, Ballet Nuevo Mundo de Caracas, Riverside for Alvin Ailey Am. Dance Theatre, (Operas) Boito's Mefistofele, Opera Co. Phila.; author: Dancing Spirit, 1993. Recipient Dance Mag. award, 1972, Key to City, N.Y.C., 1976, Spirit of Achievement award Nat. Women's Divsn., Yeshiva U. Albert Einstein Coll. Medicine, 1992, Golden Plate award, Am. Acad. Achievement, 1993. Address: Alvin Ailey Am Dance Theater 211 W 61st St Fl 3 New York NY 10023-7832

JAMISON, PEGGY LOUISE, elementary school educator; b. Hamilton, Ohio, May 13, 1951; d. Thomas Patrick and Rita Frances (Kelly) Glynn; m. Steven Charles Jamison, Dec. 29, 1979; children: Christopher, Kevin. BA in Speech Comm., Marquette U., 1973; elem. cert., Miami U., Oxford, Ohio, 1976; MEd in Reading, Xavier U., 1980. Cert. tchr., Ohio. Elem. tchr. St. Richard's Sch., Cin., 1976-77; reading tchr., tutor Princeton Jr. High Sch., Cin., 1978-79; elem. tchr., reading dept. coord. Fairfield (Ohio) Mid. Sch., 1979-1984, Eng. tchr. Mem. NEA, Ohio Edn. Assn., Fairfield Classroom Tchrs. Assn. Avocations: music, photography, sailing, quilting. Home: 16 Carrie Cir Oxford OH 45056-9203 Office: Fairfield City Schs 1111 Nilles Rd Fairfield OH 45014-3006

JAMISON, PHILIP, artist; b. Phila., July 3, 1925; s. Philip Duane and Daisy (McCadden) J.; m. Jane B. Gray, Oct. 11, 1950; children: Philip Duane III, Terry Jane, Linda B. Student, Phila. Mus. Sch. Art, 1946-50. Instr. Phila. Coll. Art, 1961-63. Author: Capturing Nature in Watercolor, 1980, Making Your Paintings Work, 1984, A Painting Without Spirit is Like Flat Beer, 1988, I Hate People Who Refer to Works of Art as "Pieces!", 1995; one-man shows Hirschl & Adler Galleries, N.Y.C., 1959, 63, 65, 67, 69, 71, 74, 76, 80, Sessler Gallery, Phila., 1963, 72, Duke U., 1969, Del. Art Mus., 1973, Janet Fleisher Gallery, Phila., 1977, Grand Gallery, Wilmington, Del., 1977, Whistler's Daughter Gallery, Basking Ridge, N.J., 1981, Newman Galleries, Bryn Mawr, Pa., 1982, 84, 86, 88, 90, 93, Patricia Carega Gallery, Washington, 1985, 87, Ruthven Gallery, Lancaster, Ohio, 1986, Hahn Gallery, Phila., 1998, 2002; represented in permanent collections Pa. Acad. Fine Arts, NAD, Wilmington Soc. Fine Arts, U. Del., Boston Mus. Fine Arts, Nat. Air and Space Mus., Washington, Brandywine River Mus., Pa., others; NASA artist for Apollo-Soyuz, for Space Shuttle Mission 51-G, 1985. Served with USNR, 1943-46. Recipient Dawson medal Pa. Acad. Fine Arts, 1959, 77, Dana medal, 1961, first award Nat. Arts Club, N.Y.C., 1961; Lena A. Mason prize NAD, 1962, Samuel Finley Breese Morse medal NAD, 1969, Walter Biggs Meml. award NAD, 1982, William Church Osborn prize Am. Watercolor Soc., 1961, 79, medal of Honor Knickerbocker Artists, N.Y.C., 1961, Bainbridge award Allied Artists Am., 1958, 60, first prize Wilmington Soc. Fine Arts, 1957, 59, 61, M.W. Zimmerman Meml. prize Phila. Watercolor Club, 1963, Gold medal honor Allied Artists Am., 1964, Childe Hassam Fund purchase prize AAAL, 1965; C.F.S. award, 1966, Edgar A. Whitney award, 1971, High Winds award, 1972, Whitney award, 1973; Ted Kautzky Meml. award, 1974, Ranger Fund purchase prize NAD, 1962, prize, 1967, Alfred Easton Poor award, 1999, Zella W. Pike award, 2003, Pike prize, 2003; Adolph and Clara Obrig award, 1974, Thornton Oakley Meml. prize Phila. Watercolor Club, 1967, Gold medal Franklin Mint Gallery Am. Art, 1974, Merit award Nat. Watercolor Exhbn., Springfield (Ill.) Art Assn., 1979, Mem. N.A.D. (academician), Am. Watercolor Soc. (Lily Saportas award 1965, Mary S. Litt medal 1978, Larry Quackenbush Meml. award 1982, Edgar A. Whitney award 1984, Dale Meyers Cooper medal 1985, Bronze medal of honor 1994, Saunders/Waterford award, 1996), Phila. Water Color Club (Dawson Meml. prize 1977, George Gansworth Meml. prize 1981).

JAMISON, ROGER W., pianist, piano educator; b. Marion, Ohio, June 18, 1937; s. Harold Theodore and Martha Louise (Haas) J.; m. Caroline R. Hansley, Jan. 26, 1957; children: Lisa Renee, Eric Karl. BS, Ohio State U., 1959, MA (scholar), 1961; postgrad. Oberlin Conservatory, Oakland U.; student George Haddad, Columbus, Ohio, Mischa Kottler, Detroit. Piano faculty mem. Detroit Conservatory of Music, 1964-68, Cranbrook Schs., Bloomfield Hills, Mich., 1981-84; performer in one-man mus. presentation Spirits of Great Composers, 1979—; dir. music Birmingham Temple, Farmington Hills, Mich., 1984-95; soloist Brunch with Bach series Detroit Inst. Arts., Detroit Symphony Orch.'s Internat. Brahms Festival; regular soloist Christ Ch., Cranbrook, 1982-95; concert tour of Eng., 1991; condr. All Ohio Piano Ensemble, 1997; cons. Royal Oak Arts Council; adjudicator Am. Coll. Musicians. Mem. Nat. Guild of Piano Tchrs. (past pres. Oakland-Macomb chpt.) Address: 173 W Heffner St Delaware OH 43015-1258

JAMMALAMADAKA, PAPA RAO, molecular biologist; b. Pedamiram, Andhra Pra, India, Aug. 10, 1952; came to U.S., 1986; s. Lakshmi Narasimha Murty and Venkata Satyavati Jammalamadaka; m. Srilakshmi S.P.P. Jammalamadaka, May 3, 1986; 1 child, Sai Teja. MSc, Madurai Kamaraj U., Madurai, 1976; MPhil, U. Hyderabad, 1979, PhD, 1985. Postdoctoral fellow Wayne State U., Detroit, 1986-89, Victoria U. of Wellington, N.Z., 1989-91; sr. postdoctoral fellow Waite Agrl. Rsch. Inst., Adelaide, South Australia, 1991-94; postdoctoral fellow Med. Coll. Ga., Augusta, 1995-99; sr. rsch. scientist Wayne State U., Detroit, 1999—. Contbr. articles to profl. jours. Avocations: reading, meditation, international travel. Office: Wayne State U Immunology and Microbiol 540 E Canfield Rm 7233 Detroit MI 48201 Home: 24467 Bethany Way Novi MI 48375-2821 E-mail: pjammala@hotmail.com.

JAMMER, LYNN REYNOLDS, physician; b. Syracuse, N.Y., Dec. 27, 1929; d. Loren H. and Patricia I. (Seely) Reynolds; m. Louis A. Jammer, Sept. 9, 1950; children: Dana, Sherry, Holly, Tad. AB, BS, Syracuse U., 1952; MEd, Trenton State U., 1972; MS in Pathology, Temple U., 1976; MD, Autonoma de Guadalajara, 1980. Intern then resident Jersey Shore Med. Ctr., Neptune, N.J., 1980-83; med. dir. Long Beach Island Med. Ctr., Ship Bottom, N.J., 1991—. Active RPIF, Washington, 1976—. Republican. Episcopalian. Avocations: microscopy, reading, gourmet cooking, travel medicine. Home: 3709 Ocean Blvd Beach Haven NJ 08008-4126

JAMPOLE, MICHAEL, music educator, composer; b. NYC, Jan. 12, 1953; s. Sidney and Anita Prager Jampole; m. Jane Hutten, Dec. 30, 1979; 1 child, Jaime Kikpole. MusB in Edn., Northwestern U., 1973; MS in Edn., No. Ill. U., 1983. Music Teaching, grades K-12 State of Ill., 1973, Classroom Teaching, grades K-9 State of Ill., 1984. Band dir. Wilmette (Ill.) Pub. Schools, 1974—, chair dept. music, 1995—2005; band dir. Rockford (Ill.) Pub. Schools, Rockford, 1973. Condr., musician, Beach Park, Ill., 1969—; composer, arranger, Beach Park, 1970—; clinician, lectr., Beach Park, 1995—. Contbr. First Lessons on Each Instrument, The Instrumentalist, The Creative Band and Orchestra, First Lessons on Eath Instrument. Vol. Northwestern U. Sch. of Music, Evanston, Ill., 1993—; mem. Waukegan (Ill.) Mcpl. Band. Mem.: NEA, Ill. Edn. Assn., Am. Sch. Band Dirs. Assn., Music Educators Nat. Conf., Ill. Music Educators Assn. (Cert. Outstanding Service 2000), Northwestern U. Marching Band Alumni. Democrat. Avocations: guitar, singing, computers. Office: Wilmette Public Schools 569 Hunter Road Wilmette IL 60091 Business E-Mail: jampolem@wilmette39.org.

JAMRICH, JOHN XAVIER, retired university administrator; b. Muskegon Heights, Mich., June 12, 1920; s. John and Mary (Mudry) J.; m. June Ann Hrupka, June 26, 1944; children: June Ann, Marna Mary, Barbara Sue. Student, Milw. State Tchrs. Coll., 1939-40, Ripon Coll., 1940-42; BS, U. Chgo., 1942-43; MS, Marquette U., 1946-48; PhD, Northwestern U., 1951; LHD (hon.), No. Mich. U., 1968. Instr. math. Marquette U., 1946-48; asst. instr. math. U. Wis., 1948-49; asst. dean men Northwestern U., 1949-51; dean students Coe Coll., Cedar Rapids, Iowa, 1951-55; dean faculty, prof. math. Doane Coll., Crete, Nebr., 1955-57; assoc. dir. Legis. Survey Higher Edn. in Mich., 1957-58; prof. higher edn., dir. Center for Study Higher Edn., Mich. State U., 1957-63, assoc. dean Coll. Edn., prof. higher edn., 1963-68; pres. No. Mich. U., 1968-83, adj. prof., 1983—. Cons.-examiner N. Central Assn. Colls. and Secondary Schs., 1962—; cons. in field, 1959—; Ford Found. cons. for devel. U. Nigeria, 1964; cons. higher edn. Govt. of Thailand, 1967; dir. Lake Superior & Ishpeming R.R.; chmn. Nat. Adv. Council Fin. Aid to Students, 1975 Author numerous articles in field; co-author several books; piano and vocal music composer. Bd. dirs. Mich. Joint Council on Econ. Edn., 1977—; trustee Marquette (Mich.) Gen. Hosp.; bd. dirs. Bay Cliff Health Camp, Marquette; mem. Mich. Council for Arts, 1969-73; vol. pianist Mayo Clinic, 2004- Served to capt. USAAF, 1942—46. Decorated Order Lion Finland; recipient City of Peace award (Israel), World War II Victory medal Russian Govt., 1997, Disting. Svc. medal U.S. Dept. Army, 1983. Mem. Newcomen Soc. N.Am. Home: 13971 Croton Ct Jacksonville FL 32224

JAN, CHWU-CHING HWANG, environmental chemistry consultant; b. Taipei, Taiwan, July 10, 1956; d. Chau-Ching and Hsiu-Mei (Lin) Huang; m. Deng-Yang Jan; 1 child, Avery. BS, Nat. Cheng-Kung U., 1978; MBA, U. Chgo., 1995; PhD, Ohio State U., 1986. Rsch. asst. Nat. Sci. Found., Taipei, Taiwan, 1978-79; lab. mgr. Nat. Tsing Hua U., Hsinchu, Taiwan, 1979-81; sr. rsch. chemist UOP, Des Plaines, Ill., 1986-92; cons. IRIS DC Inc., Elk Grove Village, Ill., pres., 1993—. Advisor tech. CASDAY Co., Ltd., Hsinchu, Taiwan, 1993—. Contbr. articles to profl. jours. including Jour. Electro.-analytical Chem., Interfacial Electrochem., Analytical Chemistry. Mem.: Am. Chem. Soc. (Internat. Student grant 1985). Achievements include patents for hydrotreating processes for organic and halogenerated organic feedsocks containing undesirable olefinic and/or halogen components and/or organic materials, process for decomposing peroxide impurities in a tertiary butyl alcohol feedstock. Office: IRIS DC Inc 1644 Von Braun Trl Elk Grove Village IL 60007-3100 Office Phone: 847-891-8760. E-mail: dyccjan@aol.com.

JAN, CONCHITA T., music educator; b. Taipei, Taiwan, Apr. 15, 1941; arrived in U.S., 1971; BA, Towson (Md.) State U., 1982, postgrad.; cert., Royal Conservatory in Madrid, 1973. Pvt. piano tchr., 1978—; accompanist Tung-Hsin Choral Soc., Potomac, Md., 1982—90; condr. Hua Sheng Women's Chorus, Washington, 1990—98. Judge Am. Coll. Musicians, 2001—. Mem.: Md. Music Tchrs. Assn. (chmn. piano ensemble festival 1983—96, chmn. piano concerto competition 1996—2000, chmn. piano solo festival 2000—, v.p. student activities 2001—). Home: 10 Boat House Ct North Potomac MD 20878 E-mail: ctjan@yahoo.com.

JAN, GEORGE POKUNG, political science professor; b. Peking, Jan. 6, 1925; arrived in US, 1955; s. Yunan and Tehchieh (Lee) J.; m. Norma Yingchiang Wen, Sept. 28, 1946; children: Gregory, David, Daniel. BA, Nat. Chengchi U., Nanking, China, 1949; MA, So. Ill. U., 1956; PhD, NYU, 1960. Various positions including editor newspaper/mag., tchr., writer, dean, 1949-55; instr. Chinese NYU, N.Y.C., 1959-60; asst. prof. polit. sci. No. Ill. U., DeKalb, 1961; asst. to full prof. of govt. U. S.D., Vermillion, 1961-68, dir. Summer Inst. for Asian Studies, 1964-66; prof. polit. sci. U. Toledo, 1968-93, prof. emeritus, 1993—, chmn. Asian studies program, 1970-93, dir. Inst. for Asian Studies, 1990-93; pres. Am. Inst. Tech., Toledo, 1993-00. Vis. prof. polit. sci. Beijing U., China, 1988; hon. rsch. fellow Rsch. Ctr. for Contemporary China, Beijing U., 1988—; adviser to China U. Geol. Scis., Beijing, 1993—; hon. chmn. bd. Second H.S., Wenzhou Tchr's. Coll., China, 2000—, frequent commentator on Radio Free Asia,2000— Author: The Chinese Commune Experiment, 1964, A Practical English Grammar for Junior Middle Schools, 1953, A Study of English Words, 1955, How to Do Business with China, 1994, Introduction to Political Science, 2000, Understanding Contemporary China, 2004, The Chinese Commune, 2004, others; editor: Government of Communist China, 1966, The International Politics of Asia, 1969, China Bus. Newsletter, 1993-98, International Relations of Asia, 1998, Political Development of China, 1998; mem. editl. bd. Asian Profile Jour., 1983-86, Jour. Econs. and Internat. Rels., 1986—, The New World of Politics, 1991—; contbr. articles to profl. jours., ency. and books. Pres. Chinese Assn. Greater Toledo, 1983-84; bd. dirs. Toledo Coun. on World Affairs, 1969-76; chmn. keynote session, Symposium on Chinese Ams. in the 1990s, Detroit, 1987; hon. chmn. bd. Second H.S. Wenzhou Tchrs. Coll., 2000—. Recipient Outstanding Svc. award The Internat. Inst. of Greater Toledo, 1983, teaching grants Asia Found., Japan Soc., 1964, 65, 66, rsch. grants U. Toledo, U. S.D., U. Mich., U. Chgo. numerous years, Significant Contribution award Pacific Cultural Found., Republic of China, 1988; named Hon. Rsch. Fellow, Rsch. Ctr. for Contemporary China, Beijing U., 1988, others. Mem. AAUP, Am. Polit. Sci. Assn., Midwest Polit. Sci. Assn., Assn. Asian Studies, Ohio Chinese Acad. and Profl. Assn. (bd. dirs. 1991—, pres. 1994-95), Mich. Chinese Acad. and Profl. Assn. (outstanding leadership award 1992), Am. Assn. Chinese Studies, Internat. Studies Assn., Ohio Internat. Edn. Assn. (chmn. planning and program com. 1976-77), Chinese Acad. and Profl. Assn. of Mid-Am. (bd. dirs. 1986-89), Am. Biog. Inst., Inc. (rsch. bd. advisors 1996—), Internat. Biog. Ctr. (hon. adv. coun.), Phi Beta Kappa, Pi Sigma Alpha, Phi Kappa Phi, Pi Gamma Mu, Phi Beta Delta. Avocations: gardening, photography, travel, swimming, chess. Home: 3041 Valley View Dr Toledo OH 43615-2237 Personal E-mail: aitje@aol.com.

JANA, SADHAN C., engineering educator, researcher; s. Surendra Nath and Snehalata Jana; m. Soma Dasadhikari, Dec. 11, 1987; children: Subhra Jyoti, Sanhita. B, U. of Calcutta, 1983—86; M, Indian Inst. of Tech., 1986—88; PhD, Northwestern U., 1991—93. Postdoctoral fellow CUNY, 1993—94; sr. engr. Gen. Electric Rsch. Ctr., Schenectady, NY, 1994—98; asst. prof. U. Akron, Ohio, 1998—2004, assoc. prof., chmn. dept., 2004. Mem. summer faculty NASA Glenn Rsch. Ctr., Cleve., 1999—2005; rsch. asst. U. Mass., Amherst, 1988—91, Northwestern U., Evanston, Ill., 1991—93. Named Disting. Young Alumnus, U. of Calcutta, 2001; recipient NSF Career award, 2002—, Gold medal, U. of Calcutta, 1986; Nat. Merit scholar, Govt. of India, 1977—86, NASA/OAI Summer Faculty fellowship, NASA Glenn Rsch. Ctr., 1999. Mem.: Polymer Processing Soc. (assoc.), Am. Chem. Soc. (assoc.), Soc. Plastics Engrs. (assoc.). Achievements include patents for process for multi-layer polymeric articles with surface conductivity; on process for making composite materials with thermoplastic and thermosetting polymers; on process for shear isolation of rubber latex particles without chemicals; on design of chaotic single extrusion screws for chaotic mixing of immiscible polymers. Office: U Akron 250 S Forge St Akron OH 44325-0301 Office Phone: 330-972-8293. Business E-Mail: janas@uakron.edu.

JANAK, EDWARD ADAM, III, language educator; b. Buffalo, N.Y., Oct. 3, 1970; s. Edward Adam Jr. and Linda Lee (Grotke) J. BA English, SUNY, Fredonia, 1992. Cert. provisional tchr. English 7-12, N.Y.; ann. cert. English, S.C. Tchr. self-contained classroom North Collins (N.Y.) Jr. High, 1993; drama/English tchr. Marlboro County High Sch., Bennettsville, S.C., 1993—. Student tchr. Cassadaga Valley Jr./Sr. High Sch., Sinclairville, N.Y., 1992; substitute tchr. Baker Hall, Inc., Lackawanna, N.Y., 1992-93; drama club/stage crew sponsor Marlboro County High Sch., 1993—, journalism dept. co-sponsor, 1993—, varsity soccer coach, 1993—, crisis intervention team, 1993—. Editorialist: (TV) Prime Time, WNYF-TV, 1992; author poetry. Team leader Act - 135 Sch. Improvement, Marlboro County High Sch., 1993—; mem. Village Action Coalition, Hamburg, N.Y., 1992. Mem. Nat. Coun. Tchrs. English, Arts Coun. Co-op Interlochen, Internat. Soc. Poets. Lutheran. Avocations: music appreciation, performance art, visual art appreciation, cooking. Home: 701 W Main St Apt 11 Bennettsville SC 29512-3857 Office: Marlboro County High Sch 951 Fayetteville Avenue Ext Bennettsville SC 29512-4151

JANAK, PETER HAROLD, automotive company executive; b. Detroit; BS in Aerospace Engring., Miss. State U., 1963; grad. exec. program, Stanford U., 1994. Rsch. fluid amplifiers dept. aerospace engring. Miss. State U., State College, 1962—63; propulsion engr. space disvn. Chrysler Corp., New Orleans, 1963—65; from sr. engr. to chief performance analysis sect. Teledyne-Brown Engring., Hunstville, Ala., 1965—68; head propulsion tech. sect. TRW Def. and Space Sys. Group, Houston, 1968—71, mgr. surveillance sys. engring. McLean, Va., 1972—78, mgr. signal processing sys. dept., 1978—79, mgr. SURTASS engring., 1979—80, mgr. undersea surveillance projects and combat sys., 1980—83, mgr. def. sys. ops. Fairfax, Va., 1987—90, mgr. tax modernization program, 1990—92, dep. gen. mgr. divsn. info svcs., 1992—94, v.p., gen. mgr. divsn. info. svcs., 1994—95; mgr. propulsion sys. dept. Technologieforschung, GmbH, Stuttgart, Germany, 1971—72; v.p., dep. gen. mgr. ea. divsn. PRC Sys. Svcs., McLean, 1983—84, pres., gen. mgr. divsn. sys. engring. and analysis, 1984—87; v.p., chief info. officer TRW Inc., Cleve., 1995—98; chief info. officer Delphi Automotive Sys., Troy, Mich., 1998—99; v.p., chief info. officer Delphi Corp., Troy, 1999—. Mem. external rsch. adv. bd. Miss. State U. Mem.: IEEE, Conf. Bd., Working Coun. Chief Info. Officers, Soc. Automotive Engrs., Soc. Mfg. Engrs. Office: Delphi Corp 5725 Delphi Dr Troy MI 48098-2815

JANC, JOHN J., language educator; b. Blue Island, Ill., July 24, 1945; BA in French Lang. and Lit., English Lang. and Lit., U. Wis., Eau Claire, 1967; MA in French Lang. and Lit., U. Mich., 1968; MA in Comparative Lit., U. Wis., Madison, 1974, PhD in French Lang. and Lit., 1981; diplôme de méthodologie audio-visuelle, U. Poitiers, France, 1975; Doctorat, U. La Sorbonne Nouvelle, Paris, 1977; diplôme supérieur de Français des Affaires, C. of C. and Industry Paris, 1981. Instr. French St. Benedict Coll., Ferdinand, Ind., 1968—69, U. Wis. Stout, Menomonie, 1969—72; lectr. English CAREL, Royan, France, 1972—74; prof. French Minn. State U., Mankato, 1979—. Spkr. numerous workshops and seminars; tester Internat. Baccalaureate Exam, Mpls., St. Paul and Owatonna, Minn., 1990—95. Author: (edit. critique) Les Deux Trouvailles de Gallus, 1983, (series) Que se passe-t-il en France in Minn. Lang. Rev., 1987—, (edit. critique) Victor Hugo: Torquemada, 1989, Faisons des progrès: Manuel de conversation, 1997, (edit. critique) Victor Hugo: Hernani, 2001; contbr. articles to profl. jours., papers to profl. confs. Decorated chevalier in l'Ordre des Palmes Académiques; named CASE Univ. Prof. of Yr., State of Minn., 1988; recipient Founders award, Ctrl. State Conf., 1999; grantee, U. Wis., Madison, 1976, Minn. State U., 1980, 1982, 1987, 2000, NEH, 1990; Woodrow Wilson fellow, 1967—68, E.B. Fred fellow, U. Wis., Madison, 1976—77, Fulbright fellow, 1976—77. Mem.: Ctrl. States Conf. (pub. rels. com. 1990—91, pub. awareness com. 1991—92, leadership mentor 1996—97, state svcs. com. 1997—98, grants and fiscal devel. com. 1998—2002, bd. dirs. 2000—01, rev. bd. ann. report 2001—, leadership program 2002, awards and scholarships com. 2002, 2002, bd. dirs. 2002—03, local chair ann. conf. 2003, awards and scholarships com. 2004, awards and scholarship com. 2005, mem. rev. bd. for ann. Report of Ctrl. States 2001—03, 2005), Am. Assn. Tchrs. French (pres. 2001—03, Minn. chpt.), Minn. Coun. Tchg. Langs. and Cultures (v.p. 1987—90, co-chair fall conf. 1990, chair fall conf. 1991, pres. 1991—92, exhibits chair fall conf. 1991—, co-chair fall conf. 1992, campus coord. French lang. contest 1994—96, advt. editor Minn. Lang. Rev. 1997—, Emma Birkmaier award 1994), Soc. des Etudes Romantiques et Dix-Neuvièmistes, Am. Coun. Tchg. Fgn. Langs., Assn. des Amis de Victor Hugo, Sigma Tau Delta, Pi Delta Phi, Phi Kappa Phi, Kappa Delta Pi, Alpha Mu Gamma. Office: Minn State U AH 227 Mankato MN 56001 E-mail: john.janc@mnsu.edu.

JANCUK, KATHLEEN FRANCES, educational administrator; b. Balt., Apr. 1, 1950; d. Joseph Frank and Dorothy Jane (Lowry) J. BA in Elem. Edn., Notre Dame Coll., Balt., 1974; MEd in Reading, Towson State U., 1985; MEd in Adminstrn., Loyola Coll., Balt., 1992. Cert. tchr., reading specialist, adminstr. and supr., Md. Substitute tchr. St. Wenceslaus, Balt., 1970-72; tchr. 5th grade St. Boniface, Phila., 1972-77, Cath. C.C., Balt., 1977-82, reading specialist K-5, 1982-88; reading specialist K-8 St. Mary's Elem. Sch., Annapolis, Md., 1988-91; prin. St. Clare Sch., Balt., 1991-97, St. John Neumann Sch., Cumberland, Md., 1997—2002; dir. elem. sch. Bishop Walsh Sch., Cumberland, 2002—04, reading specialist k-12, 2004—. Non-voting mem. St. Clare Sch. Bd., Balt., 1991-97, St. John Neumann Sch. Bd., 1997-2002; mem. Sch. Sisters of Notre Dame, 1991—; mem. area pastoral coun., 1993-97. Recipient Recognition of Svc. award Archdiocese of Balt., 1993. Mem. ASCD, Elem. Sch. Prins. Assn. (exec. bd. dirs. 1994-97), Nat. Cath. Ednl. Assn., Internat. Reading Assn., Mid. States Assn. Sch. Evaluation Teams. Democrat. Roman Catholic. Avocations: collecting clowns, puppetry, swimming, singing, playing guitar and piano. Office: Bishop Walsh School 700 Bishop Walsh Rd Cumberland MD 21502 E-mail: kjancuk@allconet.org.

JANCZAK, ANDREW ANTHONY, executive; b. Buenos Aires, Feb. 20, 1950; came to U.S., 1955; s. Zygmunt and Gertrude (Sierocki) J.; m. Helen Mary Gimber, Jan. 27, 1973; children: Andrew S., Jeanette M. BS in Aerospace Engring., Polytech. Inst. Bklyn., 1972, MS in Mgmt., 1976. Mktg. dir. Telsonic/Trescott, Inc., L.I. City, NY, 1973-76; pres. Belzona, Inc., Uniondale, 1976-83; pres., owner Molecular Systems, Inc., Edgewood, 1983-90; pres. Enecon Corp., Bethpage, 1990—. Patentee in field. Avocations: golf, boating. Office: Enecon Corp 700 Hicksville Rd Ste 110 Bethpage NY 11714-3496 Office Phone: 516-349-0022. Business E-Mail: andy@enecon.com.

JANDA, CHRISTOPHER CRISCO, actor; b. Greenbrae, Calif., July 17, 1955; s. Frank Albert and Christina Teenie Janda; m. Lori Kaye Janda; children: Christina Virginia, Michael Joseph, Matthew Jeremy. Musician, Tiburon, Calif., 1966—; bartender Larkspur, Calif., 1976—; actor San Francisco, 1986—; drummer, ptnr. Ed Earley Band, Tiburon, 1994—; owner Lunamitz Prodns., Tiburon, 2001—. Primary actor in movie Blood in Blood Out, 1991, TV series Jesse Hawks, 1992, also commls. With U.S. Army, 1974-76. Mem. SAG, E. Clampis Vitis, Am. Legion. Avocations: ridng harley's, shooting, pool, camping, travel. Office: PO Box 689 Larkspur CA 94977-0689 Office Phone: 415-789-1014. E-mail: criscoandlori@comcast.net.

JANDA, LUBOMIR MIRO, organic chemist; b. Handlova, Slovakia, Feb. 8, 1953; s. Jan and Elena (Klinovska) J.; m. Jana Rothova, July 15, 1978; 1 child, Petra Jandova. MS in Organic Chemistry, Slovakian Inst. Tech., Bratislava, 1976; PhD in Organic Chemistry, Slovakian Acad. Scis., Bratislava, 1984. Synthetic organic chemist Pharm. Rsch. Inst., Bratislava, 1977-84; mgr. Slovakian Dept. Sci. and Tech., Bratislava, 1984-90; postdoctoral rsch. assoc. Ga. State U., Atlanta, 1990-92; scientist Aldrich Chem. Co., Inc., Milw., 1992—. Contbr. articles to profl. jours. including Jour. Organic Chemistry, Tetrahedron, and European Jour. Medicinal Chemistry. Officer Czechoslovakia Mil., 1976-77. Mem. DCP Club Slovakia. Avocations: bow hunting, fly fishing, beekeeping. Mailing: Aldrich Chem Co Inc 940 W St Paul Ave Milwaukee WI 53233-2681 Home: Sulekova 22 811 03 Bratislava Slovakia E-mail: mjanda@sial.com.

JANDES, KENNETH MICHAEL, superintendent of schools; b. Berwyn, Ill., Aug. 6, 1943; s. George Jerry and Dorothea Frieda Clara (Grabow) J.; m. RoseMary Patricia Klingebiel, June 18, 1966; children: Michael Jon, Kenneth Mark. BS in Edn., Ill. State U., 1966; MEd, Loyola U., Chgo., 1972; EdD, No. Ill. U., 1984. Cert. tchr., chief sch. bus. official, gen. adminstrv., supt., Ill. Math. tchr. Brook Park Sch. Sch. Dist. 95, LaGrange Park, Ill., 1966-69, sci. tchr. Brook Park Sch., 1969-74, acting prin. Brook Park Sch., 1972-74; prin. Waterman Sch. Sch. Dist. 149, South Holland, Ill., 1974-79; prin. Berger-Vandenberg Sch., Dolton, Ill., 1979-95; supt. Lincoln Sch. Dist. # 156, Calumet City, Ill., 1995—2001, Ridgeland Sch. Dist. # 122, Oak Lawn, Ill., 2001—. Chmn. dept. applied saxophone Am. Conservatory Music, Chgo., 1968-78; owner, operator Midwest Music Mart, Riverside, Ill., 1968-73; primary sci. cons. Instructor Mag., Dansville, N.Y., 1969-73; adj. prof. Govs. State U., University Park, Ill., 1985—; performing saxophonist Ken Jandes Dance Orch., Andy Tecson Jazz Ensemble, Pk. Ridge Symphony Orch. Composer of numerous choral, band, and orchestral works, 1961—; contbr. articles to profl. jours. Bd. dirs. Cmty. Family Svc. and Mental Health Ctr. La Grange, 1968-74; pres. bd. dirs. ECHO Spl. Edn. Coop., 1999-2001; bd. dirs. Thornton Fractional Area Ednl. Coop., v.p., 1998-99, pres. 1999-2001; mem. bd. supts. AERO Spl. Edn. Coop., 2001--; mem. com., treas. Boy Scouts Am., Woodridge, 1985-96; baseball coach Woodridges Athletic Assn., 1980-89; active com. on youth traffic safety Ill. Sec. of State, 1987-91; chmn. Thornton Twp. Regional Action Planning Project, 1996-97; mem. chancel choir St. Luke Presbyn. Ch., Downers Grove, Ill., 1976—, elder, 1980-86, 92-98. Named one of Outstanding Young Men Am. Jaycees, 1970. Mem. ASCD, Am. Assn. Sch. Adminstrs. (mem. govs. task force edn. in Ill., award 1986), Ill. Assn. Sch. Adminstrs. (legis. chmn. South Cook County divsn. 1997—, pres. 1999—), Ill. Assn. Sch. Bus. Ofcls. (fed. litig. ins. com. 2003—), Ill. Congress Parents and Tchrs. (hon. life), South Cook County Elem. Sch. Supt.'s Assn. (pres. 1997-98), Oak Lawn and Calumet City of C., Bus. Assocs. Calumet City, South Coop. Orgn. Pub. Edn., MENSA, Lions, Kappa Delta Pi, Phi Mu Alpha Sinfonia, Phi Delta Kappa. Avocations: astronomy, tennis, mathematics, computers, scientific reading, wine and fine dining. Home: 6671 Wheatfield St Woodridge IL 60517-1715 Office: Ridgeland Sch Dist 122 6500 W 95th St Oak Lawn IL 60453 Office Phone: 708-599-5550.

JANECZKO, JEFF M., music educator, musician; b. Evergreen Park, Ill., Apr. 1, 1973; s. Michael F. Janeczko and Gerogiann M. Gibson; life ptnr. Kristin L. Grogan. BA, Met. State Coll. Denver, Colo., 2001. Pvt. tchr., Aurora, Colo., 1997—. Musician (keyboardist): (CD) Reconceive, 2000, Introspect, 1997. Mem.: Music Tchrs. Nat. Assn. Home: 1380 N Laurel Ave #24 West Hollywood CA 90046-4605 Personal E-mail: jeff@thequietroom.com.

JANES, BRANDON CHAISON, lawyer; b. Uvalde, Tex., Oct. 9, 1951; s. Brandon Chaison and Phyllis (Collins) J.; children: Margaret, Michael, Brandon. BBA, Baylor U., 1972; JD, U. Tex., 1976. Bar: Tex. 1976, U.S. Dist. Ct. (we. dist.) Tex. 1978, U.S. Tax Ct. 1981, U.S. Ct. Appeals (5th cir.) 1981, U.S. Supreme Ct. 1981. Assoc., then ptnr. Grambling & Mounce, El Paso, Tex., 1976-80; ptnr. Small, Craig & Werkenthin, Austin, Tex., 1981-97, Akin, Gump, Strauss, Haver & Feld, Austin, Tex., 1997—. Contbr. articles to profl. jours. Mem. ABA (taxation sect.), State Bar Tex., Tex. Soc. CPAs. Home: 901 Forest View Dr Austin TX 78746-4521 Office: Akin Gump Strauss Haver & Feld 816 Congress Ave Ste 1900 Austin TX 78701-4042 E-mail: bjanes@akingump.com.

JANES, JACKSON, research institute executive; b. Washington, Aug. 25, 1947; s. Roth and Lois Janes; m. Marlis Rohwer, Sept. 7, 1979; children: Tanya, Nicolas. BA in Sociology, Colgate U., 1969; MA in Theology, U. Chgo., 1971; PhD in Internat. Studies, Claremont Grad. Sch., 1981. Instr. English and Am. studies U. Giessen, Germany, 1971-74; dir. German-Am. Inst. Tuebingen, Germany, 1977-80; dir. European Office, German Marshall Fund U.S., Bonn, 1980-85; dir. program devel. Univ. Ctr. for Internat. Studies, U. Pitts., 1986-88; dep. dir. Am. Inst. Contemporary German Studies at The Johns Hopkins, Washington, 1989-94, exec. dir., 1994—. Trustee Bundestag Internship Alunni, Bonn, 1998—; mem. adv. bd. Allied Mus., Berlin, 1998—. Author: Mixed Messages: The Study of Contemporary Germany in the United States, 1986, Priming the Pump: The Making of Foreign Area Experts, 1992. Recipient friendship award Fed. Rep. Germany, 1987. Mem. German Studies Assn. Office: Am Inst for Contemporary German Studies at Johns Hop 1755 Massachusetts Ave NW Ste 700 Washington DC 20036-2121 Fax: 202-265-9531. E-mail: jjanes@aicgs.org.

JANES, JOSEPH W., library and information science educator; b. Oneida, NY, Oct. 22, 1962; s. Donald L. and Jeannette M Janes; life ptnr. Janette Hartley. AB in Math., Syracuse U., 1982, MLS, 1983, PhD Info. Transfer, 1989. Asst. prof. U. Mich., Ann Arbor, 1989—97; dir. Internet Pub. Libr., Ann Arbor, Mich., 1995—99; asst. prof. U. Wash., Seattle, 1999—2003, assoc. prof., 2003—, assoc. dean for academics, 2004—. Author: Internet Public Library Handbook, 1999, Online Retrieval: A Dialogue of Theory and Practice, 1999, The Internet Searcher's Handbook, 1996, Introduction to Reference in the Digital Age, 2003. Rsch. grantee, Libr. Congress, 2000, Andrew W. Mellon Found., 1996, U.S. Dept. Edn., 1993, Online Computer Libr. Ctr., 2003. Mem.: ALA, Am. Soc. for Info. Sci. and Tech. Office: U Wash Info Sch Box 352840 Seattle WA 98195

JANES, ROBERT ROY, museum director, archaeologist, editor; b. Rochester, Minn., Apr. 23, 1948; m. Priscilla Bickel; children: Erica Helen, Peter Bickel. Student, Lawrence U., 1966—68, BA in Anthropology cum laude, 1970; student, U. of the Ams., Mexico City, 1968, U. Calif., Berkeley, 1968—69; PhD in Archaeology, U. Calgary, Alta., Can., 1976. Postdoctoral fellow Arctic Inst. N.Am., U. Calgary, 1981-82; founding dir. Prince of Wales No. Heritage Centre, Yellowknife, 1976-86, project dir. Dealy Island Archaeol. and Conservation Project, 1977-82; founding exec. dir. Sci. Inst. of N.W.T.; sci. advisor Govt. of N.W.T., Yellowknife, 1986-89; exec. dir., pres., CEO Glenbow Mus. Art Gallery Libr. and Archives, Calgary, 1989-2000; fellow Glenbow-Alta. Inst., 2000—. Mus./heritage cons., 2000—; adj. prof. archaeology U. Calgary, 1990—. Author: Preserving Diversity-Ethnoarchaeological Perspectives on Culture Change in the Western Canadian Subarctic, 1991, Museums and the Paradox of Change, 1995, 2d edit., 1997, Looking Reality in the Eye: Museums and Social Responsibility, 2005; (with others) The Arctic Institute of North America Technical Paper No. 28, 1983; editor-in-chief Jour. Mus. Mgmt. and Curatorship, 2003; contbr. articles to profl. jours. Mem. First Nations/CMA Task Force on Mus. and First Peoples, 1989-92, Banff. Kootenay and Yoho Nat. Pks. Devel. Adv. Bd.; nat. adv. bd. Ctr. for Cultural Mgmt., U. Waterloo, chair, 2003; chair bd. dirs. Friends of Banff Nat. Pk., 2003; vice-chair, chair bd. dirs. Biosphere Inst. of Bow Valley, 2003. Recipient Nat. Parks Centennial award Environ. Can., 1985, Can. Studies Writing award Assn. Can. Studies, 1989, Disting. Alumni award Alumni Assn. of U. Calgary, 1989, L.R. Briggs Disting. Achievement award Lawrence U., 1991, Queen Elizabeth II Golden Jubilee Commemorative medal 2003; Can. Coun. doctoral fellow, 1973-76; rsch. grantee Govt. of Can., 1974, Social Scis. and Humanities Rsch. Coun. Can., 1988-89. Fellow Arctic Inst. N.Am. (bd. dirs. 1983-90, vice chmn. bd. 1985-89, hon. rsch. assoc. 1983-84, chmn. priorities and planning com. 1983-84, exec. com. 1984-86, assoc. editor Arctic jour. 1987-97), Can. Mus. Assn. (hon. life, cert. accreditation 1982, Outstanding award in Mus. Mgmt., Outstanding Achievement award for publ. 1996), Am. Anthrop. Assn. (fgn.); mem. Can. Archaeol. Assn. (v.p. 1980-82, pres. 1984-86, co-chmn. fed. heritage policy com. 1986-88), Can. Art Mus. Dirs. Orgn. (mem.-at-large bd. dirs. 1992-95), Alta. Mus. Assn. (moderator seminars 1990, Merit award 1992, Merit award for Museums and the Paradox of Change 1996), Assn. Cultural Execs. (bd. dirs. 1999--2002, ACE award for Can. Cultural Mgmt. 1998), Sigma Xi. Home: 104 Prendergast Pl Canmore AB Canada T1W 2N5

JANES, WILLIAM SARGENT, real estate company executive; b. Cambridge, Mass., Mar. 24, 1953; s. G. Sargent and Ann (Brown) J.; m. Alice Maxine Rowley, June 19, 1982; children: Pack Sargent, Maxine Cotton. BA, Bowdoin Coll., 1976. Sr. sales cons. Coldwell Banker, Washington, 1976-84; ptnr. Lincoln Property Co., Washington, 1984-89; pres. Rock Creek Ptnrs., Inc., Washington, 1990—; prin. RMB Realty, Washington, 1990—. Bd. dirs. Am. Skiing Co., Brazos Advisors, Brazos Fund L.P., CapStar Hotel Co. Carr Real Estate Svcs., DaVinci Advisors Max/FW, L.L.C., The Mendik Co., Inc., MeriStar Hospitality Corp., MeriStar Investments Ptnrs., L.P., Paragon Group, Inc. Tristee Bpwdpom Coll., Washington Nat. Cathedral Found.; mem. circles bd. Kennedy Ctr. Mem. NAREIT, SIOR, Urban Land Inst. Home: PO Box 1204 Middleburg VA 20118-1204 Office: RMB Realty Inc 1133 Connecticut Ave NW Washington DC 20036-4305

JANEWAY, RICHARD, retired academic administrator; b. LA, Feb. 12, 1933; s. VanZandt and Grace Eleanor (Bell) Janeway; m. Katherine Esmond Pillsbury, Dec. 23, 1955; children: Susan Kent, David VanZandt, Elizabeth Anne. AB, Colgate U., 1954; MD, U. Pa., 1958. Diplomate Am. Bd. Psychiatry and Neurology. Intern Hosp. U. Pa., 1958—59; resident N.C. Baptist Hosp., Winston-Salem, 1963—66; mem. faculty Bowman Gray Sch. Medicine (now Wake Forest U. Sch. Medicine), Winston-Salem, 1966—; prof. neurology Wake Forest U., Winston-Salem, 1971—2003, prof. medicine and mgmt., 1997—2003, prof. emeritus, 2003—, dir. Cerebral Vascular Rsch. Ctr., Bowman Gray Sch. Medicine, 1969—71; dean Bowman Gray Sch. Medicine, Wake Forest U., Winston-Salem, 1971—85, exec. dean, 1985—94, v.p. health affairs, 1983—90, exec. v.p. health affairs, 1990—97, ret., 1997—. Mem. exec. com. So. Nat. Bank, Winston-Salem, NC, 1982—95; dir. BB&T Corp., 1995—2003, bd. dirs., mem. exec. com., chmn., 2001—03; mem. nat. adv coun. regional med. programs HEW, 1974—77; mem. -at-large Nat. Bd. Med. Examiners, 1979—87; mem. N.C. Joint Conf. Com. on Med. Care, Inc., 1983—2003; dir. N.C. Inst. Medicine. Mem. Winston-Salem Forsyth Co. Bd. Edn., 1970—73; trustee Winston-Salem State U., 1991—95, Colgate U., 1988—95; bd. dirs. Nat. Assn. for Biomed. Rsch., 1993—96, Ams. for Med. Progress, Inc., 1993—97, Winston-Salem Found., 1994—2002, chmn., 1997, 1998. Capt. USAF, 1959—63, flight surgeon, 1962—63. Recipient fellow, USPHS, 1956, Markle scholar, 1968—73. Fellow: ACP, Am. Heart Assn. (coun. on stroke), Am. Acad. Neurology; mem.: AMA, Soc. Med. Adminstrs., Greater Winston-Salem C. of C. (bd. dirs. 1985—89, 1991—95, chmn. 1992), Inst. Medicine of NAS, Am. Clin. and Climatol. Assn., Assn. Am. Med. Colls. (exec. coun. 1977—86, mem. accreditation coun. on grad med. edn. 1981—85, chmn. coun. of deans 1982—83, exec. com. 1982—86, chmn. 1984—85), Am. Neurol. Assn., Rotary (dir. 1977—80, v.p. 1981—82, pres. 1982—83), Alpha Omega Alpha, Sigma Xi, Phi Beta Kappa. Republican. Episcopalian. Avocations: photography, golf, flower arranging, reading. Business E-Mail: rjaneway@triad.rr.com.

JANG, JEONG, professional golfer; b. Taejeon, Korea, June 11, 1980; Attended, JoongBoo U. Winner Korea Women's Open, 1997, Korea Women's Amateur, 1998. Mem. Korea Women's Nat. Team, 1997—98, World Amateur Championship Team, 1998. Achievements include five top-ten finishes, 2002; six top-ten finishes, 2003; seven top-ten finishes, 2004. Avocations: skiing, nintendo. Office: c/o LPGA 100 International Golf Dr Daytona Beach FL 32124-1092

JANG, SOOCHEONG (SHAWN), education educator; arrived in US, 1998; s. Kilyong Jang and Youngjoo Kim; m. Soyeon Park, Nov. 26, 1993; 1 child, Jiwoong. PhD, Purdue U., West Lafayette, Ind., 2002. Asst. prof. Kans. State U., Manhattan, Kans., 2002—05, Purdue U., West Lafayette, Ind., 2005—. Dep. gen. mgr. LG Mcht. Banking Corp., Seoul, Korea (South), 1995—98. Recipient Best Paper Award, CHRIE, 2004, 2005, Best Travel Grant Award, TTRA, 2003, Best Paper Award, ISTTE, 2002, HTM Grad. Edn., 2002. Achievements include research in Hospitality and Tourism Mgmt. Home: 3358 Putnam St West Lafayette IN 47906 Office: Purdue Univ Stone Hall 700 W State St West Lafayette IN 47907-2059 Office Phone: 765-496-3610. Business E-Mail: jang12@purdue.edu.

JANIAK, ANTHONY RICHARD, JR., investment banker; b. Pitts., Sept. 21, 1946; s. Anthony R. and Ann Theresa Janiak; m. Anne Marie McDevitt, Aug. 23, 1969; children: Brian Richard, Carolyn Marie. BS, Pa. State U., 1968; MBA, U. Chgo., 1970. Assoc. Smith Barney & Co., N.Y.C., 1970-74; v.p. Smith Barney Internat., Tokyo, 1974-77, Smith Barney, Harris Upham & Co., N.Y.C., 1977-78, mng. dir., 1980—; v.p. Smith Barney, Harris Upham Internat., Paris, 1978-80; mng. dir., dir. internat. Smith Barney Inc., N.Y.C., 1995-98; mng. dir. Smith Barney Citigroup, N.Y.C., 1998—. Bd. dirs. Global Wrap Cons. Group, Tokyo, 1997-2001, Soditic Fin., Geneva, 1998-2004, Fubon Securities, Taipei, Taiwan, 2001-03; chmn. bd. dirs. Genesis Energy LLC, 1999-2002; mem. adv. com. bus. coun. UN, 1984-90, N.Y.C.; mem. task force on fin. svcs. U.S.-Japan Businessmen's Coun., 1982-83; mem. adv. com. on pub. affairs Japan Soc., N.Y.C., 1986-88; mem. emerging markets adv. com. SEC, 1991-93; exch. ofcl. Am. Stock Exch., 1992—, NASDAQ listing com., 1999-2000. Bd. dirs. Town and Village Civic Club of Scarsdale, 1992-95, 98-2001, A Better Chance, 2003—; trustee Scarsdale Hist. Soc., 1999-2001. Republican. Roman Catholic. Avocations: tennis, coin collecting/numismatics, music, golf. Home: 172 Woodbrook Rd White Plains NY 10605 Office: Smith Barney 388 Greenwich St New York NY 10013-2339 Office Phone: 212-816-7608. Business E-Mail: a.r.janiak@citigroup.com.

JANICAK, PHILIP GREGORY, psychiatrist, educator; b. Chgo., Aug. 2, 1946; s. Edward and Josephine (Raskauskas) J.; m. Mary Judith Cray, Oct. 16, 1976; 1 child, Matthew Cray. BS in Psychology with honors, Loyola U., Chgo., 1969, MD, 1973. Diplomate Am. Bd. Psychiatry and Neurology. Asst. clin. prof. dept. psychiatry Loyola U., Maywood, Ill., 1976-78; rsch. assoc. U. Chgo., 1979-81; asst. prof. U. Ill., Chgo., 1982-85, assoc. prof., 1986-92, prof., 1992—2004, Rush U., 2004—. Chief rsch. unit Ill. State Psychiat. Inst., Chgo., 1984-96; med. dir. psychiat. clin. rsch. ctr. U. Ill., 1996-2004, Rush U., 2004--. First author: Principles and Practice of Psychopharmacotherapy, 1993, 4t edit., 2001. NIMH grant co-investigator, 1986, 91, 93; NIMH grant prin. investigator, 1990; NIH grant assoc. program dir. 2000-2004. Fellow Am. Psychiat. Assn. (disting. fellow). Roman Catholic. Avocation: voice. Business E-Mail: pjanicak@rush.edu.

JANICK, JULES, horticultural scientist, educator; b. N.Y.C., Mar. 16, 1931; s. Henry Spinner and Frieda (Tullman) Janick; m. Shirley Reisner, June 15, 1952; children: Peter Aaron, Robin Helen Janick Weinberger. BS, Cornell U., 1951; MS, Purdue U., 1952, PhD, 1954; DS in Agr. (hon.), U. Bologna, Italy, 1990; Doctor (hon.), Tech. U., Lisbon, Portugal, 1994. Instr. Purdue U., West Lafayette, 1954-56, asst. prof., 1956-59, assoc. prof., 1959-63, prof., 1963-88, James Troop Disting. prof. in horticulture, 1988—; dir. Purdue Ctr. for New Crops and Plant Products, 1990—. Cons. Food and Agrl. Orgn., Rome, Italy, 1988. Author: Horticultural Science, 4th edit., 1986, Classical Papers in Horticultural Science, 1989; co-author: Plant Science: An Introduction to World Crops, 3d edit., 1981; co-editor: Advances in Fruit Breeding, 1975, Methods in Fruit Breeding, 1983, Advances in New Crops, 1990, New Crops, 1993, Fruit Breeding (3 vols.), 1996; editor: Hort. Revs., Plant Breeding Revs., Progress in New Crops, 1996, Perspectives on New Crops and New Uses, 1999, Trends in New Crops and New Uses, 2002. Fellow AAAS, Portuguese Hort. Assn., Am. Soc. Hort. Sci. (pres. 1986-87), Internat. Soc. Hort. Sci. Jewish. Avocation: drawing. Home: 420 Forest Hill Dr West Lafayette IN 47906-2316 Office: Dept Horticulture and Landscape Architecture Purdue U 625 Agriculture Mall Dr West Lafayette IN 47907-2010 E-mail: janick@purdue.edu.

JANICKI, ROBERT STEPHEN, retired pharmaceutical executive; b. Manette, Wash., Dec. 7, 1934; s. Stephen Walter and Elizabeth Caroline (Gorman) J.; m. I. Jane Betcher, Aug. 18, 1956; children: Robert, Beth, David. BS, Grove City Coll., 1956; MD, Temple U., 1961. Diplomate Nat. Bd. Med. Examiners. Intern U.S. Naval Hosp., Phila., 1961-62; resident in occupl. medicine USN, 1962-63; assoc. dir. clin. rsch. Dow Pharms., Indpls., 1966-68; assoc. med. dir. Neisler divsn. Union Carbide Corp., Sterling Forest, N.Y., 1968-69; assoc. med. dir. regulatory affairs Abbott Labs., North Chicago, Ill., 1969-70, dir. clin. rsch. pharm. products divsn., 1970-71, v.p. med. affairs pharm. products divsn., 1971-79, v.p. research pharm. products divsn., 1979-83, corp. v.p. R & D pharm. products divsn., 1983-89, sr. v.p., 1989-90. Bd. dirs. Osprey Pharms., Jacksonville, Fla.; cons. New Drug Devel

Contbr. articles to profl. jours. Trustee Grove City (Pa.) Coll., 1995-99. Lt. comdr. M.C., USN, 1961-66. Fellow Am. Coll. Clin. Pharmacology; mem. Am. Soc. Clin. Pharmacology and Therapeutics, Sigma Xi, Alpha Omega Alpha. Home: 138 Anchor Dr Vero Beach FL 32963-2941 Personal E-mail: rsjanicki@aol.com.

JANICKI, THOMAS I., gynecologist; s. Danuta Janicka and Stanley Janicki; m. Anna J. Solowij; children: Oscar T., Arthur A. MD, Med. Acad. Warsaw, 1974. Cert. Ob-Gyn Am. Bd. Ob-Gyn, 1982, Advanced Operative Laparoscopy and Hysteroscopy Accreditation Coun. of Gynecologic Endoscopy, 1995. Asst. clin. prof. ob-gyn Case We. Res. U., Cleve., 1982—86, assoc. clin. prof. reproductive biology, 1986—; attending physician U. Hospitals Cleve., 1980—. Dir. pelvic pain ctr. MacDonald Women's Hosp. U. Hospitals Cleve., 2003—; mem. sci. adv. bd. FemmePharma, Inc., Wayne, Pa., 2000—; bd. dirs. Internat. Pelvic Pain Soc., 2003—, U. Suburban Health Ctr., South Euclid, Ohio, 2004—; bd. trustees Cleve. Pub. Radio — WCPN 90.3, 1990—96. Contbr. articles to profl. jours. Recipient Attending Physician of Yr. Award, Macdonald Women's Hosp., 1986, Attending Physician of Yr. award, MacDonald Women's Hosp., 1987, 1989, 1996, Ronald Golden, MD award for Med. Excellence, Macdonald Women's Hosp., 1993, MacDonald Women's Hosp., 2001, Dean's Award for saving life of prof. of Forensic Medicine, Med. Acad. of Warsaw, 1974. Fellow: Am. Coll. Obstetricians and Gynecologists; mem.: Am. Soc. Reproductive Medicine, Am. Pain Soc., World Endometriosis Soc., Internat. Assn. for Study of Pain, Internat. Pelvic Pain Soc. (bd. of directors memeber 2003—05), Am. Assn. Gynecologic Laproscopists. Achievements include patents for "Veress Needle System and Method"; research in Autonomic Dysfunction in Patients Suffering from Chronic Pelvic Pain; Use of vaginal danazol in treatment of pelvic pain associated with endometriosis; Local neurogenic inflammation as a mechanism of chronic visceral pain conditions; Treatment of Interstitial Cystitis with Local Danazol. Office: Green Road Obstetrics and Gynecology 1611 South Green Rd #216 Cleveland OH 44121 Office Phone: 216-381-2223. Office Fax: 216-381-5975. Personal E-mail: tij@att.net.

JANICOT, DANIEL CLAUDE EMMANUEL, foundation administrator; b. Neuilly Sur Seine, France, May 20, 1948; s. Francois-Xavier and Antoinette (Mauxion) J.; previously married to Monique Bibal; children: Laetitia, Mathilde; m. Catherine Lachenal; 1 child, Thomas. Law Degree, Faculte de Droit de Paris, 1972; Grad. Degree, Inst. D'Etudes Politiques, Paris, 1971; Postgrad. Degree, Ecole Nationale D'Adminstrn., Paris, 1975. Auditor State Coun., Paris, 1975—, dep. sec.-gen., 1978-82, maitre des requetes, 1979; maitre de confs. Inst. D'Etudes Politiques, 1976-78, Ecole Nationale des Ponts et Chausees, Paris, 1977-78; gen. rapporteur Commn. D'Acces Aux Documents Adminstrn., Paris, 1979; v.p. Nat. Libr., Paris, 1981; maitre de seminaire Ecole Nationale D'Adminstrn., Paris, 1982-93; dir. exec. office of dir. gen. UNESCO, Paris, 1991-94, asst. dir. gen., 1994—. State councillor, State Coun., Paris, 1995—. Author: (book) La Cooperation Internationale. Bd. dirs. Pompidou Ctr. Libr., Paris, 1979; del. gen. Union Centrale des Arts Decoratifs, Paris, 1982-86, Am. Ctr., Paris, 1980-90; chmn. bd. dirs. Ctr. Nat. d'art contemporain, Grenoble, 1995; vice-chmn. bd. dirs. Inst. franÇais de gestion, 1996—. Chevalier Ordre Nat. du Merite, France, 1988, Ordre Nat. Des Arts et Des Lettres, France, 1985, Chevalier Ordre Nat. Légion d'Honneur, 1999 Home: 6 Rue Casimir Perier Paris 75007 France Office: Conseil d'Etat Palais Royal 75100 Paris France

JANIGA-PERKINS, CONSTANCE GABRIELLE, language educator; d. Edward John and Margaret (Mihalovic) Janiga; m. Michael Allen Perkins, Mar. 8, 1992; 1 child, Gabrielle Janiga Perkins. PhD, Ind. U., 1987; BA, Douglass Coll., 1977. Assoc. prof. of hispanic lang. and lit. Modern Languages and Classics, Tuscaloosa, Ala., 1987—; asst. prof. Spanish SUNY, Oswego, 1986—87. Co-editor (with Dr. Heitor Martins): (critical edition) Dialogo Entre o Deus Momo e o Censor. VII Anuario do Museu da Inconfidencia e do Grupo de Museus e Casas Historicas de Minas Gerais. Brasilia: Ministerio da Educacao e Cultura, 1985.; contbr. critical articles, studies to profl. publs.; author: (book) Immaterial Transcendence: The Process of the Colonial Writing Subject in Brazil's Letter of Discovery, 2001. V.p. Univ. Pl. Sch. PTA, 1999—2004; active Girl Scouts U.S. Fellow, NEH, 1991, 1992; grantee, Fulbright Found., 1983, U.S. Dept. Edn./Fulbright Found., 1995—97, 1986; Fulbright Rsch./Tchg. grantee, Costa Rica, 1991, Arts & Sciences Tchg. fellow, Coll. of Arts and Scis., 1997—2001. Mem.: South Ea. Coun. on L.Am. Studies, South Ea. MLA, Nat. Fulbright Assn., Parent Tchr. Assn., Phi Beta Kappa, Sigma Delta Pi, Sigma Beta Delta. Avocation: 2d degree blackbelt. Office: Modern Langs and Classics BB Comer 200 Tuscaloosa AL 35487-0246 Office Fax: 205-348-9909. E-mail: cgjaniga@msn.com.

JANIS, ALLEN IRA, retired physicist, educator; b. Chgo., Sept. 11, 1930; s. David M. and Rosa (Ginsburg) J.; m. Phyllis Meyer, Sept. 6, 1953; children: Stuart, Wynne. BS, Northwestern U., 1951; postgrad., Cornell U., Ithaca, N.Y., 1951-53; PhD, Syracuse U., 1957. Mem. faculty U. Pitts., 1957-92, assoc. prof. physics, 1963-68, prof., 1968-92, prof. emeritus, 1993—, sr. research assoc. Philos. Sci. Center, 1967-75, assoc. dir. Philos. Sci. Center, 1975-92; fellow emeritus Philos. Sci. Center, 1993—. Mem. Fedn. Am. Scientists (sec. 1964-65), Am. Phys. Soc., Am. Assn. Physics Tchrs., AAAS, AAUP, Philosophy of Sci. Assn. Home: 425 Garden City Dr Monroeville PA 15146-1258 Office: Univ Pitts Dept Physics and Astronomy Pittsburgh PA 15260 E-mail: aij@pitt.edu.

JANIS, CONRAD, actor, musician, art dealer; b. N.Y.C. s. Sidney and Harriet J.; children: Christopher, Carin; m. Maria Grimm, Nov. 30, 1987. Appeared in numerous Broadway plays including Junior Miss, 1942, Dark of the Moon, 1945, The Next Half Hour, 1945, The Brass Ring, 1951 (World Theater award), Time Out for Ginger, 1952, Visit to a Small Planet, 1957, Sunday in New York, 1961, Marathon '33, 1963, The Front Page, 1969, Same Time Next Year, 1975-76; films include Snafu, 1945, Margie, 1946, That Hagen Girl, 1947, Let's Rock, 1958, Airport '75, The Duchess and the Dirtwater Fox, 1976, The Buddy Holly Story, 1977, Roseland, 1977, Oh, God! Book II, 1979, Nothing in Common, 1987, Sonny Boy, 1987, Mr. Saturday Night, 1992, The Gods Must Be Crazy III, 1992; star, dir. The Feminine Touch, 1995, The Cable Guy, 1995, Addams Family Reunion, 1998; actor, dir. The November Conspiracy, 1996; appeared in over 350 major network TV shows including Suspense, 1950, Philco Play House, 1951, Studio One, 1952, Armstrong Circle Theater, 1953, Highway to Heaven, 1986, Golden Girls, 1987, 89, Murder, She Wrote, 1988, 91, Baywatch, 1996, The New Rockford Files, 1997, Frasier, 1997, 2000, 02, Diagnosis Murder, 1998, (recurring role) Family Law, 1999-2000; numerous TV movies including Miracle on 34th Street, 1973, The Virginia Hill Story, 1974, The Magnificent Magnet of Santa Mesa, 1977, The Gossip Columnist, 1984, The Red Light Sting, 1984, Asimov's Probe, 1987, Caddie Woodlawn, 1988, Time After Time, 2002; TV series include I Bonino, Quark, Mork and Mindy, 1978-82; spokesperson TV series on modern art, Appreciating Art, 1991; leader jazz group, 1951—; TV appearances with Johnny Carson, Diana Shore, Mike Douglas, The Late Show with Ross Schaeffer, David Letterman Show, spls. include Burt Convy, Juke Box Hits, Jerry Lewis Telethons, others; appeared in major jazz clubs throughout US, jazz festivals, Monterey, Calif., Palm Springs, Calif., Sacramento, L.A. Classic and many others, concerts at N.Y. Carnegie Hall, Town Hall, Phila. Acad. Music, Nugget Jazz Festival, Playboy Jazz Festival, 1997, others; jazz trombonist with various artists including Roy Eldredge, Coleman Hawkins, Buddy Rich, Bobby Hackett, Hot Lips Page, Wild Bill Davison; leader Beverly Hills Unlisted Jazz Band, 1978- (subject of PBS spl. titled That's A Plenty 1981), The Tuxedo Junction, (PBS spl.) This Joint is Jumpin, 1997; writer, producer, star: (with others) (video spl.) This Joint Is Jumpin', 1997, numerous recs. for many jazz labels; co-owner. Sidney Janis Gallery, N.Y.C.; co-founder with Maria Grimm, producer Golden Era Pictures (co. now titled MiraCon Pictures), 1988—. Recipient Theatre World award, 1952; named to Playboy Jazz Poll, 1960, 61; Silver Theatre award, 1950 Mem. SAG, AFTRA, Acad. Motion Picture Arts and Scis., Actors Equity Assn., Am. Fedn. Musicians, Nautico Club (Bilbao, Spain), Bohemian Club (San Francisco). Fax: (310) 273-0180. Office Phone: 310-820-9225. E-mail: traid43@aol.com.

JANIS, ELINOR RAIDEN, artist, educator; b. N.Y.C., Dec. 8, 1934; d. Edward and Lea Raiden; m. Leon Janis, July 14, 1957 (div. Jan. 5, 1970); children: Madeline, Richard, Cheryl. BA in Elem. Edn., UCLA, 1957; MFA, Instituto Allende, 1975. Instr. elem. schs., 1957—66, Woman's Workshop, Granada Hills, Calif., 1971—73; painting instr. Instituto Allende, 1974, 1976—77, Santa Monica Pks. and Recreation, Calif., 1977; instr. L.A. City Schs., 1978—86; profl. artist, 1986—. One-woman shows include Galeria Conde, San Miguel de Allende, Mex., 1974, Beyond Baroque Gallery, Venice, Calif., 1977, Canyon Cafe, Glendale, Calif., 2000—01, exhibited in group shows at Barnsdall Pk., L.A., 1972, Emerson Gallery, 1972, Brentwood (Calif.) Art Ctr., 1973, McCaffery Galleries, L.A., 1973, Ryder Gallery, 1973, Galeria Pintora de Jovenes, Mexico City, 1974, Powerhouse Gallery, Montreal, Can., 1975, Woman's Bldg., L.A., 1975, Woman's Ctr., Ridgefield, Con., 1975, Assn. Humanist Artists, San Francisco, 1975, Museo de Arte Contemporaneo, San Miguel de Allende, 1977, Viva Gallery, Sherman Oaks, Calif., 2000—05, others. Mem. Amnesty Internat., L.A., 1995—2001, NOW, 1985—2001, Handgun Control, 1990—2001. Recipient scholarship, Instituto Allende, 1974, 2d prize, Burbank Creative Arts Ctr. Show, 2001. Mem.: Valley Artists Guild, L.A. County Mus. Art. Democrat. Jewish. Avocations: pottery, stone carving, etching. Office: Elinor Janis Studio 14417 Chase St # 298 Panorama City CA 91402 Personal E-mail: erjanis@aol.com.

JANIS, F. TIMOTHY, technology company executive; b. Chgo., Apr. 11, 1940; s. Fabian M. and Phyllis (Underwood) Janiszewski; m. Kathryn Dickey; children: Mark David, Paul Joseph, Melissa Ann. BS in Chemistry, Wichita State U., 1962, MS in Chemistry, 1963; PhD in Chemistry, Ill. Inst. Tech., 1968. Asst., then assoc. prof. chemistry Ill. Benedictine Coll., Lisle, Ill., 1969-74; asst. acad. dean Franklin (Ind.) Coll., 1974-77; divn. dir. Indpls. Ctr. for Advanced Rsch., 1977-92; founder and pres. ARAC, Inc., Franklin, Ind., 1992—. Cons. Argonne (Ill.) Nat. Lab., 1968-74, Office Pers. Mgmt., Denver, 1988-94; mem. adv. bd. R&D Enterprise Asia Pacific, 1999. Co-author: Moving R&D to Marketplace, 1993, rev. edit., 1995, 25 publs. on tech. transfer; internat. editor Tech. Bus. Mag., 1998-2000. Mem. Lisle Cmty. High Sch. Bd., 1970-72; bd. dirs. Near North Devel. Corp., Indpls., 1990-94. Named Sagamore of the Wabash, Gov. of State of Ind., 1990. Mem. Tech. Transfer Soc. (treas., pres. 1990-92, exec. dir. 1993-96). Roman Catholic. Avocations: golf, reading, sightseeing. Office: 604 Davis Dr Franklin IN 46131-7682 Office Fax: 317-738-3980. Business E-Mail: tjanis@aracinc.com.

JANIS, MICHAEL JON, molecular biologist, entrepreneur; b. Meadville, Pa., June 6, 1970; s. Richard Joseph and Kathleen Ann (Conlin) J. BS in Biology, Northeastern U., 1994; MS in Biochemistry, Johns Hopkins U., 2001; postgrad. in Molecular Biology and Biochemistry, UCLA, 2001—. Cert. in emergency disaster response ARC. Biochem. technologist intern Ciba-Corning Diagnostics, Medfield, Mass., 1991-92; rsch. perfusion intern dept. cardiothoracic surgery Boston U. Hosp., 1992-93; founder, pres. Structural Design Concepts, Boston, 1994-96; molecular rsch. assoc. Geron Corp., Menlo Park, Calif., 1996-99; founder, pres. MOLECULIM, Menlo Park, Calif., 2001; assoc. scientist, molecular rschr. Affymetrix, Inc., Santa Clara, Calif., 1999—. Patentee in field. Vol. ARC, Palo Alto, Calif., 1999-2001. Mem.: Am. Chem. Soc., Am. Assn. Cancer Rsch. (assoc.). Avocations: rowing, sculling, music, mountain climbing, skiing. Office: Affymetrix Inc 3380 Central Expressway Santa Clara CA 95051 Home: #217 10918 Strathmore DR Los Angeles CA 90024-2412 E-mail: mjanis@chem.ucla.edu.

JANIS, WILLIAM R., lawyer, state legislator; b. Chgo., Oct. 15, 1962; m. Rose Ann Hunter; children: Rachel Ann, Robert Keith. BA in History and Eng., Va. Mil. Inst., 1984; JD, U. Va., 1999. Commd. officer USN, 1984, advanced through grades to lt. comdr., 1993, ret., 1995; pvt. practice; state del. dist. 56 Va. House of Dels., 2002—. Mem.: Federalist Soc., NRA, Order of the Arrow, U.S. Navy League, Am. Legion, VFW, K.C. Republican. Roman Catholic. Office: Gen Assembly Bldg RM 705 PO Box 406 Richmond VA 23218 Address: Dist Office PO Box 3703 Glen Allen VA 23058 Office Phone: 804-726-5856. E-mail: del_janis@hoose.state.va.us.

JANISCHEWSKYJ, WASYL, electrical engineering educator; b. Prague, Czechoslovakia, Jan. 21, 1925; s. Ivan and Hanna (Ravych) J.; m. Emilia Miszczuk; children: Roxolana, Marko. Student, Tech. U. Hannover, Fed. Republic of Germany, 1948-50; B of Applied Sci., U. Toronto, 1952, M of Applied Sci., 1954; Hon. Doctor, Natl. Tech. U. of Ukraine Polytechnical Inst., Kyiv, 1998. Registered profl. engr., Ont. Testing engr. Moloney Electric Co., Toronto, Can., summer 1952; demonstrator/instr. U. Toronto, 1952-55, lectr. to prof., 1959-90, prof. emertius, 1990—, asst. dept. head elec. engring., 1964-70, assoc. dean faculty of applied sci. and engring., 1978-82; elec. engr. Aluminium Labs., Kingston, Ont., 1955-59; elect. engr. NRC, Ottawa, Ont., Can., summer 1961, Ont. Hydro, Toronto, Can., summers 1962-65. Contbr. over 100 articles to profl. jours. Fellow IEEE; mem. Am. Soc. for Engring. Edn., Internat. Elec. Commn., Internat. Conf. on Large High Vol. Elec. Systems, Can. Elec. Assn., Assn. Profl. Engrs. Ont., Taras Shevchenko Sci. Soc., Ukrainian Free Acad. Scis. Mem. Ukranian Orthodox Ch. Home: 65 Humbercrest Blvd Toronto ON Canada M6S 4K6 Office: Univ Toronto Dept Elec/Computer Engring Toronto ON Canada M5S 3G4 Office Phone: 416-978-3116. Business E-Mail: janisch@ecf.utoronto.ca.

JANKE, JOHN ERIC, secondary educator; b. Longview, Wash., Mar. 30, 1960; s. John Charles and Rose Kathryn (Albertson) Janke. AA, Lower Columbia Coll., 1982; BA in History, Ctrl. Wash. U., 1984, MEd, 1999; BA in Edn., Western Wash. U., 1986. Cert. tchr. Wash. Jr. sch. high tchr. Bd. Edn., Kelso, Wash., 1986-94, jr. high tchr. Longview, 1986-94, Spannaway, Wash., 1994-2000. Named Alumni of the Yr., Ctrl. Wash. U., 1997. Mem.: NEA, Kelso Edn. Assn., Wash. Edn. Assn. Avocations: golf, stamp collecting/philately, pool. Home: 912 Elizabeth St Kelso WA 98626-2817 E-mail: johnjanke@yahoo.com.

JANKE, KENNETH, investment consultant; b. Ft. William, Ont., Can., May 13, 1934; s. Adolf Earthman and Julianna (Dika) J.; m. Sally Mildred Roach, June 29, 1957; children: Kenneth Stuart, Laura Lynn, Julie Ann. Student, Mich. State U., 1952-56. Asst. mgr. Household Fin. Co., Detroit, 1958—60; gen. mgr. Nat. Assn. Investors, Royal Oak, Mich., 1960—76, pres., CEO, 1976—2002, chmn., CEO, 2002—. Bd. dirs. Investment Edn. Inst., Royal Oak, pres. 1995-2002, chmn., 2002—; bd. dirs. World Fedn. Investors, Brussels, pres., 1995—. Author: Ask Mr. Naic, 1982, Golf Is A Funny Game (But It Wasn't Meant To Be), 1992, Starting and Running a Profitable Investment Club, 1996; co-author: Wit and Wisdom of Golf, 1997; columnist mag. Better Investing. Chmn. Mich. Golf Hall of Fame, Lake Orion; pres. Am. Cancer Soc.-Oakland County, Southfield, Mich., 1974-75; pres., bd. dirs. NAIC Growth Fund, Royal Oak; bd. dirs. AFLAC, Inc., Columbus, Ga.; bd. advisors Mich. PGA, West Bloomfield. With US Army, 1956-58, ETO. Recipient Disting. Svc. award Investment Edn. Inst., 1972, Founder award Am. Cancer Soc., 1970; inductee Dearborn Sports Hall of Fame, Mich., 2002. Fellow Fin. Analysts Soc. Detroit (pres. 1984—), Fin. Analysts Fedn.; mem. Nat. Investor Rels. Inst. (pres. Detroit 1985—), We. Golf Assn. (bd. dirs., pres.), Indianwood Golf and Country Club (Lake Orion), Renaissance Club (Detroit), NFL Alumni (Lauderdale, Fla.), Scalawag's Country Club (Mt. Clemens, Mich.), Masons. Republican. Episcopalian. Avocations: golf, golf collecting. Home: 4305 W Maple Rd Bloomfield Hills MI 48301-2901 Office: Nat Assn Investors Corp 711 W 13 Mile Rd Madison Heights MI 48071-1806 Office Phone: 248-583-6242. Business E-Mail: naicinvest@aol.com.

JANKE, NORMA E., nursing consultant; b. Chgo. d. Cornel and Sylvia Louise Wohlberg; m. Louis P. Janke. B Univ. Studies in Biology, U. N.Mex., 1976; BSN, U. Ala., Huntsville, 1979; student in Paralegal Studies, Arapahoe CC, Littleton, Colo., 1992—93. RN Tex., Colo. Emergency rm. nurse intravenous therapy, radiology Swedish Med. Ctr. & Porter Meml. Hosp., Englewood, Denver, Colo., 1980—90; nurse, med. specialist Am. Family, Englewood, Colo., 1990—94; nurse, asst. mgr. utilization rev. compliance Gt. West Life, Englewood, Colo., 1994—96; nurse, claims med. specialist Nationwide, Englewood, Colo., 1996—2000; nurse, risk mgmt. specialist Exempla Health Care, Wheat Ridge, Colo., 2001—02. Pres. Merevan Legal Nurse Cons. Svcs., Argyle, Tex., 1994—, Sedalia, Colo., 1994—; instr. Am. Heart ACLS & BCLS, Englewood, Colo., 1984—94. Vol. Metroport Meals-On-Wheels, Roanoke, Tex., 2004—. Mem.: Am. Assn. Legal Nurse Cons. (cert., sec. Denver chpt. 2001). Avocations: dog breeding, hiking, photography. Office Phone: 817-308-1960.

JANKE, RONALD ROBERT, lawyer; b. Milw., Mar. 2, 1947; s. Robert Erwin and Elaine Patricia (Wilken) J.; m. Mary Ann Burg, July 3, 1971; children— Jennifer, William, Emily. B.A. cum laude, Wittenberg U., 1969; J.D. with distinction, Duke U., 1974. Bar: Ohio 1974. Assoc. Jones Day, Cleve., 1974-83, ptnr., 1984—. Served with U.S. Army, 1970-71, Vietnam. Mem. ABA (chmn. environ. control com. 1980-83), Ohio Bar Assn., Greater Cleve. Bar Assn., Environ. Law Inst. Office: Jones Day N Point 901 Lakeside Ave E Cleveland OH 44114-1190 Office Phone: 216-586-7279. Business E-Mail: rrjanke@jonesday.com.

JANKLOW, MORTON LLOYD, lawyer, literary agent; b. N.Y.C., May 30, 1930; s. Maurice and Lillian (Levantin) J.; m. Linda Mervyn LeRoy, Nov. 27, 1960; children: Angela LeRoy, Lucas Warner. AB, Syracuse U., 1950; JD, Columbia U., 1953. Bar: NY 1953, DC 1961, U.S. Dist. Ct. (so. and ea. dists) NY, U.S. Ct. Appeals (2d cir.), U.S. Supreme Ct. Chmn., CEO Morton L. Janklow Assocs., Inc., 1977-89; of counsel Janklow & Ashley, LLP, N.Y.C., 1989—; sr. ptnr. Janklow & Nesbit Assocs., 1989—. Trustee Managed Accts. Svcs., PaineWebber PACE funds, 1996-2003; chmn. Janklow & Nesbit (U.K.); bd. dirs. Revlon, Inc., 1997-2000, Orbis Comm., Inc., N.Y.C., 1986-89; bd. dirs., mem. finance com. McCaffrey & McCall, Inc., N.Y.C., 1962-87; chmn. exec. com. Harvey Group, Inc., N.Y.C., 1968-71, Cable Funding Corp., N.Y.C., 1971-73; mem. exec. com. Sloan Commn. Cable Comm., 1970-71, Andrew Wellington Cordier fellow Columbia U. Sch. Internat. Affairs; vis. lectr. Radcliffe Coll., Columbia U. Law Sch., NYU; bus. and fin. adv. bd. NYU Press and NYU Sch. Arts, 1977—; donor, founder Morton L. Janklow Professorship of Lit. and Artistic Property, Columbia U. Sch. Law; life mem., Harlan Fiske Stone fellow of Columbia U. Law Sch.; founder Morton L. Janklow Program for Advocacy in the Arts, Columbia U. Law Sch.; mem. dean's coun. Columbia U. Law Sch., 1992—. Bd. dirs., exec. com., devel. chmn. City Center Music and Drama, 1971-75; bd. dirs. Film Soc., Lincoln Ctr., 1972-75, Am. Cinematheque, 1971-75; bd. govs. Jewish Mus., 1969-75; dir., chmn. Janklow Found.; trustee Mr. and Mrs. Harry M. Warner Found., 1965—, Sidney Sheldon Found.; mem. Council of Friends, Whitney Mus. Am. Art, 1973-82, also mem. com. on paintings and sculptures; ad hoc com. on pub. and merchandising activities Met. Mus. Art, 1998-2003; bd. advisors Princeton U. Art. Mus., 1984-89; mem. adv. bd. Guggenheim Mus., 1980-86; adv. council Sch. Arts, NYU; mem. Ind. Com. on Arts Policy; bd. advisors Columbia U. Jour. Art and the Law; assn. of fellows Pierpoint Morgan Libr., N.Y.C. Served with AUS, 1953-55. Decorated chevalier l'Ordre des Arts et des Lettres de la Republique Française. Mem. ABA, N.Y. Bar Assn., Assn. of Bar of City of N.Y. (membership com. 1967—), N.Y. County Lawyers Assn., Fed. Comms. Bar Assn., Am. Judicature Soc., Coun. on Fgn. Rels., Com. on the Rsch. Librs., N.Y. Pub. Libr: chmn. Arthur Ross Book award Jury. Office: 445 Park Ave New York NY 10022-2606 Office Phone: 212-421-1700. E-mail: mjanklow@janklow.com.

JANKOVIC, JOSEPH, neurologist, educator; b. Teplice, Czechoslovakia, Mar. 1, 1948; came to U.S., 1965; m. Cathy Sue Inselberg, May 26, 1973; children: Jason, Daniel, Zachary. MD, U. Ariz., 1973. Diplomate Am. Bd. Neurology. Med. intern Baylor Coll. Medicine, Houston, 1973-74, asst. prof. neurology, 1977-84, assoc. prof., 1984-88, prof., 1988—; resident in neurology Columbia U., N.Y.C., 1974-76, chief resident in neurology, 1976-77. Dir. Parkinson's Disease Ctr. and Movement Disorder Clinic, Houston, 1977—; sr. attending physician Meth. Hosp., Houston, 1988—. Author over 500 articles and book chpts. in field; editor/co-editor 16 med. books; mem. editorial bd. jours. Movement Disorders, Clin. Neuropharmacology, Neurology Jour., Jour. Neurology Psychiatry. Chmn. sci. adv. bd. Blepharospasm Rsch. Found.; mem. adv. bd. Dystonia Med. Rsch. Found., Internat. Tremor Found., Tourette's Syndrome Med. Adv. Bd. Grantee disease rsch. founds., pharmaceutical cos., NIH Fellow Am. Acad. Neurology; mem. AMA, Am. Neurol. Assn., Soc. for Neurosci., Movement Disorders Soc. (pres.-elect 1991-94, pres. 1994-96). Avocations: tennis, family activities, music. Office: Baylor Coll Medicine 6550 Fannin St Ste 1801 Houston TX 77030-2744

JANKOWSKI, ROBERT, management consultant; BA in English, Iona Coll., 1970; MBA, Almeda U., 1999. Dir. ops. A.T. Hudson and Co., 1989—92; dir. spl. projects Heller Fin., 1992—2000; COO, v.p. ops. and project mgmt. Dynamic Svcs. Internat., Inc., 2000—02. Home: 26 Mead St Stamford CT 06907 Office Phone: 845-721-3080. Personal E-mail: bobj13@aol.com.

JANKOWSKI, THEODORE ANDREW, artist; b. New Brunswick, N.J., Dec. 14, 1946; s. Theodore Andrew and Lois (Amarescu) J.; m. Rebecca Buck, July 23, 1983; 1 child, Tito Henry. Student, McMurrough Sch. Art, Indialantic, Fla., 1956-58, 74-75, R.I. Sch. Design, 1972, Cape Sch. of Art, Provincetown, Mass., 1975-76, 79-87, Cen. Fla. U., 1976-77. One-man shows include Eye of Horus Gallery, Provincetown, 1985; exhibited in group shows at Provincetown Art Assn. Mus., 1984, Bethlehem (Pa.) City Hall, 1988, Michael Ingbar Gallery, N.Y.C., 1988, 91; represented in permanent collections at State Mus. at Palace of Peter the Gt., Leningrad, USSR, Cigna Mus. and Art Collection, Phila., Mishkan Olemanut Mus. Art, Israel, Novosibirsk (Russia) Picture Gallery, CIGNA Mus., Phila., Johns Hopkins U., Balt., Vassar Coll. portrait collection, Hiroshima Peace Meml. Mus., Hiroshima Japan - Hunter Mus. of Am. Art, Chattanooga, Holyoke (Mass.) Mus. Art, McGill U., Montreal, Que., Can., Downey (Calif.) Mus. Art, Ark. Art Ctr., Little Rock, Muzeum Niepoldlegosi, Warsaw, Poland, Nat. Mus. Bosnia, Sarajevo, Yad Vashem The Holocaust Martyrs and Heroes Art Mus., Jerusalem, Beloit Coll. Wright Mus. ARt, Pradd Sch. Design, N.Y.C., Mt. Holyoke Coll. Art Mus., Kokoiki Bapt. Ch. (mural), others Home: PO Box 791 Kapaau HI 96755-0791

JANKOWSKY, JOEL, lawyer; BBA, U. Okla., 1965, JD, 1968. Bar: Okla. 1968, US Mil. Appeals 1968, US Supreme Ct. 1971, DC 1976. Legis. asst. to Speaker Carl Albert U.S. Ho. of Reps., 1972—77; joined Akin Gump Strauss Hauer & Feld LLP, Washington, 1977, now ptnr., public policy dept. and mem. mgmt. com. Bd. dirs. Closeup Found., Washington, Cancer Rsch. Found. Am., Alexandria, Va.; trustee Potomac Sch., McLean, Va., 1984-90; mem. bd. advisors Carl Albert Ctr. U. Okla.; mem. Page Rev. Commn. for US Ho. Reps., 1982. Capt. JAGC U.S. Army, 1968—72. Office: Akin Gump Strauss Hauer & Feld LLP Ste 400 1333 New Hampshire Ave NW Washington DC 20036-1564 Office Phone: 202-887-4082. Office Fax: 202-887-4288. Business E-Mail: jjankowsky@akingump.com.

JANNERS, ERIK NIKOLAS, music educator, conductor; b. Ft. Sam Houston, San Antonio, Jan. 8, 1972; s. Sigurds and Martha Janners. MusB, Alma Coll., 1994; MusM, U. Utah, 1997; D in Musical Arts, U. Ala., 2001. Dir. bands U. Regina, Canada, 2001—04, St. Xavier U., Chgo., 2004—. Dir. condr.'s workshop St. Xavier U., Chgo., 2004—. Contbr. articles to profl. publs. Mem. at large Sask. Band Assn., Canada, 2002—04. Mem.: Music Educators Nat. Conf. Avocations: hiking, reading, travel, sports, fitness. Home: 6005 Stewart Dr Apt #613 Chicago IL 60527 Office: Saint Xavier University 3700 W 103rd St Chicago IL 60655 Office Phone: 773-298-3422. Home Fax: n/a. Personal E-mail: nikolas1972@hotmail.com. E-mail: janners@sxu.edu.

JANNETTA, PETER JOSEPH, neurosurgeon, educator; b. Phila., Apr. 5, 1932; s. Samuel and Frances (Alfano) J.; m. Diana R. Jannetta, Sept. 9, 1989; children: Susan, Carol, Joanne, Peter, Elizabeth, S. Michael. AB, U. Pa., 1953, MD, 1957. Diplomate Am. Bd. Surgery, Am. Bd. Neurol. Surgery. Intern Hosp. U. Pa., 1957-58, resident in surgery, 1958-63; resident in neurosurgery, asso. UCLA Center for Health Scis., 1963-66; asst. instr. U. Pa., 1958-62, instr., 1960-63, instr. surgery, 1962-63; assoc. prof., chmn. surgery La. State

U., 1966-71, prof., chmn. neurosurgery, 1971; prof. neurosurgery U. Pitts., 1971-76, Francis Sergeant Cheever Disting. prof., 1976-98, chmn. dept. neurol. surgery, 1976-2000, dir. divsn. neurol. surgery, 1973-2000; active staff Presbyn.-Univ. Hosp., Pitts., Children's Hosp. Pitts.; sr. attending staff Montefiore Hosp., Pitts.; sr. cons. VA Hosp., Pitts.; prof., vice chmn. dept. neurosurgery Allegheny Gen. Hosp. Sec. of health Commonwealth of Pa., 1995-96. Co-editor: The Cranial Nerves, 1981, Trigeminal Neuralgia, 1990; contbr. numerous articles to profl. jours. Mem. A.C.S., AMA, AAAS, Am. Surg. Assn., Allegheny County, Pa. med. socs., Assn. Academic Surgery, Am. Assn. Neurol. Surgeons, Congress Neurol. Surgeons, Fellowship Acad. Neurosurgeons, Internat. Assn. Study Pain, Internat. Soc. Pediatric Neurosurgery, Mid-Atlantic, Pa., Pitts. neurosurg. socs., N.Y. Acad. Scis., Pitts. Acad. Medicine, Pitts. Surg. Soc., Ravdin-Rhoads Surg. Soc., Research Soc. Neurol. Surgeons, Soc. Critical Care Medicine, Soc. Neurol. Surgeons, Soc. Neurosci., Soc. Neurosurg. Anesthesia and Neurol. Supportive Care. Office: Allegheny Gen Hosp Dept Neurosurgery 420 E North Ave Ste 302 Pittsburgh PA 15212

JANNEY, ALLISON, actress; b. Dayton, Ohio, Nov. 19, 1960; BA, Kenyon Coll.; pvt. studies in acting, Neighborhood Playhouse, N.Y.C. Appeared in feature films: Big Night, 1996, Private Parts, 1997, Primary Colors, 1998, Six Days, Seven Nights, 1998, The Ice Storm, 1997, Celebrity, 1998, 10 Things I Hate About You, 1999, Drop Dead Gorgeous, 1999, Nurse Betty, 2000, American Beauty, 1999, Leaving Drew, 2000, Finding Nemo (voiceover), 2003, How to Deal, 2003; plays (on Broadway) A View From The Bridge (Tony award nominee 1998, Outer Critics Circle award,Drama Desk award); appearances on TV: The West Wing (role C.J. Gregg), 1999-, (Emmy award Outstanding Lead Actress in a Drama Series, 2004), A Girl Thing (TV mini), 2000 Recipient Outstanding Featured Actress in a Play for "A View From the Bridge", Drama Desk Award, 1998, Outstanding Supporting Actress in a Drama Series for "The West Wing", Emmy Award, 1999, 2000, Best Actress in a Television Series Drama for "The West Wing", Golden Satellite, 2000, Best Ensemble Cast Performance for "The West Wing", 2000, Outstanding Female Actor in a Drama Series for "The West Wing", The Actor Awards, 2000, Outstanding Ensemble in a Drama Series for "The West Wing", 2000, Outstanding Supporting Actress in a Drama Series for "The West Wing", Emmy Awards, 2001, Outstanding Female Actor in a Drama Series for "The West Wing", The Actor Awards, 2001, Outstanding Ensemble in a Drama Series for "The West Wing", 2001, Outstanding Female Actress in a Drama Series for "The West Wing", Emmy Awards, 2002.

JANNEY, CHRISTOPHER G., lawyer; b. Bethesda, Md., Feb. 14, 1964; BA summa cum laude, U. Md., 1986; JD cum laude, Harvard U., 1991. Bar: Md. 1991, DC 1993. Analyst Nat. Drug Policy Bd. US Dept. Justice, Washington, 1986—88; assoc. to ptnr. Shaw Pittman LLP, Washington; ptnr., health care group Sonnenschein Nath & Rosenthal LLP, Washington, 2003—. Mem.: ABA (mem. health law sect.), Am. Health Lawyers Assn. Office: Sonnenschein Nath & Rosenthal LLP Ste 600, E Tower 1301 K St NW Washington DC 20005 Office Phone: 202-408-6399, 202-408-9151. Business E-Mail: cjanney@sonnenschein.com.

JANNEY, DANIEL S., health products executive; BA, Georgetown U.; MBA, UCLA. V.p. health care and biotech. investment banking group Montgomery Securities, 1993—96; mng. dir. Alta Ptnrs., 1996—; chmn. bd. dirs. Dynavax Technologies Corp., Berkeley, Calif., 1996—, Corgentech, Inc. Mem. adv. bd. Rebecca and John Moores Cancer Ct., U.C.S.D. Office: Dynavax Technologies Corp 717 Potter St #100 Berkeley CA 94710*

JANNEY, DONALD WAYNE, lawyer; b. Clinton, N.C., Jan. 9, 1952; s. Wayne Columbus and Bernice (Talley) J.; m. Sydney Louise Rhame, May 28, 1977; children: Taylor Columbus, Camden St. Clair. BA, Furman U., 1974; JD, U. Va., 1978. Bar: Ga. 1978, U.S. Dist. Ct. (no. dist.) Ga. 1978, U.S. Ct. Appeals (11th cir.) 1982. Assoc. Troutman Sanders, Atlanta, 1978-85; ptnr. Troutman Sanders and predecessor firm, Atlanta, 1985—. Bd. dirs. State YMCA Ga., Atlanta, 1980-91. Mem. ABA, Ga. Bar Assn., Atlanta Bar Assn., Phi Beta Kappa. Baptist. Home: 705 E Morningside Dr Atlanta GA 30324-5220 Office: Troutman Sanders Ste 5200 600 Peachtree St NE Atlanta GA 30308-2216 Office Phone: 404-885-3000. E-mail: donald.janney@troutmansanders.com.

JANNEY, OLIVER JAMES, lawyer; b. N.Y.C., Feb. 11, 1946; s. Walter Coggeshall and Helen Jennings (James) Janney; m. Suzanne Elizabeth Lenz, June 21, 1969; children: Elizabeth Flower, Oliver Burr. BA cum laude, Yale U., 1967; JD, Harvard U., 1970. Bar: Mass. 1970, N.Y. 1971, Fla. 1991. With Walston & Co., Inc., N.Y.C., 19770-73, asst. v.p., 1971-73; assoc. Cleary Gottlieb, Steen & Hamilton, N.Y.C., 1973-76; with RKO Gen., Inc., N.Y.C., 1976-90, asst. sec., 1977-85, asst. gen. atty., 1978-82, asst. gen. counsel, 1982-85, sec., gen. counsel, 1985-89; exec. v.p., gen. counsel, sec. Uniroyal Tech. Corp., Sarasota, Fla., 1990—2003; ptnr. Janey & Curd, LLP, 2005—. 1st lt. USAR, 1969—77. Mem.: ABA, Fla. Bar Assn., Sarasota County Bar Assn., Assn. Bar of City of N.Y., N.Y. State Bar Assn., Am. Corp. Counsel Assn. Republican. Home: 1684 Peregrine Point Dr Sarasota FL 34231-2331 Office: Janney & Curd LLP c/o Uniroyal Engineered Products 290 Cocoanut Ave Ste 1A Sarasota FL 34236-4949 Office Phone: 941-684-3314. Personal E-mail: oliverjanney@aol.com.

JANNEY, STUART SYMINGTON, III, investment company executive; b. Balt., Aug. 30, 1948; s. Stuart Symington and Barbara (Phipps) J.; m. Lynn Mary Buchheit, Oct. 28, 1975; children: Emily, Matthew. BA, U. N.C., 1970; JD, U. Md., 1973. Bar: Md. 1973. Legis. asst. Sen. Charles Mathias U.S. Senate, Washington, 1973-75, fgn. policy asst. Sen. Howard Baker, 1976-77; spl. asst. U.S. Sec. State U.S. State Dept., Washington, 1975-76; ptnr. Niles, Barton & Wilmer, Balt., 1977-86; mng. dir. Alex Brown & Sons, Balt., 1986-94; head Alex. Brown Asset Mgmt., Balt., 1986-93; chmn. bd. Bessemer Trust Co., N.Y.C., 1994—, Bessemer Securities Corp., N.Y.C., 1994—. Bd. dirs. Johns Hopkins U., Balt., 1988—, vice chmn., 1995-2002; chmn. bd. dirs. Applied Physics Lab., 1991—, Md. Zool. Soc., Balt., 1979—; bd. dirs. Md. Horsebreeders, 1991-98; bd. dirs. Thoroughbred Owners and Breeders Am.; bd. dirs. Keeneland Assocs., Nat. Audubon Soc., N.Y.C., 1982-92; steward Jockey Club U.S. Mem.: NY Racing Assn. (bd. dirs.). Office: Bessemer Trust Co 630 5th Ave New York NY 10111-0100

JANNINI, RALPH HUMBERT, III, electronics executive; b. Boston, Dec. 30, 1932; s. Humbert P. and Marian H. (Roman) J.; m. Pauline T. Occhinto, Feb. 16, 1957; children: Ralph H. IV, Mark L., Lisa M. BS in Acctg., Bentley Coll., 1957. CPA, Mass. Auditor New Eng. Electric System, Westboro, Mass., 1957-68, mgr. rates and statistics, 1968-73; asst. to pres. Gas Inc.-Colonial, Lowell, Mass., 1973-76; v.p. Colonial Gas Co., Lowell, 1976-87; pres. James Millen Electronics, Malden, Mass., 1988—. Cons. Antennas Etc., Andover, Mass., 1980—; prin. Unadilla/Reyco/InLine Products, 1986—, Andover Book and Collaborative, 1995—. Served with U.S. Army, 1952-53, Korea. Republican. Roman Catholic. Office: James Millen Electronics 87 Belmont St North Andover MA 01845-2304

JANNOT, MARK ALLEN, magazine publishing executive; s. Kenneth and Maureen Jannot; m. Liza Schoenfein, Sept. 18, 1993. BS in journalism, MS in journalism, Medill Sch. Journalism, Northwestern U., 1987. Dep. editor Men's Jour.; contbg. editor Chgo. Mag.; exec. editor Nat. Geographic Adventure, 1998—2003; dep. editor Popular Sci., 2003—04, editor-in-chief, 2004—. Office: Popular Science 2 Park Ave 9th Fl New York NY 10016

JANNOTTI, GENE PATRICK, business consultant, telecommunications professional; b. Newburgh, NY, Oct. 10, 1946; s. Pellegrino and Anne J. BS in Math., Siena Coll., 1968; MA in Math., St. John's U., 1970; MS in Bus. Policy, Columbia U., 1981. Cert. sys. profl. Asst. programmer N.Y. Tel., N.Y.C., 1971-72, computer ops. mgr., 1973-80, staff mgr., 1980-84; programmer Bell Labs., Greensboro, N.C., 1972-73; dist. mgr. Bell Comm. Rsch., Piscataway, N.J., 1984-87; staff dir. NYNEX Corp. Comm., N.Y.C., 1987-89, NYNEX Videoteleconferencing, N.Y.C., 1989-91; dir. ops. NYNEX Computer Ops., Pearl River, N.Y., 1991; dir. NYNEX Software Devel., N.Y.C., 1992-95; founder, pres. LCA, Llewellyn Cons. Assocs., Westfield, N.J., 1995-98; dir. Computer Scis. Corp., 1998—; founder Unique Cruise and Travel, 2000—, prin., owner Garwood, N.J., 2000—. Capt. USAR, 1968-74. Mem. Data Processing Mgmt. Assn. (bd. dirs. N.Y. chpt. 1980-84, exec. v.p. 1984), Project Mgmt. Inst., Germania Corinthian Union Lodge # 11, Free and Accepted Masons. Roman Catholic. Avocations: travel, gardening, photography. Home and Office: PO Box 267 Garwood NJ 07027-0267 Office Phone: 908-301-1123. E-mail: genej@homemail.com, gjanott@csc.com.

JANNUZI, F. TOMASSON, economics professor; b. Pitts., Apr. 23, 1934; s. Frank Humbert and Angela Mary (Tomasson) J.; m. Barbara Lucille Gallagher, Sept. 15, 1957; children: Buell Tomasson, Frank Sampson. AB, Dartmouth Coll., 1955; PhD in Econ., U. London, 1958. Field rep. for So. Asia, E. Africa Found. For Youth and Student Affairs, N.Y.C., 1959-61; asst. rep. The Asia Found., N.Y.C., 1961-62, program officer for So. Asia div. San Francisco, 1962-65, asst. rep. for India, 1965-68; vis. lectr. in econs. U. Tex., Austin, 1968-72, dir. at the Ctr. for Asian Studies, Nat. Resource Ctr. for So. Asia, 1972-86, assoc. prof. of econs., 1973-79, prof. of econs. and Asian studies, 1979-98, assoc. chmn. dept. econs., 1995-97, prof. emeritus econs., 1998—. Pres. Asia Rsch. Assoc. Inc., Austin, Tex., 1985-99; vis. fellow Internat. Devel. Ctr. U. Oxford, Eng., 1989-92; sr. assoc. St. Antony's Coll. Oxford, 1989; vis scholar Ctr. for South Asian Studies, U. Va., 1999—; cons. USAID, Dept. State, Def. Intelligence Coll., World Bank, 1973—. Author: Agrarian Crisis in India: The Case of Bihar, 1974, India in Transition: Issues of Political Economy in a Plural Society, 1988; India's Persistent Dilemma: The Political Economy of Agrarian Reform, 1994; co-author: (with James T. Peach) The Agrarian Structure of Bangladesh, 1980; contbr. articles to profl. jours. Dir. Austin Coun. on Fgn. Affairs Inc., Tex., 1987-98; mem. Inst. of Current World Affairs, Hanover, N.H., 1987—98; trustee Am. Inst. of Indian Studies, Chgo., 1973-87, chmn. 1979-81. Fellow Ford Found.; mem. Phi Beta Kappa. Democrat. Avocation: travel. Home: 1835 Mountainside Dr Blacksburg VA 24060-9203 Personal E-mail: ftjannuzi@msn.com.

JANNUZZI, LUIGI, playwright, educator; b. Bound Brook, NJ, Nov. 12, 1952; s. Louis and Virginia Jannuzzi; m. Patricia Christensen, June 21, 1987; children: Louis III, Mark. BA, Salem U., 1975; MA, Notre Dame Univ., 1977. Tchr., drama, creative writing, pub. speaking Immaculata H.S., Somerville, NJ; tchr. St. Peter's H.S., New Brunswick, NJ; claims adj. Allstate Ins., NJ; with Weichert Realtor. Author: (one-act play) A Bench at the Edge, 1982 (Grand Prize Drama League Ireland, Moat Club from Naas., 1999, Grand Prize Assn. Ulster Drama Festivals Scotland, U.K. Wick Players Scotland, 2001), The Barbarians are Coming, 1986, The Appointment, 1995, With or Without You, 1996, (plays) Night of the Foolish Moon, 1998, For the Love of Juliet, 2004; comic monologue: Anthem, Nat. Pub. Radio, 1999. Mem. N.J. Rep. Finalist Nat. Playwrights Conf. at the Eugene O'Neill Theatre Ctr., Waterford, Conn., 1987, 1999; recipient Samuel French Play award, 1981, 1995, 1996; grantee Playwriting fellowships, N.J. State Arts Coun., 1999, Nat. Endowments for the Humanities, Univ. Vt., 1995, Columbia Univ., 1998, Rutgers Univ., 2000; grant, Walt Whitman Cultural Arts Ctr., 2001, Geraldine R. Dodge Found., 1995, 2001, Playwriting fellowships, N.J. State Arts Coun., 1987. Mem.: N. J. Theatre Educators Coalition, Dramatists Guild, Genesis Rep., Waterfront Ensemble, Met. Theatre Co. Achievements include fourteen time finalist in Samuel French One Act Competition in NYC, finalist in Turnip Theatre American Globe Theatre Festival in NYC, finalist in the Orlando Shakespeare Festival; winner, Goshen Playwriting Peace prize, 1986. Office: C/O Alleen Hssung/Samuel French 45 W 25th St New York NY 10010 Office Phone: 908-268-3600. Personal E-mail: LJannuzzi@hotmail.com.

JANOLLARI, DAVID, television broadcasting executive, cable producer, television producer; With Nederlander TV Prodn., NY; dir. comedy devel. Fox Broadcasting; v.p. comedy devel. Warner Bros. TV Network, 1991—93, sr. v.p. comedy devel., 1993—95, exec. v.p. creative affairs, 1995—97, pres. entertainment, 2004—; co-founder, pres. Greenblatt Janollari Studio, 1997—2004. Exec. prodr.: (TV series) The Hughleys, 1998—2002, To Have & to Hold, 1998, Maggie Winters, 1998—99; exec. prodr.: (TV series) Off Grow Up, 1999; exec. prodr.: (TV series) Heat Vision and Jack, 1999, Chicks, 1999, The Chronicle, 2001—02, One on One, 2001—, Definitely Maybe, 2001; exec. prodr.: (TV series) Six Feet Under, 2001—; exec. prodr.: (TV series) American Family, 2002—04, Platinum, 2003, Eve, 2003—. Office: WB Network 4000 Warner Blvd Burbank CA 91522

JANOO, JABIN, obstetrician, gynecologist; b. Nairobi, Kenya, Aug. 26, 1969; arrived in U.S., 1997; d. Tajdin Kassam and Jenab Ismail Janoo; m. Farrukh Mamfuz Jalisi; children: Inara Farrukh Jalisi, Alina Sanniya Jalisi. MB, BChir, Aga Khan U.; Karachi, Pakistan, 1994; MD, U.S. Med. Licensing Examination, 1997. Lic. physician W.Va., cert. Am. Bd. Ob-gyn. Ho. officer Aga Khan U. Hosp., Karachi, 1995—96, rsch. officer, 1996—97; resident in internal medicine W.Va. U. Hosp., Morgantown, 1997—98, resident in ob-gyn., 1999—2002, chief resident, 2002—. Organizer, designer health survey Aga Khan Found./UNICEF, Tajikistan, 1995—96; facilitator, advisor Aga Khan U., 1995. Contbr. articles to profl. jours. Scholar Aga Khan Found., 1989. Fellow: Am. Coll. Ob-Gyn.; mem.: ACP (Best Rschr. award 1999). Avocations: swimming, reading, writing, walking. Office: WVa Univ Hosp Dept ObGyn Stadium Dr Morgantown WV 26506 Office Phone: 304-293-5632. Office Fax: 304-293-2131. E-mail: jajezfj@hotmail.com.

JANOS, ELLEN L., lawyer; b. 1951; BA with honors, Simmons Coll., 1973; JD magna cum laude, New Eng. Sch. Law, 1977. Bar: Mass. 1977, US Supreme Ct. 1984, US Ct. Appeals (1st Cir.). Adminstrv. counsel Mass. Atty. Gen. Office; asst. atty. gen. Commonwealth of Mass.; ptnr., Health Care Sect. Mintz Levin Cohn Ferris Glovsky & Popeo PC, Boston, coord., Fraud & Abuse & Corp. Compliance Practice Group. Contbr. editor Health Care Fraud & Abuse Newsletter, NY Law Pub. Co., spkr. in field. Mem. Mass. Bd. Medicine Task Force, 1992. Office: Mintz Levin Cohn Ferris Glovsky & Popeo PC One Financial Ctr Boston MA 02111 Office Phone: 202-348-1662. Office Fax: 202-542-2241. Business E-Mail: ejanos@mintz.com.

JANOS, JAMES See VENTURA, JESSE

JANOS, JAMES DONALD, security and safety consultant; b. Martins Ferry, Ohio, Apr. 29, 1949; s. James and Susie Janos; m. Janet L. Smith, Feb. 2, 1980; children: Janelle N., Justin K. AAS in Indsl. Security, W.Va. No. C.C., 1987; BA in Criminial Justice-BOR, West Liberty State Coll., 1987; MS in Safety Mgmt., W.Va. U., 1995; postgrad., Internat. U., Grandview, Mo., 2005—. Security cons. Diebold Inc., Wheeling, W.Va., 1979-80, Day and Night Security, Wheeling, 1981-83; broadcast engr. Sta. WOMP Radio, Bellaire, Ohio, 1983-86; electronics cons. Bethany (W.Va.) Coll., 1987-89; safety intern Vandenberg AFB, Lompoc, Calif., 1990; broadcast engr. Sta. WKWK-Radio Inc., Wheeling, 1991—96, sports broadcaster, 1991—96. Broadcast engring. cons., Bridgeport, Ohio, 1990—. Vol. disaster svcs. ARC, Wheeling, 1990; libr. asst. OCPL, Wheeling, 1996—2004; comms. officer Ohio County CAP; nuc. safety specialist State W.Va., 2004—. With USN, 1975—78, with USAF, 1967—74. Master Mason; mem. Am. Soc. Safety Engrs., Nat. Assn. Radio and Telecommunications Engrs. Avocations: photography, research investigation, amateur astronomy. Home and Office: 400 Jacquette St Bridgeport OH 43912-1012

JANOSKI, HENRY VALENTINE, investment advisor, former banker; b. Nanticoke, Pa., Feb. 14, 1933; s. Bruce and Marie (Rozmarek) J.; m. Rita Rosemary Ruane, Sept. 27, 1980; children: Maria, Elizabeth. BA magna cum laude, Yale U., 1955; MBA, U. Pa., 1960, CFA, CSA. Sr. credit analyst Nat Bank Detroit, 1960-63; asst. cashier First Nat. Bank, Wilkes-Barre, Pa., 1963-65; sr. v.p. Northeastern Bank, Scranton, Pa., 1965-80; investment counselor, fin. planner Clarks Summit and Scranton, Pa., 1980-92; realtor assoc. Clarks Summit, 1992; chief trust investment officer Penn Security Bank and Trust Co., Scranton, 1992—2001; sr. investment officer Linden Asset Mgmt., Inc., Scranton, 2002—05; sr. investment advisor Northeastern Fin. Cons., Inc., Clarks Summit, 2005—. Instr. fin. Marywood Coll., Scranton, 1983. Bd. dirs. Cmty. Med. Ctr., Scranton, 1974-97, asst. treas., 1976-91; bd. dirs. Emergency Med. Svcs. Northeastern Pa., Pittston, 1976—, pres., 1985-87, Polish Am. Congress No. Pa. divsn., Scranton, 1972—, v.p., 1972-89, pres., 1989-2004, Ethics Inst. N.E. Pa., Dallas, 1991-96, Keystone chpt. Am. Heart Assn., Scranton, 1968-74, treas., 1968-74; chmn. Campaign for Yale U., Northeastern Pa., 1976-78; incorporating dir. Lackawanna County U.S. Constn. Bicentennial Commn., 1987-88; mem. Lackawanna County Commrs. Transition Task Force for Fin./Budget, 2003-04; treas. Grove St. Home Sch. Assn., Clarks Summit, 1987-90; lectr. Christ the King Ch., Dunmore, 1982-87, Our Lady of the Snows Ch., Clarks Summit, 1987—, Ch. of St. Benedict, Newton Twp., 1991—; allocations vol. United Way, 1988-91, 2002-05. 1st lt. AUS, 1955-57. Recipient Assn. U.S. Army award, 1954, Disting. Mil. Student award, 1955, Am. Legion award, 1947, 51, Cert. Leadership Lackawanna, 1989. Mem. Fin. Analysts Phila., CFA Inst., Soc. of Cert. Sr. Advisors, Estate Planning Coun. Northeastern Pa., Experiment in Internat. Living (France), Le Cercle Francais (treas. 1994-2004), Ecologia/Ekologiya, Luzerne County Hist. Soc., Nanticoke Hist. Soc., Greater Scranton C. of C., Esperanto League for N.Am., Universala Esperanto Asocio, Polish Nat. Alliance, Polish Falcons Am., Polish Am. Hist. Assn., Kosciuszko Found., Assn. Yale Alumni (rep. 1988-91), Aircraft Owners and Pilots Assn., Schultzville Airport Pilots Assn., Westmoreland Club (Wilkes-Barre), Scranton Club, Yale Club of Northeastern Pa. (sec. 1985-88, alumni sch. com. interviewed applicants 1965-98), U. Pa. Alumni Club of Northeastern Pa., Leadership Lackawanna Alumni Assn., Phi Beta Kappa. Republican. Roman Catholic. Avocations: travel, languages. Home: 107 Carteret Dr Clarks Summit PA 18411-1009 Office: Northeastern Fin Cons Inc 3 Abington Exec Park Ste 1 Clarks Summit PA 18411 Office Phone: 570-586-1064. Personal E-mail: HJanoski@aol.com.

JANOWITZ, JAMES ARNOLD, lawyer; b. N.Y.C., Sept. 2, 1946; s. Arnold and Erna (Frankel) J.; m. Katherine Eva Sborovy, Aug. 6, 1967; children: Jessie Elizabeth, William Aaron. BA, Haverford Coll., 1967; JD, NYU, 1971. Bar: N.Y. 1972, U.S. Dist Ct. (so. dist.) N.Y. 1972. Tchr. St. David's Sch., N.Y.C., 1968-72; assoc. Guzik & Boukstein, N.Y.C., 1972-73, Reavis & McGrath, N.Y.C., 1973-74, Pryor, Cashman & Sherman, N.Y.C., 1974-76; ptnr. Pryor, Cashman, Sherman & Flynn, N.Y.C., 1977—. Adj. prof. Cardozo Law Sch., Yeshiva U., N.Y.C., 1992; bd. dirs. Avenue Entertainment, 1986-99. Editor NYU Jour. Internat. Law and Politics, 1970-71. Mem. N.Y. State Bar Assn., Assn. of Bar of City of N.Y. Office: Pryor Cashman Sherman & Flynn 410 Park Ave Fl 10 New York NY 10022-4407

JANOWSKI, THADDEUS MARIAN, architect; b. Cracow, Poland, Aug. 16, 1923; came to U.S., 1960, naturalized, 1972; s. Stanislaw and Maria (Kijak) J.; m. Zofia K. Owinski, Apr. 19, 1949 (div.); 1 child, Barbara Margaret MCP in Architecture, Poly. Acad., Cracow, 1949; MArch, U. Ill., 1962; PhD (hon.), Inst. Three Dimensional Perception, 1987. Chief architect Miastoprojekt Cracow, 1949-58; chief cons. So. Poland K.U.A., Warsaw, 1958-60; lectr. Poly Acad. Cracow, 1947-50, 1958-60; instr. U. Ill., 1960-62; assoc. prof. U. Man., Can., 1962-65, Iowa State U., Ames, 1965-71; prof. Syracuse U., N.Y., 1971—; proprietor, dir. Mus. Archtl. Graphics Internat., 1994—. Pres. Inst. Three Dimensional Perception, Inc., 1985; chief arch. for Saudi royal family estates, Ga., 1983-89; prin., dir. Mus. Archtl. Graphics Internat., 1991—; chmn. hon. doctorates com. Syracuse U. Senate, 1978-81. Numerous exhbns. in U.S. and Europe, 1949—; built over 6 million sq. ft. constrn. commns. include Interstate Farm Devel., Des Moines, 1967, Settlement of town houses, East Des Moines, 1969. Co-author: Sacred Art in Poland, 1955; The Urban Scale, 1968. Patentee in field. Recipient numerous prizes nat. or internat. competitions including prize Polish Embassy bldg., Peking, China, 1955, 1st prize Polish Pavillion, Brussels, Belgium, 1956, 1st prize astronomy obs. and planetarium Warsaw, 1956, award exptl. bldg., Moscow, 1959, 1st prize sch. bldgs., Poland, 1960, prize Red Rock Hill Devel., San Francisco, 1961, 2d prize campus, Dublin, Ireland, 1964, 1st prize Olympic Stadium, Banff, Can., 1962, 2d and 3rd prizes fall out shelters Office Civil Defense, 1964, 2d prize, 1966; 1st prize Bicentennial medal Iowa, 1972; 1st prize for U.S. Stamp Copernicus Quincentennial; 1st prize and commn. for monument commemorating victims of Katyn Massacre, Toronto, 1979, Syracuse, N.Y., 1985. Fellow World-Wide Acad. Scholars New Zealand, Intercontinental Biographical Assn. (U.K.); mem. Assn. Polish Architects, Assn. Painters, Sculptors and Artists in Poland, Assn. Scientists Hist. Armament, Canadian Assn. U. Tchrs., NRA, Am. Legion. Address: 575 Reynolds Bend Rd SE Rome GA 30161-2546 *On our beautiful planet, architecture is one of the necessary evils. It is a sensor of society's cultural level, therefore the architect determines the dignity of environment by restraint, simplicity, honesty, obviousness, and antiexhibitionism.*

JANSEEN, FAMKE, actress; b. Amsterdam, Noord-Holland, Netherlands, Nov. 5, 1965; m. Tod Williams, 1995 (div. 2000). Actor: (films) Fathers and Sons, 1992, Relentless IV: Ashes to Ashes, 1994, Lord of Illusions, 1995, GoldenEye, 1995, Dead Girl, 1996, City of Industry, 1997, Snitch, 1998, The Gingerbread Man, 1998, Deep Rising, 1998, RPM, 1998, Celebrity, 1998, Rounders, 1998, The Adventures of Sebastian Cole, 1998, The Faculty, 1998, House on Haunted Hill, 1999, Love and Sex, 2000, Circus, 2000, X-Men, 2000, Made, 2001, Don't Say a Word, 2001, I Spy, 2002, X2: X-Men United, 2003, Eulogy, 2004, Family of the Year, 2004, Hide and Seek, 2005; (TV films) Model by Day, 1994; TV appearances include: Star Trek: The Next Generation, 1992; Melrose Place, 1994; The Untouchables, 1994; Ally McBeal, 2000, 2001; Dinner for Five, 2002, 2003; Nip/Tuck, 2004. Office: Creative Artist Agency 9830 Wilshire Blvd Beverly Hills CA 90212-1825*

JANSEN, ANGELA BING, artist, educator; b. N.Y.C., Aug. 17, 1929; d. Lester and Jean Bing; m. Gunther Jansen, Mar. 8, 1956; children— Edmund, Douglas. BA, Bklyn. Coll., 1951; MA, NYU, 1953; student, Bklyn. Mus. Art Sch., 1947-50, Atelier 17, N.Y.C., 1950-52. Tchr. art, public schs., N.Y.C., 1954-60. One-man shows: Madison (Wis.) Art Center, 1977, Gimpel & Weitzenhoffer, N.Y.C., 1974, 78, group shows: Bklyn. Mus., 1950, 70, 76, Library of Congress, Washington, 1969, 71, Ljubljana Internat. Print Biennale, Yugoslavia, 1971, 73, 75, 77, Venice Biennale, 1972, Internat. Exhbn. Drawing, Rejeka, Yugoslavia, 1972 (award), Internat. Print Biennale, Cracow, Poland, 1978; represented in permanent collections: Mus. Modern Art, N.Y.C., Met. Mus. Art, N.Y.C., N.Y. Pub. Library, Art Inst. Chgo., Tate Gallery, London, Victoria and Abert Mus., London, Bibliotheque Nationale, Paris, Bklyn. Mus., Phila. Mus. Art, Fonds d'Art Contemporain, Centre de Recherche et d'Etude de la Sculpture Contemporaine, Mauberge, France, Musée du Petit Format, Couvin, Belgium, Bklyn. Mus., Francine Tyler Art Forum, summer, 1979. Nat. Endowment for Arts grantee, 1974—75.

JANSEN, DANIEL ERVIN, former professional speedskater, marketing professional, former Olympic athlete; b. Milw., June 17, 1965; s. Harry William and Geraldine (Grajek) J.; m. Robin Wicker, Apr. 28, 1990 (div.); children: Jane Danielle, Olivia Renee. Student, U. Wis., Milw., 1986, 87, 89. Speed skater U.S. Olympic Com., Colorado Springs, Colo.; pro tour speedskater; sports mktg. profl. Miller Brewing Co., Milw., 1988—; skating coach Chicago Blackhawks, 2005—. Overall World Cup Champion Internat. Skating Union, 1986, 87, 92, 93, 94, World Sprint Champion, 1988, 94; recipient Gold medal for 1000m men's speedskating Lillehammer Winter Olympic Games, 1994. Roman Catholic. Achievements include 46 World Cup victories, 75 World Cup medals, setting world record for 1000m race in 12.43 seconds, Lillehammer Winter Olympic Games, 1994; inducted into US Olympic Hall of Fame, 2004.*

JANSEN, DONALD ORVILLE, lawyer; b. Odessa, Tex., Nov. 17, 1939; s. Orville Charles and Dolores Elizabeth (Olps) J.; m. E. Janice Law; children: Donald Orville, Lauren, Christine, David, Margaret BBA magna cum laude, Loyola U., New Orleans, 1961, JD cum laude, 1963; LLM, Georgetown U., 1966. Bar: La. 1963, Tex. 1965. Ptnr. Fulbright and Jaworski, Houston, 1966—. Served to capt. JAGC, U.S. Army, 1963-66 Mem. ABA, Fed. Bar Assn. State Bar Tex., La. Bar Assn., Am. Coll. Trust and Estate Counsel Roman Catholic. Home: 5212 Sagesquare St Houston TX 77056-7041 Office: Fulbright & Jaworski 1301 Mckinney St Ste 5100 Houston TX 77010-3031 Office Phone: 713-651-5479. Personal E-mail: djansen@fulbright.com.

JANSEN, G. THOMAS, dermatologist; b. Manitowoc, Wis., July 16, 1926; s. Gerald M. and Sarah (Grady) J.; m. Frances Bovick, Sept. 6, 1952; children: Mark, Kurt, Anne, Drew, Fran. BS, U. Wis., Madison, 1948, MD, 1950. Diplomate: Am. Bd. Dermatology (pres. 1985-86). Intern Med. Coll. of Va., 1950-51; resident in dermatology U. Wis., 1953-54, U. Mich., 1954-56; practice medicine specializing in dermatology Little Rock, 1956—2004; pres. Little Rock Dermatology Clinic, 1968—2004; ret., 2004. Mem. faculty U. Ark. Med. Center, 1956—2004, prof. dermatology, 1965—2004, prof. emeritus, 2004—, chmn. dept., 1965-82; mem. staff Doctors Hosp., U. Ark. Hosp., St. Vincent Infirmary, Bapt. Hosp.; pres. Am. Dermatology Found., 1980-81 Served as officer M.C. USNR, 1951-54. Recipient Disting. Svc. award, Am. Bd. Dermatologists, 1987, Finnerud award, 1996, Alumni citation, U. Wis. Med. Sch., 2002. Mem. AMA, Am. Dermatol. Assn. (pres. 1993), Am. Acad. Dermatology (asst. sec.-treas. 1980-83, sec.-treas. 1983-85, pres.-elect 1987, pres. 1988, hon. 1991, Master in Dermatology 1991, Everett C. Fox Lectureship award 1995, Gold medal 1997), Soc. Investigative Dermatology, Nat. Program Dermatology, Am. Coll. Chemosurgery, So. Med. Assn. (pres. 1976-77, Disting. Svc. award 1991), Ark. Med. Soc., Ark. Dermatol. Soc., Pulaski County Med. Soc. (A Lifetime of Outstanding Contbns. to Medicine award 2004), Alpha Omega Alpha. Roman Catholic. Home: 6601 Pleasant Pl Little Rock AR 72205-2868 Office: 500 S University Ave Ste 501 Little Rock AR 72205-5307

JANSEN, JAMES STEVEN, lawyer; b. Marshalltown, Iowa, Mar. 16, 1948; s. Virgil Charles and Virginia Rae (Hiatt) J.; m. Patricia Jean Beard, Nov. 24, 1984; children: Katherine, Emily, Ashley, Kristen. BS in Edn., U. Nebr., 1970; JD, Creighton U., 1973. Bar: Nebr. 1974, U.S. Dist. Ct. Nebr. 1974. Dep. county atty. County of Douglas, Omaha, 1974-78, county atty., 1991—2003; assoc. Naviaux, Kinney, Jansen and Dosek, Omaha, 1979-83; from assoc. to ptnr. Stave, Coffey, Swenson, Jansen and Schatz, Omaha, 1984—90; assoc. atty. McGrath, North, Mullin and Kratz PC LLO, Omaha, 2003—. Bd. dirs. Domestic Violence Coord. Coun. Greater Omaha, 1996-2003, co-chair, 1996-97, chmn., 1997-98; bd. dirs. Omaha Cmty. Partnership, 1991-2003, chmn., 2000-01; mem. Nebr. Drug and Violent Crime Policy Bd., Lincoln, 1991-98, bd. dirs. Project Harmony Child Protection Ctr., 1996—, chmn., 1998. Mem. Nebr. State Bar Assn., Omaha Bar Assn., Nebr. County Atty.'s Assn. (bd. dirs. 1991—98, pres. 1997-98). Democrat. Roman Catholic. Avocations: golf, reading. Office: McGrath North Mullin and Kratz PC LLD 3700 First National Tower 1601 Dodge St Omaha NE 68102 Office Phone: 402-341-3070. Business E-Mail: jjansen@mnmk.com.

JANSEN, MARY FRANCES, minister; b. Fullerton, Calif., Feb. 21, 1970; d. James Russell and Martha Brockman Jansen. BA in English, U. Calif., Irvine, Calif., 1995; MA in Theology, U. San Francisco, 2004. Mem. mktg. staff Rainbow Technologists, Irvine, Calif., 1992—96; asst. young adult ministry Archdiocese San Francisco, 1999—2003, dir. young. adult ministry, 2004—. Mem.: Cath. Profls. and Bus. Club (bd. dirs. 2003—04). Democrat. Roman Cath.

JANSEN, MEREDITH ANN, youth ministry and catechesis coordinator; b. Wichita Falls, Tex., Oct. 13, 1975; d. Adolph William and Lauren Andrea Jansen. BM, Midwestern State U., Wichita Falls, 2003. Coord. youth ministry and adolescent catechesis Sacred Heart Cath. Ch., Wichita Falls, 1999—. Roman Catholic. Home: 3211 Grant St Wichita Falls TX 76308 Office: Sacred Heart Cath Ch 1504 10th St Wichita Falls TX 76301 Office Phone: 940-723-5288. Office Fax: 940-767-0160. Personal E-mail: meredith_jansen@yahoo.com. E-mail: mjansen@sacredheartwf.org.

JANSEN, MICHAEL JOHN, health facility administrator; b. Swannanoa, N.C., July 24, 1945; s. Edward John and Mary Bernadette (Haughian) J.; m. Roxanne Shellenberger, June 27, 1970 (div. May 1992); m. Linda Kathryn Hughes, Aug. 21, 1993; children: Kathryn Anne, Victoria Elizabeth. BS in BA, U. S.C., 1967; M. Health Adminstrn., Duke U., 1976. Adminstrv. asst. Watts Hosp., Durham, N.C., 1976-77; asst. dir. Durham County Gen. Hosp., 1977-80; asst. adminstr. St. Joseph's Hosp., Atlanta, 1980-83, sr. v.p., COO, 1983-89; group v.p. SunHealth, Charlotte, N.C., 1989-90; sr. assoc. adminstr., COO Cape Fear Valley Health Sys., Fayetteville, NC, 1991-2001; CEO MedAccom, Research Triangle Park, NC, 2001—03; adminstr. Breezewood Family Healthcare, Fayetteville, NC, 2003—. Bd. dirs. St. Joseph's Hosp., Atlanta, 1985-89, Fayetteville Symphony Orch., 1993-95, United Way of Cumberland County, Fayetteville, 1993-95; chmn. bd. dirs. Shared Svcs. for So. Hosps., Atlanta, 1986-87. Capt. USAF, 1967-72, Col. USAFR, 1990-96. Recipient Falcon award/Spaatz award Civil Air Patrol, 1967. Fellow Am. Coll. Healthcare Execs. Office: Breezewood Family Healthcare PA PO Box 87448 Fayetteville NC 28304-7448

JANSEN, ROBERT BRUCE, consulting civil engineer; b. Spokane, Wash., Dec. 14, 1922; s. George Martin and Pearl Margaret (Kent) J.; m. Barbara Mae Courtney, Sept. 18, 1943. BSCE, U. Denver, 1949; MSCE, U. So. Calif., 1955. Registered profl. engr., Calif., Colo., Wash. Chief Calif. Div. Dam Safety, Sacramento, 1965-68; chief of ops. Calif. Dept. Water Resources, Sacramento, 1968-71, dep. dir., 1971-75, chief design and constrn., 1975-77; asst. commr. U.S. Bur. Reclamation, Denver, 1977-80; cons. civil engr., 1980—. Cons. TVA, Chattanooga, 1981—2003, So. Calif. Edison Co., Rosemead, 1982—2002, Pacific Gas and Electric, San Francisco, 1982—93, Hydro-Quebec, Montreal, 1986—98, Ala. Power Co., Birmingham, 1986—, Ga. Power Co., 1989—94. Author: Dams and Public Safety, 1983; editor: Safety of Existing Dams, 1983; co-author: Development of Dam Engineering in the United States, 1988; editor, co-author: Advanced Dam Engineering for Design, Construction, and Rehabilitation, 1988. Mem. U.S. Soc. on Dams (chmn.1979-81), ASCE, NAE (elected). Home and Office: 509 Briar Rd Bellingham WA 98225-7811

JANSON, JULIA S., utilities executive; m. Chip Janson; children: Jennifer, Rachel. BA in Am. Studies, Georgetown Coll.; JD, U. Cin., 1988. Bar: Ohio 1988. Law clk. Adams, Brooking, Stepner, Wolterman & Dusing, Covington, Ky., Cin. Gas & Electric Co., 1987—88, supr. securities processing, transfer agt. common and preferred stock, 1988—93; corp. atty., key mem. legal team responsible for completing merger of Cin. Gas & Electric Co. and PSI Energy Cinergy Corp., 1993—94, mgr. investor rels., 1995—96, counsel, 1996—98, sr. counsel, 1998—, corp. sec., sr. counsel, 2000—. Bd. dirs. Lighthouse Youth Svcs., 2000—01. Office: Cinergy Corp 139 E 4th St Cincinnati OH 45202

JANSON, PATRICK, vocalist, educator, actor; b. Cleve., Oct. 10, 1967; s. Robert L. and Gloria Ann (Dominguez) J.; m. Christine Marie Fondaw, June 8, 1991; children, Emma Susanne, Madison Ann. MusB, Baldwin-Wallace Coll., 1990. Singer, actor, dir., mus. dir., condr. various theatres and opera cos., 1990—; tchr. music St. Joseph Acad., Cleve., 1990-91, 98—, Univ. Sch., Hunting Valley, Ohio, 1991-92; tchr. Perry-Mansfield Performing Arts Camp, Steamboat Springs, Colo., summer 1993, 95, Usdan Ctr. for the Creative and Performing Arts, L.I., N.Y., summer 1998. Prodn. asst. Broadway musical The Life. Recipient 1st pl. prize Profl. Artists Devel. Competition, 1990. Mem. Actors Equity Assn., Alpha Sigma Phi (pres. interfraternity coun. 1988-89, pres. chpt. 1989-90). Address: 4018 Shelley Dr North Olmsted OH 44070 Personal E-mail: pjanson02@aol.com.

JANSON, RICHARD ANTHONY, plastic surgeon; b. Passaic, N.J., Nov. 30, 1945; m. Mary Ann Janson, 1971; children: Sarah, Matthew. BA, Rice U., 1967; MD, Med. Coll. Wis., 1971. Diplomate Am. Bd. Plastic Surgery. Intern St. Joseph Hosp., Denver, 1971-72, resident in gen. surgery, 1972-76; resident in plastic surgery U. Tex. Med. Branch, Galveston, 1976-79; pvt. practice Grand Junction, Colo., 1979—. Fellow ACS, Am. Soc. Plastic & Reconstructive Surgeons; mem. Colo. Soc. Plastic & Reconstructive Surgeons. Office: 1120 Wellington Ave Grand Junction CO 81501-6129 Office Phone: 970-243-6200.

JANSSEN, CARRON JOYCE, elementary school educator, music educator; b. Chgo., Aug. 28, 1955; d. Howard Armstrong and Shirley Lois Turpin; m. Uwe Detlof Janssen, June 18, 1983; children: Noel Uwe, Rachel Frances, Erica Heather. AA, William Rainey Harper Coll., 1980; MusB, Elmhurst Coll., 1997; MA in Tchg., Aurora U., 2002. Cert. tchr. State of Ill., 2002. Elem. music specialist Sch. Dist. U-46, Elgin, Ill., 1997—. Music dept. com. Sch. Dist. U-46, Elgin, 1999—, Sunnydale bldg. com., 2004—, dist. stds. and reporting com., 2000—04. Clk. course Hanover Pk. Pk. Dist. Swim Team, Ill., 1998—2004. Mem.: NEA, Elgin Tchrs. Assn., Ill. Edn. Assn., Ill. Music Educators Assn., Nat. Assn. Music Edn., Music Educators Nat. Conf., Lambda Sigma Psi, Kappa Delta Pi, Phi Kappa Phi. Mem. United Church Christ. Avocations: various musical instruments, singing, reading, swimming. Home: 216 Carver Ln Schaumburg IL 60193-1219 Office Phone: 630-213-5610. Personal E-mail: carronuwe6183@sbcglobal.net. E-mail: carronjanssen@u-46.org.

JANSSEN, JAMES ROBERT, consulting software engineer; b. Frederick, Md., June 14, 1959; s. Robert James and Kathryn Doris (Randolph) J.; m. Deborah June Dellwo, Mar. 15, 1986 (div. Sept. 20, 1988). BSEE, Stanford U., 1981, MSEE, 1982. Simulation technician Varian Assocs., Palo Alto, Calif., 1981; hardware design engr. Fairchild Test Systems, San Jose, Calif., 1982-86, Factron Test Systems, Latham, N.Y., 1986-87; software, sys. designer Schlumberger Technologies Labs., Palo Alto, 1988; software engr. Photon Dynamics, Inc., San Jose, 1989-90, ADAC Labs., Milpitas, Calif., 1990-92, software, system designer Aalborg, Denmark, 1992, Milpitas, 1992-94; consulting software engr. self-employed, Sunnyvale, Calif., 1994-96; mem. tech. staff Netscape Comms. Corp., Mountain View, Calif., 1996-99, Am. Online Inc., Mountain View, 1999-2001; pres., founder MouseMine, Inc., Scotts Valley, Calif., 2001—03. Pres., founder Digital Studio Systems, Inc., Sunnyvale, 1990-93. Patentee multiple timing signal generator. Civic vol. City of Sunnyvale, 1993. Mem. Tau Beta Pi. Avocations: motocross racing, auto race driving, auto race spectating, composing and recording pop music, piano. Home and Office: 721 Wolverine Way Scotts Valley CA 95066-2923 E-mail: jimj@ihwy.com. *I know enough to know how little I know.*

JANSSEN-PELLATZ, EUNICE CHARLENE, healthcare facility administrator; b. Urania, La., Mar. 23, 1948; d. Luther Clarence and Eunice Bobby (Pendarvis) Smith. BS in Nursing, Humboldt State U., 1970; MS in Nursing, Calif. State U., Fresno, 1980. Dir. nurses, asst. adminstr., coord. patient care svcs. Mad River Community Hosp., Arcata, Calif.; nursing supr. Fresno (Calif.) Community Hosp.; emergency response coord. Humboldt County Pub. Health Dept. Home: 824 Diamond Dr Arcata CA 95521-8212 Office Phone: 707-268-2133. E-mail: pellatz@sbcglobal.net.

JANSSENS, JOE LEE, controller; b. Alpine, Tex., Apr. 13, 1964; s. Charles Louis Janssens and Sue Ellen (Cheairs) Ticknor; m. Diana Bookout, Sept. 9, 1995; children: Ryan, Stephanie. BBA in Fin., Tex. A&M U., 1986; BA in Spanish, U. Houston, 1996, MA in History, 2004. CPA Tex., cert. mgmt. acct. Staff auditor Price Waterhouse, Houston, 1988-89; consol. acct. Energy Ventures, Inc., Houston, 1989-92; sr. internat. acct. Ashland Exploration, Inc., Houston, 1992-95; contr. Peak Svcs. USA Ltd., Texas City, Tex., 1996-97, Peak USA Energy Svcs., Ltd., Houston, 1997, Tube-Alloy Corp., Houston, 1997-98; fin. dir. Grant Prideco SA de C.V. Veracruz, Mexico, 1998-2000; fin. svcs. rep. IBM (formerly PriceWaterhouseCoopers), Houston, 2001—04; project contr. BP, Houston, 2005—. Mem.: AICPA, Inst. Mgmt. Accts., Phi Kappa Phi. Roman Catholic. Avocations: western history, linguistics, scuba diving. Home: 7803 Braesdale Ln Houston TX 77071-1303 Office: BP 200 Westlake Pk Blvd Ste 871 Houston TX 77079 E-mail: jansssejl@bp.com.

JANSSON, JOHN PHILLIP, architect, consultant; b. Phila., Nov. 27, 1918; s. John A. and Isabelle (Ericson) Jansson; m. Ann C. Winter, Apr. 8, 1944 (div. Oct. 1970); children: Linda Ann, Lora Jean; m. Elizabeth Clow Peer, Jan. 21, 1978 (dec. May 1984). BArch, Pratt Inst., 1947; postgrad., SUNY, 1949. Registered arch., N.Y., lic. Nat. Coun. Archtl. Registration Bd.s. Architect various firms, 1949—54; pvt. practice N.Y.C., 1949—; cons. mktg. products, materials and svcs. to bldg. and constrn. industry, 1949—; exec. v.p. Archtl. Aluminum Mfrs. Assn., N.Y.C., 1954—58; mgr. market devel. Olin-Metals Div., N.Y.C., 1958—62; dir. Pope, Evans & Robbins, cons. engrs., 1970—82; ptnr. Morris Ketchum, Jr. and Assocs., Archs., 1964—68; exec. dir. N.Y. State Coun. Architecture, 1968—73; dir. Gruzen & Ptnrs., 1972—74; pres. Bldg. Constrn. Tech., 1975—78; v.p. Ehrenkrantz Group, 1974—82. Cons. N.Y. State Pure Waters Authority, 1968—69; chmn. N.Y. State Architecture-Constrn. Interagency Com., 1968—74; sec. N.Y. State Gov.'s Adv. Com. State Constrn. Programs, 1970—71; dir. U.S. trade mission leader to Nigeria Dept. of Commerce, 1981. Mem. N.Y. State Citizens Com. Pub. Schs., 1952—55; v.p. citizens adv. com. Housing Authority, Town of Oyster Bay, NY, 1966—68; bd. dirs. Bldg. Industry Data Adv. Coun., 1976—78, Park Ten Coop., 1981—82; instr. Outward Bound, Hurrican Island, Rockland, Maine, 1982—; media specialist Image Ctr. Am.'s Cup, 1987. Served to capt. USMCR, 1943—46. Mem.: AIA (mem. archs. govt. com. 1971—77), Soc. Mil. Engrs. Soc. N.Y.C., Am. Mgmt. Assn., Associated Coun. Arts, Nat. Trust Historic Preservation, Soc. Archtl. Historians, N.Y. State Assn. Archs. (dir.), N.Y. Bldg. Congress, Archtl. League N.Y., Nat. Inst. Bldg. Scis., BRAB Bldg. Rsch. Inst., Nat. Inst. Archtl. Edn., Constrn. Specialist Inst., Am. Arbitration Assn., Fleety Res. Assn., Victorian Soc. Am., Mus. Modern Art, U.S. Naval Acad. Officers and Faculty Club, Md. Capital Yacht Club (bd. dirs. 1993—94). Home: 6301 River Crescent Dr Annapolis MD 21401-7721 Personal E-mail: jpjansson@yahoo.com.

JANURA, JAN AROL, apparel manufacturing executive; b. Chgo., May 12, 1949; s. Cornel Harold Charles and Violet Mary Janura. BS, Colo. State U., 1971; MA, Fuller Theol. Sem., 1973; postgrad., Harvard Bus. Sch., 1997. Area dir. Young Life Campaign, Seattle, 1973-76; CEO, dir. Carol Anderson, Inc., L.A., 1977—2002; CFO Fresh Retail Chain, 1988—, Outdoor Videos Inc., 1988—; CEO Old Maui Brand, Rancho Dominguez, Calif., 2000—. Dir. Camp Anderson; pres. L.A. Electric Motorcar Co., 1979-80; prin., dir. Pheasant Hill Orchards, Connel, Washington; founder, CEO Old Maui Brand men's shirt co.; bd. dirs. C.A., Inc., catalog mfg. Nordstrom, Neiman Marcus, Coldwater Creek; founder Feather Chuckers Brand clothing, Carol Anderson's By Invitation; bd. chmn. CAbi Women's Home Clothing Sales; founder oldmaui.com, cabionline.com. Mem. Rep. Nat. Com., 1986, Rep. Presdl. Task Force, 1984-86; trustee Janura Libr., Glendale; founder Smiling Moose Lodge, Cameron, Mont. Weyerhaeuser fellow, 1972-73, Glendale Fellowship Found.; bd. dirs. Palos Verdes Leadership Found., We. Leadership Found., Starr Leadership Found., SW Leadership Found., NW Fellowship, Rivergate Fellowship, Crested Butte, Colo., Glendale (Calif.) Young Life Found. Fellowship (bd. mem.), Oaks Christian H.S. (bd. dirs.), Westlake Village, Calif.; commence spkrs. Colo. State U., Fort. Collins, 2003. Recipeint Salesman of Yr. award, 1983, 84; Carpenteria fellow, 2002. Mem. Fly Fishermen Am. (life), Trout Unlimited (life), Henrys Fork Found., Calif. Trout, 11-99 Found. (life), Pvt. Aircraft Owners Assn., Beechcraft Owners' Club, Montana and Land Reliance, Friends of Montana Land Reliance, Mammoth Lakes Fly Fisherman, Young Pres.'s Orgn. (L.A. chpt., Beta Forum), World Pres. Orgn., Friends of Norris Theater, Snowcreek Athletic Club, L.A. Athletic Club, Wash. Athletic Club, N.Y. Athletic Club, Pres. Pointe Assn. (pres. 1991-96), Juniper Ridge Assn., Admirals Club (life), Solomon Hill Hunt Club, Scootney Farms Hunting Club, Ironwood Country Club, Fly Fisherman Club, Virginia Country Club (Long Beach, Calif.; winner 50th Intergalactic Golf Tournament 1999). Office: 18915 S Laurel Park Rd Rancho Dominguez CA 90220-6005 Business E-Mail: jjanura@oldmaui.com.

JANUS, JUDITH, artist; b. Phila. With Martha Graham Dance Co., 1949—50; mem. CCF Ceta Artists Project, 1978—79. One-woman shows include St. Agnes Br. Libr., N.Y.C., 2001, Donnell Libr. Ctr., 2003, exhibited in group shows at Broome St. Gallery, 1995, 1997—98, 2004, Cork Gallery at Lincoln Ctr., 1995, 1997, Salmagundi Club, 1995, Pen and Brush, 1995, 1997, 2001, Cardozo Law Sch., Lever House, 1995, Alliance of Queens Artists, 1996 (Sculpture 1st prize), 93 South Art Gallery, N.Y., 1997, Pace University Arts Center, N.Y.C., 1997, Lever House, 1998, Allied Artists of America, Nat. Arts Club, 1998, Am. Artists Profl. League, 1999—2000, Art54 Gallery, 1999, Brewster Gallery, 2000, Internat. Comm. Design, Seoul, 2000, Ceres Gallery, N.Y.C., 2000, Noho Gallery, 2001, Met. Artists, Cork Gallery, 2001, 2003, at Met. Artists, Cornell Gallery, 2002, at Venezuelan Consulate Gallery, 2003—04; dancer, choreographer Mohonk, Symphony Space, N.Y.C., 1978, Am. Mus. Natural History, 1978, Smithsonian Baird Auditorium, 1981, Becky Perces Scholarship Fund, Sarah Lawrence Coll., 1984; Bklyn. Mus., 1978, over 30 juried exbhns.; dancer, choreographer (solo program) Songs that Dance, Dancer in an Art Gallery. Bugs, Celebration, and others. Recipient first prize in sculpture, Alliance Queens Artists, 1996; scholar, Art Students League, Art Students League. Fellow: Am. Artists Profl. League (Oehler Meml. award 2000); mem.: Met. Artists, Burr Artists (1st v.p.). E-mail: judithjanus@yahoo.com.

JANUZZI, JAMES LOUIS, physician, internist, gastroenterologist; b. N.Y.C., Feb. 2, 1941; s. Fred and Alexandra (Calogera) J.; m. Louise Marie Carini, June 27, 1964; children: Marisa, James, Louis. AB, St. Peter's Coll., 1962; MD, N.Y. Med. Coll., 1966. Diplomat of Am. Bd. Internal Medicine and Gastroenterology. Pres. med. staff St. Vincent's Hosp., N.Y.C., 1989-91. Bd. Trustees St. Vincent's Hosp., N.Y.C., 1989-93. Capt. U.S. Army, 1968-70. Office: 29 Washington Sq W New York NY 10011-9180 Office Phone: 212-982-5551.

JANZEN, NORINE MADELYN QUINLAN, medical technologist; b. Fond du Lac, Wis., Feb. 9, 1943; d. Joseph Wesley and Norma Edith (Gustin) Quinlan; m. Douglas Mac Arthur Janzen, July 18, 1970; 1 son, Justin James. BS, Marian Coll., 1965; med. technologist, St. Agnes Sch. Med. Tech., Fond du Lac, 1966; MA, Ctrl. Mich. U., 1980. Med. technologist Mayfair Med. Lab., Wauwatosa, Wis., 1966-69; supr. med. technologist Dr.'s Mason, Chamberlain, Franke, Klink & Kamper, Milw., 1969-76, Hartford-Parkview Clinic, Ltd., 1976-94; patient svc. ctrs. supr. Med. Sci. Labs., Wauwatosa, Wis., 1994-97, Poole Med. Tech. Med. Sci. Labs, 1997-98; clin. mgr. Planned Parenthood Wis., 1997-99; coord. health in bus. Hartford Parkview Clin., 1990-91, drug program coord., 1991-94; outreach coord. Cmty. Meml. Hosp., Menomonee Falls, Wis., 2000—. Co-chair joint mtg. Clin. Lab. Mgrs. Assn. and Wis. Assn. for Clin. Lab. Scientists, 1993-94. Coord. Warhawk Band Booster Uniform Project, 1997—99; mem. Dem. Nat. Com., 1973—; substitute poll worker Fond du Lac Dem. Com., 1964—65; post card ministry coord. Meth. Ch., 1996—2001, cmty. league youth col., recognition coord.; focus team leader Coll. Youth Ministries, Meth. Ch., 2000—; mem. Post Card Ministry Bd., 1998—2001; lay mem. to ann. conf. United Meth. Ch., Menomonee Falls, 2004—; bd. dirs. Menomonee Falls Teen Ctr., 2001—, Iowa State Parents Assn., 2001—04. Mem.: AAUW (corr. sec. 1994—96, rec. sec. 1996—98, pub. policy chair 1998—2001, chair Evening of Literary Excellence 2001—02, pres. 2001—03, treas. 2003—, state, dist. 2 coord. 2003—, co-chair ann. meeting 2004—05), Southeastern Suprs. Group (co-chmn. 1976—77), Milw. Soc. Clin. Lab. Scientists (pres. 1971—72, bd. dirs. 1972—73, exec. sec. 1999—), Clin. Lab. Mgmt. Assn. (co-chair joint meeting 1993—94), Wis. Assn. Clin. Lab. Scientists (chmn. awards com. 1976—77, treas. 1977—81, dir. 1977—84, pres.-elect 1981—82, pres. 1982—83, chmn. awards com. 1984—85, dir. 1985—87, chmn. awards com. 1986—87, chair ann. meeting 1987—88, exec. sec. 1991—, Mem. of Yr. award 1982, 1995, numerous svc. awards), Nat. Soc. Clin. Lab. Scientists (awards com. chair 1984—87, 1988—91, nominations com. 1989—92), Am. Soc. Clin. Lab. Scientists (people to people clin. lab. scientist del. to People's Rep. China 1989, Mem. of Yr. award 1997), Warhawk Band Boosters (uniform fundraiser chair 1996—98, chair Trysting Place tent party fundraiser 1997—2000), Comms. of Wis. (chmn. 1977—79, originator), LWV, Cmty. League, Alpha Mu Tau, Alpha Delta Theta (nat. dist. chmn. 1967—69, nat. alumnae dir. 1969—71). Home: N101 W17383 Tanglewood Dr Germantown WI 53022 Office: Cmty Meml Hosp W180 N 8085 Town Hall Rd Menomonee Falls WI 53051 Office Phone: 262-257-3453. Personal E-mail: nmjanzen@aol.com.

JANZEN, PETER S., lawyer; b. Apr. 1959; BA in polit. sci., JD, Hamline U. With Land O' Lakes Inc., 1993, v.p., gen. counsel, 2003—. Office: Land O Lakes Inc 4001 Lexington Ave N Saint Paul MN 55126 Home: 6439 Fawn Ln Lino Lakes MN 55014-5420 Office Fax: 651-481-2000, 651-481-2222.

JAOUDI, MARIA M., religious studies educator, humanities educator; BA in Philosophy summa cum laude, Bloomfield Coll., 1974; MA in Asian Studies summa cum laude, Seton Hall U., 1984; PhD in Hist. Theology, Fordham U., 1992. Tchg. asst. Bloomfield Coll., 1975; asst. prof. Seton Hall U., 1987—89; spiritual dir. Ctr. for Religious Studies and Spirituality, Tenafly, NJ, 1984—90; assoc. prof. Calif. State U., Sacramento, 1996—. Adj. lectr. Pace U., 1989-91; pres. N.Am. Conf. on Christianity and Ecology, 1985-88; chair document com. N.Am. Conf. on Christianity and Ecology/UN, fall 1987; lectr. in field of world religions and ecology. Author: Christian and Islamic Spirituality, 1993, (book chpts.) The Jesus Prayer and Modern Pilgrims, 1988, Christian Ecology: Building an Enivoronmental Ethic for the Twenty-first Century, 1988, Christian Mysticism West and East: What the Masters Teach Us, 1998; contbr. articles and book revs. to profl. jours. Office Fax: 530-278-7483. E-mail: jaoudim@csus.edu.

JAOUEN, RICHARD MATTHIE, plastic surgeon; MD, U. Autonoma de Guadalajara, Jalisco, Mexico, 1975. Intern St. Joseph Hosp., Denver, 1976-77, surgeon, 1977-81; plastic surgeon Ind. U. Med. Sch., Indpls., 1981-83, North Colo. Med. Ctr., Greeley, Colo., 1983—. Office: 1640 25th Ave Greeley CO 80634-4959

JAQUA, RICHARD ALLEN, pathologist; b. Fort Dodge, Iowa, Apr. 15, 1938; s. John Franklin and Esther J.; m. Mary Joanne Stewart, Dec. 29, 1969 BA magna cum laude, Yale U., 1960; MD, Harvard U., 1965. Diplomate: Am. Bd. Pathology, Am. Bd. Nuclear Medicine. Teaching fellow pathology Harvard Med. Sch., 1965-67; resident clin. pathology NIH, 1967-69; intern pathology Mass. Gen. Hosp., Boston, 1965-66; fellow tumor pathology Meml.-Sloane Kettering Cancer Center, N.Y.C., 1969-70; asst. prof. pathology U. S.D. Sch. Medicine, Vermillion, 1970-73, asso. prof., 1973-74, asso. prof., acting chmn. dept. lab. medicine, 1974-77, prof., chmn. dept. lab. medicine, 1977—2002, dir. Electron Microscopy Lab. and Clin. Virology Lab., 1979—2002; pathologist VA Hosp., Sioux Falls, SD, 1978—2002; physician Lab. Clin. Medicine, Sioux Falls, 1970—2002. Part-time prof. pathology Sch. Medicine U. S.D., 2003—; prof. emeritus U. S.D. Sch. Medicine. Served with USPHS, 1967-69. Recipient Outstanding Prof. awards U. S.D. Med. Students, 1971, 75, 77, 90; VA grantee, 1980-82. U. S.D. Faculty Recogition award, 1986. Fellow Coll. Am. Pathologists, Am. Soc. Clin. Pathologists; mem. AAAS, Sigma Xi, Alpha Omega Alpha. Home: 27546 483rd Ave Canton SD 57013-5511 Office: USD Health Sci Ctr 1400 W 22nd St Sioux Falls SD 57105-1505 Business E-Mail: rjaqua@usd.edu.

JAQUESS, JAMES FLETCHER, lawyer, consultant; b. Evansville, Ind., Mar. 25, 1948; s. John Roberts and Sybil L. Jaquess; children: Karen Renee, Regina Kathryn. BS, Ind. State U., 1971, MBA, 1975; JD, Ga. State U., 1987. Diplomate, Metallurgical Analysis, Metals Engring. Inst., Sr. Reactor Operator, Babcock & Wilcox Co., Nuc. Power Ops. Tng., Babcock & Wilcox Co., Quality Engr., Am. Soc. Quality, Quality Auditor, Am. Soc. Quality, Project Manager, ABB, Nuc. Welding Ops., Babcock & Wilcox, Non Destructive Testing, Babcock & Wilcox. Sr. quality engr. Babcock & Wilcox, Mt. Vernon, Ind., 1971—74, resident quality mgr., nuc. pressure vessel mfg., 1974—76, quality mgr., nuc. constrn. Lynchburg, Va., 1976—77, program mgr., internat. nuc. projects, 1977—79, bus. devel. mgr., european ops., 1980—82; project mgr. ABB Impell, Atlanta, 1982—84, mgr., nuc. ops. quality assurance, 1984—89, mgr., nuc. power tech. svcs., 1989—90; bus. devel. mgr. ABB Combustion Engring., 1990—94; dir., bus. devel. Wais & Assocs. Engring., 1994—95; bus. devel. mgr., global ops. Lockwood Greene Engrs., 1995—99; mgr., cons. svcs., Europe So. Co., 1999—2000; dir., Caribbean project devel. Mirant, 2000—02; acct. exec. Electric Power Rsch. Inst., 2003—. Legal cons., Atlanta, 2000—05; dir. USA Water Ski, 2003—05; editl. rev. bd. Am. Soc. Quality, Milw., 1992—2005, Quality Press, 1995—2005; pres. Ga. Water Sports, Inc., Atlanta, 1998—2005. Contbr. articles to profl. jours.

Trustee Am. Water Ski Ednl. Found., Winter Haven, Fla., 1994—98; mem. SAR, Atlanta, 2000—05, Sons Union Vets.Civil War, Atlanta, 1998—2005, SCV, Lawrenceville, 1997—2005. Recipient Am. Jurisprudence award, 1987, Wall St. Jour. Student Achievement award, 1972. Fellow: Am. Soc. Quality (editl. rev. bd. 1992—95); mem.: ABA, ASME (assoc.), Southeastern Econ. Devel. Coun., Am. Nuc. Soc. (chmn. Atlanta sect. 1984—85), Soc. Mfg. Engrs., Am. Waterski Assn. (dir. 1993—2005, exec. v.p. 2002—05), Theta Chi, Alpha Kappa Psi (life). Achievements include first to Statistical Analysis of Nuclear Steam Generator Tube Failures. Avocations: water-skiing, motor sports. Office: Electric Power Rsch Inst 3554 Suwanee Creek Rd Suwanee GA 30024 Office Phone: 678-475-3997. Personal E-mail: jjaquess@bellsouth.net.

JAQUISS, NIGEL, reporter; married; 3 children. BA in English, Dartmouth Coll., 1984; MA in Journalism, Columbia U., 1997. Oil trader, NY, Signapore Cargill, Morgan Stanley and Goldman Sachs, 1984—95; reporter Willamette Week, Portland, Oreg., 1998—. Recipient Pulitzer Prize for investigative reporting, 2005, 3 first place awards, Nat. Edn. Writers Assn. Office: Willamette Week 820 SW Tenth Ave Portland OR 97205 Office Phone: 503-243-2122.*

JARAMILLO, CARLOS ALBERTO, civil engineer; b. Medellin, Colombia, Dec. 5, 1952; came to the U.S., 1986; s. Alberto and Maria Jaramillo; m. Celeste Jaramillo; children: Daniel J., Nicolas, Diego A. BCE, U. Nacional, Medellin, 1978; MS, U. Minn., 1980. Registered profl. engr., Wis., Colombia. Engr. Integral S.A., Medellin, Colombia, 1977-79, sr. design engr., 1980-86; rsch. asst. St. Anthony Falls Lab., Mpls., 1979-80; civil engr. Mead & Hunt Inc., Madison, 1986-89; sr. geotech. engr. Harza Engring. Co., Chgo., 1989—2001, jr. ptnr., 1998—2001; sr. geotech. engr., ptnr. MWH Global, 2001—. Prof. Escuela de Ingenieria de Antioquia, Medellin, 1981-86; designer numerous dams & underground structures. Cons. to public utilities, various countries 1994—; contbr. articles to profl. jours. Mem. ASCE (rock mechanics com.), U.S. Soc. on Dams, U.S. Nat. Soc. Soil Mechanics and Found. Engring., Phi Kappa Phi. Avocations: jogging, photography, stamp collecting/philately, astronomy. Office: MWH Global Ste 1900 175 W Jackson Blvd Chicago IL 60604 Business E-Mail: carlos.a.jaramillo@mwhglobal.com.

JARAMILLO, MARI-LUCI, retired federal agency administrator; b. Las Vegas, N.Mex., June 19, 1928; BA magna cum laude, N.Mex. Highland U., 1955, MA with honors, 1959; PhD, U. N.Mex., 1970. Tchr., Albuquerque and Las Vegas, N.Mex., 1955-65; asst. prof. U. N.Mex., 1965-72, assoc. prof., chmn. dept. elem. edn., 1972-75, assoc. prof. edn., 1976-77, prof., 1977, spl. asst. to pres., 1981-82, assoc. dean Coll. Edn., 1982-85, v.p. for student affairs, 1985-87; amb. to Republic of Honduras U.S. Dept. State, 1977-80, dep. asst. sec. for Inter-Am. affairs Washington, 1980-81; asst. v.p., dir. Ednl. Testing Service, Emeryville, Calif., 1987-93; dep. asst. sec. for Inter-Am. affairs Dept. Def., Washington, 1993-95. Bd. trustees Tomas Rivera Nat. Policy Ctr., Claremont (Calif.) Coll. Grad. Sch., 1985-93; minority recruiter Dept. State, Washington, 1990-2000; commr. Calif. Commn. of Post-Secondary Edn., Sacramento, 1990-93; active Coun. Am. Ambs., Washington, 1983-; bd. dirs. Latin Am. Scholarship Program for Am. Univs., Boston, Children's TV Workshop, N.Y.C.; cons. for curriculum, tchr. tng. and sch. reform, 1960-; vice chair, bd. regents, N.Mex. Highlands U., 2001—. Author: Madame Ambassador; The Shoe Maker's Daughter, 2002; contbr. articles to jours., chpts. to books. Bd. dirs. Internat. House, U. Calif., Berkeley, 1989-93; scholar panelist Nat. Latino Comm. Ctr., L.A., 1990—; active Bay area Network L.Am. Women, San Francisco, 1987-93; regent N.Mex. Highlands U., 2003—, vice chair, 2000—. Decorated Order Francisco Morazan (Honduras), Order of Great Silver Cross (Honduras); recipient Cubberly award Stanford U., 1975, N.Mex. Disting. Svc. award, 1977, Anne Roe award Harvard U. Grad. Sch. Edn., 1986, PRIMERA award Mex. Am. Women's Nat. Assn., 1990; named Outstanding Chicana, 1975, Hon. Honduran Citizen, Govt. of Honduras, 1980, Disting. Woman of Yr., U. N.Mex. Alumni Assn., 1985, Disting. Hispanic lectr. Calif. State U. at Fullerton, 1988, Outstanding Hispanic Educator, 1988, Outstanding Leader in Edn. to Hispanic Cmty., 1991. Mem. Nat. Assn. Bilingual Edn., Latin Am. Assn., Am. Assn. Colls. for Tchr. Edn., Nat. Council La Raza. Home: 10501 Lagrima de Oro NE Apt 342 Albuquerque NM 87111

JARANILLA, SARAH J., critical care nurse, consultant; arrived in U.S., 1976; d. Angelo C. and Leonor J. Jaranilla; children: Christine Joy Reynoso, Jerome Jay Laguilles, Sarah Joy Laguilles. BSN, Philippine Union Coll., Manila, 1973. RN Tex. Head nurse med./surg. unit Bacolod (The Philippines) Sanitarium & Hosp., 1973—75; charge nurse med./surg. unit Hansford Hosp., Spearman, Tex., 1976—77; critical care RN Monterey Park (Calif.) Hosp., 1978—80; DON, owner Sarnel Nurse Registry, West Covina, Calif., 1980—85; DON CJS Nursing Svcs., West Covina, 1985—93; adminstr., dir. patient svcs. Alpha Omega Home Health Svcs., Inc., Glendora, Calif., 1994—96; adminstr., owner Alternative Staffing, Inc., Torrance, Calif., 1997—2002; adminstr., dir. patient svcs. Gen. Home Health Care, Glendale, Calif., 2003—. Recipient Virgo Nurse of the Yr. award, Virgo Prodn., 2000. Mem.: Philippine Nurses Assn. So. Calif. (assoc.). Office Phone: 323-899-1698. Personal E-mail: sjaranilla@aol.com.

JÄRBE, TORBJÖRN ULF CHRISTIAN, psychologist, educator; b. Kristianstad, Sweden, May 6, 1946; came to the U.S., 1991; s. Bengt O. and Kajela E. (Lochner) J.; m. Esta R. Kroon (div.); children: John, Shamalee; m. Diane A. Mathis, Dec. 28, 1991 (dec.). BA in Psychology, U. Uppsala, 1969, MS, 1972, PhD, 1977. Project leader dept. psychology U. Uppsala, Sweden, 1972-91; vis. scientist ctr. for addiction rsch. U. Medicine and Dentistry N.J., 1991; vis. assoc. prof. divsn. addiction rsch. and treatment Hahnemann U., Phila., 1991-92, rsch. assoc. prof., 1992—; prof. dept. psycol. Temple U., Phila., 1999—. Postdoctoral fellow in pharmacology U. N.C., 1977-78. Referee numerous scientific jours.; contbr. articles to profl. jours. Björnström-Stephenson fellow Am.-Sweden Found., 1977-78. Mem. European Neurosci. Assn., Internat. Brain Rsch. Orgn., Swedish Soc. for Alcohol and Drug Rsch., Soc. for Stimulus Properties of Drugs (pres. 1990), European Behavioral Pharmacology Soc., Internat. Cannabis Rsch. Soc., Internat. Behavioral Neurosci. Soc., Coll. on Problems in Drug Dependence, Am. Psychol. Assn. Office: Temple U Coll Liberal Arts 265 67 Weiss Hall Psych Dep 1701 N 13th St Philadelphia PA 19122-6011 Home: 2303 N Cuthbert Dr Lindenwold NJ 08021-2661 Office Phone: 215-204-6977. Business E-Mail: tjarbe@temple.edu.

JARBOE, MARK ALAN, lawyer; b. Flint, Mich., Aug. 19, 1951; s. Lloyd Aloysius and Helen Elizabeth (Frey) J.; m. Patricia Kovel, Aug. 20, 1971; 1 child, Alexander. Student, No. Mich. U., 1968-69; AB with high distinction, U. Mich., 1972; JD magna cum laude, Harvard U., 1975. Bar: Minn. 1975, U.S. Dist. Ct. Minn. 1975, U.S. Ct. Appeals (8th cir.) 1975, U.S. Ct. Appeals (7th cir.) 1993. Law clk. to presiding justice Minn. State Ct., St. Paul, 1975-76; from assoc. to ptnr. Dorsey & Whitney LLP, Mpls., 1976-81, ptnr., 1982—, and chmn., Indian law practice group and Indian & gaming practice group, mem. policy com., 1991, 2005—. Lectr. U. Minn. Law Sch., Hamline U. Sch. Law. Contbr. articles to profl. jours. Pres. parish coun. Ch. of Christ the King, Mpls., 1981-83. Mem. Minn. Am. Indian Bar Assn., Mensa, Phi Beta Kappa. Republican. Roman Catholic. Office: Dorsey & Whitney LLP 50 S 6th St Ste 1500 Minneapolis MN 55402-1498 Office Phone: 612-340-2686. Office Fax: 612-340-2868. E-mail: jarboe.mark@dorsey.com.

JARDELEZA, LOLITA LEDESMA, secondary school educator; b. Manila, Philippines, Mar. 18, 1932; came to U.S., 1951; d. Romeo Gil and Dorotea Severino (Gamboa) Ledesma; m. Magdaleno Laganzda Jardeleza Jr., Sept. 18, 1951; children: Christine, Madeleine, Madgaleno III, Melanie, Tomas Jose, Ann, Mary, Daniel, Roberto. BA, Assumption Coll., 1951; MA, Regis Coll., 1984. Facilitator Washington Duaconate Program, 1973; dir. resource ctr. Holy Cross Acad., Kensington, Md., 1980-84, tchr., campus minister, 1984—. Newsletter editor Teams of Our Lady, Washington; missionary, Papua New Guinea, 2001; tchr. St. Francis Sch., Philippines, 2003; retreats to couples, ladies, young mothers group. Author: Compost Makes the Strawberries Grow, 1991. Mem. Deacons' Adv. Bd., Washington, 1972-81; mem., co-chmn. Family Life Adv. Bd., Washington, 1980-83; counselor engaged couples Archdiocese Washington. Republican. Roman Catholic. Avocations: calligraphy, banner making, poetry. Home: 1913 Locust Grove Rd Silver Spring MD 20910-1304 Office: Acad Holy Cross 4920 Strathmore Ave Kensington MD 20895-1299

JARDETZKY, OLEG, medical educator, researcher; b. Yugoslavia, Feb. 11, 1929; came to U.S., 1949, naturalized, 1955; s. Wenceslas Sigismund and Tatiana (Taranovsky) J.; m. Erika Albensberg, July 21, 1975; children by previous marriage: Alexander, Theodore, Paul. BA, Macalester Coll., 1950, D.Sc. (hon.), 1974; MD, U. Minn., 1954, PhD (Am. Heart Assn. fellow), 1956; postgrad., U. Cambridge, Eng., 1965-66; LL.D. (hon.), Calif. Western U., 1978; MD (hon.), U. Graz, Austria, 1994; Doctorate (hon.), U. Aix-Marseille II, 1998. Research fellow U. Minn., 1954-56; NRC fellow Calif. Inst. Tech., 1956-57; asso. Harvard U., 1957-59, asst. prof. pharmacology, 1959-66; dir. biophysics and pharmacology Merck & Co., 1966-68, exec. dir., 1968-69; prof. Stanford U., 1969—, dir. Stanford Magnetic Resonance Lab., 1975-97, dir. NMR Center, Sch. Medicine, 1983-84; dir. emeritus Stanford Magnetic Resonance Lab., 1998—. Vis. fellow Merton Coll., Oxford (Eng.) U., 1976; cons., vis. prof., lectr. in field; chmn. Internat. Coun. on Magnetic Resonance in Biology, 1972-74; dir. Internat. Sch. on Magnetic Resonance in Biology, Ettore Majorana Ctr., Sicily, 1993—; chmn. biotech. panel World Fedn. Scientists, 1998—. Contbr. articles to profl. jours.; mem. editorial bd. Jour. Theoretical Biology, 1961-88, Molecular Pharmacology, 1965-75, Jour. Medicinal Chemsitry, 1970-78, Biochimica Biophyica Acta, 1970-86, Revs. on Bioenergetics, 1972-89, Biomembrane Revs., 1972-80, Jour. Magnetic Resonance in Biology and Medicine, 1986—2000, Jour. Magnetic Resonance, 1993—2000. Recipient career devel. award USPHS, 1959-66, Kaiser award, 1973, Von Humboldt award, 1977, Pauling medal, 1984, Grand Gold Honor insignia (Austria), 1993, Founder's gold medal Internat. Coun. Magnetic Resonance in Biology, 1994, Prix Marianne Dessewffy Internat. Conf. of Genealogy and Heraldry, 1998; grantee NSF, 1957—, NIH, 1957—; travel fellow Am. Physiol. Soc., 1959. Fellow AAAS; mem. Am. Chem. Soc., Am. Soc. Biol. Chemistry and Molecular Biology, Biophys. Soc., Assn. Advanced Tech. in Biomed. Scis. (pres. 1981-88), Internat. Soc. Magnetic Resonance (chmn. divns. of biology and Medicine 1986-89), Phi Beta Kappa, Sigma Xi, Alpha Omega Alpha. Home: 950 Casanueva Pl Stanford CA 94305-1068 Office: Stanford U CCSR 269 Campus Dr Rm 3155-B Stanford CA 94305-5174 Office Phone: 650-723-6153. Business E-Mail: jardetzky@stanford.edu.

JARDINE, CINDY M., music educator; b. Tucson, Ariz., May 26, 1953; d. Lawrence Ralph Crouch, Arlene Ione (Fish) Crouch; m. Herald J. Jardine, Aug. 7, 1971; 1 adopted child, Brian P. Lima children: Robbi Ann, Tony, Nanette, Miken, Barbara, Janni. Cert. baton/dance tchr., Sharonlee's Sch. Dance, Elko, Nev., 1971. Tchr. choir and drill team Buhl Sch. Dist., Buhl, Idaho, 1981—84; tchr. choir, string, drill team Butte County Sch. Dist., Arco, Idaho, 1993—. Owner, operator Cindy's Majorettes, Arco, Idaho, 1971—; pvt. music tchr., Arco, 1971—; music cons. State of Idaho, 1993—. Author: (plays) What Goes Beyond "Z". Dir. Murtaugh Little Theatre, Murtaugh, Idaho, 1986—90; pres. Lost Rivers Cmty. Arts, Arco, Idaho, 1998—; bd. dirs. Lost Rivers Cmty. Choir and Theater, Arco. Mem.: Music Tchr. Assn. (6th dist. Idaho, Music Tchr. of Yr. 1996, 1998), Music Educators Nat. Conf. Mem. Lds Ch. Home: RR 1 Box 480 Arco ID 83213-9753

JARECKI, HENRY GEORGE, physician, financial planner; b. Stettin, Germany, Apr. 15, 1933; s. Max Jarecki and Gerda Kunstmann; m. Gloria Friedland, 1957; children: Andrew, Thomas, Eugene, Nicholas. MD, U. Heidelberg, Germany, 1957. Diplomate Am. Bd. Psychiatry and Neurology. Dir. Mocatta Metals Corp., N.Y.C., 1970-89, Mocatta & Goldsmid Ltd., London, 1973-89, Mocatta Hong Kong Ltd., 1975-89; chmn. Brody, White & Co. Inc., N.Y.C., 1971-95, Brody White Ltd, London, 1989-95, Guana Island Hotel Corp., British Virgin Islands, 1975—, Falconwood Corp., N.Y.C., 1976—, MovieFone, Inc., N.Y.C., 1989-99, PsychoGenics, Inc., Hawthorne, NY, 1998—. Asst. clin. prof. dept. psychiatry Sch. Medicine Yale U., New Haven, 1970—; gov. BVI Cmty. Coll., British Virgin Islands, 1989—; bd. dirs. Sotheby's Holdings, Inc., 2000-03; dir. tourist bd. British Virgin Islands, 2003-; trustee Inst. Internat. Edn., 2000-, vice-chmn., 2003—; chmn. Scholar Rescue Fund, 2002—; dir. Classical Theatre of Harlem, 2005—. Author: Modern Psychiatric Treatment, 1971; dir. (film) Gardeners of Eden, 1997, Cuba, Island of Music, 2000; contbr. articles to profl. jours. Adv. coun. Princeton U., Yale U. Sch. Medicine Dept. Psychiatry, 1992—; trustee Am. Mus. Natural History, 1991-99; bd. dirs. Botanic Soc. Brit. V.I., 1986—, Chgo. Bd. Trade, 1993-96; internat. liaison com. Food Corps Program, 1987-95, Island Resources Found., Tortola, Brit. Virgin Is., 1988— Mem. Nat. Futures Assn. (bd. dirs. 1979-93), Am. Psychiat. Assn. (Presdl. Commendation 1984). Office: Falconwood Corp 67 Irving Pl 12th Fl New York NY 10003 Business E-Mail: hj@falconefone.com. E-mail: hj@jarecki.com.

JARECKIE, STEPHEN BARLOW, museum curator; b. Orange, N.J., Feb. 18, 1929; s. Eugene Albert and Doris Condit (Brittin) J.; m. Gretchen Kinsman Fillmore, Aug. 10, 1959. BA, Lehigh U., 1951; MA, Syracuse U., 1961. Installation asst. Munson-Williams-Proctor Inst., Utica, N.Y., 1955-60, edn. asst., 1960-61; registrar Worcester (Mass.) Art Mus., 1961-83, assoc. in photography, 1962-69, assoc. curator photography, 1969-73, curator photography, 1973-94, curator of photography emeritus, 1995—; photo. adv. Fitchburg (Mass.) Art Mus., 1996—. Author: WAM catalogue, The Early Republic: Consolidation of Revolutionary Goals, 1976, American Photography: 1840-1900, 1976, Photographers of the Weimar Republic, 1986; contbr. to catalogue, pamphlets, articles to mus. lit. With AUS, 1951-53. Guest Fed. Republic of Germany for study of republic's museums, 1967. Mem. U.S. Naval Inst. (assoc.) Episcopalian. Achievements include building scale model original bldgs., grounds of Proctor Inst., 1957-60. Home: 47 Mount View Dr Holden MA 01520-2137 Office: 185 Elm St Fitchburg MA 01420-7503

JARES, DANIEL JOHN, secondary school educator; b. Berwyn, Ill., Nov. 7, 1948; s. Laddie Joseph Jares and Ethel Jenny Hemmer. BA in Social Studies Edn., U. Ill., 1970; MAT, U. Fla., 1974. Tchr. social studies Addison Trail H.S., Addison, Ill., 1970—2004; tchr. cert. officer Elmhurst (Ill.) Coll., 2004—. Mem.: Nat. Coun. Social Studies. Mem. United Church Of Christ. Home: 1331 S Finley Rd # 407 Lombard IL 60148 Office: Elmhurst Coll 190 Prospect Ave Elmhurst IL 60126 E-mail: jaresd@elmhurst.edu.

JARES, TIMOTHY E., finance educator, consultant, associate dean; b. Mitchell, S.D., May 7, 1963; s. Wayne R. and Donna L. Jares; m. Jayne E. Clausen, June 5, 1963; children: Caleb, Mitchell, Ryan. BS, U. S.D., 1985; MBA, U. Nebr., 1994, PhD, 1998. Software technician Land Bank Nat. Data Processing Ctr., Omaha, 1985—86; sr. software engr. Harris Corp., Bellevue, 1986—88; task mgr. Sterling Software, Bellevue, 1988—91; cons., sys. engr. Hughes Aircraft Co., Bellevue, Nebr., 1991—97; asst. prof. fin. U. North Fla., Jacksonville, 1997—2001, U. No. Colo., Greeley, 2001—, asst. dean, assoc. dean, assoc. prof. Cons. Bus. Valuation, Inc., Jacksonville, 1998—. Mem.: So. Fin. Assn., Fin. Mgmt. Assn. Avocations: golf, outdoor activities. Office: U No Colo MCB Fin CB #128 501 20th St Greeley CO 80639 Business E-Mail: tim.jares@unco.edu.

JARGOWSKY, PAUL A., economics professor; b. Sea Isle City, N.J., June 30, 1958; s. Bernard Andrew and Lucy Joanna Jargowsky; m. Marie Isabelle Chevrier, Sept. 13, 1987; children: Isabelle Chevrier, Sophia Chevrier. AB magna cum laude, Princeton U., 1980; M in Pub. Policy, Harvard U., 1986, PhD in Pub. Policy, 1991. Assoc. prof. polit. economy U. Tex., Richardson, 1997—; dir. The Bruton Ctr., U. Tex., 2002—, Tex. Schools Project, U. Tex., 2003—. Mem., sci. adv. com. Ctr. Urban Environ. Rsch. and Edn., U. of Md. Balt. County, 2001—; mem., nat. adv. bd. Inst. Rsch. Poverty, U. Minn. Law Sch., 1999—; elected mem., policy coun. Assn. Pub. Policy Analysis and Mgmt., 2001—04. Author: Poverty and Place: Ghettos, Barrios, and the American City; contbr. articles to profl. jours. Mem. cmty. needs assessment com. United Way of Met. Dallas, 2001, mem. cmty. assessment tech. adv. com., 2002—03. Recipient Recipient Manuel C. Carballo award, Harvard U., 1986, Best Book award, Urban Affairs Assn., 1999; grantee, Twentieth Century Fund, 1997, Russell Sage Found., 1998, 2002, Brookings Instn., 2002. Mem.: Am. Sociol. Assn. (assoc.), Urban Affairs Assn. (assoc.), Assn. Pub. Policy Analysis and Mgmt. (assoc.), Assn. Am. Geographers (assoc.). Office: U Tex P O Box 830688 MS GC31 Richardson TX 75083-0688 Office Phone: 972-883-2992. Office Fax: 972-883-2551. E-mail: jargo@utdallas.edu.

JARLES, RUTH SEWELL, education educator; d. Nashville Clyde Sewell and Zetta Marie Hurt; m. Terry Waters Milligan, June 16, 1990; m. Marion Evert Jarles, Dec. 19, 1957 (div. Mar. 1980); children: Leslie Marie Murphy, Eva Colleen Wakeley, Brian Keith. AA, Western Okla. State Coll., 1976; BA magna cum laude, U. Colo., Colorado Springs, 1982; MDiv, Iliff Sch. Theology, 1985; PhD, U. Denver, 1993. Dir. Christian edn. Patrick Henry Village Army Chapel, Heidelberg, Germany, 1973—74; dir. curriculum Grace Child Devel. Ctr., Altus, Okla., 1976—77; dir. Christian edn. First Congl. Ch., Colorado Springs, Colo., 1980—84; asst. to the dir. joint PhD program U. Denver, Iliff Sch. Theology, 1991—92; adj. faculty, tchg. or rsch. asst. U. Denver, Iliff Sch. Theology, Front Range and Auraria C.C., 1983—98; asst. materials sci. br. Nat. Renewable Energy Lab., Golden, Colo., 1994—95; exec. dir. Colo. Libr. Assn., Denver, 1995—98; gen. edn. faculty Art Inst. Colo., Denver, 1998—. Seminar leader Gender Differences in Comm. in the Workplace; session convenor, panel mem. Women in Religion; lectr. U. Colo., Boulder, 2002—04. Contbr. articles to profl. jours. Student senate Iliff Sch. Theology, Denver, 1984—86; mentor students cmty. svc. projects Art Inst. Colo., Denver, 1997—; chair/mem. South Africa task force, race and religion com., women's com. Iliff Sch.Theology, Denver, 1984—92; mem. publs. com. Colo. Women's Agenda, Denver, 1993—95, 2005; chair/mem. edn., fin., adminstrv. bd., music and fine arts, peace with justice coms. Trinity United Meth. Ch., Denver, 1984—92; mem. exec. com. Nat. Renewable Energy Lab. Women's Network, Golden, 1994—95; active Art Inst. Colo. Christmas project Denver Safe Ho., 2001—. Recipient E. Craig Brandenburg award, United Meth. Ch.; scholar Ea. Star Tng. awards for Religious Leadership, The Grand Chpt. Colo., Order Ea. Star, 1984—86; Oliver Read Whitley scholar, Iliff Sch. Theology, Seminarian scholar, Ctr. for Biblic Studies, Jerusalem, Israel, Ga. Harkness scholar, United Meth. Ch. Mem.: AAUW, Denver Art Mus., Nat. Women's History Mus., Nat. Mus. for Women in the Arts. Office: Art Inst Colo 1200 Lincoln St Denver CO 80203 Home: 6240 W 24th Ave Edgewater CO 80214-1034 Office Phone: 303-824-2151.

JARMAN, BETH S., small business owner; d. Wayne David and Jean (Marshall) Smith; m. George Land, Nov. 3, 1987; children: Alex, Jarman Michelle. BA cum laude, U. Utah, 1963, MS, 1970, PhD, 1977. Pub. sch. tchr. Twenty Nine Palms H.S., Twenty Nine Palms, Calif., 1964—65, Davis County Sch. Dist., Bountiful, Utah, 1971—74; dir. Utah Dept. of Commerce, Salt Lake City, 1964—65; mem. State Ho. of Rep., Salt Lake City, 1974—77, Utah State Ho. of Rep., Salt Lake City, 1974—76; chairperson Utah Housing Fin. Agy., Salt Lake City, 1976—82; pres. Site Devel. Corp., Scottsdale, Ariz., 1980—82; asst. dir. dept. of health svcs. Ariz. State Govt., Phoenix, 1984—85, dir. ariz. dept. of commerce, 1985—88; founding pres. Phoenix City Club, Phoenix, 1987—; pres. The Farsight Group, Scottsdale, Ariz., 1988—. Asst. dir. Dept. of Health Svcs., Phoenix, 1984—85. Author: (book) Breakpoint and Beyond, You Can Change Your Life by Changing Your Mind. Pres. Charter 100. Recipient Outstanding Tchr. in the Social Studies, Utah Coun. for the Social Studies, 1975, Recogntion for courage and decication for sponsoring the ERA, YWCA, 1976, Outstanding Svc. award, Utah Housing Fin. Agy., 1978, Recognition for Founding the Phoenix City Club, Phoenix City Club Bd., 1987; Clarrissa Abrelia Hinckley Grad. Fellowship, Hinckley Inst. of Politics, 1975, Grad. Fellowship, U. Utah, 1977. Mem.: Charter 100 (program chair 2004—05, pres. 2005—). Office: Farsight Group 6619 N Scottsdale Rd Scottsdale AZ 85250 Office Phone: 480-945-8765. Office Fax: 480-945-8765. Personal E-mail: bethjarman@cox.net.

JARMAN, MARK FOSTER, language educator; b. Mt. Sterling, Ky., June 5, 1952; s. Donald Ray and Bo Dee (Foster) J.; m. Amy Lynn Kane, Dec. 28, 1974; children: Claire Marie, Zoe Anne. BA, U. Calif., Santa Cruz, 1974; MFA, U. Iowa, 1976. Instr. Ind. State U., Evansville, 1976-78; vis. lectr. U. Calif., Irvine, 1979-80; asst. prof. English Murray (Ky.) State U., 1980-83, Vanderbilt U., Nashville, 1983-86, assoc. prof. English, 1986-92, prof. English, 1992—. Mem. Associated Writing Programs, Norfolk, Va., 1980—, Poets' Prize Com., NYC, 1988—2002. Author: Iris, 1992, The Black Riviera, 1990, 2d edit., 1995, Far and Away, 1985, The Rote Walker, 1981, North Sea, 1978, 2d edit., 1989, The Reaper Essays, 1996, Questions for Ecclesiastes, 1997, Unholy Sonnets, 2000, The Secret of Poetry, 2001, Body and Soul: Essays on Poetry, 2002, To the Green Man, 2004; editor: Rebel Angels: 25 Poets of the New Formalism, 1996. Winner Poets' prize, 1991, Lenore Marshall Poetry prize, Acad. of Am. Poets and The Nation Mag.,1998; John Simon Guggenheim Meml. Found. poetry fellow, 1991-92, Robert Frost fellow, Bread Loaf Writer's Conf., 1985; NEA grantee, 1977, 83, 92; recipient Joseph Henry Jackson award SF Found., 1974. Mem.: Nat. Book Critics Cir. Mem. Christian Ch. Office: Vanderbilt U Dept English Nashville TN 37235 Office Phone: 615-322-2541. E-mail: mark.jarman@vanderbilt.edu.

JARMUSCH, JIM, film director, actor; b. Akron, Ohio, Jan. 22, 1953; m. Sara Driver. Attended, Columbia U. Actor: (films) American Autobahn, 1984, Straight to Hell, 1987, Helsinki Napoli All Night Long, 1987, Leningrad Cowboys Go to America, 1989, The Golden Boat, 1990, In The Soup, 1992, Iron Horsemen, 1994, Tigrero: A Film That Was Never Made, 1994, Blue in the Face, 1995, Typewriter, the Rifle & the Movie Camera, 1996, Cannes Man, 1996, Sling Blade, 1996, Divine Trash, 1998, (TV series) Fishing With John, 1991, American Cinema, 1994; writer, dir., editor, prodr., composer: Permanent Vacation, 1982 (Joseph von Sternberg prize Mannheim, Internat. Critics prize Figueira da Foz, Portugal 1981); dir., writer, editor: Stranger Than Paradise, 1984 (Camera D'Or Cannes Film Festival 1984, Best Picture of Yr. Nat. Soc. Film Critics 1984), Coffee and Cigarettes, 2003; dir., editor: Coffee and Cigarettes III, 1993 (Golden Palm Cannes Film Festival 1993); dir., writer: Down By Law, 1986 (Best Film award Locarno, Best Fgn. Film Norway, Denmark and Israel), Mystery Train, 1989 (Highest Artistic Achievement prize Cannes Film Festival), Dead Man, 1995 (World Premiere Cannes Film Festival 1995, Felix award Best Non-European Film 1996, Best Cinematography award N.Y. Critics Cir. 1996); dir., writer, prodr.: Night on Earth, 1991 (Grand award Best Feature Film Houston Internat. Film Festival 1992, Ind. Spirit award Best Cinematography 1993), Ghost Dog: The Way of the Samurai, 1999, Broken Flowers, 2005; exec. prodr.: When Pigs Fly, 1993; dir., cinematographer: Year of the Horse, 1997; cinematographer: You Are Not I, 1981.*

JAROFF, LEON MORTON, magazine editor; b. Detroit, Feb. 27, 1927; s. Abraham and Ruth (Rockita) J.; m. Claire Lynn Fox, Aug. 15, 1954 (div. Nov. 1975); children: Peter, Jill, Susan, Nicholas, Jennifer; m. Mary Katherine Moran, Jan. 10, 1976. BS in Elec. Engring. and Math., U. Mich., 1950. Writer Materials and Methods Mag., N.Y.C., 1950-51; researcher, reporter, corr. Life Mag., N.Y.C., Detroit, Chgo., 1951-58; corr., assoc. editor, sr. editor Time Mag., N.Y.C., Detroit, Chgo., 1958-79, scis. editor N.Y.C., 1985-87, contbr., 1988—, Time.com columnist, 2002—; founder, mng. editor Discover Mag., N.Y.C., 1980-84. Co-chair bd. for student publs. U. Mich., 1992-98; cons. Internat. Astron. Union's Working Group on Near-Earth Objects. Author: The New Genetics, 1991, also 44 Time mag. cover stories. Trustee Neurosci. Rsch. Found., La Jolla, Calif.; bd. dirs. Rogosin Inst., N.Y.C.; mem. Coun. Media Integrity, 2001-. With USN, 1944-45. Recipient Robert S. Ball Meml. award Aviation Space Writers Assn., 1978, Excellence award, 1989; Sci. Writing award AAAS/Westinghouse Corp., 1978, Sci. Writing award Am. Inst. Physics/U.S. Steel Corp., 1976, 82-83; named Asteroid 7829 Jaroff in his honor Fellow AAAS, Com. for Sci. Investigation of Claims of the Paranormal; mem. Am. Soc. Mag. Editors (exec. com. 1984-85), Am. Inst. Physics (adv. com. 1982—). Jewish. Avocations: tennis, computers, chess. Home: PO Box 1080 East Hampton NY 11937-0901 Office: Time Mag Time & Life Bldg 1271 Avenue Of The Americas New York NY 10020-1300 Office Phone: 212-522-3747. Personal E-mail: neonleo@aol.com.

JARON, DOV, biomedical engineer, educator; b. Tel Aviv, Oct. 29, 1935; came to U.S., 1958, naturalized, 1972; s. Meir and Sara (Levit) Yarovsky; m. Brooke E. Boberg, Sept. 16, 1978; children: Shulamit, Tamara. BS magna cum laude, U. Denver, 1961; PhD, U. Pa., 1967. Sr. research asso. Maimonides Med. Center, Bklyn., 1967-70; dir. surg. research Sinai Hosp. of Detroit, 1970-73; asso. prof. elec. engring. U. R.I., Kingston, 1973-77, prof., 1977-79, coordinator biomed. engring., 1973-79; prof. biomend. engring. and sci. Drexel U., Phila., 1979—, dir. Biomed. Engring. and Sci. Inst., 1979-96. Calhoun disting. prof., 1998—; vis. prof. elec. engring. Rutgers U., New Brunswick, N.J., 1968-73; adj. prof. biomed. engring. Wayne State U., 1971-73; adj. prof. physiology Temple U. Sch. Medicine, 1980—; adj. prof. radiology Jefferson Med. Coll., 1983—; dir. Div. Biol. and Critical Systems, NSF, 1991-93; assoc. dir. Nat. Ctr. Rsch. Resources, dir. biomedical tech. NIH, 1996-98. Contbr. articles to sci. jours. NSF, NIH, Office Naval Research, pvt. founds. research grantee. Fellow AAAS, IEEE, Am. Inst. for Med. and Biol. Engring.; mem. AAUP, Internat. Fedn. for Med. and Biol. Engring. (pres. 2000-2003), Internat. Union for Phys. and Engring. Scis. in Medicine (v.p. 2003—), Biomed. Engring. Soc., Am. Soc. for Engring. Edn., Assn. for Advancement Med. Instrumentation, Internat. Soc. Artificial Organs, Am. Soc. for Artificial Internal Organs, Biophys. Soc., N.Y. Acad. Scis., Engring. in Medicine and Biology of IEEE (pres. 1986-87), Sigma Xi, Tau Beta Pi, Eta Kappa Nu. Achievements include research of cardiac assist devices, cardiovascular dynamics and modeling, microcirculation, biomed. instrumentation. Home: 122 Bethlehem Pike Philadelphia PA 19118-2815 Office: Drexel U Sch Biomed Engring Sci and Health Systems 32nd and Chestnut St Philadelphia PA 19104 Business E-Mail: dov.jaron@drexel.edu.

JARQUE, CARLOS M., former federal official; b. Mexico City, Oct. 18, 1954; Actuary Degree, U. Anáhuac, 1976; diploma, M in Econs. and Polit. Sci., London Sch. Econs., 1978; postgrad., U. Oslo, 1978; PhD in Econs., Nat. U. Australia, 1982; postgrad., Harvard U., 1984. Pres. Nat. Inst. for Stats., Geography and Informatics; gen. dir. stats. Dept. Programming and Budget; pres. Interdeptmental Pub. Fin. Com.; gen. dir. Internat. Stats. Inst.; world pres. UN Stats. Commn.; pres. UN Cartographic Conf.; sec. of social develop. Govt. of Mexico, 1999—2000; mgr. sustainable develop. Inter-Amer. Develop. Bank, 2001—. Sec. Nat. Devel. Plan, 1995-2000; vis. prof. Harvard U. Contbr. articles to profl. jours. Recipient Nat. Sci. and Tech. award, Nat. Actuaries' award, Benito Juárez medal of merit, Henri Willen Methorst medal, Adolf Quetelet medal. Office: 1300 New York Ave NW Washington DC 20577

JARRAH, ABDUL SALAM, mathematician; arrived in U.S., 1996; PhD, N.Mex State U., 2002; degree in math. and computer sci., Yarmonk U., Jordan, 1992. Asst. prof. math. E. Tenn. State U., Johnson City, 2002—04; sr. rsch. assoc. Va. Tech, Blacksburg, 1998—. Mem.: Am. Math. Soc. (assoc.), Soc. Math. Biology (assoc.), Soc. Indsl. and Applied Math. (assoc.). Office: Va Bioinformatics Inst Washington St Blacksburg VA 24061 Office Phone: 540-231-9456. E-mail: ajarrah@ut.edu.

JARRARD, LEONARD EVERETT, psychologist, educator; b. Waco, Tex., Oct. 23, 1930; s. Thomas Ivan and Levis Everett (Lasswell) J.; m. Janet Grier Shoop, Aug. 16, 1958; children: Alice Grier, David Frazier, Hugh Everett. BA, Baylor U., Waco, 1955; MS, Carnegie Inst. Tech., Pitts., 1957, PhD, 1959. Asst. to asso. prof. psychology Washington and Lee U., 1959-66; assoc. prof. to prof. psychology Carnegie-Mellon U., 1966-71; Robert L. Telford prof. psychology Washington and Lee U., Lexington, Va., 1971-2001, prof. emeritus, 2001—. Vis. lectr., prof. exptl. psychology U. Oxford, Eng., 1975-76; interim assoc. prof. anatomy U. Fla., 1965-66; acad. visitor Inst. Psychiatry, U. London, 1988-89. Editor: Cognitive Processes of Nonhuman Primates, 1971; cons. editor: Jour. Comparative and Physiol. Psychology, 1970-75, Behavioral Neurosci. Psychology, 1995-2001. Served with USAF, 1952-54. Fellow AAAS, APA, APS; mem. Soc. for Neurosci., Psychonomics Soc., Va. Acad. Sci. So. Soc. Philosophy and Psychology, Phi Beta Kappa, Omicron Delta Kappa, Sigma Xi. Home: RR 5 Box 1067 Lexington VA 24450-9805 Office: Washington and Lee U Dept Psychology Lexington VA 24450

JARRELL, CHARLES MICHAEL, bishop; b. Opelousas, La., May 15, 1940; Student, Immaculata Minor Sem., Cath. U. Ordained priest Roman Cath. Ch. 1967, bishop 1993. Bishop Diocese of Houma (La.)-Thibodaux, 1993—2002, Diocese of Lafayette, La., 2002—.*

JARRELL, TIM, travel guide publishing executive; Mktg. Quality Paperback Book Club, Meredith Book Group; with Children's TV Workshop, 1996—99; v.p., pub. dir. Sports Illustrated for Kids, 1999—2004; v.p., pub. Fodor's Travel Publishing, NYC, 2004—. Office: Fodor's Travel Publishing 1745 Broadway New York NY 10019

JARRETT, CHARLES ELWOOD, insurance company executive, lawyer; b. Abilene, Tex., Apr. 11, 1957; s. Jerry Vernon and Martha (McCabe) J.; m. Stephanie J. Baker, Apr. 16, 1988; 1 child, Megan McCabe. AB, Dartmouth Coll., 1980; JD, U. Mich., 1983. Bar: Mass. 1984, US Dist. Ct. Mass. 1984, Ohio 1986, US Dist. Ct. No. Dist. Ohio 1986, US Ct. Appeals 6th cir. 1987, US Supreme Ct. 1988. Assoc. Choate Hall & Stewart, Boston, 1984-86, Baker & Hostetler, Cleve., 1986-90, ptnr., 1990—2000; chief legal officer The Progressive Corp., Ohio, 2000—, sec., v.p., 2001—. Office: Progressive Corp 6300 Wilson Mills Rd Mayfield OH 44143

JARRETT, DALE, race car driver; b. Conover, N.C., Nov. 26, 1956; m. Kelley Jarrett; children: Jason, Natalee, Karsyn. Named winner, Daytona 500, 1993, 1996, 2000, Mello Yello 500, 1994, Miller 500, 1995, Coca-Cola 600, 1996, Goodwrench 400, 1996, Brickyard 400, 1996, 1999, Pa. 500, 1997, Goody's Headache Powder 500, 1997, Exide NASCAR 400, 1997, VAW-GM 500, 1997, Dura-Lube 500, 1997, Transouth Fin. 500, 1997, 1998, MBNA Platinum 400, 1998, Winston 500, 1998, Pontiac Excitement 400, 1999, KMart 400, 1999, Pepsi 400, 1999. Office: DAJ Racing Inc PO Box 564 Conover NC 28613-0564

JARRETT, LEOTTA ESTHER, elementary school educator, minister; b. Nassau, Bahamas, Nov. 27, 1930; arrived in U.S., 1953; d. Arthur and Esther Louise Pinder; m. Arthur LeRoy Jarrett, July 1, 1950; children: Valencia, Freneau, Sibyl, Arthur L. Jr. BA, Notre Dame Nemur U., 1970; MS, Calif. State U., 1974, MS, 1996; EdD, U. San Francisco, 2000. Sec. elem. sch. Joseph E. Smith, Chattanooga, 1958—63; sec. personnel dept. Langston U., Okla., 1963—65; adminstrv. sec. Pacific Bell Telephone Co., San Francisco, 1965—66, San Mateo Elem. Sch. Dist., 1966—69; tchr., quasi adminstr. San Mateo-Foster City Sch. Dist., 1970—2002; assoc. min. Trinity Bapt. Ch., 1996—2003. Tchr., sponsor, counselor Adopt-A-Student Program, San Mateo, 1990—98; dir., proprietor Lee Jarrett Sch. Personal Devel. and Modeling, 1980—96. Mem. adv. bd. ARC, Burlingame, Calif., 1990—92; advisor, coord., judge North Ctrl. San Mateo Adv. Com., 1990—2000; chair clergy com. Health Adv. Com.; charter mem. African Am. Cmty., San Mateo, 1996—. Mem.: NEA, ASCD, Internat. Assn. Mins. Wives and Mins. Widows, Inc., Alpha Kappa Alpha, Phi Delta Kappa, Delta Theta Sigma. Baptist. Avocations: travel, poetry, storytelling, antiques. Home: 117 Success Mine Loop Grass Valley CA 95945-9764 Fax: 530-477-8750.

JARRETT, MARK PAUL, rheumatologist, health facility administrator; b. Bklyn., Dec. 29, 1949; s. Irving and Claire Jarrett; m. Michele Jonas, Aug. 15, 1974; children: Matthew, Nicole, Tyler. BS, Muhlenberg Coll., 1971; MD, NYU, 1975; MBA, Wagner Coll., 1994. Bd. cert. Am. Bd. Internal Medicine, Am. Bd. Rheumatology, Am. Bd. Geriatrics, Am. Bd. Quality Assurance and Utilization Rev. Physicians. Intern in internal medicine Montefiore Hosp., Bronx, 1975; resident in internal medicine, 1976—78; rheumatology fellow Montefiore Hosp./Albert Einstein Coll. Medicine, 1978-80; asst. prof. medicine Northwestern U. Med. Sch., Chgo., 1980-82; dir. rheumatology S.I. U. Hosp., 1982-98; sr. med. dir. Care Mgmt. Group Greater N.Y., Lake Success, N.Y., 1999-2000, pres., 2000-2001; chief med. officer S.I. Univ. Hosp., 2001—. Clin. asst. prof. medicine SUNY Health Scis. Ctr.-Downstate, Bklyn., 1982—. Bd. dirs. Cmty. Cable TV, S.I., 2000-2001, Physician Health Svcs. N.Y., N.Y.C., 1998-2001. Fellow ACP, Am. Coll. Rheumatology; mem. AMA, Am. Fedn. Rsch., Am. Geriatrics Soc., Am. Mgmt. Assn., Chief Med. Officers Soc., Richmond County Med. Soc. (pres. 1990), Phi Beta Kappa. Avocations: travel, gourmet food. Office: Staten Island Univ Hosp 475 Seaview Ave Staten Island NY 10305 E-mail: mjarrett@si.rr.com.

JARRETT, NOEL, chemical engineer, researcher; b. Long Eaton, Eng., Nov. 17, 1921; came to U.S., 1926, naturalized, 1942; s. John Richard and Lena Eliza (Hexter) J.; m. Violet E. Dipner, Sept. 24, 1949; children: Robert, Kenneth, James, Thomas. BS in Chem. Engring, U. Pitts., 1949; MS in Chem. Engring, U. Mich., 1951. Lubrication sales engr. Freedom-Valvoline Co., Freedom, Pa., 1949-50; rsch. engr., group leader, asst. chief Alcoa Labs., Aluminum Co. Am., 1951-65, chief div. process metallurgy, 1965-69, asst. dir. metal prodn. labs., 1969-81, tech. dir. smelting rsch. and devel., 1981-82, tech. dir. chem. engring. rsch. and devel., 1982-87; ret., 1987; prin. Noel Jarrett Assocs. Patentee smelting, melting and purification of alumninum. Served with U.S. Army, 1942-45. Fellow Am. Soc. Metals; mem. NAE, Am. Isnt. Chem. Engrs., Minerals, Metals and Materials Soc., VFW, Am. Legion, Masons, Elks, Sigma Xi. Episcopalian. Home and Office: 149 Jefferson Dr New Kensington PA 15068-3127 Office Phone: 724-335-6880. *I have found that the one who performs the tasks immediately at hand so well that his work cannot be ignored will reap society's rewards without asking.*

JARRETT, OLGA SOFIA SEASTROM, education educator, researcher; b. Easton, Pa., Sept. 22, 1940; d. Erik Gunnar Seastrom and Rida Norma Collmar Seastrom; m. Robert Earl Jarrett, June 20, 1966; children: Andrew David Jarrett (deceased at age 25), Christopher Samir Jarrett (age 35), Erik George Jarrett (age 22). BA, Pa. State U., 1962, MA, 1966; PhD, Ga. State U., 1980. Civil rights intern YWCA, Atlanta, 1963—64; instr. Pa. State U., New Kensington, Pa., 1965—68; supr. of preschool programs Belize Christian Social Coun., Belize, 1973—74; project dir. Ga. State U., Atlanta, 1980—83, asst. prof., 1994—2000, assoc. prof., 2000—; adj. asst. prof. Overseas Program Boston (Mass.) U., Heidelberg, Germany, 1985—91. Specialist edn. program Army Child Devel. Svcs., Heidelberg, 1985—91; cons. in field. Contbr. articles to profl. jours. Founder Parent Edn. for Devel., Bridgetown, Barbados, 1971—72; mem. edn. com. Atlanta (Ga.) Aquarium, 2003—05. Grantee, NSF, 1999—2005. Mem.: Am. Ednl. Rsch. Assn. (mem. exec. bd. 2003—05, mem. peace edn. spl. interest group), Nat. Assn. Rsch. in Sci. Tchg. (mem. awards subcommittee 2003—05), The Am. Assn. Child's Right to Play (sec. 2001—), The Assn. Study of Play (pres. 2004—, co-editor). Democrat. Avocations: travel, rock, mineral, and fossil collecting, reading. Home: 1070 Ashbury Drive Decatur GA 30030 Office: ECE Georgia State University University Plaza Atlanta GA 30303 Office Phone: 404-651-0959. Office Fax: 404-651-1495. E-mail: ojarrett@gsu.edu.

JARRETT, POLLY HAWKINS, secondary education educator, retired; b. Columbia, S.C., May 6, 1929; d. William Harold and Ann Beatrice (Carson) Hawkins; m. Nov. 21, 1953 (dec. Aug. 1984); children: William Guy Jr., Henry Carson. Student, Montreat Coll., 1947-49; BS in Secondary Edn., Longwood Coll., 1951. Tchr. 7th grade McDowell County Schs., Marion, N.C., 1951-52; tchr. 8th grade Marion City Schs., 1952-53, Burke County Schs., Morganton, N.C., 1954-56; tchr. 7th grade Wake County Schs., Raleigh, N.C., 1956-58, Durham (N.C.) County Schs., 1958-59; tchr. 7th and 8th grade Raleigh City and Wake County Schs., Raleigh, 1959-79; tchr. social studies Wake County Pub. Schs., Raleigh, 1979-90, ret., 1990. Adv. bd. State Employees Credit Union, Raleigh, 1988—92, Raleigh, 1994—2000. Mem. United Daus. of the Confederacy (chpt. pres. 1978-81, 91-96, divsn. historian 1981-83, dist. VI dir. 1983-85, divsn. chaplain 1986-90, divsn. parliamentarian 1994-96, chmn. bd. trustees 1990-91), Delta Kappa Gamma (chpt. pres. 1988-90, regional dir. 1990-92, state 2d v.p. 1997-99, chmn. N.C. divsn. State Conv. 2001, mem. S.E. regional steering com. 2003), Kappa Delta Pi, Pi Delta Epsilon, Pi Gamma Mu. Democrat. Methodist. Avocations: travel, growing roses, reading, pets. Home: 3405 White Oak Rd Raleigh NC 27609-7620

JARRETT, VALERIE BOWMAN, real estate company executive; b. Shiraz, Iran, Nov. 14, 1956; d. James Edward and Barbara (Taylor) B.; 1 child, Laura Allison. BA, Stanford U., 1978; JD, U. Mich., 1981. Bar: Ill. 1981, U.S. Dist. Ct. (no. dist.) Ill. 1981. Assoc. Pope, Ballard, Shepard & Fowle Ltd., Chgo., 1981-84, Sonnenschein, Carlin, Nath & Rosenthal, Chgo., 1984; dep. corp. counsel for fin. and devel. City of Chgo., dep. chief of staff for Mayor Richard Daley, commr., dept. planning and devel.; exec. v.p., mng. dir. The Habitat Co., Chgo. Dir. USG Corp., Joyce Found., Met. Planning Coun.; chmn. The Chgo. Stock Exch., Local Initiative Support Corp. Dir. RREEF Am. II, Navigant Cons., Inc.; pres. Southeast Chgo. Commn., Chicago-land C. of C.; trustee Mus. Sci. and Industry, Windows to the World Comm., U. Chgo.; vice chmn. U. Chgo. Hosps. Leadership Greater Chgo. fellow, 1985-86. Mem. Econ. Club, Comml. Club. Democrat. Avocation: travel. Office: The Habitat Co 350 West Hubbard St Chicago IL 60610 Office Phone: 312-527-5400.

JARRETT, WILLIAM JAY, theater educator, costume designer; s. Jefferson Henry and Wilton Amy (Haynie) Jarrett. MusB, U. Ga., 1973, MFA in Drama, 1985. Lic. cosmetologist Ga., 1973. Co-owner VJ's Headline, Athens, Ga., 1976—78; owner, stylist Jay Jarrett's Salon, Athens, Ga., 1978—82; hair stylist Joel & Co., Savannah, Ga., 1986—90; drama tchr. Savannah/Chatham County Sch., 1990—93, chmn. Dept. Drama, 1992—93; band dir. Dekalb (Ga.) County Sch., 1993—99; h.s. drama tchr. Fulton County Sch., Atlanta, 1999—. Freelance costume designer, Atlanta, 1993—; costume designer Aurora Theatre, Daluth, Ga., 2000—01. Singer (tenor): Savannah Symphony Chorale, 1987—93, Athens Choral Soc., 1973—93. Mem.: U.S. Inst. Theatre Tech., Ga. Theatre Conf., S.E. Theatre Conf., Phi Mu Alpha. Libertarian. Avocations: British mystery novels, cocker spaniels, musical theatre dramaturgy, chicken memorabilia. Home: PO Box 8296 Atlanta GA 31106 Office: North Springs High Sch 7447 Roswell Rd Atlanta GA 30328

JARROW, ROBERT ALAN, economist, educator; b. Hackensack, N.Y., June 16, 1952; s. Benjamin Charles and Irene Elizabeth (Kozniewski) Jaworowski; m. Gail Dian Goundry; children: Kyle, Tate, Heather. BA, Duke U., 1974; MBA, Dartmouth Coll., 1976; PhD, MIT, 1979. Prof. fin. and econs. Cornell U., Ithaca, N.Y., 1979—. Cons. Bank of Am., San Francisco, 1987-89, Merrill Lynch, 1994, Kamakura Corp., 1995—, FDIC, 2003—. Author: Option Pricing, 1983, Finance Theory, 1988, Modelling Fixed Income Securities and Interest Rate Options, 1996, 2d revised edit., 2002, Derivative Securities, 1996, 2000; contbr. articles; assoc. editor: Rev. Derivatives Rsch., 1997—; editor: Math. Fin., 2002; co-editor: Jour. Derivatives, 1999—2002. Recipient Pomerance prize Chgo. Bd. Options Exch., 1982; named Fin. Engr. Yr., 1997; named to Fixed Income Security Analysts Hall of Fame, 2004. Mem. Am. Fin. Assn., Econ. Soc., Ops. Rsch. Soc., Soc. for Promotion Econ. Theory, Math. Assn. Am. Avocations: jogging, soccer, Karate. Office: Cornell U Sage Hall Ithaca NY 14853 Business E-Mail: RAJ15@cornell.edu.

JARSMA, CYNTHIA LYNN, secondary school educator; d. John Truman and Joyce Marilyn Taylor; m. Brian Matthew Jarsma, Aug. 27, 1988. BA in English, Nazareth Coll., Kalamazoo, Mich., 1989; MA in Edn., Saginaw Valley U., Mich., 2000. Cert. tchr. State of Mich., 1990. Tchr. L'Anse Creuse Pub. Schs., Chesterfield, Mich., 1994—99, East China Sch. Dist., Mich., 1999—. Intake worker Macomb St. Clair Pvt. Industry Coun., Mount Clemens, Mich. Avocations: travel, photography, scrapbooks.

JARVI, NEEME, conductor; b. Tallinn, Estonia, June 7, 1937; arrived in U.S., 1980; s. August and Elss Jarvi; m. Liilia Jarvi, Sept. 2, 1961; children: Paavo, Kristjan, Maarika. Diploma in Music and Conducting, St. Petersburg (USSR) State Conservatorium, 1960; hon. doctorate, U. Aberdeen, Scotland, Music Conservatory of Talinn, Estonia, Gothenberg (Sweden) U., U. Mich. Condr. Estonian Radio Symphony Orch., 1960-63, chief condr., 1963-76, Estonian State Opera, 1963-76, Estonian State Symphony, 1976-80; prin. condr. Gothenburg (Sweden) Symphony Orch., 1982—; prin. condr., music dir., condr. laureate Royal Scottish Orch., Glasgow, 1984-88; music dir. Detroit Symphony Orch., 1990—, now music dir. emeritus. Prin. guest condr. Birmingham Symphony Orch., England, 1980—83; guest condr. N.Y. Philharm. Orch., Boston Symphony Orch., Phila. Orch., Chgo. Symphony, Royal Concertgebow, Amsterdam, Philharmonia London, London Symphony, Scandinavian Orch., Met. Opera House, N.Y.C. Decorated Knight Comdr. North Star Order Sweden; recipient 1st prize in conducting, Accademia Nazionale di Santa Cecilia, 1971.*

JARVI, PAAVO, conductor; b. Tallinn, Estonia, 1963; U.S., 1980; Studied at, Curtis Inst. of Music, Los Angeles Philharm. Inst. Prin. guest condr. Royal Stockhkolm Philharm., City of Birmingham, Eng.; condr. Cin. Symphony Orch., 2001—. Condr. UBS Verbier Youth Orch. (summer series); artistic adv. Estonian Nat. Symphony Orch., 2002—. Named Editor's Choice, Feb. 2003 edit. of Gramophone; recipient Kultuurkapital award, Estonian Min. of Culture. Office: CSO Administrative Offices Music Hall 1241 Elm St Cincinnati OH 45202*

JARVIK, MURRAY ELIAS, psychiatry, pharmacology educator; b. N.Y.C., June 1, 1923; s. Jacob and Minnie (Haas) J.; m. Lissy, Dec. 19, 1954; children— Laurence Ariel, Jeffrey Gil. BS, CCNY, 1944; MA, UCLA, 1945; MD, U. Calif., San Francisco, 1951; PhD, U. Calif., Berkeley, 1952. Research technician phys. chemistry Rockefeller Inst., N.Y.C., 1943-44; research assoc. neurophysiology neurology dept. Mt. Sinai Hosp., 1953-55; research assoc. psychopharmacology L.I. Biol. Assn., Cold Spring Harbor, N.Y., 1955-56; asst. prof. pharmacology Albert Einstein Coll. Medicine, 1956-60, assoc. prof., 1960-68, prof., Sadie Danciger Distinguished scholar, 1968, prof. psychiatry, 1969-72; prof. psychiatry, pharmacology U. Calif. at Los Angeles, 1972—; chief psychopharmacology unit Brentwood VA Hosp., 1972—. Vis. asst. prof. physiol. psychology U. Calif. at Berkeley, 1955; adj. asst. prof. N.Y. U., 1957; vis. physician Bellevue Hosp., N.Y.C., 1960; research scientist N.Y. U. Med. Center, 1936-65, sr. research scientist, 1965; mem. adv. com. on abuse of stimulant and depressant drugs Bur. Drug Abuse Control, FDA, 1966—; mem. adv. com. on tobacco habituation Am. Cancer Soc., 1967— Mng. editor Psychopharmacologia, 1966-71; mem. editorial adv. bd. Behavioral Biology. Recipient Career Scientist award NIMH, 1971, Career Scientist award, 1971-72; fellow Ctr. for Advanced Study in Behavioral Scis. Stanford U., 1988-89. Fellow AAAS, N.Y. Acad. Scis., Am. Psychol. Assn. (div. pres. 1966-68); mem. Am. Coll. Neuropsychopharmacology, Collegium Internationale Neuro-Psychopharmacologium, Internat. Brain Research Orgn., Am. Psychopath. Assn., Phi Beta Kappa, Sigma Xi. Office: VA Med Ctr Brentwood Los Angeles CA 90073 E-mail: mjarvik@ucla.edu. *A guiding principle in my life has been that psychiatry can and should be a science and not merely an art. The principles of validation and control should be applied to psychiatry just as they are to any other science. I have felt that psychopharmacology and the study of the brain are the pathways one must follow to learn more about behavior. Although great progress is occuring in the understanding of molecular mechanisms, the molar study of behavior is indispensable for a complete knowledge of psychiatry and psychology.*

JARVIK, ROBERT K., biomedical research scientist; b. Midland, Mich., May 11, 1946; m. Elaine Levin, 1968 (div. 1985); 2 children; m. Marilyn Vos Savant, 1987. BA, Syracuse U., 1968, DSc (hon.), 1983; MA, NYU, 1971; MD, U. Utah, 1976; Dr sc (hon.), Hahnemann U., 1985. Rsch. asst. Div. Artificial Organs U. Utah, Salt Lake City, 1971-76, asst. dir. exptl. labs. Div. Artificial Organs, 1976-82, asst. rsch. prof. surgery, 1979-87; pres. Symbion, Inc., Salt Lake City, 1981-87, Jarvik Rsch., Inc., N.Y.C., 1987—; mem. nat. selection panel NASA Tchr. in Space Project, Washington, 1985. Sect. editor Internat. Jour. Artificial Organs, 1979-88; inventor repeating hemostatic clip instruments and cartridges, total artificial hearts powered by electrohydraulic energy and Jarvik-7; patentee in field. Named Inventor of Yr. Intellectual Property Owners, 1983, named John W. Hyatt award Soc. Plastics Engrs., 1983; recipient Golden Plate Am. Acad. Achievement, 1983, Gold Heart award Utah Heart Assn., 1983, Nat. Hero award, 1992. Mem. Am. Soc. Artificial Internal Organs Achievements include invention of the Jarvik-7, the first permanent implantable artificial heart. The first Jarvik-7 was implanted into Barney Clark in 1982 - he survived 112 days; the Jarvik 2000, a thumb sized battery operated pump that fits directly into the left ventricle and pushes oxygenated blood throughout the body.

JARVIS, BARBARA ANNE, lawyer; b. Kansas City, Mo., Apr. 14, 1934; d. Herman Edward and Marjorie Maude (Graber) Spitzenfeil; A.A., Kansas City Jr. Coll., 1953; B.S. in Polit. Sci. magna cum laude, Ariz. State U., 1976, J.D., 1979; m. Thomas B. Jarvis, Sept. 9, 1965; 1 son, Kenneth Mark. Technologist Menorah Med. Center, Kansas City, Mo., 1955-56, Ariz. State U. Student Health Service, 1960-62, Scottsdale (Ariz.) Bapt. Hosp., 1962-65; chief technologist Skyline Lab., Globe, Ariz., 1967-72; practice law, Phoenix, 1979—; pro tem judge Ashland (Oreg.) Municipal Ct., 1990—. Sec. Globe Planning and Zoning Commn., 1970-75; assoc. coordinator Women's Polit. Caucus Ariz.; 1st vice chmn. Ariz. Democratic Com.; mem. Dem. Nat. Com. from Ariz.; chmn. neighborhood rehab. com. Phoenix Urban Form, 1976-77, mem. steering com., 1976-79; mem. Phoenix Bd. Adjustment, 1977-82, chmn., 1980-81; chmn. Village 4 Planning Com., City of Phoenix; chmn. citizens adv. com. Ariz. Dept. Corrections, 1983-85, Paradise Corridor, 1986-88; chmn. planning commn. City of Ashland, Oreg., 1992—; bd. dirs. Salvation Army, Globe, Gila Pueblo campus Eastern Ariz. Coll., Gila County Guidance Clinic, On Track, Medford, Oreg., 1990—; mem. gov's. com. on alcohol and drug abuse, 1994—, chmn. Oreg. Hanford Cleanup Bd., 2004-2005. Mem. State Bar Ariz., State Bar Orge., Maricopa County Bar Assn. (co-chmn. alternatives to sentencing com. 1980-81), Ariz. Assn. Criminal Justice, Nat. Orgn. Criminal Def. Lawyers, Oreg. Criminal Def. Lawyers Assn., Ariz. Women Lawyers, Women in Law (chmn.), Jackson County Bar Assn., Ariz. State U. Law Sch. Alumni Assn., Charter 100, Pi Sigma Alpha, Phi Kappa Phi. Office: 1159 Emma St Ashland OR 97520-3470

JARVIS, CHARLENE DREW, university administrator, former scientist; b. Washington, July 31, 1941; two children. BA, Oberlin (Ohio) Coll., 1962; MS in Psychology, Howard U., 1964; PhD in Neuropsychology, U. Md., 1971; DSc (hon.), Amherst Coll., 1994, George Washington U., 2001. Supr. statis. lab. Howard U., 1965-66, prof. psychol. Washington, 1970-71; rsch. psychologist NIMH, 1971-78; coun. mem. Coun. of the D.C., 1979-2000; chair com. on housing and econ. devel. coun. of the D.C., 1981-2000; chair pro temp Coun. of the D.C., 1994-2000; pres. Southeastern Univ., Washington, 1996—. Chair bd. dirs. Met. Washington Coun. of Govts.; bd. dirs. Pa. Ave. Devel. Corp., Nat. Health Mus., Fed. City Coun., BB&T Regional Bank, Washington office; mem. steering com. Greater Washington Mktg. Partnership of the Greater Washington Bd. of Trade, 1993—; mem. coms. NIMH, adv. coun., 1993—; mem. breast cancer task force, 1993—; mem. Ronald Reagan Ctr. for Emergency Medicine, George Washington U. Hosp., 1993—. Bd. dirs. Girl Scouts Am., Pvt. Industry Coun., 1986—; mem. Leadership Washington, 1991-92; chair transp. subcom. D.C. chpt. ARC; del. Nat. Dem. Conv., 1980, 84, 88, 92; nat. co-chair Mondale for Pres., 1984, Clinton/Gore campaign, 1992; candidate for mayor, D.C., 1982, 90; chair pro tempore Coun. D.C., 1997—; chair cmty. bus. partnership com. Greater Washington Bd. of Trade; chair, bd. dirs. Washington D.C. Conv. and Tourism Corp., 2001—. Recipient Howard U. Alumni award, 1993, over 100 others; Named one of 50 Most Powerful Women in the Washington Area Washington Bus. Jour., 1985, 100 Most Powerful Women in the Washington Area, Washingtonian Mag., 1989, 94, Washingtonian of Yr. Washingtonian Mag., 1999. Mem. Nat. Assn. Ind. Colls. and Univs. (bd. dirs.), D.C. C. of C. (pres.-elect). Home: 1789 Sycamore St NW Washington DC 20012-1030 Office: Southeastern Univ 501 I St SW Washington DC 20024-2715 E-mail: president@admin.seu.edu.

JARVIS, DONALD BERTRAM, judge; b. Newark, N.J., Dec. 14, 1928; s. Benjamin and Esther (Golden) J.; m. Rosalind C. Chodorcove, June 13, 1954; children: Nancie, Brian, Joanne. BA, Rutgers U., 1949; JD, Stanford U., 1952. Bar: Calif. 1953. Law clk. to justice John W. Shenk Calif. Supreme Ct., 1953-54; assoc. Erskine, Erskine & Tulley, 1955, Aaron N. Cohen, 1955-56; law clk. Dist. Ct. Appeal, 1956; assoc. Carl Hoppe, 1956-57; adminstrv. law judge Calif. Pub. Utilities Commn., San Francisco, 1957-91, U.S. Dept. of Labor, San Francisco, 1992—. Mem. exec. com. Nat. Conf. Adminstrv. Law Judges, 1986-88, sec. 1988-89, vice-chair, 1990-91, chair-elect, 1991-92, chair 1992-93; pres. Calif. Adminstrv. Law Judges Coun., 1978-84; mem. faculty Nat. Jud. Coll., U. Nev., 1977, 78, 80; mem. U.S. Bd. of Alien Labor Cert. Appeals, 1995—. Chmn. pack Boy Scouts Am., 1967-69, chmn. troop 1972; class chmn. Stanford Law Sch. Fund, 1959, mem. nat. com., 1963-65; dir. Forest Hill Assn., 1970-71; patron San Francisco Opera. Served to col. USAF Res., 1949-79. Decorated Legion of Merit. Mem. ABA (mem. ho. of dels. 1993-99, vice chair jud. divsn. 1997-98, chair elect 1998-99, chair 1999-2000), State Bar Calif., Bar Assn. San Francisco, Calif. Conf. Pub. Utility Counsel (pres. 1980-81), Air Force Assn., Res. Officers Assn., Ret. Officers Assn., San Francisco Gem and Mineral Soc., Stanford Alumni Assn., Rutgers Alumni Assn., Phi Beta Kappa (pres. No. Calif. 1973-74), Tau Kappa Alpha, Pi Alpha Theta, Phi Alpha Delta. Home: 530 Dewey Blvd San Francisco CA 94116-1427 Office: 50 Fremont St San Francisco CA 94105-2230

JARVIS, ELBERT, II, (JAY JARVIS), employee benefits specialist; b. Washington, N.C., Sept. 20, 1944; s. Elbert J. Sr. and Laura F. (Lilley) J.; m. Anita Kleinfeld, Nov. 28, 1968 (div. Nov. 1983); 1 child, Elbert J. III; m. Audrey H. Liebross, July 28, 1991; 1 child, Benjamin Grover. A of Bus. Adminstrn., No. Va. C.C., 1972; BSBA, George Mason U., 1974. Sales mgr. Baumgarten Co., Washington, 1970-71; sales rep. Mass Mut., Washington, 1974-84; pres. The Pers. Dept., Inc., Annandale, Va., 1983—2001, Jarvis Consulting Ltd., 2001—. Founder No. Va. Group Health Alliance, No. Va. C. of C., 1998. Editor: (student handbook) Focal Point, 1973, Beth El Temple 1995-97, bd. dirs. Directory chair, 1990, 91, 92, 94, web master, 1999-2000, fund chair, 2000—; v.p. Brotherhood, 1999—. Scoutmaster, cubmaster, Webelos leader Boy Scouts Am., Clifton, Annandale and Arlington, Va., 1970-71, 85-86; mem. county com., state del. Arlington Rep. Party, 1975-85; pres., sec. Arlington Jaycees, 1980-82; pres., bd. dirs. Lafayette Village Cmty. Assn., Annandale, Va., 1994-95; bd. dirs. Beth El Hebrew Congregation, v.p. 2000-01, 1st v.p. Brotherhood Beth El, 1999-2001, Brotherhood pres., 2001-2003, webmaster, 1999-2000, chmn. permanent endowment fund, 2000—, v.p., treas. 2003—; bd. dirs. Annadale Sq. Office Condominium, 1999. Mem. Am. Compensation Assn., Health Underwriters Assn. (sec. No. Va. chpt. 1996-97), Washington chpt. Cert. Employee Benefit Specialists (assoc.), Arlington C. of C. (chmn. comms. com. 1983, bd. dirs. 1988-92, 92-94, chmn. sml. bus. coun. 1990, 92, chmn. expo com. 1991, chmn. awards and small bus. week 1994, Disting. Svc. awards 1989), Soc. Employee Benefits Profls., Alexandria C. of C. (mem. advantage program com. 1993-96), Fairfax County C. of C. (vice chmn. small bus. awards 1993-94, mem. team captain 1996), Northern Va. C. of C. (founder, bd. chair 1998—), Lafayette Village Comm. Assn. (pres.). Jewish. Avocations: canoeing, camping, photography. Home: 7828 Ashley Glen Rd Annandale VA 22003-1556 Office: Jarvis Cons Ltd PO Box 1650 Annandale VA 22003 Office Phone: 703-560-2737. E-mail: jay@jarvisconsulting.org.

JARVIS, ERICH DAVID, neurobiologist; b. N.Y.C., May 6, 1965; s. James Reginald Jarvis and Sasha Valeria (Monk) McCall; m. Miriam Virtudes Rivas, May 1984; children: Electra Riva, Syrus Chaske. BA in Biology and Mathematics, Hunter Coll., 1988; PhD in Molecular Neurobiology & Animal Behavior, Rockefeller U., 1995, postdoc. in Molecular Neurobiology & Animal Behavior, 1995—98. Asst. prof. Rockefeller U., NY, 1998—, Duke U., NC, 1999—. Pres. coun. black affairs Duke U., 1999—2002, grad. students admissions com., 1999—, grad. student steering com., 1999—, dir. minority recruitment, 2000—, mem. steering com. black collective, 2001—, mem. molecular biology com., 2001—. Contbr. genetic rsch. articles in learning and memory to sci. publs. Recipient First Pl. award Excellence in Biomed. Rsch., NIH, 1986, George H. Hitching New Investigator award, Triangle Cmty. Found., 2000—01, award, Esther & Joseph Klingenstien Fund., 2000—03, Whitehall Found., 2000—, Alan T. Waterman award, NSF, 2002—; grantee, 2000—03, NIH, 2001—02. Democrat. Avocations: dance, genealogy. Office: Duke U Med Ctr Dept Neurobiology Box 3209 Durham NC 27710

JARVIS, GILBERT ANDREW, humanities educator, writer; b. Chelsea, Mass., Feb. 13, 1941; s. Vernon Owen and Angeline M. (Burkard) J.; m. Carol Jean Ganter, Jan. 26, 1963; children: Vicki Lynn, Mark Christopher. BA, St. Norbert Coll., De Pere, Wis., 1963; MA, Purdue U., 1965, PhD, 1970. Prof. Ohio State U., Columbus, 1970-95, chmn. humanities edn., 1980-83, assoc. chmn. dept. ednl. theory and practice, 1983-87, chmn. dept. ednl. studies, 1987-95, dir. ESL programs, 1994-2000, chmn. prof. emeritus, 1995—. Cons. Internat. Edn. Program, U.S. Dept. Edn., Washington, 1977-84, others. Author: Et Vous?, 1983, 3d edit., 1989; Invitation, 1979, 4th edit., 1993, Y tu?, 1986, 2d edit., 1988, Connaitre et se connaitre, 3d edit., 1986, Invitation Essentials, 1991, 2d edit., 1995, Invitation au monde francophone, 2000, 2d edit., 2005; editor: The Challenge for Excellence, 1984; mem. editl. bd. Modern Lang. Jour., 1979-86; adv. bd. Can. Modern lang. Rev., 1982—. Mem. Am. Coun. Tchg. Fgn. Langs. (editor Rev. Fgn. Lang. Edn. 1974, 75, 76, 77), Phi Delta Kappa. Avocations: travel, photography. Home: 8337 Evangeline Dr Columbus OH 43235-1136

JARVIS, IRENE, retired medical/surgical nurse; b. Bronx, NY, Aug. 24, 1924; d. John Henry and Ella Harrison Jarvis; 1 child, Yvonne Marie Johnson. MA, BA, Bklyn Coll., Brooklyn, NY, 1978. RN NY State Edn. Dept., 1950. Child abuse expert NYC Dept. of Human Resouces, New York, NY, 1973—92; hosp. investigator NYC Dept. of Hospitals, New York, NY, 1960—73; head nurse Cumberland Hosp., New York, NY, 1950—59. Adventist. Avocations: travel, reading.

JARVIS, JAMES HOWARD, II, judge; b. Knoxville, Tenn., Feb. 28, 1937; s. Howard F. and Eleanor B. J.; m. Martha Stapleton, June 1957 (div. Feb. 1962); children: James Howard III, Leslie; m. Pamela K. Duncan, Aug. 23, 1964 (div. Apr. 1991); children: Ann, Kathryn, Louise; m. Gail Stone, Sept. 4, 1992. BA, U. Tenn., 1958, JD, 1960. Bar: Tenn. 1961, U.S. Dist. Ct. (ea. dist.) Tenn. 1961, U.S. Ct. Appeals (6th cir.) 1965. Assoc. O'Neil, Jarvis, Parker & Williamson, Knoxville, Tenn., 1960-68, mem., 1968-70, Meares, Dungan, Jarvis, Knoxville, Tenn., 1970-72; judge Law & Equity Ct., Blount County, Tenn., 1972-77, 30th Jud. Ct., Blount County, Tenn., 1977-84, U.S. Dist. Ct. (ea. dist.) Tenn., Knoxville, 1984—, chief judge, 1991-98. Bd. dirs. Maryville (Tenn.) Coll., 1991-98; past chmn. fin. com. St. Andrews Episc. Ch.; past bd. dirs. Detoxification Rehab. Inst. Knoxville; past com. codes of conduct Jud. Conf. U.S. Named Trial Judge of Yr., Am. Bd. Trial Advs., 2004. Mem. Tenn. Bar Assn. (bd. govs. 1983-84), Am. Judicature Soc., Tenn. Trial Judges Assn. (pres. exec. com.), Tenn. Jud. Conf. (pres. 1983-84), Blount County Bar Assn., Knoxville Bar Assn. (Judicial Excellence award 2002), Great Smoky Mountains Conservation Assn., Phi Delta Phi, Sigma Chi (significant Sigma Chi). Republican. Home: 6916 Stone Mill Rd Knoxville TN 37919-7431 Office: Howard H Baker Jr US Courthouse 800 Market St Knoxville TN 37902-2327

JARVIS, JOSEPH BOYER, retired university administrator; b. Springville, Utah, June 1, 1923; s. Joseph Smith and Mildred (Boyer) J.; m. Patricia Ann Potts, Dec. 17, 1955; children: Seth N., Nathan Y., Mary Beth. Student, Harvard U., 1942; BA, U. Ariz., 1947; MA, Ariz. State U., 1950; PhD, Northwestern U., 1958; HHD, U. Utah, 1989. Instr. speech U. Ariz., 1950-52, Dartmouth Coll., 1954-55; asst. prof. U. Utah, 1956-63, asso. prof., 1963-68, prof. speech, 1968-72, prof. communication, 1972-89, asst. dean Coll. Letters and Sci., 1958-60, assoc. program dir. sta. KUED-TV, 1957-60, asst. to pres., 1962-64, adminstr. univ. theatre, 1963-64, dean summer sch., 1962-67, dean admissions and registration, 1965-71, assoc. v.p. acad. affairs, 1967-88. Spl. asst. to US Commr. Edn., Washington, 1961—62. Bd. dirs. Salt Lake City Pub. Libr., 1976-91, pres., 1978-80, 84-86; bd. dirs. Youth Inc., Salt Lake City, 1969-77, chmn., 1970-71; vice chmn. Alberta Henry Edn. Found., 1973-80; bd. dirs. Utahns United Against the Nuclear Arms Race, 1984-92, chmn., 1985-86; bd. dirs. Utah Com. for Am.-Soviet Rels., 1987-91, chmn., 1989-91; bd. dirs. ACLU Utah, 1989-90, pres., 1990; bd. dirs. Utah Children, 1989-95, Utah Heritage Found., 1990-95, Utah Found. for Open Govt., 1993-95, Utah Region Nat. Conf. for Cmty. and Justice, 1998—; Cmty. adv. coun., Salt Lake City YWCA, 1992-98; Human Svcs. adv. coun. Salt Lake County, 1992-96. Mem.Parents, Families and Friends of Lesbians and Gays (bd. dirs. Salt Lake chpt., 1993-2005), UN Assn. Utah (v.p. 1978-80, pres. 1980-82), NAACP (bd. dirs. Salt Lake br. 1986-94), Phi Beta Kappa, Phi Kappa Phi. Home: 2357 Blaine Ave Salt Lake City UT 84108-3034

JARVIS, PETER R., lawyer; b. N.Y.C., July 19, 1950; BA in Econs. magna cum laude, Harvard U., 1972; MA in Econs., JD, Yale U., 1976. Bar: Oreg. 1976, U.S. Dist. Ct. Oreg. 1976, U.S. Ct. Appeals (9th cir.) 1977, Wash. 1983, U.S. Dist. Ct. (we. dist.) Wash. 1983, U.S. Dist. Ct. (ea. dist.) Wash. 1985, U.S. Tax Ct. 1991. Assoc. Stoel Rives LLP, Portland, Oreg., 1976—82, ptnr., 1982—2003; ptnr.-in-charge, Portland, legal ethics, risk mgmt. Hinshaw & Culbertson LLP, Portland, Oreg., 2003—. Author: (with others) Oregon Rules of Professional Responsibility (updated annually); editor, author: (with others) The Ethical Oregon Lawyer, 1991, 98; ethics columnists: Oregon Law Jour.; spkr. on legal ethics issues. Mem. ALI (Harrison Tweed Spl. Merit award 1993), Oreg. State Bar (former mem. legal ethics com., Pres.'s Membership Svcs. award 1991), Wash. State Bar (mem. profl. conduct com.), Assn. Profl. Responsibility Lawyers (bd. dir., 1999-,pres. 2005), Phi Beta Kappa. Office: Hinshaw & Culbertson LLP Ste 1950 1000 SW Broadway Portland OR 97205-3078 Office Phone: 503-243-3243. Office Fax: 503-243-3240. Business E-Mail: pjarvis@hinshawlaw.com.*

JARVIS, RICHARD S., academic administrator; b. Nottingham, Eng., Feb. 13, 1949; came to U.S., 1974; s. John Leslie and Mary Margaret (Dodman) J. BA in Geography, Cambridge (Eng.) U., 1970, MA, 1974, PhD in Geography, 1975. Lectr. Durham (Eng.) U., 1973-74; assoc. prof. SUNY, Buffalo, 1975-87, asst. to pres., 1986-87, v.p. acad. Fredonia, 1987-90, prof. geoscis., 1987-90; vice provost SUNY Sys., Albany, 1990-94; chancellor Univ. and C.C. Sys. Nev., Reno and Las Vegas, 1994-99, U.S. Open U., Aurora, Colo., 1999—2002, Oreg. U. Sys., 2002—04; provost U. Tex., El Paso, 2005—. Mem. adv. bd. Bechtel Nev., Las Vegas, 1995-97, NTS Devel. Corp., Las Vegas, 1997. Editor: River Networks, 1983; contbr. articles to profl. jours. Trustee United Way, Reno, 1996-99, EDAWN, Reno, 1996-99. Office: U Tex El Paso 500 W University Ave El Paso TX 79968 Office Phone: 915-747-7885. Business E-Mail: rsjarvis@utep.edu.

JARVIS, ROBERT MARK, law educator; b. NYC, Oct. 17, 1959; s. Rubin and Ute (Hacklander) J.; m. Judith Anne Mellman, Mar. 3, 1989. BA, Northwestern U., 1980; JD, U. Pa., 1983; LLM, NYU, 1986. Bar: N.Y. 1984, Fla. 1990. Assoc. Haight Gardner Poor & Havens, N.Y.C., 1983-85, Baker & McKenzie, N.Y.C., 1985-87; asst. prof. law ctr. Nova Southeastern U., Ft. Lauderdale, Fla., 1987-90, assoc. prof., 1990-92, prof., 1992—. Chmn. bd. dirs. Miami Maritime Arbitration Bd., 1993-94; vice chmn. bd. dirs. Miami Internat. Arbitration and Mediation Inst., 1993-94; mem. adv. bd. Carolina Acad. Press, 1996- Co-author: AIDS: Cases and Materials, 1989, 3d edit, 2002, AIDS Law in a Nutshell, 1991, 2d edit., 1996, Notary Law and Practice: Cases and Materials, 1997, Travel Law: Cases and Materials, 1998, Sports Law: Cases and Materials, 1999, Art and Museum Law: Cases and Materials, 2002, Gaming Law: Cases and Materials, 2003, Theater Law: Cases and Materials, 2004, Admiralty: Cases and Materials, 2004; author: Careers in Admiralty and Maritime Law, 1993, An Admiralty Law Anthology, 1995; editor: Maritime Arbitration, 1999, Law of Cruise Ships, 2000; co-editor: Prime Time Law: Fictional Television as Legal Narrative, 1998, Bush v. Gore: The Fight for Florida's Vote, 2001, Amicus Humoriae: An Anthology of Legal Humor, 2003; mem. editl. bd. Washington Lawyer, 1988-94, Jour. Maritime Law and Commerce, 1990-92, 2001—, assoc. editor, 1993-95, editor, 1996-2000, Maritime Law Reporter, 1991-99, Hospitality Law, 1999-2001; adv. bd. Transnat. Lawyer, 1991-2004, World Arbitration and Mediation Report, 1990—, U. San Francisco Maritime Law Jour., 1992-95, 2002—; contbg. editor Preview U.S. Supreme Ct. Cases, 1990-95, 99-2002 Mem.: ABA (vice chmn. admiralty law com. young lawyers divsn. 1992—93, chair 1993—94), Phi Delta Phi (province pres. 1989—91, coun. 1991—93), Assn. Am. Law Schs. (chmn.-elect maritime law sect. 1991—93, chmn. 1993—94), Maritime Law Assn. U.S., Fla. Bar Assn. (admiralty law com. 1988—95, vice chmn. 1991—92, chmn. 1992—93, exec. coun. internat. law sect. 1992—96), Acacia, Northwestern U. Club South Fla. (v.p. 1992—93, pres. 1993—95), Phi Beta Kappa. Democrat. Jewish. Office: Nova Southeastern U Law Ctr 3305 College Ave Fort Lauderdale FL 33314-7721 Office Phone: 954-262-6172. Business E-Mail: jarvisb@nsu.law.nova.edu.

JARVIS, TERESA LYNN, art educator, artist; b. Huntington, W.Va., May 10, 1956; d. Thomas Richard and Lovetta (Qualls) McComas; m. Roger Dale Jarvis, July 28, 1992; children: Richard Allen, Sarah Elizabeth. BA, Marshall U., 1979, MA, 1988. Cert. art and elem. tchr., W.Va. Tchr. St. Joseph Grade Sch., Huntington, 1979-88, Crum (W.Va.) Elem. and Mid. Schs., 1988—. Editl. cartoonist (newspaper) The Martin County-Tug Valley Mountain Citizen, 1991. Mem. ASCD, Nat. Art Educators Assn., Internat. Reading Assn., Am. Fedn. Tchrs., W.Va. Edn. Assn., Wayne County Reading Coun., Delta Kappa Gamma (Sigma chpt.). Democrat. Baptist. Avocations: drawing, painting, reading, walking, country line dancing. Home: PO Box 483 Kermit WV 25674-0483

JARVIS, WILLIAM DAVID, cellular pharmacologist, researcher; s. Floyd Eldridge and Pauline Lemon Jarvis. BA in English, U. Va., Charlottesville, 1984, PhD in Neurosci., 1991. Postdoctoral fellow U. Va., Charlottesville, Va.; rsch. assoc cancer biology Massey Cancer Ctr., Richmond, Va., 1996—99; asst. prof., then assoc prof. integrative biology and pharmacology U. Tex. Health Sci. Ctr., Houston, 1999—2003; chief tech. officer Dominion Diagnostics, Inc., North Kingstown, RI, 2003—. Author over 70 reports, revs., chpts., articles in field. Recipient Howard Temin Rsch. Scientist Devel. award, NIH/Nat. Cancer Inst., 1999—; Individual Nat. Rsch. Svc. fellow, 1993—95, Specialized Program of Excellence in Cancer Rsch. grantee, 2004—. Mem.: Endocrine Soc., Soc. Neuroscience, Am. Soc. Biochemistry and Molecular Biology, Am. Soc. Pharmacology and Exptl. Therapeutics, Am. Cancer Soc. Episcopalian. Achievements include research in pharmaceutical development and mechanistic investigations of multiple anti-neoplastic drugs; discovery of delineated the ceramide signaling pathway for initiating cell death in human cancers; development of effective drug interactions for more powerful anti-cancer treatments (Leukemia, Lymphoma); discovery of multiple protective signaling systems that allow cancers to thwart various modern treatment strategies; research in complex and interrelated signaling networks that centrally regulate tumor cell survival. Avocations: historical / architectural rennovation, collecting antiques, rare books, ephemera, travel, writing, photography. Office: Dominion Diagnostics Inc 211 Circuit Dr North Kingstown RI 02852-7440 Office Phone: 401-667-0892. E-mail: wdjarvis@dominiondiagnostics.com.

JARVIS, WILLIAM ROBERT, epidemiologist, educator; b. Oakland, Calif., June 2, 1948; s. John James and Mattie Belle (Steele) J.; m. Janine M. Jason, July 4, 1982; children: Danielle Kristin, Ashley Alana. BS in Psychology with honors, U. Calif., Davis, 1970; MD, U. Tex., Houston, 1974. Intern U. Tex. Med. Ctr., Houston, 1974-75; resident in pediat. Children's Hosp., L.A., 1975-77; pediatric infectious disease fellow Toronto Hosp. for Sick Children, 1977-78; fellow pediat. infectious diseases, virology, pub. health Yale U. Sch. Med., 1978-80; commd. med. officer USPHS, 1980, advanced through grades to capt., 1990, ret., 2003; asst. chief Nat. Nosocomial Infections Surveillance Systems Ctrs. for Disease Control, Atlanta, 1981-90, asst. chief epidemiology br., 1984-87, chief epidemiology br. hosp. infections program, 1987-91, chief investigation, prevention br. hosp. infections program, 1991-2000, acting dir. hosp. infections program, 1996-98, assoc. dir. program devel. Divsn. Healthcare Quality Promotion, 2001—02; dir. Office Extramural Rsch. Nat. Ctr. for Infectious Diseases, Atlanta, 2002—03. Asst. prof. pediat. infectious disease and immunology Emory U., Atlanta, 1985-96, assoc. prof., 1996—; asst. prof. Rollins Sch. Pub. Health, 1999—, pvt. cons., 2003—. Contbr. over 500 articles to profl. jours., chpts. to books. Mem. Infectious Diseases Soc. Am., Am. Soc. Microbiology, Soc. Hosp. Epidemiologists Am. (pres. 2001-02), Sigma Xi. Roman Catholic. Avocations: stock market, gardening, tennis, travel. Office: Jason &Jarvis Assoc 135 Dune Ln Hilton Head Island SC 29928 Address: 4483 23rd St Unit 1 San Francisco CA 94114 Office Phone: 843-686-3750. Personal E-mail: wrjmj@aol.com.

JARZAVEK, JOHN BRIAN, English and art history educator; b. Middletown, Conn., Sept. 18, 1941; s. John Celestin and Stephanie Teresa (Kaminski) J. Carte de assiduité, Sorbonne, Paris, 1961; BA, Wesleyan U., Conn., 1963; MA, Yale U., 1965. English dept. tchr. Rivers Sch., Weston, Mass., 1965—98, art history tchr., 1968—, chmn. English dept., 1970-84. Reader advanced placement art history exam., Ednl. Testing Svc., Princeton, 1987—, reader English achievement, 1986-91. Fulbright fellow Bristol U., England, 1963, Woodrow Wilson fellow Wilson Found., 1964. Mem. Phi Beta Kappa. Democrat. Roman Catholic. Avocation: vocal classical record collecting. Office: Rivers Sch 333 Winter St Weston MA 02493-1071 E-mail: j.jarzavek@rivers.org.

JASEN, MATTHEW JOSEPH, lawyer, retired judge; b. Buffalo, Dec. 13, 1915; s. Joseph John and Celina (Perlinski) Jasinski; m. Anastasia Gawinski, Oct. 4, 1943 (dec. Aug. 1970); children: Peter M., Mark M., Christine, Carol Ann; m. Gertrude O'Connor Travers, Mar. 25, 1972 (dec. Nov. 1972); m. Grace Yungbluth Frauenheim, Aug. 31, 1973 (dec. Nov. 13, 2003). BA, Canisius Coll., 1937; LLB, U. Buffalo, 1939; postgrad., Harvard U., 1944; LLD (hon.), Union U., 1980, N.Y. Law Sch., 1981. Bar: N.Y. 1940. Ptnr. firm Beyer, Jasen & Boland, Buffalo, 1940-43; pres. U.S. Security Rev. Bd., Wurttemberg-Baden, Germany, 1945-46; judge U.S. Mil. Govt. Ct., Heidelberg, Germany, 1946-49; sr. ptnr. firm Jasen, Manz, Johnson & Bayger, Buffalo, 1949-57; justice N.Y. Supreme Ct. (8th jud. dist.), 1957-67; judge N.Y. Ct. Appeals, 1968-85; U.S. Supreme Ct. spl. master S.C. v. U.S., 1987-88; spl. master Ill. vs. Ky. U.S. Supreme Ct., 1989-95; of counsel Moot & Sprague, Buffalo, 1986-90; counsel Jasen, Jasen & Sampson, P.C., Buffalo, 1990-99, Jasen & Jasen, P.C., Buffalo, 1999—. Mem. N.Y. State Jud. Screening Com., 1996—. Contbr. articles to profl. jours. Mem. council U. Buffalo, 1963-66; trustee Canisius Coll. Chair of Polish Culture, also, Nottingham Acad. Served to capt. AUS, 1943-46, ETO. Fellow Hilbert Coll.; recipient Disting. Alumnus award SUNY-Buffalo Sch. Law, 1969, Disting. Alumnus award Alumni Assn., 1976, Disting. Alumnus award Canisius Coll., 1978, Edwin F. Jaeckle award SUNY-Buffalo Sch. Law, 1982. Mem. Nat. Conf. Appellate Judges, State U. N.Y. at Buffalo Law Sch. Alumni Assn. (pres. 1964-65), Am., N.Y. State, Erie County bar assns., Am. Law Inst., Am. Judicature Soc., Lawyers Club Buffalo (pres. 1961-62), Nat. Advocates Club, Profl. Businessmen's Assn. Western N.Y. (pres. 1952), Phi Alpha Delta, DiGamma Soc. Roman Catholic (mem. Bishop's Bd. Govs., Buffalo diocese 1951—). Clubs: K.C. (4 deg.). Home: 26 Pine Ter Orchard Park NY 14127-3928 Office: Ste 700 69 Delaware Ave Buffalo NY 14202-3805 Office Phone: 716-848-9500. Personal E-mail: jjatts@buffnet.net.

JASHEL, LARRY STEVEN (L. STEVEN ROSE), entrepreneur, media consultant; b. Dayton, Ohio, Jan. 21, 1950; s. Joseph John and Ruth Margarete (Race) Jashel. Student, Harper Coll., Palatine, Ill., 1968—70. Pub.'s asst. Pub.'s Devel. Corp., Chgo., 1971-73; pub. rels. dir. Ill. Entertainer/Chgo. Star/Bankers' Guide, Chgo., 1973-76; v.p. Internat. Media Prodns., Inc., Chgo., 1976-78, Microdynamics Corp., Chgo., 1978-80; exec. v.p. Calif. Aqua Tech, Inc., The Solar Generation, L.A., 1980-82; pres., CEO Ra-Tel Comms. Corp., Ra-Tel Entertainment Corp./Cable Radio, Chgo., 1982-88; founder Steven Rose Prodns. and L.S. Jashel Assocs., Chgo., 1988-98; founder, CEO Spuppets, Ltd., 1996, Children's Cultural Network, 2000—; exec. dir. Superior Benefit Solutions, 1998-2000. TV prodr., dir., writer Ind. Broadcasting, Chgo., 1982—; radio prodr., on-air personality Nat. Pub. Radio, Chgo., Washington, 1982—, Sta. WJRC-AM, Chgo., 1987—88; music prodr. ind. rec. artists, Chgo., 1982—; cons. Corp. Pub. Broadcasting, 1982—; spkr. in field. Author: Song of a New Age, 1990, A Bakers Dozen, 1995, The Best Poems of 1997, Planet Medieval, 1998, Mystic Blue and the Z-Generation, 2001, Beyond Dreams, 2002, Discovery of Earf, 2003, (book and TV script) Lovestar--The Exciting Adventures, 1994—95; author: (prodr. and dir.) Spuppets (puppets in space), 1997; co-author: Morning Song, 1997; musician: (musical acts) The Detours, Sudden, The Amboy Dukes, The Yellow Brick Road, J.J. Lee and the Radiants, 1964—72, Mystic Blues, 2002—; actor: (films) Sore Losers, 2001, Road to Perdition, 2002, Insanity, 2003—. Named del. rep. to Presdl. Inauguration Ball, Washington, D.C., 1980; recipient Blue Ribbon award, Midwest Sports Assn., 1968, Film Festival award, 1984, Am. Svc. award, Am. Svc. Corp., 1988, Nat./Internat. award of Distinction for Children's Video and Packaging, 1998, Videographer award, 1998, Telly award, 2000, Omni award, 2001, Music Video award, 2003, Golden Telly award, 2004. Mem.: NARAS (Grammy awards 1982—), ASCAP (award 1998—99, 2000), Children's Entertainment Assn., Internat. Assn. Bus., Nat. Cable TV Assn., Nat. Assn. Pvt. Enterprise, Higher Consciousness Soc., Chgo. C. of C., Smithsonian Instn. (assoc.). Avocations: writing for children, bicycling, camping, hiking. Office: PO Box 435 Willow Springs IL 60480-0435

JASINSKI, GEORGE JOHN, lawyer; b. Chgo., Dec. 12, 1954; s. George Ambrose and Geraldine Marie (Orowick) J.; m. Kathy Mary Procenti, Nov. 8, 1980; children: George Ambrose, David Francis, Gabrielle Kathryn. BS, Bradley U., 1976; JD, John Marshall Law Sch., 1979. Bar: Ill. 1979, U.S. Dist. Ct. (no. dist.) Ill. 1979, U.S. Ct. Appeals (7th cir.) 1979. Assoc. Law Offices of Phillip F. Maher, Chgo., 1979-80; ptnr. Barrett, Sramek & Jasinski, Palos Heights, Ill., 1980-98; owner Law Offices George J. Jasinski, Palos Heights, Ill., 1998—. Mem. ABA, Assn. Trial Lawyers Am., Ill. Bar Assn. (torts sect. 1980—, civil practice and procedure sect. 1980—, workers compensation sec. 1980—), Ill. Trial Lawyers Assn., Chgo. Bar Assn., Am. Arbitration Assn., S.W. Suburban Bar Assn., Palos Heights C. of C. Roman Catholic. Avocations: all sports, travel, music. Home: 12311 S Pine Pl Palos Heights IL 60463-1885 Office: Law Offices George J Jasinski 7330 W College Dr Ste 101 Palos Heights IL 60463-1160 also: 77 W Washington St Ste 600 Chicago IL 60602-2803

JASINSKI, KENNETH M., energy executive; Exec. v.p., gen. counsel Energy East Corp., New Gloucester, Maine, 1998—2000, exec. v.p., gen. counsel, sec., 2000—02, exec. v.p., CFO, 2002—. Office: Energy East Corp 52 Farm View Dr New Gloucester ME 04260-5116*

JASINSKI-CALDWELL, MARY L., insurance company executive; b. Chester, Pa., May 8, 1959; d. A. Robert and Helen M. Jasinski; m. William A. Caldwell, Aug. 4, 1990; children: Helaina M., Anna L. Student, student, Loyola Coll., Balt., 1980; AS, Goldey Beacom Coll., Wilmington, Del., 1982, BS, 1983. Registered orthotic fitter; cert. sr. pharmacy technician. Gen. mgr. pension plan City Pharmacy of Elkton (Md.), Inc., 1975-96, treas., 1987-96, jr. ptnr., 1994, v.p., 1996—; founder, pres. City Home Health Care, Inc., Elkton, 1997—. Disc jockey, promoter Garfield's Restaurant, Elkton; editl. writer local newspapers; pro-life columnist KC newsletter; nat. bd. advisors McKesson Drug Co., 2001—. Creator ednl. program PARTICIP.A.A.T.E. For Life. Advisor Cecil County Pregnancy Ctr., Cecil County Bd. Edn. Textbook Adubtion Policy Com., 1995; pro-life educator City of Elkton, Inc.; varsity I coach Christian Youth Orgn., 2004—05, coach youth volleyball, 2002—; chmn. arts and environment com. Immaculate Conception Parish, 2004—; bd. dirs. Cecil County chpt. ARC, 1996—2001, fin. devel. chmn. Cecil County chpt., 2000—01; bd. dirs. Mission Am., Inc., Md. Right to Life, 1993—94, co-chair Cecil County chpt., 1993—94. Alpha Chi scholar, Lindback scholar; recipient J.W. Miller award, Outstanding Achievement in Excellence award K.C., 1994, Ralph and Eleanor Hicks Outstanding Vol. svc. award ARC, Cecil County, Md., 1999-2000; named Family of Yr., 1995; named to Honor Roll of Best 250 Independents in U.S., Drug Topics, 1992, Cecil County Md.'s "Favorite Pharmacy" Cecil Whig's Reader's Poll, 2002, 03, 04. Mem. NAFE, NRA, Am. Pharmacists Assn. (assoc.), Am. Mgmt. Assn., Nat. Fedn. Ind. Bus., Bd. Orthotic Cert., Am. Assn. Pharm. Technicians, Nat. Right to Life Com., Am. Life League, Internat. Platform Assn., Pro-Life Md., Christian Coalition, Cath. Alliance, Cecil County C. of C., Stopp Internat., Human Life Internat., Concerned Women for Am., Pharmacists for Life, Goldey Beacom Coll. Alumni Assn., Movement for a Better Am., Cath. League, Liberty

Alliance, Epic Pharmacies, Inc., Susan B. Anthony List, Alpha Chi. Republican. Roman Catholic. Avocations: home improvement, gardening, social concerns, pro-life education, reading. Office: City Pharmacy Inc 723 N Bridge St Elkton MD 21921-5398 Office Phone: 410-398-4383. Personal E-mail: williamandmarycaldwell@msn.com. Business E-Mail: citypharmacy@dol.net.

JASIUNAS, BONNIE LOU, psychologist, educator; b. Cleve., Nov. 13, 1948; d. Lillian Mary Ann Kosley and John Anthony Parker; m. Gary Wayne Jasiunas, Nov. 27, 1970; children: J. Banning, Chad Aaron. BS in Edn., U. Akron, 1970, MS in Edn., 1988. Cert. sch. psychologist Ohio Bd. of Edn., 1986, lic. Ohio Bd. of Psychology, cert. Nat. Assn. Sch. Psycholgists, 2004, tchr. Ohio Bd. of Edn., 1970. Tchr. Copley-Fairlawn City Sch., Ohio, 1970—75; sch. psychologist Medina (Ohio) City Sch., Medina, Ohio, 1986—88, Shaker Heights (Ohio) City Sch., Shaker Heights, Ohio, 1988—. Author: Fine and Gross Motor Checklist, Steps to Peacemaking, Banana Splits; HEARTS, Mending Hearts, Friendship Club, C.A.R.E. Bear Program; contbr. articles to profl. jours. Mem. sch. psychology exam. com. Ohio Bd. Psychology, Columbus, 2003—. Ednl. Enrichment grant, Shaker Found., 1996, 2000, 2001, 2004, Ednl. Grant, Shaker Heights PTO, 1998, 2001, 2002, 2003. Mem.: Shaker Heights Tchr. Assn. (assoc.), Ohio Sch. Psychologist Assn. (assoc.; spl. edn. com. chmn. 1988—92, Pete Gross Best Practices award 1994), Alpha Gamma Delta (pres. Omega chpt. 1970). Office: Shaker Heights City Sch 15600 Parkland Dr Shaker Heights OH 44120 Office Phone: 216-295-4020. Office Fax: 216-295-4019. E-mail: jasiunas_b@shaker.org.

JASKOT, JOHN JOSEPH, retired insurance company executive; b. Allentown, Pa., Dec. 5, 1921; s. George W. and Anna (Kuzma) J.; m. Joyce Ranck, May 25, 1946; children: Lisa Anne, Philip Ross. Student, Muhlenberg Coll., Allentown, 1947-49; JD with honors, George Washington U., 1951, LL.M., 1953. Bar: D.C. 1951. Exec. v.p., gen. counsel, corp. sec. United Svcs. Life Ins. Co., Washington, 1953-88; v.p., legal counsel United Svcs. Gen. Life Co., 1968-87; v.p. Bankers Security Life Ins. Soc., 1985-88, also bd. dirs.; sec. Provident Life Ins. Co., 1983-86, United Olympic Life Ins. Co., 1984-86; sec., sr. v.p. USLICO Corp., 1984-88; ret., 1988. With USCGR, 1942-46, PTO. Mem. Am. Arbitration Assn. (arbitrator 1988—). Home: 15101 Interlachen Dr # 920 Silver Spring MD 20906-5620 *True success should only be measured by an individual's own assessment of his accomplishments.*

JASKOT, RICHARD D., academic administrator, career military officer; BS, Ill. Inst. Tech.; grad., Navel Flight Officer Sch., 1977; MS in Nat. Resource Strategy, Industrial Coll. Armed Forces. Enlisted USN, 1975; advanced through grades to rear adm.; assigned to Black Falcons, Va.; test dir. Air Test and Evaluation Squadron Five, China Lake, Calif.; staff strike ops. and weapons officer for comdr. Carrier Group Four; with VA-75 Sunday Punchers; comdr. Medium Attack Weapons Sch., Atlantic; comdr. sea VA-34 Blue Blasters, Carrier Air Wing SEVEN, 1991—92; head Aviation Placement Office Bureau of Navy Personnel; chief Evaluation Branch Joint Staff J-7, Operational Plans and Training Directorate; combating terrorism dep.-directorate chief Training, Doctrine and Assessments Div.; dep. comdr. Carrier Air Wing Seven, 1997; fellow Chief of Navel Ops. Strategic Studies Group, Newport, RI, 2001; dep. dir. Plans and Policy US European Command, 2001—03; comdt. Nat. War Coll., 2003—. Promoted to Flag Officer rank USN, 2001. Decorated Defense Superior Svc. Medal, Legion of Merit, Meritorious Svc. Medal (with gold star), Air Medal (with bronze star), Navy and Marine Corps Commendation Medal (with 2 gold stars). Office: Nat War Coll Fort Lesley J McNair 300 5th Ave Washington DC 20319-6000 Office Phone: 202-685-3937.*

JASKOWSKI, TROY D., immunologist, researcher; b. Mpls., Jan. 17, 1968; s. John Edward Jaskowski and Betty Earline Teal; m. Maria Consuelo Fierro, Sept. 6, 1993; children: Milagros Lorenza, Marisa Athena. Student, Weber State U., 1988—96. Rsch. scientist, immunology ARUP Inst., Salt Lake City, 1990—. Contbr. articles to profl. jours. Mem.: Assn. Med. Lab. Immunologists. Achievements include development of Serologic and Protein assays. Office: ARUP Inst 500 Chipeta Way Salt Lake City UT 84108 Business E-Mail: jaskowtd@aruplab.com.

JASON, JACK I., film producer, interpreter; s. Benjamin Joseph and Sarah Shemaria Jason. BA, Calif. State U., Hayward, 1978; MA, NYU, 1984. Grad. fellow NYU, N.Y.C.; acad. advisor U. Calif., Berkeley; prodr. Solo One Prodns., L.A. Presenter Acad. Awards, 1987, 88; voice over artist/sign language interpreter for Marlee Matlin. Exec. prodr.: (films) Where the Truth Lies, 1999; exec. prodr.: (films) Eddies Million Dollar Cookoff, 2003 (NCFR, 2004); author: (films) Eddies Million Dollar Cookoff, 2003 (NCFR, 2004); actor: (films) The Player, 1991; (TV series) The Larry Sanders Show, 1994, Arrested Development, 2005. Recipient Award of Merit, Nat. Victim Ctr., 1994, Child Quest Internat., 1994, Hon. Mention, NCFR Media Awards, 2004. Mem.: AFTRA, SAG. Jewish. Office: Solo One Prodns 8205 Santa Monica Blvd Los Angeles CA 90046

JASON, KYLE, radio personality, musician; Host The Kyle Jason Show, Air Am. Radio, NYC, 2005—. Singer: (albums) Revenge, Identify, The Vault Vol. 1, The Vault Vol. 2, The Vault Vol. 3, Red Pill, Generations, 1997, Love, Sex, and Magic, 2002. Avocations: Karate, boxing, singing. Office: Air Am Radio 3 Park Ave New York NY 10016*

JASPAN, STANLEY S., lawyer; b. N.Y.C., Apr. 13, 1946; BS, Cornell U., 1968; JD, Yale U., 1971. Bar: Wis. 1971. Mng. ptnr. Foley & Lardner LLP, Milw., 1999—. Lectr. in law, adj. assoc. prof. Marquette U. Law Sch., 1978-88. Mng. editor: Yale Law Jour., 1970-71. Mem. ABA, State Bar Wis., N.Y. State Bar Assn., Milw. Bar Assn. Office: Foley & Lardner LLP Firstar Ctr 777 E Wisconsin Ave Ste 3800 Milwaukee WI 53202-5367 Office Phone: 414-297-5814. Business E-Mail: sjaspan@foley.com.

JASPER, JOHN A., writer, lawyer; b. Latonia, Ky., Feb. 26, 1954; s. John A. and Adraw C. Jasper; m. Alexandra Powers Everhart; children: Caitlin, Taulbe. BA, North Ky. U., Highland Heights, KY, 1976; MA, U. of Cinncinati, Cinncinati, OH, 1979; JD, Antioch Law Sch., Washington, DC, 1982. Factory worker UPS, Cincinnati, Ohio, 1972—76; asst. city mgr. Covington, Ky., 1976—77; city mgr. Chevy Chase, Friendship Heights, Md., 1977—79; legis. asst. U.S. Senate Judiciary Commn., Washington, 1980—82; prosecutor State of Ky., Luoisville, 1983—88; sr. atty. US Govt., Washington, 1988—. Panelist Mystery Writers Conf., 2000—01, Va. Festival of the Book, 2000—01. Author: (novels) Sweet Poison of Misused Wine. Campaign mgmt. Ky. Governer race, Congress race, County Exec. race, Ky., 1983—87. Independent. Avocation: rugby. Home: 4101 Cathedral Avenue Washington DC 20016 Personal E-mail: jasperbook@aol.com.

JASPER, NORMAN HANS, engineer; b. Detmold, Germany, May 10, 1918; came to U.S., 1932; s. Friedrich and Hannah (Franzmeier) J.; m. Wilma L. Knief, Aug. 1940; children: Norma, Richard. BME, CCNY, 1941; MS, U. Md., 1952; Dr. Engring., Catholic U. Am., 1956. Naval architect Puget Sound Naval Shipyard, Bremerton, Wash., 1941-46; with David Taylor Model Basin U.S. Navy, Washington, 1946-61, spl asst. David Taylor Model Basin, 1960-61, tech. dir. U.S. Navy R&D Lab. Panama City, Fla., 1961-72, sci. adviser comdr. operational test evaluation force Norfolk, Va., 1972-73; pres. Lagoon Investment Co., Tallahassee, 1972—. Mem. U.S. Navy Anti-Submarine Warfare Coun., 1961-68. Author numerous tech. papers and reports. Sloan Inst. Advanced Engring. Studies fellow MIT, 1971-72; recipeint Disting. Civilian Svc. awards U.S. Navy Dept., Def. Dept., 1962. Fellow ASME; mem. Am. Soc. Naval Architects and Marine Engrs. (mem. tech. panels and coms.), Elks, Sigma Xi. Achievements include development of patented explosion-resistant ship design for minesweeping; development and installation of a solution for silencing nuclear submarines, for computing temperature induced stresses i ships, for dynamic slamming loads on high-speed boats. Avocations: tennis, camping, travel, rare coin collecting, art collecting. E-mail: normanjasper@aol.com.

JASPERSEN, FREDERICK ZARR, economist; b. Phila., Sept. 23, 1938; s. Frederick Franklin and Jean Lorraine (Zarr) J.; m. Margie C. Trainor, Oct. 10, 1965. BA in Internat. Relations, Dartmouth Coll., 1961; MA Peace Corps fellow, Ind. U., 1965, PhD in Econs., 1969. Mem. Peace Corps, Colombia, 1961-63; teaching asst. fellow Ind. U., Bloomington, 1964-65; Harvard U. econ. advisor Ministry Fin., Chile, 1968-69; economist Standard Oil N.J., N.Y.C., 1969-70, Am. Embassy Brazil, 1970-71; sr. economist World Bank, Washington, 1978-86, lead economist macroecon. adjustment policy and growth, 1987-91; chief devel. policy rsch. divsn. Inter-Am. Devel. Bank, Washington, 1991-95; sr. advisor Internat. Fin. Corp., Washington, 1995-98; dir. Latin Am. Inst. of Internat. Fin., Washington, 1999—. Lectr. econs. Chile, Brazil, Ind. U. Contbr. author: World Development Report, 1981, Adjustment Experience and Growth Prospects of the Semi-Industrial Countries, 1981; co-editor: Pathways to Growth: Comparing Latin America and East Asia, 1997. V.p. Sidwell Friends Sch. Alumni Assn., 1978-80. Ford Found. Latin Am. teaching fellow Fletcher Sch., Tufts U., 1967-68 Mem. Am. Econ. Assn., World Affairs Coun. Clubs: Dartmouth (Washington), Cosmos (Washington). Home: 5013 Randall Ln Bethesda MD 20816-1959 Office: Ste 8500 2000 Pennsylvania Ave NW Washington DC 20006-1852

JASSO, GUILLERMINA, sociologist, educator; b. Laredo, Tex., July 22, 1942; d. José Jasso-Rodríguez and Guillermina de los Santos-Lozano. BA, Our Lady of the Lake Coll., 1962; MA, U. Notre Dame, 1970; PhD, Johns Hopkins U., 1974. Asst. prof. Barnard Coll. and Columbia U., N.Y.C., 1974-77; spl. asst. to commr. U.S. Immigration and Naturalization Svc., Washington, 1977-79; dir. rsch. U.S. Select Commn. on Immigration and Refugee Policy, Washington, 1979-80; asst. prof. U. Mich., Ann Arbor, 1980-82; assoc. prof. U. Minn., Mpls., 1982-86, prof., 1986-87; prof., dir. theory workshop U. Iowa, Iowa City, 1987-91; prof. NYU, N.Y.C., 1991—, dir. methods workshop, 1991-97. Mem. study sect. on social sci. and population NIH, 1991-95; mem. U.S. Com. for Internat. Inst. for Applied Sys. Analysis, 1993-2001; mem. various programs NSF, 1987-96, 98-99; panel on demographic and econ. impacts of immigration NAS, 1995-97; population rsch. subcom. Nat. Inst. Child Health and Human Devel., NIH, 1998-2002, adv. com. SBE Directorate, NSF, 2003—; mem. com. on redesign of U.S. naturalization test NAS, 2004-05; vis. prof. Zentrum Umfragen, Methoden, und Analysen, Mannheim, Germany, 1995, U. Leipzig, Germany, 1996; core rsch. team bination study on migration between Mex. and US, U. Commn. on Immigration Reform, 1995-97; disting. alumni lectr. U. Notre Dame, 1987; pub. lectr. Our Lady of Lake U., 1989; disting. lectr. NSF, 2003; keynote spkr. Oldendorff Inst., Tilburg (The Netherlands) U., 2004, Swedish Sociol. Soc., 2005. Author: The New Chosen People, 1990; mem. editl. bd. Social Justice Rsch., 1985—, Jour. Math. Sociology, 1985—, Rationality and Society, 1999—, European Sociological Review, 2001-, Internat. Jour. Comparatine Sociology, 2001-; dep. editor Am. Sociol. Rev., 1996-99; contbr. articles to profl. jours. Grantee Russell Sage Found., 1983-85, Rockefeller Found., 1985-86, NSF, 1994-97, 2000-02, NIH, 1995-99, 2000-, PEW, 2001-; fellow Ctr. for Advanced Study in Behavioral Scis., Stanford, Calif., 1999-2000; rsch. fellow Inst. for the Study of Labor (IZA), Bonn, Germany. Fellow Johns Hopkins Soc. Scholars; mem. Am. Sociol. Assn. (chair internat. migration sect. 1996-99, chair theory sect. 1996-99, chair rational choice sect. 2000-03, chair soc. psychol. sect. 2002-04), Sociol. Rsch. Assn. Office: NYU Dept Sociology 269 Mercer St 4th Fl New York NY 10003-6633 E-mail: gj1@nyu.edu.

JASSY, EVERETT LEWIS, lawyer; b. N.Y.C., Feb. 4, 1937; s. David H. and Florence A. (Pollak) J.; m. Margery Ellen Rose; children: Katherine Savitt Lennon, Andrew Ralph, Jonathan Scott. AB, Harvard U., 1957, JD, 1960. Bar: N.Y. 1960, D.C. 1975. Assoc. Dewey Ballantine, N.Y.C., 1960—68, ptnr., 1968—, chmn. mgmt. com., 1991—2003. Mem. ABA, N.Y. State Bar Assn., Assn. Bar City N.Y., The Tax Club, Harmonie Club (bd. govs. 1999-2001), Fairview Country Club (Greenwich, Conn.), Stockbridge (Mass.) Golf Club. Avocations: golf, travel. Home: 20 Tompkins Rd Scarsdale NY 10583-2838 Office: Dewey Ballantine LLP 1301 Avenue Of The Americas New York NY 10019-6022 Office Phone: 212-259-6200. Business E-Mail: ejassy@dbllp.com.

JASTROW, KENNETH M., financial executive; Pres., CEO Lumbermen's Investment Corp.; chmn. Capital Mortgage Bankers; CFO Temple-Inland Corp., Austin, Tex., 1991—99, group v.p., 1995—98, pres., COO, 1998—99, chmn., CEO, 2000—. Bd. dir. MGIC Investment Corp., KB Home. Office: Temple-Inland Corp 1300 S Mopac Expressway Austin TX 78746*

JASZCZAK, RONALD JACK, physicist, researcher, consultant; b. Chicago Heights, Ill., Aug. 23, 1942; s. Jacob and Julia (Gudowicz) J.; m. Nancy Jane Bober, Apr. 15, 1967; children: John, Monica. BS with highest honors, U. Fla., 1964, PhD, 1968. Staff physicist Oak Ridge Nat., 1969-71, AEC postdoctoral fellow, 1968-69; prin. rsch. scientist Searle Diagnostics, Inc., 1971-73, sr. prin. rsch. scientist, 1973, rsch. group leader, 1973-77, chief scientist, 1977-79; assoc. prof. radiology Duke U. Med. Ctr., Durham, N.C., 1979-89, prof., 1989—, assoc. prof. biomed. engring., 1986-91, prof., 1992—. Rsch. prof. Inst. of Stats. and Decision Scis., 1991-93; founder, chmn. bd. dirs. Data Spectrum Corp., Hillsborough, N.C.; investigator Nat. Cancer Inst. Grant, 1983—, Dept. Energy Grant, 1989—. Contbr. articles to profl. jours.; patentee in field. Recipient Outstanding Alumni award U. Fla. Dept. Physics, 2004; NASA fellow, 1964-67, U. Fla. fellow, 1967-68; RCA scholar, 1963-64. Fellow IEEE; mem. IEEE Nuc. and Plasma Scis. Soc. (pres. 1997-98), AAAS, Soc. Nuc. Medicine (Paul C. Aebersold award 2000), Am. Phys. Soc., Am. Assn. Physicists in Medicine, Soc. Photo-Optical Instrumentation Engrs., Sigma Xi, Phi Beta Kappa, Phi Kappa Phi, Tau Sigma, Sigma Pi Sigma. Office: Duke U Med Ctr Dumc 3949 Durham NC 27710-0001

JATLOW, PETER I., pathologist, medical educator, researcher; b. New Brunswick, NJ, Feb. 12, 1936; s. Daniel and Anne (Davis) J.; m. Stephanie Bea Yager, Dec. 22, 1959; children: Allison, Julia. BS, Union Coll., Schenectady, N.Y., 1957; MD, SUNY Downstate Med. Ctr., Bklyn., 1961; MS (hon.), Yale U., 1976. Intern Montefiore Hosp., Bronx, NY, 1961-62; resident Yale-New Haven Hosp., 1962-66; asst. prof. lab. medicine Yale U., New Haven, 1968-73, assoc. prof. lab. medicine, 1973-76, prof. lab. medicine, 1976—, chmn. dept. lab. medicine, 1984—. Cons. FDA, Washington, 1978-82; mem. biomed. rsch. rev. com. USPHS, Nat. Inst. Drug Abuse, Rockville, Md., 1982-86; mem. test material devel. subcom. FLEX Program Nat. Bd. Med. Exam., Phila., 1990-91. Editor: Methodology in Analytical Toxicology, vol. II, 1982; editl. bd. Clin. Chemistry, 1973-83, Selected methods in Clin. Chemistry, 1976-79, Jour. Analytical Toxicology, 1978-79, Therapeutic Drug Monitoring, 1979-86, 90—, Clinica Chimica Acta, 1984-90, Am. Jour. Clin. Pathology, 1988—; contbr. numerous articles to profl. jours. Served to surgeon USPHS, 1966-68. Recipient Irving Sunshine award in clin. toxicology Internat. Assn. Therapeutic Drug Monitoring and Toxicology, 1993, Jean R. Oliver award/Master Tchr. in Pathology, Alumni Assn., SUNY Health Sci. Ctr., Bklyn., 2001. Fellow AAAS (award for rsch. and leadership in lab. medicine 1997), Coll. Am. Pathologists; mem. Acad. Clin. Lab. Physicians and Scientists (pres. 1983-84, Gerald T. Evans award 1988), Am. Soc. Clin. Pathology, Am. Assn. Clin. Chemistry (award for outstanding contbns. to clin. chemistry in selected area of rsch. 1985, award for outstanding contbns. in edn. 1995). Home: 617 Saddle Ridge Rd Orange CT 06477-2024 Office: Yale U Sch Medicine Dept Lab Medicine PO Box 208035 New Haven CT 06520-8035

JATRAS, JAMES GEORGE, lawyer; b. 1955; m. Kathy Jatras; 2 children. BA, Pa. State U., 1974; JD, Georgetown Univ., 1978. Bar: Pa. 1978. Consular officer US State Dept., Tijuana, Mexico, 1979—81, fgn. svc. officer, Russian affairs, 1981—85; policy analyst US Senate Republican Policy Com., 1985—2002; ptnr., legis. practice Venable LLP, Washington, 2002—. Office: Venable LLP 575 7th St NW Washington DC 20004 Office Phone: 202-344-8308. Office Fax: 202-344-8300. Business E-Mail: jgjatras@venable.com.

JAUDES, RICHARD EDWARD, lawyer; b. St. Louis, Feb. 22, 1943; s. Leo August, Jr. and Dorothy Catherine (Schmidt) Jaudes; m. Mary Kay Tansey, Sept. 22, 1967; children: Michele, Pamela. BS, St. Louis U., 1965, JD, 1968. Bar: Mo. 1968, U.S. Dist. Ct. (ea. dist.) Mo. 1973, U.S. Ct. Appeals (8th cir.) 1973, U.S. Supreme Ct. 1990. With Peper, Martin, Jensen, Maichel & Hetlage, St. Louis, 1973-97, mng. ptnr., 1990-93; ptnr., chair labor and employment practice group Thompson Coburn LLP, St. Louis, 1997—, mem. mgmt. com., 1997—2000. Bd. dirs. Baldor Electric Co. Vol. counsel St. Louis chpt. MS Soc., 1990—. Lt. USN, 1968—73, comdr. USNR. Office: Thompson Coburn LLP One US Bank Plz Saint Louis MO 63101-1693 Office Phone: 314-552-6431. E-mail: rjaudes@thompsoncoburn.com.

JAUDON, VALERIE, artist; b. Greenville, Miss., Aug. 6, 1945; d. Baize R. and Gladys E. (Hill) J.; m. Richard Kalina, Oct. 23, 1979. Student, Miss. State Coll. for Women, 1963—65, Memphis Acad. Art, 1965, U. of Americas, Mexico, 1966—67, St. Martins Sch. Art, London, 1968—69. One-woman shows of paintings include Holly Solomon Gallery, N.Y.C., 1977-79, 81, Pa. Acad. Fine Arts, Phila., 1977, Galerie Bishofberger, Zurich, Switzerland, 1979, Galerie Hans Strelow, Dusseldorf, Fed. Republic Germany, 1980, Corcoran Gallery, L.A., 1981, Sidney Janis Gallery, N.Y.C., 1983, 85, 86, 88, 90, 93, 96, Quadrat Mus., Bottrop, Fed. Republic Germany, 1983, Amerika Haus, Berlin, 1983, Dart Gallery, Chgo., 1983, Fay Gold Gallery, Atlanta, 1985, Macintosh/Drysdale Gallery, Washington, 1985, Barbara Scott Gallery, Bay Harbor Islands, Fla., 1994, Miss. Mus. Art, Jackson, 1996, Betsy Senior Gallery, N.Y.C., 1998, Stadel Mus., Frankfurt, Germany, 1999-2000, Von Lintel Gallery, N.Y.C., 2003, 05; numerous group shows including, Mayor Gallery, London, 1979, Galerie Habermann, Cologne, Germany, 1979, Galerie Hans Strelow, Dusseldorf, 1979, Galerie Modern Art, Vienna, Austria, 1980, Mus. Modern Art, Oxford, Eng., 1980, Greenberg, Gallery, St. Louis, 1980, Sidney Janis Gallery, N.Y.C., 1980, San Francisco Art Inst., 1980, Mus. Modern Art, N.Y.C., 1980, Leo Castelli Gallery, N.Y.C., 1980, Thomas Segal Gallery, Boston, 1980, Venice (Italy) Biennale, 1980, Nat. Gallery of Art, Washington, 1980, Chgo. Art Inst., 1981, Mus. Fine Arts, Boston, 1982, Neuberger Mus., Purchase, N.Y., 1982, Hudson River Mus., Yonkers, N.Y., 1983, Berkshire Mus., Pittsfield, Mass., 1983, La Jolla Mus., Calif., 1983, Margo Leavin Gallery, L.A., 1984, Bronx Mus., 1985, Am. Ctr., Paris, 1986, Dayton Art Inst., 1987, Cin. Art Mus., 1989, Tel Aviv Mus. Art, 1992, Robert McClain Gallery, Houston, 1996, Turner/Runyon Gallery, Dallas, 1997, Kunsthallen Brandts Kaledefabrik, Odense, Denmark, 2001, Angel Row Gallery, Nottingham, England, 2001, Porin Taidemuseo, Eteläranta, Finland, 2002; executed ceramic mural Equitable Bldg., N.Y.C., 1988, brick and granite plaza Police Plaza, N.Y.C., 1989; Blue Pools Courtyard Birmingham (Ala.) Mus. Art, 1993; mosaic floor Washington Nat. Airport, 1997, grass garden Thomas Eagleton Courthouse, St. Louis, 2004; represented in permanent collections including Hirshhorn Mus., Washington, Mus. Modern Art, N.Y.C., Albright-Knox Art Gallery, Buffalo, N.Y., Fogg Art Mus., Cambridge, Mass.,Sammlung-Lugwig Mus., Aachen, Fed. Republic Germany, Dayton (Ohio) Art Inst., Nat. Museum of Women in the Arts, Washington, St. Louis Art Mus., Ludwig Mus., Budapest, Hungary, Miss. Mus. Art, Jackson. Recipient 1st prize award So. Contemporary Arts Festival, 1967, Art award Miss. Inst. Arts and Letters, 1981, 97, Excellence in Design award N.Y.C. Art Commn., 1988, civic Spirit award Women's City Club of N.Y., Merit award Am. Soc. Landscape Architects Ala. chpt., 1994; named Honored Artist from State of Miss. Nat. Mus. Women in Arts, Washington; N.Y. State CAPS grantee for graphics, 1980; Visual Arts Fellowship grant Nat. Endowment Arts, 1988; N.Y. Found. for Arts grantee in painting, 1992. Address: 795A Accabonac Rd East Hampton NY 11937-1807 E-mail: vjaudon@earthlink.net.

JAURON, DICK (RICHARD M. JAURON), former professional football coach; b. Peoria, Ill., Oct. 7, 1950; m. Gail Jauron; children: Kacy, Amy. Degree in History, Yale U. Profl. football player Detroit Lions, 1973-77, Cin. Bengal, 1978-80; co-owner health and fitness ctr. Cin.; with Nautilus; secondary coach Buffalo Bills, 1985; defensive backs coach Green Bay Packers, 1986—94; defensive coord. Jacksonville Jaguars, 1995—98; head coach Chgo. Bears, 1999—2003; defensive coord. Detroit Lions, 2004—. Active numerous charities. Named 1974 Pro Bowl selection, NFL Coach of the Yr., 2002 Avocation: golf. Office: c/o Detroit Lions 222 Republic Drive Allen Park MI 48101

JAUSSI, LINDA ANN, music educator; b. Idaho, July 6, 1961; d. Norman Leon Jaussi and Lyda Jeanene Miller; children: Dalen Hansen, Daline Hansen, Krista Hansen, Trevor Hansen, Ashley Hansen. AAS, Ricks Coll., Rexburg, Idaho, 1997; BA in Music, Utah State U., 1999. Cert. entrepreneurial tng. program SBA. Freelance composer/arranger, Scottsdale, Ariz., 1979—2001; writer, columnist, photographer Leader & Cache Citizen Newspapers, Tremonton & Garland, 1989—95; vocal instr. music dept. Utah State U., Logan, 1997—99; photographer PCA, Logan, 1997—98; tchr. Farmington (N.Mex.) Mcpl. Schs., 1999—2001; dir. youth musical theater San Juan Coll. and local groups, Farmington, 2000—01; with ABC Music, Scottsdale, Ariz., 2003, Linda Jaussi Studios, 2003—. Asst. dir. univ. choirs Utah State U., Logan, 1997. Composer: (choral works, works for voice) Just In Time, 2001. Bd. dirs. spl. needs PTA, Garland, 1992—93; career exploration chairwoman Ricks Coll. Acad. Coun., Rexburg, 1980—81; dist. capt. Reps., Scottsdale, 2001; com. mem. Logan Mayoral Coun., 1995. Named Soloist, Garland Regional Messiah Performance, 1993; recipient Choral Special Merit award, Utah State Music Dept., 1998, Certificate of Achievement, Ricks Coll. Acad. Coun., 1980—81. Mem.: No. Utah Choral Soc. (tour choir 1995—96), Nat. Music Educators Assn., Choral Union Ariz. State U. Mem. Lds Ch. Avocations: sightseeing, boating, kayaking, hiking. Personal E-mail: liberty10@hotmail.com.

JAVID, MANUCHER J., retired neurosurgery educator; b. Tehran, Iran, Jan. 11, 1922; came to U.S., 1944, naturalized, 1957; s. Asdolah and Touba (Ahdiyeh) J.; m. Lida Emma Fabbri, Oct. 19, 1951; children— Roxane, Daria, Jeffrey, Claudia. MD, U. Ill., 1946. Diplomate: Am. Bd. Neurosurgery. Intern Augustana Hosp., Chgo., 1946-47, resident gen. surgery, 1947-48, resident neurosurgery, 1948-49; asst. in neuropathology Ill. Neuropsychiat. Inst., Chgo., 1948-49; fellow in neurosurgery Lahey Clinic, Boston, 1949; resident neurosurgery New Eng. Med. Center, Boston, 1950; clin. research fellow neurosurgery Mass. Gen. Hosp., Boston, 1950, asst. resident, 1951, chief resident neurosurgery, 1952; teaching fellow in surgery Harvard, 1952; instr. Med. Sch. U. Wis., Madison, 1953-54, asst. prof., 1954-57, asso. prof., 1957-62, prof. neurosurgery, 1962-98, endowed named prof. neurol. surgery, 1998, emeritus prof., 1998—, chmn. dept. neurosurgery, 1962—95. Cons. neurosurgeon VA Hosp., Madison, 1956-98. Contbr. articles profl. jours. Mem. AMA, ACS, AAUP, AAAS, Soc. Neurol. Surgeons, Am. Assn. Neurol. Surgeons, Am. Assn. Med. Colls., Soc. for Neurosci., Central Neurosurg. Soc. (pres. 1964), Internat. Intradiscal Therapy Soc. (treas. 1987-90, pres.-elect 1990—, pres. 1991, hon. mem. 1999), N.Y. Acad. Scis., Xeiron, Sigma Xi, Phi Beta Pi, Alpha Omega Alpha. Mem. Baha'i Faith. Club: Rotarian. Achievements include introduction of osmotherapy in neurosurgery and ophthalmology by the clin. use of urea for reduction intracranial and intraocular pressure. Home: 4750 Lafayette Dr Madison WI 53705-4865 Personal E-mail: mjavid@facstaff.wisc.edu. *Since I was a small child, I wanted to be a doctor and help the sick. As I grew older, the Baha'i Faith, served as a guideline to achieve this goal. Its teachings have helped me to appreciate the oneness of God, the oneness of religion, the oneness of humanity, and the sanctity of life.*

JAVITS, ERIC MOSES, lawyer, diplomat; b. N.Y.C., May 24, 1931; s. Benjamin A. and Lily Javits; m. Margaretha Espersson, May 24, 1979; children from previous marriage: Jocelyn Ingrid, Eric Jr. Student, Stanford U., 1948-49; AB, Columbia U., 1952, JD, 1955. Bar: N.Y. 1955, U.S. Supreme Ct. 1959. Temp. cons. Office Def. Moblzn., Washington, 1951; assoc. firm Javits & Javits, N.Y.C., 1955-58, mem. firm to ptnr., 1958-82; sr. ptnr. Javits, Robinson, Brog, Leinwand & Reich, P.C. (and successor firms), 1984-89; cons. to Dept. State, amb.-designate to Venezuela, 1989-90; sr. counsel Robinson, Brog, Leinwand, Reich, Genovese & Gluck, P.C. (and successor firms), 1993—2001; U.S. perm. rep. and amb. to Conf. on Disarmament in Geneva, 2002—03, Orgn. Prohibition Chem. Weapons, The Hague, 2003—. Ind. gen. ptnr. ML Venture Ptnrs., 1982-96; spl. dep. to N.Y. Atty. Gen. Elections Frauds Bur., 1958-59; counsel N.Y. Senate Com. on Affairs of City

N.Y., 1959; mem. N.Y.C. Commn. for Protocol, 1994-2001; bd. dirs. N.Y. State Conv. Ctr. Oper. Corp., 1995-2001; past dir. N.Y. Stock Exch., Am. Stock Exch., over the counter cos. Author: SOS New York, 1961. Mem. numerous charitable coms.; bd. govs. N.Y. Young Rep. Club, 1955-58, v.p., 1957-58, bd. advisers, 1958-64; trustee French Inst./Alliance Francaise, 1995-2001, Cardozo Law Sch., 1997-2001; mem. exec. com. Jacob K. Javits campaigns, 1954-80; mem. N.Y. Rep. County Com., 1960-64; mem. exec. com. Nat. Rep. Club, 1962-70; exec. sec. U.S. Paper Exporters Coun., Inc., 1964-72; mem. bd. Spain-U.S.A. C. of C., 1993-2001; chmn. emeritus Spanish Inst., N.Y.C.; bd. dirs. Fair Return League, Inc., pres., 1975—; chmn. Republican Eagles, 1999-2001. Decorated Order of Isabel La Catolica (Spain), 1981, 89; recipient Spanish Inst. Gold medal, 1994. Mem.: Nacoms, U. Club N.Y.C., Phi Alpha Delta, Beta Theta Pi, Phi Beta Kappa. Jewish.

JAVITS, JOSHUA MOSES, lawyer; b. N.Y.C., Jan. 2, 1950; s. Jacob Koppel and Marian (Borris) J.; m. Sabina Paula Golding, May 25, 1985. BA, Yale U., 1972; JD, Georgetown U., 1978. Bar: D.C. 1979, Calif. 1983. Trial atty. NLRB, L.A., 1978-83; assoc. Mullholland & Hickey, Washington, 1983-85, Cades, Schutte, Fleming & Wright, Washington, 1985-87; arbitrator Washington, 1985-88; mem., chmn. Nat. Mediation Bd., Wshington, 1988-93; ptnr. Ford & Harrison, Washington, 1993—2001; arbitrator and mediator, 2001—. Mem. ABA, Nat. Acad. Arbitrators, Indsl. Relations Rsch. Assn., Soc. Fed. Labor Relations Profls., Soc. Profls. in Dispute Resolution. Office Phone: 202-237-2044. E-mail: jjavits@aol.com.

JAVITT, JONATHAN C., ophthalmologist; b. NYC, Nov. 7, 1956; s. Norman B. and Suzanne (Markovits) J.; m. Marcia C. Fishman, June 29, 1986; children: Zachary, Matthew, Gabrielle. AB with honors, Princeton U., 1978; MD, Cornell U., 1982; MPH, Harvard U., 1984. Diplomate Am. Bd. Ophthalmology. Intern Lenox Hill Hosp., N.Y.C., N.Y., 1982-83; resident Wills Eye Hosp., Phila., 1984-87; fellow Johns Hopkins Hosp., Balt., 1988-89; instr. Johns Hopkins U., 1987-90, asst. prof., 1990-99, prof. Balt., 1999—; asst. prof. Georgetown U., Washington, 1990-93, assoc. prof., 1993-96, prof. Sch. Medicine, prof. sch. Pub. Policy, 1996—; founder, chmn. Certitude, Inc., Mpls., 1994—; sr. v.p., nat. med. dir. United Health Care/Applied Health Care Informatics, Mpls., 1997-98; chmn. Health Directions LLC, Bethesda, 1998—; founder, pres., vice chmn. EMEDX, Inc., 1999—. Founder Coderyte, Inc., 2000; bd. dirs. Acad. Homeland Security; expert cons. Health Care Fin. Adminstrn., Balt., 1987—; spl. employee The White House Health Reform Task Force, Washington, 1992; cons. Nat. Eye Inst./NIH, 1990—, Nat. Inst. Diabetes Digestive and Kidney Disease/NIH, 1991—, Agy. for Health Care Policy Rsch., 1994—, The World Bank, Washington, 1993—, Swedish Coun. on Tech. Improvement, 1997, Japanese Min. of Health, 1993, Australia Min. of Health, 1994—; apptd. Pres.'s Info. Tech. Adv. Com., 2003—. Sect. editor Archives of Ophthalmology, 1993—, Ophthalmology Times, 1993—; author more than 200 books, chpts., articles; patentee in field. Com. chair Nat. Health Policy Coun., Washington, 1992—; cmty. spkr. on health care The White House, 1992—; trustee Md. Rep. Party, 2000—; mem. campaign com. Bush for Pres., 2000; mem. Rep. Presdl. Roundtable; bd. dirs. Washington Jewish Fedn., Brookdale Inst., Am. Joint Distbn. Com.; active Johns Hopkins Pres.'s Club, Weill Cornell Med. Coll. Deans Cir., Rep. Senatorial Trust; fin. dir. Erlich for Gov., 2002. Recipient Cert. of Appreciation, USAF, 1991, Physician Scientist award Nat. Eye Inst., 1988; U.S. Presdl. Letter of Appreciation, 1993; Kellogg Found. fellow, 1983, sr. fellow Potomac Inst. for Policy Studies, 2001—; named guest of honor Japanese Glaucoma Soc., 1996, New England Ophthalmologic Soc., 1997. Fellow Am. Acad. Ophthalmology (Honor award 1990, Sr. Recognition award 2000), Am. Glaucoma Soc.; mem. AMA, AOPA, NBAA, Assn. for Rsch. in Vision and Ophthalmology, Assn. for Health Svc. Rsch., Am. Glaucoma Soc., Kehilath Jeshurun, Royal Ocean Racing Club, Princeton Club, Harvard Club, Cosmos Club. Avocations: sailing, aviation. Office: Health Directions LLC 4733 Bethesda Ave Ste 720 Bethesda MD 20814 E-mail: jjavitt@healthdirections.net.

JAVITT, NORMAN B., medical educator, researcher; b. N.Y.C., Mar. 9, 1928; s. Bernard and Zara (Hillman) Jakubovitz; m. Suzanne Markovits, June 5, 1955; children: Jonathan Chaim, Daniel Coleman, Joel Israel, Gail Hannah. AB cum laude, Syracuse U., 1947; PhD in Physiology, U. N.C., 1951; MD, Duke U., 1954. Diplomate Am. Bd. Internal Medicine; lic. physician, N.Y. Predoctoral fellow USPHS, Chapel Hill, N.C., 1949-51; intern Mt. Sinai Hosp., N.Y.C., 1954-55, asst. resident, 1957-58, chief resident, 1959-60, Sara Welt fellow in medicine, spl. USPHS, 1961-62; asst. physician, advanced fellow Am. Heart Assn. Vanderbilt Clinic, Columbia Coll. Physicians and Surgeons, N.Y.C., 1957-58; instr. dept. medicine NYU Sch. Medicine, 1962-64, asst. prof., 1964-68; assoc. prof. Cornell U.Med. Coll., N.Y.C., 1968-73, prof., 1973-83; assoc. attending physician N.Y. Hosp., N.Y.C., 1968-73, attending physician, 1973-83; prof. medicine, prof. pediatrics NYU Med. Ctr., N.Y.C., 1983—, dir. divsn. hepatic diseases, 1983-2000; guest investigator Nat. Inst. Child Health and Development, Nat. Insts. of Health, Bethesda, Md., 2000—; assoc. dir. clin. rsch. unit NYU Med. Ctr., N.Y.C., 1985-90. Cons. Meml. Sloan-Kettering Cancer Ctr., N.Y.C., 1970-83; vis. prof. Rockefeller U. Hosp., 1970-76; cons. medicine VA Hosp., Bklyn., 1977-83; chief divsn. gastroenterology Cornell-N.Y. Hosp. Med. Ctr., 1973-81, chief divsn. hepatic diseases, acting chief divsn. gastroenterology, 1981-83; cons. Tisch Hosp., NYU Med. Ctr., 1983—; mem. tng. grant study sect. Nat. Inst. Arthritis, Metabolic & Digestive Diseases, NIH, 1978-85; mem. steering com. Nat. Cooperative Gallstone Study, 1973-80, chmn. clin. mgmt. com., 1974-78; gen. medicine study Section A, NIH, 1976-80. Mem. editl. adv. bd. Hosp. Practice, 1969-93; assoc. editor Jour. Lipid Rsch., 1977-78, 86—, editl. bd., 1983—; author, editor 2 books; contbr. articles to profl. jours. Capt., M.C., U.S. Army, 1955-57. Fellow ACP; mem. Am. Physiol. Soc., Am. Soc. Pharmacology and Exptl. Therapeutics, Am. Fedn. Clin. Rsch., Am. Soc. Clin. Investigation, Am. Assn. Study of Liver Disease, Am. Gastroenterol. Assn., Am. Soc. Clin. Pharmacology and Therapeutics, Am. Soc. Biol. Chemists, Am. Pediatric Soc., Am. Soc. Parenteral and Enteral Nutrition, Harvey Soc., Sigma Xi, Alpha Omega Alpha. Jewish. Avocation: grandparenting. Home: 501 E 79th St New York NY 10021-0735 Office: NYU Med Ctr Divsn Hepatic Disease New York NY 10016 Business E-Mail: norman.javitt@med.nyu.edu.

JAVOSKY, RUDOLPH V., retail executive; b. Toronto; m. Carole Javosky; 3 children. Grad, McGill U. Sr. design ptnr. Bregman + Hamann Architectural and Engring. Firm, Toronto; exec. v.p. design and constrn. Campeau Corp., 1987—88; sr. v.p., store design and constrn. Federated Dept. Stores, 1988—. Mem.: AIA, Inst. Store Planners, Royal Archtl. Inst. Canada, Nat. Assn. Store Fixture Manufacturers. Office: Federated Dept Stores Inc 7 West 7th St Cincinnati OH 45202

JAW, ANDREW CHUNG-SHIANG, software analyst; b. Tainan, Taiwan, Feb. 10, 1953; came to U.S., 1978; s. Ping-Tsen and Pey-Yuh Jaw; m. Amy Chi, July 30, 1979; children: Andrew, Anfin, Audrey. BS in Mech. Engring., Tatung Inst. Tech., Taipei, Taiwan, 1974; MS in Metall.Engring., Poly. Inst. N.Y., 1981; MSEE, Syracuse U., 1987. Engr. Tatung Co., Taipei, Taiwan, 1976-78; sr. assoc. engr. IBM Corp., Endicott, NY, 1980-89, Rochester, Minn., 1990-91; software cons. A BOC Health Care Co., Madison, Wis., 1991-92; sr. software engr. A Rockwell Internat. Co., Milw., 1992-94; staff software assurance analyst ARDIS Co., Lincolnshire, Ill., 1994-96, lead tech. programmer analyst, 1996-98, Am. Mobile Satellite Corp., Lincolnshire, Ill., 1998-2000; sr. network mgmt. sys. engr. Motient Corp., Lincolnshire, Ill., 2000—03, project mgr., 2004—. Adj. prof. info. sys. ITT Tech. Inst., Greenfield, Wis., 2003—04, Concordia U., Mequon, Wis., 2003—. Patentee in field. Recipient Cert. of Merit, Assembly of the State of NY, 1985; rsch. fellow Poly. Inst. NY, 1979. Mem. IEEE Computer Soc. Business E-Mail: Andrew.Jaw@Computer.org.

JAWAD, SAID TAYEB (SAID TAYEB DJAWAD), ambassador, commentator, writer; b. Kandahr, Afghanistan, Feb. 27, 1958; came to U.S., 1986; s. Mir Hussain and zakia Shah; m. Shamim Rahman, Nov. 16, 1986. Student, Kabul (Afghanistan) U., 1976-80, Wilhelms U., Muenster, Germany, 1984-86, Long Island U., 1986; MBA, Golden Gate U., San Francisco, 2001. With Lehnardt & Bauman, N.Y.C., 1988-89, Steefel, Levitt & Weiss, San Francisco, 1989—2002; chief of staff, spokesman Pres. Afghanistan, Kabul, Afghanistan, 2002—03; dir. Office Internat. Rels., 2001—03; Afghan amb. to U.S., 2003—. Writer, polit. commentator various newspapers, radio and TV stas. including BBC. Columnist OMAID, 1992-95; pub. Substratum of Human Rights Violations in Afghanistan, Modern Dictatorship, The United States and the Afghan Resistance, Soviets Expansion to the South, Fundamentalism in Central Asia; contbr. articles to BBC World Reports (London) and to polit. jours. throughout world. Bd. dirs. Afghanistan Cultural Soc., San Francisco, 1990-92; mem. Internat. Soc. for Human Rights, Frankfort, Germany, 1983-86; mem. nat. adv. bd. Info. Am., Atlanta, 1991-94; active Amnesty Internat., N.Y.C., 1987—. Mem. World Affairs Coun. Office: Embassy of Afganistan 2341 Wyoming Ave NW Washington DC 20008 Home: 2341 Wyoming Ave NW Wash DC Office Phone: 202-483-6410. E-mail: info@embassyofafghanistan.org.

JAWAHAR, AJAY, neurosurgeon, educator; b. India, Mar. 14, 1965; arrived in U.S., 1997; s. Hingorani Joseph and Saudine C. Jawahar; m. Lisa Louise Smith, June 21, 2003; children: Dylan Wayne, Stuti Celeste, Eleanor Clarice. MD, U. Rajasthan, Jaipur, India, 1987, M of Surgery, 1992; MS in Med. Physics, Haywood U., London, 2004. Diplomate Nat. Bd. Neurosurgeons India. Leskell fellow in radiosurgery U. Pitts., 1997—99; postdoctoral fellow in radiosurgery La. State U., Shreveport, 2000—01, lectr. in neurosurgery, 2001, asst. prof. neurosurgery, 2004—. Mem. instnl. rev. bd. for human rsch. La. State U., Shreveport, 2004—; cons. on brain tumors Guilford Pharms., Balt., 2003—. Author: Saunder Manual of Neurosurgical Practice, 2003; contbr. articles to profl. med. jours. Mem. Think First, Shreveport, 2003. Recipient Jason Cardelli Award for Exellence in Cancer Rsch., Feist-Weiler Cancer Ctr., 2003, Mahaley Award for Best Clin. Rsch. in Brain Tumors, Nat. Brain Tumor Soc., 2005. Mem.: Internat. Stereotactic Radiosurgery Soc., Am. Assn. Neurol. Surgeons, Congress of Neurol. Surgeons, KC (1st deg.). Roman Catholic. Avocations: reading, music, travel, movies. Office: La State U Health Scis Ctr 1501 King's Hwy Shreveport LA 71103 Office Phone: 318-675-6195.

JAWIDZIK, EDWARD MARK, priest; b. New Brunswick, N.J., Apr. 25, 1954; s. Edward John and Phyllis Jean (Kaczmarek) Jawidzik. BA in Humanities, St. Mary's Sem.Coll., Balt., 1976; MDiv, Immaculate Conception Sem., Mahwah, N.J., 1980. Ordained priest Roman Catholic Church, 1981. Deacon intern Saint Joan of Arc Ch., Marlton, NJ, 1980—81; parochial vicar St. Mary of the Lake Ch., Lakewood, NJ, 1981—86, Our Lady Star of the Sea Ch., Long Branch, NJ, 1986—87, St. Ann's Ch., Keansburg, NJ, 1987—94; pastor Our Lady of Perpetual Help Ch., Highlands, NJ, 1994—95; parochial vicar St. Rose Ch., Belmar, NJ, 1995—2001, St. Robert Bellarmine Ch., Freehold, NJ, 2001—. Mem. liturgy com. Emmaus Program for Priestly Spirituality, 1982—83; Rep. for Bayshore Deanery Priest's Coun., Trenton, NJ, 1992—95; pro-life chaplain Monmouth County, NJ, 1995—; rep. for Coastal Monmouth Deanery Priest's Coun., Trenton, 1995—2001. Author: Historical Houses of Worship in the Freehold Area, 2005. Mem Keansburg Alliance on Substance Abuse, 1987—94; chaplain KC Bayshore Coun., East Keansburg, 1987—92, KC St Catharine's Coun., Spring Lake, NJ, 1999—2001; Faithful Friar assembly KC Monsignor Kivelitz, Freehold, NJ, 2004—; chaplain KC Freehold Coun., 2005—; mem. commemorative book com. Diocese Trenton 125th Ann., 2004—. Recipient Proclamation of Acclaim, Mayor and Borough Coun., Keansburg, 1991, Proclamation award, 1994. Mem.: Freehold Twp. Hist. Preservation Commn., Acton Inst. Study of Religion and Liberty, Freehold Interfaith Clergy Assn. (Diocese of Trenton 125th Anniversary commemorative book com. 2004—). Roman Catholic. Achievements include founding mem., Nat. Campaign for Tolerance, 2004. Avocations: baseball, history, music. Home: 61 Woodstock Pl Freehold NJ 07728 Office: St Robert Bellarmine Ch 61 Georgia Rd Freehold NJ 07728 Office Phone: 732-462-7429.

JAWIN, ANN JULIANO, human resource specialist; b. Barnesboro, Pa. d. Santo and Benedetta (Vanchiere) Giuliano; m. Edward Henry Jawin; children: Ronald, Paul. BA, Hunter Coll., 1943; profl. diploma, St. John's U., 1976. Asst. personnel dir. Davis & Geck, N.Y.C., 1945-52; guidance counselor h.s. divsn. N.Y.C. Bd. Edn., 1962-86; dir. guidance Bramson Tech. Coll., N.Y.C., 1986-89; pres., founder Ann J. Jawin Assocs., N.Y.C., 1990—; founder, chair bd. dirs. Ctr. Women N.Y., N.Y.C., 1987—. Author: A Women's Guide to career Preparation, 1979, Report on Sex Bias in N.Y. Public Schools, 1977, Where's the Money for College?, 1985. Founder, chair bd. dirs. Dougbay Manor Civic Assn., Douglaston, N.Y., 1966—; pres. Bay Terrace Cmty. Coun., Bayside, Queens, N.Y., 1955-66; N.Y. State Committeewoman N.Y. State Dem. Party. Recipient Susan B. Anthony award NOW, 1985, Ralph Bunche award UN Assn., 1996, Vol. Svc. award Mayor Rudolph Giuliani, N.Y.C., 1997, Citation of Merit Fernando Ferrer Bronx Borough Pres., 1998; named Humanitarian of Yr. Dems. for New Politics, 1995, Hunter Coll. Hall of Fame, 1993. Mem. AAUW (Leadership award 2001), N.Y. State Guidance Assn., Ams. of Italian Heritage (founder, chair bd. dirs. 1987—, Woman of Yr. 1998, Disting. Leadership award 2002). Avocations: walking, reading, swimming, gardening. Office: Center for Women of New York 12055 Queens Blvd Rm 325 Jamaica NY 11424-1015 Office Phone: 718-793-0672. E-mail: centerwny@yahoo.com.

JAWORSKA, TAMARA, artist; b. Archangel, Russia; arrived in Can., 1969; d. Antoni Jankowski; m. Tadeusz Jaworski, 1957; children: Ewa, Piotr. BFA in Painting, State Acad. Fine Arts, Lodz, Poland, 1950, MFA in Design and Weaving Art, 1952; M of Painting (hon.), Accademia Italia, 1982. From asst. prof. to sr. asst. prof., lectr. State Acad. Fine Arts, Poland, 1952-58. One-woman shows include State Gallery of Textiles, Lodz, 1965, State Gallery of Fine Arts, Warsaw, 1965, Pushkin Nat. Mus., Moscow, 1966, Fine Arts Mus., Plymouth, U.K., 1968, Scottish Woolen Gallery, Galashields, 1968, Richard Demarco Gallery, Edinburgh, Scotland, 1968, Rothman's Art Gallery, Stratford, 1970, Merton Gallery, Toronto, 1970, London Art Gallery, 1971, Glendon Art Gallery, Toronto, 1972, Nienkamper Art Gallery, Toronto, 1979, Art Gallery of Hamilton, 1980, Nat. Museums and Art Galleries in Spain, 1980-81, Can. Cultural Ctr., Paris, 1981, Galerie Inard, Paris, 1981, Munich Art Gallery, Germany, 1982, Galerie Inard, Toulouse, France, 1982, 91, Galerie Inard, Paris, 1984, 91, Leo Kamen Gallery, Toronto, 1987, 89, John B. Aird State Gallery, Toronto, 1992, Peak Gallery, Toronto, 1997, Solo Gallery, Toronto, 2003, 04, 05, also exhibits in France, Germany, Belgium, Switzerland, Luxembourg, U.K., Spain, Austria, Poland, Russia, Hungary, U.S., Mex., Can., Paris, Eng., Scotland, Holland, Austria, Spain, Moscow, Poland, Hungary, Can., U.S., others; group exhbns. include Warsaw and Lodz art galleries, Pushkin Mus., European Art Gallery, Moscow, Richard Demarco Gallery, Edinburgh, Fine Art Mus., Plymouth, Eng., Merton Gallery, Toronto, Hermitage Leningrad Mus., USSR, Nat. Art Gallery, Teheran, Mus. Modern Art, Mexico City, Art Gallery of Ont., RCA-Art 2000, Toronto and Stratford, 2000; exhibited tapestries at New Coll., Galerie Inard, Ctr. Nat. de la Tapisserie d'Abusson, Paris, later in Madrid, Barcelona, Valencia, San Sebastian, Paris, Munich, Zurich, others; works in permanent collections of Pushkin Nat. Mus., European Art Gallery, Moskau, Russia, Nat. Mus., Warsaw, Nat. Mus. of Textile Arts, Lodz, Poland, Nat. Mus. of Home Army, King City, Krakow, Poland, Galashields Art Inst., Scotland, Bank of Montreal, Toronto, Bell Can., Ottawa, Molson Canadian, Toronto, Mut. Ins. of Can., Toronto, First Can. Pl. Main Lobby, Gulf Can. Sq. Main Lobby, and many corp. and pvt. collections in Europe, Am., Mid. East, Centre Nat. de la Tapisserie D'Aubusson Galerie Inard, Paris; subject of articles in art books and mags. Decorated Order of Can.; recipient Gold medal-Triennial di Milano, Interior Design and Architecture, Milan, 1957, award for excellence Wool Gathering, Montreal, 1974, Gold medal Academia Italia delle Arti, 1980, Gold Centaur, Academia Italia delle Arti, 1982, Gold medal and 1st prize Internat. Art Competition, N.Y.C., 1985, Commemorative medal Gov. Gen. Can., 1993, Highest Civilian Recognition for Achievements in Field of Creative Visual Arts, 1994, Golden Jubilee medal Her Majesty Elizabeth II, 2002. Fellow York Univ.; mem. Royal Can. Acad. Art, Academia Italia delle Arti, Ontario Soc. Artists. Home: 49 Don River Blvd Toronto ON Canada M2N2M8 E-mail: tamtad@ica.net, qts@gallery.solo.com.

JAY, CHRISTOPHER EDWARD, stockbroker; b. Walla Walla, Wash., May 2, 1949; s. Orville Elmo and Juanita Hope (Beckius) J.; m. Mardra Marguerite Jones, July 25, 1981; children: Pohaku Kepano, Hope Lauren, Christopher James. BS, Lewis and Clark Coll., 1972; MA, U. Nev., 1975. 1st v.p. Merrill Lynch & Co., Anchorage, 1975—. Dist. chair Rep. Cen. Com., Anchorage, 1980-81; bd. trustees Lewis and Clark Coll., Portland, Oreg., 1988—; bd. dirs. Anchorage Mus. History and Art Found., 1988-90, KSKA Pub. Radio, Anchorage, 1991-93, Alaska Pub. Broadcasting Inc., Anchorage, Providence Hosp. Found., Anchorage; bd. dirs., treas. Anchorage Symphony Orch.; active 1st Presbyn. Ch., Anchorage, apptd. by Anchorage mayor to sit on the Investment Adv. Bd. for the Mcpl. of Anchorage Endowment Fund, 2003 Named one of nation's top brokers Registered Rep. mag., 1995, 1998 Broker Hall of Fame, Rsch. Mag., 1998; recipient Disting. Alumni award Lewis and Clark Coll., 1996. Mem. Rotary (pres. Anchorage chpt. 1989-90, Paul Harris fellow 1989, co-chmn. dist. conv. 1997, elected del. to Nat. Rep. Conv. 2000, elected aternate to Nat. Rep. Convention). Republican. Presbyterian. Avocations: reading, walking, travel, civic activities. Home: 11060 Hideaway Lake Dr Anchorage AK 99507-6141 Office: Merrill Lynch & Co 3601 C St Fl 14 Anchorage AK 99503-5925

JAY, DAVID JAKUBOWICZ, management consultant; b. Dec. 7, 1925; came to U.S., 1938, naturalized, 1944. s. Mendel and Gladys Gitta (Zalc) Jakubowicz; m. Shirley Anne Shapiro, Sept. 7, 1947; children: Melvin Maurice, Evelyn Deborah. BS, Wayne State U., 1948; MS, U. Mich., 1949, postgrad., 1956-57, U. Cin., 1951-53, MIT, 1957. Registered profl. engr., Calif., Mich., Ohio. Supr. man-made diamonds GE Corp., Detroit, 1951-56; instr. U. Detroit, 1948-51; asst. to v.p. engring. Ford Motor Co., Dearborn, Mich., 1956-63; project mgr. Apollo environ. control radiators N.Am. Rockwell, Downey, Calif., 1963-68; staff to v.p. corp. planning Aerospace Corp., El Segundo, Calif., 1968-70; founder, pres. PBM Sys. Inc., 1970-83; pres. Cal-Best Hydrofarms Coop., Los Alamitos, 1972-77, Inkmarks Corp., 1989—95. Cons. in field. Patentee in air supported ground vehicle, others. Pres. Cmty. Design Corp., Los Alamitos, 1971-75; life master Am. Contract Bridge League. With USNR, 1944-46. Fellow Inst. Advancement Engring.; mem. Art Stamp and Stencil Dealers Assn. (pres. 1993-95), Inst. Mgmt. Sci. (chmn. 1961-62), Western Greenhouse Vegetable Growers Assn. (sec.-treas. 1972-75), Tau Beta Pi. Jewish. Home: 13441 Roane Santa Ana CA 92705-2271 Office: 137 W Bristol Ln Orange CA 92865 Office Phone: 714-998-9471. E-mail: djay@biznetsyscorp.com.

JAY, FRANK PETER, retired writer, lexicographer, educator; b. Bklyn., Feb. 12, 1922; s. Frank G. and Harriet Ann (Niffer) J.; m. Jayne Marie Charles, Aug. 15, 1947; children— Jennifer, Christopher, Alison, Angela, Jonathan, Melissa, Bryan, Nicole, Matthew. AB, Fordham U., 1943; MA, Columbia U., 1946. Mem. faculty Fordham U., 1946-92, prof. English, 1948-92; editor-in-chief reference books Funk & Wagnalls, N.Y.C., 1963-65, exec. editor, 1968-73; editor-in-chief reference books Reader's Digest, N.Y.C., 1965-66; editor-in-chief IEEE Dictionary, 1977, 84, 88. Author: Jack: The Story of a Pretty Good Donkey, 1970, also articles, short stories; editor-in-chief: The New Internat. Year Book, 1963, 64, 65, Internat. Everyman's Ency., 20 vols, 1970. Served with USAAF, 1942-43. Mem. Overseas Press Club (N.Y.C.), Princeton Club (N.Y.C.), Manhasset Bay Yacht Club, Kappa Delta Pi. Home: 3 Huntington Rd Port Washington NY 11050-3510

JAY, NORMA JOYCE, artist; b. Wichita, Kans., Nov. 11, 1925; d. Albert Hugh and Thelma Ree (Boyd) Braly; m. Laurence Eugene Jay, Sept. 2, 1949; children: Dana Denise, Allison Eden. Student, Wichita State U., 1946-49, Art Inst. Chgo., 1955-56, Calif. State Coll., 1963. Illustrator Boeing Aircraft, Wichita, 1949-51; co-owner Back Door Gallery, Laguna Beach, Calif., 1973-88. Guest artist Coos Art Mus., 2003. One-woman shows include Milcir Gallery, Tiburon, Calif., 1978, Newport Beach City Gallery, 1981, exhibited in group shows at Am. Soc. Marine Artists ann. exhbns., 1978—2001, Peabody Mus., Salem, Mass., 1981, Mystic Seaport Mus. Gallery, Conn., 1992—95, Grand Ctrl. Gallery, N.Y., 1979—84, The Back Door Gallery, Laguna Beach, 1973—88, Mariners' Mus., Newport News, Va., 1985—86, Nat. Heritage Gallery of Fine Art, Beverly Hills, Calif., 1988—, Md. Hist. Mus., 1989, Kirsten Gallery, Seattle, 1991—97, R.J. Schaefer Gallery Mystic (Conn.) Seaport Mus., 1992, Vallejo Gallery, Newport Beach, 1992, Caswell Gallery, Troutdale, Oreg., 1994—95, Columbia River Maritime Mus., Astoria, Oreg., 1994, Arnold Art Gallery, Newport, Conn., 1994, Mystic Internat. Exhbn., 1995, Lu Martin Galleries, Laguna Beach, 1996—, Frye Art Mus., Seattle, 1997, Cummer Mus. Art & Gardens, Jacksonville, Fla., 1997—98, Cape Mus. Fine Arts Inc., Dennis, Mass., 2001, Coos Art Mus., Coos Bay, Oreg., 2003, Newport (R.I.) Art Mus., 2003, Maine Maritime Mus., Bath, 2003, Connecticut River Mus., Essex, 2004, Vero Beach Mus. of Art, Fla., 2004, Represented in permanent collections James Irvine Found., Newport Beach, Niguel Art Assn., Laguna Niguel, Calif., Deloitte, Haskins & Sells, Costa Mesa, Calif., M.J. Brock & Sons Inc., North Hollywood, Calif., others. Recipient Best of Show award Ford Nat. Competition, 1961, First Pl. award Traditional Artists Exhbn., San Bernadino County Mus., 1976, artist award Chriswood Gallery Invitational Exhbn., Rancho California, Calif., 1973, Dirs. Choice award, People's Choice award Coos Art Mus. Marine Exhbn., 1996, featured guest artist, 1998, Coos Art Mus., 2003, 1st Pl. award Maritime Art Exhibit, Newport Harbor Nautical Mus., Newport Beach, 1998-99. Fellow Am. Soc. Marine Artists (charter); mem. Niguel Art Assn. (first pres. 1968, hon. life mem. 1978), Artists Equity, Am. Artists Profl. League. Democrat.

JAYAKRISHNAN, RAJARAMAN, civil engineer; m. Srividya Sankaranarayanan. BE, Tamil Nadu Agrl. U., 1991; MCE, Asian Inst. Tech., 1993; PhD, Tex. A&M U., 2001. Registered profl. engr., Fla., 2004. Rsch. assoc. Asian Inst. of Tech., Bangkok, 1993—95; grad. rsch. asst. Tex. A&M U. Sys., Temple, Tex., 1995—98, specialist, 1999—2001; assoc. engr. Boyle Engring. Corp., Sarasota, Fla., 2001—. Contbr. articles to profl. jours. Grantee, State Tex., 2001. Mem.: ASCE, Am. Geophys. Union, Am. Water Resources Assn., Am. Soc. Agrl. Engrs., Gamma Sigma Delta. Hindu. Avocations: classical music, nature, travel, astronomy, books. Home: 10023 Reagan Dairy Trail Bradenton FL 34212 Personal E-mail: guruguhan@yahoo.com.

JAYARAM, PRATHIBA, researcher, educator; BS in Pharmacology, Govt. coll., India, 1988, MS in Pharmacology, 1990; PhD in Pharmacology, Manipal Acad. Higher Edn., India. Asst. prof. Manipal Acad. Higher Edn., India, 1990—97; post doc rschr. U. Tenn. Health Sci. Ctr., Memphis, 2002—. Contbr. articles in neuroscience. Recipient Disting. Alumni Award, Manipal Acad. Higher Edn., 2000. Office: Univ Tenn Health Ctr 874 Union Ave Memphis TN 38163 Office Phone: 901-448-4583. Personal E-mail: prathiba_nc@yahoo.com.

JAYASANKAR, SUBRAMANYAN, orthopaedic surgeon; Grad., Elphinstone Coll., Mumbai, Grant Medical Coll. Gen. surgery & orthopaedic surgery residency Grant Medical Coll. & Sir J.J. Group of Hospitals, Mumbai; orthopedic residency Harvard U. & Mass. Gen. Hosp., Mass., prof. orthopedic surgery, 1974—, New England Baptist Hosp., 1974—. Pres. Boston Medical Library; volunteer consulting orthopaedic surgeon Mass. Dept. of Mental Health & Dept. of Corrections, Eunice Kennedy Shriver Ctr., Fernald State Sch., Monson State Sch., Lemuel Shattuck Hosp. Bd. dirs. Mass. Medical Soc. Charitable Found., Network of Indian Professionals, Internat. Health Org. Mem.: AMA (health Internat. Medical Grad. Section), Mass. Medical Soc. (chair com. on medical svc., vice chair com. on professional liability), Indian Medical Assn. of New England (former bd. trustees chair), Am. Assn. of Physicians of Indian Origin (former pres.). Office: Harvard Medical Sch 74 Country Dr Weston MA 02493*

JAYMAN, JANETTA J., director; b. Westminster, Md., Apr. 3, 1963; d. Richard Will and Helen Aileen Long; m. John R. Jayman, June 23, 1990; children: John Richard, Joseph Anthony. BA, U. MD., 1985; MEd, Loyola Coll., 1991. Tchr., dept. chair English Balt. County Pub. Schs., 1985—97;

asst. prin. Carroll County Pub. Schs., Westminster, 1997—2001, supr. English, 2001—05. Presenter in field. Mem.: ASCD, Nat. Coun. Tchrs. English. Office: Carroll County Pub Schs 125 N Court St Westminster MD 21157

JAYNE, CRISTINA MARSH, retired elementary education educator; b. Mar. 15, 1935; BS in Elem. Edn., Ohio U., 1958; student, Rio Grande Coll., Bowling Green (Ky.) U., Ashland Coll., Ohio U. Cert. elem. tchr., Ohio. Tchr. grade 2 Kingston (Ohio) Sys., 1956-59; tchr. grade 3 and 4 Chillicothe City, Ohio, 1960-67, tchr. grade 5, 1974-98; ret., 1998. Recipient Educator Emeritus award, Chillicothe Edn. Assn., 2005. Address: 459 W 5th St Chillicothe OH 45601-3014

JAYNE, EDWARD RANDOLPH, II, executive search consultant; b. Kirksville, Mo., Sept. 24, 1944; s. Edward Randolph and Marietta (Jonas) J.; m. Nancy Elizabeth King, June 18, 1966; children: Kathryn Eden, Matthew Randolph. BS, USAF Acad., 1966; PhD, MIT, 1969. Officer, pilot USAF, 1966-77; staff nat. security coun. The White House, Washington, 1976-77; assoc. dir. nat. security and internat. affairs Office of Mgmt. and Budget The White House, Washington, 1977-80; v.p. Gen. Dynamics Corp., St. Louis, 1980-87; pres. McDonnell Douglas Missile Sys. Co., St. Louis, 1987-93; pres., COO, bd. dirs. Insituform Mid-Am., St. Louis, 1993-94; sr. ptnr. Heidrick & Struggles, McLean, Va., 1996—. Bd. dirs. C.A.E., Inc., Toronto, The Falcon Found., USAF Acad., Colo., MetricVision, Inc., Inst. Def. Analysis. Maj. gen. Air Nat. Guard; ret. NSF fellow, 1966-69, White House fellow, 1973-74. Office: Heidrick & Struggles Inc 1750 Tysons Blvd Ste 300 Mc Lean VA 22102-4243 Office Phone: 703-848-2500. E-mail: rjayne@heidrick.com.

JAYNE, THOMAS R., lawyer; m. Patti Jayne; 4 children. BA, Westminster Coll., 1973; JD, U. Mo., 1976. Bar: Mo. 1976, Ill. 1979, Tex. 1995. Ptnr. Thompson Coburn LLP, St. Louis. Pres. bd. mgrs. Ctrl. Inst. for the Deaf; mem. Knowles Found. Bd.; bd. govs. Truman State U., Kirksville, Mo., 2000—. Office: Thompson Coburn LLP One US Bank Plz Saint Louis MO 63101

JAYSON, MELINDA GAYLE, lawyer; b. Dallas, Sept. 29, 1956; d. Robert and Louise Adelle (Jacobs) J. BA, U. Tex., 1977, JD, 1980. Bar: Tex. 1980, U.S. Dist. Ct. (no. dist.) Tex. 1980, U.S. Ct. Appeals (5th and 11th cirs.) 1981, U.S. Dist. Ct. (so. dist.) Tex. 1989, U.S. Ct. Appeals (8th cir.) 1990, U.S. Supreme Ct. 1991. Assoc. Akin, Gump, Strauss, Hauer & Feld, Dallas, 1980-86, ptnr., 1987-96, Melinda G. Jayson, P.C., 1996—; gen. counsel Hall Fin. Group, Dallas, 1999—. Comml. arbitrator, mem. regional adv. coun. Am. Arbitration Assn.; arbitrator, mediator N.Y. Stock Exch., NASD Regulation, Inc., Nat. Arbitration Forum, CPR Inst. Dispute Resolution; mediator U.S. EEO Commn., 1999-2000; arbitrator Nat. Arbitration Forum, 2000—. Named one of Outstanding Young Women Am., 1983. Mem.: Am. Health Lawyers Assn. (arbitrator, mediator), Tex. Bar Assn., Dallas Bar Assn., State Bar of Tex. (mem. dist. 6A grievance com. 1997-99, mem. professionalism enhancement com. 1997-99). (mem. dist. 6A grievance com. 1997—99, mem. professionalism enhancement com. 1997—99). Office: Ste 2015 5445 Caruth Haven Ln Dallas TX 75225-8166 Office Phone: 972-377-1145. Business E-Mail: mjayson@hallfinancial.com.

JAY-Z, (COREY SHAWN CARTER), rap artist, music company executive; b. Bklyn., Dec. 4, 1969; Founder Roc-A-Fella Records, N.Y.C., 1995—, Roc-A-Fella Films, Rocawear, 1999—; prin., owner 40/40 Club, N.Y.C.; pres. Def Jam Record Co., 2005—. Singer: (albums) Reasonable Doubt, 1996 (Platinum), In My Lifetime, Vol. I, 1997 (Platinum), Vol. 2: Hard Knock Life, 1998 (Platinum 5 times, Grammy award, 1998), Vol. 3: Life and Times of S. Carter, 1999 (Platinum 3 times), The Dynasty: Roc la Familia, 2000 (Platinum 2 times), MTV Unplugged, 2001 (Gold), The Blueprint, 2001 (Platinum 2 times), The Blueprint, Vol. 2: The Gift & The Curse, 2002 (Platinum 2 times), Best of Both Worlds, 2002 (Platinum), Blueprint 2.1, 2003 (nominated 6 Grammy awards, 2003), The Black Album, 2003 (MTV Video Music awards Best Rap Video for the song 99 Problems, MTV Video Music award Best Direction In a Video for the song 99 Problems, 2004, MTV Video Music awards Best Editing In a Video for the song 99 Problems, 2004, MTV Video Music awards Best Cinematography In a Video for the song 99 Problems, 2004), (TV series) Unplugged Blueprint, 2001, Jay-Z LIVE, 2003; composer: (films) Space Jam, Soul Food, Rush Hour, Nutty Professor II: The Klumps, Training Day, Paper Soldiers, Austin Powers in Goldmember, Barbershop, Bad Boy II; actor, prodr., writer Streets Is Watching, 1998; actor: (films) Paper Soldiers, 2002, (TV guest appearances) Saturday Night Live, 2000, 2002, 2003, Mad TV, 2001, Ashlee Simpson Show, 2004. Founder Team Roc, Shawn Carter Scholarship Fund, Annual Jay-Z Santa Claus Toy Drive. Named Sammy Davis Jr. Entertainer of Yr., Soul Train, 2001, Favorite Male Rap/Hip Hop Artist, Am. Music Awards, 2004; named one of World's 100 Most Influential People, Time Mag., 2005; recipient Best Rap Video award, MTV Music Video Awards, 1999, Rap Artist of Yr. award, Billboard Music, 1999, Lyracist of Yr., Solo award, Source, 1999, Best Hip Hop Artist, Solo award, 2001, Best Male Hip Hop Artist award, BET, 2001, 2004, R&B/Soul or Rap Album of Yr. for The Blueprint, Soul Train, 2002. Achievements include creating the urban clothing line "Roca Wear"; first rapper to have his own signature sneaker, the S. Carter by Reebok. It went on to become one of the biggest-selling sneakers of 2003. Office: Roc A Fella Records 825 8th Ave 19th Floor New York NY 10019-7416 also: Def Jam Recording Simmons 89 Bradhurst Ave New York NY 10039-3314

JE, CHUNG-HWAN, engineering educator, researcher; b. Masan, Kyungnam, South Korea, May 20, 1963; s. Bong-Ho Je and Il-Kyu Na; m. Hee-Kyung Yeom, June 27, 1993; children: Robin, Michelle. BS, Ajou U., Suwon, Korea, 1989, MS, 1991, U. Colo., 1994; PhD, U. Utah, 1998. Registered profl. engr., Utah. Post-dr. U. Utah, Salt Lake City, 1998—99; environ. engr. Moutain States Analytical, Salt Lake City, 1999—2001; sr. environ. engr. Encore Environ., Salt Lake City, 2001; adminstrv. faculty U. Nev., Reno, 2001—, grad. faculty, 2004—. Internat. activity com. U. Nev., 2004—; chpt. pres. Korean-Am. Scientists, Salt Lake City, 1999—2001. Author: several jour. articles in field. Recipient Student Paper award, Water Environ. Assn. Utah, 1998, Travel Grant award, Assn. Lab. Automation, 2004. Mem.: Water Environment Fedn., Am. Water & Works Assn., Am. Chem. Soc. Avocations: reading, classical music, fishing. Office: Univ Nevada Dept Environ Health & Safety MS 328 Reno NV 89557

JEAN, CLAUDETTE R., retired elementary school educator; b. Nashua, N.H., Sept. 26, 1930; d. Thomas Noel and Elise Marie (Archambault) J. BA, Rivier Coll., 1952; MA, Fitchburg (Mass.) Coll., 1956. Cert. tchr. Elem. tchr. Donald St. Sch., Beford, N.H., 1952-53, Arlington St. Sch., Nashua, N.H., 1953-56, J.B. Crowley Sch., Nashua, N.H., 1956-65, Sunset Heights Sch., Nashua, N.H., 1965-91, Nashua; ret. Rep. N.H. Gen. Ctr., Concord, 1992—. Negotiating team Nashua Tchrs. Union, 1969—; state Dem. com. N.H. Dems., Concord, 1992; Hillsborough County com. County Delegation, Manchester, N.H., 1992. Recipient Toland award AFL-CIO, 1991. Mem. Nashua Tchrs. Union (cons. 1991-94), Sr. Citizens Club, Retired Tchrs. Assn., Nashau Coll. Club. Roman Catholic. Avocations: golf, travel, reading.

JEAN, RAYMOND A., vehicle, building products manufacturing executive; b. Aug. 23, 1942; BS in Engring. Physics, Univ. Maine; MBA, Univ. Chgo. With Allis Chalmers, 1965—73, Evans Products Co., 1974—75, 1979—83, Gulf & Western, 1976—78, I.C. Industries, 1983—87; group v.p. Varlen Corp., 1988—96, COO, 1993—98, pres., 1997—99, CEO, 1999; corp. v.p. Amsted Industries, 1999—2001; chmn., pres., CEO Quanex Corp., Houston, 2001—. Office: Quanex Ste 1500 1900 W Loop S Houston TX 77027 Office Phone: 713-961-4600. Office Fax: 713-439-1016.*

JEAN, WYCLEF, musician, recording industry executive; b. La Plaine, Haiti, Oct. 17, 1972; m. Marie Claudinette Jean, 1994. Rap singer with the Fugees; albums include: Blunted on Reality, 1993, The Score, 1996; music videos include: To All the Girls, Gone Till November, Gon Till November - Remix, Gone Til November (live), Guantanamera, Guantanamera II, We Trying to Stay Alive, Wyclef on Production (English), Wyclef Welcome (Creole); remixes include: Cheated - (To All the Girls), What's Clef Got to Do With It, We Trying to Stay Alive Remix, Gone Till November Remix; songs include: Carnival, Yele, Jaspora, Enter the Carnival (interlude), Gunpowder, We Yrying to Stay Alive, Street Jeopardy, Mona Lisa, Fresh Interlude, Son Fezee, Year of the Dragon, Words of Wisdom (interlude), Gone Till November, Anything Can Happen Down Lo Ho (interlude) To All the Girls, Prelude to "To All the Girls" (interlude), Bubblegoose, Pablo Diablo (interlude), Guantanamera, Apocalypse, Intro/Court/Clef/Intro (skit/interlude); composer (films) When We Were Kings, 1996, Love Jones, 1997, Life, 1999, Next Friday, 2000, Dr. Dolittle 2, 2001, Shottas, 2002, The Agronomist, 2003, The Manchurian Candidate, 2004; Film appearances include Shottas, 2002, Be Cool, 2005. Office: c/o Columbia Records 550 Madison Ave New York NY 10022-3211 also: c/o Columbia Records PO Box 4450 New York NY 10101-4450*

JEAN-BAPTISTE, TRICIA, public relations executive; married; 1 child, Nicholas. Pub. rels. positions Le Parker Meridien Hotel, NY, Doral Hotels and Resorts; mgr. corp. comm. Days Inn Am., Parsippany, NJ, 1998; founder Tricia Jean-Baptiste Comm., 1998—. Recipient Golden Bell Bronze award, Hotel Sales and Mktg. Assn. Mem.: NY Women in Comm. (past bd. mem.). Office: Tricia Jean-Baptiste Comm 375 Greenwich St Ste 804 New York NY 10013 Office Phone: 212-941-3988. Office Fax: 212-941-3989. Business E-Mail: trica@tricapr.com.

JEANDRON, CAROL ADRAGNA, academic administrator; d. William Joseph and Lillie Mae Borne Adragna; children: Laurie Ann, Gerald Joseph, Mark Andrew, Nicole Christine. BA, Tulane U., New Orleans, 1965; MEd, U. of New Orleans, 1976; PhD, U. of So. Miss., 1983. English tchr. Orleans Parish Sch. Sys., New Orleans, 1965—68; tchr./counselor/adminstr. St. Bernard Parish Pub. Sch. Sys., Chalmette, La., 1968—84; instr. St. Bernard Parish C.C., Chalmette, La., 1984—92; prof./dean/vice chancellor of academic affairs/provost Nunez C.C., Chalmette, La., 1992—2001; dir., office of svc. learning Loyola U. New Orleans, 2001—. Cons. Am. Assoc. Cmty. Colls., Washington DC, 2001—. Facilitator - establishment La. Campus Compact, La., 2002—04. Grantee Cmty. Colls. Broadening Horizons through Svc. Learning, Am. Assoc. Cmty. Colls., 1997—2003, Coun. of Ind. Colls. grantee, 2001—03; scholar, Gus Mayer and Tulane U. scholar, 1961—65. Mem.: Nat. Soc. for Exptl. Edn. (bd. dir.). Office: Loyola University New Orleans 6363 St Charles Ave Campus Box 115 New Orleans LA 70118

JEAN-LOUIS, GIRARDIN, psychologist, educator, researcher; b. Port-Au-Prince, Haiti, Dec. 7, 1967; s. Jean-Louis Girardin and Marie L. Beaugris. BA, CUNY, 1992, MA, 1997, PhD, 1997. Instr. CUNY, Staten Island, 1994-97; rsch. psychologist U. Calif., San Diego, 1997-2000; asst. prof. L.I. U., Bklyn., 2000—, SUNY, Bklyn., 2000—. Co-dir. sleep lab. Coll. L.I., 1994-97; clin. dir. Kingsbrook Jewish Med. Ctr., N.Y., 2000—. Contbr. articles to profl. jours. Postdoctoral fellow NIH-NHLBI, 1997. Mem. Am. Acad. Sleep Medicine (Trainee fellow 1997), Sleep Rsch. Soc. (Rsch. Merit award 1999). Avocations: music, hiking, reading, jogging. Office: SUNY Down State Med Ctr, Box 58 450 Clarkson Ave Brooklyn NY 11203 E-mail: jeanlouisg@yahoo.com.

JEANLOZ, RAYMOND, geophysics educator; b. Winchester, Mass., Aug. 18, 1952; BA, Amherst Coll, 1975; PhD in Geology and Geophysics, Calif. Inst. Tech., 1979. Asst. prof. Harvard U., 1979-81; from asst. prof. to assoc. prof. U. Calif., Berkeley, 1982-85, prof., 1985—. Exec. dir. Miller Inst. for Basic Rsch. in Sci., 1998-2003; chair bd. on earth scis. and resources NRC, 1999-2003; chair internat. security and arms control NAS Com, 2004-. Editor Ann. Rev. Earth and Planetary Sci., 1996—. Recipient Mineral. Soc. Am. award, 1988, life fellow, 1988; MacArthur grantee, 1988. Fellow AAAS, Am. Geophysics Union (J.B. Macelwane award 1984); mem. NAS, Am. Acad. Arts and Scis. Office: U Calif Dept Earth & Planetary Sci Berkeley CA 94720-4767

JEANLOZ, ROGER WILLIAM, biochemist, educator; b. Berne, Switzerland, Nov. 3, 1917; came to U.S., 1947, naturalized, 1953; s. William M. and Rose (Poisat) J.; m. Dorothea A.H. de Passavant, Dec. 20, 1945; children: Patrick Marc (dec.), Claude-André, Raymond François, Danielle Renée, Sylvie Anne. Baccalaureate, Coll. Geneva, Switzerland, 1936; Chem.E., U. Geneva, 1941, D.Sc., 1943; A.M. (hon.), Harvard, 1961; D.Sc. (hon.), U. Paris, 1980. Rsch. assoc. U. Geneva, 1943-45, U. Basel, 1945-46; asst. U. Montreal, 1946-47; sr. research fellow NIH, 1947-48; sr. scientist Worcester Found. Exptl. Biology, 1948-51; asso. biochemist Mass. Gen. Hosp., Boston, 1951-61, biochemist, 1961—2003; rsch. assoc. Harvard Med. Sch., 1951-57, assoc. organic chemistry, 1957-60, asst. prof. biol. chemistry, 1960-61, assoc. prof., 1961-69, prof., 1969-88, emeritus prof. biol. chemistry and molecular pharmacology, 1988—. Mem. bd. tutors biochem. scis. Faculty Arts and Scis., Harvard U., 1960—; mem. study sect. physiol. chemistry div. research grants NIH, 1964-68, 69-70; mem. physiol. chemistry B. research study com. Am. Heart Assn., 1971-74. Author: (with Balazs) The Amino Sugars, 3 vols, 1965, (with Gregory) Glycoconjugate Research, 2 vols, 1979; Editor: Carbohydrate Research; editorial bd.: Connective Tissue Research, Molecular Biology, Biochemistry and Biophysics, Biochimie, Glycoconjugate Jour.; contbr. articles to profl. jours. Recipient medal Société de Chimie Biologique de France, 1960, medal U. Liege, 1964, Prix Jaubert U. Geneva, 1973, Stratton award Am. Friends of Switzerland, 1981, Alexander von Humboldt Sr. Scientist award, 1983; Guggenheim fellow, 1976-77. Fellow AAAS; mem. Am. Soc. Biol. Chemists, Am. Chem. Soc., Swiss Chem. Soc., Royal Chem. Soc. (London), French Biochem. Soc., Biochem. Soc., Soc. for Glycobiology, Am. Coll. Rheumatology. Home: 42 Ruthven Rd Newton MA 02458-2316 Personal E-mail: jeanloz@fas.harvard.edu.

JEANNE, ROBERT LAWRENCE, entomologist, educator; b. NYC, Jan. 14, 1942; s. Armand Lucien and Ruth (Stuber) Jeanne; m. Louise Grenville Bluhm, Sept. 18, 1976; children: Thomas Lucien, James McClure. BS in Biology, Denison U., 1964; postgrad., Justus-Liebig U., Giessen, Fed. Republic Germany, 1964-65; MA, Harvard U., 1968, PhD in Biology, 1971. Instr. biology U. Va., Charlottesville, 1970-71; asst. prof. biology Boston U., 1971-76; asst. prof. entomology U. Wis., Madison, 1976-79, assoc. prof., 1979-83, prof., 1983—. Rschr.: numerous publs. on social insects. Fellow Rotary Found., 1964—65, Guggenheim Meml., 1986—87. Fellow: AAAS; mem.: Wis. Acad. Scis., Arts and Letters, Animal Behavior Soc., Internat. Union Study Social Insects (chmn. protempore, sec.-treas. 1979—80, pres. western hemisphere sect. 1981, assoc. editor Insectes Sociaux 1986—2002), Assn. Tropical Biology, Phi Beta Kappa, Sigma Xi. Achievements include numerous discoveries relating to nest construction, nest architecture, communication, defense, caste polymorphism, polyethism, social organization, and life histories in social wasps. Office: U Wis Dept Entomology 1630 Linden Dr Madison WI 53706-1520 Office Phone: 608-262-0899. Business E-Mail: jeanne@entomology.wisc.edu.

JEANSON, CEDRIC, film company executive; b. Paris, Jan. 6, 1965; came to U.S., 1989; s. Dominique and Nicole (Jansse) J. MS in Internat. Mgmt., Internat. Mgmt. Inst. Paris, 1987; MBA, Northwestern U., Evanston, Ill., 1991. Mgr. internat. distbn. Dino de Laurentiis Comm., Beverly Hills, Calif., 1991-93; dir. internat. Miramax Film Corp., L.A., 1993-95, v.p. internat. sales, 1995-97, sr. v.p. N.Y.C., 1997-99, exec. v.p., 1999—. Mem. Brit. Acad. Film and TV Arts, Am. Film Mktg. Assn., Am. Film Inst. Avocations: film, music, soccer, tennis, skiing. Office: Miramax Film Corp 99 Hudson St New York NY 10013-2815

JEBEJIAN, SARKIS, lawyer; b. NYC, Nov. 14, 1969; BA, Columbia Univ., 1991, JD, 1994. Bar: NY 1995. Assoc. Cravath Swaine & Moore LLP, NYC, 1994—96, 1998—2002, Hong Kong, 1996—98, ptnr., corp. NYC, 2002—. Prodn. editor Columbia Bus. Law Rev. Mem.: Assn. of Bar of City of NY. Office: Cravath Swaine & Moore LLP Worldwide Plz 825 Eighth Ave New York NY 10019-7475 Office Phone: 212-474-1188. Office Fax: 212-474-3700. Business E-Mail: sjebejian@cravath.com.

JEBSEN, HARRY ALFRED ARTHUR, JR., history educator; b. Chgo., Apr. 8, 1943; s. Harry Alfred Arthur Jebsen; m. Elaine Claire Melchert, Sept. 5, 1964; children— Timothy Paul, Christopher Warren. B.A., Wartburg Coll., 1965; M.A., U. Cin., 1966, Ph.D., 1971. Prof. history Texas Tech U., Lubbock, 1969-81, dir. urban studies, 1972-81, assoc. dean arts and scis., 1980-81; dean Coll. of Arts and Scis., Capital U., Columbus, Ohio, 1981-88, provost, 1988-95, prof. history, 1995—. Author: History of Dallas, Texas Park System, 1971. Contbr. articles to profl. jours. Bd. dirs. Luth. Council for Community Action, Lubbock, 1970-78, U. Ministries of Lubbock, 1971-81, Luth. Social Services of Central Ohio, Columbus, 1984-92. Recipient Fish and Loaves award Luth. Council for Community Action, Lubbock, 1977; NDEA fellow, Cin., 1966-69. Mem. Am. Assn. Higher Edn., N.Am. Soc. Sport Historians. Democrat. Avocations: golf, reading. Home: 1397 Goldsmith Dr Westerville OH 43081-4526 Office: Capital U 2199 E Main St Columbus OH 43209-2394 E-mail: hjebsen@capital.edu.

JECKLIN, LOIS UNDERWOOD, art corporation executive, consultant; b. Manning, Iowa, Oct. 5, 1934; d. J.R. and Ruth O. (Austin) Underwood; m. Dirk C. Jecklin, June 24, 1955; children: Jennifer Anne, Ivan Peter. BA, U. Iowa, 1992. Residency coord. Quad City Arts Coun., Rock Island, Ill., 1973-78; field rep. Affiliate Artists Inc., N.Y.C., 1975-77; mgr., artist in residence Deere & Co., Moline, Ill., 1977-80; dir. Vis. Artist Series, Davenport, Iowa, 1978-81; pres. Vis. Artists Inc., Davenport, 1981-88; pres., owner Jecklin Assocs., Davenport, 1988—2004. Asst. to exec. dir. Walter W. Naumburg Found., N.Y.C., 1990-2004; cons. writer's program St. Ambrose Coll., Davenport, 1981, 83, 85; mem. com. Iowa Arts Coun., Des Moines, 1983-84; panelist Chamber Music Am., N.Y.C., 1984, Pub. Art Conf., Cedar Rapids, Iowa, 1984; panelist, mem. com. Lt. Gov.'s Conf. on Iowa's Future, Des Moines, 1984. Trustee Davenport Mus. Art, 1975-98, hon. trustee, 1998-2003; regional bd. nat. adv. coun., Figge Art Mus., Davenport, 2005—; trustee Nature Conservancy Iowa, 1987-88; steering com. Iowa Citizens for Arts, Des Moines, 1970-71; bd. dirs. Tri-City Symphony Orch. Assn., Davenport, 1968-83; founding mem. Urban Design Coun., HOME, City of Davenport Beautification Com., 1970-72; bd. govs. Mus. Arts and Design, NYC, 1995—; devel. coun. U. Iowa Mus. Art, 1996-2002. Recipient numerous awards Izaak Walton League, Davenport Art Gallery, Assn. for Retarded Citizens, Am. Heart Assn., Ill. Bur. Corrections, many others; LaVernes Noyes scholar, 1953-55. Republican. Episcopalian. Home and Office: 1232-27th St NW Washington DC 20007

JEDLICKA, ALLEN DEAN, finance educator, consultant; s. Waldemar John and Elnora Ethel Jedlicka; 1 child, Sierra Delores Glonek. BA, San Diego State U., 1965; PhD, Northwestern U., 1973. Vol. Peace Corps, Chilijchi, Bolivia, 1965—67; full prof. mgmt. internat. bus. U. No. Iowa, Cedar Falls, Iowa, 1973—. Cons. Jedlicka Assocs., Hudson, Iowa, 1976—; cons. in field. Author: Organization and Rural Development, 1978, Organization Change and the Third World, 1987, Volunteerism and World Development, 1990; contbr. articles to profl. jours. Active City of Cedar Falls. Fellow, NSF, 1970—73; Sr. Fulbright scholar, 1978. Avocations: hiking, backpacking, beach walking, gardening. Office: Dept Mgmt Univ No Iowa Cedar Falls IA 50614

JEFFCOAT, MARJORIE K., dental educator, dean; Degree, MIT; DMD, Harvard U. Sch. Dental Med., 1976. Faculty mem. Harvard U. Sch. Dental Med.; asst. dean rsch. U. Ala. Sch. Dentistry, prof., chair dept. periodontics, prof. biomedical engring., James Rosen Endowed chair of dental rsch., interim chair dept. oral biology; dean U. Penn. Sch. Dental Med., 2003—. Mem. adv. com. rsch. on women's health Nat. Inst. Dental and Craniofacial Rsch., NIH. Editor-in-chief: Journal of the American Dental Assoication, 2001—. Recipient President's Achievement award, U. Ala., Birmingham. Mem.: Am. Acad. Periodontology (Clin. Rsch. award, Gies award), Internat. Assn. Dental Rsch. (past pres.), Am. Assn. Dental Rsch. (past pres.). Office: U Penn Sch Dental Med Robert Shattner Ctr 240 S 40th St Philadelphia PA 19104-6030

JEFFCOTT, JANET BRUHN, statistician, consultant; b. Madison, Wis., Dec. 5, 1939; d. Hjalmar Diehl and Janet H. (Weber) Bruhn; m. Robert Gordon Jeffcott, Apr. 20, 1963. BA, U. Wis., 1962, MA, 1968. Asst. librarian Madison Area Tech. Coll., 1968-83, dist. librarian, 1983—91, adminstr. instructional media, telecommunications, 1988—91, media tech. adminstr., 1989—91. Pres. and treas. Fidelity & Assocs., Madison, 1982—; prin. J.B. Jeffcott & Assocs., Madison, 1989—, Edumetrics, Manistique, Mich., 2003-; sec.-treas. Manistique (Mich.) Mfg. & Tech., Inc., 1990-99, pres., treas., 1999-2002. Home and Office: Edumetrics 711 Oak St Manistique MI 49854

JEFFE, DONNA B., medical educator; b. St. Louis, Oct. 7, 1951; d. Jacob D. and Paula F. Lite; m. James S. Jeffe, Jan. 2, 1972; children: Jennifer E., Joel M. BA in Biology, Washington U., 1972, MA in Edn., 1990, PhD in Edn., 1993. Analytical chemist Sigma-Aldrich Chem. Co., St. Louis, 1973—75; prin. dancer and founding mem. St. Louis Ballet Co., 1980—87; substitute tchr. Pky. Sch. Dist., Chesterfield, Mo., 1988—90; tchg. asst. Washington U., St. Louis, 1990—92; post-doctoral fellow medicine Washington U. Sch. Medicine, St. Louis, 1993—96, rsch. assoc., 1996—98, instr. medicine, 1998—99, rsch. asst. prof. medicine, 1999—. Contbr. articles to profl. jours. Grantee, Nat. Cancer Inst., 2001—02, Siteman Cancer Ctr., 2001—02, Nat. Cancer Inst. and the Breast Cancer Stamp Fund, 2003—, Longer Life Found., 2003, Barnes-Jewish Hosp. Found., 2003. Mem.: APA, Am. Psychosicial Oncology Soc., Soc. Behavioral Medicine, N.Am. Menopause Soc. Achievements include research in Social Support in Older Lung Cancer Patients; Quality of Life over Time: DCIS vs. Early Breast Cancer; Psychosocial Factors Associated with Delay in Diagnosis among Locally Advanced Breast Cancer Patients - a Pilot Study. Avocations: travel, reading, walking, running. Office: Washington Univ Sch Medicine Ste 6700 4444 Forest Park Ave Saint Louis MO 63108 Office Phone: 314-286-1914. E-mail: djeffe@wustl.edu.

JEFFE, ROBERT ALLAN, diversities technology and services company executive; b. Highland Park, Mich., May 12, 1950; s. Sidney David and Lorraine Rhea (Lashkowitz) J.; m. Elizabeth Rohn, Nov. 20, 1976; children: Alison Elizabeth, Peter Edmond. AB in Econs. summa cum laude, Dartmouth Coll., 1972; MBA with honors, Stanford U., 1974. Assoc. Morgan Stanley & Co., Inc., N.Y.C., 1974-78, v.p., 1979-80, prin., 1981-85, mng. dir., 1986—94; mng. dir., global natural resources unit Smith Barney Inc., 1994—96; mng. dir. Credit Suisse First Boston, 1996—2001; sr. v.p., corp. bus. devel. GE Corp., 2001—. Mem. Phi Beta Kappa. Mem. Unitarian Ch.

JEFFE, SIDNEY DAVID, automotive executive, engineer; b. Chgo., May 6, 1927; s. J.I. Jeffe; children: Robert A., Leslie A. BSME with honors, Ill. Inst. Tech., 1950; MS in Automotive Engring. with honors, Chrysler Inst. Engring., 1952; postgrad., Carnegie-Mellon U., 1968. With Chrysler Corp., 1950-80, v.p. engring. and rsch., 1976-80; sr. v.p. ops. Sheller Globe Corp., Detroit, 1982-86; prof. mech. engring. Ohio State U., 1980-82; sr. v.p. internat. bus. and tech. devel. and implementation, head customer and govt. rels. activities Sheller Globe Corp., Detroit, 1986-90; v.p. internat. bus. and tech. devel. Mesnel S.A.- Schlegel Corp., Madison Heights, Mich., 1990-92; internat. bus. and tech. cons., expert witness, 1992—. Exec. dir. Transp. Rsch. Ctr. Ohio, E. Liberty; sec.-treas. Transp. Rsch. Bd. Ohio, 1980-82; sr. v.p. internat. bus. and tech. devel. United Tech. Engineered Sys. Divsn., 1990; bd. dirs. J.L. French Automotive Castings Inc.; engring. and bus. cons. Energy Conversion Devices, Inc., 2000—. Responsible for devel. Chrysler's first front-wheel drive cars- Omni, Horizon, K cars and Minivans, 1976-80; author papers in field. Served with AUS, 1945-47. Fellow Engring. Soc. Detroit, Soc. Automotive Engrs. (Russell Springer award 1957, Coll. Fellows 1985); mem. Tau Beta Pi (Outstanding New Mem. award 1948), Pi Tau Sigma (Outstanding New Mem. award 1949). Clubs: DC Ranch Country (Scottsdale, Ariz.), Orchard Lake Country, Detroit Athletic, Ren Cen. Unitarian Universalist. Home: 41120 Fox Run Rd #110 Madison Green Novi MI 48377 Office Phone: 248-669-1861.

JEFFERDS, WILLIAM JOHN, military officer; b. Stockton, Calif., Sept. 26, 1929; s. Wallace Vincent and Margaret (Moreing) J.; m. Patricia Ann, Aug. 16, 1949; children: Jerilyn Ann, Janelle Kay, Mark Christian. BA, San Jose State U., 1952; EdD, U. Calif., Berkeley, 1966; grad., Harvard U., 1984. Cert. tchr., Calif. Advanced through grades to maj. gen., 1985; commd. U.S. Army, 1964-68; bn. comdr. 2/159 inf. bn., 1974-75; brigade comdr. 49th MP brigade, 1977-82; comdg. gen. 40th CA task force, 1979-82; comdg. gen. 40th mech. ifn. divsn., 1985-88; tchr. Alum Rock Sch. Dist., San Jose, Calif., 1952-56; asst. prin., 1956-58; prin., 1958-62; asst. supt., 1962-68; supt., 1968-87; comdr. Calif. Army Nat. Guard, Sacramento, 1987-89; spl. asst. chief nat. guard bur. Pentagon, Washington, 1990-2000; sr. mil. advisor Gov. of Calif. and dir. of office of mil. support, 2000—. Dir. Calif. Dept. Gen. Svcs., 2003—04; apptd. Com. Coun. on Mil. Support, 1985. Chmn. March of Dimes Walkathon, Santa Clara County, 1972. Decorated Disting. Svc. medal, Legion of Merit, Order of Calif. Mem. Nat. Guard Assn. U.S., Nat. Guard Assn. Calif. Republican. Roman Catholic. Home: 124 Gold Rock Ct Folsom CA 95630 E-mail: wjefferds@aol.com.

JEFFERIES, FRANCES (PAM JEFFERIES), elementary school educator; b. Jellico, Tenn., Aug. 6, 1949; d. John and Lucille (Taylor) Allen; m. Johnny Lynn Jefferies; children: Johnny Lynn Jr., Melanie Dawn. BS, Lincoln Meml. Coll., Harrogate, Tenn., 1991; MEd in Counseling and Guidance, Lincoln Meml. Coll., 1995. Elem. tchr. East LaFollette Elem. Sch., LaFollette, Tenn., 1991-95; sch. counselor K-8 East and West LaFollette, 1995—. Baptist. Home: 225 Fincastle Dr La Follette TN 37766-9200 Office Phone: 423-566-7325.

JEFFERIES, JOHN TREVOR, astrophysicist, observatory administrator; b. Kellerberrin, Australia, Apr. 2, 1925; came to U.S., 1956, naturalized, 1967; s. John and Vera (Healy) J.; m. Charmian Candy, Sept. 10, 1949; children: Stephen R., Helen C., Trevor R. MA, Cambridge (Eng.) U., 1949; DSc, U. Western Australia, Nedlands, 1962. Sr. research staff High Altitude Obs., Boulder, Colo., 1957-59, Sacramento Peak Obs., Sunspot, N.Mex., 1957-59; prof. adjoint U. Colo., Boulder, 1961-64; prof. physics and astronomy U. Hawaii, Honolulu, 1964-83, dir., Inst. Astronomy, 1967-83; dir. Nat. Optical Astronomy Obs., Tucson, 1983-87, astronomer, 1987-92. Cons. Nat. Bur. Stds., Boulder, 1960-62; disting. vis. scientist Jet Propulsion Lab., 1991-94. Author: (monograph) Spectral Line Formation, 1968; contbr. articles to profl. jours. Guggenheim fellow, 1970-71. Mem. Internat. Astron. Union, Am. Astron. Soc. Home: 1652 E Camino Cielo Tucson AZ 85718-1105 E-mail: jtjeff@comcast.net.

JEFFERIES, WILLIAM MCKENDREE, internist, educator; b. Richmond, Va., Oct. 1, 1915; s. Richard Henry and Mary Adeline (Harris) J.; m. Jeanne Telfair Mercer, Dec. 28, 1946 (dec. Dec., 1991); children: Richard Mercer, Scott McKendree, Colin Tucker, Leslie McLaurin. BA summa cum laude, Hampden Sydney Coll., 1935; MD, U. Va., 1940. Diplomate Am. Bd. Internal Medicine. Instr. in Math., Physics, Chemistry McGuires Univ. Sch., Richmond, Va., 1936; resident Mass. Gen. Hosp., Boston, 1940-42; flight surgeon San Antonio Aviation Cadet Ctr., 1942; post surgeon India China Div. Air Transport Command, 1943-45, divsn. med. inspector, 1945; rsch. fellow Am. Cancer Soc. Com. on Growth NRC Harvard Med. Sch., Boston, 1946-49; from instr. to asst. prof. medicine Case Western Reserve Med. Sch., Cleve., 1949-92; clin. prof. medicine U. Va. Sch. of Medicine, Charlottesville, 1993—. Mem. internship com. Univ. Hosps., Cleve., 1955-65; bd. dirs. Brush Found., 1966-67; mem. com. for human investigation Luth. Med. Ctr., Cleve., 1977-92; chmn. diabetes adv. com. Euclid Gen. Hosp., Cleve., 1979-82. Author: (med. books) Safe Uses of Cortisone, 1981, Safe Uses of Cortisol, 1996; contbr. articles to profl. jours., chpts. to books. Com. mem. Boy Scouts Am., Shaker Heights, Ohio, 1957-68; past chmn. coun. of deacons, bd. of ministry and fellowship Plymouth Ch. of Shaker Heights. Lt. col. med. corps U.S. Army (attached to air force) India Burma Theatre. Fellow ACP; mem. AAAS, SAR, AMA, N.Y. Acad. Scis., Albemarle County Med. Soc., Am. Thyroid Assn. (Van Meter award 1949), Clin. Immunology Soc., Endocrine Soc., Am. Fertility Soc., Am. Fedn. for Clin. Rsch., Ctrl. Soc. for Clin. Rsch., Friends of Nat. Libr. of Medicine, Am. Legion, Cheshire Cheese Club, Raven Soc., Phi Beta Kappa, Omicron Delta Kappa, Alpha Omega Alpha, Kappa Alpha, Phi Beta Pi. Avocations: golf, fly fishing, skiing. *Anything worth doing is worth doing to the best of your ability.*

JEFFERS, EVE JIHAN See EVE

JEFFERS, LAURIE TOOLEY, psychologist; b. Syracuse, NY, Feb. 21, 1968; d. John Gary and Yolanda Estelle Tooley; m. Troy Marlin Jeffers, Dec. 31, 1999; children: Tyler, Jonathan. BA, U. Rochester, 1990; MS, Rochester Inst. of Tech., 1993. Cert. nat. cert. sch. psychologist, sch. psychologist NY State. Sociotherapist Hillside Children's Agy., Rochester, NY, 1990—94; sch. psychologist Gates Chili Ctrl. Sch., Rochester, NY, 1993—2005. Volleyball coach Gates Chili Schs., Aqunas Inst., Rochester, NY, 1994—2004; softball coach Gates Chili Schs., Rochester, NY, 1994—2003. Mem.: Nat. Assn. of Sch. Psychologists, NY State Assn. of Sch. Psychologists. Avocations: softball, golf, skiing, beach volleyball. Office: Gates Chili Ctrl Sch Dist 910 Wegman Rd Spencerport NY 14559 Office Phone: 585-247-5050.

JEFFERS, MICHAEL BOGUE, lawyer; b. Wenatchee, Wash., July 10, 1940; s. Richard G. and Betty (Ball) J. BA, U. Wash., 1962, LLB, 1964; LLM in Taxation, NYU, 1970. Bar: Wash. 1964, N.Y. 1970, Calif. 1988. Coun. Dechert LLP, Newport Beach, 2002—. Sec. Thornburg Mortgage Inc. Mem. ABA, Calif. Bar Assn., Orange County Bar Assn., Wash. State Bar Assn., U. Wash. Alumni Assn. (pres. Greater N.Y. chpt. 1972-88), Pacific Club, Nat. Wild Turkey Fedn., Ballet Pacifica, Explorers Club, Phi Gamma Delta. Office: Dechert LLP 4675 MacArthur Ct Ste 1400 Newport Beach CA 92660 Office Phone: 949-442-6084. Business E-Mail: michael.jeffers@dechert.com.

JEFFERS, TRELLIE LEE JAMES, language educator, dean; b. Eatonton, Ga., Dec. 12, 1933; d. Charlie and Florence (Paschal) James; m. Lance F. Jeffers, May 26, 1959 (dec. July 1985); children: Valjeanne Jeffers Thompson, Sidonie Jeffers Jones, Honorée F. BA, Spelman Coll., 1955; MA, Calif. State U., 1970; DA, Atlanta U., 1986. Cert. adminstrn. and supervision. Tchr. high schs., Ga., Ill., N.C., Fla., 1955-66; asst. prof. Calif. State U., Long Beach, 1969-71; freelance writer Carolina Times, Durham, N.C., 1979-82; coord. Learning Resource Ctr., chmn. Resource Ctr. Clark Coll., Atlanta, 1983-85; prof. English Talladega (Ala.) Coll., 1985—, dean divsn. humananities and fine arts, 1998—. Vis. lectr. N.C. Ctrl. U., Durham, 1975-81, chair English component acad. skills, 1977-78. Author: poems; contbr. article to book. Fellow NEH, 1988, 93. Mem. Libr. Congress, Coll. Lang. Assn., So. Conf. on African Am. Studies (mem. adv. bd. 1992, 99), Ala. League Advancement Edn., George Moses Horton Soc., Pi Lamda Theta, Kappa Delta Pi. Democrat. Roman Catholic. Avocations: sewing, creative writing, cooking, singing, gardening. Home: 219 Edgewood Ave Talladega AL 35160-3021 Office: Talladega Coll 627 Battle St W Talladega AL 35160-2354 E-mail: tjeffers@talladega.edu.

JEFFERSON, CHARLES E., state representative; b. Waco, Tex., Mar. 31, 1945; children: Carl Edward, Curtis Lamar, Charles Jr. Student, Paul Quinn Coll. Mem. Ill. Ho. of Reps., 2001—. Past v.p. United Way; mem. Winnebago County Bd. With U.S. Army. Mem.: Rockford Sportsmen Golf Assn. (past pres.), Lions (past pres.), Masons. Democrat. Office: 281-S Stratton Office Bldg Springfield IL 62706 Address: EJ Zeke Giorgi Ctr 200 S Wyman # 304 Rockford IL 61107

JEFFERSON, DENISE, dance school director; b. Chgo. Studied ballet with, Edna L. McRae; BA, Wheaton Coll.; MA, NYU; Ph.D. (hon.), Wheaton College, 2000. Co-founder, co-dir. Chgo. Dance Ctr.; tchr. dance U. Ill., Chgo.; with Pearl Lang Dance Co.; mem. dance faculty Sch. Arts NYU, Alvin Ailey Dance Ctr., 1975—80; dir. Alvin Ailey Am. Dance Ctr. Scholarship program, 1980-84, Alvin Ailey Dance Sch., 1984—; v.p. Nat. Assoc. of Schools of Dance. Remedial writing tchr. Seek program Hunter Coll.; developed modern dance program Benedict Coll.; guest tchr. U.S., internat.; mem. internat. team dance profls. Dutch govt. to evaluate Dance acads. in Holland, 1990; adjudicator Arts Recognition, Talent Search Confederation Nat. de Danse, Fedn. Interprofl. de la danse, 1992. Mem. adv. bd. Profl. Children's Sch.; mem. adv. com. dance dept. U. Okla.; trustee Elisa Monte Dance Co. Grantee Nat. Endowment Arts and Humanities; scholar Martha Graham Sch. Contemporary Dance. Mem. Nat. Assn. Schs. Dance (bd. dirs. 1989-91, program evaluator, mem. commn. accredation), N.Y. State Coun. Arts (dance panel, appeal panel). Office: Alvin Ailey Am Dance Ctr 211 W 61st St Fl 3 New York NY 10023-7832

JEFFERSON, JAMES WALTER, psychiatrist, educator; b. Mineola, NY, Aug. 14, 1937; s. Thomas Hutton and Alice (Withers) J.; m. Susan Mary Cole, June 25, 1965; children: Lara, Shawn, James C. BS, Bucknell U., 1958; MD, U. Wis., 1964. Diplomate Am. Bd. Psychiatry and Neurology, Am. Bd. Internal Medicine. Asst. prof. psychiatry U. Wis. Med. Sch., Madison, 1974-78, assoc. prof., 1978-81, prof., 1981-92; disting. sr. scientist Dean Found. for Health, Rsch. and Edn., Madison, 1992-98; clin. prof. psychiatry U. Wis. Med. Sch., Madison, 1992—; disting. sr. scientist Madison Inst. Medicine, 1998—. Pres. Healthcare Tech. Sys., Madison, 1998—; co-dir. Lithium Info. Ctr., Madison, 1975—, Obsessive Compulsive Info. Ctr., Madison, 1990—; dir. Ctr. Affective Disorders, Madison, 1983-92. Co-author: Neuropsychiatric Features of Medical Disorders, 1981, Lithium Encyclopedia for Clinical Practice, 1983, 2nd edit., 1987, Depression and Its Treatment, 1984, 2nd edit., 1992, Anxiety and Its Treatment, 1986, Handbook of Medical Psychiatry, 1996. Served to maj. U.S. Army, 1968-71. Fellow ACP, Am. Psychiat. Assn.; mem. Collegium Internat. Neuropsychopharmacologium, Am. Soc. Clin. Psychopharmacology (nat. bd. trustees 1996—). Avocations: bicycling, travel. Office: Madison Inst Medicine 7617 Mineral Point Rd Madison WI 53717-1623 Office Phone: 608-827-2451. Business E-Mail: jjefferson@healthtechsys.com.

JEFFERSON, JONATHAN KENNETH, dean; BS in Math., Morehouse Coll., 1982; M in Engring., Cornell U., 1983. Comprehensive cert. coach Ga., cert. behavioral co ns. Ga., behavioral analyst in bus. perspectives Ga., leadership coach Ga. Ptnr. CSC Cons. Sys., Bridgewater, NJ, 1992—94; exec. dir. BellSouth Corp., Atlanta, 1994—96; ptnr. Computer Scis. Corp., Atlanta, 1996—97; v.p. A.T. Kearney, Atlanta, 1997—2004; dean, sch. bus. adminstrn. Clark Atlanta U., 2004—. Internat. treas. Ch. of Our Lord Jesus Christ, NYC. Featured in Article, Black Enterprise Mag., 2002. Mem.: Christian Coaches Network (assoc.), Internat. Coaching Fedn. (assoc.), Beta Kappa Chi, Pi Mu Epsilon. Office: Clark Atlanta Univ Sch Bus 223 James P Brawley Dr Atlanta GA 30314

JEFFERSON, JOSEPH MURRAY, banker; b. Heilwood, Pa., July 9, 1919; s. Ernest Maloy and Edith (Morris) J.; m. Mary Margaret Kerr, May 27, 1943 (dec. Mar. 1991); children: James Murray, Sharon Lee; m. Mary Jo Greenly, Dec. 11, 1999; 1 stepchild, Traci Romedy. BS, Waynesburg (Pa.) Coll., 1943; postgrad., Ind. U., 1949—51, Dartmouth Coll., 1963—64. Laborer Buckeye Coal Co., Nemacolin, Pa., 1936-41; sec. First Fed. S&L Assn., Waynesburg, Pa., 1945-52; exec. v.p., CEO Provident Fed. S&L Assn., Pitts., 1953-61; v.p. First Fed. S&L Assn. of Pitts., 1961-68; pres., CEO Washington (Pa.) Fed. Savs. Bank, 1968-86, dir. emeritus, 1995—; dir., vice chmn. Fed. Home Loan Bank of Pitts., 1986-91. Bd. dirs. Pa. Indsl. Devel. Agy., Harrisburg, 1963-64, Pa. Econ. League, Harrisburg, 1985-95, YMCA, Washington, 1968-85. With U.S. Army Aircorps, 1941-42, lt. USN, SubPac, 1943-46. Named to Pa. Cmty. Bankers Hall of Fame, 1992. Mem. U.S. S&L League (dir. exec. com. 1968-71), Pa. S&L League (pres. 1963-64), Masons (32 deg.), Lions (Melvin Jones fellow). Avocations: golf, public speaking. Home: 320 Olympia St Pittsburgh PA 15211-1367

JEFFERSON, RALPH HARVEY, international affairs consultant; b. Rochester, N.Y., Aug. 6, 1927; s. Charles Frederic and Mabel Florence (Thomas) J.; m. Jenny Chaapel Clark, Oct. 29, 1960; children: Edward Clark, Jenny Chaapel, Alexandra Victoria. BA, Yale U., 1949; LLB, Harvard U., 1952; cert., Inst. d'Etudes Politiques, Paris, 1956. Bar: N.Y. 1952. Treas. Harvard Legal Aid Bur., 1950-52; atty. Root, Ballantine, Harlan, Bushby and Palmer, N.Y.C., 1952-55; legal adviser to def. adviser U.S. Mission to NATO, Paris, 1960-63; atty. Office of Asst. Gen. Counsel, Office Sec. of Def., Washington, 1957-60, 63-66; acting spl. adviser for prisoner of war affairs Office of Asst. Sec. Def., Washington, 1970-71, dep. dir. in Europe-NATO Directorate, 1967-70, 72-78; civil dep. comdt., dir. studies NATO Def. Coll., Rome, 1978-82; dir. for NATO policy Office Asst. Sec. Def., Washington, 1982-88; sr. rsch. fellow Nat. Def. U., Washington, 1988-89; internat. affairs cons. Washington, 1994—. Bd. dirs. Chol Chol Found. for Human Devel. With USN. Mem.: Diplomatic and Consular Officers Ret. (assoc.). Avocations: piano, tennis, sailing. Home and Office: 507 Epping Forest Rd Annapolis MD 21401-6562 E-mail: rhjefferson@comcast.net.

JEFFERSON, RICHARD, professional basketball player; b. LA, June 21, 1980; Grad., U. Arizona, 2001. Player NJ Nets, 2001—. Mem. USA Basketball Men's Sr. Nat. Team, 2003, US Olympic Basketball Team, Athens, Greece, 2004. Office: NJ Nets 390 Murray Hill Pkwy East Rutherford NJ 07073

JEFFERSON, SANDRA TRAYLOR, choreographer; b. Tarboro, N.C., Feb. 28, 1942; d. Charles Labon and Doris Vivian (Parker) Traylor; m. Milton Franklin Jefferson, July 2, 1960; children: Mark Franklin, Todd Christopher. Student, Parks Sch. Dance, Petersburg, Va., 1947-58, Sch. of the Richmond (Va.) Ballet, 1958-60; diploma, Julia Mildred Harper Sch. Dance, Richmond, 1960; studied with Robert David Brown, Sterling, Va., 1978-80. Soloist Ballet Impromptu, Richmond, 1958-60; freelance dance instr. Chantilly, Va., 1968-70; ballet coach Artistic Skating Club of Sterling, 1980; founder, dir. Ballet for Skaters, Manassas, Va., 1980-89; artistic dir., cons. in choreography No. Va. Artistic Skating Club, Manassas, 1986-89. Artistic dir. Skating Club of Manassas, 1989; founder, dir. Ballet for Skaters, Seabrook, Md., 1989-94; choreographer, ballet coach Nat. Capitol Dance and Figure Club, Seabrook and Washington, 1989-94; founder, dir. Ballet for Figure Skaters, Sterling, Va., 1993-94; students include nat. medalists in the U.S. and Can. and mems. Can. World Team, U.S. Olympic Sports Festival Team; freelance choreographer, ballet coach, Sterling, 1993—. Developer Brosano Technique Vocabulary of Movement, 1986, Free Form Ballet, 1993, co-developer (artistic skating technique) Brosano Technique, 1981. Social dir. Jaycee-ettes, Winchester, Va., 1963—67. Recipient Achievement award Jaycee-ettes, 1963, 64, 65, 66, 67, U.S. S.E. Soc. Roller Skating Tchrs. Am. award, 1988, World Decoration of Excellence award Am. Biog. Inst., 1989. Mem.: Profl. Dance Tchrs. Assn. United Methodist. Avocations: art, music. Home and Office: 507 S Maple Ct Sterling VA 20164-2710

JEFFERSON, THOMAS EDWARD, JR., military officer; b. Cleve., Mar. 23, 1963; s. Thomas Edward Jefferson, Sr. and Frances Louise Hurdle; m. Bridget Lashon Ward, Dec. 13, 2003; children: Tiarra, Bijan, Haila. BA, Va. State U., 1984; postgrad., Park Coll., Columbus, Ohio, 2003—05. Enlisted USMC, advanced through grades to master sgt., 1984; sta. comdr. Recruiting Sub Sta. E. Columbus, 1994—96, Recruiting Sub Sta. N. Columbus, 1996—98, Recruiting Sub Sta. S. Columbus, 2002—04; mil. entry processing sta. head marine liaison Recruiting Sta., Cin., 1998—99, Gahanna, Ohio, 2004—, asst. recruiting instr. Charleston, W.Va., 1999—2002. Recruiter Recruiting Sub Sta. W. Columbus, 1992—94. Mem. editl. com. Marine Corps Opportunity Book, 1996 (Commdg. Gen. cert. of Commendation). Named Recruiter of the Yr., Recruiting Sta. Cin., 1992, 1993, Sta. Comdr. of the Yr., 1994, 1997, Recruiting Sta. Charleston, 2002. Office: USMC MEPS Columbus 775 Taylor Rd Rm 118 Gahanna OH 43230

JEFFERSON, WALLACE B., state supreme court justice; s. William and Joyce Jefferson; m. Rhonda Jefferson; 3 children. BA in Political Philosophy, 1985, JD U. Tex., 1988. Cert.: Tex. Bd. Legal Specialization (in civil appellate law). With Groce, Locke & Hebdon, San Antonio, 1988—91; ptnr. Crofts, Callaway & Jefferson, San Antonio, 1991—2001; justice Tex. Supreme Ct., Austin, 2001—04, chief justice, 2004—. Mem. Tex. Supreme Ct. Advisory Com., Tex. State Commn. on Jud. Conduct; chair host com. Fifth Circuit Jud. Conference, 2000. Mem. bd. dirs. San Antonio Pub. Libr. Found., Alamo Area Big Bros./Big Sisters.; mem. edn. com. San Antonio Area Found. Named 40 Under 40 Rising Star, San Antonio Bus. Jour., 1996, Texas Lawyer, 2001, Outstanding Young Lawyer, San Antonio Young Lawyers Assn., 1997. Mem.: William S. Sessions Am. Inns of Ct. (past pres.), San Antonio Bar Assn. (pres. 1998—99, President's award 2000). Office: 201 W 14th St Austin TX 78701 also: PO Box 12248 Austin TX 78711

JEFFERSON, WILLIAM J. (JEFF JEFFERSON), congressman; b. Lake Providence, La., Mar. 14, 1947; BA, Southern Univ., 1969; JD, Harvard U., 1972; LLM, Georgetown U., 1996. U.S. Fed. Dist. Ct. law clerk; ptnr. Jefferson, Bryan and Gray; legis. asst. to Sen. Johnston; state sen., 1981-90; mem. U.S. Congress from 2nd dist. La., 1991—. Mem. ways and means com., Dem. steering com., subcoms. select revenue and trade. Served AUS, Judge Advocate General Corps. Democrat. Office: US Ho of Reps 240 Cannon House Ofc Bldg Washington DC 20515-1802*

JEFFERY, GEOFFREY MARRON, medical parasitologist; b. Dundee, N.Y., May 13, 1919; s. Joseph Ewart and Augusta (Knapp) J.; m. Jane Wicker, Aug. 16, 1941; children: Janet A. Harrison, Thomas W., Sarah V. Houghton, Susan E. Tosh. AB, Hobart Coll., 1940; MA, Syracuse U., 1942; ScD, Johns Hopkins U., 1944; MPH, Yale U., 1961. Biol. aide health and safety dept. TVA, 1944; commd. officer USPHS, 1944, scientist dir., 1960; tech. aid, cons. malaria control in war areas TVA, 1944-45; assigned divsn. lab. svcs. Communicable Disease Ctr., 1945-46, charge br. lab. Sch. Tropical Medicine San Juan, P.R., 1946-47; asst. prof. biology U. Bridgeport, Conn., 1947-48; charge Malaria Rsch. Lab., NIH, Milledgeville, Ga., 1948-54; mem. staff Lab. Tropical Diseases-Lab. Parasite Chemotherapy, NIAID, NIH, Columbia, S.C., 1954-63, head sect. epidemiology, 1961-63; asst. chief Lab. Parasite Chemotherapy, NIAID, NIH, Bethesda, 1963-66, acting chief, 1966, chief, 1967-69, C.Am. Malaria Rsch. Sta., San Salvador, El Salvador, 1969-74; asst. dir. Bur. Tropical Diseases, Ctr. Disease Control, Atlanta, 1974-75; dir. vector biology and control div. Bur. Tropical Diseases, 1975-81; asst. dir. divsn. parasitic diseases Ctr. for Infectious Diseases, Ctrs. for Disease Control, 1982-84. Mem. expert adv. panel on malaria WHO, 1963—99; assoc. mem. commn. malaria Armed Forces Epidemiol. Bd., 1965-69, mem., 1969-73; Del. Internat. Congress Tropical Medicine and Malaria, Lisbon, 1958, Rio de Janeiro, 1963, Teheran, Iran, 1968; Del. Internat. Congress Parasitology, Rome, Italy, 1964, Washington, 1969; Del. Internat. Conf. on Protozoology, London, 1965, Latin Am. Congress Parasitology, Medellin, Colombia, 1973; mem. sci. group on chemotherapy of malaria WHO, Geneva, 1967, mem. sci. group on parasitology, Teheran, 1968; cons. on status of malaria in Africa AID, 1979; mem. sci. working group on applied field rsch. in malaria WHO, Geneva, 1979, mem. steering com., 1981-86; cons. on malaria U.S.-China Health Agreement, 1980; del. Asia and Pacific Conf. on Malaria, Honolulu, 1985; temp. advisor meetings WHO, Kuala Lumpur, 1981, Albuquerque, 1982, Nairobi, 1983, Bangkok, 1984; invited participant concerted action 1st plenary meeting on malaria modelling European Union, Tuebingen, Germany, 1998. Contbr. numerous articles to sci. jours. tropical medicine and parasitology. Recipient Pub. Health Svc. Commendation medal, 1966, Dept. Army cert. of appreciation patriotic civilian svc., 1973 Fellow Royal Soc. Tropical Medicine (local sec. 1984-89); mem. Am. Soc. Tropical Medicine and Hygiene (sec.-treas. 1961-67, v.p. 1971, pres. 1975, Bailey K. Ashford award 1959), Am. Soc. Parasitologists, Assn. Southea. Biologists (editor bull. 1959-60, exec. com. 1962-66), Tropical Medicine Assn. Washington, Southea. Soc. Parasitologists, S.C. Acad. Sci. (mem. council 1960, 62, Jefferson award 1952, 56, 60), Commd. Officers Assn. USPHS, Sigma Xi, Kappa Sigma. Presbyterian. Home: 1085 Blackshear Dr Apt B Decatur GA 30033-2612 Office: Center Disease Control Atlanta GA 30333 Personal E-mail: gjeffery2@comcast.net.

JEFFERY, REUBEN, III, federal agency administrator; BA, Yale U., 1975; MBA, JD, Stanford U., 1981. Atty. Davis, Polk & Wardwell LLP; ptnr., mng. dir. Goldman Sachs; spl. adv. to the pres. for lower Manhattan Develop. Exec. Office of the Pres.; rep. and exec. dir., Coalition Provisional Authority US Dept. Defense, 2003—04; spl. asst. to pres., sr. dir. internat. economic affairs, Nat. Security Coun. Exec. Office of Pres., 2004—05; commr., chmn. Commodity Futures Trading Commn., 2005—. Office: Commodity Futures Trading Commn Three Lafayette Ctr 1155 21st St NW Rm 9060 Washington DC 20581-0001 Office Phone: 202-418-5050. Office Fax: 202-418-5533.

JEFFERY, WILLIAM RICHARD, developmental biology educator, researcher; b. Chgo., June 9, 1944; s. William and Marjorie (Gross) J. BS, U. Ill., Chgo., 1967; PhD, U. Iowa, 1971. Rsch. assoc. U. Wis., Madison, 1971-72, Sch. Medicine, Tufts U., Boston, 1972-74; asst. prof. biophysics U. Houston, 1974-77; asst. prof. zoology U. Tex., Austin, 1977-80, assoc. prof., 1980-85, prof., 1985-87, J.F. Miescher Regents prof., 1987-90; prof. zoology U. Calif., Davis, 1990-93, prof. molecular and cellular biology, 1993-96; prof., head biology Pa. State U., University Park, 1997-99; prof., chair biology U. Md., College Park, 1999—2004. Co-dir. embryology course Marine Biology Lab., Woods Hole, Mass., 1983-87, active, 1975—. Mem. editl. bd. Devel., 1987-98, Jour. Exptl. Zoology, 1989—, Seminars in Devel. Biology, 1990-96, Seminars in Cell and Devel. Biology, 1997—, Biol. Bull., 1985-90, Cell Motility and the Cytoskeleton, 1985-86, Internat. Jour. Devel. Biology, 1989-2002, Animal Biology, 1991—, Internat. Rev. of Cytology, 1999—, Molecular Biol. Evolution, 2000—, Internat. Jour. Devel. Biology, 2002-; N.Am. editor Zygote, 1993-96 Fellow AAAS; mem. Am. Soc. Zoologists (divsn. chmn. 1988-90, Outstanding Svc. award 1990), Soc. Devel. Biologists (trustee 1987-89, 1995-97, pres. 1995-96), Am. Soc. Cell Biology, Sigma Xi. Home: 1530 Thursto Rd Dickerson MD 20842 Office: Univ Md Dept Biology 1200 Bio Psych Bldg College Park MD 20742-0001 E-mail: Jeffery@umd.edu.

JEFFORDS, JAMES MERRILL, senator; b. Rutland, Vt., May 11, 1934; s. Olin Merrill and Marion (Hausman) J.; m. Elizabeth Daley; children: Leonard Olin, Laura Louise. BS, Yale U., 1956; LLB, Harvard U., 1962. Bar: Vt. 1962. Law clk. to Judge Ernest Gibson Vt. Dist., 1962; ptnr. Bishop, Crowley & Jeffords, Rutland, 1963-66, Kenney, Carbine & Jeffords, Rutland, 1966-69; atty. gen. State of Vt., 1969-72; ptnr. George E. Rice, Jr. and James M. Jeffords, 1973-74; mem. 94th -100th Congresses from Vt.; mem. agr. com., ranking minority mem. edn. and labor com., chmn. environ. study conf., 1978-79; a founder Congl. solar coalition, mem. Congl. tourism caucus, mem. Nat. Commn. on Employment and Unemployment Stats., 1979-89; U.S. Senator from Vt., 1989—; ranking mem. environ. and pub. works, health, edn., labor and pensions com., vet. affairs com., fin. com. Mem. spl. com. on aging; mem. New Eng. Congl. Caucus, N.E.-Midwest Coalition; town agt. Shrewsbury, 1964-68, zoning adminstr., 1966-68; mem. Jud. Selection Bd., 1967-68; chmn. Hwy. Dept. Investigating Com., 1968; mem. Vt. Senate, 1967-68. With USNR, 1956-59; capt. Res. (ret.). Mem. ABA, Vt. Bar Assn., Rutland County Bar Assn., Am. Judicature Soc. (dir. 1973-76), VFW, Lions, Elks. Independent. Conglist.(Trustee). Office: US Senate 413 Dirksen Senate Ofc Bldg Washington DC 20510-4503 Office Phone: 202-224-5141. E-mail: vermont@jeffords.senate.gov.*

JEFFRESS, WILLIAM H., JR., lawyer; b. Birmingham, Ala., July 17, 1945; s. William H. and Dorothy (Grubbs) J.; m. Judith Ray Jones; children: Amy, Jonathan, William. BA, Washington & Lee U., 1967; LLB, Yale U., 1970. Bar: D.C. 1971, U.S. Dist. Ct. D.C., U.S. Ct. Appeals 5th Cir., U.S. Supreme Ct. 1975. Law clk. to Judge Gerhard A. Gesell U.S. Dist. Ct. D.C., Washington, 1970-71; law clk. to Justice Potter Stewart U.S. Supreme Ct., Washington, 1971-72; atty. Miller, Cassidy, Larroca & Lewin, Washington, 1972—2000; ptnr. litigation dept. & mem. exec. com. Baker Botts LLP, Washington, 2000—. Chmn. adv. bd. Am. Criminal Law Review, 1984-86.

Editor in chief, Yale Law Jour.; vice-chmn. editorial bd. Criminal Justice Mag., 1986—. Named one of 75 Best Lawyers in Washington, Washingtonian survey mag., 2002. Fellow Am. Coll. Trial Lawyers, Am. Bar Found.; mem. ABA (past chmn. Criminal Justice Standards Com.). Democrat. Office: Baker Botts LLP The Warner 1299 Pennsylvania Ave NW Washington DC 20004-2400 Office Phone: 202-639-7751. Office Fax: 202-585-1087. Business E-Mail: william.jefress@bakerbotts.com.

JEFFREY, DAVID KENNETH, dean, educator; b. Englewood, N.J. s. Kenneth Milton and Alice (Black) Jeffrey; m. Anne Elizabeth Badgett, Aug. 18, 1961; m. Rhoda Settle (div.); children: David, Elizabeth; m. Martha Langley (div.); children: Robert, Scott, David. BA, Hobart Coll., 1963; MA, U. Va., 1965; PhD, U. N.C., 1972. Policeman Richmond (Va.) City, 1963—64; reporter Richmond (Va.) News Leader, 1964; instr. English U. N.C., Greensboro, NC, 1965—67; asst. prof. Auburn (Ala.) U., 1970—74, assoc. prof., 1974—83; prof. English, U. La., Monroe, 1983—90, head dept. English, 1990—95, assoc. dean, 1995—2004; interim dean James Madison U., Harrisonburg, Va., 2004—. Avocation: fly fishing. Office: James Madison Univ 800 Main St Harrisonburg VA 22807 Office Phone: 540-568-7044.

JEFFREY, JUDY, school system administrator; BA, U. of No. Iowa, 1963; MA, Creighton U., 1981. With Council Bluffs Cmty. Sch. Dist.; adminstr. Early Childhood, Elementary and Secondary Edn. div. Iowa Dept. Edn., 1996—, dir. edn., 2004—. Tchr. Cedar Falls and Goldfield dists., Iowa; instr. Creighton U.; pres. Coun. of Chief State Sch. Officers Dep. Commn., 2001—03, bd. dirs. Office: Iowa Dept Edn Grimes State Office Bldg Des Moines IA 50319-0146 Office Phone: 515-281-5294. Office Fax: 515-242-5988.*

JEFFREY, ROBERT GEORGE, JR., manufacturing executive; b. Bronx, N.Y., Oct. 2, 1933; s. Robert George and Ethel Ruth (Rohrbeck) J.; m. Linda L. Nardone; children: Diana, Christine, Jennifer, Joseph. BBA, Pace U., 1959; MBA, NYU, 1966. CPA, N.Y., N.J. Sr. acct. Deloitte & Touche, N.Y.C., 1959-65; asst. mgr. corp. acctg. Union Camp Corp., Wayne, N.J., 1965-66, asst. to comptr., 1966-69, mgr. corp. acctg., 1969-70, dir. fin. planning, 1970-72, corp. comptr., 1972-79; exec. v.p. Huntington Mgmt. Corp., 1980-82; v.p. fin. Rudco Industries Inc., 1982-84, sr. v.p., 1984-87; ptnr. R.G. Jeffrey, CPA, Wayne, 1987—. Adj. prof. taxation William Paterson U., 1993—; bd. dirs. The Corby Group. Trustee Wayne Twp. Bd. Edn., 1975-78. Served with USAF, 1952-56. Mem. AICPA, N.Y. State Soc. CPAs, N.J. Soc. CPAs (bd. dirs. Passaic County chpt.), Fin. Execs. Inst. Home: 28 Pelham Rd Wayne NJ 07470-2873 Office: 61 Berdan Ave Wayne NJ 07470-3229 Office Phone: 973-628-0022.

JEFFREY, SHERI, lawyer; BS cum laude, Loyola Marymount U., 1982, JD, 1985; LLM, NYU, 1986. Bar: Calif. 1985. Ptnr. Corp. & Fin. Dept., mem. Entertainment Group Kaye Scholer LLP, LA. Mem.: State Bar Calif. Office: Kaye Scholer LLP Ste 1700 1999 Ave of the Stars Los Angeles CA 90067 Office Phone: 310-788-1270. E-mail: sjeffrey@kayescholer.com.

JEFFREY, THERBER KENT, music educator; s. Marvin Kent and Linda Richardson Therber; m. Dawn Monuwella Therber, Dec. 29, 2001. MusB, U. Tenn., Knoxville, 1988. Band dir. Red band H.S. Hamilton County Dept. Edn., Chattanooga, 1999—2002; band dir. Armuchee H.S. Floyd County Ga. Dept. Edn., Rome, Ga., 2002. Bass trombonist Jericho Brass, Rome, 2000. Recipient Dir.'s award, performing arts consultants, Chgo., 2002. Mem.: Ga. Music Educator's Assn. (assoc.), Tenn. Music Edn. Assn. (assoc.), Phi Mu Alpha Sinonia (assoc.). Baptist. Avocations: gardening, music performance. Office: Armuchee HS 4203 Martha Berry Hwy NW Rome GA 37379 E-mail: bassbene1@att.net.

JEFFREY, WILLIAM ALAN, federal agency administrator, physicist; b. Arlington Heights, Ill., Jan. 13, 1960; s. Lynn Ann Engelking Jeffrey. BSc, MIT, 1982; MA, Harvard U., 1984, PhD, 1988. Rsch. analyst Strategic Planning Assocs., Washington, 1982-83; rsch. staff mem. Inst. for Def. Analyses, Alexandria, Va., 1988-91; sr. rsch. scientist Grumman Aerospace, Herndon, Va.; dep. dir. Advanced Tech. Office, chief scientist Tactical Tech. Office, Def. Advanced Rsch. Projects Agy. US Dept. Def., asst. dep. for tech. Def. Airborne Reconnaissance Office; sr. dir. for homeland & nat. security, asst. dir. for space & aeronatics Office Sci. & Tech. The White House, Washington; dir. Nat. Inst. Standards & Tech, US Dept. Commerce, Gaithersburg, Md., 2005—. Tutor Boston Dept. Edn., 1984, Alexandria Dept. Edn., 1989—. Contbr. articles to profl. jours. Danforth Ct. Excellence in teaching award, 1985, Am. Astron. Soc. Solar Physics studentship, Harvard Grad. Sch. Arts and Sciences award, 1985; NASA fellow, 1985, 86, 87. Mem. Am. Phys. Soc., Am. Astron. Soc., Sigma Xi, Sigma Pi Sigma. Office: Nat Inst Standards & Tech 100 Bureau Dr Stop 1000 Gaithersburg MD 20899 E-mail: william.jeffrey@nist.gov.*

JEFFREYS, ALBERT LEONIDAS, lawyer; b. Chase City, Va. m. Lee H. Hickson. AB in History and Govt., Fla. So. Coll.; JD, So. Meth. U., 1969. Bar: Tex. 1971. Tech. writer Collins Radio, Dallas, 1959-60; contract negotiator LTV Electro Systems, Dallas, 1960-71; corp. atty., asst. sec. Earth Resources Co., Dallas, 1971-73; gen. counsel, asst. sec. Liquid Paper Corp., Dallas, 1973-80; gen. counsel, dir. of contracts Electrospace Systems, Inc., Richardson, Tex., 1980-81; pvt. practice Richardson and Dallas, 1981—; gen. counsel Ratheal Cos., Garland, Tex., 1991-92; referral counsel to office of econ. devel. City of Dallas, 1999—2003. Sgt. U.S. Army. Mem. ABA, Tex. Bar Assn., Dallas Bar Assn. Home: 328 Huffhines St Richardson TX 75081-4113 E-mail: jstrpt@aol.com.

JEFFREYS, ARCELIA TAYLOR, education educator; b. Oxford, NC, Dec. 10, 1944; d. Irene Taylor Allen. BS, NC Ctrl. U., 1968, MS, 1970; EdD, U. NC, Greensboro, 1989. Instr., advisor Shaw U., Raleigh, NC, 1970—72; tchr., coach Wake County Pub. Schs., Raleigh, NC, 1972—83; supr. student tchrs. NC Ctrl. U., Durham, 1989—. Cons. Durham Pub. Sch. Tchrs., 1995—. Chmn. fundraising ADA, Raleigh, NC, 1995—96. Fellow U. Coll. fellow, 2003; grantee Minorities Presence grantee, U. NC, 1984—87. Mem.: NCAHPERD (assoc.; com. mem. 2002—). Baptist. Avocations: golf, travel. Home: 1137 Shonele Lane Stem NC 27581 Office: North Carolina Central University 1801 Fayetteville Street Durham NC 27707-3129 Personal E-mail: ajeffreys16@aol.com. E-mail: ajeffrey@wpo.nccu.edu.

JEFFREYS, ELYSTAN GEOFFREY, petroleum engineer, consultant; b. Apr. 26, 1926; s. Geoffrey and Georgene Frances Theodora (Littell) J.; m. Pat Rumage, May 1, 1946 (div.); children: Jeri Lynn, David Powell; m. Peggi Villar, Feb. 28, 1975 (div. 2000); m. Sandra H. Garthwait, Aug. 5, 2002. Geol. Engr., Colo. Sch. Mines, 1951, grad. in Econ. Evaluation and Investment Decision Methods, 1972, grad. in Econ. Evaluation and Investment Decision Methods, 1991. Registered profl. engr., Miss., land surveyor, Miss, profl. geologist, Ala.; cert. sr. appraiser of oil and gas properties Am. Soc. Appraisers, 1993. Ptnr. G. Jeffreys & Son, 1951-53, Jeffreys & Launius, 1953-55; pvt. practice petroleum exploration, 1954-77; exploration mgr. Arrowhead Exploration Co., Mobile and Brewton, Ala., 1977-83; cons. petroleum geologist and appraiser, 1984—. Pres., chmn. bd. dirs., CEO Major Oil Co., Jackson, Miss., 1961—84, v.p., 1984—98, The Jeffreys Co., Inc., Mobile, 1976—96, pres., CEO, 1996—2001; asst. mgr. Kee Energy Co., LLC, 1996—2005. Vestryman Trinity Episcopal Ch., Mobile, 1989-92, 94-96, sr. warden, 1991-92; bd. trustees The Appraisal Found., 1993-94. With 3d U.S. Army, 1944-46, ETO. Mem. Miss. Geol. Soc., Ala. Geol. Soc., New Orleans Geol. Soc. Am. Assn. Petroleum Geologists (50 Yr. Membership 2001), Fla. Ind. Petroleum Prodrs. Assn., Gulf Coast Assn. Geol. Socs. (treas. 1960, Cert. of Svc. 1971), Miss. Assn. Petroleum Landmen, Assn. Petroleum Landmen of Ala., Masons (32 degree), Pi Kappa Alpha. Address: 115 Fairway Dr Daphne AL 36526-7401 Office Phone: 251-621-1850. Personal E-mail: EGJeffreys@aol.com.

JEFFREYS, JOE E., theater educator, writer; s. Edward Osmond and Nancy Wall Jeffreys. BA in English, Wake Forest U., 1986; MFA in Dramaturgy, Stony Brook U., 1989; PhD in Performance Studies, NYU, 1996. Adj. prof. Stony Brook U., NY, 1996—, NYU, N.Y.C., 2000—. Judge Lambda Lit. Awards, 1998, N.Y. Internat. Fringe Theatre Festival, N.Y.C., 2000—. Contbg. author: Art, Glitter & Glitz, 2004. Hedonist.

JEFFRIES, JOHN CALVIN, JR., dean, law educator; b. 1948; BA, Yale U., 1970; JD, U. Va., 1973. Bar: Va. 1973, D.C. 1974. Law clk. to Hon. Justice Powell U.S. Supreme Ct., 1973-74; asst. prof. U. Va., Charlottesville, 1975-79, assoc. prof., 1979-81, prof. law, 1981—, Emerson Spies prof., 1986—, acad. assoc. dean, 1994—99, Arnold H. Leon prof. law, dean Sch. Law, 2001—. Prof. FBI Acad., Quantico, Va., 1976—; vis. asst. prof. Stanford U., fall 1977; vis. prof. Yale U., 1981-82, So. Calif. U., fall 1986, 89, 93; John V. Ray rsch. prof. 1989-1991; Horace W. Goldsmith rsch. prof. 1992-1995; William L. Matheson and Robert M. Morgenthau disting. prof. 1996-2001. Author: Justice Lewis F. Powell, Jr.: A Biography, 1994, (with Low) Model Penal Code and Commentaries, 3 vols., 1980, (with Karlan, Low and Rutherglen) Civil Rights Actions: Enforcing the Constitution, 2000, Federal Courts and the Law of Federal-State Relations, 4th edit., 1998, (with Low and Bonnie) Cases and Materials on Criminal Law, 1982, 2d edit., 1986; editor-in-chief Va. Law Rev. Mem. Am. Law Inst., Va. State Bar (com. for oversight of bar activities). Office: U Va Sch Law Charlottesville VA 22903 Office Phone: 434-924-7343. Business E-Mail: jcj3w@virginia.edu.*

JEFFRIES, MICHAEL S., apparel executive; b. Elk City, Okla., July 13, 1944; m. Susan Jeffries; 1 child, Andrew. BA in Econs., Claremont McKenna Coll., 1966; MBA, Columbia U., 1968. With Abraham and Straus, 1968; exec. v.p. merchandising Bullock's, 1980-83; pres., CEO Alcott & Andrews, 1983-89; exec. v.p. merchandising Paul Harris, 1990-92; pres., CEO Abercrombie & Fitch Co., Ohio, 1992—, chmn., 1998—. Office: Abercrombie & Fitch Co 6301 Fitch Path New Albany OH 43054*

JEFFRIES, ROBERT JOSEPH, retired engineer, information technology executive, educator; b. Norwalk, Conn., Jan. 6, 1923; s. Charles William and Christine (Jacobsen) J.; m. Anna Darling Cumming, Oct. 13, 1945; children: Christine Darling, Bruce Cumming. BS, U. Conn., 1944, MS, 1946; DEng, Johns Hopkins U., 1948. Engr. NACA, 1944-46; instr. Johns Hopkins U., 1946-48; research assoc. N.C. State Coll., 1948-49; assoc. prof. Mich. State U., 1949-54; tech. planning adviser Schlumberger Instrument Co., 1954-55; asst. to pres. Daystrom, Inc., 1955-57; pres., founder Data-Control System, Inc., 1957-66, chmn. bd., 1966-68; prof. U. Bridgeport, Conn., 1968-75, ret.; founder, dir. Ednl. & Tech. Cons., Inc., 1953-57. V.p., dir. TJB Resources Inc., 1972-88; dir. emeritus Evergreen Fund Family; v.p., founder Found. Instrumentation Edn. and Rsch., 1958-66; fellow-in-residence Edgar Cayce Found., Virginia Beach, Va., 1981-88; prof. Atlantic U., 1986-90. Editor Jour. Instrument Soc. Am., 1953-54; contbr. tech. papers. Trustee Am. Unitarian Assn., Cmty. Ch. Coll., Sun City Ctr., Tampa Bay Cmty. Found., SCC coun. Recipient Disting. Alumnus award U. Conn., Disting. Alumnus award John Hopkins U. Fellow NRC; mem. Instrument Soc. Am. (pres. 1957-58), Assn. Rsch. and Enlightenment (trustee), Conn. Commn. for Higher Edn. (vice chmn.), U. Conn. Enginrg. Alumni Assn. (pres. 1969-71), Sigma Xi, Tau Beta Pi, Eta Kappa Nu. Home: 1010 American Eagle Blvd Apt 502 Sun City Center FL 33573-5284 E-mail: rjjeff@tampabay.rr.com.

JEFFRIES, RUSSELL MORDEN, communications company official; b. Carmel, Calif., July 15, 1935; s. Herman M. and Louise (Morden) J.; m. Barbara Jean Borcovich, Nov. 24, 1962; 1 child, Lynne Louise. AA, Hartnell Coll., 1971. Sr. communications technician AT&T, Salinas, Calif., 1955-91. Mayor City of Salinas, 1987-91. Pres. El Gabilan Sch. PTA, Salinas, 1971-74, Salinas Valley Council PTA, 1975-76; mem. Salinas City Sch. Bd., 1975-81; mem. Salinas City Council, 1981-87; bd. dirs. Community Hosp. Salinas Found., 1987—, Salinas-Kushikino Sister City, 1987—, pres. 1992-93, John Steinbeck Ctr. Found., 1987-96, Food Bank for Monterey County, 1992-96; hon. bd. dirs. Monterey Film Festival, 1987-96, Calif. Rodeo Assn., 1987; mem. ctrl. bd. Calif. Regional Water Quality, 1992—; commr. Moss Landing Harbor, 1996. Recipient hon. service award PTA, Salinas, 1976; cert. of appreciation Calif. Dept. Edn., 1980, Salinas City Sch. Dist., 1981, Calif. Sch. Bds. Assn., 1981, Steinbeck Kiwanis, Salinas, 1987; named hon. mem. Filipino community Salinas Valley, 1988. Mem. Salinas C. of C., Native Sons Golden West, K.C. Republican. Roman Catholic. Avocations: fishing, hunting, bowling, golf. Home: 204 E Curtis St Salinas CA 93906-2804

JEFFRIES, TELVIN, human resources specialist, retail executive; With Best Products, 1987—93; various human resources positions including sr. v.p. Kohl's Corp., Menomonee Falls, Wis., 1993—2003, exec. v.p., 2003—. Com. chmn. Holy Redeemer Institutional Church of God in Christ Ednl. complex project. Office: Kohls Corp N56 W17000 Ridgewood Dr Menomonee Falls WI 53051 Office Phone: 262-703-7000. E-mail: telvin.jeffries@kohls.com.*

JEFFS, THOMAS HAMILTON, II, retired bank executive; b. Grosse Pointe Farms, Mich., July 11, 1938; s. Thomas Raymond and Geraldine (Bogan) J.; m. Patricia Lucas, June 20, 1964; children: Leslie, Laura, Caroline BBA in Gen. Bus., U. Mich., 1960, MBA, 1961. With NBD Bank, 1962-99, pres., COO, until 1999; vice chmn., bd. dirs. First Chgo. NBD Corp., 1995-98. Bd. dirs. MCN Energy Group, Inc., Detroit, Intermet Corp., Local Initiatives Support Corp. Bd. dirs. Detroit Symphony, Econ. Club Detroit; chmn. New Detroit, Inc.; dir. Detroit Renaissance, Inc. With U.S. Army, 1960-62. Mem. Bankers Roundtable, Detroit Athletic Club, Detroit Club (pres. 1982), Detroit Country Club, Yondotega Club, Grosse Pointe Club. Republican. Episcopalian. Home: 27 Fair Acres Dr Grosse Pointe Farms MI 48236-3101 Office: NBD Bank 611 Woodward Ave Detroit MI 48226-3408

JEFIC, DIJANA, nephrologist; b. Travnik, Bosnia-Herzegovina, Jan. 20, 1973; arrived in US, 2001; d. Ljubo and Visnja Bozic; m. Dane Jefic, Oct. 2, 1997. MD, U. Novi Sad Med. Sch., Novi Sad, Serbia, 1996. Diplomate Internal Medicine Am. Bd. of Internal Medicine, 2004, cert. ECFMG Ednl. Comittee for Fgn. Med. Graduates, 2000. Internal medicine resident St John Hosp. and Med. Ctr., Detroit, 2001—04, nephrology fellow, 2004—. Mem.: ACP (assoc.). Office: St John Hosp and Med Ctr 22201 Moross Rd #150 Detroit MI 48236 Office Phone: 313-886-8787 1248. Office Fax: 313-886-4103. Business E-Mail: dijana.jefic@stjohn.org.

JEGEN, SISTER CAROL FRANCES, religious studies educator; b. Chgo., Oct. 11, 1925; d. Julian Aloysius and Evelyn W. (Bostelmann) J. BS in History, St. Louis U., 1951; MA in Theology, Marquette U., 1958, PhD in Religious Studies, 1968; degree (hon.), St. Mary of the Woods, Terra Haute, Ind., 1977. Elem. tchr. St. Francis Xavier Sch., St. Louis, 1947-51; secondary tchr. Holy Angels Sch., Milw., 1951-57; coll. tchr. Mundelein Coll., Chgo., 1957-91; prof. pastoral studies Loyola U., Chgo., 1991—. Adv. coun. U.S. Cath. Bishops, Washington, 1969-74; trustees Cath. Theol. Union, Chgo., 1974-84. Author: Jesus the Peace Maker, 1986, Restoring Our Friendship with God, 1989; co-author: (with Byron Sherwin) Thank God, 1989; editor: Mary According to Women, 1985. Participant Nat. Farm Worker Ministry, Fresno, Calif., 1977—; mem. Pax Christi, U.S.A., 1979—, Jane Addams Conf., Chgo., 1989. Recipient Loyola Civic award Loyola U., Chgo., 1981, Chgo. medallion for Excellence in Catechesis, 1996, Sor Juana award Hispanic Ministry, 2000; named one of 100 Women to Watch Today's Chgo. Woman, 1989. Mem. Cath. Theol. Soc. Am., Coll. Theology Soc., Cath.-Jewish Scholars Dialog, Liturgical Conf. Democrat. Roman Catholic. Avocations: music, gardening. Home: Wright Hall 6364 N Sheridan Rd Chicago IL 60660-1700

JEGEN, LAWRENCE A., III, law educator; b. Chgo., Nov. 16, 1934; s. Lawrence A. and Katherine M. Jegen; children: Christine M., David L. BA, Beloit Coll., 1956; JD, U. Mich., 1959, MBA, 1960; LLM, NYU, 1963. Bar: Ill. 1959, U.S. Dist. Ct. (no. dist.) Ill. 1959, U.S. Dist. Ct. (so. dist.) Ind. 1962, Ind. 1966, U.S. Tax Ct. 1966, U.S. Ct. Appeals (7th cir.) 1980, U.S. Supreme Ct. 1980. Tax cons. Coopers & Lybrand, N.Y.C., 1960-62; asst. prof. law Ind. U., Indpls., 1962-64, assoc. prof., 1964-66, prof., 1966—, Thomas F. Sheehan prof. tax law and policy, 1982—, prof. philanthropic studies Ctr. Philanthropy, 1992—, external tax counsel, 1997—. Ind. U. rep. to Nat. Assn. Coll. and Univ. Attys.; co-founder Annual Tax Inst. for Colls. and Univs.; bar rev. lectr., vis. prof. in field; spl. counsel Ind. Dept. Revenue, 1963-65, Gov.'s Commn. on Med. Edn., 1970-72; mem. commr.'s adv. com. IRS, 1981-82; advisor Notre Dame Estate Planning Inst.; mem. Ind. Corp. Law Survey Commn.; State Tax Notes corr. for Tax Analysts; contbg. editor Inst. Bus. Planning's Tax Planning Svc.; bd. dirs., officer Ind. Continuing Legal Edn. Forum; 1st chmn. bd. dirs. Baccalaureate Edn. Sys. Trust of Ind.; mem. Ind. Gen. Assembly Study Commn.-Ind. Gen. Corp. Act; mem. Ind. Corps. Survey Commn., 1965—; commr. Nat. Conf. Uniform State Laws, 1981-91; dir. N.Am. Wildlife Assn., 1981-90. Author: Indiana Will and Trust Manual, 1967-95; Lifetime and Estate, Personal and Business Planning, 1987; Estate Planning and Administration in Indiana, 1979, numerous other books, articles, chpts. Chmn. bd. dirs. Ind. Bar Ednl. Sys. Tchrs., 1988-89; mem. adv. bd. Ind. U. Ctr. on Philanthropy. Named hon. sec. of state, State of Ind., 1967, 1980, hon. dep. atty. gen., 1968, hon. state treas., 1969, Ford fellow, 1963; recipient Spl Alumni Tch. award, Ind. U. Alumni Assn., 1970, 1976, 1980, 1985, Excellence in Taxation award for improvement tax adminstrn., State of Ind. Quality for Ind. Taxpayers, Inc., 1990, The Thomas Hart Benton Mural medallion, 1993, 1994, 3 Sagamore of the Wabash awards, State Ind., Internat. award, Assn. Continuing Legal Administrators for Excellence in Continuing Legal Edn., Ind. U. Most Outstanding Law Prof. award 6 times, Pres.'s Cir. Commemorative medallions Ind. U. Disting. Tchg. award, Tchr. of Significance, Ind. U. Fellow Am. Bar Found. (life), Am. Coll. Probate Counsel, Am. Coll. Tax Counsel; mem. ABA, FBA, Mid-West Inst. Estate and Tax Planning (adv. bd.), Ind. Bar Assn. (chmn. taxation sect. 1969-70, presdl. citation 1971), Indpls. Bar Assn. (Dr. Morton Finney Jr. Excellence in Legal Edn. award), Ind. Trial Lawyers Assn. (corp. taxation, estate taxation, state and local taxation). Office: Indiana Univ Sch Law 530 W New York St Indianapolis IN 46202-3225 Office Phone: 317-251-5300. Personal E-mail: profjegen@aol.com.

JEHLE, MICHAEL EDWARD, financial advisor, lawyer; b. Lawrence, Kans., Apr. 2, 1954; s. Edwin Paul and Catherine Claire (Cragoe) J.; m. Kimberly Ellen Davis, Aug. 4, 1979; children: Kathryn Anne, Christine Michelle. BS, S.W. Mo. State U., 1976; JD, Stanford U., 1979. Bar: Calif., Ill., Pa. Atty. The First Nat. Bank of Chgo., 1979-84, sr. atty., 1984-86; v.p., gen. counsel Equibank, Pitts., 1986-87, sr. v.p., gen. counsel, sec., 1987, Equimark Corp., Pitts., 1987-89, exec. v.p., chief fin. officer, 1989-90; pres. Strategic Adv. Group, Pitts., 1990-95, Strategic Healthcare Advisors, Pitts., 1993-95; dir. rsch. MED 3000 Group, Inc., Pitts., 1995-96; pres. THI, Inc., Pitts., 1996—. Co-author: Sovereign Lending, 1984. Mem. ABA, Nat. Health Lawyers Assn., Healthcare Fin. Mgmt. Assn. Republican. Methodist. Avocations: Karate, wine collecting. Home: 411 Maple Ln Sewickley PA 15143-1021 Office: THI Inc 411 Maple Ln Sewickley PA 15143-1021 Office Phone: 412-749-8959. Personal E-mail: mejehle@hotmail.com.

JEHLEN, PATRICIA D., state legislator; b. Austin, Tex., Oct. 14, 1943; d. Paul Kindred Jr. and Ruth Miller (Zumbrunnen) Deats; m. Alain Peter Jehlen, Aug. 29, 1969; children: Nicholas, Wendy, Peter. BA, Swarthmore Coll., 1965; MA in Teaching, Harvard U., 1969. Rschr. Harvard Sch. Edn., Cambridge, Mass., 1966-67; tchr. history Brookline (Mass.) H.S., 1968-71; mem. Somerville (Mass.) Sch. Com., 1976-91, Mass. Ho. of Reps., Somerville, 1991—. VISTA vol. Cook County Migrant Coun., Chicago Heights, Ill., 1965-66. Democrat. Home: 67 Dane St Somerville MA 02143-3730 Office: Mass Ho of Reps Rm 275 Boston MA 02133 Office Phone: 617-722-2676. Business E-Mail: rep.patricia.jehlen@hon.state.ma.us.

JELALIAN, ALBERT V., electrical engineer; b. Bridgewater, Mass., June 30, 1933; s. Siragan and Zarouhi (Tanelian) J.; m. Mary B. Karoghlanian; children: Alan H., Leslie K. BSEE, Northeastern U., 1957. Reg. profl. engr., Mass. Engr. Raytheon Co., Lexington, Mass., 1957-81, mgr. electro-optics lab Sudbury, Mass., 1981-86, asst. dir., 1986-91, asst. mgr. equipment devel. labs. (electro optics), 1991-92; pres. Jelalian Sci. & Engring., Bedford, Mass., 1992—. Inventor: holds ten patents relating to aviation safety and mil. products; contbr. articles to profl. jours.; author: Laser Radar Systems, 1992; guest editor IEEE Procs. Spl. Issue on Laser Radar Sys., 1995-96. Recipient Recognition award NASA, Washington, 1974, Group Achievement award, 1975, Disting. Svc. award IRIS, 1993, Nat. Sci. and Tech. award IRIS, 1998; fellow Mil. Sensing Symposium. Mem. IEEE (sr.), Infrared Info. Symposium (vice chmn. active systems 1989-91, nat. chmn. 1991-93), Optical Soc. Am. Office: Jelalian Sci & Engring 3 Reeves Rd Bedford MA 01730-1334 Office Phone: 781-271-0208. Personal E-mail: jsne@aol.com.

JELEN, TED G., political scientist; b. Evergreen Park, Ill., Apr. 30, 1952; s. Thaddeus Andrew and Frances Jelen; m. Marthe Atwater Chandler, June 14, 1982; children: Christopher Michael Chandler, Robert Martin Chandler. BA, Knox Coll., 1970—74; PhD, Ohio State U., 1974—79. Prof., polit. sci. Benedictine U., Lisle, Ill., 1981—97, U. Nev., Las Vegas, 1997—. Editor Jour. Sci. Study Religion, 1999—2003. Author: (book) Between Two Absolutes: Public Opinion and the Politics of Abortion, 1992, Public Atitudes Toward Church and State, 1995, A Wall of Separation? Debating Church-State Relations in the United States, 1998, To Serve God and Mammon, 2000; editor: Religion and Politics in Comparative Perspective, 2002. Mem.: Midwest Polit. Sci. Assn., Soc. for the Sci. Study of Religion, Am. Polit. Sci. Assn. Avocation: guitar. Office: Univ Nev 4505 Maryland Pkwy Las Vegas NV 81954-5029 Office Phone: 702-895-3355. E-mail: jelent@unlv.neveda.edu.

JELINEK, FREDERICK, electrical engineer, educator; b. Prague, Czechoslovakia, Nov. 18, 1932; arrived in U.S., 1949, naturalized, 1955; s. William and Trudy (Kocmanek) J.; m. Milena Tobolova, Feb. 4, 1961; children—Hannah, William. BS, MIT, 1956, MS, 1958, PhD, 1962; DS Math. and Physics (hon.), Charles U., Prague, 2001. Instr. MIT, Cambridge, 1959-62; lectr. Harvard U., Cambridge, 1962; asst. prof. Cornell U., Sch. Elec. Engring., Ithaca, N.Y., 1962-66, assoc. prof., 1966-72, prof., 1972-74; vis. scientist MIT, Lincoln Lab., 1964, 65, IBM, 1968-69; sr. mgr. continuous speech recognition IBM, T.J. Watson Research Center, Yorktown Heights, N.Y., 1972-93; prof., dir. Ctr. Lang. and Speech Processing Whiting Sch. Engring. Johns Hopkins U., Balt., 1993—. Author: Probabilistic Information Theory, 1968, Statistical Methods for Speech Recognition, 1998; contbr. articles to profl. jours. Chmn. Liberal Party, Ithaca, N.Y., 1970-72, mem. state exec. com., 1971-73. Recipient Outstanding Achievement in the Field of Speech Comm. European Speech Comm. Assn., 2000; named One of top 100 innovators in speech recognition by Tech. Mag., 1981. Fellow IEEE (life; pres. Info. Theory Group 1977, bd. govs. 1970-79, 81-86, Info. Theory Group best paper award 1971, Soc. award Signal Processing Soc. 1998, Golden Jubilee Paper award Info. Theory Soc. 1998, Third Millennium medal 2000, Computer, Speech and Lang. paper award 2002). Office: Johns Hopkins U Ctr Lang and Speech Processing Barton Hall 3400 N Charles St Baltimore MD 21218 Office Phone: 410-516-7730. Business E-Mail: jelinek@jhu.edu.

JELINEK, JOHN JOSEPH, public relations executive; b. San Pedro, Calif., Sept. 3, 1955; s. Joseph Francis and Patricia Valerie (Powers) J.; m. Christl Michele Schneider, June 1986 (div. July 1997). BA, Loyola U., 1977; MA, Loyola-Marymount U., 1983; postgrad., Syracuse U. Assoc. editor E-Go Enterprises, Sherman Oaks, Calif., 1976-77; advt. dir. Select Promotions, Irvine, Calif., 1977-78; editor SCORE Internat., Westlake Village, Calif., 1978-79; exec. editor Petersen Pub. Co., L.A., 1979-82, editor, 1982-85; pub. rels. account exec. Hill and Knowlton Inc., L.A., 1985-87; acct. supr. Freeman/McCue Pub. Rels., Newport Beach, Calif., 1987-88; account supr. tech. div. Fleishman Hillard Inc., L.A., 1988-89; rep. pub. affairs corp. news dept. Ford Motor Co., Dearborn, Mich., 1989-90; product info. mgr. Ford of Can., Oakville, 1990-92; car product devel., pub. affairs mgr. Ford Motor Co., Dearborn, Mich., 1993-96, product devel., pub. affairs mgr., 1996-98, dir. car strategy comm., 1998-2001, Ford brand comm. mgr., 2001—02; v.p. pub. affairs Ford of Can., Oakville, 2002—. Author: (with others) Consumer's Guide to 1978 Trucks, 1978, Consumer's Guide to 1980 Trucks, 1979,

Complete Guide to Used Cars, 1981, How to Buy the Best Compact Truck, 1984; columnist Guns & Ammo Mag., 1980-84, Petersen's Hunting Mag., 1986-87. Capt. Calif. State Mil. Res. 1982-89. Recipient 1st place award Calif. Newspaper Pub. Assn., 1977 Mem. NRA (life), L.A. County Mus. Natural History-Automobile Collection Coun., Aircraft Owners and Pilots Assn., Nat. Aeronautical Assn., Detroit Inst. Art. Republican. Roman Catholic. Avocations: travel, flying, skiing, cooking. Office: Ford Motor Co Can The Canadian Rd Oakville ON Canada L6J 5E4 E-mail: jjelinek@ford.com.

JELINEK, VERA, dean; b. Kosice, Czechoslovakia, Dec. 16, 1935; came to U.S., 1947; d. Joseph and Margit (Lefkovits) Schnitzer; m. Josef E. Jelinek, June 19, 1960; children: David, Paul. BA in History, CUNY, 1956; MA, Johns Hopkins U., 1958; PhD in Modern European History, NYU, 1977; diploma, Sch. Advanced Internat. Study, Bologna, Italy. Translator Rockefeller Bros. Fund, N.Y.C., 1958-59; exec. dir. U.S. Youth Coun., N.Y.C., 1959-63; dir. internat. programs, social and natural scis. NYU, N.Y.C., 1985—, dir. Lillian Vernon Ctr. for Internat. Affairs, 2000—04, dir. The Energy Forum, 2000—, asst. dean, dir. Ctr. Global Affairs, 2004—. Mem. adv. com. N.Y.C.-Budapest Sister City Program, 1991-94; prin. dir. pilot tng. program for new UN diplomats NYU, 1996-97. Author audio cassette: Before You Go-Italy, 1985. Mem. edn. com. Mus. Am. Folk Art, N.Y.C.; edn. co-chair The Am. Antiques Show, 2002—03. Recipient fellowship Ford Found., 1960, grant NYU Curriculum Challenge Fund, 1989, 90, 99, Phillip E. Frandson award Nat. Univ. Continuing Edn. Assn., 1991. Mem. Am. Folk Art Soc., Carnegie Coun. on Ethics and Internat. Affairs, Women's Fgn. Policy Group, Phi Beta Kappa. Democrat. Avocations: tennis, jogging, folk art, cooking, travel. Office: Woolworth Bldg 15 Barclay St New York NY 10007 Office Phone: 212-992-8380.

JELKS, GLENN WILLIAM, plastic surgeon; b. South Gate, Calif., Oct. 21, 1943; s. William Harry and Parthena Imogene Jelks; m. Elizabeth Anne Brady, Sept. 4, 1965; children: Jennifer, Deborah, Michael. BA, U. Calif., Berkeley, 1965; MS, Mich. State U. Coll., 1973; MD, Mich. State U. Coll. Human Medicine, 1973. Diplomate Am. Bd. Ophthalmology, 1979, Am. Bd. Plastic and Reconstructive Surgery, 1982, Nat. Bd. Med. Examiners. With med. edn., mktg. and sales dept. Merck, Sharp and Dohme divsn. Merck and Co., Inc., San Francisco, 1965-69; med. rsch. fellow dept. interdepartmental curriculum Mich. State U.-Biomed. Comm. Ctr., East Lansing, 1971-73; grad. asst., clin. sci. instr. Mich. State U., East Lansing, 1973; intern straight surgery UCLA, 1973-74, resident gen./orthopaedic surgery, 1974-75; resident ophthalmology UCLA-Jules Stein Eye Inst., 1975-78; resident Inst. Reconstructive Plastic Surgery, NYU Med. Ctr., NYC, 1978-80. Assoc. prof. ophthalmology, assoc. prof. plastic surgery NYU Med. Ctr., NYC, 1980-; attending plastic surgeon NYU Med. Ctr., NY, 1980-, Bellevue Hosp., NYC, 1980-, Manhattan Eye, Ear and Throat Hosp., NYC, 1980-, The Valley Hosp., Ridgewood, NJ, 1991-; adj. attending in ophthalmology and plastic surgery NY Eye and Ear Infirmary-Lenox Hill Hosp., NYC, 1995-; examiner Am. Bd. Plastic Surgeons, 1995, 96; mem. continuing med. edn. adv. com., surg. case rev. com., oper. rm. com. NY Eye and Ear Infirmary; mem. laser com. NYU Med. Ctr.; mem. audiovisual com. Manhattan Eye, Ear and Throat Hosp.; vis. prof. Mass. Eye and Ear Infirmary, Boston, 1989, Robert H. Ivy Soc., Phila., 1990, UCLA, 1992, Yale U., New Haven, Conn., 1992. Consulting editor Ophthalmic Plastic and Reconstructive Surgery, Plastic Surgery Outlook, Ophthalmic Plastic and Reconstructive Surgery Jour; assoc. editor Annals of Plastic Surgery, 1995-96. Recipient Rsch. Travel award Am. Coll. Cardiology, 1970, Sci. Exhibit award AMA Conv., San Francisco, 1972, Lester T. Jones award for excellence in surg. anatomy Am. Soc. Ophthalmic Plastic and Reconstructive Plastic Surgeons 1986, Arthur L. Garnes Lectr. award Harlem Hosp., N.Y., 1987; NIH Cardiovas. trainee Mich. State U., 1969; Student Rsch. fellow Mich. Heart Assn., 1970, 71; Plastic Surgery Ednl. Found. traveling prof., 2000-01. Fellow Am. Acad. Ophthalmology; mem. AMA (Continuing Edn. award 1976, 79, 82, 85, 88), Internat. Soc. Craniofacial Surgeons, European Soc. Opthalmic Plastic and Reconstructive Surgery, Am. Acad. Ophthalmology, Am. Soc. Plastic and Reconstructive Surgeons, Am. Coll. Surgeons, Am. Soc. Maxillofacial Surgeons (mem. continuing med. edn. com. 1995-96), Am. Soc. Aesthetic Plastic and Reconstructive Surgery (mem. edn. commn. 1994, traveling prof. 1995), Am. Assn. Plastic Surgeons (mem. time and place com. 1995-96), Northeastern Soc. Plastic Surgeons (chmn. membership com. 1994-95, mem. nominating com. 1994-95, sec. 1995-99, pres. 1999-2000), NY State Med. Soc., NY County Med. Soc., NY Regional Soc. Plastic and Reconstructive Surgeons, NY Acad. Medicine, NY Orbit Soc. Avocations: boating, fishing, golf, skiing, tennis. Office: 875 Park Ave New York NY 10021-0341 Address: FPT 8 8V 550 First Ave New York NY 10016 E-mail: gwj@jelksmedical.com.

JELKS, MARY LARSON, retired pediatrician; b. Galva, Ill., 1929; MD, U. Nebr., 1955. Diplomate Am. Bd. Pediats., Am. Bd. Allergy and Immunology. Intern Johns Hopkins Hosp., Balt., 1955-56, resident, 1956-57, 58-60, Grace-New Haven Hosp., 1957; fellow U. Fla. Tchg. Hosp., 1960-61; clin. asst. prof. U. South Fla.; ret.; active aerobiology, 1985—. Fellow Am. Acad. Allery and Immunology, Am. Acad. Pediats.; mem. AMA. Achievements include active research in aerobiology. Home: 1930 Clematis St Sarasota FL 34239-3813 E-mail: mjelks99@cs.com.

JELLICORSE, JOHN LEE, communications and theatre educator; b. Bristol, Tenn., Nov. 1, 1937; s. Harold Lee and Kathleen J.; m. Lenah Mary Lawrence, July 21, 1961 (div. 1980); 1 child, Jennifer Lee; m. Delayna Maxine Jordan, June 28, 1992; 1 child, John Adam. AB, U. Tenn., 1959; PhD, Northwestern U., 1967. From instr. to assoc. prof. Northwestern U., Evanston, Ill., 1962-69; assoc. prof. U. Tenn., Knoxville, 1969-74; prof., head dept. communication and theatre U. N.C., Greensboro, 1974-88, dir. theatre divsn., 1988-90, dir. broadcasting/cinema divsn., 1990-91; dean Sch. Comm. Hong Kong Bapt. U., 1991-94; prof. U. N.C., Greensboro, 1994—2001, head dept. broadcasting and cinema, 2001—. Cons. Wroclaw Tech. U., Poland. Contbr. chapters to books, articles to profl. jours. Recipient Outstanding Tchr. award Northwestern U., 1968; So. Fellowship Fund fellow, 1959-62. Mem. Assn. for Comm. Adminstrn., Am. Film Inst., Internat. Comm. Assn., Nat. Comm. Assn., Univ. Film and Video Assn. Office: U NC Greensboro 209 Brown PO Box 26170 Greensboro NC 27402-6170 Office Phone: 336-334-3846. Business E-Mail: jljellic@uncg.edu.

JELLINEK, GEORGE, broadcast executive, music educator, writer; b. Budapest, Hungary, Dec. 22, 1919; came to U.S., 1941; s. Daniel and Jolan Jellinek; m. Hedy Dicker, July 29, 1942; 1 child, Nancy Berezin. Student, Lafayette Coll., 1943; MusD (hon.), L.I. U., 1984. Dir. program services SESAC, Inc., N.Y.C., 1955-64; rec. dir. Muzak, Inc., N.Y.C., 1964-68; music dir. Sta. WQXR, N.Y.C., 1968-84; asst. prof. music NYU, N.Y.C., 1976-91. Author: Callas, Portrait of a Prima Donna, 1960, 2d edit. 1986, The Magic Chair, 1966, The Scarlet Mill, 1968, History Through the Opera Glass, 1994; contbg. editor: Stereo Rev. mag., 1958-74, Ovation mag., 1974-88; contbr. articles to the N.Y. Times, Musical America, The Opera Quar.; host (radio show) The Vocal Scene, 1969-2004. Trustee Bagby Found. Served to 1st lt. M.I., U.S. Army, 1942-46. Recipient Maj. Armstrong Broadcast award, 1978, Ohio State award, 1978, Gabriel award, 1982, George Washington award Am. Hungarian Found., 1986, Gold medal Internat. Radio Festival, 1995, Grammy award, 1996. Mem. ASCAP, AFTRA. Office: Sta WQXR 122 5th Ave New York NY 10011-5605

JELLINEK, MICHAEL STEVEN, psychiatrist, pediatrician; b. N.Y.C., Sept. 30, 1948; s. Kurt and Kate (Jacoby) J.; m. Barbara A. Jellinek, June 14, 1970; children: David M., Abraham R., Isaiah T., Hanna R. BA, Columbia Coll., 1970; MD, Albert Einstein Coll. Medicine, 1973. Diplomate Nat. Bd. Med. Examiners, Am. Bd. Pediatrics; diplomate in psychiatry and child psychiatry Am. Bd. Psychiatry and Neurology. Instr. pediatrics Montefiore Hosp. & Med. Ctr., N.Y.C., 1976—79; chief child psychiat. svcs. Mass. Gen. Hosp., Boston, 1979—, asst. in pediat., 1979—81, asst. pediatrician, 1981—83, dir. outpatient psychiatry, 1984—93, assoc. pediatrician, 1984—86, assoc. psychiatrist, 1984—86, pediatrician, 1986—, psychiatrist, 1986—, asst. gen. dir. ambulatory svcs., 1992—, sr. v.p. ambulatory svcs., 1994—2001, sr. v.p. adminstrn., 1995—2001; pres. Newton Wellesley Hosp., 2001—; assoc. prof. psychiatry (pediatrics) Harvard U., Boston, 1987—96, prof. psychiatry and pediatrics, 1996—. Asst. instr. Columbia U., N.Y.C, 1970; cons. Shriner Burns Inst., Boston, 1979—. Dir. Camp Rainbow, Croton-on-Hudson, 1977-81. Fellow Am. Acad. Pediat., Am. Acad. Child Psychiatry (treas. 1991-93, Simon Wile award 1993); mem. Am. Pediat. Soc., Am. Psychiat. Soc. (Ittleson award 1999), Soc. Prof. Child Psychiatry, New Eng. Coun. Child Psychiatry. Democrat. Jewish. Avocations: running, soccer coach, carpentry. Home: 132 Pleasant St Newton MA 02459-1828 Office: Mass Gen Hosp Fruit St Bulfinch 351 Boston MA 02114 Office Phone: 617-293-6255. Business E-Mail: mjellinek@partners.org.

JELLINEK, MILES ANDREW, lawyer; b. Dec. 27, 1947; s. Alfred Marquis and Rena Elizabeth (Felberg) J.; m. Annabelle Francis O'Leary, Apr. 9, 1976; children: Beth Elise, Laura Anne. BA, U. Pa., 1969, JD, 1974. Bar: Pa. 1974, N.J. 1987. Law clk. Ct. Common Pleas, Phila., 1974-75; sr. mem. Cozen O'Connor, Phila., 1975—. Adj. instr. dept. legal studies Temple U., 2001—. Mem. Germantown Cricket Club (Phila.). Democrat. Jewish. Avocations: tennis, squash, golf, singing. Office: Cozen O'Connor 1900 Market St Philadelphia PA 19103-3527 Office Phone: 215-665-2038. E-mail: Mjellinek@cozen.com.

JELLINEK, PAUL S., foundation executive, health economist; b. Madison, Wis., Dec. 25, 1951; s. Joseph S. Jellinek and Elvira Myers; m. Janice Susan Kissling, Dec. 23, 1972; children: Lisa, Michael, Amy, Robert. BA, U. Pa., 1972, U. So. Fla., 1978; MS in Pub. Health, U. N.C., 1980, PhD, 1983. Copy editor Sarasota (Fla.) Herald-Tribune, 1973; reporter Wayne County Reporter, Monticello, Ky., 1974; med. health tech. St. Joseph's Hosp., Tampa, Fla., 1975-78; program officer Robert Wood Johnson Found., Princeton, N.J., 1983-91, v.p., 1991—. Dir. Grantmakers in Health, Washington, 1993-99; bd. dirs. student pugwash U.S.A., 2000; mem. Gov.'s Task Force on Child Abuse, Trenton, N.J., 1988-94. Contbr. articles to profl. jours. Mem. social justice com. Our Lady of Sorrows Ch., Mercerville, N.J., 1989—. Bush Inst. for Child and Family Policy fellow, 1982-83. Mem. Am. Econ. Assn., Am. Pub. Health Assn. Avocation: blues band. Office: Robert Wood Johnson Foundation PO Box 2316 Princeton NJ 08543-2316

JELLINEK, ROGER, editor; b. Mexico City, Jan. 16, 1938; came to U.S., 1961; s. Frank Louis Mark and Marguerite Lilla Donne (Lewis) J.; m. Margherita DiCenzo, Dec. 22, 1963 (div. 1984); children: Andrew Mark, Claire; m. Eden-Lee Murray, 1984; 1 child, Everett Peter Murray. Student, Bryanston Sch., Dorset, Eng., 1951—56; MA, Cambridge (Eng.) U., 1961. Assoc. editor Random House, 1963-64; editor Walker & Co., NYC, 1964—65, NY Times Book Rev., NYC, 1966—70, dep. editor, 1970—73; editor-in-chief Times Books, Quadrangle/NY Times Book Co., NYC, 1974—78, sr. editor, 1978—81, editor Lamont newsletter and yearbook Palisades, 1981—91; pres. Clairemark, Ltd., 1981—, Jellinek & Murray Lit. Agy. Editor Atlantic Realm Project, 1983-93; editl. dir. Inner Ocean Pub., 2000-03; pub. Hawaii map series. Pres. ArtMaps Ltd., 1996—; program chair Hawaii Book and Music Festival, 2006. With Royal Marines, 1956-57; 2d lt. Brit. Intelligence Corps, 1957-58. Mellon fellow Yale U., 1961-63. Home and Office: 2024 Mauna Pl Honolulu HI 96822-1102 Office Phone: 808-521-4057.

JELLISON, KATHERINE KAY, historian, educator; b. Garden City, Kans., Jan. 5, 1960; d. Billy Dean and Margaret Ruth (Brown) Jellison; m. David John Winkelmann, Aug. 10, 1985. BA, Ft. Hays (Kans.) State U., 1982; MA, U. Nebr., 1984; PhD, U. Iowa, 1991. Asst. prof. Memphis State U., 1991-93, Ohio U., Athens, 1993-96, assoc. prof. history, 1996—. Author: Entitled to Power: Farm Women and Technology, 1913-1963, 1993. Named Outstanding Young Alumni Ft. Hays State U., 1994; recipient Excellence in Feminist Pedagogy award Ohio U., 1994; Smithsonian Instn. fellow, 1989. Mem. NOW, Am. Hist. Assn., Orgn. Am. Historians, Berkshire Conf. on History of Women, Social Sci. History Assn., Ohio Acad. History. Democrat. Methodist. Avocations: hiking, watching old movies. Office: Ohio University Dept History Bentley Annex Athens OH 45701 Business E-Mail: jellison@ohio.edu.

JEMBERIE, ALEMAYEHU LAKEW, seismologist, researcher; m. Menbere Ejigu Getu, June 25, 1990; children: Befekadu Alemayehu Lakew, Wossenyelesh Alemayehu Lakew, Biruh Alemayehu Lakew. BSc, Addis Ababa U., Ethiopia, 1988, MSc, 1993; PhD, St. Louis U., 2002. Lectr. Arbaminch Water Tech. Inst., Ethiopia, 1988—97; postdoctoral rsch. fellow U. Memphis, 2003—. Head physics lab. Arbaminch Water Tech. Inst., North Omo, 1989—97. Bd. mem., acct. Kidist Mariam Ethiopian Orthodox Tewahido Ch., Memphis, 2004. Scholar, St. Louis U., 1997—2002; Rsch. and Tng. in Italian Labs. fellow, Internat. Ctr. for Theoretical Physics, 1995—96. Mem.: Internat. Ctr. for Theoretical Physics (assoc.), Seismol. Soc. of Am. (assoc.), Am. Geophys. Union (assoc.). Ethiopian Orthodox Tewahido Church. Achievements include development of first attenuation map of China and surrounding regions. Home: 2322 Ceylon Ct Memphis TN 38119 Office: U Memphis CERI 3876 Central Ave Memphis TN 38152 Office Phone: 901-678-1728. Office Fax: 901-678-4734. Personal E-mail: ajemberi@memphis.edu.

JEMELIAN, JOHN NAZAR, management consultant; b. N.Y.C., May 10, 1933; s. Nazar and Angel (Jizmejian) Jemelian; m. Rose Melkonian, Nov. 22, 1958; children: Steri, Lori, Brian, Joni. BS, U. So. Calif., 1956. CPA Calif., 1961. Mgr. audit staff Price Waterhouse & Co., LA, 1958-64; treas. The Akron, LA, 1964-82, v.p. fin., 1976, exec. v.p., 1977-82; v.p., gen. mgr., dir. Acromil Corp., City of Industry, Calif., 1982-85; sr. v.p. fin. and adminstrn., CFO, sec., treas. World Vision Inc., 1985-98; pres. Claremont Facilities Corp., 1990—2005, Pasadena Resources Corp., 1990-94. Dir. D.I. Engring., Inc.; fin. advisor African Enterprises, 1966—68. Bd. dirs. Pasadena Christian Sch., 1965—67, 1969—70, treas., 1965—67; chmn. bd. Donor Automation, 1975—2001; trustee Haigazian Coll., Beirut, 1974—78; deacon Lake Ave. Congl. Ch., 1964—68, trustee, 1970—73, chmn. bd. trustees, 1972—73, chmn. ch. com., 1974; chmn. bd. Media Ministries, Inc., 1975—95; trustee Narramore Christian Found., 1976—93, Met. Ministries, 1979—80; chmn. Christian Bus. Men's Com., 1979—81, 1986—87, Sahag Mesrob Armenian Christian Sch., 1980—85; deacon, elder Ch. on the Way, 1980—95; chmn. bd. dirs. Armenian Gospel Mission, 1999—; bd. dirs. Forest Home Christian Conf. Ctr., 1972—75, 1978—81, 1984—88, 1992—95, 2001—04. With F.A. U.S. Army. Named Boss of Yr. Beverly Hills chpt., Nat. Secs. Assn., 1970. Mem.: AICPA, Retail Contr. Assn. (dir. 1973—74), Calif. Soc. CPA, Toastmasters-Windjammers LA (pres. 1963), LA Athletic Club, Beta Gamma Sigma, Beta Alpha Psi, Delta Sigma Pi. Home: 261 Sharon Rd Arcadia CA 91007-8044 Office: 800 West Chestnut Monrovia CA 91016-3198 Fax: 626-301-1128. E-mail: jjemelia@worldvision.org.

JEMELLA, BRIAN, research scientist; b. N.J., 1981; s. Donald and Sheila Jemella. BS in Physics, U. Md., 2003. Client assoc. JP Morgan Chase Bank, Mt. Kisco, NY, 2000—02; rsch. asst. Inst. Rsch. Elects. and Applied Physics, College Park, Md., 2002—05. Author: (guest column) Iraq Veterans Need a Thank You, Tax Criticism Makes No Cents; contbr. articles to profl. jours. Mem.: Am. Phys. Soc. Conservative. Avocations: scuba diving, swimming, reading, investing.

JEMIELITY, THOMAS JOHN, language educator; b. Cleve., Dec. 17, 1933; s. Joseph Henry and Margaret Anne (Wielgus) Jemielity; m. Barbara Gray, Aug. 7, 1965; children: David Christopher, Samuel Andrew, Sarah Margaret. MA, John Carroll U., Cleve., 1958; PhD, Cornell U., 1965. Lectr. English Carleton U., Ottawa, Canada, 1962-63; instr. U. Notre Dame, Ind., 1963-65, asst. prof. English, 1965-70, assoc. prof., 1970-90, prof., 1990—2003, prof. emeritus, 2003—. Vis. lectr. Lancaster (Eng.) U. Author: (book) Satire and the Hebrew Prophets, 1992; contbr. articles to profl. jours. Summer fellow, Ind. Com. Humanities, 1988. Mem.: Johnson Soc. Ctrl. Region (pres. 1985), Johnson Soc. London, Johnson Soc. (Lichfield, Eng.), Jane Austen Soc. N.Am., Am. Soc. 18th Century Studies. Home: 20408 Kern Rd South Bend IN 46614-5046 Office: U Notre Dame Dept English Notre Dame IN 46556 Business E-Mail: thomas.j.jemielity.1@nd.edu.

JEMISIN, NOAH, artist, educator; b. Birmingham, Ala., Apr. 7, 1943; s. Noah Sr. and Blanche (McDolle) J.; m. Janice Erlin Finklea, 1968 (div. 1977); 1 chld, Nora K. BS in Fine Arts, Ala. State U., Montgomery, 1966; MA, U. Iowa, 1972, MFA, 1974. Exec. dir., curator Bronx River Art Ctr. and Gallery, Bronx, N.Y., 1986-90; adj. prof. C.W. Post Coll./L.I. U., Brookville, N.Y., 1992-94; master artist City Arts, N.Y.C., 1994—; artist, cons. Charter Sch., Lansing, Mich., 1996—; master artist Arts Connection, N.Y.C., 1999; instr. El Puente Acad., Bklyn., 1995—. Adj. prof. Purchase Coll.-SUNY, 1999; mem. adv. bd. Bronx River Art Ctr. and Gallery, 1986-92; mem. panel N.Y. Found. for the Arts, N.Y.C., 1997; mem. 20th Century Art panel Met. Mus. Art, N.Y.C., 1986, 87; vis. artist Parsons Sch. Design, N.Y.C., 1985. Recipient award for sculpture Pollock-Krasner Found., 1997, award for painting, 1994, 2000; award for painting N.Y. Found. for the Arts, 1994; Arts Internat. travel grantee to West Africa, 1992, 95. Avocations: reading, running, film, music (jazz). Home: 315 Berry St Brooklyn NY 11211-5130

JEMISON, MAE CAROL, physician, engineer, entrepreneur, philanthropist, educator, former astronaut; b. Decatur, Ala., Oct. 17, 1956; d. Charlie and Dorothy (Green) J. BS in ChemE, BA in African-Am. Studies, Stanford U., 1977; MD, Cornell U., 1981. Physician Peace Corps, Sierra Leone, Western Africa, 1983—85; pvt. practice L.A.; mission specialist NASA, Houston, 1987—93, astronaut on space shuttle Endeavor, 1992; prof. Dartmouth Coll., 1995—2002; mem, bd. dirs. Scholastic Inc.; national sci. literary advocate Bayer Corp., 1995—. Founder, pres. BioSentient Corp., The Jemison Group, Inc., 1993—, The Earth We Share Internat. Sci. Camp; A.D. White prof.-at-large Cornell U.; founder, pres. The Dorothy Jemison Foundation for Excellence, 1994—; mem., bd. dirs. Scholastic, Inc.; national sci. literary advocate Bayer Corp., 1995—; bd. dirs. Valspar Corp., Kimberly-Clark Corp. Author: Find Where The Wind Goes, 2001; TV host Discovery Channel, World of Wonder, 1994—95. Named one of World's 50 Most Beautiful People, People Mag., 1993. Mem.: NAS Inst. Medicine. Achievements include being first woman of color to fly in space. Office: Jemison Group Inc PO Box 591455 Houston TX 77259

JEN, FRANK CHIFENG, finance and management educator; b. Shanghai, May 15, 1931; came to U.S., 1957; s. Seybold E. and Susan (Lin) J.; m. Daisy Chi, Aug. 26, 1962; children: Amy K., Wendy K., Edward K. BS, N. Central Coll., 1959; MBA, U. Wis., 1960, PhD, 1963. Asst. prof. finance SUNY, Buffalo, 1964-66, assoc. prof., 1966-68, prof., 1968-97, chmn. dept. fin., 1967-70, Mfrs. & Traders Trust Co.'s prof. banking/fin. to emeritus, 1972-97, 97—, Univ. rsch. scholar, 2002—, chmn. dept. fin., 1967-70, chmn. dept. operating analysis, 1970-77, dir. bank mgmt. inst. and advanced comml. lending program, 1977-97, co-dir., dir. China MBA program, 1984-91, univ. rsch. scholar, 2002—. Vis. prof. Dalian (China) U. Tech., 1980—. Contbr. articles to profl. jours. Mem. Am. Fin. Assn., Am. Econ. Assn., Soc. Econ. and Fin. Mgmt. in China (pres. 1985-88), Pi Gamma Mu, Beta Gamma Sigma. Office: SUNY Buffalo Sch Mgmt Jacobs Ctr Amherst NY 14260-0001 E-mail: frankjen@buffalo.edu.

JEN, JOSEPH JWU-SHAN, federal agency administrator; b. Chung King, Sichuan, China, May 8, 1939; arrived in U.S., 1962; s. H.C. and Lucia (Chang) J.; m. Salina Fond, Sept. 4, 1965; children: Joanne Pauline, Jeffrey Jay. BS, Nat. Taiwan U., 1960; MS, Wash. State U., 1964; PhD, U. Calif., Berkeley, 1969; MBA, So. Ill. U., 1986. Asst. prof. Clemson (S.C.) U., 1969-74; rsch. food technologist U.S. Dept. Agr., Beltsville, Md., 1975; assoc. prof. Clemson (S.C.) U., 1974-79, prof., 1979; assoc. prof. Mich. State U., East Lansing, 1979-80; mgr. Campbell Soup Co., Camden, N.J., 1980-83, dir., 1983-86; chmn. divsn. food sci. and tech. U. Ga., Athens, 1986-92; dean Coll. Agr. Calif. Poly. State U., San Luis Obispo, 1992—2001; under sec. rsch., edn. and econ. USDA, Washington, 2001—. Vis. prof. Nat. Taiwan U., 1976. Editor: Chemistry and Function of Pectin, 1986, Quality Factors of Fruits and Vegetables, 1989; contbr. articles to profl. jours. Recipient Cert. of Merit, Ministry of Econ. Affairs, Rep. of China, 1980, Ministry of Agr., Rep. of China, 1988, Disting. Educator award, Nat. Assn. Coll. Tchrs. Agr., 1999, Grad. Alumni achievement award, Wash. State U., 2002, Leadership Citation, Coun. Sci. Soc. Presidents, 2005. Fellow Inst. Food Technologists (chmn. fruits and vegetable products 1988-89); mem. Am. Chem. Soc., Chinese Am. Food Soc. (pres. 1977, Profl. Achievement award 1986), Sigma Xi. Achievements include first to use hydrophobic chromatography in food enzyme research; development of high quality dehydrated vegetable pieces; establishment of teaching and research program in food processing in China and Taiwan; established innovative public/private partnership programs at Calif. Poly. State U. Office: USDA Research, Edn & Econ 1400 Independence Ave SW Washington DC 20250 Office Phone: 202-720-5923. Business E-Mail: joseph.jen@usda.gov.

JENCKS, CHRISTOPHER SANDYS, sociologist, educator; b. Balt., Oct. 22, 1936; s. Francis Haynes and Elizabeth (Pleasants) J. BA, Harvard U., 1958, M.Ed., 1959; postgrad., London Sch. Econs., 1959-61; LL.D., Kalamazoo Coll., 1969; D.Litt., Columbia Coll., 1983. Assoc. editor New Republic mag., 1961-63; fellow Inst. Policy Studies, Washington, 1963-67; mem. faculty Harvard U., 1967-80, 96—, prof., 1973-80, 96—, Malcolm Wiener prof. social policy, 1998—; John D. MacArthur prof. sociology and urban affairs Northwestern U., Evanston, Ill., 1980-96; vis. prof. U. Chgo., 1994-95. Author: (with David Riesman) The Academic Revolution, 1968, (with others) Inequality, 1972, Who Gets Ahead?, 1979, (with Paul Peterson) The Urban Underclass, 1991, Rethinking Social Policy, 1992, The Homeless, 1994, (with Meredith Phillips) The Black-White Test Score Gap, 1998. Guggenheim fellow, 1967-68, 82-83, Inst. for Advanced Study fellow, 1985-86, Russell Sage Found. fellow, 1991-92, Ctr. for Advanced Study in Behavioral Scis., 1997-98, 2001-02. Mem.: Am. Philos. Soc., Nat. Acad. Scis. Office: Harvard U Kennedy Sch Govt Cambridge MA 02138

JENCKS, PENELOPE, sculptor; b. Balt., Mar. 23, 1936; d. Gardner Platt and Ruth DeWitt (Pearl) J.; m. Sidney Jack Hurwitz, Dec. 20, 1958; children: Edwin David, Adam Gardner, Erica Ruth. Student, Swarthmore Coll., 1954-56, Hans Hoffmann Sch., 1955, Skowhegan Art Sch., 1956, 57, Stuttgart (Germany) Kunstakademie, 1959; BFA, Boston U., 1958. Instr. Braintree (Mass.) Art Assn., 1971-72, Art Inst. Boston, 1975-79, Boston Coll., Newton, Mass., 1978; prof., Saltzman vis. artist Brandeis U., Waltham, Mass., 1981-83. Resident MacDowell Colony, 1975, 76, 78, 87; guest lectr. in field. One-woman shows include Fitchburg (Mass.) Art Mus., 1976, Landmark Gallery, N.Y.C., 1977, 81, Art Inst. Boston, 1978, Helen Shlein Gallery, Boston, 1981, 85; exhibited in group shows at U.S.I.S. Amerika Haus, Freiburg, Germany, 1960, Nat. Inst. Arts & Letters, N.Y.C., 1966, Mass. Coun. Arts & Humanities, Boston, 1966, Thayer Acad., Braintree, 1971, Boston Visual Artists Union, 1974, Pa. State Univ. Mus. Art, 1974, Kennedy Galleries, N.Y.C., 1977, GVW Smith Art Mus., Springfield, Mass., 1977, Clark Univ. Mus., Worcester, Mass., 1978, Mass. Artists Found. Fed. Res. Bank, Boston, 1980, Danforth Mus., Framingham, Mass., 1980, 84, Rose Art Mus. Brandeis U., 1982, MacDowell Colony Benefit, Cambridge, Mass., 1983, Brockton (Mass.) Art Mus., 1983, Currier Gallery Art, Manchester, N.H., 1984, Fitchburg Art Mus., 1984, Newton Arts Ctr., 1985, Boston U., 1986, Alchemy Gallery, Boston, 1987, Helen Bumpus Gallery, Duxbury, Mass., 1989, Rising Tide Gallery, Provincetown, Mass., 1989, Contemporary Sculpture, Chesterwood, Stockbridge, Mass., 1989. Recipient Mass. Artists Found. award, 1977, Commendation for Design Excellence, NEA, 1981, Henry Hering Meml. medal Nat. Sculpture Soc., 1988; winner numerous competitions and commns.; grantee Brandeis U., 1983. Office: 175 Parker St Newton MA 02459-2549 Mailing: c/o National Academy Design 1083 Fifth Ave New York NY 10128*

JENDERS, ROBERT ALLEN, medical educator, researcher; s. Raymond Steven and Audrey Cecilia Jenders. BS, Marquette U., 1984; MD, U. Wis., 1988; MS, Northeastern U., 1993. Diplomate Am. Bd. Internal Medicine, 1991, Am. Bd. Internal Medicine, 2001, Fellow Am. Coll. Physicians, 2004.

Med. resident U. Wis. Hosp. and Clinics, Madison, 1988—91; clin. and rsch. fellow in medicine Mass. Gen. Hosp. and Harvard U., Boston, 1991—94; asst. prof. medicine and med. informatics Columbia U., N.Y.C., 1994—2002; assoc. prof. clin. medicine U. Calif., L.A. and Cedars-Sinai Med. Ctr., 2002—. Co-chair clin. decision support tech. com. Health Level Seven, Ann Arbor, Mich., 1998—; mem. tech. working group Nat. Immunization Program, Ctrs. for Disease Control and Prevention, Atlanta, 1999—. Contbr. articles to profl. jours. Mem.: ACP, Am. Med. Informatics Assn. Achievements include leadership in continuing development of the Arden Syntax, the only recognized standard for procedural medical knowledge representation. Office: Cedars-Sinai Med Ctr 8700 Beverly Blvd SSB-309 Los Angeles CA 90048-1804 Business E-Mail: jenders@ucla.edu.

JENERALCZUK, JOANNA MARIA, statistician, educator, mathematician; b. Bialystok, Poland, Aug. 15, 1962; d. Maria Teresa Wilkon and Jaroslaw Jeneralczuk; m. Thurlow Adrean Cook, Jan. 13, 1996; children: Michael Piotr, Thomas John Jeneralczuk Cook. M in Math., U. Warsaw, Bialystok, Poland, 1986; M in Math. and Stats., U. Mass., Amherst, 1998, postgrad., 1999—. Math. tchr. Liceum 0golnoksztalcace, Bialystok, 1986—87; tchr. dept. math. and stats. U. Mass., Amherst, 1998—. Tchr., lectr. U. Mass Statis. Consulting Ctr., Amherst, 2002; lectr. Bay Path Coll., 2001—02. Contbr. chapters to books. Mem.: Am. Math. Soc. Roman Catholic. Home: 160 Summit St Belchertown MA 01007 Office: Univ Mass Dept Math and Stats Amherst MA 01003 E-mail: jeneral@math.umass.edu.

JENES, THEODORE GEORGE, JR., retired military officer; b. Portland, Oreg., Feb. 21, 1930; s. Theodore George and Mable Marie (Moon) Jenes; m. Beverly Lorraine Knutson, Jan. 29, 1953; children: Ted, Mark. BS, U. Ga., 1956; MS, Auburn U., 1969; grad., Army Command and Gen. Staff Coll., Armed Forces Staff Coll., Air War Coll.; LLD (hon.), U. Akron, 1986. Enlisted U.S. Army, 1951, commd. 2d lt., 1953, advanced through grades to lt. gen., 1984, various assignments, 1953-75, combat duty, 1965—66; comdr. 3d Brigade, 2d Inf. Divsn., Republic of Korea, 1975-76, 172d Inf. Brigade, Ft. Richardson, Alaska, 1978-81; dep. commdg. gen. U.S. Army Tng. Ctr., Ft. Dix, NJ, 1976-78; comdr. 4th Inf. Divsn., Ft. Carson, Colo., 1982-84; dep. commdg. gen. U.S. Army Combined Arms Combat Devel. Activity, Ft. Leavenworth, Kans., 1981-82; comdg. gen. 3d U.S. Army, Ft. McPherson, Ga., 1984-87; comdr. U.S. Army Forces Ctrl. Command, Ft. McPherson, Ga., 1984-87; dep. commdg. gen. hdqrs. U.S. Army Forces Command, Ft. McPherson, Ga., 1984-87, ret., 1987; cons. Burdeshaw and Assocs., 1987-88; gen. mgr. Seattle Tennis Club, 1988-94. Decorated D.S.M., Legion of Merit, Bronze Star, Meritorious Sevc. medal, Air medal, Army Commendation medal, Vietnamese Cross of Gallantry with Silver Star, Combat Infantry Badge. Mem.: Am. Hellenic Ednl. Progressive Assn., Assn. U.S. Army, Rotary. United Methodist. Avocations: reading Biblical and military history, golf. Home: 809 169th Pl SW Lynnwood WA 98037-3307 E-mail: tedbevjen2@comcast.net.

JENG, HELENE WU, retired administrative librarian; b. Taipei, Taiwan, July 23, 1938; came to U.S., 1966; d. Shou-Li and Mei-Tze (Huang) Wu; m. Bih-Jing Jeng, Nov. 27, 1971; children: Henry David, Lana Keren. BA, Soochow U., Taipei, 1962; MLS, Appalachian State U., 1968. Asst. to dir. Nat. Sci. Mus., Taipei, 1962-64; pub. asst. Taiwan Power co., Taipei, 1964-66; head libr. Lancaster Extension/U. S.C., 1968-73, Villa Julie Coll., Balt., 1974-78; libr. Mt. Wilson State Hosp., Balt., 1978-81; reference libr. U.S. Army Med. Rsch. Inst., Edge, Md., 1981-83; adminstrv. libr. Md. Dept. of Planning, Balt., 1983—2003. Elder, Balt. Taiwanese Presbyn. Ch., Randallstown, Md., 1997; pres. Taiwanese Am. Assn., Balt. and Columbia, Md., 1986. Mem. ALA, Md. Libr. Assn. Republican. Avocations: reading, classical music, performing arts, travel, sightseeing. Office: Md Dept of Planning Libr 301 W Preston St Ste 1101 Baltimore MD 21201-2392 Home: 4420 Summer Grape Rd Pikesville MD 21208-6322

JENICEK, ALICIA JOANNE, nursing consultant; d. John Andrew and Alice Jeanette Jenicek; children: James Josef Wong, John Daniel Wong. BS in Biology, Tex. A&M U., 1982; BSN, U. Tex. Med. Br., 1984. Cert. legal nurse cons., Med.-Legal Consulting Inst., Inc., RN Tex.; cert. massage therapist Dept. Health, Tex., massage therapy instr. Dept. of Health, Tex. Staff nurse U. Tex. Med. Br., Galveston, 1984—85, La. State U. Med. Ctr., Shreveport, 1986, Hosp. Corps. Am. Highland Hosp., Shreveport, 1986—87, Highland Clinic, Shreveport, 1987, Schumpert Med. Ctr., Shreveport, 1987—92; tchr. San Jacinto Med. Ctr., Baytown, Tex., 1992—2001; massage therapist Healing With Feeling, Taylor Lake Village, 1997—, massage therapy instr., 1998—; legal nurse cons. Med.-Legal Consulting, Taylor Lake Village, 2001—; paramed. technician Exam One, Houston, 2004—. Instr. European Massage Therapy Inst., Houston, 1999—2001; cons. James M. Andersen, Esquire, Houston, 2002—, Sanes, Matthews and Forester, Houston, 2004—. Editor: (newsletter) Medical-Legal Consulting. Mem. St. Paul Cath. Cmty., Houston, 1992—2005. Mem.: U. Tex. Med. Br. Aux., Internat. Massage Assn., Healing Arts Network, Am. Specialty Health Networks, Am. Assn. Legal Nurse Cons., Nat. Alliance Cert. Legal Nurse Cons., Bay Area Aggies Former Student Assn. (scholarship reviewer 2003—04), Massage and Bodywork Educators Alliance. Roman Catholic. Avocations: art, crafts, reading. Home and Office: Med-Legal Consulting 1126 Live Oak Ln Taylor Lake Village TX 77586 Office Phone: 281-460-8239. Personal E-mail: ajajenicek@cs.com. Business E-Mail: ajenicekwongclnc@cs.com.

JENKIN, JAMES THOMAS, video editor; b. Montclair, N.J., Apr. 28, 1964; s. David Alan and Dolores Ann (Hyland) J.; m. Evelyn Lebron. Student, Raritan Valley Coll., Somerville, N.J., 1987-88; cert. advanced non-linear editing, Avid Sch. Forman Rising Sun Coatings, Flemington, N.J., 1985-89; with dept. videotape playback Picsonic Prodns., N.Y.C., 1989-91, videotape editor, 1991—; sr. editor program Headliners and Legends MSNBC, 1999—2002, sr. editor primetime unit, 2002—; pres. TBM Prodns., Hoboken, NJ. Pres. Thought Bubble Media. Contbr. articles to mags. Recipient various Telly awards, 1991, 92, 95, Communicator award, 1997, Videographer award, 1998, Silver medal NY Festival, 2001. Mem. Internat. TV Soc. Avocations: music composition, softball, tennis, movie research. Office Phone: 201-583-4000. E-mail: jtj909@aol.com.

JENKINS, ALBERT FELTON, JR., lawyer; b. Madison, Ga., Jan. 18, 1941; s. A. Felton and Jimmie Lucille (Davis) J.; m. Julie Richardson Green, Apr. 16, 1966; children: A. Felton III, Emily Green, Alan Davis. AB, U. Ga., 1963, LLB, 1965. Bar: Ga. 1965, U.S. Dist. Ct. (no. dist.) Ga. 1965, U.S. Ct. Appeals GA. 1965, U.S. Ct. Appeals (4th cir.) 1981, U.S. Ct. Appeals (5th cir.) 1966, U.S. Ct. Appeals (11th cir.) 1981, U.S. Ct. Appeals (D.C. cir.) 1987, U.S. Supreme Ct. 1968. Assoc. King & Spalding, Atlanta, 1965-70, ptnr., 1971-92, ret. ptnr., 1992—. Chmn. bd. visitors U. Ga. Law Sch., Athens, 1974; mem. Gov.'s Appellate Jud. Selection Com., Atlanta, 1972-73, Gov.'s Jud. process Rev. Com., Atlanta, 1984-85, Ga. Joint Study Commn. on Revenue Structure, 1992-95, Ga. Agrl. Exposition Authority; dir. Dundee Mills, Inc., 1994-95. Co-author: (2 vol. treatise) Georgia Civil Procedure Forms-Practice, 1988. Sec. U. Ga. Bd. Trustees, 1979-85; chmn., pres. Atlanta Unit Am. Cancer Soc., 1982-83; trustee Atlanta Fulton Pub. Libr. Sys., 1995-97. Sgt. Air Nat. Guard, 1965-71. Fellow Am. Bar Found.; mem. State Bar of Ga. (pres. Young Lawyers 1972-73, bd. govs. 1983-91), Piedmont Driving Club (Atlanta), Phi Beta Kappa, Omicron Delta Kappa. Methodist. Office: King & Spalding 191 Peachtree St SW Ste 4100 Atlanta GA 30303-1763 Office Phone: 706-342-3564.

JENKINS, ALEXANDER, III, consumer products company executive, consultant; b. Weymouth, Mass., Feb. 17, 1934; s. Alexander and Eva Gladys (Price) J.; m. Judith H. Switzer, Jan. 4, 1975; children: Alexander Tuxbury, Edith Garland, Charles Jordan. BS, Yale U., 1956; MBA, Harvard U., 1961. Rsch. asst. Harvard Bus. Sch., Boston, 1961-62; treas. Ocean Rsch. Equip., Inc., Falmouth, Mass., 1962-65, 77-78, Orion Rsch., Inc., Cambridge, Mass., 1962-70, exec. v.p., 1970-71; pvt. practice cons. Cambridge, Mass., 1971-79; v.p. Adcole, Cambridge, Mass., 1972-77; pres. Jenkins Trading, Inc., Chelsea, Mass., 1973-91; prin. Sormani Calendars divsn., Chelsea, 1991—. Treas., dir. Pintek, Inc., 1979-81; div. mgr. Spectra Physics, 1980-81; pres., CEO Orion Rsch., Inc., Cambridge, 1981-88, chmn., chief exec. officer, 1988-89; pvt. cons., 1989—, treas. Jenkins Trading Inc. (dba Sormani Calendars) 1991—. With USN, 1956-59. Episcopalian. Home: 37 Breakwater Dr Chelsea MA 02150-4024 Office: 121 Webster Ave Chelsea MA 02150 Office Phone: 617-889-9300. Personal E-mail: sormani@mindspring.com.

JENKINS, ALYCE MITCHEM, writer, educator; b. Harvard, Ill., Nov. 3, 1935; d. John Foster and Queenie Black Mitchem; m. Reese Valmer Jenkins, Dec. 27, 1962; children: David William, Elizabeth Ann Jenkins Manfredi. BA, U. Colo., 1957; MS, U. Wis., 1961. Cert. tchr. Ill., Wis., Ohio, N.J. English tchr. Crystal Lake (Ill.) H.S., 1957—60; demonstration tchr. No. Ill. U., DeKalb, 1961—62; English, social studies tchr. H. Schenk Jr. H.S., Madison, Wis., 1962—66; homebound tchr. Cleve. Pub. Schs., 1971—76, 1977—78; tchr. social studies Laurel Sch., Shaker Heights, Ohio, 1977—78; English instr. Kean U., Union, NJ, 1980; social studies, English tchr. Middlesex (N.J.) H.S., 1980—85, 1993—94; freelance writer, 1985—. Founder, leader Rainbow Writers, Bridgewater, 1992—95. Author: Lost in a Blizzard, 2001; co-author: College Board Achievement: English Composition, 1988; contbr. over 100 articles to adult and juvenile periodicals. Founder, leader Connected Hearts Adoption Triad Support, North Plainfield, NJ, 1997—; instr., mentor Sisters Aftercare, Bridgewater, NJ, 2001—; mem. adv. bd. N.J. Adoption Resource Clearing House, 2003—; mem. Presbyn. Women, 1997—. Fellow Knapp Grad., U. Wis., 1960—61. Mem.: Bound Brook Writers, Soc. Children's Book Writers and Illustrators (award com., Mag. Merit awards 1999, Mag. Merit award 1996), Pi Lambda Theta, Kappa Delta Pi, Phi Beta Kappa. Democrat. Presbyterian. Avocations: genealogy, reading, gardening, correspondence, grandchildren. Home: 11 Clifton Ave New Brunswick NJ 08901 Personal E-mail: alycemj@aol.com.

JENKINS, ANTHONY JEROME, prosecutor; U.S. atty. V.I. US Dept. Justice, 2005—. Office: US Attys Office US Courthouse and Fed Bldg 5500 Veterans Dr Ste 260 St Thomas VI 00802-6424 Office Phone: 340-774-5757. Office Fax: 340-776-3474.

JENKINS, ANTONIO DEWAN, exercise specialist; b. Chgo., June 9, 1979; s. Vera L. Jenkins, Martha Mae and Edward Jenkins. BS in Social Sci., Delta State U., Cleveland, Miss., 1997—2002; MS in Edn., Alcorn State U., Miss., 2002—04. Cert. exercise instr. NETA, 2004. Compliance asst. Alcorn State U. Athletics, Miss., 2003; exercise specialist Meth. Healthcare, Tunica, Miss., 2004—. Cons., project dir. Computers Etc., Clarksdale, Miss., 2003—05; founder, CEO Coaching To Excellence, Clarksdale, Miss., 2004—05. Chmn. African Am. Student Coun., Delta State U., Miss., 2001—02. Mem.: Phi Beta Sigma (life; Miss. state sec. 2004—). Baptist. Avocations: running, model building, reading, chess, weightlifting. Office Phone: 662-621-9005. Office Fax: 662-621-1572. E-mail: at_jenkins79@yahoo.com.

JENKINS, BECKI EUNICE, medical products executive, writer; b. Connersville, Ind., Oct. 6, 1965; d. Bailey Eugene Jenkins, Sr. and Annie Mae Stikeleather. Cert. in Surg. Tech., Ball Meml. Sch., 1986; RN, Distance Learning-Excellsior, Indpls., 2004. Cert. surg. technologist. Surg. technologist St. Vincent Hosp., Indpls., 1991—, ctrl. svc. technician, 1996—; writer Infection Control Today, Indpls., 1999—; pres., CEO Sterilization By Design, Inc., Indpls., 2000—. Care group steward New Wineskin Ministries, Indpls., 2000—04; cons. Assn. for Advancement of Med. Instrumentation, Balt., 2001—; med. missions dir. New Wineskin Ministries, Indpls., 2003—; rep. Voice of the Martyrs, Bartlesville, Okla., 2004—; bd. dirs., med. missions, supply coord. Missionary Connection; coord. Computers for the Third World, Living Bread to the World. Author: (handbook) Sterilization By Design: processing/reprocessing of instrumentation in medical devices; application of basic principles, 2002, What Kind of Love is This?, 2004, (lyrics) Gospel One, 2000, Way Out Gospel One, 2000; contbr. articles to profl. jours. Coord. C-Moble; active Voice of the Martyrs, Bartleville, Okla., 2003; pastor New Wine Minsitries; active New Wineskin Ministries, Indpls., 2003; internat. surg. team Cutting Edge Found., Bartleville, Okla., 2004. Recipient Healthcare Heroes award, Ind. Bus. Jour., 2000, St Louis De Marrilac award, St. Vincent Hosp., 2001. Mem.: Internat. Assn. Healthcare Ctrl. Svc. Materials Mgmt., Assn. for Advancement of Med. Instrumentation (assoc.; sterilization working group 2000, AAMI Becton Dickinson Career achievement Award 2003), Internat. Assn. of Healthcare Ctrl. Svc. Materials Mgmt. (assoc.; instr., spkr. 1996, pres. Ind. chpt. 2005, cert. ctrl. svc. technician), Assn. of Surg. Technologist (assoc.). Achievements include design of sterilization trays; development of cleaning brushes for healthcare use; discovery of problem in healthcare that presented patient safety risk. Avocation: writing poems, lyrics, articles and Christian books. Personal E-mail: becki5789@msn.com.

JENKINS, BRENDA GWENETTA, pre-school administrator, special education educator; b. Durham, NC, Aug. 11, 1949; d. Brinton Alfred and Ophelia Arden (Eaton) Jenkins. BS, Howard U., 1971, MEd, 1972, cert. advanced grad. studies, 1975; postgrad., Trinity Coll., Am. U., U. DC, Marymount Coll., 1976—. Cert. tchr., Washington; cert. Advanced Grad. Studies Spl. Edn., aerobics instr., Nat. Dance Exercise Instr.'s Tng. Assn. Cheerleading coach Howard U., Washington, 1971-86; tchr. DC Pub. Schs., Washington, 1972—, aerobics instr., 1982-97, Goals 2000 English, lang. arts, history writer, 1995-96; v.p. Nerdlihc Corp., Washington, 1985—; ptnr. Jenkins, Trapp-Dukes and Yates Partnership, Washington, 1984; co-owner Fantasia Early Learning Acad., Washington, 1985-98; instr. aerobics Washington Dept. Recreation, Washington, 1988—93; instr. You Fit, Inc. Nat. Children's Ctr. Washington, 1991-93, Anthony Bowen YMCA, Washington, 1992-93; instr. health, nutrition support Rockville, Md., 1992; instr., coach Maryvale PomPom/cheerleaders, Montgomery County, Md., 1992-94, asst. chmn. tchr. collaborative program, 1992-94, co-chair program com. tchr. collaborative, 1995-96; fitness instr. Oxedine Performing Arts Acad., Prince George's County, 1995-96. Aerobic instr. Coun. Exceptional Children, Washington, 1982, recreation svcs., City of Rockville, 1986—; developer My Spl. Friend program, 1984, BJ's Thinking Cap, 1991, Learning Creations, 1994, Girlfriends; bldg. rep. Washington Tchrs. Union AFT, AFL-CIO, 1987-89, 91-94, 1996-2004, asst. bldg. rep., 1990-91, 94-95, 2004-; supr. Foster Grandparent program Sharpe Health Sch., 1988—; trainer AIDS in Workplace, 1990, Early Childhood Substance Abuse Project Tng., 1992-93, Substance Abuse Prevention Edn., 1995, Metro Foster Grandparent Program Adv. Bd., Washington, 1992; mem. preschool adv. bd. DC Pub. Schs., 1992-93, coordinating curriculum coun., 1994-96; master tchr. Coop. Tchr. Corp., 1993; curriculum writer, 1993; v.p. spl. edn. Washington Tchrs. Union Local 6, 1994-2004; stds. specialist, 1997—; convention del. Am. Fed. Tchrs., 1998, 2004; adv. bd. Supt.'s Tchr. Affairs, 1999-; mem. Spl. Edn. State Adv. Panel, Washington, 1998-2000, D.C. Parent Tng. and Info. Ctr., ARC, Inc. Adv. Panel; exec. bd. dirs. Assembly of Petworth, 1998—; DC Pub. Schs. recruiter Nat. Alliance Black Sch. Educators, Nashville, 1999, resident mentor tchr., 1999-2004; mem. Disting. Educators Roundtable, 1998-2004; supt. search com. D.C. Pub. Schs., 2004; pre-test participant Corp. for Nat. and Cmty. Svc., 2004; presenter, spkr. in field Singer: 2000 Voices Lincoln Meml., 2000. Active DC Spl. Edn. State Adv., 1998, Internat. Space Camp, Huntsville, Ala., 1998; mem. Martin Luther King Tribute Choir, 2005 Recipient Outstanding Svc. award Kappa Delta Pi, 1978-79, 81-82, 84, citation Washington Tchr. Union, 1985, State winner Elem. Level Nat. Citizenship Edn. Tchr.'s award Ladies Aux. VFW, Washington, 2002, 03; named DC Tchr. of Yr. Coun. Chief State Sch. Officers, 1998, U. DC Cooperating Tchr., 2004; grantee spl. edn. DC Pub. Sch. state office, 1993, Citibank, 1994; named to Hall of Fame Bison Found. Inc., Howard U., 1995; Washington Post grant in the arts, 1999-04, Masonic Scottish Rite Educator Excellence award, 2001. Mem.: ASCD, Am. Fedn. Tchrs. (presiding officer WTU Spl. Educator and Svc. Provider Forums 1998—, sch. to careers tchr. extern 2001, DCPS new tchr. orientation trainer 2001—04, new tchr. orientation trainer 2001—04, new tchr. coord. 2001—04, WTU Positive Tchr. ad campaign 2004, DCPS stds. facilitator 2005), Coun. Exceptional Children, Howard Alumni Cheerleaders Assn. (co-founder 1977, pres. 1990—94, v.p. 1998—, Outstanding Recognition award 1984, Recognition award named Brenda G. Jenkins Outstanding Cheerleader award 1987), DC Parents and Friends of Children with Spl. Needs (critical ptnrs. group/supts. task force 2003, bd. dirs., DCPS leadership/anchor stds. team mem. 2005—), Pi Lambda Theta, Kappa Delta Pi (exec. com. Theta Alpha chpt.). Democrat. Avocations: alumni cheerleading, fashion design, cooking, dance, poetry. Office Phone: 202-576-6161.

JENKINS, BRUCE STERLING, federal judge; b. Salt Lake City, Utah, May 27, 1927; s. Joseph and Bessie Pearl (Iverson) J.; m. Margaret Watkins, Sept. 19, 1952; children— Judith Margaret, David Bruce, Michael Glen, Carol Alice. BA with high honors, U. Utah, 1949, LLB, JD, U. Utah, 1952. Bar: Utah 1952, U.S. Dist. Ct. 1952, U.S. Supreme Ct. 1962, U.S. Circuit Ct. Appeals 1962. Pvt. practice, Salt Lake City, 1952-59; assoc. firm George McMillan, 1959-65; asst. atty. gen. State of Utah, 1952; dep. county atty. Salt Lake County, 1954-58; bankruptcy judge U.S. Dist. Ct., Utah, 1965-78, judge, 1978—, chief judge, 1984-93. Adj. prof. U. Utah, 1987-88, 95-99. Research, publs. in field; contbr. essays to Law jours.; bd. editors: Utah Law Rev, 1951-52. Mem. Utah Senate, 1959-65, minority leader, 1963, pres. senate, 1965, vice chmn. commn. on orgn. exec. br. of Utah Govt., 1965-66; Mem. adv. com. Utah Tech. Coll., 1967-72; mem. instl. council Utah State U., 1976. Served with USN, 1945-46. Named Alumnus of Yr. award Coll. Law Univ. Utah, 1985; recipient Admiration and Appreciation award Utah State Bar, 1995, Emeritus Merit of Honor award U. Utah Alumni Assn., 1997. Fellow Am. Bar Found.; mem. ABA, Am. Inn Ct., Utah State Bar Assn. (Judge of Yr. 1993), Salt Lake County Bar Assn., Fed. Bar Assn. (Disting. Jud. Svc. awrd Utah chpt. 1993), Order of Coif, Phi Beta Kappa, Phi Kappa Phi, Phi Eta Sigma, Phi Sigma Alpha, Tau Kappa Alpha. Democrat. Mem. Lds Ch. Office: US Dist Ct 462 US Courthouse 350 S Main St Salt Lake City UT 84101-2106

JENKINS, CHARLES H., JR., retail company executive; m. Dorothy Chao; children: Jennifer, Anthony. BBA in bus. administrn., Emory U., 1964, MBA in bus. administrn., 1965; PhD, Havard Bus. Sch. Asst. to real estate v.p. Publix, 1969, v.p., 1974, exec. v.p., 1988, chmn. exec. com., 1990—2000, COO, 2000, CEO, 2001—. Pres. Lakeland C. of C. Mem.: Boston Symphony Orch. Bd. of Overseers.*

JENKINS, DARRELL LEE, librarian; b. Roswell, N.Mex., Aug. 12, 1949; s. Lindon C. and Joyce (King) J.; m. Susan Jenkins. BA, Ea. N.Mex. U., 1971; MLS, U. Okla., 1972; MA, N.Mex. State U., 1976. Asst. edn., psychology, gift libr. N.Mex. State U., Las Cruces, 1972—73, edn. psychology libr., 1973—74, asst. reference libr., 1974—75, asst. catalog libr., 1975—76, asst. serials libr., 1976—77, acting head reference dept., 1977; adminstrv. svcs. libr. So. Ill. U., Carbondale, 1977—82, dir. libr. svcs., 1982—91, head social scis. divsn., 1992—2001. Cons. U.S. Naval Base, So. Ill. U., Groton, Conn., 1985-91; chmn. bd. dirs. CEC Comm., Inc., 1997-99. Author: Specialty Positions in ARL Libraries, 1982; co-author: Library Development and Fund Raising Capabilities, 1988; contbr. articles to profl. jours. Mem. ALA (chmn. libr. orgn. mgmt. sect. 1985-86), Am. Soc Info. Sci., Assn. Christian Librs., Ill. Libr. Computer System Orgn. (pres. 1985-86), Phi Kappa Phi, Beta Phi Mu, Phi Alpha Theta (Outstanding Libr. award 2002). Republican. Mem. Ch. Assembly God. Avocations: tennis, swimming, bicycling. E-mail: dj779@hotmail.com.

JENKINS, DAVID RAY, lawyer; b. Hammond, La., Sept. 6, 1955; s. Harlan Herbert Jenkins and Lilly Ann (Miller) Seitter; m. Francis Ann Radnich Brandenburg, June 11, 1977 (div. Oct. 1988); m. Katrina Lee Weatherson, Dec. 3, 1993; children: Daniel Harlan, Andrew James. BA in Integrated Liberal Arts, St. Mary's Coll. Calif., Moraga, 1977; JD, U. Calif., Davis, 1980. Bar: Calif. 1980, U.S. Dist. Ct. (ea. dist.) Calif. 1980. Staff atty. Alaska Code Revision Project, Davis, 1980-81; law clk. U.S. Bankruptcy Ct., Modesto, Calif., 1981-83; assoc. Rutan & Tucker, Costa Mesa, Calif., 1983-85, Fullerton, Lang, Richert & Patch, Fresno, Calif., 1985-87; shareholder Lang, Richert & Patch, Fresno, 1987-95; ptnr. Motschiedler, Michaelides & Wishon, Fresno, 1995—2004; pres. David R. Jenkins, PC, 2004—. Mem. Calif. Bankruptcy Forum (dir. 2002-03), Ctrl. Calif. Bankruptcy Assn. (dir. 1995-98, 2002-, pres. 2003). Democrat. Roman Catholic. Avocations: tennis, bicycling, hiking, gardening. Office: David R Jenkins PC 2444 Main St #120 Fresno CA 93721 Office Phone: 559-264-5695. Personal E-mail: drjbklawyer@sbcglobal.net.

JENKINS, DAWN, special education educator, dancer; b. Harrisburg, Pa., Sept. 12, 1955; d. Reese Walls and Catherine Verbos Jenkins. EdB magna cum laude, U. Miami, Fla., 1977, EdM, 1978. Cert. profl. educator Fla., cert. assoc. master tchr. Fla. Tchr. of mentally challenged Holmes Elem. Sch., Miami, 1978—79; tchr. of deaf and hard of hearing Auburndale Elem. Sch., Miami, 1979—80; tchr. elem. deaf and hard of hearing Arcola Lake Elem., Miami, 1980—93; tchr. of deaf and hard of hearing Palm Springs Mid. Sch., Hialeah, Fla., 1993—. Choreographer and tchr. South Fla. Theatre of the Deaf, Miami, 1990—96; presenter Very Spl. Arts movement workshop, incorporating dance into curriculum Mid. Sch. Conv., Ft. Lauderdale, Fla., 1997; conf. presenter What's Up in Deaf Education; choreographer, dance tchr. for deaf students Very Spl. Arts program VSA Internat., Brussels; adj. prof. Interpreters Deaf program Miami Dade Coll., 1998—2000. Mem. Homeowners' Assn., Miami Lakes, Fla., 1995—98; founding mem. local club for the deaf Optimist Internat., Miami Lakes, 1996—97; fund raising sponsor Am. Cancer Soc., Miami, 1995—2003. Recipient Outstanding ESE tchr., Miami-Dade County, 1996; grantee, Impact II Com. of Miami Dade Schs., 2000; scholar, U. Miami Marching Band, 1973—77. Mem.: Nat. Dance Edn. Orgn., Fla. Educators of Hearing Impaired, Fla. Registry Interpreters, Nat. Dance Edn. Orgn., Nat. Assn. of the Deaf, Coun. Exceptional Children, Conv. Am. Instrs. Deaf. Presbyterian. Achievements include development of dance program for the deaf, research project for MDCPS, 1991; students performing The Wind That Blew at Internat. Very Spl. Arts Festival, representing Fla., Belgium, 1994. Avocations: dance, exercise, travel, reading, yoga. Office: Palm Springs Mid Sch 1025 W 56th St Hialeah FL 33012 E-mail: dawnjenkins@mindspring.com.

JENKINS, DONALD JOHN, museum administrator; b. Longview, Wash., May 3, 1931; s. John Peter and Louise Hazel (Pederson) J.; m. Mary Ella Bemis, June 29, 1956; children: Jennifer, Rebecca. BA, U. Chgo., 1951, MA, 1970. Mus. asst. Portland (Oreg.) Art Mus., 1954-56, asst. curator, 1960-69, curator, 1974-75, dir., 1975-87, curator Asian art, 1987—2003, chief curator, 1998-2001, curator emeritus, 2004—; assoc. curator Oriental art Art Inst. Chgo., 1969-74. Mem. gallery adv. com. Asia House Gallery, NYC, 1977-91; application reviewer NEH, Washington, 1984-86; lectr. various museums and art orgns., 1969—. Author: (exhbn. catalogues) Ukiyo-e Prints and Paints, 1971, The Ledoux Heritage, 1973, Masterworks in Wood/China and Japan, 1976, Images of Changing World, 1983, The Floating World Revisited, 1993, Mysterious Spirits, Strange Beasts, Earthly Delight and Early Chinese Art from the Arlene and Harold Schultzer Collections, 2005 Mem. Pittock Mansion Adv. Com., Portland, 1975-87, chmn., 1983-84; chmn. N.W. Regional China Coun., Portland, 1980-89; mem. art selection com. Performing Arts Ctr., Portland, 1983-89; bd. dirs. Classical Chinese Garden, Portland, 2000—. Recipient Uchiyama Susumu Meml. award Japan Ukiyo-e Soc., 1993, Order of Rising Sun with gold rays and rosette Japanese Govt., 1994, Flying Horse Cmty. Svc. award N.W. China Coun., 1996. Mem. Soc. for Japanese Arts, Assn. Asian Studies, Ukiyo-e Soc. Am., Japan-Am. Soc. Oreg. (chmn. cultural affairs com. 1987-98), The Internat. House of Japan. Home: 16418 NW Rock Creek Rd Portland OR 97231-2406 Office: Portland Art Mus 1219 SW Park Ave Portland OR 97205-2486 Business E-Mail: donald.jenkins@pam.org.

JENKINS, EDWARD BEYNON, research astronomer; b. San Francisco, Mar. 20, 1939; s. Francis Arthur and Henrietta Beynon (Smith) J.; m. Myrna Dean Stewart, June 29, 1963; children: Brian Francis, Eric Dean. AB, U. Calif., Davis, 1962; PhD, Cornell U., 1966. Rsch. assoc. Princeton (N.J.) U., 1966-67, mem. rsch. staff, 1967-73, rsch. astronomer, 1973-79, sr. rsch. astronomer, 1979—. Mem. mgmt. and ops. working group NASA, Washington, 1976-79, 88-91, mem. astrophysics subcom., 1992-93; mem. com. on space astronomy and astrophysics NAS, Washington, 1986-89; co-investigator Space Telescope Imaging Spectrograph, 1985—, Far Ultraviolet

Spectroscopic Explorer, 1989—; prin. investigator Interstellar Medium Absorption Profile Spectrograph, 1980-2002. Contbr. numerous articles to Astrophys. Jour. Recipient Rsch. award Alexander von Humboldt Found., 1992-93. Mem. Am. Astron. Soc. (v.p. 1996-99), Internat. Astron. Union (pres. Commn. 44, 1988-91). Democrat. Unitarian Universalist. Office: Princeton U Obs Astronomy Dept Princeton NJ 08544-1001 Office Phone: 609-258-3826. Business E-Mail: ebj@astro.princeton.edu.

JENKINS, ELIZABETH ANN, federal judge; b. 1949; BA, Vanderbilt U., 1971; JD, U. Fla. Coll. Law, 1976. Bars: Fla. 1977, D.C. 1978. Atty. advisor U.S. Dept. of Justice, 1976-78; asst. U.S. atty. Middle Dist. of Fla., Orlando, FLa., 1978-82, Southern Dist. of Fla., West Palm Beach, Fla., 1983-85; magistrate judge U.S. Dist. Ct. (mid. dist.) Fla., 1985—. Office: US Courthouse 801 N Florida Ave Ste U32 Tampa FL 33602-3849 Office Phone: 813-301-5774.

JENKINS, ERIC E., financial analyst, writer; b. LA, Oct. 15, 1965; s. Elson and Sarah O. Jenkins; m. Trina Y. Chambers; children: Latrice S., Timothy E., Derrick M., Sabrina M. Student, U. So. Calif., 1982—84; A in Acctg., Career Inst., 1998. Cert. Acct., Calif., 1998. Fin. analyst Sony Pictures Entertainment, Culver City, Calif., 1999—. Author: (novel) Get it Today - A Jarvis Holiday Mystery. Personal E-mail: ericej@hotmail.com.

JENKINS, EVERETT WILBUR, JR., lawyer, writer, historian; b. Oklahoma City, Nov. 28, 1953; s. Everett Wilbur and Lillie Bell (Ingram) J.; m. Monica Lynn Endsley, June 3, 1978 (div. Aug. 13, 2003); children: Ryan, Camille, Jennifer, Cristina. BA cum laude, Amherst Coll., 1975; JD, U. Calif., Berkeley, 1978. Bar: Calif. 1979. Dep. county counsel Contra Costa County, Martinez, Calif., 1980-81; dep. city atty. City of Richmond, Calif., 1981-84, asst. city atty., 1984—2004, interim city atty., 2004—; bd. atty. West County Agy., Richmond, 1981-90; authority atty. Solid Waste Mgmt. Authority West Contra Costa, Richmond, 1985-87, 88-91. Legal rep. tech. adv. com. Contra Costa County Solid Waste Commn., Martinez, Calif., 1986-87, pub. mem., 1987-88; adv. atty. West Contra Costa Transp. Adv. Com., San Pablo, 1994—; bd. atty. Richmond Housing Authority, 1992-99; bd. dirs. Contra Costa Co. Hazardous Materials Commn., Martinez, 1987-88. Author: Pan-African Chronology, 1996, Pan-African Chronology II, 1998, Pan-African Chronology III, 2001, The Muslim Diaspora, 1999, The Muslim Diaspora, vol. 2, 2000, The Creation, 2003. Bd. dirs. YMCA of the East Bay, Oakland, 1996—; bd. dirs. West Contra Costa YMCA, Richmond, 1987—, chair program com., 1991-92, vice chair bd. dirs. 1992-96, chair bd. dirs., 1996-98, chair cmty. gifts campaign, 1992-94 (named Rita Davis Vol. of the Yr., 1993); umpire Little League Baseball, 1997—, ASA Softball, 1997—. Mem. ABA, State Bar Calif. (exec. bd. pub. law sect. exec. com. 1987-91, editor Pub. Law News 1988-91, liaison to bd. govs. 1991-92), Continuing Edn. Bar (joint adv. com. 1993-96), Contra Costa County Bar Assn., Charles Houston Bar Assn., Nat. Assn. Sports Officials. Independent. Office: City Atty's Office 1401 Marina Way South Richmond CA 94804-1654 Office Phone: 510-620-6509.

JENKINS, FRED WILLIAM, librarian; b. Cin., Apr. 13, 1957; s. Frederick Edwin and Ethel Mae Jenkins; m. Nancy Diane Courtney, Oct. 31, 1992. BA in Classics, U. Cin., 1979; AM in Classics, U. Ill., 1981, PhD in Classical Philology, 1985, MS in Libr. and Info. Sci., 1986. Historical collections cataloger Coll. of Physicians of Phila., 1986-87; catalog/rare book libr. U. Dayton, Ohio, 1987-96, coord. and head of collection mgmt., 1996—. Author: Classical Studies: A Guide to the Reference Literature, 1996 (Choice Outstanding Acad. Book 1996, Ohio Libr. Found. Rsch. award 1997); contbr. articles to profl. jours. Mem. Am. Philol. Assn., Am. Soc. Papyrologists, Acad. Libr. Assn. Ohio (mem. program com. 1991-93, Rsch. award 1993), Assn. Coll. and Rsch. Librs. (WESS classical, medieval and renaissance discussion group 1994, 98), Phi Beta Kappa. Home: 2771 Green River Dr Columbus OH 43228-8130 Office: U Dayton 300 College Park Ave Dayton OH 45469-0001

JENKINS, HERMAN ARTHUR, otologic educator, otolarynologist; b. Glenwood, W.Va., Apr. 24, 1945; s. Melva Winson and Sarah (Qualls) J.; m. Karen Hull Jenkins, June 22, 1974; children: Lee Vincent, Kelly Hull. BS in Zoology, Marshall U., 1966; MD, Vanderbilt U., 1970. Diploma Am. Bd. Otolaryngology (assoc. examiner 1994), Nat. Bd. Med. Examiners. Straight surg. intern UCLA Ctr. for Health Scis., 1970-71, resident in surgery, 1971-72; resident in otolaryngology UCLA Ctr. for Health Scis. and affiliated hosps., 1974-77; clin. and rsch. fellow in neurotology U. Hosp. Zurich, Switzerland, 1979-80; asst. prof. UCLA Ctr. for Health Scis., 1977-81; prof. otolaryngology Baylor Coll. Medicine, Houston, 1981—, vice chmn. dept. otorhinolaryngology and communicative scis., 1989—; active staff Meth. Hosp., Houston, 1981—, Harris County Hosp. Dist., Houston, 1981—; attending physician VA Med. Ctr., Houston, 1981—. Mem. courtesy staff Meml. Med. Ctr., Corpus Christi, Tex., 1981—, St. Luke's Epis. Hosp., Houston, 1981—; sci. exhibitor; frequent presenter in field; lectr., guest speaker in field, 1978—; reviewer med. jours., 1986—; mem. sci. rev. com. Deafness Rsch. Found., 1985-88; cons. panel on devices in otolarngology FDA, 1985-89, mem., 1989—; mem. task force Nat. Inst. on Deafness and Other Communication Disorders, 1989; mem. CDRC; cons. Nat. Inst. for Aging, NIH, 1985—, Nat. Eye Inst., 1986—; also others. Mem. editorial bd. Microsurgery, 1986—, Internat. Jour. Base of Skull Surgery, 1989—, Skull Base Surgery, 1989—; contbr. numerous articles and abstracts to med. jours., chpts. to books. Maj. M.C., USAF, 1972-74. I.N.C.O. scholar, 1961-66; grantee Nat. Inst. Neurol. and Communicative Disorders and Stroke, NIH, 1977-81, 84—, Clayton Found. for Rsch. Neurotology, 1981—, Union Pacific Found., 1985-89. Mem. AMA, ACS, Am. Acad. Otolaryngology-Head and Neck Surgery, honor award 1986, award for exhibits 1986, 87, 91), Am. Laryngol., Rhinol. and Otol. Soc., Barany Soc., Am. Neurotology Soc., Am. Otol. Soc., Assn. for Rsch. in Otolaryngology, Internat. Skull Base Soc., Soc. Univ. Otolaryngologists-Head and Neck Surgeons, Acoustic Neuroma Assn., Am. Auditory Soc., Internat. Soc. Posturography, Tex. Med. Assn. (best sci. exhibit award 1987), Harris County Med. Soc., also others. Office: Baylor Coll Medicine Otol Dept One Baylor Plz Houston TX 77030

JENKINS, HOWARD M., supermarket executive; b. 1951; MBA, Emory U. With Publix Supermarkets, Inc., Lakeland, Fla., 1966—, v.p. rsch., exec. v.p., 1976-90, CEO, 1990—2001, chmn. bd. dirs., 1990—. also: 1936 George Jenkins Blvd Lakeland FL 33815-3760*

JENKINS, JAMES ROBERT, lawyer, chemicals executive; b. Waukegan, Ill., June 10, 1945; s. William Ivy and Louise Elnora (Lampkins) J.; m. Anita Louise Horne, June 29, 1968; children: James R. II, Andrea Louise. AB in Philosophy, U. Mich., 1967, JD, 1973. Bar: Mich. 1973, Ill. 1974. Law clk., then assoc. Koster and Bullard, Ann Arbor, Mich., 1971-73; law clk. to Justice Seidenfeld 2d Dist. Ill. Ct. Appeals, Waukegan, 1973-74; asst. defender State of Mich. Appellate Defender Office, Detroit, 1974-75; dep. defender Fed. Defender Office, Detroit, 1975-76; v.p., sec., gen. counsel, counsel sec. to corp. bd. dirs., counsel to exec. com., mem. fin. com. Dow Corning Corp., Midland, Mich., 1976—2000; sr. v.p., gen. counsel Deere & Co., Moline, Ill., 2000—. Trustee Alma Coll., 1985—. 1st lt. U.S. Army, 1967-70, Vietnam. Decorated Bronze Star. Fellow Mich. State Bar Found.; mem. Mich. State Bar Assn., Am. Law Inst., Am. Arbtration Assn. (bd. dirs.), Assn. Corp. Counsel (chmn, 2005-, vice chmn. bd. dirs.). Office: Deere Co 1 John Deere Pl Moline IL 61265-8098

JENKINS, REV. JOHN I., academic administrator; PhB, Notre Dame U., 1976, MPhil, 1978; PhB, Oxford U., 1987, PhD, 1989; MDiv, Jesuit Sch. Theology, Berkeley, 1988; licentiate in Sacred Theology, Jesuit Sch. Theology, Berekeley, 1988. Ordained a priest Basilica of the Sacred Heart, Notre Dame U., 1983. Mem. faculty Notre Dame U., 1990—, prof. ancient philosophy, medieval philosophy, philosophy of the religion, adj. prof. London program, 1988—89, religious superior of Holy Cross priests, fellow, trustee, 1997—2000, v.p. and assoc. provost, 2001—05, pres., 2005—; dir. Old Coll. program for Notre Dame undergraduate candidates for Congregation of Holy Cross, 1991—93. Author: Knowledge and Faith in Thomas Aquinas, 1997, (articles published in) The Jour. Philosophy, Medieval Philosophy and Theology, The Jour. of Religious Ethics; spkr. Ann. Aquinas Lecture, U. Dallas, 2000. Recipient Lilly Teaching Fellowship, Notre Dame U., 1991—92. Office: Office of the President Notre Dame U Main Bldg Notre Dame IN 46556*

JENKINS, JOHN SMITH, retired dean, lawyer; b. Pittston, Pa., Dec. 11, 1932; s. Walter Hershel and Mildred (Lewis) J.; m. Marilyn Lewis, Aug. 23, 1958; 1 child, John Smith Jr. BA, Lafayette Coll., Easton, Pa., 1954; JD with honors, George Washington U., 1961; MA, Am. U., 1967. Bar: Va. 1961, U.S. Ct. Appeals for the Armed Forces, 1964, U.S. Supreme Ct. 1982. Commd. ensign U.S. Navy, 1955, advanced through grades to rear admiral, 1978; stationed at naval communications sta. Pearl Harbor, Hawaii, 1955—56; duty on U.S.S. Rochester, 1956-57; with Bur. Naval Personnel Washington, 1957-62; with Hdqrs. 1st Naval Dist. Boston, 1962-64; staff Office Navy JAG, 1964-65; staff Office Legis. Affairs Washington, 1969-71; staff Office of Asst. Sec., 1971-73; spl. counsel to sec. Office of Sec., 1973-76; asst. civil law JAG, 1976-78; dep. JAG, 1978-80; JAG, 1980-82; asst. dean Nat. Law Ctr. George Washington U., Washington, 1982-86, assoc. dean, 1986-2000, sr. assoc. dean, 2000—01, sr. assoc. dean emeritus, 2001. Decorated D.S.M. Legion of Merit. Fellow Am. Bar Found.; mem. ABA (ho. of dels., 1987-2005, chair standing com. on lawyers in the armed forces 1991-94, standing com. on delivery of legal svcs. 1997-2001, standing com. on legal assistance for mil. pers. 2001-05, chair, 2003-05), FBA, Judge Advs. Assn., Army and Navy Club (gov. 1988-98), George Washington U. Club. Episcopalian. Home: 5809 Helmsdale Ln Alexandria VA 22315-4138 Office Phone: 703-971-5421. Personal E-mail: jsjmlj@aol.com.

JENKINS, JUDITH ALEXANDER, bank consultant; b. Fort Sill, Okla., Oct. 14, 1940; d. James Buchanan and Gerry Lee (Gibbs) Permenter; m. Robert Miles Turner, Oct. 28, 1962 (div. 1972); m. Clarence Withers Alexander, Dec. 19, 1975 (div. Jan. 1987); m. David Claude Jenkins, Apr. 23, 1994. Student, U. Okla., 1958-59; BA in English, U. Tulsa, 1962; MBA, U. Okla., 1969; postgrad., U. St. Thomas, 1975-78. Asst. cashier So. Nat. Bank of Houston, 1971-73, asst. contr., 1973-74, asst. v.p. and asst. contr., 1974, v.p., contr., 1974-77, sr. v.p., contr., 1977-79; cons., 1979—. Mem. Beta Gamma Sigma, Gamma Phi Beta. Office: 16218 Wrangler Rd Rosharon TX 77583 Office Phone: 281-595-2030. E-mail: calikino@msn.com. *Learning, discipline, and independence are my goals and the major contributors to my success in business and personal life.*

JENKINS, KENNETH VINCENT, literature educator, writer; b. Elizabeth, N.J. s. Thomas Augustus and Rebecca Meredith (Williams) J.; 4 children. AB, MA, Columbia Coll.; postgrad., Columbia U. Tchr. South Side Sr. High Sch., Rockville Centre, N.Y., 1953-72, chmn. dept. English, 1965-72. Prof. English, Afro-Am. lit. Nassau Community Coll., Garden City, N.Y., 1972—, chmn. Afro Am. studies dept., 1975—, supr. adj. faculty, 1974-82; cons. in English, N.Y. State Dept. Edn., Albany, 1965-72; mem. Regents Question Com. in English, Albany, 1966-71; owner Black Books and Artifacts. Author: Teaching African Literature, 1960, Last Day in Church, 1965; contbr. revs., poems to profl. publs. Chmn. bd. dirs., founder Target Youth Ctrs., Inc., 1973-76, African-Am. Book Ctr., 1982—; mem. nat. bd. Pacifica Found., 1973-79, chmn., 1975-76, pres., 1976-78; bd. dirs. Sta. WBAI-FM, N.Y.C., 1972-85, Nassau County Youth Bd., 1976-2000, chmn., 1978-99, chair emeritus 1999—; mem. N.Y. Gov.'s Commn. on Youth, 1984-94; bd. dirs. L.I. Cmty. Found., 1989-98, N.Y. State Youth Support, Inc., 1990-93; mem. bd. Schomburg Ctr., N.Y.C., 1990-98. Recipient cmty., county, state awards, M.L. King Award, Celebration Com. Nassau County, 1990, Special Svc. Award One Hundred Black Men, 1994, Nat. Coun. of Negro Women, Inc. Award, 2003; Pennington grantee, 1953. Mem.: Afro-Am. Inst., Assn. Study of Afro-Am. Life and History, Mensa, Phi Delta Kappa. Office: Nassau C C Garden City NY 11530

JENKINS, LYNN M., state official, former state legislator; b. Topeka, June 10, 1963; m. Scott M. Jenkins; children: Hayley, Hayden. AA, Kans. State U., 1984; BS, Weber State Coll., 1985. CPA. CPA, 1985—; rep. Kans. State Ho. Reps., 1998—2000; mem. Kans. State Senate, 2000—03, mem. gen. govt. budget com., ins. com., post audit com., govt. orgn. and elections com., taxation com.; treas. State of Kans., 2003—. Mem. adv. bd. Ct. Apptd. Spl. Advocate; bd. dirs. YMCA Metro, Family Svc. and Guidance Ctr.; treas., bd. dirs. Prince of Peace Presch.; active Jay Snideler PTO, Susanna Wesley United Meth. Ch. Mem. Kans. Soc. CPAs. Republican. Methodist. Office: 900 SW Jackson St Ste 201 Topeka KS 66612-1235

JENKINS, MARC DELANO, music educator; s. John David and Alma Elizabeth Holley Jenkins; 1 child, Marc Delano Jr. MusB in Voice, Temple U., 1978, MusM, 1981. Cert. profl. tchr. Pa. Mem. voice faculty Settlement Music Sch., Phila., 1978—79; baritone soloist Bryn Mawr (Pa.) Presbyn. Ch., 1979—83; mem. adj. voice faculty Temple U., Phila., 1983—87; mem. voice faculty Freedom Theatre, Phila., 1986—88; music tchr. Phila. Sch. Dist., 1988—; min. of music Mother Bethel A.M.E. Ch., Phila., 1989—2005; voice and piano instr. Chestnut Hill (Pa.) Summer Arts Camp, 1991—93. Soloist Pa. Pro Musica, Phila., 1978—87, asst. musical dir., 1982—87; soloist U. Pa. Collegium Musicum, Phila., 1983—86; musical dir. The New Skyliters Jazz Chorale, Phila., 1992—95, Del Art Chorale, Phila., 1996—; dir. Benjamin Franklin Cluster Choir, Phila., 2000—02; artistic dir. W. Russell Johnson Music Guild, Nat. Assn. Negro Musicians, Phila., 2001—04; condr. W. Russell Johnson Music Guild Chorus, Phila., 2003—. Scholar Blossom Festival Vocal Chamber Ensemble, Kent. Ohio, 1980, Berkshire Music Festival, 1997. Mem.: Am. Choral Dirs. Assn., Phi Mu Alpha (life). Home: 6901 Old York Rd A-411 Philadelphia PA 19126 Personal E-mail: mdjdac@att.net.

JENKINS, MARGARET BUNTING, human resources executive; b. Warsaw, Va., Aug. 3, 1935; d. John and Irma (Cookman) Bunting; children: Sydney, Jr., Terry L. Student, Coll. William and Mary, 1952, AA in Bus. Adminstrn., 1973; BA in Human Resource Devel., St. Leo Coll., 1979; M in Adminstrn., George Washington U., 1982; PhD in Human Rsch. Mgmt., Columbia Pacific U., 1986. Rehab. counselor, tchr. York County Schs., Yorktown, Va.; mgr. Waterfront Constrn. Co., Seafood Corp., Seaford, Va., 1960—72; labor rels. specialist Naval Weapons Sta., Yorktown, 1974—77, staffing specialist, 1977—78, position classification specialist, supr. shipbuilding, conversion and repair Newport News, Va., 1978-81, supr. pers. mgmt. specialist, supr. shipbuilding, conversion and repair, 1981—90, pers. mgmt. specialist Yorktown and Cheatham, Va., 1990—94. Bd. dirs. various health orgns.; owner Jenkins Consulting. Author: Organizational Impact on Human Behavior, 1996; (poetry) Heron Haven Reflections, 1996; poetry published in Mists of Enchantment, 1995, Treasured Poems of America, 1996, Poets of the 90's, A Celebration of Poets, Showcase Edit., 1998, 99, The Best Poems of Poets award 2001; featured in: Cancer Has Its Privileges, Stories of Hope and Laughter (Christine K. Clifford), 2002 (Best Poets award 2002, 03, 04, Internat. Poetry award 2003, 04). Decorated Meritorious Civilian Svc. award USN, 3 Navy commendations; recipient award Newport News, 1990, Alumni medallion Coll. William and Mary, 1994, 95, 96, 97, 98, 99, 2000, 01, 02, 03, 04, 05. Mem.: Chesapeake Writers Assn., Classification and Compensation Soc. (pres. 1984), Soc. for Human Resource Mgmt., Long Ridge Writers Group, Toastmasters Internat. (pres. 1985—87, various offices, award), Nature Conservancy, Audubon Soc., 4-Alumni Assn., Internat. Soc. of Poets (Disting. mem. 1996), Sierra Club, Fedn. Women's Clubs. Methodist. Avocations: reading, creative writing, art. Home: PO Box 203 Seaford VA 23696-0203 *Excel beyond the norm. Be a risk-taker, and blaze a trail so others may follow. Allow creativity to flourish.*

JENKINS, MARGARET LUDMILLA, choreographer, dancer; b. Berkeley, Calif., Dec. 1, 1942; d. Hyman David and Edith Arnstein J.; m. Albert J. Wax, Apr. 2, 1972; 1 dau., Leslie Marissa. Student, Juilliard Sch. Music, 1960-61, UCLA, 1961-63. Dancer Jack Moore Dance Co., N.Y.C., 1960, Al Huang Dance Co., 1961, Gus Solomons Jr. Dance Co., 1963-65; tchr. Merce Cunningham Sch., N.Y.C., 1965-70; asst. to Merce Cunningham, N.Y.C., Boston, Stockholm, La Rochelle, France, 1965-74; dancer Twyla Tharp Dance Co., 1965-67, Viola Farber Dance Co., 1967-70; tchr. Paris, London, Stockholm, 1967; artistic dir. Margaret Jenkins Dance Co., San Francisco, 1972—; panelist NEA, Nat. Endowment for Arts, 1977-80; vice-chmn. DANCE/USA, also bd. dirs. Mem. challenge ct. panel and final rev. panel NEA, 1986, Rockefeller Choreography Project, 1986, Sundance Inst., 1986. Choreographer: Videosongs, 1976, Copy, 1977, About The Space In Between, 1977, Into Three, 1978, Red Yellow Blue, 1978, No One But Whittington, 1978, Straight Words, 1979, Invisible Frames, 1979, Duets, 1980, Versions By Turns, 1980, Harp, 1981, Cortland Set, 1982, In the Round I, 1982, In the Round II, 1982, First Figure, 1984, Max's Dream, 1984, Inside Outside (Stages of Light), 1985, Pedal Steal, 1985, Home Pt. 1, 1986, Home Pt. 2, 1986, Shelf Life, 1987, Georgia Stone, 1987, Shorebirds Atlantic, 1988, And So They, 1988, Rollback, 1988, Light Fall, Miss Jacobi Weeps, 1989, Woman Window Square, 1990, Age of Unrest, 1991, Sightings, 1991, Strange Attractors, 1992, The Gates (Far Away Near), 1993, Liquid Interior, 1995, Fault, 1996. Active Andrew W. Mellon Found., 1995, Nat. Dance Project, 1996, Nat. Dance Residency Program, 1996. Guggenheim fellow, 1980; Nat. Endowment for Arts fellow, 1978-79, 80, 81; recipient San Francisco award of Honor in Dance, 1984. Mem. San Francisco Bay Area Dance Coalition., Am. Arts Alliance (trustee) Office: Margaret Jenkins Dance Co 3973 25th St # A San Francisco CA 94114-3812

JENKINS, MAYNARD, automotive executive; With Orchard Supply Hardware, pres., CEO, 1986-97; chmn., CEO CSK Auto Corp., Phoenix, 1997—. Office: CSK Auto Corp 645 E Missouri Ave Ste 400 Phoenix AZ 85012*

JENKINS, MELVIN LEMUEL, lawyer; b. Halifax, NC, Oct. 15, 1947; s. Solomon Green and Minerva (Long) Jenkins; m. Wanda Joyce Holly, May 20, 1972; children: Dawn, Shelley, Melvin, Holly Rae-Ann. B.S., N.C. Agrl. and State U., 1969; J.D., U. Kans., 1972. Bar: Nebr. 1973, US. Dist. Ct. Nebr. 1973. Atty. Legal Aid Soc., Kansas City, Mo., 1972, HUD, Kansas City, Mo., 1972—73; regional atty. U.S. Commn. on Civil Rights, Kansas City, Mo., 1973—79, regional dir., 1979—2002; atty. Stennis and Assocs., Omaha, 2002—. Chmn. A.M. Roundtable, Kansas City, 1981—83; mem. Kansas City Human Relations Commn., 1980. Mem. Mo. Black Adoption Adv. Bd., Kansas City, 1981—; bd. dirs. Joan Davis Spl. Sch. Mem.: ACLU, ABA, Fed. Bar Assn., Nat. Bar Assn., Nebr. Bar Assn., Urban League, Masons (master mason for civil rights 1979). Mem. Ame Ch. Home: 8015 Sunset Cir Grandview MO 64030-1461 Office: 300 S 19th St Ste 216 Omaha NE 68102 Office Phone: 402-342-4093.

JENKINS, MICHAEL GRADY, judge; b. Millen, Ga., Apr. 25, 1961; s. Solomon Leslie and Marjorie (McBride) Jenkins; m. Yvonne M. Wiley, Apr. 28, 2001. BS, Ga. So. Coll., 1984; JD, John Marshall Law Sch., 2000. Newspaper reporter Statesboro (Ga.) Herald, 1985—87; ins. agt. Sylvania, Ga., 1987—93; chief magistrate judge Screven County, Sylvania, 1993—2002; adminstrv. law judge State of Ga., 2002—. Comml. timber and livestock prodr. Mem. First Christian Ch., Sylvania, Ga.; bd. dirs. Neil McCauley Found. Mem.: Gideons Internat., Rocky Branch Hunting Club (pres. 1997—), Pinnacle Club, Sylvania Rotary (sec., v.p., pres.). Mem. Christian Ch. Avocations: hunting, fishing.

JENKINS, NORMAN, accountant; m. Cammye Jenkins; children: Nicholas, Alexandra. Undergraduate bus. admin., Howard Univ.; graduate bus. admin., George Washington Univ. Vice-pres. Marriott Internat., Inc.; pres., CEO Nat. Assn. Black Accts. Office: Nat Assn Black Accts 7249-A Hanover Pkwy Greenbelt MD 20770 Office Phone: 301-474-6222. Office Fax: 301-474-3114.*

JENKINS, PATTY, film director, scriptwriter; Student in Painting, Cooper Union; degree in Dir.'s Program, Am. Film Inst. Dir.: (films) Just Drive, 2001; author: (films) Just Drive, 2001; dir.: (films) Velocity Rules, 2001 (Short Film award Telluride Indiefest, 2001); author: (films) Velocity Rules, 2001; dir.: (films) Monster, 2003 (nominated Golden Bear award Berlin Internat. Film Fest, 2004, nominated Ind. Spirit award, 2004); author: (films) Monster, 2003. Office: Creative Artists Agency 9830 Wilshire Blvd Beverly Hills CA 90212-1825

JENKINS, PAUL, artist; b. Kansas City, Mo., July 12, 1923; s. William Burris and Nadyne (Fellers) J.; m. Esther Ebenhoe, 1944 (div.); 1 child, Hilarie Paula; m. Alice Baber, 1964 (div.); m. Suzanne Donnelly, 1979. Student, Art Students League, N.Y.C., 1948-52; Hum.D., 1973, 96. Author: (plays) Strike the Puma, 1966; co-author: Observations of Michel Tapie, 1956, Shaman to the Prism Seen, 1987, Anatomy of a Cloud, 1983, Seven Aspects of Amadeus and the Others, 1992, Shaman to the Prism Moon, 1994, articles, (films) The Ivory Knife, 1965; exhibitions include Studio Paul Facchetti, Paris, 1954, Gimpel Weitzenhoffer Gallery, N.Y.C., Karl Flinker Gallery, Paris, Georges Fall Gallery, Galerie Patrice Trigano, Galerie Sapone, Nice, Gimpel Fils Gallery, London, Gallery Art Point, Tokyo, Martha Jackson Gallery, N.Y.C., Assoc. Am. Artists, NY, Galerie Proarta, Zurich, Chateau-Musée de Cagnes Sur Mer, Joseph Rickards Gallery, N.Y., Redfern Gallery, London, one-man shows include Mus. Fine Arts, Houston, San Francisco Mus. Art, Palm Springs Desert Mus., Musée Picasso, Antibes, Mus. Nice, France, Hofstra Mus., Hempstead, N.Y., Butler Inst. Am. Art, Youngstown, Ohio, Basilica Palladiana Vicenza, Centre D'Art Contemporain Bouvet Ladubay, Saumur, Represented in permanent collections Mus. Modern Art, Whitney Mus., Guggenheim Mus., NY, Corcoran Gallery, Washington, Tate Gallery, London, Musee D'Art Moderne, Paris, Centre Georges Pompidou, Fondation Maeght, St-Paul-de-Vence, Musee Picasso, Antibes, Stedelijk Mus., Amsterdam, Netherlands, Mus. Western Art, Tokyo. Served with USNR, 1943-45. Decorated Commandeur des Arts et Lettres France; recipient Silver medal Corcoran Gallery Art, 1967, Art Dir.'s award for Anatomy of a Cloud, 1984, Life Achievement award Butler Inst. Am. Art, 1997, medal City of Paris, 1997, Benjamin West Clinedinst medal Artists' Fellowship N.Y., 2000. Mem. Royal Cambrian Acad. (hon.; Wales), Nat. Acad. N.Y. (elected). Studio: Imago Terrae PO Box 6833 Yorkville Sta New York NY 10128

JENKINS, PEGGY ANNE, special education educator; b. Detroit, Sept. 27, 1954; d. Hollis Burton and Marian Ellen Mackinder; children: Jeffrey Scott, Gregory James, Steven Michael. BS, Ea. Mich. U., 1976; MA, Oakland U., 1979. Tchr. trainable mentally impaired Detroit Pub. Schs., 1977; mid. sch. spl. edn. tchr. Oak Pk. (Mich.) Schs., 1977—87; secondary spl. edn. tchr. cons. Lahser H.S., Bloomfield Hills, Mich., 1987—. Supervising tchr. Bloomfield Hills Sch., 2000—01. Sunday sch. tchr. Pine Hill Congl. Ch., West Bloomfield, Mich., 1998—2005. Mem.: ASCD. Avocations: golf, flute, bridge, travel. Home: 2839 Colonial Trl Bloomfield Hills MI 48304 Office: Lahser HS 3456 Lahser Rd Bloomfield Hills MI 48302 Office Phone: 248-341-5723. Personal E-mail: consultantpeggy@aol.com. E-mail: pjenkins@bloomfield.org.

JENKINS, REESE V., historian, educator; b. Muncie, Ind., June 28, 1938; s. John Thomas and Vada Arline Fraze Jenkins; m. Alyce Jeanette Mitchem Jenkins, Dec. 27, 1962; children: David William, Elizabeth Ann Manfredi. BA, U. Rochester, 1960; MS, U. Wis., 1963, PhD, 1966. Tchr. history and math. Madison (Wis.) Ctrl. Univ. H.S., 1963—64; asst. prof. history No. Ill. U., Dekalb, 1966—67; from asst. to assoc. prof. history of sci. and tech. Case Western Res. U., Cleve., 1967—78; dir., editor Thomas A. Edison Papers Rutgers U., New Brunswick, NJ, 1978—95, prof. history, 1978—. Harvard-Newcomen Bus. History fellow Harvard U., Boston, 1969—70; vis. assoc. prof. history U. Rochester, NY, 1976—77; hist. cons. Eastman Kodak Co., Rochester, 1993, Fuji Photofilm Co., Ashagara, Japan, 1995—99; participant PBS-TV programs on Thomas Edison, 1979—95; prin., cons., participant PBS-TV Am. Experience: George Eastman, 2000—01. Author: Images & Enterprise, 1975 (award N.Y. Photo Soc., 1976, Choice award, 1976), Japanese edit., 1998; editor-in-chief Papers of Thomas A. Edison, Vols. 1-3, 1989—94 (award Assn. Am. Pubs., 1989), microfilm edit., 1985—95; contbr. articles to profl. jours.; mem. editl. bd.: N.J. History, 1980—. Trustee Wesley Found., Rutgers U., New Brunswick, 1984—90, chair, 1987—89. Recipient award of recognition, N.J. Hist. Commn., Trenton, 1991; grantee NSF, NEH,

NEA, numerous others. Mem.: Soc. for History of Tech. (exec. coun. 1980—82, 1992—94, chair various coms. 1977—, Dexter prize 1978), Assn. for Documentary Editing (chair various coms. 1991—96, commendation 1996), History of Sci. Soc. (pres. Mid-West Junta 1978—79, coun. 1973—75). Democrat. Presbyterian. Avocations: reading, photographica, family history, women's collegiate basketball, walking. Home: 11 Clifton Ave New Brunswick NJ 08901-1503 Office: Dept History Rutgers U College Ave Campus New Brunswick NJ 08903-5059 Personal E-mail: Reese638@aol.com.

JENKINS, RICHARD DALE, actor, theatre director; b. DeKalb, Ill., May 4, 1947; s. Dale Stevens and M. Elizabeth (Wheeler) J.; m. Sharon R. Friedrick, Aug. 23, 1969; children: Sarah Pamela, Andrew Dale. BFA, Ill. Wesleyan U., 1969, LHD (hon.), 1991. Actor Trinity Repertory Co., Providence, R.I., 1970-84, stage dir., 1984-90, artistic dir., 1990-94. Appeared in (plays) The Suicide, The Iceman Cometh, In the Belly of the Beast, American Buffalo, Waiting for Godot, Of Mice and Men, True West, Fool for Love, others, (films) Silverado, Hannah and Her Sisters, The Witches of Eastwick, Stealing Home, Little Nikita, Blue Steel, Sea of Love, Blaze, Wolf, The Indian in the Cupboard, Flirting With Disaster, There's Something About Mary, The Mod Squad, Snow Falling on Cedars, Me, Myself & Irene, One Night at McCool's, The Man Who Wasn't There, many others (TV movies) Double Crossed, Afterburn, And The Band Played On, Into Thin Air, others (TV Series) Six Feet Under, 2001-2005; dir. Billy Bishop Goes to War, Tartuffe, The Crucible, The Lady from Maxim's, Camino Real, Golden Boy, The School for Wives, The Lower Depths, Other People's Money, The Glass Menagerie, Macbeth, The Seagull, The Hope Zone, Twelfth Night or What You Will, A Christmas Carol, others. Recipient Spl. Recognition award New Eng. Theatre Conf., 1991, Achievement in Theatre award, 1991; named Best Dir., Boston Theatre Critics, 1982.*

JENKINS, RICHARD ERIK, patent lawyer; b. Newport News, Va., Jan. 12, 1946; s. Willard Erette and Ina Beatrice (Porter) J.; m. Susan Rankin Thurston, Aug. 24, 1968 (div. Nov. 1991); 1 child, Anna; m. Lisa Joanne Weavers, Nov. 11, 2003. BS, N.C. State U., 1968, M in Stats. and Econs., 1971; JD, U. N.C., 1975. Engr. Celanese Corp., Charlotte, N.C., 1971-72; assoc. atty. Stevens, Davis, Miller & Mosher, Washington, D.C., 1975-76, Bell, Seltzer, Park & Gibson, Charlotte, N.C., 1976-78; ptnr. Adams &Jenkins, Charlotte, 1978-80; asst. patent counsel Burlington Industries, Inc., Greensboro, N.C., 1980-84; sr. ptnr. Jenkins, Wilson & Taylor, Durham, NC, 1984—. Adj. assoc. prof. Duke U., Durham, 1989—, N.C. State U., Raleigh, N.C., 1992-95. Trustee N.C. Ctrl. U., Durham, 1992-95, Peace Coll., Raleigh, 2001—; bd. govs. Univ. Club, Durham, 1994-98; bd. dirs. Coun. Entrepreneurial Devel., 1988-90, N.C. State Found., 2002—. Mem. AMA, N.C. Bar Assn., Rotary, Hope Valley Country Club, Univ. Club, Carolina Club. Republican. Presbyterian. Avocations: golf, yard, reading. Office: Jenkins Wilson & Taylor 3100 Tower Blvd Ste 1400 Durham NC 27707-2563 Office Phone: 919-489-4393. E-mail: rjenkins@jenkinswilsontaylor.com.

JENKINS, RICHARD LEE, manufacturing executive; b. Lynchburg, Va., July 20, 1931; s. Robert Julian and Beulah Vivian (Crews) J.; m. Doris E. Rucker, Dec. 24, 1958; children: Terena M., Richard C. BA, Lynchburg Coll., 1957; MBA, U. Mass., 1970. Various fin. mgmt. positions Gen. Electric Co., Lynchburg, Schenectady, N.Y., and Pittsfield, Mass., 1957-72; controller, mgr. Mfg. Transformer div. Allis-Chalmers, Pitts., 1972-75; gen. mgr. Indsl. Pump div. Allis-Chalmers, Cin., 1975-79; sr. v.p. Lynchburg Foundry, 1979-81; gen. mgr. service div. Siemens-Allis, Inc., Atlanta, 1981-84; sr. v.p. adminstrn. and internat. ops., chief fin. officer Diversified Products Corp., Opelika, Ala., 1984—. Treas., bd. dirs. Micah Corp. of Berkshire County, Pittsfield, 1968-72; bd. dirs. Va. Nat. Bank, Lynchburg, 1979-81. Auditor ARC, Pittsfield, 1966; bd. dirs., exec. on loan United Community Services, Pittsfield, 1972; campaign chmn. Piedmont Heart Assn., Lynchburg, 1980. Served with USN, 1950-54, Korea. Mem.: Cherokee Country (Atlanta), Saugahatchee Country (Opelika). Home: 2245 Springwood Dr Auburn AL 36830-7231 Office: Diversified Products Corp 309 Williamson Ave Opelika AL 36804-7313 E-mail: richardjenkins@charter.net.

JENKINS, ROBERT BERRYMAN, real estate developer; b. Evanston, Ill., Oct. 11, 1950; s. Clive Ridley and Genevieve (Brown) Crawford J.; m. Carol Lynn Kealey, Sept. 22, 1984; children: Paul Brown, Leighanne Kealey. BEE, Cornell U., 1972; postgrad., U. W. Fla., 1974. Cert. Profl. Solar Technology, 1984. Owner Fothergill's Outdoor Sportsman, Aspen, Colo., 1978-81; owner, engr. Sophisticated Solar, Aspen, 1983-85; owner/pres. Sandhill Devels., Gulf Breeze and Aspen, 1985—; owner, pres. Roaring Fork Liquors, Inc., Glenwood Springs, Colo., 1992-2000. Grad. Leadership Santa Rosa County, Fla., 1988-89. Recipient U.S. Dept. Energy Nat. Award for Energy Innovation, 1987, Gov.'s Energy award Fla. Gov., 1987; named Man of Yr., Gulf Breeze, 1991. Mem. Internat. Coun. Shopping Ctrs., Trout Unltd. (life). Republican. Methodist. Avocations: snowskiing, flyfishing, whitewater rafting. Address: PO Box 14 200 Doc Henry Rd Woody Creek CO 81656

JENKINS, ROBERT GORDON, retired military officer, federal official; b. Charlottesville, Va., Dec. 14, 1941; s. Charles Gordon and Rosa Lee (Berry) J.; m. Nicki Jean Mitchell, Aug., 1966; children: Lara Elizabeth, Christopher Scott. BS, Va. Poly. Inst. and State U., 1964; MS, W.Va. U., 1967. Commd. USAF, 1968—, advanced through grades to brig. gen., fighter pilot, 1968-75; comdr. 22d Tactical Fighter Squadron, Bitberg Air Base, Germany, 1981-82; asst. chief staff AOC Allied Air Forces Ctrl. Europe, Boerlink, Germany, 1982-84; dep. comdr. for ops. Tactical Air Warfare Ctr., Eglin AFB, Fla., 1984-85; comdr. Air Forces Iceland, Keflavik, 1985-87; vice comdr. 354 Tactical Fighter Wing, Myrtle Beach, S.C., 1987-88, comdr., 1988-90; dep. dir. gen. purposes forces HQ USAF, Pentagon, Washington, 1990-92, dep. dir. ops., 1992; comdr. 51st Fighter Wing, Osan Air Base, Korea, 1992-94; vice comdr. 7th Air Force, Osan Air Base, Korea, 1994-95; dir. logistics HQ Pacific Air Force, 1995-97; pres. Exco Techs. Inc., 1997-2000; dir. aviation mgmt. U.S. Dept. Energy, 2000—. Decorated Legion of Merit with cluster, DFC, 2 Meritorious Svc. medals, 12 Air medals, 2 Commendation medals, DFC with cluster, Disting. Svc. medal. Mem. Order of Daedalians. Home: 9853 Hidden Estates Cv Vienna VA 22181-6090 E-mail: RandNJenk@aol.com.

JENKINS, ROBERT H., steel company executive; BBA, U. Wis. Pres., CEO Sundstrand Corp. (now Hamilton Sundstrand Corp.), Rockford, Ill., 1995—97, chmn., pres., CEO, 1997—99. Bd. dirs. Clarcor Inc., 1999—, Sentry Ins., Solutia, Inc., Visteon Corp., AK Steel Holding Corp., Jason Inc. Office: AK Steel Holding Corp 703 Curtis St Middletown OH 45043-0001 also: Clarcor Inc 840 Crescent Centre Dr Franklin TN 37067*

JENKINS, ROBERT NORMAN, reporter, editor; b. Washington, Oct. 22, 1943; s. Jack Julian and Mina Lorraine (Katz) J.; m. Dianne Ruth Lang, June 1966 (div. June 1973); children: Kirsten Rose, Joshua Matthew; m. Dianne Carol Dearmin, Dec. 14, 1974; children: Michael Robert, Ryan Robert. BA in Journalism, Mich. State U., 1965. Newspaper reporter Grand Rapids (Mich.) Press, 1965-67; newspaper reporter, editor Newsday, Garden City, N.Y., 1967-69, St. Petersburg (Fla.) Times, 1969—. Recipient 1st Place News Section Design, Fla. Soc. Newspaper Editors, 1974. Mem.: Soc. Am. Travel Writers (nat. v.p. 1999—2001, Lowell Thomas Travel award Gold 1996, 2000, Lowell Thomas Travel award Silver 1996, 1999, Lowell Thomas Travel award Bronze 1999, 2000, 2001, 2002), Hon. Coaches Mich. State U. Office: St Petersburg Times 490 1st Ave S Saint Petersburg FL 33701-4204 Business E-Mail: jenkins@sptimes.com.

JENKINS, RONALD WAYNE, lawyer, engineer, mediator; b. Johnson City, Tenn., Aug. 14, 1950; s. James Herman and Peggy Sue (Hutchison) J.; children: April Chalice, Kimberly Michelle, Robert Herman, Ronald Wayne II. BSEE, U. Tenn., 1972, JD, 1980. Bar: Tenn. 1980, U.S. Supreme Ct. 1986, U.S. Ct. Appeals (6th cir.) 1986, U.S. Dist. Ct. (ea. dist.) Tenn. 1986. Assoc. M. Lacy West, P.C., Kingsport, Tenn., 1980-83, Herndon, Coleman, Brading & McKee, Johnson City, 1984-86, ptnr., 1985—2001, Herrin, Booze, Rambo, Jenkins & Wheeler, Jonesborough, Johnson City, 2001—. Instr. rsch. and writing III U. Tenn. Coll. Law, 1979; mediator Tenn. Supreme Ct. Rule 31. Rsch. editor Tenn. Law Rev., 1978-79, editor-in-chief, 1979. With Ubon Royal AFB, 1972—73, Thailand Eglin AFB, 1973—74, Fla. Hahn AFB, 1974—75, Germany Spangdahlem AFB, 1976—77 Royal AFB, 1977, England Andrews AFB, 1983—84, Md. Mem. ABA, Tenn. Bar Assn., Washington County Bar Assn., Fed. Bar Assn., Nat. Aeronautic Assn., Aircraft Owners and Pilots Assn., Am. Bd. Trial Advs. (assoc. 1999), Tau Beta Pi (Tenn. col., engring. honor), Eta Kappa Nu (electrical engring. honor), Spangdahlem AB Aero Club (pres. 1976-77). Avocations: agriculture, aviation. Office: Herrin Booze Rambo Jenkins & Wheeler PO Box 308 806 E Jackson Blvd Jonesborough TN 37659-0308

JENKINS, RUBEN LEE, chemicals executive; b. Beggs, Okla., Nov. 27, 1929; s. William Arnold and Myrtle (Kimble) J.; m. Sylvia Griffin, July 17, 1956; children: Amy, Kimble Lee, William Griffin. BA, U. Okla., 1952, LLB, 1956; LLM, NYU, 1959. Bar: Okla. 1956. Law clk. to presiding justice U.S. Dist. Ct. (we. dist.) Okla., Oklahoma City, 1956; clk. U.S. Ct., Oklahoma City, 1956-58; research asst. in internat. law NYU, N.Y.C., 1958-59; assoc. Allende & Brea, Buenos Aires, Argentina, 1959-60; exec. v.p., gen. counsel White Eagle Internat., Midland, Tex., 1960-65; v.p. corp. devel. Plough, Inc., Memphis, 1965-71, dir, 1970, sr. v.p. hdqrs., 1972-73, exec. v.p., 1973-76, pres., 1976-89; dir. Schering-Plough Corp., Madison, N.J., 1971-89, sr. v.p., 1976-80, exec. v.p., 1980-89. Bd. dirs. Chickasaw coun. Boy Scouts Am., Memphis; hon. trustee Memphis U. Sch. Capt. USMC, 1952-54. Mem. ABA, Tenn. Bar Assn., Okla. Bar Assn., Non-Prescription Drug Mfrs. Assn. (bd. dirs. 1976-89), Palm Beach Polo and Country Club. Methodist. Address: 2886 Winding Oaks Ln West Palm Beach FL 33414 E-mail: rljenkins1@adelphia.net.

JENKINS, SHERRY L., state insurance program administrator; b. San Diego, Aug. 2, 1956; children: Shannon D., Adam D. AAS, Oscar Rose Jr. Coll., Midwest City, Okla., 1978; BS in Acctg. and Fin., Harrington U., London, 1981, MBA, 2000; BS, Oklahoma City U., 1999. Cert. flexible compensation Employers Coun. on Flexible Compensation. Accounts specialist II State of Okla. - Employees Benefits Coun., Oklahoma City, 1996—99, FSA claim supr., 1999—2000, mgr. members accounts, 2000—03, ins. program adminstr., 2004—. Recipient Govenor's Commendation award, State of Okla. - Gov,. Frank Keating, 2000. Mem.: Delta Mu Delta (assoc.; Zeta Omega chpt.), Alpha Sigma Lambda (assoc.; Omicron Chi). Office: OK Employees Benefits Council Ste 1200 200 N Harvey Oklahoma City OK 73102 Business E-Mail: sjenkins@ebc.state.ok.us.

JENKINS, SPEIGHT, performing company executive, writer; b. Dallas, Jan. 31, 1937; s. Speight and Sara (Baird) J.; m. Linda Ann Sands, Sept. 6, 1966; children: Linda Leonie, Speight. BA, U. Tex.-Austin, 1957; LL.B., Columbia U., 1961; DMus (hon.), U. Puget Sound, 1992; HHD, Seattle U., 1992. News and reports editor Opera News, N.Y.C., 1967-73; music critic N.Y. Post, N.Y.C., 1973-81; TV host Live from the Met, Met. Opera, N.Y.C., 1981-83; gen. dir. Seattle Opera, 1983—. Classical music editor Record World, N.Y.C., 1973—81; contbg. editor Ovation Mag., N.Y.C., 1980—87. Served to capt. U.S. Army, 1961-66. Recipient Emmy award for Met. Opera telecast La Boheme TV Acad. Arts and Scis., 1982 Mem. Phi Beta Kappa Assocs. Presbyterian. Office: Seattle Opera PO Box 9248 Seattle WA 98109-0248

JENKINS, THOMAS H., lawyer; b. Washington, Oct. 25, 1951; BA, Davidson Coll., 1974; MS, Pa. State U., 1976; JD, U. Va., 1979. Bar: NY 1980, DC 1984, lic.: US Dist. Ct. (Ea. Dist.) NY, US Dist. Ct. (So. Dist.) NY, registered: US Patent & Trademark Office. Ptnr. Finnegan, Henderson, Farabow, Garrett & Dunner LLP, Washington, mng. ptnr., 1996—2001, leader, Bio./Pharm. Practice Group. Mem.: Bar Assn. DC, DC Bar Assn. Office: Finnegan Henderson Farabow Garrett & Dunner LLP 901 New York Ave NW Washington DC 20001-3315 Office Phone: 202-408-4000. Office Fax: 202-408-4400. Business E-Mail: tom.jenkins@finnegan.com.

JENKINS, THOMAS LLEWELLYN, physics professor; b. Cambridge, Mass., July 16, 1927; s. Francis A. and Henrietta (Smith) J.; m. Glen Pierce, July 8, 1951; children: Gale F., Phillip P., Matthew A., Sarah E. BA, Pomona Coll., 1950; PhD, Cornell U., 1956. Physicist Lawrence Radiation Lab., Livermore, Calif., 1955-60; faculty Case Western Res. U., Cleve., 1960—, prof. physics, 1968-94, prof. emeritus physics, 1994—. Sci. and Engring. Research Council fellow Southampton U., (Eng.), 1983 Mem. Am. Phys. Soc., AAAS, Phi Beta Kappa, Sigma Xi. Home: 869 Belwood Dr Cleveland OH 44143-3239 Office: Case Western Res Univ Physics Dept Cleveland OH 44106

JENKINS, TONY DEAN, salesman; b. Dallas, Jan. 26, 1961; s. Frank Jr. Jenkins and Leotha Hamilton; m. Adriana Rodriguez Jenkins, Aug. 6, 1983; children: Tony D. Jr., Benjamin D. BS, Dallas Bapt. U., 1983. Asst. mgr. Church's Chicken, Dallas, 1990-91; sales rep. Mut. of Omaha, Dallas, 1992-94; driver Schneider Nat., Greenbay, Wis., 1994-96; dispatcher Glazer's Wholesale, Dallas, 1996-99; spl. rep. George S. May Internat. Co., Park Ridge, Ill., 1999-2000; ind. sales rep. Dallas, 2000—; agt. Farmers Ins., Addison, Tex., 2002—. 1st lt. U.S. Army, 1984-87 Mem. Alpha Phi Alpha. Avocations: golf, tennis, jogging. Office: PO Box 380863 Duncanville TX 75138-0863 Office Phone: 214-704-6150. E-mail: JTDJenkins1@aol.com.

JENKINS, WILLIAM L. (BILL JENKINS), congressman; b. Detroit, Nov. 29, 1936; m. Mary Kathryn Myers; 4 children. BA Tenn. Tech. U., 1958, JD U. Tenn., 1961. Farmer, Rogersville; atty.; circuit ct. judge 3d jud. dist. State of Tenn., 1990-96; mem. 105th-108th Congress from 1st Tenn. Dist., Washington, 1997—; mem. judiciary com. Former dir. Home Fed. Savs. and Loan, Tenn. Bd. dirs. TVA, 1972-78; mem. Tenn. Ho. of Reps., 1963-71, spkr. of House, 1969-71; commr. Tenn. Dept. Conservation; policy advisor energy and legis. issues to gov. State of Tenn.; chmn. Tenn. Heart Assn., Cancer Crusade. Mem. Hawkins County Farm Bur., Am. Legion, Masons. Republican. Baptist. Avocations: hunting, fishing. Office: US House of Reps 1207 Longworth House Office Bl Washington DC 20515-4201 also: PO Box 769 320 W Center St Kingsport TN 37660-3658*

JENKINS, WILLIAM L., academic administrator; b. South Africa; arrived in US, 1978; m. Peggy Jenkins; children: Sharon, Gwynn, Anthea, Warren. Professional vet. medicine degree, U. Pretoria, South Africa, 1958, vet. specialist credentials, 1968; PhD, U. Missouri, Columbia, Mo., 1970; D (hon.), U. Pretoria, 2004. Various positions over several years to prof. and head, Dept. of Vet. Physiology, Pharmacology and Toxicology U. Pretoria, South Africa, 1971—78; faculty, Dept. of Vet. Physiol. and Pharmacology Texas A&M U., College Station, Tex., 1978—88; dean of Sch. of Vet. Medicine La. State U., Baton Rouge, 1988—93, provost and vice chancellor, 1993—96, chancellor, 1996—99; pres. La. State U. Sys., Baton Rouge, 1999—. Mem. NIH's Alcohol Abuse and Misuse on Coll. Campuses Com., La. Blue Ribbon Commn. for Teacher Quality. Pub. more than 60 scientific articles and 15 textbook chapters; co-author of vet. pharmacology textbook. Bd. dir. Greater Baton Rouge C. of C., Baton Rouge Ctr. for World Affairs, Coun. for a Better La., Arts Coun. of Greater Baton Rouge, La. Endowment for the Humanities, Academic Distinction Fund; mem. Baton Rouge board of Nat. Conf. for Cmty. and Justice. Named Communicator of Yr., PublicRelations Assn. of La., 1997, Disting. Alumnus, U. Mo., 1997; recipient Communication and Leadership award, Toastmasters Internat., 1999, Vision of Excellence award, New Orleans Regional C. of C., 2000. Mem.: Am. Academy of Vet. Nutrition, Internat. Assn. of Forensic Toxicologists, World Assn. of Vet. Physiologists, Pharmacologists and Biochemists, Am. Coll. Vet. Clin. Pharmacology, Am. Vet. Medical Assn. Office: Office of Chancellor 156 Thomas Boyd Hall La State Univ Baton Rouge LA 70803

JENKINS-ANDERSON, BARBARA JEANNE, pathologist, educator; b. Chgo. d. Carlyle Fielding and Alyce Louise (Walker) Stewart; m. Sidney Bernard Jenkins, Sept. 22, 1951 (div. June 1970); children: Kevin Jenkins, Judy Kelly, Sharolyn Sanders, Marc Jenkins, Kayla French; m. Arthur Eugene Anderson, Sept. 30, 1972. BS, U. Mich., 1950; MD, Wayne State U., 1957. Diplomate Am. Bd. Pathology. Intern Providence Hosp., Detroit, 1958-59, resident in psychiatry, 1959-60; resident in pathology Henry Ford Hosp., 1961-62, U. Mich. Affiliated Program, 1962-65; staff pathologist Wayne County Hosp., 1966-70, Detroit Receiving Hosp., 1970-72; asst. prof. pathology Wayne State U. Med. Sch., Detroit, 1970—72, assoc. prof. pathology, 1973—; adminstrv. med. dir. Detroit Med. Ctr. Univ. Labs., Detroit, 1988—; chief pathology Detroit Receiving Hosp./Univ. Health Clinic, Detroit, 1990—. Instr. U. Mich., 1966-70. Recipient Leonard Sain award U. Mich., 1980. Mem. Alpha Omega Alpha. Avocations: golf, interior design. Office: DMC Univ Labs 4201 Saint Antoine St Detroit MI 48201-2153 Office Phone: 313-993-0539. Business E-Mail: banderso@dmc.org.

JENKINS-BRADY, TERRI LYNN, publishing executive, journalist; b. Albuquerque, Sept. 19, 1952; d. Hubert Arnold Jenkins and Helen Hope Zumwalt; m. Timothy Daniel Brady, July 4, 2000; stepchildren: Cori Danielle Brady, Colt Mitchell Brady. Student, U. Albuquerque, 1971—75, U. N.Mex., 1976. Pub. rels./fund-raiser March of Dimes, 1980; asst. to editor Prime Time, Albuquerque, 1995—2000, columnist, 2000—02; editor Al Bowl Querque Times, Albuquerque, 2000; editor in chief, ptnr. Write Up The Road Pub., Kenton, Tenn., 2002—; retail sales rep., freelance writer, 1974—79. Co-author: Romancing the Road, 2002, You Know You're Married To A Trucker When..., 2003; editor: Driven 4 Profits Fin. Newsletter, 2003, Oh, Pegasus: A Work of Love Thoughts, 2003, Driven Profits, 2002, Plonk Goes the Weasel, 2004, Gearing Up 4 Profits, 2004, Death Had A Yellow Thumb, 2005, Simpatico Patio!, 2005, Billy Beaver's Traveler, 2001—04, Reflerctions Thru My Windshield, 2005. Mem. adv. bd. Hiland Sr. Ctr., Albuquerque, 1996—97; co-founder Further Up the Road scholarship Rotary Club, Union City, Tenn., 2002. Recipient Bronze and Silver medals, Imperial Soc. Tchrs. Ballroom Dance, 1981. Mem.: Small Pubs. Assn. N.Am., Writer's Ink. Avocations: travel, writing, designing wearable art, ballroom dancing. Office: Write Up The Road Pub PO Box 69 Kenton TN 38233-0069 Office Phone: 731-749-8567. Business E-Mail: terrijenkins-brady@writeuptheroad.com.

JENKS, CARL M., lawyer; b. Cleve., 1945; BA, Carleton Coll., 1967; MA, Duke Univ., 1973, PhD, 1979; JD, Harvard Univ., 1980. Bar: Ohio 1982. Law clk. Judge Walter R. Mansfield, US Ct. of Appeals, Second Cir., 1980—81; ptnr., chair, general tax practice Jones Day, Cleve. and NYC. Author (numerous articles): profl. publications. Named to Best Lawyers in America. Fellow: Am. Coll. of Bankruptcy, Am. Coll. of Tax Coun.; mem.: Am. Law Inst. Fluent in Portuguese. Office: Jones Day North Point 901 Lakeside Ave Cleveland OH 44114-1190 also: Jones Day 222 E 41st St New York NY 10017-6702 Office Phone: 216-586-7173, 212-326-8321. Office Fax: 216-579-0212, 212-755-7306. Business E-Mail: cmjenks@jonesday.com.

JENKS, THOMAS EDWARD, lawyer; b. Dayton, Ohio, May 31, 1929; s. Wilbur L. and Anastasia A. (Ahern); m. Marianna Fischer, Nov. 10, 1961; children: Pamela (dec.), William, David, Christine, Daniel, Douglas Student, Miami U., Oxford, Ohio, 1947-50; JD cum laude, Ohio State U., 1953; hon. grad., U.S. Naval Sch. Justice, 1953. Bar: Ohio 1953, U.S. Dist. Ct. (so. dist.) Ohio 1961, U.S. Supreme Ct. 1971, U.S. Ct. Appeals (6th cir.) 1984. Pvt. practice, Dayton, 1955—; atty. Jenks, Pyper & Oxley, Dayton. Lectr. in med. malpractice law. Served to 1st lt. USMC, 1953-55 Fellow Am. Coll. Trial Lawyers, Ohio Bar Found.; mem. ABA (ho. of dels. 1985-88), Am. Bar Found. (life), Dayton Bar Assn. (life, pres. 1978-79), Ohio Bar Assn. (life, bd. govs. litig. sect., 1990-98), Internat. Assn. Def. Counsel, Ohio Assn. Civil Trial Attys., Am. Bd. Trial Advs. (adv.), Kettering C. of C. (past pres.), Kettering Holiday at Home Found. (past pres.), Order of Coif, Dayton Lawyers Club (pres. 1999-2002), Optimist Club (past pres. Oakwood chpt.), Phi Delta Phi, Sigma Chi. Republican. Roman Catholic. Office: Jenks Pyper & Oxley Courthouse Plz SW 10 N Ludlow St Dayton OH 45402 Office Phone: 937-223-3001. Business E-Mail: tjenks@jpolawyers.com.

JENKS, ZOYA ELAINE, retired librarian; b. Chgo., Mar. 13, 1933; d. Abraham and Anna (Frumkin) Hochstein; m. George Merritt Jenks, Mar. 7, 1957; children: Darrell, Mark, Andrew. BA, UCLA, 1956; MLS, Clarion U., 1983. Prin. lit. asst. UCLA, 1956-57; tutor history U. Tasmania, Hobart, Australia, 1963-66; lectr. music Bucknell U., Lewisburg, Pa., 1967-83, catalog libr., 1983-89, head catalog dept., 1990-96; ret., 1996. Reviewer Australian Broadcasting Commn., Hobart, 1963-66. Mem. ALA, Pa. Libr. Assn. (chair acad. and rsch. 1988, bd. dirs. 1995-97). Democrat. Avocations: music, travel, reading. Home: 202 N 2nd St Lewisburg PA 17837-1518 Business E-Mail: zjonks@bushnell.edu.

JENKYN, ADRIAN JOHN, computer company executive; b. Milford Haven, Wales, July 19, 1939; s. Reginald John Mantell and Alice Thora (Laugharne) J.; m. Elizabeth Jane Hatton, Mar. 11, 1961 (div. 1989); children: David Adrian, Anthony Graham; m. Joyce Faye Brazier, Oct. 27, 2001. Higher nat. cert. in elec. engring., Rugby (Eng.) Coll. Tech., 1960. Supervising engr. ICL Ltd., Worcester, Eng., 1964-68, sr. engr. Cairo and Berlin, 1967-68, field mgr. Norwich, Eng., 1968-72, project mgr. Cairo, 1972-75, engring. mgr. Moscow, 1975-77, sr. mgr. Bracknell, Eng., 1977-82, br. mgr. Tokyo, 1982-88; pres. JAI Computer Tech., Tokyo, 1988-98; Y2K tech. coord. AARP, Washington, 1998—; specialist in bus., 1999; continuity and disaster prevention and recovery, 2003; bus. continuity mgr. Ill. Dept. Pub. Health, 2005. Chmn. St. David's Soc. Wales, Tokyo, 1992. Decorated Most Excellent Order Brit. Empire. Fellow Brit. Computer Soc., Instn. Inc. Elec. Engrs.; mem. Inst. Dirs., Brit. C. of C. in Japan (exec. com. 1992), Tokyo Brit. Club (founder, chmn. 1986). Avocations: contract bridge, photography, community theater. E-mail: jenkyn@earthlink.net.

JENNE, ARTHUR KIRK, secondary school educator; b. Pikeville, Ky., Jan. 15, 1942; s. William Kendrick and Robina Laurie (Kirk) J.; m. Linda Louise Morris; children: Karen Jenne Stevens, Arthur Kirk II. BS, Towson (Md.) State Coll., 1970; MEd, Western Md. Coll., 1973. Instr. Balt. County Pub. Schs., Towson, 1970—. Designer computer learning ctr. Balt. County Pub. Schs., 1986. Author: Read, Study, Think...Reading Comprehension, 1973, Computer Utilization of T.G., 1987. Pres. St. Matthew's Ch. Coun., Pleasant Valley, Md., 1994, Carroll County U.C.C. Lay fellowship, 1994-96. With USMC, 1961-65. Mem. Md. Instructional Computer Coord., State of Md. Internat. Reading Assn., Marine Corps. League, Valley Lions (pres. 1991-92), Am. Legion. Home: 2110 Hughes Shop Rd Westminster MD 21158-2923

JENNERICH, EDWARD JOHN, academic administrator, dean; b. Bklyn., Oct. 22, 1945; s. William James and Anna Johanna (Whicker) J.; m. Elaine Zaremba, May 27, 1972; children— Ethan Edward, Emily Elaine BA, Trenton State Coll., 1967; MSL.S., Drexel U., 1970; PhD, U. Pitts., 1974. Cert. tchr., learning resources specialist. Tchr. U.S. history Rahway High Sch., N.J., 1967-70; librarian Westinghouse High Sch., Pitts. Pub. Sch., 1970-74; adminstrv. intern U. Pitts, 1973; chmn. dept. library sci. Baylor U., Waco, Tex., 1974-83; dean Sch. Library Sci. So. Conn. State U., New Haven, 1983-84; v.p. acad. affairs Va. Intermont Coll., Bristol, 1984-87; grad. dean Seattle U., 1987-89; assoc. provost for acad. adminstrn., dean Grad. Sch., 1989-97; pres. Knowledge N.W. Inc., 1997—. Mem. rev. panel Fulbright Adminstrv. Exch., 1983-86. Co-author: University Administration in Great Britain, 1983, The Reference Interview as a Creative Art, 1987, 2d edit., 1997; contbr. articles to profl. jours. Bd. dirs. Waco Girls Club, Tex., 1977-83 Mem. ALA (office for libr. pers. resources 1980-82), Am. Assn. Univ. Adminstrs. (bd. dirs. 1980-82, 83-86, 89-93, 94—, v.p. 1996—, exec. com. 1982-87, chmn. overseas liaison com. 1982-87, Eileen Tosney Adminstrv. Excellence award 1985), Assn. for Coll. and Rsch. Librs. (exec. bd. dirs. 1984-88), Phi Delta Kappa. Republican. Episcopalian. Avocations: collecting and painting military miniatures, reading, travel, outdoor sports, sailing. Home: 6935 NE 164th St Kenmore WA 98028-4282 E-mail: jennerich@mindspring.com.

JENNESS, JAMES, grocery manufacturing company executive; b. Chgo., May 15, 1946; m. Sharon Jenness; 3 children. B in Mktg., M in Bus. Adminstrn., DePaul U., Chgo. Vice chmn., COO Leo Burnett Co., mem. exec.

com., bd. dirs.; CEO Integrated Merchandising Sys. LLC; bd. dirs. Kellogg Co., Battle Creek, Mich., 2000—, chmn. CEO, 2005—. Co-trustee W.K. Kellogg Found. Trust; bd. dirs. Grocery Mfrs. Am., Schwarz Paper Co.; guest lectr. DePaul U., Chgo. Bd. dirs. exec. com. mem., chair mktg. com. Children's Meml. Hosp.; bd dirs. Mercy Home for Boys and Girls; bd. trustees DePaul U., Chgo., chmn. coll. commerce advisory coun. Mem.: Econs. Club Chgo. Office: Kellogg Co 1 Kellogg Sq Battle Creek MI 49016-3599*

JENNETT, JOSEPH CHARLES, retired academic administrator, engineering educator; b. Dallas, June 11, 1940; s. James C. and Rita (Gavin) Buchanan; m. Linda Ellis, Aug. 2, 1963; children: Erin, Brian. BS in Civil Engrng., So. Meth. U., 1963, MS in Civil Engrng., 1966; PhD, U. N.Mex., 1969. Registered profl. engr. Mo., N.Y., S.C., Tex. Field engr. Pitometer Assocs., U.S., Can., 1964-65, 69; instr. civil engrng. U. N.Mex., Albuquerque, 1965-66; asst. prof. civil engrng. U. Mo., Rolla, 1969-73, assoc. prof. civil engrng., 1973-75; assoc. prof., chmn. civil engrng. Syracuse (N.Y.) U., 1975-78, prof., chmn. civil engrng., 1978-81; prof. environ. systems engrng. Clemson (S.C.) U., 1981—, dean engrng., 1981—96, provost, v.p. acad. affairs, 1991—96; pres. Tex. A&M U., Laredo, Tex., 1996—2001, pres. emeritus, 2001—. Adj. prof. civil engrng. Syracuse U., 1981-87; constr. engr. Dept. of Water Resources, State of Calif., 1963-64, Projects in N. Sydney, New Waterford, Halifax, Can., 1969; cons. Pitometer Assocs., Pa., Ga., Mich., Ky., 1964-65, Calspan Corp., Litton Industries, Schwitzer Corp., Dow Chem., Union Carbide, Martin Marietta, 1969, 85—. Co-author: Lead in the Environment, Geochemistry and the Environment; contbr. articles to profl. jours. Vol. troop 235 Boy Scouts Am., Clemson; adviser Water and Wastewater Treatment Authorities, Natal, Brazil, Wesley Found.; patron Greenville (S.C.) Theatre on the Green. Named Outstanding Young Engr. of Yr. Mo. Soc. Profl. Engrs., 1974. Fellow ASCE; mem. NAS, NSPE, Am. Soc. Engring. Edn. (bd. dirs. 1986-89), Am. Acad. Environ. Engrs. (bd. dirs. 1988-91), S.C. Soc. Profl. Engrs. (pres. Piedmont chpt. 1987-88, Outstanding Engr. of Yr. Piedmont chpt. 1990, S.C. Engr. of Yr. 1990), U. N.M. Outstanding Coll. Engring. Alumni, Water Pollution Control Fedn., Nat. Rsch. Coun. Commn. (life scis. com.), Order of Engr. (bd. dirs. 1988-91). Episcopalian. Avocations: photography, travel, camping, fishing, reading, skiing. Home: PO Box 2761 Wimberley TX 78676

JENNEWEIN, JAMES JOSEPH, architect; b. New Rochelle, N.Y., July 20, 1929; s. Carl Paul and Gina (Pirra) J.; m. Edith Joan Wilson, Nov. 28, 1953; children: James Christopher, Gina Louise, Donald Andrew, Jonathan Paul. BArch, Syracuse U., 1952. Fulbright scholar Stuttgart U. (Technische Hochschule), Federal Republic of Germany, 1955-56; draftsman McCoy & Blair Architects, White Plains, N.Y., 1956-57; designer Harrison & Abramovitz Architects, N.Y.C., 1957-60; prin./ptnr. Jennewein Architects, N.Y.C., 1961-62; prin. McElvy, Jennewein, Stefany & Howard, Architects, Tampa, Fla., 1962-84, Jennewein, Archtl. Planning, Tampa, 1984; prin., ptnr. Jennewein Schemmer and Assocs., Tampa, 1985-91; ptnr. Ruyle Hayes Plus Jennewein, Architects, P.A., Tampa, 1992—. Pres. Fla. State Bd. Architecture, 1969-72. Trustee Brookgreen Gardens, Murrells Inlet, S.C., 1983—; chmn. Gasparilla Art Show, Tampa, 1977, Tampa C. of C. Environ. Com., 1987; pres. Tampa Bay Art Ctr., 1975, Tampa Mus. Art, 1985. Lt. (j.g.) USN, 1952-55. Recipient House of Yr. award Archtl. Record, N.Y.C., 1963, Ybor Sta. P.O. award Hillsborough County Planning Commn., Tampa. 1989. Fellow AIA; mem. Fla. Assn. AIA (pres. 1985-86, Pullara award 1985), Fla. Cen. Chpt. AIA (pres. 1967-68, Honor medal 1985), Nat. Sculpture Soc. (allied profl.), Tampa Yacht Club, Ye Mystic Krewe of Gasparilla, Tampa. Republican. Episcopalian. Avocations: fishing, sailing. Home: 4710 W Clear Ave Tampa FL 33629-5512 Office: Ruyle Hayes Plus Jennewein Archs 3333 W Kennedy Blvd Ste 203 Tampa FL 33609-2959 Office Phone: 813-879-6633.

JENNINGS, CAROL, marketing executive; b. Marion, Ohio, Oct. 2, 1945; d. Richard P. and Mary (LeMaster) J.; m. John Putnam Merrill Jr., Jan. 3, 1981. BA, Miami U., Oxford, Ohio, 1967. News editor Penton Pub. Inc., Cleve., 1967-69; pub. rels. exec. Cen. Nat. Bank, Cleve., 1969-71; dir. pub. rels. New Eng. Conservatory of Music, Boston, 1971-74, Bklyn. Acad. Music, N.Y.C., 1974-75; account exec., supr. Hill and Knowlton, N.Y.C., 1975-81, from v.p. to mng. dir., 1981-87; sr. v.p., gen. mgr. Hill, Holliday, Connors, Cosmopolus, Boston, 1987, Hill and Knowlton, Boston, 1987-90; dir. corp. communications Bain and Co., Boston, 1991-93; dir. mktg. Heidrick and Stiuggles, Inc., Atlanta, 1995-97; mktg. and pub. rels. cons. Palm Beach, Fla., 1997—.

JENNINGS, DEAN THOMAS, lawyer; b. Mar. 17, 1951; s. Paul Alyosis and Bonnie Mae; m. Kathleen Kay Kiefer, June 15, 1973; children: Matthew Thomas, Margaret Jo. BS in English, Iowa State U., 1973; JD, Creighton U., 1976. Bar: Iowa 1976, Nebr. 1982, U.S. Dist. Ct. (so. dist.) Iowa 1976. Tchr., coach Boone H.S., Iowa, 1972-73; ptnr. McGinn, McGinn, Jennings & Springer, Council Bluffs, Iowa, 1974—. Adj. faculty mem. Creighton U. Law Sch., 2004—. Mem. ABA, Assn. Am. Trial Lawyers, Iowa Bar Assn., Nebr. Bar Assn. Office: McGinn McGinn Jennings & Springer 25 Main Pl Ste 500 Council Bluffs IA 51503 E-mail: mmjs@cbiowa.com.

JENNINGS, DEBORAH E., lawyer; b. Washington, Feb. 8, 1949; BA with honors, U. Md., 1970; JD, Georgetown U., 1974. Bar: Md. 1974, D.C. 1984. Asst. state's atty. Montgomery County, Md., 1975-77; asst. atty. gen., 1977-80; chief Criminal Investigations Divsn., 1978-80; mem. Piper & Marbury, Balt.; ptnr. Piper Marbury Rudnick & Wolfe, 1999—2004; ptnr., chmn. Environ. practice group DLA Piper Rudnick Gray Cary, Washington, 2005—. Co-author: Md. Handbook on Environ. Law. Mem. & past pres. Network 2000. Fellow Am. Bar Found. Office: DLA Piper Rudnick Gray Cary 1200 19th St NW Washington DC 20036-2412 Office Phone: 202-861-3842. Office Fax: 202-223-2085. Business E-Mail: deborah.jennings@dlapiper.com.

JENNINGS, FREDERIC BEACH, JR., economist, saltwater flyfishing guide; b. Boston, Dec. 29, 1945; s. Frederic Beach III and Ellen (Osgood) J.; m. Lucille Candace Giglio, Aug. 15, 1975; children: Frederic Beach V, Thomas Chapin. BA magna cum laude, Harvard U., 1968; MA in Econs., Stanford U., 1980, PhD in Econs., 1985. Jr. medicare acct. Blue Cross-Blue Shield, Boston, 1968-69; ind. rsch. fellow Inst. Humane Studies, Menlo Park, Calif., 1969-71, 77-78; asst. mgr. Globe Bag Co., South Boston, 1972-73; rsch. asst. Charles River Assocs., Cambridge, Mass., 1973-74; rsch. and teaching fellow Stanford (Calif.) Dept. Econs., 1974-79; instr. econs. Tufts U., Medford, Mass., 1979-83; asst. prof. Bentley Coll., Waltham, Mass., 1985-87; sr. econ. cons. The Mac Rsch. Group, Cambridge, 1987-88, Charles River Assocs., Boston, 1988-91; sr. mgr. Econ. Analysis Group Office of Fed. Tax Svcs. Arthur Andersen & Co., Washington, 1991-92; pres. EconoLogistics, Ipswich, Mass., 1992—; owner Peak Dawn Anglers, Ipswich, 1996—; founder Ctr. Ecol. Econ. and Ethical Edn., Ipswich, 1998—. Chmn., rep. Stanford Grad. Student Coun., 1974-76; senator Stanford Student Senate, 1975-76; co-pres. Associated Students Stanford U., 1976-77; founder Stanford Grad. Students Assn., 1978-79, The Bentley Participants, Waltham, 1986-87, Full Circle Discussion Group Tufts U., Medford, 1981-84; resident assoc. Residential Edn., Stanford, 1978-79. Author: Democracy in Disarray, 1978, Mystical Tides, 1996, (paper) Value, Exchange and Profit, 1966, (essays) Academy, Society and Personal Growth, 1983, Whither Our Education?, 1983; co-author Greenpeace Study on Fisheries Mgmt., 1999. Mem. joint Greenpeace Study on Fisheries Mgmt., 1999. Mem. Am. Econ. Assn., Cliometrics Soc., Indsl. Orgn. Soc., Western Econ. Assn., Atlantic Econ. Soc., Kress Soc., Harvard Travellers Club, Rotary. Avocations: fly fishing, sailing, skiing, tennis, golf. Home: 261 Argilla Rd Ipswich MA 01938-2615 Office: EconoLogistics PO Box 946 Ipswich MA 01938-2212 also: Peak Dawn Anglers PO Box 946 Ipswich MA 01938-0946 Office Phone: 978-356-2188. Business E-Mail: Fbj@Fohe.zzn.com.

JENNINGS, GABRIELLE, artist; b. San Francisco, Dec. 23, 1966; Student, U. Paris, 1988; BFA, U. Calif.-San Diego, La Jolla, 1990; MFA, Art Ctr. Coll. Design, Pasadena, Calif., 1994. Artist-in-residence 200 Gertrude Street, Melbourne, Australia, 1996, Künstlerhaus Bethanien, Berlin, 1997-98. Solo exhbns. include Künstlerhaus Bethanien, 200 Gertrude Street, Art Ctr. Coll. Design, Pasadena, Guardshack, Bergamot Sta., Santa Monica; exhibited in group shows Rutgers U., New Brunswick, N.J., MFA Gallery, Art Ctr. Coll. Design, 1991, 94, Guggenheim Gallery, Chapman U., Orange, Calif., 1994, L.A. Ctr. for Photog. Studies, Hollywood, Calif., 1994, 95, Calif. State U., L.A., 1994, Mark Moore Gallery, Santa Monica, Calif., 1994, Bergamot Sta., Santa Monica, 1995, David Zwirner Gallery, N.Y.C., 1996, U. Chgo., 1996, Post, L.A., 1997, W139, Amsterdam, 1997, La. Mus. Art, Humlebaek, 1997, OSMOS, Berlin, 1998, West Space, Melbourne, 1998, Para/Site, Hong Kong, Castello di Rivoli, Turin, Sunshine and Noir Art, L.A., 1960-97, Artists Space, N.Y., 2000, Kunst-Und Kunstgeweberevien, Pforzheim, 2001, Mus. New Art, Detroit, 2002, others; videography includes She Disappeared First, 1993, Agapanthus Lapsus, 1994, To Whom It May Concern, 1994, Momentary Suspension, 1995, The Kiss, 1996, (prelude) Eight Minutes, 1995, The Kiss, 1996, A Small Fortune, 1996, Here and There, 1998, Triptych, 1999, Motion Studies, 2000, Rainbow, 2001, Circus Series, 2002-2003, others. Fellow Art Matters Inc., 1996. Avocations: fiction, video, painting, installation art. E-mail: tv3d@sbcglobal.net.

JENNINGS, GERALD D. (JERRY JENNINGS), mayor; b. Albany, NY, July 31, 1948; 1 child, Gerald Joseph. BA, SUNY, Brockport, 1970; MEd, SUNY, Albany, 1975. Tchr. Philip Schuyler High Sch., Albany, 1971-73, Albany High Sch., 1973-79, vice prin.; mayor City of Albany, 1993—. Former mem. Dem. com.; former alderman Common Coun. City Albany, 1979-93. Recipient City Livability award, US Conf. of Mayors, 1998, Pub. and Private Partnership Outstanding Achievement award, 1999, Pub.-Private Partnership Program award, Nat. Coun. for Urban Economic Develop., 1998. Mem. Ft. Orange Vets. Post, KC. Office: City Hall Albany NY 12207 Office Phone: 518-434-5100. Office Fax: 518-434-5013.*

JENNINGS, HAMLIN MANSON, materials scientist, educator; b. N.Y.C., N.Y., Aug. 4, 1946; s. Addison Llewellyn and Bojan Hamlin Jennings; m. Glenys Nell Robinson; 1 child, Ashley. MS, Tufts U., 1969; PhD, Brown U., 1975. Cert. chartered engr. U.K., 1994. Rsch. fellow U. of Cape Town (South Africa), 1975—76, lectr., 1976; rsch. asst. Imperial Coll., London, 1977—79, lectr., 1979—82, sr. vis. fellow, 1983; phys. scientist Nat. Inst. of Stds. and Tech., Gaithersburg, Md., 1983—87; prof. civil and environ. engrng. and materials and sci. engrng. Northwestern U., Evanston, Ill., 1987—, chair civil & environ. engrng. dept., 2002—; pres. Evanston Materials Consulting Corp., Wilmette, Ill. Editor Cement and Concrete Rsch., 1998—; assoc. editor Jour. of the Am. Ceramic Soc., 1999—; adv. bd. Jour. of Advanced Concrete Tech., Japan, 2001—. Author over 200 pubs., 12 patents. Fellow: Inst. of Materials, U.K., Am. Ceramic Soc.; mem.: ASCE, Am. Concrete Inst. Avocations: sailing, squash, outdoors. Office: Northwestern Univ Dept Civil and Environ Engring A236 Tech Inst 2145 Sheridan Rd Evanston IL 60208-3109 Office Phone: 847-491-4858. Office Fax: 847-491-4011. Business E-Mail: h-jennings@northwestern.edu.

JENNINGS, HENRY SMITH, III, cardiologist; b. Atlanta, May 16, 1951; s. Henry Smith Jr. and Elizabeth (Martin) J.; m. Polly Cooper; 1 child, Mary Bailey. BS summa cum laude, Davidson Coll., 1973; MD, Vanderbilt U., 1977. Diplomate Am. Bd. Internal Medicine, subspecialty cardiovascular diseases and interventional cardiology, Nat. Bd. Med. Examiners; lic. physician and surgeon, Tenn., Ky. Intern internal medicine Vanderbilt U. Affiliated Hosps., Nashville, 1977-78, resident internal medicine, 1978-80; fellow clin. cardiology divsn. cardiology dept. medicine Vanderbilt U., Nashville, 1980-82; clin. instr. medicine Vanderbilt U. Sch. Medicine, Nashville, 1982-89, asst. clin. prof. medicine, 1989-97, assoc. clin. prof. medicine, 1997—; med. dir. Cardiac Rehab. Ctr. St. Thomas Hosp., Nashville, 1984—2001, assoc. chief cardiac scis., 2001—05, pres.-elect med. staff, 2005—; chmn. steering com. St. Thomas Heart Inst., 2002—04. Mem. active staff St. Thomas Hosp., Nashville; affiliate staff Vanderbilt U. Med. Ctr., Nashville; mem. courtesy staff Centennial Med. Ctr., Nashville; mem. cons. staff Bapt. Hosp., Nashville. Contbr. articles to profl. jours. Bd. dirs. Heart Inst., St. Thomas Hosp., Nashvile, 1992-94, Tenn. Heart Inst., 1989-91. Justin Potter med. scholar Vanderbilt U. Sch. Medicine, Nashville, 1973-77. Fellow ACP, Am. Coll. Cardiology, Am. Coll. Chest Physicians, Coun. Clin. Cardiology Am. Heart Assn., Soc. Cardiac Angiography and Interventions; mem. AMA, Am. Assn. Cardiovasc. and Pulmonary Rehab., Internat. Soc. Heart Transplantation, Am. Heart Assn., So. Med. Assn., Tenn. Med. Assn., Nashville Acad. Medicine, Gottlieb Friesinger Soc. (pres.-elect 2001, pres. 2002). Methodist. Home: Northumberland 3 Castle Rising Nashville TN 37215-4126 Office: Saint Thomas Cardiology Cons PC 4230 Harding Pike Ste 530 Nashville TN 37205-2013 Fax: 615-292-2763. Office Phone: 615-515-2100. E-mail: hjennings@stcardiology.com.

JENNINGS, JAMES BURNETT, oil company executive; b. Temple, Tex., Sept. 20, 1940; s. William Donald and Ruth Imogene (Dodson) J.; m. Sharon Marie Lewis, Aug. 7, 1964 (div. 1982); 1 child, James Christopher; m. Regina Ann Richter, Nov. 5, 1983; 1 child, Michael Thomas. AA, Del Mar Coll., Corpus Christi, Tex., 1961; BS, Trinity U., 1963; MS, Purdue U., 1966; postgrad., Cornell U., 1967. Tchr. Burbank High Sch., San Antonio, 1963-65; tchr., coach Munster (Ind.) High Sch., 1965-69; geophysicist Shell Oil Co., Houston, 1969-74; chief geophysicist Columbia Gas Devel. Corp., Houston, 1974-79; exploration mgr. Hunt Oil Co., Houston, 1979-84, sr. v.p. Dallas, 1984-88, group v.p. worldwide exploration, 1988-91, exec. v.p., dir., 1991—99, pres., 1999—2004, chmn., 2004—. Contbr. articles to mags. Mem. Soc. Exploration Geophysicists, Am. Assn. Petroleum Geologists, Assn. Internat. Petroleum Negotiators. Republican. Office: Hunt Oil Co 1445 Ross Ave Ste 1400 Dallas TX 75202-2739 Business E-Mail: jjennings@huntoil.com.

JENNINGS, JAMES WILSON, JR., lawyer; b. Temple, Tex., Aug. 10, 1943; s. James W. and Mary Lee (Patton) J.; m. Anne Rita Moran, Aug. 9, 1969; children: Helene, Anne Conway, Mary. BA in English, Washington and Lee U., 1965, JD, 1972. Bar: Va. 1972, U.S. Dist. Ct. (we. dist.) Va. 1972, U.S. Ct. Appeals (4th cir.) 1980, U.S. Supreme Ct. 1991. Law clk. Supreme Ct. of Va., Richmond, 1972-73; ptnr. Woods, Rogers & Hazlegrove, Roanoke, Va., 1973—. Adj. prof. Washington and Lee Sch. of Law, 1999. Chmn. bd. editors Jour. Civil Litig., 1990-94, Mcpl. Liability Reporter, 1990-93; bd. editors Def. Coun. Jour.; contbr. articles to profl. jours. Co-chmn. drive for attys. United Way, 1975; chmn. fund drive for attys. Am. Cancer Soc., 1976; bd. dirs. Art Mus. of Western Va., 1990-96, v.p., 1995-96; bd. dirs. Opera Roanoke, 1988-96, pres., 1996; trustee Funds of Diocese of Southwestern Va.; v.p. Art Mus. of Western Va., 1995-96; bd. dirs. North Cross Sch. Lt. (j.g.) USN, 1965-69. Fellow Va. Law Found., 1997. Mem. ABA, Nat. Assn. Ry. Trial Counsel, Am. Bd. Trial Advocates (pres. Va. chpt. 1995-96), Va. Bar Assn., Va. Assn. Def. Attys. (pres. 1988-89), Roanoke City Bar Assn. (medical-legal liaison com. 1990-94, bd. dirs. 2003—), Internat. Assn. Def. Counsel, Assn. Def. Trial Attys. (exec. coun. 1997-2003, pres. 2002), Def. Rsch. Inst. (bd. dirs. 2001-03, Exceptional Performance citation 1989), Assn. Internat. de Droit des Assurances, Downtown Roanoke Inc. (bd. dirs. 1981-89), Ted Damon Inn of Ct., Washington and Lee Alumni Assn. (bd. dirs. 1984-88), Roanoke Regional C. of C. (bd. dirs. 1989-93), Order of Coif, Roanoke Country Club (bd. govs.), Shenandoah Club. Episcopalian. Home: 2710 Rosalind Ave SW Roanoke VA 24014-2330 Office: Woods Rogers & Hazlegrove 10 S Jefferson St Ste 1400 Roanoke VA 24011-1331 Office Phone: 540-983-7615. E-mail: jennings@woodsroyen.com.

JENNINGS, JERRY D., federal agency administrator; b. Flint, Mich., July 2, 1940; s. C. Oren and Retha S. (Wood) J.; m. Misako Sonoda, Oct. 10, 1976; children: Catherine, Victoria, Elizabeth. Student, Mott Community Coll., Flint, Mich., 1958-59, U. Mich., 1960; BS, Ea. Mich. U., 1961; student, John Jay Coll., CUNY, 1970-71, Harvard U., 1987. Intelligence officer CIA, Washington and S.E. Asia, 1965-68; spl. agt. FBI, Memphis, N.Y.C., 1968-72; spl. asst. to dir. Office Nat. Narcotics Intelligence Dept. Justice, Washington, 1972-73; staff mem. NSC, Washington, 1973-82; exec. dir. Office of Sci. and Tech. Policy and White House Sci. Coun., Washington, 1982-86; acting dir. Selective Svc. Sys., Washington, 1987, dep. dir., 1988—90; acting dir. Fed. Emergency Mgmt. Agy., Washington, 1990, dep. dir., 1991-92; chmn., chief exec. officer Phoenix Comm. and Rsch. Co., McLean, Va., 1993—2000; deputy asst. sec. def and dir. Def. POW/Missing Personnel Office, 2001—. Served to Capt. USMC, 1961-65. Mem.: SAR, VFW (life), Mil. Order Carabao, Am. Legion (life), Army and Navy Club (Washington). Baptist. Avocations: tennis, skiing, chess. Office: OASD Internat Security Affairs 2400 Defense Pentagon Washington DC 20301-2400

JENNINGS, JON PAUL, non-profit foundation executive; b. Richmond, Ind., Oct. 2, 1962; s. Paul Nathan and Alice Belle Jennings. MPA, Harvard U., 2000. Scout, video coord. Boston Celtics, 1986-90, asst. coach, scouting coord., 1990-97; White House fellow The White House, Washington, 1997-98, sr. asst. to Cabinet Sec., 1998-99; acting asst. atty. gen. U.S. Dept. of Justice, Washington, 1999-2000; sr. advisor to Cabinet Sec., The White House, 2000-01; co-founder, pres. Team Harmony Found., Cambridge, Mass., 1993—. Winner NBA World Championship, 1986; named NBA All Star Coach, Boston Celtics, 1990-91, one of 10 Most Outstanding Young Leaders, Boston Jaycees, 1996. Roman Catholic. Avocations: flying, reading, basketball. Office: Team Harmony Found 401 Park Dr Boston MA 02215 Home: 6788 River Ridge Dr Newburgh IN 47630-9739 Fax: 617-425-6300. E-mail: info@teamharmony.org, jennings@teamharmony.org.

JENNINGS, JOSEPH ASHBY, banker; b. Richmond, Va., Aug. 12, 1920; s. Joseph Ashby and Leone (Bishop) J.; m. Anne Barrow Hatcher, Oct. 29, 1960; children: Joseph Ashby III, Ashby Anne. BS, U. Richmond, 1949, DSc (hon.), 1980; grad. certificate, Stonier Grad. Sch. Banking, Rutgers U., 1952; LLD (hon.), Va. Union U., 1991. With United Va. Bank, Richmond, 1949-85, v.p., 1956-66, sr. v.p., 1966-67, exec. v.p., 1967-71, pres., 1971, chmn. bd., 1972-85; also dir.; vice chmn. bd. United Va. Bankshares, Inc., 1972-75, pres., 1975-76, chief adminstrv. officer, 1972-76, chmn. bd., chief exec. officer, 1976-85, chmn. bd., 1985-86. Served with USAAF, 1942-46. Mem. Fin. Analysts Fedn. (past exec. v.p., dir.), Phi Beta Kappa, Omicron Delta Kappa, Phi Delta Theta, Beta Gamma Sigma. Presbyterian.

JENNINGS, KAREN, human resources specialist; b. Mich. BA, U. Ark. Various positions Southwestern Bell, Ark., 1972—95; chmn. SBC Asset Mgmt, Inc., 1995—96; assoc. v.p. chmn.'s office SBC Comm., Inc., 1995—96; pres. Southwestern Bell, Mo., 1996—97; v.p., gen. mgr., operator svcs. SBC Telecomm., Inc., 1997—98; sr. v.p. human resources SBC Comm. Inc., 1998—99, sr. exec. v.p. human resources, 1999—2002, sr. exec. v.p. human resources and comm., 2002—. Bd. dirs. SBC Found. Bd. dirs. Elizabeth Glaser Pediatric AIDS Found. Mem.: Leaders Forum. Office: SBC Comm Inc 175 E Houston San Antonio TX 78205-2233 Office Phone: 210-821-4105. Office Fax: 210-351-2071.*

JENNINGS, KENNETH W., Jeopardy champion, software engineer; b. Edmonds, Wash., May 23, 1974; m. Mindy Jennings; 1 child, Dylan. BA in English, BS in Computer Sci., Brigham Young U. Missionary LDS Ch., Spain; software engineer CHG Companies, Salt Lake City. Mem., edits lit. and mythology questions Nat. Academic Quiz Tournaments LLC. Presented Top Ten List: Late Show With David Letterman, 2004; appeared on: The Tonight Show, 2004; appeared in a TV advertisement for Cingular Wireless, 2005, appeared in an ad for Allstate Ins. Co., 2005, contestant Tournament of Champions, Jeopardy, 2005. Named Person of the Week, ABC World News Tonight, 2004; named one of 10 Most Fascinating People in 2004, Barbara Walters Spl. Mem. Lds Ch. Achievements include Highest winning Jeopardy! contestant; most consecutive Jeopardy! appearances; top TV game show winner. Avocations: painting, hiking.*

JENNINGS, LOUIS BROWN, retired humanities educator; b. Lancaster, S.C., May 5, 1917; s. Arthur Ewart and Selma Helms Jennings; m. Grace Irene Allen, May 24, 1943 (dec.); children: Carolyn Jennings Sautter, Sharon Jennings Moore. AB, Duke U., Durham, N.C., 1938; BD, Crozer Theology Sem., Chester, Pa., 1945; grad. studies, U. Pa., Phila., 1942—45; PhD, U. Chgo., 1964. Ordained minister United Ch. of Christ, 1956. From instr. to prof. Marshall U., Huntington, W.Va., 1948—79; assoc. prof. Ohio U., Portsmouth, 1961—69, prof. Ironton, 1965—72. Dept chmn. Marshall U., 1948—79. Co-author: (Book) Biography of Edgar Johnson Goodspeed, 1948; author: Biography of Shirley Jackson Case, 1949, The Function of Religion, 1978. Fellow Crozer Theol. Sem., 1947—48, Univ. of Chgo., 1947—48; grantee Ford Found. for Advancement of Edn., 1951—52. Democrat. United Ch.Of Christ. Avocation: walking. Home: care Sharon J Moore 7 Hillendale Ct Huntington WV 25705

JENNINGS, MEGHAN YOUNG, music educator; b. Oswego, N.Y., May 1, 1978; d. Elizabeth Young and Robert Paul Jennings. Bachelor magna cum laude, Syracuse U., 2000, Master, 2002—02. Cert. tchr. N.Y., 2000. Band, chorus, gen. music tchr. Bridgeport Elem. Sch., NY, 2002—; ch. organist Holy Family-St. Michael's Parish, Fulton, NY, 2003—. Piano tchr., Fulton/Bridgeport, NY, 2000—; Irish dance instr. Bridgeport Elem. Sch., NY, 2002—; music dir. Fulton Cmty. Theater, NY, 2003; voice tchr., Fulton, NY, 2003—; youth choir dir. Holy Family-St. Michael's Parish, Fulton, NY, 2004—. Coord. elem. sch. entry in ann. Chittenango Wizard of Oz Parade, Bridgeport Elem. Sch., NY, 2003—04. Recipient Chancellor's scholarship, Syracuse U., 1996-2000, Music award, 1996-2000, Richard J. and Joann Olson Fay scholarship, 1999-2000, Harwood Simmons award, Syracuse U. Wind Ensemble, 2002. Mem.: Pi Eta Sigma, Phi Kappa Phi, Golden Key Nat. Honor Soc., Pi Kappa Lambda, Sigma Alpha Iota. Roman Catholic. Achievements include Established After School Irish Dancing Program at Bridgeport Elementary School; Established School-Wide Piano Recital at Bridgeport Elementary School. Avocations: playing musical instruments, Irish dancing, N.Y. Yankees baseball fan, Syracuse U. basketball fan, researching on the internet. Home: 46 West 4th St Fulton NY 13069 Office Phone: 315-633-9611. Personal E-mail: irishdancer23@yahoo.com.

JENNINGS, PAUL CHRISTIAN, civil engineering educator, academic administrator; b. Brigham City, Utah, May 21, 1936; s. Robert Webb and Elva S. (Simonsen) J.; m. Millicent Marie Bachman, Aug. 28, 1981; m. Barbara Elaine Morgan, Sept. 3, 1960 (div. 1981); children: Kathryn Diane, Margaret Ann. BSCE, Colo. State U., 1958; MSCE, Calif. Inst. Tech., 1960, PhD, 1963. From prof. civil engring., applied mechanics to prof. emeritus Calif. Inst. Tech., Pasadena, 1966—2002, prof. emeritus, 2002—, provost, 2004—. Mem. faculty bd. Calif. Tech. Inst., 1974-76, steering com., 1974-76, chmn. nominating com., 1975, grad. studies com., 1978-80; cons. in field. Author: (with others) Earthquake Design Criteria. Contbr. numerous articles to profl. jours. 1st lt. USAF, 1963-66. Recipient Honor Alumnus award Colo. State U., 1992, Achievement in Academia award Coll. Engring., 1992; Erskine fellow U. Canterbury, New Zealand, 1970, 85. Fellow AAAS, New Zealand Soc. Earthquake Engring.; mem. ASCE (Walter Huber award 1973, Newmark medal 1992), Seismol. Soc. Am. (pres. 1980), Earthquake Engring. Rsch. Inst. (pres. 1981-83), Athenaeum Club. Avocations: fly fishing, hiking. Home: 640 S Grand Ave Pasadena CA 91105-2423 Office: Calif Inst Tech Mail Code 206-31 Pasadena CA 91125-0001 Business E-Mail: pcjenn@caltech.edu.

JENNINGS, PERRY G., retail executive; BBA, Concord Coll., Athens, W.Va.; MBA, Va. Tech. U. Compensation mgr. Lowe's Cos., Inc., 1984, v.p. ops. and merchandising support, 1998—99, sr. v.p. human resources, 1999—. Office: Lowes Co Inc 1605 Curtis Bridge Rd Wilkesboro NJ 28697

JENNINGS, RICHARD MILBURN, resort developer; b. Washington, Nov. 7, 1927; s. Maurice Edgar J. and Norma Milburn; m. Nini Bjonness, Mar. 21, 1964 (div. 1986); children: Lynn Urban, Stephanie, Jan. Student, Stanford U., 1944-46; BA, Ariz. State U., 1955; MA, Georgetown U., 1968, PhD in Govt., 1975. Commd. 2d lt. U.S. Army, 1947, advanced through grades to brigade comdr., 1969; asst. to Sec. of Def., 1971—72; retired U.S. Army, 1975; pres. Western Colo. Investments, Aspen, 1982-89; sr. v.p. Preferred Resorts, Aspen, 1989-95; pres. Western Resorts Internat., Aspen, 1995-98, chmn., 1998—2004. Author: U.S./Soviet Arms Competition, 1975; contbr. articles to profl. jours. Pres. Anderson Ranch Arts Ctr., Showmass Village, Colo.,

1979-82; nat. coun. mem. Aspen Theater in the Park, 1997-99. Decorated Legion of Merit with oak leaf cluster, Korean Silver Star, Bronze Star with 3 oak leaf clusters, Air medal with 7 oak leaf clusters, Vietnamese Gallantry Cross. Mem. Nat. Assn. Realtors, Stanford Alumni Assn., Indian Wells Tennis Club. Avocations: writing, skiing, tennis. Office: Western Resorts Internat 1004 Vine St Aspen CO 81611 E-mail: dickjennin@aol.com.

JENNINGS, SAM, II, academic administrator; b. Orofino, Idaho, Oct. 16, 1972; s. Sam and Linda Jennings; m. Lisa Connolly, June 28, 1997; 1 child, Ella. BA, Lewis-Clark State Coll., 1996; MA, Portland State U., 1999; PhD, Capella U., 2005. Coord. residence life Lewis-Clark State Coll., Lewiston, Idaho, 1994—98; resident dir. Lewist & Clark Coll., Portland, Oreg., 1998—2000; area coord. NW Mo. State U., Maryville, Mont., 2000—. Mem.: Assn. Coll. & U. Housing Officers Internat. (regional com. mem. 2000—04), Assn. Coll. Pers. Adminstrs., Nat. Assn. Student Pers. Administrators.

JENNINGS, STEPHEN GRANT, academic administrator; b. Indpls., Dec. 6, 1946; s. Grant Orville and Helen Zura (MacDonald) J.; m. Sarah Ferguson, Apr. 26, 1969; children: Amy Jennings Bishop, Meredith Jennings Poole. BA, Trinity U., 1968; MS, Miami U., Oxford, Ohio, 1970; PhD, U. Ga., 1976; diploma in ednl. mgmt., Harvard U., 1982; LLD, Coll. Ozarks, Point Lookout, Mo., 1997; LHD, Simpson Coll., 1998. Asst. dean for resident life So. Meth. U., Dallas, 1970-73; asst. dir. housing U. Ga., Athens, 1973-76; assoc. dean students Tulane U., New Orleans, 1976-80; v.p. student svcs. Furman U., Greenville, S.C., 1980-83; pres. Coll. of Ozarks, Point Lookout, Mo., 1983-87, Simpson Coll., Indianola, Iowa, 1987-98, Oklahoma City U., 1998-2001, U. Evansville, Ind., 2001—. Instnl. cons. Am. Coll. in London, 1995; bd. dirs. Old Nat. Bank, Nat. Pub. Radio and TV (WNIN). Mem. Coun. Ind. Colls., Nat. Assn. Schs., Colls. and Univs. (bd. dirs. 1993—), Nat. Assn. Intercollegiate Athletics (coun. of pres. 1983-87), So. Assn. Colls. and Schs. (vis. teams 1982—), North Cen. Assn. Colls. and Schs. (vis. teams 1989—), So. Assn. Coll. Student Pers. (pres. 1983), Harvard U. Alumni Assn. (class rep.), Rotary, Evansville Club, Sigma Alpha Epsilon. Avocations: racquet sports, golf, reading. Office: U Evansville Office of President 1800 Lincoln Ave Evansville IN 47722-0001

JENNINGS, SUSAN, middle school educator; b. N.Y.C., May 1949; d. Manson and Deborah J. BA, Adelphi U., 1971, MA, 1974. Cert. math. and history tchr. Math. tchr. Beach St. Middle Sch., West Islip, NY, 1972—2004; ret., 2004; pvt. practice tax acct. Babylon, NY, 1983—. Episcopalian. Avocations: travel, gardening, crafts, photography.

JENNINGS, THOMAS PARKS, lawyer; b. Alexandria, Va., Nov. 16, 1947; s. George Christian and Ellen (Thompson) J.; m. Shelley Corrine Abernathy, Oct. 30, 1971; 1 child, Kathleen Eayre. BA cum laude with honors in History, Wake Forest U., 1970; JD, U. Va., 1975. Bar: Va. 1975. Assoc. Lewis, Wilson, Lewis & Jones, Arlington, Va., 1975-78; atty. First Va. Banks, Inc., Falls Church, 1978-80, gen. counsel, 1980—2003, sec., 1993-99, sr. v.p., 1995—2003; sr. atty. advisor Fed. Housing Fin. Bd., 2004—. Adj. prof. George Mason U. Sch. Law, Arlington, 1987—88. Trustee Arlington Cmty. Found., 1998-2003, treas., 2001-03; dir. Rixey St. Found., Inc., 1997—; deacon Georgetown Presbyn. Ch., Washington, 1980-82, elder, 1983-85, 95-97, trustee, 1988-90, dir. Bd. Pensions, Presbyn. Ch. USA, 2001—. With U.S. Army, 1970-71. Mem. Va. State Bar Assn. Presbyterian. Avocations: bridge, kayaking. Personal E-mail: stkj123@aol.com. Business E-Mail: jenningst@fhfb.gov.

JENNINGS, TONI, lieutenant governor; b. Orlando, Fla., May 17, 1949; d. Jack C. and Margaret (Murphy) J. BA, Wesleyan Coll., Macon, Ga., 1971; postgrad., Rollins Coll., 1972-73. Pres. Jack Jennings and Sons, Inc., Gen. Contractors, Orlando, 1973—; mem. Fla. Ho. of Reps., 1976-80, Fla. Senate, 1980—2000, pres., 1996—2000; lt. gov. Florida, 2003—. Republican leader pro tempore, 1982-83, 85, 86, Rep. leader, 1984, 86-88. legis. del. Orange County, 1980-82, 86-88. Bd. dirs. Salvation Army; active Rep. Women's Federated Club of Winter Park, Orlando Women's Rep. Club Federated. Recipient Spl. Commendation award Fla. Restaurant Assn., 1979, Meritorious Svc. award Fla. Fedn. Humane Socs., 1979, Disting. Alumni awrd Wesleyan Coll., 1981, Freedom award Women for Responsible Legislation, 1982, Support of Law Enforcement award Fla. Sheriffs Assn., Outstanding Efforts award Tampa Missing Children Help Ctr., 1983, Outstanding Svc. award Grocers' Assn. Fla., 1983, Legis. award Fla., 1983, Legis. award Fla. Chiropractic Assn., 1983, 86, Appreciation award Fla. Med. Assn. and Physicians of Fla., 1983, 2d Ann. Frank J. Fahrenkopf, Jr. Outstanding State Minority Leader award, 1988, Ann. Legis. award for Leadership in Econ. Devel. Legislation award Fla. C. of C., 1987; named Legislator of Yr., Orange County Young Rep. Club, 1980-81. Mem. Orlando Area Bd. Realtors (Friend of Realtors award 1989), Builders and Contractors, Ctrl. Fla. Builders Exch., Delta Kappa Gamma, Phi Kappa Phi, Kappa Delta Epsilon. Republican. Office: Lt Gov The Capitol PL-05 Tallahassee FL 32399-0001*

JENNINGS, SISTER VIVIEN, literature and language professor; b. Jersey City; d. Eugene O. and Alice (Smith) J. BA, Caldwell Coll.; MA in English, Cath. U. Am.; MS in Telecommunications, Syracuse U.; PhD in English, Fordham U.; postgrad., Oxford (Eng.) U., 1994; EdD (hon.), Providence Coll.; LittD (hon.), Caldwell Coll.; DHL (hon.), St. Peter's Coll. Prof. English Caldwell Coll., 1960-69; major supr. Dominican Sisters-Caldwell, 1969-79; instr. broadcasting writing Syracuse U., 1979-80; with community affairs dept. Sta. WIXT TV, Syracuse, N.Y., 1980; dir. telecommunications Barry U., 1982-83; dir. pub. affairs Cath. Telecommunications Network Am., 1983-84; pres. Caldwell Coll., 1984-94, prof. English, 1995-99; prin. St. Dominic Acad., Jersey City, 1999—. Originator, designer campus TV studios Caldwell Coll., Barry U.; curriculum planner, coord. new grad.-level curriculum in telecommunications Barry U.; lectr. on ednl. and media issues. Producer: Centenary Journey, 1981, Advent Vesper Chorale, 1981, American Immigrant Church, 1982, Las Casas: Ministry of Presence, 1987; co-producer: The Boat People, 1980. Founder, dir. Children's TV Experience; founder Project Link Ednl. Ctr., Newark. Recipient Gov.'s Pride N.J. Albert Einstein award for edn., 1989. Office: St Dominic Acad 2572 Kennedy Blvd Jersey City NJ 07304-2107

JENNINGS, WIRT HOLMAN, JR., retired marketing executive; b. Newberry, S.C., Oct. 5, 1927; s. Wirt Holman and Dorothy Elizebeth (Suber) J.; m. Carrie Lucille Braswell, Oct. 26, 1947; children: Michael Earl, Martha Jane, Dorothy Elizebeth. BS in Math. and Chemistry, Newberry Coll., 1949; grad., Lynhurst U., 1958. Area rep. to mgr. T.A. Edison, Inc., West Orange, N.C., 1949-52; sales trainee Esso Std. Oil, N.J., Columbia, S.C., 1952-55, sales rep. Bennettsville, S.C., 1955-56; sales supr., asst. dist. mgr. Esso, Humble, Enco, Columbia, 1956-64, dist. mgr. Birmingham, Ala., 1964-67, project coord. Memphis, 1967-68; nat. project coord. Exxon Co. USA, Houston, 1968-75, innovative project coord. Charlotte, N.C., 1975-80, Memphis, 1980-83, Houston, 1983-85; pres. Mktg. Expeditors, Inc., Houston, 1985-93; councilman Newberry County Coun., 1997-2001. Co-founder, pres. Cayce/West Columbia (S.C.) Jaycees, 1956; pres. Ala. Petroleum Coun., Birmingham, 1966; pres. AARP, Newberry, 1997—; chmn. Rep. Party, Newberry, 1997—; mem. founding bd. dirs. Nat. Ins. Automotive Svc. Excellence, Washington, 1972-74; bd. trustees Newberry Coll., 2000—; bd. dirs. Houston Water and Sewer, 1971-75. With USN, 1945-46. Mem. Newberry Coll. Home Guard (commdr. 1997—), Columbia Exxon Annuitant Club (ex-officio, pres. 1998—). Avocations: fishing, hunting, golf. Home: 51 Jennings Pt Prosperity SC 29127-8842 E-mail: jennings@scmail.com.

JENNISON, BRIAN (LESTER), environmental specialist; b. Chelsea, Mass., June 13, 1950; s. Lewis L. and Myra S. (Piper) J. BA, U. N.H., 1972; PhD, U. Calif., Berkeley, 1977; cert. hazardous materials mgr., U. Calif., Davis, 1986. Tchg., rsch. asst. U. Calif., Berkeley, 1972-77; staff rsch. assoc. Dept. of Molecular Biology, Berkeley, 1978-80; instr. dept. biology Calif. State U., Hayward, 1977; sr. biologist San Francisco Bay Marine Rsch. Ctr., Emeryville, Calif., 1980-81; inspector I Bay Area Air Quality Mgmt.Dist., San Francisco, 1981-83, inspector II, 1983—87; enforcement program specialist Bay Area Air Quality Mgmt. Dist., San Francisco, 1987—92; dir. air quality mgmt. divsn. Washoe County Dist. Health Dept., Reno, 1992-2000; dir. Lane Regional Air Pollution Authority, Springfield, Oreg., 2000—05. Cons. U.S. Army C.E., L.A., 1980, San Francisco, 1981; instr. U. Calif., Berkeley, 1990-93, Assoc. Bay Area Govs., 1990-92; adj. prof. U. Nev., Reno, 1994-2003; planning specialist NH Dept. Environ. Svcs., Air Resources Divsn., 2005—. Contbr. articles to profl. jours. Harbor Br. Found. fellow, 1977-78. Mem.: Assn. Local Air Pollution Control Officers (bd. dirs. 2001—05), Air and Waste Mgmt. Assn. (chmn. Ea. Sierra chpt. 1994—96), Navy League U.S. (life), Phi Beta Kappa. Avocations: railroad history, photography. E-mail: bljennison@comcast.net.

JENNY, CAROLE, physician, researcher; b. St. Louis, June 4, 1946; d. Vance Buescher and Alice Emelie Jenny; m. Thomas Allen Roesler, Mar. 16, 1974; children: Laura Alice Roesler, Amelia Martha Roesler. BA, U. Mo., 1968; BMS, Dartmouth Med. Sch., 1970; MD, U. Wash., 1972; MBA, Wharton Sch., U. of Pa, 1976. Pediatrics Am. Bd. of Pediat., NC, 1977. Prof. of pediat. Brown Med. Sch., Providence, 1996—; dir., child protection team Hasbro Children's Hosp., Providence. Com. on child abuse and neglect Am. Acad. of Pediat., Elk Grove Village, Ill. Mem. Am. Profl. Soc. on the Abuse of Children, Chgo., 1991—. Recipient Outstanding Svc. to Maltreated Children, Am. Acad. of Pediat., 1999, Ray Helfer award, Nat. Coalition of Children's Trust Funds, 2002. Achievements include research in child abuse, head trauma, sexual abuse. Office: Brown Medical School 593 Eddy St Potter-005 Providence RI 02903 Business E-Mail: cjenny@brown.edu.

JENRETTE, THOMAS SHEPARD, JR., music educator, choral director; b. Roanoke, Va., Feb. 1, 1946; s. Thomas Shepard and Virginia Catherine (Harris) J. BA, U. N.C., 1968, MusM, 1970; D of Mus. Arts, U. Mich., 1976. Choral dir. Cummings H.S., Burlington, NC, 1969—72; dir. cultural arts Burlington City Schs., NC, 1972—73; dir. choral activities S.W. State U., Marshall, Minn., 1976—79, East Tenn. State U., Johnson City, 1979—. Dir. music First Christian Ch., Johnson City, 1981-84, Covenant Presbyn. Ch., Johnson City, 1991—; dir. East Tenn. State U. Chorale European Tour, 1985, 98, 2001; guest condr. choral festival N.C. High Sch., Raleigh, 1987, 2002, Govs. Sch. for Arts, Murfreesboro, Tenn., 1987, Nat. Seminar of Intercollegiate Men's Choruses, Inc., 1992, 2004; guest condr. N.C. All-State Male Choir, 1997, All-East Tenn. H.S. Male Choir, 1998, Tenn. All-State H.S. Male Choir, 2001, S.C. All-State Male Choir, 2002, Ga. All-State H.S. male choir, 2003, We. Carolina Choral Festival, 2005, Nat. Condrs. Conf., U. So. Miss., 2000 Grantee East Tenn. State U., 1988, 90, 96, 99. Mem. Am. Choral Dirs. Assn. (life; condr. 1986, 88, 94, 2000, 04, so. divsn. convs., 89, 99 nat. conv., so. divsn. repertoire and stds. chair for male choirs 1999—), Tenn. Music Educators Assn. (conductor state convs. 1990, 91, 94, 2000, dir. White House, Christmas 1989, 2001, Canticum Novum Festival, Caracas, Venezuela, 1996), Internat. Fedn. Choral Music, Nat. Assn. Tchrs. Singing, Coll. Music Soc. (life), Music Educators Nat. Conf. (condr. so. divsn. conv. 1997), Phi Mu Alpha (hon.), Omicron Delta Kappa, Pi Kappa Lambda. Home: 2734 E Oakland Ave Apt C-25 Johnson City TN 37601-1887 Office Phone: 423-439-6949. Business E-Mail: jenrette@etsu.edu.

JENSEN, ADOLPH ROBERT, former chemistry educator; b. Elmhurst, Ill., Apr. 14, 1915; s. Adolph George William and Marie (Diener) J.; m. Nelle B. Willams, Sept. 5, 1950; children— Robert, Margaret. BS, Wheaton Coll., Ill., 1937; MS, U. Ill., 1940, PhD, 1942; postgrad., Ohio U., summer 1959, Rensselaer Poly. Inst., summer 1962, Purdue U., summer 1970, Duke, summer 1971. Head analytical chemistry sect. Lewis Flight Propulsion Lab., NASA, Cleve., 1942-46; prof. chemistry Baldwin-Wallace Coll., Berea, Ohio, 1946-83, prof. emeritus, 1983—, chmn. dept. chemistry, 1956-71. Vis. scientist Ohio Acad. Sci., 1960—64. Fellow AAAS; mem. Am. Chem. Soc., Ohio Acad. Sci. (v.p. chemistry sect. 1969-70), AAUP, Lutheran Acad. Scholarship, Sigma Xi, Phi Lambda Upsilon, Sigma Pi Sigma. Home: 2018 Atkins Ave Lakewood OH 44107-5404

JENSEN, ARTHUR ROBERT, psychologist, educator; b. San Diego, Aug. 24, 1923; s. Arthur Alfred and Linda (Schachtmayer) J.; m. Barbara Jane DeLarme, May 6, 1960; 1 child, Roberta Ann. BA, U. Calif., Berkeley, 1945; PhD, Columbia U., 1956. Asst. med. psychology U. Md., 1955-56; research fellowInst. Psychiatry U. London, 1956-58; prof. ednl. psychology U. Calif., Berkeley, 1958-94; prof. emeritus, 1994—. Author: Genetics and Education, 1972, Educability and Group Differences, 1973, Educational Differences, 1973, Bias in Mental Testing, 1979, Straight Talk about Mental Tests, 1981, The g Factor, 1998, Clocking the Mind: Mental Chronometry and Individual Differences, 2005; contbr. to profl. jours., books. Guggenheim fellow, 1964-65, fellow Ctr. Advanced Study Behavioral Scis., 1966-67 Fellow AAAS, Am. Psychol. Assn., The Galton Inst., Am. Psychol. Soc.; mem. Psychonomic Soc., Am. Soc. Human Genetics, Soc. for Social Biology, Behavior Genetics Assn., Psychometric Soc., Sigma Xi. Office: U Calif Sch Edn Berkeley CA 94720-0001

JENSEN, ARTHUR SEIGFRIED, consulting engineering physicist; b. Trenton, NJ, Dec. 24, 1917; s. Emil Anthony and Emma Anna (Lund) J.; m. Lillian Elizabeth Reed, Aug. 9, 1941; children: Deane Ellsworth, Alan Forrest, Nancy Lorraine. BS, U. Pa., 1938, MS, 1939, PhD in Physics, 1941; diploma in advanced engring., Westinghouse Sch. Applied Sci., 1972, diploma in computer sci., 1977. Registered profl. engr., Md. Research physicist U.S. Naval Research Labs., Washington, 1941; research physicist RCA Labs., Princeton, N.J., 1945-57; mgr. spl. electron devices Westinghouse Electronic Tube Div., Balt., 1957-65; sr. adv. physicist Electronics Systems Ctr., Balt., 1965-91; cons. physicist Westinghouse Electronic Systems Ctr., Balt., 1991-94; co-owner, chief engr. Jensen Cons. Engring., 1994—. Mem. Md. State Bd. Registration Profl. Engrs., 1979-86, vice chmn., 1983-86; cons. Nat. Acad. Sci., 1970 Contbr. articles to profl. jours. Mem. Endowed Sons of Norway Found., Nancy Lorraine Jensen Meml. Scholarship Fund. Served to capt. USN, 1941-46, USNR, 1946-77, ret., 1977—. Hector Tyndale fellow, 1939, George Lieb Harrison fellow, 1940; recipient Outstanding Svc. award Engrs. Coun. Md., 1986, Gov.'s citation, 1986, Westinghouse spl. patent award, 1972. Fellow IEEE (life), Washington Acad. Scis.; mem. AAAS, AIAA, Res. Officers Assn., Ret. Officers Assn., Naval Res. Assn., Am. Phys. Soc., Am. Assn. Physics Tchrs., Soc. Photo-Optical Instrumentation Engrs., Optical Soc. Am., N.Y. Acad. Scis., Md. Acad. Scis. (chmn. awards com.), Nat. Coun. Engring. Examiners (chmn. internat. rels. com.), Infrared Info. Symposium, Am. Legion, Fleet Res. Assn., Sons of Norway, Nat. Eagle Scout Assn., Vigil Honor Order of Arrow, Sigma Xi, Pi Mu Epsilon, Kappa Phi Kappa. Clubs: U.S. Naval Acad. Officers and Faculty. Achievements include patents in field; invention of the first practical random access memory (RAM) electron tube, used in early computers, first computerized telephone central office, over-the-horizon radar; airborne moving target radar, and DEW line radar analysis; the infrared TV camera tube which aided aerodynamic design of SR-71 supersonic plane; micro-mirror matrix TV projection light modulator that projected large, bright, live TV picture display; digital light processing using the same micro-mirror projections; low noise integrated circuit for camera photoplane detector chip; research in conceptual designs of military meteorological satellite sensor sys. Home and Office: Chapel Gate 1104 Oak Crest Village 8820 Walther Blvd Parkville MD 21234-9022

JENSEN, BARBARA WOOD, interior design business owner; b. Salt Lake City, Apr. 30, 1927; d. John Howard and Loretta (Sparks) Wood; m. Lowell N. Jensen, June 26, 1947 (dec. Aug. 2000); children: Brent Lowell, Robyn Lynn, Todd Wood; m. Thomas A. Mackey, Feb. 24, 2001. Interior decorator paint and wall paper co., 1947-49; cons., interior designer, 1950-60; pres., treas. Barbara Jensen Interiors, Inc., Salt Lake City, 1960-79; interior designer, 1979—; owner Barbara Jensen Designs, St. George, Utah and Las Vegas; lectr. in field. Lectr. in field; dir. 1st Women's Bancorp, Utah. Chmn. Utah Legis. Rep. Ball, 1970, Utah Symphony Ball, 1979. Fellow Inst. Profl. Designers (London); mem. Assistance League, Com. Fgn. Affairs, Interior Design Soc. (assoc.), Ft. Douglas Country Club, Knife and Fork Club, Hi-Steppers Dance Club, Ladies Lit. Club, Pres.'s Club of Utah, Bloomington Country Club, Elks. Mem. Lds Ch. Home: 2575 Kuhio # 1504 Honolulu HI 96815

JENSEN, BILL, artist; b. Mpls., Nov. 26, 1945; m. Margrit Lewczuk; 1 child, Russell Lewczuk. BA, U. Minn., 1968, MFA, 1970. Exhibitions include Fischbach Gallery, NYC, 1973, 1975, Washburn Gallery, NYC, 1980, 1981, 1982, 1984, 1986, 1987, 1988, 1989, 1991, 1992, 1994, 1996, Mus. Modern Art, NYC, 1986, The Phillips Collection (travelling exhbn.), Washington, DC, 1987, Margo Leavin Gallery, LA, 1991, Mary Boone Gallery, NYC, 1993, 1995, 1998, 2001, 2003, Nielsen Gallery, Boston, 1994, Joseloff Gallery, U. Hartford, Conn., 1999, Danese Gallery, NYC, 2000, 2002, 2004, Tex. Gallery, Houston, 2003. Active in Creative Artists Pub. Svc. Program, 1979. Nat. Endowment for the Arts fellow, 1985-86. Mailing: c/o Danese Gallery 41 E 57th St New York NY 10022-1908*

JENSEN, D. LOWELL, judge, lawyer, federal official; b. Brigham, Utah, June 3, 1928; s. Wendell and Elnora (Hatch) J.; m. Barbara Cowin, Apr. 20, 1951; children: Peter, Marcia, Thomas. AB in Econs, U. Calif.-Berkeley, 1949, LL.B., 1952. Bar: Calif. 1952. Dep. dist. atty., Alameda County, 1955-66; asst. dist. atty., 1966-69; dist. atty., 1969-81; asst. atty. gen. criminal div. Dept. Justice, Washington, 1981-83, assoc. atty. gen., 1983-85, dep. atty. gen., 1985-86; judge U.S. Dist. Ct. (no. dist.) Calif., Oakland, 1986—. Mem. Calif. Council on Criminal Justice, 1974-81; past pres. Calif. Dist. Atty.'s Assn. Served with U.S. Army, 1952-54. Fellow Am. Coll. Trial Lawyers; mem. Nat. Dist. Atty.'s Assn. (victim/witness commn. 1974-81), Boalt Hall Alumni Assn. (past pres.) Office: US Dist Ct 1301 Clay St Rm 490C Oakland CA 94612-5217

JENSEN, DALLIN W., lawyer; b. Afton, Wyo., June 2, 1932; s. Louis J. and Nellie B. Jensen; m. Barbara J. Bassett, Mar. 22, 1958; children: Brad L., Julie N. BS, Brigham Young U., 1954; JD, U. Utah, 1960. Bar: Utah 1960, U.S. Dist. Ct. Utah 1962, U.S. Supreme Ct. 1971, U.S. Ct. Appeals (10th cir.) 1974, U.S. Ct. Appeals D.C. 1980. Asst. atty. gen. Utah Atty. Gen., Salt Lake City, 1960—83, solicitor gen., 1983—88; shareholder Parsons, Behle & Latimer, Salt Lake City, 1988—. Alt. commr. Upper Colo. River Commn., 1983—; mem. Colo. River Basin Salinity Adv. Coun., 1975—; commr. Utah Reclamation Mitigation and Conservation Commn., 2003—; spl. legal cons. Nat. Water Commn., Washington, 1971—73. Author (with Wells A. Hutchins): The Utah Law of Water Rights, 1965; mem. editl. bd. Rocky Mountain Mineral Law Found., 1983—85; contbr. articles on water law and water resource mgmt. to profl. jours. Served with U.S. Army, 1955—57. Mem. Lds Ch. Home: 3565 S 2175 E Salt Lake City UT 84109-2902 Office: PO Box 45898 Salt Lake City UT 84145-0898 Office Phone: 801-532-1234. E-mail: djensen@pblutah.com.

JENSEN, DAVID GRAM, management consultant; b. New Britain, Conn., Jan. 24, 1955; s. Robert and Vera (Ericksen) J. BS, Cen. Conn. State U., 1977; MS, U. Wis., 1979. Assoc. dir. phys. dept. New Britain (Conn.) YMCA, 1975-77; grad. asst. LaCrosse (Wis.) Exercise Program, 1978-79; staff rsch. assoc. U. Calif., San Diego, 1979-81, coord. rsch. cardiology, 1981-83; med. application cons. Med. Data Systems, San Diego, 1983-84; med. sales specialist Siemens Med. Systems, Mission Viejo, Calif., 1984-90; chief adminstrv. officer UCLA, 1990-95; pres. Scientific Selling Systems, L.A., 1993—. Cons. Western Imaging, Denver, 1991—. Contbr. articles to profl. jours. Mem. Nat. Speakers Assn., Inst. for Mgmt. Cons. Avocations: pub. speaking, exercise, motivational books and tapes. Home and Office: 3518 Barry Ave Los Angeles CA 90066-2802

JENSEN, DAVID WILLIAM, management consulting executive; b. Fairfield, Mont., May 17, 1943; s. Ray and Berniece (Pixton) J.; m. Loretta Searle Jensen, May 26, 1967; children: Lara, Camille, Teresa, Garrett, Steven, Rachel, Carrie. BS in Mech. Engring., Brigham Young U., 1969; MBA in Fin., Mktg., Lindenwood Coll., 1984. Sr. planner Atlantic Richfield, Richland, Wash., 1974-76; maintenance engr. Deer and Co., Waterloo, Iowa, 1976-78; cons. Ralston Purina Co., St. Louis, 1978-80, prin., 1980-88; pres., chief exec. officer Mgmt. Adv. Group, St. Louis, 1988—. Adj. prof. Washington U., St. Louis, 1990—, mem. indsl. adv. bd. Sch. Tech. and Info. Mgmt., 1986-87. Author: (manual) International Maintenance, 1984. Orgnl. sponsor St. Louis coun. Boy Scouts Am., 1987. Capt. USAF, 1969-74. Decorated Disting. Flying Cross, 11 air medals, Vietnamese Cross of Galantry (Vietnam). Mem. Soc. Mfg. Engrs. (sr. mem.), Inst. Indsl. Engrs. (sr. mem.). Mem. Lds Ch. Avocations: flying, church work, counseling. E-mail: jensen@magcare.com.

JENSEN, DICK LEROY, lawyer; b. Audubon, Iowa, Oct. 25, 1930; s. A.B. and Bernice (Fancher) J.; m. Nancy Wilson, June 30, 1956; children: Charles F., Sarah R. (dec.). LL.B., U. Iowa, 1954. Bar: Iowa 1954. Practice in, Audubon, Iowa, 1958-60; gen. counsel, sec. Walnut Grove Products, Co., Atlantic, Iowa, 1960-64; legal staff W.R. Grace & Co., Atlantic, 1964-66; gen. counsel, v.p., sec. Spencer Foods, Inc., Iowa, 1966-72, dir., 1968-72; mem. Dreher, Simpson and Jensen, Des Moines, 1972—. Notes and legis. editor Iowa Law Rev., 1953—54. Pres. S.W. Iowa Mental Health Inst., 1964-66. Served to lt. USNR, 1955-58. Mem.: Masons, Phi Delta Phi, Sigma Nu. Republican. Presbyterian. Home: 4823 Cedar Dr West Des Moines IA 50266 Office: Dreher Simpson & Jensen The Equitable Bldg Ste 222 Des Moines IA 50309-3723 Office Phone: 515-288-5000. Business E-Mail: djensen@dreherlaw.com.

JENSEN, DOUGLAS BLAINE, lawyer; b. Fresno, Calif., Feb. 10, 1943; s. Rodger Blaine and Margaret Mae J.; m. Lesley S. Smith, Sept. 4, 1967 (div.); children— Clayton B., Kelly E.; m. Patty Stocking Telles, Aug. 5, 1988. AB, Stanford U., 1964, JD, 1967. Bar: Calif. 1967, U.S. Dist. Ct. (ea. dist.) Calif., U.S. Dist. Ct. (no. dist.) Calif., U.S. Ct. Appeals (9th cir.). Clk. to judge U.S. Ct. Appeals 9th Cir., Fresno and San Francisco, 1967-68; Internat. Legal Ctr. fellow, Santiago, Chile, 1968-70; assoc. Miller, Groezinger, Pettit, Evers & Martin, San Francisco, 1970-72, Baker, Manock & Wanger, Fresno, Calif., 1972-74; ptnr. Baker, Manock & Jensen, Fresno, 1974—; adj. prof. water law San Joaquin Coll. Law, 1980-83. Chmn. Valley Children's Hosp., 1976-93. Mem. ABA, State Bar Calif., Fresno County Bar Assn. (pres. 1982-83). Club: Rotary (pres. 1992-93). Contbr. article to legal publ. Office: 5260 N Palm Ave Ste 421 Fresno CA 93704-2217

JENSEN, EDMUND PAUL, retired bank holding company executive; b. Oakland, Calif., Apr. 13, 1937; s. Edmund and Olive E. (Kessell) J.; m. Marilyn Norris, Nov. 14, 1959; children: Juliana L., Annika M. BA, U. Wash., 1959; postgrad., U. Santa Clara, Stanford U., 1981. Lic. real estate broker, Oreg., Calif. Mgr. fin. plan and evaluation Technicolor, Inc., Los Angeles, 1967-69; group v.p. Nat. Industries & Subs, Louisville, 1969-72; v.p. fin. Wedgewood Homes, Portland, 1972-74; various mgmt. positions U.S. Bancorp, Portland, 1974-83; pres., COO U.S. Bancorp, Inc., Portland, 1983-93; vice chmn., COO U.S. Bancorp, Inc., Portland, 1993-94; pres., CEO Visa Internat., 1994-99; ret., 1999. Bd. dirs. U.S. Nat. Bank of Oreg., U.S. Bank Washington, Phoenix Tech.; trustee Tax Free Trust Oreg.; chmn. Portland Family Funds. Chmn. United Way, 1986, N.W. Bus. Coalition, 1987; bd. dirs. Saturday Acad., Portland, 1984—, Visa U.S.A., Visa Internat., Marylhurst Coll., Oreg. Bus. Coun., Oreg. Downtown Devel. Assn., Oreg. Ind. Coll. Found., 1983—, treas., 1986—, chmn., 1988—; bd. dirs. Portland Art Mus., 1983—, vice chmn., 1989—. Mem. Portland C. of C. (bd. dirs. 1981—, chmn. 1987), Assn. Res. City Bankers, Assn. for Portland Progress (pres. 1988), Waverly Country Club, Multnomah Athletic Club, Arlington Club, Olympic Club.

JENSEN, ELWOOD VERNON, biochemist; b. Fargo, ND, Jan. 13, 1920; s. Eli A. and Vera (Morris) J.; m. Mary Welmoth Collette, June 17, 1941 (dec. Nov. 1982); children: Karen Collette, Thomas Eli; m. Hiltrud Herborg, Dec. 21, 1983 AB, Wittenberg U., 1940, DSc (hon.), 1963; PhD, U. Chgo., 1944; DSc (hon.), Acadia U., 1976, Med. Coll. Ohio, 1991; MD (hon.), U. Hamburg, 1994, U. Athens, 2005. Faculty U. Chgo., 1947-90, assoc. prof. biochemistry Ben May Inst. Cancer Rsch., 1954-60, prof., 1960-63, Am. Cancer Soc. rsch. prof. physiology, 1963-69, dir. Ben May Inst., 1969-82, dir. Biomed. Ctr. Population Research, 1972-75, prof. physiology, 1969-73, 77-84, prof. biophysics, 1973-84, prof. biochemistry, 1980-90, Charles B. Huggins disting. svc. prof., 1981-90, emeritus prof., 1990—; rsch. dir.

Ludwig Inst. for Cancer Rsch., 1983-87; scholar-in-residence Fogarty Internat. Ctr. NIH, 1988, Cornell U. Med. Coll., 1990—91; prof. Inst. for Hormone and Fertility Rsch. U. Hamburg, Germany, 1992—97. Adv. coun., GM Cancer Rsch. Found.; Nobel vis. prof. Karolinska Inst., Huddinge, Sweden, 1998, STINT vis. scientist, 1998-99, prof. emeritus, 1999-2001; John and Gladys Strauss chair for cancer rsch. U. Cin., 2002-03, George and Elizabeth Wile chair in cancer rsch. and disting. prof., 2004—; vis. scientist NICHD/NIH, 2001; vis. prof. Max-Planck-Inst. for Biochemie, Munich, 1958; chemotherapy rev. bd. Nat. Cancer Inst., 1960-62, bd. sci. counselors, 1969-72; mem. Nat. Adv. Coun. Child Health and Human Devel., 1976-80; adv. com. biochemistry and chem. carcinogenesis Am. Cancer Soc., 1968-72, coun. for rsch. and clin. investigation, 1974-77; mem. assembly life scis. NRC, 1975-78; com. on sci., engring. and pub. policy Nat. Acad. Scis., 1981-82; rsch. adv. bd. Clin. Rsch. Inst. of Montreal, 1987-96, Klinik for Tumor Biologie, Freiburg, 1993-2002, Strang Cancer Prevention Ctr., 1994-98; cons. Rockefeller U. Hosp., 1990-92; internat. adv. bd. Fundazione Giovanni Lorenzini, Milan, 2001—. Mem. editl. bd. Perspectives in Biology and Medicine, 1966—, Archives of Biochemistry and Biophysics, 1979-84, Biochemistry, 1969-72, Life Scis., 1973-78, Breast Cancer Rsch. and Treatment, 1980—, Endocrine-Related Cancer, 1994-2004, Jour. Biol. Markers, 1998—, Internat. Jour. Oncology, 2004-; assoc. editor: Jour. Steroid Biochemistry, 1974-94; contbr. articles to profl. jours. Recipient D.R. Edwards medal, 1970, La Madonnina prize, 1973, Pap award, 1975, prix Roussel, 1976, Nat. award Am. Cancer Soc., 1976, Gregory Pincus Meml. award, 1978, Gairdner Found. award, 1979, Lucy Wortham James award, 1980, Charles F. Kettering prize, 1980, Golden Plate award, 1980, Nat. Acad. Clin. Biochemistry award, 1981, Scientist of Yr. award Achievement Rewards for Coll. Scientists Found., 1981, Pharmacia award, 1982, Hubert H. Humphrey award, 1983, Rolf Luft medal, 1983, Renzo Grattarola medal, 1984, Fred C. Koch award, 1984, Axel Munthe award, 1985, Humboldt Sr. Rsch. prize, 1992, Joseph Bolivar DeLee award Chgo. Lying-In Hosp., 1995, Brinker Internat. award for breast cancer rsch. Susan G. Komen Found., 2002, Albert Lasker award for Basic Med. Rsch., Albert and Mary Lasker Found., 2004; citations: Ohio State Senate and Ho. Reps., 2004; Guggenheim fellow, 1946-47. Mem. NAS (coun. 1981-84), AAAS (Amory prize 1977), Am. Soc. Biochemistry and Molecular Biology, Am. Chem. Soc., Am. Assn. Cancer Rsch. (G.H.A. Clowes award 1975, Dorothy P. Landon prize 2002), Endocrine Soc. (pres. 1980-81), Am. Gyn/Ob Soc. (hon.), St. Paul Surg. Soc. (hon.), EORTC Receptor and Biomarker Group (hon.), Honorable Order Ky. Cols. Office: U Cin Dept Cell Biology Vontz Ctr Molecular Studies 3125 Eden Ave Cincinnati OH 45267-0521 Office Phone: 513-558-5750. Business E-Mail: elwood.jensen@uc.edu.

JENSEN, ERIC REINHARD, music educator; s. Ernest Anton and Elsa Minna Jensen. B of Music, U. Colo., 1955; MA, U. Denver, 1956; PhD, Mich. State U., 1970. Tchr. choral, music appreciation Shorewood Pub. Schs., 1960—65; chmn. dept. music Coll. Artesia, 1965—68; dean Milton Coll., 1970—73; assoc. dir. Colegio Americano, Monterrey, Mexico, 1973—77; choral condr. Eunice Pub. Schs., 1977—78; v.p. Am. Home Security Life Ins. Co., 1978—81; faculty Nova U., 1990—95; tchr. piano pvt. practice, 2005—. Arranger, pianist: Marriage of Figaro, Godspell, condr., pianist: Amahl, condr.: Annie, chorus condr.: Fidelio; composer: Chautauqua; condr.: Bye Bye, Birdie, Music Man, Babes in Arms, Li'l Abner, How to Succeed in Business, Calamity Jane, others. Pres. Artesia Libr. Bd., Friends of Libr., Las Cruces; mem. Literacy Coun., Artesia; dir. music St. Paul's Episcopal Ch. Scholar, U. London, U. Colo. Mem.: Am. Guild Organists, Coun. Grad. Students. Avocations: running, bicycling. Home and Office: 703 W Mann Artesia NM 88210 Office Phone: 505-748-4025.

JENSEN, EVA MARIE, medical/surgical nurse; b. Santa Maria, Calif., Sept. 2, 1956; d. Paul Cabello and Dolores Margaret Gutierrez; m. Royal George Jensen, Mar. 22, 1986 (div. Mar. 15, 1993). AA, Cuesta Coll., 1977; lic. vocation nurse, Hartnell Coll., 1980. RN Calif., 1982, cert. psychiat. and mental health nurse, Calif., 1995. Nurse Atascadero (Calif.) State Hosp., Atascadero, 1986—2003, Twin Cities Hosp., Templeton, 1982—86, 2003—. Participant nurses' health study Harvard Med. Sch., Boston, 1992—. Democrat. Roman Catholic. Avocation: adopting and rescuing abandoned animals.

JENSEN, HANNE MARGRETE, pathology educator; b. Copenhagen, Dec. 9, 1935; came to U.S., 1957; d. Niels Peter Evald and Else Signe Agnete (Rasmussen) Damgaard; m. July 21, 1957 (div. Apr. 1987); children: Peter Albert, Dorte Marie, Gordon Kristian, Sabrina Elisabeth. Student, U. Copenhagen, 1954—57; MD, U. Wash., 1961. Resident and fellow in pathology U. Wash., Seattle, 1963-68; asst. prof. dept. pathology U. Calif. Sch. Medicine, Davis, 1969-79, assoc. prof., 1979—2001, dir. transfusion svc., 1973—, prof., 2001—. McFarlane prof. exptl. medicine U. Glasgow, Scotland, 1983. Mem. No. Calif. Soc. for Electron Microscopy, U.S. and Can. Acad. of Pathology, Am. Cancer Soc., Am. Soc. Clin. Pathologists, AAAS, Am. Assn. of Blood Banks, Calif. Blood Bank Sys., People to People Internat., Internat. Platform Assn; fellow Pacific Coast Obstetrician and Gynecol. Soc., Coll. of Am. Pathologists. Office: U Calif Sch Medicine Dept Pathology Davis CA 95616 Office Phone: 530-752-7229. Business E-Mail: hmjensen@ucdavis.edu.

JENSEN, HANS WILLIAM, library director; b. Sept. 8, 1953; BA in Math, History, U. Wis., 1975, MALS, 1977. Asst. dir. Sun Prairie (Wis.) Pub. Libr., 1978-83; dir. Portage (Wis.) Pub. Libr., 1983—. Office: Portage Pub Libr 253 W Edgewater St Portage WI 53901-2117 E-mail: hjensen@scls.lib.wi.us.

JENSEN, HAROLD LEROY, medical liability insurance administrator, physician; b. Mpls., Aug. 17, 1926; s. Harold Hans and Nell Irene (Cameron) Jensen; m. Nancy Elizabeth Scharff, Sept. 9, 1950 (div. 1976); children: Eric Richard, Kris Ann, Beth Susan; m. Sandra Lee Steinel, Oct. 18, 1976. BS, U. Ill., 1950, MD, 1955. Intern Ill. Ctrl. Hosp., Chgo., 1955-56, resident, 1956-57; pvt. practice in internal medicine Ill., 1957—87; mem. staff Ingalls Meml. Hosp., Harvey, Ill., dir. continuing med. edn., 1979-87, v.p. med. affairs, 1987-2000, cons. med. affairs, 2000—. Asst. clin. prof. medicine U. Ill.; guest lectr. Gov.'s State U., University Park, Ill.; bd. gov. ISMIE Mut. Ins. Co., 1986—. Mem. editl. bd.: Chgo. Healthcare, 1990—93; contbr. articles to profl. jours. Chmn. Med. Polit. Action Com., 1990—92; pres. bd. dirs. Homewood (Ill.) Pub. Libr., 1970—76; mem. policy bd. Cook County Healthcare Summit, 1990; chmn. Met. Chgo. Health Info. Network, 1995—2000. With U.S. Army, 1944—46. Mem.: AMA (del. 1983—95), Ill. Med. Physicians' Svc. Orgn. (bd. dirs. 1995—96), Am. Coll. Utilization Rev. Physicians (bd. dirs. 1985—89, cert.), ACP Execs., Chgo. Health Econ. Coun. (vice chmn. 1981—85), Ill. Med. Soc. (trustee 1983—86, sec., treas. 1986, chmn. bd. trustees 1988—90, treas. 1988—96), Chgo. Med. Soc. (pres. 1985—86), Flossmoor Country Club (pres. 1972—73). Republican. Office: ISMIE Mutual Ins Co 20 N Michigan Ave Chicago IL 60602-4811

JENSEN, KATHRYN PATRICIA (KIT), broadcast executive; b. Fairbanks, Alaska, June 20, 1950; d. Edward Leroy and Doris Patricia (Fee) Bigelow; 1 child, Alexander Morgan. BA, U. Alaska, 1974. Sta. mgr., program dir. Sta. KUAC-FM, U. Alaska, Fairbanks, 1976-82; gen. mgr. Sta. KUAC-FM-TV, U. Alaska, Fairbanks, 1982-87; pres., gen. mgr. Sta. WCPN-FM, 1987—2001; COO Stas. WVIZ/PBS and 90.3 WCPN Ideastream, Cleve., 2001—. Founding mem. Alaska Pub. Radio Network, 1978-85; bd. dirs. Nat. Pub. Radio, 1983-89, Pub. Radio Internat., 1997—. Bd. dirs. United Way, Cleve., 2001—04. Recipient Elaine B. Mitchell award Alaska Pub. Radio Network, 1988, Oebie award, 1992, 95, William H. Kling Innovation and Entrepreneurship award Pub. Radio Internat., 1995, Leadership in Non-profit Mgmt. award Case We. Res. U., Mandel Ctr. Non-Profit Orgns., 1999; named Pub. Radio Gen. Mgr. of Yr., DEI/PRADO, 1999. Episcopalian. Avocations: reading, gardening. Office: Stas WVIZ & WCPN 3100 Chester Ave Ste 300 Cleveland OH 44114-4604

JENSEN, KENNETH R., data processing executive; BA in Econs., Princeton U.; MBA in Acctg. and Econs., PhD in Acctg. and Econs., U. Chgo. Exec. v.p. Fiserv, Inc., Brookfield, Wis., 1984—86, CFO, sec., treas., dir., 1984—, sr. exec. v.p., 1986—. Office: Fiserv Inc 255 Fiserv Dr Brookfield WI 53045*

JENSEN, LAURA SMIETANKA, political scientist, educator; b. Chgo., Sept. 26, 1955; d. Leonard Lambert and Marilyn Ann (Fuehlen) Smietanka; m. Roderick V. Jensen, Aug. 4, 1979; children: Katharine, Roderick. BA, Wellesley Coll., 1977; MFA, Princeton U., 1979; MPA, U. Conn., 1991, PhD, 1996. NEH fellow U. Conn., Storrs, 1993-94; CFH fellow, vis. instr. Wesleyan U., 1995-96; asst. prof. U. Mass., Amherst, 1996—2003, assoc. prof., 2003—. Author: Patriots, Settlers and the Origins of American Social Policy, 2003. Selectman Town of Clinton, Conn., 1989-95, commr. Planning and Zoning Commn., 1985-89. Mem. Phi Beta Kappa. Avocations: orienteering, landscape gardening, violinist. Home: 9 Harkness Rd Pelham MA 01002-9704 Office: U Mass Dept Polit Sci Amherst MA 01003

JENSEN, LYNN EDWARD, retired medical association administrator, economist; b. Rock Springs, Wyo., May 27, 1945; s. Glen and Helen (Anderson) J.; m. Carol Jean Lombard, June 10, 1967 (dec. Dec. 2001); children: Chelsea, Kara; m. Janet Gayle Clash, Jan 24, 2004. BA, Idaho State U., 1967; PhD, U. Utah, 1979. Rsch. assoc. Dept. Commerce, Washington, 1967, U. Utah, 1971-74, Utah State Planning Office, 1971-74; economist AMA Rsch. Ctr., Chgo., 1974-75, dir., 1975-85; v.p. health policy AMA, Chgo., 1985-96, group v.p. strategic mgmt. and devel., 1996-97, COO, 1997-2000, interim exec. v.p., 1998, ret., 2000. Mem. Robert Wood Johnson Found. Adv. Com., Princeton, N.J., 1983-84, Johnson & Johnson Cmty. Health Program, 1985-88; health adv. com. GAO. Editor-in-chief Intermountain Econ. Rev., 1972-73; assoc. editor Jour. Bus. and Econ. Stats., 1981-85; contbr. articles to profl. jours. With U.S. Army, 1968-70. Mem. AMA, Assn. Am. Med. Soc. Execs., Am. Soc. Assn. Execs., Am. Econ. Assn., Nat. Assn. Bus. Economists. Presbyterian. Avocations: reading, computers, swimming, photography, biking. Home: 1310 W Francis Dr Arlington Heights IL 60005-2210 E-mail: lejensen@comcast.net.

JENSEN, MARGARET, real estate broker; b. Payson, Utah, Aug. 12, 1948; d. Basil D. Broadbent and V. Merlene Ellsworth; m. Don E. Jensen, Sept. 27, 1997; children: Chad, Troy, Kristin, Dean, Debbie, Sean, Julie. AS, Casper Coll., 1968; BS with distinction, Colo. State U., 1989, postgrad., 1990. Grad. Realtor Inst., CRB, CRS, EMT. Clk. Colo. 8th Jud. Dept., Loveland; owner, CEO Lil Rascals, Ft. Collins, 1980-96; real estate salesperson Hometown Advantage, Loveland, 1996, Century 21, Ft. Collins, 1996; pres. Home Sweet Home Realty, Inc., Ft. Collins, 1997—; owner Home Sweet Home Bakery, Inc., Home Sweet Home Knitted Creations, Inc. Rental cons. Ft. Collins, 1985-99; tax cons., Ft. Collins, 1975-90; family cons. Ft. Collins, 1990-97. Finalist Miss Am. Pageant, 1968; instr. ARC, Ft. Collins, 1975-85; tax preparer for VITA IRS, Ft. Collins, 1975-90; supr. trip to Russia People to People, 1990. Mem. Lions Club Internat., Mortar Bd., Golden Key Nat. Honor Soc., Colo. Assn. of Realtors, Nat. Assn. of Realtors, Omicron Nu, Alpha Gamma Delta, Phi Kappa Phi. Avocations: piano, baking (3 Blue Ribbons, Larimer County Fair 2004). Home and Office: 2205 Stonecrest Dr Fort Collins CO 80521-1318 Office Phone: 970-482-2320. E-mail: buycolorado@aol.com.

JENSEN, MARK A., lawyer; BA summa cum laude, Ind. Univ., 1994; JD cum laude, Harvard Univ., 1997. Bar: Ill. 1998, D.C. 1999, US Dist. Ct. No. Ill. 1998, US Dist. Ct. So. Ind. 1999, US Ct. Appeals, 7th Cir. 1999. Law clk. Chief Judge Sarah Evans Baker, US Dist. Ct. So. Ind.; ptnr., Spec. Matters & Govt. Investigations, hiring ptnr. Washington King & Spalding LLP, Washington. Office: King & Spalding LLP 1700 Pennsylvania Ave NW Washington DC 20006 Office Phone: 202-626-5526. Office Fax: 202-626-3737. Business E-Mail: mjensen@kslaw.com.

JENSEN, MARVIN ELI, retired agricultural engineer, science administrator; b. Clay County, Minn., Dec. 23, 1926; s. John M. and Inga C. (Haugness) J.; m. Doris A. Lundberg, Sept. 4, 1947; children: Connie, Jeffrey, Eric. BS in Agr., N.D. State U., 1951, MS in Agrl. Engring., 1952, DSc (hon.), 1988; PhD in Civil Engring., Colo. State U., 1965. Instr., asst. prof. N.D. State U., Fargo, 1952-55; agrl. engr. Soil and Water Rsch. divsn. USDA, Bushland, Tex., 1955-58, head irrigation and drain sect. Ft. Collins, Colo., 1959-61, investigation leader Ft. Collins and Kimberly, Idaho, 1961-68; dir. Snake River Conservation Rsch. Ctr. Agrl. Rsch. Service USDA, Kimberly, 1969-78, nat. program leader Ft. Collins and Beltsville, Md., 1979-87; dir. Colo. Inst. for Irrigation Mgmt. Colo. State U., Ft. Collins, 1987—92; ret. Pres. Internat. Commn. Irrigation and Drainage, New Delhi, 1984-87. Editor: (monograph) Design and Operation of Farm Irrigation Systems, 1980; sr. editor: (manual) Evapotranspiration and Irrigation Water Requirements, 1990. Recipient Disting. Svc. award USDA, 1983, W.E. Morgan Alumni Achievement award, 1990, Disting. Svc. award Colo. State U., 1994; named to USDA-ARS Sci. Hall of Fame, 2000. Fellow Am. Soc. Agrl. Engrs. (tech. v.p. 1983-86, John Deere Gold medal 1982); mem. NAE, ASCE (hon., chmn. irrigation and drainage div. 1976-77, Tipton award 1982, Arid Lands Hydraulic Engring. award 1990, State-of-the-Art award, 1992). Avocations: golf, photography.

JENSEN, MICHAEL CHARLES, journalist, lecturer, author; s. Stanley Charles and Billie Jane (Cooke) J.; m. Jane Rice Woodruff, July 23, 1960; children: Heidi, Michael Charles Jr. AB, Harvard U., 1956; MS, Boston U., 1961. Reporter Boston Herald-Traveler, 1960-63, exec. fin. editor, 1963-64; reporter, editor N.Y. Times, N.Y.C., 1970-78; chief. fin. corr. NBC Nightly News, Today program, N.Y.C., 1978-2000. Lectr. in field. Author: The Financiers, 1976; contbg. author: Corporations and Their Critics, 1980; contbr.: articles to Saturday Rev., Harvard Bus. Rev. Served to lt. (j.g.) USNR, 1957-60. Recipient Page One award Newspaper Guild N.Y., 1973, Deadline Club award N.Y.C. profl. chpt. Sigma Delta Chi, 1976, media awards for econ. understanding, 1980, Janus awards for excellence in fin. broadcasting, 1981, 88, award for best news documentary San Francisco Film Festival, 1984, Gabriel awards Assn. Cath. Broadcasters, 1988, 89, 93, Disting. Alumnus award Boston U., 1989, EDI award Nat. Easter Seal Soc., 1991, Nat. News Emmy, 1993; named best econs. and bus. corr. in Am., TV Guide, 1988; named Luminary, 1999. Mem. Am. Soc. Bus. Press Editors (pres. N.Y. chpt. 1965-66), Am. Bus. Press (dir. 1967). E-mail: mikejensencom@aol.com.

JENSEN, MIKE, information scientist; b. Montevideo, Minn., May 16, 1962; s. Richard Charles and Virginia Dee Jensen; m. Beth Geller-Jensen, Mar. 3, 2001. MBA, U. St. Thomas, Mpls., 1996. Program mgr. TUI Cons., Tacoma, 2003—04; sr. project mgr. Carter & Burgess, San Antonio, 2004—. Mem.: Assn. Info. Tech. Profls. (assoc.), Americas SAP Users Group (assoc.), Am. Soc. Quality (assoc.), Project Mgmt. Inst. (corr.). Office: Carter & Burgess Inc 55 Waugh Dr Ste 800 Houston TX 77007 Office Phone: 713-803-2107. Office Fax: 210-494-4525.

JENSEN, NANCY DAGGETT, music educator; b. LA, Sept. 10, 1942; d. Daniel Thomas and Louise Helen (Kuljian) Daggett; m. Sven Oxfeldt Jensen, Nov. 19, 1978; children: Lori, Brian. BA, San Jose State U., 1964, MA, 1967. Cert. master tchr. in music. Pvt. piano tchr., Los Altos, Calif., 1967—. Mem. Music Tchrs. Assn. of Calif. (pres. 1972-74, 82-83, 85-86, 93-94, state chmn. cert. of merit 1974-79), Calif. Assn. of Profl. Music Tchrs., Steinway Soc. (bd. dirs.). Personal E-mail: nanchopin@sbcglobal.net.

JENSEN, PAUL ALLEN, mechanical engineer; b. Chgo., Aug. 27, 1936; BS, U. Ill., 1959; MS, U. Pitts., 1963; PhD in Ops. Rsch. and Indsl. Engring., Johns Hopkins U., 1967. Engr. surface div. Westinghouse Electric Corp., 1959-63, from asst. prof. to assoc. prof., 1967-73; prof. indsl. engring. ops. rsch. U. Tex., Austin, 1973—, Cullen prof. of mech. engring., 1991. Mem. Inst. Ops. Rsch. and Mgmt. Sci. Office: U Tex Dept Mech Engring Austin TX 78712-1063

JENSEN, PAUL EDWARD TYSON, business educator, consultant; b. New Orleans, Apr. 27, 1926; s. Paul Christian and Nena Laura (Robertson) J.; m. Jule Valerie Geisenhofer, Jan. 10, 1953; children: Christian, Elena, Constance. BS in Physics, Tulane U., 1947, BBA, 1949; MBA, Golden Gate U., 1976. Asst. mgr. Cuban Atlantic Sugar Co., Lugareño, Cuba, 1952-55; sr. engring. specialist GTE, Mountain View, Calif., 1955-82; sr. staff engr. TRW, Inc., Sunnyvale, Calif., 1982-92; dean Sch. of Bus., Northwestern Poly. U., Fremont, Calif., 1988—, also bd. trustees. Cons. geog. info. sys. TRW, Inc., Sunnyvale, 1993-94. Capt. USMCR, 1945-61, WWII, Korea. Fellow Soc. Tech. Comm. (assoc.); mem. IEEE (life, sr. mem.), Am. Phys. Soc., Internat. Soc. Computer Modeling and Simulation, World Future Soc., Assn. Old Crows. Presbyterian. Avocations: amateur radio, jogging, photography, travel. Home: 8033 Regency Dr Pleasanton CA 94588-3131 Office: Northwestern Poly U 47671 Westinghouse Dr Fremont CA 94539-7474 Business E-Mail: jensen@npu30.npu.edu.

JENSEN, REUBEN ROLLAND, former automotive company executive; b. Ainsworth, Nebr., Dec. 22, 1921; s. Jens Christian and Amy Caroline (Boyer) J.; m. Janet A. McCann, Oct. 19, 1974; children: Shannon (Mrs. Roger Santora), Bruce. Student, U. Nebr., 1938-41. With Gen. Motors Corp., Detroit, 1946, jr. engr. Hydra-Matic div., 1965-67, gen. mgr. Hydra-Matic div., 1967-70, gen. mgr. Allison div., 1970-72, v.p., group exec., 1972-74, exec. v.p., 1974-84. Mem. adv. bd. Chem. Bank Internat., 1973-86. Served with USNR, 1943-45. Recipient Silver Beaver, Disting. Eagle, Silver Buffalo, Boy Scouts Am., 1973 Mem. Assn. U.S. Army, Navy League U.S., Am. Ordnance Assn., Quail Ridge Country Club (Boynton Beach, Fla.), Meadowbrook Country Club (Northville, Mich.), Masons. Home: 3609 Chinaberry Ter Boynton Beach FL 33436-4528 also: 14016 Eaton Dr Plymouth MI 48170

JENSEN, RICHARD A., economics professor; m. Gay N. Dannelly, Dec. 30, 1993. PhD, Northwestern U., Evanston, Ill., 1980. Asst. prof. Ohio State U., Columbus, Ohio, 1980—88; assoc. prof., prof. U. Ky., Lexington, Ky., 1988—2000; prof. U. Notre Dame, Notre Dame, Ind., 2000—. Fellow: Internat. Jour. of Indsl. Orgn.; mem.: Phi Beta Kappa, Am. Econ. Assn. Office: Univ Notre Dame 434 Flanner Notre Dame IN 46556-5611 Office Phone: 574-631-7698. Business E-Mail: jensen.24@nd.edu.

JENSEN, RICHARD DENNIS, librarian; b. Payson, Utah, Oct. 20, 1944; s. Ruel Whiting and Ethel Josepha (Otte) J.; m. Maxine Swasey, Apr. 21, 1966; children: Shaun, Craig, Todd, Jana, Brad, Kristine, April, Lynne. BS in Zoology, Brigham Young U., 1971, MLS, 1976. From asst. sci. libr. to pub. svc. coord. Brigham Young U., Provo, Utah, 1971—2001, reference svc. coord., 2001—03, life sci. libr., 2003—. Co-author: Agricultural and Animal Sciences Journals and Serials: An Analytical Guide, 1986, (indexes) Great Basin Naturalist, 50 Year Index, 1991, BYU Geology Studies, Cumulative Index, vol. 1-37, 1954-1991, 1992. Mem. Lds Ch. Avocations: farming, sports, camping. Office: Brigham Young U Libr Sci & Maps Dept 2324 HBLL Provo UT 84602-2734 Office Phone: 801-422-6012. Business E-Mail: Richard_Jensen@byu.edu.

JENSEN, RICHARD JORG, biologist, educator; b. Sandusky, Ohio, Jan. 17, 1947; s. Aksel Carl and Margaret (Wolfe) Jensen; m. Faye Robertson, May 30, 1970. BS, Austin Peay State U., 1970, MS, 1972; PhD, Miami U., 1975. Asst. prof. Wright State U., 1975-79; prof. St. Mary's Coll., 1979—. Guest prof. U. Notre Dame, Ind., 1981—, dir. Greene-Nieuwland Hebarium, 1988—; sr. rsch. fellow Ctr. field Biology, Austin Peay State U., 1986—88; vis. scholar dept. botany Miami U., 1987; panelist systematic biology program NSF, 1983—87; exec. com. Am. Midland Naturalist, 1990—. Assoc. editor: Am. Midland Naturalist, 1989—2004; mem. editl. bd. Plant Systematics and Evolution, 1990—96; assoc. editor: Systematic Botany, 1996—2000. Named to Acad. Hall of Fame, Austin Peay State U., 1998; grantee, NSF, 1973, 1979, 1985, 1987, 1995, Rsch. Corp., 1984, Eli Lilly, 1990. Fellow: Ind. Acad. Sci. (co-chair program com. 1988, fellow com., biol. survey com., publ. com., grantee 1983, 1991); mem.: Internat. Oak Soc. (bd. dirs. 1997—, membership chair 1997—, webmaster 2000—), Soc. Systematic Biology, Internat. Assn. Plant Taxonomy, Bot. Soc. Am., Am. Soc. Plant Taxonomists (rsch. com. 1987—90, chmn. 1989—90, treas. 1991—96, honors and awards com. 2000—02, coun. mem. at large 2000—03, chair 2001, pres.-elect 2004, Disting. Svc. award 1996), Sigma Xi (grantee 1974). Democrat. Avocations: reading, computing, genealogy research. Home: 2044 Carrbridge Ct South Bend IN 46614-3514 Office: St Mary's Coll Dept Biology Notre Dame IN 46556 also: Greene-Nieuwland Herbarium Univ of Notre Dame Dept Biol Scis Notre Dame IN 46556 Office Phone: 574-284-4674. Business E-Mail: rjensen@saintmarys.edu.

JENSEN, RICHARD (DICK) K., retired literature educator; b. Jacksonville, Fla., Sept. 1, 1935; s. Kenneth M. and Marguerite Sidel Jensen; m. Martha Prater Jensen, June 1, 1959; children: Carol, David. BA, Maryville Coll., 1957; MA, U. Memphis, 1989. Broadcast journalist various companies, 1966—81; prof. Rust Coll., Holly Springs, Miss., 1990—95, U. Memphis, Memphis, 1995—97, N. Greenville Coll., Greenville, SC, 1997—2001, U. SC, Spartanburg, SC, 2001—02; ret., 2002. Bd. dirs. C. of C., Black Mt., NC, 1970—72, First Foundations, Inc., SC, 1997—2005. Author: The Billy Pulpits, 1996, Pearl Survivors, 2001, Normandy Survivors. 2004. Sch. bd. Greenville County Sch. Bd., Greeville, SC, 2004; press sec. State Atty. Gen., NC, 1974—75; field office mgr. Gov. Office, NC, 1975—77; press sec. Billy Graham, 1970; founding, pres. First Foundations, Inc. Recipient Green Eyeshade award, Sigma Delta Chi, 1968, Excellence in Tchg. award, Bush Found., 1992. Independent. Avocations: writing, pub. spkg. Office: First Founds Inc PO Box 991 Travelers Rest SC 29690 Office Phone: 864-834-2300. E-mail: ffi113@bellsouth.net.

JENSEN, ROBERT FREDERICK, management consultant; b. Oakland, Calif., Sept. 6, 1945; s. Robert F. Jensen, Sr. and Gertrude L. Lonergan; m. Karen M. Jost, June 26, 1965; children: Julie Ann, Sara Christine, Patrick James. BBA, Loras Coll., 1967. CPA, CMC, CDPA. Staff auditor McGladrey, Davenport/Des Moines, 1967-71, mgmt. cons., 1971-78, mgmt. cons., coord. Chgo., 1978-82, exec. ptnr., 1982-86, regional mng. ptnr., 1986-96, chief ops. officer/econ. units, 1996-99, exec. v.p., mergers and acquistions, 1999-2000, sr. v.p., mergers & integration, 2000—01, exec. v.p. mergers, 2001—. Office: RSM McGladrey Inc 1699 E Woodfield Rd Ste 300 Schaumburg IL 60173-4957 E-mail: bob_jensen@rsmi.com.

JENSEN, ROBERT TRYGVE, retired lawyer; b. Chgo., Sept. 16, 1922; s. James T. and Else (Uhlich) J.; m. Marjorie Rae Montgomery, Oct. 3, 1959 (div. June 1973); children: Robert Trygve, James Thomas, John Michael; m. Barbara Mae Wilson, Aug. 5, 1974. Student, U. N.C., 1943; LL.B., JD, BS, Northwestern U., 1949; LL.M., U. So. Calif., 1955. Bar: Calif. 1950. Asst. counsel Douglas Aircraft Co., Inc., 1950-52, 58-60, counsel El Segundo div., 1952-58; gen. counsel Aerospace Corp., El Segundo, 1960-84, asst. sec., 1961-67, sec., 1967-85. Founding mem. World Assn. Lawyers of World Peace Through Law Center. Served with AUS, 1942-46, PTO. Mem. Alpha Delta Phi, Phi Delta Phi. Fax: 310-475-0445. E-mail: rtjsr@aol.com.

JENSEN, RONALD L., insurance company executive; Chmn. bd. dirs. UICI and predecessor co., Dallas, 1983—, mem. exec. and compensation coms.; pres., CEO UICI, Dallas, 1993-94, 97-99. Office: #300 2301 W Plano PKWY Plano TX 75075-8436*

JENSEN, RYAN R., geographer, educator; m. Tricia L. Jensen. BS in Cartography and Geographic Info. Sys., Brigham Young U., 1996, MS in Geography, 1997; PhD, U. Fla. Asst. prof. Ind. State U., Terre Haute, 2000—. Grantee, NSF, NASA. Office Phone: 812-237-2258.

JENSEN, SAM, lawyer; b. Blair, Nebr., Oct. 30, 1935; s. Soren K. and Frances (Beck) J.; m. Marilyn Heck, June 28, 1959 (div. Jan. 1987); children: Soren R., Eric, Dana; m. Carmen Patton, Apr. 7, 1990. BA, U. Nebr., 1957, JD, 1961. Bar: Nebr. 1961. With Smith Bros., Lexington, Nebr., 1961-63, Swarr, May, Smith and Andersen, Omaha, 1963-83, Erickson & Sederstrom, P.C., Omaha, 1983—2005, Berens and Tate, P.C., L.L.O., Omaha, 2005—. Chmn. bd. dirs., v.p. bd. dirs. Omaha Public Power Dist., 1979-81; chmn. Nebr. Coordinating Commn. for Postsecondary Edn., 1976-78. Del. Nat. Rep. Conv., 1960, mem. Nebr. Rep. Ctrl. Com., 1968-70; mem. Regents Commn. Urban U., U. Nebr., Omaha, chmn. Task Force on Higher Edn.; mem. Hwy Commn. State of Nebr., 1989-95; vice chmn. Opera Omaha, 1992-95, v.p., 1994-96. Recipient Disting. Service award U. Nebr., 1981 Mem. Omaha Bar

Assn. (past exec. com.), Nebr. Bar Assn. (chmn. com. public relations 1973-76), Am. Bar Assn., U. Nebr. Alumni Assn. (pres. 1976-78), Rotary Club, Omaha Club, Beta Theta Pi, Phi Delta Phi. Clubs: Rotary, Omaha, Racquet. Office: Berens and Tate PC LLO 10050 Regency Cir Ste 400 Omaha NE 68114 Office Phone: 402-391-1991. Personal E-mail: Jensen@cox.net. Business E-Mail: samj@berenstate.com.

JENSEN, THOMAS C., lawyer; b. Pasadena, Calif., 1958; BA, U. So. Calif., 1980; JD, Lewis & Clark Coll., Portland, Oreg., 1983. Bar: Oreg. 1984, DC 1998. Dep. exec. sec. US-Can. Pacific Salmon Commn., 1987—89; majority counsel US Senate Com. on Energy and Natural Resources, Subcom. on Water and Power, 1989—92; exec. dir. Grand Canyon Trust, 1992—95; assoc. dir. natural resources White House Coun. on Environ. Quality, 1995—97; of counsel to ptnr. Troutman Sanders LLP, Washington, 1997—2004, head environ. and natural resources practice; ptnr., environ. & energy group Sonnenschein Nath & Rosenthal LLP, Washington, 2004—. Chair Nat. Environ. Conflict Resolution Adv. Com. US Inst. for Environ. Conflict Resolution, 2002—; mem. leadership coun. Pew Inst. for Oceans Sci. Trustee William D. Ruckelshaus Inst. for Environment and Natural Resources U. Wyo. Named Disting. Environ. Law Grad., Lewis & Clark Coll. Office: Sonnenschein Nath & Rosenthal LLP Ste 600, E Tower 1301 K St NW Washington DC 20005 Office Phone: 202-408-3956. Office Fax: 202-408-6399. Business E-Mail: tjensen@sonnenschein.com.

JENSEN, TOMMY GERT, oceanographer; b. Copenhagen, Mar. 4, 1954; came to U.S., 1985; s. Knud Erik and Paula Bertha (Rasmussen) J.; m. Louise Marie Mattacchione, Oct. 18, 1989; 1 child, Gianna Majbritt Mattacchione. BS, U. Aarhus, Denmark, 1978; Cand. Sci. in Phys. Oceanography, U. Copenhagen, 1981, Lic. Sci. in Phys. Oceanography, 1986; PhD in Geophys. Fluid Dynamics, Fla. State U., 1989. Asst. Greenland Geol. Inst., Copenhagen, 1978; rsch. asst. Nordic Coun. for Phys. Oceanography, various, Scandinavia, 1979-83; rsch. fellow U. Copenhagen, 1983-85, lectr., 1985; rsch. asst. Fla. State U., Tallahassee, 1985-89; rsch. assoc. Colo. State U., Fort Collins, 1989-96, rsch. scientist, 1996—. Reviewer NSF, Washington, 1991—, Gulf of Maine Regional Marine Rsch. Program, 1993—, Nat. Oceanog. and Atmospheric Adminstrn., 1993—, Jour. Geophys. Rsch., 1987—, Jour. Oceanography, 1991—, Jour. Phys. Oceanography, 1992—, Jour. of Climate, 1994—, Monthly Weather Rev., 1996—, Pure and Applied Geophysics, 1996—, Geophys. Rsch. Letters, 1996—, NASA, 1994—, U.S. Dept. Energy, 1994—; internat. lectr. U. Sao Paulo, Brazil, 1990; mem. users exec. com. Supercomputer Computations Rsch. Inst., Fla. State U., 1987-89; mem. sci. team Computer Hardware Advance Math. and Model Physics, U.S. Dept. Energy, 1992—; Shared Memory Processing evaluation project team mem. Nat. Energy Rsch. Supercomputer Ctr., 1995; vis. sr. sci. Internat. Rsch. Ctr. for Computational Hydrodynamics, Danish Hydraulic Inst., Denmark, 1994, 95, 96. Contbg. author: Modelling Marine Systems II, 1989 (Sigma Xi award 1989); contbr. articles to profl. jours Recipient fellowships Nordic Coun. for Phys. Oceanography, 1980, U. Copenhagen, 1983, NATO Sci. Fellowship prog., 1984, NATO Advanced Study Inst., 1985, Super Computer Rsch. Inst., Fla. State U., 1987. Mem. Am. Geophys. Union, The Oceanography Soc., Phi Kappa Phi, Chi Epsilon Pi, Sigma Xi. Avocations: camping, skiing, hiking, scuba diving, tennis. Home: 1319 Clementine Ct Fort Collins CO 80526-4208 Office: Dept Atmospheric Science Colo State Univ Fort Collins CO 80523-0001

JENSEN, WALTER EDWARD, retired lawyer, educator; b. Chgo., Oct. 20, 1937. AB, U. Colo., 1959; JD, Ind. U., 1962, MBA, 1964; PhD (Univ. fellow), Duke U., 1972. Bar: Ind. 1962, Ill. 1962, D.C. 1963, U.S. Tax Ct. 1982, U.S. Supreme Ct. 1967. Asst. prof. bus. law U. Colo., Boulder, 1958-62; assoc. prof. Colo. State U., 1964-66, U. Conn., Storrs, 1966-67, Ill. State U., 1970-72; prof. bus. adminstrn. Va. Poly. Inst. and State U., beginning 1972, prof. fin., ins. and law, 1972-; with Inst. Advanced Legal Studies, U. London, 1983-84; ret.; prof. emeritus, 2005. Prof. U.S. Air Force Grad. Mgmt. Program, Europe, 1977-78, 83-85; Duke U. legal rsch. awardee, rschr., Guyana, Trinidad and Tobago, 1967; vis. lectr. pub. internat. law U. Istanbul, 1988, Roberts Coll. U. Bosporous, Istanbul, Uludag U., Turkey, 1988; rschr. U. London Inst. Advanced Legal Studies, London Sch. Econs. and Inst. Commonwealth Studies, 1969, 71-74, 76; Ford Found. Rsch. fellow Ind. U., 1963-64; faculty rsch. fellow in econs. U. Tex., 1968; Bell Telephone fellow in econs. regulated pub. utilities U. Chgo., 1965. Recipient Dissertation Travel award Duke U. Grad. Sch., 1968; Ind. U. fellow, 1963, 74, scholar, 1963-64. Mem. D.C. Bar Assn., Ill. Bar Assn., Ind. bar Assn., ABA, Am. Polit. sci. Assn., Am. Soc. Internat. Law, Am. Judicature Soc., Am. Bus. Law Assn., Alpha Kappa Psi, Phi Alpha Delta, Pi Gamma Mu, Pi Kappa Alpha, Beta Gamma Sigma. Contbr. articles to profl. publs.; staff editor Am. Bus Law Jour., 1973—; vice chmn. assoc. editor for adminstrv. law sect. young lawyers Barrister (Law Notes), 1975-83; book rev. and manuscript editor Justice System Jour: A Mgmt. Rev., 1975—; staff editor Bus. Law Rev., 1975— . Home: 3358 Glade Creek Blvd 5 Roanoke VA 24012 Office: Va Poly Inst and State U Blacksburg VA 24060

JENSEN-RUOPP, HELGA SPITKO, school program administrator, consultant; b. Kosterchan, May 24, 1946; came to US, 1954. d. George and Greta Maria Spitko; m. John Martin Jensen, June 9, 1968 (div. May 1984); children: John-Karl, Caroline, Michael, Heidi; m. James Martin Ruopp, Apr. 9, 1988. BA, Adelphi U., 1968, MA, 1970, We. Conn. State U., 1992; EdD, Columbia U., 1992, 2000. Biology tchr. Danbury (Conn.) High Sch., 1986-98; coord. K-12 sci. Danbury Pub. Schs., 1998—. Tchr. German German Lang. Sch. Danbury; adj. instr. Western Conn. State U., Danbury, 1993—, cons., 1998-2000; instr. Coop. Program for Superior High Sch. Students, 1993; scientist, tchr. drug metabolism Boehringer Ingelheim Pharm., 1989-90; ecologist Key Issues Inst.: Keystone Sci., 1997; mem. Goals 2000 Grant Implementation; presenter in field. Mem. Candlewood Lake Authority, Danbury, 1993. Fellow Conn. Sci. Tchrs. Assn., N.Y. Acad. Scis., Phi Delta Kappa, Kappa Delta Pi; mem. AAUW, Conn. Sci. Suprs. Assn., Assn. Supervision and Curriculum Devel. Lutheran. Avocations: excercising, walking, mountain biking, painting, sculpting. Office: Danbury Bd Edn Beaver Brook Rd Danbury CT 06810

JENSH, RONALD PAUL, retired anatomist; b. NYC, June 14, 1938; s. Werner G. and Dorothy (Hensle) J.; m. Ruth Eleanor Dobson, Aug. 18, 1962; children: Victoria Lynn, Elizabeth Whitney BA, Bucknell U., 1960, MA, 1962; PhD, Jefferson Med. Coll., 1966. From instr. anatomy to prof. Thomas Jefferson U., Phila., 1966—68, prof. anatomy, 1982—2004, course coord. histology, 1988—2004, ret., 2004. Staff Op. Concern Inc., Cherry Hill, N.J., 1970-72; cons. reproductive biology Bio-Search Inc., Argus Rsch. Lab. Inc., Ortho Rsch. Found. Contbr. articles to sci. jours. Task force com. on comm. S. Jersey Methodist Conf., 1974-80; chmn. Learning Resources Ctr., Haddonfield United Meth. Ch., NJ, 1976-79. Recipient Christian R. and Mary F. Lindback Found. Disting. Teaching award, 1978, Disting. Alumnus award, 1985, Faculty Achievement award Burlington Northern Found., 1989, Jefferson Med. Coll. Portrait, 1994, Award for Disting. Alumnus in a Chosen Profession, Bucknell U., 1997. Mem. AAAS, Am. Soc. Zoologists, N.Y. Acad. Scis., Teratology Soc. (treas. 1989-92), Behavioral Teratology Soc. (pres. 1985-86), Am. Assn. Anatomists, Soc. Am. Mus. Natural History, Inst. Social Ethics and Life Scis., Jefferson Med. Coll. Alumni Assn. (hon. life), Phi Beta Kappa, Sigma Xi, Psi Chi, Phi Sigma. Home: 230 E Park Ave Haddonfield NJ 08033-1835 Personal E-mail: histdoc@comcast.net.

JENSON, JON EBERDT, metal products executive; b. Madison, Wis., Aug. 1934; s. Theodore Joel and Gertrude Beatrice (Eberdt) J.; m. Jeannette Marie Hasman, May 1, 1976; children: James, Peter. BS, U. Wis., 1956; postgrad., Goethe U., Frankfort, Germany, 1956; diploma, U. Cologne, West Germany, 1957. From staff rep. to dir. mktg. and tech. svcs. Forging Industry Assn., Cleve., 1959-75; exec. v.p., sec. Am. Metal Stamping Assn., Cleve., 1975-80; pres. Precision Metalforming Assn., Independence, Ohio, 1980-2000, pres. emeritus, 2000—; interim dir. Precision Machined Products Assn., Brecksville, Ohio, 2001—02. Exec. dir., sec. Forging Industry Ednl. and Rsch. Found., Cleve., 1967-75; lectr. NYU, 1973-75; Ohio bd. advisors Liberty Mut. Ins. Co. Author: Forging Industry Handbook, 1966; editor: Metal Forming mag, 1975-90, pub. 1990-2000. Bd. regents Insts. Orgn. Mgmt., U.S. C. of C., 1977-83, vice chmn., 1982, chmn., 1983; mem. bd. regents Marycrest Sch., Independence, Ohio, 1979-86; bd. dirs. Cleve. Conv. and Visitors Bur., 1988; chmn. Consuming Industries Trade Action Coalition, 1999-2004; mem. U.S. adv. trade com. With USNR, 1958-59. Rotary Internat. fellow, 1956 Mem. Am. Soc. Assn. Execs. (cert. assn. exec.), Cleve. Soc. Assn. Execs., Rockwell Springs Trout Club. Home: 5700 Brookside Rd Cleveland OH 44131-6013 E-mail: jjenson@pma.org.

JENSON, WILLIAM G., federal agency administrator; b. Hartford, Conn. BA in History, Hobart Coll., 1970; JD, Suffolk U., 1975. Bar: Mass. 1975. Atty. Office Gen. Counsel USDA, Washington, 1976-96, jud. officer, 1996—. Instr. USDA, 1980—, mem. grad. sch.'s paralegal com., 1987. Mil. intelligence specialist1970 U.S. Army, 1970—72, Vietnam. Mem.: ABA (vice chairperson adminstrv. law and regulatory practice-agr. sect. 1996—), Mass. Bar Assn. Office: Dept Agr Office Jud Officer S Bldg Rm 1449 Washington DC 20250-0001 E-mail: william.jenson@usda.gov.

JENSSEN, WARREN DONALD, microbiologist, consultant; b. Woodbridge, N.J., Aug. 23, 1942; s. Joseph and Lillian (Anderson) J.; m. Donna M. Larson; children: Kirsten E., Erik C. BA, Rutgers U., 1965, PhD, 1970; MS, Purdue U., 1966. Diplomate Am. Acad. Microbiology, Am. Bd. Bioanalysis. Tchg. fellow Purdue U., W. Lafayette, Ind., 1965-66; rsch. fellow Rutgers U., New Brunswick, N.J., 1966-70; postdoctoral fellow Rutgers Med. Sch., New Brunswick, N.J., 1983-84; rsch. fellow Robert Wood Johnson Med. Sch., 1984-87; adj. prof. Union County Coll., Cranford, N.J., 1969-70, asst. prof., 1970-74, assoc. prof., 1974-79, prof., 1979-85, sr. prof., 1985—; adj. prof. Kean Coll., Union, N.J., 1972-75. Clin. microbiology cons. JFK Med. Ctr., Edison, N.J., 1973-76, Raritan Bay Med. Ctr., Perth Amboy, N.J., 1976-98, VA Med. Ctr., Lyons, N.J., 1989-96; dir. health svcs. lab. Union County Coll., 1974-82; dir. Union County Pub. Health Lab., 1977-82; pub. health bacteriologist N.J. Dept. Environ. Protection, 1973—; assoc. med. staff Raritan Bay Med. Ctr., 1985—; clin. lab. dir. N.J. Bd. Med. Examiners, 1985—; adj. clin. instr. Robert Wood Johnson Med. Sch., 1985-91; adj. prof. biomed. careers program Univ. Medicine and Dentistry of N.J., 1999—2002; recycling coord., Califon, 1988-92, Hunterdon County Health Adv. Com., 1985-88, Hunterdon County Mcpl. Officers Assn., 1987-89. Contbr. articles to profl. jours. Den leader, asst. scoutmaster Boy Scouts Am., Califon, N.J., 1980-84; vice chmn. Bd. Health, Califon, 1983-89; mem. Environ. Comm., Califon, 1985-89. Mem. Theobald Smith Soc., Am. Soc. Microbiology, N.J. Link for Microbiology (program chair 1983-85), AAUP (exec. bd. 1973-98). Achievements include antibiotic action on membrane-associated polyribosomes of Streptococcus faecalis, photoinduction of sporulation in Trichoderma viride, computerized compilation of antimicrobial susceptibility data, fatal septicemia due to CDC-DF2 in a splenectomized patient, a novel insertion of a resistance transposon in methicillin-resistant Staphylococcus aureus, prevalence of MLS resistance and erm gene classes among clinical strains of staphylococci and streptococci, molecular epidemiology of MLS resistance in staphylococus aureus and coagulase-negative staphylococci. Home: 83 River Rd Califon NJ 07830-4371 Office: Union County Coll 1033 Springfield Ave Cranford NJ 07016-1528 Office Phone: 908-709-7562. Business E-Mail: jenssen@ucc.edu.

JENTSCH, LYNDA JEANNE, language educator; b. Harlingen, Tex., Nov. 9, 1953; d. Theodore Werner Jentsch and Elinor Jean Elwert; m. Bart Grooms, Aug. 4, 1979; children: Walker Elwert, Owen Michael. BA, Kutztown State Coll., 1975; MA, Vanderbilt U., 1979, PhD, 1983. Tchg. asst., sr. tchg. fellow Vanderbilt U., Nashville, 1978—79; instr. Jefferson C.C., Louisville, 1979—81; from instr. to asst. prof. Spanish U. Ala., Birmingham, 1982—92; from asst. prof. to assoc. prof. Spanish Samford U., Birmingham, 1992—. Author: Exile and the Process of Individuation, 1986. Mem.: Am. Lit. Translators Assn., Ala. Assn. Fgn. Lang. Tchrs., Am. Assn. Tchrs. Spanish & Portugese.

JENTZ, GAYLORD ADAIR, law educator; b. Beloit, Wis., Aug. 7, 1931; s. Merlyn Adair and Delva (Mullen) Jentz; m. JoAnn Mary Hornung, Aug. 6, 1955; children: Katherine Ann, Gary Adair, Loretta Ann, Rory Adair. BA, U. Wis., 1953, JD, 1957, MBA, 1958. Bar: Wis. 1957. Pvt. practice law, Madison, 1957-58; from asst. prof. to assoc. prof. bus. law U. Okla., 1958-65; assoc. prof. U. Tex., Austin, 1965-68, prof., 1968-98, Herbert D. Kelleher prof. bus. law, 1982-98, prof. emeritus, 1998—, chmn. gen. bus. dept., 1968-74, 80-86. From vis. instr. to vis. prof. U. Wis. Law Sch., Wis., 1957—65. Author (with others): Texas Uniform Commercial Code, 1967; author: rev. edit., 1975; author: (with others) Business Law Text and Cases, 1968, Business Law Text, 1978, Legal Environment of Business, 1989, Texas Family Law, 7th edit., 1992, Business Law Today-Alternate Essentials Edition, 4th edit., 1997, Fundamentals of Business Law, 6th edit., 2005, West's Business Law: Text and Cases, 9th edit., 2004, West's Business Law: Alternate Edition, 9th edit., 2005, Law for E-Commerce, 2002, West's Business Law-Extended Case Study, 2003, Business Law Today-Interactive Text, 6th edit., 2003, Business Law Today-The Essentials, 6th edit., 2003, Business Law Today-Comprehensive Edition, 6th edit., 2004; dep. editor: Social Sci. Quar., 1966—82, mem. editl. bd.:, 1982—94, editor-in-chief: Am. Bus. Law Jour., 1969—74, adv. editor:, 1974—. With U.S. Army, 1953—55. Named to CBA Hall of Fame, 1999; recipient Outstanding Tchr. award, U. Tex. Coll. Bus., 1967, Jack G. Taylor Tchg. Excellence award, 1971, 1989, Joe D. Beasley Grad. Tchg. Excellence award, 1978, CBA Found. Adv. Coun. award, 1979, Grad. Bus. Coun. Outstanding Grad. Bus. Prof. award, 1980, James C. Scorboro Meml. award for outstanding leadership in banking edn., Colo. Grad. Sch. Banking, 1983, Utmost Outstanding Prof. award, 1989, CBA award for excellence in edn., 1994, Banking Leadership award, Western States Sch. Banking, 1995, Civitatis award, U. Tex., 1997. Mem.: So. Bus. Law Assn. (pres. 1967), Wis. Bar Assn., Tex. Assn. Coll. Tchrs. (pres. Austin chpt. 1967—68, mem. exec. com. 1979—80, state pres. 1971—72), Acad. Legal Studies Bus. (pres. 1971—72, mem. exec. com. 1989—94), Am. Arbitration Assn. (nat. panel 1966—96), Southwestern Fedn. Adminstrv. Disciples (v.p. 1979—80, pres. 1980—81), Phi Kappa Phi (pres. 1983—84), Omicron Delta Kappa. Home: 4106 N Hills Dr Austin TX 78731-2826 Office: U Tex IROM Dept B6500 McCombs Sch Bus CBA 5 202 1 U Sta Austin TX 78712

JEON, SUNG-EOK, computer scientist; s. Hakbong Jeon and Myunghun Park; m. Hyeseon Kim, Oct. 28, 1972; children: Kaylin, Layney. BS with honors, Yonsei U., Seoul, Korea, 1996; MS, KAIST, Taejeon, Korea, 1999, Ga. Tech, 2002. Grad. rsch. asst. EE/KAIST, Taejeon, Republic of Korea, 1997—99, ECE/Ga. Tech, Atlanta, 2000—. Recipient Excellent Academic Achievement awards, Yonsei U., 1993—96. Achievements include research in computer networks (internet, wireless network).

JEONG, SEONG-IL, aerospace engineer, researcher; b. Kwangju, South Korea, May 9, 1968; s. Doo-Sung and Hyo-Yeon (Oh) Jeong; m. Guk-Hee Kim, June 20, 1998; 1 child, Alexander. BS, Seoul Nat. U., Republic of Korea, 1990, MS, 1992; PhD, Tex. A&M U., 2002. From jr. rsch. engr. to sr. rsch. engr. Samsung Aerospace Industries, Ltd., Seoul, Republic of Korea, 1992—97; commd. rschr. Korea Inst. Sci. & Tech., Seoul, 1997—98; rschr., tchg. asst. Tex. A&M U., College Station, 1998—2002; rsch. assoc. NRC, Washington, 2003—. Contbr. articles to profl. jours. Recipient Innovation and Creativity Prize Paper award, IEEE Industry Application Soc., 2004. Avocations: golf, soccer. Home: 8471 Charmed Days Laurel MD 20723 Office: NASA Goddard Space Flight Ctr Code 545 Bldg 4 Rm 119 Greenbelt MD 20771 Business E-Mail: sjeong@mscmail.gsfc.nasa.gov.

JEPPSON, ROGER WAYNE, lawyer; b. San Francisco, June 26, 1936; s. Wayne O. and Maude (Josephson) J.; m. Janet Strong, Nov. 27, 1957; children: Jennifer, Jill. B.S. in Polit. Sci., Brigham Young U., 1958; J.D., Duke U., 1961. Bar: Oreg. 1961, Nev. 1961. Law clk. Justice Kenneth J. O'Connell of Oreg. Sup. Ct., 1961-62; assoc. Woodburn, Wedge and Jeppson and predecessors, Reno, 1962-65, ptnr., 1965-91; shareholder Jeppson & Lee, Reno, 1991-98; ptnr. Van Cott, Bagley, Cornwall & McCarthy, 1991-98; shareholder Hale Lane Peek Dennison Howard and Anderson, 1998—. Contbr. various profl. jours., Mem. Nev. State Bar Assn. (chmn. ethics com. 1979-82, del. 9th cir. judicial conf. 1979-82), Oreg. State Bar Assn., Washoe County Bar Assn. (pres. 1974-75), Rocky Mountain Mineral Law Found. (trustee 1985-2003). Democrat. Office: 5441 Kietzke Ln Reno NV 89511

JEPSON, HANS GODFREY, investment company executive, director; b. Spencer, W.Va., July 24, 1936; s. Hans G. and Juanita Imogene (Shears) J.; m. Barbara Gayle Keller, Dec. 3, 1966. AB magna cum laude, Princeton U., 1958. Exec. editor Arnold Bernhard & Co., NYC, 1961—68; v.p., rsch. dir. Dominick & Dominick, Inc., NYC, 1968—70; dir., sr. v.p., rsch. dir. Alliance Capital Mgmt. Corp., NYC, 1970—76; exec. v.p., chief investment officer U.S. Trust Co. NY, NYC, 1976—80; pres. Valquest Assocs., Inc., NYC, 1980—, Lafayette Enterprises, Inc., NYC, 1983—, The Stanton Corp., Del., 1994—. Bd. dirs. J. Aron Charitable Found.; trustee Am. Bible Soc. 2d lt. U.S. Army, 1958—59, capt. USAR, 1959—66. Mem. CFA Inst., NY Soc. Security Analysts, Dial, Elm and Cannon Club (Princeton, NJ), Princeton Club (NYC), Econ. Club (NYC), La Boule New Yorkaise (NYC), Fedn. Petanque USA, Inc. Home: 11 5th Ave New York NY 10003-4342 Office: Lafayette Enterprises Inc 126 E 56th St Fl 23 New York NY 10022-3639

JEPSON, ROBERT SCOTT, JR., bank executive; b. Richmond, Va., July 20, 1942; m. Alice Finch Andrews, Dec. 28, 1964; children: Robert Scott, John Steven. BS, U. Richmond, 1964, M of Commerce, 1975; JD (hon.), Gonzaga U., 1986; DCS (hon.), U. Richmond, 1987; DH (hon.), Hamline U., 1988; LLD (hon.), Tusculum Coll., 1989, Ashland U., 1990, Elmhurst Coll., 1991; DSC in Bus. Adminstrn., Franklin U., 1996. With Va. Commonwealth Bankshares, Richmond, 1966-68; v.p. corp. fin. Birr Wilson & Co., Inc., San Francisco, 1968-69; pres. Calif. Capital Mgmt. Corp., Irvine, 1970-73; v.p., dir. corp. fin. Cantor Fitzgerald & Co., Beverly Hills, Calif., 1973-75; dir. corp. planning and devel. Campbell Industries, San Diego, 1975-77; v.p., mgr. merger and acquisition divsn. Continental Ill. Bank, Chgo., 1977-82; sr. v.p., group head U.S. Capital Markets Group, 1st Nat. Bank Chgo., 1982-83; chmn., CEO The Jepson Corp., Chgo., 1983-89, Jepson Assoc. Inc., Savannah, Ga., 1989—. Chmn. Jepson Vineyards Ltd., Ukiah, Calif., 1985—, Coburn Optical Industries Inc., Tulsa, 1992-98; chmn., CEO Kuhlman Corp., Savannah, Ga., 1993-99; bd. advisors Jepson Found., Chgo., 1988—; bd. dirs. AGL Resources, Inc., Atlanta, Dominion Resources, Inc., Richmond, Va.; asst. prof. fin. Nat. U., 1976; lectr. U. Richmond, U. Chgo., Northwestern U., Kansas U., Luther Coll., Wake Forest U. Bd. trustees Gonzaga U., Spokane, Wash., 1982—86, Hamline U., St. Paul, 1987—92; bd. trustees, vice rector U. Richmond, 1992—95; mem. bd. advisors Franklin U., Columbus, 1996—; chmn., bd. dirs. Ga. Cancer Coalition, 2004—; chmn., bd. visitors Savannah Coll. of Art and Design, 2001—. 1st lt. U.S. Army, 1964—66. Recipient Citation Honor Founders medal Elmhurst Coll., Ill., 1994, Volunteerism and Philanthropy award Coun. Ind. Colls., 1997. Mem. Commonwealth Club (Richmond), Savannah Yacht Club, Oglethorpe Club (Savannah), Chatham Club (Savannah), Plantation Club (Savannah), Omicron Delta Kappa, Alpha Kappa Psi, Beta Gamma Sigma (Entrepreneur of Yr. medallion 1996), Phi Gamma Delta. Republican.

JERACE, CHARLOTTE LOUISE, writer, consultant; b. Rockland, Maine, Nov. 17, 1942; d. Max and Ida (Shapiro) Gopan; m. Harvey Cohen, Aug. 22, 1964 (div. Oct. 1971): children: Scott, Melissa; m. Michael Crawley Jerace, July 12, 1986. MEd, Antioch U., 1981. pres. Coast-to-Coast Prodns., Truro, Mass., 1990—. Agt. Aetna Life Ins. Co., Boston, 1975-80; mng. editor Employee Comm. Svcs., Natick, Mass., 1980-85; sr. mgr. KPMG Peat Marwick, Boston, 1985-94; prin. Buck Consultants, Boston, 1994—2004. Author: A Survivor's Manual, 1978, Facing the Future, 1980, Secret Hiding Places, 1994, Sweet Talk, 1997, Kentucky Rain, 2000, Daring Dog, 2004, Dancing Dog, 2004. Chmn. Truro Beach Commn., 1993—; pres. Boston chpt. Eleanor Roosevelt group Hadassah, 1968-70, mem., 1966—. Recipient Telly award, 1990, 91, 92, 99, Award of Excellence Bus. Ins. Mag., 1993, Am. Film Video award, 1999. Mem. Internat. Assn. Bus. Communicators (Award of Excellence 1992), New. Eng. Employee Benefits Coun. Democrat. Jewish.

JERDEE, SYLVIA ANN, minister; b. Alpine, Tex., Apr. 18, 1941; d. Rolf Walter and Marjorie O. Kaasa; m. Joseph C. Jerdee, June 15, 1963; children: Jonathan, Peter, Theodore. BA, Luther Coll., 1963; EdM, Boston U., 1978; MDiv, Luther Seminary, 1995. Ordained min. Evang. Luth. Ch. Am., 1995. Tchr. Washington H.S., Sioux Falls, SD, 1963—64, Army Edn. Ctr., Dept. of Def., Germany, 1974—78, Frankfurt (Germany) Am. H.S., 1978—85, guidance counselor, 1985—91; pastor Calvary LUth. Ch., Orr, Minn., 1995—99, Faith Little Norway Luth. Parish, Mentor, Minn., 1999—. Pastor Calvary Luth. Ch. Avocations: travel, reading. Office: Faith Little Norway Luth Parish Box 186 Mentor MN 56736

JERDEE, THOMAS HARLAN, business administration educator, researcher; b. Mpls., Aug. 30, 1927; s. Thomas Elias and Agnes (Christensen) J.; m. Marian Alice Raether, July 26, 1953; children— William Hans, Robert Gustaf BA, Gustavus Adolphus Coll., 1950; MA, U. Minn., 1956, PhD, 1960. Asst. prof. bus. adminstrn. U. N.C., Chapel Hill, 1959-63, assoc. prof., 1963-68, prof., 1968—. Prof. emritus U. N.C., Chapel Hill, 1991—. Co-author: Older Employees, 1985, Becoming Aware, 1976. With USN, 1952-54. Avocations: hiking, bicycling, canoeing, skiing. Home: 206 Spring Ln Chapel Hill NC 27514-3540 E-mail: ujerdr@mindspring.com.

JEREZ-FARRAN, CARLOS, language educator; b. Barcelona, Feb. 14, 1950; arrived in U.S., 1980; s. Baltasar Jerez-Soler and Josefa Farran-Mir. BA, Sheffield (Eng.) U., 1980; PhD, U. Mass., 1986. Asst. prof. U. Notre Dame, Ind., 1986—92, assoc. prof. Spanish, 1992—. Contbr. articles to profl. jours. Fellow, NEH, 1992. Mem.: MLA, Nanovic Inst. European Studies, Am. Assn. Tchrs. Spanish and Portuguese. Office: Dept Romance Languages Univ Notre Dame Notre Dame IN 46556 Home: 54213 Terrace Ln South Bend IN 46635

JERGE, MARIE CHARLOTTE, minister; b. Mineola, NY, Dec. 26, 1952; d. Charles Louis and Helen Marie (Scheld) Scharfe; m. James Nelson Jerge, Aug. 27, 1977. AB, Smith Coll., 1974; MDiv, Luth. Theol. Sem. of Phila., 1978. Pastor St. Mark Evang. Luth. Ch., Mayville, NY, 1978-88; co-pastor Zion Evang. Luth. Ch., Silver Creek, 1983-88; asst. to the bishop Upstate NY Synod, Buffalo, 1988—2002; dir., bd. dirs. Acad. of Preachers, Phila., 1995-99; bishop Upstate NY Synod, ELCA, Syracuse, 2002—; v.p. NY State Coun. of Chs., 2003—. Bd. dirs. Acad. Preachers, Phila., 1982-99. Chairperson Chautauqua County Commn. of Family Violence and Neglect, Mayville, 1981-82, bd. dirs., 1978-88. Named one of outstanding Young Women in Am., 1980. Avocations: needlecrafts, aerobics, golf, cross country skiing. Home: 370 Borden Rd Buffalo NY 14224-1713 Office: Upstate NY Synod 890 E Brighton Ave Syracuse NY 13205

JERGER, EDWARD WILLIAM, engineering educator, dean; b. Milw., Mar. 13, 1922; s. Nickolaus and Ann (Huber) J.; m. Dorothy Marie Post, Aug. 2, 1944 (dec. 1981); children: Betty Ann Murphy, Barbara Lee Smyth; m. Elizabeth Cordiner Sweitzer, Mar. 27, 1982. BS in Mech. Engring, Marquette U., 1946; MS, U. Wis., 1948; PhD, Iowa State U., 1951. Registered profl. engr., Iowa, Ind. Process engr. Wis. Malting Co., Manitowoc, 1946-47; asst. prof. mech. engring. Iowa State U., 1948-55; asso. prof. mech. engring. U. Notre Dame, 1955-61, prof., head mech. engring., 1961-68, asso. dean, 1968-82, prof. mech. engring., 1982-97, prof. emeritus, 1989—. Cons. U. Madre De Maestra Santiago, Dominican Republic, 1965-71 Bd. dirs. Beaufort County Schoolbook Found. Served with USAAF, 1943-46. Mem. ASME, Am. Soc. Engring. Edn., Nat. Soc. Profl. Engrs., Nat. Fire Protection Assn., Sigma Xi, Phi Kappa Phi, Pi Tau Sigma (nat. v.p. 1969-74, pres. 1974-78), Tau Beta Pi. Home: 4 Coburn Ct Bluffton SC 29909-4560 Personal E-mail: profjerger@islc.net.

JERNIGAN, CHRISTOPHER BRUCE, men's college basketball coach; s. David Paul and Camilla Jernigan; m. Camilla Viertel Randrup; 1 child, Christopher. AA, Met. State U., 1990. Basketball player and coach, Fjellhamar, Norway, 1998—99, Innsbruck, Austria, 1999—2000, H.E.I. Denmark,

Aarhus, 2000—01; basketball coach Hesser Coll., Manchester, Mass., 2004—; supr. GCA Svcs., Newmarket, NH, 2004—. Recipient Golden Poet award, Worldwide Poetry, 1998, 1999. Home: 9 River St Apt E22 Newmarket NH 03857 Personal E-mail: dskywalkerj@hotmail.com.

JERNIGAN, DONALD, hospital administrator; BS in chemistry, U. Tex., Arlington; PhD, Baylor U. Former pres. Metroplex Hosp., Killeen, Tex., Tennessee Christian Med. Ctr.; former CEO, Multi-State Hosp. Divsn. Adventist; former sr. v.p. Adventist Health Sys., currently exec. v.p.; CEO, pres. Fla. Hosp. Ctr., 1999—. Diplomat Am. Coll. Healthcare Execs. Office: 111 N Orlando Ave Winter Park FL 32789

JEROME, JERROLD V., retired insurance company executive; BS, Linfield Coll., 1952; MBA, Stanford U., 1959. V.p. Teledyne, Inc., L.A., 1962-90; pres., CEO Unitrin, Inc., Chgo., 1990-92, vice chmn., 1992-94, chmn., 1994-99; ret., 1999. Office: Unitrin Inc 1 E Wacker Dr Chicago IL 60601-1802

JEROME, JOHN JAMES, lawyer; b. N.Y.C., Oct. 17, 1933; s. Eugene George and Gladys Odette (Conterno) J.; children by previous marriage: Christopher J., Jennifer T.; m. Maureen M. Murphy, Sept. 19, 1981; children: Mairin Ashling, Emily Campbell. BBA, St. John's U., N.Y.C., 1958, LLB, 1961. Bar: N.Y. 1962, U.S. Dist. Ct. (so. dist.) N.Y. 2d cir., 3d cir., U.S. Supreme Ct., U.S. Dist. Ct. (ea. dist.) N.Y. 1964. Assoc. Milbank, Tweed, Hadley & McCloy, N.Y.C., 1962-70, ptnr., 1970-98; pres. Jerome Advisors, LLC, N.Y.C., 1999—. Adj. prof. N.Y. Law Sch., 1978-81; lectr. Am. Law Inst., Corp. Strategies, Inc., N.Y. State Bar Assn., Nat. Law Jour., Oreg. Law Sch., Ky. Law Sch. With U.S. Army, 1954-57. Mem. ABA (program chmn.), N.Y. State Bar Assn., Assn. of Bar of City of N.Y. (chmn. com. on bankruptcy and corp. reorgn. 1990-93), Nat. Bankruptcy Conf. Clubs: N.Y. Athletic, Sharon and Norfolk Country. Home: 1165 5th Ave New York NY 10029-6931 Office: 245 Park Ave 24th Fl New York NY 10167

JEROME, JOSEPH WALTER, mathematics professor; b. Phila., June 7, 1939; s. Joseph Walter and Hermena Josephine (Ostertag) J.; m. Sara Tobin, July 2, 1999. BS in Physics, St. Joseph's U., 1961; MS, Purdue U., 1963, PhD, 1966. Vis. asst. prof. U. Wis., Madison, 1966-68; asst. prof. Case Western Res. U., Cleve., 1968-70; faculty Northwestern U., Evanston, Ill., 1970—, assoc. prof., 1972, prof. math., 1976—. Vis. fellow Oxford (Eng.) U., 1974—75; vis. prof. U. Tex., Austin, 1978—79, Rush Med. Coll., Chgo., 1994—97; cons. Bell Labs., NJ, 1981—87; vis. scientist, 1982—83; vis. scholar U. Chgo.1, 1985; mem. adv. panel Internat. Workshops on Computational Electronics, 1990—; reviewer in field. Author (with S. Fisher): Springer Lecture Series Math. 479, 1975, Approximation of Nonlinear Evolution Systems, 1983, Analysis of Charge Transport, 1995; editor: Modelling and Computation for Applications, 1998; editor: (with G.Q. Chen and G. Gasper) Nonlinear Partial Differential Equations, 2005; mem. editl. bd.: Jour. Nonlinear Analysis, Jour. Computational Electronics; contbr. more than 120 articles to profl. jours. Br. Sci. Coun. sr. vis. fellow Oxford, 1974-75; NSF rsch. grantee, 1970—; recipient disting. alumnus award Purdue U. Sch. Sci., 1996. Mem. Am. Math. Soc., Soc. for Indsl. and Applied Math. Roman Catholic. Office: Northwestern U 2033 Sheridan Rd Evanston IL 60208-0830 Office Phone: 847-491-5575. Business E-Mail: jwj@math.northwestern.edu.

JEROME, KATHLEEN A., writer, retired publishing executive; b. Biloxi, Miss., May 14, 1955; d. Clarence and Marianne M. Boehm; children: Lindsay, Eric. BS in Biology Edn., Miami U., Oxford, Ohio, 1977. High sch. biology tchr., Ill., 1978-79; home tutor Fed. Homebound Program, Ill., 1980; from sci. editor to pres. Scott Foresman & Co., Glenview, Ill., 1981—95; pvt. practice Daniel Island, SC, 1996—. Mem. Nat. Sci. Tchrs. Assn., Internat. Reading Assn., Trident Literacy Assn. (bd. dirs. 2003—). Office Phone: 843-856-3532. E-mail: kjerome@verticalconnectpress.com.

JEROME, MARY MICHAELA DOYLE, retired middle school educator; b. Bklyn., Apr. 28, 1947; d. George A. and Elise (Sullivan) Doyle; children: Dennis Michael, Peter Gregory. BA in Math., Anna Maria Coll., 1968. Cert. in secondary math., R.I. Tchr. math. Thompson Mid. Sch., Newport, 1968—2003, chmn. dept. math., 1991—94; ret., 1994; editor website R.I. Math. Tchrs. Assn., 1995—. Coord. TIMES 2, Newport, 1980-2002, 8th grade leader, 1994-2003. Recipient Presdl. award for excellence in teaching math. and sci. Nat. Sci. Tchrs. Assn., 1992. Mem. NEA, Nat. Edn. Assn. R.I., Nat. Coun. Tchrs. Math, R.I. Mid. Level Educators, Delta Kappa Gamma (chpt. pres. 1984-88, state treas. 1988-90, state legis. chair 1991-93, state yearbook editor 1985-2003), RI Math. Tchrs. Assn. (tech. chair of bd., web editor). Roman Catholic.

JEROME, NORGE WINIFRED, nutritionist, anthropologist, educator; b. Grenada, Nov. 3, 1930; arrived in U.S.A., 1956, naturalized, 1973; d. McManus Israel and Evelyn Mary (Grant) Jerome. BS magna cum laude (hon.), Howard U., 1960; MS, U. Wis., 1962, PhD, 1967. Cert. nutrition splty.; fellow Am. Coll. Nutrition. Asst. prof. U. Kans. Med. Sch., Kans. City, 1967—72, assoc. prof., 1972—78, prof., 1978—95, dir. cmty. nutrition divsn., 1981—95; dir. Office of Nutrition, AID, Washington, 1988—91; sr. rsch. fellow Univ. Ctr., AID, Washington, 1991—92; interim assoc. dean minority affairs U. Kans. Med. Sch., Kans. City, 1996—98, prof. emerita, 1996—. Tech. adv. group The Nat. Ctr. for Minority Health; dir. ednl. resource centers U. Kans. Med. Center, 1974-77, head cmty. nutrition lab., 1978-95; cons. Children's TV Workshop, 1974-77; chair adv. bd. Teenage Parents Ctr., 1971-75; planning and budget coun., children and family svc. United Cmty. Svc., 1971-80; panel on nutrition edn. White House Conf. on Food, Nutrition and Health, 1969; bd. dir., health care com. Prime Health, 1976-79; bd. dir. Coun. on Children, Media and Merchandising; consumer edn. task force Mid Am. Health Systems Agy., 1977-79; commr. N. Am. working group Commn. Anthropology Food and Food Habits, Internat. Union Anthrop. and Ethnol. Sci., 1979-80; chmn. com. nutritional anthropology Internat. Union Nutritional Sci., 1979-80; lipid metabolism adv. com. NIH, 1978-80; nat. adv. panel multi-media campaign to improve children's diet U.S. Dept. Agrl., 1979-81; bd. advisers Am. Coun. on Sci. and Health, 1985-88; cons. in field. Sr. author: Nutritional Anthropology, 1980; asso. editor: Jour. Nutrition Edn., 1971-77; adv. council, 1977-80; editor: Nutritional Anthropology Communicator, 1974-77; mem. editl. bd.: Med. Anthropology: Cross Cultural Studies in Health and Illness, 1976-88, Internat. Jour. Nutrition Planning, 1977-88, Nutrition and Cancer: An Internat. Jour, 1978-2000, Jour. Nutrition and Behavior, 1981-86; contbr. articles to profl. journals. Mem. com. man food sys. NRC, 1980-83; bd. dir. Kans. City Urban League, 1969-77, Crittenton Ctr., Kans. City, Mo., 1979-80; mem. awards com. in nutrition edn. Met. Life Found., 1983-85; pres. Assn. for Women in Devel., 1991-93; trustee U. Bridgeport, Conn., 1992—; trustee Child Health Found., 1992-2000, chmn. bd. dir., 1996-98; v.p., bd. trustees U. Bridgeport, Conn., 1997—; bd. dir. Black Health Care Coalition of Kans. City, 1993-2002, Solar Cookers Internat., 1992-2000, pres., 1998-99, Johnson County, Kans. Found. on Aging, 2001-04, Health Care Found. Greater Kans. City, 2004—; mem. Commn. on Aging, Johnson County, Kans., 1997—; bd. dirs., vice chair cmty. adv. com. Kansas City Health Care Found., 2004. Decorated Dau. Brit. Empire; recipient First Higuchi Irvin Youngberg Rsch. Achievement award U. Kans., 1982, Excellence in Academia award Inst. Caribbean Studies, 2002. Fellow Am. Soc. for Nutritional Sci., Am. Anthrop. Assn. (chair com. nutritional anthropology 1974-77, founder com. nutritional anthropology 1974), Soc. Applied Anthropology, Am. Coll. Nutrition, Soc. Med. Anthropology, Am. Soc. Nutritional Sci., 1998; mem. Am. Public Health Assn. (food and nutrition coun. 1975-78, governing coun. 1982-85), Am. Inst. Nutrition (program com. 1983-86), Am. Soc. Clin. Nutrition, Am. Men and Women of Sci., Nat. Acad. Sci. (world food and nutrition study panel), N.Y. Acad. Sci., Inst. Food Technologists, Am. Dietetic Assn., Assn. for Women in Devel. (pres. 1991-93), Soc. Behavioral Medicine, Club of Rome (U.S. assoc.) Office: U Kans Med Ctr 3901 Rainbow Blvd Mail Stop 1008 Kansas City KS 66160-7313 Business E-Mail: njerome@kumc.edu. *Creative blending appears to have been the key for me--the melding of multiple traditions and styles, the melding of philosophies and strategies, and most importantly, the melding of ancient and modern thought and practices.*

JERRITTS, STEPHEN G., management consultant; b. New Brunswick, N.J., Sept. 14, 1925; s. Steve and Anna (Kovacs) J.; m. Audrey Virginia Smith, June 1948; children: Marsha Carol, Robert Stephen, Linda Ann; m. 2d, Ewa Elizabet Rydell-Vejlens, Nov. 5, 1966; 1 son, Carl Stephen. Student, Union Coll., 1943-44; B.M.E., Rensselaer Poly. Inst., 1947, MS Mgmt., 1948. With IBM, various locations, 1949—58, IBM World Trade, N.Y.C., 1958—67, Bull Gen. Electric divsn. Gen. Electric, France, 1967—70, merged into Honeywell Bull, 1970—74; v.p., mng. dir. Honeywell Info. Sys. Ltd., London, 1974—76; group v.p. Honeywell U.S. Info. Sys., Boston, 1977—80; pres., COO Honeywell Info. Sys., 1980—82; pres., CEO Lee Data Corp., 1983—85; with Storage Tech. Corp., 1985—88, pres., COO, 1985—87, vice-chmn., 1987—88; pres., CEO NBI Corp., 1988—92; cons., advisor Price Waterhouse and Wang Labs Creditors Comm., 1992—93; corp. sr. v.p., pres. Latin Am. Wang Labs., Inc., 1993—98. Interim CEO Zapotec Inc., 1999; bd. dirs. Honeywell, Inc., Storage Tech. Corp., NBI Corp., Wang Labs., Lee Data Corp. Bd. dirs. Guthrie Theatre, 1980-83, Charles Babbage Inst., 1980-92, Minn. Orch., 1980-85; trustee Rensselaer Poly. Inst., 1980-85, mem. adv. bd. Lally Sch. Mgmt., 1994—2003, Rensselaer Poly. Inst. With USN, 1943-46, lt. USNR, 1946-57. Mem. Computer Bus. Equipment Mfrs. (dir. exec. com. 1979-82), Assoc. Industries Mass. (dir. 1978-80).

JERRY, ROBERT HOWARD, retired education educator; b. Brazil, Ind., July 25, 1923; s. Floyd W. and Zetta (Hoffman) J.; m. Marjorie O. Collings, July 23, 1950; children: Robert Howard II, E. Claire. BS, Ind. State U., 1949, MS, 1951; EdD, Ind. U., 1963; postgrad., Colo. U., 1951. Tchr. elem. sch., Fowler, Ind., 1949—50; tchr. h.s. Delphi, Ind., 1951—57; prin. Covington H.S., Ind., 1957—60; supt. Worthington Schs., Ind., 1961—63; mem. faculty Ind. State U., Terre Haute, 1963—85, prof. edn., 1974—85, rep. Sch. of Grad. Studies, 1986—98; ret., 1998. Dep. state supt. public instrn., Ind., 1967-69; active North Central Assn. Colls. and Schs. Co-author: Legal Rights and Responsibilities of Indiana Teachers. Bd. dirs. Vigo County Friends of Libr. Served with USNR, 1943—46. Mem. Ind. Ret. Sch. Adminstrs., Kiwanis, Exch. Club (pres. 1973174), Blue Key, Theta Alpha Phi, Pi Gamma Mu, Phi Delta Kappa, Phi Delta Theta. Home: 2908 Crawford St Terre Haute IN 47803-2848

JERRY, ROBERT HOWARD, II, dean, law educator; b. Lafayette, Ind., July 11, 1953; s. Robert Howard and Marjorie (Collings) J.; m. Lisa Nowak, Sept. 4, 1982; children: John Robert, James Martin, Elizabeth Catherine. BS, Ind. State U., 1974; JD, U. Mich., 1977. Bar: Ind. 1977, U.S. Ct. Appeals (D.C. cir.) 1978, U.S. Ct. Appeals (7th cir.) 1980, U.S. Ct. Appeals (10th cir.) 1989. Law clk. to Hon. George MacKinnon U.S. Ct. Appeals (D.C. cir.), Washington, 1977-78; assoc. Barnes, Hickam, Pantzer & Boyd, Indpls., 1978-81; assoc. prof. law U. Kans., Lawrence, 1981-85, prof., 1985-94, dean sch. law, 1989-94; prof., Herbert Herff chair of excellence law Cecil C. Humphreys Sch. Law U. Memphis, 1994—98; dean Levin Coll. Law, U. Fla., 2003—. Author: Understanding Insurance Law, 1987, 2d edit., 1996, 3rd edit., 2002; (with Roger C. Henderson) Insurance Law: Cases and Materials, 2d edit., 1996, 3rd edit., 2001; contbr. numerous articles to profl. jours., chpts. to books. Fellow Am. Bar Found.; mem. ABA, Am. Law Inst. Democrat. Episcopalian. Office: Levin College of Law PO Box 117620 Gainesville FL 32611 Office Phone: 352-392-9238. Business E-Mail: jerryr@law.ufl.edu.

JERVIS, JANE LISE, academic administrator, historian; b. Newark, N.J., June 14, 1938; d. Ernest Robert and Helen Jenny (Roland) J.; m. Kenneth Albert Pruett, June 20, 1959 (div. 1974); children: Holly Jane Pruett, Cynthia Lorraine Pruett; m. Norman Joseph Chonacky, Dec. 26, 1981; children: Philip Joseph Chonacky, Joseph Norman Chonacky. AB, Radcliffe Coll., 1959; MA, Yale U., 1974, MPhil, 1975, PhD in History of Sci., 1978. Freelance sci. editor and writer, 1962-72; lectr. in history Rensselaer Poly. Inst., 1977-78; dean Davenport Coll., lectr. in history of sci. Yale U., 1978-82; dean students., assoc. prof. history Hamilton Coll., 1982-87; dean coll., lectr. in history Bowdoin Coll., 1988-92; pres. Evergreen State Coll., Olympia, Wash., 1992-2000; acad. dean Goddard Coll., 2004—. Cons. in field. Author: Cometary Theory in 15th Century Europe; contbr. articles to profl. jours.; book reviewer; presenter in field. Trustee Maine Hist. Assn., 1991-92, Stonehill Coll., 1996-02, Providence St. Peter's Hosp., 1997-2000; chair Maine selection com. Rhodes Scholarship Trust, 1990-92, chair N.W. selection com., 1992-93; commr. N.W. Assn. Schs. and Colls. Commn. on Colls., 1994-99. Office: Goddard College 123 Pitkin Road Plainfield VT 05667 Business E-Mail: jane.jervis@aya.yale.edu. E-mail: jjervis99@comcast.net.

JERVIS, ROBERT, political science professor; b. N.Y.C., Apr. 30, 1940; s. Herman and Dorothy J.; m. Kathe Weil, June 19, 1967; children: Alexa, Lisa. BA, Oberlin Coll., 1962; MA, U. Calif.-Berkeley, 1963, PhD, 1967. Asst. prof. govt. Harvard U., 1968-73, assoc. prof., 1973-75; vis. assoc. prof. polit. sci. Yale U., 1974-75; prof. polit. sci. UCLA, 1975-80, Columbia U., N.Y.C., 1980—, Adlai E. Stevenson prof. of internat. rels., 1989—, chair exec. com. of faculty arts and scis., 1993-94, acting assoc. v.p. arts and scis. for planning, 1994-95. Lady Davis vis. prof. Hebrew U., Jerusalem, spring 1977 Author: Perception and Misperception in International Politics, 1976, The Illogic of American Nuclear Strategy, 1984, Psychology and Deterrence, 1985, The Logic of Images in International Relations, 2d edit., 1989, The Meaning of the Nuclear Revolution, 1989, System Effects: Complexity in Political and Social Life, 1997, American Foreign Policy in a New Era, 2005; editor: Perspectives on Deterrence, 1989, Dominoes and Bandwagons, 1990, Soviet American Relations after the Cold War, 1991, Coping with Complexity in the International System, 1992; contbr. articles to prof. jours. Guggenheim fellow, 1978-79; recipient Grawemeyer award Ideas Improving World Order, Nevitt Sanford Career Achievement award Internat. Soc. Polit. Psychology, 1992, Lionel Trilling award, 1998. Fellow AAAS; mem. Am. Polit. Sci. Assn. (v.p. 1988-89, pres. 2000-01, Best Book in Polit. Psychology award 1998), Internat. Studies Assn. (Security Studies award 1996), Coun. on Fgn. Rels. (fellow 1970-71). Democrat. Home: 1170 5th Ave New York NY 10029-6527 Office: Columbia U Dept Polit Sci New York NY 10027 E-mail: RLJ1@columbia.edu.

JERVIS-HERBERT, GWENDOLYN THERESA, mental health services professional; b. N.Y.C., July 15, 1950; d. Nehemiah (Stepfather) and Margaret Rose Campbell; m. Samuel A. Herbert, Sept. 13, 1970 (div. May 1984). BS in Edn., SUNY, Buffalo, 1976, MS, 1989. Coord. case mgr., counselor Geneva B. Scruggs HEalth Care Ctr., Buffalo, 1983—87; counselor mental health Kaleida Health, 1987—2001, med. social worker, 2001—02, sr. counselor, 2002—. Clin. liaison Women Human Rights & Dignity, Buffalo, 1993—2001; clins. cons., conf. planner Mental Health Assn., 1997. Multicultural diversity com. Kalieda Health, Buffalo, 1995—99; cons., presenter Strive for Women, Inc., 2002. Scholar, Neighborhood Youth Corp., Bronx, 1968. Democrat. Avocations: reading, jazz, travel, mentoring. Home: 347 Florida St Buffalo NY 14208 Office Phone: 716-859-2886.

JESBERG, ROBERT OTTIS, JR., educational consultant, science educator; b. Springfield, Ill., Nov. 17, 1947; s. Robert O. Sr. and Catharine I. (Patton) J.; m. Ruth Marie Andreas, Aug. 21, 1971; children: Kate Debra, Amy Lyn. BA in Biology, Susquehanna U., 1969; MEd, Temple U., 1971, secondary prin. cert., 1974. Cert. secondary biology and gen. sci. tchr., secondary sch. prin. Sci. tchr. Centennial Schs., Warminster, Pa., 1969—99, asst. prin., 1979, 85, 88; sci. cons. K'NEX Industries, Inc., Hatfield, Pa., 1994—; sci. coord. Centennial Schs., Warminster, Pa., 1996-98; mem. adv. com. Gov.'s Sci. Inst. Carnegie Mellon U., 1999—; cons. edn. K'nex Edn., Hatfield. Site dir., instr. Lawrence Hall of Sci., NSF Summer Insts., U. Calif., Berkeley, 1990-92; sci. cons. Singapore Am. Schs., 1993; dir. adult edn. Centennial Schs., Warminster, Pa., 1984-97, staff devel. trainer, 1985—; instr. Pa. Commonwealth Excellence in Sci. Tchg. Alliance, Franklin Inst. Mus., Phila., 1996—. Author: (with others) K'NEX Racer Energy Educator Guide, 1996, K'NEX Bridges Educator Guide, 1996. Elder Lenape Valley Presbyn. Ch., New Britain, Pa., 1988—. Recipient Outstanding Sci. Supr. in Pa. Pa. Sci. Suprs. Assn., 1989; named Outstanding Educator in Bucks County, Pa. Bucks County ASCD, 1987, Outstanding Contbn. and Svc. to Bucks County ASCD, 1987. Mem. Nat. Sci. Tchrs. Assn., Pa. Math/Sci. Eisenhower Consortium (chairperson 1997-98, 2003-2005), Bucks County Sci. Tchrs. Assn. (pres. 1992-99). Republican. Home: 116 Blue Jay Rd Chalfont PA 18914-3104 Office: K'Nex Edn 2990 Bergey Rd Hatfield PA 19440-0700 Office Phone: 215-996-4229. E-mail: rjesberg@knex.com.

JESIOLKIEWIC, JILL MARIE, interior designer; b. St. Petersburg, Fla., Sept. 15, 1978; d. Joseph Edward and Sally Anne Jesiolkiewic. BS magna cum laude, Fla. State U., 2000. Fider & Nasad accredited Fla. State U., 2000. Interior designer Tidmore Henry and Assocs., Sarasota, Fla., 2000—. Contbr. articles to publs. Mem.: Nat. Soc. Collegiate Scholars, C. of C., Home Builders Assn., Am. Soc. Interior Designers, Golden Key Honor Soc., Phi Theta Kappa. Avocations: surfing, ballet, art. Office: Tidmore Henry and Assocs 1014 East Ave N Sarasota FL 34237 Office Phone: 941-954-4454. Office Fax: 941-955-4427.

JESKE, HOWARD LEIGH, retired insurance company executive, lawyer; b. York, Nebr., Sept. 25, 1917; s. Charles W. and Sina (Hanna) J.; m. Bettyclaire Barton, Nov. 23, 1943; children: Vaughn C., Craig B., Lynn Ellen Braziel, Laurel Claire McFarland. AB, Cornell Coll., Mt. Vernon, Iowa, 1940; LL.B., McGeorge Coll. Law, Sacramento, 1951. Bar: Calif. 1951. Capt. USAAF, 1942-45. Mem. ABA, Calif. Bar Assn., Sutter Club (Sacramento). Republican. Home: 4035 Eagles Nest Auburn CA 95603-5922

JESKE, MARC R., lawyer; b. 1952; m. Laura Jeske; 2 children. BA, U. Ill., Champaign, 1974; JD, MBA, Northwestern U., 1979. Bar: Ill. 1979. In-house counsel Chgo. and Northwestern Transp. Co., 1979—87, Inland Steel Industries, 1987—2001; gen. counsel & corp. sec. Ispat Inland Inc., 2001—. Avocation: running. Office: Ispat Inland Inc 3210 Watling St East Chicago IN 46312 Office Phone: 219-399-5528.

JESKY, T. J., pharmaceutical products executive; b. Chgo., Feb. 15, 1947; s. Henry J. and Joan F. (Lalko) J.; m. Jackeline Vasquez, Feb. 28, 2004; 1 child, Julia Alexandra. Lic. in derecho, Nat. U. Autónoma Mexico, Mexico City, 1968—70; BA Mktg. and Retailing, Bradley U., 1969. Field rep. Morton Norwich, Chgo., 1973-76, major account rep., 1976-79; Chgo. dist. mgr. Norwich Eaton Pharms., N.Y., 1979-80; N.Y.C. dist mgr. Norwich Eaton (A Procter & Gamble Co.), N.Y., 1980-83; mgr. Midwest and P.R. divsn. Norwich Eaton, Oak Brook, Ill., 1983-90; mgr. P.R. divsn. nat. accounts, mgr. nat. hosp. divsn. Procter & Gamble Pharms., Norwich, N.Y., 1990-93, mgr. divsn. Cin., 1994-95; pres., CEO Studebaker's, Inc., Scottsdale, Ariz., 1995-97, Ionosphere, Inc., Scottsdale, 1997-98, Barrington Labs., Inc., Las Vegas, 1998-2000; CEO Eaton Labs., Inc., Las Vegas, 2000—. Contbr. articles to profl. jours. Mem. Pharm. Mfr. Assn., Am. Mgmt. Assn., Nat. Pharm. Coun. Home: PO Box 8744 Scottsdale AZ 85252-8744

JESPERSEN, JOHN KRESTEN, librarian, architectural historian; b. Seattle, Wash., Feb. 11, 1946; s. Johannes Kresten and Josephine Mae Jespersen; m. Heather Bruce Pattison, June 14, 1986. BA, Providence Coll., 1969—73; AM, Brown U., 1973—77, PhD, 1977—84; MLIS, U. RI, 1998—2000. Vis. lectr. MIT, Dept. of Architecture, Cambridge, Mass., 1984, Yale U., Sch. of Architecture, New Haven, 1984—88; vis. asst. prof. Mary Wash. Coll., Fredericksburg, Va., 1986—87, The Coll. of William and Mary, Williamsburg, 1987—88; asst. prof. S.W. Mo. State U., Springfield, 1988—89; lectr. ornament Tech. U. of N.S., Sch. of Architecture, Halifax, 1989—90; reference libr. Curry Coll., Milton, Mass., 2001—02; evening reference libr. RISD, Providence, 2001—02; tech. services supr. Curry Coll., Milton, Mass., 2002—05; cataloging libr., asst. prof. R.I. Coll., Providence, 2005—. Author (co-author): (exhibition) Rubenism; co-author: (Direct Imagination CD-ROM) "Owen Jones, The Grammar of Ornament., 1856"; contbr. articles to profl. jours. Scholar Samuel H. Kress Travel Fellowship, Samuel H. Kress Found., 1979. Mem.: ALA (assoc.), Beta Phi Mu. Avocations: guitar, silversmith. Office: Rhode Island College 600 Mount Pleasant Ave Providence RI 02908 Office Phone: 401-456-2820. E-mail: jjespersen@ric.edu.

JESPERSEN, ROBERT RANDOLPH, legal association administrator; b. N.Y.C., June 17, 1936; s. Randolph Foyen and Marie (Larsen) J.; m. Shirley Dubber, Dec. 20, 1958; children: Robert Randolph Jr., Craig Christopher. AB, Columbia U., 1958, AM, 1964; JD, U. Houston, 1975; LLM, U. Tex., 1987. Bar: Tex. 1975, Ark. 1981, U.S. Supreme Ct., U.S. Ct. Appeals (5th and 8th cirs.), U.S. Dist. Ct. (so. dist.) Tex., U.S. Dist. Ct. (ea. dist.) Ark., U.S. Ct. Mil. Appeals. Pvt. practice law, 1975—. Moderator Am. Arbitration Assn. conf., Little Rock, 1987; asst. atty. gen. Tex., 1975-76; apprentice banker The Bank of N.Y., N.Y.C., 1964-66; mgmt. analyst U.S. Govt., Washington, 1961-62; hon. consul Kingdom of Lesotho, Jurisdiction of Tex., 1972-75; legal cons., 1995—; adj. prof. law U. Ark.-Little rock, 1987-91, prof. bus. law, 1980-95, prof. emeritus, 1995—; vis. prof. law U. Auckland, 1993; vis. sr. lectr. bus. law Massey U., N.Z., 1991; vis. disting. lectr. internat. bus. Calif. State U., Long Beach, 1987; vis. prof. bus. law U. Tex., Austin, 1987; part-time instr. Houston C.C., 1975-76; part-time tchg. fellow U. Houston, 1974-75; sr. advisor Assn. African Univs., Accra, Ghana, 1971-72; headmaster Kurisini Internat. Edn. Ctr., Dar-es-Salaam, Tanzania, 1969-71; dir. devel. African-Am. Inst., N.Y.C., 1967-69; assoc. dir. career svcs. Princeton U., 1966-67; asst. dir. univ. placement Columbia U., 1962-64. Co-author: Business Law: Comprehensive Edit., 1987, Business Law: Text and Cases, 1984, 8th edit., 1996, American Legal System, 1986; editor, contbr.: Industrial Laws, 1980; editl. bd. Jour. Legal Studies Edn., 1983-85, The Houston Lawyer, 1978-80; editor: Proc. of Internat. Legal Studies Assn. Ann. Mtg., 1988; contbr. numerous articles to profl. jours. 1st lt. USMC, 1958—61, col. res. USMC, 1961—88. Recipient Tchg. Excellence award Nat. Conf. of Acad. Bus. Adminstrn., 1993, Faculty Excellence award Coll. Bus. Adminstrn., U. Ark.-Little Rock, 1992; Sam M. Walton Free Enterprise fellow, 1995, Peace Rsch. fellow U. Auckland Ctr. for Peace Studies, 1992. Mem. Nat. Assn. Scholars, The Federalist Soc. for Law and Pub. Policy Studies (lawyers divsn. Ark. chpt. dir. 1992-93, 94-95, pres. 1991-92), Am. Bus. Law Assn. (pres. 1988-89), So. Reg. Bus. Law Assn. (pres. 1983-84), Ark. Bar Assn. (mem. alternative dispute resolution com. 1987-88, 92-93, internat. law com. 1983-84), State Bar of Tex. (exec. com. mil. law sect. 1978-80), Southwestern Fedn. Adminstrv. Disciplines (bd. dirs. 1982-84), Internat. Consular Acad., Am. Arbitration Assn., Assn. Law Tchrs. G.B., Assn. of Attenders and Alumni of the Hague Acad. Internat. Law, Nat. Arbitration Forum, Order of Barristers, Order of Advocates, Golden Key, Beta Gamma Sigma (chpt. pres. 1985-86), Phi Kappa Phi (chpt. pres. 1984-85), Phi Alpha Delta, Alpha Kappa Psi, Alpha Phi Omega. Republican. Home: 3208 C-108 E Colonial Dr Orlando FL 32803

JESSELL, THOMAS M., medical educator; PhD in Neurobiology, Cambridge U., Eng. Rsch. fellow Trinity Coll., Cambridge U., England; postdoctoral fellow Gerald Fishbach Lab. Harvard Med. Sch., Boston, asst. prof. neurobiology; prof. biochemistry and molecular biophysics and mem. Ctr. for Neurobiology and Behavior Columbia U. Coll. Physicians and Surgeons, 1985—; investigator Howard Hughes Med. Inst. Contbr. articles to profl. jours.; co-editor (with others): Principles of Neural Science; mem. editl. bd. several jours. Co-recipient (with Corey Goodman) March of Dimes prize in developmental biology, March of Dimes, 2001; recipient Bristol-Myers Squibb award for disting. achievement in neurosci. rsch., 2000. Fellow: cad. Arts and Scis., Royal Soc. London; mem.: Inst. of Medicine of NAS. Achievements include research in on early development of the vertebrate central nervous system; the molecular mechanisms that determine the identities of neurons generated in the spinal cord; on the guide the axons of sensory and motor neurons to their targets that permit them to form functional neuronal circuits. Office: Columbia Univ Coll Physicians and Surgeons 630 W 168th St New York NY 10032*

JESSEN, DAVID WAYNE, accountant; b. Albuquerque, Jan. 13, 1950; s. Irving Matthew and Lucille Barbara (Huber) J.; m. Melissa Meyer, Oct. 4, 1975; children: Jennifer Leigh, Kimberly Paige. BBA in Acctg., U. N.Mex., 1972. CPA N.C., N.Mex., S.C. Staff acct. local CPA firm, Albuquerque, 1971-74, jr. ptnr., 1974-75; mgr. in charge Santa Fe office Ernst & Young, 1975-80, prin. in charge Santa Fe office, 1980—86, dir. taxes N.Mex. offices

Albuquerque, 1980-86, tax ptnr. N.Mex. offices, 1986, ptnr., mgr. N.C. offices Raleigh, NC, 1987-89. Mem. Arthur Young Nat. Real Estate Com., 1988, mem. nat. hightech com., 1988-94; ptnr., dir. entrepreneurial svcs. Ernst & Young, Raleigh, 1989-2002, S.E. region dir. entrepreneurial svcs., 1992-94, dir. tax dept., 1995—, dir. tax entrepreneurial svcs., 1998-2003. Asst. scoutmaster Boy Scouts Am.; bd. dirs. St. Joseph Hosp. Health Care Found., 1986—87, N.C. Mus. Art Found., 1992—, treas., 1994—2001, Kiwanis Found. Eagle Scout, Bus. Friends Coun., N.C. Soc. to Prevent Blindness; chmn. pres.'s cir. Wake Med. Ctr. Found., 1996—2001, bd. dirs., 1997—; bd. dirs., chmn. fin. com., exec. com. WakeMed, treas., 2005—; bd. dirs. Food Bank of N.C., 2001—, chmn. fin. com., treas.; mem. parents coun. U. N.C., Chapel Hill, 2000—03; mem. Ch. Congregation at Duke U. Chapel; mem. bus. sch., acctg./MSA adv. bd. U. N.C., Wilmington; treas. bd. dirs. N.C. Mus. Art, 2003—. Mem. AICPA (nat. com. small bus. taxation), Coun. for Entrepreneurial Devel. (treas. 1989-92, bd. dirs.), Nat. Assn. Accts. (Raleigh chpt., v.p., bd. dirs. 1989-91), N.Mex. Estate Planning Coun., N.Mex. Soc. CPAs (taxation com., pub. rels. com., v.p. Santa Fe chpt. 1980), N.C. Assn. CPAs, Santa Fe C. of C., Albuquerque C. of C., Raleigh C. of C., Santa Fe Jaycees, Albuquerque Jaycees, Elks, Kiwanis, West Raleigh Rotary, Alpha Kappa Psi. Home: 4921 Misty Oak Dr Raleigh NC 27613-6349 Office Phone: 919-981-2905.

JESSEN, JOEL ANNE, not-for-profit executive, art educator; b. Seattle, Sept. 7, 1940; d. John Paagard and Anne Vilma Jessen. BA, U. Wash., 1962, MFA, 1964. Instr. Cornish Coll. Arts, Seattle, 1965—76; pres., CEO Kappeler Inst., Inc., Seattle, 1975—. Instr. U. Wash., Seattle, 1970—71, Highline Coll., Seattle, 1970—71. Author: The Imperative Step, 1972, The Physical, The Mental, and The Spiritual, 1978. Recipient Patrick Gavin Meml. prize, Boston Printmakers, 1965. Mem.: U. Wash. Alumni. Avocation: art. Office: Kappeler Inst Inc PO Box 99735 Seattle WA 98139-0735 Business E-Mail: joel@kappelerinstitute.org.

JESSEPH, STEVEN AUSTIN, risk management consultant; b. Seattle, June 26, 1951; s. John Ervin and Marley Mary (Austin) J.; m. Bonnie Lynn Fogle, July 4, l981; children: Jason Todd, Lane Nolan, Bethany Lynn, Blaire Ashley. BA in Psych., Otterbein Coll., 1973; MS in Corrections, Xavier U., 1977; postgrad., Ohio State U., 1979-81. Adminstrv. specialist Franklin County Welfare Dept., Columbus, Ohio, 1974; probation officer Franklin County Mcpl. Ct., Columbus, 1974-81; v.p. Promark Co., Cin., 1981-83; mgr. corp. outplacement Fox-Morris Assoc., Charlotte, N.C., 1983-86, v.p. career transition svcs., 1987-90, sr. v.p. nat. accts., 1991-92, sr. v.p. southeast region gen. mgr., 1992-94; exec. dir. job replacement svcs. Sara Lee Corp., Chgo., 1994—97, exec. dir. global workplace values and safety, 1997—2003; v.p. compliance and risk mgmt. Sara Lee Branded Apparel, Winston-Salem, NC, 2003—. Bd. dels. Nat. Safety Coun., bd. trustees; bd.dirs. Worldwide Responsible Apparel Prodn. Program. Contbr. articles to profl. jours. Bd. dels. Nat. Safety Coun.; chair social responsibility com. Am. Apparel & Footware Assn. Avocations: golf, fishing, travel. Office: Sara Lee Branded Apparel 1000 E Hanes Mill Rd Winston Salem NC 27105 Office Phone: 336-519-8888.

JESSOR, RICHARD, psychologist, educator; b. Bklyn., Nov. 24, 1924; s. Thomas and Clara (Merkin) J.; m. Shirley Glasser, Sept. 27, 1948 (div. 1982); children: Kim, Tom; m. Jane Ava Menken, Nov. 13, 1992. Student, CCNY, 1941-43; BA, Yale U., 1946; MA, Columbia U., 1947; PhD, Ohio State U., 1951. Intern, clin. psychology trainee VA/Ohio State U., Columbus, 1947-50; asst. prof. psychology U. Colo., Boulder, 1951-56, assoc. prof., 1956-61, prof., 1961—, dir. rsch. program problem behavior Inst. Behavioral Sci., 1966-97, dir. Inst. Behavioral Sci., 1980—2001, dir. rsch. program in health behavior Inst. Behavioral Sci., 2001—. Dir. MacArthur Found. Rsch. Network on Successful Adolescent Devel. Among Youth in High Risk Settings, 1987-96; cons. Nat. Inst. on Drug Abuse, 1975-76, Nat. Inst. on Alcohol Abuse and Alcoholism, 1976-80, WHO, Geneva, 1976-80; cons. in field. Author: (with T.D. Graves, R.C. Hanson & S.L. Jessor) Society, Personality, and Deviant Behavior: A Study of a Tri-Ethnic Community, 1968, (with S.L. Jessor) Problem Behavior and Psychosocial Development: A Longitudinal Study of Youth, 1977, (with J.E. Donovan and F. Costa) Beyond Adolescence: Problem Behavior and Young Adult Development, 1991; co-editor: Contemporary Approaches to Cognition, 1957, Cognition, Personality and Clinical Psychology, 1967, Ethnography and Human Development: Context and Meaning in Social Inquiry, 1996; editor: New Perspectives on Adolescent Risk Behavior, 1998, Perspectives on Behavioral Science: the Colorado Lectures, 1991; cons. editor Jour. Cons. and Clin. Psychology, 1975-77, Cmty. Mental Health Jour., 1974-78, Alcohol Health and Rsch. World, 1981-90, Alcohol, Drugs and Driving, 1985-92, Adolescent Medicine: State of the Art Revs., 1989—; mem. editl. bd. Prevention Sci., 1999—; cons. editor Sociometry, 1964-66, assoc. editor, 1966-69; contbr. articles to profl. jours. Served with USMC, 1943-46, PTO. Decorated Purple Heart; Social Sci. Rsch. Coun. pre-doctoral fellow Ohio State and Yale U., 1950-51; Social Sci. Rsch. Coun. fellow Ohio State U., 1954, Social Sci. Rsch. Coun. postdoctoral fellow U. Calif.-Berkeley, 1956-57, NIMH spl. rsch. fellow Harvard-Florence Rsch. Project, Italy, 1965-66, Ctr. for Advanced Study in the Behavioral Scis. fellow Stanford U., 1995-96; recipient Faculty Rsch. Lectureship award U. Colo., 1981-82; Gallagher lectr. Soc. Adolescent Medicine, 1987, Outstanding Achievement in Adolescent Medicine award, 2005; named Highly Cited Rsch. in Social Scis., Inst. for Sci. Inf., 2003. Fellow APA, Am. Psychol. Soc. (charter fellow); mem. Soc. for Psychol. Study of Social Issues, Soc. for Study of Social Problems. Avocations: mountain climbing, running marathons. Home: 1303 Marshall St Boulder CO 80302-5803 Office: U Colo Inst Behavioral Sci Cb 483 Boulder CO 80309-0001 Office Phone: 303-492-8148. Business E-Mail: jessor@colorado.edu.

JESSUP, CLIFTON R., JR., lawyer; b. Detroit, Mar. 12, 1955; BA summa cum laude, Oakwood Coll., 1976; JD, U. Mich., 1978. Bar: Neb. 1979, Tex. 1990, US Ct. Appeals, Sixth Circuit, US Ct. Appeals, Ninth Circuit, US Dist. Ct., Dist. Neb., US Dist. Ct., No. Dist. Tex., US. Dist. Ct., We. Dist. Tex., US. Dist. Ct., So. Dist. Tex. Shareholder Greenberg Traurig LLP, Dallas. Bd. trustees Oakwood Coll.; served on North Tex. Regional Mental Health Bd. Named one of Am. Top Black Lawyers, Black Enterprise Mag., 2003, Tex. Super Lawyers, Tex. Monthly, 2003, 2004; recipient Master, John C. Ford Am. Inns Ct. Mem.: ABA, Neb. State Bar Assn., State Bar Tex. Office: Greenberg Traurig LLP 600 Three Galleria Tower 13155 Noel Rd Dallas TX 75240 Office Phone: 972-419-1280. Business E-Mail: jessupc@gtlaw.com.

JESSUP, JAN AMIS, arts volunteer, writer; b. Chgo., Aug. 10, 1927; d. Herman Harvey and Anita (Lincoln) Sinako; m. Everett Orme Amis, Dec. 20, 1970 (dec. Nov. 1981); m. Joe Lee Jessup, Apr. 16, 1989. BA, U. Minn., 1948; postgrad., Rutgers U., 1969-70. Bd. dirs., mem. exec. com. Broward Ctr. Performing Arts Pacers, Ft. Lauderdale, Fla., 1985—88, pres., 1987—88; spkr. U. Internat. Bus., Beijing, 1985. Active not-for-profit orgns. including Girl Scouts U.S., Boy Scouts Am., Presbyn. Ch.; active beautification com., Lighthouse Point, Fla., 1978—89, sec., 1988—91; rep. to Fla. Art Orgns., 1987—88; bd. dirs. Archways, Ft. Lauderdale, 1987—91, Fla. Grand Opera, 1993—; trustee Miami City Ballet, 1991—94; adv. bd. Guild of the Palm Beaches, 1994—95; bd. govs. Fla. Philharm. Orch., 1981—98, v.p. representing all affiliates, 1985—87, 1992, 1994—96, exec. com., 1989—93, v.p. individual giving, 1991—92, Boca Raton bd. dirs., 1994—2002, chmn. affiliate com., 1994—95; mem. program com. Boca Raton Ctr. for Arts, 2002—; trustee Harid Conservatory, 1997—; founding pres. Harid Guild, 1997—99; pres. symphony soc., bd. dirs. Symphony of the Ams., 2004—; bd. adv. Youth Automotive Tng. Co.; bd. advisors Youth Automotive Tng. Corps, 2004—; bd. dirs. Master Chorale South Fla.; leadership coun. Boca Raton (Fla.) Philharmonic Symphonia. Mem.: Symphony of Am. Soc. (pres. 2004—), Royal Dames Cancer Rsch. (trustee 1995—97), Gold Coast Jazz Soc. (bd. dirs. 1992—98, v.p. 1994—98), Ft. Lauderdale Philharm. Soc. (bd. dirs. 1986—2003), Opera Soc. (sec. 1986—87, bd. dirs. 1986—, v.p. pub. rels. 1987—88), Royal Palm Dinner Theatre (bd. dirs. 1998—2000), The Opus Soc. (chmn. 1981—85, bd. dirs., mem. exec. com. 1981—96, pres. 1989—93), Am. Symphony Orch. League (bd. dirs. 1998—, liaison and com. mem. Nat. Youth Orch. Festival 2000 Com. 2000—01), Internat. Game Fish Assn. (adv. coun. 2001—), Nat. Soc. Arts and Letters, Am. Symphony Orch. League Vol. Coun. (sec. 1986—87, bd. dirs. 1986—92, v.p. 1987—88, vice chmn. 1989—90, pres. 1989—90, advisor 1990—91, assoc. Resource Devel. Inst. 1996—98), Centre For The Arts (program com. 2002—04), Ocean Reef Club, Sea Grape Garden Club (past pres.), Royal Palm Yacht and Country Club Women's Club, Boca Raton Resort and Club. Republican. Avocations: music listening, boating, fishing, writing, bridge. Home: 133 Coconut Palm Rd Boca Raton FL 33432-7975 Personal E-mail: janjessup@aol.com, amisj@bellsouth.net.

JESSUP, JOE LEE, business educator, management consultant; b. Cordele, Ga., June 23, 1913; s. Horace Andrew and Elizabeth (Wilson) J.; m. Janet Amis, Apr. 16, 1989. BS, U. Ala., 1936; MBA, Harvard U., 1941; LLD (hon.), Chung-Ang U., Seoul, Korea, 1964. Sales rep. Proctor & Gamble, 1937-40; liaison officer bur. pub. rels. U.S. War Dept., 1941; spl. asst. and exec. asst. Far Ea. div. and office exports Bd. Econ. Warfare, 1942-43; exec. officer to chief of staff Svcs. of Supply-Europian Theatre, 1943-44; exec. officer, office deptl. adminstrn. Dept. State, 1946; exec. sec. adminstr.'s adv. coun. War Assets Adminstrn., 1946-48; v.p. sales Airken, Capitol & Service Co., 1948-52; assoc. prof. bus. adminstrn. George Washington U., 1952, prof., 1952-77, prof. emeritus, 1977—, asst. dean Sch. Govt., 1951-60; pres. Jessup and Co., Ft. Lauderdale, Fla., 1957—2002. Bd. dirs. Giant Food, Inc., Washington, mem. audit com., 1971—75; bd. dirs. Hunter Assn. Labs., Fairfax, Va., mem. exec. com., 1966—69, exec. v.p., 1967, coord. Air Force Regources Mgmt. program, 1951—57; del. in edn. 10th Internat. Mgmt. Conf., Sao Paulo, Brazil, 1954, 11th Internat. Mgmt. Conf., Paris, 1957, 12th Internat. Mgmt. Conf., Sydney and Melbourne, Australia, 1960, 13th Internat. Mgmt. Conf., Rotterdam, The Netherlands, 1966, 14th Internat. Mgmt. Conf., Tokyo, 1969, 15th Internat. Mgmt. Conf., Munich, 1972; mem. Md. Econ. Devel. Adv. Commn., 1973—75. Mem. Civil Svc. Commn., Arlington County, Va., 1973—75; trustee Tng. Within Industry Found., Summit, NJ, 1954—58; mem. bd. overseers Lynn U., Boca Raton, Fla., 1991—2002; mem. adv. bd. Youth Automotive Tng. Ctr., Hollywood, Fla., 1993—; trustee Philharm. Orch., Fla., 1986—91; mem. nat. adv. coun. Ctr. Study of Presidency, 1974—99; mem. Atlanta regional panel selection of White House fellow, 1990—95, mem. Miami regional panel. Decorated Bronze Star; recipient cert. of appreciation Sec. of Air Force, 1957 Mem.: Royal Palm Yacht and Country Club, Univ. Club (Washington), Harvard Club (N.Y.C.). Home: 133 Coconut Palm Rd Boca Raton FL 33432-7975

JESSUP, JOHN MILBURN, surgical oncologist; b. New Haven, Aug. 4, 1946; s. John Baker and Dorothy (Milburn) J.; m. Kathleen Amy Foxen, May 7, 1977; children: Katherine, John, James. BA, Yale U., 1968; MD, N.Y. Med. Coll., 1972. Diplomate Am. Bd. Surgery; lic. physician Mass., Tex. Intern, jr. asst. resident N.Y. Hosp.-Cornell Med. Ctr., N.Y.C., 1972-74; clin. assoc. surgery Nat. Cancer Inst./NIH, Bethesda, Md., 1974-76; resident in gen. surgery U. Tex. Med. Sch., Houston, 1977-80, faculty assoc. dept. gen. surgery Anderson Hosp. and Tumor Inst., 1980-81, asst. surgeon, 1981-86, assoc. surgeon, 1986-89; assoc. prof. surgery New England Deaconess Hosp., Boston, 1989—. Vis. scientist basic rsch. program Frederick Cancer Rsch. Ctr., Litton Bionetics, Inc., Frederick, Md., 1976-77; vis. prof. dept. gen. surgery U. Mo., Kansas City, 1982; faculty assoc. dept. gen. surgery Anderson Cancer Ctr., Houston, 1980-81, asst. prof., 1981-86; from asst. to assoc. prof. dept. gen. surgery U. Tex. Med. Sch., Houston, 1982-89; from asst. to assoc. prof. U. Tex. Health Sci. Ctr., Houston, 1983-89; from asst. to assoc. prof. dept. immunology Anderson Hosp. and Tumor Inst., 1984-89, assoc. prof. dept. surgery, 1986-89; assoc. prof. surgery Harvard Med. Sch., Boston, 1989—; cons. in surgery Dana-Farber Cancer Inst., Boston, 1989—; mem. provisional staff New England Bapt. Hosp., Boston, 1990—, Cardinal Cushing Gen. Hosp., Brockton, Mass., 1990—; mem. courtesy staff Goddard Meml. Hosp., Stoughton, Mass., 1990—, Southwood Community Hosp., Norfolk, Mass., 1991—; cons. microgravity scis. divsn. NASA, Clear Lake, Tex., 1988—; vis. prof. Eastern Maine Med. Ctr., Bangor, 1991, dept. surgery U. Vt., Burlington, 1991, McGill U. and U. Montreal, 1993; Curts vis. prof. Dartmouth Med. Ctr., Hanover, N.H., 1991; vis. faculty Ont. Cancer Inst., Toronto, 1992; ad hoc spl. rev. group upper gastrointestinal cancer NIH, 1991, site visitor program-project rev. Wistar Inst., 1991, mem. spl. rev. coms., 1992, 93; site visitor program-project rev. Thomas Jefferson U., 1993; mem. MIR sci. panel Nat. Aeronautics and Space Adminstrn., Washington, 1993, mem. shuttle-MIR working group, 1993; mem. biotech. facility rev. panel space sta. NASA Johnson Space Ctr., Houston, 1993, biotech. sci. discipline working group, 1992—; lectr. in field Author (with others): Neoplasm Immunity: Mechanisms, 1976, Immuno-aspects of the Spleen, 1976, Biology and Treatment of Colorectal Cancer, 1986, Colon Cancer Cells, 1986, 90, General Surgical Oncology, 1992, Atlas of Surgical Oncology, 1992, Surgical Decision Making, 3d edit., 1993, Current Therapy in Oncology, 1993, others; sub-editor Yr. Book of Cancer, 1985-87; mem. editorial bd. Jour. Clin. Oncology, 1988-93, Yr. Book of Cancer, 1991—; guest editor Surg. Oncology Clinics N.Am., 1991; contbr. articles to profl. jours. Lt. comdr. USPHS, 1974-76. Fellowship Tng. grant Am. Cancer Soc., 1979-80, Surg. Oncology Rsch Tng. grant., NASA, 1991—, Immunomedics, Inc. grantee. Fellow ACS (commn. on cancer mem. 1992—); mem. AAAS, AMA, AIAA, Am. Assn. Cancer Rsch., Assn. Acad. Surgery (program com. mem. 1984-86), Soc. for Surg. Oncology (govt. rels. com. mem. 1991, local arrangements com. 1993—, clin. rsch. and govt. rels. com. 1991-92), Am. Soc. Clin. Oncology (program com. mem. 1991), Am. Soc. Cell Biology, Soc. Univ. Surgeons, Aerospace Med. Assn. (program com. mem. 1988-90, space medicine rsch. 1992—), Soc. for Biol. Therapy, Metastasis Rsch. Soc., N.Y. Acad. Scis., Tex. Med. Assn., Southern Med. Assn., Surg. Biology Club, Houston Surg. Soc., Harris County Med. Soc., Alpha Omega Alpha. Office: New England Deaconess Hosp 110 Francis St # A Boston MA 02215-5501

JESSUP, KAREN LOUISE, historic preservation educator, consultant; b. Detroit, Mar. 20, 1945; d. Robert LeRoy and Vera Louise (Krieghoff) Crispin; m. Richard Jessup Jr., June 24, 1967; children: Dana Leigh, Amy Krieghoff, Kara Buntin. BA, Allegheny Coll., 1967; MA in Preservation Studies, Boston U., 1983. Caseworker Child Welfare Services of Allegheny County, Pitts., 1968-70; pvt. practice cons. Providence, 1983—. Mem. faculty Roger Williams Coll., Bristol, R.I., 1985—; adj. assoc. prof. grad. program in historic preservation Boston U., 1987—. Contbr. articles to profl. jours. Mem. distbn. com. Citizens Bank Community Found., Providence, 1986—; sec. R.I. Legis. Commn. on Preservation Law, 1986—; trustee Heritage Found. Rhode Island; panelist Mass. Council on the Arts. Alden scholar Allegheny Coll., 1967; named Providence Disting. Citizen, 350 Yr. Celebration. Mem. Providence Preservation Soc. (exec. com. 1982—, bd. dirs. 1982—, pres. revolving fund 1985—), Preservation Action (nat. bd. dirs. 1984—), Nat. Trust for Historic Preservation (bd. dirs. Antoinette Downing Fund 1986—).

JESSUP, LYNNE KATIE, minister; b. Ithaca, N.Y., Sept. 14, 1951; d. John Fitzgerald and Ruth Elizabeth (Hoerber) Dixon; m. Robert Keith Jessup, Sept. 14,1985. BA, Wittenberg U., 1973; BTh, Gulf Coast Bible Coll., 1978. Ordained to ministry Ch. of God, 1981. Pastor Ch. of God, Saratoga, Ind., 1978-92, Olive Bethel Ch. of God, Akron, Ind., 1992—; postmaster Zanesville, Ind., 1999—. Del. Ch. of God Gen. Assembly, Anderson, Ind., 1978—; forwarding agt. Friends of Turkey, 1984-86; alumni recruiter Gulf Coast Bible Coll., 1982-86; bd. dirs. Haven Ministries, 1984-85; chaplain Randolph County Hosp., 1985-90. Columnist From the Chaplain's Desk, local newspaper, 1985-86. Pres. R.E.A.C.H. Svcs., Inc., Winchester, Ind., 1982-82; chmn. Cystic Fibrosis Bike-a-thon, Saratoga, 1981, 82. Mem. Winchester Area Ministerial Assn. (pres. 1981-82, sec.-treas. 1983-85, 91), Randolph County Hosp. Chaplains Assn. (pres. 1982-83), Youth Explosion, Alumni in Action, Mid-Am. Bible Coll. Republican. Home: 514 Bittersweet Ln Ossian IN 46777-9310 Office: Olive Bethel Ch of God 8515 E 200 N Akron IN 46910-9423 *Living in this world can keep us so busy "doing" things that we fail to take time to develop who we "are". God calls us first to "be" His people and to "be" the kind of people He desires, and if we will seek after this, the "doing" will take care of itself.*

JESSUP, PAUL FREDERICK, financial economist, educator; b. Evanston, Ill., Apr. 16, 1939; s. Paul S. and Gertrude (Strohmaier) J.; m. Johanna A.M. Friesen, June 27, 1970; children: Christine Marieke, Paul Charles Friesen. BS, Northwestern U., 1960, PhD, 1966; AM, Harvard U., 1963; BA, U. Oxford, Eng., 1963; MA, U. Oxford, 1983. Economist com. banking and currency U.S. Ho. of Reps., Washington, 1963-64; faculty U. Minn., Mpls., 1967-82, prof. fin., 1973-82; with Jessup & Co., Inc., St. Paul, 1982—; William Kahlert prof. mgmt. and econs. Hamline U., St. Paul, 1988—. Dir. Gerbill Inc.; Sabbatical prof. in residence Fed. Res. Bank, Mpls., 1973-74 Author: The Theory and Practice of Nonpar Banking, 1967, (with Roger B. Upson) Returns in Over-the-Counter Stock Markets, 1973, Competing for Stock Market Profits, 1974, Modern Bank Management: A Casebook, 1978, Modern Bank Management, 1980, Invest To Win: A Coach's Guide to Stocks, Bonds and Mutual Funds, 2001; editor: Innovations in Bank Management: Selected Readings, 1969; contbr. articles to profl. jours. Mem. Midwest Fin. Assn. (past pres.), Univ. Club. Home: 1979 Shryer Ave W Saint Paul MN 55113-5414 Office: Hamline U 1536 Hewitt Ave Saint Paul MN 55104-1284

JESSUP, PHILIP CARYL, JR., retired lawyer; b. Utica, N.Y., Aug. 30, 1926; s. Philip C. and Lois K. (Kellogg) J.; m. Dorothy A. Kerr, Jan. 15, 1951 (div.); children: Timothy, Nancy, Margaret; m. Helen I. Ibbitson, Jan.24, 1969; stepchildren: Genevieve, Lucinda, Francesca, Alexander. BA, Yale Coll., 1949; JD, Harvard U., 1952. Bar: N.Y. 1954. Atty. Whitman, Ransom & Coulson, N.Y.C., 1952-58; legal officer Internat. Nickel Co., Inc., N.Y.C., 1958-63; gen. solicitor internat. Inco Ltd., N.Y.C., 1963-68; chief legal officer, sec., dir. Inco Europe Ltd., London, 1968-72; pres., mng. dir. P.T. Internat. Nickel Indonesia, Jakarta, 1972-78; v.p., gen. counsel and sec. Inco Ltd., N.Y.C., Toronto, Can., 1978-84; sec., gen. counsel Nat. Gallery Art, Washington, 1985-2000. Dir. Bignore N.V., Geneva, 1981-85; chmn. bd. Inco Gulf, E.C., Bahrain, 1980-84; chmn. bd. Am. Friends Nat. Gallery Art Australia, N.Y.C., 2001—; bd. dirs. Norfolk Land Trust, Norfolk, Conn., 2002—, v.p., 2003—. Trustee Obor, Internat. Book Inst. Inc., Phila., 1978—2001, sec.-treas., 1989-96, chmn. bd., 1996-2001; mem. adv. commn. H.H. Humphrey Fellowship Program, 1984-89; trustee Asia Soc., 1991-99, sec., 1993-99, mem. adv. com. Washington Ctr., 1985-2000, chmn. adv. com., 1989-2000; pres. Friends of Hosp. for Sick Children, Toronto, 1985—; mem. Coun. on Fgn. Rels., N.Y.C., 1972—; pres. West Brooklyn Ind. Dems., 1956-58. Served to staff/sgt. C.E., U.S. Army, 1944-46. Mem. ABA, Assn. of Bar of City of N.Y., Century Assn. (N.Y.C.). Democrat. Home: 97 Gamefield Rd Norfolk CT 06058-1272

JESSUP, R. JUDD, health science association administrator; b. San Francisco, Oct. 15, 1947; s. R. Bruce and Adaline (Brown) J.; m. Jeanne (Bannash), Sept. 7, 1968 (div. Dec. 1987); children: Jarrett, Jody, Rik, Alycia; m. Charlene (Massei), May 19, 1990. BA, Knox Coll., 1969; MBA, U. Denver, 1971. Dir. mktg. svc. Blue Cross Blue Shield, Denver, 1972-78, dir. alt. delivery sys., 1978-80; pres. HMO Colo., Inc., Denver, 1980—87, Take Care Health Plan, Concord, Calif., 1987-94, Take Care, Inc., Concord, Calif., 1991-94; pres., HMO divsn. F. H. P. Internat., Fountain Valley, Calif., 1994-96; pvt. investor Calif., 1996—2002; CEO US Labs, Irvine, Calif., 2002—. Bd. dir. Corvel Corp., Novamed Eyecare Svc. Avocation: golf. Home: 30962 Via Serenidad Trabuco Canyon CA 92679-4002

JESTY, JOLYON, biochemist, researcher; b. Poole, Dorset, United Kingdom, Aug. 10, 1946; s. John Bedford and Pauline Jesty; m. Jennifer Slater; children: Gillian, Sophy, Justin; m. Joan K. Kiely. BA in Biochemistry, Oxford (Eng.) U., 1968, DPhil, 1972. Postdoctoral Yale U., New Haven, Conn., 1972—75; faculty of medicine and pathology Stony Brook U., Stony Brook, NY, 1975—. Prof. biochemistry, hemostasis, bioethics; pres., u. senate Stony Brook U., 1996—97; lectr., bioethics & policy, 1991—. Grantee Rsch. grants, NIH, Am. Heart Assn., NATO, NSF, 1978—. Mem.: Internat. Soc. for Thrombosis & Haemostasis. Achievements include Tchg. devel.: ethics and policy. Avocations: Austin Healeys, woodworking, piano. Office: Stony Brook Univ Health Sci Ctr Stony Brook NY 11794-8151 Office Phone: 631-444-2059.

JETER, DEREK SANDERSON, professional baseball player; b. Pequannock, NJ, June 26, 1974; s. Charles and Dorothy Jeter. Student U. Mich., 1992. Baseball player NY Yankees, 1995—. Author (with Jack Curry): The Life You Imagine: Life Lessons For Achieving Your Dreams, 2001. Founder Turn 2 Foundation, 1996. Named Minor League Player of Yr., The Sporting News, 1994, Am. League Rookie of Yr., Baseball Writers Assn. of Am., 1996, World Series MVP, 2000, MLB All-Star Game MVP, 2000; named to Am. League All-Star Team, 1998—2002, 2004; recipient Am. League Gold Glove Award, 2004. Achievements include being a mem. of World Series Champions, 1996, 98, 99, 2000; led Am. League in hits (219), 1999; MLB record for post-season hits (123), 2003; guest host, Sat. Night Live, 2001. Office: NY Yankees Yankee Stadium E 161st and River Ave Bronx NY 10451

JETER, HOWARD F., former ambassador; b. Union, S.C., Mar. 6, 1947; m. Donice M. Jeter; 2 children. BA, Morehouse Coll.; MA, Columbia U., UCLA. Legis. intern Ga. Ho. Reps.; with Fgn. Svc.; with bur. oceans and internat. environ. and sci. affairs Dept. State, 1977-78; econ., comml. and consular officer Maputo, Mozambique, 1979-82; polit. officer Dar es Salaam, Tanzania, 1983-86; dep. dir. U.S. Liaison Office, Windhoek, Namibia, 1984; dep. chief of mission Maseru, Lesotho, 1987-88; charge d'affaires, 1989-90; dep. chief of mission Windhoek, 1990-93; amb. to Botswana Dept. State, 1993-96, spl. presdl. envoy to Liberia, 1997—99; amb. to Nigeria Lagos, 2001—03; exec. v.p. Goodworks Internat., 2004—. Recipient Superior Honor award, Sr. Performance award; Internat. fellow Columbia U., fellow Ford Found., Merrill Overseas Study-Travel fellow. Mem. Am. Fgn. Svc. Assn., Coun. Fgn. Rels., Phi Beta Kappa. Office: Goodworks International 303 Peachtree Street NE Ste 4420 Atlanta GA 30308 Office Phone: 404-527-8484. Office Fax: 404-527-3827.

JETER, JAMES YANDELL, freelance/self-employed musician; s. Yandell and Nelle Jeter; life ptnr. Keith Westerfield. MusB, The U. Tex., 1971; MusM, The Juilliard Sch., 1974; DMA, SUNY, Stony Brook, 2000. Prin. bassoon N.Y.C. (N.Y.) Orch., 1980—88; sub bassoon, contra Met. Opera Orch., N.Y.C., 1986—88; prin. bassoon Westfield (N.J.) Symphony Orch., 1990—; solo bassoon Virtuosi Quintet, Inc., N.Y.C.; prin. bassoon St. Cecilia Orch., N.Y.C. Instr. bassoon Sewanee (Tenn.) Summer Music Festival, Kinhaven Music Sch., Weston, Vt.; affiliate artist Sarah Lawrence Coll., N.Y., tchr. Scholar, The Juilliard Sch., 1971—74, SUNY, Stony Brook, N.Y., 1997—2000. Mem.: Chamber Music Am., Am. Fedn. of Musicians, Internat. Double Reed Soc. (contbr. articles). Personal E-mail: chleojet@yahoo.com.

JETER, WAYBURN STEWART, retired microbiology educator, microbiologist; b. Cooper, Tex., Feb. 16, 1926; s. Joseph Plato and Beulah (Stewart) J.; m. Margaret Ann McDonald, May 30, 1947; children— Randall Mark, Monette Ann, Marcus Kent. BS, U. Okla., 1948, MS, 1949; PhD, U. Wis., 1950. Diplomate: Am. Bd. Microbiology. Mem. faculty U. Iowa, 1950-63, assoc. prof., 1958-63; prof. microbiology U. Ariz., Tucson, 1963-89, prof. microbiology emeritus, 1989—, prof. pharmacology and toxicology, 1983-91, prof. pharmacology and toxicology emeritus, 1991—, head dept. microbiology and med. tech., 1967-83, dir. lab. cellular immunology, 1976-91, dir. med. tech. program, 1976-79. Vis. prof. immunology and med. microbiology U. Fla., 1980; pres. Scientific Rels. Svcs., Inc., 1988—99. Contbr. articles profl. jours. Served with USNR, 1943-46. Fellow AAAS; mem. Am. Acad. Microbiology, Am. Assn. Immunologists, Ariz. Acad. Sci., Am. Soc. Microbiology (mem. council 1975-77), Soc. Exptl. Biology and Medicine, Sigma Xi. Democrat. Presbyterian. Home: 5140 N Via Sempreverde Tucson AZ 85750-5966 E-mail: wayjeter@peoplepc.com.

JETLEY, KARUN, software company executive, consultant; s. Baldev Krishan and Shobhna Jetley. BS, Houston Bapt. U., 1985—90; MBA, U. of Houston, 1990—92. Dir. software devel. BKI, Houston, 1993—97; data arch. Reliant Energy, Houston, 1998—99; pres. effesoft, Houston, 2000—03; global data arch. BMC Software Inc., Houston, 2002—03, BindView Devel.

Corp., Houston, 2004—; panel mem. EDC, 2005. Bd. mem. CMP Adv. Bd., Houston, 2002—; mem. IDE Rsch. Panel; mem. panel on rsch. Evans Data Corp., 2004—. Founding mem. Nat. Campaign for Tolerance, 2004. Mem.: SQL Server Group, Houston Advt. Fedn. (corr.). Achievements include creation of new product segment in software industry by inventing first request/requirements software suite; invented, copyrighted, trademarked first request/metadata tool in the world - effesoft. Personal E-mail: knvrqut@sbcglobal.net.

JETT, BRENT W., astronaut, military officer; b. Pontiac, Mich., Oct. 5, 1958; m. Janet Leigh Lyon, 1992. BS in Aerospace Engring., U.S. Naval Acad., Annapolis, Md., 1981; MS in Aero. Engring., U.S. Naval Postgrad. Sch., Monerey, Calif., 1989. Commd. ensign USN, Annapolis, Md., 1981, advanced through grades to capt., 2002; naval aviator USN Fighter Squadrons 101 and 74, Naval Air Sta. Oceana, Va. Beach, 1983—86; student Naval Postgrad. Sch., Monterey, Calif., 1986—89; project test pilot USN Strike Aircraft Test Directorate, 1989—91; F-14B pilot USN USS Saratoga, 1991—92; astronaut USN Johnsoon Space Ctr., Houston, 1992—. Decorated Disting. Flying Cross USN, 3 space flight medals, Exceptional Svc. medal NASA. Mem.: Soc. Exptl. Test Pilots, U.S. Naval Acad. Alumni Assn., Assn. Space Explorers, Assn. Naval Aviation. Achievements include 3 space flights, 4000 flight hours in over 30 different aircraft and 450 carrier landings. Office: Asromaut Office NASA Johnson Space Ctr Houston TX 77058*

JETT, ERNEST CARROLL, JR., paper company executive, lawyer; b. Liberty, Tex., July 10, 1945; m. Janene L. Jett. BA cum laude, Baylor U., 1967; MA, La. State U., 1969; JD, U. Tex., 1973. Bar: Tex. 1973, U.S. Dist. (so. dist.) Tex. 1979, U.S. Ct. Appeals (5th cir.) 1979, U.S. Supreme Ct. 1979, Mo. 1980. Mem. legal staff Cooper Industries, Inc., 1973-75, Tenneco, Inc., 1975-79; v.p., gen. counsel, sec. Leggett & Platt, Inc., Carthage, Mo., 1979—. Editor Tex. Internat. Law Jour. 1972-73. Mem. ABA, Am. Corp. Coun. Assn., Am. Soc. Corp. Secs., State Bar Tex., Mo. Bar Assn., Phi Alpha Theta, Alpha Chi, Phi Eta Sigma, Phi Delta Phi, Pi Gamma Mu. Office: Leggett & Platt Inc 1 Leggett Rd Carthage MO 64836-9649 Home: 4702 S Jackson Ave Joplin MO 64804-4837 Office Phone: 417-358-8131. E-mail: ernest.jett@leggett.com.

JETT, JOAN (JOAN LARKIN), musician; b. Phila., Sept. 22, 1960; Guitarist, vocalist The Runaways, 1975—79, Joan Jett & the Blackhearts, 1981—; signed with Mercury Records, 1976. Musician (with The Runaways): (albums) The Runaways, 1976, Queens of Noise, 1977, Live in Japan, 1977, Waitin' For The Night, 1977, Little Lost Girls, 1981, I Love Playing With Fire, 1982, And Now...The Runaways, 1978, Flaming Schoolgirls, 1980, Best Of The Runaways, 1987, Born To Be Bad, 1993, Neon Angels, 1991, The Runaways featuring Joan Jett and Lita Ford, 1998; musician: Joan Jett, 1981, Bad Reputation, 1981, I Love Rock 'n' Roll, 1981, Album, 1983, Glorious Results Of A Misspent Youth, 1984, I Need Someone, 1984, Good Music, 1986, Up Your Alley, 1988, Hit List, 1990, Notorious, 1991, Flashback, 1993, Do You Wanna Touch Me, 1993, Pure & Simple, 1994, Fit To Be Tied: Great Hits, 1997, Fetish, 1999, Naked, 2004; prodr.(by The Germs): (album) G.I.; co-author: (songs) House of Fire performed by Alice Cooper on album Trash, 1989; actor: (films) Light of Day, 1987, Talking About the Weather, 1994, Boogie Boy, 1997, By Crook or By Hook, 2001, The Sweet Life, 2003, (guest appearances): (TV series) Highlander, 1992, Walker, Texas Ranger, 2000,: (Broadway plays) The Rocky Horror Picture Show, 2001. Nominee Grammy award for best rock performance by a group for single I Hate Myself for Loving You, 1989. Office: Blackheart Records 636 Broadway New York NY 10012

JETT, STEPHEN CLINTON, geography and textiles educator, researcher; b. Cleve., Oct. 12, 1938; s. Richard Scudder Jett and Miriam Ida (Horn) Greene; m. Mary Frances Manak, Aug. 7, 1971 (div. 1977); 1 child, Jennifer Frances; m. Lisa Sue Roberts, June 17, 1995. AB, Princeton U., 1960; postgrad., U. Ariz., 1962—63; PhD, Johns Hopkins U., 1964. Instr. geography Ohio State U., Columbus, 1963-64; asst. prof. geography U. Calif., Davis, 1964-72, assoc. prof., 1972-79, prof., 1979—2000, prof. textiles and clothing, 1996—2000, prof. emeritus geography, textiles and clothing, 2000—, chmn. geography dept., 1978-82, 87-89. Author: Navajo Wildlands, 1967 (1 of 50 Books of Yr., Am. Inst. Graphic Arts 1967, 1 of 20 Merit Award Books, Western Book Pubs. Assn. 1969), House of Three Turkeys, 1977, Navajo Architecture, 1981 (1 of Outstanding Acad. Books, Choice mag. ALA 1981), Navajo Placenames and Trails of the Canyon de Chelly System, Arizona, 2001, France, 2004; (monograph) Tourism in the Navajo Country, 1966; editor jour. Pre-Columbiana; contbr. numerous articles to profl. jours. and chpts. to books. Mem. Hist. and Landmarks Commn., Davis, 1969-73; vice chmn. Gen. Plan Noise Element Study Com., Davis, 1974-76, chmn. ad hoc citizens noise com., 1997-98; mem. exec. coun. Univ. Farms Unit Number 1 Neighborhood Assn., Davis, 1987-90. Fellow: Am. Geog. Soc., Explorers Club; mem.: AAAS, Found. Rsch. Ancient Maritime Explorations (bd. dirs., treas. 2002—), Inst. for Study of Am. Cultures (bd. dirs. 1996—), Epigraphic Soc. (bd. dirs. 1996—, v.p. 2003—), Soc. Am. Archaeology, Assn. Am. Geographers (chair Am. Indian splty. group 1989—91). Avocations: travel, photography, textiles and other ethnographic arts, French language and culture. E-mail: scjett@hotmail.com.

JETTER, ARTHUR CARL, JR., insurance company executive; b. Omaha, Oct. 9, 1947; s. Arthur Carl and Virginia Ann (Turner) J.; m. Jennifer Ann Jochim, Mar. 30, 1974; children: Arthur Carl III, Sarah Ann. BBA, Dana Coll., 1974. Registered health underwriter; CFP, CLU; registered employee benefits cons.; FLMI, LTCP. Sales rep. life ins. Guarantee Mut., Omaha, 1974-81; pres. Art Jetter & Co., Omaha, 1981—, Employers Mut. Acceptance Co., Omaha, 1981—. Capt., helicopter pilot inf. U.S. Army, 1968-72, Vietnam. Fellow Life Mgmt. Inst.; mem. Life and Health Ins. Found. for Edn. (life; dir. 2004-), CLU (cert., edn. chmn. Omaha chpt. 1984-91), Nat. Assn. Ind. Life Brokerage Agencies (chmn. 2000), Nat. Assn. Health Underwriters (pres. 1991-92, Gordon Meml. award 1995, Health Ins. Industry person of yr. 1995), Mass Mktg. Ins. Inst. (Person of Yr. award 1993). Republican. Lutheran. Home: 13624 Parker Cir Omaha NE 68154-3829 Office: Art Jetter and Co 11305 Chicago Cir Omaha NE 68154-2636 Office Phone: 402-330-2900. E-mail: art@jetter.com.

JETTON, C. LORING, JR., lawyer; b. Pitts., Feb. 10, 1943; s. Clyde Loring and Barbara (Lewis) J.; m. Marion Luyken, Feb. 19, 1966; children: Ada Elizabeth, Christopher Loring. AB, Harvard U., 1964; JD, Columbia U., 1969. Bar: N.Y. 1969, D.C. 1970. Law clk. to Hon. W. Feinberg U.S. Ct. Appeals (2d. cir.), 1969-70; assoc. Wilmer, Cutler & Pickering, Washington, 1970-76, ptnr., 1977—. Lt. U.S. Army, 1964-66. Mem. ABA, D.C. Bar. Office: Wilmer Cutler & Pickering 2445 M St NW Ste 500 Washington DC 20037-1487

JETTON, GIRARD REUEL, JR., lawyer, retired oil industry executive; b. Washington, Feb. 19, 1924; s. Girard Reuel and Hallie (Grimes) J.; m. Mera Riddell, Sept. 4, 1948 (dec. Dec. 1997); children: Mera Elizabeth, Robert Girard, James Thomas. BS in Engring., George Washington U., 1945, BA, 1947; JD, Harvard U., 1950. Bar: D.C. 1951, Md. 1959, Ohio 1960. Elec. engr. in rsch., 1944-45; patent atty. Washington, 1950-51; atty. IRS, Washington, 1951-54; trial atty. Dept. Justice, Washington, 1954-55; atty. then ptnr. McClure & McClure, Washington, 1955-60; with Marathon Oil Co., Findlay, Ohio, 1960-85, asst. to chmn. bd., 1969-73, corp. sec., 1973-85; pvt. practice Findlay, 1985—. With USNR, 1945-46. Mem. Bar Assn. D.C., Findlay/Hancock County Bar Assn., Met. Club (Washington). Home and Office: PO Box 813 Leland MI 49654-0813

JETTON, STEVE, newspaper editor; Met. editor Houston Chronicle. Office: Houston Chronicle 801 Texas St Houston TX 77002-2996

JEUB, MICHAEL LEONARD, financial consultant; b. Mpls., Mar. 2, 1943; s. Leonard M. and Florence J.; m. Alice Ann Linden (div. 1980); children: Christopher Michael, Annette Michelle; m. Julia Jean Stephenson, Feb. 4, 1983; children: Michael Leonard Jr., Robert. BS in Acctg., Calif. State Poly. U., 1966. CPA, Tex., Calif. Staff acct. Ernst & Whinney, L.A., 1966-70; CFO Internat. Clin. Lab., Inc., Nashville, 1970-85, pres. east, 1985-88; pres. August Enterprises, 1988-91; pres., COO, CFO MICA, San Diego, 1991-93; exec. v.p., CFO, treas. Nat. Health Labs., Inc., 1993-94; sr. v.p., CFO Jenny Craig Internat., 1994-2000; fin. cons. La Jolla, Calif., 2000—01; ptnr. Tatum CFO, 2000—; CFO The Immune Response Corp., San Diego, 2002—03, Road Runner Sparts, 2005—. Home: 12959 Chaparral Ridge Rd San Diego CA 92130-2454 Office: 5549 Copley Dr San Diego CA 92111 E-mail: MikeJeub@aol.com.

JEVTIC, MILOMIR, artist, sculptor; b. Valjevo, Yugoslavia; s. Sreten Jevtic and Milena Mitrovic; m. Ana Sonc, July 7, 1977; children: Damjan, Matija. MA in Art, U. Lubljana, Yugoslavia, 1973. Engr. artist Wausau (Wis.) Tile, 1995-96, Strescon Industries, Balt., 1997-98. Prin. works include sculpture Woodely Garden Pk., monument Reverend Matej Nemadovic, sculpture U. Student Housing Devel. Achievements include patent in method of casting materials using flexible resilient mold. Home: 1 Knoll Mist Ln Gaithersburg MD 20879 E-mail: jevticart@cs.com.

JEVTOVIC-TODOROVIC, VESNA, physician, researcher; d. Dragomir Jeftimije and Milka Radisav Jevtovic; m. Slobodan Milenko Todorovic, Oct. 6, 1984; children: Marko Slobodan Todorovic, Nikola Slobodan Todorovic, Katarina Vesna Todorovic. MD, U. Belgrade Sch. Medicine, Yugoslavia, 1980—85; PhD, U. Ill. Sch. Medicine, Chgo., 1986—2000. Cert. Mo., 1992, Va., 2001. Asst. prof., anesthesiology Wash. U. Sch. Medicine, St. Louis, 1998—2001; assoc. prof. U. Va., Dept. Anesthesiology, Charlottesville, 2001—. Grantee, NIH, 2000—. Mem.: Va. Soc. Anesthesiology (life), Assn. U. Anesthesiologists (life), Soc. for Neuroscience (life), Mo. Soc. Anesthesiologists (life), Am. Soc. Anesthesiologists (life). Achievements include patents for the role of NMDA antagonists in the management of chronic painful conditions. Avocations: piano, needlepoint, gardening. Office: U Va Dept Anesthesiology PO Box 800710 Charlottesville VA 22908-0710 Business E-Mail: vj3w@virginia.edu.

JEW, HENRY, pharmacist; b. Hong Kong, June 10, 1950; BS in Pharmacy, U. Ga., 1974. Preceptor to externship program So. Sch. of Pharmacy, U. Ga., 1974-78; researcher Brompton's Mixture, 1977-78; pharmacist VA Med Ctr, Decatur, Ga., 1984—89, VNS Inc., Atlanta, 1992—99, Kaiser Permanent, 2000—02, VA Med. Ctr., 2003—.

JEWEL, (JEWEL KILCHER), folk singer, songwriter; b. Payson, Utah, May 23, 1974; d. Lenedra Carroll and Atz Kilcher. Grad., Interlochen Arts Acad., Mich., 1992. Co-founder/owner Magic Lantern Entertainment, 2002—. Musician: (albums) Pieces of You, 1995, Spirit, 1998, Joy: A Holiday Collection, 1999, This Way, 2001, 0304, 2003, (singles) Woman to Woman, 1994, For the Last Time, 1995, Who Will Save Your Soul, 1996, (performs on soundtracks) I Shot Andy Warhol, 1996, The Craft, 1996, Phenomenon, 1996, Wizard of Oz in Concert: Dreams Come True, 1996, Batman & Robin, 1997, Ride with the Devil, 1999, Life or Something Like It, 2002, Sweet Home Alabama, 2002; actor: (films) Ride With the Devil, 1999; author: (book of poetry) A Night Without Armor, 1998, (memoir) Chasing Down the Dawn, 2000. Co-founder Higher Ground for Humanity, 1998—. Recipient Am. Music Award for Favorite Pop/Rock New Artist, 1997.

JEWELL, GEORGE HIRAM, lawyer; b. Fort Worth, Jan. 9, 1922; s. George Hiram and Vera (Lee) J.; m. Betty Jefferis, July 21, 1944 (dec. Feb. 2000); children: Susan Jewell Cannon, Robert V., Nancy Jewell Wommack; m. Nancy Hart Glanville, May 19, 2001. BA, U. Tex., 1942, LLB, 1950. Bar: Tex. 1950. With Baker & Botts, LLP, Houston, 1950—; sr. ptnr. Baker & Botts, Houston, 1960-90, counsel, 1990—. Trustee Tex. Children's Hosp., Houston, 1977—, pres., 1982-83, chmn., 1984-86; bd. dirs. Schlumberger Ltd., N.Y.C., Paris, 1975-90; M Corp, M Bank, Houston, 1974-1982; Pogo Producing Co., Houston, 1978-1990; Schlumberger Found., N.Y.C., 1982-90. Lt. USNR, 1943-46, 50-53. Fellow Am. Coll. Tax Counsel, Am. Bar Foun.; mem. ABA, Houston Country Club, Coronado Club, Old Baldy Club, Eldorado Country Club, Blind Brook Club, Order of Coif, Phi Beta Kappa, Phi Delta Phi. Home: 1000 Uptown Park Blvd Houston TX 77056

JEWELL, KENNETH CARL, music educator; s. Carl and Nancy Jewell; m. Jennifer Mary McLaughlin, June 17, 2001. BSc in Music Edn., Clarion U. Pa., 1992; MA in Edn. Adminstrn., Westmnster Coll., 2004. Cert. Instrnl. Prin. Pa. Dept. Edn. Dir. bands Thomas Stone HS, Waldorf, Md., 1993—94; elem. instr. music Charles County Pub. Sch., La Plata, Md., 1994—99; music educator, dir. bands Commodore Perry Sch. Dist., Hadley, Pa., 1999—, yearbook advisor, 1999—. Asst. dir. Mercer Cmty. Band, Pa., 1999—. Mem.: Nat. Assn. Secondary Sch. Prins., Pa. State Edn. Assn. Avocations: music, photography, woodworking, bicycling, skiing. Home: 219 Drake Rd New Wilmington PA 16142 Office: Commodore Perry Sch Dist 3002 Perry Hwy Hadley PA 16130

JEWELL, MARK LAURENCE, plastic surgeon; b. Kansas City, Mo., Oct. 26, 1947; s. James Lemley and Martha (Bullock) Jewell; m. Mary Rita Lind, Nov. 30, 1975; children: Mark II, James, Hillary. BS in Zoology, U. Kans., 1969, MD, 1973; postgrad., UCLA, 1977, U. Tenn., 1979. Cert. Am. Bd. Plastic Surgery, 1981. Resident in surgery UCLA, 1973—76; fellow, burn surgery U. So. Calif., L.A., 1976—77; resident, plastic surgery U. Tenn., Chattanooga, 1977—79; practice medicine specializing in plastic surgery Eugene, Oreg., 1979—; plastic surgeon Inamed Aesthetics. Contbr. articles to profl. jours. Lt. USNR, 1970—79. Recipient Rsch. award, Am. Soc. Clin. Pathologists, 1972, U. Kans. Sch. Medicine, 1973. Mem.: Am. Soc. for Aesthetic Plastic Surgery (v.p.), Am. Med. Joggers Soc., Lane County Med. Soc., Oreg. Med. Soc., Am. Soc. Plastic Surgeons. Episcopalian. Avocations: skiing, running, art, cooking, computers. Home: 4080 Spring Blvd Eugene OR 97405-4450 Office: 630 E 13th Ave Eugene OR 97401-3625

JEWELL, ROBERT V., lawyer; b. Houston, 1954; BBA in Fin., U. Tex., 1975; JD, So. Meth. U., 1978. Bar: Tex. 1978. Ptnr., Corp./Securities Dept. Andrews & Kurth LLP, Houston, mem. mgmt. com. Editor: Southwestern Law Jour., 1978. Mem.: ABA, Tex. Bus. Law Found., State Bar Tex. (corp. law com., Corp. Banking & Bus. Law Sect.), Houston Bar Assn., Phi Delta Phi. Office: Andrews & Kurth LLP 600 Travis St Ste 4200 Houston TX 77002-3090 Office Phone: 713-220-4358. Office Fax: 713-238-7135. Business E-Mail: bjewell@andrewskurth.com.

JEWELL-SHERMAN, DEBORAH, school system administrator; m. Cornelius Sherman; 2 stepchildren. EdB, NYU, 1976; EdM, Kean U., 1981, Harvard U., 1992, EdD, 1995. Former tchr., N.Y.C., Newark, Fairfax County, Va., former guidance counselor, asst. prin., prin.; prin. Hampton, Va., 1989—92; asst. supt. Virginia Beach, Va., 1992—95; assoc. supt. Richmond, Va., 1995—2002; supt., 2002—. Office: Richmond Pub Schs 301 N 9th St Richmond VA 23219

JEWETT, GEORGE FREDERICK, JR., forest products company executive; b. Spokane, Wash., Apr. 10, 1927; s. George Frederick and Mary Pelton (Cooper) J.; m. Lucille Winifred McIntyre, July 11, 1953; children: Mary Elizabeth, George Frederick III. BA, Dartmouth Coll., 1950; MBA, Harvard U., 1952. Asst. sec., asst. treas. Potlatch Corp., 1955-62, v.p. adminstrn., 1962-68, corp. v.p. adminstrn., 1968-71, sr. v.p., 1972-77, vice chmn. bd. adminstrn., 1977-78, vice chmn., 1979-99, retired, 1999. Trustee Calif. Pacific Med. Found. Mem.: NY Yacht Club, Pacific Union Club, Bohemian Club, St. Francis Yacht Club. Home: 2990 Broadway St San Francisco CA 94115-1062 Office: 1 Maritime Plz Ste 1640 San Francisco CA 94111-3506 Office Phone: 415-981-3390.

JEWETT, JACK, educational association administrator; B, U. Ariz. Sr. v.p. pub. policy TMC Healthcare, Tucson; mem., majority whip Ariz. Ho. Reps., 1982—92; mem. Ariz. Bd. Regents, 1998—, pres., 2002—03. Bd. dirs. United Way of Greater Tucson, Tucson 30, Jr. Achievement, Ariz. Internat. Campus Adv. Com. Mem.: Assn. of Governing Bds. of Univs. and Colls. (bd. dirs. 2005—, Disting. Svc. Award in Trusteeship 2004). Mailing: Assn of Governing Bds of Univs and Colls One Dupont Cir Washington DC 20036*

JEWETT, THOMAS O., science educator, writer; b. Belleville, Ill., Apr. 6, 1949; s. Robert Wayne and Mamie Louise Jewett; m. Laura Lorraine Lloyd, May 20, 1995; children: Sean Thomas, Jefferson Travous. BS, So. Ill. U., Edwardsville, 1971, MS, 1976; EdS, St. Louis U., 1984, PhD, 1985. Cert. tchr. K-6 Ill., tchr. 6-12 Ill., gen. adminstr. K-12 Ill., supervisory adminstr. K-12 Ill. Tchr. Wolf Br. Sch. Dist., Belleville, 1971—87, prin. and asst. supt., 1987—92; adj. instr. Southwestern Ill. Coll., Belleville, 1976—86; prof. So. Ill. U., Edwardsville, 1992—2001, emeritus prof., 2001—; prof. McKendree Coll., Lebanon, Ill., 2001—. Curriculum cons. and author Met. Area Urban Resources Partnership, St. Louis, 1995—96; cons. Project Concern-Ill. Dept. Edn., Springfield, 1995—96, Met. Profl. Devel. Sch. Consortium, St. Louis, 1995—97. Author: Outdoor Environmental Learning Activities (Ill. Environ. Conservation Tchr. of the Yr., 1986), First Impressions: 200 Years of St. Clair County History, The Belleville Germans; contbg. author: Prairie For the Prairie State; contbr. articles to numerous profl jours. Bd. dirs. St. Clair County Hist. Soc., Belleville, 1983—86; mem. exec. com. Met. Profl. Devel. Sch. Consortium, St. Louis, 1995—97. Recipient Outstanding Young Educator award, Belleville Jaycees, 1984, Tchr. of Yr. award, Ill. Conservation Dept., 1986, Generations of Success award, Southwestern Ill. Coll., 1996, Sch. of Edn. Gt. Tchr. award, So. Ill. U., Edwardsville, 1996; Sch. of Edn. rsch. grantee, So. Ill. U., 1999 to 2001. Mem.: Ill. Sci. Tchrs. Assn., Nat. Sci. Tchrs. Assn., Ill. State Acad. Sci., Kappa Delta Pi (counselor 1992—96). Avocations: scuba diving, triathlons, fiction writing, gardening. Office: McKendree College 701 College Road Lebanon IL 62254 Business E-Mail: tojewett@mckendree.edu.

JEWISON, NORMAN FREDERICK, film producer, director; b. Toronto, Ont., Can., July 21, 1926; s. Percy Joseph and Irene (Weaver) J.; m. Margaret Ann Dixon, July 11, 1953; children: Kevin Jefferie, Michael Philip, Jennifer Ann. Student, Malvern Collegiate Inst., Toronto, 1940-44; BA, Victoria Coll., U. Toronto, 1944; LLD (hon.), U. Western Ont., 1974, U. Trent, 1985, Ryerson Inst., 1986. With CBC, 1952-58, CBS, 1958-61, Universal Studios, 1961-64; freelance film dir., producer, exec. producer, 1965—. Presenter student film award CNE, 1980-81; dir. Harry Belafonte, Jackie Gleason, Andy Williams, Judy Garland, Danny Kaye TV shows; produced 1981 Acad. Awards; pres. of jury Avoriaz Film Festival, France, 1981. Dir.: (TV films) 40 Pounds of Trouble, The Thrill of it All, 1963, Send Me No Flowers, 1964, (feature films) Art of Love, The Cincinnati Kid, 1965, In the Heat of the Night, The Thomas Crown Affair, 1967, Gaily, Gaily, 1968; producer, dir.: (films) The Russians are Coming, 1966, Fiddler on the Roof, 1970, Jesus Christ Superstar, 1972, F.I.S.T., 1977, And Justice For All, 1979, Best Friends, 1982, Only You, 1994; producer: (films) The Landlord, 1969, Billy Two Hats, 1972, Rollerball, 1974; exec. producer: (films) Dogs of War, 1980, Iceman, 1983, The January Man, 1988; exec. producer, dir.: (films) A Soldiers Story, 1984, Agnes of God, 1985, Moonstruck, 1988, In Country, 1989; co-producer, dir.: (film) Other People's Money, 1991; author: This Terrible Business Has Been Good to Me, 2005. Served with Royal Can. Navy, 1945-46. Decorated companion Order of Can., 1982; named Dir. of Yr., Nat. Assn. Theatre Owners, 1982, Best Dir. Berlin Film Festival, 1988; recipient Can. Liberty award, 1958, Irving G. Thalberg Meml. award, 1999, Emmy award, 1960, Emmy award nominations, 1961-62, TV Dirs. award, 1961, Golden Globe award, 1966, Acad. award nominations, 1966-67, 72, 74, 84, 88; honored by Calif. ACLU, 1984. Mem. Can. Ctr. for Advanced Film Studies (founder, co-chmn. 1986), Dirs. Guild Am. (goals and purposes com. 1982, award nominations 1966, 67, Outstanding Directorial Achievement award nomination 1984). Avocations: skiing, yachting, tennis. Office: Yorktown Prodns Inc Bldg 2465 3000 Olympic Blvd Santa Monica CA 90404-5073*

JEYDEL, RICHARD K., lawyer; b. Livingston, N.J., Jan. 10, 1950; m. Ellen C. Ebert, Aug. 30, 1981; children: Patricia, Peter. AB, Sarah Lawrence Coll., 1972; JD, Harvard U., 1975. Bar: N.J. 1975, N.Y. 1983, U.S. Ct. Appeals (3d and 5th cirs.) 1983. Assoc. McCarter & English, Newark, 1976-79; corp. counsel Kanematsu-Gosho (USA), Inc., N.Y.C., 1979-85, v.p., gen. counsel, 1985-91; sr. v.p., sec., gen. counsel Kanematsu USA Inc., N.Y.C., 1991—. Past mem. ethics com. Supreme Ct. Dist. XIII; mem. panel of arbitrators and mediators, large complex case program arbitrator and pres. panel mediator Am. Arbitration Assn. Capt. U.S. Army, 1975-76. Mem. ABA, Am. Corp. Counsel Assn. (bd. dirs. 1996-2002), N.J. Bar Assn., N.J. Corp. Counsel Assn. (bd. dirs. 1986-90, 93—, past pres.), Am. Arbitration Assn. (panel arbitrators and mediators, bd. dirs. 1996—). Office: Kanematsu USA Inc 75 Rockefeller Plaza 22nd Fl New York NY 10019 Business E-Mail: rjeydel@kanematsuusa.com.

JEYNES, MARY KAY, college dean; b. Miami, Fla., Oct. 31, 1941; d. Nasrallah and Martha Demetry; m. Paul Jeynes, Sept. 30, 1978. BS, Fla. State U., 1963. Program dir. Orange County YMCA, Orlando, Fla., 1964-69, Ea. Queens YMCA, Belrose, N.Y., 1970-73; regional coord. N.Y. State Park and Recreation Commn., N.Y.C., 1974-77; dir. health, fitness and recreation YWCA of N.Y.C., 1978-79; dean continuing edn. and adult programs Marymount Manhattan Coll., N.Y.C., 1980—. Mem.: Manhattan (N.Y.) C. of C. (hon.; pres. 1996—97, chmn. bd. dirs. 1998—2002). Office: Marymount Manhattan Coll 221 E 71st St New York NY 10021-4532

JEYNES, WILLIAM HETTICH, education educator; b. NYC, Mar. 27, 1957; s. Paul Hettich and Enid Phillips Jeynes; m. Hyelee Jung Jeynes, June 17, 1986; children: Isaiah, Elisha, Luke. BA, U. Wis., 1979; DMin, Freedom U., 1986; PhD, Freedom Sem., 1992; EdM, Harvard U., 1993; PhD, U. Chgo., 1997. Lectr. Northea. Ill. U., Chgo., 1996—99, U. Chgo., 1996—99, Roosevelt U., Schaumburg, 1999, Nat. Louis U., Evanston, 1999; asst. prof. Hillsdale Coll., Mich., 1999—2001; assoc. prof., prof. Calif. State U., Long Beach, 2001—. Advisor, spkr. Harvard Family Rsch. Project, Cambridge, Mass., 2005—. Author: Divorce, Family Structure and the Academic Success of Children, 2002, Religion, Education and Academic Success, 2003, American Educational History: A Journey Through Time, 2006. Prfes. Gd's Love Ministries, Huntington Beach, Calif., 1978—. Recipient Rosenberger award, U. Chgo., 1994. Mem.: APA, Am. Ednl. Rsch. Assn. (chair religion and edn. spl. interest group 2004—). Avocations: football, baseball, walking, weightlifting, chess. Home: 16712 Saybrook Ln #109 Huntington Beach CA 92649 Office: Calif State U 1250 Bellflower Blvd Long Beach CA 90840

JEZUIT, LESLIE JAMES, manufacturing executive; b. Chgo., Nov. 4, 1945; s. Eugene and Tillie (Fleszewski) Jezuit; m. Janet Diane Bushlus, Oct. 12, 1968; children: Douglas Blake, Kevin Lane. BS in Mech. and Aerospace Engring., Ill. Inst. Tech., 1969, MBA, 1974. Mgr. engring. graphic systems group Rockwell Internat., Chgo., 1968-74, dir. comml. systems Cicero, Ill., 1974-75; v.p. mktg. and sales Mead Digital Sys., Dayton, Ohio, 1975-80; v.p. mktg. and sales Signal divsn. Fed. Signal Corp., University Park, Ill., 1980-81, pres. Signal divsn., 1981-85, v.p. corp. devel. Oak Brook, Ill., 1985-86; div. mgr. power distbn. div. Eaton Corp., Milw., 1986-87, gen. mgr. indsl. control and power distbn. div., 1987-88, v.p., 1988-91; pres., COO Robertshaw Controls Co., Richmond, Va., 1991-95; pres., CEO, chmn. bd dirs. Quixote Inc., Chgo., 1995—; chmn. Transp. Mgmt. Techs., LLC, Chgo., 1998-2001, Quixote Corp., 2001. Instr. Keller Sch. Mgmt., Chgo., 1982—83. Active United Way, Chgo., 1983—85; mem. Chgo. Crime Commn.; bd. dirs. Better Bus. Bur. Milw., 1986, United Performing Arts Found. Milw., 1986, Greater Milw. Com., 1991—92. Mem.: Gas Appliance Mfrs. Assn. (bd. dirs. 1994—96), Am. Hwy. Users Assn. (bd. dirs. 2001—, vice chmn. 2003), Monee C. of C., Will County Local Devel. Co. (v.p. 1984—85, Bus. Man of the Yr. award 1985), S. Surburban C. of C., Met. Club (Chgo.). Republican. Achievements include patents in field. Avocations: boating, fishing, cross country skiing, photography. Home: 26576 Countryside Lake Dr Mundelein IL 60060-3342 Office: Quixote Inc 35 E Wacker Dr Chicago IL 60601-2108 Office Phone: 312-467-6755.

JHA, AKHILESH KUMAR, engineer; s. Maya Kant Jha and Lata Devi; m. Anjali Mishra, Aug. 8, 2002; 1 child, Eshani. PhD, Va. Poly. Inst. and State U., Va., 2002. Rsch. assoc. Aerospace and Ocean Engring., Blacksburg, Va., 1998—2000, Ctr. for Intelligent Material Systems and Structures, Blacksburg, Va., 2000—02; sr. engr. NextGen Aeronautics, Torrance, Calif., 2002—. Session chair SPIE Smart Structures Conf., San Diego, 2003; reviewer AIAA, SPIE, ASME Conf. and Jour.; session chair AIAA-SDM Conf., 2003—03. Athelete (long distance runner) Intra-IIT Competition (4 Silver and One Gold Medal);, musician flutist. Sec. Associataionfor India's Devel., Blacksburg, Va., 1999—2000; student rep. Commn. on Classified Staff Affairs, Blacksburg, Va., 1998—99; grad. student rep. Aerospace and Ocean Engring. Dept, Blacksburg, Va., 1998—99; gen. sec. Rajendra Prasad Hall of Residence, Kharagpur, India, 1996—97. Recipient Def. Rsch. Devel. Orgn. award, Ministry of Def., India, 1994—98, Outstanding Student Mem. with Highest Honor, Outstanding Student Honor Soc., 2003; grantee Small Bus. Innovation Rsch., US Army, 2003, NASA, 2003, Grad. Rsch. Asst., Aerospace and Ocean Engring., 1998—2000, Mech. Engring., 2000—02, Rsch. Grant, Air Force Office of Sci. Rsch., 2002; scholar State Merit Scholarship, Bihar State Govt., 1986—90. Mem.: ASME (corr.), AIAA (corr.), Internat. Soc. for Optical Engrs. (corr.). Achievements include invention of A Morphing Aircraft with variable sweep, area, and span; research in Free vibration analysis of an Inflated Toroidal Shell; Piezoelectric Actuator and sensor models for an Inflated Toroidal Shell; Knowledge-based tools for predicting rd.-induced vibrations; first to Vibration of dynamic systems under Cyclostationary Excitations; research in Morphing Aircraft concepts, classifications, and challenges; Viration control of a smart composite plate using neural network and Genetic Algorithm; Cyclostationary random vibration of a ship propeller and a rd. vehicle; Vibration nalysis and control of an infltable Toroidal Satellite Component using Piezoelectric actuatotrs and sensors; Sliding mode contr. and observer for vibration control of a gossamer structure; Importance of geometric nonlinearity and follower pressure load in the dynamic analysis of a gossamer structure; Cyclostationary random vibration of a ship propeller; Optimum placement of Piezoelectric actuators and sensors on an inflated Torus; A lit. survey of ultra-light and inflated Toroidal Satellite Components. Office: NextGen Aeronautics 2780 Skyaprk Dr Ste 400 Torrance CA 90505 Office Phone: 310-626-8374. Home Fax: 310-891-2825; Office Fax: 310-891-2825. Business E-Mail: ajha@vt.edu.

JHA, GAUTAM GOPALJI, medical researcher; b. Mumbai (Bombay), Maharashtra, India; s. Gopalji Jagdish and Sudha Gopalji Jha; m. Vaishali Sawant Jha, Jan. 1, 1974. MBBS, Terna Med. Coll., Navi Mumbai, India, 1998; MS in Pharmacology and Toxicology, U. R.I., 2002. Cert. Med. Coun. India, 1998, Maharashtra Med. Coun., 1998. Asst. lectr. Terna Med. Coll. & Hosps., Navi Mumbai, India, 1998; resident dr. BAM Hosp., Mumbai, 1998—99; tchg. asst. U. R.I., Kingston, 1999—2001; rsch. scientist Arqule Inc., Woburn, Mass., 2001—02, Millennium Pharm. Inc., Cambridge, Mass., 2002—03; rsch. fellow North Ctrl. Bronx Hosp., N.Y., 2003—. Author: (poster presentation) 30th Annual Meeting New Eng. Pharmacologists, New Eng. Regional Medicinal Chemistry and Pharmacognosy Meeting, 8th Internat. Conf. Carcinogenic/Mutagenic N-Substituted Aryl Compounds; contbr. (poster presentation) SBS Annual Meeting; author (jour. article) European Jour. Drug Metabolism & Pharmacokinetics. Recipient Nestle Young Investigator award for genuine rsch., 2001. Mem.: Maharashtra Med. Assn., Med. Soc. N.Y. Home: 7 Hegeman Ave Apt 20G Brooklyn NY 11212 Personal E-mail: jhagautam@hotmail.com.

JHABVALA, FARROKH, lawyer, educator; b. Bombay, May 2, 1945; arrived in U.S., 1972; s. Pheroze and Freny Jhabvala; m. Margarita Gutierrez, Aug. 25, 1978. PhD, Tufts U., 1977; JD, U. Miami, 1988. Bar: Fla. 1988, D.C. 1989, U.S. Dist. Ct. (so. dist. Fla.) 1989, U.D. Dist. Ct. (mid. dist. Fla.) 2000, U.S. Ct. Appeals (11th cir.) 1996, U.S. Ct. Appeals (5th cir.) 1997, U.S. Ct. Appeals (4th cir.) 2001, U.S. Ct. Appeals (7th cir.) 2002, U.S. Ct. Appeals (8th cir.) 2004. Asst., assoc. prof. Fla. Internat. U., Miami, 1976—84, prof. Internat. Rels., 1984—98; assoc. Jorden Burt LLP, Miami, 1988—97, ptnr., 1997—. Contbr. articles to profl. jours. Recipient Francis Deak prize, Am. Soc. Internat. Law, 1979. Mem.: ABA. Avocations: history, gardening. Office: Jorden Burt LLP 777 Brickell Ave Ste 500 Miami FL 33131 Office Phone: 305-371-2600. Office Fax: 305-372-9928. Business E-Mail: fj@jordenusa.com.

JHABVALA, RUTH PRAWER, writer; b. Cologne, Germany, May 7, 1927; lived in India, 1951-75; came to U.S., 1975; d. Marcus and Eleonora (Cohn) Prawer; m. Cyrus S. H. Jhabvala, 1951; 3 children. MA, London U., 1951, DLitt (hon.), 1986, LHD (hon.), 1995, D Arts (hon.), 1996. Author: To Whom She Will, 1955, The Nature of Passion, 1956, Esmond in India, 1957, The Householder, 1960, Get Ready for Battle, 1962, A Backward Place, 1965, A New Dominion, 1972, Heat and Dust, 1975 (Booker award for fiction Nat. Book League 1975), In Search of Love and Beauty, 1983, Three Continents, 1987, Poet and Dancer, 1993, Shards of Memory, 1995; (short story collections) Like Birds, Like Fishes and Other Stories, 1964, A Stronger Climate: Nine Stories, 1968, An Experience of India, 1971, How I Became a Holy Mother and Other Stories, 1976, Out of India: Selected Stories, 1986, East Into Upper East, 1998, My Nine Lives, 2004; (film scripts) The Householder, 1963; (with James Ivory), Shakespeare Wallah, 1965, The Guru, 1968, Bombay Talkie, 1970, Autobiography of a Princess, 1975, Roseland, 1977, Hullabaloo over Georgie and Bonnie's Pictures, 1978, The Europeans, 1979, Jane Austen in Manhattan, 1980, Quartet, 1981, Heat and Dust, 1983, The Bostonians, 1984, A Room With a View, 1986 (Writers Guild of Am. award for best adapted screeplay 1986, Acad. award for best adapted screenplay 1986); (with John Schlesinger) Madame Sousatzka, 1988, Mr. and Mrs. Bridge, 1990, Howards End, 1992 (Acad. award for best adapted screenplay 1992), Remains of the Day, 1993 (Acad. award nomination for best adapted screenplay 1993), Jefferson in Paris, 1995, Surviving Picasso, 1996; (with James Ivory) A Soldier's Daughter Never Cries, 1998, The Golden Bowl, 2000. Decorated comdr. Brit. Empire; Guggenheim fellow, 1976; Neil Gunn. Internat. fellow, 1979; MacArthur Found. fellow, 1984-89. Home: 400 E 52d St New York NY 10022-6404

JHINGRAN, ANUJA, oncologist, educator; b. India, Nov. 15, 1962; arrived in U.S., 1980; BA, Smith Coll., 1984; MD, Tex. Tech. U., 1988. Intern Baylor Coll. Medicine, Houston, resident in radiation oncology, 1993; radiation oncologist John Sealy Hosp., Galveston, Tex., 1993-95, Rosewood Med. Ctr., Houston, 1995-96, Columbia Spring Br. Hosp., Houston, 1995-96, Brazosport Hosp., Lake Jackson, Tex., 1995—, Columbia West Houston Hosp., 1996. Asst. prof., clin. dir. U. Tex. Med. Br., Galveston, 1993-95; asst. prof. U. Tex. MD Anderson Cancer Ctr., Houston, 1996—. Contbr. articles to profl. jours. Mem. AMA, Am. Radiol. Soc., Am. Assn. Women Radiologists, Am. Radium Soc., Am. Soc. Therapeutic Radiation Oncology, Tex. Med. Assn., Tex. Radiol. Soc. Office: UT MD Anderson Cancer Ctr Box 97 1515 Holcombe Blvd Houston TX 77030

JIA, JUNHUI, urologist, researcher; s. Jia Mengzhen and Yang Aiying; m. Junfang Junfang, May 1, 1992; 1 child, Jia Bingzhou. MD, Zhangjiakou Med. Sch., China, 1991; MS, Beijing Med. U., 1999. Diplomate China, 1991. Resident Handan Ctr. Hosp., China, 1991—96, vice chmn. dept. urology, 2000—02. Vis. scientist U. Tex. Med. Br., Galveston, 2002—. Recipient Outstanding Student award, Beijing Med. U., 1998. Fellow: ASM (corr.); mem.: Assn. of Urology in China. Home: 7400 Jones Dr #3813 Galveston TX 77551 Office Phone: 409-772-4911.

JIA, WEITAO, dental products executive, researcher; b. Shanghai, May 14, 1959; s. Kexi Jia and Xianchai Cheng; m. Shari Xiafei Chang, Jan. 11, 1988; children: Irene, Ricky. Diploma in stomatology, Shanghai, China, 1981; MSc, NYU, 1988; PhD, Kennedy Western U., Thousand Oaks, Calif., 1999. Rsch. asst. Shanghai Second Med. U. Sch. Stomatology, 1981-87; rsch. asst., instr. NYU, N.Y.C., 1987-89; rschr. Jeneric/Pentron, Inc., Wallingford, Conn., 1989-95, mgr. composite R&D, 1995-97, dir. R&D, 1997-99, v.p. dental product R&D, 1999—2001; v.p. R&D, Pentron Clin. Techs., LLC, 2001—. Bd. dirs. CJ Multi Tech Enterprises, Inc. Wallingford, 1997—. Patentee in field. Mem. AAAS, Am. Assn. Dental Rsch., Am. Chem. Soc., Acad. Dental Materials, Internat. Assn. Dental Rsch., N.Y. Acad. Scis. Office: Pentron Clin Techs LLC 68 N Plains Industrial Rd Wallingford CT 06492 Personal E-mail: weitaojia@hotmail.com. Business E-Mail: wjia@pentron.com.

JIA, XIAOCHUAN, engineer; b. Taiyuan, Shanxi, China, Feb. 28, 1966; arrived in US, 1999; s. Qingdong Jia and Dexiang Niu; m. Zhimin Mu, Apr. 12, 1967; children: Mengyun, Melinda. Bachelor, Taiyuan U. Tech., 1986, Master, 1991; PhD, Xi'an (China) Jiaotong U., 1996. Rsch. assoc. Xi'an Jiaotong U., 1992—96; prof. Taiyuan U. Tech., 1997—99; vis. prof. Va. Poly. Inst. and State U., Blacksburg, 1999—2001; chief R&D engr. Leeson Electric, Motor Technologies Group, Regal-Beloit Corp., Grafton, Wis., 2001—. Cons. Beijing Heavy Electric Machine Works, 1996—99, Beijing Caichi Power Electronics Ctr., 1996—99, Yongji Rlwy. Electric Machine Works, Yongji, Shanxi, China, 1997—98; fellow Crown Internat., 1999—2000, MagneTek, Inc, 2000—01. Recipient Outstanding Paper award, Shanxi Chinese Soc. for Elec. Engring., 1996, First class rsch. project award, Shanxi Chinese Sci. and Tech. Commn., 1997, Outstanding paper award, Chinese Linear Electric Machine Soc., 1998, Excellent Young Scientist award, Shanxi Edn. Com., 1998, Outstanding Paper award, Shanxi Young Rschr. Devel. Conf. Mem.: IEEE Power Electronic Soc., IEEE Magnetic Soc., IEEE Industry Application Soc. Achievements include invention of 15 Phase Induction Motor And Drive System; development of High frequency inductor model; Integrated magnet design; High breakdown torque high speed induction motor; High power density low cogging torque permanent motor; design of High efficiency Induction motor; Synchronous reluctant motor; invention of 11 Phase Brushless Exciter; development of 3 phase DC output rectified generator; design of Brushless DC motor; High frequency multi-winding transformer. Avocations: fishing, travel, swimming. Office: Leeson Electric Regal-Beloit Corporation 2100 Washington St Grafton WI 53024 Office Phone: 262-387-5201. Personal E-mail: xiaochj2003@yahoo.com. Business E-Mail: jia.xiaochuan@rbcmtg.com.

JIAN, CHEN, international organization official; b. Feb. 2, 1942; married; 1 child. Attaché Dept Internat. Orgn. and Conf. Fgn Min., 1977—80; asst. Office Exec. Dir. representing China at Internat. Monetary Fund., 1984—85; dir. to counselor to dep. dir-gen Dept. of Internat. Orgn. and Conf. of Fgn Min., 1985—92; dir. - gen. Dept. Info., 1994—96; asst. min. Fgn. Affairs, 1996—98; spokesman Fgn. Min.; amb. extraordinary and plenipotentiary of China to Japan, 1998—2001; dip. Chinese Fgn. Min.; attaché, Chinese Permanent Mission UN, 1972—77, third sec., second sec., and then first sec., 1980—84, amb. extraordinary and plenipotentiary and dep. permanent rep., 1992—94, under sec.-gen. gen. assembly affairs and conf. svc., 2001—. Rep. Gen. Assembly, Sec. Coun., Econ. and Soc. Counc., UN Environ. Program, Econ. and Soc. Commn. for Asia and Pacific. Office: UN Headquarters First Ave at 46th St New York NY 10017

JIAN, CUI, research scientist; s. Guangxue Cui and Yulan Yang; m. Wu Yingzi, Apr. 3, 1969; children: Melissa Cui, David Cui. M.D., Ph.D., China Med. U., Shenyang, 1998. Asst. prof. Liver Cancer Inst., Zhongshan Hosp., Shanghai, 1998—2000, clin. assoc. prof. Liver Cancer Inst., 2000—. Rsch. assoc. Kimmel Cancer Ctr., Phila., 2001—05. Mem.: Am. Assn. Cancer Rsch. Achievements include discovery of mechanism of JNK autophosphorylation; research in Wnt pathway in hepatocellular carcinoma. Office: Kimmel Cancer Ctr 1002/BSLB 233 S 10th St Philadelphia PA 19107

JIANG, BING-HUA, science educator; arrived in U.S., 1991; s. Guilin Jiang and Yueying Zheng; m. Jenny Z. Zheng, Jan. 21, 1986; children: Lisa L., Rena Z. PhD, Miss. State U., 1994; BS in Tropical Crops, S. China U. Postdoctoral rsch. assoc. Johns Hopkins U. Sch. Medicine, Balt., 1994—97; rsch. assoc. Scripps Rsch. Inst., La Jolla, Calif., 1997—2000; asst. prof. cell signaling W.Va. U., Morgantown, 2000—. Mng. editor Frontiers in Bioscience, Albertson, NY, 2000—; prof. Chinese Acad. of Sci., Shanghai, 2003—. Contbr. articles to profl. jours. Grantee, Am. Heart Assn., Am. Cancer Soc., NIH, 2000—. Mem.: Am. Assn. for Cancer Rsch. (life). Achievements include patents in field. Office: Cancer Ctr W Virginia Univ 1801 Health Sciences South Morgantown WV 26506 E-mail: bhjiang@hsc.wvu.edu.

JIANG, HAO, pharmacologist; b. Shenyang, Liaoning, China, June 22, 1974; s. Zuozhou Jiang and Fengqin Liu; m. Jing Lu, Mar. 22, 1976. BSc, China Pharm. U., 1996; MSc, Shenyang Pharm. U., 1999; PhD, MD, Peking Union Med. Coll., 2002. Tchg. asst. Shenyang Pharm. U., China, 1997—97, rsch. asst., 1996—99, Peking Union Med. Coll., 1999—2002; rsch. scientist U. of Pa. Sch. of Medicine, Phila., 2002—. Contbr. articles to profl. jours.; mem. editl. bd. Jour. Biol. Scis., 2003—04; mem. editl. bd.: Internat.Jour. Pharm. Scholar Outstanding grad., Peking Union Med. Coll., 2002, Shenyang Pharm. U., 1999. Mem.: Am. Chem. Soc., Am. Soc. for Mass Spectrometry, China Pharm. Assn. (1st prize in alaytical chemistry rsch. 1998), Am. Assn. for Cancer Rsch. (assoc.), Soc. of Toxicology (assoc.). Achievements include research in novel biomarker in urine and plasma for individual fluoropyrimidine drug chemotherapy; circadian rhythm of dihydropyrimidine dehydrogenase in humans; identification of novel omeprazole metabolites in human urine samples by HPLC/MS; novel activation pathway of benzopyrene in human lung carcinoma cells. Home: 324 S 43rd St Apt 2rear Philadelphia PA 19104 Office: 135 JMB Pharmacology Univ of Penn 3620 Hamilton Walk Philadelphia PA 19104 Office Fax: 215-537-2236. Personal E-mail: haojiangus@yahoo.com. E-mail: haojiang@mail.med.upenn.edu.

JIANG, HONG, information scientist; b. Beijing, Dec. 30, 1969; d. Zikang Jiang and Yuehua Fang; m. Xuefeng Wang. BA, Renmin U. of China, Beijing, 1996; MS in Biostats., U. Nebr., 2000. Statistician Tsinghua U., Beijing, 1991—96; rsch. asst. U. Nebr., Lincoln, 1999—2000; data analyst Douglas County Health Dept., Omaha, 2000—. Cons. on stats. and SAS programming U. Nebr., Lincoln, 1999—2000; cons. database, immunization assessment, medicaid and managed care childhood immunization measurement Douglas County Health Dept., Nebr., 2000—; state immunization assessment coord. CDC and Prevention. Contbr. articles to profl. jours. Mem.: Nat. Assn. for Pub. Health Stats. and Info. Sys., Am. Statis. Assn. Office: Douglas County Health Dept 1819 Farnam St Omaha NE 68183 Office Phone: 402-444-3284. Business E-Mail: hjiang@co.douglas.ne.us.

JIANG, HONG, spatial analyst, metallurgical engineer; s. Zhixing Jiang and Ning Wang; m. Yanli Zhang, Dec. 14, 1963; children: Zishan, Jessica Zhang, Tom Zhang. PhD, NE Forestry U., Harbin, China, 1989. Assoc. prof. Inst. Botany Chinese Acad. Sci., Beijing, 1992—93, prof. Inst. Botany, 1994—95, prof. Inst. Geography and Resources Sci., 1995—96; prof. (courtesy) Oreg. State U., Corvallis, 1995—96; vis. prof. U. Alta., Edmonton, Canada, 1997—98; assoc. rsch. scientist Natural Resources Can., Edmonton, 1997—2001; sr. scientist Conservation Biology Inst., Corvallis, Oreg., 2001—; prof. Nanjing U., China, 2004—05, SW Normal U., Chongqing, China, 2004—05. Named Outstanding Youth Scientist of China, Assn. Sci. and Tech., China, 1993. Mem.: Internat. Assn. Conservation Biology (assoc.). Achievements include development of the world's first successful spatial database of Chinese forest productivity using remote sensing and ecological modeling high technology; major contributions to the carbon cycle modeling of terrestrial ecosystem, especial boreal forests, one of world's largest forests; significant contribution to the establishment of the forest age classification in the Pacific Northwest; co-founder of Chinese Ecosystem Research Network (CERN); development of new theory and methods in population dynamics and environmental filter effects of plant endangering process. Office: Conservation Biology Inst 260 SW Madison Ave Ste 106 Corvallis OR 97333 Office Fax: 541-752-0518. E-mail: hongjiang@consbio.org.

JIANG, HONGXING, physics professor, researcher; s. Yulong Jiang and Zhen Xie; m. Jingyu Lin, Nov. 23, 1983; children: Frank, Andrew, Kelly. PhD, Syracuse U., 1981—86. Various edn. positions to assoc. prof. physics Kans. State U., Manhattan, Kans., 1993—98, prof. physics; dir. Kans. Advanced Semiconductor Coord. Lab., Manhattan, Kans., 1999—. Advisor PhD program; vis. scientist Sandia Nat. lab., Albuquerque. Author: (Teaching, Researching, invention) Micro-size light emitters, 2001. Grantee Research Grants, 1992—. Mem.: Materials Rsch. Soc., Internat. Optical Soc., Am. Phys. Soc. Office: Kansas State U Cardwell Hall Manhattan KS 66506 Business E-Mail: jiang@phys.ksu.edu.

JIANG, RUIHUA JOY, finance educator; d. Fuhan Jiang and Yujuan Ho; m. Jiayou Tian, July 8, 1988; children: Shuyun Tian, Henri Tian. PhD, The U. of Western Ont., Can., 2003. Lectr. of English lit. East China Normal U., China, 1988—93; asst. prof. of mgmt. Lehigh U., Bethlehem, Pa., 2003—. Contbr. articles to profl. jours. Mem.: Acad. of Mgmt. Office: Lehigh University 621 Taylor St Bethlehem PA 18015 Office Phone: 610-758-3419.

JIANG, TAO, mathematician, educator; arrived in U.S., 1994; s. Chaoshi Jiang and Shugui Xia. PhD, U. of Ill., 2000. Asst. prof. Mich. Technol. U., Houghton, Mich., 2000—01, Miami U., Oxford, Ohio, 2001—. Spkr. at internat. and nat. profl. meetings. Contbr. more than 25 articles to profl. jours. Recipient Hohn-Nash award, U. of Ill. math. dept., 2000. Mem.: Phi Kappa Phi (hon.).

JIANG, WEILIN, physicist; s. Peizhong Jiang and Yulan He; m. Shurong Liu; 1 child, Siduo. BSc in Physics, Zhejiang U., Hanzhou, China, 1982; MS in Physics, China Inst. Atomic Energy, Beijing, 1987; Phd in Physics, Tech. U. Dresden, Germany, 1997. Asst. prof. Hefei (China) Poly. U., China, 1982—84; asst. rschr. Inst. Physics. Chinese Acad. Scis., Beijing, 1987—93; rsch. asst. Rsch. Ctr. Rossendorf, Dresden, 1993—97; postdoctoral fellow Pacific NW Nat. Lab., Richland, Wash., 1997—2000, rsch. scientist, 2000—01, sr. rsch. scientist, 2002—. Judge Mid Columbia Sci. Fair; organizer confs., spkr., presenter, reviewer in field. Contbr. articles to profl. jours., chpts. to books. Recipient Outstanding Rsch. Project award, Fundamental Sci. Directorate, Pacific NW Nat. Lab., 2004, Outstanding Performance award, 2003. Mem.: Materials Rsch. Soc. Achievements include research in ion-beam irradiation effects in ceramic materials. Avocations: travel, table tennis, photography. Office: Pacific Northwest Nat Lab PO Box 999 MSIN K8-93 Richland WA 99352 Office Phone: 509-376-5471.

JIANG, WENHUI, materials scientist; s. Yongkui Jiang and Rongzhen Gao; m. Shu Feng, Feb. 9, 1965; 1 child, Han. BS, Northeastern U., Shenyang, China, 1984, MS, 1987; PhD, Inst. Metal Rsch., Chinese Acad. Scis., Shenyang, China, 1999. Tchg. asst. Shenyang U. Tech., 1987—89, assoc. prof., 1997—2000, prof., 2000—01; vis. scholar Polytechnico di Turino, Italy, 1994—95; vis. rsch. investigator U. Mich., Ann Arbor, 2001—03, vis. prof., 2004—05; rsch. assoc. So. Meth. U., Dallas, 2003—04, U. Tenn., Knoxville, Tenn., 2005—. Named Excellent Tchr., Govt. of Shenyang City, 2001, Shenyang U. Tech., 2001, 2000; Shi Changxu fellow, Inst. Metal Rsch., Chinese Acad. Scis., 1999, Wei Hua Sci. and Tech. fellow, Chinese Acad. Scis., 1999. Mem.: The Sci. Rsch. Soc. (hon.). Home: 1800 W Clinch Ave Apt 8 Knoxville TN 37916 Office: Univ Tenn 210 SERF Bldg Knoxville TN 37996 Office Phone: 734-764-5290. Personal E-mail: whjiangf@hotmail.com, whjiangf@yahoo.com. Business E-Mail: wjiang5@utk.edu.

JIANG, WENXIN, statistician, researcher; b. Chang zhou, China, June 8, 1967; s. Yaoming and Yun (Xu) Jiang. BS, Nanjing U., China, 1988; MS, Cornell U., 1995, PhD, 1996. Asst. prof. Northwestern U., Evanston, Ill., 1996—2002, assoc. prof., 2002—. Contbr. articles to profl. jours. Office: Northwestern U Dept Statistics 2006 Sheridan Rd Evanston IL 60208-0852 E-mail: wjiang@northwestern.edu.

JIANG, WILLIAM YUYING, business educator, consultant, researcher; b. Hengyang, Hunan Province, China, Jan. 18, 1955; s. Rongguang Jiang and Hongkang Lei; m. Leslie Rongqui Yi, Sept. 5, 1988; children: Cosmo Yi, Cordelia Yi. BA in English, Hunan Normal U., Changsha, China, 1981; MA in English Lexicology, Xiamen U., China, 1984; MA in Comparative Lit., U. Ill., 1985, MS, 1986; MPhil in Bus., PhD in Bus., Columbia U., 1991. Asst. prof. San Jose State U., 1991—94, assoc. prof., 1994—97, prof., 1997—. Mng. dir. JS Cresvale Securities (US) Inc., Cupertino, Calif., 1999—2001; chancellor First Light Acad., Centreville, Va., 2002—. Translator: (novel) The Egoist, To Kill a Mockingbird; contbr. articles to profl. jours. Recipient Acad. Rsch. award, Chinese NSF, 1997, 2000; scholar, Pres. Fellowship, 1984—86, Columbia U., 1987, 1988, 1989, 1990; Marjorie Hope Nicolson scholar, 1987, Provost's Internat. scholar, San Jose State U., 2003. Mem.: Internat. Mgmt. Assn. Human Resource (chmn. mgmt. divsn. 1995—96), The Asian Am. Mfg. Assn., Chinese Economist Soc., Monte Jade Soc. Sci. and Tech., Indsl. Rels. Rsch. Assn., The Am. Econ. Assn., Assn. Chinese Profs. U.S. (dir. bd. 2001—03, dir. mem. 2001—03), Acad. Mgmt. (participation com. chair 1999—2002). Avocations: skiing, travel, foreign languages learning, reading. Home: 19901 La Mar Dr Cupertino CA 95014-3377 Office: San Jose State Univ One Washington Sq San Jose CA 95192-0070 Office Phone: 408-924-2450. Personal E-mail: jiang_w11@hotmail.com. E-mail: jiang_w@cob.sjsu.edu.

JIANG, YONG PING, research scientist; b. China, July 11, 1956; came to U.S., 1983; s. Hepei and Xudai J.; m. Xiao Fang, June 22, 1985; children: Alexandra, Barbara F. BS, Nanjing U., China, 1982; MS, Rutgers U., 1985, PhD, 1988. With Nat. Hosp., Arlington, Va., 1988-90; asst. prof. Temple Med. Sch., Phila., 1990-92; rsch. investigator U. Mich. Med. Ctr., Ann Arbor, 1992-95; assoc. scientist Harvard Med. Sch., Boston, 1995-98; CEO ABTEK, Inc., Malden, Mass., 1996—. Vice chmn. bd., pres. Bio-Pharm. Co., Beihan, China, 1996—. Patentee in field. Recipient rsch. award Am. Heart Assn., 1994-95. Mem. AAAS, Am. Assn. Hematology (rsch. award 1993). Avocations: fishing, music, travel. Office: ABTEK Inc 376 Washington St Malden MA 02148 E-mail: yjiang9999@aol.com.

JIAO, ALLAN Y., law educator; M in Econ. Law, Jinan U., Guangzhou, China, 1988; MPA, Lewis & Clark Coll., 1991; PhD in Criminal Justice, Rutgers U., Newark, 1996. Prof., chair law and justice studies Rowan U., Glassboro, NJ, 1995—. Vis. scholar City U. of Hong Kong, 2001—02. Fulbright scholar, 2001—02. Mem.: Acad. Criminal Justice Scis. (assoc.). Office: Rowan U Law & Justice Studies 201 Mullica Hill Rd Glassboro NJ 08028 Office Phone: 856-256-4838. Business E-Mail: jiao@rowan.edu.

JIBBEN, LAURA ANN, state agency administrator; b. Peoria, Ill., Oct. 1, 1949; d. Charles Otto and Dorothy Lee (Skaggs) Becker; m. Michael Eugene Hagan, July 7, 1967 (div. Apr. 1972); m. Louis C. Jibben, July 14, 1972. BA in Criminal Justice, Sangamon State U., 1984; MBA, Northwestern U., 1990. Asst. to chief of adminstrn. Ill. Dept. Corrections, Springfield, 1974-77, exec. asst. to dir., 1977-80, dep. dir., 1980-81; mgr. toll services Ill. Tollway Dept., Oak Brook, 1981-86; chief adminstrv. officer Regional Transp. Authority, Chgo., 1986-90, fund mgr. loss financing plan, 1987-90, also, chmn. pension trust, exec. dir., 1990-96; v.p., gen. mgr. MTA, Inc., Chgo., 1996-99; ptnr. Hanson Engrs., Inc., Oak Brook, Ill., 1999-2000; sr. project mgr., cons. mgmt. Alfred Benesch & Co., 2000—02, v.p., 2002—. Cons. labor studies Sangamon State U., Springfield, 1981; bd. dirs. Chgo. Found. for Women. Mem. surface tranps. adv. panel U. Ill., 1997—2000; apptd. mem. transp. adv. bd. City of Naperville, 1988—90; bd. dirs. Family Shelter Svcs., 1990—91; bd. dirs., chair devel. com. Govt. Assistance Program, 1997—2000, sec. bd., 1999; mem. nat. adv. bd. Women's Transp. Seminar, 1996—2004; mem. Peoria Women's Fund Grants Com., 2003—; mem. Midwest Traffic Conf. program com. Bradley U., 2002—; acting pres. Ctrl. Ill. chpt. WTS, 2004—, pres., 2004—05. Recipient Appreciation award VFW, Chgo., 1983, award Ill. State Toll Hwy. Authority, 1986; named Woman of Yr., Nat. Women's Transp. Seminar, 1991, AAUW, 1991. Mem. NAFE, Women's Transp. Seminar (Woman of Yr. award Chgo. chpt. 1991, Nat. Woman of Yr. 1991), Beta Sigma Phi (treas., v.p., corr. sec. Naperville and Easton, Ill. chpts.), Lambda Alpha. Avocations: reading, jogging, gardening, golf. Office: Alfred Benesch & Co 205 N Michigan Ave Ste 2400 Chicago IL 60601 Office Phone: 312-565-0450. Business E-Mail: ljibben@benesch.com.

JIE, LIAN, research scientist; b. Qinhuangdao, Hebei, China, July 18, 1973; s. Chuiren Lian and Yuelan Chen; m. Fan Zhang, Apr. 19, 1980. BE, YanShan U., Qinhuangdao, 1994; ME, Tsinghua U., Beijing, 1998; MSE, U. Mich., 2002, PhD, 2003. Rsch. asst. Tsinghua U., Beijing, 1995—98, U. Mich., Ann Arbor, 1998—2003, rsch. fellow, 2003—. Contbr. articles to sci. jours. Rackham Predoctoral Honor fellow, U. Mich., 2003. Mem.: Materials Rsch. Soc. (corr.), Microbeam Analysis Soc. (corr. Disting. Scholar award 2002), Am. Phys. Soc. (corr.), Alpha Nu Sigma (corr.; Mich. Alpha chpt.), Sigma Xi (corr.). Achievements include contributed to discovery of radiation resistant materials, zirconate pyrochlore, awarded by DOE as 101 most important discovery in last 25 years; research in understanding radiation response of pyrochlore compounds to ion beam damage; contributed to novel plasma process method for the functionalization of nanoparticles and carbon nanotubes. Home: 1129 McIntyre Dr Ann Arbor MI 48105 Office: U Mich 2355 Bonisteel Blvd Ann Arbor MI 48109-2104 Office Phone: 734-936-3129. Personal E-mail: jlian2002@yahoo.com. E-mail: jlian@umich.edu.

JIE, MIN, mechanical engineering educator, researcher; b. Wuhan, Hubei, China, Nov. 29, 1963; s. Fangzuo Jie and Shizheng Han; m. Rong Xie, Sept. 13, 1966; 1 child, Meng. BS, U. Sci. and Tech. of China, 1985; MS, Peking U., 1988. Rsch. asst. Peking U., 1985-88; asst. prof. then assoc. prof. Huazhong U. Sci. and Tech., Wuhan, 1988-97; guest rschr. The Hong Kong Poly. U., 1997-98; rsch. asst. U. Mich., Dearborn, 1998—. Contbr. articles to profl. jours. Mem. Hubei Soc. Theoretical and Applied Mechs. (acad. sec. solid mechs. com. 1995-97), Am. Soc. Civil Engrs., Am. Soc. Mech. Engrs. Office: U Mich 4901 Evergreen Rd Dearborn MI 48128 Home: # 201bld2 8176 Brooke Park Dr Canton MI 48187-5114 also: 37825 Joy Rd Apt 103 Westland MI 48185-1055 Fax: 313-593-3851. E-mail: mjie@umich.edu.

JIECHI, YANG, ambassador; b. Shanghai, May 1950; m. Le Aimei; 1 child. Student, Bath U., England; grad., London Sch. Econs. and Polit. Scis., 1975. Staff mem., 2d sec. Translation and Interpretation Dept., Fgn. Ministry, 1975—83, counselor and divsn. dir.; 2d sec. then 1st sec., counselor Chinese Embassy in U.S., 1983—87; counselor, divsn. dir., dept. dir.-gen. Dept. Am. and Oceanian Affairs, Fgn. Ministry, 1990—93; min. Chinese Embassy in U.S., 1993—95, asst. fgn. min., 1995—98, vice fgn. min., 1998—2000, amb. extraordinary and pleinpotentiary, 2001—. Office: Embassy of Peoples Republic of China 2300 Connecticut Ave NW Washington DC 20008

JIL, MARIE LUYK, music educator; d. Kenneth E. and Lois C. Luyk. B of Music Edn., Temple U., 1984. Tchr. music Archdiocese Washington, Darnestown, Md., 1996—. Mem.: MENC. Office Phone: 301-869-0940.

JILCOTT, REBECCA ANN, music educator; b. Ahoskie, N.C., Feb. 20, 1965; d. Lanny Edward and Rebecca Sue Jilcott. B in Music Edn., James Madison U., 1988. Cert. instrumental and vocal instr. Dir. orch. Chester Mid. Sch. Chesterfield (Va.) Pub. Schs., 1988—91, head music dept., 1991—2005, dir. orch. L.C. Bird H.S., 1988—97; dir. orch. Carver Mid. Sch., 1991—2005, head music dept., 2000—05; condr. Richmond Symphony Youth Orch.-Sinfonietta; music dir. Matoaca Mid. Sch., Ettrick, Wash., 2005—. Violist Petersburg Symphony, 1996; dir. summer strings program Va. Music Camp staff, 1995, 96; condr. Richmond Symphony Youth Orch.-Sinfonietta. Named James River PTA Dist. Vol. of Yr., 2004—05. Mem.: NEA, Va. Edn. Assn., Chesterfield Educators Assn. (mem. bd. dirs. 2000—04), Music Educators Nat. Conf., Thespian Soc., Chesterfield Womens Soccer Assn. (registrar 1998—2000), Sigma Alpha Iota (life). Baptist. Avocations: soccer, reading, gardening, travel, guest conductor. Office: Matoaca Mid Sch 6001 Hickory Rd Ettrick VA 23803 Office Phone: 804-524-3620 ext. 117. Personal E-mail: BJilcott@aol.com.

JILER, LINDA CERISE, retired fire and aviation program support specialist, fire emergency dispatcher, consultant, researcher, writer; b. Santa Monica, Calif., Dec. 30, 1956; d. Milton John "Jack" Jiler and Peggy Jean Williams. AA, Lassen Coll., 1979, Cert. Forestry Technician, 1980. Cert. Calif. Dept. Forestry and Fire Protection Fire Acad., 1990. Fire clk./firefighter-wildland Lassen Coll. Contract Crew, Susanville, Calif., 1976-77; forestry technician (fire) U.S. Forest Svc. Lassen Nat. Forest/Eagle Lake Ranger Dist./Bogard Ranger Sta., Susanville, Calif., 1977-80; dist. personnel technician U.S. Dept. Interior-Bur. Land Mgmt., Susanville Dist., Calif., 1981-86; pub. contact rep. U.S. Dept. Interior Bur. Land Mgmt. Susanville Dist., Susanville, Calif., 1986; wildland firefighter/dispatcher Lassen Coll. Contract Fire Crew, Susanville, Calif., 1986-87; fire, aviation program asst., lightning detection specialist U.S. Dept. Interior Bur. Land Mgmt., Calif. State Office, Sacramento, 1988-93; 9-1-1 interagy. fire dispatcher Calif. Dept. Forestry and Fire Protection, Camino, 1988-93; 9-1-1 interagency emergency commd. ctr. Calif. Dept. Forestry and Fire Protection, Camino Interagency Emergency Command Ctr., 1988-93; cons. info. svcs. Sacramento, 1993—. Speaker in field; pub. info. officer USDA-FS, U.S. Dept. Interior-Bur. Land Mgmt., CDF, 1983-93. Author: How to Get A Job with the Federal Government, 1983, rev. edit., 1985, 86, Injury and Claim Processing Manual, 1985, Demobilization Training Guide, 1985, Train-the Trainer Wildland Fire Timekeeping Procedures, 1985, (manual) California State Office SOP for Intelligence Gathering, 1987-88; co-author: (manual) California Interagency Mobilization Guide, 1988, Bur. of Land Management's State Policy for Handling of Burn Victims, 1988. Recipient Cert. of Appreciation, Lassen County Bd. Suprs., 1986, 87, Cert. of Appreciation and Cert. of Recognition for Outstanding Performance, U.S. Forest Svc. Pacific S.W. Region, 1987, Nat. Wildland Coord. Group award for Outstanding Performance, U.S. Forest Svc. Pacific N.W. Region and Wallow Whitman Nat. Forest, 1986, Superior Achievement and Profl. Contbns. award U.S. Dept. Agriculture Forest Svc. and U.S. Dept. Interior Bur. Land Mgmt., 1990; cert. Appreciation Eldorado Bd. Suprs. U.S. Forest Svc., 1992, Recognition award Oakland Athletics Baseball Club, 1987, Recognition award San Diego Padres Baseball Club, 1988. Mem. ACLU, Am. Soc. for Prevention of Cruelty to Animals, The Humane Soc. U.S., World Wildlife Fedn., Calif. State Employees Assn. (classification rep. 1989-93), Calif. Profl. Firefighters, Chronic Fatigue Immune Dysfunction Syndrome Assn. Am., Chronic Fatigue Immune Dysfunction Syndrome and Fibromyalgia Support Groups, Nat. Trust for Hist. Preservation, Nat. Conf. Incident Command System Fin. Officers, Nat. Australian Shepherd Club Am., Sigma Kappa (alumni past pres.), Sierra Club. Democrat. Avocations: australian shepherds, calligraphy, sociology studies, social justice, civil rights. Home: 919 Laurelhurst Dr Eugene OR 97402-1735

JILER, WILLIAM LAURENCE, publisher; b. Bridgeport, Conn., Oct. 16, 1925; s. Jacob and Sarah J.; m. Jan Gardner, Oct. 14, 1956; children: Wendy Jo, James Paul. BS, Bates Coll., Lewiston, Maine, 1948; postgrad., U. So. Calif., 1950. With E.R. Squibb & Co., New Brunswick, N.J., 1948-50; with Commodity Research Bur., Inc., N.Y.C., now Jersey City, 1950-64, 69-85, pres., 1969-85; with Standard & Poor's Corp., 1964-69, dir., 1964-69. Mem. econ. adv. com. Commodity Futures Trading Commn., 1975-76; founder, pres. Trendline Corp. Author: How Charts Can Help You in the Stock Market, 1962; assoc. editor: Commodity Year Book, 1951-80; created the CRB Commodity Futures Index Traded as a Futures Contract on the New York Futures Exchange. Served to 2d lt. USAAF, 1943-45. Mem. Nat. Assn. Bus. Economists, Market Technicians Assn., N.Y. Soc. Security Analysts. E-mail: bjiler@aol.com. *Find a need and fulfill it to the best of your ability.*

JILES, DAVID COLLINGWOOD, physicist, materials science educator; b. London, Sept. 28, 1953; s. Kenneth Gordon and Vera Ellen (Johnson) J.; m. Helen Elizabeth Graham, Oct. 29, 1979; children: Sarah Jane, Elizabeth Anne, Andrew John, Richard David. BSc, Exeter (Eng.) U., 1975; MSc, Birmingham (Eng.) U., 1976, DSc, 1990; PhD, Hull (Eng.) U., 1979. Registered profl. engr.; chartered engr. Postdoctoral fellow Victoria U., Wellington, New Zealand, 1979-81; rsch. assoc. Queens U., Kingston, Canada, 1981-84; rsch. fellow Iowa State U., Ames, 1984-86, assoc. physicist, 1986-88, physicist, 1988-90, assoc. prof., 1988-90, sr. physicist, 1990—, prof., 1991—, Anson Marston disting. prof., 2003—; prof. magnetics, dir. Wolfson Ctr. U. Cardiff, Wales, 2005—. Chmn. Conf. on Properties and Applications of Magnetic Materials, Chgo., 1985-2001; pres. Magnetics Tech. Inc., Ames, 1989—; dir. Magnetics Tech. U.K., Ltd., 2004—; cons. engr. State of Iowa, Des Moines, 1996; sci. advisor Brit. Admiralty, 1991-92, NATO, 1992-2000, U.S. NRC, 1996-97; vis. prof. U. Hull, Eng., 1991, 94, U. Saarland, Germany, 1992, 97, Tech. U. Vienna, 2000, 03, Cardiff (Wales) U., 2004; vis. scientist Czech Acad. Sci., 1999. Author: Introduction to Magnetism and Magnetic Materials, 1991, 2d edit., 1998, Introduction to Electronic Properties of Materials, 1994, 2d edit., 2001; editor: IEEE Transactions on Magnetics, 1992—2004, editor-in-chief, 2004—; editor Nondestructive Testing and Evaluation, 1988-2005, Jour. of Materials Sci. Materials in Electronics, 2002; contbr. more than 450 articles to profl. jours. Recipient Fed. Lab. Consortium award U.S. Dept. Energy, 1994, Magnetics Soc. Disting. Lectr. award, 1997. Fellow IEEE, Inst. Elec. Engrs. U.K., Inst. Physics, Am. Phys. Soc. (chair topical group on magnetism and its applications, 1997-99), Magnetics Soc. (adminstrv. com. 1995-2001, 03-), Inst. Math. and its Applications; mem. AAAS. Achievements include 14 patents; developer of various models relating to non-linear effects and theory of ferromagnetic hysteresis. Office: Cardiff U Wolfson Ctr Magnetics Ames IA 50010-0001

JILHEWAR, ASHOK, gastroenterologist; b. Nanded, Maharashtra, India, Jan. 30, 1947; came to U.S., 1977; naturalized 1987; BS, MB, Marathwada U., 1970; MD, Govt. Med. Coll., Aurangabad, 1970. Diplomate Am. Bd. Internal Medicine, Am. Bd. Gastroenterology, Am. Bd. Geriatric Medicine, Am. Bd. Quality Assurance and Utilization Rev. Physicians. Rotating intern Med. Coll. Hosp., Aurangabad, India, 1968—70; resident St. Luke's Hosp. and Royal infirmary, Huddersfeild, England, 1970—72; med. registrar internal medicine Gen. Hosp., Sligo, Ireland, 1973—77; chief resident PG1 and internal medicine U. Health Scis.-Chgo. Med. Sch. and VA Hosp., 1977—79; clin. instr. U. Health Scis.-Chgo. Med. Sch., 1978—79; fellow in gastroenterology Michael Reese Hosp., Chgo., 1980—81; mem. exec. com. Meth. Hosp., Chgo., 1985—90, chmn. med. dept., 1988—90; mem. staff dept. medicine Grant Hosp., Chgo., 1986—. Lectr. preventive and social medicine Med. Coll., Aurangabad, 1970; mem. exec. com. Meth. Hosp. Chgo., 1985-90, v.p. med. staff, 1987-88, treas., sec. 1985-87, chmn. dept. medicine, 1988-90; med. dir. approved home for intermediate care nursing home, 1986-95; med. advisor Office Hearings and Appeals, HHS, 1985—; med. reviewer Ill. Med. Rev. Orgn., 1993—, Crescent Cmty. Found. for Med. Care, 1994—. Fellow Royal Coll. Physicians Can., Am. Coll. Internat. Physicians; mem. AMA, ACP, Am. Headache Soc., Am. Gastroenterol. Assn., Royal Coll. Physicians U.K., Royal Coll. Physicians Ireland, Ill. State Med. Assn., Chgo. Med. Soc. (PRO study com., fee mediation subcom. 1992) Office: North Park Stomach Clinic 5393 N Milwaukee Ave Chicago IL 60630-1251 Office Phone: 773-775-9500. Personal E-mail: ajilhewar@hotmail.com.

JILK, LAWRENCE T., JR., banker; b. Charleston, W.Va., Oct. 5, 1938; s. Lawrence T. and Frances E. Jilk; m. Marcia Bryans, Nov. 20, 1965; children: Linda, Karen. BA, U. Del., 1960; MBA, Drexel Inst. Tech., 1966. Sr. v.p. Provident Nat. Bank, Phila., 1960-77; pres., CEO Nat. Penn Bank, Boyertown, Pa., 1980-90, chmn., 1990—; pres., CEO Nat. Penn Bancorp, Boyertown, Pa., 1990—. Instr. Stonier Grad. Sch. Banking; chmn., founding dir. East Ctrl. Pa. chpt., Robert Morris Assocs. Bd. dirs., sec. Berks Minority Devel. Corp.; bd. dirs. Reading Emergency Shelter, pres., 1993; pres., dir., founder Boyertown Area Creative Housing; bd. dirs. Reading/Berks Human Rels. Commn., chair strategic planning com.; vol. Big Bros.; chmn. Frontier Dist. Hawk Mountain coun. Boy Scouts Am., dir.; chmn., dir. Boyertown United Way, Boyertown Area YMCA; bd. dirs. Reading and Berks County YMCA, Boyertown YMCA Real Estate Holding Co., Boyertown Area Sports Complex, STEPS Home, Reading/Berks Human Rels. Coun., chair, strategic planning com., Hispanic Ctr., chair strategic planning com., Neighborhood Housing Svcs., chair operation facelife com., Pa. Housing Econ. and Devel. Corp., Harrisburg, Cmty. Housing Resource Bd., pres., 1993; chmn. adv. coun. Interfaith Cmty. Devel. Corp., Pottstown; chmn. fin. com. St. Columbkill's Ch.; founding dir. Boyertown Cmty. Coun, Boyertown Means Bus. Recipient Gold Crest award Humanitarian of Yr., Salvation Army, 1991, Outstanding Vol. Fund-Raiser in Northeastern Pa., award, 1991, Father Wilfred Penny award Alternatives Family Resources, 1991, Community Svc. award Pa. Dirs. Assn. for Community Action, 1992; named Citizen of Yr., Boyertown Area Jaycees, 1991, Humanitarian of Yr., Tri-County C. of C., 1993. Mem. Pa. Bankers Assn. (bd. dirs., exec. com., founding chmn., mem. community reinvestment task force, chmn. group II, chmn. sch. comml. lending, lectr.), Am. Bankers Assn., Nat. Bankers Assn. Office: National Penn Bancshares Inc PO Box 547 Boyertown PA 19512-0547

JILLETTE, ARTHUR GEORGE, JR., school system administrator, educator; b. Malden, Mass., May 1, 1937; s. Arthur George and Esther Harriett (Peachey) J.; m. Janet Downs White, June 20, 1960 (div. 1973); 1 child, Joseph Arthur; m. Beatrice Miriam Ellis, May 3, 1975; children: Grace Harder, Andrew Hopkins, Timothy Hopkins. BS, Boston U., 1960, MRE, 1964; cert. in audio communicative disability, NYU, 1967. Cert. tchr., N.H., community coll. adminstr., Calif. Assoc. rsch. scientist NYU Deafness Rsch. Ctr., N.Y.C., 1965-67; cons. spl. edn. N.H. Dept. Edn., Concord, 1967-74, 85-88, 1997-99, acting dir. spl. edn., 1974-75; dir. planning and devel. N.H. Div. Vocat. Rehab., Concord, 1975-79; dean spl. svcs. N.H. Tech. Coll., Claremont, 1979-83, dean students, 1983-85; dir. spl. svcs. Sch. Admnstrv. Unit #43, Newport, NH, 1988—91, asst. supt. schs., 1991-94; dir. spl. svcs. Sch. Adminstrv. Unit 32, Lebanon, N.H., 1994-97; dir. spl. edn. Lyme N.H. Sch. Dist., 1999—2000; coord. spl. edn. svcs. Goshen-Lempster Coop. Sch. Dist., 2000—. Dir. Lake Sunapee Mediation Program, Newport, 1990—, pres., 1996—; mem. state adv. coun. Individuals with Disabilities Edn. Act., 1989-94; consumer mem. N.H. State Bd. Hearing Care Providers, 2001—; pres., dir. Sullivan County Rehab. Ctr., Claremont, 1980-83. Editor: Denominational Work With the Deaf, 1966. Moderator Town of Goshen, N.H., 1980—, planning bd. chmn., 1985-89, zoning bd. chmn., 1986-89; mem. Goshen-Lempster Coop. Sch. Bd., 1975-80, 95-2000, chmn., 1979-80, 97-2000; mem., sec. Newport Revitalization Com., 2002—. Social and Rehab. Svcs. fellow U.S. Dept. Edn., 1964-65. Mem. Nat. Stereoptician Assn., Nat. Assn. Watch and Clock Collectors, N.H. Assn. Spl. Edn. Adminstrs., Elks, Odd Fellow, Masons. Democrat. Mem. Soc. Of Friends. Avocations: house restoration, stereo photography, clock restoration, computers. Home: PO Box 1016 Goshen NH 03752-1016 Office: Sch Adminstrv Unit # 71 School Rd Lempster NH 03605

JILOT, RICHARD FRANK, project manager, educator; b. Green Bay, Wis., Apr. 8, 1952; s. Richard J. and Ann Marie Jilot; m. Wanelle T. (Tatum) J., Oct. 16, 1993. BSCE, Mich. Tech. U., 1978; MBA, Miss. State U., 1984; project mgmt. program, Ga.-Pacific/Clemson U. Contrn., 1995; cert., Coll. for Fin. Planning, Denver, 1998. Lic. registered rep. Nat. Assn. Securities Dealers; lic. class C-life and health La. Ins. Constrn. supt. lumber products divsn. Am. Can Co., Bellamy, Ala., 1979-83; project engr. paper converting James River Corp., Green Bay, Wis., 1983-88, mgr. engring. and maintenance Ypsilanti, Mich., 1988-91; sr. staff engr. paper converting Ga.-Pacific Corp., Crosset, Ark., 1991-96; core team leader Walk Haydel (A Dames & Moore Co.), Pine Bluff, Ark., 1996-97, sr. project mgr. North Little Rock, Ark., 1997; personal fin. advisor, registered rep. Am. Express Fin. Advisors, West Monroe-Shreveport, La., 1998; asst. dist. mgr. H&R Block, Monroe, La., 1999—2002, dist. mgr., 2002—. Adj. prof. dept. engring. and bus. So. Ark. U., Magnolia, 1996-98. Pres. Holy Cross Parish Coun., Crossett, 1992; mem. comty. involvement team Leadership Crossett, Ark., 1992-96. Mem. KC. Republican. Roman Catholic. Avocations: private pilot, model railroading, swimming, reading, computers. Home: 139 Lomaland Dr West Monroe LA 71291-2341 Office: 1603 Louisville Ave Monroe LA 71201 E-mail: rjilot@hrblock.com.

JIMENEZ, CARLOS, Spanish language educator; b. Jerez, Andalusia, Spain, Aug. 16, 1963; arrived in U.S., 1987; s. Domingo Jimenez and Manuela Lopez; m. Mercedes Juliá, June 2, 1987. MA, Villanova U., 1990; PhD, U. Pa. Asst. prof. Spanish Cabrini Coll., Radnor, Pa., 1999—. Coord. study abroad Cabrini Coll., Radnor, 1999—, dir. study abroad program in Spain, 1999—. Author: (books) Aventura, 1993, Album, 2002; contbr. poetry to revs. Mem.: MLA, Asociacion de Licenciados y Doctores en Estados Unidos Espanoles, Am. Assn. Tchrs. of Spanish and Portuguese. Home: 1524 County Line Rd Bryn Mawr PA 19010 E-mail: jcjimenez@cabrini.edu.

JIMÉNEZ, CARMEN JULIA, language educator; d. Roberto Jiménez and Petra Pizarro; m. Angel D. Mejías, May 24, 1987; 1 child, Victor Cortés Herrera. BA, U. PR, 1987; MA, U. Utah, 1994; PhD, Pa. State U., 2002. Health educator Congreso Latinos Unidos, Phila., 1999—2000; lectr., asst. prof. U. Utah, Salt Lake City, 2000—01; asst. prof. Salisbury (Md.) U., 2001—. Tchg. asst. U. Utah, Salt Lake City, 1992—94; grad. asst. Pa. State U., University Park, 1994—98. Advisor Latino Students Assn. Salisbury U., 2001—03. Recipient Cert. of Recognition, The Puerto Rican Students Assn., 1995—97; fellow Sparks Dissertation fellow, Pa. State U., 1998; grantee, 1997. Mem.: MLA, Phi Sigma Iota. Avocations: reading, travel. Office: Salisbury Univ 1101 Camden Ave Salisbury MD 21801

JIMENEZ, DANIEL, music educator; b. Hialeah, Fla., Oct. 16, 1978; s. Jorge Lius and Liana Maria Jimenez. B in Music, U. Miami, 2000. Cert. profl. tchr. Fla., music tchr. Fla. Bookkeeper Arch. Libr., U. Miami, Coral Gables, Fla., 1996—2000; band tchr. Doral (Fla.) Mid. Sch., Doral, Fla., 2001—. Trumpet player Orch Am., Miami, 1995—. Mem.: Music Educators Nat. Conf., Fla. Bandmasters Assn. Avocations: music, golf, reading, fishing, boating. Office: Doral Mid Sch 5005 NW 112th Ave Doral FL 33178

JIMENEZ, JESUS ALEJANDRO, engineering educator; s. Lorenzo Monico Jimenez and Maria Eugenia Dominguez de Jimenez; m. Marcia Veronica Lopez, Nov. 3, 2000; 1 child, Jesus Alejandro. BS in Indsl. Engring., U. Tex., El Paso, 1997, MS in Indsl. Engring., 1999. Rschr. asst. The U. of Tex. at El Paso, 1996—99, Ariz. State U., Tempe, Ariz., 2000—04, instr., 2004—. Recipient Rotary Youth Leadership award, Club Rotario de Cd. Juarez, Mex., 1993; fellow Preparing Future Faculty fellow, Ariz. State U., 2001—03. Mem.: Inst. for Ops. Rsch. and the Mgmt. Scis., Omega Rho. Office Phone: 480-965-7835. Personal E-mail: ljimene0@msn.com.

JIMENEZ, MARCOS DANIEL, former prosecutor; b. Havana, Cuba, Dec. 15, 1959; came to U.S., 1961; s. Frank T. and Daisy (D'Clouet) J.; m. Michelle Ann; 3 children. BA, U. Miami, Fla., 1980, JD, 1983. Bar: Ill. 1983, U.S. Dist. Ct. (no. dist.) Ill. 1983, Fla. 1984, U.S. Dist. Ct. (so. dist.) Fla. 1984, U.S. Ct. Appeals (11th cir.) 1985. Assoc. Phelan, Pope and John, Ltd., Chgo., 1983-84, Greenberg, Traurig et al, Miami, 1984-89; asst. U.S. atty. (So. dist.) Fla. U.S. Dept. Justice, Miami, 1989—92, US atty., 2002—05; ptnr. White & Case LLP, 1992—2002. Contbr. articles to profl. jours. Mem. ABA, Fla. Bar Assn. (com. mem.), Dade County Bar Assn. (com. mem.), Hurricane Club. Republican. Baptist. Avocations: basketball, saxophone.

JIMENEZ, MERCY, corporate financial executive; BA, Northwestern U.; MBA, Harvard Grad. Sch. Bus. Mgr. fin. product lines Citigroup-Global Payments Products; v.p. corp. devel. Chase Manhattan Mortgage Corp., Tampa, Fla., 1994—96; joined Fannie Mae, 1996, v.p. corp. devel. Wash., DC, 1996, v.p. sr. products, 1998, v.p. mktg. Southwestern region Dallas, 2000, sr. v.p. Southwestern region, 2000—02, sr. v.p. bus. and product devel., 2002—. Bd. dirs. Nat. Assn. Hispanic Real Estate Profl., Tex. Mortgage Bankers Assn., Atlantic Coun. Office: Two Galleria Tower 13455 Noel Rd Ste 600 Dallas TX 75240-5003 Office Phone: 972-773-7444.

JIMENEZ, SERGIO A., internist, educator, rheumatologist; b. Cuzco, Peru, Feb. 21, 1942; s. Julio Alexandre and Bertha Margarite (Astete) J. BS, Nat. U. San Marcos, Lima, Peru, 1959, MD, 1964; MS, U. Pa., 1984. Diplomate Am. Bd. Internal Medicine. Asst. prof. dept. medicine U. Pa., Phila., 1974-80, asst. prof. dept. orthop. surgery, 1978-80, assoc. prof. medicine and orthop. surgery, 1980-86, prof., 1986-87; prof. medicine, dir. rheumatology rsch. Thomas Jefferson U., Phila., 1987-92, prof. biochemistry and molecular biology, 1987—, dir. divsn. rheumatology, 1992—, Dorrance H. Hamilton prof. medicine, 1992—, vice-chmn. rsch. dept. medicine, 1999—2003. Hon. adj. fellow Benjamin Franklin Inst., Phila., 1981—; chmn. med. adv. bd. Scleroderma Rsch. Found., Mid-Atlantic Chpt., 1979—; mem. rsch. scholarships com., Ea. Pa. chpt. Arthritis Found., 1981-84; mem. med./sci. bd. Scleroderma Fedn., 1994—; mem. Nat. Inst. Health Gen. Medicine A Study Sect., 1990-94, mem. spl. rev. com., 1995—; mem. NIH Peer Review Oversight Group, 1998-2000; bd. sci. councellors Nat. Inst. Arthritis Musculoskeletal Diseases, NIH, 1999-2000; acting chmn., bd. councellors Nat. Inst. Arthritis Musculoskeletal Diseases NIH, 2000-02; chmn. bd. sci. councellors Nat. Inst. Arthritis Musculoskeletal Disease, NIH, 2002-05. Author over 270 articles to med. jours., 450 abstracts in procs. worldwide sci. jours., 90 editls., revs., and chpts. to jours. and books. Bd. dirs. Washington Square West Civic Assn., Phila., 1978-82, v.p., 1981-82, trustee, 1988—; mem. Phila. Hispanic C. of C., 1990—. Capt. Peruvian Army Res., 1964-65. Recipient Gerald P. Rodnan award for excellence in scleroderma rsch., U. Pitts., 1986, Joseph Lee Hollander award for excellence in rheumatology Ea. Pa. Arthritis Found., 2000; program project for rsch. on osteoarthritis, NIH, 1992—. Fellow Soc. for Molecular Medicine; mem. Am. Coll. Rheumatology, Am. Soc. Biol. Chemistry and Molecular Biology, Osteoarthritis Rsch. Soc. (exec. bd. 1994—, pres.-elect 1997-2000, pres. 2000-02), Internat. Soc. for Matrix Biology (founding mem.), Am. Soc. Matrix Biology. Republican. Roman Catholic. Avocations: fine arts, sculpture, opera, anthropology, archeology. Home: 900 Spruce St Philadelphia PA 19107-6131 Office: Thomas Jefferson Univ 233 S 10th St Ste 509 Philadelphia PA 19107-5541 Office Phone: 215-503-5042. Business E-Mail: sergio.jimenez@jefferson.edu.

JIMENEZ-SUAREZ, CARMEN, librarian; b. Bklyn., June 26, 1959; d. Manuel and Maria L. (Suarez) Jimenez. BA, U. P.R., 1983, MLS magna cum laude, 1991. Cert. secondary tchr., libr., P.R. Tchr. Colegio Ntra. Sra. de Guadalupe, Rio Piedras, P.R., 1985-87; libr. Academia Perpetuo Socorro, Santurce, P.R., 1987-88, Academia San Ignacio, Rio Piedras, 1988-91, Conservatory Music P.R., Hato Rey, 1990—, Bonneville Sch., Rio Piedras, 1996—. Mem. ALA, ASCD, Sch. Libr. Assn., Am. Assn. Sch. Librs. Office: Conservatory of Music of PR Apartado 41227 Minillas Sta Santurce PR 00940-1227 Office Phone: 787-751-0160 244.

JIMMERSON, JERROLD PHILLIP, retired music educator, conductor; s. Noress L. (Stepfather) and Dorothy L. Larson; m. Alice C. Diersen, Sept. 1, 1965; children: Kevin B., Bryan P., Deron M. BA, Buena Vista Coll., 1966; MusM Edn., Drake U., 1976. Cert. instrumental music tchr. Iowa, instrumental music instr. Instrumental music instr. Crestland Cmty. Schs., Early, Iowa, 1966—71, Nevada (Iowa) Cmty. Schs., 1971—74; instrumental tchr. Manson N.W. Webster Schs., Manson, Iowa, 1974—90; instrumental music instr. Manson N.W. H.S., 1990—2003; ret., 2003. Profl. musician, condr. Karl L. King Mcpl. Band, Fort Dodge, Iowa, 1960—.

JIN, DEBORAH, physicist, educator; AB, Princeton U., 1990; PhD, U. of Chgo., 1995. Rsch. assoc. Nat. Inst. of Standards and Tech., 1995—97, physicist, 1997—; fellow, and asst. prof. adjoint U. of Colo., Boulder, 1997. Recipient Pres. Early Career for Sci. and Engr., 2000, Maria Goeppert-Meyer prize, Am. Phys. Soc., 2002, Nat. Acad. of Sci. award for initiatives in rsch., 2002; fellow MacArthur Found., 2003. Office: Univ of Colo JILA 440 UCB Boulder CO 80309

JIN, HA See JIN, XUEFEI

JIN, HAIPENG, engineer; PhD, U. Calif., San Diego, La Jolla, Calif., 2003. Sr. engr. Qualcomm Inc., San Diego, Calif., 2003—. Achievements include research in wireless IP standards. Office: Qualcomm Inc 5775 Morehouse Dr San Diego CA 92121 Office Phone: 858-651-6181. Business E-Mail: hjin@qualcomm.com.

JIN, XIAOYING, electrical engineer, computer engineer, researcher; d. Jingrang Jin and Musen Xiong; m. Yuanfang Gao; 1 child, Jason Deli Gao. BS, Wuhan U., Hubei, 1996, MS, 1999; PhD, U. Missouri, Columbia, 2005. Software engr. Huawei Tech. Co. Ltd., China, 1999—2000; rsch. asst. U. Missouri, Columbia, 2000—. Session chmn. ann. meeting Soc. of Photo-Optical Instrumentation Engrs., Denver, 2004. Contbr. articles to profl. jours. Recipient Rsch. Excellence award, SPIE Soc. and Newport, 2004; Gui & Xu acad. scholar, Wuhan U., 1997—98, 1994—95, First-Class scholar,

1992—96. Mem.: IEEE (reviewer Transactions on Geosci. and Remote Sensing, reviewer Geosci. and Remote Sensing Letters), Internat. Soc. Optical Engring., Tau Beta Pi. Achievements include development of registered letter image analysis and database management system; multimedia broadcasting-on-demand system. Office: U Missouri-Columbia 349 Engineering Bldg West Columbia MO 65211 Office Phone: 573-884-6400. Personal E-mail: jinxiaoying@gmail.com. E-mail: xje4e@mizzou.edu.

JIN, XUEFEI (HA JIN), literature educator, writer; b. Jinxian, China, Feb. 21, 1956; s. Danlin Jin and Yuanfen Zhao; m. Lisha Bian, July 6, 1982; 1 child, Wen. BA, Heliongjiang U., 1981; MA, Shandong U., 1984; PhD, Brandeis U., 1993. Lectr. Boston U., 1992-93, prof. English, 2002—; asst. prof. Emory U., Atlanta, 1993—2002. Author: (poetry collections) Between Silences, 1990, Facing Shadows, 1996, Wreckage, 2001, (short story collections) Ocean of Words: Army Stories, 1996 (PEN/Hemingway Award, 1997), Under the Red Flag, 1997 (Flannery O'Connor Award for Short Fiction, 1997), (novels) In the Pond, 1998, Waiting, 1999 (Nat. Book Award for Fiction, 1999, PEN/Faulkner Award for Fiction, 2000), The Bridegroom, 2000, The Crazed, 2002, War Trash, 2004 (Named one of 10 Best Books of Yr., NY Times Book Rev., 2004, PEN/Faulkner Award for Fiction, 2005). Served People's Liberation Army, China. Guggenheim Fellowship, 1999. Avocations: reading, walking. Office: Boston U Dept English 236 Bay State Rd Boston MA 02215 Business E-Mail: xjin@bu.edu.

JIN, YAN, adult education educator; b. Nanjing, Jiangsu Province, China, July 13, 1959; s. Zhen Jin, Qican Qian; m. Jannie Jiaying Wu; children: Emily, Jessica. Doctor of Engineering, University of Tokyo, Tokyo, Japan, 1985—88. Rsch. assoc. Stanford U., Palo Alto, Calif., 1991—94, sr. rsch. scientist, 1994—96; asst. prof. U. So. Calif., LA, 1996—99, assoc. prof., 1999—. Founder, v.p.l Vite Corp., Mountain View, Calif., 1996—, dir. bd., 1996—99; chief cons. Jinteck, Arcadia, 1994—; dir. IMPACT Lab. U. S.C., LA; tech. advisor ePM LLC, Austin, Tex., 2002—. Inventor Virtual Design Team - Organization Simulator, 1995; editor: Multimedia Technology for Collaborative Design and Manufacturing, 1997; author: Data Mining for Design and Manufacturing, 2001, Coordination Theory and Collaboration Technology, 2001, Universal Design Theory, 1998, Computational Organization Theory, 1993, (Conference publication) 5th World Multiconference on Systems, Cybernetics and Informatics, 2001; contbr. articles to profl. jours. and papers to confs. Recipient Faculty Career award, NSF, 1998, Rsch. award, Toyota Motor Corp., 1993—2002, Ford Motor Co., 1998, Best Paper award, 14th Internat. Conf. on design theory and methodolgy, 2002; Monbusho scholar, Ministry of Edn., Japan, 1983—88. Mem.: ASME, Am. Assn. Artificial Intelligence. Office: U So Calif 3650 McClintock Ave OHE-430 Los Angeles CA 90089-1453 E-mail: yjin@usc.edu.

JIN, ZHENRONG, electrical engineer, researcher; arrived in U.S., 1999; s. Jiaxi Jin and Shuhua Chao; m. Xue Li, Dec. 18, 2002; 1 child, Alex. BS, SE U., Nanjing, China, 1996, MS, 1999; PhD, Ga. Inst. Tech., 2004. Grad. rsch. asst. Auburn (Ala.) U., Auburn, 1999—2002, Ga. Inst. Tech., Atlanta, 2002—04; adv. engr. IBM Microelectronics, Essex Junction, Vt., 2004—. Contbr. articles to profl. jours. Scholar, BASF, 1999; Presdl. fellow, Auburn U., 1999—2002. Mem.: IEEE, Sigma Xi. Achievements include research in silicon germanium (SiGe) hetero-junction bipolar transistors (HBTs); discovery of small size effects on low-frequency noise in SiGe HBTs; new low-frequency noise mechanisms in SiGe HBTs; development of low-frequency noise model in SiGe HBTs in radiation enviroments; low-frequency noise simulations in SiGe HBTs. Office: IBM Microelectronics 1000 River St MS 972F Essex Junction VT 05452 Office Phone: 802-769-3161. Business E-Mail: zhenrjin@us.ibm.com.

JIN, ZHONGHAI, physicist; b. Taihu, China, Jan. 26, 1963; arrived in U.S., 1990; s. Fu-You Jin and Tao-Mei Yin; m. Qingyu Chen, July 20, 1987; children: Pongyang, Lucy Ahren. BS, U. Sci. China, 1984; MS, Chinese Acad. Sci., Hefei, China, 1987; PhD, U. Alaska, 1995. Postdoctoral rschr. U. Alaska, Fairbanks, 1995-96, Scripss Inst. Oceanography, La Jolla, Calif., 1996-99; rsch. scientist U. Calif., San Diego, 1999—2000; sr. scientist AS&M, Inc., Hampton, Va., 2000—. Mem. Am. Geophys. Union, Am. Meteorol. Soc. Achievements include development of a coupled atmosphere-ocean radiative transfer model and its research applications. Avocations: basketball, soccer, music. Office: Ste 300 1 Enterprise Pky Hampton VA 23666

JINDAL, BOBBY PIYUSH, congressman; b. Baton Rouge, La., June 10, 1971; s. Amar Jindal, Raj Jindal; m. Supriya Jolly; children: Selia, Shaan. ScB in Biology, Brown U., 1991; MLitt in Politics, Oxford U., England, 1994. Assoc. McKinsey & Co., Washington, 1994—96; sec. La. Dept. of Health and Hosps., Baton Rouge, 1996—98; exec. dir. Nat. Bipartisan Commn. Future of Medicare, Washington, 1998—99; pres. U. La. Sys., Baton Rouge, 1999—2001; asst. sec. Dept H.H.S., Washington, 2001—03; mem. U.S. Ho. Reps., 109th Congress, 1st Dist. La., 2005—. Bd. dirs. Our Lady of the Lake Hosp., Baton Rouge, 2000—01, Edn. Commn. of States, 2000—01. Bd. dirs. Nat. Conf. Cmty and Justice, Baton Rouge chpt., 2000—01, Teach for Am., Baton Rouge chpt., 1997—98, BBB, Baton Rouge, 1987—88, Salvation Army, Baton Rouge, 1986—87. Named La.'s Most Outstanding Young Man, Junior C. of C., 1995; named to All-USA First Acad. Team, USA Today, 1992; recipient Jefferson award, Nat. Inst. Pub. Svc., 1998; scholar, Rhodes Trust, 1992—94. Mem.: Phi Beta Kappa. Republican. Roman Catholic. Office: 1205 Longworth House Office Bldg Washington DC 20515-1801 Office Phone: 202-225-3015.*

JINDRA, CHRISTINE, editor; b. Cleve., Sept. 18, 1947; d. Lad Joseph and Ann Frances (Makar) J.; m. Peter J. Junkin, Aug. 1, 1970 (div. Dec. 1987); children: William Patrick, Michael Lad. BS in Journalsim, Ohio State U., 1969. City reporter Buffalo News, 1969-70; metro reporter Plain Dealer, Cleve., 1970-82, assignment editor, nat. reporter, 1982-84, state editor, 1984-86, metro editor, 1986-88, feature editor, 1988-92, asst. mng. editor, 1992-2001, Sunday editor, 2001—. Mem.: Women's Cmty. Found., Women's City Club. Avocations: skiing, gardening, travel, cooking. Office: Plain Dealer 1801 Superior Ave E Cleveland OH 44114-2198 Office Phone: 216-999-4839. E-mail: cjindra@plaind.com.

JINES, MICHAEL L., utilities executive; JD, U. Houston. Bar: Tex. Joined Reliant Energy, 1982; sr. v.p., gen. counsel Reliant Resources' Wholesale Group; dep. gen. counsel Reliant Energy, Inc.; dep. gen. counsel, gen. counsel wholesale group Reliant Resources, Inc., Houston, sr. v.p., gen. counsel, 2003—. Mem. Pro Bono Coll. State Bar Tex. Editor: Houston Law Rev.; mem. adv. bd.: Houston Jour. Internat. Law. Fellow: Houston Bar Found. (life); mem.: Houston Bar Assn. (co-chair LegalLine com. 1996—97). Office: Reliant Energy Exec Offices PO Box 1384 Houston TX 77251-1384 Office Phone: 713-497-7465. Business E-Mail: mjines@reliant.com.

JING, ZHIGANG, electrical engineer; arrived in US, 2000, naturalized; s. Liangyun Jing and Xianxiu Wang. BSEE, U. Electronic Sci. and Tech. China, 1993, MSEE, 1996, PhD, 1999; postgrad., Columbia U./Poly. U., 2004. Sr. rsch. assoc. Dept. of Elec. Engring. Tsinghua U., Beijing, 1999—2000; rsch. scientist NY State Ctr. for Advanced Tech., 2000—04; sr. staff engr., sys. engring. MeshNetworks Inc., Maitland, Fla., 2004; prin. staff engr. sys. Motorola Inc., Maitland, 2004—. Mem. patent com. Motorola Inc., Maitland, 2004—; spkr. in field. Author: QOS control in high-speed networks, 2001, Broadband Packet Switching Technologies-A Practical Guide to ATM Switches and IP Routers, 2001; contbr. articles to profl. jours. Recipient Best Paper awards, U. Tex., Austin., 2004. Mem.: IEEE (jour. editor). Achievements include design of a packet-switching system, Petastar, which is based on an innovative multi-dimensional multiplexing scheme. Petastar provides as much as 1, 000 times the capacity as traditional switch; development of MAC, a new class of distributed matching algorithms for a large-dimensional switching system that solves the scheduling and routing problem in much less time than traditional scheme; invention of round robin-based dispatching schemes for a multi-stage switch, which outperform Lucent ATLANTA switch in achieving 100% throughput without an internal bandwidth expansion. Office: Motorola Inc 485 N Keller Road Suite 250 Maitland FL 32751 Business E-Mail: zhigang.jing@motorola.com.

JINKS, ROBERT LARRY, retired newspaper publisher; b. Mt. Pleasant, Tex., Jan. 26, 1929; s. Leon Carlton and Mary (Cunnyngham) J.; m. Anne Claire van Ravesteyn, May 8, 1971; children by previous marriage: Laura Beth, Daniel Carlton, Beau Pottorff. BJ, U. Mo., 1950; MS, Columbia, 1956. News editor Muskogee (Okla.) Times-Democrat, 1950-51; reporter Greensboro (N.C.) Daily News, 1953-55; reporter, city editor Charlotte (N.C) Observer, 1956—60; mem. staff Miami (Fla.) Herald, 1960-77, mng. editor, 1966-72, exec. editor, 1972—76; editor, v.p. San Jose (Calif.) Mercury News, 1977-81; sr. v.p. news and ops. Knight-Ridder Corp., Miami, Fla., 1981-89; pub. San Jose (Calif.) Mercury News, 1989-94, ret., 1994. Pres. AP Mng. Editors, 1975—76, Fla. Soc. Newspaper Editors, 1975; bd. dirs. McClatchy Newspapers, Inc. With AUS, 1951-53. Named to 50th anniversary honors list Columbia Grad. Sch. Journalism, 1963, Disting. Grad., 1983; Disting. Grad. award U. Mo., 1990. Mem. Am. Soc. Newspaper Editors (dir. 1980-86).

JINRIGHT, NOAH FRANKLIN, vocational school educator, security firm executive; b. Banks, Ala., Dec. 5, 1936; s. William Carroll and Ila Marie (Garrett) J.; m. Sarah Ann (Graham) Nickolson, Nov. 21, 1959 (div. Sept. 1974); children: Charlene M., Lisa A., Michael D.; m. Frances Lenora (Gaskins), June 11, 1978; children: Diana Carol, Jonathan Franklin. Ed., Columbus (Ga.) Tech. Lic. ins. agt., Ga; cert. security officer; cert. archtl. and mech. drafting; cert. plate and pipe welder. Operator scale Bibb Textiles, Columbus, Ga., 1954-56; operator press and share Columbus Iron Works, Columbus, Ga., 1957-58; ins. agt. Interstate Life, Columbus, Ga., 1958-61; operated winder, starter, generator Joe Hooten, Inc., Columbus, Ga., 1960; fireman City of Columbus, Columbus, Ga., 1960-66; ins. agt. Murray Meadows Ins. Agy., Columbus, Ga., 1960—67; advt. rep. Jinright Enterprises, Columbus, Ga., 1966; ins. agt. Security Life of Ga., Columbus, Ga., 1966; operator share and press Pascoe Steel, Columbus, Ga., 1966-67; machinist Goldens' Foundry and Machine Works, Columbus, Ga., 1967; carpenter, roofer Muscogee County Sch. Dist., Columbus, Ga., 1968-72; pattern maker Pekor Iron Works, Columbus, Ga., 1972-78; instr. metals tech. Spencer H.S., Columbus, Ga., 1978-91, Carver H.S., Columbus, Ga., 1991-94; security officer Sizemore Security Internat., 1994-95, 97-99; instr. metals tech. Kendrick H.S., Columbus, Ga., 1994-99; ret., 1999; security officer Sizemore Security Internat., 1999-2001, The Wackenhut Corp. Security Internat., 2001—03, Securitas Security Svc., USA, Inc., 2003—. Past mfg. rep. printing and advtg. specialties; cons. Voc. Tng. and Rsch. Inst., Seoul, Korea, 1989-90; instr., ptnr. with M. Davis; fire protection supr. 9311th A.F.Rescuer Squadron Columbus, Ga., (Tech. Sgt.). Contbg. articles to local newspapers. Sponsor Spencer H.S. AWS Club, 1979-81; exec. trainer Precision Metalforming Assn., 1996-99; past trustee Epworth United Meth. Ch., ch. usher; mem. Columbus Confederate Drill Team; adv. bd. Am. Biog. Inst., 1999—. Staff sgt. Ga. Army Nat. Guard, 1954-63; tech. sgt. USAFR, 1963-65. Mem. NEA, Internat. Soc. Welding Educators (1st symposium program adv. bd.), Am. Foundry Soc., Am. Welding Soc. (adv. bd.), Vocat. Indsl. Clubs Am. (advisor, cert. of appreciation region VIII 1996), Trade and Indsl. Educators Ga. (mem. West Ga. Sch. to work-evaluation team 1994-99), Muscogee Edn. Assn., Ga. Assn. Educators, Ga. Vocat. Assn., Am. Vocat. Assn., Precision Metalforming Assn., Am. Foundrymen's Soc., Ga. Tchrs. Union, So. Assn. Colls. and Schs., Ga. Assn. Educators. Methodist. Avocations: fishing, hunting, camping, model building, photography. Home: PO Box 63 Columbus GA 31902-0063 Office: 2040 Lee Rd 427 Phenix City AL 36867 Office Fax: 334-297-7545.

JIRAK, SARAH REED, secondary school educator; b. Washington, Iowa, Oct. 21, 1963; d. Cletus Constant and Audrey Jean Reed; m. Donald Myles Jirak, Dec. 29, 1989; 1 child, Shawn Douglas. BA in Religion World History, U. Iowa, 1987. Lic. secondary edn. Tchr. religion St. Mary's Jr.-Sr. HS, Sleepy Eye, Minn., 1987—. Parish music liturgist St. Mary's Parish, Sleepy Eye, 2003—; mem. worship com. New Ulm Diocese, 2005—. Mem.: Nat. Pastoral Musicians Assn., Phi Beta Kappa. Avocations: music, piano. Office: Saint Marys Jr Sr HS 104 Saint Marys St NW Sleepy Eye MN 56085

JIRAUCH, CHARLES W., lawyer; b. St. Louis, Apr. 27, 1944; m. Sally J. Costello, 1968 (div. Mar. 1977); m. Dana K. Bowen, 1980; children: Melissa, Mathew, Kathleen. BSEE, Washington U., 1966; JD, Georgetown U., 1970. Bar: Ill. 1971, Ariz. 1975, Nev. 1991, Calif. 1993, Colo. 1993, U.S. Patent Office 1970, U.S. Supreme Ct. 1978. Atty. Leydig, Voit & Mayer, Chgo., 1970-71, McDermott, Will & Emery, Chgo., 1971-75, Streich Lang, Phoenix, 1975-2000, Quarles & Brady Streich Lang, Phoenix, 2000—; examiner U.S. Patent Office, 1968—70. Bd. dirs. Valley Big Bros./Big Sisters, 1980-86, pres. bd. dirs., 1985-86; pres., bd. dirs. Valley Big Bros./Big Sisters Found., 1988-92; mem. Gov.'s Coun. on Workforce Policy, 2004; mem. bd. advisors to dean Ariz. State U. Sch. Engring., 1998—; bd. dirs., mem. exec. com., gen. counsel, v.p. Ariz. Bus. and Edn. Coalition, 2002—; mem. Ariz. Dem. Coun. Mem. ABA, Internat. Bar Assn., Fed. Cir. Bar Assn., Calif. Bar Assn., Ariz. Bar Assn. and Found., Maricopa County Bar Assn. and Found. (tech. law sect. bd. dirs. 2000-04, chmn. 2001-04), Am. Judicature Soc., Am. Intellectual Property Law Assn., Ariz. Civil Liberties Union, Am. Electronic Assn. (exec. com. Ariz. chpt. 1999-2003), Ariz. Tech. Coun. (bd. dirs. 2000—, chair workforce devel. com. 2001—), Ariz. C. of C. (edn. and tech. comms. 2002—). Democrat. Roman Catholic. Office: Quarles & Brady Streich Lang 2 N Central Ave Phoenix AZ 85004-2345 Office Phone: 602-229-5503. Business E-Mail: cjirauch@quarles.com.

JIRMASEK, KRISTY ANN, school psychologist, counselor; d. Joseph Edward and Marion LaBella; m. Ryan Patrick Jirmasek, Aug. 31, 2002. BA magna cum laude, Mount Union Coll., 1997; MEd, John Carroll U., 1999. Lic. sch. psychologist, sch. counselor, psychology and sociology tchr. Ohio Dept. Edn. Sch. psychologist Strongsville (Ohio) City Schs., 2000—04; sch. counselor Lucas County Ednl. Svc. Ctr., Toledo, 2004—, sch. psychologist, 2004—. Mem.: NEA, Ohio Sch. Counseling Assn., Ohio Sch. Psychologists Assn., Ohio Counseling Assn., Ohio Edn. Assn., Nat. Assn. Sch. Psychologists (cert. sch. psychologist), Am. Sch. Counseling Assn. Roman Cath. Avocations: exercise, sports, reading.

JISCHKE, MARTIN C., academic administrator; b. Chgo., Aug. 7, 1941; m. Patricia Fowler; children: Charles, Marian. BS in Physics with honors, Ill. Inst. Tech., 1963; MS in Aeronautics and Astronautics, MIT, 1964, PhD in Aeronautics and Astronautics, 1968. Engr. Rand Corp., Santa Monica, Calif., 1965; research engr. Battelle N.W. Lab., Richland, Washington, 1970; research fellow Donald W. Douglas Lab., Richland, 1971, Nat. Aeronautics and Space Adminstrn., Moffett Field, Calif., 1973; from asst. prof. to prof. aerospace, mech. and nuclear engring. U. Okla., 1968-75, prof., dir. Sch. Aerospace, Mech. and Nuclear Engring., 1977-81, interim pres., 1985, dean Coll. Engring., 1981-86, mem. various coms., 1985; White House fellow, spl. asst. to sec. of transp. U.S. Dept. Transp., Washington, 1975-76; chancellor U. Mo., Rolla, 1986-91; pres. Iowa State U., Ames, 1991-2000, Purdue U., 2000—. Bd. dirs. Kerr McGee Corp., Wabash Nat. Corp., Duke Realty Corp., Ctrl. Ind. Corp. Partnership, Assn. Am. Univs., NCAA, Nat. Assn. State Univs. and Land Grant Colls., Mo. Alliance for Sci., 1987-91; The Keystone Found., 1984-90, Mo. Corp. for Sci. and Tech., vice-chmn., 1990-91; participant Japanese Econ. Found. Vis. Leaders Program, 1983; mem. Gov.'s Coun. on Sci. and Tech. State of Okla., 1983-84, Gordon Rsch. Conf. on Geophysics; mem. planning com. for 80's Okla. State Regents for Higher Edn.; mem. organizing com. 14th Midwestern Mechanics Conf.; mem. adv. com. for engring. sci. NSF Engring. Directorate, 1985-88; mem. com. on statewide postsecondary telecomm. policy Mo. Coordinating Bd. for Higher Edn., 1987-91; chmn. Congrl. Aero. Adv. Com., 1987-89; sci. adviser to Gov. of Mo., 1990-91; mem. Am. Coun. on Edn. Com. on Math. and Sci., 1990-91. Contbr. articles and reports to profl. publs. Civilian aide Sec. of Army, State of Mo. East, 1987-91; bd. dirs. Bankers Trust, 1995—, Iowa Spl. Olympics, Am. Coun. on Edn., 1996—, Nat. Merit Scholarship Corp., 1997—99; mem. Kellogg Commn. on the Future of State and Land-Grant U., 1995—2000; founding pres. Global Consortium of Higher Edn. and Rsch. for Agr., 1999. Recipient Ralph Teetor award Soc. Automotive Engrs., 1971, Brandon H. Griffith award U. Okla., U. Okla. Regents award for superior teaching, 1975, IIT Prof. Achievement award, 1992, Delta Tau Delta Achievement award, 1992, Engrs. Club St. Louis Achievement award, 1991, Dept. Army Outstanding Civilian Svc. medal, 1991; NASA fellow, 1966; NSF fellow, 1965; AEC/NORCUS summer faculty fellow, 1970-71, NASA/ASEE fellow, 1973. Fellow AAAS, AIAA (assoc., sec.-treas. Okla. chpt., vice chmn., chmn.); mem. ASME, AAUP (v.p., pres. Okla. chpt.), NSPE, Am. Phys. Soc., Am. Soc. Engring. Edn. (Centennial Medallion 1993), Nat. Assn. State Univs. and Land Grant Colls. (bd. dirs., chair 1997-98), Assn. Big Twelve Univs. (pres. 1994-96), Mo. Soc. Profl. Engrs., Rotary, Phi Beta Kappa, Tau Beta Pi, Sigma Xi, Pi Tau Sigma, Sigma Gamma Tau, Sigma Pi Sigma, Phi Eta Sigma. Home: 500 McCormick Rd West Lafayette IN 47906 Office: Purdue U Office of the Pres West Lafayette IN 47906

JIUYONG, SHI, judge; b. Zhejiang, China, Sept. 1926; BA in Govt. and Pub. Law, St. John's U., Shanghai, 1948; MA in Internat. Law, Columbia U., 1951, postgrad., 1951-54. Asst. rsch. fellow Internat. Law Inst. Internat. Rels., Beijing, 1956-58; sr. lectr., assoc. prof. Internat. Law Fgn. Affairs Coll., Beijing, 1958-64; rsch. fellow Internat. Law Inst. Internat. Law, Beijing, 1964-73, 73-80; tchr. Internat. Econ. Law Dept. Law Peking U., 1980-85; prof. Internat. Law Fgn. Affairs Coll., Beijing, 1984-93; prof. Law Fgn. Econ. Law Tng. Ctr. Min. Justice People's Republic China, Beijing, 1987-88; judge Internat. Ct. of Justice, The Hague, The Netherlands, 1994—, v.p., 2000—03, pres., 2003—. Adviser Chinese Soc. Internat. Law, Beijing, Chinese del. 35th session Gen. Assembly UN, China's Alt. Rep. Sixth Com. to 35th session, Chinese del. to 36th, 37, 38th sessions UN Gen. Assembly and China's del. Sixth Com. at same sessions, 1981-83; legal adviser Ministry Fgn. Affairs People's Republic China, 1980-93, Office Chinese Sr. Rep. Sino-Brit. Joint Liaison Group on Hong Kong plenary sessions, 1985-93, Chinese Ctr. Legal Consultancy, Beijing, 1989-93, Chinese del. 1980 Ann. Meeting Bd. Govs. Internat. Monetary Fund and Internat. Bank Reconstruction and Devel., del. Ministry Fin. People's Republic China Internat Bank Reconstruction and Devel., Chinese del. talks between Govt. China and Asian Devel. Bank, 1986, Chinese side Working Group Sino-Brit. Negotiations regarding Hong Kong, 1984, Chinese del. Disarmament Conf., 1991-92; del. Chinese del. to sessions Asian-African Legal Consultative Com., 1981, 85, 93, Chinese del. legal consultations between Ministry Fgn. Affairs of People's Republic China and Dept. State U.S. Am., 1983, 1984, Chinese del. negotiations between Govt. People's Republic China and Govt. U.S. Am. on Mut. Promotion and Protection of Investment Agreement, 1983, 1984; expert sr. legal experts meeting rev. Montevideo program, UN Environ. Program, Geneva, 1991, Nairobi, 1991; lectr. internat. fin. instns. Nat. Bureau Oceanography, People's Republic China, 1986, protection of private fgn. investment Hague Acad. Internat. Law Regional Program, Beijing, 1987, Grad. Inst. Internat. Studies, Geneva, 1988, autonomy in Internat. Law Sem. UN Office, Geneva, 1988, certain issues relating to legal status of Hong Kong Spl. Adminstrv. Region, internat. trade regulation, 1985-86, others; chmn. panel discussions new internat. econ. order Beijing Conf. Law of the World Peace through Law, 1990; participant symposium internat. law arms control and disarmament, Geneva, 1991, Seminar Draft Code Crimes and internat. criminal jurisdiction, symposium on tchg., dissemination and rsch. internat. law in devel. countries, Beijing, 1992. Mem. Am. Soc. Internat. Law, Internat. Law Commn. (rep. to 45th session UN gen. Assembly 1990, 30th meeting of Asian-African Legal Consultative Conf. 1991, mem. 1987-93, rapporteur, 1988, chmn. 1990, lectr. 1991), Inst. Hong Kong Law Chinese Law Soc., Standing Com., Beijing Com., Eighth Ann. Com., Chinese People's Polit. Consultative Conf., Fgn. Econ. and Trade Arbitration Commn., China Coun. Promotion Internat. Trade, Steering Com. Office: Internat Ct of Justice Peace Palace 2517 KJ The Hague Netherlands

JIVETIN, ALEXANDER, geophysicist, educator; b. Tashkent, Uzbekistan, USSR, June 8, 1952; arrived in U.S., 1992; s. Anatoly Vasilievich and Anna Vasilievna Jivetin; m. Stella Gensirovskaia, Oct. 21, 1975; children: Sergey, Julia. M of Geophysics, Tashkent U., 1974; PhD in Geology and Minerology, Moscow Geoprospecting Inst., 1983. Sr. lab. technician Ctrl. Asia Inst. Geology and Mineral Resources, Tashkent, 1974-76; main engr. sci. dept. Uzbekistan Ministry of Geology, Tashkent, 1976-79; sr. rschr. Inst. of Oil and Gas Geology, Tashkent, 1979—92; pvt. tutor math., physics chemistry and earth sci. Bklyn., 1992—2005; tchr. Ohr Eliezer Sch., Bklyn., 1998—2003. Acad. sec. govt. seismol. com., Tashkent, 1978—79; expert Ministry of Geology, 1984—92. Author: How Gods Dodged the Big Bang, or Is Life Preprogrammed?, 2001; creator Combined Anthropic Principle; contbr. over 25 articles to profl. jours.; patent for lottery game methods. Organizer, pres. Nature Conservation Soc. Uzbekistan, 1986-92. Mem. N.Y. Acad. Scis. Office: 8640 Bay Pkwy Brooklyn NY 11214 Office Phone: 718-265-6977. Personal E-mail: sciencestreamjivetin@hotmail.com.

JO, YOUNG GYUN, nuclear engineer; b. Cheong Ju City, Republic of Korea, June 10, 1961; s. Yijoon and Ohran Jo; m. Miae Jo; children: Eunji, Enuyong. BS in Nuc. Engring., Seoul Nat. U., 1984, MS in Nuc. Engring., 1986; PhD in Nuc. Engring., U. Tex., Austin, 1998. Level I nuc. engr., Korea, 1984. Rschr. Korea Atomic Energy Rsch. Inst., Taejon, Republic of Korea, 1986—89, sr. rschr., 1990—94; tchg. asst. U. Tex., Austin, 1994—98; sr. engr. So. Nuc. Oper. Co., Birmingham, Ala., 1998—. Rsch. adviser Korea Atomic Energy Rsch. Inst., Taejon, 2003—. Contbr. numerous articles to profl. confs. and proceedings. Ch. treas. St. Luke Hwang Korean Cath. Ch., Birmingham, 2001—03. Mem.: Am. Nuc. Soc. Roman Catholic. Achievements include designed and developed a thermal neutron imaging system for real time neutron radiography and computed tomography; principal investigator and project mamager of Korea's technical self reliance in the area of probabilistic safety assessment of nuclear power plants. Avocations: gardening, writing poems. Office: So Nuc Operating Co 40 Inverness Ctr Pky Birmingham AL 35242 Office Phone: 205-992-7305. E-mail: ygjo@southernco.com.

JOANIDHI, ZHANI, mathematician, educator; b. Tirana, Albania, Sept. 17, 1965; arrived in U.S., 2000; s. Tasho and Meri Joanidhi; m. Ornela Gambeta, Apr. 30, 1995; children: Nei, Patris. BS in Math., State U. Tirana, 1988; MA in Math. Edn., CUNY, 2004. Cert. math. tchr. NY. Shareholder, mktg. mgr. Extra Ltd., Korca, Albania, 1993—2000; math tchr. John Adams H.S., Ozone Park, NY, 2002—; math instr. Interboro Inst., N.Y.C., 2004—. Advisor of math team John Adams H.S., 2003—; instr. math. State U. Albania, Korca, 1999—2000. Mem. coun. St. Nicolas Albanian Ch., Jamaica Estates, NY, 2001—05. Tchg. fellow, Americorps, 2002—05. Mem.: Nat. Coun. Tchrs. Math., Math. Assn. Am. Avocations: tennis, chess, travel, gardening, reading. Home: 47-10 188 St Flushing NY 11358 Office: John Adams HS 101-01 Rockaway Blvd Ozone Park NY 11417 Office Phone: 718-322-0500. Office Fax: 718-738-9077. Personal E-mail: joanidhizh@msn.com.

JOB, AMY GRACE, librarian, educator; b. Orange, N.J., Mar. 8, 1942; d. George Calvert and Amy Clark (Barret) Segear; m. Kenneth A. Job, Nov. 8, 1968; children: Karen, Annmarie, Kenneth Jr. BA, Montclair State Coll., 1964, MEd, 1978; MLS, Rutgers U., 1966; EdD, Seton Hall U., 1987. Cert. ednl. media specialist, N.J. Libr. Potsdam (N.Y.) State Coll., 1965-67, William Paterson U., Wayne, N.J., 1968—, instr., 1968—, Kean State Coll., Union, N.J., 1969-70. Cons. Pompton Lakes (N.J.) Schs., 1993, Pub. Schs., Paterson, 1992-94. Author: (with others) Selection Bibliography, 1994; co-author: Reference Work in School Libraries, 1996, School Library Media Specialist as Manager, 1997, Now What Do I Do?, 2001; contbr. articles to profl. jours. Mem. West Milford (N.J.) Bicentennial com. West Milford Hist. Soc., 1974-76, mem. 150th Celebration com., 1983-85. Recipient Disting. Svc. award, NJ Libr. Assn. Colls. and Univs., 1992, N.H. Hist. Day Outstanding Educator award, 2001, Faculty Svc. award, 2004, Pres. award, NJ Libr. Assn., 2005. Mem. N.J. Libr. Assn. (chair coms. 1972—, Pres. award 2005), ALA, Ednl. Med. Assn. (chair N.J. sect. 1980—, Spl. award 2005). Avocations: reading, gardening. Home: 5 Navajo Trail West Milford NJ 07480-3609 Office Phone: 973-720-2140. Business E-Mail: joba@wpu.edu.

JOBE, ANGELA FRANCINE, postmaster, writer; b. Independence, Mo., Dec. 18, 1962; d. William Clay and Lela Alice Bryant; children: Brittney Jenae, Brady Jordan. Grad. HS, Lexington, Mo. Clerk US Postal Svc., Wellington, Mo., Higginsville, Mo., postmaster Dover, Mo. Author: Illegal Goodbye, 2004. Sgt. USAF, 1982—84, Germany. Recipient Achievement award, USAF, Germany, 1984. Home: PO Box 44 Dover MO 64022

JOBE, ANN CONNOR, dean, educator; B Biology, Secondary Edn., Middlebury Coll.; RN, Col. St. Catherine, 1976; MSN Med.-Surg. Nursing/Edn., U. Minn., 1978; MD, U. Nevada, 1986. Asst. prof. dept. family medicine, asst. dean student affairs Sch. Medicine, assoc. dean student affairs, 1992—94, assoc. prof., 1993—97, assoc. dean student affairs, acad. programs, 1994—95, sr. assoc. dean, 1995—2001, prof., 1997—, asst. vice chancellor health scis., 1998—2001; instr. dept. family medicine East Carolina U.'s Brody Sch. Medicine, 1989; resident in family practice Fla. Hosp., Orlando; instr. nursing U. Nevada, Las Vegas, Nev.; nurse in neurosurgery U. Hosps., Minneapolis; interim vice chancellor health scis. East Carolina U., Greenville, NC, adj. clin. prof. Sch. Nursing, 1994—; dean Mercer U.-Sch. Medicine, 2001—. Spkr. in field. Contbr. articles to nat. jours. including Am. Jour. Clin. Nutrition, multimedia edn. projects, Family Medicine, Jour. Nutrition Edn., Acad. Medicine, Archives Family Medicine, Family Community Health. Founding bd. chmn. non-profit orgn. Common Ground Solutions. Grantee Nat. Cancer Inst., W.K. Kellogg Found., U.S. Dept. Health and Human Svs., Am. Acad. Family Physicians Found.

JOBE, LARRY ALTON, finance company executive; b. Knox City, Tex., Jan. 12, 1940; s. Lloyd Alton and Georgia (Swift); m. Suzanne Marie Storch, Aug. 2, 1980; 1 dau., Jennifer Marie; children by previous marriage: Lorrie Aileen, Lezlie Amee, Lowell Alton, Lloyd Alan, Leland Austin, Llewyn. BBA, U. North Tex., 1961, postgrad., 1961-65. CPA, Tex. Joined Grant Thornton, Dallas, 1961, mgr., 1967-69, ptnr., 1968-69, mng. ptnr., mem. exec. com. Dallas, 1973—, S.W. regional mng. ptnr., 1983-91; chmn. Legal Network, Inc., 1991—; pres. Nat. Corporate Network, 1997—; chmn. Ind. Bank Tex., 2002—; asst. sec. commerce Washington, 1969-72; v.p. fin. Dart Industries, 1972-73. Mem. acctg.adv. bd. U. North Tex., U. Tex.; bd. dirs. Ind. Nat. Bank. Contbr. articles to profl. jours. Bd. dirs. Dallas Citizens Coun., Eisenhower World Affairs Inst.; chmn. bd. trustees Dallas Theol. Sem.; mem. Chief Execs. Roundtable; chmn. bd. Dallas Alliance for Minority Enterprise, Dallas Minority Bus. Ctr., Profl. Devel. Inst. of U. North Tex.; mem. pres.'s coun. North Tex. State U. Recipient Excellence in Acctg. award Haskins and Sells Found., 1960; Outstanding Alumni award U. North Tex., 1965, Pres.' Svc. award, 1986; U.S. Interagy. Audit Tng. award, 1970, Outstanding Svc. award, 1st Place Author's award Fed. Govt. Accts. Assn., 1970. Mem. AICPA, Tex. Soc. CPAs, Fed. Govt. Accts. Assn., Dallas C. of C. (dir., vice chmn.), Blue Key, Phi Eta Sigma, Alpha Chi, Alpha Lambda Pi, Beta Alpha Psi. Office: 600 N Pearl St Ste 2100 Dallas TX 75201-2825 E-mail: ljobe@legaljobnet.com.

JOBS, STEVEN PAUL, computer company executive; b. Feb. 24, 1955; s. Paul J. and Clara J. Jobs; m. Laurene Powell, Mar. 18, 1991; 4 children. Student, Reed Coll. With Hewlett-Packard, Palo Alto, Calif.; designer video games Atari Inc., 1974; co-founder Apple Computer Inc., Cupertino, Calif., 1976, chmn. bd., 1976—85, interim CEO, 1997, dir., 1997—, CEO, 1998—; pres. NeXT Computer, Redwood City, Calif., 1985—97; CEO NeXT Computer (acquired by Apple Computer Inc.), 1985—97; co-founder, chmn., CEO Pixar Animation Studios Inc., Emeryville, Calif., 1986—. Exec. prodr.: (films) Toy Story, 1995. Nominee Rave award in Business, WIRED, 2005; named one of 100 Most Influential People, Time Mag., 2005, 50 Most Powerful People in Hollywood, Premiere mag., 2002—05; recipient Nat. Medal Tech., presented by Pres. Ronald Reagan, 1985, Jefferson award for pub. svc., 1987, Entrepreneur of the Decade award, Inc. Mag., 1989. Achievements include co-designer (with Stephan Wozniak) Apple I Computer; development of Apple II computer in 1977; iMac in 1998; iPod portable music player in 2001, iTunes in 2002 and iTunes Music Store, 2003. Office: Pixar Animation Studios 1200 Park Ave Emeryville CA 94608-3677 Address: Apple Computer Inc 1 Infinite Loop Cupertino CA 95014 Office Phone: 510-752-3000, 408-996-1010. Office Fax: 510-752-3151, 408-974-2113.*

JOCHIM, MICHAEL ALLAN, archaeologist; b. St. Louis, May 31, 1945; s. Kenneth Erwin and Jean MacKenzie (Keith) J.; m. Amy Martha Waugh, Aug. 12, 1967; children: Michael Waugh, Katherine Elizabeth. BS, U. Mich., 1967, MA, 1971, PhD, 1975. Lectr. anthropology U. Calif., Santa Barbara, 1975-77, asst. prof., 1979-81, assoc. prof., 1981-87, prof., 1987—, dept. chmn., 1987-92; asst. prof. Queens Coll. CUNY, Flushing, 1977-79. Mem. archaeology rev. panel NSF, Washington, 1988-90. Author: Hunter-Gatherer Subsistence and Settlement, 1976, Strategies for Survival, 1981, A Hunter-Gatherer Landscape, 1998; editor (series) Interdisciplinary Contributions to Archaeology, 1987—; editor Am. Antiquity, 2004—. Chmn. Community Adv. Com. for Spl. Edn., Santa Barbara County, 1980-82. Grantee NEH, 1976, NSF, 1980, 81, 83, 89, 91, 94, 2002, Nat. Geog. Soc., 1987, 97, Wenner-Gren, 1999. Fellow Am. Anthrop. Assn.; mem. Soc. for Am. Archaeology, Sigma Xi. Office: U Calif Dept Anthropology Santa Barbara CA 93106 Office Phone: 805-893-4396. Business E-Mail: jochim@anth.ucsb.edu.

JOCHUM, JAMES J., federal agency administrator; BA in Polit. Sci. with high distinction, U. Iowa, 1987, JD, 1990. Atty. Foley & Lardner, Milwaukee, 1990—92; asst. v.p. Brenton Bank, Cedar Rapids, Iowa, 1992—94; internat. trade counsel Office of Sen. Charles E. Grassley, 1994—97, legis. dir., 1997—99; majority counsel U.S. Senate Banking Com.; sr. mgr. govt. rels. Accenture L.L.P., 2000—01; asst. sec. export adminstrn. U.S. Dept. Commerce, Washington, 2001—03, asst. sec., import adminstrn., 2003—. Mem.: Order of Coif. Republican. Office: Dept Commerce Import Adminstrn 14th St & Constitution Ave NW Rm 9099B Washington DC 20230

JOCHUM, PAM, state representative; b. Dubuque, Iowa, Sept. 26, 1954; AA, BA, Loras Coll. Pub. info. and mktg. dir. Loras Coll.; instr. N.E. Iowa C.C.; mem. Iowa Ho. Reps., Des Moines, 1993—, mem. various coms. including judiciary, mem. state govt. ways and means com. Chair Alzheimer Memory Walk, CROP Walk; del. Dem. Nat. Conv., 1980, floor whip, 1984; chair Dubuque County Dem. Ctrl. Com., 1982; statewide co-chair U.S. Senator Tom Harkin's Re-Election Com.; former bd. dirs. Dubuque County Assn. for Retarded Citizens, Dubuque County Compensation Bd., Loras Coll. Arts and Lectr. Series, Nat. Cath. Basketball Tournament, Sacred Heart Cath. Ch., Women's Recreation Assn., Mississippi Valley Promise, LWV. Democrat. Office: State Capitol East 12th and Grand Des Moines IA 50319 also: 2368 Jackson St Dubuque IA 52001 E-mail: pam.jochum@legis.state.ia.us.

JOCHUM, VERONICA, pianist; b. Berlin; d. Eugen and Maria (Montz) J.; m. Wilhelm V. von Moltke, Nov. 15, 1961. MusM, Staatliche Musikhochschule, Munich, 1955, Concert Diploma, 1957; pvt. study with Edwin Fischer, Josef Benvenuti, 1958—59, Rudolf Serkin, Phila., 1959—61. Faculty Settlement Sch. Music, Phila., 1959-61, New Eng. Conservatory Music, Boston, 1965—, Berkshire Music Center, Tanglewood, 1974, Radcliffe Inst., Cambridge, Mass. Recs. with Laurel, Deutsche Grammophon, Philips, Golden Crest, Pro Arte, GM Recs., CRJ, Tahra recs., Tudor; Numerous tours, throughout N. and S. Am., Asia, Europe and, Africa; as soloist with world renowned orchs., including Boston Symphony, Balt. Symphony, London Philharmonic, Los Angeles Chamber Orch., London Symphony, Mpls. Symphony, Berlin, Hamburg and Munich Philharmonics, Bavarian and Bamberg Symphonies, Munich Chamber Orch., radio orchs. of Hamburg, Munich, and Frankfurt, Orch. Maggio Musicale, Florence, La Fenice Orch., Venice, RAI-Orch., Naples, Mozarteum Orch., Salzburg, Concertgebouw Orch., Amsterdam, The Hague Philharmonic, Venezuelan Symphony, Caracas, Jerusalem Symphony, others; appearances on radio and TV, recitals in more than 50 countries on 4 continents; participant, Marlboro Music Festival, Montreux Festival, Bregenz Festival, Mecklenburg Festival, Festival de Vallonie (Belgium), Tanglewood, N.W. Bach Festival, Spokane, Ea. Music Festival, Chambermusic East. Bd. mem. Berkshire Inst. Theology and the Arts. Recipient cross Order of Merit (Germany); Bunting fellow Harvard U., 1996-97. Office: New Eng Conservatory Music 290 Huntington Ave Boston MA 02115-5018

JOCK, KATHERINE ANN, art educator; b. Midland, Mich., Aug. 10, 1967; d. Donald S. High and Evelyn M. Wells; m. Nicolas Dean Jock, Aug. 20, 1994; children: Zachary D., Jaron D. AA (hon.), Delta Coll.; BA with hons. in Art Edn., Saginaw Valley State U. Asst. kindergarten class Zion Luth. Sch., Bay City, Mich., 2000—01. Day camp program dir. Lake Huron Boy Scouts of Am., Auburn, Mich., 1999—; mural program dir. Zion Luth. Sch., Bay City, Mich., 2002—; vol. art tchr. Zion Luth. Ch., Bay City, Mich., 2001—02; vol. coord. and fundraiser Bay City Pub. Sch., Bay City, Mich., 1999—2002. Charcoal drawing, Untitled (Second Nat. Bank Art Purchase Award, 1992), sculpture, Candor (Merit Cert., League of Innovation Nat. Juried Student Art Completion, 1996). Coord. event decoration Zion Luth. Ch., Bay City, Mich., 2001—02. Recipient Outstanding Grad. award in Art, Delta Coll., 1997; scholar, Saginaw Valley State U., 2002—04; Roberts fellowship, Saginaw Valley State U. and Donna Roberts, 2003—04. Mem.: MAEA (assoc.), Alpha Chi (hon.), Phi Theta Kappa (hon.). Democrat. Lutheran. Avocations: travel, hiking, pottery, cross country skiing, theater. Home: 5546 Christopher Ct Bay City MI 48706-3462 Office: Studio 23 901 N Water Street Bay City MI 48708 Office Phone: 989-894-2323.

JOCK, PAUL F., II, lawyer; b. Indpls., Jan. 25, 1943; s. Paul F. and Alice (Sheehan) J.; m. Gail A. Webre, Sept. 16, 1967; children: Craig W., Nicole L. BBA, U. Notre Dame, 1965; JD, U. Chgo., 1970. Bar: Ill. 1970, N.Y. 1990. Ptnr. Kirkland & Ellis, Chgo. and N.Y.C., 1970-2001; sr. v.p., gen. counsel GM Asset Mgmt., N.Y.C., 2000—05; ptnr. Jenner & Block LLP, N.Y.C. and Chgo., 2005—. V.p. legal affairs Tribune Co., Chgo., 1981. Assoc. editor U. Chgo. Law Rev., 1969-70. Served to lt. USN, 1965-67. Mem. ABA, Chgo. Bar Assn., Assn. of the Bar of City of N.Y. Home: 2 Columbus Ave Unit 2913 New York NY 10023 Office: Jenner & Block LLP One IBM Plaza Ste 4400 Chicago IL 60611 E-mail: paul.jock@gm.com.

JOCKERS, ETHEL CATHERINE, mathematics and computers educator; b. Bklyn., May 4, 1932; d. Frank and Ethel (Ostrovsky) Gudanek; m. Kenneth Martin Jockers, June 26, 1954; children: Kenneth, Claudia, Cynthia. BA, Bklyn. Coll., 1953, MA, 1956; MA in Liberal Studies, SUNY, Stony Brook, 1977. Tech. asst. Bell Tel. Labs., N.Y.C., 1953-55; tchr. math. Bushwick High Sch., Bklyn., 1955-57; tchr. math. and computers Massapequa (N.Y.) High Sch., 1957-93; retired, 1993. Author: Computer Programming in BASIC, 1980. Mem. AAUW (v.p. 1968-72, 80-84, sec. 1988-92), Chi Epsilon Delta. Roman Catholic. Avocations: reading, boating, travel. Home: 247 Sunset Blvd Massapequa NY 11758-8545

JODOCK, DARRELL HARLAND, minister, educator; b. Northwood, N.D., Aug. 15, 1941; s. Harry N. and Grace H. (Hansen) J.; m. Janice Marie Swanson, July 8, 1972; children: Erik Thomas, Aren Kristofer. BA summa cum laude, St. Olaf Coll., 1962; BD with honors, Luther Theol. Sem., 1966; postgrad., Union Theol. Sem., N.Y.C., 1966-67; PhD, Yale U., 1969. Ordained to ministry Am. Luth. Ch., 1973, Luth. Ch. in Am., 1978. Instr. Luther Theol. Sem., St. Paul, 1969-70, asst. prof., 1970-73, 75-78; asst. pastor Grace Luth. Ch., Washington, 1973-75; prof. dept. religion Muhlenberg Coll., Allentown, Pa., 1978-99, head dept. of religion, 1978-92, Class of 1932 rsch. prof., 1989; disting. prof. religion Gustavus Adolphus Coll., St. Peter, Minn., 1999—. Chmn. various coms. N.E. Pa. Synod Evang. Luth. Ch. in Am., 1979-99, del. to nat. assembly, 1995, 97, 99, 2005; adv. bd. Berman Ctr. for Jewish Studies, 1985-92; founder, chmn. bd. Inst. for Jewish-Christian Understanding, 1988-99; bd. Inst. for Ecumenical and Cultural Rsch., Collegeville, 1999—; chair Assn. Tchg. Theologians of the Evang. Luth. Ch. Am., 2002—. Evang. Luth. Ch. Am. Consultative Panel Luth.-Jewish Rels., 2005—. Author: The Church's Bible: Its Contemporary Authority, 1989; translator: Luther and the Peasants' War (Hubert Kirchner), 1972; editor and co-author: Ritschl in Retrospect: History, Community and Science, 1995, Catholicism Contending with Modernity: Roman Catholic Modernism and Anti-Modernism in Historical Context, 1999; contbr. articles to profl. jours. Recipient Paul C. Empie Meml. award Muhlenberg Coll., 1987; Danforth Found. fellow 1962-69, Inst. for Ecumenical and Cultural Rsch. fellow, 1982-83. Mem. Am. Acad. Religion (pres. 19th Century theology group 1981-86, 1997-2001), Am. Soc. Ch. History, Soc. for Values in Higher Edn., Internat. Schleiermacher Soc., Internat. Bonhoeffer Soc., Søren Kierkegaard Soc., Phi Beta Kappa, Omicron Delta Kappa (campus leadership 1985—). Office: Gustavus Adolphus Coll Dept Religion 800 W College Ave Saint Peter MN 56082-1485

JOE, BINA, chemistry professor, geneticist, researcher; d. Joseph Puthumana and Annamma Joseph; m. Venkatesha Basrur; 1 child, Basrur Abhijith. PhD in biochemistry, U. Of Mysore, 1990—96. Vis. scientist NIH, Bethesda, Md., 1997—2001; asst. prof. Med. Coll. Of Ohio, Toledo, Ohio, 2001—04. Editl. bd. mem. Physiol. Genomics (Jour.), 2004—. Author: 28 scientific manuscripts. Fogarty Internat. fellowship, Fogarty Ctr.,NIH, 2002. Office: Med Coll Of Ohio 3035 Arlington Ave Toledo OH 43614 Office Phone: 419-383-4415. Office Fax: 419-383-6168. Business E-Mail: bjoe@mco.edu.

JOE, DON W., lawyer; b. Dallas, Mar. 13, 1959; s. David Tsetling and Shoo Hoi (Kwan) J. BA in Polit. Sci., Columbia U., 1981, JD, 1984. Bar: N.Y. Atty. Fed. Savings and Loan Insurance Corp., Washington, RadioShack Corp. Mem. Asian-Am. Legal Defense Fund, Citizens Against Govt. Waste. Recipient 1st Place award Gen. Motors Intercollegiate Bus. Competition, 1981. Mem. ABA, Fed. Bar Assn., Asian-Pacific Am. Bar Assn., Am. Corp. Counsel Assn., Orgn. Chinese-Ams.; mem, co-founder Dallas Asian-Am. Bar Assn. (pres., 1988-90, treasurer). Republican. Roman Catholic. Office: RadioShack Corp 300 RadioShack Circle Fort Worth TX 76102*

JOEL, AMOS EDWARD, JR., telecommunications consultant; b. Phila., Mar. 12, 1918; s. Amos Edward and Anna (Potsdamer) J.; m. Rhoda Ethel Fenton (dec.); children: Jeffrey (dec.), Stephanie, Andrea. BEE, MIT, 1940, MEE, 1942. Registered profl. engr., N.Y. Mem. tech. staff Bell Tel. Labs., N.Y. and N.J., 1940-52, supr. Whippany, N.J., 1952-54, dept. head, 1954-61, dir. Holmdel, N.J., 1961-67, cons., 1967-83, ret., 1983; cons., 1983—. Cons. AT&T Bell Comm. Rsch., GTE, IBM, Contel, Pacific Tel.; lectr. in field of switching sys. Author: Electronic Switching Central Office Systems of the World, 1976, Electronic Switching: Digital Central Office Systems of the World, 1982, History of Science and Technology in the Bell System-Switching Technology, 1982; author: (with others) Fundamentals of Digital Switching, 1983, 2d edit., 1990, Electronics, Computers and Telephone Switching, 1990, Future of the Central Office, 1991; contbr. articles to encys. and profl. jours.; holder more than 70 patents. Co-recipient Outstanding Patent award N.J. R & D Coun., 1972, Stuart Ballantine medal Franklin Inst., 1981, Centary prize Internat. Telecom. Union, 1983, Columbian medal City of Genoa, Italy, 1984, Kyoto prize in advanced tech., 1989, Nat. Med. of Tech., 1993; named N.J. Inventor of Yr., 1989. Fellow IEEE (life, co-recipient Alexander Graham Bell medal 1976, IEEE medal of honor 1992, nat. medal tech. 1993, 3d Millennium medal 2000), Am. Acad. Arts and Scis.; mem. NAE, AAAS, Comm. Soc. of IEEE (pres. 1973-75), Sigma Xi, Eta Kappa Nu (Karapetoff eminent members' award 2000). Avocations: organ and keyboard music, railroading. Home: Winchester Gardens One Turnberry Ct Maplewood NJ 07040-2423 E-mail: a.joel@ieee.org.*

JOEL, BILLY (WILLIAM MARTIN JOEL), musician; b. Bronx, NY, May 9, 1949; s. Howard and Rosalind (Nyman) Joel; m. Elizabeth Webber, 1972 (div. 1982); m. Christie Brinkley, Mar. 23, 1985 (div. Aug. 1994); 1 child, Alexa Ray; m. Kate Lee, Oct. 2, 2004. LHD (hon.), Fairfield U., 1991; HMD (hon.), Berklee Coll. Music, 1993; Mus D (hon.), Southampton Coll., 2000. Joined band The Hassles, LI, 1968, Attila, 1970; solo rec. artist, 1972—; performed in piano bars under name Bill Martin LA, 1973; co-founder LI Boat Co., 1996. Albums: (with The Hassles) The Hassles, 1967, Hour of the Wolf, 1968, (with Attila) Attila, 1970, (solo) Cold Spring Harbor, 1971, Piano Man, 1973, Streetlife Serenade, 1974, Turnstiles, 1975, The Stranger, 1977, 52nd Street, 1978 (Grammy Award for album of yr., 1979, Grammy Award for best male pop vocal performance, 1979), Glass Houses, 1980 (Grammy Award for best male rock vocal performance, 1980), Songs in the Attic, 1981, The Nylon Curtain, 1982, An Innocent Man, 1983, Greatest Hits, Vols. I and II, 1985, Vol. III, 1997, The Bridge, 1986, Kohuept: Live from the Soviet Union, 1987, Storm Front, 1989, River of Dreams, 1993, 2000 Years: Millenium Concert, 2000, Essential Billy Joel, 2001, Fantasies & Delusions, 2001; songs include Just the Way You Are, 1978 (Grammy Award for record of yr., 1978, Grammy Award for song of yr., 1978); summer tour with Elton John, 1994, spring tour with Elton John, 1995, Asian and European tour with Elton John, 1998; author, children's book, Goodnight My Angel: A Lullabye, 2005. Established The Rosalind Joel Scholarship CCNY, 1996. Grammy Legend Award, 1990, Humanitarian Award, Cathedral of St. John the Divine, 1990, Billboard Century Music Award, 1994, ASCAP Founder's Award, 1997, Am. Music Awards Award of Merit, 1999, James Smithson Bicentennial Medal of Honor, 2000, Johnny Mercer Award, Songwriter's Hall of Fame, 2001, Music Cares Person of Yr., 2002; inducted into Songwriter's Hall of Fame, 1992, Rock and Roll Hall of Fame, 1999. Achievements include premiering first prodn. tour of the USSR by an Am. popular artist, 1987; inspiring Broadway musical Movin' Out, 2002. Office: Maritime Music Inc PO Box 628 Glen Cove NY 11542-0628

JOEL, RICHARD MARC, academic administrator, law educator, dean; b. NYC, Sept. 9, 1950; s. Avery Joel and Annette (Bloom) Ashwal; m. Esther Duora Ribner, Nov. 11, 1973; children: Penina, Avery, Arielle, Noam. BA, NYU, 1972, JD, 1975. Bar: N.Y. 1976, U.S. Dist. Ct. (ea. dist.) N.Y. 1976. Asst. dist. atty. Borough of Bronx, NY, 1975-78; dir. alumni affairs Yeshiva U., NYC, 1978-80, asst. dean Cardozo Sch. Law, 1980-82, assoc. dean Cardozo Sch. Law, 1982, adj. prof. law, 1985, pres., 2003—. Pres. Hillel, Found. for Jewish Campus Life. Sec. Hebrew Acad. Long Beach, N.Y., 1983—; bd. dirs. Jewish Community Council Oceanside, N.Y., 1977-81, Young Israel Oceanside, 1986—. Root-Tilden scholar NYU, 1972-75. Mem. ABA. Democrat. Jewish. Avocations: music, youth work. Office: Yeshiva U Cardozo Sch Law 55 5th Ave New York NY 10003-4301*

JOEL, WILLIAM LEE, II, interior and lighting designer; b. Richmond, Va., Feb. 23, 1933; s. J. Alton and Dorothy Joel; m. Merry Pick, June 5, 1955; children: Taryn, Dana, Wendy, Holly. Student, R.I. Sch. Design, 1953-55; AB, Brown U., 1955; postgrad., N.Y. Sch. Interior Design, 1956, Pratt Inst., 1958-61. Cert. interior designer Commonwealth of Va. Draftsman Mills Denmark Inc., N.Y.C., 1957-58; with sales and interior design Lord & Taylor's Inc., N.Y.C., 1958-61; pres., interior designer Richmond (Va.) Art Co. Inc. Instr. Va. Commonwealth U. (formerly Richmond Profl. Inst.), 1963-67; set designer Barksdale Theatre, Hanover, Va., 1977-88; mem. adv. bd. interior design program Va. Poly. Inst and State U., 1986-90; speaker numerous orgns., radio and TV programs. Prin. works include Culpepper (Va.) Hosp., The Curles Neck Pl., Richmond, Dominion Nat. Bank, Richmond, Gary, Stoch, Walls offices, Richmond, Gov.'s Exec. Mansion, Commonwealth Va., 1976, Hello Inc., Richmond, Hill Bldg., Richmond, Hunter House Mus., Norfolk, Va., Richmond, Fredericksburg and Potomac R.R. Co. corp. hdqrs., Rolph Clark Stone Packaging Co. offices, Straub and Dalch office complex, Westminster Canterbury House, Richmond, Wickham Valentine House, Willow Oaks Country Club, Continental Cablevision, Richmond, St. Paul Episcopal Ch., Richmond, numerous residences; author: articles published bi-monthly in Rich Art website. Co-chmn. com. for cert. Va. Interior Designers, 1982-90; mem. Downtown Mktg. Com., chmn. subcom. Xmas Sound and Lighting, Richmond, 1988-91, mem. prodn. Richmond Forum sets and lighting design, 1989-95; bd. visitors Found. for Interior Design Edn. and Rsch., 1977-84, mem. accreditation com., 1984-88; mem. Va. Mus. Fine Arts, City of Richmond Christmas Candlelight Com., edn. com. Retail Mchts. Assn., 1980-85; mem. urban design com. Ctrl. Richmond Assn., 1993. 1st lt. USMC, 1952-57. Recipient award Va. Mus. Fine Arts, Richmond, 1970, Cert. Distinction, 1973; named contest winner Richmond Symphony Orch., 1975. Fellow Am. Soc. Interior Designers (cert., pres. Va. chpt. 1970-72, 80-81, mem. nat. bd. 1972-74, 76-77, regional v.p. 1976-77, nat. com. 1976); mem. Nat. Fire Protection Assn. Avocations: sailing, canoeing, electronics, sport cars. Home: 8905 Sierra Rd Richmond VA 23229-7828 Office: Richmond Art Co 530 E Main St Ste 600 Richmond VA 23219-2431 Office Phone: 804-644-0733.

JOELSON, MARK RENÉ, lawyer; b. Paris, Oct. 23, 1934; came to U.S., 1941, naturalized, 1947; s. Michael and Helen (Streicher) J.; m. Anastasia Whelan, June 4, 1967; children: Helen, Daniel, Marisa. BA, Harvard U., 1955, LLB, 1958; diploma in law, Oxford U., Eng., 1962. Bar: D.C. 1958, U.S. Supreme Ct. 1959. Atty. U.S. Dept. Justice, Washington, 1958-63; assoc., then ptnr. Arent, Fox, Kintner, Plotkin & Kahn, Washington, 1963-80; ptnr. Wald, Harkrader & Ross, Washington, 1980-85, Morgan, Lewis & Bockius LLP, Washington, 1986-97; pvt. practice, 1998—. Mem. adv. com. internat. investment, tech. and devel. U.S. Dept. State, 1978-87; cons. UN Conf. Trade and Devel., 1977-79; adj. prof. Georgetown U. Law Ctr., Washington; panelist N.Am. Free Trade Agreement, Am. Arbitration Assn., Nat. Arbitration Forum, NASD, mediator US Dist. Ct., DC, 2001-. Author (with Earl W. Kintner): An International Antitrust Primer, 1974; author: An International Antitrust Primer, 2d edit., 2001; editor (with others): Current Legal Aspects of Doing Business in the E.E.C., 1978; editor: Enterprise Law in the 80's, 1980, Joint Ventures in the United States, 1988. Fulbright scholar Oxford U., 1961-62. Mem. ABA (chmn. sect. internat. law and practice 1983-84, del. Internat. Bar Assn. coun. 1984-92), Internat. Bar Assn., Fed. Bar Assn. (pres. D.C. chpt. 1976-77), DC Bar Assn. (chmn. internat. dispute resolution com., internat. sect., 2001-2003), Washington Inst. Fgn. Affairs, Cosmos Club (Washington), Order of Brit. Empire. Office Phone: 202-626-6815. Personal E-mail: joelsonmr@msn.com.

JOERN, CHARLES EDWARD, JR., lawyer; b. Oak Park, Ill., Apr. 27, 1951; s. Charles Edward and Eleanor Joern; m. Christine Mary Lake, July 28, 1973; children: Jessica, William, Marisa, Angela, Alexandra. BA, Knox Coll., 1973; M in Urban Affairs, U. Colo., 1976; JD, De Paul U., 1980. Bar: Ill. 1980, U.S. Dist. Ct. (no. dist.) Ill. 1980, U.S. Ct. Appeals (7th cir.) 1981, U.S. Supreme Ct. 1995. Asst. to planning cons. J.R. Crowley and Assocs., 1973-74; sys. analyst Aravada, Colo. Bldg. Inspection Divsn., U. Colo. sponsorship, 1974-75; student intern divsn. comprehensive health planning Colo. Dept. Health, 1976; law clk. Cook County Legal Assistance Found., Chgo., 1978; consumer fraud divsn. Office Ill. Atty. Gen., 1979-80; assoc. Pope, Ballard, Shepard & Fowle, Ltd., Chgo., 1980-94, Burke, Weaver & Prell, Chgo., 1994-2000, Holland & Knight, Chgo., 2000—. Panel atty. Chgo. Vol. Legal Svcs. Found. Bd. advisors N.C. Outward Bound Sch., Morgantown, 1983-99; bd. dirs. Richport YMCA, LaGrange, Ill., 1984—, chmn., 1990-93; village trustee LaGrange Park, 1997—. Fellow in pub. affairs U. Colo., 1979. Mem. ABA (litigation sect.), Ill. State Bar Assn., Chgo. Bar Assn. (chmn. child abuse and neglect com. 1985-86), Pi Alpha Alpha. Republican. Roman Catholic. Office: Holland & Knight LLC 131 S Dearborn Chicago IL 60603 E-mail: charles.joern@hklaw.com.

JOERRES, JEFFREY A., staffing company executive; BS, Marquette U. Various mgmt. positions IBM; v.p. sales and mtkg. ARI Network Svcs.; v.p. mktg. Manpower, Inc., Milw., from 1993, sr. v.p. European ops. and global account mgmt. and devel., until 1999, pres., CEO, 1999—, chmn., 2001—. Bd. dirs. Artisan Funds, Johnson Controls, Nat. Assn. Mfr.; Bd. of Trustees Comm. for Econ. Devel. Mem. Commn. Tech. & Adult Learning Nat. Gov. Assn. Mem.: Am. Soc. for Tng. & Devel. Office: Manpower Inc 5301 N Ironwood Rd Milwaukee WI 53217-4982*

JOERSZ, FRAN WOODMANSEE, secondary school educator; b. Bismarck, N.D., Apr. 29, 1954; d. Joe G. and Winnie (McGillic) Woodmansee; m. Jon D. Joersz; children: Brett, Ben, Courtney. Student, Bismarck State Coll., 1972; BA in Edn., U. Wyo., 1975. Tchr. 3rd grade Deer Trail (Colo.) Pub. Sch., 1975-76; tchr. 8th grade remedial reading Mandan (N.D.) Jr. High Sch., 1976-78; tchr. title I reading Saxvik St. Mary's Grade Sch., Bismarck, 1979; tchr. 8th grade devel. reading Wachter Jr. High Sch., Bismarck,

1979-81; tchr. 7th grade devel. reading written and oral communications Hughes Jr. High Sch., Bismarck, 1981—. Bd. dirs. Rape Victim Adv. Program; founding bd. dirs. Our Kids Need to Know; state bd. dirs. Make A Wish Found. Recipient Milken award, 1994; named Edn. alumna of Yr., U. Wyo., 2003. Mem. PEO, N.D. Edn. Assn. (Tchr. of Yr. 1991, Profl. Courage award 1994), Internat. Reading Assn., Nat. Assn. Student Activity Advisers. Avocations: walking, reading, volleyball, writing, travel. Home: 520 N Mandan St Bismarck ND 58501-3748 Office: Horizon Mid Sch 500 Ash Coulee Dr Bismarck ND 58503 Office Phone: 701-221-3555. Business E-Mail: fran_joersz@educ8.org.

JOESTEN, MELVIN DUANE, retired chemistry professor; b. Rochelle, Ill., Oct. 27, 1932; s. Allen and Hattie Joesten; m. Maribel May Joesten, Dec. 19, 1953; children: Jo Ellen Frick, Charles David. BA in edn., No. Ill. U., 1954; PhD, U. of Ill., 1962. Chemistry tchr. Oswego (Ill) HS, 1956—58; asst. prof., chemistry So. Ill. U., Carbondale, Ill., 1962—66; assoc. prof. chemistry Vanderbilt U., Nashville, 1966—75, prof., chemistry, 1975—98, retired Nasvhille, Tenn., 1998—. Fulbright lectr. Trinity Coll., Dublin, 1972—73; chmn. Vanderbilt U., Chemistry Dept., Nashville, 1976—82. Author: Hydrogen Bonding; co-author: World of Chemistry, World of Chemistry: Essentials; contbr. articles various profl. rsch. jours. Specialist 2nd class U.S. Army, 1954—56, United States and Germany. Grantee Alliance for Enhancement of Sci. Edn. and Tech., NSF, 2000 - 2005, Use of Multimedia in Introductory Chemistry, 1994-1997. Mem.: Am. Chem. Soc. Office: Vanderbilt U VU Station B 351822 Nashville TN 37235-1822 Office Phone: 615-322-2699. E-mail: melvin.d.joesten@vanderbilt. edu.

JOFEN, JEAN, foreign language educator; BA, Bklyn. Coll., 1943; MA, Brown U., 1945; PhD, Columbia U., 1960; MS, Yeshiva U., 1961. Cert. sch. psychologist, N.Y. Teaching fellow Brown U., 1943-44; lectr. adult edn. Bklyn. Coll., 1951-61; assoc. prof. Yeshiva U., N.Y.C., 1955-62; assoc. prof., chmn. dept. Germanic and Slavic langs. Bernard M. Baruch Coll., N.Y.C., 1962-77, prof., 1977—, chmn. dept. modern langs., 1977-83, chmn. dept. Germanic, Hebraic and Oriental langs., 1983—, bd. govs., 1973—. Mem. adv. bd. Jewish Studies CUNY, 1986; lectr., speaker various sci., civic and religious orgns. and socs. in U.S. and Europe; scholar abroad, Vienna, Austria, 1991. Author: A Linguistic Atlas of Eastern European Yiddish, 1964, rev. edit., 1967, Das letzte Geheimnis (in German), 1972, The Jewish Mystic in Kafka, 1987, (textbooks) Yiddish for Beginners, 1963, Yiddish Literature for Beginners, 1972, (with Y. Kerstein) Hebrew for Beginners, 1975, (with E. Mok) Chinese for Beginners, 1980; editor Elizabethan Concordance series: The Concordance of The Works of Christopher Marlowe, 1979, A Concordance to The Shakespeare Apocrypha, 3 Vols., 1987; Nat. Endowment for Humanities; assoc. editor Jour. Evolutionary Psychology; contbr. numerous articles to profl. jours. Recipient Nat. Jewish Culture Found. award, 1963, Kohut Found. award, 1966, Bernard M. Baruch Coll. medal for 35 yrs. svc., AAUW award, 1968, 69, others; fellow Inst. for Yiddish Lexicological Rsch. CUNY, 1963—; grantee Ford Found., 1970, Population Coun. Rockefeller Inst., 1970-71, Rsch. Found. CUNY, 1985, Lucius N. Littauer Found., 1986, Austrian Fed. Ministry for Sci. and Rsch., 1991. Fellow Jewish Acad. Arts and Scis.; mem. Am. Assn. Tchrs. German, MLA, AAUP, Am. Assn. Profs. Yiddish (pres.), Am. Psychol. Assn., Marlowe Soc. Am. (founder 1975, pres. 1975-84, organizer 1st. Internat. Congress in Eng. 1983), Mich. Acad. Arts and Scis., Acad. Scis. and Humanities CUNY, Sigma Alpha. Address: 409 Avenue I Brooklyn NY 11230-2619

JOFFE, BARBARA LYNNE, computer management professional, computer artist; b. Bklyn., Apr. 12, 1951; d. Lester L. and Julia (Schuelke) J.; 1 child, Nichole. BA, U. Oreg., 1975; MFA, U. Mont., 1982. Cert. project mgr. IBM; cert. project mgmt. profl. Project Mgmt. Inst. Applications engr., software developer So. Pacific Transp., San Francisco, 1986-93; computer fine artist Barbara Joffe Assocs., San Francisco, Englewood, Colo., 1988—; instr. computer graphics Ohlone Coll., Fremont, Calif., 1990-91; adv. programmer, project mgr.-client/server Integrated Sys. Solutions Corp./IBM Global Svcs. So. Pacific/Union Pacific Railroads, Denver, 1994-97; applications sys. mgr. IBM Global Svcs./CoBank, Greenwood Village, Colo., 1997-99; exec. project mgr. IBM/GM Web Hosting, 2000—01, IBM/Cendant, 2001—. Artwork included in exhibits at Calif. Crafts XIII, Crocker Art Mus., Sacramento, 1983, Rara Avis Gallery, Sacramento, 1984, Redding (Calif.) Mus. and Art Ctr., 1985, Euphrat Gallery, Cupertino, Calif., 1988, Computer Mus., Boston, 1989, Siggraph Traveling Art Shown, Europe and Australia, 1990, 91, 4th and 7th Nat. Computer Art Invitational, Cheney, Wash., 1991, 94, Visual Arts Mus., N.Y.C., 1994, 96, IBM Golden Circle, 1996. Recipient IBM Project Mgmt. Excellence award, 1998. Mem. Project Mgmt. Inst. (cert.), Assn. Computing Machinery. Avocations: art, gardening, hiking. Personal E-mail: joffeb@aol.com.

JOFFE, ROBERT DAVID, lawyer; b. NYC, May 26, 1943; s. Joseph and Bertha (Pashkovsky) Joffe; m. Virginia Ryan, June 20, 1981; stepchildren: Elizabeth DeHaas, Ryan DeHaas;children from previous marriage: Katherine, David. AB, Harvard U., 1964, JD, 1967. Bar: NY 1970, US Dist. Ct. (so. and ea. dists.) NY 1971, US Ct. Appeals (2d cir.) 1972, US Supreme Ct. 1973. Maxwell Sch. Africa Pub. Svc. fellow (funded by Ford Found.), Republic of Malawi, 1967-69; state counsel, 1968-69; assoc. Cravath, Swaine & Moore, NYC, 1969-75; ptnr. Cravath, Swaine & Moore LLP, NYC, 1975—, dep. presiding ptnr., 1998, presiding ptnr., 1999—. Apptd. bd. dirs. Pres. Clinton Romanian Am. Enterpise Fund, 1994—2003. Chair Harvard Law Sch. Nat. Fund, 1995—97, dean's adv. bd., 1997—; vice chmn. Fiduciary Trust Co. Internat., 2005—; bd. dirs. Jericho Project, 1985—97, Human Rights First (formerly The Lawyers Com. for Human Rights), 1988—, Fiduciary Trust Co. Internat., 1999—, Franklin Resources, 2003—, After Sch. Corp., 2001—. Recipient Disting. Leadership Recognition award, Lawyers Com. Civil Rights, 1992, Learned Hand award, Am. Jewish Com., 2004, John J. McCloy award, Fund for Modern Courts, 2005. Mem.: ABA, Coun. Fgn. Rels., Assn. Bar City NY (chmn. trade regulation com. 1980—83, mem. exec. com. 1995—99, mem. nominating com. 2001—02, v.p. 2003—04), NY Bar Assn., Human Rights Watch/Africa (mem. adv. com.), Century Assn. Club, Harvard Club. Achievements include recognition by the The Lawyers' Committee for Civil Rights Under Law for distinguished leadership in helping secure the passage of the Civil Rights Act of 1991. Home: Apt 13A 300 W End Ave New York NY 10023-8156 Office: Cravath Swaine & Moore LLP Worldwide Plz 825 8th Ave Fl 46 New York NY 10019-7475 Office Phone: 212-474-1448. Office Fax: 212-474-3700. Business E-Mail: rjoffe@cravath.com.

JOFFE, RUSSELL T., dean; BS, U. Witwatersrand, Johannesburg, S. Africa, 1977. Diplomate Am. Bd. Psychiatry and Neurology, 1984. Intern Mount Sinai Hosp., Toronto, Canada; resident in psychiatry Royal Ottawa Hosp., U. Ottawa, McMaster U.; fellow NIH, Bethesda, Md., 1983—85; mem. dept. psychiatry U. Toronto; chair dept. psychiatry and behavioral neurosciences McMaster U., 1994—97, dean faculty of health scis.; dean U. Medicine and Dentistry N.J. - N.J. Med. Sch., 2001—05. Mem. Expert Adv. Com. on Psychiatric Illness of U.S. Pharmacopoiea, 1990—. Contbr. of more than 250 articles in profl. jours.; author: more than 30 chpts. for med. textbooks about depression. Recipient Award of Excellence, Depressive and Manic Depressive Assn. Ont.; grantee of more than 50 rsch. grants. Fellow: Royal Coll. Physicians and Surgeons Can., Am. Psychiatric Assn. (Gold award for Academically Sponsored Programs). Office: 185 S Orange Ave Newark NJ 07103*

JOFFE, STEPHEN NEAL, surgeon, medical educator; b. Springs, Transvaal, Republic of South Africa, Jan. 11, 1943; came to U.S., 1980; s. Hirshy N. and Pearl (Cohen) J.; m. Sandra Noche, Dec. 18, 1966; children: Heidi, Craig. BS, U. Stellenbosch, Cape Province, South Africa, 1963, MD, 1976; B in Medicine and Surgery, U. Witwatersrand, Johannesburg, South Africa, 1967. Fellow Coll. of Surgeons of South Africa, 1972, Royal Coll. Physicians and Surgeons of Glasgow, 1973, Royal Coll. of Surgeons of Edinburgh, 1973, Am. Coll. Surgeons, 1983; Diplomate Am. Bd. Laser Medicine and Surgery, 1986. Rotating registrar surgery Groote Schuur Hosp. Univ. of Capetown (South Africa), 1970-72, sr. registrar in surgery, 1972-73; sr. registrar 3 tutor in surgery dept. of surgery Hammersmith Hosp. and Royal Postgrad. Med. Sch., London, U.K., 1973-75, resident surg. officer, 1974-75; hon. cons. surgeon, sr. lectr. in surgery Univ. of Glasgow (Scotland), 1975-80, Dept. of Surgery Glasgow Royal Infirmary, 1975-80; prof. of surgery U. Cin. Coll. of Medicine, 1980-90; esteemed quondam prof. surgery and medicine U. Cin. Med. Ctr., 1990—. House surgeon, house physician Johannesburg Gen. Hosp., 1968; resident surg. officer Hammersmith Hosp., 1974; courtesy staff and cons. surgeon various U.S. Hosps.; chmn. bd., dir. Surg. Laser Techs. (Japan) Co., Ltd., 1986, 88; pres. Laser Ctrs. Am., Inc., Cin., 1985—. Editor numerous med. books; contbr. articles to numerous publs., mags. and jours. Recipient Nash Meml. Prize, 1966, 1989 Enterprise award Cin. Bus. Courier; Barnes Agranat scholar, 1967. Mem. AASS, AMA, Internat. Assn. Endocrine Surgeons, Internat. Duodenal Club, Internat Fedn. Surg. Colls., Internat. Nd;Laser Soc. (chmn., founder 1983, co-chmn. 1985), Collegium Internat. Chirurgiae Digestivae, Internat. Soc. Surgery, Internat. Soc. Optical Engring. (co-chmn. Lasers in Medicine 1986, 87), Internat. Hosp. Fedn., European Soc. Surg. Rsch., Assn. Surgeons Great Britain and Ireland, British Soc. Gastroenterology, Pancreatic Soc. Great Britain, Surg. Rsch. Soc. (U.K.), Caledonian Soc. Gastroenterology, Scottish Soc. for Exptl. Medicine, Indian Soc. Gastroenterology, Assn. for Advancement Med. Instrumentation, Assn. for Gnotobiotics, Soc. U. Surgeons, Soc. for Surgery of Alimentary Tract, Royal Soc. Medicine, Endocrine Soc., Assn. Acad. Surgeons, Pancreas Club, Am. Assn. Clin. Anatomists, Am. Assn. Endocrine Surgeons, Am. Bd. Laser Surgery (examiner 1986), Am. Coll. Gastroenterology, Am. Coll. Healthcare Adminstrs., Am. Coll. Healthcare Mktg. Inst., Am. Coll. Med. Staff Affairs Inst., Am. Fedn. Clinic Rsch., Am. Gastroent. Assn., Am. Inst. Physics, Am. Physiol. Soc., Am. Soc. Gastrointestinal Endoscopy, Am. Soc. Laser Medicine and Surgery, N.Y. Acad. Scis., numerous others. Home: 8750 Red Fox Ln Cincinnati OH 45243-3731

JOFFE, STEVEN, hematologist, oncologist, pediatrician, ethicist; s. Leonard and Marcelle Joffe; m. Elizabeth Haas, Apr. 17, 1967; children: Sonia Leah, Elijah Simon. MD, U. of Calif., San Francisco, 1988—92; AB, Harvard Coll., 1984—88; MPH, U. of Calif. at Berkeley, 1995—96. Bd. Cert. Diplomate Am. Bd. of Pediat., 1995, Bd. cert. Diplomate Am. Bd. of Pediat., Hematology/Oncology sub-board, 2000. Attending physician Dana-Farber Cancer Inst., Boston, 2000—, Children's Hosp., Boston; asst. prof. pediat. Harvard Med. Sch., Boston. Mem.: Am. Soc. Bioethics and Humanities, Am. Soc. Clin. Oncology. Office: Dana-Farber Cancer Inst 44 Binney St Boston MA 02115 Office Phone: 617-632-5295. Business E-Mail: steven_joffe@dfci.harvard.edu.

JOGLAR, FRANCISCO, academic administrator; Dean U. P.R., Sch. Medicine, San Juan, 1999—. Office: A-878 Main Bldg PO Box 365067 San Juan PR 00936-5067 Office Phone: 787-765-2363. Business E-Mail: fjoglar@rcm.upr.edu.

JOHAL, DHARAMPAL SINGH, physician; b. Amritsar, Punjab, India, Apr. 10, 1960; came to U.S., 1992; s. Bhajan S. and Bhupinderpal K. (Tur) J.; m. Palwinder K, Mar. 1, 1990; 1 child, Gurnaj S. BSc in Zoology with honors, Delhi (India) U., 1978; pre-med., Guru Nanak Dev U., Amritsar, Punjab, India, 1979; MBBS, Govt. Med. Coll., Amritsar, 1984; MD, Govt. Med. Coll., 1988, U. Medicine and Dentistry N.J., 1996. Diplomate Am. Bd. Internal Medicine. Jr. resident in medicine and surgery Govt. Med. Coll./Hosp., Amritsar, Punjab, India, 1985; pvt. practice Amritsar, 1986; med. resident Govt. Med. Coll., Amritsar, 1987-88; med. cons., dir. Guru Nanak Mission Hosps., Punjab and Haryana, India, 1989-92; med. resident U. Hosp. U. Medicine and Dentistry N.J., Newark, 1993-96; physician Fresno, Calif., 1996—. Resident dir. Medivisa Internat Practitioner, Australia, 1986-92; dir. primary care Chief Khalsa Dewan Hosp., Tarn Taran, Punjab, India, 1991; presenter, researcher in field. Organizer St. John Mission Ambulatory Med. and Eye Camps, Punjab and Haryana, India, 1990-92; vol. blood donation and health hygiene camps, Punjab and Haryana. Mem. AMA, ACP, Am. Profession Practice Assn. Office: 7011 N Howard St Ste 201 Fresno CA 93720 Address: 10168 N Rowell Ave Fresno CA 93720-3491

JOHANN, ANNE DOROTHY, visual artist, painter, graphic artist; b. North Tarrytown, N.Y., Feb. 24, 1957; d. John Thomas and Elizabeth Keay (Hamilton) Sekelsky; m. Thomas Richard Johann, Aug. 28, 1982. BFA with highest honors, Pratt Inst., 1980. Printer asst. Solo Press, Inc., N.Y.C., 1980—82; tchr. oil painting Croton-Cortlandt Ctr. for Arts, Cortlandt Manor, NY, 1994, 1995, 2001—, tchr. watercolor painting, 1998—, tchr. drawing, 2001—. Summer instr. Croton-Cortlandt Ctr. Arts, 2004; guest instr. watercolors Putnam Arts Coun., 2004, tchr. oil, acrylic painting, 2004—; summer guest instr. Watercolors Putnam Arts Coun., 2004, 05. Open edit. print, The Old Mill as seen from the Charles Bridge, Prague, N.Y. Graphic Soc., 2001. Recipient award, N.Y. State Art Tchrs., 1975, residency grantee, Vt. Studio Ctr., Johnson, Vt., 2000, artist grantee, Vt. Studio Ctr., 2000, Award of Excellence, Manhattan Arts Internat. mag., 1999, Vasari Oil Colors award, Art of N.E. U.S.A., Silvermine Guild Galleries, New Canaan, Conn., 2000, Westchester Arts Coun. Mcpl. Challenge grant, CCCA/Town of Cortlandt, 2001—02. Mem.: Croton Coun. on Arts, N.Y. Artists Equity Assn., Nat. Assn. Women Arts (France Lieber Meml. award 2002), New Haven Paint and Clay Club (David T. Langrock Found. prize for landscape 2001, honorable mention active mems. exhibit 2001). Home: 316 Grand St Croton On Hudson NY 10520-3500 Office Phone: 914-806-4067. Personal E-mail: johann@bestweb.net.

JOHANNES, JOHN ROLAND, political science professor, dean; b. Milw., Dec. 15, 1943; s. Jerome Fridolin and Teresa (Stoiber) J.; m. Frances Virginia Slater, Aug. 5, 1967; children: Teresa, Michael, James. BS, Marquette U., 1966; AM, Harvard U., 1968, PhD, 1970. Asst. prof. polit. sci. Marquette U., Milw., 1970-75, assoc. prof., 1975-84, prof., 1984-95, chmn. dept. polit. sci., 1980-88, dean Coll. Arts and Scis., 1988-93; v.p. acad. affairs Villanova (Pa.) U., 1995—. Chmn. Bradley Inst. for Democracy and Pub. Values, 1988-93. Author: Policy Innovation in Congress, 1972, To Serve the People, 1984; co-editor and contbr. editor Money, Elections, and Democracy, 1990; contbr. articles to profl. jours. Am. Philos. Soc. grantee, 1978; Everett Dirksen Ctr. grantee, 1981, 82, NEH grantee, 1972. Mem. Am. Polit. Sci. Assn., Midwest Polit. Sci. Assn., So. Polit. Sci. Assn., Assn. Am. Colls. and Univs. Home: 840 Galer Dr Newtown Square PA 19073-3517 Office: Villanova U Office Acad Affairs 800 E Lancaster Ave Villanova PA 19085-1603 Office Phone: 610-519-4521. E-mail: john.johannes@villanova.edu.

JOHANNES, KAY L., insurance company executive; b. Milw., July 3, 1952; d. James Ben and Evelyn (Horne) J.; m. Thomas A. Rozek, June 13, 1972 (div. Oct. 1975); m. Alexander David Bub, Jan. 5, 1982; 1 child, David A. AAS in Visual Comm., Milw. Area Tech. Coll., 1972; BS in Instrnl. Tech., Rochester Inst. Tech., 1977. Audio visual tech. Nicolet H.S., Glendale, Wisc., 1972-75; visual designer, animator Pohlman Studios, Milw., 1977-79; designer multimedia AV Centrum AB, Stockholm, 1979-80; owner, prodr. Johannes, Milw., 1980-82; audio visual prodr. Photography Unltd., Milw., 1982-87; sr. salestrack specialist Northwe. Mut. Life Ins. Co., Milw., 1987—. Chair visual comm. adv. bd. Milw. Area Tech. Coll., 1990—2005. Vol. Big Brothers/Big Sisters, Ozaukee County, Wisc., 1978-91. Mem. order of Amaranth (royal matron), White Shrine Jerusalem (worthy high priestess). Methodist. Avocations: motorcycles, computer web design. Home: W4802 Knuth Rd Random Lake WI 53075 Office: Northwestern Mut Life Ins Co 720 E Wisconsin Ave Milwaukee WI 53202 E-mail: kayj@myexcel.com.

JOHANNS, MICHAEL OWEN, secretary of agriculture, former governor; b. Osage, Iowa, June 18, 1950; s. John Robert Sr. and Adeline Lucy (Royek) J.; m. Constance J. Weiss, June 10, 1972 (div. Dec. 1985); children: Justin Michael, Michaela Susan; m. Stephanie A. Suther, Dec. 24, 1986. BA, St. Mary's Coll., Winona, Minn., 1971; JD, Creighton U., 1974. Law clk. to Hon. Hale McCown Nebr. Supreme Ct., Lincoln, 1974-75; assoc. Cronin & Hannon, O'Neill, Nebr., 1975-76; ptnr. Nelson, Johanns, Morris, Holdeman & Titus, Lincoln, 1976-91; mayor City of Lincoln, 1991-98; gov. State of Nebr., 1999—2005; sec. USDA, Washington, 2005—. Econ. devel & commerce com. chmn. Nat. Govs. Assn., 2000-03 Mem. Lancaster County Bd., Lincoln, 1983-87; mem. City Coun. Lincoln, 1989-91. Mem. Nebr. Bar Assn. Republican. Roman Catholic. Avocations: skiing, biking, reading. Office: Office Sec USDA 1400 Independence Ave SW Washington DC 20250*

JOHANNSEN, MARC ALAN, lawyer; b. Victorville, Calif., Feb. 14, 1964; s. Gerald W. and Sharon K. J.; m. Kimberly Kriss, Sept. 29, 1990. BSBA magna cum laude, Carroll Coll., 1986; JD cum laude, U. Minn., 1989. Bar: Minn. 1989, U.S. Dist. Ct. Minn. 1990, Wis. 1997. Jud. clk. Hennepin County Dist. Ct., Mpls., 1989-90, Minn. Ct. Appeals, St. Paul, 1990-91; atty., shareholder Lommen, Nelson, Cole & Stageberg, Mpls., 1991—. Vol. pro bono atty. Vol. Lawyers Network, Mpls., 1991—; mem. city coun. City of Vadnais Heights, Minn., 1995—. AV Rating, Martindale Hubbell. Mem. ABA, Minn. Bar Assn., Hennepin County Bar Assn. Avocations: hiking, gardening, computers, politics. Office: Lommen Nelson Cole & Stageberg 80 S 8th St 2000 IDS Center Minneapolis MN 55402 Office Phone: 612-339-8131. Business E-Mail: marc@lommen.com.

JOHANSEN, ERLING, retired dental educator, dean; b. Overhalla, Norway, Apr. 8, 1923; came to U.S., 1945; s. Trygve Vilmar and Jenny Marie (Gansmo) J.; m. Inger Marie Nordback, July 4, 1952; children: Erling Trygve, Erik Bjarne, Steven Douglas. DMD cum laude, Tufts U., 1949; PhD, U. Rochester, 1955; DSc (hon.), Athens (Greece) U., 1981; HHD (hon.), New Eng. Sch. Law, 1993. Eastman/Squibb fellow, dental rsch. Rochester (N.Y.) U., 1950-55, asst. prof. dentistry, 1955-58, assoc. prof. dentistry, 1958-61, prof. dental rsch., 1961-66, Welcher prof. dental rsch., 1966-78, chair dept. dentistry and dental rsch., 1955-78; prof. general dentistry Tufts U. Sch. Dental Medicine, Boston, 1979-95, acting chmn. oral health svc. dept., 1979-86, dean, 1979-95, dean emeritus, Disting. Prof. emeritus, 1995—. With Norwegian Armed Forces Dental Corps, 1949-50, Norwegian Pub. Health Svc., 1950; cons. Strong Meml. Hosp., Rochester, 1958-79, Eastman Dental Ctr., Rochester, 1967-78, Genesee Hosp., Rochester, 1967-78, Monroe Cmty. Hosp., Rochester, 1968-75; project supr. Rochester Neighborhood Health Ctr., 1965-70, Migrant Dental Program, Rochester, 1965-70; coord. dental program, U. Rochester Cancer Ctr., 1974-78; cons. Highland Hosp., 1975-78; numerous coms. and consultantships, including AMA Coun. on Drugs, USPHS, Bur. Environ. Health, Nat. Inst. Dental Rsch., King Abdulaziz U., Jeddah, Saudi Arabia, Ministry of Health, Kuwait, Union of 11 faculties State of Planalto Ctrl., Brasilia, Brazil, others; internat. lectr. and presenter in field. Contbr. articles to profl. jours.; editor Jour. Dental Edn., 1974-76, AAAS Symposium 11, 1979, AAAS Symposium on Oral Health of Elderly, 1987; patentee in field of remineralizing solution; reviewer, mem. editl. bds. various jours. Bd. dirs., chair, fundraising com., pres., trustee-advisor Scandinavian Charitable, West Newton, Mass., 1995—, pres., 2003; Gavel lectureship com., Forsyth Inst., Boston, 1997—. Lt., Norwegian Army, 1949-50. Disting. Lectr. Pan Am. Health Orgn., WHO, 1973; Dr. Erling Johansen Endowed Professorship, Tufts U., 1994; recipient Leif Erikson Day Citation award Sons of Norway, 2004. Fellow AAAS (coun. mem. 1963-67, 72-77), Am. Coll. Dentists (chmn. We. N.Y. sect., New Eng. sect.), Internat. Coll. Dentists, Pierre Fauchard Dental Honor Soc.; mem. ADA (internat. com., 7th dist., N.Y., 1969-76, Coun. Scientific Rsch., N.Y., 1971-78, 83-87; various coms. and task forces; presenter testimony U.S. Ho. of Reps. 1986), Am. Assn. Dental Schs. (chmn. sect. advanced edn. 1968-69, v.p. advanced edn. programs 1970-74, exec. com. 1970-74, adminstrv. bd. coun. deans 1989-93, chair 1992-93, various other coms. and subcoms.), Am. Assn. Dental Rsch. (sec.-treas., bd. dirs. 1976-79), Internat. Assn. Dental Rsch. (coun. mem. 1958-61, 69-76, bd. dirs. 1974-75, various coms. and subcoms.), Greater N.Y. Dental Soc. (Dr. Irving E. Gruber award 1998), Mass. Dental Soc. (rsch. awards com. 1980—), Dental Soc. Norway, Korean Dental Assn. (hon.), Tufts U. Alumni Assn. (Disting. Svc. award 1994), Sigma Xi, Omicron Kappa Upsilon. Avocations: fishing, skiing, photography, historical research. Home: 69 Windsor Rd Needham MA 02492-1440 Office: Tufts U Sch Dental Medicine One Kneeland St Boston MA 02111 E-mail: ejimj@rcn.com.

JOHANSEN, IRIS, writer; 2 children. Author: (novels) The Forever Dream, 1985, The Wind Dancer, 1991 (Rita award winner), Storm Winds, 1991, Reap the Wind, 1991, Golden Barbarian, 1992, Last Bridge Home, 1992, Tiger Prince, 1993, Magnificent Rogue, 1993, Beloved Scoundrel, 1994, Midnight Warrior, 1994, Dark Rider, 1995, Lion's Bride, 1996, Ugly Duckling, 1996, Long After Midnight, 1997, The Face of Deception, 1998, And Then You Die, 1998, Killing Game, 1999, The Search, 2000, Final Target, 2001, Body of Lies, 2002, No One to Trust, 2002, Dead Aim, 2003, Fatal Tide, 2003, Firestorm, 2004, Blind Alley, 2004 (NY Times and USA Today Bestseller lists), Countdown, 2005 (Publishers Weekly Hardover Bestseller list), Delaney series, 34 books in Bantam Loveswept series. Recipient Career Achievement award, Romantic Times. Mailing: c/o Author Mail Bantam Dell Publ 1745 Broadway New York NY 10019 E-mail: mail@irisjohansen.com.

JOHANSEN, JOHN MACLANE, architect; b. NYC, June 29, 1916; s. John Christen and Jean (MacLane) J.; m. Beate Gropius; children from previous marriage: Deborah, Christen BS, Harvard U., 1939; MArch, Harvard Grad. Sch. Design, 1942. Draftsman Marcel Breuer; rschr. Nat. Housing Agy., Washington; with Skidmore, Owings, & Merrill, NYC; founder pvt. practice, New Canaan, Conn., 1948; prin. Johansen-Bhavnani, NYC, 1973-89; pvt. practice NYC, 1989—. Co-author: A Life in the Continuum of Modern Architecture, 1996. Fellow AIA (honor award 1972, medal of honor NY 1976); mem. Am. Acad. in Rome, NAD, Am. Acad. Arts and Letters (Brunner award 1968), Archtl. League (NY pres. 1968-70) Address: 821 Broadway New York NY 10003-4702*

JOHANSEN, MARJORIE HARKINS, librarian; b. Salem, Oreg., Sept. 9, 1938; d. Lewis Charles Harkins and Marjorie (Fossum) Boring; 1 child, Christopher. BA, Oreg. State U., 1960; MLS, San Jose State U., 1981. Reference libr. Burlingame (Calif.) Pub. Libr., 1982-86, San Francisco (Calif.) State U., 1987-90; bus. reference libr. San Mateo (Calif.) Pub. Libr., 1990-94; owner retail franchise Anokhi, 1994—2000. Libr. San Francisco Pub. Libr. Govt. Info. Ctr., 1996—; mem. libr. editl. bd. Greenwood Press. Mem. ALA, Calif. Libr. Assn. Democrat. Episcopalian.

JOHANSON, DONALD CARL, physical anthropologist; b. Chgo., June 28, 1943; s. Carl Torsten and Sally Eugenia (Johnson) Johanson; 1 child, Tesfaye Meles. BA, U. Ill., 1966; MA, U. Chgo., 1970, PhD, 1974; DSc (hon.), John Carroll U., 1979; D.Sc. (hon.), Coll. of Wooster, 1985. Mem. dept. phys. anthropology Cleve. Mus. Natural History, 1972-81, curator, 1974-81; pres. Inst. Human Origins, Berkeley, Calif., 1981-97, dir. Tempe, Ariz., 1997—. Prof. anthropology Stanford U., 1983-89, Ariz. State U., 1997, Virginia M. Ullman chair human origins, 2000; adj. prof. Case Western Res. U., 1978-81, Kent State U., 1978-81. Co-author: (with M.A. Edey) Lucy: The Beginnings of Humankind, 1981 (Am. Book award 1982), Blueprints: Solving the Mystery of Evolution, 1989, (with James Shreeve) Lucy's Child: Discovering a Human Ancestor, 1989, (with Kevin O'Farrell) Journey from the Dawn: Life with the World's First Family, 1990, (with Lenora Johanson and Blake Edgar) Ancestors: In Search of Human Origins, 1994, (with Blake Edgar) From Lucy to Language, 1997, (with Giancarlo Ligabue) Ecce Homo, 1999, (with W.H. Kimbel and Y. Rak) The Skull of Australopithecus afarensis, 2004; host PBS Natures Series; prodr. (film) Lucy in Disguise, 1982; host, narrator NOVA series In Search of Human Origins, 1994 (Emmy nomination 1995); contbr. numerous articles to profl. jours. Recipient Jared Potter Kirtland award for outstanding sci. achievement Cleve. Mus. Natural History, 1979, Profl. Achievement award U. Chgo., 1980, Gold Mercury Internat. ad personem award Ethiopia, 1982, Humanist Laureate award Acad. of Humanism, 1983, Disting. Svc. award Am. Humanist Assn., 1983, San Francisco Exploratorium award, 1986, Internat. Premio Fregene award, 1987, Alumni Achievement award U. Ill., 1995, Anthropology Media award Am. Anthropol. Assn., 1999, Webby award for best sci. web site, 2002; named Endowed Chair Virginia Ullman Chair in Human Origins, Webby award Internat. Acad. Digital Arts and Scis., 2002; grantee Wenner-Gren Found., NSF, Nat. Geog. Soc., L.S.B. Leakey Found., Cleve. Found., George Gund Found., Roush Found. Fellow AAAS, Calif. Acad. Scis., Rochester (N.Y.) Mus., Royal Geog. Soc.; mem. Am. Assn. Phys. Anthropologists, Internat. Assn. Dental Rsch., Internat. Assn. Human Biologists, Am. Assn. Africanist Archaeologists, Soc.

Vertebrate Paleontology, Soc. Study of Human Biology, Societe de l'Anthropologie de Paris, Centro Studi Ricerche Ligabue (Venice), Founders' Coun., Chgo. Field Mus. Natural History (hon.), Assn. Internationale pour l'etude de Paleontologie Humaine, Mus. Nat. d'Histoire Naturelle de Paris (corr.), Explorers Club (hon. dir.), Nat. Ctr. Sci. Edn. (supporting scientist). Office: Inst Human Origins Ariz State U PO Box 874101 Tempe AZ 85287-4101 Office Phone: 480-727-6580. Business E-Mail: johanson.iho@asu.edu.

JOHANSON, GREGORY JOHN, psychotherapist, minister; b. Portland, Ore., Jan. 29, 1947; s. Knut Harry and Liv Angel (Einarsen) J.; m. Cherith Hope Hansen, May 20, 1967; 1 child, Leif Nathan. BA in Psychology and Philosophy, Willamette U., 1969; MDiv Pastoral Care, Emory U., 1972; postgrad., Pacific U. Grad. Sch., 1979—82; MPhil, Drew Grad. Sch., 1994, PhD, 1997. Lic. profl. counselor N.J., clin. counselor N.J. Pastor United Meth. Chs., Oreg. and N.J., 1969—; pvt. practice as pastoral psychotherapist Oreg. and N.J., 1979—; dir. counseling svcs., chaplain Plz. Santa Maria Hosp., Baja, Calif., 1980—81; lectr. in psychology Western State Chiropractic Coll., Portland, Oreg., 1981—82; lectr. Nat. Coll. Naturopathic Medicine, Portland, 1981—82, Mt. Hood C.C., 1981—82; contract therapist Luth. Family Svcs., Klamath Falls, Oreg., 1982—; psychotherapy trainer, founding trainer Hakomi Inst., Boulder, Colo., 1982—, also bd. dirs.; clin. assoc. prof. marriage and family therapy Ctrl. Conn. State U., New Britain, 1998—. Editor Hakomi Forum, Hakomi Inst., Boulder, 1982—; faculty tutor PhD students Union Grad. Sch., Yellow Springs, Ohio, 1989—; book rev. editor pastoral care sect. Pulpit Digest, San Francisco, 1986-91; guest lectr. Western Oreg. State Coll. Psychology Hons. Program, Monmouth, Oreg., 1980, Drew U. DMin Program, Madison, N.J., summer 1996, Columbia Coll. Master's Program, Chgo., 1993, Australian Sch. of Applied Psychology, Sydney, Australia, 1996, counseling masters program Pace U., White Plains, N.Y.; adj. prof. pastoral counseling Drew U., 2001—; bd. dirs. U.S. Assn. for Body Psychotherapy; rsch. faculty Santa Barbara Grad. Inst. Author: Grace Unfolding, 1991, Sanfte Stärke: Heilung im Geiste des Tao te King, 1993, Revelacion de la Gracia: Psicoterapia en el Espiritu de el Tao-te King, 1994; editor: Feed My Sheep, 1984, Pastoral Care Issues In the Pulpit, 1984; co-editor The Jour. of Self-Leadership; mem. editl. bd. The Jour. of Pastoral Care, 2000—; contbr. numerous articles to books and periodicals. Ordained elder United Meth. Ch., 1974; mem. peer rev. com. U.S. Assn. for Body Psychotherapy, bd. dirs. Lelia S. Bortzmeyer scholar Willamette U., 1966, Dean's award scholar Emory U., 1970, Shirley Sugerman scholar Drew Grad. Sch., 1987; postdoctoral fellowship Princeton U., 1999—. Fellow Am. Assn. Integrative Medicine (diplomate Coll. Pastoral Counselors); clin. mem. Assn. for Clin. Pastoral Edn., Clin. Theology Assn. (editl. bd., profl., Eng.), Am. Assn. Pastoral Counselors, Am. Psychotherapy Assn. (diplomate, editor and rev. bd.), Soc. for Pastoral Theology, Internat. Pastoral Care Network for Social Responsibility, Assn. for Transpersonal Psychology, Am. Acad. Religion, Forge Inst. for Spirituality and Social Change, Integral Inst. of Spirituality, Am. Psychological Assn. (divsn. 24 and 32). Republican. United Methodist. Avocations: stained glass work, sailing, wood construction, sports, Aikido. Home and Office: PO Box 625 Branchville NJ 07826-0625 Office Phone: 973-875-5643 4.

JOHANSON, PATRICIA MAUREEN, artist, parks designer; b. N.Y.C., Sept. 8, 1940; d. Alvar Einar and Elizabeth (Deane) J.; m. E.C. Goossen (dec.); children: Alvar Deane, Gerrit Hull, Nathaniel James. Student, Bklyn. Mus. Art Sch., 1958, Art Students League, 1961; AB, Bennington Coll., 1962; MA, Hunter Coll., 1964; BS, BArch, City Coll. Sch. Architecture, 1977; DFA (hon.), Mass. Coll. of Art, 1995. Vis. prof. art SUNY-Albany, 1969; vis. artist MIT, 1974, Oberlin (Ohio) Coll., 1974, Alfred (N.Y.) U., 1974, West Tex. State U., 1988, Yale U., 1989, Mass. Coll. Art, Boston, 1994, Calif. State U., Monterey Bay, 1997, 99; Southworth lectr. Colby Coll., Waterville, Maine, 1981; cons. Mitchell-Giurgola Assocs., architects, N.Y.C., Phila., 1972—, Oikos, Seoul, South Korea, 1996, Yukong Ltd., Ulsan, South Korea, 1996, Seoul Devel. Inst., Seoul, 1999, Millenium Park, Seoul, 1999, Nat. Endowment for Arts, Washington, 1988, City of Petaluma, Calif., 1999, Carollo Engrs., 2001, The Murie Ctr., Moose, Wyo., 2001—; artist-in-residence N.Y. Found. for Arts, 1987—; del. Survival and the Arts, Sundance Inst., Utah, 1991; del. Global Forum Gen. Assembly, Kyoto, Japan, 1993, Art & Environ., Ankara, 1997, Year 2000 Symposium, Dumbarton Oaks, Washington, keynote spkr. Internat. Fedn. of Landscape Architects, Belem, Brazil, 2002, Wuhan U., China, 2004, Art in Embassies program U.S. Dept. State; mem. grants selection com. NEA, 2000. Solo shows Tibor de Nagy Gallery, N.Y.C., 1967, SUNY at Albany, 1969, Montclair (N.J.) State Coll., 1974, Rosa Esman Gallery, N.Y.C., 1978, 79, 81, 83, Dallas Mus. Art, 1982, Philippe Bonnafont Gallery, San Francisco, 1984, New Arts Program, Kutztown, Pa., 1987, Albany Acad., 1987, Painted Bride Art Ctr., Phila., 1991; National Museum of Kenya, Nairobi, 1996—, Salina Art Ctr., Kans., 2001; retrospectives, Bennington Coll., 1973, 91, Twining Gallery, N.Y.C., 1987, Berkshire Mus., Pittsfield, Mass, 1987, Coll. St. Rose, Albany, N.Y., 2004; numerous group shows including most recently Gallery Route One, Point Reyes, Calif., 1999, The Presidio, San Francisco, 1999, Villa Medici, Rome, 2000, Mass. Coll. Art, 2000, French Cultural Svcs. Gallery, N.Y.C., 2000, Institut Francais D' Architecture, Paris, 2000, Contemporary Arts Ctr., Cin., 2002, Mus. of Contemporary Art, L.A., 2004, Armory Ctr. Arts, Pasadena, Calif., 2004, The Natural World Mus., San Francisco, 2004; represented in permanent collections, Detroit Inst. Arts, Dallas Mus. Art, Mus. Modern Art, Met. Mus. Art, N.Y.C., Nat. Mus. Women in Arts, Washington, Herbert F. Johnson Mus., Cornell U., Berkshire Mus., N.Y. State Coun. on Arts Film Collection, Syracuse, Storm King Art Ctr., Mountainville, N.Y., Crawford and Chester Sts. Park, Cleve., Oberlin Coll., Bennington Coll., Brandeis U., U. Mass., Amherst, Dumbarton Oaks Contemporary Landscape Design Collection, Washington, pvt. collections; films The Art of the Real, USIA, 1968, Stephen Long, CBS-TV, 1968, Patricia Johanson: Cyrus Field, 1974, The City Project: Cleveland, 1977, A Conversation with Patricia Johanson, Heritage Cablevision, 1985, Patricia Johanson, Berks (Pa.) Community TV, 1990, Patricia Johanson: The Leonhardt Lagoon, 1992, Patricia Johanson: A Sense of Place, 1992, Patricia Johanson: Multilevel Designs, Aesthetic, Ecological, Functional, Cedar Arts Forum, Iowa, 1994, Q&A with Patricia Johanson, PBS, 1998, Chicken Scratch with Patricia Johanson, Petaluma, California Cmty. TV, 1999, Johanson interview The Environment Show Nat. Pub. Radio, 2000, Patricia Johanson: Zhang Jia Jie National Forest Park, Wulingyuan-TV, China, 2004; author: Art and Survival: Creative Solutions to Environmental Problems, 1992; co-author: (with Caffyn Kelley) Art and Survival: Patricia Johanson's Environmental Projects, 2005; works include park design, sculpture, ecol. landscapes, street furniture, pavement designs, site planning for Consol. Edison Co., Yale U., Columbus East H.S., Ind., House and Garden mag., Internat. Yr. of Child Commn., Fair Park Lagoon, Dallas, Corning Preserve, Albany, Cathedral Sq., Sacramento, Pelham Bay Pk., N.Y.C., Candlestick Pt. State Park, San Francisco, Omame Project, Brasilia, Brazil, Park for the Amazon Rainforest, Brazil, Nairobi River Park, Kenya, Ulsan Dragon Park, Ulsan, Korea, The Rocky Marciano Trail, Brockton, Mass., Millenium Park, Seoul, French Cultural Svcs. Garden, N.Y., South Ninth St. Corridor, Salina, Kans., Ellis Creek Water Recycling Facility and Tidal Wetlands Park, Petaluma, Calif., Pub. Art Master Plan, Rockland County, N.Y., 1990, Ecol. Master Plan Greater Boston Met. Region, 1994—, Sugarhouse Pedestrian Crossing, Salt Lake City, Stormwater Purification Garden, Duluth, Minn. Bd. dirs. New Arts Program, Pa., 1988—, Islands Inst. of Interdisciplinary Studies, 2005; bd. advisors Artists Representing Environ. Arts, Inc., N.Y.C., 1991—. Guggenheim fellow, 1970, 80, NEA fellow, 1975, Olesen fellow Bennington Coll., 1991; Adolph & Esther Gottlieb Found. grantee, 1998; recipient 1st prize Environ. Design Competition, Montclair State Coll., 1974, Internat. Womens Yr. award, 1976, Gold medal Acad. Italia delle Arti, Parma, 1979, Townsend Harris medal CCNY, 1994, Arts and Healing Network award, 2003, Gov.'s Quality Growth Grand Achievement award Envision Utah, 2004; named to Hunter Coll. Hall of Fame, 1987; named to Mepham H.S. Hall of Fame, 1998. Mem. Global Forum Arts Group. Home: 179 Nickmush Rd Buskirk NY 12028-3202 Personal E-mail: johansonsite@aol.com. *Let problems be your inspiration.*

JOHANSSON, ALICIA BARBARA, musician; b. Warsaw, May 21, 1941; d. Boleslaw Bielik and Halina Helena Napiorkowska; m. Evert Johansson, May 13, 1972 (div. 1978); m. Kjell Johansson, Jan. 2, 1980 (div. 1986); 1 child, Sandra; m. James McClung, Nov. 29, 1986 (div. 1995). BA in Piano Solo, Conservatory of Warsaw, 1961, MA in Musical Sci., 1968; cert. organist, U. Stockholm, 1984. Radio anchor Polish Radio and TV, Warsaw, 1959—63; piano accompanist Royal Opera, Stockholm, 1973—78, Cramer and Cullberg Ballet, Stockholm, 1974—80, Opera Ballet Sch., Stockholm, 1973—86, various concerts, Stockholm, 1978—86, Cleve. Ballet, 1986—90, Colo. Ballet, Denver, 1990—2000; organist various chs., Cleve. and Denver, 1987—; pvt. accompanist; tchr. piano and organ Denver, 1990—; organist, choir dir. Jefferson Ave. United Meth. Ch., Denver, 2003—. Performer: numerous organ and piano concerts; composer ch. music, 1973—. Organizer Royal Opera and Ballet Club, Stockholm, 1975—86. Mem.: Music Tchrs. Assn., Am. Guild Organists, Musicians Union. Democrat. Avocations: investing, hiking, travel, nature. Home and Studio: 7165 S Gaylord St E-6 Littleton CO 80122 Personal E-mail: AliciaJohansson@ricochet.com.

JOHANSSON, NILS A., information services executive; b. 1948; Grad., U. Uppsala, Sweden, 1972; MBA, U. Ill., 1975. With Am. Hosp. Supply Corp., 1973-81; group contr. Bell & Howell Co., Skokie, Ill., 1981-87, treas., 1987-88, treas., v.p., 1988-89, bd. dirs., 1990—, v.p. fin., CFO, 1989—, bd. dirs., 1990, sr. v.p. fin., CFO, 1992-94. Office: Bell & Howell 3400 W Pratt Ave Lincolnwood IL 60712

JOHANSSON, SCARLETT, actress; b. N.Y.C., Nov. 22, 1984; Student, The Lee Strasberg Theatre Inst., N.Y.C.; Grad., Profl. Children's School, 2002. Actor: (films) North, 1994, Just Cause, 1995, If Lucy Fell, 1996, Manny & Lo, 1996, Fall, 1997, Home Alone 3, 1997, The Horse Whisperer, 1998, My Brother the Pig, 1999, Ghost World, 2000 (award for best actress Toronto Film Critics Assn., 2001), The Man Who Wasn't There, 2001, An American Rhapsody, 2001, Eight Legged Freaks, 2002, Lost in Translation, 2003 (award for best actress Boston Soc. Film Critics, 2003, Upstream prize for best actress Venice Film Festival, 2003), Girl with a Pearl Earring, 2003, The Perfect Score, 2004, A Love Song for Bobby Long, 2004, A Good Woman, 2004, (voice only) The SpongeBob Squarepants Movie, 2004, In Good Company, 2004, Match Point, 2005, The Island, 2005; (TV series) Entourage, 2004. Office: Artists Mgmt Group 9465 Wilshire Blvd #519 Beverly Hills CA 90212-2604*

JOHN, CÉDRIC MICHAEL, geologist, researcher; b. Geneva, Sept. 10, 1974; s. Franz Michael John and Monique Hahni; m. Sidonie Wicky, Nov. 14, 2003. PhD, U. Potsdam, Germany, 2003. Geology diplomate U. Neuchâtel, Switzerland, 1999. Rschr. U. Calif., Santa Cruz, 2003—. Staff scientist Integrated Ocean Drilling Program, College Station, Tex., 2005—. Grantee, Land Baden-Württemberg, 1999-2002; Fond Margerith Würtrich et Mattey Dupraz grant, U. Neuchatel, 1997, Bourse pour jeunes chercheurs grant, Swiss NSF, 2004-2005. Mem.: Soc. for Sedimentary Geology, Am. Geophys. Union. Achievements include research in past climate changes.

JOHN, CHRISTOPHER CHARLES, former congressman; b. Crowley, Acadia Parish, La., Jan. 5, 1960; m. Payton Smith; children Hays, Harrison BA, La. State U., 1982. Aide to John N. John, Jr. La. Ho. of Reps., 1974—82, mem., 1988—96, U.S. Congress from 7th La. dist., 1997—2005, mem. energy and commerce com. Bd. aldermen City of Crawley, 1984—88. Democrat. Roman Catholic.

JOHN, SIR ELTON HERCULES (REGINALD KENNETH DWIGHT), musician; b. Pinner, Middlesex, Eng., Mar. 25, 1947; s. Stanley and Sheila Eileen (Farebrother) Dwight; m. Renate Blauel, Feb. 14, 1984 (div. Nov. 18, 1988). Student, Royal Acad. Music, London, 1959-64. Singer, songwriter, musician, began playing piano, 1951, joined group Bluesology, 1965, appeared (films) Tommy, 1975, Spice World, 1997, The Country Bears, 2002, appearances Live Aid, 1985, Freddie Mercury Tribute Concert, 1992, voice (films) The Road to El Dorado, 2000, toured America 10 times, 1970—76; composer: (broadway musical) Aida, 2000 (Tony award for Best Original Score); composer, performer Empty Sky, 1969, Elton John, 1970, Tumbleweed Connection, 11.17.70, Friends, Madman Across The Water, 1971, Honky Chateau, 1972, Don't Shoot Me I'm Only The Piano Player, Goodbye Yellow Brick Road, 1973, Caribou, Greatest Hits, 1974, Empty Sky, Captain Fantastic and the Brown Dirt Cowboy, Rock of the Westies, 1975, Here and There, Blue Moves, 1976, Greatest Hits Vol. II, 1977, A Single Man, 1978, Victim of Love, 1979, 21 at 33, 1980, Jump Up, 1982, Hearts, 1984, Ice on Fire, 1985, Leather Jackets, Your Songs, 1986, Live in Australia, 1987, Reg Strikes Back, 1988, Sleeping with the Past, The Thom Bell Sessions, 1989, To Be Continued, 1990, The One, 1992, Duets, 1993, Made in England, 1995, Love Songs, 1996, The Big Picture, 1997, Elaborate Lives: The Legend of Aida, 1998—99, The Road to El Dorado, 2000, composer, performer singles Lady Samantha, 1969, From Denver to L.A., Take Me to the Pilot/Your Song, Border Song, 1970, Friends, Levon, 1971, Tiny Dancer, Rocket Man, Honky Cat, Crocodile Rock, 1972, Daniel, Saturday Night's Alright for Fightin', Goodbye Yellow Brick Road, Step into Xmas, 1973, Bennie and the Jets, Don't Let the Sun Go Down on Me, The Bitch Is Back, Lucy in the Sky with Diamonds, 1974, Philadelphia Freedom, Someone Saved My Life Tonight, Island Girl, 1975, I Feel like a Bullet (In the Gun of Robert Ford), Don't Go Breaking My Heart, Sorry Seems to Be the Hardest Word, 1976, Bite Your Lip (Get Up and Dance), 1977, Ego, 1978, Mama Can't Buy You Love, Victim of Love, Part-Time Love, Johnny B Goode, Little Jeannie, Song for Guy, Are You Ready for Love, 1979, Song for Guy, 1979, Little Jeannie/Conquer the Sun, Don't Ya Wanna Play This Game No More?, 1980, Chloe, 1981, Empty Garden (Hey Hey Johnny), Blue Eyes, 1982, I'm Still Standing, Kiss the Bride, I Guess That's Why They Call It the Blues, 1983, Sad Songs (Say So Much), Who Wears These Shoes, 1984, Wrap Her Up, Nikita, Heartache All Over the World, 1986, Candle in the Wind, 1987, I Don't Wanna Go on with You Like That, Town of Plenty, Candle in the Wind (live), A Word in Spanish, 1988, Healing Hands, 1989, You Gotta Love Someone, Easier to Walk Away, Don't Let the Sun Go Down on Me, 1991, The One, 1992, Believe, Made in England, 1995; composer (singer): (album) The Muse, 1999, The Road to El Dorado, 2000, One Night Only: The Greatest Hist Live, 2000, Songs From the West Coast, 2001, Live at the Ritz, 2002, Peachtree Road, 2004; composer music (film) The Lion King, 1994 (Best Original Song Acad. award for Can You Feel the Love Tonight?). Established Elton John Aids Found., 1993—; Chmn. Watford Football Club, 1976—90, pres., 1990—. Named to Rock & Roll Hall of Fame, 1994; recipient Gold Discs for all albums composed, Best British Male Artist Brits award, 1991, Grammy award, 1981, Grammy Legend award, 2000, Kennedy Ctr. Honors, John F. Kennedy Ctr. Performing Arts, 2004. Achievements include played to over 2 million people across 4 continents, 1984, 86; first popular Western singer to perform in USSR, 1979; knighted February 24, 1998. Address: Twentyfirst Artists Ltd 1 Blythe Rd London W14 OH9 England

JOHN, GEER G., political science professor; b. Johnstown, Pa., Jan. 13, 1958; s. James H. and Jean A. Geer; children: Megan R. Geer, James D. Geer. PhD, Princeton U., 1986; BA, Franklin and Marshall U., 1980. Assoc. prof. Ariz. State U., 1986—95; prof. Vanderbilt U., Nashville, 1996—. Author: In Defense of Negativity, From Tea Leaves to Opinion Polls, Nominating Presidents, Public Opinion and Polling, Politicians and Party Politics; editor-in-chief: Jour. Politics, 2005—. Coach Lipscomb Green Hills Baseball League, Nashville, 1997—2002. Mem.: Phi Beta Kappa. Home: 5875 E Ashland Dr Nashville TN 37215 Office: Vanderbilt U Nashville TN 37235 Office Phone: 615-322-6222.

JOHN, HUGO HERMAN, natural resources educator; b. Natoma, Kans., Feb. 13, 1929; s. Lorenz Louis and Clara Marie (Doehrmann) J.; m. Prudence Patricia Shuck, Sept. 9, 1950; children: Patrick, Peter, Sarah. BS, U. Minn., 1959, MS, 1961, PhD, 1964. From asst. prof. to assoc. prof. Coll. Forestry U. Minn., St. Paul, 1964-69, prof., 1969-72; prof. Coll. Forestry, Wildlife and Range Scis., assoc. dean U. Idaho, Moscow, 1972-74; dean, prof. Sch. Natural Resources U. Vt., Burlington, 1974-83; dean Coll. Agriculture and Natural Resources, dir. Agrl. Expt. Sta. and Coop. Extension U. Conn., Storrs, 1983-87, prof. natural resources, 1987-94, prof. emeritus, 1994—. Forestry expert UN Food and Agr. Orgn., Puerto Cabezas, Nicaragua, 1965-66, Nat. Univ. Medellin, Colombia, 1969-71; cons. Taconic Found., N.Y.C., Internat. Paper Co., N.Y.C., 1981-84; sr. cons. UN Devel. Programme, Humane Soc. of U.S., 1993—; devel./planning cons. Internat. Exec. Svcs. Corps., Zimbabwe, 1996, Ukraine, 1998; Minn. conf. moderator UCC, 2002—. Contbr. articles to profl. jours. Mem., treas. bd. dirs. Smokey House Project, Danby, Vt., 1976—; bd. dirs. Merek Forest Found., Rupert, Vt., 1980-83, Ea. States Expn., West Springfield, Mass, 1989—, mem. Conn. trustees, 1984—, chmn., 1989-94. With U.S. Army, 1950-52. Mem. Soc. Am. Foresters (chmn. accreditation com. 1981-84), Am. Forestry Assn. Avocations: gardening, woodworking. Home: Box 732 501 4th Ave SE Mapleton MN 56065-9782 Personal E-mail: hugohoya@hickorytech.net.

JOHN, JASON CHRISTOPHER, artist, educator; b. Detroit, Mar. 5, 1980; s. Joseph Charles and Rose Leah John. AS, Luzerne County CC, Nanticoke, Pa., 2000; studied with Anthony Waichvus, 2000—02; BFA, Kutztown U., 2002; MFA, Indiana U. Pa., 2005. Salesman J and J Crewing, Wilkes-Barre, Pa., 1992—2002; asst. instr. Wyoming Valley Art League, Kingston, Pa., 2001—02; instr. color theory Indiana U. Pa., 2003—04, instr. drawing/painting, 2004—; tchr. Arin HS, Indiana, 2004. Recipient 3d pl., Artist's Mag., 2003. Mem.: Wyoming Valley Art League (3d pl. 2002), Student Art Assn., Phi Kappa Phi. Democrat. Avocations: weightlifting, snowboarding, skiing. Home: 44 W Broad St Nanticoke PA 18634

JOHN, MERTIS, JR., record company executive; b. Detroit, May 22, 1932; s. Mertis and Lillie G. (Robinson) J.; m. Essie M. Wincher, June 16, 1957; 1 child, Darryl E. AA, Wayne Coll., 1978; student, Marygrove Coll., 1999—2000. Songwriter, prodr. King Records, Cin. and N.Y.C., 1955-67; founder Mertis Music Co., Detroit, 1962—; founder, pres. Meda Records, 1980—. Corr. mem. Broadcast Music Inc. Speaking from the Heart, 1996; author: My Life and My Experiences in the Entertainment World, 1999, poetry; co-prodr.: Inside Music, 1977; songwriter: This Is Your Day, 1996 (presented to Rock and Roll Hall of Fame, 1996); songwriter, prodr., singer (the family group) The United Fice w/ Mable Haywood, Mildred and Little Willie John; composer: over 300 songs. With U.S. Army, 1952—54, Korea. Recipient Golden Poet award World of Poetry, 1989, 90; inducted into the Rock and Roll Hall of Fame, 1996. Mem. Detroit Soc. Musicians and Entertainers (chmn. bd. dirs. 1984—), Nat. Acad. Rec. Arts and Scis., Am. Fedn. Musicians, Masons (32d degree). Baptist. Fax: 313-862-5882. Office Phone: 313-862-5880.

JOHN, PETER C., lawyer; b. Albany, NY, Dec. 25, 1941; BA, Cornell Univ., 1963; JD, Villanova Univ., 1966. Bar: Ill. 1966, US Dist Ct. (no. dist. Ill.) 1969, US Ct. Appeals (5th, 7th cir.). Atty. Isham Lincoln & Beale, 1966—79; ptnr. Phelan Pope & John, 1979—94, Hedlund Hanley & John, 1994—2000; ptnr., comml. litigation, product liability practices Williams Montgomery & John Ltd., Chgo., 2000—. Mem. adv. council Nat. Judicial Coll.; mem. Ill. Supreme Ct. Com. on Jury Instructions, 1967—76. Contbr. articles to profl. jours. Served USMC, 1966—67, served to comdr. USNR, 1967—76. Named an Ill. Super Lawyer, Chgo. Mag., 2004. Fellow: Am. Coll. Trial Lawyers, Internat. Soc. Barristers; mem.: Internat. Acad. Trial Lawyers (pres. 2001—02), ABA, Am. Bd. Trial Advocates, Soc. Trial Lawyers, Ill. State Bar Assn., Chgo. Bar Assn. Office: Williams Montgomery & John Suite 2100 20 N Wacker Dr Chicago IL 60606 Office Phone: 312-443-3210. Office Fax: 312-630-8510. Business E-Mail: pcj@willmont.com.

JOHN, RICHARD C., enterprise development organization executive; b. Milw., Mar. 17, 1950; s. Richard C. and Mary W. (Widrig) J.; m. Carolyn H. Finn, June 2, 1973; children: Catherine M., Yuri G., Meredith C. BBA, U. Wis., 1972; MBA, Northwestern U., 1982. CPA. Supr. sr. acct. Price Waterhouse, N.Y.C., 1972-78; with Amoco Corp., Chgo., 1978-83; supr. fin. contr. Amoco Prodn. Co. Internat., Chgo., 1983-84; mgr. acctg. Amoco Oil Co., Chgo., 1984-85; staff dir. budgets Amoco Corp., Chgo., 1985-87; mgr. fin. & adminstrn. Amoco Chem. Co., Houston, 1987-89; contr. Amoco Performance Products, Atlanta, 1989-93; mgr. Amoco Corp., Chgo., 1993-96; v.p. fin. and adminstrn., CFO Opportunity Internat., Oak Brook, Ill., 1996—. Bd. dirs., treas. Opportunity Transformation Investments, Oak Brook, Opportunity Microcredit Fund, Oxford, Eng.; bd. dirs. Oportunidad Microfinanzas, Guadalajara, Mexico, 2003—. Bd. dirs., treas. Flagstaff Mission to the Navajos, 1996—; deacon 4th Presbyn. Ch., 1979-87; elder, treas. Clear Lake Presbyn. Ch., 1988-89; officer, mem. choir Johnson Ferry Bapt. Ch., 1990-93; missions com. small group leader Wheaton Bible Ch., 1994—, elder, 2003—, treas., 2004—. Mem. AICPA, Fin. Execs. Internat. Office: Opportunity Internat 2122 York Rd Oak Brook IL 60523-1930 Business E-Mail: rjohn@opportunity.org.

JOHN, RICHARD RODDA, transportation executive; b. Berlin, Mar. 31, 1929; came to U.S., 1938; s. Richard R. and Margaret G. (Howard) J.; m. Suzanne L. Heckman, June 7, 1958; children: Richard Rodda, Margaret Louise, Robert Edward. BS in Engring. Physics magna cum laude, Princeton U., 1951, MSME, 1952, MS in Aero. Engring., 1953, PhD in Aero. Engring., 1957. Dir. Aerophysics lab. AVCO Corp., Wilmington, Mass., 1958-70, chief mech. engring. div., 1971-76, dir. Office Energy and Environment, 1976-82, dep. dir., chief scientist, 1982-89; dir. John A. Volpe Nat. Transp. Systems Ctr., Cambridge, Mass., 1989—2004, sr. sci. and tech. advisor, 2004—. Mem. adv. com. on space power and electric propulsion, NASA, 1965-70, aero. engring. dept. adv. coun. Princeton U., 1972-78. Contbr. articles to profl. jours. Recipient Presdl. Meritorious Rank award, 1987 Pres. Reagan, Presdl. Disting. Rank award from Pres. Bus., 1990, from Pres. Clinton, 2000; Howard C. Phillips fellow Princeton U., 1952, Guggenheim fellow, 1953. Mem. AIAA (assoc., chmn. electric propulsion com. 1965-70); Soc. Automotive Engrs. (rsch. exec. bd. 1978-85), Phi Beta Kappa, Sigma Xi. Congregationalist. Avocations: gardening, golf, 20th century print collecting, classical music. Home: 19 Saddle Club Rd Lexington MA 02420-2102 Office: Dept Transp John A Volpe Nat Transp Systems Ctr 55 Broadway-Kendall Sq Cambridge MA 02142 Office Phone: 617-494-3333. Business E-Mail: john@volpe.dot.gov.

JOHN, RICKY, state official; b. Chaguanas, Trinidad, May 2, 1957; BSEE, N.J. Inst. Tech., 1981, MS in Mgmt., 1992; PhD in Engring. Mgmt., Kennedy-Western U., 2000. Space shuttle flight test engr. NASA, Kennedy Space Ctr., Fla., 1981-82; lectr. John Donaldson Tech. Inst., Trinidad, West Indies, 1982; systems engr. FAA, N.Y.C., 1983-84; adminstr. divsn. energy N.J. Bd. Pub. Utilities, Newark, 1985-96, tech. adviser, 1996—. Developer space shuttle tech. launch procedures, 1981. Judge and presenter of NASA award, North N.J. Regional Sci. Fair, 1993—; mem. edn. com. N.J. Martin Luther King, Jr. Commn., 1987-90; bd. dir. N.J. Inventor's Hall Fame. Named Energy Mgr. of Yr. N.J. Assn. Energy Engrs., 1994, N.J. Aviation Hall Fame; recipient Nat. Cert. of Recognition U.S. Dept. Energy, 1995. Mem. IEEE (sr.), N.J. Inst. Tech. Alumni Assn. (trustee 1991—, treas. 1994-96, v.p. pub. rels. 1996-98). Home: 350 Davis Ave Kearny NJ 07032-3558

JOHN, SELENA LATRICIA, systems analyst; b. Savannah, Ga., Feb. 18, 1972; d. Gloria W. John. B in Social Work, Savannah State Coll., 1995; MPA, Savannah State U., 1999. Med. social svcs. profl. Meml. Health U., Savannah, 1997-98; adolescent counselor Tidelands Cmty. Svc. Bd., Savannah, 1999; grad. intern. Chatham County Fin. Dept., Savannah, 1999; logistics acct. analyst Diamond Crystal Brands, Savannah, 1999—. Intern, vol. Boys and Girls Clubs of Am., Savannah, 1993-95; vol. ARC, 1998-99, campaign com. Mayor, Savannah, 1997; coord., organizer Voter Registration, Savannah, 1998-99; vol. Buckle-up Am., St. Joseph's Candler Hosp., Habitat for Humanity. Grad. Students scholar Ga. Regents Bd. Acad. Scholarship, 1998-99. Mem. NASW, Coalition Minority Pub. Adminstrs., Am. Soc. Pub. Adminstrs., Sigma Gamma Rho. Office: 3000 Tremont Rd Savannah GA 31405-1500 E-mail: slj1922@hotmail.com.

JOHN, SUSAN V., state representative; b. Nov. 20, 1957; BA, George Washington U.; JD, Syracuse U. Bar: N.Y. Assoc. Phillips, Lytle, Hitchcock, Huber and Blaine, 1983—; mem. N.Y. State Assembly, mem. jud. com., edn. com., also mem. energy com., librs. and edn. tech. com., chair labor com. Chair Legis. Commn. on Solid Waste Mgmt., 1995—97, Alcholism and Drug Abuse Com., 1997—99, Govtl. Ops. Com., 1999—2000; served on First Legis. Joint Budget Conf. Com. on Mental Health, 1998, Joint Budget Conf. Com. on Edn., 1999—2000. Chair Majority Steering Com.; serves on Judiciary, Edn., Energy, Libraries and Tech. and Social Svcs. Coms. Mem. Greater Rochester Assn. Women Attys. Office: 840 University Ave Rochester NY 14607 also: NY State Assembly LOB Rm 522 Albany NY 12248-0001 Business E-Mail: johns@assembly.state.ny.us.

JOHNA, SAMIR, surgeon; b. Baghdad, Iraq, Nov. 22, 1958; s. Denkha Johna and Doris Bercham; m. Layla Nano, Apr. 14, 1992; 1 child, Kristin Ishtar. M.B.Ch.B., Baghdad Coll. of Medicine, Iraq, 1983. Diplomate Am. Bd. Surgery ACS, 1999. Asst. prof. of surgery Loma Linda U. Sch. of Medicine, Loma Linda, Calif., 1999—; assoc. dir. for surg. residency program Loma Linda U. Med. Ctr., 2002—. Attending surgeon So. Calif. Permanente Med. Group, Fontana, Calif., 2002—; assoc. prof. surgery Loma Linda U., 2003. Contbr. articles to profl. jours. Fellow: ACS; mem.: Assyrian Med. Soc. (founder). Home: 1616 W Olive Ave Redlands CA 92373 Office: Southern California Permanente Medical 9961 Sierra Ave Fontana CA 92335 Personal E-mail: s.johna@verizon.net.

JOHNS, BEVERLEY ANNE HOLDEN, special education administrator; b. New Albany, Ind., Nov. 6, 1946; d. James Edward and Martha Edna (Scharf) Holden; m. Lonnie J. Johns, July 28, 1973. BS, Catherine Spalding Coll., 1968; MS, So. Ill. U., 1970; postgrad., Western Ill. U., 1973—74, postgrad., 1979—80, postgrad., 1982, U. Ill., 1984—85. Cert. adminstr., tchr. Ill. Demonstration tchr. So. Ill. U., Carbondale, 1970-72; instr. MacMurray Coll., Jacksonville, Ill., 1977—79, 1990—93, 2002—; intern Ill. State Bd. Edn., Springfield, 1981; program supr. Four Rivers Spl. Edn. Dist., Jacksonville, 1972—2003; learning and behavior cons., 2003—. Chair Ill. Spl. Edn.; conf. coord. Ill. Alliance, Champaign, 1982-94; lectr., cons. in field. Author: Report on Behavior Analysis in Education, 1972; author: (with V. Carr) Techniques for Managing Verbally and Physically Aggressive Students, 2002, Reduction of School Violence: Alternatives to Suspension, 2005; author: (with B. Johns, E. Crowley & E. Guetzloe) Effective Curriculum for Students with Behavioral Disorders, 2002; author: (with J. Keenan) Techniques for Managing a Safe School, 1997; author: (with E. Crowley) Students with Disabilities & General Education: A Desktop Reference for School Personnel, 2003; author: (with E. Paula Crowley) (book) Students with Disabilities and General Education: A Desktop Reference for School Personnel; editor: Position Papers of Ill. Council for Exceptional Children, 1981; contbr. articles to profl. jours.; author: Getting Behavioral Interventions Right, 2005. Bd. dirs. Jacksonville Area Assn. Retarded Citizens, v.p., 1993-94, sec. 1996-99; govt. rels. chair Internat. Coun. Exceptional Children, 1984-87; fed. liason Ill. Adminstrs. Spl. Edn., 1985-86. So. Ill. U. fellow, 1968; resolution honoring Beverly H. Johns Internat. Coun. for Exceptional Children Conv., 1982; recipient Recognition cert. Ill. Atty. Gen., 1985, Outstanding Leadership award Internat. Coun. Exceptional Children, 2000; named Jacksonville Woman of Yr., Bus. and Profl. Women, 1988, Unsung Hero Jacksonville Jour.-Courier, 1993. Mem. ASCD, Assn. Retarded Citizens (com. 1982-85), Ill. Coun. for Children with Behavioral Disorders (founder, past pres., pres. Ill. divsn. for learning disabilities 1991-92, Presdl. award 1985), Ill. Alliance for Exceptional Children (v.p. 1982-94), Learning Disabilities Assn. (bd. dirs., pres. 2000-03), Ill. Coun. Exceptional Children (past pres., chair govt. rels. com. 1982-95, 97-98, 2002—, governing bd. 1984-95, Presdl. award 1983, Lifetime Achievement award 1989, First Lady 1993), Internat. Coun. for Children with Behavioral Disorders (pres. 1997), West Ctrl. Assn. for Citizens with Learning Disabilities (founder, com. chair 1997), Internat. Pioneer Press (editor CEC pioneer divsn., pres. internat. pioneers divsn.), Internat. Divsn. Learning Disabilities (exec. bd.), Delta Kappa Gamma (chpt. pres. 1988-90, state exec. bd. 1991—), Phi Delta Kappa. Roman Catholic. Avocation: world travel. Home: PO Box 340 Jacksonville IL 62651-0340 Office Phone: 217-245-5781. Personal E-mail: bevjohns@juno.com.

JOHNS, CHRISTOPHER GEORGE, photojournalist, editor; b. Medford, Oreg., Apr. 15, 1951; s. George Arthur and Joanne Harriet (Utz) J.; m. Pamela Jean Formick, Sept. 11, 1976 (div.); m. Elizbeth Johns, 3 children. BS in Tech. Journalism, minor in Agriculture, Oreg. State U., 1974; M in Photojournalism, U. Minn. Sch. Journalism and Mass Communications, 1975. Staff photographer Albany (Oreg.) Democrat-Herald, 1973-74; teaching asst. U. Minn. Sch. Journalism, Mpls., 1974-75; staff photographer Topeka Capital-Jour., 1975-80, Seattle Times, 1980-84; freelance contract photojournalist Nat. Geog., 1985—95, staff photographer, 1995—2003, assoc. editor, 2003—05, editor-in-chief, 2005—. Photographer/author Valley of Life: Africa's Great Rift, Hawaii's Hidden Treasures, Our Inviting Eastern Parklands, Wild at Heart: Man and Beast in Southern Africa. Named Photographer of Yr., Region 7, Nat. Press Photography Assn., 1977, 1978, Photographer of Yr., Photographer of Yr. Competition, 1978, Nat. Newspaper Photographer of Yr., 1979; named one of world's 25 most important photographers, Am. Photo mag., 2003. Mem.: Nat. Press Photographers Assn., Sigma Delta Chi. Office: Nat Geographic 1145 17th St NW Washington DC 20036-4688*

JOHNS, DIANA, secondary school educator; BS, Mich. State U.; MS, U. Mich. Jr. high school tchr. Crestwood Dist. Schools, Dearborn Heights, Mich., sr. high sch. tchr., sci. dept. chair. Outstanding Earth-Sci. Tchr. award, 1992, Tchr. of the Year award Crestwood Sch. Dist., Scholarship award Crestwood High Sch. Chpt. NHS. Mem. Nat. Assn. Geology Tchrs., Mich. Earth Sci. Tchrs. Assn. Office: Crestwood Sr High Sch 1501 N Beech Daly Rd Dearborn Heights MI 48127-3403

JOHNS, JANET SUSAN, physician; b. Chgo., July 18, 1941; d. Nicholas C. and Doris Ann (Douglas) J.; m. Harlan R. Bullard; children: George, Sam. AB, Ind. U., 1963, MD, 1966. Diplomate Am. Acad. Family Practice. Intern Meml. Hosp., South Bend, Ind. Office: Purdue U Student Health 1826 Push West Lafayette IN 47905 Home: 22526 N Hermosillo Dr Sun City West AZ 85375-3045

JOHNS, JASPER, artist; b. Allendale, SC, May 15, 1930; s. Jasper and Jean (Riley) J. Student, U. S.C., 1947-48. One-man exhbns. include, Leo Castelli Gallery, N.Y.C., 1958, 60, 61, 63, 66, 68, 76, 81, 84, Minami Gallery, Tokyo, 1965, 75, Galerie Rive Droite, Paris, 1959, 61, Galleria D'Arte Del Naviglio, Milan, 1959, Ileana Sonnabend, Paris, 1963, Columbia Mus. Art (S.C.), 1960, Jewish Mus., N.Y.C., 1964, White-chapel Gallery, London, 1964, Pasadena Mus. (Calif.), 1965, Smithsonian Instn. Nat. Collection Fine Arts, 1966, Arts Council Gt. Britain, 1974-75, Whitney Mus. Am. Art, 1977, Kunsthalle, Cologne, 1978, Centre Pompidou, Paris, 1978, Hayward Gallery, London, 1978, Seibu Mus., Tokyo, 1978, San Francisco Mus. Modern Art, 1978, Kunstmuseum, Basel, 1979, Des Moines Art Ctr., 1983, St. Louis Art Mus., 1985, Mus. Modern Art, 1986, Kunsthalle, 1986, Wight Art Gallery UCLA, 1987, Galerie Daniel Templon, Paris, 1987, Mus. Contemporary Art, L.A., 1987, Venice Biennale, 1958, 64, 78, Phila. Mus. Art, 1988, Walker Art Ctr., Mpls., 1990, Mus. Fine Arts, Houston, 1990, Fine Arts Mus. San Francisco, 1990, Montreal Mus. Fine Arts, 1990, Nat. Gallery Art, Washington, 1990, Kunstmus. Basel, 1990, Hayward Gallery, London, 1990, St. Louis Art Mus., 1991, Ctr. for Fine Arts, Miami, 1991, Denver Art Mus., 1991, Brooke Alexander Edits., N.Y.C., 1991, Whitney Mus. Am. Art, N.Y.C., 1991, Harvard U. Art Mus., 1992, San Diego Mus. Art, 1992, Cana Art Gallery, Seoul, 1991, Gagosian Gallery, N.Y., 1992, Palaus de Luppe, La Fondation Vincent Van Gogh, Arles, France, 1992, Milw. Art Mus., 1992, Galeria Weber Alexander Cobo, Madrid, 1992, Nat. Acad. Design, N.Y.C., 1996, Phila. Mus. of Art, 1999, Art Inst. Chgo., 1999, others; represented in permanent collections Mus. Modern Art, Albright-Knox Art Gallery, Buffalo, Tate Gallery, London, Moderna Museet, Stockholm, Stedelijik Mus., Amsterdam, The Netherlands, Whitney Mus., N.Y.C., Kunstmuseum, Basel, Centre Pompidou, Art Inst. Chgo., Balt. Mus. Art, Cleve. Mus. Art, Kunsthaus Zurich, Mpls. Inst. Art, Nat. Gallery Art, San Francisco Mus. Modern Art, Va. Mus. Fine Arts, Richmond, Walker Art Ctr., others; illustrator (book) In Memory of My Feelings, 1967. With U.S. Army, 1949—51, Japan. Recipient 1st prize Print Biennale Ljubljana, Yugoslavia, prize IX Sao Paulo (Brazil) Biennale, Skowhegan medal for painting Skowhegan Sch. of Painting and Sculpture, Skowhegan medal for graphics, Mayors award of Honor for Arts and Culture City of N.Y., Wolf prize for painting, Wolf Found., Internat. prize Venice Biennale, 1988, Nat. Medal of Arts, The White House; named to S.C. Hall of Fame, 1989. Mem. Am. Acad. Arts and Letters (Gold medal for graphic art), Royal Acad. Arts, Nat. Inst. Arts and Letters, Am. Acad. Arts and Scis. Address: PO Box 642 Sharon CT 06069-0642*

JOHNS, JOHN D., insurance company executive, lawyer; BA, U. Ala.; MBA, JD, Harvard U. Ptnr. Cabaniss, Johnston, Gardner, Dumas & O'Neal; founding ptnr. Maynard Cooper & Gale; v.p., gen. counsel Sonat Inc., 1988—93; from exec. v.p., CFO to pres., CEO Protective Life Corp., Birmingham, Ala., 1993—2002, pres., 2002—, CEO, 2002—, chmn. bd. dirs. Office: Protective Life Corp 2801 Hwy 280 S Birmingham AL 35223*

JOHNS, JULYE MATTHEWS, lawyer; b. Biloxi, Keesler AFB, Miss., Sept. 16, 1974; d. Ralph Hagood Johns, Jr. and Sallie (Matthews) Johns. BA in Arts and Scis., U. S.C. Honors Coll., 1996; JD, Vanderbilt U. Sch. Law, 1999. Bar: Ga., U.S. Ct. Appeals (11th cir.), U.S. Dist. Ct., no. and middle dists., Ga. Assoc. Love, Willingham, Peters, Gilleland & Monyak, Atlanta, 1999—2002, Weinberg, Wheeler, Hudgins, Gunn & Dial, Atlanta, 2003—04, Huff, Powell & Bailey, Atlanta, 2004—. Guardian ad litem Atlanta Vol. Lawyers Found., 2000—. Mem. Jr. League Atlanta, 2002—. Recipient Algernon Sydney Sullivan award, The So. Soc., U. S.C., 1996, Best Brief award, Vanderbilt Intramural Moot Ct. Competition. Mem.: Def. Rsch. Inst., Lawyers Club Atlanta, Vanderbilt Moot Ct. Bd. (exec. assoc.), Mortar Bd., Moot Ct. Bd., Phi Eta Sigma, Gamma Beta Phi, Alpha Lambda Delta, Omicron Delta Kappa, Order of Omega, Phi Delta Phi. Episcopalian. Office: Huff Powell & Bailey 1355 Peachtree St Ste 2000 Atlanta GA 30309 Office Phone: 404-892-4022. Office Fax: 404-892-4033. Business E-Mail: jjohns@huffpowellbailey.com.

JOHNS, MARY E., law librarian; b. Davenport, Iowa, Apr. 27, 1953; d. Donald S. and Elizabeth C. Blackman; m. Christopher K. Johns, Aug. 25, 1973; 1 child, Eric Robert. AB, U. Calif., Berkeley, 1977; MLS, La. State U., 1982. Cataloger La. State U. Law Libr., Baton Rouge, 1982-84, head cataloging, 1984—87, 1989—2001, acting head tech. svcs., 1987-89, electronic info. svcs. libr., 2001—. Mem. Am. Assn. Law Librs. Home: 864 Albert Hart Dr Baton Rouge LA 70808-5807 Office: La State U Law Libr Baton Rouge LA 70803-1010 Office Phone: 225-578-6530. Business E-Mail: mary.johns@law.lsu.edu.

JOHNS, MICHAEL DOUGLAS, health facility administrator, retired government agency administrator; b. Allentown, Pa., Sept. 8, 1964; s. Glenn Franklin and Nancy Louise (Hummel) J.; m. Nicole Denise Miles, Sept. 30, 1995 (div. 1999); 1 child, Michael Douglas Jr. Student, Cambridge (Eng.) U., 1984; BBA in Econs., U. Miami, 1986. Editl. intern Nat. Journalism Ctr., Washington, 1983; Lyndon Baines Johnson intern Congressman Don Ritter, Washington, 1984; asst. editor Policy Rev. Mag., Washington, 1986-88; fgn. policy analyst The Heritage Found., Washington, 1988-91; spl. asst. to pres. Drew U., Madison, N.J., 1991-92; speechwriter to Pres. of U.S. The White House, Washington, 1992; speechwriter to U.S. Sec. Commerce U.S. Dept. Commerce, Washington, 1992-93; dir. rsch. Internat. Rep. Inst., Washington, 1993-94; mgr. corp. comm., sr. writer Eli Lilly and Co., Indpls., 1994-95; aide to U.S. Senator Olympia J. Snowe U.S. Senate, Washington, 1996-97; sr. assoc. S.R. Wojdak & Assocs., Phila., 1997-2000; v.p. Gentiva Health Svcs., Melville, NY, 2000—. Fgn. policy group advisor Dole for Pres., Inc., Washington, 1996; sr. advisor to global devel. projects Internat. Rep. Inst., Kuwait, Turkey, other nations, 1993-94; mgr. mktg., promotion and communication strategies cancer, cardiovasc., endocrine, infectious and ctrl. nervous sys. pharm. products Eli Lilly and Co., 1994-95; guest polit. and pub. policy analyst MacNeil/Lehrer News Hour, C-SPAN, CNBC, PBS Nightly Bus. Report, Fox Morning News, Voice of Am., BBC, others; sr. mgmt. and mgr. mktg., comms. and investor rels. for Fortune 1000 health svcs. co., 2000—; guest lectr. UN, Vassar Coll., U. N.C., Chapel Hill, others. Author: Seventy Years of Evil in the Soviet Union, 1988, U.S. and Africa Statistical Handbook, 1990, U.S. and Africa Statistical Handbook, 2d edit., 1991; co-author: Freedom in the World: The Annual Survey of Political Rights and Civil Liberties, 1993, Finding Our Roots, Facing Our Future: America in the 21st Century, 1997; contbg. editor: USSR Monitor newsletter, The Heritage Found., 1989—91; contbr. articles to Wall St. Jour., Christian Sci. Monitor, Nat. Rev., others. Active Luth. Ch. of the Holy Spirit, Emmaus, Pa Recipient Century III Leadership award, Shell Oil Co., 1981, Svc. award, Kiwanis, 1982, Cert. appreciation, Spl. Olympics, 1983, award of appreciation, Lao Vets Am., 1995, numerous citations, Congl. Record, U.S. Congress, Web awards of Long Island, 2001. Mem.: Washington Ind. Writers, Bush/Quayle Alumni Assn., Reagan Alumni Assn., Nat. Journalism Ctr. Alumni Coun., Am. Assn. Homecare (pub. affairs com.), Am. Med. Writing Assn., Pub. Rels. Soc. Am., Internat. Assn. Bus. Comminicators, Nat. Investor Rels. Inst., Assn. on Third World Affairs, Iron Arrow Honor Soc. of U. Miami, Lambda Chi Alpha (Internat. Hall of Fame 1996). Republican. Lutheran. Home: 219 Cabot Ct Deptford NJ 08096-5114 Office Phone: 856-853-8672. E-mail: mjohns8@aol.com.

JOHNS, MICHAEL MARIEB EDWARD, otolaryngologist, academic administrator; b. Detroit, Jan. 27, 1942; s. Trini Lou DelCampo; children: Christina, Michael. BS, Wayne State U., 1964, Grad. Biol. Sci., 1965; MD with distinction, U. Mich., 1969. Diplomate Am. Bd. Otolaryngology. Intern Univ. Hosp., Ann Arbor, Mich., 1968—70, resident in otolaryngology, 1971—75; resident in gen. surgery St. Joseph's Mercy Hosp., Ann Arbor, 1970—71; asst. prof. U. Va. Med. Ctr., Charlottesville, 1977—79, assoc. prof., 1979—82, prof., 1982—84, Johns Hopkins U. Sch. Medicine, Balt., 1984—96, dean med. faculty, v.p. medicine, 1990—96; exec. v.p. health affairs Emory U., Atlanta, 1996—. Co-chmn. Md. Sci. Week Blue Ribbon Panel, Balt., 1992—; chmn.-elect Coun. of Deans. Co-author: Head and Neck Cancer, 1990; contbr. articles to profl. jours.; editor: Archives of Otolaryngology; contbg. editor: Journal of American Medical Association. Grantee, Robert Wood Johnson Found., 1992, NIH, 1995. Mem.: Inst. of Medicine, Ctr. Club, Cosmos Club. Office: Emory U Robert W Woodruff Health Scis Ctr 1440 Clifton Rd NE Ste 400 Atlanta GA 30322-1053*

JOHNS, RICHARD JAMES, physician, educator; b. Pendleton, Oreg., Aug. 19, 1925; s. James Shanard and Pearl (McKenna) Johns; m. Carol Greacen Johnson; children: Richard Clark, Robert Shanard, James Ashmore. BS, U. Oreg., 1947; MD, Johns Hopkins U., 1948. Diplomate Am. Bd. Internal Medicine. Intern Johns Hopkins Hosp., Balt., 1948—49, asst. resident, 1951—53, fellow in medicine, 1953—55, resident, 1955—56, instr., 1955—57, physician, 1956—, asst. prof., 1957—61, assoc. prof., 1961—66, asst. dean admissions, 1962—66, prof. medicine, 1966—, dir. subdept. biomed. engrng., 1966—70, mem. adv. bd., prin. prof. staff Applied Physics Lab., 1967—, prof., dir. dept. biomed. engrng., 1970—91, disting. svc. prof., 1991—. Bd. dirs. Sparton Corp. Bd. visitors Sch. Engring., Duke U., 1986—; chmn. adv. com. Divsnl. Health Scis. and Tech., Harvard-MIT, 1987—92; mem. com. sci., engring. and pub. policy NAS, 1988—90; mem. sci. adv. com. GM, 1991—97; sec., vice chmn., chmn. med. bd. Myasthenia Gravis Found.; trustee Am. Bd. Clin. Engrng., pres., 1976—83; bd. dirs. Whitaker Found., 1991—94. Capt. M.C. U.S. Army, 1949—51. Fellow: Royal Soc. Medicine, Am. Inst. for Biol. and Med. Engrng. (founding), AAAS, ACP; mem.: Inst. Medicine-NAS (coun. 1987—90), IEEE (pres. group on engring. in medicine and biology 1970—72), Biomed. Engrng. Soc. (bd. dirs. 1972—75, pres. 1978—79), Assn. Am. Physicians, Am. Soc. Clin. Investigation, Am. Clin. and Climatol. Assn. (v.p. 1977—78, sec.-treas. 1979—85, pres. 1986—87), Sparton Corp. (dir. 2002—), Annapolis Yacht Club, Caduceus Club, Elkridge Club, Johns Hopkins Club (v.p. 1969—70), Peripatetic Club, Interurban Clin. Club (pres. 1980—81), Johns Hopkins Med. Soc. (pres. 1968—69), Tau Beta Pi, Nu Sigma Nu, Phi Kappa Psi, Alpha Omega Alpha, Sigma Xi. Home: 203 E Highfield Rd Baltimore MD 21218-1105 Office: Johns Hopkins U Sch Med 1830 E Monument St Ste 501 Baltimore MD 21287 E-mail: rjohns@jhmi.edu.

JOHNS, SARA KELLY, school librarian; b. Plattsburgh, N.Y., July 31, 1949; d. Richard Walter and Lita Vance Lynch Kelly; m. Frank Robert Johns, Aug. 18, 1991; m. Robert Frederick Brenizer, July 10, 1977 (dec. July 23, 1987); children: Anthony Francis, Robin Lynn Brenizer, Robert Douglas Brenizer, Tyler Jacob, Ryan Kelly Brenizer. BA in English, SUNY, Plattsburgh, 1971; MLS, SUNY, Albany, 1972. Cert. sch. libr. media specialist Bd. of Regents, N.Y. State, 1972. Seconday sch. libr. media specialist Beekmantown Mid./Sr. H.S., Plattsburgh, 1972—99; secondary libr. media specialist Lake Placid (N.Y.) Mid./Sr. H.S., 1999—. Adj. prof. for libr. rsch. methods Feinbrug Libr., SUNY, Plattsburgh, 1990—; cons. libr. media program evaluation, 2004—. Mem. capital campaign com. Saranac Lake Free Libr., NY, 2001—05, pres. bd. trustees, 1998—2002. Recipient Excellence in Librarianship, North Country Reference and Rsch. Libr. Resources, 1996; grantee, AASL and 3M® Corp., 2004. Mem.: ALA (councilor-at-large 2001—04), Nat. Bd. for Profl. Tchg. Standards Libr. Media Standards Writing Com. (mem. writing com. 1997—2001), N.Y. Online Virtual Libr., Regents Commn. Libr. Svc. for 21st Century (rep. building-level sch. libr. media specialists 1998—2000), AASL (mem. com. 1994—96, adv. ad hoc task force 1996—97, mentoring ad hoc task force 1996—97, chair leadership forum planning com. 2001—), N.Y. Libr. Assn. (bd. dirs., sch. libr. career awareness network sch. libr. media sect. 1985—90, pres. sch. libr. media sect. 1993—94, program dir., summer leadership retreats 1993—, chair ednl. leadership com. 1994, mem. com. co-chair 1994—96, sr. councilor-at- large 2003—05), No. Adirondack Libr. Assn. (charter mem., past pres. 1986), Delta Kappa Gamma (chpt. pres., co-pres.). Baptist. Avocations: travel, reading, needlecrafts. Home: 67 Canaras Ave Saranac Lake NY 12983 Office: Lake Placid Mid/Sr High Sch 34 School St Lake Placid NY 12946 Office Phone: 518-523-2474 4132. Office Fax: 518-523-4861. E-mail: sjohns@lakeplacidcsd.net.

JOHNS, WARREN LEROI, retired lawyer; b. Nevada, Iowa, June 9, 1929; s. Varner Jay and Ruby Charlene (Morrison) J.; m. Elaine C. Magnuson, July 24, 1955 (div. June 1983); children: Richard Warren, Lynn Cherie Johns-Pence; m. Ruth Page Scott, Sept. 29, 1985. BA, La Sierra U., 1950; MA, Andrews U., 1951; JD, U. So. Calif., 1958. Bar: Calif. 1959, U.S. Dist. Ct. (cen. dist.) Calif. 1959,U.S. Supreme Ct. 1963, Md. 1976, D.C. 1976, U.S. Dist. Ct. Md. 1976, U.S. Dist. Ct. D.C. 1976, U.S. Tax Ct. 1976, U.S. Ct. Appeals (4th cir.) 1976, U.S. Ct. Appeals (10th cir.) 1977, U.S. Ct. Customs and Patent Appeals 1979. Gen. counsel So. Calif. Conf. Seventh-day Adventists, Glendale, 1959-63, Pacific Union Conf. Seventh-day Adventists, Glendale and Sacramento, 1964-69; pvt. practice Sacramento, 1969-75; gen. counsel Gen. Conf. Seventh-day Adventists, Washington, 1975-92, trustee; pvt. practice Brookeville, Md., 1992-98; ret., 1998. Mem. adv. bd. Ctr. for Ch./State Studies, De Paul U. Coll. Chgo., 1987-93, spl. counsel to gen. conf., 1992-95; spl. counsel Adventist HealthCare Corp., Columbia Union Health-Care Corp., 1992-97. Author: Dateline Sunday USA, 1967, Ride to Glory, 1999; editor CreationDigest.com, 2001, Creation Equation Newsletter, 2002; founding editor JD, 1978-92. Chmn. bd. dirs., pres. Sacramento Area Econ. Opportunity Coun., 1974; co-founder CH. State Coun., 1963; founder CMT scholarship fund for H.S. srs., 2005. Recipient Frank Yost award Ch. State Coun., Glendale, Alumnus of Achievement award Andrews U., 1981, Alumnus of Yr. award La Sierra U., 1994. Mem. AAAS, ABA (vice-chmn. com. on torts, non-profit, charitable and religious orgns., sect. of tort and ins. practice 1990-91). Democrat. Avocations: sports, photography, book collecting. Personal E-mail: wj1929@dtccom.net.

JOHNS, WILLIAM DAVID, nuclear medicine physician, internist; b. Waterbury, Conn., 1955; BS, Brown U., Providence, RI; MS, Yale U., New Haven, Conn.; MD, U. Conn., Farmington, 1983. Diplomate Am. Bd. Nuclear Medicine, Am. Bd. Internal Medicine. Resident internal medicine Danbury Hosp., 1983-86; resident nuclear medicine Brigham Womens Hosp., Boston, 1986-88; nuclear medicine physician, internist Danbury Hosp., Conn., 1988—. Asst. clin. prof. U. Conn. Med. Sch. Mem. Am. Coll. Physicians, Soc. Nuclear Medicine, Am. Coll. Nuclear Physicians. Office: Danbury Hosp Nuclear Medicine 24 Hospital Ave Danbury CT 06810-6099

JOHNS, WILLIAM HOWARD, psychiatrist, neurologist; b. Hamilton, Ohio, Apr. 18, 1941; s. Howard William and Martha (Sleigh) J.; m. Catherine Marie O'Keefe, May 30, 1982; children: Howard William II, Stephanie Marie. AB, Princeton U., 1963; MS in Anatomy, U. Cin., 1968; DO, Kirksville (Mo.) Coll. Osteo. Medicine, 1973; ed. spl. student program, Topeka Inst. for Psychoanalysis, 1984-90. Instr. anatomy Kirksville Coll. Osteo. Medicine, 1967-73; intern Grandview Hosp., Dayton, 1973-74; resident in neurology Cleve. Clinic Hosp., 1974-77; asst. prof. neurology Ohio U. Coll. Osteo. Medicine, Athens, 1977-78; pvt. practice neurology Dayton, Ohio, 1978-82; resident psychiatry The Menninger Found., Topeka, Kans., 1982-85, psychiatrist, staff psyciatrist, 1985-96, asst. team leader, 1985-89, comprehensive out-patient evaluations, 1985-89; faculty mem. Karl Menninger Sch. Psychiatry, Topeka, 1990-95; pvt. practice psychiatry, 1995—. Dir. Psychotic Disorders Study Program, 1993-95, neuropsychiatry consultations, 1992-95; clin. asst. prof. neurology Wright State U. Sch. Medicine, Dayton, 1979-82, Ohio U. Coll. Osteo. Medicine, Athens, 1979-82, W.Va. Sch. Osteo. Medicine, Lewisburg, 1979-82; staff psychiatrist St. Francis Hosp. and Med. Ctr., Topeka, 1995—; med. dir. adult unit Parkview Hosp., Topeka, 1996, v.p. med. staff, 1996, pres., 1997-98. Recipient Outstanding Clin. Faculty award Dayton region Ohio U. Coll. Osteo. Medicine, 1982, Sydney M. Kanev Meml. award Am. Coll. Neuropsychiatrists, 1985, Outstanding Clun. Faculty award Dayton region Ohio Coll. Osteo. Medicine. Mem. Am. Acad. Neurology, Am. Neuropsychiatric Assn. Avocations: family, reading, sports, travel. Home: 517 SW Danbury Ln Topeka KS 66606-2229 Office: The Menninger Found 2709 SW 29th St Topeka KS 66614-2000

JOHNSEN, BARBARA PARRISH, writer, educator; b. Fort Madison, Iowa, Feb. 21, 1933; d. Lloyd Lynn and Genevieve Agnes (Peter) P.; m. James Cotten Johnsen (dec.); 1 child, Holly Ann. BA, Fla. So. Coll., 1959; MEd, Boston U., 1964. Cert. tchr., Calif. Account exec. Ledger Pub. Co., Lakeland, Fla., 1954-62; tchr., counselor Long Beach (Calif.) Unified Sch. Dist., 1965-74; owner Ednl. Counseling and Cons., Cazenovia, N.Y., 1990-2000. Mem. Madison County Coun. on Alcohol and Substance Abuse, 1986-92. Chair Madison County Cmty. Svcs. Bd., 1987-95; v.p. LWV N.Y. State, Albany, 1993-97. Avocations: writing, poetry, travel. Office Phone: 315-655-2947. E-mail: BarbJ.Johnsen@aol.com.

JOHNSEN, DAVID C., dean, dentistry educator; BS, U. Mich., 1965, DDS, 1970; MS in Pediat. Dentistry, U. Iowa, 1973. Diplomate Am. Bd. Pediat. Dentistry. Pediat. dentistry instr. U. Iowa, Iowa City, 1972-73, prof. pediat. dentistry, dean, 1995—; from asst. to assoc. prof. W.Va. U. Hosp., 1974-80, Case Western Res. U., Cleve., 1980-95, interim dean, 1993-95, dir. pediat. dentistry residency program, 1990-95. Contbr. articles to profl. jours. Mem. Head Start, World Vision, QualChoice Managed Health Care, Ctrs. for Disease Control, HHS Bur. Maternal and Child Health. Recipient numerous grants. Mem. Monongalia (Ohio) County Dental Soc., Iowa Pediat. Dentistry Alumni Assn., Am. Assn. for Dental Rsch., Am. Assn. Dental Schs., Am. Acad. Pediat. Dentistry, Am. Dental Education Assn. (past pres.). Office: U Iowa Coll Dentistry Rm 308 Iowa City IA 52242

JOHNSEN, EUGENE CARLYLE, mathematician, educator; b. Mpls., Jan. 27, 1932; s. Bernhardt Thorwald and Esther Elvira (Eklund) J.; m. Marjorie Marie Wacklin, Aug. 31, 1957. BChem, U. Minn., 1954; PhD, Ohio State U., 1961. NAS/NRC Rsch. Assoc. Nat. Bur. Stds., Washington, 1962-63; lectr. math. U. Calif., Santa Barbara, 1963-64, asst. prof., 1964-68, assoc. prof., 1968-74, prof., 1974-94, prof. emeritus, 1994—, dir. summer sessions, 1981-94, 94-97, cons. rschr., 1994—. Vis. lectr. in math. U. Mich., Ann Arbor, 1968-69; vis. scholar in sociology Harvard U., Cambridge, Mass., 1984-85; mathematician Sperry Rand, St. Paul, 1956, 57; instr. chem. and math. U.

Minn., 1956-57; instr. math. Ohio State U., Columbus, 1962; organizer and co-organizer of math. social sci. confs.; reviewer NSF. Contbr. numerous articles to profl. jours.; referee numerous profl. jours.; mem. editl. bd. Jour. Math. Sociology. Mem. Los Angeles County Mus. Art, 1985—, L.A. Music Ctr. Opera League, 1986—; mem. Santa Barbara C. of C./U. Calif. Santa Barbara Bus. Adv. Com., 1979-84. Grantee USAFOSR, NSF, Dept. Edn.; Fulbright travel award fellow U. Tübingen, 1969; fellow NSF, 1959. Mem. AAAS, Am. Math. Soc., Math. Assn. Am., Am. Statis. Assn., Soc. Indsl. and Applied Math., Internat. Network for Social Network Analysis, Am. Sociol. Assn. (acting chair, then chair math. sociology sect. 1995-97), U. Calif. Santa Barbara Faculty Club, Channel City Club, Am.-Scandinavian Found. (bd. dirs. Santa Barbara chpt. 2005—), Sons of Norway (pres. Ivar Aasen Lodge 1999-2001, 03—), Phi Beta Kappa, Sigma Xi, Phi Lambda Upsilon, Pi Mu Epsilon, Alpha Chi Sigma. Avocations: music, opera, tennis, travel. Home: 1603 Paterna Rd Santa Barbara CA 93103-1826 Office: U Calif Dept Math Santa Barbara CA 93106-3080 Business E-Mail: johnsen@math.ucsb.edu.

JOHNSEN, KAREN KENNEDY, marketing professional; b. Easton, Pa., June 28, 1939; d. Charles Edward and Gladys Swensen Kennedy; m. Henry Lehmann Johnsen, May 26, 1962; children: Erik Lehmann, Elisa Beth Johnsen Peters. BS in Bus. cum laude, Russell Sage Coll., Troy, N.Y., 1961; MS in Bus. Edn., SUNY, Albany, 1970. Cert. bus. tchr. N.Y., 1970. With account svc. divsn. McCann-Erickson, Inc., N.Y.C., 1961—62; exec. asst. pub. rels. Johnson & Johnson, New Brunswick, NJ, 1962—65; staff writer investment divsn. Glens Falls Ins. Co., NY, 1965—66; exec. sec. to pres., sec.-treas. Glens Falls Portland Cement Co., 1966—69; dir. devel. (funding and audience) Lake George Opera Festival, Glens Falls, 1970—73; publicity dir. fund raising campaign Glens Falls YMCA; freelance writer, adminstrn./media/mktg. cons., 1974—; exec. asst., media dir., staff writer Kimberly Comm., Inc., Chatham, NJ, 1974—82; sales mgr. Lifelines Gifts & Cards, N.Y.C., 1982—84; entrepreneur mktg., sales and mgmt. KJ Assocs., 1985—; ind. Mary Kay beauty cons., 1994—. Charter sec. pub. relations Scotch Plains Assn. Concerning Environment, 1999—; former bd. dirs. Plainfield Symphony Soc.; sec. Lake George Opera Guild, 1970—73, Edvard Grieg Soc., 1996—2000; charter sec. adv. bd. Project 2000, Norwegian Immigration Assn., 1996. Mem.: NAFE, AAUW (chpt. treas., comm. chmn.), Vesterheim Norwegian-Am. Mus., Am. Scandinavian Found., Scandinavian Am. Heritage Soc., Russell Sage Coll. Alumnae Assn. (class agt., alumnae admissions liaison 1995—, class reunion chair 2001, 2006), Vasa Order of Am. (past dist. sec., cultural leader, supr. children's clubs, N.J. dist., past sec., past chmn., cultural leader, supr. children's clubs local lodge), Order Ea. Star, Delta Pi Epsilon. Presbyterian. Avocations: skiing, singing, writing, folk-art painting. Home and Office: 109 Glenside Ave Scotch Plains NJ 07076 Office Phone: 908-928-9061. E-mail: kkjohnsen@comcast.net.

JOHNSEN, MELISSA C., information technology executive; BA in History, U. Calif., Davis, 1979. Paralegal, 1979—86; support rep. and network mgr. Barrister Info. Sys., 1986—88; MIS mgr. Streich Lang, 1988—91; mgr. microcomputer svcs. McKesson Corp./PCS, Inc., 1991—92; dir. computer networks Oreg. Health Scis. U. and Hosp., 1995; dir. presentation svcs. dept. Nationwide Ins. Enterprise, Columbus, Ohio, 1992—98; v.p. prodn. svcs. Starbucks Coffee Co., Seattle, 1998—2000; chief tech. officer Netstock Direct Corp., Bellevue, 2000; v.p. web hosting SBC Comm., Dublin, Ohio, 2000—02; CIO - Worldwide Targus Group Internat., Inc., Anaheim, Calif., 2002; v.p. info. sys. svc. delivery Express Scripts, Inc., St. Louis, 2002—. Adv. bd. re-entry workers Bates Tech. Coll., 1999—2000; adv. bd. diversity students Puget Sound Ctr. Tech. Inst., 1999—2000; spkr. at profl. confs. Author: (user Manual) SUMMATION, 1988. Vol. Mid-Ohio Food Bank, Columbus, Ohio, 1995—96, Windsor Acad., 1996—98; participant U. Wash. MBA Mentor Program, 1999—2000; mem. St. Louis Infrastructure Coun., 2004—; mem. tech. com. St. Louis United Way, 2004—; bd. mem. Cystic Fibrosis of St. Louis, 2005. Mem.: Women in Tech. Internat., Soc. Info. Mgmt. Address: 312 E Adams Ave Kirkwood MO 63122

JOHNSON, ABIGAIL PIERREPONT, investment company executive; b. Boston, Dec. 19, 1961; d. Edward C. Johnson; m. Christopher J. McKown; 2 children. BA in Art History, Hobart and William Smith Coll., 1984; MBA, Harvard U., 1988. Rsch. assoc. Booz, Allen and Hamilton; portfolio mgr. Fidelity Investments, Boston, 1988—, assoc. dir., 1994—, sr. v.p., 1998—, pres. Fidelity Mgmt. & Rsch., 2001—05, pres., Fidelity Employers Services, 2005—. Bd. dirs. FMR Corp. Recipient Most Powerful Women, Forbes mag., 2005. Office: Fidelity Investments 82 Devonshire St Boston MA 02109-3605*

JOHNSON, ADDIE COLLINS, secondary education educator, former dietitian; b. Evansville, Ind., Feb. 28; d. Stewart and Willa (Shamell) Collins; m. John Q. Johnson, Sept. 6, 1958 (dec. Aug. 1991); 1 child, Parker. BS, Howard U., 1956; MEd, Framingham State Coll., Mass., 1967. Registered dietitian, Mass. Dietitian Boston Lying-In Hosp., 1957-61; dietitian Diet Heart Study, Harvard U. Sch. Pub. Health, Boston, 1962-63; tchr. Foxboro (Mass.) Pub. Sch., 1968-2000; dietitian Sch. Medicine Boston U., 1975-77, Westinghouse Health Systems, Boston; faculty Dept. Nursing Boston State Coll., 1979-82; real estate sales assoc. Century 21, Sharon, Mass., 2001—. Nutrition cons. Head Start program Westinghouse Sch., Boston, 1979-82; instr. dept. nursing U. Mass., 1981-89, Bridgewater (Mass.) State Coll., 1982-97; mem. state adv. coun. Dept. Edn Bur. Nutrition Edn., 1981-83; participant NSF Project Seed, 1992; chmn. edn. com., bd. dirs. Consumer Credit Counseling Svcs. of Mass., Inc., 1996-99; scorer licensure tests Mass., 2000—. Bd. dirs. Norfolk-Bristol County Home Health Assn., Walpole, Mass., 1975-78; presenter Nat. Social Studies Assn., Boston, 1984-85; instr./trainer health svcs. edn. ARC, 1987-90. Nominated for Mass. Tchr. of Yr., 1999. Mem.: AAUW, NAACP (life), Consumer Credit Counseling Svc. (bd. chair edn. com. 1998—99), Mass. State Dept. Edn. (adv. bd. 1995—98), Soc. Nutrition Edn., Mass. Tchrs. Assn. (higher edn. com. 1984—87), Ea. Mass. Home Econs. Assn. (bd. dirs. 1978), Am. Home Econs. Assn., Am. Dietitic Assn., Delta Kappa Gamma (journalist Iota chpt. 1986—88, membership com. 1988—92, v.p. 1994, pres. Iota chpt. 1996—98, state world fellowship chairperson, Internat. Area Achievement award 2001). Avocations: travel, bicycling. Home: 92 Morse St Sharon MA 02067-2719 Office Phone: 781-784-6771. E-mail: johnsoa1@rcn.com.

JOHNSON, ALAN ARTHUR, physicist, educator, consultant; b. Beckenham, Eng., Aug. 18, 1930; came to U.S., 1962; s. Frederick W. and Dorothy (Tew) S.; m. Elizabeth Ann Banks, June 22, 1958 (div. Dec. 1981); children: Stephen Graham, Michael Andrew, David Nicholas, Brian Philip, Susan Christine; m. Barbara Davidson Pinkerton, Mar. 11, 1990. B.Sc. with spl. honours in Physics, Reading (Eng.) U., 1952; MA in Physics, U. Toronto, 1954; Ph. D. in Metal Physics, U. London, Eng.; diplomate, Imperial Coll., London, 1960. Sci. officer Royal Naval Sci. Service, Eng., 1954-56; lectr. metallurgy Imperial Coll. Sci. and Tech., U. London, 1960-62; dir. rsch. Materials Rsch. Corp., Orangeburg, N.Y., 1963-65; prof. phys. metallurgy Bklyn. Poly. Inst., 1965-71, head dept. phys. and engring., metallurgy, 1967-71; prof. materials sci., chmn. dept. Wash. State U., 1971-75; dean Grad. Sch. U. Louisville, 1975-76, prof. materials sci., 1975—2002. Cons. to govt. and industry, 1960—; pres. Metals Rsch., Inc., 1988—. Recipient Kentuckiana Metroversity award for innovative tchg., 1995, Disting. Citizen of Louisville, 1996, Cmty. Svc. award U. Louisville, 2001. Fellow AAAS, Inst. Materials, Inst. Physics, Am. Soc. for Metals (nat. nominating com. 1980-81, chmn. Louisville chpt. 1981-82, 89-90, 96-97, chmn. metals engring. inst. com. 1982-83); mem. Coun. Engring. Instns. (chartered engr.), Tau Beta Pi, Phi Kappa Phi. Office: Metals Rsch Inc 101 W Chestnut St Louisville KY 40202-0001 E-mail: barbalan@bellsouth.net.

JOHNSON, ALBERT WESLEY, retired political science professor; b. Insinger, Sask., Can., Oct. 18, 1923; s. Thomas William and Louise Lillian J.; m. Ruth Elinor Hardy, June 27, 1946; children: Andrew, Frances, Jane, Geoffrey. BA, U. Sask., 1942; MA, U. Toronto, Ont., Can., 1945; MPA (Littauer fellow), Harvard U., 1950, PhD (Littauer fellow), 1963; LLD (hon.), U. Regina, 1977, U. Sask., 1978, Mt. Allison U., 1982, Queen's U., 1992, Carleton U., 1999. Dep. provincial treas. Govt. of Sask., Regina, 1952-64; asst. dep. minister fin. Govt. of Can., Ottawa, Ont., 1964-68, econ. adviser to prime minister on constn., 1968-70, sec. treasury bd., 1970-73, dep. minister nat. welfare, 1973-75; pres. CBC, Ottawa, 1975-82; Skelton-Clark fellow Queens U., 1982-83; prof. polit. sci. U. Toronto, 1983-89; sr. fellow Can. Centre for Mgmt. Devel., Ottawa, 1989-91; prof. emeritus U. Toronto. Cons. on governance IMF, Indonesia, 1988, 91, South Africa, 1992-99; chmn. task force on univ. programs, Sask., 1992-93. Author: Dream No Little Dreams: A Biography of the Douglas Government of Saskatchewan, 1944-1961, 2004; contbr. articles to profl. publs.; editorial bd.: Can. Public Policy, 1974-75. Bd. dirs. Nat. Film Bd., 1970-82, U. Sask. Hosp., 1957-64; mem. Nat. Arts Centre, 1975-82; bd. govs. U. Sask., Saskatoon, 1952-63. Recipient Gold medal Profl. Inst. of Pub. Svc. of Can., 1975; decorated Companion of the Order of Can., 1997; A.W. Johnson Disting. Chair established Sask. Dept. Fin., 2000. Mem. Ottawa Polit. Economy Assn. (pres. 1969-70), Inst. Public Adminstrn. Can. (pres. 1962-63, Vanier medal 1976, nat. council 1951-69), Can. Polit. Sci. Assn. (exec. council 1963-64) Mem. United Ch. of Can. Home Fax: 613-225-3313.

JOHNSON, ALBERTA CLARK, psychology professor; b. Chattanooga, Apr. 19, 1942; d. William Ross and Helen W. Clark; m. John Burlin Johnson, Mar. 12, 1965; children: Sonya K., Roxanne Johnson Dingman. BA, U. N.C., Greensboro, 1964; MS, U. Ariz., 1979, PhD, 1988. Cert. family life educator, Nat. Coun. Family Rels. Membership dir. Tucson Area Coun. Camp Fire, 1981—83; asst. dir. Ext. Winter Sch., Tucson, 1984—87; human devel. specialist U. Ariz. Coop. Ext. Svc., Tucson, 1983—87; assoc. faculty Pima C.C., Tucson, 1987—88; family life specialist U. Ariz. Coop. Ext. Svc., 1989—92, U. Ark. Coop. Ext. Svc., Little Rock, 1989—92; cons. Little Rock, 1992—93; asst. prof. psychology and edn. Ga. Highlands Coll. (formerly Floyd Coll.), Rome, 1993—97, assoc. prof. psychology, 1997—2002, prof. psychology, 2002—, study abroad coord., 2003—05. Sec., governing state bd. dirs. Parents Anonymous of Ariz., Phoenix, 1983-84; mem. Gov.'s Coun. on Children, Youth and Families, Phoenix, 1983-84; pres. bd. dirs. Pima County chpt. Parents Anonymous, Tucson, 1985-86; v.p. Women's Info. Network, Inc., Rome, 1997-99; bd. dirs. Ga. Breast Cancer Coalition, 2000-03. Named Woman of Excellence, 1998, Women in Mgmt. and Greater Rome C. of C. Mem.: SEPA, APA, AAUP, Coun. Tchrs. of Undergrad. Psychology, Am. Psychol. Soc., Nat. Coun. on Family Rels., Pi Lambda Theta, Kappa Omicron Nu, Psi Beta (v.p., pres.-elect). Avocations: photography, hiking, reading, travel. Office: Ga Highland Coll 3175 Highway 27 N Rome GA 30162-1864 Business E-Mail: ajohnson@highlands.edu.

JOHNSON, ALEX MOORE, dean, law educator; b. Portland, Oreg., Oct. 5, 1953; s. Alex M. and Margaret Johnson; m. Karen J. Anderson. BA, Claremont U., 1975; JD, UCLA, 1978. Bar: Calif. 1978, U.S. Dist. Ct. (cen. and so. dists.) Calif. 1978. Atty. Latham & Watkins, L.A., 1978-80, 82-84; assoc. prof. law U. Minn., Mpls., 1980-82, William S. Pattee prof. law, dean, law sch. Mpls., 2002—; asst. prof. U. Va., Charlottesville, 1984—88, prof. law, 1989-93, Mary and Daniel Loughran prof. law, 1993—2002, vice provost for faculty, 1995—2002; chair Law Sch. Admissions Coun., 2001—03. Vis. prof. U. Tex., Austin, 1988-89, Stanford Law Sch., 1991. Contbr. articles to profl. jours. Mem. Law Sch. Admission Coun. (bd. trustees 1994, minority affairs com. 1989-94, chmn. 2001-2003), Assn. Am. Law Schs. (chair curriculum and rsch. com. 1993—), U. Va. Alumni Assn. (chmn. career counseling panel 1987—). Office: U Minn Sch Law Walter F Mondale Hall Rm 381 229-19th Ave S Minneapolis MN 55455 Office Phone: 612-625-4841. E-mail: alexjohn@umn.edu.

JOHNSON, ALLEN E., music educator; b. Columbia, SC, Jan. 3, 1955; s. Darrell E. and Lorena McDonald Johnson. MusB, U. SC, 1977. Grad. foreman Fred Gretsch Co., Ridgeland, SC, 1979; pvt. instrn. and music performer Coosawhatchie, SC, 1979—83; hist./organology lectr. pvt., Florence, SC, 1995—2005; music edn. Coker Coll., Hartsville, SC, 2000; store mgr. Parker Music Co., 1983—98; orch. tchr. Wilson H. Williams Mid., 2000—03; pvt. instrn. Florence, SC, 2005. Bd. mem. Florence Area Arts Coun., 1999—2000; cons. Florence Dist. 1 Schools, 1985—2005. Performer: Florence Symphony Orch., 1997—2005. Recipient Vol. of the Quarter, Southside Mid. Sch., 1990—91. Democrat. Home: 321 Warley St Florence SC 29501 Personal E-mail: eajokra@netzero.net.

JOHNSON, ALLEN HALBERT, surgeon; b. Atascadero, Calif., Jan. 23, 1922; s. Halbert Theodore and Julia Hallock (Kommers) J.; m. Mary Marchant McGee, Oct. 21, 1945 (dec. July 1983); children: Kathryn, Martha, Elizabeth, Kenneth; m. Darlyn Richardson, June 17, 1990. AB, U. Calif., Berkeley, 1943; MD, U. Calif., San Francisco, 1946. Diplomate Am. Bd. Surgery. Intern U. Calif., San Francisco, 1946-47, asst. resident, 1947-48, asst. resident surgery, 1950-54, chief resident, 1954-55; pvt. practice San Jose, Calif., 1955-91; clin. prof. surgery U. Cal., San Francisco, 1991—. Chief of staff Santa Clara (Calif.) Valley Med. Ctr., 1969-72, San Jose (Calif.) Hosp., 1980-82; clin. prof. surgery Stanford U., 1970—; instr. in field. Contbr. articles to profl. jours. Bd. dirs. Boys & Girls Clubs, San Jose, 1962—, YMCA, San Jose, 1964—, Vis. Nurses Assn., San Jose, 1964-70, ARC, San Jose, 1960-72. Capt. Med. Corps, U.S. Army, 1948-50. Mem. ACS (bd. govs. 1974-80), San Jose Surg. Soc. (pres. 1963-64), U. Calif. Med. Alumni Assn. (pres. 1981-82), Nafziger Surg. Soc. (pres. 1973-74), Pacific Coast Surg. Assn. (sec.-treas. 1980-86, pres. 1990-91), Calif. Acad. Medicine (pres. 1992), San Jose Country Club (bd. dirs. 1975-78), Gustine Gun Club. Republican. Avocations: music, photography, golf, duck hunting, camping. Home: 1655 Emory St San Jose CA 95126-1909

JOHNSON, ALLISON, corporate communications specialist, marketing executive; b. Pa. B.J, U. Fla. With Chem. Banking Corp., Wells Fargo Bank, Apple Computer Co.; dir. corp. comm. Netscape, IBM; v.p. global brand and comm. Hewlett-Packard Co., Palo Alto, Calif., sr. v.p. global brand and comm., 2001—05; v.p. global mktg. comm. Apple Computer Inc., Cupertino, Calif., 2005—. Office: Apple Computer Inc 1 Infinite Loop Cupertino CA 95014

JOHNSON, A(LYN) WILLIAM, chemistry professor, writer, researcher, consultant; b. Calgary, Alta, Can., Dec. 16, 1933; came to U.S., 1954, naturalized, 1981; s. Alyn C. and Irene (Johnston) J.; m. Joan Auger, July 26, 1956; children: Patricia, Nancy, Robert, Katherine. BS, U. Alta., 1954; PhD, Cornell U., 1957. Research fellow Mellon Inst., Pitts., 1957-60; asst., then asso. prof. chemistry U. N.D., 1960-65; asso. prof., chmn. dept. chemistry U. Sask. Regina, 1965-67; dean Grad. Sch., prof. chemistry U. N.D., Grand Forks, 1967-75, 77-88, dir. R & D, 1967-75, prof. chemistry, 1988-94, emeritus prof., 1995—. Vis. prof. U.S. Mil. Acad., West Point, N.Y., 1994-95, U. Mass., Amherst, 1989; dir. N.D. regional environ. assessment program N.D. Legis. Coun., Bismarck, 1975-77. Author: Ylid Chemistry, 1966, Ylides and Imines of Phosphorus, 1993, Invitation to Organic Chemistry, 1998, also over 50 articles to profl. jours. Fellow: AAAS, Chem. Inst. Can.; mem.: Am. Chem. Soc. (cons. C3S program), Rotary, Sigma Xi. Episcopalian. Home: 9 Tanyard Ln Bella Vista AR 72714-2450

JOHNSON, AMY LYNN, elementary school educator; b. Roanoke, Va., July 10, 1979; d. Ricky Lee and Sonya Allen Carter; m. Michael Bryan Johnson, Aug. 3, 2002. BS, Radford U., 2001; MS, U. Va., 2005. Lic. coll. tchr. Va. Tchr. Franklin County Pub. Schools, Rocky Mount, Va., 2001—. Tech. rep. Franklin County Pub. Schools, Rocky Mount, Va., 2002—. Named Tchr. of Yr., Henry Elem. Sch., 2005. Mem.: ASCD (corr.), Roanoke Valley Reading Assn. (corr.). Democrat. Baptist. Avocations: travel, shop. Home: 71 Roselawn Ln Boones Mill VA 24065 Office: Henry Elem Sch 200 Henry School Rd Henry VA 24102 Office Phone: 540-483-5676. Personal E-mail: amy.johnson@frco.k12.va.us.

JOHNSON, ANGELA, children's book author; b. Tuskegee, Ala., June 18, 1961; d. Arthur and Truzetta (Hall) J. Degree, Kent State U. Child develop. worker Vol. in Svc. to Am., 1981—82; freelance writer, 1989—. Author: Tell Me a Story, Mama, 1989 (Sch. Libr. Jour. Best Books list 1989), Do Like Kyla, 1990, When I Am Old with You, 1990 (Ezra Jack Keats award U.S. Bd. on Books for Young People 1990, Coretta Scott King Book award 1990), One of Three, 1991, The Leaving Morning, 1992, The Girl Who Wore Snakes, 1993, Julius, 1993, Toning the Sweep, 1993 (Young Adult Libr. Svcs. Assn. Best Book for young adults list 1994), Shoes Like Miss Alice's, 1994, Joshua By the Sea, 1994, Joshua's Night Whispers, 1994, Mama Bird, Baby Bird, 1994, Rain Feet, 1994, Heaven, 1998 (Coretta Scott King Author award 1998), Gone from Home, 2000, Looking for Red, 2002, The First Last Part, 2003 (Michael L. Printz Award 2004); (poetry) The Other Side: Shorter Poems, 1998 (Coretta Scott King award 1999). Child development worker, vol. Svc. to Am., Ravenna, Ohio, 1981-82. MacArthur fellowship, 2003. Mem.: MacArthur Found.

JOHNSON, ANNE HALE, educational association administrator, director; b. Rochester, N.Y., Oct. 12, 1923; d. Ezra Andrews and Josephine (Booth) Hale; m. Arthur William Johnson, July 20, 1957; children: Joy Sanborn, Randall, Christiane Brooks (dec.). BA, Smith Coll., 1945; MA, Columbia U., 1952; MDiv, Union Theol. Sem., N.Y.C., 1956. Exec. dir. Rochester Assn. for the UN, 1946-49; asst. to dir. World Fedn. UN Assns./Internat. Student Movement for UN, Paris, 1950-51; exec. dir. Citizens for Ike, Rochester, 1951-52; midwest field rep. U.S. Com. for UNICEF, Chgo., 1953; dir. Christian edn. Swarthmore (Pa.) Presbyn. Ch., 1956-57; tchr. and coord. adult edn. issues Georgetown Presbyn. Ch., Washington, 1957-72, 85—; tchr. Old and New Testament courses Madeira Sch., McLean, Va., 1961-62. Spkr. in fields of fgn. policy, religious activities, women's issues. Contbr. articles to newspapers. Mem. bd. Union Theol. Sem., 1990—, chair, 1996—; mem. bd. Madeira Sch., 1993-97, Faith and Politics Inst., Washington, 1992—, Presbyn. Women, Washington, 1992-96; v.p. bd. The Living Pulpit, Bronx, N.Y., 1991—; sec.-treas. Safe Travel Am., Potomac, Md., 1987—; founding bd. mem. Rep. Coalition for Choice, Washington, 1989—, bd., 2002—; mem. Montgomery County Rep. Ctr. Com., 1994-2002; mem. steering com. Covenant Network of Presbyns., 1998, mem. adv. com., 2002; mem. Planned Parenthood Found., 1998—. Republican. Presbyterian. Home: 10600 Red Barn Ln Potomac MD 20854-1953

JOHNSON, ANNE STUCKLY, retired lawyer; b. Axtell, Tex., Jan. 8, 1921; d. Arnold Joseph and Angeline (Morris) Stuckly; m. Edward James Johnson, Oct. 9, 1943 (dec. 1967); children: Edward M., Ronald J., Dennis L., Shawn T., Rozlynn Jan, Anne J'lynn, Kevin J, Karal Ian, Donna Lynn. BA, Baylor U., 1940; MA in Econs., St. Mary's U., 1974, JD, 1980. Bar: Tex. 1980. Claims clk. Social Security Adminstrn., Amarillo, Tex., 1940-42; asst. chief divsn. pers. Pantex Ordnance Plant, Amarillo, Tex., 1942-43; chief divsn. pers. Cactus Ordnance Works, Dumas, Tex., 1943-44; citations unit supr. Gen. Hdqrs. Far East Command, Tokyo, 1950-51; v.p., treas. Drive-Safe Corp., San Antonio, 1967-69; counseling psychologist ARC, San Antonio, 1968-69, Divsn. Pers. Office, Ft. Sam Houston, 1969, pers. mgmt. specialist, 1969-77; pvt. practice Oliver B. Chamberlin Offices, San Antonio, 1981-86, San Antonio, 1987-93; ret., 1994. Active Am. Heart Assn., 1983—. Mem. ABA, San Antonio Bar Assn., Tex. Bar Assn., Am. Trial Lawyers Assn., Assn. Social Econs., Tex. Trial Lawyers Assn., Phi Alpha Delta, Pi Gamma Mu, Omicron Delta Epsilon. Home: 3714 Hunters Point San Antonio TX 78230

JOHNSON, ANTHONY, automotive executive; Pres., CEO Onan Corp.; CEO Pentair Inc.; founder Hidden Creek Inustries, Mpls.; mng. ptnr. J2R Partners. Office: Tower Automotive 27175 Haggerty Rd Novi MI 48377-3626*

JOHNSON, ANTHONY O'LEARY (ANDY JOHNSON), meteorologist, consultant; b. Tampa, Fla., Apr. 19, 1957; s. Paul Bryan and Katie Hobbs (Nunez) J. BS in Meteorology, Fla. State U., 1979. Cert. cons. meteorologist, broadcast meteorologist. Courthouse runner Gregory, Cours, et. al., Tampa, 1977; water resources planner S.W. Fla. Water Mgmt. Dist., Brooksville, 1978; staff meteorologist Sta. WTVT-TV, Tampa, 1979-82, systems mgr., 1982-89, weather office mgr., 1989—. Meterol. cons. Gulf Coast Weather Svc.-Weather Vision, Tampa, 1979—; software devel. mgr. TTI Techs. Inc., Tampa, 1989-92; site coord. Space Sci. and Engring. Ctr. U. Wis., Madison, 1989—. Active capital improvements com. Plantation Homeowners Assn., Tampa, 1991; judge Hillsborough Regional Sci. Fair, Tampa, 1990, 91, 92, 96; fundraiser Dunedin Youth Guild, 1992, Northside Mental Health Hosp. Aux., 1993, 94, Children's Home, Pinellas Aux., 1993, 94, 95; vol. Sch. Enrichment Vols. in Edn. (SERVE), 1992. Mem. AAAS, Am. Meteorol Soc. (Seal of Approval for TV weathercasting 1982—, v.p. West Fla. chpt. 1984-85, pres. 1989-92, 94—), Internat. Platform Assn., Phi Beta Kappa, Pi Mu Epsilon, Chi Epsilon Pi. Republican. Achievements include development of quantitative predictive methods of energy delivery interruption in severe Florida freezes; research on temporal and spatial climatological anomalies on landfalling hurricanes in West Central Florida. Office: Sta WTVT-TV Weather Svc 3213 W Kennedy Blvd Tampa FL 33609-3006 Home: 3912 W Dale Ave Tampa FL 33609-4405 Office Phone: 813-870-9696. Personal E-mail: andyccm@aol.com.

JOHNSON, ANTONIA AXSON, food products executive; b. Sept. 6, 1943; d. Axel Axson and Antonia Johnson; m. P. Göran Ennerfelt; children: Alexandra Mörner, Caroline Mörner, Axel Mörner, Sophie Mörner. Student, Radcliffe Coll., 1963-64; MA in Psychology and Econs., U. Stockholm, 1971. With Nordstjernan AB, 1971—79, Axel Johnson AB, Stockholm, 1979—, chair, 1982—. Chmn. bd. Axel Johnson Inc., Stamford, Conn., City Mission of Stockholm; bd. dirs. The Axel and Margaret Axson Johnson's Found.; bd.dirs. NCC Nordic Constrn. Co.; bd. dirs. World Childhood Found.; mem. IVA-Royal Swedish Acad. Engring. Scis.; bd. dirs. Axfood AB, Nordstjernan AB, Axel Johnson Internat., Sweden. Named Profl. Woman of Yr., 1987, Fin. Woman of Yr., 1988; named # 1 of Am.'s Top 25 Women Bus. Owners, Nat. Found. for Women Bus. Owners and Working Woman, 1992, named # 4 of Am.'s Top 50 Women Bus. Owners, 1993, named one of most powerful women, Forbes mag., 2005. Office: Axel Johnson AB Villagatan 6 PO Box 26008 S-100 41 Stockholm Sweden also: Axel Johnson Inc 300 Atlantic St Stamford CT 06901-3522

JOHNSON, ARNOLD RAY, public relations executive; b. Baton Rouge, Sept. 15, 1955; came to U.S., 1954; s. Hillery and Sedonia (Celestine) J. BA, Xavier U., 1977. Chmn., CEO U.S.A. Pub. Rels., Baton Rouge, 1989—, Inter-Continental Transp., New Orleans, 1989—. Pres. Nat. Contractors, Inc., 2005—, Diamond "J" Ranch, Tex., United Internat. Found., Inc.; active internat. program on negotiation Harvard U., internat. forum Wharton Sch. Active Knights Peter Clare Cath. Orgn., UN Internat. Drug Program. Named Amb. of Goodwill; recipient Regional Businessman of Yr. Ernest & Young. Mem. Internat. Plimsoll Club, Internat. Club, World Trade Assn. (v.p.), Beta Rho Omega. Republican. Roman Catholic. Home: 6214 Plank Rd Baton Rouge LA 70805 Office: Inter-Continental Transport Inc 1 Canal St Ste 2500 New Orleans LA 70130-1152

JOHNSON, ARTHUR GILBERT, microbiology educator; b. Eveleth, Minn., Feb. 1, 1926; s. Arthur Gilbert and Selma (Niemi) J.; m. Mildred Louise Anderson, June 15, 1951; children: Susan, Sally, Gary, Peter. BA, U. Minn., 1950, M.Sc., 1951; PhD, U. Md., 1955. Biochemist Walter Reed Army Inst. Rsch., Washington, 1952-55; asst. prof. U. Mich., 1956-62, asso. prof., 1962-66, prof. microbiology, 1966-78; prof., head dept. med. microbiology/immunology U. Minn. Sch. Medicine, Duluth, 1978-99, prof. emeritus, 1999—. Mem. pre, postdoctoral and spl. fellowships study sect. NIH, 1968-70; mem. nat. adv. dental rsch. coun. NIH, 1972-75; mem. Nat. Bd. Med. Examiners, 1980-84; mem. bacteriology and mycology study sect. NIH, 1983-87, chmn., 1986-87; cons. microbiology. Editor Infection and Immunity, 1977-86. Served with US Merchant Marine, 1943-46. Mem. Am. Assn. Immunologists, Am. Soc. Microbiology, Infectious Diseases Soc. Am., Soc. Biol. Therapy, Immunocomprised Host Soc., Internat. Endotoxin Soc., Assn. Med. Sch. Microbiology and Immunology Chairs (pres. 1991-92). Achievements include research on immunology. Home: 209 Rockridge Cir Duluth MN 55804-1857 Office: U Minn Sch Medicine Dept Microbiology/Immunology Duluth MN 55812

JOHNSON, ARTHUR WILLIAM, JR., retired research scientist; b. Steubenville, Ohio, Jan. 8, 1949; s. Arthur William and Carol (Gilcrest) J. BMus, U. So. Calif., 1973. Lectr. Griffith Obs. and Planetarium, 1969-73; planetarium writer, lectr. Mt. San Antonio Coll. Planetarium, Walnut, Calif., 1970-73; dir. Fleischmann Planetarium U. Nev., Reno, 1973-2001; ret., 2001. Apptd. Nev. state coord. NSTA/NASA Space Sci. Student Involvement Program, 1994. Writer, prodr. films (with Donald G. Potter) Beautiful Nevada, 1978, Riches: The Story of Nevada Mining, 1984. Organist, choirmaster Trinity Episcopal Ch., Reno, 1980—; bd. dirs. Reno Chamber Orch. Assn., 1981-87, 1st v.p., 1984-85. Nev. Humanities Com., Inc. grantee, 1979-83. Mem. Am. Guild Organists (dean No. Nev. chpt. 1984-85, 96-99, 2002-05), Assn. Anglican Musicians, Internat. Planetarium Soc., Cinema 360 (treas. 1985-90, pres. 1990-98), Pacific Planetarium Assn. (pres. 1980), Lions (pres. Reno Host Club 1991-92), Large Format Cinema Assn. (v.p. 1996-99). Republican. Episcopalian. Office Phone: 775-322-9001. E-mail: arthurj@unr.edu.

JOHNSON, AUSTON GILBERT, III, auditor; m. Mary Bosworth; 3 children. BS, Utah State U., 1976. CPA, Utah. Auditor State of Utah, Salt Lake City, 1996—. Mem. acctg. adv. bd. U. Utah Sch. Acctg., 1993; mem. sch. accountancy adv. coun. Utah State U., 1994—. With USN, 1969-73. Mem. AICPA (Outstanding Discussion Leader 1993), Utah Assn. CPAs (vice-chmn. state and local govt. com. 1987-88). Office: Office Utah State Auditor Utah State Capitol Complex East Office Bldg Ste 310 Salt Lake City UT 84114-2310 E-mail: austonjohnson@utah.gov.

JOHNSON, BADRI NAHVI, social studies educator, real estate company officer; b. Tehran, Iran, Dec. 1, 1934; came to U.S., 1957; d. Ali Akbar and Monir Khazraii Nahvi; m. Floyd Milton Johnson, July 2, 1960; children: Rebecca, Nancy, Robert. BS, U. Minn., 1967, MA, 1969, PhD, 2001. Stenographer Curtis 1000, Inc., St. Paul, 1958-62; lab. instr. U. Minn., Mpls., 1966-69, teaching asst., 1969-72; chief exec. officer Real Estate Investment and Mgmt. Enterprise, St. Paul, 1969—; prof. emeritus sociology Anoka-Ramsey C.C., Coon Rapids, Minn., 1973—2003. Pub. speaker, bd. dirs., sponsor pub. radio KFAI, Mpls., 1989-93; established an endowed scholarship for women Anoka Ramsey C.C., 1991. Radio talk show host KCW, Brookline Parks, Minn., 1993. Organizer Iranian earthquake disaster relief, 1990; bd. dirs. dist. 7 Cmty. Coun., 1996-98. Recipient Earthquake Relief Orgn. citation Iranian Royal Household, 1968, Islamic Republic of Iran citation for organizing earthquake disaster relief, 1990. Mem.: NEA, Sociologists of Minn., Minn. Edn. Assn., Women's Leadership Forum, Nat. Social Scis. Assn., U. Minn. Alumni Assn. Avocations: world travel, classical and historical novels, exotic food, gardening. Home: 1726 Iowa Ave E Saint Paul MN 55106-1334 Office Phone: 651-771-8000. Business E-Mail: john1800@tc.umn.edu.

JOHNSON, BARBARA ANN, health services educator; b. Rochester, N.Y., July 3, 1953; d. Ray Clifford and Helen Frances (Lindgren) J.; m. William A. Perison, Feb. 28, 1986 (dec. 1998); 1 child, Alyssa Ann. BSEd, Worcester State COll., 1975; MA, U. Mass., 1977; PhD, U. Fla., 1982. Lic. speech-lang. pathologist, Tex., La., N.Y., Calif. Speech therapist Killingly Pub. Schs., Danielson, Conn., 1975-76; grad. tchg. asst. dept. comm. disorders U. Mass., Amherst, 1976-77; level II trainee VA Med. Ctr., Gainesville, Fla., 1977-78; grad. tchg. asst. Eng. Lang. Inst. U. Fla., Gainesville, 1978-79, grad. tchg. asst. speech dept., 1980-81; pvt. practice speech-lang. pathologist North Ctrl. Fla., 1980-81; asst. prof. speech sci., pathology and audiology dept. St. Cloud (Minn.) State U., 1983-84; dir. speech-lang. pathologist South County Speech-Hearing-Learning Ctr., Gilroy, Calif., 1984-85; vis. asst. prof. speech dept. Nat. Inst. for Deaf Rochester (N.Y.) Inst. Tech., 1985-90; asst. prof. speech dept. La. Tech. U., Ruston, 1990-92; assoc. prof., chair/dir. dept. comm. disorders U. Tex.-Pan Am., Edinburg, 1992-96, interim dean, assoc. prof. Coll. Health Scis. & Human Svcs., 1996-98, prof., chair dept. comm. disorders, 1998-99; prof., chair dept. speech pathology and audiology Ithaca (N.Y.) Coll., 2000—04, prof. speech lang. pathology, 2000—. Presenter, mentor in field. Author: Language Disorders in Children: An Introductory Clinical Perspective, 1996; contbr. articles to profl. publs. Grantee Crippled Children's Soc. Santa Clara County, 1985, U.S. Dept. Edn., 1993, 94, U. Tex.-Pan Am., 1994, Pro-Tec Equipment, 1995, Health Career Opportunity Program, 19965. Mem. Am. Speech-Lang.-Hearing Assn. (cert. clin. competence, Svc. Recognition award 1993, mem. profl. svcs. bd. 1991-93, multi-site com. 1991-93), Tex. Speech-Lang.-Hearing Assn., Coll. Health Deans, Tex. Soc. Allied Health Professions, Coun. Grad. Programs in Comm. Scis. and Disorders, Coun. Suprs. in Speech-Lang. Pathology and Audiology (pres. 1997), Kappa Delta Pi. Office Phone: 607-274-3165. Business E-Mail: bjohnson@ithaca.edu.

JOHNSON, BARBARA ELIZABETH, lawyer; b. Des Moines, Aug. 2, 1957; d. William Frederick and Dorothy Jane (Colvin) Spotz; m. Richard Gordon Johnson, Mar. 4, 1984. BS, Grove City (Pa.) Coll., 1979; JD, Coll. of William and Mary, 1984. Bar: Pa. 1984, U.S. Dist. Ct. (we. dist.) Pa. 1984, U.S. Ct. Appeals (3d and Fed. cirs.) 1984. Patent agt. NASA-Langley Rsch. Ctr., Hampton, Va., 1982-84; assoc. atty. The Webb Law Firm, Pitts., 1984-92, shareholder, dir., 1992—. Mng. dir. The Webb Law Firm, 2001-04; bd. dirs. Precision Staffing Svcs., Inc., Metro Family Practice. Recipient Alumni Achievement award, Grove City Coll., 2004. Mem.: Pitts. Intellectual Property Law Assn. (pres. 2000—01), Am. Chem. Soc. (chmn. Pitts. sect. 1995), Pitts. Chemists Club. Republican. Avocations: piano, writing, figure skating, auto repairing. E-mail: bjohnson@webblaw.com.

JOHNSON, BARBARA JEAN, retired judge, lawyer; b. Detroit, Apr. 9, 1932; d. Clifford Clarence and Orma Cecile (Boring) Barnhouse; m. Ronald Mayo Johnson, June 24, 1965; 1 child, Belinda Etezad. BS, U. So. Calif., 1953, JD, 1970. Bar: Calif. 1971. Ptnr. Angela, Burford, Johnson & Tookay, Pasadena, Calif., 1970-77; judge L.A. Mcpl. Ct., 1977-81, L.A. Superior Ct., 1981-97; ret., 1997. Lectr. U. So. Calif. Law Sch. profl. program; adj. prof. Southwestern U. Law Sch. Recipient Ernestine Stahlhut award, 1981. Mem. Calif. Judges Assn., 1977-98, Nat. Assn. Women Judges, 1980-98, Calif. Women Lawyers Assn. (pres. 1976-77), Women Lawyers Assn. LA (pres. 1975-76), Christian Legal Soc. Home: 1000 Prospect Blvd Pasadena CA 91103-2810

JOHNSON, BARBARA PIASECKA, philanthropist, art historian and collector, business investor; b. Staniewicze, Poland; d. Pelagia and Wojciech Piasecki; m. J. Seward Johnson 1971 (dec.1983). Grad., U. Wroclaw. Chair., dir. trustee Barbara Piasecka Johnson Found., 1974—. Owner extensive art collection, Barbara Piasecka Johnson Collection; mem. bd. mgrs. Wistar Inst., Phila., 1989-91; mem. chmn.'s coun. Met. Mus. Art, N.Y.C., 1986; mem. adv. com. Nat. Gallery Art, Washington, 1980-91; bd. dirs. Inst. for Polish-Jewish Studies, Oxford, Eng.; mem. fine arts com. U.S. Dept. State, 1978-85; mem. strategic adv. com. dept. molecular genetics and microbiology Robert Wood Johnson Med. Sch., U. Medicine and Dentistry N.J. Trustee, bd. dirs. Atlantic Found., 1972-85, Harbor Br. Found., 1972-85; trustee, chair Paderewski Ctr.; mem. coun. Found. for U. Wroclaw, 1991-92. Recipient Heritage award Polish Am. Congress, 1989, Nat. Citizen of Yr. award Am-Pol Eagle, 1989, Disting. Svc. award Am. Coun. for Polish Culture, 1990, Award St. Brother Albert Chmielowski, 1990, Hon. Citizen award State of Calif., 1990, Appreciation diploma Min. Fgn. Affairs Republic Poland, 1991, Gold medal U. Wroclaw, 1991, Sci. Devel. award Acad. Agriculture Wroclaw, 1991, Crystal Heart award Found. for Devel. Cardiac Surgery Zabrze, 1992, Merit cert. Pres. Coun. N.Y.C., 1993, Champion of Democracy award Coll. Democracy Washington, 1993, Waclaw Nizynski medal Polish Artists Agy, 1994, Living Legacy award Women's Internat. Ctr., 1994, The Order of Saint Charles Officer decoration conferred by H.S.H. Prince Rainier III in recognition of svcs. rendered to the Principality of Monaco, 1995. Mem. Am. Assn. for Polish-Jewish Studies (hon. chmn.), Rotary Internat. (Paul Harris fellow 1988). Office: BPJ Holding Corp 4519 Province Line Rd Princeton NJ 08540-2211*

JOHNSON, BENJAMIN F., VI, economist, consultant; b. Kingston, NY, Sept. 17, 1952; s. Benjamin F. and Alice (Terry) J. BA in Econs., U. South Fla., 1974; MS in Econs., Fla. State U., 1977, PhD in Econs., 1982. Sr. utility analyst Office of Pub. Counsel, State of Fla., 1974-77; pres., cons. economist Ben Johnson Assocs., Inc., Tallahassee, Fla., 1977—. Contbr. articles to N.Y. Times, Pub. Utilities Fortnightly, profl. jours. Mem. Am. Econ. Assn. Office: 2252 Killearn Center Blvd Tallahassee FL 32309-3573 Office Phone: 850-893-8600.

JOHNSON, BERNETTE JOSHUA, state supreme court justice; b. Ascension Parish, La. d. Frank Joshua Jr. and Olivia W. Johnson. BA, Spelman Coll., Atlanta, 1964; JD, La. State U., 1969; LLD (hon.), Spelman Coll., 2001. Bar: La. Law intern Civil Rights divsn. U.S. Dept. Justice; judge La. Civil Dist. Ct., 1984-94, chief judge, 1994; assoc. justice La. Supreme Ct., New Orleans, 1994—. Legal svc. atty. New Orleans Legal Assistance Corp.; community organizer NAACP Legal Defense & Educational Fund, NYC; chair New Orleans Chapter So. Christian Leadership Conference. Bd. dirs. YMCA, New Orleans; chmn. bd. Learning Ctr., Greater St. Stephen Full Gospel Bapt. Ch.; bd. dirs. NOLAC, 1992-99. Named Woman of Yr., LaBelle chpt. Am. Bus. Women's Assn., 1994; Named one of Outstanding Women on Bench New Orleans Assn. Black Women Attorneys; recipient Ernest N. Morial award NOLAC, Daniel Byrd award NAACP, A.P. Tureaud Citizenship award NAACP, Margaret A. Brent Women Lawyers of Achievement award ABA. Office: La Supreme Ct 400 Royal St New Orleans LA 70130*

JOHNSON, BETSEY LEE, fashion designer; b. Hartford, Conn., Aug. 10, 1942; d. John Herman and Lena Virginia J.; m. John Cale, Apr. 4, 1966; 1 child, Lulu; m. Jeffrey Olivier, Feb. 7, 1981. Student, Pratt Inst., N.Y.C., 1960-61; BA, U. Syracuse, 1964. Editorial asst. Mademoiselle mag., 1964-65; prin. designer Paraphernalia (owned by Puritan Fashions, Inc.), 1965—69; ptnr., co-owner Betsey, Bunky & Nini, N.Y.C., 1969; designer Alvin Duskin Co., San Francisco, 1970; head designer Alley Cat by Betsey Johnson (div. LeDamor, Inc.), 1970—74; freelance designer jr. women's div. Butterick Pattern Co., 1971—75; designer Betsey Johnson's Kids Children Wear, Shutterbug, Inc., 1974—77, Jeanette Maternities, Inc., 1974-75, 1974—75; designer first line womens clothing Gant Shirtmakers, Inc., 1974—75; designer Tric-Trac by Betsey Johnson, Womens Knitwear, 1974—76; head designer jr. sportswear Star Ferry by Betsey Johnson and Michael Milea, 1975—77; owner, head designer B.J., Inc., N.Y.C., 1978—; owner retail stores N.Y.C., L.A., San Francisco, Coconut Grove, Fla., Venice, Calif., Boston, Chgo., Seattle, London, Eng., Vancouver, B.C. Hon. chair. Fashion Targets Breast Cancer initiative, CFDA, 2004. Named to Fashion Walk of Fame, 2002; recipient Coty award, 1972, Timeless Talent award, CFDA, 1999. Mem. Coun. Fashion Designers Am., Women's Forum. Office: Betsey Johnson Co 251 E 60th St New York NY 10022

JOHNSON, BOINE THEODORE, manufacturing executive, mayor; b. N.Y.C., Dec. 17, 1931; s. Boine Theodore and Emma (Hall) J.; children: Boine Theodore III, Marc Ian, Jordan James, Jann Louise; m. Kathleen Piaggesi, July 11, 1992. BA cum laude, Williams Coll., 1953; MBA with high distinction (Baker scholar), Harvard, 1958. Instr. Harvard Bus. Sch., Cambridge, Mass., 1958—59; asst. to dir. corporate planning AMF Corp., N.Y.C., 1959—62; mgr. mgmt. cons. div. Commonwealth Services Inc., N.Y.C., 1962—66; mgr. corporate planning Gen. Electric Co., 1966—68; sr. v.p. corporate devel., gen. mgr. chem. div. Technicon Corp., Tarrytown, NY, 1968—79; v.p. Perkin Elmer Corp., Norwalk, Conn., 1979—81; v.p., gen. mgr. Capintec, Inc., Montvale, NJ, 1981—82; pres. Voland Corp., Hawthorne, NY, 1982—88; chmn. bd. Texture Techs. Corp., Scarsdale, NY, 1988—. Dir. Datamedic, Inc., Peoples Bank for Savs. of New Rochelle, Meditron, Inc. Trustee, mayor Village of Scarsdale, N.Y., 1971-77; bd. dirs., vice chmn. Westchester County Assn. Served to lt., C.E. USNR, 1953-56. Mem. Sci. Apparatus Makers Assn., Theta Delta Chi (trustee edn. found. 1968-72, pres. Founders' Corp. 1966-87, pres. grand lodge 1969-71), Williams Club, Amateur Comedy Club (N.Y.C.), Town Club (Scarsdale), St. Botolph Club (Boston). Republican. Presbyterian. Home and Office: 18 Fairview Rd Scarsdale NY 10583-2136

JOHNSON, BRAD, professional football player; b. Marietta, Ga., Sept. 13, 1968; m. Nikkie Johnson. Postgrad in phys. edn., Fla. State Univ. Quarterback Tampa Bay Buccaneers, 2001—04, Wash. Redskins, 1999—2000, Minn. Vikings, 1992—98, 2005—. Involved Muscular Dystrophy Assn., Children's Miracle Net., Children's Hosp., Toys for Tots. Achievements include mem. Super Bowl XXXVII Champion Tampa Bay Buccaneers, 2002. Office: 9520 Vikings Dr Eden Prairie MN 55344

JOHNSON, BRAD, state official; b. Lake Forest, Ill., Mar. 6, 1952; s. Kenneth A. and Claire Rabe Johnson; m. Lisa Storey. Dist. rep. to Congressman Ron Marlenee, 1983—84; mgr. Gallatin County Fairgrounds, 1985—89; sec. state State of Mont., Helena, 2005—. Co-chmn. Young Voters for the Pres. (Nixon), Ill., 1972; volunteer John Connally for Pres, Tex., 1980. Mem.: Mont. Rep. Party (exec. bd. 1984—89, 2003—). Republican. Office: Office of Sec of State State Capitol Rm 260 PO Box 202801 Helena MT 59620-2801

JOHNSON, BRIAN DOUGLAS, physician, school system administrator; b. Detroit, Jan. 29, 1960; s. Claude and Irene Johnson; m. Donna Annette Dresher, July 21, 1984; children: Garrett, Joel. BA, Youngstown State U., 1982; MD, Ohio State U., 1986. Physician Ctrl. Okla. Med. Group, Oklahoma City, 1994—2001; aerospace medicine physician FAA, Oklahoma City, 2001—. V.p., pres. adv. bd. S.W. Christian Acad., Moore, Okla., 1999—. Capt. USAF, 1986—89. Fellow: Am. Acad. Family Physicians. Republican. Lutheran. Avocations: baseball, sports, painting, reading. Office: FAA CAMI AAM 310 Rm B36 6700 S MacArthur Blvd Oklahoma City OK 73169

JOHNSON, BRIAN KEITH, electrical engineering educator; b. Madison, Wis., Mar. 11, 1965; s. Alton Cornelius and Virginia Rae (Korener) Johnson; m. Elizabeth M. Williams, Jan. 3, 1998; children: Erica Pearl, Mark Macrae, Cora Mane. BS, U. Wis., 1987, MS, 1989, PhD, 1992. Registered profl. engr., Wis., Idaho. Teaching asst. U. Wis., Madison, 1988, rsch. asst., 1988-92; engr. Lawrence Livermore Nat. Labs., Livermore, Calif., 1989; asst. prof. U. Idaho, Moscow, 1992-97, assoc. prof., 1997—2004, prof., 2004—. Instr. Coll. Engring. Tchg. Asst. Tng., U. Wis., Madison, 1988, Engring. profl. devel., 1992-98; co-advisor Iron Cross Leadership Soc., Madison, 1988-92, U. Idaho IEEE Student Chpt., 1995—; dir. Western Virtual Engring., 1996-99. Lodge chief Order of the Arrow, Boy Scouts Am., 1982-84, dir. Brownsea Double 2Course, Madison, 1987, advisor, 1990-92. Recipient Vigil Hon. Membership, Order of the Arrow, Boy Scouts Am., 1988, Leadership award, Exploring Boy Scouts Am., 1986, Outstanding Young Faculty award U. Idaho Coll. Engring., 1995. Mem. IEEE (chair working group on utility applications of supercondrs. 1999—, sec. working group on modeling and simulation of distributed resources, 2001—, mem. AdCom intelligent transp. systems coun., ITS coun.), Am. Soc. Engring. Edn., Internat. Coun. on Large Electric Sys. Roman Catholic. Avocations: cross country skiing, bicycling, backpacking. Office: U Idaho Dept Elec Engring Moscow ID 83844-0001 E-mail: b.h.johnson@ieee.org, bjohnson@eskimo.com.

JOHNSON, BROOKE BAILEY, consultant, former television executive; b. L.A., May 12, 1951; d. Edwin Beauvais and Jeanne (Foote) Bailey; m. Peter Michael Johnson, Sept. 18, 1982; children: Bailey Peter, Lee Keating. BA, Northwestern U., 1973, MS in Journalism, 1974. Promotion dir. Sta. KGUN-TV, Tucson, 1975-77; asst. programming dir. Sta. WLS-TV, Chgo., 1977-82; dir. programming Sta. WABC-TV, N.Y.C., 1982-89; became v.p. programming Arts & Entertainment Network, N.Y.C., 1989, sr. v.p. programming and production, 1989—2000; cons. A&E; sr. v.p. and gen. mgr. The Food Network, N.Y.C., 2003—. Mem. NOW. Mem. Nat. Cable Acad., Cable TV Assn., NATAS, Nat. Assn. TV Program Execs. (Iris award), Kappa Alpha Theta. Office: The Food Network 1180 Avenue of the Americas New York NY 10036

JOHNSON, BRUCE, engineering educator; b. Hawarden, Iowa, Sept. 4, 1932; s. York and Dorothy Ellen (DeBruce) J.; m. Dorothy Jane Rylander, Aug. 27, 1955; children: Sharon Hilgart, Kristen Aiken. BS in Mech. Engring., Iowa State U., 1955; MS in Mech. Engring., Purdue U., 1962, PhD, 1965. Instr. U.S. Naval Acad., Annapolis, Md., 1957-59, assoc. prof., 1964-70, project dir. model basin, 1968-76, prof., 1970-99, Naval Sea Systems Command prof. hydrodynamics, 1975-87, dir. Hydromechanics Lab., 1976-87, dir. ocean engring. program, 1996-99, dir. spl. projects hydromechanics lab., 2000—, prof. emeritus, 2001—. Instr. Purdue U., 1959-64; chmn. 18th Am. Towing Tank Conf., 1977, U.S. Rep. Info. Com. Internat. Towing Tank Conf., 1975-84, chmn. symbols and terminology group, 1985-99, editor, pub. ITTC Symbols and Terminology List, 1996-99. Author: (with T. Gillmer) Introduction to Naval Architecture, 1982, (with D. Newman) Engineering Economic Analysis, 1994, (with J. Womack) A Guide to Fishing Vessel Stability, 2004; editor: (with B. Nehrling) Proc. of 18th Am. Towing Tank Conf, 1977; contbr. articles to profl. publs. Trustee Bauman Bible Telecasts, 1970-93, fin. chmn., 1990-93; mem. Bowie State U. Found., 1995-97. Served with USN, 1955-59. Recipient award for excellence in engring. teaching Western Electric Fund, 1971, Navy Meritorious Civilian Svc. award, 1994, 96, Navy Superior Civilian Svc. award, 1998, 00, Svc. Excellence award Naval Acad. Alumni Assn., 1998, Meritorious Pub. svc. award USCG, 2002; Ford Found. grantee, 1962-64. Fellow Soc. Naval Archs. and Marine Engrs. (chmn. Chesapeake Sailing Yacht Symposium 1985, 87, chmn. electronic media com. 2000-03, exec. com. 2000-03, chmn. fishing vessel ops. and safety panel 2001-05, co-chmn. small working vessel ops. and safety panel 2005-); mem. ASME, Am. Soc. Naval Engrs. (chmn. scholarship com. 1983-89, nat. coun. 1986-88, 89-91), Md. Capital Yacht Club (bd. dirs. 1986-93, commodore 1992), Naval Acad. Sailing Squadron, Chesapeake Bay Yacht Racing Assn. (pres. 1990). Unitarian Universalist. Achievements include rsch. in naval architecture, hydrodynamics. Home: 7101 Bay Front Dr Apt 523 Annapolis MD 21403 Office: Dept Naval Architecture and Ocean Engring US Naval Acad Annapolis MD 21402 E-mail: aronj@bellatlantic.net.

JOHNSON, BRUCE E., lieutenant governor, former state legislator; b. Telpoli, Libya, May 25, 1960; m. Kelley Johnson; children Shane, Megan, Connor, Morgan Christine BS, Bowling Green State U.; JD, Capital U. Mem. Ohio Senate from 3rd dist., Columbus, 1994—2001; chmn. Senate Judiciary Com.; chmn. Ways & Means Com.; mem. counsel Chester, Wilcox & Saxbe, Columbus; dir. OH Dept. Devel., Columbus, 2001—; lt. gov. State of OH, Columbus, 2005—. Recipient Watchdog of the Treasury, Crime Victims Witness Assn award for Outstanding Legis. Mem. Columbus Bar Assn., Ohio Bar Assn. Republican. Office: Office Lt Gov 77 High St 23rd Fl Columbus OH 43215

JOHNSON, BRUCE EDWARD HUMBLE, lawyer; b. Columbus, Ohio, Jan. 22, 1950; s. Hugo Edward and M. Alice (Humble) J.; m. Paige Robinson Miller, June 28, 1980; children: Marta Noble, Winslow Collins, Russell Scott. AB, Harvard U., 1972; JD, Yale U., 1977; MA, U. Cambridge, Eng., 1978. Bar: Wash. 1977, Calif. 1992. Atty. Davis Wright Tremaine LLP, Seattle, 1977—. Mem. oversight com. King County Gov. Access Channel, 1996—2001. Co-author: Advertising and Commerical Speech, A First Amendment Guide, 2d edit., 2004. Bd. dirs. Seattle Repertory Theatre, 1993—, pres., 1999-2001, chair, 2004—; bd. dirs. Huntington's Dis. Soc. of Am., N.W. chpt., 2001—. Mem. ABA (tort and ins. practice sect., media law and defamation torts com. chair 1999-2000). Home: 711 W Kinnear Pl Seattle WA 98119-3621 Office: Davis Wright Tremaine LLP 2600 Century Sq 1501 4th Ave Seattle WA 98101-1688 Office Phone: 206-628-7683. E-mail: brucejohnson@dwt.com.

JOHNSON, BRUCE MARVIN, language educator; b. Chgo., Apr. 29, 1933; s. George A. and Elsie L. (Clausing) J.; m. Jean C. Kruger, June 29, 1957; 1 son, Abram. BA, U. Chgo., 1952, Northwestern U., 1954, MA, 1955, PhD, 1959. Instr. English U. Mich., 1958-62; asst. prof. English U. Rochester (N.Y.), 1962-68, assoc. prof., 1968-76, prof., 1976-92, prof. emeritus, 1992—, chmn. dept. English, 1981-84. Author: Conrad's Models of Mind, 1971, True Correspondence: A Phenomenology of Thomas Hardy's Novels, 1983. Sr. fellow NEH, 1974-75; fellow Guggenheim Found., 1977-78 Democrat. Home: Apt 407 16540 Heron Coach Way Fort Myers FL 33908-5523 Office: U Rochester Dept English Rochester NY 14627 Office Phone: 585-275-4092.

JOHNSON, BRUCE ROSS, elementary school educator; b. La Porte, Ind., May 18, 1949; s. Egbert Johannes Daniel and Ruth Elvera (Johnson) J. BS, Ball State U., Muncie, Ind., 1971; ME, Valparaiso U., 1975; postgrad., Nat. Coll. Edn., Evanston, Ill., 1974, Beijing Normal U., 1988, Western Mich. U., U. Va., Ind. U. Purdue, Antioch U., Seattle, Calif State U. Cert. elem. sch. tchr., Ind. Vol. tchr. Peace Corps, St. Vincent, W.I., W.I., 1971-72; tchr. South Ctrl. Sch., Union Mills, Ind., 1972-76, 77—; tchr. gifted and talented Purdue U., 1995—. Missionary tchr. Luth. Ch., Liberia, West Africa, 1976-77; vis. instr. U. London, 1974, U. Moscow, 1974, U. Paris, 1974; ednl. seminar China, 1988, Japan, 1990, Australia, 1993; guest lectr. dept. edn. Purdue U., 1995-2002. Contbr. articles to newspapers. Pres. People to People Internat., La Porte, Ind., 1981-83, trustee, Kansas City, Mo., 1983-88, 2005; bd. dirs. La Porte County Libr. Leasing Corp., 1988—; mem. ch. coun. Bethany Luth. Ch., La Porte, 1983-86, 90-93; LaPorte County Bicentennial Commn., 1975-76; v.p. Friends of La Porte County Libr., 1984-86, pres., 1986-88, 2005; chmn. books and coffee meet the author series LaPorte County Pub. Libr., 1985—; trustee La Porte County Hist. Soc., 1985-92, 94—; v.p. N.W. Ind. Geneal. Soc., 1981-82; pres. Cmty. Concert Assn., La Porte, 1984; mem. Pan Am. Games Com., 1986-87; mem. steering com. La Porte County Spelling Bee, 1979-91, chmn., 1981, 85, 90, 99, 2004, LaPorte County Leadership, Inc., 1986-87; chmn. Miss. Valley coun. People-to-People, 1983-88; mem. bicentennial com. Bill of Rights, 1989-90; bd. dirs. LaPorte Literacy Coalition, 1997—2002. Named to Outstanding Young Men Am., 1985, State finalist NASA Tchr.-in-Space project, 1985; Ind. State Tchrs. Assn. scholar, 1970; recipient Dean Earl A. Johnson Outstanding Svc. award Ball State U., 1971, Lifetime Achievement award People to People, cert. of merit Ind. Dept. Edn., 1985. Mem. NEA (life), Ind. State Tchrs. Assn., Amateur Music Club (pres. 1982-83), Little Theater Club (bd. dirs. 1980-83, 89-92), Lions (pres. 2000-01, bd. dirs. 1983—), Phi Delta Kappa (life). Avocations: performing in musical theater, collecting foreign coins, travel, gardening. Home: 2012 Village Rd La Porte IN 46350-7874 Office: South Cen Community Schs 9808 S 600 W La Porte IN 46382-9600

JOHNSON, C. NICHOLAS, dance company executive; b. Jan. 15, 1955; MFA in Dance/Drama, U. Ariz.; studied with, Stefan Niedzialkowski, Frank Hatchett, Richard Levi, De Marco, N.Y.C. Assoc. artistic dir. Goldston & Johnson Sch. of Mimes; chief officer Mid-Am. Dance Theatre, Wichita, Kans.; asst. prof., dir. dance, modern dance, jazz, mime Coll. Fine Arts Wichita State U. Freelance tchr., dir., choreographer and performer various U.S. ballet schs. and univs. Performer Marcel Marceau World Ctr. Mime, Invisible People Mime Theatre, Internat. Children's Theatre Festival, Hong Kong. Kans. Arts Commn. fellow, 1999. Office: Wichita State U Sch Performing Arts-Dance PO Box 101 Wichita KS 67260-0001 Office Phone: 316-978-3645. Personal E-mail: alltheacreations@cox.net. Business E-Mail: nick.johnson@wichita.edu.

JOHNSON, C. TERRY, lawyer; b. Bridgeport, Conn., Sept. 24, 1937; s. Clifford Gustave and Evelyn Florence (Terry) J.; m. Suzanne Frances Chichy, Aug. 24, 1985; children: Laura Elizabeth, Melissa Lynne, Clifford Terry. AB, Trinity Coll., 1960; LLD, Columbia U., 1963. Bar: Ohio 1964, U.S. Ct. Appeals (6th cir.) 1966, U.S. Dist. Ct. (so. dist.) Ohio 1970. Legal dep. probate ct. Montgomery County, Dayton, Ohio, 1964-67; head probate dept. Coolidge Wall & Wood, Dayton, 1967-79, Smith & Schnacke, Dayton, 1979-89, Thompson, Hine and Flory, Dayton, 1989-92; head estate planning and probate group Dayton office Porter, Wright, Morris & Arthur, Dayton, 1992—. Frequent lectr. on estate planning to various profl. orgns. Contbr. articles to profl. jours. Fellow Am. Coll. Trust and Estate Counsel; mem. Ohio Bar Assn. (bd. govs. estate planning, trust and probate law sect., chmn. 1993-95), Dayton Bar Assn. (chmn. probate com. 1992-94), Ohio State Bar

Found. (trustee 1995-2000), Ohio CLE Inst. (trustee 1995-99, chair 1998-99), Dayton Legal Secs. Assn. (hon.), Dayton Bicycle Club. Home: 8307 Rhine Way Centerville OH 45458-3017 Office: Porter Wright Morris & Arthur 1 S Main St Ste 1600 Dayton OH 45402-2028 Office Phone: 937-449-6701. E-mail: cjohnson@porterwright.com.

JOHNSON, CAGE SAUL, hematologist, educator; b. New Orleans, Mar. 31, 1941; s. Cage Spooner and Esther Georgianna (Saul) J.; m. Shirley Lee O'Neal, Feb. 22, 1968; children: Stephanie, Michelle. Student, Creighton U., 1958-61, MD, 1965. Intern U. Cin., 1965-66, resident, 1966-67, U. So. Calif., 1969-71, instr. L.A., 1971-74, asst. prof., 1974-80, assoc. prof., 1980-88, dir. Comprehensive Sickle Cell Ctr., 1991—, prof., 1988—. Chmn. adv. com. Calif. Dept. Health Svcs., Sacramento, 1977—; dir. Hemoglobinopathy Lab., L.A., 1976—; bd. dirs. Sicke Cell Self-Help Assn., L.A., 1982-86. Contbr. numerous articles to profl. jours. Dir. Sickle Cell Disease Rsch. Found., L.A., 1986-94; active Nat. Med. Fellowships, Inc., Chgo., 1979—; chmn. rev. com. NIH, Washington, 1986-91; chmn. adv. com., 1995-97, mem. adv. coun., 1997-2002. Major U.S. Army, 1967-69, Vietnam. Fellow N.Y. Acad. Scis., Am. Coll. Angiology; mem. Am. Soc. Hematology, Am. Fedn. Clin. Rsch., Western Soc. Clin. Investigation, Internat. Soc. Biorheology, E.E. Just Soc. (sec.-treas. 1985-93, pres. 1994-95, sec. 1996—). Avocation: restoring antique automobiles. Office: 2025 Zonal Ave Los Angeles CA 90089-0110 Office Phone: 323-442-1259. E-mail: cagejohn@usc.edu.

JOHNSON, CAMMARIE, behavior analyst; b. Detroit, June 15, 1960; d. Charles Warren and Norine Carroll (Goode) J.; m. Charles Jonathan Burlile, July 24, 1993; children: Kathryn Johnson Burlile, Charles Evan Johnson Burlile. BA in Psychology, BA in English, Pitzer Coll., 1982; MA in Psychology, Northeastern U., 1992. Lic. mental health counselor, Mass.; bd. cert. behavior analyst. Psychologist I W.E. Fernald State Sch., Waltham, Mass., 1984—88; clin. ednl. specialist New Eng. Ctr. for Children, Southborough, Mass., 1988—92, dir. edn., 1992—95; program dir. New Eng. Ctr. for Autism, Southborough, 1995—; assoc. psychologist E.K. Shriver Ctr., Waltham, 1993—99; faculty MS program in applied behavior analysis Northeastern U., Boston, 1994—. Chairperson curriculum com. New Eng. Ctr. for Children, 1992—; presenter (original rsch.) local, nat. and internat. confs. Contbr. articles to profl. jours. Mem. human rights com. New Eng. Ctr. for Children, 1989-96. Recipient fellowships Northeastern U., 1986, 87, 88. Mem. Assn. for Behavior Analysis, Berkshire Assn. for Behavior Analysis and Therapy. Avocations: travel, creative writing, hiking, quilting, bird watching. Home: 86 Adams St Westborough MA 01581 Office: The New Eng Ctr for Children 33 Turnpike Rd Southborough MA 01772-2108 Office Phone: 508-481-1015 3138. E-mail: cjohnson@necc.org.

JOHNSON, CANDICE ELAINE BROWN, pediatrics educator; b. Cin., Mar. 21, 1946; d. Paul Preston and Naomi Elizabeth Brown; m. Thomas Raymond Johnson, June 30, 1973; children: Andrea Eleanor, Erik Albert. BS, U. Mich., 1968; PhD Microbiology, Case Western Reserve U., 1973, MD, 1976. Diplomate Am. Bd. Pediat., 1981. Intern, resident in pediat. Rainbow Babies and Children's Hosp./Met. Gen. Hosp., Cleve., 1976-78; fellow in ambulatory pediatrics Met. Gen. Hosp., 1978-79; asst. prof. pediat. Case Western Res. U., Cleve., 1980-90, assoc. prof., 1990-97; prof. pediat. U. Colo., Denver, 1997—; pediatrician Children's Hosp., Denver, 1997—. Mem. rev. panel NIH, Washington, 1993; faculty sen. Case Western Res. U., 1988-91. Contbr. articles profl. jours. Mem. Am. Acad. Pediat., Pediat. Infectious Disease Soc., Soc. for Pediatric Rsch., So. Utah Wilderness Alliance, Sierra Club. Home: 2290 Locust St Denver CO 80207-3943 Office: Child Health Clinic B032 1056 E 19th Ave Denver CO 80218-1007 Office Phone: 303-861-6007.

JOHNSON, CARL FREDERICK, marriage and family therapist; b. July 18, 1947; BA in Psychology, Northwestern U., 1969; MA in Clin. Psychology, Ga. State U., 1975. Lic. marriage and family therapist, Ga. Grad. tchg. asst. Ga. State U., Atlanta, 1972-73; family therapist Bridge Family Ctr., Atlanta, 1973-80; pvt. practice The Family Workshop, Atlanta, 1979—. Adj. instr. Dekalb C.C., Clarkston, Ga., 1981-82; appointee Ga. Composite Bd. Profl. Counselors, Social Workers and Marriage and Family Therapists, 1985-93; exec. dir. Ga. Assn. Marriage and Family Therapy, Atlanta, 1997—. Contbr. articles to profl. jours. Fellow: Am. Assn. for Marriage and Family Therapy (Divsnl. Contbn. award 1993, Outstanding Contbn. to Marriage and Family Therapy award 2001); mem.: Assn. Marital and Family Therapy Regulatory Bds. (founder, pres. 1987—91, coord. devel. nat. licensing exam in marital and family therapy 1989—92), Ga. Assn. for Marriage and Family Therapy (chair legis. affairs com. 1980—85, 1993—95, Outstanding Contbn. award 1983, 1985, 1993, Lifetime Achievement/Disting. Svc. award 1996). Home: 751 N Parkwood Rd Decatur GA 30030-5023 Office: Family Workshop Ste 200 2200 Century Pkwy NE Atlanta GA 30345 Office Phone: 404-633-3347.

JOHNSON, CARL RANDOLPH, chemist, educator; b. Charlottesville, Va., Apr. 28, 1937; BS, Med. Coll. Va., 1958; PhD in Chemistry, U. Ill., 1962. NSF rsch. fellow chemistry Harvard U., 1962; from asst. to prof. chemistry Wayne State U., Detroit, 1962—90, Disting. prof., 1990—2001, chair dept. chemistry, 1997—2001, Disting. prof. emeritus, 2002—. Humboldt sr. scientist, 1991; bd. dirs. Organic Syntheses, Inc. Mem. adv. bd.: Jour. Organic Chemistry, 1976—81. Alfred P. Sloan fellow, 1965-68. Mem. Am. Chem. Soc. (assoc. editor jour. 1984-89, Harry and Carol Mosher award 1992, Arthur C. Cope Sr. Scholar award 2002). Achievements include research in organic sulfur chemistry, especially sulfoxides and sulfoximines, exploratory synthetic chemistry, synthesis of compounds of potential medicinal activity, organometallic chemistry, synthesis of natural products, enzymes in synthesis. Home: 118 Wilton Coves Dr Hartfield VA 23071 E-mail: crj@chem.wayne.edu.

JOHNSON, CAROLINE JANICE, insurance company executive; b. Chgo., Jan. 6, 1941; d. LeRoy Paine and Johnetta Louise (Brock) Collins; m. Charles Robert Rice (divorced); 1 child, Robert Michael; m. James Arthur Lunningham (divorced); 1 child, Mark LeRoy; m. George Bolds (div. 1970); 1 child, Troy Andrew; m. Howard Edward Johnson Sr., May 4, 1985 (div. 2004). Sec. Roosevelt U., Chgo., 1959-60; police steno Chgo. Police Dept., Chgo., 1960-62; sec., dental asst. Dr. Lucien Holman, Joliet, Ill., 1962-64; sec. Amoco Chems., Joliet, Ill., 1964-68; ins. sales Allstate, Joliet, Ill., 1978-85; dept. mgr., ins. sales Beneficial Ins. Co., Chgo., 1985-86; agy. mgr. Heritage Agy. Inc., Chgo., 1987-88; owner Ins. Coun., Inc., Chgo., 1988—. Mem. Chgo. Assn. Ins. Women (bd. dirs. communication Chgo. chpt. 1989—), Internat. Horsemen's League (Chgo. pres. 1987-88, 97—, bus. mgr. 1988-97, pres. 1997—). Democrat. Avocation: riding and showing horses. Home and Office: 7695 E 625S Knox IN 46534 Office Phone: 574-542-2709. E-mail: cjohnson@insurancecouncillinc.com.

JOHNSON, CAROLYN ELIZABETH, librarian; b. Oakland, Calif., May 29, 1921; d. Ferdinand Orin and Clara Wells (Humphrey) Hassler; m. Benjamin Alfred Johnson, Feb. 12, 1943; children: Robin Rebecca, Anne Elizabeth, Delia Mary. BA, U. Calif.-Berkeley, 1946; cert. libr., Calif. State U. Fullerton, 1960; MLS, Immaculate Heart Coll., 1968. Cert. libr. Calif. Asst. children's libr. Fullerton Pub. Libr., 1951—59, coord. children's svcs., 1959—81, city libr., 1981—90, ret., 1990, apptd. curator Mary Campbell collection hist. children's lit., 1990. Part-time instr. Rio Hondo City Coll., Whittier, Calif., 1970—72, Calif. State U.-Fullerton, 1972—77; vice chmn. 3d Pacific Rim Conf. Coun., 1983—86; mem. Korczak award com. U.S. Bd. Books for Young People, 1988. Author: (book) The Art of Walter Crane, 1988. Founding bd. dirs. Youth Sci. Ctr., Fullerton, 1958; mem. Libr. Tech. Tng. Adv. Com., Fullerton Coll., 1970; chmn. adv. bd. YWCA Child Devel. Ctr., 1992—; bd. dirs. Fullerton Pub. Libr. Found., mem. endowment fund, 1994, sec., 1995; bd. dirs. Friends of the Fullerton Pub. Libr. Named Profl. Woman of Yr., North Orange County YWCA, 1986, Woman of Yr., Fullerton C. of C., 1990, North Orange County YWCA, 2003. Mem.: LWV, AAUW, ALA, PTA (life), So. Calif. Coun. on Lit. for Children and Young People (pres. 1979—81, Dorothy C. McKenzie award 1987), Orange County Libr. Assn. (v.p.), Calif. Libr. Assn. (chmn. children's service div.), Theta Sigma Phi, Phi Beta Kappa. Methodist. Home: 644 Princeton Cir E Fullerton CA 92831-2728

JOHNSON, CAROLYN JEAN, retired law librarian; b. Beaver Dam, Wis., Nov. 7, 1938; d. Henry William and Bernice Mae (Haas) Krueger; m. Robert Edward Johnson, June 19, 1960; children: Eric Steven, Kristin Elizabeth. BS in Edn., Wartburg Coll., 1960. Tchr., various locations, 1960-64, Hennepin County Library, 1972-81; libr. 3M Tech. Libr., St. Paul, 1981-86; law libr. 3M Ctr. Law Libr., St. Paul, 1986-2000; ret., 2000. Mem. Am. Assn. Law Libraries, Minn. Assn. Law Libraries. Lutheran. Avocations: reading, walking, cooking.

JOHNSON, CAROLYN M., librarian, writer; b. Bklyn., Apr. 3, 1949; AA in Liberal Arts, Queensborough C.C., Bayside, N.Y., 1970; BA in English and Am. Lit., Hunter Coll., 1973; M Libr. and Info. Sci., St. John's U., Jamaica, NY, 1975, MA in English and Am. Lit., 1980. Cataloging libr. Pace U. Libr., N.Y.C., 1978—79, N.Y. Bot. Garden Libr., Bronx Park, NY, 1979—81; libr., web rschr., writer Greenwood Press, Westport, Conn., 1980—2002, Librs. Unltd. mem. Greenwood Pub. Group, Westport, 2002—. Online libr., ednl. writer THE BOOK BAG on Am. Online, N.Y.C., 1996—2001; web site rschr., evaluator, site summary writer studyweb.com, San Diego, 1999—2000; web site evaluator Ctr. for Montessori Tchr. Edn., White Plains, NY, 1997—99. Author: Discovering Nature with Young People: An Annotated Bibliography and Selection Guide, 1987, Using Internet Primary Sources to Teach Critical Thinking Skills in the Sciences, 2003; contbr. articles to profl. jours., articles to lit. mags., children's ednl. mags. and to ednl. websites; asst. host AOL Children's Writers Online Chat/Workshop, 2005. Mem.: Soc. Children's Book Writers and Illustrators. Avocations: photography, reading, genealogy, classical music. E-mail: WriterLibr@aol.com.

JOHNSON, CARYN ELAINE See GOLDBERG, WHOOPI

JOHNSON, CHANNEY, elementary school educator; b. Chgo., Ill., Dec. 2, 1963; d. Mary Hampton and Michael Edgar Johnson; 1 child, Christina Flowers. BA, Grinnell Coll.; MS, Barry U.; EdD, Fla. Internat. U. Fla. Educator's Certificate Fla., 1986. Tchr. Miami-Dade County Pub. Schools, Fla., 1985—92, Mus. of Sci., Miami, 1987—88; asst. prin. Miami-Dade County Pub. Schools, Fla., 1992—98, prin., 1998—; adj. prof. Fla. Internat. U., 2002—. Cons. Barry U.-Annenberg Challenge, Miami Shores, Fla., 2001. Multicultural recruitment Grinnell Coll., Grinnell, Iowa, 1987—2003; founding dir. TLC in Action, a 501(c)3 nonprofit corp.; campaign worker DNC, Miami, Fla., 2000—02; voters' registration vol. NAACP, Miami-Dade, Fla., 2000—01; accreditation com. New Birth Bapt. Ch., Miami, Fla., 1997—99, charter sch. com., 2001—, bd. trustees, 2003—. Recipient Prin. of the Yr. Nominee, Dade Counseling Assn., 1998—99, Asst. Prin. of the Yr., Region Finalist, Miami-Dade County Pub. Schools, 1997—98, Tchr. of the Yr., Ludlam Elem. Sch., 1989—90; Delores Auzenne fellow, Fla. Internat. U., 1993—97, Citibank Tchr. Mini-grant, Citibank Success Fund, 1987—88. Mem.: Magnet Schools of Am., United Way Leadership Cir. (assoc.). Achievements include research in comparative study of high-achieving and low-achieving African-American students in an urban setting. Home: 1651 NE 115 St #33C Miami FL 33181 Personal E-mail: doc63chan@aol.com.

JOHNSON, CHANNING D., lawyer; BA in econ., Stanford U., 1972; JD, Harvard U., 1975. Bar: Calif. 1978, US. Dist. Ct., Central Dist. Calif. 1978. Ptnr. Akin Gump Strauss Hauer & Feld LLP, LA. Mem. Pasadena Planning Commn., 1982—86, Calif. State Bar Judicial Nominees and Evaluation Commn., 1992—94. Named one of Am. Top Black Lawyers, Black Enterprise Mag., 2003. Mem.: State Bar Calif. (mem. bus. law section). Office: Akin Gump Strauss Hauer & Feld LLP 2029 Century Pk E Ste 2400 Los Angeles CA 90067-3012 Office Phone: 310-229-1075. Business E-Mail: cjohnson@akingump.com.

JOHNSON, CHARLES BARTLETT, portfolio manager; b. Montclair, N.J., Jan. 6, 1933; s. Rupert Harris and Florence (Endler) J.; m. Ann Demarest Lutes, Mar. 26, 1955; children: Charles E., Holly, Sarah, Gregory, William, Jennifer, Mary (dec.). BA, Yale U., 1954. With R.H. Johnson & Co., N.Y.C., 1954-55; pres. Franklin Distbrs., Inc., 1957-97; chmn. Franklin Resources, Inc., 1969—, CEO, 1969—2004. Bd. dirs. various Franklin and Templeton Mut. Funds; bd. govs. Investment Co. Inst., 1973-88. Trustee Crystal Springs Uplands Sch., 1984-92; bd. dirs. Peninsula Cmty. Found., 1986-96, San Francisco Symphony, 1984-2002; bd. overseers Hoover Instn., 1993—. 1st lt. U.S. Army, 1955—57. Mem. Nat. Assn. Securities Dirs. (bd. govs. 1990-92, 95-96, chmn. 1992), Commonwealth Club of Calif. (bd. dirs. 1995-97). Office: Franklin Resources Inc One Franklin Pkwy San Mateo CA 94403-1906

JOHNSON, CHARLES E., federal agency administrator; married; 6 children. BS, Brigham Young U., 1960. CPA. Various positions in public acctg. KPMG; dir. planning and budget Office of Gov., Utah, 1991—92, chief of staff to Gov., 1992—97; vice chmn. bd. strategic direction Garff-Warner Orgn., 1997—2001; chmn. Utah State Bd. Regents, 1997—2002, mem., 1997—2004; v.p. Huntsman LLC, 2001—04; pres. Huntsman Cancer Found., 2001—04; asst. sec. budget, tech. and fin. US Dept. Health and Human Svcs., Washington, 2005—. Office: US Dept Health and Human Svcs Hubert H Humphrey Bldg 200 Independence Ave SW Rm 514G Washington DC 20201 Office Phone: 202-690-6396. Office Fax: 202-690-5405. E-mail: Charles.Johnson@hhs.gov.*

JOHNSON, CHARLES E., II, technology company executive; b. Muskegon, Mich., Feb. 22, 1936; s. Paul C. and Anne (Lovelace) Johnson; m. Patricia Bell, Aug. 2, 1958; children: Charles, Julia, Peter. BA, Colgate Coll., 1958; LL.B., U. Wis., 1961; A.M.P., Harvard U., 1983. Bars: Mich., 1961, Wis. 1961. Group v.p. replacement Sealed Power Corp., Muskegon, 1970-72, group v.p. internat., 1972-82, group v.p. gen. products, 1982-84, exec. v.p., 1984-85, pres., chief operating officer, 1985—, also dir.; dir. SPX Corp., Charlotte, NC, 1976—, bd. chmn., 2004—. Dir. First of Am. Bank, Muskegon Gen. campaign mgr. YFCA, Muskegon, 1978; bd. dirs. Muskegon Bus. Coll., 1984—; trustee Wayland Acad., Beaver Dam, Wis., 1984—, Hackley Hospital. Served with USAR, 1962-68 Named Bus. Leader of Yr., Muskegon C. of C., 1979 Mem.: Century, Muskegon Country. Republican. Roman Catholic. Avocations: boating; golf; tennis. Office: SPX Corporation 13515 Ballantyne Corp Pl Charlotte NC 28277*

JOHNSON, CHARLES FLOYD, television executive, producer; b. Camden, NJ, Feb. 12; s. Orange Maull and Bertha Ellen (Seagers) J.; m. Sandra Brashears, June 4, 1966 (div. 1971); m. Anne Burford, June 18, 1983; 1 child, Kristin. BA, Howard U., 1962, JD, 1965; student, U. Del., 1960. Bar: D.C., 1968. Atty., advisor US Copyright, Washington, 1967-70; assoc. Howard Berg Law Offices, Wilmington, Del., 1970-71; prodn. coordinator Universal TV, Universal City, Calif., 1971-74, assoc. producer The Rockford Files and Baa Baa Black Sheep, 1974-76, producer The Rockford Files, Simon and Simon (pilot), Hellinger's Law, 1976-80, supervising producer Magnum P.I., 1982-86, co-exec. producer Magnum P.I., 1986-88, exec. producer Revealing Evidence, 1990; producer Bret Maverick Warner Bros. TV, Burbank, Calif., 1981-82; prod. Voices of Our People (In Celebration of Black Poetry) Sta. KCET/Pub. Broadcasting Sys., LA, 1981-82; co-exec. prodr. B.L. Stryker Blue Period Prodn., LA, 1988-90; co-exec. prodr. JAG Paramount Studios, LA, 1996—. Vice chmn. Media Forum, LA, 1980-85; bd. dir. Comm. Bridge, LA, 1981-89. Author: (bull.) Copyright & Developing Countries, 1967; co-author: Black Women in Television, 1990; co-exec. producer Quantum Leap, 1992-93, JAG, 1996—, (pilot) First Monday, 2001; exec. producer The Rockford Files movies, 1993-96, co-exec. Prod. Nary CIS pilot and series, 2003. Bd. dir. Ind. Video and Filmmakers, 1985-90, Kwanza Found., 1985—, Crossroads Theatre Acad., 1990-98, Mediascope, 1994—, Santa Clarita Film Festival, 1997—. With US Army, 1965-67. Recipient Stony Brook Coll. Preparatory award, 1979, Horward U. Alumni Assn. award, 1982, 85, Outstanding, Achievement Minorities in Broadcasting Award, 2000. Mem.: SAG, AFTRA, Am. Film Inst., Prodrs. Guild Am. (treas. 1996—98, sec. 1998—2001), Caucus for Prodrs., Writers and Dirs., Acad. TV Arts and Scis. (student activities com., Emmy award 1978, 1981, 7 Emmy nominations), Writers Guild Am., Omega Psi Phi (chpt. treas. 1961—62). Democrat. Methodist. Avocations: bicycling, travel. Office: Sunset Gower Studios 1438 N Gower St Bldg 35 4th Fl Los Angeles CA 90038

JOHNSON, CHARLES JOHNSON, music educator; b. Hendricks, Minn., Feb. 4, 1950; s. Carvell A. Johnson and Clara G. (Digre)Johnson; m. Rhonda Rae Bovee, June 29, 1974; children: Sarah, Emily. BA, Concordia Coll., Minn., 1972. Tchg. Lic. Minn., 1972. Jr. high sch. band, 8th grade English tchr. Fosston Pub. Sch., Minn., 1972—73; k-12 music dir. Kensington Pub. Sch., Minn., 1973—78; band dir. Starbuck H.S., Minn., 1978—91; dir. of bands Minnewaska Area H.S., Glenwood, Minn., 1991—. Choir. Mem.: Minn. Music Educators Assc. (licentiate; region rep. 1994—96), Minn. Band Dirs. Assn. (assoc.; bd. mem. 1999—2002). Office Phone: 320-239-1341.

JOHNSON, CHARLES L., II, military officer; BSCE, USAF Acad., 1972; MS in Engring. Adminstrn. and Law, George Washington U., 1976; grad., Air Command and Staff Coll., 1986, Air War Coll., 1991, Def. Sys. Mgmt. Coll., 1993; grad. in Exec. Devel., U. Ill., 1995. Commd. 2d lt. USAF, 1972, advanced through grades to maj. gen., 1999; UH-1N/CH-3E instr. pilot, chief scheduling and tng. 89th Mil. Airlift Wing, Andrews AFB, Md., 1973-78; AB-212 instr. pilot Joint DOD Helicopter Tech. Asst. Field Team Royal Saudi Air Force, Taif Air Base, Saudi Arabia, 1978-79; C-141 flight examiner, chief pilot, chief current ops. 60th Mil. Airlift Wing, Travis AFB, Calif., 1980-83; chief spl. actions and studies group Airlift and Trainers Sys. Program Office, Wright-Patterson AFB, Ohio, 1983-85; chief C-17 program divsn. Mil. Airlift Command, Scott AFB, Ill., 1986-90; mil. asst. to asst. sec. of Air Force for acquisition The Pentagon, Washington, 1991-92; comdr. 97th Ops. Group 97th Air Mobility Wing, Altus AFB, Okla., 1992-93; dir. C-141 Sys. Program Office Warner Robins Air Logistics Ctr., Robins AFB, Ga., 1993-96; program dir. C-17 Sys. Program Office Aero. Sys. Ctr., Wright-Patterson AFB, Ohio, 1996-99; dir. logistics, Hdqrs. Air Mobility Command Scott AFB, Ill., 1999; dir. plans and programs, Hdqrs. Air Mobility command, 1999-2000; comdr. Oklahoma City Air Logistics Ctr., Tinker AFB, Okla., 2000—03, Hanscom AFB, Mass., 2003—. Decorated Legion of Merit with one oak leaf cluster, Meritorious Svc. medal with 5 oak leaf clusters. Office: Hanscom AFB 9 Eglin St Hanscom Afb MA 01731-2109 E-mail: charles.johnson@tinker.af.mil.

JOHNSON, CHARLES LESLIE, aerospace physicist, consultant; b. Ashland, Ky., Mar. 1, 1962; s. Charles Leslie and June Mays (Gesling) J.; m. Carol Elaine Peck, May 7, 1988; children: Carl Stuart, Leslie Arlene. BA in Chemistry and Physics, Transylvania U., 1984; MS in Physics, Vanderbilt U., 1986; grad., Internat. Space U., 1991. Rsch. physicist Gen. Rsch. Corp., Huntsville, Ala., 1986-90; aerospace physicist NASA-Marshall Space Flight Ctr., Huntsville, 1990-98; mgr. Interstellar Propulsion Rsch. NASA, Huntsville, Ala., 1998-2000, mgr. In-Space Transp. Techs., 2000—. Cons. Gen. Rsch. Corp., Huntsville, 1990-91; co-chmn. space symposium Tech. and Bus. Exhbn. and Symposium, 1994; chmn. STEDTRAIN (Sci. Tech. Edn. and Tng.) symposium, 1995. Tech. cons.: (motion picture) Lost in Space, 1998; contbr. articles to profl. jours. Deacon lst Christian Ch., Huntsville, 1989-91. Named Sci. Guest of Honor, LibertyCon Sci. Fiction Conv., 1996, MidSouth-Con Sci. Fiction Conv., 2001, Profl. of Yr., Huntsville Assn. Tech. Socs., 1998. Mem. AIAA (chmn. space programs and techs. conf., advanced techs. and applications symposium 1996), Nat. Space Soc., World Future Soc. (pres. North Ala. chpt. 1998-99, prin. investigator propulsive small expendable deployer space experiment 1998-2003). Republican. Baptist. Achievements include patents in field of laser pulsed fiber optic neutron detector in 1994; combination solar sail and electrodynamic tether propulsion system in 2003. Avocations: genealogy, reading. Personal E-mail: lesjohnsonastp@yahoo.com.

JOHNSON, CHARLES OWEN, retired lawyer; b. Monroe, La., Aug. 18, 1926; s. Clifford U. and Laura (Owen) Johnson. BA, Tulane U., 1946, JD, 1969; LLB, Harvard U., 1948; LLM, Columbia U., 1955. Bar: La. 1949. Pvt. practice, Monroe, 1949-50; mem. law editl. staff West Pub. Co., St. Paul, 1953; atty. Office of Chief Counsel, IRS, Washington, 1955-79, chief Ct. Appeals br. Tax Ct. divsn., 1968-79. Author: (book) The Geneology of Several Allied Famillies, 1961. With AUS, 1950—52. Fellow: Samuel Victor Constant Soc.; mem.: SCV, S.R. (past pres. D.C. soc.), SAR (past pres. D.C. soc.), FBA, Va. Hist. Soc., Miss. Hist. Soc., Nat. Gavel Soc. (past treas., past pres.), Nat. Lawyers Club, La. Bar Assn., New Eng. Ancestry Alliance (pres.), St. David's Soc. N.Y., St. Nicholas Soc. City of N.Y., Va. Geneal. Soc., Round Table Club of New Orleans, Harvard Club of Boston, Army and Navy Club Washington, Order of Scions of Colonial Cavaliers 1640-1660 (gov., founding gov.), Soc. Cin., Mil. Order Stars and Bars (past judge adv. gen.), Soc. Desc. Jersey Settlers, Huguenot Soc. La. (past pres.), Huguenot Soc. S.C., Sons and Daus. of Pilgrims (past treas., 2d dep. gov. gen.), Royal Soc. St. George, St. Andrew's Soc. Washington, Sons Union Vets, Nat. Soc. Desc. Early Quakers (past nat. presiding clk.), Soc. Colonial New Eng. (past gov. gen. nat. soc.), Soc. of 1812 (past pres. D.C. soc.), Soc. Colonial Wars (past dep. gov. D.C. soc., lt. gov., gov.), Order of the First Families of Conn., 1631-1662 (gov. gen.), Plymouth Hereditary Soc. (gov. gen.), Order Descs. Ancient and Honorable Artillery Co. (gov. gen.), The Hereditary Order of the Families of the Pres. and First Ladies of Am. (founding mem., atty. gen.), St. David's Soc. of N.Y., Nat. Soc. Sons and Daus. of Antebellum Planters 1607-1861 (past pres. gen.), Sons and Daus. Colonial and Antebellum Bench and Bar 1565-1861 (founding pres. gen. 1994—98), Order Descs. Colonial Physicians and Chirurgiens (past. pres. gen.), Order First Families R.I. and Providence Plantations 1636-1647 (past gov. gen.), Hereditary Order First Families of Mass. (past registrar gen., gov. gen.), Order First Families Miss. 1699-1817 (gov. gen. 1967—69), Order Founders and Patriots of Am. (past gov. D.C., past geneal. gen., past dep. historian gen.), First Families of Ga. (past chancellor gen.), Hereditary Order Descs. Colonial Govs. (past gov. gen.), Soc. Descs. Colonial Clergy (past chancellor gen.), Order Ams. of Armorial Ancestry (past pres.), Soc. Descs. Old Plymouth Colony, Jamestowne Soc., Sons and Daus. of Province and Republic of West Fla. 1763-1810 (past gov.), La. Colonials. Home: Apt 809S 2111 Jefferson Davis Hwy Arlington VA 22202-3121 Home (Winter): Patrician Condominiums Apt 223 3450 S Ocean Blvd Palm Beach FL 33480

JOHNSON, CHARLES ROBERT, lawyer; b. Dallas, July 30, 1934; s. Calvin Thor and Lula Martha Pool Johnson; m. Agnes McGuire, Jan. 1957; children: Erin, Hunter, Thor. BBA, Tex. A&M U., 1955; JD, So. Meth. U., 1961. Bar: Tex. 1961; bd. cert. estate planning and probate law Tex. Bd. Legal Specialization. Assoc., ptnr. Locke Purnell, Dallas, 1961-68; ptnr. Stalcup Johnson, Dallas, 1968-77, Johnson Smith Kourney, Dallas, 1977-78, Coke & Coke, Dallas, 1978-81, Pettit & Martin, Dallas, 1981-88, Shank Irwin, Dallas, 1988-91, Johnson & Steinberg, Dallas, 1991-94, Johnson Jordan Nipper & Monk, Dallas, 1994—. Assoc. editor Southwestern Law Jour., 1960-61; guest instr. fed. income taxation and estate planning So. Meth. U. Sch. Law, 1964-65; vis. prof. fed. income taxation, corp. taxation and bus. assns. I and II So. Meth. U. Sch. Law, 1976-77. Chmn. Joni and Friends Ministries, Dallas; 1st lt. aircraft artillery U.S. Army, 1957-58. Fellow Am. Coll. Trust & Estate Coun., Nat. Assoc. Estate Planning Coun.; mem. Dallas Bar Assn., Am. Bar Assn., State Bar Tex., Estate Planning Coun. N. Tex. (former pres., bd. dirs.), Order of Woolsack, Barristers, Delta Theta Phi. Avocations: reading, walking, gardening. Office: Johnson Jordan Nipper & Monk 1050 Three Galleria Twr 13155 Noel Rd LB3 Dallas TX 75240-1531 Office Phone: 972-392-1123. E-mail: cjohnson@jjnmlaw.com.

JOHNSON, CHARLES S., III, lawyer; b. Nashville, Oct. 31, 1948; BA, Bard Coll., Annandale-on-Hudson, NY, 1970; JD, Fisk U. Boston Coll. Law Sch., 1973. Bar: Ga. 1973, US Tax Ct. 1988, US Supreme Ct., US Cts. of Appeals (4th, 5th, and 11th Circuits). Candidate US Ho. of Rep. (5th Congl. Dist. Ga.), 1986; ptnr. Holland & Knight LLP, Atlanta, mem. dirs. com. Adj.

prof., antitrust U. Ga. Law Sch., 1976; chmn. Atlanta Jud. Commn., 1977—97; mem. Ga. State Bd. Bar Examiners, 1983—87, chmn., 1987; bd. dir. Techwood Park, Inc.; pres. Southern Reg. Coun. Mem. Boston Coll. Indsl. and Commercial Law Review, 1971—73; contbr. articles to profl. jours. Trustee Bard Coll., Annandale-on-Hudson, NY, 1979—84, Simon's Rock Coll., Great Barrington, Mass., 1979—84; former bd. dir. Atlanta Bus. League, Bard Coll., Metropolitan Atlanta Red Cross, Alliance Theater/Alliance Children's Theater, Simon's Rock Coll., So. Christian Home for Children, Young Democrats Ga.; former chmn. Atlanta Urban League, Atlanta Legal Aid Soc., Atlanta Exchange, Atlanta Region Open Housing Coalition. Named one of Ten Most Outstanding Young People in Atlanta, 1985; recipient Martin Luther King, Jr. Peace and Justice award, King Ctr., 1985. Mem.: Gale City Bar Assn. (pres. 1978), Atlanta Bar Assn. (bd. dir. 1999—2000), State Bar Ga. (mem. state disciplinary bd. 1981—82), Nat. Bar. Assn. (v.p. 1984—86), ABA (mem., antitrust sect. com. on insurance, energy and transportation, chair, conf. of minority ptnrs. in majority.corp. law firms, vice-chair torts & ins. practice sect. com. pub. regulation ins. law). Office: Holland & Knight LLP 1201 W Peachtree St NE 1 Atlantic Ctr Ste 2000 Atlanta GA 30309 Office Phone: 404-817-8530. Business E-Mail: cjohnson@hklaw.com.

JOHNSON, CHARLES WILLIAM, state supreme court justice; b. Tacoma, Wash., Mar. 16, 1951; m. Dana Johnson. BA in Economics, U. Wash., 1974; JD, U. Puget Sound, 1976. Bar: Wash. 1977. Former atty. priv. practice; justice Wash. Supreme Ct., 1991—, assoc. chief justice. Adjunct prof. Seattle U. Law Sch., 1977—91; co-chair Wash. State Minority and Justice Commn., Equal Civil Justice Funding Task Force. Mem. bd. dirs. Wash. Assn. Children and Parents; mem. vis. com. U. Wash. Sch. Social Work; bd. visitors Seattle U. Sch. Law; liaison ltd. practice bd., co-chair BJA subcom. on juv. svcs.; mem. Am. Inns of Ct., World Affairs Coun. Pierce County. Mem. Wash. State Bar Assn., Tacoma-Pierce County Bar Assn. (Liberty Bell award young lawyers sect. 1994). Avocations: sailing, downhill skiing, bicycling. Office: Wash State Supreme Ct PO Box 40929 Olympia WA 98504-0929

JOHNSON, CHERLYN ANN, education educator; b. New Orleans, La., Dec. 27, 1969; d. Isadore and Kathleen Marie Johnson. BA, Dillard U., 1992; MA, U. Akron, 1995; PhD, Syracuse U., 2000. Tchg. asst. U. Akron, 1993—95, English tchr., 1994—95; instr. Syracuse U., 1995—99; tchr. English, summer supr. Syracuse Ednl. Opportunity Ctr.-SUNY, 1999—2000; asst. prof. Va. State U., 2001—. Rev. Multicultural Perspectives Jour., 2002—; author: Guests at an Ivory Tower: The Challenges Black Students Experience While Attending a Predominantly White University, 2005. English Edn. Cultural Diversity grant, Nat. Coun. of Tchrs. of English, 1999. Mem.: Am. Edn. Rsch. Assn., Nat. Coun. of Tchrs. of English, Nat. Assn. of Multicultural Edn. Dem. Bapt. Avocations: reading, writing, travel. Office: Va State U PO Box 9072 Petersburg VA 23806 Business E-Mail: cajohnso@vsu.edu.

JOHNSON, CHEVALIER RUTHERFORD BARRY, economist, consultant; s. Chevalier Barry and Marianne Faircloth. BS with honors, Ga. Inst. Tech., 2000, MS, 2003. Assoc. R. Barry Johnson, Cons., Huntsville, Ala., 1996—. Contbr. scientific papers to profl. jours. Operational auxilarist (highest status) US Coast Guard Aux.; unit commr. Blue Grass Coun., Boy Scouts Am., Lexington, Ky.; mem. Cath. Com. Scouting for Diocese Lexington, Lexington, Ky., 2003. Decorated Meritorious Team Commendation Operational O US Coast Guard, Unit Commendation with Operational O. Mem.: Internat. Soc. for Philos. Enquiry, US Lipizzan Registry, The Lafayette Club, Mil. Soc. of the Wild Geese Noble Officer Corps, Noble Soc. of Celts (sec. 2002), Omicron Delta Epsilon, Nat. Eagle Scout Assn. Roman Catholic. Avocations: yachting, music, dance, history.

JOHNSON, CHRISTINE VAUGHN, secondary educator; b. Bremerton, Wash., Mar. 14, 1951; d. Roy Vaughn and Florence Mae (Cleveland) J.; m. Jay Herbert Gainer, Feb. 25, 1989. BA in Math. and Secondary Edn., Western Wash. U., Bellingham, 1970-74, postgrad., 1974-75. Tchr. corps intern Neah Bay (Wash.) Sch., 1972-73; secondary math instr. Forks (Wash.) High Sch., 1975-77; middle and upper sch. math. tchr. Bush Sch., Seattle, 1977-91; curriculum specialist Wash. Math. Engring. Sci. Achievement U. Wash. Coll. Engring., Seattle, 1991-93, 1996—98; math instr. Univ. Prep. Acad., Seattle, 1992-93; mem. founding com. Hyla Middle Sch., Bainbridge Island, Wash., 1993—; mid. sch. math. tchr. Hyla Mid. Sch., Banbridge Island, Wash., 1998—. Tchr. math. engring. and sci. achievement U. Wash., 1988, workshop coord., 1986; instr. Upward Bound, Western Wash. U., Bellingham, 1975-77; pres. Nat. Nuclear Free and Ind. Pacific Network Bd., 1983-84; tchr. math. ednl. enrichment program Lakeside Sch. Contbg. author (book) Quilting with Kids, 1997; author: curriculum materials for mid. sch. students. Recipient award Wash. Environ. Edn. Assn. Home: 5864 Old Mill Rd NE Bainbridge Island WA 98110-3139 E-mail: chris@hylamiddleschool.org.

JOHNSON, CHRISTOPHER D., lawyer; b. Little Rock, Ark., 1952; BA magna cum laude, Princeton U., 1974; JD, U. Va., 1977. Bar: Ariz. 1977, registered: US Dist. Ct., Ariz. 1977, US Ct. Appeals (9th cir.) 1978. Ptnr. Squire, Sanders & Dempsey LLP, Phoenix, chmn., Corp. Fin. Practice Group. Contbr. articles to profl. jours.; spkr. in field. Bd. dir. Enterprise Network, Ariz. Tech. Incubator. Mem.: Ariz. Software & Internet Assn., State Bar Ariz. (exec. coun. mem. 1979—95, chmn. Securities Regulation Sect. 1994—95), Order of Coif. Office: Squire Sanders & Dempsey LLP Two Renaissance Sq 40 N Central Ave Ste 2700 Phoenix AZ 85004-4498 Office Phone: 602-528-4046. Office Fax: 602-253-8129. Business E-Mail: cjohnson@ssd.com.

JOHNSON, CHRISTOPHER HOWARD, historian; b. Washington, Ind., Nov. 22, 1937; s. Austin F. and Janice (Thompson) Johnson; m. Lois Ann Sebree, June 10, 1960; children: Leslie C. Giordani, Abigail E. Kercorian. BA, Wabash Coll., Crawfordsville, Ind., 1960; MS, U. Wis., Madison, 1962, PhD, 1968. Asst. prof. Wayne State U., Detroit, 1966—70; vis. lectr. U. E. Anglia, Norwich, England, 1970—71; asst. prof. Wayne State U., Detroit, 1971—74, assoc. prof., 1974—80, prof., 1980—2003, mem., acad. scholars, 1997—, prof. emeritus, 2003—. Mem. bd. editors French Hist. Studies, 1983—90; vis. prof. U. Mich., Ann Arbor, 1989; residential fellow Camargo Found., Cassis, France, 1999. Author: Utopian Communism in France: Cabet and the Icarians, 1839-1851, 1974 (Nat. Book Award nominee, 1975), Maurice Sugar: Law, Labor, and the Left in Detroit, 1912-1950, 1989, The Life and Death of Industrial Languedoc, 1700-1920, 1995. Bd. trustees Ferndale Ednl. Found., Mich., 2004—; mem. Pleasant Ridge Planning Commn., Mich., 2004—. Fellow, Social Sci. Rsch. Coun., 1964—65, NEH, 1975, Guggenheim Found., 1981—82. Mem.: 18th Century Studies Assn., Soc. for French Hist. Studies, Am. Hist. Assn. Democrat. Avocations: golf, violin. Business E-Mail: aa4307@wayne.edu.

JOHNSON, CHRISTOPHER TODD, music educator, music minister; m. Sonia Johnson, Apr. 27, 2002. B in Music Edn., BS in Computer Sci., Iowa State U., 2000. Dir. worship ministries Grand Ave. Bapt. Ch., Ames, Iowa, 1999—; vocal music tchr. Roland-Story Mid. Sch., Roland, Iowa, 2001—. Mem.: Iowa Choral Dirs. Assn. (website designer 2002—05). Avocations: singing, gigging with jazz musicians, travel. Home: 2319 Jensen Ave Ames IA 50010

JOHNSON, CLARENCE TRAYLOR, JR., state judge; b. Trenton, Fla., Aug. 16, 1929; s. Clarence Traylor and Jessie Granade (Wilson) J.; m. Shirley Ann Traxler, Aug. 30, 1957; children: James Waring, Robert Dale, Douglas Earl, Jan Elizabeth. BSBA, U. Fla., 1955, JD, 1958. Ptnr. Cone, Wagner, Nugent, Johnson, McKeown & Dell, West Palm Beach, Fla., 1958-71; sr. cir. ct. judge 18th Jud. Cir. of Fla., Brevard and Seminole Counties, 1971-92. Chmn. Fla. Conf. of Cir. Judges, 1990-91; mem. Fla. Bench Bar Commn., State of Fla., 1990-92; faculty Fla. Jud. Coll., 1988-90; mem. Fla. Fed.-State Jud. Coun., 1989-91, Jud. Coun. Fla., 1989-91. Pres. Jr. C. of C., Cocoa, Fla., 1963-64; chmn. bd. Cen. Brevard YMCA, Cocoa, 1965-66; pres. YMCA, Brevard County, 1968-71, Rotary, Cocoa, 1965-66; charter pres. Vassar B. Carlton Am. Inn of Ct., 1992-93. With USAF, 1950-54. Recipient Disting. Svc. award Cocoa Jaycees, 1965, Jud. Achievement award Acad. Fla. Trial Lawyers, 1987. Mem. ABA, Brevard County Bar Assn. (pres. 1969-70), The Fla. Bar (bd. govs. 1970-71). Lutheran. Avocation: fishing. Home: 600 Heron Dr Merritt Island FL 32952-4022

JOHNSON, CLARK CUMINGS, lawyer, educator, dean; b. Traverse City, Mich., Nov. 19, 1940; s. Harold Eugene and Mary Delight (Cummings) Johnson; m. Kerry Jane Spencer, May 1, 1990; children: Asher, James, Christopher, Spencer, Sterling, Iris. BA, U. Mich., 1963; JD cum laude, Wayne State U., 1970, MS, 1985, PhD, 1990; LLD (hon.), Mich. State U., 2002. Bar: Mich. 1970, U.S. Dist. (ea. dist.) Mich. 1970, U.S. Supreme Ct. 1974, U.S. Ct. Appeals (6th cir.) 1998. Asst. atty. gen., Mich., 1970—71; ptnr. Schmidt, Nahas, Coburn & Johnson, Mount Clemens, 1971—74; prof. law Mich. State U., 1974—, assoc. dean, 1984—85. Home: 1687 Quarton Rd Birmingham MI 48009-1037 Office: Mich State U 83 E Shaw Ln East Lansing MI 48824-1300 Office Phone: 248-258-0700. Business E-Mail: drclarkjohnson@law.msu.edu.

JOHNSON, CLARK EVERETTE, JR., judge; b. Jacksonville, Ala., Oct. 2, 1923; s. Clark Everette and Nora Lee (Kelley) J.; m. Arlene Washam, Feb. 23, 1952; children: David Terrel, Paul T., Clark Everette III. BS in Commerce, U. Ala., 1947, LLB, 1948. Bar: Ala. 1948. Pvt. practice, Albertville, Ala., 1948-71; asst. dist. atty. Marshall County, 1952-53; cir. judge 27th Jud. Cir., Marshall County, 1971-88. Tchr. Sunday sch. local Meth. ch., 1950—; candidate for Ala. legislature, 1958, 62. With AUS, 1943-46. Decorated Purple Heart. Mem. Ala. Bar Assn., Marshall County Bar Assn. Home: 5 Wright Rd Albertville AL 35951-4130

JOHNSON, CLARKE COURTNEY, financial consultant, educator; b. Wisconsin Rapids, Wis., July 11, 1936; s. Julius and Esther (Larsen) L. BSEE, U. Wis., 1958; MSIM, Purdue U., 1962, PhD, 1972. Asst. prof., asst. dean U. Wis.-Milw., 1966-72; vis. prof. Boston U. Sch. Mgmt., 1973-75; assoc. prof., assoc. dean DePaul U. Coll. Commerce, Chgo., 1975-77; prof., dean Iona Coll. Sch. Bus., New Rochelle, N.Y., 1977-79; prof. fin. Pace U. Grad. Sch. Bus., N.Y.C., 1979-98, chmn. dept., 1985-98, chmn. faculty coun. Sch. Bus., 1996-98; ret., 1998; pres. C. Johnson and Assocs., 1998—. Cons. in field Contbr. articles to profl. jours. Served with USAF, 1958-61. Mem. Am. Fin. Assn., Am. Econs. Assn., Fin. Mgmt. Assn., Eta Kappa Nu, Beta Gamma Sigma. Home: 333 E 79th St Apt 20Y New York NY 10021-0961 Office: 333 E 79th St Apt 20Y New York NY 10021-0961 Office Phone: 212-535-9411. E-mail: ckcjohnson@aol.com.

JOHNSON, CLAUD H., sales executive, consultant; BA in Bus. Adminstrn., U. Colo., Boulder. Mgr.-distr. sales to nat. sales mgr., sr. tech. rep. Miles Labs., Inc., Elkhart, Ind., 1976—82; U.S. sales mgr. Bartek Ingredients, Inc., Stoney Creek, 1983—2002; pres. Claud H. Johnson, Inc. Sales Agency, USA, Cherry Hill, NJ, 2002—05. Recipient awards, Nat. Inst. Food Technologists, Am. Assn. Cereal Chemists, Nat. Assn. Candy Technologists, Chgo. Drug and Chem. Assn. Address: 11 Candlewick Way Cherry Hill NJ 08003

JOHNSON, CLEVELAND THOMAS, music historian, church musician; b. Norfolk, Va., Nov. 3, 1955; s. Thomas Butt Jr. and Hilda Faith (Shelton) J.; children: Kimberly Elizabeth, Anneke Marie, Nicholas Vasek. BMus, Oberlin (Ohio) Coll., 1977; DPhil, Oxford (Eng.) U., 1984. Music librarian Old Dominion U., Norfolk, 1984-85; assoc. prof. music DePauw U., Greencastle, Ind., 1985—. Author: Vocal Compositions in German Organ Tablatures, 1550-1650: A Catalogue and Commentary, 1989; editor: (music edit.) Heinrich Scheidemann 12 Orgelintavolierungen, 3 vols., 1990-93; recs. (6 CDs) Complete Organ Works of Heinrich Scheidemann. Bd. dirs. Habitat for Humanity, Putnam County, Ind., 1990-91, 94, 95. Lilly Endowment grantee, 1989, NEH grantee, 1987, 89, DAAD/Fulbright grantee, Germany, 1980-81 Am. Inst. Indian Studies grantee, 2001, ASIA Network greantee, 2003; Thomas J. Watson fellow. Mem. Am. Musicol. Soc., Westfield Ctr. for Early Keyboard Studies, Early Music Am., Am. Guild of Organists (dean DePauw U. chpt. 1985-87). Avocations: gardening (antique roses), antique hunting, calligraphy. Home: 425 Anderson St Greencastle IN 46135 Office: DePauw U Sch Music Greencastle IN 46135-0037 Office Phone: 317-658-4396. E-mail: cjohnson@depauw.edu.

JOHNSON, CLIFTON HERMAN, retired historian, retired archivist, retired director; b. Griffin, Ga., Sept. 13, 1921; s. John and Pearl (Parrish) Johnson; m. Rosemary Brunst, Aug. 2, 1960; children: Charles, Robert, Virginia. Student, U. Conn., 1943—44; BA, U. N.C., 1948, PhD, 1959; MA, U. Chgo., 1949; postgrad., U. Wis., 1951. Tutor LeMoyne Coll., Memphis, 1950—53, asst. prof., 1953—56, prof., 1960—61, 1963—66; asst. prof. East Carolina Coll., 1958—59; asst. libr. and archivist Fisk U., 1961—63; exec. dir. Amistad Rsch. Ctr., New Orleans, 1966—92, emeritus, 1992. Author (with Carroll Barber): The American Negro: A Selected and Annotated Bibliography for High Schools and Junior Colleges, 1968; author: A Legacy of La Amistad: Some Twentieth Century Black Leaders, 1989, Abolitionism in the Antislavery Movement, 1997; editor: God Struck Me Dead: Religious Conversions and Experiences and Autobiographies of Ex-Slaves, 1969. Exec. bd. dirs. All Congregations Together, 1997—2002; bd. dirs. La. World Expn., 1980—82, Lillie Carroll Jackson Mus., 1978—89, Countee Cullen Found., 1981—87, Friends of Archives La., 1978—90, La. Folklife Commn., 1982—85, Ctr. for Black Music Rsch., 1986—, New Orleans Urban League, 1994—2001; cons. DreamWorks Prodns., 1997. With AUS, 1940—45. NEH fellow, 1994. Mem.: Am. Cival Liberties Union, Lane Co. Com. for Defense of Bill of Rights, So. Poverty Law Ctr., Beyond War, Amistad Am. Business E-Mail: clifton@peak.org.

JOHNSON, CONOR DEANE, mechanical engineer; b. Charlottesville, Va., Apr. 20, 1943; s. Randolph Holaday and Louise Anna (Deane) J.; m. Laura Teague Rogers, Dec. 20, 1966; children: William Drake, Catherine Teague. BS in Engring. Mechanics, Va. Poly. Inst., 1965; MS, Clemson U., 1967, PhD in Engring. Mechanics, 1969. Registered profl. engr., Calif. With Anamet Labs., Inc., 1973-82, sr. structural analyst Dayton, Ohio, 1973-75, prin. engr. San Carlos, Calif., 1975-81, v.p., 1981-82; program mgr. Aerospace Structures Info. and Analysis Ctr., 1975-82; co-founder, pres. CSA Engring., Inc., Mountain View, Calif., 1982—. Tech. dir. damping conf., exec. com. N.Am. Conf. on Smart Materials and Structures. Contbr. articles to profl. jours.; patentee in field. Capt. USAF, 1969-73 Mem. AIAA (structural dynamics tech. com.), ASME (adaptive structures tech. com., structures and materials award 1981), N.Am. Smart Structures and Materials Conf. (mem. exec. com., tech. chmn. Damping confs. 1991, 93, 95, 96), Gourmet Cooking Club, Sigma Xi. Methodist. Home: 3408 Beresford Ave Belmont CA 94002-1302 Office: CSA Engring Inc 2565 Leghorn St Mountain View CA 94043-1613 Office Phone: 650-210-9000. Business E-Mail: cjohnson@csaengineering.com.

JOHNSON, CORNELIUS RAYMOND, prosecutor; b. Waco, Tex., Jan. 20, 1963; s. Virgil O. Howard and Beatrice Earline Johnson; m. Gay Lanell Pasley (div. Dec. 1999). AA, Tarrant County Jr. Coll., 1990; BS, Tex. Christian U., 1991; JD, U. Tulsa, 1995. Bar: Okla. 1996, U.S. Ct. Appeals (10th cir.) 1996, U.S. Dist. Ct. (no. and ea. dists.) Okla. 1997, U.S. Dist. Ct. (we. dist.) Okla. 1998, U.S. Supreme Ct. 2000. Assoc. atty. Law Firm of Riggs, Abney, Tulsa, 1996-99; asst. city atty. Tulsa City Atty.'s Office, Tulsa, 1999—. Bd. dirs. Leadership Tulsa, 1999. Maj. USAR. Mem. ABA, Okla. Bar Assn., Spl. Forces Assn., 1st Calvalry Divsn. Assn., 1st Infantry Divsn. Assn., Internat. Churchill Soc., Nat. Black Prosecutors Assn. Democrat. Unitarian Universalist. Avocations: weightlifting, jogging, reading, cooking, horseback riding. Office: Tulsa City Attys Office 200 Civic Ctr Tulsa OK 74103-3856 Office Phone: 918-596-7717. Business E-Mail: crjohnson@ci.tulsa.ok.us.

JOHNSON, CRAIG N., management consultant; b. Warren, Pa., Jan. 8, 1942; s. Norman Andrew and Edice (Riedel) J.; m. Sally Van Dusen, May 23, 1969; children: Maria Pepper, Anna Sergeant, Samantha Bennett. BS, U. Pa., 1963, MBA, 1968. Cert. mgmt. cons. Inst. Mgmt. Cons. Prin. William E. Hill & Co. Inc., N.Y.C., 1968-72; v.p. INA Properties, Phila., 1972-75; sr. prin. Hay Assocs., Phila., 1975-80; pres. Lavino Shipping Co., Phila., 1980-90, Maritrans, Inc., Phila., 1990—94; mng. dir., adv. dir. Glenthorne Capital Inc., 1994—; chmn. Blair Corp., 2003—. Bd. dirs. The Phila. Contributorship; chmn. Blair Corp., 2003—; bd. trustees Chestnut Hill Healthcare Found. Mem. Com. of Seventy, Phila., 1975-97; bd. dirs. Acad. Natural Scis., Phila.; trustee Springside Sch., 1994-98; assoc. trustee U. Pa., 1990-96. Repubican. Episcopalian. E-mail: craig.johnson74@verizon.net.

JOHNSON, CRAIG W., lawyer; b. Pasadena, Calif., Dec. 28, 1946; BA magna cum laude, Yale U., 1968; JD, Stanford U., 1974. Bar: Calif. 1974. Atty. Wilson, Sonsini, Goodrich & Rosati, Palo Alto, Calif. Bd. visitors Stanford U. Law Sch., 1974-77. Mem. State Bar Calif. Office: Wilson Sonsini Goodrich & Rosati Two Palo Alto Sq Palo Alto CA 94306

JOHNSON, CRANE, writer, lawyer; b. Bayard, Nebr., June 30, 1921; s. Carl Arthur and Pearl (Haskins) J. MA, U. So. Calif., 1948; postgrad., Stanford U., 1949; PhD, Case We. Res. U., 1960; LLB, N.Y. Law Sch., 1960; LLM, NYU, 1968. Bar: N.Y., 1962. Vol. legal aid lawyer. Author: Past Sixty, 1953, The Withered Garland, 1956, Seven Short Plays, 1965, Tiger In Crystal, 1966, Seven Shorter Plays, 1966, Seven Strange Plays, 1966, Twenty-Five One Act Plays, 1966, Ten One Act Plays, 1967, Thirty-Five One Act Plays, 1967, Venus Preserved, 1971, The Locusts, 1971, Dracula, 1976, Presque Isle Village, 1995, Three Jacumba Tales, 1998, Ten Stories, 1999, Twelve Jacumba Tales, 1999, Jacumba Heidi, 2000, Buckboard to Jacumba, 2001, Mountain Springs Saga, 2002, Seven Jacumba Tales, 2003, Letters From Miss Ellen, 2004, author of over 50 plays. U.S. rep. at ednl. confs. in London and Vienna. Served with AUS, WWII. Mem. N.Y. Bar Assn. Address: PO Box 158 Jacumba CA 91934-0158

JOHNSON, CURTIS LEE, publishing executive, editor, writer; b. Mpls., May 26, 1928; s. Hjalmar N. and Gladys (Goring) J.; m. Jo Ann Lekwa, June 30, 1950 (div. 1974); children: Mark Alan, Paula Catherine; m. Rochelle Miller Hickey, Jan. 11, 1975 (div. 1980); m. Betty Axelrod Fox, Aug. 28, 1982 (div. 1990). BA, U. Iowa, 1951, MA, 1952. Mag. and ency. editing and writing, Chgo., 1953-60; textbook and ednl. editing and writing, 1960-66; editor, pub. December Press, 1962—, pres., 1985—; free-lance editing and writing, 1966-72, 78—; mng. editor Aldine Pub. Co., 1972-73; v.p. St. Clair Press, 1973-77; sr. writer Bradford Exchange, 1978-81; mng. editor Regnery Gateway, 1981-82. Author: (with George Uskali) How to Restore Antique and Classic Cars, 1954; Hobbledehoy's Hero, 1959, Nobody's Perfect, 1973, Lace and a Bobbitt, 1976, The Morning Light, 1977, Song for Three Voices, 1984; The Mafia Manager, 1991, (with R. Craig Sautter) Wicked City Chicago, 1994, Thanksgiving in Vegas, 1995, 500 Years of Obscene...and Counting, 1997; editor: (with Jarvis Thurston) Stories from the Literary Magazines, 1970, Best Little Magazine Fiction, 1970, (with Alvin Greenberg), 1971, (with Jack Conroy) Writers in Revolt, 1973, (with Diane Kruchkow) Green Isle in the Sea, 1986, Who's Who in Writers, Editors & Poets, 1985-96; essays The Forbidden Writings of Lee Wallek, 1978; (with R. Craig Sautter) 26 Martyrs, 2004, Little by Little, 2004, Salud: Selections and Interview, 2005; contbr. articles to profl. jours.; cons. editor Panache mag, 1967-76. With USN, 1946—48, with USNR, 1948—53. Nat. Endowment Arts writing grantee, 1973, 81 Mem. Nat. Writers Union, Phi Beta Kappa, Club d'Ronde. Office: December Press PO Box 302 Highland Park IL 60035-0302 Office Phone: 847-940-4122.

JOHNSON, CURTIS LILDON, retired oil industry executive; b. La Mesa, Tex., May 11, 1922; s. William Marion and Annie Mary (Pearson) J.; married Feb. 21, 1945; children: Sarah Ann, Rebecca Sue, Richard Curtis. BBA, U. Tex., 1949, JD, 1948. Agt. Bur. Internal Revenue, Corpus Christi, Tex., 1949-50; civil svc. dir. NAS Hosp., Corpus Christi, 1950-51; wire line operator Otis Pressure Control, Corpus Christi, 1951-52; directional driller Houston Oil Field Material Co., Corpus Christi, 1952-60, dist. svc. mgr. Alice, Tex., 1960-64; v.p. svcs. D&W Oil Tools, Corpus Christi, 1964-67; owner, pres. Target Directional Drilling and Petroleum Cons., Corpus Christi, 1967-79, 80-85; v.p., ops. mgr. Goldston Oil Co., Houston, 1979-80; pres. J.O. Resources Devel. Co., Corpus Christi, 1985-93; acct. mgr., sales rep. Multi-Shot (a BWWC Co.), Corpus Christi, 1993—2003; ret. Sgt. USAF, 1942-45, PTO. Recipient award Pres. of Tunisia, 1980. Mem. Soc. of Petroleum Engrs., Internat., Corpus Christi Am. Petroleum Inst., Victoria Am. Petroleum Inst., Masons. Democrat. Avocations: golf, hunting, sports officiating.

JOHNSON, CYNDA ANN, physician, educator; b. Girard, Kans., July 16, 1951; BA in Biology and German with honors, Stanford U., 1973; MD, UCLA, 1977; MBA, U. Mo., Kansas City, 1999. Diplomate Am. Bd. Family Medicine (bd. dirs., pres. 1999-2000). Tchg. fellow U. N.C., Chapel Hill, 1980-81; intern U. Kans. Med. Ctr., Kansas City, 1977-78, 1978-80, prof., acting chair dept. family medicine, 1998—99; prof., head dept. family medicine U. Iowa Coll. Medicine, Iowa City, 1999—2003; dean Brody Sch. Medicine East Carolina U., Greenville, NC, 2003—. Mem. Am. Acad. Family Physicians, Soc. Tchrs. Family Medicine, N.C. Acad. of Family Physicians, N.C. Med. Soc. Office: E Carolina U Brody Sch Medicine Brody AD52 600 Moye Blvd Greenville NC 27834 Office Phone: 252-744-2201. E-mail: johnsoncyn@mail.ecu.edu.

JOHNSON, DANIEL D., music educator; b. Hettinger, N.D., Oct. 7, 1952; BA, Concordia Coll., 1974; M in Music Edn., Northwestern U., 1980. Music educator Terry H.S., 1974—76, Bishop Ryan H.S., 1976—79, Dickinson H.S., 1980—86, Perry Hall H.S., 1986—90, Capital H.S., 1991—96, Skyview H.S., Nampa, Idaho, 1996—2004. Mem.: Nampa Edn. Assn., Idaho Music Educator's Assn., NEA, Nat. Band Assn., Music Educators Nat. Conf., Coll. Mus. Soc., World Assn. Symphonic Bands and Ensembles. Lutheran. Avocations: music, genealogy. Home: 406 E Michigan Ave Nampa ID 83686

JOHNSON, DARRYL NORMAN, retired ambassador; b. Chgo., 1938; m. Kathleen Desa Forance; 3 children. BA cum laude in English Literature, U. Wash., 1960. With Boeing Co., Seattle, 1962; vol. Peace Corps, Thailand, 1963—65; fgn. svc. officer US Dept. State, Bombay, 1966-68, Hong Kong, 1969-73, Moscow, 1974-77, officer-in-charge Yugoslav affairs Washington, 1977-79, China, 1979-81; Pearson fellow Office Senator Claiborne Pell, Washington, 1981-82, spl. asst. to Under Sec. Polit. Affairs, 1982-84; fgn. counselor for polit. affairs US Dept. State, Beijing, 1984—87, dep. chief of mission Warsaw, 1988—91, US amb. to Lithuania Vilnius, 1991—94, dep. coord. for asst. and former Soviet Union, 1994—96, dir. Am. Inst., 1996—99, polit. adv. to chief and naval ops., 1999—2000, dep. asst. sec. state for East Asian and Pacific affairs, 2000—01, US amb. to Thailand Bangkok, 2001—04; ret., 2004.

JOHNSON, DARYL DIANE, oil painter; b. N.Y.C., Aug. 28, 1953; d. Wilbur Henry and Dorothy (Hinton) J.; m. C. Roth Benson, May 8, 1982; children: Sven Hardy Benson, Astrid Posey Benson. BFA, Hope Coll., 1975; postgrad., U. Cin., 1976, Art Student's League, N.Y.C., 1978. Vt. Studio Sch., Johnson, 1988. Paintings in permanent collections of: Aetna Ins. Co., Hartford, Conn., Delta Airlines, Boston, Gen. Electric, Greenwich (Conn.) Hosp., Mariott Hotels, N.Y.C. and St. Louis, Pepsico, Purchase, N.Y., WMUR-TV, Manchester, N.H. One-man shows: Bell Gallery, Stamford, Conn., 1983, Cityarts Gallery, New Haven, 1987, Hatfield Gallery, Manchester, 1989, McGowan Gallery, Concord, N.H., 1990. Author commd. works Mary Immaculate Hosp., 1983, mural "New Hampshire Triptych" WMUR-TV, 1992. Recipient painting award Conn. Painters and Sculptors Show, Stamford Mus., 1981. Mem. N.H. Art Assn. (in juried shows recipient 1st prize 1989, 90, Miriam Sawyer award 1989, Connor award 1990), N.H. Creative Club. Avocation: motorcycling. Home and Office: 31 Storybrook Ln Amherst NH 03031-2604 Office Phone: 603-672-4422.

JOHNSON, DAVID, medical association administrator; Dir. divsn. oncology, hematology Vanderbilt U., Nashville. Office: Vanderbilt U 777 Preston Research Bldg Hematology/Oncology Nashville TN 37232-6307 Office Phone: 615-343-9454.

JOHNSON, DAVID CHESTER, academic administrator, sociologist, educator; b. Jan. 21, 1933; s. Chester Laven and Olga Henriett (Resnick) J.; m. Jean Ann Lunnis, Sept. 10, 1955 (dec. 1996); children: Stephen, Andrew, Jennifer. BA, Gustavus Adolphus Coll., 1954; MA, U. Iowa, 1956, PhD, 1959; LLD, Luther Coll., 1993. Instr. to prof. sociology Luther Coll., Decorah, Iowa, 1957-69; dean arts and scis. East Stroudsburg (Pa.) U., 1969-76; v.p. acad. affairs St. Cloud (Minn.) State U., 1976-83; dean Gustavus Adolphus Coll., St. Peter, Minn., 1983-90; chancellor U. Minn., Morris, 1990-98; cons. to Scandinavian univs., 1999—. Leader of numerous hiking groups to Norwegian and Transylvanian mountains. Mem. bd. Friends of Libr., U. Minn. Librs., 2003—. NSF sci. faculty fellow Inst. Social Rsch., Oslo, 1965-66, adminstrv. fellow Am. Coun. Edn., Luther Coll., 1968-69, Summer Leadership fellow Bush Found., Inst. Edn. Mgmt., Harvard U., 1981; Kennedy Swedish Fund grantee, 1976. Mem. Elder Learning Inst. U. Minn. (bd. dirs., pres.), U. Minn. Retirees Assn. (pres.), Am. Swedish Inst., Friends of the Libr. Democrat. Lutheran. Home: 1235 Yale Pl Apt 1705 Minneapolis MN 55403-1948

JOHNSON, DAVID D., lawyer, game company executive; b. Sioux City, Iowa, Aug. 17, 1951; BA in Polit. Sci., U. Nev., 1975; JD, Creighton U., 1978. Chief dep. atty. gen. Gaming Divsn. Nev. Atty. Gen. Office, 1985—87; ptnr. Schreck, Jones, Bernhard, Woloson & Godfrey, 1987—95; sr. v.p., gen. counsel, sec. Alliance Gaming Corp., 1995—2000; gen. counsel Anchor Gaming, 2000—01; ptnr. Bernhard, Bradley & Johnson, Las Vegas, 2001—03; sr. v.p., gen. counsel, sec. Internat. Game Technology, Reno, 2003—. Office: International Game Technology 9295 Prototype Dr Reno NV 89521*

JOHNSON, DAVID J., JR., lawyer; b. Huntington, NY, 1956; BA, U. Va., 1979, JD, MBA, U. Va., 1985. Bar: Calif. 1985, US Dist. Ct., Ctrl. Dist. Calif. 1985. Ptnr. corp./securities O'Melveny & Myers LLP, LA, head transactions dept., mem. policy com., ptnr. Washington. Office: O'Melveny & Myers LLP 400 S Hope St Los Angeles CA 90071-2899 Address: O'Melveny & Myers LLP 1625 Eye St NW Washington DC 20006-4001 Office Phone: 213-430-6605. Office Fax: 213-430-6407. Business E-Mail: david_johnson@omm.com.

JOHNSON, DAVID KENNETH, historian; b. Keene, N.H., Dec. 31, 1960; s. Kenneth R. and Julia (Lewis) J. BA, Georgetown U., 1983; MA, U. Chgo., 1987; PhD candidate, Northwestern U., 1992—. Historian History Assocs. Inc., Rockville, Md., 1988-92; fellow history dept. Northwestern U., Evanston, Ill., 1992-96, adj. lectr., fellow history dept., 1997—; fellow Smithsonian Instn., Washington, 1996-97. Author: (with others) Creating a Place for Ourselves, 1997, Leaders From the 1960s, 1994; contbr. articles to profl. jours. Pres. Northwestern U. Gay & Lesbian Univ. Union, 1995-96. Fellow Smithsonian Instn., 1996-97; Dissertation Year fellow Northwestern U., 1997-98. Mem. Orgn. Am. Historians, Am. Hist. Assn. Office: Northwestern Univ Dept Hist Harris Hall 202 Evanston IL 60208-0001

JOHNSON, DAVID M., finance company executive; Bachelor's Degree with honors, Harvard U., 1982; M in Econs., Yale U., 1986. Mng. dir. investment banking divsn. Merrill Lynch, Pierce, Fenner and Smith, 1986—98; exec. v.p. fin. Cendant Corp., 1998, sr. v.p., CFO, 1998—2001; exec. v.p., CFO The Hartford Fin. Svcs. Group, Inc., 2001—. Named one of top tech. innovators, Info. Week mag., 2004; named one of leading U.S. CFO's under age 40, CFO Mag., 2000. Office: The Hartford Fin Svcs Group Inc Hartford Plaza 690 Asylum Ave Hartford CT 06115

JOHNSON, DAVID PAUL, music educator; b. Madison, Wis., Jan. 25, 1950; s. Paul Strepper and Shirley Johnson; m. Mary Lea Bowers, Aug. 21, 1971; children: Scott David, Kimberly Matie. BA Music Edn., U. Wis. Madison, 1972. Cert. Tchr. DPI Madison, Wis., 1972. Trip dir. YMCA, Madison, Wis., 1966—68; first sgt. Wis. N.G. Band, Madison, Wis., 1972—2002; adjudicator Wis. Sch. Music Assn., Madison, 1972—. Adjudicator Wis. Sch. Music Assn., Madison, Wis., 1975—. None (none) None (none, none). None none, None, None. 1sg Army N.G., 1972—2002, Madison, WI. Decorated Army Commendation Medal Wis. N.G. Mem.: Phi Beta Mu (assoc.; none, none none). Conservative. Catholic. Achievements include patents for None. Avocations: gardening, fishing, none, none, none. Home: 431 Fairview Dr Viroqua WI 54665 Office: Cashton Oublic Schools 540 Coe St Cashton WI 54619 Business E-Mail: johnsond@cashton.k12.wi.us.

JOHNSON, DAVID PAUL, writer, poet, publishing executive; b. Mpls., Sept. 26, 1941; s. Arthur Gerald and Elizabeth Louise Johnson; m. DoRayne Lee Hendrickson, Sept. 13, 1969; children: Arthur Gerald, Andrew Paul. BA, U. Minn., 1964. Pres. Am. Comml. Properties, Edina, Minn., 1981—90; exec. v.p. JBL Cos., Eagan, Minn., 1990—2000; owner, founder Bristlecone Pub., New Hope, Minn., 2000—. Author (pen name David Paul): Liberate Me, Lord - Trilogy, 2002—04. Dir. Downtown Y, Mpls., 1979—93, chmn. of bd., 1990—91, vice chmn., 1988—89; dir. Cir. of Discipline, Mpls., 1999—2005. Office: Bristlecone Pub Co 3527 Hillsboro Ave New Hope MN 55427 Office Phone: 763-746-3805. E-mail: dpaulbristlecone@comcast.net.

JOHNSON, DAVID PAUL, music educator; b. Pullman, Wash., Oct. 8, 1957; s. Robert Owen and Barbara Anderson Johnson; m. Vickie Galster Reinwald (div.); children: Isaac, Claire, Celeste; m. Nadya Stepanova Johnson, June 5, 2004. BA, Whitman Coll., 1980; MA, U. Oreg., 1992, PhD, 1997. Music specialist Grant Union High Sch., John Day, Oreg., 1984—90, Yoncalla Sch. Dist., 1998—2004; CEO Three Jewels Music, Republic, 2001—; music specialist Republic Sch. Dist., Wash., 2004—05. Composer-in-residence Corp. Yaddo, Saratoga Springs, NY, 1992. Composer: (CD's) David Paul Johnson 5x5, 1996, Songs to the Silent Moon, 2001. Fellow, U. Oreg., Eugene, 1991—94. Mem.: Am. Soc. Composers, Authors and Pubs., Music Educators Nat. Conf. Home: PO Box 1196 680 Leo Gaffney Republic WA 99166 Office: Three Jewels Music PO Box 1196 Republic WA 99166

JOHNSON, DAVID RAYMOND, lawyer; b. Bartlesville, Okla., Sept. 12, 1946; s. Lloyd Theodore and Mary Pauline (Auten) J.; m. Marion Frances Monroe, May 14, 1977; children: Marc, Meredith. BA, Tulane U., 1968; JD, U. Va., 1971. Bar: Tex. 1971, D.C. 1977, U.S. Dist. Ct. D.C. 1979, U.S. Ct. Appeals (D.C. cir.) 1981, U.S. Supreme Ct. 1982, U.S. Claims Ct. 1984. Assoc. Fulbright & Jaworski, Houston, 1971-72, Washington, 1974-78, ptnr., 1978-87; atty.-advisor Office of Gen. Counsel of Air Force, Washington, 1972-74; ptnr. Gibson, Dunn & Crutcher LLP, Washington, 1987—2003, adv. counsel, 2004—. Trustee Washington Episcopal Sch., 1991-93, McLean Sch. Md., 1994-96. Capt. USAF, 1972-74. Mem. D.C. Bar Assn., Phi Beta Kappa, Raven Soc., Order of Coif, Congressional Country Club. Office: Gibson Dunn & Crutcher LLP 1050 Connecticut Ave NW Ste 900 Washington DC 20036-5306 Office Phone: 202-955-8662. Business E-Mail: djohnson@gibsondunn.com.

JOHNSON, DAVID TIMOTHY, diplomat; m. Scarlett M. Swan, May 23, 1981; children: Carrie, Rachel, Andrew. BA in Econs., Emory U., 1976; postgrad., Can. Nat. Def. Coll., 1989-90. Asst. nat. trust examiner US Treasury Dept.'s Office of the Comptroller of Currency, prior to 1977; various assignments US Fgn. Svc., 1977—; econs. officer U.S. Embassy in Berlin US Dept. State, 1981-83, desk officer, NATO, 1983—87, dep. spokesman for dep. asst. sec. state, 1993-95; dep. press sec. for fgn. affairs, sr. dir. pub. affairs, Nat. Security Coun. White House, 1995-97; amb. to Orgn. for Security and Cooperation in Europe US Dept. State, Vienna, 1998—2001; min. US Embassy, London, 2003—; chargé d'affaires ad interim Am. Embassy, London, 2004—05. Office: 8400 London Pl Washington DC 20521-8400 Office Phone: (44)(20) 7894 0225.

JOHNSON, DAVID WILFRED, JR., ceramics engineer, researcher; b. Windber, Pa., Sept. 23, 1942; s. David W. Sr. and Vanessa J. (Shoff) Johnson; m. Bonnie Kay Respet, June 20, 1964; children: Analee J., Bradley D. BS in Ceramic Sci., Pa. State U., 1964, PhD in Ceramic Sci., 1968. Tech. staff Bell Tel. Labs., Murray Hill, NJ, 1968-83; supr. advanced ceramic processing AT&T Bell Labs., Murray Hill, 1983-88; dir. metallurgy and ceramics rsch. dept. Bell Labs Lucent Techs., Murray Hill, 1988-2000; dir. materials rsch. dept. Agere Sys., New Providence, NJ, 2001—02; editor Jour. of Am. Ceramic Soc., 2002—. Adj. prof. Stevens Inst. Tech., Hoboken, NJ, 1982—; Taylor lectr. Pa. State U., University Park, 1989. Contbr. articles to profl. jours. Chmn. Bedminster Twp. Zoning Bd. Adjustment, NJ, 1991—94, 1996—. Fellow: Am. Soc. Materials, Am. Ceramic Soc. (v.p. 1990—92, treas. 1992, pres. 1994, Ross Coffin Purdy award 1978, Fulrath award 1984, John Jeppson award 1998, Indsl. Rsch. prize 2000, Orton Lecture 2004); mem.: AAAS, NAE, Electrochemical Soc., Acad. Ceramics, Materials Rsch. Soc., The Materials Soc. Achievements include patents in field; research in in ceramic powder processing as applied to ferrites, ceramic substrates, sol-gel silica glass and high temperature superconductors. Business E-Mail: johnsond@stevens.edu.

JOHNSON, DEANNA KAY, music educator; b. Hastings, Nebr., July 20, 1948; d. Harlan Dean and Twila Mae Mack; children: Eric Len, Amanda Kay Ledin. BMusEdn, Hastings Coll., Nebr., 1971. Tchr. Geneva North Rehab., Fairfield, Nebr., 1968—2004. Trainer: c.l.o.w.n, developing capable people, student assistance program team Drug Free Nebr./W.I.N Cadre, Hastings, Nebr., 1981—2004; speech coach Nelson Cmty. Schs., Nelson, Nebr., 1985—2001, choir dir., 1985—2001. Pres. Cmty. Theater Assn., Clay Center, 2002—04; mem. staff devel. advsory ESU, Hastings, 1985—2004; EMT Clay Center City Ambulance Crew, 1978—88; deacon United Ch. of Christ, Clay Center, 2003—04; bd. dirs. Ednl. Svc. Agy., Hastings, Nebr., 2000—04; pres. (aux.) N.A.M.I.C., Indianapolis, Ind., 2002—03. Mem.: Music Edn. Assn. (assoc.), Nebr. Edn. Assoc. (assoc.; local pres. 1990—2001), Nebr. Music Teachers (assoc.). Home: 228 nParkside Ln Lincoln NE 68521 Personal E-mail: djohnson@esu9.org.

JOHNSON, DEBRA DENISE, finance company executive; b. Wilmington, Del., Aug. 13, 1966; d. John Gutherie and Deloris Bell Osborne; m. Michael Allen Johnson, Mar. 25, 1995; children: Theodore Roosevelt Handy, III, Michael Allen Johnson, Jr. Assocs. Degree, Wilmington Coll., 2002. Credit clk. Wildupco Fed. Credit Union, Wilmington, 1982—84; mgr. Discover Fin. Svcs., New Castle, Del., 1985—. Author, counselor, Christian writer: Excerpts on Life Volumes I and II. Marriage counselor Spirit Life Ministries Internat., Wilmington, 1997. Avocations: reading, writing, cooking. Office Phone: 302-323-7028. Personal E-mail: thecovenantinnkeeper@comcast.net.

JOHNSON, DEBRA JOLYN, plastic surgeon; b. Geeter, Calif., Jan. 11, 1955; d. James Weldon and Hazel Knox Johnson; m. Mario Francisco Gutierrez, May 7, 1983; children: Gabriela, Pablo. BS, U. Calif., Irvine, 1977; MD, Stanford U., 1981. Diplomate Am. Bd. Plastic Surgery. Plastic surgeon Plastic Surgery Ctr., Sacramento, 1989—. Dir. Sutter Cleft Lip/Palate Panel, Sacramento, 2001—; mem. adv. bd. Y Me Save Ourselves, Sacramento, 1995—; lectr. in field. Vol. lectr., surgeon, bd. dirs. Interplast, Rotaplast, Cirjuanos Platikos Mundi, Amref, 1980—. Mem.: Calif. Med. Assn. (chmn. plastic surgery 2002—), Am. Soc. Plastic Surgeons, Calif. Soc. Plastic Surgeons (treas. 2003—). Avocations: cooking, gardening. Office: 95 Scripps Dr Sacramento CA 95825 Business E-Mail: tpsc@pscoffice.com.

JOHNSON, DEBRA POPE, education educator; b. Denver, Colo., Aug. 10, 1958; d. Ural Pope; m. Frank Johnson, Apr. 26, 1982; children: Tolaison Monique, Ashley Michele. EdD, U. Sarasota, Sarasota, Fla., 2005. Cert. Edn. Profl. Standards Commn., 2005. Instrnl. tech. specialist Ga. Southwestern State U., Americus, Ga., 1999—2001; 6th grade tchr. Merry Acres Mid. Sch., Albany, Ga., 2004—. Dir. clin. experiences Ga. Southwestern State U., Americus, Ga., 2001—03. 2nd v.p. Delta Sigma Theta Sorority, Inc., Albany, Ga., 2000—02. Recipient Tchr. of the Yr., Dougherty County Sch. Sys. Radium Mid. Sch., 1998. Mem.: Ga. Assn. of Educators. Home: 2525 Betty's Dr Albany GA 31705 Office: Merry Acres Mid Sch 1601 Florence Dr Albany GA 31707 Office Phone: 229-431-3338. Personal E-mail: debrapj@prodigy.net. Business E-Mail: debra.johnson@dougherty.k12.ga.us.

JOHNSON, DENISE LOUISE (BELL), newspaper reporter, photographer, paralegal, librarian, life agent; b. Washington, Nov. 27, 1967; d. Richard Keith Bell and Kay Lorraine (Sutherland) Reynolds. Student, Inst. Adventiste du Saleve, Collonges, France, 1988; BA in French, Loma Linda U., 1990. Yearbook editor Loma Linda U., La Sierra, Calif., 1989-90, desk technician Loma Linda, Calif., 1990-92; staff writer Inland Empire Cmty. Newspapers, Colton, Calif., 1990-91, city editor San Bernardino, Calif., 1991-94; asst. circ. supr. Del Webb Meml. Libr. Loma Linda (Calif.) U., 1994-2000; reporter City Newspaper Group, Colton, Calif., 1995-99; life agt. Denise Bell Life Agt., Redlands, Calif., 2000—01; paralegal Law Offices Don Featherstone, Corona, Calif., 2001—. Asst. leader Girl Scouts U.S., Walla Walla, Wash., 1986; co-leader Girl Scouts Switzerland, Geneva, 1987, Girl Scouts U.S., Loma Linda, 1988-93. Mem.: San Bernardino County Bar Assn. Avocations: photography, writing, archery. Home: 391 N Main St Ste 204 Corona CA 92880 E-mail: natashabelle@hotmail.com.

JOHNSON, DENISE REINKA, state supreme court justice; b. Wyandotte, Mich., July 13, 1947; Student, Mich. State U., 1965-67; BA, Wayne State U., 1969; postgrad., Cath. U. of Am., 1971-72; JD with honors, U. Conn., 1974; LLM, U. Va., 1995. Bar: Conn. 1974, U.S. Dist. Ct. Conn. 1974, Vt. 1980, U.S. Ct. Appeals (2d cir.) 1983, U.S. Dist. Ct. Vt. 1986. Atty. New Haven (Conn.) Legal Assistance Assn., 1974-78; instr. legal writing Vt. Law Sch., South Royalton, 1978-79; clerk Blodgett & McCarren, Burlington, Vt., 1979-80; chief civil rights divsn. Atty. Gen.'s Office, State of Vt., 1980-82; chief pub. protection divsn. Atty. Gen.'s Office, Montpelier, Vt., 1982-88; pvt. practice Shrewsbury, Vt., 1988-90; assoc. justice Vt. Supreme Ct., Montpelier, 1990—. Chair Vt. Human Rights Commn., 1988-90. Mem. Am. Law Inst., Am. Judicature Soc. Office: Vt Supreme Ct 109 State St Montpelier VT 05609-0001

JOHNSON, DEWEY, JR., retired biochemist; b. Sapulpa, Okla., Sept. 23, 1926; s. Dewey and Maude (Hickey) Johnson; m. Patricia R. Rodgers, Feb. 14, 1953 (dec. Mar. 1997); children: Joseph D., Paul D., Mary Ann, Richard E.; m. Carol S. Martin, Sept. 25, 1999. BS, Colo. State U., 1950; MS, U. Conn., 1955; PhD, Rutgers State U., 1958. Nutritionist Limecrest Rsch. Lab., Newton, N.J., 1958-63; biochemist Equitable Life, N.Y.C., 1963-79, Met. Life, N.Y.C., 1980-90, disability underwriter, 1990-92; chemist EPA, Edison, NJ, 1993—2001; ret., 2001—. Contbr. Avocation: Avocations: gardening, woodworking. Home: 59 Dunnell Rd Maplewood NJ 07040-1333

JOHNSON, DIANA ATWOOD, business owner, innkeeper; b. Rochester, N.Y., Nov. 3, 1946; d. Edwin Havens and Barbara (Field) A.; m. Kenneth Durant Milne, June 10, 1967 (div. Apr. 1982); m. Howard Samuel Tooker, May 5, 1985 (div. Aug. 1994); m. John Samuel Johnson, June 2, 1996. BA, Skidmore Coll., 1968. Owner, innkeeper Old Lyme (Conn.) Inn, 1976-2001; dir. Bank of Southeastern Conn., 2005—. Vice-chmn., bd. dirs. Maritime Bank & Trust, Essex, Conn., 1995-99; adv. bd. Webster Bank, 1999-2001; incorporator Lawrence Meml. Hosp., New London, Conn., 1990-95; bd. dirs. Bank of Southeastern Conn., 2004-05 Trustee Conn. River Mus., Essex, 1976-98, pres., 1989-94, chmn., 1994-96; trustee Lyme Hist. Soc., Old Lyme, 1985-87, Lyme Acad. Fine Arts, Old Lyme, 1980—, chmn. 1996—2003, chmn. emeritus, 2003—, treas., 1992-96; trustee Mystic Coast Travel and Leisure Coun., 1992—, chmn. 1994-96; bd. dirs. Conn. chpt. Nature Conservancy, 1994—2004, sec., 2001, chair govt. rels. com. 2001-04; chmn. Town of Old Lyme Open Space Com., 1998-2000, mem., 1998—; mem. State of Conn. Natural Heritage, Open Space and Watershed Land Acquisition Rev. Bd., 1998—; mem. adv. bd. Norwich Navigators, 1995-99, Tidewater Inst., 2004-; dir. Southeastern Conn. Enterprise Region, 1995-2001; del. Rep. Nat. Conv., San Diego, 1996; chmn. Rep. Town Com., 2000-02, vice chmn., 1998-99; mem. Conn. Rep. Fin. Com., 1997-2003; mem. Congressman Simmons Fin. Com., 1999; state ctrl. committeewoman 20th Dist. Conn. Rep. Party, 2001-03. Recipient Disting. Adv. for the Arts award Conn. Commn. on the Arts, 1999. Mem. Nat. Restaurant Assn., Conn. Restaurant Assn. (bd. dirs. 1991-93, 99-2001), Prof. Assn. Innkeepers, Gray Gables Croquet Club (founder), U.S. Croquet Assn. Republican. Presbyterian. Avocations: american antiques, antique house restoration, croquet. Home: 12 Tantummaheag Rd Old Lyme CT 06371-1137 Office: 75 Crystal Ave New London CT 06320 also: PO Box 787 Old Lyme CT 06371 E-mail: dianaajohnson@aol.com.

JOHNSON, DIANE JONES, librarian; b. Youngstown, Ohio, Oct. 23, 1956; d. Wilbur Hudson and Barbara Jean Jones; m. Paul David Taylor, Sept. 27, 1975 (div. Nov. 1989); children: Noel Thomas Taylor, Sara Elizabeth Taylor; m. Ray Johnson, Dec. 30, 1989. BS summa cum laude, Youngstown State U., 1978; MLS, East Carolina U., 1985. Cert. libr. assoc., Md.; cert. pub. libr., N.C. Print svcs. Canfield (Ohio) H.S., 1978-80; media specialist Poland (Ohio) Mid. Sch., 1980-82; libr. Sheppard Meml. Libr., Greenville, N.C., 1982-90; catalog technician St. Mary's Coll., St. Mary's City, Md., 1990-93; pub. svcs. libr. Charles County Pub. Libr., La Plata, Md., 1993-97, acting dir., 1997, br. mgr., 1997—. Cons.: (book) Senior High School Catalog, 1985-89. Youngstown Edn. Found. scholar Youngstown State U., 1975-78. Mem. Md. Libr. Assn. Baptist. Avocations: reading, walking, travel, needlecrafts. Home: 1309 Leicester Dr La Plata MD 20646-3550 Office: Charles County Pub Libr 2 Garrett Ave La Plata MD 20646-5959

JOHNSON, DIANE LAIN, writer, critic; b. Moline, Ill., Apr. 28, 1934; d. Dolph Lain and Frances Eloise (Elder) Lain; m. John Frederic Murray, Nov. 9, 1969; children: Kevin, Darcy, Amanda, Simon Johnson. AA, Stephens Coll., 1953; BA, U. Utah, 1957; MA, PhD, UCLA, 1968. Mem. faculty dept. English U. Calif., Davis, 1968-87. Author: Fair Game, 1965, Loving Hands at Home, 1968, Burning, 1970, The Shadow Knows, 1975, Lying Low, 1978, Lesser Lives, 1972, Terrorists and Novelists, 1982, Dashiell Hammett, 1983, Persian Nights, 1987, Health and Happiness, 1990, Natural Opium, 1993, Le Divorce, 1997, Le Mariage, 2000, L'Affaire, 2003. Woodrow Wilson grantee, 1967; AAUW fellow, 1968; Guggenheim Found. fellow, 1977-78; Nominee Nat. Book Awards, 1973, 79; recipient Rosenthal award Am. Acad. Arts and Letters, 1979, Mildred and Harold Strauss Living, Am. Acad. & Inst. Arts and Letters, 1988. Mem. MLA, PEN.

JOHNSON, DIANE LYNN, publishing consultant, management consultant; b. N.Y.C., Apr. 26, 1945; d. Lawrence Schlesinger and Rita (Gorman) Kingsley (dec. May 1996); m. Arnold Krull, Mar. 6, 1969 (div. Mar. 1973); m. Martin A. Johnson, Aug. 19, 1981. Student, New Sch. of Social Rsch., N.Y.C., 1967-69. Ops. mgr. Cambist Films, Inc., N.Y.C., 1963-69; pres. Fantasy Jewelry, Inc., N.Y.C., 1973-75; v.p., media Dynamic House/Tele House, Inc., N.Y.C., 1973-75; v.p., gen. mgr. Columbia Communications, Inc., N.Y.C., 1975-80; pres. Pub. Dynamics, Inc., Boca Raton, Fla., 1982—2003. Cons. Key Pub., Inc., Katonah, N.Y., 1978-80, Milan Schuster, Inc., N.Y.C., 1980-81; tchrs. aide/spl. edn. Omni Middle Sch., Boca Raton, Fla., 1999-2003. Mem. Literacy Vols. Am., N.Y.C., 1973-75; big sister Big Sister Program, N.Y.C., 1973-75; tchrs. aide Jewish Community Ctr. Nursery Sch., Stamford, 1981-82; group leader Smokers Anonymous, Stamford, 1988-93; vol. Morikami Mus., Delray Beach, Fla.; asst. lectr. Weight Watchers Palm Beach County, 1999—. Mem. Landmark Club (Stamford, Conn.), Hadassah Brandeis U. Nat. Women's Com. Jewish. Avocations: cooking, gardening, reading, creative writing, antique collecting (oriental and middle east deco). Home: 9506 Lantern Bay Cir West Palm Beach FL 33411-5171 E-mail: djrainbow1@aol.com.

JOHNSON, DOLORES DEBOWER, consultant; b. Schuyler, Nebr., Nov. 8, 1932; d. Ernest Edward and Edna Cecelia (Stone) DeBower; m. Richard Allan Johnson, Sept. 3, 1952 (dec. 1983); children: Erik, Kristi, Kurt. BA summa cum laude, U. Minn., 1972; cert., Harvard U., 1975. Mgr. St. Paul Chamber Orchestra, 1973-77, Houston Symphony, 1977-80; gen. mgr. Minn. Opera, St. Paul, 1980-81; dir. devel. Walker Art Ctr., Mpls., 1981-84; mng. dir. Houston Grand Opera, 1984-96. Adj. lectr. Goucher Coll., Balt., 1998—. Bd. dirs. Cultural Arts Coun. Houston, 1986-90, Bus. Vol. in Arts, 1991-96. Bush Found. fellow, 1975. Mem. Minn. Composers Forum (pres. 1982-84). Office: PO Box 162 Schuyler NE 68661-0162 Home: PO Box 162 Schuyler NE 68661-0162 Fax: 402-352-2598.

JOHNSON, DOLORES ESTELLE, retired small business owner; b. Phila., Dec. 2, 1932; d. William Johnson Bellamy and Sadie Louise (Waddell) Messado; m. Edward Harding Johnson Jr., Aug. 29, 1953 (dec. Feb. 1981); children: Louise P., Edward A., Marie E., Michael G. Parking enforcement officer City of Phila. Police Dept., 1957—59; jeweler, owner LuBelle Jewelers, Phila., 1963—83; originator, owner, baker Pizzarama, Phila., 1965—67; armed guard Globe Security Corp., Phila., 1977—79; artist, jeweler, owner Piercing Eyes Indian Crafts, Phila., 1982—97; ret., 1997. Recipient Outstanding Cmty. Svc. award, Pepsi Cola Co., 1966, award, Chapel of the Four Chaplains for humanitarian works. Mem. United Am. Indians of Delaware Valley, Amerindian Soc. (v.p.), Atlantic City's Garden Ctr. Mus. Art (life). Episcopalian. Avocations: poetry, art, music, camping.

JOHNSON, DONALD CLAY, librarian, curator; b. Clintonville, Wis., Aug. 19, 1940; s. Everett Clay and Gertrude Edna Dorthea J. BA, U. Wis., 1962, PhD, 1980; MA, U. Chgo., 1967. Curator S.E. Asia Collection Yale U., New Haven, 1967-70; head reference libr. No. Ariz. U., Flagstaff, 1971-72; asst. libr. reader svcs. Nat. U. Malaysia, Kuala Lumpur, 1972-74; head reader svcs. Coll. William and Mary, Williamsburg, Va., 1980-87; curator Ames Libr. South Asia, U. Minn., Mpls., 1987—. Author: Southeast Asia: A Bibliography, 1970, Guide to Reference Materials on Southeast Asia, 1970, Index to Southeast Asian Journals, 1982, Agile Hands and Creative Minds, a Bibliography of Textile Traditions in Afghanistan, Bangladesh, Bhutan, India, Nepal, Pakistan, and Sri Lanka, 2000, Wedding Dress Across Cultures, 2003. Ford Found. scholar, 1963-64; Rsch. grantee Am. Inst. Indian Studies, 1989-90, 94; Fulbright fellow, 2003-04. Mem. ALA (life), Assn. for Asian Studies (editor Resources for Scholarship series 1997-98). Avocation: textiles in South and Southeast Asia. Office: U Minn Ames Libr South Asia 309 19th Ave S Minneapolis MN 55455-0438 Office Phone: 612-624-5801. Business E-Mail: d-john4@tc.umn.edu.

JOHNSON, DONALD EDWARD, JR., lawyer; b. Denver, Sept. 24, 1942; s. Donald Edward and Miriam Bispham (Chester) J.; m. Charlotte Marie Hassett, Aug. 15, 1964; children: Julie Anna, Jenny Marie. Student, Lewis and Clark Coll., 1960-62; BA in History, U. Ariz., 1968; JD, U. Wyo., 1971. Bar: Wyo. 1971, Colo. 1971, U.S. Dist. Ct. Colo. and Wyo. 1971, U.S. Supreme Ct. 1978. Assoc. Hammond and Chilson, Loveland, Colo., 1971-72; dep. dist. atty. 8th Jud. Dist., Loveland and Fort Collins, Colo., 1972-80, chief dep. dist. atty., 1977-80; assoc. Allen, Rogers, Metcalf and Vahrenwald, Ft. Collins, 1980-82, ptnr., 1982—. Asst. city atty., prosecutor City of Loveland, 1971-72; asst. mcpl. judge, Loveland, 1972; instr. bus. law Ames Coll., 1972-74; lectr. Regional Homocide Sch., 1977. Author: Criminal Conspiracy—The Colorado District Attorney's Evidence Manual, 1976; student editor ABA Law Student Jour. Chmn. 45th Republican House Dist., 1977-82; mem. Colo. Rep. Central Com., 1980-85; mem. Loveland Open Space Adv. Bd., 1977-78; bd. dirs. Loveland United Way, 1977-84, pres., 1981-83; bd. dirs. Loveland Midget Athletic Assn., sec., 1974-78; mem. ctrl. com. Parlimentarian Larimer County Rep., 1992-96; mem. local adv. bd. McKee Med. Ctr., Loveland, 1992—, pres., 1995—; mem. adv. bd. Banner Health Sys., Colo., 1996—, pres., 1999-2002; mem. adv. bd. Cmty. Found. No. Colo., Loveland, 2003—; treas. 8th Jud. dist. Victims Assistance Law Enforcement Fund, 1990-96 (8th judicial dist.), mem. nominating commn., 1998—; mem. Larimer County Bench-Bar Commn., 1993-95. Served to sgt. USMC, 1966-68. Mem. ABA (Gold Key award 1970), Larimer County Bar Assn. (exec. com. 1990-2002, pres. 1995-96), Colo. Bar Assn. (bd. govs. 1997-2002), Colo. Trial Lawyers Assn. Episcopalian. Office: Allen Vahrenwald & Johnson LLC Key Bank Bldg 125 S Howes St 1100 Fort Collins CO 80521

JOHNSON, DONALD LEE, retired agricultural materials processing company executive; b. Aurora, Ill., Mar. 9, 1935; s. Leonard F. and Fern J. (Johnson) J.; m. Virginia A. Wesoloski, Sept. 3, 1960; children: Joyce E., Janis M., Jolene G., Jay R. AS, Joliet Jr. Coll., 1959; BS, U. Ill., 1962; DSc,

Washington U., 1966. Devel. engr. Petrolite Corp., Webster Groves, Mo., 1962-64; sr. devel. engr. A.E. Staley Co., Decatur, Ill., 1965-67, rsch. mgr. chem. div., 1967-75, dept. dir. rsch. div., 1975-87; v.p. product and process tech. Grain Processing Corp., Muscatine, Iowa, 1987-2000. Adv. coun. adult vocat. edn. State of Ill., Springfield, 1983—87; mem. organizing com. Ann. Symposium on Biotech. for Fuels and Chems., 1985—97; departmental vis. com. botany dept. U. Tex., Austin, 1986—99; mem. applied sci. adv. coun. Miami U., Oxford, Ohio, 1987—97; chmn. rev. com. Solar Energy Rsch. Inst., Golden, Colo., 1988—89; mem. Sci. and Industry Adv. Bd., Nat. Renewable Energy Lab., Golden, Colo., 1993—99; mem. Bd. on Higher Edn. in the Workforce NRC, 2001—. Contbr. sci. papers to profl. jours.; patentee in field. Staff sgt. USAF, 1953-57. Mem. AAAS, AIChE, Am. Chem. Soc., Nat. Acad. Engring., Am. Legion, Rotary. Republican. Avocations: sailboat racing, running. Home: 106 Cape Fear Dr Hertford NC 27944-9218 Office Phone: 252-426-6499. E-mail: virdon@mchsi.com.

JOHNSON, DONALD WAYNE, lawyer; b. Memphis, Feb. 2, 1950; s. Hugh Don and Oline (Rowland) J.; m. Jan Marie Mullinax, May 12, 1972 (div. 1980); 1 child, Scott Fitzgerald; m. Cindy L. Walker, Dec. 10, 1988; children: Trevor Christian, Mallory Faith. Student, Memphis State U., 1968, Lee Coll., 1968-72; JD, Woodrow Wilson Coll. Law, 1975. Bar: Ga. 1975, U.S. Dist. Ct. (no. dist.) Ga. 1975, U.S. Ct. Appeals (5th cir.) 1976, U.S. Ct. Appeals (11th, 9th, DC cirs.) 1984, U.S. Ct. Claims 1978, U.S. Tax Ct. 1978, U.S. Supreme Ct. 1979. Ptnr. Barnes & Johnson, Dalton, Ga., 1975-77, Johnson & Fain, Dalton, 1977-80; pvt. practice Dalton, 1975-85, Atlanta, 1985—; city atty. City of Forest Park, Ga., 1996-97. Bd. dirs. Pathway Christian Sch., Dalton, 1978-85, Jr. Achievement of Dalton, 1978-84, Dalton-Whitfield County Day Care Ctrs., Inc.; legal counsel Robertson for Pres. Com., Ga., 1988; bd. chmn. Ga. Family Coun., 1990-97; Rep. chmn. Clayton County, 1993-95; Rep. gen. counsel 3rd Congl. Dist., 1993-95, Clayton County Rep. Com., 1995-96; Rep. candidate for Ga. Senate, 1998; emcee, community prayer breakfast, Proj. Cor. Angel Tree, 1999-. Recipient Power of One award Ga. Family Coun., 1997. Mem. State Bar Ga., Fayette County Bar Assn., Ga. Trial Lawyers Assn., Christian Legal Soc. Mem. Ch. of God. Office: PO Box 187 Fayetteville GA 30214-0187 Personal E-mail: djohnson1@msn.com. E-mail: jlfpc@mindspring.com.

JOHNSON, DORIS JEAN, social worker; b. Raymond, Miss., July 16, 1946; AA, Wayne County C.C., Detroit, 1986; BSW, U. Detroit, 1989; MSW, Wayne State U., 1993. Supr. Ren, Detroit, 1993—94; psychiat. social worker Aurora Healthcare, Inc., Detroit, 1994—2001, Detroit Cmty. Health Connection, 2002—; clin. social worker Psychiat. and Behavioral Medicine Profls., 2003—. Author: (novel) A Reflection of Memories, 2003. Pres. Slum Lord Fighters, Detroit, 1981, Human Svcs. Orgn./Wayne County C.C., 1984; v.p. social work orgn./Univ. Detroit, 1988. Recipient cert. Appreciation, Detroit Police Athletic League, 1989, award of Recognition, Detroit City Coun., 1989, cert. appreciation, 36th Dist. Ct., Detroit, 1997. Mem.: Black Expression Club. E-mail: doris0716@aol.com.

JOHNSON, DOROTHY CURFMAN, elementary school educator; b. Smithsburg, Md., Nov. 21, 1930; d. Paul Frank and Rhoda Pearl (Witmer) Curfman; m. Robert Nelson Johnson, Jan. 24, 1953 (div. Dec. 1965); children: Gregory Nelson, Eric Paul. Student, Gettysburg Coll., 1948-50, Waynesboro Bus. Coll., 1950, Broward C.C., Ft. Lauderdale, Fla., 1967; BS in Edn., Fla. Atlantic U., 1969, postgrad., 1975-76. Cert. tchr., Fla. Sec. to prodn. mgr. Westinghouse Elec. Corp., Sunbury, Pa., 1951-53; sec. to v.p., sales Metal Carbides Corp., Youngstown, Ohio, 1966; tchr. Sch. Bd. of Broward County, Ft. Lauderdale, Ohio, 1969-93, curriculum specialist, 1993-96. Masters in Edn. Prog., 1973-74, team coord. Sanders Park Elem., Pompano Beach, Fla., 1985-96; mem. North Area Adv. Bd., Pompano Beach, 1990-96; sec. Sanders Park PTA, Pompano Beach, 1994-96. Sec.-treas. Georgen Arms Bd. of Dirs., Pompano Beach, 1997—; dir. Georgen Arms Condo, Inc., Pompano Beach, 1974—; active Jr. League, Youngstown. Recipient Master Tchr. award State of Fla., 1981-82. Mem. Alpha Xi Delta. Lutheran. Home: 280 S Cypress Rd Apt 5 Pompano Beach FL 33060-7038

JOHNSON, DOUG, advertising executive, public relations executive; b. Watertown, N.Y., Aug. 16, 1919; s. H. Douglas and Clare (Lane) J.; m. Geraldine Evans, Aug. 11, 1943; children: Andrew (dec.), Molly E., Faith D. Student pub. schs. Pres. Doug Johnson Assos. (pub. relations), Syracuse, N.Y., 1949-61, Barlow/Johnson, Inc. (advt. and pub. relations), Syracuse, 1961-80, Johnlow Corp., Fayetteville; chmn. bd. Nowak Barlow Johnson, Fayetteville, 1980-82; v.p. mktg. Edward Joy Co., Inc., Syracuse, 1982-84. Pres. 10 Co. Mktg.; dir. Agway Indemnity Ins. Co., Dewitt, N.Y., Key Bank of Central N.Y., Syracuse, Syracuse Baseball Club, Inc.; chmn. exec. com. Agway Ins. Co., Dewitt. Home sec. to congressman, 1949-65; bd. dirs., v.p. Community Gen. Hosp. Syracuse, N.Y. State Coll. Forestry Found.; bd. dirs., past pres. Syracuse Boys Club; v.p. N.Y.C. Assoc. Artists; pres. L.W. Artists Assn., 1997-98; bd. dirs., past pres. USO of CNY, nat. bd. dirs., USO. Served with AUS, 1941-45. Decorated Purple Heart with 3 oak leaf clusters, Bronze Star, Combat Infantry Badge with Silver Star. Mem. Pub. Rels. Soc. Am. (cert. bus. communicator), Syracuse C. of C. (pres. 1968-69) Clubs: Century (gov.). Home and Office: 1444 Leisure World Mesa AZ 85206-2304

JOHNSON, DOUGLAS BLAIKIE, lawyer; b. Chgo., Sept. 13, 1952; s. Marvin Melrose and Anne Stuart (Campbell) J.; m. Pamela Jane Tomlinson, Aug. 1, 1975; children: Richard Aaron, Lauren Stuart, Diana Blaikie, Scott Nathaniel, Catherine Joan. BSME, U. Nebr., 1974; JD, Seton Hall U., 1980. Bar: Nebr. 1980, U.S. Dist. Ct. Nebr. 1980; registered profl. engr., Nebr., Ark. Project engr. DuPont, Cleve., 1974-75, Exxon Chems., Linden, N.J., 1975-78, cost engr., 1978-80; sr. engr. InterNorth, Inc., Omaha, 1980-82, market planner, 1982-84, corp. planner, 1984-85, bus. mgr., 1985-86; program mgr. Brunswick Corp., Lincoln, Nebr., 1987-95; product devel. mgr. Lincoln Composites, 1995-98, sr. bus. devel. mgr., 1999-2000, dir. oilfield products, 2000—02; mgr. Gen. Dynamics, 2003—. Mem. ABA, ATLA, Nebr. Bar Assn., Lincoln Bar Assn., Triangle, Sigma Tau, Pi Tau Sigma, Phi Eta Sigma. Republican. Presbyterian. Home: 4600 Birch Hollow Dr Lincoln NE 68516-5107 Office: Gen Dynamics 4300 Industrial Ave Lincoln NE 68504-1107 Office Phone: 402-465-6575. Business E-Mail: djohnson2@gdatp.com.

JOHNSON, DOUGLAS WELLS, lawyer; b. May 31, 1949; s. Robert Douglas and Mildred Irene J.; m. Kathryn Ann Hoberg, Oct. 18, 1980. BA, U. Denver, 1971, JD, 1974. Ptnr. Mellman, Mellman & Thorn, Denver, 1974-80; sr. atty. Amoco Corp., Chgo., 1980-91; mgr. real estate Amoco Oil Co., Chgo., 1991-94; sr. atty. Amoco Corp., Chgo., 1994-98; mng. atty. BP Am. Inc., Warrenville, Ill., 1998—. U. Denver Alumni scholar, 1967—71. Mem. ABA, Ill. Bar Assn., D.C. Bar Assn., Chgo. Bar Assn., Kappa Delta Pi. Home: 3040 Indianwood Rd Wilmette IL 60091 Office: BP America Inc 4101 Winfield Rd Warrenville IL 60555 Office Phone: 630-836-3451. Business E-Mail: johnsodw@bp.com.

JOHNSON, DOUGLAS WILLIAM, radiologist; b. Westpoint, NY; s. Andrew Larson and Barbara Joan (Rosborough) J.; m. Susan Mary Friedman, July 23, 1977; children: Danielle, Michael. BS in Biology, Va. Tech., Blacksburg, Va., 1976; MD, Med. Coll. Va., Richmond, 1979. Chmn. radiation oncology David Grant USAF Med. Ctr., Travis AFB, Calif., 1983-87; ptnr. Fla. Radiation Oncology Group, Jacksonville, Fla., 1987—. Asst. prof. radiation-oncology Stanford Med. Ctr., Stanford U., Calif., 1983-87; asst. prof.-oncology Mayo Clinic Med. Sch., Rochester, Minn., 1995—; fellow Am. Coll. Radiology, Phila., 1995. Patentee in field. Col. USAF, 1975-. Fellow Am. Coll. Radiology; mem. Am. Soc. Therapeutic Radiology & Oncology. Avocation: aviation. Office: Baptist Cancer Inst 1235 San Marco Blvd Ste 3 Jacksonville FL 32207-8560 Office Phone: 904-202-7020.

JOHNSON, DWAYNE DOUGLAS (THE ROCK), professional wrestler, actor; b. Hayward, Calif., May 2, 1972; s. Rocky and Ata Johnson; m. Dany Garcia, May 3, 1997; 1 child, Simone Alexandra. Degree in criminology, U. Miami. Actor: (films) The Mummy Returns, 2001, The Scorpion King, 2002, The Rundown, 2003, Walking Tall, 2004, Be Cool, 2005; wrestler (TV series) WWF Superstars of Wrestling, 1996, WWF Monday Night Raw, 1996—97, Sunday Night Heat, 1998—2004, Raw is War, 1997—2004, WWF Smackdown, 1999—2002, TV appearances include That 70s Show, 1999, The Net, 1999, Star Trek: Voyager, 2000. Achievements include 7 time World Wrestling Fedn. champion. Office: c/o WWF Titan Tower 1241 E Main St Stamford CT 06902*

JOHNSON, DWIGHT ALAN, lawyer; b. Huntington, W.Va., Sept. 26, 1945; s. Oliver Frederick and Garnette (Taylor) J.; m. Bonny Libbey, Nov. 15, 1969; children: Claire L., Daniel F., Philip T. BA, Princeton U., 1968; JD, Yale U., 1974. Bar: Conn. 1975, D.C. 1975, U.S. Ct. Appeals (D.C. cir.) 1976. Assoc. Jones, Day, Reavis & Pogue, Washington, 1974-77, Murtha Cullina LLP, Hartford, Conn., 1977-80, ptnr., 1980—, chmn. exec. com., 1990-95. Bd. dirs. Phonon Corp., Simsbury, Conn. Sec., bd. dirs. Conn. Capitol Region Growth Coun., Hartford, 1992-97; bd. dirs. Conn. Sci. Mus., 1978-84, pres., 1982-83; bd. dirs. Parents Anonymous Conn., Inc., 1981-87, pres., 1983-85; bd. dirs. Tutu Found. Devel. and Relief South Africa, 1986-89, Lyme Disease Found., 1990-94; bd. dirs. Hartford Symphony Orch., 1991—, pres., 1994-96; trustee World Affairs Coun., 1998-2001, Conn. Energy Found., 1984-90, Conn. Policy Econ. Coun., 1996-98; bd. dirs. Conn. Charter Oak chpt. ARC, 2000—. With U.S. Army, 1968-71, Vietnam. Decorated Bronze Star. Mem. Conn. Bar Assn. (mem. exec. com. pub. utilities law sect. 1979—). Office: Murtha Cullina LLP City Pl 185 Asylum St Hartford CT 06103 Office Phone: 860-240-6024.

JOHNSON, E. DIANE, librarian; b. Columbia, S.C., June 21, 1956; d. Clark R. and C. Estelle (Graham) J. BA magna cum laude, U. Wis., 1978; MA, U. Minn., 1980. Libr. Health Scis. Libr./Univ. Mo., Columbia, 1980-85, head info. svcs., 1986—. Designated instr. Med. Libr. Assn., 1990—; del. Citizen Ambassador Prog. Med. Librs. Delegation to China, 1989; active various clinics and workshops in field; others. Contbr. articles to profl. jours. Recipient grad. sch. tuition scholarship U. Minn., 1979, Libr. Sci. Acad. award U. Wis., Oshkosh, 1978, Ida and George Eliot prize Med. Libr. Assn., 1998, Estelle Brodman award Med. Libr. Assn., 1999, Hetzner award for excellence in acad. health sci. librarianship, 1999, others. Office: U Mo J Otto Lottes Health Scis Libr Columbia MO 65212-0001 Business E-Mail: johnsone@health.missouri.edu.

JOHNSON, E. ERIC, insurance executive; b. Chgo., Feb. 7, 1927; s. Edwin Eric and Xenia Alice (Waisanen) J.; m. Elizabeth Dewar Brass, Sept. 3, 1949; children: Christal L. Johnson Neal, Craig R. BA, Stanford U., 1948. Dir. group annuities Equitable Life Assurance Soc., San Francisco, 1950-54, div. mgr. L.A., 1955-59; v.p. Johnson & Higgins of Calif., L.A., 1960-67, dir., 1968-87, chmn., 1986-87, TBG Fin., L.A., 1988—. Bd. dirs. Am. Mutual Fund; exec. v.p. Johnson & Higgins, N.Y.C., 1984-87, Law Environ. Group, Showscan Corp. Bd. dirs. Sta. KCET, pub. TV, L.A., chmn., 1992-94; mem. adv. bd. UCLA Med. Ctr., chmn. 1995-97; bd. dirs. Jonsson Comprehensive Cancer Ctr., UCLA, Stanford U. Grad Sch. Bus.; trustee Nuclear Decommissioning Trust, Rosemead, Calif., Calif. State Dept. Mental Hygiene, Calif. Coun. for Econ. Edn., William H.Parker Police Found., 1992—. Mem. Calif. Club, L.A. Country Club, Vintage Club, Links Club N.Y.C., Beach Club, So. Calif. Tennis Assn. (v.p.), Tehama Golf Club. Avocations: golf, tennis, contemporary art, spectator sports. Office: TBG Fin 2029 Century Park E Los Angeles CA 90067-2901

JOHNSON, E. PERRY, lawyer; b. Pa., 1943; BA, W. Va. U., 1965, JD, 1968. Bar: W. Va. 1968, D.C. 1981, Mo. 1983. Instr. Boston U. Sch. Law, 1973-74, asst. dir., 1977-79, bur. competition, exec. asst. to chmn., 1979, dep. dir., 1979-80, dir., 1980-81; ptnr. Bryan Cave LLP, St. Louis. Vis. asst. prof. W. Va. U., 1972-73; adj. prof. St. Louis U. Sch. Law, 1985-86. With USN, 1968-72. Mem. ABA. Office: Bryan Cave LLP One Metropolitan Square 211 N Broadway Ste 3600 Saint Louis MO 63102-2733 E-mail: epjohnson@bryancave.com.*

JOHNSON, E. SCOTT, lawyer; b. Washington, June 28, 1951; s. William and Dorothy (Young) J.; m. Karen Colaianni, May 15, 1969 (div. 1972); 1 child, Scott Adrian; m. Cindy Ward, Feb. 14, 1986; 1 child, Tracy Elizabeth. BA summa cum laude, Md. U., 1985; JD cum laude, Georgetown U., 1988. Bar: U.S. Ct. Appeals (Md.), U.S. Dist. Ct. (Md. dist.). Studio musician Blue Seas Studios, Balt., 1973-75; record producer Flite III Studios, Balt., 1975-80; atty. Ober, Kaler, Grimes & Shriver, Balt., 1988—, chmn. intellectual property practice group. Legal intern Nat. Assn. Broadcasters, 1987. Editor-in-chief Public Domain Report, 1993—99; contbr. articles to profl. jours.; producer LP's including Portal of Antrim, 1976, Rivers of Memory, 1979, Portraits, 1978; Doncha Hide It, 1978, co-producer North Mountain Velvet, 1978. Pres. Md. Lawyers for the Arts, Balt., 1990—98; pres. Young Audiences Md., Balt., 1994-97; bd. dirs. Creative Alliance, 2004-; mem. Md. State Arts Coun., 2004—. Recipient First Prize: Nathan Burkan Copyright Law Competition ASCAP, Georgetown, 1987, Second Prize: Stephen G. Thompson Nat. Writing Competition Communications Law; named one of 115 Best Lawyers, Balt. Mag., 1995, Top Attorneys, 2003. Mem. ABA, ASCAP, NARAS, Washington Area Music Assn., Md. Bar Assn., Copyright Soc. U.S.A., Mid-Atlantic Arts Found., Inc. (v.p. 2001-03, pres. 2003-04), Wash. Area Music Assn. (bd. dirs. 1993-). Office Fax: 443-263-7588. E-mail: johnson@ober.com.

JOHNSON, EARL, JR., judge, author; b. Watertown, SD, June 10, 1933; s. Earl Jerome and Doris Melissa (Schwartz) J.; m. Barbara Claire Yanow, Oct. 11, 1970; children: Kelly Ann, Earl Eric, Agaarn Yanovitch. BA in Econs., Northwestern U., 1955, LL.M., 1961; JD, U. Chgo., 1960. Bar: Ill. 1960, US Ct. Appeals (9th cir.) 1964, DC 1965, US Supreme Ct. 1966, Calif. 1972. Trial atty., organized crime sect. Dept. Justice, Washington, Miami, Fla. and Las Vegas, Nev., 1961-64; dep. dir. Neighborhood Legal Svc. Project, 1964-65, OEO Legal Svc. Program, 1965-66, dir., 1966-68; vis. scholar Ctr. for Study of Law and Soc. U. Calif., Berkeley, 1968-69; assoc. prof. U. So. Calif. Law Ctr., LA, 1969-75, dir. clin. programs, 1970-73, prof. law, 1976-82, dir. Program Study Dispute Resolution Policy, Social Sci. Rsch. Inst., 1975-82; assoc. justice Calif. Ct. Appeal, 1982—; co-dir. Access to Justice Project European U. Inst., 1975-79. Vis. scholar Inst. Comparative Law, U. Florence, Italy, 1973, 75; Robert H. Jackson lectr. Nat. Jud. Coll., 1980; adv. panel Legal Svc. Corp., 1976-80; legis. impact panel Nat. Acad. Sci., 1977-80; faculty Asian Workshop on Legal Svcs. to Poor, 1974; mem. Internat. Legal Ctr., Legal Svcs. in Developing Countries, 1972-75; founder, bd. mem. Action for Legal Rights, 1971-74; pres., trustee Western Ctr. on Law and Poverty, 1972-73, 76-80; v.p., chmn. exec. com. Calif. Rural Legal Assistance Corp., 1973-74; exec. com. Nat. Sr. Citizens Law Ctr., 1980-82; sec. Nat. Resource Ctr. for Consumers of Legal Svc., 1974-82; chair Nat. Equal Justice Libr. Com., 1989-92; pres., Consortium for Nat. Equal Justice Libr., Inc., 1992-95, bd. dir., 1995—; chair Calif. Access to Justice Working Group, 1993-96; mem. Calif. Commn. on Access to Justice, 1997—2004, co-chmn., 2002-03. Author: Justice and Reform: The Formative Years of the Am. Legal Svc. Program, 1974, 2d edit., 1978, Toward Equal Justice: A Comparative Study of Legal Aid in Modern Soc., 1975, Outside the Courts: A Survey of Diversion Alternatives in Civil Cases, 1977, Dispute Processing Strategies, 1978, Dispute Resolution in Am., 1985, Calif. Trial Guide, 8 vols., 1986, Tex. Trial Guide, 6 vols., 1989, NY Trial Guide, 5 vols., 1990, Fla. Civil Trial Guide, 5 vols., 1990, Ill. Civil Trial Guide, 5 vols., 1991, Fed. Trial Guide, 5 vols., 1992, Ind. Civil Trial Guide, 5 vols., 1992, Calif. Family Law Trial Guide, 5 vols., 1992, Pa. Civil Trial Guide, 5 vols., 1992, Mich. Trial Guide, 5 vols., 1993, NC Civil Trial Guide, 5 vols., 1993, Calif. Criminal Trial Guide, 3 vols., 1994, Murder on Appeal (as Holmes Marshall), 2001; editor U. Chgo. Law Rev, 1960; mem. editl. bd. Jour. Law and Social Inquiry, 1987—; contbr. articles to books and periodicals. Bd. dir. Beverly Hills Bar Found., 1972-73, Nat. Legal Aid and Defenders Assn., 1987-91; trustee LA Legal Aid Found., 1969-71; mem. LA County Regional Planning Commn., 1980-81; bd. visitors U. San Diego Law Sch., 1983-86. Served with USNR, 1955-58. Recipient Dart award for acad. innovation U. So. Calif., 1971, Loren Miller Legal Svc. award Calif. State Bar, 1977, Appellate Justice of the Yr. award LA Trial Lawyers Assn., 1989, Outstanding Jud. Achievement award Calif. Trial Lawyers Assn., 1991, Legal Svc. Pioneer award LA Legal Aid Found., 1999, Appelate Judge of the Yr. award, Consumer Attorneys of Calif., 2003; named So. Calif. Citizen of Week, 1978; Ford Found. fellow, 1960; Dept. State lectr., 1975; grantee Ford Found.; grantee Russell Sage Found.; grantee Law Enforcement Assistance Adminstrn.; grantee NSF. Fellow Am. Bar Found. (rsch. adv. com. 1996-2001, chair 1999-2002); mem. ABA (com. chmn. 1972-75, spl. com. resolution minor disputes 1976-83, coun. sect. of individual rights and responsibilities 1990-91, consortium on legal svc. and the pub. 1991-94), Calif. Bar Assn., LA Bar Assn. (neighborhood justice ctr. com. 1976-81), Law and Soc. Assn., Nat. Legal Aid and Defender's Assn. (bd. dir. 1968-74), Am. Acad. Polit. and Social Sci., Calif. Judges Assn. (appellate cts. com. 1983-87, 98-99, ethics com. 1985-89), Internat. Assn. Procedural Law, Internat. Legal Aid Group, 1999, Order of Coif. Democrat. Office: Ct Appeals Calif 2d Appellate Dist 300 S Spring St Los Angeles CA 90013-1230 E-mail: justej@aol.com. *I have profound faith in the power of ideas to shape American society and in the special significance of one fundamental concept— equal justice, in its full meaning.*

JOHNSON, EARVIN See JOHNSON, MAGIC

JOHNSON, EDDIE BERNICE, congresswoman; b. Waco, Tex., Dec. 3, 1935; d. Lee Edward and Lillie Mae (White) J.; m. Lacy Kirk Johnson, July 5, 1956 (div. Oct. 1970); 1 child, Dawrence Kirk. Diploma in Nursing, St. Mary's Coll. of South Bend, 1955; BS in Nursing, Tex. Christian U., 1967; MPA, So. Meth. U., 1976; LLD (hon.), Bishop Coll., 1979, Jarvis Coll., 1979, Tex. Coll., 1989, Houston-Tillotson Coll., 1993, Paul Quinn Coll., 1993. Chief psychiat. nurse psychotherapist Vets. Hosp., Dallas, 1956-72; state rep. Tex. Ho. Reps. Dist. 33-0, Dallas, 1972-77; regional dir. HEW, Dallas, 1977-79, exec. asst. to adminstr. for primary health care policy Washington, 1979-81; v.p. Vis. Nurse Assn. of Tex., Dallas, 1981-87; mem. Tex. State Senate, dist. 23, 1986-93, U.S. Congress from 30th Tex. dist., Washington, 1993—, mem. sci., transp. and infrastructure coms.; chair Black caucus 107th U.S. Congress. Cons. div. urban affairs Zales Corp., Dallas, 1976-77; exec. asst. personnel div. Neiman-Marcus, Dallas, 1972-75; pres. Eddie Bernice Johnson & Assocs., Inc., Metroplex News, Dallas-Ft. Worth Airport. Bd. dirs. ARC. Recipient Citizenship award Nat. Conf. Christians and Jews, 1985; named an Outstanding Alumnus St. Mary's Coll. of Nursing, 1986. Mem. Alpha Kappa Alpha. Democrat. Office: US Ho of Reps 1511 Longworth HOB Washington DC 20515-4330 Office Phone: 202-225-8885. Business E-Mail: rep.e.b.johnson@mail.house.gov.

JOHNSON, EDGAR MCCARTHY, psychologist; b. Jacksonville, Fla., Oct. 29, 1941; s. James Mack Johnson and Dorothy (Vickers) Logue; m. Fatima Nunes, Sept. 9, 1967; children: Victoria C., David M. BS in Applied Psychology, Ga. Inst. Tech., 1964; MS in Exptl. Psychology, Tufts U., 1967, PhD in Exptl. Psychology, 1969. Rsch. psychologist U.S. Army Rsch. Inst., Alexandria, Va., 1970-78, chief human factors sect., 1978-80, dir. systems rsch. lab., 1980-82, tech. dir., 1982-93, dir., 1993—2002; chief psychologist U.S. Army, 1982—2002; mem. rsch. staff Inst. Def. Analyses, Alexandria, Va., 2002—. Served to capt. U.S. Army, 1968-70. NDEA fellow, 1965-67. Fellow APA, Am. Psychol. Soc., Human Factors and Ergonomics Soc., Washington Acad. Sci. (Sci. Achievement award 1980); mem. Cosmos Club (Washington), Sigma Xi. Office: Inst for Def Analyses 4850 Mark Ctr Dr Alexandria VA 22311-1882 Home: 1384 Mission San Carlos Dr Amelia Island FL 32034 Business E-Mail: emjohnso@ida.org. E-mail: emj1@sigmaxi.org.

JOHNSON, EDITH SCOTT, language educator, writer, consultant; b. Nashville, Ga., Mar. 25, 1943; d. James O'Leary and Edith Scott (Strother) Fuller; m. David James Moore, Feb. 4, 1962 (div. Sept. 1968); children: Meg Moore Bragdon, Marijim Moore Reeves; m. James Carter Johnson, Nov. 22, 1969 (div. June 1975); 1 child, James Carter III. BA in Art and English, Valdosta (Ga.) State Coll., 1968; MA in English, U. Nev., Reno, 1990; PhD in English, Ga. State U., Atlanta, 1997. Test code writer Westinghouse Air Brake Co., Lexington, Ky., 1962-64; rsch. asst. U. Ky., Lexington, 1964-67; songwriter, recording artist Dove and Commanchee Records, Nashville, 1967-74; adminstrv. coord. devel. studies Ga. State U., Atlanta, 1976-80; asst. dir. PACE program U. Nev., Reno, 1985-88, asst. dir. writing ctr., 1988-90, adj. instr. English, 1989-91; asst. prof. English Abraham Baldwin Coll., Tifton, Ga., 1991—; instr. English Moultrie (Ga.) Tech. Coll., 2002—. Writing cons. Crisp Area Arts Alliance, Cordele, Ga., 1996-97; resident poet Abraham Baldwin Coll., 1995-97; rschr. Ga. State U., Atlanta, 1991-97. Author: Driftwood and Wintergreen, 1996 (Internat. Poet award Internat. Soc. Poets), Cold Hearts and Glass Eyes, 1997 (1st class award Ga. State U.), Images of Love and Ice, 1998, The Evening Wolves, 1998, The Toolbox, 2002; contbg. poet: World of Poetry, 1985 (Golden Poet award 1985), Iliad Press, 1995-96 (Poet of Yr. award 1995-96); performer Arts Experiment Sta., Tifton, 1996-97; poetry reader The Magpie Shop, Art Dept. Cornwall (Eng.) Coll., 1996. Tchr. bible Trinity United Meth. Ch., Tifton, 1997. Collected works dedicated in her honor Crisp Area Arts Alliance, Cordele, 1997. Mem. Nat. Coun. Tchrs. English, Nat. Assn. for Devel. Edn. (presenter, presider 1991-97), Nat. Authors' Registry. Avocations: dulcimer, piano, guitar, singing, landscape and portrait art. Office: 361 Industrial Blvd Moultrie GA Home: 315 15th St SE Apt G2 Moultrie GA 31768-5063

JOHNSON, EDNA RUTH, editor; b. Sturgeon Bay, Wis., Dec. 23, 1918; d. Charles Frederick and Georgina (Knutson) Johnson; m. Al Larson, 1955. BA, U. So. Fla., 1971. With The Churchman, 1950-89; editor The Human Quest (formerly The Churchman), St. Petersburg, Fla., 1958—98. Tchr. ballroom dancing to Eckerd Coll. Students, St. Petersburg, Fla., 1995-96. Co-author (with Antoni Gronowicz): Sergei Rachmaninoff, 1946; editor: Friendship News (USA-USSR), 1975—88; mem. editl. bd. The Humanist, Amherst, N.Y., 1980—. Bd. dirs. ACLU, Nat. Emergency Civil Liberties Com., N.Y.C. Named Fla. Humanist of Yr. Am. Humanist Assn. Fla., 1975, Pres. Soc. of Fine Arts Arts, Pinellas Park, Fla., 1970-90. Mem. Acad. Sr. Profls. at Eckerd Coll. Avocations: ballroom dancing, ballet, painting. Home and Office: 411 First Ave N Princess Martha Apt 901 Saint Petersburg FL 33701 Office Phone: 727-894-0097.

JOHNSON, EDWARD MICHAEL, molecular biologist, educator; b. Kenosha, Wis., Apr. 9, 1945; s. Edward and Mary Margaret (Pratch) J.; m. Elizabeth Buckingham Childs, June 14, 1969; 1 son, Nathaniel Livingston. B.A., Pomona Coll., 1967; Ph.D., Yale U., 1971. Postdoctoral fellow Rockefeller U., N.Y.C., 1971-73, asst. prof. molecular biology, 1975-81, assoc. prof., 1981—; research assoc. Sloan-Kettering Cancer Ctr., N.Y.C., 1973-75; adj. assoc. prof. Cornell U. Grad. Sch. Med. Sci., N.Y.C., 1981—; prof. molecular biology and pathology Mt. Sinai Med. Sch., 1984— . Contbr. numerous articles to sci. publs. Jane Coffin Childs fellow in molecular biology, 1971; Leukemia Soc. Am. Spl. Fellow, 1974; recipient Faculty Rsch. award Am. Cancer Soc. Mem. Am. Soc. Biolchem. and Molecular Biology, Am. Soc. for Pharmacology and Exptl. Therapeutics, Am. Soc. for Cell Biology, N.Y. Acad. Scis., AAAS. Home: 531 E 88th St Apt 4B New York NY 10128-7756 Office: Mt Sinai Sch Medicine 1 Gustave L Levy Pl # 1194 New York NY 10029-6500

JOHNSON, ELAINE LUCILLE, artist, director; b. New Orleans, La., Oct. 1, 1957; d. Lionel Lloyd Johnson, Sr. and Lucille (Green) Johnson; children: Keva, Kima, Kori Richard. Attended, Univ. of New Orleans, N.O., La., 1977—79, St. Bernard Comm. Coll., Chalmette, La., 1984, Nunez Comm. Coll., 2002. Cert. Nurse aide, Nursing Home/ St. Bernard, La., 1984. Nurse aide Nursing Home, St. Bernard, La., 1984—2003; dir. Boogie's Art Gallery, St. Bernard, La., 1999—. Dir. art and craft Vacation Bible Sch., First Bapt. Ch., Verret, La. Author: (coloring book) Color with Boogie, 2002, (craft, annual project) New Yr. Craft, (picture book) Picture Perfect Book "00", 2000. Mem.: New Orleans Art Coun. Achievements include open first Art Gallery in St. Bernard, La. with Joan Sloan, 1999. Now a non-profit Gallery/Studio.

JOHNSON, ELIZABETH DIANE LONG, retired lawyer; b. Pasadena, Calif., Nov. 16, 1945; d. Volney Earl and Sylvia Irene (Drury) Long; m. Lynn Douglas Johnson, Oct. 22, 1966; 1 child, Barbara Annette. BA, U. of Houston, 1967; JD, Rutgers U., 1980. Bar: N.J. 1980, U.S. Dist. Ct. N.J. 1980, Pa. 1984, U.S. Supreme Ct. 1986. Pvt. practice, Riverside, NJ, 1980—96; ret., 1996. Pub. defender Riverside Twp., 1988-91; speaker Comprehensive Justice Ctr. Burlington County, 1987-89. Del. Women in Law to Peoples Republic of China Citizen Amb. Program of People to People Internat., 1989; mem. Orchid Found., 1989-97, rec. sec., 1991-97; mem. Tenby Chase Civic Assn., Delran, N.J., 1972-87, treas., 1976, v.p., 1974; trustee Drenk Mental Health Ctr., 1988-95, pres., 1991-94, chair bd. trustees, 1993-94, vice chair bd. trustees, 1995. Mem.: Burlington County Bar Found. (trustee 1988—91, treas. 1988—90, v.p. 1990—91, pres. 1991—92), Burlington County Bar Assn. (chmn. bench and bar com. 1989—91), N.J. Women Lawyers Assn., Mensa, Soc. for Right to Die, Rotary (sec. Riverside 1991—92, v.p. 1992—93, pres.-elect 1993—94, pres. 1994—95, dir. 1995—96, Dist. 7500 area rep. 1995—96, sec. Beverly 2000—01, 2003—, v.p. 2001—02, pres. 2002—03, Dist. 7500 sec. 2004—05, Outstanding Dist. Officer 2004—05), Delta Gamma. Methodist.

JOHNSON, ELIZABETH MISNER, health services executive; b. Lewiston, Idaho, May 16, 1939; d. Gervase Arthur and Blenda N. (Westerlund) Misner; m. Dohn Robert Johnson, Oct. 13, 1962; children: Dohn Robert Jr., Kevin Arthur. BS in Acctg., U. Idaho, 1961. CPA, Calif., Wash. Audit staff Randall, Emery, Campbell & Parker (now Pricewaterhouse Coopers), Spokane, Wash., 1961—62; audit staff, sr. Price Waterhouse, L.A., 1962-65; CPA L.A., 1966-73; CFO KLP, Inc. dba Call-America, Mesa, Ariz., 1995-98; gen. mgr. Life Line Screening, Phoenix, 2001—. Treas., pres., hon. life mem. Arts Coun. Calif. State U., Northridge, 1975—; internat. dir. alumnae devel. Alpha Gamma Delta (recipient unusually outstanding svc. award, 1993), U.S. and Can., 1988-98; chmn. bd. trustees Alpha Gamma Delta Found., 1998-2001, trustee, 1998—. Pres. Soroptimist Internat., Coeur d'Alene, Idaho, 1991-92, regional nominating com., 1993-94. Mem. Ariz. Soc. of CPAs. Home: 14839 S 47th Way Phoenix AZ 85044-6881 E-mail: liz@mtparkranch.org.

JOHNSON, ELMER WILLIAM, lawyer; b. Denver, May 2, 1932; s. Elmer William and Lillian Marie (Nelson) J.; m. Constance Dorothy Mahon, June 18, 1955; children: Julianne Marie, Valerie Lynn, Garrett Douglas. BA, Yale U., 1954; JD, U. Chgo., 1957. Bar: Ill. 1957. Assoc. Kirkland & Ellis, Chgo., 1956-62, ptnr., 1962—99; v.p., group exec. gen. counsel Gen. Motors Corp., Detroit, 1983-87, exec. v.p., dir., 1987-88; gen. counsel Internat. Harvester, Chgo., 1982-83; spl. counsel to chmn. of Ameritech Corp., Chgo., 1982-83; pres., CEO Aspen Inst., Washington, 1999—2002; ptnr. Jenner & Block, Chgo., 2002—. Mem. legal adv. com. N.Y. Stock Exch., 1987-91; v.p., dir. The Econ. Club of Chgo.; chmn. bd. govs. Chgo. Lighthouse for Blind. Author: Avoiding the Collision of Cities and Cars, 1993, Chicago Metropolis 2020, 2001. Trustee U. Chgo., 1977-89, Aspen Inst., Colo., 1988-2002, pres. CEO, 1999-2002. Fellow Am. Acad. Arts and Scis.; mem. ABA, Ill. Bar Assn., Chgo. Club, Old Elm. Republican. Presbyterian. Office: Jenner & Block 1 IBM Plaza Chicago IL 60611

JOHNSON, ERIC B., state legislator; b. New Orleans, Aug. 20, 1953; m. Kathryn Johnson; children: Marcus, Righton. Degree in architecture, Tulane U. Architect North Point Real Estate; mem. Ga. Ho. of Reps., 1993-94; senator 1st dist. Ga. State Legislature, 1994—, pres. pro tem, 2003—, mem. appropriations com., ethics com., fin. com, natural resources/environment com., rules com., vice chmn. regulated industries and utilities com. Sponsor, mem. joint senate-house study com. on cert. of need health care facilities Ga. State Senate. Regional dir. former U.S. Senator Mack Mattingly, 1981-83; alumnus Leadership Savannah; active Inner City Night Shelter. Named Ga.'s Young Rep. of Yr., 1980. Mem. AIA, Exec. Assn. of Savannah. Mem. Savannah Christian Ch. Address: 128 Baymeadow Point Savannah GA 31405 Business E-Mail: ejohnson@legis.state.ga.us.

JOHNSON, ERIK REID, lawyer; b. L.A., Jan. 13, 1950; BA in Psychology magna cum laude, UCLA, 1973; JD, Loyola U., 1978. Bar: Calif. 1978, Nev. 1984. Dep. dist. atty. L.A. County, 1979-86; dep. state pub. defender State of Nev., Carson City, 1986-89; pvt. practice Carson City, 1989—. 1st lt. USAR, 1973-79. Office: 711 E Washington St Carson City NV 89701-4063

JOHNSON, ERMA JEAN, human services administrator; b. Little Rock, Dec. 20, 1951; d. Odessa Johnson; m. Willie R. Johnson, June 19, 1977 (div. Apr. 6, 1985); 1 child, Preya D. AA, Lamar (Colo.) Coll., 1970; BA, Chgo. State U., 1973; MS, Almeda Coll. and Univ., Boise, Idaho, 2002. Social worker, coord. East Ctr. Cmty. Mental Health, Toledo, 1977—78; social worker Toledo Mental Health Ctr., 1979—80, social program coord., 1980—84, mental health adminstr., 1984—85; supt. Ohio Dept. Youth Svcs., Warrensville, 1985—87, regional adminstr. Toledo, 1987—2002; pres., CEO New Hope Recovery Ctr., Holland, Ohio, 2002—. Mem. adv. bd. Children and Family First, Toledo, 1985—2002, Lourde Coll., Sylvania, Ohio, 1999—2001; v.p. Am. Bus. Women Am., Toledo, 1995—97. Recipient Humanitarian award, Youth Svc. Cmty. Svcs., 1999, recognition for vol. counseling ex-offenders, Lucas County Adult Probation Dept., Toledo, Operation DARE, Chgo.; grantee, Target Stores, 1999—2000. Mem.: NAFE. Baptist. Avocations: walking, bowling, flower arranging, creating community programs. Office Phone: 419-356-3320.

JOHNSON, ERNEST FREDERICK, chemical engineer, educator; b. Jamestown, N.Y., Apr. 4, 1918; s. Ernest Frederick and Esther Marie (Engstrom) J.; m. Marjorie Ruth McMullin, July 15, 1944 (dec. Dec. 2003); children: David S. (dec.), Carolyn L. Walton, Arthur B., Melissa A. Bonner. BS, Lehigh U., 1940; PhD, U. Pa., 1949. Rsch. engr., tech. supr. synthetic organic chem. mfr. Barrett div. Allied Chem. Corp., Phila., 1940-46; asst. prof. dept. chem. engring. Princeton U., 1948-54, assoc. prof., 1954-59, prof., 1959-86, acting chmn. dept. chem. engring., 1959-60, chmn. dept., 1977-78, assoc. dean faculty, 1962-66, clk. of faculty, 1983-86, assoc. Plasma Physics Lab., 1955-86, prof. emeritus, 1986—, sr. advisor to pres., 1988-91. Cons. petroleum, chem., engring., environ., food processing firms, govt. agys., 1949—; bd. dirs. Autodynamics Inc. 1968-85; mem. adv. bd. Indsl. and Engring. Chemistry, 1964-67. Author: Automatic Process Control, 1967; contbr. Advances in Chemical Engineering, 1958, Ency. Chemistry, Chemistry of Fusion Power Development, 1972; contbr. articles to sci. jours. Trustee Associated Univs., Inc., 1962-68, chmn. bd., 1965-67; trustee Westminster Found., 1973-79. Recipient Nat. Engrs. Week Engring. Edn. award, 1994, Lehigh U. Alumni Assn. award, 2000, Eugene G. Grace Class of 1889 award Lehigh U., 2001; named hon. mem. Princeton Class of 1962. Fellow AAAS, AIChE (exec. com. Cen. Jersey sect. 1972—), Am. Inst. Chemists; mem. Am. Chem. Soc. (exec. com. div. indsl. and engring. chemistry 1965-67, coun. 1976-78), Princeton Engring. Assn. (sec.-treas. 1954-57, exec. com. 1954—), Adirondack Mountain Club, Appalachian Mountain Club, Tärnavrå Yacht Club, Sigma Xi, Tau Beta Pi, Phi Eta Sigma. Presbyterian (elder). Home: 39 Pleasant Hill Rd Freeport ME 04032 also: 212 Indian Point Rd Stonington ME 04681-9702

JOHNSON, EUGENE CLARE, data processing company executive; b. Whitehall, Wis., Nov. 19, 1940; s. Paul Reuben and Clara Theresa (Severson) J.; m. Livia Ann Baynes, Sept. 23, 1967; children: Andrew Paul, Anthony Alexander. Student, Madison Coll., 1959, Pasadena Coll., 1961, Purdue U., 1962, Harvard U., 1974. Vol. Peace Corps, Chile, 1962-64; acct. Am. Ins. Underwriters, N.Y.C., 1964-66; advanceman to Pres. Richard M. Nixon N.Y.C., 1966-68; asst. treas. Bristol-Myers Co., N.Y.C., 1968-69; spl. asst. to Gov. Nelson Rockefeller N.Y.C., 1969—70; mgr. advanced systems div. U.S. Postal Service, Washington, 1971-80; mgr. govt. relations dept. ITT, Washington, 1980-85; exec. v.p., chief operating officer TCom Systems, Inc., Washington, 1985-88; v.p. market devel. Diversified Data and Communications Inc., Washington, 1988-90; pres., chief exec. officer Bus. Mail Express, Inc., Washington, 1990-95, Mail 2000, Washington, 1995—2003; vice-chmn., founder Global Mail Strategies. Founder Electronic Funds Transfer Assocs., Washington, 1977. Patentee performance analyzer. Sr. adviser Reagan Presdl. Transition Team, 1980; presdl. appointee U.S. Archtl. and Transp. Barriers Compliance Bd., 1988-90; adv. bd. Peace Corps., 1990-92. Mem.: Kenwood Golf and Country (Bethesda, Md.) (chmn. bd. dirs. 1987). Avocations: tennis, golf, jogging. Home: 5525 Chamberlin Ave Chevy Chase MD 20815-6643 Office: Ste 300 7316 Wisconsin Ave Bethesda MD 20814-2976 E-mail: genecjohnson@hotmail.com.

JOHNSON, EUGENE LAURENCE, lawyer; b. Wisconsin Rapids, Wis., Nov. 30, 1936; s. Elmer Hilding and Claribel May Johnson; m. Barbara Dell Braley, June 18, 1960; children: Mark, Ben, Christopher. BSCE, U. Wis., 1960, JD, 1962. Bar: Minn. 1963, Calif. 1965, U.S. Patent Office 1963. Atty. Pillsbury Co., Mpls., 1962-64; assoc. Mellin, Hanscom & Hursh, San Francisco, 1964-66; ptnr. Dorsey & Whitney, Mpls., 1966-98, Eugene L. Johnson, PA, Wayzata, Minn., 1998—. Program founder, adj. prof. intellectual property law William Mitchell Coll. Law, 1967-75. Capt. USAR, 1960. Mem. Minn. Bar Assn. (past bd. govs.), Am. Intellectual Property Law Assn., Minn. Intellectual Property Law Assn. (past pres.), Am. Swedish Inst. (bd. trustees), Mpls. Athletic Club, Lafayette Country Club. Republican.

JOHNSON, EVA JO, educational consultant; b. Chattanooga, Aug. 9, 1941; d. Joseph Saddler and Wilma (Logue) Scruggs; m. Richard Louis Spence, Apr. 4, 1959 (div. Mar. 1967); children: Gail, Richard, Donald Lamarion, Stephani. BS, So. Conn. State U., 1975, MS, 1978; postgrad., Fairfield U., 1983. Cert. in spl. edn. and adminstrn. and supervision. Tchr. spl. edn. Hamden (Conn.) Pub. Schs., 1975-87, supr. alternative program, 1987-91; instr. psychology South Ctrl. C.C., New Haven, 1988-89; educator spl. edn. resources Hamden Pub. Schs., 1991—. Chairperson Profl. Devel., Hamden, 1984-85; cons. Hamden Pub. Schs., 1976-87, coord. ann. ethnic celebration, 1978-89 Devel. curriculum project Celebration of Excellence, 1990 (Edn. award 1990). Chairperson membership com. N.H. Urban League, New Haven, 1985-88; mem. League Women Voters, Hamden, 1988-91; v.p. Conn. Afro Am. Hist. Soc., New Haven, 1992—; vol. in missions. Recipient Prudence Crandall award Conn. Edn. Assn., 1987, John Rogers Meml. award Conn. Edn. Assn., 1989, Woman in Leadership award YWCA, 1989, Cmty. Svc. award Bus. and Profl. Women, 1992, So. Conn. State U. Alumni Citation award, 2001. Mem. Phi Delta Kappa, Alpha Kappa Alpha (pub. rels. chair 1992—, Svc. award). Mem. United Methodist Ch. Avocations: foreign travels, writing, walking, cooking, decorating. Home and Office: 3 Fern Ln Branford CT 06405-3352 E-mail: evajo7@yahoo.com.

JOHNSON, EVA MARIA, retired translator; b. Ludwigshafen, Rhine, Germany, Jan. 19, 1920; came to U.S., 1951; naturalized 1955; d. George and Maria Regina (Wurzel) Lenz; m. Martin L. Johnson, June 8, 1952 (dec. Jan. 1994); 1 child, Michael Andrew. Student, Ludwigshafen, 1938, Vorbeck Lang. Sch., 1940-43. Interpreter, translator German, English and French, Police, Lampertheim, Germany, 1945-46; reporter Deutsche Presse Dienst, Wiesbaden, Germany, 1946-48; editl. specialist U.S. Mil. Govt., Wiesbaden, Germany, 1948-51; bilingual sec. Embassy of Austria, Washington, 1951-53; translator Internat. Affairs Dept. CIO, Washington, 1953—55; translator Combat Ops. Rsch. Group, CDC, Fort Belvoir, Va., 1965-70; freelance translator top secret clearance Dept. Def., Washington, 1970-72; sr. sect., translator Holman & Stern, Patent Law Office, Washington, 1972-85; ret., 1985. Key-note spkr. Surviving POWs VA Hosp., Martinsburg, W.Va., 1996. Anti-Nazi activist, 1943-45. Mem.: The Ret. Mil. Officer Assn. (life). Avocations: photography, writing, eggeury, gardening, reading. Home: 352 Monastery Ridge Rd Stephenson VA 22656 Personal E-mail: rjohnson@visuallink.com.

JOHNSON, EVELYN BRYAN, airport terminal executive; b. Corbin, Ky., Nov. 4, 1909; d. Edward William and Myme Estelle (Fox) Stone; m. Wyatt J. Bryan, Mar. 21, 1931 (dec. 1963); m. Morgan N. Johnson, Feb. 25, 1965 (dec. Mar. 1977). Grad., Tenn Wesleyan Jr. Coll., 1929; student, U. Tenn., 1930—32. With Morristown (Tenn.) Flying Svc., Inc., 1947-97, designated pilot examiner, 1952—2005, sec.-treas., 1949-62, pres., 1962-82; mgr. Moore Murrell Airport, 1962—. Gov.'s appointee Tenn. Aero. Commn., 1983—2001, vice-chmn., 1987—89, chmn., 1989—91, 1994—96. Recipient Carnegie Hero medal, 1958, Svc. to Mankind award Morristown Sertoma Club, 1981, Kitty Hawk award, FAA, 1991, Friends of Aviation award Tenn. Aviation Assn., 1992, Stewart G. Potter Aviation Edn. award Aviation Distbrs. and Mfrs. Assn., 1992, Elder Statesman of Aviation award Nat. Aeronautics Assn., 1993, Katherine Wright Meml. award Nat. Aeronautics Assn. and the Ninety Nines, 2002; named Flight Instr. of Yr., Nashville Dist. 1973, 79, So. region 1979, Nat., 1979 (all FAA), Outstanding Alumnus Tenn. Wesleyan Coll., 1981, Tenn. Divsn. Aviation Airport Mgr. of Yr., 2004; named to Women in Aviation Pioneers Hall of Fame, 1994, Hamblen Women Hall of Fame, 1997, Flight Instr. Hall of Fame, EAA Air Venture Mus., Oshkosh, 1997, Ky. Aviation Hall of Fame, 2000, Tenn. Aviation Hall of Fame, 2002, Kathryn Wright Meml. award Nat. Aeronautics Assn., 2002; holder of record most flying time for women pilots Guiness Book of Records 1995— Mem. CAP, Morristown Area C. of C., Nat. Assn. Flight Instrs. (bd. dirs., treas 1987-88, award 1992), Ninety-Nines (Award of Merit 1994), Whirly Girls (plaque 1992, Livingston award 2004, Airport Mgr. of the Yr. 2004, Wright Bros. Master Pilot award 2004), Aircraft Owners and Pilots Assn., Silver Wings (bd. dirs. 1987-2002, Woman of Yr. 1981, Carl Fromhagen award 1992), United Flying Octogenarians. Republican. Baptist. Home: 775 Commanche Dr Jefferson City TN 37760 Office: PO Box 1013 Morristown TN 37816-1013 Office Phone: 423-586-2483.

JOHNSON, EVELYN PORTERFIELD, journalist, educator; b. Kansas City, Mo., Jan. 7, 1937; d. Roy LaVerne and Lorraine (Lardie) Porterfield; m. Robert Luck Johnson, June 30, 1962 (div. 1972); children: Jennifer, Lara, Tracey, Virginia. BA, Ea. Bapt. Coll., St. Davids, Pa., 1958. Tchr. Lower Merion Sch. Dist., Ardmore, Pa., 1958—60, Prince Georges County, Md., 1961—62, Loudoun County Sch., Leesburg, Va., 1977—92; freelance journalist local newspapers and mags. Chmn. Regional English Tchrs. Conf., Leesburg, 1991. Author: book, 2003. Founder Bluemont (Va.) Fair, 1970—, Friends of Bluemont, 2002—; mem. Keep Loudoun Beautiful; mem. Blue Ridge Dist. Loudoun's Women Commn.; Blue Ridge rep. Loudoun County Archtl. Rev. Com., 1992. Mem.: Preservation Soc. Loudoun County (founder, pres. 1974—), Democrat. Baptist. Avocations: reading, collecting local history, antiques, old house tours. Home: PO Box 247 Bluemont VA 20135

JOHNSON, FAYE M., medical educator; d. Fred Tulloch Johnson and Faye Maxine Vincent; m. Ajay Kwara, Oct. 24, 1993; children: Sean, Megan. BA, Johns Hopkins U., 1989; MD, PhD, U. Tex., 1996. Cert. internal medicine 2000, med. oncology 2003, lic. Tex. Resident Baylor Coll. Medicine, Houston, 1997—99; asst. prof. thoracic, head and neck med. oncology U. Tex. M.D. Anderson Cancer Ctr., 2003—. Contbr. articles to profl. jours., chapters to books. Recipient Cmty. Svc. award, CIBA-GEIGY, 1991; fellow, U. Tex. M.D. Anderson Cancer Ctr., 2000—02, 2002—03, Tng. Acad. Oncology, 2001—03, ASCO/AACR, Vail, Colo., 2001; grantee, Nat. Inst. Child Health and Hukan Devel., 1993—95, MD Anderson Cancer Ctr., 2003—; Leventhal scholar, Women in Cancer Rsch., 2003. Mem.: AMA, Tex. Med. Assn., Am. Assn. Cancer Rsch., Am. Soc. Clin. Oncology. Office: MD Anderson Cancer Ctr 1515 Holcombe Houston TX 77030

JOHNSON, FRANCIS SEVERIN, physicist; b. Omak, Wash., July 20, 1918; s. Ralston Severin and Elizabeth (Gruenes) J.; m. Maurine Marie Green, Sept. 12, 1943; 1 dau., Sharan Kaye. B.Sc. with honors in Physics, U. Alta., Can., 1940; MA in Physics and Meteorology, UCLA, 1942, PhD in Meteorology, 1958. Head, high atmosphere research sect. U.S. Naval Research Lab., Washington, 1946-55; mgr. space physics research Lockheed Missiles & Space Co., 1955-62; head, atmospheric and space scis. div. S.W. Center Advanced Studies, Dallas, 1962-64, dir. earth and planetary scis. lab., 1964-69; acting pres. U. Tex. at Dallas, 1969-71; dir. Center for Advanced Studies, 1971-74, Cecil H. and Ida M. Green honors prof. natural sci., 1974-89, prof. emeritus, 1989—2003, exec. dean grad. studies and research, 1976-79; asst. dir. astron., atmosphere, earth and ocean scis. NSF, Washington, 1979-83. Cons. ionospheric physics subcom., space scis. steering com. NASA, 1960-62, mem. planetary atmospheres subcom., space scis. steering com., 1962-67, chmn. lunar atmospheric measurements team, Apollo sci. planning teams, 1964-67, mem. adv. bd. Mars space missions, 1964-67, mem. lunar and planetary missions bd., 1967-71; mem. adv. panel atmospheric scis. NSF, 1962-67; mem. working group IV COSPAR, 1965-80, v.p., 1975-80; mem. Nat. Acad. Scis. panel adv. to central radio propagation lab. Nat. Bur. Standards, 1962-65, mem. panel weather and climate modification Nat. Acad. Scis., 1964-70, mem. space sci. bd., 1969-81, mem. geophysics research bd., 1971-77, mem. bd. on atmospheric scis. and climate, 1984-87, mem. Nat. Acad. Scis. com. adv. to NOAA, 1966-71, mem. climate research bd., 1977-79; mem. adv. com. research to coordinating bd. Tex. Coll. and Univ. System, 1966-67; mem. sci. advisory bd. USAF, 1968-79; mem. nat. adv. com. Oceans and Atmosphere, 1971-73; pres. Spl. Com. on Solar Terrestrial Physics, 1974-77; mem. Aerocibo adv. bd. and vis. com. Nat. Astronomy and Ionsphere Ctr. Cornell U., 1985-88. Author: Satellite Environment Handbook, 1965; also numerous articles. Served with USAAF, 1942-46. Decorated Bronze Star medal; recipient Henryk Arctowski award NAS, 1972, Exceptional Sci. Achievement medal NASA, 1973, Meritorious Civilian Service award USAF, 1979, Disting. Tex. Sci. award Tex. Acad. Scis., 1984, Disting. Alumni award U. Alta., 2001. Fellow Am. Geophys. Union (vice chmn. sect. geomagnetism and aeronomy 1964-68, pres. sect. solar planetary relationships 1970-72, John Adam Fleming award 1977), AAAS (council mem. 1968-72), Am. Meteorol. Soc. (councilor 1976-78), IEEE, AIAA (chmn. tech. com. space and atmospheric physics 1961-64, Space Sci. award 1966); mem. Internat. Assn. Geomagnetism and Aeronomy (exec. com. 1967-71), Internat. Union Radio Sci. (chmn. U.S. Commn. IV 1964-67, sec. U.S. nat. com. 1967-70, vice chmn. 1970-73, chmn. 1973-76), Internat. Union Geodesy and Geophysics (U.S. nat. com. 1973-76).

JOHNSON, FRANK, educator, retired state official; b. Ogden, Utah, Mar. 12, 1928; s. Clarence Budd and Arline (Parry) J.; m. Maralyn Brewer, Aug. 15, 1950; children: Scott, Arline, Laurie, Kelly, Edward. BS, U. Utah, 1955; MS, U. Ill., 1958, PhD, 1960. Instr. U. N.D., Grand Forks, 1955-56; teaching asst. U. Ill., Urbana, 1956-59; rsch. asst. prof. U. Del., Newark, 1959-60; prof. U. Utah, Salt Lake City, 1960-93, assoc. dean, 1970-77; dir. divsn. pub. utilities State of Utah, Salt Lake City, 1989—97. Cons. Gen. Foods, Sears, Magnavox, Albertsons, Zion Bank, Nat. Food Brokers Assn., others; part-owner Old Post Office Bldg., Ogden, Utah, Seventeenth St. Storage. Legis. Utah House of Reps., Salt Lake City, 1982-88; mem. Humanitarian Svc. Mission, eastern Europe, 1998-99; trainer vols. Salt Lake City Winter Olympics, 2002. Republican. Avocations: mountains, travel, reading, public and church service. Home: 1048 E Fairway Dr North Salt Lake UT 84054-3056

JOHNSON, FRANK EDWARD, surgeon educator; b. Evanston, Ill., Oct. 28, 1943; s. Frank E. and Beryl Madeline (Johnson) J.; m. Tamiko Asato, Jan. 24, 1976; children: Mariko, Michael, Eric, David. BA, U. Minn., 1964, MD, 1967. Diplomate Am. Bd. Surgery. Intern UCLA affiliated hosps., 1967-78; resident in surgery U. Wash., Seattle, 1972-74, U. Colo., 1974-77; rsch. fellow U. Calif., San Francisco, 1975-76; fellow in surg. oncology Meml. Sloan-Kettering Cancer Ctr., N.Y.C., 1977-79; rsch. prof. Guy's Hosp., London, 1986-87; clin. instr. surgery Cornell U., N.Y.C., 1977-79; asst. prof. St. Louis U. Med. Ctr., 1979-84, assoc. prof., 1984-89, prof., 1989—. Editor: Cancer Patient Follow-up, 1997, The Bionic Human, 2005, author 15 med. films; contbr. articles to profl. jours. Co-founder Children's Heart Fund, Mpls., 1969. Lt. comdr. USN, 1969-71, Vietnam. Decorated Bronze Star; grantee NIH, Am. Cancer Soc., Royal Coll. Surgeons Found., VA Merit Rev. Mem. ACS, Am. Gastroent. Assn. AMA, Soc. Surg. Oncology, Am. Soc. Clin. Oncology, Am. Assn. Cancer Edn., Am. Paraplegia Soc., Am. Assn. Cancer Rsch., Am. Radium Soc., Am. Soc. Preventive Oncology, Ctrl. Surg. Assn. (grantee), Southwestern Surg. Congress, Am. Head and Neck Soc., Am. Physiol. Soc., Soc. Univ. Surgeons, Soc. Surgery of the Alimentary Tract, Assn. Acad. Surgeons, Assn. Surgeons of Gt. Britain and Ireland. Office Phone: 314-577-8316.

JOHNSON, FRANK(LIN) LENARD, former professional basketball coach; b. Weirsdale, Fla., Nov. 23, 1958; m. Amy Johnson; children: Lindsay, Natalie. Postgrad, Wake Forest U., 1981. Guard Wash. Bullets, 1981—88, Houston Rockets, 1988—89, Varese & Rimini, Italy, 1989—92, Phoenix Suns, 1992—94, asst. coach, cmty. rels. dept., head coach, 2002—03. Named NBA All-Rookie honors, 1982.

JOHNSON, FRANKLYN ARTHUR, academic administrator; b. Rochester, NY, Nov. 6, 1921; s. Robert Barnes and Olyve Cole (Eckler) J.; m. Emily Bernetta Lingle, Aug. 15, 1945 (div. Aug. 1978); children: Franklyn Arthur Jr.(dec.), Terri A. Cochran, Sandra C. Fox; m. Elena Senese, Sept. 27, 1991. BA, Rutgers U., 1947; MA, Harvard U., 1949, PhD, 1952; LHD (hon.), Jacksonville U., 1961; DLitt (hon.), Mt. Senario Coll., Ladysmith, Wis., 1971; LLD (hon.), Flagler Coll., St. Augustine, Fla., 1976; DCL (hon.), Drury Coll., Springfield, Mo., 1976; HHD (hon.), Mo. Valley Coll., 1978. Intelligence officer CIA, Washington, 1949-51; asst., assoc. prof. govt. Rollins Coll., Winter Park, Fla., 1952-56; pres., prof. govt. Jacksonville U., Fla., 1956-63, Calif. State U., Los Angeles, 1963-65; asst. sec., dir. Job Corps OEO, Washington, 1965-67; pres., chmn., trustee Wm. H. Donner Found., N.Y.C., 1967-70; dir. Arthur Vining Davis Founds., Coral Gables, Fla., 1970-78; prof. adminstrn. Fla. Atlantic U., Boca Raton, 1970-87; pres., prof. mgmt. S.W. Fla. Coll., Naples, 1987—. Trustee Inst. for Am. Univs., Aix-en-Provence, France, 1967—97, Eckerd Coll., St. Petersburg, Fla., 1978—90; chmn. S.E. Coun. Founds., Atlanta, 1975—77. Author: Defence by Committee, 1960, Defence by Ministry, 1980, 81, One More Hill, 1949, rev. edits., 1982, 88, Santori, 1990, Castro: The Last Hurrah, 1992, The Periled Presidency, 1995, Here and There, 1995, After Thoughts, 1996, D. S. Nemenoff, Maestro, 1996, A Chance Encounter, 1996, Odds and Ends, 1996, The Gods That Failed, 1997, Pearls Are a Girl's Best Friend, 1997, The 22nd Amendment, 1998, The Reluctant Presidents, 1999, Santori Island of Evil, 1999, Key West to Cuba, 2000, The Mismated, 2001, Triangle of Terror: Trauma in Everglades City, 2003, Dynasty of Deceit: 2015, The Last of the 3 Castros, 2004, Eyes Only: Countdown to Chaos, 2005; also articles on def., civil and mil. rels., adminstrn. Mem. U.S. Com. United World Colls., N.Y.C., 1975-85, Fla. Gov.'s Coun. on Indian Affairs, Tallahassee, 1975-80, exec. adv. coun. Fla. Atlantic U., chmn.; bd. dirs. Collier Cultural and Ednl. Ctr., Naples; v.p., dir. Beachwood Assn., Inc., 1992-94; pres. Francobollo Press, 1998—. Lt. U.S. Army, 1942-45, ETO. Decorated Disting. Svc. medal, Jubilee of Liberty, Croix deGuerre, Diplome de la Liberation de Normandie (France); Prisoner of War medal, Silver Star, 5 Bronze Stars, 3 Purple Hearts, Conspicuous Svc. Cross; recipient George Washington honor medal Freedoms Found., Valley Forge, 1956, Profl. Achievement award Barry U., Miami, Fla., Eric Fenby lectr., 1991; named Champion Ind. Higher Edn. in Fla., Ind. Colls. Fla., 1992 Svc. Medallion, N. Fla. Jr. Coll., Madison, Fla. Fellow Inter-U. Seminar on Armed Forces and Soc.; mem. Delius Assn. Am. (life, founding pres.), Can. Inst. Strategic Studies, Phi Beta Kappa, Phi Alpha Theta, Pi Alpha Alpha (pres.), Phi Kappa Phi. Republican. Presbyterian. Avocations: classical music, writing fiction. Home: PO Box 1873 Bonita Springs FL 34133-1873 Office Phone: 239-992-5190. Personal E-mail: el-francobollo@webtv.net.

JOHNSON, FREDA S., financial analyst, consultant; b. N.Y.C., Mar. 17, 1947; m. J. Chester Johnson, May 7, 1989. BA in Polit. Sci., CUNY, 1968; grad. Advanced Mgmt. Program, Harvard U., 1986. Analyst mcpl. div. Dun & Bradstreet Corp., N.Y.C., 1968-71; sr. analyst Moody's Investor Svc., Inc. (subs. Dun & Bradstreet), N.Y.C., 1972, v.p., assoc. dir. mcpl. dept., 1973-79, sr. v.p., dir. mcpl. dept., 1979-81, exec. v.p., 1981-90; pres. Govt. Fin. Assocs., Inc. pub. fin. adv. co., 1992—. Mem. Anthony Commn. for Pub. Fin.; former sr. credit advisor Ecolink, joint Soviet-Am. pub. fin. project; Congl. testifier U.S. Senate Com. on Banking, Housing and Urban Affairs, subcom. fiscal affairs and health U.S. Ho. of Reps., U.S. Senate Com. Govtl. Affairs, Joing Econ. Com. Congress; Nat. Assn. Ind. Pub. Fin. Advisors, 1993-95, Queens Coll. Corp. Adv. Bd., 1994-99; bd. govs. Coun. Mcpl. Performance, 1984-86; instr. New Sch. for Social Rsch., 1982-83; mem. adv. bd. City Almanac, 1982-84; trustee Citizens Budget Com.; spkr. numerous profl. orgns., univs.; adj. prof. Grad. Sch. Bus. Adminstrn. Columbia U., spring 1991. Avocations: theater, museums.

JOHNSON, G. CAROL, finance company executive; b. Hamilton, Ohio, Sept. 7, 1942; d. Carlace A. Tipton; m. Robert L. Braddock (div. 1984); children: Ryan Braddock, Lauren Braddock; m. Ed. Johnson, Feb. 17, 1985; children: Meryl, Erica. BA, U. Cin., 1965, MA, 1976. V.p. Fed. Home Loan Bank Cin., 1973-85; pres. PENN Mortgage Corp., Cin., 1985-87; dir. comms. Neighborhood Reinvestment Corp., Washington, 1989-91; dir. affordable housing investments Fed. Home Loan Mortgage Corp., Vienna, Va., 1991-94; sr. v.p. GMAC Mortgage Corp., Horsham, Pa., 1995—. Bd. dirs. MERL Holdings Inc. Active Jr. League, Cin. and Washington, 1980-92, Johnson House Historic Site; chair bd. dirs. Habitat for Humanity Internat., 1997—. Mem. Am. Homeowners (chair 1999-2000), Edn. Counseling Inst. (bd. dirs., vice chair 1997-99), Links, Inc. Office: GMAC Mortgage Corp 100 Witmer Rd Horsham PA 19044

JOHNSON, GARRETT BRUCE, lawyer; b. Akron, Ohio, Sept. 15, 1946; s. Vincent Hadar and Elizabeth Irene (Garrett) J.; m. Barbara Peters Silver, May 31, 1969; children: Emily Peters, Adam Garrett. A.B., Princeton U., 1968; J.D., U. Mich., 1971. Bar: Ill. 1973, U.S. Dist. Ct. (no. dist.) Ill. 1973, U.S. Ct. Appeals (7th cir.) 1979, U.S. Supreme Ct. 1990. Fellow Max Planck Inst. for Fgn. and Internat. Criminal Law, Freiburg, Germany, 1971-72; assoc. Kirkland & Ellis, Chgo., 1973-78, ptnr., 1978— . Article and book review editor Mich. Law Rev. 1970-71. Humboldt scholar, 1971-72. Office: Kirkland & Ellis 200 E Randolph Dr Fl 58 Chicago IL 60601-6636 Office Phone: 312-861-2268. Business E-Mail: gjohnson@kirkland.com.

JOHNSON, GARY KEITH, pediatrician; b. Chgo., Aug. 26, 1951; s. John Edward and Dorothy Lucille (Rudder) J. AB, Dartmouth Coll., 1973; MD, U. Ill., Chgo., 1979, MPH, 1985. Diplomate Am. Bd. Med. Examiners, Am. Bd. Pediatrics. Intern Columbus Hosp., Chgo., 1980, resident in pediatrics, 1980-83; fellow in ambulatory pediatrics Cook County Hosp., Chgo., 1983-85; dir. ambulatory pediatrics Hurley Med. Ctr., Flint, Mich., 1986-92; clin. pediatrician McCree North Health Ctr., Flint, 1992-95; participant scholars program Mich. Pub. Health Leadership Inst., Flint, 1995-96; med. dir. Genesee County Health Dept., 1995—. Asst. prof. pediatrics Mich. State U., East Lansing, 1986—, tchr. med. ednl. program Coll. Human Medicine and U. Affiliated Hosp. of Flint (Mich.), Inc., 1986—; presenter in field. Contbr. numerous articles to profl. jours. and cmty. newspapers. Chairperson Early On program Genesee County, 1993-94. Primary Care Faculty Devel. fellow Mich. State U., 1988-89. Fellow Am. Acad. Pediatrics (Mich. chpt. exec. com. cmty. access to child health, state facilitator 1990-98); mem. AMA, Genessee County Med. Soc., Mich. State Med. Soc., Ambulatory Pediatric Assn., Am. Pub. Health Assn. Democrat. Presbyterian. Avocations: swimming, bicycling. Office: Genesee County Health Dept 630 S Saginaw St Flint MI 48502-1525

JOHNSON, GARY L., publishing executive; b. Mpls., Aug. 19, 1938; s. Maurice Fred and Alta Elizabeth J.; m. Carol Ann Schlisler, Sept. 8, 1962. Diploma, Bethany Coll. of Missions, Mpls., 1959; student, Augsburg Coll., 1960-63. Mgr. Bethany Book Shop, Mpls., 1960-63, Bethany Printing Divsn., Mpls., 1963-76; pres. Bethany House Pubs., Mpls., 1963—. Avocation: songwriting. Office: Bethany House Pubs 11400 Hampshire Ave S Minneapolis MN 55438-2852

JOHNSON, GARY M., lawyer; b. 1947; BS, Gustavus Adolphus Coll., 1969; JD, NYU, 1973. Law clk. to justice U.S. Ct. Appeals (3d cir.), Phila., 1973-74; assoc. Dorsey & Whitney, Mpls., 1974-79, ptnr., 1980—. Fellow Am. Coll. Trust and Estate Counsel; mem. Minn. Bar Assn., Hennepin County Bar Assn., Order of Coif. Office: Dorsey & Whitney Ste 1500 50 South Sixth Street Minneapolis MN 55402-1498 Office Phone: 612-340-2774. Business E-Mail: johnson.gary@dorsey.com.

JOHNSON, GARY THOMAS, lawyer; b. Chgo., July 26, 1950; s. Thomas G. Jr. and Marcia Johnson; m. Susan Elizabeth Moore, May 28, 1978; children: Christopher Thomas, Timothy Henry, Anna Louisa. AB, Yale U., 1972; Hons. BA, Oxford U., 1974, MA, 1983; JD, Harvard U., 1977. Ba: Ill. 1977, NY 1993, US Dist. Ct. (no. dist.), Ill. 1977, US Ct. Appeals (7th cir.) 1985, US Supreme Ct. 1986, Supreme Ct. Eng. and Wales 2004. Assoc. Mayer, Brown & Platt, Chgo., 1977-84, ptnr., 1985-94, Jones Day, Chgo., 1994—. Trustee Lawyers' Com. for Civil Rights Under Law, 1992-94, exec. com., 1998-, regional co-chair, 1996-2001, co-chair, 2001-2003, bd. dirs. 1994-; mem. Ill. Supreme Ct. Spl. Commn. on the Adminstrn. of Justice, 1992-94; mem. Spl. Commn. on Adminstrn. of Justice Cook County, Chgo., 1984-88; v.p. Criminal Justice Project of Cook County, 1987-91. Bd. dirs. Chgo. Lawyers' Com. for Civil Rights Under Law, 1981-90, Legal Assistance Found., Chgo., 1987-96, pres., 1994-96. Rhodes scholar Oxford U., 1972-74. Fellow Am. Bar Found. (life; state chair 2003—), Ill. Bar Found. (life); mem. ABA (Ho. of Dels. 1991-97), Am. Judicature Soc. (bd. dirs. 1987-91), Ill. State Bar Assn., Chgo. Bar Assn., Chgo. Coun. Lawyers (pres. 1981-83), Internat. Bar Assn., Law Soc. Eng. and Wales. Office: Jones Day 77 W Wacker Dr Chicago IL 60601-1692 Office Phone: 312-269-1599. Personal E-mail: gary.johnson.bk.72@aya.yale.edu.

JOHNSON, GARY WILLIAM, environmental scientist, consultant; b. Warwick, R.I., Feb. 23, 1957; s. Donald Milton and Elaine Carin (Soderlund) J.; m. Diane Lynn Farrell, Aug. 1, 1992; children: Danielle Lynn, Kelsey Ann. BA in Biology, U. R.I., 1979; MS in Environ. Sci., U. New Haven, 1987. Cert. instr. Inst. Nuclear Power Operators; OSHA cert. safety trainer. Rschr. Nat. Marine Fisheries Svc., Narragansett, RI, 1978—79; asst. scientist N.E. Utilities, Waterford, Conn., 1979—84, assoc. scientist Berlin, Conn., 1984—86, scientist Rocky Hill, Conn., 1986—97; sr. scientist, environ. coord. N.E. Nuc. Energy Co., Waterford, Conn., 1997—2000; supr. environ. programs Millstone Nuc. Power Sta. Dominion Nuc. Conn., Waterford, 2000—; pres. Sci. Epicenter and DNA Learning Ctr., New London, Conn., 2001—. Prin. scientist Ecologic Risk Mgmt. Svcs., Monroe, Conn., 1989-94; guest lectr. U. New Haven, 1990-96; lectr. in field. Contbr. articles to profl. jours. Vol. sci. guide East Lyme (Conn.) Jr. High Sch., 1983-96; guide, lectr. Audubon Soc., Jamestown, R.I., 1983-85; chmn. Waterford Conservation Commn., 1997—; v.p. Meadow Green Homeowners Assn., 1999—; mtn. guide Okemo Mtn. Resort, Ludlow, Vt., 1998—. Mem. Edison Electric Power Industry Biologists, Nat. Environ. Tng. Assn. Achievements include obtaining ISO 14001 environmental management systems certification for Millstone Nuclear Power Facility, Waterford, Conn.; development of state of the art computer models to perform quantitative analysis of ecologic and human health risk from exposure to toxic materials; research in condenser biofouling control efforts for the nuclear power industry; coordinated all environmental issues to support the decommissioning of a nuclear power plant. Home: 2 Melanie Dr Waterford CT 06385-1600 Office: Dominion Nuclear Conn Millstone Nuclear Power Sta PO Box 128 Waterford CT 06385-0128 Office Phone: 860-447-1791 ext. 0757. E-mail: gary_william_johnson@dom.com.

JOHNSON, GEOFFREY MCCLURE, lawyer; b. Princeton, N.J., May 2, 1951; s. Edward Dudley and Laurie (Vance) J.; m. Barbara Lee Sloan. Student, Sorbonne, Paris, 1972; AB, Princeton U., 1973; JD, Georgetown U., 1976. Bar: N.J. 1976, N.Y. 1978, U.S. Dist. Ct. (ea. and so. dists.) N.Y. 1978, U.S. Ct. Appeals (11th cir.) 1992. Assoc. McCarter & English, Newark, 1976-78, Phillips, Nizer, N.Y.C., 1978-84; ptnr. Lewis & McKenna, Saddle River, N.J., 1984—. Office: Johnson & Conway LLP 18 Sycamore Ave Ho Ho Kus NJ 07423

JOHNSON, GEORGE AXIL, III, television producer; b. Hastings, Mich., Nov. 14, 1974; s. George Axil, Jr. and Judy Lynn Johnson; m. Karen Gwen Hynes, June 26, 1999; children: George Axil IV, Hannah Joy, Grace Alynn. Diploma, Hollywood Scriptwriting Inst., Calif., 1994—96. Videographer, editor Two Legs Prodns., Lake Odessa, Mich., 1998, Alliance Prodns., Grand Rapids, Mich., 1999—2000; program dir. WKTV TV-25, Wyoming, Mich., 1998—2000; news editor WZZM TV-13, Grand Rapids, Mich., 2000; prodn. mgr. WINM TV-63, Edgerton, Ohio, 2000—; pres., founder Allegory Pictures, Waterloo, Ind., 2000—. TV prodn. instr. WKTV TV-25, Wyoming, Mich., 1998—2000; writer WINM TV-63, Edgerton, Ohio, 2000—. Author: (screenplays) Dreamer: The Movie, 2001; dir., prodr. (films) Dreamer: The Movie, 2004 (Internat. Film Festival Outstanding Dramatic Comedy, 2005). Recipient Lifetime Achievement award, Hollywood Scriptwriting Inst. Republican. Avocations: writing, films. Office: Allegory Pictures 875 Plank Rd Waterloo IN 46793 Office Phone: 260-837-7874.

JOHNSON, GEORGE H., finance company executive; b. Boston, Aug. 30, 1941; s. Harry G. and Josephine (Grenda) J.; m. Marguerite Anne Harrington, Aug. 12, 1967; 1 child, Heather Diana. BS, Northeastern U., Boston, 1966. CLU, ChFC; cert. internal auditor; enrolled agt. IRS; cert. tax preparer; fellow life office mgmt. Sr. internal auditor U.S. Life Corp., N.Y.C., 1970-76; dir. internal audit, treas. Consumers United Group, Inc., Washington, 1976—, also bd. dirs. Former bd. dirs., chair World Hunger Edn. Svc., Washington. Participant blood bank donor program ARC, Washington, 1977—. Mem. Inst. Internal Auditors, Md. Soc. Accts., Am. Soc. CLU and ChFC, Cert. Tax Preparers, Washington Inst. Internal Auditors. Home: 11805 Bunchberry Ln Gaithersburg MD 20878-2315

JOHNSON, GEORGE WARNER, gifted and talented educator, consultant; b. Logan, Ohio, June 16, 1949; s. George Bernard and Martha Ann Johnson; m. Jean Ann Hutchison, Oct. 31, 1971 (dec. Mar. 5, 1988); children: Melissa Renee Johnson-Stokes, George Christopher, Bryan Michael; m. Jeanne Christina Hohman, Sept. 9, 1989; 1 child, Mark Hohman. EdB, Ohio U., 1971; MEd, Ashland (Ohio) U., 2001, postgrad., 2002—. Cert. secondary edn-history Ohio, elem. edn. grades 1-8 Ohio, gifted edn. K-12 Ohio, elem./mid. sch. prin. Ohio. Elem. tchr. So. Local Sch. Dist., Hemlock, Ohio, 1974—85, tchr., dir. gifted program and svcs., 1986—. Bd. govs. Southea. Ohio Odyssey of the Mind, Athens, 1986—87, Southea. Ohio Regional Scholars, Athens, 1987; dir., coord. sch. trips to Washington and Europe So. Local Schs., Hemlock, 1987—; dir. ednl. svcs. for Ohio Soc. for Creative Anachronism, Inc., Milpitas, Calif., 1989—92, regional v.p. orgnl. devel. Midwestern U.S. and Can., 1989—91, corp. dir., 1992—94, chmn. internat. edn. com., 1994—95; orgnl. pres. for N.Am. Regia Anglorum, Bristol, England, 2000—; judge Southea. Ohio Power of the Pen Competition, Logan, 2003—; ednl. cons. for staff devel. Literacy Curriculum Alignment Project, Reynoldsburg, Ohio, 2003—05; adj. prof. Ashland U., 2005—. Author: Christmas Ornaments, Lights, and Decorations, Vol. I, 1987, 1990, 1995, 1998, Christmas Ornaments, Lights, and Decorations, Vol. II, 1997, Christmas Ornaments, Lights, and Decorations, Vol. III, 1997, Pictorial Guide to Christmas Ornaments and Collectibles, 2004, 2005; curator (mus. exhibit) Memories of Halloween Past, 2003, Christmas Through the Ages, 2004. Bd. dirs. Bowen Ho. Cultural Arts Ctr., Logan, 2001—05, Acad. Achievement Scholarship Fund, So. Local Schs., Hemlock, 1985—2005. Named Featured Tchr., Ohio Schs. Mag., 1999; named to Gifted Edn. Hall of Fame, Ohio U., 2003; recipient award for outstanding svc. to edn. of children, Soc. for Creative Anachronism, Inc., 1984, 1989, 1990, author's commendation, Ohio State Senate, 1987, Contbns. to Success of Gifted Students award, Southea. Ohio Spl. Edn. Regional Resource Ctr., 1987, 1992, 1996, Excellence in Talented and Gifted Programming award, S.E. region Ohio Sch. Bds. Assn., 1993; Martha Holdings Jennings scholar, 1985—86. Mem.: NEA, ASCD, Ohio Mid. Sch. Assn., Ohio Assn. Elem. Sch. Administrs., Am. Edn. Rsch. Assn., European Coun. on High Achievement, Nat. Assn. Gifted Children, Ohio Assn. Gifted Children, Ohio Edn. Assn., So. Local Edn. Assn. (pres. 1976, 1999), Masons, Order of Ea. Star (patron 1980—82). Avocations: antiques, historical reenactment, old house restoration, European travel, educational presentations. Home: 18 E Hunter St Logan OH 43138 Office: So Local Sch Dist 10397 State Rte 155 SE Hemlock OH 43743 Office Phone: 740-394-1173. Personal E-mail: taly@ohiohills.net.

JOHNSON, GERALD LEE, health facility administrator; b. May 7, 1952; MHA, Kennedy Western U., 1993, PhD, 2001. Cert. Am. Coll. Healtcare Execs. Adminstr. Heart Ctr. Manatee Meml. Hosp., Bradenton, Fla., 1983-88; dir. imaging St. Mary's Med. Ctr., Racine, Wis., 1988-90; dir. off site devel. Hardin Meml. Hosp., Etown, Ky., 1990-96; adminstr., dir. U. Louisville Hosp., 1996-2000; dir. diagnostic and therapeutic svcs. Danville (Va.) Regional Med. Ctr., 2000—. Fellow Am. Healthcare Radiol. Adminstrs., Am. Coll. Cardiology, Lions (pres.). Address: PO Box 2397 Danville VA 24541-0397 E-mail: cherhealth@gcronline.com, johnsong@drmc.drhsi.org.

JOHNSON, GERTRUDE COOGAN, educational consultant, elementary school educator; b. Pitts., Mar. 7, 1938; d. John Patrick and Gertrude Quinn Coogan. BS in Edn., Duquesne U., Pitts., 1960; MEd, U. Ill., Urbana, 1971. Tchr. Pitts. Pub. Schs., 1960—63, Dept. Def. Europe, Washington, 1963—65, Dept. Def. Japan, Washington, 1965—66; coord., tchr., gifted students Oak Park Sch. Dist. 97, Ill., 1966—94; cons. West 40 Intermediate Svc. Ctr., La Grange Park, Ill., 1994—. Coord. Reading First Program West Cook County. Mem.: ASCD, Nat. Staff Devel. Coun., Phi Delta Kappa. Home: 203 N Kenilworth 3J Oak Park IL 60302 Office: West 40 Intermediate Svc Ctr 928 Barnsdale Rd La Grange Park IL 60526 Office Phone: 708-482-4350. Business E-Mail: gjohnson@west40.k12.il.us.

JOHNSON, GLENDON E., retired insurance company executive; b. 1924; BS, U. Utah, 1948; JD, Harvard U., 1952. In charge Wash. office Am. Life Convention, Washington, 1959-68; pres. Great Southern Life Ins. Co., Houston, 1968-70; pres., chmn. bd. dirs., CEO Am. Nat. Ins. Co. Inc., Galveston, Tex., 1970-77; law ptnr. Routier & Johnson P.C., Washington, 1978-84; CEO Cathend Valley Ranch, LLC, 1979—; pres., CEO John Alden Ins. Co., Inc., 1984-87; chmn. bd., CEO John Alden Fin. Corp., Miami, Fla., 1987-98; pres., chmn. bd., CEO John Alden Life Ins. Co., 1984-98. Mem. nat. bd. Boy Scouts Am., 1971-77, 1981—, nat. exec. com., 1981—, nat. v.p., chmn. audit com., mem. nominating com., 1994—, mem. exec. bd. Fla. coun., chmn. nat. Cub Scout com., 1981-83, chmn. nat. program group, 1983-86, chmn. mktg. and relationships com., 1987-91, chmn. pers. com., 1992-93 (Silver Beaver award 1971, Silver Antelope award 1974, Silver Buffalo award 1993, Good Scout award 1993); regional rep. to quorum LDS Ch., 1971-76.

JOHNSON, GLENN THOMPSON, retired judge; b. Washington, Ark., July 19, 1917; s. Floyd and Reola (Thompson) J.; m. Elaine Bailey, May. 26, 1993; children: Evelyn A., Glenn T. BS, Wilberforce U., 1941; JD, John Marshall Law Sch., 1949, LL.M., 1950; grad., Nat. Coll. State Trial Judges, 1971, Appellate Ct. Judges Seminar, N.Y. U., 1974; LL.D. (hon.), Ark. Bapt. Coll., 1978. Bar: Ill. 1950. Pvt. practice law, 1950-57; asst. atty. gen., 1957-63; sr. asst. atty. Met. San. Dist. Chgo., 1963-66; assoc. judge Cir. Ct., Cook County, Chgo., 1966-68, judge, 1968-73; justice Ill. Appellate Ct., Chgo., 1973—. Trustee John Marshall Law Sch. Served with AUS, 1942-46. Recipient merit award John Marshall Law Sch., 1970; Merit award Beatrice Caffrey Youth Service, 1976 Mem. Nat. Bar Assn. (merit award 1970), ABA, Ill. Bar Assn., Chgo. Bar Assn., Cook County Bar Assn. (awards 1967, 73, pres. 1964-66), Am. Acad. Matrimonial Lawyers (gov.) Methodist. Home: 5050 S Lake Shore Dr Apt 2517 S Chicago IL 60615-3217

JOHNSON, GLORIA, labor union administrator; m. David Johnson; children: Toni, David. Bookkeeper Internat. Union Electronic, Elec., Salaried, Machine and Furniture Workers, 1954, chmn. Women's Coun.; coord. women's activities Internat. Union Electronic, Elec., Salaried, Machine and Furniture Workers-CWA; v.p. AFL-CIO, 1993; treas., founding mem. Coalition Labor Union Women, pres., 1993—. Rschr., spkr. in field. Named Pres.'s Commn. Celebration Women in Am. History, Pres. Bill Clinton, 1998; recipient Op. PUSH award Outstanding Women in Labor Movement, Econ. Equity award, Women's Equity Action League, 1981, award, So. Christian Leadership Conf., 1985, Achievement award, A. Philip Randolph Inst., 1994, Wise Women award, Ctr. Women Policy Studies, 1995, Ann. Pathway to Excellence award, NAACP, 1995, Eugene V. Debbs Labor award, 1999, Nat. Black Caucus State Legis. Labor Leader award, 2000, Nat. Com. Pay Equity's Winn Newman award, 2000. Office: 1925 K St NW Ste 402 Washington DC 20006

JOHNSON, GOODYEAR See O'CONNOR, KARL

JOHNSON, GORDON GILBERT, theology studies educator, minister; b. St. Paul, Nov. 19, 1919; s. Gilbert Oliver and Myrtle Isabel (Bjorklund) J.; m. Alta Fern Borden, May 21, 1945; children: Gregg A., Gayle E. Johnson Hyames. Cert., Moody Bible Inst., 1941; AA, Bethel Coll., St. Paul, 1943; student, Harvard U., 1944, 45; BA, U. Minn., 1945; BD, Bethel Theol. Sem., 1946; ThM, Princeton Theol. Sem., 1950; ThD, No. Bapt. Theol. Sem., 1960. Ordained to ministry Bapt. Gen. Conf., 1946. Pastor 1st Bapt. Ch., Milltown, Wis., 1946-48, Bethel Bapt. Ch., Montclaire, N.J., 1948-51, Central Ave. Bapt. Ch., Chgo., 1951-59; v.p., dean, prof. preaching Bethel Theol. Sem., St. Paul, 1959-84; interim sr. pastor Trinity Bapt. Ch., St. Paul, 1972-73; assoc. pastor, interim sr. pastor College Ave. Bapt. Ch., San Diego, 1984-89; interim dean Bethel Sem. West, San Diego, 1990-91; interim sr. pastor Clairemont Emmanuel Bapt. Ch., San Diego, 1990-91, First Bapt. Ch., Lakewood, Long Beach, Calif., 1991-92, New Life Ch., Woodbury, Minn., 1993, Elim Bapt. Ch., Mpls., 1995-96. Chmn. bd. publ. Bapt. Gen. Conf., Chgo., 1948-53, pres. bd. trustees, 1953-55, chmn. world mission bd., 1955-60, moderator, 1957-58, 85-86; mem. gen. coun. Bapt. World Alliance, Washington, 1965-85; lectr. in field; del. to World Congress on Evangelism, Berlin, 1965; educator for elderhostels for Bethel Coll., Minn., 1992-98; vis. prof. Regent Coll., Vancouver, 1976; pres. Minn. Sem. Consortium, 1979-81. Author: My Church, Making God Known Through Story; contbr. articles to profl. jours. With USN, 1944-45. Rsch. scholar Yale U. Div. Sch., 1969. Mem. Acad. Homileticians, Religious Speech Assn. Personal E-mail: johgor@bethel.edu. *In a capricious and sometimes explosive world an underlying confidence in the gracious providence of a loving God gives peace and wholeness of life. That makes possible an optimism about life.*

JOHNSON, GORDON JAMES, performing company executive, conductor; b. St. Paul, 1949; BS, Bemidji State U., 1971; MS, Northwestern U., 1977; D in Mus. Arts, U. Oreg.; studied with Leonard Bernstein, Erich Leinsdorf, Herbert Blomstedt. Music dir., condr. Great Falls (Mont.) Symphony Assn., 1981—, Glacier Orch. and Chorale, Mont., 1982-97; artistic dir., condr. Flathead Music Festival, Mont., 1987-96; music dir., condr. Mesa (Ariz.) Symphony Orch., 1997—. Grad. tchg. fellow U. Oreg, 1979—81; artist in residence Condr's Guild Inst., W.Va. U., 1984; condr. Spokane Symphony at The Festival at Sandpoint; guest condr. St. Paul Chamber Orch., 1971, Spokane Symphony, 1983, 86, Dubuque Symphony, Iowa, 1985, Charlotte Symphony, NC, 1985, Lethbridge Symphony, Alberta, Canada, 1986, Cheyenne Symphony, Wyo., 1986, West Shore Symphony, Mich., 1988, Bozeman Symphony, Mont., 1989, Kumamoto Symphony, Kyshu, Japan, 1991, Kankakee Symphony, Ill., 1993, Toulon Symphonies, France, 1994, Guam Symphony, 1995, Tokyo Lumiere Orch., 1995, Fort Collins Symphony, Colo., 1995, Wilmslow Symphony Orch., England, 1997; guest ballet condr. Alberta Ballet, 1986, Oakland Ballet, Calif., 1988, Eugene Ballet, Oreg., 1993, David Taylor Ballet, Colo., Colo., 1994, St. Petersburg Ballet, Russia, 1995, Western Ballet Theater, Oreg., 1996; spkr. regional conf. Am. Symphony Orch. League, 1987, spkr. nat. conf., 88; mem. adj. faculty U. Great Falls, 1981—, U. Mont., 1996—; lectr. U. Guam, 1995; condr. seminars L.A. Philharmonic Inst., 1983, Condr.'s Guild Inst., 1984, Festival at Sandpoint, Condr.'s Program, 1986, Am. Symphony Orch. League's Am. Condr.'s Program, N.Y. Philharmonic, 1987, Condr.'s Guild "Bruckner Seminar", Chgo. Symphony Orch., 1989, Carnegie Hall Tng. Program for Condrs., Cleve. Orch., 1993. Named to Highland Park High Sch. Hall of Fame, St. Paul, 1997; Philharmonic Condr.'s scholar St. Paul Chamber Orch., 1971, L.A. Philharmonic Inst. fellow, 1983. Mem.: ASCAP. Office: Great Falls Symphony Assn PO Box 1078 Great Falls MT 59403-1078 Office Phone: 406-453-4102. E-mail: gordon@gfsymphony.org.

JOHNSON, GORDON SELBY, consulting electrical engineer; b. Petersburg, Ind., July 25, 1918; s. Basil Orvil and Lillian May (Selby) J.; m. Frances Marie Overstreet, June 15, 1940; children: Lowell, Anne, Judith, Martha, Carol, Gordon, Mary; m. Alice Woods, 2002. BSEE, Purdue U., 1939. Registered profl. engr., Wis. Engr. Sunbeam Electric Mfg. Co., Evansville, Ind., 1939-41, Kohler (Wis.) Co., 1941-48, dept. head, 1948-55, chief engr., 1955-65, mgr. engring., 1965-76, sr. staff engr., 1976-85, cons. engr., 1985-87; pvt. practice cons. Winter Haven, Fla., 1987—. Dir. communications and tech. assistance Elec. Generating Systems Assn., Boca Raton, Fla., 1986-92, tech. dir., 1993-99, pres., 1983-84. Author: Kohler Tech. Series, 1976-85; editor: Elec. Grounding, 1992, On-Site Power Generation, 1990, 2d edit., 1993, 3rd edit., 1998; editor Powerline mag., 1986-92, tech. editor, 1993-99; contbr. numerous articles to profl. jours. Pres. Sheboygan (Wis.) County Coun. of Chs., 1965-67; lay leader N.E. Wis. Dist. United Meth. Ch., 1975-76; chmn. adv. com. Lakeshore Tech. Coll., Sheboygan, 1970-80; adv. high sch. sci. seminars. With U.S. Mcht. Marine, 1944-45, ETO, NATOUSA. Recipient L.H. Carpenter Outstanding Svc. award Elec. Generating Systems Assn., 1973; named Athlete of Yr., Fla. Sr. Games, 1999. Fellow IEEE (sect. chmn. 1953-54); mem. NSPE, Soc. Automotive Engrs., Nat. Fire Protection Assn. Avocations: competitive running, bicycling, gardening. Home and Office: 421 Flagler Rd SE Winter Haven FL 33884 Office Phone: 863-324-3711. E-mail: johnsonjogs@aol.com.

JOHNSON, GREGORY E., diversified financial services company executive; b. Orange, N.J., 1961; BBA, Washington and Lee U., 1983. CPA. Former sr. acct. Coopers & Lybrand; with Franklin/Templeton Distributors, Inc., San Mateo, Calif., 1986—, pres., 1999—, co-CEO, 2003—, also chmn.; pres. FranklinTempleton Investment Svcs.; v.p. Franklin Advisers, Inc. Bd. dirs. Fiduciary Trust Co. Internat. Office: Franklin Resources Inc 1 Franklin Pky Bldg 970 1st Fl San Mateo CA 94403

JOHNSON, HANSFORD TILLMAN, former civilian military employee; b. Aiken, S.C., Jan. 3, 1936; s. Wade Hansford and Julia Johnson; m. Linda Ann Whittle, June 21, 1959; children: Richard, Elizabeth, David. BS in Thermodynamics and Aerodynamics, U.S. Air Force Acad., 1959; MS in Aeros., Stanford U., 1967; MBA in Bus. Sci., U. Colo., 1970; postgrad., Nat. War Coll., 1975-76. Registered profl. engr., Colo.; lic. Nat. Assn. Securities Dealer Prin. Commd. 2d lt. USAF, 1959, advanced through grades to 4-star gen., 1989; asst. prof. U.S. Air Force Acad., Colorado Springs, Colo., 1968-71; comdr. 22d Bomb Wing USAF, March AFB, Riverside, Calif., 1979-81; plans staff officer USAF Hdqrs., Washington, 1972-75; asst. dep. for plans Strategic Air Commd., Omaha, 1981-82; dir. programs USAF Hdqrs., Washington, 1982-85, dep. ops. Offutt AFB, Neb., 1985-86; vice comdr. in chief Pacific Air Forces USAF, Hickam AFB, Hawaii, 1986-87; dep. comdr. in chief U.S. Cen. Command, MacDill AFB, Fla., 1987-88; dir., moved forces to and from Persian Gulf Joint Chiefs of Staff, Washington, 1988-89; comdr. in chief U.S. Transp. Command, Mil. Airlift Command (now Air Mobility Command), Scott AFB, Ill., 1989-92; ret. USAF, 1992; bd. dirs. USAA, San Antonio, 1987-92, chief of staff, 1993, vice chmn., 1993—95; pres., CEO USAA Capital Corp., 1993—95; v.p., CEO Credit Union Nat. Assoc., Madison, Wis., 1995—2001; asst. sec. USN, Washington, 2001—02, 2003—04, acting sec., 2003. Mem. Tex. Rsch. and Tech. Found., Decorated DFC with 2 oak leaf clusters, Legion of Merit, Silver Star, DSM, Def. DSM with 2 oak leaf clusters, Def. Meritorious Svcs. medal, Meritorious Svc. medal, Air medal with 22 oak leaf clusters, Air Force DSM with oak leaf cluster; Republic of Vietnam Armed Forces Honor medal 1st class with one svc. star, Gallantry Cross with palm. Mem. AIAA, Order of Daedalians (flight capt. 1975, 84, 85), Soc. Mil. Engrs.

JOHNSON, HARDWICK SMITH, JR., school psychologist; b. Millen, Ga., Aug. 13, 1958; s. Hardwick Smith Sr. and Louise (Joiner) J. BA, Atlanta Christian Coll., 1981; MEd, Ga. So. Coll., 1984; EdS, Ga. State U., 1988; DSc (hon.), Holy Trinity Coll.; DD (hon.), St. Ephrem's Inst.; EdD, Nova Southeastern U., 2002. Cert. spl. edn. tchr., Ga.; cert. sch. psychologist. Ga. Spl. edn. resource tchr. Claxton (Ga.) High Sch., 1983-86; sch. psychologist, 1986—. Genealogist, 1980—; supervising tchr. Author: The History of the Johnson Family and Johnson Church, 1976, The Aaron Family, 1986, Some Descendants of James and Rachel Oglesby, 1785-1991, 1991. Organizing club pres. Young Reps. Coweta County. Named Tchr. of the Yr., Coun. for Exceptional Children, Claxton, 1985, Hon. Order Ky. Col., 1986, hon. admiral Tex. Navy Gov. of Tex., 1987, lt. col. a.d.c. Gov. of Ga., 1987, citizen State of Okla., citizen of L.A., col. Gov. La., lt. col. Gov. Ala., hon. mem.

Coweta Tribal Town of the Creek Indian Nation (now Okla.); recipient Liberty medal with oak lead cluster SAR, Meritorious Svc. award SAR, Silver Good Citizenship medal SAR, medal of honor NSDAR, medal of honor NSDAC, Minuteman medal NSSAR, 1994. Fellow Am. Coll. Genealogists; mem. SAR (v.p. chpt. 1985-86, pres. Statesboro chpt. 1986-87, state sec. 1987—, Meritorious Service medal Ga. soc. 1987, state pres., v.p. gen. South Atlantic dist. 1991-92), SCV, Nat. Soc. Sons of Am. Colonists (nat. v.p. 1986—, gov. Ga. soc. 1987—, gov. gen. 1989-91, Mil. Order of the Stars and Bars), Coun. for Exceptional Children (pres.-elect, v.p. 1985-86), Ga. Assn. Educators (sch. rep. 1985—, pres.-elect 1986-87), NEA (sch. rep.), Ga. Assn. Sch. Psychologists, Continental Soc. Sons Indian Wars (founding gov. gen., nat. pres.), The Nat. Gavel Soc., Jamestowne Soc., Gen. Soc. Colonial Wars, Colonial Order Acorn, First Families Ga. (founding sec./treas. gen., gov. gen. 1993—), Nat. Huguenot Soc., Gen. Soc. War 1812 (former v.p. gen.), Sons Revolution in State of Ga., Hereditary Order Descendants Colonial Govs. (gov. gen. 1999—), Nat. Soc. Descs. Early Quakers, Nat. Soc. Ams. of Royal Descent (1st v.p.), Order Indian Wars of U.S., Order Ams. Armorial Ancestry, Hereditary Order Descs. Loyalists and Patriots Am. Revolution (dep. gov. gen.), Order Colonial Lords of Manors in Am., Baronial Order of Magna Charta, Order of The Three Crusades,(1096-1192), Order of The Crown of Charlemagne in the U.S.A. (1st v.p), The Colonial Soc. Pa., Descendants Washington's Army at Valley Forge (organizing cmdr. Ga. brigade), Aztec Club of 1847-Mil. Soc. of the Mex. War (former v.p.), Baronial Order of Magna Charta, St. George's Soc. (Jacksonville, Fla.), Nat. Soc. Sons and Daus. of Pilgrims (gov. gen. 1993-95), Sons and Daughters of the Colonial, Antebellum Bench and Bar, Order of Scions of Colonial Cavaliers (dep. gov. gen.), The Old Guard (Atlanta), Sons and Daus. of Antebellum Planters, DeMolay (master councilor 1977-78), Am. Priory Most Venerable Order of Hosp. of St. John of Jerusalem (comdr.), Order Merovingian Dynasty (founder mem., founding v.p.), Charlotte Manigalt Soc., Soc. for the Preservation of Early Am. Art, City Tavern Club, Kappa Delta Pi (historian 1983—), Phi Delta Kappa. Republican. Avocations: heraldry, travel, writing, reading. Home: 1317 Winburn Drive East Point GA 30344

JOHNSON, HAROLD EARL, human resources specialist; b. Lincoln, Nebr., July 11, 1939; s. Earl W. and Evelyn Jean (Sipp) J.; m. Carol Louise Schmidt, Aug. 17, 1971 (div.); children: Andrew Brian, Daniel Earl; m. Janet Gaillard, May 30, 2004. BS, U. Nebr., 1961. From indsl. relations trainee to mgr. profl. employment Am. Can Co., 1961—68; dir. recruitment/devel. metal mining div. Kennecott Copper Corp., 1968—73; v.p. personnel Am. Medicorp Inc., 1973—75; v.p. employee relations. devel., then sr. v.p. employee relations and corp. adminstrn. INA Corp., 1975—79; sr. v.p. human resources Federated Dept. Stores, Inc., Cin., 1979—85; sr. v.p. corp. personnel and adminstrn. The Travelers Cos., Hartford, Conn., 1985—89; mng. ptnr. Korn/Ferry Internat., N.Y.C., 1989—92; exec. search and human resources Norman-Broadbent Internat., N.Y.C., 1992—96; sr. ptnr., bd. dirs. The Cabot Group, Washington, 1996—2002; sr. ptnr. TMP Worldwide, 1997—2001; chmn. global human resources practice Heidrick and Struggles, Internat., Denver, 2002—. Bd. dirs. Snowfly Inc., Laramie, Wyo. Mem. Sky Club (N.Y.C.), Univ. Club (N.Y.C.), Winged Foot Golf Club (Mamoroneck, N.Y.), Ptarmigan Country Club, Ft. Collins/Colo., Assn. Exec. Search Cons., Ft. Collins Country Club, Ptarmiean Golf Club (Ft. Collins). Republican. Presbyterian. Office: Heidrick and Struggles Internat 1400 Sixteenth St Denver CO 80202 Office Phone: 212-984-9465. Business E-Mail: hal.johnson@kornferry.com.

JOHNSON, HARRY A., III, lawyer, finance company executive; b. Memphis, Jan. 30, 1949; s. Harry A. Jr. and Penny (Pentecost) J.; m. Patricia Jane Reynolds; children: McKenzie, Kelly. BBA, So. Meth. U., 1971, JD, 1974. Bar: Tenn., 1974, U.S. Dist. Ct. (we. dist.) Tenn. 1974. Counsel First Tenn. Nat. Corp., Memphis, 1974-79, sr. v.p., div. mgr., 1979-84; ptnr. Glankler, Brown, Gilliland, Chase, Robinson & Raines, Memphis, 1984-88; exec. v.p., gen. counsel First Horizon Nat. Corp. (formerly First Tenn. Nat. Corp.), Memphis, 1988—. Bd. dirs. Brooks Mus. Art, Inc., Memphis, 1990—, chmn. bd., 1996—; bd. dirs. LeBonheur Children's Med. Ctr.; chmn. bd. Christ Meth. Day Sch., Memphis, 1989-92; sr. exec. programs Stanford U., 1999. Mem. ABA, Tenn. Bar Assn., Memphis and Shelby County Bar Assn., Fin. Svcs. Roundtable (lawyer's com.). Methodist. Office: First Horizon Nat Corp 165 Madison Ave Memphis TN 38103-2723

JOHNSON, HARRY STERLING, lawyer; b. Havre de Grace, Md., Nov. 10, 1954; s. Harry Durwood and Sarah Gladys (Rice) J.; m. Janet Amanda Thomas, May 14, 1988; 1 child, Amanda Sterling. BA, U. Md., Catonsville, 1976; JD, U. Md., Balt., 1979. Bar: Md. 1979, U.S. Dist. Ct. Md. 1979, U.S. Dist. Ct. D.C. 1986. Assoc. Whiteford, Taylor & Preston, Balt., 1979-86, ptnr., 1986—. Instr. U. Md., Baltimore County, Catonsville, 1982-87; bd. dirs. Bedco Devel. Corp., The Chapman Funds, The Afro Am. Newspapers; mem. com. Rules of Practice and Procedure, Ct. Appeals Md., Annapolis, 1986—. Mem. exec. bd. Balt. Area coun. Boy Scouts of Am., 1990—; pres., chair New Community Coll. Balt. Found., 1988, Greater Balt. Com., 1989, chair Balt. County Md. Human Relations Commn., 1998-2003; mem. bd. trustees Balt. Ednl. Scholarship Trust, 1993-, Greater Balt. Med. Ctr., 2001-, Center Stage, 2002-. Named to Am.'s Top Black Lawyers, Black Enterprise mag., 2003; recipient Disting. Black Marylander Award, Towson U., 2003, Leadership in Law Award, The Daily Record, 2003. Mem. ABA, Md. State Bar Assn. (bd. govs. 1987-89, 91—, treas. 1999-2002, pres.-elect 2002-03, pres. 2003-04), Bar Assn. Baltimore City, Nat. Bar Assn., Monumental City Bar Assn. (Founder's award 1987), DC Bar Assn. Avocations: music, sports, tennis. Office: Whiteford Taylor & Preston 7 St Paul St Ste 1400 Baltimore MD 21202-1626 E-mail: hjohnson@wtplaw.com.

JOHNSON, HAYNES BONNER, journalist, writer, commentator; b. N.Y.C., July 9, 1931; s. Malcolm Malone and Ludie (Adams) J.; m. Julia Ann Erwin, Sept. 21, 1954 (div.); m. Kathryn A. Oberly, June 29, 2002; children—Katherine Adams, David Malone, Stephen Holmes, Sarah Brooks, Elizabeth Haynes. BJ, U. Mo., 1952; MS, U. Wis., 1956; HHD (hon.), Wheeling Jesuit U., 1997; LHD (hon.), U. Mo., 1999. Reporter Wilmington (Del.) News-Jour., 1956- 57; with Washington Star, 1957-69, reporter, copy editor, to asst. city editor, night city editor to spl. assignments corr.; nat. corr. Washington Post, 1969-73, asst. mng. editor, 1973-77, columnist, 1977-94; prof. polit. comm. and journalism George Washington U., Washington, 1994-96; Knight chair, prof. journalism U. Md., 1998—. Ferris prof. journalism and pub. affairs Princeton U., 1975-78; TV commentator PBS Washington Week in Rev., 1967-94, The News Hour with Jim Lehrer, 1994—2004; guest scholar Brookings Instn., 1987-91; Regents lectr. U. Calif., Berkeley, 1992; lectr. in field. Author: Dusk at the Mountain, 1963, The Bay of Pigs, 1964, (with Bernard M. Gwertzman) Fulbright: The Dissenter, 1968, (with George C. Wilson) Army in Anguish, 1972; (with Richard Harwood) Lyndon, 1973, The Working White House, 1975, In the Absence of Power, 1980; (with Howard Simons) The Landing, 1986, Sleepwalking Through History, 1991, Divided We Fall, 1994, (with David S. Broder) The System, 1996, The Best of Times, 2001, The Age of Anxiety: McCarthyism to Terrorism, 2005; editor: The Fall of a President, 1974. Bd. dirs. Herbert Block Found. Served to 1st lt. AUS, 1952—55. Recipient Pub. Svc. prize and Grand award for reporting Washington Newspaper Guild, 1962, 68, Interpretive Reporting award, 1965, Nat. Reporting award, 1968, Pulitzer prize for nat. reporting, 1966, Headliners award for nat. reporting, 1968, Sigma Delta Chi gen. reporting award, 1969; fellow in comm. Duke U., 1973-74; profl. in residence Annenberg Sch., 1993. Mem. Nat. Acad. Pub. Adminstrn. Clubs: Gridiron (Washington); Nassau (Princeton); Fed. City (Washington). Home: 2812 Woodland Dr NW Washington DC 20008-2742 Office: Coll Journalism U Md Journalism Bldg College Park MD 20742-0001 E-mail: haynesjohnson@hotmail.com.

JOHNSON, HENRY FRED, clergy; b. Colorado Springs, Aug. 23, 1948; s. Nathan Eugene Johnson Sr. and Jessie Bell (Stovall) Crowder; m. Christine Johnson, May 20, 1967; children: Diedre M., Tina D., Tevin AA in Social Work, Pikes Peak C.C., Colorado Springs, 1990; B in Biblical Studies, Nazarene Bible Coll., Colorado Springs, 1993, B in Christian Edn., 1995; M in Bibl. Studies, Andersonville Bapt. Sem., 1998, PhD in Bibl. Studies, 2000. Ordained Baptist Min. Personnel sr. sgt. U.S. Army, 1967-87; program coord. Martin Luther Home, Colorado Springs, 1988—2000; youth pastor Friendship Missionary Bapt. Ch., Colorado Springs, 1991-99; co-pastor Chapel Pueblo (Colo.) Minimum Ctr., 1993—2001; writer Henry Johnson Min., Colorado Springs, 1995—; instr. Nat. Bapt. Youth Convention, New Orleans, 1995—2000; cmty. coord. Resource Exch., Colorado Springs, 2000—; interim pastor Friendship Missionary Bapt. Ch., 2001—04. Dir. Christian edn. Gen. Missionary Bapt. Conv. of Colo., 1999-2002, dean of congress, 2002-; assoc. editor, adv. Praisenet.org, 2002- Author: Challenge of the Teens in the 90's and Beyond, 1995, Book of James, 1998, Arise and Rebuild, 1997, Book of Revelation, 2000. Baptist. Office: Henry Johnson Ministries PO Box 17922 Colorado Springs CO 80935-7922 E-mail: reverendhenry@aol.com.

JOHNSON, HENRY LOUIS, federal agency administrator, former school system admnistrator; b. Tuscaloosa, Ala. married; 3 children. BS in Biology, Livingston Coll., Salisbury, N.C., 1968; MA in Tchg., U. N.C., Chapel Hill., 1975; DEd in Sch. Adminstrn., N.C. State U., 1990. Tchr. Wake County Pub. Schs., 1969—75, prin. elem. sch., 1975—78, middle sch. dir., 1979—81; asst. supt. for curriculum and instrn. Johnston County Schs., 1986—92; assoc. state supt. instruction and accountability svcs. N.C. Dept Edn., 1997—2002; supt. of edn. Miss. State Dept. Edn., 2002—05; asst. sec. elementary & secondary edn. US Dept. Edn., Washington, 2005—. Named to Livingston Coll. Hall of Fame, 2002; recipient N.C. Disting. Alumnus award, N.C. State U., 1994, Presidl. citation, Livingstone Coll., 1999. Office: US Dept Edn 400 Maryland Ave SW Rm 3W315 Washington DC 20202*

JOHNSON, HERBERT ALAN, historian, lawyer, department chairman; b. Jersey City, Jan. 10, 1934; s. Harry Oliver and Magdalena Gertrude (Diemer) J.; m. Barbara Arlene (Balcerak), Sept. 24, 1955 (dec. Nov. 1980); children: Amanda Blair, Vanessa Paige.; m. Jane (McCue), June 4, 1983. AB, Columbia U., 1955, MA, 1961, PhD (Schiff fellow), 1965; LLB, N.Y. Law Sch., 1960; postgrad., Luth. Theol. So. Sem., 1981-84. Bar: N.Y. 1960; U.S. Supreme Ct. 1965; D.C. 1967; S.C. 1983; ordained vocat. deacon, The Episcopal Ch., 1991. Jr. clk. First Nat. City Bank of N.Y., N.Y.C., 1955; adminstrv. asst. Chase Manhattan Bank, N.Y.C., 1957—60; practiced law in N.Y.C., 1960—67; rsch. asst. Papers of John Jay, Columbia U., 1961—63; lectr. Hunter Coll., N.Y.C., 1964—65, asst. prof. history, 1965—67; assoc. sem. on history of legal polit. thought Columbia U., 1966—77, assoc. sem. on early Am. history, 1967—77; assoc. editor Papers of John Marshall, Inst. Early Am. History and Culture, Williamsburg, Va., 1967—70, co-editor, 1970—71, editor, 1971—77; prof. law and history U. S.C., Columbia, 1977—90, Ernest F. Hollings prof. constl. law, 1991—2002, disting. prof. law emeritus, 2002—. Lectr. Coll. William and Mary Williamsburg, 1967-77; Bostick vis. rsch. prof. So. studies program U. S. C., 1976, 77; mem. com. rsch., publ. Heritage '76 Com. Am. Revolution Bicentennial Commn., 1972-73; mem. bd. adjustments, appeals, Williamsburg, 1970-77; trustee Fund for Preservation of John Marshall House, 1972-74; Fund Coop. Editl. Rsch. Am. Antiquarian Soc., 1972-76; mem. profl. adv. bd. Angel Home Health & Hospice, 2002-. Author: The Law Merchant and Negotiable Instruments in Colonial New York, 1664-1730, 1963; John Jay, 1745-1829, 1970; Imported Eighteenth Century Law Treatises in Am. Libraries 1700-1799, 1978; Essays on New York Colonial Legal History, 1981; History of Criminal Justice, 1988, 3d edit., 2002; John Jay: Colonial Lawyer, 1989; The Chief Justiceship of John Marshall, 1997; Wingless Eagle: U.S. Army Aviation Through World War I, 2001; co-author: Historical Courthouses of New York State-18th and 19th Century Halls of Justice Across the Empire State, 1977; Foundations of Power, John Marshall, 1801-15, vol. 2, History of the Supreme Court of the U.S., 1981; editor: The Papers of John Marshall, Vol. 1, 1974, Vol. II, 1977, South Carolina Legal History, 1980; Am. Legal and Constitutional History: Cases and Materials, 1994, 2d edit., 2000; gen. editor Chief Justiceships of the U.S. Supreme Court Series, 1989—; contbg. articles to profl. jour. Chaplain assoc. Bapt. Med. Ctr., Columbia, 1983-2002; hospice legal svc. vol., 1986-2000; chaplain Angel Hospice, Franklin, N.C., 2002-2004; mem. ethics com. S.C. Episcopal Home, Still Hopes, 1989-99; 1st lt. USAF, 1955-57; ret. col., Res. Recipient: William P. Lyons Masters' Essay Award Loyola U., 1962; Paul S. Kerr History prize N.Y. State Hist. Assn., 1970, Rsch. award Faculty of Law U. S.C., 2001; U. S.C. Edn. Found. Rsch. Award profl. sch., 2000; Am. Council Learned Soc. Fellow, 1974-75; Inst. Humane Studies Fellow, 1981, 85; vis. fellow Centre for Comparative Constl. Studies, U. Melbourne Law Faculty, 1992; vis. rsch. scholar U. Toronto Law Faculty, 1995; vis. prof. Univ. of Birmingham, (Eng.), 1998. Mem. Am. Hist. Assn. (Littleton-Griswold com. 1976-81, interim com. Bicentennial era 1976-77), Selden Soc. (state corr. for S.C. 1988-2002), Stair Soc., Air Force Assn., Am. Law Inst., Assn. Am. Law Sch. (chmn. legal history sect. 1979), Am. Soc. Legal History (pres. 1974-75, del. Am. Coun. Learned Soc. 1977-80, bd. dirs. 1999-2001), U. South Caroliniana Soc., Res. Officers Assn., Assn. Profl. Chaplains, Nat. Eagle Scout Assn. Episcopalian. Home: 245 Laurel Falls Rd Franklin NC 28734-9527 Office Phone: 828-524-8032. Personal E-mail: janeherb@dnet.net.

JOHNSON, H(ERBERT) FISK, manufacturing executive; AB, Cornell U., 1979, ME, 1980, MS, 1982, MBA, 1984, PhD, 1986. With S.C. Johnson & Son, Inc., Racine, Wis., 1987—, pres., gen. mgr. Canada, mng. dir. corp. new products and tech. Racine, Wis., vice chmn., 1999—2000, chmn., 2000—, CEO, 2004—. Mem. Pres. Adv. Com. Trade Policy and Negotiation, 2002—, World Bus. Coun. Sustainable Devel., 2002—; trustee emeritus Cornell U., 2002—; bd. dirs. Conservation Internat., mem. exec. bd. ctr. environ. leadership in bus.; former trustee nat edn. trust Phi Psi. Office: SC Johnson & Son Inc 1525 Howe St Racine WI 53403-2236 Office Phone: 262-260-2000. Office Fax: 262-260-6004.

JOHNSON, HERBERT FREDERICK, sales executive, retired academic administrator, librarian; b. St. Paul, Minn., Aug. 1, 1934; s. Herbert Oscar and Hazel Grace (Otto) J.; m. Delores Elaine Madson, Aug. 21, 1955; children: Steven F., Eric L., Kirsten M. BA, U. Minn., 1957, MA, 1959; postgrad., Kursverksamheten Vid Lunds Universitet, Betyg, 1975. Libr. U.S. Govt., Washington, 1959-61; asst. bus. libr. Columbia U., 1961-64; head libr., assoc. prof. Hamline U., 1964-71; dir. librs., prof. Oberlin Coll., 1971-78; libr. dir. Oberlin Pub. Libr., 1971-78; dir. librs. Emory U., 1978-88, mem. faculty adv. com. Jimmy Carter Ctr. for Policy Studies, 1982-84; sales & svc. rep. Active Mobility of Ga., Marietta, 1988-91; sr. regional mgr. Williams/Howard Assocs., 1989-91; regional v.p. Primerica Fin. Svcs., Marietta, Ga., 1991—2002, sr. regional mgr., 2003—; registered prin. PFS Investments, Inc., 1991—; project dir. Nat. Drug Info. Ctr. Nat. Families in Action Inc., 1989-90. Lectr. U. Minn. Libr. Sch., 1967; vis. prof. Atlanta U. Sch. Libr. Svcs., 1979; charter bd. Cooperating Librs. in Consortium, St. Paul, 1969-71; libr. adv. com. Minn. Higher Edn. Coordinating Commn., 1970-71; mem. com. input standards Ohio Coll. Libr. Ctr., 1972-73, chmn. com. patron input, 1973-75; chmn. Ohio Multitype Interlibr. Cooperation Com., Ohio State Libr. Bd., 1976-78; mem. adv. and steering com. Ohio Pre-White House Conf. on Libr. and Info. Svcs., 1977-78; bd. dirs. Assn. Rsch. Librs., 1983-88, pres., 1987-88; chmn. librs. adv. com. Univ. Ctr. in Ga., Atlanta, 1979-80, 85-86; del. users coun. OCLC Online Computer Libr. Ctr. Inc., 1981-83, 85-88; bd. dirs. Southeastern Libr. Network, 1980-83, chmn. bd., 1981-83; bd. govs. Rsch. Librs. Group, 1986-87. Contbr. articles to profl. jours. Mem. com. on internat. programs Nat. Student YMCA's, 1962-64; mem. Minn. Rep. Task Force on Edn., 1966; pres., treas. Lord of Life Luth. Ch., Lorain, Ohio, 1972-75; mem. Lorain Coop. Luth. Ministry Bd., 1976-78; v.p. St. Luke Luth. Ch., Atlanta, 1979-80, 81-82; bd. dirs. Nat. Families in Action, 1979-89, 90—, pres. 1987-88, v.p., 1990-93, mem. Parent Corps U.S.A., 2004—; mem. adv. com. DeKalb/Rockdale counties of Met. Atlanta chpt. ARC, 1981-88, Cobb/Douglas counties of Met. Atlanta chpt. ARC, 1988-92, emergency cmty. svcs. com., 1990-94; bd. dirs. Scandinavian Am. Found. Ga., 1983-, v.p. 1993-2000, chmn. bd., 2000-02; bd. dirs. Swedish Coun. Am. 1987—, chair Glenn T. Seaborg Nobel prize travel award com., 1990-2002, jr. achievement classroom cons., 1993-94. Lt. col. USNR, 1957—78. Decorated Army Commendation medal, Meritorious Svc. medal; George Williams fellow, 1957; Coun. on Libr. Resources fellow, 1974-75; NSF grantee, 1967-71. Mem. ALA, Nat. Family Caregivers Assn. (nat. caregivers adv. panel 2000—), Am. Scandinavian Found., Am. Swedish Inst., Ga. Libr. Assn., Southeastern Libr. Assn., Atlanta Zool. Soc., Chattahoochee Nature Ctr., Common Cause, Minn. Libr. Sch. Alumni Assn. (chmn. 1967), Wildlife Preservation Trust, Nat. Trust Hist. Preservation, Scandinavian Am. Found. Ga., Sierra Club, High Mus. Art, Rotary (dist. 6900 youth exch. com. 1994-97, treas. 1995-97, group study exch. team leader to dist. 2360 Sweden 2002, dist. group study exch. com. 2003—, chair 2003—, club sec. 1981-82, club pres. 1984-85, club dir. North Dekalb, Ga. 1998-2001, 2002-04, Ga. Rotary Internat. student program host family 1998—, Svc. Above Self award 2001, Dist. Svc. award 2002), East Cobb (Ga.) Bus. Assn. (bd. dirs. 1996-2000), Mil. Officers Assn. Am., Vasa Order Am. (bd. dirs. Am. Nordic Lodge 708, 2003—), Beta Phi Mu. *Too many folks have given up realizing their dreams, yet with the Lord's help, anyone has the capacity to make their dreams a reality. The toughest part of the struggle is winning the battle between the ears- that is in believing in ones self. There is no greater thrill than having helped another win that struggle and having made a difference in that person's life!.*

JOHNSON, HERBERT MICHAEL, publisher; b. Leipzig, Germany, Mar. 19, 1936; came to U.S., 1940; s. Walter J. Johnson; m. Susan Armstrong, July 9, 1960; children: Walter J. II, Matthew G., Herbert M. Jr., Miranda S., George F. BS, Duke U., 1958. Mgr. domestic sales Acad. Press, Inc., N.Y.C., 1958-66; v.p., founder Greenwood Press, Inc., Westport, Conn., 1967-72; pres., pub., founder Johnson Assocs, Inc., Greenwich, Conn., 1972-80; founder, CEO, JAI Press, Inc., Greenwich, 1975-99; founder, pres., pub. Armstrong Pub. Co., 1993-97; pres. Ablex Pub. Co., 1997-99; dir. Nutmeg Investment Ptnrs. LLC, Greenwich, Conn., 1998—; chmn. Info. Age Pub. Inc., 2001—. Mem. council Boy Scouts Am., Greenwich, 1967-80; bd. dirs. Arch St. Teen Ctr., 1999—, United Way Greenwich, 2004— Home: Augustus Ln Greenwich CT 06830-7040 Office: Nutmeg Investment Ptnrs LLC 80 Mason St PO Box 4967 Greenwich CT 06831-0419 E-mail: hmjnutmeg@aol.com.

JOHNSON, HERMAN LEONALL, retired research nutritionist, researcher; b. Whitehall, Wis., Apr. 1, 1935; s. Frederick E. And Jeanette (Severson) J.; m. Barbara Dale Matthews, July 3, 1960 (dec. May 1971); m. Barbara Ann Badger, Apr. 3, 1976. BA in Chemistry, North Cen. Coll., Naperville, Ill., 1959; MS in Biochemistry and Nutrition, Va. Poly. Inst. and State U., 1961, PhD in Biochemistry and Nutrition, 1963. Rsch. biochemist S.R. Noble Found., Ardmore, Okla., 1963-65; nutrition chemist U.S. Army Med. Rsch., Denver, 1965-74; nutrition physiologist Letterman Army Rsch., Presidio San Francisco, 1974-80, Western Human Nutrition Rsch. Ctr. USDA, Presidio San Francisco, 1980-95, ret., 1995. Contbr. numerous articles to profl. jours. Trustee 1st Meth. Ch., Ronnert Park, Calif., 1985-94, mem. fin. com., 1994—. With Med. Svc. Corps U.S. Army, 1954-56. Named one of Outstanding Young Men of Am., 1975; NIH traineeship Va. Poly. Inst. and State U., Blacksburg, 1961-63. Mem. AAAS, Am. Inst. Nutrition, Am. Soc. Clin. Nutritionists, Am. Coll. Nutritionists, Am. Coll. Sports Medicine, Sebastopol Spinners, Sigma Xi, Phi Lambda, Phi Sigma. Republican. Achievements include research on human nutrition. Home: 256 Alden Ave Rohnert Park CA 94928-3704 Home Fax: 707-795-7465. E-mail: barbherm@inreach.com.

JOHNSON, HORTON ANTON, pathologist; b. Cheyenne, Wyo., Nov. 12, 1926; s. Horton Antonius and Katharine Mary (Tidball) J.; m. Caryl Abell Daly, Nov. 20, 1970; children by previous marriage: Katherine, Kristin, Margaret, Ann, Gregory, Marjorie. AB, Colo. Coll., 1949; MD, Columbia U., 1953. Diplomate: Am. Bd. Pathology. Intern Univ. Hosp., Ann Arbor, Mich., 1953-54, resident in pathology, 1954-57, Pondville Cancer Hosp., Walpole, Mass., 1957-58; scientist Brookhaven Nat. Lab., 1958-60, 63-70; asst. prof. pathology U. Utah, 1960-63; prof. pathology SUNY, Stony Brook, 1970-72, Ind. U., 1972-75; prof., chmn. dept. pathology Tulane U., New Orleans, 1975-84; prof. pathology Columbia U., N.Y.C., 1984-91; dir. pathology St. Luke's-Roosevelt Hosp. Ctr., N.Y.C., 1984-91. Docent Met. Mus. Art, 1993—. Served with USNR, 1944—46, USS Atlanta. Recipient Lederle Med. Faculty award, 1961 Fellow: Royal Soc. Medicine, Coll. Am. Pathologists; mem.: Soc. Health and Human Values, Assn. Clin. Scientists, N.Y. Acad. Scis., Radiation Rsch. Soc., Biophys. Soc., Internat. Acad. Pathology, Am. Soc. Exptl. Pathology, Alpha Omega Alpha, Phi Beta Kappa. Achievements include rsch. on radiation injury, aging, theoretical biology. Home: 39 N Cove Rd Old Saybrook CT 06475-2538 Office: 3 Lincoln Ctr Ste 47C New York NY 10023-6566 E-mail: horton_johnson@hotmail.com.

JOHNSON, HOWARD WESLEY, retired academic administrator, finance company executive; b. Chgo., July 2, 1922; s. Albert H. and Laura (Hansen) J.; m. Elizabeth J. Weed, Feb. 18, 1950; children: Stephen Andrew, Laura Ann, Bruce Howard. BA, Central Coll., Chgo., 1943; MA, U. Chgo., 1947; cert., Glasgow (Scotland) U., 1946; LLD (hon.), Harvard U., U. Miami, 1966, U. Mass., 1969, Oklahoma City U., 1970, U. Cin., 1973, Babson Coll., 1978; ScD (hon.), Lowell Tech. Inst., Tufts U., Bryant Coll., 1967; LHD (hon.), Northea. U., 1966, Roosevelt U., 1969; LittD (hon.), Clarkson Coll. Tech., 1973. From asst. to assoc. prof., dir. mgmt. rsch. U. Chgo., 1948-51, 53-55; asst. to v.p. pers. adminstrn. Gen. Mills, Inc., 1952-53; assoc. prof., dir. exec. programs, assoc. dean Sloan Sch. Mgmt., MIT, 1955-59, prof., dean, 1959-66; pres. MIT, 1966-71; chmn. corp., 1971-83; hon. chmn. corp., 1983-90; life mem. corp., 1983-97; life mem. emeritus, 1997—. Exec. v.p. Federated Dept. Stores, 1966; chmn. Fed. Res. Bank Boston, 1968-69; trustee Putnam Funds, 1961-71; mem. Pres.'s Adv. Com. on Labor-Mgmt. Policy, 1966-68; chmn. Environ. Studies Bd. NAS-NAE, 1973-75; mem. sci. adv. com. Mass. Gen. Hosp., 1968-70; mem. Nat. Manpower Adv. Com., 1967-69, Nat. Commn. on Productivity, 1970-72; trustee Com. Econ. Devel., 1968-71, Wellesley Coll., 1968-86, trustee emeritus 1986—; trustee Radcliffe Coll., 1973-79; hon. trustee Aspen Inst. for Humanistic Studies, Inst. Deaf Analyses, 1971-79; mem. corp. Woods Hole (Mass) Oceanog. Instn. Author: Holding the Center: Memoirs of a Life in Higher Education, 1999. Trustee WGBH Ednl. Found., 1966-71, Henry Francis du Pont Winterthur Mus., 1984-87, Dibner Inst., 1992-97; mem. corp. Mus. Sci., Boston; overseer Boston Symphony Orch, 1968-72; mem.-at-large Boy Scouts Am.; pres. Boston Mus. Fine Arts, 1975-80, trustee 1971-72, chmn. bd. overseers, 1980-83, chmn. exec. com., 1983-87, hon. life trustee 1992—; trustee Alfred P. Sloan Found., 1982-95, chmn. bd. 1988-95; bd. dirs. Nat. Arts Stablzn. Found., 1983-87, Museo de Arte de Ponce, 1983-87. With AUS, 1943-46. Recipient Alumni medal U. Chgo., 1970, Gyorgy Kepes Fellowship prize MIT, 1999. Fellow AAAS, Am. Acad. Arts and Scis.; mem. Coun. Fgn. Rels., Am. Philos. Soc., Nat. Acad. Scis. (Pres.'s Circle), Nat. Acad. Engring. (Pres.'s Cir.), Inst. of Medicine (Pres.'s Cir.), Century Assn. (N.Y.C.), Comml. Club (Boston), Tavern Club (Boston), St. Botolph Club (Boston), Phi Gamma Delta. Office: MIT 77 Massachusetts Ave Cambridge MA 02139-4307 Office Phone: 617-253-0636. Business E-Mail: hwj@mit.edu.

JOHNSON, IRVING STANLEY, pharmaceutical executive, research scientist; b. Grand Junction, Colo., June 30, 1925; s. Walter Glen and Frances Lucetta (Tuttle) J.; m. Alwyn Neville Ginther, Jan. 29, 1949; children: Rebecca Lyn, Bryan Glenn, Kirsten Shawn, Kevin Bruce. BS, Washburn U., Topeka, 1948; PhD, U. Kans., 1953. With Lilly Rsch. Labs., Indpls., 1953-88, v.p. rsch., 1973-88; mem. profl. edn. com. Am. Cancer Soc., 1972-82. Rschr. cancer, virus, genetic engring.; mem. UCLA Symposia Bd., 1988-; bd. dirs. Allelix Biopharms., Ligand Pharms.; sci. adv. bd. Elan Corp., 1996-; trustee La Jolla Cancer Rsch. Found., 1990-93; advisor to biomed. rsch. cos., venture capital groups; mem. Recombinant Adv. Com., NIH; indep. biomedical rsch. cons. Mem. sci. adv. bd. Biotech., 1986—; mem. editorial bd. Chemico-Biol. Interactions, 1968-73; contbr. articles to profl. publs.; patentee in field. With USNR, 1943-46. Recipient 1st ann. Congl. award for sci. and tech., 1984, Coll. Liberal Arts and Scis. Alumni Disting. Achievement award U. Kans., 2005. Fellow AAAS; mem. Am. Assn. Cancer Rsch. (Cain Meml. award for outstanding preclin. rsch. in cancer chemotherapy 1986), Am. Soc. Cell Biology (mem. pub. policy com.), Environ. Mutagen Soc., Internat. Soc. Chemotherapy, N.Y. Acad. Scis., Soc. Exptl. Biology and Medicine, Am. Soc. Immunologists (mem. sci. adv. bd. biotech), Soc. for Neurosci., Sigma Xi, Phi

Sigma. Episcopalian. Achievements include being widely acknowledged for leadership team which led to the production and approval of the first health care product manufactured by recombinant DNA/genetic engineering techniques.

JOHNSON, J. CHESTER, corporate financial executive, consultant, writer; b. Chattanooga, Sept. 28, 1944; m. Freda Stern; children: Juliet Christina, Guilbert Roland. Student, Harvard U., 1962-65; BSE, U. Ark., 1967. Sr. analyst Moody's Investors Svc., 1968-71; head pub. fin. rsch. and adv. group The Morgan Bank, 1972-77; dep. asst. sec. U.S. Treasury Dept., Washington, 1977-78; chmn., prin. Govt. Fin. Assocs., Inc., N.Y.C., 1979—. Bd. dirs., chair fin. com. N.Y. State Environ. Facilities Corp., 1991-95; chmn. Fed. Task Force to create Nat. Devel. Bank; chmn. Fed. Inter-agy. Task Force for Improvement Govtl. Fin. Reporting; chmn. Fund to Assure Pub. Infrastructure Fin., Nat. Infrastructure Bond Coalition, 1988-91; interviewed on pub. fin. Cable News Network, ABC Morning News Feature, PBS News Roundup, NBC Nightly News, others. Author: (poetry) OH America!, January 12th, 1967, 2d edit., 1975, Family Ties, Internecine Interregnum!, 1981, For Conduct and Innocents, 1982, Shorts: For Fun, Not for Instruction, 1985, It's a Long Way Home, An American Sequence, 1985, Shorts: On Reaching Forty, 1985, Exile/Martin, 1986, The Professional Curiosity of a Martyr, 1987, Freda's Appetite, 1991, Lazarus, Come Forth, 1993, Plain Bob (Unbehaved), 1993; (with W.H. Auden) revised psalms in The Book of Common Prayer of The Episcopal Church, 1971-77; co-author: Original Disclosure Guidelines for Securities' Offerings by State and Local Governments, 1976, The Future of Boston's Capital Plant, 1980, Mayor's Financial Management Handbook, 1985: contbr. numerous articles to profl. jours. and poetry to anthologies. Mem. vestry Trinity Wall St. Ch., 2001—. Mem. Nat. Assn. Ind. Pub. Fin. Advisors (pres. 1989-91), Nat. Soc. Mcpl. Analysts, Nat. Fedn. Mcpl. Analysts (Disting. Lifetime Contbn. award 1988). Office: Govt Fin Assocs Inc 590 Madison Ave 21st Fl New York NY 10022 Office Phone: 212-521-4090. Personal E-mail: jchester.gfa@prodigy.net.

JOHNSON, J. M. HAMLIN, manufacturing executive; b. Ridgway, Pa., Oct. 10, 1925; s. Manferd H. and Esther (Hallstrom) J.; m. Sara N. Richardson, Sept. 11, 1948; children: Stephanie (Mrs. William G. Cox), Robert H., Elizabeth E., Lara D. (Mrs. Ellwyn A. Reynolds Jr.), David L., Christine M. (Mrs. Thomas Syzmanski), Shawn J. BS, Grove City Coll., 1949; student, Pa. State U., 1969. With Stackpole Corp., St. Mary's, Pa., 1950—, supr. acctg., to 1960, operational auditor, 1960-64, mgr. acctg., 1964-68, asst. treas., 1968-71, treas., asst. sec., 1971-79, v.p., treas., asst. sec., 1979-84, v.p., treas. asst. sec., dir., 1984-88, v.p., treas., sec., dir., 1988; ret., 1990. Bd. dirs. Hamlin Bank & Trust Co., past bd. dirs. Cmty. Nurses of Elk & Cameron Counties Inc., Home Health Svcs. Past mem. Ridgway Area Sch. Bd.; trustee Stackpole-Hall Found., 1983—; past chmn., bd. dirs. St. Marys Regional Med. Ctr.; bd. dirs., past treas., past pres. ELCAM Vocat. Rehab. Ctr.; past bd. dirs. United Fund St. Marys; past bd. dirs. Elk County Regional Med. Ctr.; bd. dirs., treas. Elk County Cmty. Found., 1999—. With USAAF. Mem. Nat. Assn. Accts. (pres. 1958-59), Bavarian Hills Club. Home: 517 Center St Saint Marys PA 15857-1001

JOHNSON, J. MITCHELL, communications executive; b. Dallas, May 12, 1951; s. J. Edward and Blanche (Dabney) J.; 1 child, Philip Louis. BS, U. Tex.; MS, U. So. Calif. Prodn. asst. Guggenheim Prodns., Washington, 1975-77; pres. Ft. Worth Prodns., 1977—; CEO J. Mitchell Johnson Prodns., Ft. Worth, 1986—; publisher Fodor's Video Guides, Ft. Worth, 1986-93; CEO Abamedia, LP, Ft. Worth and Moscow, 1995—; pres. Archive Media Project, Ft. Worth and Moscow, 1996—. Official trade rep. Russian State Film and Photo Archives, Krasnogorsk. Producer 14 films for Fodor's, 1986-93; 20 TV programs for Ostankino Russian TV; Co-production ABC News N.Y. 1994-95; Producer, dir. TV films including Gymnast, Pub. Broadcasting System, 1980 (JQ award 1981), Artist and Athlete, ABC, 1980; producer TV films Moses Pendleton Presents Moses Pendleton, ABC, 1983 (1st place award San Francisco Film Festival 1984), Mondale for America, 1984, Yanks for Stalin (History Channel) 1999, Red Files (PBS Series) 1999. Exec. producer Mondale for Am.-Cons. '84, Washington, 1984; chmn. Budapest, Hungary-Ft. Worth Sister Cities Internat. Com., chmn. media panel Tex. Commn. for Arts and Humanities, Austin, 1986, chmn. Citizens Cable Bd., City of Ft. Worth, 1990-91. Recipient Gold award N.Y. TV Film Festival, 1981, Golden Eagle award Council on Internat. Nontheatrical Events, Washington, 1983, Best Documentary and Film awards N.Mex. Film Festival, Albuquerque, 1984, Best Documentary award USA Film Festival, Dallas, 1984. Mem. Internat. Music Ctr. (pres. 1987-88), Motion Picture Producers Tex. (pres. 1987-88), Found. for Social Innovations Moscow-N.Y. (bd. dirs.), Ft. Worth Club. Democrat. Methodist. Avocations: travel, music, electronics. Office: J Mitchell Johnson Prodns Inc PO Box 125 Fort Worth TX 76101-0125

JOHNSON, J. STEWART, curator, art consultant; Curator dept. decorative arts Cooper-Hewitt Nat. Design Mus., Smithsonian Instn., NYC, 1974—76; named curator of design Mus. Modern Art, NYC, 1976; cons. design and architecture dept. modern art Met. Mus. Art, NYC. Author: American Modern 1924-1940: Design for a New Age, 2000. Co-recipient Award for Best Architecture or Design Show, Internat. Assn. Art Critics/USA, 2005. Office: Met Mus Art 1000 5th Ave New York NY 10028-0198*

JOHNSON, JAMES A., finance company executive; b. Benson, Minn., Dec. 24, 1943; s. Alfred I. and Adeline (Rasmussen) J.; m. Katherine Marshall, Feb. 15, 1969 (div. 1973); m. Maxine Isaacs, Jan. 12, 1985; 1 child, Alfred Isaacs. BA, U. Minn., 1965; MA, Princeton U., 1968. Spl. asst. to Sen. Walter Mondale U.S. Senate, Washington, 1972; dir. pub. affairs Dayton Hudson Corp., Mpls., 1973-76; exec. asst. to v.p. Walter Mondale The White House, Washington, 1977-81; pres. Pub. Strategies, Washington, 1981-85; mng. dir. Lehman Bros., N.Y.C., 1985-89; vice-chmn. Fannie Mae, Washington, 1990-91, chmn., CEO, 1991-98, chmn. exec. com. bd. dirs., 1999; chmn., CEO Johnson Capital Ptnrs., Washington, 2000-01; vice chmn. Perseus, 2001—. Bd. dirs. Target Corp., Goldman Sachs Inc., Temple-Inland, Gannett, Inc., KB Home, United HealthGroup. Chmn. John F. Kennedy Ctr. for Performing Arts, 1996-2004; chmn. bd. trustees The Brookings Instn., 1994-2003. Democrat. Avocations: tennis, golf, travel. Office: Perseus LLC 2099 Pennsylvania Ave NW Washington DC 20006 Office Phone: 202-752-6790.

JOHNSON, JAMES D., lawyer; b. LeMars, Iowa, Apr. 12, 1943; BS, U. Iowa, 1965, JD, 1967. Bar: Iowa 1967, Ill. 1970, NY 1994. Law clk. to Hon. George C. Edwards U.S. Ct. Appeals (6th cir.), 1967-68; ptnr. corp. and securities law Sidley Austin Brown & Wood LLP, NYC, and mem. exec. com. Note editor U. Iowa Law Review, 1966-67. Mem. ABA, Chgo. Bar Assn., Phi Delta Phi. Office: Sidley Austin Brown & Wood LLP 787 Seventh Ave New York NY 10019 Office Phone: 212-839-7350. Office Fax: 212-839-5599. Business E-Mail: jjohnson@sidley.com.

JOHNSON, JAMES DAVID, concert pianist, organist, educator; b. Greenville, SC, Aug. 7, 1948; s. Theron David and Lucile (Pearson) J.; m. Karen Elizabeth Jacobson, Feb. 1, 1975. MusB, U. Ariz., 1970, MusM, 1972, D of Mus. Arts, 1976; MusM, Westminster Choir Coll., 1986. Concert pianist, organist Pianists Found. Am., Boston Pops Orch., Royal Philharm., Nat. Symphony Orch., Leningrad Philharmonic, Victoria Symphony, others, 1961—; organist, choirmaster St. Paul's Episcopal Ch., Tucson, 1968-74, First United Meth. Ch., Fairbanks, Alaska, 1974-89, All Saints Episc. Ch., Omaha, 1995—; prof. music U. Alaska, Fairbanks, 1974-96, chair music dept., 1991-94; Isaacson prof. of music U. Nebr., Omaha, 1994—2001, chair dept. music, 1999—2001, Robert M. Spire chair in music, 2002—. Recordings include Moszkowski Etudes, 1973, Works of Chaminade Dohnanyi, 1977, Mendelssohn Concerti, 1978, Beethoven First Concerto, 1980, Beethoven, Reinecke, Ireland Trios with Alaska Chamber Ensemble, 1988, Kabalevsky Third Concerto, Muczynski Concerto, Muczynski Suite, 1990, Beethoven Third Concerto, 1993 (2002). Recipient Record of Month award Mus. Heritage Soc., 1979, 80, Excellence in Tchg. award U. Nebr. at Omaha, 2001; named Tchr. of Yr., Nebr. Music Tchrs. Assn., 2005. Fellow Music Tchrs. Nat. Assn.; mem. Am. Guild Organists, Phi Kappa Phi, Pi Kappa Lambda, Omicron Delta Kappa. Episcopalian. Avocations: painting, woodworking, icon writing. Office: U Nebr Dept Music Omaha NE 68182-0001 Personal E-mail: jjpiano@cox.net.

JOHNSON, JAMES DOUGLAS (JIM JOHNSON), lawyer; b. Crossett, Ark., Aug. 20, 1924; s. Thomas William and Maudie Myrtle (Long) J.; m. Virginia Morris, Dec. 21, 1947; children: Mark Douglas, John David and Joseph Daniel (twins). LL.B., Cumberland U., 1947. Bar: Ark. 1948. Practice in, Crosset, 1948-58; assoc. justice Supreme Ct. Ark., 1958-66; practice law Little Rock, 1966—; Ark. Senate 22d Senatorial Dist., 1950-54. Served with USMCR, World War II. Mem. Ark. Jud. Council, Lamda Chi Alpha. Republican. Christian Scientist. Home: PO Box 1086 Conway AR 72033-1086 Office Phone: 501-329-8383. Fax: 501-329-8383.

JOHNSON, JAMES ERLING, insurance executive; b. Waseca, Minn., May 19, 1942; s. Erling Olaf and Geneva Eleanor (Nyberg) J. BA cum laude, Carleton Coll., 1964; MS, U. Iowa, 1966. Sr. asst. health svcs. officer USPHS, 1966—68; with Minn. Life Ins. Co., St. Paul, 1968—, 2d v.p., actuary, 1976—79, v.p., actuary, 1979—90, sr.v.p., actuary, 1990—; pres., CEO Minn. Fire & Casualty, Minnetonka, 1984—97, also bd. dirs.; pres., CEO Adjustable Life Ins. Co., St. Paul, 1988—93, also bd. dirs. Mem. alumni bd. Carleton Coll., Northfield, Minn., 1987-90, coun., 1988-89, bd. trustees 1999-2003; campaign cabinet St. Paul United Way, 1988-89; bd. dirs. Minn. Landmarks, 1988—, treas., 1989-91, chmn., 1991-96; trustee ECH Found., 1989-95, asst. treas., 1990-91, treas., 1991-95; bd. dirs. Alliance of Am. Insurers, 1994-95, vice chmn., 1994-95, Saint Paul Chamber Orch., 1998—, co-chair indivdual gifts com., 1998-2000, vice chair devel., 2000—; mem. adv. bd. Minn. Ctr. for Ins. Rsch., 1995—. U. Iowa fellow, 1964-66; recipient Exceptional Svc. award St. Paul United Way, 2004 Fellow Soc. Actuaries; mem. Am. Acad. Actuaries, Twin Cities Actuarial Club (chmn. 1978-79), Mpls. Club, Univ. Club (St. Paul), Minn. Assn. of Mutual Ins. Cos. (bd. dirs. 1984-97, pres. 1992-94), Nat. Assn. of Secondary Sch. Prins. (trustee Trust to Reach Edn. Excellence 1999—), Am. Coun. of Life Ins. (chair group ins. com., 2003-05), Calhoun Beach Club, Phi Beta Kappa, Pi Mu Epsilon. Episcopalian. Avocations: travel, reading, running, swimming. Home: 2034 Lower Saint Dennis Rd Saint Paul MN 55116-2833 Office: Minn Life Ins Co 400 Robert St N Saint Paul MN 55101-2015 E-mail: james.johnson@minnesotamutual.com.

JOHNSON, JAMES HARDING, advertising executive; b. Perry, Iowa, Sept. 26, 1940; s. Richard Harding and Dorothy Margarite (Nelson) J.; m. Kathy Novak, Dec. 27, 1980; children: Ann Katherine, Alexander Simon, Elizabeth Ashely; children by previous marriage: Jennifer Lynn, James Harding. BA, U. Wash., 1963; PHD, U. Minn., 1972. Lic. psychologist, Utah, Va., Ill. Asst. prof. psychology U. Utah, Salt Lake City, 1975-77, dir. divsn. psychology Med. Sch., 1976-77; assoc. prof., vice chmn. dept. psychiatry Ea. Va. Med. Sch., Norfolk, 1977-79; chmn. Va. Consortium for Profl. Psychology, Norfolk, 1978-79; prof., dir. clin. psychology Ill. Inst. Tech., Chgo., 1979-83; pres. Human Edge Software, Inc., San Mateo, Calif., 1983-87, Text Generations Techs., San Mateo, 1987-89, Johnson Direct Advt., Palo Alto, Calif., 1988-89; CEO Connected Brands, 1989—. Author: Mental Health in the 21st Century, 1979, Technology in Mental Health Care Delivery Systems, 1980, How to Buy Almost Any Drug Legally Without a Prescription, 1990; co-author: Mind Prober, 1985; mem. editl. bd. Computers in Psychiatry and Psychology, Computers in Human Service, Behavior Rsch. Methods and Instrumentation, 1977, Computers in Psychiatry and Psychology, Computers and Behavioral Sci.; contbr. articles to profl. jours. Recipient Rush bronze medal Am. Psychiat. Assn., 1975. Mem. APA. Office: Connections 220 Twin Dolphin Dr Ste A Redwood City CA 94065-1488

JOHNSON, JAMES HAROLD, lawyer; b. Galesburg, Ill., May 3, 1944; s. Harold Frank and Marjorie Isabel J.; m. Judith Eileen Moore, June 5, 1966; children: Todd James, Tiffany Nicole. BA, Colo. Coll., 1966; JD, U. Tex., 1969. Bar: N.Y. 1970, Colo. 1971, Tex. 1975. Assoc. Winthrop, Stimson, Putnam & Roberts, N.Y.C., 1969-70, Sherman & Howard, Denver, 1970-72; corp. counsel Tex. Instruments, Inc., Dallas, 1972-85; v.p., gen. counsel, sec. Am. Healthcare Mgmt., Dallas, 1985-86, Ornda Healthcorp, Dallas, 1986-94; shareholder Jenkens & Gilchrist, PC, Dallas, 1994-97; ast. gen. counsel Sulzer Medica Inc., Houston, 1997—2002; sr. counsel Sherder & Welch, Dallas, 2003—. Mem. ABA, Tenn. Bar Assn., Tex. Bar Assn., Am. Health Lawyers Assn. Republican. Methodist. Avocations: skiing, horseback riding. Home: 3907 N Kimball Ct Missouri City TX 77459-6230 Office: Ste 630 Founders Sq 900 Jackson St Dallas TX 75202 Home: 9204 Old Veranda Rd Plano TX 75024-7082

JOHNSON, JAMES I., lawyer; b. 1948; BS, U. Minn., 1972; JD, William Mitchell Coll. Law, 1976. Bar: Minn. 1976. Asst. gen. counsel Control Data Corp., 1978—90; gen. counsel, sec. Norand Corp., 1990—97; v.p., gen. counsel, sec. HNI Corp., Muscatine, Iowa, 1997—, sec. bd. dirs. Bd. dirs. Assn. Bus. and Industry. Mem.: Assn. Corp. Counsel Iowa Chpt. Office: HNI Corp 414 E Third St PO Box 1109 Muscatine IA 52761-0071 Office Phone: 563-264-7186. Office Fax: 563-264-7217. E-mail: johnsonji@HNICorp.com.

JOHNSON, JAMES J., lawyer; b. Beacon, NY, Nov. 5, 1946; BA, Mich. State U., 1969; JD, Ohio State U., 1972. Bar: Ohio 1972. Atty, legal divsn. Procter & Gamble Co., Cin., 1973—76, counsel, legal divsn., 1976, asst. brand mgr, PS&D, 1976—79, sr. counsel, legal divsn., 1979—81, divsn. counsel, indsl. divsn., 1981—85, divsn. counsel, PS&D and BS&HCP divsn., 1985—88, assoc. gen. counsel, 1988—90, dep. gen. counsel, 1990—91, v.p., gen. counsel, 1991—92, sr. v.p., gen. counsel, 1992—99, chief legal officer, 1999—2004, chief legal officer, sec., 2004—. Mem.: Chief Legal Officer Roundtable (exec. com.), Ohio Legal Assistance Found. (bd. trustees), Nat. Legal Aid and Defender Assn. (corp. adv. com.), Civil Justice Reform Group (steering com.), Assn. of Gen. Counsel (exec. com.), Queen City Club, Camargo Club, Commonwealth Club. Office: Procter & Gamble Co 1 Procter And Gamble Plz Cincinnati OH 45202-3393

JOHNSON, JAMES L., telecommunications industry executive; With Southwestern Associated Telephone Co., 1949—88; chmn, CEO GTE Corp., 1988—92, chmn. emeritus, 1992—; dir. CellStar Corp., Carrollton, Tex., 1994—, non-exec. chmn. bd., 2001—. Bd. dir. Harte Hanks Comms., Inc., Mutual N.Y., Inc. Office: CellStar Corp 1730 Criercroft Ct Carrollton TX 75006

JOHNSON, JAMES MARTIN, state supreme court justice, lawyer; b. Seattle; married; 2 children. BA in Economics, Harvard U., 1967; JD, U. Wash., 1970. Bar: Wash. 1970, U.S. Supreme Ct., Wash. Supreme Ct., Fed. Ct. of Appeals Eighth Circuit, Fed. Ct. of Appeals Ninth Circuit, Fed. Ct. of Appeals D.C. Circuit. Counsel Wash. Legislative Joint Com. on Banking Insurance & Transportation, 1970—71; chief atty. for fisheries/game div. Wash. State, 1973—83; chief special litigation div., sr. asst. atty. gen. fish & wildlife div. Wash. Atty. Gen. Office, 1983—93; atty. priv. practice, 1993—2004; justice Wash. Supreme Ct., 2005—. Lt., chief administrative services Ninth Infantry Div. U.S. Army, 1971—73. Avocations: scuba diving, sailing, fishing, hunting, opera. Office: Wash Supreme Ct 415 12th Ave SW PO Box 40929 Olympia WA 98504-0929

JOHNSON, JAMES MYRON, psychologist, educator; b. Sauk Centre, Minn., Aug. 4, 1927; s. Walfred and Sophie Catherine (Koelzer) J.; m. Constance Mary Blodgett, Apr. 15, 1950; children: Kathryn, Peter, Donna, Daniel, Amy, Linda, Eric, Christian. BA, U. Minn., 1948; MA, Clark U., 1950; PhD, Columbia, 1958; ME (hon.), Stevens Inst. Tech., 1986. Staff psychologist Lever Bros. Co., 1955-64; Adj. prof. Grad. Sch. Indsl. Engring., N.Y.U., 1963-66; dep. dir. lab. psychol. studies Stevens Inst. Tech., 1964-67, dir., 1967-73, prof. mgmt. sci. and psychology, 1966-89, prof. emeritus, 1989—, assoc. dean acad. affairs, 1972-76, dir. tech. and soc. curriculum, 1972-75; dir. Center for Mgmt. of Organizational Resources, 1976-81; sr. partner Organizational Scis. Assocs., 1980-88; v.p. G. W. Fotis Assocs., Inc., 1982-88, head, dept. of mgmt., 1988-89. Cons. to industry. Prodr.: (film) The Man Who Revolutionized Management: Frederick Winslow Taylor; co-editor: Parish Life; editor: Lyme Cath. Observer. Pres. Darien (Conn.) Mental Health Assn., 1961-64, 68-70; mem. Darien Democratic Town Com.; bd. dirs. Gateway, Inc., 1979-86. Served with USNR, 1945-46. Mem. Am. Psychol. Soc., Met. N.Y. Assn. Applied Psychology (pres. 1963-64), Sigma Xi (treas. 1984-89), Old Lyme Country Club. Democrat. Roman Catholic. Home: 4 Tantummaheag Rd Old Lyme CT 06371-1137

JOHNSON, JAMES ROBERT, physicist, consultant; b. Dallas, Apr. 9, 1951; s. Samuel Robert Johnson and Shirley Lee Melton; m. Anita Miller, June 8, 1948; m. Cynthia Mary Moritz, Sept. 23, 1976 (div.); children: Elizabeth Mary, Robert Joseph. PhD, Tex. A&M U., 1979. Rsch. assoc. U. Ariz., Lunar and Planetary Lab., Tucson, 1979—84; sr. engr. E-Systems Sci. and Tech., Garland, Tex., 1984—86, mgr. infrared exploitation group, 1986—96; dir. Sci. and Tech. Raytheon, 1996—99; chief scientist Raytheon Intelligence and Info. Systems, 1999—2003; pres., chief scientist ADB Consulting, Santa Fe, 2003—; advisor to Collin coun. dir. homeland security Collin County Homeland Security, McKinney, Tex., 2003—. Mem. U. Tex., Grad. Rsch. Adv. Com., Richardson, 2001—; advisor dir. Smithsonian, Washington, 2002—02; advisor to dir. Measurements and Signatures Analysis, Arlington, Va., 2000—02. Mem. Planning Bd., McKinney, Tex., 1984—87, City Coun., Murphy, 1985—87. Recipient Departmental Physics award, Navarro Jr. Coll., 1971, Departmental French award, 1971. Achievements include discovery of Methane atmosphere on Pluto (1980); patents for Estimation of surface temperatures using mutli-angle satellite infrared imagery; Estimation of surface temperatures using multi-spectral satellite imagery; research in Raytheon Highest Achievment Award (1996); Research Project of the Year Award from Raytheon (1995); Publish first infrared spectrum of a comet (1982); Generated first absolutely calibrated spectrum of a comet from 0.1 to 5.5 microns wavelength, used to select filters for International Halley Watch; discovery of Water in clay material on Asteroid Ceres (1982); development of first all hazards homeland security intelligence capability at a local level in the United States. Avocations: computers, tennis, travel, investment. Office Phone: 505-741-0699. Personal E-mail: james_r_johnson@earthlink.net.

JOHNSON, JAMES TERENCE, lawyer, educator, minister; b. Springfield, Mo., Oct. 25, 1942; s. Clifford Lester and Margaret Jeanne (Wallace) Johnson; m. Martha Susan Mitchell, May 2, 1964; children: Jennifer Jeanne, Emily Jill. BA, Okla. Christian Coll., 1964; JD, So. Meth. U., 1967; LLD (hon.), Pepperdine U., 1980. Min., Okla., Tex., 1961—; staff counsel, asst. prof. Okla. Christian Coll., Oklahoma City, 1968-72; pvt. practice Oklahoma City, 1969—2000; v.p. Okla. Christian U., 1972-73, exec. v.p., 1973-74, pres., 1974-95, chancellor, 1995—2000. Co-founder Enterprise Sq., 1982, Cascade Coll., 1993. Elder Marble Falls (Tex.) Ch. Christ, 2004. Named to Okla. Higher Edn. Hall of Fame, 2000. Mem.: Okla. Bar Assn., Phi Delta Theta.

JOHNSON, JAN KINSLEY, artist; b. South Paris, Maine, Apr. 14, 1929; d. Chester C. and Ruth Sawin (Holt) Kinsley; m. Richard E Johnson, Feb. 3, 1951. Grad., Sch. of Mus. of Fine Arts, Boston, 1981, 5th yr. cert., 1982; BFA, Tufts U., 1986. Artist, Harwich, Mass., 1977—. One woman shows include Harvard Law Sch., Cambridge, Mass., 1984, Higgins Gallery, Cape Cod C.C., Barnstable, Mass., 1990; exhibited in group shows at Berkshire Mus., Pittsfield, Mass., 1982, Copley Soc., Boston, 1988. Recipient Drawing award Cape Cod Conservatory, 1973. Mem. Women's Caucus for Art. Home: 5 Sugar Pine Cir Mashpee MA 02649-3437

JOHNSON, JANE J., artist; b. Lusk, Wyo., Sept. 11, 1951; m. Michael W. Johnson. AA, Oklahoma City CC, 1999; BA in Graphic Arts, U. Ctrl. Okla., Edmond, 2001, MS in Gen. Edn., 2002. Instr. ARC, Oklahoma City, 1992—2005; artist-in-residence Okla. Arts Coun., 2000—05; registrar Photography Hall of Fame & Mus., Oklahoma City, 2000—03; instr., photography Oklahoma City CC, 2004. Artist in residence Okla. Arts Coun., 2000—05, Art Council of Okla. City, 2005; instr. Studio Mid, Midwest City, Okla., 2004—05. Bd. mem. Girl Scouts Sooner Coun., Chickasha, Okla., 2000—05; instr. Am. Red Cross, 1992—2005. Recipient 1st Place - Photography, Cleve. County Fair, Norman, Okla., 2003. Mem.: Metro Camera Club, Okla. Art Guild, Okla. Visual Art Coalition, Okla. Mus. Assn., Boy Scouts, Girl Scouts. Avocations: art, photography.

JOHNSON, JANET HELEN, literature educator; b. Everett, Wash., Dec. 24, 1944; d. Robert A. and Jane N. (Osborn) J.; m. Donald S. Whitcomb, Sept. 2, 1978; children: J.J., Felicia. BA, U. Chgo., 1967, PhD, 1972. Instr. Egyptology U. Chgo., 1971-72, asst. prof., 1972-79, assoc. prof., 1979-81, prof., 1981—; dir. Oriental Inst., 1983-89; research assoc. dept. anthropology Field Mus. of Natural History, 1980-84, 94-99, 2003—; Morton D. Hull disting. svc. prof. U. Chgo., 2003—. Author: Demotic Verbal System, 1977, Thus Wrote Onchsheshonqy, 1986, 3d revised edit., 2000, (with Donald Whitcomb) Quseir al-Qadim, 1978, 80; editor: (with E.F. Wente) Studies in Honor of G.R. Hughes, 1977, Life in a Multi-Cultural Society, 1992. Recipient Morton D. Hall disting. svc., 2003; grantee, Smithsonian Instn., 1977—83, NEH, 1978—81, 1981—85, Nat. Geog. Soc., 1978, 1980, 1982. Mem. Am. Rsch. Ctr. in Egypt (bd. govs. 1979—, exec. com. 1984-87, 90-96, v.p. 1990-93, pres. 1993-96). Office: U Chgo Oriental Inst 1155 E 58th St Chicago IL 60637-1540 Office Phone: 773-702-9530. Business E-Mail: j-johnson@uchicago.edu.

JOHNSON, J(ANET) SUSAN, psychologist; b. Ramey AFB, P.R., Mar. 24, 1948; d. Wesley Roger and Marie Dolores (Stecher) J. BA in Psychology, San Diego State U., 1970, Ma in Psychology, 1974. Coord. nat. exec. lab. Navy Nat. Elec. Lab., San Diego, 1970—72; assoc. dir. clin. decisions Navy Health Rsch. Ctr., San Diego, 1972—78; exec. dir. Edwards Assocs., San Diego, 1978—; clin. intern in clin. psychology TRI Cmty. Svcs. Outpatient Clinic, San Diego, 1978—80; pres. Strategic Vision, San Diego, 1983—. Cons. in field; co-founder Ctr. for Value Centered Life, 1999; key spkr., program coord. for nat. presidencies, prime mins., Fortune 100 CEO's, 1978—; pvt. practice on theoretical devel. of value centered psychology, 1972—; rschr. in U.S., U.K., France, Germany, Hungry, Bulgaria, Japan, Brazil, Italy, Greece, Russia and numerous other countries. Contbr. articles to profl. publs. Avocations: skiing, boating, scuba diving, gardening. Office Phone: 858-576-7141. Business E-Mail: susan.johnson@strategic.vision.com.

JOHNSON, JAY WITHINGTON, former congressman; b. Bessemer, Mich., Sept. 30, 1943; s. Ruben W. and Catherine W. (Withington) J.; m. Jane Sholtz (div.); m. Jo Lee Works, June 26, 1982; stepchildren: Christopher, Joanna AA, Gogebic Community Coll., 1963; BA, No. Mich. U., 1965; MA, Mich. State U., 1970. Disk jockey Sta. WFMK, Lansing, Mich., 1968-69; news anchorman Sta. WILX-TV, Lansing, 1969-70; radio news reporter Sta. WOWO, Ft. Wayne, Ind., 1970-73; news anchorman Sta. WPTV-TV, West Palm Beach, Fla., 1973-76; radio news reporter Sta. WVCG/WLVE-FM, Miami, Fla., 1976; TV producer Sta. WPLG-TV, Miami, 1976; news anchorman, mng. editor Sta. WPEC-TV, West Palm Beach, 1977-80; news anchorman Sta. WOTV-TV, Grand Rapids, Mich., 1980-81, Sta. WFRV-TV, Green Bay, Wis., 1981-87, Sta. WLUK-TV, Green Bay, 1987-96; mem. 105th Congress from 8th Wis dist., 1997-98, mem. agrl., transp. and infrastructure coms.; acting dep. asst. sec. congl. rels. USDA, 1999-2000; dir. U.S. Mint, Washington, 2000-2001. Vol. Big Bros./Big Sisters, Green Bay, 1982-87 (Vol. of Yr. 1985); pres., bd. dirs. Family Violence Ctr., Green Bay, 1982-87; v.p. communications United Way, Green Bay, 1987—; adv. bd. Libertas Alcohol Treatment Ctr., 1989—. With U.S. Army, 1966-68. Recipient Gov's award Gov. Tommy Thompson, 1988; named Citizen of Yr. Masons, 1987.

JOHNSON, JEAN ELAINE, nursing educator; b. Wilsey, Kans., Mar. 11, 1925; d. William H. and Rosa L. (Welty) Irwin. BS, Kans. State U., 1948; MS in Nursing, Yale U., 1965; MS, U. Wis., 1969, PhD, 1971; DS (hon.), Univ. Wis., 1998. Instr. nursing, Iowa, 1948—58; staff nurse Swedish Hosp., Englewood, Colo., 1958—60; in-svc. edn. coord. Gen. Rose Hosp., Denver, 1960—63; rsch. asst. Yale U., New Haven, 1965—67; assoc. prof. nursing

Wayne State U., Detroit, 1971—74, prof., 1974—79; dir. Ctr. for Health Rsch., 1974—79; assoc. dir. oncology nursing Cancer Ctr. U. Rochester, NY, 1979—93, prof. nursing, 1979—95, prof. emerita, 1995—. Rosenstadt prof. health rsch. Faculty Nursing, U. Toronto, 1985; vis. prof. U. Utah Coll. Nursing, 1996—97, U. Wis., Madison, 1998. Author: Self-Regulation Theory: Applying Theory to Your Practice, 1997; contbg. author Handbook of Psychology and Health, vol. 5, 1984; contbr. articles to profl. jours. Recipient Bd. Govs. Faculty Recognition award, Wayne State U., 1975, award for disting. contbn. to nursing sci., Am. Nurses Found. and ANA Coun. for Nurse Rschrs., 1983, Grad. Tchg. award, U. Rochester, 1991, Disting. Rschr. award, Oncology Nursing Soc., 1992, Outstanding Contbns. to Nursing and Psychology award, divsn. of health psychology APA, 1993; grantee, NIH, 1972—95. Fellow: AAAS, Am. Psychol. Soc., Acad. for Behavioral Medicine Rsch.; mem.: ANA (chmn. coun. for nurse rschrs. 1976—78, commn. for rsch. 1978—82), Inst. Medicine of NAS (com. on patient injury compensation 1976—77, membership com. 1981—86, gov. coun. 1987—89), Phi Kappa Phi, Omicron Nu, Sigma Xi. Home: 4924 Whitecomb Dr Apt 15 Madison WI 53711-2661 Personal E-mail: jean_joh@msn.com.

JOHNSON, JEFFREY M., publishing executive; b. July 23, 1959; married; 3 children. BS in accountancy, U. Ill.; M in ops. mgmt., U. Chgo. With KPMG Peat Marwick, 1981—84; mem. corp. office staff Tribune Co., Chgo., 1984—86; various ops. positions Chgo. Tribune, 1986—92; v.p. & dir. ops. Orlando Sentinel, 1992—98; exec. v.p., gen. mgr. & COO Landoll Inc., 1998—2000, pres. & CEO, 2000; sr. v.p. & gen. mgr. LA Times, 2000—05, exec. v.p. & gen. mgr., 2005, pub., pres. & CEO, 2005—. Bd. dirs. YMCA of Met. LA, United Way of Greater LA, Orange County Performing Arts Ctr. Co-recipient Tribune Mgmt. Award, 1992. Office: LA Times 202 W 1st St Los Angeles CA 90012*

JOHNSON, JEH CHARLES, lawyer; b. N.Y.C., Sept. 11, 1957; s. Jeh Vincent and Norma (Edelin) J.; m. Susan M. DiMarco, Mar. 18, 1994. BA, Morehouse Coll., Atlanta, 1979; JD, Columbia U., 1982. Bar: N.Y. 1983, D.C. 1999. Litig. assoc. Sullivan & Cromwell, N.Y.C., 1982—84; assoc. Paul, Weiss, Rifkind, Wharton & Garrison, N.Y.C., 1984-88, 92-93; asst. U.S. atty. So. Dist. N.Y., 1989-91; ptnr. Paul, Weiss, Rifkind, Wharton & Garrison, N.Y.C., 1994-98, 2001—; gen. counsel USAF, Washington, 1998—2001. Adj. lectr. law Columbia U. Law Sch., N.Y.C., 1995—97. Mem.: Coun. Fgn. Rels. Office: Paul Weiss Rifkin Wharton & Garrison 1285 Ave of Americas New York NY 10019 Business E-Mail: jjohnson@paulweiss.com.

JOHNSON, JEH VINCENT, architect; b. Nashville, July 8, 1931; s. Charles Spurgeon and Marie Antoinette (Burguette) J.; m. Norma Edelin, Dec. 28, 1956; children— Jeh Charles, Marguerite Marie. AB, Columbia U., 1953, M.Arch., 1958. Architect/designer Paul R. Williams, Los Angeles, 1956; designer Adams & Woodbridge, N.Y.C., 1957-62; asso. Gindele & Johnson (P.C. Architects and predecessors), Poughkeepsie, N.Y., 1967-69, partner, 1969-71, pres., 1971-80; ptnr. LeGendre Johnson McNeil Assos., 1980-90; pvt. practice architecture Wappingers Falls, N.Y., 1990—. Sr. lectr. in art Vassar Coll., 1964—2001, lectr. in urban studies, 1995—2000, lectr. emeritus, 2001-; mem. N.Y. State Bd. for Architecture, 1974-84, chmn., 1980-82; mem. Nat. Commn. Urban Problems, 1967-69; nat. master grader Nat. Coun. Archtl. Registration Bds., 1984-91. Designer: Dutchess County (N.Y.) Mental Health Ctr., 1969, Lagrange (N.Y.) Town Hall, 1969, Newburgh (N.Y.) Houses on the Lake, 1970, Whitney Young Health Ctr., Albany, N.Y., 1973, St. Simeon Apts. for Elderly, Poughkeepsie, 1973, 93, Bedford-Stuyvesant Comml. Ctr., N.Y.C., 1978, Camp of Tomorrow, Girl Scouts U.S.A., Mt. Pleasant, N.Y., 1985, Millbrook (N.Y.) Ch. Alliance Housing, Ctrl. Bapt. Ch., Salt Point, N.Y., Hillcrest House, Poughkeepsie, 1992, The Intercultural Ctr. at Vassar Coll, 1993, St. Anna Apts., Poughkeepsie, 1996. Mem. Dutchess County Planning Bd., 1988-92; bd. dirs. Scenic Hudson, Inc., 1995—. William Kinne Fellows traveling fellow, 1958 Fellow AIA (nat. task force on affordable housing, Students medal 1958); mem. Nat. Orgn. Minority Architects (charter), AAUP, NAACP, Sigma Pi Phi. Clubs: Masons. Home and Office: 14 Edgehill Rd Wappingers Falls NY 12590-1228 Office Phone: 845-297-5524.

JOHNSON, JENNIE, chaplain, social worker; b. Houston, Sept. 18, 1952; d. James L.C. and Marilyn Mildred (Frazier) J.; children: Alan, David. BS in Social Work, Tex. Woman's U., 1976; postgrad., Bishop's Sch. Theology, Denver, 1979—81, Samaritan Theol. Sem., L.A., 1982—84, Episcopal Theol. Sem., Austin, Tex., 1986—87, Episcopal Theol. Sem., 2004. Cert. social worker, Tex.; oblate Order of St. Benedict, 1998; mem. Daus. of the King, 2003—. Comdr. 94th Ord. Det. USAR, Ft. Carson, Colo., 1978—80, evaluator 1st maneuver tng. command Denver, 1980—81; planner prodn. control Elmo Semiconducter, L.A., 1981—83; planner quality control TRW Def. and Space Guidance, L.A., 1983—84; dir. chpt. svcs. Greater Amarillo Red Cross, Tex., 1985—86; chaplain Austin State Hosp., 1987—88, Brackenridge Hosp., Austin, 1988—91, Hospice Austin, 1992—95; asst. dir. Centex Chpt. ARC, Austin, 1995—96; chaplain Seaton Med. Ctr., Austin, 1998—. Conveener Integrity Austin, 1989-90, 92-94, 96-97; conf. presenter Nat. Episcopal AIDS Coalition, Cin., 1990-2005; self-employed musical instrument woodwork, 2005. Founding bd. dirs. Out Youth Austin/YWCA, 1990-92; mem. Tex. AIDS Network, Austin, 1992-2001; foster parent Casey Family Program, Austin, 1992-94; diocesan del. St. Michael's Episcopal Ch., Austin, 1988—, jr. warden, 1993-95, mem. vestry, 1993-97, mem. divsn. for spiritual devel. of diocese 1997-2000, Mentor Edn. for Ministry, 1980-2000; mem.-at-large Women for Social Witness Network, Nat. Episcopal Ch., 1992-96; mem. Episcopal Womens Caucus, 1993—, Nat. Hospice Orgn., 1993-2000, Tex. Hospice Orgn., 1992-2000, presenter state conf., 1995, Order of St. Luke the Physician, 1984—, 1st lt. U.S. Army, 1975-80. Democrat. Avocations: paleontology, needlecrafts, reading, woodworking, camping. Office Phone: 512-799-1187. E-mail: johnsonjk@austin.rr.com.

JOHNSON, JENNIFER J., federal official; Dep. sec., bd. mems. office Fed. Res. Sys., Washington. Office: Fed Res Sys Bd Mems Office 20th And C Sts NW Ofc Washington DC 20551-0001

JOHNSON, JENNIFER ROSE, lawyer; b. Springfield, Mo., Dec. 24, 1959; d. LeRoy Vincent Johnson and Jewell Faye Tykeson. BS in Psychology, Evangel Coll., 1984; AA in Nursing, Mesa C.C., 1987; JD, U. Ariz., 1992. Bar: Calif. 1992, U.S. Ct. Appeals (9th cir.) 1998, U.S. Dist. Ct. (ctrl. dist.) Calif. 1998; RN Ariz. Nurse Mesa Gen. Hosp., Ariz., 1987—89, Tucson Gen. Hosp., 1989—92; assoc. Tuverson & Hallyand, Palm Springs, Calif., 1992—98, Lafollette, Johnson et al, Santa Ana, 1998—99; ptnr. Tuverson & Hillyard, Newport Beach, 1999—2000; atty. Lopez, Hodes et al, 2000—. Mem.: ATLA, Trial Lawyers for Pub. Justice, Consumer Attys. Calif. (at-large bd. dirs. 2001—), Orange County Trial Lawyers Assn. Avocations: church choir, exercise, piano, sports. Office: Lopez Hodes Restaino Milman & Skikos 450 Newport Ctr Dr 2d Fl Newport Beach CA 92660 Office Phone: 949-640-8222. Business E-Mail: jjohnson@lopez-hodes.com.

JOHNSON, JENNIFER TOBY, military officer; b. Syracuse, N.Y., May 23, 1976; d. Norman Edward and Barbara Catherine Johnson. BS, U.S. Mil. Acad., 1998; attended, U.S. Army Flight Sch., 1998—2000, U.S. Army Capt. Career course, 2003—04; student, Harvard Bus. Sch. and John F. Kennedy Sch. Govt., 2005—. Commd. 2d lt. U.S. Army 1st Battalion (Attack), 3d Aviation Regiment, 3d Inf. Divsn. (Mechanized), Ft. Hood, Tex., 2000—01, advanced through grades to capt., 2001—, served at Hunter Army Airfield, Ga., 2000—03, served Iraq, 2003—, 2003—. Decorated Presdl. Unit Citation Pres. George W. Bush. Republican. Lutheran. Avocations: golf, skiing, violin. Home: 6004 Bay Hill Cir Jamesville NY 13078 Office: 38 Ellery St Cambridge MA 02138 Office Phone: 912-596-3228, 254-338-9232.

JOHNSON, JEROME LINNÉ, cardiologist, educator; b. Rockford, Ill., June 19, 1929; s. Thomas Arthur and Myrtle Elizabeth (Swanson) J.; m. Molly Ann Rideout, June 27, 1953; children: Susan R. Johnson, William Rideout. BA, U. Chgo., 1951; BS, Northwestern U., 1952, MD, 1955. Diplomate Nat. Bd. Med. Examiners. Intern U. Chgo. Clinics, 1955-56; resident Northwestern U., Chgo., 1958-61; chief resident Chgo. Wesley Meml. Hosp., 1960-61; mem., v.p. Hauch Med. Clinic, Pomona, Calif., 1961-88; pvt. practice cardiology and internal medicine Pomona, 1988—. Clin. assoc. prof. medicine, U. So. Calif., L.A., 1961—; mem. staff Pomona Valley Hosp. Med. Ctr., chmn. coronary care com. 1967-77; mem. staff L.A. County Hosp. Citizen ambassador, People to People; mem. Town Hall of Calif., L.A. World Affairs Coun. Lt. USNR, 1956-58; bd. dirs. Claremont chpt. ARC, 1993-2000; bd. dirs., health com. Mt. San Antonio Gardens Retirement Home, 1993-2000. Fellow: Am. Coll. Cardiology, Am. Geriatrics Soc., Royal Soc. Health; mem.: Galileo Soc., Am. Heart Assn. (bd. dirs. L.A. County div. 1967-84, San Gabriel div. 1963-89), Am. Soc. Internal Medicine, Inland Soc. Internal Medicine, Pomona Host Lions. Avocations: photography, swimming, bicycling, medical and surgical antiques, travel. Home: 648 Delaware Dr Claremont CA 91711-3457 Personal E-mail: linne1@aol.com.

JOHNSON, JILL ANN, lyricist, actress; b. Larchmont, NY, Nov. 10, 1943; d. Anthony Francis and Rita Hume Johnson; m. Thomas William Green (div.); children: Gwendolyn Harris, Kevin Green. Student, Butler Bus. Sch., 1995. Sec. Scripps-Howard News, NYC, 1961—67, Paul Pulley Atty., Durham, NC, 1973—74; rsch. asst. Sun Rsch., Norwalk, Conn., 1994; receptionist Consol. Mgmt., Westport, Conn., 1995; prodn. specialist Greenwood Publ., Westport, 1996—97. Freelance writer; guest poet Sta. WOMR-Radio, Provincetown, 2003. Singer: Cape Cod Cable TV Christian Program, 2003; actor: various sr. ctrs.; author: numerous poems; composer: (CD) America, 2002, (songs) White Cap Wave; contbr. articles to profl. jours.; contbr. Best Song to album dedicated to 9/11 victims: Ellis Island Farewell, 2002; actor: (films) Lost in Yonkers, 2002. Recipient People's Choice award, Chatham Fine Arts, 2001, award, Hilltop Records, Inc. Mem.: ASCAP, Cape Cod Women's Orgn., King Wasa Swedish Lodge. Avocations: dance, bicycling, ice skating, singing, poetry. Home: 218 Jonathans Way Brewster MA 02631 Office Phone: 508-896-5274.

JOHNSON, JIMMY, sports broadcaster, former professional football coach; b. Port Arthur, Tex., July 16, 1943; BA, U. Ark., 1965. Asst. coach Louisiana Tech. U., LA, 1965, Wichita State U., KS, 1967, Iowa State U., IA, 1968-68, U. Oklahoma, Norman, OK, 1970-72, U. Arkansas, AR, 1973-76, U. Pittsburg, 1977-78; head coach Oklahoma State U., OK, 1979-83, U. Miami, Miami, FL, 1983-88, Dallas Cowboys, Dallas, 1989-94; sports commentator, football analyst Fox Network, 1994-95; head coach, gen. mgr. Miami Dolphins, 1996-99; co-host NFL Sunday, Fox, 2002—. Coach NCAA Divsn. I championship team, 1987, Super Bowl (XXVII, XXVIII) championship team, 1992-93; named Coach of Yr. Walter Camp Found., 1986-87, NFL Coach of Yr. Coll. & Pro Football Newsweekly, 1990, UPI, 1990, AP, 1990, Football Digest, 1991; recipient Seattle Gold Helmet award, 1986.*

JOHNSON, JOAN BRAY, insurance company consultant; b. Kennett, Mo., Nov. 19, 1926; d. Pleas Green and Mary Scott (Williams) Bray; m. Frank Johnson Jr., Nov. 6, 1955; 1 child, Victor Kent. Student, Drury Coll., Springfield, Mo., 1949-51, Cen. Bible Inst. and Coll., 1946-49. Staff writer Gospel Pub. Co., Springfield, Mo., 1949-51; sec. Kennett Sch. Dist. Bd. Edn., 1951-58; spl. features corr. Memphis Press-Scimitar, 1959-60; sec. to v.p. Cotton Exchange Bank, Kennett, Mo., 1959-60; proposal analyst Aetna Life Ins. Co., El Paso, Tex., 1960-64, pension adminstr., 1964-71, office mgr. Brokerage div. Denver, 1971-78, office adminstr. Life Consol. div. Oakland, Calif., 1979-82, office adminstr. PFSD div. Walnut Creek, Calif., 1983-86, office adminstr. PFSD-Health Mktg. div. Sacramento, 1986-89, regional adminstr. Hartford, Conn., 1989-91, cons. Santa Ana, Calif., 1991—, Met-Life Ins. Co., Dallas, 1998—, Transamerica Life, LA, 1999—, Reliar Star Ins., 1999—. Officer local PTA, 1964-71; pres. Wesley Svc. Guild, 1968-71; den mother Boy Scouts Am.; fin. sec. Green Valley United Meth. Ch., 1992—. Recipient Tex. Life Svc. award PTA, 1970. Fellow Life Office Mgmt. Assn. (instr. classes); mem. DAR (regent Silver State Nev. chpt. 1994-96, Nev. state treas. 1998—01, bd. dirs. Nev. 1996—, Nev. state chaplain 2003-2004, Nev. vice regent 2004—), Assn. Bus. and Profl. Women, Life Underwriters Assn., Clark County Heritage Mus., Last Monday Club, Opti-Mrs., Allied Arts Club. Democrat. Home: 2415 La Estrella St Henderson NV 89014-3608 E-mail: ojbjohnson1@juno.com.

JOHNSON, JOAN (JAN) HOPE VOSS, communications executive, photojournalist, public relations executive; b. Exira, Iowa, Nov. 18, 1922; d. George Carl Alfred Voss and Evelyn Hope Rendleman; m. Conrad Loren Johnson, Jan. 5, 1955 (div. Mar. 29, 1982); children: Scott Conrad, Dawn Ann Bissell, Lisa Ann Lewis; m. James Francis Pressnall, Nov. 23, 1941 (div. Nov. 15, 1952). Traffic/continuity dir., broadcaster KJAN Radio, Atlantic, Iowa, 1952—53; dir. of women's programming KVTV-TV, Sioux City, Iowa, 1953—57; prodr., dir., broadcaster, women's programming tv WMT-TV/WMT Radio, Cedar Rapids, Iowa, 1957—70; consumer cons. a.k.a. Bette Schaper, 1st lady of games industry Schaper Mfg. Co., Minneapolis, Minn., 1966—67; dir. publ. and cmty. rels. Grant Wood Area Edn. Agy., Cedar Rapids, Iowa, 1970—76; mktg./ins. coord. Perpetual Savs. and Loan, Cedar Rapids, Iowa, 1977—82; audio-visual cons., dir. of fund raising Muree Christian Sch., Jhika Gali, Pakistan, 1982—84; dir. pub. rels./devel. McKean Leprosy Inst., Chiang Mai, Thailand, 1984—85; dir. of devel./ Murree Christian Sch., Jhika Gali, Pakistan, 1986—88; profl. spkr. Jan Voss Johnson Enterprises, Atlantic, Iowa, 1988—. Nat. v.p. Am. Women in Radio and TV, Cedar Rapids, Iowa, 1966—67. Contbr. articles; author: (family history, paternal) Quo Fata Vocant; editor: (illustrated poetic anthology) Poems My Mother Taught Me. Dem. candidate for pub. office Iowa State Legislature, Cedar Rapids, Iowa, 1969—70. Seaman, second class S 2/C WAVES USN, 1942—43, N.Y. Mem.: Iowana Coun. (exec. bd.), Camp Fire Girls (bd. mem. 1966—67). D-Liberal. United Ch.Of Christ. Avocations: family, photography, cooking, travel, history of eastern cultures. Home: 1200 Brookridge Cir 401 Atlantic IA 50022-2304

JOHNSON, JOANN MARDELLE, federal agency administrator; b. Massena, Iowa, Feb. 24, 1949; BA in Edn., U. No. Iowa, 1971. Former tchr.; grain and livestock prodr.; mem. Iowa Senate from 39th dist., Des Moines, 1994—2000; mem. appropriations com., mem. commerce com.; chair ways and means com.; chair commerce com.; mem. Nat. Credit Union Admin., Alexandria, Va., 2002—, vice chair, 2003—. Mem. 4-H, Local Devel. Bd.; vol. various cmty. orgns.; campaign mgr. Rep. Dwight Dinkla, 1992, Congressman Jim Lightfoot, 1990, orgn. dir., 1986-88. Mem. Am. Legis. Exch. Coun., Farm Bur., Cattleman's Assn. Republican. Office: Nat Credit Union Admin Off of the Bd 1775 Duke St Alexandria VA 22314-3428 E-mail: boardmember.johnson@ncua.gov.

JOHNSON, JOANNE CAROL, elementary school educator; b. Fort Atkinson, Wis., Jan. 1, 1954; d. Harold Otto and Jessie (Leona) Schroeder; m. David E. Johnson, May 30, 1982 (div. Jan. 1999); children: David, Allan. BSE, So. Coll. Seventh Day Adventist, 1983. Tchr. Seventh Day Adventist Ch., Cambridge, Wis., 1983-88, Roan Mountain, Tenn., 1989—95. Republican. Avocations: stamps, crafts, gardening. Home: 1357 Little Elk Rd Elk Park NC 28622-9132

JOHNSON, JOEL W., food products executive; With General Foods Corp.; exec. v.p. sales and mktg. Hormel Foods Corp., 1991-92, pres., 1992-93, COO, CEO, 1993-95, chmn. bd., CEO, pres. Austin, Minn., 1995—. Bd. dirs. Overseers of The Carlson Sch. Mgmt. U. Minn.; trustee Hamilton Coll. Office: Hormel Foods Corp 1 Hormel Pl Austin MN 55912-3680

JOHNSON, JOHN, broadcast journalist, artist; b. NYC, June 20, 1938; s. John Edward and Irene Elizabeth (Tutt) J. BA, CCNY, 1961, M Art Edn., 1963; DHL (hon.), St. Thomas Aquinas Coll., 1991. Tchr., asst. prin. N.Y.C. Bd. Edn., 1960-67; assoc. prof. fine arts Lincoln U., 1967-68; prodr., dir., writer documentary unit ABC News, N.Y.C., 1968-71; corr. ABC Evening News, N.Y.C., 1971-72; reporter WABC-TV News, N.Y.C., 1972-85, sr. corr., anchor, 1985-95; anchor WCBS-TV News, N.Y.C., 1995-96; anchor, sr. corr. WNBC-TV News, N.Y.C., 1996-97; ret., 1997. Essayist: The Black Power Revolt, 1968; author: Only Son: A Memoir, 2002; one-man shows include Walter Wickiser Gallery, Soho, NY, 2003, 04; appeared in films Copland, 1997, 54, 1996. Recipient Best Enterprise Reporting award AP, 1977, Emmy award for Best Sports Programming, 1978, Best Documentary award AP, 1979, Emmy award for Best Investigative Reporting, 1983, Emmy award for Best Spot News, 1982, Emmy award for Best Svc. News, 1982, Nat. Broadcast award for Outstanding Spot News, UPI, 1982, Lifetime Achievement award in broadcast journalism N.Y. Assn. Black Journalists, 1997; named to CCNY Comm. Hall of Fame, 2000. Mem. AFTRA, Dirs. Guild Am. Office Phone: 845-638-2898. E-mail: Gaspard2j@aol.com.

JOHNSON, JOHN A., communications company executive; b. Milw., 1915; s. John W. and Amy (Nelson) J.; m. Harriet Nelson, Sept. 11, 1938; children: Barbara (Mrs. James A. Groff), John Vance, Susan (Mrs. Don H. Boatwright), Richard Bailey. AB, DePauw U., 1937; JD, U. Chgo., 1940; LLM, Harvard U., 1946. Bar: Ill. 1946, D.C. 1979. Gen. counsel USAF, 1952-58, NASA, 1958-63; v.p. internat. Comm. Satellite Corp. (COMSAT), 1964-73, sr. v.p., 1973-74; pres. COMSAT Gen. Corp., 1973-77, chmn. bd., CEO, 1977-80; chmn. Satellite TV Corp., 1980-81. U.S. rep. interim comm. satellite com. INTELSAT, 1964-73, chmn. 1964-69, bd. govs., 1973-74, INMARSAT Coun., 1979; dir. World Christian Broadcasting Corp., 1981-91. Contbr.: articles to profl. jours., also to Ency. Brit. Active Falls Church (Va.) Sch. Bd., 1949-56, chmn. 1951-56; mem. exec. bd. Va. Sch. Bds. Assn., 1953-56; trustee Northeastern Christian Jr. Coll., 1955-85, chmn. bd. trustees, 1958-73; bd. visitors Coll. of U. Chgo., 1966-71, Western Res. Law Sch., 1964-67; bd. dirs. Pan Am. Devel. Found., 1986-92, Health Talents Internat., 1992-99. Lt. (j.g.) USNR, 1943-46. Recipient Exceptional Civilian Service award Dept. Air Force; Outstanding Leadership medal NASA; Alumni citation for pub. service U. Chgo.; Alumni citation DePauw U. Mem. Am. Soc. Internat. Law, Inter-am Bar Assn., Internat. Acad. Astronautics. Mem. Ch. of Christ. Home: 12158 Clipper Dr Woodbridge VA 22192-2209

JOHNSON, JOHN D., grain company executive; b. Rhame, N.D. BBA, Black Hills State U. Feed cons. GTA divsn. Cenex Harvest States Cooperatives, Inver Grove Heights, Minn., 1976, regional sales mgr., dir. sales and mktg., gen. mgr. GTA Feeds, group v.p. Farm Mktg. and Supply, 1992, pres., gen. mgr., 1998—, pres., CEO, 2000—. Bd. dirs. Ventura Foods, Sparta Foods. Mem. Nat. Coop. Refinery Assn. (bd. dirs.), Nat. Coun. Farmer Coops. (bd. dirs.) Office: Cenex Harvest States 5500 Cenex Dr Inver Grove Heights MN 55077*

JOHNSON, JOHN D., JR., neurosurgeon; b. Ft. Belvoir, Va., July 1, 1966; m. Kim Floyd. BS magna cum laude, Auburn U., 1988; MD U. Ala., 1992. Diplomate Am. Bd. Neurol. Surgery. Surg. intern U. Ky. Med. Ctr., Lexington, 1992—93, neurosurg. resident, 1993—98; neurosurgeon North Ala. Neurol., P.A., Huntsville, 1998—; active staff Huntsville Hosp. Systems, Crestwood Med. Ctr., Huntsville, Surgery Ctr. Huntsville; cons. staff HealthSouth Rehab. Hosp. of North Ala., Huntsville, Decatur (Ala.) Gen. Hosp. Clin. instr. U. Ala. Sch. Medicine, 1998—; presenter in field. Contbr. articles to med. jours. Mem.: AMA (v.p. univ. chpt. 1989—90), Madison County Med. Soc., Congress of Neurol. Surgeons, Am. Assn. Neurol. Surgeons, Med. Assn. State of Ala., Phi Eta Sigma, Alpha Lambda Delta, Omicron Delta Kappa, Phi Kappa Phi, Phi Gamma Delta. Avocations: travel, reading, football, golf, biking. Office: North Ala Neurol PA 105 Rand Ave Huntsville AL 35801

JOHNSON, JOHN DAMIAN, music educator; b. Wichita, Kans., Sept. 28, 1976; s. John Henry and Debra Ann Johnson. BM in Music Edn., Washburn U., 1999. Cert. tchr. Kans., provisional tchg. cert. Mo. Sales assoc. Manning Music, Topeka, 1995—97, low brass instr., 1995—99; dir. music SW Charter Sch., Kansas City, Mo., 2000—. Pastoral coun. sec. St. Monica Cath. Ch., Kansas City, 2000—02. Mem.: Music Educators Nat. Conf. Democrat. Roman Catholic. Office: Southwest Charter Sch 6512 Wornall Rd Kansas City MO 64113 Home: 108 Hiawatha Ave Hiawatha KS 66434-1915 Business E-Mail: djohnson@swcharterschool.org.

JOHNSON, JOHN FRANK, professional recruitment executive; b. Bklyn., Apr. 23, 1942; s. John Henry and Sirkka (Keto) J.; m. Martha Lear Fryer, Aug. 31, 1963 (div. Apr. 1988); children: Kristin Lin, Heather Alane; m. Virginia K. Yeaser, Nov. 16, 1989 BA in Econs., Tufts U., 1963; MBA in Indsl. Relations, Columbia U., 1964. Indsl. relations analyst Ford Motor Co., Dearborn and Livonia, Mich., 1964-67; various human resources positions Gen. Electric Co., Chgo. and Louisville, Ky., 1967-76; successively assoc., v.p., mng. dir., exec. v.p. and mng. dir. Lamalie Amrop Internat., Cleve., 1976-84; pres. LAI Ward Howell (formerly Lamalie Amrop Internat.), N.Y.C. and Cleve., 1984-95, pres., CEO Cleve., 1987-94, chmn., 1995-99; vice chmn. TMP Worldwide Exec. Search, Cleve., 1999—; sr. client ptnr. Korn/Ferry Internat., Cleve., 2003—. Mem. Human Resource Planning Soc., The Planning Forum, Assn. for Corp. Growth, Internat. Assn. Corp. and Profl. Recruiters, The Club (Cleve.), Union Club (Cleve.), Internat. Game Fishing Assn., Kirtland Country Club, Calusa Pines Golf Club. Avocations: big game fishing, golf, travel, wine collecting, thoroughbred racing. Office: Korn Ferry Internat 600 Superior Ave Ste 1300 Cleveland OH 44114 Office Phone: 216-479-6818.

JOHNSON, JOHN GRAY, retired university chancellor; b. Irwin, Pa., Aug. 8, 1924; s. John Arthur and Elizabeth (Gray) J.; m. L. Jane Wyncoop, Aug. 28, 1948; children: Scott Raymond, Lynn. BS, Carnegie Mellon U., 1949; LL.D. (hon.), U. Indpls., 1980. Alumni dir. Carnegie Mellon U., 1955-60; exec. dir. Am. Alumni Council, Washington, 1960-64; v.p. devel. Butler U., Indpls., 1964-66, pres., 1978-88, chancellor, 1989-90; v.p. for devel. Carnegie Mellon U., Pitts., 1966-78. Mem. adv. bd. Splendido Cmty. With AUS, 1943-46. Decorated Air medal; named Sagamore of the Wabash. Mem. Ind. C. of C. (life), Sun City Found. (pres.), Oro Valley Country Club, Phi Kappa Phi, Omicron Delta Kappa. Home: 14326 N Green Meadow Ln Tucson AZ 85755-7120

JOHNSON, JOHN H., lawyer; b. Raleigh, NC, 1948; BA, Univ. NC, 1970, JD, 1976. Bar: NC 1976, Ga. 1987. Staff atty., legal br., enforcement divsn., region 4 EPA, 1977—80, chief, air and toxics law br., office of regional counsel, region 4, 1980—83, chief, hazardous waste law br., office of regional counsel, region 4, 1983—86; assoc. Troutman Sanders LLP, Atlanta, 1986—90, ptnr., environ., natural resources, 1990—, and practice group leader, environ. and natural resources. Named a Super Lawyer, Atlanta Mag., 2004. Mem.: ABA, NC State Bar, State Bar Ga. Office: Troutman & Sanders LLP One Logan Sq Ste 5200 600 Peachtree St NE Atlanta GA 30308-2216 Office Phone: 404-885-3166. Office Fax: 404-962-6594. Business E-Mail: john.johnson@troutmansanders.com.

JOHNSON, JOHN J., historian, educator; b. White Swan, Wash., Mar. 26, 1912; s. George E. and Mary (Whitford) J.; m. Maurine Amstutz, June 8, 1942; 1 son, Michael G. BA, Central Wash. Coll., 1940; MA, U. Calif.-Berkeley, 1943, PhD, 1947; postgrad., U. Chgo., 1943-44, U. Chile, 1946. Tchr. pub. schs., Wash., 1935-39; mem. faculty Stanford U., 1946-78, prof. history, 1958-78, emeritus prof., 1977—; chmn. com. Latin Am. studies, 1966-72; prof. U. N.Mex., Albuquerque, 1980-85. Acting chief S. Am. br., div. research Am. Republic, State Dept., 1952-53; lectr. U. Ariz. Summer Sch., Guadalajara, Mex., 1955, 58, 61; cons. to industry and govt., 1959—; Fulbright lectr. U. Auckland, New Zealand, 1974; vis. prof. U. N.Mex., 1977, 79, Ariz. State U., 1980 Mng. editor Hispanic Am. Hist. Rev., 1980-85. Author: Pioneer Telegraphy in Chile, 1948, Political Change in Latin America; The Emergence of the Middle Sectors, 1958, The Military and Society in Latin America, 1964, Simon Bolivar and Spanish American Independence: 1783-1830, 1967, 2d edit., 1992, Latin America in Caricature, 1980, 2d edit., 1993, A Hemisphere Apart: The Foundations of United States Policy Toward Latin America, 1990; editor, contbr.: Role of the Military in Underdeveloped World, Continuity & Change in Latin America, 1964. Recipient Bolton prize Conf. Latin Am. History, 1959, Disting. Alumnus award Cen. Wash. U., 1977, Disting. Service award Conf. Latin Am. History,

1987; fellow Nat. Humanities Ctr., 1985-86. Mem. Am. Hist. Assn. (mem. council 1976-79, chmn. conf. Latin Am. history 1961), Latin Am. Studies Assn. (pres. 1970, 1st Kalman Silvert Pres.'s prize 1983) Home: PO Box 2506 Crested Butte CO 81224-2506

JOHNSON, JOHN PHILIP, geneticist, researcher; b. Wabash, Ind., June 6, 1949; s. Melvin Leroy and Cleo Pauline (Aldrich) J.; m. Sheryl Kay Kennedy, June 3, 1978; children: Craig Eric, Lindsay Sara. BS, U. Mich., 1971, MD, 1975. Diplomate Am. Bd. Pediatrics, Am. Bd. Med. Genetics. Intern, 2d-yr. resident Children's Hosp. Los Angeles, 1975-77; 3d yr. resident in pediatrics U. Utah, Salt Lake City, 1977-78, fellow in genetics, 1980-82, asst. prof. pediatrics, 1982-85; pediatrician Family Health Program, Salt Lake City, 1978-80; assoc. dir. med. genetics, attending/active staff physician Children's Hosp. Oakland, Calif., 1985-92; dir. med. genetics attending/active staff physician Children's Hosp., Oakland, 1992-94; dir. med. genetics Shodair Children's Hosp., Helena, Mont., 1994—, active mem. staff, 1995—. Clinic physician Utah State Tng. Sch., American Fork, 1982-85; attending and staff physician Primary Children's Med. Ctr., Salt Lake City, 1978-80. Assoc. editor Am. Jour. Med. Genetics, 1995-97; contbr. articles to med. jours. Recipient William J. Branstrom award U. Mich., 1967. Fellow Am. Acad. Pediatrics; mem. Am. Soc. Human Genetics, Soc. for Pediatric Rsch., Alpha Omega Alpha. Avocations: skiing, hiking, camping, piano, jazz. Home: 2604 Gold Rush Ave Helena MT 59601-5625 Office: Shodair Childrens Hosp PO Box 5539 Helena MT 59604-5539 Office Phone: 406-444-7530. Business E-Mail: jjohnson@shodair.org.

JOHNSON, JOHN PRESCOTT, retired philosophy educator; b. Tumalo, Oreg., Apr. 24, 1921; s. John Edward and Caroline Prescott (Eaton) J.; m. Mable Alice Dougherty, June 9, 1943; children: Grace Beth Johnson Booth), John Paul, Carol Ruth Johnson Hull. AB, Pitts. State U., 1947, MS, 1948; PhD, Northwestern U., 1959. Asst. prof. philosophy Bethany (Okla.) Nazarene Coll., 1949-57; asst. prof. U. Okla., Norman, 1957-62; assoc. prof. philosophy Monmouth (Ill.) Coll., 1962-69; prof. philosophy Monmouth (Ill.) Coll., 1969-86; chmn. dept. philosophy Monmouth (Ill.) Coll., 1967-86, emeritus prof. philosophy, 1986—; ret., 1986. Vis. asst. prof. Northwestern U., summer 1961; Cons. research project student values U.S. Office Edn., 1967 Author: The Value Philosophy of Wilbur Marshall Urban, 1988, The Reality of Faith, 1996, The Gates of Light, 2000, The More Excellent Way, 2000, The Living Fountain: The Symbolism of Grace, 2003; contbr. articles to philos. jours. Mem. Am. Philos. Assn., Ill. Philos. Assn. (sec.-treas. 1967-69, pres. 1971-73).

JOHNSON, JOHN WALTER, III, lawyer; b. Nashville, Mar. 3, 1947; s. John Walter and Nancy Thornton (Pierce) J.; m. Margaret Hamilton Mebane, Oct. 5, 1973 (div. June 1980); m. Susan T. Johnson, May 18, 1985; children: Virginia Hamilton, Margaret Peyton, John Walter IV. BS, U. Tenn., Knoxville, 1969, JD, 1973. Bar: Tenn. 1973, Ga. 1976, U.S. Dist. Ct. (no. dist.) Ga. 1976, U.S. Dist. Ct. Tenn. 1974, U.S. Tax Ct. 1974. Assoc. Grant, Clements & Bower, Chattanooga, 1973-74; ptnr. Anderson & Johnson, Chattanooga, 1975-83, Hatcher & Johnson, Chattanooga, 1983-85, Hatcher, Johnson & Meaney, Chattanooga, 1985—. Bd. dirs. Multiple Sclerosis, Chattanooga, 1978; pres. Luth. Ch. of the Good Shepherd, Chattanooga, 1983, Chattanooga Cerebral Palsy, 1978-81; housing trustee Kappa Sigma Fraternity, Chattanooga, 1992; mem. Univ. Alumnae Coun., Chattanooga, 1990—. Bd. dirs. Walter E. Boehm Birth Defects Ctr. Mem. Tenn. Trial Lawyers Assn., Chattanooga Trial Lawyers (treas., v.p., pres. 1977-81). Republican. Avocations: golf, skiing, football. Home: 210 Blackwell Farm Rd Chattanooga TN 37421 Office: Hatcher Johnson & Meaney 2901 E 48th St Chattanooga TN 37407-3303

JOHNSON, JOHN WARREN, retired professional society administrator; b. Mpls., Jan. 29, 1929; s. Walter E. and Eileen L. J.; m. Marion Louise Myrland; children: Daniel Warren, Karen Louise, Nancy Marie. BA, U. Minn., 1951. CEO Am. Collectors Assn., Inc., Mpls., 1955-96; ret., 1996. Bd. dirs. Western Nat. Ins. Group, Western Nat. Ins. Co., Mpls. and Seattle. Author: Political Christians, 1979, You Can Manage Your Money, 1981, 38 Days to Cape Town, 1981, Credit Guide for Collectors, 1984, The Pearls of Saigon, 1987, The Use of Humor in Public Speaking Is No Joke!, 1991, 53 Days to Beijing, 1991, The Strange Blood of East Africa, 1995. Mem. Mpls. City Coun., 1963-67; mem. Minn. State Ho. of Reps., 1967-74, asst. majority leader, 1972-74; Rep. candidate for Gov. of Minn., 1974; v.p. Mt. Olivet Luth. Ch. With USNR, 1947-53. Mem. Am. Soc. Assn. Execs. (chmn. bd. 1986-87), U.S. C. of C. (chmn. bd. regents 1973, bd. dirs. 1990-92), Minn. Soc. Assn. Execs. (past pres.). Lutheran. Office: 5108 James Ave S Minneapolis MN 55419

JOHNSON, JOHN WILLIAM, JR., executive recruiter; b. St. Petersburg, Fla., Dec. 10, 1932; s. John William and Elizabeth (Lowitz) J.; m. Cecelia Lynn Wescott, Feb. 6, 1960; children: William Wescott, James Robert, Gayle McCrimmon. AB, Wesleyan U., Middletown, Conn., 1954; postgrad., NYU, 1958-59. With Benton and Bowles, Inc., N.Y.C., 1958-82, v.p., account supr., 1963-70, sr. v.p., mgmt. supr., 1970-82, adminstr. profit sharing plan, 1969-82, dir., 1977-82; with Webb, Johnson Assocs., N.Y.C., 1982—2002, founder, former pres., 1982-95, mng. dir., 1995-2000, sr. mng. dir., 2000—02; co-founder, mng. dir. Johnson & Norinsky Assocs., 2002—. Mem. Scarsdale Planning Bd., 1984-88, Scarsdale Non-Partisan Jud. Qualifications Com., 1987-92, Scarsdale Bd. Ethics, 1995-2000; pres. Rainsford House Assn., N.Y.C., 1964-66, bd. dirs., 1962-70; bd. mgrs. Jacob Riis Settlement, 1963-89; bd. dirs. St. Christopher's Inc., 1965-2000, hon. bd. dirs., 2000—; mem. parents steering com. Coll. William and Mary, 1987-91; warden Ch. St. James the Less, Scarsdale, 1993-95; trustee Healthcare Chaplaincy, 1999-2005. Pilot USNR, 1954-58 Decorated China Def. Ribbon; co-honoree Scarsdale Hist. Soc. award, 1996. Mem. Winged Foot Golf Club, Sky Club, Mid Ocean Club, Harbour Ridge Club. Office: 1 Dag Hammarskjold Plaza 34th Fl New York NY 10017 Home: 24 Stonygate Oval New Rochelle NY 10804 Office Phone: 212-224-7477.

JOHNSON, JOHNNY, research psychologist, consultant; b. Clarksdale, Miss., Jan. 10, 1938; s. Eddie B. and Elizabeth (Ousley) J.; children: Tonya, Anita. Student, Coahoma Jr. Coll., 1957, Hunter Coll., 1964, N.Y.U., 1963; BS, Tenn. State U., 1970, MS, 1974; postgrad., Saybrook Inst., 1987-89. Instr. Dept. of the Navy, Millington, Tenn., 1976-80, edn. specialist, 1980-87, curriculum advisor, 1987-88; prof. human resources mgmt. Pepperdine U., L.A., 1975-77; prof. psychology Shelby State C.C., Memphis, Tenn., 1985—. Actor: (films) Elvis, 1989, Memphis, 1990, The Firm, 1993, A Family Thing, 1995; recording artist with releases in jazz, blues and Latino. With USN, 1957-63. Mem. APA (assoc.), Am. Psychol. Soc., Soc. Psychol. Study of Social Issues, Assn. Black Psychologists, Soc. Psychol. Study Gay and Lesbian Issues, Internat. Platform Assn. Avocations: golf, dog breeding, music, foreign languages, pocket billiards. Home: 773 Margie Dr Memphis TN 38127-2727 Office Phone: 901-357-5613. E-mail: JJuanCool@aol.com.

JOHNSON, JOHNNY RAY, retired mathematics professor; b. Chatham, La., Dec. 19, 1929; s. Dave Ernest and Bessie (Morris) J.; m. Betty Ann Moore, Oct. 21, 1960 (div. May 1982); children: Todd Michael, John Fitzgerald, Shauna Renee; m. Barbara F. Kennedy, June 1, 1990. BS, La. Tech U., 1951; MS, Auburn U., 1953, PhD, 1959. Registered profl. engr., La. Asst. prof. math. La. Tech U., 1958-62; assoc. prof. math. Appalachian State U., 1962-63; prof. elec. engring. La. State U., Baton Rouge, 1963-83, prof. emeritus, 1983—; prof. math. U. North Ala., 1984-95, prof. emeritus, 1995—. Adj. prof. elec. engring. U. Fla., Gainesville, 1976-77; mem. staff Combat Ops. Research Group, Ft. Monroe, Va., summer 1957; mathematician Boeing Co., New Orleans, summer 1965; engring. specialist Gen. Dynamics, 1983-84 Author: (with David E. Johnson) Mathematical Methods in Engineering and Physics, 1965, Graph Theory with Engineering Applications, 1972, Introductory Electric Circuit Analysis, 1981, Linear Systems Analysis, 1975; (with David E. Johnson and John L. Hilburn) Basic Electric Circuit Analysis, 1978, 3d edit., 1986, 4th edit., 1990, (with David E. Johnson, John L. Hilburn and Peter D. Scott) 5th edit., 1995, (with David E. Johnson and Harry P. Moore) A Handbook of Active Filters, 1980, (with David E. Johnson) A Funny Thing Happened on the Way to the White House, 1983, revised edit., 2004, (with David E. Johnson and John L. Hilburn) Electric Circuit Analysis, 1989, 2d edit., 1991, Introduction to Digital Signal Processing, 1989, (with David E. Johnson, John L. Hilburn & Peter D. Scott) Electric Circuit Analysis, 3d edit., 1997. Pres. Wildwood PTA, 1973-74. Served with AUS, 1954-56. Mem. IEEE (sr. 1968-93, Centennial medal 1984), U. North Ala. Inst. for Learning in Retirement (v.p., chmn. curriculum com. 1997-98, treas. 1998-99), Sigma Xi, Tau Beta Pi, Phi Kappa Phi, Eta Kappa Nu, Pi Mu Epsilon, Kappa Mu Epsilon. Home: 209 Wesley Ct Florence AL 35630-1486 Personal E-mail: jjohnson66@sprynet.com.

JOHNSON, JON L., advertising executive; Chmn., CEO, dir. Publicis, Salt Lake City. Office: 132 Pierpont Ave STE 200 Salt Lake City UT 84101-1905

JOHNSON, JONATHAN EDWIN, II, lawyer; b. Whittier, Calif., May 1, 1936; s. Roger Edwin and Louise (Thompson) J.; m. Clare Hardy, June 23, 1963 (dec. 1995); children: Jonathan III, Hardy, Benjamin, Adam, Rufus, Bradford, Roger, Ralph; m. Garnet Kalsched, June 17, 2000. BChemE, Cornell U., 1959, MBA, 1960; JD with honors, George Washington U., 1963. Bar: Calif. 1964; cert. specialist family law, Calif. Assoc. Tuttle & Taylor, L.A., 1963-65; pvt. practice L.A., 1965-67; ptnr. Johnson & Jarvis, L.A., 1967-68, Johnson, Poulson, Coons & Slater, L.A., 1968—. Instr. paralegal probate U. West L.A. Sch. Law, 1974; mem. clergy adv. com. to supt. edn., City of L.A., 1978-81. Named Outstanding Lawyer, J. Reuben Clark Law Soc.-L.A. Chpt., 2000, a So. Calif. Super Lawyer, 2004, 2005. Fellow Am. Acad. Matrimonial Lawyers (counsel So. Calif. chpt. 1998-99); mem. Calif. State Bar Assn. (legis. com. family law sect. 1978-88, chmn. 1980), Beverly Hills Bar Assn. (exec. com. family law sect. 1977-82, 86-88, 91—, chmn. 2003-2004), Inter-stake Bus. and Profl. Assn. L.A. (pres. 1974), Cornell Club of So. Calif. (pres. 1966-68), Order of Coif, Sigma Chi, Phi Delta Phi. Lds Ch. Home: 1094 Acanto Pl Los Angeles CA 90049-1604 Office: Johnson Poulson & Coons 10880 Wilshire Blvd Ste 1100 Los Angeles CA 90024-4112 Office Phone: 310-475-0611.

JOHNSON, JOSEPH CLAYTON, JR., lawyer; b. Vicksburg, Miss., Nov. 15, 1943; s. Joseph Clayton and Rose Butler (Levy) J.; m. Cherrian Frances Turpin, Oct. 24, 1970; children: Mary Clayton, Erik Cole. BS, La. State U., 1965, JD, 1969. Bar: La. 1969, U.S. Dist. Ct. (ea. and mid. dists.) La. 1969, U.S. Dist. Ct. (we. dist.) La. 1979, U.S. Ct. Appeals (5th cir.) 1982. Ptnr. Taylor, Porter, Brooks & Phillips, Baton Rouge, 1969—. Mem. civil justice reform act com. U.S. Dist. Ct. (mid. dist.) La., 1995-97, chmn. 1996-97; mem. La. Atty. Disciplinary Bd., 1997-99. Bd. editors Oil and Gas Reporter, 1988—2005. Pres. Baton Rouge area Am. Cancer Soc., 1987—88; mem. adv. bd. Ctr. for Energy Law, 2000—05. With U.S. Army, 1969—75. Recipient John Rogers award, 1999, Ctr. for Am. and Internat. Law. Master: Dean Henry George McMahon Am. Inn of Ct.; mem.: Ctr. for Am. and Internat. Law (bd. editors Oil and Gas Reporter), Baton Rouge Bar Assn., La. State Law Inst. (mineral code com.), La. Bar Assn. (mem. ho. of dels. 1979—92, coun. rep. mineral law sect. 1986—94, chmn. mineral law sect. 1992—93). Republican. Methodist. Office: PO Box 2471 Baton Rouge LA 70821-2471 Office Phone: 225-387-3221. E-mail: clay.johnson@taylorporter.com.

JOHNSON, JOSEPH EGGLESTON, III, physician, educator; b. Elberton, Ga., Sept. 17, 1930; s. Joseph Eggleston Jr. and Marie (Williams) J.; m. Judith H. Kemp, Jan. 21, 1956; children: Joseph Eggleston IV, Judith Ann, Julie Marie. BA cum laude, Vanderbilt U., 1951, MD, 1954. Diplomate Am. Bd. Internal Medicine (bd. govs. 1977-83, exec. com. 1981-83), Am. Bd. Allergy and Immunology. Intern Johns Hopkins Hosp., Balt., 1954-55, resident, 1957-61, physician, 1961-66; mem. faculty Johns Hopkins Med. Sch., Balt., 1961-66, asst. dean, 1963-66; chief infectious diseases U. Fla. Coll. Medicine, Gainsville, 1966-72, assoc. dean, 1970-72; prof., chmn. dept. Bowman Gray Sch. Medicine, Winston-Salem, N.C., 1972-85; chief med. service N.C. Baptist Hosp., mem. residency rev. com. internal medicine, 1978-83, chmn. residency rev. com. internal medicine, 1983-85; dean Med. Sch., prof. medicine U. Mich., Ann Arbor, 1985-90, prof. internal medicine, 1985-93; accreditation commn. on grad. med. edn., 1988-93; sr. v.p. membership and spl. advisor to exec. v.p. Am. Coll. Physicians, Phila., 1993—, interim exec. v.p., 1994-95. Adj. prof. of medicine U. Pa., 1994—. Contbr. articles to profl. jours. Served to lt. USNR, 1955-57. John and Mary R. Markle scholar, 1962-67; Mead-Johnson postgrad. scholar, 1960-61 Fellow ACP (sci. program com. 1979-85, chmn. sci. program com. 1982-85, chmn. elect bd. govs. 1985, chmn. bd. govs., bd. regents 1985-93, gov.-elect N.C. 1981-82, gov. N.C. 1982-86, treas. 1991-93, interim exec. v.p. 1994-95), Am. Acad. Allergy, Royal Soc. Medicine (travelling fellow 1970-71); mem. AMA (chmn. Med. Sch. sect. 1990-91, alternate del. 1996-2003), Internat. Soc. Internal Medicine (pres. 2000-02), Am. Fedn. Clin. Rsch., Assn. Am. Physicians, Infectious Diseases Soc. Am., Soc. Exptl. Biology and Medicine, N.Y. Acad. Scis., Am. Assn. Immunologists, So. Soc. Clin. Investigation, Am. Soc. for Microbiology, Assn. Profs. Medicine (sec.-treas. 1978-81, pres.-elect 1981-82, pres. 1982-83), Am. Clin. and Climatol. Assn., Société Française de la Tuberculose et des Maladies Respiratoires, Assn. Program Dirs. in Internal Medicine (exec. coun. 1980-83), Assn. Am. Med. Colls. (exec. coun. 1983-85), Coun. Acad. Socs. (adminstrv. bd. 1978-85), Federated Coun. for Internal Medicine (vice chmn. 1981-82, chmn. 1982-83), Johns Hopkins Soc. Scholars, Phi Beta Kappa, Sigma Alpha Epsilon, Phi Chi, Omicron Delta Kappa, Alpha Omega Alpha. Office: Am Coll Physicians Independence Mall West 6th St at Race Philadelphia PA 19106 E-mail: jjohnson@mail.acponline.org.

JOHNSON, JOY ANN, diagnostic radiologist; b. New Richmond, Wis., Aug. 16, 1952; d. Howard James and Shirley Maxine (Eidem) J.que BA in Chemistry summa cum laude, U. No. Colo., 1974; D of Medicine, U. Colo., 1978. Diplomate Am. Bd. Radiology, Nat. Bd. Med. Examiners; cert. added qualification pediatric radiology. Resident in radiology U. Colo., 1978-81, fellow in pediat. radiology, 1981-82; asst. prof. diagnostic radiology and pediatrics, chief sect. pediatric radiology Clin. Radiology Found. U. Kans. Med. Ctr., Kansas City, 1982-87; radiologist Radiology Assocs. Ltd., Kansas City, Mo., 1987-92; mem. staff Bapt. Med. Ctr., Kansas City, Mo., 1987-92; radiologist Children's Mercy Hosp., Kansas City, 1992-95, Leavenworth-Kansas City Imaging, 1996—; assoc. prof. U. Mo., Kansas City, 1992—; chief of staff Cushing Mem. Hosp., 2002—04. Speaker Radiol. Soc. Republic of China, 1985, RSNA 2000 panel mem. Contbr. articles to med. jours. Nat. Cancer Inst. fellow, 1982. Mem. AMA, Am. Coll. Radiology, Radiol. Soc. N.Am., Am. Inst. Ultrasound in Medicine (mem. program com. Kansas City 1984), Soc. Pediatric Radiology (mem. com. for cmty. bsed pediat. radiologists 1998-2003), Am. Assn. Women in Radiology, Lambda Sigma Tau. Avocations: horseback riding, physical fitness, sports, reading. Office: Leavenworth-Kansas City Imaging 9201 Parallel Pkwy Kansas City KS 66112-1528

JOHNSON, JOY NOREEN, artist, construction executive; b. Iron Mountain, Mich., Mar. 8, 1937; d. Walter George and Martha Martina J.; m. William Louis Johnson, Aug. 8. 1959; children: Jody Noreen, Cheryl Christine. Nursing Diploma, Northwestern U., 1958; BA magna cum laude, Calif. State U., 1981, MA with distinction, 1983. V.p. Staiger Constrn., Fresno, Calif., 1976-94, sec., treas., 1994—; presenter, spkr., lectr. in field. One woman shows include Calif. State U., Fresno, 1978, 83, 94, Gallery 25, Fresno, 1980, 82, 84, 85, 86, 91, 93, 97, Plums Gallery, Fresno, 1989, 92, 99, Clarks Gallery, Bakersfield, Calif., 1991, Gallery M, Fresno, 1991, Fresno Art Mus., 1995, Lincoln Art Ctr., Colo., 1996, Merced (Calif.) Art Ctr., 1996, Bakersfield Coll., 1998; group shows include Fresno Art Mus., 1978, 86, 91-93, Gallery 25, 1980, 81, 82, 83, 84, 85, 92, 94, 96, 97, 98, 00, Matrix Gallery, Sacramento, 1981, Calif. State U., Fresno, 1981, 94, Long Beach, 1990, Fresno County Pub. Health Bldg., 1982, Gina B., Beverly Hills, Calif., 1988, Pieces Gallery, Highland Park, Ill., 1989, Taylor Gratzer Gallery, West Hollywood, Calif., 1989, Sidney Rothman Gallery, N.J., 1990, Beach Vision Gallery, 1991, Gallery M., 1991; represented in permanent collections including Fresno Art Mus.; featured in numerous catalogues, mags., tv interviews including San Joaquin Valley Mag., Artists of Central and Northern California, Next Wave, Artists to Watch in the 90's, West Art, Fresno Art Mus. preview, Channel 30, Channel 47, Channel 18, numerous others. Participant Fresno (Calif.) Interfaith, 1997—; mem. selection com. women's coun. Fresno Art Mus., 1990—, bd. dirs. Women's Coun. of 100, 1994—, pres., 1995-97; mem. Gallery 25, Fresno, 1978—, pres., 1982, lectr. Artist, interpreter A-Z grantee Fresno Art Mus., 1994; recipient Winners Circle award Am. Cancer Soc., 1995. Mem. Coalition of Women's Art Orgns. (nat. bd. dirs. 1983), Phi Kappa Phi.

JOHNSON, JOYCE, retired military officer; m. Jim Calderwood; 1 child, James. DO, Mich. State U., 1980; DSc (hon.), Des Moines U., 2002. Commd. into US Pub. Health Svc.; various positions US Food and Drug Adminstrn., Nat. Inst. Mental Health, Substance Abuse and Mental Health Svcs. Adminstrn.; chief med. officer, surgeon gen. US Coast Guard, 1997—2003, dir. health and safety, 1997—2003, ret., 2003; v.p. health scis. Battelle Meml. Inst., Arlington, Va., 2004—. Bd. trustees US Coast Guard Acad. Named Physician Exec. Yr.; recipient Dr. Nathan Davis award for outstanding govt. svc., Am. Med. Assn. Achievements include among the first to do AIDS rsch. with Ctr. Disease Control, Atlanta; first female flag officer with USCG; first woman to serve on bd. trustees Coast Guard Acad. Avocations: cooking, travel.

JOHNSON, JOYCE ANN, elementary school educator; b. Phila., Dec. 7, 1950; d. Walter Scott and Marie Therese (Uhlman) J. BA in Elem. Edn., Bethany (W.Va.) Coll., 1973. Elem. tchr. Avalon (N.J.) Bd. Edn., 1973—; ret., 2005. Named Avalon Tchr. of Yr., Gov.'s Tchr. Recognition Program, 1993. Mem. NEA, N.J. Edn. Assn. Cape May County Edn. Assn. (chmn. fund raising 1987-90), Avalon Edn. Assn. (pres. 1985-90), Embroiderers Guild Am., Country Shore Woman's Club (trustee 1989-90, treas. 1990-92, 1st v.p. 1993-95, pres. 1995-97, 3d v.p. 1997-99). Democrat. Episcopalian. Avocations: travel, reading, handwork. Home: 46 Jill Ave # 986 Marmora NJ 08223-1152

JOHNSON, JUDITH A., educational administrator; b. Bklyn., July 17, 1939; d. Charles Washington and Gwendolyn (Allen) Lockley; divorced; children: Pamela Johnson, Paul Johnson. BA, Bklyn. Coll., 1961; MA, NYU, 1966; 6th yr. cert., SUNY, New Paltz, 1981; postgrad., Columbia U., 1984—. Tchr. N.Y.C. Pub. Schs., 1960-62, asst. prin., guidance counselor, 1964-66, coord. guidance, 1971-73; prin. Mamaroneck (N.Y.) Pub. Schs., 1974-79; dir. instrnl. svcs. So. Westchester Bd. Coop. Ednl. Svcs., Portchester, N.Y., 1979-85; dir. curriculum K-12 Nyack (N.Y.) Pub. Schs., 1985-90; asst. supt. for curriculum and instrn. White Plains (N.Y.) Pub. Schs., 1990-97; dep. asst. secy Office of Elementary and Secondary Edn., Washington, DC, 1997—. Co-author curriculum guides. Recipient cert. of appreciation Phi Delta Kappa, 1982, Founder's award Westchester Prins. Ctr., 1988, One of 100 Exec. Educator's N.Am. award Nat. Sch. Bd. Assn., 1990, achievement award Nyack Bd. Edn., 1990; also numerous grants and awards in field. Mem. Assn. for Supervision and Curriculum Devel. (nat. bd. dirs. 1986-88), N.Y. State Assn. for Supervision and Curriculum Devel. (sec., bd. dirs. 1986—), Am. Ednl. Rsch. Assn., NAACP. Avocations: theater, concerts, walking, tennis. Home: 48 Fessler Dr Spring Valley NY 10977-2004

JOHNSON, JUDY M., artist, writer; b. Marquette, Mich., Aug. 11, 1946; d. Lowell Kenneth and Helen C. (Heath) Johnson; children: Jenny R. Taliadoros, Kenneth R. Taylor. Student, Mich. State U., 1964-66. Cert. EFT energy practitioner, hypno-therapist and past-life regressions. Artist B. Shackman Pub., N.Y.C., 1984-90, Dover Publs., N.Y.C., 1986—; writer miscellaneous nat. publs., 1984—; lead artist Magicloth Toys, Concord, Mass., 1995—2000; owner Judy's Place Online Mail Order, Skandia, Mich., 1978—; artist Schilling Toys, Bowling, Mass., 2001—. Writer of verse Marion Heath Greeting Cards, Wareham, Mass., 1994-95; chmn. Art on the Rocks, Marquette, 1994, 2001; mng. editor Original Paper Doll Artists Guild "OPDAG Paper Doll Studio", Kingfield, Mass., 1984—. Author, artist paper dolls; author, editor 2 Twp. Centennial History Books, 1992, 95, pictorial archives; author, pub. herb books, humor books; pub. Lake Superior Art Assn. newsletter KIOSK,1993-2001, self publish, paper doll art mail order and website. Cmty. activist in ecology and art, Mich., 1960—; lay spkr. United Meth. Ch., Alma and ctrl. Mich., 1983-88. Mem. Lake Superior Art Assn. (chair arts show 1994—2001). Avocations: herbs, creative cooking, reading, family. Home: PO Box 216 Skandia MI 49885-0216 Office: PO Box 216 Skandia MI 49885-0216 Office Phone: 906-942-7865. Personal E-mail: judyspapergoods@charter.net.

JOHNSON, JULIA A., writer; b. Des Plaines, Ill., Sept. 8, 1961; d. John J. and Margaret J. Roarty; m. Quinten R. Johnson; 1 child, Raymond. BA English, Mount St. Mary's Coll., Emmitsburg, Md., 1983. Office svcs. pers. First Boston Corp., N.Y.C., 1984—86; fixed income trader Kidder Peabody, Inc., N.Y.C., 1986—88; mergers & acquisitions staff Scott-Macon, Ltd., N.Y.C., 1991—92; brokerage asst. Paine Webber, Hackensack, NJ, 1997—98; pub. rels. writer In House, Inc., Vienna, Va., 2000—01; freelance writer, pub. rels. cons. Julie Johnson, Leesburg, Va., 1993—. Writer, cons. Issue Action Publs., Leesburg, Va., 1999—2000. Author: (novels) Loudoun County: Blending Tradition with Innovation, 2000; contbr. articles to profl. jours. Mem.: Loudoun C. of C., Loudoun County C. of C. Democrat. Roman Catholic. Avocations: running, travel, hiking, biking, reading. Office: PO Box 285 Leesburg VA 20178-0285

JOHNSON, JULIA F., bank executive; Sr. v.p. Banc One Corp, Columbus, Ohio, 1993—; with Bank One, Columbus, 1985—99, dir., office of info. and policy, 1999—2003. Office: Banc One Corp Dept OH-0152 100 E Broad St Dept Oh-152 Columbus OH 43215-3607

JOHNSON, JULIE MARIE, lawyer, lobbyist, judge; b. Aberdeen, S.D., Aug. 7, 1953; d. Howard B. and Jerauldine (Dilly) J.; m. Bryan L. Hisel. BA in Govt., Comm., U. S.D., 1974, MA in Polit. Sci., JD, U. S.D., 1976. Bar: S.D. 1977, U.S. Dist. Ct. S.D. 1977. Assoc. Siegel, Barnett Law Firm, Aberdeen, 1977; law clk. Fifth Judicial Circuit Ct., Aberdeen, 1977-78; ptnr. Maloney, Kolker, Fritz, Hogan & Johnson, Aberdeen, 1978-84; dep. sec. S.D. Dept. Labor, Aberdeen, Pierre, 1983-84, sec. Gov.'s Cabinet, 1985-87; pres. Industry and Commerce Assn. of S.D., Pierre, 1987-95; sec., Gov.'s Cabinet S.D. Dept. Revenue, Pierre, 1995; exec. dir. S.D. Rural Devel. Coun., Pierre, 1995—2003; acting exec. dir. S.D. Math., Sci. and Tech. Coun., 2002—03; adminstrv. law judge State of S.D., 2003—; chair Govs. Red Tape Task Force, 2004—. Adj. faculty S.D. State U., 1996—. Treas. S.D. Cmty. Found., Pierre, 1987-95; mem. Pvt. Industry Coun., 1985-87, S.D. Coun. on Vocat. Edn., 1985-87; bd. dirs. Mo. Shores Women's Resource Ctr., Pierre, 1988-89; chmn. S.D. Main St. Adv. Coun., 1987-91; bd. dirs. United Way, 1988-96, chmn., 1991; mem. Shortgrass Arts Coun., 1987—, South Dakotans for the Arts, 1981—, Solid Waste Mgmt. Plan Task Force, 1990, S.D. Citizens Adv. Coun. on Hazardous Waste, 1991-92, gov.'s adv. coun. on health care reform, 1992-93, gov.'s Homestate Underground Lab adv. coun., 2002-04; bd. dirs. Hist. S.D. Found., 1996-99; founding mem., legal counsel Outdoor Women of S.D., Inc., 1995—; bd. trustees USD Found., 1992—; trustee, mem. bus. affairs com., 1996—, com. on trustees, Kelley Ctr. for Entrepreneurship adv. bd., presdl. search com. Dakota Wesleyan U., 1999-2000; founding mem., treas. S.D. Discovery Ctr. and Aquarium, Inc., bd. dirs., 1988-92; mem. S.D. Water Congress, 1990-97, bd. dirs., 1987-95; bd. dirs. Nyoda Girl Scout Coun., 1997-99; mem. adv. bd. W.O. Farber Ctr. for Excellence in Civic Leadership, 1998—; bd. dirs. Farber Fund, 1987—; founding mem. S.D. Chambers and Econ. Devel. Coun., 1989—; mem. Network Mgmt. Team Nat. Rural Devel. Partnership, 1998-2001; course leader Leadership Ctrl. S.D., 1996—; mem. Children's Care Hosp. and Sch. Found. Bd., 1997—, vice chair, 2005—, investment com., 1999—, joint exec. com., 2003—, devel. com., 2004—, chair governance com., 2005—; mem. Nat. Rural Devel. Partnership Presdl. Transition Team, 2000-01, Agr. and Econ. Devel. Task Force, 2001, S.D. Habitat for Humanity Bd., 2001—, vice chair, 2005—; bd. dirs. Historic S.D. Found., 1995-98, Genesis of Innovation, 2000-03; acting exec. dir. S.D. Math., Sci. and Tech. Coun., 2000-03; vol. chmn. S.D. WWII Meml. Dedication, 2001; vol. chair S.D. Korean War Meml. Dedication Com., 2003-04, seating/decorating co-chair, 2003-04; chmn. Govs. Red Tape Task Force, 2004—, vice chiar, 2005—; bd. dirs. S.D. Habitat for Humanity, 2001—, vice chair, 2005—; founder, treas. Friends of Discovery Ctr., S.D.;

trustee, mem. coms. Dakota Wesleyan U., Children's Care Hosp. Found., U. S.D. Found.; active S.D. Vietnam War Meml., 2005—, chair dignitaries, 2005—, legal counsel, 2005—. RJR Nabisco fellow Women Execs. in State Govt., Harvard, 1986; named Outstanding Young Citizen Jaycees, Aberdeen, 1982, S.D. Jaycees, 1983. Mem. S.D. Bar Assn. (chmn. adminstrv. law com. 2001-04, chair adminstrv. law sect., 2004—, mem. CLE com., Worker's compensation com., chmn. ad law sect. 2004—), Industry and Commerce Assn. S.D. (bd. dirs. 1985-87), U. S.D. Alumni Assn. (exec. com. 1987-96, pres. 1990-92), AAUW, Bus. and Profl. Women U.S.A. (nat. legis. chmn. 1987-88, 92-94, nat. chmn. issues mgmt. 1991-93, pres. S.D. 1984-85, Woman of Yr. award Aberdeen chpt. 1982), Women Execs. in State Govt. (bd. didrs. 1985-87), Coun. State Mfrs. Assn., S.D. Mining Assn. (bd. dirs. 1991-95, Gold PAC, 1995-), Nat. Indsl. Coun., Coun. State C.'s of C., Ducks Unltd., Rotary, Zonta, WIG Investment Club, Women's Investment Group, Rocky Mountain Elk Found. Republican. Lutheran. Address: 1100 E Church St Apt 352 Pierre SD 57501-2354 Office: 210 E 4th St Pierre SD 57501 Home: 1414 Sharpstone Dr Mitchell SD 57301-6250 Business E-Mail: juliem.johnson@state.sd.us.

JOHNSON, JULIE WEST, secondary school educator, writer; b. Fargo, N.D., Apr. 19, 1947; d. Edmund Elwell and Lillian Lindbergh (Christie) Johnson; m. Lance Jeffrey Rips, Apr. 18, 1976; 1 child, Eve Clare Johnson Rips. BA, Swarthmore Coll., 1969; MA, Stanford U., 1972. Cert. secondary tchr. (life). Editorial asst. New Yorker mag., N.Y.C., 1969-70; English tchr. Notre Dame Acad., Belmont, Calif., 1972-74; tchr. English New Trier High Sch., Winnetka, Ill., 1974—; free-lance writer McDougal, Littell Pubs., Evanston, Ill., 1980—. Author: Literature 9, 1983, 2d rev. edit., 1987, 91, Literature 11, 1984, 2d rev. edit., 1987, 91. Mem. Nat. Council Tchrs. English, Ill. Assn. Tchrs. English, New Trier Tchrs. Assn. Avocations: fiction writing, theater, classical music, cinema. Home: 1801 Asbury Ave Evanston IL 60201-3503 Office: New Trier High Sch 385 Winnetka Ave Winnetka IL 60093-4238 Office Phone: 847-784-6522.

JOHNSON, KAREN, professional society administrator; b. Jersey City, N.J. BS, Loretto Heights Coll., 1977; MS, Yale U., 1984. Cert. mental health clin. nurse specialist. Commd. nurse officer USAF, advanced through grades to lt. col., ret., 1992; from mem. staff to v.p. NOW, Washington, 1975—90, co-chair, nat. com. on racial diversity, 1990—93, v.p. Washington, 1993—2001, exec. v.p., 2001—. Mem., nat. bd. dirs, NOW, 1986-90; adv. bd. Cornell U. Peace Studies Program's Women in the Military Project. Contbr. articles to mags. Vol. soup kitchens, New Haven, Conn., Dayton, Ohio, San Antonio Free Clin., San Antonio Battered Women's Shelter; sr. ptnr. Partners Program, Denver; bd. mem. Am. Cancer Soc., Greene County, Ohio. Recipient Keeper of the Flame award State of Ohio, 1990; decorated Air Force Commendation medal 1992. Mem. Kappa Gamma Pi, Sigma Theta Tau. Office: NOW 733 15th St NW 2nd Fl Washington DC 20005

JOHNSON, KAREN ELAINE, secondary school educator, tax preparer; b. San Diego, Feb. 7, 1957; d. Alan Jerome and Clarex Irene Johnson. AA, Mesa Coll., San Diego, 1978; BA, San Diego State U., 1981; MA, Calif. State U, San Bernardino, 1985; MS, Nat. U., Vista, Calif., 1993. Cert. tchr., reading specialist, adminstrv. svcs. Calif. Tchr. William S. Hart Union H.S. Dist., Newhall, Calif., 1982, San Jacinto (Calif.) Unified Sch. Dist., 1982—85, Grossmont Union H.S. Dist., La Mesa, Calif., 1985—86, Oceanside Unified Sch. Dist., 1986—; tax preparer H & R Block, Encinitas, Calif., 1996—2001. Mem. Oceanside Unified Sch. Dist. Strategic Plan Com., 1996—; chair-8th grade lang. arts/social studies Oceanside Unified Sch. Dist., 1989—99. Mem.: AAUW (Carlsbad bd. dirs. 1992—2004, legal advocacy v.p. 2000—04, Carlsbad bd. dirs. 2002—05, named Gift Honoree 1993, 1996, 1999), Delta Kappa Gamma (Carlsbad chpt. rec. sec. 1993—95, 1997—99, corr. sec. 2000—04, chpt. pres. 2004—). Avocations: crocheting, knitting, music, reading. Home: 2651 Regent Rd Carlsbad CA 92008-6413 Office: Oceanside Unified Sch Dist 2111 Mission Ave Oceanside CA 92054 Personal E-mail: bigbodaciousbabe@yahoo.com.

JOHNSON, KATHARINE DECKER, artist; b. Piqua, Ohio, Apr. 24, 1951; d. Richard Patrick and Joan Decker; m. Gary William Johnson, May 21, 1994. BA, Xavier U., 1974; masters cert. scientific illustration, U. Calif., Santa Cruz, 1996. Graphic artist G&S Typesetters, Austin, 1985-86; tech. illustrator Tektronix, Inc., Beaverton, Oreg., 1987-90; illustrator Holt, Reinhart & Winston, Austin, 1990-91; tech. illustrator Nat. Instruments Corp., Austin, 1991-94; artist, illustrator EE Design, Livermore, Calif., 1994—; scientific illustrator Livermore Area Recreation and Park Dist., 1995—. Illustrator LabView Graphical Programming, 1994, 2d edit., 1997, LabView Power Programming, 1998, Modern Physics, 1991, World Geography Today, 1991, Biology 2000, 1991; exhibited in group shows Buffalo Mus. of Sci., 1997, Chgo. Bot. Garden, 1997, Mus. of Art and History, 1997, Smithsonian Instn., 1996, No. Ariz. U., 1995, Washington State Conv. Ctr., 1993, 94, 95, 96. Mem. Guild of Nat. Sci. Illustrators, Am. Soc. of Botanical Artists. Office: EE Design 4086 Compton Ct Livermore CA 94550-3453

JOHNSON, KAY DURBAHN, real estate manager, consultant; b. Crookston, Minn., Apr. 4, 1937; d. Wilbert John and Frieda (Johnson) Durbahn; m. Ray Arvin Johnson, May 14, 1960; children: Sherry Kay Johnson Johnston, Diane Rosalind Johnson Peterson, Laura Faye Johnson Gill. BA, U. Minn., 1959. Reference analyst Indsl. Rels. Ctr. U. Minn., Mpls., 1959-61; real estate mgr. Minnetonka, Minn., 1976—; ptnr. Broadmoor Plantation Investors, Fargo, ND, 1976—2005; v.p. D&T Property, Inc., Minnetonka, 1990—, also bd. dirs.; v.p. Comreco, LLC, 2002—, bd. dirs. Tax reduction cons. R.A. Johnson & Assocs., Minnetonka, 1985—; bd. dirs. Empire Aggregate, Inc., 2001—. City of Minnetonka Planning Commn., 1972-74, vice chair, 1973-74; mem. Land Use Task Force, 1972-74; liaison Ridgedale Devel.; mem. choir, various coun. positions Minnetonka Luth. Ch. Mem. Mpls. Inst. Arts. Republican. Avocations: art, music, travel. *For greater happiness try to balance your life by making time for all aspects of living, including activities to meet social, spiritual, physical, family, work, and intellectual needs.*

JOHNSON, KEITH LIDDELL, chemical company executive; b. Darlington, England, July 22, 1939; came to U.S., 1948, naturalized, 1958; s. Arthur Henry and Beatrice (Liddell) J.; m. Margaret Elaine Meston, Aug. 29, 1959; children: Leslie Margaret, Kevin Liddell, Gregory Norman, Kathleen Elaine; 1 ward, Ann Louise Warwick. BA, U. Mich., 1960. Chem. technician Ajem Labs., Livonia, Mich., 1956-60; rsch. chemist labs. Swift & Co., Chgo., 1960-63, project mgr., 1963-67, group leader R&D ctr. Oak Brook, Ill., 1967-71, adminstrv. asst. to exec. v.p. Chgo., 1971-72, quality assurance dir., 1974-78, group mgr. plant quality assurance, 1978-82; quality assurance mgr. refinery divsn. Swift Edible Oil Co. subs. Swift & Co., Chgo., 1972-73, corp. quality assurance mgr., 1973-74; tech. dir. Norman Fox & Co., L.A., 1982-83, br. mgr., 1983-88, gen. mgr., 1988—, exec. v.p., dir., 1989—, pres., 1993—2003, vice chmn., 2003—. Bd. dirs. Lexard Corp., L.A., v.p. 1990-94; bd. dirs. Chem. Distbn. Network, Des Plaines, Ill.; mem. Chgo. Manpower Area Planning Com., 1971; mem. industry adv. bd. South Coast Air Quality Mgmt. Dist., Calif., 1982-84. Contbr. articles to profl. jours. V.p., dir. St. Martha's Sr. Care Ctr., West Covina, Calif., 1993—, chmn. bd., 1995-99, vestry St. Martha's Epsicopal Ch., sr. warden 1991-96, 98-2001; bd. dirs. St. Martha's Episcopal Sch., 1999-2001. Mem. Chgo. Chemists Club, Chem. Art Forum Chgo. (v.p. 1980, pres. 1981), Am. Chem. Soc. (chair elect so. Calif. sect. 2000-01, chair 2001—, mem. exec. com. 2000—), Soc. Cosmetic Chemists (membership chmn. Bay area chpt. 1985, chmn. 1987-88), Am. Oil Chemists Soc., Chem. Mktg. Assn. So. Calif., Internat. Union Pure and Applied Chemistry. Episcopalian. Achievements include 17 U.S. and 25 fgn. patents. Home: 342 Amberwood Dr Walnut CA 91789-2473 Office: Ste 150 200 Citadel Dr City Of Commerce CA 90040-1554 E-mail: keithjohnson@prodigy.net, kjohnson@norfox.ws.

JOHNSON, KELLY A., federal agency administrator; BS in Environ. Mgmt., with high honors, Rutgers U., Cook Coll.; MPA in Environ. Mgmt., Ind. U. Sch. Pub. and Environ. Affairs; JD magna cum laude, Ind. U. Sch. Law. Assoc. Holland & Hart, 1990—95; mem. Bush-Cheney transition team, US Dept. Interior; sr. counsel Senate Energy and Natural Resources Com.; primary adv. to asst. atty. gen., Environ. & Natural Resources divsn. US Dept. Justice, Washington, 2001—05, acting asst. atty. gen., Environment & Natural Resources divsn., 2005—. Office: US Dept Justice Environl and Natural Resources Divsn 950 Pennsylvania Ave Washington DC 20530*

JOHNSON, KELLY OVERSTREET, lawyer; b. Tallahassee, Fla., May 3, 1958; m. Hal Johnson; 2 children. BS in Real Estate and pre-Law, Fla. State Univ., 1979, JD with honors, 1982. Civil litigator Fla. Dept. of Legal Affairs, 1983—85; atty. Ervin, Varn, Jacobs, Odom & Kitchen, 1985—88; pvt. practice, 1988—90; ptnr. Broad and Cassel, Tallahassee, 1990—. Mem.: Am. Bar Assn. (Ho. of Del. 1992—94, 2003—), Tallahassee Women Lawyers (pres.), Tallahassee Bar Assn. (pres. 1990—91), Fla. Bar Assn. (young lawyers divsn. bd. gov. 1986—90, bd. of gov. 1997—, pres. 2004—05), Guardian Ad Litem Program, Legal Aid Found., Jr. League of Tallahassee. Office: Broad & Cassel 215 S Monroe St Ste 400 PO Box 11300 Tallahassee FL 32302-1300 Office Phone: 850-681-6810. Business E-Mail: kjohnson@broadandcassel.com.

JOHNSON, KENNETH F., lawyer; b. Ft. Bragg, Calif., June 10, 1938; s. Frank W. and Gertrude Johnson; m. Jane Perry Drennan, June 11, 1961; children: Erik, Mark. BSCE, U. Calif., Berkeley, 1962; JD, U. Calif., Hastings, 1969. Bar: Calif. 1970. Atty. Crosby Heafey Roach & May PC, Oakland, Calif., 1997—2003; of counsel ReedSmith LLP, Oakland, 2003—. Note and comment editor: Hastings Law Jour., 1968-69. Officer USNR, 1962—66. Scholar U. Calif. Hastings, 1967-68, 68-69. Mem. Calif. Bar Assn., Alameda County Bar Assn., Contra Costa County Bar Assn., Bar Assn. San Francisco, Assn. Bus. Trial Lawyers Assn., Order of Coif. Office: Reed Smith LLP 1999 Harrison St Fl 24 Oakland CA 94612-3520 Office Phone: 510-466-6724.

JOHNSON, KENNETH HARVEY, veterinary pathologist; b. Hallock, Minn., Feb. 17, 1936; s. Clifford H. and Alma (Anderson) J.; Sept. 17, 1960; children: Jeffrey, Gregory, Sandra. BS, U. Minn., 1958, DVM, 1960, PhD, 1965. Jr. asst. health officer NIH, Bethesda, Md., 1958; practice vet. medicine Edina, Minn., 1960; USPHS-NIH non-service fellow U. Minn., St. Paul, 1960-65, asst. prof. dept. vet. pathology and parasitology, 1965-69, assoc. prof., 1969-73, prof., 1973-98, prof. emeritus dept. vet. pathobiology, 1998—, head, sect. pathology, dept. vet. biology, 1974-76, chmn. dept. vet. pathobiology Coll. Vet Medicine, 1976-83. Cons. Minn. Mining & Mfg. Co., Medtronic Inc., Natural-Y Surg. Specialties; principle and co-investigator several NIH grants, 1965-98. Mem. editl. bd. Amyloid, the Internat. Jour. of Exptl. and Clin. Investigation; contbr. chpts.: Veterinary Clinics of North America, 1971, Spontaneous Animal Models of Human Disease, 1979, Kirk's Current Veterinary Therapy; contbr. articles to sci. jours. Councilman Nativity Lutheran Ch., St. Anthony Village, Minn., 1972-75. Recipient Tchr. of Yr. award, 1968-69, Norden award for disting. tchr. in vet. medicine, 1970, Beecham award for rsch. excellence, 1989, Ralston Purina Small Animal Rsch. award, 1990, Phi Zeta faculty achievement award, 1992, Outstanding Achievement award Bd. of Regents of U. Minn., 2001. Mem.: AAUP, Am. Soc. Investigative Pathology, Am. Coll. Veterinary Pathologists (hon.), Gamma Sigma Delta, Phi Zeta, Sigma Xi. Home: 3510 Skycroft Dr Minneapolis MN 55418-1780 E-mail: johns049@tc.umn.edu.

JOHNSON, KENNETH OSCAR, retired oil industry executive; b. Center City, Minn., Apr. 11, 1920; s. Oscar W. and Sigrid (Hollsten) Johnson; m. Margery Wheeler, Apr. 18, 1945; 1 child, Eric W. BSChemE, U. Minn., 1942. With Exxon Corp., Houston, 1942-74, heavy fuels mgr. supply dept., 1968-72, wholesale fuels sales mgr., mktg. dept., 1972-74; chmn., CEO Belcher Oil Co., Miami, Fla., 1974—88; bd. dirs. Coastal Corp., 1988—2001; ret., 2001. Cons., 2001—. Achievements include patents in field. Home: 845 Admiralty Parade Naples FL 34102-7874

JOHNSON, KENNETH PETER, neurologist, researcher; b. Jamestown, N.Y., Mar. 12, 1932; s. Kenneth Peter and Nina (Bengtson) Johnson; m. Jacquelyn Johnson, June 23, 1956; children: Peter, Thomas, Diane, Douglas. BA, Upsala Coll., East Orange, N.J., 1955; MD, Jefferson Med. Coll., Phila., 1959. Diplomate: Am. Bd. Psychiatry and Neurology. Intern Buffalo Gen. Hosp., 1959-60; resident Hosp. of Cleve., 1963-65; asst. prof. neurology Case Western Res. U., Cleve., 1968-71, assoc. prof., 1971-74; prof. U. Calif., San Francisco, 1974-81; prof., chmn. U. Md., Balt., 1981—, chmn., 1981—2002; chief neurology VA Hosp., Balt., 1981-83. Editor: Neurovirology, 1984; contbr. numerous articles in field to profl. jours. Served to lt. U.S. Navy, 1961-63. Recipient Weil award Am. Assn. Neuropathology, 1967, Research Ctr. Devel. award NIH, 1968-73, John J. Dystal prize, 2000; Zimmerman lectr. Stanford U., 1981 Fellow Am. Neurol. Assn.; mem. Am. Acad. Neurology, Am. Soc. Virology, Am. Congress Rehab. Medicine, Am. Soc. Neurorehab., Internat. Soc. for Neuroimmunology. Lutheran. Office: Md Ctr for MS 11 S Paca St 4th Fl Baltimore MD 21201

JOHNSON, KENNY, architecture educator; s. Jocelyn and Kenny Johnson; m. Allison Mullins, June 8, 2000; 1 child, Carter Grant. Grad. in Engring. Tech., MDI, Springfield, Va., 1997. American Design Drafting Assocation (ADDA) Certificate, Am. Design Drafting Assocation (ADDA)/VA, 2001; AutoCAD 2004 Certified AutoDesk/VA, 2005, AutoCAD 2000 Certified AutoDesk/VA, 2002, AutoCAD R14 Certified AutoDesk/VA, 1998, A+ Certified CompTia/VA, 2000, Network + CompTia/VA, 2001; Gemstone Certified Gemological Institure of Am. (GIA), 1997, Diamond Certified Gemological Institure of Am. (GIA), 1997. Jewelry mgr. Svc. Mdse., Fredericksburg, Va., 1996—99; drafter FACE Assocx., Tyson's Corner, Va., 1997—98; project mgr. Fredericksburg Glass and Mirror, Va., 1998—99; drafting instr. North Stafford H.S., Va., 1998—; lead drafter Herlong Assocs., Inc., Fredericksburg, Va., 1999—. Advisor SkillsUSA, Stafford, Va., 1992—2005; mem. Hist. Fredericksburg Found., Inc, Va., 2003—05; founding bd. mem. The Fredericksburg Regional Preservation Trust, Va., 2003—05. Named Drafter of Yr., Stafford County & MDI, 1992, 1993, 1997, Tchr. of Yr., TrueValue All Am., 1999. Avocations: billiards, 3d computer animation. Office: North Stafford HS 839 Garrisonville Rd Stafford VA 22554 Office Phone: 540-658-6150.

JOHNSON, KERMIT DOUGLAS, minister, retired military officer; b. Mpls., Sept. 2, 1928; s. J. Anton Uno and Anna Judith (Goranson) J.; m. Carolyn Marie Johanson, Dec. 22, 1951; children: Karin Joy, Christopher Douglas. BS, U.S. Mil. Acad., 1951; MDiv, Princeton Theol. Sem., 1960; grad., Command Gen. Staff Coll., 1969, U.S. Army War Coll., 1976. Ordained to ministry, Presbyn. Ch., 1960. Commd. 2d lt. U.S. Army, 1951, infantry co. comdr., 1952-53, resigned, 1955, recommd. as chaplain, 1960, advanced through ranks to maj. gen., 1979, served in Vietnam, two tours Federal Republic of Germany, dep. chief of chaplains Washington, 1978-79, chief of chaplains, 1979-82, ret., 1982; assoc. dir. Ctr. for Def. Info., Washington, 1983-86. Author: Realism and Hope in a Nuclear Age, 1988, Ethics and Counterrevolution: American Involvement in Internal Wars, 1997, chpts. in 5 books on mil. ethics, nuclear issues and just war; contbr. articles to various periodicals. Decorated Bronze Star with oak leaf cluster. Home and Office: 4520 Grattan Price Dr Unit 6 Harrisonburg VA 22801 *In this world so full of tragedy, I believe the only cure for an inhuman aloofness from suffering is in our attempt to discern the good news and join with it.*

JOHNSON, KEVIN MAURICE, professional basketball player; b. Sacramento, Calif., Mar. 4, 1966; Student, U. Calif., 1987. Basketball player Cleve. Cavaliers, 1987—88, Phoenix Suns, 1988—. Mem. Dream Team II, 1994. Named NBA Most Improved Player, 1989; named to All-NBA 2d team, 1989—91, All-NBA 3d team, 1992, All-NBA 2d team, 1994. Office: care Phoenix Suns 201 E Jefferson St Phoenix AZ 85004-2412

JOHNSON, KEYSHAWN, professional football player; b. L.A., July 22, 1972; Student, W. L.A. Coll., U. So. Calif. Wide receiver N.Y. Jets, 1996—2000, Tampa Bay Buccaneers, 2000—03, Dallas Cowboys, 2004—. Named wide receiver coll. All-Am. first team, The Sporting News, 1995; named to Pro-Bowl, 1998, 1999, 2001. Achievements include first round draft pick (1st pick overall) NFL, 1996; mem. AFC Ea. Conf. championship team, 1998. Office: c/o Dallas Cowboys 1 Cowboys Pkwy Irving TX 75063

JOHNSON, KRAIG NELSON, lawyer, arbitrator, mediator; b. Landstuhl, Germany, July 8, 1959; arrived in US, 1966; s. Howard Arthur Sr. and Joy Anne (Nelson) J.; m. AmberJade F. Leca, Nov. 13, 1993. BA with honors, Eckerd Coll., 1981; M in Internat. Mgmt., Am. Grad. Sch. Internat. Mgmt., Glendale, Ariz., 1982; JD, Baylor U., 1992. Bar: Fla. 1993; cert. mediator and arbitrator Supreme Ct. of Fla. Mktg. mgr. Jack Eckerd Corp., Clearwater, Fla., 1982-85; mktg. systems mgr. NCS, Inc., Houston, 1985-87; dir. ops. Petro, Inc., El Paso, 1987-90; atty. and shareholder Zimmerman, Shuffield, Kiser & Sutcliffe, P.A., Orlando, Fla., 1992—2003; atty., founding and mng. ptnr. Goodman McGuffey Lindsey & Johnson LLP, Orlando, Fla., 2003—. Editor: Florida Workers' Compensation Practice, 1994; contbr. articles to profl. jours. Mem. internat. trade and investment adv. bd. Econ. Devel. Commn. of Mid-Fla., Orlando, 1997—; mem. Task Force on Title IX, Baylor U. Bd. of Regents, Waco, 1992-93; bd. dirs. Asian-Am. C. of C., Orlando, 1994-95. Fellow Soc. of Antiquaries of Scotland; mem. Am. Immigration Lawyers Assn., St. Andrew's Soc. of Ctrl. Fla. (bd. dirs., v.p. 1996-98, pres. 1998-2000), Fla. Bar Assn. (sect. on internat. law and litig.), Order of Barristers. Avocations: sailing, flying, shooting sports, mandarin chinese and german languages. Home: 509 N Hampton Ave Orlando FL 32803-5516 Office: Goodman McGuffey Lindsey & Johnson LLP Ste 200 1245 W Fairbanks Ave Winter Park FL 32789 Office Phone: 407-478-1247.

JOHNSON, LADY BIRD (MRS. CLAUDIA ALTA TAYLOR), former First Lady of the United States; b. Karnack, Tex., Dec. 22, 1912; d. Thomas Jefferson Taylor; B.A., U. Tex., 1933, B.Journalism, 1934, D.Letters, 1964; LL.D., Tex. Woman's U., 1964; D.Letters, Middlebury Coll., 1967; L.H.D., Williams Coll., 1967, U. Ala., 1975; H.H.D., Southwestern U., 1967; m. Lyndon Baines Johnson (36th Pres. U.S.), Nov. 17, 1934 (died Jan. 22, 1973); children: Lynda Bird Johnson Robb, Luci Baines. Mgr. husband's congl. office, Washington, 1941-42; owner, operator radio-TV sta. KTBC, Austin, Tex., 1942-63, cattle ranches, Tex., 1943—, First Lady of the U.S., 1963-68. Hon. chmn. Nat. Headstart Program, 1963-68, Town Lake Beautification Project; also cotton and timberlands, Ala. Mem. Advisory council Nat. Parks, Historic Sites, Bldgs. and Monuments; bd. regents U. Tex., 1971-77, mem. internat. conf. steering com., 1969; trustee Jackson Hole Preserve, Am. Conservation Assn., trustee emeritus Nat. Geog. Soc.; founder Nat. Wildflower Research Ctr., Austin, 1982. Recipient Togetherness award Marge Champion, 1958; Humanitarian award B'nai B'rith, 1961; Businesswoman's award Bus. and Profl. Women's Club, 1961; Theta Sigma Phi citation, 1962; Disting. Achievement award Washington Heart Assn., 1962; Industry citation Am. Women in Radio and Television, 1963; Humanitarian citation Vols. of Am., 1963; Peabody award for White House TV visit, 1966; Eleanor Roosevelt Golden Candlestick award Women's Nat. Press Club; Damon Woods Meml. award Indsl. Designers Soc. Am., 1972; Conservation Service award Dept. Interior, 1974; Disting. award Am. Legion, 1975; Woman of Year award Ladies Home Jour., 1975; Medal of Freedom, 1977; Nat. Achievement award Am. Hort. Soc., 1984. Life mem. U. Tex. Ex-Students Assn. Episcopalian. Author: A White House Diary, 1970. Address: LBJ Libr and Mus 2313 Red River St Austin TX 78705-5702

JOHNSON, LAEL FREDERIC, lawyer; b. Yakima, Wash., Jan. 22, 1938; s. Andrew Cabot and Gudney M. (Fredrickson) Johnson; m. Eugenie Rae Call, June 9, 1960; children: Eva Marie, Inga Margaret. AB, Wheaton Coll., 1960; JD, Northwestern U., 1963. Bar: Ill. 1963, U.S. Dist. Ct. (no. dist.) Ill. 1964, U.S. Ct. Appeals (7th cir.) 1966. V.p., gen. counsel Abbott Labs., Abbott Park, Ill., 1981-89, sr. v.p., sec., gen. counsel, 1989-94; of counsel Schiff Hardin LLP, Chgo., 1995—. Mem., past chmn. Law Sch. bd. Northwestern U. Mem.: ABA, Assn. Gen. Counsel. Office: Schiff Hardin LLP 6600 Sears Tower Chicago IL 60606 Office Phone: 312-258-5536.

JOHNSON, LARRY WALTER, lawyer; b. Princeton, Minn., May 21, 1934; s. Alfred Herbert and Lillian Martha (Wetter) J.; m. Mary Ann Lindstrom, June 14, 1958; children: Lawrence W. II, Kristin Jane. BS in Law, U. Minn., 1957, LLB, 1959. Bar: Minn. 1959. Assoc. Dorsey & Whitney, Mpls., 1961-66, ptnr., 1967-95, of counsel, 1996—. Bd. dirs. Remmele Engring., Inc. Co-author, co-editor Minnesota Estate Administration, 1968. Bd. dirs. Minn. Bus. Found. Excellence in Edn., St. Paul. 1981-85, Walker Sponsor's Fund, Mpls., 1987; trustee Walker Meth. Residence and Health Services, Inc., Mpls., 1985-86. Served to 1st lt. U.S. Army, 1959-61. Mem. Minn. Bar Assn., Hennepin County Bar Assn., Mpls. Athletic Club. Republican. Congregationalist. Avocation: handball. Home: 5400 W Highwood Dr Minneapolis MN 55436-1225 Office: Dorsey and Whitney 50 S 6th St Ste 1500 Minneapolis MN 55402-1553

JOHNSON, LAURA STICHNOTH, music educator, secondary school educator; b. Watseka, Ill., June 27, 1966; d. Marvin Lee and Sherrill Lou Koch Stichnoth; m. Mark Alan Johnson, July 16, 1988; children: Kyle Alan, Kelly Ruth, Kevin Lee. BS, U. Ill., 1989; M in Music. Edn., Vandercook Coll. Music, 1992. Tchr. Glenbard North H.S., Carol Stream, Ill., 1989—. Asst. choir dir. First United Meth. Ch., Elgin, Ill., 1995—, children's choir dir., 2004—; mem. St. Charles (Ill.) Singers, 1990—. Mem.: Music Educator Nat. Conf., Am. Choral Dir. Assn. Methodist. Home: 4031 Lakeside Dr Hanover Park IL 60133 Office: Glenbard North High Sch 990 Kuhn Rd Carol Stream IL 60188

JOHNSON, LAURENCE F., college executive; b. Corpus Christi, Tex., Dec. 17, 1950; s. Howard E. and B. Louise (Franklin) J.; m. Maria Guadalupe Cisneros-Solís, Dec. 15, 1979; children: Alexis Elizabeth, Laurence Alejandro. BA, U. Tex., 1975, PhD, 1993; MBA, S.W. Tex. State U., San Marcos, 1988. Divsn. chair Austin C.C., 1983-93; assoc. dir. League for Innovation in the C.C., Mission Viejo, Calif., 1994-96; exec. v.p. Terra C.C., Fremont, Ohio, 1996—. Mem. adv. bd. Invest Learning, Inc., San Diego, 1994-96; postdoctoral trainee Inst. for Edml. Mgmt., Harvard U., 1998. Author: Embracing the Tiger, 1997; contbr. articles to profl. jours.; editor: Leadership Abstracts, 1994-96, Learning Without Limits, 1996, Common Ground, 1996; gen. editor C.C. Jour. Rsch. and Practice, Denton, Tex., 1994-97. Mem. Tri-County Mental Health Bd., Fremont, Ohio. Recipient Sloan Rsch. award Am. Assn. C.C.s, Washington, 1996, Goodman Malamuth award Am. Assn. Univ. Adminstrs., Washington, 1994, Internat. Tchg. Excellence award Nat. Inst. for Staff and Orgnl. Devel., 1991; named to Exec. Leadership Inst., League for Innovation, Costa Mesa, Calif., 1995. Mem. Nat. Coun. Instrnl. Adminstrs., Continuous Quality Improvement Network (instl. rep.), Nat. Learning Infrastructure Initiative (instl. rep.), Phi Kappa Phi, Kappa Delta Pi. Avocations: music, scuba, skiing, reading. Office: Terra C C 2830 Napoleon Rd Fremont OH 43420-9814

JOHNSON, LAURENCE MICHAEL, lawyer; b. N.Y.C., Feb. 8, 1940; s. Edgar and Eleanor (Kraus) Johnson; m. Margie Serrano, Mar. 15, 2003; children: Mark Steven, Lisa Arienne, Laura Elizabeth, Daniel Milton, Miguel L., Daniel B. AB cum laude, Harvard U., 1961; LL.B. cum laude, Columbia U., 1964. Bar: Mass. 1964. Research asst. Columbia U., 1962-64; law clk. Supreme Jud. Ct. Mass., 1964-65; from assoc. to ptnr. firm Nutter, McClennen & Fish, Boston, 1965-77; ptnr. firm Newman & Meserve, Boston, 1977-78, Palmer & Dodge, Boston, 1978-83; sole practice law Boston, 1983-85; ptnr. firm Johnson & Polubinski, Boston, 1985-86, Johnson & Schwartzman, Boston, 1986—91; of counsel Fordham & Starrett, Boston, 1991—96; ptnr. Mahoney, Hawkes & Goldings, Boston, 1996—2001, Davis, Malm & D'Agostine, Boston, 2001—. Arbitrator Am. Arbitration Assn., 1976—; tchg. team Harvard Trial Adv. Workshop, 1976—; mem. trial adv. faculty Mass. Contg. Legal Edn. of New Eng. Law Inst., 1979—. Author: 20 Years of Civil Rights: Epilogue and Prologue, Boston Bar Journal, 1988; contbr. articles to profl. jours. Group chmn. larger law firms United Way of Mass. Bay, 1976; mem. Sudbury Human Rights Council, 1964-68, pres., 1965-66, Recipient Patriot award, 1976 Fellow: Am. Coll. Trial Lawyers (complex litigation com. 1994—99), Mass. Bar Found. (life; trustee 2005—); mem.: ABA (jud. adminstrn. divsn., litigation and anti-trust sects.), Mass. Bar

Assn., Am. Law Inst., Boston Bar Assn. (steering com. lawyers com. for civil rights under law 1976—), Harvard Varsity Club, Harvard Club N.Y., Harvard Club Boston. Democrat. Home: 11 Northway Rd Randolph MA 02368-2913 Office Phone: 617-367-2500. Personal E-mail: ljohnson@davismalm.com. *The trial lawyer's art requires a combination of knowledge, both specialized and general, experience (and the judgment that comes with it), energy, determination, uncompromising self-appraisal and receptivity to the ideas of others. Its object is effective communication and to achieve it, it draws upon not only the law, but every area of human interest. It provides boundless opportunities for creative achievement, but they are realized only in proportion to the effort actually expended.*

JOHNSON, LAURIE LYNN, history educator; b. Sussex, N.J., May 25, 1966; d. Richard L. Johnston and Nancy B. Johnson. BA, James Madison U., Harrisonburg, Va., 1988; MA, Boston Coll., Chestnut Hill, Mass., 1990. Cert. tchr. social studies and German NJ. Dept. of Edn. Grad. tchg. asst. Boston Coll., Chestnut Hill, Mass., 1989—90; social studies tchr. Hackettstown H.S., NJ, 1990—91; history tchr. Phillipsburg Bd. of Edn., NJ, 1991—; Lincoln-douglas debate coord. Met. Forensics Inst., South Orange, NJ, 2000—; forensics coach Phillipsburg and Ridge H.S. forensics teams, Phillipsburg and Basking Ridge, NJ, 1996—; German tchr. Warren County Adult Edn., Broadway, NJ, 1994—96; adj. history faculty Warren County C.C., Broadway, NJ, 1995; track and field coach Phillipsburg and Nazareth H.S., Phillipsburg, and Nazareth, Pa., 1992—. Site team mem. Advancement Via Individual Determination Nat. Orgn., Phillipsburg, NJ, 2003—; mentor Phillipsburg Sch. Dist. Mentoring Program, 2003—04. Recipient Diamond Key award, Nat. Forensic League, 2004, Gov.'s Tchr. Recognition award, State of N.J., 1999; scholar Barton scholar, Nat. Debate Coaches Assn., 1999. Mem.: NEA (assoc.), Nat. Coun. for the Social Studies (assoc.), Am. Assn. of Tchrs. of German (assoc.), Nat. Forensic League (assoc.; nfl dist. committe mem. 2001—04), Nat. Debate Coaches Assn. (assoc.). D-Liberal. Presbyterian. Avocations: running, travel, reading, independent films, gardening. Home: 208 South Third St Phillipsburg NJ 08865 Office: Phillipsburg Board of Education 445 Marshall St Phillipsburg NJ 08865 Office Phone: 908-454-6551. Personal E-mail: fraulaurie@hotmail.com.

JOHNSON, LAWRENCE ALAN, cereal technologist, educator, administrator; b. Columbus, Ohio, Apr. 30, 1947; s. William and Wyoma (Swift) J.; m. Bernice Ann Miller, June 15, 1969; children: Bradley, David. BS, Ohio State U., 1969; MS, N.C. State U., 1971; PhD, Kans. State U., 1978. Rsch. chemist Durkee Foods div. SCM Corp., Strongsville, Ohio, 1973-75; assoc. rsch. chemist Food Protein R&D Ctr. Tex. A&M U., College Station, 1978-85; dir. Ctr. for Crops Utilization Rsch. Iowa State U., Ames, 1991—. Mem. rsch. com. Am. Soybean Assn., St. Louis, 1987-91, Nat. Corn Grower's Assn., St. Louis, 1990-91. Author: (with others) Handbook of Cereals, 1991; editor: (book/procs.) Technologies for Value-Added Products from Proteins and Co-Products, 1989, Corn Chemistry and Technology; contbr. more than 150 articles to profl. jours. 1st lt. U.S. Army, 1971-73. Recipient Rsch. award Corn Refiners Assn., 1998. Mem. Am. Assn. Cereal Chemists (assoc. editor jour. 1982-85, dir. 2002-04), Am. Soc. Agrl. Engrs., Am. Oil Chemists Soc. (assoc. editor jour. 1989—, v.p. 2003-04, pres. 2004-05, Archer Daniels Midland Rsch. award 1986, 92, 99, 2001, 02), Royal Swedish Acad. Agr. and Forestry (fgn. mem. 1999), Inst. Food Techs. Republican. Lutheran. Achievements include 11 patents. Home: 2226 Buchanan Dr Ames IA 50010-4368 Office: Ctr Crops Utilization Rsch Iowa State U Ames IA 50011-0001 Office Phone: 515-294-4365. Business E-Mail: ljohnson@iastate.edu.

JOHNSON, LAWRENCE EUGENE, lawyer; b. Morrison, Ill., Sept. 26, 1937; s. Frederick Eugene and Ruth Helen (Lorke) J.; m. Debby Karen McCaleb, June 17, 1961; children: Mark Lawrence, Eric Eugene, Lori Ann Johnson Purtzer. BS, No. Ill. U., 1960, MS, 1962; JD, U. Ill., 1965. Bar: Ill. 1965, U.S. Dist. Ct. (ctrl. dist.) Ill. 1965, U.S. Ct. Appeals (7th cir.) 1965; lic. pilot. Pvt. practice, 1965-68; states atty. County of Champaign, Ill., 1968-72; pvt. practice Champaign, 1972—. Spl. asst. atty. gen. litigation Ill. Dept. Revenue, 1982-86, Ill. Dept. Labor, 1982-86, Ill. Dept. Transp., 1986-90, Ill. Dept. Conservation, 1988-90, Ill. Dept. Nuclear Safety, 1989-90. Bd. mem. Ill. State Bd. Elections, 1990-95, vice chmn., 1993-95; chmn. Ill. Liquor Control Commn., 1972-73; hearing officer Ill. State Bd. Elections, 1988-90; mem. airport hazard zoning task force divsn. aeronautics Ill. Dept. Transp., 1987-88. With U.S. Army, 1955-57. Mem. U.S. Pilots Assn. (bd. dirs. 1989—), Ill. Pilots Assn. (pres. 1991-93, v.p., bd. dirs. 1989-91), Illini Area Pilots Assn. (pres. 1989-91), Ill. Trial Lawyers Assn., Champaign Urbana Kiwanis Early Risers, Champaign Urbana Ambucs, AMVETS (life). Office: Johnson & Assocs PO Box 1127 202 W Hill St Champaign IL 61824-1127 E-mail: lejai@shout.net.

JOHNSON, LAWRENCE M., retired bank executive; b. 1940; Student, U. Hawaii. With Bank of Hawaii, Honolulu, 1963-2000, exec. v.p., 1980-84, vice chmn., 1984-89, pres., 1989-2000, now chmn. bd., CEO, until 2000, ret., 2000. Address: Ste # 230 130 Merchant St Honolulu HI 96813 Office Phone: 808-537-8200.

JOHNSON, LAYMON, JR., management analyst; b. Jackson, Miss., Sept. 1, 1948; s. Laymon and Bertha (Yarbrough) Johnson; m. Charlene J. Johnson, Nov. 13, 1982. B in Tech., U. Dayton, 1970; MS in Sys. Mgmt., U. So. Calif., 1978. Mem. tech. staff Rockwell Internat., Canoga Park, Calif., 1975-77; sr. dynamics engr. Gen. Dynamics, Pomona, Calif., 1978-83; fin. sys. specialist Northrop Corp., Pico Rivera, Calif., 1983-90; utility budget analyst dept. water and power City of L.A., 1991-97; mgmt. analyst L.A. Police Dept., 1997—. Lt. comdr. USNR, 1970—92. Mem.: So. Calif. Crime and Intelligence Analysts Assn., Internat. Assn. Crime Analysts, Inst. Safety and Sys. Mgmt. Triumvirate, Calif. Crime Analysts Assn., Internat. Assn. Law Enforcement Intelligence Analysts, Vietnam Vets. Am., Los Angeles County Mus. Art, Am. Philatelic Soc., Trojan Club, Tau Alpha Pi. Democrat. Roman Catholic.

JOHNSON, LEANNE, lawyer; b. Shreveport, La., Oct. 18, 1961; BS magna cum laude, So. Ark. U., 1983; JD with high honors, U. Ark., 1986. Bar: Ark. 1986, Tex. 1987, U.S. Dist. Ct. (so. and ea. dists.) Tex. 1987; bd. cert. in personal injury trial law Tex. Bd. Legal Cert. Clk. to Hon. Nauman Scott U.S. Dist. Ct. (we. dist.) La., Alexandria, 1986-87; from assoc. to ptnr. Orgain, Bell & Tucker, LLP, Beaumont, Tex., 1987—. Former dir., sec., officer Beaumont YMCA. Mem. Jefferson County Young Lawyers Assn. (former officer, dir.), Jefferson County Bar Assn. Office: Orgain Bell & Tucker LLP 470 Orleans St Ste 400 Beaumont TX 77701-3076

JOHNSON, LENNART INGEMAR, materials engineering consultant; b. Mpls., Dec. 23, 1924; s. Sixten Richard Wilhem and Marie Augusta Johnson; m. Muriel Grant, Oct. 7, 1961; 1 child, Sandra Lee. BS in Chem. Engring., U. Minn., 1948. Petroleum engr. Northwestern Refining Co., New Brighton, Minn., 1948-49; sr. engr. Ordnance Div. Honeywell, Hopkins, Minn., 1949-67, prin. materials engr. Def. Sys. Div., 1967-69, supr. engring. Def. Sys. Div., 1969-87; staff engr. Armament Sys. Div. Honeywell Inc., Hopkins, Minn., 1987-88; cons. Soc. Automotive Engring., Warrandale, Pa., 1989-99. Cons. Ecubed Assocs., Inc., 1993-97; forum leader and presenter, U. Wis. Engring. Inst., Madison, 1965. Contbr. numerous articles to profl. jours. Mem. credentials com. Hennepin County Rep. Conv., Minn., 1972, alt. del., 1974. Recipient Prize Paper award, Inst. Elec. Engrs. Fellow Am. Inst. Chemists (emeritus); mem. Soc. Automotive Engrs. (sec. aerospace composites com. 1986-87, chmn. 1987-89). Achievements include development of injection molding technology, urethane and epoxy casting resins, and urethane foaming resins. Home and Office: 14109 Mount Ter Minnetonka MN 55345-3826

JOHNSON, LEONARD MORRIS, retired pediatrician, surgeon; b. Gowanda, N.Y., June 11, 1931; s. Leonard Brynolf and Helen Berdena (Morris) J.; m. Ann Marie Homer, Mar. 30, 1968; children: H. Leif B. Johnson, Nils A.C. Johnson. BA, Haverford Coll., 1954; MD, U. Pa., 1958; MS in Surgery, U. Minn., Mayo Grad. Sch., Rochester, 1966. Diplomate Am. Bd. Gen. Surgery; cert. special competence in pediatric surgery. Intern Colo. Gen. Hosp., Denver, 1958-59; fellow in gen. surgery Mayo Clinic, Rochester, 1959-63; fellow in pediatric surgery Children's Mercy Hosp., Kansas City, Mo., 1964-65; vis. pediatric surgeon Acad. Hosp., Uppsala, Sweden, 1967; registrar in pediatric urology Alder Hey Children's Hosp., Liverpool, Eng., 1967-68; gen. surgeon SS Hope (Project Hope), Guayaquil, Ecuador, 1964, gen. and pediatric surgeon Conakry, Guinea, 1965, Nicaragua, Colombia, Sri Lanka, 1965-68; pediatric surgeon Children's Hosp., Oakland, Calif., 1969-97, ret., 1997, chief of dept. of surgery, 1989-92. Bd. dirs. Children's Hosp., Oakland, Calif., 1982-91; bd. trustees Children's Hosp. Found., Oakland, 1986-95; mem. exec. bd. Mt. Diablo-Silverado Coun. Boy Scouts Am., 1996—. Recipient Order Ruben Dario, Pres. Republic of Nicaragua, Managua, 1966; recipient Bronze Bambino award Children's Hosp., Oakland, 1990. Fellow Am. Coll. of Surgeons, Surgical fellow Am. Acad. of Pediatrics; mem. Am. Trauma Soc. (founding mem.), Am. Pediat.-Surg. Assn., Pacific Assn. Pediatric Surgeons, Brit. Assn. Pediat. Surgeons, Alameda-Contra Costa Med. Assn. Avocations: photography, hiking, skiing, travel, music. Personal E-mail: lmj2544219@aol.com.

JOHNSON, LESTER FREDRICK, artist; b. Mpls., Jan. 27, 1919; s. Edwin August and Helma Marie (Holmes) J.; m. Josephine Valenti, Feb. 12, 1949; children: Leslie Maria, Anthony Edwin. Student, Mpls. Art Inst., 1939-41, St. Paul Art Sch., 1939-41, Art Inst. Chgo., 1943. Prof. painting Yale U., 1964—, dir. studies, 1968—. Mem. Milford (Conn.) Fine Arts Council, 1972-73; mem. art adv. com. Housatonic Community Coll., Stratford, Conn., 1969-87 One-man shows, Zabriskei Gallery, N.Y.C., Martha Jackson Gallery, N.Y.C., Donald Morris, Detroit, Walter Moos Gallery, N.Y.C., Toronto, Can., David Barnett Gallery, Milw., Mpls. Art Inst., Dayton Art Inst., Fort Worth Art Inst., Yale Univ. Mus., Gimpel Fils Gallery, London, Gimpel Hanover Gallery, Zurich, Switzerland, Westmoreland Mus. Art. Greenburg, Pa. (traveling), Augustana Coll. Centennial Hall Gallery, Pa. Acad. Fine Arts, Newport Harbor Art Mus., Edward Thorpe Gallery, N.Y.C., Gimpel-Weitzenhofer Gallery, N.Y.C., Peter Findley Gallery, N.Y.C., Denise Dade' Gallery, N.Y.C., Joseph Rickards Gallery, N.Y.C., Jim Goodman Gallery, N.Y.C.; exhibited in numerous group shows; represented in permanent collections, Albright Knox Mus., Dayton Art Inst., Met. Mus. Art, N.Y.C., Mus. Modern Art, New Sch. for Social Research, Phoenix Art Mus., U. Nebr., Walker Art Mus. Recipient Creative Arts award Brandeis U., 1978, Jimmy Ernest award in art Am. Acad. Arts and Letters, 2003; Trumbull Coll. fellow, 1996—; Guggenheim fellow, 1973. Mem. Nat. Acad. Design (coun.), Am. Acad. Letters. Home: PO Box 7582 Greenwich CT 06836-7582 Office: Yale U Sch Art York And Chapel St New Haven CT 06520

JOHNSON, LESTER LARUE, JR., artist, educator; b. Detroit, Sept. 28, 1937; s. Lester L. and Haroldine M. (Stanley) J. BFA, MFA, U. Mich. Prof. Coll. for Creative Studies, Detroit. Participant dept. art and art history 3d Ann. African Am. Lecture Series, Wayne State U., 2000, internat. conf. on African Influences in the Visual Arts of the Ams., 2001. Exhibitions include Whitney Mus. Art, Nat. Acad. Design, N.Y.C., Kalamazoo Inst. Arts, Mich., Saginaw Art Mus., Detroit Inst. Arts, Univ. Mich. Mus. Art, Ann Arbor, Centro de Memoria e Cultura dos Correios, Salvador, Bahia, Brazil, Detroit Pretty City at G.R. N'Namdi Gallery and the Univ. Cultural Assn., 2003, Klemm Gallery, Siena Heights U., Adrian, 2004, Buckham Gallery, Flint, 2005, Represented in permanent collections Osaka U. Arts, Japan, Mus. Afro-Brasileiro at Fed. U. of Bahia, Salvador, Brazil, prin. works include Bishop Internat. Airport, Flint. Recipient John S. Newberry Purchase prize, 54th Exhibit Mich. Artists, Detroit Inst. Arts, 1964, recognition award African-Am. Music Festival; grantee Andrerw W. Mellon Found. Office: Coll for Creative Studies 201 E Kirby St Detroit MI 48202-4034 Office Phone: 313-664-7486. E-mail: ljohnson@ccscad.edu.

JOHNSON, LISA PARRISH, medical/surgical nurse; b. Goldsboro, N.C., Jan. 28, 1962; d. Dennis Wilbert Parrish and Margie Mae Daughtry; m. Tony Allen Johnson, July 30, 1982; children: Jamie Shay, Christy Lynn. ADN, Johnston C.C., Smithfield, N.C., 1982. ACLS, BCLS, cert. mobile intensive care nurse, pediatric advanced life support; ACLS, RN. Emergency RN Johnston Meml. Hosp., Smithfield, NC, 1981—92, 2001—; staff RN Home Health and Hospice, Smithfield, NC, 1992—2001. Avocations: reading, kayaking, attending soccer games. Home: 1860 Braswell Rd Smithfield NC 27577

JOHNSON, LOLA NORINE, retired advertising and public relations executive, educator; b. Austin, Minn., Dec. 28, 1942; d. Alton E. and Evelyn M. (Quast) Milbrath; m. Dennis D. Johnson, June 15, 1963 (div. July 1973); children: Brenda J., Erik B. Attended, Coll. of St. Thomas. Pub. rels. account rep. Kerker & Assocs. Advt. and Pub. Rels., Bloomington, Minn., 1973-78; comm. mgr. Norwest Bank Mpls., 1978-83; dir. media rels., account supr. Edwin Neuger & Assocs. Pub. Rels., Mpls., 1983-85; v.p., mng. dir. The Richards Group, Mpls., 1985-86; owner, pres. PR Plus, Edina, Minn., 1986-2000; ret., 2000. Mem. cmty. faculty, instr., counselor Met. State U., Mpls., St. Paul, 1980-93. Cons. comm. United Way, Mpls., 1982. Recipient Gold award United Way Mpls., 1982. Home: 7151 York Ave S Apt 807 Minneapolis MN 55435-4435

JOHNSON, LON. M., JR., lawyer; b. Pikeville, Ky., May 21, 1950; s. Lon M. Sr. and Edith Bentley Johnson. BS, Pikeville Coll., 1972; JD, U. Ky., 1977. Bar: Ky. 1977, U.S. Dist. Ct. (ea. dist.) Ky. 1981. Assoc. Baird & Baird, Pikeville, 1977-78; pvt. practice Pikeville, 1978—. Republican. Southern Baptist. Home: 5105 Collins Hwy Pikeville KY 41501-6843 Office: Weddington Bldg Second Fl 209 Second St Ste 201 Pikeville KY 41501-3843 Office Phone: 606-437-0911. Office Fax: 606-437-0911 51. E-mail: lmjjesq@hotmail.com.

JOHNSON, LONNIE L., JR., information specialist; b. Bridgeton, N.J., May 16, 1964; s. Lonnie L and Ivory M. Johnson; m. B.J. F. Brown Johnson, Aug. 7, 1987; children: Nima Warfield, Nashad Warfield. BA in Bus., Kean U., 1996; MA in Libr. Sci., Rutgers U., 2000. Acct. Ortho Biotech (Johnson and Johnson), Raritan, NJ, 1996—98; CEO/pres. Calenture Pub., Plainfield, NJ, 1999—. Bd. dirs. JBW, Plainfield, NJ. Avocation: chess. Office: Calenture Publishing PO Box 2812 Plainfield NJ 07062 Personal E-mail: mbalj@hotmail.com.

JOHNSON, LOREN CHARISSE, publishing executive, writer; b. Hackensack, N.J., Sept. 6, 1960; d. Larry Lee and Peggy Garris (Stepmother), Patrick Charles (Stepfather) and Barbara Jean Lauder; m. Dennis Johnson, Jan. 24, 1992 (div. Aug. 1996); 1 child, Leah; m. Sandy Simmons, June 1982 (div. Oct. 1985); 1 child, Charisse; m. Dennis Johnson, Sept. 15, 1997. Student, Hunter Coll., 1982; AA, U. Fla., 1981. Editl. sec. Harcourt Brace Jovanovich Pub., N.Y.C., 1982—84; adminstrv. asst. Chem. Bank, N.Y.C., 1984—88; personnel cons. Office Personnel Search, N.Y.C., 1988—91; prin., owner Licensing By Loren, Inc., NJ, 1994—; freelance mtg. loan officer Stroudsburg, Pa., 2000—. Prin., owner The Dreamers, 1996—. Author: The Dreamers, 1996, Jesus & Me, 1998, Misunderstood, 1998. Recipient 1st Runner Up, N.J. Jr. Miss Pageant, 1977. Avocations: reading, writing, movies, sports, children. Office: Licensing by Loren Inc PO Box 936 Marshalls Creek PA 18335

JOHNSON, LOYD, agricultural engineer, researcher; b. Mar. 18, 1927; s. Iley Benford and Ruth (Humphrey) J.; m. Ester Banegas, Dec. 24, 1952; children: Theresa Ann, Thomas Patrick, Loyd Carl. BS, Auburn U., 1950, MS, 1954. Registered profl. engr., Calif. Sr. project engr. United Fruit Co., Tiquisate, Guatemala, La Lima, Honduras, Almirante, Panama, 1951—60; agrl. engr. Rockefeller Found., 1960-82; mem. rsch. staff Internat. Rice Rsch. Inst., Los Banos, Philippines, 1960-68, Centro Internacional de Agricultura Tropical, Cali, Colombia, 1968-77, Internat. Agrl. Devel. Svc., Guayaquil, Ecuador, 1977-81, Internat. Fertilizer Devel. Ctr., Florence, Ala., 1981-82. Cons. agrl. engr. Internat. Agrl. Devel. Svcs., Dhaka, Bangladesh, 1982-83, Bogor, Indonesia, 1984-85, WINROCK, Pyinmana, Myanmar, 1986-88, Islamabad, Pakistan, 1990, 94. With USNR, 1945-46. Mem. Am. Soc. Agrl. Engrs. (Kishida Internat. award), Indian Soc. Agrl. Engrs. (life), Bangladesh Soc. Agrl. Engrs. Roman Catholic. Achievements include development of agricultural experimental station fields and research support facilities. Home: 287 Herman Bailey Rd Somerville AL 35670-5231 Personal E-mail: stoutox@hiwaay.net.

JOHNSON, LUAN, disaster management consultant; b. Provo, Utah, Apr. 27, 1956; d. Jack R. and Colleen (Kesler) J. BA, Brigham Young U., 1981, MA, 1984; PhD, U. Wash., 1994. Dir. Tchg. Resource Ctr., Provo, 1980-84; tchg. asst. comms. dept. Brigham Young U., Provo, 1982-83; counselor Master Acad., Salt Lake City, 1985; ednl. designer, program mgr. City of Sunnyvale, 1986-90; tchg. asst., rsch. asst., speech comm. dept. U. Wash., Seattle, 1991-93; program mgr. City of Seattle, 1993—2005; dir. SPAN disaster, svcs. a non-profit disaster preparedness & response orgn., 2004—. Recipient Best Ednl. Campaign award Internat. Assn. Emergency Mgrs., 1998, Nat. Coord. Coun. of Emergency Mgmt. Best Newsletter award, 1996, 98, 2002, 1st pl.-best ednl. campaign Internat. Assn. Emergency Mgrs., 1998, Outstanding Pub. Svc. award Seattle Police Dept., 1999, 1st pl.-best ednl. video Internat. Assn. Emergency Mgrs., 1999. Mem.: Phi Kappa Phi. Mem. Lds Ch. Avocation: collecting and flying kites. Home: 4014 A Midvale Ave N Seattle WA 98103

JOHNSON, LYNN BARBARA, artist, civic worker; b. N.Y.C., Jan. 23, 1933; d. Carl Lincoln (stepfather) and Mary Catherine (Albert) Nelson; m. Frederick Hannan Johnson, Dec. 14, 1957; children: Christopher H., Laura B., Thor A. AA with honors, Stockton Jr. Coll., 1952; BFA, BA, U. Wash., 1954. With Standard Oil Co., San Francisco, 1956-57; tchr. Menlo Park (Calif.) Pvt. Sch., 1957-58, Niantic (Conn.) Pub. Sch., 1961-63; pvt. tchr. art San Diego, 1968-69; art dealer Kenneth Behm Galleries, Seattle and Bellevue, Wash., 1981-84. Juror N.W. Internat. Women's Conf. Art Exhbn. One-woman shows include Menlo Park Show, 1958-59, Hartford Conn. Amory Show, 1965, Converse Gallery Annual Show, 1965, San Diego Watercolor Annual, 1967, Northwest Watercolor Annual, 1972. Founder Niantic (Conn.) Outdoor Art Show, 1962; co-founder Bellevue Jazz Festival, 1977; mem. Bellevue Centennial Steering Com., 1998; steering com. Race Talks exhibn. Wing Lake Mus.; western region rep. global network com. Virginia Gildersleeve Found.; mem. citizens' coord. com. King County Centennial, 1988; chmn. Bellevue City Arts Commn, 1983; co-founder and pres. Seattle-King County Cmty. Arts Network, 1986—87; co-founder Bellevue Allied Arts Coun., 1981, Wash. State Art Alliance, 1979; v.p. Found. Internat. Understanding Through Sutdents, 1987—88; founding mem. Women Together U.S./U.S.S.R., 1990—; vol. KCTS-TV, 1991—; founding chmn. Bellevue Cmty. Diversity Awards, 1993—; active, Pacific Sci. Ctr.; mem. art exhbn. and media coms. N.W. Women's Conf., 1993—95; chmn. Bellevue City Arts Com.; advisor MAP/UW Alumni Assn., 1995—2003, bd. dirs., 2003—; mem. Bellevue Regional Tourist Ctr. Commn., 1998—99, Bellevue Sch. Dist. Citizens' Task Force, 1979—80, Wash. State Ad Hoc Com. on Arts, 1977—79, Bellevue Sch. Dist. Affirmative Action Com., 1989—; chmn. King County Transit Commn., Bellevue City Arts Commn, 1980—81; del. Wash. Rep. Com., 1987—88; active City of Bellevue Transit Adv. Group, 1993—94; bd. dir. Seattle Opera Guild, 1990—94, Seattle Group Theatre, 1990—93; pres. Bel Canto Opera Group, 1990—; advisor MAP/UW Alumni Assn; bd. dirs. Seattle Group Theatre. Recipient numerous awards for watercolors, Calif., N.Y., Conn.; World of Difference award Sta. KIRO-TV, 1990; finalist Priz de Paris, Vogue mag., 1954; Nat. Assn. Fgn. Student Affairs travel grantee, 1987; named gift honoree AAUW, 1990. Mem.: Am. Assn. Univ. Women (Wash. State cultural rep., chair nominating com.), Wash. Arts Alliance, San Diego Watercolor Soc. (profl.), Nat. Mus. Women Arts (charter mem.), Bellevue Art Mus. (founding docent, founding patron 1978), Seattle Art Mus. (native arts coun.), Native Am. Studies Assn., Seattle Opera Guild (bd. dir. 1990—94), Overlake Rep. Women's Club, U. Wash. Alumni Assn. (life; class of 1954 40th reunion com., class of 1954 50th reunion com.), Women's U. Club, Lambda Rho. Home: 2202 102nd Pl SE Bellevue WA 98004-7003 E-mail: jcedarhouse@aol.com.

JOHNSON, M. GLEN (MAURICE GLEN JOHNSON), political science professor; b. Pikeville, Ky., Nov. 18, 1936; s. Marvin Forrest and Norcie (Wicker) J.; m. Sipra Bose, July 13, 1963; children: Denise Bose, Robert Alexander. BA, Georgetown Coll., Ky., 1958; MA, U. N.C., Chapel Hill, 1961, PhD, 1966. Instr. polit. sci. U. Ky., Lexington, 1963-64; from instr. to prof. Vassar Coll., Poughkeepsie, NY, 1964—2002, prof. emeritus, 2002—, acting pres., 1997—98, 2003—04; dir. Am. Studies Rsch. Ctr., Hyderabad, India, 1990-93; disting. vis. prof., exec. dir. Prince Alwaleed Bin Talal Bin Abdulaziz Alsaud Ctr. Am. Studies and Rsch. Am. U., Cairo, 2004—. Author: (with others) Beyond the Water's Edge, 1975, Consensus at the Crossroads, 1972, La Dèclaration Universelle des Droits de l'Homme, 1991, Ah, Columbus! The Indian Discovery of America, 1993, The Universal Declaration of Human Rights 1948-1993, 1994, The Universal Declaration of Human Rights: A History of its Creation and Implementation, 1998; editor Indian Jour. Am. Studies, 1990-1993; contbr. articles to profl. jours. Trustee Poughkeepsie Day Sch., 1968-72, 85-88, 99—2004, pres. bd. trustees, 1986-88; trustee Eleanor Roosevelt Ctr. at Val-Kill, 1986-90, 94-2002, v.p., 1989-90, 95-97, pres., 1997-2000; bd. dir. Friends of Fulbright in India, 1995—, chmn. bd., 2003-04; bd. dir. World Affairs Coun. Mid Hudson Valley, 2003-. Named Sr. Fulbright lectr. U. Poona, India, 1977-78, sr. Fulbright lectr. India, 1990-93. Mem. Am. Polit. Sci. Assn., Assn. for Asian Studies, Internat. Studies Assn. Home: 39 Garfield Pl Poughkeepsie NY 12601-4321 Office: Vassar Coll Box 376 124 Raymond Ave Poughkeepsie NY 12604-0376 also: Ctr American Studies American U Cairo 113 Kasr el Aini St PO Box 2511 Cairo 11511 Egypt Business E-Mail: johnsong@vassar.edu, gjohnson@aucegypt.edu.

JOHNSON, MADGE RICHARDS, business owner, fundraiser, consultant; b. Washington, Oct. 4, 1952; d. Benjamin Ellsworth and Virginia (Oliver) Richards; m. Jeffrey Leonard Johnson, June 25, 1977; children: Jared Benjamin, Jessica Lauren. B.S. in Bus. Mgmt., Strayer Coll., 1973; MBA Columbia Union Coll. 2004. Nat. govt. sales rep. G.F.C. Mfg. Co., Bklyn., 1972-75; ter. sales rep. John H. Breck, Am. Cyanamid, Wayne, N.J.; ter. sales mgr. Drackett Products Co., Cin., 1977-81, E.J. Brach & Sons., Chgo., Annapolis, Md., 1981-87, owner, pres. Madge Johnson Ltd., 1987—; sec.-treas. Recreation Environments Co., Annapolis, Md., 1988-90, asst. dir. Columbia Union Coll. Takoma Park, MD, 1999—; Treas. Martin Barr Sch., 1989-90 Mem. NAFE, Grocery Mfrs. Reps., Women in Consumer Product Sales. Home and Office: 17205 Magruders Ferry Rd Brandywine MD 20613-8358

JOHNSON, MAGIC (EARVIN JOHNSON JR.), professional sports team executive, development company executive, former professional basketball coach and player; b. Lansing, Mich., Aug. 14, 1959; s. Earvin and Christine Johnson; m. Earleatha "Cookie" Kelly, Sept. 1991; children: Earvin III, Elisa; 1 child, Andre. Student, Mich. State U., 1976-79. Basketball player LA Lakers, 1979—91, 1996, head coach, 1994, v.p., co-owner, 1994—; sportscaster NBC-TV, 1993-94; chmn., CEO Johnson Devel. Corp., 1993—; chmn. Magic Johnson Entertainment, Magic Johnson Productions & Magic Johnson Enterprises, 1997—; co-chmn. exec. steering com. for diversity NASCAR, 2004—. Author: (autobiography) Magic, 1983; (with Roy S. Johnson) Magic's Touch, 1989; What You Can Do to Avoid AIDS, 1992; My Life, 1992. Established the Magic Johnson Found., 1991. Named Most Outstanding Player, NCAA Divsn. I Tournament, 1979, NBA Finals MVP, 1980, 1982, 1987, NBA MVP, 1987, 1989, 1990, NBA All-Star Game MVP, 1990, 1992, Player of Yr., Sporting News, 1987; named one of 50 Greatest Players in NBA History, 1996; named to All-NBA first team, 1983—91, All-NBA Second Team, 1982, NBA All-Rookie Team, 1980, NBA All-Star Team, 1980, 1982—92, Mich. State U. Athletics Hall of Fame, 1992, Naismith Meml. Basketball Hall of Fame, 2002; recipient All-Around Contributions to Team Success Award, IBM, 1984, Schick Pivotal Player Award, 1984, J. Walter Kennedy Citizenship Award, NBA, 1992. Achievements include being mem. of NCAA Championship Team, 1979, NBA Championship Team, 1980, 82, 85, 87, 88, US Olympic Basketball gold medal winning team, 1992; chosen first overall in 1979 NBA Draft; holder of career record for highest assists-per-game avg. (11.2), career playoff record for most assists (2346), NBA Finals single-series record for highest assists-per-game avg. (14.0), 1985, NBA Finals single-series highest assists-per-game avg. by a rookie (8.7), 1980, NBA Finals single-game record for most points by rookie (42), 1980. Office: Johnson Devel Corp & Magic Johnson Found 9100 Wilshire Blvd Beverly Hills CA 90212-3415

JOHNSON, MARCIA J., dental hygienist; b. Cleve., Dec. 16, 1949; d. Bernard Exsall and Aletha Odessa (Mason) Baker; m. Gregory Carl Johnson, Apr. 24, 1987; children: Bernard, Cecelia. Grad. dental hygienist, U. Minn., Mpls., 1972. Cert. Registered Dental Hygienist Wash., Nat. Bd. Cert. Minn. Dental hygienist Children's Hosp., Mpls., 1972—74, Dr. McDonald and Dr. Kinneberg, St. Paul, 1974—77, Dr. Lorenzo Patelli, Seattle, 1978—82, Dr. Terry Thomas, Seattle, 1983—90, Dr. Charles Wallace and Dr. Al. Solhaug, Seattle, 1991—98, Dr. Kathy Curtis and Dr. John Larsen, Seattle, 1999—2003, Dr. Linda FuKuda, Seattle, 2000—. Author: (poetry) Expressions from My Heart, 2004. Vol. Planned Parenthood, Seattle, 1984—87; pres. PTA, Seattle, 1996—97; Sunday sch. tchr. Grace United Meth. Ch., Seattle, 1997—99, chair women, 2001—03. Recipient Vol. Cert., John Muir Elem. Sch., 1996—2002. Mem.: Seattle Dental Hygiene Soc. Democrat. Methodist. Avocations: flower arranging, poetry, reading, writing, walking. Home: 9212 39th Ave S Seattle WA 98118-4827

JOHNSON, MARGARET ANDERSON, writer, publishing executive, agricultural products executive; b. Knoxville, Tenn., Apr. 19, 1927; d. Samuel Waller and Laura Lewis (Lawhon) Anderson; m. Thomas Carlisle Johnson, Jan. 9, 1949; children: James Scott, Wendy, Laura Lynn. Student, U. Tenn. and U. Fla., 1945—49. Writer, artist Water Oak Pub., Tallahassee, pub., 1990—. Author, illustrator: Berber, A Lamb's Tale, 1998. Past pres. Ednl. TV Coun., Tampa, Tampa Jr. Women's Club; past advisor parliamentary procedure Jr. League of Tallahassee, past bd. dirs.; past v.p. Christian Women's Club, Tampa; past pres. PTA; tchr. Sunday sch., 50 yrs. Tallahassee Bible Ch.; tchr. Sunday sch. First Bapt. Ch., Tampa, Fla., Grace Ch., Christ Cmty. Ch., Tampa, writer, illustrator Sunday sch. materials. Named Most Outstanding Sustainer, Jr. League, Tallahassee, 1989. Mem.: Alpha Omicron Pi (coll. chpt. pres., alumni chpt. pres., Tampa). Republican. Avocations: painting, writing, horseback riding, providing a haven for needy animals. Home and Office: Water Oak Pub 2984 Water Oak Plantation Dr Tallahassee FL 32312 Personal E-mail: majwopub@yahoo.com.

JOHNSON, MARGARET ANN (PEGGY), library administrator; b. Atlanta, Aug. 11, 1948; d. Odell H. and Virginia (Mathiasen) Johnson; m. Lee J. English, Mar. 4, 1978; children: Carson J., Amelia J. BA, St. Olaf Coll., 1970; MA, U. Chgo., 1972; MBA, Met. State U., 1990. Music cataloger U. Iowa Librs., Iowa City, 1972-73; analyst Control Data Corp., Bloomington, Minn., 1973-75; br. libr. St. Paul Pub. Librs., 1975-77; head tech. svcs. St. Paul Campus Librs., U. Minn., 1977-86; collection devel. officer Univ. Librs., U. Minn., Mpls., 1987-90; asst. dir. St. Paul Campus Librs., U. Minn., 1987-95; planning officer U. Librs. U. Minn., Mpls., 1993-97, asst. univ. libr., 1997—2003, interim univ. libr., 2002, assoc. univ. libr., 2003—. Libr. cons. Mekerere U., Kampala, Uganda, 1990, U. Nat. Rwanda, 1990, Inst. Agr. and Vet. Hassan II, Rabat, Morocco, 1992—, Ecole Nat. Agr., Meknes, Morocco, 2000, China Agrl. U., Beijing, 2001—. Author: Automation and Organizational Change in Libraries, 1991, The Searchable Internet, 1996, Fundamentals of Collection Development and Management, 2004; editor: New Directions in Technical Services, 1997; editor Technicalities Jour., 2000—, Libr. Resources and Tech. Svcs., 2003—; editor Guide to Tech. Svcs. Resources, 1994, Recruiting, Educating and Tng. Librarians for Collection Devel., 1994, Collection Mgmt. and Devel., 1994, Virtually Yours, 1998; contbr. articles to profl. jours. Recipient Samuel Lazerow Rsch. fellowship Assn. Coll. and Rsch. Librs., Inst. for Sci. Info., 1987; Blackwell scholar Assn. for Libr. Collections and Tech. Svcs., 2005 Mem. ALA, Internat. Assn. Agrl. Librs. and Documentatists, U.S. Agrl. Info. Network, Assn. for Libr. Collections and Tech. Svcs. (pres. 1999-2000). Office: U of Minn Librs 499 Wilson Libr 309 19th Ave S Minneapolis MN 55455-0438 Office Phone: 612-624-2312. Business E-Mail: m-john@umn.edu.

JOHNSON, MARGARET H., welding company executive; b. Chgo., June 3, 1933; d. Harold W. and clara J. (Pape) Glavin; m. Odean Jack Johnson, Nov. 18, 1950; children: Karen Ann, Dean Harold. Student, Moody Bible Inst., 1976-78. V.p., sec. Seamline Welding, Inc., Grayslake, Ill., 1956-96, also bd. dirs. Author: Living Faith, 1973, 80, Lord's Ladder of Love, 1976, God's Rainbow, 1982; contbr. articles to religious mags. Trustee SWCEPS, Grayslake, 1963-99; life mem. Rep. presdl. Task Force, 1982—; trustee, 1986-88; charter founder Ronald Reagan Rep. Ctr., 1987; mem. lake View Neighborhood Group, Chgo., Small Group Ch. Cmty.; active Mary, Seat of Wisdom Cath. prayer groups, 1970-90, renew facilitator, 1986-88, co-chairperson, 1986-88; Sunday sch. tchr.; mem. parish coun. St. Gilbert parish, 1995-2000, evangelization chair, 1995-99, hospitality chair, 1995-99, welcome home program, 1998-99; mem. St. Raymond Cath. Ch., Mt. Prospect, 2000—; mem. spiritual life com. The Moorings of Arlington Heights, 2001—, mem. operating bd., 2005. Recipient Internat. Peace Prize, United Cultural Convention of Am. Biog. Inst., 2005. Mem. AARP, ASCAP, Fedn. Ind. Small Bus., Internat. Platform Assn., Women's Aglow Fellowship, Grayslake c. of C., Exch. Club of Grayslake, Grayslake Devel. Corp. Home: Apt 415 811 E Central Rd Arlington Heights IL 60005-3279

JOHNSON, MARGARET KENNARD, artist, educator; b. Madison, Wis., Feb. 3, 1918; d. Dwight Clinton and Florence June (Lott) Kennard; m. Edward Oscar Johnson, Sept. 1, 1947; children: Lonni Sue, Aline Marie. BFA, Pratt Inst., 1941; M in Design, U. Mich., 1943; studied with Josef Albers, 1944. Cert. tchr., Mich. Art. supr. Ypsilanti (Mich.) Schs., 1941-42; acting asst. prof. Drake U., Des Moines, Iowa, 1943-45; asst. prof. Tex. State Coll. for Women, Denton, 1945-46; instr. adult classes Mus. Modern Art, N.Y.C., 1946-71; art. instr. Tokyo American Club, 1981-83; instr. Princeton Art Assn., 1960-75, 85—. Instr. found. classes The Art Sch. Pratt Inst., Bklyn., 1946-49; instr. Princeton Adult Sch., 1965-74. Work exhibited in one woman shows Internat. Print Soc., New Hope, Pa., 1983, Gallery Tapies, Kobe, Japan, 1985, Norske Grafikere, Oslo, 1985, Am. Ctr., Tokyo, 1986, N.J. State Mus., Trenton, 1988, The Tolman Collection, Tokyo, Japan, 1995, 2002, Artworks, Trenton, N.J., 1996, Rider U., Lawrenceville, N.J., 2004, The Nassau Club, Princeton, N.J., 2005; group exhibits include Sao Paulo Mus., Brazil, 1973, Tochigi Prefectural Art Mus., Utsunomiya, Japan, 1980, Coll. Womens' Assn. Japan show, Tokyo, 1976-79, 81, 83-88, 2001, 02, 03, 04, Met. Mus., Tokyo, 1976-79, 83-88, Pratt Graphs Ctr., N.Y.C., 1986, Milberg Gallery, Firestone Libr. Princeton U., 1988-89, Genkan Gallery, Am. Club, Tokyo, 1989, Princeton Artists Alliance Show, Newark (N.J.) Mus., 2002, Cleve. Art Mus., 2004, N.J. State Mus., Trenton, 2005; work exhibited in permanent collections British Mus., London, 1986, Tochigi Prefectural Mus., Japan, 1980; co-author Japanese Prints Today, 1980; contbr. articles to Am. and Japanese art jours. Mem. Princeton Artists Alliance, Printmaking Council of N.J., Montgomery (N.J.) Ctr for the Arts. Avocations: hiking, travel, classical music, museums, world culture. Home: 231 Snowden Ln Princeton NJ 08540-3629

JOHNSON, MARGUERITE ANNIE See ANGELOU, MAYA

JOHNSON, MARIE-LOUISE TULLY, dermatologist, educator; b. N.Y.C., July 26, 1927; d. James Henry and Mary Frances (Dobbins) Tully; m. Kenneth Gerald Johnson, June 10, 1950. AB, Manhattanville Coll., 1948; PhD, Yale U., 1954, MD, 1956. Intern, then resident Yale-New Haven Med. Ctr., 1956-59; asst. prof. medicine, dermatology Yale U., 1961-67, clin. prof. dermatology, 1980—; chief dermatologist med. svc. Atomic Bomb Casualty Commn., Hiroshima, Japan, 1964-67; assoc. prof. dermatology NYU, 1967-70, 74-76, prof. dermatology, 1976-80; assoc. prof. dermatology, coord. continuing med. edn. Dartmouth Coll., Hanover, NH, 1971-74; chief dermatology Bellevue Hosp., N.Y.C., 1974-80; dir. med. edn. Benedictine Hosp., Kingston, NY, 1980-93. Cons. Health and Nutrition Exam. Survey I, II, Health Stats., Washington, 1967-84. Contbg. author: Cecil's Textbook of Medicine, 15th edit., 1979, 16th edit., 1982, 17th edit., 1985, Dermatology in General Medicine, 2d edit., 1979. Mem. Cardinal Cooke Pro-Life Commn., Albany, N.Y., 1986-87; bd. dirs. Maternity and Early Childhood Found., Albany, 1984-2001, pres., 1987-2001; bd. dirs. Sulzberger Inst. for Dermatologic Edn., 1986-93; pres. Mid-Hudson Consortium for the Advancement of Edn. for Health Professions, 1989-92; bd. govs. Yale U. Alumni Assn., 1991-94; v.p. Assn. Yale U. Alumni in Medicine, 1991-93, pres., 1993-95. Named Disting. Alumna, Manhattanville Coll., 1977, Rose Hirschler award Women's Dermatologic Soc., 1993, Papal Cross Pro Ecclesia et Pontifice Pope John Paul II, 1994, Clark W. Finnerud award Dermatology Found., 1997. Fellow Am. Acad. Dermatology (master 1995, bd. dirs. 1976-80, Presdl. citation 1999); mem. Am. Dermatol. Assn. (bd. dirs. 1986-92, v.p. 1991-92, pres. 2000-01), Inst. Medicine of NAS, Internat. Physicians for Prevention of Nuc. War (del. 1982, 83, 87, 88, 89). Roman Catholic. Home: 15 Strawberry Bank Rd High Falls NY 12440-5128 Office: Kingston Hosp Med Arts Bldg Ste 202 368 Broadway Kingston NY 12401-5159 Office Phone: 845-338-7472.

JOHNSON, MARILYN, retired obstetrician, retired gynecologist; b. Houston, May 7, 1925; d. William Walton and Marilyn (Henderson) J. BA, Rice Inst., 1945; MD, Baylor U., 1950. Intern New Eng. Hosp. Women and Children, Boston, 1950-51; resident Meth. Hosp., Houston, 1951-53; fellow in gynecol. pathology Harvard Med. Sch., 1952-53; resident in gynecology M.D. Anderson Tumor Inst., Houston, 1954, fellow, 1955; practice medicine specializing in ob-gyn. Houston, 1954-81, Fredericksburg, Tex., 1981-97; ret., 1997. Mem. staffs St. Joseph's, Meml., Meth., Park Plaza, Hill Country Meml. Rosewood, South Austin Cmty., Comfort (Tex.) Cmty. hosps.; clin. instr. ob-gyn Coll. Medicine, Baylor U., 1954—, Postgrad. Sch. Medicine, U. Tex., 1954—; gynecologist De Pelchin Faith Home, Houston, 1954—, also Rice U., Richmond State Sch.; med. dirs. Birthright, Inc., Houston, 1973—; chief med. staff Hill Country Meml. Hosp., Fredericksburg, Tex., 1990-92; cons. Tex. bd. Blue Cross Blue Shield; pro-life public spkr. Bd. dirs. Right to Life, Houston, Found. for Life. Grantee Sandoz Labs., 1973, 75, Delbay Pharm. Co., 1977. Fellow Am. Coll. Obstetricians and Gynecologists; mem. AMA, Am. Soc. Colposcopic Pathologists, Tex. Med. Assn., Am. Med. Women's Assn., Internat. Infertility Assn., Harris County Med. Soc., Postgrad. Med. Assembly South Tex., Houston Ob-Gyn. Soc., Tex. Folklore Soc., Zonta, Fredericksburg Rockhounds. Republican. Baptist. Home: 2301 Lakeside Ct Rockport TX 78382-3519

JOHNSON, MARK ALAN, lawyer; b. Marysville, Ohio, June 5, 1960; s. Neil Raymond and Elizabeth Johnson; m. Deborah Anne Hillis, Sept. 21, 1984. BA, Otterbein Coll., 1982; JD, Ohio State U., 1985. Bar: Ohio 1985, U.S. Dist. Ct. (so. dist.) Ohio 1985, U.S. Ct. Appeals (6th cir.) 1987, U.S. Dist. Ct. (no. dist.) Ohio 1991, U.S. Ct. Appeals (5th cir.) 1998. Assoc. Baker and Hostetler LLP, Columbus, Ohio, 1985-92, ptnr., 1993—. Mem. ABA (litigation sect., mem. bus. torts litigation com., comml. and banking litigation com.), Ohio Bar Assn., Columbus Bar Assn. Office: Baker & Hostetler LLP 65 E State St Ste 2100 Columbus OH 43215-4215 Office Phone: 614-228-1541. Business E-Mail: mjohnson@bakerlaw.com.

JOHNSON, MARK ANDREW, lawyer; b. Plainville, Kans., Feb. 27, 1959; s. Delton Lee and Margaret Ellen (McCracken) J. BA in Chemistry, Reed Coll., 1982; JD, U. Calif., Berkeley, 1987. Bar: Oreg. 1987, U.S. Supreme Ct. 1991. Jud. clk. U.S. Dist. Ct. Oreg., Portland, 1987-88, Oreg. Ct. of Appeals, Salem, 1988-89; assoc. Gevurtz, Menashe, Larson, Kurshner & Yates, PC, Portland, 1989-93; ptnr. Findling & Johnson LLP, Portland, 1993-99; of counsel Bennett Hartman Morris & Kaplan, LLP and predecessor, Portland, 1999—. Mem. ABA, Nat. Lesbian and Gay Law Assn. (co-chmn. 1994-95), Oreg. Gay and Lesbian Law Assn. (co-chair 1990-92), Oreg. State Bar (pres. 1998-99). Office: Bennett Hartman Morris & Kaplan LLP 851 SW 6th Ave Ste 1600 Portland OR 97204-1307 E-mail: johnsonm@bennetthartman.com.

JOHNSON, MARK EUGENE, lawyer; b. Independence, Mo., Jan. 8, 1951; s. Russell Eugene and Reatha (Nixon) J.; m. Vicki Ja Lane, June 11, 1983. AB with honors, U. Mo., 1973, JD, 1976. Bar: Mo. 1976, U.S. Dist. Ct. (we. dist.) Mo. 1976, U.S. Ct. Appeals (8th cir.) 1984, U.S. Supreme Ct. 1993. Ptnr. Stinson Morrison Hecker LLP, Kansas City, Mo., 1976—. Editor Mo. Law Rev., 1974-76. Pres. Lido Villas Assn., Inc., Mission, Kans., 1979-81. Mem. ABA, Mo. Bar Assn., Kansas City Bar Assn., Lawyers Assn. Kansas City, Def. Rsch. Inst., Internat. Assn. Def. Counsel, Mo. Orgn. Def. Lawyers, Carriage Club, Order of Coif, Phi Beta Kappa, Phi Eta Sigma, Phi Kappa Phi, Omicron Delta Kappa. Republican. Presbyterian. Home: 4905 Somerset Dr Shawnee Mission KS 66207-2230 Office: Stinson Morrison Hecker LLP 1201 Walnut St Ste 2900 Kansas City MO 64106-2150 Office Phone: 816-691-2724. Business E-Mail: mjohnson@stinsonmoheck.com.

JOHNSON, MARK HAROLD, lawyer; b. Grants Pass, Oreg., June 12, 1956; s. Harold R. and Dorothy A. Johnson; m. Susan M. Johnson, June 16, 1979; children: Eric M., Sarah S. BA, Harvard U., 1978; JD, U. Calif. Hastings Coll. Law, San Francisco, 1981. Bar: Calif. 1981. Ptnr. Fenton & Keller (formerly Hoge, Fenton, Jones & Appel, Inc.), Monterey, Calif., 1981-97, Johnson, Gaver & Leach, LLP, Monterey, 1997—. Office: Johnson Gaver & Leach LLP 2801 Monterey Salinas Hwy Ste B Monterey CA 93940-6401 E-mail: mjohnson@jglllp.com.

JOHNSON, MARK J., mining executive; Degree in Engring., Montana Tech. From engr. to sr. v.p., COO ops. Freeport-McMoRanCopper & Gold Inc., New Orleans, 1986—2003, sr. v.p., 2003—, COO ops., 2003—. Office: Freeport McMoRan Copper & Gold Inc 1615 Poydras St New Orleans LA 70112

JOHNSON, MARK MATTHEW, museum administrator; b. Dec. 10, 1950; s. Charles Michael Jr. and Jean Lee (Reid) J.; m. Amy Joy Schneider, March 10, 1984; children: Rachel Amelia, Sarah Jean. BA, U. Wis., Whitewater, 1974; cert. Art Mus. Studies, MA in Art History, U. Ill., 1976. Rsch. assoc. Krannert Art Mus., Champaign, Ill., 1975, asst. dir., curator, 1981-85; lectr. dept. mus. edn. Art Inst. Chgo., 1975-77; curator dept. art history and edn. Cleve. Mus. Art, 1977-81; dir. Muscarelle Mus. Art. Coll. William and Mary, Williamsburg, Va., 1985-94; lect. dept. fine arts Coll. William and Mary, 1985-94; dir. Montgomery (Ala.) Mus. Fine Arts, 1994—. Author: Idea to Image: Preparatory Studies from the Renaissance to Impressionism, 1980, Romeyn de Hooghe, 1989, Literacy Through Art, 1990, Nissan Engel: Nouvelles Dimensions, 1994, Hans Grohs: An Ecstatic Vision, 1996, (English and French edits.) Nissan Engel, 1998, Ginny Ruffner, 2003; organized, curated numerous exhbns., 1980—. Rsch. and travel grantee various mus. Mem. Assn. Art Mus. Dirs., Internat. Coun. Mus., Coll. Art Assn., Am. Assn. Mus. (accreditation com.). Office: Montgomery Mus Fine Arts PO Box 230819 One Museum Dr Montgomery AL 36123-0819 Office Phone: 334-240-4333. Business E-Mail: mjohnson@mmfa.org.

JOHNSON, MARK P., lawyer; b. Billings, Mont., Aug. 14, 1955; BA cum laude, Yale U., 1977; JD, Harvard U., 1980. Bar: Mo. 1980, US Dist. Ct. We. Dist. Mo. 1980, US. Ct. Appeals 10th Cir. 1982, US Ct. Appeals 8th Cir. 1982, US Supreme Ct. 1985. Ptnr. Spencer Fane Britt & Browne, Kansas City, Mo., 1987—94, Sonnenschein Nath & Rosenthal LLP, Kansas City, Mo., 1994—. Counsel Am. Strokes Found. Mem.: ABA, Racial Justice Collaborative, Kansas City Met. Bar Assn., Mo. Bar, Assn. Yale Alumni. Office: Sonnenschein Nath & Rosenthal LLP Ste 1100 4520 Main St Kansas City MO 64111 Office Phone: 816-460-2424. Office Fax: 816-531-7545. Business E-Mail: mjohnson@sonnenschein.com.

JOHNSON, MARLENE M., nonprofit executive; b. Braham, Minn., Jan. 11, 1946; d. Beauford and Helen (Nelson) J.; m. Peter Frankel. BA, Macalester Coll., 1968. Founder, pres. Split Infinitive, Inc., St. Paul, 1970-82; pres., bd. dirs. Face to Face Health and Counseling Clinic, 1977-78; with Working Opportunities for Women, 1977-82; lt. gov. State of Minn., St. Paul, 1983-91; sr. fellow Family Support Project, Ctr. for Policy Alternative, 1991-93; assoc. adminstr. for adminstrn. GSA, Washington, 1994-95; v.p. for people and strategy Rowe Furniture Corp., McLean, Va., 1995-97; CEO NAFSE: Assn. Internat. Educators, 1998—. Founder, past chmn. Nat. Leadership Conf. Women Execs. in State Govt.; mem. exec. com., midwestern chair Nat. Conf. Lt. Govs.; bd. dirs. AFS-USA, Inc., 1992-98, Nat. Capitol Region coun. Girl Scouts U.S., 1997-2004, bd. trustees AFS Internat. programs, 1998-2002; mem. adv. bd. Comm. Consortium Media Ctr., 2000-, Ctr. for Children in Poverty, Columbia U., 2002. Chmn. Minn. Women's Polit. Caucus, 1973-76, Dem.-Farmer-Labor Small Bus. Task Force, 1978, Child Care Task Force, 1987; dir. membership sect. Nat. Women's Polit. Caucus, 1975-77; vice chmn. Minn. Del. to White House Conf. on Small Bus., 1980; co-founder Minn. Women's Campaign Fund, 1982; bd. dirs. Nat. Child Care Action Campaign; chair Children's 2000 Commn., 1990; candidate for Mayor St. Paul, 1993. Recipient Outstanding Achievement award St. Paul YWCA, 1980, Disting. Svc. award St. Paul Jaycees, 1980, Disting. Citizen citation Macalester Coll., 1982, Disting. Contbns. to Families award Minn. Coun. on Family Rels., 1986, Minn. Sportfishing Congress award, 1986, Royal Order of Polar Star Govt. Sweden, 1988, Children's Champion award Def. Fund, 1989, Jane Preston award Minn. State Coun. on Vocat. Tech. Edn., 1989, Legis. Leadership award Am. Fedn. Tchrs., 1991; named One of Ten Outstanding Young Minnesotans, Minn. Jaycees, 1980; Swedish Bicentennial Commn. grantee, 1987. Mem. Nat. Assn. Women Bus. Owners (past pres.). E-mail: marlenej@nafsa.org.

JOHNSON, MARSHALL HARDY, investment company executive; b. Raleigh, NC, Sept. 7, 1923; s. William Thompson and Evie (Barnes) J.; m. Mary Lynn Lewis, June 24, 1947 (div. 1977); children: Marshall Hardy, Lynn Lewis Johnson-Titchener, Carter Johnson Overton; m. Beverly Ray Johnson, June 2, 1984. Student, U. N.C., 1942-43, 45-46; grad. in banking, U. Pa., 1957. Reporter, analyst Dunn & Bradstreet, Raleigh, 1946-47; chmn., pres., CEO McDaniel Lewis & Co., Greensboro, N.C., 1947—; v.p. Scott & Stringfellow, Inc., Richmond, Va., 1993-96. Mem. Midwest Stock Exch., Chgo., 1960-77; dir. emeritus First Citizen Bank & Trust, Greensboro, Mcpl. Coun., Raleigh; adv. dir. Friends Home, 1985-93; freelance writer. Contbr. articles to profl. jours. Dir. Young Dems., Greensboro, 1962-66, Jr. C. of C., Greensboro, 1964-70; deacon, tchr. First Bapt. Ch., Greensboro. With USN, 1942-46. Fellow: Fin. Fedn. Am.; mem.: Securities Dealers of Carolinas (pres. 1976), Securities Industries Assn. (Mid-Atlantic exec. com. 1986—93), Nat. Assn. Securities Dealers, Am. Arbitration Assn., Greensboro Country Club, Kiwanis (Hixon award 1998), Odd Fellows, Magna Charta Barons, VFW, Alpha Tau Omega. Avocations: tennis, golf, swimming. Home: 310 Kimberly Dr Greensboro NC 27408-5018 Office: McDaniel Lewis & Co PO Box 9 Greensboro NC 27402-0009 E-mail: zipjohnson@triad.rr.com. *I've learned that our quality of life is largely determined by our own choices.*

JOHNSON, MARTIN ALLEN, publishing executive, artist; b. Bklyn., Aug. 20, 1931; s. Ellis A. and Estelle (Rudnick) Johnson; m. Suzanne Cornbleet, Dec. 12, 1964 (div. Feb. 1979); 1 child, Sarah; m. Diane Schlesinger Krull, Aug. 19, 1981. AB, Bard Coll., 1954. Assoc. editor Am. Printer and Lithographer mag., N.Y.C., 1956-57, mng. editor, 1957-58, editor, 1958; mng. editor Printing Impressions mag., Phila., Delaware Valley Printing Impressions, 1958-61; pub. PTM mag., Chgo., 1959-67; v.p. Ednl. Screen and Audio Visual Guide, Chgo., 1962-67; pres. Trade Periodical Co., Chgo., 1967—, Pub. Dynamics, Inc., Stamford, Conn., 1968—, U.S. Indsl. Publs., Inc., Stamford, 1971—, U.S. Graphics Corp., Stamford, 1974—, Landmark Comms. Corp., Stamford. Spl. coor. Sun-Sentinal, Chgo. Tribune. Contbr. articles to profl. jours. With U.S. Army, 1954—56. Recipient Justin P. Allman award, Wallcoverings Assn., 1993. Mem.: ArtSource, Cornell Mus. Art Guild, Fla. Watercolor Soc., Boca Raton Mus. Artist Guild (profl.), Am. Watercolor Soc. (sustaining), Am. Soc. Interior Designers, Typophiles (N.Y.C.), Norton Mus. Art, Am. Music Libr. Israel, Wellington Club (London), Landmark Club (Stamford), Exec. Club (Chgo.), Chgo. Press Club. Jewish. Avocations: poetry, objective biblical history, painting. Office: Pub Dynamics Inc 9506 Lantern Bay Cir West Palm Beach FL 33411 Office Phone: 561-204-3883. E-mail: mjtalk2me@aol.com.

JOHNSON, MARTIN CLIFTON, physician; b. Santa Fe, Nov. 16, 1933; s. Henry J. and Dorothy (Clifton) J.; m. Priscilla Bollam, June 13, 1959; children: Martin Clifton II, Kurt B., Kirsten L. Ustach, Katharine E. AB, Stanford U., 1955, MD, 1959. Diplomate Am. Bd. Neurol. Surgery, Am. Bd. Pediat. Neurosurgery, Am. Bd. Forensic Examiners, Am. Bd. Forensic Medicine; cert. Homeland Security Level III. Intern in surgery Palo Alto (Calif.) Stanford U. Hosp., 1959-60; fellow in neurosurgery Mayo Found., Rochester, Minn., 1960-61; asst. resident gen. surgery Presbyn. Med. Ctr., San Francisco, 1963-64; asst. resident, sr. resident, chief resident in neurosurgery U. Cin., 1964-68; pvt. practice neurosurgery/pediat. neurosurgery Portland, Oreg., 1968-99. Col. M.C. AUS, ret.; lt. comdr. M.C. USNR, 1961-63. Fellow ACS, Am. Acad. Pediats.; mem. AMA, Portland Met. Med. Soc., Oreg. Med. Soc., Congress Neurol. Surgeons, Am. Assn. Neurol. Surgeons, Am. Assn. Pediatric Neurosurgery, Multnomah Athletic Club, Columbia Aviation Club. Office: Pacific Northwest Neurol Assocs PC 31870 SW Country View Ln Wilsonville OR 97070-7476 Office Phone: 503-694-5900. Personal E-mail: martinc33@hotmail.com.

JOHNSON, MARV ANTHONY, school psychologist; b. Rome, N.Y., Nov. 9, 1968; s. Jay Leslie and Helen Catherine Johnson; m. Betsy Joan Becraft. AA, Mohawk Valley C.C., 1989; BA cum laude, SUNY, Plattsburgh, 1990; MA, U. Colo., 1997, cert. in edn. specialist, 2001. Cert. sch. psychologist Colo. Dept. Edn. Caseworker, investigator Oneida Coutny Dept. Social Svcs., Utica, NY, 1992—94; sr. social caseworker Denver County DHS, 1995—2000; sch. psychologist Edison Sch. Inc., Colorado Springs, 2001—04, Pueblo Sch. Dist., 2004—. Recipient Profl. of yr. awad, Pikes Peak ARC, 2004. Mem.: Colo. Soc. Sch. Psychologists, Nat. Assn. Sch. Psychologists. Office: Pueblo Sch Dist 60 29 Lehigh Ave Pueblo CO 81005 Office Phone: 719-549-7853.

JOHNSON, MARVIN RICHARD ALOIS, architect, consultant; b. Humphrey, Nebr., Aug. 13, 1916; s. Otto Henry and Reenste (Berends) J. AB, BA in Architecture, U. Nebr., 1943; M.Architecture, Harvard U., 1948. Designer, draftsman firm Clark & Enersen, Lincoln, Nebr., 1946-47, 48-50; cons. architect div. sch. planning N.C. Dept. Public Instrn., Raleigh, 1950-80; architect, cons. ednl. facilities, 1981—. Cons. HEW, Washington, 1960 Contbr. articles to profl. jours. Served with USNR, 1943-46. Fellow AIA (recipient Distinguished Service citation N.C. chpt. 1960, v.p. N.C. chpt. 1977-78, pres.-elect 1979, pres. 1980); mem. Council Ednl. Facility Planners, Am. Assn. School Adminstrs., Phi Beta Kappa. Democrat. Lutheran. Home: 3500 Faulkner Dr Apt D303 Lincoln NE 68516-6639 E-mail: mramrajohn@aol.com.

JOHNSON, MARY ELIZABETH, music educator, musician; b. Tyler, Tex., Mar. 29, 1933; d. Robert Edward and Mamie Oberia (Walters) Spaulding; m. George Devereaux Johnson, Mar. 31, 1955; children: Bradford D., Robin Elizabeth. BFA, So. Meth. U., 1955; pvt. studies with Bomar Cramer, Dallas, 1964—69. Music tchr. Dallas Country Day Sch., 1955; tchr. Dayton Pub. Schs., Ohio, 1956—57; pvt. tchr. piano Dallas, 1962—; profl. accompanist, 1985—; duo-pianist, 1965—; sponsor, tchr. creative and performing arts program Dallas Ind. Sch. Dist., 1981—82, 1983, 1984. Sponsor Jr. Melodie and Jr. Harmonie. Mem. Northwest Bible Ch. Dallas, 3-score com. N.W. Bible Ch. Named to Hall of Fame, Am. Coll. Musicians, 1981. Mem. Nat. Guild Piano Tchrs. (cert., named to honor roll 1971), Tex. Fedn. Music Clubs (historian 1974-76, state chmn. music svc. in cmty. 1971-73, dist. jr. counselor 1971-78, dist. chmn. music svc. in cmty. 1971-78, rec. sec. 5th dist. 1975-76, 1st v.p. 1977-78, jr. festival chmn. 1977-80, dist chmn. Jr. Gold Cup awards 1980, 84, 85, 86, 87, 88, asst. chmn. North Dallas divsn. 5th dist. jr. festival 1981-82), Music Tchrs. Nat. Assn., Jr. Pianists Guild Dallas (chmn. jr. recitals 1983, chmn. sr. recitals 1984, treas. 2003-2005), Tex. Music Tchrs. Assn., Dallas Music Tchrs. Assn., Music Study Club Dallas (chmn. piano program 1981-82), Music Study Club, Dallas Fedn. Music Clubs (del. 1969-78, 1st v.p. 1977), Daus. Republic Tex. (1st v.p. Bonham chpt. 1975-76), Alpha Delta Pi, Melodie Club (pres. 1969-71, 2d v.p. 1977—, 1st v.p. 2003-04, 2006-06, choral accompanist, counselor jr. club, historian, press sec. 1981-82, 1st v.p. 2003-2004, 2004—), Kalista Club (yearbook chmn. 1983-

2000, v.p. 1984-85, pres. 1986-87), Park Cities Club, Tower Club, Kermis Club, Rondo-Carrousel Club, Trippers Club, Steinway Hall's Ptnrs. in Performance, Mu Phi Epsilon (patron). Home: 3848 Cedarbrush Dr Dallas TX 75229-2701

JOHNSON, MARY KATHERINE (KATIE JOHNSON), elementary school educator; b. Prescott, Wis., June 12, 1945; d. Walter Frank and Mary Jane (Larson) Johnson; m. William F. Hilton, June 23, 1968 (div. 1985); children: Bradley Eric, Karin Louise. BA, Mich. State U., 1967, MA, 1970; postgrad., U. Calif., Berkeley, 1970—. Cert. elem. tchr., Calif. Tchr. East Lansing (Mich.) Pub. Schs., 1967-68, Hall's Crossroads Sch., Aberdeen, Md., 1968-69, Oakland (Calif.) Pub. Schs., 1970-82; tchr., cons. Bay Area Writing Project, Berkeley, 1978—, Bay Area Math. Project, Berkeley, 1994—, Bay Area Calif. Arts Project, Berkeley, 1997—; cons. Child Devel. Project, San Ramon, Calif., 1985; tchr. Berkeley Unified Sch. Dist., 1986—, support provider, beginning tchr. support and assessment program, 2000—, tchr math leader, 2003—; coord. pub. programs, math. edn. program Lawrence Hall of Sci., U. Calif., Berkeley, 1996-98; curriculum developer, writer U. Calif. Bot. Gardens, 2001—, tchr. trainer, 2003—. Mem. MATHTEQ U. Calif, Berkeley, 1987—90; mem. com. of credentials Commn. for Tchr. Preparation and Licensing, Sacramento, 1974—76; mem. program com. Asilomar Math. Conf., 1995—2000; rep. No. Regional Spl. Edn. Local Plan Area Com., 1994—98, Region III Full Inclusion Task Force for State of Calif., 1994—98; participant Calif. Rsch. Inst., 1992; mem. adv. task force on tchr. preparation in mainstreaming Calif. Commn. on Tchr. Credentialling, 1996; adv. bd. Profl. Internship Program., U. Calif., Berkeley; tchr. leader Profl. Insvc. for New and Experienced Tchrs., 1997—; mem., tchr.-leader Profl. Instrn. for New and Established Tchrs., 1998—2002; math tchr. leader Berkeley Unified Sch. Dist., 2003—04, mem. spl. edn. task force, 2004—; spkr. in field. Contbg. author: Portfolio Assessment in Mathematics, 1990, Teacher Handbook on Homework, C.M.C. Communicator, 1993. Coord. children's coun. Epworth Meth. Ch., Berkeley, 1985-88, 96-98, Youth Coun., 1993-95; cert. lay spkr. Bay View dist. Calif.-Nev. United Meth. Ch., Berkeley, 1989—, trustee, 1994-96, 98-2002; pres. bd. trustees Maya's Music Therapy Fund, 1994-2004; mentor tchr. Berkeley Unified Sch. Dist., 1996, 99; mem. adv. bd. Calif. Urban Partnership program U. Calif., Berkeley, 1999-2004. Recipient Outstanding Alumni K-12 Tchr. award Mich. State U. Coll. Edn. Alumni Assn., 2002; named Math. Tchr. of Yr. Alameda/Contra Costa Counties Math. Educators, 1996; Berkeley Pub. Edn. Found. grantee, 1988, 89, 90, 92, 94, 95, 98, 2000-03, 2004, In Dulce Jullibo Inc. grantee, 1989, 90, 92, 94, 95, 99, 2003, BAMP grantee, 1995, Calif. Math. Coun. grantee, 1995; fellow Bay Area Math. Project, 1994, Oakland-Bay Area Writing Project, 1977, Bay Area Writing Project, 1978, 98, Bay Area Calif. Arts Project, 1997. Mem. Nat. Coun. Tchrs. English, Nat. Coun. Tchrs. Math., Calif. English Coun., Calif. Math. Coun., P.E.O., Profl. Instr. for New and Established Teacher; bd. dirs. CA Chpt. Assn. Persons with Severe Handicaps (bd. dirs. 1997-2005), Alameda-Contra Costa County Math. Educators (pres. 2000-04, bd. dirs.). Democrat. Avocations: singing, jogging, swimming, gourmet cooking, sewing. Home: 1016 Keeler Ave Berkeley CA 94708-1404 Office: Oxford Sch 1130 Oxford St Berkeley CA 94707-2624

JOHNSON, MARY LOU, lay worker, educator; b. Moline, Ill., July 15, 1923; d. Percy and Hope (Aulgur) Sipes; m. Blaine Eugene Johnson, May 30, 1941 (dec.); children: Vivian Johnson Sweedy Maday, Michael D. (dec.), Amelia Johnson Harms Thomas, James Michael (dec.). Grad. high sch., Moline. From chmn. Christian edn. to dir. 1st Christian Ch., Moline, 1971—88, dir. Christian edn., 1988—93, ret., 1993, chmn. Christian edn., 2001—03. Sunday sch. tchr. 1st Christian Ch., Moline, 1958-84; cluster del. Christian Chs. Ill. and Wisc., Moline, 1988-89. Author: (poem) What Is A Mother?, 1965. Officer various positions PTA, Moline, 1972-75, hon. life mem. State of Ill., 1972; leader, dist. chair Girl Scouts U.S., Moline, 1955-65; skywatcher USAF Ground Observer Corps, Moline, 1955-57; vol. telethon coord. Muscular Dystrophy Assn., Moline, 1971-94; del. lt. gov.'s Commn. on Aging, Springfield, Ill., 1990; historian 1st Christian Ch., Moline, 1996—, libr., 2000—; vol. C.A.R.E. Ministry, 1999—, Ring for Care, 1999-2002, We. Ill. Area Agy. on Aging, 1998-2003; bd. dirs. Wee Care Day Care Ctr., 2003—. Recipient Appreciation award Muscular Dystrophy Assn., 1964-94. Republican. Home: 2014 9th St Moline IL 61265-4779 Personal E-mail: grmalou624@aol.com. *Life hands us many challenges. I find them interesting and always have been willing to accept them. Not all my efforts have been successful; however, each attempt has helped me grow to be a better person.*

JOHNSON, MARY MARGARET DICKENS, researcher, consultant; b. Ottumwa, Iowa, July 10, 1955; d. Donald Milton and Maxine Margaret Dickens; m. Donald Hampton Johnson, July 30, 1944; children: Laurie Anne Davidson, Donald, Jr. Hampton. *Mother, Maxine (Kinsinger) Dickens, graduated Phi Theta Kappa from Ottumwa Heights Women's College on Scholarship during the Depression. Brother, Rex, was an Air force captain and pilot and flew 100 combat missions in Vietnam. Brother, John, Graduated Iowa State Phi Beta Kappa and head of aerospace engineering class. He received a PhD from Berkley. Brother, Bruce, patented a windowing technique in 2000. Both Bruce and Rex hold a BS in Chemical Engineering from ISU, and an MBA from Pepperdine University and the University of Iowa respectively.* M, U. Hawaii, 1979; B, Iowa State U., 1976; M, Johns Hopkins Sch. Advanced Internat. Studies, 1986; cert. of Completion, U. Va., 1988—92; postgrad. in pub. affairs, Fla .Atlantic U., 2003—. Cert. purchasing mgr., cert. profl. contracts mgr., scuba diver 1974. Media asst. dept. entomolgy Iowa State U., Ames, 1973—74, rsch. asst. dept. sociology & anthropology, 1974—76; rsch. grantee East West Ctr., Honolulu, 1976—78; fgn. affairs specialist U.S. Dept. of State/Agy. for Internat. Devel., Washington, 1980—81; fed. summer intern U.S. Dept. of Commerce/Nat. Telecom. and Info. Adminstrn., Washington, 1980—80; export adminstrn. specialist U.S. Dept. of Commerce, Washington, 1982—85; English lang. tchr. INTERAC, Tokyo, 1985; tchr., pub. rels. officer Overseas Devel. Co., Kowloon, Hong Kong, 1986—87; English lang. tchr. Philips Lang. Learning Systems, Tokyo, 1986; sr. contracts mgr. Systems Flow, Inc., Rockville, Md., 1997—98; with HSI Geotrans, Sterling, Va., 1992; contract specialist U.S. GSA, Washington, 1987—94, Wash. Suburban San. Commn., Laurel, Md., 1996—97; grad. asst. Fla. Atlantic U., Ft. Lauderdale, 2003—. Workshop/seminar leader Nat. Contract Mgmt. Assn., Idaho Falls, Idaho, 2002; third v.p. Alpha Chi Omega Sorority, Ames, Iowa, 1975—76; outstanding scholar U.S. GSA, Washington, 1987—94; workshop leader Nat. Contract Mgmt. Assn. World Congress, Long Beach, Calif., 2002; author Nat. Def. Coll. Symposium, Rockville, Md., 1998; field study grant for ind. rsch. in Bangladesh, India and Sri Lanka, East West Ctr. Communication Inst., Honolulu, 1977; student project for amity among nations rschr. in Nigeria and Ghana, Iowa State U., Ames, Iowa, 1974; workshop/seminar leader Nat. Contract Mgmt. Assn., Idaho Falls, Idaho, 2002, West Palm Beach, Fla., 00, Nat. Assn. of Purchasing Managers, Boca Raton, Fla., 2002; pres. Nat. Contract Mgmt. Assn., South Fla. Chpt., Boca Raton, Fla., 2003—04; author Nat. Contract Mgmt. Assn., Contract Mgmt. Mag., McLean, Va., 1996—; fellow Nat. Contract Mgmt. Assn., McLean, Va., 2003—; mem. Mortar Bd., Iowa State U., Ames, Iowa, 1976—2003; pres. Alpha Lamda Delta, Ames, Iowa, 1973—74; rsch. asst. Pub. Procurement Rsch. Ctr., 2003—04; mem. faculty continuing studies online studies Villanova U., 2004—; presenter in field; mem. planning com. Internat. Pub. Empowerment Conf. Author: (article contract mgmt. mag.) Planning for Y2K: What the Government Did Right; contbr. articles and book revs. to profl. jours. Mem. CARE Women's Group, St. John's Anglican Cath., Hong Kong, 1986—87, St. Paul's by the Sea Episc. Ch., Ocean City, Md., 1988—, Chapel St. Andrew, Boca Raton, Fla., 1998—2003, St. James Episc. Ch., Islamorada, Fla., 2000—, St. Nicholas Episc. Ch., Pompano Beach, Fla., 2004—05; mem. altar guild St. Albans Anglican Ch., Tokyo, 1985; adj. mem. St. Andrew's Anglican Cath., Honolulu; eucharistic min. Truro Episcopal Ch., Fairfax, Va., 1989—90; mem. edn. for ministry St. Patrick's Episcopal Ch., Falls Church, Va., 1995—96. Home Fellowship, Truro Episcopal Ch., 1987—94. Fellow: Nat. Contract Mgmt. Assn. (cert. profl. contracts mgr. 2002, cert. assoc. contracts mgr. 2002, pres. 2003, grant to participate in World Congress 2002); mem.: Nat. Assn. Purchasing Mgmt. (workshop leader 2002, Monetary award presentation 2002), 4-H Club, Tau Kappa Epsilon, Alpha Chi Omega. Avocations: bicycling, walking, needlepoint, cooking, gardening. Home: 1926 NE 2nd St Deerfield Beach FL 33441 Office: Florida Atlantic U 111 East Las Olas Blvd Fort Lauderdale FL 33301 Office Phone: 954-547-3204. Personal E-mail: conchcontracts@aol.com. Business E-Mail: mjohn110@fau.edu.

JOHNSON, MARY PAULINE (POLLY JOHNSON), nursing administrator; b. Ohio, May 23, 1940; BSN summa cum laude, Ohio State U., 1962; MSN, Duke U., 1980. RN, N.C. Staff nurse psychiatry unit Univ. Hosps., Ohio, 1963-64; pediatric office nurse Gaithersburg, Md., 1971-73; clin. nurse coord. N.C. Meml. Hosp., Chapel Hill, 1973-86; grant coord. N.C. Assn. Home Care, 1988; practice cons. N.C. Bd. Nursing, Raleigh, 1988-96, assoc. dir. practice, 1996-97, exec. dir., 1997—. Adv. com. PREP Project Citizens Advocacy Ctr. Fellow: Am. Acad. Nursing; mem.: ANA, NC Inst. Medicine (bd. dirs.), Nat. Coun. State Bds. Nursing (bd. dirs., v.p.), NC Nurses Assn., NC Orgn. Nurse Leaders, Sigma Theta Tau. Office: NC Bd of Nursing 3724 National Dr Raleigh NC 27612-4070 Office Phone: 919-782-3211 ext. 250. E-mail: polly@ncbon.com.

JOHNSON, MARYL RAE, cardiologist; b. Fort Dodge, Iowa, Apr. 15, 1951; d. Marvin George and Beryl Evelyn (White) Johnson. BS, Iowa State U., 1973; MD, U. Iowa, 1977. Diplomate Am. Bd. Internal Medicine, Am. Bd. Cardiovasc. Diseases. Intern U. Iowa Hosps., Iowa City, 1977-78, resident, 1978-81, fellow, 1979-82; assoc. in cardiology U. Iowa Hosps. and Clins., Iowa City, 1982-86, asst. prof. medicine cardiovasc. divsn., 1986-88; asst. prof. medicine Med. Ctr. Loyola U., 1988-92, assoc. prof., 1992-94, Rush. U., 1994-97, Northwestern U. Med. Sch., 1998—2002; prof. medicine U. Wis. Med. Sch., Madison, 2002—. Med. dir. cardiac transplantation U. Iowa Hosp., 1986—88; assoc. med. dir. cardiac transplantation Loyola U., 1988—94, assoc. med. dir. Rush Heart Failure and Cardiac Transplant Program, 1994—97; dir. heart failure cardiac transplant program Northwestern U. Med. Sch., 1998—2001, dir. heart failure program, 2001—02; med. dir. heart failure and transplantation U. Wis. Hosp. and Clinics, 2002—. Editor (assoc. editor): Jour. Heart and Lung Transplantation, 1995—99; mem. editl. bd.:, 2000—. Mem. Nat. Heart Lung and Blood Adv. Coun., Bethesda, Md., 1979—83; mem. biomed. rsch. tech. rev. com. NIH, 1990—93, chairperson, 1992—93, chair biomed. rsch. tech. spl. emphasis panel, 1999—2002. Recipient Jane Leinfelder Meml. award, U. Iowa Coll. Medicine, 1977, Clin. Investigator award, NIH, 1981, New Investigator Rsch. award, 1981, 1986; Barry Freeman scholar, 1974. Mem.: ACP, AAAS, AMA, United Network for Organ Sharing (Thoracic Organ Com. 2005—), Am. Soc. Transplantation (chair membership com. 2003—04, bd. dirs. 2004—), Am. Coll. Cardiology (heart failure and cardiac transplant com. 2002—, chair 2004—), Am. Heart Assn., Ctrl. Soc. Clin. Rsch., Internat. Soc. Heart and Lung Transplantation, Order of Rose, Alpha Omega Alpha, Iota Sigma Pi, Phi Kappa Phi, Alpha Lambda Delta. Office: U Wis Madison E5/582D CSC 5710 600 Highland Ave Madison WI 53792 Office Phone: 608-263-0080. Business E-Mail: mrj@medicine.wisc.edu.

JOHNSON, MATTIEDNA, medical/surgical nurse; b. Amite County, Miss., Apr. 7, 1918; d. Isaac and Minnie (Ramsey) J.; m. Robert William Kelley, Oct. 19, 1943 (div. May 1980); children: Bobby Lou, Robert William Jr., Patricia Elaine, Frances Minette. RN, Terrell Meml. Hosp.; postgrad., Homer G. Phillips Hosp.; MA, Ashland Theol. Sem. RN, Tenn., Mont., Minn.; diaconal min. United Meth. Ch. Head nurse Jane Terrell Hosp., Memphis; staff nurse Homer G. Phillips Hosp., St. Louis; lab. tech. U.S. Army U. Minn., Mpls.; pvt. duty nurse Mpls. Dist. Minn. State, Mpls.; medical missionary Gbarnga (Liberia) Meth. Mission; pvt. duty night nurse Mo., Tenn., Ohio. Author: Tots Goes to Gbarnga, 1994, Johnson's Instructors Guide, 1949, Johnson's Manual-Church Nursing, 1994. Created ch. nursing Am. Red Cross., 1949—, vol. instr. Recipient Last Living Natural Scientist of 2000 Millennium award. Mem. ANA, Nat. Black Nurses Assn. (sec. 1970—). Achievements include crystallization of penicillin mold for gun shot wounds; tests of staphlococcus germs and terriable mice mold against streptococcus hymolyticus germ of scarlet fever; developed R13 Mold penicillin crystals for the injectable IV-Intra Muscular. Home: 13606 Abell Ave Cleveland OH 44120-3954

JOHNSON, MELODY, school system administrator; BS in Sociology, Phillips U.; Masters, TWU; PhD in Ednl. Adminstrn., U. Tex., Austin. Tchr., Okla., Dallas, Selma, San Antonio, 1975—82; asst. prin. Meridith Magnet Sch., Tex., 1983—85; prin. Travis Mid. Sch., Tex., 1985—89; state sr. dir. Mid. Sch. Edn. for Tex., 1992—95; dist. area supt. for San Antonio, 1995—97; assoc. supt. for curriculum, instrn. and student support San Antonio Ind. Sch. Dist., 1997—2000; dep. supt. Providence Schs., 2000—02, supt., 2002—05, Fort Worth Ind. Sch. Dist., 2005—. Pres. Coop. Superintendency Exec. Leadership Program, U. Tex. Named R.I. Woman of the Yr. for Edn., 2004; fellow Broad Found. Nat. Supt.'s Acad., 2002, Coop. Superintency, 1989. Achievements include commended by State Comptr. of Tex. for excellent curriculum frameworks and stds. documents; acknowledged by Carnegie Corp. N.Y. for having served as one of 15 state dirs. of nat. mid. sch. initiative. Office: Fort Worth ISD Office of the Superintendent 100 N University Dr Fort Worth TX 76107-1360 Office Phone: 401-456-9221.

JOHNSON, MELVIN N., academic administrator, economist; s. William Thomas and Vernedia Rosemary Johnson; m. Marcelite Elaine Dingle, Dec. 22, 1968; children: DeAndra Chanet Martin, Monet Nichelle Bloodworth, Melvin Roschaun. BS in Econs., N.C. Agrl. and Tech. State U., 1968; MA in Econs., Ball State U., 1974; MBA in Bus. Econs., Ind. U., 1979, DBA in Bus. Econs., 1983. Commd. 2d lt. USAF, 1968, advanced through grades to lt. col., officer Soesterberg Air Base, Netherlands, 1968—90; assoc. prof. econs. N.C. Agrl. and Tech. State U., Greensboro, 1990—92, chair bus. adminstrn., 1992—97, interim dean grad. sch., 1997—98, assoc. vice chancellor, 1998—2000; provost, vice chancellor Winston-Salem (N.C.) State U., 2000—05; pres. Tenn. State U., Nashville, 2005—. Bd. dirs., chair strategic planning Piedmont Triad Ctr. Advanced Mfg., Greensboro, NC, 1994—99, Simon Green Atkins Cmty. Devel. Corp., Winston-Salem, NC, 2000—; bd. advisors Harvard Inst. Higher Edn., Cambridge, Mass., 1999—2002; bd. dirs., chair U. N.C. Tchg. and Learning with Tech., Chapel Hill, 1999—2001; commr. NC State Banking Commn., Raleigh, NC, 1999—2002; bd. dirs., chair investments N.C. Bapt. Hosp., Winston-Salem, 2002—; bd. dirs. Carolina Ctr. Internat. Understanding, Winston-Salem Downtown Devel. Corp., IdeAlliance Rsch. Pk. Devel., WINSTONET; co-chair bd. directors Ctr. Cmty. Safety. Co-author: Balance of Payments Adjustment: Macro Facets of International Finance Revisited, Empirical Evidence for the Traditional Approach to the Capital Account, A Monetary Model of the Mexican Balance of Payments; contbr. articles to profl. jours. Bd. dirs., chair planning Multiple Sclerosis Soc., Greensboro, 1999—2002; chair tech. coun. Winston-Salem C. of C., 2000—03. Named Outstanding Young Men of Am., 1975; Millennium Leadership Inst. Protégé fellow, Am. Assn. State Colls. and Univs., 2001, Nissan fellow, Nissan USA, 1993, Ayres fellow, Am. Banking Assn., 1995, NAFEO Kellogg Leadership fellow, Nat. Assn. Equal Opportunity Higher Edn., 2003—04, Future Focus 2020 Sr. fellow, Babcock Sch., Wake Forest U., 2003—. Mem.: Piedmont Club (mem. wine com. 2003—04), Rotary (mem. program com. 2001—04), Golden Key, Alpha Sigma Lambda, Omicron Delta Epsilon, Beta Gamma Sigma, Alpha Phi Alpha (life). Office: Tenn State Univ 3500 John A Merritt Blvd Nashville TN 37209*

JOHNSON, MICHAEL, retired Olympic athlete; b. Dallas, Sept. 13, 1967; m. Kerry Johnson; 1 child. Student, Baylor U., 90. Ret., 1991. BBC sports commentator. Recipient Gold medal 200 meters Goodwill Games, 1990, 94, 4 x 100 relay Barcelona Olympics, 1992, 200 meters and 400 meters Summer Olympics, Atlanta, 1996; winner 200 meters World Athletic Championships, 1991, 400 meters, 1993; U.S. Nat. champion 200 meters, 1990-92, 95; named Athlete of Yr. USA Track & Field, 1993-94, Male Athlete of Yr. AP, 1996; world record holder indoor 400 meters, 200 meters at 1996 Olympics; gold medal for 400 meters World Championship, 1997., gold medalist, 400m & 4 x 400m, Sydney Olympic Games, 2000; first athlete to be ranked no. 1 in the world in both the 200m and 400m; 3 time recipient of the Jesse Owens award.*

JOHNSON, MICHAEL DENNIS, lawyer; b. Upper Darby, Pa., Sept. 2, 1948; s. Peter Joseph and Gloria Veronica (Magro) Caruso; 1 child, Monica Ann. BA in political sci., Washington State Univ., 1970; JD, Univ. Washington, 1973. Bar: Wash., Ct. of Appeals Bar (5th cir.), Ct. of Appeals Bar (8th cir.), U.S. Supreme Ct. Trial lawyer Civil Rights Divsn., Washington, 1973-76; sr. trial lawyer Criming Sect. Civil Rights Divsn., Washington, 1976-84; sr. litigation counsel U.S. Dept. Justice, Little Rock, 1984-93, first asst. U.S. atty., 1993-2000; U.S. atty., 2001—03; adj. prof. U. Ark., Little Rock, 1985—. Instr. Nat. Inst. of Trial Advocacy, So. Bend, Ind., 1988—, U.S. Dept. Justice Advocacy Inst., Washington, 1980—, Criminal Justice Inst., Little Rock, 1993-97. Author: Management of Civil Rights Allegation, 1994. Recipient Cert. of Appreciation ATF, 1986, 88, 97, Spl. Recognition award, 1988, LECC, 1993, Outstanding Svc. award IRS, 1992, Exceptional Svc. award FBI, 1989, Cert. of Achievement award Ark. Trial Lawyers Assn., 1991, Ark. Investigation, 1990, DOJ Trial Advocacy, 1987, Outstanding Achievement award Secret Svc., 1998, Recognition of Outstanding Prosecution award FBI, 1999, 2000. Mem. William R. Overton Inn of Ct. Avocations: photography, travel, athletics. Mailing: 1404 E Glass Ave Spokane WA 99207

JOHNSON, MICHAEL KENNETH, chemistry professor; b. Tonbridge, Kent, Eng., Mar. 8, 1953; came to U.S., 1980; s. Thomas Sydney and Eileen J.; m. Carole Ann Woodhouse, Aug. 21, 1976; children: Caroline Louise, Thomas Michael. BA, Cambridge U., 1974, MA, 1977; MSc, U. East Anglia, 1975, PhD, 1977. Postdoctoral fellow U. East Anglia, Norwich, 1977-80; postdoctoral rsch. assoc. Princeton (N.J.) U., 1980-82; asst. prof. chemistry La. State U., Baton Rouge, 1982-86; assoc. prof. chemistry U. Ga., Athens, 1987-91, prof. chemistry, 1991-98, disting. rsch. prof. chemistry, 1998—, dir., 1993—. Biophysics grant rev. panel NSF, Washington, 1990-95; biophysics study sect. NIH, Washington, 2000—. Editor: Electron Transfer in Biology and the Solid State, 1990; contbr. articles to profl. jours. Alfred P. Sloan fellow, 1986; Rsch. grantee NIH, 1984, 87, 94, 2000, 04, NSF, 1986, 90, 94, 98. Mem.: Am. Chem. Soc., Phi Kappa Phi. Home: 1100 Double Bridges Rd Winterville GA 30683-4830 Office: U Ga Dept Chemistry Athens GA 30602 Office Phone: 706-542-9378. Business E-Mail: johnson@chem.uga.edu.

JOHNSON, MICHAEL LEWIS, psychiatrist; b. Louisville, May 17, 1941; s. Ralph L. and Bee (Burr) J.; children: Kirstin, Aaron, Jessica; m. Frances Bourne. AB, Earlham Coll., Richmond, Ind., 1963; MD, Ind. U., 1968. Diplomate Am. Bd. Psychiatry and Neurology. Intern Marion County Gen. Hosp., Indpls., 1968-69; resident in psychiatry Wash. U. Barnes Hosp., St. Louis, 1969-72; staff psychiatrist U.S. Naval Hosp., Portsmouth, Va., 1972-74, South Cen. Community Mental Health Ctr., Bloomington, Ind., 1974-80; psychiatrist pvt. practice, Bloomington, Ind., 1974-83; unit dir. Milford-Whitinsville (Mass.) Regional Hosp., 1983-85; staff psychiatrist Harvard Vanguard Med. Assocs., Cambridge, Mass., 1985-2000, Peabody, Mass., 1997-2000, Boston, 2000—. Instr. in psychiatry Harvard Med. Sch., Boston, 1985—, mem. comm. skills task force, 2001--; instr. in psychiatry Cambridge Hosp., 1985-92, Brigham and Women's Hosp., 1993—; mem. credentials com. Harvard Pilgrim Health Care; mem. psychopharmacology com. and ctrl. psychiat. consultation svc. Harvard Vanguard Med. Assocs., mem. com. skills task force, Harvard Med. Sch., cons. psychiatrist Pain Program Harvard Vanguard Med. Assocs.; sci. adv. bd. mem. Ott Light Sys., Santa Monica, Calif.; bd. dirs. Lenair Healing Found., Inc., Newbury, Mass. Author: (book chpt.) Psychotherapists Guide to Pharmacotherapy, 1989; subject of docudrama Virtuoso, 1991. Recipient Robert H. Ebert tchg. award Harvard Vanguard Med. Assocs., 1999; Harvard Macy fellow, 2003. Mem. Soc. Of Friends. Achievements include being subject of stage play and docudrama Virtuoso, 1996. Office: Harvard Vanguard Med Assocs 147 Mil Stt Boston MA 02109

JOHNSON, MICHAEL PAUL, historian, educator; b. Ponca City, Okla., July 6, 1941; s. Howard W. and Maybelle P. (Fetrow) J.; m. Anne E. Thompson, June 2, 1962; children: Ian Michael, Sarah Elizabeth. AB in Chemistry cum laude, Knox Coll., 1963; MA in History, Stanford U., 1967, PhD in History, 1973. Asst. prof. LeMoyne Coll., Memphis, 1967-68; instr. San Jose (Calif.) State U., 1970-71; asst. prof. history U. Calif., Irvine, 1971-77, assoc. prof., 1977-84, prof., 1984-94, Johns Hopkins U., Balt., 1994—. Author: Toward a Patriarchal Republic, 1977, Black Masters, 1984, No Chariot Let Down, 1984, The American Promise, 1998, Reading the American Past, 2 vols., 1998, Abraham Lincoln, Slavery and the Civil War, 2000. Am. Coun. Learned Socs.fellow, 1977; NEH fellow, 1982; Ctr. for Advanced Study in Behavioral Scis. fellow, 1999-00; Time Mirror Found. disting. rsch. fellow, 2004-05. Mem. Am. Hist. Assn., Orgn. Am. Historians (ABC Clio Am. History and Life award 2003), So. Hist. Assn., Am. Antiquarian Soc., Soc. Am. Historians, Phi Beta Kappa. Office: Johns Hopkins U Dept History Baltimore MD 21218 Office Phone: 410-516-7575.

JOHNSON, MICHELLE L., lawyer; BSBA, U. Calif. Berkeley, 1975; JD, U. Denver, 1985. Bar: Calif. 1986. Ptnr., exec. dir. Thelen Reid & Priest LLP, San Francisco, mng. ptnr. adminstr. Spkr. in field. Mem.: Bar Assn. San Francisco (Bus. Law Sect.), State Bar Calif. (Bus. Law Sect.), ABA (Corp., Banking & Bus. Law Sect.), Order of St. Ives. Office: Thelen Reid & Priest LLP 101 Second St Ste 1800 San Francisco CA 94105-3601 Office Phone: 415-369-7101. Office Fax: 415-371-1211. Business E-Mail: mljohnson@thelenreid.com.

JOHNSON, MIKKEL BORLAUG, physicist; b. Waynesboro, Va., Jan. 2, 1943; s. Wallace A. and Anne D. (Davies) J.; m. Lynne McFadden, June 14, 1966; children: Kara Marit, Krista Lynne. BS, Va. Poly. Inst., 1966; MS, Carnegie Mellon U., 1968, PhD, 1970. Rsch. assoc. Cornell U., Ithaca, N.Y., 1970-72; staff mem., fellow Los Alamos (N.Mex.) Nat. Lab., 1972—. Vis. prof. SUNY, Stony Brook, 1981-82, Carnegie Mellon U., 1997-98. Editor: Relativistic Dynamics and Quark-Nuclear Physics, 1986, Nuclear and Particle Physics on the Light Cone, 1989, LAMPF Workshop on (Pi,K) Physics, 1991; assoc. editor Nuclear Physics, 1975-97. Lab. fellow Los Alamos Nat. Lab, 1991; recipient Humboldt award for Sr. U.S. Scientist, Humboldt Found., 1986. Fellow Am. Phys. Soc. Home: 118 Piedra Loop Los Alamos NM 87544-3828 Office: Los Alamos Nat Lab P divsn Ms H846 Los Alamos NM 87545-0001 E-mail: mbjohnson@lanl.gov.

JOHNSON, MILLARD WALLACE, JR., mathematics professor, mechanical engineer, educator; b. Racine, Wis., Feb. 1, 1928; s. Millard Wallace and Marian Manilla (Rittman) J.; m. Ruth Pugh Gifford, Dec. 26, 1953; children: Millard Wallace III, Jeannette Marian Brooks, Charles Gifford, Peter Allen. BS in Applied Math. and Mechanics, U. Wis., 1952, MS, 1953; PhD in Math, MIT, 1957. Rsch. asst. MIT, 1953-57, lectr., 1957-58; mem. staff Math. Rsch. Ctr. U. Wis., Madison, 1958-94, prof. mechanics, 1958-63, prof. mechanics and math., 1964-94, mem. staff Rheology Rsch. Ctr., 1970—, mem. Engine Rsch. Ctr., 1985—, prof. emeritus Madison, 1994—. Contbr. articles to profl. jours. Adv. bd. Internat. Math. and Statis. Librs. (IMSL), 1971-92. With USN, 1946-48. Fellow ASME; mem. Soc. Rheology, Soc. Indsl. and Applied Math., Am. Acad. Mechanics, Brit. Soc. Rheology, Wis. Acad. Scis., Arts and Letters, Phi Beta Kappa. Home: 802 Blue Ridge Pkwy Madison WI 53705-1148 Office: U Wis Dept Eng Phys 1500 Engineering Dr Madison WI 53706-1609 E-mail: mwjohns1@wisc.edu.

JOHNSON, MURRAY H., optometrist, researcher, consultant, lecturer; b. Montreal, Que., Can., Jan. 29, 1956; arrived in U.S., 1980; s. William and Leah (Bedzowski) J.; m. Linda Fluxman, Apr. 30, 1978; children: Warren Natan, Tanya Yael, Arielle Carly. Diploma in Optometry, Witwatersrand Coll., Johannesburg, 1977; postgrad., U. Montreal, 1980; BS, OD, U. Houston, 1981, MSc in Physiol. Optics and Vision Sci., 1984; postgrad., U. Tex. Health Ctr., 1983. Lic. optometrist, Tex., 1983, therapeutic lic., Tex., 1992; cert. ocular therapeutics for treatment and mgmt. ocular disease U. Houston, 1992; cert. optometric glaucoma specialist, U. Houston, 2002. Clin. instr. U. Houston, 1981-85, postdoct. fellow, 1981-84; researcher Inst. contact Lens Rsch., Houston, 1983-88; pvt. practice optometry specializing in contact lenses Eye & Contact Lens Assocs. North Tex., Dallas, 1985—. Vis. asst. prof. U. Houston, 1984-85, adj. asst. prof., 1985-89; cons., clin. investigator Metro Optics, Inc., Dallas, 1989—; premktg. clin. evaluator, cons. and investigator to various contact lens and pharm. mfrs., 1989—; clin. investigator Paragon Optical, Mesa, Ariz., 1992; cons. Unilens Corp., Largo, Fla., 1989; clin. examiner Nat. Bd. Clin. Skills Exam., Nat. Bd. Examiners in Optometry, 1997—; cons. Johnson & Johnson Vision Care, Inc. Vistakon Divsn, Jacksonville, Fla., 2005—. Contbr. articles to profl. jours. Mem. clin. care com. Global Vision Inst., Global Vision Dallas, 1996; mem. edn. com. Akiba Acad. Dallas, 1986—88, bd. dirs., 1986—97, long range planning com., 1987—88, devel. com., 1993, v.p., treas, 1993—94, budget com., 1993—96, scholarship com, 1994—2002; bd. dirs. Congregation Share Tefilla, Dallas, 1988—92; steering com. B'nai B'rith, 1986—88, treas., 1987—88; mem.-at-large Jewish edn. com. Jewish Fedn. Dallas, 1998—99; mem. Jewish identity and values experiences com. Jewish Edn. Dept., 1999—2003, chair, 2000—01; local beneficiaries subcom., allocations com. Jewish Fedn. Greater Dallas, 1999—2000, mem. renaissance and renewal subcom. planning and allocations com., 2000—03; chair Jewish identity and values experiences subcom. Jewish Edn. Com., 2000—01. Postdoctoral fellow U. Houston, 1981-84, grantee 1981, 82; Ezell Rsch. fellow Am. Optometric Found., 1983. Fellow Am. Acad. Optometry; mem. AAAS, Assn. Rsch. in Vision and Ophthalmology, Am. Pub. Health Assn. (vision care sect.), Am. Optometric Assn. (contact lens sect.), Tex. Optometric Assn., Dallas County Optometric Soc., Am. Optometric Found. (Ezell fellows club), Sigma Xi. Jewish. Avocations: walking, swimming, racquetball. Office: Eye & Contact Lens Assocs N Tex 18111 Preston Rd Ste 180 Dallas TX 75252-6009

JOHNSON, MYRTLE ALICE HARRIS, elementary and secondary school educator; b. Phila., Aug. 10, 1947; d. James and Margaret (Robinson) Harris; m. Ronald Walter Johnson, May 24, 1975; 1 child, Craig Noel. BS in Edn., Temple U., 1977; MDiv, New Brunswick Theological Seminary, 2000; postgrad., Andersonville Theol. Sem., 2005. Cert. tchr., Pa., N.J. Tchr. Pine Hill Bd. Edn., NJ, 1977—84; lang. tchr. Passaic Bd. Edn., NJ, 1986—88. Creative bible instr. preachers kids Internat. Assn. of Min. Wives and Min. Widows, Inc., 1986—92, chair preachers kids, 1993—2002, coord. Nat. Stand Against Violence, 2001. Author: Teaching Tools/Materials: Bringing God's Word to Children, 2005. Sunday sch. tchr. Jones Meml. Bapt. Ch., Phila., dir., tchr. Vacation Bible Sch.; Sunday sch. tchr. Union Bapt. Ch., Passaic, N.J., organizer, dir. Vacation Bible Sch., coord., dir. summer program Recipient Outstanding Leadership award Vacation Bible Sch., Jones Meml. Bapt. Ch., Phila., Muriel Lemon Johnson Internat. award, 2001; crowned Queen Women's Convention, Nat. Bapt. Convention, 2002-03. Mem. Internat. Interdenominational Min.'s Wives and Min.'s Widows, Inc., N.J. Dist. Missionary Bapt. Assn., Inc. (1st v.p. women's aux. N.J. dist. 2001-05, pres. 2005—). Achievements include developed and coordinated six-week summer camp program Jones Meml. Bapt. Ch., 1989-. Home: 219 Myrtle Ave Passaic NJ 07055-3212

JOHNSON, NAN, retired academic administrator; b. Pitts., Jan. 12, 1930; d. Vernon Eugene Heffelfinger and Kathryn Jennings Reed; m. James William Johnson, Oct. 5, 1957; children: Miranda Johnson Haddad, Reed Vann. AB, Barnard Coll., 1952; postgrad., Cornell U., 1952-53; MA, U. Rochester, 1960. Legislator Monroe County Legislature, Rochester, N.Y., 1976-95; founding dir. Susan B. Anthony U. Ctr., U. Rochester, 1995-99; ret. Trustee SUNY, 1976-90; adj. assoc. prof. polit. sci. U. Rochester, 1984-99. Pres. AAUW Rochester, 1997. Mem. Nat. Women's Hall Fame (trustee, bd. mem. 1987—), Friends Women's Rights Nat. Park, Inc. (pres., founder). Democrat. Home: 308 Sea Oats Trail Kitty Hawk NC 27949 E-mail: heriand@aol.com.

JOHNSON, NANCY ELIZABETH, bookseller; b. Des Moines, July 21, 1953; d. Walter Eugene and Frances Goodman (Eaton) J. BS, Drake U., 1975. Page Legislature State of Iowa, Des Moines, 1967-69, asst. bill clk., 1970-71; pub. rels. Conv. and Visitors Bur., Des Moines, 1975-76; antique show promoter Collector's Extravaganza, Denver, 1976—; bookseller The Library, 1977—; owner, mgr. The Libr., Des Moines, 1997—2002; owner Nancy Johnson, Bookseller, 2003—; prodr. Antiques at Wings, Denver, 2003—, Antiques at the Fairgrounds, Des Moines, 2005—. Pres., CEO Collectors Extravaganza Corp., 1996—; dir. The Frances Goodman Johnson Found., 1998—. Mem. Internat. Booksellers Fedn., Mountains & Plains Booksellers Assn., Profl. Show Mgrs. Assn. (bd. dirs. 1999-, v.p. 2001-02, pres. 2003-), Internat. Assn. Exhbn. Mgmt. (bd. dirs., Rocky Mtn. chpt., 2004-), Cyclone Corvettes, Inc. (bd. dirs. 1998), Alpha Kappa Delta, Kappa Delta Pi, Psi Chi. Republican. Protestant. Avocations: languages, competition driving. Home: 1020 15th St # 37G Denver CO 80202 Office: PO Box 692 Des Moines IA 50303-0692 Office Phone: 515-262-6714.

JOHNSON, NANCY LEE, congresswoman; b. Chgo., Jan. 5, 1935; d. Noble Wishard and Gertrude Reid (Smith) Lee; m. Theodore H. Johnson, June 27, 1932; children— Lindsey Lee, Althea Anne, Caroline Reid BA, Radcliffe Coll., 1957; postgrad., U. London, 1957-58. Vice chmn. Charter Commn. New Britain, Conn., 1976-77; mem. Conn. Senate from 6th dist., 1977-82, U.S. Congress from 5th Conn. dist., Washington, 1983—, mem. ways and means com., chmn. health subcom., com. on taxation. Pres. Friends of Libr., New Britain Pub. Libr., 1973-76, Radcliffe Club Northern Conn., 1973-75; bd. dirs., pres. Sheldon Cmty. Guidance Clinic, 1974-75; dir. religious edn. Unitarian Universalist Soc. New Britain, 1967-72; bd. dirs. United Way New Britain, 1976.79. Recipient Outstanding Vol. award United Way, 1976; English Speaking Union grantee, 1958-59 Republican. Home: 141 S Mountain St New Britain CT 06052-1511 Office: Ho of Reps 2113 Rayburn Bldg Washington DC 20515-0705 Office Phone: 202-225-4476.

JOHNSON, NANCY PLATTNER, secondary school educator; b. Milw., July 1, 1938; d. Paul and Mary (Kalns) Plattner; m. Orville Johnson, III, July 1, 1978. BS, U. Chgo., 1960; postgrad., Ohio State U., 1965; M, U. Cen. Fla., Orlando, 1974; PhD, U. Wis., 1979. Cert. elem. tchr., secondary math Nat. Bd. Tchr. Harvard Sch. Boys, Chgo., 1960-61; math. tchr. Boone County Schs., Columbia, Mo., 1962-64, Columbus, Ohio, 1964-66; math. instr. U. Wis., Stevens Point, 1966-72; math. educator Orange County, Orlando, Fla., 1972-76; rsch. grad. asst., instr. U. Wis., Madison, 1976-79; vis. assoc. prof. Stetson U., Orlando, 1980-81; math. educator Seminole County Sch. Bd., Sanford, Fla., 1982—. Contbr. articles to profl. jours. Bd. dirs. Crown Oaks Springs Cmty. Assn., 1974—. Named Math. Tchr. of the Yr., 1999—2000; NSF grantee, Ohio State U., 1964—65, NSF fellow, U. Wis., 1976—79. Mem.: NEA, Seminole County Edn. Assn., Seminole County Math. Coun., Fla. Math. Coun., Fla. Tchg. Profl., Nat. Coun. Tchrs. Math., Math. Assn. Am. Avocations: art, music, writing. Home: 212 Jasmine Ln Longwood FL 32779-4908

JOHNSON, NEAL FREDERICK, psychologist, educator; b. Willmar, Minn., May 1, 1934; s. Malcolm Ruben and Helen Laura Johnson; m. Kathleen A. Crimmins, Sept. 9, 1960 (dec. Jan. 2000); children: Neal, Margaret (dec. Sept. 1999), Elizabeth, Michael. BA, U. Minn., 1956, PhD, 1961. Prof. psychology Ohio State U., Columbus, 1961—. Vis. prof. U. Calif., Berkeley, 1965, Berkeley, 74, Berkeley, 75, Berkeley, 77, Berkeley, 78, Berkeley, 83. Contbr. articles to profl. jours.; assoc. editor Jour. Memory and Lang., 1984-88; consulting editor Jour. Verbal Learning and Verbal Behavior, 1965-84, Memory & Cognition, 1972-82, Jour. Exptl. Psychology: Human Perception and Performance, 1978-82, Jour. Exptl. Psychology: Learning, Memory and Cognition, 1982-89, Jour. Memory and Lang., 1988-94, Gen. Psychology Rev., 1996—. Mem. com. Troop 312 Boy Scouts Am., Columbus, 1974-81. Rsch. scholar Tozer Found., Stillwater, Minn., 1959; grantee U.S. Office Edn., NIH, NSF. Fellow APA (pres. Soc. Gen. Psychology 1995, pres. divsn. exptl. psychology 1996), AAAS (governing coun. 1998-2000, presiding officer psychology sect. 2002-04); mem. Psychonomic Soc. (pres. 1997), Coun. Sci. Soc. Presidents, Midwestern Psychol. Assn. (pres. 1987). Presbyterian. Avocations: downhill skiing, fencing. Home: 5478 Rockwood Rd Columbus OH 43229-4324 Office: Dept Psychology Ohio State U Columbus OH 43210 Office Phone: 614-292-3093. Business E-Mail: johnson.64@osu.edu.

JOHNSON, NICHOLAS, writer, lawyer, educator; b. Iowa City, Sept. 23, 1934; s. Wendell A.L. and Edna (Bockwoldt) Johnson; m. Karen Mary Chapman, 1952 (div. 1972); children: Julie, Sherman, Gregory, Alexander; m. Mary Eleanor Vasey, 1991. BA, U. Tex., 1956, LL.B., 1958; L.H.D., Windham Coll., 1971. Bar: Tex. 1958, D.C. 1963, U.S. Supreme Ct. 1963, Iowa 1974; lic. radio amateur. Law clk. to judge John R. Brown, U.S. 5th Circuit Ct. Appeals, 1958-59; law clk. to U.S. Supreme Ct. Justice Hugo L. Black, 1959-60; acting assoc. prof. law U. Calif. at Berkeley, 1960-63; assoc. Covington & Burling, Washington, 1963-64; adminstr. Maritime Adminstrn., chmn. Maritime Subsidy Bd. U.S. Dept. Commerce, 1964-66; commr. FCC, 1966-73; adj. prof. law Georgetown U., 1971-73; Poynter fellow Yale U., 1971; vis. prof. U. Ill., Champaign-Urbana, 1976, U. Okla., Norman, 1978, Ill. State U., Normal, 1979, U. Wis., Madison, 1980, Newhouse Sch., Syracuse U., 1980, U. Iowa Coll. Law, 1981—; vis. prof. dept. communications studies U. Iowa, 1982-85; vis. prof. Western Behavioral Scis. Inst., U. Calif., San Diego, 1986-91. Vis. prof. Calif. State U., Los Angeles, 1986, New Sch. Soc. Resource ConnectEd, 1990, U. Iowa dept. theater arts, 1999; regents prof. U. Calif., San Diego, 2000; co-dir. U. Iowa Inst. for Health, Behavior and Environ. Policy, 1990-93; chmn., dir. Nat. Citizens Comm. Lobby, 1975—, Nat. Citizens Com. for Broadcasting, 1974-78; pub. access, 1975-77; commentator Nat. Pub. Radio, 1975-77, 83-86, Sta. WRC-AM, Washington, 1977, Sta. WSUI, Iowa City, 1982-87; presdl. advisor White House Conf. on Libraries and Info. Services, 1979; exec. com. World Acad. Art and Sci., 1993-97. Author: Cases and Materials on Oil and Gas Law, 1962, How to Talk Back to Your Television Set, 1970, Japanese transl., 1971, Life Before Death in the Corporate State, 1971, Test Pattern for Living, 1972, Broadcasting in America, 1973, Cases and Materials on Communications Law and Policy, 1981, 82, 83, 84, 85, 86, Readings for Law of Electronic Media, 1993-94, (with David Loundy) Law of Electronic Media in a Cyberspace Age, 1996; syndicated columnist: Gannett News Service, 1982-84, Register and Tribune Syndicate, 1984, Cowles Syndicate, 1985-86, King Features Syndicate, 1986, Iowa City Press Citizen, 1998-2001; contbr. to legal, gen., internat. publs.; contbg. editor, host PBS The New Tech Times, 1983-84. Dem. candidate for U.S. Ho. of Reps. from 3d Iowa Dist., 1974; bd. dirs. Ctr. for Study Commercialism, 1991-96, Citizens Ind. Pub. Broadcasting, 1999-2002, Common Cause, 1990-96, Internat. Soc. Gen. Semantics, 1960-2000, Iowa City Cmty. Sch. Dist., 1998-2001, Virtual Classroom Project, 1990-91, Vol. in Tech. Assistance, 1994-2000; mem. adv. bd. Ctr. Media Edn., 1993-, Cultural Environ., Movement, 1992-, Fairness and Accuracy in Reporting, 1996—, Inst. Pub. Accuracy, 1997-, Open Soc. Inst. Media Group, 1999-2000, Project Censored, 1976-, U. Iowa Info. Arcade, 1991-92, War and Peace Found., 1988-, Working Assets Long Distance, 1992-96; mem. Broadband and Telecom. Commn., Iowa City, 1981-87. Named One of 10 Outstanding Young Men in U.S., U.S. Jaycees, 1967, recipient New Republic Pub. Defender award, 1970, Civil Liberties Award Ga. ACLU, 1972, DeWitt Carter Reddick award U. Tex., 1977, George Stoney award Nat. Fedn. Local Cable Programmers, 1987; fellow World Acad. Art and Sci., 1991—. Mem. D.C., Iowa Bar Assn. (Citizenship award 1951), State Bar Tex., Golden Key, Order of Coif, Phi Beta Kappa, Phi Delta Phi, Phi Eta Sigma, Pi Sigma Alpha. Democrat. Unitarian Universalist. Home and Office: PO Box 1876 Iowa City IA 52244-1876 Office Phone: 319-337-5555. E-mail: njohnson@inav.net.

JOHNSON, NICHOLE SHARESE, school nurse practitioner, basketball coach; b. NYC, Nov. 13, 1975; d. Lorelei Davis. BSN, Coll. New Rochelle, 1997; MSN, U. Phoenix, 2005. RN. Staff nurse NYU Med. Ctr., NYC, 1997—98; contract nurse Theracare, 1998—99; contract nursing Allcare Nursing, Hicksville, 1999—2000; sch. nursing NYC Dept. Edn., 1999—; homecare nursing Visting Nurse Svc. NY, Bronx, 2002—03. Jr. h.s. head basketball coach Rainbow Basketball Assn., Bronx, 2002—05. Named Coach of Yr., Rainbow Basketball Assn., 2004—05. Mem.: ANA (licentiate), NY State Sch. Nurse Assn. (licentiate), Nat. Assn. Sch. Nurses (licentiate), NY State Nurse Assn. (licentiate), Sigma Theta Tau.

JOHNSON, NOBLE MARSHALL, research scientist; b. San Francisco, Feb. 23, 1945; BSEE cum laude, U. Calif., Davis, 1967, MSEE, 1970; PhD, Princeton U., 1974. Rsch. staff SRI Internat., Menlo Park, Calif., 1974—76; from rsch. staff to sr. rsch. staff Xerox Palo Alto Rsch. Ctr., Palo Alto, 1976—87, prin. scientist Electronic Materials lab., 1987—; mgr. Optoelectronic Materials and Devices, 1999—. Vis. lectr. Princeton (NJ) U., 1986, U. Erlangen-Nürnberg, Germany, 1988; presenter in field. Co-editor 5 books; contbr. over 330 articles to profl. jours.; patentee in field. Recipient Disting. Sr. U.S. Scientist award Alexander von Humboldt Found., Germany, 1987; Nat. Def. Grad. fellow, Princeton U., 1969-72. Fellow Am. Phys. Soc., IEEE; mem. Sigma Xi. Office: Palo Alto Rsch Ctr Electronic Materials Devices Lab 3333 Coyote Hill Rd Palo Alto CA 94304-1314 Business E-Mail: njohnson@parc.com.

JOHNSON, NOEL LARS, biomedical engineer; b. Palo Alto, Calif., Nov. 11, 1957; s. LeRoy Franklin and Margaret Louise (Lindsley) J.; children: Margaret Elizabeth, Kent Daniel. BSEE, U. Calif., Berkeley, 1979; M of Engring., U. Va., 1982, PhD, 1990. Mgr. R & D Hosp. Products divsn. Abbott Labs., Mountain View, Calif., 1986-99; founder HealtheTech., Inc., 1999—2004; pres., CEO Novashunt, Inc., Saratoga, Calif., 2004—. Contbr. articles to profl. jours. Fellowship NIH 1980-85; rsch. grantee Abbott Labs. 1989. Mem. IEEE, Biomed. Engring. Soc., Delta Chi (founder, 1st pres. chpt. U. Calif. at Berkeley). Achievements include invention of metabolic monitor, patented automated drug delivery system, pharmacokinetic drug infusion, and critical care disposables. Business E-Mail: njohnson@novashunt.com. E-mail: noeljo@aol.com.

JOHNSON, NORMAN TERRY, public relations executive, writer; s. Samuel and Francis E. (Morse) Johnson; children: Robin, Denise, Lisa. Degree, San Diego (Calif.) Jr. Coll., 1956. Pub. rels. exec. various hotels, Las Vegas, 1967—77; prin., owner Johnson Agy., Las Vegas, 1978—. Author: History of Off-Road Racing, 1976, Magellan's of the Sky, 2004. Sgt. USAF, 1950—53, Korea. Recipient Lifetime Achievement award, Las Vegas (Nev.) Entertainment, 2004. Mem.: C.A.S.T. Achievements include creator of world famous Mint 400 Off-Road Race 1968-93. Avocations: sculpting, auto racing. Office Phone: 702-798-5210. Personal E-mail: racenorm@cox.net.

JOHNSON, OMOTUNDE EVAN GEORGE, economist; b. Freetown, Sierra Leone, Mar. 27, 1941; came to U.S., 1961; s. Evan George and Elizabeth O. (Allen) J.; m. Octavia Olayemi John, Oct. 30 1965; children: Olatunde Cheryl, Omoyemi Evan, Olubayo Darryl. BA, UCLA, 1965, MA, 1967, PhD, 1970. Lectr. in econs. Calif. State U., Long Beach, 1967-69; lectr. U. Sierra Leone, Freetown, 1969-73; vis. asst. prof. U. Mich., Ann Arbor, 1973-74; economist IMF, Washington, 1974-79, sr. economist, dep. divsn. chief, 1979-92, advisor, 1992-94, divsn. chief, 1994-98, asst. dir., 1998-2000; econ. rschr. and cons. McLean, Va., 2000—. Vis. rsch. fellow U. Oxford, Eng., 1996-97; resident rep. IMF, Ghana, 1987-90. Contbr. numerous articles to profl. jours. Mem. Am. Econ. Assn., U.S. Chess Fedn., Royal Econ. Soc. U.K., Nat. Symphony Orch. Assn., Met. Opera Guild. Episcopalian. Avocations: chess, piano, classical music, reading. Home and Office: 6401 Oak Meadow Way Mc Lean VA 22101-5342 Personal E-mail: oegjohnson@aol.com.

JOHNSON, OPAL BURTON, retired elementary school educator; b. Mercer County, W.Va., May 30, 1929; d. Martin Luther and Annie Elizabeth (Gentry) Burton; m. Eugene Hunter Johnson, Mar. 13, 1948; children: Eugene Hunter Jr., Nancy Gayle Johnson Canady. BA, King Coll., Bristol, Tenn., 1966; MA in Teaching, East Tenn. State U., 1977. Cert. elem. tchr., Va. Tchr. Bristol (Va.) Sch. System, 1966—2005, ret., 2005. Named Tchr. of Yr., Bristol (Tenn.-Va.) Rotary Club, 1989 Mem. NEA, Va. Edn. Assn., Bristol Edn. Assn., Phi Kappa Phi, Phi Delta Kappa. Presbyterian. Achievements include Developed second grade curriculum in math., science, health, and social studies. Avocations: rose gardening, crafts. Home: 1011 Carolina Ave Bristol TN 37620-3905

JOHNSON, OWEN VERNE, historian, educator; b. Madison, Wis., Feb. 22, 1946; s. Verner Lalander Johnson and Marianne Virginia (Halvorson) Muse; m. Marta Kucerova, July 17, 1969 (div. Jan. 26, 2001); children: Eva, Hana; m. Ann Coonradt Tyron, May 12, 2001. BA in History with distinction, Wash. State U., 1968; MA in History, U. Mich., 1970, cert. in Russian Ea. European studies, PhD in History, U. Mich., 1978. Reporter Pullman (Wash.) Herald, 1961-67; reporter, announcer Sta. KWSU Radio-TV, Pullman, 1965-68; reporter, editor, producer Sta. WUOM, Ann Arbor, Mich., 1969-77; adminstrv. asst. Ctr. Russian and Ea. European Studies U. Mich., Ann Arbor, 1978-79; asst. prof. Sch. Journalism So. Ill. U., Carbondale, Ill., 1979-80; asst. prof. Ind. U., Bloomington, 1980-87, assoc. prof., 1987—, dir. grad. studies, 1990-91, acting dir. Polish studies, 1989-90, 2004—05, dir. Russian and Ea. European Inst., 1991-95. Mem. Modern Sweden Seminar, Uppsala, 1967; mem. Studia Academica Slovaca Comenius U., Bratislava, 1973; field advisor journalism Am. Coun. Tchrs. Russian, 1993—96; adj. prof. history Ind. U., Bloomington, 1996—. Author: (book) Slovakia 1918-38: Education and the Making of a Nation, 1985; co-author: Eastern European Journalism Before, During and After Communism, 1999; contbr. articles to profl. jours.; mem. editl. bd., Slovakia, 1978—89, Journalism Monographs, 1986—88, Kosmas, 1996—, Media Rsch., 2002—; corr. editor: Journalism History, 1985—2000, cons. editor: Slavic Rev., 1985—91, corr.: Slovak Spectator, 2004—. Capt. USAR, 1971—79. Recipient Excellence in Journalism award, Sigma Delta Chi, 1966; grantee, Nat. Coun. Soviet and E. European Rsch., 1988—90, Am. Coun. Learned Socs./Social Sci. Rsch. Coun. Joint Com. Ea. Europe, 1983, Internat. Rsch. and Exchs. Bd., 1973—74, 1982, 1989, 2003—04. Mem.: Slovak Studies Assn. (pres. 1988—91), Orgn. Am. Historians, Czechoslovak History Conf. (editor newsletter 1980—84, mem. exec. com. 1988—92, Stanley Pech award 1987—88), Assn. Edn. Journalism and Mass. Comm. (head history divsn. 1985—86), Am. Assn. Advancement Slavic Studies (mem. edn. com. 1988—90), Am. Hist. Assn. Democrat. Presbyterian. Office: Ind U Sch Journalism 200 Ernie Pyle Hall Bloomington IN 47405 Fax: 812-855-0901. Office Phone: 812-855-9247. E-mail: johnsono@indiana.edu.

JOHNSON, PATRICK THOMAS, military officer; b. Clarence, N.Y., Mar. 23, 1978; s. Richard Douglas Johnson and Ruth Helen Johnson-Souder; m. Crystal M. Miller, Dec. 21, 1998; 1 child, Amelia Jane. AA, Hilbert Coll., 1998; BA, Pk. U., 2004. Commd. ensign USMC, advanced through grades to staff sgt., ops. chief New River, NC, 1999—2002, liaison officer White House Quantico, Va., 2002—. Decorated Navy and Marine Corps Achievement medal USMC, Good Conduct medal, Global War on Terrorism Expeditionary award, Kosovo Campaign medal, NATO (Kosovo) medal, Good Conduct medal, Global War on Terrorism Svc. medal, Joint Meritorious Unit award White Ho. Mil. Office, Presdl. Svc. badge. Mem.: Hilbert Coll. Student Govt. Assn. (assoc.; freshmen rep. 1996—98), Presdl. Svc. Assn. (assoc.), Phi Beta Lambda Assn. (assoc.). Baptist. Avocations: weightlifting, travel, classic cars. Office Phone: 703-784-2364. Personal E-mail: ptj7041@yahoo.com.

JOHNSON, PAUL EDWARD, poet, writer; b. Northfield, Conn., July 30, 1921; s. Philip Edward and Dorothy Marie (Swanson) Johnson; m. Nina Anikienko Zelinsky, Nov. 19, 1961; stepchildren: Eugene Anikienko, Alexander Anikienko, Ludmila Anikienko. Grad. h.s. Ins. salesman Bankers Life & Casualty, Waterbury, Conn., 1949; machine operator Torrington (Conn.) Co., 1966—86; ret., 1986. Inventor Scribendi-Intellect Game; author: numerous poems. Fin. officer Clausson Raught Post, Copake Falls, NY, 1990. With U.S. Army, 1944—48. Recipient Hon. mention, Iliad Lit. Awards, 1996, Editor's Choice award for Outstanding Achievement in Poetry, Nat. Libr. Poetry, 1996. Avocations: antiques, art, music, reading, poetry. Home: 132 Lincoln Rd Copake NY 12516-1022

JOHNSON, PAUL OREN, lawyer; b. Mpls., Feb. 2, 1937; s. Andrew Richard and LaVerne Delores (Slater) J.; children: Scott, Paula, Amy. BA, Carleton Coll., 1958; JD cum laude, U. Minn., 1961. Bar: Minn. 1961. Atty. Briggs & Morgan, St. Paul, 1961-62, Green Giant Co., Le Sueur, Minn., 1961-66, asst. sec., 1967-74, sec., 1975-79, v.p., gen. counsel, 1971-79, v.p. corporate rels., 1973-79, mem. mgmt. com., 1976-79; gen. counsel H.B. Fuller Co., St. Paul, 1979-84, sr. v.p., sec., 1980-90, mem. mgmt. com., 1981-90. Bd. dirs. The Fulcrum Group, chmn. bd. dirs. Bd. dirs. Boy Scouts Am.; bd. dirs. Rep. County Com., 1965; bd. dirs. Minn. State U., 1979-82, v.p., 1980-82; chmn. bd. dirs. Minn. Com. Serving Deaf and Hard of Hearing, 1992-98; bd. dirs. vice chair Minn. Acads.; bd. dirs., mem. exec. com., treas. Self Help for Hard of Hearing. Office: Lexington-Riverside 403-1077 Sibley Meml Hwy Saint Paul MN 55118-3680

JOHNSON, PETER FORBES, transportation executive, business owner; b. Salem, Mass., May 7, 1934; s. William Bennett and Sarah Loraine (Nee) J.; m. Mikell Kraus, Oct. 11, 1958; children: Krista, Todd, Karyn, Jennifer. BS, U.S. Mcht. Marine Acad., 1957. Deck officer Texaco, Port Arthur, Tex., 1958-63; from deck officer to master Reynolds Metals Co., Corpus Christi, Tex., 1963-65, port capt., 1965-68, operating mgr., 1968-71; internat. marine mgr. Gulf Miss. Marine Corp., New Orleans, 1971-72; cons. Peter F. Johnson & Assocs., New Orleans, 1972-73; exec. v.p. Pyramid Marine, Inc., New Orleans, 1973-76; pres., owner, chmn. bd. Pacific-Gulf Marine, Inc., New Orleans, 1976—. Trustee U.S. Mcht. Marine Acad., Kings Point, NY. Lt. (j.g.) USNR, 1959-63. Mem. Coun. Am. Master Mariners, Soc. Naval Architects and Marine Engrs., Propeller Club U.S. (Maritime Man of Yr. 1986), U.S. Navy League, Southern Yacht Club, English Turn Country Club. Republican. Roman Catholic. Avocations: fly fishing, golf, hunting, sailing. Home: 3 Lakeway Ct New Orleans LA 70131-3322 Office: Pacific Gulf Marine Inc PO Box 6479 New Orleans LA 70174-6479 Office Phone: 504-362-8121. E-mail: pfj@pac-gulf.biz.

JOHNSON, PETER JAMES, JR., lawyer, legal analyst; b. NYC; BA, JD, Columbia U., 1982. Bar: NY 1987, NJ 1988, US Dist. Ct (so., ea. districts) NY, US Dist. Ct. NJ. Former sr. advisor to Mayor David Dinkins City of NY; former sr. v.p. NY State Urban Devel. Corp.; pres. Leahey & Johnson, PC, NYC; legal analyst FOX news channel. Chmn. NY Appellate Divsn., Com. on Character & Fitness; mem. NY State Jud. Screening Panel. Mem.: Assn. Trial Lawyers Am., NY County Lawyers Assn., NY State Bar Assn., NJ State Bar Assn., Assn. Bar of the City of NY. Office: Leahy & Johnson PC 120 Wall St Ste 2220 New York NY 10005

JOHNSON, PHILIP LEIGH, geologist; b. 1959; s. Paul Christian and Genevieve Johnson; m. Suzanne Hecker, Sept. 25, 1999; 1 child, Erik. BA, San Francisco State U., 1987; MS, San Jose State U., 1990. Registered geologist Calif., cert. engring. geologist Calif. Staff geologist Earth Sci. Assocs., Palo Alto, Calif., 1990—92, Dames and Moore, San Francisco, 1992—95; supervising geologist Cotton Shires and Assocs., Los Gatos, Calif., 1995—. Contbr. articles to profl. jours. Mem.: Soc. for Sedimentary Geology, Assn. Engring. Geologists (field trip chair 2004—), Geol. Soc. Am. Office: Cotton Shires and Assocs 330 Village Ln Los Gatos CA 95030

JOHNSON, PHILIP LESLIE, lawyer; b. Beloit, Wis., Jan. 24, 1939; s. James Philip and Christabel (Williams) J.; m. Kathleen Rose Westover, May 12, 1979; children: Celeste Marie, Nicole Michelle. AB, Princeton U., 1961; JD, U. South Calif., 1973. Bar: Calif. 1973, U.S. Ct. Appeals (9th cir.) 1975, U.S. Ct. Mil. Appeals 1978, U.S. Supreme Ct. 1980. Pilot U.S. Marine Corps., 1961-70; assoc. Law Office Wm. G. Tucker, L.A., 1973-78; ptnr. Engstrom, Lipscomb & Lack, L.A., 1978-92; judge pro tem Calif. State Bar Ct., 1990-95; ptnr. Lillick & Charles, Long Beach, Calif., 1993-99, Shaw, Terhar & LaMontagne, L.A., 2000—. Chmn. aerospace law com. Def. Rsch. Inst. Contbr. articles to profl. jours. Pres., bd. dirs. U. So. Calif. Legion Lex, 1992-93; chmn. com. to nom. alumni trustees Princeton U., 1996-97, exec. com. of alumni coun., 1996-97; chmn. Marine Corps Scholarship Found. LA Ball, 1997-99, bd. dirs. 1999-2005. Mem. ABA, Nat. Bar Assn., Langston Bar Assn., Princeton Club So. Calif. Avocations: flying, skiing, jazz. Home: 5340 Valley View Rd Palos Verdes Peninsula CA 90275-5089 Office: Shaw Terhar & LaMontagne 707 Wilshire Blvd Ste 3060 Los Angeles CA 90017 Office Phone: 213-614-0400. Office Fax: 212-628-4534. Business E-Mail: pjohnson@stl.lawoffices.com. E-mail: avnlawyer@aol.com.

JOHNSON, PHILIP MCBRIDE, lawyer; b. Springfield, Ohio, June 18, 1938; BA with honors, Ind. U., 1959; LLB, Yale U., 1962. Bar: Ill. 1962, DC 1983, NY 1984. Ptnr. Kirkland & Ellis, Chgo., 1962-81; chmn. Commodity Futures Trading Commn., Washington, 1981-83; ptnr. Wiley, Johnson & Rein, Washington, 1983-84; ptnr., now of counsel, commodities, futures and options Skadden, Arps, Slate, Meagher & Flom, Washington, 1984—; lectr. on commodities regulation U. Va. Law Sch., 1993—. Spkr. panelist on Commodity Exch. Act Fed. Bar Assn., others; mem. adv. com. definition and regulation Commodity Futures Trading Commn., adv. com. state jurisdiction and responsibility; adv. com. regulatory coordination, adv. com. fin. products, adv. com. tech., adv. com. global markets Commodity Futures Trading Commn.; chair, Commodity Futures Trading Commn., 1981-83 Author: Derivatives Regulation, 3 vols., 1997, Derivatives: A Manager's Guide to the World's Most Powerful Financial Instruments, 1999; mng. editor Yale U. Law Jour, 1962, Agrl. Law Jour; bd. editors, International Financial Law Review; contbr. articles to legal jours. Mem. ABA (founder, first chmn. com. on regulation of futures and derivative instruments 1976-81, mem. governing coun. sect. on bus. law 1981-83), Futures Industry Assn. (bd. dirs. 1980-81, 86-87), Internat. Bar Assn. (founder, first chmn. subcom. on commodities, futures and options law 1987-90), NY Stock Exch. (mem. regulatory adv. com. 1989—2004). Office: Skadden Arps Slate Meagher & Flom 1440 New York Ave NW Ste 700 Washington DC 20005-2111 Office Phone: 202-371-7340. Office Fax: 202-661-9081. Business E-Mail: pjohnson@skadden.com.

JOHNSON, PHILIP WAYNE, judge; b. Greenwood, Ark., Oct. 24, 1944; s. John Luther and Flora (Joyce) J.; m. Carla Jean Newsom, Nov. 6, 1970; children: Betsy, Carl, Jeff, Laura, Philip. BA, Tex. Tech. U., 1965, JD, 1975. Bar: Tex. 1975, U.S. Dist. Ct. (no. and we. dists.) Tex. 1976, U.S. Ct. Appeals (5th cir.) 1984, U.S. Supreme Ct. 1984; cert. in civil trial and personal injury trial law, Tex. Bd. Legal Specialization. Assoc. Crenshaw Dupree & Milam, Lubbock, Tex., 1975-80, ptnr., 1980-98; justice Tex. State Ct. of Appeals (7th dist), Amarillo, 1999—2002, chief justice, 2003—05; justice Tex. Supreme Ct., Austin, Tex., 2005—. Bd. dirs., pres. Lubbock County Legal Aid Soc., Tex., 1977-79; bd. dirs., chmn. Trinity Christian Schs., Lubbock, 1978-83, 85-89; bd. dirs., pres. S.W. Lighthouse for Blind, Lubbock, 1978-85. Served to capt. USAF, 1965-72. Decorated Silver Star, D.F.C.; Cross of Gallantry (Vietnam). Fellow: Tex. Bar Found. (life), Am. Bar Found. (life); mem.: Austin (Tex.) Bar Assn., Lubbock County Bar Assn. (pres. 1984—85), Amarillo Bar Assn., Tex. Bar Assn., Order of Coif, Phi Delta Phi. Mailing: PO Box 12883 Austin TX 78711 Home: 5604 Southwest Pkwy Austin TX 78701 Office: Texas Supreme Ct 201 W 14th St Rm 104 Austin TX 78701

JOHNSON, PHILLIP EDWARD, lawyer; b. Cleve., Mar. 19, 1950; s. Donald Marquis and Jeannette (Tetinek) Johnson; m. Priscilla Dwinnell, Sept. 12, 1981. BA, Miami U., Oxford, Ohio, 1972; JD, Case Western Res. U., Cleve., 1975. Bar: Ohio 75, U.S. Dist. Ct. (no. dist.) Ohio 75, Maine 77, U.S. Dist. Ct. Maine 77. Assoc. Arter & Harden, Cleve., 1975—77, Pierce, Atwood, Schriber, Allen, Smith & Lancaster, Augusta and Portland, Maine, 1977—82, ptnr., 1983—92, Johnson & Webbert, LLP, Augusta, 1992—. Vice chmn. Maine Bd. of Property Tax Rev., 1992—; mem. Maine Profl. Ethics Commn., 2001—, chmn., 2003—. Mem.: ABA, Kennebec County Bar Assn. (pres. 1983—85), Maine Trial Lawyers Assn. (bd. govs. 1993—2003), Maine State Bar Assn., Lawyer-Pilots Bar Assn. Republican. Home: 66 Hemlock Ter Augusta ME 04330-6248 Office: PO Box 79 160 Capitol St Augusta ME 04332-0079 E-mail: pjohnson@johnsonwebbert.com.

JOHNSON, PHILLIP MURRAY, treasurer, paper company executive, consumer products company executive; b. Terril, Iowa, Jan. 7, 1940; s. Martin R. and Elnora Gertrude (Mills) J.; m. Marion Elizabeth Banister, Dec. 26, 1970; children: Benjamin, Peter. BS in Econs., Iowa State U., Ames, Iowa, 1963, MS in Econs., 1965. Instr., econs. and bus. fin. Pahlavi U., Shiraz, Iran, 1966—68; v.p. Chase Manhattan Bank, NYC, 1968-83, Mellon Bank, NYC, 1983—89; sr. v.p. Mitsui Trust Bank, NYC, 1989-95; sr. dir. internat. devel. Georgia-Pacific Corp., Atlanta, 1995—99, v.p. and treas., 1999—. Dir. Georgia-Pacific Masisa Resinas (Chile) SRL, Conception. Mem. US Peace Corps, 1966-1968, US Returned Peace Corps. Vols., Chastain Park Civic Assn., Fin. Execs. Internat. Avocations: tennis, skiing. Home: 31 Darbrook Rd Westport CT 06880-3611 Office: Georgia-Pacific Corp 133 Peachtree St NE Atlanta GA 30303 Office Phone: 404-652-4467, 404-652-4000.

JOHNSON, PHYLLIS MARIE, clergywoman; b. Snohomish, Wash., Apr. 21, 1918; d. Arthur Abel and Alta Campbell (Cochran) J. BA, U. Wash., 1941; M Religious Edn. cum laude, San Francisco Theol. Sem., 1950. Commd. Christian educator Presbyn. Ch., 1950; ordained minister Presbyn. Ch., 1978. Dir. Christian edn. First Presbyn. Ch., Aberdeen, Wash., 1950-55, Northminster Presbyn. Ch., Seattle, 1955-56, United Chs. of Olympia (Wash.), 1956-65, Millwood Presbyn. Ch., Spokane, Wash., 1966-69, Pullman (Wash.) Presbyn. Ch., 1969-77, assoc. pastor, interim, 1978; interim pastor Community Presbyn. Ch., Rigby, Idaho, 1979; interim assoc. pastor Emmanuel Presbyn. Ch., Spokane, Wash., 1980-81; ednl. cons. Covenant Christian Ch., Spokane, 1988-89. Horizons rep. Presbyn. Women Inland Empire, Spokane, 1988-93; chaplain Ecumenical Ch. Secretarial Group, Spokane, 1980-90. Author, illustrator: Trees for Sharing, 1984, Christmas Cache: A Storehouse of Christmas Treasures, 1990; editor newsletter Com. on Women, Presbytery of Inland Empire, Spokane, 1982-89. Mem. Proclaim Liberty Day Care and Low Cost Housing Unit Bd. Named Hon. life mem. Pullman Presbyn. Ch. Women, 1978, Millwood Community Presbyn. Ch.-Presbyn. Women, Spokane, 1989. Mem. UN Assn., Spokane Valley Ch. Women United (pres.), Spokane Valley Minister's Fellowship, Nat. Assn. Presbyn. Ch. Educators, Nat. Assn. Presbyn. Clergywomen, Internat. Assn. Women Ministers. Avocations: writing, gardening.

JOHNSON, QUANDA DAWNYELL, performing artist, writer, producer; b. Phila. d. Olin Chester and Vernetta Dudley Johnson. BA, U. Del. Performance cert. The Am. Musical And Dramatic Acad. Founder, pres. The Qwest Factor, N.Y.C., 1999—. Prodr.(singer, actor): (theatrical events) Lyrical Langston: His Muse For Music, My Lord, What A Morning! The Story of Marian Anderson in Her Own Words, Beyond the Veil of the Sorrow Songs: W.E.B. DuBois Sings the Souls fo Black Folks; actor(singer, dancer): various Broadway, regional, European and concert prodns. and film appearances; contbg. author (poetry) Anthology of Am. Poets. Sponsor Compassion Internat., Peru, 2002—. Recipient acad. scholarship, U. Del., Best Actress Nomination, Audelco Awards, 2003. Mem.: Am. Guild Mus. Artists, Am. Fedn. TV and Radio Artists, Actors' Equity Assn., N.Y. Women in Film and TV, Theater Comms. Group. Avocations: travel, writing poetry and short stories, all aspects of fine art, particularly oil pastels and drawing, reading, spa excursions. Office: The Qwest Factor 5E 1194 1st Ave New York NY 10021-7113 Office Phone: 212-769-8593.

JOHNSON, RANDALL CLYDE, mortgage company executive; b. Tulsa, Okla., Feb. 12, 1949; s. Clyde O. and Barbara Grace Johnson; m. Mary Dan Peck, June 25, 1971 (div. Aug. 1981); 1 child, Paul C.; m. Frances Evelen Wigelious, Oct. 1, 1982; 1 child, Tyler B. BA, U. Miami, Coral Gables, Fla., 1971. V.p. Baker Mortgage Co., Miami, Fla., 1971-75; S.E. U.S. regional mgr. Gen. Electric Credit Corp., Coral Gables, Fla., 1975-77; pres., CEO Equitable Mortgage Resources, Inc., Clearwater, Fla., 1977-89; chmn., CEO Market St. Mortgage Co., Clearwater, 1989—. Mem. adv. bd. Avondale Funding Corp., Chgo., 1998—2000, Residential Funding Corp./GM Acceptance, Bloomington, Minn., 1999, Fannie Mae Corp., Washington, 2000—02. Contbr.: Real Estate Financing Desk Book, 1977. Pres. Mental Health Assn. Pinellas County, Clearwater, 1986-89; participant Leadership Pinellas, Clearwater, 1988-98; dir. Clearwater Marine Sci. Ctr., 1990-91; vice chmn. Mortgage Bankers Polit. Action Com., Washington, 1996-98; hon. chmn. Pinellas County March of Dimes, 2000; mem. pres.'s coun. U. Miami, 1998—, bd. trustees 2005-; bd. trustees All Children's Hosp. Found., 2003. Recipient Schumacher-Bolduc award, 1999; named Outstanding Young Men in Am., JCs Internat., 1979, Floridans to Watch in the Next Ten Years, Fla. Trend Mag., Miami, 1980, Significant Sig, Sigma Chi Nat. Fraternity, Evanston, Ill., 1998; faculty fellow Sch. Mortgage Banking, Washington, 1988. Fellow Soc. Cert. Mortgage Bankers (master CMB, mem. CMB commn. 2001-); mem. Mortgage Bankers Assn. Am. (profl. mem., bd. govs. 1995—, Legion of Honor 1999), Mortgage Bankers Assn. Fla. (profl. mem., pres. 1987-88), Carlouel Yacht Club, Wade Hampton Golf Club, Cypress Run Golf Club. Republican. Episcopalian. Avocations: spending time with my family, golf, fishing. Home: 887 Royal Birkdale Dr Tarpon Springs FL 34688-6302 Fax: 727-791-4136. Business E-Mail: randy.johnson@msmcorp.com.

JOHNSON, RANDY (RANDALL DAVID JOHNSON), professional baseball player; b. Walnut Creek, Calif., Sept. 10, 1963; Student, U. So. Calif. Pitcher Montreal Expos, 1985—89, Seattle Mariners, 1989—98, Houston Astros, 1998, Ariz. Diamondbacks, 1999—2004, New York Yankees, 2005—. Named Pitcher of Yr., Sporting News, 1995, Am. League Strikeout Leader, 1992—95, Am. League Earned Runs Average (ERA) Leader, 1995, Nat. League Strikeout Leader, 1999—2002, 2004, Nat. League Earned Run Average (ERA) Leader, 1999, 2001—02, Nat. League Wins Leader, 2002, Co-MVP, World Series, 2001; named to All-Star Team, 1990, 1993—95, 1997, 1999—2002, 2004; recipient Am. League Cy Young award, 1995, Nat. League Cy Young award, 1999—2002. Achievements include mem. World Series Champion Arizona Diamondbacks, 2001; pitched a no-hitter vs. Detroit Tigers, 1990; pitched a perfect game vs. Atlanta Braves, 2004; holds MLB record for career strikeouts by a left-handed pitcher; ranks 3rd all-time for career strikeouts. Office: c/o New York Yankees Yankee Stadium E 161 st and river ave Bronx NY 10452

JOHNSON, RAYMOND K., information technology manager; b. Texas City, Tex., Jan. 25, 1959; s. Raymond Knight and Gertrude Delores Johnson; m. Sandra D. Meaux, Nov. 7, 1957; 1 child, Matthew Kee. BSEE, U. Houston, 1983. Instrumentation and elec. specialist Brown & Root, Houston, 1978—85; sr. customer svc. rep. Honeywell, Houston, 1985—89; pres., chief sicentist Kingwood (Tex.) Tech. Group, 1989—97; mgr. info. tech. San Jacinto River Authority, Conroe, Tex., 1997—. Contbr.: ANSI Standard, Application of Safety and Instrumentation Systems for the Process Industries, 1996. Leader Boy Scouts Am., Houston, 1991—. Recipient Excellence in Engring. award, Chevron Chem. Co., 1991, Project award, Chevron Info. Tech. Co., 1992, Comdr.'s award for civilian Svc., U.S. Army, 1993, St. George award, Episcopal Ch., 2000, Cert. of Achievement, FEMA, 2005. Mem.: NRA, Instrumentation, Sys. and Automation Soc., Am. Radio Relay League (life). Republican. Avocations: hunting, camping. Office: San Jacinto River Authority 1577 Damsite Rd Conroe TX 77304 Office Phone: 281-367-9511. Personal E-mail: w7rkj@yahoo.com. Business E-Mail: drrayj@sjra.net.

JOHNSON, RAYMONDA THEODORA GREENE, retired humanities educator; b. Chgo., Jan. 12, 1939; d. Theodore T. and Eileen (Atherley) Greene; m. Hulon Johnson, June 27, 1964; children: David Atherley, Theodore Cassell, Alexander Ward. BA in English, DePaul U., 1960; MA in English, Loyola U., Chgo., 1965. Cert. high sch. English tchr., Ill. Tchr. high sch. English, Chgo. Pub. Schs., 1960-65; instr. English, Harold Washington Coll. (formerly Loop Coll.), City Coll., Chgo., 1965-66, asst. prof., 1966-91, assoc. prof., 1991-96, faculty advisor coll. newspaper, 1989-92, 96-98, pres. faculty coun., 1990-92, mem. faculty coun., 1990-94, chair English and speech dept., 1992—2004, coord. coll. assessment plan com., 1995-99, prof., 1996—2004, prof. emeritus, 2004—. Mem. Brit. Partnership Articulation team, 1997—. Middle sch. v.p. parents coun. Latin Sch., Chgo., 1974-76, trustee, 1987-93; adv. bd. high jump program Latin Sch. Chgo., 1989-98; cubmaster, leader Boys Scouts Am., Chgo., 1974-81; black creativity adv. com. Mus. Sci. and Industry, Chgo., 1984-96; steering com. St. Thomas the Apostle Anti-Racism Ethnic Sensitivity, 1999—; chair St. Thomas the Apostle Parish Diversity Dinners, 1999—. Recipient Svc. award St. Thomas the Apostle Ch., Chgo., 1984. Mem. Twigs Mothers Club (pres. 1982-84), Alpha Kappa Alpha. Democrat. Roman Catholic. Avocations: reading, sewing, modern dance, theater, music. Home: 6747 S Bennett Ave Chicago IL 60649-1031 E-mail: rajohnson@ccc.edu.

JOHNSON, RENA MARIE, physician; b. Wash., DC, June 9, 1961; d. Paul Colonius Johnson III and Amy Virginia (Smith) Johnson. BA, Wellesley Coll., 1981, Howard U., 1983; MD, Howard U., Med. Sch., 1987; MPH, George Wash. U., 2000. Residency Temple U., Pitts., 2000; pres. Amelia Dove, LLC, Silver Spring, Md., 2000—. Adv. bd. Pres.'s Commn. on Health Care Reform, Wash., 1993. Vol. Md. Nat. Capital Park and Planning Commn., Montgomery County, Md. Mem.: Am. Bd. of Family Practice, Montomery County Med. Soc., Am. Acad. of Family Physicians. Avocations: golf, genealogy, horticulture. Home: 1022 Gadsden Ave Silver Spring MD 20905 Office: Amelia Dove Family Practice 1111 Spring St Ste G2 Silver Spring MD 20910 Office Phone: 301-565-2882. Office Fax: 301-565-2992. E-mail: rmjmd@yahoo.com.

JOHNSON, REVERDY, lawyer; b. NYC, Aug. 24, 1937; s. Reverdy and Reva (Payne) J.; children: Deborah Ghiselin, Reverdy Payne AB cum laude, Harvard U., 1960, LLB, 1963. Bar: Fla. 1963, Calif. 1964, N.Mex. 1997. Assoc. Brobeck, Phleger & Harrison, San Francisco, 1963-66; from assoc. to ptnr. Pettit & Martin, San Francisco, 1966-95; of counsel Steinhart & Falconer LLP, San Francisco, 1995-97, Scheuer Yost & Patterson, Sante Fe, NMex., 1996—, Fenwick and West, LLP, Mountain View, Calif., 1999—2003. Co-owner Johnson Turnbull Vineyards, Napa Valley, Calif., 1977-93; tech. adv. com., com. open space lands Calif. Joint Legislature, 1968-69, chmn., 1969-70 Bd. dirs. Planning and Conservation League, 1966—72, League to Save Lake Tahoe, 1972—77, Found. for San Francisco's Archtl. Heritage, 1975—84, San Francisco Devel. Found., 1986—96, Santa Fe Shakespeare Co., 2001—03, pres., 2002—03. Mem. Urban Land Inst. (vice-chmn. recreational devel. council 1975-78, comml. and retail devel. council 1980-99), Napa Valley Vintners Assn. (bd. dir. 1985-88, v.p. 1987, pres. 1988), Am. Coll. Real Estate Lawyers, Lambda Alpha. also: Scheuer Yost & Patterson 125 Lincoln Ave Ste 223 Santa Fe NM 87501-2053 Office Phone: 505-989-7500. E-mail: reverdyj@santafelawyers.com.

JOHNSON, RICHARD A., lawyer; b. Mar. 23, 1950; AB, Brown Univ., 1972; MS, MIT, 1973; JD, Yale Univ., 1976. Bar: Calif. 1977, D.C. 1978. Law clk. Judge Eugene A. Wright, US Ct. Appeals, 9th Cir., Seattle, 1976—77; assoc. gen. counsel, internat. trade US Dept. Commerce, 1980—81; ptnr., Internat. Trade Practice Group Arnold & Porter, Washington. Editor: Yale Law Journal. Chmn., Biotech. Com. & vice chmn., Tech. & Innovation Com. OECD/BIAC; chmn. OECD Intellectual Property Task Force; mem. bd. vis. MIT Corp. Nat. Fellow, Nat. Sci. Found., 1973. Mem.: Am. Soc. of Internat. Law (mem., exec. bd., past chmn., annual meeting), U.S. Council for Internat. Bus., Bus.-Univ. Forum. Office: Arnold & Porter 555 Twelfth St NW Washington DC 20004-1206 Office Phone: 202-942-5550. Office Fax: 202-942-5999. Business E-Mail: richard.johnson@aporter.com.

JOHNSON, RICHARD ARNOLD, statistics educator, consultant; b. St. Paul, July 10, 1937; s. Arnold Verner and Florence Dorothy J.; m. Roberta Anne Weinard, Mar. 21, 1964; children— Erik Richard, Thomas Robert B.E.E., U. Minn., Mpls., 1960, MS in Math., 1963, PhD in Stats., 1966. Asst. prof. stats. U. Wis., Madison, 1966-70, assoc. prof., 1970-74, prof. stats, 1974—, chmn. dept. stats., 1981-84; head Greentree Statis. Consulting, Madison, Wis., 1978—. Cons. industry, Dept. Energy; cooperating scientist Dept. Agr. Co-author: Statistical Concepts and Methods, 1977, Applied Multivariate Statistical Analysis, 1982, 5th edit., 2002, Probability and Statistics for Engineers (4th edit. 1990, 5th edit. 1994, 6th edit. 2000, 7th edit. 2005), Statistics-Principles and Methods, 1985, 5th edit., 2005, Business Statistics-Decision Making with Data, 1997, Statistical Reasoning and Methods, 1998. Recipient Frank Wilcoxon prize, 1991; NATO sr. postdoctoral fellow, 1972; numerous grants NSA, NSF, ONR, Air Force, NASA. Fellow Inst. Math. Stats. (program sec. 1980-86, mem. of council 1980-86), Am. Statis. Assn. (sect. rep. to council 1980-82), Royal Statis. Soc.; mem. Internat. Statis. Inst. Lutheran. Avocations: fishing, cross country skiing. Office: Greentree Statis Cons 7122 Valhalla Trl Madison WI 53719-3039 Business E-Mail: rich@stat.wisc.edu.

JOHNSON, RICHARD AUGUST, literature and language professor; b. Washington, Apr. 18, 1937; s. Cecil August and Esther Marie (Nelson) J.; m. Michaela Ann Memelsdorff, Aug. 20, 1960; children— Nicholas, Patrick, Hong, Loeun. BA, Swarthmore Coll., 1959; PhD, Cornell U., 1965. Instr. English U. Va., Charlottesville, 1963-65; asst. prof. Mt. Holyoke Coll., South Hadley, Mass., 1965-71, assoc. prof., 1971-74, prof., chmn. dept., 1974-80, 1988-91, prof. Alumnae Found., 1980-86, Lucia, Ruth and Elizabeth MacGregor prof. English, 1986—2004, emeritus prof., 2004—. Vis. prof. Amherst Coll., 1979, 84-88. Author: Man's Place: An Essay on Auden, 1973; co-author: Common Ground: Personal Writing and Public Discourse, 1992, Finding Common Ground, 1996; contbr. articles to profl. jours. Mem. MLA, AAUP, Phi Beta Kappa Democrat. Episcopalian. Home: 1214 Noyes Dr Silver Spring MD 20910-2717 E-mail: rjohnson@mtholyoke.edu.

JOHNSON, RICHARD DARRELL, management consultant; b. Columbus, Ohio, Aug. 1, 1935; s. Darrell Dean and Gretchen Price (Motz) Johnson; m. Ann Elizabeth Sektnan, Apr. 9, 1960; children: Julie Ann, Jennifer Lynn, Douglas Richard. B in Indsl. Engring., Ohio State U., 1958, MBA, 1962. CPA Ohio, Ill.; cert. in computer processing Inst. Cert. Computer Profls.; registered profl. engr., Ohio. Consulting staff Arthur Andersen & Co., Cleve., 1962-65, consulting mgr., 1965-70, consulting ptnr., 1970, consulting mng. ptnr., 1971-75, cons. retail industry head, 1969-75, chmn. adv. coun., 1976-78, country mng. ptnr. Iran, Afghanistan and Pakistan Tehran, Iran, 1975-77, mng. ptnr. profl. edn. Chgo., 1977-79, mng. ptnr. edn. consulting, 1979-86; mng. ptnr. change mgmt. Andersen Consulting, Chgo., 1986-91, ret. ptnr., 1991; pres. VIA Internat. Ltd., Chgo., 1992-99; chmn. VIA Internat. LLC, Chgo., 1998-99; pres. RDJ Ltd. Mgmt. Conss., 1999—. Mem. Ill. Dist. 67 Bd. Edn., Lake Forest, 1984—90, sec., 1984—85, chmn. edn. com., 1987—90, chmn. strategic planning com., 1989—90, v.p., 1989—90; trustee Ravinia Festival Assn., Highland Pk., Ill., 1988—2004, vice chmn., 1998—2002, chmn. devel. com., 1998—2002, long range planning com., 1996—; treas. Lake Forest (Ill.) Symphony Assn., 1979—81, v.p., 1981—83, exec. v.p., 1983—89, adv. bd., 1989—; gen. coord. Chgo. campaign Am. Cancer Soc., 1983; dir. United Way Lake Forest, Lake Bluff, Ill., 1981—, treas., 1984—86, pres., 1986—88; mem. Chgo. adv. bd. Coll. Engring., Ohio State U., 1988—91, alumni adv. coun., 1996—99; mem. Alumni Assn. Bd., 1999—2004, vice chmn., 2001—04; mem. Coll. Bus. Adv. Coun., 1976—83, 1st v.p., 1978—79; mem. Ruth Weimer Mt. Leadership Initiatives Fund, 1997—2001. 1st lt. USAF, 1958—61. Recipient Internat. Disting. Svc. award, Assn. Sys. Mgmt., 1976, Gerlach award, 1998, Alumni Citizenship Award, OSU Alumni Assoc., 1998, Disting. Alumni award, Fisher Coll. of Bus., 2002. Mem.: Chgo. Coun. Fgn. Rels., Sloane Gardens Club (London) (treas. 1993—94), Pelican Marsh Golf Club (Naples), Exec. Club Chgo., Pelican Isle Yacht Club (Naples, Fla.), Sigma Chi (Significant Sig award 2002). Avocations: skiing, boating, tennis, golf, classical music. Home: 351 Sussex Ln Lake Forest IL 60045-2057 Office: RDJ Ltd 351 Sussex Lane Lake Forest IL 60045-2057 E-mail: rdjltd@earthlink.net.

JOHNSON, RICHARD DAVID, retired librarian; b. Cleve., June 10, 1927; s. Robert Emanuel and Emma (Lindhorst) J.; m. Harriett Herzog, Sept. 8, 1956; children: Ruth Ellen, Royce Emanuel. BA, Yale U., 1949; MA in Internat. Rels., U. Chgo., 1950, MALS, 1957. Libr. Nat. Opinion Rsch. Ctr. U. Chgo., 1956-57; reference libr. Stanford, 1957-59; cataloger Stanford U., 1959-60, 61-62, adminstrv. asst. to dir., 1960-61, head acquisitions, 1962-64, chief undergrad. libr. project, 1964-67, chief libr. tech. svcs., 1967-68; dir. librs. Claremont (Calif.) Colls., 1968-73, SUNY, Oneonta, 1973-94; ret., 1994. Editor: Calif. Libr., 1966-68, Coll. and Rsch. Librs., 1974-80, Choice, 1982, Lexington Books series on librs., 1981-87, N.Y. Libr. Assn. Bull., 1986-91, Assn. Libr. Collections and Tech. Svcs. Newsletter, 1989-91, Glimmerglass Opera Guild Newsletter, 1995—; mng. editor: Jour. Libr. Automation, 1980. Trustee Four County Libr. System, Binghamton, N.Y., 1978-88, South Cen. Rsch.Libr. Coun., Ithaca, 1986-90. With inf. AUS, 1952-54. Decorated Bronze Star; recipient Acad./Rsch. Libr. of Yr. award Assn. Coll. and Rsch. Librs., 1984, Trustees award for outstanding svc. South Ctrl. Rsch. Libr. Coun., 1994, Ptnr. in Excellence award Opera Vols. Internat., 2000. Mem. ALA, Calif. Libr. Assn. (pres. 1972), N.Y. Libr. Assn. (pres. acad. and spl. librs. sect. 1981-82, 2d v.p. 1982, Spirit of Librarianship award 1992), Beta Phi Mu. Presbyterian. Home: 2 Walling Blvd Oneonta NY 13820-1918

JOHNSON, RICHARD DEAN, pharmaceutical consultant, educator; b. DeKalb, Ill., July 8, 1936; s. Arthur Dean Johnson and Evelyn Alice (Telford) Williams; m. Paula Marcellus Jennings, Nov. 3, 1942; children: Janet Telford Bijur, Julie Johnson McVeigh, Richard Dean Jr., Jennings Brodie. BS, U. Calif., Berkeley, 1960; PharmD, U. Calif., San Francisco, 1961, MS, 1962, PhD, 1965; MBA, Rockhurst Coll., 1984. Cert. tchr. Calif., lic. pharmacist Calif. Sect. head R&D Allergan Inc., Irvine, Calif., 1965—67; dir. regulatory affairs Syntex Labs., Inc., Palo Alto, Calif., 1967—73; mng. dir. licensing Marion Labs., Inc., Kansas City, Mo., 1973—79, v.p. licensing, 1980—82, v.p. corp. devel., 1983—87, v.p. bus. alliances, 1987—88; corp. v.p. Marion Merrell Dow, Inc., Kansas City, Mo., 1989—91, ret., 2003; prin., owner KC Pharma, LLC, Kansas City, Mo., 1991—. Adj. prof. Sch. Pharmacy, U. Mo., Kansas City, 1991-95, R&D coun., 1993—, adj. grad. prof., 1995—; bd. dirs. Dey Labs., Inc., Concord, Calif., Tanabe-Marion Labs., Kansas City, U.S. Biosci., Inc., Blue Bell, Pa., ImmunoPharmaceutics, Inc., San Diego, Lovelace Respiratory Rsch. Inst., Albuquerque, Micrologix Biotech Inc., Vancouver, B.C., mem. comp. and audit coms., Tima Tech., Inc., Kansas City, AusAm Biotech., Inc., Santa Monica, Calif., mem. comp. and intellectual property coms.; guest lectr. U. S.C. Sch. Bus. Adminstrn., Columbia, 1975-79; pharm. analyst SunTrust Robinson Humphrey, 2002, Cottonwood Capital Mgmt., LLC, 2002-04. Contbr. articles to profl. jours. Presdl. exch. exec. White House, Washington, 1970-71, U.S. Pharmacopeia Com. of Rev., 1990-2001; trustee U. Mo., Kansas City Pharmacy Found., 1993—, v.p., 1994-96, pres., 1996-98, fin. com., 1996—2000, pres. emeritus, 1998—, chmn. devel. com., 1994-96, chmn. exec. and fin. coms., 1996-98, dean's adv. bd., 1995—; trustee Johnson Family Fund, Kansas City Cmty. Found., 1993—, U. Kansas City Bd., Mo., 1996-2001, U. Mo., Kansas City, 2001—; fin., real estate and life scis. coms., 1998—; mem. Kansas City Life Sci. Initiative and Undergrad. Rsch. coms., 2001—; dean's adv. bd. Sch. Pharmacy U. Calif., San Francisco, 1994-97, bd. counsellors, 1997-2001; dean's adv. bd. Sch. Pharmacy U. Mo., Kansas City, 1995-2001, 2003—; trustee Conservatory of Music, U. Mo., Kansas City, 1998-2002; Henry W. Bloch Sch. Bus. and Pub. Adminstrn. exec. roundtable U. Mo., Kansas City, 1998-2003; active Internat. Rels. Coun., Kansas City, 1998—; active De La Salle Sch. Devel. Com., 1993-2001, St. Lukes Hosp. Stroke Com., 1993—, U.S. Pharmacopeia Drug Nomenclature Com., 1990-2001, vet. drug com., 1998-2001, ARC, Kirkwood Soc. Recipient Grad. award Borden Co., 1962; NIH Pub. Health Svc. Tng. grant, 1962-65; Am. Found. for Pharm. Edn. fellow, 1962-65, Sir Henry S. Wellcome Meml. fellow, 1962-63, Am. Inst. Chemists fellow, 1965-70. Mem.: ACS, AAAS, Licensing Exec. Soc., Fedn. Internat. Pharmacy, Pharm. Mfrs. Assn., N.Y. Acad. Sci., Acad. Pharm. Sci., Am. Pharm. Assn., Am. Assn. Pharm. Scis., Am. Found. for Pharm. Edn. Centurion, ARC Kirkwood Soc., Mission Hills Country Club, La Jolla Country Club, River Club (Kansas City), Carriage Club (Kansas City, Mo.), Hallbrook Country Club (Leawood, Kans.), Balboa Bay Club (Newport Beach, Calif.), La Jolla (Calif.) Beach and Tennis Club, Sigma Xi, Phi Lambda Sigma, Rho Chi. Home: 5330 Ward Pky Kansas City MO 64112-2369 Office: KC Pharma LLC 222 W Gregory Blvd Kansas City MO 64114-1110 also: 8486 El Paseo Grande La Jolla CA 92037-3013 Address: 4000 N Lake Blvd Tahoe City CA 96145-5303 Office Phone: 816-444-5556. E-mail: kcpharma@webtv.net.

JOHNSON, RICHARD FRED, lawyer; b. July 12, 1944; s. Sylvester Hiram and Naomi Ruth (Jackson) Johnson; m. Sheila Conley, June 26, 1970; children: Brendon, Bridget, Timothy, Laura. BS, Miami U., Oxford, Ohio, 1966; JD cum laude, Northwestern U., 1969. Bar: Ill. 1969, Ind., 2004, U.S. Dist. Ct. (no. dist.) Ill. 1969), U.S. Dist. Ct. (ctrl. dist.) Ill. 2000, U.S. Ct. Appeals (7th cir.) 1977, U.S. Ct. Appeals (2d cir.) 1980, U.S. Ct. Appeals (9th cir.) 1991, U.S. Ct. Appeals (5th cir.) 1993, U.S. Supreme Ct. 1978. Law clk. U.S. Dist. Ct. (no. dist.) Ill., Chgo., 1969-70; assoc. firm Lord, Bissell &

Brook, Chgo., 1970-77, ptnr., 1977—2004, Gessler, Hughes, Socol, Piers, Resnick and Dym, Ltd., Chgo., 2004—. Lectr. legal edn. Contbr. articles to profl. jours. Recipient Am. Jurisprudence award 1968. Mem. Chgo. Bar Assn., Union League. Home: 521 W Roscoe St Chicago IL 60657-3518 Office: Gessler Hughes Socol Piers Resnick & Dym Ltd 70 W Madison Chicago IL 60602 Office Phone: 312-604-2618. Business E-Mail: rjohnson@ghsltd.com.

JOHNSON, RICHARD JAMES VAUGHAN, retired publishing executive; b. San Luis, Potosi, Mex., Sept. 22, 1930; s. Clifton Whatford and Myrtle Louise (Hinman) Johnson; m. Belle Beraud Griggs, Aug. 6, 1955; children: Shelley Beraud, Mark Hinman. BBA, U. Tex., Austin, 1954. Asst. to exec. dir. Tex. Daily Newspaper Assn., 1955—56; with Houston Chronicle Pub. Co., 1956—2002, chmn., 2000—02, ret., 2002. Chmn., CEO, dir. Robert A. Welch Found.; bd. visitors M.D. Anderson Cancer Ctr.; bd. dir. Tex. Med. Ctr. With U.S. Army, 1952—54. Mem.: Am. Newspaper Pubs. Assn. (past pres. and chmn.), Tex. Daily Newspaper Assn. (pres. 1978), Houston Club, River Oaks Country Club. Unitarian Universalist. Office: Houston Chronicle 801 Texas Ave Houston TX 77002-2996

JOHNSON, RICHARD KENT, publishing executive; b. Moberly, Mo., Mar. 22, 1952; s. Edward and Elizabeth Johnson; m. Susan Fersh, Sept. 4, 1976; children: Alexis, Claire. BA, Am. U., 1974. TV prodn. specialist Smithsonian Inst., Washington, 1974-77; dir. pub. rels. Congl. Info. Svc., Bethesda, Md., 1977-80, dir. advt. and promotion, 1980-83, dir. communications, 1983-89, dir. mktg., 1989-90, v.p. mktg., 1990-96, Univ. Publs. Am., Bethesda, 1990-96; sr. v.p. Congl. Info. Svc. and Univ. Pubs. Am., 1997-98; exec. dir. Scholarly Pub. and Acad. Resources Coalition, Washington, 1998—. Bd. dirs. BioOne, Stichting SPARC Europe; mem. adv. bd. Project Euclid Cornell U., 2002—; mem. nat. adv. com. NIH PubMed Ctr., 2003—05; mem. steering com. SPARC Europe, 2001—03. Recipient Echo Leader award Direct Mktg. Assn., 1986, Mktg. Achievement award Info. Industry Assn., 1985, 89, 90. Home: 5622 Lamar Rd Bethesda MD 20816-1350 Office: 21 Dupont Cir NW Ste 800 Washington DC 20036-1543 Business E-Mail: rick@arl.org.

JOHNSON, RICHARD TENNEY, lawyer; b. Evanston, Ill., Mar. 24, 1930; s. Ernest Levin and Margaret Abbott (Higgins) J.; m. Marilyn Bliss Meuth, May 1, 1954; children: Ross Tenney, Lenore, Jocelyn. AB with high honors, U. Rochester, 1951; postgrad., Trinity Coll., Dublin, Ireland, 1954-55; LLB, Harvard, 1958. Bar: D.C. 1959. Trainee Office Sec. Def., 1957-59; atty. Office Gen. Counsel. Dept. Def., 1959-63; dep. gen. counsel Dept. Army, 1963-67, Dept. Transp., 1967-70; gen. counsel CAB, 1970-73, mem., 1976-77; gen. counsel NASA, 1973-75, ERDA, 1975-76; chmn. organizational integration Dept. Energy Activation, Exec. Office of Pres., 1977; ptnr. firm Sullivan & Beauregard, 1978-81; gen. counsel Dept. Energy, 1981-83; ptnr. Zuckert, Scoutt, Rasenberger & Johnson, 1983-87; prin. Law Offices of R. Tenney Johnson, Esq., Washington, 1987-2001; gen. counsel Assn. of Univs. for Rsch. in Astronomy, 1987—. Lt. USNR, 1951-54. Mem. ABA, Fed. Bar Assn., Cosmos Club, Phi Beta Kappa, Theta Delta Chi. Office Phone: 202-483-2101. E-mail: marandten@starpower.net.

JOHNSON, RICHARD TIDBALL, neurology, microbiology and neuroscience educator, research virologist; b. Grosse Pointe, Mich, July 16, 1931; s. Horton and Katharine (Tidball) J.; m. Frances W. Johnson, Sept. 18, 1954; children: Carlton, Erica, Matthew, Nathan. AB cum laude, U. Colo., Boulder, 1953; MD, U. Colo., Denver, 1956. Diplomate Am. Bd. of Psychiatry and Neurology. Intern Stanford U. Hosp., San Francisco, 1956-57; clin. pathologist dept. virus diseases Walter Reed Army Inst. of Research, Washington, 1957-58, asst. chief dept. of virus diseases, 1959; asst. resident in neurology Mass. Gen. Hosp., 1959-60, clin. fellow neuropathology, 1959-61, sr. resident neurology, 1961-62; teaching fellow in neurology Harvard Med. Sch., Boston, 1959-60, teaching fellow neuropathology, 1959-61, teaching fellow neurology, 1961-62; exchange teaching fellow, 1st asst. in neurology Med. Sch. of King's Coll., U. Durham, Newcastle-Upon-Tyne, 1962; hon. fellow dept. microbiology Australian Nat. U., Canberra, 1962-64; assoc. neurologist Cleve. Met. Gen. Hosp., 1964-69; asst. prof. neurology Case Western Res. U., Cleve., 1964-68, assoc. prof. neurology, 1968-69; assoc. prof. microbiology Johns Hopkins U. Sch. of Medicine, Balt., 1969-74, Dwight D. Eisenhower prof. neurology, 1969-88, prof. microbiology, 1974—, prof. neurosci., 1983—; joint appointment dept. molecular microbiology & immunology Johns Hopkins U. Bloomberg Sch. Pub. Health, 1984—. Neurologist Johns Hopkins Hosp., Balt., 1969—, neurologist-in-chief, 1988-97, prof., dir. dept. neurology, 1988-97; cons. neurology Balt. City Hosp., 1974; vis. prof. U. Peruana Cayetano Heredia, Lima, Peru, 1971, Imperial Coll. of Health Sci., Teheran, Iran, 1974, Inst. fur Virologie und Immunobiologie, U. Wurzburg, 1976; vis. prof. neurology and neuropathology Mahidol U., Bangkok, 1984; vis. sci. Armed Forces Research Inst. of Med. Sci., Bangkok, Thailand, 1984; founding dir. Nat. Neurosci. Inst., Singapore, 1997-2000. Author (with others): Amotrophic Lateral Sclerosis: Recent Research Trends, 1976; author: Infections of the Nervous System, 1987, Viral Infections and the Developing Nervous System, 1988, Viral Infections of the Nervous System, 1982, 1998, Current Therapy in Neurologic Diseases, Vol. 2, 1987, Current Therapy in Neurologic Diseases, Vol. 3, 1990, Current Therapy in Neurologic Diseases, Vol. 4, 1993, Current Therapy in Neurologic Diseases, Vol. 5, 1997, Current Therapy in Neurologic Diseases, Vol. 6, 2001; mem. editl. bd. 10 profl. jours.; editor: Annal. Neurol., 1988—. Mem. adv. bd. Nat. Multiple Sclerosis Soc., 1971—, exec. com., 1981—, chmn., 1985—89; spl. cons. to NIH on transmissible spongiform encephalopathis, 2001—; mem. adv. coun. James A. Baker Inst. for Animal Health, Cornell U., 1977—89; program dir. Pew Neurosci. Program, Pew Charitable Trusts, 1985—91. Decorated comendador Order of Hipolito Unanue; recipient Jean Martin Charcot aard Internat. Fedn. of Multiple Sclerosis Soc. 1985, Smadel medal Infectious Disease Soc. of Am., 1986, Multiple Sclerosis Soc. medal Assn.of Brit. Neurologists, 1986,; Pioneer award Int. Soc. Neuroviro, 1999, fellow Royal College of Physicians of London (hon), 2003, numerous others. Fellow Am. Acad. Neurology (2d v.p. 1975-77), Royal Coll. Medicine (London); mem. Assn. Am. Physicians, Am. Soc. for Virology, Australian Assn. Neurologists (hon.), Interurban Clin. Club, Acad. Brasileira de Neurologia, Assn. for Rsch. in Nervous and Mental Diseases, Internat. Brain Rsch. Orgn., Peripatetic Club, Soc. for Neurosci., Soc. Peruana de Psiquiatria, Johns Hopkins Med. Soc. (pres. 1970-71), Balt. Neurol. Soc. (pres. 1973-74), Am. Soc. for Clin. Investigation, Am. Neurol. Assn. (councillor 1977-81, v.p. 1984-85, pres. 1986-87), Am. Assn. Neuropathologists (assoc.), World Fedn. Neurology (chmn. research group on neuroimmunology and virology 1979—), Am. Soc. for Microbiology, AAAS, Philippine Neurol. Assn. (hon. fellow), Internat. Soc. for Antiviral Rsch., Inst. of Medicine/NAS, Am. Fedn. Clin. Rsch., Alpha Omega Alpha, Phi Beta Kappa. Avocations: photography, travel. Office: Johns Hopkins U Sch Medicine Dept Neurology 600 N Wolfe St Meyer 6-181 Baltimore MD 21205 E-mail: rtj@jhmi.edu.

JOHNSON, ROBERT, airport terminal executive; Mgr. Ft. Smith (Ark.) Regional Airport, Ft. Smith, AR, 1997—.

JOHNSON, ROBERT ALAN, lawyer; b. Harrisburg, Pa., June 18, 1944; s. Harry Andrew and Minna Melissa (Ebert) J.; m. Selina Braham Pedersen, Aug. 25, 1979; children: Isabella P., Robert A. Jr. BA, Washington and Jefferson Coll., 1966; JD, Harvard U., 1969. Bar: Pa. 1969. Assoc. Buchanan Ingersoll, Pitts., 1969-76, ptnr., 1977—. Contbr. legal articles to profl. jours. Pres. Bach Choir Pitts., 1979—81; bd. dirs. Presbyn. Assn. of Chautauqua, 2005—, Pitts. Opera, 1985—94, River City Brass Band, Pitts., 1986—95, Renaissance and Baroque Soc., Pitts., 1994—, Friends of the Music Libr., Carnegie Libr. of Pitts., 1995—, CTC Found., 1999—, River City Brass Band Charitable Endowment, Pitts., 2000—, Early Music Am., 2002—, Chatham Baroque, Pitts., 2004—. Fellow Am. Coll. Tax Counsel, Am. Coll. Employee Benefits Counsel; mem. ABA, Allegheny County Bar Assn., Allegheny Tax Soc. (chmn. 1982-83), Pitts. Tax Club, Duquesne Club. Republican. Presbyterian. Avocation: avid collector classical music recs. Home: 601 St James St Pittsburgh PA 15232-1434 Office: Buchanan Ingersoll 301 Grant St Ste 20 Pittsburgh PA 15219-1410 Office Phone: 412-562-8832. Business E-Mail: johnsonra@bipc.com.

JOHNSON, ROBERT ALLISON, life insurance company executive; b. Canandaigua, N.Y., Sept. 8, 1928; s. Allison Fisher and Thelma Marie (Beers) J.; m. Suzanne Amundsen Stone, Dec. 18, 1951; children: Pamela Suzanne, Carol Alison, Elizabeth Stone, Cynthia Marie. BA in History, Harvard U., 1950; MBA, Western New Eng. Coll., 1963. With Mass. Mut. Life Ins. Co., Springfield, 1951—, employment mgr., 1958-72, dir. pers., 1972-76, sr. v.p., 1976—. Author: This Violent Land, 2005. Active ARC. Served with U.S. Army, 1951-53. Mem. Life Office Mgmt. Assn., Am. Soc. CLU's. Home: 181 Windjammer Dr Leesville SC 29070 Office: 1295 State St Springfield MA 01111-0001 E-mail: rallisonj@pbtcomm.net.

JOHNSON, ROBERT BRUCE, historic preservationist; b. Salina, Kans., Dec. 14, 1941; s. Robert Alexander and Virginia Belle (Keen) J.; m. Dora Koundakjian, May 14, 1966 (div. May 1986); children: Martin, Alicia; m. Genevieve Whittemore, Oct. 18, 1986; 1 child, James Trevor Johnson. BA, Wheaton Coll., 1964; JD, Cath. U. Sch. of Law, Washington, 1976. Orgnl. sales leader The Southwestern Co., Nashville, 1963-65; asst. housing mgr. Nat. Capitol Housing Authority Housing Urban Devel., Washington, 1966-67; project dir. Archdiocese of Washington Office of Edn., Washington, 1967-70; dep. dir. Dept. Labor Youth Svcs., Washington, 1970-75; pres. Intown Properties Inc., Washington, 1977-81, Mt. Vernon Realty Inc., Washington, 1981-86, Premier Realty Svcs. Inc., Washington, 1986-90; sr. v.p. AmeriFund Inc., Washington, 1990-95; devel. dir. Patrick Henry Inst., Lynchburg, Va., 1995-98; pres. Monument Real Estate Historic Properties, 1994—; 576992. Cons. Nat. Trust for Hist. Preservation, Washington, 1982-83, New Covenant Schs., Lynchburg, Va.; prin. Towne Ctr. Assocs., Staunton, Va., 1979-92, Capitol Link Devel. Assocs., Washington, 1986-89, Coolidge House Assocs., Washington, 1987-94. Contbr. articles to profl. jours. Treas., co-founder New City Montessori Sch., Washington, 1969—73; mem. Cmty. Advisors on Equal Employment, Washington, 1967—70; patron Nat. Children's Choir, 1979—89; treas., initiator Bottle Bill Initiative Campaign, Washington, 1985—86; hon. chmn. Bus. Adv. Coun., 2002; commr. Presdl. Bus. Commn., 2002. Recipient Silver Palm Eagle Scout Boy Scouts Am., 1957. Mem. Nat. Trust for Hist. Preservation, Hist. Staunton Found. (ann. preservation award 1982, 83), Victorian Soc. Am., Lynchburg Acad. Music Theatre (co-chmn. bus. adv. coun.). Home: Villa Mozart 517 Washington St Lynchburg VA 24504 Personal E-mail: oscarlilly1@aol.com.

JOHNSON, ROBERT D., aerospace transportation executive; m. DeDe Johnson; 3 children. Graduate, Miami U., Oxford, Ohio. Pres., mng. dir. GE Aircraft Engines, Singapore, 1983—93; v.p., gen. mgr., mfg. and svcs. AAR Corp., Chicago, 1993—94; v.p., gen. mgr., global repair and overhaul operations AlliedSignal Aerospace, Phoenix, 1994—96, v.p., gen. mgr., aerospace svcs., 1996—97, pres., CEO, mktg., electronic and avionics systems, 1997—99, pres., CEO, mktg., sales, & svcs., 1997—99, pres., CEO, 1999—2001, Honeywell Aerospace, Phoenix, 2001—04, chmn., 2005—. Bd. trustee Embry-Riddle Aeronautical U., 2002, Ariz. State U. Pres. Club; bd. Aviation Safety Alliance, Entrada Software. Bd. dirs. Scottsdale Home Nat. Bank, The Zanesville, Ohio. Mem.: Aerospace Inductries Assn. (exec. com.), Devel. and Flight Safety Edu. Com., U. Ariz. (adv. bd.), Miami U. of Ohio (adv. bd.), Conquistadores Del Cielo. Office: Honeywell Aerospace PO Box 52181 Phoenix AZ 85072 Office Phone: 602-365-3099, 973-445-2000. Office Fax: 973-455-4807.

JOHNSON, ROBERT EUGENE, historian, academic administrator; b. NYC, Aug. 7, 1943; s. Robert E. and Eileen Mary (Holden) J.; m. Laura Zoe Climenko; children: Byron, Alexander. BA, Antioch Coll., 1965; PhD, Cornell U., 1975. History lectr. Erindale Coll. U. Toronto, 1971-74, asst. prof. history, 1975-79, assoc. prof. history, 1979-95; prof., 1995—; dir. Ctr. for Russian and East European Studies U. Toronto, 1989-2000. Author: Peasant and Proletarian, 1979, The Seam Allowance, 1982, Contadini e Proletari, 1993; editor: The 1937 Census of USSR, 1992. Rsch. grantee Social Sci. and Humanities Rsch. Coun. Can., Toronto and Moscow, 1994-99. Mem. Am. Hist. Assn., Am. Assn. for Advancement of Slavic Studies, Can. Assn. Slavists (v.p. 1985-86). Avocations: mycology, cross country skiing, canoeing. Office: U Toronto CREES Munk Ctr 1 Devonshire Pl Toronto ON Canada M5S 3K7 E-mail: johnson@chass.utoronto.ca.

JOHNSON, ROBERT GRAHAM, surgeon, educator, researcher; b. Norman, Okla., July 28, 1953; s. William Froman Johnson and Mary Elizabeth Davison; m. Cindy Snodgrass, Aug. 2, 1975; children: Chase, Rainey. MD, U. Okla., 1978. Diplomate Am. Bd. Surgery, Am. Bd. Thoracic Surgery. Resident in gen. surgery U. Okla., Oklahoma City, 1978-83, resident in cardiothoracic surgery, 1983-85; fellow in cardiac surgery Mass. Gen. Hosp., Boston, 1980-81; mem. faculty Harvard U. Med. Sch., Boston, 1985—89, assoc. prof., 1989—99; prof., chair dept. surgery St. Louis U., 1999—. Fellow ACS, Am. Coll. Cardiology, Am. Coll. Chest Physicians (pres. 2001); mem. AMA, Soc. Univ. Surgeons, Alpha mega Alpha. Episcopalian. Office: St Louis U 3635 Vista at Grand Blvd Saint Louis MO 63110 Office Phone: 314-577-8352. E-mail: johnsorg@slu.edu.

JOHNSON, ROBERT HENRY, political science educator; b. Hannaford, N.D., Jan. 23, 1921; s. Albert Idan and Alma (Peterson) J.; divorced; children: Mark Olin, Eric Lowell, Hilary Jean. BA, Concordia Coll., Moorhead, Minn., 1942; MS, Syracuse U., 1943; PhD, Harvard U., 1949. Tchg. fellow Harvard U., 1948-49, instr. govt., 1949-51; asst. to exec. sec. NSC, 1951-54, mem., sec. spl. staff, 1954-59, dir. planning bd. secretariat, 1959-61, mem. sr. staff, 1961-62; mem. policy planning coun. State Dept., 1962-67; sr. fellow Brookings Instn., 1966-68, guest scholar, 1970, 71, 73, 80; Harvey Picker prof. internat. rels. Colgate U., 1968-71, 80-84, Charles Evans Hughes prof. govt., 1971-80, chmn. dept. polit. sci., 1979-82, 83-84. Vis. fellow Overseas Devel. Coun., 1974-75, 76-77, 84-86, 87-88; sr. fellow Nat. Policy Assn., 1988—; cons. to dir. internat. divsn. GAO, 1978-82; resident assoc. Carnegie Endowment for Internat. Peace, 1982-83, 86-87. Author: Improbable Dangers, U.S. Conceptions of Threat in the Cold War and After, 1994; contbr. articles to profl. jours. and newspapers. With USNR, 1943-46. Recipient Rockefeller Pub. Svc. award, 1958; Alumni Achievement award Concordia Coll., 1975; fellow Social Sci. Rsch. Coun., 1948-49; Ford Found. grantee, 1966 Mem. Am. Polit. Sci. Assn., Coun. on Fgn. Rels. Congregationalist. Home: 8400 Carderock Dr Bethesda MD 20817 Office: Nat Policy Assn 1424 16th St NW Washington DC 20036-2211

JOHNSON, ROBERT HERSEL, journalist; b. Colorado City, Tex., May 28, 1923; s. Robert Hersel and Leah (Sikes) J.; m. Luise Putcamp, Jr., Feb. 24, 1945; children: Robert Hersel, III, Luise Robin, Jan Leah, Stephanie Neale, Jennifer Anne, Ann Tapia. BS in Journalism, So. Methodist U., 1947. Reporter Phoenix Gazette, Ariz., 1940-42; asst. sports editor Ariz. Republic, Phoenix, 1942-43; newscast writer Sta. KOY, Phoenix, 1943; reporter Dallas Times-Herald, 1946; with AP, 1946-88, UT/ID bur. chief, 1954-59, Ind. bur. chief, 1959-62, Tex. bur. chief, 1962-69, gen. sports editor, 1969-73, mng. editor, 1973-77, asst. gen. mgr., spl. asst. to pres., 1977-84, N.Mex. bur. chief, 1984-88; prof. journalism N.Mex. State U., Las Cruces, N.Mex., 1988, U. N.Mex., Albuquerque, 1989; exec. dir. N.Mex. Found. for Open Govt., Albuquerque, 1989—. Mem. Newspaper Readership Coun., 1977-82. Mem. N. Mex. Hist. Records Adv. Bd., 1993-2002. Capt. USMCR, 1943-46, 51-52. Named to N.Mex. Press Hall of Fame, 2000, Heroes of the 50 States: The Open Govt. Hall of Fame, 2003; recipient Liberty Bell award, Albuquerque Bar Assn., 2002, Working for the Best in Govt. award, Common Cause N.Mex., 2004. Home: 2740 Tramway Cir NE Albuquerque NM 87122-1205 Office Phone: 505-345-7808. Personal E-mail: nmfog@aol.com. *The kind of journalism that is likely to bring about change for the better is journalism that is painfully honest, painfully clear, that illuminates large issues with small details, and in which the reporter is not a participant or an advocate but a dispassionate observer who keeps his own emotions at bay until the story is told.*

JOHNSON, ROBERT LEE, JR., physician, educator, researcher; b. Dallas, Apr. 28, 1926; s. Robert L. and Doris (Miller) J.; m. Aileen Johnson, 1952; children: Stephen Lee, Robert Edward. BS, So. Meth. U., 1947; MD, Northwestern U., 1951. Intern Cook County Hosp., Chgo., 1951-52; resident in internal medicine Parkland Meml. Hosp., Phila., 1952-55; fellow nat. foun. infantile paralysis and clin. instr. U. Tex. Southwestern Med. Ctr., Dallas, 1955-56; fellow dept. physiol. and pharmacology Grad. Sch. Medicine U. Pa., Phila., 1956-57; asst. prof. U. Tex. Southwestern Med. Ctr., Dallas, 1959-65, assoc. prof., 1965-69, prof. medicine, 1969—; John Butler Meml. lectr. U. Wash., Seattle, 2001. Vis. staff Parkland Meml. Hosp., Dallas, 1957—, Zale Lipshy U. Hosp., Dallas, 1989—, St. Paul Hosp., Dallas, 2000-; cons. chest diseases VA Hosp., Dallas, 1966—; dir. sarcoidosis clinic Parkland Meml. Hosp., 1983—; mem. parent rev. com. Nat. Heart, Lung, and Blood Inst. for Spl. Ctrs. of Rsch. proposals, 1983-85; mem. Nat. Heart, Lung, and Blood Rsch. Rev. Com., 1985-89; mem. respiratory and applied physiology study sect. NIH, 1991-94. Mem. editl. bd.: Jour. Clin. Investigation, 1972—77, Jour. Applied Physiology, 1980—82, Circulation, 1996—, guest referee editor: Jour. Applied Physiology, —, Am. Jour. Physiology, —, Chest, —, Circulation, —, Circulation Rsch., —, Am. Jour. Med. Sci., —, Am. Jour. Respiration and Circulation Medicine, —, Jour. Clin. Investigation, —, Early Human Devel., —, Kidney Internat., —. With Naval ROTC, 1945-46; with USNR, 1944-46; maj. USAR, 1962. Mem. Am. Heart Assn. (cardiopulmonary coun. exec. com. mem. 1990-92, nominating com. cardiopulmonary coun. 1989-93, chmn. 1990-92), Am. Thoracic Soc. (planning com. mem. 1987-90, com. proficiency standards 1985-94, Scientific Accomplishment award 1996), Am. Coll. Chest Physicians, Am. Fedn. Clin. Rsch., Am. Physiol. Soc., Am. Soc. Clin. Investigation, Assn. Am. Physicians, Cen. Soc. Clin. Rsch., So. Soc. Clin. Rsch., Soc. Sigma Xi. Office: UT Southwestern Med Ctr 5323 Harry Hines Blvd Stop 9034 Dallas TX 75390-9034

JOHNSON, ROBERT LOUIS, cable television company executive, professional sports team owner; b. Hickory, Miss., Apr. 8, 1946; s. Archie and Edna Johnson; m. Sheila Crump, Jan. 19, 1969. BA in History, U. Ill., 1968; M in Pub. Affairs, Princeton U., 1972. Press. sec. Hon. Walter E. Fauntroy, Congl. del. from Washington, 1973—76; v.p. govt. rels. Nat. Cable TV Assn., 1976—79; founder Black Entertainment TV, Washington, 1979, pres., 1979—93; founder, pres. Dist. Cablevision, Inc., 1980—; chmn., pres., CEO BET Holdings, Inc. (formerly Black Entertainment TV sold to Viacom), Washington, 1993—2001; CEO BET Holdings, Inc., 2001—05, chmn., 2005; founder RLJ Companies, 2001—; majority owner NBA expansion team Charlotte Bobcats, 2002—; owner WNBA team Charlotte Sting, 2003—. Bd. dirs. US Airways, Hilton Hotels, General Mills; bd. governors Rock and Roll Hall of Fame, Cleveland, Ohio; appointed social security commn. Pres. Bush, 2001—. Bd. dirs. United Negro Coll. Fund, Am. Film Inst.; bd. govs. The Grammy Found.; bd. dirs. Jazz at Lincoln Ctr., Strayer Edn., Inc., Johns Hopkins U. Recipient Image award, NAACP, 1982, Bus. of Yr. award, D.C. C. of C., 1985, Exec. Leadership Coun. award, Turner Broadcasting, 1993, 20/20 Vision award, Cablevision Mag., 1995, Hall of Fame award, Broadcasting and Cable Mag., 1997, Good Guys award, Nat. Women's Polit. Caucus, 1998, Disting. Alumni award, Princeton U., 1998. Democrat. Office: BET Holdings Inc 1900 W Pl NE Washington DC 20018-1211

JOHNSON, ROBERT MAX, lawyer; b. Thomas, Okla., Aug. 20, 1942; s. Claude L. and Jesse C. (Stimmel) J.; m. Virginia A. LeForce, May 31, 1964; children: Kelli Brook, Brent Matthew. BS, Okla. State U., 1964; JD, U. Okla., 1967; LLD (hon.), Oklahoma City U., 2001. Bar: Okla. 1967. Shareholder Crowe & Dunlevy, Oklahoma City, 1967—, pres., 1985-87, exec. com., 1992—. Spl. lectr. in land fin. and real estate contracts U. Okla. Coll. of Law, Norman, 1973, 84. Mng. editor: Oklahoma Environmental Law Handbook, 1992-96; contbr. to book: The Law of Distressed Real Estate, 1987; case editor Okla. Law Rev., 1966. Bd. dirs. Redbud Found., Oklahoma City, 1987-96, Myriad Gardens Conservatory, Oklahoma City, 1987-89, Myriad Gardens Found., 1993-96, ARC, 1994-96, Arts Coun. Oklahoma City, 1994—, Am. Heart Assn., 1999—; chmn. Oklahoma City Festival of Arts, 1993-94, Murrah Fed. Bldg. Meml. Task Force, 1995-96, Oklahoma City Nat. Meml. Found., 1996-98, Oklahoma City Nat. Meml. Trust, 1998-2001. Capt. U.S. Army, 1968-70. Recipient Outstanding Svc. to the Pub. award Okla. Bar Assn., 1998, Cmty. Svc. award, 2000, Disting. Svc. award, Oklahoma City/County Hist. Soc., 2000, Robert M. Johnson award, Am. Coll. Mortgage Attys., 2001; named King, Oklahoma City Beaux Arts Ball, 2001. Fellow Am. Coll. Mortgage Attys. (bd. regents, pres. 1994-95, chmn. exec. com. 1995-96); mem. Am. Coll. Real Estate Lawyers, Oklahoma City Golf and Country Club (bd. dirs. 1981-82, sec. 1982), Order of Coif, Phi Delta Phi (magister 1966-67), Lambda Alpha. Avocations: golf, quail hunting, fly fishing. Home: 1608 Mulholland Dr Edmond OK 73003-4114 Office: East Wharf Plz Ste 102 9225 Lake Hefner Pkwy Oklahoma City OK 73120 Office Phone: 405-755-1650. E-mail: RMJohnson@coxinet.net.

JOHNSON, ROBERT WOOD, IV, (WOODY JOHNSON), sports team executive, philanthropist; b. New Brunswick, NJ, Apr. 1947; m. Nancy Sale Frey (div. 2001); 3 children. B.A. in History, U. Ariz., 1972. Major shareholder Johnson & Johnson; acquired Am. Video Corp.; founder, chmn., CEO The Johnson Co. Inc., 1984—; owner N.Y. Jets, Hempstead, 2000—. Advisory coun., Nat. Diabetes and Digestive and Kidney Diseases NIH, 1992—94. Co-author (with Sale Johnson): Managing Your Child's Diabetes, 1994. Founder, chmn. Alliance for Lupus Rsch.; chmn. Juvenile Diabetes Rsch. Found. Internat.; co-chmn., rsch. partnership Juvenile Diabetes Rsch. Found.; bd. dirs. Robert Wood Johnson Found. Office: NY Jets 1000 Fulton Ave Hempstead NY 11550-1030

JOHNSON, RODNEY, writer, crime artist; b. Nyack, N.Y., July 26, 1971; s. Randy Reed and Rebecca Cole. Author: (book) Promise You'll Love Me For Ever, 2000, Crime Fame Fortune and Glory, 2003, Crime Artist, 2004. Home: 94 Fed St Apt #4 Springfield MA 01105 Office: 1stt Books Libr 1663 Liberty Dr Ste 200 Bloomington IN 47403

JOHNSON, RON, information technology executive; BA in econ., Stanford U.; MBA, Harvard U. Buying and inventory mgr. Mervyn (divsn. of Target Corp.); mgmt. exec. positions Target Corp., 1984—2000; sr. v.p. retail Apple Computer Inc., Cupertino, Calif., 2000—. Office: Apple Computer Inc 1 Infinite Loop Cupertino CA 95014 Office Phone: 408-996-1010.

JOHNSON, RONALD, academic administrator; DDS, U. Pitts., 1961; cert. pedodontics, Harvard U., 1967. Dental accreditation ADA. Faculty U. Iowa, UCLA, Charles R. Drew Postgrad. Med. Sch., U. Pa.; prof., chmn. pediat. dentistry U. So. Calif., L.A., clin. prof. pediat. Med. Sch., assoc. dean clin. affairs Dental Sch.; v.p. strategic affairs U. Tex. HSC, Houston. Hon. chair profl. studies Marquette U., Milw.; coun. mem. Nat. Adv. Dental Rsch. Coun., NIH. Contbg. editor Jour. Endodontics and Dental Traumatology. Fellow Am. Coll. Dentists, Internat. Coll. Dentists; mem. ADA, Am. Assn. Hosp. Dentists, Am. Assn. Dental Schs. Office: U Tex HSC-H 7000 Fannin St Ste 1530 Houston TX 77030 E-mail: ronald.johnson@uth.tmc.edu.

JOHNSON, RONALD CARL, chemistry professor; b. Milw., Sept. 5, 1935; s. Carl Walter and Valeska Ella (Schulz) J.; m. Susan Nancy Anderson, Aug. 27, 1960; children: Erica Susan, Laura Karen. BS, Lawrence Coll., 1957; PhD, Northwestern U., 1961. From asst. prof. to prof. Emory U., Atlanta, 1961-75, prof., 1975-2001, prof. emeritus, 2001—. Author: Coordination Chemistry, 1964, 2d edit. 1987; Descriptive Chemistry, 1965, General Chemistry, 1974. Mem. AAAS, AAUP, Am. Chem. Soc. (chair Ga. sect. 1974-75, counselor 1977-80), Ga. Acad. Sci. (pres. 1977-78), Phi Beta Kappa, Sigma Xi. Presbyterian. Avocations: walking, racquetball, bridge. Office: Emory U Dept Chemistry Atlanta GA 30322-0001 Business E-Mail: rjohn04@emory.edu.

JOHNSON, RONALD GLENN, arts administrator; b. L.A., Dec. 3, 1949; s. Edward Andrew and Elizabeth Jane (Freeman) J.; m. Jane E. Walker, Aug. 16, 1969; children: Andrew Edward, Robin Winfield. MusB, W.Va. U., 1975, MusM, 1977. Freelance musician, L.A., 1977-85; edn. coord. San Diego Symphony Orch., 1985-86, artistic adminstr., 1986-87, mgr., 1987-89; ops. mgr. Mainly Mozart Festival, San Diego, 1989-90; exec. dir. Eugene (Oreg.)

Symphony Orch., 1990—. Sgt. U.S. Army, 1970-73. Mem. Am. Symphony Orch. League, Northwest Assn. Symphony Orchs. (pres.). Avocations: golf, outdoor recreation. Office: Eugene Symphony Orch 45 W Broadway Ste 201 Eugene OR 97401-3002

JOHNSON, RONALD KAY, retail company executive; b. Abilene, Tex., Feb. 26, 1939; s. Vernon Floyd and Mattye Sue (Milburn) J.; m. Sally Ann Fleet, Nov. 22, 1962 (div.); 1 child, Sheri May. AA, Spokane Falls Coll., 1970; BA in Theatre Arts with honors, Eastern Wash. State U., 1971; AS with honors, Portland C.C., 1992. Divsn. mgr. Nutrition Ctrs. Fred Meyer, Inc., Portland, Oreg., 1971—. V.p. Nutrition Ctrs. Divsn., 1979-87; owner, mgr. Valley Mist Farm, San Diego, 1957-65; med. massage therapist, 2003. Actor Lake Oswego Cmty. Theatre, 1979—, Portland Civic Theatre. Recipient Best Supporting Actor award Spokane Civic Theatre, 1967-68, Best Actor award Oreg. Theatre Soc., 1980-81. Avocation: raising Appaloosa show horses. Home: 2319 Old Maypearl Rd Waxahachie TX 75167 Personal E-mail: ronaldkjohnson@hotmail.com.

JOHNSON, RONALD LEONARD, health facility administrator, consultant; b. Escanaba, Mich. s. Leonard John and Edith Brerland Johnson; m. Nancy C. Johnson, Oct. 5, 1968; children: Susan, Steven, Scott, Sarah, Sharon. BSME, Purdue U., 1957; MBA, Ind. U., 1959. Sales rep. IBM, Ind., 1961—72; dir. sales McDonnell Dooliso Auto Co., Palo Alto, Calif., 1973—81; dir. mktg. Tecnilon Data Sys., Santa Clara, Calif., 1981—82; prin., owner R.L. Johnson & Assocs., Tracy, Calif., 1982—. Author: Deceit & Vengance, 2004, Retribution, 2004, Vigillance & Pressure, 2004; contbr. articles to profl. jours. Lt. capt. USAF, 1958—61. Fellow: Heller Info. Mgmt. Soc. Home and Office: RL Johnson & Assocs 1241 Citadelle St Tracy CA 95304

JOHNSON, ROSEMARY S., elementary school educator; b. Spickard, Mo., Feb. 1, 1948; d. John R. Prims and Lillian F. Dunbar; m. Alan L. Johnson, Apr. 15, 1947; children: Sean Lee, Brian Keith. BS in Elem. Edn., BHSU, 1981; MS, S.D. State U., 1994, MS in Edn., 2000. Tutor Douglas Sch. Sys., Box Eider, SD, 1980—84; tchr. 1st grade Dept. Def. Dep. Sch., Madrid, 1985—87; substitute tchr. Rapid City Area Schs., SD, 1987—88, tchr. 6th grade, 1988—91, tchr. 5th grade, 1991—98, tchr. 8th grade, 1998—2001, dean students, 2001—02, tchr. math., 2002—. Co-author: Best Classroom Practices, 1999. Mem.: Kappa Delta Phi, Phi Kappa Phi. Republican. Lutheran. Home: 6201 Long View Rd Rapid City SD 57703

JOHNSON, ROY RAGNAR, electrical engineer, researcher; b. Chgo., Jan. 23, 1932; s. Ragnar Anders and Ann Viktoria (Lundquist) J.; m. Martha Ann Mattson, June 21, 1963; children: Linnea Marit, Kaisa Ann. BSEE, U. Minn., 1954, MS, 1956, PhD, 1959. Rsch. fellow U. Minn., 1957-59; from rsch. engr. to sr. basic rsch. scientist Boeing Sci. Rsch. Labs., Seattle, 1959-72; prin. scientist KMS Fusion, Inc., Ann Arbor, Mich., 1972-74, dir. fusion expts., 1974-78, tech. dir., 1978-91, dept. head for fusion and plasmas, 1985-88; tech. dir. Innovation Assocs., Inc., Ann Arbor, 1992; Inertial Confinement Fusion classification/records mgr. Lawrence Livermore (Calif.) Nat. Lab., 1992—. Vis. lectr. U. Wash., Seattle, 1959-60; vis. scientist Royal Inst. Tech., Stockholm, 1963-64; cons. Dept. Edn., Washington, 1995, 98, 2000, 03, 04, 05. Author: Nonlinear Effects in Plasmas, 1969, Plasma Physics, 1977, Research Trends in Physics, 1992; contbr. articles to profl. publs.; patentee in field. Bd. advisors Rose-Hulman Inst. Tech., 1982-. Decorated chevalier Order of St. George; comdr. Order of Holy Cross of Jerusalem. Fellow: Am. Phys. Soc.; mem.: AIAA, IEEE (life), AAAS, N.Y. Acad. Scis., Am. Def. Preparedness Assn., Nuc. Plasma Scis. Soc. of IEEE (exec. com. 1972—75), Swedish Club Detroit, Swedish Coun. Am., Am. Swedish Inst., Swedish Am. Hist. Soc., Commonwealth Club Calif., Assn. Old Crows, Torpar Riddar Orden, Vasa Order Am. (past chmn. Svea lodge), Gamma Alpha, Eta Kappa Nu. Lutheran. Home: PO Box 166 Livermore CA 94551-0166 Office: Livermore Nat Lab PO Box 808 Livermore CA 94551-0808 Office Phone: 925-422-7254. Business E-Mail: johnson3@llnl.gov.

JOHNSON, RUFUS WINFIELD, lawyer; b. Montgomery County, Md., May 1, 1911; s. Charles L. and Margaret (Smith) J.; m. Rosena L. Allen, June 21, 1939 (div. May 1971); m. Vaunda Louise Griffith, May 29, 1971; step-children: Yvonne, Jackie, Karen, Rodney, Michelle. AB, Howard U., 1934, postgrad., 1934-36, LLB, 1939. Bar: Calif., Ark., Supreme Ct. Ark., Supreme Ct. Calif., D.C. Dist. Ct., U.S. Ct. Appeals, D.C., U.S. Supreme Ct., Supreme Ct. of South Korea; cert. counsel Judge Advocate Gen. Sch., Washington. Pvt. practice, D.C., Calif., Ark., 1945—. Originator Lawyer's Pro Bono Svc. Ret. lt. col. USAR. Decorated Combat Inf. badge, Purple Heart, Bronze Star with 2 oak leaf clusters, Spl. Citation for Bravery. Mem. VFW (life), Am. Judicature Soc., Am. Acad. Polit. and Social Sci., Mil. Order Purple Heart, Internat. Soc. Poets, Am. Kempo Karate Assn., Sr. Citizens Coalition, Ret. Officers Assn., Am. Legion, Masons, Am. Karate Assn. (5th degree Shorin-Ryu Black Belt), Lions. Baptist. Home: 1202 Barbara Ann St Kerrville TX 78028-3411

JOHNSON, S. CURTIS, chemicals executive; BA econ., Cornell Univ.; MBA, Northwestern Univ. Dir. worldwide bus. JohnsonDiveresy; vice-pres., mng. dir. Mexican Johnson; vice-pres., mng. dir. bus. devel. Johnson Diversey, chmn. Office: Johnson Diversey 8310 16th St Sturtevant WI 53177-0902*

JOHNSON, SALLY A., nurse, educator; b. Rockford, Ill., Apr. 24, 1923; d. Herbert A. and Aileen (Peyton) Johnson; m. Bert Klackle; children: Ann Elizabeth Scannell, Stacey Aileen Lerager. RN Good Samaritan Hosp., 1945; nurse obstetrics delivery Women's Hosp., N.Y.C., 1947-49, St. Francis Hosp., Evanston, Ill., 1953; charge, head nurse Broward Gen. Hosp., Ft. Lauderdale, Fla., 1968; night supr. Ashbrook Convalescent and Nursing Hosp., Scotch Plains, N.J., 1968—. Owner Thomas A. Edison Brick Co., Sally Johnson Enterprises. Coun. chmn. Betty Merit Tchrs. Scholarship, 1962; area nat. organizer Girl Scouts U.S.A., 1962-65; Westfield (N.J.) Round-Up and Health chmn., 1962-63; pres. Tamaques Sch., 1965, adviser Parent Tchr. Orgn., 1966, fgn. relationship chmn., 1967-68; exec. bd. chmn. Westfield HS PTA Newsletter, 1968-70; chmn. Nat. Space Edn., Westfield, 1964; Westfield chmn. fgn. nurses Overlook Hosp., Summit, N.J., 1964-69. Recipient scholarship to Harvard U. Coll. Bus. Mem. Nat. Assn. Investors Corp., Nat. Dist. Nurses Assn., NOW (N.J. coord. 1967-68), Am. Contract Bridge League, Bridge Tchrs. Assn., Naples Investment Club (sec. 1995-96). Republican. Achievements include patent for marking devices. E-mail: sallyjohnson@comcast.net.

JOHNSON, SAMIRA EL-CHEHABI, marketing professional; b. Niagara Falls, NY, Mar. 2, 1958; d. Munzir and Ismat (Zakaria) El-Chehabi; m. Kenneth M. Johnson, Sept. 21, 1991; 1 child, Davis B. BS in Med. Tech. magna cum laude, SUNY, Buffalo, 1980. Component lab. supr. ARC, Detroit, 1982-85; sr. med. technologist Rush Presbyn. St Lukes Med. Ctr., Chgo., 1985-86; tech. cons. Baxter Internat., Deerfield, Ill., 1986-88, ednl. svcs. mgr., 1988-89, market mgr., 1989-93, sr. market mgr., 1993-99; dir. mktg. Cerus Corp., Concord, Calif., 1999—2003; freelance cons., 2003—. Assoc. editor Continuous Flow, 1988-90, Component Therapy Digest, 1988-90; patentee in field. Mem. Nat. Blood Data Resource Ctr., 1996—. Mem. ANA (program adminstr. 1988-98), Am. Soc. Clin. Pathologists, Am. Soc. Med. Technologists (program adminstr. 1988-98), Am. Assn. Blood Banks, Internat. Soc. Blood Transfusion. Avocations: sailing, scuba diving, theater, horseback riding, rollerblading. Home and Office: 159 Chestnut Cir Northport NY 11768 Office Phone: 847-812-4081. Personal E-mail: samira_johnson13@yahoo.com.

JOHNSON, SAMUEL (SAM JOHNSON), congressman; b. San Antonio, Tex., Oct. 11, 1930; m. Shirley L. Melton; children: James R., Gini Mulligan, Beverly Briney. BBA, So. Meth. U., 1951; M in Internat. Affairs, George Washington U.; grad., Armed Forces Staff Coll., Nat. War Coll. Joined USAF, 1950, fighter pilot, prisoner of war, 1966-73, former dir. Air Force Fighter Weapons Sch., former mem. Thunderbirds, wing commdr., air div. commdr., ret., 1979; founder home bldg. co., 1979; mem. Tex. Ho. of Reps., 1984-91, U.S. Congress from 3d Tex. dist., Washington, 1991—; mem. ways and means com.; mem. edn. and the workforce com., chmn. employer-employeerels. subcom. Edn. and the workforce com., early childhood, youth and families subcom. Chmn. Conservative Action Team. Decorated 2 Silver Stars, Disting. Flying Cross, 4 Air medals, 2 Purple Hearts. Republican. Office: 1211 Longworth Ho Office Bldg Washington DC 20515-0001 also: 801 E Campbell Rd Ste 425 Richardson TX 75081-1867*

JOHNSON, SANDRA HANNEKEN, law educator; b. St. Louis, Jan. 20, 1952; d. Clarence F. and Mary Rose (Uykosky) Hanneken; m. Robert G. Johnson, 1973; children: Emily, Kathleen. AB summa cum laude, St. Louis U., 1973; JD, NYU, 1976; LLM, Yale U., 1977. Bar: N.Y. 1978. Asst. prof. law N.Y. Law Sch., 1977-78, St. Louis U., 1978-81, assoc. prof. law, 1981-84, prof. of law, 1984—, Tenet prof. health care law & ethics, 2000—, assoc. dean, 1979—81, 1985—88, interim dean, 1991—92, provost, 1998—2002; vis. prof. Univ. Houston Law Ctr., 1991, Washington U. Sch. Law, 1995. Dir. Ctr. for Health Law Studies, St. Louis, 1982-85, 88-91; cons. Inst. of Medicine Project on Nursing Homes, N.Y., 1985; mem. Hastings Ctr. Project on Ethics in Nursing Homes, N.Y., 1988-91. Co-author: Nursing Homes and the Law, 1985, Health Law, 1987, 2nd edit., 1991, Health Law Cases Materials & Problems, 4th edit.; mem. bd. editors Law, Medicine and Health Care, 1985—; contbr. articles to profl. jours. Participant St. Louis Leadership Devel. Program, 1980-81; bd. mem. Inst. for Peace & Justice, St. Louis, 1988-90; mem. Instl. Rev. Bd., St. Louis U., 1989-90. Grantee Nat. Inst. of Dispute Resolution, 1985, AARP, 1988; Edmund Pellegrino medal, 2003, HEAL Inst.; Woman of the Year 2002, St. Louis Daily Record; fellow, Hastings Ctr. Mem. ABA, Am. Soc. Law Medicine & Ethics (dir. Mayday Project on Legal & Regulatory Issues in Pain Relief, Disting. Health Law Tchr. award, William J. Curran award), Midwest Bioethics Roundtable, St. Louis Health Lawyers Assn. (chmn.), Phi Beta Kappa, Alpha Sigma Nu. Office: St Louis U Sch of Law 3700 Lindell Blvd Saint Louis MO 63108-3412

JOHNSON, SANDRA K., electrical engineer; b. Fukuoka, Japan, Sept. 19, 1960; arrived in U.S., 1961; d. George Garland and Gloria Dean (Hagger) Johnson. BSEE, So. U., Baton Rouge, La., 1982; MSEE, Stanford U., 1984; PhD, Rice U., 1988. Rsch. staff mem. T.J. Watson Rsch. Ctr. IBM, Yorktown Heights, NY, 1988—2000; mgr. Websphere database devel. IBM Silicon Valley Lab., San Jose, 2000—02; mgr. Linux Performance IBM, Austin, Tex., 2002—03, sr. tech. staff, 2003—; chief tech. officer global small and med. bus. IBM Sys. and Tech. Group, 2004—. Mem.: IEEE, Computing Rsch. Assn. (com. on status of women in computing sci. 1990—96), Assn. Computing Machinery, IEEE Computer Soc. Office: IBM 11501 Burnett Rd Austin TX 78758 Office Phone: 512-838-4983.

JOHNSON, SANKEY ANTON, manufacturing executive; b. Bremerton, Wash., May 14, 1940; s. Sankey Broyd and Alice Mildred (Norum) J.; m. Carolyn Lee Rogers, Nov. 30, 1968; children: Marni Lee, Ronald Anton. BS in M.E, U. Wash.; MBA, Stanford U. V.p., gen. mgr. Cummins Asia Pacific, Manila, Philippines, 1974-78; v.p. automotive Cummins Engine Co., Columbus, Ind., 1978-79; v.p. North Am. Bus., 1979-81; pres., chief exec. officer Onan Corp., Mpls., 1981-85; exec. v.p. Pentair Inc., St. Paul, from 1985, chief operating officer, 1985—, pres., 1986-89; chmn. Hidden Creek Industries, Mpls., 1989—2004; mng. ptnr. OG Ptnrs., Mpls., 2004—. Trustee Mfr.'s Alliance. Bd. advisors Stanford Grad. Sch. Bus. Mem. Lafayette Club. Home: 2310 Huntington Point Rd W Wayzata MN 55391-9743 Office: OG Partners 294 Grove Ln E Wayzata MN 55391 Office Phone: 952-404-4100.

JOHNSON, SARAH D., historical society director; b. Topeka, Kans., Aug. 18, 1978; d. Donald Jerry and Janet Christina Johnson. BA, Baker U., 2000; MA, Eastern Ill. U., 2002. Collections intern Pk. City. Hist. Soc., Pk. City, Utah, 2001; education program coord. Manitowne County Hist. Soc., 2001—03, exec. dir., 2004. Author/editor various web sites and web pages. Adv. com. Wis. Hist. Soc., 2004—. Mem.: Assn. of Midwest Mus., Wis. Fedn. of Museums, Assn. for State and Local History. Office: Manitowoc County Hist Soc 1701 Mich Ave Manitowoc WI 54220 Business E-Mail: mchistoc@lakefield.net.

JOHNSON, SARAH LYNN (LEWIS), librarian, editor; b. New Britain, Conn., Oct. 21, 1969; d. Stephen Harry and Judith Ann (Orman) Lewis. BA in French, Drew U., 1991; MA in Linguistics, Ohio State U., 1992; M Info. and Libr. Studies, U. Mich., 1994. Reference and sys. libr. Bridgewater (Mass.) State Coll., 1995—2002; asst. prof. libr. svcs. Ea. Ill. U., Charleston, 2002—; book rev. editor Pub. Svcs. Quar., 2004—. N.Am. regional editor jour. Reference Revs., 2001—04; coord. editor Hist. Novels Rev., 2000—; hist. fiction editor NoveList Readers Adv. Svc., 2001—, Electronic Resources Rev., 2000. Co-author: The Information Professional's Guide to Career Development Online, 2002; author: Historical Fiction: A Guide to the Genre, 2005. Mem. ALA, Assn. Coll. and Rsch. Librs. Office: Eastern Illinois Univ Booth Library Charleston IL 61920 Office Phone: 217-581-7538. E-mail: cfsln@eiu.edu.

JOHNSON, SCOTT STUART, merchant banker; s. Tod Stuart and Cindy Schwartz Johnson. BA, Columbia U., 1994, M in Internat. Affairs, MBA, Columbia U., 1997. Equity rsch. assoc. Salomon Smith Barry, Inc., 1997—99; equity rsch. analyst Merrill Lynch & Co., Inc., 1999—2000; CFO, bd. dirs. BrandAid Comm., N.Y.C., 2000; CEO SJ Partners, LLC, N.Y.C., 2001—. Book reviewer Jour. Internat. Affairs. Sit on term mem., advisory com. Coun. on Fgn. Rels., N.Y.C., 2002—. Recipient First Pl. award, Montauk Sprint Relay Triathalon, 2003; Martin Fischbein fellow, Fischbein Found., 1992. Mem.: Atlantic Coun., Am. Enterprise Inst., Assn. for Corp. Growth, Ctrl. Pk. Track Club (life). Republican. Jewish. Avocation: competitive marathon running. Office: SJ Ptnrs LLC 60 W 66th St Ste 32C New York NY 10023 Business E-Mail: scott@sjpartners.com.

JOHNSON, SHANE RICHARD, research scientist, consultant; s. Richard Dorvald and Lois Gail Johnson; m. Heather Dianne Johnson; children: Bobbi Jo Heather, Ryan Shane. BSc, Simon Fraser U., Can., 1987—91; PhD, U. B.C., Can., 1991—96. Rsch. asst. U. B.C., Vancouver, Canada, 1991—96; rsch. scientist Ariz. State U., Tempe, 1996—. Cons. Lytek Corp., Phoenix, 2000—04. Contbr. articles to profl. jours. Organizing chair North Am. Conf. on Molecular Beam Epitaxy, Tempe, Ariz., 2000. Fellow, Natural Sci. and Engring. Rsch. Coun. Can., 1996—98; scholar, 1991—95, Sci. Coun. B.C., 1993—96. Mem.: IEEE, Am. Phys. Soc. Office: Ariz State Univ Box 876206 Tempe AZ 85287-6206 Office Phone: 480-965-2565. Business E-Mail: shane.johnson@asu.edu.

JOHNSON, SHANNON, professional basketball player; b. Aug. 18, 1974; Grad., U.S.C., 1996. Mem. 2 ABL Champion Columbus Quest; profl. basketball player Valencia, Spain, Orlando Miracle (now Conn. Sun), 1999—2002, Conn. Sun, 2003, San Antonio Silver Stars, 2004—. Named All-WNBA 2nd Team, 1999, 2000, Inaugural WNBA All-Star Team, 1999, WNBA All-Star Team, 2000, 2002, 2003. Achievements include mem. US Women's Basketball Team, Athens Olympics, 2004. Office: c/o San Antonio Silver Stars 1 SBC Center San Antonio TX 78219

JOHNSON, SHARI, early childhood educator; b. Phila., Apr. 5, 1955; d. Solomon and Evelyn (Spector) Haas; m. Andrew Johnson, Aug. 6, 1989; children: Jessica Ariel, Benjamin Paul. BS, Pa. State U., 1975; MEd, Chestnut Hill Coll., Phila., 1985; postgrad., U. of the Arts, Phila., 1993-94, C.C. of Phila., 1993-94. Cert. in early childhood edn., elem. edn., Pa. Tchr. Phila. Housing Authority, 1977-82; sr. career tchr. pre-kindergarten Head Start Sch. Dist. Phila., 1982—. Bd. dirs. Multiple Opportunities for Many Youths. Mem. Nat. Assn. for Edn. of Young Children, Assn. for Childhood Edn. Internat., World Orgn. for Early Childhood (France). Avocations: dance, sewing, swimming, basket weaving. Office: Sch Dist Phila Cook-Wissahickon Sch 201 E Salignac St Philadelphia PA 19128

JOHNSON, SHARON ELAINE, elementary school educator; b. Grant County, Wis., Dec. 31, 1936; d. Ralph Philip and E. Blanche (Fry) Long; m. Edward Dean Johnson, Apr. 15, 1961; 1 child, Perry Edward; 1 stepchild, David Dwight. B Music Edn., Coe Coll., Cedar Rapids, Iowa, 1959; M Elem. Edn., Murray (Ky.) State U., 1965; M Spl. Edn., U. Mo., Kansas City, 1980. Cert. elem. and music tchr., Kans., Iowa, Ky.; cert. elem., music and spl. edn. tchr., Mo. Elem. tchr. Kans. City (Kans.) Bd. Edn., 1959-63, 65-66; tchr. vocal music Marshall County Bd. Edn., Benton, Ky., 1963-65; elem. tchr. Consol. Sch. Dist. 1, Hickman Mills Bd. Edn., Kansas City, Mo., 1966-79, tchr. kindergarten, 1980—93; sub. tchr. Sunshine Ctr. for Handicapped Pre-Sch., 1993—. Mem. NEA, ASCD, Internat. Reading Assn. (historian 1985-86), Mo. Edn. Assn. (bldg. rep. 1976—). Avocations: needlepoint, reading education journals, word puzzles, helping children learn, spectator sports. Home: 1022 S Park Ave Independence MO 64050-4225

JOHNSON, SHEILA CRUMP, entrepreneur; b. Pa. m. Robert L. Johnson (div. 2002); children: Paige, Brett. Music tchr. Sidwell Friends Sch., Washington, 1973—89; former cultural liaison to Middle East U.S. Info. Agency; co-founder Black Entertainment TV; owner Salamander Farms, Middleberg, Va.; developer Salamander Inn and Spa, Middleberg, Va.; co-owner Lincoln Holdings, LLC; team pres. Washington Mystics WNBA; designer of luxury linens. Bd. dirs. Parsons Sch. Design; pres. Washington Internat. Horse Show; established first Nat. Music Conservatory, Amman, Jordan. Achievements include first Black female to be certified as billionaire. Avocations: horseback riding, music, violin. Office: c/o Lincoln Holdings LLC 401 9th St NW Washington DC 20004*

JOHNSON, SHERI LOUISE, clinical psychologist; b. Carey, N.C., July 21, 1965; d. Robert M. and Virginia (Hunt) J. BA, Salem Coll., 1982; MS, U. Pitts., 1986, PhD, 1992. Postdoctoral fellow Brown U., Providence, 1992-93, asst. clin. prof., 1993-95; asst. prof. U. Miami, Coral Gables, 1995—. Expert rater DSM-IV trials for inter-rater reliability, 1994. Contbr. articles to profl. jours. Grantee Nat. Alliance for Schizophrenia and Depression, 1993-95, NIH, 1995-96. Achievements include research on life events in bipolar and unipolar depression. Office: U Miami Dept Psychology PO Box 249229 Coral Gables FL 33124-9229

JOHNSON, SHIRLEY AMAGNA, health system executive; b. Santa Rosa, The Philippines, Apr. 16, 1959; came to U.S., 1980; d. Federico Fontalera Amagna Jr. and Lourdes Dayan Barriga; m. Mark James Johnson, Mar. 25, 1982; children: Farrell, Mark Jr., Craig. BS in Commerce, Ctrl. Philippines U., Iloilo City, 1980; MBA, Drury Coll., 1990; postgrad., U. So. Calif., 1994—. Acct. U. Mo., Rolla, 1987-90; acctg. sys. analyst County of San Luis Obispo, Calif., 1990-99; project mgr. Wellpoint Health Networks, Inc., Thousand Oaks, Calif., 1999—. Bd. dirs. Ctrl. Coast Women's Polit. Com., San Luis Obispo, 1995-96; founding mem. Clean Campaign Com., San Luis Obispo, 1996—; mem. adv. bd. Citizens Transp. Adv. Com., San Luis Obispo, 1998-99; mem. San Luis Obispo Leadership Program, 1999—. Mem. ASPA, Inst. Mgmt. Accts. Office: 1 Wellpoint Way Thousand Oaks CA 91362-3893 E-mail: shirley.johnson@wellpoint.com.

JOHNSON, SILAS R., JR., retired military officer; b. Ft. Worth, Jan. 29, 1945; s. Silas Robert and Lucille (Burns) J.; m. Paulette Kamykowski, Apr. 12, 1968; children: Jennifer, Tyler. BBA, U. Miami, Coral Gables, Fla., 1967; MPA, Pepperdine U., 1979; postgrad., Air U., Montgomery, Ala., 1975, 83, 89. Commd. 2d lt. USAF, 1968, advanced through grades to major gen., 1998; co-pilot, aircraft comdr. 416 Bombardment Wing, Griffiss AFB, N.Y., 1969-74; spotlight officer, chief of tanker assigments Strategic Air Command, Offutt AFB, 1974-77; RF-4C pilot 363d Tactical Reconnaissance Wing, Shaw AFB, S.C., 1977-80; co-pilot, aircraft comdr., flight comdr. 60th Bombardment Squadron, Anderson AFB, Guam, 1981-83; air staff action officer to asst. dir. air force issues team USAF Hdqrs./The Pentagon, Washington, 1983-86; comdr. 46th Bombardment Squadron/319th Bombardment Wing, Grand Forks AFB, N.D., 1986-88; dir. Joint Flag Officer Warfighting Course, Maxwell AFB, Ala., 1989-90; asst. dep. comdr. maint., later vice comdr. 319th Bombardment Wing, Grand Forks AFB, 1990-91; vice comdr. 4th Wing, Seymour Johnson AFB, N.C., 1991-92; comdr. 93d Bomb Wing, Castle AFB, Calif., 1992-94, 552d Air Control Wing, Tinker AFB, Okla., 1994-96; dep. dir. ops. joint chiefs of staff The Pentagon, Washington, 1996-98; vice comdr. 21st Air Force, McGuire AFB, N.J., 1998-99; comdr. Air Mobility Warfare Ctr. USAF, Ft. Dix, N.J., 1999-2000; chief U.S. Mil. Tng. Mission, Riyadh, Saudi Arabia, 2000—02; ret. USAF, 2002; pres. SRJ Cons. Inc., 2002—; v.p. Burdeshaw Assocs., Bethesda, Md., 2002—. Decorated Def. Disting. Svc. medal, Def. Superior Svc. medal, Legion of Merit with 2 oak leaf clusters, Air medal with 2 oak leaf clusters, Air Force Commendation medal, Vietnam Svc. medal; recipient Moeller Trophy for outstanding wing comdr. in air combat command, 1996. Mem. Daedalians (chpt. pres.), Sigma Chi. Avocations: golf, reading.

JOHNSON, SPENCER, physician, writer; BA in Psychology, U. Southern Calif.; MD, Royal Coll. of Surgeons. Dir. comm. Medtronic; research physician Inst. for Inter-Disciplinary Studies; consultant The Center for Study of the Person. Medical clerkship The Mayo Clinic, Harvard Med. Sch.; leadership fellow Harvard Bus. Sch. Co-author (with Kenneth Blanchard): The One Minute Manager, 1982; author: The One Minute Mother, 1995, Who Moved My Cheese?: An A-Mazing Way to Deal with Change In Your Work and Life, 1998, One Minute for Yourself, 1999, The Present: The Gift That Makes You Happier and More Successful, Today!, 2003. Office: Who Moved My Cheese? LLC 1775 W 2300 S Ste B Salt Lake City UT 84119

JOHNSON, STANFORD LELAND, finance educator; b. Mapleton, Utah, July 31, 1924; s. Leland Stanford and Mary Alice (Thompson) J.; m. Lucy E. Watts, Sept. 14, 1945 (div. 1976); children: Janet, Debbie, Stanford Leland, Robert, Gregory, Kent; m. Heidi G. Ivanoff, Jan. 1977 (div. 1996); m. Linda M. Sartain, Oct., 1998 (dec. Dec. 13, 2001). BS in Bus. and Social Sci., Utah State U., 1949; MS in Mktg. and Retailing, NYU, 1950; PhD in Bus, N.Y. U., 1965. Cert. comml. pilot. Field research Dept. Commerce, 1949-51; asst. mgr. Wickel's Men's Wear Store, Logan, Utah, 1951-52; asst. prof. Sch. Bus., Utah State U., 1951-54; asst. dean, instr. N.Y. U., 1954-64; mem. faculty San Francisco State U., 1964-89, prof. mktg., transp. and world bus., 1968-89, chmn. dept., 1972-76. Cons. to industry, 1960—; lectr. U. Calif. Med. Sch., Pharm. Adminstrn., 1969-85. Editorial cons., McGraw-Hill Book Co., Houghton Mifflin Co., Wadsworth Pub. Co., Sci. Research Assos. Bd. dirs., acad. adviser Schiller Internat. U., Heidelberg, Germany, 1969— . Served as pilot USAAF, 1943-45. Ins. fellow Am. Assn. U. Tchrs., 1953; Forum and Finance fellow, 1954; Found. for Econ. Edn. fellow, 1955; recipient Founder's Day award NYU, 1965. Mem. Sales and Mktg. Execs. Assn. Republican. Mem. Ch. of Jesus Christ of Latter Day Saints. Home: 4609 Park Woods Dr Pollock Pines CA 95726-9508 Personal E-mail: pllstanford@aol.com.

JOHNSON, STEPHANIE L. B., small business owner, office manager; b. Colorado Springs, Colo., Sept. 29, 1945; d. George Edgar and Anne Eastwood Bates; m. Johnny B. Johnson, Dec. 26, 1964; 1 child, Jennifer L. B. Johnson-Bahr. A, Blair Coll., 1964. Office mgr., girl Friday W. E. Nash, Arch., Bryan, Tex., 1965—69; owner, mgr. Bates Enterprises, Colorado Springs, Colo., 1991—; office mgr. Becker-Johnson, Inc., 1991—. Chair Platte Ave. Improvement Dist. Maintenance Adv. Bd., Colorado Springs, 2000—; chairperson The RIDER Com. NSA Oversight Com., 2002—. Editor (creator): (newsletter) The Gold Std. (Sertoma Dist. Newsletter of the Yr., 2003), Knob Hill Neighbor. Pres. Platte Ave. Bus. & Neighborhood Assn., Colorado Springs, 1999—2003; v.p. Police Adv. Com., 2002—03. Mem.: History Day Scholars, Inc. (assoc.; sec.-treas. 1985—2003), Cheyenne Mountain Sertoma Club (assoc.; bd. mem. 1999—2003, Ben Franklin award 1996, Sertoman of Yr. award 2002), Rocky Mountain Youth Leadership Found., Inc. (assoc.; pres. 1989—99, Stephanie L. B. Johnson award 1995), Mil. Order of World Wars (life; treas. 1997—99, Patrick Henry Silver medal 1990). Conservative. Methodist. Avocations: historical preservation, travel, antique toy collecting, old english sheepdogs, classic & special interest cars. Home: 116 E Columbia St Colorado Springs CO 80907 Office: Becker-Johnson Inc 2601 Platte Pl Colorado Springs CO 80909 Office Phone: 719-473-5653. E-mail: oneblonde1@prodigy.net.

JOHNSON, STEPHEN, architectural firm executive; Student, Columbia U. Joined Hardy, Holzman, Pfeiffer Assocs. LLP, 1981, mng. dir. L.A., 2003—. Spkr. in field. Mem.: ALA, AIA, Soc. for Cull. and Univ. Planning, Nat. Trust for Hist. Preservation, Calif. Preservation Found., Western Mus. Assn., L.A. Conservancy (former v.p.). Office: HHPA Ste 430 811 W 7th St Los Angeles CA 90017

JOHNSON, STEPHEN L., federal official; b. Washington, Mar. 21, 1951; s. William Arrett and Nell (Easler) J.; m. Deborah Lynn Jones, Aug. 5, 1972; children: Carrie, Matthew, Allison. BA, Taylor U., 1972; MS, George Washington U., 1976. Dir. tech. ops. Litton Bionetics, Kensington, Md., 1976-80; sr. sci. advisor EPA, Washington, 1980-84, 86-88, dir. field ops. divsn., 1984-86, dep. dir. hazard evaluation divsn., 1988-90, dir. registration divsn., dep. dir., pesticide programs, 1997—99, asst. adminstr. prevention pesticides & toxic substances, 2000—03, acting dep. adminstr., 2003—04, dep. adminstr., 2004—05, acting adminstr., 2005, adminstr., 2005—. Dir. tech. ops. Hazleton Labs. Corp., Falls Church, Va., 1984-86; chmn. FIFRA sci. adv. panel EPA, Washington, 1988-90; exput cons. WHO, Geneva, 1988-90. Contbr. articles to profl. jours. Bd. dirs. Frederick (Md.) County Crisis Pregnancy Ctr., 1987; deacon Fredricktown Bapt. Ch., Walkerville, Md., 1991; commr. USTA Jr. League, Frederick County, 1993; bd. dirs. Frederick Tennis Patrons. Mem. USTA (bd. dirs., v.p. Md. dist.). Avocation: tennis. Office: EPA Ariel Rios Fed Bldg 1200 Pennsylvania Ave NW Rm 3000 Washington DC 20460 E-mail: johnson.stephen@epa.gov.*

JOHNSON, STEPHEN PATRICK HOWARD, lawyer; b. Holmfirth, England, Feb. 23, 1957; came to U.S., 1982; s. Herbert Edward Johnson; 1 child, Graham Johnson. BA in genetics, Cambridge (Eng.) U., 1978, MA (hon.), 1993; solicitors final exam. with honors, Coll. of Law, London, 1980; JD with high honors, Ill. Inst. Tech., 1984. Bar: Ill. 1984, N.Y. 1991, Calif. 2002; solicitor Supreme Ct. Eng. 1982. Solicitor, trainee Bird & Bird, London, 1980-82; assoc. Kirkland & Ellis, Chgo., 1982-88, ptnr., 1988-90, N.Y.C., 1990—2003, ptnr., mem. mgmt. San Francisco, 2003—. Contbr. chpt. to book. Office: Kirkland & Ellis LLP 555 California St San Francisco CA 94104 Office Phone: 415-439-1439. Office Fax: 415-439-1500. Business E-Mail: sjohnson@kirkland.com.

JOHNSON, STERLING, JR., federal judge; b. 1934; BA, Bklyn. Coll., 1963; LLB, Bklyn. Sch. Law, 1966. With N.Y.C. Police Dept., 1957-67; asst. U.S. atty. U.S. Atty. Office (ea. dist.) N.Y., 1967-70; atty. civilian complaint rev. bd. U.S. Atty. Office (so. dist.) N.Y., 1970-74, atty. drug enforcement adminstrn., 1974-75, spl. narcotics prosecutor, 1975-91; fed. judge U.S. Dist. Ct. (ea. dist.) N.Y., Bklyn., 1991—. Commr, US Sentencing Commn., DC, 1991-; active Second Cir. Task Force on Gender, Racial, and Ethnic Fairness in Cts.; mem. Nat. Conf. Fed. Trial Judges Exec. Com. Bd. dirs. Bedford Stuyvesant Restoration Corp., Cardinal Cook Com. on Substance Abuse; active Police Athletic League, Pres. Drug Adv. Coun. With USMC, 1952-55, USNR, 1975—. Mem. ABA, N.Y. State Bar Assn., Nat. Black Prosecutors Assn., Nat. Orgn. Black Law Enforcement Execs., N.Y. State Dist. Attys. Assn. Office: US Dist Ct Ea Dist NY 225 Cadman Plz E Rm 432 Brooklyn NY 11201-1818*

JOHNSON, STEVEN M., food service executive; CPA. With Ernst & Young LLP; contr. Fugate Enter., Inc., 1985—91; COO Coulter Enterprises, Inc., 1992—98; dir. Total Entertainment Restaurant Corp., 1998—, CEO, 1999—. Office: 9300 E Ctrl Ave Ste 100 Wichita KS 67206

JOHNSON, STEWART WILLARD, civil engineer; b. Mitchell, SD, Aug. 17, 1933; s. James Elmer Johnson and Grace Mahala (Erwin) Johnson Parsons; m. Mary Anis Giddings, June 24, 1956; children: Janelle Chiemi, Gregory Stewart, Eric Willard. BSCE, SD State U., 1956; BA in Bus. Adminstrn. and Polit. Sci., U. Md., 1960; MSCE, PhD, U. Ill., 1964. Registered profl. engr., Ohio. Commd. 2d lt. USAF, 1956, advanced through grades to lt. col., prof. mechs. and civil engring. Air Force Inst. Tech. Dayton, Ohio, 1964-75, dir. civil engring. Seoul, Republic of Korea, 1976-77, chief civil engring. research div. Kirtland AFB, N.Mex., 1977-80, ret., 1980; prin. engr. BDM Corp., Albuquerque, 1980-94, Johnson and Assocs., Albuquerque, 1994—; engr. Northrop Grumman, Albuquerque, 2003—04. Cons. in site surveys, found. design, constrn. of ground stas. for satellite comm. sys., 1992-2001; cons. space sci. and lunar basing NASA, U. N.Mex., N.Mex. State U. and Los Alamos Nat. Lab., 1987-92; adj. prof. civil engring. U. N.Mex., 1987-92; prin. investigator devel. concepts for lunar astron. obs. U. N.Mex., N.Mex. State U., NASA, 1987-94; tech. chmn. Space '88, Space '90, Space '94, Space '96, Space '98, Space 2000, Space 2002, Internat. Confs., Albuquerque; vis. lectr. Internat. Space U., Japan, 1992, Huntsville, Ala., 1993, Barcelona, Spain, 1994, Stockholm, 1995; mem. panel on siting lunar base European Space Agy., 1994; gen. chair Space 96 and RCEII Conf., Albuquerque, 1996; gen. chmn. Space Conf., Albuquerque, 1998, 2000, Robotics Conf., Albuquerque, 1998, 2000. Editor Engineering, Construction, and Operations in Space, I, 1988. II, 90, V, 96, Space 2000 Procs., Space 2002 Procs.; contbr. articles to profl. jours. Pres. ch. coun. Ch. of Good Shepherd United Ch. of Christ, Albuquerque, 1983-85, chmn. bd. deacons, 1991-93, 2000, moderator, 1996-97, clk., 2002; S.W. Conf. (United Ch. Christ) del. to Gen. Synod XIX, St. Louis, 1993, Gen. Synod XX, Oakland, Calif., 1995, Gen. Synod XXI, Columbus, Ohio, 1997; trustee Lunar Geotech. Inst., 1990—; mem. adv. bd. Lab. for Extraterrestrial Structures Rsch., Rutgers U., 1990—. Fellow Nat. Acad. Scis. NRC, 1970-71; recipient World Bar Assn. Space Humanitarian award, 1996. Fellow: ASCE (chmn. exec. com. aerospace divsn. 1979, tech. activities com. 1984, chmn. com. space engring. and constrn. 1987—, mem. nat. space policy com. 1988—96, chmn. 1990—96, Outstanding News Corr. award 1981, Aerospace Scis. and Tech. Applications award 1990, Edmund Friedman Profl. Recognition award 1989); mem.: AAAS, AIAA (space logistics com., Engr. of Yr. Region IV 1990), Nat. Space Soc., Am. Geophys. Union, Soc. Am. Mil. Engrs., Sigma Xi, Pi Sigma Alpha. Republican. Mem. United Ch. Of Christ. Avocations: photography, swimming, walking, gardening, hiking. Personal E-mail: stwjohnson@aol.com.

JOHNSON, SUS O'NEILL, retired library and information scientist; b. Chgo., Ill., Sept. 23, 1939; d. William Stanford and Ruth Irwin Snyder; m. Richard Patrick O'Neill (div.); children: Terence William O'Neill, Paul Staunton O'Neill, Debra O'Neill Flynn; m. Douglas Lee Johnson, Feb. 10, 1990. Attended, Conn. Coll., 1960; BA, Boston U., 1961; MLS, U. Pitts., 1964; MPA, Am. U., 1989. Sci. tech. ref. libr. Libr. of Congress, Wash., DC, 1984; libr., ref. divsn. Georgetown U. Med. Libr., Wash., 1984—87; libr., DOD contract IIT Rsch. Inst., Arlington, Va., 1987—88; libr. James Defense Info. Group, Alexandria, Va., 1988—89, World Bank, Wash., DC, 1989—2001, info. officer, 1994—98, sr. info. projects officer, 1999—2001; ret., 2002; cons. Sand Swab & Assoc., Bethesda, Md., 2002—05. Co-editor: Leadership and Management Principles in Libraries, 2002, International Information and Library Review, 2001—02; contbr. articles various profl. jours. Accordianist Mighty Spl. Music Makers, Bethesda, Md., 1992—; chair archives preservation project Bach Consort, 2003—05; fundraiser for libr. Sousa Mid. Sch., Wash., DC, 2003—05. Named SIG Mem. of Yr., ASIST, 2003, 2000—02; recipient President's award, Spec. Libr. Assn., 2001. Mem.: Am. Soc. for Info. Sci. & Tech. (chair 2000—03), Spl. Libr. Assn., DC Chpt. (pres. 2001—02), Phi Kappa Phi, Pi Alpha Alpha. Democrat. Episc. Avocations: tennis, golf, swimming, writing, music. Home: 8505 Victory Ln Potomac MD 20854 Home Fax: 320-306-1652. E-mail: sueojohnson@hotmail.com.

JOHNSON, SUSAN ELEANOR, writer, sociologist; b. Rockford, Ill., Apr. 3, 1940; d. Harold Adams and Margaret Dale (Madden) J.; life ptnr. Constance Wolfe. AB, Bryn Mawr Coll., 1962; MA, U. Wis., 1965, PhD, 1974. Instr. U. Wis., Madison, 1967-69; lectr., instr. U. Minn., Duluth, 1971-73, 76, 77; asst. prof. Cook Coll., Rutgers U., New Brunswick, N.J., 1974-75; adj. faculty Antioch U. West, Seattle, 1982, 84, 86; pvt. practice writer, rsch. cons. Anchorage, 1991—. Author: Staying Power: Long Term Lesbian Couples, 1990, When Women Played Hardball, 1994, For Love and For Life, 1995, Lesbian Sex: An Oral History, 1996. Mem. NOW, Am. Sociol. Assn., Soc. for Am. Baseball Rsch., All-Am. Girls Profl. Baseball League Players Assn. Unitarian Universalist. Avocations: conversation, reading, sports fan, walking. Office: 565 Olympic View Dr Coupeville WA 98239-9597

JOHNSON, SUZANNE M. NORA, diversified financial services company executive, lawyer; b. Chgo., 1957; BA magna cum laude, Univ. So. Calif., 1979; JD, Harvard Univ. Bar: Calif. 1983. Law clk. Judge Francis Murnaghan, US Ct. Appeals, Balt.; atty. Simpson Thacher & Bartlett; with Goldman Sachs Group, NYC, 1985—, ptnr., 1992—, head global healthcare, investment banking div., 1994—2002, head global investment rsch. div., 2002—, mem. mgmt. com., 2002—, chmn. Global Markets Inst., 2004—, vice chmn., 2004—. Henry Crown Fellow Aspen Inst. Trustee Brookings Institution, Carnegie Institution, RAND Health, TechnoServe, Univ. So. Calif.; dir. Children Now; mem. adv. bd. of councilors Harvard Med. Sch. Mem.: Council Fgn. Rels. Office: Goldman Sachs Group 85 Broad St New York NY 10004*

JOHNSON, SYLVIA SUE, university administrator, educator; b. Abiline, Tex., Aug. 10, 1940; d. SE Boyd and Margaret MacGillivray (Withington) Smith; m. William Ruel Johnson; children: Margaret Ruth, Laura Jane, Catherine Withington. BA, U. Calif., Riverside, 1962; postgrad., U. Hawaii, 1963. Elem. edn. credential, 1962. Chmn. bd. regents U. Calif., 2000—. Mem. bd. regents U. Calif.; mem. steering com. Citizens Univ. Com., chmn., 1978-79; bd. dirs., charter mem. U. Calif.-Riverside Found., chmn. nominating com., 1983—; pres., bd. dirs. Friends of the Mission Inn, 1969-72, 73-76, Mission Inn Found., 1977—, Calif. Bapt. Coll. Citizens Com., 1980—; bd. dirs. Riverside Comty. Hosp., 1980—, Riverside Jr. League, 1976-77, Nat. Charity League, 1984-85; mem. chancellors blue ribbon com., devel. com. Calif. Mus. Photography; state bd. dirs. C. of C., 2003. Named Woman of Yr., State of Calif. Legislature, 1989, 91, Citizen of Yr., C. of C., 1989; recipient Golden Key award Soroptomist Internat., 2000, Chancellor's medal U. Calif. Riverside, 2002, Trustees award for extraordinary svc. U. Calif. Riverside, 2004, Silver Raincross medal Jr. League Riverside, 1993, Spirit of Excellence award Calif. Bapt. Coll., 2004, Annual Frank Miller Civic Achievement award, Mission Inn Found., 2005. Mem. U. Calif.-Riverside Alumni Assn. (bd. dirs. 1966-68, v.p. 1968-70), Calif. C. of C. (bd. dirs. 2003—). Business E-Mail: ssj@johnson-machinery.com.

JOHNSON, TERESA RENE', research scientist; d. James Kenneth and Linda Kaye Johnson. BS, Liberty U., 1985; MS, Med. Coll. Va./Va. Commonwealth U., 1990; PhD, Vanderbilt U., 1999. Rsch. assoc. Med. Coll. Va., Richmond, 1990—94, Vanderbilt U. Sch. Medicine, Nashville, 1999—2000; staff scientist NIH, Bethesda, Md., 2000—. Scientist NIH Vaccine Rsch. Ctr. Animal Care and Use Com., Bethesda, 2002—; mem. NIH NIAID Promotion Action Com., 2004—; reviewer numerous sci. jours., 2002—. Outreach and recruitment specialist NIH NIAID Vaccine Rsch. Ctr., Bethesda, 2001—05; educator Vanderbilt U. AIDS Outreach Program, 1996—2000. Recipient Sidney P. Colowick award Sci. Achievement, Vanderbilt U. Sch. Medicine, Dept. Microbiology and Immunology, 1999, Disting. Svc. award, NIH, 2002—04; grantee, Vanderbilt U. Sch. Medicine, Dept. Microbiology and Immunology, 1999; scholar, Liberty U., 1981—82, Commonwealth of Va., 1986—87. Mem.: Chesapeake Cytometry Consortium, Internat. Cytokine Soc., Am. Soc. Microbiology, Am. Assn. Immunologists (AAI-Huang Found. Trainee Achievement award 1999), Microbes and Def. Academic Soc. (sr. advisor 1999—2000, events coord. 1996—99). Office: NIH 40 Convent Dr Bldg 40 Rm 2614 Bethesda MD 20892-3017 Office Phone: 301-594-8570. Office Fax: 301-480-2771. Personal E-mail: teresaj@nih.gov.

JOHNSON, THEODORE MEBANE, brokerage house executive; b. Denver, Jan. 25, 1934; s. Harold Theodore and Flora Luella (Cunningham) J.; m. Sandra Hall, May 23, 1970 (dec.). BS, U. Denver, 1956; postgrad. Advanced Mgmt. Program, Harvard U. Partner, Hornblower Weeks-Hemphill, Noyes, 1961-78, sr. v.p., dir., exec. com., until 1978; exec. v.p., divsn. dir. PaineWebber, Inc., N.Y.C., 1978—2003. Chmn. bd. dirs., CEO Cross Match Techs., 1997—. Co-founder, past dir. N.Am. Housing Corp. Served to lt. (j.g.) USNR, 1956-57. Mem. Securities Industry Assn. (govt. rels. com., past chmn. Mid-Atlantic chpt.), Bond Club (Washington), Congl. Country Club (Washington), Univ. Club (Washington), City Tavern Club (Washington), N.Y. Athletic Club, Robert Trent Jones Country Club (Manasas, Va.), Pine Tree Country Club (Boynton Beach, Fla.). Presbyterian. Home: 140 Atlantic Ave Palm Beach FL 33480-3707

JOHNSON, THOMAS FLOYD, former academic administrator, educator; b. Detroit, June 1, 1943; s. Edward Eugene and Adella Madeline (Norton) J.; m. Michele Elizabeth Myers, Mar. 26, 1965; children: Jason, Amy, Sarah. BPh, Wayne State U., 1965; BD, Fuller Theol. Sem., 1968; ThM, Princeton Sem., 1969; PhD, Duke U., 1979. Pastor Presbyn. Ch. U.S.A., Pa., Mich., 1969-76; asst. prof. U. Sioux Falls, S.D., 1978-83; acad. dean Sioux Falls (S.D.) Coll., 1981-83, pres., 1988-97; prof. N.Am. Baptist Sem., Sioux Falls, 1983-88; dean George Fox Evang. Sem., Portland, Oreg., 1997—2001; interim pres. George Fox U., Newberg, 1997-98, prof. bibl. theol., 1997—. Contbr. 9 articles to Internat. Standard Bible Ency., 1988; author: 1, 2, and 3 John New International Biblical Commentary, 1993. Bd. dirs. Children's Home Soc. S.D., Sioux Falls, 1980-86, S.D. Symphony Orch., 1988-92, Carroll Inst., 1989-93, Coalition Christian Colls. and Univs., 1992-97. Mem. Am. Bapt. Assn. Colls. and Univs. (pres. 1992-94), Soc. Bibl. Lit., Sioux Falls C. of C. (bd. dirs. 1992-95), Rotary (bd. dirs. Downtown Club 1991-95, pres. 1993-94). Office: George Fox Univ 414 N Meridian St Newberg OR 97132 Office Phone: 503-554-2663. Personal E-mail: tmj365@yahoo.com. *Every day, with all its tasks and relationships, is a gift from God. Our response is to live thankfully, in service to God and God's world.*

JOHNSON, THOMAS S., electronics executive; b. 1946; BS, U. Fla., 1972; MBA, Harvard U., 1976. With IKON (formerly Alco Std. Corp.), 1975-89, v.p. ops. office products group; COO Danka, 1989-90; office imaging industry cons., 1991-94; dir., pres., CEO Global Imaging Sys., Inc., Tampa, Fla., 1994—. Office: Global Imaging Sys Inc Ste 200A 820 Northdale Blvd Tampa FL 33624 also: PO Box 273478 Tampa FL 33688-3478

JOHNSON, THOMAS STEPHEN, banker; b. Racine, Wis., Nov. 19, 1940; s. H. Norman and Jane Agnes (McAvoy) Johnson; m. Margaret Ann Werner, Apr. 18, 1970; children: Thomas Philip, Scott Michael(dec.), Margaret Ann. AB in Econs., Trinity Coll., 1962; MBA, Harvard U., 1964. Instr. Grad. Bus. Sch. Ateneo de Manila U., Philippines, 1964-66; spl. asst. to contr. U.S. Dept. Def., Washington, 1966-69; with Chem. Bank, N.Y.C., 1969-89, pres., dir., 1983-89, Mfrs. Hanover Trust Co., N.Y.C., 1989-91; pres., chmn., CEO, bd. dirs. GreenPoint Fin. Corp., GreenPoint Bank, N.Y.C., 1993—2004. Bd. dirs. North Fork Bancorp., Alleghany Corp., R.R. Donnelley & Sons, Inc., The Phoenix Cos., Inc., Lower Manhattan Devel. Corp., Freddie Mac. Chmn., bd. trustees US Japan Found.; chmn. bd. dirs. Inst. Internat. Edn.; bd. dirs. Cancer Rsch. Inst., United Way NYC, World Trade Ctr. Meml. Found.; past chmn., trustee Trinity Coll.; past chmn. bd. dirs. Union Theol. Sem. Mem.: Coun. Fgn. Rels., Harvard Club N.Y.C., Links N.Y.C., River Club N.Y.C., Palm Beach Polo and Country Club, Montclair Golf Club. Roman Catholic. Office: care of North Fork Bank 90 Park Ave Fl 4 New York NY 10016-1301 Business E-Mail: Thomas.Johnson@GreenPoint.com.

JOHNSON, THOMAS STUART, lawyer; b. Rockford, Ill., May 21, 1942; s. Frederick C. and Pauline (Ross) J. BA, Rockford Coll., 1964, LLD, 1989; JD, Harvard U., 1967. Bar: Ill. 1967. Ptnr., past pres. Williams & McCarthy, Rockford, 1967—. Lectr. in field. Contbr. numerous articles to profl. jours. Chmn. bd. trustees Rockford Coll., 1986—89; trustee Eastern Ill. U., 1996—2000, Emanuel Med. Ctr., Turlock, Calif., 1984—86, Swedish Covenant Hosp., Chgo., 1984—86, Lincoln Acad. of Ill., 1999—; chmn. bd. dirs. Ill. Inst. Continuing Legal Edn., Chgo., 1984—86; treas. Lawyers Trust Fund of Ill., Chgo., 1984—86; bd. govs. Regent's Coll., London, 1985—89; bd. dirs., mem. benevolence bd. Covenant Ch. Am., Chgo., 1984—86; chmn. Regent's Found. for Internat. Edn., London; chancellor Ill. Acad. Lawyers, 1999. With U.S. Army, 1968—70. Fellow Am. Bar Found., Am. Coll. Trust and Estate Counsel; mem. ABA (ho. of dels. 1982-89, chmn. commn. on advt. 1984-88), Ill. Bar Assn. (bd. govs. 1976-82, sec. 1981-82, medal of honor 1997), Winnebago County Bar Assn. (pres. 1990), Am. Judicature Soc. (bd. dirs. 1986-90), Rotary (pres. Rockford 1992-93), Univ. Club Rockford. Republican. Home: 913 N Main St Rockford IL 61103-7068 Office Phone: 815-987-8920. E-mail: tjohnson@wilmac.com.

JOHNSON, TIMOTHY AUGUSTIN, JR., lawyer; b. Clearwater, Fla., Dec. 17, 1945; s. Timothy Augustin and Ruth (Brown) J.; m. Clair Smith, Aug. 23, 1967; children: Chester Wolcott, Kathryn Elizabeth. BA, U. Fla., 1966, JD, 1969. Bar: Fla. 1969, U.S. Dist. Ct. (mid. dist.) Fla. 1970, U.S. Ct. Appeals (5th cir.) 1972, U.S. Supreme Ct. 1972. Assoc. Carlton, Fields et al., Tampa, Fla., 1969-73; ptnr., shareholder Johnson, Pope, Bokor, Ruppel & Burns LLP, Clearwater, 1973—. Mem. Fla. Bd. Bar Examiners. Pres. PACT, 1986-88; mem. Leadership Fla., 1983-84; chmn. Clearwater Long Range Econ. Devel. Commn., 1988-89; mem. bd. trustees Tampa Prep. Sch., 1985-90; trustee, chmn. investment subcom. U. South Fla. Found.; chmn. Clearwater Charter Rev. Com. Name 1 of 5 Outstanding Young Men, Jr. C. of C., Fla., 1979, Friend of the Arts, Arts Coun., Pinellas County, Fla., 1986. Mem. Fla. Bar (pres. young lawyers sect., bd. govs.). Republican. Avocations: exercise, hiking, boating. Office: Johnson Pope Bokor Ruppel & Burns LLP 911 Chestnut St Clearwater FL 33756-5643 Office Phone: 727-461-1818. Business E-Mail: timj@jpfirm.com.

JOHNSON, TIMOTHY D., music educator, composer, poet; b. Salina, Kans., June 8, 1943; s. Dwight Howard and Lucy Polly Johnson; m. Vickie Ellen Ohmer, Aug. 19, 1972; children: Michael Anthony, Brandon Curtis, Rae Ann Rachelle. BME, Kans. State Teachers Coll., 1966; MME, Emporia State U., 1997. Cert. music tchr. Ariz., 1997. Mem., formerly brass contractor/rd. mgr. Jerry Presley Band, Lenexa, Kans., 1985—; dir. bands Wickenburg H.S., Ariz., 2002—. Performer (arranger, composer): A Prairie Lullaby, The TreeTop, author of poems. Freelance musician, spkr., entertainer various religious, youth, prisons, 1970—2002. Mem.: Music Educators Nat. Conf., Ariz. Music Educators Assn. R-Conservative. Protestant. Avocations: travel, reading. Personal E-mail: victims@localnet.com.

JOHNSON, TIMOTHY JOHN, writer, educator; s. Burton Freeman and Muriel Catherine Johnson; m. Agnieszka Skwarska. BA in Theology, St. Louis U., 1974—78; STB in Scred Theology, Pontifical Faculty St. Bonaventure, Rome, 1980; STL in Sacred Theology, Pontifical Gregorian U., Rome, 1982, STD in Sacred Theology, 1989. Assoc. prof., religion and chair, liberal studies dept. Flagler Coll., St. Augustine, Fla., 1998—. Bd. mem., Bonaventure texts in transl. series St. Bonaventure U., Olean, NY, sr. co-editor of franciscan studies. Author: (book) Iste Pauper Clamavit: St. Bonaventure's Mendicant Theology of Prayer; editor: Bonaventure: Mystic of God's Word; author: The Soul in Ascent: Bonaventure on Poverty, Prayer and Union with God; contbr. articles to profl. jours. Fulbright Scholar, 2003—04. Mem.: Soc. for the Study of Christian Spirituality, Internat. Medieval Sermon Studies, Am. Acad. Religion. Office: Flagler Coll 74 King St Saint Augustine FL 32085 Office Phone: 904-819-6266. Office Fax: 904-826-0094. E-mail: johnsont@flagler.edu.

JOHNSON, TIMOTHY PATRICK, health and social researcher; b. Batavia, N.Y., July 14, 1954; s. Elmore Thomas and Sara (McKinsey) J.; m. LuEllen Doty, June 20, 1988; children: Sara Elizabeth, Elliott William. BA, Western Ky. U., 1977; MA, U. Wis., Milw., 1978; PhD, U. Ky., 1988. Rsch. analyst dept. medicine U. Ky., Lexington, 1980-82, rsch. coord. survey rsch. ctr., 1982-88; staff assoc. for psychometrics Am. Bd. Family Practice, Lexington, 1988-89; asst. rsch. prof. epidemiology and biostatistics sch. pub. health U. Ill., Chgo., 1991—, project coord. survey rsch. lab., 1989-91, asst. dir. survey rsch. lab., 1991-93, assoc. dir., 1993-96, acting dir., 1996-98, dir., 1998—, assoc. prof. pub. adminstrn., 1996—2003, prof. pub. adminstrn., 2003—, assoc. rsch. prof. pub. health, 2002—03, rsch. prof. public health, 2003—. Contbr. articles to profl. jours. Mem. APHA, AAAS, Am. Sociol. Assn., Am. Assn. Pub. Opinion Rsch., Am. Statis. Assn., Am. Coll. Epidemiology, Am. Assn. for the Advancement of Sci. Roman Catholic. Office: U Ill Survey Rsch Lab 412 S Peoria St Chicago IL 60607-7063 Business E-Mail: timj@uic.edu.

JOHNSON, TIMOTHY PETER, senator; b. Canton, SD, Dec. 28, 1946; s. Vandal Charles and Ruth Jorinda (Ljostveit) J.; m. Barbara Brooks, June 6, 1969; children: Brooks Dwight, Brendan Vandal, Kelsey Marie. BA, U. S.D., 1969, MA, 1970, JD, 1975; postgrad., Mich. State U., 1970-71. Bar: S.D. 1975, U.S. Dist. Ct. S.D. 1976. Fiscal analyst Legis. Fiscal Agy., Lansing, Mich., 1971-72; pvt. practice Vermillion, S.D., 1975-86; mem. S.D. Ho. of Reps., 1979—82, S.D. Senate, 1983—86, U.S. Ho. of Reps., 1987-97; U.S. senator from S.D., 1997—. Adj. inst. U. S.D., Vermillion, 1974-83; mem. S.D. Code Commn., Pierre, 1982-86. Mem. Vermillion City Planning Commn., 1977-78; treas. Clay County Dem. Com., Vermillion, 1978; del. Dem. Nat. Conv., 1988, 92, 96. NSF grantee, 1969-70. Mem. S.D. Bar Assn., Clay County Bar Assn., Phi Beta Kappa, Omicron Delta Kappa. Democrat. Lutheran. Office: 136 Hart Senate Ofc Bldg Washington DC 20510-0001 also: 320 S First St Ste 103 Aberdeen SD 57401-1554*

JOHNSON, TIMOTHY VINCENT, congressman, lawyer; b. Champaign, Ill., July 23, 1946; 9 children. Attended, US Military Academy, 1964; BA, U. Ill., 1969; JD, U. Ill. Coll. of Law, 1972. Alderman Urbana City Council, 1971—75; atty. priv. practice, 1972—; mem. from 104th Dist. Ill. Ho. of Reps, 1977—2000; mem. U.S. Congress from 15th Ill. dist., Washington, 2001—, mem. agr. com., sci. com., transp. and infrastructure com. Mem. Congressional Fire Services Caucus, Congressional Internet Caucus, Congressional Rural Caucus, Legislative Audit Commn. Mem. U.S. Army, 1964—65. Recipient Order of the Coif. Mem.: Phi Beta Kappa (Bronze tablet). Republican. Assembly Of God. Office: US Ho of Reps 1229 Longworth Ho Office Bldg Washington DC 20515-1315*

JOHNSON, TOD STUART, market research company executive; b. Mpls., June 6, 1944; s. David Z. and Helen R. (Connor) J.; m. Cindy Schwartz, Aug. 28, 1966; children: Scott, Stacey BS, Carnegie Mellon U., 1966, MSIA, 1967. Vice pres. Market Sci. Assocs., Inc., Des Plaines, Ill., 1967-71; pres., chief exec. officer NPD Research, Inc., Port Washington, N.Y., 1971-89, Home Testing Inst., Inc., Port Washington, N.Y., 1980-89, OPOC Computing, Inc., Port Washington, N.Y., 1980-89, NPD Group, Port Washington, N.Y., 1982—, The NPD Group Inc. (merger of NPD Rsch. Inc., Home Testing Inst. Inc., and OPOC Computing), Port Washington, N.Y., 1989—; chmn., dir. NPD/Nielsen, Inc., 1987-91; chmn. ISL Internat. Surveys Ltd., Toronto, 1990-98; mng. dir. GFK Mktg. Svcs. Europe GmbH, 1995-99; chmn., CEO Jupiter Media Metrix, N.Y.C., 1998—2001. Bd. dirs. Advt. Rsch. Found., N.Y.C., sec., 1988, vice chmn., 1989, chmn., 1990; founding co-chmn. Coun. Mktg. and Opinion Rsch., 1992-94. Contbr. articles to profl. jours.; patentee in field Trustee Carnegie-Mellon U., Pitts., 1980—, chmn., trustee student affairs com., 1982-85, co-chmn. devel. com., 1993-2000. Mem. Young Pres. Orgn. Republican. Jewish. Home: 10 Heathcote Rd Scarsdale NY 10583-4414 Office: NPD Group 900 W Shore Rd Port Washington NY 11050-4624

JOHNSON, TOM MILROY, dean, physician, educator; b. Northville, Mich., Jan. 16, 1935; s. Waldo Theodore and Ruth Jeanette (Christensen) J.; m. Emily Chapin Rhoads, June 13, 1959 (div. Aug. 1983); children— Glenn C., Heidi R.; m. Jane Susan Robb, June 10, 1987; 1 stepchild, Elizabeth K. BA in Psychology with honors, Coll. of Wooster, 1956; MD, Northwestern U., 1961; postgrad. in health systems mgmt., Harvard U., 1974. Rotating intern Detroit Receiving Hosp., 1961-62; resident in internal medicine U.

Mich. Med. Ctr., Ann Arbor, 1962-65, fellow in pulmonary disease, 1967-68; asst. prof. internal medicine Mich. State U., East Lansing, 1968-71, assoc. prof., asst. dean Coll. of Medicine Grand Rapids, 1971-77; prof. medicine, dean Sch. of Medicine U. N.D., Grand Forks, 1977-88; prof., assoc. dean Coll. Human Medicine, Mich. State U., 1988-94; campus dean, CEO Kalamazoo Ctr. for Med. Studies Mich. State U., 1994-98, prof. emeritus medicine East Lansing, 1999—; cons. in med. edn. Fla. State U., 1999—2001. Bd. dirs. No. Mich. Regional Health Svcs., Petosky, 1991—2001. Contbr. articles to profl. jours. Capt. M.C., USAF, 1965-67. A. Blaine Brower Traveling scholar ACP, 1977; Tom M. Johnson lecture hall named in his honor Grand Rapids Med. Ctr., 1982; recipient Physician Leadership award Mich. Hosp. Assn., 1999, Disting. Alumni award Coll. of Wooster, 2003. Fellow ACP (Laureate award Mich. chpt.); mem. AMA, Mich. State Med. Soc., Studebaker Drivers Club, Antique Automobile Club of Am., Alpha Omega Alpha. Avocation: restoration of antique automobiles and older farm houses. Home and Office: 4815 Barton Rd Williamston MI 48895-9305 E-mail: tmilroyjohnson@yahoo.com.

JOHNSON, VAHE DUNCAN, lawyer; b. Providence, Dec. 18, 1938; s. Vahe D. and Katharine (Simpson) J.; m. Diana E. Lepow, Apr. 13, 1964; children: Alexandra, Mark Adam. AB, Harvard U., 1960, LLB, 1963. Bar: R.I. 1964. From assoc. to ptnr. Edwards & Angell, Providence, 1963—. Bd. dirs. Fleet Nat. Bank, Fleet Bank of Mass., N.A., Fleet Bank, N.A. Trustee Providence Found., 1985, Providence Pub. Libr, 1988, Miriam Hosp., Providence, 1990, Lifespan Corp., Capitol Ctr. Commn., Tufts Vet. Sch., 1999, R.I. Sch. Design, 2005. Office: Edwards & Angell 2800 Fin Plz Providence RI 02903 Office Phone: 401-276-6477. Business E-Mail: johnson@EdwardsAngell.com.

JOHNSON, VAN R., health facility administrator; b. Idaho; BS, Brigham Young U.; MS, U. Minn. Sr. mgr. Intermountain Healthcare Corp., Salt Lake City; pres., CEO Sutter Community Hospitals, Sacramento, 1990—95; sr. v.p., COO Sutter Health, Sacramento, 1990—95, pres., CEO, 1995—. Bd. dirs. Boy Scouts Am. Golden Empire Coun. Recipient award of distinction Hosp. Coun. No. and Ctrl. Calif., 1996. Office: Sutter Health 2200 River Plaza Dr Sacramento CA 95833-4134

JOHNSON, VERDIA E., marketing professional; B in Mktg., Howard U.; MBA in Mktg., NYU. With Colgate Palmolive Co., Standard Brands, Nabisco Brands; dir. advt. Black Enterprise Mag.; v.p. bus. devel. and sales Gannett Outdoor; v.p., gen. mgr. Stedman Graham & Ptnrs.; pres., founding ptnr. Footsteps, LLC, NYU, NY, 2000—. Named 25 Most Black Influential Women in Bus., Network Mag.; recipient Outstanding Women in Mktg. and Comm. award, Ebony Mag., 2001, Urban Wheels award, 2002. Office: Footsteps LLC 200 Varick St Rm 610 New York NY 10014-7487 Office Phone: 212-924-6432.

JOHNSON, VERONICA ANN WILKERSON, library director; b. Detroit, Aug. 5, 1952; d. James Henry and Alberta (Dixon) Wilkerson; m. Melvin Lee Johnson, Nov. 3, 1973; children: Dichondra Rosalyn, Christopher Lee, Jonell Henry. BA, Wayne State U., 1975; MA, U. Mich., 1977. Lab technician Project Prescad Wayne County Health Dept., 1978—79; children's libr. Inkster (Mich.) br. Wayne Oakland Libr. Fedn., 1979, head cmty. libr., 1979—85; govt. rels. specialist State Libr. Mich., 1985—87, dir. info. and govt. svcs., 1987—. Owner Verondee Cons. Co., East Lansing, Mich.; spkr., presenter workshops in field; v.p. Info. Movers, Inc., Mich. Newspaper columnist: Library Lines; author: manuals on mktg. govt. publs., cost effective methods and cmty. needs/pub. libr. Adviser City of Inkster; vol. Tng. Youth Leadership Devel., Sister Cities Internat.; sec. Inkster Cmty. Project Pride, 1979—80; mem. City of Inkster Cable TV Task Force, 1981—; chmn. workshop com. Inkster Internat. Friendship Force Exch., 1981—; mem. East Lansing Planning Commn., 1995—; apptd. Selective Svc. Bd., Mich., 2002—; adminstrv. aide State Rep. Hansen Clarke, Mich.; legis. liaison Gov. James J. Blanchard; bd. dirs. U. Mich. Lansing Svc. Ctr., 1993—. Recipient Young Libr. of the Yr. award, 1982; fellow, U. Mich. Sch. Libr. Sci., 1976—77. Mem.: ALA (chmn. ASCLA/SLAS com., mem. ASCLA planning com. 1986—87), NAACP, Coun. State Agy. Librs. (sec./treas.), Mich. Libr. Assn., Med. Libr. Assn., Gamma Phi Delta. Mem. Ch. Of Christ. Home: 915 Darlington Ave East Lansing MI 48823-1882 Office: Dir Univ Mich Lansing Svc Ctr 101 S Washington Sq Lansing MI 48933 Office Phone: 517-372-7801. Business E-Mail: veronicj@umich.edu.

JOHNSON, VICKIE, professional basketball player; b. Apr. 15, 1972; B of Sociology & Psychology, La. Tech. Inst., 1996. Guard-forward Tarbes, France, 1996—97, WMBA - N.Y. Liberty, N.Y.C., 1997—. Named NCAA Tournament All-Final Four, 1994, Sun Belt Conf. Player of Yr., MVP, Kodak All-Am., 1995, Street & Smith All-Am., 1996; recipient La. Player of Yr., 1996. Avocations: movies, shopping, friends, tennis. Office: NY Liberty 2 Penn Plz New York NY 10121-0101

JOHNSON, VICTOR LAWRENCE, banker, director; b. Phila., Feb. 8, 1928; s. Paul J. and Eleanor (Moskowitz) J.; m. Joan Markovitz, Dec. 4, 1955; children: Linda E., Sally A. Grad., Phillips Exeter Acad., 1945; BA, Haverford Coll., 1949; MBA, Wharton Sch. of U. Pa., 1951. Vice pres. Ocean City Mfg. Co., Phila., 1953-58; pres. Johnson Computing Co., Phila., 1958-68, chmn. bd., dir., 1968—; with Provident Nat. Bank, Phila., 1969—, sr. v.p., 1971—; pres., dir. Allen Data Systems, Inc., Phila., 1970; pres. JCI Data Processing Inc., 1976—. Bd. dirs. Sircom Knitting Co., Spring City, Pa., pres., 1980-81; chmn. Wordco Data Systems Inc., 1992. Bd. dirs., mem. budget com. Phila. United Fund, 1954-67; bd. dirs. Nicetown Club Boys and Girls, Phila., 1954-57, Huntingdon Valley (Pa.) Civic Assn., 1956-64; bd. dirs., exec. com. Rydal/Meadowbrook (Pa.) Civic Assn., 1969—; mem. planning and devel. com. Germantown Friends Sch., 1970-73; vol. trustee Not-For-Profit Hosps. Bd., v.p., 1984-87, chmn. planning com., 1987-89; vice chmn., 1989-96, trustee, exec. com. Albert Einstein Med. Ctr., 1973—, vice chmn., 1980, chmn. bd. govs. No. divsn., 1981-84, chmn. bd. dirs., 1987-90; chmn. bd. trustees Health Care Found., 1987-90; dir. Jefferson Health System, 1998; sec., treas. Delaware Valley Hosp. Couns., 1982-95; chmn. bd. Delaware Valley Health, Edn. and Rsch. Found., 1982-85; bd. dirs. Phila. Festival Theatre for New Plays, 1989-94. With U.S. Army, 1951-52. Fellow Coll. Physicians Phila. (trustee 2002—); mem. Pa. Bankers Assn., Bank Automation Assn. Delaware Valley, Am. Hosp. Assn. (coun. governing bds. 1989, del. 2004), Hosp. Trustees Assn. Pa. (vice chmn. bd. 1991-92, chmn. bd. 1992), Locust Club (Phila.), Philmont Country Club (Huntingdon Valley) (bd. dirs., exec. v.p.). Home: Hidden Glen Jenkintown PA 19046

JOHNSON, VICTORIA HOUSTON, elementary school educator, poet; b. Cleve., Dec. 6, 1961; s. Daniel Arron and Margaret Mildred Houston; m. Clyde Bowman Johnson, Nov. 15, 1980; children: Lamont Anthony, Ronald Clyde. AA, Social Svc. Tech. Sch., 1997. Cert. day care Cuyaga County Child Care, 80. Day care adminstr., youth leader Greater Love Bapt. Ch., Cleve., 1996—; tchr. extended learning program Cleve. City Schs., 2000—01; co-owner C.J. Famous Angus, Cleve. Noon-time supr. Cleve. City Schs., 1995—2000. Contbr. poetry to lit. publs. (Hon. Mention, Nat. Libr. Poetry, 99, Editor's Choice award, 98). Named Poet of Merit, Nat. Libr. Poetry, 1997; recipient Pres.' Recognition of Lib. Excellence award, Nat. Authors Registry. Avocations: reading, writing, dog shows. Office: Greater Love Missionary Bapt Ch 3630 E 116th St Cleveland OH 44105

JOHNSON, W. CLAYTON, lawyer; b. Roanoke, Va., Sept. 14, 1955; BA, Univ. Va., 1977, JD, 1980. Bar: Calif. 1980, NY 1985. Atty., Calif., 1980—84; assoc. Cravath Swaine & Moore LLP, NYC, 1984—88, ptnr., corp., 1988—, ptnr. Hong Kong, 1994—2003. Mem. Va. Law Rev. Mem.: ABA, NY State Bar Assn. Office: Cravath Swaine & Moore LLP Worldwide Plz 825 Eighth Ave New York NY 10019-7475 Office Phone: 212-474-1160. Office Fax: 212-474-3700. Business E-Mail: cjohnson@cravath.com.

JOHNSON, W. DONALD, research and development company executive; b. 1947; m. Pat Johnson; 4 children. Grad. in Applied Math., Engring., N.C. State U., 1974. With DuPont, Kinston, NC, 1974, Richmond, Va., asst. site mgr. Seaford, Del., with European Nonwovens Geneva, global bus. dir. Kevlar Richmond, Va., 1994, mng. dir., gen. mgr. Advanced Fibers Systems, 1996, v.p., gen. mgr., 1997, v.p., gen. mgr. Nylon (N.Am.), 1997, group v.p. Nylong Worldwide, 1999—2001, group v.p. ops. and svcs. Wilmington, Del., 2001—. Office: DuPont DuPont Bldg 1007 Market St Wilmington DE 19898

JOHNSON, W. TAYLOR, physician; b. Suffolk, Va., Jan. 17, 1936; s. Walter Taylor and Ethel (Storey) Johnson; m. Bettie Ann Orendueff; children: Elizabeth Ann, Patricia Ellen. Grad., Duke U., 1957, MD, 1961. Diplomate Am. Bd. Dermatology, Am. Bd. Dermatopathology. Commd. ensign USN, 1954; advanced through grades to capt. Nat. Naval Med. Ctr., 1975, intern Bethesda, Md., 1961-62; resident in dermatology U.S. Naval Hosp., San Diego, 1964-66; fellow in dermatopathology Armed Forces Inst. Pathology, Washington, 1967-68; staff physician U.S. Naval Tng. Ctr., San Diego, 1962-64; staff dermatologist Nat. Naval Med. Ctr., Bethesda, 1967-72, asst. chief dermatology, 1972-78, chief dermatology, 1978-81; asst. prof. medicine Georgetown U., Washington, 1969-88; pvt. practice Gaithersburg, Md., 1981—98. Contbr. articles to profl. jours. Mem.: AMA, Internat. Soc. Dermatol. Surgery, Med. and Chirurgical Faculty Md., Montgomery County Med. Soc., Am. Soc. Dermatology, Am. Acad. Dermatology, Washington Soc. Dermatology (pres. 1983), Assn. Mil. Dermatologists (pres. 1979). Republican. Presbyterian. Avocations: tennis, computers. Home: 516 Moss Tree Dr Wilmington NC 28405-5246 E-mail: taylor.johnson@alumni.duke.edu.

JOHNSON, WAINE CECIL, dermatologist; b. Mt. Vernon, Tex., Sept. 30, 1928; s. Tulley Bell and Lizzie J.; m. Deanna Glutz, Dec. 1973; children: Susan Lynn, Carol Ann, Sandra Kay. BS, E. Tex. State U., 1949; MD, U. Tex., 1953. Intern Brooke Army Hosp., 1953-54; resident in dermatology Walter Reed Army Hosp., 1955-58; fellow in dermal pathology Armed Forces Inst. Pathology, 1960-61; mem. staff Skin and Cancer Hosp., Phila., 1962-78, asst. dir. lab., 1962, dir., 1970-78; mem. faculty Temple U. Med. Sch., Phila., 1962-78, prof. dermatology, 1970-78; clin. prof. U. Pa. Med. Sch., 1978—; chmn. dept. dermatology Grad. Hosp. U. Pa., 1978-98; mng. ptnr. Delaware Valley Dermatopathology LLP, 1998—2000; co-mng. dir. Delaware Valley Dermatopathology divsn. Inst. for Dermatopathology, Conshohocken, Pa., 2001—. Author numerous papers in field.; Co-editor: Dermal Pathology, 1974. Served to maj. M.C. USAR, 1953-62. Recipient Gold medal sci. exhibit Am. Soc. Clin. Pathologists-Coll. Am. Pathologists, 1962 Mem.: ACP, AMA, Coll. Physicians of Phila. (chmn. dermatology sect. 1994—97), Atlantic Dermatol. Conf. (pres. 1979—80), Phila. Dermatol. Soc. (pres. 1979—80), Histochem. Soc., Soc. Investigative Dermatology, Am. Soc. Dermatopathology (pres. 1988), Am. Registry Pathology (pres. 2003—05), Internat. Acad. Pathology, Am. Dermatol. Assn., Am. Acad. Dermatology (chmn. pathology com. 1976—80). Home: 744 Crosswicks Rd Rydal PA 19046-3004 Office: Ste 310 20 Ash St Millenium 1 Conshohocken PA 19428 E-mail: wjohnson@ameripath.com.

JOHNSON, WALLACE, retired army officer; b. Oklahoma City, Aug. 8, 1939; s. Carroll Wallace and Pauletta (Bibbs) J.; m. Lela Mae Johnson, Dec. 25, 1959; children: Wallace, Steven, Valerie Lynne, Sharon Denise. BS, U. Okla., 1961; MBA, Ala. A&M U., 1973. Commd. 2d lt. U.S. Army, 1961, advanced through grades to lt. col., 1978; lt. inf. platoon leader, exec officer 1/58th Inf. (Mech), Ft. Benning, Ga., 1962-64; detachment comdr. Co. A-29 C 10th spl. forces Bad Tolz, West Germany, 1964-66, detachment comdr. A333, 5th spl. forces group, Republic Vietnam, 1966-67; br. chief instr. USAMMCS Redstone Arsenal, Ala., 1969-71; security plans, ops. officer 23d support group, Republic Korea, 1971-72; chief orgn. br. USAMMCS, Redstone Arsenal, 1973-75; exec. officer 101st Ordnance Bn., Heilbronn, W. Ger., 1976-78; surety insp. Office of Insp. Gen., Heidelberg, W. Ger., 1978-79; sr. logistics instr. Command and Gen. Staff Coll., Ft. Leavenworth, Kans., 1979-84; chief materiel and logistics systems div. Army Ordnance Missile and Munition Ctr. and Sch., 1984-85; sr. program analyst CAS, Inc., 1985-86; mgr. logistics integration Acustar, Inc. Mil.-Pub. Electronic Systems, 1986-88, mgr. bus. devel. dept., automatic test equipment (ATE)/test program sets (TPS) and electroluminescent display products Chrysler Corp., 1986-91; dir. mktg. Automation Rsch. Systems Ltd., 1991-93, program mgr., 1993-94 GMU, 1994—; dir., mentor-protege program; instr. U.S. Army service shcs.; sr. parachutist, jump master. Decorated Combat Inf. Badge, Bronze Star. Mem. Assn. U.S. Army, Am. Def. Preparedness Assn., Internat. Platform Assn., Soc. Logistics Engrs., Unmanned Vehicle Assn., Spl. Forces Assn., Nat. Def. Industry Assn. Republican. Baptist. Club: Jaywalkers of Ft. Leavenworth (v.p. 1980-81), Kiwanis, Nat. Space Club (vice chmn.). Lodge: Sertoma (Leavenworth chpt. pres. 1981-84). Home: 9513 Retriever Rd Burke VA 22015-4515 Office: George Mason U Fairfax VA 22030-3409

JOHNSON, WALLACE STEPHEN, JR., Asian languages educator; b. Hampton, Va., Nov. 6, 1932; s. Wallace Stephen and Ellen Virginia (Weston) J.; m. Diantha Sibley Haviland, June 3, 1970; 1 child, Wallace Stephen III BA, Johns Hopkins U., 1957; PhD. U. Pa., 1968; postgrad., Harvard U. Law Sch., 1970-71. Prof. Asian langs. U. Kans., Lawrence, 1965—. Translator: The T'ang Code: General Principles, 1979; editor: A Concordance to the T'ang Code, 1965, An Index to the Pien-tzu lei-pien, 1967, A Concordance to the Kuan-tzu, 1970, A Concordance to the Han-fei tzu, 1975, A Reader in Chinese Literature, 1976, A Reader in Chinese Anthropology-Sociology, 1976, A Reader in Chinese International Relations, 1976, A Reader in Chinese Art History, 1976, (with Grace Wan) A Reader in Chinese History, 1972; editor Jour. Asian Legal History. Fellow Am. Council Leared Soc., 1970, Harvard U. Law Sch., 1970, Howard Found., 1972, Humboldt Found., 1972 Mem. Assn. for Asian Studies Home: 1633 Stratford Rd Lawrence KS 66044-2529 Office: U Kans Dept East Asian Langs Lawrence KS 66045-0001

JOHNSON, WALTER EARL, geophysicist; b. Denver, Dec. 16, 1942; s. Earl S. and Helen F. (Llewellyn) J.; m. Ramey Kandice Kayes, Aug. 6, 1967; children: Gretchen, Roger, Aniela. Grad. in Geophys. Engring., Colo. Sch. of Mines, 1966. Registered profl. engr., Colo.; cert. geologist, Colo. Geophysicist Pan Am. Petroleum Corp., 1966-73; seismic processing supr. Amoco Prodn. Co., Denver, 1973-74, marine tech. supr., 1974-76, divsn. processing cons., 1976-79; geophys. supr. No. Thrust Belt, Denver, 1979-80; chief geophysicist Husky Oil Co., Denver, 1981-82; exploration mgr. Rocky Mountain and Gulf Coast divsn., Denver, 1982-84; geophys. mgr. ANR Prodn. Co., Denver, 1985-99; pres. Exploration GeoCons., Inc., Denver, 2000—. Pres. Sch. Lateral Ditch Co.; cons. engr. Bd. dirs. Rocky Mountain Residence. Mem. Denver Geophys. Soc., Soc. Exploration Geophysicists. Republican. Baptist. Office: 1645 Court Pl Ste 309 Denver CO 80202-4507

JOHNSON, WALTER KLINE, civil engineer; b. Mpls., Aug. 28, 1923; s. Horace Edward and Ida Axelina (Kline) J.; m. Geneva Lorraine Olson, Sept. 2, 1950; children: Kristine Idelle, Karen Margaret, Konstance Louise. BCE, U. Minn., 1948, MS, 1951, PhD, 1963. Registered profl. engr., Minn. With Greeley and Hansen, Chgo., 1948-49, Infilco, Inc., Tucson, 1951-52, Toltz, King, Duvall, Anderson & Assocs., St. Paul, 1952-55; faculty U. Minn., Mpls., 1955—, assoc. prof. civil engring., 1965-74, prof., 1974-75; dir. planning Met. Waste Control Commn., St. Paul, 1975-89; mgmt. cons. in environ. engring. St. Paul, 1989—. Patentee wastewater sampler. Capt. USAAF, 1943-46. EPA rsch. fellow Brit. Water Pollution Rsch. Lab., 1971. Fellow ASCE (pres. N.W. sect. 1972-73), Am. Water Works Assn., Cen. State Water Environment Assn.; mem. Am. Acad. Environ. Engrs. (diplomate). Lutheran. Achievements include rsch. on biol. waste water treatment, sludge bulking, nitrogen removal by denitrification. Home: 5321 29th Ave S Minneapolis MN 55417-2010 E-mail: WKJ1@JUNO.COM.

JOHNSON, WARREN DOUGLAS, infectious diseases physician, researcher; b. Mt. Vernon, N.Y., Oct. 9, 1937; s. Warren D. and June Marie (Lavezzi) J.; m. Barbara Florence Bean, June 14, 1969; children: Christopher, Sarah, David, Matthew. BS, Carrol Coll., 1958; MD, Columbia U., 1962. Diplomate Am. Bd. Med. Examiners, Am. Bd. Internal Medicine with subspecialty in infectious diseases. Instr. in medicine Cornell U. Med. Coll., N.Y.C., 1967-69, asst. prof., 1969-74, dir. rsch. and tng. program at U. Bahia, 1969-79, assoc. prof. medicine, 1974-81, prof. medicine, 1981, dir. internat. health svcs., 1986—, chief divsn. internat. medicine, 1986, chief divsn. internat. medicine and infectious diseases, 1995—, B.H. Kean prof. tropical medicine, 1990—; from asst. to attending physician N.Y. Hosp., N.Y.C., 1969—. Mem. nat. adv. allergy and infectious diseases coun. NIAID, NIH, Washington, 1995-99, chmn. micro and infectious diseases rsch. coun., 1987-90; chmn. subspecialty bd. infectious diseases Am. Bd. Internal Medicine, 1996-00, bd. dirs. Contbr. over 200 sci. articles to profl. publs., chpts. to books. Mem. Demerest (N.J.) Sch. Bd., 1984-90. Capt. USAF, 1964-66. Recipient Emilio Ribas medal in infectious diseases Brazil Soc. Infectious Diseases, 1992; named Prof. Hon. Fed. U. Bahia, Brazil, 1989. Fellow ACP, N.Y. Acad. Scis., Infectious Disease Soc. Am., Royal Soc. Tropical Medicine; mem. Am. Soc. Tropical Medicine, Am. Clin. Climatology Assn., Assn. Am. Physicians. Lutheran. Avocations: gardening, cooking. Office: Cornell U Med Coll A421 1300 York Ave New York NY 10021-4805

JOHNSON, WAYNE D., gas industry executive; b. Winterset, Iowa, Sept. 20, 1932; s. Leslie E. and Ruth N. J.; m. Lynne Alice Brouwer, June 15, 1963; children: Christopher W., Kevin B. BA, U. Nebr., 1954; LLB, Harvard U., 1959. Bar: Ill. bar 1959. Assoc., then ptnr. Ross, Hardies, O'Keefe, Babcock & Parsons, Chgo., 1959-72; asst. gen. counsel Peoples Gas Co., Chgo., 1972-75; sr. v.p., gen. counsel Entex, Inc., Houston, 1975-78, pres., 1978-86, utility cons., 1986-87; pres. United Tex. Transmission Co., 1987-93, Am. Natural Gas Power, Inc., Houston, 1993-97; utility cons., 1997—. Dir. Simmons & Co., Internat., 1980—. Past chmn. Galveston Bay Found.; vice chmn. Sam Houston Area Coun., Boy Scouts Am.; mem. data integration team and demand task force Nat. Petroleum Coun., Com. on Natural Gas, 1998-2000. With U.S. Army, 1954-56. Woodrow Wilson fellow, 1954 Mem. Am. Gas Assn., So. Gas Assn. (past chmn.), Lawyer's Club (Chgo.). Home: 5517 Cedar Creek Houston TX 77056

JOHNSON, WAYNE HAROLD, librarian, retired municipal official; b. El Paso, Tex., May 2, 1942; s. Earl Harold and Cathryn Louise (Greeno) J.; m. Patricia Ann Froedge, June 15, 1973; children: Meredith Jessica (dec.), Alexandra Noëlle Victoria. BS, Utah State U., 1968; MPA, U. Colo., 1970; MLS, U. Okla., 1972. Circulation libr. Utah State U., Logan, 1968, adminstrv. asst. libr., 1969; with rsch. dept. Okla. Mgmt. and Engring. Cons., Norman, 1972; chief adminstrv. svcs. Wyo. State Libr., Cheyenne, 1973-76, chief bus. officer libr. archives and hist. dept., 1976-78, state libr., 1978-89; county grants mgr. Laramie County, Wyo., 1989-2001. Cons. in field. Trustee Bibliog. Ctr. for Rsch., Denver, pres., 1983, 84; mem. Cheyenne dist. Longs Park coun. Boy Scouts Am., 1982-86; active Cheyenne Frontier Days, 1975—; mem. admissions and allocation com. United Way, 1991-94; mem. Ho. of Reps., Wyo. Legislature, 1993-2004; mem. senate Wyo. Legis., 2005—; chmn. Transp. Hwys. Com., 1999-2004. With USCG, 1960—64. Mem. Aircraft Owners and Pilots Assn., Cheyenne C. of C. (chmn. transp. com. 1982, 83, mil. affairs com. 1994—), Am. Legion, Masons (Grand Lodge libr. 2001-, master Cheyenne Lodge No. 1, 2005-06), Kiwanis (bd. dirs. 1986-87), No. Colo. Yacht Club. Republican. Presbyterian.

JOHNSON, WEYMAN THOMPSON, JR., lawyer; b. Atlanta, July 13, 1951; s. Weyman Thompson Sr. and Dixie LaNé (Peevy) J.; m. E. Allison Forkner, July 13, 1974; children: Chloe Forkner, Willa Rose. BA, Mercer U., 1973; JD, U. Ga., 1979. Bar: Ga. 1979, U.S. Dist. Ct. (no. dist.) Ga. 1979, U.S. Ct. Appeals (4th and 11th cir.) 1983, U.S. Supreme Ct. 1989. Reporter Columbus (Ga.) Ledger Newspaper, 1973-75; assoc. Fisher & Phillips, Atlanta, 1979-83, ptnr., 1984; assoc. Paul, Hastings, Janofsky & Walker, Atlanta, 1984-88, ptnr., 1988—, mem. policy com., vice chmn. employment law dept. Adj. prof. U. Ga., Sch. Law, Ga. State U. Coll. Law. Author: Plant Closing Law, 1989, Negligence in Employment Law, 2002. Bd. deacons First Bapt. Ch., Decatur, 1984—, chmn., 1998, 2002; bd. dirs. Nat. Multiple Sclerosis Soc., 1995—, chmn. Ga. chpt. Atlanta, 1990—94; chair Governance Com., 2001—. Mem. ABA, State Bar Ga. (sec.-treas. labor sect. 1999-2000), Atlanta Bar Assn. (chmn. labor sect. 1989-90, bd. dirs. 1991-92), Indsl. Rels. Rsch. Assn., Ga. Def. Lawyers Assn., Nat. M.S. Soc. (bd. dirs. 1995—, v.chmn. 1998—), Eagles Landing Country Club. Office: Paul Hastings Janofsky & Walker 600 Peachtree St NE Fl 24 Atlanta GA 30308-2265 Office Phone: 404-815-2209. Business E-Mail: weymanjohnson@paulhastings.com.

JOHNSON, WILLARD RAYMOND, political science professor; b. St. Louis, Nov. 22, 1935; s. Willard and Dorothy (Stovall) J.; m. Vivian Robinson, Dec. 15, 1957; children: Caryn L., Kimberly E. BA, UCLA, 1957; MA, Johns Hopkins U., 1961; PhD, Harvard U., 1965. Asst. prof. polit. sci. MIT, Cambridge, Mass., 1964-69, assoc. prof., 1969-73, prof. polit. sci., 1973-96, prof. emeritus, 1996—. Vis. assoc. prof. Harvard U. Sch. Bus., Cambridge, 1969; exec. dir. Circle Inc., Roxbury, Mass., 1968-70; adj. prof. Fletcher Sch., Medford, Mass., 1971-82; cons. U.S. Nat. Commn. for Minority Enterprise, Washington, 1969; chmn. bd. Circle Inc. subs. Devel. Corp., 1970; mem. U.S. Commn. for UNESCO, Washington, 1960-66, Coun. Fgn. Rels., 1977-95. Author: The Cameroon Federation, 1970, (with Vivian R. Johnson) West African Governments and Volunteer Development Organizations, 1990; contbr. articles to Daedalus, 1973-82; New Eng. dir. Jour. African Civilizations, 1979-82, Jour. Modern African Studies, 1983, Negro History Bull., 2001; mem. editl. bd. Africa Today, 175-2001. Bd. dirs. TransAfrica and TransAfrica Forum, Washington, 1978-95, chmn., 1984-86, pres. Boston chpt., 1980-84, 89-90, Greater Roxbury Interfaith Housing Corp., Boston, 1970; chmn. Africa Policy Task Force, McGovern for Pres. campaign, 1972; sr. adv. bd. Boston Pan-African Forum, Inc., 1997—; pres. Kans. Inst. African Am. and Native Am. Family History, 1997—. Recipient M.L. King Jr. award MIT Pres.'s Office, 1982, YMCA Black Achiever's award, 1988; fellow and grantee Ford Found.; grantee Social Sci. Research Council, 1975, Rockefeller Found., 1977; Fulbright grantee, 1987; resident fellow Rockefeller Study Ctr., Bellagio, Italy, Sept. 1987; Fulbright scholar Indonesia, summer 1991. Mem. Assn. Concerned African Scholars (bd. dirs. 1977—, nat. co-chmn. 1984-89), African Studies Assn., Nat. Conf. of Black Polit. Scientists. Democrat. Baptist. Office: MIT Dept Polit Sci 30 Wadsworth St Cambridge MA 02142-1320 *I believe that personal and social health is based on responsible engagememt, creative action, reflective credulity, disciplined energy, and mutual respect.*

JOHNSON, WILLIAM ALEXANDER, clergyman, theology studies educator; b. Bklyn., Aug. 20, 1934; s. Charles Raphael and Ruth Augusta (Anderson) J.; m. Carol Genevieve Lundquist, June 11, 1955; children—Karin Ruth, Karl William, Krister Frederick. BA, Queens Coll., City U. N.Y., 1953; B.D. (Univ. fellow, Morrow Meml. fellow, Daniel Delaplaine fellow), Union Theol. Sem., 1956; Teol. Kand., Lund U., 1957, Teol. Lic., 1958, Teologie Doktor, 1962; MA, Columbia U., 1958, PhD (Univ. fellow, Rockefeller Bros. fellow), 1959. Ordained deacon Meth. Ch., 1955, priest Episcopal Ch., 1968. Profl. baseball player N.Y. Giants, 1949-51; dir. Boys Club, Salvation Army, Jamaica, N.Y., 1952-54; minister Mt. Hope and Teabo Meth. chs., Wharton, N.J., 1954-56; elder Meth. Ch., 1956; minister Immanuel and Union Meth. chs., Bklyn., 1957-59; asst. in instrn. Columbia U., N.Y.C., 1957, Union Theol. Sem., N.Y.C., 1958; instr., asst. prof. religion Trinity Coll., Hartford, Conn., 1959-63; lectr. philosophy and theology Hartford Sem. Found., 1961-62; assoc. prof. religion, chmn. dept. religion Drew U., Madison, N.J., 1963-66; research prof. religion NYU, N.Y.C., 1966; vis. lectr. Union Theol. Sem., N.Y.C., 1966; vis. prof. religion Princeton (N.J.) U., 1966-68; prof., chmn. dept. religion Manhattanville Coll., Purchase, N.Y., 1967-71; vis. prof. Christian ethics Gen. Theol. Sem., N.Y.C., 1970; Albert V. Danielsen prof. Christian thought, prof. philosophy and history of ideas Brandeis U., Waltham, Mass., 1971—, prof. Near Ea. and Jewish studies, 1988—; canon residentiary Cathedral Ch. of St. John The Divine, N.Y.C., 1973—. Vis. Prof. Protestant theology N.Am. Coll., Vatican City, 1969-75; vis. prof., Tokyo, Stockholm, 1979, U. Gothenburg, Sweden, 1979, U. Copenhagen, 1994-95, Univ. Perth, Australia, 1997, 99, 2001; examining chaplain Diocese of Arctic, 1982; lectr. in field. Author: The Philosophy of Religion of Anders Nygren, 1958, Christopher Polhem: The Father of Swedish Technology, 1963, Nature and the Supernatural in the Theology of Horace Bushnell, 1963, On Religion: A Study of Theological Method in

Schleiermacher and Nygren, 1964, Problems in Christian Ethics, 1965 (with Nels F.S. Ferré) Swedish Contributions to Modern Theology, 1966, The Search for Transcendence, 1974, The Christian Way of Death, 1974, Invitation to Theology, 1979, Philosophy and the Gospel, 1979, (with Moorhead Kennedy) Christianity and Terrorism, 1986, O Boundless Salvation, 1987; also articles; debut as Popolo in Aida, Met. Opera, 1989, Tosca, 1990, La Boheme, 1992. Democratic committeeman Hartford, 1960-63; mem. exec. com. Am. Friends Service Com., Coll. Div., 1966-70; bd. dirs. Queens Coll. CUNY; priest-in-charge Korean Episc. Ch., N.Y.C., 1992—. Recipient David F. Swenson-Kierkegaard Meml. award, 1964, Harbison award for Tchr. of Yr. Danforth Found., 1965; named Outstanding Young Man in Am. Jr. C. of C., 1964; Disting. Alumnus Queens Coll., 1980; Scandinavian-Am. Found. fellow, 1956, 85; Fulbright scholar U. Copenhagen, 1957-58; Dempster Grad. fellow Meth. Ch., 1958; Am. Philos. Soc. fellow, 1971, 85. vis. rsch. fellow Princeton, 1972; Guggenheim fellow for study in Rome, Italy, 1972; NSF grantee, 1978; Rockefeller fellow Aspen Inst., 1978, fellow Aspen Inst., Jerusalem, 1982; Nat. Endowment Humanities grantee, 1978, 86; grantee Arthur Vining Davis Found., 1981; grantee Trinity Ch. of N.Y.C., 1982, 84; grantee Tauber Inst. Study of European Jewry; named All-Am. Baseball Player, Amateur Athletic Assn., 1952, 53, All-Am. Soccer Player, Amateur Athletic Assn., 1953. Mem. Am. Acad. Religion, Asia Soc., Japan Soc., Scandinavian-Am. Heritage Soc., Am. Philos. Assn., Danforth Assos., Soc. for Sci. Study Religion, Soc. for Religion in Higher Edn. (Kent fellow 1959), Australian-Am. Assn., Shakespeare Soc. of Am. (academic advisor), Soc. Anglican Theologians, Vasa Order Am., Am. Soc. Christian Ethics, Swedish Pioneer Hist. Soc., Soc. for Scandinavian Study, Danish-Am. Soc., Australian-Am. Soc., Willa Cather Pioneer Meml. Found., Authors Guild, Episcopal Churchmen for South Africa, New Haven Theol. Group, Westchester Inst. Psychiatry and Psychoanalysis (dir.), Ecumenical Found. for Christian Ministry, English Speaking Union, Ch. Soc. for Coll. Work, Paris Am. Club, Columbia University Club, Met. Opera Club, The Pilgrims, Shakespeare Soc. Am. (acad. advisor), The Coffee House, Lotos Club (medal of hon., medal of merit 2004), Century Club, Explorer's Club, Phi Beta Kappa, Pi Gamma Mu, Phi Sigma Tau. Democrat. Episcopalian. Office: 27 Fox Meadow Rd Scarsdale NY 10583-2903 also: 44 Pascal Ave Rockport ME 04856-5918 Office Phone: 914-723-6389. *I have attempted in my life to fulfill the simple prayer of St. Francis: Lord, make me an instrument of your peace/Where there is hatred ... let me sow love/Where there is injury ... pardon/Where there is doubt ... faith/Where there is despair ... hope/Where there is darkness ... light/Where there is sadness ... joy. For it is giving that we receive; it is pardoning that we are pardoned; and it is dying that we are born to eternal life.*

JOHNSON, WILLIAM DAVID, retired academic administrator; b. Bloomington, Ind., Aug. 9, 1924; s. Ben and Ida Grace (Garlock) J.; m. Audrey Aelise Thurston; 1 child, Sheryn Aelise Johnson Peters BS, Ind. U., 1946. Asst. bursar U. Va., Charlottesville, 1947-54; comptroller George Washington U., 1954-69, dir. planning and budgeting, 1969-82, assoc. provost, 1982-84, provost, 1984-89. Served to 1st lt. U.S. Army, 1943-46; ETO Mem. Fin. Exec. Inst. (chpt. pres. 1969-70), Eastern Assn. Coll. and Univ. Bus. Officers, Nat. Assn. Coll. and Univ. Bus. Officers, Omicron Delta Kappa, Delta Chi Republican. Presbyterian. Avocations: woodworking, golf, skeet shooting. Home: 3440 S Jefferson St Apt 705 Falls Church VA 22041-3125

JOHNSON, WILLIAM DEAN, power company executive; b. Pa., Jan. 9, 1954; BA, Duke U., 1978; JD, U. N.C., 1982. Law clk. Hon. J.D. Philips Jr., U.S. Ct. Appeals, 4th Cir., 1982-83; assoc. Hunton & Williams, 1983-90, ptnr., 1990-92; assoc. gen. counsel Carolina Power & Light, Raleigh, 1992-95, v.p., corp. sec., 1995-1999, sr. v.p., corp. sec., 1999-2001; pres., CEO, Progress Energy Svc. Co., Raleigh, 2002—03; exec. v.p., gen. counsel, sec. Progress Energy, Inc., Raleigh, 2001—02, group pres. energy delivery, 2004—05, pres., COO, 2005—. Mem. ABA, N.C. Bar Assn. Office: Progress Energy Inc 411 Fayetteville Street Mall Raleigh NC 27601-1748 Office Phone: 919-546-6463. E-mail: bill.johnson@pgn.mail.com.

JOHNSON, WILLIAM G., neurologist, educator; MD, Columbia U., N.Y.C., 1967. Diplomate Am. Bd, Psychiatry and Neurology, 1977. Intern Medicine N.Y. Hosp. Cornell Med. Ctr., N.Y.C., 1967—68, resident medicine, 1968—69; fellow in Biochem. Genetics NIH, Bethesda, Md., 1969—72; physician dept. neurology Robert Wood Johnson U. Med. Group, New Brunswick, NJ, 1991—. Prof. neurology UMDNJ- Robert Wood Johnson Med. Sch., Piscataway, 1991—; dir. lab. neurogenetics, Piscataway, 1991—. Office Phone: 732-235-4508. Business E-Mail: wjohnson@umdnj.edu.

JOHNSON, WILLIAM HOWARD, agricultural engineer, educator; b. Sidney, Ohio, Sept. 3, 1922; s. Russell Earl and Dollie (Gamble) J.; m. Wyoma Jean Swift, Oct. 2, 1943; children: Lawrence Alan, Cheri Ellen, Dana Sue. BS, Ohio State U., 1948, MS, 1953; PhD, Mich. State U., 1960. Registered profl. engr. Mem. faculty Ohio Agrl. Expt. Sta., Wooster, 1948-64, Ohio Agrl. Rsch. and Devel. Ctr., Wooster, 1964-70, prof., assoc. chmn. dept. agrl. engring., 1959-70; part-time prof. Ohio State U., 1964-70; prof., head dept. agrl. engring. Kans. State U., Manhattan, 1970-81, dir. Engring. Expt. Sta., 1981-87. Cons. farm equipment cos. Author: (with B.J. Lamp) Principles, Equipment and Systems for Corn Harvesting, 1966; also articles. Recipient Disting. Alumnus award Coll. Engring., Ohio State U., 1974; named to Coll. Engring. Kans. State U. Hall of Fame, 1992. Fellow Am. Soc. Agrl. Engrs. (pres. 1986-87, McCormick-Case Gold Medal award 1994), Kans. Engring. Soc. (pres. 1985-86), Sigma Xi, Tau Beta Pi. Achievements include research on soil-plant-machine relationships, harvesting, design for soiltillers, planters, harvesters. Home: 2121 Meadowlark Rd #131 Manhattan KS 66502 Office: Kans State Univ Dept Agrl Engring Seaton Hall Manhattan KS 66506 Business E-Mail: wjohnson@ksu.edu.

JOHNSON, WILLIAM MICHAEL, physician; b. Olean, N.Y., Nov. 20, 1940; s. Loren Edward and Ann Elizabeth (Van Dyke) J.; m. Marlene Elsie Brill, June 26, 1965; children: Michael Scott, Susan Kim, Amy Marlene, Linda Marie. AB, Stanford U., 1963, MD, 1968; MPH, Harvard U., 1970, M in Indsl. Health, 1971. Diplomate Am. Bd. Internal Medicine, Am. Bd. Preventive Medicine. Intern, SUNY-Buffalo Hosps., 1968-69; resident in occupational medicine Harvard Sch. Public Health, Boston, 1969-71; acting dep. dir. div. field studies and clin. investigations Nat. Inst. Occupational Safety and Health Cin., 1971-73; resident in internal medicine U. Ariz. Hosps., Tucson, 1973-75, fellow in pulmonary disease, 1975-77; asst. prof. environ. health, adj. asst. prof. medicine U. Wash., Seattle, 1977-80; commd. lt. col. U.S. Army, 1980, advanced through grades to col., 1986; chief pulmonary disease svc. Dwight David Eisenhower Army Med. Ctr., Fort Gordon, Ga., 1983-93, staff, 1980-83; staff physician dept. Vet. Affairs Med. Ctr., Augusta, Ga., 1993-2004; pvt. cons., 2004; asst. clin. prof. medicine Med. Coll. Ga., Augusta, 1981-88, assoc. clin. prof. of medicine, 1988-1993, assoc. prof. medicine, 1995-2004. Contbr. articles on pulmonary disease and occupational cancer to profl. jours. Served as surgeon USPHS, 1971-73. Fellow Am. Coll. Chest Physicians; mem. Am. Thoracic Soc., Soc. Occupational and Environ. Health, N.Y. Acad. Scis. Home: 2948 Foxhall Cir Augusta GA 30907-3647 Office Phone: 706-863-4270. Business E-Mail: wmjohnson@knology.net.

JOHNSON, WILLIAM POTTER, publishing executive, director; b. Peoria, Ill., May 4, 1935; s. William Zweigle and Helen Marr (Potter) J.; m. Pauline Ruth Rowe, May 18, 1968; children: Darragh Elizabeth, William Potter. AB, U. Mich., 1957. Gen. mgr. Bureau County Rep., Inc., Princeton, Ill., 1961-72; pres. Johnson Newspapers, Inc., Sebastopol, Calif., 1972-75, Evergreen, Colo., 1974-86, Canyon Commons Investment, Evergreen, 1974—, Johnson Media, Inc., Granby, Colo., 1987—. Author: How the Michigan Betas Built a $1,000,000 Chapter House in the '80s. Alt. del. Rep. Nat. Conv., 1968. Lt. USNR, 1958-61. Mem.: Nat. Newspaper Assn., Colo. Press Assn., Vero Beach Yacht Club, Beta Theta Pi. Home: 8820 S Sea Oaks Way #204 Vero Beach FL 32963 Office: PO Box 409 Granby CO 80446-0409

JOHNSON, WILLIAM R., food products executive; m. Suzie Johnson; children: Brad, Tracy. Grad., UCLA; MBA, U. Tex. Asst. prod. mgr. Behold Furniture Polish, 1974; gen. mgr., new businesses, Heinz USA H.J. Heinz Co., Pitts., 1982—84, v.p., new businesses, Heinz USA, 1984—88, pres., CEO, pet products, 1988—92, head, Starkist, 1992, sr. v.p., pet products, Starkist, Asia/Pacific oper., 1993—96, pres., COO, 1996—98, pres., CEO, 1998—, chmn., 2000—. Bd. dirs. H.J. Heinz Co., 1993—, Clorox Co., Ga.-Pacific Corp., Grocery Mfr. Am. Bd. dirs. Extra Mile Found.; mem. Athena Awards Com.; chair, ann. campaign United Way Western Pa., 2001. Office: PO Box 57 600 Grant St Pittsburgh PA 15219-2702*

JOHNSON, WILLIAM STANLEY, metal distribution company executive; b. Elmhurst, Ill., May 11, 1957; s. Raymond J. and Nancy A. (Zinns) J.; m. Lisa Ann Grundy, July 14, 1990; 1 child, William Chase. BS in Bus. and Acctg., Ind. U., 1979; MBA in Fin., Mercer U., 1986. CPA, Calif.; CFP. Auditor, sr. auditor Ernst & Young, CPA's, Indpls., 1979-80; various fin. and acctg. positions Am. Hosp. Supply Co., Evanston, Ill., 1980-86; v.p. fin., dir. acctg. Abbey Med./Beaverbrook Group, Costa Mesa, Calif., 1987-91; corp. fin. mgr. Severin Group, Ivrine, Calif., 1991-94; corp. contr., CFO, Earle M. Jorgensen Co., Brea, Calif., 1994—. Mem. adj. faculty U. Phoenix, Fountain Valley, Calif., 1998—. Mem. FEI, AICPA, Calif. Soc. CPA's. Home: 744 Via Lido Soud Newport Beach CA 92663-5558*

JOHNSON, WILLIAM T., religious organization administrator, organist; s. Gerald T. and Elaine K. Johnson. BA, Edgecliff Coll. Xavier U., 1982. Cert. organist Meth. Theol. Sch. Ohio, 2004. Music dir., organist Holy Name Cath. Ch., Columbus, Ohio, 1995—98, St. Mary Cath. Ch., Delaware, 1998—2004; organist Our Lady Victory Cath. Ch., Columbus, 2002—04; asst. organist St. John Bapt. Cath. Ch., 2000—04; music dir., organist St. Peter Cath. Ch., Mansfield, 2004—. Organist, Columbus, 1998—; instr. music, Mansfield, 2004—. Mem.: Nat. Assn. Pastoral Musicians, Am. Guild Organists, Ohio Geneal. Soc., New Eng. Hist. Geneal. Soc., Hon. Order Ky. Cols., Chi Phi. Democrat. Roman Catholic. Avocation: genealogy. Office: St Peter Cath Ch 104 West First St Mansfield OH 44902 Office Phone: 419-524-2572 2113.

JOHNSON, WYLIE PIERSON, electric utility executive; b. Montgomery, Ala., Mar. 28, 1919; BSME, Auburn U., 1942; postgrad., Cornell U., 1943, Ga. Inst. Tech., 1959. Registered profl. engr., Ala. Engr. Ala. Power Co., Montgomery, 1946-52, supr. transmission lines Birmingham, 1952-58, supt. transmission, 1958-66, supt. spl. svcs., 1966-74, mgr. gen. svcs., 1974-76, ret., 1976. Chmn. transmission and large substation com. Southeastern Electric Exchange, Atlanta, 1962-66. Contbr. articles to profl. jours. Chief insp. Election Ofcls., Montgomery County, Ala., 1980-93; pres. Pike Rd. Vol. Fire Dept. Bd., 1985-86. Served to lt. USS Grainger, USNR, 1943-46, PTO. Mem. IEEE (chmn. Ala. sect. 1962-63), ASME, Montgomery Geneal. Soc. (v.p.), SAR (pres. Richard Montgomery chpt. 1989-91, pres. Ala. State soc. 1997, nat. trustee 1998), Birmingham Engrs. Club (chmn. budget and fin. 1961), Green Valley Country Club, The Club, Young Men's Bus. Club, Exch. Club (pres. Vestavia Club 1974-75), Capital City Club, Rotary (pres.-elect Tuskegee club 1998), Masons, Shriners, Lambda Chi Alpha. Baptist. Avocation: wild life preservation. Home: 1991 Shades Crest Rd Birmingham AL 35216-1429

JOHNSON, YVONNE AMALIA, elementary school educator, consultant; b. DeKalb, Ill., July 1, 1930; d. Albert O. and Virginia O. (Nelson) J. *Albert and Virginia spent their lifetimes farming. Albert's father returned to DeKalb after the Gold Rush. He homesteaded land which later became the family farm. Albert's mother was charter member of 1st Lutheran Church in DeKalb in 1858. Virginia's father was a blacksmith and made one of the first firewagons for DeKalb. Albert was a charter member of the DeKalb County Farm Bureau when it was established in 1912. Virginia did missionary work for Lutheran Church. Elaine, sister, was teacher and worked in the poultry division of DeKalb Agricultural Association, with Kenneth, brother. Elaine's husband, Leo, was the communications director for DeKalb Agricultural Association and developed the company logo.* BS in Edn., No. Ill. State Tchrs. Coll., 1951; MS in Edn., No. Ill. U., 1960. Tchr. Love Rural Sch., DeKalb, 1951-53, West Elem. Sch., Sycamore, Ill., 1953—2002; coord. Media Ctr. West Sch. Ill. honors sci. tchr., ISU, 1985-87. Contbr. articles to profl. publs. Bd. dirs. Sycamore Pub. Libr., 1974-98, pres. bd. dirs., 1984-98, chmn. maj. fund drive for addition to libr., 1994-98; founder Dekalb County Excellence in Edn. award, 1999; bd. trustees Midwest Mus. Natural History, 2002—Named DeKalb County Conservation Tchr., 1971, Gov.'s Master Tchr., State of Ill., 1984, Outstanding Agrl. Tchr. in the Classroom Dekalb County Farm Bur., 1993; grantee NSF, 1961, 62, 85, 86, 87, NASA, 1988; Sci. Lit. grantee State of Ill., 1992-94. Mem. NEA, NSTA (cert. in elem. sci.), Ill. Sci. Tchrs. Assn., Ill. Edn. Assn., Sycamore Edn. Assn., Coun. for Elem. Sci. Internat. Office: West Elem Sch 240 Fair St Sycamore IL 60178-1641

JOHNSON-BROWN, LINDA LEE, music educator; b. Anchorage, Alaska, Dec. 19, 1952; d. Charles Arthur Johnson and Marion Lorraine Bancroft-Johnson; m. Raymond Lee Brown, July 5, 1980; children: Michelle, Lorri, Joshua, Jennifer, Jacqui, Daniel; m. Robert Michael Arnold, Dec. 22, 1976 (div. Jan. 15, 1979); 1 child, Lorraine Marie. MusB, Ill. State U., 1976; MEd, Marygrove Coll., 2000. Tchr. Joliet (Ill.) Pub. Schs., 1976—79, Herscher (Ill.) Cmty. Schs., 1979—80, Watseka (Ill.) Cmty. Schs., 1980—81, St. Anne (Ill.) Pub. Schs., 1981—82, Donovan (Ill.) Cmty. Schs., 1985—90, Shelby County Pub. Schs., Memphis, 1990—94; tchr. Dillon Elem. Carman-Ainsworth Cmty. Schs., Flint, Mich., 1994—. Mem. curriculum devel. fine arts com. State of Ill., Watseka, 1989; mem. task force Gov. Jennifer Grandholms, Flint, 2003. Pres. Kid's for Am. America's Fund Afghan Orphans, Flint, 2001—02; min. music Assemblies of God, 1995—2003. Mem.: DAR, Music Educators Nat. Conf., Music Educators Assn. Republican. Avocations: reading, history, writing, music, singing. Home: 13490 Lakebrook Drive Fenton MI 48430 Office: Carman Ainsworth Community Schs Dillon Elem 1197 E Schumacher Ave Burton MI 48529

JOHNSON-COHEN, YEVONNE B., minister, counselor; b. Flint, Mich., July 22, 1951; d. Andrew L. and Barbara Elizabeth Johnson; m. Benton Kline Cohen, May 31, 2004; 1 child, Nevlynn L. Johnson. BA, MA, Mich. State U., 1982; MDiv, Louisville (Ky.) Presbyn. Sem., 1997. LCSW Mich. Bd. Social Work, 2002; lic. profl. counselor Mich. Dept. Cmty. Health, 2002. Min. additions counselor God's Ho. Mission, Owings Mills, Md., 2000—. Author: A Miracle in the House; co-prodr.: (films) Women and Addiction. Urban counselor God's Ho. Mission, Owings Mills, Md., 2000—04. Grantee, Profl. Bus. Women Flint, Mich., 1979. Mem.: NCADD (assoc.), Counselors Networking Assn. (assoc.), Sarasota Acad. Christian Counseling (assoc.). Achievements include development of female specific clinical addictions program; spiritual enrichment program for addictions program; clinical library for female addictions program. Avocations: travel, cooking, reading, community outreach. Office: Gods House Mission 8705 Groffs Mill Drive Owings Mills MD 21117 Office Phone: 410-654-5442. Personal E-mail: ybcohen@comcast.net. E-mail: ghmission@comcast.net.

JOHNSON-D'ALESSIO, ANNA, writer, poet; b. Villa Littoria, Italy, June 19, 1959; arrived in Canada, 1964; d. Frank and Rosa D'Alessio; m. Robert Johnson, June 29, 1985. Student, St. Clair Coll., 1980—81, Internat. Corr. Sch., 1984, Lifetime Career Schs., 1986, Nat. Edn. Corp., 1990—91. Waitress, hostess, cashier La Cusine Restaurant, Windsor, 1979—82; hostess Viscount Hotel, Windsor, Canada, 1982—83; sales agt. Jacobson's, Grosse Pointe, Mich., 1989—99. Author: (poetry) A Place Within, 2001, (anthology) Be Content, Poet Speaks Out; contbr. poems to lit. publs.; rec. artists: CD You Don't Really Know. Recipient Golden Poet award, 1989, Poet of Yr. medallion, 2003, Wall of Tolerance award, 2004, Internat. Poet of Merit award, 2004, Shakespeare Trophy of Excellence award, 2004, Outstanding Achievement in Poetry, 2004, High Merit award, 2004, Silver Award Bowl, Commemoreate Award Mediallion, Internat. Soc. of Poets, others. Mem.: Wayne State U. Alumni Assn., Detroit Inst. Arts, Famous Poet Soc. (award 1990—, trophy of excellence 2002), Internat. Soc. Poetry (award 1989—, Poet of Merit award 2003, Bronze Commemorative award medallion 2002). Roman Catholic. Avocations: interior decorating, crafts, knitting, dance, music. Home: 665 W Warren Ave Apt 312 Detroit MI 48201 Office: Authorhouse Ste 200 1663 Liberty Dr Bloomington IN 47403

JOHNSON-LEIPOLD, HELEN P., outdoor recreation company executive; b. 1957; V.p. consumer mktg. svcs. worldwide SCJ, 1992-95, exec. v.p. N.Am. businesses, 1995-97, v.p. personal and home care products, 1997-98, v.p. worldwide consumer products-mktg., 1999; chmn., CEO Johnson Outdoors (formerly Johnson Worldwide Assocs. Inc.), Miami Beach, Fla., 1999—. Office: 555 Main St Racine WI 53403 Office Fax: 262-631-6601.

JOHNSON-MORAN, KELLY KATHLEEN, health facility administrator, writer; b. Milw., Wis., Sept. 10, 1977; d. Clay Phillip Johnson; m. Darren Michael Moran, Aug. 17, 2002. Cert. CNA, Aurora Health Care, 1999. Asst. mgr. CNA Brotoloc Health Care Sys., Muskego, Wis., 1999—2001; caregiver CNA Luth. Soc. Svcs., Waukesha, Wis., 2002—03; resident coord. Creative living Environ., Milw., 2003—. Author: Forty-Second Street, 2002, An Insomniac's Dream, 2005, When the Leaves Stop Falling, 2005. Vol. Big Brothers/Big Sisters, Milw., 2002—, Spl. Olympics, Milw., 2004—. Recipient Editor's Choice award, Nat. Libr. of Poetry, 1993. Democrat. Roman Cath. Avocations: reading, writing, crafts, films, volunteer work. E-mail: authorkellymoran@aol.com.

JOHNSON OF THE LATERAN SEE, BARON RUTHERFORD BARRY, economist; s. Chevalier Ralph Barry and Lady Marianne Faircloth Johnson. BS in Applied Physics with Honor, Ga. Inst. Tech., 2000, MS, 2003. Assoc. R. Barry Johnson Cons., Huntsville, Ala., 1996—. Contbr. articles to profl. jours.; composer: (piano and organ music) Birthday Music for Archduke Otto von Habsburg. Operational auxiliarist (highest status) USCG Aux. - Dept Homeland Security, 1995. Recipient Knight Comdr. of the Order of San Marino, The Most Serene Republic of San Marino, 2005, Knight of the Order of St. Sylvester, Pope and Martyr, Vatican City-State, 2004, Eagle Scout with Bronze Palm, Boy Scouts of Am., 1992; fellow, Soc. Antiquaries Scotland, 2001. Fellow: Internat. Soc. Philos. Enquiry (sec. 2002—05); mem.: Soc. Colonial Wars, Gamma Sigma Delta, Omicron Delta Epsilon. Irish Catholic. Avocations: sailing, horseback riding, ballroom dancing, music, history.

JOHNSON-PAYTON, LORI RENEE, systems engineer; b. Jacksonville, N.C., Dec. 27, 1967; d. Robert Russa and Louise Margaret Johnson; m. Daryl Spencer Payton, June 8, 1996; 1 child, Joshua Payton. BS in Sys. Engring., U. Va., 1991; MS in Indsl. Engring., Ga. Inst. Tech., 1992; M Cert. in Project Mgmt., George Washington U., 1998; PhD, U. of Va., 1997. Solutions/product planner desktop sys. pers. computing divsn. IBM Corp., Research Triangle Park, NC, 1997—99, program mgr. desktop sys., 2000; spl. bids and ops. program mgr. desktop sys. IBM Corp., Research Triangle Park, NC, 2000—01; engring. cons. bid re-engring. group IBM Corp., Research Triangle Park, 2001—. Contbr. articles to profl. jours. Fellow, GEM Found., 1991—92; scholar, NSF, 1993—95. Mem.: PMI Inst., Inst. For Ops. Rsch. and the Mgmt. Sci., Soc. of Risk Analysis, Nat. Soc. of Black Engineers, Tau Beta Pi, Delta Sigma Theta, Alpha Kappa Psi. Avocations: running, travel, swimming, aerobics, piano. Home: 101 Covewood Court Durham NC 27713 Office: IBM Corporation 3039 Cornwallis Rd Bldg 002/JJ326 Research Triangle Park NC 27709 Personal E-mail: ljohnson_payton@hotmail.com. E-mail: ljp@us.ibm.com.

JOHNSON VELAZCO, NANCY RUTH, marketing professional; b. Phila., Feb. 4, 1948; d. Samuel Blaine and Ruth Dorothy (Carpenter) Johnson; m. Julio Horacio Velazco, Dec. 6, 1982 (div. Oct. 1984); 1 child, Cristine. BA in Spanish, Ursinus Coll., Collegeville, Pa., 1970; MA in Spanish, Villanova U., 1974; MBA, The Wharton Sch. U. Pa., 1978. Secondary tchr. Spanish, William Penn Sch. Dist., Lansdowne, Pa., 1970-76; indsl. rsch. analyst indsl. rsch. unit Wharton Sch., U. Pa., Phila., 1976-78; sales rep. pharma. Eli Lilly & Co., Providence, 1978-79, market rsch. analyst Indpls., 1979-80, mktg. mgr. Buenos Aires, 1980-82; Intron product mgr., bus. devel. mgr. Schering Plough Corp., Miami, Fla., 1983-84, regional mktg. dir. for L.Am., 1984-89, dir. respiratory, dermatology and antifungals Kenilworth, N.J., 1989-90, sr. mktg. dir. global mktg., 1991—2003; sr. dir. Global Profl. Svcs., 2003—. Author: The Political, Economic and Labor Climates in Mexico, 1977, The Political, Economic and Labor Climates in Peru, 1978; patentee # 6, 297, 227 B1. Chmn. party events Children's Specialized Hosp., Mountainside, N.J., 1994—; mem. bd. trustees Meadowland Hosp., Secaucus, N.J. Mem. Nat. Soc. DAR (treas. Westfield chpt. 1995-2002). Republican. Office: Schering-Plough Corp 2000 Galloping Hill Rd Kenilworth NJ 07033-1328 E-mail: nancy.johnson@spcorp.com.

JOHNSTON, BERNARD FOX, foundation executive, writer; b. Taft, Calif, Nov. 19, 1934; s. Bernard Lowe and Georgia Victoria (Fox) J.; m. Audrey Rhoades, June 9, 1956 (div. Sept. 1963); 1 child, Sheldon Bernard. BA in Creative Arts, San Francisco State U., 1957, MA in World Lit., 1958. Lectr. philosophy Coll. of Marin, Kentfield, Calif., 1957-58; lectr. humanities San Francisco State U., 1957-58, 67-68; instr. English Contra Costa Coll., San Pablo, Calif., 1958-63; Knowles Found. philosophy fellow, 1962; fellow Syracuse U., 1964-66; freelance writer Piedmont, Calif., 1968-77; pres. Cinema Repertory, Inc., Point Richmond, Calif., 1978-89; pres., exec. dir. Athena Found., Tiburon, Calif., 1990—, Incline Village, Nev., 1990—. Exec. prodr. (TV series) The Heroes of Time, (TV documentary) The Shudder of Awe; CEO The Athena Found., Inc., 1997, Mahler Festival, U. Colo., Boulder, 1998; guest lectr. Sierra Nev. Coll., 2005; lectr. in field Author: (screenplay) Point Exeter, 1979, Ascent Allowed, 1988 (award); author, editor: Issues in Education: An Anthology of Controversy, 1964, The Literature of Learning, 1971; festival pianist Lake Tahoe Internat. Film Festival, 1998; resident pianist Tahoe-Chrysler Corp., 1998; pianist (CD) Time Remembered; musical dir., featured pianist Lake Tahoe Summer Music Series, 2000, piano soloist Sierra Nevada Coll. Presdl. Dinner, 2000; featured pianist Lake Tahoe Hebrew Assn. Concert, 2001, Tahoe Forest Hosp. benefit, Lake Tahoe, Lake Tahoe Wildlife Benefit, 2003; pianist San Francisco State U. Athletic Awards Ceremony, 2001, Squaw Creek Resort, Lake Tahoe Forest Benefit, concert, featured pianist, 2001, 03; featured pianist Thunderbird Lodge, Lake Tahoe, 2003, (North Tahoe Jury Arts award 2004), Roseville Art Exhibit, 2004; essay Bound for Glory. Arts grantee Silicon Valley Cmty. Found., 1998; recipient TV Arts award Krisch Found., 2001; Bell-Brook Talent TV Award, 1950. Mem. Dirs. Guild Am., Writers Guild Am., Coun. for Basic Edn., Wilson Ctr. Assocs., Assn. Lit. Scholars and Critics, Smithsonian Instn., Donner Land Trust, Nat. Assn. Scholars, Calif. Assn. Scholars, San Francisco State Alumni Assn., Commonwealth Club of Calif. Avocations: classical and jazz piano, backpacking, softball. Office: 845 Southwood Blvd Ste 50 Incline Village NV 89451-9463 Personal E-mail: athenaprods@powernet.net.

JOHNSTON, CARDEN, emergency physician, pediatrician; b. Birmingham, Ala., Nov. 23, 1936; MD, U. Ala., 1961. Intern Wilford Hall Meml. Hosp., Lackland AFB, Tex., 1961-62; resident Charity Hosps. La., New Orleans, 1964-66; resident pediat. Hosp. Sick Children, London, 1966-67; active staff Children's Hosp., Birmingham, 1975—. Prof. pediat. U. Ala., Birmingham, 1992-95, emeritus prof., 1995—. Fellow RCP; mem. AMA, Am. Acad. Pediat. (pres. 2003-04), Am. Coll. Emergency Physicians. Office: Childrens Hosp Ala 1600 7th Ave S Ste 1 Birmingham AL 35233-1785

JOHNSTON, CAROLYN JUDITH, construction engineer; b. Atlanta, Nov. 24, 1961; d. Lynn H. and Doris S. (Lacy) J.; m. Paul William Miller, July 20, 1996; 1 child, Savannah Lee. BS in Constrn. Mgmt., So. Tech. U., 1990; MS in Constrn. Mgmt., Clemson U., 1997. Cert. profl. constructor. Journeyman plumber Quality Mech., Norfolk, Va., 1984-86; asst. supt. R.G.Moore Bldg., Virginia Beach, Va., 1986-87; asst. field engr. Holder Constrn., Atlanta, 1987-89; clk. of works Sharondale Constrn., Atlanta, 1989-90; constrn. engr. Bechtel, Aiken, S.C., 1990-95; project engr. R.W. Allen & Assocs., Augusta, Ga., 1995-97; project mgr. York Internat., Aiken, S.C., 1997-99; sr. project mgr. ACTS, Inc., New Ellenton, S.C., 2000; Bell Co. project engr. U.S. Dept.

Energy Project/Tritium Extraction Facility, Aiken, SC, 2001—02; planner, scheduler Handscomb, Faithful & Guild Honda Mfg. Plant, 2002—05; spl. projects mgr. Atlanta airport multiple projects Limbach, Inc., 2005—. Nat. Assn. Women Constrn. scholar, Atlanta, 1990. Mem. Am. Inst. Constructors, Profl. Constrn. Estimators (sec. 1996-98, newsletter editor 1996-98), Nat. Mgmt. Assn., Constrn. Specification Inst. Office: Limbach Inc 600 Bohannon Rd Fairburn GA 30213-2898 Home: 1415 Brawley Cir NE Atlanta GA 30319 Office Phone: 678-479-1000. Personal E-mail: carolyn.johnston@limbachinc.com.

JOHNSTON, CATHERINE VISCARDI, former magazine publisher; Grad., Manhattanville Coll., 1975. With House & Garden mag., 1977; acct. exec. GQ mag., 1980; former pub. Mirabella mag., N.Y.C.; pub. Mademoiselle mag., N.Y.C., 1995-96; sr. v.p. sales & mktg. Conde Nast Publs., 1996—97, exec. v.p. sales & mktg. N.Y.C., 1997—99. Recipient Disting. Alumni award, Manhattanville Coll., 2000.

JOHNSTON, CYNTHIA FAE, elementary school educator; b. Ogden, Utah, Aug. 26, 1948; d. Francis H. and Idamay (Lindsay) Johnston. BS, Weber State Coll., 1970; postgrad., U. Utah, Utah State U., Galludet U. Tchr., grade 1 Weber Sch. Dist., Ogden, Sch. Dist. 1, Rock Springs, Wyo.; tchr., grade 2 Weber Sch. Dist., Ogden; ret., 2004. Mem.: Ret. Tchrs. Assn., Delta Kappa Gamma.

JOHNSTON, CYRUS CONRAD, JR., medical educator; b. Statesville, NC, July 16, 1929; m. Marjorie Tarkington, Feb. 20, 1960; 2 children. BA, Duke U., 1951, MD, 1955. Diplomate Am. Bd. Internal Medicine. Intern Duke Hosp., Durham, N.C., 1955-56; resident in medicine Barnes Hosp., St. Louis, 1956-57; rsch. fellow in endocrinology and metabolism Ind. U., Indpls., 1959-61, instr. medicine, 1961-63, asst. prof., 1963-67, assoc. prof., 1967-69, prof. medicine, 1969-97, disting. prof. medicine, 1997—2002, disting. prof. emeritus, 2002—; assoc. dir. Gen. Clin. Rsch. Ctr. Ind. U. Med. Ctr., Indpls., 1962-67, program dir., 1967-72, prin. investigator, 1968-88, dir. divsn. endocrinology and metabolism, 1968-94. Mem. aging rev. com. Nat. Inst. Aging, 1982-85, chmn. geriatrics rev. com., 1985-86; mem. nursing sci. rev. com. NIH, 1988-89; mem. com. for protection of human subjects Ind. U.-Purdue U., Indpls., 1966—, chmn., 1978—; chmn. Nat. Osteoporosis Found. Sci. Adv. Bd., 1992-96; med. adv. panel Paget's Disease Found., 1989—; bd. trustees Nat. Osteoporosis Found., 1992—, pres., 1996-2001; mem. Nat. Adv. Coun. on Aging, 1992-95. Assoc. editor Bone and Mineral, 1985-94, Bone, 1995-2004; editl. bd. Jour. Bone and Mineral Rsch., Jour. Clin. Endocrinology and Metabolism, 1988-91. Capt. USAF, 1957-59. Recipient Career Rsch. Devel. award USPHS, 1963-68, Sandoz prize Internat. Assn. Gerontology, 1993, Experience Excellence Recognition award Glenn W. Irwin, Jr., MD, 2001. Mem. ACP, AAAS, AMA, Am. Assn. Clin. Endocrinologists (Yank D. Coble, Jr. M.D. Disting. Svc. award 1998), Am. Fedn. Clin. Rsch., Am. Soc. for Bone and Mineral Rsch. (Frederic C. Bartter award 1996), Am. Clin. and Climatological Soc., Ctrl. Soc. for Clin. Rsch., Endocrine Soc., Sigma Xi. Office: Indiana U Dept Medicine 541 N Clinical Dr CL 459 Indianapolis IN 46202-5112 E-mail: cjohnsto@iupui.edu.

JOHNSTON, DAVID CARTER, performing company executive, theater educator; b. Moline, Ill., Dec. 20, 1951; s. Clayton Eugene and Doris Elaine Johnston; m. Sally Kathleen Sefton, June 13, 1992; 1 child, Anneka Kathleen. BA in Speech and Theatre, Augustana Coll., Rock Island, Ill., 1973; MFA in Theatre and Directing, U. Oreg., Eugene, 1981. Secondary edn. tchg. cert. Augustana Coll., 1973. Freelance theatre dir., 1973—90; grad. tchg. fellow U. Oreg., Eugene, 1979—81; co-founder Essential Theatre Alliance, Eugene, 1980—82; acting tchr. Lane C.C., Eugene, 1982—82; co-founder Circa 21 Children's Theatre, Rock Island, Ill., 1983; artistic dir. Maui Acad. of Performing Arts, Wailuku, Maui, Hawaii, 1992—. Ops. mgr. Circa 21 Dinner Theatre, Rock Island, Ill., 1976—78. Dir.: over 80 theatrical prodns.including profl., univ. and coll., summer stock, touring and children's theatre shows throughout US. Bd. dirs. Haleakala Waldorf Sch., 2000—04; steering com. mem. Kauleo: Maui Arts Edn. Advocates, 2004—05. Recipient Donald Tornquist Excellence in Theatre award, 1973. Avocations: golf, walking, nature, reading. Home: 2832 Kekaulike Ave Kula HI 96790 Office: Maui Acad Performing Arts 81 N Church St Wailuku HI 96793 Office Phone: 808-244-8760. Home Fax: 808-244-6530; Office Fax: 808-244-6530. Personal E-mail: david@mauiacademy.org. E-mail: david @mauiacademy.org.

JOHNSTON, EDWARD ALLAN, lawyer; b. Balt., Sept. 25, 1921; s. William Henry and Hattie Frisby (Sanner) J.; m. Dorothy Janet Swart, June 23, 1951 (dec. Jan. 1994); children: Elizabeth Janet, Jean Taylor; m. Mary Ellen Kinnaird, Apr. 15, 1995. BBA, U. Balt., 1942, BS, 1947, LLB, 1949, LLM, 1957. Bar: Md. 1949; CPA, Md. Assoc. Whiteford, Taylor & Preston, Balt., 1954-62, ptnr., 1962—. Lectr. taxes U. Balt., 1948-65; bd. dirs. Dunbar Armored Express Inc. Pres. Dickeyville Assn., 1960; bd. dirs. Contact-Balt., 1974-80, chmn. bd., 1976-80; trustee Asbury Found., 1970—; trustee The Wesley Home, Inc., 1985-92; v.p., gen. counsel Soc. of Srs., 1983—; gen. counsel Ea. Srs. Golf Assn., Inc., 1988—; chmn. of adminstrv. bd. Meth. Ch., 1965-69, 88-90, trustee, chmn. bd., 1977-87. Recipient Alumnus of Yr. award U. Balt., 1980; named into Athletic Hall Fame, U. Balt., 2004. Mem. U. Balt. Alumni Assn. (pres. 1975-76), Md. Golf Assn. (v.p. 1960-67, pres. 1968), Mid. Atlantic Golf Assn. (v.p. 1978-81, pres. 1982, gen. counsel 1983—), Balt. Country Club (golf com., house commn., bd. govs. 1989-95, exec. com., treas. fin. com. 1991-95, v.p. 1992-93, pres. 1993-95). Home: 4104 Ravenhurst Cir Glen Arm MD 21057-9767 Office: Whiteford Taylor & Preston 210 W Pennsylvania Ave Ste 400 Baltimore MD 21204-5332 Office Phone: 410-832-2029. Business E-Mail: ejohnston@wtplaw.com.

JOHNSTON, FRANCIS CLAIBORNE, JR., lawyer; b. Richmond, Va., Jan. 6, 1943; s. Francis Claiborne and Virginia (Williams) J.; m. Carolyn Satterfield, Dec. 5, 1970; children: Angier Williams, Francis Claiborne III. AB magna cum laude, Princeton U., 1964; LLB, U. Va., 1967. Bar: Va. 1967, U.S. Dist. Ct. (ea. dist.) Va. 1968, U.S. Ct. Appeals (4th cir.) 1968. Assoc. Mays & Valentine, Richmond, 1968-72; ptnr. Mays & Valentine LLP, Richmond, 1972—; mng. ptnr. Mays & Valentine, Richmond, 1987-91. Adj. asst. prof. T.C. Williams Sch. Law, U. Richmond, 1974-76. Mem. session and diaconate 1st Presbyn. Ch., Richmond; bd. dirs. 1st Presbyn. Ch. Endowment Fund, Inc., 1972—, pres., 1993—; bd. dirs. Westham Civic Assn., 1984-86, Westminster-Canterbury Found., 1986-91, Westminster-Canterbury Corp., 1996-2000, vice-chmn. 1999; bd. dirs. Va. Post-Conviction Assistance Project, 1991-2000, pres., 1996-98; bd. dirs. Libr. of Va., 1997—, vice-chmn., 2000; trustee Valentine Mus., Richmond, 1980-89; bd. dirs. Westminster Presbyn. Homes Inc., 2000—. Fellow Am. Bar Found., Va. Law Found. (bd. dirs. 1991-94); mem. ABA (Ho. Dels. 1992-98), Va. Bar Assn. (chmn. exec. com. 1988, pres. 1990), Richmond Bar Assn., Assn. of Bar of City of N.Y., Am. Law Inst., Commonwealth Club, Country Club Va., Forum Club, Farmington Country Club. Home: 7009 Lakewood Dr Richmond VA 23229-6933 Office: Troutman Sanders Mays & Valentine 1111 E Main St Richmond VA 23219-3531 also: PO Box 1122 Richmond VA 23218-1122

JOHNSTON, FRANK MARION, retired general practice physician; b. Macon, Ga., Dec. 6, 1928; s. Thomas Allen and Frances Marion (Driggers) J.; m. Eugenia Elliott, Jan. 10, 1950 (div. 1975); children: Allene, Eugenia, Frank Marion Jr.; m. Margaret Moore, Dec. 31, 1975 (dec. 1989); m. Carol Lasell Hoskins, July 31, 1993 (div. 2001). BA, Emory U., Atlanta, 1953; MD, Med Coll. Ga., 1959. Diploamte Am. Bd. Psychiatry and Neurology. Intern Emory U. Hosp., Atlanta, 1959-60; resident Med. Coll. Ga. Hosps., 1960-63; pvt. practice psychiatry and gen. medicine Savannah, Ga., 1965-77; pvt. practice gen. medicine Spring Hill, Fla., 1983-97; med. dir. Community Mental Health Ctr. of Middle Ga., Dublin, 1977-80, Charter Broad Oaks Hosp., Savannah, 1972-76; chief of staff H.C.A. Oak Hill Hosp., Spring Hill, Fla., 1986-88; ret., 1997; med. dir. Recovery Place, 2003—. Chmn. bd. trustees H.C.A. Oak Hill Hosp., 1993-96. Recipient Mental Health Bell award, Savannah Mental Health Assn., 1973; Paul Harris fellow, 1989. Fellow Am. Psychiat. Assn. (disting. life fellow, del. 1968-76); mem. Ga. Psychiat. Assn. (pres. 1975-76), Hernando County Med. Soc. (pres. 1989-90), Med. Assn. Ga. (del. 1968-78), Rotary, Masons, Shriners. Republican. Presbyterian. Avocations: fishing, boating, cooking. Office Phone: 912-355-1440.

JOHNSTON, GEORGE W., lawyer; b. Syracuse, NY, Aug. 8, 1950; s. Norman Fero and Mary Jane (Innes) J. BA, Johns Hopkins U., 1972; JD, Georgetown U., 1975. Bar: Md. 1975. Law clerk U.S. Dist. Ct., Balt., 1975-76; atty. Venable, Baetjer & Howard, Balt., 1976—; chief oper. officer Venable, Baetjer & Howard, LLP, 1999—2001. Lectr. in field. Author: BNA Aids Guide, 1990, Affirmative Action Workbook, 1992, Maryland Employer's Guide, 1991; contbr. articles to profl. jours. Chmn. Md. Citizens for the Arts; bd. dirs. Walters Art Mus. Mem. ABA, FBA, Md. Bar Assn., Balt. City Bar Assn. Office: Venable LLP 1800 Mercantile Bank 2 Hopkins Plz Ste 1800 Baltimore MD 21201-2982 Office Phone: 410-244-7585. Business E-Mail: gwjohnston@venable.com.

JOHNSTON, GERALD E., manufacturing company executive; b. Whittier, Calif. BS, Cal. St. Fullerton. V.p. corp. devel. and planning Procter and Gamble; with Clorox Co., Oakland, Calif., 1981—, v.p., corp. devel and planning, 1992—93, v.p., gen mgr., Kingford Products Div., 1993—96, group v.p. Oakland, Calif., 1996—99, pres., COO, 1999—2003, pres., CEO, 2003—. Office: Clorox Co 1221 Broadway Oakland CA 94612-1888

JOHNSTON, GLADYS STYLES, university official; b. St. Petersburg, Fla., Dec. 23, 1942; d. John Edward and Rosa (Moses) Styles; m. Hubert Seward Johnston, July 30, 1966. BS in Social Sci., Cheney U., 1963; MEd in Ednl. Adminstrn., Temple U., 1969; PhD in Ednl. Adminstrn.-Orgnl. Theory, Cornell U., 1974. Tchr. Chester (Pa.) Sch. Dist., 1963-66, West Chester (Pa.) Sch. Dist., 1966-67, asst. prin., elem. prin., dir. Summer Sch., 1968-71; dir. Head Start Chester County Bd. Edn., West Chester, 1967-69; teaching asst., rsch. asst. Cornell U., Ithaca, N.Y., 1971-74; asst. prof. ednl. adminstr. and supervision Rutgers U., New Brunswick, N.J., 1974-79, assoc. prof., chmn. dept. Grad. Sch. Edn., 1979-83, chmn. dept. mgmt. Sch. Bus., 1983-85; dean, prof. Coll. Edn., Ariz. State U., Tempe, 1985-91; provost, v.p. for acad. affairs DePaul U., Chgo., 1991-93, chancellor, 1993—. Disting. Commonwealth vis. prof. Coll. William and Mary Sch. Edn., Williamsburg, Va., 1982-83; manuscript reviewer Jour. Higher Edn., Jour. Ednl. Leadership, Prentice Hall Pub. Co., Englewood Cliffs, N.J.; speaker and conf. presenter in field; cons. AT&T, Ednl. Testing Svc., Prentice-Hall Pub. Co.; cons. to coordinating bd. Tex. Coll. and Univ. System. Author: Research and Thought in Administration Theory, 1986; mem. editorial bd. Ednl. Evaluation and Policy Analysis, Ednl. Adminstrn. Quar., Ednl. and Psychol. Rsch. Jour.; contbr. articles and book revs. to profl. jours., chpts. to books. Bd. dirs. Edn. Law Ctr., 1979-86, Sta. KAET-TV, Phoenix, 1987—, Found. for Sr. Living, 1990-91; mem. adv. coun. to bd. trustees Cornell U., 1981-86; trustee Middlesex Gen. Univ. Hosp., 1983-86. Recipient Outstanding Alumni award Temple U.; Andrew D. White fellow Cornell U. Mem. ASCD, Am. Assn. Colls. for Tchr. Edn., Nat. Conf. Profs. Ednl. Adminstrn., Am. Ednl. Rsch. Assn. (proposal reviewer 1979—, chmn. task force for participation and membership 1981—, chmn. E.F. Linquist award com. 1985, mem. govt. rels. com. 1986—, publ. com. 1986—), Phi Kappa Phi, Phi Delta Kappa, Alpha Phi Sigma. Office: U of Nebraska at Kearney Office of Chancellor 905 W 25th St Kearney NE 68845-4238

JOHNSTON, GWINAVERE ADAMS, public relations consultant; b. Casper, Wyo., Jan. 6, 1943; d. Donald Milton Adams and Gwinavere Marie (Newell) Quillen; m. H.R. Johnston, Sept. 26, 1963 (div. 1973); children: Gwinavere G., Gabrielle Suzanne; m. Donald Charles Cannalte, Apr. 4, 1981. BS in Journalism, U. Wyo., 1966; postgrad., Denver U., 1968-69. Editor, reporter Laramie (Wyo.) Daily Boomerang, 1965-66; account exec. William Kostka Assocs., Denver, 1966-71, v.p., 1969-71; exec. v.p. Slottow, McKinlay & Johnston, Denver, 1971-74; pres. The Johnston Group, Denver, 1974-92; chair, CEO JohnstonWells Pub. Rels., Denver, 1992—. Adj. faculty U. Colo. Sch. Journalism, 1988-90. Bd. dirs. Leadership Denver Assn., 1975-77, 83-86, Mile High United Way, 1989-95, Colo. Jud. Inst., 1991-2000, Denver's 2% Club, chair, 1996—, Spring Inst., 1997-2000, Lower Downtown Denver, Inc., Inst. for Internat. Edn., 1998-99, U. Wyo. Found., 2000—, Wyo. Bus. Coun., 2001- Recipient Athena award Colo. Women's C. of C., 1999. Fellow Am. Pub. Rels. Soc. (pres. Colo. chpt. 1978-79, bd. dirs. 1975-80, 83-86, nat. exec. com. Counselor's Acad. 1988-93, sec.-treas. 1994, pres.-elect 1995, pres. 1996, profl. award Disting. Svc. award 1992); mem. Colo. Women's Forum, Denver Athletic Club, Denver Press Club. Republican. Home: 717 Monaco Pky Denver CO 80220-6040 Office: JohnstonWells Pub Rels 1512 Larimer St Ste 720 Denver CO 80202-1610

JOHNSTON, JAMES R., lawyer; b. Seattle, Aug. 19, 1953; BS magna cum laude, U. Wash., 1975, JS, 1978. Bar: Wash. 1978, US Ct. Appeals (9 Cir.), US Dist. Ct. (We. Dist.) Wash., Us Dist. Ct. (Ea. Dist.) Wash., US Tax Ct., Yakama Tribal Ct. Asst. atty. gen., Natural Resources Divsn. State of Wash., 1978—83; assoc. Bogle & Gates, PLLC, 1983—87, ptnr., 1988—97, chmn., Forest Resources Practices Group, 1994—97; ptnr., Envirn./Natural Resources/Land Use Practice Area Perkins Coie LLP, Seattle. Trustee Wash. Rsch. Coun. Mem.: Soc. Am. Foresters, ABA (vice chmn. forest resources com., Environ., Energy & Resources Sect. 1994—), Wash. State Bar Assn. Office: Perkins Coie LLP 1201 Third Ave Ste 4800 Seattle WA 98101-3099 Office Phone: 206-359-8626. Office Fax: 206-359-9000. Business E-mail: jjohnston@perkinscoie.com.

JOHNSTON, JAMES ROBERT, library director; b. Wheaton, Ill., June 3, 1947; s. Robert W. and Elizabeth S. (Townsend) J.; m. Carol Ann Trezza, June 14, 1969; children: Steven J., Julie M. BA, U. Notre Dame, 1969; MLS, Fla. State U., 1973. Head librarian Grande Prairie Library Dist., Hazel Crest, Ill., 1973-76; chief librarian Joliet (Ill.) Pub. Library, 1976—; pres. bd. dirs. Ill. Library Employees Benefit Plan. Mem. automation com. Heritage Trail Libr. Sys., Shorewood, Ill.; pres. Ill. Libr. Employees Benefit Plan, Joliet; bldg. cons. Co-author: Illinois Library Trustees Association Booklet "Selecting Consultants", 1986; contbr. speeches and articles in field. V.p. Joliet/Will County Project Pride; mem. events com. C. of C. Mem. Ill. Libr. Assn. (pub. libr. sect. 1977-78, legis. devel. com. 1977-82, jr. mems. roundtable 1976-77, regional planning com. 1996, Title III rev. com. 1996—, interlibr. coop. subcom., intellectual freedom com.), Kiwanis, Beta Phi Mu. Avocations: ho guage model railroading, softball, bowling, golf. Home: 2208 Graystone Dr Joliet IL 60431-8785 Office: Joliet Pub Library 150 N Ottawa St Joliet IL 60432-4192 Office Phone: 815-740-2670. Business E-Mail: jrjohnston@joliet.lib.il.us.

JOHNSTON, JAMES WESLEY, retired consumer products company executive; b. Chgo., Apr. 11, 1946; s. Ted and Irma (Hacker) J.; children: Amanda E., Emily S. BS in Accountancy, U. Ill., 1967; MBA, Northwestern U., 1971. C.P.A., Ill. Fin. analyst Ford Motor Co., 1967-69; with N.W. Industries, 1969-79, dir. corp. devel., 1973-75, v.p. mktg., 1975-79; exec. v.p. Asia/Pacific R.J. Reynolds Tobacco Internat. Inc., 1979, pres., chief exec. officer Asia/Pacific Hong Kong, 1979-81; exec. v.p. R.J. Reynolds Tobacco Co., U.S., 1981-84; divsn. exec. consumer banking N.E. U.S. Citicorp, N.Y.C., 1984-89; chmn. CEO R.J. Reynolds Tobacco Co., Winston-Salem, N.C., 1989-95; chmn. R.J. Reynolds Tobacco Worldwide, Winston-Salem, N.C., 1993-96; vice chmn. RJR Nabisco, Inc., 1995-96, ret., 1996. Bd. dirs. Sealy Corp., Trinity, N.C., RemoteLight.com, Inc., Research Triangle Park, N.C. Treas., trustee, pres. Village of Bolingbrook, Ill., 1973-75; bd. dirs. Winston-Salem Bus. Inc., 1989—; active N.C. Bus. Coun. Mgmt. and Devel., Raleigh, 1989—; trustee Wake Forest U., Winston-Salem, 1991—; mem. bd. visitors Wake Forest U. Bapt. Med. Ctr., Winston-Salem, 1991—. Mem.: Piedmont Club, Old Town Club. Office: 115 Eastbend Ct Mooresville NC 28117 Office Phone: 704-660-5466.

JOHNSTON, JASON SCOTT, law educator; married; 1 child. AB summa cum laude, Dartmouth Coll., 1978; JD cum laude, U. Mich., 1981, PhD in Econs., 1984. Law clk. to Hon. Gilbert S. Merritt US Ct. Appeals (6th cir.), 1984—85; asst. to assoc. prof. law Vermont Law Sch., 1985—89; assoc. prof. to prof. Vanderbilt Law Sch., 1989—94; prof. U. Pa. Law Sch., Phila., 1995—2001, Robert G. Fuller Jr. prof., 2001—, dir. Program on Law and Environment, 1998—. Olan vis. fellow U. So. Calif. Law Ctr.; vis. prof. U. Va. Sch. Law, 2001. Contbr. articles to law jours. Office: U Pa Law Sch 3400 Chestnut St Philadelphia PA 19104 Office Phone: 215-898-6911. Office Fax: 215-573-2025. E-mail: jjohnsto@law.upenn.edu.*

JOHNSTON, JOAN LAWLER, director, consultant; d. Robert John and Patricia (Zimmermann) Lawler; m. Thomas Russell Johnston, July 31, 1965; children: Timothy Robert, Christopher Thomas. BA, Rosary Hill Coll., 1965; MA, SUNY Buffalo, 1973; MS, Canisius Coll., 1990; EdD, Columbia U., 2000. School District Administrator NY State Bd. of Regents, 1990. Tchr. English Hamburg H.S., NY, 1975—87; coord. staff devel. Hamburg Ctrl. Sch. Dist., 1987—90; 9-10 prin. Grand Island H.S., NY, 1990—91; asst. prin. Lancaster H.S., NY, 1991—92; dir. curriculum Clarence Ctrl. Sch. Dist., NY, 1992—. Bd. dirs. N.Y. State ASCD, Albany, 2000—, v.p., 2002—; bd. dirs. ASCD, Alexandria, Va., 2000—03, W. N.Y. Women in Adminstrn., Buffalo, 1993—96; leadership coun. ASCD, Alexandria, 2003—. Mem. pub. broadcasting cmty. task force WNED-Ch 17, Buffalo, 2000—; mrm. instl. assessment project Erie C.C., Buffalo, 2001—02; mrm. ednl. adminstrn. and supervision coun. Canisius Coll., Buffalo, 1990—95. Recipient Disting. Educator award, Harcourt Brace Pub., 1997, William Meyer award, N.Y. State Assn. for Comprehensive Edn., 1996. Fellow: Inst. for Devel. Ednl. Activities (Disting. Educator award 1986, 1991); mem.: Nat. Staff Devel. Coun., Harvard Prin.'s Ctr., China Light Yacht Club, Wanakah Country Club, Phi Delta Kappa (Read Travel Scholarship to China 2002, Fellow in Ednl. Leadership 1998). Roman Catholic. Avocations: travel, golf, cultural activities, skiing. Home: 5268 Lakeshore Rd Hamburg NY 14075 Office: Clarence Central Sch Dist 9625 Main St Clarence NY 14031 Office Phone: 716-407-9109.

JOHNSTON, JOHN DEVEREAUX, JR., retired law educator; b. Asheville, N.C., Oct. 1, 1932; s. John D. and Marion R. (Green) J.; m. Beryl R. Watson, Dec. 21, 1952; m. Diana Armatage, June 10, 1972; children: Catherine, Patricia, Sharon, Laura, Jackie, John. AB, Duke U., 1954, LL.B., 1956. Bar: N.C. 1956, U.S. Ct. Appeals (4th cir.) 1969, U.S. Supreme Ct. 1969. Mgmt. trainee J.P. Morgan & Co., 1956-58; pvt. practice Asheville, 1959-62; asst. prof. Duke U. Law Sch., Durham, N.C., 1963-64, asst. dean, 1963-65, assoc. prof., 1965-67, prof., 1968-69; prof. law NYU Law Sch., N.Y.C., 1969-89, prof. law emeritus, 1990—. Vis. prof. Vanderbilt U., 1972, UCLA, 1975, Washington U., St. Louis, 1981, Hastings Coll. Law U. Calif., San Francisco, 1984. Author: (with G. Johnson) Land Use Control, 1977; contbr. articles to profl. jours. Home: 21 Stuyvesant Rd Asheville NC 28803-3022 E-mail: jdjjr@worldnet.att.net. *As a young law teacher, I was mentored by two wise elders. One emphasized preparation: Don't ever go into class without knowing where you intend to take it. The other counselled flexibility: Be prepared for anything, and let student input determine how the class will unfold. A third elder provided a synthesis: Never overestimate what your students already know, nor underestimate what they are capable of learning.Applying that maxim, I determined to introduce new subjects slowly and carefully, even spoon-feeding the students for a while. Thereafter, development of the topic proceeded at their speed. After they reached a level of sophistication well beyond my expectations, I concluded that the third elder was the wisest.*

JOHNSTON, JOSEPHINE ROSE, chemist; b. Cranston, RI, Aug. 9, 1926; d. Robert and Rose (Varca) Forte; m. Howard Robert Johnston, Mar. 7, 1949 (dec.); 1 child, Kevin Howard. Student, Carnegie Inst., 1945-47; BS, Mich. State U., 1972, MA, 1973; postgrad., MIT, 1973—. Med. technologist South Nassau Community Hosp., Rockville Centre, N.Y., 1947-50, Mich. State U., East Lansing, 1950-53, faculty specialist, 1966-76; dept. pathology Albany (N.Y.) Med. Ctr., 1953-54; med. lab. supr. Bulova Watch Co., Jackson Heights, N.Y., 1954-57; sr. chemistry technologist Mid Island Hosp., Bethpage, N.Y., 1958-66; sr. rsch. assoc. Uniformed Svcs. Univ., Bethesda, Md., 1976-78, asst. to chmn. dept. physiology, 1978-82, assoc. to chmn., 1982-96; sr. scientist NASA-Spaceline/Archive, Bethesda, 1997-99; owner, operator Slipstream II, 1997—. Author: Patriarch: The Life of T.J. Haddy, 1994; contbr. articles to profl. jours. With Danzinger Found., Lauderdale, Fla., 1990-91; vol. tech. com. fundraising Twinridge Elem. Sch., 1997-98. Mem. Analytical Chem. Soc., Data and Electronic Soc., Internat. Platform Assn., Kiwanis (bd. dirs.). Lutheran. Office: Slipstream II 6813 Woodville Rd Mount Airy MD 21771-7611 Office Phone: 301-829-3509. E-mail: zzman@msn.com.

JOHNSTON, LAURANCE SCOTT, foundation director; b. St. Paul, Aug. 4, 1950; s. Scott D. and Laura L. (Wallace) J. BS, Hamline U., 1972; MS, Northwestern U., 1973, PhD, 1976; MBA, George Mason U., 1985. Postdoctoral fellow Chgo. Med. Sch., 1977-78; regulatory scientist Bur. Foods, FDA, Washington, 1978-81; exec. sec. NIH, Bethesda, Md., 1981-86; dir. div. sci. rev. Nat. Inst. Child Health and Human Devel., NIH, Bethesda, 1986-92; dir. spinal cord rsch. and edn. founds. Paralyzed Vets. of Am., 1992-97; health educator, grantee, writer and nat. and internat. speaker in biomed. and disability rsch., 1997—. Contbr. articles to mags. and profl. jours. Damon Runyon/Walter Winchell Cancer Found. fellow, 1978. Home: 637B S Broadway St PMB 241 Boulder CO 80305 Office Phone: 303-449-0639. Personal E-mail: laurancejohnsto@aol.com.

JOHNSTON, LAWRENCE R., food products executive; b. Corning, NY, Aug. 29, 1948; married; 2 children. BA in Bus. Adminstrn., Stetson U., Deland, FL, 1972. Merchandising mgr. GE Appliances; region mgr. GE; gen. mgr. Eastern Sales & Distbn. Opers., GE Appliances; pres. Internat. GE Puerto Rico; gen. mgr. Domestic Sales Opers., GE; v.p. sales & distbn. GE Appliances, 1989; pres. & CEO GE Med. Sys., Europe, Paris, 1997; sr. v.p. GE, 1999; pres. & CEO GE Appliances, 1999—2001; chmn. bd. & CEO Albertson's, Inc., 2001—. Chmn. GE's European Exec. Coun.; bd. mem. Food Mktg. Inst., Washington, CIES World Food Forum, Paris; co. officer GE, 1989. Office: Albertsons Inc 250 Parkcenter Blvd Boise ID 83706*

JOHNSTON, LLOYD DOUGLAS, social sciences educator; b. Boston, Apr. 18, 1940; s. Leslie D. and Madeline B. (Irvin) J.; 1 child, Douglas Leslie. BA in Econs., Williams Coll., 1962; MBA, Harvard U., 1965, postgrad., 1965-66; MA in Social Psychology, U. Mich., 1971, PhD, 1973. Research asst. Grad. Sch. Bus. Adminstr., Harvard U., Boston, 1965-66; asst. study dir. Inst. Social Research, U. Mich., Ann Arbor, 1966-73, asst. research scientist, 1973-75, assoc. rsch. scientist, 1975-78, sr. rsch. scientist and program dir., 1978-98; disting. sr. rsch. scientist, rsch. prof. Inst. Social Rsch., U. Mich., Ann Arbor, 1998—; chmn. exec. com. U. Mich. Substance Abuse Rsch. Ctr. Excellence, 1990-95, acting dir., 1994-95. Prin. investigator Monitoring the Future: A Continuing Study of Lifestyles and Values of Am. Youth, 1975—, Youth, Education and Society, 1996—, also other nat. and internat. survey studies; cons. to WHO, UN, EEC, Coun. of Europe, Pan Am. Health Orgn., White House, U.S. Congress, various founds., numerous fgn. govts., fed. agys., univs., rsch. insts., TV networks, Nat. Partnership for Drug Free Am., 1978—; chmn. tech. planning group; mem. Resource Group for Goal Seven, Nat. Edn. Goals Panel, 1991-2002; mem. extramural sci. adv. bd. Nat. Inst. on Drug Abuse, 1990-94; mem., also chmn. prevention subcom., Nat. Adv. Coun. on Drug Abuse, 1982-86, Presdl. appointee White House Conf. for a Drug-Free Am., 1987-88, Presdl. appointee Nat. Commn. for Drug Free Schs., 1989-90; chmn. drug epidemiology sect. Internat. Coun. on Alcohol and Addictions, 1982-2002; mem. Com. on Problems of Drug Dependence, 1982-86; mem. or chmn. various adv. coms. various univs., founds.; mem. various working groups NAS; mem. various coms. and adv. groups Nat. Inst. Drug Abuse, 1975—; mem. or chmn. 7 working groups WHO, 1975—; invited lectr. nat. and internat. confs. and convs.; testimony before Congress and fed. regulatory agys. Author: Drugs and American Youth, 1973, Student Drug Use in America, 1975-81, 82, Monitoring the Future Nat. Survey Results on Drug Use 1975-2003, vol. 1 and 2, 2004, 53 other books and monographs on drug use and lifestyles of Am. secondary sch. students and young adults, 1972—, 27 reference vols.; editor: Conducting Follow Up Research on Drug Treatment Programs, 1977; contbr. more than 120 chpts. to books, articles to profl. jours. Recipient Nat. Pacesetter award in rsch. Nat. Inst. on Drug Abuse, 1982, 1st Sr. Rsch. Scientist award and lectureship U. Mich., 1987, Regents award for disting. pub. svc., 1998, Disting. Rsch. Scientist award, 1998. Fellow Coll. on Problems of Drug Dependence; mem. APA, Soc. for Psychol. Study Social Issues (sec.-treas. 1976-79), Am. Sociol. Assn., Am. Pub. Health Assn. Home: 5538 Lawrence Ct Pinckney MI 48169-9257 Office: U Mich Inst Social Rsch Ann Arbor MI 48109 Business E-Mail: lloydj@umich.edu.

JOHNSTON, LYNN BEVERLEY, animator; b. Collingwood, Ont., Can., May 28, 1947; d. Mervyn and Ursula (Bainbridge) Ridgway; m. Rod Johnston; children: Aaron, Katherine. Student, Vancouver Sch. Art, 1964-67. Med. illustrator McMaster U. Cartoonist, For Better or For Worse, 1979—; author: David We're Pregnant 1974, Hi, Mom, Hi, Dad, 1975, Do They Ever Grow Up?, 1977, Growing Like a Weed, 1997; 18 collections of comic strips including Middle Age Spread, 1998. Recipient Reuben award Nat. Cartoonist's Soc., 1985; named to disting. Order of Can., 1992; nominated Pulitzer prize for editl. cartooning, 1994. Mem. Nat. Cartoonists Soc. (pres. 1988). Office: Universal Press Syndicate 4520 Main St Kansas City MO 64111 Business E-Mail: businessinfo@fborfw.com.

JOHNSTON, MALCOLM (CALUM), bank executive; b. Glasgow, Scotland, July 10, 1934; s. Malcolm and Margaret Brown (MacPherson) J.; m. Anna Maria Bindels, Sept. 7, 1963; children: Margareta J.M., Malcolm H.A. Grad., Kelvinside Acad., Glasgow. With Standard Bank of Ghana Ltd, 1955-62, Standard Bank of Nigeria Ltd., 1962-69, The Bank of Nova Scotia, 1969-97, asst. agt. N.Y.C., 1969-72, spl. rep. Hong Kong, 1972-74, mgr. Kuala Lumpur, Malaysia, 1974-76, Kingston, Jamaica, 1976-78, from asst. gen. mgr. to gen. mgr. Caribbean region, 1979-83, sr. v.p. comml. credit Toronto, 1983-86, exec. v.p. internat. banking, 1986-97; also bd. dirs.; pres., CEO Bank NT Butterfield, 1997—. Mil. Svc. The Royal Highland Regiment, The Black Watch. Fellow Inst. Can. Bankers (gold medal 1983); mem. Nat. Club (Toronto), Hong Kong Club, Kelvinside Academicals, Glasgow, Coral Beach and Tennis Club (Bermuda). Office: Bank of Butterfield PO Box HM 195 Hamilton HM AX Bermuda E-mail: calumjohnston@bntb.bm.

JOHNSTON, MARGUERITE, retired journalist; b. Birmingham, Ala., Aug. 7, 1917; d. Robert C. and Marguerite (Spradling) J.; m. Charles Wynn Barnes, Aug. 31, 1946; children: Susan, Patricia, Steven, Polly. AB, Birmingham-So. Coll., 1938. Reporter Birmingham News, 1939-44; Washington corr. Birmingham News, Birmingham Age-Herald, London Daily Mirror, 1945-46; columnist Houston Post, 1947-69, fgn. news editor, mem. editorial bd., 1969-85, assoc. editor editorial page, 1972-77, asst. editor editorial page, 1977-85; ret., 1985. Lectr. in field, 1947—; instr. creative writing U. Houston, 1946-47, lectr. feature writing, 1965-66; lectr. Baker Coll., Rice U., 1977-78; del. Asian Am. Women Journalists Conf., Honolulu, 1965, 1st World Conf. Women Journalists, Mexico City, 1969 Author: Public Manners, 1957, A Happy Worldly Abode, 1964, Houston: The Unknown City, 1836-1946, (Winedale Historical Ctr. Ima Hogg award, Otis Lock award East Tex. Historical Assn.), 1991. Mem. Mcpl. Art Commn., 1971—76, Houston Com. Fgn. Rels.; bd. dirs. Tex. Bill of Rights Found., 1962—64, Planned Parenthood, 1953—55, Population Inst., 1985—91. Recipient Theta Sigma Phi Headliner award, 1954, 1st ann. award of merit Houston Com. Alcoholism, 1956, cert. of merit Gulf Coast chpt. Am. Soc. Safety Engrs., 1960, Agnese Carter Nelms award Planned Parenthood, 1968, Sch. Bell award Tex. State Tchrs. Assn., 1974, 75, Gold Key award Nat. Council Alcoholism, 1975, Global award Population Inst., 1981. Mem. Tex. Soc. Architects (hon.), Philos. Soc. Tex., Phi Beta Kappa, Pi Beta Phi Home: 2929 Buffalo Speedway Houston TX 77098

JOHNSTON, MARILYN FRANCES-MEYERS, physician, educator; b. Buffalo, Mar. 30, 1937; BS, Dameon Coll., 1966; PhD, St. Louis U., 1970, MD, 1975. Diplomate Am. Bd. Pathology, Diplomate Nat. Bd. Med. Examiners. Fellow in immunology Washington U., St. Louis, 1970-72; resident in pathology Washington U. Hosp., St. Louis, 1975-77, St. John's Mercy Med. Ctr., St. Louis, 1977-79; research fellow hematology St. Louis U. Sch. Medicine, 1979-80; instr. biochemistry St. Louis U., 1972-75, asst. prof. pathology, 1980-87, assoc. prof., 1987-92, prof., 1992-99, prof. emeritus, 1999—, dir. transfusion svcs., 1980-99; staff pathologist Christian Hosp. Barnes Jewish Christian Hosps., St. Louis, 1999—. Med. dir. Mo./Ill. Regional Red Cross, 1983-88; area chmn. for inspection and accreditation Am. Assn. Blood Banks, Arlington, Va., 1984; med. dir. transfusion svc. Christian Hosps., Barnes-Jewish-Christian Hosp. Sys., St. Louis, 1999—. Author: Transfusion Therapy, 1985. Named Goldberger fellow, AMA, 1979; recipient Transfusion Medicine Acad. award, Nat. Heart, Blood and Lung Inst., 1984—. Mem. Am. Assn. Blood Banks, Am. Assn. Immunologists, Internat. Soc. Blood Transfusion, Am. Soc. Clin. Pathologists, Sigma Xi.

JOHNSTON, MARK DAVID, language educator; b. Puyallup, Wash., Nov. 23, 1952; s. Arthur David and Carol Mae Johnston; m. Anne Clark Bartlett, Nov. 19, 1960; children: Matthew Augustine Johnston-Urey, Benjamin Gregory Johnston-Urey. BA, U. Oreg., 1974; PhD, The Johns Hopkins U., 1978. Asst. prof. Spanish Wash. U., St. Louis; asst. prof. English Ill. State U., Normal, 1982—83, from assoc. prof. to prof. Spanish, 1983—97; corp. desktop support supr. US Cellular Corp., Chgo., 1998—99; info. tech. dir. The Newberry Libr., 1999—2003; prof. Spanish DePaul U., Chgo., 2003—. Vis. prof. history and Spanish St. Xavier U., Chgo., 2000; vis. prof. comparative lit. U. Iowa, Iowa City, 1990. Author: The New Rhetoric of Ramon Llull (Hermagoras Press), The Book of the Lover and the Beloved of Ramon Llull (Aris & Phillips), (scholarly monograph) The Spiritual Logic of Ramon Llull (Oxford, Clarendon Press), The Evangelical Rhetoric of Ramon Llull (Oxford University Press). Pres. Independence Pk. Adv. Coun., Chgo., 2000—03. Recipient John Nicholas Brown prize Outstanding First Book, Medieval Acad. Am., 1991; fellow, Am. Coun. Learned Societies, 1979, 1982, NEH, 1980, 1998, 1994—95. Mem.: Ill. Medieval Assn. (pres. 2001—02), Midwest MLA, MLA Am. D-Liberal. Lutheran. Avocations: old house renovation, greyhound rescue, bagpiping. Office: Dept Modern Langs DePaul U 802 W Belden Chicago IL 60614 E-mail: mjohnst4@depaul.edu.

JOHNSTON, MAXINE, retired librarian; b. Gillham, Ark., Dec. 21, 1928; Student, Lamar Coll., 1946-51; BS, Sam Houston State U., 1953; MLS, U. Tex., 1958. Adminstrv. asst. Beaumont Pub. Libr. (formerly Tyrrell Pub. Libr.), 1947-53; asst. libr. South Park H.S., 1953-55; reference libr. Lamar U., 1955-68, acting dir., 1968-69, assoc. dir., 1970-80, dir., 1980-88. Contbr. articles to profl. jours. Mem. ALA (life), Tex. Libr. Assn. (life, dist. vice chair 1960-61, nominating com. chair 1965-66, reference round table 1967-69, vice chair, chair 1967-69, legis. com. 1973-75, coll. & univ. divsn. vice-chair, chair 1984-86), Tex. Info. Exch. (bd. chair 1971-72), Tex. Coun. State Univ. Librs. (state contract com. chair 1983-86), Big Thicket Assn. (life, com. mem. 1966-81, v.p. 1971-73, pres. 1973-75, 94-98, newsletter editor 1971-81, 99—), Big Thicket Conservation Assn. (bd. dirs. 1993-99), Tex. Com. Natural Resources (task force chair 1987-92), LWV, Nat. Parks and Conservation Assn. (Margery Stoneman Douglas Citizen Conservationist of Yr. award 1996), Sierra Club (exec. com. Lone Star chpt. 1994-96, Spl. Svc. award 1989), Tex. Folklore Soc., Tex. Gulf Hist. Soc., Nature Conservancy, Alpha Chi, Beta Phi Mu, Phi Kappa Phi. Home: 9715 Main St Batson TX 77519-7938

JOHNSTON, MICHAEL (WILLIAM JOHNSTON), political science educator, university administrator; b. Omaha, Nebr., Nov. 1, 1949; s. William M. and Margaret Mary (Ryan) J.; m. Bette Bennett, 1976; children: Michael Joseph, Patrick Brendan Ryan. BA in Polit. Sci summa cum laude, Macalester Coll., St. Paul, 1971; MPhil in Polit. Sci., Yale U., 1974, PhD in Polit. Sci., 1977. Teaching fellow, acting instr. Yale U., 1972-76; instr. U. Pitts., 1976-77, asst. prof., 1977-82, assoc. prof., 1982-86; from assoc. prof. to prof. Colgate U., Hamilton, NY, 1986—2003, Charles A. Dana prof. polit. sci., 2003—, divsn. dir. for the social sci., 2004. NEC fellow, mem. Sch. Social Sci., Inst. for Advanced Study, Princeton, NJ, 2002—03; vis. lectr. politics, vis. fellow Ctr. Urban and Regional Rsch. U. Glasgow, Scotland, 1983—84; vis. fellow dept. politics and Inst. Rsch. in Social Scis. U. York, England, 1991; vis. fellow St. Aidan's Coll., 1997; vis. fellow dept. politics U. Durham, England, 1997; rsch. assoc. Cogen, Holt and Assocs., New Haven, 1974—75; cons. to numerous U.S. govt. and internat. orgns., 1992—; spkr., cons., presenter in field. Author: Political Corruption and Public Policy in America, 1982, Fraud, Waste and Abuse in Government, 1986; author: (co-editor) Political Corruption: A Handbook, 1989; co-editor: Political Corruption, 2002; contbr. articles to profl. jours.; editor: Civil Society and Corruption, 2005. NSF fellow, 1972-76; grantee U. Pitts., 1983, Nuffield Found., 1984, Fulbright/British Coun. Higher Edn., 1984, Colgate U. Rsch. Coun. Maj. Grants com., 1987, New Liberal Arts program Colgate U./Sloan Found., 1988, 90, Leverhulme Trust/Social and Cmty. Planning Rsch., 1998, NEH fellow 2002-03. Mem. Am. Polit. Sci. Assn., Phi Beta Kappa, Pi Sigma Alpha Democrat. Roman Catholic. Avocations: computing, baseball, trains. Home: 41 W Main St Earlville NY 13332-1900 Office: Colgate U Dept Polit Sci 13 Oak Dr Hamilton NY 13346-1383 Fax: 315-228-7883. Office Phone: 315-228-7756. E-mail: mjohnston@mail.colgate.edu.

JOHNSTON, MICHAEL FRANCIS, auto parts company executive; b. Concord, Mass., May 21, 1947; s. Harold William and Julia Theresa (May) J.; children: Scott, Evon, Meghan. BS, Lowell U., 1969; MBA, Mich. State U., Troy, 1987. Asst. mgr. ops. analysis Western Union, N.Y.C., 1969-71; fin. analyst Microdot, Greenwich, Conn., 1971-72, asst. to gen. mgr. Detroit Diamond div. Wyandotte, Mich., 1972-73, asst. to gen. mgr. Wittek Mfg. div. La Grange Park, Ill., 1973-75, plant mgr. Detroit Diamond div. Wyandotte, 1976-78, v.p., gen. mgr. Internat. div. Mt. Clemens, Mich., 1978-87; v.p., gen. mgr. Kaynar div. Microdot, Fullerton, Calif., 1987-89; fin. analyst United Tech.-Otis, N.Y.C., 1975-76; v.p., gen. mgr. SLI div. Johnson Controls Inc., Milw., 1989-93, v.p. and gen. mgr. battery group, 1993—96, pres., North America/Asia Pacific, 1997—99; pres., COO Visteon Corp., 2000—04, bd. dir., 2002—, CEO, 2004—. Mem. bd. dir. Flowserve Corp., Dallas, Whirlpool Corp., Mich. Office: Visteon Corp 17000 Rotunda Dr Dearborn MI 48120*

JOHNSTON, MICHAEL WAYNE, lawyer; b. Houston, Mar. 23, 1955; m. M. Katherine Johnston, June 2, 1979; children: K. Elizabeth, M. Phillip. BA, Trinity U., San Antonio, 1977; JD, Baylor U., 1980. Bar: Tex. 1980, U.S. Dist. Ct. (no. dist.) Tex. 1980, U.S. Ct. Claims 1981, U.S. Supreme Ct. 1988, U.S. Dist. Ct. (so. dist.) Tex. 1988, U.S. Dist. Ct. (we. dist.) Tex. 1989; bd. cert. civil trial law; bd. cert. consumer law. Shareholder Simon, Anisman, Dobey & Wilson, Fort Worth, 1980-86; ptnr. Thompson, Coe, Cousins & Irons, Dallas, 1986-89, Knox, Beadles & Johnston, Dallas, 1989-94, Broude, Nelson & Harrington, Ft. Worth, 1994-97, Johnston & Assocs., Ft. Worth, 1997—. Contbr articles to profl. jours. Pres. Univ. West Neighborhod Assn., Ft. Worth. Mem. Def. Rsch. Inst., Tarrant Bar Assn., Dallas Bar Assn., Legal Network for Deaf, Coll. State Bar of Tex. Office: Johnston & Assocs LLP Ste 800 307 W 7th St Fort Worth TX 76102-5108

JOHNSTON, NICKLETT ROSE, research nurse, clinical perfusionist; d. Robert Nick Moriana and Melba Grohe, Roger E. Grohe (Stepfather); m. Roy Edwin Johnston, Aug. 5, 1995; m. Michael Minnella, 1979 (div. 1992); children: Michael Paul Minnella, Anita Marie Minnella. ADN, Cochise Coll., Douglas, AZ, 1979; BSN, U. Phoenix, 2002; MSN, Graceland U., 2005. Cert. clin. perfusionist Tex., 1989, ACLS, Tex., 2002. RN Tucson Med. Ctr., 1982—87; clin. perfusionist, RN, Cardiovasc. Support Svcs., Dallas, 1988—89; clin. perfusionist, RN dept. cardiovascular and thoracic surgery U. Tex. Southwestern Med. Ctr., Dallas, 1989—2003, sr. rsch. nurse dept. cardiovascular and thoracic surgery, 2003—. Mem. ANA, Washington, 1979—90, Am. Soc. for Extra Corporeal Tech., Hattiesburg, Miss., 1989—, knowledge base com., 1999—2000; instr. Am. Heart Assn., Dallas, 1994—95. Author: The Emergency use of Recombinant Hirudin in Cardiopulmonary Bypass (Am. Soc. for Extra Corporeal Tech. Case Report award, 2000), Argatroban in Adult Extracorporeal Membrane Oxygenation, Simplified Solution to Eliminating Electrical Noise During Cardiac Surgery. Mem.: Am. Bd. Perfusionists, Am. Bd. Nursing (licentiate), Theta Tau. Home: 324 Harbor Landing Dr Rockwall TX 75032 Office: Cardiothoracic Surgery 5909 Harry Hines Blvd Dallas TX 75390 Office Phone: 214-645-7728. Personal E-mail: johnstonr@sbcglobal.net.

JOHNSTON, NORMAN JOHN, retired architecture educator; b. Seattle, Dec. 3, 1918; s. Jay and Helen May (Shultis) J.; m. Lois Jane Hastings, Nov. 22, 1969. BA, U. Wash.-Seattle, 1942; B.Arch., U. Oreg., 1949; M. in Urban Planning, U. Pa.-Phila., 1959, PhD, 1964. Registered architect, Wash. City planner Seattle City Planning Commn., 1951-55; asst. prof. arch. U. Oreg.-Eugene, 1956-58; assoc. prof. architecture and urban planning U. Wash.-Seattle, 1960-64, prof., 1964-85, prof. emeritus, 1985—, assoc. dean, 1964-76, 79-84, chmn. dept. architecture, 1984-85. Mem. nat. exams. com. Nat. Coun. Archtl. Registration Bds., Washington, 1970-81, 88-99; vis. prof. Tokyo Inst. Tech., 1991, 98; Fulbright prof. Istanbul Tech. U., 1968-69; mem. Wash. State Archtl. Registration Bd., 1989-2000, chmn., 1988-89. Author: Cities in the Round, 1983, Washington's Audacious State Capitol and its Builders, 1988 (Gov.'s Book award 1984, 89), The College of Architecture and Urban Planning, 75 Years at the University of Washington: A Personal View, 1991, The Fountain and the Mountain - The University of Washington Campus, 1895-1995, 1995-2003, National Guide Series: The University of Washington, 2001; editor: NCARB Architectural Registration Handbook, 1980; contbr. articles to profl. jours. Mem. King County Policy Devel. Commn., Seattle, 1970-76; mem. Capitol campus design adv. com. State of Wash., Olympia, 1982-2000, chmn., 1980-88, 96; trustee Mus. History and Industry, 1997-2000. Recipient Wash. Disting. Citizen award, 1987, Barney award AIA Coll. of Fellows, 2003. Fellow AIA (pres. Seattle chpt. 1981, AIA medal Seattle chpt. 1991, Wash. Coun. medal 1997); mem. Phi Beta Kappa, Sigma Chi, Tau Sigma Delta. Presbyterian. Home: 900 University St Apt Au Seattle WA 98101-1778 Office: U Wash C Architecture & Urban Planning PO Box 355726 Seattle WA 98195-5726 E-mail: njjo@u.washington.edu.

JOHNSTON, OSCAR BLACK, III, lawyer; b. Tulsa, Oct. 1, 1941; s. Oscar Black Jr. and Carol (VanDerwiele) J.; m. Ruth Archdeacon Darrough; children: Eric Oscar, David Darrough. BBA, Baylor U., 1963; JD, U. Tulsa, 1966. Bar: Okla. 1966, U.S. Dist. Ct. (no., ea., we. dists.) Okla., U.S. Ct. Claims, U.S. Ct. Appeals (10th cir.), U.S. Supreme Ct. Asst. U.S. attorney U.S. Dist. Ct. (we. dist.) Okla., 1970-76; ptnr. Logan & Lowry, L.L.P., Vinita, Okla., 1979—. Assoc. editor Tulsa Law Review, 1964-66. Presiding judge divsn. 54 Okla. Temp. Ct. Appeals, 1980-81, judge divsn. XIV, 1991-93; presiding judge panel VI Lawyer-Staffed Ct. Appeals, 1992. Capt. JAGC, U.S. Army, 1966-70. Fellow Am. Bar Found. (state chair 2001-03), Okla. Bar Found. (trustee 1988-96, pres. 1995); mem. ABA (sects. litigation, family law and criminal), Fed. Bar Assn. (pres. Oklahoma City chpt. 1975), Craig County Bar Assn. (pres. 1986-88), Okla. Bar Assn. (mem. fin. com. 2003—, assoc. editor, mem. bd. editors Okla. Bar Jour. 2000—), Okla. Trial Lawyers Assn., Rotary (pres. Vinita 1983-84), Phi Alpha Delta. Republican. Methodist. Office: Logan & Lowry PO Box 558 Vinita OK 74301-0558 Home: 116 Westwood Ave Vinita OK 74301-2703

JOHNSTON, PHILIP CONNELLY, lawyer; b. N.Y.C, June 6, 1968; s. John Martin and Suzanne (Shephardson) J. AB, U. Mich., 1990; MA in Internat. Studies, Johns Hopkins U., 1994; JD, Columbia U., 2000. Corr. UPI, Moscow, 1995-97; law clk. to Hon. Joan A. Lenard, U.S. Dist. Ct. for So. Dist. Fla., Miami, Fla., 2000—02; assoc. Skadden, Arps, Slate, Meagher & Flom, NYC, 2002—. Avocations: languages, travel. Office: US Dist Ct for So Dist Fla 301 N Miami Ave 7th Fl Miami FL 33121 Home: 400 E 57th St Apt 8R New York NY 10022-3023

JOHNSTON, RICHARD ALAN, lawyer; b. Buffalo, Mar. 18, 1950; s. Richard W. and Virginia (Holmes) J.; m. Patricia Downing, Aug. 28, 1971; children: Matthew, Sarah, Elizabeth, Michael. BA, Cornell U., 1972; JD, Harvard U., 1976. Bar: Mass. 1977, U.S. Dist. Ct. Mass. 1977, U.S. Ct. Appeals (1st cir.) 1977. Law clk. to presiding justice Mass. Ct. Appeals, Boston, 1976-77; assoc. Hale and Dorr LLP, Boston, 1977-82, sr. ptnr., 1982—. Co-chmn. North Area Task Force, Charlestown, Mass., 1981—; trustee Dennis (Mass.) Conservation Trust, 1988—, pres., 1995—; mem. transition team Mass. Gov. William Weld, 1990-91; internat. election observer Internat. Human Rights Law Group, Nepal, 1991; dir. Friends of City Square Park, 1993—2001; trustee Hockey Humanitarian Award Found., 1997—; pres. Friends of Tanzanias Schs., Inc., 1997—, Compact of Cape Cod Conservation Trusts, 2001—. Mem. ABA, Internat. Bar Assn., Boston Bar Assn., Nat. Health Lawyers Assn., Mass. Bar Assn. Home: 43 Monument Ave Charlestown MA 02129-3323 Office: Wilmer Cutler Pickering Hale and Dorr LLP 60 State St Boston MA 02109-1816 Office Phone: 617-526-6282. Business E-Mail: richardjohnston@wilmerhale.com.

JOHNSTON, RICHARD BOLES, JR., pediatrician, educator, biomedical researcher; b. Atlanta, Aug. 23, 1935; s. Richard Boles and Jane (Dillon) Johnston; m. Mary Anne Claiborne, Aug. 13, 1960; children: Richard B. III, S. Claiborne, Kristin M. BA, Vanderbilt U., 1957, MD, 1961; MS (hon.), U. Pa., 1986. Diplomate Am. Bd. Pediat., Am. Bd. Pediat. Infectious Disease. Resident in pediat. Vanderbilt U., 1961-63, Harvard U., 1963-64, fellow pediat. immunology, 1967-70; asst. prof., assoc. prof. depts. pediat. and microbiology U. Ala. Med. Ctr., Birmingham, 1970-76; vis. assoc. prof. Rockefeller U., N.Y.C., 1976-77, vis. prof., 1983-84; prof. pediat. U. Colo. Sch. Medicine, Denver, 1977-86; chmn. dept. pediat. Nat. Jewish Ctr. Immunology and Respiratory Medicine, Denver, 1977-86, U. Pa. Sch. Medicine, Phila., 1986-90, Wm. H. Bennett prof. pediat., 1986-92; physician-in-chief Children's Hosp. of Phila., 1986—90; med. dir. March of Dimes Birth Defects Found., White Plains, N.Y., 1992-98. Adj. prof. pediat., chief sec. pediat. immunology Yale U. Sch. Medicine, 1992—98; prof. pediat. Sch. Medicine U. Colo., Denver, 1999—, assoc. dean rsch. devel., 2001—; exec. v.p. acad. affairs Nat. Jewish Med. & Rsch. Ctr., 2004—; trustee Internat. Pediat. Rsch. Found., 1983—87, 1995—98, chmn., 1984—87, 1997—98; chmn. adv. bd. for vaccines and related biols. FDA, Bethesda, Md., 1990—93, chmn. com. vaccine safety, Inst. Medicine, 1992—93, chmn. com. new rsch. in vaccines, 1993—94, chmn. forum vaccine safety, 1995—98, chmn. com. asthma and indoor air, 1998—99, bd. health promotion disease prevention, 1994—2001, chmn. com. rsch. in multiple sclerosis, 1999—2001, chmn. com. health implications of perchlorate, 2003—05. Mem. editl. bd. 7 profl. jours., 1978—; contbr. 260 articles to profl. jours.; editor Current Opinion in Pediatrics, 1997—. Capt. M.C., U.S. Army, 1964-66. Faculty scholar Josiah Macy Jr. Found., 1976-77; recipient Commr. citation and Wiley medal FDA, 1994. Fellow AAAS; mem. Inst. Medicine NAS, Am. Soc. Clin. Investigation, Am. Pediat. Soc. (pres. 1996-97), Assn. Am. Physicians, Soc. Pediat. Rsch. (pres. 1980-81). Office: Office of Dean C-290 U Colo Sch Medicine 4200 E 9th Ave Denver CO 80262 Office Phone: 303-315-6792. Business E-Mail: richard.johnston@uchsc.edu.

JOHNSTON, RICHARD FOURNESS, biologist, educator; b. Oakland, Calif., July 27, 1925; s. Arthur Nathaniel and Marie (Johnson) J.; m. Lora Lee Bliler, Feb. 7, 1948; children: Regan, Janet, Cassandra. BA, U. Calif., Berkeley, 1950, MA, 1953, PhD, 1955. Asst. prof. dept. biology N.Mex. State U., 1956-58; mem. faculty depts. zoology and ecology U. Kans., Lawrence, 1958—, prof., 1968-92, prof. emeritus, 1992—, chmn., 1979-82, editor mus. publs., 1974-76, 86-91; program dir. systematic biology NSF, Washington, 1968-69; editor Ann. Rev. Ecology and Systematics, 1968-92, Current Ornithology, 1981-87. Mem. adv. panel biol. scis. Smithsonian Fgn. Currency Program, 1969-71 Served with AUS, 1943-46. Am. Acad. Arts and Scis. grantee, 1957; nat. Acad. Sci. grantee, 1959-83. Fellow Am. Ornithol. Union (Coues award 1975), AAAS, mem. Ecol. Soc. Am., Soc. Systematic Zoology (editor jour. 1967-70, pres. 1977), Soc. Study Evolution. Home: 615 Louisiana St Lawrence KS 66044-2337 E-mail: rfj@ku.edu. *Variability or heterogeneity or pluralism is present in nearly everything humans do or to which they are exposed.*

JOHNSTON, ROBERT FOWLER, venture capitalist; b. Phila., Aug. 15, 1936; s. William S. and Elinor (Fowler) J.; m. Lynn Dixon, Feb. 5, 1972; children: William McCord, Bradford Dixon, Alexandra Fowler. BA, Princeton U., 1958; MBA, NYU, 1964. With F.S. Smithers & Co., N.Y.C., 1960-61, Smith Barney & Co., N.Y.C., 1963-67; pres. Johnston Assocs. Inc., Princeton, N.J., 1967—. Bd. dirs. Vela Pharm., Inc., Trenton, N.J., Targent Inc., Princeton, ExSAR Corp., Princeton, Ctr. for Edn. Reform, Washington, 2004—. Co-author: Entrepreneurial Science: New Links Between Corporations, Universities and Government. Mem. adv. coun. Princeton U. Dept. Molecular biology, 1983—; mem. exec. com. Friends of Inst. Advanced Study, Princeton, 1992—, chmn., 1998—2002; founder Edn. Ventures Found. With USAF, 1961-62. Mem. Nat. Venture Capital Assn., Univ. Club of N.Y.C. Avocations: archaeology, art. Home: Sycamore Creek 48 Elm Ridge Rd Pennington NJ 08534 Office: Johnston Assoc Inc 181 Cherry Valley Rd Princeton NJ 08540-7911 Office Phone: 609-924-3131. Business E-Mail: rjohnston@jaivc.com.

JOHNSTON, RONALD LEE, lawyer; b. Topeka, Feb. 6, 1948; s. Harry Clayton and Ruth Winifred (Stanley) J.; m. Joan Louise Lesser, Mar. 9, 1975; children: Ryan, Lauren. BA, Calif. State, Fullerton, 1970; JD, U. So. Calif., 1973. Bar: Calif. 1973, U.S. Dist. Ct. (cen. dist.) Calif. 1975, U.S. Dist. Ct. (no. dist.) Calif. 1980, U.S. Ct. Appeals (9th cir.) 1984, (fed. cir.) 1996. Ptnr. Irell & Manella, L.A., 1974-80, Blanc Williams Johnston & Kronstadt, L.A., 1980-2000; with Arnold & Porter, L.A., 2000—. Lectr. various insts., contbr. numerous articles to profl. jours. Editor in chief: The Computer Lawyer, 1984—; mem. U.S.C. Law Rev. Mem. Computer Law Assn. (bd. dirs. 1988—), U.S.C. Computer Law Inst. (chmn. 1979—), Order of Coif. Office: Arnold & Porter 777 S Figueroa St 44th Fl Los Angeles CA 90017

JOHNSTON, STANLEY HOWARD, JR., curator, rare book dealer; b. Cleve., Apr. 28, 1946; m. Carol Ann Lewis, June 19, 1976. BA, Columbia Coll., 1968; MA, U. Western Ont., London, Can., 1970, PhD, 1977; MS in LS, Case Western Res. U., 1979. Tchg. asst. U. Western Ont., London, 1971-72; asst. to editors Spenser Newsletter, London, 1972-73; bibliographer Cleve. Herbals Project, Cleve., 1984-90; curator of rare books Holden Arboretum, Kirtland, Ohio, 1990—. Internet columnist Coun. on Bot. and Hort. Librs., 1995—; libr. adv. com. The Herb Soc. Am., Kirtland, Ohio, 1997-99. Author: The Cleveland Herbal, Botanical and Horticultural Collections, 1992, Cleveland's Treasures from the World of Botanical Literature, 1998; contbr. articles to profl. jours.; internet columnist. Recipient Charles Robert Long award of Extraordinary Merit. Mem. MLA, Bibliog. Soc. Am., Soc. for History of Natural History, ALA (rare books and manuscripts sect.), The Bibliog. Soc., Coun. on Bot. and Hort. Librs. (mem. publs. com., electronic comm. com., 1996—, documentation strategy com. 1996-2001, long term planning com., 1997-2001, preservation and access com. 2001—, steering com. 2001—), Medieval Acad. Am., Am. Philatelic Soc., No. Ohio Bibliophilic Soc. Republican. Presbyterian. Avocations: philatey, collecting mystery, science-fiction and fantasy books. Home: 7226 Grant St Mentor OH 44060-4704 Office: The Holden Arboretum 9500 Sperry Rd Kirtland OH 44094-5149 Office Phone: 440-602-3829. E-mail: stanley177@aol.com.

JOHNSTON, STEVEN ROY, music educator; b. Franklin, Pa., May 25, 1970; s. Beryle Lee and Myrna Suzanne Johnston; m. Tracie Renee Galla, Nov. 20, 1976. MusB in Edn., Baldwin-Wallace Coll., Conservatory of Music, Ohio, 1992; MusM in Music Edn., Youngstown State U., Ohio, 2001. Tchg. Cert. Pa. Dept. of Edn., 1995. Band dir., instrumental music Strongsville City Schs., Strongsville, Ohio, 1993—95, Franklin Area Sch. Dist., Pa., 1995—. Trombonist Franklin Silver Cornet Band, Pa., 1984—; prin. trombonist Venango Chamber Orch., Franklin, Pa., 1995—; prin. tenor horn, baritone horn Wildcat Rgt. Band, Home, Pa., 1998—; sub. trombonist Butler Symphony Orch., Butler, Pa., 2003—; performing arts coord. Venango County Young Peoples Arts Festival, Franklin, Pa., 2004—; presenter in field. Composer: (composition for symphonic band) The 63rd Pennsylvania Regimental March (Citation from the Pa. Ho. of Reps., 1996); composer: (arranger) (symphonic band) Oil Fever Galop, Crazy On Oil, American Petroleum Polka, Oil On The Brain, Petroleum Galop, Pa Has Struck Ile, Petroleum Court Dance, (recording) Music of the Oil Boom, 2005. Civil war re enactor 150th Pa. Bucktail Rgt., Meadville, Pa., 2002—05. Mem.: Internat. Assn. of Jazz Educators, Internat. Trombone Assn., Nat. Band Assn., Music Educators Nat. Conf., Pa. Music Educators Assn. Home: 108 Hemlock Dr

Franklin PA 16323 Office: Franklin High Sch 246 Pone Ln Franklin PA 16323 Office Phone: 814-432-2121. Office Fax: 814-432-5031. Personal E-mail: srjohnston105@yahoo.com. E-mail: johnston@fasd.k12.pa.us.

JOHNSTON, SUSAN A., lawyer; b. Dec. 16, 1953; BA, Wellesley Coll., 1975; JD, Harvard Univ., 1978. Bar: Mass. 1978. Assoc. Ropes & Gray, Boston, 1978—87, ptnr., 1987—, head tax & benefits dept. Contbr. articles to profl. jours. Mem. Tax Adv. Bd. Investment Co. Inst., 1988—. Mem.: ABA (chmn. Com. Regulated Investment Cos. 1987—89), Boston Bar Assn. (chmn. tax sect. 1985—87, chmn. Internat. Tax Com. 1985—87, chmn. State Tax Com. 1987—89). Office: Ropes & Gray 1 International Pl Boston MA 02110-2624 Office Phone: 617-951-7301. Office Fax: 617-951-7050. Business E-Mail: susan.johnston@ropesgray.com.

JOHNSTON, THOMAS E., prosecutor; b. 1967; BA, JD, W.Va. U. Atty. Schrader, Byrd and Companion, 1994—96; assoc. Flaherty, Sensabaugh and Bonasso, 1996—98; ptnr. Bailey, Riley, Buch and Harmon, Wheeling, W.Va., 1998—2001; U.S. atty. no. dist. W.Va. U.S. Dept. Justice, 2001—. Office: PO Box 591 Wheeling WV 26003-0011

JOHNSTON, THOMAS MCELREE, JR., retired church administrator; b. Coral Gables, Fla., June 10, 1934; s. Thomas McElree and Lorine (Davis) J.; m. Anna Youel Armstrong, July 2, 1960; children: Kathryn Armstrong, Timothy Armstrong, Sara Helen. BA, Amherst Coll., 1956; MDiv, Yale U., 1959; ThM, Princeton Theol. Sem., 1963; D of Ministry, San Francisco Theol. Sem., 1978. Ordained to ministry Presbyn. Ch., 1959. Assoc. coord. religious affairs NC State U., Raleigh, NC, 1959-62; min. community svc. Tabernacle Presbyn. Ch., Phila., 1963-66; organizer, head of staff Ch. of the Reconciler, Clearwater, Fla., 1966-78; assoc. Presbytery devel. Synod of the Covenant, Columbus, Ohio, 1978-85, assoc. exec., 1985-88; exec. Synod of the Trinity, Camp Hill, Pa., 1988-2000; ret. Pres. Pa. Coun. Chs., Harrisburg, 1995-98; chair Synod Exec. Forum, 1997; chmn. gen. assembly Synod Staff Forum, 1997; corr. mem. Gen. Assembly Coun., Louisville, 1993-94. Publisher: (newspaper) Trinitarian. Pres., organizer Religious Cmty. Svcs., Inc. Clearwater, 1968-70; pres. Pinellas County Head Start, Inc., Clearwater, 1968-72; mem. Pinellas County Sch. Bd., Pinellas County Coun., Clearwater, 1972-76; bd. dirs. Cmty. Svc. Found., Largo, Fla., 1969-78, Drug Free Pa., Inc., 1999-2002. Named Vol. of Yr., Civic Coun., Pinellas County, Fla., 1972; recipient Humanitarian award Lions Club, 1975. Mem. Rotary Internat. (club. pres. 2003-04, pres. Harrisburg Found. 2004-05). Presbyterian. Home: 1041 Country Club Rd Camp Hill PA 17011-1049 E-mail: tom.johnston@paonline.com.

JOHNSTON, VAN ROBERT, finance educator; b. Sudbury, Can., Feb. 23, 1945; s. Olaf Wesley and Bernice Everlyn (Mullen) J.; m. Suzanne Marie Simpson, July 26, 1969; children: David A., Erik W., Jacqueline M. BA in Polit. Sci., Loyola U., L.A., 1967; M of Pub. Adminstrn., U. Southern Calif., 1974, PhD, 1976. Sr. lifeguard, trainer, instr. L.A. County, 1963-68; rsch. assoc., instr. U. Southern Calif., L.A., 1975-76; dir. prof. mgmt. program U. Denver, 1986-88, chair bus. and pub. policy, 1986-91, prof. mgmt. policy, 1976—. Disting. vis. prof. mgmt. strategy USAF Acad., Colorado Springs, 1991-93; faculty assoc. Intermodal Transp. Inst., Denver, 1997—; profl. cons., trainer, rschr. numerous orgns., 1975—. Co-editor Policy Studies Rev., 1997—; contbr. numerous articles to profl. jours. Marshall internat. golf tournament Profl. Golf Assn., 1986, 87; coach, soccer Cherry Creek Soccer Assn., 1977-84; active Boy Scouts Am., 1979-89. Recipient Outstanding Young Men of Am. U.S. Jaycees, 1979, Program and Mgmt. award Nat. Am. Soc. of Pub. Adminstrs., 1984, Univ. Tchg. award Mortar Bd. Nat. Honor Soc., U. Denver, 1997. Mem. Am. Soc. for Pub. Adminstrs. (exec. com. 1997-98, nat. coun. 1997-98, sect. chair 1997—, publs. com. 1996—, Outstanding Svc. award 1998), Pinery County Club, Colo.-Am. Soc. for Pub. Adminstrn. (pres., v.p., Leadership award 1983). Avocations: golf, ranch, siberian husky, photography, exercise. Office: U Denver Daniels Coll of Bus Dept Of Mgmt Denver CO 80208-0001

JOHNSTON, VIRGINIA EVELYN, retired editor; b. Spokane, Wash., Apr. 26, 1933; d. Edwin and Emma Lucile (Munroe) Rowe; m. Alan Paul Beckley, Dec. 26, 1974; children: Chris, Denise, Rex. Student, Portland C.C., 1964, Portland State U., 1966, 78-79. Proofreader the Oregonian, Portland, 1960—62, teletypesetter operator, 1962—66, operator Photon 200, 1966—68, copy editor, asst. women's editor, 1968—80, spl. sects. editor, 1981—83, editor FOOD day, 1982—2001; ret., 2002. Pres. Matrix Assocs., Inc., Portland, 1975—, chmn. bd., 1979—; past pres. Bones & Brew, Inc. Editor Principles of Computer Systems for Newspaper Mgmt., 1975-76. Cons. Portland Sch. Dist. No. 1, 1978, Dem. Party Oreg., 1969. Democrat. Home: 4140 NE 137th Ave Portland OR 97230-2624

JOHNSTON, WILLIAM DAVID, lawyer; b. Aberdeen, Md., Jan. 31, 1957; s. David Irvine and Nancy (Smith) J.; m. Mary Teresa Miller, May 29, 1983; children: Ellen Christine, Amy Elizabeth. AB, Colgate U., 1979; JD, Washington and Lee U., 1982. Bar: Del. 1982, U.S. Dist. Ct. Del. 1983, U.S. Ct. Appeals (3rd cir.) 1991, U.S. Supreme Ct. 1991. Judicial law clk. to chief justice Daniel L. Herrmann Del. Supreme Ct., Wilmington, 1982-83; assoc. Potter, Anderson and Corroon, Wilmington, 1983-85, Young, Conaway, Stargatt and Taylor, Wilmington, 1985-89, ptnr., 1990—. Contbr. articles to profl. jours. Mem. choir, adminstrv. bd. lay leadership Aldersgate United Meth. Ch., Wilmington, 1970—, chmn. religion and race commn., 1987-89; com. chmn. Boy Scouts of U.S. troop 67, 1982-85, Del. Human Rels. Commn., 1986—; trustee The Pilot Sch., 1995—. Best Brief Worldwide award Am. Soc. Internat. Law, Washington, 1980. Mem. ABA (chmn. indemnification and ins. subcom. 1997—, Am. Judicature Soc. (bd. dirs. 2002—), Del. State Bar Assn. (award for pub. svc. 1991, 93, 99, pres.-elect 2000-2001, pres. 2001-02), Sigma Chi (pres. Colgate U. chpt. 1984-88), Phi Delta Phi, Univ. and Whist Club (bd. govs. 1990-95), Lincoln (Del.) Club, Wilmington Country Club. Methodist. Avocations: running, squash, reading, travel, golf. Office: Young Conaway Stargatt and Taylor The Brandywine Bldg 1100 West St PO Box 391 Wilmington DE 19899-0391 Office Phone: 302-571-6679. Business E-Mail: wjohnston@ycst.com.

JOHNSTON, WILLIAM DAVID, biotechnologist, director; b. Chgo., Nov. 5, 1944; s. Samuel David and Jeanne (Williams) J.; m. Susan Diane Ward, Aug. 19, 1966; children: Kimberly Dawn Sites, Kirk David, Tiffany Dee Hansen, Kyle Donald, Ryan Daryl. BS in Chemistry, Brigham Young U., 1969, PhD in Organic Chemistry, 1974. V.p. Parish Chem. Co., 1973-75; mgr. materials control Baxter Healthcare Corp., 1975-80; group mgr., polymer rsch. and material control Travenol Labs., Inc., 1980-84, v.p. Material and Membrane Tech. Ctr., 1984-86, v.p. applied scis., 1987-93; v.p., gen. mgr. gene therapy div. Baxter Healthcare Corp., Round Lake, Ill., 1993-97; pres., CEO Inhibitex, Inc., Atlanta, 1997—. Mem. adv. bd. Ill. Jr. Acad. Sci., Springfield, 1984-86, Ga. Dept. Econ. Devel., 2003; bd. dirs. Ga. Biomed. Ptnrs., 1999—, vice chmn., 2005—; mem. emerging co. sect. governing bd. Biotech. Industry Orgn., 2002—, bd. dirs., 2004—; co-chair BioSci. Coun. for Metro Atlanta; mem. adv. bd. Coll. Engring., U. Ill., Chgo., 1988-92, dept. chem. engring. Northwestern U., Evanston, Ill., 1989-98. Contbr. articles to profl. jours.; patentee in field. Stake pres. LDS Ch., Buffalo Grove, Ill., 1988-97; exec. coun. N.E. Ill. coun. Boy Scouts Am., 1989-97; chmn. bd. LDS Social Svcs., Naperville, Ill., 1990-97. Brigham Young U. scholarship. Mem. AAAS, Am. Chem. Soc., Internat. Soc. for Artificial Organs, Internat. Soc. Blood Purification (exec. bd. 1991-96), Soc. for Biomaterials, Internat. Soc. of Cell Transplantation, Sigma Xi. Home: 1422 Spyglass Hill Dr Duluth GA 30097-5948 Office: Inhibitex Inc 9005 Westside Pky Alpharetta GA 30004 E-mail: bjohnston@inhibitex.com.

JOHNSTON, WILLIAM J., JR., neurosurgeon; b. Sept. 11, 1945; BS, U. Southwestern La., 1969; MD, La. State U., 1973. Neurol. surgeon Neurosurg. Assocs., Metairie, La., 1979—; chief staff East Jefferson Gen. Hosp., Metairie, 1992. Office: 4228 Houma Blvd Ste 220 Metairie LA 70006-3006 Office Phone: 504-456-9393, 504-456-9393.

JOHNSTON, WILLIAM P., health facility administrator; BA, Vanderbilt Univ., 1966, JD, 1969. Ptnr. Waller Landsden Dortch & Davis; mng. dir., mem. bd. dir., CEO Equitable Securities Corp., 1995—97; vice-chmn. SunTrust Capital Markets, Inc., 1998—2001, CEO, 1998—2000; mng. dir. SunTrust Robinson Humphrey, 2001—02; mem. bd. dir. Renal Care Group, 2002—, also chmn., 2003—. Office: Renal Care Group Ste 600 2525 West End Ave Nashville TN 37203 Office Phone: 615-345-5500. Office Fax: 615-345-5505.*

JOHNSTON, WILLIAM WEBB, pathologist, educator; b. Statesville, N.C., Aug. 26, 1933; s. Jesse Clyde and Pauline Elizabeth (Massey) J. BS, Davidson Coll., 1954; MD, Duke U., 1959. Diplomate Am. Bd. Pathology, Am. Bd. Cytopathology, Internat. Bd. Cytopathology. Intern Duke U., 1959-60, resident in pathology, 1960-63, mem. faculty, 1963—, prof. pathology, 1972-97, dir. div. cytopathology and cytotechnology tng. program, 1966—; ret., 1996. Bd. dirs. Anatomical Pathology Svc.; cons. pathologist Durham VA Hosp., Duncan County Hosp.; chmn. Internat. Bd. Cytopathology, 1992-98. Author: (with W.J. Frable) Respiratory Cytopathology, 1974; Diagnostic Respiratory Cytopathology, 1979; (with S.H. Bigner) The Cytopathology of the Central Nervous System, 1981, 2d edit., 1994, Pulmonary Cytology (with James Linder), 1992; assoc. editor Acta Cytologica, 1978—, sr. mem. editorial bd., 1992; editor: Masson Monographs in Cytopathology; mem. editorial bd. Am. Jour. Clin. Pathology, 1986; editorial cons. Masson Publs., N.Y.C.; mem. editorial adv. bd. Jour. Nat. Cancer Inst. Fellow Internat. Acad. Cytology (Maurice Goldblatt award 1995), Am. Soc. Clin. Pathologists, Coll. Am. Pathologists, Royal Soc. Medicine; mem. AMA (del. 1982-96), Am. Soc. Cytology (rev. bd., pres. 1981-82, Papanicolaou award 1986), Am. Assn. Pathologists, Arthur Purdy Stout Soc. Surg. Pathology, Internat. Acad. Pathology, Am. Assn. for Cancer Rsch. Republican. Presbyterian (organist). Home: 8200 Bromley Rd Hillsborough NC 27278-9709

JOHNSTON, YNEZ, artist, educator; b. Berkeley, Calif., May 12, 1920; BFA, U. Calif., Berkeley, 1941, MFA, 1946. Lectr. art U. Calif., Berkeley, 1950—51, Colorado Springs Fine Arts Ctr., 1954—55, Chouinard Art Inst., 1956, Calif. State U., LA, 1966—67, U. Judaism Sch. Fine Arts, LA, 1967, Otis Art Inst., LA, 1978—81; artist-in-residence Fullerton Coll., Calif., 1982. One-man exhbns. include: San Francisco Mus. Art, 1943, Redlands U., 1947, Santa Barbara (Calif.) Mus. Art, 1952, 57, Pasadena (Calif.) Mus. Art, 1955, 62, Colorado Springs (Colo.) Fine Arts Center, 1955, Calif. Palace Legion of Honor, 1956, The O'Hana Gallery, London, 1958, Paul Kantor Gallery, Los Angeles, 1952, 53, 55, 57, 58, 61-62, 63, Beloit (Wis.) Coll., 1961, Barbara Cecil Gallery, New Orleans, 1963, Mex., 1959, Occidental Coll., L.A., 1955, Esther Bear Gallery, 1967, Ball State U., 1967, Stewart-Verde Galleries, San Francisco, 1966, San Francisco Mus. Art, 1967, Mekler Gallery, L.A., 1970-82, 84, 89, Tokyo Shoten Gallery, N.Y.C., 1976, Mitsukoshi Gallery, Tokyo, 1977, Wiener Gallery, N.Y.C., 1977, Worthington Gallery, Chgo., 1982, 85, 88, Mekler Gallery, 1987, 89, Tomlyn Gallery, Fla., 1990-99, 2003, Fresno Mus. Art, 1992, Tortue Gallery, Santa Monica, 1994-96, Tobey Moss Gallery, L.A., 1994, 2003, Kennedy Museum, Athens, Ohio, 1997, Lyman Allyn Mus, New London, Conn., 1998, Schmidt-Bingham Gallery, N.Y.C., 1998, 99, 2001, Santa Cruz Mus., Calif. 1998, Norton-Simon Mus., Pasadena, Calif., 2004; also exhibited numerous group shows including: Whitney Mus. Am. Art, 1953-56, Mus. Modern Art, 1952, 54, Carnegie Inst., 1951, 55, I.F.A. Gallery, Washington, 1963, 100 Prints of the Year, N.Y.C., 1963, Bklyn. Mus., 1966, Vancouver (B.C., Can.) Print Internat., World Print Competition, San Francisco, 1977, Met. Mus., 1978, L.A. County Mus., 1980-81, Drawings from Their Collection, Nat. Gallery Smithsonian, Washington, Wight Gallery UCLA, 1988, Nat. Gallery Modern Art, New Delhi, 1988, Memory Gallery, Nagoya, Japan, 1990, Gallery IV, L.A., 1990, Worcester Art Mus., 1991, Amon Carter Mus., 1991, Women's Art Mus., Washington, 1994, Met. Mus. Fresno, Calif., 1994, Brigitie Haasner Gallery, Wiesbaden, Germany, Norton-Simon Mus., 1999, Traveling Show in China, Macao, Municipal Gallery, Rio Honda Coll., L.A., Taiwan, 2001, Norton Simon Johnston Collection, 2005, Metrospective Show, Worthington Gallery, Chgo., 2005, others; represented in permanent collections numerous museums including, Santa Barbara Mus. Art, Mus. Modern Art, Philbrook Art Center, Los Angeles County Mus., City Art Mus. St. Louis, Whitney Mus. Am. Art, Phila. Mus. Art, San Diego Mus. Art, U. Ill., Met. Mus. Art, Hirshhorn Collection, Herbert F. Johnson Collection (Cornell U.), San Francisco Mus. Art, Otis Art Inst., Milw. Art Center, Worcester Art Mus. (travelling print exhbn. to Terra Mus., Chgo., Amon Carter Mus., Ft. Worth, 1990), Santa Fe Mus. of Fine Art, The Nat. Mus. Israel, Jerusalem, Gift Gardens Bot./Sculpture Pk., Fla., Norton-Simon Mus., numerous schs. and colls., other museums, also pvt. collections. Recipient San Francisco Mus. Art award oil painting, 1946; awards Calif. State Fair, 1951, 61, 62; award etching Los Angeles County Mus., 1950; exhbn. first award Met. Mus. Art, 1952; purchase award Exhbn. Fgn. Artists, Rome, Italy, 1952; purchase award Otis Art Inst., 1963; purchase award Los Angeles Municipal Art Dept., 1967; also commns.; John Simon Guggenheim Found. grantee, 1952; Louis Comfort Tiffany grantee, 1955, 56; Huntington Hartford grantee, 1957; James Phelan grantee, 1958; MacDowell Colony grantee, 1959; Tamarind workshop fellow, 1966; Nat. Endowment Arts painting grantee, 1976, 85 Home and Studio: 579 Crane Blvd Los Angeles CA 90065-5019

JOHNSTON-COLLINS, ROBIN, director; b. Phila., July 7, 1968; d. William Charles and Patricia Mary Johnston; m. James Penman Collins, Oct. 8, 2004. BA in Elem. Edn., BA in Psychology, Glassboro State Coll., 1990; MA in Ednl. Leadership, St. Joseph's U., 2002. Tchr. 6th grade Evesham Twp. Pub. Schs., Marlton, NJ, 1992—93, tchr. 5th grade, 1993—2003; supr. instrn. Medford Twp. Pub. Schs., 2003—04; curriculum supr. Evesham Twp. Pub. Schs., 2004—. Mem.: ASCD, Burlington County Curriculum Consortium, N.J. Prins. & Suprs. Assn., West Jersey Reading Coun. (bd. dirs. 2003—). Avocation: yoga. Home: 3 Colebrick Ct Shamong NJ 08088 Office: Evesham Twp Pub Schs 25 S Maple Ave Marlton NJ 08053

JOHNSTONE, CRAIG S., elementary school educator; Tchr. Page (Ariz.) Mid. Sch., 1992-94. Recipient Tchr. Excellence award Internat. Tech. Edn. Assn., Ariz., 1992. Home: 7811 East Lindon St Tucson AZ 85715

JOHNSTONE, D. BRUCE, university administrator; b. Mpls., Jan. 13, 1941; s. D. Bruce and Florence Morton (Elliott) J.; m. Gail Eberhardt, July 30, 1965; children: Duncan Bruce, Cameron. BA, Harvard U., 1963, M.A.T., 1964; PhD, U. Minn., 1969; D (hon.), Towson St U., 1995, D'Youville Coll., 1995, Calif. State U., San Diego, 1997. Tchr. econs. and history, Westport, Conn., 1964-65; asst. dir. U. Minn. Center for Econ. Edn., 1966-69; adminstrv. asst. to Sen. Walter F. Mondale, 1969-71; project specialist Ford Found., 1971-72; exec. asst. to pres. U. Pa., 1972-77, assoc. prof. edn., 1976-79, v.p. for adminstrn., 1977-79; pres. State U. Coll. at Buffalo, 1979-88; chancellor SUNY Sys. Office SUNY, Albany, 1988-94, prof. Buffalo, 1994—. Author: New Patterns for College Lending, 1973, Sharing the Costs of Higher Education, 1986; co-editor: The Funding of Higher Education: International Perspectives, 1993, In Defense of American Higher Education, 2001; contbr. articles to profl. jours. Bd. dirs. Buffalo Arts Commn.; bd. trustees D'Youville Coll. Democrat. Episcopalian.

JOHNSTONE, DOUGLAS INGE, retired state supreme court justice; b. Mobile, Ala., Nov. 15, 1941; s. Harry Inge and Kathleen (Yerger) J.; m. Mary Jayne Baynes (div.); 1 child, Francis Inge. BA, Rice U., 1963; JD, Tulane U., 1966. Bar: Ala. 1966, U.S. Dist. Ct. Ala. 1966, U.S. Ct. Appeals (5th cir.) 1968, U.S. Supreme Ct. 1969. Pvt. practice, Mobile, 1966-84; dist. judge Ala. Dist. Ct., Mobile, 1984-85, presiding dist. judge, 1985, cir. judge, 1985-99; justice Supreme Ct. Ala., Montgomery, 1999—2005; ret., 2005. Mem. House of Reps. State of Ala., 1974-78. Mem. bd. advisors Salvation Army, Mobile, 1989—; bd. dirs. Mental Health Assn., Mobile, 1990-92. Capt. U.S. Army, 1963-72. Elected Outstanding Freshman Rep., Capital Prses Corps., 1975; recipient Meritorious Svc. award Mobile County Bd. of Health, 1968, Humanitarian Svc. award Mobile Cerebral Palsy Assn., 1973. Mem. ABA, Am. Judges Assn., Ala. Bar Assn., Mobile Bar Assn., Internat. Acad. Trial Judges. Democrat. Episcopalian. Avocations: hunting, boating, flying. Office: PO Box 191379 Mobile AL 36619-6379 E-mail: djohnstone@bellsouth.net.

JOHNSTONE, IAIN MURRAY, statistician, educator, consultant; b. Melbourne, Victoria, Australia, Dec. 10, 1956; s. Samuel Thomas Murray and Pamela Beatrice (Kriegel) J. BS with honors, Australian Nat. U., Canberra, 1978, MS, 1979; PhD, Cornell U., 1981. Asst. prof. stats. Stanford (Calif.) U., 1981-85, assoc prof. stats., 1986-92, assoc. prof. biostatistics, 1987-92, prof. stats., biostatistics, 1992—, dept. chmn., 1994—97, sr. assoc. dean for natural scis., 2003—. Contbr. articles to profl. jours. Bd. dirs. Bd. on Math. Scis. and its Applications, Washington, 1999—2002; pres. Inst. Math. Stats., 2001—02. Recipient Presdl. Young Investigator award, NSF, 1985—91; Alfred P. Sloan Rsch. fellow, Sloan Found., 1988—90, Guggenheim fellow, John Simon Guggenheim Found., 1997—98. Fellow: AAAS; mem.: NAS.

JOHNSTONE, JOHN WILLIAM, JR., retired chemical company executive; b. Bklyn., Nov. 19, 1932; s. John William and Sarah J. (Singleton) J.; m. Claire Lundberg, Apr. 14, 1956; children: Thomas Edward, James Robert, Robert Andrew. BA, Hartwick Coll., Oneonta, N.Y., 1954; DSc (hon.), Hartwick Coll., 1990; grad. advanced mgmt. program, Harvard U., 1970. With Hooker Chem. Corp., 1954-75, group v.p., 1973-75; pres. Airco Alloys divsn. Airco, Inc., 1976-79; v.p., gen. mgr. indsl. products, then sr. v.p. chems. group Olin Corp., 1979-80, corp. v.p., pres. chems. group Norwalk, Conn., 1980-85, pres., 1985-87, chief operating officer, 1986-87, chmn., pres., CEO, 1988-96, chmn. of bd., 1996, bd. dirs., ret., 1996. Bd. dirs. Arch Chem. Inc. Trustee Hartwick Coll., 1983-91, 92—. Mem. Soc. Chem. Industry, Soap and Detergent Assn. (former chmn. bd. dirs.), Chem. Mfrs. Assn. (chmn. bd. dirs. 1991), Woodway Country Club, Blind Brook Club. Episcopalian.

JOHNSTONE, MARTIN E., state supreme court justice; b. 1949; BA, Western Ky. U.; JD, U. Louisville. Bar: Ky. Judge 3d Magisterial Dist., Ky., 1976-78; dist. judge Jefferson County, Ky., 1978-83; chief judge, 1987-93; circuit judge, 1985-87; justice Ky. Ct. Appeals, 1993-96, chief judge pro tem, 1996; justice Ky. Supreme Ct., 1996—. Recipient Outstanding Trial Judge award Ky. Acad. Trial Attys., 1991. Mem. Louisville Bar Assn. (Judge of Yr. 1981). Office: Ky Supreme Ct Capital Bldg 700 Capitol Ave, Suite 1000 Frankfort KY 40202-2761 also: Ky Supreme Ct Ste 1000 700 W Jefferson St Louisville KY 40202-4737 Office Phone: 502-595-3199.*

JOHNSTONE, MURRAY A., ophthalmologist, researcher; m. Jeanie Johnstone; children: Amy Lighthall, Laura. MD, Wash. U., St. Louis, 1967. Cert. med. dr. Mo., 1967. Glaucoma cons. Swedish Med. Ctr., Seattle, 1973—; dir. glaucoma rsch. Pacific NW Rsch. Found., 1977—80. Glaucoma rsch. activities Swedish Med. Ctr., Seattle, 1973—. Contbr. articles to profl. jours. With USCG, 1961—62, Alameda California. Recipient Goldberger award Nutritional Rsch., Johns Hopkins U., 1965; fellow, Harvard Med. Sch./Mass. Eye and Ear Infirmary, 1971—72; grantee, Nat. Eye Inst., 1977—80. Mem.: Am. Soc. Cataract and Refractive Surgery, Am. Eye Study Club, Wash. Assn. Eye Physicians and Surgeons, Am. Acad. Ophthalmology (Honor award 1991, 2001), Assn. Rsch. Vision Ophthalmology, Chandler and Grant Glaucoma Soc., Am. Glaucoma Soc., Alpha Omega Alpha. Achievements include discovery of Hair Growth by Prostaglandins; patents for Hair Growth by Prostaglandins; discovery of Valves in Outflow System of Eye; Dynamic Movement of Outflow Structures of Eye; Pump Controlling Aqueous Outflow in Eye. Avocation: glaucoma research. Office: Glaucoma Consultants Northwest 1221 Madison St Seattle WA 98104 Office Phone: 206-682-3447. Home Fax: 206-682-8219; Office Fax: 206-682-8219.

JOHNSTONE, QUINTIN, law educator; b. Chgo., Mar. 29, 1915; s. Quintin and Wegia (Metsker) Johnstone; m. Nancy McMullen; children: Robert Dale, Katherine Mary. AB, U. Chgo., 1936, JD, 1938; LLM, Cornell U., 1941; JSD, Yale U., 1951; DHL, Quinnipiac Coll., 1993. Bar: Ill. 1939, Oreg. 1948. Pvt. practice, Chgo., 1939-41; atty. OPA, 1941-47; mem. law faculty Willamette U., 1947—49, U. Kans., 1950-55, Yale U., New Haven, 1955—, Justus S. Hotchkiss prof., 1969-85, prof. emeritus, 1985—; dean law, prof. Haile Selassie I U., Ethiopia, 1967-69. Prof. N.Y. Law Sch., 1985—2000. Author (with D. Hopson): Lawyers and Their Work, 1967; author: (with C. Berger) Land Transfer and Finance, 4th edit., 1993; author: (with M. Wenglinsky) Paralegals, 1985; contbr. articles to profl. jours. Mem.: ABA, Oreg. Bar Assn., Conn. Bar Assn. Home: 22 Morris St Hamden CT 06517-3423 Office: Yale Law Sch PO Box 208215 New Haven CT 06520-8215 Office Phone: 203-432-4931. Business E-Mail: quintin.johnstone@yale.edu.

JOHNSTONE, ROBERT PHILIP, retired lawyer; b. Bellefonte, Pa., Dec. 1, 1943; s. B. Kenneth and Helene (Hetzel) J.; m. Susan Alice Hardy, June 22, 1968; children: Natalie, Nancy. BS with honors, Denison U., 1966; JD magna cum laude, U. Mich., 1969. Bar: Ind. 1969. Assoc. Barnes, Hickam, Pantzer & Boyd, Indpls., 1969-75, ptnr., 1976-82, Barnes & Thornburg, Indpls., 1982—2004; ret., 2004. Chmn. litigation dept. Barnes & Thornburg, 1988-89, mem. mgmt. com., 1988-89; bd. dirs. Protective Order Pro Bono Porject, 2004—; lectr., panelist legal seminars and trial advocacy programs. Sec.-treas. Contemporary Art Soc. of Indpls. Mus. Art, 1983—84; v.p., bd. dirs. Friends of Herron Gallery, Herron Sch. Art, 1981—85; bd. dirs. Eagle Creek Park Found., 2001—04. Fellow Am. Coll. Trial Lawyers (state com. 1992-97, state chair 1995-96); mem. Ind. Bar Assn., Order of the Coif, Woodstock Club (Indpls., bd. dirs. 1988-90, v.p. 1989, pres. 1990), Indpls. Art Ctr. (bd. dirs. 1991-97), Dramatic Club (Indpls.), Phi Beta Kappa, Omicron Delta Kappa. Home: 1065 W 52nd St Indianapolis IN 46228-2463 Office: Barnes & Thornburg 11 S Meridian St Indianapolis IN 46204-3535 Office Phone: 317-231-7230. Business E-Mail: bob.johnstone@btlaw.com.

JOHNSTONE, ROSE MAMELAK (MRS. DOUGLAS JOHNSTONE), biochemistry educator; b. Lodz, Poland, May 14, 1928; d. Jacob Shea and Esther (Rotholz) Mamelak; m. Douglas Johnstone, Aug. 9, 1953; children: Michael, Eric. BSc, McGill U., 1950, PhD, 1953. Nat. Cancer Inst. of Can. fellow Nat. Inst. for Med. Rsch., London, Strangeway Rsch. Lab., Cambridge, England, 1954-56; rsch. assoc. McGill-Montreal Gen. Hosp. Rsch. Inst., 1956-60; faculty McGill U., Montreal, 1961-97, assoc. prof. biochemistry, 1967-76, prof., 1977-97, prof. emeritus, 1997—, chmn. dept., 1980-90. Gilman Cheney chair biochemistry McGill U., Montreal, 1985-96, emeritus chair, 1997-98. Contbr. articles to profl. jours. Grantee Nat. Cancer Inst. Can., 1965-67, Med. Rsch. Coun. of Can., 1965-2001, NIH, 1987-90, 92-96. Fellow Royal Soc. Can. (treas. 1991-94); mem. McGill Assn. U. Tchrs. (membership sec. 1967-70, treas. 1995-96), Biol. Chemists Am., Can. Biochem. Soc. (pres. 1985-86), Internat. Assn. Women Bioscientists (sec. 1985-88). Home: 4064 Oxford Montreal PQ Canada H4A 2Y4 Office: McGill U McIntyre Med Sci 3655 Sir Wm Osler Promenade #804 Montreal PQ Canada H3G 1Y6 Office Phone: 514-398-7264. Business E-Mail: rose.johnstone@mcgill.ca.

JOHNSTONE, SALLY MAC, educational association administrator, psychology educator; b. Macon, Ga., Dec. 8, 1949; d. Ralph E. and Maxine A. J.; m. Stephen R. Tilson, 1977; 1 child, Emma. BS, Va. Poly. Inst., 1974, MS, 1976; PhD, U. N.C., 1982. Lectr. European div. U. Md., Heidelberg, Germany, 1982-84, instr. psychology College Park, 1984-89, asst. dean, 1984-86, dir. Ctr. for Instructional Telecom., 1986-89; dir. Western Coop. for Ednl. Telecom., Boulder, Colo., 1989—. Cons. Northwest Legis. Leadership Forum, Seattle, 1990, Pacific Northwest Econ. Region, Whistler, B.C., 1991, Calif. State U. System, 1993; invited panelist U.S. Dept. Edn., Washington, 1990, 97, Aspen Inst., Washington, 1990, Pacific Northwest Econ. Region, 1991-92; presenter Pacific Rim Pub. U. Pres. Conf. Asia Found., Bangkok, Thailand, 1990, Workshops Pacific Telecom Coun., Honolulu, 1991, 99; spkr. edn. commn. states' Legislator's Workshop, Cin., 1992; meeting Nat. Assn. State Univs. & Land Grant Colls. Distance Edn. & Telecomm. Working Group; witness U.S. Senate Subcom. Edn., Humanities and Arts, Washington, 1991; study advisor Corp. Pub. Broadcasting, 1993; spkr. So. Assn. Schs. and Colls., 1997, Nat. Assn. State Univs. and Land Grant Colls., 1997, Asia Pacific Learning Forum, 2000-01, Hispanic Assn. Colls. and Univs., 2004, UNESCO, 2002, 2004, LearnTec, Germany, 2005; council Regional Accrediting Commns., 2000, Higher Edn. Accrediting, 2003; internat. coun. for Open & Distance Learning, 2000, 01; advisor Western Govs. U., 1996-98. Author: Lessons on Accommodations for Colleges and Rural High Schools Linking Electronically, 1996; co-author: (with Witherspoon and Wasem) Rural TeleHealth: Telemedicine, Distance Education and Informatics, 1993;

co-editor: (with Markwood) New Pathways to a Degree: Technology Opens the College, 1994, Distance Learner's Guide, 2005; columnist: Syllabus, 2001-2004; editl. bd. Open Learning Journal, Americal Journal of Distance Education. Judge sci. fair U. Hills Elem. Sch., Md., 1986-89; mem. adv. com. Boulder Valley Sch. Bd., 1999; bd. trustees US Open Univ., 1998-2002; adv. com. Nat. Info. Ctr. Hispanic Edn., 1999, Consortium Advancement Pvt. Higher Edn., 1998-2001; com. co-chair Nat. Postsecondary Edn. Coop., 1998-99. Grantee Annenberg/CPB Project, 1988, 91-96, U.S. Dept. Edn., 1991, 99, Ford Found., 1991, Fund for Improvement of Postsecondary Edn., 1993, 96, Dept. Commerce Nat. Telecomms. and Info. Adminstrn., 1994, Western Assn. Schs. and Colls., 1997, Hewlett Found., 2001, 02, Lumina Found., 2004; recipient Disting. Rsch. award Nat. U. Continuing Edn. Assn., 1989, Lifetime Achievement award, Nat. U. Telecomms. Network, 2003. Mem. Am. Psychology Assn., Am. Assn. Higher Edn. (bd. mem. 1998-2002). Avocations: hiking, cross country skiing. Home: 4876 10th St Boulder CO 80304-4319

JOHNS-TREAT, CORINNE V., management consultant; b. San Francisco, Nov. 9, 1953; d. Joseph Sal and Mildred (Balisha) Johns; m. Harold Kenneth Treat, June 4, 1982; children: Nicolas, Rachel. BS in Bus., San Jose State U., 1976; MA in Mgmt., U. Phoenix, San Jose, Calif., 1986. Mgr. dept. mdse. Capwells, Fremont, Calif., 1976—77; records auditor Ford Motor Corp., Milpitas, Calif., 1977—80; sr. analyst Xerox Corp, Hayward, Calif., 1980—81; mgr. advanced products project Amdahl Corp., Sunnyvale, Calif., 1981—87, mgr. engrng. change control, 1983—85, mgr. advanced products planning, 1985—87; mng. prin. CINTAM Cons., San Jose, 1987—. Author: Project Management, 1986; contbr. articles to profl. jours., including San Jose Bus. Jour. Team mgr. Ctrl. Valley Youth Soccer Assn., San Jose, 1997—; active 1st Congl. Ch., San Jose, 1998-99. Avocations: singing, guitar, soccer, golf. Personal E-mail: consulheintam@yahoo.com.

JOHNTING, WENDELL, law librarian; b. Winchester, Ind., Aug. 30, 1952; s. Ernest K. and Jewell G. (Browning) J. AB, Taylor U., 1974; MLS, Ind. U., 1975. Cataloging and govt. documents libr. Ind. U. Sch. Law Libr., Indpls., 1975—. Project dir. Indpls. Law Cataloging Consortium, 1980-92; vis. libr. Cambridge U., Squire Law Libr., Cambridge, Eng., 1985; founding mem. Info. Online Project Leaders, 1987-90; spkr. in field; mem., sec. Ind. U. Librs. Faculty Coun., 2001-02. Libr. vol. Beech Grove (Ind.) Pub. Libr., 1993-95; reader, vol. Marion County Health Care Home, Indpls., 1989. Mem.: Indpls. Law Librs. Assn. (sec.-treas. 1999—2001), Ind. Libr. Fedn. (pers. com. 2000—), Christian Legal Soc. (faculty adv. 2001—), Ind. U. Librs. Assn. (exec. bd. 1982—85, v.p. 1986—87, treas. 1999—2001, exec. bd. 2004—05), Ohio Region Assn. Law Librs. (sec. 1982, exec. bd. 1982—85), Knights of Pythias, Dramatic Order Knights of Khorassen, Alpha Phi Gamma, Chi Alpha Omega, Beta Phi Mu. Republican. Baptist. Avocations: gardening, astronomy, cooking. Home: 420 N 23rd Ave Beech Grove IN 46107-1032 Office: Ruth Lilly Law Libr Ind U Sch Law 530 W New York St Indianapolis IN 46202 Office Phone: 317-278-1874. Business E-Mail: wjohntin@iupui.edu.

JOHNTZ, JOHN HOFFMAN, JR., lawyer; b. Alva, Okla., Apr. 26, 1937; s. John H. and Veenetia E. (Burchfiel) J.; m. Linda B. Dover, June 9, 1962; children: John H., Jason Dover. BA, Harvard U., 1959; JD, U. Kans., 1965. Bar: Kans. 1965, U.S. Supreme Ct. 1971. Ptnr. Payne & Jones, P.C., Overland Park, Kans., 1965—. Mem. family adv. com. Kans. Jud. Coun.; mem. Kans. Bd. Law Examiners; head draftsman Kans. Domestic Rels. Law; bd. dirs. Brookside Bank, Olathe Fin. Svcs. Corp.; spkr. domestic rels. law. Co-author: Tax Aspects of Litigation; contbr. articles to profl. jours.; bd. editors Kans. Bar Jour. Pres. Kemper Mus. Contemporary Art; bd. dirs. mem. coun. Soc. Fellows Nelson-Atkins Mus. Art; bd. dirs. Kansas City-Xion, China Sisters City Com., Kans. Citizens for the Arts, Mid-Am. Arts Alliance, Kansas City Artists Coalition, Arts Coun. Johnson County, Kans. City Repertory Theatre. Lt. (j.g.) USN, 1959—61. Named Shawnee Mission North Disting. Alumnus. Fellow: Am. Acad. Matrimonial Lawyers; mem.: ABA, Kans. State Hist. Soc. (bd. dirs.), Phi Beta Kappa, Phi Delta Phi (grad. of yr. 1965). Home: 4424 W 84th St Shawnee Mission KS 66207-1811 Office: Payne & Jones Chartered PO Box 25625 Shawnee Mission KS 66225-5625 Office Phone: 913-469-4100. E-mail: jjohntz@paynejones.com, johntz@aol.com.

JOHRI, SHILPA, pulmonologist, internist; d. Harish Chandra and Manju Asthana; m. Pankaj Kumar; children: Manavi, Mohini, Ashwin. MBBS, Rajendra Med. Coll., Ranchi, India, 1991; MD, Sarojini Naidu Med. Coll., Agra, India, 1996. Diplomate Am. Bd. Internal Madicine, in pulmonary disease Am. Bd. Internal MedicinE. Resident med. officer Sarojini Naidu Med. Coll., India; sr. resident Deen Dayal Upadhyay Hosp.; housestaff, internal medicine Lincoln Med. Ctr. - Cornell U., Bronx, NY, adminstrv. chief resident, internal medicine; clin. fellow, divsn. of pulmonary and critical care medicine NY Presbyn. Hosp. - Weill Cornell Med. Ctr., N.Y.C., 2000—03; pulmonologist, intensivist, internist Health Care on the Sq., Boydton, Va., 2003—, Halifax Regional Hosp., South Boston, Va., 2003—. Presenter in field. Contbr. articles to profl. jours. Grantee, Va. Primary Care Assn., 2004; State Merit scholar, Ranchi U., 1987—89. Mem.: ACP (licentiate; mem. 1997—, Regina McGuinn Meml. award 2002, finalist 1999—2000, 2002—03), AMA (licentiate), Indian Med. Assn. (licentiate; mem. 1991), Am. Coll. Chest Physicians (licentiate). Achievements include research in bronchoalveolar lavage findings in patients undergoing complex spinal surgeries; hypoxic encephalopathy from anemic anoxia; pyothorax associated lymphoma; bilateral pneumothorax after transthoracic needle biopsy of a right lung nodule; Non-Hodgkin's Lymphoma presenting as a pelvic mass and Hydronephrosis; massively elevated CSF protein (6667 mg/dl) in a case of Transverse Myelitis; lactic acidosis syndrome with nucleoside analog antiretroviral therapy; ciprofloxacin induced renal failure; evaluation of nti-BCG antiserum based immunometric assay for tubercular antigen and comparison with adenosine deaminase levels in the diagnosis of tuberculosis. Home: 4380 Brentwood Dr South Boston VA 24592 Office: Health Care on the Sq 380 Washington St Boydton VA 23917 Office Phone: 434-738-6102 242. Office Fax: 434-738-6982. Personal E-mail: sjohri@pol.net.

JOINER, GARY DILLARD, cartographer, writer, history professor; b. El Dorado, Ark., Aug. 30, 1951; s. Frank Dillard and Rudy Rachel Joiner; m. Marilyn Murrell Segura, Aug. 7, 1982. BA, La. Tech. U., 1973; postgrad., Lancaster (Eng.) U., 1999—, La. Tech. U., 2000—02. Pres. Precision Cartographics, Shreveport, La., 1982—; instr. history La. State U., Shreveport, 1996—, dir. Red River Regional Studies Ctr., 1999—. Author: (journal) Civil War Regiments, 1994, Red River Steamboats, 1999, Historic Shreveport-Bossier, 2000, One Damn Blunder from Beginning to End: The Red River Campaign - 1864; editor: Historians of the Western Theater of Civil War, 2000—. Pres. North La. Civil War Roundtable, Shreveport, 1994-98; bd. dirs. North La. Stroke Assn., Shreveport, 1998—; treas., bd. dirs. Oakland Cemetery Preservation Soc., Shreveport, 1999—; bd. dirs. McNeill Street Pumping Sta. Preservation Soc., Shreveport, 1998—. Mem. Mem. Am. Hist. Assn., Soc. Hist. Assn., Soc. for Mil. History, The Hist. Soc., North La. Hist. Soc. (bd. dirs. 1996—, jour. editor 2000—), DeSoto Parish Hist. Soc. (pres. Mansfield 2000—), Tarshar Soc. Methodist. Avocations: reading, travel, writing, archaeology. Home: 1039 Blanchard Pl Shreveport LA 71104 Office: La State U One University Pl Shreveport LA 71115 also: Precision Cartographics 1029 Blanchard Pl Shreveport LA 71104 Fax: 318-222-0662. E-mail: gjoiner@pilot.lsus.edu, gdjoiner@bellsouth.net.

JOISH, VIJAY N., pharmacoeconomics and outcomes researcher; b. Guntakal, Andhra Pradesh, India, Dec. 1, 1974; s. Nagaraj K. and Sushila N. Joish. BS in pharm., U. Bombay, India, 1993—97; postgrad., U. Ariz., 1999—. Grad. tchg. asst. Idaho State U., Pocatello, 1997—99; grad. rsch. asst. U. Ariz., Tucson, 1999—. Statis. cons. U. Ariz., Tucson, 2002—. Grad. senator Associated Students of Idaho State U., Pocatello, 1998—99. Mem.: Internat. Soc. Pharmacoeconomics and Outcomes Rsch. (student chpt. pres. 2000—02, Disting. Svc. award 2002). Achievements include research in methodological issues in economic assessments of healthcare programs and outcomes research; epidemiology, pharmaceutical policy and regulation affairs affecting medical services and the healthcare market. Office: U Ariz PO Box 210207 Tucson AZ 85721-0207 Business E-Mail: Joish@Pharmacy.Arizona.Edu.

JOKLIK, WOLFGANG KARL, biochemist, virologist, educator; b. Vienna, Nov. 16, 1926; s. Karl F. and Helene (Giessl) J.; m. Judith Vivien Nicholas, Apr. 9, 1955 (dec. Apr. 1975); children: Richard G., Vivien H.; m. Patricia Hunter Downey, Apr. 23, 1977. B.Sc. with 1st class honors, U. Sydney, Australia, 1948, M.Sc., 1949; D.Phil. (Australian Nat. U. scholar), U. Oxford, Eng., 1952. Australian Nat. U. research fellow, Copenhagen, Denmark, 1953, Canberra, Australia, 1954-56; fellow, 1957-62; assoc. prof. cell biology Albert Einstein Coll. Medicine, Bronx, N.Y., 1962-65, prof. cell biology, 1965-68, Siegfried Ullmann prof. biochem. virology, 1966-68; prof., chmn. dept. microbiology and immunology Duke U. Med. Ctr., Durham, N.C., 1968-92, James B. Duke Disting. prof. microbiology and immunology, 1972-92, James B. Duke prof. microbiology, 1992-96, James B. Duke prof. emeritus, 1996—. Sr. author: Zinsser Microbiology, 15th, 16th, 17th, 18th, 19th, 20th edits.; editor-in-chief Virology, 1975-93, Microbiological Rev., 1991-95; contbr. articles to profl. jours. Recipient Sr. U.S. award Alexander Humboldt Found., 1985, ICN Internat. prize for virology, 1991. Mem. NAS, Inst. Medicine of NAS, Am. Soc. Virology (pres. 1982-83), Am. Soc. Microbiology, Am. Soc. Biol. Chemists. Address: Duke U Med Ctr Dept Molecular Genetics and Microbiology PO Box 3020 Durham NC 27710-0001 Office Phone: 919-684-2042. Personal E-mail: joklikb@aol.com.

JOLAS, BETSY, composer, educator; b. Paris, Aug. 5, 1926; d. Eugene and Maria (MacDonald) J.; m. Gabriel Illouz, Aug. 27, 1949; children: Frederic, Claire, Antoine. BA, Bennington Coll., 1946; student, Conservatoire Nat. Paris, 1946. Replaced Olivier Messiaen Paris Conservatory, 1971-74, prof. advanced analysis and composition, 1975—. Prof. composition Tanglewood, 1976-77, SUNY, Buffalo, 1976, Yale U., 1979, 82, Boston U., 1985, Darius Milhaud prof. Mills Colls., Fromm prof. Harvard, 1994; resident Am. Acad. Rome, 1999; Berlin Prize fellow Am. Acad. Berlin, 2000; vis. prof. composition U. Mich., 2003-05, 05-. Compositions include Points d'or for one saxophonist playing four saxophones and ensemble, 1982, Episode Sixiéme pour alto, 1983; Trois Duos Pour Tuba et Piano, 1983; O Wall, for wind quintet, 1976; Well Met, for ensemble, 1973; Tales of a Summer Sea, for orch., 1977, Stances, for piano and orch., 1978, Points D'Aube, for ensemble and viola solo, 1968; Préludes Fanfares Interludes Sonneries, for wind orch. and percussion, 1983; Trois Rencontres, for string trio solo and orch., 1973, Sonate á 12, for 12 voice soloists a capella, 1970; Motet II, for choir and orch., 1965; Caprice á deux voix, for soloists without accompaniment, 1978; Quatuor II for solo voice and string trio, 1964; Le pavillon au bord de la rivière, chamber opera in 4 acts, 1975; Le Cyclope, chamber opera in one act, 1986; Schliemann opera in 3 acts, 1989; Frauenleben 9 Lieder for viola and orch., 1992, Sigrancia Ballade for baritone and orch., 1995, Lumor 7 sacred lieder for saxophone and orch., 1996, Petite Symphonie Concertante for violin and orch., 1997, Quatvor VI avec clarinette, 1997, Sonate ä 8, for cello octet, 1998, Motet III, for 5 soloists, chorus and baroque orch., 1999, Trio Sopra, for clarinet, violin and piano, 2000, Concerto-Fantaisie, for piano and mixed chorus, 2001, Motet IV for soprano, flute, clarinet, violin, cello and harp, 2002; Wanderlied for cello and ensemble, 2003; many recs.; contbr. articles to profl. jours. Performer French Radio, Paris, 1955-65. Decorated Chevalier de la Legion d'Honneur, Officier de l'Ordre Nat. du Mérite, Commandeur des Arts et Lettres; recipient Internat. Conducting Competition prize, Besançon, 1953, Copley Found. Chgo. award, 1954, ORTF award, 1961, Am. Acad. Arts award, 1973, Grand Prix de la Music, 1974, Grand Prix de la Ville de Paris, 1981, Grand Prix de la SACEM, 1982, Koussevitsky Found. award, 1974, Prix Internat. Maurice Ravel, 1992, Personnalité de l'année, 1993, Prix SACEM de la Meilleure Création, 1994. Mem. Am. Acad. Arts and Letters, Am. Acad. Arts and Scis. Office: Conservatoire Nat Supérieur de Musique 209 Ave Jean Jaurés 75019 Paris France Personal E-mail: betsyjolas@noos.fr.

JOLEY, LISA ANNETTE, lawyer; b. Centralia, Ill., Mar. 30, 1958; BS magna cum laude, Murray State U., 1980; JD magna cum laude, So. Ill. U., 1983. Bar: Ill. 1983, Mo. 1984. Sr. assoc. gen. counsel litig. Anheuser-Busch Companies Inc., St. Louis, v.p., dep. gen. counsel litig., 2000—02, v.p., dep. gen. counsel, 2002—04, v.p., gen. counsel, 2004—. Mem.: Mo. Bar Assn., Ill. State Bar Assn., St. Clair County Bar Assn., Bar Assn. Met. St. Louis, ABA, Pi Sigma Alpha. Office: Anheuser-Busch Companies Inc One Busch Pl Saint Louis MO 63118

JOLICOEUR, PAUL, molecular biologist; b. Beauceville, Que., Can., Jan. 4, 1945; s. Philippe Jolicoeur and Eva Rodrigue; m. Claudine Tremblay, Apr. 10, 1976. BA, Laval U., Que., 1964, MD, 1968, PhD, 1973. Intern Royal Victoria Hosp., Montreal, Canada, 1968—69; med. dir Lama-Kara Hosp. (SUCO), Togo, 1969—70; pvt. practice Gaspésie, Canada, 1970; postdoctoral fellow MIT, Cambridge, 1973-76; dir. lab. molecular biology Clin. Rsch. Inst. Montreal, 1976—. Contbr. articles to profl. jours. Recipient medal Lt. Gov. of Que., 1964. Mem. Med. Rsch. Coun. (study sect. 1978-81, Centennial fellow 1975-76), Nat. Cancer Inst. (study sect. 1982-84, 96-98, adv. com. on rsch. 1984-88), Royal Soc. Can. (Can.'s chair 2000). Home: 5296 Durocher Outremont PQ Canada H2V 3Y1 Office: Montreal Inst Clin Rsch 110 W Ave des Pins Montreal PQ Canada H2W 1R7 Office Phone: 514-987-5569. Office Fax: 514-987-5794.

JOLIE, ANGELINA, actress; b. LA, June 4, 1975; d. Jon Voight and Marcheline Bertrand; m. Jonny Lee Miller, 1995 (div. Feb. 1999); m. Billy Bob Thornton, 2000 (div. 2003); adopted children: Maddox, Zahara Marley. Student, Strasberg Theatre Inst.; Grad. in Film, NYU. Actress. Former profl. model, London, NYC, LA; good will amb. UN High Commr. for Refugees, Geneva, 2001—. Actor: (films) Lookin' to Get Out, 1982, Cyborg 2, 1993, Angela & Viril, 1993, Hackers, 1995, Without Evidence, 1995, Foxfire, 1996, Mojave Moon, 1996, Love Is All There Is, 1996, True Women, 1997, George Wallace, 1997 (Goldon Globe award for best supporting actress, 1998, nominated Emmy award outstanding supporting actress, 1998), Playing God, 1997, Gia, 1998 (Grand Jury Award for best actress, 1998, Outfest award for outstanding actress, 1998, nominated Emmy award outstanding lead actress, 1998, SAG award for best actress, 1999, Golden Globe for best actress, 1999, Golden Satellite award for best actress, 1999), Hell's Kitchen, 1998, Playing by Heart, 1998 (Nat. Bd. of Rev. award for breakthrough performance, 1998), Pushing Tin, 1999, The Bone Collector, 1999, Girl, Interrupted, 1999 (Academy Award for best supporting actress, 2000, Golden Globe award for best supporting actress, 2000, SAG Award for best supporting actress, 2000, Broadcast Film Critics award for best supporting actress, 2000), Dancing in the Dark, 2000, Gone in Sixty Seconds, 2000, Original Sin, 2001, Life or Something Like It, 2002, Lara Croft Tomb Raider: The Cradle of Life, 2003, Beyond Borders, 2003, Taking Lives, 2004, Shark Tale (voice), 2004, Sky Captain and the World of Tomorrow, 2004, Alexander, 2004, Mr. and Mrs. Smith, 2005, (music videos) Meat Loaf, Lenny Kravits, Antonello Venditti, The Lemonheads. Recipient ShoWest Award for supporting actress of yr., 2000, Cambodian citizenship for conservation work, King Norodom Sihamoni, 2005. Office: Creative Artists Agy 9830 Wilshire Blvd Beverly Hills CA 90212

JOLIN, DIANE LOUISE, elementary school educator; d. Dudley and Dolores Keech; m. Kenneth R. Jolin, June 9, 1968; children: Todd, Robyn, Sara. BA, Dakota Wesleyan U., Mitchell, S.D., 1968. Lic. Educator's Profl. ND Dept. of Instrn. Title 1 reading instr. Granada/Huntley Pub. Sch., Huntley, Minn., 1970—72, Edgeley Pub. Sch., Edgeley, ND, 1979—. Mem.: Prairie Reading Coun. (pres. 2003—05), ND Reading Assn., Internat. Reading Assn. Home: 8108 Hiway 13 Edgeley ND 58433-0958 Office: Edgeley Pub Sch 307 6th St Edgeley ND 58433-7434 Office Phone: 701-493-2292.

JOLLES, BERNARD, lawyer; b. N.Y.C., Oct. 5, 1928; s. Harry and Dora (Hirschorn) J.; m. Lenore Madison Jolles, Oct. 11, 1953 (div. Jan. 1984); children: Abbe, Jacqueline, Caroline. BA, N.Y.U., 1951; LLB, Lewis & Clark Coll., 1961. Bar: Oreg. 1963, U.S. Dist. Ct. Oreg. 1964, U.S. Dist. Ct. (no. dist.) Miss. 1968, U.S. Ct. Appeals (9th cir.) 1965, U.S. Supreme Ct. 1979. Assoc. Anderson Franklin Jones & Olsen, Portland, Oreg., 1963-68; ptnr. Franklin Olsen Bennett & Desbarsay, Portland, Oreg., 1968-79, Jolles, Sokol & Bernstein and successor firms, Portland, Oreg., 1979—, Jolles Bernstein & Garone and predecessor firms Jolles Sokol & Bernstein, Portland, Oreg., 1979—. Editor: Damages, 1974. Bd. dirs. ACLU, Portland, Oreg., 1975—. Fellow Am. Coll. Trial Lawyers; mem. Oreg. State Bar Assn. (pres. 1986-87), Am. Inns of Ct. (sr. barrister 1985—). Avocations: cooking, reading. Office: Jolles & Bernstein 721 SW Oak St Fl 2 Portland OR 97205-3712 Office Phone: 503-228-6474. E-mail: berniej@jollesbernstein.com.

JOLLEY, SAMUEL DELANOR, JR., academic administrator; b. Fort Valley, Ga., Feb. 1, 1941; s. Samuel Delanor Sr. and Mary Louise (Breazele) J.; m. Jimmye Christine Hambry, Dec. 24, 1963; children: Terena, Samuel III. BS, Ft. Valley State Coll., 1962; MS, Atlanta U., 1965; EdD, Ind. U., 1974. Tchr. math. Ballard Hudson Sr. H.S., Macon, Ga., 1962-67; instr. math. Ft. Valley (Ga.) State Coll., 1967-70, asst. prof. math., 1970-75, assoc. prof. math., 1975-82, coord. student teaching, 1980-83, chmn. divsn. edn., 1983-85; prof. math. Fort Valley (Ga.) State Coll., 1982-93, dean Sch. Arts and Scis., 1985-93; exec. dir., CEO, Atlanta Univ. Ctr., Inc., 1998—2004; pres. Morris Brown Coll., Atlanta, 1993—97, 2004—. Mem. adv. bd. Salvation Army, Atlanta, 1995-97; bd. dirs. AUC Coun. Pres.'s, Atlanta, 1993—, Atlanta Paralympics Organizing Com., 1994-97, Univ. Ctr. Ga., Atlanta, 1993—97, Univ. Cmty. Devel. Corp., Atlanta, 1993—2004; nat. bd. dirs. Fund for Improvement of Post Secondary Edn. Mem. NAACP, Am. Assn. Higher Edn., Omega Psi Phi, Sigma Pi Phi. Democrat. Methodist. Avocations: chess, swimming, tennis. Office: Morris Brown Coll 643 Martin Luther King Jr Dr N Atlanta GA 30314-4140 Office Phone: 404-739-1010. E-mail: sjolleyjr@aol.com.

JOLLIE, SUSAN BARBARA, lawyer; b. Milw., May 23, 1950; d. Harry William and Dolores Eleanor (Schlueter) J. BA, Marquette U., 1972; JD, Georgetown U., 1976. Bar: D.C. 1976; U.S. Ct. Appeals (D.C. cir.) 1985, U.S. Ct. Appeals (8th cir.) 1991. From trial atty. to assoc. gen. counsel antitrust, litigation Civil Aeronautics Bd., Washington, 1977-83; gen. counsel SMC Internat., Washington, 1984-85; assoc. Galland, Kharasch, Morse & Garfinkle pc, Washington, 1985-87, ptnr., 1987—96; pvt. practice law Annandale, Va., 1996—. Rep. McLean (Va.) Civic Assn., 1991-92; pres. Nat. Women's History Mus., 2001—. Mem. Wisc. State Soc. (v.p. 1980—), Internat. Aviation Club, Aero Club. Home: 7503 Walton Ln Annandale VA 22003-2558 Office: 7503 Walton Ln Annandale VA 22003 Office Phone: 703-354-8450. E-mail: sjollie@cox.net.

JOLLS, CHRISTINE MARGARET, law educator; b. White Plains, NY, Oct. 1, 1967; d. Robert Talcott and Cecelia (Thurmaier) Jolls; m. Ranier Gavlilk; 2 children. BA in English & Quantitative Economics, Stanford U., 1989; JD, Harvard U., 1993; PhD in Economics, MIT, 1995. Bar: Mass. 1997. Jud. clk. to Judge Stephen F. Williams U.S. Ct. Appeals DC Cir., 1995—96; jud. clk. to Justice Antonin Scalia US Supreme Ct., 1996—97; asst prof. law Harvard Law Sch., Cambridge, Mass., 1994—95, 1997—2001, prof., 2001—, named vice dean scholarship & intellectual life, 2003. Contbr. articles to univ. law reviews Stanford U., Harvard U., U. Chicago, 1998—2001; mem. editl. bd. Am. Law and Economics Rev., New Haven, 1999—; reporter Restatement of Employment Law, Phila., 2001—; fellow Mind/Brain/Behavior Interfaculty Initiative Harvard U. Fellow: Nat. Bur. Econ. Rsch. Office: Harvard Law Sch 1563 Massachusetts Ave Cambridge MA 02138 Office Phone: 617-496-4643. Office Fax: 617-495-4299.

JOLLY, BRUCE DWIGHT, manufacturing executive; b. Wheeling, W.Va., Aug. 27, 1943; s. Edward and Martha Elizabeth (Glass) J.; m. Alice Marie O'Beirne, May 25, 1974 (div. Sept. 1997); children— Mara O'Beirne, Brock Thomas; m. Anne Caroline Rist, Dec. 22, 2001. AB, Dartmouth Coll., 1965; MBA, U. Va., 1967. Systems engr. IBM Corp., Richmond, Va., 1967-68; fin. analyst Keystone Consol. Industries, Peoria, Ill., 1970-73; contr. HON Industries, Inc., Muscatine, Iowa, 1973-76, sec., treas., 1976-79; v.p. fin. Hawkeye Steel Products, Inc., Waterloo, Iowa, 1979-83, Cosco, Inc., Columbus, Ind., 1983-90; chief fin. officer Kiel Bros. Oil Co. Inc., Columbus, Ind., 1990-96; v.p. fin. Riverton Investment Corp., Winchester, Va., 1996—2004; ptnr. Tatum CFO Ptnrs., Charlottesville, 2004—. With AUS, 1968-70, Vietnam. Decorated Bronze Star. Mem. Rotary, Phi Kappa Psi. Republican. Presbyterian. Office: Tatum FCO Ptnrs 9775 Seminole trl PMB 335 Charlottesville VA 22901-2824

JOLLY, BRUCE O., lawyer; BA, Univ. NC, 1969, JD, 1973. Bar: NC 1973, Va. 1974, DC 1976, Md. 1988. Washington counsel Credit Union Nat. Assn.; fed. regulatory counsel Independent Bankers Assn.; atty. Shook, Hardy & Bacon LLP, Washington; ptnr., banking, fin. svcs. practice Venable LLP, Washington, 2003—. Contbr. articles in field. Mem.: ABA, Md. Bar Assn., DC Bar Assn., Va. Bar Assn., NC Bar Assn. Office: Venable LLP 575 7th St NW Washington DC 20004 Office Phone: 202-344-4818. Office Fax: 202-344-8300. Business E-Mail: bojolly@venable.com.

JOLLY, CHARLES NELSON, lawyer, pharmaceutical executive; b. New Brunswick, N.J., Aug. 14, 1942; s. Nelson Frederick and Marie Mercedes (Montemayor) J.; div.; children: T. Christopher, Susan Noel. BS, Holy Cross Coll., 1964; LLB, George Washington U., 1967. Bar: D.C. 1968, Tenn. 1984. Counsel Swift & Co., 1966—70, Miles Labs., 1970—71, dir. legis. affairs Washington, 1971—75, assoc. gen. counsel Elkhart, Ind., 1975—77; v.p., sec., gen. counsel, bd. dirs. Chattem Inc., Chattanooga, 1977—94; of counsel Baker, Donelson, Bearman, Caldwell & Spencer, Chattanooga, 1999—. Corp.sec Prestige Brands Holdings Inc., Irivngton, NY. Cand. for U.S. Congress, 1994, 96; past bd. dirs. Sr. Neighbors of Chattanooga, Inc., Tenn. Conservation League. Mem.: ABA, Van Buren County C. of C. (past bd. dirs.), BBB Chattanooga (past chmn., past bd. dirs.), Coun. Better Bus. Burs. U.S. (past bd. dirs.), Non-Prescription Drug Mfrs. Assn. (past bd. dirs., vice chmn. exec. com.), DC Bar Assn., Chattanooga Bar Assn., Tenn. Bar Assn., Chattanooga Retriever Club (past bd. dirs., past sec.), Mid. Tenn. Amateur Retriever Club (past sec.). Office: 172 College St Spencer TN 38585-1301 Office Phone: 914-524-6892. E-mail: cjolly@bakerdonelson.com.

JOLLY, DANIEL EHS, dental educator; b. St. Louis, Aug. 25, 1952; s. Melvin Joseph and Betty Ehs (Koehler) Jolly; m. Paula Kay Haas, 1972 (div.); 1 child, Farrell. BA in Biology and Chemistry, U. Mo., Kansas City, 1974, DDS, 1977. Diplomate Am. Bd. Special Care Dentistry. Resident in hosp. dentistry VA Med. Ctr., Leavenworth, Kans., 1977-78; pvt. practice Newcastle, Wyo., 1978-79; asst. prof. U. Mo., Kansas City, 1979-87; chief restorative dentistry Truman Med. Ctr., Kansas City, 1979-87; dir. dental oncology Trinity Luth. Hosp., 1982-87; assoc. prof., dir. gen. practice residency program Ohio State U., Columbus, 1987—, prof., dir. gen. practice residency program, 1993—. Dir. Honduras Clinic Project, 1992—; bd. dirs. Rinehart Found. U. Mo. Dental Sch., Kansas City, 1985—87; cons. Lee's Summit (Mo.) Care Ctr., 1984—87, Longview Nursing Ctr., Grandview, 1986—87; sec. Combined Hosp. Dental Staff, Columbus, 1989—90, v.p., 1990—91, pres., 1991—92. Author: (manual) Hospital Dental Hygiene, 1984, Hospital Dentistry, 1985, OSU Manual Hospital Dentistry, 1989—, (booklet) Nursing Home Dentistry, 1986, Dental Oncology, 1986. Mem. profl. adv. coun. Easter Seal Soc., 1986—92, sec. bd. dirs. Easter Seal Rehab. Ctr. Columbus, 1990—93, mem. regional coun. Kansas City, 1985—87; pres. Health Profls. Serving Humanity. With U.S. Naval Sea Cadet Corps, 1998—99. Recipient Alumni Achievement award in dentistry, U. Mo., Kansas City, 1995. Fellow: Pierre Fauchard Acad., Am. Coll. Dentistry, Acad. Dentistry Handicapped (pres. 1992), Acad. Gen. Dentistry, Acad. Dentistry Internat., Am. Soc. Dentistry Children, Am. Assn. Hosp. Dentists (regional v.p. 1993—, sec., pres.-elect 2002—03, pres. 2003—), Am. Soc. Geriatric Dentistry; mem.: ADA, Am. Bd. Special Care Dentistry (pres. 2004—, diplomate 2004), Ohio Dental Assn. (Humanitarian award 1998), Internat. Soc. Oral Oncology, S.W. Oncology Group, Fedn. Spl Care Orgns. Dentistry (chmn. 1992—93), Greater Kansas City Dental Soc., Internat. Assn. Dentistry handicapped (pres. 1994—96, past pres. 1996—98, editor 1998—), Magna Charta Barons Club. Avocations: photography, skiing, scuba diving, swimming, horses. Home: 1601 W Fifth Ave # 118 Columbus OH 43212-2310 Office: Ohio State U Coll Dentistry PO Box 182357 305 W 12th Ave Columbus OH 43218-2357 E-mail: djolly82552@cs.com.

JOLLY, E. GRADY, federal judge; b. Oct. 3, 1937; BA, U. Miss., 1959, LLB, 1962. Trial atty. NLRB, Winston-Salem, NC, 1962—64; asst. U.S. atty. No. Dist. Miss., 1964—67; trial atty. Dept. Justice Tax Div., Washington, 1967—69; pvt. practice Jolly, Miller & Milam, Jackson, Miss., 1969—82; judge U.S. Ct. Appeals (5th cir.), Jackson, 1982—. Office: James O Eastland US Courthouse 245 E Capitol St Rm 202 Jackson MS 39201*

JOLLY, JAMES LOUIS, JR., academic administrator; b. Gadsden, Ala., Nov. 5, 1947; s. James Louis Jolly and Judy Jewel Antoinette Bruce-Jolly; m. Joyce Theresa Vance, Aug. 18, 1973; children: Bryan Eugene Marchant, Jon Kyser McGee, James Edward. AS, Gadsden State Jr. Coll., 1968; BS, U. Ala., 1970, MA, 1972, PhD, 1987; theology degree, U. of the South, Sewanee, Tenn., 2003. Tchr. Litchfield Jr. High, Gadsden, 1970—71; instr. Brewer State Jr. Coll., Tuscaloosa, Ala., 1972—79, Shelton State C.C., Tuscaloosa, 1979—88, instr., divsn. chair, 1988—2000; dean instrnl. svcs. Gadsden State C.C., 2000—. Mem. Leadership Tuscaloosa, 1999—; moderator, bd. dirs. Ala. Pub. Policy Inst., 1995—; 2d v.p. Cababa coun. Girl Scouts, 2004—; field dir. Miss Ala. Orgn.; mem. allocation com. United Way of Etowch County. Fulbright fellow, 2005. Mem.: Instrnl. Officers of Ala., Southea. Conf. Svc. Learning, Am. Assn. C.C.s, Postsecondary Assn. Ala. (pres. 2001—02), Ala. Coll. English Tchrs. Assn. (pres. 2002—03). Episcopalian. Home: 906 4th St SW Attalla AL 35954 Office: Gadsden State CC 1000 George Wallace Dr Gadsden AL 35402 Office Phone: 256-549-8256.

JOLLY, JEFFREY RUSSELL, music educator, musician; b. Amarillo, Tex., Oct. 19, 1953; s. M Russell and Joyce Doctor Jolly; m. Diane Marie Knobl, July 6, 1974; children: Joshua Russell, Rebecca Anne. MusB in Classical Guitar Performance, U. So. Calif., 1978; MusM in Edn., U. N.Mex, 1988. Cert. K- 12 music tchr. N.Mex. Dept. Edn., 1981. Dir. bands Belen H.S. and Mid. Sch., N.Mex., 1981—, Covenant Presbyn. Ch., Albuquerque, 1981—. Clinician, music ensembles, N.Mex., 1987—; guitar and vocal performer, 1973—; coord. participatory murder mysteries St. James Hotel, Cimarron, 1987—; workshop clinician Presbyn. Assn. Musicians, Albuquerque, 1996—99; tchr., clinician Hummingbird Music Camp, Jemez Springs, 1987—; guitar accompanist De Profundis Men's A Cappella Choral Ensemble, Albuquerque, 2000—03. Composer: (stage musical) Earthstar, (incidental music) See Mommy Cry, (choral anthem) A Word to the Wise, And Ransom Captive Israel, (choral setting) Be Thou My Vision, (incidental music) A Company of Pilgrims; author: (play) The Winter People, The Wrong Game, All That Glitters, The Ace of Hearts, A Murderous Past Time; composer: (choral) The Birth of God (A Service of Carols); musician: (compact disc) Reverberations, Vol. 1, Reverberations, Vol. 2; composer: (incidental music) Frontiers of Faith (Commn., Gen. Assembly of the Presbyn. Ch. (USA), 1994, 1994); musician: (compact disc) The Green Man; composer: (incidental music) Dandelion Wine, (stage musical) Posada de Amor, (choral anthem) Hymn to the Holy Spirit, (incidental music) The Boys Next Door, (television theme music) News 101, News 101Nambe Award Show (Rocky Mountain Emmy Award, 1993), Adventure Rio. Advocate, fund raiser Health Care for Homeless, Albuquerque; various coms. Presbyn. Ch., 1979—2005. Recipient N.Mex. Quality in Edn. award, 2001; grantee, McCune Found., 1993. Mem.: Presbyn. Assn. Musicians, N.Mex. Music Educators Assn., Music Educators Nat. Conf., Phi Kappa Phi (Quality in Edn. award 2001). Presbyterian. Avocations: beer brewing, fly fishing, travel, gardening. Home: 100 Vissing Pl Los Lunas NM 87031 Office: Belen Consolidated Sch Dist 520 N Main Belen NM 87002 Office Phone: 505-966-1619. Home Fax: 505-865-6177; Office Fax: 505-966-1650. Personal E-mail: vonjolly@aol.com. E-mail: jollyj@belen.k12.nm.us.

JOLLY, MEENAKSHI, rheumatologist; m. Neeraj Jolly. MBBS, Med. Coun. of India, India, 1991; MS in clin. profl., U. Chgo., 2004. Cert. Am. Bd. Internal Medicine (cert. in rheumatology), Clin. rsch. trng. program U. Chgo., 2003. Sect. chief, rheumatology Christ Med. Ctr., Chicago, 2003—; asst. prof. of clin. medicine U. Ill. at Chgo., Chicago, Ill. Cons., tchg., clin. rsch., mentoring Christ Med. Ctr., Oaklawn, Ill., 2003—. Mem.: Arthritis Found., Lupus Found., Am. Coll. of Rheumatology. Achievements include research in rheumatic issues. Office: Christ Medial Ctr U Illinois 4440 W 95th St Oaklwan IL 60453 Office Phone: 708-684-5405. Office Fax: 708-684-2500. Personal E-mail: meenakshijolly_1@hotmail.com. E-mail: meenakshi.jolly-md@advocatehealth.com.

JOLLY, RAJESH, management consultant; B in Comm. magna cum laude, U. Bombay, 1970; MBA in Mktg. and Fin., U. Memphis, 1974; postgrad., U. So. Calif., 1991. From v.p. ops. and mktg. to exec. v.p. fin. Pancho's, Inc., Memphis, 1974—80, pres., CEO, 1988—93; regional mgr. Pepsico, Inc., Irvine, Calif., regional v.p. Wichita, Kans., 1980—88; pres., co-founder Centrex Venture Group, Raleigh, NC, 1993—95; v.p. Asia/Pacific Wendy's Internat., Honolulu, 1995—98; v.p. N.Am. ops. Budget Rent-a-Car, Daytona, Fla., 1999—2001; cons., owner Jolly & Assoc., Chgo., 2001—03; sr. v.p., pres. internat. Fedex Kinko's, Dallas, 2004—. Home: 228 Orchard Ln Glen Ellyn IL 60137

JOLLY, TODD B., music educator, minister; b. Wichita, Kans., Apr. 1, 1961; s. M Russell and Joyce Doctor Jolly; m. Judith Joan Yamamoto, Oct. 19, 1996; m. Yvette Marie Maraffi, June 30, 1984 (div. Feb. 2, 1992); children: Amber Lea, Nicole Marie, Bryan Todd. BA, Trenton State Coll., Hillwood Lakes, N.J., 1984; MDiv, San Francisco Theol. Sem., San Anselmo, Calif., 1993. Ordained minister of word and sacrament Presbytery of San Francisco, 1993. Interim assoc. pastor Lakeside Presbyn. Ch., San Francisco, 1993—95; pastor Clayton Presbyn. Ch., Clayton, Ind., 1996—97; music tchr./choirmaster Stuart Hall, San Francisco, 1997—; dir. of liturgical music Seventh Ave. Presbyn. Ch., San Francisco, 1997—; apprentice dir. San Francisco Boys Chorus, 2000—02. Composer in residence San Francisco Sch. of the Arts, 2004; music dir. San Francisco Renaissance Voices, 2005—. Composer: (choral music) Rise and Shine, (jazz mass) Mazz, (art song) The Oath, (choral work) To Be Read at a Funeral. Mem.: Am. Choral Dirs. Assn. D-Liberal. Presbyterian. Avocations: hiking, snowshoeing, gardening, cooking. Office: Stuart Hall Broadway San Francisco CA 94115 Office Phone: 415-563-2900.

JOLLY, WILLIAM THOMAS, language educator; b. Helena, Ark., Apr. 8, 1929; s. Sidney Eugene and Eva (Jones) J. BA, Southwestern at Memphis, 1952; MA, U. Miss., 1958; PhD, Tulane U., 1968. Assoc. ancient langs., chmn. dept. Millsaps Coll., Jackson, Miss., 1959-65; assoc. prof. Greek and Latin Rhodes Coll., Memphis, 1965-75, prof., 1975-94, chmn. dept. fgn. langs., 1975-79, prof. emeritus, 1994—. With USN, 1953-55. Recipient Clarence Day award Day Found., 1991. Mem. Am. Philol. Assn/, Linquistic Soc. Am., Archaeol. Inst. Am., Classical Assn. Mid. West & South, Tenn. Classical Assn., Tenn. Philol. Assn., Am. Classical Legue. Democrat. Methodist. Home: 697 University St Memphis TN 38107-5138 Office: Rhodes Coll 2000 N Parkway Memphis TN 38112-1690

JONARIS, GEORGE G., electrical engineer, computer engineer; b. Cairo, Egypt, Egypt, Feb. 2, 1962; arrived in U.S., 1988; s. Jonaris G Kreiz, Nawal L Morcos; m. Lily I. Jonaris, June 10, 1995; children: Christine, Claire. PhD, N.C. State U., 1992. Sr. software engineer Cadence Design Systems, San Jose, 1992—2004, project leader, 1999—2004; staff engr. Synopsys, Mountain View, Calif., 2004—. Recipient Student Achievement award, Syndicate of Engineers, Cairo, Egypt, 1984. Mem.: IEEE, Toastmasters Internat., Phi Kappa Phi. Achievements include patents for circuit layout technique with template-driven placement using Fuzzy logic. Office: Synopsys 700 E Middlefield Rd Mountain View CA 94043 Personal E-mail: gjggig111@sbcglobal.net.

JONAS, GARY FRED, healthcare executive; b. N.Y.C., Apr. 26, 1945; s. Otto and Hilde (Levy) Jonas; m. Rosalyn Ethel Levy; children: Lauren, Rachel. BS in Ops. Rsch., Columbia U., 1966; MBA, Harvard U., 1968. Mgmt. cons. Fry Cons., Washington, 1968-69; divsn. dir. Univ. Rsch. Corp. Ctr. Human Svcs., Chevy Chase, Md., 1970-73, exec. v.p., 1973-75, pres., CEO, 1975-85, chmn., CEO, 1985-88, also bd. dirs.; pres., COO The Earle Palmer Brown Cos., Bethesda, Md., 1988-93, also bd. dirs.; pres., CEO 20/20 Laser Ctrs., Inc., Bethesda, 1993-97, also bd. dirs.; exec. v.p., dir. TLC Laser Eye Ctrs., Inc., Bethesda, 1997-2000; mng. ptnr. Venture Philanthropy Ptnrs., Inc., Reston, Va., 2000—02; CEO Strategic Planning Advisors, Inc., 2002—; pres. Alase Laser Hair Removal Ctrs., 2002—. Faculty assoc. Johns Hopkins U., 1999—; adj. faculty Am. U., Washington. Contbr. articles to profl. jours. Mem.: Young Pres.'s Orgn. (exec. com., chmn. Washington metro chpt. 1987—88), Washington Bd. Trade, Am. Soc. Tng. and Devel., Conf. Bd., Nat. Contract Mgmt. Assn., Profl. Svcs. Coun. (past bd. dirs., v.p.), Inst. Mgmt. Cons. (cert.), Woodmont Country Club, Harvard Club. Home: 6716 Melody Ln Bethesda MD 20817-3115 Office Phone: 301-469-1945. E-mail: gary@jonas.com.

JONAS, GILBERT, public relations and fund raising executive; b. July 22, 1930; s. Harry and Mitzi (Rosenstein) J.; m. Barbara L. Selby, Sept. 1953 (div. Nov. 1961); 1 child, Susan; m. P. Joyce Theise, Dec. 27, 1964; children: Jillian, Stephanie. BA, Stanford U., 1951; grad. cert. Chinese studies, Columbia U., 1953, MA in Internat. Affairs, 1955. Pub. rels. counsel African Independence movements and East Asian govts., 1955-67; exec. sec. Am. Friends of Vietnam, N.Y.C., 1956-57; v.p. Harold L. Oram, Inc., N.Y.C., 1958-61; exec. sec. Am. Med. Ctr. for Burma, N.Y.C., 1959-61; cons., acting dir. Far East, Peace Corps, Washington, 1961; pres., owner Gilbert Jonas Co., Inc., N.Y.C., 1962—2003. Author: One Shining Moment-A History of the Student World Federalist Movement, 1942-1953, 2000, Freedom's Sword: The NAACP and the Struggle Agaist Racism in America, 1909-1969, 2004. Dir. pub. info. N.Y. Youth for Stevenson, 1956; mem. exec. com. N.Y. Com. for Dem. Voters, 1959-62; pres. Reform Ind. Dem. of N.Y., 1958-59; mem. civil rights staff Nat. Citizens for Kennedy-Johnson, 1960; devel. and pub. rels. counsel NAACP, 1965-95, mem. exec. com. Mid-Manhattan br., 1997-2000, life mem.; mem. steering com. N.Y. Citizens for Humphrey-Muskie, 1968; nat. coord. Biracial Democrats Miss. Democratic Convention, 1968, Charles Evers for Gov. Miss., 1971; co-founder N.Y.C. Reform Movement, Dem. party, 1958-63; bd. dirs. Am. Com. on Africa, 1955-59, League Indsl. Democracy, 1972-91, Harlem Youth Devel. Found., 1998—2002; nat. coord. Holy Land Conservation Fund, 1977-82; cons. Internat. Civil Rights Ctr. and Mus., Greensboro, N.C., 1996-97, Chinese Dissidents; founding bd. mem., treas. The Wei Jingsheng Found., 1998-2002; chmn. World Federalist Assn. Greater Metro N.Y., 2001-2002; mem. nat. bd. World Federalist Assn., 2002-04; mem. coun. World Federalist Movement, 2001-03. With U.S. Army, 1953-55. Recipient Ann. Freedom award Miss. NAACP, 1970, Ann. Humanitarian award Manhattan NAACP, 1989. Mem. Phi Beta Kappa, Sigma Delta Chi. Home: 215 E 80th St Apt 5L New York NY 10021-0545 E-mail: partisanme@aol.com.

JONAS, HARRY S., medical education consultant; b. Kirksville, Mo., Dec. 3, 1926; s. Harry S. and Sarah (Laird) J.; m. Connie Kirby, Aug. 6, 1949; children— Harry S., III, William Reed, Sarah Elizabeth. BA, Washington U., St. Louis, 1949, MD, 1952. Intern St. Luke's Hosp., St. Louis, 1952-53; resident Barnes Hosp., St. Louis, 1952-56; practiced medicine specializing in ob-gyn., Independence, Mo., 1956-74; prof. ob-gyn, chmn. dept. ob-gyn Truman Med. Center; asst. dean U. Mo-Kansas City Sch. Medicine, 1975-78, dean, 1978-87, med. edn. cons., 2000—, spl. cons. to the dean; asst. v.p. med. edn. AMA, Chgo., 1987-2000. Mem. Independence City Council, 1964-68; mem. Jackson County (Mo.) Legislature, 1973-74. Mem. ACOG (pres. 1986-87), Ctrl. Assn. Obstetricians and Gynecologists, Assn. Profs. Gynecology and Obstetrics, Assn. Am. Med. Colls., A.C.S., AMA, Mo. Med. Assn., Jackson County Med. Soc., Kansas City Gynecol. Soc., Chgo. Gynecol. Soc. Home: 207 NW Spruce St Lees Summit MO 64064-1430 Office: U Mo-Kansas City Sch Medicine 2411 Holmes St Kansas City MO 64108-2741 Office Phone: 816-235-5284. Business E-Mail: jonash@umkc.edu.

JONAS, HOWARD, communications executive; BA economics, Harvard U. Founder Jonas Publishing Corp, 1979—; chmn IDT Corp, 1990—, CEO, 1991—2001, pres., 1991—96, treas., 1990—2002; chmn. IDT Telecom., 1999—2002; co-chmn. IDT Media, 2002—; chmn. bd. dir. Net2Phone, 2001—. Office: c/o IDT Corp 520 Broad St Newark NJ 07102*

JONAS, JIRI, chemist, educator; b. Prague, Czechoslovakia, Apr. 1, 1932; arrived in US, 1963; s. Frantisek and Jirlna (Vondrak) Jonas; m. Ana M. Masiulis, June 1, 1968. BSc, Tech. U. Prague, 1956; PhD, Czechoslovak Acad Sci., 1960; D honoris causa (hon.), U. Rio de Janeiro, 2003. Research assoc. Inst. Organic Chemistry, Czechoslovak Acad. Sci., Prague, 1960-63; vis. scientist, dept. chemistry U. Ill., Urbana, 1963-65, from asst. to assoc. prof., 1966-72, prof., 1972—2001, prof. Ctr. for Advanced Study, 1996-2001, prof. emeritus, 2001—, sr. staff mem. Materials Research Lab., 1970-93, dir. sch. chem. scis., 1983-93, dir. Beckman Inst. Advanced Sci. and Tech., 1993—2001, dir. emeritus, 2001—. Mem. editl. bd. Jour. Magnetic Resonance, 1975—2000, Jour. Chem., 1980—83, Jour. Chem. Physics, 1986—89, Accts. Chem. Rsch., 1990—93, Ann. Rev. Phys. Chemistry, 1991—95; contbr. articles to profl. jours. Recipient U.S. Sr. Scientist award, Alexander von Humboldt Found., 1988; Alfred P. Sloan fellow, 1967—69, J. S. Guggenheim fellow, 1972—73, Sr. scholar, U. Ill., 1985—88. Fellow: AAAS, Am. Phys. Soc., Am. Acad. Arts and Scis.; mem.: NAS, Materials Rsch. Soc., Am. Chem. Soc. (assoc. editor. Jour. Am. Chem. Soc., Joel Henry Hildebrand award 1983), Am. Philos. Soc., NBTC Club (Naples, Fla.), U. Ill. Tennis Club. Roman Catholic. Office: Univ of Ill 166 Roger Adams Lab 600 S Mathews Urbana IL 61801 E-mail: j-jonas@uiuc.edu.

JONAS, JOAN (JOAN AMERMAN EDWARDS), artist; b. NYC, July 13, 1936; m. Gerald Jonas, 1959. BA in art history, Mt. Holyoke Coll., 1958; studied sculpture, Boston Mus. Fine Arts, 1958—61; MFA in sculpture, Columbia U., 1965. Joined faculty MIT, Cambridge, Mass., 2000, prof. dept. architecture, prof., acting dir. visual arts program. Exhibitions include Aspects de l'art actuel presentes par la Galerie Sonnabend, Musee Galliera, Paris, 1973, Stage Sets, Inst. Contemporary Art, U. Pa., Phila., 1976, Three Tales, Documenta 6, Kassel, Germany, 1977, Joan Jonas: The Juniper Tree, Stedelijk Mus., Amsterdam, 1979, Whitechapel Art Gallery, London, 1979, Music, Sound, Language Theater, Stedelijk Mus., Amsterdam, 1981, Double Lunar Dogs, Contemporary Arts Mus., Houston, 1981, Other Realities - Installations for Performance, 1981, Upside Down and Backwards, Documenta 7, Kassel, Germany, 1982, He Saw Her Burning, DAAD Galerie, Berlin, 1984, Revolted by the thought of known places...Sweeney Astray, Kunst-Werke, Berlin, 1992, Joan Jonas: Works 1968-1994, Stedelijk Mus., Amsterdam, 1994, Props: Works 1994-1997, Pat Hearn Gallery, NYC, 1997, In the Shadow a Shadow, 1999, Drawings, Reinhard Hauff Gallery, Stuttgart, Germany, 2000, Joan Jonas: Film and Video Work, 1968-76, Dia Ctr. for Arts, NYC, 2000, Joan Jonas: Performance, Video, Installation, 1968-2000, Galerie der Stadt, Stuttgart, Germany, 2000—01, Neue Galerie fur Bilden Kunst, Berlin, 2003, Joan Jonas: Video Retrospective, Mus. Carillo Gil, Mex. City, 2003, Joan Jonas: Five Works, Queens Mus. Art, NYC, 2003 (Award for Best Exhbn. of Time Based Art, Internat. Assn. Art Critics/USA, 2005), Lines in the Sand, Rosamund Felsen Gallery, Santa Monica, 2003, The Renaissance Soc., Chgo., 2004, The Shape, the Scent, the Feel of Things, 2004, film and videography, Wind, 1968, Paul Revere, 1971, Mirror Check, 1971, Vertical Roll, 1972, Organic Honey's Visual Telepathy, 1972, Duet, 1972, Left Side Right Side, 1972, Songdelay, 1973, Three Returns, 1973, Barking, 1973, Two Women, 1973, Disturbances, 1974, Merlo, 1974, Glass Puzzle, 1974, May Windows, 1976, Good Night, Good Morning, 1976, I Want to Live in the Country (And Other Romances), 1977, Upside Down and Backwards, 1981, Double Lunar Dogs, 1983, He Saw Her Burning, 1983, Big Market, 1984, Brooklyn Bridge, 1988, Volcano Saga, 1989. Recipient Polaroid Award for Video, 1987, Maya Deren Award for Video, Am. Film Inst., 1988, Hyogo Prefecture Mus. Modern Art Prize, Japan Internat. Video Art Festival, Anonymous Was a Woman Award, 1998. Office: MIT Visual Arts Program 265 Massachusetts Ave N51-315 Cambridge MA 02139*

JONAS, JOHN FRANCIS, lawyer; b. St. John's, Que., Can., May 3, 1950; s. Hans and Lora Jonas; m. Sheila Coplan, Sept. 26, 1977; children: Benjamin, David. BA, Clark U., 1972; JD, Cornell U., 1976. Bar: D.C. 1976. Atty. HHS, Washington, 1976-78; legis. asst. Office Congresswoman Liz Holtzman, Washington, 1978-80; legis. dir. Office Congressman Bob Shomansky, Washington, 1980-81; tax counsel Com. on Ways and Means U.S. Congress, Washington, 1981-86; ptnr. Patton Boggs LLP, Washington, 1986—, chmn. Public Policy dept. & Regulatory dept. Office: Patton Boggs LLP 2550 M St NW Washington DC 20037-1350 Office Phone: 202-457-5624. Office Fax: 202-457-6315. Business E-Mail: jjonas@pattonboggs.com.

JONAS, RAYMOND ANTHONY, education educator, writer; b. San Mateo, Calif., July 12, 1954; s. Carl and Lucille Jonas; m. Patricia Scarlett Jonas; children: Anthony, Elizabeth, Katherine. PhD, UC Berkeley, Berkeley, Calif., 1985. Prof. U. Wash., Seattle, 1985—. Vis. prof. Universite de Nantes, Nantes, France (incl. Monaco), 1993—93, Universite de Montpellier, 1992—92. Author: The Tragic Tale of Claire Ferchaud and the Great War, France and the Cult of the Sacred Heart: An Epic Tale for Modern Times, Industry and Politics in Rural France; Peasants of the Isère, 1870-1914. Fellow Howard Found. Fellowship, George A. and Eliza Howard Found., 1997-8, NEH Fellowship, Nat. Endowment for the Humanities, 2004-2005; scholar Fulbright Sr. Scholar, Fulbright Commn., 1993-4. Mem.: Am. Hist. Assn. Avocations: photography, rowing. Office: Univ Wash Box 353560 Seattle WA 98195-3560 Office Phone: 206-543-5790. Business E-Mail: jonas@u.washington.edu.

JONAS, RICHARD ANDREW, medical educator; b. Adelaide, South Australia, Nov. 28, 1951; came to US, 1982; s. Lyall Richard Jonas; m. Dianne E. Wearne, Apr. 12, 1980 (div. May 1996); children: Andrew William, Michael Richard; m. Katherine Vernot, Nov. 6, 1999; 1 child, Nicole Sofia. MBBS with honors, U. Adelaide, 1974; MA, Harvard U., 1994. Gen. surgery resident Royal Melbourne Hosp., Australia, 1975-79; cardiac surgery resident Green Ln. Hosp., Auckland, New Zealand, 1980-82; resident in cardiac surgery Brigham & Women's Hosp., Boston; surg. fellow Brigham and Women's Hosp., Boston, 1982-83; chief resident in cardiac surgery Children's Hosp., Boston, 1983-84; prof. surgery Harvard Med. Sch., Boston, 1994—; chief of cardiac surgery Children's Hosp., Boston, 1994—2004; chief cardiovasc. surgery, co-dir. Congenital Heart Inst., Children's Nat. Med Ctr., Washington, 2004—. Author: Cardiopulmonary Bypass in Neonates and Infants, 1994, Comprehensive Surgical Management of Congenital Heart Disease, 2004. Fellow ACS, Soc. of Neurosci.; mem. Am. Assn. of Thoracic Surgery v.p., Soc. of Thoracic Surgery, Am. Surg. Assn. Episcopalian. Avocations: skiing, mountain trekking. Office: Children's Nat Med Ctr 111 Michigan Ave NW Washington DC 20010 Office Phone: 202-884-2811. E-mail: rjonas@cnmc.org.

JONAS, SARAN, neurologist, educator; b. N.Y.C., June 24, 1931; s. Myron and Margaret (Wurmfeld) J.; m. Ruth Haber, Sept. 16, 1956; children: Elizabeth Ann, Frederick Jonathan. BS, Yale U., 1952; MD, Columbia U., 1956. Diplomate Am. Bd. Psychiatry and Neurology, Am. Bd. Internal Medicine. Intern Bellevue Hosp., N.Y.C., 1956-57, resident and fellow in medicine and neurology, 1957-62; practice medicine specializing in neurology N.Y.C., 1964—; from clin. instr. to assoc. prof. clin. neurology NYU Sch. Medicine, 1964-77, prof. clin. neurology, 1977—, acting chmn. dept. neurology, 1987-91. Assoc. dir. neurology NYU Hosp., 1970-87, dir., 1987-91, dir. electroencephalography, 1969-94; acting dir. neurology Bellevue Hosp., N.Y.C., 1987-91, assoc. dir., 1991—, dir. electroencephalography, 1994—. Served with USN, 1962-64. N.Y. State fellow in rheumatic diseases, 1962-64 Mem. Am. Acad. Neurology, Assn. for Rsch. in Nervous and Mental Diseases, Am. Heart Assn. (Stroke Coun., Epidemiology Coun.), Am. Epilepsy Soc. Office: 530 1st Ave New York NY 10016-6402

JONAS, STEPHEN P., investment company executive; b. 1953; BA in Math. magna cum laude, Boston U., 1974, MBA with highest honors, 1975. CFO, Graphic Sys., Inc., Hudson, N.H., 1975-78; from head of fin. to divsn. CFO, Wang Labs., Lowell, Mass., 1978-87; v.p. fin. investor info. svcs. Fidelity Investments, Boston, 1987, various fin. mgmt. positions, sr. v.p., CFO Personal Investments and Brokerage Group, sr. v.p., CFO, 1998, exec. dir., Fidelity Mgmt. and Rsch., 2005—. Office: Fidelity Investments 82 Devonshire St Boston MA 02109*

JONAS, STEVEN, preventive medicine physician, writer, public health service officer; b. N.Y.C., Nov. 22, 1936; s. Harold Jacob and Florence Jane (Kyzor) J.; m. Josephine Gear, June 19, 1964 (div.); m. Linda Sue Friedman, Nov. 23, 1971 (div.); children: Jacob Henry, Lillian Sara. BA cum laude, Columbia Coll., 1958; MD, Harvard U., 1962; MPH, Yale U., 1967; MS, NYU, 1997. Diplomate Am. Bd. Preventive Medicine-Pub. Health. Intern Lenox Hill Hosp., N.Y.C., 1962-63; postdoctoral rschr. Univ. Coll. London and London Sch. Econs., 1963-65, resident in preventive medicine and pub. health, 1965—67; dist. health officer N.Y.C. Dept. Health, 1967-68, dir. ambulatory care planning and devel., 1969; dir. dept. social medicine Morrisania City Hosp., Bronx, NY, 1969-71; asst. prof. Albert Einstein Coll. Medicine, Bronx, 1969—71; lectr. Mt. Sinai Sch. Medicine, N.Y.C., 1969-89, asst. prof. dept. cmty. medicine, 1971—74; coord. ambulatory svcs. Univ. Hosp., 1971-74, assoc. prof. dept. cmty. and preventive medicine, 1974-83; prof. dept. preventive medicine Stony Brook U. Sch. Medicine, 1983—, prof. Grad. Program in Pub. Health, 2004—; attending physician Nassau County Med. Ctr., East Meadow, NY, 1973-86. Cons. dept. medicine Winthrop-U. Hosp., Mineola, N.Y., 1979-93; adj. assoc. prof. Columbia U. Sch. Architecture, 1977-79; adj. assoc. prof. med. edn. Tex. Coll. Osteo. Medicine, Ft. Worth, 1980-85; adj. prof. legal edn. Touro Coll. Sch. of Law, Huntington, N.Y., 1998—; mem. N.Y. State Bd. Medicine, 1979-88. Author: Quality Control of Ambulatory Care: A Task for Health Departments, 1977, Medical Mystery: The Training of Doctors in the United States, 1978, Triathloning for Ordinary Mortals, 1986, revised, 1999, An Introduction to the U.S. Health Care System, 5th edit., 2003, The New Americanism, 1992, Take Control of Your Weight, 1993, Regular Exercise: A Handbook for Clinical Practice, 1995, The Essential Triathlete, 1996, Talking About Health and Wellness with Patients, 2000; editor, co-author: Health Care Delivery in the United State (Book of Yr. award Am. Jour. Nursing 1982), 1977, 81, 86, co-editor, 1999, 2002, Health Promotion and Disease Prevention in Clinical Practice, 1996; co-author: Pacewalking: The Balanced Way to Aerobic Health, 1988, The "I Don't Eat (But I Can't Lose)" Weight-Loss Program, 1989, Just the Weigh You Are, 1997, Help Your Man Get Healthy, 1999, 30 Secrets of the World's Healthiest Cuisines, 2000; chief editor: (Springer series) Health Care and Society, 1976-79, Medical Education, 1978-2000; assoc. editor Preventive Medicine, 1983-2005; mem. editl. bd. ACSM's Health & Fitness Jour., 1999—, Am. Jour. Preventive Medicine, 1987-99; book rev. editor Am. Jour. Preventive Medicine, 1991-92; mem. editl. bd. Am. Med. Athletic Assn. Quarterly, 1988—, columnist, 1999—, editor-in-chief (J), 2002—; staff writer, Am. TRI, 2002-2004; contbr. articles to profl. jours.; reviewer in field. Sr. advisor U.S. Preventive Svcs. Task Force, 1984-89. Fellow Am. Pub. Health Assn., Am. Coll. Preventive Medicine (com. chmn. 1979-82), N.Y. Acad. Medicine (med. edn. com. 1983-92); mem. AMA, Am. Hosp. Assn. (life), NY Acad. Scis., Profl. Ski Instrs. Am. (cert. level I 1995), Assn. Tchrs. Preventive Medicine (pres. 1977-78), Am. Mensa, Phi Beta Kappa. Democrat. Jewish. Avocations: bicycling, pacewalking and running, weightlifting, triathlon competition, skiing. Home: 105 Washington Ave Port Jefferson Station NY 11777-2003 Office: Stony Brook U Sch Med Stony Brook NY 11794 Office Phone: 631-444-2147. Business E-Mail: steven.jonas@stonybrook.edu.

JONAS, TINA WESTBY, federal agency administrator; BA, Ariz. State U.; MA, Georgetown U. Sr. budget examiner, intelligence br. nat. security divisn. U.S. Dept. Def., Washington, 1991—95; mem. appropriations com., def.

subcom. Ho. of Reps., Washington, 1995—2001; dep. undersec. def. fin. mgmt. U.S. Dept. Def., Washington, 2001—02; asst. dir. fin., CFO FBI, Washington, 2002—04; undersec. def. (comptr), CFO U.S. Dept. Def., Washington, 2004—. Recipient Disting. Pub. Service medal, US Dept. Def. Office: US Dept Def 1100 Defense Pentagon Washington DC 20301*

JONAS, TONY, television executive; Dir. dramatic series Aaron Spelling Prodns.; v.p. dramatic series and long form programming MGM/UA TV Group; sr. exec. in charge of devel. Winkler/Rich Prodns., Paramount; v.p. devel. Disney TV; sr. v.p. drama devel. Warner Bros. TV (previously Lorimar TV), 1989-91, exec. v.p. creative affairs, 1991-95, pres., 1995-98, Tony Jonas Prodns., Burbank, Calif., 1999—. Exec. prodr.: (TV series) Queer as Folk, 2000—, Leap Years, 2001—02; (TV films) Lost at Home, 2003.

JONASON, WILLIAM A., lawyer; b. 1958; BA in Econ. with honors, St. Olaf Coll., 1980; JD with distinction, Univ. Iowa, 1983. Bar: Minn. 1983. Law clk., Chief Judge Donald Lay US Ct. of Appeals (8th cir.), 1983—84; ptnr., corp. group; co-chair, closely held businesses group Dorsey & Whitney LLP, Mpls., and mem., policy com. Adj. prof. law Hamline Law Sch., 1988—89, St. Thomas Law Sch., 2004. Sr. articles editor Iowa Law Rev., 1982—83. Bd. dir. Volunteer Connection, Rochester Pub. Libr. Found., Rochester Pub. Sch. Found., YMCA Camp Olson. Mem.: Minn. Bar Assn., Hennepin Co. Bar Assn. Office: Dorsey & Whitney LLP Ste 1500 50 S Sixth St Minneapolis MN 55402-1498 Office Phone: 612-340-2600, 612-492-6111. Office Fax: 612-340-7800. Business E-Mail: jonason.bill@dorsey.com.

JONASSEN, JAMES O., architect; b. Aberdeen, Wash., July 23, 1940; s. James E. and Marjorie E. (Smith) J.; m. Patricia E. Glen, June 9, 1958 (div. Oct. 1975); m. Marilyn Joan Kampa, June 11, 1977; children: Christian A., Steven E. BArch, U. Wash., 1964; MS in Architecture, Columbia U., 1965. Registered architect Ala., Alaska, Ariz., Calif., Colo., Fla., Ga., Idaho, Ill., Kans., La., Minn., Mo., Mont., Nebr., Nev., N.Mex., N.C., Ohio, Okla., Oreg., S.D., Tex. Wash., Utah., Wis., D.C., Del. Mass. Miss., N.H., N.Y., R.I., Vt., P.R., British Columbia, Can. Designer NBBJ Group, Seattle, 1965-70, ptnr., 1970—; CEO NBBJ West, 1983-96, mng. ptnr., 1997—. Bd. dirs. Health Insights Found. Prin works include Bettelle Meml. Lab., Richland, Wash., 1965 (lab of yr. award 1968), Heath Profl. Bldg., 1970, Children's Orthopedic Hosp., Seattle, 1972 (AIA Honor award 1976), St. Mary's Hosp., Surg. Pavilion, Rochester, Minn., 1982, St. Vincent Med. Office Bldg., Portland, Oreg., 1983, Scottsdale Meml. Hosp. N., Ariz., 1984, Seattle VA Hosp., 1985, Stanford U. Hosp., 1986, St. Joseph Host. Med. Ctr., 1988, Providence Med./ Ctr., Seattle, 1990 (AIA Merit award), David Grant Med. Ctr., Fairfield, Calif., 1986 (USAF Honor award 1989, Spl. citation DOD 1988, Type i Honor award USAF 1989, Excellence in Design award DOD 1991), Alaska Native Med. Ctr., 1997, Kangbuk Med. Ctr., Seoul, Korea, 1998, Capital Coast Health Med. Ctr., Wellington, New Zealand, 2000. Bd. dirs. Health Facilities Rsch. and Edn. Project, 1991—98, Swedish Med. Ctr. Found., 1993—, Sch. Zone Inst., 1990—; pres.bd. Architecture and Children project, 1990; mem. vis. com. U. Washington Sch. Medicine, 2001—. Recipient Seattle Newsmaker Tomorrow award, Time Mag., 1978, Modern Health Care award, Swedish Med. Ctr., 1997—2000, Seattle Archtl. Found. Bd., 2000—; fellow fellow, Naramore Found., 1969; scholar Columbia U. scholar, 1964. Fellow AIA (chmn. steering com. 1983-85, nat. com. architecture for health, mem. Nat. Life Cycle Task Force 1977, bd. dirs. Seattle chpt. 1985-87, Modern Healthcare award 1998); mem. Sr. Coun. Archs. (pres. 1999, 2000), Wash. Athletic Club, Columbia Tower Club, Rotary. Office: NBBJ 111 S Jackson St Seattle WA 98104-2881 Business E-Mail: jjonassen@nbbj.com.

JONASSON, RALPH GEORGE, research chemist; b. Hamilton, Ont., Can., July 8, 1957; s. Werner and Cecilia (Liedtke) Jonasson. BSc, McMaster U., Hamilton, 1980; PhD, U. Western Ont., London, Can., 1986. Postdoctoral fellow McMaster U., Hamilton, 1986-87, rsch. assoc., 1987-88; rsch. officer Alta. Rsch. Coun., Edmonton, Can., 1989-98; rsch. chemist Vulcan Performance Chems., Columbus, Ga., 1998—2002. Author: (book chpt.) Advances in Lignocellulosics Characterization, 1999; inventor in field; contbr. articles to profl. jours. Mem. AAAS, Internat. Assn. Water Quality (reviewer 1998-2001), Chem. Inst. Can. (chair Edmonton local sect. 1996, past chair Edmonton local sect. 1997), Am. Chem. Soc., Royal Soc. Chemistry, Geochem. Soc. Avocations: history, philosophy, silviculture, wine appreciation. Home: 62 Juanita Dr Hamilton ON Canada L9C 2G3

JONCKHEERE, ALAN MATHEW, physicist; b. Howell, Mich., Feb. 12, 1947; s. August Peter and Elizabeth Gertrude (Nash) Jonckheere; m. Barbara Jean Minter, Aug. 16, 1969; children: Jessica, Susan, Laura Jean and Amanda Jean (twins). BS, Mich. State U., 1969; MS, U. Wash., 1970, PhD, 1976. Instr. physics dept. Fermi Nat. Accelerator Lab., Batavia, Ill., 1976-78, staff physicist, 1978—, assoc. dept. head meson dept., 1981-83, assoc. dept. head exptl. areas, 1983-84, Beams group coordinator, 1984-85, accelerator div. exptl. support dept., 1985-89, researcher div. D0 dept., 1989—. Researcher elem. particle physics Stanford Linear Accelerator Ctr., Lawrence Berkeley Lab., Calif. Contbr. papers to physics publs. Office: Fermi Natl Accelerator Lab PO Box 500 Batavia IL 60510-0500 Business E-Mail: Jonckheere@fnal.gov.

JONDAHL, LYNN, foundation administrator; BA, Iowa State U., 1958; MDiv, Yale U., 1962. Ordained min. United Ch. of Christ, 62. Mem. ho. reps. State of Mich., Lansing, 1972—94, chmn. taxation com., mem. coll. and univ, consumers and judiciary coms., mem. juvenile justice subcom.; exec. dir. Mich. Prospect for Renewed Citizenship, Flint. Campus pastor Calif. State Coll., L.A.; co-dir. Christian Faith and Higher Edn. Inst. Mich. State U. Active Foster Grandparent Program, Student Advocat. Ctr., Ctr. Handicapped Affairs; corp. mem. United Ch. Bd. Nomeland Ministries. Named Legislator of Yr., Mich. Fedn. Pvt. Child and Family Agys., 1985, Mich. Twp. Assn., 1987, Citizens Alliance to Uphold Spl. Edn., 1990, Assn. Retarded Citizens Mich., 1990, Outstanding Legislator, AAUP, 1985, Outstanding Legislator of Yr., Mich. Assn. Deaf, Hearing and Speech Svcs., 1990; recipient Consumers Advocate award, Mich. Citizen's Lobby, 1974, Philip Hart award, Consumer Educators Mich., 1980. Mem.: ACLU, Mich. Women's Studies Assn., Mich. China Coun. Office: Northpart Center Ste 406 432 N Saginaw St Flint MI 48502

JONDAHL, TERRI ELISE, importing and distribution company executive; b. Ukiah, Calif., May 6, 1959; d. Thomas William and Rebecca (Stewart) J. AA in Bus. Adminstrn., Mendocino Coll., 1981; BA in Adminstrn. and Mgmt., Columbia Pacific U., 1993. Office systems analyst County of Mendocino, Ukiah, 1980-83; micro systems analyst Computerland of Annapolis, Md., 1983-84; controller Continental Mfg. Inc., Nacogdoches, Tex., 1984-87, mktg. mgr., 1987-89, dir. sales and mktg., 1989-95; exec. v.p., chief oper. officer CAB Inc., Oakwood, Ga., 1995—2002; CEO Cab Inc., 2002—. Co-author: National Federation of Business & Professional Women Local Organization Revitalization Plan, 1989. Fellow: Hall County C. of C.; mem.: NAFE, Am. Bus. Women's Assn., Ukiah Bus. and Profl. Women (pres. 1981—82), Nacogdoches Bus. and Profl. Women (pres. 1987—88), Tex. Fedn. Bus. and Profl. Women (state pres. 1994—95), Com. of 200 Orgns., Gwinnett Chamber Chmn.'s Club, Leadership Gwinnett, Gwinnett County C. of C. (CEO exec. roundtable), Nacogdoches County C. of C. (small bus. adv. com. 1990). Home: 6009 Lanier Heights Cir Buford GA 30518 Office: CAB Inc 4161 Chamblee Rd Oakwood GA 30566-3518 E-mail: tjondahl@cabinc.com.

JONES, ABBOTT C., investment company executive; b. Lexington, Ky., Aug. 14, 1934; s. John Catron and Lois (Sauters) J.; m. Carol Donahue, June 29, 1957; children: Cynthia, Alison, Hilary. BA, Principia Coll., 1956; MBA, Harvard U., 1958. Salesman Carnation Co., 1959-60; account exec. Benton & Bowles, N.Y.C., 1960-63; with Ogilvy & Mather, N.Y.C., 1963-77, sr. v.p., dir., 1973-77; sr. v.p., gen. mgr. Foote, Cone & Belding, N.Y.C., 1977-82; pres. Foote, Cone & Belding, Associated Communications Cos., N.Y.C., 1982-86; pres., chief operating officer Foote, Cone, Belding Communications, Inc., N.Y.C., 1986-89; pvt. cons. practice Greenwich, Conn., 1989-90; founder, mng. dir. AdMedia Ptnrs. Inc., NYC, 1990—. Served with U.S. Army, 1958-59. Mem.: Boca Grande, Belle Haven. Office: 19th Flr 444 Madison Ave New York NY 10022-6903 Business E-Mail: ajones@admediapartners.com.

JONES, AIDAN DREXEL, lawyer; b. Wilmington, Del., Dec. 17, 1945; s. Richard Leonard and Dorothy Drexel (Walsh) J.; m. Kathleen Dellert, Aug. 19, 1972; 4 children. BA, Wesleyan U., 1967; JD, Georgetown U., 1974. Bar: D.C. 1975, U.S. Supreme Ct. 1984, Md. 1996. Law clk. U.S. Dist. Ct., Washington, 1974—75; assoc. Edward Greensfelder Jr. P.C., Washington, 1975—77, Haight, Gardner, Poor & Havens, Washington, 1977—83; ptnr. Finley, Kumble, Wagner, Heine, Underberg, Manley, Myerson & Casey, Washington, 1983—87, Laxalt, Washington, Perito & Dubuc, Washington, 1988—90, Washington, Perito & Dubuc, Washington, 1990—91, Graham & James, Washington, 1991—95; pvt. practice, 1995—. Contbr. articles to profl. jours. Mem. nat. alumni com. Wesleyan U., Middletown, Conn., 1987-89, 1967 class agt., 1985-92; trustee River Road Unitarian Ch., 1992-94; co-treas. Sidwell Friends Sch. Parents Assn., 1995-97, v.p., 1997-98, pres. 1998-99. Lt. USN, 1968-71. Mem. ABA (vice chmn. aviation and space law com. 1985-91). Office: 1818 N St NW Ste 700 Washington DC 20036-2477 Office Phone: 202-293-2386. Personal E-mail: ajones2506@aol.com.

JONES, ALAN PORTER, JR., food manufacturing executive; b. Milw., Feb. 27, 1925; s. Alan Porter and Eleanor Pratt (Bright) J.; m. Jean Drummond, Sept. 12, 1953; children: Richard, Susan, Cynthia, Alexandra. BA cum laude, Harvard U., 1948, MBA, 1950. With Jones Dairy Farm, Ft. Atkinson, Wis., 1950—, asst. treas., 1953-61, treas., 1961-74, v.p., treas., 1974-93, bd. dir. Pres. Uncle Josh Bait Co., 1978—2002; bd. dirs. Johnson Bank. Bd. dir. Dwight Foster Pub. Libr., 1952-87, Wis. Livestock and Meat Coun., 1981-97, Ft. Atkinson C. of C., 1985-88; mem. Ft. Atkinson Sch. Bd., 1968-69, Wis. Gov.'s Adv. Com. on Internat. Trade, 1981-97, Wis. Internat. Trade Coun., 1997-2003, Wis. Citizens Environ. Coun., 1980-84, Wis. Radioactive Waste Policy Coun., 1984-87; trustee Ripon Coll., Wis., 1974-77; bd. dirs. Wis. Nature Conservancy, 1992-95. With inf. U.S. Army, 1943-45. Decorated Bronze Star, Combat Inf. badge. Mem.: Internat. Crane Found., Nat. Audubon Soc., Gathering Waters, Nature Conservancy. Republican. Home: 433 Adams St Fort Atkinson WI 53538-1401 Office: Jones Dairy Farm PO Box 808 Fort Atkinson WI 53538-0808

JONES, ALEX S., reporter, writer; b. Greeneville, Tenn., Nov. 19, 1946; m. Susan E. Tifft, Sept. 21, 1985. BA, Washington and Lee U., 1968. Editor Greeneville (Tenn.) Sun, 1978-83; press reporter N.Y. Times, 1983-92; host On the Media Nat. Pub. Radio, 1993-97; host, exec. editor Media Matters PBS, 1995—; Eugene C. Patterson prof. Practice Journalism Duke U., 1998—2000. Sr. fellow Media Studies Ctr., 1996-97; dir. Joan Shorenstein Ctr. on the Press, Politics, and Pub. Policy, Harvard U., 2000—. Author: (with Susan E. Tifft) The Patriarch: The Rise and Fall of the Bingham Dynasty, 1991, The Trust: The Private and Powerful Family Behind The New York Times, 1999. Recipient Pulitzer prize for specialized reporting, 1987; Nieman fellow, 1981-82. Home: Apt 61 1 Waterhouse St Cambridge MA 02138-3612 Business E-Mail: alex.jones@harvard.edu.

JONES, AMELIA SUSAN, retired anesthesiologist; b. Kansas City, Mo., Nov. 2, 1930; d. John Thomas and Amelia (Coyner) Creegan; m. Warren Collins (dec.); children: Daniel W. Collins, Stephen D. Collins; m. Thomas J. Swann (dec.); m. Howard P. Jones (dec.); 1 child, John R. B in Nursing, St. Marys; postgrad., U. St. Louis. Anesthetist staff Meth. Hosp., Houston, 1951—53; anesthetist staff, head of svc. North Houston Hosp., Houston; anesthetist staff Hermann Hosp., Houston, Galveston County Hosp., Texas City, USPHS Hosp., Galveston, Tex.; head nurse Ben Taub Hosp., Houston; anesthetist, head svc. Cleve. Hosp.; ret. Author: The Unrepentent, 2007, Teddy Gave, 2000. Democrat. Avocations: painting, poetry, art, reading.

JONES, ANDREW WILLIAM, pharmaceutical executive; b. Midland, Mich., Feb. 15, 1970; s. William Clarence Jones, Mary Constance Jones; m. Christine Marie Cullen. BS, U. Del., 1992. Assoc. dir. quality assurance Cardinal Health, Somerset, NJ, 2001—; tech. mgr. RTP Region KMI / PAREXEL, Durham, NC, 1998—2001; sr. assoc. Biogen, INC, Cambridge, Mass., 1997—98; scientist /engr. Nanosystems (Kodak), Collegeville, Pa., 1993—97. Presenter in field. Author: My Sophomore Year, 2001, Signed Books and spoke on work at a variety of stores in the Raleigh, NC area., 2001, Signed books in the Princeton, NJ., 2002; contbr. numerous articles to profl. jours. Mem.: Internat. Pharm. Acad., Am. Assn. Pharm. Scientists, Inst. of Validation Tech., Parenteral Drug Assn., Internat. Assn. of Pharm. Engrs. Office: Cardinal Health 14 School House Rd Somerset NJ 08873 Business E-Mail: andrew.jones@cardinal.com.

JONES, ANDRUW RUDOLF, professional baseball player; b. Willemstad, Curacao, The Netherlands, Apr. 23, 1977; Outfielder Atlanta Braves, 1996—. Named to Nat. League All-Star Team, 2000, 2002—03; recipient Nat. League Gold Glove Award, 1998—2004. Office: Atlanta Braves PO Box 4064 Atlanta GA 30302 Fax: 404-614-1391.

JONES, ANITA JOYCE, musician, composer, music educator; b. Taylor, Tex., Feb. 13, 1933; d. Johnnie Cavitt Gilstrap and Jessie Lee Stiles; m. Robert Carmon Jones, Aug. 28, 1953; children: Robin Lisette, Janet Carol, Jeffrey Carr. Mus B summa cum laude, Univ. Tex., Austin, 1952, Mus M, 1953; MA sacred music, Southwestern Bap. Theol. Sem., Ft. Worth, Tex., 1957; Mus D, Univ. Tex., Austin, 1970. Piano instr. Tex. Wesleyan Coll., Ft. Worth, 1953—54; piano & organ instr. Mary Hardin Baylor Coll., Belton, Tex., 1957—59; prof. organ and organist in residence Baylor Univ., Waco, Tex., 1969—. Concert organist worldwide Mgmt. Rosenhaus Enterprises, Waco, Tex., 1958—; recording artist Motette, Word, and Rosenhaus Records. Composer: (music book) King of Instruments, 2000, Organ Preludes on Favorite Hymns, 1996, Three for Lent, 2000; performer: Riverside Ch., Mormon Tabernacle, Notre Dame Cathedral. Named to Walter Gilewicz Hall of Fame, 2001; recipient award of Merit, Mu Phi Epsilon, 1998, Nat. Citation, Nat. Fed. of Music Clubs, 1997, Collegiate Tchr. of the Yr., Tex. Music Tchrs. Assn., 2003. Fellow: Am. Guild of Organists; mem.: Am. Rose Soc. (cons. rosarian). Achievements include first to woman to play on the inaugural concert series at the Crystal Cathedral and the only woman to play at the opening gala of the San Francisco Symphony's new organ in Davies Symphony Hall. Home: 3525 Carondolet Waco TX 76710 Office: Baylor Univ Sch Music One Bear Pl Box 97408 Waco TX 76798-7408 Office Phone: 254-710-1417.

JONES, ANITA KATHERINE, computer scientist, educator; b. Ft. Worth, Mar. 10, 1942; d. Park Joel and Helene Louise (Voigt) J.; m. William A. Wulf, July 1, 1977; children: Karin, Ellen. AB in Math., Rice U., 1964; MA in English, U. Tex., 1966; PhD in Computer Sci., Carnegie Mellon U., 1973, PhD in Sci. and Tech. (hon.), 2000. Programmer IBM, Boston, Washington, 1966-69; assoc. prof. computer sci. Carnegie-Mellon U., Pitts., 1973-81; founder, v.p. Tartan Labs. Inc., Pitts., 1981-87; free-lance cons. Pitts., 1987-88; prof., head computer sci. dept. U. Va., Charlottesville, 1988-93, prof., 1997—, univ. prof., 1998—, Lawrence A. Quarles prof. engring. and applied sci., 1999; dir. def. rsch. and engring. Dept. Def., Washington, 1993-97. Mem. Def. Sci. Bd., Dept. Def., 1985-93, 98—; mem. sci. adv. bd. USAF, 1980-85; governing bd. Nat. Sci. Found.; vice-chair governing bd. NSF, 1998-2004; bd. dirs. Sci. Applications Internat. Corp., InQTel; trustee Mitre Corp., 1989-93, chair Va. Rsch. and Technology Adv. Commn., 1999-2002, Commonwealth of Va. Advs. Commn.; mem. corp. Charles Stark Draper Labs., 1999—; bd. dirs. BBN Techs. Editor: Perspectives on Computer Science, 1977, Foundations of Secure Computation, 1971. Recipient Air Force Meritorious Civilian Svc. award, 1985, Medal for Disting. Pub. Svc. Dept. of Def., 1996, Disting. Svc. award Computing Rsch. Assn., 1997, Augusta Ada Lovelace award, Assn. Women in Computing, 2004. Fellow IEEE, AAAS, Assn. Computing Machinery (editor-in-chief Transactions on Computer Sys. 1983-91), Am. Acad. Arts and Scis.; mem. Nat. Acad. Engring., MIT Corp., Sci. Found. of Ireland (bd. dirs. 2000-2003), Sigma Xi. Avocation: gardening. Office Phone: 434-982-2224. Business E-Mail: jones@virginia.edu.

JONES, ANN, writer, photographer; b. Eau Claire, Wis., Sept. 3, 1937; d. Oscar Trygve and Miriam Berenice (Rufsvold) Slagsvol. BS, U. Wis., 1960, PhD, 1970; MA, U. Mich., 1961. Tchr. writing and womens studies CCNY, N.Y.C., 1970-73, U. Mass., Amherst, 1973-75, Mt. Holyoke Coll., South Hadley, Mass., 1986-97. Author: Uncle Tom's Campus, 1973, Women Who Kill, 1980, Everyday Death, 1985, Next Time, She'll Be Dead, 1994, 2d edit., 2000, Looking for Lovedu, 2001; co-author: When Love Goes Wrong, 1992 (Literary Guild); contbr. articles to profl. jours. Mem. Authors Guild, PEN Am. Ctr., Nat. Writers Union, Nat. Book Critics Circle. Home and Office: PO Box 26 Esopus NY 12429-0026

JONES, ANTHONY RAY, military career officer; b. Wash., Ind. m. Nancy Erwin; children: Regan, Erin, Holly. BS in Bus., Ind. U., 1970; M in Sys. Mgmt., U. So. Calif., L.A., 1982; grad., Army Command/Gen. Staff Coll., U.S. Army War Coll. Commd. 2nd lt. US Army Infantry, 1970, advanced through grades to lt. gen., 1998, inf. platoon leader, co. exec. officer 1st bn. 30th Inf. Schweinfurt, Germany, aviation platoon leader, HHC co. comdr. 9th inf. divsn. Ft. Lewis, Wash., exec. officer 213th Aviation Co. Camp Humphreys, co. comdr. E Co., task force 160, exec. officer 160th Spl. Ops. Aviation Group Ft. Campbell, Ky., comdr. 3d bn., 227th Aviation Regiment, 3d Armored Divsn. Ft. Hood, Tex., comdr. Combat Aviation Brigade, 24th Inf. Divsn. Ft. Stewart, Ga., chief ops. and contingency plans, dep. chief staff ops. Washington, dep. dir. ops. J3 Joint Staff, asst. divsn. comdr.-forward 1st Armored divsn. Tuzla, Bosnia-Herzegovina; asst. ops. officer, test concepts and project officer US Army Aviation Bd., Ft. Rucker; ops. rsch., sys. analysis for force modernization office US Army Mil. Pers. Ctr., Alexandria, Va.; aviation ops. officer Spl. Ops. Office, dep. chief of staff US Army, Washington; dep. commdg. gen., chief of staff, headquaters US Army Tng. and Doctrine Command, Wash., DC, 2003—; chief investigator, mil. intelligence in the abuse of prisoners at Abu Ghraib in Irag, 2004; acting comdr. training and doctrine command US Army, 2005—. Decorated Def. Superior Svc. medal, Legion of Merit with oak leaf cluster, Bronze Star, Meritorious Svc. medal with seven oak leaf clusters, Air medal, Army Commendation medal with oak leaf cluster, Nat. Def. Svc. medal with oak leaf cluster, Armed Forces Expeditionary medal, S.W. Asia Svc. medal, Kuwait Liberation medal, Joint Meritorious Unit award with oak leaf cluster. Office: Office Army Chief of Staff TRADOC 1500 Army Pentagon Washington DC 20310-1500

JONES, ARTHUR EDWIN, JR., library director, literature educator; b. Orange, N.J., Mar. 20, 1918; s. Arthur Edwin and Lucy Mabel (Alpaugh) J.; m. Rachel Evelyn Mumbulo, Apr. 24, 1943; 1 child, Carol Rae Jones Jacobus BA, U. Rochester, 1939; MA, Syracuse U., 1941, PhD in English, 1950; MLS, Rutgers U., 1964. Instr. English Syracuse U., N.Y., 1946-49, Drew U., Madison, N.J., 1949-52, asst. prof., 1952-55, assoc. prof., 1955-60, prof. English and Am. lit., 1960-86, dir. libraries, 1956-85, prof., libr. emeritus, 1986—. Evaluator Middle States Assn. Colls., Phila., 1955-85. Author: Darwinism and American Realism, 1951; contbr. articles to profl. jours.; book reviewer Library Jour., 1956-75, Choice, 1969— Trustee Madison Pub. Library, N.J., 1958-79, pres., 1976-79. Served to 1st lt. U.S. Army, 1941-46 Named to U. Rochester Athletic Hall of Fame, 1997; Lilly Endowment scholar Am. Theol. Libr. Assn., 1963-64 Mem. MLA, Nat. Coun. Tchr. of Eng., ALA (councillor 1970-71), Am. Theol. Libr. Assn. (pres. 1967-68), AAUP, Lions Club, Habitat for Humanity. Democrat. Home: 400 Avinger Ln Apt 409 Davidson NC 28036-9718

JONES, ARTHUR FREDERICK, art university administrator, educator; b. Queens, NY, Dec. 20, 1945; s. Arthur and Theresa (Schnabel) Jones; m. Crystal Hui-Shu Yang, Oct. 4, 2000; children: Mark Bennett, Meredith Lynn, Leo Wen-Shu. BA, SUNY, New Paltz, 1967; MA, Case-Western Res. U., 1970, PhD, 1974. Lectr. dept. art history Case-Western Res. U., Cleve., 1970; lectr. fine arts dept. John Carroll U., University Heights, Ohio, 1970—71; lectr. Cleve. State U., 1970; lectr. dept. art history and edn. Cleve. Mus. Art, 1971; instr., asst. prof., assoc. prof. dept. art U. Ky., Lexington, 1971—93; dir. U. Ky. Ctr. Contemporary Art, 1984—93, Art Other Side St. Gallery, Cin., 1987—90; chair, prof. dept. art Radford U., Va., 1993—2003; curator modern and contemporary art, co-curator Kolla Landwehr Found. collection Huichol art Radford U. Art Mus., 1998—2003; chair, prof. dept. art U. ND, Grand Forks, 2003—, dir. u., art collections, 2005—. Humanities cons. Ky. Humanities Coun., Frankfort, 1978; mem., bd. dirs. Endowment Appalachian Artists, Lexington, 1983—86; traveling scholar Appalachian Ctr. Traveling Scholars Program, Lexington, 1983—87; v.p. Folk Art Soc. Ky., Lexington, 1983—92; assoc. Appalachian Studies Ctr. U. Ky., Lexington, 1990—93; scholar in residence Pollock-Krasner Ho. and Study Ctr., East Hampton, NY, 1992—93; mem. com. to establish guidelines for coll. and univ. galleries and museums Southeastern Coll. Art Conf., 1999—2000; mem. Greater Grand Forks Mktg. Svcs. Partnership Adv. Bd., 2003—; bd. dirs. Artwise, 2005—. Author: The Art of Paul Sawyer, 1976, Audrey Flack: Love Conquers All, 1996, Adolf Dehn: Works on Paper from the Radford University Art Museum Collection, 2003, Kentucky Tradition in American Landscape Painting, 1983, (textbook) Introduction to Art, 1992; author, co-author Ibram Lassaw: Deep Space and Beyond, 2001, Radford University Art Museum: Selections from the Permanent Collection, 1999, The Kentucky Painter: From the Frontier Era to the Great War, 1981, author, art critic (art exhbn. revs.) New Art Examiner, regional editor Ky., New Art Examiner, Chgo., 1990—93; exhibitions include NOTORO Internat. Art Symposium, Gniew Castle, Poland, 1995, Elaine Benson Gallery, Bridgehampton, NY, 1994, Huntington Mus. Art, WV (Exhbn. award, 1992), Chautauqua Art Assn. Galleries, Chautauqua Instn., NY (Exhbn. award, 1991); curator (exhibitions) U. Ky. Art Mus., 1981, Owensboro Mus. Fine Art, 1983, Art Mus. Western Va., Roanoke, 1996. Recipient Radford U. Found. award for Creative Scholarship, 2003; Project grantee, Ky. Arts Commn., 1980, Spl. Exhibitions grantee, Nat. Endowment Arts, 1980, Pub. Humanities Program grantee, Ky. Humanities Coun., 1985, Project grantee, Ky. Arts Coun., 1992. Mem.: Nat. Coun. Art Adminstrs., Nat. Assn. Schs. Art and Design, Southeastern Coll. Art Assn., Nat. Art Edn. Assn., Mid. Am. Coll. Art Assn., Coll. Art Assn. Avocations: travel, collecting art. Home: 6525 Woodcrest Rd Grand Forks ND 58201 Office: U ND PO Box 7099 Grand Forks ND 58202 Office Phone: 701-777-2907. Office Fax: 701-777-2903. Personal E-mail: art.jones@und.nodak.edu.

JONES, BARBARA ELLEN, neurologist, educator; b. Phila., Dec. 19, 1944; d. Charles and Ella (Yeager) J.; m. John Gordon Galaty, Aug. 12, 1972; 1 child, James Gordon. BA, U. Del., 1966, MA, 1969, PhD, 1971. Rsch. assoc., asst. prof. U. Chgo., 1972-77; asst. prof. dept. neurology and neurosurgery McGill U., Montreal, 1977-82, assoc. prof., 1982-88, prof., 1989—. Vis. lectr. U. Nairobi, Kenya, 1974-75; vis. scientist Oxford U., Eng., 1984-85; vis. prof. U. Geneva, 1991-92, 98-99. Contbr. articles to profl. jours. Postdoctoral fellow Coll. de France, Paris, 1970-72. Mem.: Am. Neurosci. Soc., Sleep Rsch. Soc. Avocations: horseback riding, skiing. Home: 97 Arlington Ave Westmount PQ Canada H3Y 2W5 Office: McGill Univ 3801 Univ St Montreal PQ Canada H3A 2B4 Office Phone: 514-398-1913. Business E-Mail: barbara.jones@mcgill.ca.

JONES, BARBARA S., federal judge; b. 1947; BA, Mount St. Mary's, 1968; JD, Temple, 1973. Special atty. honors prog. Manhattan Strike Force Against Organized Crime and Racketeering US Dept. Justice, 1973—77, asst. US atty. Office US Atty. (So. Dist. NY), 1977—83, asst. US atty. chief gen. crimes unit (So. Dist. NY), 1983—84, asst. US atty. chief organized crime unit (So. Dist. NY), 1984—87; chief asst. DA County of NY, NYC, 1987—96; judge US Dist. Ct. (So. Dist. NY), 1996—. Adj. prof. trial advocacy Fordham U. Sch. Law. Trustee Vera Inst. Justice, 2000—. Mem.: NY County Lawyers Assn., Assn. Bar City NY, American Coll. Trial Lawyers. Office: US Courthouse 40 Foley Sq Room 2103 New York NY 10007*

JONES, BARCLAY GIBBS, III, investment banker; b. Berkeley, Calif., Oct. 14, 1960; s. Barclay Gibbs and Anne (Tompkins) J.; m. Jean Murray Dyer, Nov. 11, 1989; children: Barclay, Katherine, August. BS in Econs., U. Pa., 1982. Asst. to pres. W.P. Carey & Co., Inc., N.Y.C., 1982-86, v.p., 1986-87, sr. v.p., 1987-88, mng. dir., 1988-97, vice chmn., 1997-99; mng. dir. Barlow Ptnrs., N.Y.C., 1999—; mng. ptnr., exec. v.p. Star Fin. Inc. (N4C), N.Y.C. Mem. Racquet and Tennis Club, The Brook Club, St. Elmo Club, Cold Spring Harbor Beach Club, Piping Rock Club. Office: Star Fin Inc 1114 Ave of the Americas New York NY 10036 Office Phone: 212-930-9409. Business E-Mail: bjones@istarfinancial.com.

JONES, BEN F., artist, educator; b. Paterson, N.J. s. Ormsby Francis and Elise (North) Jones. BA, William Paterson U., Wayne, N.J., 1959—63; MA, NYU, 1963—67; MFA, Pratt Inst., Bklyn., 1981—83. Art tchr. Passaic Bd. Edn., Bklyn., 1963—67; art prof. N.J. City U., Jersey City, 1967—. Represented in permanent collections Studio Mus., Harlem, N.Y., N.J. State Mus., Newark Mus., N.J., Jose Marti Nat. Libr., Havana, Cuba, Montclair Art Mus., N.J. Grantee, NEA, 1982, N.J. Coun. on Arts, 1985, Puffin Found., 2002, Joan Mitchell Found., 2003. Mem.: Nat. Conf. Artists. Socialist. Home: 117 Kensington Ave Apt 206 Jersey City NJ 07304 Office: NJ City Univ 2039 Kennedy Blvd Jersey City NJ 07304

JONES, BILL T., dancer, choreographer; b. Bunnell, Fla., Feb. 15, 1952; Student, SUNY, Binghampton, 1970; PhD (hon.), Bard Coll., 1996; PhD (hon.), Art Inst. of Chicago, Bard Coll., Columbia Coll., The Juilliard Sch., Swarthmore Coll., SUNY Binghamton. Co-founder Am. Dance Asylum, 1973; co-founder, artistic dir. Bill T. Jones/Arnie Zane & Co. (now Bill T. Jones/Arnie Zane Dance Co.), 1982—. Author: Last Night on Earth, 1995; choreographer, soloist Negroes for Sale, 1973, Track Dance, 1974, (with Arnie Zane) Pas de Deux for Two, 1974, Across the Street, 1975, Everybody Works/All Beasts Count, 1976, WhosedebabedoIbabedoll, 1977, De Sweet Streak to Loveland, 1977, The Runner Dreams, 1978, Stories, Steps and Stomps, 1978, Progresso, 1979, Echo, 1979, Naming Things Is Only the Intention to Make Things, 1979, Floating the Tongue, 1979, Monkey Run Road, 1979, Blauvelt Mountain, 1980, Sisyphus, Act I and II, 1980, Open Spaces, 1980, Tribeca, Automation, Three Wise Men, Christmas, 1980, Secret Pastures, 1984, History of Collage, 1988, D-Man in the Waters, 1989 (Bessie Award 1989), Dances 1989, Last Supper at Uncle Tom's Cabin/The Promised Land, 1991, Love Defined, 1991, Aria, 1992, Last Night on Earth, 1992, Fête, 1992, Achilles Loved Patroclus, 1993, War Between the States, 1993, Still/Here, 1994, We Set Out Early...Visibility Was Poor, 1997, dir., choreographer (operas) New Year, 1990, The Mother of Three Sons, Lost in the Stars, dir. (with Rhodessa Jones) Perfect Courage, 1990 (Izzy award 1990). Named an Irreplaceable Dance Treasure, Dance Heritage Coalition, 2000; recipient (with Arnie Zane) N.Y. Dance and Performance award (Bessie) choreographer/creator category, given for freedom of information, 1986, Dorothy B. Chandler Performing Arts award, 1991, Dance Mag. award, 1993, Edinburgh Festival Critics' Award (presented to company), 1993, Creative Artists Public Svc. Award, 1979, MacArthur Genius fellowship, 1993, Izzy award, 2001, Dorothy & Lillian Gish prize, 2003, Wexner Prize, Wexner Ctr. for the Arts, 2005. Office: Bill T Jones/Arnie Zane Co 853 Broadway Ste 1706 New York NY 10003-4703

JONES, BILLY ERNEST, retired dermatology educator; b. Daytona Beach, Fla., Jan. 29, 1933; s. Bibb Ernest and Marjorie (Eyre) J.; m. Hannah Warren, June 12, 1958; children: Alan W., Lawrence W., Marjorie E. BS, The Citadel, 1954; MD, Duke U., 1958. Diplomate Am. Bd. Dermatology. Commd. 2d lt. U.S. Army, 1958, advanced through grades to maj., 1964, intern William Beaumont Hosp. El Paso, Tex., 1958-59, gen. med. officer Henry Barracks Cayey, P.R., 1959-61, resident in dermatology The Presidio San Francisco, 1961-64, chief dermatology Ft. Gordon, Ga., 1964-67, resigned, 1967; practice medicine specializing in dermatology Greenville, N.C., 1967-80; prof. medicine East Carolina U., Greenville, 1991-97, ret., 1997, 1997. Recipient Clin. Tchr. award Sr. Class, 1983, 84, 88, Teaching Recognition award 1st yr. residents, 1982, 3d yr. residents, 1985 Med. Sch. East Carolina U. Fellow Am. Acad. Dermatology; mem. AMA, N.C. Med. Soc. Republican. Episcopalian. Avocations: tennis, horticulture.

JONES, BOB, III, academic administrator; b. 1939; m. Beneth Jones; 3 children. BA, MA, Bob Jones U.; D (hon.), Pillsbury Bapt. Bible Coll., San Francisco Bapt. Theological Seminary, Maranatha Bapt. Bible Coll. Various positions with Bob Jones U., pres. Greenville, SD, 1971—. Mem. exec. com., bd. trustees Bob Jones U.; v.p. bd. dirs. Gospel Fellowship Assn. Office: Bob Jones U Office Of Pres Greenville SC 29614-0001

JONES, BOISFEUILLET, JR., publishing executive; b. Atlanta, Nov. 14, 1946; s. Boisfeuillet and Laura (Coit) J.; m. Barbara Frost Pendleton, Sept. 13, 1969; children: Lindsay Pendleton, Theodore Boisfeuillet. AB, Harvard U., 1968, JD, 1974; D.Phil., Oxford U., 1981. Bar: Mass. 1974, D.C. 1979. Law clk. Judge Levin H. Campbell, US Ct. Appeals (1st cir.), Boston, 1974-75; atty. Hill and Barlow, Boston, 1975-80; v.p., counsel Washington Post, DC, 1980-95, pres., gen. mgr., 1995-2000, pub., CEO, 2000—. Dir. Bowater Mersey Paper Co., Ltd., N.S., Assoc Press, NY, Robinson Terminal Warehouse Corp., Alexandria, Va., Fed. City Coun., Washington, Eugene & Agnes Meyer Found., Washington, Newspaper Assn. Am. Rhodes scholar Rhodes Trust, 1968. Episcopalian. Home: 4331 Forest Ln NW Washington DC 20007-1137 Office: Washington Post 1150 15th St NW Washington DC 20071-0002 Office Phone: 202-334-7141.

JONES, C. PAUL, lawyer, educator; b. Grand Forks, N.D., Jan. 7, 1927; s. Walter M. and Sophie J. (Thorton) J.; m. Helen M. Fredel, Sept. 7, 1957; children— Katherine, Sara H. BBA, JD, U. Minn., 1950; LLM, William Mitchell Coll. of Law, 1955. Assoc. Lewis, Hammer, Heaney, Weyl & Halverson, Duluth, Minn., 1950-51; asst., chief dep. Hennepin County Atty., Mpls., 1952-58; asst. U.S. atty. U.S. Atty's. Office, St. Paul, 1959-60; assoc. Maun & Hazel, St. Paul, 1960-61; ptnr. Dorfman, Rudquist, Jones, & Ramstead, Mpls., 1961-65; state pub. defender Minn. State Pub. Defender's Office, Mpls., 1966-90. Adj. prof. law William Mitchell Coll. of Law, St. Paul, 1953-70, prof. law, 1970—2001, prof. emeritus, 2001-. assoc. dean for acad. affairs, 1991-95; adj. prof. U. Minn., Mpls., 1970-90; mem. adv. com. on rules of criminal procedure Minn. Supreme Ct., 1970—. Author: Criminal Procedure from Police Detention to Final Disposition, 1981; Jones on Minnesota Criminal Procedure, 1955, 64, 70, 75; Minnesota Police Law Manual, 1955, 67, 70, 76 Mem. Minn. Gov.'s Crime Commn., St. Paul, 1970s, Minn. Fair Trial-Free Press Assn., Mpls., 1970s, Citizens League, Mpls., 1955—, Mpls. Aquatennial Assn., Mpls., 1955-60, Minn. Coun. on Crime and Justice, 1991—. Recipient Reginald Heber Smith award Nat. Legal Aid and Defender Assn., 1969 Fellow Am. Coll. Trial Lawyers; mem. Am. Bd. Trial Advs., ABA, Minn. State Bar Assn., Hennepin County Bar Assn., Ramsey County Bar Assn., Nat. Legal Aid & Defender Assn. Clubs: Suburban Gyro of Mpls. Lodges: Rotary. Democrat. Lutheran. Avocations: fishing, hunting, golf, desert watching. Home: 5501 Dewey Hill Rd Edina MN 55439-1906 Office: William Mitchell Coll Law 875 Summit Ave Saint Paul MN 55105-3030

JONES, CARL E., JR., bank executive; m. Ann Karpinski Jones. BS in Banking and Finance, U. of Ala., 1962. Joined Merchant Nat. Bank (predecessor bank of Regions Bank), Mobile, Ala., 1962; pres. First Ala. Bancshores, Inc., Mobile, 1978; chmn, CEO First Ala. Bancshores, Inc. (now Regions Bank), Mobile, Ala., 1981—95; regional pres. Ala. operations First Ala. Bank, Ala., 1984—97; regional pres. La. First Ala. Bank (merged to become Regions Financial Corp. in 1994), 1993—97; COO Regions Financial Corp., Birmingham, Ala., 1997-98, pres., 1998—2004, CEO, 1998—2005, chmn., 2001—. Bd. dirs. Ala. Power Co. Mem. president's cabinet U. of Ala. Office: Regions Fin Corp 417 N 20th St PO Box 10247 Birmingham AL 35202-0247*

JONES, CARLETON SHAW, information technology executive, lawyer; b. N.Y.C., Sept. 8, 1942; s. Carlyle Herman and Virginia Ann (Sloat) J.; m. Dona Baker VanArsdale, July 15, 1972; children: Emily Baker, Timothy Dustin. BA, Denison U., 1964; LLB, Yale U., 1967. Bar: Ohio 1967, Fla. 1971, D.C. 1973. Law clk. to chief judge U.S. Ct Appeals (6th cir.), Akron, Ohio, 1967; dep. gen. counsel Price Commn., Exec. Office of Pres., Washington, 1971-73; assoc. Shaw, Pittman Potts & Trowbridge, Washington, 1973-77, ptnr., 1978-91; sr. v.p., counsel Sysorex Info. Sys., Fairfax, Va., 1992, pres., 1992-97, also bd. dirs.; pres. Vanstar Govt. Sys. (formerly Sysorex Info. Sys.), Fairfax, 1997-99; advisor, bd. mem. high tech. cos., 1999—; pres. Info Ops Govt. Solutions, Arnold, Md., 2000—01; pres., COO Multimax, Inc., Landover, Md., 2001—. Spkr. on fed. high-tech. procurement issues. Lt. (j.g.) USNR, 1967-71. Mem. ABA, Chevy Chase Club, Met. Club. Office Phone: 301-925-8222. Personal E-mail: csjchch@aol.com.

JONES, CAROLYN, dean, law educator; 1 child, Alison. BA, U. Iowa, 1976, JD, 1979; LLM, Yale U., 1982. Bar: Iowa. Asst. city atty. Sioux City, 1979—80; assoc. Klass, Whicher and Mishne, 1981—82; prof. St. Louis U. Sch. Law, 1982—90, U. Conn. Law Sch., 1990—2004, assoc. dean academic affairs; dean U. Iowa Coll Law, 2004—. Vis. prof. law U. Exeter, Washington U., U. Iowa, 1986—87, 1989, Moritz Coll. Law, Ohio State U., 2004. Recipient Sanxay Prize, Order of Coif. Office: U Iowa Coll Law 276 Boyd Law Building Iowa City IA 52242 E-mail: carolyn-jones@uiowa.edu.

JONES, CAROLYN JANE, minister; b. Grove City, Pa., Jan. 28, 1937; d. Hester Clark and Winifred Eleanor (Hoag) J.; m. Thomas Woodward Golightly. BA, Westminster Coll., 1958; MA in Edn., Syracuse U., 1963; MDiv, Pitts. Theol. Sem., 1977, D Ministry, 1989. Ordained to ministry Presbyn. Ch. (U.S.A.), 1977. Tchr. Am. Coll. for Girls, Cairo, 1958-61, Bethel Park High Sch., Pa., 1963-68; asst. dean women Syracuse U., N.Y., 1968-71; dir., asst. dir. activities and orgns. Office Student Affairs, Syracuse U., 1971-74; assoc. in Christian edn. Pebble Hill Presbyterian Ch., DeWitt, NY, 1971—74; dir. Christian edn. Newlonsburg United Presbyn. Ch., Murrysville, Pa., 1975-77; assoc. pastor Glenshaw Presbyn. Ch., Pa., 1977-84; interim minister at large Pitts. Presbytery, 1984-90; exec. presbyter Washington Presbytery, Presbyn. Ch. (U.S.A.), 1990—98; interim assoc. synod exec. Synod of the Trinity, Presbyn. Ch. (U.S.A.), 1999—2003. Bd. dirs. Pitts. Theol. Sem.; bd. mgrs. New Wilmington Missionary Conf.; bd. trustees Westminster Coll., Pa. Recipient Thomas Jamison scholar, 1977; Sylvester S. Marvin Meml. fellow, 1977. Mem. Cleric of Pitts., Internat. Assn. Women Ministers, Assn. Presbyn. Interim Ministry Specialists, Presbyn. Clergywomen's Assn. Home: 106 Farmview Pl Venetia PA 15367-1300

JONES, CHARLES CALHOUN, estate and business planning consultant; b. Bedford, Pa., Jan. 12, 1940; s. Charles Stauffer and Marjorie Vesta (Calhoun) J.; m. Patricia Jean Diehl, Aug. 12, 1960; children: Kathryn Lynn, Suzanne Elizabeth, Christopher Andrew. BS in Econs., Widener U., 1961. CLU; chartered fin. cons.; registered investment advisor. Field dir. Bus. Men's Assurance, Kansas City, Mo., 1970—76; pres. Agrl. Bus. Adminstrn., Kansas City, 1976—78; br. mgr. E.F. Hutton, Raytown, Mo., 1978—79; pres. C.C.J. Inc., Kansas City, 1979—90; chmn. coun. John Hancock Mut. Life Ins. Co., 1992—98, mem. agts. adv. com., mktg. chmn., 1992—99. Chmn. bd. dirs. Pentrust LLC; advisor Nat. Cattleman's Assn., Denver, 1976-79. Author: Financial Management Pentrust, 1987; contbr. articles to profl. jours. Gov. Am. Royal, Kansas City, 1981; mem. adminstrv. bd. and coun. Luth. Ch., Kans.; bd. dirs. Povidence/ St. John Hosp. Found., 1999—, Endowment Found. The Am. Coll. Investment and Pension Com., Bryn Mawr, Pa.; found. bd. dirs. Am. Coll. Bryn Mawr, 2005—. Mem. Lees Summit C. of C. (econ. devel. com. 1982-85), Soc. Fin. Svc. Profls. (bd. dirs. 1998-2002), Assn. Internat Fin. Planners (bd. dirs. 1976-80), Planned Giving Coun. (charter), Rotary Internat., Soc. of Fin. Svc. Profls., Loch Lomond Club (Luss, Scotland), Blue Hills Country Club, Reynolds Plantation Nat.Golf Club. Avocation: golf. Office: Pentrust LLC PO Box 481993 Kansas City MO 64148-1993 Office Phone: 816-941-0513. Business E-Mail: chuck@pentrust.com.

JONES, CHARLES E., retired state supreme court chief justice; b. June 12, 1935; BA, Brigham Young U., 1959; JD, Stanford U., 1962. Bar: Calif. 1963, Ariz. 1964, US Dist. Ct. Ariz. 1964, US Ct. Appeals (9th cir.) 1963, US Ct. Appeals (10th cir.) 1974, US Supreme Ct. 1979. Law clk. to Hon. Richard H. Chambers U.S. Ct. Appeals (9th cir.), 1962-63; assoc., ptnr. Jennings, Strouss & Salmon, Phoenix, 1963-96; apptd. justice Ariz. Supreme Ct., Phoenix, 1996, vice chief justice, 1997—2002, chief justice, 2002—05; ret., 2005—. Bd. visitors Brigham Young U. Law Sch., 1973-81, chmn., 1978-81, Univ. Arizona Coll. Law, 2003—. Named Avocat du Consulat-Gen. de France, 1981—; Alumni Dist. Svc. award Brigham Young U., 1982; recipient Aaron Feuerstein award U. Ariz., 1998, Pub. Svc. award Ariz. Alumni Assn., 2005, Career Achievement award State Bar Ariz., 2005, Chapman award Ariz. League of Women Voters, 2005, Pub. Svc. award, U. Ariz. Fellow Am. Bar Found., Ariz. Bar Found.; mem. ABA, State Bar Ariz. (Career award, 2005), Fed. Bar Assn. (pres. Ariz. chpt. 1971-73), J. Reuben Clark Law Soc. (nat. chmn. 1994-97), Maricopa County Bar Assn., Am. Coll. Labor and Employment Lawyers (former dir.), Pi Sigma Alpha. Office: Ariz Supreme Court 1501 W Washington St Phoenix AZ 85007-3222

JONES, CHARLES HILL, JR., banker; b. July 14, 1933; s. Charles Hill and Susan Roy (Johnston) J.; m. Hope Haskell, Jan. 28, 1961; children: Hope H., Charles Hill III, Henry M.T. Grad., Groton (Mass.) Sch., 1952; BA in Econs., U. Va., 1956. With Wood, Struthers & Winthrop, Inc., N.Y.C., 1956-73, gen. ptnr., 1968-69, v.p., dir., dir. rsch., 1969-73; sr. v.p., chief investment officer Midlantic Nat. Bank, Edison, 1974-87; gen. ptnr. Edge Ptnrs., 1987—. Bd. dirs. N.J. Title Ins. Co., chmn., 2000-01; bd. dirs. NJT Holdings, chmn., 2000-. Author: (with Joseph D. Davis) Toll Road Bonds, 1959, The Growth Rate Appraiser, 1968. Treas. N.Y. chpt. R.E. Lee Meml. Found., 1964-69; trustee, chmn. fin. com. Monmouth Med. Ctr., 1975-81; pres. bd. trustees Rumson (N.J.) Country Day Sch., 1982-85; trustee Hampden-Sydney Coll., 1995-99, 2002-03. Mem. Inst. Chartered Fin. Analysts, Bond Club, City Midday Club (trustee, treas. 1965-71, v.p. 1972-74). Office: NJ Title Co 400 Lanidex Plaza 2nd Fl Parsippany NJ 07054

JONES, CHARLES IRVING, bishop; b. El Paso, Tex., Sept. 13, 1943; s. Charles I. Jr. and Helen A. (Heyward) J.; m. Ashby MacArthur, June 18, 1966; children: Charles I. IV, Courtney M., Frederic M., Keith A. BS, The Citadel, 1965; MBA, U. N.C., 1966; MDiv, U. of the South, 1977, DD, 1989. CPA. Pub. acctg. D.E. Gatewood and Co., Winston-Salem, N.C., 1966-72; dir. devel. Chatham (Va.) Hall, 1972-74; instr. acctg. U. of the South, Sewanee, Tenn., 1974-77; coll. chaplain Western Ky. U., Bowling Green, 1977-81; vicar Trinity Episcopal Ch., Russelville, Ky., 1977-85; archdeacon Diocese of Ky., Louisville, 1981-86; bishop Episcopal Diocese of Mont., Helena, 1986-2001. Bd. dirs. New Directions Ministries, Inc., N.Y.C.; mem. standing com. Joint Commn. on Chs. in Small Communities, 1988-91, Program, Budget and Fin., 1991-94; v.p. province VI Episcopal Ch., 1991-94, mem. Presiding Bishop's Coun. Advice, 1991-94. Author: Mission Strategy in the 21st Century, 1989, Total Ministry: A Practical Approach, 1993; bd. editors Grass Roots, Luling, Tex., 1985-90; contbr. articles to profl. jours. Founder Concerned Citizens for Children, Russelville, 1981; bd. dirs. St. Peter's Hosp., Helena, 1986-2001; bd. dirs. Christian Ministry in Nat. Parks, 1992—2001. With USMCR, 1961-65. Mem. AICPA, Mont. Soc. CPAs. Episcopalian. Avocations: running, flying, writing, skiing. Office: PO Box 4926 Helena MT 59604 Office Phone: 406-442-0345. E-mail: bpci@aol.com.

JONES, CHARLES W., labor union executive; b. Gary, Ind., Apr. 29, 1923; s. Charles Browning and Inez (Teegarden) J.; m. Ursula M. Wilden, Aug. 25, 1950; children: Charles Alan, Newton Browning, Donna Ruth, Doris Ursula. Grad. high sch., Gary. Boilermaker various constrn. contractors; organizer, then staff rep., rsch. & edn. dir., internat. v.p. Internat. Brotherhood of Boilermakers, Iron Ship Builders, Blacksmiths, Forgers and Helpers, Kansas City, Kans., now internat. pres.; ret. Chmn. bd. dirs. BB&T Co.; v.p. bldg. constrn. trades dept., v.p. metal trade dept. AFL-CIO. Office: Internat Brotherhood Boilermaker Iron Ship Bldrs Blacksmiths 753 State Ave Ste 570 Kansas City KS 66101-2511

JONES, CHARLES WILLIAM, lawyer; b. Spartanburg, S.C., Apr. 7, 1951; s. Charles Andrew and Elizabeth (Bridgeman) J.; m. Helen Elizabeth Bell, Jan. 28, 1972; children: Charlotte Elizabeth, Erika Caroline. BA, Wofford Coll., Spartanburg, 1973; student, U. Vienna, 1971-72; JD, U. S.C., 1976. Bar: S.C. 1976, U.S. Dist. Ct. S.C. 1976, U.S. Ct. Appeals (4th cir.) 1976. Page S.C. Senate, Columbia, 1975-76; instr. Spartanburg Meth. Coll., 1987; atty. The Whiteside-Smith Firm, Spartanburg, 1976—. Bd. dirs. Spartanburg Office of the Pub. Defender. Mem. Rotary Club (Paul Harris fellow), Phi Alpha Delta, Alpha Phi Delta. Avocations: flying, sports car racing. 1st degree black belt U.S. Tang Soo Do Moo Duk Kwan Fedn., Inc. Office: The Whiteside-Smith Firm 220 N Church St Ste 3 Spartanburg SC 29306-5104

JONES, CHERRY, actress; b. Paris, TN, Nov. 21, 1956; Founder Amer. Rep. Theatre, Cambridge, Mass., 1980—; guest artist Arena Stage, Washington, D.C., 1983-84. Stage appearances include: (with Amer. Rep. Theatre) King Lear, Twelfth Night, Major Barbara, Caucasian Chalk Circle, The Serpent Woman, Platonov, Life Is a Dream, The School for Scandal, The Three Sisters, As You Like It, Baby with the Bathwater, A Midsummer Night's Dream, Journey of the Fifth Horse, (Off Broadway) Desdemona, Goodnight Desdemona, Baltimore Waltz (Obie award), And Baby Makes Seven, Light Shining in Buckinghamshire, Big Time, Ballad of Soapy Smith, I Am a Camera, The Philanthropist, The Importance of Being Earnest, (Broadway) Angels in America, Our Country's Good, Macbeth, Stepping Out, The Heiress (Tony award Best Actress 1995), The Night of the Iguana, 1996, Doubt, 2005 (Outer Critics Cir. award, outstanding actress in a play, 2005, Lucille Lortel award, outstanding lead actress, 2005, Tony award, best performance by a leading actress in a play, 2005, Drama Desk award, outstanding actress in a play, 2005, Obie award, The Village Voice, 2005); television appearances include: (movies) Alex: The Life of a Child, 1986; film appearances include: The Big Town, 1987, Light of Day, 1987, Housesitter, 1992, The Tears of Julian Po, 1997, (voice) Out of the Past, 1998, The Horse Whisperer, 1998, Murder in a Small Town, 1999, Cradle Will Rock, 1999, The Perfect Storm, 2000, Erin Brockovich, 2000, Signs, 2002. Office: The William Morris Agy 151 S El Camino Dr Beverly Hills CA 90212-2775*

JONES, CHERYL BROMLEY, English language and humanities educator; b. Attleboro, Mass., Apr. 12, 1947; d. C. Chester and Lillian P. (Griffin) Bromley; married, Aug. 5, 1972. BA in English, State Coll. Bridgewater, 1969, MAT; postgrad., Lesley Coll., Boston Coll. Tchr. English Oliver Ames H.S., North Easton, Mass., 1968—70, Easton Jr. H.S., North Easton, 1970—88; tchr. English. social studies Sandwich H.S., Mass., 1988—94; tchr. English, writing, humanities Plymouth North H.S., Mass., 1994—2004; assoc. prof. U. Mass., Boston, 1998; ret., 2004. Assoc. cons. Rsch. Better Tchg./Tchrs., Acton, Mass., 1997—; tchr., facilitator summer residency Poetry ALive!, Asheville, N.C., 1990—; literacy cons., Buzzard's Bay, Mass., 1988—; creator, dir. student poetry reading Lang. Art Consortium Educator Student Celebratory Poetry Reading, 1989-2003 Author: (book series) Teaching with Panache, 1991. Lucretia Cocker fellow Mass. Dept. Edn., 1989-90; recipient Peter Faraldy award MASCD, 1995-96. Mem. Nat. Coun. Tchrs. English (election com., support tchg. & learning English 1991), Mass. Coun. Tchrs. English (liaison 1996—, pres. 1992-96), Lucretia Crocker Acad. Tchg. Fellows (bd. alt. 1995-98). Roman Catholic. Avocations: race walking, cooking, travel. Home: 12 Woodside Ave Buzzards Bay MA 02532-4727

JONES, CHIPPER (LARRY WAYNE JONES JR.), professional baseball player; b. De Land, Fla., Apr. 24, 1972; s. Larry Wayne and Lynne Jones; m. Karin Fulford, 1992 (div. 1999); m. Sharon Jones, Mar. 26, 2000; 2 children. Student, Stetson U. Shortstop Jacksonville Jaguars, 1990—95; third base Atlanta Braves, 1995—2001, 2004—, leftfield, 2002—03. Founder Chipper Jones Family Found., 2001—. Named Atlanta Brave's Team MVP, 1996, Nat. League MVP, 1999; named to Nat. League All Star team, 1996—98, 2000—01; recipient Florida High Sch. baseball player of the year, 1990, Nat. League Silver Slugger award, 1999. Achievements include first Round MLB pick, Atlanta Braves, 1990; member of World Series Champion Atlanta Braves team, 1995. Avocation: hunting. Office: Turner Field PO Box 4064 Atlanta GA 30302-4064

JONES, CHRISTINE MASSEY, retired furniture company executive; b. Columbus, Ga., Nov. 7, 1929; d. Louis Everett and Donia (Spivey) Massey; divorced; children— James Raymond, Jr., James David. Student, Ga. Southwestern Coll., 1947-48. With Muscogee Mfg. Co., Columbus, Ga., 1948-56, Haverty Furniture Cos., Atlanta, 1956—97, v.p., corp. sec., 1978—97; ret., 1997. Deacon First Presbyn. Ch., Columbus, Ga., 2004—. Mem. Am. Soc. Corp. Secs. (securities industry com.)

JONES, CHRISTOPHER DON, lawyer; b. Longview, Tex., Jan. 23, 1964; s. Donald and Audrey Gale Jones; m. Michelle McCullough, Feb. 16, 1991; children: Catherine Abigail, Christopher Andrew, Michael Adam. BBA, Baylor U., 1987, JD, 1989. Bar: Tex. 1989; cert. personal injury trial law Tex. Bd. Legal Specialization. Assoc. Worsham, Forsythe, Sampels & Wooldrige, Dallas, 1989-92, Misko, Howie & Sweeney, LLP, Dallas, 1992-95, Howie & Sweeney, LLP, Dallas, 1995-96, Erskine, McMahon & Stroup, LLP, Longview, Tex., 1996-97; ptnr. Stroup & Jones, LLP, Longview, Tex., 1997-2000, Jones & Jones, LLP, Longview, Tex., 2000—. Bd. dirs. Atty. Info. Exchange Group, 2002—. Asst. mng. editor Baylor Law Rev., 1989. Mem. Leadership Longview, 1998-99. Named Kiwanian of Yr., Kiwanis Club Dallas, 1993. Mem. ABA, Tex. Bar Assn., Tex. Trial Lawyers Assn. (sustaining). Democrat. Avocations: golf, hunting, running. Office: Jones & Jones LLP 420 N Green St Ste C Longview TX 75601-6443 E-mail: cjones@joneslawyers.com.

JONES, CHRISTOPHER PRESTIGE, classicist, educator, historian, consultant; b. Kent, U.K., 1940; s. William Prestige and Irene May (McCreddie) J. BA, Oxford U., 1962; PhD Classical Philology, Harvard U., 1965. From lectr. to prof. U. Toronto, Can., 1965-92, chair dept. classics, 1986-90; prof. classics and history Harvard U., Cambridge, 1992-97, George Martin Lane prof. classics and history, 1997—. Vis. lectr. Harvard U., 1968; assoc. prof. Ecole Normale Supérieure de Jeunes Filles, Paris, 1979, Ecole Normale Supérieure, Paris, 1992; acting vice dean Faculty Arts and Scis., U. Toronto, 1985-86. Author: Philostratus: Life of Apollonius of Tyana, 1971, Plutarch and Rome, 1971, The Roman World of Dio Chrysostom, 1978, Culture and Society in Lucian, 1986, Kinship Diplomacy in the Ancient World, 1999; co-editor: Le Martyre de Pionios, prêtre de Smyrne, 1994; editor, translator: Philostratus: Life of Apollonius, 2 vols., 2005; contbr. numerous articles to profl. jours. Fellow Royal Soc. Can., Am. Numismatic Soc.; mem. Am. Philol. Assn. (chair subcom. epigraphical bibliog. 1981-89, subcom. cartography 1986-90), Am. Acad. Arts and Scis., German Archeol. Inst. (corr. mem. 1992—), Am. Philos. Soc. Home: 130 Mount Auburn St Apt 107 Cambridge MA 02138-5757 Office: Harvard U Boylston Hall Cambridge MA 02138 Office Phone: 617-496-3823. Business E-Mail: cjones@fas.harvard.edu.

JONES, CHRISTOPHER WILLIAM, music educator; b. Elyria, Ohio, Jan. 28, 1972; s. Ronald William and Rose Marie Jones; m. Laura Lynn Frank; 1 child, Katherine Elizabeth. BA in music edn., U. Of Akron, 1990—96, MusM in edn., 1999—2004. Music education K-12 Ohio. Music educator Cleve. Pub. Schools, 1996—97; instrumental music educator Orrville City Schools, Ohio, 1997—. Mem.: IAJE, OMEA, MENC, Canton Bluecoats Drum & Bugle Corps. (life; alumni 1993). Home: 1969 Lakeview Dr Orrville OH 44667 Office: Orrville City Schools 841 North Ella St Orrville OH 44667 Office Phone: 330-682-4448. Personal E-mail: cljones@bright.net. E-mail: orvl_jones@tccsa.net.

JONES, CINDY SMITH, research scientist; b. Lawrenceville, Ga., Jan. 31, 1969; d. Leroy J. Smith and Margie Smith Barnette. AA in Tech., Athens (Ga.) Tech. Coll., 1996. Rsch. tech. lab. U. Ga., Athens, Ga., 1997—. Coauthor (published presentation) INTC Conference. Named Outstanding Rsch. Lab. Tech. Student, Athens Tech. Coll., 1995; Presdl. scholar, 1994; 1995; 1996, All-American scholar, 1995. Mem.: Phi Theta Kappa (life). Home: PO Box 297 Winterville GA 30683 Office: U Ga TMI Dept 360 Dawson Hall Athens GA 30602 Office Phone: 706-542-0908. E-mail: cjones@fcs.uga.edu.

JONES, CLAIRE BURTCHAELL, artist, educator, writer; b. Oakland, Calif. d. Clarence Samuel and Florence Mallett (Hinchman) Burtchaell; m. E.C. Jones; children: Holland Mallett, Lela Claire, S. Evan. AB, Stanford U.; postgrad., Laguna Beach Sch. Art, 1972-73, San Diego Art Acad., 1980-82. Freelance art tchr., Park Ridge, Ill., 1967; tchr. Jade Fon Group, Pacific Grove, Calif., 1972-73, Merced Coll., Sierra Mountains, Calif., 1973; freelance pvt. workshop, painting for commns. and galleries Calif., 1973—. Bd. reviewers Dorland Mountain Arts Colony, 1990—. Author: First The Blade (ann. collection), 1939, Arrows in the Air, 1947-51, Utah Sings, 1953; editor: Watercolor West Newsletter, 1978-83; contbr. articles to profl. jours. Bd. reviewers Dorland Mountain Arts Colony, Temecula, Calif., 1985—. Recipient numerous awards for artwork. Founding mem. Nat. Mus. Women in the Arts, Assn. Western Artists (bd. dirs. 1970-71), Watercolor West (bd. dirs. 1978-81, 86—, membership chmn. 1988-96), Stanford Alumni Assn., Literati West (founder, sec.-treas. 1994—).

JONES, CLAYTON M., computer and electronics company executive; b. Nashville; BS, U. Tenn.; MS, George Washington U. Former fighter pilot USAF; various exec.-level positions aerospace industry; with Rockwell Internat. Corp., Cedar Rapids, Iowa, 1995—, sr. v.p., pres. Rockwell Collins, 1999—, chmn., CEO. Mem. AIAA (bd. dirs.), Gen. Aviation Mfrs. Assn. Office: Rockwell Internat Corp 400 Collin Rd NE Cedar Rapids IA 52498-0001

JONES, CLYDE RAY, historian, consultant; s. Weston Eugene and Rozeltha Elizabeth Jones; m. Susan Carol Crosier, Oct. 11, 1969; children: Amanda Montgomery children: Graham Crosier, Perry Loomis. BS, Iowa State U., 1961; MA, SUNY, Oneonta, 1965, MA, 1976, cert. of Advanced Study, 1977. Mus. dir. Concord Antiquarian Soc., Concord, Mass., 1965—68; assoc. curator NY State Hist. Assn., Cooperstown, NY, 1968—75, conservator, 1975—. Adj. prof. SUNY, Cooperstown Grad. Program, 1969—. Author: (exhibit catalog) Memento Mori, (book) Charles City, Iowa; its Architectural Heritage; contbr. articles to profl. jours. Advisor Planning Bd., Cooperstown, NY; trustee and elder First Presbyn. Ch., Cooperstown; dir. and officer Assn. for Gravestone Studies, Greenfield, Mass.; bd. dirs. and officer The Cook Found., Cooperstown, NY, 1988—; dir. and officer Cooperstown Art Assn., 1975—; dir. Hyde Hall, Inc., Cooperstown, 1989—. Fellow: Am. Inst. for Conservation (life); mem.: Lower Hudson Conf. (assoc.), Floyd County Hist. Soc. (assoc.), Theatre Hist. Soc. of Am. (assoc.). Avocations: architectural restoration, landscaping and gardening, photography of gravestones. Office: New York state Historical Association Lake Rd Cooperstown NY 13326 Office Phone: 607-547-1442. E-mail: jones2@telenet.net.

JONES, COBI, professional soccer player; b. Detroit, June 16, 1970; Student, UCLA. Midfielder Coventry City, 1994—95, Vasco da Gama, 1995—96, L.A. Galaxy, 1996—, U.S. Nat. Team, 1996—. With gold medal U.S. team Pan Am. Games, 1991; with U.S. Olympic Team, 1992, U.S. Nat. Team, 1992—95, including victory over Ivory Coast, 1992. Host (TV series) Megadose (MTV), guest appearance Beverly Hills 90210, 1994. Achievements include tied for all-time assist lead, with 11. Office: c/o US Soccer Fedn 1801-1811 S Prairie Ave Chicago IL 60616*

JONES, CORA CHANDLER, librarian; b. Lenoir, N.C., 1952; d. Wilborn Pinkney and Thelma Greene Chandler; m. Gary Duran Jones, May 4, 2002; 1 child from previous marriage, Matthew Glenn Miller. BA in History, Univ. N.C., Greensboro, N.C., 1980; MLS, Emory Univ., Atlanta, Ga., 1981. Cert. pub. libr. N.C. Libr. tech. Davidson Co. Cmty. Coll., Lexington, NC, 1972—80; br. mgr. Caldwell Co. Pub. Libr., Lenoir, NC, 1981—88; tech. svc. supr. Hickory Pub. Libr., Hickory, NC, 1988—90, asst. dir., 1990—2000, dir., 2000—. Chair N.C. Pub. Libr. Cert. Commn., Raliegh, NC, 2001—; bd. mem. Hickory Metro Sports Commn., Hickory, NC, 2000—04; treas. N.C. Pub. Libr. Dirs. Assn., Hickory, NC, 2002—04. Mem. Hickory Kiwanis Club, Hickory, NC, 2000—; budget com. Catawba Co. United Way, Hickory, NC, 2002—; mem. Small Bus. Devel. Network, Hickory, NC, 2004—. Mem.: Am. Libr. Assn., N.C. Libr. Assn. Avocations: web design, storytelling, genealogy. Office: Hickory Pub Libr 375 Third St NE Hickory NC 28601 Office Phone: 828-304-0500. Business E-Mail: cjones@ci.hickory.nc.us.

JONES, CRAIG WARD, lawyer; b. Pitts., June 14, 1947; s. Curtis Edison and Margaret (McFarland) J.; m. Sarah Dowding; children: Laura McFarland, Rebecca Long, Nancy Harper. BA, Carleton Coll., 1969; JD, U. Pitts., 1976. Bar: Pa. 1976, U.S. Dist. Ct. (we. dist.) Pa. 1976, U.S. Ct. Appeals (3d cir.) 1981. Ptnr. Reed Smith LLP, Pitts., 1976—2004. Served to lt. USNR, 1969-73. Mem. Allegheny County Bar Assn. Presbyterian. Home: 208 Cornwall Dr Pittsburgh PA 15238-2639 Office Phone: 412-288-3020.

JONES, CURLEY CLEVELAND, librarian; b. Feb. 23, 1941; s. Cleve and Susie J. AA, Sts. Jr. Coll., Lexington, Miss., 1965; BA, Tougaloo (Miss.) Coll., 1969; MLS, SUNY, Geneseo, 1971; MEd, U. Utah, 1975; Cert. of Advanced Study in Librarianship, U. Ill., 1977. Cert. tchr., N.Y. Librarian U. Utah, Salt Lake City, 1972—. Editor Black Bibliography, 1977, supplement, 1981. Adv. to mayor Salt Lake City Cmty. Coun., 1989-96; bd. dirs. Ctrl. City Cmty. Coun., 1998—. Mem. ALA, Assn. Study of Negro Life and History, Mt. Plains Libr. Assn., Utah Libr. Assn., High Marine Lodge.

JONES, CYNTHIA RECTOR, artist; b. Washington, Apr. 27, 1951; d. George Harry and Patricia (Twohy) Rector; m. Kelly Chapman Jones, June 12, 1971; children: Grace, Kelly, Laura. BA, Stratford Coll., 1971. Tchr. North Shore Pvt. Sch., Norfolk, Va., 1971-73, First Presbyn. Presch., Norfolk, 1985-90. Exhbns. include Edenton Gallery, Norfolk, 1994, Smithfield Gallery, Norfolk, 1994, Suffolk Mus., Norfolk, 1994, Agora Gallery, 1997, Va. Wesleyan Coll. City union rep. King's Daughters Hosp., Norfolk, 1976, 80, 95; parish coun. Sacred Heart Catholic Ch., Norfolk, 1983-85; pres. St. Mary's Infant Home, Norfolk, 1993-95. Mem. Jr. League Norfolk, Harborfront Garden Club (pres. 1987-88).

JONES, D. PAUL, JR., bank executive, lawyer; b. Birmingham, Ala., Sept. 26, 1942; s. D. Paul and Virginia Lee (Mount) J.; m. Charlene Dale Angelich, Aug. 1964; children: Holly, Allison, Paul, III. BS, U. Ala., 1964, JD, 1967; LL.M., N.Y. U., 1968. Bar: Ala. Mem. firm Balch, Bingham, Baker, Hawthorne, Williams & Ward, Birmingham, 1970-78, of counsel, 1978-86; exec. v.p., gen. counsel, dir. Compass Bancshares, Inc., Birmingham, 1978-84, vice chmn., 1984-89, pres., COO, 1989-91, chmn., CEO, 1991—. Bd. dirs. Compass Bank, Russell Lands Co., Bus. Coun. Ala., Compass Bancshares, Inc.; exec. com. Pub. Affairs Rsch. Coun. Ala.; mem. Internat. Fin. Conf. Chmn. Ala. Bus. Charitable Trust Fund; mem. adv. bd. Better Bus. Bur. Birmingham; adv. bd. Salvation Army, Birmingham; bd. visitors Sch. Commerce and Bus. Adminstrn., U. Ala.; mem. pres.'s coun. U. Ala., Birmingham, Ala. Inst. Deaf and Blind; ptnr. Econ. Devel. Partnership Ala.; grad. bd. trustees Leadership Birmingham; grad. Leadership Ala.; mem. adv. bd. Juvenile Diabetes Found., Ala., corp. chmn. Walk to Cure Diabetes, 1999; co-chmn. Advantage 21 Leadership Coun.; mem. adv. coun. Nat. Multiple Sclerosis Soc.; bd. dirs. Region 2020, Inc., Fed. Res. Bank Atlanta; dinner chmn. 32d ann. awards dinner Nat. Conf. for Cmty. and Justice, 2000; adv. bd. Svc. Corp. Ret. Execs. Mem. ABA, Ala. Bar Assn. (chmn. sect. corp., banking and bus. law 1973-75, bd. bar examiners 1975-78), Birmingham Bar Assn., Am. Bankers Assn. (mem. govt. rels. coun. 1985-88), Ala. Bankers Assn. (pres. 1989-90, chmn. fin. com. 1990-91, exec. coun.), Fin. Svcs. Roundtable (bd. dirs., banking and fin. markets com.), Soc. Internat. Bus. Fellows, Newcomen, Birmingham C. of C., Birmingham C. of C. Found., Birmingham Bus. Leadership Group, Svc. Corps Ret. Execs. (adv. bd.), The Club, Old Overton, Country Club Birmingham, Willow Point Golf and Country Club (Alexander City), Rotary. Home: 2010 Garden Pl Birmingham AL 35223-1156 Office: Compass Bancshares Inc PO Box 10566 Birmingham AL 35296-0001 also: Compass Bancshares Inc 15 20th St S Birmingham AL 35233-2000*

JONES, DAN LEWIS, psychologist; b. Halifax, Va., Oct. 8, 1951; s. Ernest Lewis and Mary Elizabeth (Francis) J.; m. Temple Kiger Jones, Aug. 17, 1974; children: Natalie Temple, Layla Michelle. BA, Appalachian State U., 1974; MA, West Ga. Coll., 1976; PhD, U. Kans., 1986. Lic. psychologist, N.C., Calif., Va.; diplomate in counseling psychology Am. Bd. Profl. Psychology; cert. treatment of alcohol and other psychoactive substance use disorders, APA Coll. of Profl. Psychology. Instr. psychology N.C. Ctrl. U., Durham, 1976-79; counselor Adult Life Resource Ctr., U. Kans., Lawrence, 1979-84; psychology intern Counseling Ctr. U. Calif., Irvine, 1984-85; acting dir. adult life resource ctr. U. Kans., 1985-86; staff psychologist Counseling Ctr. Utah State U., Logan, 1986-88; psychologist Counseling Ctr. East Tenn. State U., Johnson City, 1988-89; sr. psychologist, dir. tng., asst. dir. Counseling and Psychol. Svcs., Appalachian State U., Boone, N.C., 1989-97, dir., 1996—; part-time pvt. practice. Cons. IRS, 1985, Bristol (Tenn.) Mental Health Ctr., 1989, N.C. Ct. Counseling Svcs., 1979. Author: (with others) Counseling Adults, 1985, editor; author (manual) The Stress management Workshop, 1985, (with others) AACD Stress Workshop Manual, 1985; ad hoc reviewer Jour. Psychotherapy Integration, Jour. Coll. Student Devel., Jour. of Am. Coll. Health, others. Fellow Acad. of Counseling Psychology; mem. APA (chmn. spl. interest group on coll. counseling ctrs. divsn. 17, mem. program com. divsn. 29), ACA, Am. Coll. Counseling Assn., NC Psychol. Assn., Am. Coll. Pers. Assn. (directorate commn. VII), Internat. Assn. Counseling Svcs. (bd. dirs., pres.); Assn. Univ. and Coll. Counseling Ctrs. (governing bd.). Democrat. Avocation: racquetball. Home: 357 Fawn Dr Boone NC 28607-8461 Office Phone: 828-262-3180.

JONES, DANIEL L., manufacturing executive; b. 1964; m. Donna Jones; children: Trevor, Katelynn, Reagen. BBA, East Tex. State Univ. Pres., COO Encore Wire Corp., McKinney, Tex., interim CEO, 2005—, also bd. dirs. Treas. Prosper Christian Men's Fellowship; mem. McKinney C. of C. Mem.: Prosper Sports Assn. Office: Encore Wire Corp 1410 Millwood Rd Mc Kinney TX 75069*

JONES, DANIEL W., construction executive; Pres., chief operating officer Zaring Nat. Corp., Cin., 1989—. Office: Zaring National Corp 625 Eden Park Dr #1250 Cincinnati OH 45202-6024

JONES, DAVID A., consumer products company executive; Pres., CEO The Regina Co., 1989—94; chmn., CEO, COO Thermoscan, Inc., 1995—96, pres., 1996—98; chmn., CEO Rayovac, 1996—98. Office: Rayovac 601 Ray O Vac Dr Madison WI 53711 Office Phone: 608-275-3340.*

JONES, DAVID A., JR., insurance company executive; BA in History magna cum laude, Yale U., 1980, JD, 1988. English tchr. Hunan Med. Coll., Changsha, China; with internat. divsn. First Nat. Bank Boston; atty.-adviser Bur. East Asian and Pacific Affairs U.S. Dept. State, 1988-92; assoc. Hirn Reed & Harper, Louisville; chmn., mng. dir. Chrysalis Ventures, LLC, Louisville, 1993—; vice chmn. Humana, Louisville, 1996—2005, chmn., 2005—. Adj. prof. Georgetown U. Law Ctr., Washington; former chmn. Greater Louisville Health Enterprises Network; mem. adv. com. Brookings Ctr. on Health Policy; bd. mem. Nat. Com. on US-China Relations. Office: Humana Inc 500 W Main St Louisville KY 40202 also: Chrysalis Ventures LLC 1650 Nat City Tower 101 S Fifth St Louisville KY 40202*

JONES, DAVID ALLEN, health benefits company executive; b. Louisville, Aug. 7, 1931; s. Evan L. and Elsie F. (Thurman) Jones; m. Betty L. Ashbury, July 24, 1954. BS, U. Louisville, 1954; JD, Yale U., 1960. Bar: Ky. 1960. Founder Humana Inc. (formerly Extendicare Inc.), Louisville, 1961, CEO, 1961—97, chmn., dir. Louisville, 1997—; ptnr. Greenebaum, Doll and McDonald and predecessor, Louisville, 1965—69, of counsel, 1969—74. Dir. Abbott Labs. Lt. (j.g.) USN, 1954—57. Mem.: Louisville Area C. of C. Office: Humana Inc 500 W Main St Ste 300 Louisville KY 40202-4268*

JONES, DAVID CHARLES, retired air force officer, former chairman Joint Chiefs of Staff; b. Aberdeen, S.D., July 9, 1921; s. Maurice and Helen Alice (Meade) J.; m. Lois M. Tarbell, Jan. 23, 1942; children: Susan Jones Coffin, Kathy Jones Franklin, David Curtis. Student, U. N.D., Minot State Coll.; grad., Flying Sch., Roswell, N.Mex., 1943, Nat. War Coll., Washington, 1960; H.L.D., U. Nebr., 1974, La. Tech. U., 1975, Minot State Coll., 1979, Boston U., 1980, Troy State U. Commd. 2d lt. U.S. Air Force, 1943, advanced through grades to gen., 1971; dep. comdr. ops. Vietnam; vice comdr. 7th Air Force; comdr.-in-chief U.S. Air Force Europe; comdr. 4th Allied Tactical Air Force; chief of staff U.S. Air Force, Washington, 1974-78; chmn. Joint Chiefs of Staff, Dept. Def., Washington, 1978-82, ret., 1982. Former bd. dirs. GE, RCA, NBC, US Airways, Kemper Ins., SRA Internat., USX, Servus Fin.; chmn. Nat. Edn. Corp., Hay Sys. Decorated Def. D.S.M., Air Force D.S.M., Navy D.S.M., Army D.S.M., Legion of Merit, D.F.C., Bronze star, Air medal, numerous others. Mem. Air Force Assn., Falcon Found., Mgmt. Execs. Soc., Coun. on Fgn. Rels., Alfalfa Club. E-mail: dcji@aol.com.

JONES, DAVID CHARLES, international financial and management consultant; b. Cowes, Eng., Feb. 8, 1935; came to U.S., 1970; s. Charles Alfred and Alice Elizabeth (Rickman) J.; m. Gabrielle Clara Mabey, Sept. 28, 1957; children: Stephen Charles, Philip Simon (dec.), Catherine Claire. Cert. in acctg. and fin. mgmt., Chartered Inst. Pub. Fin. and Accountancy, London, 1961. Cert. acct., Eng. Clk. Brit. Rail, London, 1951-55, Isle of Wight (Eng.) County Coun., Newport, 1955-56; acct. Petworth (Eng.) Dist. Coun., 1956-59; chief acct. Kingswood (Eng.) Dist. Coun., 1959-61; sr. acct. Luton (Eng.) Borough Coun., 1961-63; tech. asst. Govt. of U.K., Entebbe, Uganda, 1963-68, Blantyre, Malawi, 1968-70; sr. fin. analyst World Bank, Washington, 1970-80, fin. adviser, 1980-87; cons. Internat. Fin. and Mgmt. Cons., Annandale, Va., 1987—, World Bank, Internat. Monetary Fund, 1987—. Vis. lectr. Grad. Sch. Design, Harvard U., Cambridge, Mass., 1987—, rsch. fellow, 1994—, Grad. Sch., George Mason U., Fairfax, Va., 1990—; v.p. Internat. Devel. Tng. Inst., Washington, 1988-95; sr. assoc. cons. Internat. Mgmt. Cons. Ltd., Eng.; expert testimony D.C. Com., U.S. Ho. of Reps. Author: Municipal Accounting for Developing Countries, 1984; contbr. articles to profl. jours. Cpl. R.A.F., 1953-55, Eng. Fellow Assn. of Chartered Cert. Accts.; mem. Chartered Inst. Pub. Fin. and Accountancy, Internat. Consortium on Govtl. Fin. Mgmt. (bd. dirs. 1980—). Episcopalian. Avocations: amateur poet, music composer, classical music, meditation, railways. Home: 4936 Andrea Ave Annandale VA 22003-4180

JONES, DAVID KEITH, education educator; b. Santa Monica, Calif., Dec. 10, 1962; s. David Elwyn and Brenda Jones; m. Marjorie Kathleen Smith, Oct. 6, 2002; 1 child, Ethan David. PhD, U. of So. Calif., 1980—91. Assoc. prof. of psychology Westminster Coll., Fulton, Mo., 1995—; asst. prof. of psychology Lyon Coll., Batesville, Ark. Dir. of assessment Westminster Coll., Fulton, Mo. Author: (textbook instructor supplements) Instructor supplements for Passer/Smith Psychology: Frontiers and Applications (Haynes Fellowship, 1987); contbr. articles to profl. jours. Bd. dirs. Family Counseling Ctr., Columbia, Mo., 2002—05. Grant, U.S. Dept. of Labor, 2002. Mem.: Soc. for the Tchg. of Psychology, Soc. for Personality and Social Psychology, Midwestern Psychol. Assn., Internat. Assn. for Relationship Rsch., Coun. of Teachers of Undergraduate Psychology, Assn. of Am. Colleges and Universities, AAUP (Westminster coll. chpt. pres. 2001—03), Phi Beta Kappa, Psi Chi. Office: Westminster College 501 Westminster Ave Fulton MO 65251 Office Phone: 573-592-6118. E-mail: jonesd@westminster-mo.edu.

JONES, DAVID M., zoological park administrator; b. Cheshire, Eng., Aug. 14, 1944; arrived in U.S., 1994; m. Janet Jones; 3 children. BSc in Zoology, Royal Vet. Coll., London, 1966; B in Vet. Medicine, Royal Veterinary Coll., London, 1969. 1st resident vet. surgeon Whipsnade pk. Zool. Soc. London, 1969-75, sr. vet. officer, 1975, responsible for animal collection London and Whipsnade, 1981, dir. zoos London and Whipsnade, 1984, CEO, 1991; dir. conservation and consultancy London and Whipsnade, 1993; dir. N.C. Zool. Pk., Asheboro, 1994—, Dept. Environ. Natural Resources State of N.C., 1994—. Chmn. Fauna and Flora Internat., London, 1987—94; chmn. conservation com. World Wide Fund Nature UK, 1988—94, trustee; chmn. Brooke Hosp. Animals, London, Pakistan, 1990—98, India, 2000—02, Yadkin Pee-Dee Lakes Project, 1998—; mem. coun. World Wildlife Fund U.S., 1996—2002; bd. mem. Nat. Audubon N.C., 2002—, Environ. Def. N.C., 2003—. Contbr. articles to profl. jours. Fellow: Inst. of Biology; mem.: Royal Coll. Vet. Surgeons. Home: 1688 Sylvan Way Asheboro NC 27205-2546 Office: 4401 Zoo Pkwy Asheboro NC 27205-1425 Office Phone: 336-879-7102. Personal E-mail: david.m.jones@ncmail.net.

JONES, DAVID MILTON, economist, educator; b. Newton, Iowa, June 22, 1938; s. Charles Raymond and Mary Evelyn (Corrough) J.; m. Becky Ann Jones Strait, Aug. 4, 1962; children: David, Jennifer, Stephen. BA with honors, Coe Coll., 1960; MA, U. Pa., 1961, PhD, 1969. Economist Fed. Res. Bank N.Y., N.Y.C., 1963-68; v.p., fin. economist Irving Trust Co., N.Y.C., 1968-72; vice-chmn., chief economist, bd. dirs. Aubrey G. Lanston & Co., Inc., N.Y.C., 1972-2000; owner DMJ Advisors LLC, Denver, 2000—, Crystal Lake Resort, Pine, Colo. Advisor panel Fed. Res. Bank N.Y., 1982-93, cons. bd. govs., 1996—; mem. bd. vis. U. Pa.; former dir. pub. interest Suffolk County Savs. and Loan, Centerreach, N.Y.; bd. dirs. Aubrey G. Lanston & Co., Inc., Coe Coll., Union Theol. Sem.; lectr. AIMR security analysts seminar, Northwestern U.; chmn. bd. Investors' Security Trust Co., Ft. Myers, Fla., 2004—. Author: Fed Watching and Interest Rate Projections: A Practical Guide, 1986, The Politics of Money: The Fed under Alan Greenspan, 1991, The Buck Starts Here: How the Federal Reserve Can Make or Break Your Financial Future, 1995, Unlocking the Secrets of the Fed: How Monetary Policy Affects the Economy and Your Wealth Creation Potential, 2002. Chmn. fin. and investment com. United Ch. Bd. for World Ministries, N.Y.C., 1975-86; mem. bond com. Twp. of Montclair, 1982-83. Woodrow Wilson Found. fellow, 1960; NDEA fellow, 1960 Mem. Nat. Assn. Bus. Economists, Econ. Club of N.Y., Nat. Econ. Club (bd. dirs.). Office: PO Box 529 Pine CO 80470 Personal E-mail: dmj@allabouttrust.com.

JONES, DAVID RHODES, editor, consultant; b. Connellsville, Pa., Sept. 13, 1932; s. David Rhodes and Ruth Elizabeth (Dillon) J.; m. Mary Lee Lauffer, Oct. 8, 1955; 1 dau., Elizabeth Lee. BA, Pa. State U., 1954; MA, N.Y. U., 1961. Reporter Wall Street Jour., N.Y.C., 1957-61, bur. chief Pitts., 1961-63; with N.Y. Times, 1963—97, corr., Detroit, 1963-65, nat. labor reporter, Washington, 1965-68, asst. nat. editor, N.Y.C. N.Y.C., 1969-72, nat. editor, 1972-87, editor nat. editions, 1987-97, asst. mng. editor, 1989-97. Trustee Pa. State U. Served to 1st lt. USAF, 1955-57. Mem.Tau Kappa Epsilon.

JONES, DAVID ROBERT, zoology educator; arrived in Can., 1969; s. William Arnold and Gladys Margery Jones; m. Valerie Iris Gibson, Sept. 15, 1962; children: Melanie Ann, Vivienne Samantha. BSc, Southampton U., 1962; PhD, U. East Anglia, Norwich, Eng., 1965. Rsch. fellow U. East Anglia, 1965-66; lectr. zoology U. Bristol, 1966-69; prof. zoology U. BC, Vancouver, Canada, 1969—, Disting. U. scholar, 2004—, Killam Univ. prof., 2005—. Contbr. numerous articles to profl. jours. Decorated Order of Can.; recipient Killam Rsch. prize, 1993, Murry A. Newman award significant achievement aquatic rsch., 2004; fellow, Killam Found., Can., 1973, 1989; scholar, Peter Wall Inst. Advanced Studies, Vancouver, 2002. Fellow Royal Soc. Can. (Flavelle medal 2000); mem. Soc. Exptl. Biology, Am. Physiol. Soc., Can. Zool. Soc. (Fry medal 1992). Avocations: opera, music, theater. Office: Zoology Animal Care U BC 6199 S Campus Rd Vancouver BC Canada V6T 1W5 Office Phone: 604-822-2180. Business E-Mail: jones@zoology.ubc.ca.

JONES, DAVID ROBERT **See BOWIE, DAVID**

JONES, DIANA WYNNE, writer; b. London, Aug. 16, 1934; d. Richard Aneurin Jones and Marjorie (Jackson) Hughes; m. John Anthony Burrow, Dec. 22, 1956; children: Richard, Michael, Colin. BA, St. Anne's Coll. U. Oxford, Eng., 1956. Free-lance writer part-time, Essex, Oxford, Eng., 1944-70; full-time writer Oxford, Bristol, Eng., 1970—. Panel judge Guardian Award for Children's Books, London, 1979-83, Whitbread Prize for Lit., Children's Sect., London, 1988; judge World Fantasy Awards, 2001. Author: Wilkins' Tooth (in U.S. Witch's Business), 1973, The Ogre Downstairs, 1974, Eight Days of Luke, 1975, Cart and Cwidder, 1975, Dogsbody, 1975, Power the Three, 1976, Drowned Ammet, 1977, Charmed Life, 1977 (Guardian award 1978), Who Got Rid of Angus Flint, 1978, The Spellcoats, 1979, The Magicians of Caprona, 1980, The Homeward Bounders, 1981, The Time of the Ghost, 1981, Witch Week, 1982, Warlock at the Wheel, 1984, Archer's Goon, 1984 (Boston Globe/Horn Book award), Fire and Hemlock, 1985 (Phoenix award, 2005), Howl's Moving Castle, 1986 (Boston Globe/Horn Book award), A Tale of Time City, 1987, The Lives of Christopher Chant, 1988, Chair Person, 1989, Wild Robert, 1989, Hidden Turnings, 1989, Castle in the Air, 1990, Black Maria, 1991, A Sudden Wild Magic, 1992, The Crown of Dalemark, 1993, Stopping for a Spell, 1993, Hexwood, 1993, Fantasy Stories, 1994, Everard's Ride, 1995, The Tough Guide to Fantasyland, 1996, Minor Arcana, 1996, Deep Secret, 1997, Dark Lord of Derkholm, 1998, (retelling of) Puss n' Boots, 1999, Mixed Magics, Year of the Griffin, 2000, The Merlin Conspiracy, 2003, Unexpected Magic, 2004, Changeover, 2004, Conrad's Fate, 2005; animated film: Howl's Moving Castle, 2004. Recipient, Mythopoaic Soc. award, 1995, 99, Joseph Wagner award Brit. Fantasy Soc., 1999. Mem. Soc. of Authors, Brit. Fantasy Soc. Avocations: cooking, owning a cat. Home: 9 The Polygon Bristol BS8 4PW England Office: care Greenwillow Books 105 Madison Ave New York NY 10016-7418

JONES, DONALD LEIGH, retired music educator; b. St. Louis, July 2, 1935; s. Norman R.D. and Esther Hamilton Jones; m. Pamela Smith, Aug. 12, 1961; children: Carole Anne, Patricia Annette Doerr, Donna Leigh Ashmore. AB in Music, Monmouth Coll, Ill., 1957; EdM in Music, U. Mo., Columbia, 1961. Cert. tchr. Ill. Dir. band Warren County Grade Sch. Dist. #222, Monmouth, Ill., 1956—57; asst. band dir. Monmouth Coll., 1957; tchr. band and vocal music grades 1-12 Stronghurst Cmty. Grade and H.S., 1957—58; dir. vocal music Belleville Twp. H.S. and Jr. Coll. (now Belleville West H.S., 1961—90; ret., 1990. Music dir. Theta Chi Fraternity Monmouth Coll., Ill., 1953—57; dir. U.S. Army Warner Kaserne Protestant Chapel Choir, Munich, 1959—60; minister of music and chancel choir Hillcrest Christian Ch., Belleville, Ill., 1961—72; substitute tchr. music dept. Belleville West H.S., 1990—98. Performer (All Am. Festival Choir): Carnegie Hall, N.Y.C., 1991, Trybonyn Hall, Moscow, 1991, Glinka Amolney Sabor Hall, St. Petersburg, 1991; composer: (songs) Oh Belleville West, Born for Us This Day, Alleluia, Christ Lives, Glory Hallelu; arranger and lyricist: And Then There Was Song; author: (software) Music Contest Aids program, 1986—97. Mem. cmty. chorus So. Ill. U., Edwardsville, Ill., 1992—93; dir. chancel choir Stronghurst Presbyn. Ch., Stronghurst, Ill., 1957—58, St. Matthew United Meth. Ch., 1972—80, mem. With U.S. Army, 1958—60. Mem.: St. Clair County Retired Tchrs. Assn. (life), Ill. Retired Tchrs. Assn. (life), Am. Choral dir. Assn. (life). Republican. Home: 1737 W Belle St Belleville IL 62226-6109

JONES, DONNA LEE NOBLE, emergency nurse; b. Bryan, Tex., Feb. 4, 1953; d. Kathryn MacLean Noble; m. Alan Jones. ADN with honors, North Shore Community Coll., Beverly, Mass., 1982. RN, Mass., Calif.; CEN, cert. trauma nurse, mobile intensive care nurse. Med.-surg. nurse Salem (Mass.) Hosp., 1982-86; emergency nurse Beverly Hosp., 1986-90; neurol. nurse Mass. Gen. Hosp., Boston, 1990-91; emergency nurse Level I Trauma Ctr. Valley Med. Ctr., Fresno, Calif., 1991-93, Petaluma Valley, 1993-96, 98—, Sonoma Valley, 1993—, San Francisco Gen. Hosp., 1997—. Med. advisor Human Rights Com. Bass River, Beverly, 1983-84; adj. faculty paramedic edn. Northeastern U., Boston, 1989-90. Educator Project RAP, Unit Against Sexual Assault, Beverly, 1988-90; EMT educator North Shore Ambulance, Salem, 1989; educator Emergency Nurses Care Program, Mass., 1987, Calif. 1998—. Mem. Emergency Nurses Assn. (sec. Mariner chpt. 1989-90), Sonoma County Bar Assn, Alpaca Owners Breeders Assn. (citizen ambassador del. emergency medicine 1990, 93). Avocations: photography, travel, forensics, medical legal issues, alpacas.

JONES, DORIS LOGAN, artist, art educator; b. Billings, Mont, May 5, 1926; d. William Ernest and Florence Mabel (Snow) Logan; m. Edward Evans Jones, Aug. 23, 1947; children: Mark, Kent, Stanton, Clifton, Konni; 7 foster children. BA, Brigham Young U., 1949, MA, 1950; student, Washburn U., 1946-47, Denver U., 1944-45; BA, Brigham Young U., 1949; postgrad., Ea. Mont. State Coll., 1954-55. One-woman shows in Mont., Wyo., Colo., Ga., Calif., Tex., Paris, Pa. Mem. Billings Arts Assn., Cody Country Art League, Billings Book Club, West Extension Club (pres. 1992-93), Machine Knitting Club. Avocations: genealogy, organ music, sewing, knitting, architecture, portrature and Indians from many tribes I visit. Home: 1032 N 29th St Billings MT 59101-0730

JONES, DOROTHY F., judge; b. Sept. 3, 1946; d. Birl Floyd Madden and Aszie (Brown) Madden Simpson; m. Raymond Wilkerson (div. Jan. 1972); 1 child, Vicky; m. Allen J. Jones, Aug. 15, 1987 (dec. Aug. 1997); 1 stepchild, Felicia. BA, DePaul U., 1974, JD, 1979. Bar: Ill. 1979, U.S. Dist. Ct. (no. dist.) Ill. 1980, U.S. Supreme Ct. 1983. Acct. Allied Radio, Chgo., 1962-68, Atlantic Richfield, Chgo., 1968-72; tchr. Chgo. Pub. Schs., 1974-80; asst. pub. defender Cook County Pub. Defender's Office, Chgo., 1980-92; elected cir. judge Daley Ctr. Cir. Ct. Cook County, Chgo., 1992—, retained, 1998. Legal adviser 28th Ward alderman, Chgo., 1982-83. Chmn. prin.'s com. Suder Sch., Chgo., 1978, rec. sec. cmty. coun., 1979; adviser Westside People for Progress, Chgo., 1982; bd. dirs. Chgo. Youth Ctrs.; founder Concerned Citizens, Mother's House. Recipient certs. merit Clemente H.S. Bilingual Dept., Chgo., 1979, Kinsey Elem. Sch., Chgo., 1980, Kennedy H.S., Chgo., 1980. Mem. ABA, Ill. State Bar Assn., Chgo. Bar Assn., Cook County Bar Assn. (bd. dirs. 1982-84, rec. sec. young lawyers sect. 1982-83, Merit award 1982, cert. of appreciation 1998), Am. Arbitration Assn., Nat. Assn. Criminal Def. Attys., Ill. Judges Assn., Ill. Jud. Coun., Austin Cmty. Club, Mix Bowling League. Democrat. Methodist. Home: 133 S Waller Ave Chicago IL 60644-3948 Office: Richard J Daley Ctr Cir Ct Cook County 50 W Washington St Chicago IL 60602-1305

JONES, DOUGLAS GORDON, retired literature educator; b. Bancroft, Ont., Can., Jan. 1, 1929; s. Gordon Wilfred and Arlene (Ford) Jones; m. Betty Jane Kimbark, Sept. 23, 1950 (div.); children: Stephen, Skyler, Tory Joanne, North; m. Monique Baril, Dec. 1, 1976; 1 stepchild, Nicolas Grandmangin. BA in English, McGill U., 1952; MA in English, Queen's U., 1954; DLitt (hon.), Guelph U., 1982. Instr. Royal Milit. Coll., Kingston, Ont., 1954-55, Ont. Agrl. Coll., Guelph, 1955-61, Bishop's U., Lennoxville, 1961-63; prof. dept. letters and comm. U. Sherbrooke, Que., Can., 1963-94. Vis prof Univ Victoria, BC, Canada, 1978, Univ Canadienne en France, Villefranche-sur-Mer, 1987; mem arts adv panel, juries Can Coun. Author: (poetry) Frost on the Sun, 1957, The Sun is Axeman, 1961, Phrases from Orpheus, 1967, Under the Thunder the Flowers Light Up the Earth, 1977 (Gov Gen Award for Poetry, 1977, A J M Smith Award for Poetry, 1977), A Throw of Particles: New and Selected Poems, 1983, Balthazar and Other Poems, 1988 (QSPELL Prize for Poetry, 1989), A Thousand Hooded Eyes, 1991, The Floating Garden, 1995 (QSPELL Prize for Poetry, 1995), Wild Asterisks in Cloud, 1997, Grounding Sight, 1999; translator: The Terror of the Snows: Selected Poems of Paul-Marie Lapointe, 1976, The Fifth Season: Poems by Paul Marie Lapointe, 1995, Normand de Bellefeuille Categorics, One, Two & Three, 1993 (Gov Gen Award for Translation, 1993), Emile Martel, For Orchestra and Solo Poet, 1996; ed, contbg translator: poetry The March to Love: Selected Poems of Gaston Miron, 1986, Esprit de Corps: Quebec Poetry of the Late Twentieth Century in Translation, 1997; contbr. articles to profl jours. Mem.: League Canadian Poets, Royal Soc Can, Asn for Can and Que Literatures. Home and Office: 120 Houghton St North Hatley PQ Canada J0B 2C0 E-mail: dgjones@abacom.com.

JONES, DOUGLAS WILEY, lawyer; b. Fort Lauderdale, Fla., 1948; AB, Princeton U., 1970; JD, Harvard U., 1973. Bar: (N.Y.) 1974. Ptnr. Milbank, Tweed, Hadley & McCloy LLP, N.Y.C., 1982—2004, cons. ptnr., 2005—. Mem.: Assn. Bar NYC, Am. Bar Assn. Office: Milbank Tweed Hadley & McCloy LLP 3 Darby Cir East Hampton NY 11937

JONES, E. STEWART, JR., lawyer; b. Troy, N.Y., Dec. 4, 1941; s. E. Stewart and Louise (Farley) J.; m. Constance M., Dec. 28, 1968; children: Christopher, Brady, Erin. BA, Williams Coll., 1963; JD, Albany Law Sch., 1966. Bar: N.Y. 1966, U.S. Dist. Ct. (no. dist.) N.Y. 1966, U.S. Ct. Appeals (2d cir.) 1976, U.S. Supreme Ct. 1976, U.S. Dist. Ct. (we. dist.) N.Y. 1987, U.S. Claims Ct. 1991, U.S. Dist. Ct. (so. and ea. dist.) N.Y. 1994, U.S. Dist. Ct. Vt. 2004. Asst. dist. atty. Rensselaer County (N.Y.), 1968-70, spl. prosecutor, 1974; ptnr. E. Stewart Jones, Troy, 1974—. Lectr. in field; mem. com. on profl. standards of 3d jud. dept. State of N.Y., 1977-80, mem. 3d jud. screening com., Albany County; mem. merit selection panel for selection and appointment of U.S. magistrate for No. Dist. N.Y., 1981, 91; bd. dirs. Univ. Found. at Albany, trustee Troy Savs. Bank. Contbr. numerous articles to profl. jours. Trustee The Albany Acad., Albany Law Sch.; active Nat. Alumni Coun. Albany Law Sch. With USNG. Fellow: Am. Bar Found., N.Y. Bar Found., Inner Circle Advs., Internat. Soc. Barristers (chmn. Upstate N.Y. 1988—), Am. Bd. Trial Lawyers, Am. Inns. of Ct., Internat. Acad. Trial Lawyers, Am. Coll. Trial Lawyers, Am. Bd. Profl. Liability Attys. (diplomate), Internat. Soc. Barristers; mem.: ABA (numerous coms.), Acad. Trial Profls., Fed. Ct. Bar Assn., Coll. Master Advs. and Barristers (sr. counsel), Saratoga County Bar Assn., Am. Coll. Barristers (sr. counsel), Internat. Acad. Litigators (diplomate), Civil Justice Found. (founding sponsor), Trial Lawyers for Pub. Justice (founder), Inst. Injury Reduction (founder), Am. Bd. Trial Advs. (adv.), N.Y. State Assn. Criminal Def. Lawyers, Nat. Assn. Criminal Def. Lawyers, Nat. Bd. Trial Advocacy (diplomate), Fed. Bar Coun., Dispute Resolutions, Inc. (nat. panel of arbitrators), Am. Arbitration Assn. (nat. panel of arbitrators), N.Y. State Defenders Assn., Albany County Bar Assn., Am. Soc. Law and Medicine, Rensselaer County Bar Assn., Am. Judicature Soc. (sustaining), Practising Law Inst., Capital Dist. Trial Lawyers Assn. (bd. dirs. 1973—76), N.Y. State Trial Lawyers Assn. (bd. dirs. 1982—91, dir. emeritus 1991), N.Y. State Bar Assn. (mem. exec. com. trial lawyers sect. 1977—90, 1981—94, mem. spl. com. med. malpractice, other coms., Outstanding Practitioner award 1980), Williams Club (N.Y.C.), Stone Horse Yacht Club (Harwich Port, Mass.), Ft. Orange Club, Schuyler Meadows Club. Home: 46 Schuyler Rd Loudonville NY 12211-1447 Office: 28 2nd St Troy NY 12180-3986 E-mail: info@esjlaw.com.

JONES, EDGAR ALLAN, JR., law educator, lawyer, arbitrator; b. Bklyn., Jan. 8, 1921; s. Edgar Allan and Isabel (Morris) J.; m. Helen Callaghan, Sept. 15, 1945; children: Linda Marie, Anne Marie, Carol Marie, Edgar Allan III, Denis James, Robert Morris, David Llewellyn, Therese Marie, Catherine Marie, Nancy Marie, Daniel Anthony. BA, Wesleyan U., 1942; LLB, U. Va., 1950. Bar: Va. 1948. Faculty UCLA, 1951—, prof. law, 1958-91, emeritus, 1991—, asst. dean, 1957-58; dir. Law-Sci. Rsch. Ctr., 1963-66; labor dispute arbitrator, mediator, fact finder for pvt. and pub. employers and unions, 1953—. Appeared as judge ABC-TV network programs Accused, 1958-59, Traffic Ct., 1958-61, Day in Court, 1958-64; moderator ednl. TV program Forum West, 1966; author: (novels) Mr. Arbitrator, 2000, Break a Leg, Professor, 2005; editor: Law and Electronics: The Challenge of a New Era, 1960; founding editor Va. Law Weekly, 1948-50, NAA Chronicle, 1977-78; contbr. numerous labor law, arbitration and polygraph articles to law revs. Pres. Creddalt Rsch., Inc., 1959-90; dir. Deauville Restaurant, Inc. (Jimmy's 1978-94); pub. mem. Calif. Commn. Manpower Automation and Tech., 1963-67, Calif. Manpower Adv. Com., 1964-67; nat. enforcement commr. WSB, 1951; sec. Californians for Kennedy, 1960. 1st lt. USMC, 1942-45. Mem. ABA, Nat. Acad. Arbitrators (pres. 1981). Home: PO Box 1347 Pacific Palisades CA 90272-1347 E-mail: tedjones@ucla.edu.

JONES, EDITH HOLLAN, federal judge; b. Phila., Apr. 7, 1949; m. Sherwood (Woody) Jones; 2 children. BA Cornell U., 1971; JD with honors, U. Tex., 1974. Bar: Tex. 1974, U.S. Supreme Ct. 1979, U.S. Ct. Appeals (5th and 11th cirs.), U.S. Dist. . (so. and no. dists.) Tex. Assoc. Andrews & Kurth, Houston, 1974—82, ptnr., 1982—85; judge U.S. Ct. Appeals (5th cir.), Houston, 1985—. Gen. counsel Rep. Party of Tex., 1981—83. Master: ABA; mem.: Houston Bar Assn., State Bar Tex. Presbyterian. Office: 12505 US Courthouse 515 Rusk Ave Houston TX 77002-2655*

JONES, EDITH IRBY, physician; b. Conway, Ark., Dec. 23, 1927; d. Robert and Mattie (Buice) Irby; m. James Beauregard Jones, Apr. 16, 1960 (dec. Oct. 1989); children: Gary Ivan, Myra Vonceil Jones Romain, Keith Irby. BS, Knoxville Coll., 1948; MD, U. Ark., 1952. Intern Univ. Hosp., Little Rock, 1952-53; gen. practice medicine Hot Springs, Ark., 1953-59; resident in internal medicine Baylor Coll. Medicine, Houston, 1959-62; practice medicine specializing in internal medicine Houston, 1962—; mem. staff Meth. Hosp., Houston, Hermann Hosp., Houston, Riverside Gen. Hosp., Houston, St. Elizabeth Hosp., Houston, St. Anthony Ctr., Houston, St. Joseph Hosp., Houston, Thomas Care Ctr., Houston, Town Park, Houston, chief of staff. Clin. asst. prof. medicine Baylor Coll. Medicine, U. Tex. Sch. Medicine, Houston; dir. Prospect Med. Lab.; bd. dirs., sec. Mercy Hosp. Comprehensive Health Care Group; ptnr. Jones, Coleman and Whitfield; grand med. examiner Ct. Calanthe Jurisdiction, Tex.; cons. Social Security Agy., Tex. Pub. Welfare Dept., Vocat. Rehab. Assn., Tex. Rehab. Commn.; bd. dirs. Std. Savs. Assn., Houston; others. Contbr. articles to profl. jours. Bd. dirs. Houston Internat. U., Drug Addiction Rehab. Enterprise, March of Dimes, Houston, Odessey House, Houston; adv. bd. Houston Coun. on Alcoholism; com. for revising justice code, Harris County, Tex.; chmn. bd. trustees Knoxville Coll.; impartial hearing officer Houston Ind. Sch. Dist.; trustee Mut. Assn. for Profl. Svc.; mem. Cmty. Welfare Planning Assn., Friends of Youth, Human Svcs. Adv. Coun., Houston; bd. visitors U. Houston; others. Dr. Edith Irby Jones Day proclaimed by State of Ark., 1985, City of Little Rock, 1985, City of N.Y.C., 1986; named one of 30 Most Influential Black Women Houston, 1984; named to Tex. Black Women's Hall of Fame, 1986; commended by Calif. Senate, 1969; proclamation by city coun., Houston, 1985, Mayor of Houston, 1986; recipient cert. of citation Ho. of Reps. State of Tex., 1986, Volunteerism and Cmty. Svc. award Tex. Acad. Internal Medicine, 2000, Scroll of Merit award Nat. Med. Assn., 2001; portrait placed in entrance hall U. Ark. for Med. Scis., 1985; others; named one of 100 Leading Black Physicians Black Enterprise mag., 2001. Fellow Am. Coll. Medicine, Am. Soc. Internal Medicine (Oscar E. Edward award 2001); mem. AMA, Am. Med. Women's Assn. (v.p. Houston chpt.), Nat. Med. Assn. (past pres., Scroll of Merit 2001), Lone Star Med. Assn., Harris County Med. Assn., Houston Med. Forum, Tex. Assn. Disability Examiners, Bus. and Profl. Women, Nat. Coun. Negro Women, Inc. (v.p. Dorothy Height chpt.), NAACP, PTA, YMCA, Alpha Kappa Mu, Delta Sigma Theta, Eta Phi Beta. Clubs: Links, Inc., Top Ladies of Distinction, Girl Friends, Inc., Women of Achievement, Inc. (Hall of Fame 1985). Lodges: Order Eastern Star. Democrat. Avocations: travel, walking, swimming. Home: 3402 S Parkwood Houston TX 77021 Office: 2601 Prospect St Houston TX 77004-7737 Office Phone: 713-529-3145. E-mail: eijones@advmed.com.

JONES, EDWARD GEORGE, neuroscience educator, neurologist; b. Upper Hutt, Wellington, N.Z., Mar. 26, 1939; came to U.S., 1972; s. Frank Ian and Theresa Agnes (Riordan) J.; m. Elizabeth Suzanne Oldham, Apr. 27, 1963; children: Philippa Emilie, Christopher Edward. MD, U. Otago, Dunedin, New Zealand, 1962; PhD, U. Oxford, Eng., 1968. Med. and surg. intern Tauranga Hosp., New Zealand, 1963; demonstrator to assoc. prof. dept. anatomy U. Otago Med. Sch., Dunedin, New Zealand, 1964-72; Nuffield Dominions demonstrator and lectr. Balliol Coll., U. of Oxford, England, 1964-72; assoc. prof. to prof., dept. anatomy and neurobiology Washington U. Sch. Medicine, St. Louis, 1972-84, George H. and Ethel Ronzini Bishop scholar, 1981-84, dir. divsn. exptl. neurology, 1981-84; prof. and chmn. dept. anatomy and neurobiology U. Calif., Irvine, 1984-98, dir. Ctr. Neurosci. Davis, 1998—, prof. psychiatry, 1998—, Disting. prof. psychiatry, 2003—. Cons. NIH, 1972—; dir. Neural Systems Lab., Frontier Rsch. Program in Neural Mechanisms of Mind and Behavior, Riken, Japan, 1988-96; vis. sr. rsch. fellow St. John's Coll. at U. Oxford, Eng., 1989-90. Author: The Thalamus, 1984, 2d edit. 2005; co-author: Thalamus, 1997, The Thalamus and Basal Telencephalon, 1982; co-editor: (book series) Cerebral Cortex, 1984-2001; author, reviewer numerous sci. and hist. articles, chpts. in books, 1964—. Mem. Pres.'s Adv. Bd. Calif. State U., Long Beach, 1986-90. Named one of 100 most cited biol. scientists, Sci. Citation Index, 1982, 151 Thompson scientific highly cited scientist database, 2001; recipient Rolleston Meml. prize, U. Oxford, 1970, Lashley award, Am. Philos. Soc., 2001; grantee rsch. grantee, NIH, 1971—. Fellow: AAAS; mem.: Nat. Acad. Scis., Anat. Soc. Gt. Britain and Ireland (Symington Meml. prize 1968), Am. Assn. Anatomists (Cajal medal 1999, Henry Gray award 2001), Soc. Neurosci. (com. chair 1978—81, 1988—89, pres.-elect 1997—98, pres. 1998—99). Democrat. Avocations: reading, writing, carpentry. Office: U Calif Ctr Neurosci 1544 Newton Ct Davis CA 95616-4859 Office Phone: 530-757-8747.

JONES, EDWARD LOUIS, historian, educator; b. Georgetown, Tex., Jan. 15, 1922; s. Henry Horace and Elizabeth (Steen) Jones; m. Dorothy M. Showers, Mar. 1, 1952 (div. Sept. 1963); children: Cynthia, Frances, Edward Lawrence; m. Lynn Ann McGreevy, Oct. 7, 1963; children: Christopher Louis, Teresa Lynne. BA in Philosophy, BA in Far East, U. Wash., 1952, BA in Speech, 1955, postgrad., 1952—54; JD, Gonzaga U., 1967. Social worker Los Angeles Pub. Assistance, 1956-57; producer, dir. Little Theatre, Hollywood, Calif. and Seattle, 1956-60; research analyst, cons. to Office of Atty. Gen., Olympia and Seattle, Wash., 1963-66; coordinator of counseling SOIC, Seattle, 1966-68; lectr., advisor, asst. to dean U. Wash., Seattle, 1968—. Instr. Gonzaga U., Spokane, Wash., 1961—62, Seattle CC, 1967—68; dir. drama workshop Driftwood Players, Edmonds, Wash., 1975—76. Author: Black Zeus, 1972, Profiles in African Heritage, 1972, Tutankhamon: Son of the Sun, King of Upper and Lower Egypt, 1978, Black Orators' Workbook, 1982, The Black Diaspora: Colonization of Colored People, 1988, From Rulers of the World to Slavery, 1990, President Zachary Taylor and Senator Hamlin: Union or Death, 1991, Why Colored Americans Need an Abraham Lincoln in 1992, Forty Acres and a Mule: The Rape of Colored Americans, 1994, Mister Moon Goes to Japan, a children's story, 2001, Black Zeus II, 2005; editor, pub.: various jours. V.p. Wash. Com. Consumer Interests, Seattle, 1966—68. Served to 2d lt. U.S. Army, 1940—45. Recipient Appreciation award, Office Minority Affairs, 1987, Fla. chpt. Nat. Bar Assn., 1990, Acad. Excellence award, Nat. Soc. Black Engrs., 1987; Frederick Douglass scholar, Nat. Coun. Black Studies, 1985, 1986. Mem.: Western Polit. Sci. Assn., Nat. Acad. Advising Assn. (bd. dirs. 1979—82, editor Jour. 1981—, award for Excellence 1985), Am. Acad. Polit. and Social Sci., Nat. Assn. Student Pers. Adminstrs., Smithsonian Inst. (assoc.). Democrat. Baptist. Avocations: travel, research, chess. Office: U Wash Ethnic Cultural Ctr Seattle WA 98195-0001 Office Phone: 206-524-7627.

JONES, EDWARD PAUL, writer, editor; b. Washington, Oct. 5, 1950; s. Aloysius and Jeanette Majors Jones. BA, Holy Cross Coll., 1972; MFA, U. Va., 1981. Editor, columnist Tax Analysts, Arlington, Va., 1983—2002; prof. Princeton U., George Mason U., U. of Maryland. Author: Lost in the City, 1992 (PEN/Hemingway award for fiction, 1993), The Known World, 2003 (Nat. Book Critics Circle award for fiction, 2004, Pulitzer Prize for fiction, 2004, Internat. IMPAC Dublin Literary award, 2005). Recipient Lannan Literary award Lannan Found., 1995, Nat. Endowment for the Arts fellowship, MacArthur Fellow, 2004. Mem. PEN Avocation: stamp collecting/philately.*

JONES, ELAINE HANCOCK, humanities educator; b. Niagara Falls, N.Y., Feb. 17, 1946; d. Roy Elmer and June Edna (Clark) Hancock; m. Ralph Jones III, Oct. 9, 1971 (div. June 1981). AAS in Comml. Design, U. Buffalo, 1962; BFA, SUNY, Buffalo, 1971, MFA in Painting, 1975; postgrad., Fla. State U., 1993—. Med. illustrator Roswell Park Meml. Inst., Buffalo, 1967—70; designer, animator Acad. McLarty Film Prodns., Buffalo, 1970—73; publs. designer Buffalo/Erie County Hist. Soc., 1974—78; dir. publs. Daemen Coll., Amherst, NY, 1978—80; owner, art dir. Plop Art Prodns., Melbourne, Fla., 1981—86; instr. humanities Brevard C.C., Melbourne, 1986—; prof. humanities Brevard campus Rollins Coll., Melbourne, 1995—2004. One-woman shows include SUNY, Buffalo, 1974, Upton Gallery, N.Y., 1975, Gallery Wilde, Buffalo, 1978; exhibited in group shows at Fredonia Coll., N.Y., 1975, Upton Gallery, 1975, Brevard Art Mus., Melbourne, Fla., 1987. Mem. docent program Art Mus./Sci. Ctr., Melbourne, 1983-84, mem. edn. com., 1995—; officer Platinum Coast chpt. Sweet Adelines Internat., 1984-90. Nat. Merit scholar, 1971-75; recipient cert. of merit Curtis Paper Co., 1977; N.Y. State Coun. on Arts grantee, 1975. Republican. Home: 2240 Sea Ave Indialantic FL 32903-2524 Office: Brevard CC Liberal Arts Dept 3865 N Wickham Rd Melbourne FL 32935-2310 Office Phone: 321-632-1111 x5744.

JONES, ELAINE R., former legal association administrator, civil rights advocate; b. Norfolk, Va., Mar. 2, 1944; AB, Howard U., 1965; LLB, U. Va., 1970. Spl. asst. to sec. William T. Coleman Jr. US Dept. Trans., Washington, 1975—77; pres., dir.-counsel, atty. NAACP Legal Def. and Ednl. Fund, Washington, 1993—2004. Mem. panel arbitration Am. Stock Exch. Recipient Recognition award Black Am. Law Student Assn, 1974, Spl. Achievement award Nat. Assn. Black Women Attys., 1975, Olender Found. Peacemaker award, 2000, Lamplighter Award for Equity and Justice, Black Leadership Forum, 2003, Lifetime Achievement award, Am. Law mag., 2005 Mem. Nat. Bar Assn., Internat. Fedn. Women Lawyers, Old Dominion Bar Assn., Va. trial Lawyers Assn., Delta Sigma Theta.

JONES, ELI, III, marketing/sales educator; b. Houston, Nov. 24, 1961; s. Eli Jones, II and Elvira Jones; m. Fern Cecilia Walker; children: Necia, Tracia, Christopher, Elicia. BS in Journalism, Tex. A & M U., 1979—82, MBA, 1985—86, PhD in Mktg., 1993—97. Key acct. mgr. Quaker Oats, Houston, 1986—88, zone sales planning mgr. Jacksonville, Fla., 1988—89, key accts. exec. Charlotte, NC, 1989—90; sales mgr. Nabisco, Houston, 1990—92; zone mgr. Frito Lay, Houston, 1992—93; instr. Tex. A & M U., College Station, 1993—97; assoc. prof. mktg. U. Houston, 1997—. Dir. Program for Excellence in Selling, Houston, 1997—; faculty advisor Program for Excellence in Selling Alumni Assn., Houston, 1998—; chair doctoral dissertation U. Houston, 1997—; pres., CEO Eli Jones & Assoc., Inc., Houston, 2001—; mentor, charter mem. KPMG's PhD Project mktg. chap., 1997—; adv. bd. The Fischer Inst., Akron, 1999—; sales coach Baylor U. Nat. Collegiate Sales Competition, Waco, 1999—2002; exec. sales instr., rschr., cons. various nat. and local firms and orgns., 1997—; keynote spkr. Cougar Preview, Houston, 1997—; adv. bd. Charter Sch., Victoria, 2000—; guest spkr. Sales & Mktg. Execs. Assn., Houston, 1999—2000. Dir.: (Sales Certification Program) Program for Excellence in Selling, —; co-editor: Sales Professional Network, 2001—; editl. rev. bd.: Indsl. Mktg. Mgmt., 2001—, Jour. Personal Selling and Sales Management, 2000—. Judge H.S. DECA competition, Humble, 2001; instr. Seeds of Life Ministry Workshop, Houston, 1999. Mem.: Nat. Conf. in Sales Mgmt., Southwestern Mktg. Assn., Acad. Mktg. Sci. (Outstanding Mktg. Tchr. 2001), Am. Mgmt. Assn., Alpha Mu Alpha. Avocations: Contemporary Christian Music Ministry, A/V technology, travel, basketball. Office: University of Houston 4800 Calhoun Rd Houston TX 77204-6028 Personal E-mail: eli-fern-jones@msn.com. Business E-Mail: eli-jones@uh.edu.

JONES, ELIZABETH (A. ELIZABETH JONES), former federal agency administrator; b. Munich, May 6, 1948; d. William Charles Jones and Sara Demarest (Ferris); m. Thomas Anthony Homan, 1977; m. Donald Andrew Ruschman, 2000; 2 children. BA in history, Swarthmore Coll., 1970; studied Arabic, in Beirut, Tunis and Cairo, 1975—77; in Internat. Rels., Boston U., 1986. Joined Fgn. Svc., 1970; fgn. svc. post Kabul, Afghanistan, 1971—72; pub. affairs officer Near East and South Asia Bur., 1972—73; polit. officer Cairo, 1973—75, Amman, Jordan, 1977—79; dep. prin. officer U.S. Interests Sect., Baghdad, Iraq, 1979—80; dep. chief mission Islamabad, Pakistan, 1988—92; Lebanon desk officer, 1981—83; dep. dir. for Lebanon, Jordan, Syria, and Iraq, 1983—84; head econ./comml. sect. U.S. Mission, West Berlin, 1985—88; dep. chief mission Bonn, Germany, 1992—93; exec. asst. to sec. state US Dept. State, Washington, 1993—94, US amb. Rep. of Kazakhstan, 1995—98, prin. dep. asst. sec. Bur. Near Eastern Affairs Washington, 1998—2000; sr. advisor Caspian Basin Energy Diplomacy, 2000—01; asst. sec. for European and Eurasian affairs U.S. Dept. of State, Washington, 2001—05; dir. AE Jones LLC, 2005—.

JONES, ELIZABETH WINIFRED, biology professor; b. Seattle, Mar. 8, 1939; d. Kenneth Clifford Harris and Dorothea (Dowty) J. BS, U. Wash., 1960, PhD, 1964. Postdoctoral fellow MIT, Cambridge, 1964-67, instr. in biology, 1967-69; asst. prof. Case Western Res. U., Cleve., 1969-74; assoc. prof. Carnegie Mellon U., Pitts., 1974-82, prof., 1982—, dept. head, 2000—, Frederick A. Schwertz Disting. Prof. of Life Scis., 2000—. Vis. scientist Sch. Medicine Wash. U., 1981-82; adj. prof. in psychiatry U. Pitts., 1985—; mem. genetics tng. com. NIH, Bethesda, Md., 1972-73, mem. genetics study sect., 1976-80, 84-86, chair, 1990-93. Co-author: (with D.L. Hartl) Genetics: Principles and Analysis, 1998, (with D.L. Hartl) Essential Genetics, 1999, Genetics: An Analysis of Genes and Genomes, 2000, 04; editor: Molecular Biology of the Yeast Saccaromyces, 2 vols., 1981, 82, Molecular and Cellular Biology of the Yeast Saccaromyces, 3 vols., 1991, 92, 97; assoc. editor Genetics, 1980-96, editor-in-chief 1997—; assoc. editor Yeast, 1984—, Ann. Rev. of Genetics, 1990—; mem. editl. bd. Molecular Biology of the Cell, 1992-2000. Recipient Rsch. Career Devel. Award, NIH, 1971—74, 1975—77; grantee professorship, Howard Hughes Med. Inst., 2002—. Fellow AAAS; mem. Am. Soc. Microbiology, Am. Acad. of Microbiology, Am. Soc. Cell Biology (coun. 1992-95), Genetics Soc. Am. (pres. 1987), Am. Soc. Human Genetics. Office: Carnegie Mellon U 4400 5th Ave Pittsburgh PA 15213-2617 Business E-Mail: ej09@andrew.cmu.edu.

JONES, EMIL, JR., state legislator; b. Chgo., Oct. 18, 1935; s. Emil Sr. and Marilla (Mims) J.; m. Patricia Sterling, Dec. 14, 1974 (dec.); children: Debra, Renee, John, Emil III. A in Bus. Adminstrn., City Coll. Chgo., 1970. Mem. Ill. Ho. Reps., Springfield, 1972-82, Ill. Senate, Springfield, 1982—, Senate Dem. leader, 1992—2002, mem. exec. com., pres., 2002—05, senate pres., 2003—, bd. dirs. pres.' forum, 2004—. Active Task Force on Long Term Care, Morgan Pk. Civic League, Chgo. Recipient Legis. of the Yr. award, Keep Chgo. Beautiful, 2002, Outstanding Legis. award, Chgo. Prin. & Adminstr. Assn., 2003, Small Victories award, Chgo. Assn. for Retarded Citizens, 2003, Legis. of the Yr., Ill. Assn. of Minorities in Govt., 2003, Humanitarian of the Yr., Abraham Lincoln Ctr., 2003, Social Action award, Nat. Assn. of Black Social Workers, 2003, Dem. Legis. of the Yr., Ill. State Crime Commn., 2003, Champion Justice award, Ill. Equal Justice Coalition, 2003, Nat. Winn Newman Econ. Equity award, Svc. Employee Internat. Union, 2003, Person of the Yr. award, United Food & comml., 2003. Mem. Nat. Black Caucus State Legislators, Nat. Conf. State Legislators, Knights of St. Peter Claver, Shriners. Democrat. Roman Catholic. Home: 11357 S Lowe Ave Chicago IL 60628-4714 Office: 507 W 111th St Chicago IL 60628-4019 also: James R Thompson Ctr 100 W Randolph St Ste 16 600 Chicago IL 60601-3220 Office: 327 State Capitol Springfield IL 62706

JONES, ERIC S., lawyer; b. Lansing, Mich., Sept. 28, 1967; s. Stephen Albert and Judith H. J. BA, U. Richmond, 1989; JD, Emory U., 1992. Bar: Ga. 1992, U.S. Dist. Ct. (no. dist.) Ga. 1992. Assoc. Zirkle & Smith, Atlanta, 1992-93, Zirkle & Hoffman, Atlanta, 1993-97, ptnr., 1997—. Mem. ABA, Ga. Bar Assn., Atlanta Bar Assn., Def. Rsch. Inst., Atlanta Claims Assn., Ga. Self Insurers Assn. Avocation: coaching soccer. Office: Zirkle & Hoffman Ste 2900 Five Concourse Pkwy Atlanta GA 30328 E-mail: esj@zirklaw.com.

JONES, ERIK REID, choral conductor; s. Robert Thomas Jones and Joline Nan Matheson; m. Rochelle Marie Myers, June 3, 2001. MusB summa cum laude, U. Mass., 1992; MusM, U. Cin., 1994; D of Musical Arts, U. Md., 2003. Artistic dir. Master Singers of Va., Ashburn, 1994—; chief arch. washingtonpost.com, Arlington, Va., 1998—2002. Composer: (choral music) I'm Gonna Sing 'til the Spirit Moves Me in my Heart, Ukrainian Bell Carol, Miserere mei, Deus, Three Meditations on Snow. Chancellor's Talent scholar, U. Mass., 1988—92, grad. fellow, U. Md., 2003—05. Democrat. Jewish. Home: 7503 Palmer Ln Takoma Park MD 20912 Personal E-mail: erik@choralmusic.org.

JONES, EUGENE GORDON, pharmaceutical company executive; b. Lookout, W.Va., June 26, 1929; s. Alphus Raymond and Mona Blanche (Bobbitt) J.; m. Nancy Lee Hall, Aug. 19, 1951; children: Gene Douglas, Michael Gordon, Rebecca Lee, Jody Lynn. BS, Va. Tech. U., 1951. Med. rep. The Upjohn Co., Charlottesville, Va., 1956-60, profl. svcs. mgr. Washington, 1960-63, sr. med. rep. Roanoke, Va., 1963-68, hosp. med. rep. Richmond, Va., 1968-70, dist. sales mgr. Va., 1970-73, tng. specialist Kalamazoo, Mich., 1973-76, tng. mgr., 1976-87, nat. tng. dir., 1987-90; pres., owner Global Meeting Planners, 1991—. Bd. dirs. Kalamazoo Specialty Plants. Author: (self instrn. course) Managed Health Care, 1985, Arthritis Primer, 1976. Foudner, pres. Am. Diabetes Assn., Roanoke chpt., 1967, Richmond chpt., 1971, state del. ADA, 1970; bd. dirs. United Way, Kalamazoo, 1990-91, Mich. Diabetes Assn., Detroit, 1979; deacon River Rd. Presbyn. Ch.; mem. Rep. Presdl. Task Force. Lt. U.S. Army, 1951-53, Korea, capt. USAR, 1953-60. Mem. Korean War Vets. Assn. (founder of the Kalamazoo Mi Korea War chpt., life), Nat. Soc. Pharm. Sales Trainers (hon., pres. Western chpt. 1980-81, pres. nat. orgn. 1987-88, dir. 1985-90, founder newsletter 1987), Meeting Planners Internat., Internat. Meeting Planners, Mil. Order World Wars (treas. 1964-68), Kalamazoo Aviation History Mus., Charles Garfield Group (hon.), Korean War Vets. Assn. Res. Officers Assn. of U.S. (life), PGA Assocs. (life), Am. Legion, Vets. of Fgn. Wars. Avocations: volunteering, golf, reading, walking, travel.

JONES, EVERETT BRUCE, retired civil engineer, hydrologist; b. Ft. Collins, Colo., Sept. 23, 1933; s. Donald Lee and Muriel Virginia (Gwynn) J.; m. Margie Raben, May 27, 1956; children: Elizabeth Gwynn, Janet Lee. BS, U. Wyo., 1955; MS, Pa. State U., 1957; PhD, Colo. State U., 1964. Registered profl. engr., Wyo., Colo., Mont., Alaska. Chief of water devel. State of Wyo., Cheyenne, 1959-61; engr., hydrologist D.W. Barr Assocs., Mpls., 1964-65; asst. dir. inst. land/water rsch. Pa. State U., University Park, 1965-68; coord. water resources EG&G, Inc., Boulder, Colo., 1968-70; v.p. M.W. Bittinger and Assocs., Ft. Collins, 1970-77; pres. Resource Cons., Inc., Ft. Collins, 1977-87; regional mgr. spl. projects ESE, Inc., Englewood, Colo., 1987-88; outside dir. N.Am. Weather Cons., Salt Lake City, 1987-88; assoc. Bisop-Brogden Assocs., Lakewood, Colo., 1988-90; dist. mgr., dir. midwest regional govt. svcs. Groundwater Tech., Inc., Englewood, 1990-91; with Jacobs Engrng. Group, Inc., Denver, 1991—94. V.p., bd. dirs. Wyo. Well Svc., Inc., Cody, 1965-71; v.p. rsch. Land and Water Cons., Inc., Ft. Collins, 1972-75; pres. Aetech West, Inc., Ft. Collins, 1982-83; v.p. Altair, Inc., Lakewood, 1989-90. Contbr. numerous articles to tech. jours.; editor tech. procs. Vol., Wyo. Presbytery Coms., Habitat for Humanity, Cody C. of C.; mem. emeritus adv. coun. for geoscis. dept. Colo. State U. 1st lt. U.S. Army, 1955-57. NDEA fellow, 1961-64. Mem. ASCE, Am. Geophys. Union, Wyo. Engrng. Soc., Rotary Internat., Sigma Xi, Phi Kappa Phi, Xi Sigma Pi, Sigma Gamma Epsilon. Republican. Presbyterian. Avocations: fishing, amateur radio, western history.

JONES, EVERETT RILEY, JR., oil industry executive; b. Leitchfield, Ky., July 28, 1918; s. Everett Riley and Margie (Hatfield) J.; m. Lois Gibbins, July 15, 1950; children: Stacey Rae, Rande Leigh. Student, Spencerian C.C., 1936-37, U. Louisville, 1946-47. Lic. pub. acct., Ky. Sec. treas., dir. Lafitte Oil Corp., Louisville, 1947-49; ptnr. Fryer & Hanson Drilling Co., Dallas, 1950-58; pres., dir. Bengal Producing Co., Dallas, 1959—. Dir. Dallas County Small Bus. Devel. Ctr., Inc. Contbr. articles/stories to newspapers, publs. Trustee S.W. Engring. Found. Served to capt. USAAF, 1942-45. Decorated D.F.C., Air medal with 4 oak leaf clusters. Mem. Engrs. Club Dallas (past pres.) Dallas Petroleum Club (past pres.), Royal Air Force Club in London, Northwood Country Club Dallas. Episcopalian. Office: 8080 N Central Expy Dallas TX 75206-1838

JONES, FERDINAND TAYLOR, JR., psychologist, educator; b. N.Y.C., May 15, 1932; s. Ferdinand Taylor and Esther (Haggie) J.; m. Antonina Laub, Sept. 26, 1953 (div. Mar. 1967); children: Joanne Esther, Terrie Lynn; m. Myra Jean Rogers, Nov. 25, 1967. AB, Drew U., 1953; PhD, U. Vienna, Austria, 1959. Staff psychologist Riverside Hosp., Bronx, N.Y., 1959-62; chief psychologist Westchester County Community Mental Hosp. Bd., White Plains, N.Y., 1962-67; tng. cons. Lincoln Hosp. Mental Health Services, Bronx, 1967-69; tchr. psychology Sarah Lawrence Coll., Bronxville, N.Y., 1968-72; prof. psychology Brown U., Providence, 1972-97, prof. emeritus, 1997, dir. psychol. svcs., 1972-1992; clin. lectr. Emeritus in Psychiatry and Human Behavior, 2002. Scholar-in-residence The Schomburg Ctr. for Rsch. in Black Culture, 1987; cons. St. Peter's Head Start, Yonkers, N.Y., 1967-71, Bronx State Hosp., 1969-72; vis. prof. U. Dar es Salaam, Tanzania, 1993, Oberlin Coll., 1997, 98, U. Cape Town, 1999, Sarah Lawrence Coll., 2001. Co-editor: The Triumph of the Soul: Cultural and Psychological Aspects of African American Music. Bd. dirs. Am. Orthopsychiat. Assn., 1984-87. Served with AUS, 1953-56. Mem. APA, Am. Orthopsychiat. Assn. (pres. 1989-90), Ea. Psychol. Assn., Westchester County Psychol. Assn. (past pres.), Assn. Black Psychologists, Soc. Psychol. Study Social Issues, Internat. Assn. for Jazz Edn. Achievements include developing (with Myron W. Harris) small group method for reduction of distance and dissonance in interracial communication. Office: Brown U 79 Waterman St Providence RI 02912-9079 Business E-Mail: ferdinand_jones@brown.edu. *Dedicated to channeling a lifelong fascination with people into skilled understanding of human behavior and the alleviation of problems in human functioning.*

JONES, FLETCHER, JR., automotive company executive; CEO Fletcher Jones Mgmt., Las Vegas, Nev., pres. Office: Fletcher Jones Mgmt Group Inc 7300 W Sahara Ave Las Vegas NV 89117-2756

JONES, FLORENCE M., music educator; b. West Columbia, Tex., Apr. 11, 1939; d. Isaiah and Lu Ethel (Baldridge) McNeil; m. Waldo D. Jones, May 29, 1965; children: Ricky, Wanda, Erna. BS, Prairie View A&M U., 1961, MEd, 1968; postgrad., U. Houston, 1980, Rice U., 1988. Cert. tchr. elem. edn., math. Tchr. English and typing Lincoln H.S., Port Arthur, Tex., 1961-62; tchr. grades three and four Houston Ind. Sch. Dist., 1963-90, tchr. gifted and talented, 1990-94; tchr. piano Windsor Village Liberal Arts Acad., Houston, 1994—. Dist. tchr. trainer Houston Ind. Sch. Dist., 1985-90; shared decision mem. Sch. decision Making Team, 1993-94; coord. gifted/talented program, Petersen Elem. Sch., Houston, 1990-94; participant piano Recital Hartzog Studio, 1985-88; film previewer Houston Media Ctr. Curriculum writer Modules to Improve Science Teaching, 1985; author sci. pop-up book, 1980, gifted/talented program, 1994; contbr. poems to lit. jours. Youth camp counselor numerous non-denominational ch. camps, U.S., 1961-89; active restoration of Statue of Liberty, Ellis Island Found., NYC, 1983-85; lay min. Ch. of God, 1961-94; charter founder The Am. Family History Immigration Ctr., Ellis Island, NYC; charter mem. Wall of Tolerance; co-chair Rosa Parks Commn. Recipient Letter of Recognition for Outstanding Progress in Edn., Pres. Bill Clinton, 1994, Congresswoman Sheilia Jackson Lee, Tex. Gov. George Bush, State Rep. Harold V. Sutton Jr., Houston Mayor Bob Lanier, Tex. Gov. Ann Richards; Gold Cup/Highest Music award Hartzog Music Studio, 1987, Diamond Key award Nat. Women of Achievement, 1995, Editors Choice award Nat. Libr. Poetry, 1995, cert. recognition Quaker Oats Co. and NCNW Inc., 1999, Youth Advisors trophy and New Millennium Leader plaque Nat. Women Achievement, 2001, others; named Grandparent of Yr. Nat. Women of Achievement Youth Divsn., 2003; named to The Internat. Poetry Hall of Fame; recipient Humanitarian trophy NCNW, Inc., 2005; Wall of Tolerance honoree, 2005 Mem. NEA, Houston Assn. Childhood Edn. (v.p. 1985-88), Assn. for Childhood Edn. (bd. dirs. 1979-91), Houston Zool. Soc., World Wildlife Fund, Nat. Storytelling Assn., Tejas Storytelling Assn. (life), Soc. Children's Book Writers and Illustrators, Nat. Audubon Soc., Am. Mus. Natural History, Tex. Ret. Tchrs. Assn. (life), Internat. Soc. Poets (disting. life mem., Silver Cup award for outstanding poetry achievement 2003), Smithsonian Instn., Nat. Mus. Am. Indian, Nat. Mus. Women in Arts Democrat. Avocations: writing, reading, storytelling, collecting sea shells, arts and crafts. Home: 3310 Dalmatian Dr Houston TX 77045-6520

JONES, F(RANCIS) WHITNEY, fund raising executive, consultant; b. Waterford, N.Y., May 10, 1944; s. Francis Whitney and Katherine (Draper) J.; m. Robyn Abrams, June 11, 1966 (div. 1984); children: Lindsay Draper, Christopher Austin; m. Suzanne Mewborn, Dec. 28, 1985; children: Alexander Whitney, Spencer Elliott. Student, U. Paris, 1964-65; AB, Hamilton Coll., 1966; PhD, U. N.C., 1971. Instr. English U. N.C., Chapel Hill, 1970-71; asst. prof. English St. Andrews Coll., Laurinburg, N.C., 1971-77; devel. dir. Old Salem, Inc., Winston-Salem, N.C., 1977-80; sr. cons. Ampersand, Inc., Winston-Salem, 1980-81; pres. Whitney Jones, Inc., Winston-Salem, 1981—. Pres. Triad Fund-Raising Execs. Coun., Winston Salem, 1989-91. Active United Way cmty. program solving com., Winston-Salem, 1989-93, Arts Advocates of N.C., Raleigh, 1991-96; chmn. Family Found. N.Am., 1998-2000; mem. Family Svc. Am., 1998-2000. Younger Humanists fellow Nat. Endowment for the Humanities, Washington, 1975. Mem. The Jargon Soc. (pres. 1977-96), Green Hill Ctr. for N.C. Art (v.p. 1990), Nat. Soc. Fund Raising Execs. (pres. N.C. Triad chpt. 1991-95), Am. Assn. of Fund Raising Counsel (trust for philanthropy). Democrat. Episcopalian. Office: Whitney Jones Inc 119 Brookstown Ave Winston Salem NC 27101-5245 Home: 4125 Birch Creek Trl Winston Salem NC 27106-6510

JONES, FRANK A., JR., psychiatrist, educator; MD, Case Western U., Cleve., 1972. Diplomate Am. Bd. Psychiatry and Neurology, 1977. Psychiatry intern Boston State Hosp., Dorchester, Mass., 1972—73; resident in psychiatry Worcester State Hosp., 1973—75; physician dept. psychiatry Univ. Behavioral Health Ctr., Piscataway, NJ, 1977—2002. Prof. psychiatry Robert Wood Johnson Med. Sch., 1977—. Office: 3055 Rte 27 Franklin Park NJ 08823 Office Phone: 732-422-0800.

JONES, FRANK CATER, retired lawyer; b. Macon, Ga., June 19, 1925; s. Charles Baxter and Carolyn (Cater) J.; m. Annie Gantt Anderson, Mar. 31, 1951; children: Eugenia Anderson Henderson, Annie Gantt Blattner, Carolyn Corley, Frank Cater. BBA, Emory U., 1947; LLB, Mercer U., 1950, LLD (hon.), 1996. Bar: Ga. 1950. Pvt. practice, Macon, 1950—77; mem. firm Jones, Cork & Miller (and predecessor), 1950—77, King & Spalding, Atlanta, 1977—2001; of counsel Jones, Cork & Miller, Macon, Ga., 2005—. Bd. dirs. So. Trust Corp. Trustee Wesleyan Coll., Macon, 1966—, chmn. bd. dirs., 1981-86; pres. Atlanta Symphony Orch. League, 1982-84; chmn. Ga. Gt. Park Authority, 1980-83, Ga. Pub. Telecom. Commn., 1983-98, Met. Atlanta chpt. ARC, 1987-88; bd. dirs. Carter Ctr., Emory U., 1987—; chmn. Michael C. Carlos Mus., 1991-96; trustee Emory U., Atlanta, 1991-95, trustee emeritus, 1995—. Fellow: ACTL (bd. regents 1986—, sec. 1990—92, pres. 1993—94); mem.: ABA (ho. of dels. 1972—94), U.S. Supreme Ct. Hist. Soc. (pres. 2002—), State Bar of Ga. (pres. 1968—69), Ga. Bar Assn. (pres. young lawyers sect. 1956—57), Macon Bar Assn. (pres. 1954), Greater Macon C. of C. (pres. 1965), Rotary. Home: 4957 Wellington Dr Macon GA 31210-4427 Office: Jones Cork & Miller PO Box 6437 435 Second St Macon GA 31208-6437 Office Phone: 478-745-2821. Personal E-mail: frank.jones@jonescork.com.

JONES, FRANK GRIFFITH, lawyer; b. Houston, Sept. 11, 1941; s. A. Gordon and Grace (Griffith) Jones; m. Deborah Ann Young, July 5, 1969; children: Russell G., Sarah G., Christopher Y. BS, Rice U., 1963; JD, U. Tex., 1966. Bar: Tex. 1966, U.S. Dist. Ct. (so., no. and ea. dists.) Tex., U.S. Ct. Appeals (5th and 8th cirs.), cert.: (civil trial specialist). Ptnr. Fulbright & Jaworski, L.L.P., Houston, 1966, co-ptnr. in charge Houston office, 2001—. Chmn. Fulbright & Jaworski Employment Commn., 1988—92. Chmn. troop com. Boy Scouts Am., Houston, 1986—88; chair Environ. Adv. Com., 2004—, Govtl. Relations Com., 2005; bd. dirs. exec. com. Greater Houston Partnership; bd. dirs. Houston Symphony, Holly Hall Retirement Cmty., Friends Fondren Llbr.; mem. Rice U. Fund Coun., Houston, 1987—93; pres. Baker Coll. Rice U., 1962—63. Lt. (j.g.) USNR, 1967—72. Keeton Fellow, U. Tex. Law Sch., 1993—. Fellow: Internat. Acad. Trial Lawyers, Am. Coll. Trial Lawyers (ADR com. 1986—96, chmn. 1992—94, ethics com. 1996—2001, moot ct. com. 2004—); mem.: ABA, Chartered Inst. Arbitrators, Tex. Gen. Counsel Forum, Products Liability Adv. Coun., Def. Rsch. Inst., Am. Counsel Assn., Tex. Assn. Def. Counsel, Am. Bar Found., Houston Bar Found. (chmn. 2003), Tex. Bar Found., Tex. Bar Assn., Houston Young Lawyers Assn. (pres. 1972—73), Internat. Assn. Def. Counsel, Am. Bd. Trial Advs., Greater Houston Partnership (exec. com. 2003—), Houston City Club, Rotary, Phi Delta Phi (past pres.). Avocations: tennis, travel. Office: Fulbright & Jaworski LLP 1301 Mckinney St Ste 5100 Houston TX 77010-3095 Office Phone: 713-651-5473.

JONES, FRANK JOSEPH, insurance company executive; BA, U. Notre Dame, 1960, BS, 1961; MS in Nuclear Engring., Cornell U., 1963; MBA, U. Pitts., 1964; PhD in Econs., Stanford U., 1971. Sr. economist U.S. Gen. Acctg. Office/Office Program Analysis, Washington, 1975-76, various to expert cons., 1976-78; sr. economist SRI Internat., Menlo Park, Calif., 1976-78; v.p. rsch., chief economist Chgo. Mercantile Exch., 1978-79; exec. v.p., chief operating officer N.Y. Futures Exch., 1979-82; sr. v.p., mgr. Index and Options Products Div. N.Y. Stock Exch., 1982-83; mng. dir. Fin. Dept. Kidder, Peabody, & Co., Inc., N.Y.C., 1983-88; dir. Barclays de Zoete Wedd Gov. Securities, Inc., N.Y.C., 1988-89; assoc. dir. Global Securities Rsch., dir. Fixed Income Rsch. Merrill Lynch & Co., N.Y.C., 1989-91; exec. v.p., chief investment officer Guardian Life Ins. Co. of Am., N.Y.C., 1991—. Bd. dirs. Internat. Securities Exch., N.Y.C., 2000--; assoc. prof. Sch. of Bus., San Jose U., 1973-78; fin. faculty Stern Sch. Bus., NYU, 1995—; spkr. in field. Author several books including: Global Government Bonds, 1992, The Futures Game: Who Wins, Who Loses and Why?, 1987, Marco Finance--The Financial System and the Economy, 1978, (with Frank J. Fabozzi, Franco Modigliani and Michael Ferri) Foundations of Financial Markets and Institutions, 3d edit., 2002; contbr. articles and book chpts. to profl. publs.

JONES, FRANK N., chemist, researcher, educator, consultant; b. Columbia, Mo., Dec. 27, 1936; s. Frank Norton and Sara Bay (Neale) J.; m. Nancy H. Jones, Jan. 1960 (div. Aug. 8, 1982); 1 child, David S. AB, Oberlin Coll., 1958; PhD, Duke U., 1962. Instr. Duke U., Durham, N.C., 1961-62; postdoctoral fellow MIT, Cambridge, 1962-63; staff chemist, rsch. supr. Ctrl. Rsch. Fabrics and Finishes E.I. duPont de Nemours, Inc., Wilmington, Del., 1963-73; R&D mgr. Celanese, Louisville, 1973-79; rsch. mgr. Cargill, Inc., Mpls., 1979-83; prof., chair polymers and coatings N.D. State U., Fargo, 1983-90; prof. Ea. Mich. U., Ypsilanti, 1990—, dir. NSF Industry/Univ. Rsch. Ctr. in Coatings, 1990—2001. Cons. Exxon, 1984-98, Monsanto, 1983-92. Author: (with others) Organic Coatings: Science and Technology, Vol. I, 1992, Vol. II, 1994, 2d edit., 1999; editor: Proceedings of the American Chemical Society Division of Polymeric Materials: Science and Engineering, Vol. 73, 1995, Vol. 74, 1996; contbr. numerous articles to profl. jours. including Jour. Applied Polymer Sci., Macromolecules, Jour. Coatings Tech., among others. Recipient awards Roon Found., 1986, 87, 91; NSF fellow, 1960-61; grantee NSF, 1990-2001, Exxon Chem. Co., 1985-98, Ford Motor Co., 1995-98. Mem. Am. Chem. Soc. (divsn. polymeric materials sci. and engrng. chmn. sec. 1993-94, vice chmn. 1995, chmn. elect 1996, chmn. 1997), Fed. Socs. for Coatings Tech. (Matiello lectr. 1995). Achievements include publications and patents in compounds with liquid crystalline properties and coating binders based thereon, polymeric vehicle for coatings, solventless liquid coatings, coatings with improved mar resistance, polymer nanoparticles., among others. Office: East Mich U Nat Sci Found Coatings Rsch 430 W Forest Ave Ypsilanti MI 48197-2453 Office Phone: 734-487-2203. E-mail: frankjones@comcast.net.

JONES, FRANK WYMAN, management consultant, director, mechanical engineer; b. Ironton, Ohio, Jan. 20, 1940; s. Kylius and Kathleen (McDonald) J.; m. Margaret Kwitek, Sept. 1, 1962; children: Kelly, Connie, Katie, Colleen, Carolyn. BSME, U. Cin., 1963; MBA, Ind. U., 1965. V.p., gen. mgr. G & L Machine Tool Divsn., Fond du Lac, Wis., 1976-80; exec. v.p. Giddings & Lewis Inc., Fond du Lac, Wis., 1980-81, pres., CEO, 1982-86; mgmt. cons. Tucson, 1987—. Bd. dirs. Modine, Racine, Wis., Star Cutter Co., Farmington Hills, Mich., Gardner Publs., Inc., Cin. Gen. Tool Co., Cin. Mem. Am. Mgmt. Assn., Nat. Assn. Corp. Dirs. Republican. Roman Catholic. Home: 6740 N Saint Andrews Dr Tucson AZ 85718-2619

JONES, FRANKLIN ROSS, education educator; b. Charlotte, NC, Jan. 3, 1920; s. William Morton and Olive Ruth (Moser) J.; divorced; children: Franklin Ross, C. Morton, Susan Noel. AB, Lenoir Rhyne Coll., 1941; MA, U. NC, 1951; DEd, Duke U., 1960. Tchr., NC, 1944-48; prin. Jr. H.S., Henderson, NC, 1948-54; dist. sch. prin. Wake County, NC, 1954-56; dist. supt. Roxboro (NC) schs., 1956-58; chmn. dept. edn. Randolph-Macon Coll., Ashland, Va., 1959-64; interim dean U. Richmond (Va.), 1962; dean Sch. Edn. Old Dominion U., 1964-69, Eminent prof., 1974-94; founder Child Study Ctr., 1965, disting. prof., 1969—, social founds. program leader, 1973-77, doctoral program liaison rep., 1974-77, faculty chmn., 1981—. Dir. Forest Ridge Corp., 1985; vis. rsch. scholar Duke U., 1967; cons. HEW, State Sch. Sys. and Colls.; lectr. in field; mem. com. White house Conf. Children and Youth, 1968-71, Ea. regional chmn., 1968-71; mem. Va. Gov.'s Com. Implementation, 1971-73; spkr. 25th Internat. Congress of Psychology, Brussels, 1992; symposium chmn. European Congress of Psychology, Athens, Greece, 1995; cons. to dean on test score stats., Old Dominion U., 1995—; adj. prof. U. Va., 1959-64. Author: Psychology of Human Development, 1969, 3d edit. 1992, Handbook on Testing, 1972, Understanding the Middlescent Years, 1978, Theory of Adult Development, 1980, Jack, 2002, How to Survive Middle Age, 2005; Radio series Sta. WTAR, Norfolk, 1973-75; test item writer for NY Regency exams, 1987, Ednl. Testing Svc., 1989; guest editor Education, 1990—, Jack, 2002, How to Survive Middle Age, 2005. Mem. Norfolk Urban Coalition, 1969-73; chmn. March of Dimes, Person County, NC, 1956-57; mem. adv. bd. Tidewater Rehab. Ctr., 1967-69; chmn. Hull Scholarship Fund, 1983-85; coord. U. Joy Fund Drive, 1974-95; univ. chmn. United Fund, 1982, 84; chmn. assessment com. Va. Reading to Learn Program, 1990-91; cons. to sch. systems, ETS, HEW, Coll. 1966—; dir. Praxis Ctr., 1993—; adminstr. Nat. Bd. for Cert. Counselors Ctr., Nat. Lang. and Music Bd. of Certification; chmn. scholarship fund Brewton Parker Coll., Mt. Vernon, Ga., 1999-2004; chmn. drive for low-paid faculty Old Dominion U., 2002-. Recipient Heritage Found. award, 1996, Football recognition and scholar Brewton Parker Coll., Ga., 1999; Va. Golden Olympnics tennis doubles champion, 1982-84, 880 meter run Gold medal, 1983, 100 meter dash Silver medal, 1984. Mem. Am. Psychol. Soc. (charter), S.E. Psychol. Assn., Va. Assn. U. Profs. (dir. 1962-64), South Atlantic Philosophy Edn. Soc. (pres. 1966-69, dir. 1969—), Va. Assn. Rsch. in Edn. (Disting. Rsch. awards 1972, 73, 78), NC Edn. Assn. (pres. North Ctrl. chpt. 1951, pres. North Ctrl. Prins. 1956), Ea. Ednl. Rsch. Assn., Nat. Urban Edn. Assn., Alpha Tau Kappa, Kappa Delta Pi, Phi Delta Kappa, Phi Kappa Phi, Pi Gamma Mu (sec. 1962-64), Harbor Club (Norfolk), Lions, Rotary. Achievements include being member of Bicycle Relay Jr. Marathon World's Record team, 1933. Home: 1026 Manchester Ave Norfolk VA 23508-1243 Office Phone: 757-683-3238.

JONES, GALEN RAY, physician assistant; b. Salt Lake City, Feb. 1, 1948; s. Leonard Ray and Veda (Whitehead) J.; m. Patricia Ann Poulson, Jan. 21, 1972; children: Brian, Marci, Natalie. Grad. with honors, Med. Field Svc. Sch. Ft. Sam Houston, San Antonio, 1971; grad. Medex Demonstration Program Physician Asst. cert. program magna cum laude, U. Utah, 1976, BS, 1982. Missionary Ch. of Jesus Christ of Latter Day Saints, Alta., Sask., Can., 1967-69; asst. mgr. Cowan's Frostop Hamburger Stand, Salt Lake City, 1969-70; with Safeway Stores, Inc., Salt Lake City, 1970; o.r. tech. Latter Day Saint Hosp., Salt Lake City, 1973-75; physician asst. Lovell Clinic Inc., Lovell, Wyo., 1975-77, Family Health Care, Inc., Tooele, Utah, 1977-86, West Dermatology and Surgery Med. Grp., Redlands, Calif., 1986-95; with blood and marrow transplant program Univ. Hosp. and Primary Childrens Med. Ctr. U. Utah, Salt Lake City, 1996-98; physician asst. D. Edgar Allen Dermatology, Ogden, 1998—. Maturation lectr. Tooele Sch. Dist., 1978-86; course dir., instr. EMT, North Big Horn County Search and Rescue, 1976; instr. EMT, Grantsville Ambulance Inc., 1979-85; lectr. on skin care and changes to sr. citizen groups, hosp. auxs., health fairs, 1986—; Boy Scouts Am. scoutmaster 1987-89, scout com. chair, 2001—; high sch. sophomore sem. tchr. religion, 1991-96; owner Adventureland and TopHat Video, Magna, Utah, 1982-96. Author: (with others) The P.A. Clinical Practice, 1995. Chmn. County Health Teen Pregnancy Prevention Project, Tooele, 1980-81; adv. bd. State Dept. Health-Rural Health Network, Salt Lake City, 1985-86; health lectr. County Health & Edn. Dept. Progs., Tooele, 1977-86; mormon bishop/pastor Lakeview Ward, Latter Day Saints Ch., Tooele, 1982-86; mem. Utah Acad. Physician Assts. (pres. 1980-81, editor newsletter 1979-80); mem. People to People Ambs. P.A. del. to China, Beijing, Xian, Guillin, Yangshou, Hong Kong, 2000-01. With U.S. Army, 1971-73. U. Utah grantee, 1966, 67, 69. Fellow Am. Acad. Physician Assts., Utah. Acad. Physicians Assts., Utah Soc. Dermatol. Physician Assts. (bd. dirs. 2004), Soc. Dermatology Physician Assts. Republican. Mem. Lds Ch. Avocations: gardening, hiking, camping, skiing, photography, travel. Home: 2670 Willow Wick Dr Sandy UT 84093-1929 Office: D Edgar Allen Dermatology 3860 Jackson Ave Ogden UT 84403-1956

JONES, GENIA KAY, critical care nurse, consultant; b. Dallas, Dec. 21, 1954; d. Joe and Juanita Sue (White) Self; m. Paul L. Jones, June 1, 1986. ADN, Tarrant County Jr. Coll., 1976; mgmt. cert., Cedar Valley Coll., 1980; sci. update, Mountain View Coll., Dallas, 1984; BSN, Regent's U., 2001. RN; cert. emergency nurse; cert. BLS, ACLS, ACLS instr. Instr. Steven's Pk. Hosp., Dallas, 1972-77; asst. dir. nursing svcs. Four Season's Conv. Ctr., Dallas, 1977-78; with surgery dept. Dallas/Ft. Worth Med. Ctr., 1978-80; dir. nursing Med. Staffing Svcs., Dallas, 1980, Reproductive Svcs., Inc., Dallas, 1981; adminstrv. supr. Dallas Family Hosp., 1982-85; patient care coord., emergency dept. Dallas S.W. Med. Ctr., 1985-90, staff nurse, emergency dept., 1990-99; medical consultant Needham, Johnson, Lovelace, and Johnson, 1992—; emergency nurse dir. Rockwall Minor Emergency Ctr., 1999—2001; emergency nurse Virtual Healthcare Svcs. Meth. Med. Ctrs. Dallas, 2001—03, Med. Ctr. of Arlington, 2002—. Internat. flight nurse Air Ambulance Network, Inc., Dallas, 1987—; instr. intravenous therapy, 1980—; cons., adv., 1980—; medico-legal cons., 1990—; clin. instr. Edn. Am., 1999—2001. Recipient Citizens award, Certs. Apprecition, HOSA Nat. Leadership Conf., Silver medal of Honor; Internat. Biog. Assn. fellow, 1990. Mem. NAFE, Am. Heart Assnb., Nurses' Svc. Orgn., Tex. Nurses' Assn., Emergency Nurses' Assn. Home: 108 Burkett Ln Red Oak TX 75154-7602

JONES, GEOFFREY MELVILL, physiology research educator; b. Cambridge, Eng., Jan. 14, 1923; s. Benett and Dorothy Laxton (Jotham) J.; m. Jenny Marigold Burnaby, June 21, 1953; children: Katharine, Francis, Andrew, Dorothy. BA, Cambridge U., 1944, MA, 1947, MB, BCh, 1949. House surgeon Middlesex Hosp., London, Eng., 1949-50; sr. house surgeon Addenbrookes Hosp., Cambridge, Eng., 1950-51; sci. med. officer Royal Air Force Inst. Aviation Medicine, Farnborough, Eng., 1951-55; sci. officer Med. Rsch. Coun., Eng., 1955-61; assoc. prof. physiology, dir. aviation med. rsch. unit McGill U., Montreal, Que., Can., 1961-68, prof., dir., 1968-88, Hosmer rsch. prof., 1978-91, emeritus prof. physiology, 1991—. Rsch. prof. clin. neuroscis. U. Calgary, Alta., Can., 1991—, Coll. France, 1979, 95; vis. prof. Stanford U., 1971-72. Author: (with another) mammalian Vestibular Physiology, 1979; editor: (with another) Adaptive Mechanisms in Gaze Control, 1985; contbr. numerous articles to profl. jours. Served to squadron leader Royal Air Force, 1951-55. Sr. rsch. assoc. Nat. Acad. Sci., 1971-72; recipient Skylab Achievement award NASA, 1974, 1st recipient Dohlman medal Dohlman Soc. Toronto U., 1987, Quinquennial Gold medal Barany Soc. Internat., 1988, Ashton Graybiel award U.S. Naval Aerospace Labs., 1989, Wilbur Franks Annual award Can. Soc. Aerospace Medicine, Buchanan-Barbour award Royal Aeronautical Soc., 1991, Mc Laughlin Medal, 1991, Royal Soc. Can. Fellow Can. Aeronautics and Space Inst., Aerospace Med. Assn. (Harry Armstrong award 1968, Arnold D. Tuttle award 1971), Royal Soc. Can. (McLaughlin medal 1991), Royal Soc. London, Royal Aeronautical Soc. London (Stewart Meml. award 1989, Buchanan Barbour award 1990); mem. U.K. Physiol. Soc., Can. Physiol. Soc., Can. Soc. Aerospace Med. Soc., Internat. Collegium Otolaryngology, Soc. Neurosci. Avocations: tennis, sailing, outdoor activities, reading, piano and violin playing/composition. Office: U Calgary Dept Clin Neuroscis 3330 Hospital Dr NW Calgary AB Canada T2N 4N1

JONES, GEORGE FLEMING, international consultant; b. San Angelo, Tex., June 27, 1935; s. George Fleming and Cora (Brewer) J.; m. Maria Rosario Correa, Apr. 23, 1960; children: George III, Robert, Michael, Mary Louise. AB magna cum laude, Wabash Coll., 1955; AM, Tufts U., 1956; MA, Stanford U., 1967; LLD, Wabash Coll., 2000. Joined Fgn. Svc., Dept. State, 1956; with Econ. Bur., Dept. State, Washington, 1956-58; with Am. Embassy Ecuador, 1958-60, Ghana, 1961-63, Venezuela, 1963-66; officer in charge Venezuelan affairs Dept. State, Washington, 1967-69, officer in charge Colombian affairs, 1969-71; polit. advisor U.S. Mission to IAEA, Vienna, 1971-74; counselor for polit. affairs Am. Embassy, Guatemala, 1974-77; student Nat. War Coll., Washington, 1977-78; Latin Am. adviser U.S. del. U.S.-Soviet Conventional Arms Talks, 1978; dep. dir. office Latin Am. regional polit. affairs Dept. State, 1978-80, dir., 1980-82; dep. chief of mission Am. Embassy Costa Rica, 1982-85, Chile, 1985-89; sr. adviser for Latin Am. and Caribbean affairs U.S. del. UN Gen. Assembly, N.Y.C., 1990, 95; amb. to Republic of Guyana, 1991-95; dir. programs for the Ams., Internat. Found. for Election Sys., Washington, 1996-99. Dir. Democracy and Governance Ctr. Devel. Assocs., Inc., 2000-05. Recipient Superior Honor award Dept. State, 1987. Mem. Am. Fgn. Svc. Assn. (v.p. 1989-90, 2003-05, bd. dirs. 1999-2001), Sr. Fgn. Svc. Assn. (bd. dirs. 1990-92). Home: 3804 Acosta Rd Fairfax VA 22031-3804 E-mail: georgejones@cox.net.

JONES, GEORGE STEVEN, civil engineer; b. Belgrade, Yugoslavia, June 2, 1927; m. Sofia Jones, 1960; 1 child, Appta. BSCE, Northwestern U., 1951, MSCE, 1956, PhD in Bus. Adminstrn., 1958; PhD, Hamilton State U.; PhD (hon.), U. Fla., 1972. Civil engr. Hollabird & Root, Chgo., 1956—57; profl. engr., gen. mgr. Arcadia Enging. Internat., Inc., 1956—70, chmn. bd., 1970—. Civil engr. US C.E., 1951—54; prof. structural enging. Northwestern U., Evanston, Ill.; chmn. dept. econs. U. Ill., Chgo.; legis. asst. Gen. Assembly, Ill.; pres. Tetrakear & Assocs., Inc.; bd. dirs. 1st Nat. Bank of Chgo., Skokie (Ill.) Cmty. Hosp. Author: The Pneumatic Tube Goes Modern, 1958, Opportunities in Construction, 1960, Management and Labor, 1962; contbr. articles to profl. jours. Bd. chmn. Oakton Coll.; pres. Hamilton State U. Maj. U.S. Army. Mem.: NSPE, ASCE. Avocation: swimming. Address: Box 462 Osprey FL 34229 Office Phone: 941-926-0964.

JONES, GEORGE WASHINGTON, JR., lawyer; b. Balt., July 27, 1953; s. George W. and Mattie Alice (Reed) Jones; m. Loretta Phylis Pleasant, Aug. 5, 1978; children: Melissa Grace, George Charles, Jessica Michelle. BA, U. Chgo., 1975; JD, Yale U., 1980. Bar: DC 1980, US Dist. Ct. DC 1980, US Ct. Appeals (DC. cir.) 1983, US Supreme Ct. 1986. Law clk. to judge Philip W Tone U.S. Ct. Appeals (7th Cir.), Chgo., 1978-79; assoc. O'Melveny & Myers, Washington, 1979-80; asst. to solicitor gen. U.S. Dept. Justice, Washington, 1980-83; assoc. Sidley & Austin, Washington, 1983-87, ptnr., 1988—2001, Sidley Austin Brown & Wood LLP, Washington, 2001—. Mem.: ABA, DC Bar (pres. 2002—03, bd. gov., gen. counsel). Office: Sidley Austin Brown & Wood LLP 1501 K St NW Washington DC 20005 Office Phone: 202-736-8158. Office Fax: 202-736-8711. Business E-Mail: gjones@sidley.com.

JONES, GERALD PAUL, information technology educator; b. South Gate, Calif., July 11, 1946; AB, U. So. Calif., L.A., 1968, MSEd, 1978, PhD, 1985. Mem. staff U. So. Calif., L.A. Contbr. articles to profl. jours. Mem. Phi Beta Kappa. Home: PO Box 18425 Los Angeles CA 90018-0425 Office: U So Calif JEF 214 1020 W Jefferson Blvd Los Angeles CA 90089-0251 E-mail: gpjones@usc.edu.

JONES, GERALDINE ANN JOHNSON, secondary school educator; b. Seaford, Del., July 30, 1939; d. Thomas E. and Marion Frances (Walker) Johnson; 1 child, Monica. BA, Del. State Coll., 1961; MBA, Cen. Mich. U., 1978; postgrad., Temple U., 1986—; PhD in Edn., Capella U., 1999; MDiv, Ea. Bapt. Theol. Seminary, 2005. Caseworker Div. Social Services, Dover, Del., 1962-64; tchr. English William C. Jason Sch., Georgetown, Del., 1966-67; vis. tchr. Capital Sch. Dist., Dover, 1967—. Home and sch. coord. migrant edn. program, Dover, 1967; paraprofl. Title I, Dover, 1964, 65; supr. Head Start Program, Camden, Del., 1970; speaker in field Active local polit. coms.; lay leader; pres. United Meth. Women, Whatcoat, pres. Peninsula conf., gen. bd. global ministries Peninsula-Del. conf., bd. laity, Dover dist. nominating com., com. on episcopacy/superintendency, coun. on ministries., del. to gen. conf. and jurisdicitonal conf., 1992; mem. nominating com. Upper Atlantic regional sch., dir. summer day camp, asst. dean; mem. Yesterdays Youth Choir, Seaford; min. Outreach Ministries United Meth. Ch.; pastor Union Wesley Unites Meth. Ch., Claresville, Del., 2005; pastor Union Wesley United Meth. Ch., Clarksville, Del., 2005— Named Woman of Yr., Whatcoat Ch., 1986; recipient Young award 2003. Mem. NEA, Internat. Assn. Pupil Pers. Workers, Del. Assn. Cert. Vis. Tchrs. (sec.-treas. 1984), Capital Educators Assn., Del. State Coll. Alumni Assn. (pres. Kent County chpt., Alumni of Yr. 1985, Ms. Alumni 1986-87), Nat. Alumni Assn. (pres.), William C. Jason Alumni Club (treas.), Delta Sigma Theta, Sigma Iota Epsilon. Democrat. Avocations: singing, writing, sewing, cooking, piano. Office: Capital Sch Dist 945 Forest St Dover DE 19904-3498 E-mail: gerryej@aol.com, gjones@capital.k12.de.us.

JONES, GILBERT LEED, retired law enforcement officer, coroner, author; b. Inglewood, Calif., Mar. 22, 1947; s. Vernal and Gwendolyn Helen J.; m. JoAnne Lynn Stang-Jones, June 4, 1966; children: Natalie Lynn Jones-Henderson, Dean Leed Jones. AS, Mt. San Antonio Coll., Walnut, Calif., 1978. Advanced cert. for peace officer stds. in tng., Calif. Dep. sheriff Los Angeles County Sheriff's Dept., L.A., 1969-80; dep. sheriff, coroner Mendocino County Sheriff's Dept., Ukiah, Calif., 1980-2000. Search and rescue mem. mounted posse Mendocino County Sheriff;s Dept., 1981-96, mounted enforcement officer, 1994-2000, critical incident negotiator, 1995-2000, property mgmt. officer, 1996-2000. Author: (novels) Journey to Horse Heaven, 1997, A Case of Corruption, 1997, Eleven Ninety-Nine! Officer Down!, 1998, In The Company of Their Own Kind, 1998. Sgt. U.S. Army, 1966-69. Republican. Avocations: wilderness horseback riding, horse training. Office: 1266 Soda Lake Rd Fallon NV 89406-6322 E-mail: wordcraft@cccomm.net.

JONES, GLENN EARLE, property management executive; b. Greensboro, N.C., May 11, 1946; s. Harold Clifford and AnnaBelle (Goodwin) Jones. BS in Hotel and Restaurant Mgmt., Cornell U., 1968. Asst. to gen. mgr. Warwick Hotel, Houston, 1968—69; Northwestern Ohio sales rep. L.G. Balfour Co., Attleboro, Mass., 1969—72; resident mgr. Chase Park Plaza Hotel, St. Louis, 1972—74; gen. mgr. Holiday Inn, Steamboat Springs, Colo., 1974, Santa Fe Hilton Inn, 1975, Sheraton Inn, New Orleans, 1976—79; pres. Landmark Systems Inc., New Orleans, 1979—. Chmn. Sheraton So. Regional Owners and Mgrs. Coun., 1981—. Mem. com. memberships Greater New Orelans Tourist and Conv. Commn.; mem. dist. com. United Fund. Mem.: Am. Hotel Mgmt. Assn. (cert., mem. fund devel. com. Ednl. Inst.), Cornell Soc. Hotelmen, New Orelans Hotel and Motel Assn. (treas.). Episcopalian. Home: 3101 Rue Parc Fontaine # 1408 New Orleans LA 70131-

JONES, GLOWER WHITEHEAD, lawyer; b. Atlanta, May 4, 1936; s. Samuel L. and Alma (Powell) Jones; m. Joanna Dayvault, Apr. 5, 1980; children: Jeff, Tom, Frank, Michael; 1 child, Mark. Grad., Dartmouth Coll., 1958; JD, Emory U., 1963. Bar: Ga. 1962, U.S. Dist. Ct. Ga. 1963, U.S. Ct. Appeals (5th and 11th cirs.), U.S. Ct. Claims, U.S. Supreme Ct. Assoc. Smith, Swift, Currie, McGhee & Hancock, Atlanta, 1963—65; ptnr. Smith Currie & Hancock, Atlanta, 1967—99, of counsel, 2000—. Author: Legal Aspects of Doing Business in North America and Canada, 1987, Alternative Clauses to Standard Construction Contracts, 1990; editor: 2d edit., Construction Subcontracting: A Legal Guide for Industry Professionals, 1991, Wiley Construction Law Update, 1992, 1993, 1994, Construction Contractors: The Right To Stop Work, 1992, Remedies for International Sellers of Goods, 1993; mem. editl. bd. Ga. State Bar Jour.; contbr. articles to profl. jours. Exec. bd. Met. Atlanta Boys' & Girls' Clubs, Inc., asst. sec., 1973—80, sec., 1980—83; trustee, past pres. Atlanta Florence Crittendon Svcs., Inc.; treas. IBA Found.; bd. dirs. Samuel L. Jones Boys' & Girls' Club, Inc., So. Region Boys Clubs Am., Carrie Steele Pitts Home, Gate City Day Nursery Assn. Recipient Golden Boy award, Met. Atlanta Boys' Club, 1971. Fellow: Chartered Inst. Arbitrators; mem.: ABA, Fed. Bar Assn., Internat. Bar Assn. (chmn. internat. sales com., chmn. UNCITRAL subcom., chmn. membership com., mem. governing coun. sect. bus. law), Ga. Bar Assn., State Bar Ga., Atlanta Bar Assn. (former chmn. prepaid legal svcs. com., engr. lawyers rels. com.), Lawyers Club Atlanta, Am. Judicature Soc., Assn. Trial Attys. Am., Ga. Assn. Trial Lawyers, Dartmouth Coll. Alumni Club, Emory U. Alumni Club, Ansley Park Golf Club, World Trade Club, Dartmouth Club, Atlanta Athletic Club, Baylor Alumni Club, Phi Delta Theta. Home: 195 14th St PH401 Atlanta GA 30309 Office: Smith Currie & Hancock Harris Tower 233 Peachtree St NE Ste 2600 Atlanta GA 30303-1530

JONES, GORDON KEMPTON, dentist; b. Rochester, NY, July 22, 1946; s. Joseph Kempton and Eunice (Patten)J.; m. Kathleen Anne FitzSimmons, July 24, 1971; children: Bryan Kempton, Brendan Austin, Graeme Meghan, Michael Cameron, Meredith Hunter, Mallory Sterling. BA in Chemistry, U. N.C., 1968, DDS, 1976; MS in Restorative Dentistry, U. Mich., 1984. Lic. dentist, Ill., N.C. Commd. lt. USN, 1976, advanced through ranks to capt., 1993; resident Naval Regional Med. Ctr., Camp Pendleton, Calif., 1977; dentist U.S.S. Holland USN, Holy Loch, Scotland, 1977-80; head dept. operative dentistry Naval Dental Clinic, Great Lakes, Ill., 1984—90, 1993—97, cons. operative dentistry, 2000—05; dentist regional med. ctr. USN, Great Lakes, Ill., 1980-82; head dept. operative dentistry Naval Dental Ctr., Norfolk, Va., 1990-93, dir. managed care Great Lakes, Ill., 1993-97, clinic dir., 1996-97; comdg. officer Naval Dental Rsch. Inst., 1997-99; splty. leader for dental rsch. USN, 1997-2000, program mgr. mercury abatement Great Lakes, 2001—03, head comprehensive dentistry, 2003—. Cons. Naval Hosp. Great Lakes, 1984—86, 1993—2002, asst. dir. advanced edn. in gen. dentistry, 2002—04, USN Surgeon Gen.'s area coord. for rsch. integrity, 2003—05, mem. exec. com. med. staff, 2004—, naval medicine dep. spl. asst. human subjects protection, 2003—05; asst. clin. prof. Northwestern U. Dental Sch., Chgo., 1985—90, Chgo., 1995—98; quality assurance coord., head advanced clin. program in gen. dentistry, Norfolk, 1990—93; com. chmn. Am. Bd. Operative Dentistry, 1987—, pres., 1996—2000, exec. coun., 1996—2002, chair exam. com., 2000—; cons. ADA Comm. Accreditation, 2003—; VISN-12 rsch. com. U.S. VA, 1998—. Contbr. articles to profl. jours.; speaker in field. Course dir. ARC, Great Lakes, 1984-90. Fellow Internat. Coll. Dentists; mem. ADA, Acad. Operative Dentistry (mem. jour. editl. bd. 1993-95, 96—), Am. Assn. Dental Rsch. (pres. Chgo. sect. 2000-01, chair local organizing com. 2000-01), Am. Dental Edn. Assn., Internat. Assn. Dental Rsch., Acad. Gen. Dentistry, Am. Assn. Dental Schs., Am. Legion, Omicron Kappa Upsilon, Alpha Phi Omega, Delta Sigma Delta. Avocations: computer science, reading, walking. Home: 1541 N Mckinley Rd Lake Forest IL 60045-1377 Office Phone: 847-688-3620. Personal E-mail: gjones1541@sbcglobal.net. E-mail: gkjones@gl.med.navy.mil.

JONES, GRACE MEREDITH, music educator; b. Roseburg, Oreg., Dec. 22, 1956; d. James Rexford and Mary Frances Jones; 1 child, Mejak. BS, Western Oreg. U., 1981; MusM in Performance-Choral Conducting, U. Ariz., 1991. Cert. tchr. Ariz., 1981, Wash., 1999. Music and art tchr. Apache Reservation, Ariz., Mex. border; music and art tchr. ranch children Oreg.; music tchr. Paisley Sch. Dist., Oreg., 1981—82, Whiteriver Sch. Dist., Ariz., 1982—83, Blueridege Sch. Dist., Pinetop-Lakeside, Ariz., 1983—87, Douglas Sch. Dist., Ariz., 1992—99, Burlington Edison Sch. Dist., Wash., 2000—; choir dir. Edison Choir, Bow, Wash., 2001—. Actor: local theater prodns., 1978—80 (First Adult Divsn. award, 1980), various prodns., 1987—91, Bisbee Theatre Guild, 1992—98; artist, dir. artist (murals with at risk youth exhibitions), Douglas, Ariz. Mem.: Musicans Ednl. Nat. Conv. (corr.). Avocations: artistic design, music compositions, directing childrens productions, African drumming, acting. Office Phone: 360-757-3375.

JONES, GRANT RICHARD, landscape architect; b. Seattle, Aug. 29, 1938; s. Victor Noble and Iona Belle (Thomas) J.; m. Ilze Grinbergs, 1965 (div. 1983); 1 child, Kaija. Student in liberal arts, Colo. Coll., 1956-58; BArch, U. Wash., 1962; M in Landscape Arch., Harvard U., 1966, postgrad. (Frederick Sheldon fellow), 1967-68. Draftsman Jones Lovegren Helms & Archs., Seattle, 1958-59; designer Landscape Archs., Seattle, 1961-65, state conservation planner Honolulu, 1968-69; rsch. assoc. landscape architecture rsch. office Harvard U., 1966-67; prin. Archs. and Landscape Archs., Ltd., Seattle, 1969—. Instr., vis. critic U. Oregon, U. Washington, U. Calif. at Berkeley, CSN Calpoly, U. Va., Harvard U.; lectr. and spkr. in field 30 univs., U.S.; chmn. landscape archtl. registration bd., State of Wash., 1974-79; mem. coun. Harvard U. Grad. Sch. Design, 1978-82, 91-96; vis. com. Harvard U. Grad. Sch., 1993—; bd. visitors U. Oregon Sch. Arch. and Allied Artists; bd. dirs. Scenic Am., Stewardship Ptnrs., Landscape Arch. Found. Author: The Nooksack Plan: An Approach to the Investigation and Evaluation of a River System, 1973; (with B. Gray and J. Burnham) A Method for the Quantification of Aesthetic Values for Environmental Decision Making, 1975, Design as Ecogram, 1975; (with J. Coe and D. Paulson) Woodland Park Zoo: Long Range Plan, Development Guidelines and Exhibit Scenarios, 1976, Landscape Assessment...Where Logic and Feelings Meet, 1978, Design Principles for Presentation of Animals and Nature, 1982, What Are Zoos?, 1984, An Arboretum on a Landfill, 1984, Beyond Landscape Immersion to Cultural Resonance, 1989, Some Thoughts on Power and Influence, 1993; prin. works include Nooksack River Plan, Bellingham, Wash.; Yakima (Wash.) River Regional Greenway, Union Bay Teaching and Research Arboretum, U. Wash., Seattle, Newhalem Campground, North Cascades Nat. Park, Woodland Park Zool. Gardens, Seattle, Washington Park Arboretum, U. Wash., Seattle, zoo master plans for Kansas City, Roanoke, Va., Detroit and Honolulu, Dallas Arboretum and Bot. Garden, Toledo Zoo African Savannah Complex, Thai Elephant Forest at Woodland Park Zoo, Singapore Bot. Gardens, Paris Pike Hist. Hwy, Denver Commons Park, others. Recipient Nat. award Am. Zoo Assn., 1981-84. Fellow Am. Soc. Landscape Architects (chmn. Wash. chpt. 1972-73, trustee 1979—, v.p., 1988-90, Merit award in community design 1972, Honor award in regional planning 1974, Merit award in regional planning 1977, Merit award in park planning 1977, Merit award in instnl. planning 1977, Pres.'s award of excellence 1980, merit awards in landscape planning), Nature Conservancy, Am. Hort. Soc., Am. Assn. Bot. Gardens and Arboreta, Audobon, Sierrra Club, Phi Gamma Delta, Diet, Rainier Club. Office: Jones & Jones Archs and Landscape Archs Ltd 105 S Main St Ste 300 Seattle WA 98104-2578

JONES, GREGORY ROBERT, lawyer; b. San Marcos, Tex, Apr. 12, 1952; s. Robert Calvin and Dorothy Jeanne J.; m. Julia Ann Paris, Mar. 23, 1985; children: Richard, Andrew, Michael. BS cum laude, W.Va. U., 1974; MBA, Ala. A&M U., 1977; JD, Samford U., 1981. Bar: Ala. 1981, Ga. 1981. Atty. Humphrey & Smith, P.C., Huntsville, Ala., 1981, Thrasher & Whitley, P.C., Atlanta, 1982-85; atty., mgr. contracts Sci. Atlanta, Inc., Atlanta, 1986-88, Thiokol Corp., Huntsville, 1988-91; v.p., gen. counsel QMS, Inc., Mobile, Ala., 1991-96; atty. Hand Arendall, L.L.C., Mobile, 1996—. Bd. dirs., sec. German Ala. Partnership, Birmingham, 1998. 1st lt. U.S. Army, 1974-78. Mem. Japan Am. Soc. Ala. (bd. dirs. 1997—), Ala. Export Coun. (treas. 2000—), Fairhope Yacht Club (youth sailing advisor 1996-97). Republican. Episcopalian. Avocations: sailing, writing. Office: Hand Arendall LLC PO Box 123 Mobile AL 36601-0123 Fax: 334-694-6375. E-mail: gjones@handarendall.com.

JONES, GWENYTH ELLEN, information technology executive; b. Omaha, Sept. 21, 1952; d. Robert Lester and Mary Ellen (Ouren) J.; m. William F. Knoff Jr. BA, U. Va., 1974, MA in English, 1982. Mktg. dir. John Wiley & Sons, N.Y.C., 1986-89, pub., 1989-90, dir. info. systems and tech., 1990-97, exec. dir. pub. info. systems and techs., 1997—2001; v.p. Pub. Info. Sys. and Techs., 2001—. Mem. Assn. Am. Pubs. Avocations: dance, tennis. Office Phone: 748-850-6109.

JONES, HAROLD ANTONY, banker; b. Bklyn., Nov. 5, 1943; s. Harold Edward and Marie Albertine (Schwietering) J.; m. Jo Ann T. Titone, Oct. 8, 1966; children: Christopher, Gregory. BA, Pace Coll., 1968; postgrad., Am. Inst. Banking, 1970; AAS., Grad. Sch. Savs. Banking, Brown U., 1975; grad., Exec. Mgmt. Program, U. Mass., 1977. With Mfrs. Trust Co., N.Y.C., 1961-64; with Lincoln Savs. Bank, N.Y.C., 1964-90, dir. mktg., 1978-79, sr. v.p., corp. sec., 1979-81, dir. retail banking div., 1980-90; sr. v.p. bank adminstrn. Ridgewood Savs. Bank, N.Y.C., 1990—. Guest lectr. money and banking NYU; guest lectr. corp. social responsibility Columbia U.; pres. N.Y. Savs. Banks Life Ins. Council, 1985 Decorated knight Holy Sepulchre of Jerusalem; named Outstanding Banker in Cmty. Revitalization Brighton Beach Neighborhood Assn., 1978, Banker of Yr. Manhattan C. of C., 1990. Mem. Fin. Advt. and Mktg. Assn. N.Y. (dir.), Bank Mktg. Assn., Cmty. Bankers Assn. NY State (com. on pub. info.), Thrift Inst. Mktg. (chmn. exec. com.), Harbour Green Assn. (pres. 1992). Office: Ridgewood Savings Bank 71-02 Forest Ave Ridgewood NY 11385

JONES, H(AROLD) GILBERT, JR., lawyer; b. Fargo, N.D., Nov. 2, 1927; s. Harold Gilbert and Charlotte Viola (Chambers) J.; m. Julie Squier, Feb. 15, 1964; children: Lenna Lettice Mills Jones Carroll, Thomas Squier, Christopher Lee. B of Engring., Yale U., 1947; postgrad., Mich. U., 1948-49; JD, UCLA, 1956. Bar: Calif. 1957. Mem., ptnr. Overton, Lyman & Prince, L.A., 1956—61; founding ptnr. Bonne, Jones, Bridges, Mueller & O'Keefe, L.A., 1961—89, of counsel, 1990—92, Lewis, Brisbois, Bisgaard & Smith, 1992—; pvt. practice, 2001—. Bd. dirs. Wilshire YMCA, 1969-75. With U.S. Army, 1950-52. Fellow Am. Coll. Trial Lawyers, Am. Bd. Trial Advs. (nat. pres. 1988-89, nat. exec. com. 1990, 92, 96, nat. bd. dirs. 1977—, pres. L.A. chpt. 1980, Calif. Trial Lawyer of Yr. 1999), Internat. Acad. Trial Lawyers; mem. ABA, Calif. Bar Assn., Los Angeles County Bar Assn. (past. chmn. legal-med. rels. com.), Orange County Bar Assn., So. Calif. Assn. Def. Counsel, Jonathan Club, Transpacific Yacht Club (commodore 1996-98), Newport Harbor Yacht Club (commodore 1998), Cruising Club Am., L.A. Yacht Club (Blue Water Cruising award, 1985), Univ. Athletic Club. Home: 818 Harbor Island Dr Newport Beach CA 92660-7228 Office: 650 Town Center Dr Ste 1400 Costa Mesa CA 92626-7020 Office Phone: 714-668-5516. E-mail: hg5150@aol.com, gjones@lbbslaw.com.

JONES, HARRY EDWARD, diplomat, writer; b. Phila., Feb. 19, 1938; s. Harry Edward and Helen Jean (Spoon) Jones; m. Patricia Anne Pascoe, Oct. 13, 1964; children: Michael Sumner, Christopher Steven, Anne Pelton. BS, Pa. State U., 1959, MPA, 1975. Sr. fgn. svc. officer. min. counselor US Dept. of State, Washington, 1965—2002; contractor CIA, McLean (Langley), Va., 2002—, dir. nat. intelligence. Polit. econ. min. Consul Gen. Author: (novel) Shadow In A Weary Land. Specialist 5th class (e-5) U.S. Army, 1960—62, Washington, DC (Pentagon). Mem.: Diplomatic and Consular Officers Ret. (DACOR). Episcopalian. Avocations: gardening, painting. Home: 208 Caroline St Fredericksburg VA 22401

JONES, HARRY GORDON, electronics company executive; b. New Orleans, Nov. 1, 1950; s. Harry G. and Jessie Mae (Alexis) J.; m. Judith D. Pitts, April 16, 1971 (dec. Feb. 1982); children: Kristina, Kimberly. AA, Pensacola Jr. Coll., 1981; student, Southeast La. U., 1975-78. Engr. Xerox Corp., New Orleans, 1975-78, Lear Siegler, Inc., Denver, 1978-81; pres., chief exec. officer Spectrum Systems, Inc., Pensacola, Fla., 1981—. Mem. engring. adv. coun. U. West Fla. Past chmn. adv. bd. Small Bus. Devel. Ctr., U. West Fla. Coll. Bus. Mem. Instrument Soc. Am. (emissions monitoring stds. com.), Air Pollution Control Assn., Am. Mgmt. Assn., Pensacola C. of C. (cluster industry task force). Republican. Assembly of God. Office: Spectrum Systems Inc 3410 W Nine Mile Rd Pensacola FL 32526-7808

JONES, HENDREE EVELYN, research scientist, psychologist; b. Richmond, Mar. 11, 1972; d. Clinton Edward Jones and Hendree Fitzgerald Mason; m. Erik Matthew Lensch, June 28, 1997; 1 child, Ashley Carter Lensch. BA, Randolph-Macon Coll., 1992; MA, U. Richmond, 1994; PhD, Va. Commonwealth U., 1997. Postdoctoral fellow Johns Hopkins U., Behavioral Pharm. Rsch. Unit, Balt., 1997—98; instr. Johns Hopkins U., Behavioral Biology, Dept. Psychiat., 1998—99; rsch. dir. Johns Hopkins U., Ctr. for Addiction and Pregnancy, 1998—; asst. prof. Johns Hopkins U., Behavioral Biology, Dept. Psychiat., 1999—; program dir. cornerstone Johns Hopkins U., 2000—. Rsch. panel mem. Ctr. for Substance Abuse Treatment, Chevy Chase, Va., 2000; grant reviewer Nat. Inst. Drug Abuse, Washington, 2002, standing reviewer, 2004—; reviewer Nat. Registry for Effective Treatment Programs, Washington, 2003—. Contbr. articles various profl. jours. Vol. Hopkins House, Alexandria, Va., 2000—. Recipient Young Psychopharmacologist award, 1999. Fellow: Md. Psychol. Assn.; mem.: APA (Early Career Contbn. to Applied Psychology award), Coll. on Problems of Drug Dependence, Phi Beta Kappa. Achievements include development of animal model of abused inhalants during pregnancy; behavioral therapy for treating drug abusing partners of pregnant drug dependent women; research in pharmacotherapies for pregnant women. Avocations: reading, scuba diving, exercising, scrapbooks. Office: Johns Hopkins Bayview Med Ctr 4940 Eastern Ave D 3 E Baltimore MD 21224 Home: 318 Woodlawn Rd Baltimore MD 21210 Office Phone: 410-550-7684. Business E-Mail: hejones@jhmi.edu.

JONES, HERMAN OTTO, JR., corporate professional; b. Jacksonville, Fla., Dec. 1, 1933; s. Herman Otto Sr. and Esther (Powell) J.; m. Marjorie Seaver, June 4, 1955 (dec. June 1996); two children (dec.); m. M. Beth Seaver, May 10, 1997. BSA, U. Fla., 1956. V.p. Oak Crest Hatcheries, Inc., Jacksonville, 1956-71; exec. v.p. Oak Crest Enterprises, Inc., Jacksonville, 1958-71; dir. sales Diversified Imports, Inc., Lakewood, N.J., 1971-73, BEC Ltd., Winchester, Eng., 1973-78; sales rep. Paul Revere Ins. Co., Jacksonville, 1978-81; v.p. Anitox Corp., Buford, Ga., 1981-85; pres. Gateway Suppliers, Inc., Jacksonville, 1986-98; v.p. Sales Agritek Bio Ingredients Corp., Montreal, Quebec, Can., 1993-97; pres. Gateway Bio-Nutrients, Inc., 1998—. Contbr. articles to profl. jours. Vice chmn. bd. deacons Riverside Bapt. Ch., 1988-89, deacon, 1991-94, sec. of deacons, 1991-92, dir. Sunday Sch., 1992-93; bd. dirs. South Shore Condos, 1998-2001, treas., 1998-2001, 2003, pres., 2001—03; past pres. Duval Co. Farm Bur., 1964, Fla. Poultry Assn., 1964, Fla. Hatchery, 1964, Fla. Breeders Assn., 1965, Fla. Poultry Fedn., 1965; mem. Duval County Rep. Exec. Com., 2003—. Named Outstanding Mem., Fla. Poultry Fedn., 1965, Southeastern Poultry and Egg Assn., 1963, State Outstanding Young Farmer, Fla. Jaycees, 1968; recipient Disting. Service award, Jacksonville Jaycees, 1970. Mem.: Fla. Feed Assn., U.S. Poultry and Egg Assn., Greater Jacksonville Agrl. Fair Assn. (bd. dirs. 2002—, vice chmn. 2004), Mandarin Mus. and Hist. Soc., Beaches Sea Turtle Patrol, Gainesville Quarterback Club, Order of DeMolay (Chevalier degree state master councilor state of Fla. 1953), Order Ea. Star (past patron), Jesters, Shriners, Masons (master), Rotary (bd. dirs. South Jacksonville 1989—91, Paul Harris fellow). Republican. Avocations: golf, travel. Home: CND #703 1551 1st St S Jacksonville FL 32250-6360 Address: 1125 NW 33d Ave Gainesville FL 32609 E-mail: hjones@gatewaybio-nutrients.com.

JONES, HOBERT W., health physics and radiochemistry consultant; b. Lexington, Ky., Aug. 12, 1957; s. John E., Jr. and Peggy Ann (Pickle) J. BS in Physics, U. Ky., 1980; MS in Health Physics, Ga. Inst. Tech., 1985. Cert. health physicist; registered radiation protection technologist. Radiochem. lab. analyst Tenn. Valley Authority, Soddy-Daisy, 1981-84; health physicist Am. Electric Power Svc. Corp., Columbus, Ohio, 1985-91; sr. health physicist EG&G Mound Applied Techs., Miamisburg, Ohio, 1991-92, tech. specialist health physics, 1992-93; health physicist, radiochemist Labyrinth Group, Dayton, Ohio, 1993-95; health physicist Internat. Cons., Inc., 1997-98; health physics and radiochemistry cons. Enercon Svcs., Inc., 1998—2002, Horizon Environ. Group, Inc., 2002—03; health physicist Ohio Environ. Protection Agy., Utility Radiol. Safety Bd., Citizens Adv. Coun. Nuc. Safety, 2003—, Oak Ridge Associated Univs., 2003. Mem. Am. Nuclear Soc. (assoc.), Health Physics Soc. (plenary), Cin. Radiation Soc. (bd. dirs. 1993-94, pres.-elect 1993-95, pres. 1994-95), Ky. Cols. Home: 550 E Whipp Rd Centerville OH 45459-2256 Office: Cin Ops Ctr 2100 Sherman Ave Ste 250 Norwood OH 45212 E-mail: hobertjones@yahoo.com.

JONES, HOUSTON GWYNNE, history professor; b. Yanceyville, N.C., Jan. 7, 1924; s. Paul Hosier and Lemma Sue (Fowlkes) J. BS, Appalachian State Coll., 1949; MA, George Peabody Coll., 1950; postgrad., NYU, 1951—52; cert. archival adminstrn., Am. U., 1957; PhD, Duke U., 1965. Prof. history Oak Ridge (N.C.) Mil. Inst., 1950-53; chmn. div. soc. scis. West Ga.

Coll., Carrollton, 1955-56; state archivist of N.C. State Dept. Archives & Hist., Raleigh, N.C., 1956-68; dir. State Dept. Archives & History, Raleigh, N.C., 1968-74; adj. prof. history U. N.C., Chapel Hill, 1974-94, dir. N.C. Coll., 1974-94, Thomas W. Davis rsch. historian, 1994—. Mem. Nat. Hist. Publs. and Records Commn., Washington, 1978-86, N.C. Hist. Commn., Raleigh, 1977—. Author: Books For History's Sake, 1966, The Records of a Nation, 1969, Local Government Records, 1980, North Carolina Illustrated, 1983, North Carolina History: An Annotated Bibliography, 1995, Historical Consciousness in the Early Republic, 1995, Scoundrels, Rogues and Heroes of the Old North State, 2004; editor-in-chief N.C. Hist. Rev., 1968-74; gen. editor: North Caroliniana Society Imprints, 1978—. Chmn. Am's. 400th Anniversary Com., Raleigh, 1978-80; founder, sec.-treas. North Caroliniana Soc., Chapel Hill, 1975—; sec. Joint Commn. on Status of Nat. Archives, Washington, 1967-68. Served with USN, 1942—46. Recipient Disting. Alumnus award Appalachian State U., 1971, Cannon Cup hist. preservation N.C. Soc. for Preservation of Antiquities, 1971, Univ. Svc. award U. N.C. Gen. Alumni Assn., 1990, Disting. Svc. award in documentary publ. and preservation Nat. Hist. Publs. and Records Commn., Washington, 1990, John Tyler Caldwell award in humanities N.C. Humanities Coun., 2001, N.C. awrd State of N.C., 2002. Fellow Soc. Am. Archivists (pres. 1968-69, Waldo G. Leland prize 1967, 81), Soc. North Caroliniana (Soc. award 1994); mem. N.C. Literary and Hist. Assn. (sec. 1969-75, pres. 1975-76, Crittenden Meml. award 1977), N.C. Writers Conf. (chmn. 1982, Conf. award 1994), Am. Assn. for State and Local History (sec. 1978-82, award of merit 1968, award of distinction 1989), Nat. Assn. State Hist. Preservation Officers (com. chmn. 1972-74), Hist. Soc. N.C. (pres. 1979-80, R.D.W. Connor award 1956), Soc. History Discoveries (coun. 2003—), Carolina Club. Office: U NC Libr NC Collection Chapel Hill NC 27599-3930 Home: PO Box 127 Chapel Hill NC 27514-0127

JONES, INGRID SAUNDERS, food products executive; b. Detroit; EdB, Mich. State U.; EdM, Ea. Mich. U., 1973; HHD (hon.), Mich. State U., Atlanta Coll. Art, Morris Brown Coll. Tchr. pub. sch. sys., Detroit, Atlanta; exec. dir. Detroit/Wayne County Child Care Coordinating Coun.; legis. analyst to the pres. Atlanta City Coun.; exec. asst. to Mayor Maynard Jackson; asst. to v.p. for urban and govtl. affairs The Coca-Cola Co., 1982—86, mgr. urban projects, 1986—87, dir. urban affairs, 1987—88, asst. v.p., 1988—91, v.p., mgr. corp. external affairs, 1991, sr. v.p. corp. external affairs Atlanta, 2000—. Chair The Coca-Cola Found.; bd. dirs. Girls, Inc., Mich. State U. Found., Andrew Young Sch. Policy Studies, Ga. State U., Desmond Tutu Peace Found., Coca-Cola Scholars Found., Cmty. Found. Greater Atlanta, 1994—, Nat. Black Arts Festival, Coun. on Founds., Woodruff Arts Ctr., United Way Met. Atlanta, chair. Named to Hall of Fame, Ga. State U. Sch. Bus., 1998; recipient Pres. award, Morehouse Coll., 1988, Nat. Equal Justice award, NAACP Legal and Edn. Fund, 1997, Jondelle Johnson Legacy award, NAACP-Atlanta Chpt., 1998, Woman of Achievement award, YWCA Greater Atlanta, 1998, John B. Gerlach Devel. award, Ohio State U. Found., 1998, Nat. Action Networker's Keepers of the Dream award, 2001. Mem.: Soc. Internat. Bus. Fellows, Atlanta Rotary Club. Office: The Coca-Cola Co PO Box 1734 Atlanta GA 30301

JONES, ISOLA CHARLAYNE, mezzo soprano, voice educator; b. Chgo., Dec. 27, 1949; B in Music Edn., Northwestern U., Ill., 1971; D in Musical Arts (hon.), Providence (R.I.) Coll., 1991; M in Gen. Edn., Capella U., Mpls., 2003. Mezzo-soprano Met. Opera, Lincoln Ctr., NY, 1977—91, Nat. Opera, Washington, 1983, Palm Beach (Fla.) Opera, 1986, Cin. Opera, 1987, Seattle Opera, 1987, Spoletto (Italy) Festival, Italy, 1989, Seoul (Rep. of Korea) Opera, 1995—97, Ariz. Opera, Tucson / Phoenix, 2001—. Singing artist Ariz. Interfaith Movement, Phoenix, 1999—2002. Mem.: Sigma Alpha Iota (hon.). Office: South Mt Cmty Coll 7050 S 24th St Phoenix AZ 85040 Home Fax: 602-336-0578. Personal E-mail: isola@cox.net.

JONES, J. GILBERT, private investigator; b. San Francisco, June 1, 1922; s. Enoch Roscoe (L.) Jones, Sr. and Remedios (Ponce de Leon) Jones. Student, U.S. Mcht. Marine Acad., 1942—44, San Francisco City Coll., 1941—42, student, 1946—47; AB, U. Calif., Berkeley, 1949, MA, 1952. Pvt. investigator. Ins. insp. Ins. Cos. Insp. Bur., San Francisco, 1959—62; pub. rels. cons. San Francisco, 1962—67; ins. insp. Am. Svc. Bur., San Francisco, 1967—72; propr., mgr. Dawn Universal Internat., San Francisco, 1972—, Dawn Universal Security Svc., San Francisco, 1983—. Mem.: SAR, Libr. Congress Assocs., U. Calif. Alumni Assn., World Affairs Coun. N. Calif., Commonwealth Club of Calif., Sons Spanish-Am. War Vets. Soc. Republican. Office: PO Box 424057 San Francisco CA 94142-4057

JONES, J. KENLEY, journalist; b. Greenville, S.C., Feb. 24, 1935; s. J. Clyde and Mildred Idel (Smith) J.; m. Margaret Jean McPherson, Dec. 11, 1965; children— Stephanie, Jason, Eleanor. Student, Furman U., 1953-55; BS in Speech, Northwestern U., 1957, MS in Journalism, 1963; postgrad., Columbia U., 1964-65. Reporter City News Bur. of Chgo., 1962; reporter, cameraman KRNT-TV, Des Moines, 1963-64, WSB-TV, Atlanta, 1965-69; fgn. corr. NBC News, Asia, 1969-72; corr. NBC News (Southeast Bur.), Atlanta, 1972-98. Served with USNR, 1958-61. Recipient Overseas Press Club award for best television reporting from abroad, 1970 Mem. AFTRA, Nat. Acad. Television Arts and Scis. Presbyterian. Office: 1175 W Peachtree St NW Atlanta GA 30309-3432

JONES, JAMES A., III, lawyer; b. Miami, Fla., June 16, 1944; BA, Yale U., 1966; JD, U. Va., 1973. Bar: Va. 1973, N.Y. 1984. Mem. Hunton & Williams LLP, Richmond, Va., ptnr., head, bus. practice group NYC. With USN, 1966—70. Mem. ABA (com. on devel. in bus. fin. corp. banking and bus. law sect. 1978—), N.Y. State Bar Assn., Va. State Bar Assn. Office: Hunton & Williams LLP 43rd Fl 200 Park Ave New York NY 10166-0136 Office Phone: 212-309-1140. Office Fax: 212-309-1100. Business E-Mail: jjones@hunton.com.

JONES, JAMES EARL, actor; b. Arkabutla, Miss., Jan. 17, 1931; s. Robert Earl and Ruth (Williams) J.; m. Cecilia Hart, Mar. 15, 1982; 1 child, Flynn Earl. BA, U. Mich., 1953, LHD (hon.), 1970; diploma, Am. Theatre Wing, 1957; studied with Lee Strasburg, Ted Danielewsky; DFA (hon.), Princeton U., 1980, Yale U., 1982; LHD (hon.), Columbia Coll., 1982; ArtsD (hon.), NYU, 1994. Appeared in plays: Much Ado About Nothing, 1955-59, 1961, Stalag 17, 1955-59, The Caine Mutiny, 1955-59, Arsenic and Old Lace, 1955-59, The Desperate Hours, 1955-59, Othello numerous appearances (Drama Desk award for best performance, 1964, Vernon Rice award, 1965), Egghead (Broadway debut), Sunrise at Campobello, 1958, The Big Knife, 1959, King Henry V, 1960, Measure for Measure, 1960, Richard II, 1961, A Midsummer Night's Dream, 1961, The Apple (Obie award best actor) 1961, Clandestine on the Morning Line (Obie award best actor) 1961, Richard III, 1961, Taming of the Shrew, 1961, Moon on a Rainbow Shawl (Obie award best actor) 1962, The Merchant of Venice, 1962, The Tempest, 1962, Toys in the Attic, 1962, Macbeth, 1962, The Winter's Tale, 1963, The Emperor Jones, 1964, 1967, Baal (Obie award best performance) 1965, Coriolanus, 1965, Troilus & Cressida, 1965, The Great White Hope, 1969 (Drama Desk award outstanding performance 1969, Golden Globe award new male star of yr. 1971, Tony award for best actor, Antoinette Perry award best actor in a dramatic play, 1969), Les Blancs (Drama Desk award outstanding performance) 1970, Hamlet (Drama Desk award outstanding performance) 1973, King Lear, 1973, The Cherry Orchard (Drama Desk award outstanding performance) 1973, The Iceman Cometh, 1973, Of Mice and Men, 1974, Paul Robeson, 1977, Hedda Gabler, 1980, Master Harold and The Boys, 1982-83, Fences, 1985-87 (Drama Desk award, Antoinette Perry award, Outer Critics Circle award for Best Actor, 1987, Tony award for Best Actor, Drama Critics award), On Golden Pond, 2005; appeared in movies: Dr. Strangelove, 1963, The Great White Hope, 1970 (Acad. Award nom. best actor 1970, Golden Globe award new male star of 1971), King: A Filmed Record Montgomery to Memphis, 1970, The Man, 1972, Malcolm X, 1972, Claudine, 1973 (Image award best actor NAACP, 1974, Golden Glove award non. best actor in a musical or comedy, 1974) The River Niger, 1975, The Bingo Long Traveling All-Stars and Motor Kings, 1976, Star Wars, 1977 (voice of Darth Vader), The Greatest, 1977, A Piece of the Action, 1978, The Empire Strikes Back, 1980 (voice of Darth Vader), Conan the Barbarian, 1982, Return of the Jedi, 1983 (voice of Darth Vader), Soul Man, 1986, Allan Quartermain & the Lost City of Gold, 1987, Matewan, 1987, Gardens of Stone, 1987, Coming to America, 1988, Field of Dreams, 1989, The Hunt For Red October, 1990, Sneakers, 1991, Patriot Games, 1992, Meteor Man, 1993, Sommersby, 1993, The Sandlot, 1993, (voice) The Lion King, 1994, Clear and Present Danger, 1994, Cry The Beloved Country, 1995, A Family Thing, 1996, Looking for Richard, 1996, Gang Related, 1997, Summer's End, 1998, (voice) The Lion King II: Simba's Pride, 1998, Undercover Angel, 1999, On the Q.T., 1999, Finder's Fee, 2001, (voice) Recess Christmas: Miracle on Third Street, 2001, (cameo in trailer) The Spongebob Squarepants Movie, 2004, (voice) Robots, 2005, The Sandlot 2, 2005, Star Wars: Episode III Revenge of the Sith, 2005 (voice of Darth Vader); TV movies include: The Cay, 1974 (Golden Gate award, Golden Hugo award, Gabriel award, 1975), King Lear, 1974, Jesus of Nazareth, 1977, Roots: The Next Generation, 1979, Guyana Tragedy: The Story of Jim Jones, 1980, The Atlanta Child Murders, 1985, The Last Elephant (Ace nomination) 1990, Heatwave, 1990 (Ace award, best actor in a supporting role, Emmy award best supporting actor in a spl. or mini-series 1991), By Dawn's Early Light, 1990 (Emmy award nomination outstanding supporting actor 1991), The Vernon Johns Story, 1993, What the Deaf Man Heard, 1997, Summer's End, 1999, Santa and Pete, 1999, (voice) 2004: A Light Knight's Odyssey, 2004; TV series: (narrator) Malcolm X, 1972, (host) Black Omnibus, 1973, (host) Vegetable Soup, 1975, Sojourner, 1975, Third and Oak (Ace award), Business World News, 2003-; star TV series Paris, 1979-80, Gabriel's Fire, 1990 (Outstanding Lead Actor in Dramatic Series Emmy award 1991), Pros & Cons, 1991 (Emmy award bestactor in a drama series, Best Actor NAACP), Under One Roof, 1995; appeared on TV shows GuidingLight, As The World Turns, The Defenders, East Side, West Side, Dr. Kildare, Tarzan, Highway to Heaven, L.A.Law, Homicide: Life onthe Street, Lois & Clark: The New Adventures of Superman, Frasier, Law & Order, Touched by an Angel, Picket Fences, (voice) The Simpsons, Garfield and Friends; appeared, narrated TV specials including Black Omnibus: Negro in the Arts, 1973, (narrator) Beauty & The Beast CBS Library Misunderstood Monsters, 1981, Aladdin & His Wonderful Lamp Fairie Tale Theatre, 1986, Wonderworks, 1986, Soldier Boys CBS Schoolbreak Special, 1987, The 41st Annual Tony Awards, 1987, Square One Television, 1987, America Picks The All-Time Favorite Movies, 1988, Teach 109 American Playhouse, 1988, (narrator) A Hard Road to Glory: The Black Athlete, 1988, (narrator) Michael Jackson: Motown on Showtime, 1988, (host, narrator) The Way We Hear Smithsonian World, 1988, (host narrator) Who Lives Who Dies, 1988, Saturday Night with Connie Chung, 1989, Third and Oak: The Pool Hall American Playwrights Theatre, 1989, The 43rd Annual Tony Awards, 1989, Reflections on the Silver Screen with Prof. Richard Brown, 1990, America's All Star Tribute to Oprah Winfrey, 1990, World Series, 1990, 44th Annual Tony Awards, 1990, Golden Glove awards, 1990, Nat. Meml. Day Concert, 1990, 42d Annual Primetime Emmy Awards, 1991, A Party for Richard Pryor, 1991, 17th Annual People's Choice Awards, 1991, 12th Annual Ace Awards, 1991, (narrator) Visitors from the Unknown, 1991, Muhammad Ali, Biography, 1991, Portrait of Castro's Cuba, 1991, Twenty-Third Annual NAACP Image Awards, 1991, When It Was A Game, 1991, (narrator) The Creative Spirit, 1992, AFI Salute to Sidney Poitier, 1992, Shelly Duvall's Bedtime Stories, 1992, (narrator) Ivory Wars: Lincoln Memorial Day Concert, 1993, 47th Annual Tony Awards, 1993, The Second Civil War, 1996, Alone, 1997, Lincoln Memorial Day Concert, 1997; recordings include: Great American Documents (with Orsen Welles, Henry Fonda, Helen Hayes), 1976, The People Could Fly, Oedipus Rex, To be Young, Gifted and Black, Poems from Black Africa, The Emperor Jones, Native Son, The Great White Hope, John Henry, The New Testament, Portraits of Freedom; appeared in Bell Atlantic Commercials; the voice behind CNN Lincoln Portrait, 1993; vocal introduction 3rd Rock from the Sun; co-author: (with Penelope Niven) James Earl Jones: Voices and Silences, 1993. Recipient The Village Voice Off-Broadway award, 1962, Theatre World award, 1962, Hon. Doctoral Degree Black Am. Culture Festival, 1969, Grammy award, 1976, medal for spoken lang. Am. Acad. Arts and Letters, 1981, Office of Black Ministries Toussaint medallion, 1982, Theater Hall of Fame award, 1985, Emmy award for performance in children's programming, Soldier Boys, CBS Schoolbreak Spl., 1987-88, L.A. Film Tchrs. Assn. Jean Renoir award, 1990, Commonwealth award Disting. Svc. in the Dramatic Arts, Bank of Del., 1991, Nat. Medal of Arts for outstanding contbn. to cultural life of country, 1992, Hall of Fame Image award for great contbn. to arts, NAACP, 1992, UCLA medal, 1993; named Disting. Artist, L.A. Music Ctr. Club, 1994, John Houseman award The Acting Co., 1995; numerous other acting awards, nominations-Obie, Drama Desk, Tony, Golden Globe, Outer Critics Cir., ACE, others. Mem. Nat. Council of Arts (Presdl. appt. to adv. bd. 1962, presdl. appointee 1970-76), Actors' Equity Assn., SAG, Am. Fedn. TV and Radio Artists, Theatre Comm. Group (bd. dirs. 1962). Can commonly be seen on TV commericals for Verizon (formerly Bell Atlantic). Address: Horatio Prodns PO Box 610 Pawling NY 12564-0610*

JONES, JAMES FLEMING, JR., academic administrator, language educator; b. Atlanta, Apr. 9, 1947; s. James F. and Sarah Kate (Smith) J.; m. Jan Sheets, Nov. 15, 1969; children:Jennifer, Justin, Jason BA, U. Va., 1969; MA, Emory U., 1972; cert., U. Paris-Sorbonne, 1972; MPhil, Columbia U., 1974, PhD, 1975. Tchr., chmn. dept. fgn. langs. Woodward Acad., College Park, Ga., 1969-72; preceptor Columbia U., 1973-75; prof. Romance langs. and lit. Washington U., St. Louis, 1975-91, chmn. dept. Romance langs., 1982-91; vice provost, dean Dedman Coll., So. Meth. U., Dallas, 1991-96; pres. Kalamazoo Coll., 1996—2004, Trinity College, 2004—. Sr. visitor for Hilary term, Oxford, 1987. Precentor, Ch. of St. Michael and St. George, Clayton, Mo., 1978-91. Decorated chevalier Ordre des Palmes Académiques; recipient Avis Blewett award Am. Guild Organists, 1989, Faculty award Washington U., 1990, Disting. Alumnus award Ga. Mil. Acad.-Woodward Acad. Alumni Assn., 1990; NEH fellow, 1976, Folger Inst. fellow, 1982. Mem. MLA, Am. Assn. Tchrs. of French, Am. Soc. 18th Century Studies, Soc. Rousseau Studies, Soc. Prévost d'Exiles Office: Trinity College 300 Summit St Hartford CT 06106

JONES, JAMES L., JR., career military officer; b. Kansas City, Mo., Dec. 19, 1943; BS Sch. Fgn. Svc., Georgetown U., 1966; student, Amphibious Warfare Sch., Quantico, Va., 1973-74; grad., Nat. War Coll., 1985. Commd. 2d lt. USMC, 1967, advanced through grades to gen., 1999; platoon and co. comdr. Vietnam, 1967-68; co. comdr. Camp Pendleton, Calif., 1968-70, Marine Barracks, Washington, 1970-73, 3d Marine Divsn., Okinawa, Japan, 1974-75; served in officer assignments sect. Marine Hdqrs., Washington, 1976-79; liasion officer to U.S. Senate Washington, 1979-84; comdr. 3d bn. 9th Marines 1st Marine Divsn., Camp Pendleton, 1985-87; from sr. aide to comdt. to mil. sec. to comdt. Hdqrs. Marine Corps., Washington, 1987-89; comdg. officer 24th Marine Expeditionary Unit, Camp Lejeune, N.C., 1990-92; dep. dir. U.S. European Command, Stuttgart, Germany, 1992-94; comdg. gen. 2d Marine Divsn., Camp Lejeune, 1994-96; dep. chief of staff plans, policies, and ops. Hdqrs. Marine Corps, Washington, 1996-99, sr. mil. aide to Sec. of Def., 1997-99; 32d commdt. USMC, Washington, 1999—2003; comdr. U.S. European Command, 2003—; supreme allied comdr. Europe, 2003—. Decorated D.S.M., Silver Star, Legion of Merit with 3 gold stars, Bronze Star with Combat V. Office: NATO Hdqs Blvd Leopold III 1110 Brussels Belgium*

JONES, JAMES M., lawyer; b. Chgo. AB magna cum laude, Miami Univ., Ohio, 1983; JD with honors, Ohio State Univ., 1986. Atty. Jones Day, Columbus, Ohio, adminstrv. ptnr. Pitts. Named Nation's Urban Pro Bono Publico Atty. of Yr., Legal Services Corp., 1992; named one of Columbus' Ten Outstanding Young Citizens, Columbus Jr. C. of C.; recipient Cmty. Svc. award, Columbus Bar Assn. Fellow: Columbus Bar Found.; mem.: ABA, Allegheny County Bar Assn., Pa. Bar Assn., Order of Coif, Phi Beta Kappa. Office: Jones Day One Mellon Bank Ctr 31st Fl 500 Grant St Pittsburgh PA 15219 Office Phone: 412-394-7230. Office Fax: 412-394-7959. Business E-Mail: jmjones@jonesday.com.

JONES, JAMES PARKER, federal judge; b. Tampa, Fla., July 3, 1940; s. Edmund Leroy and Nellie (Parker) J.; m. Mary Duke Trent, June 24, 1964; children: J. Trent, Benjamin P., Jonathan E. AB, Duke U., 1962; LLB, U. Va., 1965. Bar: Va. 1965. Asst. atty. gen. Va. Atty. Gen., Richmond, 1965-66; law clk. US Ct. Appeals, Richmond, 1966-68; atty. Penn, Stuart, Eskridge & Jones, Abingdon and Bristol, Va., 1968-96; judge US Dist. Ct. (We. Dist.) Va., Abingdon, 1996—2004, chief judge, 2004—. Bd. dirs. Va. Ctr. for Innovative Tech., Reston, Va., 1987-90. State senator Commonwealth of Va., 1983-88; mem. Dem. Nat. Com., 1982-92; mem. State Bd. Edn., 1990-96, pres., 1992-96. Fellow Am. Coll. Trial Lawyers (mem. Va. state com. 1995-96); mem. The Nature Conservancy (trustee Va. chpt. 1988-96). Democrat. Espicopalian. Office: US Dist Ct 180 W Main St Abingdon VA 24210-2844

JONES, JAMES RICHARD, business administration educator; b. Saginaw, Mich., May 25, 1940; s. George B. and Rena Jones; m. Sheila I. Jones; children: Kimme Ann, Kriste Gay, Kelle Lyn, Karme Jill. BA, Mich. State U., 1962, MBA, 1964; PhD, Ariz. State U., 1969. Research analyst Mich. Public Service Commn., Lansing, 1962; systems analyst Allis-Chalmers Mfg. Co., West Allis, Wis., 1964-65; asst. prof. transp. U. Houston, 1967-70; asso. prof. mktg. U. Ga., Athens, 197— 72; spl. asst. Dept. Transp., Washington, 1972-74, transp. economist, 1974-76; Disting. prof. transp. Memphis State U., 1976-81; George R. Brown Disting. prof. bus. Trinity U., San Antonio, 1981—. Cons. in field. Author books in field; contbr. articles to profl. jours.; bd. editors: Jour. Mktg. Theory and Practice, 1992—. Keeshin fellow, 1963. Mem. Am. Soc. Traffic and Transp., Am. Mktg. Assn., Council Logistics Mgmt., Transp. Research Forum, Transp. Research Bd., So. Mktg. Assn., Assn. Mktg. Theory and Practice, Am. Inst. Decision Scis. Home: 1711 Brush Creek Dr San Antonio TX 78248-2003 Office: Trinity U One Trinity Pl San Antonio TX 78212-3104 Office Phone: 210-999-7230. Business E-Mail: jjones@trinity.edu.

JONES, JAMES ROBERT, ambassador, retired congressman, lawyer; b. Muskogee, Okla., May 5, 1939; m. Olivia Barclay, 1968; children: Geoffrey Gardner, Adam Winston. AB in Journalism and Govt., U. Okla., 1961; LLB, Georgetown U., 1964. Bar: Okla. 1964, D.C. 1964. Legis. asst. Congressman Ed Edmondson, 1961-64; spl. asst. Pres. Lyndon Johnson, 1965-69; mem. 93d-99th congresses from 1st Dist. Okla., Washington, 1973-87; chmn. budget com. 97th and 98th Congress, Washington; chmn. social security subcom. 99th Congress, Washington; ptnr. Dickstein, Shapiro & Morin, Washington, 1987-89; chmn. bd., chief exec. officer Am. Stock Exch., N.Y.C., 1989-93; U.S. amb. to Mexico, 1993-97; pres. Warnaco Internat., 1997-98; CEO Manatt, Jones Global Strategies, Washington. Bd. dirs. Kaiser Family Found., Grupo Modelo, Kansas City So. Ind., Anheuser Busch, Keyspan, Inc.; co-chmn. U.S.-Mex. Bus. Com.; chmn. Meridian Internat. Ctr., World Affairs Couns. of Am. Served to capt. CIC AUS, 1964—65. Mem.: D.C. Bar Assn., Okla. Bar Assn. Office: 700 12th St NW Ste 1100 Washington DC 20005 Office Phone: 202-585-6560. E-mail: jjones@manatt.com. *In essence, I try to follow the admonition of Thomas Aquinas, "To work as if everything depends upon you, and pray as if everything depends on God.*

JONES, JAMES THOMAS, state supreme court justice, former attorney general; b. Twin Falls, Idaho, May 13, 1942; s. Henry C. and Eunice Irene (Martens) J.; m. Nancy June Babson, Nov. 25, 1972; 1 dau., Katherine A. Student, Idaho State U., 1960-61; BA, U. Oreg., 1964; JD, Northwestern U., 1967. Bar: Idaho 1967. Legis. asst. to U.S. Senator, Washington, 1970-72; law practice Jerome, Idaho, 1973-82; atty. gen. State of Idaho, Boise, 1973-91; pvt. practice law Boise, 1991—2005; assoc. justice Idaho Supreme Ct., Boise, 2005—. Capt. U.S. Army, 1967-79, Vietnam. Decorated Bronze Star; decorated Air medal with 4 oak leaf clusters, Cross of Gallantry (Vietnam), Army Commendation medal Mem. Idaho Bar Assn., Am. Legion, VFW. Republican. Lutheran. Office: Idaho Supreme Ct PO Box 83720 Boise ID 83720*

JONES, JANET LEE, psychology educator, cognitive scientist; b. Scottsdale, Ariz., Apr. 4, 1957; d. Gerry L. and Alicia M. (Coppes) J.; m. Alan M. Krajecki, 1986. BA in Psychology magna cum laude, Pomona Coll., 1984; MA in Higher-Order Cognition, UCLA, 1985, PhD in Cognitive Psychology/Psycholinguistics, 1989. Artist, designer Ruth Downs Ltd., 1973-74; text editor Text Craft, Inc., 1975-76; bookkeeper Verde Ind. Newspaper, 1976-77; exec. asst. to v.p. Honeywell, 1978-81; teaching asst. psychology dept. Pomona Coll., Claremont, Calif., 1982-84; teaching fellow and assoc. UCLA, 1985-89; vis. asst. prof. Pitzer Coll., Claremont, 1990; prof. psychology Ft. Lewis Coll., Durango, Colo., 1990—. Horse trainer, riding instr., 1973-77; lectr. Calif. State U., Long Beach, 1989; presenter in field. Author: Understanding Psychological Science, 1995, The Psychotherapist's Guide to Human Memory, 1999; contbr. articles to profl. jours. Scholar Pomona Coll., 1981-84; grad. fellow UCLA, 1984-85; recipient Gengerelli Disting. Dissertation award, 1989. Mem. APA, Am. Psychol. Soc. (charter), Western Psychol. Assn., UCLA Psychology Alumni Assn., Internat. Alliance of Tchr. Scholars, Assn. Am. Colls. and Univs., Phi Beta Kappa, Sigma Xi. Office: Ft Lewis Coll Dept Psychology 1000 Rim Dr 274 EBH Durango CO 81301

JONES, JANICE COX, elementary school educator, writer; b. Jackson, Miss., Nov. 4, 1937; d. Eugene Debs and Thelma Corelli (Beard) Cox; m. June 20, 1959 (div. June 1985); children: Allison Jones Griffiths, Tamara Jones McKee. BS with highest distinction, Miss. Coll., 1959; MEd magna cum laude, U. Miami, 1968. Cert. elem. edn. Tchr. Jackson Pub. Sch., 1959-60, Arlington (Tex.) Pub. Schs., 1960-63, Houston Pub. Schs., 1963-64, Miami-Dade County Pub. Schs., 1967-1980, 1988—97; pres. Palm Tree Prodns., Ltd., 1980-88. Tchr. English ESOL Say Sch., Tokyo, 1985; tutor, child welfare worker CBS, Twentieth Century Fox, N.Y.C., Miami, 1981-; pvt. tutor, owner Think, Ink!, Miami, 1983-; piano tchr. MDCPS Cmty. Sch., Miami, 1991-; participant Miss. Gov.'s Edn./Econ. Task Force, 1990-91; workshop presenter Children's Cultural Coalition & Arts for Learning; speaker/poet in field; usher Coconut Grove Playhouse, Actor's Playhouse, Gablestage, Biltmore. Author several books of poetry, Geography Fun Facts: A Trip Across the U.S.A. in Poetry, Numbered & Named: A Preventive for Math Anxiety in Children and Adults. Dist. exec. adv. com. to sch. bd. for gifted edn. Miami-Dade County Pub. Schs., 1987-91; adv. bd. Metro-Dade Rapid Transit, 1974-77; parent sponsor Olympics of the Mind Team, 1984; parent sponsor Queen's Ct., Jr. Orange Bowl, Coral Gables, Fla., 1983; vol. pianist, organist, music dir. Village Green Baptist Mission, Miami, 1973; vol. Habitat for Humanity, 1991-. Recipient nat. poetry award, Byline Mag., 2002, ann. conf. scholarship, World Future Soc.; grantee, NEA, 1973. Mem. Am. Fedn. Tchrs., Dade Heritage Trust (edn. com., writer), Miami Writer's Club, Fla. Freelance Writers Assn., Nat. Writers Assn. South Fla. chapt. (bd., exec. sec. 1997-, nat. writing contest chair, 1998-2001), United Tchrs. Dade (bldg. steward 1976-78), Tropical Audubon Soc., Coun. for Internat. Visitors, Internat. Platform Assn. (red carpet com.), Soc. Children's Book Writers and Illustrators, Miami Arts Exch., Nature Conservancy, Sierra Club. Avocations: Broadway plays and musicals, museums, fishing, photography, travel, accordion. Home: 6301 SW 93rd Ct Miami FL 33173-2317

JONES, JAY ROBERT, music educator; b. Richmond, Mo., Jan. 28, 1968; s. J. W. and Paula Jones. B in Music Edn., Ctrl. Meth. Coll., Fayette, Mo., 1990; MS in Edn., N.W. Mo. State U., 1997. Tchg. cert. Mo. Dir. bands So. Boone County, Ashland, Mo., 1990—92, Stewartsville (Mo.) C-II Schs., 1992—98, Platte County R-3 Sch. Dist., Platte City, Mo., 1998—. Condr., clinician Mid Mo. Ednl. Music Festivals, 1996—; condr., band dir. N.W. Mo. State U. Music Camp, 1997—2001, 2005; coord. Wilson Ctr. Performing Arts Platte County Sch. Dist., 2002—; adminstrv. asst. Platte County HS, 2004—05. *He is currently All-But-Dissertation (ABD) on a Doctor of Education degree from University of Missouri-Columbia where his research efforts are focused on developing a dialogic evaluation model for assessing student teacher perceptions of preparedness at the university level.* Co-editor: Building Better Bands, 2002; contbg. author: Mo. Sch. Music Mag., 2002—. Asst. scoutmaster Stewartsville troop 222 Boy Scouts Am., 1993—98. Recipient proclamation, Gov. Mo., 2001. Mem.: Nat. Band Assn., N. Ctrl. Mo. Bandmasters Assn. (pres. 2000—01), Music Educators Nat. Conf., Mo. State Tchrs. Assn., Mo. Music Educators Assn. (v.p. N.W. dist. 2000—02, pres. N.W. dist. 2002—), Mo. Bandmasters Assn. (membership chmn. 2000—), Phi Mu Alpha, Phi Beta Mu. Avocations: travel, photography. Home: 8109 N Stoddard Ave Kansas City MO 64152 Office: Platte County R3 Schs 1501 Branch Platte City MO 64079

JONES, JEANNE PITTS, pre-school administrator; b. Richmond, Va., Oct. 19, 1938; d. Howard Taliaferro and Anne Elizabeth (Warburton) Pitts; m. Jack Hunter Jones, Nov. 17, 1962; children: Jack Hunter, Jr., Judith Anne, James Howard, Jon Martain. BA, Marshall U., 1961, postgrad., 1962, Presbyn. Sch. Christian Edn., Richmond, 1974, 94; MEd in Early Childhood Edn., Va. Commonwealth U., 2000. Cert. tchr. Va. Tchr. Richmond Pub. Schs., 1961-65; founder Bon View Sch. Early Childhood Edn., Richmond, 1971, tchr., 1971-91, dir., 1971—. Acad. affairs chmn. Good Shepherd Episcopal Sch. Bd., Richmond, 1985-88; mentor Ecumenical Child Care Network Nat. Coun. Chs., Washington, 1990-92. Chmn. room parents Crestwood Sch. PTA Bd., Richmond, 1974-80; publicity chmn. Va. Swimming, Richmond, 1978-88, children's coord. Bon Air United Meth. Ch., Richmond, 1985-93, v.p. Bon Air United Meth. Women, 1991-94; dir. Camp Friendship, Bon Air UMC, Richmond, 1992-2004; Va. Children's Action Network, Va. Conf. of United Meth. Ch., rep., 1993-95; Va. Conf. United Meth. Ch., weekday com. 1992-94. Recipient Spl. Mission recognition Bon Air United Meth. Women, Richmond, 1987. Mem.: Nat. Assn. Edn. for Young Children (validator 1993—, mentor 1994—98, accreditation chair 2005—), Va. Assn. for Early Childhood Edn. (affiliate pres. 2002—04, 3d v.p. liaisons 2004—05), Chesterfield Coalition Early Childhood Educators (bd. dirs. 1993—97), Presch. Assn. Ch. Ednl. Dirs. (pres. 1993—95), Richmond Early Childhood Assn. (mem.-at-large 1994—96, rec. sec. 1996—98, 1998—2000, v.p. membership 2000—02, pres.-elect 2001—02, pres. 2002—04, past pres. 2004—, Richmond Early Childhood Adv. of the Yr. 2002). Republican. Avocations: aerobics, reading. Home: 9103 Whitaker Cir Richmond VA 23235-4053 Office: Bon View Sch Early Childhood Edn 1645 Buford Rd Richmond VA 23235-4274

JONES, JEFFREY FOSTER, lawyer; b. Phila., Apr. 24, 1944; s. Richard L. and Dorothy A. (Shaw) J.; m. Susan Craft, Aug. 22, 1970; children: Amanda, Michael. BA, Williams Coll., 1966; JD, Harvard U., 1973. Bar: Mass. 1973, U.S. Dist. Ct. Mass. 1974, U.S. Dist. Ct. Appeals (1st cir.) 1974. Law clk. Supreme Jud. Ct., Boston, 1973-74; assoc. Palmer & Dodge, Boston, 1974-80, ptnr., 1980-88, mng. ptnr., 1998—. Chmn. bd. Law Firm Resources Project, 1981—96; dir. Mass Inc., Mass. Bus. Roundtable. Overseer Boys and Girls Clubs of Boston, 1974-93, sec., bd. dirs., 1993-2000, chair, bd. dirs., 2002—; trustee Radcliffe Coll., 1995-99, Sterling and Francine Clark Art Inst., 1995-98; bd. dirs. Willow Hill Sch., 1991—. Lt. USN, 1966-70. Mem. ABA, Nat. Assn. Coll. and Univ. Attys., Boston Bar Assn., Mass. Bar Assn., Greater Boston C. of C. (dir. 1998—). Democrat. Avocations: racquetball, golf, reading. Office: Palmer and Dodge LLP 111 Huntington Ave 19th Fl Boston MA 02199-7613 Office Phone: 617-239-0246. Business E-Mail: jjones@palmerdodge.com.

JONES, JENK, JR., editor, educator; b. Tulsa, June 24, 1936; s. Jenkin Lloyd and Juanita Rose (Carlson) J.; m. Carol Beatrice Jaros, June 27, 1959; children: Janette Lloyd Jones Strickland, Landon Lloyd. BA in Polit. Sci., U. Colo., 1958. Sports writer Mpls. Tribune, 1959; reporter, news editor Anchorage Times, 1959-61; state capital corr. Tulsa Tribune, Oklahoma City, 1961-62, Washington corr., 1962-63, copy editor Tulsa, 1963-64, chief copy desk, 1964-65, asst. city editor, 1965-66, asst. mng. editor, 1966-67, mng. editor, 1968-74, exec. editor, 1974-88, editor, 1988-91, editor, pub., 1991-92; chief copy editor, writer, photographer South Ctrl. Golf Mag., Tulsa, 1993—, Hurricane Tracker Mag., 1995—2001. Prof. journalism Okla. State U., 1993-95, prof. polit. sci. U. Ctr., Tulsa, Okla., 1995-96; cons. editor The Tulsa Sentinel, 1992-93; juror Pulitzer Prize, 1982-83. With USAFR, 1958-64. Unitarian Universalist. Home: 6447 S Louisville Ave Tulsa OK 74136-1532 Office: South Ctrl Publs 2723 S Memorial Dr Tulsa OK 74129 E-mail: jonesjenk@cox.net.

JONES, JERRY (JERRAL WAYNE JONES), professional football team executive; b. L.A., Oct. 13, 1942; m. Gene Jones; children: Stephen, Charlotte, Jerry Jr. Grad., U. Ark., 1965, MBA, 1970. Exec. v.p. Modern Security Life, Springfield, Mo., 1965-69; prin. oil and gas bus., 1970—; pres., gen. mgr. Dallas Cowboys, 1989—. Nat. Paralysis Assn.; Boys Clubs Am. Avocations: hunting, fishing, tennis, water-skiing, skiing. Office: Dallas Cowboys 1 Cowboys Pkwy Irving TX 75063-4999*

JONES, JEWEL, social services administrator; b. Oklahoma City, Okla., Dec. 7, 1941; d. Joseph Samuel and Jewell (Hathyel) Fisher; m. Maurice Jones, July 17, 1976; children: Anthony, Carmen. BA in Sociology, Langston (Okla.) U., 1962; MA in Pub. Adminstrn., U. Alaska, Anchorage, 1974. Tchr. Seidman Sch., L.A., 1962; correctional oifcer State of Calif. Dept. Corrections, Corona, 1963-65; probation officer County of San Bernardino, Calif., 1965-67; dep. exec. dir. Cmty. Action Agy., Anchorage, 1967-70; social svcs. dir. City of Anchorage, 1970-87; social svcs. mgr. Municipality of Anchorage, 1987-2000, dir. health & human svcs., 2000—. Chmn. bd. Alaska Housing Fin. Corp., Anchorage, 1995—; pres. Anchorage KidsPlace Project, 1994-95; chair Alaskan of the Yr. Scholarship Com., 1985—; chmn. bd. Janet Helen Tolan Gamble and Toby Gamble Ednl. Trust, 1998—. Mem. adv. bd. Salvation Army, Anchorage, 1982-87, Alaska R.R., Anchorage, 1990—; trustee United Way of Anchorage, 1990-97; bd. dirs Alaska Ctr. for Performing Arts, 1987-97. Recipient Pres.'s award Alaska Black Caucus, 1984, Employment of Handicapped award Mayor of Anchorage, 1979, Execs. in Profile award Region X Blacks in Govt. award, 1998. Mem. NAACP (Harambe award 1973), Alaska Black Leadership Conf. (Cmty. Svc. award 1979-80), Links Inc., Quota Club Intenrat., Valli Vue Homeowners Assn. (v.p.), Zeta Phi Beta. Democrat. Avocations: cooking, reading, gardening. Office: Municipality Anchorage PO Box 196650 Anchorage AK 99519-6650

JONES, JOEL MACKEY, academic administrator; b. Millersburg, Ohio, Aug. 11, 1937; s. Theodore R. and Edna Mae (Mackey) Jones; children: Carolyn Mae, Jocelyn Corinne. BA, Yale U., 1960; MA, Miami U., Oxford, Ohio, 1962; PhD, U. N.Mex., 1966. Dir. Am. studies U. Md., Balt., 1966-69; chmn. Am. studies U. N.Mex., Albuquerque, 1969-73, asst. v.p. acad. affairs, 1973-77, dean faculties, assoc. provost, prof. Am. studies, 1977-85, v.p. adminstrn., 1985-88; pres. Ft. Lewis Coll., Durango, Colo., 1988-99, pres. emeritus, 1999—; interim supr. of schs. Durango Pub. Schs., 1999; interim pres. Salisbury State U., 1999—2000. Bd. dirs. 1st Nat. Bank. Contbr. numerous essays, articles and chpts. to books. Founder Rio Grande Nature Preserve Soc., Albuquerque, 1974—; bd. dirs., mem. exec. com. United Way, Albuquerque, 1980-83; na. bd. cons. NEH, 1978—; bd. dirs. Mercy Hosp., 1990-94; mem. ACE Commn. on Leadership. Farwell scholar Yale U., New Haven, 1960; sr. fellow NEH, 1972; adminstrv. fellow Am. Coun. Edn., Washington, 1972-73. Mem. Am. Studies Assn., Am. Assn. Higher Edn., Am. Assn. State Colls. and Univs. (chair com. on cultural diversity, Colo. state rep. 1994—). Home: 2319 County Road 205 Durango CO 81301-8555

JONES, JOHN ARTHUR, lawyer; b. San Antonio, Fla., Oct. 9, 1921; s. Charles Garfield and Catherine Magdalene (Smith) J.; m. Margarette Lorraine (Sally) Johnson, Sept. 17, 1949; children: Matthew, Lisa, Malcolm, Darby. AA, U. Fla., 1947, JD with honors, 1949. Bar: Fla. 1949, U.S. Dist. Ct. (so. dist.) Fla. 1952, U.S. Ct. Appeals (5th cir.) () 1959, U.S. Ct. Appeals (11th cir.) 1982, U.S. Supreme Ct. () 1978. Assoc. Holland & Knight and predecessors, Tampa, Fla., 1949-54, ptnr., 1954—. Faculty Fla. Sch. of Banking, 1969-81. Editor, contbr.: How to Live and Die with Florida Probate, 1972, Practice Under Florida Probate Code, 1976-2002. Served in U.S. Army, 1940-46; lt. col. USAR. Decorated Bronze Star; recipient Robert C. Scott Meml. award, Fla. Bar Assn., William S. Belcher Lifetime Professionalism award, 2003. Fellow Am. Coll. Trust and Estate Counsel; mem. ABA, Fla Bar Assn. (cert. wills, trusts and estates, chmn. real property probate and trust law sect. 1980-81), Hillsborough County (Fla.) Bar Assn., Internat. Acad. Estate and Trust Lawyers, Am. Coll. Real Estate Lawyers, Am. Bar Found., Masons, Shriners, Tampa Club, Univ. Club. Home: 5027 W San Miguel St Tampa FL 33629-5428 Office: Holland & Knight LLP PO Box 1288 100 N Tampa St Ste 4100 Tampa FL 33602 E-mail: jajones@hklaw.com.

JONES, JOHN ELLIS, real estate broker; b. Odum, Ga., Oct. 28, 1941; s. Roland Warnell and Agnes Carridean (Brown) J.; m. Nellie Ann Dougherty, June 21, 1963; children: John Richard, Katherine Ann. BSBA, U. Fla., 1967. Cert. residential broker. With FBI, Washington, D.C., 1959-64; mgr. Fed. Res. Bank, Jacksonville, Fla., 1967-69; asst. mgr. Blue Cross/Blue Shield of Fla., Jacksonville, 1969-72; mgr. Heavener Realty Co., Jacksonville, 1972-75; pres., owner John Jones Realty Inc., Jacksonville, 1975-77, ERA Mid. Ga., Macon, 1977-79, ERA-Jones Realty Co., Macon, 1979-81; assoc. broker McNair Realty Co., Macon, 1981-89, Sheridan Solomon Kernaghan Realtors, Macon, 1989-91; with Fickling and Co., Macon, Ga., 1991—. Instr. real estate Macon Coll., 1980—, instr. real estate sales seminar, 1988—. Deacon San Jose Bapt. Ch., Jacksonville, 1975; Bible tchr. Vineville Bapt. Ch., Macon, 1979, deacon, trustee, 2004—. Mem. Nat. Assn. Realtors (nominee Educator of Yr. 1996), Ga. Assn. Realtors (bd. dirs. 2004—), Mid. Ga. Assn. Realtors (bd. dirs., sec. 1995, v.p. 1996, pres. elect 1997, pres. 1998, past pres. 1999, Realtor of Yr. 1996), Ga. Realtors Inst., Realtors Nat. Mktg. Inst., Real Estate Educators Assn., Ga. Real Estate Educators Assn., Macon C. of C. (hon. life, bd. dirs. 1996-98, amb. 1989, Ambs. award 1995), River North Country Club (bd. dirs. 1992-94), Cert. Residential Specialists (Ga. chpt. sec. 1995, pres.-elect 1996, pres. 1997, Realtor of Yr. 1997, Pres. award 2004). Republican. Avocations: bible study, self development. Home: 193 Rivoli Lndg Macon GA 31210-8633 Office: Fickling & Co 2960 Riverside Dr Macon GA 31204-1275 Office Phone: 478-757-9600 x156.

JONES, JOHN FRANK, retired lawyer; b. Feb. 24, 1922; s. Dwight Frank and Veronica Esther (Sheehy) Jones; m. Sally Oppegard; children: Janna Jones Bellwin, John M., Jeramy Ridder, Jill Jones Nester, Julie, Jeffrey, J. David. BS, U. N.D., 1946; MS in Organic Chemistry, U. Wis., 1953; JD, U. Akron, 1956. Bar: Ohio 1956, U.S. Patent Office, U.S. Ct. Appeals. Patent atty. B.F. Goodrich Co., Akron, Ohio, 1956—62; sr. patent atty. Standard Oil Co., Cleve., 1962—70, patent counsel, 1970—81, food and drug atty. Vistron Corp. subs., 1968—81; ret., 1981. Cons. Standard Oil Co., Cleve., 1981—95, Ashland Chem. Co. (div. Ashland Oil Co.), Columbus, Ohio, 1981—95, B.F. Goodrich Co. Contbr. articles to profl. jours. Served with USAAF, 1943—46. Decorated D.F.C., Air medal. Mem.: ABA, Cleve. Intellectual Property Law Assn., Ohio Bar Assn., Am. Chem. Soc., CBI Hump Pilots Assn. Republican. Achievements include patentee in chem. and polymer fields. Home and Office: 2724 Cedar Hill Rd Cuyahoga Falls OH 44223-1226

JONES, JOHN HARDING, photographer; b. Pitts., Apr. 28, 1923; s. John F. and Emma Eleanor (West) Jones; m. Teresa Watras, June 23, 1999 (div.); 1 child, Blair Harding. BFA, Rochester Inst. Tech., 1949; MBA, Pepperdine U., 1978; PhD, U. London, 1983; M in Photography (hon.), Brantridge Forest, Eng.; DLitt (hon.), Ky. Christian U.; EdD, St. John's U. Seaman U.S. Naval Air, 1940, advanced through grades to comdr., 1948; ret., 1963; chief photographer U.S. Steel Corp., Pitts.; mgr. art & photo dept. Magnavox Corp., Urbana, Ill.; chief photographer rehab. medicine sect. U.S. Vet. Adminstrn., L.A.; coord. rehab. medicine domiciliary sect. Wadsworth VA Hosp., L.A. Tchr. Carnegie Mellon Inst., Pitts., Earl Wheeler Schs., Pitts., Seattle U., Art Inst. Pitts.; dir., owner The Little Studio, Panorama City, Calif., 1989—, The Little Studio West, Panorama City, 1994—; owner The Little Studio, Pitts., The Little Studio West, The Howling Publ. Author: Photography, 1972, The Correspondence Educational Directory, 1976, 79, 84, 94, Correspondence Courses for High School Credit & GED Preparation, 1994. Recipient award Writers Guild, 1977, Merit award Cooking, 1986; elected to Am. Police Hall of Fame, 1996 Mem. Profl. Photographers Am., Masons, Shriners, Order of the Eastern Star (worthy patron 1986). Presbyterian. Avocations: bowling, writing, travel, civic activities, stamp collecting/philately, publishing. Office Phone: 559-305-0396. Personal E-mail: jonesusn@yahoo.com. Business E-Mail: jjones2823@coarsegold.us.

JONES, JOHN HARRIS, lawyer; b. New Blaine, Ark., Apr. 9, 1922; s. Ira Burton and Byrd (Harris); m. Marjorie Crosby Hart, 1983. AB, U. Central Ark., 1941; postgrad., George Washington U. Law Sch., 1941-42; LL.B., Yale, 1947. Bar: Ark. 1946, U.S. Supreme Ct. 1963. Comms. clk. FBI, 1941-42; practice in Pine Bluff, 1947—; spl. judge Circuit Ct., 1950; spl. chief justice Ark. Supreme Ct., 1997. Chmn. bd. Pine Bluff Nat. Bank, 1964-77, pres., 1966-76; Mem. Ark. Bd. Law Examiners, 1953-59; Republican nominee for U.S. Senate, 1974; Rep. presdl. elector, 1980; v.p., dir. John Rust Found., 1953-60. Served to 1st lt. USAAF, 1943-45. Decorated Purple Heart, Air medal. Mem. Ark. Bar Assn., Jefferson County Bar Assn. (pres. 1959-60). Mem. Christian Ch. (elder 1963-65, trustee 1965-71, 78-84). Clubs: Eden Park (Pine bluff), Little Rock Club. Home: 4001 S Cherry St Pine Bluff AR 71603-7156

JONES, JOHN MARTIN, JR., lawyer; b. Balt., Dec. 31, 1928; s. John Martin and Nannalee (Rogers) J.; m. Dayle Fort Nesbitt, July 27, 1969; children— David Mallory, Kelly Anne, Jeffrey Wallace Arthur, Kathleen Celeste; stepchildren— Martha Nesbitt Dewey, William Fort Nesbitt, Howard Scott Nesbitt. AB, U. Md., 1951, LL.B, 1953. Bar: Md. 1953, U.S. Dist. Ct. Md. 1953, U.S. Ct. Appeals (4th cir.) 1954, U.S. Supreme Ct. 1959. Assoc. Piper & Marbury, Balt., 1954-59, ptnr., 1960-86; pvt. practice, 1986-99; asst. atty. gen. State of Md., 1959-60; counsel Wilmer, Cutler & Pickering, Balt., 2000-01; legal cons. to law firms, 2001—02; of counsel Kirkland & Ellis, 2003—. Mem. Md. Gov.'s Commn. to Study Tax Laws. Mem. Balt. Area council Boy Scouts Am.; publ. adv. Regional Planning Council, Greater Balt., 1977. Mem. ABA, Md. Bar Assn., Bar Assn. Balt. City, Am. Judicature Soc. (life), Am. Law Inst. (life), Center Club, Yale Club of N.Y.C., Order of Coif, Delta Theta Phi, Delta Kappa Epsilon. Clubs: Center, Yale of N.Y.C, DKE of N.Y.C. Achievements include being a mem. adv. com. in drafting and preparation of Am. Law Inst.'s Model Land Development Code, 1970-77. Office: 200 Saint Paul Pl Ste 2121 Baltimore MD 21202-2004 Office Phone: 410-539-2700. E-mail: johnmartinjo1967@aol.com. *Palma Non Sine Pulvere.*

JONES, JOHN P., III, chemicals executive; b. 1950; With Air Products and Chem. Inc., Allentown, Pa., 1972—, v.p. and gen. mgr. Environ. & Energy Divsn., 1988—92, group v.p. Process Sys. Group, 1992—93, exec. v.p. Gases & Equipment, 1996—98, pres., COO, 1998—2000, chmn., pres., CEO, 2000—; pres. Air Products Europe Inc., 1993—96. Dir. ADP Inc., Am. Chemistry Coun.; exec. com. Soc. Chem. Industry Am. Sect. Office: Corp Secretary's Office Air Products & Chemicals Inc 7201 Hamilton Blvd Allentown PA 18195-1501*

JONES, JOHN WESLEY, entrepreneur; b. Wenatchee, Wash., Nov. 15, 1942; s. Richard F. and Hazel F. (Hendrix) J.; m. Melissa L. Meyer, June 22, 1968 (div. 1982); children: John E., Jennifer L.; m. Deborah G. Matthews, Apr. 24, 1993. BA in Bus./Econs., Western Wash. U., Bellingham, 1966. Trainee Jones Bldg., Seattle, 1967-69, mgr., 1969-78; owner/mgr. N.W. Inboards, Bellevue, Wash., 1974-78, Jones Bldg., Seattle, 1978-86; pvt. investor Bellevue, 1987—; owner/mgr. J. Jones Enterprises, 1994—. Trustee BOMA Health & Welfare Trust, 1982-86, chmn. 1986; mem. Seattle Fire Code Adv. Bd., 1979-86. With USMCR, 1966-72. Mem. Seattle Bldg. Owners Mgrs. Assn. (trustee 1979-86), Bldg. Owners Mgrs. Internat., N.W. Marine Trade Assn., Am. Assn. Individual Investors, Composite Fabricators Assn., Soc. Naval Architects Marine Engrs., Boat US, Seattle Yacht Club, NRA, Internat. Show Car Assn., Nat. Street Rod Assn., Specialty Equipment Mktg. Assn. Republican. Avocations: boating, water-skiing, skiing, automobiles, photography. Home and Office: PO Box 2088 Port Townsend WA 98368

JONES, JOHN WILLIAM (BUZZ JONES), music educator, conductor; b. Bryn Mawr, Pa., Aug. 11, 1950; s. Pual Revere and Dorothea Ann Jones; m. Gail Marie Peters, June 25, 1981. BS in Music Edn., Lebanon Valley Coll., 1972; MusM in Edn., Towson U., 1975; D in Musical Arts, Temple U., Phila., 1994. Music tchr. Howard County Pub. Schs., Ellicott City, Md., 1973—79; owner Cumberland Music, Carlisle, Pa., 1979—81; instr. music Dickinson Coll., Carlisle, 1980—89; sales mgr. Menchey Music Svc. Inc., Hanover, Pa., 1981—89; prof. Gettysburg (Pa.) Coll., 1989—. Composer: Wales: Land of My Fathers, 1997, Glory Ridge: A Cantata for the New, 2001, Axiom Asunder, 2004. Recipient Std. award, ASCAP, 1996—, Creative Arts Achievement award, Lebanon Valley Coll., 2002, Pa. Ptnrs. in the Arts award, 2003. Mem.: Internat. Assn. Jazz Edn. (pres. 2003—), Phi Beta Mu. United Ch. Of Christ. Avocations: travel, golf, walking. Home: 70 Windbriar Ln Gettysburg PA 17325 Office: Gettysburg Coll Box 403 400 N Washington St Gettysburg PA 17325

JONES, JOIE PIERCE, entrepreneur, educator, acoustician, writer; b. Brownwood, Tex., Mar. 4, 1941; s. Aubrey M. and Mildred K. (Pierce) J.; m. Kay Becknell, June 12, 1965. BA, U. Tex., 1963, MA, 1965; PhD, Brown U., 1970. Sr. scientist Bolt Beranek & Newman, Inc., Cambridge, Mass., 1970-75; assoc. prof., dir. ultrasonics rsch. lab. Case Western Res. U. Sch. Medicine, Cleve., 1975-77; prof., chief med. imaging, dir. grad. studies, dept. radiol. scis. U. Calif., Irvine, 1977—. Cons. acoustics; pres. Computer Sci. Systems, 1978—; founding gen. ptnr. Of Food and Wine, 1982—, Meditherm Assocs., Ltd., 1983-85, Spar Techs., 1987-90, Surgisonics Inc., 1991—, Dermasonics, Inc., 2002-; proposal reviewer NSF/NIH, 1974—; appointee sci. and tech. adv. com. Pres. Carter, 1977-81. Author: Acoustical Imaging, 1995, Acoustics and Society: Applications of Ultrasound in Medicine, 1972; co-author (with Z.H. Cho, M. Singh): Foundations of Medical Imaging, 1993; mem. editl. bd. Ultrasound in Medicine and Biology, 1976—; contbr. more than 300 articles to profl. jours. Active vol. local govt. Jr. fellow, U Tex., Austin, 1961—63. Fellow Am. Inst. Ultrasound in Medicine, IEEE, Acoustical Soc. Am., Am. Phys. Soc.; mem. AAAS, Am. Assn. Physicists in Medicine, Calif. Wine and Food Soc., Phi Beta Kappa. Democrat. Achievements include more than 50 patents in field. Home: 2094 San Remo Dr Laguna Beach CA 92651-2628 Office: U Calif Dept Radiol Sci Irvine CA 92697-5000 Office Phone: 949-824-6147. Business E-Mail: jpjones@uci.edu.

JONES, JOLENE REBECCA, medical transcriptionist, educator; b. Rush City, Minn., Nov. 2, 1947; d. Adrian Moses Sr. and Norma Mae Sauer; m. Gary Luverne Kerg, Aug. 6, 1966 (div. May 31, 1969); m. Orie Austin Jones, Aug. 29, 1999; children: Todd Michael Kerg, Marie Norma Jane Kerg-Frazier. BS in English, History, Ea. N. Mex U., 1999. Lic. Techg. N. Mex, 1999. Tchr. Clovis (N.Mex.) HS, 1999—2000; instr. English Ea. N.Mex U., Portales, N.Mex., 2000—02; med. transcriptionist Sparrow Family Med. Clinic, Portales, N.Mex., 2002—; owner Mo-Mac Enterprises Typing Svc., The Kitchen Table Baking and Candy Making. Author: A Christmas Collection, 1978, Simply Poetic, 1982, Expressions, 1993, True? Texas Tales, 1994, Hearts Entwined, Credit for an Angel: A Collection of Christmas Stories and Poems, 2004, Santa's Christmas Miracle, 1992; Winter in Minnesota (Third Pl., 1998). Mem. Ladies Aux. VFW, Isle, Minn., 1990—. Recipient Poet of Merit, Internat. Soc. of Poets, 2002—04, Am. Poetry Assn., 1987, 1989, 1990, Third Pl. poetry, El Portal, 1997, Cert. of Appreciation, Gov. Raul H. Castro, Ariz., 1976, Parker Women's Civic Club, Ariz., 1976, Outstanding Acheivement in English Undergrad. Studies, Outstanding Acheivement in History and Social Studies. Mem.: Portales C. of C. (assoc.), VFW Ladies Aux., Parker Women's Civic Club (assoc.; arts chairperson 1976—77), Friends of the Libr. (assoc.), History Guild (assoc.; sec./treas. 1998—99), Phi Alpha Theta (assoc.; sec./treas. 1998—99), Blue Key Honor Frat. (life). Independent. Presbyterian. Avocations: writing, crocheting, jewelry making/design, cake decorating, sewing. Office Phone: 505-226-0177. Personal E-mail: jrmoses@wtrt.net.

JONES, JOSEPH LOUIS, retired manufacturing company executive; b. Farmville, Va., Feb. 27, 1923; s. Joseph Louis and Edna (Elcan) J.; m. Dorothy Jeanne Jennings, June 21, 1949; children: Joseph, Catherine, Carolyn. BA, Va. Poly Inst., 1947. With Armstrong World Industries, Lancaster, Pa., 1947-88, prodn. mgr., 1961-66, v.p. carpet ops., 1966-74, exec. v.p., dir., 1974-83, chmn., pres., chief exec. officer, 1983-88, bd. dirs. Bd. dirs. Carpenter Technology, Reading, Pa., Armstrong World Industries. Trustee Lancaster Gen. Hosp. Served to capt., inf. AUS, 1943-46. Decorated Bronze Star. Mem. Lancaster C. of C., NAM (dir.), The Club Pelican Bay (Naples, Fla.). Republican. Presbyterian (trustee). Club: Lancaster Country. Home (Summer): 618 Willow Valley Lakes Dr Willow Street PA 17584-9648 Home (Winter): 8420 Abbington Cir 331 Naples FL 34108

JONES, JOSEPH SEYMOUR, small business owner, poet; b. Gadsden, Ala., July 4, 1962; s. Jimmie and Sallie Carstarphen Jones. AS in Bus., Bishop State Jr. Coll., Mobile, Ala., 1983; BS in Bus., U. Mobile, 1986; MA in Tchg., Spring Hill Coll., 1994. Cert. elem. tchr. Ala. Dept. Edn. Acctg./engring. support staff U.S. Army Corps Engrs., Mobile, 1979—87; parts clk. Mobile County Pub. Schs., 1988—90, fuel specialist, 1990—94, cert. elem. tchr., 1994—98; owner, mng. founder Believe Enterprises, LLC, Mobile, 2001—. Author: A Poet's Poetic Expressions: Mustard Seeds, 2001, Lady! The World Forever Thanks You!, 1998, Lady! Le Monde à Jamais Vous Remercie!, 1999, numerous poems. Recipient Poet of Merit awards, Internat. Soc. Poets, Washington, 1998—2000. Avocations: restoring classic cars and antique homes, fishing, photography. Office: Believe Enterprises LLC PO Box 40216 Mobile AL 36640-0216

JONES, JUDITH MILLER, director; BA, George Washington U., 1965; student, Georgetown U., 1965—67; MA in Edn. Tech., Cath. U., 1969. With IBM, 1969—71; legis. asst. Sen. Winston L. Prouty Vt., 1971—72; spl. asst. Office Dep. Asst. Sec. Legis. Dept. Health, Edn. and Welfare, Washington, 1971—72; dir. Nat. Health Policy Forum The George Washington U., Washington, 1972—. Mem. Nat. Com. Vital and Health Stats., 1988—91, chmn., 1991—96; lectr. The George Washington U. Office: National Health Policy Forum 2131 K Street NW Ste 500 Washington DC 20037 Business E-Mail: jmjones@gwu.edu.

JONES, KAREN FITZGERALD, literature educator; d. Cole Younger and Dorothy R Fitzgerald; m. William Noyel Jones, June 15, 1974; 1 child, William Blake. AA, Emmanuel Coll., 1974; BA, Tift Coll., 1978; MA, Piedmont Coll., 2004. Tchr. Elbert County Mid. Sch., Elberton, Ga., 1978—93, Elbert County Comp. H.S., 1994—; tchr./adj. prof. Emmanuel Coll., Franklin Springs, Ga., 2005. Bldg. rep. PAGE, Elberton. Recipient Tchr. of the Yr., Elbert County Bd. Edn., 1999. Mem.: Nat. Coun. of Teachers of English, Profl. Assn. Ga. Educators. Republican. Pentecostal. Office: Elbert County Comprehensive HS 600 Abernathy Circle Elberton GA 30635

JONES, KATHERINE R., nursing educator; BSN, MS in Med.-Surgical Nursing, U. Mich.; PhD in Adminstrn. & Policy Analysis, Stanford U., 1983; post-doctoral studies in Healthcare Fin. & Quality, Johns Hopkins U. Asst./assoc. prof. Coll. Health Related Professions U. Fla., 1983—88, UCLA Sch. Nursing, 1988—91; assoc. prof. U. Mich. Sch. Nursing, 1991—98, dir. divsn. nursing & health care adminstrn.; prof. nursing U. Colo. Health Sciences Ctr., Denver, 1999—2003, sch. nursing faculty chair; prof. Yale Sch. Nursing, New Haven, 2003—, acting dean, 2004—, dir. Yale Program for the Advancement of Chronic Wound Care. Office: Yale U Sch Nursing PO Box 9740 100 Church St S New Haven CT 06536 Office Phone: 203-737-1791. Office Fax: 203-737-5034. Business E-Mail: katherine.jones@yale.edu.

JONES, KATHRYN CHERIE, pastor; b. Breckenridge, Tex., Nov. 26, 1955; d. Austin Thomas and Margaret May (Mohr) J. BA, U. Calif., San Diego, 1977; MDiv, Fuller Theol. Sem., 1982. Assoc. pastor La Jolla (Calif.) United Meth. Ch., 1982-84; pastor in charge Dominguez United Meth. Ch., Long Beach, Calif., 1984-88, San Marcos (Calif.) United Meth. Ch., 1988-90; dir. The Walk to Emmaus, Upper Rm. Ministries, Nashville, 1990-98, Resource Initiatives & Interpretation, Upper Rm. Ministries, Nashville, 1998—. Coord. chaplains Pacific Hosp., Long Beach, 1986-88. Bd. dirs. So. Calif. Walk to Emmaus Cmty., L.A., 1987-88, San Diego chpt., 1988-90; vol.

victim advicacy groups, including You Have the Power, Forever Group. Mem. Christian Assn. Psychol. Studies, Evangs. for Social Action. Democrat. Office: The Upper Room 1908 Grand Ave PO Box 340004 Nashville TN 37203-0004

JONES, KEITH ALDEN, lawyer; b. Tulsa, July 11, 1941; s. Leonard Virgil and Bernadine (Hutchison) J.; m. Renata Skuta, June 15, 1974; children: Emily Isobel, Alden Rivendale. BA, Harvard U., 1963, LLB, 1966. Bar: Mass. 1966, D.C. 1978, U.S. Supreme Ct. 1972. Asst. prof. Boston U. Law Sch., 1966-67; lectr. Harvard U. Law Sch., 1967-68; assoc. Ropes & Gray, Boston, 1968-70; minority counsel U.S. Senate Select Com. on Small Bus., 1970-72; asst. to Solicitor Gen. of U.S., 1972-75; dep. solicitor gen., 1975-78; ptnr. Fulbright & Jaworski, Washington, 1978-94; of counsel Beck, Redden & Secrest, Houston, 1995—. Mem. ABA, Am. Law Inst.

JONES, KELSEY A., lawyer, educator; b. July 15, 1933; m. Virginia Bethel Ford; children: Cheryl Darlene Jones Campbell-Smith, Eric Andre, Claude Anthony; 1 child, Kelsey A. II. AB magna cum laude, Miss. Indsl. Coll., 1955, D.D., 1969; MDiv, Northwestern U., 1959; postgrad., U. Mich., 1960; cert. in clin. pastoral care and counselling, Wesley Med. Ctr., Wichita, Kans., 1967. Staff counselor State Prison So. Mich., Jackson, 1959—62; chmn. Kans. Bd. Probation and Parole, 1965—70; prof. social scis. U. D.C. (Van Ness Campus), Washington, 1972—77, chmn. dept. social/behavioral scis., 1977—78, prof. criminal justice, 1978—79, assoc. prof., 1978—82, chmn., 1979—91, prof., 1982—94, spl. asst. to pres. for environ. health, occupl. safety and instl. security, 1984—86, justice prof. emeritus, 2003—. Resident facilitator The Think Tank at Emeritus Manor, Takoma Park, Md.; vis. lectr. in Black history Fed City Coll. U. DC, Mt. Vernon, 1973—75; INTER/MET, dir. Bacc & Liason Consult, 1973—77; spkr., lectr. and presenter in field. Contbr. articles to profl. jours. Sec. KS/MO ann. conf. Vis. Chapel Meth. Pop Cook County Jail, 1962—70; apptd. staff Reception Diag Ctr. MI Correct Commn., 1961; del. Gen Conf. of Christ Meth. Episcopal Ch., 1966, Centennial Session Gen. Conf., 1970; bd. dirs. D.C. Corrections Found., Bros Inc; dean Leadership Edn. of 3d Episcopal Dist.; bd. trustee Washington Internat. Coll.; sec. NY/WA ann. conf. Vis. Chapel Meth. Pop Cook County Jail, 1956—58; first pres. Wichita Urban League, LEAP com. Desegration of Pub. Sch. Recipient Presdl. citation, Nat. Assn. Equal Opportunities in Higher Edn., 1979, Alumnus of Yr. Disting. Svc. award, Howard U., Washington, 1980, Disting. Svc. award, Lorton Student Govt. Assn. U. D.C., 1980, cert. for workshop on crime prevention for coll. and univ., Campus Crime Prevention Programs, 1985. Mem.: ASHE, Am. Soc. Pub. Adminstrn., Nat. Assn. Chief of Police, Am. Soc. Indsl. Security, Northeastern Assn. Criminal Justice Educators, Nat. Criminal Justice Assn., Inst. Criminal Justice Ethics, North Atlantic Conf. Criminal Justice Educators, Acad. Criminal Justice Scis., Alpha Phi Alpha, Phi Alpha. Achievements include development of curriculum at pre-coll., undergraduate and gradate levels; research in an environ. approach to environ. health; implications for accountability in crime, drug, public, and social policy. Office: Justice Prof Emeritus Resident Facilitator Think Tank at Emeritus Manor Takoma Park PO Box 60379-0379 Washington DC 20039-0379

JONES, KENNETH B., JR., surgeon; b. Shreveport, La., 1940; MD, Tulane U., 1966. Diplomate Am. Bd. Surgery. Intern Confederate Meml. Med. Ctr., Shreveport, 1966-67; resident in gen. surgery La. State U. and affiliated hosp., Shreveport, 1969-73; fellow in pediat. surgery Ala. Children's Hosp., 1973; chief of staff Christus Schumpert Med. Ctr., Shreveport, 1999-2001; clin. asst. prof. surgery La. State U. Med. Ctr., 1984—. Fellow: ACS; mem.: AMA, Internat. Fedn. Surgery Obesity, Surg. Assn. La., Am. Soc. Gen. Surgeons (nomination com. 2004), Am. Soc. Bariatric Surgery (chmn. surg. access com. 1997—2000, sec. treas. 1998—2000, pres. 2001—02, chmn. surg. access com. 2002—04), Southeastern Surg. Congress, Brazilian Soc. Bariatric Surgery (hon.). Office: 1801 Fairfield Ave Ste 408 Shreveport LA 71101-4468 Home: 950 McCormick St Shreveport LA 71104 Office Phone: 318-222-7584. Personal E-mail: pbsurgkj@aol.com.

JONES, KENNETH BRUCE, surgeon; b. Scottsville, Ky., Apr. 17, 1953; s. Kenneth C. and Betty (Miller) J.; m. Carol Jean Munger, June 28, 1980; children: Daniel, Christopher, Elizabeth. BS, U. Ky., 1974; MD, Vanderbilt U., Nashville, 1978. Diplomate Am. Bd. Surgery; cert. advanced trauma life saving. Surg. intern and resident U. Louisville Med. Sch., 1978-80; resident in surgery East Tenn. U. Med. Sch., Johnson City, 1980-82, chief resident, 1983; surgeon Claiborne Surg. Group, Tazewell, Tenn., 1983-84, N.E. Ark. Surg. Clinic, Jonesboro, Ark., 1984—; sec. med. staff Meth. Hosp., 1986-87, chief of surgery, 1988-90, vice chief of staff, 1989-91, chief of staff, 1992-94; chief of surgery St. Bernard's Regional Med. Ctr., 1996-97; mem. hosp. bd. Regional Med. Ctr. N.E., 1997. Asst. clin. prof. surgery U. Ark. Area Health Edn. Ctr., Jonesboro, 1985—; cancer liaison of ACS Commn. on Cancer to St. Bernard's, 1996—; alumni bd. Vanderbilt Med. Sch., 2005—. Contbr. articles to profl. jours. Active sch. bd., 1993-98; deacon So. Bapt. Ch. Justin Potter med. scholar, 1974-78. Fellow: ACS; mem.: NRA, Am. Soc. Bariatric Surgery, Soc. Am. Gastrointestinal Endoscopic Surgeons, Am. Soc. Gen. Surgery, Am. Cancer Soc. (pres. Craighead County unit 2000—01), Nat. Wild Turkey Fedn., Dove Sportsman Soc., Ducks Unltd., Phi Beta Kappa. Baptist. Avocations: hunting, sporting clays shooting, jogging, toy trains. Home: 2600 Nix Lake Dr Jonesboro AR 72404-0917 Office: NE Ark Surg Clinic 800 S Church St Ste 104 Jonesboro AR 72401-4154 Office Phone: 870-932-4875. E-mail: jonesfamily@cox-internet.com.

JONES, KENSINGER, advertising executive; b. St. Louis, Oct. 18, 1919; s. Walter C. and Anna (Kensinger) Jones; m. Alice May Guseman, Oct. 7, 1944; children: Jeffrey, Janice A. Jones Geary. Student, Washington U., St. Louis, 1938-39. TV writer, advt. agy. supr. Leo Burnett Co., 1952-57; exec. v.p., creative dir. Campbell-Ewald Co., Detroit, 1957-68; sr. v.p., creative dir. D.P. Brother & Co., Detroit, 1968-70; sr. v.p., exec. creative dir. Leo Burnett Co., Inc., Chgo., 1970-73; regional creative dir. Leo Burnett Pty. Ltd., Sydney, Australia, 1973-75, Leo Burnett, SE Asia, 1975-77; creative supr. Biggs/Gilmore, 1981-83; lectr. Mich. State U., 1982-95; emeritus, 1996. Vis. lectr., China, 1988, Taipei, Taiwan, Jakarta, Indonesia, 90, Dalhousie U., N.S., 1992. Author: Enter Singapore, 1974, Looking for the Best, 1994; author: (as R. N. Lake) Not Guilty, Just Dead, 1999; co-author: Cable Advertising-New Ways to New Business, 1986, A Call From the Country, 1989, Love Poems of a Business Man, 1997, Case Histories in Co-operation, 1999; author: (radio series) Land We Live In, 1945—52; contbr. poems and articles to mags.; exhibitions include Detroit Hist. Mus., 2004, Represented in permanent collections Hartman Collection, Duke U. Bd. dirs. World Med. Relief, Inc., 1961—92, dir. emeritus, 1993; chmn. Barry County Planning and Zoning Commn., Pks. and Recreation Commn.; mem. comm. com. Nat. Coun. Boy Scouts Am., 1966—92; county grants coord. Barry County, 1977—78, mem. futuring steering com., 1988—; mem. Econ. Devel. Action Group, 1988—96; mem. dean's cmty. coun. arts Mich. State U., 1993—96, mem. coop. ext. adv. coun., 1993—95. With U.S. Army, 1940—44. Named Barry County Sr. Citizen of the Yr., 1999; recipient Silver Beaver award, Boy Scouts Am., Silver salute, Mich. State U., 1982, award, Freedoms Found., 1984, Positive Action for Tomorrow award, Barry County, 1995. Mem.: Adcraft Club Detroit, Circumnavigators Club, Players Club. Home: 425 Pritchardville Rd Hastings MI 49058-9328 *The opportunity to absorb, examine, synthesize and then utilize facts and experience is what makes creative endeavor fascinating. Somehow the individual mind finds new and meaningful relationships between previously unrelated data. An idea is born. It becomes an advertising campaign, a book or movie, a new product. Trying to find those new relationships makes life rewarding in so many ways. Dissatisfaction with the status quo is the prod toward all progress. Use your talents broadly. Not just to make a living, but to improve your life, your environment, your society. By doing so you'll improve your talents.*

JONES, KERRI-ANN, director scientific organization; AB, Barnard Coll., 1975; MA in Molecular Biophysics and Biochem., Yale U., 1981, PhD in Molecular Biophysics and Biochem., 1985. Fellow AAAS, 1985-96; indep. cons., 1986-89; program officer NIH Fogarty Internat. Ctr. Internat. Health, 1989-92; staff NSF Tchr. Enhancement program, 1982-89; from science officer to chief coordn. U.S. AID, 1989-95; dep. to assoc. dir. Nat. Sec. and Internat. Affairs, 1995-96; assoc. dir. Internat. Sec. and Internat. Afffairs, 1996-98, acting dir., 1998; analyst White House Off. Science and Tech. Pol., 1995—. Contbr. articles to profl. jours.; presenter in field. Vol. My Sister's Place, 1989-92 (bd. dirs. 1991-92). Mem. AAAS, Coun. For. Rels. Office: Apt 611 2032 Belmont Rd NW Washington DC 20009-5443

JONES, KRISTEN GAE, chemistry educator; b. Lemmon, S.D., May 13, 1959; d. Jack Martin and Barbara Harriet (Olson) Wanstedt; m. Bruce G. Henry, May 22, 1982 (div. Aug. 1995); children: Karissa, Kelli; m. Samuel J. Jones, June 14, 1997; 1 child, Samuel. BS, S.D. State U., 1980; MS, Tex. A&M U., 1982. Chemistry tchr. A&M Consol. H.S., College Station, Tex., 1985—. Cons. in advanced placement chemistry, 1992—. Contbr. articles to profl. jours. Recipient S.W. Regional award in H.S. Chemistry Tchg., Am. Chem. Soc., 1993, AP award S.W. Region Coll. Bd., 1995. Mem. Sci. Tchr.'s Assn. of Tex., Assn. Chemistry Tchrs. of Tex. Lutheran. Avocations: reading, science, children. Home: 2905 Colton Pl College Station TX 77845-7719 Office: A&M Consol HS 1801 Harvey Mitchell Pkwy S College Station TX 77840-5146

JONES, KRISTIE KAYE, mathematics educator; b. Dallas, June 18, 1973; d. Harold Gene Jones and Dorothy Kaye McCoy. BS cum laude in Math., U. Tex., 1995; MS in Human Devel., U. N.Tex., 2001; postgrad., U. Md., 2001—. Cert. secondary math. Tex. Dance tchr. Kid's Dance Co., Plano, Tex., 1990—95; math. specialist Project SEED, Dallas, 1996—2000; math tchr. Highland Pk. (Tex.) H.S., 2000—01; instr. U. Md., College Pk., 2003—04, rsch. asst., 2002—. Profl. devel. Arlington (Va.) Pub. Sch., 2004. Ad hoc reviewer: Contemporary Ednl. Psychology, 2004. Fellow, U. Md., 2001—03; scholar, Richardson's Women's Club, 1991—95, S.W. Bell, 1992—95. Mem.: APA, Am. Ednl. Rsch. Assn., Nat. Coun. Tchrs. Math., Phi Kappa Phi.

JONES, KRISTIN ANDREA, artist; b. Washington, Aug. 1, 1956; d. Frank W. and Arlene (Swift) Jones; m. Andrew Ginzel, June 14, 1986. Student, St. Martins Sch. Art, London, 1978-79; BFA, R.I. Sch. Design, 1979; MFA, Yale U., 1983. Artistic cons. Hudson River Park Conservancy, N.Y.C., 1997. Executed art works for Oreg. Conv. Ctr., Portland, 1990, Battery Park City, N.Y.C., 1992, Pa. Conv. Ctr., 1994, Olympic Arts Festival, Atlanta, 1996, MTA, N.Y.C., 1999, Metronome Union Sq. S., N.Y.C., 1999, Tevereterno, 2002—, Kansas City Internat. Airport, 2004. Recipient Pollack-Krasner Found. award, 1994, Louis Comfort Tiffany Found. award, 1991; Visual Arts fellow Nat. Endowment for the Arts, 1986, 94; Fulbright fellow, 1983-84, 2001-02; Am. Acad. in Rome fellow, 1994-95. Home: 289 Bleecker St New York NY 10014-4106 E-mail: kristin@jonesginzel.com.

JONES, L. Q. See MCQUEEN, JUSTICE

JONES, LAUREN EVANS, lawyer; b. Lawrence, Kans., Jan. 10, 1952; s. Kevin Rice and Marcia Jo Ann (Peterson) J.; m. Vivien Craig Long, Mar. 26, 1978; children: Dylan Tyler, Hayden Blake, Carson Reed. BA in History, U. Mich., 1973; JD, Duke U., 1977. Bar: R.I. 1978, U.S. Dist. Ct. R.I. 1978, U.S. Ct. Appeals (1st cir.) 1985, U.S. Ct. Appeals (9th cir.) 1994, U.S. Supreme Ct. 1991. Assoc. Lovett, Morgera, Schefrin & Gallogly, Providence, R.I., 1979-83; ptnr. Jones & Aisenberg, Providence, 1983-89; owner Jones Assocs., Providence, 1990—. Mem. Jud. Performance Eval. Commn., 1993—; mem. R.I. Supreme Ct. Com. on Profl. and Civility, 1995-96. Editor R.I. Bar Jour., 1989-95, 2002-; contbr. articles to profl. jours. Nominee R.I. Supreme Ct., 1993, 95, 96, 97. Mem. R.I. Bar Assn. (exec. com. 1989-2000, 2002—, sec. 1995, v.p. 1996, pres. elect 1997, pres. 1998-99). Office: Jones Assocs 72 S Main St Providence RI 02903-2907 Office Phone: 401-274-4446. E-mail: ljones@appeallaw.com.

JONES, LAURIE LYNN, magazine editor; b. Kerrville, Tex., Sept. 2, 1947; d. Charles Clinton and Jean Laurie (Davidson) J.; m. C. Frederick Childs, June 26, 1976; children: Charles Newell (Clancy), Cyrus Trevor; 1 stepchild, Ariel Childs. BA, U. Tex., 1969. Asst. to dir. coll. admissions Columbia U., N.Y.C., 1969-70; asst. to dir. Office Alumni-Columbia U., N.Y.C., 1970-71; asst. advt. mgr. Book World, 1971-72, Washington Post-Chgo. Tribune, 1971-72; editl. asst. N.Y. Mag., N.Y.C., 1972-74, asst. editor, 1974, sr. editor, 1974-76, mng. editor, 1976-92, Vogue Mag., N.Y.C., 1992—. Mem. Am. Soc. Mag. Editors, Women in Coummunication, Advt. Women N.Y. Republican. Methodist. Home: 40 Great Jones St New York NY 10012-1109 Also: 62 Giles Hill Rd Redding Ridge CT 06876 Office: Vogue Magazine 4 Times Sq New York NY 10036-6561 Office Phone: 212-286-6910. Personal E-mail: Laurie_Jones@vogue.com.

JONES, LAWRENCE NEALE, retired dean, minister; b. Moundsville, W.Va., Apr. 24, 1921; s. Eugene Wayman and Rosa (Bruce) J.; m. Mary Ellen Cooley, Mar. 29, 1945 (dec. Aug. 2003); children: Mary Lynn, Rodney Bruce. B.Ed., W. Va. State Coll., 1942, LL.D., 1965; MA, U. Chgo., 1948; B.D., Oberlin Grad. Sch., 1956; PhD, Yale U., 1961; LL.D., Jewish Theol. Sem., 1971. Ordained to ministry United Ch. Christ, 1956; student Christian Movement Middle Atlantic Region, 1957-60; dean chapel Fisk U., 1960-65; dean students Union Theol. Sem., N.Y.C., 1965-71; prof. Union Theol. Sem. (Afro-Am. ch. history), 1970; dean Union Theol. Sem., 1971-74, acting pres., 1970; dean Sch. Div. Howard U., Washington, 1975-91, ret., 1991. Pres. Civil Rights Coordinating Council, Nashville, 1963-64 Bd. dirs. Sheltering Arms and Children's Svc., 1970-75, Inst. Social and Religious Studies Jewish Sem., United Ch. Bd. for World Ministries, 1969-75; bd. dirs., sec. exec. com. Assn. Theol. Schs., U.S. and Can.; chmn. exec. com. Fund for Theol. Edn., 1978—. With AUS, 1943-46, 47-53. Rockefeller Doctoral grantee; Lucy Monroe scholar; Rosenwald scholar; Am. Assn. Theol. Schs. Study grantee. Mem. Am. Ch. History Soc., Am. Acad. Religion, Soc. Study Black Religion (pres. 1973-75), Nat. Com. Black Churchmen.

JONES, LAWRENCE TUNNICLIFFE, lawyer; b. Mineola, N.Y., Jan. 20, 1950; s. Carroll Hudson Tunnicliffe and Florence Virginia (Greene) J. BA, U. Va., 1972; JD, U. Richmond, 1975. Bar: Va. 1975, D.C. 1976, N.Y. 1976, U.S. Dist. Ct. (ea. and so. dist.) N.Y. 1976, U.S. Supreme Ct. 1986. Bus. mgr. law review U. Richmond, Va., 1974-75; ptnr. Carroll Hudson Tunnicliffe Jones and Lawrence Tunnicliffe Jones Attys. at law, Mineola, 1976-91; owner, 1992—. Trustee Nassau County Hist. Soc., 1976—, pres., 1983-89; bd. dirs. Friends of Hist. St. George's Ch., Hempstead, N.Y., 1982—, v.p., 1990-92, pres., 1992-94; bd. dirs. St. Mary's Devel. Fund, Garden City, N.Y., 1983-89, pres., 1987-89; pres. coun. Cathedral Sch. St. Paul Alumni Fund, Inc., Garden City, 1984—; bd. govs. Cathedral Sch. St. Mary, Garden City, 1983-86. Recipient Mineola Bus. Person of Yr. award, 2000. Mem. ABA, Nat. Acad. Elder Law Attys., Va. State Bar Assn., N.Y. State Bar Assn., Nassau County Bar Assn., Nassau County Tax and Estate Planning Coun., Univ. Club (N.Y.C.), Univ. Club (L.I., pres. 1986-87, 93-94, bd. dirs. 1983-86, 89—), Mineola C. of C. (dir. 1993—), Garden City Golf Club, Mineola-Garden City Rotary (dir. 1991-94), Garden City Fellowship (pres. 1993-94, dir. 1994—), Cathedral Club (Garden City) (pres. 1993-95), Garden City C. of C. Episcopalian. Avocation: historic building preservation. Home: 158 Cathedral Ave Hempstead NY 11550-1140 Office: Jones & Jones 1000 Franklin Ave Ste 302 Garden City NY 11530-2910

JONES, LAWRENCE WILLIAM, retired physicist; b. Evanston, Ill., Nov. 16, 1925; s. Charles Herbert and Fern (Storm) J.; m. Ruth Reavley Drummond, June 24, 1950; children: Douglas Warren, Carol Anne, Ellen Louise. BS, Northwestern U., 1948, MS, 1949; PhD, U. Calif. at Berkeley, 1952. Research asst. U. Calif. Radiation Lab., Berkeley, 1950-52; mem. faculty U. Mich., Ann Arbor, 1952—, prof. physics, 1963-98, chmn. dept. physics, 1982-87, prof. emeritus, 1998—. Physicist Midwestern U. Rsch. Assn., 1956-57; vis. physicist Lawrence Radiation Lab., Berkeley, 1959—, cons., 1964-66; vis. scientist CERN, Geneva, Switzerland, 1961-62, 65, 85—, assoc., 1988—; vis. physicist Brookhaven Nat. Lab., Upton, N.Y., 1963—, Fermi Nat. Accelerator Lab., Batavia, Ill., 1971—; vis. prof. Tata Inst. Fundamental Rsch., Bombay, India, 1979, U. Sydney Australia, 1991; elem. particle physics panel of physics survey com. NRC, 1984; cons. ctrl. design group Superconducting Super Collider Nat. Lab., 1985-87, vis. physicist, 1991-94; cons. NASA, 1974-81, 2002; trustee Univs. Rsch. Assn., 1982-87; disting. vis. scholar U. Adelaide, 1991; vis. scientist U. Auckland, 1991; co-chmn. sci. adv. com. Mich. Environ. Coun., 2000—; mem. internat. adv. com. Bolivian Obs. of Mt. Chacaltaya, 2001—. Mem. adv. panel for Cosmic Rays Jour. of Physics G., 1991-95. Guggenheim fellow, 1965; Sci. Rsch. Coun. fellow, 1977. Fellow Am. Phys. Soc. Home: 2666 Parkridge Dr Ann Arbor MI 48103-1731 Office: U Mich Dept Physics Ann Arbor MI 48109-1120 Business E-Mail: lwjones@umich.edu.

JONES, LAWRENCE WORTH, poet, editor, performance art producer, songwriter; b. Norman, Okla., Jan. 5, 1950; s. Walter Neil and Jane Elizabeth (McCauley) J. BA in English, CUNY, 1991, MFA in creative writing, 2005. Supr. Fidelity Svc. Co., Boston, 1978-83; compliance dir. Alliance Fund Svcs., N.Y.C., 1985-88; dir. Cafe Nico, artists, writers, photographers collective, N.Y.C., 1991-2000. Advisor ABC No Rio, N.Y.C., 1991—. Author: We Become a Picnic, 1994; contbr. poetry to Downtown Poets, 1999, CUNY Arts, 2004. Coord. Gay Liberation Front, N.Y.C., 1970; plaintiff Gay Cmty. Alliance, Norman, Okla., 1972; campaign coord. Nader NYC '96, 1996. Recipient alumni scholarship, CUNY, 2002, tchg. fellowship, 2004—05. Mem. Poets and Writers, Poetry Project, Acad. Am. Poets (assoc.) Avocations: art history, watercolors, collage. Home: 994 Bushwick Ave Apt 4R Brooklyn NY 11221-3749 E-mail: ljones11221@yahoo.com.

JONES, LEE BENNETT, chemistry professor, educator, academic administrator; b. Memphis, Mar. 14, 1938; s. Harold S. and Martha B. J.; m. Vera Kramar, Feb. 8, 1964; children: David B., Michael B. BA magna cum laude, Wabash Coll, 1960; PhD, M.I.T., 1964; DSC (hon.), Wabash Coll., 1992. Faculty U. Ariz., Tucson, 1964-85, prof. chemistry, 1972-85, asst. head dept. chemistry, 1971-73, head dept., 1973-77, dean Grad. Coll., 1977-79, provost Grad. Studies and Health Scis., 1979-82, v.p. rsch., 1982-85; prof. chemistry, exec. v.p., provost U. Nebr., Lincoln, 1985—2002, exec. v.p., provost emeritus, 2002—. Chmn. bd. dirs. Coun. Grad. Schs., 1986; mem. Grad. Records Exam. Bd., 1986-91; mem. Midwest Higher Edn. Commn., 1995—. Mem. editl. bd. Jour. Chem. Edn, 1975-79; contbr. numreous articles to sci. jours. Mem. Nebr. R&D Authority, 1985—, Midwest Higher Edn. Commn.; vice chmn. Nebr. Ednl. Telecomm. Commn., 1987-88, 91-92. NSF fellow, 1961-63, 64— Mem. AAAS, AAUP, Am. Chem. Soc., Chem. Soc. (London), N.Y. Acad. Scis., Phi Beta Kappa. Home: 1611 Kingston Rd Lincoln NE 68506-1526 Office: U Nebr 106 Varner Hall 3835 Holdrege St Lincoln NE 68503-1435 E-mail: LBJones@nebraska.edu.

JONES, LEONADE DIANE, media publishing company executive; b. Bethesda, Md., Nov. 27, 1947; d. Leon Adger and Landonia Randolph Jones. BA with distinction, Simmons Coll., 1969; JD, MBA, Stanford U., 1973. Bar: Calif. 1973, DC 1979. Summer assoc. Davis Polk & Wardwell, NYC, 1972; securities analyst Capital Rsch. Co., LA, 1973-75; asst. treas. Washington Post Co., 1975-79, 86-87, treas., 1987-96; dir. fin. svcs. Post-Newsweek Stas., Inc., Washington, 1979-84, v.p. bus. affairs, 1984-86; ind. mgmt. cons., pvt. equity investor, 1997-99, 2001—; CFO, sec. VentureThink, LLC, 1999-2001; exec. v.p., CFO Versura, Inc., 2000-01. Ind. chmn., bd. dirs. Am. Balanced Fund, Inc., Income Fund Am., Inc., Fundamental Investors, Growth Fund Am., Inc., The New Economy Fund, Smallcap World Fund, Inc.; mem. investment mgmt. subcom. of benefit plans com. Am. Stores Co., 1992—99; mem. investment adv. com. NY State Tchrs. Retirement Sys., 1999—; mem. investment mgmt. subcom. Albertson's Inc., 1999—. Bd. dirs. The Women's Found., 2000—03. Named to D.C. Women's Hall of Fame, 1992; recipient Candace award for bus., 1992, Serwa award, 1993. Mem.: DC Bar Assn., Calif. Bar Assn., Nat. Bar Assn., Stanford U. Bus. Sch. Alumni Assn. (bd. dirs. 1986—88, pres. Washington-Balt. chpts. 1984—85). Personal E-mail: leonade@att.net.

JONES, LEWIS ARNOLD, JR., physician, radiologist, consultant; b. Detroit, Sept. 16, 1950; s. Lewis Arnold, Sr. and Berlene (Irish) J.; m. Pamela Denise Jennings, Nov. 14, 1992; children: Jennifer Tiffany, Alicia Dawn, Lewis Alexander. Student, Highland Park Coll., 1968-69, Wayne State U., 1969-72; MD, U. Mich., 1978. Diplomate Am. Bd. Radiology. Radiology residency Providence Hosp., Southfield, Mich., 1978-82; diagnostic radiologist Tri-County Radiology, P.C., West Bloomfield, Mich., 1983-84; clin. instr. of radiology Wayne State U. Sch. of Medicine, Detroit, 1984-91; clin. asst. prof. radiology, 1991-97; physician cons. Mich. Dept. Cmty. Health, Lansing, 1997-2000; radiologist Henry Ford Hosp., Detroit, 2000—02, Genesys Physicians Integrated Diagnostics, Burton, Mich., 2002—04; breast radiologist Karmanos Cancer Inst., Detroit, 2004—. Mem. cmty. adv. com. Karmanos Cancer Inst., Detroit, 1994-97; adv. bd. African Am. anti-platelet stroke prevention Wayne State U., 1996-97; co-investigator Women's Health Initiative, Detroit, 1996-97; co-chmn. 1997 Mich.'s Year of Women's Health, Mich. Dept. Cmty. Health, Lansing, 1997-98. Vol. spkr. Am. Cancer Soc., 1986—. Co-creator, co-presenter seminars Ptnrs. for Life, A women's health empowerment program, Mich., 1996—; bd. dirs. Oakland County Am. Cancer Soc., 1988—. Recipient Life Saver award Am. Cancer Soc., Southfield, Mich., 1990, Frederick Douglass award Nat. Assn. Negro Bus. and Profl. Women's Clubs, New Met. Detroit Club, 1996; winner "What a Man" contest, Essence Mag./ Preferred Stock Cologne, N.Y.C., 1995. Mem. AMA, Mich. State Med. Soc., Wayne County Med. Soc., Am. Coll. Radiology, Assn. Univ. Radiologists, Soc. Breast Imaging. Avocation: jazz and classical music collector. Home: 4951 Champlain Cir West Bloomfield MI 48323-3529

JONES, LIAL A., museum director; BA, U. Del., 1979; attended, Mus. Mgmt. Inst., U. Calif., Berkeley, 1996. Asst. dir. Del. Art Mus., Wilmington, 1979, dep. dir., CEO; dir. Crocker Art Mus., Sacramento, 1999—. Recipient Art Educator of Yr., Art Educators of Del., 1993, Paul Getty Trust Scholarship, 1996. Office: Crocker Art Mus 216 O St Sacramento CA 95814 E-mail: ljones@cityofsacramento.org.*

JONES, LINCOLN, III, army officer; b. Ft. Benning, Ga., Jan. 23, 1933; s. Lincoln and Doris G. (Baltz) J.; m. Alexandra Ann Archbald, June 21, 1958; children: Peter L., Patricia A. BS, U.S. Mil. Acad., 1958; MS, Auburn U., 1969. Commd. 2d lt. U.S. Army, 1958; advanced through grades to maj. gen.; brigade comdr. 9th Inf. Div., 1978-79, chief staff div. and Ft. Lewis, 1980, asst. div. comdr., 1980-82; dep. chief of staff LANDSOUTH, Verona, Italy, 1982-85; dep. comdg. gen. V Corps, Frankfurt, Germany, 1985-87; comdg. gen. USASETAF, Vicenza, Italy, 1987-90; pres., CEO ENRON Power Corp., Houston, 1991-93; pres. ENRON Engring. and Constrn. Co., Houston, 1994-96; vice chmn. ENRON Europe Ltd., London, 1996-98; pres. Lincoln Assocs. Inc., Houston, 1999—, Internat. Bus. and Energy Devel. Corp. for Pakistan; chmn. World Wide Strategic Ptnrs. Corp., Houston, 2003—, Internat. Spectrum Develop. Corp. Inc., Houston, 2005—. Exec. prof. U. Houston. Mem. Com. on Fgn. Rels., Houston; bd. dirs. World Coun. Fgn. Affairs; vice chmn. Nat. Def. U. Found. Decorated D.S.M. with oak leaf cluster, Def. Superior Svc. Medal, Legion of Merit with oak leaf cluster, D.F.C., Bronze Star for valor with oak leaf cluster, others. Mem. Assn. U.S. Army (vice-chmn.), Assn. Grads. U.S. Mil. Acad. Episcopalian. Home: 9 Fernglen Dr The Woodlands TX 77380-3957

JONES, LINDA, communications educator; BA in English, U. Mich., 1972; MS in Journalism with distinction, Northwestern U., 1985. Reporter The Chelsea (Mich.) Standard, 1973-75; county govt., police reporter The Marshall (Mich.) Evening Chronicle, 1975-77; edn. reporter The Bay City (Mich.) Times, 1977--79, asst. met. editor, 1979-81, met. editor, 1981-86; vis. asst. prof. dept. journalism Roosevelt U., 1986-88; asst. prof. Medill Sch. Journalism Northwestern U., 1988-92, dir. tchg. newspaper program, 1992—; assoc. prof. journalism Roosevelt U., Chgo., 1992—, dir. Sch. Comm., 1995—. Acting dir. Multicultural Journalism Ctr., Urban Journalism Ctr.; tchr. workshop sessions Journalism Edn. Assn./Nat. Scholastic Press Assn. convs., 1992-96, chair Multicultural Scholarship Com., 1996. Contbr. articles to profl. jours.; judge and lectr. in field. Office: Roosevelt Univ 505 E Ctr for Profl Advancement 430 S Michigan Ave Chicago IL 60605-1394 E-mail: ljones@roosevelt.edu.

JONES, LINDA MAY, tour guide, writer; b. El Dorado, Kans., Nov. 9, 1937; d. Forrest Edward and Edith May Carlson; m. William Stanley Conard, Sept. 1, 1957 (div. Nov. 1970); children: Chris Dale Conard, Carin Dene Conard, Curtis Dean Conard; m. Verl Ray Jones, Nov. 6, 1982. Student, U. Kans., 1955-57, U. Colo., 1970-71. Tour guide Queen City Tours, Denver, 1976-84, tour guide coord., 1977-84, Am. Travel Brokers, Denver, 1977-84; owner Columbine Tours, Denver, 1984-92; tour dir. Backyard Tours, Englewood, Colo., 1993—2002, Mountains and More Tour Co., Golden, Colo., 1993—, Colo. Conv. Assocs., 1998—. Mem. tourism adv. com. Metro Denver Conv. and Visitors Bur., 1990; seminar presenter; staff writer Colo. Gambler, 1994—. Co-author: Mile High Denver, A Guide to the Queen City, 1981, Up the Gulch-Historic Walking Tours of Black Hawk, Central City and Nevadaville, 2005; contbr. hist. articles to mags. V.p. Rep. Ctrl. Com., Gilpin County, Colo., 1983-93; v.p. Gilpin County Hist. Soc., Central City, Colo., v.p. 1988-90, pres., 1990—. Mem. Mt. Lookout DAR, Rotary, Alphi Phi. Methodist. Avocations: hiking, horseback riding, snowshoeing. Home: PO Box 615 Black Hawk CO 80422 E-mail: linda@fairburnmountain.com.

JONES, LINDA R. WOLF, company executive; b. Jersey City, Sept. 4, 1943; d. Eugene Leon and Lottie (Pinkowitz) Rubin; m. Frank Paul Jones, Oct. 21, 1973 (div. Nov. 1987); 1 child, Elisabeth Noel. AB, Bryn Mawr Coll., 1964; MA, Yale U., 1968; DSW, Yeshiva U., N.Y.C., 1985. Dir. planning and tng. N.Y.C. Dept. Employment, 1971-77; dir. legislation N.Y.C. Community Devel. Agy., 1977-78; supervisory legis. analyst N.Y.C. Human Resources Adminstrn., 1978; sr. policy analyst Community Svc. Soc. N.Y., 1978-85; dir. pub. policy YMCA Greater N.Y., 1985-89; dir. spl. projects Phoenix House, N.Y.C., 1990-92; dir. income security policy Community Svc. Soc., N.Y.C., 1992-94; exec. dir. Therapeutic Communities Am., Washington, 1994—2002; dir. internat. ops. Conwal divsn. Axiom Resource Mgmt., Falls Church, Va., 2002—. Adj. extension faculty Cornell U./NY State Sch. Indsl. and Labor Rels., NYC, 1975-80; dir. Nonprofit Coord. Com. NY, NYC, 1986-94, Govt. Affairs Profls., NYC, 1989-94. Author: Eveline M. Burns and the American Social Security System 1935-60, 1991; mem. editl. bd. New Eng. Jour. Human Svcs., 1981—; contbr. articles to profl. jours. Active Civic Affairs Forum, NYC, 1985-94; legis. task force NY State Gov.'s Office Vol. Svc., NYC, 1987-90. Mem. Women in Govt. Rels., Am. Pub. Welfare Assn. (dir. 1982), Bryn Mawr Club Westchester (bd. dirs., past pres. 1974-94), Bryn Mawr Club Washington. Home: 6621 7th Pl NW Washington DC 20012 Office: Conwal Divsn Axiom Resource Mgmt Inc Ste 703 5111 Leesburg Pike Falls Church VA 22041

JONES, LOUIS, JR., (BUCKY JONES), academic administrator; Dir. Fayetteville (Ark.) regional campus Webster U. Mem. Ark. Bar Assn. (pres. 1999—). Office: Webster U 3448 N College Ave Fayetteville AR 72703-5105

JONES, LUPE SIRENA, insurance agent; b. Pasadena, Calif., Jan. 12, 1970; d. Luis Prado and Antonia Diaz Ixta; m. Anthony Laschint Jones-Carroll, June 13, 1992 (div. Aug. 1999).

JONES, LYLE VINCENT, psychologist, educator; b. Grandview, Wash., Mar. 11, 1924; s. Vincent F. and Matilda M. (Abraham) Jones; m. Patricia Edison Powers, Dec. 17, 1949 (div. 1979); children: Christopher V., Susan E., Tad W. Student, Reed Coll., 1942—43; BS, U. Wash., 1947, MS, 1948; PhD, Stanford U., 1950. Nat. Research fellow, 1950—51; asst. prof. psychology U. Chgo., 1951—57; vis. assoc. prof. U. Tex., 1956—57; assoc. prof. U. N.C., 1957—60, prof., 1960—69, Alumni disting. prof., 1969—92, rsch. prof., 1992—, dir. L.L. Thurstone Psychometric Lab., 1957—74, 1979—92, vice chancellor, dean Grad. Sch., 1969—79. Pres. Assn. Grad. Schs., 1976—77; cons. in field. Author: Studies in Aphasia: An Approach to Testing, 1961, The Measurement and Prediction of Judgment and Choice, 1968, An Assessment of Research-Doctorate Programs in the United States, 5 vols., 1982, Indicators of Precollege Education in Science and Mathematics, 1985, The Nation's Report Card: Evolution and Perspectives, 2004; Psychometrika, 1956—61, mem. editl. com. for psychology Mc-Graw-Hill, 1965—77; contbr. articles to profl. jours. Mng. trustee J. McKeen Cattell Fund, 1974—. With Air Corps U.S. Army, 1943—46. Recipient Thomas Jefferson award, U. N.C., 1979; fellow, Ctr. Advanced Study in Behavioral Scis., 1964—65, 1982—83; grantee, NIH, 1957—63, NSF, 1960—63, 1971—74, 1982—84, 1993—97, NIMH, 1963—74, 1979—87. Fellow: AAAS, APA (pres. divsn. 1963—64), Am. Statis. Assn., Am. Psychol. Soc., Am. Acad. Arts and Scis.; mem.: Psychometric Soc. (pres. 1962—63), Inst. Medicine, Nat. Coun. Measurement Edn., Am. Ednl. Rsch. Assn. Home: 6578 US Highway 15 501 N Pittsboro NC 27312-7793 Office: U NC CB 3270 Davie Hl Chapel Hill NC 27599-0001 E-mail: lvjones@email.unc.edu.

JONES, M. DOUGLAS, JR., pediatrician, educator; b. San Antonio, Apr. 22, 1943; BA, Rice U., 1964; MD, U. Tex., 1968. Diplomate Am. Bd. Pediat. Intern U. Colo. Sch. Medicine, Denver, 1968-69, resident, 1969-71, fellow neonatal-perinatal medicine, 1973-75; pediatrician-in-chief Children's Hosp., U. Hosp., Denver; prof., chmn. pediatrics U. Colo. Sch. Medicine. Mem. Am. Bd. Pediat., Am. Acad. Pediat., Am. Pediat. Soc., Soc. for Pediat. Rsch. Office: Childrens Hosp 1056 E 19th Ave Denver CO 80218-1088

JONES, MALLORY See DANAHER, MALLORY

JONES, MARIE MILIE, lawyer; b. Greensburg, Pa., Jan. 27, 1963; d. Robert John and Josephine Mary (Cirucci) Milie; m. Cameron W. Jones. BA, Duquesne U., 1985, JD, 1987. Bar: Pa. 1987, U.S. Supreme Ct. 1991, W. Va. 1994. Assoc. Meyer, Darragh, Buckler, Bebenek & Eck, PLLC, Pitts., 1987-92, ptnr., 1992—, mng. atty., 1998—. Chair hearing com. Disciplinary Bd. of the Supreme Ct. of Pa. Mem. devel. com. Allegheny County Bar Found.; grad. Leadership Pitts. XVI, 2001; bd. dir. Duquesne U., 1997—2001, 2003—. Mem.: Federation of Defense and Corp. Coun., Pa. Def. Inst. (pres. 2002—03), Allegheny County Bar Assn., W.Va. Bar Assn., Pa. Bar Assn., Alumni Assn. Duquesne U. (pres. 1997—2001). Republican. Roman Catholic. Office: Meyer Darragh Buckler Bebenek & Eck PLLC US Steel Tower 600 Grant St STe 4850 Pittsburgh PA 15219 Office Phone: 412-553-7103. E-mail: mjones@mdbbe.com.

JONES, MARION, track and field athlete; b. L.A., Oct. 12, 1975; m. C.J. Hunter, 1998 (div. 2001); 1 child, Timothy Montgomery. Graduate, U. NC. Named Women's Athlete of the Yr., Track and Field News, 1997, 1998, 2000, Athlete of the Year, ESPN, Reuters, and the IAAF, 2000, Female Athlete of Yr., AP, 2000; recipient AP and USOC Female Athlete of the Yr., 2000, Jesse Owens award winner, 1997—98, 2002. Achievements include won 100m gold, World Championships, 1997; ranked #1 in the world at 100m & 200m by T&FN, 1997-2002; won 100m, 200m, World Cup, 1998; USA Outdoor 200m champ US title in the event, 1998-2001, 100m and long jump, 1997; undefeated in every competition until her last one of the year, 35 of 36 total, 1998; won Goodwill Games 100m, 1998, 2001, 200m, 1998; ran anchor on 4x200m USA team that set the world record (1:27.46) at USA vs. THE WORLD at the Penn Relays, 2000; ran anchor in gold medal winning 4x100m relay at Worlds, 2001; World 200m champion, 2001; 100m, 200m champion, USA, 2002; won World Cup 100m, which completed the first undefeated season of her career, 2002; won 3 gold medals for 100, 200, 4x100, Sydney Games, 2000. Office: c/o USA Track & Field 1 Rca Dome Ste 140 Indianapolis IN 46225-1023*

JONES, MARK A., music educator, musician; BS in Music, Dana Coll., 1976; MusM in Edn., VanderCook Coll. Music, 1994. Cert. std. tchr. Nebr., 1977. Organist Luther Meml. Luth. Ch., Omaha, 1975—87; dir. bands Ft. Calhoun Cmty. Schs., 1977—. Clinician Mid-Am. Music Enterprises, Lincoln, Nebr., 1985—; music adjudicator various orgns.; dir. music Luther Meml. Luth. Ch., 1984—86, Kountze Meml. Luth. Ch., 1993—94, organist, 2002—. Composer exercises for young band instruction. Recipient Disting. Svc. award, Ft. Calhoun Schs., 1998. Mem.: NEA, Nat. Band Assn., Nebr. State Bandmasters Assn., Nebr. State Edn. Assn., Ft. Calhoun Edn. Assn. (pres. 1982—83), Phi Beta Mu. Avocations: running, motorcycling, travel. Office: Fort Calhoun High Sch 1506 Lincoln St Fort Calhoun NE 68023 Office Phone: 402-468-5591. Office Fax: 402-468-5593.

JONES, MARK LOGAN, educational association executive, educator; b. Provo, Utah, Dec. 16, 1950; s. Edward Evans and Doris (Logan) J.; m. Catherine A. Bailey. BS, Ea. Mont. Coll., 1975; postgrad. in labor rels., Cornell U.; postgrad., SUNY, Buffalo. Narcotics detective Yellowstone County Sheriff's Dept., Billings, Mont., 1972-74; math tchr. Billings (Mont.) Pub. Schs., 1975-87; rep. Nat. Edn. Assn. of N.Y., Buffalo, Jamestown, 1987-91, Nat. Edn. Assn. Alaska, Anchorage, 1991—. Mem. Alaska Tchr. Licensure Task Force, Tchr. Edn. Adv. Coun., Adv. Com. on Tchr. Stds., Alaska Partnership Tchr. Enhancement; bd. mem. Alaska staff Devel. Network; mem. various coms. Alaska Dept. Edn. Photographs featured in 1991 N.Y. Art Rev. and Am. Artist. Committeeman Yellowstone Dem. Party, Billings, 1984-87; exec. com. Dem. Cen. Com., Billings, 1985-87; bd. dirs. Billings Community Ctr., 1975-87; concert chmn. Billings Community Concert Assn., 1980-87; bd. dirs. Chautauqua County Arts Coun.; bd. dirs. Big Brothers and Big Sisters Anchorage. With U.S. Army, 1970-72. Recipient Distinguished Svc. award, Billings Edn. Assn., 1985, Mont. Edn. Assn., 1987. Mem. ACLU, Billings Edn. Assn. (bd. dirs. 1980-82, negotiator 1981-87, pres. 1982-87), Mont. Edn. Assn. (bd. dirs. 1982-87), Ea. Mont. Coll. Tchr. Edn. Project, Accreditation Reviewer Team Mont. Office Pub. Edn., Big Sky Orchard, Masonic, Scottish Rite. Avocations: bonsai, photography, reading, classical and jazz music, hunting, fishing. Home: PO Box 102904 Anchorage AK 99510-2904 Office: 4100 Spenard Rd Anchorage AK 99510 Office Phone: 907-274-0536. E-mail: cabaileymljones@gci.net.

JONES, MARSHALL BUSH, education educator, researcher; b. Portchester, NY, Jan. 25, 1928; s. Donald and Muriel Marshall Jones; m. Beverly Ratner, Mar. 7, 1952; children: Donald Ratner, Susan Story Marshall. BA, Yale U., 1946—49; PhD, Univ. of Calif. at LA, 1950—53. Lt. j.g. (med. svc. corps) U.S. Naval Sch. of Aviation Medicine, Pensacola, Fla., 1953—55, rsch. psychologist, 1956—62; asst. prof. of psychiatry U. of Fla., 1962—68; assoc. prof. of behavioral sci. Penn State Coll. of Medicine, Hershey, Pa., 1968—72, prof. of behavioral sci., 1973—2003, prof. and chair of behavioral sci., 1979—. Chair, bd. of directors Keystone Human Services, Harrisburg, Pa., 1996—. Contbr. articles to profl. jours. Pres. ACLU of Fla., Gainesville, Fla., 1966—68; chair, bd. of directors Keystone Human Services, Harrisburg, Pa., 1996—2003. Lt. j.g. Navy Med. Svc. Corps, 1956—62, Pensacola, Fla. Recipient McLaughlin Vis. Prof., McMaster U., 1985. Mem.: AAAS (assoc.). D-Liberal. Achievements include development of isoperformance methodology; the theory of behavioral contagion; the risk-factor model of complex genetic diseases. Home: 41 West Caracas Ave Hershey PA 17033 Office: Penn State Coll of Medicine 500 University Dr Hershey PA 17033 E-mail: mbj1@psu.edu.

JONES, MARY EMMA B., psychologist; b. Izmir, Turkey, Nov. 10, 1944; came to U.S., 1946; d. Lawrence Hartwell Brown and Erma Marie (Carl) Macfie; m. Robin Dee Jones, Sept. 11, 1966; children: Darcy Marie, Samuel Evan. BA in English, Campbell U., 1967; MEd in Mid. Grades, North Ga. Coll., 1984; EdS in Sch. Counseling, U. Ga., 1990, PhD in Counseling Psychology, 1997. lic. psychologist, Ga. Tchr. high sch. Harnett County Schs., Lillington and Buies Creek, N.C., 1967-69; craftsperson (weaver) Jugtown Pottery, Seagrove, N.C., 1969-70; designer, weaver Wolf Pen Crafts, Young Harris, Ga., 1970-78; instr. weaving Campbell Folk Sch., Brasstown, N.C., 1977-78; tchr. Union County Mid. Sch., Blairsville, Ga., 1978-90; sch. counselor St. Joseph Sch., Athens, Ga., 1990-94; intern in counseling psychology Park Ctr., Ft. Wayne, Ind., 1994-95; therapist Laurelwood Mental Health/Substance Abuse divsn. Northeast Ga. Med. Ctr., Gainesville, 1995-97; dir. Laurelwood Partial Hospitalization Program, Blairsville, Ga., 1997-98; pvt. practice lic. psychologist Blairsville, 1998—. Active PTA, Harnett County, N.C., 1967-69, Union County, 1978-90; active St. Joseph Sch. PTA, Athens, 1990-94. Named STAR Tchr., Union County Schs., C. of C. and Bus. Coun. Ga., 1984. Mem. APA, Ga. Psychol. Assn. Avocations: camping, swimming, hiking, sketching, tennis. Home: PO Box 141 Young Harris GA 30582-0141 Office: PO Box 881 Blairsville GA 30514-0881 Office Phone: 706-745-2872.

JONES, MARY GARDINER, lawyer, educator, consumer products company executive; b. N.Y.C., Dec. 10, 1920; d. Charles Herbert and Anna Livingston (Short) Jones. BA, Wellesley Coll., 1943; JD, Yale U., 1948. Bar: N.Y. 1949. Intern tchr. George Sch., Newtown, Pa., 1943—44; rsch. analyst, rsch. and analysis br. Internat. Law sect. OSS, Washington, 1944—46; assoc. Donovan, Leisure, Newton and Irvine, N.Y.C., 1948—53, Webster, Sheffield, Fleischmann, Hitchcock & Chrystie, N.Y.C., 1961—64; trial atty. antitrust divsn. Dept. Justice, N.Y.C., 1953—61; commr. FTC, Washington, 1964—73; prof. Coll. Commerce and Bus. Adminstrn. and Coll. Law U. Ill., Urbana, 1973—75; v.p. for consumer affairs Western Union Telegraph Co., Washington, 1975—82; pres. Consumer Interest Rsch. Inst., Washington, 1983—2001; dir. MCA, Inc., Universal City, Calif. Mem. com. on sci. and tech. Fed. Coun. Sci. and Tech., non-trustee mem. rsch. and policy com.; mem. bd. Coun. Econ. Priorities, 1976—84, Inst. Future, 1977—; dir. Coun. Better Bus. Burs., 1982—; mem. Pres.'s Panel on Antitrust Laws, 1977—78. Bd. editors Jour. Consumer Affairs, editl. rev. bd. Jour. Consumer Interest; contbr. articles to profl. jours. Trustee Colgate U., 1966—80, Wellesley Coll., 1971—89; nat. adv. coun. Hampshire Coll. Mem.: AAUW (2d v.p. Washington br. 1968—69, adv. coun.), Yale Law Sch. Assn. (v.p. D.C. 1969—70, exec. com. 1971—76), Am. Arbitration Assn., Assn. Bar City of N.Y., Internat. Law Assn., Fed. Bar Assn. E-mail: mgjones@cgi.com.

JONES, MARY LAURA, developer, fundraiser; b. Mpls., 1946; d. William Ray and Emily H. Jones; children: Donald Aaron, Justin David, Mark Joseph Bushman. BA in English, U. S.C., 1968; MA in History, Northwestern U., 2004. Vol. U.S. Peace Corps, 1968—71; assoc. dir. Funding & Devel., Chgo., 1971-75, The Inst. of Cultural Affairs, Chgo.; dir. Cleve. Region, 1975-79, Pacific, Oceania Region, Apia, Western Samoa, 1979-83. Co-creator Cmty. Devel. Tng. Curriculum, 1984—85. Mem. bd. dirs. Uptown Cmty. Resource Ctr. Inst. Cult. Affairs, Chgo., 1986-04, Uptown C. of C., Uptown Cmty. Devel. Corp., UPCORP Econ. Devel. Corp.; mem. coun. Ebenezer Luth. Ch. Mem. Uptown C. of C. (bd. dirs.). Lutheran. Home and Office: Inst Cultural Affairs 4750 N Sheridan Rd Chicago IL 60640-5042 Office Phone: 773-769-6363 x 202. E-mail: mljones@ica-usa.org.

JONES, MARY M., landscape architect; Student, U. Tex., Austin, 1974—75; B of Landscape Arch. magna cum laude, Tex. A&M, 1979. Registered landscape arch., Mass., Calif., Tex., Ohio, Ariz., Mich., Minn. Arch. Johnson Johnson & Roy, Inc., Ann Arbor, Mich.; prin. Hargreave Assocs., 1983—. Mem. Mayor's Inst. on City Design, 2002, 03; mem. Sch. Arch. found. adv. coun. U. Tex., Austin, 2002; mem. dean's external adv. coun. Sch. Arch. Tex. A&M, 2001—02; co-chair Landscape Arch. CEO Roundtable, 2000—01; mem. landscape adv. coun. dept. landscape arch. and environ. planning U. Calif., Berkeley; mem. adv. bd. and publ. com. Designed Landscape Forum; mem. design rev. bd. Bay Conservation Devel. Commn.; lectr. in field; vis. critic landscape arch. Harvard Design Sch. Contbr. articles to profl. jours. and mags.; prin. works include Sydney Olympics Master Concept Design, U. Cin. Master Plan, Guadalupe River Pk., Byxbee Pk., Crissy Field, San Francisco. Mem.: Am. Soc. Landscape Artists (Honor award for excellence in the study of landscape arch. 1979), San Francisco Planning and Urban Rsch. Assn., Am. Acad. Rome (Prince Charitable Trusts fellow 1997—98). Office: Hargreaves Assocs 118 Magazine St Cambridge MA 02139 also: Hargreaves Associates 398 Kansas Street San Francisco CA 94103

JONES, MARY OLIVE, academic administrator; b. Pitts., Jan. 8, 1979; d. David A and Catherine M Jones. BA, Goucher Coll., Balt., 2000; MA, Columbia U., 2002; PhD, Capella U., Mpls., 2003—. Admissions' asst. Columbia Law Sch., N.Y.C., 2002; student svc. asst. Barnard Coll., N.Y.C., 2002; record's specialist U. of Mich., Ann Arbor, 2002—04; career ctr. coord. Ross Sch. of Bus., U. of Mich., Ann Arbor, Mich., 2004—. Ballroom/ ballet/ yoga instr. Dance Steps Studio, Ypsilanti, Mich., 2004—. Dance performance, Time (Am. Coll. Dance Festival, 1st Pl., 2002). Choreographer Whitmore Lake H.S., Whitmore Lake, Mich., 2004. Scholar Internat. Study Abroad scholar, Goucher Coll., 1999. Avocations: travel, teaching ballroom/ ballet, ice skating, reading.

JONES, MARYANNA THERESA, music educator, soprano; b. Hazleton, Pa., Aug. 7, 1952; m. Michael David Jones, Nov. 1, 1974; children: Shawn Michael, Christopher Aaron. Degree in liberal arts, Corning (N.Y.) C.C., 1971; BA, W.Va. Wesleyan Coll., 1974; cert. music tchr., Coe Coll., 1976; Med, Nat. Louis U., Evanston, Ill., 1990; elem. classroom cert., Hampton (Va.) U., 1994. Cert. tchr Ky. Music tchr. Urbana (Iowa) Schs., 1978—79, Walcott (Iowa) Schs., 1979—82; adult edn. educator Big Bend Coll., Germany, 1982—84; presch. tchr. Army Cmty. Svcs., Germany, 1982—84; music tchr. Zweibruecken (Germany) Am. Elem. Sch., 1984—87, Pirmasens (Germany) Am. Elem. Sch., 1987—95, Landstuhl (Germany) Am. Schs., 1995—98, Walker Intermediate Sch./Scott Mid. Sch., Fort Knox, Ky., 1998—. Named Tchr. Who Made A Difference, U. Ky., 2004, Ky. Col., 2005, Ky. Dist. Tchr. of Yr., Dept. of Def. Dependent's Schs., 2005; named one of Women Who Change Am., Nat. Women's History Month, 2005; recipient Excellence in Tchg. award, Campbellsville U., 2004, cert. of honor and recognition, Ky. Ho. Reps., 2005, citation/proclamation, 2005. Mem.: Music Educators Nat. Conf., Nat. PTSA/PTO (life), Alpha Kappa Delta. Avocations: travel, reading, writing, scrapbooks, singing. Home: PO Box 51 Elizabethtown KY 42702 Office: Scott Mid Sch 7474 Mississippi St Fort Knox KY 40121 Office Phone: 502-624-2236. Office Fax: 502-624-5433. Personal E-mail: mdmtjones2@cs.com. Business E-Mail: maryanna.jones@am.dodea.edu.

JONES, MAURICE D., lawyer; b. 1959; BS, Brigham Young U.; JD, U. Ill. Bar: 1988. Ptnr. Davis & Kuelthau, S.C.; legal counsel Banta Corp.; sec., gen. counsel Manitowoc Co., Manitowoc, Wis., 1999—2002, v.p., gen. counsel, sec., 2002—04, sr. v.p., gen. counsel, sec., 2004—. Office: Manitowoc Co Inc 2400 S 44th St Manitowoc WI 54221-0066 Office Phone: 920-684-4410. Office Fax: 920-683-8129.

JONES, MELBA KATHRYN, elementary school educator, librarian; b. Marshall, Ark., Mar. 13, 1924; d. Willie Claud and Bessie Kathryn (Mason) Holder; m. Rex Gene Jones, Aug. 9, 1947; children: Mickey Gene, Terry John, Cathryn Jayne. BA, Coll. Ozarks, 1972. Tchr. Everton (Ark.) Pub. Schs., 1942-47; libr. Valley Springs (Ark.) Pub. Schs., 1966-85. Mayor City of Everton, 1979-87, council woman, 1988-91; bd. govs. North Ark. Regional Med. Ctr., 1993—; mem. bd. Ark. Cattlemen's Assn., 1993; mem. city coun., Everton, Ark., 1996—; dir. Cmty. Ctr., 2004; chmn. adminstrn. bd. Meth. Ch., 1980-2003. Grantee, Ark. Indsl. Devel. Commn., 1985, Ark. Dept. Econ. Devel., 1999, 2000, 2003. Democrat. Methodist. Avocations: painting, reading, sewing, crafts, cooking. Home: PO Box 12 Everton AR 72633-0012

JONES, MICHAEL D., lawyer; BA summa cum laude, Dillard U., 1982; JD cum laude, Georgetown U., 1985. Bar: Ga. 1986, DC 1989. Law clk. Eleventh Cir. Ct. Appeals, 1985—86; ptnr., co-chair firm diversity com. Kirkland & Ellis LLP, Washington. Bd. dirs. Legal Aid Soc. Named One of Top 10 Trial Attys. in the Nation, Nat. Law Jour., 2001, 75 Best Lawyers in Washington, Washington Mag., 2002, America's Top Black Litigators, Black Enterprise, 2003; recipient Thurgood Marshall award. Achievements include author, "Lie-tery Winners" & "Old Assumptions Die Hard" in Nat. Law Journ. Office: Kirkland & Ellis LLP 655 Fifteenth St NW Washington DC 20005 Office Phone: 202-879-5294. Office Fax: 202-879-5200. E-mail: mjones@kirkland.com.

JONES, MICHAEL LYNN, financial consultant, branch operations manager; b. Tulsa, Okla., Aug. 24, 1967; s. Leonard A. and Loretta F. (Howard) J.; m. Renee D. Carter, Aug. 2, 1986; 1 child, Jonah Jacob. Student, U. Okla., 1985-88, Am. Coll., 1997-98. CFP, Internat. Bd. Cert. Fin. Planners. Retail mgr. The Finish Line, Broken Arrow, Okla., 1985-88; stockbroker Stuart James Co., Tulsa, 1988-89; rep. Am. Bank and Trust, Tulsa, 1989-91; fin. advisor Am. Express Fin. Advisors, Tulsa, 1991-97; fin. cons. PrimeVest Fin. Svcs., Tulsa, 1997-98, Wachovia Securities, Tulsa, 1998—. Mem. Young Dems., Tulsa, Promise Keepers, Tulsa; vol. Soc. for Prevention of Cruelty to Animals, Salvation Army, Boys Club, Broken Arrow, 1987-92; mem. Jr. C. of C., Tulsa. Mem. Internat. Assn. for Fin. Planning (regional chpt. v.p. 1995-99), Inst. of CFP, Okla. U. Alumni Assn., Tulsa Running Club, Green Country Classic Mustangs, Tulsa Optimist Club, Toastmasters Internat. Tulsa, Mensa, Forest Ridge Country Club, Jr. C. of C. Democrat. Avocations: reading, music, physical fitness, family activities. Home: 9226 S Maplewood Ave Tulsa OK 74137-4123 Office: s/b Wachovia Securities 6120 S Yale Ave Ste 1650 Tulsa OK 74136-4218

JONES, MICHAEL STUART, music educator; b. East Point, Ga., Aug. 9, 1964; s. Charles Kenneth and Sue Hinton Jones. B in Music Edn., U. S.C., 1986. Cert. tchr. S.C., 1987. Band dir. Johnsonville (S.C.) HS, 1987—91, West Florence HS, Florence, SC, 1991—. Mem.: Am. Sch. Band Dir.'s Assn., Internat. Assn. Jazz Educators, S.C. Music Educator's Assn., S.C. Band Dir.'s Assn. (region chmn. 1995—), Music Educator's Nat. Conf., Phi Beta Mu, Phi Mu Alpha Sinfonia (life), Kappa Kappa Psi (life). Office: West Florence High Sch 221 N Beltline Dr Florence SC 29501 Office Phone: 843-664-8473. Office Fax: 843-664-8475. E-mail: msjones@FSD1.org.

JONES, MICHELE ANN, accountant; b. Jamestown, N.Y., Apr. 17, 1970; d. Douglas Lowell and Sharon Elyse Tibbitts; m. David Carl Jones, June 1, 1991; child. Elyse Anna. AS, Jamestown (N.Y.) C.C., 1990; BS, SUNY, Fredonia, 1992. CPA-Inactive, Wash. Part-time clk. Country Woods Country Store, Jamestown, 1986-93; adminstrv. asst. Cummins Engine Co., Lakewood, N.Y., 1989-90; acct. Deluxe Storage Sys., Warren, Pa., 1993-94; gen. ledger act. MRC Bearings, Jamestown, 1994-96, cost acct., 1996—. Recipient Recognition for Leadership Ability and Achievements, Allen Park Womens Club, 1985; USA scholar Jamestown C.C., 1988-90. Mem. AICPA, Inst. Mgmt. Accts. (dir. pub. rels. 1996—). Avocations: swimming, gardening, antiquing, crafting, quilting. Home: 1740 Warren Jamestown Blvd Jamestown NY 14701-9209 Office: MCR Bearings 402 Chandler St Jamestown NY 14701-3802 Office Phone: 716-661-2696. Business E-Mail: michele.a.jones@skf.com.

JONES, MILTON BENNION, retired agronomist; b. Cedar City, Utah, Jan. 15, 1926; s. William Lunt and Claire (Bennion) Jones; m. Grace Elaine Guymon, Sept. 8, 1951; children: Milton B., Jr., Richard W., Jo Layne, Tamera, Sherilee, Karolyn. BS, Utah State U., 1951; PhD, Ohio State U., 1955. Successively jr. agronomist, asst. agronomist, assoc. agronomist, agronomist, lectr. emeritus U. Calif., Hopland, Davis, 1955—. Cons. IRI Rsch. Inst., Campinas, Brazil, 1963—65, CSIRO, Australia, 1974, BLM, Ukiah, Calif., 1970—77, Sulphur Inst., Washington, 1967—88, AID U., Evora, Portugal, 1984, Basque Govt., Bilbao, Spain, 1987, MAF, Invernay, New Zealand, 1990. Contbr. articles to profl. jours. Humanitarian mission, Scotland, 1991—93, 1997—2000; mem. sch. bd. Ukiah Elem. Sch. Dist., 1962—63; scout leader local chpt. Boy Scouts Am., Ukiah, 1962—70. With USN, 1944—47. Fellow: Soil Sci. Soc., Agronomy Soc. Office: U Calif 4070 University Rd Hopland CA 95449-9717 Home: 1501 East 1500 N Provo UT 84604 Personal E-mail: miltgrace@adelphia.net.

JONES, MILTON H., JR., bank executive; BS in Acctg., Notre Dame U. Sr. planning analyst Bank of Am., various positions, fin. group, 1977—90, exec. v.p., group mgr., fin. and adminstrn. of the Ga. bank, 1990—97, chmn., diversity adv. coun., mem., mgmt. opers. com., group exec., tech. & opers., tech. solutions exec., quality and productivity exec., consumer and comml. bank, quality and productivity exec., 2003—; fin. exec. NationsBanc Svcs., Greensboro, NC, 1994—97, pres., dealer fin. svc. group, 1997. Mem. Leadership Atlanta, Leadership Ga.; mem. exec. com. YMCA of Metro. Atlanta; mem. bd. trustees Meharry Med. Coll., Nashville; mem. exec. com. Metro. Atlanta C. of C. Recipient Career Achievement award, Nat. Assn. of

Black Accts., Corp. Trailblazer award, Dollars and Sense Mag., Best and Brightest award, Pioneer award, Atlanta Urban Banker's Assn. Office: Bank of Am Corp 100 N Tryon St Charlotte NC 28255

JONES, MILTON WAKEFIELD, publisher; b. Burbank, Calif., Apr. 18, 1930; s. Franklin M. and Lydia (Sinclair) J.; m. Rita Strong, May 4, 1959; 1 son, Franklin Wayne. AA, Santa Monica City Coll., 1950; BS, U. So. Calif., 1952. V.p. mktg. Sav-Ink Co., Newport Beach, Calif., 1956-58; account exec. KDES-Radio, Palm Springs, Calif., 1958-60; pres. Milton W. Jones Advt. & Pub. Rels. Agy., Palm Springs, 1960—, Desert Publs., Inc., Palm Springs, 1965—, Riverside Color Press, Inc., Palm Springs, Olman Travel Svc., Palm Springs, 1979-84. Pres. Franklin Comms. (Sta. KPSL-Radio), 1987-98, Airport Displays Ltd., 1972—; vice chmn. Palm Springs Savings Bank, 1981-96; bd. dirs., treas. Canyon Nat. Bank. Pub. Palm Springs Life Mag., 1965—, Wheeler Bus. Letter, Palm Springs, 1969-77, San Francisco mag., 1973-79, Guest Life, Orange County, N.Mex., Carmel/Monterey, St. Petersburg/Clearwater, Vancouver, Can., El Paso, Houston, 1978—, Orange County mag., 1987-89, McCallum Theatre Program, 1989—, Ofcl. Guide to Houston, 1993, El Paso Guest Life, 1993, Pebble Beach, The Magazine, 2002, Pub. Record newspaper, 1996, Official Guide to Ontario, 2001, Official Guide to Galveston Island, 2003. Mem. Desert Press Club (pres. 1965). Home: 422 N Farrell Dr Palm Springs CA 92262-6559 also: 206 Abalone Ave Newport Beach CA 92662-1304 Office: 303 N Indian Canyon Dr Palm Springs CA 92262-6015 E-mail: milt@palmspringslife.com.

JONES, MONICA LANEE', secondary school educator, writer; b. Detroit; d. Howard and Arene Jones. BA, Oakland U., 1992, EdM, 1999; postgrad., Howard U., 1992—93; MA, Ea. Mich. U., 2003. Educator Cass Tech. H.S., Detroit, 1998—. Author: Better Late Than Never, 2001. Mem.: Am. Counseling Assn., Alpha Kappa Alpha.

JONES, NICHOLAS P., civil engineering educator; b. New Zealand; BCE with honors, U. Auckland, New Zealand, 1980; MCE, Calif. Inst. Tech., 1981, PhD in civil engring., 1986. Engr. Edwards, Clendon & Partners, New Zealand, 1979—80; asst. prof. civil engring. Johns Hopkins U., Balt., 1986—91, assoc. prof., 1991—95, prof., 1995—2002, 2004—, chair dept. civil engring., 1999—2002, dean Whiting Sch. Engring., 2004—; prof., head dept. civil and environ. engring. U. Ill., Urbana-Champaign, 2002—04. Internat. editor Jour. Wind Engring. and Indsl. Aerodynamics. Named a Presdl. Young Investigator, NSF, 1989; named Young Engr. of Yr., Md. Soc. Profl. Engineers, 1988; recipient George Owen Tchg. Award, Johns Hopkins U., 1987, Robert Pond Tchg. Award, 1991, Excellence in Teaching Award, Johns Hopkins U. Alumni Assn., 2001; Erskine Fellow, U. Canterbury, New Zealand, 1999. Mem.: Internat. Assn. Bridge Aerodynamics (founding exec. sec.), Earthquake Engring. Rsch. Inst., Am. Assn. Wind Engring., ASCE (nat. infrastructure policy com. 2000—03, dir. Md. sect. 1995-97, Walter Huber Civil Engring. Rsch. prize 1997), Sigma Xi, Tau Beta Pi. Office: The Johns Hopkins U Whiting Sch Engring 3400 N Charles St Baltimore MD 21218-2681 Business E-Mail: npjones@jhu.edu.

JONES, NORAH, vocalist, musician; b. N.Y.C., Mar. 30, 1979; d. Ravi Shankar and Sue Jones. Student, U. North Tex. With Blue Note Records, 2001—. Musician: (albums) First Sessions, 2001, Come Away With Me, 2002 (Grammy awards: Album of Yr., 2002, Record of the Yr., 2002, Best New Artist, 2002, Best Female Pop Vocal Performance, 2002, Best Pop Vocal Album, 2002), Feels Like Home, 2004 (Best Female Pop Vocal Performance for Sunrise song, 2005); musician: (with Ray Charles) Genius Loves Company, 2004 (Grammy award: Record of Yr. for Here We Go Again song with Ray Charles, 2005, Best Pop Collaboration with Vocal for Here We Go Again song with Ray Charles, 2005); musician: (recording) A Very Special Acoustic Christmas, Where We Live: Stand For What You Stand On, Remembering Patsy Cline, Just Because I'm a Woman (tribute to Dolly Parton), (soundtrack for film) Love Actually, 2003. Named Best Young Female Singer, VH1, 2002. Office: Macklam Feldman Mgmt Ste 200 1505 W 2d Ave Vancouver BC V6H 3Y4 Canada

JONES, OLIVER HASTINGS, consulting economist; b. Altoona, Pa., Dec. 9, 1922; s. Oliver Hastings and Mary (Herman) J.; m. Margaret Ann Vogel, July 4, 1942; children: Thomas, William, David, Robert, Richard. BA, St. Francis Coll., Loretto, Pa., 1948; MA, Pa. State U., 1949, PhD, 1961. Analyst, divsn. bank ops., bd. govs. Fed. Res. System, 1951-55; sr. economist, rsch. dept. Fed. Res. Bank, Cleve., 1955-59; assoc. rsch. economist, real estate rsch. program Grad. Sch. Bus. Adminstrn., U. Calif., L.A., 1959-61; economist Stanford Rsch. Inst., 1961-62; dir. rsch. Mortgage Bankers Assn. Am., 1962—68, exec. v.p., 1968—77; cons. economist Oliver Jones & Assocs., 1977—. Professorial lectr. Am. U., 1967— Author: (with Leo Grebler) The Secondary Mortgage Market, 1961, Financial Futures Market, 1983. Served with AUS, 1942-45. Mem. Am. Statis. Assn., Am. Econ. Assn., Am. Finance Assn., Nat. Assn. Bus. Economists, Conf. Bus. Economists, Lambda Alpha. (internat. pres. 1976-77) Clubs: Cosmos (Washington), Metropolitan (Washington). Home: 67 Greenfield Dr Carlisle PA 17013-7682

JONES, ORA MCCONNER, retired foundation administrator; b. Augusta, Ga., Jan. 2, 1929; d. Landirs and Mamie (Elderidge) Williams; m. Walter R. McConner, June 27, 1953 (div.); 1 child, Susan L.; m. Courtney P. Jones, Feb. 14, 1991. BA, Paine Coll., Augusta, 1949; MA, Boston U., 1951; EdD, Nova U., Ft. Lauderdale, Fla., 1982. Instr. Paine Coll., Augusta, 1951-55; tchr. Chgo. Pub. Schs., 1956-66, adminstr., 1966-79, asst. supt., 1979-89, supt. dist. 6, 1989-91; exec. dir. Branch County Comty. Found., Coldwater, Mich., 1991—. Pres., bd. trustees Paine Coll., 1996; mem. Profl. Women's Aux. Provident Hosp.; bd. dirs. Ryerson Libr. Found., Aquinas Emeritus Coll., YWCA, Clark Retirement Found. Danforth study grantee, 1955; recipient Image award League of Black Women, 1974, Silver Beaver award Boy Scouts Am., 1985; named Educator of Yr. Chgo. Black Sch. Educators, 1984; recipient Outstanding Educator's award Beatrice Coffee's, 1989. Mem. Am. Assn. Sch. Adminstrs., Nat. Alliance of Black Sch. Educators, Coun. for Exceptional Children, Altrusa Club, Beta Sigma Phi, Phi Delta Kappa, Alpha Gamma Psi. Episcopalian. Home: 4956 N Quail Crest Dr SE Grand Rapids MI 49546-7539 E-mail: JonesOraB@aol.com.

JONES, ORLO DOW, retired lawyer, retired pharmaceutical executive; b. Logan, Utah, June 10, 1938; s. Orlo Elijah and Joyce (Lewis) Jones; m. Ilarene Balls, July 9, 1958; children: Monica, Orlo Courtney. BS, Utah State U., 1960; LL.B., U. Calif., Berkeley, 1963. Bar: Calif. 1964. Atty. Carlson, Collins & Bold, Richmond, Calif., 1968-69, AT&T, San Francisco, 1969-71, Longs Drug Stores, Inc., Walnut Creek, Calif., 1971-76, sec., gen. counsel, 1976—, v.p., 1979-87, sr. v.p., 1987—. Lectr. comml. leases Continuing Edn. Bar U. Ext., U. Calif., Berkeley. Served to capt. JAGC U.S. Army, 1964—68. Republican. Mem. Lds Ch. Home: 156 Santiago Dr Danville CA 94526-1941

JONES, OSCAR CALVIN, minister, dean; b. San Antonio, Sept. 1, 1932; s. Oscar Sr. and Nonnie Lee (Cunningham) Jones Simpson; m. Peggy Ann Helm, June 12, 1977; children: Dennis Ray, Shawntelle Janora. BTh, Am. Sch. Divinity, 1968, ThM, 1971; PhD, Trinity Theol. Sem., 1981, DMin, 1982, postgrad., 1982—. Ordained to ministry Am. Bapt. Chs., 1957. Pastor, counselor St. John Bapt. Ch., Long Beach, Calif., 1965-69; exec. dir. M.A.T.E., Inc., L.A., 1969-71; area rep. ABC, N.Y.C., 1971-83; pastor, counselor Shiloh Bapt. Ch., Sacramento, 1983-85; pres. Guardalupe Coll., San Antonio, 1995-97; dean Am. Internat. Theol. Inst. & Sem., San Antonio, 1996—, acad. dean, 1998—; pastor Corinthian Bapt. Ch., Fairbanks, Ak., 1998; interim pastor New Union Missionary Bapt. ch., San Antonio, 1999, Martin Luther King Jr. Meml. Bapt. Ch., Renton, Wash., 2000—01; ret., 1995. Prof. Calif. State U., Sacramento, 1985; instr. golden age srs. Greater Corinth Bapt. Ch., San Antonio; we. rep. M&M benefit bd. Am. Bapt. Chs. U.S.A., N.Y.C., 1985-95; mem. supr. com. Am. Bapt. Credit Union, 1986-95; mem. We. Commn. on Ministry, Oakland, 1986-94. Author: The Preacher's Dilemma, 1978, The 10 Crowns of the Bible, 1974, The Psychological View-Point on Counseling The Black American, 1982, Motifs for Ministry, The Call to the Ministry. Mem. exec. com. Am. Bapt. Black Chs., Valley Forge, Pa., 1969-84; mem. exec. bd. Inter-Faith Svc. Bur., Sacramento, 1983-84; trustee Am. Bapt. Sem. West, Oakland, Calif., 1985—, Am. Bapt. Homes of West, pastoral clin. edn., fellow, 1982-84. Mem. Alpha Phi Alpha. Democrat. Office: New Union Missionary Bapt Ch 818 N Mittman San Antonio TX 78202-1507

JONES, PATRICIA L., lawyer; BA, U. Minn.; JD, William Mitchell Coll. Law. Sr. v.p., chief accounting officer, gen. counsel, sec. H.B. Fuller Co., 2000—. Office: HB Fuller Co 1200 Willow Lake Blvd PO Box 64683 Saint Paul MN 55164-0683 Office Phone: 651-236-5900.

JONES, PAUL TUDOR, II, investment executive; b. Memphis, 1954; m. Sonia Jones; 4 children. BA in Economics, U. Va., 1976. Acct. exec. Dunavant Commondity Co., Inc., N.Y.C., 1977; with E.F. Hutton and Co., Inc., N.Y.C., 1976-77, acct. exec., 1978-80, v.p., 1980-82; formed Tudor Investment Corp., N.Y.C., 1983—; founder, chmn. bd. Bellwether Ptnrs., Inc., N.Y.C., 1986. Chmn. NY Cotton Exchange (NYCE), 1992—95, bd. dirs., 1992—99, NY Bd. of Trade, 1992—99. Co-founder (with Jann Wenner) Robin Hood Found., 1988; bd. dirs. Everglads Found., Nat. Fish and Wildlife Found.; co-chair Save Our Everglades Campaign; sponsor I Have a Dream program, Bedford-Stuyvestant Sch.Sys., 1986—. Achievements include Instrumental in the creation of FINEX, the fin. futures div. of the NY Cotton Exchange, and the devel. of the US Dollar Index futures contract; designed and implemented the first ethnics training course that became standard for exchange membership on all future exchanges in the US in 1989; sponsored Bedford-Stuyvesant students in the I Have a Dream program by pledging to further the education of the students with fin. and other support. Over 100 students received a college education; organizer of the Madison Square Garden concert raising $33 million for victims of the September 11th attacks.

JONES, PETER D'ALROY, historian, writer, retired educator; b. Hull, England, June 9, 1931; arrived in U.S., 1959, naturalized, 1968; s. Alfred and Madge (Rutter) D'Alroy; m. Johanna Maria Hartinger, Feb. 20, 1987; 1 child, Heather Marie; children from previous marriage: Kathryn Beauchamp Fly Ebert, Barbara Collier Rosenberg. BA, Manchester (Eng.) U., 1952, MA, 1953; postgrad. rsch. in collective bargaining, Inst. Solvay U. Brussels, 1954; PhD, London U. Sch. Econ., 1963. Freelance editor, London, 1953-56; linguist RAF, 1956—57; lectr. U.S. history dept. Am. studies Manchester U., 1957-58; vis. asst. prof. econs. Tulane U., 1959-60; from asst. to full prof. Smith Coll., 1960-68; William R. Kenan Jr. prof. Am. instns. and values Trinity Coll., Hartford, 1980—81; prof. history U. Ill., Chgo., 1968-98, prof. emeritus, 1998—. Vis. prof. Columbia U., U. Mass., U. Hawaii, U. Düsseldorf, Fed. Republic Germany; Fulbright prof. U. Warsaw, Poland, UNAM, Mexico City, U. Salzburg, Austria; mem. com. examiners Grad. Record Exams. Ednl. Testing Svc., Princeton, N.J., 1966-70; mem. Am. studies com. Am. Coun. Learned Socs., 1973-75; lectr. cultural affairs U.S. Dept. State, Bur. Cultural Affairs and USIA, 1973-87; adv. to publs. Author: Economic History of U.S.A. Since 1783, 1956, 2nd edit., 1965, The Story of the Saw, 1961, America's Wealth, 1963, The Consumer Society, 1965, 2d edit., 1967, The Christian Socialist Revival, 1968, The Robber Barons Revisited, 1968, Robert Hunter's Poverty: Social Conscience in the Progressive Era, 1965, La Sociedad Consumidora, 1968, Since Columbus: Poverty and Pluralism in the History of the Americas, 1975, The U.S.A.: A History of Its People and Society, 2 vols., 1976, Henry George and British Socialism, 1991; co-editor: Biographical Dictionary of American Mayors, 1820-1980, 1981, Ethnic Chicago, 1981, rev. and enlarged edit., 1984, 4th edit., 1995; contbr. several entries to Ency. World Biography, 1988, 94; contbr. numerous articles and book revs. to profl. jours., popular newspapers. R.W. Emerson prize com Phi Beta Kappa, 1991—94. Mem. London Sch. Econs. Soc. (life). Personal E-mail: verdi1901@aol.com.

JONES, PHILIP HOWARD, broadcast journalist; b. Marion, Ind., Apr. 27, 1937; s. Thomas Howard and Charline (Shugart) J.; m. Paricia Ann Powell, June 4, 1961; children: Pamela Lynn, Paul Howard. BS in Arts and Scis., Ind. U., 1959. Dir. news Sta. WTHI-TV, Terre Haute, Ind., 1960-61; polit. corr. Sta. WCCO-TV, Mpls., 1961-69; White House corr. CBS News, Washington, 1974-76, Capitol Hill corr., 1977-89, nat. corr., 1989-90; corr. 48Hrs. Broadcast, 1990-95; Washington corr. CBS News, 1995—2001, Washington polit. corr., 1996—2001; contbg. corr. PBS Religion Ethics News Weekly, 2001—. Lectr. in field. With USAF, 1961—62. Recipient Internat. News award Radio-TV News Dirs. Assn., 1965, award for Vietnam war reporting, 1966, Emmy award for CBS Indochina air war coverage NATAS, 1971, (6) Emmy awards CBS News 48 Hours Broadcast Coverage, 1992. Home: 5105 Westport Rd Chevy Chase MD 20815-3713 Personal E-mail: phil.jones@verizon.net.

JONES, PHILIP KIRKPATRICK, JR., lawyer; b. Baton Rouge, June 26, 1949; s. Philip Kirkpatrick and Mary Jane (Kincade) J.; m. Serena Catherine Cockayne, Apr. 5, 1980; children: Veronica Cockayne, Nicola Kincade, Clare Kirkpatrick, Philip Carruth Elliot. BA in Govt., Dartmouth Coll., 1971; JD, La. State U., 1974; LLB, diploma in legal studies, Cambridge (U.K.) U., 1976. Bar: La. 1974, U.S. Dist. Ct. (ea. and we. dist.) La. 1980, U.S. Ct. Appeals (5th and 11th cirs.) 1981, U.S. Dist. Ct. (mid. dist.) La. 1987, U.S. Supreme Ct. 1992. Law clk. to John A. Dixon Jr. Supreme Ct. La., New Orleans, 1974-75; staff atty. Presdl. Clemency Bd., Washington, 1975; lectr. U. Singapore, 1977-79; from assoc. to ptnr. Liskow & Lewis, New Orleans, 1980—. 1st lt. USAF, 1975. Republican. Presbyterian. Office: Liskow & Lewis PC 50th Fl One Shell Square New Orleans LA 70139 Office Phone: 504-556-4132. E-mail: pkjones@liskow.com.

JONES, PHILIP NEWTON, internist, educator; b. Billings, Mont., May 27, 1924; s. Robert Newton and Edith (Woodbury) J.; m. Rebecca Ann Means, June 13, 1948; children: Robert Newton II, Rebecca Ann, Margaret Jane. Student, Stanford, 1942-43, U. Wis., 1944; MD, Washington U., St. Louis, 1948. Diplomate Am. Bd. Internal Medicine. Intern St. Luke's Hosp., Chgo., 1948-49, resident in internal medicine, 1949-51; rssch. fellow internal medicine Northwestern U., Chgo., 1953, clin. asst. medicine, 1954-57; practice medicine, specializing in internal medicine and hepatology Chgo., 1954-94; clin. asst. medicine U. Ill., Chgo., 1957-58, from clin. instr. to clin. assoc. prof. medicine, 1958-71; assoc. prof. medicine Rush Coll. Medicine Chgo., 1971-75, prof. medicine, 1975-94, prof. emeritus, 1994—. Sr. attending physician Presbyn.-St. Luke's Hosp., Chgo., 1954-94, treas. med. staff, 1960-62, mem. exec. com., med. staff, 1960-62, 72-77, sec. med. staff, 1972-73, pres. med. staff, 1973-75; mem. exec. bd. Rush-Presbyn.-St. Luke's Med. Ctr., Chgo., 1973-75, trustee, 1973-77. Contbr. articles to books and profl. jours. Mem. bd. edn., Kenilworth, Ill., 1962-68, pres., 1965; mem. Welfare Council Met., Chgo., 1965-66; bd. dirs. Presbyn. Home, Evanston, Ill., 1978-88, 93—. Served with AUS, 1943-46, to capt. USAF, 1951-53. Fellow Am. Coll. Physicians, Inst. Medicine Chgo.; mem. Am. Assn. Study Liver Disease, Chgo. Soc. Internal Medicine, Am. Fedn. Clin. Research, AMA, Ill. Med. Assn., Chgo. Med. Soc., Nu Sigma Nu. Republican. Congregationalist (pres. bd. trustees). Clubs: Comml. (Chgo.); Indian Hill. Home: 868 Pembridge Dr Lake Forest IL 60045-4200 Personal E-mail: pnjrmj1@yahoo.com.

JONES, PHILLIP JOHN, librarian; b. Inglewood, Calif., May 27, 1968; s. John Luther Jones and Shirley Ann Sharp. BA, Univ. Calif., Santa Barbara, 1990; MA, Univ. Calif., Irvine, 1991; MS, Univ. Ill., 1994. Reference libr. Baylor U., Wao, Tex., 1994—2003; head reference, assoc. libr. U. Ark., Fayetteville, 2003—. Contbr. articles pub. to profl. jour. Mem.: Resource and User Svcs. Assn., Assn. of Coll. and Rsch. Librs., ALA (life), Phi Beta Kappa. Roman Catholic. Avocation: travel. Home: 4406 W Cheyenne Dr Fayetteville AR 72704-5549 Office: Univ Ark Librs 365 N Ozark Ave Fayetteville AR 72701-4002 Office Phone: 479-575-3081.

JONES, PHYLLIS EDITH, nursing educator; b. Barrie, Ont., Can., Sept. 16, 1924; d. Colston Graham and Edith Luella (Shand) J. BScN, U. Toronto, 1950, MSc, 1969; DNSc (hon.), U. Turku, Finland, 1993. With Victorian Order Nurses, Toronto, 1950-53, asst. dir., 1959-63; supr. Vancouver Dept. Health, 1953-58; prof. nursing U. Toronto, 1963-89, dean Faculty Nursing, 1979-88, prof. emeritus, 1989—. Cons. WHO, 1985, 86 Contbr. articles to profl. jours. Can. Nurses Found. fellow, 1967-69; recipient grants Nat. Health Research and Devel.; recipient grants Ont. Ministry Health. Fellow Am. Public Health Assn.; mem. Coll. Nurses Ont., Registered Nurses Assn. Ont., Can. Public Health Assn., Can. Soc. Study Higher Edn., N.Am. Nursing Diagnosis Assn. (charter), ProNursing Finland (hon.). Home: RR 2 Owen Sound ON Canada N4K 5N4 Office Phone: 519-372-2517.

JONES, PHYLLIS GENE, judge; b. Fargo, N.D., May 29, 1923; d. Joseph C. and Rosina Belle (Pinkham) Bambusch; m. Dwight Bangs Jones, May 29, 1945 (dec.); children: Stephanie Martineau, Jacqueline Ridge, Kent Carroll; m. David D. Norman, Oct. 9, 1970 (dec.). BA, Macalester Coll., 1944; JD, William Mitchell Coll. Law, 1960. Bar: Minn. 1960. Wirephoto operator AP, St. Paul, 1943-45; reporter St. Paul Pioneer Press, 1945-46; asst. county atty. Ramsey County, St. Paul, 1960-71; gen. counsel Minn. Urban County Attys. Bd./Minn. County Attys. Coun., St. Paul, 1971-75; pvt. practice St. Paul, Cottage Grove, Minn., 1975-84; judge Minn. Dist Ct. 10th Jud. Dist., Anoka, 1984-93. Mem. Minn. Adv. Coun. to State Investment Bd., 1983-84; mem. Washington County Pers. Com., Stillwater, Minn., 1982-84. Supr. Grey Cloud Town Bd., Minn., 1971—75. Mem. ABA, Minn. State Bar Assn. (chmn. victimless crimes com. 1974-75, co-chair sr. lawyers com. 1997-99), Ramsey County Bar Assn. (exec. com. 1982-83), Washington County Hist. Soc. (dir. 2000—). Achievements include distinction of being the first full-time female prosecutor in Minnesota.

JONES, PIRKLE, photographer, educator; b. Shreveport, La., Jan. 2, 1914; s. Alfred Charles and Wilie (Tilton) J.; m. Ruth-Marion Baruch, Jan. 15, 1949 (dec. Oct. 1997). Grad., Calif. Sch. Fine Arts, 1949; PhD in Fine Arts (hon.), San Francisco Art Inst, 2003. Profl. free-lance photographer, 1949—; asst. to Ansel Adams, 1949—53; faculty Calif. Sch. Fine Arts, 1953-58, San Francisco Art Inst., 1971-97. Tchr. Ansel Adams Workshops, Yosemite.; Mem. Archtl. Adv. Com., Mill Valley, Calif., 1963-67 Exhibited in leading art mus.; photographic archive established Spl. Collections Libr., U. Calif., Santa Cruz; author: Portfolio One, 1955, (with Dorothea Lange) Death of a Valley, 1960, Portfolio Two, 1968; (with Ruth-Marion Baruch) Black Panthers, 1968, 2002, The Vanguard, A Photographic Essay on the Black Panthers, 1970; author: Berryessa Valley, The Last Year, 1995, Pirkle Jones California Photographs, 2001. Nat. Endowment for Arts photography fellow, 1977; recipient award of honor for exceptional achievement in field of photography Arts Commn. of City and County of San Francisco, 1983 Home: 663 Lovell Ave Mill Valley CA 94941-1086 Office Phone: 415-383-0877. E-mail: pirkle@earthlink.net.

JONES, RANDAL R., lawyer; b. 1961; BBA magna cum laude, Pacific Lutheran Univ., 1983; JD with honors, Duke Univ., 1987. Bar: Wash. 1987. Atty., corp. fin. securities practice group Bogle & Gates PLLC, 1987—95, ptnr., corp. fin., securities practice group, 1995—99; co-chair, ptnr., corp. group Dorsey & Whitney LLP, Seattle, 1999—, mem. mgmt. com. Mem.: ABA, Wash. State Bar Assn., King Co. Bar Assn., Phi Delta Phi, Beta Gamma Sigma. Office: Dorsey & Whitney LLP Ste 3400 US Bank Ctr 1420 Fifth Ave Seattle WA 98101-4010 Office Phone: 206-903-8814. Office Fax: 206-903-8820. Business E-Mail: jones.randal@dorsey.com.

JONES, RAYFORD SCOTT, surgeon, educator; b. Dallas, Aug. 24, 1936; MD, U. Tex., Galveston, 1961. Diplomate Am. Bd. Surgery. Intern U. Tex., 1961-62; resident U. Pa. Hosp., Phila., 1962-67; mem. staff Duke U. and VA Hosp., Durham, N.C.; then prof. surgery Duke U., U. Va., Charlottesville; now dir. divsn. rsch. of optimal patient care Am. Coll. Surgeons, Chgo. Mem. ACS, Am. Surg. Assn., Soc. Clin. Surgery, So. Surg. Assn., Soc. Univ. Surgeons. Office: Am Coll Surgeons 633 N Saint Clair St Chicago IL 60611-3211

JONES, RAYMOND EDWARD, JR., brewing executive; b. New Bern, N.C., Jan. 27, 1927; s. Raymond Edward and Ellen LaVerne (Mallard) J.; children: Leslie Anne, Raymond Edward III. BS, U. Md., 1953; LL.B., U. Balt., 1962. Bar: Md. 1962. Office mgr. Hopkins Furniture Co., Annapolis, Md., 1953-55; sr. v.p. legal, sec. Nat. Brewing Co., Balt., 1956-75; (merged with Carling Brewing Co. 1975); sr. v.p. legal and indsl. relations, dir. Carling Nat. Breweries, Inc., 1975-78; sec., assoc. gen. counsel Miller Brewing Co., 1978-84, v.p., gen. counsel, sec., 1984-89. House counsel and/or officer Divex, Inc., Laco Products, Inc., Laco Corp., C.W. Abbott, Inc., Pompeian, Inc., Interhost Corp., Solarine Co., Balt. Baseball Club, Inc., 1967-75 Bd. dirs. Soc. Preservation Md. Antiquities, 1969-71. Served with USNR, 1942-45. Mem. ABA, Md. Bar Assn., Balt. Bar Assn., Sigma Chi, Sigma Delta Chi. Presbyterian. Home: 24848 Deepwater Point Dr Saint Michaels MD 21663-2324

JONES, RAYMOND MOYLAN, strategy and public policy educator; b. Phila., Dec. 28, 1942; s. Raymond and Elizabeth (Shaw) J.; m. Barbara Ann Donaghue, May 22, 1965; children: Andrea Marie, Audra Marie. BS, U.S. Mil. Acad., 1964; MBA, Harvard U., 1971; JD, U. Tex., 1973; PhD, U. Md., 1993. Bar: Tex. 1973, U.S. Supreme Ct. 1993. Commd. 2d lt. U.S. Army, 1964, advanced through grades to capt., 1966, ret., 1969; legal asst. to chmn. Occidental Petroleum Corp., L.A., 1973-75; pres. Oxy Metal Industries Internat., Geneva, 1975-77, Occidental Resource Recovery Corp., Irvine, Calif., 1978-81; v.p. Hooker Chem. Corp., Houston, 1977-78; pvt. practice cons. Austin and Irvine, 1981-86; lectr. Calif. State U., Long Beach, 1986, U. Md., College Park, 1986-90, Loyola Coll., Balt., 1990—. Cons. to multinational and domestic orgns. Author: Strategic Management in a Hostile Environment: Lessons from the Tobacco Industry, 1998; contbr. articles, book rev. to profl. publs. Mem. Friends of Austin Symphony Orch.; mem. Ludwig Von Mises Inst., Burlingame, Calif., 1987—, Intercoll. Studies Inst., Bryn Mawr, Pa., 1987—; mgmt. con. ARC, Balt., 1988—. Grantee U. Md. 1987, Loyola Coll. 1993. Mem. Am. Econ. Assn., Acad. Internat. Bus., Strategic Mgmt. Soc., Acad. Mgmt., State Bar Tex., Harvard Club. Roman Catholic. Home: 305 Kerneway Baltimore MD 21212-4714 Office: Loyola Coll Sellinger Sch Bus Mgmt Baltimore MD 21210-2699 Office Phone: 401-617-2377. E-mail: rjones@loyola.edu.

JONES, REBA (BECKI) PESTUN, elementary school educator, music educator; b. Logan, W.Va., Apr. 30, 1949; d. John Rohac and Carolyn Kelly Pestun; m. Edgar Roger Jones, Aug. 22, 1968; 1 child, Karaleah Sabina Reichart. MusB in Edn., W.Va. U., 1970; EdM in Music Edn., U. Md., 1986; DMA, Shenandoah U., 2003. Cert. postgrad. prof. in music edn. grades K-12 Va., 1986, tchr. Am. Orff Schulwerk Assn., 1986. Choir dir. Asbury United Meth. Ch., Charles Town, W.Va., 1976—86; music tchr. grades K-5 Columbia Elem. Sch. - Fairfax County Pub. Schs., Annandale, Va., 1986—2002; music tchr. grades K-6 Herndon (Va.) Elem. - Fairfax County Pub. Schs., 2002—. Musician (composer/educator): (creative musical unit) A Musical Physical Fitness Workout (Semi-Finalist for the Nat. Music Found., 2000), (creative music units for grades k-3) Rabbit on My Mind (Winner of Impact II Nat. Grant and Va. Commn. for the Arts Grant for Outstanding Achievement, 1999), (original musical for grades k-6) Coal Mining Musical (Impact II Nat. Award Winner, 2001), (original musical unit for grades k-3) Sea Turtle Rhapsody (Impact II Nat. Award Winner, 2002), (original music unit for grades k-6) A True Whale Story (Winner Outstanding Achievement from the Va. Commn. for the Arts, 1998), (original musical with appalachian songs) Journey From the Mountain to the Sky (Hon. Mention from Nat. Music Found., 1999), (original music teaching unit) Musical Manatees (Impact II Nat. Grant Award Winner, 2003), (musical teaching unit and performance) Forever Free (Wash. Post Grant in Edn. Winner, 1998); musician: The Bully Butterfly, 2004 (winner Va. Commn. of Arts Grant, 2004). Mem.: Music Educator's Nat. Conf., Appalachian Studies Assn., Am. Orff Schulwerk Assn., Fairfax Gen. Music Educators Assn., Fairfax Edn. Assn. Office: Herndon Elem Sch 630 Dranesville Rd Herndon VA 20170 Office Phone: 703-326-3162. Business E-Mail: becki.jones@fcps.edu.

JONES, RENEE MAUREEN, freelance/self-employed writer; b. N.Y.C., Jan. 31, 1962; d. Morris Donald Jones and Joan Loretta (Bennett) Murrell; 1 child, Eric Denzel. BA, Hunter Coll., 1985, MS in Edn., 1993. Cert. early childhood and elem. tchr., Ga., N.Y. Art tchr. Abyssinian Bapt. Ch., N.Y.C., 1985—97; tech. writer, 1997—. Author: Reading Strategies: A Guide for Parents and Caregivers, When I Was Young in Harlem. Mem. Schomburg Soc. for Rsch. in Black Culture. Office Phone: 678-860-4343. E-mail: readingstrategies@yahoo.com.

JONES, RICHARD HENRY, ambassador; b. Shreveport, La., Aug. 26, 1950; m. Joan Jones; 4 children. BS in Math., Harvey Mudd Coll., 1972; MS in Bus., U. Wis., 1976, PhD in Bus. and Stats., 1980. With U.S. Fgn. Svc., 1976—, petroleum attache, econ. advisor Riyadh, Saudi Arabia, 1984—86, counselor polit. affairs, 1989—92; dir., Office of Developed Country Trade, Bur. Econ. & Bus. Affairs US Dept. State, Washington, 1987—89, dir. office Egyptian affairs, 1993—95, U.S. amb. to Lebanon Beirut, 1996—98, U.S. amb. to Kazakhstan Almaty, 1998—2001, U.S. amb. to Kuwait Kuwait City, 2001—04; chief policy officer, dep. adminstr. Coalition Provisional Authority, Baghdad, Iraq, 2003—04; sr. adv. and policy coord. on Iraq, Office of Sec. of State US Dept. State, Washington, 2005—, U.S. amb. to Israel Tel Aviv, 2005—. Mem. U.S. mission Orgn. for Econ. Coop. and Devel., Paris, 1980—83. Office: US Embassy 9700 Tel Aviv Pl Washington DC 20521-9700*

JONES, RICHARD K., information technology executive; Student in Computer sci., Univ. of Waterloo, Ontario, Can. Sr. cons. ptnr. JNL EFT Cons. Inc.; pres. & CEO Bethany Computer Sys. Inc.; dir. computing and comm. & CTO Technicolor Inc.; joined Countrywide Financial Corp., Calabasas, Calif., 1995—, sr. v.p., infrastructure, IT divsn., exec. v.p. of enterprise arch., IT, sr. mng. dir. & chief info. officer. Office: Sr Mng Dir & CIO Countrywide Fin Corp 4500 Park Granada Calabasas CA 91302-1613

JONES, RICHARD LAMAR, entomology educator; b. Charleston, Miss., May 31, 1939; s. Raymond Lee and Tyna Louise (Holland) J.; m. Anne Marchman, June 6, 1964; children: Katherine Mathis, Margaret Holland; m. Joan Marie Wood, Nov. 29, 1997. BS, Miss. State U., 1963, MS, 1965; PhD, U. Calif., Riverside, 1968. Rsch. entomologist Agrl. Rsch. Svc., USDA, Tifton, Ga., 1968-77; assoc. prof. entomology U. Minn., St. Paul, 1977-84, prof., head dept., 1984-91, dean Coll. Agr., 1991-95; dean of rsch., dir. Fla. Agrl. Expt. Sta. U. Fla., Gainesville, Fla., 1995—. Editor, author: Semiochemicals, 1974; also over 70 articles. With USN, 1958-60. Scholar NIH, 1965-68, Fulbright scholar, Leiden, The Netherlands, 1980. Mem. AAAS, Entomol. Soc. Am. (fin. com. 1989-96), Am. Chem. Soc. Avocations: golf, fishing. Office: U Fla PO Box 110810 Gainesville FL 32611-0180

JONES, RICHARD MELVIN, bank executive, director, former retail executive; b. Eldon, Mo., Nov. 26, 1926; m. Sylvia A. Richardson, 1950; 3 children. BSBA, Olivet Nazarene Coll., 1950, LLD (hon.), 1983; grad. advanced mgmt. program, Harvard U., 1973. With Sears, Roebuck & Co., 1950-89, store mgr., 1963-68, gen. mgr. Washington and Balt., 1974, exec. v.p.-East, 1974-80, corp. v.p., 1980, vice-chmn., CFO, 1980-85, pres., CFO, 1986-88; chmn., CEO Guaranty Fed. Savs. Bank, Dallas, 1989-91. Trustee Field Mus. Natural History, Northwestern Univ. Assocs., Chgo.; adv. coun. J.L. Kellogg Grad. Sch. Mgmt. Northwestern U.

JONES, RICHARD MICHAEL, lawyer; b. Chgo., Jan. 16, 1952; s. Richard Anthony and Shirley Mae (Wilhelm) J.; m. Catherine Leona Ford, May 25, 1974. BS, U. Ill., 1974; JD, Harvard U., 1977. Bar: Colo. 1977, U.S. Dist. Ct. Colo. 1977. Assoc. Davis, Graham & Stubbs, Denver, 1977-81; corp. counsel Tosco Corp., Denver, 1981-82; asst. gen. counsel Anschutz Corp., Denver, 1982-88, gen. counsel, v.p., 1989—. Mem. ABA, Colo. Bar Assn., Denver Bar Assn. Office: Anschutz Corp 555 17th St Ste 2400 Denver CO 80202-3987

JONES, RICHARD WALLACE, interior designer; b. Canandaigua, N.Y., Dec. 6, 1929; s. William Wallace and Maybelle Louise (Smith) J.; m. Patricia Hardwick, June 24, 1957 (div. 1973). Student, Hobart Coll., 1946-47; tchr.'s cert., Longy Sch., Cambridge, Mass., 1952; postgrad., Yale U. Sch. Music, 1952-53. Owner, operator Richard W. Jones studios, Boston, Hartford, Conn., 1954-63; designer, mgr. House of Good Taste Pavilion, N.Y. World's Fair, 1963-66; design editor Redbook Mag., N.Y.C., 1967-72; sr. design editor Better Homes & Gardens mag., Des Moines, 1972-76; pres., dir. Circanow Interior Design Firm, Des Moines, N.Y.C., 1974-90; designer, mgr. D.H. Hershel Inc., Nantucket, Mass., 1978-81; ptnr., designer, buyer Portobello, Nantucket, 1981-83; dir. design Laura Ashley Inc., Ridgewood, N.J., 1989-90; interior designer Godfrey & Assocs., Naples, Fla., 1994-97; prin. Richard W. Jones Designs, Naples, Fla., 1997—. Curator Hammond Mus., Gloucester, Mass., 1950-60, Hill-Stead Mus., Farmington, Conn., 1962; del. Internat. Fedn. Interior Designers, Amsterdam, The Netherlands, 1975-76. Editor in chief Interiors mag., Residential Interiors, 1976-78. Mem. Pres.' Com. on Barrier Free Design, Washington, 1972-74. Recipient Dorothy Dawe award Sr. Design Editor, 1974. Fellow Am. Soc. Interior Designers (nat. pres. 1976. Disting. Svc. medal 1977); mem. Nat. Soc. Interior Designers (nat. pres. 1972-74), Nantucket C. of C. (bd. dirs. 1980-82, sign approval com. 1982-84). Presbyterian. Avocations: collecting contemporary and african art, travel. Home and Office: PO Box 1139 Naples FL 34106-1139

JONES, ROBERT ALFRED, retired clergyman; b. Buffalo, July 19, 1930; s. Ralph A. and Edna Mae (Carver) J.; m. Helen T. Webster, July 20, 1957; children: Marc E., Paul R., Nancy L. BA, Houghton Coll., 1953; MA, Alfred U., 1959. Ordained to ministry United Meth. Ch., 1959. Assoc. pastor University United Meth. Ch., Buffalo, 1959-63; campus min. SUNY, Buffalo, 1963-67; pastor Woodside United Meth. Ch., Buffalo, 1967-74; sr. pastor Baker Meml. United Meth. Ch., East Aurora, N.Y., 1974-80; supr. Rochester dist United Meth. Ch., 1980-86; sr. pastor Ctrl. Park United Meth. Ch., 1986-89; asst. to bishop N.Y. west area United Meth. Ch., Syracuse, 1989-91; sr. pastor Williamsville (N.Y.) United Meth. Ch., 1991—99. Home: 146 Farber Ln Williamsville NY 14221-5754

JONES, ROBERT ALONZO, economist; b. Evanston, Ill., Mar. 15, 1937; s. Robert Vernon and Elsie Pierce (Brown) J.; m. Ina Turner Jones; children: Lindsay Rae, Robert Pierce, Gregory Alan, William Kenneth. AB, Middlebury Coll., 1959, LLD, 1992; MBA, Northwestern U., 1961. Economist Hahn, Wise & Assocs., San Carlos, Calif., 1966-69; sr. rsch. officer Bank of Am., San Francisco, 1969-74; v.p., dir. fin. forecasting Chase Econometrics, San Francisco, 1974-76; chmn. bd. Money Market Svcs., Inc., Belmont, Calif., 1974-86, MMS Internat., Redwood City, Calif., 1986-89, chmn. emeritus, 1989-2000; chmn. bd. dirs. Market News Internat., N.Y.C.; chmn. emeritus Geonomics Inst., Middlebury, Vt., 1995—, chmn. bd., 1986-95, Jones Interant., 1990—, Digital Integrator, Inc., Incline Village, Nev., 1993—. Chmn. bd. Jones Fin. Network, Inc., Incline VIllage; dean coun. Harvard U. Div. Sch., Cambridge, Mass., 1991—; mem. Kellogg Alumni Adv. Bd., Northwestern U., 1993—; trustee Middlebury Coll., 1998—; instr. money and banking Am. Inst. Banking, San Francisco, 1971, 72. Author: U.S. Financial System and the Federal Reserve, 2974, Power of Coinage, 1987. Councilman, City of Belmont, Calif., 1970-77, mayor, 1971, 72, 75, 76; dir. San Mateo County Transit Dist., 1975-77; chmn. San Mateo County Coun. Mayors, 1975-76; trustee Incline Village Gen. Improvement Dist., 1984-85, Carlmont United Meth. Ch., 1978-81. 1st lt. USAR, 1961-68. Recipient Ernst & Young Entrepreneur of the Yr. award, 1986, Stanton Recognition award North Shore Country Day Sch., 1996; named Hon. life mem. Calif. PTA, ordo honorum Kappa Delta Rho Nat. Frat.; John Harvard fellow Harvard U., 1996. Mem. Nat. Assn. Bu. Economists, San Francisco Bond Club. Republican. Methodist. Office: Jones Internat Inc PO Box 7498 Incline Village NV 89452-7498 *The entrepreneurial spirit is distinguished by passion, creativity, and the fulfillment of mission through other people.*

JONES, ROBERT CLAIR, middle school educator; b. Norfolk, Va., Apr. 9, 1949; s. Leon Herbert and Barbara Dean (Jones) J.; m. Geri Lee Siebels, Feb. 13, 1977; children: Adam, Matthew, Aaron, Lee. BS, Old Dominion U., 1971, MS, 1981. Tchr. Virginia Beach (Va.) Jr. High Sch., 1971-73, Kempsville Jr. High Sch., Virginia Beach, 1973—. Adj. faculty Old Dominion U., Norfolk, Va., 1990—; co-chmn. faculty coun. Kempsville Mid. Sch., 1992-93, curriculum coord., grade level chair, 1993—; program devel. com. for mid. schs., Virginia Beach City Schs., 1990-91, chmn. social studies curriculum adv. com., 1990-91, instr. staff devel., 1989-91; speaker in field. Contbr. articles to profl. jours.; featured in Oasis mag. Baseball coach Pony Colt League, Virginia Beach, 1991-92; vol. Make A Wish Found., Virginia Beach, 1990-92. Named Tchr. of Yr., Va. Coun. Social Studies, 1987—. Mem. ASCD, NEA, Nat. Coun. Social Studies, Va. Edn. Assn., Va. Coun. Social Studies, Virginia Beach Edn. Assn. Avocations: collecting records, collecting Beatles memorobilia, professional musician. Home: 812 Yearling Ct Virginia Beach VA 23464-3214 Office: Kenpsville Mid Sch 260 Churchill Dr Virginia Beach VA 23456

JONES, ROBERT EDWARD, federal judge; b. Portland, Oreg., July 5, 1927; s. Howard C. and Leita (Hendricks) J.; m. Pearl F. Jensen, May 29, 1948; children— Jeffrey Scott, Julie Lynn BA, U. Hawaii, 1949; JD, Lewis and Clark Coll., 1953, LHD (hon.), 1995; LLD (hon.), City U., Seattle, 1984. Bar: Oreg. Trial atty., Portland, Oreg., 1953-63; judge Oreg. Circuit Ct., Portland, 1963-83; justice Oreg. Supreme Ct., Salem, 1983-90; judge U.S. Dist. Ct. Oreg., Portland, 1990—. Mem. faculty Nat. Jud. Coll., Am. Acad. Jud. Edn., ABA Appellate Judges Seminars; former mem. Oreg. Evidence Revision Commn., Oreg. Ho. of Reps.; former chmn. Oreg. Commn. Prison Terms and Parole Stds.; adj. prof. Northwestern Sch. Law, Lewis and Clark Coll., 1963—, Willamette Law Sch., 1988-90. Author: Rutter Group Practice Guide Federal Civil Trials and Evidence, 1999—. Mem. bd. overseers Lewis and Clark Coll., mem. bd. visitors to Northwestern Sch. Law. Served to capt. JAGC, USNR. Recipient merit award Multnomah Bar Assn., 1979; Citizen award NCCJ, Legal Citizen of the Yr. award Law Related Edn. Project, 1988; Service to Mankind award Sertoma Club Oreg.; James Madison award Sigma Delta Chi; named Disting. Grad., Northwestern Sch. Law; Outstanding Profl. Achievement Alumnus award, U.S. Merchant Marine Acad., 1998; Judge Robert E. Jones Oreg. Justice award, Am. Judicature Soc., 1999, Lifetime Commitment to Jury Trial Sys. award Am. Bd. Trial Advs., 2004. Mem. Am. Judicature Soc. (bd. dirs. 1997-2001), State Bar Oreg. (past chmn. Continuing Legal Edn.), Oreg. Circuit Judges Assn. (pres. 1967-1968), Oreg. Trial Lawyers Assn. (pres. 1959, chair 9th cir. edn. com. 1996-97). Office: US Dist Ct House 1000 SW 3rd Ave Ste 1007 Portland OR 97204-2944 Office Phone: 503-326-8340. E-mail: robert_jones@ord.uscourts.gov.

JONES, ROBERT EMMET, language educator, humanities educator; b. N.Y.C., Sept. 16, 1928; s. Robert Emmet and Lois Kathryn (UpdeGrove) J. AB, Columbia U., 1948, PhD, 1954; certificat de phonetique Sorbonne, Paris, 1949. Vis. instr. French Columbia U., 1953-54; asst. prof. French U. Ga., Athens, 1954-61, U. Pa., 1961-67; assoc. prof. French and humanities M.I.T., 1967-71, prof. French and humanities, 1971-92, prof. emeritus, 1992—; tchr. French cooking, 1976—. Author: The Alienated Hero in Modern French Drama, 1961, Panorama de la nouvelle critique en France, 1968, Gerard de Nerval, 1974, H.R. Lenormand, 1984, Botticelli's Face, 2002; contbr. articles to profl. jours. Mem. MLA, Am. Assn. Tchrs. French, French Library Boston. Clubs: St. Anthony, St. Botolph. Episcopalian. Home: 452 Beacon St Boston MA 02115-1001 E-mail: r.e.jones@comcast.net.

JONES, ROBERT GEAN, religion educator; b. Magnolia, Ark., Feb. 17, 1925; s. Emless Bunyan and Eunice (Gean) J.; m. Marian Laverne Alexander, July 23, 1946; 1 dau., Carolyn Ann. BA cum laude, Baylor U., 1947; B.D. cum laude, Yale, 1950, MA, 1957, PhD, 1959. Ordained to ministry Bapt. Ch., 1946; minister Deep River (Conn.) Bapt. Ch. and; First Bapt. Ch. of, Saybrook, 1950-59; asst. prof. religion George Washington U., Washington, 1959-61, asso. prof., 1961-64, prof., 1964-91, prof. emeritus, 1991—, chmn. dept. religion, 1963-79, univ. marshal, 1969-89. Adj. prof. U. Tenn., Chattanooga, 1991-93, Maryville Coll., 1993-95. Author: The Rules for the War of the Sons of Light With the Sons of Darkness, 1957, The Manual of Discipline (1QS), The Old Testament and Persian Religion, 1964. Mem. Soc. Bibl. Lit. and Exegesis, Am. Acad. Religion, Alpha Chi, Omicron Delta Kappa. Home: 307 Amohi Ln Loudon TN 37774-3013 Personal E-mail: robgjones@aol.com.

JONES, ROBERT GERARD, lawyer; b. Latrobe, Pa., Nov. 13, 1956; BSME, W. Va. U., 1979; JD, St. Louis U., 1987. Bar: Mo. 1987, DC 1988. Sr. engr. Exxon Coal U.S., 1979—84; assoc. Crowell & Moring, Washington, 1987—91; of counsel Arch Mineral Corp., 1991—94; sr. counsel Arch Coal, Inc., St. Louis, 1994—2000, v.p. law, gen. counsel, 2000—. Office: Arch Coal Inc One City Place Dr Ste 300 Saint Louis MO 63141 Office Phone: 314-994-2700.

JONES, ROBERT GRIFFITH, law educator, mayor; b. State Coll., Pa., Mar. 25, 1936; s. Edward H. and Dorothy (Griffiths) J.; m. Carolyn E. Hazard, Aug. 29, 1959; Robert Griffith Jr., Chester H. AB, Davidson (N.C.) Coll., 1958; MDiv, Yale U., 1961; PhD, Duke U., 1966; JD, U. Va., 1974. Bar: Va. 1974, U.S. Supreme Ct. 1977. Asst. prof. Davidson (N.C.) Coll., 1964-65; assoc. prof. Lehigh U., Bethlehem, Pa., 1965-71; prof. U. Va., Charlottesville, 1971-74; mayor City of Virginia Beach, Va., 1986-88; chmn. Jones, Marcari, Russotto, Walker & Spencer, P.C., Virginia Beach, 1991—. Adv. bd. mem. Cenit Bank, 1997—. Vice-chmn. Tidewater Transp. Dist. Commn., 1987-88, chmn., 1988; councilman City Council of Virginia Beach, 1982-88, chmn. Va. Beach Econ. Devel. Authority. Mem. ABA, Va. Bar Assn., Virginia Beach Bar Assn. Democrat. Presbyterian. Home: 2716 Robin Dr Virginia Beach VA 23454-1814 Office: 128 S Lynnhaven Rd Virginia Beach VA 23452-7417 E-mail: rgjvbva@aol.com.

JONES, ROBERT HENRY, automotive distribution executive; b. Willow Springs, N.C., Dec. 31, 1935; s. Kenneth Tomas and China Christiana (Blalock) J.; m. Margaret Ann Page; children: Julie Beth, Jeffrey Bert, Jay Brent. AA in Acctg., Kings Coll., 1960. Acct. Jones & Guerrero Co., Inc., Agana, Guam, 1961-63, gen. mgr., 1963-67, v.p., 1967-73, exec. v.p., 1973-84; pres., chief exec. officer Triple J Enterprises, Tamuning, Guam, 1984—. Chmn. bd. Guam Visitors Bur., 1974-76, bd. dirs., 1968-89; chmn. Pacific Asia Travel Assn., Micronesia chpt., 1988-89; v.p. Boy Scouts Am., Hawaii, 1968—. Served with U.S. Army, 1957-59. Recipient Silver Beaver award Boy Scouts Am., 1975, Silver Antelope award, 1991; Mr. Tourism award Guam Visitors Bur., 1976. Mem. Guam C. of C. (chmn. 1980, Bus. Man of Yr. award 1983); Guam Hotel and Restaurant Assn. (pres., founder 1969-71). Lodges: Rotary (bd. dirs. Guam). Republican. Presbyterian. Avocations: skiing, dirt bike riding, travel.

JONES, ROBERT JEFFRIES, lawyer; b. Atlantic City, N.J., Sept. 7, 1939; s. Robert Lewis and Mildred Laura (Jeffries) J.; m. Joan Mary Feichtner, Aug. 17, 1963; children: Christopher, Kendall, Stephen. BA, Colgate U., 1961; LLB with honors, U. Pa., 1964. Bar: Pa. 1965, U.S. Dist. Ct. (ea. dist.) Pa. 1965, U.S. Ct. Appeals (3d cir.) 1965. Assoc. Saul, Ewing LLP, Phila., 1964-71, ptnr., 1971—. Mem. steering com. Bond Atty.'s Workshop, Chgo., 1980. Mem. Montgomery County Rep. Com., Norristown, Pa., 1967-71; chmn. Whitpain Twp. Park and Recreation Bd., Blue Bell, Pa., 1980-84; bd. dirs. Phila. YMCA Camps, 1970-76; trustee Colgate U., 1999-2005; mem. gen. counsel alumni corp., 1993-99, pres. Phila. chpt., 1980-84. Fellow Am. Coll. Bond Counsel (founder); mem. ABA, Phila. Bar Assn. (chmn. tax exempt fin. com. 1985-86), Pa. Bond Lawyers Assn. (founder Harrisburg, Pa. 1987), Pa. Economy League (bd. dirs. 1994—). Avocations: golf, history. Office: Saul Ewing LLP 3800 Centre Sq W Philadelphia PA 19102 Office Phone: 215-972-7802. E-mail: rjjboilerplate@aol.com, rjones@saul.com.

JONES, ROBERT RUSSELL, retired magazine editor; b. Topeka, Oct. 19, 1927; s. Russell Alonzo and and Marie (Carter) J.; m. Dorothy Jean Vincent, Sept. 3, 1947; children— Daniel Robert, Mark Alan. AB in Polit. Sci. and History, Washburn U., Topeka, 1949; MS in Tech. Journalism, Kans. State U., Manhattan, 1959. Expt. sta. editor, asst. prof. agrl. econs. Kans. State U., 1957-60; asst. editor Agrl. Pubs. Inc., Milw., 1960-67; sci. editor, asst. prof. expt. sta. U. Mo., Columbia, 1967-72; assoc. editor Indsl. Research mag., Chgo., 1972-74, editor, 1974-78; editorial dir. Indsl. Research & Devel. mag., Barrington, Ill., 1978-83; editor, editorial dir. Research & Devel. Mag., Barrington, 1984-89, exec. editor Des Plaines, Ill., 1989-91; editorial dir. Chromatography Forum Mag., Barrington, 1986, Chromatography Mag., Barrington, 1987; ret., 1991. Chmn. R & D Scientist of Yr. award ann. program, 1974-91, I-R 100 new products awards ann. program, 1974-87, R & D 100 new product awards ann. program, 1988-91; pres., CEO, editl. dir. Applied Sci. Communications, 1991—. Editor: The Unsettled Earth, 1975, Foresight mag., 1991-93, First Notes mag., 1991-95, The Spire mag., 1995—. Served with USNR, 1945-46. Mem. AAAS, Am. Bus. Press (Jesse H. Neal Editorial Achievement award 1976), Am. Soc. Bus. Press Editors, Nat. Assn. Sci. Writers. Democrat. Baptist. Home: 1213 Main St Evanston IL 60202-1650 Office Phone: 847-328-8133.

JONES, ROGER ALAN, chemistry professor, researcher, consultant; b. York, Pa., Mar. 25, 1947; s. Galen Victor and Frieda (Shaull) J. BS, U. Del., 1969; PhD, U. Alberta, 1974. Postdoctoral fellow MIT, Cambridge, Mass., 1974-77; asst. prof. chemistry Rutgers U., New Brunswick, NJ, 1977-82, assoc. prof., 1982-88, prof. Piscataway, NJ, 1988—, chmn. dept. chemistry and chem. biology, 1996—. Contbr. articles to profl. jours. NIH rsch. grantee, 1982—; faculty rsch. awardee Am. Cancer Soc., 1986-91. Fellow AAAS, Am. Chem. Soc. Part of 30 member research team (with Edward Arnold) developing a trio of drugs that are believed to destroy HIV, the virus that causes AIDS, tenifovir, or the DAPY (diarylpyrimidine) at Rutgers University at the Center of Advanced Biotechnology and Medicine. Office: Rutgers U Chemistry & Chemical Biology 610 Taylor Rd Office WL-A104/A103 Piscataway NJ 08854 Office Phone: 732-445-4900. Office Fax: 732-445-5866. E-mail: jones@rutchem.rutgers.edu.*

JONES, RONALD ARTHUR, physician, composer; b. Balt., Aug. 2, 1952; m. Arthur John Jones and Joyce Irene (Cooper) Smith; m. Leslie Joan Farrington, Feb. 22, 1973 (div.); children: Sarah Leslie, Hannah Renee, Naomi Carolyn; m. Regina Louise Van Nostrand, Mar. 21, 1997; 1 stepchild, Raymond Van Nostrand. BA, Johns Hopkins U., 1974; MD, Tufts U., 1980. Intern Walter Reed Hosp., 1980-81, resident, 1981-83; intern Jefferson Hosp., Arlington, Va., 1984-85; resident in emergency medicine Long Island Jewish Hosp., N.Y.C., 1985-92; pvt. practice N.Y.C., 1992—. Vol. staff attending physician St. Luke's/Roosevelt Med. Ctr., N.Y.C., 1993—; faculty Columbia Univ., N.Y.C., 1995—, instr. Coll. Physicians and Surgeons, 1995—; lectr. Harvard Univ., Boston, 1985. Author: Discover, 1984; composer: Jones Beach, 1992; contbr. articles to Integral Geometry, Quantum Math. Physics, 1992. Capt. U.S. Army, 1980-84. Faculty tchg. award John Simon Guggenheim Found., 1994, Faculty Dispensary Tchg. award L.I. Jewish Emergency Medicine, 1989. Democrat. Lutheran. Avocations: guitar, piano, chess, writing, math.

JONES, RONALD DAVID, retired lawyer; b. Oneida, N.Y., Jan. 2, 1930; s. Keith Walton and Winnie (Thomas) J.; children: Susan D., Stephen T.; m. Hildegard Vetter, June 9, 1984. BS, Yale U., 1951; JD cum laude, Harvard U., 1958. Bar: N.Y. 1958, U.S. Ct. Appeals (1st, 2nd, 4th, 5th, 6th and D.C. cirs.), U.S. Supreme Ct. 1980. Assoc. LeBoeuf, Lamb, Leiby & MacRae, N.Y.C., 1958-64, ptnr., 1965-89, of counsel, 1990—2002. Pres. Coun. Econ. Regulation, 1988-92; chmn. United Distbn. Cos., 1990-97; chmn. Upper Housatonic Valley Nat. Heritage Area, Inc., 2000—. Served to lt. USNR, 1951-55 Mem. ABA (chmn. sect. on pub. utilities law 1986-87), Internat. Bar Assn. (chmn. SBL com. on utility law 1988-90), Univ. Club (N.Y.C.). Avocations: running, writing, history. Office: 27 Woodcrest Ln PO Box 1942 Lakeville CT 06039 Personal E-mail: rdj655@earthlink.net.

JONES, RONALD WINTHROP, economics professor; b. Louisville, July 5, 1931; s. August F. and Bess (White) J.; m. Sarah Jay-Smith, July 20, 1956 (div. 1964); 1 child, Deane; m. Catherine L. Maitland, June 14, 1969; children: Laura, Dylan, Brenn, Polly. AB, Swarthmore Coll., 1952; PhD, MIT, 1956. Instr. MIT, 1955-56, Swarthmore Coll., 1956-57; prof. econs. U. Rochester (N.Y.), 1958—. Co-author: World Trade and Payments; author: International Trade-Essays in Theory, 1979, Globalization and the Theory of Input Trade, 2000. Fellow NAS, Econometric Soc., Am. Acad. Arts and Scis. Office: U Rochester Dept Econs Rochester NY 14627 Office Phone: 585-275-2688. Business E-Mail: jonr@troi.cc.rochester.edu.

JONES, RONNELL ANDERSEN, lawyer, educator; m. K. C. Jones; 1 child, Max. BA, Utah State Univ., 1995; JD, Ohio State Univ., 2000. Assoc. Jones Day, Columbus, Ohio, 2000—02, San Francisco, 2002—03; law clk. U.S. Ct. Appeals (9th cir.), San Francisco, 2002; law clk. to Hon. Sandra Day O'Connor U.S. Supreme Ct., 2003—04; vis. faculty fellow Univ. Ariz. Coll. Law, 2004—. Mem.: Ohio State Univ. Alumni Assn. (Thomson award 2003), Order of the Coif. Office: University of Arizona Rogers College of Law PO Box 210176 Tucson AZ 85721-0176

JONES, ROY, JR., professional boxer; b. Pensacola, Fla., Jan. 16, 1969; Student, Pensacola Jr. Coll.; trains under, Coach Alton Merkerson. Profl. matches include Jorge Vaca, 1992, Art Serwano, 1992, Jorge Castro, 1992, Glen Thomas, 1992, Percy Harris, 1992, Glenn Wolfe, 1993, Bernard Hopkins (won IBF Middleweight Title), 1993, Thulane Malinga, 1993, Fermin Chirino, 1993, Daniel Garcia, 1994, Thomas Tate, 1994, James Toney (won IBF Super Middleweight Title, 1994, Antoine Byrd, 1994, Vinny Pazienza, 1994, Tony Thornton, 1994, Merqui Sosa, 1996, Eric Lucas, 1996, Bryant Brannon, 1996, Mike McCallum (won WBC Light Heavyweight Title), 1996, Montell Griffen (regained WBC Light Heavyweight Title), 1997, Virgil Hill, 1998, Lou Del Valle (won WBA Light Heavyweight Title), 1998, Otis Grant, 1998, Richard Frazier, 1999, Reggie Dwayne Johnson (won IBF Light Heavyweight Title, Unified belts), 2000, Richard Hall, 2000, Eric Harding, 2000, Derrick Harmon, 2001, Julio Cesar Gonzalez, 2001, Glenn Kelly, 2002, Clinton Woods, 2002, John Ruiz (won WBA Heavyweight Title), 2003, Antonio Tarver (regained WBC Light Heavyweight Title), 2003. Recipient exclusive endorsement contract Nike Sports Mgmt.; WBC light heavyweight champion, 1997—2004. Recipient Silver medal, Olympic Games, Seoul, 1988, Val Barker Trophy award, 1988. Avocations: playing basketball, speaking to children on the value of education and the perils of drugs.

JONES, RUSSEL CAMERON, civil engineer, educator; b. Tarentum, Pa., Oct. 18, 1935; s. Frederick Russel and Helena Doris (Elliot) J.; m. Sharon Ann Keillor; children: Amy Sue, Kimberly Nicole, Tamara Melissa. BS, Carnegie Inst. Tech., 1957, MS, 1960, PhD, 1963; MALS, U. Del., 1994. Structural engr. Hunting, Larsen & Dunnels, Pitts., 1957-59; asst. prof. civil engring. M.I.T., 1963-66, assoc. prof., 1966-71; prof., chmn. dept. civil engring. Ohio State U., Columbus, 1971-76; dean Sch. Engring., U. Mass., Amherst, 1977-81; v.p. acad. affairs Boston U., 1981-87, v.p. acad. devel., 1985-87; pres. U. Del., Newark, 1987-88, univ. rsch. prof., 1988-95; exec. dir. NSPE, Alexandria, Va., 1995-98; mng. ptnr. World Expertise LLC, Falls Church, Va., 1998—. Named Del. Engr. of Yr., 1994; recipient Collingwood prize, ASCE, 1966, Edmund Friedman profl. recognition award, 1981, Internat. medal for disting. contbns. to engring. edn., Australasian Assn. Engring. Edn., 1993, Chair's award, Am. Assn. Engring. Socs., 2005; fellow, NDEA, 1959—62, ASCE, 1962—63. Fellow AAAS, ASCE (hon.; bd. dirs. 1969-71, 72-75, v.p. 1976-77), NSPE, Am. Soc. Engring. Edn., Accreditation Bd. Engring. and Tech. (bd. dirs. 1983-86, pres. 1987-88), Royal Soc. for Encouragement of Arts, Mfrs. and Commerce, Instn. of Engrs. of Ireland; mem. IEEE, Am. Assn. Higher Edn., Nat. Assn. for Sci., Tech. and Soc. (bd. dirs. 1992-95), Sigma Xi, Tau Beta Pi, Phi Kappa Ph, Chi Epsilon, Sigma Nu. Office: 2001 Mayfair Mclean Ct Falls Church VA 22043-1761 Personal E-mail: rcjonespe@aol.com.

JONES, RUTH SCHUESSLER, academic administrator, political science professor; 1 child, Mark P. BS, Ind. State U., 1963; PhD, Georgetown U., 1969. Instr. Kans. State U., 1967-69; from asst. prof. to assoc. prof. U. Mo., St. Louis, 1969-81; prof. Ariz. State U., Tempe, 1981—, loan exec. bd. regents, 1989-90, chair polit. sci., 1985-92, dir. Univ. for the Next Century, 1994-96, exec. asst. to pres., 1996—2002; v.p. office of provost, 2002—. Author: (with others) Campaign and Party Finance in North American and Western Europe, 1993, The Parties Respond: Changes in the American Party System, 1993, Comparative Political Finance Among Democracies, 1994; mem. editl. bd. Polit. Behavior, 1986-90, Election Politics, 1987-89, Western Polit. Quar., 1988-90, Am. Rev. Politics, 1993-96, Dilemmas in Am. Politics, 1993—, Social Sci. Quar., 1994—; contbr. articles to profl. jours. Commr. Ariz. Clean Elections Commn., 1999—; bd. dirs. Ariz. Girls Ranch, Inc., 1995—; bd. dirs. Neighborhood Ptnrs., Inc., 1998—. Recipient Disting. Alumni award Ind. State U., 1990, Nat. Woman of Achievement award Alpha Omicron Pi, 1997. Mem. AAUW, Am. Polit. Sci. Assn. (Mentor of Distinction 1993). Office: Ariz State U PO Box 877805 Tempe AZ 85287-7805 Office Phone: 480-965-6605. Business E-Mail: ruth.jones@asu.edu.

JONES, SALLY DAVIESS PICKRELL, writer; b. St. Louis, June 4, 1923; d. Claude Dildine Pickrell and Marie Daviess (Pittman) Pickrell; m. Charles William Jones, Sept. 2, 1943 (dec.); 1 child, Matthew Charles (dec.). Student, Mills Coll., Oakland, Calif., 1941-43, U. Calif.-Berkeley, 1945, Columbia U., 1955-58. Author: (novels) Lights Burn Blue, 1947. Mem. Met. Mus. Art, Nat. Coun. Women, Asia Soc., Fgn. Policy Assn., UN Assn. Episcopalian. Address: 1525 Pelican Point Dr Apt HA101 Sarasota FL 34231-6774

JONES, SAMUEL COLIN, minister, religious studies educator; b. Northport, Ala., Dec. 27, 1943; s. Colin and Sarah Anders Jones; m. Laura Fisher Jones, Dec. 21, 1969; children: Mark(dec.), Jonny, Susanne. AA, Bapt. Bible Inst., 1965; BA, William Coll., 1970; MA, New Orleans Bapt. Sem., 1984. Pastor New Hope Bapt. Ch., Brundridge, Ala., 1966—70, Unity Bapt. Ch., Leakesville, Miss., 1970—72, Moselle Bapt. CH., 1972—76, Foxworth Bapt. Ch., 1977—78, Vanee Bapt. Ch., Vanee, Ala., 1978—82, Unity Bapt. Ch., Pascagoula, Miss., 1982—90; maintenance dir. Pascagoula Schs., 1989—. Pres. pastor's conf. Jackson County Bapt., Pascagoula, 1983—84, dir. misson, 1985. Pres. Jaycees, Moselle, 1974—75; mem. Moselle Fire Dept., 1973—76; v.p. New Hope PTA, Brundridge, 1967—68. Named hon. mayor, Westmoreland, Tenn., 1976. Home: 1222 11th St Pascagoula MS 39567

JONES, SAMUEL LEANDER, conductor; b. Inverness, Miss., June 2, 1935; s. Samuel Leander and Ella Mae (Spencer) J.; m. Nancy Ruth Peacock, Jan. 29, 1957 (div.); children: Rachel Ann, Alison Frances; m. Kristin Barbara Schutte, Dec. 22, 1975. BA, Millsaps Coll., 1957; MA, U. Rochester, 1958, PhD, 1960; D (hon.), Millsaps Coll., 2000. Dir. instrumental music Alma (Mich.) Coll., 1960-62, instr., 1960-61, asst. prof., 1961-62; music dir. Saginaw Symphony Orch., 1962-65; asst. condr. Rochester Philharm. Orch., N.Y., 1965-67, assoc. condr., 1967-69, resident condr., 1969-70, condr., 1970-72; dean Shepherd Sch. of Music Rice U., Houston, 1973-79, prof. of conducting and composition, Shepherd Sch. Music, 1973-97, prof. emeritus, 1997—; prof. of conducting and composition, dir. orchestral studies Carnegie-Mellon U., Pitts., 1988-89. Assoc. dir. Am. Symphony Orch. League Inst. of Orchestral Studies, Orkney Springs, Va., 1966-76; mus. advisor Flint Symphony Orch., 1974-76; guest condr. Pitts. Symphony, Detroit Symphony, Houston Symphony, Buffalo Philharm., Prague Symphony; composer-in-residence Seattle Symphony Orch., 1997—. Founder Alma Symphony, 1961; condr., Saginaw (Mich.) Symphony, 1962-65, also, dir., Saginaw Choral Soc., composer-in-residence, Delta Coll., Univ. Ctr., Mich., 1964-65; founder, conductor: Festival Orch, Univ. Ctr., 1964-65; guest condr., Pitts. Symphony, Buffalo Philharmonic, Shenandoah Valley Music Festival, Naumberg, Iceland symphonies. others.; Composer: Symphony 1, 1960, In Retrospect, 1959, Overture for a City, 1964, Festival Fanfare (commd. Am. Symphony Orch. League), 1964, Elegy in Memory of John Fitzgerald Kennedy, 1917-63, 1963, Let Us Now Praise Famous Men (commd. Shenandoah County Bicentennial Commn.), 1972, Spaces, 1974, Contours of Time, 1975, Fanfare and Celebration (commd. Houston Symphony), 1980, A Symphonic Requiem (commd. Sioux City Symphony), 1983, The Trumpet of the Swan (commd. Millsaps Coll.), 1985, Listen Now, My Children (commd. Midland-Odessa Symphony), 1985, (opera) A Christmas Memory, 1982, Canticles of Time, Symphony No. 2 (commd. Millsaps Coll.), 1990, Symphony No. 3 (commd. Amarillo Symphony), 1991, The Seas of God (commd. Greensboro Choral Soc.), 1992, (oratorio) The Temptation of Jesus (commd. 2d Presbyn. Ch. Richmond), 1995, Cello Sonata, 1997, Janus (commd. Seattle Symphony), 1998, (commd. Amarillo Symphony) Roundings, 1999-2000, Aurum Aurorae (commd. ASCAP Found. and Meet The composer), 2001, Eudora's Fable: The Shoe Bird (commd. Miss. Boychoir), 2002, Chorale--Overture for Organ and Orchestra (commd. Seattle Symphony), 2003, Concerto for Tuba and Orchestra, 2005; orchestral works, 1958—, solos, songs, chamber works, 1958—; writer/narrator: ednl. TV series for N.Y. State Dept. Edn. The World of Music. Recipient Founders medal Millsaps Coll., 1957, rec. publ. award Ford Found., 1976; Woodrow Wilson fellow, 1958; Martha Baird Rockefeller Found. grantee, 1973; music award Miss. Inst. Arts and Letters, 1986, 91, 2003; Internat. Angel award, 1997; named to Miss. Musicians Hall of Fame, 2000. Mem. ASCAP, Am. Music Ctr., Condrs. Guild (pres. 1987-89), Meet the Composer, Am. Symphony Orch. League, Omicron Delta Kappa, Lambda Chi Alpha. Methodist. Avocations: birding, reading. Home: 35247 34th Ave S Auburn WA 98001-9034 Office: Seattle Symphony Orch Benaraya Hall PO Box 21906 200 University St Seattle WA 98111-3906 E-mail: campanile@earthlink.net, sj@samueljones.net.

JONES, SARA SUE FISHER, librarian; b. Rupert, Idaho, May 2, 1962; d. Richard Sherman and Dana Louise Fisher; m. Martin R. Jones, Jan. 7, 1984; children: Russel, Elaine. BA in Comms., Boise State U., 1983; MLS, Syracuse U., 1999; postgrad., U. North Tex. Libr. dir. Stanley (Idaho) Cmty. Libr., 1984-86; English tchr. Minidoka County Schs., Rupert, Idaho, 1986-88; children's librarian Elko (Nev.) County Libr., 1988-95, libr. dir., 1995-2000; state libr., divsn. adminstr. Nev. State Libr. and Archives, 2000—. Commr. State Nev. Commn. on Ednl. Tech. Elko County Libr. Bd. scholar, 1997-99; IMLS scholar Mem. Nev. Libr. Assn. (pres. 2000—, pub. trustee, chair, Dorothy McAlindin award 1995, scholar 1997-98), Nev. Libr. Orgn. (chair N.E. dist.), Philanthropic Edn. Orgn., Soroptimist Internat. (pres. 1995-96). Avocations: reading, camping, golf. Office: 100 N Stewart St Carson City NV 89701

JONES, SCHUYLER, museum director, anthropologist; b. Wichita, Kans., Feb. 7, 1930; s. Schuyler and Ignace (Mead) J.; m. Lis Margit Søndergaard Rasmussen, Dec. 20, 1955; children: Peter R., Hannah L.; m. Lorraine da'Luz Vieira, Aug. 4, 1998. MA in Anthropology with honors, Edinburgh (Scotland) U.; MA in Anthropology, DPhil in Anthropology, Oxford (Eng.) U. Asst. curator Pitt Rivers Mus., U. Oxford, 1970-71, asst. curator, univ. lectr. ethnology, 1971-85, dir., 1985-97; fellow Linacre Coll., Oxford U., 1970-97, prof. emeritus, 1997—. Anthropol. expdns. to Atlas Mountains, So. Algeria, French West Africa, 1951-52, Belgian, Congo, 1952-53, Morocco High Atlas, Algeria, Sahara, Niger River, 1954, East Africa, 1953, Turkey, Iran, Afghanistan, Pakistan, India, Nepal, 1958-59; ten expdns. to Nuristan in the Hindu Kush, 1960-70, Chinese Turkestan, 1985, Tibet and Gobi Desert, 1986, So. China, Xinjiang and Pakistan, 1988, Western Greenland, 1991, Greenland and East Africa, 1993; mem. coun. Royal Anthropol. Inst., 1986-89. Author: Sous le Soleil Africain, 1955, Under the African Sun (revised French version), 1956, Annotated Bibliography of Nuristan (Kafiristan) and the Kalash Kafirs of Chitral, part 1, 1966, part 2, 1969, The Political Organization of the Kam Kafirs, 1967, Men of Influence in Nuristan, 1974, Tibetan Nomads: Environment, Pastoral Economy & Material Culture, 1996; co-author: Nuristan, 1979, Afghanistan, 1992; contbr. numerous articles to profl. jours. Trustee Horniman Mus., 1989—95; bd. govs. Kans. State Hist. Soc., 2004—. Decorated Comdr. Brit. Empire. Avocations: travel in remote areas, browsing in second-hand bookstores. Address: 1570 N Ridgewood Wichita KS 67208 E-mail: drschuylerjones@cs.com.

JONES, SCHUYLER ELIZABETH, community health nurse; b. Tampa, Fla., June 5, 1963; d. Bennet Spencer Jones and Sharon Widincamp Royal; children: Rayna Elizabeth, Roy Widincamp. Degree in nursing, Hillsborough County Sch. of Nursing, 1984. Lic. LPN Fla. Nurse St. Josephs Womans Hosp., Tampa, Fla., 1984—89, Dacco, Inc., Tampa, Fla., 1990—94, USA Med. Staffing, St. Petersburg, Fla., 1996—99; owner LadyBugs Lawnscape, Newport Richey, Fla., 2000—05; nurse Sunshine Youth Svcs., Fla. Dept. Juvenile Justice, Lutz, Fla., 2005—. Cons. landscape design Am. Assn. of Handymen, New Port Richey, Fla., 2004—; adv. bd. DACCO, Inc., Tampa, Fla., 1992—94. Vol. Big Brothers/Big Sisters, Tampa, Fla., 1986—87. Democrat. Avocations: writing, photography, camping, sugargliders, real estate investment. Home: 4924 Cherry Ct New Port Richey FL 34652 Office: LadyBugs Lawnscape 4924 Cherry Ct New Port Richey FL 34652 Office Phone: 813-766-5366. E-mail: eyeofagypsy@yahoo.com.

JONES, SHELDON ATWELL, lawyer; b. Melrose, Mass., Apr. 20, 1938; s. Sheldon Atwell and Hannah Margaret (Andrews) J.; m. Priscilla Ann Hatch, Sept. 10, 1966; children: Sarah Percy, Abigail Atwell. BA, Yale U., 1959; LLB, Harvard U., 1965. Bar: Mass. 1965, U.S. Dist. Ct. Mass. 1967, Calif. 2001. Assoc. Gaston, Snow, Motley & Holt, Boston, 1965-72; ptnr. Gaston Snow & Ely Bartlett, Boston, 1972-87, Dechert LLP, Boston, Newport Beach, 1987—2003, of counsel Boston, 2003—. Past sec. H&Q Healthcare Investors, Boston. Contbr. articles to profl. jours. Lt. (j.g.) USN, 1959-62. Mem. ABA (past chmn. subcom. on investment cos., state regulation of securities com.), Mass. Bar Assn., Boston Bar Assn. (past co-chmn. subcom. on investment cos. and investment advisers), Calif. State Bar Assn., Yale Club, Harvard Club. Avocations: skiing, sailing. Home: 19 Eagle Trace Wolfeboro NH 03894 Office: Dechert LLP 200 Clarendon St Boston MA 02116 Office Phone: 617-728-7123. E-mail: sheldon.jones@dechert.com.

JONES, SHERMAN J., academic administrator, investment company executive, educator; b. Newport News, Va., Jan. 12, 1946; s. Sherman Edward and Leola Mae (Pryer) J.; children: Kimberly, Sherman Edward. BA in Am. Studies with honors, Williams Coll., 1968; MBA, Harvard U., 1970, EdD, 1978. Woodrow Wilson adminstrv. intern, asst. to pres. Cen. State U., Ohio, 1970-71; asst. dir. Office Coop. Acad. Planning Inst. for Svc. to Edn., Washington, 1971-72; mgmt. cons. Cresap, McCormick & Paget, Inc., Washington, 1972-75; mgmt. cons. mgmt. div. Acad. for Ednl. Devel., Inc., Washington, 1975-77; v.p. for adminstrn. Fisk U., Nashville, 1977-80, v.p., acting dean, 1980-82; exec. v.p., prof. mgmt. Tuskegee (Ala.) U., 1982-84, prof. mgmt., exec. v.p., provost, 1984-91; prof. mgmt., provost, v.p. for acad. affairs Clark Atlanta U., 1991-93; pres., headmaster So. Normal Sch., Brewton, Ala., 1993-96; investment rep. Edward D. Jones & Co., 1996-99; fin. advisor Prudential Securities, Inc., Atlanta, 1999—2002; v.p. devel. Knoxville (Tenn.) Coll., 2000—03; prin., owner Jones Fin. Svcs., Knoxville, 2002—; assoc. prof. bus. adminstrn. Tenn. Wesleyan Coll., Athens, 2005. Bd. dirs. Better Bus. Bur. Nashville/Middle Tenn., 1978-82; mgmt. bd. John A. Andrew Community Hosp., 1982-85; adv. bd. St. Andrews Sewanee Sch., Tenn., 1986-92, bd. trustees, 1993-97; mem. Nashville Coun. on Fgn. Rels., Kiwanis, 1997-.; bd. trustees YMCA, Brewton, Ala., 1995—97. Harvard Grad. Sch. Edn. teaching fellow in edn., 1976-77. Mem. Alumni Coun. Harvard Grad. Sch. Edn., Williams Coll. Exec. Coun. Alumni Soc, Kiwanis. Republican. Episc. Avocations: sports, reading, tennis, weightlifting, cooking. Home: PO Box 11222 Knoxville TN 37939 Office: Raymond James 6555 Chapman Hwy Knoxville TN 37920 Office Phone: 865-579-2776. Business E-Mail: sherman.jones@raymondjames.com.

JONES, SHIRLEY, actress, singer; b. Smithton, Pa., July 31, 1934; d. Paul and Marjorie (Williams) J.; m. Jack Cassidy, Aug. 5, 1956 (div. 1975); children: Shaun, Patrick, Ryan; m. Marty Ingels, 1977. Grad. high sch., 1952; student, Pitts. Playhouse. Appeared with chorus South Pacific, 1953, in Broadway prodn. Me and Juliet, 1954; other state appearences include The Beggar's Opera, 1957, The Red Mill, 1958, Maggie Flynn, 1968, On a Clear Day, 1975, Show Boat, 1976, Bitter Suite, 1983; films include role of Laurey in Oklahoma, 1954, later stage tour Paris and Rome, sponsorship U.S. Dept. State, Carousel, 1956, April Love, 1957, Never Steal Anything Small, 1959, Bobbikins, 1959, Elmer Gantry, 1960 (Acad. Best Supporting Actress award 1961), Pepe, 1960, The Two Rode Together, 1961, The Music Man, 1962, The Courtship of Eddie's Father, 1963, A Ticklish Affair, 1963, Bedtime Story, 1964, The Secret of My Success, 1965, Fluffy, 1965, The Happy Ending, 1969, The Cheyenne Social Club, 1970, Beyond the Poseidon Adventure, 1979, Tank, 1984, There Were Times, Dear, 1985; night club tour with husband, 1958, later TV and summer stock; star TV series The Partridge Family, 1970-74, Shirley, 1979; guest star: TV series McMillan, 1976; starred with Patrick Cassidy (Broadway): 42nd Street; Silent Night, Lonely Night, 1969, But I Don't Want To Get Married!, 1970, The Girls of Huntington House, 1973, The Family Nobody Wanted, 1975, The Lives of Jenny Dolan, 1975, Winner Take All, 1975, Yesterday's Child, 1977, Evening in Byzantium, 1978, Who'll Save Our Children, 1978, A Last Cry for Help, 1979, The Children Of An Lac, 1980, Inmates: A Love Story, 1981, There Were Times Dear, 1987, Carousel, 2005; one-woman concert: TV series Shirley Jones' America 1981; author: Shirley and Marty: An Unlikely Love Story, 1990. Nat. chairwoman Leukemia Found. Named Mother of Yr. by Women's Found., 1978. Office Phone: 818-278-0123. Business E-Mail: suiteone@earthlink.net.

JONES, SHIRLEY JOYCE, small business owner, fashion designer; b. Chgo., Aug. 13; d. Roman C. Carpen and Mary A. Mleczko; m. William T. Jones, May 2, 1959; children: Debra Ann, Lisa Courtney. Student, Wright Coll., 1955-56, Triton Coll., 1963-64; grad., Ippolito Beauty Sch., 1973. Lic. cosmetologist, Ill. Pres. St. Vincent Ferrer, River Forest, Ill., 1973-74; owner Shirley Jones Beauty Studio, Chgo., 1979-93, Flare Schaumburg, 1983-87, Surprise Boutique, Oakbrook, Ill., 1988-96, Shirley Jones Boutique, Chgo., 1993-96; founder, chmn. gala cancer charity September Surprise, Oak Brook, Burr Ridge, Ill., 1990—. V.p. Oak Brook Republican Womens Club, 1999; active Dupage Fedn. Republican Women, Nat. Fedn. Republican Women, Ill. Fed. Repub. Women (chief of protocol, vice chmn., chaplain). Grantee Ippolito Beauty Sch., 1973. Mem. Fashion Group Internat., Chgo. Fashion Group, Nat. Arts and Letters Soc., Oakbrook, Ill. Roman Catholic. Avocations: golf, dance, travel, antiques, gourmet cooking. Home and Office: 6812 Fieldstone Dr Burr Ridge IL 60527-6967

JONES, SIDNEY LEWIS, economist, researcher, educator; b. Ogden, Utah, Sept. 23, 1933; s. Lewis W. and Anna Vernal (Evans) J.; m. Marlene Stewart, Nov. 24, 1953; children— Randall Sidney, Stanna, Bryan Lewis, Blake Stewart, Allyson. BS with honors in Econs, Utah State U., 1954; MBA, Stanford, 1958, PhD, 1960. Asst. prof. finance Northwestern U., Evanston, Ill., 1960-64, asso. prof., 1964-65; prof. finance U. Mich., Ann Arbor, 1965-69, 71-72; sr. staff economist Pres.'s Council Econ Advisers, 1969-71, spl. asst. to chmn., 1970-71; minister-counselor for econ. affairs to NATO, Brussels, Belgium, 1972-73; asst. sec. for econ. affairs Dept. Commerce, Washington, 1973-74; dep. asst. to Pres., also; dep. counsellor for econ. policy White House, 1974-75; counselor to sec. Treasury, Washington, 1975; asst. sec. for econ. policy Dept. Treasury, 1975-77; fellow Woodrow Wilson Internat. Center for Scholars, Washington, 1977-78; asst. to bd. govs. FRS, 1978; research scholar Am. Enterprise Inst.; Public Policy Research and lectr. Georgetown U., 1979-84; under sec. for econ. affairs Commerce Dept., Washington, 1984-86; prof. Georgetown U., Washington, 1986-89; assoc. faculty Brookings Inst., Washington, 1986-89; asst. sec. for econ. policy U.S. Dept. of the Treasury, Washington, 1989-93; vis. prof., rsch. assoc. Carleton Coll., 1993—. Vis. prof. Cornell U., 1994-95, Dartmouth Coll., 1993, Ariz. State U., 1996, U. North Carolina, 1999. Co-author: The Generalist-Specialist Dichotomy in the Management of Creative Personnel, 1960, Managerial Problems in Finance, 1964, Financial Institutions, 4th edit. 1966, The Development of Economic Policy, 1980, Public and Private Economic Adviser: Paul W. McCracken, 2000. Served to 1st lt. Q.M.C. AUS, 1954-56. Recipient Distinguished Alumni award Utah State U., 1971; Newell scholar; McKinsey fellow; Ford Found. fellow, 1957-60 Home: 8505 Parliament Dr Potomac MD 20854-4001

JONES, STANLEY BOYD, retired researcher; b. Balt., July 27, 1938; s. Arthur Boyd and Lillian Ailene (Powell) J.; m. Judith K. Miller, Mar. 9, 1981; children— Andrew, Jeffrey, Lisa, Julia. BA, Dartmouth Coll., 1960; postgrad., Yale U., 1960-63. Ordained Episc. priest., 1992. Mem. profl. staff, staff dir. Subcom. on Health, U.S. Senate, Washington, 1970-76; program devel. officer Inst. of Medicine, Nat. Acad. Scis., Washington, 1976-78; v.p. Fullerton, Jones & Wollkstein (Health Policy Alternatives), Washington, 1978-80; v.p. for Washington representation Nat. Assns. Blue Cross and Blue Shield Plans, 1980-83; prin. Health Policy Alternatives, 1983-86; pres. Consol. Healthcare, 1986-89; ind. cons. on health policy Washington, 1989—; clergyman Diocese of W.Va., 1992—2004; dir. Health Ins. Reform Project George Washington U., 1994-99. Commr. D.C. Gen. Hosp. Mem. Inst. of Medicine of Nat. Acad. Scis. Office: 2021 K St NW Washington DC 20006-1003 E-mail: stan@stanleyjones.com.

JONES, STANTON WILLIAM, management consultant; b. New Orleans, May 24, 1939; s. Albert DeWitt and Clara Arimenta (Stanton) J.; m. Gladys Marina Caceres, Aug. 22, 1990; children: Hazel Nathalye, Albert Stanton, 1 child from a previous marriage, Ellen Marie. BS, Embry-Riddle Aero. U., Daytona Beach, Fla., 1973; MBA, Syracuse (N.Y.) U., 1977. Cert. internal auditor. Commd. 2d lt. U.S. Army, 1963, advanced through grades to lt. col., 1979, fixed wing pilot Ft. Rucker, Ala., 1965-72, rotary wing pilot, 1972; mgmt. cons. Stanton W. Jones & Assocs., San Francisco, 1987—. Joint venture ptnr. Budget Analyst to Bd. Suprs., San Francisco, 1988—. Bd. dirs. Hunter's Point Boys & Girls Club, San Francisco, 1987—. Decorated Meritorious Svc. medal. Mem. Alpha Phi Alpha (pres. 1988-90). Roman Catholic. Avocations: chess, reading, jogging. Home: 1948 Cortereal Ave Oakland CA 94611-2632 Office: Stanton W Jones & Assocs 57 Post St Ste 713 San Francisco CA 94104-5025 Office Phone: 415-399-1013. Personal E-mail: stantonj@aol.com.

JONES, STEPHANIE TUBBS, congresswoman, lawyer, prosecutor; b. Cleve., Sept. 10, 1949; BA, Case Western Res. U., 1971, JD, 1974. Bar: Ohio 1974, U.S. Dist. Ct. (no. dist.) Ohio 1975, U.S. Ct. Appeals (6th cir.) 1981, U.S. Supreme Ct. 1981. Asst. gen. counsel, EEO adminstr. N.E. Ohio Regional Sewer Dist., 1974-76; asst. prosecutor Cuyahoga County Prosecutor's Office, 1976-79; trial atty. Cleve. dist. office EEO, 1979-81; judge Cleve. Mcpl. Ct., 1982-83, Cuyahoga County Ct. of Common Pleas, 1983-91; prosecutor Cuyahoga County, Cleve., 1991-98; mem. U.S. Congress from 11th Ohio dist., 1999—; mem. banking and fin. svcs. com., 1999—2002; mem. com. on small bus., 1999—2002; mem. ways and means com., 2003—. Mem. Stds. Ofcl. Conduct, 1999-; vis. com. bd. overseers Franklin Thomas Backus Sch. Law, Case Western Res. U. Bd. trustees Comty. Re-entry Program; bd. trustees class of 1984 Leadership Cleve. Alumnae; mem. Task Force on Violent Crime, Substance Abuse Initiative; trustee Cleve. Police Hist. Soc.; bd. trustees Bethany Bapt. Ch. Recipient Outstanding Vol. Svcs. in Law and Justice award Urban League Greater Cleve., 1986, Women of Yr. award Cleve. chpt. Nat. Assn. Negro Bus. and Profl. Women's Clubs, Inc., 1987, award in recognition of outstanding svc. to judiciary and black comty. Midwest region Nat. Black Am. Law Student Assn., 1988, Career Women of Achievement award YWCA, 1991, Disting. Svc. award Cleve. chpt. NAACP, 1997; named Black Profl. of Yr., Black Profl. Assn. Cleve., 1995, 1994 Ohio Dem. of Yr., Ohio Dem. Party, 1995; inductee Collinwood H.S. Hall of Fame, 1994, Soc. Benchers of Case Western Res. U. Sch. of Law, 1996. Mem. ABA, Nat. Black Prosecutor's Assn., Nat. Dist. Atty.'s Assn. (met. prosecutor's com.), Nat. Coun. Negro Women, Nat. Coll. Dist. Attys. (bd. regents), Ohio State Bar Assn. (Nettie Cronise Lutes award 1997), Ohio Prosecuting Attys. Assn. (exec. com.), Cleve. Bar Assn. (trustee), Norman S. Miner Bar Assn. (past treas.), Cuyahoga Women's Polit. Caucus, Delta Sigma Theta (Greater Cleve. Alumnae chpt., Althea Simmons award 1993). Democrat. Office: Ho of Reps 1009 Longworth Hob Washington DC 20515-3511 also: Dist Office 3645 Warrensville Ctr Rd Ste 204 Shaker Heights OH 44122*

JONES, STEPHEN, lawyer; b. Lafayette, La., July 1, 1940; s. Leslie William and Gladys A. (Williams) J.; m. Virginia Hadden (dec.); 1 child, John Chapman; m. Sherrel Alice Stephens, Dec. 27, 1973; children: Stephen Mark, Leslie Rachael, Edward St. Andrew. Student, U. Tex., 1960—63; LLB, U. Okla., 1966. Sec. Rep. Minority Conf., Tex. Ho. of Reps., 1963; personal asst. to Richard M. Nixon N.Y.C., 1964; adminstrv. asst. to Congressman Paul Findley, 1966-69; legal counsel to gov. of Okla., 1967; spl. asst. U.S. Senator Charles H. Percy and U.S. Rep. Donald Rumsfeld, 1968; mem. U.S. del. to North Atlantic Assembly NATO, 1968; staff counsel censure task force Ho. of Reps. Impeachment Inquiry, 1974; spl. U.S. atty. No. Dist. Okla., 1979; spl. prosecutor, spl. asst. dist. atty. State of Okla., 1977; judge Okla. Ct. Appeals, 1982; civil jury instrn. com. Okla. Supreme Ct., 1979-81; adv. com. ct. rules Okla. Ct. Criminal Appeals, 1980; now mng. ptnr. Stephen Jones & Assoc., Enid, Okla. Adj. prof. U. Okla., 1973—76; instr. Phillips U., 1982—90; bd. dirs. Coun. on the Nat. Interest Found. Author: Oklahoma and Politics in State and Nation, 1907-62, 1974, Others Unknown: The Oklahoma City Bombing Case and Conspiracy, 1998; co-author: France and China, The First Ten Years, 1964-74, 1991, Vernon's Oklahoma Forms 2d Criminal Practice & Procedure Vols. I, II, 1999; contbr. articles to various jours. Bd. dirs., coun. mem. Nat. Interest Found.; acting chmn. Rep. State Com., Okla., 1982; Rep. nominee Okla. atty. gen., 1974, U.S. Senate, 1990; spl. counsel to Gov. Okla., 1995; apptd. chief def. counsel by U.S. Dist. Ct., Oklahoma City, U.S. vs. Tim McVeigh, Oklahoma City Bombing Case, 1995-97; mem. vestry St. Matthews Episc. Ch., 1974, sr. warden, 1983-84, 89-90. Mem.: ABA, Okla. Bar Assn., Garfield County Bar Assn., Beacon Club. Office: PO Box 472 Enid OK 73702-0472 Office Phone: 580-242-5500. Business E-Mail: sjones@stephenjoneslaw.com.

JONES, STEPHEN B., academic administrator; m. Judy Jones; 2 children. BS, PhD in resources mgt, SUNY, Syracuse. Dir. Ala. Cooperative Extension Sys., 1997—2001; vice chancellor, prof. Coll. Nat. Resources NC State Univ., 2001—04; chancellor Univ. Alaska, Fairbanks, 2004—. Office: University of Alaska Chancellor's Office PO Box 757500 Fairbanks AK 99775*

JONES, STEVE See JONES, W.

JONES, SUSAN DORFMAN, real estate broker, writer; b. N.Y.C., Oct. 4, 1939; d. Joseph and Sarah (Sorrin) Dorfman; m. William Harry Jones, Sept. 18, 1960; children: Jeffrey Scott, Eric David, Timothy Mark BA, Syracuse U., 1961. Pres., owner Antiques Corp. Am., 1972—77, Susan & Sons Antiques, 1977—; comm. officer Riggs Bank, Washington, 1978—81; mgr. publs. Potomac Electric Power Co., Washington, 1981—82; sr. mgr. corp. comm. MCI Corp., Washington, 1982—83; dir. corp. comm. Sears World Trade, Washington, 1983—85; dir. corp. comm. and govt. rels. Oxford Devel. Corp., Bethesda, Md., 1985—87; comm. expert pub. health svc./health and human svcs. U.S. Alcohol, Drug Abuse, Mental Health Adminstrn., Rockville, Md., 1989—91; real estate broker Weichert Realtors, Washington, 1991—. Vol. staff Cleve. Clinics, Cleve. H.S. of Arts, 2003—; free-lance writer, cons., Washington, 1975-92; radio personality Sta. 4KQ, Brisbane, Australia, 1962; adj. prof. comms. Am. U., Washington, 1978-82. Author, editor, project mgr. corp. ann. reports. Recipient 1st pl. award for columns N.Y. Press Assn., 1961, Gold Quill award Internat. Assn. Bus. Communicators, 1980. Mem.: Greater Capital Area Assn. Realtors, Nat. Assn. Realtors, Pub. Rels. Soc. Am., Women in Telecommunications, Nat. Assn. Bank Women, Internat. Assn. Bus. Communicators, Jewish Cmty. Ctr. Cleve., Nat. Press Club. Democrat. Jewish. Home and Office: 30650 Jackson Rd Orange Village OH 44022-1731 Office: 5035 Wisconsin Ave NW Washington DC 20016-4113 E-mail: suebillj@yahoo.com.

JONES, SUSAN EMILY, fashion educator, administrator, educator emeritus; b. N.Y.C., Sept. 9, 1948; d. David and Emily Helen (Welke) J.; m. Henry J. Titone, Jr., Oct. 21, 1974 (div. 1980); m. Douglas S. Robbins, Aug. 21, 1985. BFA, Pratt Inst., Bklyn., 1970. Designer Sue Brett, N.Y.C., 1970-74, St. Tropez, 1975; prof. fashion Pratt Inst., Bklyn., 1972-2000, chairperson fashion dept., 1981-2000, chairperson merchandising and design programs fashion dept., 1983-2000; computer software cons., 1988-89; owner, designer Sej Wearable Artworks, 1992—. Internat. observer Jeunes Createurs de Mode,

Paris, 1987, judge, 1988; U.S. rep. SAGA Internat. Design Ctr., Copenhagen, 1992, serdesigns, Hawaii, 2001—. Tech. book reviewer, 1994—. Recipient Young Am. Designer award Internat. Ladies Garment Workers Union, 1970, Ptnr. in Edn. award N.Y.C. Pub. Sch. Sys. Chancellor, 1992-93. Mem. Fashion Group (regional com. 1983-87, mem. com. 1990-93, ednl. com. 1995-96, co-chair ednl. com. 1996-98), Nat. Retail Fedn., Under Fashion Assn. Home: 79-7199 Mamalahoa Hwy 351 F Holualoa HI 96725 Office: Pratt Inst Dept of Fashion Design 200 Willoughby Ave Brooklyn NY 11205-3899 Personal E-mail: sejpratt@aol.com. Business E-mail: sjones@pratt.edu, serdesigns@aol.com.

JONES, SUSAN MCGOWAN, gifted and talented educator; b. Alameda, Calif., May 12, 1959; d. Thomas and Gladys Mae (Prutzman) McG.; m. Warren Howard Jones, Oct. 31, 1980 (div.); children: Kelly Hardcastle, Reilly James; m. Barry William McLaughlin, May 22, 2004 AS in Edn., No. Va. Community Coll., 1988; BA in Russian Area Studies, George Mason U., 1991; MEd, Marymount U., 1994; EdD candidate, Coll. William & Mary, 2003—. Cert. nat. bd. cert. tchr. Va. State Lic. Data processor Tracor, Inc., Virginia Beach, Va., 1982-83; computer operator Hughes, Bendix, Holmes and Narver, Virginia Beach, 1983-84; data analyst Tracor, Inc., Virginia Beach, 1984; systems analyst Advanced Tech., Inc., Virginia Beach, 1984-85, computer programmer Reston, Va., 1986-87; tech. writer Swiger Group, Reston, 1987; tchr. 3rd grade Loudoun Country Day Sch., Leesburg, Va., 1991-93; tchr. 4th and 5th grade Loudoun County Pub. Schs., 1994—2000, Va. Beach City Pub. Sch., 2001—. Master tchr. Nat. Tech. Tchr. Inst., WNVT, Fairfax, 1998-99; cand. Nat. Bd. for Profl. Teaching Certification, 1999; translation cons. Systems Ctr., Inc., Reston, 1990—. Recipient Gov.'s Sch. Outstanding Educator, 2005. Mem. ASCD, World Affairs Coun., Golden Key, Phi Theta Kappa, Alpha Chi. Business E-Mail: smmcgo@wm.edu. E-mail: smjones59@aol.com.

JONES, SUZANNE FRANCIS, music educator; b. Lexington, Ky., Oct. 29, 1950; d. William Cleveland and Velma Warren Francis; m. James Curtis Jones, Apr. 4, 1975; children: William Nathan, Natalie Kara, Katie Suzanne, Curtis Tanner. BA in Music Edn., U. Ky., 1972; MA in Music Edn., Ea. Ky. U., 1980. Cert. Nat. Bd. Profl. Tchg. Stds. Itinerant music tchr. Mary Todd/No. Elem. Schs., Lexington, 1972—74; tchr. music Breckinridge Elem. Sch., Lexington, 1974—77; pvt. piano instr. Lexington, 1977—93; ch. organist Tates Creek Christian Ch., Lexington, 1980—90; choral dir. Winburn Mid. Sch., Lexington, 1990—92; gen. music instr. Crawford Mid. Sch., Lexington, 1992—93; music and choral tchr. Tates Creek Elem. Sch., Lexington, 1993—. Mem. com. for choral workshop Fayette County Music Educators, Lexington, 2002—05. Youth choir dir. Tates Creek Christian Ch., Lexington, 1980—90, So. Acres Christian Ch., Lexington, 1995—97; children's dir. Southland Christian Ch., Lexington, 1969—74, youth leader, 1999—2004. Mem.: Orff-Schulwerk Assn., Ky. Music Educators, Ctrl. Ky. Music Educators, Music Educations Nat. Assn. Democrat. Avocations: travel, music. Home: 524 Grove Ln Lexington KY 40517 Office: Tates Creek Elem 1113 Centre Pky Lexington KY 40517 E-mail: cjones4350@alltel.net.

JONES, TAD, state representative; b. Tucson, Ariz., Sept. 23, 1972; s. Ted and Corky (Burkert) Jones; m. Samantha Hamilton Jones; 1 child, Logan Benjamin. BS in Mktg., U. Tulsa, 1996. Sec., treas. Green Country Oil and Gas Co., Inc.; intern Senator Don Nickles; co-founder Miket Ads Sign Corp.; mem. Okla. Ho. of Reps., 1999—, vice chmn. econ. devel. com., minority whip; chair A & B Edn. Sub Com., 2005—. Mem.: Am. Legis. Action Coun., Fellowship Christian Athletes, Oologah Sch. Found., Rotary (Sgt. at Arms). Republican. Office: State Capitol 2300 N Lincoln Blvd Rm 3014 B Oklahoma City OK 73105

JONES, TERRELL B., travel company executive; b. 1948; Grad., Denison U., Granville, Ohio. Travel agt. Vega Travel, Chgo.; v.p. Travel Advisors, Sabre Applications and Devel., Fort Worth; v.p. product devel. Sabre Travel Info. Network; pres. Sabre Decision Techs.; dir. product devel. Am. Airlines, 1978, pres. Sabre Computer Svcs., 1993-96; pres. Sabre Computer Svcs., 1996-99, Sabre Interactive, 1996-99; sr. v.p. Sabre Inc.; pres. (ret. 2002) Travelocity.com; mng. ptnr. Essential Ideas, 2002—. Mem. customer adv. bd. Intel, Lotus; mem. The Rsch. Bd.; bd. dir., La Quinta Corp.; bd. dir, Earthlink

JONES, TERRENCE DALE, foundation administrator, consultant; b. Kansas City, Mo., Jan. 11, 1948; s. Bobby J. and Ida Lorene (Overstreet) Jones; m. Polly Nell McDowell, 1992; 1 child, Eryn. BS, U. Kans., 1970, MA, 1972; MFA, U. Ga., 1971. Mgr., dir. Bradford Repertory Theatre, Vt., 1970-71; designer, instr. Miami-Dade CC, Fla., 1972-74; designer, asst. prof. Grinnell Coll., Iowa, 1974-76; mng. dir., asst. prof. Kirkland Fine Arts Ctr., Millikin U., Decatur, Ill., 1976-81; gen. mgr., asst. dean Clowes Meml. Hall/Jordal Coll. Fine Arts, Butler U., Indpls., 1981-86; dir. Krannert Ctr. for Performing Arts U. Ill., Urbana, 1986-96; pres., CEO Wolf Trap Found. Performing Arts, Vienna, Va., 1996—. Arts cons., Ohio, Tex., Wis., Ind., Ill.; mem. arts midwest adv. panel NEA, end. conf. chmn.; mem. theater and film. profl. adv. bd. U. Kans., WGMS Peforming Arts Fund. Prodr.: (plays) Achilles: A Kabuki Play, 1991. Mem. panel performing arts touring program Va. Commn. Arts; bd. dirs. Cultural Alliance Greater Washington, 1997—; bd. dirs., exec. com. Ill. Arts Alliance, Ill. Presenters Network. Recipient Best Lighting Design award, Univ. Theatre, U. Kans., Lawrence, 1970, Dawson Arts Mgmt. award, 1989; Study grantee, Ford Found./Grinnell Coll., 1975—76, Assn. Coll., Univ. and Cmty. Arts Adminstrs./NEA, 1978, 1981, 1985, 1986, 1988, 1990. Mem.: Ill. Arts Coun. (presenters panel), Assn. Performing Arts Presenters (bd. dirs. 1986—88), Dance/USA, Chamber Music Am., Am. Arts Alliance, Internat. Soc. Performing Arts (mem. edn. com. 1997—), Internat. Assn. Auditorium Mgrs., Fairfax County C. of C. (bd. dirs.), Champaign County C. of C., Rotary. Methodist. Avocations: golf, historical novels, classic films, welsh heritage. Office: Wolf Trap Found for Performing Arts 1645 Trap Rd Vienna VA 22182-2063 Office Phone: 703-255-4043.

JONES, THOMAS CLABURN, poet, educator; s. Thomas and Margaret Jones; m. Karin K. Krueger, Nov. 29, 1980; children: Thomas Claburn, Caroline Hollingsworth, Elizabeth Anderson, Drew Bartholomew Vandervelde, Margaret Alfaretta; m. Catherine Schlumberger, Aug. 29, 1964 (div. 1980). BA, Harvard U., 1964; diploma of French Civilization Studies, Sorbonne U. Paris, 1962; diploma of German Lang. and Lit.-Oberstufe, Goethe Inst., 1963; JD, Columbia U., 1968; MFA in Creative Writing, George Mason U., 1992. Bar: State Bar Wis. 1980. Rep. Amnesty Internat., Washington, 1972—79; tchr. Greyhills Acad. H.S., Tuba City, Ariz., 1994—98, dean, lang. arts dept., 1997—98; tchr., lang. arts Tuba City H.S., 1998—. Mission del. Egypt Amnesty Internat., London, 1979, mission del. Malaysia, Singapore, Brunei, 78, mission del. Philippines, 75, mission del. Spain, 75; vis. prof. poetry Visva Bharati U., Santiniketan, India, 1992; adj. prof. Navajo C.C., Tuba City, 1993—94. Writer (collections of poems) No Prisoners, 1976, Footbridge to India, 1990, Madmen and Bassoons, 1992, (collections of poems) Green Lake, 1996, Rez Dreamtime, 2001, Writing on Horseback, 2004, India Poems: Songs of Sarasvati, 2004; translator: (collections of poems) Book of Fragments, poems by Rei Berroa, co-translated with the author, Songbook of Absences, poems by Miguel Hernandez. Dist. atty. Green Lake County, Wis., 1983—84.

JONES, THOMAS OWEN, computer industry executive; b. Phila., Apr. 6, 1932; s. Paul John and Katharine (McCahey) J.; m. Mary Louise Russell, Sept. 19, 1959 (div. Aug. 1979); children: SusanR., Thomas H., Andrew S. BS in Engring., U. Pa., 1954, MBA, 1958. Account mgr. IBM Corp., Phila., 1958-66; asst. to sec. HEW, Washington, 1966-67; v.p. Donaldson, Lufkin & Jenrette, Inc., N.Y.C., 1967-72; pres. Jones/Hosplex Sys., N.Y.C., 1973-84, Carnegie-Madison Inc., N.Y.C., 1984-87, Fifth Generation Computer Corp., N.Y.C., 1987—, Golden Enterprises, Inc., Melbourne, Fla., 1999. Lectr. fin. Temple U. Evening Sch. Bus., 1959-66; cons. to sec. HEW, Washington, 1967-68; mem. Edn. Commr.'s Adv. Coun. on Copyright Policy, Washington, 1967-70. Mem. N.Y. State Adv. Coun. on Edn., Albany, 1970-75; mem. N.Y.C. #4 Cmty. Planning Bd., 1973-75. With U.S. Army, 1954-56. White House fellow U.S. Commn. on White House Fellows, Washington, 1966-67; named Outstanding Young Man of the Main Line, Jr. C. of C., Bryn Mawr, Pa., 1966. Mem.: IEEE, NY Acad. Scis., Wharton Alumni Assocs. (exec. bd. 1993—2000), Am. Legion, Union League Club Phila., NY Athletic Club. Avocations: tennis, travel. Office Phone: 212-756-0964. Personal E-mail: tojones@aol.com. Business E-Mail: tojones@fifthgen.com.

JONES, THOMAS OWEN, JR., finance educator, military officer; b. Washington, June 24, 1935; s. Thomas Owen Jones and Annie May Bell; m. Jasie Barringer, Nov., 1982 (div. Nov. 1989); m. Phyllis Stepp Cage, Oct. 10, 1990; stepchildren: Rebecca Lynn, Julie Gayle Cage. BSME, U. Pa., 1957; BSBA, U. Southwestern La., 1966; MBA, George Washington U., 1968, D of Bus. Adminstrn., 1972. Lic. comml. pilot, bldg. contractor, N.C.; cert. flight instr. Officer (ret.), naval aviator USN, 1958-2000; asst. and acting dean Coll. Bus. Loyola U., New Orleans, 1971-74; dean Sch. Bus. Eastern Ill. U., 1974-78; pres., CEO Galleries One, N.Y.C., 1978-85; founder, chmn. TJA Consulting, Washington, 1976-85; founder, CEO, chmn. BillPayers, Inc., Greensboro, N.C., 1985-99; chmn. divsn. bus. Greensboro Coll., 1986—, Fred L. Proctor Sr. prof. bus. Founding ptnr. Boston Consulting Group, Cambridge, Mass., 1966. Bd. dirs. Prison Ministry of N.C., 1998-2000. Rear admiral USNR, 1958-2000, ret. Recipient Gold medal Pan Am. Games, Mexico City, 1955, Gold medal Am. Canoeing Assn., 1957, Silver medal Olympic Games, Melbourne, Australia, 1956; 12 rowing championships Am. Rowing Assn., 1952-61., Fellow Acad. Mgmt.; mem. Assn. Exptl. Test Pilots, Greensboro City Club, Kiwanis, Beta Gamma Sigma. Republican. Presbyterian. Avocations: home building, teaching sunday school, demonstration piloting, coaching rowing. Home: 3614 Pinetop Rd Greensboro NC 27410 Office: Greensboro Coll 815 W Market St Greensboro NC 27401 Office Phone: 336-272-7102 289. E-mail: billpayers@aol.com.

JONES, THOMAS WADE, financial services executive; b. Phila., May 17, 1949; s. Edward Wilfred and Marie (Carter) J.; m. Stephanie Susan Bell, Aug. 1, 1968 (div. 1972); 1 child, Nigel; m. Adelaide Emma Knox, June 14, 1975; children: Evonne, Michael, Victoria. BA, Cornell U., 1969, M in Regional Planning, 1972; MBA, Boston U., 1978. CPA, Mass., N.Y. Lectr. Cornell U., Ithaca, N.Y., 1971-72; contract mgr. Abt Assocs., Inc., Cambridge, Mass., 1972-73; prin., mgr. Arthur Young & Co., Boston, Ma., 1973-81; pres. Atlantic TV Corp., Boston, 1981-82; from 2nd v.p. to sr. v.p., treas. John Hancock Mut. Life Ins. Co., Boston, 1982-89; exec. v.p., CFO Tchrs. Ins. & Annuity Assn., N.Y.C., 1989-93, pres., COO, 1993—97; vice chmn. Traveler's Group, 1997; chmn., CEO Smith Barney Asset Mgmt., 1997—98; chmn., CEO, Global Investment Mgmt. Citigroup, Inc., 1999—2004, chmn., CEO, Citigroup Asset Mgmt., 1999—2004. Project mgr. N.Y.-Pa. Health Planning Coun., Binghamton, N.Y., 1971-72; bd. dirs. Thomas & Betts Corp., Bridgewater, N.J.; trustee, bd. dirs. Ea. Enterprises Inc., Boston. Trustee Boston Ballet, 1976—, Brookings Instn., Washington, 1992—, Cornell U., Ithaca, N.Y., 1993—, Cmty. Econ. Devel., N.Y.C., 1993—; mem. vestry Trinity Ch., Boston, 1987—; bd. dirs. Nellie Mae, Inc., Boston, 1987—. Fellow AICPA, Mass. Soc. CPAs, World Affairs Coun. Boston (bd. dirs. 1988—). Avocation: tennis. Office: Citigroup Inc 399 Park Ave New York NY 10043

JONES, THORNTON KEITH, research chemist; b. Brawley, Calif., Dec. 17, 1923; s. Alfred George and Madge Jones; m. Evalee Vestal, July 4, 1965; children: Brian Keith, Donna Eileen. BS, U. Calif., Berkeley, 1949, postgrad., 1951-52. Research chemist Griffin Chem. Co., Richmond, Calif., 1949-55; western product devel. and improvement mgr. Nopco Chem. Co., Richmond, Calif., 1955; research chemist Chevron Research Co., Richmond, 1956-65, research chemist in spl. products research and devel., 1965-1982; product quality mgr. Chevron USA, Inc., San Francisco, 1982-87, ret. Patentee in field. Vol. fireman and officer, Terra Linda, Calif., 1957-64; mem. adv. com. Terra Linda Dixie Elem. Sch. Dist., 1960-64. Served with Signal Corps, U.S. Army, 1943-46. Mem. Am. Chem. Soc., Forest Products Research Soc., Am. Wood Preservers Assn., Alpha Chi Sigma. Republican. Presbyterian. Avocations: music, gardening, wine and food.

JONES, TOM, singer; b. Pontypridd, Wales, June 7, 1940; s. Thomas and Freda (Jones) Woodward; m. Melinda Trenchard, 1956; 1 son, Mark. Student, Treforrest Secondary Modern Sch. Bricklayer, factory and constrn. laborer. Pub. singing debut at age 3 in village stores of Wales; sang in local pubs; changed name to Tom Jones, 1963; organized backup group the Playboys to sing in London clubs; first hit record was It's Not Unusual, 1964; appeared on Brit. radio and TV; toured U.S. in 1965, 68; appeared on Ed Sullivan Show; star of TV show This is Tom Jones, 1969-71; regular appearances in nightclubs, concert halls and on TV; songs recorded include What's New Pussycat, 1965, Thunderball, 1965, Green Green Grass of Home, 1966, Delilah, 1968, Love Me Tonight, 1969, Can't Stop Loving You, 1970, She's A Lady, 1971, Letter to Lucille, 1973, Say You'll Stay Until Tomorrow, 1976; albums Darlin, 1981, Move Closer, 1989, Carrying A Torch, 1990 (includes collaborations with Van Morrison); sang score for mus. play Matador; hit single A Boy From Nowhere, 1987, Kiss (in collaboration with Art of Noise), 1988, The Complete Tom Jones, 1993, Reload, 1999 (multi-platinum world-wide), Best of Tom Jones, 2000; film Mars Attacks, 1996, Agnes Brown, 1999, The Emperor's New Groove, 2000; TV appearances include Here, There and Everywhere: a Concert for Linda, 1999, Jerry Springer on Sunday, 1999, An Audience with Tom Jones, 2000, Millenium Celebrations at the White House, 2000, Queen's Jubilee Concert, 2002; TV series The Morecambe & Wise Show, The Sonny and Cher Show, (voice) The Simpsons, The Fresh Prince of Bel-Air, Russell Gilbert Live, The Panel, 20/20. Recipient Grammy award as Best New Artist, 1965, Brit. Best Male Vocalist award, 2003, Brit. Outstanding Contbn. award, 2003. Office: c/o Tom Jones Enterprises 10100 Santa Monica Blvd Ste 2035 Los Angeles CA 90067-4100

JONES, TOM GEORGE, lawyer; b. Defiance, Ohio, Oct. 21, 1934; s. Russell George and Edith (Guinn) J.; m. Annette Huttmacher, June 14, 1959 (div. Mar. 1979); children: Amy Jones Welsh, Mary Margaret Goss, Russell Nicholas, Jennifer Jones Auger; m. Susan Lee Crawford Whitacre, Sept. 17, 1982; stepchildren: Robert Parker Whitacre, James Alan Whitacre, Elizabeth Lee Whitacre. BS in Mktg., Ind. U., 1956; JD, Ind. U., Indpls., 1961. Bar: Ind. 1961, U.S. Dist. Ct. (so. dist.) Ind. 1961, U.S. Ct. Appeals (7th cir.) 1961; cert. personal injury mediator, Indiana Trial Cts. Ptnr. Jones, Hoffman & Admire, Franklin, Ind., 1961—. Dep. pros. atty. Johnson County, 1960-61; lectr. Ind. Continuing Legal Edn. Forum, Indpls., 1982—; mem. faculty Nat. Inst. Trial Adv., Washington, 1985—; lectr. U. Mich. Ann. Advocacy Inst., 1991-92; litigation atty., Johnson County Commr. Contbr. articles to profl. jours. Atty. Johnson County Planning Commn. and Zoning Bd., Ind., 1961-66. Fellow Ind. Trial Lawyers Assn. (chmn. criminal law sect. 1981-83, bd. dirs., 1982-95), Roscoe Pound Found.; mem. ABA, Indpls. Bar Assn., Johnson County Bar Assn.(sec. 1962, pres. 1974), Am. Bd. Trial Advocates (pres. Ind. chpt. 1990-95, nat. bd. dirs. 1990-96), Internat. Soc. Barristers, Nat. Assn. Criminal Def. Lawyers, Assn. Trial Lawyers Am. (sustaining), Tex. Trial Lawyers Assn., Melvin N. Bellie Soc., Phi Kappa Psi, I-Mans Assn. Lodges: Elks, Shriners, Masons, Scottish Rite. Mem. Christian Ch. (Disciples Of Christ). Office: Jones Hoffman & Admire 150 N Main St Franklin IN 46131-1721 Fax: 317-736-4440. E-mail: tommygjones@hotmail.com.

JONES, TOM J., music educator; b. Pascagoula, Miss., Apr. 15, 1947; s. Johnnie Amos and Josephine Jackson Jones; m. Barbara Linda Thompson (div.). BA, Prairie View A&M U., 1971; postgrad., Calif. State U., Haywood, 1976—78, Golden Gate U., 1978—80. Choral tchr. Oklahoma City Pub. Sch., 1971—72; race rels., comm. cons. Tinker AFB, Okla., 1972—74; music, English tchr. Oakland (Calif.) Unified. Sch., 1974—94; English, journalism instr. Forest Brook H.S., Houston, 1994—98; prin. Hope Charter Sch., Houston, 1998—99; music instr. Houston Sch. Dist., 1999—. Asst. registrar Golden Gate U., San Francisco, 1978—80; conductor, CEO Ebony Opera West, Oakland, 1978—88, Oakland Boys Choir, 1988—94. Author: (short stories) (poems, essays) Words From the Heart, 2002, Protocol for the Church Music, 1976. Min. music Faith Presbyn. Ch., Mills Grove Christian Ch.; asst. music dir. Allen Temple Bapt. Ch, Star Bethel Bapt. Ch., 1975—94. Recipient Am. Spirit award, Am. Savings Bank, Oakland, 1987, Outstanding Alumni award, Prairie View A&M U., 2002. Mem.: Nat. Assn. Negro Musicians, Tex. Choral Dirs., Omega Psi Phi. Democrat. Baptist. Avocations: photography, weightlifting. Home: 200 Treasure Ln Kingwood TX 77339

JONES, TOMMY LEE, actor; b. San Saba, Tex., Sept. 15, 1946; s. Clyde L. and Lucille Marie (Scott) J.; m. Kate Lardner, 1971 (div. 1978); m. Kimberlea Gayle Cloughley, May 30, 1981 (div. 1996); m. Dawn Laurel Mar. 19, 2001. BA cum laude in English, Harvard U., 1969. Broadway debut in A Patriot for Me, 1969; other stage appearances include Fortune and Men's Eye's, 1969, Four on a Garden, 1971, Blue Boys, 1972, Ulysses in Nighttown, 1974, True West, 1981; film debut in Love Story, 1970; other film appearances include Eliza's Horoscope, 1972, Life Study, 1972, Jackson County Jail, 1976, Rolling Thunder, 1977, The Betsy, 1978, Eyes of Laura Mars, 1978, Coal Miner's Daughter, 1980, Back Roads, 1981, Nate and Hayes, 1983, River Rat, 1984, Black Moon Rising, 1986, The Big Town, 1987, Stormy Monday, 1988, The Package, 1989, Fire Birds, 1990, JFK, 1991 (Acad. award nominee), Under Siege, 1992, The Fugitive, 1993 (Golden Globe award for best supporting actor 1994, Acad. award for best supporting actor 1993, Oscar for Best Actor in a Supporting Role, 1994), House of Cards, 1993, Heaven and Earth, 1993, Blown Away, 1994, The Client, 1994, Natural Born Killers, 1994, Blue Sky, 1994, Cobb, 1994, Batman Forever, 1995, Men in Black, 1997, Volcano, 1997, U.S. Marshals, 1997, (voice) Small Soldiers, 1998, Rules of Engagement, 2000, Double Jeopardy, 1999, Space Cowboys, 2000, Men in Black II, 2002, The Hunted, 2003, The Missing, 2003, Man of the House, 2005; TV movies include Smash-Up on Interstate 5, 1976, Charlie's Angels, 1976, The Amazing Howard Hughes, 1977, The Rainmaker, 1982, The Executioner's Song (Emmy award), 1982, The Park is Mine, 1985, Yuri Nosenko, KGB, 1986, Broken Vows, 1987, Stranger on My Land, 1988, April Morning, 1988, Gotham, 1988, The Good Old Boys (also dir., writer), 1995; appeared in TV miniseries, Lonesome Dove, 1989.*

JONES, TONY, academic administrator; Dir. Glasgow Sch. Arts, 1980—86; pres. Sch. Art Inst. Chgo., 1986—92; dir. Royal Coll. Art, London, 1992—96; pres. & co-CEO Sch. Art Inst. Chgo., 1996—. Named Hon. Dir. Bd., Osaka U. Arts (Japan), 2000, Hon. Prof., U. Wales, 1995; recipient Scotland's Newbery Medal, 1986. Fellow: Royal Coll. Art (sr.); mem.: Am. Inst. Architects (hon.). Office: School of Art Institute of Chicago Office of the President 37 South Wabash Ave Chicago IL 60603*

JONES, TRACEY KIRK, JR., retired minister, educator; b. Boston, Mar. 16, 1917; s. Tracey Kirk and Marion (Flowers) J.; m. Martha Clayton, Sept. 12, 1942 (dec. June 1975); children: Judith Grace Watson, Tracey Kirk Jones, III, Deborah Anita Jones Breitenbach; m. Junia K. Moss, July 1, 1978. BA, D.D., Ohio Wesleyan U.; B.D., Yale Div. Sch., 1942. Ordained to ministry Meth. Church, 1945; missionary Meth. Ch., China, 1946-50, 1952-55, exec. bd. mission, 1955; exec. sec. S.E. Asia, 1955-62; assoc. gen. sec. div. world missions, 1962-64; assoc. gen. sec. world div., 1964-68; gen. sec. bd. missions, 1968-72; gen. sec. bd. global ministries, 1972-80. Adj. prof. Drew Theol. Sch., Madison, N.J., 1980-89; mem. governing bd. Nat. Coun. Chs., 1st v.p., 1978-80. Author: Our Mission Today, 1963. Home: 700 John Ringling Blvd Apt W308 Sarasota FL 34236-1588

JONES, TRACY WEBB, lawyer; b. Lexington, Jan. 14, 1965; s. John Morland and Carol Tracy Webb; m. Robert Bondurant Jones, June 3, 1995. BA in Polit. Sci., U. Ky., 1987, JD, 1990. Bar: Ky. 1990, U.S. Dist. Ct. (we. dist.) Ky. 1991, U.S. Dist. Ct. (ea. dist.) Ky. 1992, U.S. Ct. Appeals (6th cir.) 1996. Staff atty. Fruit of the Loom, Bowling Green, Ky., 1990-91; assoc. Gallion, Baker & Bray, Lexington, 1991-98; atty. pvt. practice, Versailles, Ky., 1998-99; sen. atty. lexington-Fayette Urban County Govt., Lexington, Ky., 1999—. Bd. dirs. Visually Impaired Presch. Svcs., Lexington, 1994—. Office: 200 E Main St Lexington KY 40507 Home: 808 Royal Ridge Ct Versailles KY 40383-1922

JONES, TREVOR OWEN, biomedical industry executive, management consultant; b. Maidstone, Kent, Eng., Nov. 3, 1930; came to U.S., 1957, naturalized, 1971; s. Richard Owen and Ruby Edith (Martin) J.; m. Jennie Lou Singleton, Sept. 12, 1959; children: Pembroke Robinson (dec.), Bronwyn Elizabeth. Higher Nat. Cert. in Elec. Engring., Aston Tech. Coll., Birmingham, Eng., 1952; Ordinary Nat. Cert. in Mech. Engring., Liverpool (Eng.) Tech. Coll., 1957. Registered profl. engr., Wis.; chartered engr., U.K. Student engr., elec. machine design engr. Brit. Gen. Electric Co., 1950-57; project engr., project mgr. Nuc. Ship Savannah, Allis-Chalmers Mfg. Co., 1957-59; with GM, 1959-78, staff engr. in charge Apollo computers, 1967, dir. electronic control sys., 1970-72, dir. advanced product engring., 1972-74; dir. GM Proving Grounds, 1974-78; v.p. engring., automotive worldwide TRW Inc., Cleve., 1978-80, v.p. transp. electronics group, 1980-87, chmn. bd. dirs. Libbey-Owens-Ford Inc., 1987-94; chmn., CEO Internat. Devel. Corp., 1987—; from vice chmn. to chmn. Echlin Inc., 1995-98, chmn. bd. dir., interim pres. and CEO, 1997; chmn., founder, CEO Biomec Inc., 1998—. Chmn. emeritus Ohio Fuel Cell Coalition; vice chmn. Motor Vehicle Safety Adv. Coun., 1971; chmn. Nat. Hwy. Safety Adv. Com., 1976. Author, patentee automotive safety and electronics. Trustee Lawrence Inst. Tech., 1973-76; exec. bd. Clinton Valley coun. Boy Scouts Am., 1975; bd. govs. Cranbrook Inst. Sci., 1977; mem. Sec. of Def. Def. Sci. Bd. Task Force on Internat. Arms Devel. Cooperation, 1995-98; chmn. Nat. Rsch. Coun. Com. Partnership for a New Generation Vehicle, 1994-2001; vice chair bd. trustees Cleve. State U., 2001. Officer Brit. Army, 1955-57. Recipient Safety award for engring. excellence U.S. Dept. Transp., 1978. Fellow Brit. Instn. Mechanical Engrs. (hon.), Brit. Instn. Elec. Engrs. (Hooper Mem. prize 1950), IEEE (life, exec. com. vehicle tech. soc. 1977-81), Royal Soc. of the Arts, Mfg. and Commerce, Soc. Automotive Engrs. (Arch T. Colwell paper award 1974-75, Vincent Bendix Automotive Electronics award 1976, Edward N. Cole award 1988), Engring. Soc. Detroit, Engring. Soc. Cleve., Instn. Mech. Engrs. (hon.); mem. NAE, Union Club, Royal Poinciana Country Club (Naples, Fla.) Republican. Episcopalian. Home: Two Bratenahl Pl Bratenahl OH 44108 also: Ste 2001 4151 Gulf Shore Blvd N Naples FL 34103 Office Phone: 216-937-2800 x222. Business E-Mail: tojones@biomec.com. *Innovation and the acceptance of change are fundamental seeds of progress, and only hard work and an open mind will permit you to harvest its fruits.*

JONES, VALERIE MARIE, art educator; b. Pitts., Dec. 11, 1958; d. John Arthur Jones and Mary Jo Daniels; life ptnr. William Jay Stephens. BS, Kutztown State U., 1981; cert., U. Ala., Huntsville, 1992; MA, U. Ala., Tuscaloosa, 2001. Cert. tchr. art Nat. Bd. for Profl. Tchg. Stds., 2004. Maitre de Glover Restaurant, Guntersville, Ala., 1988—90; restaurant dir. Hilton, Huntsville, Ala., 1990—97; elem. educator second grade Hampton Cove (Ala.) Acad., 1997—98; visual arts educator Guntersville City Schools, 1998—. Restaurant cons. Huntsville Hilton, 1998—2000. 200 ft. long mural on permanent display, Guntersville History Mural. Mem. Guntersville Mus. and Cultural Ctr., 1999—2005, Mountain Valley Arts Coun., Guntersville, 1998. Named Educator of the Yr., Guntersville C. of C., 2001; grantee, Apple Found., 2003, 2003, 2004; G.I.F.T.S Mini grantee, Guntersville C. of C., 2002. Mem.: NEA (assoc.), Ala. Coun. for Tech. in Edn. (assoc.), Ala. Edn. Assn. (assoc.), Ala. Art Edn. Assn. (assoc.), Nat. Art Edn. Assn. (assoc.), Nat. Art Honor Soc. (assoc.; tchr./sponsor 1998). Office: Guntersville High School 14227 US Highway 431 South Guntersville AL 35976 Office Phone: 256-582-2046. Office Fax: 256-582-4742. Personal E-mail: vjones1211@charter.net.

JONES, VAUGHAN FREDERICK RANDAL, mathematician, educator; b. Gisborne, New Zealand, Dec. 31, 1952; m. Martha Weare Myers, Apr. 7, 1979; children: Bethany Martha, Ian Randal, Alice Collins. BSc, U. Auckland, New Zealand, 1972, MSc with first class honors, 1973; DSc in Math., Ecoles Mathematiques, Geneva, 1979; DSc (hon.), U. Auckland, 1992, U. Wales, 1993. Asst. lectr. U. Auckland, New Zealand, 1974; asst. U. Geneva, 1975—80; E.R. Hedrick asst. prof. math. UCLA, 1980—81; asst. prof. U. Pa., Phila., 1981—84, assoc. prof., 1984—85; prof. math. U. Calif., Berkeley, 1985—. Vis. lectr. U. Pa., Phila., 1981—82; dir. New Zealand Math. Rsch. Inst. Recipient F W W Rhodes Meml. Scholarship, Swiss Govt. Scholarship, 1973, Vacheron Constantin Prize, 1980, Guggenhein fellowship, 1986, Fields medal Internat. Congress, Kyoto, Japan, 1990, New Zealand Govt. Sci. medal, 1991, Onsager medal, Trondheim U., 2000. Fellow: Royal Soc.; mem.: Norwegian Royal Soc. Letters & Scis., U.S. Nat. Acad. Scis., London Math. Soc. (hon.), Am. Acad. Arts & Scis. Achievements include index theorem for von Neumann algebras; discovery of a new polynomial invariant for knots which led to surprising connections between apparently quite different areas of mathematics. Office: U Calif Berkeley Dept Math 970 Evans Hall Berkeley CA 94720-3841

JONES, VAUGHN PAUL, construction marketing executive; b. Johnstown, Pa., Apr. 25, 1947; s. Gordon Kenneth and Luella Jane (Seesholtz) Jones; m. Karen Tolbert, Nov. 22, 1985; children: Shelly Marie, Stewart Conway. BS in Acctg., Ferris State U., 1971; MBA, Capital U., 1985; grad., Columbus (Ohio) Area Leadership Program, 1985-86. Lic. health care risk mgr. Fla. Auditor John W. Galbreath, Columbus, 1972-74; mgmt. analyst State of Ohio, Columbus, 1974-76; contr. Functional Planning, Inc., Columbus, 1976-82; pres. N. Area Mental Health Svcs., Inc., Columbus, 1982-87; assoc. exec. dir. Lakeside Alternatives, Inc., Orlando, Fla., 1987-90; adminstrv. svcs. mgr. Prog. Cos. Fla. Divsn., Tampa, 1991-92; v.p. corp. svcs. Harbor Behavioral Health Care Inst., Inc., New Port Richey, Fla., 1992-98; dep. devel. officer Fla. Housing Fin. Corp., Tallahassee, 1998; project mgr. Itasca Constrn. Assocs., Tampa, 1998—2001, dir. bus. devel. healthcare divsn., 2001—05; dir. mktg. Superior Constrn Greenville LLC, Tampa, 2005—. Vol. United Way Campaign; chmn. polit. letterwriting com. gubernatorial campaign Columbus, 1985. Recipient Senatorial citation, State of Ohio, 1985, Ho. of Reps. citation, 1986. Mem.: Fla. Soc. Healthcare Risk Mgrs., MBA Execs., Rotary (v.p. Capital City West Club 1981). Avocations: collecting antique tools, collecting bamboo fly rods, fly fishing, fly tying. Home: 1648 Parker Point Blvd Odessa FL 33556 Office: Itasca Constrn Assocs 7884 Woodland Center Blvd Tampa FL 33614-2409 Office Phone: 813-975-8909. Business E-Mail: vjones@superiorconstruction.com.

JONES, VELITA YVETTE, music educator; b. Greenville, SC, Sept. 25, 1967; d. Claude S and Nettie Francis Jones; 1 child, Christopher Brandon. BS, SC State U., 1990; M in Music Edn., Converse Coll., Spartanburg, SC, 2000. Nat. bd. cert. tchr. 2004. Music specialist Greenbrier Elem. Sch., Greenville, SC, 1995—; facilitator Curriculum Leadership in the Arts, Columbia, SC, 2000—. Outreach cons. Arts in Basic Curriculum, Rock Hill, SC, 2003—. Mem. NAACP, Greenville, SC, 2003—04. Grantee, Kraft Foods, 2003. Mem.: Pi Delta Kappa, SCMEA (spl. learners chmn. 2003—05), Pi Kappa Lambda Music Soc., Delta Sigma Theta Sorority, Inc. Democrat. Seventh Day Adventist. Avocations: traveling, singing, composing, reading, watching television. Home (Summer): 167 Oakvale Drive Piedmont SC 29673 Office: Greenbrier Elem Sch 853 Log Shoals Rd Greenville SC 29607 Office Phone: 864 355300. Personal E-mail: vjones@greenville.k12.sc.us.

JONES, VERNON QUENTIN, surveyor; b. Sioux City, Iowa, May 6, 1930; s. Vernon Boyd and Winnifred Rhoda J.; m. Rebeca Buckovecz, Oct. 1981; children: Steve Vernon, Gregory Richard, Stanley Alan, Lynn Sue. Student, UCLA, 1948-50. Draftsman III, city engr. City of Pasadena, Calif., 1950-53; sr. civil engring. asst. L.A. County Engrs., L.A., 1953-55; v.p. Treadwell Engring. Corp., Arcadia, Calif., 1955-61, pres., 1961-64, Hillcrest Engring. Corp., Arcadia, 1961-64; dep. county surveyor Ventura County, Calif., 1964-78; propr. Vernon Jones Land Surveyor, Bullhead City, Ariz., 1978—; city engr. City of Needles, Calif., 1980-87. Instr. Mohave Community Coll., 1987-90. Chmn. graphic tech. com. Ventura Unified Sch. Dist., 1972-78, mem. career adv. com., 1972-74; mem. engring. adv. com. Pierce Coll., 1973; pres. Mgmt. Employees of Ventura County, 1974; v.p. Young Reps. of Ventura County, 1965; pres. Marina Pacifica Homeowners Assn., 1973. Mem. League Calif. Surveying Orgns. (pres. 1975), Am. Congress on Surveying and Mapping (chair so. Calif. sect. 1976), Am. Soc. Photogrammetry, Am. Pub. Works Assn., County Engrs. Assn. Calif. Home: PO Box 20761 Bullhead City AZ 86439-0761

JONES, VERNON RORY, computer company executive, consultant; s. Gordon Jones and Janet Douglas; m. Janet Sandona. BSc (hon.), City U., London, 1986; MBA, U. Chgo., 1991. New product mgr. Thomson Consumer Electronics, London, 1986—89; sr. assoc. Marakon Assocs., Stamford, Conn., 1991—95; ptnr. strategy consulting PricewaterhouseCoopers, NYC, 1995—2000; v.p. strategy and bus. devel. Nextera, LA, 2000—02; prin. Bus. Intelligence Assocs., San Francisco, 2002—. Office: Business Intelligence Assocs 1 St Francis Pl San Francisco CA 94107 Office Phone: 650-218-4000. Personal E-mail: mail@v-rory-jones.org. Business E-Mail: roryjones@biassociates.com.

JONES, VILLIE, music educator; b. N.Y.C., Mar. 3, 1973; s. Willie and Jacqueline Diane Jones; m. Dawn Linette Jones; 1 child, Villie II. BA in Music with Edn. Cert., Savannah (Ga.) State U., 1997. Lic. tchr. N.C., cert. educator Ga. Choral dir. Red Springs (N.C.) Mid. Sch., 1998—99, Reid Ross Classical Sch., Fayetteville, NC, 1999—2000; dir. of bands S.W. Mid. Sch., Savannah, 2000—01, Westover Mid. Sch., Fayetteville, 2001—03, Westover H.S., Fayetteville, 2003—. Named New Tchr. of Yr., S.W. Mid. Sch., 2001. Mem.: N.C. Music Educators Assn., Music Educators Nat. Conf., Southea. Dist. Bandmasters Assn., Alpha Phi Alpha (cmty. svc. advisor 1997—98, Outstanding Cmty. Svc. award 1998). Avocations: travel, cultural outings, exercise, dining out, mentoring. Office: Westover HS 277 Bonanza Dr Fayetteville NC 28303 Home: 2910 Coachway Dr Fayetteville NC 28306 Office Phone: 910-864-0190. Personal E-mail: vjones_apa1@hotmail.com. E-mail: villiejones@ccs.k12.nc.us.

JONES, VIRGINIA MCCLURKIN, retired social worker; b. Anniston, Ala., Mar. 13, 1935; d. Louie Walter and Virginia Keith (Beaver) McClurkin; m. Charles Miller Jones, Jr., Mar. 16, 1957; children: Charles Miller III, V. Grace. BA, Agnes Scott Coll., 1957; MA, U. Tenn., 1965, MSSW, 1979. English instr. U. Tenn., Knoxville, 1967-71; religious edn. dir. Oak Ridge Unitarian Ch., 1972-73, 76-78; co-owner, mgr. The Bookstore, 1973-76; English instr. Roane State C.C., 1975-80; pvt. practice clin. social work Oak Ridge, 1980-98. Cons. Mountain Cmty. Health Ctr., Coalfield, Tenn., 1980-83, Valley Ridge Hospice, 1987-89. Contbr. articles to newspapers. Mem.: NASW, Concord Yacht Club, Rotary. Democrat. Episcopalian. Office: 969 Oak Ridge Turnpike Oak Ridge TN 37830-6554

JONES, VIVIAN EILENE, music educator; b. Tulsa, Okla., Oct. 13, 1948; d. Lucius and Vivian Dotson Jones. BS in Music Edn., Morgan State U., Balt., 1970; EdM in Spl. Edn., Coppin State Coll., Balt., 1974. Cert. educator S.C., tchr. Mo. Tchr. Balt. City Pub. Schs., 1970—74, St. Louis Pub. Schs., 1974—84, Oakland (Calif.) Unified Sch. Dist., 1984—90, Kirkwood (Mo.) R-7 Sch. Dist., 1990—94, Charleston (S.C.) County Sch. Dist., 1994—2000, 2004—, Dorchester Dist. 2, Summerville, SC, 2000—04. Dir. Charleston Symphony Orch. Gospel Choir, 2000—; music coord. Charleston Devel. Acad. Charter Sch., 2004—; choral clinician B.E.A.C.H. Gifted and Talented Program, Georgetown, SC, 1999—. Composer: (radio comml.) It's Cajun Delight, (program theme song) If You Gear Up; arranger (Negro spirituals). Scholarship grantor Coastal Cmty. Found., Charleston, 2001—05. Recipient Key to the City, Jefferson City, Mo., 1989, Outstanding Contbn. in the Arts award, Moja Arts Festival Com., 2002. Mem.: Music Educators Nat. Conf., Am. Choral Dirs. Assn., Alpha Kappa Alpha (Neophyte of Yr. 1968). Avocations: travel, puzzles, swimming. Home: 8093 Shadow Oak Dr Charleston SC 29406 Office: Burke HS 244 President St Charleston SC 29403 Office Phone: 843-724-7757. Office Fax: 843-720-2359. E-mail: vivian_jones@charleston.k12.sc.us.

JONES, W. S. (STEVE JONES), dean; b. Elkin, NC; m. Lisa Jones; 4 children. BA in econ., U. NC, 1974; MBA, Harvard Bus. Sch., 1978; Doctorate (hon.), Queensland U. Tech., 2002. Mgmt. cons. McKinsey & Co., Atlanta, 1984—90, Melbourne, Australia, 1984—90; joined as cons. ANZ Banking Group, Australia, 1990, mng. dir. retail ops., 1993—95, New Zealand mng. dir., 1995—96; mng. dir., chief exec. Suncorp Metway Ltd., Brisbane, Australia, 1997—2002; dean Kenan-Flagler Bus. Sch., U. NC, Chapel Hill, 2003—. Named one of Top 50 CEOs in Australia, The Bulletin mag., 2001; recipient Centenary Medal for svc. to bus. and commerce through banking and fin, Australian Govt., 2003. Office: Kenan-Flagler Bus Sch U NC Chapel Hill Campus Box 3490 McColl Bldg Chapel Hill NC 27599-3490

JONES, WALTER BEAMAN, congressman; b. Pitt County, N.C., Feb. 10, 1943; m. Joe Anne Jones; 1 child. BA in History, Atlantic Christian Coll., 1967. Mgr. Walter B. Jones Office Supply Co., 1967-73; salesman Dunn Assoc., 1973-82; pres. Benefit Reserves, Inc., 1989-94, Judson Co., 1990-94; rep. N.C. Ho. of Reps., 1983-92; mem. 104th-108th Congress from 3d N.C. dist., 1995—; mem. armed srvc. com., resources com., banking & financial com. Republican. Office: US House Reps 422 Cannon Bldg Ofcbldg Washington DC 20515-0001*

JONES, WALTER HARRISON, chemist, educator; b. Griffin, Sask., Can., Sept. 21, 1922; s. Arthur Frederick and Mildred Tracy (Walter) J.; m. Marion Claire Twomey, Oct. 25, 1959 (dec. Jan. 1976); m. Dorothy-Lynne Byrne, 1979 (div. 1981, remarried 1994, div. 1997). BS with honors, UCLA, 1944, PhD in Chemistry, 1948. Rsch. chemist Dept. Agr., 1948—51; sr. rsch. engr. N.Am. Aviation, 1954—56; rsch. chemist Los Alamos Sci. Lab., N.Mex., 1951—54; mgr. chemistry dept. Ford Motor Co., 1956—60; sr. staff and program mgr., chmn. JANAF-ARPA-NASA Thermochem. panel Inst. Def. Analyses, 1960—63; head propulsion dept. Aerospace Corp., 1963—64; sr. scientist, head advanced tech. Hughes Aircraft Co., 1964—68; prof. aero. sys., dir. Corpus Christi Ctr. U. West Fla., Pensacola, 1969—75, prof. chemistry, 1975—95; vis. rsch. chemist UCLA, 1994—. AEC fellow UCLA, 1954; vis. prof. U. Toronto, 1979, 92, U. Queensland, 1998; cons. pvt., fed. and state agys. Author: (novels) Prisms in the Pentagon, 1971; contbr. articles to tech. jours., chpts. to books. Mem. Gov.'s Task Force on Energy, Regional Energy Action Com., Fla. State Energy Office, adv. com. Tampa Bay Regional Planning Coun.; judge regional and state sci. fairs. Grantee, NSF, 2000—; fed. and state grantee, rsch. corp. grantee. Fellow ASEE/ONR, NATO, Am. Inst. Chemists; mem. AIAA, AAUP, AAAS, Am. Astron. Soc. (propulsion com.), Am. Chem. Soc. (chmn. Pensacola sect.), NY Acad. Scis., Am. Phys. Soc., Internat. Solar Energy Soc., Combustion Inst. World Assn. Theoretical Organic Chemists, Am. Ordnance Assn., Air Force Assn., Philos. Soc. Washington, Pensacola C. of C., Phi Beta Kappa, Sigma Xi (pres. local chpt.), Pi Mu Epsilon, Phi Lambda Upsilon (sec. local chpt.), Alpha Mu Gamma, Alpha Chi Sigma (pres. local chpt.). Achievements include patents in field. Home and Office: 355 Calle Loma Norte Santa Fe NM 87501-1256 Office Phone: 505-983-8123.

JONES, WALTON LINTON, internist, retired government agency administrator; b. McCaysville, Ga., Dec. 4, 1918; s. Walton Linton and Pearl Josephine (Gilliam) J.; m. Caroline Wells Schachte, June 5, 1943; children—Walton Linton III, Francis Stephen, Kathleen Caroline BS, Emory U., 1939, MD, 1942. Diplomate Am. Bd. Preventive Medicine. Commd. lt. (j.g.) U.S. Navy, 1942, advanced through grades to capt., 1956; rotating intern U.S. Naval Hosp., Charleston, S.C., 1942-43, aerospace medicine, 1944; flight surgeon USMC Aircraft Squadrons, 1944-47; head aero. med. safety Navy Dept., 1947-53; sr. med. officer U.S.S. Randolph, 1953-55; dir. aero. med. ops. and equipment Bur. Medicine and Surgery, Navy Dept., 1955-64; dir. biotech. and human research div. NASA, 1964-66; ret. U.S. Navy, 1966; civilian dir. biotech and human research div. NASA, Washington, 1966-70, dep., dir. life scis., 1970-75, dir. occupational medicine, 1975-82, dir. occupational health, 1982-85; cons. aerospace medicine, 1985—. Mem. exec. com. hearing and bioacoustics Nat. Acad. Scis., 1964-85, chmn., 1970, mem. exec. com. on vision, 1964-85; Kober lectr. Georgetown U., 1968 Leader, mem. com. Nat. Capital Area council Boy Scouts Am., Falls Church, Va., 1956-64 Decorated Legion of Merit; recipient Exceptional Service medal NASA, 1979, Outstanding Leadership medal NASA, 1985. Fellow Aerospace Medicine Assn. (Bauer award 1970, pres. 1980), AIAA (assoc., recipient John Jeffries award 1970), Royal Soc. Health; mem. Internat. Astronautics Acad., Assn. Mil. Surgeons (Founders award 1956), Internat. Acad. Aerospace Medicine.

JONES, WANDA FAYE (FAYE WILLIAMS JONES), retired librarian, media specialist; b. Little Rock, May 7, 1949; d. Hoyt and Marcella (Durnie) Williams; m. Robert David Jones, Nov. 22, 1978. BS in Edn., Ouachita Bapt. U., Arkadelphia, Ark., 1971, MS in Edn., 1975; MLS, Tex. Woman's U., 1980. Cert. English tchr., in libr. media, Ark. Libr. media specialist Carthage (Ark.) Pub. Sch., 1971-74, Harris Elem. Sch., North Little Rock, Ark., 1974-77, Jacksonville (Ark.) Elem. Sch., 1977-83, North Pulaski High Sch., Jacksonville, 1983—2000. Conf. and workshop presenter, 1982; adj. faculty U. Ctrl. Ark., 1995—99; cons. Little Rock Writing Project, 1999. Author poems, Grandmother Earth X, 2003, Grandmother Earth XI, 2004, co-author curriculum guides; author: (articles and revs.) Ark. News and Views, Ark. Librs. Mem. standards com. for media program Ark. State Libr., 1983; mem. Cen. Ark. Friends of Libr. Recipient award for exemplary libr. program U.S. Dept. Edn., 1986. Mem. NEA, Ark. Assn. Instrnl. Media (com. 1977—, chmn. student media festival 1987-88), Ark. Edn. Assn. (conf. chmn. libr. media div. 1982-84), Ark. Libr. Assn. (chmn. poster session 1989-92), Ark. Assn. Sch. Librs. (v.p. 1983, pres. 1984), Internat. Assn. Sch. Librianship, Pulaski Assn. Classrm. Tchrs., Nat. Fedn. of State Poetry Socs., Poets Roundtable Ark., River Mkt. Poets, Mo. State Poetry Soc., Poetry Soc. Okla. Baptist. Avocations: travel, reading, writing, photography.

JONES, WAYNE ALLEN, publisher; b. Bisbee, Ariz., Feb. 10, 1945; s. Earl Wayne and Mary Elizabeth Brown Jones; m. Susheel Dheer, Dec. 30, 1967; children: Sangita (Bete) Adrienne Pfister, Alexander Subhash. A.B. in Biology, Harvard Coll., 1967; M.A. in English, U. Mich., 1969; A.M. in English, Harvard U., 1970, PhD in English and Am. Lit. and Lang., 1974; postgrad. in Clin. profl. Psychology, Roosevelt U., 2003—. Lectr., asst. prof. U. Ill., Chgo., 1972—76; asst. prof. U. Miami, Coral Gables, Fla., 1976—80, adj. asst. prof., 1980—89; documentation specialist and other positions Digital Equipment Corp., Maynard, Mass., 1980—98; alliance mgr. Compaq Computer Corp., Marlborough, Mass., 1998—2002; global alliance mgr. Hewlett-Packard Co., Littleton, Mass., 2002—03. Adv. bd. Nathaniel Hawthorne Soc., Bloomfield Hill, Mich., 1974—77; founder, co-dir. The Snarks - A Miami Writer Workshop, 1978—80; pub. Fractal Edge Press, Chgo., 2002—. Contbr. The Nathaniel Hawthorne Calendar, editor, collaborator (three-act play) The Shift by Bernard McCabe, assoc. editor Nathaniel Hawthorne Jour., 1977—80; contbg. editor: Nathaniel Hawthorne Soc. Newsletter, 1975—76; mem. adv. bd., contbr. First Printings of Am. Authors, 1974—80; author: Stone Works, 2002, Decades of Rehearsal, 2003; author: (with Barnard McCabe) The A Poems, 2003. Juried poet Houston Poetry Fest, 2000, 2002, 2003, Chgo. Poetry Fest, 2003; pres. bd. dirs. Studio Potter, Dunbarton, NH, 2000—03. Named to Greybeard - DTR-SIG Hall of Fame, Datatrieve Spl. Interest Group, 1982; recipient award of merit, Soc. Tech. Comm., 1981, 1991, Recognition for Outstanding Partnering and Customer Presentations, Platinum Technologies Corp., 1998; fellow, U. Ill., Chgo., 1975, Huntington Libr., San Marino, CA, 1976, Am. Coun. Learned Socs., 1977; grantee, U. Ill., Chgo., 1974; Max Orovitz Summer fellow in arts and humanities, U. of Miami, 1979. Mem.: Phi Kappa Phi (chpt. sec.-tras. 1979—80). Independent. Taoist. Achievements include discovery of Nathaniel Hawthorne's first review of another author; Hawthorne's means of funding Fanshawe, his first novel; Hawthorne's income from The Token and Twice-Told Tales; a previously unknown Hawthorne love letter; 2 volumes of Manning Estate records in Nathaniel Hawthorne's hand. Avocation: photography. Personal E-mail: wayne.jones@att.net.

JONES, WELLINGTON DOWNING, III, banker; b. Topeka, Feb. 16, 1945; s. Wellington Downing Jr. and Nancy (Neiswanger) J.; m. Andrea Loftus, May 2, 1970; children: Wellington Downing IV, Heather, Lindsey. BSBA, Northwestern U., 1967; postgrad., Grad. Sch. Banking, Madison, Wis., 1980, Harvard U., 1987. Mktg. rep. IBM, Chgo., 1969-76; v.p. data processing 1st Bank & Trust (name 1st Source Bank 1981), South Bend, Ind., 1976-79, v.p. retail banking, 1979-81; sr. v.p. 1st Source Bank, South Bend, 1981-88; pres. 1st Nat. Bank Mishawaka (acquired by 1st Source Bank 1983), Ind., 1983; exec. v.p. 1st Source Corp., South Bend, 1988—98, pres., 1998—. Bd. dirs. Trustcorp Mortgage, South Bend. Bd. dirs. Neighborhood Housing Svcs., South Bend, 1986—, Entertainment Dist. Bd., South Bend, 1991—, United Way St. Joseph County, South Bend, 1991—; chmn. South Bend Mayor's Housing Forum, 1991—; pres. No. Ind. Hist. Soc., South Bend, 1991—. Sgt. USMCR, 1967-73. Mem. Signal Point Club (Niles, Mich.), Morris Park Country Club. Presbyterian. Avocations: golf, platform tennis, reading, investments. Office: 1st Source Bank 100 N Michigan St South Bend IN 46601-1630

JONES, WILLIAM ADRIAN, percussionist, education program administrator; b. Oakland City, Ind., Feb. 27, 1962; s. Rene Ardell Jones. BS in Music Mgmt., U. Evansville, 1985, BA in Spanish, 1986; MusB, U. Ky., 1990, MusM, 1993. Edn. program coord. Lexington (Ky.) Children's Mus., 1992-94; asst. counselor Calvary and Band Squadron The Culver Academies, Culver, Ind., 1996; asst. band dir. The Culver (Ind.) Academies, 1996. Profl. performer with Owensboro Symphony Orch., 1981-83, Evansville (Ind.) Philharm. Orch., 1981-83, Encore Dinner Theatre, Evansville, 1986-87, Tales and Scales Performing Arts Troupe, Evansville, 1986-87, Evansville Symphonic Band, 1983-89, Lexington Philharm. Orch., 1992; pvt. instr. percussion Carl's Music Ctr., Lexington, 1992-95; coord. children's summer program Lexington C.C., 1994; percussion instr., arranger Princeton Cmty. High Sch., Princeton, 1996. Counselor Culver Summer Upper Camps, summer 1996. Recipient various scholarships, fellowships and awards. Mem. Ky. Alliance for Arts Edn. (bd. dirs., sec. 1994-95), Percussive Arts Soc., Mortar Bd., BSU Alumni and Friends Assn. (interim pres. 1995), Golden Key, Phi Beta Kappa, Omicron Delta Kappa, Pi Kappa Lambda, Sigma Delta Pi, Phi Mu alpha. Home: CEF # 988 1300 Academy Rd Culver IN 46511-1234

JONES, WILLIAM ALLEN, lawyer; b. Phila., Dec. 13, 1941; s. Roland Emmett and Gloria (Miller) J.; m. Margaret Smith, Sept. 24, 1965 (div. 1972); m. Dorothea S. Whitson, June 15, 1973; children— Darlene, Rebecca, Gloria, David. BA, Temple U., 1967; MBA, JD, Harvard U., 1972. Bar: Calif. 1974. Atty. Walt Disney Prodns., Burbank, Calif., 1973-77, treas., 1977-81; atty. Wyman Bautzer et al, L.A., 1981-83, MGM/UA Entertainment Co., Culver City, 1983, v.p., gen. counsel, 1983-86; sr. v.p., corp. gen. counsel, sec. MGM/UA Communications Co., Culver City, Calif., 1986-91; exec. v.p., gen. counsel, sec. Metro-Goldwyn-Mayer Inc., Santa Monica, Calif., 1991-95, exec. v.p. corp. affairs, 1995-97, sr. exec. v.p., 1997—. Bus. mgr. L.A. Bar Jour., 1974-75; bd. dirs. The Nostalgia Network Inc.; mem. bd. of govs. Inst. for Corp. Counsel, 1990-93. Charter mem. L.A. Philharm. Men's Com., 1974-80; trustee Marlborough Sch., 1988-93, Flintridge Preparatory Sch., 1993-96. With USAF, 1960-64. President's scholar Temple U., 1972 Mem. Harvard Bus. Sch. Assn. So. Calif. (bd. dirs. 1985-88). Home: 1557 Colina Dr Glendale CA 91208-2412 Office: Metro Goldwyn Mayer Inc 2500 Broadway Santa Monica CA 90404-3065

JONES, WILLIAM AUGUSTUS, JR., retired bishop; b. Memphis, Jan. 24, 1927; s. William Augustus and Martha (Jones) J.; m. Margaret Loaring-Clark, Aug. 26, 1949; 4 children. BA, Southwestern at Memphis, 1948; B.D., Yale U., 1951. Ordained priest Episcopal Ch., 1952; priest in charge Messiah Ch., Pulaski, Tenn., 1952-57; curate Christ Ch., Nashville, 1957-58; rector St. Mark Ch., LaGrange, Ga., 1958-65; asso. rector St. Luke Ch., Mountainbrook, Ala., 1965-66; dir. research So. region Assn. Christian Tng. and Service, Memphis, 1966-67; exec. dir. Assn. Christian Tng. and Service, 1968-72; rector St. John's, Johnson City, Tenn., 1972-75; bishop of Mo. St. Louis, 1975-93. Adj. staff Christ Ch., Wilmington, Del., 2001. Episcopalian.

JONES, WILLIAM BENJAMIN, JR., retired electrical engineering educator; b. Fairburn, Ga., Sept. 17, 1924; s. William Benjamin and Katherine (Davenport) J.; m. Mary Pierce Hammond, Sept. 8, 1948; children: William Benjamin III, Katherine P., Joseph L. BS, Ga. Inst. Tech., 1945, MS, 1948, PhD, 1953. Mem. tech. staff Hughes Aircraft Co., Culver City, Calif., 1954-58; prof. elec. engring. Ga. Inst. Tech., 1958-67; prof. Tex. A&M U., 1967-90, head dept. elec. engring., 1967-84. Vis. prof. U. Fla., 1984-85 Author: Introduction to Optical Fiber Communication Systems, 1987. Served with USNR, 1943-46. Mem. IEEE (sr. mem., editor transactions on communication systems 1960-61, chmn. communication tech. group 1966-67, mem. tech. activities bd. 1966-69, v.p. communications soc. 1972-73, chmn. elec. engring. dept. heads assn. 1983-84), Sigma Xi, Tau Beta Pi, Eta Kappa Nu. Home: Apt 1125 3801 Village View Dr Gainesville GA 30506 E-mail: wjones1125@charter.net.

JONES, WILLIAM ERNEST, chemistry professor; b. Sackville, N.B., Can. s. Frederick W. and Jennie E. (Tuttle) J.; m. Norma Florence McKinney Reid, Aug. 9, 1958; children: Mary Ellen E., Jennifer A.J., Sarah A.L., K. Martha M. B.Sc., Mt. Allison U., 1958, M.Sc., 1959; PhD, McGill U., 1963. Asst. prof. Dalhousie U., Halifax, 1962—68, assoc. prof., 1968—73, prof. chemistry, 1973—91, chmn. dept. chemistry, 1974—83, chmn. univ. senate, 1983—89, Saint Mary's U., Halifax, 1989—91, prof. chemistry, dean faculty sci., 2001—; prof. chemistry, v.p. acad. affairs U. Windsor, 1991—98, prof. chemistry, 1991—2001; adj. prof. chemistry St. Mary's U., 2001—, acting dean faculty grad. studies and rsch., 2001—. Contbr. articles to profl. jours. Fellow Chem. Inst. Can. Home: 17 Shaw Crescent Halifax NS Canada B3P 1V2 Office: St Mary's U Office Faculty Grad Studies & Rsch Halifax NS Canada B3H 3C3 E-mail: wjones@stmarys.ca.

JONES, WILLIAM HENRY, retired military officer; b. Black Diamond, Wash., Apr. 1, 1924; s. Stanley Ernest Jones and Lena Ellenor Nott; m. Barbara Ann Liestman, May 17, 1960; 1 child, Denise; m. Shirley Ann Williams, Jan. 27, 1946 (div. May 12, 1960); 1 child, Robert. Grad. summa cum laude, Naval Sch. Hosp. Adminstrn., 1950; AA, San Diego City Coll., 1963; BA, San Diego State Coll., 1964; grad., Fed. Health Care Execs. Inst., Chgo., 1972. Apprentice seaman USN, 1942, advanced through grades to capt., combat hosp. corpsman various WWII battles, 1942—45, various enlisted assignments, 1945—50, commissioned ensign med. svc. corps, 1950, asst. fin. officer Naval Hosp. Mare Island Vallejo, Calif., 1950—54, adminstrv. officer med. dept. USS Hancock, 1954—56, asst. adminstrv. officer Naval Hosp. Bethesda, Md., 1956—58, adminstrv. officer Naval Hosp. Corps Sch. San Diego, 1958—60, dir. Amphibious Med. Indoctrination Coronado, Calif., 1960—64, chief patient affairs Naval Hosp. Oakland, Calif., 1964—66, med. adminstrn. officer Hosp. Ship USS Repose - Vietnam War, 1966—67, adminstrv. officer Naval Hosp. St. Albans, NY, 1967—69, with Naval Hosp. Yokosuka, Japan, 1969—71, dir. Health Care Adminstrn. Naval Regional Med. Ctr. Long Beach, Calif., 1971—73, exec. officer Nat. Naval Med. Ctr. Bethesda, Md., 1973—74, commanding officer Field Med. Svc. Sch. Camp Pendleton, Calif., 1974—79, officers selection bd., 1974—79, ret., 1979. Decorated Meritorious Svc. medal (2), Navy Commendation medal, Legion of Merit; recipient Poet of the Year, Famous Poet Soc., 2003. Mem.: Fleet Res. Assn., Fed. Health Care Execs., Am. Coll. Hosp. Adminstrs., Internat. Poetry Hall of Fame, Internat. Poets Soc. (disting.). Avocations: reading, walking, writing. Home: 947 San Pablo Way San Marcos CA 92078 Personal E-mail: banbjones484@msn.com.

JONES, WILLIAM O., not-for-profit fundraiser; Pres. Conf. Grand Masters Prince Hall Masons. Office: Prince Hall Masons 1630 N 4th Ave Birmingham AL 35203 Office Phone: 205-328-9078.*

JONES, WILLIAM OSBORNE, II, physician assistant; b. Corbin, Ky., May 30, 1951; s. William Osborne and Rebecca Marie (Grover) Jones; m. Patsy Jean Jones; children: Anastasia Marie Rising, William Osborne III, Thomas Adam. BS, George Washington U., 1985; MA, Webster U., 1988. Enlisted USN, 1970, advanced through grades to lt., hosp. corpsman, technician, physician asst., 1970-94, ret., 1994; pvt. practice physician asst. Gaffney, SC, 1994; with Spartanburg (S.C.) Nephrology Assocs., 1994—. Med. lectr. nephrology. Contbr. articles to profl. jours. Named to Hon. Order Ky. Cols. Fellow: Am. Acad. Physician Assts.; mem.: Naval Assn. Physician Assts., S.C. Acad. Physician Assts. (pres., v.p. 1996—99), Am. Acad. Nephrology Physician Assts. (v.p. 1997—98, sec. 1998—99), Mensa. Avocations: mountain and road cycling, motorcycling. Office: Foot Hills Nephrology 126 Disson Drive Spartanburg SC 29307 Home: 224 South Pointe Dr Cowpens SC 29330 Office Phone: 864-327-1212. Personal E-mail: wojones@aol.com. Business E-Mail: kidneypa@chesmet.net.

JONES, WILLIAM RANDOLPH, history professor; b. Little Rock, Apr. 6, 1930; s. John Riley Jones and Jewell Esther Spears; m. Anne Steed, Nov. 13, 1960; children: Anne, Brantley, Mark, Adam. AB in History and Lit., Harvard Coll., 1951; MA in History, Harvard U., 1952, PhD of History, 1958. Prof. Ga. State U., Atlanta, 1956—58, Coll. Charleston, SC, 1958—59, Ohio Wesleyan U., Delaware, 1959—62, U. N.H., Durham, 1962—95, Armstrong Atlantic State U., Savannah, Ga., 1997—2000. Cons. Testing Svc., Princeton, N.J., 1975-82; cons. in world history and silk road projects UNESCO, Paris, 1978-95; mem. seminar on legal history Columbia Law Sch., 1975-82; founder, co-dir. Internat. Conf. Group on China and Europe in the Middle Ages, 1988-95. Author: Relations of the Two Jurisdictions: Studies in Medieval and Renaissance History, 1970; contbr. articles to profl. jours. With U.S. Army, 1955-58. French Govt. fellow U. Paris, 1951, Fulbright fellow King's Coll., London U., 1958. Democrat. Home: PO Box 8606 Tucson AZ 85738 Personal E-mail: billannejone@aol.com.

JONES, WILLIAM REX, law educator; b. Murphysboro, Ill., Oct. 20, 1922; s. Claude E. and Ivy P. (McCormick) J.; m. Miriam R. Lamy, Mar. 27, 1944; m. Gerri L. Haun, June 30, 1972; children: Michael Kimber, Jeanne Keats, Patricia Combs, Sally Horowitz, Kevin. BS, U. Louisville, 1950; JD, U. Ky., 1968; LLM, U. Mich., 1970. Bar: Ky. 1969, Ind. 1971, U.S. Supreme Ct. 1976. Exec. v.p. Paul Miller Ford, Inc., Lexington, Ky., 1951-64; pres. Bill's Seat Cover Ctr., Inc., Lexington, Ky., 1952-65, Bill Jones Real Estate, Inc., Lexington, Ky., 1965-70; asst. prof. law Ind. U., Indpls., 1970-73, assoc. prof., 1973-75, prof., 1975-80; dean Salmon P. Chase Coll. Law. No. Ky. U., Highland Heights, 1980-85, prof., 1980-93, prof. emeritus, 1993—. Vis. prof. Shepard Broad Law Ctr., Nova Southeastern U., Ft. Lauderdale, Fla., 1994-95; mem. Ky. Pub. Advocacy Commn., 1982-93, 97-2000, chmn., 1986-93; chmn. Existing Structures Appeal Bd., City of Newport, Ky., 2002—. Author: Kentucky Criminal Trial Practice, 3d edit., 2001, Kentucky Criminal Trial Practice Forms, 3d edit., 2000. 1st sgt. U.S. Army, 1940-44. Cook fellow U. Mich., 1969-70, W.G. Hart fellow Queen Mary Coll. U. London, 1985. Mem. Order of Coif. Personal E-mail: wrexjones@zoomtown.com. Business E-Mail: jonesw@exchange.nku.edu.

JONES, WINONA NIGELS, retired media specialist; b. Feb. 24, 1928; d. Eugene Arthur and Bertha Lillian (Dixon) Nigels; m. Charles Albert Jones, Nov. 26, 1994; children: Charles Eugene, Sharon Ann Jones Allworth, Caroline Winona Jones Pandorf. AA, St. Petersburg Jr. Coll., 1965; BS, U. So. Fla., 1967, MS, 1968; advanced MS, Fla. State U., 1980. Libr. media specialist Dunedin Comprehensive H.S., Fla., 1967-76; libr. media specialist, chmn. dept. Fitzgerald Mid. Sch., Largo, 1976—87; dir. media svcs. East Lake H.S., Tarpon Springs, 1987—93; ret., 1993. Author: Around Palm Harbor, 2005. Dir., vol. North Pinellas Hist. Mus.; active Palm Harbor Hist. Soc., Pinellas County Hist. Soc.; del. White Ho. Conf. Libr. and Info. Svcs. Named Educator Yr. Pinellas County Sch. Bd. and Suncoast C. of C., 1983, 88, Palm Harbor Woman Yr. Palm Harbor Jr. Women's club, 1989, Palm Harbor Citizen Yr., Palm Harbor C. of C., 2002. Mem. ALA (coun. 1988-92), NEA, AAUW, ASCD, Assn. Ednl. Comm. and Tech. (divsn. sch. media specialist, coms.), Am. Assn. Sch. Librs. (com., pres.-elect 1989, pres. 1990-91, mem. exec. bd. 1991-92), Southeastern Libr. Assn., Fla. Libr. Assn., Fla. Assn. Media Edn. (pres.), U. So. Fla. Alumni Assn., Fla. State Libr. Sci. Alumni Assn., U. So. Fla. Libr. Sci. Alumni Assn. (pres. 1991-92, 92-93), Phi Theta Kappa, Phi Rho Pi, Beta Phi Mu, Kappa Delta Pi, Delta Kappa Gamma (parliamentarian 1989-90, legis. chmn. 1990, sec. 1994-96), Inner Wheel Club, Pilot Club, Civic Club, Order Ea. Star (Palm Harbor, past worthy matron). Democrat. Home: 911 Manning Rd Palm Harbor FL 34683-6344 Office Phone: 727-724-3054.

JONES, WOODSON SCOTT, pediatrician, educator; s. Robert Gene and Beverly Jones; m. Jacqueline Kay Haisler, Feb. 10, 1990; children: Rachel Elisabetta, Rebekah Kay, Valerie Nicole, Victoria Anne. BA, Baylor U., Waco, Tex., 1986; MD, U. Tex., Galveston, 1990. Diplomate Am. Bd. Pediat. Clin. asst. prof. pediat. U. Tex. Health Sci. Ctr., San Antonio, 1999—2001; asst. prof. pediat. Uniformed Svcs. U., Bethesda, Md., 2000—. Chief pediat. 31st Med. Group, Aviano AB, Italy, 1994—96, maternal child flight comdr., 1996—98; dir. med. student edn. San Antonio Military Pediat. Ctr., Lackland AFB, Tex., 1998—2000; assoc. pediatric clerkship dir. Uniformed Svcs. U., Bethesda, Md., 2000—03, program dir., pediatric clerkship, 2003—. Lt. col. USAF, 1990—2005. Decorated Medal For Svc. NATO, Air Force Meritorious Svc. Medal Lackland AFB, Tex.; named one of America's Top Pediatricians, Consumers' Rsch. Coun. of Am., 2004—05. Fellow: Am. Acad. Pediat. (exec. com. uniformed svcs. sect. 2004—05); mem.: Ambulatory Pediat. Assn. (steering com., med. student spl. interest group 2002—05, Tchg. Award 2002), Christian Med. and Dental Assn. (uniformed svcs. u. student chpt. faculty sponsor 2001—05), Alpha Omega Alpha. Achievements include development of students clinical observation of the preceptor (SCOOP): an innovative approach to use intentional modeling to teach medical students professionalism; use of video otoscopy in education to enhance medical providers educational skills. Avocations: running, skiing, travel. Office: Uniformed Svcs Univ 4310 Jones Bridge Rd Bethesda MD 20184-4799 Office Phone: 301-295-9734. E-mail: wjones@usuhs.mil.

JONES-ATKINS, DEBORAH KAYE, state official; b. Bradenton, Fla, July 2, 1958; d. Ralph and Jewelle Vanessa (Gayle) Jones; 1 child, Omari Gayle Jones-Atkins. AS with distinction, cert. in human svcs., Monroe C.C., Rochester, N.Y., 1986; BIS, Va. State U., Petersburg, 1995; postgrad., SUNY, Brockport, 1998. Credit investigator Sears Roebuck & Co., Rochester, NY, 1980; customer svc. rep. B. Forman Co., Rochester, NY, 1980-81; youth counselor Brighton Youth Agy., Rochester, NY, 1976-81; staff asst. Makro Inc., Capitol Heights, Md., 1981-82; customer svc. rep. MetroVision Inc., Capitol Hts., 1983-84; teen parent counselor Urban League of Rochester, 1985, program coord., 1988; job developer YWCA of Rochester, 1985-87; prog. support technician, sr. Dept. Med. Assistance Svc., Commonwealth of Va., Richmond, 1989-96; alt. health care supr. Commonwealth of Va. Med. Assist. Svc., 1989-96; subs. tchr. Rochester City Sch. Dist., 1996-2000; SOL tudor, subs. tchr. Henrico County Pub. Sch., 2000; social worker County of Henrico Dept. Social Svc. Mem. Women's Resource Ctr., Richmond, 1989—; heir link The Links Inc., Rochester, 1982—; vol. United Negro Coll. Fund Telethon, Rochester, 1988, N.Y. State Dept. Labor Career Edn. Expo, 1989, WXXI Auction 21, Rochester, 1989, YMCA Greater Rochester, 1989, Arts Coun., Richmond, Richmond Children's Festival, 1989, Sci. Mus. Va., Richmond, 1989, Arts Coun. Richmond 15th Ann. June Jubilee, 1990, Children's Book Festival, 1990, Maymont Found. Flower Garden Show, 1990, 91, Va. Spl. Olympics, 1990—, Jr. League Richmond 45th Book and Author Dinner, 1990, dinner asst. ticket chairperson 46th Book and Author Dinner, 1991, hostee 45th Dinner, Children's Book Festival Arts Coun. Richmond; mem. agy. svc. com. Friends Assn. for Children, 1990—; mem. student adv. com. Va. Commonwealth U. Health Svcs., 1991, Friends of Art Richmond Mus. Fine Arts, 1991; mem. membership com., audience devel. com. Richmond Profl. Women's Network; placement counselor placement com. Jr. League Richmond, 1991, mem. tng. com., 1991; mem. adv. com. Children's Mus. Richmond; mem. exec. bd. YWCA of Richmond, 1992-95, mem. fin. com., 1996—; mem. policy bd. Jr. League Richmond, 1992-93; bd. dirs. Urban League of Richmond, 1996-2001; 3rd v.p. vols. PTA Echo Lake Elem. Sch.; mem. Echo Lake Elem. PTA County Coun, 2001; mem. architect com. 2001 Springcreek Assn. Named one of Outstanding Young Women of Am., 1988. Mem. NAFE, Nat. Coun. Negro Women, Jr. League of Rochester, Nat. Trust Hist. Preservation, Richmond Profl. Women's Network (rec. sec., exec. bd. 1992—), Richmond Jaycees. Democrat. Avocations: jogging, aerobics, tennis, racquetball, the arts, reading, travel. Home: PO Box 6582 Glen Allen VA 23058 Office: 8600 Dixon Powers Rd Richmond VA 23228 Office Phone: 804-501-4042. Personal E-mail: JonesAtkins@aol.com.

JONES-GREGORY, PATRICIA, secondary art educator; b. La Grange, Ga., Apr. 15, 1944; d. Eddie Burrel Jones (dec.), Samuel Lee (stepfather) and Mildred Jones (Johnson) Turrentine; m. Bernard Gregory, Oct. 12, 1985. BFA in Art Edn., Pratt Inst., 1966; MS in Photography, Ill. Inst. Tech., 1970; postgrad. in African Studies and Rsch., Howard U., 1970—74; EdD in Ednl. Adminstrn. and Supervision, Seton Hall U., 1994. Cert. prin./supr., supr., ednl. adminstrn. and supervision, art tchr. grades K-12. Tchr. art Westfield Sch. Dist., NJ, 1966—68; instr. art Howard U., Washington, 1970—71; tchr. art Newark Sch. Dist., 1974—79, Irvington Sch. Dist., NJ, 1979—80, South Orange-Maplewood Sch. Dist., NJ, 1980—81, Montclair Sch. Dist., NJ, 1981—82; instr. art, docent Newark Mus., 1982—84; tchr. art Weequahic H.S., Newark, 1983—98. Mem. com. textbook evaluation curriculum svcs. Bd. Edn., Newark, 1983—; art dir. Ergo-Weequahic H.S., Newark, 1984-93, founder, advisor Kuumba Art Club, 1989-94, PB Graphics Design, liasion, City Without Walls Art Reach mentor program, 1997-98. Author: Many Moods of the Afro-American Woman, 1971, Multicultural Arts Exhibition Catalog, 1992, Pathways to Empowerment, 1997; editor, pub. The Harvester, 1979-83, The Beauty of Holiness, 1997, The Clarion: The Voices That Lead to Righteousness, 1999-2000, Friendship With the World, 2000, Metamorphosis of the Christian, 2001, Intermezzo in l'Italia, 2002, A Good Wife is Without Price, 2005 Rschr. Goldman and Kennedy The New York Urban Athlete, Simon and Schuster, N.Y., 1983; vol. tchr., counselor local ch. Grace B. Monroe grantee Pratt Inst., Bklyn., 1964; Grad. scholar Ill. Inst. Tech., Chgo., 1968-70; Rsch. fellow Howard U., Washington, 1972-73; recipient Cert. of Recognition, Gov.'s Tchr. Recognition Program, N.J., 1993. Mem.: ASCD, Nat. Assn. Art Educators, Nat. Assn. for Multicultural Edn., Com. to Eliminate Media Offensive to African People, Studio Mus. in Harlem, Newark Mus., Newark Art Coun., Bklyn. Mus. Art, Schomburg Ctr. Rsch. in Black Culture, Kappa Delta Pi. Avocations: art, travel, discussion, reading, writing. Home: 78 Woodland Ave East Orange NJ 07017-2006

JONES-LUKACS, ELIZABETH LUCILLE, physician; b. Norfolk, Va. d. Oliver C. and Gertrude (Layden) Jones; m. Michel J. Lukacs (dec.); children: Amanda, Laurel, Angelique, Klara. BS, Oglethorpe U., 1955. Diplomate, fellow Am. Bd. Family Practice. Intern Beth Israel Hosp., N.Y.C., 1964-65; family practice medicine Goshen, N.Y., 1965-73, Buckingham, Va., 1973-78; commd. maj. U.S. Air Force, 1978; flight surgeon Andrews AFB, Md., 1978-85, chief exec. med. program, 1991-2000; med. dir. Armed Forces Benefit Assn., Alexandria, Va., 2000—04. Unit charge physician Student Health Ctr., U. Md., College Park, 1985—91; bd. dirs. Falcon's Landing Mil. Officers Retirement Home. Author: The Curies Radium & Radioactivity, 1962, The Golden Stamp Book of Flying Animals, 1963. Col. USAFR, commd. 459th USAF Clinic. Mem. Am. Med. Womens Assn. (pres. Br. I), Md. Connemara Breeders. Episcopalian. Home: 15430 Mount Calvert Rd Upper Marlboro MD 20772-9616 E-mail: ejlukacs@juno.com.

JONES REYNOLDS, STAR (STARLET MARIE JONES), television host, lawyer, former prosecutor; b. Badin, NC, Mar. 24, 1962; m. Al Reynolds, Nov. 13, 2004. BA, Am. U.; JD, U. Houston. Bar: NY. Lawyer; sr. asst. dist. atty. Bklyn. Dist. Atty.'s Office, 1991; studio commentator Court TV, 1991; legal corrs. NBC's Today, Nightly News; host syndicated tv show Jones and Jury, 1994; former sr. corr., chief legal analyst Inside Edition, 1995; co-host ABC Daytime's The View, 1997—; nat. spokesperson Payless ShoeSource; host Live from the Red Carpet!, 2004. Notable guest appearances The Tonight Show with Jay Leno, Bravo's Celebrity Poker, Celebrity Jeopardy, The Daily Show with Jon Stewart, and The Late Show with David Letterman., honored as a subject of Lifetime TV: Intimate Portrait, 2000, hosted It's All About You With Star Jones on ShopNBC, developer of own website, featured personality for Kohl's Target, and Salon Z of Saks Fifth Avenue, featured on numerous mags. such as: Newsweek, TV Guide, Essence, Black Enterprise, and New York, host E! Entertainment Television's Live Red Carpet Arrivals of the Primetime Emmy Awards, 2004; author: You Have to Stand for Something, or You'll Fall for Anything, 1998. Bd. dir. East Harlem Sch. at Exodus House, Dress for Success, God's Love We Deliver, Girls, Inc.; launched The Starlet Fund, 2002—. Named Chief of Consumer Style, 2002; honored for work in improving the educational opportunities for low income children in East Harlem, East Harlem Sch. at Exodus House; co-recipient with co-host from "The View", Safe Horizon Champion award, 2001. Achievements include launching signature line of shoes, Starlet by Star Jones, sold exclusively at Payless ShoeSource. Office: 320 W 66th St New York NY 10023-6304

JONES-WILLS, EUNICE STEPHANIE, mental health nurse, researcher; b. Guyana, Nov. 14, 1955; came to the U.S., 1967; d. Esther (Fredericks) Elder; m. Bernard Jones, June 3, 1974 (div. Sept. 1989); m. Aloysius Ignatius Wills, May 25, 1991; children: Dwayne, Anton, Denise, Brandon, Andrew. AAS, N.Y.C. Tech. Coll., Bklyn., 1987; BS, U. Md., 1994, MS, 1996. RNC; RN, Md., D.C., Va; clin. specialist of psychiat. and mental health. Med.-surg. nurse Providence Hosp., Washington, 1987-88; charge nurse Crownsville (Md.) Hosp. Ctr., 1988-92; team leader Dept. Mental Health Svcs., Washington, 1992-96; psychiat. rsch. nurse NIH, Bethesda, Md., 1996-98; clin. nurse Bureau of Prisons Fed. Dentention Ctr., Miami, Fla., 1998—2004; with immigration and customs enforcement Dept. Homeland Security, Los Fresnos, Tex., 2004—. CPR instr. Dept. Health and Human Svcs., Washington, 1993-96; head judge sci. fair regionals Pub. Health Svc., Rockville, Md., 1997, 98, presenter pub. schs. health week, 1997, 98. Lt. comdr. USPHS, 1996—. Mem. ANA (psychiat. and mental health crt.), Res. Officer Assn., Commd. Officer Assn., Sigma Theta Tau, Phi Theta Kappa. Democrat. Roman Catholic. Avocations: reading, travel, shopping, biking. Home: 3214 Banyan Dr Harlingen TX 78550 Office: Federal Dentention Ctr 33 NE 4th St Miami FL 33132-2111

JONES-WILSON, FAUSTINE CLARISSE, retired education educator; b. Little Rock, Dec. 3, 1927; d. James Edward and Perrine Marie (Childress) Thomas; m. James T. Jones, June 20, 1948 (div. 1977); children: Yvonne Dianne, Brian Vincent; m. Edwin L. Wilson, July 10, 1981. AB, Ark. A.M.&N. Coll., 1948; AM, U. Ill., 1951, EdD, 1967; LLD, U. Ark., Pine Bluff, 2003. Tchr., sch. libr. Gary (Ind.) Pub. Schs., 1955-62, 1964-67; asst. prof. Coll. Edn., U. Ill., Chgo., 1967-69; assoc. prof. adult edn. Fed. City Coll., Washington, 1970-71; prof. edn., grad. prof. Howard U., Washington, 1969-70, 71-93, acting dean Sch. Edn., 1991-92, prof. emeritus, 1993—. Author: The Changing Mood in America; Eroding Commitment, 1977, A Traditional Model of Educational Excellence: Dunbar High School of Little Rock, Arkansas, 1981; co-author: Paul Laurence Dunbar High School of Little Rock, Arkansas: Take From Our Lips a Song, Dunbar to Thee, 2003; editor Jour. Negro Edn., 1978-91, 92-93; co-editor: Encyclopedia of African-American Education, 1996; assoc. editor Jour. of Edn. for Students Placed at Risk, 1996-2000. Chmn. East Coast steering com. Nat. Coun. on Educating Black Children, 1986—88, 1990—92, 3d v.p., 1992—94, bd. dirs., 1994—98. Recipient Frederick Douglass award Nat. Assn. Black Journalists, 1979, Disting. Scholar-Tchr. award Howard U., 1985, Exemplary Leadership award Am. Assn. Higher Edn. Black Caucus, 1988, Gertrude E. Rush award Nat. Bar Assn., 1990, Disting. Career award V.P. for Acad. Affairs, Howard U., 1993, Disting. Alumni award Coll. Edn. U. Ill., 1997; Phelps Stokes Fund sr. fellow, 1993-2000. Mem.: Soc. Profs. of Edn. (Mary Anne Raywid award 2002), Am. Ednl. Studies Assn. (pres. 1984—85), John Dewey Soc., Phi Delta Kappa (pres. Howard U. chpt. 1986—87, Svc. key 1990). Democrat. Methodist. Home: 6605 Allview Dr Columbia MD 21046-1005

JONG, ERICA MANN, writer; b. NYC, Mar. 26, 1942; d. Seymour and Eda (Mirsky) Mann; m. Michael Werthman, 1963 (div. 1965); m. Allan Jong (div. Sept. 1975); m. Jonathan Fast, Dec. 1977 (div. Jan. 1983); 1 child, Molly; m. Kenneth David Burrows, Aug. 5, 1989. BA, Barnard Coll., 1963; MA, Columbia U., 1965; PhD honoris causa, CUNY, 2005. Faculty, English dept. CUNY, 1964-65, 69-70, overseas div. U. Md., 1967-69; mem. lit. panel N.Y. State Council on Arts, 1972-74; faculty Breadloaf Writers Conf. Middlebury, Vt., 1982; mem. faculty Saltzburg Seminar, Saltzburg, Austria, 1993, 98. Author: (poems) Fruits and Vegetables, 1971, reissued edit., 1997, Half Lives, 1973, Loveroot, 1975, At the Edge of the Body, 1979, Ordinary Miracles, 1983, Becoming Light: Poems New and Selected, 1992; (novels) Fear of Flying, 1973, How to Save Your Own Life, 1977, Fanny: Being the True History of the Adventures of Fanny Hackabout-Jones, 1980, Parachutes and Kisses, 1984, Serenissima, 1987 (reissued as Shylock's Daughter, 1995), Any Woman's Blues, 1990, Inventing Memory, 1998, Sappho's Leap, 2003, (poetry and non-fiction) Witches, 1981, reissued edit., 1997, (juvenile) Megan's Book of Divorce, 1984 (reissued as Megan's Two Houses, 1995), (memoir) The Devil at Large, 1993, What Do Women Want?, 1998, (autobiography) Fear of Fifty, 1994, (non-fiction) What Do Women Want?, 2001; composer lyrics: Zipless: Songs of Abandon from the Erotic Poetry of Erica Jong, 1995, (fiction) Inventing Memory, 1997. Recipient Bess Hokin prize Poetry mag., 1971, Prix Literaire, Deauville Film Festival, 1997; named Mother of Yr., 1982; Woodrow Wilson fellow; Nat. Endowment Arts grantee, 1973. Mem. PEN, Authors Guild U.S.A. (coun. 1975—, pres. 1991-93), Poets and Writers Bd., Writers Guild Am.-West, Poetry Soc. Am. (Alice Faye di Castagnola award 1972), Phi Beta Kappa. Office: Erica Jong Prodns c/o Kenneth David Burrows 451 Park Ave S FL 8 New York NY 10016-7390 Office Phone: 212-517-2907.

JONG, SHUNG-CHANG, mycologist; b. Taipei, Taiwan, Nov. 12, 1936; came to U.S., 1965; m. Chiu-Hwa Kou, Apr. 20, 1965; children: Maria, Cynthia, Victoria. MS, Western Ill. U., 1966; PhD, Washington State U., 1969. Plant pathologist Taiwan Agrl. Rsch. Inst., Taipei, 1961—63; instr. Nat. Taiwan U., Taipei, 1963—65; tchg. asst. Western Ill. U., Macomb, 1965—66; rsch. asst. Wash. State U., Pullman, 1966—69; sr. mycologist Am. Type Culture Collection, Rockville, Md., 1969—71, curator, 1971—89, head mycology dept., 1973—, sr. staff scientist, 1989—, dir. mycology and protistology program, 1993—, dir. microbiology divsn., 1997—. Dir. Yeast Genetic Stock Ctr., 1998—; dissertation dir. George Washington U., Washington, 1975-79; tech. advisor Yamazaki Baking Co., Tokyo, Japan, 1984—; exec. bd. World Fedn. for Culture Collection, 1988-92. Contbr. articles to profl. jours. Recipient Internat. Sci. and Tech. award Ministry of Agr., 1988, Brown Hazen grant Rsch. Corp., 1974-76, J. Roger Porter award ASM/ASFCC, 1997; NSF grantee, 1975-80, 80-85, 85-90, 90-95, 95-2000, 2000—. Fellow Am. Acad. Microbiology, Washington Acad. Scis.; mem. World Fedn. for Culture Collections, Internat. Mycol. Assn. (exec. com. 1983-90), Internat. Commn. on Taxonomy of Fungi, Mycol. Soc. of Am. (com. on culture collection 1986-91). Office: Am Type Culture Collection 10801 University Blvd Manassas VA 20110-2204 Office Phone: 703-365-2742. Office Fax: 703-365-2730. Business E-Mail: sjong@atcc.org.

JONGEWARD, GEORGE RONALD, retired systems analyst; b. Yakima, Wash., Aug. 9, 1934; s. George Ira and Dorothy Marjorie (Cronk) J.; m. Janet Jeanne Williams, July 15, 1955; children: Mary Jeanne, Dona Lee, Karen Anne. BA, Whitworth Coll., 1957; postgrad., Utah State U., 1961. Sr. systems analyst Computer Scis. Corp., Honolulu, 1969-71; cons. in field Honolulu, 1972-76; prin. The Hobby Co., Honolulu, 1977-81; sr. systems analyst Computer Systems Internat., Honolulu, 1981-96, asst. v.p., 1994-96; instr. EDP Hawaii Pacific U., Honolulu, 1982-90. Mem. car show com. Easter Seal Soc., Honolulu. 1977-82; active Variety Club, Honolulu, 1978-81. Mem. Mensa (Hawaii pres. 1967-69), Triple-9. Presbyterian. Avocations: travel, professional pianist, theater, classic cars. Home: 4108 Avalanche Ave Yakima WA 98908-2915

JONKER, JEAN ELIZABETH, educational consultant; b. Holyoke, Mass., Dec. 14, 1950; d. John Edward Borowski and Jennie Elizabeth Ciszewski; life ptnr. Peter A. Kinney, 1981. BA, Coll. Our Lady of the Elms, Chicopee, Mass., 1973. Lic. secondary English Mass. Dept. Edn., 1973, cert. asst. supt. dir. — Reg. Vocat. Sch. Dist. Mass. Dept. Edn., 2002, dir. and asst. dir. Vocat. H.S. Mass. Dept. Edn., 2002, dir. and asst. dir. postsecondary tech. programs Mass. Dept. Edn., 2002, dir. vocat. program and adult vocat. program Mass. Dept. Edn., 2002. Secondary English lang. arts tchr. Holyoke Pub. Schs., 1973—99; vocat. tech. English lang. arts curriculum content specialist Mass. Dept. Edn., Malden, 1997—99, edn. specialist, 1999—. Co-author: Tech Prep English: A Collection of Unique Lesson Plans for the Technical English Teacher Vol. I, 1995, Vol. II, 1996. Mem. NAEP Achievement Levels-Setting Project for Writing, St. Louis, 1998—98; coord. State Senate Race, Holyoke, 1980—81; chairperson Holyoke H.S. Hall of Fame, 1988—2002. Named to Holyoke H.S. Hall of Fame, 1995; recipient Outstanding Tchr. award, U. Chgo., 1991, sabbatical, Mass. Dept. Edn., 1997—98; Mass. Edn. Reform Tchr. fellow, 1998. Mem.: ASCD, Nat. Tech Prep Leadership, Nat. Staff Devel. Coun., Nat. Tech Prep Network, Nat. Staff Devel. Coun., Boston Athenaeum, Mass. Alpha Delta Kappa (treas. 2003—05). Avocations: reading, genealogy, technology, theater. Home: 198 Locust St Holyoke MA 01040-3119 Office: Mass Dept Edn 350 Main St Malden MA 02148 Office Phone: 781-338-3947. Personal E-mail: jjonker@rcn.com. Business E-Mail: jjonker@doe.mass.edu.

JONKER, MARGARET N., music educator; b. Corpus Christi, Tex., Aug. 11, 1971; d. James Pomeroy and Beverly (Mozeney) Naismith; m. Randy Dwayne Jonker, July 15, 1995; children: Daniel James, Madeleine Grace, Christopher Louis. BA in Liberal Arts, Lubbock Christian U., 1992. Fin. analyst Crow Holdings, Inc., Dallas, 1994—99; piano tchr. Jonker Studio of Music, Corpus Christi, Tex., 1999—. Mem. Am. Coll. Musicians, Nat. Guild of Piano Tchrs., Tex. Music Tchrs. Assn. Republican. Avocation: piano. Home and Office: 301 Louise Drive Corpus Christi TX 78404

JONKER, PAMELA LYNN, artist; b. Denver, Apr. 25, 1947; d. William Espy and Geraldine Marie (Plumb) Ingram; m. L. Anton Jonker, Mar. 17, 1968 (div. Feb. 1994); children: Stephanie Lynn, Stacey Marie. BA in Polit. Sci., The Colo. Coll., 1969; postgrad., Calif. State U., Fresno, 1989-92. Artist-sculptor, painter, ceramist, fiber arts, Fresno, Calif. and, Espanola, N.Mex., 1979—; devel. coord. Fresno Arts Coun., 1992-93. Fiber artist/quilt hangings, 1980—; wheel-thrown manipulated ceramic bowls, 1992—; author: (exhibit catalog) Calif. State U. Fresno/Phebe Conley Gallery, 1992. Mem. Am. Quilter's Soc., Am. Craft Coun., Fresno Arts Coun., Kappa Alpha Theta. Avocations: gourmet cooking, gardening, interior design. Office: RR 3 Box 1333-9 Espanola NM 87532-9803 E-mail: pljart@netscape.net.

JONKOUSKI, JILL ELLEN, materials scientist, ceramic engineer, educator; b. Chgo. d. Joseph and Ruth Jonkouski. BS in Ceramic Engring., MS in Ceramic Engring., U. Ill. Former rschr. Battelle Meml. Inst., Columbus, Ohio; former ceramic engr. Austenal Dental, Inc., Chgo.; former rsch. scientist BIRL Indsl. Rsch. Lab. Northwestern U., Evanston, Ill.; ceramics mfg. engr., fed. project dir. Office of Sci., Office of Programs and Project Mgmt. divsn. U.S. Dept. Energy, Argonne, Ill., 1991—. Past adj. faculty Triton Coll., River Grove, Ill.; chair Internat. Gas Turbine Inst. ASME Turbo Expo, 2002, 03; chair ann. conf. on composites, materials and structures ASME, 1997—; presenter, spkr. in field. Mem. Am. Ceramic Soc. (chair Chgo.-Milw. sect. 1993-94), U. Ill. Alumni Assn. Avocations: ice skating, hiking, flying, tennis. Office: US Dept Energy Office Programs and Project Mgmt 9800 S Cass Ave Argonne IL 60439-4899 Business E-Mail: jill.jonkouski@ch.doe.gov.

JONSEN, ALBERT R(UPERT), retired medical ethics educator; b. San Francisco, Apr. 4, 1931; s. Albert R. and Helen (Sweigert) Jonsen; m. Mary Elizabeth Carolan. BA, Gonzaga U., 1955, MA, 1956; STM, U. Santa Clara, 1963; PhD, Yale U., 1967. Mem. S.J., 1949—76; ordained priest Roman Cath. Ch.; instr. philosophy Loyola U., L.A., 1956—59; asst. in instrn. Yale Div. Sch., 1966—67; asst. prof. theology and philosophy U. San Francisco, 1967—72, pres., 1969—72; prof. med. ethics Sch. Medicine, U. Calif.-San Francisco, 1972—87; adj. assoc. prof. dept. community medicine and internat. health Sch. Medicine, Georgetown U., 1977; prof. med. ethics, chmn. dept. med. history and ethics Sch. Medicine U. Wash., Seattle, 1987—99, prof. emeritus; faculty Fromm Inst. for Life-Long Learning, U. San Francisco, 2000—; co-dir. Ctr. for Medicine and Human Values, Calif. Pacific Med. Ctr., San Francisco, 2004—. Vis. prof. Yale U., 1999—2000; mem. artificial heart assessment panel Nat. Heart and Lung Inst., 1972—73, 1984—86; mem. Am. Bd. Med. Spltys., 1978—81; cons. Am. Bd. Internal Medicine, 1978—82, ACOG, 1983—88; mem. Pres.'s Commn. for Study of Ethical Problems in Medicine, 1979—82, Nat. Commn. for Protection Human Subjects of Biomed. and Behavioral Rsch., HEW, 1974—78, Nat. Bd. Med.

Examiners, 1985—87, Commn. on AIDS Rsch., NRC, 1986—92, Panel on Social Impact of AIDS (chmn.), 1989—91; chmn. nat. adv. bd. Ethics and Reprodn., 1991—96; mem. ethics adv. bd. GERON Corp., 2000—; vis. prof. Stanford U. Sch. Medicine, 2002, U. Va. Law Sch., 2002; vis. prof. dept. surgery U. Calif., San Francisco, 2004. Author: Responsibility in Modern Religious Ethics, 1968, Patterns of Moral Responsibility, 1969, Christian Decision and Action, 1970, Ethics of Newborn Intensive Care, 1976, Clin. Ethics, 1982, 6th edit., 2005, The Abuse of Casuistry: A History of Moral Reasoning, 1987, The New Medicine and the Old Ethics, 1990, The Social Impact of AIDS in the United States, 1993, Bioethics, 1997, The Birth of Bioethics, 1998, A Short History of Medical Ethics, 2000, Bioethics Behind the Headlines, 2005. Bd. trustees Inst. Ednl. Mgmt., Harvard U., 1971—74, Ploughshares Found., 1980—84; mem. San Francisco Crime Com., 1969—71; bd. dirs. Found. Critical Care Medicine, 1983—86, Sierra Health Found., 1987—. Fellow, Guggenheim, 1995—96. Fellow: The Hastings Ctr.; mem.: Am. Osler Soc. (McGovern award 1986), Am. Coll. Cardiology (Convocation Medal 1996), Am. Soc. for Bioethics and Humanities (Lifetime Achievement award 1999), Blue Cross and Blue Shield Assn. (tech. assessment program 1985—2003, med. adv. panel), Instituto de Bioetica (Madrid), Inst. Medicine (com. human values 1973, coun. 1983—85, 1990—92), Soc. Christian Ethics, Am. Soc. Law and Medicine (bd. dirs. 1986—88), Soc. Health and Human Values (pres. 1986—87). Home: 1333 Jones St # 502 San Francisco CA 94109 E-mail: arjonsen@aol.com.

JONSEN, ERIC RICHARD, lawyer; b. San Francisco, June 5, 1958; s. Richard William and Ann Margaret (Parsons) J.; m. Ida-Marie, May 8, 1982; children: Kaitlyn, Jeremy, Michelle. BA, Hartwick Coll., 1980; JD, U. Colo., 1985. Bar: Colo., N.Y., U.S. Dist. Ct. Colo., U.S. Ct. Appeals (10th cir., Fed. cir.), U.S. Ct. Appeals (fed. cir.). Assoc. William P. DeMoulin, Denver, 1986-88, Fairfield & Woods, Denver, 1988—91; ptnr. Ciancio & Jonsen PC, Denver, 1994—2001, Jonsen & Assoc. LLC, Broomfield, Colo., 2001—. Bd. dirs. Broomfield Blast Soccer Club, 2000—. Mem. ABA, Colo. Bar Assn., Rotary (pres. Broomfield Crossings 2000—). Office: Jonsen & Assocs LLC 1600 Stout St Ste 1100 Denver CO 80202 E-mail: erjonsen@jonsen.net.

JONSEN, HELEN, writer, televison producer; b. Mt. Vernon, N.Y., Dec. 10, 1957; d. Fred Carl Sr. and Catherine (Browne) Johnson; m. Mark Christopher Watkins, Oct. 27, 1985. BA in Journalism and Communications, Fordham U., 1979. With WINS Radio, N.Y.C., 1977-79; staff reporter The Daily Argus, Mt. Vernon, 1979; producer, writer WPIX-TV, N.Y.C., 1979-81; news reporter, mgr. night news WLNE-TV, Providence, 1981-84; freelance writer, TV journalist Melbourne, Australia, 1985; news reporter WNYW-TV, N.Y.C., 1986-88, WPIX-TV, N.Y.C., 1991—; ptnr. Wallapix Video, Etc., Mt. Vernon, 1988—. Adj. prof. comm. Fordham U., 1990. Author: Kangaroo's Comments and Wallaby's Words: The Aussie Word Book, Language and Travel Guide: Australia. Bd. trustees Mt. Vernon (N.Y.) Pub. Libr., 1996—. Mem. AFTRA, Women In Communications, Writers' Guild Am. Office: Wallapix Video Etc 391 Bedford Rd Chappaqua NY 10514-2207

JONSON, SONDRA LENORE, sculptor, educator; b. Phila., Dec. 28, 1954; d. George T. and Norma S. Wohl; m. James G. McHale; children: Michael G. McHale, Joseph D. McHale, Thomas C. McHale. BFA, Bryn Mawr Coll., Pa., 1975; cert. in Sculpture, Frudakis Acad. Art, Phila., 1978. Instr. drawing and sculpture U. Nev., Las Vegas, 1987—94; art workshop tchr. Las Vegas Art Mus., 1989—93; mural designer/coord. Children's Mural Project, Las Vegas, 1989—94; artist-in-residence Nebr. Arts Coun., Omaha, 1996—; sculptor S.L. Jonson Studios, Las Vegas and Cambridge, Nebr., 1985—. Lectr., judge McCook Coll., Nebr., 2004; lectr. on Sacred Art Eucharistic Congress, Washington, 2004. Prin. works include bronze monument Rachel Weeping for her Children, 2000, Sisters of Mercy Foundress, 2000, prin. works include bronze in White House Going Home war meml., 2001, prin. works include The American Farmer, Falls Pk. Sioux Falls, S.D. Asst. leader Furnas County 4-H, Cambridge, 2000—04; pres. bd. dirs. Las Vegas Art Mus., 1993; dir. Cambridge H.S. Art Club, 2002; pres. St. John's Ch. Altar Soc., Cambridge, 2001—03. Named Best Sculptor in S.W. Nebr., The S.W. Nebr. News, 2002; grantee Arts-on-Line grantee, Nebr. Arts Coun., Nat. Endowment for Art, 2000. Mem.: Nat. Assn. Art Educators, Assn. of Nebr. Art Clubs, Feminists for Life, Nat. Sculpture Soc. Republican. Roman Catholic. Avocations: horseback riding, writing, designing furniture. Home: 716 Nelson St Cambridge NE 69022 Office: S L Jonson Studios 622 Pacific St Cambridge NE 69022 Office Phone: 800-720-8574. Business E-Mail: sjonson@swnebr.net.

JONSSON, BJARNI, mathematician, educator; b. Draghals, Iceland, Feb. 15, 1920; came to U.S., 1941, naturalized, 1963; s. Jon and Steinunn (Bjarnadottir) Petursson; m. Amy Sprague, Dec. 16, 1950 (div. 1967); children: Eric M., Meryl S.; m. Harriet Parkes, Jan. 17, 1970; child, M. Kristin. BA, U. Calif. at Berkeley, 1943, PhD, 1946. Faculty Brown U., 1946-56, asst. prof., 1948-56; vis. prof. U. Iceland, 1954-55; vis. assoc. prof. U. Calif., Berkeley, 1955-56, vis. prof., rsch. mathematician, 1962-63; faculty U. Minn., 1956-66, assoc. prof., 1956-59, prof., 1959-66; disting. prof. Vanderbilt U., Nashville, 1966-93, disting. prof. emeritus, 1993—. Mem. AAUP, Am. Math. Soc. Achievements include research, publs. in lattice theory, universal algebra, founds. of algebra, group theory. E-mail: jonsson@vanderbilt.math.edu.

JONSSON, TED WILBUR, artist; b. Berkeley, Calif. s. Wilbur Henry Johnson and Laurel Marie Thomson; m. Nancy Current (div.); 1 child, Theodora Marie. BFA in Philosophy and Fine Art, U. Calif., Davis, 1957; MFA in Sculpture, U. Wash., 1965. Art curator Wash. State His. Mus., Olympia, 1967—69; art instr. Highline C.C., Midway, Wash., 1969—81, chmn. art and humanities fine performing arts, 1978—79; sculpture tech. instr. Humboldt State U., Arcada, Calif., 1989—90. Prin. works include fountain, Seattle Water Dept., Jonsherley Water Wall Sculpture, S.A. P. Plaza, Palo Alto, Calif., exhibited in group shows at Seattle Art Mus., 1964—87. Mem. adv. bd. Good Sheppard Ctr., Seattle, 1989—96; pres. bd. dirs. Wallingfor Sr. Ctr., Seattle, 1996—2000. Capt. USAR, 1957—67. Recipient Visual Arts Honor award, Gov. Wash./Wash. Arts Commn., 1979. Mem.: Artist Equity (founding mem., pres. Wash. chpt. 1989—2004), Artist Group (founding mem., pres. 1969—73). Democrat. Eastern Orthodox. Home and Studio: 805 NE Northlake Way Seattle WA 98105

JONTZ, JEFFRY ROBERT, lawyer; b. Stuart, Iowa, May 28, 1944; s. John Leo Jontz and Leora Burnette (Pittman) Myers; m. Sharyn Sue Kopriva, June 8, 1968; 1 child, Eric Barrett. BA, Drake U., 1966; JD with distinction, U. Iowa, 1969. Bar: Iowa 1969, Fla. 1971, U.S. Dist. Ct. (mid. dist.) Fla. 1971, Ohio 1972, U.S. Ct. Appeals (5th cir.) 1972, U.S. Ct. Appeals (11th cir.) 1981, U.S. Tax Ct. 1983. Law clk. to Hon. Charles R. Scott U.S. Dist. Ct. (mid. dist.) Fla., Jacksonville, 1969-70; to Hon. Bryan Simpson U.S. Ct. Appeals (5th cir.), Jacksonville, 1970-71; assoc. Jones, Day, Cockley & Reavis, Cleve., 1971-72; asst. U.S. atty. U.S. Dist. Ct. (mid. dist.) Fla., Orlando, 1972-74; pvt. practice Orlando, 1974—; ptnr. Young, Turnbull & Linscott, Orlando, 1974-79, Baker & Hostetler, Orlando, 1979, DeWolf, Ward & Morris, Orlando, 1979-84, Jontz, Russell & Hull, Orlando, 1985-86, Holland & Knight, 1986-96, Carlton Fields, Orlando, 1996—2005, Swann & Hadley, Orlando, 2005—. Contbr. articles to profl. jours.; mem. editl. bd. Iowa Law Rev., 1968. Chmn. Fed. Jud. Rels. Com., 2001—; past bd. dirs. Door Drug Rehab. Ctr. Ctrl. Fla.; bd. dirs. Fla. Symphony Orch., 1985—93, Jr. Achievement Ctrl. Fla., 1997—; mem. Rollins Coll. Tar Boosters; mem. code enforcement bd. City of Maitland, Fla., 1990—92; chmn bd. adjustment City of Winter Park, Fla., 1995—; mem. parents com. Dartmouth Coll., 1995—99; mem. long range planning com., former county commiteeman Orange County Reps., Fla.; past chmn. bd. trustees First Congl. Ch., Winter Park. Recipient Outstanding Individual Cmty. Leadership award, Vol. Ctr. Ctrl. Fla., 1991. Mem.: ABA (mem. comml. transactions litig. com., others), Am. Arbitration Assn. (comml. arbitrator 2005—), Orange County Bar Assn. (chmn. jud. rels. com. 1995—, mem. bankruptcy com.), Iowa State Bar Assn., Fla. Bar (mem. 9th cir. grievance com. 1979—82, chmn. comml. litig. com. 1981—82, mem. com. jud. adminstrn., selection and tenure 1985—86, mem. jud. nominating procedures com. 1995—96, mem. bankruptcy and creator's rights com., lectr. seminars), Ctrl. Fla. Bankruptcy Lawyers Assn., Am. Bankruptcy Inst., U. Iowa Alumni Assn. (bd. dirs. 2003—), Drake U. Nat. Alumni Assn. (bd. dirs. 1981—93, past chmn. ctrl. Fla. chpt., pres.'s cir. coun.), Citrus Club, Winter Park Racquet Club (pres. 1989—94, 1996—98, bd. govs., sec., v.p.), Tiger Bay Club Orlando, Order of Coif, Phi Delta Phi, Tau Kappa Epsilon, Omicron Delta Kappa. Office: PO Box 1870 Winter Park FL 32790-1870 Office Phone: 407-647-2777. Personal E-mail: jontz@worldnet.att.net. Business E-Mail: jjontz@swannhadley.com.

JONZE, SPIKE, film director; b. Rockville, Md., 1969; s. Arthur Spiegel III and Sandy Granzow; m. Sofia Coppola, June 26, 1999. Exec. prodr., prodr., writer, actor: (TV series) Jackass, 2000; writer, dir.: (video) Beastie Boys: Sabotage, 1994; actor: Beastie Boys: A Video Anthology, 2000; prodr.: (films) Human Nature, 2001; writer, prodr.: Jackass: The Movie, 2000; actor: Mi vida loca, 1993, The Game, 1997; actor, dir.: Being John Malkovich, 1999 (N.Y. Film Critics Cir. Award for Best First Film, 1999, Broadcast Film Critics Assn. Award for Breakthrough Performer, 1999, Online Film Critics Soc. Award for Best Debut, 1999); dir.: (video) R.E.M. Parallel, 1995, Bjork: Volumen, 1998; (films) How They Get There, 1997, Clip Cult Vol. 1: Exploding Cinema, 1999, Adaptation, 2002; actor: Three Kings, 1999 (Broadcast Film Critics Assn. Award for Breakthrough Performer, 1999). Recipient MTV Video Music Award for Best Direction for Buddy Holly, 1995. Office: Creative Artists Agy Attn Tony Metzger 9830 Wilshire Blvd Beverly Hills CA 90212-1825*

JOO, DOUGLAS D.M., newspaper and video production executive; b. Hamheung, Korea, July 14, 1945; came to U.S., 1985; s. Soo Jang and Syn Duk (Choi) J.; m. Myung Mi, Oct. 21, 1970; children: Hoon Hwi, Hoon Pal, Hoon Chul. BS, Seoul Nat. U., 1967; MA, Kyung Hee U., Seoul, 1979; MPhil, George Washington U., 1993; DPolit Sci (hon.), Sun Moon U., Korea, 2005. Pres. News World Comms., Washington, 1992—2003, Washington Times Corp., 1992—, Noticias PanAm Corp., 1996—2003; chmn., CEO Atlantic Video, Inc., 1991—; pres. U.S. Property Devel. Corp., 1991—, Nat. Hospitality Corp., 2000—; chmn., CEO UPI, 2000—03. Pres. Concept Comms., Washington, 1992—; chmn., CEO GoodLife TV Network; pres. Washington Times Aviation, 1997—. Trustee U. Bridgeport, Conn.; chmn. bd. dirs. Internat. Coalition for Religious Freedom, Washington, 1998-2003; pres. Unification Ch. Internat., 1991—. Mem. World Media Assn. (pres. 1992—), Washington Times Found. (pres. 1992—). Office: Washington Times Corp 3600 New York Ave NE Washington DC 20002-1996 Office Phone: 202-636-4841.

JOO, MICHAEL, artist, educator; b. Ithaca, N.Y., 1966; BFA, Washington U., 1989; MFA, Yale U., 1991. Adj. instr. The Cooper Union Sch. Art, N.Y.C., 1996, guest artist, 2000—. Adj. instr. The Cooper Union Sch. Art, N.Y.C., 1996, guest artist, 2000—. One-man shows include Nordanstad-Skarstedt, N.Y., 1992, Thomas Nordanstad Gallery, 1994—96, Stedelijk Mus., Amsterdam, 1995, Galerie Anne de Villepoix, Paris, 1995, Anthony D'Offay Gallery, London, 1995, Anton Kern Gallery, N.Y., 1997, exhibited in group shows at Ctr. Arts at Yerba Buena, San Francisco, 1993, Queens (N.Y.) Mus. Art, 1993, New Mus. Contemporary Art, N.Y., 1993, The Interart Ctr., 1994, Kumho Mus., Seoul, 1994, Cohen Gallery, N.Y., 1994, Serpentine Gallery, London, 1994, Inst. Contemporary Art, 1995, Randolph St. Gallery, Chgo., 1995, Mus. Contemporary Art, 1995, Kwangju Contemporary Mus., Sydkorea, 1995, Bloom Gallery, Amsterdam, 1996, The Post Office, London, 1996, Mus. Africa, Johannesburg, 1997, Anton Kern Gallery, N.Y., 1997, P.S. 1, 1998, others. Achievements include Represented Korea Venice Art Biennial, 2001. Office: care Cooper Union Sch Art 30 Cooper Sq New York NY 10003-7120*

JOO, SEUNG-HO, political scientist, educator; b. Incheon City, Republic of Korea, Dec. 6, 1959; s. Hong-Rin Joo and Soon-Hee Kim; m. Soon-Mi Hwahng, May 21, 1963; children: Esther Y.M., Danielle Y.H., Andrew Y.S. BA, Yonsei U., Seoul, 1982; PhD, Pa. State U., 1993. Asst. prof. polit. sci. U. of Minn.-Duluth, Duluth, Minn., 1994—95; assoc. prof. polit. sci. U. of Minn.-Morris, Morris, Minn., 1995—. Author: Gorbachev's Foreign Policy Toward the Korean Peninsula, 2000, Korea in the 21st Century, 2002, The Korean Peace Process and the Four Powers, 2003. Fellow Humphrey Inst. Policy Fellow, Hubert H. Humphrey Inst. of Pub. Affairs, 1997—98; grantee IREX Travel Grant, Internat. Rsch. and Exch. Bd., 2001; Disting. Rsch. fellow, Korea Inst. Nat. Unification, 1999—2000. Mem.: Internat. Studies Assn., Assn. Korean Polit. Studies (pres. 2003—), Am. Polit. Sci. Assn. Home: 4 Riverside Rd Morris MN 56267 Office: U Minn-Morris 109 Camden 601 E 4th St Morris MN 56267 Office Phone: 320-589-6203. E-mail: joos@mrs.umn.edu.

JOONDEPH, BRIAN, surgeon; b. Ridgewood, N.J., Mar. 31, 1958; m. Shirley Stroink, May 11, 1985. MD, Northwestern U., Chgo. Cert. Am. Bd. of Ophthalmology, 1990. Ptnr. Retinal Alliance PC, Denver, Colo., 2003—. Office: Retinal Alliance PC 1721 E 19th Ave Ste 550 Denver CO 80218 Office Phone: 303-894-0700. Office Fax: 303-861-5409. Personal E-mail: jooneye@hotmail.com.

JOOS, DAVID W., energy executive; BS engineering science, Iowa St. Univ., 1975, MS engineering science, 1976. With Consumer Energy, 1976, pres. and COO, 2001—04, pres. and CEO, 2004—. Mem.: Assn. Edison Illuminating Co., Michigan Coll. Found., Michigan Manufacturing Assn. (chmn. bd. dir.). Office: CMS Energy One Energy Plz Jackson MI 49201*

JOOS, FELIPE MIGUEL, mechanical engineer, researcher; b. Montevideo, Uruguay, Sept. 4, 1952; arrived in U.S., 1973, naturalized, 2003; s. Carlos Jose and Alma Elena Joos; children: Carolina Lucia, Catrina Aneliese, Celina Maria. BS in Applied Sci. and Engring., Calif. Inst. Tech., 1976; MSME, MIT, 1978, PhDME, 1983. Cert. engr., Uruguay. Engr. Ingenieros Consultores Latinoamericanos Limitada, Montevideo, Uruguay, 1978-79; mech. engr. research and devel. div. Gen. Electric Corp., Schenectady, N.Y., 1982-85; project engr. Creare, Inc., Hanover, N.H., 1985-87; tech. assoc. Eastman Kodak Co., Rochester, N.Y., 1987—. Indsl. fellow Ctr. for Interfacial Engring., U. Minn., Mpls., 1991-92; presenter in field. Contbr. articles to profl. jours.; patentee in field. Mem. ASME, Internat. Soc. Coating Sci. and Tech. (tech. session chair 1994, 98, 2000), Soc. Hispanic Profl. Engrs. (award 1993, v.p. 1989-90, treas. 1990-92, treas. Ea. Tech. and Career conf. 1991), Tau Beta Pi. Avocations: scuba diving, community affairs. Home: 75 Wood Creek Dr Pittsford NY 14534-4415 Office: Eastman Kodak Co Kodak Park Rochester NY 14652-3703 Personal E-mail: fmjoos@juno.com.

JOOSTEN, KATHRYN (KATHRYN JOOSTYN), actress; b. Dec. 20, 1939; Actor: (films) Grandview, U.S.A., 1984, The Package, 1989, Best Man, 1997, Phoenix, 1998, Kiss Toledo Goodbye, 1999, Lehi's Wife, 2002, Cojones, 2002, Halfway Decent, 2003, Red Rose and Petrol, 2003, Breaking Dawn, 2004, Win a Date with Tad Hamilton, 2004, Fathers and Sons, 2005, Hostage, 2005, Taking Your Life, 2005, Wedding Crashers, 2005; (TV films) Lady Blue, 1985, The Stranger Beside Me, 1995, The Making of a Hollywood Madam, 1996, Combustion (Silent Killer), 2004, McBride: It's Murder, Madam, 2005; (TV series) Secret Santa, 2003, Highway to Oblivion, 2003; performer: (stage) Ladies of the Corridor; actor: (video) Hellraiser:Inferno, 2000; guest appearences include General Hospital, Grace Under Fire, 1995, Roseanne, 1996, Third Rock from the Sun, 1996, ER, 1996, The West Wing (several episodes), 1996—2001, Murphy Brown, 1996, Boston Common, 1996, Frasier, 1997, Men Behaving Badly, 1997, NYPD Blue, 1997, Brooklyn South, 1997, Dharma & Greg, 1998, Dharma & Greg (several episodes), 2000—01, Just Shoot Me!, 1998, The Nanny, 1998, The Drew Carey Show, 1998, 2003, Providence, 1999, 2001, Home Improvement, 1999, Tracey Takes On, 1999, Buffy the Vampire Slayer, 2000, Becker, 2000, Ally McBeal, 2001, Scrubs, 2001, Spin City, 2001, The X Files, 2002, Judging Amy, 2003, Monk, 2003, Hope & Faith, 2003, Joan of Arcadia (several episodes), 2003—05, Charmed, 2003, Less Than Perfect, 2003, Strong Medicine, 2003, The King of Queens, 2003, A.U.S.A., 2003, Curb Your Enthusiasm, 2004, Will & Grace, 2004, Yes, Dear, 2004, Life with Bonnie, 2004, Everwood, 2004, Gilmore Girls, 2004, Desperate Housewives, 2005 (Creative Arts Primetime Emmy award for guest actress in a comedy series, 2005), Grey's Anatomy, 2005. Mem.: SAG, AFTRA, AEA.*

JOOSTYN, KATHRYN See **JOOSTEN, KATHRYN**

JORAPUR, VINOD, physician, researcher; arrived in U.S, 2001; s. Pandurang Bhimarao and Nirmala Pandurang Jorapur; m. Kshamaya Badarinarayan Panchamukhi, Feb. 4, 1999. MBBS, Sri Venkateswara Med. Coll., Tirupati, Ap, India, 1990; MD, Postgraduate Inst. Of Med. Edn. And Rsch., Chandigarh, 1994; MD in Cardiology, Sanjay Gandhi Post Grad. Inst. Of Med. Sci., Lucknow, Up, India, 1998; MD, Our Lady Of Mercy U. Hosp., Bronx, N.Y., 2002. Lic. Unrestricted Med. Med. Coun. Of India, 1990, Dm, Cardiology Sanjay Gandhi Postgraduate Inst. Of Med. Sci., Lucknow, 1998, Electrophysiology Training Course Bard South Asia Electrophysiology Tng. Program, 2001. Intern Sri Venkataramana Ruia Hosp., Tirupati, India, 1989—90; jr. resident in internal medicine Postgraduate Inst. Of Med. Edn. And Rsch., Chandigarh, India, 1991—94; chief resident in cardiology Sri Venkateswara Inst. Of Med. Sci., Tirupati, India, 1994—95; sr. resident in cardiology Sanjay Gandhi Postgraduate Inst. Of Med. Sci., Lucknow, India, 1995—98; attending cardiologist St. Stephen's Hosp., Delhi, India, 1998—98; asst. prof. of cardiology Ms Ramaiah Inst. Of Cardiology, Rajeev Gandhi U., Bangalore, India, 1998—2001; sr. housestaff Our Lady Of Mercy U. Hosp., Bronx, NY, 2002—. Cons. physician St. Stephen's Hosp., Delhi, India, 1998—98; co-dir. interventional cardiology and cardiac catheterization lab. Ms Ramaiah Inst. Of Cardiology, Rajeev Gandhi U., Bangalore, Karnataka, India, 1998—2001; co-investigator Hero-2 Internat. Multicenter Randomized Control Trial, Bangalore, Karnataka, India, 2000—01; cardiovasc. clin. rsch. fellow NYU Sch. Med., 2005. Author: (post doctoral dissertation) Transbronchial lung biopsy in sarcoidosis and relationship of histological changes to pulmonary function, (chpt.) Vascular Heart Disease, 2005; contbr. articles pub. to profl. jour. Recipient First prize in quiz contest, Indian Acad. of Pediat., 1988, Indian Coun. of Med. Rsch. award; fellow Fellowship In Cardiology, Sanjay Gandhi Postgraduate Inst. Of Med. Sci., 1995-1998; grantee Indian Coun. Of Med. Rsch. Grant, Indian Coun. Of Med. Rsch., 1987; scholar Nat. Talent Search Scholarship, Nat. Coun. of Ednl. Rsch. and Tng., India, 1982. Mem.: ACP (assoc.; assoc. mem. 2002), Am. Assn. Advancement of Sci., Med. Soc. State N.Y. (mem. heart lung cancer com. 2004—), Am. Heart. Assn., A,. Med. Assn., Indian Med. Assn. (life; life mem. 1990), Cardiol. Soc. Of India (life; life mem. 1998). Achievements include research in Echocardiographic quantification of annular dilatation and papillary muscle separation in patients of functional mitral regurgitation — role of anterior mitral leaflet length as reference; Effect of percutaneous coronary intervention on QT dispersion in acute coronary syndromes; Immunosuppressive therapy in active Takayasu's arteritis — clin., immunological and angiographic study; Clin., echocardiographic and angiographic characteristics and outcome in diabetics with acute myocardial infarction; Effect of renal transplantation on left ventricular function in chronic renal failure; Immunosuppressive therapy in aortoarteritis — clin. and angiographic follow up; Pulmonary sarcoidosis: spirometric correlation with transbronchial lung biopsy; 4. Epidemiological study of hypertension and coronary artery disease in urban and rural South India; Mitral leaflet coaptation morphology identifies mechanism of functional mitral regurgitation in heart failure: in-vitro insights for surgical strategy; Differential scallop reserve and failure mode of leaflet compensatory mechanisms in papillary displacement cardiomyopathy; Role of immunosuppressive therapy on clin., immunological and angiographic outcome in active Takayasu's Arteritis; In-vitro quantification of factors that overwhelm leaflet compensatory mechanisms for mitral regurgitation in heart failure; Influence of inter-papillary distance on mitral regurgitation in normal and myopathic hearts: implications for ventricular geometry restoration; Leaflet compensatory mechanisms for functional mitral regurgitation in papillary displacement model of heart failure; Absence of typically described electrocardiographic changes in a patient of hyperkalemia who had preexisting electrocardiographic changes; Increased intraventricular velocities — a surrogate marker for left ventricular hypertrophy in patients of hypertension; Epidemiological study of Ischemic Heart Disease; Longitudinal study of the morphologic determinants of functional mitral regurgitation in patients with post-infarction left ventricular remodeling. Avocations: travel, reading, photography. Personal E-mail: vjorapur@yahoo.com.

JORDAHL, SUSAN MARIE, music educator; b. Sebeka, Minn., Apr. 29, 1958; d. Charles Albert and Esther Ljungren; m. Delroy Alan Jordahl; children: Jessica, Jason. MEd, N.D. State U., 1980. Tchr. West Fargo (N.D.) Schs., 1985—, Trollwood Performing Arts Sch., Fargo, ND, 1995—. Bd. dirs. F-M Area Youth Symphony, Fargo, ND, 1996—98. Chmn. (program) Orchestra, 1998 (American String Teacher Recognition, 1999). Recipient Tchr. of Month award, West Fargo C. of C., 1999. Mem.: Sigma Alpha Iota (life; Variety over the years, Rose of Honor, Sword of Honor). Lutheran. Avocations: playing piano, gardening, cake decorating. Home: 1714 27th Ave S Moorhead MN 56560 Office: West Fargo HS 801 9th St E West Fargo ND 58078

JORDAK, JOHN A., JR., lawyer; b. Saginaw, Mich., Dec. 9, 1967; AB cum laude, Duke Univ., 1990; JD with distinction, Emory Univ., Atlanta, 1993. Bar: Ga. 1993. Ptnr., chmn., securities litig. group Alston & Bird LLP, Atlanta. Mng. editor Emory Internat. Law Rev., writes and lectures frequently on securities litig. and regulation. Alumni Admissions Adv. Com. Duke Univ. Office: Alston & Bird LLP One Atlantic Ctr 1201 W Peachtree St NW Atlanta GA 30309-3424 Office Phone: 404-881-7868. Office Fax: 404-881-7777. Business E-Mail: jjordak@alston.com.

JORDAN, ALEXANDER JOSEPH, JR., lawyer; b. New London, Conn., Oct. 11, 1938; s. Alexander Joseph and Alice Elizabeth (Mugovero) J.; m. Mary Carolyn Miller, Aug. 8, 1964; children: Jennifer, Michael, Stephanie. BS, U.S. Naval Acad., 1960; LLB, Harvard U., 1968. Ptnr. Gaston & Snow, Boston, 1968-91, Bingham, Dana & Gould, Boston, 1991-93, Nixon Peabody LLP, Boston, 1994—. Chmn. adv. com. Town of Hingham, Mass., 1989-95, govt. study com., 2000-01. With USN, 1960-65, capt. USNR, 1965-94, ret. Mem. ABA, Mass. Bar Assn., Boston Bar Assn., U.S. Naval Inst., Naval Res. Assn., Harvard Alumni Assn. (regional dir. 1998-2001), U.S. Naval Acad. Alumni Assn., Harvard Club Hingham (trustee, chmn. com. schs. and scholarships, past pres.), Harvard Club of Boston. Office: Nixon Peabody LLP 100 Summer St Boston MA 02110-2131 Office Phone: 617-345-1103. Business E-Mail: ajordan@nixonpeabody.com.

JORDAN, AMOS AZARIAH, JR., foreign affairs educator, retired military officer; b. Twin Falls, Idaho, Feb. 11, 1922; s. Amos Azariah and Olive (Fisher) J.; m. MarDeane Carver, June 5, 1946; children: Peggy Jordan Hughes, Diana Jordan Paxton, Keith, David, Linda Jordan Mabey, Kent. BS, U.S. Mil. Acad., 1946; BA, Oxford U., Eng., 1950, MA, 1955; PhD, Columbia U., 1961. Commd. 2d lt. U.S. Army, 1946, advanced through grades to brig. gen., 1972; instr. U.S. Mil. Acad., 1950-53, prof. social scis., 1955-72; arty. battery comdr. U.S. Army, Korea, 1954-55; asst. S-3 7th Divsn. Arty. Korea, 1955; adviser econ. and fiscal policy U.S. Econ. Mission to Korea, 1955; ret. U.S. Army, 1972; dir. Aspen Inst., 1972-74; prin. dep. asst. sec. for internat. security affairs Dept. Def., Washington, 1974-76; dep. undersec. and acting undersec. for security assistance Dept. State, Washington, 1976-77; with Ctr. for Strategic and Internat. Studies, Washington, 1977-94, pres. chief exec. officer, 1983-88, vice chmn., 1988-94, pres. Pacific Forum Honolulu, 1990-94; sr. adviser CSIS, 1994—; counselor Pacific Forum, 1994—. Mem. staff Pres.'s Com. to Study Fgn. Assistance Program, 1959; staff dir. Adv. Com. to Sec. Def. on Non-Mil. Instrn., 1962; spl. polit. advisor to U.S. amb. to India, 1963-64; cons. NSC, 1979; mem. Nat. Com. on Security and Econ. Assistance, 1983; Henry Kissinger rsch. chair in nat. security policy CSIS, 1988-92; mem. Pres.'s Intelligence Oversight Bd., 1989-93; internat. co-chmn. Coun. on Sec. Coop. in the Asia Pacific, 1993-96, chmn. U.S. com., 1993-98; co-chmn. Korean-Am. Wisemen Coun., 1991-98; Asia area adminstr. Latter Day Saint Charities, 1998-99; spl. asst. to pres. Brigham Young U., Hawaii, 2001-02; bd. dirs. Pacific Forum, Ctr. for Strategic and Internat. Studies. Author: Foreign Aid and the Defense of

Southeast Asia, 1962, Issues of National Security in the 1970's, 1967; co-author: American National Security Policy and Process, 1981, 5th edit., 1999; contbr. chpts. to books and articles to profl. jours. Decorated D.S.M., Legion of Merit with oak leaf cluster, Disting. Civilian Svc. medal Dept. Def. Mem. Coun. Fgn. Rels., Assn. Am. Rhodes Scholars, Pacific Coun. Internat. Policy, Bretton Woods Com. Office: Pacific Forum CSIS Pauahi Tower 1001 Bishop St Ste 1150 Honolulu HI 96813-3407

JORDAN, ANGEL GONI, electrical and computer engineering educator; b. Pamplona, Spain, Sept. 19, 1930; came to U.S., 1956, naturalized, 1966; s. Hilario and Perpetua (Goni) J.; m. Nieves Alfonso Cuartero, July 8, 1956; children: Xavier, Edward, Arthur. MS, PhD, Carnegie Inst. Tech., 1959; Dr. honoris causa, Poly. U. Madrid, Spain, 1985, U. Publica de Navarra, 2001. With Naval Ordnance Lab., Madrid, 1952-56; instr. elec. engring. Carnegie-Mellon U., 1956-58, asst. prof. elec. engring., 1959-62, assoc. prof., 1962-65, prof., 1965-90, univ. prof., 1990-97, U.A. and Helen Whitaker prof., 1972-80, head dept., 1969-79, dean engring. Carnegie Inst. Tech., 1979-83, provost, 1983-91, J.F and N.P. Keithley univ. prof. elec., computer engring., 1997-99, univ. prof. emeritus, 1999—. Rsch. fellow Mellon Inst. Indsl. Rsch., 1958—59; cons. to industry; bd. dirs. Magnascreen Corp., Mirror Sys., Inc., SOCINTEC. Contbr. articles to profl. jours. Dir. Pitts. High Tech. Coun., 1983-; bd. dirs. Pa. Sci. and Engring. Found, 1981-83. Recipient Enterprise award Pitts. Bus. Times, 1985; NATO sr. scientist fellow, 1976; Fulbright Disting. scholar, 1988; named Edn. Man of the Yr., Pitts., 1987. Fellow IEEE, AAAS; mem. Am. Phys. Soc., NAE, Acad. Engring. Spain, Sigma Xi, Eta Kappa Nu, Phi Kappa Phi, Tau Beta Pi. Home: 5874 Aylesboro Ave Pittsburgh PA 15217-1446 Office: Carnegie-Mellon U Wean Hall # 4618 Pittsburgh PA 15213 Office Phone: 412-268-2590. Business E-Mail: ajordan@cs.cmu.edu.

JORDAN, ANNE E. DOLLERSCHELL, journalist; b. Mpls., Mar. 30, 1964; d. Allen L. and Marcia G. (Landeen) Dollerschell; m. James Lawrence Jordan, Aug. 16, 1986; children: Davyd, Scott. BA, U. Wis., 1986. From editl. asst. to mng. editor Governing Mag., Washington, 1987—. Mem. Phi Beta Kappa, Phi Kappa Phi, Phi Theta Kappa. Office: Governing Mag Ste 1300 1100 Connecticut Ave NW Washington DC 20036-4109

JORDAN, BRUCE LESLIE, music educator, musician; b. Dayton, Ohio, Oct. 6, 1944; s. Robert Leslie and Lois Evelyn Jordan; m. Brenda Sue Jordan, July 28, 1979; children: Amanda Lynn, Robert Eugene. MusB, Miami U., 1966; MusM, Ind. U., 1969. Prof. Sinclair C.C., Dayton, 1973—. Performer (Saxophone): S.C.C. Jazz Ensemble; performer: (CD) Water Music.

JORDAN, BRYCE, retired university president; b. Clovis, N.Mex., Sept. 22, 1924; s. W. Joseph and Kittie (Cole) J.; children: Julia Cole, Christopher Joseph; m. Barbara E. Brueggebors, Oct. 28, 2000. Student, Hardin-Simmons U., 1941-42; MusB, U. Tex., 1948, MusM, 1949; PhD, U. N.C., 1956; LLD, Juniata Coll., 1985, Milliken U., 1990. Asst. prof. music Hardin-Simmons U., 1949-51; from asst. prof. to prof. music U. Md., 1954-63; prof. music, chmn. dept. U. Ky., 1963-65, U. Tex., 1965-68, v.p. student affairs Austin, 1968-70, pres. ad interim, 1970-71, pres. Dallas, 1971-81; exec. vice chancellor for acad. affairs U. Tex. System, 1981-83; pres. Pa. State U., 1983-90. Mem. faculty Salzburg (Austria) Seminar Am. Studies, 1960, 62, 98; occasional lectr. Fgn. Svc. Inst., Dept. State, 1962-63; mem. Yale Coun. on Music, 1971-73, Nat. Commn. on Higher Edn. Issues, 1982-83. Author: (with Homer Ulrich) Student Manual for Music: A Design for Listening, 1957, Designed for Listening, 1962, also articles, revs.; assoc. editor: Coll. Music Symposium, 1961-66. Bd. dirs. Dallas Grand Opera Assn., 1973-75, Pa. Econ. Devel. Ptnrship, 1987-90; trustee St. Marks Sch. Tex., 1973-81, Dallas Symphony Assn., 1972-81, Presbyn. Hosp., Dallas, 1976-83; v.p. Dallas Civic Music Assn., 1978-79, pres., 1979-80, exec. com. 1980-81; bd. dirs. Dallas County chpt. ARC, 1976-79; divsn. chmn. United Way Met. Dallas, 1979; Pa. state chmn. Am. Heart Assn., 1983-84; trustee Com. on Econ. Devel. 1988-90; adv. bd. comml. programs NASA, 1988-90; nat. chmn. higher edn. U.S. Treasury Savs. Bond Programs, 1988-89, 89-90; presiding elder Presbyn. Ch.; chmn. Austin Lyric Opera, 1991-94; vis. com. Eastman Sch. Music U. Rochester, 1991-94; chmn. fine arts adv. coun. U. Tex., Austin, 1994-96; chmn. adv. bd. U. Tex. Press, 1997-99; mem. Knight Found. Commn. on Intercollegiate Athletics, 1991-93, 2000-01. Recipient Hon. Alumni award Pa. State U., 1987, medal, 1990, Doty medal U. Tex., 1996, Presdl. citation U. Tex., 2002; named Disting. Alumnus, U. N.C., 1985, Hardin-Simmons U., 1987, U. Tex., Austin, 1991. Mem. Coll. Music Soc. (v.p. 1963-65, coun. mem. 1968-70), Am. Musicol. Soc. (chmn. greater Washington chpt. 1958-60), Music Educators Nat. Conf. (pres. Md. br. 1963), Music Tchrs. Nat. Assn., Philos. Soc. Tex., Dallas C. of C. (dir. 1979-82), So. Assn. Colls. and Schs. (commn. on colls. 1981-83), Pa. Assn. Colls. and Univs. (chmn. 1988-89), Phi Kappa Phi, Pi Kappa Lambda, Phi Mu Alpha, Golden Key. Home: 5809 Tom Wooten Cove Austin TX 78731-6512 Personal E-mail: bigbandboy@austin.rr.com.

JORDAN, CHARLES MORRELL, retired automotive designer; b. Whittier, Calif., Oct. 21, 1927; s. Charles L. and Bernice May (Letts) J.; m. Sally Irene Mericle, Mar. 8, 1951; children: Debra, Mark, Melissa. BS, MIT, 1949; grad. advanced mgmt. program, Harvard U., 1979; Doctorate (hon.), Art Ctr. Coll. Design, 1992, Ctr. for Creative Studies, 2001. With GM, Warren, Mich., 1949—, chief designer Cadillac Studio, 1957-61, group chief designer, 1961-62, exec. in charge automotive design, 1962-67, dir. styling Adam Opel A.G., 1967-70, exec. in charge Cadillac, Oldsmobile, Buick Studios, 1970-73, exec. in charge Chevrolet, Pontiac and Comml. Vehicle Studios, 1973-77, dir. design, 1977-86, v.p. design staff, 1986-92; retired, 1992. 1st lt. USAF, 1952-53. Recipient First Nat. award Fisher Body Craftsman's Guild, 1947, disting. svc. citation Automotive Hall of Fame, 1990, Wally B. Ford award Ctr. for Creative Studies, 1992; named Hon. Judge, Pebble Beach Concours d'Elegance, 1970—. Mem. Calif. Scholastic Fedn. (life), Ferrari Club Am. Address: PO Box 8330 Rancho Santa Fe CA 92067-8330 E-mail: cmjdesign@aol.com.

JORDAN, CHARLES WESLEY, retired bishop; b. Dayton, Ohio, May 28, 1933; s. David Morris and Naomi Azelia (Harper) J.; m. Margaret May Crawford, Aug. 2, 1959; children: Diana, Susan. BA, Roosevelt U., 1956; MDiv, Garrett Evangel. Theol. Sem., Evanston, Ill., 1960; LHD (hon.), Morningside Coll., 1994; DD (hon.), Rust Coll., 1995, Simpson Coll., 2000. Ordained to ministry United Meth. Ch., 1960. Pastor Woodlawn United Meth. Ch., Chgo., 1960-66; dir. of urban ministries Rockford, Ill., 1966-71; prog. staff No. Ill. Con./United Meth. Ch., Chgo., 1971-82; dist. supt. Chgo./So. Dist. United Meth. Ch., 1982-87; sr. pastor St. Mark United Meth. Ch., Chgo., 1987-92; bishop Iowa Area United Meth. Ch., Des Moines, 1992-2000; ret., 2000. Del. United Meth. Gen. Conf., 1976, 80, 84, 88, 92, Gen. Bd. Global Ministries, 1972-80, Gen. Coun. on Ministries, 1980-88; trustee Garrett Evangel. Theol. Sem., 1982-97. Commnr. Rockford Housing Authority, 1969-71; bd. dirs. Cmty. Mental Health Coun., Chgo., 1989-91, Project Image, Inc., Chgo., 1987-92, Cen. Iowa Health System, 1993-2000, Mid-Iowa coun. Boy Scouts Am., 1995-2000; pres. United Meth. Gen. Bd. Ch. and Society, 1996-2000, Ecumenical Ministries Iowa, 1999, Progressive Christians Uniting, L.A. area, 2005—. Named to Hall of Fame Wendell Phillips High Sch., Chgo., 1989. Mem. NAACP (life, chmn. religious affairs 1990-92), Kappa Alpha Psi, Sigma Pi Phi. Home: 1014 Deborah St Upland CA 91784-1206

JORDAN, CLIFFORD HENRY, management consultant; b. New Orleans, Dec. 27, 1921; s. Clifford Henry and May Rosalie (Duke) J.; m. Clara H. Nordberg, June 1, 1955. Grad. RN, Pa. Hosp. Sch. Nursing, 1949; BS in Nursing Edn., Temple U., 1954, EdD, 1975; MS in Edn., U. Pa., 1957. RN, Pa. Assoc. dir. Episc. Hosp. Sch. Nursing, Phila., 1958-63, DON, 1963-66; prof. nursing U. Pa., Phila., 1966-82, prof. emeritus, 2002—; exec. dir. Assn. Oper. Rm. Nurses, Denver, 1982-90; mgmt. cons. Phila., 1990—. Cons. in nursing adminstrn. Pa., NJ, Calif. hosps.; edn. cons. in orgnl. devel. Pa., Kans., NJ univs. Mem. Pa. Gov.'s Commn. on Health, 1975-77; bd. govs. Health Systems Agy. So. Pa., 1975-79. Recipient U. Pa. Lindbach award, 1980, Lifetime Achievement award U. Pa., 2004; named Outstanding alumni U. Pa., 1982. Fellow Am. Acad. Nursing (designated as Living Legend 1996); mem. Am. Nurses Assn. (bd. dirs.), Pa. Nurses Assn. (pres. 1962-66, 72-76), Am. Nurses Found. (v.p. 1980-82). Republican. Roman Catholic. Home and Office: The Wellington # 1610 135 S 19th St Philadelphia PA 19103-4912

JORDAN, D. BRYAN, corporate financial executive; Audit practice, 1984—91; formerly with Wachovia Corp., Charlotte NC; exec. v.p., corp. contr. Regions Fin. Corp., Birmingham, Ala., 2000—02, exec. v.p., CFO, 2002—. Mem.: Regions Asset Mgmt. Co., Rebsamen Ins. Inc. (dir.). Office: Regions Fin PO Box 10247 Birmingham AL 35202-0247

JORDAN, DANIEL PATRICK, JR., law librarian; b. Bklyn., July 15, 1951; s. Daniel Patrick and Nan (Sinnott) J. BA, Bklyn. Coll., 1975; JD, U. Pacific, 1980; MLS, Pratt Inst., 1982. Ref. librarian Touro Coll., Huntington, NY, 1982-83, head pub. services, 1983-86, head law libr., 1986—2005. Mem. ABA, Calif. Bar Assn., Am. Assn. Law Libraries. Office: Touro Coll Jacob D Fuchsberg Law Ctr 300 Nassau Rd Huntington NY 11743-4346 E-mail: DanJ@tourolaw.edu.

JORDAN, DANIEL PORTER, JR., foundation administrator, historian, educator; b. Phila., Miss., July 22, 1938; s. Daniel Porter and Mildred M. (Dobbs) J.; m. Lewellyn Lee Schmelzer, Dec. 18, 1961; children: Daniel P., Grace Dobbs, Katherine Lewellyn. BA, U. Miss., 1960, MA, 1962; PhD, U. Va., 1970; PhD (hon.), Drake U., 2005. Various tchg. positions overseas divsn. U. Md., 1962-65, Richmond, Va., 1968-69, U. Va., summers 1970-72; prof. history Va. Commonwealth U., Richmond, 1969-84, Ariz. State, 1995; dir. Stratford Hall Summer Sem., 1981-91; exec. dir. Thomas Jefferson Found. (Monticello), 1985—, pres., 1994—. Scholar in residence U. Va., 1985—. Author: Political Leadership in Jefferson's Virginia, 1983, A Richmond Reader, 1733-1983, 1983, Tobacco Merchant: The Story of Universal Leaf Tobacco Company, 1995. Mem. adv. com. Papers of Thomas Jefferson, Princeton U.; mem. Sec. of Interior's adv. bd. Nat. Pk. Sys., 1984-88, chmn., 1987-88; mem. Jeffersonian Restoration Adv. Bd., U. Va., 1985—; mem. rev. bd. Va. Hist. Landmarks Commn., 1981-92, chmn., 1989-92; mem. Nat. Pks. and Conservation Bd., 1989-92, Ea. Nat. Bd., 1991-2001; pres. Richmond Civil War Roundtable, 1983; trustee Nat. Trust for Hist. Preservation, 1999—; bd. dirs. Fund for the U.S. Capitol Visitor Ctr., 2000—; mem. adv. bd. Freedom Forum Mus., 2002—, Eudona Welty Found., 2002—; mem. curatorial adv. bd. US Senate, 2004—. Served with inf. U.S. Army, 1962-65. Thomas Jefferson Found. fellow, 1965-68; recipient award of merit Am. Assn. for State and Local History, 1977, 88, Pub. Svc. award U.S. Dept. of Interior, 1990, Medal for Va. Svc., AIA, 1993. Mem. Am. Antiquarian Soc., Va. Hist. Soc. (bd. dirs. 1986-91), Mass. Hist. Soc., So. Hist. Assn. (life), Orgn. Am. Historians (life), Walpole Soc., Phi Beta Kappa (pres. Alpha of Va. 1995-98), Omicron Delta Kappa, Sigma Chi. Methodist. Home and Office: Monticello Home of Thomas Jefferson PO Box 316 Charlottesville VA 22902-0316 Business E-Mail: djordan@monticello.org.

JORDAN, DEOVINA NASIS, administrative nurse; b. Bangued, Abra, Philippines, May 7, 1960; d. Demetrio Villamor Nacis and Francisca Bicarme Baptista; m. James Lowell Jordan, July 25, 1992. BS in Nursing, U. Perpetual Help, Rizal, Philippines, 1980; MD in Surgery, U. Santo Tomas, Philippines, 1985; M in Pub. Health, Loma Linda U., 2001; MS in Nursing, UCLA, 2004. Cert. Ednl. Comm. for Foreign Med. Grads. Phila., Pa.; Ped. Nursing, Am. Nursing Credentialing Ctr., Wash. DC. Clin. nurse Hosp. for Joint Dis. Ortho. Inst., NYC, 1987—88; clin. nurse III Mattel Children's Hosp, UCLA, L.A., 1988—; admin. nurse IV UCLA Med. Ctr., L.A., 2002—; v.p., founder Jordan Rsch. Inst., Murietta, Calif., 1994—; pres Fil-Am Assoc., Murietta, 1994—. Rsch. adv. bd. Am. Biographical Inst., 2002—. Contbr. articles various prof. jours. Recipient Outstanding Profl. Woman award, Am. Biographical Inst., 2001. Mem.: Assn. Calif. Nurse Leaders, Am. Assn. Critical Care Nurses, Calif. Nurses Asn., Am. Coll. Healthcare Execs., Alpha Tau Delta, Sigma Theta Tau.

JORDAN, EDDIE, professional basketball coach; b. Washington; Degree in health and phys. edn., Rutgers U., 1977. Basketball player Cleve. Cavaliers, 1977, N.J. Nets, 1977-80, asst. coach, 1999—2003; basketball player L.A. Lakers, 1980-84; mem. World Championship squad NBA, 1982; basketball player Portland (Oreg.) Trail Blazers; vol. asst. Rutgers U., asst. coach, 1988; part-time asst. Old Dominion; asst. coach Boston Coll., 1986; mem. coaching staff Sacramento (Calif.) Kings, 1992, head coach, 1996-99, Wash. Wizards, 2003—. Office: Wash Wizards 601 F St NW Washington DC 20004

JORDAN, EOWANA BRADLEY, retired librarian; b. Falls City, Nebr., Oct. 10, 1947; d. John G.H. and Katherine (Allard) Peters; m. Lenny A. Krieg, Apr. 30, 2005. BS in Elem. Edn., Okla. State U., 1969; MLS, Cath. U. Am., 1988. Tchr. Denver Pub. Schs., 1969-72, Am. Schs. in Europe, Wiesbaden, Fed. Republic Germany, 1972-75, Prince William Pub. Schs., Woodbridge, Manassas, Va., 1977-88, libr. Manassas, 1988—2003; ret. Mem. Gamma Phi Beta, Phi Delta Kappa. Greek Orthodox and Methodist. Home: 9110 Stonewall Rd Manassas VA 20110-2556

JORDAN, EVORA RUTH, writer, researcher, publishing executive; b. Windham, Maine, Nov. 17, 1931; d. Almon Orion and Ruth Seavey Moore; children: Barry Richard Jordon, Diane Ruth Manner. BS, Gorham State Tchrs. Coll., Gorham, Maine, 1964; MS, Univ. So. Maine, Gorham, Maine, 1966. Cert. lic. sch. counselor Univ. So. Maine, 1987. Head tchr. history dept. Falmouth Jr. high, Falmouth, Maine, 1965—74; tchr. MSAD #61, Naples, Maine, 1975—87, elem. sch. counselor, 1987—96; owner Evorabooks LLC, Canton, Conn., 2001—. Profl. spkr. in field. Author: Twenty-One Days with aVulture, 2000, Tainted Sand, 2003, Annie Love, 2003, Hannah Gray Mystery; guest spkr. (numerous radio sta.). Co-founder, vol. abuse counselor Oxford County Rape Edn. and Counseling Helpline, pres. bd. dirs.; dir. Bridgton, Maine, Child Abuse Council; chaired M.A.S.D. #61 Personal Safety Com.; ambulance attendant Casco Rescue Unit, Maine, 1981—82; candidate Maine Legis. Dist 24, 1980; chaired Town Polit. Com.; served on numerous Town Com.; selectman, chmn. Town of Casco, 1980; dedimus justice State of Maine, 1983. Recipient Extraordinary Contribution to Prevention, Cumberland County Child Abuse & Nelgect Coun., Congl. Recognition, 1996, Recognition, State of Maine, 1991, Cert. of Appreciation, Maine Dept. of Human Svcs., 1983—84, Commr. Recognition award, State of Maine, Dept. Edn., 1991, Trust Fund in her honor. Master: Am. Assn. Ret. Persons; mem.: Nat. Edn. Assn., Publ. Mktg. Assn., Maine Writerss & Publ. Alliance, Conn. Authors & Publ. Assn. (pres. 2004—, v.p., publicity chairperson, liaison to the Nat. Publ. Mktg. Assn.). Achievements include spkr. at first Russian/U.S. Conf. on Edn; helped solve tchr. shortage. Avocations: walking, swimming, singing, piano, designing book covers. Home: PO Box 397 Canton CT 06019 Office: Evorabooks LLC PO Box 397 Canton CT 06019

JORDAN, FREDERICK LEROY, trucking executive; b. Kansas City, Mo., Jan. 20, 1964; s. Thomas and Margaret Cornelia (Black) Jordan; m. Lauren Lené Ware; 1 stepchild, Letitia Lené Ware. Driving diploma, MTA Truck Driving Sch., Orlando, Fla.; AA in Electronic Engring., ITT Tech.Inst., Tampa, Fla. Longhaul driver Werner Enterprises, Omaha, 1991—93; truck driver Tampa Tribune, 1993—95; customer svc. engr. Memorex Telex Inc., Tampa, 1995—97; trucking contractor Sillman Trucking Inc., Tampa, 1997, Clarksville Refrigerated Lines, Winter Haven, Fla., 1997—2004; pres., owner Toshi Moto Express Inc., Tampa, 2004—. Crimwatch capt. Tempe Ter. Homeowners Assn., Tampa, 1993; tech. advisor 34th St. Ch. of God, Tampa, 1993. Sgt. U.S. Army, 1984—90. Decorated Svc. ribbon, Achievement medal, Good Conduct medal. Mem.: Am. Legion. Democrat. Avocations: computers, motorcycling, bicycling. Home and Office: 11718 Tom Folsom Rd Thonotosassa FL 33592

JORDAN, GLENN, film director, television director, theater director; b. San Antonio, Apr. 5, 1936; BA, Harvard U., 1957; postgrad., Yale U. Drama Sch., 1957—58. Dir. regional and stock theatre, including Cafe La Mama, late 1950s; N.Y. directorial debut with Another Evening With Harry Stoones, 1961; other plays include A Taste of Honey, 1968; Rosencrantz and Guildenstern Are Dead, 1969, A Streetcar Named Desire at Cin. Playhouse in the Park, 1973, All My Sons at Huntington Hartford Theatre, 1975; founder, N.Y. TV Theater, 1965, dir. various plays, including Paradise Lost and Hogan's Goat; dir. mini-series Benjamin Franklin, CBS, 1974 (Emmy award 1975, Peabody award); Family, ABC-TV series, 1976-77, including segment Rights of Friendship (Dirs. Guild Am. award); numerous TV plays for public TV, including Eccentricities of a Nightingale, 1976; The Displaced Person, 1976; TV movies including Shell Game, 1975, One Of My Wives Is Missing, 1975, Delta County U.S.A, 1977, In The Matter of Karen Ann Quinlan, 1977, Sunshine Christmas, 1977, Les Miserables, 1978, Son-Rise, A Miracle of Love, 1979, The Family Man, 1979, The Women's Room, 1980, Lois Gibbs and the Love Canal, 1982, Heartsounds, 1984 (Peabody award), Toughlove, 1985, Dress Gray, 1986, Something in Common, 1986, Promise, 1986 (2 Emmy awards for producing, directing, Peabody award, Golden Globe award), Echoes in the Darkness, 1987, Jesse, 1988, Home Fires Burning, 1988, Challenger, 1989, The Boys, 1990, Sarah Plain and Tall, 1990, Aftermath, 1990, O Pioneers!, 1991, Barbarians at the Gate, 1992 (Emmy award Outstanding Made for TV Movie, 1993, Golden Globe award, Best Mini-series or movie made for TV, 1994), To Dance with the White Dog, 1994, Jane's House, 1994, My Brother's Keeper, 1994, A Streetcar Named Desire, 1995, Jake's Women (Neil Simon), 1996, After Jimmy, 1996, Mary and Tim, 1996, A Christmas Memory, 1997, The Long Way Home, 1998, Legalese, 1998, Night Ride Home, 1999, Winter's End: Sarah Plain & Tall III, 1999, Midwives, 2000, Lucy, 2003; dir: feature film Only When I Laugh (Neil Simon), 1981, The Buddy System, 1983, Mass Appeal, 1984. Recipient Emmy awards for N.Y. TV Theater Plays, 1970, Actors Choice award, 1970. also: 9401 Wilshire Blvd Ste 700 Beverly Hills CA 90212-2920

JORDAN, GREGORY B., lawyer; b. Wheeling, W.Va., Aug. 10, 1959; m. Ellen Jordan; 2 children. BA magna cum laude, Bethany Coll., 1981; JD cum laude, U. Pitts., 1984. Bar: Pa. 1984, W.Va. With Reed Smith LLP, Pitts., 1984—, former dir. legal pers., former dir. practice devel., mng. ptnr., chmn. sr. mgmt. team & exec. com., 2001—. Contbr. articles to profl. journals. Bd trustees Bethany Coll., Carnegie Sci. Ctr. Named one of the top 45 lawyers in Am. under age 45, Am. Lawyer, 2003; named to The Best Lawyers in Am., 1995—. Mem.: Order of Coif, Duquesne Club. Office: Reed Smith LLP 435 Sixth Ave Pittsburgh PA 15219 Office Phone: 412-288-4124. Office Fax: 412-288-3063. Business E-Mail: gjordan@reedsmith.com.*

JORDAN, HOWARD EMERSON, retired engineering executive, consultant; b. State College, N.Mex., May 14, 1926; s. Howard E. and Elizabeth (Bruden) J.; children: Blair, Julie. BSEE, U. Wis., 1946; MS, Case Western Res. U., 1958, PhD, 1962. With Rayovac Co., Madison, Wis., 1946-52, Reliance Elec., Cleve., 1954-93, dir. corp. R & D, 1993—; pvt. cons.; rsch. scientist U. Tex. Author: Energy Efficient Electric Motors and Their Application, 1983, 2d edit., 1994; contbg. author: Handbook of Electric Machines, 1987. Served to 1st lt. USAF, 1952-54. Recipient Disting. Svc. citation U. Wis., 1989. Fellow IEEE (sr.); mem. Nat. Electrical Mfrs. Assn. (chmn. motor and generator sect. 1979). Methodist.

JORDAN, IRVING KING, university president; m. Linda Jordan; children: I. King III, Heidi. BA, Gallaudet U., 1970; MA in psychology, U. Tenn., 1971, PhD in psychology, 1973. Faculty mem. Gallaudet U., Washington, 1973, chair Dept. Psychology, 1983, dean Coll. Arts and Scis., 1986—88, pres., 1988—. Rsch. fellow Donaldson's Sch. for Deaf, Edinburgh, Scotland; vice chair President's Com. on Employment of People with Disabilities, 1990, 93. Recipient Presdl. Citizen's Medal, Washingtonian of Yr. Award, James L. Fisher Award, Coun. for Advancement and Support of Edn., Larry Stewart Award, American Psychol. Assn., Disting. Leadership Award, Nat. Assn. for Cmty. Leadership. Office: Gallaudet U Office of Pres 800 Florida Ave NE Washington DC 20002-3660 E-mail: president@gallaudet.edu.

JORDAN, JEFF, Internet company executive; BA in Polit. Sci. and Psychology, Amherst Coll.; MBA, Stanford U. From mgr. strategic planning Consumer Products Divsn. to CEO The Disney Store Worldwide The Walt Disney Corp.; exec. v.p., CFO Hollywood Entertainment; pres. website; sr. v.p. eBay U.S. eBay Inc., San Jose, Calif., gen. mgr. eBay U.S., sr. v.p. U.S. Bus., 2000—05; pres. PayPal Inc. (subs. eBay Inc.), 2005—. Office: PayPal Inc eBay Inc 2145 Hamilton Ave San Jose CA 95125*

JORDAN, JEFFREY GUY, marketing professional, consultant; b. Oshkosh, Wis., May 21, 1950; s. Berwin Russell and Delores Suzanne (Tomlitz) J. BS, U. Wis., Oshkosh, 1973; postgrad., UCLA, 1978. Analyst corp. planning and rsch. May Co. Dept. Store, L.A., 1973-77; dir. mktg. svcs. DJMC Advt., L.A., 1977-80; dir. mktg. Wienerschnitzel, Internat., Newport Beach, Calif., 1980-84, York Steakhouse Restaurants (Gen. Mills), Columbus, Ohio, 1984-85, Paragon Restaurant Group, San Diego, 1985-87; v.p. mktg. Paragon Steakhouse Restaurants, Inc., San Diego, 1987-94; owner, pres. 1-on-One Mktg. Assocs., 1994—. Cons., presenter U.S. Internat. U., San Diego, 1989. Mem. Conv. and Visitors Bur., San Diego; vol. Boys' Club of Am., Oshkosh, 1973-74; fundraising coord. Am. Cancer Soc., L.A., 1976. Mem. Am. Mktg. Assn. (treas., bd. dirs. 1996-97), Qualitative Rsch. Cons. Assn., Multi Unit Foodservice Operators Assn., San Diego Advt. Assn. (creative exec. 1986-88), San Diego C. of C. Republican. Lutheran. Avocations: sports, travel, photography. Office Phone: 858-484-2307.

JORDAN, JERRY DALE, lawyer, gas industry executive; b. Duncan, Okla., Nov. 27, 1934; s. W.F. and Leona B. (Kile) J.; m. Sally Melton, July 5, 1958; children— Mark, Anne, Whitney. B.S. in Geology, Denison U.; postgrad. U. Okla., 1960; J.D. U. Mich., 1963. Bar: Ohio 1963. Former ptnr., Vorys, Sater, Seymour & Pease, Columbus, Ohio; chmn., chief exec. officer Clinton Gas Systems Inc., 1988-98; mem. nominating com. State Ohio Pub. Utilities Commn., 1998—; mem. tech. adv. coun. Ohio Dept. Natural Resources, 2005—; bd. dirs. Nat. Petroleum Coun., Mountain States Legal Found.; dir. Knox Energy, Inc., 1989—. Chmn. Gov.'s Com. on Self-Help Natural Gas, 1976-81; mem. Franklin County (Ohio) Zoning Commn., 1985-89; adj. prof. Capital U. Law Sch., 1987-92. Mem. Ind. Petroleum Assn. Am. (vice chmn. 1997-99, chmn. 1999-2001), Ohio Oil and Gas Assn. (trustee, pres.), Eastern Mineral Law Found. (founding trustee), Columbus Bar Assn., Ohio Bar Assn., Athletic Club of Columbus (bd. dirs. 1986-92). Office Phone: 614-885-4828. E-mail: jjmaw@yahoo.com.

JORDAN, JOE J., architect; b. Phila., May 5, 1923; s. Edmund F. and Elizabeth N. (Jungkurth) Jordan; m. Sarah Jeanne Connolly, Nov. 1, 1974. BS in Architecture, U. Ill., 1949. Prin. Joe J. Jordan, FAIA, Phila., 1961-81; ptnr. Delta Group, Phila., 1972-74; prin., pres. Jordan, Mitchell Inc., Phila., 1981-93. UN tech. assistance expert Mid. E. Tech. U., Ankara, Turkey, 1958—60, acting head dept. architecture, 1959, archtl. advisor to univ. pres., 60; mem. faculty dept. architecture Drexel U., Phila., 1962, adj. prof., 64, head dept., 1965—77. Author: Senior Center Facilities, 1975, Senior Center Design, 1978, Cape May Point - The Illustrated History, 2003, Cape May Point-Three Walking Tours, 2004; contbr. articles to profl. jours. Mem. citizens coun. city planning, Phila., 1956—70; bd. dirs. Phila. Sr. Ctr., 1964—70, Reed St. Neighborhood Ho., Phila., 1968—69; mem. mayor's com. housing Phila., 1973—76; mem. Gov. Task Force Multi-Svc. Sr. Ctrs. Pa., 1975—77, N.J. Assisted Living Facilities Task Force, 1995—96; v.p. Greater Cape May Hist. Soc., 1998—2000; Cape May Point Hist. Preservation Com., 2004—. Recipient numerous archtl. awards, award of excellence, Urban Design Mag.; Fulbright fellow, 1954—55. Fellow: AIA (emeritus, Citation for Excellence, Phila. chpt. Honor award, others). Home: PO Box 22 Cape May Point NJ 08212-0022 Office Phone: 609-884-4455. Personal E-mail: joejordan@comcast.net.

JORDAN, JOHN LESTER (GAUDEAMUS), artist; b. Houston, Dec. 21, 1944; s. Jesse Peavy and Catherine Myrtle J.; m. Irena Veronika (sep.); 1 child, Najel Solomon. Student, U. Houston, 1963-65, St. Thomas U., 1974. Artist Hurlock Real Estate Co., Houston, 1963-65; salesman-designer Dennis Sleep Shop, Houston, 1967-71; dir. Jerusalem Jewels, Denver, 1979-84, Hawaii, 1985; art rep. Whitney-Morse Art Group, Saugerties, N.Y., 1988-90;

tchr. Onteora Sch. Dist., Woodstock, N.Y., 1988-91; dir. Gaudeamus-Jordan, Woodstock, 1985—; prodr. Panaramblecam Prodns., Woodstock, 1990—. Host, prodr.: (tv show) Ramble On, 1990—; exec. prodr.: Woodstock Winter Video Festival, 1994, Pete Seeger on Solar, 1997; sculptor; prodr. TV video Peter Max in Woodstock, 1994; prodr. (video) The Sand Painters of Tashi Lhunpo, 2002, The Dharma Bums in Woodstock, 2002-05; prodr. Goddess Festival Woodstock TV, 2003. Master of ceremonies Hiroshima to Now, Catskill Alliance, Woodstock, 1990; asst. organizer for Catskill Alliance for Peace, Woodstock, 1990; chmn. Earth Day, Hiroshima Day Show, 1993; organizer Woodstock UFO Network, 1998. With USAF, 1965-67. Mem. Woodstock Guild, Woodstock Artists Assn. Avocations: tv hosting and producing, recycling resource research. Home: PO Box 932 Woodstock NY 12498-0932

JORDAN, JOSEPH LOUIS, education educator, government official; Degree in bus. adminstrn. and mktg., St. Lawrence Coll.; MBA, Clarkson U. Prof. bus. St. Lawrence Coll., Brockville, Can., 1984-87, St. Lawrence Coll, Brockville, Can., 1988-93; coord. operational rev. Ministry Colls. and Univs., 1987-88; coord., prof. internat. edn. dept. St. Lawrence Coll, Brockville, Can., 1993—; owner summer retail bus. Brockville, 1990-93. Designer, implementor computer tng. courses, Africa; fulltime provincial campaign exec., 1987, 88, 92, 93, 96. Fed. mem. parliament Leeds-Grenville, 2000—02, parliamentary sec. to prime min., 2000—02. Office: 422 Confederation Bldg House of Commons Ottawa ON Canada K1A 0A6

JORDAN, JUDITH VICTORIA, clinical psychologist, educator; b. Milw., July 28, 1943; d. Claus and Charlotte (Backus) J.; m. William M. Redpath, Aug. 11, 1973. AB, Brown U., 1965; MA, Harvard U., 1968, PhD, 1973; DHL (hon.) (hon.), New Eng. Coll., 2001. Diplomate Am. Bd. Profl. Psychology. Psychologist Human Relations Service, Wellesley, Mass., 1971-73; assoc. psychologist McLean Hosp., Belmont, Mass., 1978-93, psychologist, 1993—, dir. women's studies program, 1988—, dir. tng. in psychology, 1991, dir. Women's Treatment Network, 1992—. Vis. scholar Stone Ctr. Wellesley Coll., 1985—; asst. prof. psychiatry Harvard Med. Sch., 1988—; co-dir. Jean Baker Miller Tng. Inst., Wellesley Coll. 1998; adv. bd Fox TV Network, Women First healthcare., 1998; disting. prof. Menninger Clinic, 1999. Author: Empathy and Self Boundries, 1984, Women's Growth in Connection, 1991, (with others) The Self in Relation, 1986; editor, author: Relational Self in Women; editor: Women's Growth in Diversity, 1997; editor: The Complexity of Connection, 2004. Recipient Outstanding Contbn. award, Feminist Therapy Inst., 2002. Fellow Am. Psychol. Assn.; mem. Mass. Psychol. Assn. (bd. dirs. 1983-85, Career Achievement award for outstanding contbns. to advancement of psychology as a sci. and a profession), Phi Beta Kappa. Office: McLean Hosp 114 Waltham St Lexington MA 02421-5415

JORDAN, KAREN, newscaster; b. Nashville, Tenn. d. Robert Jordan; m. Christian Farr. BA in English, Spelman Coll., Atlanta, 1994; MA in Broadcast Journalism, Medill Sch. of Journalism, Evanston, Ill., 1995. Medill News Svc. reporter WMAQ-AM, Chgo., 1995; reporter WIFR-TV, Rockford, Ill., 1995—97; weekend anchor and reporter WKEF-TV, Dayton, Ohio, 1997—99; main anchor and reporter WRGT-TV, Dayton, Ohio, 1999—2000; anchor weekend news and reporter WPHL-TV, Phila., 2000—03; co-anchor weekend news WLS-TV, Chgo., 2003—. Office: WLS-TV 190 N State St Chicago IL 60601

JORDAN, KARLA SALGE, retired primary school educator; b. Berlin, July 4, 1943; came to U.S. 1965; d. Hubert Ernst Richard and Irmgard Klara Salge; m. William Jackson Jordan, May 28, 1963 (div. 1980); 1 child, Michael Bond. BA, Berlin Tchrs. Coll., 1964, Meth. Coll., Fayetteville, N.C., 1974; MA, Fayetteville State U., 1986. Cert. tchr., N.C., ednl. supr., 1995, cert. early childhood generalist Nat. Bd. Edn., 2000. Tchr. Eastover Elem. Sch., Fayetteville, 1974-75, Montclair Elem. Sch., Fayetteville, 1975—2005; ret., 2005. Workshop presenter Cumberland County Sch., Fayetteville, spring 1983, 92-95; mem. bldg. leadership team Montclair Elem. Sch., 1992-93, chair, 1994-95, grade chair, 1980-90, 1999-2001, 2002-2003, 2003-2004, sch. improvement team chair, 1995-98, 2001-03. Treas. Montclair PTA, 1987-88, sec., 1988-90, pres. 1985, 86; youth choir dir. Eureka Bapt. Ch., Fayetteville, 1990—, min. of music, 1995—; mem., bible study leader for German fellowship Walstone Bapt. Ch., Fayetteville, German fellowship coord., 1999—. Fayetteville Jr. League mini grantee, 1991; named Tchr. of the Yr. Montclair Elem. Sch., 1987-88; recipient Fayetteville Tchr. of the Week Jr. League and the Huntington Learning Ctr., 1997. Mem. ASCD, Cross Creek Reading Coun. (rec. sec. 1990), Fayetteville Assn. for Edn. of Young Children, N.C. Assn. of Edn. (bldg. rep. 1981-83), Pi Lambda Theta. Republican. Baptist. Avocations: sewing, crafts, gardening, travel, reading. Home: 845 Mary Jordan Ln Fayetteville NC 28311-7075 Office: Montclair Elem Sch 555 Glensford Dr Fayetteville NC 28314-2326 Office Phone: 910-868-5124. E-mail: karla-sjs@msn.com, karlajordan@ccs.k12.nc.us.

JORDAN, KATE See JORDAN, KATHERINE

JORDAN, KATHERINE D. (KATE JORDAN), lawyer; BA with honors, Emory U.; JD, Vanderbilt U. Law clk. to Judge Ewing Werlein Jr. US Dist Ct., Tex.; atty. Vinson & Elkins LLP, Tex., Powell, Goldstein, Frazer and Murphy, Atlanta, 2001—03; law clk. to Chief US Magistrate Judge Gerrilyn Brill No. Dist. Ga., 2003—05; sr. counsel Southeastern Legal Found., Atlanta, 2005—. Rsch. editor Vanderbilt Jour. Transnational Law. Republican. Office: Southeastern Legal Found 6100 Lake Forrest Dr Ste 520 Atlanta GA 30328

JORDAN, KENNETH D., chemistry educator; b. Norwood, Mass., Feb. 25, 1948; s. Merrill E. and Marion F. (Smith) J.; m. Sandra D. Horwitz; children: Erin McNaughton, Kate Jordan. BA, Northeastern U., Boston, 1970; PhD, MIT, 1974. Gibbs instr. Yale U., New Haven, 1974-76, asst. prof., 1976-78, U. Pitts., 1978-80, assoc. prof., 1980-85, prof., 1985—. Program dir. NSF, Washington, 1984-85; adj. prof. Carnegie Mellon U., 1988—. Contbr. articles to profl. jours. Guggenheim fellow Guggenheim Found., 1981; Dreyfus Tchr. scholar Camille and Henry Dreyfus Found., 1977-82; fellow Alfred P. Sloan Found., 1977-79. Fellow Am Phys. Soc.; mem. Am. Chem. Soc. (chmn. theoretical chemistry subdiv. 1990-91, officer 1988-91, sec.-treas. phys. chemistry divsn. 2001—), Sigma Xi. Achievements include rsch. in methods to elucidate the role of through-bond interactions in long-range intramolecular interactions; development of techniques for theoretical studies of temporary anions, theoretical methods to characterize hydrogen bonded clusters.

JORDAN, KENT A., lawyer, educator; b. West Point, N.Y., Oct. 24, 1957; s. Amos Azariah and MarDeane (Carver) J.; m. Michelle Weaver, Apr. 25, 1981. BA in Econs. with high honors, Brigham Young U., 1981; JD cum laude, Georgetown U., 1984. Bar: Del. 1984, U.S. Dist. Ct. Del. 1985, U.S. Ct. Appeals (3d cir.) 1988, U.S. Supreme Ct. 1994, U.S. Ct. Appeals (fed. cir.) 1995, D.C. Ct. Appeals 1996. Law clk. to Hon. James L. Latchum U.S. Dist. Ct., Wilmington, Del., 1984-85; assoc. Potter Anderson & Corroon, Wilmington, 1985-87; asst. U.S. atty. U.S. Dept. Justice, Wilmington, 1987-91; chief civil divsn. U.S. Atty.'s Office, Wilmington, 1991-92; assoc. Morris, James, Hitchens & Williams, Wilmington, 1992-93, ptnr., 1994-97; v.p., gen. counsel Corp. Svc. Co., 1998—. Adj. prof. Widener U. Law Sch., Wilmington, 1995-96; mem. adv. com. U.S. Dist. Ct. Del., 1995-98, ombudsman, 1995—; sec. Bd. of Bar Examiners, Del. Supreme Ct., Wilmington, 1997, 2000—. Contbr. articles to profl. jours. Mem. Greater Hockessin Area Devel. Assn., 1991—, also past pres.; bd. dirs. Cmty. Legal Aid Soc., Wilmington, 1994-97. Mem. Am. Intellectual Property Law Assn., Del. State Bar Assn. (coun. mem. intellectual property sect. 1996-98), Fed. Bar Assn. (Del. chpt.), Richard S. Rodney Am. Inn of Ct. (sec.-treas. 1994-96, counselor 1996-98). Office: Corp Svc Co 2711 Centerville Rd Ste 400 Wilmington DE 19808 E-mail: kjordan@cscinfo.com.

JORDAN, LORNA PAULEY, artist; b. Windsor, Ont., Apr. 21, 1954; came to U.S., 1954; d. Stanely Frank and Dorothy (Ruppel) P.; m. Elverse Morris Jordan, June 25, 1983 (div. May 1986). BA, U. Va., 1976. Artist Lorna Jordan Studio, Seattle, 1979—. Artist-in-residence Seattle Pub. Utilities, 1997-98. Artist, lead designer Waterworks Gardens, 1996 (Place Design award EDRA/Places 1997); artist, co-designer Justice Garden Path, 1997; exhibited in Paine Webber Gallery, N.Y.C., Boise Art Museum, Ctr. of Contemporary Art, 1994-95. Bd. dirs., pres. On the Boards, Seattle, 1990—; commr. pub. art com., Seattle Arts Commn., 1994, vice-chair, 1995; artist, planner Longfellow Creek Habitat Improvement Project, Seattle, 1999—. Recipient Outstanding Local Achievment award ASCE, 1997; fellow N.W. Inst. Architecture and Urban Studies in Italy, Rome, 1998; resident The MacDowell Colony, Peterborough, N.H., 1994, Centrum Found., Port Townsend, Wash., 1999. Mem. Henry Contemporaries of The Henry Gallery, Contemporary Art Coun. of The Seattle Art Mus., The Uncollectors Club of The Seattle Art Mus., Ctr. on Contemporary Art. Home: 4233 Meridian Ave N Seattle WA 98103-7601 Fax: 206-634-2715.

JORDAN, LOUISE HERRON, art educator; b. Shanghai, Dec. 25, 1938; d. Edwin Warren Herron and Marie Standley; m. Michael Dean Salmon, June 21, 1958 (div. Jan. 21, 1976); m. John Patrick Jordan, June 24, 1995; children: Catherine Louise Boggess, Michael Dean Salmon, Richard Dean Salmon, Marianne Gabriel Fisher. Student, Smith Coll., 1956—58. Parish sec. St. Lawrence Cath. Ch., Alexandria, Va., 1977—80; dir. meetings and mem. Am. Inst. Biological Sci., Wash., DC, 1985—93; exec. asst. to pres. Lawrence Tech. U., Southfield, Mich., 1993—95; tchr. art Jewish Cmty. Ctr., New Orleans, 2002—. One-woman shows include The Long Gallery, Oschner Hosp., New Orleans, La., 2000, 2002, St. Tammany Art Assn., Holiday Inn, Covington, La., 2001, The Upstairs Gallery, 2001, Café Degas, New Orleans, La., 2002, exhibited in group shows at Masur Mus. Juried Show, 1997, Fest for All, Baton Rouge, La., 1997, New Orleans Art Assn. Nat. Exhibit, 1997, River Road Juried Exhibit, Baton Rouge, La., 2002, Dominican Inst. Arts Group Show, Sparkill, NY, 2003. Bd. dirs. Bancroft Pk. Civic Assn., New Orleans, 1997—; professed lay mem. Dominican Order, New Orleans, 1997—; mem. Dominican Inst. of the Arts, Adrian, Mich., 2001—. Mem.: St. Tammany Art Assn. (assoc.), New Orleans Art Assn. (assoc.), La. Watercolor Soc. (life; pres. 1998—2000, signature mem., pres. 1998—2000, chmn. internat. exhbn. 1997—99, workshop dir. 1999—), Xavier U. Alumni Assn. (hon.), Smith Coll. Alumni Assn. (assoc.). Roman Catholic. Home: 4644 Bancroft Dr New Orleans LA 70122 Office: St Anthony Studio 6218 St Anthony St New Orleans LA 70122 Personal E-mail: bayoulou222@aol.com.

JORDAN, LYNDON KIRKMAN, family practice physician; b. Mount Olive, NC, Jan. 6, 1935; s. Lyndon Kirkman and Rachael Loucille (Hazelton) J.; m. Beverly Hayes Brooks, Aug. 19, 1961; children: Lyndon III, Christopher, Patrick. BA, Duke U., 1957, MD, 1961. Diplomate Am. Bd. Family Practice. Intern Watts Hosp., Durham, N.C., 1961-62; flight surgeon Beale AFB, Marysville, Calif., 1962-64; pvt. practice Smithfield, NC, 1964—2001; dir. family medicine residency program Duke U. Sch. Medicine, Durham, 1972-74. Cons. Roche Biomed. Labs., Burlington, N.C., 1987-92, Pfizer Pharms. Co., Mahwah, N.J., 1994-92; bd. dirs. Bank of Four Oaks of Smithfield, N.C.; chmn. bd. dirs. Millennium Healthczre Network of N.C. and S.C., 1997-99; chmn. Johnston County Bd. of Health, Smithfield, 1998-2000; nat. lectr. in field of allergy. Capt. USAF, 1962-64. Named family physician of yr. N.C. Acad. Family Physicians, 1982, N.C. Tarheel of the Week, News & Observer Newspaper, Raleigh, 1983; Paul Harris fellow Rotary Internat., 1989. Fellow Am. Acad. Family Physicians. Episcopalian. Avocations: flying, hunting, fishing, painting. Home: 105 Mariah Dr Four Oaks NC 27524-8433

JORDAN, LYNNE BRANDES, ementary education educator; b. Dunkirk, N.Y., Nov. 1, 1941; d. Frank Albert and Grace Lydia Christine (Ohm) Brandes; m. John Charles Jordan, June 15, 1963; children: Julie Ann, Jeffrey Alan, Jennifer Lynne. BS in Edn., Kent State U., 1963; M in Edn., Ashland U., 2001. Tchr. Waynesville (Mo.) Schs., 1963-64, Tallmadge (Ohio) Schs., 1964-65, Streetsboro (Ohio) Schs., 1967-70; learning disabled tutor Kent (Ohio) City Schs., 1974-76, Lorain (Ohio) City Schs., 1977-79, elem. tchr., 1979—2004; ret., 2004. Vol. ARC, Lorain, 1997, Am. Cancer Soc. Reach to Recovery. Mem. AAUW, NEA, Internat. Reading Assn., Ohio Edn. Assn., Lorain Edn. Assn. Retired. Methodist. Avocations: reading, crafts, travel. E-mail: Ljordanlj@netscape.net.

JORDAN, MARTHA B., lawyer; m. David Lee; children: Stacy, Kristen. BS, Pa. State U., 1976; MBA, U. Cin., 1978; JD, U. Calif., Berkeley, 1983. Bar: Calif. 1983. With Latham & Watkins, LLP, L.A., 1983—90, ptnr., 1990—98, mng. ptnr., 1998—2004. Named one of Calif.'s Top 100 Most Influential Lawyers, Calif. Law Bus., 1999. Office: Latham and Watkins LLP Ste 4000 633 W Fifth St Los Angeles CA 90071 Office Phone: 213-485-1234.

JORDAN, MARVIN EVANS, JR., record company executive, vocalist, actor, composer; b. Muskogee, Okla., Aug. 13, 1944; s. Marvin Evans and May Elizabeth (Williams) J.; m. Suonja Summirs, Aug. 23, 1969 (div. 1983); m. Kristine Lynn Johnson, Nov. 8, 1984; children: Marvin Edwin, Mary Elizabeth, Michael Evans-Lyman; stepchildren: Daniel Noah Winger, David Paul Winger, Karen LaVohn Winger Van Hofer, Cory Brent Winger, Jay Martin Winger, Aaron Thomas Jones, Benjamin Arthur Jones Jordan, Seth Ailean Jones, Sara Jean Jones Jordan. BS, City U., Bellevue, Wash., 1981, MBA, 1983. Producer, promoter Natures Green Oratory Presents, Seattle, 1966—67; v.p. North Hollywood Releasing, Seattle, 1967-68; prin. Jordan Assocs., Seattle, 1969-89; chmn. bd. Western-Internat. Artists, Inc., 1976-78; pres. Standard Record Co., Spokane, Wash., 1989—; mem. agy. mktg. network Star Power, 1991-93; pres. Millenial Entertainment Network, 2000—; sr. ptnr., CEO Aztec Mgmt. Sys., Spokane, Wash., 2000—; owner, pres., CEO Music Mountain Studios, Spokane, 2005—. Artistic dir. Concerts Nimbus, Seattle, 1981-84; co-dir. Kids Khorus Klub, Olympia, Wash., 1985-87. Composer, lyricist, collaborator (song) Heart Songs, 1994; vocalist (album) After All, 1994; numerous unpub. songs. Asst. dist. commr. Whatcom dist. Mount Baker coun. Boy Scouts Am., 1987-91, 94-98, chmn. coun. exploring svc. team, 1993-94, membership chair Thunderbird dist. Inland N.W. Coun., 2001-2003, unit commr., 2003—04; steering com. Adult Attention Deficit Disorder Assn., 1993-94. With U.S. Army, 1963—66. Named Disting. Commr. Boy Scouts Am., 1992, recipient Wood Badge, 1990. Mem. Northwest Area Music Assn. Mem. Lds Ch. Avocations: residential design, computer programming, reading. Fax: 419-730-0308. E-mail: mejordan@myrealbox.com.

JORDAN, MARY LUCILLE, commissioner; m. Ben C. Elliott, Aug. 23, 1980; children: Elizabeth Elliott, Armando Elliott, C. Daniel Elliott. Student, Hull U., 1969-70; BA cum laude, Bonaventure U., 1971; JD, Antioch Law Sch., 1976. Bar: N.Y., 1977, D.C., 1978. Atty. Office of Fed. Register Nat. Archives & Records Adminstrn., Washington, 1976-77; sr. staff atty. United Mine Workers Am., Washington, 1977-94; chmn. Fed. Mine Safety and Health Rev. Commn., Washington, 1994—2001, commissioner, 2001—.

JORDAN, MICHAEL HUGH, information technology executive; b. Kansas City, Mo., June 15, 1936; m. Kathryn Hiett, Apr. 8, 1961 (div.); children: Kathryn, Stephen; m. Hilary Cecil, Mar. 4, 2000. BSChemE, Yale U., 1957; MSChemE, Princeton U., 1959. Cons., prin. McKinsey & Co., Toronto, London and Cleve., 1964—74; dir. fin. planning PepsiCo, Purchase, NY, 1974—76, sr. v.p. planning and devel., 1976—77; sr. v.p. mfg. ops. Frito-Lay divsn. PepsiCo Internat., Dallas, 1977—82, pres., CEO Frito-Lay divsn., 1983—85; pres. PepsiCo Foods Internat., 1982—83; exec. v.p., CFO PepsiCo Inc., Purchase, 1985—86, pres., 1986; pres., CEO PepsiCo Worldwide, Dallas, 1987—92; ptnr. Clayton, Dubilier and Rice, NYC, 1992—93; chmn., CEO Westinghouse Electric Corp./CBS, Pitts., 1993—98; ptnr. Beta Capital Group LLC; gen. ptnr. Global Asset Capital, LLC; chmn., CEO Electronic Data Systems Corp., Plano, Tex., 2003—. Bd. dirs. Aetna, eOriginal Inc.; chmn. Nat. Fgn. Trade Coun.; trustee Brookings Instn. Bd. dirs., former chmn. United Negro Coll. Fund, 1986—; bd. dirs. Ctr. for Excellence in Edn., Washington, 1988—92; mem., former chmn. US -Japan Bus. Coun.; mem. Bus. Coun.; mem. bd. trustees US Coun. for Internat. Bus.; mem. Bus. Roundtable; dir. Viventures. With USN. Recipient cert. nuclear engring., Bettis Labs. Atomic Power Labs., Pitts. Office Phone: 972-605-6000.

JORDAN, MICHAEL JEFFREY, retired professional basketball player, former professional sports team executive, retired baseball player; b. Bklyn., Feb. 17, 1963; s. James and Deloris Jordan; m. Juanita Vanoy, Sept. 1989; children: Jeffrey Michael, Marcus James, Jasmine. Student, U. N.C., 1981—84. Basketball player Chgo. Bulls, 1984—93; baseball player Chicago White Sox AA Team, 1994-95; basketball player Chgo. Bulls, 1995—98; pres. basketball ops. Washington Wizards, 1999—2000, player, 2001—03. Owner Michael Jordan's: The Restaurant, 1993—; founder Jordan Brand Clothing, 1997—. Author: RareAir: Michael on Michael, 1993; actor: (films) Space Jam, 1996, He Got Game, 1998. Named Rookie of Yr., NBA, 1985, Seagram's NBA Player of Yr., 1987, Slam-Dunk Championship winner, 1987, 1988, NBA All-Star Game Most Valuable Player, 1988, 1996, 1998, NBA Def. Player of Yr., 1988, NBA Most Valuable Player, 1988, 1991, 1992, 1996, 1998, Male Athlete of Yr., AP, 1991, 1992, 1993, NBA Finals MVP, 1991—93, 1996—98; named to Sporting News All-Am. first team, 1983—84, NBA All-Star team, 1985—93, 1996—98, 2002—03, All NBA First Team, 1987—93, 1996—98, NBA All-Def. Team, 1988—93, 1996—98; recipient Naismith award, 1984, Wooden award, 1984, IBM award, 1985, 1989, Schick Pivotal Player award, 1985, 1989. Achievements include holding record for most points in an NBA playoff game with 63; mem. NCAA divsn. 1 championship team, 1982, NBA champion Chgo. Bulls, 1991, 92, 93, 96, 97, 98, US Olympic basketball gold medal team, 1984, 92.

JORDAN, MICHELLE DENISE, judge; b. Chgo., Oct. 29, 1954; d. John A. and Margaret (O'Dood) J. BA in Polit. Sci., Loyola U, Chgo., 1974; JD, U. Mich., 1977. Bar. Ill. 1977, U.S. Dist. Ct. (no. dist.) Ill. 1978. Asst. state's atty. State's Attys. Office, Chgo., 1977-82; pvt. practice Chgo., 1983-84; with Ill. Atty. Gen.'s Office, Chgo., 1984-90, chief environ. control div., 1988-90; ptnr. Hopkins & Sutter, Chgo., 1991-93; apptd. dep. regional adminstr. region 5 U.S. EPA, Chgo., 1994—. Active Operation Push, Chgo., 1971—. Recipient Kizzy Image Achievement and Svc. award, 1990, Suzanne E. Olive Nat. EEO award 1996; named in Am.'s Top 100 Bus. and Profl. Women, Dollars and SenseMag., Chgo., 1988. Mem. Ill. Bar Assn., Chgo. Bar Assn. (bd. mgrs., chmn. criminal law com. 1987-88, mem. hearing divsn., jud. evaluation com. 1987-88, exec. coun. 1987-88), Cook County Bar Assn., Nat. Bar Assn., Alpha Sigma Nu. Democrat. Baptist.

JORDAN, NEIL PATRICK, film director, writer; b. County Sligo, Ireland, Feb. 25, 1950; BA, Univ. Coll., Dublin, Ireland, 1968. Dir. (films) Angel, 1982 (Best Film and Best Dir. awards London Critics Circle), Company of Wolves, 1984, Mona Lisa, 1986 (nomiated Best Screenplay-Motion Picture Golden Globe 1987, nominated Best Direction, Best Film, Best Original Screenplay BAFTA 1987), High Spirits, 1988, We're No Angels, 1989, The Miracle, 1991, The Crying Game, 1992 (Alexander Korda award Best British Film, NY Film Critics Cir. award Best Screenplay, 1992, Writers Guild Am. Screen award Best Screenplay Written Directly for Screen, 1993, L.A. Film Critics award, Best Fgn. Film, 1993, Oscar Best Writing, Screenplay Written Directly for Screen 1993, nominated Oscar Best Dir. 1993, nominated Best Original Screenplay, BAFTA 1993, nominated Edgar award Best Motion Picture Edgar Allen Poe Awards 1993), Interview with the Vampire, 1994, Michael Collins, 1996 (Golden Lion award Venice Film Festival 1996), The Butcher Boy, 1997 (nominated CFCA award Best Dir., Best Picture, Chgo. Film Critics Assn. Awards 1999, Silver Bear award Best Dir., Berlin Film Festival 1997), In Dreams, 1999 (Silver Raven award Brussels Internat. Festival Fantasy Film 1999), The End of the Affair, 1999 (award Best Adapted Screenplay, Brit. Acad. Film and TV Arts 2000, nominated Best Film, Best Dir., Golden Globes 2000, BAFTA 2000), Not I, 2000; writer, dir., prodr.: The Good Thief, 2002; author: A Night in Tunisia, 1976 (Guardian Fiction prize 1979), The Past, 1979, The Dream of a Beast, 1983, Sunrise With Sea Monster, 1994, Shade, 2004. Recipient Crystal Isis award Brussels Internat. Film Festival, 1998. Office: c/o Dave Wirtschafter William Morris Agency 1 William Morris Pl Beverly Hills CA 90212 also: Jenne Casarotto Casarotto Co Ltd Nat House 60 66 Wardour St London WIV 3HP England

JORDAN, NORA MARGARET, lawyer; b. Cleve., July 24, 1958; d. Thomas and Nora (Campbell) J.; m. Walter Allen Reiser, Nov. 8, 1986; children: Julia, Mary, Martha. BA, U. Notre Dame, 1980; JD, Duke U., 1983. Bar: N.Y. 1984. Ptnr. Davis Polk and Wardwell, N.Y.C., 1983—. Office: Davis Polk & Wardwell 450 Lexington Ave Fl 31 New York NY 10017-3982 Business E-Mail: njordan@dpw.com.

JORDAN, PAMELA CAROLE, librarian; b. New Haven, Jan. 13, 1949; d. Arthur Sumner and Mary Theresa (Zarnowski) J. BA, Albertus Magnus Coll., 1972. Subject and lang. specialist Sterling Library Yale U., New Haven, 1973-76, librarian Drama Library, 1976—. Mem. Ams. for Arts, New Eng. Theater Conf., Theater Library Assn., U.S. Inst. for Theater Tech. Office: 222 York St 208244 New Haven CT 06520-8244 Office Phone: 203-432-1554. Business E-Mail: pamela.jordan@yale.edu.

JORDAN, PAUL HOWARD, JR., surgeon, educator; b. Bigelow, Ark., Nov. 22, 1919; s. Paul Howard and Marie Theresa (Lewis) J.; m. Lois Regnell, Apr. 6, 1944; children: Kristine Jordan Compaglia, Craig T., Patricia Jordan Johnson. BS, U. Chgo., 1941, MD, 1944; MS, U. Ill., 1950. Intern St. Luke's Hosp., Chgo., 1944-46; resident in surgery U. Ill., Chgo., 1948-50, Hines VA Hosp., 1950-53; from instr. to clin. prof. surgery UCLA Med. Sch., 1953-58; asso. prof. U. Fla. Med. Sch., Gainesville, 1959-64; prof. surgery Baylor Coll. Medicine, Houston, 1964—2004, emeritus prof. surgery, 2004—; chief surgery VA Hosp., Houston, 1964-83, chief staff, 1969. Mem. sr. attending staff Methodist Hosp., Houston; cons. staff St. Luke's Episcopal Hosp., Houston. Author articles on gastroenterologic surgery, chpts. in books; hon. editor Centennial anniv. Jour. Am. Coll. Surgery, 2005-. Served to capt. M.C. AUS, 1946-48. Spl. NIH fellow Karolinska Inst., Stockholm, 1958-59; recipient Acrel medal Swedish Surg. Soc., 1974, Disting. Alumni Service award U. Chgo.; corr. fellow Brazilian Surg. Soc., 1976; named Disting. Houston Surgeon, 1989. Mem. ACS (chpt. councilor 1978-81), Soc. Surgery Alimentary Tract (past recorder, pres. 1983-84), Assn. VA Surgeons (past pres., Disting. Service award 1979), Am. Surg. Assn. (v.p.,1999), Soc. Internat. Chururgie, Soc. Univ. Surgeons, Am. Physiol. Soc., Am. Gastroenterol. Assn., Am. Soc. Gastrointestinal Endoscopy, Soc. Exptl. Biology and Medicine, Western Surg. Assn., So. Surg. Assn. (v.p., 2000), Tex. Surg. Soc., Harris County Med. Soc., Houston Surg. Soc. (past pres.), Houston Gastroenterol. Soc. (past pres.), U. Chgo. Med. Alumni Assn. (Disting. Sci. Service award 1984). Methodist. Office: Baylor Coll Medicine One Baylor Plaza Houston TX 77030 also: 1750 Scurlock Bldg 6560 Fannin Houston TX 77030 E-mail: p_jordan@sbcglobal.net.

JORDAN, ROBERT See RIGNEY, JAMES JR.

JORDAN, ROBERT ELIJAH, III, lawyer; b. South Boston, Va., June 20, 1936; s. Robert Elijah and Lucy (Webb) J.; m. Deborah A. Jordan; children: Janet Elizabeth, Jennifer Anne, Robert Elijah IV. SB, MIT, 1958; JD magna cum laude, Harvard U., 1961. Bar: D.C. 1962, Va. 1964, Calif. 1997. Spl. asst. civil rights Office Sec. Def., Washington, 1963-64; asst. U.S. atty. for D.C., 1964-65; exec. asst. for enforcement Office Sec. Treasury, 1965-67; dep. gen. counsel Dept. Army, 1967, acting gen. counsel, 1967-68; gen. counsel of Army, spl. asst. for civil functions to Sec. Army, 1968-71; ptnr. Steptoe & Johnson, Washington, 1971—2003, mng. ptnr., 1988-90. Mem. bd. cert. U.S. Cir. Cts. of Appeals Cir. Execs., 1987-88; pres. Langley Sch., 1981-82; mem. civil pro bono com. U.S. Dist. Ct., 1991-92. Contbr. articles to profl. jours. Mem. bd. dirs. Washington Humane Soc., 2000-03. Served to 1st lt. AUS, 1961-63. Recipient Karl Taylor Compton award, 1958, Arthur S. Flemming award, 1970, award for exceptional civilian svc. Dept. Army, 1971; Sloan Found. scholar; Edward J. Noble Found. fellow. Mem. Va. State Bar, D.C. Bar (chmn. ethics com. 1978-83, spl. com. on model rules profl conduct 1983-89, pres. 1987-88), Calif. State Bar, D.C. Bar Found. (pres. 1993-94, 97-98), Atlantic Coun. (bd. dirs. 1993—, exec. com. 1994—2001, chmn. nominating com. 1997-2001), Tau Beta Pi, Tau Kappa Alpha. Democrat. Home: 4773 Charing Cross Rd Sarasota FL 34241 Office: 1330 Connecticut Ave NW Washington DC 20036-1795 Office Phone: 202-429-6290. Personal E-mail: rjordan@steptoe.com.

JORDAN, ROBERT LEON, lawyer, educator; b. Reading, Pa., Feb. 27, 1928; s. Anthony and Carmela (Votto) J.; m. Evelyn Allen Willard, Feb. 15, 1958 (dec. Nov. 1996); children: John Willard, David Anthony BA, Pa. State U., 1948; LLB, Harvard U., 1951. Bar: N.Y. 1952. Assoc. White & Case, N.Y.C., 1953-59; prof. law UCLA, 1959-70, 75-91, prof. law emeritus, 1991—, assoc. dean Sch. Law, 1968-69. Vis. prof. law Cornell U., Ithaca, N.Y., 1962-63; co-reporter Uniform Consumer Credit Code, 1964-70, Uniform Comml. Code Articles 3, 4, 4A, 1985-90; Fulbright lectr. U. Pisa, Italy, 1967-68 Co-author: (with W.D. Warren) Commercial Law, 1983, 5th edit., 2000, Bankruptcy, 1985, 5th edit., 1999. Lt. USAF, 1951-53. Office: UCLA Sch Law 405 Hilgard Ave Los Angeles CA 90095-9000

JORDAN, ROBERT LEON, judge; b. Woodlawn, Tenn., June 28, 1934; s. James Richard and Josephine (Broadbent) J.; m. Dorothy Rueter, Sept. 8, 1956; children: Robert, Margaret, Daniel. BS in Fin., U. Tenn., 1958, JD, 1960. Atty. Goodpasture, Carpenter, Dale & Woods, Nashville, 1960-61; mgr. Frontier Refining Co., Denver, 1961-64; atty. Green and Green, Johnson City, Tenn., 1964-66; trust officer 1st Peoples Bank, Johnson City, 1966-69; v.p., trust officer Comml. Nat. Bank, Pensacola, Fla., 1969-71; atty. Bryant, Price, Brandt & Jordan, Johnson City, 1971-80; chancellor 1st Jud. Dist., Johnson City, 1980-88; dist. judge U.S. Dist. Ct. (ea. dist.) Tenn., Knoxville, 1988—2001, sr. dist. judge, 2001—. Mem. adv. com. U. Tenn. Law Alumni, 1978-80; sec. Tenn. Jud. Conf., 1987-88, mem. exec. com., 1988; del. Tenn. State-Fed. Judicial Coun., 1993—. Bd. dirs., v.p. Tri-Cities estate Planning Coun., Johnson City, 1969; bd. dirs. Washington County Tb Assn., Rocky Mount Hist. Assn., High Rock Camp, Johnson City, Jr. Achievement of Pensacola Inc.; bd. dirs., treas. N.W. Fla. Crippled Children's Assn., Pensacola; chancellor's assoc. U. Tenn. With U.S. Army, 1954-56. Named Boss of Yr. Legal Secs. Assn., Washington, Carter County, Tenn., 1982. Mem. Tenn. Bar Assn., Tenn. Bar Found., Knoxville Bar Assn. (bd. govs. 1999), Washington County Bar Assn. (pres.-elect 1980), Johnson City C. of C., Hamilton Burnett Am. Inn of Ct. (pres. 1993-94), Kiwanis (pres. Met. Johnson City Club 1969, Kiwanian of Yr. award 1986-87). Republican. Mem. Ch. Of Christ. Office: Howard H Baker US Courthouse 800 Market St Ste 141 Knoxville TN 37902-2303 Office Phone: 423-545-4224.

JORDAN, ROBERT REED, retired geologist, educator; b. N.Y.C., June 5, 1937; s. Herbert and Irene (Reed) J.; m. Jane H. Jordan, June 28, 1958; children: Richard P., Judith H. AB, Hunter Coll., 1958; MA, Bryn Mawr Coll., 1962, PhD, 1964. Cert. profl. geologist, Del.; lic. geologist, N.C., profl. geoscientist, Tex. Geologist Del. Geol. Survey, Newark, 1958-64, asst. state geologist, 1964-69, state geologist, dir., 1969—2003; state geologist emeritus, 2003—; instr. U. Del., Newark, 1962-64, asst. prof., 1964-68, assoc. prof., 1968-88, prof., 1988—2005; prof. emeritus, 2005—. Mem. Del. Air and Water Commn., Dover, 1966-73; chmn. Del. State Boundary Commn., Newark, 1971-2003; mem. Del. State Bd. Registration of Geologists, 1972-2003; mem. Outer Continental Shelf policy com. U.S. Dept. Interior, 1974-77, 85-2003, chmn., 1993-94; mem. N.Am. Commn. on Stratigraphic Nomenclature, 1978—, chmn., 1984, 92; mem. U.S. Nat. Com. on Geology, 1990-96; co-convenor Internat. Geol. Congress, Florence, Italy, 2004. Contbr. numerous articles to profl. jours. Recipient tributes Del. Gen. Assembly, 2003; named Hon. Mountaineer, State of W.Va., 1997, Ky. col., 1997. Fellow Geol. Soc. Am.; mem. Del. Acad. Sci. (pres. 1990, 2002), Am. Inst. Profl. Geologists (hon. mem. award 1996, editor 1989-90, Galey Mem. Pub. Svc. award 1992), Am. Geol. Inst. (fin. com. 1992—, treas., exec. com. 1992-93, Outstanding Svc. award 1992, 93, Ian Campbell award 1996,), Assn. Am. State Geologists (hon.; pres. 1983-84, Achievement award), Am. Assn. Petroleum Geologists (hon. mem. award 1993, Disting. Svc. award 1988, Cohee Pub. Svc. Ea. award 1990, Galey award Ea. 1995, John T. Galey Sr. meml. medal 1998, Pres.'s award divsn. environ. geology 2001).

JORDAN, ROBERT SMITH, political science professor; b. L.A., Calif, June 11, 1929; s. Ralph Burdette and Mary Wright (Smith) J.; m. Sara Jane Hatch, Sept. 19, 1961; children: Sara Jane, Mary Rebecca Leming, Robert Hatch, David Thomas. AB, UCLA, 1951; MS, U. Utah, 1955; MA, Princeton U., 1957, PhD, 1960; PhD (Fulbright scholar), St. Antony's Coll., Oxford U., Eng., 1960; Henry P. DuBois fellow. Instr. dept. politics Princeton U., 1956—57; asst. prof. pub. and internat. affairs, exec. asst. to dean Grad. Sch. Pub. and Internat. Affairs, U. Pitts., 1959—60; assoc. professorial lectr. George Washington U., 1960—62; asst. dir. Army War Coll. Center, 1960—61; dir. Air U. Center, 1961—62, assoc. prof. polit. sci. and internat. affairs, 1962—70, asst. to pres., 1962—64; dir. Ford Found. Fgn. Affairs Intern Program, Sch. Pub. and Internat. Affairs, 1968—70; dean faculty econ. and social studies, head dept. polit. sci. Fourah Bay Coll., U. Sierra Leone, 1965—67; prof. polit. sci. State U. NY at Binghamton, 1970—76, chmn. dept., 1970—74; dir. rsch. UN Inst. for Tng. and Rsch., NYC, 1975—79; Dag Hammarskold vis. prof. internat. rels. U. SC, Columbia, 1979—80; prof. polit. sci., rsch. prof. U. New Orleans, 1980—2002, dean Grad. Sch., 1980—82; rsch. prof. Coll. Urban Affairs, 2002—04, emeritus, 2004—. Disting. vis. prof. Naval War Coll., 1984-86; Fulbright prof. Cen. Study of Arms Control and Internat. Security, U. Lancaster, Eng., Jan.-June, 1988; vis. prof. internat. rels. US Air War Coll., 1992-94. Author/co-author, editor/co-editor: The NATO International Staff/Secretariat, 1967, Government and Power in West Africa, 1970, rev. edit., 1977, Europe and the Superpowers, 1971, rev. edit., 1990, International Administration, 1971, Multinational Cooperation, 1972, The World Food Conference and Global Problem Solving, 1976, Political Leadership in NATO, 1979, Changing Role and Concepts in the International Civil Service, 1980, Dag Hammarskjold Revisited: The UN Secretary-General as a Force in World Politics, 1983, Europe in the Balance: The Changing Context of European International Politics, 1986, Generals in International Politics: NATO's Supreme Allied Commander, Europe, 1987, Maritime Strategy and the Balance of Power: Britain and America in the Twentieth Century, 1989, Norstad: Cold War NATO Supreme Commander, 2000, International Organizations: A Comparative Approach of the Management of Cooperation, 2001. Served with USAF, 1951—53. Decorated Bronze Star; named Disting. Alumnus, Hinckley Inst., U. Utah, 1964; NATO rsch. fellow, 1969—70, 1990, Hooper postdoctoral fellow, U.S. Naval Hist. Ctr., 1987, 1997. Mem. ASPA (chmn. sect. on internat. and comp. adminstrn.), Assn. Princeton Grad. Alumni (pres.), Internat. Studies Assn. (v.p., chmn. sect. internat. orgn.), Acad. Coun. UN, Internat. Inst. Strategic Studies (London), Royal Inst. Internat. Affairs (London), Cosmos Club (Washington), Plimsoll Club (New Orleans), Sigma Chi (UCLA and Utah). Mem. Lds Ch. E-mail: smitty1929@charter.net.

JORDAN, RONALD P., pharmacist, pharmaceutical executive, consultant; b. Hartford, Conn., Dec. 25, 1952; s. James P. Jordan Jr. and V. Antionette Jordan; m. Karen W. Jordan, Oct. 11, 1986. BS in Pharmacy, U. R.I., 1976. Registered pharmacist. Dir. drug benefits Blue Cross & Blue Shield of R.I., Providence, 1983-87, asst. v.p., 1987-89; pres. Drug Benefit Mgmt. Systems, Inc., West Greenwich, R.I., 1989-95, HCaliber Consulting Corp., West Greenwich, 1995—2003; sr. v.p., chief info. officer Hospice Pharmacia, LLC, Phila., 1996—99; also bd. dirs.; sr. v.p., chief info. officer, bd. dirs. ExcelleRx Inc., Phila., 1999—2000. Mem. adv. bd. Allscrips Inc., Chgo., 1999-2003; spl. govt. employee HHS-HCFA, MCAC, Balt., 1999—; sr. v.p. global strategies PharmasMarket.com, 2000; pres., bd. mgrs., founder, CFO Healthation LLC, Wheaton, Ill., 2002—. Mem. Gov.'s Adv. Coun. on Health, Providence, 1998-2002. Named one of 50 Most Influential Pharmacists of Yr., Am. Druggist Mag., N.Y.C., 1997, 98, Pharmacist of Yr., R.I. Pharm. Assn., 1998; recipient Founder award N.E. Pharm. Coun., 1999, Bowl of Hygeia award A.H. Robins, R.I. Pharm. Assn., 1983. Fellow: Am. Pharm. Assn. (pres. 1998—99), Am. Soc. Cons. Pharmacists; mem.: Nat. Coun. Prescription Drug Programs (Time award 1992), Pharm. Soc. Israel (hon.), Wickford Yacht Club. Office: Healthation LLC 7955 South Cass Ave Ste 203 Darien IL 60561-5191

JORDAN, RUTH ANN, physician; b. Oct. 12, 1928; d. Willard and Esther (Fouts) J.; children: Diane J., Linda J. AB, Ind. U., 1950; MD, Columbia U., 1957. Intern St. Luke's Hosp., N.Y.C., 1957—58, asst. resident, 1958—59; physician Met. Life Ins. Co., N.Y.C., 1960—62, Standard Oil Co. of N.J., N.Y.C., 1962, MIT, Cambridge, Mass., 1963—71, New Eng. Mut. Life Ins. Co., Boston, 1963—66, asst. med. dir., 1971—74; fellow internal medicine Mass. Gen. Hosp., Boston, 1974—75; physician Simmons Coll., Boston, 1975—78, Northeastern U., Boston, 1976—78; assoc. med. dir. New Eng. Telephone Co., Boston, 1978, med. dir. clin. svcs., 1978—86; dir. occupl. medicine Gen. Med. Assn., Boston, 1986—91; assoc. med. dir. Allmerica, Worcester, Mass., 1991—97; plant med. dir. GM, Westwood, Mass., 1995—; physician Health Resource, Woburn, Mass., 1996—. Therapeutic dietitian Meth. Hosp., Indpls., 1951-53, Presbyn. Hosp., N.Y.C., part-time 1954-57; nat. coord. com. on cholesterol, 1986-2005, Mass. Adv. Coun. for Workers Compensation, 1986-89. Trustee Ind. U. Coll. Arts and Scis., 2004—. Fellow: Am. Coll. Occupl. and Environ. Medicine (health edn. com. 1984—, membership com. 1985—88, bd. dirs. 1986—92); mem.: PEO, DAR, AMA, Mass. Med. Soc. (ho. of dels. 1984—, chmn. environ. and occupl. health com. 1985—88, interspIty. com. 1985—88, nutrition com. 2001—, bylaws com. 2001—, trustee 2003—, nominating com. 2004—), Norfolk Dist. Med. Soc. (v.p. 1998—99, edn. com. 1998—, exec. com. 1998—, pres. 1999—2001, alt. rep. to Mass. Med. Soc. nominating com. 2000—03, alt. bd. trustee com. 2000—03, nominating com. 2003—), New Eng. Occupl. Med. Assn. (bd. dirs. 1980—89, pres. 1981—84), The Country Club, Columbia U. Club of New Eng. (v.p. 1981—84, bd. dirs. 1981—91, pres. 1989—91), Alpha Chi Omega. Home: 105 Rockwood St Brookline MA 02445-7408

JORDAN, SAM LATRON, minister, mediator; b. Kansas City, Mo., Feb. 6, 1925; s. Arthur William and Erma Lola Jordan; m. Laura K. Herget, July 10, 1986; children: Linda Marlyn Wells, Dana Lonnie, James Christopher Miller, David Aaron Goodwin. B, Trinity Coll., 1999; M, Trinity Sem., 2000; DDiv, Strassford U., London, 2002. Ordained Full Gospel Churches Internat., 1973; cert. Dispute Resolution Ctr., Tex., 2003. Gen. agt. Nat. Travelers Ins. Co., Des Moines, 1949—71; pastor Life Unlimited Christian Ctr., Odessa, Tex., 1971—73, Lighthouse Ch., Odessa, Tex., 1982—86, Odessa Tabernacle Ch., Odessa, Tex., 1986—2001; cert. mediator Dispute Resolution Ctr., Kerrville, Tex., 2002—. Pres. Nat. Action Crusades, Springfield, Mo., 1965—72, Jordan Constrn. Co., Odessa, 1972—90. Author: (autobiography) If I Had Only Known. Protestant. Avocations: reading, writing, ministering. Home: 305 Coyote Ridge Kerrville TX 78028 Office Phone: 830-367-3317. Personal E-mail: jordan1509@aol.com.

JORDAN, SAMANTHA KRISTINE, communications director; Student, Tex. Christian U., 1989-92; BA in History, Tex. A&M U., 1994. Intern U.S. Rep. Joe L. Barton, Washington, 1995, dist. asst., 1995, dist. asst., caseworker, dist. sys. mgr., 1996, dist. liaison, dep. press sec., 1996-97, dep. press sec., sys. mgr., legis. corr., 1997-98, press sec., 1998, comm. dir., 1998—. Mem. Leadership Press Sec. Working Group. Mem. adv. bd., alumnae club Alpha Omega Sorority; vol. Kimbell Art Mus. Mem. Rep. Commn. Assn., Tex. A&M Assn. Former Students, Tex. State Soc., 12th Man Found., Smithsonian Assocs., Libr. Congress Assocs. Home: 1020 N Stafford St Apt 312 Arlington VA 22201-4635 Office: Congressman Joe Barton 2264 Rayburn Ho Office Bldg Washington DC 20515-0001 Fax: 202-225-3052.

JORDAN, STEPHEN M., academic administrator; m. Ruth Kinnie; 3 children. BA in Polit. Sci., U. No. Colo., 1971; MPA in Fin. Adminstrn., U. Colo., Denver, 1979, PhD in Pub. Adminstrn./Policy Analysis, 1990. Vice chancellor for budgets and facilities U. Colo. Health Scis. Ctr., 1985—, asst. sec. bd. regents, 1985—; dep. exec. dir. fin. and planning, Bd. Regents Ariz. State U., 1989—; exec. dir. Kans. Bd. Regents, 1994—; pres. Ea. Wash. U., Cheney, 1998—2005, Met. State Coll. of Denver, 2005—. Mem. edn. subcom. Inland N.W. Tech. Edn. Ctr.; mem. commn. on internat. edn. Am. Coun. of Edn.; mem. com. on econ. and workforce devel. Am. Assn. State Colls. and Univs.; mem. Nat. Collaborative Adv. Group, N.W. Commn. on Colls. and Univs. Bd. dirs. Wash. Tech. Ctr., Wash. State Inst. for Pub. Policy, Coun. of Presidents; mem. exec. bd. Spokane Alliance Med. Rsch., 2003, Providence Health Svcs. Ea. Wash., Wash. Campus Compact, Air Edn. and Tng. Command, Health Industry Devel. Group, Higher Edn. Leadership Group. Mem. NCAA (mem. presdl. adv. group), Spokane Area C. of C. (bd. dirs. 2000 exec. com. 2004), Phi Kappa Phi. Office Phone: 303-556-2070.

JORDAN, THERESA JOAN, psychologist, educator; b. Irvington, N.J., Sept. 17, 1949; d. Ernest Anthony and Helen Joan (Debski) Balazs; 1 child, Theresa-Helena. BA, NYU, 1971, MA, 1972, PhD, 1979. Lic. psychologist, N.Y., N.J.; diplomate Am. Bd. Forensic Medicine, Am. Bd. Forensic Examiners, Am. Bd. Forensic Psychologists. Grad. fellow Nat. Inst. Occupational Safety and Health, N.Y.C., 1971-74; rsch. asst., rsch. coord. Project City Sci. NYU, 1974-79, assoc. dir. for rsch. Ctr. for Devel. Studies, 1979-82; asst. prof. medicine N.J. Med. Sch., Newark, 1982-92; assoc. prof. applied psychology NYU, 1992—. Dir. Ctr. for Med. Info. N.J. Med. Sch., Newark, 1989—; cons. Ctrs. for Disease Control, Atlanta, 1990; spkr. Am. Lung Assn., N.Y., 1990-96, Am. Thoracic Soc., N.Y., 1998-99; spkr. Asia-Pacific Congress on Lung Diseases, Bangkok, Thailand, Bali, Indonesia. Author: Overcoming the Fear of Riding, 1996, Understanding Medical Information, 1999; contbr. articles to profl. jours. Mem. U.S. Icelandic Demonstration Team. Mem. APA, Assn. for the Advancement Ednl. Rsch. (pres.-elect 1998—), Soc. for Med. Decision-Making, Eastern Ednl. Rsch. Assn. (2d v.p. 1985-87), Mem. Internat. Union Against Tuberculosis & Lung Disease. Avocation: rider and trainer of icelandic horses. Office: NYU Dept Applied Psychology 239 Greene St New York NY 10003-6674

JORDAN, THOMAS FREDRICK, physics professor; b. Duluth, Minn., June 4, 1936; s. Thomas Vincent and Mildred (Nystrom) J. BA, U. Minn., 1958; PhD, U. Rochester, 1962. Rsch. assoc. U. Rochester, 1961-62, instr., 1962-63; NSF postdoctoral fellow U. Bern, Switzerland, 1963-64; asst. prof. U. Pitts., 1964-67, assoc. prof., 1967-70; prof. U. Minn., Duluth, 1970—. Vis. prof., workshop participant U. Wis., 1965, Aspen (Colo.) Inst. for Humanistic Studies, 1966, Summer Inst. for Theoretical Physics, U. Colo., 1967, Internat. Ctr. for Theoretical Physics, Trieste, Italy, 1968, U. Rochester, 1976-77, Syracuse U., Nat. Inst. for Nuclear Rsch., Firenze, Italy, U. Geneva., U. Paris 1982, Internat. Ctr. for Theoretical Physics, Trieste, workshop on early universe, Erice, Italy, Geneva, U. Bern, 1986, U. Calif. at Santa Barbara, 1988, U. Tex., 1990, 94, 2003, 04, 05. Author: Linear Operators for Quantum Mechanics, 1969, Quantum Mechanics in Simple Matrix Form, 1985; contbr. numerous article to profl. jours. Rsch. fellow Alfred P. Sloan Found., 1965-67, Temple U., 1984, Bush Found. fellow U. Tex., 1994; Fulbright Rsch. grantee U. Göttingen, Fed. Republic of Germany, 1991-92, 2003.

JORDAN, V. CRAIG, endocrine pharmacologist, educator; b. New Braunfels, Tex., July 25, 1947; s. Geoffrey Webster and Sybil Cynthia (Mottram) J.; children: Helen Melissa Yvonne, Alexandra Katherine Louise; m. Monica Morrow. B.Sc. with honors, U. Leeds (Eng.), 1969, Ph.D. in Pharmacology, 1972; D.Sc. in Pharmacology, 1985, hon. MD. Research assoc. Worcester Found. for Exptl. Biology, Shrewsbury, Mass., 1972-73, vis. scientist, 1973-74; lectr. pharmacology U. Leeds, 1973-79; head endocrinology unit Ludwig Inst. for Cancer Research, U. Berne (Switzerland), 1979-80; asst. prof. human oncology and pharmacology U. Wis., Madison, 1980-81, assoc. prof., 1981-85, prof., 1985-93, visting prof. human oncology, 1993-95, also leader pharmacology group dept. human oncology; dir. Breast Cancer Research Program, Wis. Comprehensive Cancer Ctr.; prof. Cancer Pharmacology Northwestern U. Cancer Ctr., 1993—, assoc. dir. cancer control, 1993-96, dir. Lynn Sage breast cancer rsch. program, Robert H. Lurie Comprehensive Ctr.at Northwestern U., Chgo., 1993—, prof. Molecular Pharmacology and Biol. Chemistry, Northwestern U. Feinberg Sch. of Medicine, 1994—, Diana Princess of Wales Prof. of Cancer Rsch., 1999-. Mem. editorial bd. Breast Cancer Rsch. Treatment, Cancer Rsch., Cancer Letters (mng. editor), Endocrine Related Cancer (assoc. editor), European Jour. Cancer, Jour. Steroid Biochemistry, Jour. of Nat. Cancer Inst., Molecular Cell Endocrinology, Receptor, Molecular Aspects Med., assoc. editor; contbr. more than 400 articles to profl. jours. Served to capt., Intelligence Corps, Brit. Army, 1971-76; Served to capt. Spl. Air Service, 1976-78. Med. Research Council scholar, 1969-72; co-recipient Boston Obstet. Soc. prize, 1974; UICC Internat. Cancer Research Tech. Transfer grantee, 1981; Romnes Faculty fellow, 1984-85; recipient Brinker Internat. Breast Cancer award Susan G. Komen Found., 1992, Cameron prize U. Edinburgh, 1993, WL McGuire Meml. award 1994, Herbert J. Block Meml. Award for Dist. Achievement in Cancer, Ohio State U., 1996, Stang award, Cornell Med. Sch., 2000, Hon. Fellowship award and Medal, Univ. Coll., Dublin, Ireland, 2000, Bristol Myers Squibb award and Medal for Disting. Achievement in Cancer Rsch., 2001, Third Annual Breast Cancer award, European Inst. Oncology, Milan, Italy, 2001, Vivian and Meyer P. Potamkin found. award for Breast Cancer Rsch., Pa. Breast Cancer Coalition, 2001, Avon Med. Advancement award, Avon Found. 2002, Am. Cancer Society Medal of Honor, 2002, Officer of the Most Excellent Order of the British Empire for Services to Internat. Breast Cancer Rsch., Queen Elizabeth II, 2002, Charles F. Kettering award, GM Cancer Rsch. Fund, 2003, Miami Breast Cancer Conf. award of Excellence, 2003, 3rd George & Christine Sosnovsky award in Cancer Therapy, 2003-04, N. Am. Menopause Society/Eli Lilly SERM Rsch. award, 2003. Fellow Am. Inst. Chemists, Royal Soc. Chemistry, 1984; mem. Am. Assn. for Cancer Research (8th Cain Meml. award 1989, Inaugural Dorothy P. Landon Prize in Translational Rsch., 2002), Am. Soc. for Pharmacology and Exptl. Therapeutics (ASPET award 1993), Endocrine Soc., Biochem. Soc., Brit. Pharm. Soc. (Sir John Gaddum Meml. award 1993), YME Chgo. (hon. nat. bd. dir.). Research on mechanism of action of antiestrogens as anticancer agts., antiestrogen structure-activity relationships, molecular pharmacology of antiestrogens, metabolism of antiestrogens in animals and man, breast cancer therapy with tamoxifen. Office: Robert H Lurie Cancer Ctr Olson 8250 303 E Chicago Ave Chicago IL 60611

JORDAN, VERNON EULION, JR., lawyer; b. Atlanta, Aug. 15, 1935; s. Vernon Eulion and Mary (Griggs) J.; m. Shirley M. Yarbrough, Dec. 13, 1958 (dec. Dec. 29, 1985); 1 child, Vickee; m. Ann Dibble Cook, Nov. 22, 1986. BA, DePauw U., 1957; JD, Howard U., 1960; hon. degrees, DePauw U., Howard U., Boston Coll., Brandeis U., CUNY, U. Ill. Chgo. Duke U., U. Mass., NYU, Princeton U., Tulane U., Rutgers U., Tuskegee Inst., Yale U., Notre Dame U., Harvard U., plus 50 other instns. higher edn. Bar: Ga. 1960, Ark. 1964. Practice law, Atlanta, 1960-61, Pine Bluff, Ark., 1964-65; Ga. field dir. NAACP, 1961-63; dir. Voter Edn. Project So. Regional Council, 1964-68; atty. OEO, Atlanta, 1969; exec. dir. United Negro Coll. Fund, N.Y.C., 1970-71; pres. Nat. Urban League, 1972-81; sr. ptnr. firm Akin, Gump, Strauss, Hauer & Feld, LLP, Washington, of counsel, 2000—; sr. mng. dir. Lazard Freres & Co., LLC, N.Y.C., 2000—. Bd. dirs. Am. Express Co., Asbury Automotive Group, Dow Jones & Co., J.C. Penney Co., Inc., Lazard Ltd., Xerox Corp., Sara Lee Corp; chmn. Clinton Presdl. Transition Bd.; apptd. to Pres.'s adv. com. Points of Light Initiative Found., 1989. Mem. Nat. Adv. Commn. on Selective Svcs., 1966-67, Am. Revolution Bi-Centennial Commn., 1972—, Presdl. Clemency Bd., 1974; adv. coun. Social Security, 1974; trustee Ford Found., LBJ Found., Urban Inst. (life), Howard U.; mem. steering com. Bilderberg Meetings; mem. Coun. on Fgn. Rels.; adv. trustee DePauw U., bd. dirs. NAACP Legal Def. and Ednl. Fund; hon. mem. Ralph Bunche Inst. on the UN. Fellow 2Met. Applied Research Center, 1968; Fellow Harvard Inst. Politics, 1969; recipient Alexis de Tocqueville award United Way Am., 1977. Mem. ABA, D.C. Bar Assn., Nat. Bar Assn., Nat. Conf. Black Lawyers, Am. Law Inst., University Club, Board Room, Council on Fgn. Relations, Century Assn. Mem. A.M.E. Ch. Office: Lazard Freres & Co LLC 30 Rockefeller Plz New York NY 10112-0002 Office Phone: 212-632-6000.

JORDAN, W. CARL, lawyer; b. Mobile, Ala., Apr. 7, 1949; s. William Cecil and Lois Elizabeth (Smith) J.; m. Lisa Anne Gagne, Aug. 17, 1974; children: Kimberly Gardner, Hillary Elizabeth, William Christopher, Clement Nicholas. BA, Baylor U., 1971; JD, Harvard U., 1974. Bar: U.S. Dist. Ct. (so. and ea. dists.) Tex. 1975, U.S. Ct. Appeals (5th cir.) 1975, U.S. Ct. Appeals (9th cir.), Tex. 1984, U.S. Supreme Ct. 1984. Assoc. Vinson & Elkins, LLP, Houston, 1974-81, ptnr., 1981—, co-head Employment Litig. and Labor Sect., mem. Mgmt. Com. Gen. counsel, adv. dir. Tex. Employment Law Council, Austin, 1984—. Author: Developing and Enforcing Drug and Alcohol Work Rules: A Primer for Tex. Employers, 1986; contbr. articles to profl. jours. Mem. ABA (labor and employment law sect., equal employment opportunity law com., subcom. chmn. 1983-86). Home: 3722 Farber St Houston TX 77005-3714 Office: Vinson & Elkins 3300 1st City Tower 1001 Fannin St Ste 2300 Houston TX 77002-6706 E-mail: cjordan@velaw.com.

JORDAN, WILLIAM CHESTER, historian, educator; b. Chgo., Apr. 7, 1948; s. Johnnie Parker and Marguerite Jane (Mays) Jordan; m. Christine Kenyon Hershey, May 30, 1970; children: Victoria Marie, John Mark, Clare Kenyon, Lorna Janice. AB, Ripon Coll., 1969; PhD, Princeton U., 1973. Instr. Princeton U., 1973-74, lectr., 1974-75, asst. to assoc. prof. history, 1975-86, prof. history, 1986—, Behrman sr. fellow in humanities, 1990—94, Dayton-Stockton prof., 2005—; dir. Shelby Cullom Davis Ctr. for Hist. Studies, 1994-99. Vis. lectr. U. Pa., Phila., 1981-82; vis. assoc. prof. history Swarthmore (Pa.) Coll., 1985; mem. adv. com. history Grad. Records Exam, 1976-86, chmn., 1980-86; Morgan lectr. Dickinson Coll., Carlisle, Pa., 1985. Co-editor: Order and Innovation in the Middle Ages, 1976; author: Louis IX and the Challenge of the Crusade, 1979, From Servitude to Freedom, 1986, The French Monarchy and the Jews, 1989, Women and Credit, 1993, The Great Famine, 1996, The Middle Ages: An Encyclopedia for Students, 1996, The Middle Ages: A Watts Guide for Children, 2000, Europe in the High Middle Ages, 2001, Ideology and Royal Power in Medieval France, 2001, Dictionary of the Middle Ages: Supplement 1, 2004, Unceasing Strife, Unending Fear, 2005; contbr. articles to profl. jours. Recipient Behrman award Princeton U., 2003; fellow Woodrow Wilson Found., Ford Found., Danforth Found, Mellon Found., Rockefeller Found., Annenberg Rsch. Inst. Fellow Medieval Acad. Am. (Haskins medal 2000); mem. Am. Hist. Assn. (co-chair program com. 1985), Am. Coun. Learned Socs. (sec. 1986-95, bd. dirs. 1982-95), Am. Philos. Soc. (elected), Soc. French Hist. Studies, Soc. Study of the Crusades and Latin East, Haskins Soc. Office: Dept of History Princeton U Princeton NJ 08544-0001 Office Phone: 609-258-4165. Business E-Mail: wchester@princeton.edu.

JORDAN, WILLIAM DAVIS, lawyer; b. Palestine, Tex., Aug. 5, 1940; s. Henry Latimer and Evelyn (Davis) J.; m. Toby Stall Feb. 8, 1964; children: Russell Stall Jordan, Stephen Monnig Jordan. BBA with honors, U. Tex., 1963, LLB with honors, 1964. Bar: Tex. 1964; cert. estate planning and probate law Tex. Bd. Legal Specialization. Assoc., then ptnr. Jackson and Walker, Dallas, 1964—97; shareholder Johnson, Jordan, Nipper & Monk, P.C., Dallas, 1997—. Chmn. U. Tex. Tax Conf., 1977, also planning com.; spkr. in field. Contbr. articles to profl. jours. Active Dallas Estate Planning Coun.; chmn. Southwestern Legal Found. Oil and Gas Tax Inst., 1981-86, planning com.; dir., past chmn. Dallas Met. YMCA; past dir. Baylor U. Med. Ctr. Found., YMCA Rockies, Colo.; chmn. YMCA Found.; adv. dir. Cmtys. Found. Tex., Dallas Found.; past mem. Rotary, found. trustee Dallas, 1985-91. Mem. Tex. Bar Assn. (co-chmn. peer com. 1967-68), Dallas Bar Assn. (chmn. tax sect. 1977), Dallas Estate Planning Coun. (past bd. dirs.), Dallas Country Club, Beta Theta Pi. Presbyterian. Office: Johnson Jordan Nipper & Monk PC 13155 Noel Rd Ste 1050 LB3 Dallas TX 75240-1531

JORDAN, WINTHROP DONALDSON, historian, educator; b. Worcester, Mass., Nov. 11, 1931; s. Henry Donaldson and Lucretia Mott (Churchill) J.; m. Phyllis Henry, Aug. 30, 1952 (div. 1979); children: Joshua H., J. Mott, W. Eliot; m. Cora Miner Reilly, Feb. 27, 1982. AB, Harvard U., 1953; MA, Clark U., 1957; PhD, Brown U., 1960. Instr. history Phillips Exeter (N.H.) Acad., 1955-56; lectr. in history Brown U., Providence, 1959-61; fellow Inst. Early Am. History and Culture, Williamsburg, Va., 1961-63; from asst. prof. to prof. history U. Calif., Berkeley, 1963-82, assoc. dean for minority group affairs Grad. div., 1968-70; vis. prof. history and black studies U. Miss., Oxford, 1981, prof. history and Afro-Am. studies, 1982—. Vis. asst. prof. history U. Mich., Ann Arbor, 1966; vis. prof. history U. Calif., Berkeley, 1989; William F. Winter prof. history and prof. Afro-Am. studies, U. Miss., 1993—, F.A.P. Barnard Disting. prof., 1998—; vis. prof. history U. Zimbabwe, 1994. Author: White Over Black, 1968, Tumult and Silence at Second Creek, 1993; co-author: The United States, 1979, The Americans, 1982, The American People, 1986; mem. editorial bd. various scholarly jours. Council mem. Inst. Early Am. History and Culture, 1977-79. Recipient Ralph Waldo Emerson award Phi Beta Kappa, 1968, Parkman prize Soc. Am. Historians, 1969, Nat.

Book award for History and Biography Am. Book Pubs., 1969, Bancroft prize Columbia U., 1969, 94, Landry award LSU Press, 1992, Eugene M. Kayden award, 1994, Disting. Alumnus citation Brown U. Grad. Sch., 1993; fellow Charles Warren Ctr. for Study Am. History Harvard U., 1965, Social Sci. Rsch. Coun., 1966, Guggenheim Found., 1967, Ctr. for Advanced Study Behavioral Scis., Palo Alto, 1975-76; grantee NIMH, 1970-73. Mem. Am. Antiquarian Soc. (elected), Am. Hist. Assn., Orgn. Am. Historians, So. Hist. Assn., Mass. Hist. Soc. (elected), Miss. Hist. Soc., Krokodiloes Club. Home: 400 Murray St Oxford MS 38655-2914 Office: Dept History U Miss University MS 38677 Office Phone: 662-915-7148. E-mail: hsjordan@olemiss.edu.

JORDEN, ELEANOR HARZ, linguist, educator; b. NYC; d. William George and Eleanor (Funk) Harz; m. William J. Jorden, Mar. 3, 1944 (div.); children: William Temple, Eleanor Harz, Marion Telva. AB, Bryn Mawr Coll., 1942; MA, Yale U., 1943, PhD, 1950; D.Litt. (hon.), Williams Coll., 1982; D.H.L. (hon.), Knox Coll., 1985; D. Langs. (hon.), Middlebury Coll., 1991; D. Univ. (hon.), U. Stirling, Scotland, 1993. Instr. Japanese Yale U., 1943-46, 47-48; dir. Japanese lang. program and Fgn. Service Inst. Lang. Sch., Am. Embassy, Tokyo, 1950-55; sci. linguist Fgn. Service Inst., Dept. State, Washington, 1959-69; acting head Far East langs., 1961-64; chmn., 1964-67, 69; chmn. Vietnamese lang. div., 1967-69; vis. prof. linguistics Cornell U., 1969-70, prof., 1970-87, Mary Donlon Alger prof. linguistics, 1974-87, prof. emeritus, 1987—. Bernhard disting. vis. prof. Williams Coll., 1985—86, vis. prof., 1986—87, adj. prof., 1987—92; dir. Japanese FALCON program, 1972—87; prof., Disting. fellow Nat. Fgn. Lang. Ctr. Sch. Advanced Internat. Studies Johns Hopkins U., 1987—91; acad. dir. Exchange: Japan, 1988—2004; sr. cons. prep. framework Japanese lang. curriculum and Japanese coll. bd. exam, 1991—93; sr. cons. Japanese multi-media project U. Md., 1995—97, cons. Part 2, Ohio State U., 2002—; dir. SPENG Program, 1980—; co-dir. Survey on Japanese Lang. Study, 1988—92; guest scholar Wilson Ctr. Smithsonian Instn., 1982; cons., permanent disting. dir. Nat. Assn. Self-Instrnl. Lang. Programs, pres., 1977—78, 1984—85; mem. Fulbright-Hays Com. on Internat. Exch. Scholars, 1972—75; mem. area adv. com. for East Asia, 1972—76; chmn. Social Sci. Rsch. Coun. Task Force on Japanese Lang. Tng., 1976—78; mem. adv. com. Japan Found., 1979—81; mem. Lang. Attrition Project, 1981—87; advisor Ctr. for Japanese Studies, Stirling U., Scotland, 1988—92; coun. com. langs. and lit. Yale U., 1990—98; acad. dir. Alliance for Lang. Learning and Ednl. Exch., 2004—. Author: (with Bernard Bloch) Spoken Japanese, 1945, Syntax of Modern Colloquial Japanese, 1955, Gateway to Russian, 1961, Beginning Japanese, Part 1, 1962, Part 2, 1963, (with Sheehan, Quang and others) Basic Vietnamese, vols. I, II, 1965, (with Quang) Vietnamese Familiarization Course, 1969, (with Hamako Chaplin) Reading Japanese, 1976, (with Mari Noda) Japanese: The Spoken Language, part 1, 1987, part 2, 1988, part 3, 1990, (with Richard Lambert) Japanese Language Instruction in the U.S.: Resources, Practice and Investment Strategic, 1992, (with M. Noda) Japanese: The Written Language, Part 1, Vol. 1, 2005 Decorated Order of Precious Crown Emperor of Japan, 1985; recipient Superior Svc. award Dept. State, 1965, Japan Found. and Social Sci. Rsch. Coun. sr. fellow, 1976, Toyota award Twentieth Anniversary Fund grantee, 1978; Japan Found. award, 1985, Papalia award for Excellence Tchr. Tng., 1993, N.E. Conf. award Disting. Svc. and Leadership in Profession, 1994; honoree Eleanor Harz Jorden Festival, Portland State U., 1995. Mem. ALLEX (bd. dirs. 2004—), Assn. Asian Studies (v.p. 1979-80, pres. 1980-81), Linguistic Soc. Am., Am. Coun. Tchrs. Fgn. Langs., Nat. Assn. Self-Instrnl. Lang. Programs (pres. 1978, 85, permanent disting. dir. 1991—), Assn. Tchrs. Japanese (exec. com., pres. 1978-84), Japan Soc. N.Y. (bd. dirs. 1982-88), Exchange: Japan (bd. dirs., v.p., sec. 1998-2004). Office: 3300 Darby Rd Apt 1302 Haverford PA 19041-1067 Fax: 610-658-2563. Office Phone: 610-649-2409. Business E-Mail: ejorden@brynmawr.edu.

JORDEN, JAMES ROY, oil industry executive, consultant; b. Oklahoma City, Apr. 16, 1934; s. James Roy and Gordon (Peeler) J.; m. Shirley Ann Swan, Nov. 17, 1956; children: Philip Taylor, David Emerson. BS in Petroleum Engring., U. Tulsa, 1957; MA in Theol. Studies, Austin Presbyn. Theol. Sem., 2004. Engr. Shell Oil Co., various locations, 1957, 1960-81, petrophys. engr. advisor Houston, 1981-85; mgr. petroleum engring. rsch. Shell Devel. Co., Houston, 1985-88, mgr. head office prodn., tech. tng., 1988-93; mgr. CPI tng. Shell Oil Co., Houston, 1993-95; retired, 1995; cons. Quicksilver Resources, Inc., 1998—. Mem. industry adv. bd. petroleum engring. U. Tulsa, 1987-92, chmn., 1988; vis. com. petroleum engring. Colo. Sch. Mines, Golden, 1988-95. Co-author: Well Logging I, 1984, Well Logging II, 1986; co-inventor in field. 1st lt. USAF, 1957—60. Named to Hall of Fame, Petroleum Engring. Dept. U. Tulsa, 1985. Mem. Am. Inst. Mining, Metall. and Petroleum Engrs. (trustee 1983-85, 2000-02, 2004—), Soc. Petroleum Engrs. (hon., pres. 1984, Disting. Svc. award 1988, DeGolyer Disting. Svc. medal 1991, bd. dirs. 1975-79, dir. svc. corps. 1984-90, life trustee found., treas. found. 1991-92, sr. v.p. found. 1993-95, pres. found. 1995-97), Kappa Alpha. Republican. Presbyterian. Avocations: golf, reading, wine. Home: PO Box 8111 Horseshoe Bay TX 78657-8111

JORDEN, WILLIAM JOHN, writer, retired diplomat; b. Bridger, Mont., May 3, 1923; s. Hugh G. and Jane Ann (Temple) J.; m. Eleanor Harz, 1944 (div.); children: William Temple, Eleanor Harz, Marion Telva; m. V. Mildred Xiarhos, 1972. BA with honors, Yale, 1947; MS, Columbia, 1948. Instr. Japanese Yale, 1945—46; reporter Vineyard Gazette, Edgartown, Mass., 1947; radio news writer N.Y. Herald Tribune, 1948; fgn. corr. A.P., Japan and Korea, 1948—52, N.Y. Times, Japan and Korea, 1952—55, chief of bur. Moscow, 1956—58; diplomatic corr. N.Y. Times (Washington bur.), 1958-61; mem. Policy Planning Coun., State Dept., 1961-62, spl. asst. to under sec. polit. affairs, 1962-65, dep. asst. sec. state pub. affairs, 1965-66; sr. mem. staff NSC, 1966-68, 72-74; mem., spokesman Am. del. Vietnam Peace Talks, Paris, 1968-69; asst. to former Pres. Lyndon B. Johnson, 1969-72; U.S. ambassador to Panama, 1974-78. Scholar-in-residence LBJ Libr.; adj. prof. LBJ Sch. Pub. Affairs, U. Tex., 1978-80; U.S. chmn. U.S.-Panama Consultative com., 1992-95. Author: Panama Odyssey; co-author: Japan Between East and West. Served with AUS, 1943-45. Shared Pulitzer prize for internat. corr., 1958; Recipient Disting. Honor award Dept. State, 1978; Pulitzer traveling fellow, 1948-49; Council Fgn. Relations fellow, 1955-56; Decorated order of Vasco Nunez de Balboa (Republic of Panama) Mem. Coun. Fgn. Rels., Acad. Polit. Sci., Author's Guild. Clubs: Yale of Washington, Fgn. Corrs. Japan (pres. 1952-53).

JORDEN, YON YOON, health services company executive; B in Acctg., Calif. State U. V.p., controller FHP Internat. Corp.; sr. v.p., CFO, WellPoint Health Networks, Inc., Blue Cross Calif., Aera Energy LLC; exec. v.p., CFO Oxford Health Plans Inc., Norwalk, Conn., 1998—. Office: AdvancePCS 750 W John Carpenter Fwy, Ste 1200 Irving TX 75039

JORDON, ROBERT EARL, physician; b. Buffalo, May 7, 1938; s. James Wallace and Helen Viola (Sampson) J.; m. Mary Ann Michels, July 12, 1969; children: James H., Kathryn L., Marie H. BA, Hamilton Coll., 1960; MD, SUNY-Buffalo, 1965; MS, U. Minn., 1970. Diplomate: Am. Bd. Dermatology, Dermatological Immunology Diagnostic and Laboratory Immunology. Intern straight medicine Buffalo Gen. Hosp., 1965-66; resident, fellow in dermatology Mayo Clinic and Mayo Found., Rochester, Minn., 1966-69, asso. cons., 1971-73, cons. dermatology, 1973-77; instr. pathology U. Minn. Hosps., Mpls., 1971-73; Nat. Inst. Arthritis and Metabolic Diseases spl. research fellow U. Minn., Mpls., 1972-73; asst. prof. dermatology Mayo Grad. Sch. Medicine, Rochester, 1971-73, Mayo Sch. Medicine, Rochester, 1973-76, asst. prof. immunology, 1974-77, asso. prof. dermatology, 1976-77; prof. medicine, chmn. dermatology Med. Coll. Wis., Milw., 1977-82; med. career investigator VA, 1978-82; chief dermatology Froedtert Meml. Luth. Hosp., Milw., 1980-82; chmn. dept. dermatology U. Tex. Health Sci. Ctr., Houston, prof., 1983—; chief dermatology Hermann Hosp., Houston, 1983—2003; mem. study sect. NIH, 1983-86. Mem. nat. arthritis adv. bd. Nat. Inst. aRthritis and Metabolic Diseases, NIH; mem. nat. adv. bd. Arthritis, Musculoskeletal and Skin Diseases, 1989-91, chmn. 1992-93. Mem. editl. bd. Jour. Investigative Dermatology, 1977-82, Jour. Clin. and Lab. Immunology, 1977—, Archives of Dermatology, 1978-87, sect. editor Am. Jour. Dermatopathology, 1981-83, Clin. Aspects Autoimmunity, 1989-92. Elder Grace Presbyn. Ch., Houston, 1987—; bd. dirs. CAnCare of Houston, 1991-2001, pres. bd. dirs., 1997-99, chmn. bd., 1999-2001. Lt. comdr. M.C., USN, 1965-71. Recipient Bacelli Research award SUNY, Buffalo, 1965, Med. Spltys. Outstanding Achievement award Mayo Found., 1969, Marion B. Sulzberger award Am. Soc. Dermatologic Allergy and Immunology, 1983, award Am. Skin Assn., 1999, JB & Blanche Earthman award 2002. Mem. AAAS, AMA, Soc. Investigative Dermatology (com. nominations 1986—, dir. 1977-82, v.p. 1993-94), Am. Acad. Dermatology (co-chmn. com. lab. proficiency and quality control in immunodermatology 1980-83, dir. Immunopathology Symposium 1981-86, bd. dirs. 1993-98), Am. Assn. Immunologists, Am. Dermatol. Assn., Am. Fedn. Clin. Research, Am. Soc. Clin. Investigation, Assn. Profs. Dermatology (bd. dirs. 1987-89), Central Soc. Clin. Research, Dermatology Found. (chmn. med. and sci. com. 1980-81, trustee 1993-98, discovery award 2000), Soc. Exptl. Biology and Medicine, Lupus Erythematosus Soc. Wis. (mem. med. adv. bd. 1977-83), Wis. Dermatol. Soc. (pres. 1979-80), Wis. State Med. Soc., Chgo. Dermatol. Soc., Tex. Med. Assn., Houston Dermatol. Soc., Lupus Soc. Houston (adv. bd. 1986—90), Sigma Xi. Home: 376 Green Cove Dr Montgomery TX 77356-8267 Office: U Tex Health Sci Ctr Houston TX 77030

JORGENSEN, ALFRED H., retired data processing executive, retired telecommunications industry executive; b. South Gate, Calif., May 1, 1934; s. Peter Hansen and Anna Christine (Nielsen) J.; m. Carole Jean Scott, Sept. 3, 1959; children: Mark Alan, Lora Jean. AA, El Camino Coll., 1958; student, UCLA, 1958-60. Assoc. engr. Litton Industries, Beverly Hills, Calif., 1957-60; engr. Daystrom, Inc., 1960-64; with control sys. divsn. Foxboro Co., Pitts., 1964-67, dist. and regional mgr., 1967-69; with Interactive Scis., Pitts., 1969-72, v.p., 1970-71, Computeria Inc., 1971, pres., 1971-72; v.p. Interactive Scis. Corp., Braintree, Mass., 1972-77, pres., CEO, 1977-80; exec. v.p. Nat. Data Corp., Atlanta, 1980-83; v.p. nat. sales Cullinet Software Inc., 1983-85; v.p., gen. mgr. Sys. and Computer Tech., 1985-87; pres., COO Infosafe Corp., Atlanta, 1987-88; pres. Corp. Playmakers, 1988-90; dir. bus. alliances Sprint Comm., Atlanta, 1990-95; gen. mgr. Applied Tech. Ctr., 1995—2000; ret., 2000. Bd. dirs. Process Corp., Pitts., Chestatee State Bank; adj. prof. Emory U., 1998—2000. Chmn., Relay for Life Am. Cancer Soc., 2001; bd. dirs. Mass. Assn. Mental Health, 1977—79, v.p., 1978—79; bd. dirs. Satisfy (Drug Rehab. Program), Dawson Humane Soc., 2003. Mem. IEEE, Data Processing Mgmt. Assn., Assn. Iron and Steel Engrs., Instrument Soc. Am., Cash Mgmt. Assn., Am. Mgmt. Assn., Nat. Platform Assn., Pearson Yacht Club (commodore 1984). Home: 927 Liberty Church Rd Dawsonville GA 30534-7354 Personal E-mail: aljorgy@aol.com.

JORGENSEN, ERIK, forest pathologist, educator, consultant; b. Haderslev, Denmark, Oct. 28, 1921; emigrated to Can., 1955, naturalized, 1960; s. Johannes and Eva Bromberg (Hansen) J.; m. Grete Moller, June 13, 1946; children: Marianne, Birthe. M. Forestry, Royal Vet. and Agrl. Coll., Copenhagen, 1946. Forest pathologist Royal Vet. and Agrl. Coll., Copenhagen, 1948-55; forest pathologist sci. service Agr. Can., 1955-59; asst. prof. U. Toronto, 1959-63, assoc. prof., 1963-67, prof. forest pathology and urban forestry, 1967-73; chief urban forestry program Can. Forestry Service, Environ. Can., 1973-78; arboretum dir., prof. environ. biology U. Guelph, Ont., 1978-87; cons. in field, 1987-89. Author: The Development of an Urban Forestry Concept, 1967; contbr. articles to sci. jours. Served to 2d lt. Danish Army, 1946-48. Recipient Authors citation Internat. Shade Tree Conf., 1970; recipient Maple Leaf award Internat. Shade Tree Conf., 1975, Can. Patents and Devel. Ltd. Inventors cert., 1975, Trees for Tomorrow award Can. Forestry Assn., 1993. Fellow Can. Inst. Forestry; mem. Ont. Profl. Foresters Assn., Internat. Soc. Arboriculture, Ont. Shade Tree Council (life, Jaap Salm Meml. award 1975), Sigma Xi. Lutheran. Home: 172 Metcalfe St Apt 507 Guelph ON Canada N1E 6T6 *A dedication to the application of forest science to the service of mankind.*

JORGENSEN, ESTELLE RUTH, music educator; b. Melbourne, Victoria, Australia, May 28, 1945; came to US, 1986; d. Alfred Stanley and Jean Winifred (Cook) J. BA in Econs. with honors, U. Newcastle, New South Wales, Australia, 1967, Diploma in Edn., 1968; MusM, Andrews U., 1970; PhD, U. Calgary, Alta., Can., 1976. Tchr. social studies Epping Boys Sch., Sydney, Australia, 1968; tchr. social studies and music County of Newell, Brooks, Alta., Canada, 1968-69; instr. music Andrews U., Berrien Springs, Mich., 1970-71; tchr. music Milton Williams Jr. HS, Calgary, 1971-74; tchr. choral music Henry Wise Wood HS, Calgary, 1974-76; asst. prof. Sch. Edn. Notre Dame U., Nelson, BC, Canada, 1976-77; assoc. prof. music faculty McGill U., Montreal, Que., Canada, 1977-87; prof. music edn. Sch. Music Ind. U., Bloomington, 1987—. Editor: (proceedings) McGill Symposium in School Music Administration and Supervision, 1980, Philosopher, Teacher, Musician: Perspectives on Music Education, 1993, Philosophy of Music Education Review, 1993—; author: In Search of Music Education, 1997, Transforming Music Education, 2003; contbr. articles to profl. jours. Mem. Coll. Music Soc., Am. Soc. Aesthetics, Music Educators Nat. Conf., Internat. Soc. for Music Educators, Inc. Soc. Musicians, Philosophy of Edn. Soc., Internat. Soc. Philosophy Music Edn. (founding co-chair 2003-05). Avocations: travel, bicycling, photography. Office: Sch Music Ind U Bloomington IN 47405

JORGENSEN, GORDON DAVID, retired engineering company executive; b. Chgo., Apr. 29, 1921; s. Jacob and Marie (Jensen) J.; m. Nadina Anita Peters, Dec. 17, 1948 (div. Aug. 1971); children: Karen Ann, David William, Susan Marie; m. Barbara Noel, Feb. 10, 1972 (div. July 1976); m. Ruth Barnes Chalmers, June 15, 1990. BSEE, U. Wash., 1948, postgrad. in bus. and mgmt., 1956-59. Registered profl. engr., Alaska, Ariz., Calif., Colo., Nev., N.Mex., N.D., Utah, Wash., Wyo. With R.W. Beck & Assocs., Cons. Engrs., Phoenix, 1948—, ptnr., 1954-86; pres. Beck Internat., Phoenix, 1971—; ret. Project mgr. for mgmt., operation studies and reorgn. study Honduras power sys., 1969-70. Served to lt. (j.g.) U.S. Maritime Svc., 1942-45. Recipient Outstanding Svc. award Phoenix Tennis Assn., 1967, Commendation, Govt. Honduras, 1970. Mem. IEEE (chmn. Wash.-Alaska sect. 1959-60), NSPE, Am. Soc. Appraisers (sr. mem.), Ariz. Cons. Engrs. Assn., Ariz. Soc. Profl. Engrs., Internat. Assn. Assessing Officers, Southwestern Tennis Assn. (past pres.), U.S. Tennis Assn. (pres. 1987-88, chmn. U.S. Open com.), chmn. U.S. Davis Cup com., chmn. Internat. Tennis Fed., Davis Cup com.). Presbyterian (elder). Home: 74-578 Palo Verde Dr Indian Wells CA 92210-7314 Personal E-mail: gordon@jorgensens.us.

JORGENSEN, JAMES DOUGLAS, research physicist; b. Salina, Utah, Mar. 23, 1948; m. Ramona Gurr, June 6, 1970; children: Lynn Neilson, Michael Neilson, Kristeen Stenblik, Kathryn Brimball, Karen Russell, Scott Neilson. BS in Physics, Brigham Young U., 1970, PhD in Physics, 1975. Postdoctoral rsch. asst. Argonne (Ill.) Nat. Lab., 1974-77, asst. physicist solid state div., 1977-80, physicist material sci. div., 1980-89, sr. physicist, 1989—, group leader, 1988—. Mem. U.S. Nat. Com. for Crystallography, 1990-92, 94-97. Mem. editl. adv. bd. Jour. Solid State Chemistry, 1990—; contbr. over 300 articles to profl. jours. Bishop LDS Ch., Woodridge, Ill., 1984-89, stake pres., Naperville, Ill., 1998—. Recipient award for disting. performance at Argonne Nat. Lab., 1983, Barrett award, 1997; co-recipient Pacesetter award Argonne Nat. Lab., 1986, Dir.'s award, 1988; materials scis. rsch. competition award for outstanding sci. accomplishments in solid state physics U.S. Dept. Energy, 1987, 91; named honored alumnus Brigham Young U., 1992. Fellow Am. Phys. Soc.; mem. Materials Rsch. Soc., Am. Crystallographic Assn. (B.E. Warren Diffraction Physics award 1991). Office: Argonne Nat Lab Materials Sci Dv Bldg 223 Argonne IL 60439 Business E-Mail: jjorgensen@anl.gov.

JORGENSEN, PALLE E.T., mathematician, educator; b. Copenhagen, Oct. 8, 1947; came to U.S., 1973, naturalized, 1979; s. Soren A.W. and Gyrit D. (Baden) J.; m. Soon-Min Park, Jan. 4, 1975; children: Anton Y., Greta S., Tina S. AB, U. Aarhus, Denmark, 1968, MS, 1970, PhD, 1973. Asst. prof. math. Stanford (Calif.) U., 1977-79; assoc. prof. U. Aarhus, 1979-83; prof. U. Iowa, Iowa City, 1983—. Vis. assoc. prof. U. Pa., Phila., 1982-84; mem. internat. faculty Danish Govt. Rsch. Acad. Author: Operator Commutation Relations, 1984, other books on advanced math.; editor Acta Applicandae Mathematicae, 1983—, Proceedings of the Am. Math. Soc., Wavelets Through A Looking Glass, 2002; contbr. articles to profl. jours. Grantee Danish Rsch. Coun., 1976-77, NSF, 1977-79, 82—; U. Iowa faculty scholar, 1992—. Mem. Am. Math. Soc., Danish Math. Soc., Math. Assn. Am., Danish Acad. Sci. (internat. faculty), Soc. Indsl. and Applied Math. Office: U Iowa Dept Math Mlh Iowa City IA 52242 Office Phone: 319-335-0782. Business E-Mail: jorgen@math.uiowa.edu.

JORGENSEN, VIRGINIA DYER, antique dealer, museum consultant; b. Arlington, Va., Sept. 18, 1955; d. Gordon Wade and Maureen Glesner Dyer; m. Bruce Kenneth Hopkins, Feb. 21, 1987 (div. Jan. 1992); children: Lauren Pontoni, Brett Gardner, Lacy Marie Hopkins, Dustin Kenneth Hopkins; m. William Dennis Jorgensen, Sept. 30, 1994. AA, Kellogg C.C., Battle Creek, Mich., 1977; BA magna cum laude, We. Mich. U., 1998. Pub. rels., tour guide Kellogg Co., Battle Creek, 1975—80; supply publs. writer U.S. Dept. Def., Battle Creek, 1984—88; sales team leader I.I. Stanley Automotive Lighting, Battle Creek, 1990—94; devel. coord. Mich. Maritime Mus., South Haven, 1998; antique dealer Crossroads Antique Mall, Seymour, Ind., 2000—, Exit 76 Antique Mall, Columbus, Ind., 2000—03. Trustee Kentwood (Mich.) Pub. Sch. Edn. Found., 1997—99; bd. mem. Preservation Action Alliance, Battle Creek, 1994—96; mem. design consulting bd. Housing Partnership Inc., Columbus, Ind., 2000. Recipient Edith Mange award for disting. scholarship, Western Mich.U., 1998. Mem.: Colonial Williamsburg Found., Nat. Trust for Historic Preservation, Golden Key Nat. Honor Soc., Phi Alpha Theta. Presbyterian. Avocations: breeding pugs, buying and restoring old buildings. Home and Office: 1069 Redwing Dr Columbus IN 47203 E-mail: wdandvl@metinc.net.

JORGENSON, DALE WELDEAU, economist, educator; b. Bozeman, Mont., May 7, 1933; s. Emmett B. and Jewell (Torkelson) J.; m. Linda Ann Mabus, July 24, 1971; children: Eric Mabus, Kari Ann. BA, Reed Coll., 1955; AM, Harvard U., 1957, PhD, 1959; PhD (hon.), Uppsala U., 1991, Oslo U., 1991, Keio U., 2003, U. Mannheim, 2004. Mem. faculty U. Calif., Berkeley, 1959-69, prof. econs., 1963-69, Harvard U., 1969-80, Frederic Eaton Abbe prof. econs., 1980—2002, Frank William Taussig rsch. prof. econs., 1992-94, Samuel W. Morris. univ. prof., 2002—. Ford research prof. econs. U. Chgo., 1962-63 Author (with J.J. McCall and R. Radner): Optimal Replacement Policy, 1967, Econometric Studies of U.S. Energy Policy, 1975; author: (with R. Landau) Technology and Economic Policy, 1988; author: (with F.M. Gollop and B.M. Fraumeni) Productivity and U.S. Economic Growth, 1987; author: (with R. Landau) Technology and Capital Formation, 1989; author: (with Lars Bergman, Emo Zalal) General Equilibrium Modeling and Economic Policy Analysis, 1990; author: (with Kun-Young Yun) Tax Reform and the Cost of Capital, 1991; author: (with Li Jingwen, Zhang Youjing and Masahiro Kuroda) Productivity and Economic Growth in China, USA and Japan, 1993; author: (with R. Landau) Tax Reform and the Cost of Capital: An International Comparison, 1993; author: Postwar U.S. Economic Growth, 1995, International Comparisons of Economic Growth, 1995, Capital Theory and Investment Behavior, 1996, Tax Policy and the Cost of Capital, 1996; author: (with E. Hanushek) Improving America's Schools, 1996; author: Aggregate Consumer Behavior, 1997, Measuring Social Welfare, 1997, Econometric General Equilibrium Modeling, 1996, Energy, The Environment and Economic Growth, 1996, Econometric Modeling of Producer Behavior, 2000; author: (with Kun-Young Yun) Lifting the Burden: Tax Reform, the Cost of Capital, and U.S. Economic Growth, 2001; author: (with Charles Wessner) Measuring and Sustaining the New Economy, 2002; author: Economic Growth in the Information Age, 2002; author: (with Frank Lee) Industry-Level Productivity and International Competitiveness Between Canada and the United States; author: (with Charles Wessner) Productivity and Cyclicality in Semiconductors, 2004; author: Economic Growth in Canada and the United States in the Information Age, 2004; author: (with Mun S. Ho and Kevin J. Stirch) Information Technology and The American Growth Resurgence, 2005. Fellow AAAS, NAS (chair sect. 54 Econ. Scis. 2000-03), Am. Philos. Soc., Econometric Soc. (pres. 1987), Am. Statis. Assn., Am. Acad. Arts and Scis.; mem. Am. Econ. Assn. (John Bates Clark medal 1971, pres. 2000), Royal Swedish Acad. Scis. Home: 1010 Memorial Dr Cambridge MA 02138-4859 Office: Harvard U Littauer 122 Cambridge MA 02138-3001 Business E-Mail: djorgenson@harvard.edu.

JORGENSON, MARY ANN, lawyer; b. Gallipolis, Ohio, 1941; BA, Agnes Scott Coll., 1963; MA, Harvard U., 1964; JD, Case Western Res. U., 1975. Bar: Ohio 1975, N.Y. 1982. Ptnr., chair firm's corp. practice Squire, Sanders & Dempsey, 1990—. Office: Squire Sanders & Dempsey LLP 127 Public Sq Ste 4900 Cleveland OH 44114-1284 E-mail: mjorgenson@ssd.com.

JORIS-QUINTON, LIESBET, internal medicine physician; b. Antwerpen, Belgium, Oct. 2, 1958; MD, U. Instelling, 1984. Diplomate Am. Bd. Internal Medicine. Resident internal medicine U. Antwerp, 1984-87, 91-92; post doctoral fellow physiology Stanford U., Calif., 1987—88, resident internal medicine, 1993—95; post doctoral fellow physiology U. Calif. Riverside, 1988-91, 92-93; internist in hosp. medicine Scripps Clinic, San Diego, 1997—. Mem. ACP. Office: Green Hosp of Scripps Clinic 10666 N Torrey Pines Rd La Jolla CA 92037-7387 E-mail: lquinton@scrippsclinic.com.

JORTNER, JOSHUA, physical chemist, educator; b. Poland, Mar. 14, 1933; s. Arthur and Regina Jortner; m. Ruth Sanger, Jan. 26, 1960; 2 children. PhD, Hebrew U. Jerusalem; D (hon.), Ben Gurion U. Negev, Israel, 1985, Pierre and Marie Curie U., Paris, 1986; DSc (hon.), Tech. U. Munich, 1996, The Technion, Israel Inst. Tech. Instr. dept. phys. chemistry Hebrew U. Jerusalem, 1961-62, sr. lectr., 1963-65; assoc. prof. Tel Aviv U., 1965-66, prof., 1966—, head Sch. Chemistry, 1966—72, dep. rector, 1966-69, v.p., 1970-72. Rsch. assoc. U. Chgo., 1962—64, vis. prof., 1965—71, H.C. Orsted Inst., U. Copenhagen, 1974, 78, U. Calif., Berkeley, 1975; Sherman Fairchild disting. scholar, vis. prof. Calif. Inst. Tech., 1977; Hinshelwood lectr. Oxford U., 1995; Blaise Pascal prof. Ecole Normale Supérieure, Paris, 1999—2000. Contbr. over 700 articles to profl. jours.; author, editor: 23 books. Recipient award, Internat. Acad. Quantum Sci., 1972, Weizmann prize, 1973, Rothschild prize, 1976, Kolthof prize, 1976, Israel prize in Chemistry, 1982, Wolf prize, 1988, Hon. J. Heyrovsky Gold medal, 1993, August-Wilhelm-von-Hofmann medal, 1995, R.S. Mulliken medal, 1998, J.O. Hirschfelder prize, 1999, Maria Sklodowska-Curie medal, 2003, medal, Israeli Chem. Soc., 2004. Mem.: AAAS, Am. Acad. Arts and Scis., Internat. Union Pure and Applied Chemistry (v.p. 1996—97, pres. 1998—99, past pres. 2000—01), Royal Netherlands Acad. Arts and Scis. (fgn.), Learned Soc. of Czech Repub., U.S. Nat. Acad. Scis. (fgn. assoc.), Indian Acad. Sci., German Acad. Scis. Leopoldina, Romanian Acad. Scis., European Acad. Scis. and Arts, Russian Acad. Scis. (fgn.), Polish Acad. Scis., Danish Acad. Scis. and Letters (fgn. mem.), Am. Philos. Soc., Internat. Acad. Quantum Molecular Scis, Israel Acad. Scis. and Humanities (v.p. 1980—86, pres. 1986—95). Avocation: science policy. Office: Tel Aviv U Sch Chemistry Ramat-Aviv 69978 Tel Aviv Israel also: Israel Acad Scis-Humanities Einstein Sq PO Box 4040 91040 Jerusalem Israel Office Phone: +972 3 6408322. Business E-Mail: jortner@chemsg1.tau.ac.il.

JORTNER, JULIUS, materials engineer, consultant; b. Cernauti, Rumania, Mar. 3, 1936; came to U.S. 1946; s. Michael Maria (Spielvogel) J.; m. Carolee June Robbins, May 25, 1975. BME, Cooper Union, 1956; MS in Engring., UCLA, 1968. Rsch. engr. Rocketdyne divsn. North Am. Aviation, Canoga Park, Calif., 1956-68, McDonnell Douglas Astronautics Co., Huntington Beach, Calif., 1968-79, Sci. Applications, Inc., Irvine, Calif., 1979-82; pres. Jortner Rsch. & Engring. Inc., Pacific City, Oreg., 1982—2002. Lectr. in field. Editor: Thermomechanical Behavior of High-Temperature Composites, 1982, Thermostructural Behavior of Carbon-Carbon Composites, 1986; contbr. articles to profl. jours. Mem. ASME (structure and materials com. 1979-91), ASTM (mem. com. D-30 on advanced composites 1969-93), Am. Carbon Soc. (Graffin lectureship 1988, adv. com. 1995-2001), Nestucca Valley C. of C. (pres. 1996-97). E-mail: jjortner@oregoncoast.com.

JOSCELYN, KENT BUCKLEY, lawyer; b. Binghamton, Dec. 18, 1936; s. Raymond Miles and Gwen Buckley (Smith) J.; children: Kathryn Anne, Jennifer Sheldon. BS, Union Coll., 1957; JD, Albany (N.Y.) Law Sch., 1960. Bar: N.Y. 1961, U.S. Ct. Mil. Appeals 1962, D.C., 1967, Mich. 1979. Atty. adviser hdqts. USAF, Washington, 1965-67; assoc. prof. forensic studies U. Ind., Bloomington, 1967-76; dir. Inst. Rsch. in Pub. Safety, 1970-75; head policy analysis divsn. Highway Safety Rsch. Inst. U. Mich., Ann Arbor, 1976-81; dir. transp. planning and policy Urban Tech. Environ. Planning Program, Ann Arbor, 1981-84; prin. Joscelyn and Treat P.C., Ann Arbor, 1981—93, Joscelyn, McNair & Jeffrey P.C., Ann Arbor, 1993-2001. Cons. Law Enforcement Assistance Adminstrn., U.S. Dept. Justice, 1969-72; Gov.'s appointee as regional dir. Ind. Criminal Justice Planning Agy., 1969-72; vice chmn. Ind. Organized Crime Prevention Coun., 1969-72; commr. pub. safety City of Bloomington, Ind., 1974-76. Editor Internat. Jour. Criminal Justice. Capt. USAF, 1961-64. Mem. NAS, ABA, NRC, D.C. Bar Assn., N.Y. State Bar Assn., Internat. Bar Assn., Transp. Rsch. Bd. (chmn. motor vehicle and traffic law com. 1979-82), Am. Soc. Criminology (life), Assn. for Advancement Automotive Medicine (life), Acad. Criminal Justice Scis. (life), Assn. Chiefs Police (assoc.), Nat. Safety Coun., Assn. Former Intelligence Officers (life), Product Liability Adv. Coun., Sigma Xi, Theta Delta Chi Office: Kent B Joscelyn PC PO Box 130589 Ann Arbor MI 48113-0589 E-mail: kbjpc@earthlink.net.

JOSE, PEDRO A., physician; b. Dingras, Ilocos Norte, Philippines, Dec. 6, 1942; s. Urbano Llanes Jose, Filomena Andres Jose; m. Nora Doctor Doctor; children: Kristina, Maria. MD magna cum laude, U. Santo Tomas, Manila, Philippines, 1965; PhD, Georgetown U., 1976. Cert. pediatrics 1970, pediatric nephrology 1974, hypertension 1999. Prof. pediatrics, physiology and biophysics Georgetown U. Sch. Medicine, Washington, 1983—. Chair cardiovascular and renal study sect. B NIH, Bethesda, 1996—98; vis. prof. cardiovascular sci. Sun Yatsen U. Med. Scis., Guangzhou, China, 2002—; adj. prof. pediatrics George Washington U. Sch. Medicine, Washington, 2002—; dir. MD/PhD program Georgetown U., 1997—99, chair radiation safety com., 1997—; Louis K. Dahl meml. lectr. Am. Heart Assn., 2003. Contbr. scientific papers to profl. jours. Profl. and pub edn. com. Am. Heart Assn., Dallas, 2000—02; chair edn. com. Nat.Kidney Found. Capital Area, Washington. Recipient Interstate Postgrad. Med. Society award, 1972, Apolinario Mabini award, 1990. Fellow: Council High Blood Pressure Rsch.; mem.: Am. Soc. Hypertension, Am. Soc. Nephrology, Am. Heart Assn. (coun. high blood pressure rsch.), Am. Soc. Pediatric Nephrology (pres. 1990—91). Roman Catholic. Avocation: violin. Office: Georgetown U Med Ctr 3800 Reservoir Rd NW Washington DC 20007-2197 Office Phone: 202-444-8675.

JOSEFF, JOAN CASTLE, manufacturing executive; b. Alta., Can., Aug. 12, 1922; naturalized U.S. citizen, 1945; d. Edgar W. and Lottie (Coates) Castle; BA in Psychology, UCLA; widowed; 1 son, Jeffrey Rene. With Joseff-Hollywood, jewelry manufacture and rental and aircraft components and missiles, Burbank, Calif., 1939—, chmn. bd., pres., sec.-treas. Numerous TV appearances including CBS This Morning, Australia This Morning, Am. Movie Channel. Mem. Burbank Salary Task Force, 1979—, L.A. County Earthquake Fact-Finding Commn., 1981—; bd. dirs. San Fernando Valley area chpt. Am. Cancer Soc., treas., Genesis Energy Systems, Inc., 1993—; mem. Rep. Cen. Com.; del. Rep. Nat. Conv., 1980, 84, 88, 92, 96, 2000; active Beautiful People Award Com. Honoring John Wayne Carcer Clinic; appointed by Gov. Wilson to Barber and Cosmotology Bd; appointed br Pres. Clinton to Selective Svc. System. Recipient Women in Achievement award Soroptomist Internat., 1988, Rep. Congl. Com. award, 2004, Bus. Woman of Yr. award, 2004. Mem. Women of Motion Picture Industry (hon. life), Nat. Fedn. Rep. Women (bd. dir., Caring for Am. award 1986), Calif. Rep. Women (bd. dir., treas. 1986-90), North Hollywood Rep. Women (pres. 1981-82, parliamentarian), Nat. Fedn. of Rep (voting mem., program chair, 1994—, bylaws chair 1998—), Calif. Fedn. of Rep. Women (chaplain, Americanism chmn. so. div., regent chmn. Women of Achievement award 1988), L.A. County Fedn. of Rep. Women (scholarship chmn.). Home: 10060 Toluca Lake Ave Toluca Lake CA 91602-2924 Office: 129 E Providencia Ave Burbank CA 91502-1922 Office Phone: 323-849-2306.

JOSEFOWICZ, GREGORY P., retail executive; Grad., Mich. State U.; MBA, Northwestern U. Kellogg Sch. Mgmt., 1979. With Jewel-Osco (Albertson's Inc.), 1968—99; pres. Jewel-Osco, 1997—99; pres., CEO Borders Group Inc., Ann Arbor, Mich., 1999—, mem. bd. dirs., 1999—, chmn., 2002—. Mem. bd. advisors C.S. Mott Children's Hosp., Ann Arbor, Key Bank (Mich. dist.), Ann Arbor; mem. bd. dirs. Spartan Stores, Inc., Grand Rapids, Mich., Ryerson Tull, Chgo.; mem. advisory bd. Northwestern U. Kellogg Sch. Mgmt. Recipient Retailer Yr., Ill. Retail Merchants Assn., 1999. Office: Borders Group 100 Phoenix Dr Ann Arbor MI 48108*

JOSEL, MARK, physician; b. Bklyn., Jan. 26, 1928; s. Jacob and Tessie Josel; m. Anne Doolittle Josel; children: Randi, John, James, Nanci, Jack. BS, Guilford Coll., 1948; MS, Chgo. Med. Sch., 1952, MD, 1953. Physician pvt. practice, Bloomfield, Conn., 1959—. Lt. cmdr. USNR, 1953—59, Korea. Recipient Wright Brothers' 50 Yr. Safe Pilot award, FAA, 2005. Avocations: flying, skiing, kayaking. Office: Mark Josel MD 4 Northwestern Dr Bloomfield CT 06002 Office Phone: 860-243-3344. Office Fax: 860-242-2804.

JOSELL, JESSICA (JESSICA WECHSLER), public relations executive; b. Balt., June 17, 1943; d. Maury J. and Rose E. (Lodin) Snyder; m. Neil B. Josell, Apr. 30, 1965 (dec. Nov. 1967); m. Steven James Wechsler, Jan. 12, 1980. BA, U. Fla., 1965. V.p., gen. mgr. Morton Dennis Wax & Assocs., N.Y.C., 1976-81; v.p. The Raleigh Group, Ltd., N.Y.C., 1981-87; pres. Josell Comm., Inc., N.Y.C., 1981—. Exec. officer, bd. dirs. The Bridge, Inc., N.Y.C. Mem.: N.Y. Women in Film and TV. Home and Office: Josell Comm Inc 185 W End Ave Ste 22C New York NY 10023-5549 Office Phone: 212-877-5560. Business E-Mail: jessica@josellpr.com.

JOSELYN, JO ANN, space scientist; b. St. Francis, Kans., Oct. 5, 1943; d. James Jacob and Josephine Felzien (Firkins) Cram. BS in Applied Math., U. Colo., 1965, MS in Astro Geophysics, 1967, PhD in Astro Geophysics, 1978. Research asst. NASA-Manned Space Ctr., Houston, 1966; physicist NOAA-Space Environ. Lab., Boulder, Colo., 1967-78; space scientist NOAA-Space Environ. Ctr., Boulder, 1978-99; chief Geospace Branch, 1992-95; sec.-gen. Internat. Union Geodesy and Geophysics, 1999—. U.S. del. study group 6 Consultive Com. for Ionospheric Radio, 1981, 83; mem. com. on data mgmt. and computation NASA Space Sci. Bd., 1988. Mem. U. Colo. Grad. Sch. Alumni Coun., 1986-90, U. Colo. Engring. Devel. Coun., 1991-99, U. Colo. Adv. Coun. for the Women in Engring. Program, 1992-98, Grad. Sch. Adv. Coun.; bd. trustees U. Colo. Found., 2002-. Recipient unit citation NOAA, 1971, 80, 85, 86, sustained superior performance award 1985, 87-90, 92, 94; group achievement award NASA, 1983, Disting. Engring. Alumnus award U. Colo., 1987, Dir.'s award Space Environ. Lab., 1991, 95, Pacesetter award Boulder County, 1994, Sec. Commerce award for Customer Svc. Excellence, 1994, George Norlin award U. Colo. Alumni Assn., 2000; elected to U. Colo. Disting. Alumni Gallery, 1995; named Woman of Achievement, Zonta Club, Boulder, 1996; named to Colo. Women's Hall of Fame, 2002; fellow Sci. and Tech. Agy. Japan, 1990-91. Mem. AAAS, AAUW, PEO, Am. Women in Sci., Am. Geophys. Union, Union Radio Sci. Internat. (commns. G and H, membership chair of commn. H 1993-96), Internat. Assn. Geomagnetism and Aeronomy (co-chair Divsn. V on observatories, instruments, indices and data 1991-95, sec.-gen. 1995-99), Internat. Astron. Union (commns. 10 and 49), Rotary Internat., Ikebana Internat., Sigma Xi, Tau Beta Pi, Sigma Tau. Republican. Methodist. Office: Univ Colo CIRES Campus Box 216 Boulder CO 80309-0216 Business E-Mail: jjoselyn@cires.colorado.edu.

JOSEPH, ALAN LLOYD, lawyer; b. Monticello, N.Y., Dec. 28, 1953; BS in Criminal Justice magna cum laude, Wilmington Coll., 1974; JD, Cardozo Sch. Law, N.Y.C., 1979. Bar: N.Y. 1979, U.S. Dist. Ct. (so. dist.) N.Y. Atty. Baum & Shawn, Monticello, 1980; paralegal, investigator Sullivan County Legal Aid, Monticello, 1974-76; staff atty. Sullivan County legal Aid, Monticello, 1980-83; asst. dist. atty. Orange County Dist. Atty., Goshen, N.Y., 1983-85, chief asst. dist. atty., 1985-91; sole practitioner Goshen, 1991—. Mem. N.Y. State Bar Assn. Office: 261 Greenwich Ave Goshen NY 10924-2028

JOSEPH, ALLAN JAY, lawyer; b. Chgo., Feb. 4, 1938; s. George S. and Emily (Miller) Cohen; m. Phyllis L. Freedman, Sept. 1, 1958; children—Elizabeth, Susan, Katherine. BBA, U. Wis., Madison, 1959; JD cum laude, 1962. Bar: Wis. bar 1962, Calif. bar 1964. Ptnr. Pettit & Martin, San Francisco, 1965-80, Rogers, Joseph, O'Donnell & Phillips, San Francisco, 1981—. Editor: (prof. journal) Wis. Law Rev., author articles law jours. Served to capt. JACG AUS, 1962-65. Am. Bar Found. fellow, 1978—Mem.ABA (treas. 2002—, nat. chmn. pub. contract law sect. 1977-78, ho. of dels. 1980-84, bd. govs. 1995-98, chair fin. com. 1997-98), FBA, Am. Bar Retirement Assn. (trustee 1984-92, pres. 1989-90), State Bar Calif., Nat. Contract Mgmt. Assn., Order of Coif. Home: 2461 Washington St San Francisco CA 94115-1816 Office: 311 California St Fl 10 San Francisco CA 94104-2614

JOSEPH, ANNE M., lawyer, law educator; BA, Williams Coll., 1992; M.Phil., Cambridge Univ., 1995; JD, Yale Univ., 2000; PhD, Harvard Univ., 2002. Law clk. U.S. Ct. Appeals (D.C. Cir.), Washington, 2000—01; atty. U.S. Dept. Just. Civil Div., Washington, 2001—03; law clk. to Ruth Bader Ginsburg U.S. Supreme Ct., Washington, 2003—04; asst. prof. Law Sch. U. Calif., Berkeley, 2004—. Contbr. articles to prof. jour. Office: Univ Calif Berkeley Law Sch 433 North Addition Berkeley CA 94720-7200

JOSEPH, ANTHONY AARON, lawyer; b. Birmingham, Ala., Oct. 8, 1953; s. David Joseph and Lucille (Townsend) Tarver; m. Cassandra Andry, July 2, 1994; children: Kevin, Justin Gray, Aaron. BS, Vanderbilt U., 1975; M in City Planning, Howard U., 1977; JD, Cumberland Sch. Law, 1980. Bar: U.S. Dist. Ct. (mid., no. dists.) Ala. 1980, U.S. Ct. Appeals (11th cir.) 1980. Asst. dist. atty. Dist. Atty.'s Office, Bessemer, Ala., 1980—82; spl. agt. FBI, Birmingham, 1982—86; asst. U.S. atty. U.S. Atty.'s Office, Birmingham, 1986—90; ptnr. Johnston Barton Proctor & Powell, Birmingham, 1991—. Adj. prof. Miles Coll., Birmingham, 1990—94, Cumberland Law Sch., Birmingham, 1993—. Bd. dirs. ARC, Birmingham, 2001, YMCA, Birmingham, 2002—; mem. steering com. Leadership Birmingham, 2002. Mem.: ABA (mem. criminal justice coun. 2001—), Birmingham Bar Assn. (treas. 2002—), Ala. State Bar (bar commr. 2001—). Office: Johnston Barton Proctor and Powell LLP 1901 6th Ave N Ste 2900 Birmingham AL 35203 Office Phone: 205-458-9447. Business E-Mail: aaj@jbpp.com.

JOSEPH, ANTHONY BARNETT, psychiatrist; b. Bristol, England, Feb. 11, 1955; came to U.S., 1965; s. Bertram Leon and Ada Emilie (Goldschmidt) J.; m. Karen Beverly Spinks, June 20, 1980; m. James Edward, Oliver Charles. BA, MA, CUNY, 1975; BA, U. Oxford, Oxford, England, 1978; M.B., B. Chir., U. Cambridge, Cambridge, England, 1980. Diplomate Am. Bd. Psychiatry and Neurology. House surgeon Hillingdon Hosp., London, 1981; house physician Ashford Hosp., London, 1981-82; resident in psychiatry St. Elizabeth's Hosp., Boston, 1982-85; Asst. pschiatrist Inst. Law and Psychiatry, McLean Hosp., Belmont, Mass., 1985-86; dir. neuropsychiatry clinic Mass. Mental Health Ctr., Boston, 1985-89; clin. instr. psychiatry Harvard Med. Sch., Boston, 1986-88; assoc. med. dir. Medfield State Hosp., Medfield, Mass., 1986-90; sr. cons. forensic psychiatrist Mass. Dept. Mental Health, Boston, 1988-91; asst. clin. prof. psychiatry Harvard Med. Sch., Boston, 1988-95, assoc. clin. prof., 1995—, mem. continuing med. edn. faculty, 1988—; med. dir. Core Mgmt., Inc., Lexington, Mass., 1989-93; dir. neurorehab. unit N.E. Specialty Hosp., Stoughton, Mass., 1990—. Profl. adv. bd. neurobehavioral unit McLean Hosp., Belmont, Mass., 1987-90, Venture Mentoring Svc., MIT, 2000—. Contbr. articles to profl. jours.; reviewer Jour. Clin. Psychiatry, 1987—. Fellow Royal Soc. Medicine; mem. Royal Soc. Chemistry, Am. Psychiat. Assn., Boston Soc. Neurology and Psychiatry, Am. Neuropsychiat. Assn. Office: NE Specialty Hosp Neurorehab Unit 909 Sumner St Stoughton MA 02072

JOSEPH, BABU, chemical educator; b. Trivandrum, Kerala, India, Feb. 12, 1950; came to U.S., 1971; s. Thomas and Rose; m. Philomina Prasad; children: Mili, Neeraj, Sonia. BS, IIT, Kanpur, India, 1971; MS, Case Western Res. U., 1974, PhD, 1975. Rsch. assoc. MIT, Cambridge, Mass., 1975—78; asst. prof. to prof. Washington U., St. Louis, 1978—2002; chair chem. engring. dept. U. South Fla., Tampa, 2001—; vis. prof. U. of Calif., Berkeley, 1985—86. Author: Real-Time Personal Computing, 1988; editor: Wavelet Applications in Process Engineering, 1994, Model-based Process Control, 2002. Named Engring. Prof. of Yr., Washington U., 1984. Mem. Am. Inst. Chem. Engrs. (continuing edn. lectr. 1984-99), Am. Chem. Soc. Avocation: reading. Home: 5006 Devon Park Dr Tampa FL 33647-2735 Office: U South Fla Chem Engring Dept Tampa FL 33620

JOSEPH, BRIAN DANIEL, language educator; b. Nov. 22, 1951; AB cum laude, Yale U., 1973; AM, Harvard U., 1976, PhD, 1978. Asst. prof. Ohio State U., Columbus, 1979—85, assoc. prof., 1985—88, dept. chmn., 1987—97, prof. linguistics, 1988—; Kenneth E. Naylor prof. South Slavic languages and linguistics, 1997—. Session lectr. hist. linguistics U. Alberta, 1978—79; vis. prof. U. Aegean, 1989, U. Calif., Santa Cruz, 1991, U. Ill., 1999, Mich. State U., 2003; vis. tchg. fellow U. Canterbury, New Zealand, 1997; mem. cognitive sci. planning com. Ohio State U., 1989—91, mem. program rev. com. dept. Slavic languages and literatures, 1995—97, mem. eval. com. ctrl. adminstrn., 1997—98, mem. South Asia coord. com., 2001—02, mem. steering com. Ohio Tchg. Enhancement Program, 2000—01, mem. pres. and provost's adv. com., 2003—, numerous others; cons. various univs. Co-editor (with Johanna DeStefano, Neil Jacobs and Ilse Lehiste): When Languages Collide: Perspectives on Language Conflict, Language Competition, and Language Coexistence, 2003; contbr. articles to profl. jours., chapters to books. Recipient numerous fellowships and grants. Fellow: Am. Acad. Arts & Sciences; mem.: Bulgarian Studies Assn., Am. Assn. Advancement Slavic Studies, SE European Studies Assn., Am. Assn. Tchrs. Slavic and East European Languages, Modern Greek Studies Assn. (mem. exec. com. 1991—93, chmn. publications com. 1995—99, mem. symposium com. 2000—01), Linguistic Soc. Am. (mem. summer inst. fellowship com. 1995, mem. nom. com. 1996—97, chmn. nom. com. 1998, program com. cons. 1998—99, mem. ad hoc com. former inst. dirs. 1993—). Office: Dept Linguistics Ohio State Univ 222 Oxley Hall Columbus OH 43210-1298 Office Phone: 614-292-4981. Office Fax: 614-292-8833. E-mail: bjoseph@ling.ohio-state.edu.*

JOSEPH, CHARLES M., academic administrator; MusB, W.Va. U.; MusM, U. Ill.; PhD U. Cin. Mem. faculty dept. music Skidmore Coll., Saratoga Springs, NY, 1985—, William R. Kenan Endowed Chair Liberal Arts, 1995—, assoc. dean faculty, 2001—02, interim v.p. acad. affairs, dean faculty, prof. music. Chair dept. music Skidmore Coll., 1986—91, Moseley lectr., 1993; rschr. Paul Sacher Stiftung, Basel, Switzerland; Howard D. Rothschild vis. fellow Harvard U. Theatre Collection, 1999—2000; presenter in field. Author: Stravinsky and the Piano, 1983, Stravinsky Inside Out, 2001; contbr. articles to profl. jours., ency., anthologies, chapters to books. Office: Skidmore Coll 815 N Broadway Saratoga Springs NY 12866

JOSEPH, DANIEL DONALD, aeronautical engineer, educator; b. Chgo., Mar. 26, 1929; s. Samuel and Mary (Simon) J.; m. Ellen Broida, Dec. 18, 1949 (div. 1979); children: Karen, Michael, Charles; m. Kay Jaglo, Feb. 9, 1990. MA in Sociology, U. Chgo., 1950; BS in Mech. Engring, Ill. Inst. Tech., 1959, MS, 1960, PhD, 1963. Asst. prof. mech. engring. Ill. Inst. Tech., 1962-63; mem. faculty U. Minn., 1963—, assoc. prof. fluid mechanics 1965-69, prof. aerospace engring. and mechanics, 1969-90, Russell J. Penrose prof. Mpls., 1990—. Author 4 books on stability and bifurcation theory and fluid dynamics; editor 3 books; editorial bd. SIAM Jour. Applied Math, Jour. Applied Mechanics, Jour. Non-Newtonian Fluid Mechanics, others; contbr. articles to sci. jours. Guggenheim fellow, 1969-70, Timoshenko medal Am. Soc. of Mechanical Engineers, 1995. Mem. NAS, ASME, NAE, Am. Phys. Soc., Am. Acad. Arts and Scis., Soc. Engring. Sci. (G.I. Taylor medal 1990, Bingham medal Soc. of Rheology). Achievements include contbns. to math. theory of hydrodynamic stability; rheology of viscoelastic fluids. Home: 1920 S 1st St Apt 2302 Minneapolis MN 55454-1279 Office: U Minn Dept Aerospace Engring 110 Union St SE Minneapolis MN 55455-0153 Office Phone: 612-625-0309. Business E-Mail: joseph@aem.umn.edu.

JOSEPH, ELEANOR ANN, health science association administrator, consultant; b. Cleve., Mar. 6, 1944; d. Emil and Eleanor (Leelais) Dienes; m. Abraham Albert Joseph, Oct. 28, 1984 (dec.). BS in Math. cum laude, Cleve. State U., 1978, MPA in Health Care Adminstrn., 1991. Cert. profl. healthcare quality, coding specialist, accredited records technician, registered record adminstr., health info. adminstr., cert. in healthcare privacy. Asst. dir. med. records Suburban Hosp., Warrensville Heights, Ohio, 1963-77; coder Shaker Med. Ctr., Shaker Heights, Ohio, 1965, Huron Rd. Hosp., Cleve., 1965; instr. Cuyahoga C.C., Cleve., 1970-72; dir. med. records Hillcrest Hosp., Mayfield Heights, Ohio, 1977-84; med. records technician Vis. Nurse Assn., Cleve., 1985; coord. med. record svcs. Ctr. for Health Affairs Greater Cleve. Hosp. Assn., 1985-88, dir. coding svcs. Ctr. Health Affairs, 1988-89, dir. health record svcs. Ctr. Health Affairs, 1989-98; v.p. health info. mgmt. svcs. Greater Cleve. Healthcare Assn., 1999—2004, privacy officer Ctr. Health Affairs, 2001—04, v.p. revenue cycle mgmt. Ctr. Health Affairs, 2004; ind. health info. mgmt. cons., 2004—. Coding instr. cmty. edn. dept. Cleve. State U., 1998—; instr. cmty. edn. Lakeland CC, adv. task force cert. program med. office mgmt., 1992—96, coding tchr., 1999; spkrs. bur. Hillcrest Hosp., Mayfield Heights, 1978—84; adv. com. Cuyahoga CC, 1973—80, 1994—, faculty, 1999—2003; coord. seminars in field; cons. in field. Co-author: (manual) Quality Assurance Program for Medical Records Deparment, 1981, Dollars and Sense: A Reference Guide to Coding and Prospective Payment System Reimbursement Issues, 1988; co-editor: Care and Management of Health Care Records, 1988, 1992. Active Holden Arboretum, Kirtland, Ohio, 1975—, Ohio Hist. Soc., Columbus, 1975—. Recipient Outstanding Svc. award, Ctr. Health Affairs/Greater Cleve. Healthcare Assn., 1997. Mem.: N.E. Ohio Health Info. Mgmt. Assn. (chmn. coding roundtable 1993—), Ohio Health Info. Mgmt. Assn. (project leader alliances 1992—94, data quality reimbursement coun. 1992—, liaison to ambulatory sect. 1994—96, project leader developing coding seminars 1996—97, co-chmn. data quality and reimbursement coun. 1996—98, pres.-elect 1998—99, pres. 1999—2000, dir. and del. coord. 2000—01, del. to Am. Health Info. Mgmt. Assn. 2002—03, Disting. Mem. award 1997, Profl. Achievement award 2003), Ohio Assn. Healthcare Quality, Ohio Med. Record Assn. (alt. del. 1982, med. record coun. 1985—92, del. for state assn. mem. at nat. ann. mtg. 1989, legis. com. 1989—90, del. for state assn. mem. at nat. ann. mtg. 1990), N.E. Ohio Med. Record Assn. (treas. 1979, v.p. 1980, pres. 1982—83, counselor 1983, ednl. com. 1984, chmn. nominating com, 1986, ednl. com. 1987, cons. com. 1987—91, audit com., membership com., bylaws com., pub. rels. com.), East Ohio Med. Record Assn., Nat. Assn. Healthcare Quality, Am. Guild Patient Accts. Mgrs., Am. Health Info. Mgmt. Assn. (quality assurance and long term care sects., ambulatory records sec. 1992—2001, del. 1997—2000, item writing panel for cert. coding exams 1997—2003, accredited record tech. practitioner 2000—02, co-chmn. coun. cert. 2001, chair coun. on cert. 2002, nominating com. 2002—03), Am. Med. Record Assn. (cons. roster 1976, charter mem. assembly on edn. 1989), Am. Acad. Profl. Coders (treas. local chpt. 1994, endorsed as tchr. for profl. med. coder curriculum, cert.), Holden Arboretum, Northeastern Ohio Assn. for Healthcare Quality, Cleve. City Club. Lutheran. Avocations: cultural events, nature walks, golf, music. Personal E-mail: josephclvlnd@aol.com.

JOSEPH, GEORGE, insurance company executive; b. 1921; BS, Harvard Univ., 1949. CLU, CPCU. Sys. analyst, salesman Occidental Ins., 1949—54; ins. agency owner, 1954—62; founder, chmn. & CEO Mercury Ins. Group, LA, 1962—. Served as B-17 navigator USAAF, WWII. Office: Mercury Insurance Group 4484 Wilshire Blvd Los Angeles CA 90010*

JOSEPH, GREGORY NELSON, media critic, writer, actor; b. Kansas City, Mo., Aug. 25, 1946; s. Theodore Leopold and Marcella Kathryn (Nelson) J.; m. Mary Martha Stahler, July 21, 1973; children: John, Jacqueline, Caroline. AA, Met. C.C., Kansas City, 1967; BA with honors, U. Mo., Kansas City, 1969. Intern, cub reporter Kansas City Star-Times, 1965-67; feature writer, asst. city editor The Pasadena (Calif.) Union, 1971-73; investigative reporter The Pasadena Star-News, 1973-75; bus. writer The Riverside (Calif.) Press Enterprise, 1975-76; reporter, consumer writer, feature writer, TV critic The San Diego Tribune, 1976-90; TV columnist The Ariz. Republic, Phoenix, 1990-94; media critic, writer, 1994—. Recipient various writing awards Copley Newspapers, Pasadena and San Diego, 1971-73, 83, Pub. Awareness award San Diego Psychiat. Physicians, cert. of appreciation Epilepsy Soc. San Diego County, 1989. Mem.: Internat. Platform Assn., TV Critics Assn., NATAS (bd. govs. 1990—92), SAG (Ariz. br. coun., nat. com. for performers with disabilities), Phi Kappa Phi. Roman Catholic. Avocations: scriptwriting, reading, writing about hollywood, appearing at schools and on radio and tv to discuss tv and film. Home: 4864 W Alice Ave Glendale AZ 85302-5107 Address: Victoria Allen Literary Agy 1489 E Thousand Oaks Blvd Ste 2 Thousand Oaks CA 91362-6207 also: Dani's Talent Agency One E Camelback Rd Ste 550 Phoenix AZ 85012 Office Phone: 623-934-6142. Personal E-mail: kckidjoseph@msn.com.

JOSEPH, GREGORY PAUL, lawyer; b. Mpls., Jan. 18, 1951; s. George Phillip and Josephine Sheha (Nofel) J.; m. Barbara, Jan. 19, 1979. BA summa cum laude, U. Minn., 1972, JD cum laude, 1975. Bar: Minn. 1975, N.Y. 1979, U.S. Dist. Ct. Minn. 1975, U.S. Dist. Ct. (so. and ea. dist.) N.Y. 1979, U.S. Ct. Appeals (8th cir.) 1976, U.S. Ct. Appeals (2d cir.) 1979, U.S. Ct. Appeals (D.C. cir.) 1980, U.S. Supreme Ct. 1983, U.S. Tax Ct. 1987, U.S. Ct. Appeals (7th cir.) 1989, (5th cir.) 1992, (6th cir.) 1999, (11th cir.) 2002. Pvt. practice, Mpls., 1975-79; assoc. Fried, Frank, Harris, Shriver & Jacobson, N.Y.C., 1979-82, ptnr., 1982-01, chair litigation dept., 2000-01; chmn. Gregory P. Joseph Law Offices, LLC, N.Y.C., 2001—. Asst. U.S. spl. prosecutor N.Y.C., 1981—82, Washington, 1981—82; mem. adv. com. on fed. rules of evidence U.S. Judicial Conf, 1993—99; co-chair 3d Circuit Task Force on Selection of Class Counsel, 2001; chair com. of lawyers to enhance the jury process N.Y. State Cts., 1998—99, mem. adv. com. on civil practice, 1999—2002. Author: Modern Visual Evidence, 1984, Sanctions: The Federal Law of Litigation Abuse, 1989, 3rd edit., 2000, Civil RICO: A Definitive Guide, 1992, 2d edit., 2000; co-author: Evidence in America, 1987; editor: Emerging Problems Under the Federal Rules of Evidence, 1983, reporter 2d edit., 1991; co-editor: Sanctions: Rule 11 and Other Powers, 1986, 2d rev. edit., 1988; editorial bd. Moore's Fed. Practice, 1995—; contbr. articles to profl. jours. U.S. Supreme Ct. Hist. Soc., 2005—. Fellow Am. Bar Found., Am. Coll. Trial Lawyers (chmn. fed. rules of civil procedure com. 2000-02, regent 2002—); mem. ABA (chmn. litig. sect. 1997-98), Am. Law Inst., N.Y. Bar Assn. (chair trial evidence com. 1988-94), Minn. Bar Assn., N.Y. County Lawyers Assn., Assn. of Bar of City of N.Y. (chmn. profl. responsibility com. 1993-96, mem. exec. com. 1999-2003). Office: Gregory P Joseph Law Offices LLC 805 Third Ave Fl 31 New York NY 10022 Home: 845 United Nations Plz Apt 55D New York NY 10017-3536 Office Phone: 212-407-1210. E-mail: gjoseph@josephnyc.com.

JOSEPH, J. JONATHAN, interior designer; b. Gloucester, Mass., Jan. 14, 1932; s. George Stephen and Maryann (Lattof) J. Cert., Vesper George Sch. Art, Boston, 1952; student theater design, Boston Conservatory Music, 1951. Assoc. designer Reva Lewitt, Boston, 1952-67, Peter Schifando & Co., L.A., 1995—; owner interior design bus. Boston, 1967—; pres. Seraphim Galleries, Inc., L.A., 1998—. Cons. in fine arts; spl. research 19th century glass in Am., also Tiffany glass; exhibited Tiffany glass collection Mus. Fine Art, Boston, 1965, Worcester (Mass.) Art Mus., 1968. Important decorating works include: assoc. designer on the restoration of Plaza Hotel, N.Y.C., assoc. designer Ronald Reagan Presdl. Libr., Simi Valley, Calif., 1991. Author: Jane Peterson, An American Artist, 1981; co-curator: (exhbn.) Jane Peterson: An Impression, Hickory (N.C.) Mus. of Art, 1987; contbr. revs. and articles to profl. publs. Recipient award Internat. V'Soske Rug Design. Mem. Am. Soc. Interior

Designers (chmn. bd. New Eng. chpt. 1965-66, chpt. v.p. 1969-71, pres. 1971-72, bd. dirs. 1986-87), Nat. Early Am. Glass Club (1st v.p. 1967-69), Mus. Fine Arts Boston. Address: 8441 Melrose Pl Los Angeles CA 90069 Office Phone: 310-276-9594.

JOSEPH, JAMES MICHAEL, music educator; b. Springfield, Pa., July 21, 1970; s. James Lewis and Anita Louise (Iacono) Joseph. BS, Westchester U of Pa, Westchester, Pa, 1988—92; MA in Humanities, Arcadia U., 2005. Tchr. T/E Sch. Dist., Berwyn, Pa., 1992—. Band dir. Conestoga HS, Berwyn, Pa., 1997—. Avocation: travel. Office: Conestoga HS 200 Irish Rd Berwyn PA 19312 Home: Penthouse #21A1 2401 Pennsylvania Ave Philadelphia PA 19130-7008 Office Phone: 610-240-1022. E-mail: josephj@tesd.k12.pa.us.

JOSEPH, JAMES WILLIAM, political scientist, educator; b. Gilroy, Calif., Jan. 1, 1960; s. William A. and Carmina M. J.; m. Mildred P. Maxwell, July 9, 2000. BA in Polit. Sci., Calif. State U., Fresno, 1982; D, U. Calif., Riverside, 1990; MA in Internat. Rels., Calif. State U., Fresno, 1984. Calif. lifetime tchg. credential. Asst. prof. polit. sci. U. Tex., Tyler, 1993—99; prof. polit. sci., dir. model UN programs Fresno (Calif.) City Coll., 1999—. Author: Between Realism and Reality: The Reagan Administration and International Debt, 1994; polit. commentator Sta. KFSN-TV, KSEE-TV, KMPH-TV, KGPE-TV, Fresno; contbr. articles to profl. jours. Mem. Am. Polit. Sci. Assn., Internat. Studies Assn. Republican. Avocations: bicycling, reading, running. Office: Fresno City Coll 1101 E University Ave Fresno CA 93741 Home: 1871 N Hornet Ave Clovis CA 93619 Office Phone: 559-442-4600. Personal E-mail: jjospolsci@aol.com. Business E-Mail: james.joseph@fresnocitycollege.edu.

JOSEPH, JEAN, artist; b. New Rochelle, N.Y., Jan. 28, 1914; d. Barnet and Alimeta Edna (Calder) J.; m. Paul Heinz Mertens, Oct. 19, 1941 (dec. Oct. 1979); children: Bruce, Mark, Gail. Student, Art Students League, 1930-34, U. Miami, 1935. Freelance artist. One woman shows at Manhasset Libr., 1974, Unitarian Soc., 1984; computer exhibit of works; exhibited in group shows at Wildenstein Galleries, N.Y., 1952, 53-55 tour (Internat. Hallmark awards, 1952, 53-55), Nat. Acad. Design, 1953 (Allied Artists of Am. award 1953), Fire House Gallery, 1973, Port Washington Libr., 1977, Unitarian Universalists Soc., Plandome, N.Y., 1977, Lincoln House, 1980 (sculpture prize), Port Washington Libr., 1981 (hon. mention), Nassau County Mus. Fine Art, 1983, Heckscher Mus., 1986 (Top of the Eighties award 1986), Nassau County Mus. Art, 1986 (Silver award 1986), 88 (hon. mention), Discovery Gallery, N.Y., (Jurors Merit award, 1993), 1992, 62nd Ann. Mid Year Exhbn., Butler Inst. Am. Art, 1998, White Line Drawing, Fayerweather Hall, U. Va., 2001, FX Gallery, U. Va., 2002; exhibitor, lectr. Ednam Hall, Charlottesville, Va., 1999; sculpture exhbn. Newcomb Hall, U. Va., 2000. Vol. 1000 hours St. Francis Hosp., Roslyn, N.Y., 1970-75. Recipient Hon. Mention award Cannon Photo Contest, 1986. Avocations: poetry, designing clothes, carpentry, walking.

JOSEPH, JOHN, historian, educator; b. Baghdad, Iraq, Sept. 1, 1923; came to U.S., 1946, naturalized, 1961; s. Joseph Shukur and Rebecca (Alkhas) J.; m. Beatrice Paul Malick, July 20, 1956; children: Paul Faris, Lawrence John, Deena Joseph Kinsky. BA, Franklin and Marshall Coll., 1950; MA, Princeton U., 1953, PhD, 1957. Instr. Princeton U., 1956-58, lectr., 1958-59; assoc. prof. history Thiel Coll., Greenville, Pa., 1960-61; assoc. prof. Franklin and Marshall Coll., Lancaster, Pa., 1964-69, prof. history, 1969—, Lewis Audenreid prof. history, 1972, prof. emeritus, 1988—. Author: The Nestorians and Their Muslim Neighbors, 1961, Muslim-Christian Relations and Inter-Christian Rivalries in the Middle East, 1983 (named an outstanding acad. book Choice mag. 1983-84), The Modern Assyrians of the Middle East, Encounters with Western Christian missions, Archaeologists, and Colonial Powers, 2000. Recipient Excellence in Teaching award Christian R. and Mary F. Lindback Found., 1978; fellow Ford Found., 1954-56, NEH, 1979; grantee Am. Council Learned Socs.-Social Sci. Research Council Joint Com., 1966-67 Fellow Middle East Studies Assn.; mem. Phi Beta Kappa. Democrat. Home: 88 Orchard Rd Lancaster PA 17601-3228 Office: Franklin and Marshall Coll College Ave Lancaster PA 17604 Address: 88 Orchard Rd Lancaster PA 17601-3228 E-mail: j_joseph@fandm.edu.

JOSEPH, JULES K., retired public relations executive; b. Cin., Jan. 18, 1927; s. Leslie Bloch and Ellen (Kaufman) J.; m. Elizabeth Levy, Sept. 9, 1948; children— Ellen Beth, Barbara Ann, John Charles. BA in Journalism, U. Wis., 1948. Mem. press relations staff Gimbels, Milw., 1948-52; bur. chief Fairchild Publs., Milw., 1952-60; co-founder, chmn. emeritus Zigman-Joseph-Stephenson Assocs. in Pub. Rels., Milw., 1960-94; ret., 1994. Pres. Friends of Art of Milw. Art Ctr., 1961-62; v.p. Milw. County Mental Health, 1967; bd. dirs. Milw. Repertory Theatre, Camp Webb, Milw. Pks. Bd., St. John's Home for the Aged, Milw., DePaul Hosp., Charles Allis Art Libr., Wis. Olympics Com.; bd. dirs. Frank Lloyd Wright Heritage Tourism Program; adv. bd. Salvation Army. Recipient Chancellor's award for outstanding contbn. to mass communication U. Wis., 1988. Mem. Pub. Rels. Soc. Am. (accredited, treas. Wis. 1970-71, bd. dirs. counselors sect. 1991-92), Soc. for Profl. Journalists, Phi Kappa Phi. Episcopalian. Home: 10610 N Magnolia Dr Mequon WI 53092-5054 Office: 735 W Wisconsin Ave Milwaukee WI 53233-2413 Personal E-mail: jjoseph8@wi.rr.com. *During my first job (summer '47) as a reporter on the Cincinnati Enquirer I was told to leave if I did not get the story. I have translated this to mean there's no excuse for not getting the job done— or reaching your goal.*

JOSEPH, LEONARD, lawyer; b. Phila., June 8, 1919; s. Harry L. and Mary (Pollock) J.; m. Norma Hamberg, 1942; children: Gilbert M., Stuart A., Janet H. Fitzgerald. BA, U. Pa., 1941; LLB, Harvard U., 1947. Bar: N.Y. 1949. Law clk. to chief judge U.S. Ct. Appeals, Boston, 1947-48; since practiced in N.Y.C.; ptnr. and of counsel Dewey Ballantine, 1957—. Bd. dirs., exec. com. Legal Aid Soc. N.Y., 1986-89; mem. panel of disting. neutrals CPR Inst. for Dispute Resolution. Bd. editors Harvard Law Rev., 1946-47. Served with AUS, 1943-46. Fellow Am. Bar Found., Am. Coll. Trial Lawyers Office: Dewey Ballantine 1301 Avenue Of The Americas New York NY 10019-6022 Office Phone: 212-259-7180.

JOSEPH, LURA ELLEN, librarian, geologist; b. Tulsa, Jan. 24, 1947; d. Don Roscoe and Ruth Elizabeth (Taplin) Joseph. Student, St. Paul Bible Coll., 1965-67, Pan Am. Coll., 1967-68; BA in Anthropology, U. Okla., 1971, MS in Geology, 1981; MA in Psychology with honors, U. Cen. Okla., 1992; M of Libr. and Info. Studies, U. Okla., 1994. Cert. petroleum geologist. Exploration geologist Getty Oil Co., Oklahoma City, 1977-84; geologist Harper Oil Co., Oklahoma City, 1984-86, consulting geologist, 1986-88; sr. geologist Grace Petroleum, Oklahoma City, 1988-93, cons. geologist, 1993—94; phys. scis. libr. N.D. State Univ. Libr., Fargo, 1995—2001; asst. prof. libr. adminstrn. U. Ill., Urbana-Champaign, 2001—. Contbr. articles to profl. jours. Mem. Am. Assn. Petroleum Geologists, Geol. Soc. of Am., Spl. Libr. Assn., Geosci. Info. Soc. (v.p.,2003, pres. 2004), Sigma Gamma Epsilon, Psi Chi, Beta Phi Mu. Avocations: travel, photography, reading, art. Office: U Ill Geology Libr 223 Natural History Bldg 1301 W Green St Urbana IL 61801

JOSEPH, MARILYN SUSAN, gynecologist; b. Aug. 18, 1946; BA, Smith Coll., 1968; MD cum laude, SUNY Downstate Med. Ctr., Bklyn., 1972. Diplomate Am. Bd. Ob-Gyn, Nat. Bd. Med. Examiners. Intern U. Minn. Hosps., 1972-73, resident in ob-gyn, 1972-76; med. fellow specialist U. Minn., 1972-76, asst. prof. ob-gyn, 1976—, dir. women's clinic, 1984—. Med. dir. Boynton Health Svc., 1993—. Author: Differential Diagnosis Obstetrics, 1978. Fellow Am. Coll. Ob-Gyn (best paper dist. VI meeting 1981); mem. Hennepin County Med. Soc., Minn. State Med. Assn., Minn. State Ob-Gyn Soc. Avocations: cooking, bird watching, travel. Office: Boynton Health Svc 410 Church St SE Minneapolis MN 55455-0346 E-mail: mjoseph@bhs.umn.edu.

JOSEPH, MICHAEL SARKIES, accountant; b. Peoria, Ill., Dec. 10, 1950; s. Sarkas M. and Theresa I. (Kelch) J.; m. Christine L., June 28, 1975; children: Brian, Christopher, Patrick. BS, No. Ill. U., 1972. CPA. Ptnr. Ernst & Young, Cleve. and Chgo., 1972-89, ptnr. N.Y.C., 1989—; profl. acct. fellow Fed. Home Loan Bank Bd., Washington, 1981-83. Roman Catholic. Avocations: golf, swimming, youth athletic programs. Home: 38 Kellogg Hill Rd Weston CT 06883-2620 Office: Ernst & Young LLP 5 Times Sq New York NY 10036

JOSEPH, MICHAEL THOMAS, broadcast consultant; b. Youngstown, Ohio, Nov. 23, 1927; s. Thomas A. and Martha (McCarius) J.; m. Eva Ursula Boerger, June 21, 1952. BA, Case Western Res. U., 1949. Program dir. Fetzer Broadcasting, Grand Rapids, Mich., 1952-55; nat. program dir. Founders Corp., N.Y.C., 1955-57; program cons. to ABC, CBS, NBC, Capital Cities, Infinity, Cox, Entercom, Gannett, Greater Media, Tribune, Telemundo, N.Y. Times, 1958—; v.p. radio Capital Cities, N.Y.C., 1959—60; v.p. owned radio stas. NBC, N.Y.C., 1963—65. Mem. Internat. Radio and TV Soc., Nat. Assn. Broadcasters

JOSEPH, RAMON RAFAEL, internist, educator; b. N.Y.C., May 17, 1930; s. Felix R. and Helen Joseph; m. Mary Ann Kowalchik, June 16, 1956; children: Ricardo George, Maria Ann Thompson, Lisa Marie Benson. BS, Manhattan Coll., 1952; MD, Cornell U., 1956. Diplomate Nat. Bd. Med. Examiners, Am. Bd. Internal Medicine. Intern Meadowbrook Hosp., Hempstead, N.Y., 1956-57, resident, 1957, Wayne County Gen. Hosp., Westland, Mich., 1959-62, dir. gastroenterology, 1962-84, asst. dir. internal medicine, 1964-73, dir., chmn., 1973-84, pres. med. staff, 1971-72; cons. internal medicine and gastroenterology Annapolis Hosp., 1962-87; from instr. internal medicine to prof. U. Mich., 1962-85, prof. emeritus, 1998—; asst. dean U. Mich. Med. Sch., 1973-84; 1st v.p., dir. Univ. Med. Affiliates PC, 1981-84; pres., CEO Univ. Med. Affiliates (P.C.), 1985-87; med. dir. Henry Ford Hosp. Westland (Mich.) Ctr., 1987-94; sr. attending physician Henry Ford Hosp., Detroit, 1987-95. Cons. gastroenterology St. Mary Hosp., Livonia, Mich., 1966—, chmn. divsn. of gastroenterology, 1987-93. Contbr. articles to profl. jours. Mem. Community Commn. on Drug Abuse, Livonia and Westland, Mich., 1970-73; mem. Mich. Dept. Edn. Council on Drug Abuse, cons. on drug abuse public schs., Livonia, 1968-74; pres. Livonia Sch. Bd. Adv. Council, 1970-71. Capt. U.S. Army, 1957-59. Fellow ACP; mem. Am. Fedn. Clin. Research, Am. Gastroent., Assn., AAAS, Assn. Am. Med. Colls., AMA, N.Y. Acad. Sci., Detroit Gastroent. Soc. (pres. 1969-70), Mich., Wayne County Med. Socs., Am. Assn. Lab. Animal Sci., Am. Soc. Gastrointestinal Endoscopy, Am. Soc. Internal Medicine, Mich. Soc. Gastrointestinal Endoscopy (pres. 1982-86), Mich. Soc. Internal Medicine, Assn. Program Dirs. in Internal Medicine. Roman Catholic. Office Phone: 623-217-9642. Personal E-mail: rjoseph514@aol.com.

JOSEPH, ROBERT G., federal agency administrator; BA, St. Louis U., 1971; MA, U. Chgo., 1973; PhD, Columbia U., 1978. Dep. asst. sec. nuclear forces and arms control policy U.S. Dept. Def., Washington, prin. dep. asst. sec. def. internat. security policy, U.S. commr. standing consultative commn., amb. U.S.-Russian consultative commn. nuclear testing, prof. nat. security studies Nat. Def. U., 1992—2001, founder, dir. Ctr. Counterproliferation Rsch. Nat. Def. U., 1992—2001, spl. asst. to Pres., sr. dir. proliferation strategy, conterproliferation and homeland def., Nat. Security Coun., under sec. for arms control & internat. security, 2005—. Sr. scholar, dir. of studies Nat. Inst. Pub. Policy, 2004—05. Office: US Dept State Harry S Truman Bldg 2201 C St NW Rm 7208 Washington DC 20520 Office Phone: 202-647-1049. Office Fax: 202-736-4397.*

JOSEPH, ROBERT THOMAS, lawyer; b. June 12, 1946; s. Joseph Alexander and Clara Barbara (Francis) J.; m. Sarah Granger, May 22, 1971; children: Paul, Timothy. AB, Xavier U., 1968; JD, U. Mich., 1971. Bar: Mich. 1971, Ill. 1976, U.S. Dist. Ct. (no. dist.) Ill. 1976, U.S. Ct. Appeals (7th cir.) 1983. Staff atty. FTC Bur. Competition, Washington, 1971-76, asst. to dir., 1972-74; atty. Sonnenschein Nath & Rosenthal, LLP, Chgo., 1976—, ptnr., 1978—. Trustee Northbrook (Ill.) Libr. Bd., 1979-89, pres., 1983-85. Recipient Disting. Svc. award FTC, 1976. Mem. ABA (chair franchising com. of antitrust law sect. 1984-87, chair videotapes com. 1987-90, chair publs. com. 1991-94, coun. 1994-97, program officer 1997-99, com. officer 1999-2000, vice-chair 2000-2001, chair 2002-03, mem. governing bd. forum on franchising 1997-2003), Met. Club. Roman Catholic. Office: Sonnenschein Nath Rosenthal LLP 233 S Wacker Dr Ste 8000 Chicago IL 60606-6491

JOSEPH, ROSALINE RESNICK, hematologist; b. N.Y.C., Aug. 21, 1929; d. Joseph and Malca (Rosenbeg) Resnick; m. Robert J. Joseph, Jan. 2, 1954; children: Joy S., Nina B. AB, Cornell U., 1949; MD, Women's Med. Coll. Pa., Phila., 1953; MS, Temple U., 1958. Intern Kings County Hosp., Bklyn., 1953-54; resident Phila. Gen. Hosp., 1954-55, Temple U. Hosp., 1955-57; instr. dept. medicine Temple U. Med. Ctr., Phila., 1957-60, assoc. in medicine, 1960-63, asst. prof. medicine, 1963-69, assoc. prof. medicine, 1969-77; course co-coordinator Sys. Oncology Interdisciplinary Course, 1968-73; prof. medicine, dir. Med. Coll. Pa., Phila., 1977, prof. emeritus, 1999, course coordinator, 1978, prof. emeritus, 1999. Pres. med. staff Med. Coll. Pa., 1990-91. Contbr. articles to profl. jours. Del. dir. Am. Cancer Soc., 1989—. Recipient Lindback award for disting. teaching, Christian & Mary Lindback Found., 1982, Am. Cancer Soc. Div. Disting. Svc. award, 1987. Fellow ACP; mem. Am. Soc. Hematology, Am. Soc. Clin. Oncology, Alumni Assn. Med. Coll. Pa. (pres. 1988-90). Office: Med Coll Pa Hosp 3300 Henry Ave Philadelphia PA 19129-1191

JOSEPH, STACEY ANN MCGRAW, music educator, church choir director; b. Waukesha, Wis., Mar. 30, 1973; d. James William and Janet Sue McGraw; m. Timothy Lyle Joseph, July 18, 1998. MusB, U. Wis., Whitewater, 1996; postgrad., Cardinal Stritch U., Milw., 2004—. Vocal/gen. music tchr. Pepin Area Schs., Wis., 1996—98; gen. music tchr. Sch. Dist. of Janesville, 1998—99, vocal/gen. music tchr., 1998—2002, Whitewater Unified Sch. Dist., 2002—. Youth choir dir. Evang. and Ref. United Ch. of Christ, Waukesha, 1994—96, Waukesha, 2000—02, adult choir dir., 2000—; summer show choir tchr. Sch. Dist. of Milton, Wis., 1999—; dir. musicals Whitewater Unified Sch. Dist., 2002—, dir. show choir, 2002—; cooperating tchr., field studies U. of Wis. - Whitewater, 2003—; vocal and gen. music educator Whitewater Mid. Sch., 2002—. Musician soloist. Hymnal com. co-chair Evang. and Ref. United Ch. of Christ, 2001—02, chmn. pastor search com., 2002—04, music com. chmn., 2003—04. Mem.: Wis. Sch. Music Assn. (assoc.), Music Educators Nat. Conf. (assoc.), Delta Omicron (chaplain 1993—94, treas. 1993—95, 2d v.p. 1995—95). Avocations: bowling, basket weaving, card making, photography. Office: Whitewater Mid Sch 401 S Elizabeth St Whitewater WI 53190

JOSEPH, SUSAN B., lawyer; b. N.Y.C., 1958; d. Alfred A. and Bella J. BS in Econ. and Bus. Mgmt., Ramapo Coll. of N.J., 1981; JD cum laude, Seton Hall U., 1985. Bar: N.J. 1985, U.S. Dist. Ct. N.J. 1985, N.Y. 1988, U.S. Dist. Ct. (so. and ea. dist.) N.Y. 1991. Legal asst. Prudential Ins. Co. Am., Newark, 1982-85; assoc. Fox & Fox, Newark, 1985-86, Elkes, Maybruch & Weiss, P.A., Freehold, N.J., 1986-87; asst. counsel N.Am. Reins. Corp., N.Y.C., 1987-90; assoc. Mark D. Lefkowitz, Esq., 1991; mgr. GRE Ins. Group, Princeton, N.J., 1991, atty. N.Y.C., 1992-95; cons. Fin. Guaranty Ins. Co., N.Y.C., 1996-97, counsel, 1997—2001; asst. gen. counsel Am. Capital Access, 2003—04. Vol. campaign Bill Bradley for Senate, 1984, 90; vol. Starlight Found., N.Y.C., 1988—, mem. exec. com. Friends of the Maplewood (N.J.) Lib., 1995; mem Transp. Com., Twp. of Maplewood, 1999—2001; vol. Kerry-Edwards Campaign, 2004. Mem. N.J. State Bar Assn. (sect. on entertainment and arts law, newsletter editor 1992-93, bd. dirs. 1992-98, founding sec. ins. law sect. 1996-98, vice chair 1998-99, chair 1999-2000, mem. diversity com. 2003—). Democrat. Jewish. Avocations: writing, theater, photography. Address: 747 Valley St Maplewood NJ 07040-2664

JOSEPHS, BABETTE, legislator; b. N.Y.C., Aug. 4, 1940; d. Eugene and Myra A. Josephs; children: Lee Aaron Newberg, Elizabeth Master. BA, Queens Coll., 1962; JD, Rutgers U., 1976. Sole practice, Phila., 1976-78; exec. dir. Nat. Abortion Rights Action League of Pa., Phila., 1978-80, Citizens Coalition for Energy Efficiency, Phila., 1980-81; pvt. practice cons., fundraiser Phila., 1981-84; mem. Pa. Ho. of Reps., Phila., 1984—. Mem. Profl. Licensure Com., 1985—86, Ho. Health and Human Services Com., 1985—92, 1995—2002, Ho. Judiciary Com., 1987—94, 1997—2002, Ho. Appropriations Com., 1993—2002, Ho. Urban Affairs Com., 1997—98, Children and Youth Com., 2001—02, Dem. Policy Com., Common Sense Firearms Safety Caucus, Firefighters and Emergency Services Caucus, Autism Caucus, Campaign Fin. Reform Caucus, others, Pa. Commn. on Crime and Delinquency, Joint Selection Com. to Examine Election Issues, 2001—02, Agrl. and Rural Affairs Com., 2003—; mem. adv. bd. Statewide Uniform Registry of Elections, 2001—02; chair State Govt. Com., 2001—. Mem. Women's Internat. League for Peace and Freedom, LWV; hon. chair Jewish Family & Children's Services of Greater Phila.; co-founder, mem. Nat. Abortion and Reproductive Rights Action League; coord. Nat. Orgn. Women Legislators, Pa.; mem. Clean Air Coun.; Am. Jewish Com.; mem. Martin Luther King Task Force, Rebuild the Del. Valley Steering Com., Nuclear Freeze Campaign; super del. Dem. Nat. Conv., 1992; bd. dirs. ACLU; bd. mem. Save the Boyd, Franklin Paine's Skate Park. Named Legislator of Yr., Citizen Action, 1996, Dem. Woman Rep. of Yr., Capitol Area Dem. Woman's Club, 2001, Leader of Yr., Bella Vista United Civic Assn., 2004; recipient Cert. of Appreciation, AIDS WALK, 1996, President's award, Pa. Fedn. Mus. and Hist. Orgns., 1998, Disting. Pub. Svc. award, Concerned Citizens of Del. Valley, 1999, Legislator of Yr. award, Pa. Consumer Action Network, 1999, Cert. of Appreciation award, Statewide Pa. Rights Coalition, 2002, Women of Distinction award, Phila. Bus. Jour. and Nat. Assn. Women Bus. Owners, 2003, Cert. of Appreciation, Phila. 17th Police Dist., 2003, Leadership award, 2003, Disting. Achievement award, Smokefree, Pa., 2003, Spirit of Leadership award, Pathways Pa., 2004. Mem.: Center City Residents Assn., Phila. Bar Assn. (com. on civil and women's rights), Liberty City Gay and Lesbian Dem. Club. Democrat. Jewish. Office: 1528 Walnut St Philadelphia PA 19102-3604

JOSEPHSON, DIANA HAYWARD, not-for-profit executive; b. London, Oct. 17, 1936; came to U.S., 1959; d. Robert Hayward and Barbara Bailey. BA with honors, Oxford U., Eng., 1958, MA, 1962; M in Comparative Law, George Washington U., 1962. Bar: Eng. and Wales 1959, D.C. 1963. Assoc. Covington & Burling, Washington, 1959-68; asst. dir. Office of the Mayor, Washington, 1968-74; exec. dir. Nat. Capital Area ACLU, Washington, 1975-78; dep. asst. adminstr. policy and planning, satellites NOAA, U.S. Dept. Commerce, Washington, 1978-82; pres. Am. Sci. and Tech. Corp., Bethesda, Md., 1982-83, Space Am., Bethesda, Md., 1983-85; v.p. mktg. Arianespace, Inc., Washington, 1985-87; v.p. Martin Marietta Comml. Titan Inc., Washington, 1987-89; dir. bus. devel. Martin Marietta Advanced Launch Systems, Denver, 1989-90, Martin Marietta Civil Space and Communications Co., Denver, 1990-93; dep. under sec. commerce oceans and atmosphere, NOAA U.S. Dept. Commerce, Washington, 1993-97; prin. dep. asst. sec. for installations and environ. Dept. Navy, Washington, 1997-2000; sr. v.p. Environ. Def., N.Y.C., 2000—04; assoc. dir. societal-environ. rsch. & edn. Nat. Ctr. Atmospheric Rsch., 2005—. Mem. adv. coun. Nat. Ctr. for Atmospheric Rsch., 2003-05; mem. Space Applications Bd., NRC, 1988-89, Comml. Space Transp. Adv. Commn., U.S. Dept. Transp., Washington, 1984-85; mem. adv. bd. Washington Space Bus. Roundtable, 1985-87. Mem. D.C. Law Revision Commn., Washington, 1975-78, D.C. Internat. Women's Yr. State Coordinating Com., 1977. Mem. Am. Astronautical Soc. (bd. dirs. 1985-88), Nat. Space Club (bd. govs.), Women in Aerospace, Washington Space Bus. Roundtable (adv. bd. 1985-87). Avocations: sailing, reading.

JOSEPHSON, JORDAN STUART, otolaryngologist; b. Dec. 15, 1957; BS in Chemistry, SUNY, Albany, 1979; MD, SUNY Downstate Med. Sch., Bklyn., 1983. Intern gen. surgery Long Island Jewish Hosp., 1983-84, chief resident otolaygoly, 1984-88; fellow in endoscopic sinus surgery Johns Hopkins Med. Sch., Balt., 1989; otolaryngologist N.Y. Nasal and Sinus Ctr., N.Y.C., 1994—. Author, editor: Medical Clinics of North America, 1991, 2d edit., 1993; contbr. articles to profl. jours., chpt. to book. Recipient Functional Endoscopic Sinus Surgery Tchg. award, 1989, NIH Recognition for Svc. and Dedication award, 1989-94, cert. of recognition Best Drs. N.Y. Metro Area, 1994—, N.Y. Magazine Best Doctors in N.Y. Mem. AMA, Am. Rhinologic Soc., Am. Acad. Otolaryngology, Head and Neck Surgery, N.Y. State County Med. Soc. Avocations: skiing, music, reading, writing. Office: NY Nasal and Sinus Ctr 111 E 77th St New York NY 10021-1802 Office Phone: 212-717-1773.

JOSEPHSON, KENNETH BRADLEY, artist, retired art educator; b. Detroit, July 1, 1932; s. Ernest Gustav and Hilda Christine (Wick) J.; m. Carol A. Compeau, Feb. 1954 (dec. Apr. 1958); m. Sherill A. Petro, Oct. 28, 1960 (div. 1973); children: Matthew W. (dec.), Bradley J., Anissa C.; m. Sally D. Garen, Jan. 30, 1973 (div. 1978); m. Katherine R. Bateman, June 7, 1991 (div. 1998). BFA, Rochester Inst. Tech., 1957; MS, Inst. Design Ill. Inst. Tech., 1960. Photographer Chrysler Corp., Detroit, 1957-58; exch. tchr. Konstfackskolan, Stockholm, 1966-67; assoc. prof. U. Hawaii, Honolulu, 1967-68; vis. prof. Tyler Sch. Art, Temple U., Phila., 1975, UCLA, 1981-82; prof. Sch. Art Inst. Chgo., 1960-97. Fellowship panelist Nat. Endowment Arts, Washington, 1975; vis. artist Ecole Régionale des Beaux Arts De Saint-Etienne, France, fall 1995. One-person shows include Visual Studies Workshop, Rochester, N.Y., 1971, U. Iowa Mus. Art, Iowa City, 1974, 291 Galery, Milan, 1974, Cameraworks Gallery, L.A., 1976, Reicher Gallery Barat Coll., Lake Forest, Ill., 1977, Fotoforum, Kassel, Germany, 1978, Photographer's Gallery, London, 1979, Delpire Galerie, Paris, 1981, Young Hoffman Gallery, Chgo., 1981, Swen Parson Gallery No. Ill. U., 1983, Vision Gallery, Boston, 1983, Retrospective Exhbn. Mus. Contemporary Art, Chgo., 1983, Friends of Photography, Carmel, Calif, 1984, Rhona Hoffman Gallery, Chgo., 1991, 99, La Serre Gallery, Beaux-Arts de Saint Etienne, France, 1996, Retrospective Exhbn. Art Inst. Chgo., 1999, Retrospective Exhbn. Whitney Mus. Art, N.Y., 2001, Yancey Richardson Gallery, N.Y., 2001, 02, Priebe Art Gallery, U. Wis., Oshkosh, 2001, Kenneth Josephson Ctr. Photography, Lectoure, France, 2003, La Filature, Mulhouse, France, 2004, Cal Solway Gallery, Cin., 2004, Rona Hoffman Gallery, Chgo., 2004; group shows include Fla. State Mus., Gainesville, 1965, Sheldon Meml. Art Gallery, Lincoln, 1968, Fogg Art Mus., Harvard U., 1967, Eastman House, Rochester and Nat. Gallery of Can., Ottawa, 1967, Mus. Contemporary Crafts, N.Y.C., 1971, Corcoran Gallery, 1972, Art Inst. Chgo., 1973, 93, Walker Art Ctr., Mpls., 1973, Madison Art Ctr., 1973, Mus. Art, Indpls., 1973, Incontri Internazionali d'Arte Precheggio di Villa Borghese, Rome, 1973-74, Atkins Art Gallery, 1974, Kunsthaus, Zurich, 1977, Mus. Contemporary Art, Chgo., 1977, 96, Leslie Tonkonow Art Works and Projects, N.Y.C., 1998, Carol Ehlers Gallery, Chgo., 1999; Mus. Art. R.I. Sch. Design, 1978, Mus. Modern Art, N.Y.C., 1978, Light Gallery, N.Y.C., 1980, Photokina, Koln, Germany, 1980, Seibu Mus. Art, Tokyo, 1982, Barbican Art Gallery, London, 1985, L.A. County Mus. Art, Nat. Mus. Modern Art, 1989, State of Ill. Art Gallery, 1989, U. Hawaii Art Gallery, 1990, Art Inst. Chgo., 1990, Rockford Coll. Art Gallery, 1990, Catherine Edelman Gallery, Chgo., 1991, Davenport Mus. Art, 1992, Seagram Bldg. Gallery, 1992, Renaissance Soc., Chgo., Montreal Mus. of Fine Arts, 1993, Art Inst. Chgo., 1993, Chgo. Cultural Ctr., 1994, U. Ariz., 1994, Mus. Modern Art, 1995, Laurence Miller Gallery, 1995, Ehlers Caudill Gallery, Chgo., 1996, Gallery 312, Chgo., 1996, Mus. Contemporary Photography, Columbia Coll., Chgo., 1996, VIII Fotobienal Vigo (Spain), 1998, Whitney Mus. Am. Art, N.Y., 2002, 04, Art Inst. Chgo., 2002, 04, San Francisco Mus. Modern Art, 2002, Phila. Mus. Art, 2002, Stephen Daiter Gallery, Chgo., 2002, Mus. Contemporary Art, Chgo., 2002, Carl Solway Gallery, Cin., 2002, Book Light Ctr. for Book and Paper Arts, Columbia Coll., Chgo., 2004, Cin. Art Mus., 2004, Yancey Richardson Gallery, N.Y.C., 2005, others; permanent collections include Mus. Modern Art., N.Y.C., Contemporary Arts Mus., Houston, Addison Gallery Am. Art, Art Inst. Chgo., Bibliothèque Nationale, Paris, Ctr. for Creative Photography, U. Ariz., Fotografiska Museet, Stockholm, Hallmark Collections, Kansas City, Mo., Mpls. Inst. Arts, Mus. Fine Arts, Boston, Grunwald Ctr. Graphic Arts, UCLA, Nat. Mus. Art Smithsonian Instn., Washington, Nat. Mus. Modern Art, Kyoto, L.A. County Mus. Art, San Francisco Mus. Modern Art, Cartier Internat. Found., Paris, U.S. Trust Co., Art. Inst. of Chgo., Hunter Mus., Chattanooga, Tenn., Deloitte and Louche, Chgo., John D. and Catherine T. MacArthur Found., Seagram Collection,

High Mus. Art., Libr. Congress, Internat. Ctr. Photography, N.Y., Cleve. Mus. Art, Tokyo Met. Mus. Photography, Whitney Mus. Am. Art., N.Y., Spencer Mus. Art, U. Kans., Norton Simon Mus., Pasadena, Calif. Served with U.S. Army, 1953-55. Guggenheim fellow, 1972, Nat. Endowment for Arts fellow, 1975, 79, Ruttenberg Arts Found. grantee, 1983, Ill. Acad. of Fine Arts Photographer award, 1993. Mem. Soc. for Photog. Edn. (founding mem.)

JOSEPHSON, MARVIN, literary agent; b. Atlantic City, Mar. 6, 1927; s. Joseph and Eva (Rounick) J.; m. Tina Tann Chen, Apr. 12, 1973; children: Celia M., Claire A., Nancy A., Joseph T. Josephson; YiLing L.T. and YiPei R.T. Chen-Josephson. BA, Cornell U., 1949; LL.B., N.Y. U., 1952. Atty. CBS, N.Y.C., 1952-55; pres., then chmn. ICM Holdings Inc. (and predecessors), N.Y.C., 1955—. Pres., then chmn. exec. com. Internat. Creative Mgmt., Inc. subs. ICM Holdings Inc., N.Y.C., 1975. Served with USN, 1945-46. Office: ICM Holdings Inc 40 W 57th St 16th Fl New York NY 10019-4098 Fax: 212-556-6886. E-mail: mjosephson@icmtalent.com.

JOSEPHSON, RICHARD CARL, lawyer; b. Washington, Nov. 20, 1947; s. Horace Richard and Margaret Louise (Loeffler) J.; m. Jean Carol Attridge, Aug. 1, 1970; children: Lee Margaret, Amy Dorothy. AB, Case Western Res. U., 1969; JD, Coll. of William and Mary, 1972. Bar: Oreg. 1973. Law clk. Hon. John D. Butzner, Jr., U.S. Ct. Appeals, 4th Cir., Richmond, Va., 1972-73; mem. Stoel Rives LLP, Portland, Oreg., 1973—. Bd. dirs. Tucker-Maxon Oral Sch., Portland, 1987—, Vis. Nurse Assn., Portland, 1978-89, Healthlink, Portland, 1984-89, St. Mary's Acad., Portland, 1998-2001. 1st lt. U.S. Army, 1973-79. Fellow Am. Coll. Bankruptcy, Am. Coll. Comml. Fin. Lawyers; mem. ABA, Am. Bankruptcy Inst., Oreg. Bar Assn. (chmn. debtor-creditor sect. 1980-81). Avocations: skiing, white water rafting, running, bicycling, theater. Office: Stoel Rives LLP 900 SW 5th Ave Ste 2300 Portland OR 97204-1229 Office Phone: 503-294-9537. Business E-Mail: rcjosephson@stoel.com.

JOSEPHSON, WILLIAM HOWARD, retired lawyer; b. Newark, Mar. 22, 1934; s. Maurice and Gertrude (Brooks) J.; m. Barbara Beth Haws, June 18, 1995. AB, U. Chgo., 1952; JD, Columbia, 1955; commoner, St. Antony's Coll., Oxford (Eng.) U., 1958-59. Bar: NY 1956, DC 1966, US Supreme Ct. 1959. Assoc. Paul, Weiss, Rifkind, Wharton & Garrison, N.Y.C., 1955—58, Joseph L. Rauh, Jr., Washington, 1959; Far East regional counsel ICA, 1959—61; from spl. asst. to dir. to gen. counsel Peace Corps, 1961—66; from assoc. to ptnr. to counsel Fried, Frank, Harris, Shriver & Jacobson, NYC, 1966—99; asst. atty. gen. in charge charities bur. NY State Law Dept., NY, 1999—2004, ret., 2004. Adj. law tchr. George Washington U. Law Sch., 1960-61, Cardozo Law Sch., 2001, NYU, 2000-; spl. counsel NYC Human Resources Adminstrn., 1966-67, City Univ. Constrn. Fund, 1967-96, NYC Bd. Edn., 1968-71, NYC Employees' Retirement Sys., 1975-86; Nat. Dem. vice presdl. campaign coord., 1972; pres. Peace Corps Inst., 1980—; mem. NY State Gov. Task Force Pension and Investment, 1987-89, NY State Hist. Records Adv. Bd., 1990-96, NY State Archives Preservation Trust, 1994-96. Bd. editors: Columbia Law Rev, 1953-55; contbr. numerous legal publs. Trustee and treas. St. Antony's Coll. trust, 1994-99. Recipient William A. Jump award exemplary achievement pub. adminstrn., 1965, Disting. Svc. award, Valerie Kantor award, Corp. Social Responsibility award Mex. Am. Legal Def. and Edn. Fund, 1980, 81, 93. Mem. Assn. Bar City N.Y. (spl. com. on Congl. ethics 1968-70), Council on Fgn. Relations. Jewish. Home: 58 S Oxford St Brooklyn NY 11217-1305 Office Phone: 212-859-8220.

JOSEY, E(LONNIE) J(UNIUS), librarian, retired state agency administrator; b. Norfolk, Va., Jan. 20, 1924; s. Willie and Frances (Bailey) J.; m. Dorothy Johnson, Sept. 11, 1954 (div. Dec. 1961); 1 dau., Elaine Jacqueline. AB, Howard U., 1949; MA, Columbia U., 1950; MLS, SUNY, Albany, 1953; LHD, Shaw U., 1973; DPS, U. Wis., Milw., 1987; HHD, N.C. Cen. U., 1989; LittD, Clark Atlanta U., 1995; LHD (hon.), Clarion Univ. of Pa., 2001. Desk asst. Columbia U. Libraries, 1950-52; libr. tech. asst. central br. N.Y. Pub. Libr., N.Y.C., 1952; libr. I Free Libr., Phila., 1953-54; instr. social scis. Savannah State Coll., 1954-55, libr., assoc. prof., 1959-66; libr., asst. prof. Del. State Coll., 1955-59; assoc. divsn. libr. devel. N.Y. State Edn. Dept., Albany, 1966-68; chief Bur. Acad. and Rsch. Libraries, 1968-76, Bur. Specialist Libr. Svcs., 1976-86; prof. U. Pitts. Sch. Libr. and Info. Scis., 1986-95, prof. emeritus, 1995—. Mem. bd. advisors Children's Book Rev. Service, Bklyn., 1972— Editor, contbg. author: The Black Librarian in America, 1970, What Black Librarians Are Saying, 1972, New Dimensions for Academic Library Service, 1975; co-compiler, co-editor: Handbook of Black Librarianship, 1977; co-editor: A Century of Service: Librarianship in the United States and Canada, 1976, Opportunities for Minorities in Librarianship, 1977, The Information Society: Issues and Answers, 1978, Libraries in the Political Process, 1980, Ethnic Collections in Libraries, 1983, Libraries, Coalitions, And the Public Good, 1987, Politics and the Support of Libraries, 1990, Festchaift E.J. Josey: an Activist Librarian, 1992, The Black Librarian in America Revisited, 1994, Handbook of Black Librarianship, 2001; mem. editl. bd. Dictionary of Am. Library History, 1974—; mem. editl. adv. bd. ALA Yearbook, 1975-83; spl. advisor: World Ency. Black People, 1974-80; contbr. numerous articles to profl. jours. Mem. Albany Interracial Coun., 1972—86; state youth advisor Ga. Conf., 1962—66, 1st v.p., 1981—82, pres., 1982—86, life mem., 1971—, chmn. program, 1972—76, trustee; mem. tech. task force Econ. Opportunity Authority of Savannah, 1964—66; mem. adv. coun. Sch. Libr. Sci. N.C. Ctrl. U.; mem. adv. coun. Sch. Libr. and Info. Sci. SUNY, Albany, Sch. Libr. and Info. Sci. Queen's Coll. CUNY; mem. exec. bd. Savannah (Ga.) br. NAACP, 1960—66; mem. exec. bd. Albany br. Ga. Conf., 1970—72; mem. exec. bd. Albany Opportunity Authority; bd. dirs. Freedom to Read Found., 1987—91. With AUS, 1943—46. Recipient cert. of Appreciation Savannah br. NAACP, 1963, NAACP award Savannah State Coll. chpt., 1964, Merit award for work on econ. opportunity task force Savannah Chatham County, 1966, award for disting. service to librarianship Savannah State Coll. Library, 1967, Jour. Library History award, 1970, N.Y. Black Librarians Inc. award, 1979, N.J. Black Librarians Network award, 1984, Joseph W. Lippincott award, 1980, Disting. Alumnus of Yr. award SUNY Albany Sch. Library and Info. Sci. and Policy, 1981, 89, Disting. Service award Library Assn. of CUNY, 1982, Martin Luther King Jr. award for disting. community leadership SUNY, Albany, 1984, award for contbns. to librarianship D.C. Assn. Sch. Librarians, 1984, award Kenyan Library Assn., 1984, Disting. Service award Afro-Caribbean Library Assn., Eng., 1984; ALA Hon. Mem. Award, 2002. Mem.: ACLU, AAUP, ALA (hon.; founder, chmn. Black Caucus 1970—71, mem. coun. 1970—, mem. exec. bd. 1979—86, v.p./pres.-elect 1983—84, pres. 1984—85, John Cotton Dana award 1962, 1964, Black Caucus award 1979, ALA Equality award 1991, Black Caucus Demco award for disting. svc. to librarianship 1994, Wash. office award 1996—, Humphrey/OCLC/Forest Press award for contbns. to internat. librarianship 1998), Am. Soc. Info. Scis., Internat. Platform Assn., N.Y. Libr. Assn. (Disting. Svc. award 1985), Am. Acad. Polit. and Social Sci., Assn. Study Afro-Am. Life and History, Pa. Libr. Assn. (Disting. Svc. award 1996), N.Y. Libr. Club, Kappa Phi Kappa, Alpha Phi Omega. Democrat. Home: 5 Bayard Rd Unit 505 Pittsburgh PA 15213-1905 Office: U Pitts Sch Info Scis Bldg Pittsburgh PA 15260 E-mail: ejjosey@mail.sis.pitt.edu.

JOSHI, HARIHAR S., labor union administrator; b. Manjarkhed, India, Aug. 20, 1931; came to U.S., 1962; s. Sopandeo Waman and Manakarnika Narayan J.; m. Vaijayanti Pushpa Laxman Kukade, June 6, 1957; children: Chandrashekhar, Wandana, Sharad. B in Vet. Sci., M.P. Vet. Coll., 1954; MS, U. Hawaii, 1964; PhD, U. Guelph, 1971. Vet. officer Dept. Vet. & Animal Husbandry, India, 1954-58; rsch. assoc., lectr. Bombay Vet. Coll., India, 1958-62; asst. prof. U. Guelph, Ont., Canada, 1964-69; rsch. fellow Worcester Found. Exptl. Biology, Shrewsbury, Mass., 1971-75; tech. supervisor, dir. Ind. Med. Labs., Worcester and Cambridge, Mass., 1975-80; pres. Omega Med. Labs, Oxford, Mass., 1980-95. Head religious matters India Soc. Worcester, Shrewsbury, 1972-95; Hindu priest, 1972—. Mem. Am. Assn. Clin. Chemists. Home: 65 Locust Ave Worcester MA 01604-1129

JOSHI, RAKSHA, medical director; d. Manharlal Ishwarlal and Girija Joshi; m. Anoopendra Bharadwaj, Dec. 12, 1980. Dir. ambulatory ob-gyn. Monmouth Med. Ctr., Long Branch, NJ, 1998—2003, assoc. program dir., ob-gyn residency, 1998—2003; med. dir. Monmouth Family Health Ctr., Long Branch, NJ, 2004—. Adminstrn. Monmouth Family Health Ctr., Long Branch, 2004—. Recipient APGO Excellence award, 1999, CREOG Faculty award, 2000, APGO Ednl. Scholar award, 2002, Drexel U. award, 2002. Fellow: ACOG. Office Phone: 732-923-7146.

JOSHI, SANJAY, historian, educator; s. Raghunandan and Prema Joshi; m. Sanjam Ahluwalia, June 27, 1994. PhD, U. Pa., Phila., 1988—95. Asst. prof., history No. Ariz. U., Flagstaff, 1995—2002, assoc. prof., history, 2002—. Author: (history monograph) Fractured Modernity: Making of a Middle Class in Colonial North India. Fellow Fulbright-Hayes Faculty Rsch. Abroad, Dept. Edn., 2003—04. Mem.: Am. Hist. Assn., Assn. Asian Studies, Am. Inst. Indian Studies (mem. exec. com. 2003—). Avocations: travel, reading, cricket. Office: No Arizona Univ Dept History PO Box 6023 Flagstaff AZ 86001 Office Phone: 928-523-6216.

JOSHI, SURESH MEGHASHYAM, research engineer; b. Poona, India; came to U.S., 1969, naturalized 1982. B.S., Banaras U., India, 1967; M.S., Indian Inst. Tech., Kanpur, 1969; Ph.D., Rensselaer Poly. Inst., 1973. Engr., Stone & Webster Corp., Boston, 1972-73; rsch. assoc. NASA, Hampton, Va., 1973-75, sr. scientist, 1983—; rsch. prof. Old Dominion U. Research Found., Norfolk, Va., 1975-83; vis. prof. U. Va., Charlottesville, 1992-93. Author: Control of Large Flexible Space Structures, 1989, Adaptive Control of Systems with Actuator Failures, 2004; co-author: Control of Nonlinear Multibody Flexible Space Structures, 1996; contbr. articles to profl. jours. Recipient Allen B. DuMont prize Rensselaer Poly. Inst., 1973; Group Achievement award NASA, 1977, Cert. of Recognition, 1981, Quality award, 1984, 1988, 90, 91; Spl. Achievement award, 1987, 89, 94, 95; Outstanding Tech. Contributions award, 1989, 90, 92, Floyd Thompson award, 1992, Dual Career Ladder award, 1992. Fellow AIAA, IEEE (control sys. tech. award 1995, Judith A. Resnik award 2003), ASME. Avocation: amateur cartoonist. Office: NASA Langley Rsch Ctr Mail Stop 308 Hampton VA 23681

JOSHI, VYOMESH I., computer company executive; MS elec. engring., Ohio State Univ. Rsch. and devel. engring. Hewlett-Packard Co., Palo Alto, Calif., 1980—84, project mgr., 1984—89, sec. mgr., 1989—94, ops. mgr., San Diego Imaging Operatoion, 1994—95, digital copier bus., 1995—97, gen. mgr., 1997—99, v.p., gen. mgr., 1999—2002, exec. v.p. imaging & printing group, 2002—05, 2005—, exec. v.p. imaging & personal systems group, 2005. Office: Hewlett-Packard Co 3000 Hanover Rd Palo Alto CA 94304*

JOSHUA, PERCY, secondary school educator; b. Jonesville, Tex., May 5, 1952; s. Clint and Mildred (Lewis) J. BA, U. Dallas, 1974; MEd, Centenary Coll. of La., 1992, postgrad., 1996. Cert. tchr., Tex., La. Tchr. Irving (Tex.) Ind. Sch. Dist., 1975-78, Caddo Parish Schs., Shreveport, La., 1986—; chair English dept. Caddo Parish Magnet H.S., Shreveport, 1993-96. Mgr. Mr. B's, Beauty Supply, Dallas, 1978-85. Bd. dirs. Shreveport Met. Ballet; mem. Shreveport Opera, 2000-03. Fellow La. Endowment for Humanities, 1990, 92, 93, 94, 96. NEH, 1993, 2001, 04, Japanese Studies Inst., 1998. Mem. NEA, Nat. Coun. Tchrs. English (scholarship to Adelaide, Australia conf. 1993), La. Assn. Educators, La. Coun. Tchrs. English, Caddo Assn. Educators (assn. rep. 1987—), Caddo Coun. Tchrs. English (SLATE rep. 1995-2000), Shreveport C. of C. (leadership coun. 1996—). Baptist. Avocations: travel, reading, arts, chess, writing. Home: 259 Merrick St Shreveport LA 71104-2433 Office: Caddo Parish Magnet HS 1601 Viking Dr Shreveport LA 71101-5245 E-mail: percy836@bellsouth.net.

JOSKOW, JULES, economic research company executive; b. N.Y.C. s. Abraham and Mollie (Neuberg) J.; m. Charlotte Epstein, June 24, 1945; childern: Paul, Margaret, Andrew. BS, CCNY, 1941; MA, Columbia U., 1942, PhD, 1953. Mem. faculty dept. econs. CCNY, 1941-60; dir. rsch. Boni, Watkins, Jason & Co., N.Y.C., 1952-61; v.p. Nat. Econ. Rsch. Assocs., N.Y.C., 1961-70, sr. v.p., 1970-76, exec. v.p., 1976-85, pres., 1985-91, spl. cons., 1991—. Contbr. articles to profl. jours. Mem. nat. governing coun. Am. Jewish Congress, N.Y.C., 1968-71; v.p. Temple Emanuel, Great Neck, N.Y., 1974-77. Mem. Glen Head Country Club L.I. (pres. 1988-91). Home: 127 Station Rd Great Neck NY 11023-1721 Office Phone: 212-345-3000. Business E-Mail: Jules.Joskow@nera.com.

JOSKOW, PAUL LEWIS, economist, educator; b. Bklyn., June 30, 1947; s. Jules and Charlotte Joan (Epstein) J.; m. Barbara Zita Chasen, Sept. 10, 1978; 1 child, Suzanne Zoe. BA, Cornell U., 1968; M.Phil., Yale U., 1971, PhD, 1972. Asst. prof. econs. MIT, Cambridge, 1972-75, assoc. prof. econs., 1975-78, prof. econs., 1978—. Mitsui prof., 1989-96, Elizabeth and James Killian chair, 1996—, head dept. econs., 1994-98, dir. Ctr. for Energy and Environ. Policy Rsch., 1999—. Vis. prof. J.F.K. Sch. Govt., Harvard U., Cambridge, Mass., 1979-80; rsch. assoc. Nat. Bur. Econ. Rsch., 1988—; Joel Dean meml. lectr. Oberlin Coll., Ohio, 1983; cons. NERA, White Plains, N.Y., 1972-97, The World Bank, 1991-92, Rand Corp., Santa Monica, Calif., 1972-87; pub. mem. Adminstrv. Conf. U.S., Washington, 1980-82; mem. adv. coun. EPRI, Palo Alto, Calif., 1980-84; mem. acid rain adv. com. EPA, 1990-93, mem. sci. adv. bd., 1998-2002; chmn. rsch. adv. bd. Com. for Econ. Devel., 1991-94, sci. adv. bd. Inst. d'Organization Industrielle, Toulouse, France, 1991—; bd. dirs. Nat. Grid plc, London, Trans Can. Corp.; trustee Putnam Mutual Funds, Boston, 1997—. Co-author: Electric Power in the U.S., 1979, Markets For Power, 1983, Markets For Clean Air, 2000, Empirical Industrial Organization, 2003; author: Controlling Hospital Costs, 1981, Economic Regulation, 2000; also numerous articles, chpts.; co-editor, then assoc. editor Bell Jour. Econs., 1976-85; co-editor Jour. of Law, Econs. and Orgn., 1992-95; bd. editors Am. Econ. Review, 1993-98. Pres. Yale U. Coun., 1993—; mem. bd. overseers Boston Symphony Orch., 2005—. Fellow Am. Acad. Arts and Scis., Econometric Soc.; mem. ABA (assoc.), Am. Econ. Assn., Econometric Soc., Internat. Assn. for Energy Econs.(Best Paper award, 1994), Outstanding Contbns. to the Profession award 2004, Internat. Soc. for New Instnl. Econs. (v.p. 2000-2001, pres.2002-03). Home: 7 Chilton St Brookline MA 02446-3902 Office: MIT Dept Econs 50 Memorial Dr Cambridge MA 02142-1347 Office Phone: 617-253-6664. Business E-Mail: pjoskow@mit.edu.

JOSLIN, JANINE ELIZABETH, preservationist, consultant; b. Kansas City, Mo., Mar. 16, 1948; d. James Bryce and Isabel Quezon (Carr) Traner; m. Jack Leslie Joslin, Dec. 4, 1971; children: Jaclyn, Aaron, Amanda. BA in History, U. Mo., Kansas City, 1971; MA in Heritage Preservation, Ga. State U., 1992. Pvt. practice cons., Rome, Ga., 1989—92; dir. Chieftains Mus., Rome, 1992—94; pres. Gaia Walkers Inc., Leawood, Kans., 1996—99; pvt. practice cons. Leawood, 1999—. Bd. mem. Women Vision Internat., Overland Park, Kans., 1996—; pres. bd. Donnelly Internat., Kansas City, Kans., 1997—98; team leader Sci. City Mus., Kansas City, Mo., 1998—99. Contbr. articles to mags. Commr. Leawood Hist. Commn., 1998—; bd. mem. Kans. Preservation Alliance, Topeka, 2001—. Grantee, IMS, 1994, Ga. Heritage 2000, 1995, Kans. Why 150, 1999. Avocations: rowing, hiking, rafting. Home: 12508 Catalina Leawood KS 66209

JOSLIN, RODNEY DEAN, lawyer; b. Moline, Ill., May 18, 1944; s. Melvin Seth and Dorothy Ruth (Skaggs) J.; m. Ruth Anne Moody, Aug. 21, 1965 (div. July 1985); children: Amy Brooke, Eliot Dean; m. Jeanne Nowaczewski, Nov. 30, 1985; children: Benjamin Case, Cecelia Louise. AB, Augustana Coll., 1966; JD, U. Iowa, 1969. Bar: Iowa 1969, Ill. 1969, U.S. Dist. Ct. (no. dist.) Ill. 1970, U.S. Ct. Appeals (7th cir.) 1970, U.S. Supreme Ct. 1975. Assoc. Jenner & Block, Chgo., 1970-76, ptnr., 1976—. Bd. dirs. United Cerebral Palsy Assn., Chgo., 1988—, pres., 1992—; bd. dirs. Northwestern Libr. Coun., Chgo., 1988—, Augustana Coll., 1996—; chmn. Perspectives Charter Sch., 1998—. Address: 706 WHutchinson St Chicago IL 60613-1520

JOSS, PAUL CHRISTOPHER, astrophysicist, atmospheric physicist, educator; b. Bklyn., May 7, 1945; s. Everett Henry and Magda Anna (Hohorst) J.; m. Marjorie Jean Axton, Jan. 24, 1970 (div.); 1 child, Susan Elizabeth; m. Karen Elizabeth Murray, July 3, 1992 (div.); 1 child, Matthew Albert Henry. BA, Cornell U., 1966, PhD, 1971. Mem. Inst. for Advanced Study, Princeton, NJ, 1971—73; asst. prof. MIT, Cambridge, 1973—78, assoc. prof., 1978—83, prof., 1983—, mem. Ctr. for Theoretical Physics, 1973—2005, mem. Ctr. for Space Rsch., 1973—2005, assoc. head astrophysics divsn., 1983—88, mem. Kavli Inst. for Astrophysics and Space Rsch., 2005—. Vis. scientist Aspen Ctr. for Physics, 1972—, Weizmann Inst. Sci., Rehovot, Israel, 1974—75, 1978, Inst. Astronomy, Cambridge, England, 1977, 93; vis. staff mem. Los Alamos (N.Mex.) Sci. Lab., 1979—80, cons., 1980—92, Visidyne Inc., Burlington, Mass., 1979—82, 1992—93, spl. asst. to pres., 1993—; mem. adv. com. Inst. Geophysics and Planetary Physics Los Alamos Nat. Lab., 1987—92; mem. High Energy Astrophysics Mgmt. Ops. Working Group NASA, 1988—91; mem. Astronomy and Space Physics Sci. Coun. Univs. Space Rsch. Assn., 1988—92; mem. Inst. for Theoretical Physics U. Calif., Santa Barbara, 1991; pres. Joss Consulting Assocs., 1992—. Contbr. 160 articles to profl. jours. Woodrow Wilson Found. fellow, 1966; NSF fellow, 1970; Alfred P. Sloan Found. fellow, 1976. Mem. Am. Astron. Soc. (Helen B. Warner Prize 1980, exec. com. High Energy Astrophysics div. 1983-85), Am. Phys. Soc., Internat. Astron. Union, Phi Beta Kappa. Avocations: classical music, chess. Office: MIT Dept Of Physics Rm 37-607 Cambridge MA 02139 Business E-Mail: joss@space.mit.edu.

JOSS, ROBERT L., dean; m. Betty Badger Joss; children: Randall, Jennifer Joss Bradley. BA in econ. magna cum laude, U. Wash., 1963; MBA, Stanford U., 1967, PhD, 1970. Dep. to asst. sec. for econ. policy US Treas. Dept., 1968—71; asst. v.p. Wells Fargo Bank, San Francisco, 1971—72, v.p., 1972—75, sr. v.p., 1975—81, exec. v.p., 1981—86, vice chmn., 1986—93, bd. dirs., 1999—; CEO, mng. dir. Westpac Banking Corp., Australia, 1993—99; Philip H. Knight prof. and dean Stanford Grad. Sch. Bus., Stanford U., 1999—. Bd. dirs. Student Loan Mktg. Assn., 1990—93, Bus. Coun. Australia, 1998—99, Shanghai Comml. Bank, Hong Kong, 1978—93, Hong Kong, 2002—, Agilent Tech. Inc., 2003—, Epiphany Inc.; chmn. Australian Bankers Assn., 1997—99. Co-author (with Frank Blount): (book) Managing in Australia, 1999. Office: Stanford U Stanford Grad Sch Bus 518 Memorial Way Stanford CA 94305-5015

JOSSE, FABIEN J., electrical engineer, educator, computer engineer; PhD, U. Maine, 1982. Prof. Marquette U., Milw., 1982—. Achievements include research in solid state and acoustic wave device microsensors. Office Phone: 414-288-6789.

JOST, LAWRENCE JOHN, lawyer; b. Alma, Wis., Oct. 9, 1944; s. Lester J. and Hazel L. (Johnson) J.; m. Anne E. Fisher, June 10, 1967; children—Peter, Katherine, Susan. BSCE, U. Wis., 1968, JD, 1969. Bar: Wis. 1969, U.S. Dist. Ct. (ea. dist.) Wis. 1969, U.S. Ct. Appeals (7th cir.) 1969, U.S. Supreme Ct. 1980. Law clk. to judge U.S. Dist. Ct., Milw., 1969-70; assoc. firm Brady, Tyrrell, Cotter & Cutler, 1970-74; assoc. Quarles & Brady, 1974-76, ptnr., 1976—, chair real estate group, 1985—, chair real property sect., 2002—. Vis. tchr. gen. practice Wis. Law Sch. Bd. dirs. Milw. Chamber Theatre, 1998-2001, Marcus Ctr. for the Performing Arts, 2003—; pres. Vis. Nurse Assn. Milw., 1982-85, VNA, Corp., 1982-86; bd. dirs. Wis. Heritage Inc., 1980-82, Vis. Nurse Found., 1986-95, pres., 1993-94; bd. dirs. Milw. Repertory Theater, 1987-95, 2001—, pres., 1990-92; bd. dirs. United Performing Arts Fund, 1989-93. Mem. ABA, Wis. Bar Assn. (lectr. seminars), Milw. Bar Assn., Am. Coll. Real Estate Lawyers, Am. Coll. Mortgage Attys. (state chair), Nat. Assn. Indsl. and Office Properties (bd. dirs. Wis. chpt. 2003—). Mem. Plymouth United Ch. of Christ Office: Quarles & Brady LLP 411 E Wisconsin Ave Ste 2550 Milwaukee WI 53202-4497 Office Phone: 414-277-5000. Business E-Mail: ljj@quarles.com.

JOTCHAM, THOMAS DENIS, marketing communications consultant; b. Llandudno, Wales, Feb. 21, 1918; s. George James and Marion (Brand) J.; m. Margaret Jean Thirlwell, Aug. 10, 1940 (dec.); children: Patricia, Douglas, Joy, Candace (dec.), m. Thelma M. Archer, April 29, 2002. Student, Lower Can. Coll., 1929-36, McGill U., 1937-39. Sales rep. Montreal Lithographing Co., Ltd., Montreal, 1945—47; sales mgr. Wesco Waterpaints Can., Ltd., Montreal, 1947—48; advt. mgr. Pepsi-Cola Co. Can., Ltd., Montreal, 1948—52, mgr., 1952—54; asst. advt. mgr. Reader's Digest Assn., Ltd., Montreal, 1954—56; mgr., v.p. Foster Advt. Ltd., Montreal, 1956—73, exec. v.p., 1973—75, pres., 1977—81, vice chmn., 1981—83; pres. Sherwood Communications Group Ltd., Toronto, 1977—81, vice chmn., 1981—83. Mem. coun. Montreal Bd. Trade, 1973-75, v.p., 1977-78, pres., 1979, hon. chmn., 1980-81. Bd. dirs. Grace Dart Hosp., 1973-83, pres., 1979-83; bd. dirs. Can.Coun. Christians and Jews, 1978-81, Les Grands Ballets Canadien, 1976-77; mem. Venetion Condominium, Inc., pres. 1984, 88-92; treas. Freedom Found.-Broward, 1999-2000. Maj. Can. Army, 1940-45. Recipient ACA Gold medal, 1978; charter recipient McGill Mgmt. Achievement award, 1981. Fellow: Inst. Can. Advt. (pres. 1976—77); mem.: Advt. Agy. Coun. Que. (pres. 1975—76), Advt. and Sales Assocs. Montreal (pres. 1948—49), Advt. and Sales Execs. Club (pres. 1956—58), Can. Advt. and Sales Assn. (pres. 1960—61), Can.- South African Soc. (bd. dirs. 1980—89, chmn. 1983—86), Internat. Swimming Hall of Fame (chmn. 1998—99), Coral Ridge Yacht Club (gov. 1993—97, commodore 1997), St. James Club (com. chmn. 1979—81), Mt. Stephen Club (pres. 1967—68), Royal Montreal Golf Club, Ft. Lauderdale Golf and Country Club (bd. dirs. 1990—92), Thistle Curling Club (pres. 1977—78), Ont. Club, Psi Upsilon. Home and Office: 2000 S Ocean Dr #1510 Fort Lauderdale FL 33316-3813 Office Phone: 954-522-5252.

JOTHEN, MICHAEL JON, music educator, composer, conductor; b. Abington, Pa., Jan. 11, 1944; s. Marvin Carlyle and Judith Agnes Jothen; m. Gail Kristine Peterson, Aug. 19, 1967; children: Peder Joshua, Nels Matthew, Kaarn Agnes. BA, St. Olaf Coll., 1967; MA, Case-Western Res. U., 1972; PhD, Ohio State U., 1978. Tchr. k-12-vocal/gen. music Newaygo (Mich.) Pub. Schs., 1967—69; tchr. 7-9-vocal/gen. music Ashland (Ohio) City Schs., 1969—74; grad. tchg. asst. Ohio State U., Columbus, 1974—77, instr. music Newark, 1977—78; prof. music U. No. Colo., Greeley, 1978—84; supr. vocal/gen. music Balt. County Pub. Schs., Towson, Md., 1984—93; prof. music Towson U., 1993—. Cons. various pub. schs., 1985—; presenter in field. Author: (textbook) Music and You, 1987, Share the Music, 1994, Experiencing Choral Music, 2005, Spotlight on Music, 2005, composer choral compositions for varied voicings; contbr. articles to profl. jours. Musical dir. Greeley (Colo.) Chorale, 1978—85; music dir. St. Michael Luth. Ch., Balt., 1986—2005; bd. mem. Md. Music Educators Assn., Md., 1995—99. Recipient Std. award, ASCAP, 1992—2005. Mem.: Choristers Guild (bd. dirs. 1991—92, pres. bd. dirs. 1994—96, chair anniversary organizing com. 1997—98), Md. Music Educators Assn. (chair-student membership 1995—99), Music Educators Nat. Conf. (chairperson various coms.), Am. Choral Dirs. Assn. (life). Independent. Lutheran. Avocations: designing houses, museums, travel, sports. Home: 14206 Sawmill Ct Phoenix MD 21131 Office: Towson University 8000 York Rd Towson MD 21252 Office Phone: 410-704-2257. Business E-Mail: mjothen@towson.edu.

JOU, LIANGDER, research scientist; BS, Nat. Taiwan U., 1988, MS, 1986; PhD, U. Calif., Berkeley, 1995. Asst. adj. prof. U. Calif., San Francisco, 1998—. Asst. prof. U. Pitts., 2005—. Office: McGowan Inst. 3205 East Carson St Pittsburgh PA 15203 Office Phone: 415-221-4810.

JOUBERT, LORRIE B., mathematics professor; d. Thomas L. and Nancy F. Boullion; m. Lon Randall (div.); children: Tyler, Jacob; m. Bryan K. Joubert, Mar. 26, 2004. BS, La. State U., 1989; MS, U. La., Lafayette, 1995. Instr. La. State U., Eunice, 1998—2003, asst. prof., 2003—. Com. mem. La. State U., Eunice, 1998—2005; presenter regional and internat. confs. Recipient Favorite Tchr. award, Phi Theta Kappa Orgn., 2002. Mem.: Math. Assn. Am., La.-Miss. Math. Assn. 2-Yr. Colls. (sec. 2002—03, pres.-elect 2004—05). Office: La State U-Eunice PO Box 1129 Eunice LA 70535-1129

JOUKOWSKY, ARTEMIS A. W., private investor; b. Shanghai, Dec. 26, 1930; s. Artemis M.W. and Helen (Skvorzov) J.; m. Martha Content Sharp, June 9, 1956; children: Nina Lydia Koprulu, Artemis W. III, Michael A. AB,

Brown U., 1955, LLD (hon.), 1985. Dep. to dir. Am. Internat. Underwriters, Milan, 1960-66, dep. to regional dir. for Europe, 1963-66, regional v.p. for Middle East, North Africa Beirut, 1966-72, pres., regional dir. S.E. Asia Hong Kong, 1972-74, v.p. N.Y.C., 1974-77; mng. dir. Middle East Assurance and Reinsurance Co., Beirut, 1966-72; dir. Tam Sigorta, Istanbul, Turkey, 1967-72, Union Atlantique de Reassurance SA, Brussels, 1979-88, European Am. Underwriters, Vienna, 1979-87; dir., shareholder's rep. AIG Joint Ventures with Govt. Agencies, N.Y.C., 1979-87, pres. socialist countries div. and spl. world markets div., 1977-87. Founder, chmn. Brown U. Sports Found., 1983—; trustee Brown U., Providence, 1985—, vice chancellor 1988-97, chancellor, 1997-98, chancellor emeritus, 1998—, mem. bd. fellows, 1998—; chmn. campaign for rising generation for Brown U., 1991-96, chmn. campaign for Brown Med. Sch., 1997-2002; mem. bd. overseers Thomas J. Watson Inst. for Internat. Studies, 1981—; mem. vis. com. Ctr. for Old World Archaeology and Art, 1981-92; vice chmn. bd. govs. John Carter Brown Libr., 1988—; trustee Lawrenceville Sch., N.J., 1984—, pres. bd. trustees, 1997-2001; chmn. Archaeol Inst. Am., 1992—; pres. bd. trustees Am. Ctr. Oriental Rsch., Amman, Jordan, 1992—; mem. vis. com. Boston Mus. Fine Arts, 1985-92; dir. Clear Pool Camp, 1976-85; co-founder Am. Sch. Milan, 1962, bd. govs., 1961-65, pres. 1963-64, fin. com. 1962-65; trustee St. Croix Landmark Soc., Fredericksted, U.S. V.I., 1995—; trustee Internat. Rsch. and Exchs. Bd., 1998—. Decorated Order of the Cedars Govt. Lebanon, Order of Independence medal Jordan. Mem. U.S. C. of C. (gov. Hong Kong chpt.), U.S.-USSR Trade and Econ. Coun. (tourist and travel com. 1974-77), Hungarian-Am. Trade and Econ. Coun. (vce chmn. 1984-87), Exploreer's Club (N.Y.C.), India House (N.Y.C.), Hong Kong Club (life), Brown Club (N.Y.C.), Larchmont (N.Y.) Yacht Club, St. Croix Yacht Club (U.S. V.I.) Univ. Club (Providence), Hope Club (Providence), Knickerbocker Club (N.Y.C.). Office: Brown U 5 Benevolent St Providence RI 02912-9018

JOURDAN, TONI CHRISTINA, small business owner, actress, writer; b. Springfield, Oreg., Dec. 29, 1961; d. Jack Eugene and Sharon Rose Frisk; m. Charlie Nelson Jourdan, Jan. 17, 1998; 1 child, Nicholas Dawson; m. Louis Eugene Beery, Feb. 14, 1988 (div. Feb. 2, 1996). BFA, U. Idaho, 1982. Prin., owner Xanadu Theatre Co., Mesa, Ariz., 1990—, Whimsicals Character Parties, 2004—. Drama coach Ventura Pk. and Recreation, Thousand Oaks, Calif., 1995—99, Phoenix Pks. and Recreation, 1999—2002, Copper Canyon Elem. Sch., Scottsdale, Ariz., 2001—04, Washington Elem. Sch., Phoenix, 2004—05. Author: (books on tape) Little Women, Secret Garden, Dracula, Golden Bowl, Cinderella, Peter Pan, Alice in Wonderland, Moby Dick, Wizard of Oz, Huckleberry Finn, Legend of Sleepy Hollow, Joan of Arc, Anne of Green Gables, Captains Courageous; performer: Little Woman, 1998, Secret Garden, 1998, Wizard of Oz, 1998, Dracula, 1998, Cinderella, 1999, Peter Pan, 1999, Alice in Wonderland, 1999, Moby Dick, 1999, Legend of Sleepy Hollow, 1999, Joan of Arc, 1999, Captains Courageous, 1999, Huckleberry Finn, 2000, Golden Bowl, 2000, Gift of the Magi, Anne of Green Gables, 2001. Named Book Pal of Yr., Screen Actors Guild Ariz., 2004. Mem.: Soc. Children's Book Writers and Illustrators. Democrat. Buddhist. Office Phone: 480-628-2508.

JOURDREN, MARC HENRI, investment company executive; b. Paris, Dec. 28, 1960; s. Pierre Auguste Jourdren and Berthe Augustine Dubois. Diploma in econs. and fin., Essec, Paris, 1983; MBA, Harvard U., 1987. Pres., founder Essec Enterprises Internat., Paris, 1982-83; attache French Ministry of Economy and Fin., N.Y.C., 1983-85; assoc. Goldman Sachs & Co., N.Y.C. and Tokyo, 1987-88, Goldman Sachs Internat., London, 1988—2003, v.p., exec. dir., 1991—2000, head Japanese equities, 1996-99, mng. dir., 2000—03, head global products group, 1999—2003; mng. dir. Lehman Bros., 2003—, head instnl. client group, 2003—. Fgn. advisor Harvard U., Cambridge, Mass., 1989—. Mem. Wigmore Hall London, Soc. Couserans Pyrenees, Brit. Mensa Ltd. Avocations: piano, russian art, gastronomy, nature, skiing. Home: 48 Macready House Crawford St London W1H 5LP England Office: Lehman Bros 25 Bank St 29th Fl London E14 5LE England Personal E-mail: m@couzeranes.com.

JOURIAN, TRENT JACKSON, student affairs educator, activist, performer; b. Beirut, June 6, 1981; s. Berge and Marilou (Manavdjian) Jourian. BA in Gen. Mgmt., Mich. State U., East Lansing, 2002. Asst. hall dir. dept. residence life Mich. State U., East Lansing, 2003—04, asst. dir. dept. residence life, 2004; grad. asst. Office LBGT Concerns, MSU, East Lansing, 2004—05; intern Women's Ctr. Boise State U., Idaho, 2005—. Spkr., East Lansing; panelist, East Lansing; dir. rels. Student Affairs Grad. Assn., East Lansing, 2004—05; founder Phi Tau Mu (FTM) Alpha-Male chpt., East Lansing, 2004—. Performer: (gender performance, dancing and lip sync) Drag King Rebellion; columnist (campus newspaper) State News. Recipient World Gold medal Level 1 book keeping, London C. of C. and Industry, 1997, Prism award, Lansing Assn. Human Rights, 2002; scholar Cyprus-Am. Scholarship Program, Fulbright Commn., 1999. Mem.: Nat. Assn. Student Pers. Adminstrs., Am. Coll. Pers. Assn. Avocations: reading, poetry, travel, movies.

JOURNEY, DREXEL DAHLKE, lawyer; b. Westfield, Wis., Feb. 23, 1926; s. Clarence Earl and Verna L. Gilmore (Dahlke) Journey Gilmore; m. Vergene Harriet Sandsmark, Oct. 24, 1952; 1 child, Ann Marie. *Wife Vergene Journey, a registered nurse St. Mary's School of Nursing, 1947, and a member of the National Capitol Harp Ensemble, holds various concert harp performance credits, including ensemble appearances at the White House and the John F. Kennedy Center for the Performing Arts.* BBA, U. Wis., 1950, LLB, 1952; LLM, George Washington U., 1957. Bar: Wis. 1952, U.S. Dist. Ct. (we. dist.) Wis. 1953, U.S. Supreme Ct. 1955, U.S. Ct. Appeals (4th cir.) 1960, U.S. Ct. Appeals (5th cir.) 1961, U.S. Ct. Appeals (D.C. cir.) 1965, U.S. Ct. Appeals (7th and 9th cirs.) 1967, U.S. Ct. Appeals (1st cir.) 1969, D.C. 1970, U.S. Dist. Ct. D.C. 1970, U.S. Ct. Appeals (2d, 3d, 6th, 8th and 10th cirs.) 1976, U.S. Ct. Appeals (11th cir.) 1981. Counsel FPC, Washington, 1952-66, asst. gen. counsel, 1966-70, dep. gen. counsel, 1970-74, gen. counsel, 1974-77; ptnr. Schiff Hardin LLP, Washington, 1977—. Mem. mediation program U.S. Dist. Ct. (D.C. cir.), 1989—, early neutral evaluation program, 1989-95; mem. case evaluation program D.C. Superior Ct., 1991—. Author: Corporate Law and Practice, 1975; contbr. articles to profl. jours. Pres. Am. U. Park Citizens Assn., Washington, 1970-72; trustee Lincoln-Wesmoreland Housing Project, Washington, 1978-79. With Mcht. Marine Res., USNR, 1944-46, USNG, 1948-50. Knapp scholar, U. Wis., 1952. Mem.: ABA, FBA, Energy Bar Assn., Masons, Army and Navy Club, Phi Kappa Phi, Phi Eta Sigma, Theta Delta Chi. Republican. Congregationalist. Home: 4540 Windom Pl NW Washington DC 20016-2452 Office: Schiff Hardin LLP Ste 600 1101 Connecticut Ave NW Washington DC 20036-4390 Office Phone: 202-778-6420. E-mail: djourney@schiffhardin.com.

JOVANOVIC, LOIS, medical researcher; b. Mpls. BS in biology, Columbia U., 1969; B in Hebrew Lit., Jewish Theol. Seminary, 1968, M in Hebrew Lit., 1970; MD, Albert Einstein Coll. Medicine, 1973. Intern and resident NY Hosp. Cornell U. Med. Coll., 1973—76; fellow in endocrinology and metabolism Cornell U. Med. Coll., 1976—78, instr., asst to assoc. prof., 1978—86; asst. attending physician NY Hosp., 1978—85; asst. adj. prof. and physician Rockefeller U. and Rockefeller U. Hosp., 1979—85; assoc. adj. prof. U. Calif., Irvine, 1986—88; sr. scientist Sansum Med. Rsch. Found., 1985—96; dir. and chief sci. officer Sansum Diabetes Rsch. Inst., 1996—; clin. assoc. prof. medicine U. SC- LA Med. Ctr., 1986—89, prof., 1989—; rsch. biologist U. Calif., Santa Barbara, 1990—. Author numerous books and articles on diabetes and women's health. Fellow: NY Acad. Medicine, Am. Coll. Endocrinology, Am. Coll. Nutrition, ACP. Office: Sansum Diabetes Rsch Inst 2219 Bath St Santa Barbara CA 93105

JOVE, RICHARD, molecular biologist; b. Barcelona, Cataluna, Spain, Feb. 5, 1955; came to U.S., 1960; s. Ricardo and Maria Rosa (Calmet) J.; m. Hua Yu, June 21, 1984. BA, SUNY, Buffalo, 1977, MS, 1978; M in Philosophy, Columbia U., 1981, PhD, 1984. Postdoctoral fellow Rockefeller U., N.Y.C., 1984-88; asst. prof. U. Mich., Ann Arbor, 1988-94, assoc. prof., 1994-95, dir. molecular oncology program Cancer Ctr., 1992-95; prof. oncology, biochemistry and pathology U. So. Fla. Sch. Medicine, Tampa, 1995—2005; Frank and Carol Morsani prof. molecular oncology U. South Fla. Sch. Medicine, Tampa, 2003—05; dir. molecular oncology program Moffitt Cancer Ctr. and Rsch. Inst., Tampa, 1995—2005; assoc. dir. basic rsch. Moffitt Rsch. Inst., Tampa, 2003—05; prof., chair molecular medicine dept. City of Hope Nat. Med. Ctr., Duarte, Calif., 2005—, dep. dir. Comprehensive Cancer Ctr., 2005—. Recipient John S. Newberry prize Columbia U., 1984, Jr. Faculty Rsch. award Am. Cancer Soc., 1988-91; Damon Runyon-Walter Winchell Cancer Fund fellow, 1984-87; named Scientist of the Yr., Moffitt Cancer Ctr., 2002, named Frank and Carol Morsani prof. molecular oncology, 2003—. Mem. The Harvey Soc., Sigma Xi. Office: City of Hope Nat Med Ctr 1500 E Duarte Rd Duarte CA 91010 E-mail: RJove@coh.org.

JOVOVICH, MILLA (NATASHA MILITZA JOVOVICH), model, actress; b. Kiev, Ukraine, Dec. 17, 1975; d. Bogdanovitch and Galina Loginova Jovovich; m. Shawn Andrews, 1992; m. Luc Besson, 1997 (div. 1999). Appeared on mag. covers including Lei, 1987, Mademoiselle, Aerna, Harper's Bazaar, Vogue, Face, i-D, Vanity Fair, W, Marie Claire; internat. spokesmodel L'Oreal; launched line of clothing with Carmen Hawk called Jovovich-Hawk, 2003. Composer: (songs in films) Gentleman Who Fell, 1993, The Rules of Attraction, 2002, The Prince & Me, 2004; costume designer: (films) Mona Lisa Smile, 2003; actor: Two Moon Junction, 1988, Return to the Blue Lagoon, 1991, Kuffs, 1992, Chaplin, 1992, Dazed and Confused, 1993, The Fifth Element, 1997, He Got Game, 1998, The Messenger: The Story of Joan of Arc, 1999, The Million Dollar Hotel, 2000, The Claim, 2000, Zoolander, 2001, Dummy, 2002, Resident Evil, 2002, The House on Turk Street, 2002, You Stupid Man, 2002, Resident Evil: Apocalypse, 2004; (TV films) The Night Train to Kathmandu, 1988; singer: (albums) The Divine Comedy, 1994. Office: c/o Spanky Taylor 3727 W Magnolia Burbank CA 91505

JOWDY, JEFFREY WILLIAM, research and development company executive; b. New Bern, N.C., Oct. 1, 1959; s. Albert Willoughby and Millicent (McKendry) Jowdy. BA in Journalism, U. Ga., 1983, postgrad. in speech communication, 1983-85; MA in Pers. Mgmt., Troy (Ala.) State U., 1987. Cert. fund raising exec. Employee relations mgr. Phoebe Putney Meml. Hosp., Albany, Ga., 1985-87; dir. South Ga. chpt. March of Dimes Birth Defects Found., Macon, Ga., 1987-90; devel. dir. Mount de Sales Acad., Macon, 1990-94; sr. mng. dir. Jerold Panas, Linzy & Ptnrs., 1994—97; sr. v.p. YMCA of Mid. Tenn., Franklin, 1997—2003; pres. Lighthouse Counsel, 1999—. Bd. dirs. Hamilton Holt Ednl. Loan Fund, mem. Nat. Ctr. for non-profit Bds. Alumni bd. dirs. Henry Grady Coll. Journalism, U. Ga.; bd. dirs. Joe C. Davis YMCA Outdoor Ctr., Sloan Family Health Ctr.; mem. Ga. Coun. on Planned Giving; mem. Christian Stewardship Assn. Mem. Assn. Fundraising Profls. (pres. Nashville chpt.), SAR (founder, pres. Ocmulgee chpt.), Macon C. of C., Macon Heritage Found., Assn. Fundraising Profls. (pres.-elect Nashville chpt.), U. Ga. Alumni Assn. (bd. dirs.), Mid. Ga. Cedars Club (v.p., chmn. pub. rels., bd. dirs.), Kiwanis (v.p., pres. Macon chpt., Kiwanian of Yr. award 1989), Rotary Club of Nashville, Commerce Club, Phi Kappa Theta (sec. Delta Rho Found., founder, pres. Gamma Sigma Alumi chpt.). Home: PO Box 681325 Franklin TN 37068-1325 Office: 228 Circle View Dr Franklin TN 37067

JOY, BILL (WILLIAM N. JOY), venture capitalist, former computer software company executive; b. Detroit, Nov. 8, 1954; s. William C. Joy; m. Sara Joy; children: Hayden, Madison. BSEE, U. Mich., 1975, MSEE and Computer Sci., 1982. Co-founder Sun Microsystems Inc., Mountain View, Calif., 1982, v.p. rsch., 1996—98, chief scientist, 1998—2003; ptnr. Kleiner Perkins Caulfield & Byers, Menlo Park, Calif., 2005—. Bd. dirs. SpikeSource Inc., Redwood City, Calif., 2005—. Prin. designer U. Calif. (Berkeley) version of UNIX operating sys.; co-designer Java tech., SPARC microprocessor architecture. Recipient Grace Murray Hopper award, Assn. for Computing Machinery, 1986, Lifetime Achievement Award, USENIX Assoc., 1993. Mem. NAE, Am. Acad. Arts & Sciences; bd. trustees, Aspen Inst.; co-chmn., Presidential Info. Tech. Adv. Com., 1997. Achievements include the designing of Solaris, SPARC, and Java programming languages. Office: Kleiner Perkins Caulfield & Byers 2750 Sand Hill Rd Menlo Park CA 94025*

JOY, CARLA MARIE, history educator; b. Denver, Sept. 5, 1945; d. Carl P. and Theresa M. (Lotito) J. AB cum laude, Loretto Heights Coll., 1967; MA, U. Denver, 1969, postgrad., 1984-87. Instr. history Cmty. Coll., Denver; prof. history Red Rocks C.C., Lakewood, Colo., 1970—. Cons. for innovative ednl. programs; reviewer fed. grants, 1983-89; mem. adv. panel Colo. Endowment for Humanities, 1985-89. Contbr. articles to profl. publs. Instr. vocat. edn. Mile High United Way, Jefferson County, 1975; participant Jefferson County Sch. Sys. R-1 Dist., 1983-88; active Red Rocks C.C. Spkrs. Bur., 1972-89, strategic planning com., 1992-97; chair history discipline Colo. Gen. Edn. Core Transfer Consortium, 1986-96, faculty transfer curriculum coun., 1997—; mem. Colo. C.C. curriculum com., 1999—; mem. history, geography, civics stds. and geography frameworks adv. com. Colo. Dept. Edn., 1995-96; steering com. Ctr. Tchg. Excellence, 1991-92, 96-97; with North Ctrl. Self-Study Process, 1972-73, 80-81, 86-88, 96-98; with K-16 Linkages Colo. Commn. for Higher Edn., 1997-98; mem. evaluation team for Colo. Awards, edn. and civic achievement for Widefield Sch. Dist. #3, 1989; mem. Red Rocks C.C.-Clear Creek Sch. Sys. Articulation Team, 1990-91; mem. Statue of Liberty-Ellis Island Found. Inc., 1987—. Ford Found. fellow, 1969; recipient Cert. of Appreciation Kiwanis Club, 1981, Telecomm. Coop. for Colo.'s Cmty. Colls., 1990-92, Master Tchr. award U. Tex.-Austin, 1982. Mem. NEA, Am. Hist. Assn., Am. Assn. Higher Edn., Nat. Coun. Social Studies, Nat. Geog. Soc., Omohundro Inst. Early Am. History and Culture, Colo. Edn. Assn., Colo. Coun. Social Studies, World Hist. Assn., Orgn. Am. Historians, The Colo. Hist. Soc., Colo. Geog. Alliance, Soc. Hist. Edn., Phi Alpha Theta. Home: 1849 S Lee St Apt D Lakewood CO 80232-6252 Office: Red Rocks C C 13300 W 6th Ave Lakewood CO 80228-1213

JOY, EDWARD BENNETT, electrical engineer, educator, consultant; b. Troy, N.Y., Nov. 15, 1941; s. Herman Johnson and Elizabeth (Bennett) J.; m. Patricia Marie Huddleston, Aug. 27, 1966; children: Frederick Huddleston, Rebecca Elizabeth. BEE, Ga. Inst. Tech., 1963, MSEE, 1967, PhD in Elec. Engring., 1970. Asst. prof. elec. engring. Ga. Inst. Tech., Atlanta, 1970-75, assoc. prof., 1975-80, prof., 1980-98, prof. emeritus, 1998—; pres. Joy Engring. Co., Boulder, Colo., 1981—. Cons. in field. Patentee in field; contbr. to profl. publs. Lt. USNR, 1963—65, Vietnam. Recipient Continuing Edn. award, Ga. Tech., 1997. Fellow IEEE; mem. Antenna Measurements Techniques Assn. (Disting. Achievement award, 1999). Republican. Presbyterian. Avocations: amateur radio, electronics, hiking. Home and Office: 1450 Rembrandt Rd Boulder CO 80302-9478 Office Phone: 303-545-5566.

JOY, RICHARD MARKS, lawyer; b. Elmhurst, Ill., Sept. 11, 1943; s. Clifford Whitney and Phyllis Rose (Tritchler) J.; m. Diane Katherine Bound, July 21, 1967; children: Stephen Whitney, David Lee. BA, U. Mich., 1966; JD, U. Ill., 1969. Bar: Ill. 1969, U.S. Dist. Ct. (ctrl. dist.) Ill. 1970. Law clk. to Chief Justice Robert C. Underwood Ill. Supreme Ct., Bloomington, 1969-71; atty. Dobbins, Fraker, Tennant, Joy & Perlstein, Champaign, Ill., 1972—. Mem., chmn. County Bar Real Estate com., Champaign, 1983-91, 96—, City of Champaign Plan Commn., 1975-89; dir., chmn. Champaign County Mental Health Ctr., Urbana, Ill., 1977-86. Mem. Champaign West Rotary Club (bd. dirs. 1991-94). Avocation: golf. Office: Dobbins Fraker Tennant Joy & Perlstein 215 N Neil St Champaign IL 61820-4012 Office Phone: 217-356-7233. Business E-Mail: rjoy@dobbinslaw.com.

JOY, ROBERT JOHN THOMAS, medical educator; b. South Kingstown, RI, Apr. 5, 1929; s. Angelo Francis and Mary Frances (Egan) Joy; m. Beverly June Boxer, July 5, 1952 (div. May 1984); children: Robert L.F., Lisa; m. Janet Lucille Brady, July 12, 1985. BS, U. RI, 1950; MD, Yale U., 1954; MA, Harvard Coll., 1965; cert., Armed Forces Staff Coll., 1968. Commd. 1st lt. US Army, 1954, advanced through grades to col., 1970; intern, resident Walter Reed Army Med. Ctr., Washington, 1954-58; asst. dir. environ. medicine USA Med. Rsch. Lab., Fort Knox, Ky., 1959-61; comdr. USA Rsch. Inst. Environ. Medicine, Natick, Mass., 1961-62; chief comdr. USA Med. Rsch. Team, Saigon, Vietnam, 1965-66; chief med. rsch. div. Office Surgeon Gen., US Army, Washington, 1968-69; dep. med. life scis. Office Dir. Def. Rsch. Engring., Washington, 1969-71; dep. dir., dir. Walter Reed Inst. Rsch., Washington, 1971-76; prof., chmn. mil. medicine Uniformed Svcs. U. Health Scis., Washington, 1976-81, prof., chmn. med. history, 1981-96, prof. emeritus, 1996—; ret. US Army, 1981. Hon. mem. faculty Indsl. Coll. Armed Forces, Washington, 1990; faculty mem. USAF Sch. Aerospace Medicine, 1992—. Editor: Jour. History Medicine and Allied Scis., 1983—87; editor: (monographs on military medicine); contbr. Decorated Disting. Svc. medal, Legion Merit (4); recipient John Shaw Billings award, Am. Mil. Surgeons of US, 1986, William P. Clements award Uniformed Svcs., U. Health Scis., 1980. Fellow: Coll. Physicians Phila., AAAS, ACP (Davies award Med. Humanism 2002); mem.: Am. Physiol. Soc., Am. Assn. History Medicine (coun. 1979-81) (William Osler medal 1954), Osler Soc. (bd. govs. 1986-89). Home: 5821 Highland Dr Bethesda MD 20815-5531 Office: Uniformed Svcs U Dept Med History 4301 Jones Bridge Rd Bethesda MD 20814-4712

JOYCE, ANNE RAINE, editor, publications director; b. South Bend, Ind., Oct. 2, 1942; d. James Agee and Marjorie Elizabeth (Gilstrap) Raine; m. Glenn Russell Joyce, Aug. 19, 1962; 1 child, Adam Russell. AB, Cen. Meth. Coll., 1962; MA in French, U. Mo., 1966; MA in Linguistics, U. Iowa, 1979. Cert. tchr., Mo. Tchr. Centralia (Mo.) High Sch., 1962-64; instr. Coe Coll., Cedar Rapids, Iowa, 1978-79, Georgetown U., Washington, 1980-83; asst. editor Am.-Arab Affairs, Washington, 1983-84; editor, dir. publs. Mid. East Policy, Washington, 1984—; gen. sec. Mid. East Policy Coun., Washington, 1991—, v.p., 1993—. Mem. edn. com. Fairfax County (Va.) PTA Bd., 1986-88. U.S. Dept. Def. fellow, 1964-66; recipient Recognition award Am.-Arab Affairs Coun., 1988, Disting. Alumni award. Cen. Meth. Coll., 1990. Mem. Middle East Studies Assn., LWV (fin. chair Fairfax county chpt. 1981—). Home: 6916 Tulsa Ct Alexandria VA 22307-1730 Office: Middle East Policy Coun 1730 M St NW Ste 512 Washington DC 20036-4516 E-mail: ajoyce@mepc.org.

JOYCE, BERNITA ANNE, retired federal agency administrator; d. Albert A. and Margaret C. Joyce; m. Kenneth B. Lucas, Aug. 2, 1975. BA, Duchesne Coll.; MBA, U. Santa Clara, PhD, 1974. With Wolfe & Co. CPAs, Washington, 1971-72; fin. dir. Nat. Forest Products Assn., Washington, 1972-74; budget and fiscal officer ICC, Washington, 1974-77, Office Mgmt. and Budget, 1977-80; asst. dir. mgmt. svcs. Bur. Mines, Dept. Interior, 1980-85; asst. dir. Office Policy Analysis, Dept. Interior, 1985-96, asst. spl. trustee Am. Indians, 1996—99; asst. adminstr. S.J. Cmty. Georgetown U., 2000—05; pres. Rogers Sys., Inc., 2005—. Author: Financial Viability of Private Elementary Schools. Mem. AICPA, Sr. Execs. Assn., Assn. Govt. Accts., Cosmos Club, Beta Gamma Sigma. Home: 6001 Bradley Blvd Bethesda MD 20817-3807

JOYCE, BRENDAN KENNETH, pharmacist, director; s. William and Judith Joyce; m. Loralyn Nelson, Aug. 8, 1997; children: Erin children: Sean. BS, N.D. State U., 1995, PharmD, 1997. Registered Pharmacist N.D., 1997. Pharmacy practice resident St. Alexius Med. Ctr., N.D. State U., Bismarck, 1997—98; clin. pharmacist Medcenter One Health Sys., Bismarck, 1998—2001; adminstr., pharmacy svcs. N.D. Dept. Human Svcs., Bismarck, 2001—. Mem.: N.D. Soc. Health-Sys. Pharmacists (mem. at large, pres. elect, pres., immediate past pres. 1999—2003, Pres.'s Award 2002, Leadership award 2003), Nat. Coun. Prescription Drug Programs, We. Medicaid Pharmacy Adminstrs. Assn., Am. Medicaid Pharmacy Adminstrs. Assn., Am. Soc. Health-Sys. Pharmacists. Roman Catholic.

JOYCE, DIANA, psychologist, education educator; d. Donald Ray and Caroline Ann Joyce. PhD, U. Fla., Gainesville, FL, 2000. Cert. Nat. Sch. Psychologist NASP, 2001; Fla. Clin. Educator Dept. of Edn., Fla., 2002, lic. School Psychologist 2003, Psychologist 2004. Media ctr. coord. U. Fla., Tech. Transfer, Gainesville, Fla., 1995—99; outside examiner Psychol. Corp., Orlando, Fla., 2001—03; adj. instr. U. of Fla., Ednl. Psychology, Gainesville, Fla., 2002—02; sch. psychologist Hillsborough County Schools, Tampa, 2000—03; faculty U. Fla. Ednl. Psychology, Gainesville, Fla., 2003—. Mem.: NASP, NCSP, APA, Fla. Assn. of Sch. Psychologists. Meth. Achievements include research in temperament-based learning style preferences of students with oppositional defiant disorder and conduct disorder in psychiatric hospital and adjudicated youth programs; in temperament differences between gifted and nongifted children; in sex differential in self-handicapping behaviors of male and female undergraduate students. Avocations: travel, hiking, camping, theater, art. E-mail: djoyce@coe.ufl.edu.

JOYCE, FREDERICK MARK (RICK), lawyer; b. Pompton Plains, N.J., Apr. 18, 1958; s. Thomas Francis and Josephine (Kiechle) J.; m. Judy Frances Sledge, Jan. 17, 1955. BA in Polit. Sci. magna cum laude, George Washington U., 1980; JD, Georgetown U., 1984. Bar: Md. 1984, D.C. 1985, Va. 1990, U.S. Dist. Ct. Md. 1992. Assoc. Lukas McGowan, Washington, Reboul MAcMurray, Washington, Ginsburg, Feldman & Bress, Washington; ptnr. Joyce & Jacobs, Washington; ptnr., head telecom. practice group Alston & Bird, Washington; ptnr., chair, telecom. practice group Venable LLP, Washington, 2003—. Precinct capt. Fairfax (Va.) County Den. Coun., 1992—; bd. dirs. Friends of Mt. Vernon, Alexandria, Va., 1993—, vol. Washington Area Lawyers for the Arts. Recipient Leahy prize Georgetown U., 1983. Mem. ABA (litigation sect., comm. forum), D.C. Bar Assn., Alexandria C. of C. Democrat. Avocations: rowing, hiking, beer making, reading. Office: Venable LLP 575 7th St NW Washington DC 20004 Office Phone: 202-344-4653. Office Fax: 404-344-8300. Business E-Mail: rjoyce@venable.com.

JOYCE, JAMES DANIEL, clergyman; b. Spencer, Va., Jan. 12, 1921; s. James Garfield and Mary (Taylor) J.; m. Dorothy Beatrice Campbell, Aug. 2, 1946; 1 son, Kevin Campbell. AB in Religion, Johnson Bible Coll., 1945, Lynchburg Coll., 1946; BD, Butler U., 1949; MA in Biblical Theology, Yale U., 1952, PhD, 1958. Ordained to ministry Disciples of Christ Ch., 1943. Pastor Hanover Ave. Christian Ch., Richmond, Va., 1954-59; sr. student leader ecumenical inst. World Council Chs., Geneva, 1960; prof. New Testament and Bible theology Christian Theol. Sem., Indpls., 1961-62; dean grad. sem. Phillips U., Enid, Okla., 1962-74; pastor Bethany Christian Ch., Houston, 1974-80, Covenant Christian Ch., Houston, 1980—. W.E. Garrison lectr. Disciple students Yale U., 1963; Jesse M. Bader lectr. evangelism Drake U., 1968; columnist Christian Jour., 1962-80; bass soloist rec. Joy-ce Sounds, 1977; pres. World Conv. Chrs. of Christ, 1970-74, mem. exec. com., 1974—; lectr. for armed forces in Far East, 1968; adj. prof. speech and creative writing U. Houston and Houston Community Coll., 1981-82; prof. speech and writing Houston Community Coll., 1982—, also head dept. speech; mem. bd. mgrs. Pension Fund Disciples of Christ. Author: The Living Christ in Our Changing World, 1962, The Place of the Sacraments in Worship, 1967. Recipient cert. of merit Methodist Bishop of Korea, 1972. Mem. Am. Assn. Theol. Schs. (exec. com. 1966-72), Theta Phi. Home: 5211 Carew St Houston TX 77096-1319 E-mail: danbeal@sbcglobal.net.

JOYCE, JEFFREY, research scientist, consultant; b. Columbus, Ohio, Dec. 19, 1951; s. James Neal and Maxine Peterbourg Joyce; m. Sandra H. Jakobs, Feb. 15, 1997; m. Cathleen Gonzales, 1986 (div. 1995); children: Sasha Aitan, Elisabeth Allison, Dmitry Nathan. BS, U. Ill., 1977; PhD, U. Fla., 1983. Postdoctoral fellow dept. psychobiology U. Calif., Irvine, 1983—86; rsch. asst. prof. pharmacology U. Pa. Sch. Medicine, Phila., 1986—89, rsch. assoc. prof. pharmacology, 1989—95, rsch. assoc. prof. psychology and neuroscience in psychiatry, 1989—95; head and sr. scientists T.H. Christopher Ctr. for Parkinson's Disease Rsch., SHRI, Sun City, Ariz., 1995; assoc. dir. Sun Health Rsch. Inst., Sun City, 1995—. Dir. Pharm. Cons., CNS Drug Discovery and Target Devel., Scottsdale, Ariz., 1995—; bd. mem., fin. com. chair Ann. Spring Brain Conf., Gainesville, Fla., 1997—2000; adj. prof. psychology Ariz. State U., Tempe, 1998—, adj. prof. molecular and cellular biology grad. group, 1998—. Contbr. chapters to books, articles to profl. jours. Fellow: Internat. Behavioral Neuroscience Soc. (chair fin. com.), Am. Coll. Neuropsychopharmacology (fin. com. 2001—04); mem.: Internat. Soc. for Devel. Neuroscience, Soc. for Biol. Psychiatry (Ziskind-Somerfeld Research award 1997), Soc. for Neuroscience, The Movement Disorders Soc.,

European Coll. Neuropsychopharmacology, Collegium Internationale Neuro-Psychopharmacolgicum, Am. Soc. for Pharmacology and Exptl. Therapeutics. Jewish. Office: Sun Health Research Institute 10515 West Santa Fe Dr Sun City AZ 85351 Office Phone: 623-876-5439. Business E-Mail: jeff.joyce@sunhealth.org.

JOYCE, JOHN R., computer company executive; V.p. fin. and planning No. Am. IBM, controller, v.p. worldwide, pres. Asia Pacific, sr. v.p., CFO, 1999—2004, sr. v.p., group exec., global services, 2004—. Mem.: Bertelsmann AG Supervisory Bd. Office: IBM New Orchard Rd Armonk NY 10504

JOYCE, JOSEPH JAMES, lawyer, food products executive; b. Chgo., Sept. 28, 1943; s. Edward R. and Mary E. (Jordan) J.; m. Suzanne M. Sheridan, Aug. 26, 1967; children: Joseph, Michael, Peter, Kevin, Edward. BS, Xavier U., 1965; JD, Loyola U., 1968. Bar: Ill. 1968. Mem. Hill, Sherman, Meroni, Gross & Simpson, Chgo., 1968-72; atty. Pepsico, Inc., Purchase, N.Y., 1972-74, trademark counsel, 1974-77, asst. gen. counsel, 1977-86, v.p., asst. gen. counsel, 1986-98, v.p., assoc. gen. counsel, 1998—. Contbr. articles to profl. jours. Bd. mgrs. Lincoln Hall Found., Inc., 1989—. Mem. ABA, ATLA, Ill. Bar Assn., U.S. Trade Assn., Assn. Internationale pour la Protection de la Propietè Industrielle (bd. dirs.), Licensing Execs. Soc., Westchester-Fairfield Corp. Counsel Assn., Inc., Assn. Inter-Am. de la Propriedad Industrial, IIPA (exec. com. 1989—, bd. dirs.). Roman Catholic. Office: Pepsico Inc Anderson Hill Rd Purchase NY 10577

JOYCE, JOSEPH M., lawyer; b. Mpls., 1951; BSBA, U. Minn., 1973; JD, William Mitchell Coll. Law, 1977. Bar: Minn. 1977. Legal counsel Tonka Corp., Minnetonka, Minn., 1977-81, sec., gen. counsel, 1981-87, v.p., sec., gen. counsel, 1987—91; v.p. human resources, gen. counsel Best Buy Co. Inc., Mpls., 1991—97, v.p., gen. counsel, 1997—2000, sr. v.p., gen. counsel, sec., 2000—. Sec. bd. dir. Best Buy Children's Found. Office: Best Buy Co Inc PO Box 9312 Minneapolis MN 55440-9312

JOYCE, LARRY WAYNE, physician; b. Richlands, Va., June 7, 1962; s. Estil Larry and Charlotte Pearline (Dye) J. AS summa cum laude, Southwest Va. C.C., 1982; BS in Biology & Chemistry cum laude, East Tenn. State U., 1984; DO, U. Health Scis., 1989. Med. lab. tech. Mattie Williams Hosp., Richlands, Va., 1978-86; instr. biology lab. Southwest Va. C.C., Richlands, 1984-85, instr. microbiology lab., 1987, instr. chemistry, 1986; resident East Tenn. U., Quillen Coll. Medicine, Johnson City, 1989-94; asst. prof. dept. pathology East Tenn. State U., Johnson City, Tenn., 1994-98. Staff pathologist VA Med. Ctr., Mountain Home, 1994—98, Clinch Valley Med. Ctr., Richlands, Va., 1996—2003, Bloomington Med. Lab. Physicians, SC, 2003. Author: HIV Disease 1993, 94, 95, 96, 97, 98, 99, 2000, 01. HIV ednl. outreach Tri-Cities AIDS Project, Johnson City, 1990-92 (svc. awards 1990, 91); HIV educator Lambda Soc., Johnson City, 1990. Mem. Am. Assn. Med. Pers., Am. Soc. Clin. Pathologists, Coll. Am. Pathologists, Am. Osteopathic Assn., Am. Osteopathic Coll. Pathologists. Avocations: computer, tennis, hiking, movies, music. Home: 413 N Center St Ste 1 Bloomington IL 61701 E-mail: riverwayne@hotmail.com.

JOYCE, PATRICK FRANCIS, secondary school educator; s. Francis Edward Joyce; m. Ann I. Iannuzzo, July 23, 1977; children: Ryan Patrick, Shawn Patrick. AB, King's Coll., 1974; MS in Edn. and English, U. Scranton, 1983. Rxhe. English Riverside H.S., Taylor, Pa., 1978—2001, tchr. Spanish, 2001—. Dir. pub. rels. Riverside Sch. Dist., 1983—2004; yearbook advisor Riverside H.S., 1978—2002, ski club advisor, 1986—, advisor: la sociedad hispánica de riverside, 2004—, tchr. gifted edn., 1980—84. Author: (editorial commentary) The New Yorker; contbr. articles to mags. Mem.: NEA (assoc.), Riverside Edn. Assn. (assoc.), Pa. Edn. Assn. (assoc.). Democrat. Roman Catholic. Achievements include Developed school-wide multi cultural organization to help hispanic students; Advised three nationally award winning yearbooks. Avocations: bicycling, skiing, travel, reading, writing. Home: 148 Joyce Dr Moosic PA 18507 Office: Riverside High Sch 310 Davis St Moosic PA 18507 Office Phone: 570-562-2121. Office Fax: 570-562-2121. E-mail: joycep@neiu.org.

JOYCE, ROSEMARY ALEXANDRIA, anthropology educator; b. Lackawanna, N.Y., Apr. 7, 1956; d. Thomas Robert and Joanne Hannah (Poth) J.; m. Russell Nicholas Sheptak, Jan. 7, 1984. BA, Cornell U., 1978; PhD, U. Ill., 1985. Instr. Jackson (Mich.) Community Coll., 1983; lectr. U. Ill., Urbana, 1984-85; asst. curator Peabody Mus., Harvard U., Cambridge, Mass., 1985-86, asst. dir., 1986-89; asst. prof. anthropology Harvard U., Cambridge, Mass., 1989-91, assoc. prof. anthropology, 1991-94, U. Calif., Berkeley, 1994—2001, prof., 2001—. Author: Cerro Palenque, 1991, Encounters with the Americas, 1995, Gender and Power in Prehispanic Mesoamerica, 2001, The Languages of Archeology, 2002, Embodied Lives, 2003; editor: Maya History, 1993, Women in Prehistory, 1997, Social Patterns in Preclassic Mesoamerica, 1999, Beyond Kinship, 2000, Mesoamerican Archeology, 2003; contbr. articles to profl. jours. NEH grantee, 1985, 86, NSF grantee, 1989, 98, 2001, Famsi grantee, 1996, Heinz Found., Wenner-Gren Found. grantee, 1997; Fulbright fellow, 1981-82. Mem. Soc. for Am. Archaeology, Am. Anthropol. Assn. Office: U Calif Anthropology Dept 232 Kroeber Hall # 3710 Berkeley CA 94720-3710 E-mail: rajoyce@berkeley.edu.

JOYCE, STEVEN JAMES, German and comparative studies educator; b. Green Bay, Wis., Dec. 13, 1950; s. Emmett and Dolores (Remmel) J.; m. Mary Delphine Tomino; children: Alexander, Genevieve, Brendan. BA cum laude, St. Norbert Coll., De Pere, Wis., 1973; postgrad., Lawrence U., Appleton, Wis., 1973-74; MA in Comparative Lit., Purdue U., 1982; PhD in Comparative Lit., U. N.C., 1988. Assoc. prof. German, English, comparative studies Ohio State U., Mansfield, 1988—. Fulbright lectr., 2005—. Author: Transformations and Texts: G.B. Shaw's Buoyant Billions, 1992. Recipient Disting. Teaching award Ohio State U., Mansfield, 1988, 2000; Fulbright grantee, Bonn, West Germany, 1987; Fulbright Rsch. fellow, Vienna, Austria, 1983-84, 92. Mem. MLA, Fulbright Alumni Assn., Am. Assn. Tchrs. German, Phi Beta Delta. Home: 60 Stewart Ave S Mansfield OH 44906-3207 Office: Ohio State Univ 1680 University Dr 317 Ovalwood Mansfield OH 44906 E-mail: joyce.3@osu.edu.

JOYCE, WILLIAM GEORGE, JR., transportation executive; b. Oswego, N.Y., Nov. 24, 1949; s. William George and Nannette Davies J.; m. Patricia L., July 1, 1983; children: Tara, Kendra, Andrew. Student, SUNY, Oswego, 1967-71. Ops. mgr. Lake Shore Transp. Lines, Oswego, 1971-96; pres., CEO N.Y. State Motor Truck Assn., Inc., Albany, 1997—. Gen. chmn., treas. Maintenance Coun., Alexandria, Va., 1994-95; chmn. bd. dirs. N.Y. Motor Truck, Albany, 1994-96; first v.p. N.Y. Motor Carrier Conf., Buffalo, 1993-95. Mem. Am. Trucking Assn. (v.p. 1994-97), Am. Soc. Assn. Execs., Trucking Assns. (exec. coun., regional vice chair), N.Y. State Soc. Assn. Execs. Republican. Roman Catholic. Office: NYS MTA 828 Washington Ave Albany NY 12203 E-mail: bjoyce@nytrucks.org.

JOYCE, WILLIAM H., chemist; b. 1935; BS, Pa. State U., 1957; MBA, NYU, 1971, PhD, 1984. With Union Carbide Corp., Danbury, Conn., 1957—2001, past exec. v.p. ops., pres., COO, 1993—95, CEO, 1995; chmn., pres., CEO Union Carbide Corp. (merged with Dow Chemical Co.), Danbury, Conn., 1996—2001; vice chmn. bd. The Dow Chem. Co., Danbury, 2001; chmn., CEO Hercules, Inc., Willmington, Del., 2001—03, Nalco Co., Naperville, Ill., 2003—. Bd. dirs. CVS Corp., Reynolds Metals Co. Trustee U. Rsch. Assn. Inc. Recipient Nat. medal of Tech., NSF, 1993, Industry Achievement award, Plastics Acad., 1994, Lifetime Achievement award, 1997, Perkin award, Soc. Chemical Industry, 2003. Mem.: NAE, NAS (co-chmn., Gov.-Univ.-Industry Rsch. Roundtable), Am. Plastics Coun. (bd. dirs.), Soc. Chem. Industry (treas., bd. dirs.). Office: Nalco Co 1601 W Diehl Rd Naperville IL 60563-1198 Office Phone: 877-813-3523. Office Fax: 630-305-2900.

JOYCE, WILLIAM LEONARD, librarian; b. Rockville Centre, N.Y., Mar. 29, 1942; s. John Francis and Mabel Clare (Leonard) Joyce; m. Carol Gail Bertani, Aug. 13, 1967; children: Susan, Michael. BA, Providence Coll., 1964; MA, St. John's U., 1966; PhD, U. Mich., 1974. Manuscripts libr. William L. Clements Libr. U. Mich., Ann Arbor, 1968-72; curator manuscripts Am. Antiquarian Soc., Worcester, Mass., 1972-81, edn. officer, 1977-81; asst. dir. rare books and manuscripts N.Y. Pub. Libr., N.Y.C., 1981-86; assoc. univ. libr. rare books and spl. collections Princeton U., 1986-2000; Dorothy Foehr Huck chair spl. collections, prof. history Pa. State U., State College, 2000—. Lectr. Clark U., 1975—77; cons. Nat. Hist. Publs. and Records Commn., Washington, 1982, others; adj. faculty Sch. Libr. Svc., Columbia U., N.Y.C., 1984—92; vis. prof. Grad. Sch. Libr. & Info. Sci., UCLA, 1994. Author: Editors and Ethnicity: A History of the Irish-American Press, 1848-1883, 1976; editor: Catalog of Manuscripts Collections of the American Antiquarian Society, 4 vols., 1979; co-author: Evaluation of Archival Institutions, 1982, Documenting America: Assessing the Condition of Historical Records in the States, 1984; co-editor: Printing and Society in Early America, 1983; contbr. articles, revs. to profl. jours. Bd. dirs. Conservation Ctr. Art and Hist. Artifacts, 1992—2000, mem., 1995—98; chmn. J.F.K. Assassination Records Rev. Bd., 1994—98; mem. adv. com. Ctr. Jewish History, 2000—, chmn., 2001—. Fellow: Soc. Am. Archivists (coun. mem. 1981—85, pres. 1986—87); mem.: ALA (rare books and manuscripts sect., mem. publs. com. 1985—88, chmn. 1987—88), Internat. Coun. Archives (mem. com. lit. and art 1993—97), Assn. Rsch. Librs. (mem. spl. collections task force 2000—), Am. Antiquarian Soc., Orgn. Am. Historians, Bibliog. Soc. Am. (chmn. fellowship com. 1982—85), Am. Hist. Assn. (mem. profl. divsn. com. 1979—81), Grolier Club. Office: Pa State Librs 110 Paterno Library University Park PA 16802-1808 Office Phone: 814-865-1793. Business E-Mail: wlj2@psu.edu.

JOYCE, WILLIAM ROBERT, textile machinery company executive; b. Springfield, Ohio, Mar. 18, 1936; s. Robert Emmet and Christel Beatrice (Beekman) J.; m. Betty Arlene Provonsha, Aug. 29, 1959; children: Jennifer Lynn, Janet Cathleen. BA in Bus., Calif. We. U., 1982. Cert. mfg. engring. tech., Soc. Mfg. Engrs.; registered investment securities rep. Mfg. engring. Heinicke Instruments, Hollywood, Fla., 1964—68; div. mgr. Jensen Corp., Pompano Beach, Fla., 1969—72; pres. Textiles Supply, Inc., Gerton, NC, 1972—82; v.p., gen. mgr. Tex-Fab, Inc., Gerton, 1980—82; pres. Tex-nology Sys., Inc., Gerton, 1982—90, Corrib Enterprises Ltd., Automation Cons., Dana, NC, 1981—; owner The Silver Hammer Jewelry Store Chain, NC. Co-founder Assoc. Woodland Owners N.C.; mem. Hickory Nut Gorge Vol. Fire Dept., Gerton. Served with USAF, 1958—64. Recipient Innovative Devel. award, 1985, award, Optimist Club, 1953—54. Mem.: NSPE, Handmade in Am. Craft Orgn., We. Carolina Entrepreneurial Coun., Mountain Comml. Lending Consortium, Am. Inst. Design and Drafting, Soc. Mfg. Engrs., Guild Master Craftsmen (internat. mem.), Profl. Engrs. N.C., NRA. Republican. Baptist. Achievements include patents in field. Business E-Mail: wrj_keystone@msn.com.

JOYCE-BRADY, MARTIN FRANCIS, medical educator, physician, researcher; b. Wilmington, Del., Sept. 25, 1953; s. Robert Lawrence and Marjorie Theresa (Martin) Brady; m. Jean Marie Joyce, Sept. 17, 1977; children: Jessica, Erin, Emily. BA in Arts & Scis., U. Del., 1975; MD, U. Md., Balt., 1979. Medicine intern Boston City Hosp., 1979-80, medicine resident, 1980-82, chief med. resident, 1982-83; pulmonary fellow Pulmonary Ctr., Boston U. Sch. Medicine, 1982-87, asst. prof. medicine, 1987-96, assoc. prof. medicine, 1997—; dir. pulmonary function lab. Boston City Hosp., 1987-96; dir. ventilator care unit Jewish Meml. Hosp., Boston, 1988—, dir. pulmonary and respiratory therapy, 1996—. Contbr. articles to profl. jours.; peer reveiwer articles to profl. jours. H. Fletcher Brown scholar Bank of Del., Wilmington, 1975, E.L. Trudeau scholar Am. Lung Assn., 1990-92; program project grantee on lung devel. NIH, 1991-96, 97-2002, 2002—. Mem. AAAS, Am. Soc. Cell Biology, Mass. Med. Soc., Am. Thoracic Soc., Mass. Thoracic Soc. (chmn. rsch. grant com. 2003—), Am. Physiol. Soc. Democrat. Roman Catholic. Achievements include research in alternative pathway hypothesis for type I alveolar epithelial cell differentiation during lung development; lung surfactant in distributing amphipathic signal anchor proteins throughout the gas exchange surface of the lung; gamma-glutamyl-transferase and its protein isoform in an endoplasmic reticulum stress response; gamma glutamyl transferase-mediated glutatione metabolism in lung alveolar epithelial cell biology and lung redox homeostasis at the gas exchange surface of the lung; oxidant stress at birth exerts selective pressure on the expression of genes required for postnatal lung development. Office: Pulmonary Ctr 80 E Concord St Boston MA 02118-2307 Office Phone: 617-638-4860. Business E-Mail: mjbrady@bu.edu.

JOYNER, CHRISTOPHER CLAYTON, international relations educator; b. Aberdeen, Md., May 16, 1948; s. Houston Clay Joyner and Besse Hyde Sowers; m. Nancy Douglas, Dec. 27, 1972; children: Kristin Elizabeth, Clayton Douglas. BA magna cum laude, Fla. State U., 1970, MA, 1972, MA, 1973; PhD, U. Va., 1977. Co-dir. Ctr. for Peace and Environ. Studies Fla. State U., 1971-73, instr. dept. govt., 1972-73; asst. prof. polit. sci. Muhlenberg Coll., 1977-80; vis. prof. dept. govt. and fgn. affairs U. Va., 1980-81; asst. prof. polit. sci. George Washington U., Washington, 1981-85, assoc. prof., 1985-90, prof. dept. polit. sci. and Elliott Sch. Internat. Affairs, 1991-94; prof. dept. govt. sch. fgn. svc. Georgetown U., Washington, 1995—, dir. Inst. Internat. Law and Politics, 2003—. Editl. advisor Internat. Legal Materials, 1988-90; vis. prof. government, Dartmouth Coll., 1989, 91, 93, 95, 97; profl. lectr. Sch. Advanced Internat. Studies Johns Hopkins U., 1991, 92; editl. adv. bd. Rowman & Littlefield Pub., Prentice Hall Internat. Relations series, Transnat. Pubs.; editl. adv. coun. U. Tasmania Antarctic and So. Oceans Law and Policy Paper Series. Author: Antarctica and the Law of Sea, 1992, Eagle Over the Ice: The U.S. in the Antarctic, 1997, Teaching International Law, 1997, Governing the Frozen Commons: The Antarctic Regime and Environmental Protection, 1998, International Law in the 21st Century: Rules for Global Governance, 2005; editor: International Law of the Sea and the Future of Deep Seabed Mining, 1975, The Antarctic Legal Regime, 1988, The Persian Gulf War: Lessons for Strategy, Law and Diplomacy, 1990, United Nations Legal Order, 1995, The United Nations and International Law, 1997, Reining in Impunity for International Crimes and Serious Violations of Fundamental Human Rights, 1998, Governing the Frozen Commons: The Antarctic Regime and Environmental Protection, 1998, International Law in the 21st Century: Legal Rules for Global Goverance, 2005; sr. editor Va. Jour. Internat. Law, 1973-77; mem. editl. bd. Internat. Studies Rev., Ocean Yearbook Internat. Law, Va. Jour. Internat. Law, Internat. Studies Notes, Internat. Studies Quarterly, Global Governance, Case Western Res. Jour. Internat. Law, Ocean Devel. and Internat. Law, Terrorism: An Internat. Jour., 1988-92, Internat. Jour. Marine and Coastal Law, Polar Record; contbr. articles to profl. jours Governing bd., bd. dirs. Acad. Coun. on the UN Sys., 1999-2002, vice-chmn. governing bd., 2001. With USAR, 1970-76. Grantee Inst. World Order, Inc., 1971-73, Ford Found., 1989-94, Nansen Inst./Tinker Found., 1992-94, Fridtjof Nansen Inst., 1995—; rsch. fellow Antarctic Ctr. for Rsch. and Cooperation, U. Tasmania, 1994, U. Canterbury, 2001, sr. rsch. fellow Woods Hole Oceanog. Instn., 1986-87. Mem. Am. Polit. Sci. Assn., Am. Soc. Internat. Law (life, exec. com. 1984-87, 1997-2000), Antarctican Soc. (bd. dirs. 1984-87), Internat. Studies Assn. (pres. internat. law sect. 1985-86, 1997-98, mem. governing coun. 1985-86, 96-97, nat. v.p. 2004—), Internat. Law Assn., Law of Sea Inst., Nat. Eagle Scout Assn., UN Assn., Golden Key Hon. Soc., Raven Soc. Hon., Phi Beta Kappa, Omicron Delta Kappa, Phi Kappa Phi, Pi Sigma Alpha, Phi Theta Kappa, Phi Alpha Theta. Democrat. Methodist. Avocations: jogging, autograph seeking, writing. Home: 3151 Borge St Oakton VA 22124 Office: Georgetown U Dept Govt Washington DC 20057-1034 Office Phone: 202-687-5112. Business E-Mail: joynerc@georgetown.edu.

JOYNER, CLAUDE REUBEN, JR., cardiologist, educator; b. Winston-Salem, N.C., Dec. 4, 1925; s. Claude R. and Lytle (Mackie) J.; m. Nina Glenn Michael, Sept. 21, 1950; children: Emily Glenn, Claude Courtney. BS, U. N.C., 1947; MD, U. Pa., 1949. Intern Hosp. U. Pa., 1949-50; resident Bowman Grey Med. Sch., 1950, U. Pa., 1954-55, fellow in cardiology; Nat. Heart Inst. trainee, 1952-53; asst. instr. medicine Hosp. U. Pa., Phila., 1951-53, instr., 1953-56, assoc. medicine, 1956-59, asst. prof., 1959-64, assoc. prof., 1964-72; prof. medicine U. Pitts., 1972-87, Med. Coll. Pa., 1987-96, vice dean, 1989-96; chief medicine Allegheny Gen. Hosp., Pitts., 1972-96. Contbr. articles to profl. jours. Served to lt. M.C. USNR, 1950-52. Fellow Am. Coll. Cardiology, ACP, Councils on Circulation, Arteriosclerosis and Cardiovascular Radiology of Am. Heart Assn.; mem. AAAS, Am. Heart Assn., Am. Clin. and Climatol. Soc. Home: Pulpit Rock 45 Little Sewickley Creek Rd Sewickley PA 15143-8393 Office: Allegheny Gen Hosp Pittsburgh PA 15212 Office Phone: 412-359-3022.

JOYNER, DEE ANN, bank executive; b. Alton, Ill., Feb. 26, 1947; d. T. Claxton and Dorothy M. (Troeckler) Burroughs; m. Orville Joyner, Mar. 15, 1973; 1 child, Dawn L. Kotva. BA in Govt., So. Ill. U., 1971, MS in Govt., 1973; MBA, St. Louis U., 1985. Adminstrv. asst. So. Ill. U., Edwardsville, 1970-72; staff assoc. Marshall Kaplan, Gans and Kahn, Washington, 1972-73; dir. community affairs East-West Gateway Coordinating Council, St. Louis, 1973-78; exec. dir. Coro Found., St. Louis, 1978-80, St. Louis County Econ. Council, Clayton, Mo., 1985-89; planning dir. St. Louis County, 1980-84, chief of staff to county exec. Clayton, Mo., 1989-90; sr. v.p. Commerce Bank St. Louis, 1990—. Mem. Civil Svc. Bd., University City, Mo., 1984—93, Better Bus. Bur., 1991—93, Tax Increment Financing Commn./Indsl. Devel. Authority, University City, Mo., 1993—97, Alzheimers Assn., 1992—99, Girl Scout Coun. of Greater St. Louis, 1993—96, St. Louis Boundary Commn., 1999—2002; bd. dirs. Boys and Girls Town, 1994—, St. John's Mercy Med. Ctr., 1997—2000, Deaconness Found., 2002—; trustee Thomas Aquinas Inst. Theology, 2003—; bd. dirs. Metro. Assn. for Philanthropy, 2005—, Confluence, St. Louis, 1983—89, Focus St. Louis, 1996—2002, bd. chmn., 1996—98; bd. dirs. Forest Park Forever, 2003—; mem. exec. com. Automobile Club of Mo., 2003—, mem., 1995—, Delta Dental Mo., 1998—. Recipient Joseph E. Boland Meml. Outstanding Alumnus award St. Louis U., 1992, Spl. Leadership award YWCA, St. Louis, 1987, Jaint Roede Ashcroft award for Cmty. Svc., Alzheimers Assn., 1999, Above and Beyond award for cmty. svc. St. Louis Bus. Jour., 2002. Mem. Leadership St. Louis, So. Ill. U. Alumni Assn. (Alumnus of Yr. 1994), Mo Women's Forum (bd. dirs. 1989-90, 2000-02), Univ. Club (bd. dirs. 1994-97), Met. Assn. Philanthropists (bd. dirs. 2005—). Office: 8000 Forsyth Blvd Saint Louis MO 63105-1707 Office Phone: 314-746-7326. Business E-Mail: dee.joyner@commercebank.com.

JOYNER, HENRY CURTIS, airline executive; b. Baton Rouge, July 7, 1954; s. James William and Jacqueline Marie (Oliphint) J.; m. Betsy Lynne Tyler, Dec. 21, 1974; children: Sarah Hughes, Kathleen Annette. BA, La. State U., 1976; MA, U. Chgo., 1978, MA in Bus. Adminstrn., 1980. Fin. analyst Am. Airlines, Dallas/Ft. Worth, 1980, mgr. mktg. planning, 1982-84, dir. mktg. planning, 1984-87, dir. airline planning, 1987-89, v.p. personnel resources, 1989-90, v.p. mktg. planning, 1990—2000, sr. v.p. planning, 2000—. Bd. visitors TCU Neeley Sch. Internat., 2002—, Southwestern U., 2003—. Mem. corp. adv. bd. U. Chgo. Bus. Sch., 1990-91. Mem. Hurst, Evless, Bedford C. of C. (dir. 1990). Methodist. Office: Am Airlines Inc PO Box 619616 Arlington TX 76015 Office Phone: 817-967-2803.

JOYNER, J(AMES) CURTIS, judge; b. Newberry, S.C., Apr. 18, 1948; s. George C. and Joan C. (Glenn) J.; m. Mildred Ann Carter, Apr. 5, 1975; children: Jennifer Christine, Nicole Marie, Jacqlyn Ann. Student, Peirce Jr. Coll., Phila., 1967; BS in Acctg., Crtl. State U., Wilberforce, Ohio, 1971; JD, Howard U., 1974. Bar: Pa. 1975, U.S. Dist. Ct. (ea. dist.) Pa. 1981. Contr. D.C. Project, Washington, 1972-73; legal publ. specialist Fed. Register, Washington, 1974-75; asst. dist. atty. Dist. Atty. Office Chester County, West Chester, Pa., 1975-80, chief dep. dist. atty., 1980-84, 1st asst. dist. atty., 1984-87; judge Ct. of Common Pleas, 15th Jud. Dist., West Chester, 1987-92, U.S. Dist. Ct. (ea. dist.) Pa., Phila., 1992—. Mem. coun. trustees West Chester U., 1983-2000, trustee emeritus, 2001. Named Trailblazer in Law Enforcement Gov. Thornburgh, 1986; recipient Outstanding Svc. award to law enforcement Pa. Criminal Investigators, 1987, Disting. Law and Justice award County and State Detectives Assn., 1988, Donald K. Anthony Alumni Achievement Hall of Fame Crtl. State U., 1994, Pres.' Medallion for Svc. West Chester U., 2001. Mem. Fed. Bar Assn. (hon.), Chester County Bar Assn. Avocations: sports, jazz, golf. Office: US Dist Ct Rm 8613 601 Market St Philadelphia PA 19106-1714 Office Phone: 215-597-1537.

JOYNER, JOHN WESLEY, psychologist, educator; b. Memphis, Dec. 2, 1928; s. Eli Green and Ritter Mae Joyner. Student, Mich. State U., 1954-58, Ferris State U., 1958; BS, Tenn. State U., 1960, MS, 1962; PhD, Ohio State U., 1972. Lic. tchr., Tenn., counselor, Ill., Ky., Psychologist, Ohio. Mgr. Pinnacle Lanes, Nashville, 1961-63; counselor Armstrong H.S., Washington, 1963-64, Sumner H.S., Cairo, Ill., 1964-67, Cairo H.S., 1967-69, West Ky. Area Vocat. Sch., Paducah, 1969-71; rschr. assoc. Ctr. for Vocat. Edn./Ohio State U., Columbus, 1971-72; staff counselor, instr. Psychol. Ctr. Coll. Edn./Ohio State U., Columbus, 1973; assoc. prof. psychology, dir. student devel. svcs. Counseling and Testing Ctr./Tenn. State U., Nashville, 1973-84; prof. psychology Tenn. State U., Nashville, 1984—. Adv. bd. multi cultural ednl. enrichment program Tenn. State U., Nashville, 1998-2000; adminstrv. asst. Psychol. Cons. Ctr., Columbus, 1971-73; owner Test Preparation, Nashville, 1984—; cons. in field. Author: Student Self Directed Manual for the ACT, 2000. Active CORE, 1963-65, So. Poverty Law Ctr., 2000—. Staff sgt. U.S. Army, 1948-52, Germany. Recipient Rogers award for best counselor Fla. State U., 1965. Mem. NAACP, ACLU, AAUP, Am. Sch. Counseling Assn., Tenn. Counseling Assn., Phi Delta Kappa. Methodist. Avocations: politics, wildlife, sports, tv. Home: 3512 Geneva Cir Nashville TN 37209-1525 E-mail: jjoyner@tnstate.edu.

JOYNER, LORINZO LITTLE, commissioner; b. Wadesboro, N.C., May 8, 1948; BS in English Edn., N.C. A&T State U., 1969; JD, U. N.C., 1981. Tchr. English, Greensboro/Durham (NC) pub. high schs.; mem. N.C. Utilities Commn., 2001—; lawyer Office of Atty. Gen. Democrat. Office: 4325 Mail Svc Ctr Raleigh NC 27699-4325 Office Phone: 919-733-4249. Business E-Mail: ljoyner@ncuc.net.

JOYNER, MARGUERITE AUSTIN, secondary school educator; b. Memphis, Apr. 14; d. Cathey Monroe and Marguerite Victoria (Davis) Austin; m. Guy Eugene Joyner, Jr. (div. Aug. 1980); children: Marguerite Parker, Guy E. III; m. Philip O'Neil Nicar, Apr. 18, 1986. AA, William Woods Coll.; BA, So. Meth. U.; postgrad., U. Memphis, Rhodes Coll., 2003. Lic. profl. tchr. Tenn., real estate Tenn. Counselor Memphis/Shelby County Juvenile Ct., 1979—81; tchr. Briarcrest Christian Schs., Memphis, 1972—75; counselor Southaven H.S., Memphis, 1981—83; dir. recruiting ERA Sterling Realtors, Memphis, 1984—86; asst. recruiter Fed. Express/Manpower, Memphis, 1993—97; tchr. Shelby County Alt. Sch., Memphis, 2001—. Mem. Tchrs. Credit Union, Memphis; bus. cons. Melody Lane Atrium Cafe, Memphis. Trustee St. Mary's Episcopal Sch., Memphis; co-founder St. Mary's Episcopal Sch. Alumnae Assn.; asst. chmn. Rep. Precinct 44-2, Memphis. Mem.: Memphis (Tenn.) Symphony League, Les Passees Memphis, Jr. League of Memphis (chmn. day care project). Avocations: cooking, calligraphy, collecting first edition books, designing houses. Office: Shelby County Alt Sch 2911 Brunswick Rd Memphis TN 38122

JOYNER, MARK WINTON, writer, artist; b. Mt. Pleasant, Pa., Nov. 22, 1976; s. Rufus winton and Irene Fern Joyner. Student, pa. State U., 2000—. Author: Pointless Pandemonium, 2000 (Internat. Poet of Merit award Internat. Soc. of POets), Still Human, 2000. Avocations: photography, fishing, reading, travel, firearms.

JOYNER, PHILIP ANDREW, JR., musician, educator; s. Philip Andrew Joyner, Sr. and LaVerne D. Joyner; m. Joanne Sharease Palm; children: Jessica Sharease, Jasmine Patrice, Jalisa Dainease, Philip Andrew Joyner, III, Jonathan Andon. BS, U. Tenn., Chattanooga, 1981. Education State of Tenn., 1983, Commercial Pilot FAA, 1988. Tchr. Memphis City Schs., 1983—; profl. musician Peabody Hotel, Orpheum Theatre, Memphis, 1976—. Pres. Memphis Youth Symphony, Memphis, 2003—06. Recipient Outstanding Young Men of Am., 1987, 1989, 1992. Mem.: NARAS, Internat. Assn. Jazz Educators, West Tenn. Sch. Band and Orch. Assn., Tenn. Music Edn. Assn., Music Educators Nat. Conf., Kappa Delta Pi. Personal E-mail: pjoynerjr@yahoo.com.

JOYNER, WALTON KITCHIN, lawyer; b. Raleigh, N.C., Apr. 1, 1933; s. William Thomas and Sue (Kitchin) J.; m. Lucy Holmes Graves, Sept. 23, 1955; children: Sue Carson Clark, Walton K. Jr., James Y. II. AB in Polit. Sci., U. N.C., 1955, JD with honors, 1960. Bar: N.C., cert. mediator:; lic. comml. pilot. Ptnr. Joyner & Howison, Raleigh, 1960-80, Hunton & Williams, Raleigh, 1980—. Sec., treas. N.C. R.R. Co., Raleigh, 1966; bd. dirs. United Title Ins. Co., Raleigh; bd. mgrs. Wachovia Bank, N.C., 1969-98; bd. govs. U.S. Power Squadrons, 1974-81. Assoc. editor U. N.C. Law Rev. Pres. Rehab. and Cerebral Palsy Ctr. Wake County, Raleigh, 1974; trustee St. Mary's Coll., 1990-91; bd. dirs. Peace Coll. Found., 2001—. Mem.: Law Alumni Assn. U. N.C. (bd. dirs.), Wake County Bar Assn. (chmn., bd. dirs. 1977), N.C. Bar Assn. (treas. probate sect. 1983), Carolina Country Club (pres. 1983—84, 2000—01), Order of Coif, Phi Beta Kappa. Presbyterian. Avocation: flying. Home: 815 Marlowe Rd Raleigh NC 27609-7022 Office: Hunton & Williams 1 Hannover Sq PO Box 109 Fl 14 Raleigh NC 27602-0109

JOYNER KERSEE, JACKIE (JACQUELINE JOYNER KERSEE), retired track and field athlete; b. East St. Louis, Ill., Mar. 3, 1962; d. Alfred and Mary Joyner; m. Bob Kersee, Jan. 11, 1986. BA in History, UCLA, 1985; LLD (hon.), Washington U., St. Louis, 1992, Iona Coll., 1994; DHL (hon.), Harris-Stowe State Coll., 1993, Fontbonne Coll., St. Louis, 1998, Spelman Coll., 1998, Howard U., 1999, George Washington U., St. Louis, 1999. Basketball player Richmond Rage, ABL, 1996; mem. USA Track & Field Olympic Team, 1984, 1988, 1992, 1996; ret., 2001. Pres., founder JJK & Associates., Inc. Author: (autobiography) A Kind of Grace: The Autobiography of the World's Greatest Female Athlete, 1997; co-author: A Woman's Place Is Everywhere, 1994. Founder JJK Cmty. Found., 1989 (now JJK Youth Ctr. Found., 1997-), Jackie Joyner Kersee Boys & Girls Club; chmn. St. Louis Sports Commn., 1996-2000, chmn. emeritus, 2001—. Recipient Broderick Cup, 1985, James E. Sullivan Award, 1986, Jesse Owens Award, 1986, 87, Am. Black Achievement Award, Ebony mag., 1987, 1st Female Athlete of Yr. Award, Sporting News, 1988, Jim Thorpe Award, 1993, Jackie Robinson "Robie" Award, 1994, Parenting Leader Award, Parenting Mag., Jesse Owens Humanitarian Award, 1999, Humanitarian Award, Women Sports and Fitness, Pres.'s Award, Nat. Conf. Black Mayors; named Athlete of Yr., Track & Field News, 1986, Female Athlete of Yr., AP, 1987, Female of Yr., Internat. Assn. Athletics Federations, 1994, St. Louis Ambassadors Sportswoman of Yr., Hon. Harlem Globetrotter, Woman Athlete of Century, Sports Illustrated, 1999; inductee Nat. Boys and Girls Club Hall of Fame. Achievements include winner of 4 consecutive Nat. Jr. Pentathlon Championships; winner long jump, World Championships, Rome, 1987; winner Mobil Indoor Grand Prix, 1987; winner long jump, Pan Am. Games, 1987; winner heptathlon, World Championships, Stuttgart, Germany, 1993; winner hepthathlon, Goodwill Games, NYC, 1998; winner silver medal for heptathlon, LA Olympic Games, 1984; winner gold medal for heptathlon, Seoul Olympic Games, 1988; winner gold medal for long jump, Seoul Olympic Games, 1988; winner gold medal for heptathlon, Barcelona Olympic Games, 1992; winner bronze medal for long jump, Barcelona Olympic Games, 1992; winner bronze medal for long jump, Atlanta Olympic Games, 1996; set and still holds World Record for heptathlon, Seoul Olympic Games, 9/23/1988. Office: PO Box 69047 Saint Louis MO 63169-0047

JOYNES, BARBARA COLE, marketing executive; b. Rahway, N.J., Sept. 4, 1960; d. Clayton Eugene and Margaret (Fitzgerald) Cole; m. Matthew Thomas Thornhill, Oct. 15, 1983 (div. 1996); children: Allison, Clark; m. Stanley Knight Joynes III, June 24, 2000; stepchildren: Elizabeth, Alexandra. BBA in Mktg., Coll. of William and Mary, 1982. Asst. account exec. March Direct/McCann Direct, N.Y.C., 1983-84, account exec., 1984-86, account supr., 1986-87; dir. comml. client divsn. Huntsinger & Jeffer Direct, Richmond, Va., 1987-89; v.p., account supr. The Stenrich Group, Richmond, 1989-90, sr. v.p., dir. account mgmt., 1990-92, exec. v.p., dir. account mgmt., bd. dirs., 1992-95; exec. v.p. for integrated mktg. comm., mem. exec. com. The Martin Agy., Richmond, 1995-96, exec. v.p., chief adminstrv. officer, 1996—99, pnr. internat. svcs., 2000—. Mem. profit sharing com. The Martin Agy., Richmond, 1993—2003, chair mgmt. com., 1999—2002. Exec. com. bd. trustees Richmond Children's Mus., 1992-99, dir. bd. trustees, 1991-92; area coord. William and Mary Alum Admissions Network, Richmond, 1988-98; co-chair William and Mary Class of 82 Reunion com., 1997; mem. Leadership Metro Richmond Class of 1997; book fair chair Maybeury Elem. Sch., 1997—2000; cookie chair Brownie Troop #292, Girl Scouts U.S., 1996-98, bd. dirs. Commonwealth coun., 1999-2002; bd. dirs. Arts Coun. Richmond, 1998—2002; bd. dirs. Leadership Metro Richmond, 1998—2004, mem. exec. com., 1999—2004, chair devel. com., chair mem. programs com., sec. awareness/pub. rels. com., mem. recruitment com.; bd. dirs. YWCA of Richmond, 2001—, v.p., 2003-05; mem. Direct Mktg. Agy. Leaders Coun. Recipient Silver Echo award Direct Mktg. Assn., 1991, 94, Gold Echo award, 2003, Richmond Area Marketer of Yr. award Am. Mktg. Assn., 1992, 93, 94, Gold Effie award, 1992, Silver Effie award, 2000, YWCA Outstanding Woman award, 1999. Mem. Greater Richmond C. of C. (mem. exec. com. 2002-04, bd. dirs. 2000—), Willow Oaks Country Club, Farmington Country Club. Avocations: travel, family, reading, golf. Office: The Martin Agy One Shockoe Plz Richmond VA 23219-4132

JOYNT, ROBERT JAMES, academic administrator, physician; b. Le Mars, Iowa, Dec. 22, 1925; MD, 1952, PhD, 1963. Diplomate Am. Bd. Psychiatry and Neurology (past pres.). Intern Royal Victoria Hosp., Montreal, Canada, 1952—53; chief neurology Strong Meml. Hosp., Rochester, NY, 1966—84; assoc. U. Iowa, Iowa City, 1957—58, asst. prof. neurology, 1958—61, assoc. prof., 1961-66; prof. neurology U. Rochester, 1966—, chmn. dept., 1966—84; dean U. Rochester Sch. Medicine and Dentistry, 1984—89; v.p. and vice provost for health affairs U. Rochester Sch. Medicine & Dentistry, 1989—94. Named Disting. Univ. Prof., 1997; fellow, USPHS, 1954—57; scholar, Fulbright Found., 1953—54. Fellow: AAAS; mem.: AMA (chief editor Arch Neurology 1982—97), Am. Acad. Neurology (past pres.), Am. Neurol. Assn. (past pres.), Inst. Medicine, Royal Soc. Medicine, Am. Electroencephalographic Soc. Office: U Rochester Sch Medicine and Dentistry PO Box 673 Rochester NY 14642-0001 E-mail: robert_joynt@urmc.rochester.edu.

JOZWIAK, BEV ANN, artist; b. Vancouver, Wash., Jan. 18, 1953; d. thomas Whalen and Lucile Ione (Sundem) Stanfield; m. Robert Francis Jozwiak, Dec. 4, 1976; children: Kirby Mikkel, Briley Monet. BA with honors, Western Wash. U., 1976. Free-lance card designer Painted Heart & Friends, Pasadena, Calif., 1994-97, Artists of N.Am., Portland, 1994—. Tchr. watercolor painting Clark Coll., Vancouver, 1995—. Designer, artist (calendar) A Woman's Moments, 1998—, Hallmark calendar, 1999; included in Best of Watercolor, Vol. III. Mem.: S.W. Wash. Watercolor Soc., N.W. Watercolor Soc. (signature mem.), Watercolor West (juried, signature mem.), Nat. Watercolor Soc. (signature mem.), Am. Watercolor Soc. Home: 315 W 23rd St Vancouver WA 98660-2522 E-mail: paintingjoz@hotmail.com.

JU, JIANN-WEN, mechanics educator, researcher; b. Taiwan, 1958; s. Jiang and Kwai J.; m. Mali J., 1985; children: Derek, Tiffany. BS, Nat. (Taipei) Taiwan U., 1980; MS, U. Calif., Berkeley, 1983, PhD, 1986. Registered profl. engr., Calif., Ariz. Teaching asst. U. Calif., Berkeley, 1983-84, rsch. asst., 1984-86, lectr., 1986, postdoctoral rsch. engr., 1986-87; asst. prof. Princeton (NJ) U., 1987-93; assoc. prof. UCLA, 1993-98, prof., 1998—, chmn., 1999—2002, chmn., structural engr., 2001—. Cons. Air Force Engring. and Svcs. Ctr., Panama City, Fla., 1990—, Titan R&T, Chatsworth, Calif., Kasdan and Simonds, Irvine, Calif., Karagozian and Case, L.A., Miller Law, Irvine, Calif.; mem. rev. panel NSF, Washington, 1991—; chmn., organizer Symposiums; invited lectr. 130 univs. and profl. socs. Author, editor: Damage Mechanics in Engineering Materials, 1990, Recent Advances in Damage Mechanics and Plasticity, 1992, Damage Mechanics and Localization, 1992, Homogenization and Constitutive Modeling, 1993, Micromechanics and Inelasticity of Metal Matrix Composites, 1994, Damage Mechanics in Composites, 1994, Numerical Methods in Structural Mechanics, 1995, Damage Mechanics in Engineering Materials, 1998, T.H. Lin 90th Birthday Symposium on Mechanics and Materials, 2001, Symposium on Micromechanics of Heterogeneous Materials, 2002, Symposium on Micromechanics Based Materials Modeling and Simulation, 2003, Symposium on Recent Advances in Microstructural Mechanics and Damage Mechanics, 2004; mem. editl. bd. Internat. Jour. Damage Mechanics, 1992; assoc. tech. editor ASME Jour. of Engring. Materials and Technology, ASME Jour. of Applied Mechanics; contbr. articles to profl. jours.; author conf. procs. Fed. and indsl. rsch. grantee U.S. Govt., U.S. cos., Japanese cos., 1987—; recipient Presdl. Young Investigator award NSF, 1991. Fellow ASME (com. mem. 1989—, assoc. editor Jour. Engring. Materials Tech., Jour. Applied Mechanics 1995—); mem. ASCE (control group 1989-93, Walter L. Huber Civil Engring. Rsch. prize 1997), U.S. Assn. Computational Mechanics, Am. Acad. Mechanics, Am. Concrete Inst. (chmn. com. 446 fracture mechanics 2004—), Soc. Engring. Sci., Internat. Assn. for Computational Mechanics. Office: UCLA Dept Civil Engring Los Angeles CA 90095-1593 Business E-Mail: juj@ucla.edu.

JU, XIONGWEI, portfolio manager; PhD, U. Ill., 1999. Registered rep. NASD. Dir. statis. arbitrage Nomura Securities Internat., N.Y.C., 2000—02; mng. dir., portfolio mgr. Millennium Partners, LP, N.Y.C., 2002—. Contbr. articles to profl. jours. Mem.: Internat. Assn. Fin. Engrs., Am. Fin. Assn. Achievements include research in a consistent and profitable market neutral investment strategy that generates significant returns for investors. Avocations: travel, swimming. Office Phone: 212-841-4289. Personal E-mail: xwju@yahoo.com. Business E-Mail: xju@mlp.com.

JU, YOUNG KYU, structural engineer, researcher; s. Il-Ryun Ju and Soon-Ja Ohn; m. Ryu-Jin Jung, Sept. 24, 1995; children: Jae-Won, Ryu-Jung. BA, Korea U., 1991, MA, 1993, PhD, 1993—99. Rschr. Bldg. Rsch. Inst., Tsukuba, Japan, 1995; lectr. Korea U., Seoul, 1999—2003; mem. Coun. on Tall Buildings & Urban Habitat, 2000—; lectr. Kyonghee U., Suwon, Republic of Korea, 2002, Seoul Nat. U. Tech., Republic of Korea, 2001—03; sr. rschr. Daewoo Inst. Constrn. Tech., Suwon, Republic of Korea, 1995—2003; rsch. fellow Korea U., Seoul, 2003—04; rsch. scholar U. Tex., Austin, 2003—; com. mem. Korea Soc. Steel Constrn., 1999—, Archtl. Inst. Korea, 2002—, Korea Urban Disater Prevention Soc., 2002—. Cons. Daewoo Engring. & Constrn., Seoul, Republic of Korea, 1995—2003. Author: (book) Structural Design of Tall Buildings. Recipient Commendation, Ministry Edn., 1988; fellow, Japan Sci. Found., 1995. Mem.: Archtl. Inst. Korea (corr.), Korea Soc. Steel Constrn. (corr.). Achievements include patents for a folded wire mesh deck; a steel-concrete composite beam using asymmetric section steel beam; patents pending for vibration control apparatus using water tank located at top floor of a tall building; design of the Cheonan Doojung 4th Shopping Center; research in prediction & compensation of column shortening; structural analysis and design of tall buildings; nonlinear analysis of tall buildings; prediction & compensation of column shortening; evaluation of wind loads; vibration control by tuned liquid damper. Office Phone: 82 31 370 9557. E-mail: tallsite@rist.re.kr.

JUANG, HANN-MING HENRY, meteorologist; b. Kaohsiung, Taiwan, Sept. 29, 1955; came to U.S., 1980; s. Ming-Fei and Way (Hong) J.; m. Mei-Yu Lin, May 12, 1983; children: Benjamin, Belinda. BS in Atmospheric Scis., Nat. Ctrl. U., Chongli, Tawain, 1978; MS in Atmospheric Scis., U. Ill., Champaign-Urbana, 1982, PhD in Atmospheric Scis., 1988. Support scientist NOAA, Nat. Ctrs. for Environ. Prediction, Environ. Modeling Ctr. Contractor, Camp Springs, Md., 1988-98; rsch. meteorologist (GS-14) NOAA, NWS, Nat. Ctrs. for Environ. Prediction, Climate Prediction Ctr., Camp Springs, 1998—. Rsch. asst. U. Ill., Urbana-Champaign, 1980-88; cons. Ctrl. Weather Bur., Taipei, Taiwan, 1995—, Tenn. Valley Authority, U. Hawaii, U. Ill., USAF, Nat. Ctrl. U., Chongli, Nat. Taiwan U., Tapei, Ctrl. Weather Bur., Tapei, Korea Meteorol. Adminstrn., Seoul, others; presenter, lectr. in field. Contbr. articles to Monthly Weather Rev., Weather Forecasting, Bull. Amer. Meteorol. Soc., Atmospheric Sci., Meteorol. Atmospheric Physics. 2d lt. USN, 1978-80, Taiwan. Fellow Joint Inst. Marine Observation, Scripps Instn. Oceanography, 1993-95. Mem. Am. Meteorol. Soc., Am. Geophys. Union, N.Y. Acad. Scis., Sigma Xi. Achievements include development of a Regional Spectral Model, hydrostatic sigma coordinate for nonhydrostatic modeling, implementing RSM for experimental research and operational use. Fax: 301-763-8000. Ext. 7517. Office: NOAA/NWS/Nat Ctrs Environ Prediction World Weather Bldg 5200 Auth Rd Rm 806 Suitland MD 20746-4304 E-mail: henry.juang@noaa.gov.

JUAREZ, ANTONIO, psychotherapist, consultant, counselor, educator; b. El Paso, Tex., Nov. 6, 1952; s. Juan Antonio and Amelia (Rivas) J. BS in Psychology, U. Tex.-El Paso, 1976, MA in Clin. Psychology, 1982; postgrad., N.Mex. State U., 1987—, Calif. Coast U., 1990—. Cert. counselor; cert. diplomate, Am. Psychotherapy Assn., lic. profl. counselor, Tex., PhD of Martial Arts, Ea. USA Internat. Coll. Martial Arts, Pittsburgh, 2000. Caseworker asst. El Paso Mental Health Ctr., 1978-79, caseworker III, 1982-83; clin. specialist S.W. Mental Health Ctr., Las Cruces, N.Mex., 1979-80; therapist, trainer S.W. Cmty. House, El Paso, 1980-81; psychol. cons. El Paso Guidance Ctr., 1981-82, psychotherapist, 1983—, dir. N.E. svcs.; pvt. practice El Paso, 1987—. Mem. Nat. Bd. for Cert. Counselors; dir. Cross-Cultural Counseling Ctr., 1988—; instr. psychology El Paso C.C., 1988-90, faculty coord. social scis., counselor, cons.; cons. Citizens and Students Together, El Paso, 1983—; group facilitator, Tai Chi Chuan instr. Sun Valley Regional Hosp., El Paso, Tex., 1988; psychotherapist, treatment team coord. El Paso State Ctr., 1997—; adj. prof. counseling Webster U., Ft. Bliss, Tex., 1995—. Mem. Latin Am. com. N.Mex. State U., 1985. Served with USAF, 1972-76. Fellow Am. Assn. Integrative Medicine, U.S.-N.Mex. Border Health Assn., El Paso Psychol. Assn., Tex. Assn. for Counseling and Devel., Tex. Assn. for Children of Alcoholics, Golden Key, Nat. Acad. for Clin. Mental Health Counselors, Ea. U.S.A. Martial Arts Assn. (Black Belt Hall of Fame 1996, Master of Wushu 2000), Ea. U.S.A. Internat. Martial Arts Assn. (named Man of Yr. 2003, Black Belt Hall of Fame 2003). Democrat. Roman Catholic. Avocations: martial arts, playing stringed instruments. Home: PO Box 1493 Santa Teresa NM 88008-1493 Office: Cross-Cultural Counseling Ctr 2112 Trawood Dr # 3B El Paso TX 79935-3318 Business E-Mail: antonioj@epcc.edu.

JUBER, DAVID L., prosecutor; married; 2 children. BA, U. Louisville, 1965, JD, 1968. Pvt. practice, 1968—69; legis. asst. U.S. Senator Marlow W. Cook, 1969—72; asst. atty. U.S. Dist. Ct. (we. dist.) Ky., 1972—77, chief adminstrv. officer, 1978—85; second v.p., dir. govt. rels. Capitol Holding Corp., 1985—87; v.p., gen. counsel Glenmore Distilleries Co., 1987—89; gen. counsel U.S. Senator Mitch McConnell, 1990—91; asst. atty. U.S. Dist. Ct. (we. dist.) Ky., 1991—2003, atty., 2003—. Office: US Attys Office 510 West Broadway 10th Fl Louisville KY 40202

JUBINSKA, PATRICIA ANN, ballet instructor, choreographer, artist, anthropologist, archaeologist; b. Norfolk, Va. d. Joseph John and Lucy (Babey) Topping; children: Vanessa Meredith, Courtney Hilary. Student, Md. State Ballet Sch., Sch. Am. Ballet, N.Y.C.; BA, R.I. Coll.; MA, Wesleyan U.; PhD, Union Inst., 1999. Mem. N.Y.C. Ballet; freelance artist Chamber Ballet of L.A., San Antonio Ballet, Md. State Ballet; artistic dir. Blackstone Valley Ballet, Harrisville, RI, 1983, Am. Ballet, Pascoag, RI, 1984—92; asst. artistic dir. Odessa Ukrainian Dancers, Woonsocket, RI, 1991—92; freelance guest artist, 1992—; mem. Mandrivka Dancers of Boston, 1993—; mem. faculty Fine Arts West Warwick Sch., 1995—; mem. faculty Roger Williams U., 2000—. Avocation: equestrian. Home: 110 Gold Mine Rd Chepachet RI 02814 Personal E-mail: pajubinska@aol.com.

JUCEAM, ROBERT E., lawyer; b. NYC, June 16, 1940; s. Benjamin T. and Amelia B. (Spatz) J.; m. Eleanor Pam, May 24, 1970; children: Daniel, Jacquelyn, Gregory. AB cum laude, Columbia U., 1961, LLB, 1964, JD, 1972; LLM, NYU, 1966. Bar: NY 1965, US Dist. Ct. (so. and ea. dists.) NY 1966, U.S. Tax Ct. 1968, U.S. Ct. Appeals (2d cir.) 1967, U.S. Supreme Ct. 1971, U.S. Ct. Appeals (5th cir.) 1978, U.S. Ct. Appeals (DC cir.) 1980, U.S. Ct. Appeals (11th cir.) 1987, U.S. Ct. Appeals (7th cir.) 1989, U.S. Ct. Appeals (9th cir.) 1999. Law clk. US Dist. Ct., NY, 1964-66; assoc. Fried, Frank, Harris, Shriver & Jacobson, NYC, 1966-73, ptnr., 1974—. Bd. dirs. Nat. Network Def. of the Right to Counsel, Inc., 1985-89, Lawyers Com. for Human Rights, 1986-94, Bar Assurance and Reins. Ltd., 1991—, Am. Immigration Law Found., 1987—, pres., 1991-2000, treas., 2000-2003, sec., 2004-; gen. counsel U.S. Supreme Ct. Hist. Soc., 1995—, trustee, 1999—; arbitration panel U.S. Dist. Ct. (ea. dist.) NY, 1986—; mem. comml. and constrn. panels Am. Arbitration Assn., 1972-94; dir. civil rights Washington Lawyers Com., 1996-99; bd. advisors DC Bar Found., 1996-2001; treas., bd. dirs. Pro Bono Inst., 1997—. Contbr. articles to profl. jours. Trustee Mex.-Am. Legal Def. and Edn. Fund, 1986-90, chmn. program and planning com., 1988-90; adv. com. to task force on racial, gender and minority discrimination U.S. Ct. Appeals for 2d Cir., 1994-96; bd. dirs. Appleseed Found., Inc., 1997-99; bd. advisors Atlantic Legal Found., 2001-05, bd. dirs. 2005-. Recipient Lester Zazuly medal, James Madison HS, 1958, Columbia Coll. Alumni Achievement award, 1961, Edward Foxx prize Columbia Coll., 1961, Maldef Corp. Responsibility award, 1993, Valerie J. Kantor award for extraordinary achievement, 1997, Am. Immigration Law Found. hon. fellow and Founder's award, 1989, Lifetime Achievement award Ctr. for Human Rights and Constl. Law, 1993, Pro Bono Svc. award Legal Aid Soc. N.Y., 2003-04, 2004-05. Fellow Am. Bar Found. (life), NY State Bar Found., ABA (ho. of dels. 1983—, chmn. com. on immigration sect. litig. 1985-90, immigration pro bono adv. task force, 1992-98, vice chmn., 1995-96, coord. com. on immigration law 1984-87, chmn. 1989-92, mem. com. environ. controls sect. banking, 1983-86, vice chmn. com. on constrn., sec. gen. practice 1989-90, standing com. lawyers pub. svc. responsibility 1993-96, coun. fund justice and edn. 1994-2000, 2003-, adv. mem., 2000-02, chmn. major gifts com. 1997-98, Pro Bono award 1992, mem. com. Ctr. Profl. Responsibility 2004-), Royal Philatelic Soc. New Zealand; mem. Internat. Bar Assn. (chmn. Sect. Gen. Practice com. bus. migration 1987-88), Assn. Bar NYC Fund, Inc. (bd. dirs., 2004—), City Bar Fund for Justice (bd. dirs. 2004-), NY State Bar Assn., Assn. Bar City of NY (com. on trademarks and unfair competition 1983-86, com. immigration 1986-89, com. on profl. and jud. ethics 1989-92, com. Human Rights Law 1994-96), Nat. Assn. Criminal Def. Lawyers (co-chmn. com. on immigration 1988-90), Am. Judicature Soc. (life), Am. Bar Endowment, Nat. Conf. Bar Presidents (assoc.), Am. Immigration Lawyers Assn. (pres. 1982-83, bd. govt. 1971—, chmn. NY chpt. 1971-72, gen. counsel 1986-91, liaison to ABA commn. on nonlawyer practice 1993-94, editor Ann. Symposium Handbook 1985-88, assoc. editor 1989-90, Edith Lowenstein Meml. award 1981, Pro Bono award 1992), Soc. Sachems Columbia Coll., NY County Lawyers Assn. (reporter NY Equitable Distbn. Law Proposals 1968, bd. dirs. 1996-98), Def. Rsch. Inst., Assn. Fed. Def. Lawyers, Cow Neck Peninsula Hist. Soc. (life), Italy and Colonies Philat. Soc. of Gt. Brit. (life), Jack Knight Soc. (life), LI Postal History Soc. (life), Am. Helvetia Philatelic Soc. (life), Am. Philat. Soc. (life), Austrian Philatelic Soc. Internat. Fedn. Postcard Dealers, India House Club, Alpha Epsilon Pi. Home: 106 Hemlock Rd Manhasset NY 11030-1214 Office: Fried Frank Harris Shriver & Jacobson 1 New York Plz Ste 2500 New York NY 10004-1901 Office Phone: 212-859-8040. Business E-Mail: jucearo@ffhsj.com.

JUCKEM, WILFRED PHILIP, manufacturing executive; b. Sheboygan, Wis., Apr. 27, 1915; s. Arvin M. and Martha (Henning) J.; m. Dorothy Iris Dean, Dec. 8, 1941; children— Jean Audrey, Philip Dean. Grad., Sheboygan Bus. Coll., 1934. With Jenkins Machine Co., Sheboygan Falls, Wis., 1933-34, Kohler of Kohler, Wis., 1934-42, Rock Island (Ill.) Arsenal, 1942-45; with Eagle Signal Corp., Moline, Ill., 1947-63, v.p. mfg., 1958-63; asst. to pres. E.W. Bliss Co., Canton, Ohio, 1963-64, adminstrv. v.p., 1964-66, v.p. press div., 1966-67, v.p. corporate devel., 1967-68; v.p., div. mgr. E.W. Bliss Co. (Eagle Signal div.), 1968-77; chmn. bd. Sears Mfg. Co., Davenport, Iowa, 1977-86. Bd. dirs. Long Mfg. Chmn. bd. dirs. Davenport Osteo. Hosp., 1979-80, chmn., 1980-82; bd. dirs. Ridgecrest Retirement Village. Recipient Honorary Alumnus award St. Ambrose Coll., Davenport. Mem. Nat. Elec. Mfrs. Assn. (chmn. emeritus traffic control systems sect. 1972-77), Am. Ordnance Assn. (pres. Iowa-Ill. chpt. 1975-76), Asso. Employers Quad Cities (dir., past pres.) Lutheran. Home: Ridgecrest Village C-1 4130 Northwest Blvd Davenport IA 52806-4243

JUDD, ASHLEY, actress; b. Granada Hills, Calif., Apr. 19, 1968; d. Michael Ciminella and Naomi Judd; m. Dario Franchitti, Dec. 12, 2001. BA in French, U. Ky., 1990. Actor: (films) Kuffs, 1992, Ruby in Paradise, 1993, Smoke, 1995, Heat, 1995, The Passion of Darkly Noon, 1996, A Time To Kill, 1996, Normal Life, 1996, The Locusts, 1997, Kiss the Girls, 1997, Simon Birch, 1998, Eye of the Beholder, 1999, Double Jeopardy, 1999, Where the Heart Is, 2000, Someone Like You, 2001, High Crimes, 2002, Divine Secrets of the Ya-Ya Sisterhood, 2002, Frida, 2002, Twisted, 2004; (TV films) Till Death Us Do Part, 1992, Norma Jean & Marilyn, 1996, The Ryan Interview, 2000; (TV series) Sisters, 1991—93, Star Trek: The Next Generation, 1991. Named One of the 50 Most Beautiful People In The World, People Magazine, 1996. Mem.: Phi Beta Kappa. Office: William Morris Agy 1 William Morris Pl Beverly Hills CA 90212-2775

JUDD, BRIAN RAYMOND, physicist; b. Chelmsford, Eng., Feb. 13, 1931; s. Harry and Edith (Saltmarsh) J. BA, Brasenose Coll., Oxford U., 1952, MA, D.Phil., Brasenose Coll., Oxford U., 1955. Fellow Magdalen Coll., Oxford U., 1955-62; instr. U. Chgo., 1957-58; assoc. prof. U. Paris, 1962-64; staff mem. Lawrence Radiation Lab., Berkeley, Calif., 1964-66; prof. physics Johns Hopkins U., Balt., 1966-96, chmn. dept., 1979-84, Gerhard H. Dieke prof., 1992-96, prof. emeritus, 1997-98, Gerhard H. Dieke prof. emeritus, 1998—. Vis. Erskine fellow U. Canterbury, Christchurch, New Zealand, 1968; vis. fellow Australian Nat. U., Canberra, 1975; hon. fellow Brasenose Coll., Oxford U., 1983—. Author: Operator Techniques in Atomic Spectroscopy, 1963, reprinted, 1998, Second Quantization and Atomic Spectroscopy, 1967, (with J.P. Elliott) Topics in Atomic and Nuclear Theory, 1970, Angular Momentum Theory For Diatomic Molecules, 1975. Recipient Spedding award for rare-earth rsch. Rhone-Poulenc, Inc., 1988. Fellow Am. Phys. Soc. Office: Johns Hopkins U Dept Physics and Astronomy Baltimore MD 21218

JUDD, BRUCE DIVEN, architect; b. Pasadena, Calif., Sept. 28, 1947; s. David Lockhart and Martha Leah (Brown) J.; m. Diane Reinbolt, Feb. 4, 1976 (div. Oct. 1985); 1 child, Ian David. BArch, U. Calif., Berkeley, 1970, MArch, 1971. Registered arch., Calif., Nev.; cert. Nat. Coun. Archtl. Registration Bds. Designer Ribera and Sue Landscape Archs., Oakland, Calif., 1968-70, Page Clowdsley & Baleix, San Francisco, 1971-75; v.p. Charles Hall Page Assocs., San Francisco, 1975-80; prin. Archtl. Resources Group, San Francisco, 1980—. Mem. adv. bd. fed. rehab. guidelines program Nat. Inst. Bldg. Scis., HUD, 1979-80; mem. city-wide survey planning com. City of Oakland, Calif., 1979-80; cons. Nat. Main St. Program, Washington. Bd. dirs., co-founder Oakland Heritage Alliance, 1980-85; mem. Calif. Hist. Resources Commn., 1982-86, chmn., 1983-85; bd. dirs. Preservation Action, Washington, 1982-85, 90—, Friends of Terra Cotta, 1981-86, Berkeley Archtl. Heritage Assn., 1993—; mem. bd. advisors Nat. Trust for Hist. Preservation, Washington, 1981-90, advisor emeritus, 1990—; bd. trustees Calif. Preservation Found., San Francisco, 1985—, v.p., 1990-92, trustee, 1990—; active Calif. State Hist. Bldg. Safety Bd., 1991-93, also others. Recipient Excellence Honor award State of Calif., Excellence award in archtl. conservation, Spl. Restoration award Sunset Mag.; named Preservationist of Yr., Calif. Preservation Found., 1993. Fellow AIA (preservation officer No. Calif. chpt. 1978-81, hist. resources com. Calif. coun. 1979-80, nat. hist. resources com. 1981—, chmn. 1981-82), mem. Internat. Assn. for Preservation Tech. (bd. dirs. 1983-85), Park Hills Homes Assn. (chmn. archtl. com. 1992—), U.S./Internat. Coun. Monuments and Sites. Office: Archtl Resources Group Pier 9 The Embarcadero San Francisco CA 94111

JUDD, BURKE HAYCOCK, geneticist; b. Kanab, Utah, Sept. 5, 1927; s. Zadok Ray and Elva (Haycock) J.; m. Barbara Ann Gaddy, Mar. 21, 1953; children: Sean Michael, Evan Patrick, Timothy Burke. BS, U. Utah, 1950,

MS, 1951; PhD, Calif. Inst. Tech., 1954. Postdoctoral fellow Am. Cancer Soc. U. Tex., Austin, 1954-56, from instr. to prof., 1956-79, dir. Genetics Inst., 1977-79; geneticist Atomic Energy Commn., Germantown, Md., 1968-69; chief lab. genetics Nat. Inst. Environ. Health Sci., Research Triangle Park, N.C., 1979-95. Vis. asst. prof. Stanford U., Palo Alto, Calif., 1960; Gosney vis. prof. Calif. Inst. Tech., Pasadena, 1975-76; adj. prof. U. N.C., Chapel Hill, 1979-99, Duke U., Durham, 1980-2002; mem. panel genetic biology NSF, Washington, 1969-73, genetics study sect. NIH, Washington, 1974, 77, 79, 88, com. on germplasm resources NAS, Washington, 1976-77; chmn. human genome initiative rev. panel Dept. of Energy, Washington, 1988. Author: Introduction to Modern Genetics, 1980; editor: Molecular and Gen. Genetics, 1986-95; assoc. editor Genetics, 1973-78; contbr. articles to profl. jours. With U.S. Army, 1946-47. Fellow AAAS; mem. Am. Soc. Naturalists (sec. 1968-70), Genetics Soc. Am. (sec. 1974-76, v.p., pres. 1979-80). Avocations: travel, poetry, fiction. Home: 411 Clayton Rd Chapel Hill NC 27514-7613 E-mail: bjudd@bellsouth.net.

JUDD, DENNIS L., lawyer; b. Provo, Utah, June 27, 1954; s. Derrel Wesley and Leila (Lundquist) J.; m. Carol Lynne Chilberg, May 6, 1977; children: Lynne Marie, Amy Jo, Tiffany Ann, Andrew, Jacquelyn Nicole. BA in Polit. Sci. summa cum laude, Brigham Young U., 1978, JD, 1981. Bar: Utah 1981, U.S. Dist. Ct. Utah 1981. Assoc. Nielson & Senior, Salt Lake City and Vernal, Utah, 1981-83; dep. county atty. Uintah County, Vernal, 1982-84; ptnr. Bennett & Judd, Vernal, 1983-88; county atty. Daggett County, Utah, 1985-89, 91-99; pvt. practice Vernal, 1988—; county atty. Daggett County, 2000—; prosecutor City of Naples, Naples, 1996-99; legal counsel Uintah County Sch. Dist., 1996—; city atty. Naples City, Utah, 1999—, Vernal City, Utah, 2000—; atty. City of Vernal, 2000—. Mem. governing bd. Uintah Basin applied Tech. Ctr., 1991-95, v.p., 1993-94, pres., 1994-95. Chmn. bd. adjustment Zoning and Planning Bd., Naples, 1982-91, 94—; mem. Naples City Coun., 1982-91; mayor pro tem City of Naples, 1983-91; legis. v.p. Naples PTA, 1988-90; sec. Friends of Utah Field House of Natural History, 2000—; v.p. Uintah Dist. PTA Coun., 1990-92; mem. resolution com. Utah League Cities and Towns, 1985-86, small cities com., 1985-86; trustee Uintah Sch. Dist. Found., 1988-97, 2005—, vice chmn., 1991-93; mem. Uintah County Sch. Dist. Bd. Edn., 1991-95, v.p., 1991-92, pres., 1992-95; chmn. Uintah County Rep. Conv., 1998. Hinkley scholar Brigham Young U., 1977; named Oustanding County Atty. Utah, 2003. Mem. Utah Bar Assn., Uintah Basin Bar Assn., Statewide Assn. Prosecutors, Vernal C. of C. Republican. Mem. Lds Ch. Avocations: hunting, photography, lapidary. Home: 460 E 1555 S Naples UT 84078 Office: 461 W 200 S Vernal UT 84078-3049 Office Phone: 435-789-7038. E-mail: judd@easilink.com.

JUDD, JACQUELINE VOGEL, retired middle school educator; b. Edgerton, Wis., May 9, 1939; d. Ira Charles and Mabel Helen (Pratt) Vogel; m. Stanley Samual Judd, Jr., June 2, 1962; children: Gretchen Judd Cottrell, Stanley Samual III. BE, U. Wis., Whitewater, 1963, MS in Teaching, 1975. Cert. elem. tchr., Wis. Tchr. North Milton Rural Sch., Milton, Wis., 1959-61, Harmony Sch., Milton, 1961-64, Footville (Wis.) Elem. Schs., 1964-67; tchr., unit leader Madison Elem. Sch., Janesville, Wis., 1967-74; tchr., team leader Harrison Elem. Sch., Janesville, 1974-88, Marshall Mid. Sch., Janesville, 1988-91. Presenter, speaker in field. Bd. dirs., pres. Friends Janesville Libr., 1982-88; chmn. centennial com. Janesville Libr., 1986, trustee, 1987-91; bd. dirs., chmn. youth svcs. com. YWCA, Janesville, 1987—; mem. Lee County Adv. Bd. Named Woman of Distinction, YWCA, 1989. Mem. Assn. for Individually Guided Edn., Wis. Assn. Mid. Level Educators, AAUW, Rock Valley Astronomers Club, Elk Ladies (chmn. scholarship com. Janesville 1989-91, mem. exec. bd. 1996-97), Greater Pine Island Optimist Club (chair oratorical contest 1992-93), Friends of Pine Island Libr. Avocations: astronomy, reading, fishing. Home: 5190 Serenity Cv Bokeelia FL 33922-3006 E-mail: juddjs@iline.com.

JUDD, JOEL STANTON, lawyer; b. Denver, Sept. 10, 1951; s. E. James and Eleanore Judd. BA, New Coll., 1973; JD, U. Denver, 1976. Bar: Colo. 1976, U.S. Dist. Ct. Colo. 1976, U.S. Ct. Appeals (10th cir.) 1976, U.S. Supreme Ct. 1980. Assoc. Feder & Morris, Denver, 1976-77, Reckseen & Lau, Northglenn, Colo., 1977-82; sole practice Denver, 1982—; state rep. Ho. Dist. 5, Colo., 2003—. Mem. Colo. Bar Assn., Denver Bar Assn. (chair intraprofl. com. 1985-90), Colo. Trial Lawyers Assn., Allied Jewish Fedn. (chair young profls. div. 1984-86, chair Denver Jewish cmty. Israel Independence Day celebration 1987), Optimists (pres. 1980-83). Democrat. Avocations: skiing, river rafting. Home: 2904 W 24th Ave Denver CO 80211-4702 Office: # 100 2222 S Albion St Denver CO 80222-4928

JUDD, O'DEAN P., physicist; b. Austin, Minn., May 26, 1937; MS in Physics, UCLA, 1961, PhD in Physics, 1968. Staff physicist and project dir. Hughes Rsch. Lab., Malibu, Calif., 1959-67; postdoctoral fellow UCLA Dept. Physics, 1968-69; researcher Hughes Rsch. Lab., Malibu, Calif., 1969-72; researcher, group leader Los Alamos Nat. Lab., 1972-82, chief scientist for def. rsch. and applications, 1981-87; chief scientist Strategic Def. Initiative Orgn., Washington, 1987-90; energy and environ. chief scientist, lab. fellow Los Alamos (N.Mex.) Nat. Lab., 1990-93; nat. intelligence officer for sci. and tech. Nat. Intelligence Coun., Washington, 1993-94; ind. tech. advisor and cons. Los Alamos, 1995—. Mem. numerous govt. coms. related to sci. and tech., def. and nat. security policy; adj. prof. physics U. N.Mex., Albuquerque; mem. sci. adv. bd. USAF, 1999-2003. Patentee in sci. and tech.; contbr. numerous articles to sci. and def.-related jours. Fellow IEEE, AAAS, Los Alamos Nat. Lab. Inst. Advanced Engring.; mem. Am. Phys. Soc. Office: Los Alamos Nat Lab MS F650 Los Alamos NM 87544-2648

JUDD, WILLIAM ROBERT, engineering geologist, educator; b. Denver, Aug. 16, 1917; s. Samuel and Lillian (Israelske) J.; m. Rachel Elizabeth Douglas, Apr. 18, 1942; children: Stephanie (Mrs. Chris Wadley), Judith (Mrs. John Soden), Dayna (Mrs. Erick Grandmason), Pamela, Connie. AB, U. Colo., 1941, postgrad., 1941-50. Registered profl. engr., Colo., engring. geologist, Oreg. Engring. geologist Colo. Water Conservation Bd., 1941-42; supervisory engring. geologist Denver & Rio Grande Western R.R., Colo. and Utah, 1942-44; head geology sect. No. 1, acting dist. geologist-Alaska U.S. Bur. Reclamation, Office of Chief Engr., Denver, 1945-60; head basing tech. group RAND Corp., Santa Monica, Calif., 1960—66; prof. rock mechanics Purdue U., Lafayette, Ind., 1966-87, head geotech. engring., 1976-86; tech. dir. Purdue U. Underground Excavation and Rock Properties Info. Center, 1972-79, prof. emeritus civil engring., 1988—. Geotech. cons., U.S., Mexico, Cuba, Honduras, Greece, 1950-; geoscience editor Am. Elsevier Pub. Co., 1967-71; chmn. panel on ocean scis. Com. on Instl. Cooperation, 1971-85; founder and chmn. Nat. Acad. Sci. U.S. Nat. Com. on Rock Mechanics, 1963-69, co-chmn. panel on rsch. requirements, 1977-81, chmn. panel on awards, 1972-82; mem. U.S. Army Adv. Bd. on Mountain and Arctic Warfare, 1956-62, USAF Sci. Adv. Bd. Geophysics Panel Study Group, 1964-67; com. on safety dams NRC, 1977-78, 82-83; Nat. dir. Nat. Ski Patrol System, Inc., 1956-62; Alex du Toit Meml. lectr., S.Africa and Rhodesia, 1967; owner Rayanbill Galleries, 1986—. Author: (with E.F. Taylor) Ski Patrol Manual, 1956, (with D. Krynine) Principles of Engineering Geology and Geotechnics, 1957, Sitzmarks or Safety, 1960; editor: Rock Mechanics Research, 1966, State of Stress in the Earth's Crust, 1964; co-editor: Physical Properties of Rocks and Minerals, 1981; editor-in-chief: Engring. Geology, 1972-92, hon. editor, 1996—. Recipient Spl. Rsch. award NRC, 1982; named to Colo. Ski Hall of Fame, 1983; named hon. life mem. Nat. Ski Patrol System, Inc., 1988. Fellow ASCE, Geol. Soc. Am. (Disting. Practice award engring. geology divsn. 1989), South African Inst. Mining and Metallurgy; mem. Assn. Engring. Geologists (hon.), Internat. Assn. Engring. Geologists (Hans Cloos medal 1994), India Soc. Engring. Geology (life), India Acad. Scis., U.S. Com. on Large Dams (exec. coun. 1977-83, com. on earthquakes 1976-90), U.S. Ski Assn. (hon. life), U.S. Recreational Ski Assn. (hon. life). Home and Office: 1051 Cumberland Ave West Lafayette IN 47906 Personal E-mail: williamjudd@verizon.net. *Are you important? Take your thumb out of a bowl of water, then measure the hole it left.*

JUDELL, HAROLD BENN, lawyer; b. Milw., Mar. 9, 1915; s. Philip Fox and Lena Florence (Krause) J.; m. Maria Violeta van Ronzelen, May 5, 1951 (div.); m. Celeste Seymour Grulich, June 24, 1986. BA, U. Wis., 1936, JD, 1938; LLB, Tulane U., 1950. Bar: Wis. 1938, La. 1950. Mem. Scheinfeld Collins Durant & Winter, Milw., 1938; spl. agt., adminstrv. asst. to dir. FBI, 1939-44; legal attache U.S. Embassy Peru, 1942-44; ptnr. Foley & Judell, LLP, New Orleans, 1950—; v.p., dir. Dauphine Orleans Hotel Corp., 1970—, chmn. bd., 1999—, pres., 2005—. Mem. Tulane U. Bus. Sch. Coun.; trustee Greater New Orleans YMCA, 1981—; dir. Sizeler Property Investors, Inc., 1986—. Fellow Am. Coll. Bond Counsel (founding); mem. ABA, La. Bar Assn., Nat. Assn. Bond Lawyers (bd. dirs., pres. 1984-85), New Orleans Country Club, Lawn Tennis Club, Met. Club (N.Y.C.). Office: Foley & Judell LLP 365 Canal St New Orleans LA 70130-1112 Business E-Mail: hjudell@foleyjudell.com.

JUDGE, BERNARD MARTIN, editor, publishing executive; b. Chgo., Jan. 6, 1940; s. Bernard A. and Catherine Elizabeth (Halloran) J.; m. Kimbeth A. Wehrli, July 9, 1966; children: Kelly, Bernard R., Jessica. Reporter City News Bur., Chgo., 1965-66; reporter Chgo. Tribune, 1966-70, city editor, 1974-79, asst. mng. editor met. news, 1979-83; editor, gen. mgr. City News Bur. Chgo., 1983-84; assoc. editor Chgo. Sun-Times, 1984-88; from editor to pub. Chgo. Daily Law Bull., 1988—; pub. Chgo. Lawyer, 1989—; v.p. Law Bull. Pub. Co., Chgo., 1988—. Bd. dirs. Constnl. Rights Found., Chgo., 1992—, chmn. bd. dirs., 1995-97; trustee Fenwick Cath. Prep. H.S., Oak Park, Ill., 1989—; bd. dirs. Abraham Lincoln Presdl. Libr. & Mus., 2004. Named to Chgo. Journalism Hall of Fame, 2000. Mem. Sigma Delta Chi. Home: 360 E Randolph St Apt 1905 Chicago IL 60601-7335 Office: Law Bull Pub Co 415 N State St Chicago IL 60610-4631

JUDGE, CHARLES ARTHUR, academic administrator; b. Ames, Iowa, Feb. 19, 1940; s. Frank E. and Florence I. (Ivis) J.; m. Judith Ann Wolf, Aug. 25, 1973; children: Kathryn Elizabeth, Margaret Helen. BBA, U. Mich., 1962, MA, 1964, PhD, 1980. Dir. fin. aid, asst. dean men Lawrence U., Appleton, Wis., 1966-69; asst. dir. admissions Harvard Bus. Sch., Boston, 1969-71; asst. dir. Lit., Sci., Arts acad. advising U. Mich., Ann Arbor, 1972-75, dir. Lit., Sci., Arts acad. advising, 1975-95, dir. Lit., Sci., Arts acad. stds., 1995—. Chair Washtenaw County Cmty. Mental Health Bd., Ann Arbor, 1982-84. Mem. Nat. Acad. Advising Assn. Home: 1500 Barnard Rd Ann Arbor MI 48103-5928 Office: U Mich LSA Advising Ctr 1255 Angell Hall Ann Arbor MI 48109 E-mail: cjudge@umich.edu.

JUDGE, MARY FRANCES, artist; b. Mpls., July 31, 1935; d. Francis Gerald and Katherine (Moore) Judge. BA in Art, Coll. New Rochelle, 1961; M.F.A., U. Notre Dame, 1971. Mus. bd. Dallas Mus. Art, 1977-78. One woman shows include: Digital Sandbox Gallery N.Y.C. 2002-2003, Monograma Galleria, Rome, Italy 2001, Paige Gallery, Dallas, 1983, Rosenberg Library Harris Gallery, Galveston, Tex., 1983, Ross Gallery, Scottsdale, Ariz., 1981, Dolly Fiterman Gallery, Mpls., 1980, Hansen Galleries, N.Y.C., 1977, 78, Reflections Gallery, St. Louis, 1973, Contemporary Gallery, Dallas, 1973, Moody Gallery, Austin, Tex., 1972, Lee County Alliance of Arts, Ft. Myers, Fla., 1992, Oak Ridge Art Mus., Tenn., 1994; exhibited in group shows: Sotheby Parke-Bernet, N.Y.C., 1983, First Women's Bank, N.Y.C., 1982, Barbara Walter Gallery, 1982, Avery Fisher Gallery, N.Y.C., 1981, Mus. Contemporary Art, Sao Paulo, Brazil, 1980, Robinson Galleries, Houston, 1980, Dallas City Hall, 1978; permanent collections include New Brit. (Conn.) Mus. American Art; works in various Nat. and Internat. collections. Recipient 1st Nat. Award Art, Strathmore Papers Scholastic Mag., 1970; 1st Portrait award, Bixby award with St. Louis Artisans Guild, 1971. Mem. Artists Equity (dir. 1976-78), St. Louis Artists Guild (dir. 1970-71). Democrat. Roman Catholic. Studio: 376 Broadway Apt 18G New York NY 10013-3942 Office Phone: 212-227-5700.

JUDGE, MIKE, animator; b. Guayaquil, Ecuador, Oct. 17, 1962; m. Francesca Morocco, 1989; 2 children. BA in Phys. Sci., U. Calif., San Diego, 1985. Writer, dir., prodr. (TV series) Beavis and Butt-head, 1993-1997, King of the Hill, 1997—, Monsignor Martinez, 2000; (films) Beavis and Butt-head Do America, 1996, Office Space, 1999; actor (films) Inbred Jed (voice), 1991, King of the Hill (voice), 1997—, Mene Tekel (voice), 1997, Spy Kids, 2001, Spy Kids 2:Island of Lost Dreams, 2002, Serving Sara, 2002, Spy Kids 3-D:Game Over, 2003. Office: King of the Hill Watt Plaza 1875 Century Park E Fl 4 Los Angeles CA 90067-2501

JUDGE, NANCY ELIZABETH, obstetrician, gynecologist; b. Holyoke, Mass., May 21, 1951; d. Martin P. and Barbara Judge; m. David B. Wood, Oct. 30, 1982; children: David, William, Elizabeth, Meredith. AB, Smith Coll., 1973; MD, U. Mass., 1977. Intern Case Western Res. U./MetroHealth Med. Ctr., Cleve., 1977-78, resident, 1978-81; staff physician MetroHealth Med. Ctr. Case Western Res. U. Hosps., Cleve., 1981-90; dir. reproductive imaging ctr. Case Western Res. U. Hosps., 1990—, maternal-fetal medicine cons., 1990—. Asst. prof. reproductive biology Case Western Res. U., 1981—. Contbr. articles to profl. jours. Active Cleve. Art Mus., Playhouse Sq. Assn., Cleve. Garden Ctr. Fellow ACOG; mem. Cleve. Ob.-Gyn. Soc. (pres.).

JUDGE, RAJINDER, psychiatrist; b. Jullundur, India, Mar. 22, 1961; arrived in Eng., 1964, arrived in U.S., 1996; d. Sadhu and Parkash Judge. MD, U. Birmingham, Eng., 1984. Intern Wordsley Hosp. and Russells Hall Hosp., Dudley, England, 1984—85; sr. house officer psychiatry Midland Nerve Hosp., Birmingham, 1985—86; physician Riyadh, Saudi Arabia, 1986—87; psychiatry registrar North Worcester, England, 1987—89; assoc. med. dir. Smith Kline Beecham, England, 1991—96; dir., global physician for Prozac, Lilly & Co., Indpls., 1997—2000; psychiatrist Nat. Health Svc., 1991—94; registrar, sr. registrar London Charing Cross Rotation, 1989—91; v.p. neuroscience Novartis, East Hanover, NJ, 2000—03; pharm. cons., 2003—. Forensic med. examiner London Met. Police Force, 1991—. Contbr. articles to profl. jours. Mem.: ENCP, Royal Coll. Psychiatrists. Achievements include research in depression and anxiety disorders. World leader in research studies of Prozac. Responsible for establishing diagnosis of PMDD with FDA. Avocations: automobiles, movies, travel.

JUDICE, MARC WAYNE, lawyer; b. Lafayette, La., Oct. 22, 1946; s. Marc and Gladys B. Judice; m. Michelle Regan; 1 child, Renee. BS, U. La., 1969; MBA, U. Utah, 1974; JD, La. State U., 1977. Bar: La. 1977, bd. cert. civil trial law, civil trial advocacy: Nat. Bd. Trial Advocacy 2000. Ptnr. Voorhies & Labbe, Lafayette, 1977-85, Juneau, Judice, Hill & Adley, Lafayette, 1985-93, Judice & Adley, Lafayette, 1993—. Bd. dirs. Univ. Med. Ctr., Lafayette, 1991, chmn.; bd. dirs. Home Savs. Bank, Lafayette, 1996—, Women's & Childrens Hosp., Lafayette, 1992-94; bd. trustees Med. Ctr. Southwest La., 1998-2001, chmn. bd. dirs., 1999-2005. Republican. Office: Judice & Adley 926 Coolidge Blvd Lafayette LA 70503-2434 Office Phone: 337-235-2405. Business E-Mail: mwj@judice-adley.com.

JUDSON, ARNOLD SIDNEY, management consultant; b. Brockton, Mass., Mar. 29, 1927; s. Moses Joel and Fanny (Becker) J.; m. June Brenner, June 19, 1949; children: Pamela F., Jill E. BS in Chem. Engring., MIT, 1947, MS in Orgnl. Behavior, 1948. Prodn. foreman U.S. Rubber Co., Providence, 1948-50; pers. mgr., mfg. mgr., then dir. tng. and devel. Polaroid Corp., Cambridge, Mass., 1950-62; mgmt. cons. The Emerson Cons., Ltd., London, 1962-66; sr. mgmt. cons. Arthur D.Little, Inc., Cambridge, 1966-76; dir., mgmt. cons. The Berwick Group, Inc., Boston, 1976-81; pres., CEO Gray-Judson-Howard, Inc., Cambridge, 1981-90, chmn., 1990-94; pres. The Judson Co., Inc., 1994-2001. Cons. Exec. Svc. Corps. Author: A Manager's Guide to Making Changes, 1966, Making Strategy Happen, 1990, 2nd edit., 1996, Changing Behavior in Organizations, 1991; contbr. articles to bus. publs.; composer orchestral and chamber music. Chmn. bd. dirs. Greater Boston Rehab. Svcs., Cambridge, 1984-2001. With USN, 1945-46. Mem.: Univ. Club Boston. Office: The Judson Co Inc 364 Del Pond Dr Canton MA 02021 Business E-Mail: ajudson@gis.net.

JUDSON, C(HARLES) JAMES (JIM JUDSON), lawyer; b. Oregon City, Oreg., Oct. 24, 1944; s. Charles James and Barbara (Busch) Judson; m. Diana L. Gerlach, Sept. 11, 1965; children: Kevin, Nicole. BA cum laude, Stanford U., 1966, LLB with honors, 1969. Bar: Wash. 1969, U.S. Tax Ct. 1970, DC 1981. Ptnr. Davis Wright Tremaine, Seattle, 1969—. Bd. dirs. Port Blakely Tree Farms, Garrett and Ring, Joshua Green Corp., China Unicom, Lumera, Sonata Capital, Airbiquity; spkr. in field. Author: State Taxation of Financial Intitutions, 1981; contbr. articles to profl. jours. Trustee Wash. State Internat. Trade Fair, Seattle, 1981—86; mem. Assn. Wash. Bus. Tax Com., 1978—, Seattle Tax Group, 1983—; chmn. lawyers divsn. United Way, Seattle, 1986, 1987, chmn. commerce and industry divsn., 1989—91; chmn. Bus. Tax Coalition, Seattle, 1987; bd. dirs. Pacific N.W. Ballet, Pacific Sci. Ctr., Olympic Pk. Inst., 1988—, Yosemite Nat. Insts., 1993—; advisor Wash. State Dept. Revenue; tax advisor Wash. State House Reps. Dem. Caucus. Fellow: Am. Coll. Tax Counsel; mem.: ABA (chmn. com. fin. orgns. tax sect. 1978—82, chmn. excise tax com. 1983—90, interorganization coordination com. 1985—, chmn. environ. tax com. 1991—), Seattle-King County Bar Assn. (mem. tax sect. 1973—86), Wash. State Bar Assn. (chmn. tax sect. 1984—86, chmn. western region IRS/bar liaison com. 1987—88, mem. rules com. 1991—), Seattle C. of C. (mem. tax. com. 1982—), Broadmoor Golf Club (Seattle), Wash. Athletic Club (Seattle). Avocations: skiing, golf, basketball, woodworking, hiking. Office: Davis Wright Tremaine 2600 Century Sq 1501 4th Ave Seattle WA 98101-1688 Office Phone: 206-628-7686. Business E-Mail: jimjudson@dwt.com.

JUDSON, HORACE AUGUSTUS, academic administrator, chemistry educator; b. Miami, Fla., Aug. 7, 1941; s. Charles Olidge Judson and Louella Edmond; m. Beatrice Gail Shorter, Apr. 13, 1974; children: Tamara Reneé, Sonya Anita, Sojourner Maria, Jessica Gail. AB, Lincoln U., 1963, DSc (hon.), 1994; PhD, Cornell U., 1969. Asst. prof. Bethune-Cookman Coll., Daytona, Fla., 1969, Morgan State U., Balt., 1969-72, assoc. prof., 1972-74, assoc. dean, 1973-74, v.p. acad. affairs, prof., 1974-79, chmn. dept. chemistry, 1982—86; dean arts, letters and scis., prof. chemistry Calif. State U. Stanislaus, Turlock, 1986-90, provost, v.p. acad. affairs, 1991—94; pres. SUNY, Plattsburgh, 1994—2003; sr. fellow Am. Assn. State Colls. and Univs., 2003—04; pres. Grambling State U., La., 2004—. Cons. migrant edn. Md. Dept. Edn., 1977-79; evaluator sci. program Dept. Edn., Lincoln U., Pa., 1980-82; curriculum cons. several univs., Md. and Pa., 1982-86. Author: (monograph) Reflections of a Former Migrant, 1978; contbr. articles to profl. jours. Civilian aide to Sec. US Army, Md., 1975-79; mem. segmental adv. bd. Md. Bd. for Higher Edn., Annapolis, 1977-79; mem. sci. coun. Md. Acad. Scis., Balt., 1983-86; bd. dirs. Nat. Orgn. for Migrant Children, 1981-84. Recipient Outstanding Cmty. Svc. award Morgan U. Nat. Alumni Assn., 1983, Alumni Achievement award Lincoln U. Alumni Assn., 1983, Profl. Excellence award Nat. Tech. Assn., 1984, Lectureship award Fulbright Sr. Scholar Program, 1984, Disting. Citizen award, Adirondack Coun. Boy Scouts, 1999. Mem. Am. Chem. Soc., Am. Assn. for Higher Edn., Am. Assn. State Colls. and Univs. (mem. black caucus, 1995-, bd. dirs., 2003), Am. Coun. Edn., Sigma Xi. Republican. Baptist. Avocations: golf, gardening, cooking. Office: Grambling State U PO Box 607 Grambling LA 71245 Office Phone: 318-274-6117. Business E-Mail: judsonha@gram.edu.

JUDSON, HORACE FREELAND, history professor, writer; b. N.Y.C., Apr. 21, 1931; s. Freeland and Harriet Louise (Babcock) J.; m. Ann Schramm, 1953 (div.); children: Grace Louise Judson, Thomas Alexander; m. Penelope Sylvia Jones, Jan. 11, 1969 (dec. May 1993); children: Olivia Phoebe, Nicholas Matthew Freeland. AB, U. Chgo., 1948, postgrad., 1949-52, Columbia U., 1962-63. Reports writer Office of Mil. Gov. U.S., Berlin, 1948-49; various editing, advt., polit. positions N.Y.C., N.J., 1952-62; staff writer, book reviewer Time mag., N.Y.C., 1963-65; arts and scis. corr. Time-Life News Svc., London, 1965-69, Paris, 1969-72, corr. N.Y.C., 1972-73; free-lance writer Cambridge, Eng., 1973-80, Balt., 1981—; Henry R. Luce prof. writing seminars, prof. history sci. Johns Hopkins U., Balt., 1981-90; vis. prof. Stanford (Calif.) U., 1990-94; rsch. prof. History George Washington U., 1994—2003; dir. Ctr. for History of Recent Sci., 1995—2003. Cons. Philbrook Mus. Art, Tulsa, 1983-87, PBS Sta. WHYY-TV, Phila., 1985-88, Henry Luce Found., 1988-89, Harvard U. Press, 1990-95; Fred Friendly Seminars, 1999—, WNET13, N.Y.C., 2000-02; panelist and cons. Office Tech. Assessment, Washington, 1985, 86-87; lectr. U.S. and Europe; keynote spkr. 25th ann. meeting Am. Soc. Cell Biology, Atlanta, Nov. 1985, ann. meeting Pew Scholars, Feb. 1987, symposium on Genetic Experimentation and Evolutionary Change, com. on genetic experimentation Internat. Coun. Sci. Unions, U. Basel, Jan. 1988, DNA Double Helix 40 Yrs. Symposium N.Y. Acad. Scis., 1993, Am. Soc. Human Genetics, 1995; Colin Syme vis. fellow, lectr. Walter and Eliza Hall Inst. Med. Rsch., Royal Melbourne (Australia) Hosp., 1990. Author: The Techniques of Reading, 1954, 3d edit. 1971, Heroin Addiction in Britain, 1974 (Overseas Press Club prize, 1974, Med. Journalists Assn. Great Britain award, 1975), The Eighth Day of Creation, 1979 (transls. in Japanese, German, Spanish, Italian, Chinese, nominated for Nat. Book award 1980), expanded edit. 1996, 25th anniversary edit., 2004, The Search for Solutions, 1980 (transls. in Japanese, German, Dutch), The Great Betrayal:Fraud in Science, 2004; contbg. editor The Sciences, 1982-89; mem. faculty adv. bd. Johns Hopkins U. Press, 1982-84, editl. bd. The Am. Scholar, 1983-86, bd. editors Science Book Program of N.Y. Acad. Scis., 1985-90; editl. cons. various pubs. including Stanford U. Press, 1981, W.H. Freeman, 1988; author articles in The New Yorker, The Sciences, The New Republic, Harper's, The N.Y. Times Book Rev., The Spectator (London), Nature, The Lancet, Jour. AMA, Gene, Science 80, 83, 84, 85, Life, Minerva, New Eng. Jour. Med., Cell, Smithsonian, MIT Tech. Rev.; cons. editor The Eloquent Object, 1987; prodn. cons., scenarist TV films: All My Loving, BBC, 1967, Plague!, PBS, 1987-88, Our Games Our Choices, 1990-92. John Simon Guggenheim Meml. Found. fellow, 1979-80, Ctr. for Advanced Study in Behavioral Scis. (fell.), 1980-81, Prize fellow John D. and Catherine T. MacArthur Found., 1987-92, Wissenschaftskolleg zu Berlin fellow, 1987-88. Fellow AAAS; mem. History of Sci. Soc., Lansdowne Club (London), Century Assn., 14 W. Hamilton St. Club, Nat. Press Club (Washington). Democrat. Avocation: cooking. Home: 807 W University Pky Baltimore MD 21210-2911 Personal E-mail: hfjudson@speakeasy.net.

JUDSON, PHILIP LIVINGSTON, retired lawyer, consultant; b. Palo Alto, Calif., Oct. 25, 1941; s. Philip MacGregor and Elizabeth Stuart (Peck) Judson; m. Dorothy Louisa Lebohner, Sept. 6, 1963 (div. Jan. 1996); children: Wendy Patricia, Philip Lebohner, Michael Lee; m. Danielle DuPuis Kane, May 18, 1996. BA, Stanford U., 1963; JD, U. Calif., Hastings, 1969. Bar: Calif. 1970, Tex. 1999, U.S. Dist. Ct. (no. dist.) Calif. 1970, U.S. Ct. Appeals (9th cir.) 1970, U.S. Dist. Ct. (ctrl. dist.) Calif. 1984, U.S. Dist. Ct. (ea. dist.) Calif. 1985, U.S. Supreme Ct. 1987, DC 1988, U.S. Dist. Ct. (so. dist.) Calif. 1989, Tex. 1999, U.S. Dist. Ct. (no. and we. dists.) Tex. 2000, U.S. Dist. Ct. (ea. dist.) Tex. 2002. Assoc. Pillsbury, Madison & Sutro, San Francisco, 1969-76, ptnr., 1977-99, Skjerven Morrill MacPherson, LLP, San Jose, Calif., 1999, Austin, Tex., 1999—2002; shareholder Winstead Sechrest & Minick, P.C., Austin, 2002—04, ret., 2004; cons. in field. Lectr. Practicing Law Inst., U. Tex. Advanced Intellectual Property Law Inst., Inst. Am. and Internat. Law Intellectual Property Law Program. Founding mem. trustee St. Mark's Sch., San Rafael, 1980—86, pres., 1983—85; trustee Marin Acad., San Rafael, 1985—91. 1st lt. U.S. Army, 1963—65. Mem.: ABA (mem. antitrust and litig. sects.), Austin Bar Assn., Austin Intellectual Property Law Assn., Am. Judicature Soc., San Francisco Bar Assn., Order of Coif, Phi Delta Theta. Republican. Episcopalian. Home: 8004 High Hollow Dr Austin TX 78750-7872 Office Phone: 512-502-0943. Personal E-mail: pjudson@austin.rr.com.

JUELKE, ROBERT CHARLES, lawyer; b. Morristown, NJ, Oct. 27, 1968; s. Charles Vincent and Barbara Susan Juelke; m. Laura Pluschau, Jan. 2, 1993; children: Thomas Robert, Caroline Elizabeth, Eric Charles. BS, U. Va., 1990; JD, William and Mary Sch. Law, 1993. Bar: Pa. 1993, NJ 1993. Assoc. Drinker Biddle & Reath LLP, Phila., 1993—2002, ptnr., 2002—. Home: 385 Dredertown Rd Fort Washington PA 19034 Office: Drinker Biddle & Reath LLP One Logan Sq Philadelphia PA 19103 Office Phone: 215-988-2759. Office Fax: 215-988-2757. E-mail: robert.juelke@dbr.com.

JUERGENS, GEORGE IVAR, history professor; b. Bklyn., Mar. 20, 1932; s. George Odegaard and Magnhild (Julin) J.; m. Bonnie Jeanne Brownlee; children: Steven Erik, Paul Magnus. BA, Columbia Coll., 1953; BA, MA, Oxford U., 1956; PhD, Columbia U., 1965. Instr. Dartmouth Coll., Hanover, N.H., 1962-65; asst. prof. Amherst (Mass.) Coll., 1965-67; assoc. prof. Ind. U., Bloomington, 1967-80, prof. history, 1980—. Cons. Nat. Endowment Humanities, Washington, 1971— Author: Joseph Pulitzer and the New York World, 1966, News From The White House, 1981; assoc. editor: Jour. Am. History, 1968-69. With U.S. Army, 1956-58. Recipient Disting. Teaching award Amoco Found., 1982; Kellett fellow Columbia U., 1954-56; sr. faculty fellow Nat. Endowment Humanities, 1971-72; fellow Rockefeller Found., 1981-82 Mem. AAUP, Orgn. Am. Historians, Phi Beta Kappa Home: 2111 E Meadow Bluff Ct Bloomington IN 47401-6885 Office: Ind U Dept History Bloomington IN 47405 Business E-Mail: juergens@indiana.edu.

JUETTEN, GEORGE H., company executive; B in Acctg., Marquette U. Audit ptnr. Price Waterhouse, 1969—94; v.p., contr. Dresser Industries, Inc., Dallas, 1993—96, CFO, sr. v.p., treas., 1995—2001; exec. v.p., CFO Washington Group Internat., Boise, Idaho, 2001—. Office: Washington Group Internat PO Box 73 Boise ID 83729

JUGENHEIMER, DONALD WAYNE, advertising executive, communications educator, academic administrator; b. Manhattan, Kans., Sept. 22, 1943; s. Robert William and Mabel Clara (Hobert) J.; m. Bonnie Jeanne Scamehorn, Aug. 30, 1970 (dec. 1983); 1 child, Beth Carrie; m. Kaleen B. Brown, July 25, 1987. BS in Advt., U. Ill.-Urbana, 1965, MS in Advt., 1968, PhD in Communications, 1972. Advt. copywriter Fillman & Assocs, Champaign, Ill., 1963-64, 66; media buyer Leo Burnett Co., Chgo., 1965-66; asst., assoc. prof. U. Kans., Lawrence, 1971-80, prof. journalism, dir. grad. studies and rsch., 1980-85; Manship prof. journalism La. State U., Baton Rouge, 1985-87; prof., chmn. dept. communications and speech Fairleigh Dickinson U., Teaneck, N.J., 1987-89, 92-95, dean coll. liberal arts, 1989-92; chair dept. English, lang. and philosphy, 1995; prof. Sch. Journalism So. Ill. U., Carbondale, 1995—2005; prof. Coll. Mass Comm. Tex. Tech U., 2005—. Dir. Sch. Journalism So. Ill. U., Carbondale, 1995-2002; adj. faculty Turku (Finland) Sch. Econs., 1999—; adv. cons. U.S. Army, Fort Sheridan, Ill., Pentagon, Washington, 1981-90, Am. Airlines, 1989-91, IBM Corp., 1989—, U.S. Dept. Def.; cons. editor Grid Publ., Columbus, Ohio, 1974-84; grad. and rsch. dir. U. Kans., 1978-84, adv. chmn., 1974-78; adj. prof. Turku (Finland) Sch. Econs. and Bus. Adminstrn., 1998—. Author: Advertising Media Sourcebook and Workbook, 1975, 3d edit., 1989, 4th edit. 1996, Strategic Advertising Decisions, 1976, Basic Advertising, 1979, 2d edit., 1991, Advertising Media, 1980, Problems and Practices in Advertising Research, 1982, Advertising Media: Strategy and Tactics, 1992, Advertising Media Planning: A Brand Management Approach, 2004, Advertising Media Workbook and Sourcebook, 2005; bd. editors Jour. Advt., 1985-89, Jour. Interactive Advt., 2000—, Jour. Current Issues and Rsch. in Advt., 1990—. Subscription mgr. Jour. of Advt., 1971-74, bus. mgr., 1974-79; chmn. Univ. divsn. United Fund, Lawrence, 1971-72; pres. Sch.-Cmty. Rels. Coun., Lawrence, 1974-75. Recipient Hope Tchg. award U. Kans, 1977, 78, Kellogg Nat. fellow W.K. Kellogg Found., 1984-88; named Outstanding Young Men in Am. Nat. Jaycees, 1978. Mem. AAUP, Am. Acad. Advt. (pres. 1984-86, exec. sec. 2005—), Assn. For Edn. in Journalism (head advt. divsn. 1977-78), Kappa Tau Alpha, Alpha Delta Sigma. Presbyterian. Avocations: skiing, sailing, writing, travel, reading. Office: Coll Mass Comm Tex Tech Univ Box 43082 Lubbock TX 79409-3082 Home: 4015 69t St Lubbock TX 79413 Business E-Mail: donj@siu.edu.

JUHANI, ERMA, lawyer, former stock exchange executive; b. Tampere, Finland, Nov. 29, 1946; LLM, U. Helsinki, Finland, 1969, Lic. Laws, 1977. Asst. Heikki Haapaniemi Law Office, 1969; lawyer legal affairs dept. Enso-Gutzeit Oy, 1972; legal ops. mgr. Union Bank of Finland, Ltd., 1979, asst. gen. mgr. sect. for investment banking and legal ops., 1981, branch mgr. Helsinki-Etelãsatama branch, 1982; mng. dir. Unitas Ltd., 1983, Indsl. Bank Finland, Ltd., 1988; pres., CEO The Helsinki Stock Exch., 1989-97; CEO HEX Helsinki Exchs., 1997—2000; sr. advisor Borenius & Kemppinen Ltd., Helsinki, Finland, 2002—. Mem. bd. dirs. The Helsinki Stock Exchg., 1986, 88, The Finnish Found. for Share Promotion, 1989-99; chmn., mem. bd. dirs. of several Finnish Co. Office: Borenius & Kemppinen Ltd Yrjönkatu 13A FIN-00120 Helsinki Finland Office Phone: +358(0)9 615333. Business E-Mail: juhani.erma@borenius.com.

JUHL, LAURA L., elementary school educator; b. Rockford, Ill., Dec. 4, 1957; d. Richard and June Jacobson; m. Royce Juhl, Dec. 9, 1980; children: Marcus, Mitchell, Matthew. BS in Child Devel., Rockford Coll., 1997, MAT in Reading, 2002. Std. tchg. cert., Ill. Gifted coord., ESL coord., tchr. learning disabled South Beloit Consolidated Sch. Dist., Ill., 1997-98; tchr. 3d grade Harlem Consol. Sch. Dist. 122, Machesney Park, 1998—. Author: (book) Differentiation for the Gifted and Talented: Addressing Multiple Areas of Intelligence, 1997. Emerson Lathrop scholar Rockford Coll., 1995, 96, Mary Wollner award for Excellence in Diagnosis, Rockford, Coll., 2001. Mem. Internat. Reading Assn., Nat. Coun. Tchrs. of Math., Psi Chi (lifetime charter mem.), Pi Lambda Theta. Office: Olson Park Elem Sch 1414 Minahan Dr Machesney Park IL 61115 E-mail: ljuhl@harlem122.org.

JULANDER, PAULA FOIL, foundation administrator; b. Charlotte, N.C., Jan. 21, 1939; d. Paul Baxter and Esther Irene (Earnhardt) Foil; m. Roydon Odell Julander, Dec. 21, 1985; 1 child, Julie McMahan Shipman. Diploma, Presbyn. Sch. Nursing, Charlotte, N.C., 1960; BS magna cum laude, U. Utah, 1984; MS in Nursing Adminstrn., Brigham Young U., 1990. RN, Utah. Nurse various positions, Fla. and S.C., 1960-66; co-founder Am. Laser Corp., 1970-79; tchg. asst. U. Utah, Salt Lake City; exec. dir. Utah Nurses Assn., 1987—89; mem. Utah Ho. of Reps., Salt Lake City, 1989-92; Dem. nominee lt. gov. State of Utah, 1992; minority whip Utah State Senate, Dist. 1, Salt Lake City, 1998—2000; health care/polit. cons. Salt Lake City, 1992—98. Mem. adj. faculty Brigham Young U. Coll. Nursing, 1987—95; bd. dirs. Block Fin. Svcs.; mem. Utah state exec. bd U.S. West Comm., 1993—96; bd. regents Calif. Luth. U., 1994—97; 2003 trustee KUED TV, 2000—03; trustee Intermountain Health Care Hosps., 2000—. Co-author (cookbook): Utah State Fare, 1995. Pres. Utah Nurses Found., 1986—88; mem. Nat. Conf. of State Legis. Com. on Families and Children, 1999—2001, The Coun. of State Govt. Com. on Health and Aging, 1999—2001, Women's Polit.Caucus, Statewide Abortion Task Force, 1990; bd. dirs. Cmty. Nursing Svc. Home Health Plus, 1992—94; mem. Planned Parenthood Assn. Utah, 1994—2991, Utahns for Choice, 1995—2002; trustee Westminster Coll., 1994—2002, HCA-St. Mark's Hosp., 1994—95; elected sen. State of Utah, 1998—. Recipient Utah pub. health hero award, 2000, Legislator of Yr. awrd, YWCA, 2001, Jacquelyn Erbin MD award, Planned Parenthood Action Coun., 2002, Disting. Alumni award, Coll. Nursing, U. Utah, 2002, Legislator of Yr. award, Nat. Assn. Social Workers, 2002, Women's Achievement award, Utah Commn. for Women and Families, 2005, Lucy Beth Rampton award, Utah Women's Dem. Club, 2005; honored by, Govt. Commn. on Women and Families, 2005. Mem.: ANA, Women in Govt. (chair 2004), Nat Orgn. Women Legislators, Utah Nurses Assn. (legis. rep. 1987—88, Lifetime Achievement award), Phi Kappa Phi (Susan Young Gates award 1991), Sigma Theta Tau. Home: 476 B St Salt Lake City UT 84103-2544 Office Phone: 801-887-2337. Personal E-mail: paula@ulcu.com.

JULIAN, MICHAEL, grocery company executive; b. 1950; With Human Sys. Inc., Florham Pk., NJ, 1975-85, Richfood Inc., Mechanicsville, Va., 1985-87; COO, exec. v.p. Farm Fresh Inc., 1987—, chmn., CEO, 1988—; pres., CEO Jitney Jungle, Jackson, Miss., 1997-1999. Office: Jitney Jungle 1855 Lakeland Dr Ste D20 Jackson MS 39216-4947

JULIANA, JAMES NICHOLAS, manufacturing executive; b. Camden, N.J., Apr. 1, 1922; s. Nicholas and Rosa (de Noti) J.; m. Elizabeth D. Sutton, Nov. 8, 1947; children— James S., Patrick C., Mary E., Thomas E., David J., Richard S., Robert Francis, Ronald Joseph (dec.). BS, Washington Coll., Md., 1944. Spl. agt. FBI, 1947-53; asst. exec. dir., exec. dir., chief counsel to minority Senate Permanent Sub-com. on Investigations, 1953-58; exec. dir. CAB, 1958-61; pres., dir. Internat. Fact Finding Inst., 1961-62; pres. James N. Juliana Assocs., Washington, 1962-81, 84—; sec., dir. Alaska N.Am. Corp., Washington, 1970-77; v.p. fed. affairs Braniff Internat., 1977-81; prin. dep. asst. sec. for manpower, res. affairs and logistics Dept. Def., Washington, 1981-84; dir. Tround Internat., 1984-97; chmn., CEO, pres., 1993-97; dir. IX Sys., 1985-98. Mem. Pres.'s Com. on Mental Retardation, 1971-77; exec. v.p. Armed Forces Mktg. Council, Washington, 1974-81; bd. visitors, bd. govs. Washington Coll., Chestertown, Md., 1978-84. Served with USNR, 1944-46. Mem. Soc. Former Spl. Agts. of FBI, Coalition of Mil. Distbrs. (exec. dir. 1990—), Kappa Alpha, Omicron Delta Kappa. Home: 66 W 17th St Ocean City NJ 08226-2924 Office Phone: 609-399-9585.

JULIANO, JOHN LOUIS, lawyer; b. Oct. 21, 1944; s. John Carmine and Jeannette Helen (Ciotti) J.; m. Maryjane Theresa Groccia, July 4, 1966 (dec.); children: Jennifer, Jonathan; m. Edith Helen Martuscello, Aug. 21, 2004. BBA, St. John's U., 1966; JD, Bklyn. Law Sch., 1969. Bar: N.Y. 1970, U.S. Dist. Ct. (ea. and so. dists.) N.Y., U.S. Ct. Appeals (2d cir.), U.S. Supreme Ct. Ptnr. Juliano, Karlson, Weisberg, 1970-72; pvt. practice East Northport, N.Y., 1972—. Pres., dir. Hillside United Van Lines, Inc.; chair N.Y. State 10th Jud. Grievance Com., 2004—; lectr. Suffolk Acad. Law. Mem. ATLA, N.Y. State Bar Assn., Suffolk County Bar Assn. (pres. 1996-97, v.p. 1995-96, treas. 1994-95, sec. 1993-94, bd. dirs. 1998-2001), N.Y. State Trial Lawyers Assn., Criminal Bar Assn., Columbian Lawyers Assn. (sec. 1972, treas. 1973, pres. 1974-75), Am. Inns of Ct. Address: 39 Doyle Ct East Northport NY 11731-6404 Office Phone: 631-499-9300. Business E-Mail: jlj@johnljulianopc.com.

JULIBER, LOIS D., manufacturing executive; b. 1949; m. John Adams. BA, Wellesley Coll.; MBA, Harvard U. Former v.p. Gen. Foods Corp.; from gen. mgr. to pres. Far East/Can. divsn. Colgate-Palmolive Co., N.Y.C., 1988-92, chief tech. officer, 1992-94, pres. Colgate—N.Am. divsn., 1994—97, exec. v.p., chief ops. developed markets, 1997—2000, COO internat. ops., 2000—02, COO L. Am. and growth functions, 2002—, vice chmn., 2004—. Bd. dirs. DuPont Corp., 1995- Bd. trustees Brookdale Found., Wellesley Coll., Girls Inc. Recipient Luminary Award, Corp. Innovator Category, Com. 200, 2002. Mem. Harvard Bus. Sch. Club N.Y. (bd. dirs.) Avocations: tennis, gardening, cooking. Office: Colgate Palmolive Co 300 Park Ave Fl 8 New York NY 10022-7499

JULICH, NANCY C., secondary school educator; d. Robert E. and Fay Presley Conner; m. Marvin Milam Julich, June 4, 1966; children: Marvin Milam Julich, Jr., Rebecca Fay Patterson. BA in English, Music, History, U. Ala., 1966; BS in English, Music, History, Athens (Ala.) State U., 1982; MA in Secondary Edn., U. North Ala., 1989; EdS in Secondary Edn., U. Ala., 2003. Tchr. Horizen H.S., Decatur. Bd. dirs. Morgan County Adv. Bd. For At Risk Youth, Decatur, Ala.; adj. instr. English Calhoun C.C., 1989—. Child abuse prevention specialist PACT, 1984—93; bd. dirs. Decatur (Ala.) Civic Chorus, 1968—80; pres. bd. HANDS, 1992—2000. Mem.: NEA (assoc.), Decatur Ednl. Assn., Tchrs. English Jr. Coll. (assoc.), Nat. Coll. Tchrs. English (assoc.), Ala. Edn. Assn. (assoc.), Sigma Tau Delta (assoc.), Ala. Million Dollar Round Table, Jr. League. Office: Horizon High School 809 Church Street NE Decatur AL 35601 Office Phone: 256-552-3054.

JULIEN, CATHERINE, history professor; b. Palo Alto, Calif., May 19, 1950; d. Robert K. and Jean (Blaine) Julien; 1 child, Clara E.P. BA in Anthropology, U. Calif., Berkeley, 1971, MA in Anthropology, 1975, PhD in Philosophy, 1978. Dir. mus. programs Courthouse Mus., Merced, Calif.; lectr. and internat. study tour leader Smithsonian's Am. Mus. Natural History and Calif. Alumni Assn.; instr. Calif. State U., U. Bonn (Germany), U. Calif., Berkeley; assoc. prof. history We. Mich. U., Kalamazoo, 1996—. Author: Reading Inca History (Erminie Wheeler-Voegelin prize, 2000, Katherine Singer Kovacs prize MLA). Fellow, John Simon Guggenheim Meml. Found., 2003. Mem.: Phi Beta Kappa. Office: We Mich U Office Univ Rels 1903 W Michigan Ave Kalamazoo MI 49008-5433

JULIEN, CLAUDE, professional athletics coach; Profl. hockey player Am. Hockey League, 1983—92; head coach Hull Olympiques, 1996—2000, Hamilton Bulldogs, 2000—03, Montreal Canadians, 2003—. Mailing: c/o The Montreal Canadians 1275 St Antoine St West Montreal PQ Canada H3C 5L2

JULIEN, GAIL LESLIE, model, public relations professional; b. Long Island, New York, Apr. 13, 1940; d. David William Syme and Virginia Martha (Burth) Miller; m. Michael Louis Woodman, Sept. 12, 1958 (div.); children: Jho'meyr Renei and Sabrina Michelle; m. Francis Dana Julien, Dec. 24, 1977. Diploma in modeling, Coronet of Calif., 1960; grad., Am. Beauty Finishing Sch., 1961. Playboy bunny Playboy Club, Kansas City, Mo., 1970—72; Gremlin girl AMC, Kansas City, Mo., 1972; Dodge girl Dodge, Kansas City, Mo., 1972—73; owner, pres. Gail Woodman Enterprises Inc., Overland Park, Kans., 1972—76; sales rep. Kansas City Brit. Motors, Lenexa, Kans., 1976—78; dir. pub. rels., mktg. Downtown Air Ctr., Kansas City, Mo., 1978—80; dir. pub. rels., media rels. Bretney Corp., Kansas City, Mo., 1980—82; v.p. Nuwalters Co., Overland Park, Kans., 1983—84; regional mgr. aviation Multi Svc. Corp., Overland Park, Kans., 1984—2004. Rep. Nat. Bus. Aircraft Assn., 1984—2004, Can. Bus. Aircraft Assn., 1984-2004, Nat. Aircraft Transp. Assn., 1984—, Abbotsford Internat. Airshow, 1991, 93, 95, 98, Schedulars and Dispatchers Conv., 1994-2004, Internat. Operators Conf., 1998, Women in Aviation, 1998-2004, Helicopter Assn. Internat., 1994-2003; internat. v.p. Women in Corp. Aviation, 2003-04, Schedulers and Dispatchers Support Com., 1999-2000. Author: Physician's Nutritional Guide, 1984, numerous poems, self improvement and modeling course; former editor WCA Newsletter. Vol. Live On Stage '88 (AIDS), Santa Ana, Calif., 1988, St. Joseph Hosp., Kansas City, 1986-88; v.p. Young Dems., Midland, Mich., 1960; active Northshore Animal League, Christian Children's Fund, L.A. Mission, former bd. of dir., City of Hope, L.A., 1991; bd. dir., fundraiser Make A Wish of Tri Counties. Recipient Outstanding Sales Achievement award Brit. Leyland, 1976-77. Mem. Am. Bus. Womens Assn. Avocations: art, writing, swimming, acting. Home: 28129 Peacock Ridge Dr Apt 312 Palos Verdes Peninsula CA 90275-7121 Office Phone: 310-994-3094.

JULIEN, JANELLE E.D., editor, writer; b. St. Augustine, Trinidad Tobago, Dec. 20, 1978; d. Errol and Daphne Julien. BA Magna Cum Laude, Drexel U., Phila., Pa., 2003. Editl. asst. Congl. Quar. Press, Washington, 2000—00, mktg. adminstrv. asst., 2001—01, customer svc. adminstrv. coord., 2002—02; jr. editl., tech. analyst Congl. Quar. Press, Inc., 2003—05; mktg. assoc. United Press Internat., 2005—. Content developer Anamorphic Media, Washington, 2003—; conf. planning, pr com. Wash. Ind. Writers, Washington, 2003—; editl. asst. Congl. Quar. Press, Washington, 2002. Author: (novels) Lure of the Prophecy; contbr. articles to profl. jours., to newspapers and mags. Recipient Sr. First Honors, Drexel U., 2002-2003; scholar Coll. Bowl Award, 2000. Mem.: Wash. Ind. Writers (assoc.; com. mem. 2003), Phi Eta Sigma (life), Golden Key (life; project dir. 2002—03), Omicron Delta Kappa (life; pres. 2002—03). Office: United Press International 1510 H St NW Washington DC 20005 Home: 12905 Flack St Silver Spring MD 20906 Office Phone: 202-898-8005. Personal E-mail: janelle.julien@gmail.com. Business E-Mail: jjulien@upi.com.

JULIEN, ROBERT MICHAEL, anesthesiologist, writer; b. Port Townsend, Wash., Mar. 24, 1942; s. Frank Felton and Mary Grace (Powers) J.; m. Judith Dianne DeChenne, Feb. 26, 1963; children: Robert Michael, Scott M. BS in Pharmacy, U. Wash., 1965, MS in Pharmacology, 1968, PhD, 1970; MD, U. Calif.-Irvine, 1977. Intern Good Samaritan Hosp., Portland, Oreg., 1977-78; resident Oreg. Health Scis. U., 1978-80; asst. prof. pharmacology U. Calif.-Irvine, 1970-74, asst. clin. prof., 1974-77; assoc. prof. anesthesiology and pharmacology U. Oreg., Portland, 1980-83; staff anesthesiologist St. Vincent Hosp., Portland, 1983—. Author: Primer of Drug Action, 1975, 10th edit., 2004, Understanding Anesthesiology, 1984, Drugs and the Body, 1987. Recipient Svc. award Am. Epilepsy Soc., 1975. Mem. Am. Soc. Anesthesiologists, Am. Assn. Pharmacology and Exptl. Therapeutics, Soc. Neurosci., Oreg. Med. Assn., Western Pharmacology Soc. Roman Catholic. Home: 23 Becket Lake Oswego OR 97035 Office: St Vincent Hosp Dept Anesthesia 9205 SW Barnes Rd Portland OR 97225-6603 Office Phone: 503-216-2151. Personal E-mail: drsjulien@comcast.net.

JULIEN, THOMAS THEODORE, religious denomination administrator; b. Arcanum, Ohio, June 27, 1931; s. Russel Ray and Clara (Cassel) J.; m. Doris Mardella Briner, Aug. 21, 1953; children: Becky Jean, Terry Lee, Jacqueline Sue. BA, Bob Jones U., 1953; MDiv, Grace Theol. Sem., Winona Lake, Ind., 1957, DD (hon.), 1996; cert. French lang., U. Grenoble, France, 1960. Ordained to ministry Fellowship of Grace Brethren Chs., 1956. Pastor Grace Brethren Ch., Ft. Wayne, Ind., 1955-58; missionary Grace Brethren Fgn. Missions, Grenoble, 1959-64, field supt. Macon, France, 1964-78, dir. for Europe, 1964-86; exec. dir. Grace Brethren Internat. Missions, Winona Lake, 1986-2000. Author: Handbook for Young Christians, 1959, Inherited Wealth, 1976, Spiritual Greatness, 1979, Seize the Moment, 2000. Decorated chevalier de Republique (Ctrl. African Republic). Home: 545 S Circle Dr Warsaw IN 46580 Office: Grace Brethren Internat Missions PO Box 588 Winona Lake IN 46590-0588 Office Phone: 574-268-1888. E-mail: tjulien@gbim.org.

JULIUS, DAVID, biochemist; BS in life scis., MIT, 1977; PhD in biochemistry, U. Calif., Berkeley, 1984; postdoctoral rsch., Inst. Cancer Rsch., Columbia U., 1984—89. Asst. prof. U. Calif., San Francisco, 1989—96, assoc. prof., 1996—99, prof. dept. cellular and molecular pharmacology, 1999—. Mem. sci. adv. bd. Senomyx, Inc., Hydra Biosciences, Inc. Recipient First-Perl Neuroscience prize, UNC, Scholar award, McKnight Neuroscience Found., 1990, Investigator award, 1997, Syntex prize, 1997. Mem.: Nat. Acad. Scis. Office: UCSF Genentech Hall 600 16th St Box 2140 San Francisco CA 94143-2140 Business E-Mail: julius@cmp.ucsf.edu.

JULMY, CAMILLE P., real estate company executive; Degree in Bus. Adminstrn., Coll. St. Michel, Fribourg, Switzerland; Degree in Econs., U. Fribourg. With Fidinam, Lugano, Switzerland, 1973—74, sr. analyst Toronto, Canada, 1974—77, v.p. Chgo., 1977—78; vice chmn., co-founder US Equities REalty, Chgo., 1978—. Mem. exec. bd. UNICEF; bd. dirs. Roosevelt U., Pomerleau Constrn. Co., Montreal, Canada. Mem.: Swiss-Am. C. of C., Ctrl. Mich. Ave. Assn. (sec., mem. exec. bd.), Greater North Mich. Ave. Assn. (sec., mem. exec. bd.), Execs. Club Chgo. Office: US Equities Realty Ste 400 20 N Michigan Ave Chicago IL 60602

JUMA, CALESTOUS, international development educator; b. Busia, Kenya, June 9, 1953; s. John Juma Kwada and Clementina Okhubedo Juma; m. Alison Thornycroft Field, Sept. 9, 1987; 1 child, Eric Kwada Field. MSc, U. Sussex, Falmer, Brighton, U.K., 1983, DPhil, 1986. Sch. tchr., Mombasa, 1974-78; rschr., editor Environment Liaison Ctr., Nairobi, 1979-82; exec. dir., founder African Ctr. for Tech. Studies, Nairobi, 1988-95; exec. sec. UN Conv. on Biol. Diversity, Geneva and Montreal, 1995-98; rsch. fellow Kennedy Sch. Govt. Harvard U., Cambridge, Mass., 1999-2000, sr. rsch. fellow, program dir. Kennedy Sch. Govt., 2000—01; prof. Kennedy Sch. Govt., 2002—; chancellor U. Guyana, 2002—. Author: Long Run Economics, 1987, The Gene Hunters, 1989, The Adaptive Economy, 1993, Open the Social Sciences, 1996. Recipient Pew Scholars award Pew Charitable Trusts, 1991, UN Global 500 Roll of Honor, UN Environ. Program, 1993, Henry Shaw medal Mo. Bot. Garden, 2001. Fellow Kenyan Nat. Acad. Scis., N.Y. Acad. Scis., World Acad. Art and Sci.; mem. AAAS, NAS (bd. agr. and natural resources), Internat. Soc. for Study of Time. Avocations: hiking, bicycling. Home: 363 Concord Ave Cambridge MA 02138 Office: Kennedy Sch of Govt 79 JFK St Cambridge MA 02138 E-mail: calestous_juma@harvard.edu.

JUMONVILLE, FELIX JOSEPH, JR., physical education educator, real estate company officer; b. Crowley, La., Nov. 20, 1920; s. Felix Joseph and Mabel (Rogers) J.; m. Mary Louise Hoke, Jan. 11, 1952; children: Carol, Susan. BS, La. State U., 1942; MS, U. So. Calif., 1948, EdD, 1952. Assoc. prof. phys. edn. L.A. State Coll., 1948-60; prof. phys. edn. Calif. State U., Northridge, 1960-87, emeritus prof. phys. edn., 1987—. Owner Felix Jumonville Realty, Northridge, 1974-82, Big Valley Realty, Inc., 1982-83, Century 21 Lamb Realtors, 1983-86, Cardinal Realtors, 1986-87; varsity track and cross-country head coach LA State Coll., 1952-60, Calif. State U., Northridge, 1960-71. With USCGR, 1942—46. Named to, Baton Rouge H.S. Hall of Fame; recipient U.S. Commendation medal. Mem. Assn. Calif. State Univ. Profs., Pi Tau Pi, Phi Epsilon Kappa, Kappa Sigma. Home: 18427 Vincennes #36 Northridge CA 91325

JUMONVILLE, FLORENCE M., librarian, historian; b. New Orleans; d. Warren P. and Florence E. (Seither) J. BA, U. New Orleans, 1971, MEd, 1976, MA, 1988, PhD, 1997; MS, La. State U., 1972. Libr. Hist. New Orleans Collection, 1972-74, 78-82, head libr., 1982-96; libr. Belle Chasse (La.) State Sch., 1974-78; head La. and spl. collections Earl K. Long Libr., U. New Orleans, 1997—. Adj. instr. libr. sci. La. State U., Baton Rouge, 1994, 96. Author: Bibliography of New Orleans Imprints, 1764-1864, 1989, Louisiana History: An Annotated Bibliography, 2002; editor: LLA Bull., 1990—95; co-editor: A History of the Louisiana Library Association, 1925-2000, 2003; contbr. articles to profl. jours. Adv. bd. Ethel and Herman L. Midlo Ctr. for N.O. Studies, La. Hist. Records; bd. dirs. Theatre Libr. Assn. Recipient Lucy B. Foote award La. Libr. Assn., 1985, Fannie Simon award Spl. Librs. Assn. Mus., Arts and Humanities Divsn., 1997, Essae M. Culver Disting. Svc. award, La. Libr. Assn., 2005. Mem. ALA, Am. Antiquarian Soc., Am. Hist. Assn., Am. Printing History Assn., Assn. Moving Image Archivists, Bibliog. Soc. Am., Soc. for the History of Authorship, Reading and Pub., La. Hist. Assn., La. Libr. Assn. (Essae M. Culver Disting. Svc. award 2005), Beta Phi Mu, Phi Delta Kappa, Kappa Delta Pi. Avocations: needlecrafts, classic movies, reading. Office: Earl K Long Libr Univ New Orleans Lakefront New Orleans LA 70148-0001 Business E-Mail: fjumonvi@uno.edu.

JUMP, CHESTER JACKSON, JR., clergyman, church official; b. Covington, Ky., Mar. 31, 1918; s. Chester Jackson and Inez (Moore) J.; m. Margaret Elizabeth Savidge, Sept. 5, 1942; children— Karen Jane, Richard Alan, Catherine Louise, Robert Jon. AB, Albright Coll., 1938; MA, Columbia U., 1940; BD, Union Theol. Sem. N.Y.C., 1943; postgrad., Ecole Coloniale, Brussels, Belgium, 1950-51; DD, Eastern Bapt. Theol. Sem., 1965. Ordained to ministry Bapt. Ch., 1943. Pastor N.E. Larger Parish, Lyndon Center, Vt., 1943-44; missionary Belgian Congo, Republic of Congo, 1945-62; regional rep. Am. Bapt. Fgn. Mission Socs., Valley Forge, Pa., 1961-64, exec. dir., 1965-83; assoc. gen. sec. Am. Bapt. Chs., 1965-83, dir. world relief, 1983-88, interim gen. sec., 1987-88; mem. gen. bd. Nat. Council Chs., 1965-75, mem. program bd., exec. com. div. overseas ministries, 1965-83, mem. gov. bd., 1965-75, 87-88; mem. exec. com. Bapt. World Alliance, 1965-85, 87-88, v.p., 1980-85; bd. dirs., exec. com. Am. Bapt. Chs., Pa., Del., 1989-97; chmn., budget commn. Commn. on New Ch. Planting and Adminstrv. Svcs., 1989-99. Trustee Eastern Bapt. Theol. Sem.; mem. Ch. World Service Commn., 1983-88, fin. com., 1983-88; mem. Bapt. World Aid, 1970-85; mem. bd. personnel com. IMPACT. Author: (with wife) Congo Diary, 1950, Coming, Ready or Not, 1959. Mem. Pi Gamma Mu. Home and Office: 240 Applewood Dr Apt 2 Lewisburg PA 17837 E-mail: cjmsjump@ptd.net.

JUMPER, JOHN PHILLIP, retired military officer; b. Paris, Tex., Feb. 4, 1945; s. Jimmy Jumper and Maree Loretta (Jumper) J.; m. Ellen Elizabeth McGhee, Mar. 29, 1969; children: Catherine, Janet, Melissa. BSEE, Va. Mil. Inst., 1966; MBA, Golden Gate U., 1978; postgrad., Air Command and Staff Coll., Maxwell AFB, Ala., 1977-78, Nat. War Coll., Washington, 1981-82. Commd. 2d lt. USAF, 1966, advanced through grades to gen., 1997; instr. pilot 414th Fighter Weapons Squadron, Nellis AFB, Nev., 1974-77; action officer Directorate for Ops. and Tng., Washington, 1978-81; comdr. 430th Tactical Fighter Squadron, Nellis AFB, Nev., 1983; exec. officer to comdr. Hdqrs. Tactical Air Command, Langley AFB, Va., 1983-86; comdr. 33d Tactical Fighter Wing, Eglin AFB, Fla., 1986-87, 1987-88, 57th Fighter Weapons Wing, Nellis AFB, 1988-90; dep. dir. politico-mil. affairs Joint Staff, Washington, 1990-92; sr. mil. asst. for sec. def. Office Sec. Def., Washington, 1992-94; comdr. 9th AF, Shaw AFB, 1994-96; Deputy Chief of Staff, Air and

Space HAF, Washington, 1996-97; commdr. Allied Air Forces Ctrl. Europe, Ramstein AB, Germany, 1997-2000, HQ Air Combat Command, Langley AFB, 2000—01; chief of staff USAF, Washington, 2001—05. Contbr. articles to mil. pub. Decorated Def. DSM with oak leaf cluster, Legion of Merit DSM with oak leaf cluster, DFC with 2 oak leaf clusters, Air medal with 17 oak leaf clusters. Mem. Air Force Assn. Roman Catholic. Avocations: racquet ball, jogging, piano, guitar, golf, sports cars.

JUN, INSOO, nuclear scientist, researcher; b. Inchon, Republic of Korea, Oct. 3, 1963; arrived in U.S., 1983; s. Si-Won and Chan-Bok Jun; m. Seung-Ah Lee. BS, U. Mass., 1986; PhD, UCLA, 1991. Post-doctoal fellow UCLA, LA, 1992—95; scientist Hughes Space and Comm. Co., El Segundo, Calif., 1996—2000; sr. tech. staff Jet Propulsion Lab., Pasadena, Calif., 2001—. Contbr. articles to profl. jours. Mem.: Am. Geophys. Union, Americal Nuc. Soc. Office: Jet Propulsion Laboratory 4800 Oak Grove Drive Pasadena CA 91109

JUN, JONG SUP, public administration educator; b. Sunsan, Korea, July 26, 1936; s. Myung D. and Jeum S. (Pai) J.; m. Soon Y. Jun, Sept. 16, 1964; children: Eugene, Amy. LLB, Yeungnam U., Taegu, Korea, 1960; MA, U. Oreg., 1964; PhD, U. So. Calif., 1969. Prof. Calif. State U., Hayward, 1968—. Vis. prof. Hosei U., Tokyo, 1992-93, Korea U., 2000-2001; coord. Pub. Adminstrn.Theory Network, 1993—; coord. The Pub. Adminstrn. Theory Network Internat. Author: Public Administration: Design and Problem Solving, 1986, Philosophy of Administration, 1994; editor: Rethinking Administrative Theory, 2002; co-editor Globalization and Decentralization, 1996, The Social Construction of Public Administration: Interpretive and Critical Perspectives, 2005; editor: Development in the Asia Pacific, 1994, Jour. Adminstrn. Theory and Praxis, 1993—; chief editor Jour. Adminstrv. Theory and Praxis, 1994-99; editl. mem. Internat. Rev. Adminstrv. Sci., 1991. Recipient Rsch. Grant award Social Rsch.Coun., N.Y., 1979, Outstanding Acad. Achievement award Am. Soc. Pub. Adminstrn., San Francisco, 1982; Fulbright scholar Yonsei U., Korea. Fellow Nat. Acad. Public Adminstrn. Avocation: japanese gardening. Home: 18698 Mount Lassen Ct Castro Valley CA 94552-1955 Office: Calif State U Hayward CA 94552 E-mail: jongjun@csu.eastbay.edu.

JUNDI, BILAL, principal; b. Beirut, Jan. 1, 1964; s. Mohamad Amin Al Jundi and Hanife Al Bahloul; m. Rawaa Merhi, May 20, 1995. BA in edn., BA in Islamic studies, MA in edn., Aldawaa U. Lic.: Ministry of Justice, Québec, Can. (Commr. Oaths) 1998. Prin. Ecole Ali Ibn Abi Talib, St. Laurent, Canada, 1991—; orator Nation Musulmane du Québec, Montréal, Canada, 1998—. Chief exec. Muslim Cmty. of St. Laurent, St. Laurent, Canada, 1995—. Prodr.: (theatre) Shaqaek AL Noman The Coquelicot; contbr. (television documentary) Peace and Religion; participant: (film) Being Oussama, 2001. Recipient Migration Award, Ministry of Migration, 1995. Liberal. Moslem. Avocations: writing, reading, swimming, travel, arts. Office: 1610 Beauharnois W Montreal QC Canada H4N1J5 Personal E-mail: bilaljundi@ecoleali.com.

JUNEWICZ, JAMES J., lawyer; b. Oct. 1, 1950; s. John and Genevieve J.; m. Virginia Bornyas. BS, Georgetown U., 1972; JD, Duquesne U., 1976; LLM, NYU, 1978. Bar: Pa. 1977, D.C. 1978, Ill. 1984. Asst. gen. counsel SEC, Washington, 1982—84; ptnr. Mayer, Brown, Rowe & Maw LLP, Chgo., 1987—. Office: Mayer Brown Rowe & Maw LLP 190 S La Salle St Ste 3900 Chicago IL 60603-3410 Office Phone: 312-782-0600. Business E-Mail: jjunewicz@mayerbrownrowe.com.

JUNG, ANDREA, cosmetics company executive; b. Toronto, Sept. 18, 1958; m. Michael Gould, 1993 (div.); 2 children. BA magna cum laude in English Lit., Princeton U., 1979. With Bloomingdale's; sr. v.p., gen. mdse. mgr. J.W. Robinson; sr. v.p. gen. mdse. I. Magnin, San Francisco, 1987—91; exec. v.p. women's merchandising Neiman Marcus, 1991—92; cons. Avon Products, Inc., NYC, 1993, pres. product mktg. group, 1994—96, pres. global mktg., 1996—97, exec. v.p., pres. global mktg. & new bus., 1997—98, COO, 1998—99, pres., 1998—2001, CEO, 1999—, chmn., 2001—. Chmn. Cosmetic, Toiletry & Fragrance Found., 2001—; bd. dirs. GE Co., 1998—, Avon Products Inc., 1998—, Cosmetic Exec. Women. Sale Corp., Donna Karan Internat., Catalyst; mem. internat. advisory bd. Solomon Smith Barney. Mem. bd. trustees NY Presbyn. Hosp. Named one of the 50 Most Powerful Women in Bus., FORTUNE mag., 1998—, Most Powerful Women, Forbes mag., 2005. Office: Avon Products Inc 1345 Ave Americas New York NY 10105-0302*

JUNG, BETTY CHIN, epidemiologist, research analyst, educator, medical/surgical nurse; b. Bklyn., Nov. 28, 1948; d. Han You and Bo Ngan (Moy) Chin; m. Lee Jung, Oct. 1, 1972; children: Daniel, Stephanie. AA, King's Coll., 1968; BS, Columbia U., 1971; MPH, So. Conn. State U., 1993. RN, Conn., Miss., N.Y.; cert. health edn. specialist. Adminstrv. asst. Columbia U., N.Y.C., 1968-69; practical nurse Babies Hosp., N.Y.C., 1969-70, charge nurse, 1974-76; staff nurse Columbia-Presbyn. Hosp., N.Y.C., 1971-73; sch. nurse Nassau County Sch. System, Long Island, N.Y., 1984-85; grad. asst. So. Conn. State U., New Haven, 1991-92; coop. edn. intern Conn. Dept. Health Svcs., Hartford, 1991-92; intern North Ctrl. Dist. Health Dept., Enfield, Conn., 1992; epidemiologist Conn. Dept. Pub. Health, Hartford, Conn., 1992-98, health program assoc., 1998-2001, cardiovascular epidemiologist, 2003—05, cardiovascular and diabetes epidemiologist, 2005—; staff nurse Quinnipiac Coll. Student Health Svcs., 1998; mem. multicultural adv. coun. Conn. Dept. Children and Families, assoc. rsch. analyst, 2001—03. Instr. Albertus Magnus Coll., 1995—96; health columnist Baldwin Newcomers Club, NY, 1977—78; coord. Dept. Pub. Health and Svcs./Conn. EPI Info. Network, Hartford, 1994—2001; mem. Nat. Lead Info. Ctr. Spkrs. Bur., 1997—98; vol. scientist Sci.-By-Mail, 1997—98; mem. Nat. Safety Coun. Environ. Health Ctr. Spkrs. Referral Bur., 1998—2001; mem. affirmative action employee adv. com. Conn. Dept. Pub. Health, 1998—2001, mem. genetics planning com., 2004—; mem. Permanent Commn. Status of Women Talent Network, 1996—, chair news subcom., editor affirmative action newsletter, 2001; apptd. mem. multicultural adv. coun. Conn. Dept. Children and Families, 2002—03; pilot reviewer CDC Pub. Health Tng. Network, 2002—; assoc. NIH, 2004—; mem. functions workgroup EPI; dir.'s coun. pub. reps. NIH, 2004—; numerous positions So. Conn. State U., 1991—; mem. CDC CVH Inst. planning com. Conn. Dept. Pub. Health, 2005—, lead cardiovasc. epidemiology work group, 2005—; cons. in field; adj. prof., 1998—. Mem. editl. bd.: Data Quality, 1994—98, mem. manuscript rev. bd.: Jour. Clin. Outcomes Mgmt., 1995—, Pub. Health Reports, 1997—98; contbg. editor: Episource, A Guide to Resources in Epidemiology, 1998—99; editor/web pub.: SCSU Pub. Health E-News Bull., 2000—01, Public Health E-news, 2001—, Public Health Jobs Electronic Newsletter, 2000—, book proposal reviewer: Jossey Bass Pubs., 2003—; contbr. articles to profl. jours. Vol. nurse health educator, coord. Chinatown's First Ann. Health Fair, 1971-72; treas. Tenant Assn., Bronx, N.Y., 1976-77; pre-confirmation tchr. Bethlehem Luth. Ch., Baldwin, N.Y., 1981-85. Recipient numerous other grants; grantee, USPHS, 1992—98, Fed. HUD, 1995—98, U.S. Preventive Health and Health Svcs., 1998, CDC Diabetes Prevention and Control Program, 2005—; Merit scholar, Kings Coll., 1968, Columbia U. scholar, 1968—69, Women's Florist Assn. scholar, 1968, Bessie Lee Gambrill scholar, So. Alumni Assn., 1992, block grantee, Maternal Child Health, 1998—2001, Adult Blood Lead Epidemiology and Surveillance Program grantee, CDC/Nat. Inst. Occupl. Safety and Health, 1992—98, cardiovascular health grantee, CDC, 2003—. Fellow: Soc. for Pub. Health Ed.; mem.: APHA (health care reform activist network, peer assistance the model stds. project), Pub. Health Expertise Network of Mentors (program dir. 2002—), Internat. Assn. Webmasters and Designers, Boston Mus. Sci., Nat. Acad. Sci. (mentor career planning ctr. beginning scientists & engrs. 1997—98), Columbia U. Sch. Nursing Alumni Assn. (survey cons. 1994—95), Internat. Assn. IT Trainers (assoc.), So. Conn. State U. Alumni Assn. (founder pub. health chpt. 1994, interim pres, then pres. 1994—98, founder, coord. pub. health alumni mentor program 1994—2002, chair coms. 1994—, numerous other positions 1994—, editor MPH Alumni Record 1995—, founder, dir., coord. pub. health alumni spkrs. bur. 1997—, founder, program dir. pub. health expertise network of mentors 2002—, Alumni Appreciation award 1998), Conn. Pub. Health Assn., Nat. Lead Info. Ctr. Spkrs. Bur., Conn. State and Territorial Epidemiologists (alternate cons. 1996—, co-leader Healthy People 2010 1999—2001, lead cardiovasc. disease 2002—), Am. Statis. Assn. (OSPA media experts list 1997—). Avocations: reading, writing, research, web development and design, bicycling. Home: 25 Driftwood Ln Guilford CT 06437-1929 Office: Conn Dept Pub Health 410 Capitol Ave Hartford CT 06106 Office Phone: 860-509-7711. Personal E-mail: bettycjung@yahoo.com.

JUNG, DONGIL, management educator; m. Sin Young Choi, Dec. 23, 1992; children: Austin, Celeste. PhD, SUNY, Binghamton, 1997. Prof. mgmt. San Diego State U., 1997—. Office: San Diego State U 5500 Campanile Dr San Diego CA 92182 Office Phone: 619-594-0208.

JUNG, DORIS, soprano; b. Centralia, Ill., Jan. 5, 1924; d. John Jay and May (Middleton) Crittenden; m. Felix Popper, Nov. 3, 1951; 1 son, Richard Dorian. Ed., U. Ill., Mannes Coll. Music, Vienna Acad. Performing Arts; student of Julius Cohen, student of Emma Zador, student of Luise Helletsgruber, student of Winifred Cecil. Debut as Vitellia in: Clemenza di Tito, Zurich (Switzerland) Opera, 1955, other appearances with, Hamburg State Opera, Munich State Opera, Vienna State Opera, Royal Opera Copenhagen, Royal Opera Stockholm, Marseille and Strasbourg, France, Naples (Italy) Opera Co., Catania (Italy) Opera Co., N.Y.C. Opera, Met. Opera, also in Mpls., Portland, Oreg., Washington and Aspen, Colo.; soloist: Wagner concert conducted by Leopold Stokowski, 1971; with, Syracuse (N.Y.) Symphony, 1981, voice tchr., N.Y.C., 1970— . Home: 40 W 84th St New York NY 10024-4749 Office Phone: 212-873-3147. *Whether performing as a singer or teaching, attempting to understand the voice is tremendously daunting. As with life itself, the human voice defies understanding with its day to day differences and one's everchanging points of view. The secret of unflagging devotion to this life's work lies in accepting its elusiveness.*

JUNG, KWAN YEE, artist; b. Toisun, Kwang Tung, China, Nov. 25, 1932; came to U.S., 1963; s. Fred Hing and Shun Tong (Lee) J.; m. Yee Wah Yip, Sept. 10, 1962; children: Jeanne, Kathy, Laura. BA, New Asia Coll., Hong Kong, 1961. Comml. artist advt. dept. Hong Kong Soy Bean Products Co., 1961-63; owner Jung's Gallery, La Jolla, Calif., 1976-78; freelance artist, instr., demonstrator San Diego, 1978—. Exhibited in group shows including 174th ann. exhbn. NAD, 1999, Water to Women Margaret Cross Gallery, Old Pasadena, Calif., 1995, May Snow Kim's Art Gallery, Rowland Heights, Calif., 1995, Co-art Internat. Gallery, Vancouver, B.C., Can., 1996, Kruglak Gallery, Mira Costa Coll., Oceanside, Calif., 1997, San Diego Chinese Hist. Mus., 1997, The Earl and Birdie Taylor Libr., San Diego, 1998; author, Chinese Brush Painting Step By Step, 2003. Recipient First Place award San Diego Watercolor Soc., 1973, Best of Show award Sumi-E Soc. Am., 1974, Purchase award Springville Mus. Art, 1974. Mem. Nat. Acad. Design (Merit award 1992, nat. academician), Am. Watercolor Soc., Nat. Watercolor Soc. E-mail: kjung1@san.rr.com.

JUNG, LOVIEANNE, Olympic athlete; b. Fountain Valley, Calif., Jan. 11, 1980; Student, Fresno State U.; grad., U. Arizona, 2003. Mem. USA Women's Softball Team, Athens Olympics, 2004. Achievements include mem. S. Calif. Legacy ASA Championship Team, 1999; invention of mem. USA Women's Softball Gold medal Team, ISF World Championships, 2002; mem. USA Women's Gold medal Softball team, Athens Olympic games, 2004.

JUNG, TIMOTHY TAE KUN, otolaryngologist; b. Seoul, Korea, Dec. 1, 1943; came to U.S., 1969; s. Yoon Yong and Helen Chung-Hyuk (Im) J.; m. Lucy Moon Young, Sept. 10, 1972; children: David, Michael, Karen. BS, Seoul Nat. U., 1966, Loma Linda U., 1971, MD, 1974; PhD, U. Minn., 1980. Diplomate Am. Bd. Otolaryngology. Med. intern Loma Linda U. Med. Ctr., Calif., 1974—75; resident in surgery U. Minn. Med. Sch., Mpls., 1975—76, resident in otolaryngology, 1976—80, asst. prof. otolaryngology, 1980—84, clin. asst. prof., dir. prostaglandin lab., 1984—85; assoc. prof., dir. otolaryngology rsch. Loma Linda U., 1985—90, prof., dir. otolaryngology rsch., 1990—92, clin. prof., dir. otolaryngology rsch., 1992—. Mem. deafness and communications disroders rev. com. Nat. Inst. Deafness and Communications, NIH, 1989-92. Mem. editl. bd. Annals of Otology, Rhinology & Laryngology, 1994-2004, Acta Otolaryngologica, 1999—; contbr. chpts. to books, over 100 articles to profl. jours. Sec. gen. Korean-Am. Otolaryngology Soc., 1990—. Sgt. Korean Army, 1966—69. Recipient Edmund Price Fowler award. Fellow ACS, Triological Soc., Am. Acad. Otolaryngology (honor award 1990), Am. Acad. Surgeons; mem. AMA, Am. Otol. Soc., Am. Neurotol. Soc., Assn. Rsch. in Otolaryngology, Centurions, Collegium Otorhinolaryngogicum Amicetiae Sacrum, Korean-Am. Otolaryngology Soc. (sec. gen. 1990–), Alpha Omega Alpha. Seventh-day Adventist. Avocations: horticulture, photography, hiking, running. Home: 11790 Pecan Way Loma Linda CA 92354-3452 Office: 3975 Jackson St Ste 202 Riverside CA 92503-3947 Office Phone: 951-352-7920. Personal E-mail: tjung1790@aol.com.

JUNG, YEE WAH, artist; b. Canton, Quangdong, China, Sept. 4, 1936; came to U.S., 1963; d. Yeun Tsin and Shiu Fung (Poon) Yip; m. Kwan Yee Jung, Sept. 10, 1962; children: Jeanne, Kathy, Laura. Student, Chung Nam Art Sch., Wupei, China, 1954-58, New Asia Coll., Hong Kong, 1958-62. Art instr. Shiu Fung Art Studio, Hong Kong, 1958-63; art tchr. Chi-Ching Mid. Sch., Hong Kong, 1962-63; freelance artist San Diego, 1963—; owner Jung's Gallery, La Jolla, Calif., 1976-78. Solo juror Clairemont Art Guild Annual, San Diego, 1989, So. Calif. Expo Art, 1996. Exhbns. include Am. Fine Art Connection Exhbn., Poway (Calif.) Ctr. for the Performing Arts, 1995, Watercolor USA, Knoxville (Tenn.) Mus. of Art, 1995, Co-Art Gallery, Vancouver, B.C., Can., 1996, Kruglak Gallery, Mira Costa Coll., Oceanside, Calif., 1997, San Diego Chinese Hist. Mus., 1997, Taiwanese Am. Ctr., San Diego, 2000, Kim Art Gallery, Irvine, 2001, Springfield Coll., San Diego, 2002. Recipient First prize So. Calif. Expo, 1970, Watercolor USA Cash award Calif. Nat. Watercolor Soc., 1973, First Place award 25th Annual Art Festival, San Diego, 1989, Three King award Advent Fine Art 7th Annual, San Diego, 1990, award of distinction Rockport Pubs., 1997, Best Depiction of Theme award St. Mark's 42nd Annual Rel. Art Festival, 2005. Mem. Nat. Watercolor Soc., Watercolor Honor Soc., Asiatic Art Guild (panel juror 1993). Home: 5468 Bloch St San Diego CA 92122-4010 Office Phone: 858-453-5380. E-mail: kjung1@san.rr.com.

JUNGE, CHERYL MARIE, elementary school educator; b. Great Falls, Mont., Mar. 25, 1961; d. Raymond Lawrence and Elizabeth Gertrude Seerup; m. William Gordon Junge, Aug. 16, 1986; children: Rebecca Ann, Katherine Elizabeth, Bryan Christopher. BS in Elem. & Spl. Edn. with honors, Ea. Mont. Coll., 1986. Cert. tchr., Wyo., Mont. Tchr. Great Falls (Mont) Pub. Schs., 1986—91, Natrona County Schs., Casper, Wyo, 1991-92, tchr., work study coord., 1992—. Cosn. Mont. Sch. for Deaf and Blind, Great Falls, 1990. Recipient Cert. of Appreciation Indian Edn. Program, 1989, Spl. Educator's award Spl. Edn. Adv. Bd., 1993. Mem. ASCD, Wyo. Assn. for Persons in Supported Employment, Nat. Assn. Vocat. Edn. Spl. Needs Pers., Coun. for Exceptional Children (Profl. Recognition Spl. Educator 2000), Phi Detla Kappa. Republican. Roman Catholic. Avocations: dance, sewing, crafts. Home: 1150 Donegal St Casper WY 82609-3217 Office: Natrona County Schs Kelly Walsh HS 3500 E 12th St Casper WY 82609-1827 Office Phone: 307-233-2158. E-mail: cheryl_junge@ncsd.k12.wy.us.

JUNGER, MIGUEL CHAPERO, acoustics researcher; b. Dresden, Germany, Jan. 29, 1923; came to U.S., 1941, naturalized, 1946; s. José and Adrienne (Junger) Chapiro; m. Ellen Sinclair, 1960; children: M. Sebastian, A. Carlotta. BS, MIT, 1944, SM, 1946; ScD (Gordon McKay scholar), Harvard U., 1951. Postdoctoral rsch. fellow in acoustics Harvard U., 1951-55; partner Cambridge Acoustical Assocs., Inc., 1955-59, pres., 1959-89, chmn. bd. dirs., 1989-97; ret. Sr. vis. lectr. ocean engring. dept. MIT, Cambridge, 1968-78; vis. prof. U. Technologie de Compiègne, 1975, 77-82 Author: Sound, Structures and Their Interaction, 1972, 2d edit., 1986, rev. edit., 1993, Eléments d'Acoustique Physique, 1978, Handbook of Acoustic Characteristics of Turbomachinery Cavities, 1997; guest editor, author: Structural Acoustics, 1997; contbr. articles to profl. jours. Fellow ASME (Rayleigh lectr., Per Bruel Noise Control and Acoustics Gold medal 1992), Acoustical Soc. Am. (Trent-Crede medal 1987). Achievements include patents in field. Home: 90 Fletcher Rd Belmont MA 02478-2017 E-mail: ellenandmiguel@earthlink.net.

JUNGERMAN, JOHN ALBERT, physics professor; b. Modesto, Calif., Dec. 28, 1921; s. Albert Augustus and Freda (Durst) J.; m. Nancy Lee Kidwell, Oct. 23, 1948; children: Mark, Eric, Roger, Anne. AB, U. Calif., Berkeley, 1943, PhD, 1949. Research physicist Manhattan Project, Oak Ridge, Tenn. and Berkeley, 1944-45, Los Alamos, N.Mex., 1945-46, Lawrence Berkeley Lab., Berkeley, 1946-49, 50-51; asst. prof. physics U. Calif., Davis, 1951, prof. physics, 1960-91, prof. emeritus, 1991, founding dir. Crocker Nuclear Lab., 1965-80, chmn. physics dept., 1981-82, 83-87; assoc. mem. faculty Starr King Sch. for Ministry, Berkeley, Calif., 1992-93. Vis. prof. U. Grenoble, France, 1972; prin. investigator nuclear physics Atomic Energy Commn., U. Calif., Davis, 1956-71; cons. OAS U. Chile, Santiago, 1982, OAS, 1971, Internat. Atomic Energy Agy., 1982. Author: Nuclear Arms Race: Technology and Society, 1986, 2d edit., 1990, World in Process, 2000. Organizer, instr. Davis Summer Insts. on Nuclear Age Edn. for Secondary Sch. Instrs., 1986-93. NSF Nuclear Physics grantee, 1971-73, NSF Sci. Edn. grantee, 1990-93. Fellow Am. Physical Soc.; mem. Am. Solar Soc., Sigma Xi. Democrat. Avocations: piano, sailing, bicycling, painting. Office: U Calif Dept Physics Davis CA 95616 E-mail: jajungerman@ucdavis.edu.

JUNGK, JANET ETHERTON, media specialist; d. Fred Snider and Helen Florence Etherton; m. Steven E. Jungk, Mar. 10, 1979; children: Lauren E. Updike, Allison K., Kevin E., Audrey L., Lindsey K. BS in Ed, Libr. and English, Ill. State U., 1977, MS in Edn., 1979. Cert. secondary tchr. Ill., elem. tchr. Ill. Grad. asst. Office Residential Life Ill. State U., Normal, 1977—79; elem. libr. Southwestern Sch. Dist., Piasa, Ill., 1980—83; dist. libr. media specialist Carrollton (Ill.) Cmty. Unit Sch. Dist., 1994—. Author: (online professional development module) ArcVoyager- GIS for the Classroom, Microsoft Outlook, WebQuests in the Classroom. Tech. Integration grantee, Ill. State Bd. Edn., 1995—. Mem.: DAR (assoc.; historian 1983—90).

JUNIKER, ANTHONY MICHAEL, real estate developer, consultant; b. Jackson, Miss., Aug. 30, 1948; s. John and Aleen J.; m. Kathleen Akright, Oct. 9, 1982; 1 child, Margaret Aleen. BS in Acctg., Miss. State U., 1971. Cert. comm. developer. Comptroller Capital Security Svcs., Jackson, Miss., 1982-84; small bus. cons. Miss. R&D Ctr., Jackson, 1984-87, mgr. comml. bus. assistance, 1987-88; mgr. entrepreneurial devel. Miss. Dept. Econ. & Cmty. Devel., Jackson, 1988-90, mgr. cmty. ops. br., 1990-96; sr. bus. devel. officer Enterprise Corp. Delta, Jackson, 1996-2000; exec. dir. Magnolia (Ark.) Econ. Devel. Corp., 2000—. Lt. col. U.S. Army. Recipient Econ. Devel. of the Yr., Southwest Ark., 2004. Mem.: So. Econ. Devel. Coun., Comm. Devel. Coun., Golden Triangle Econ. Devel. Coun. (dir.), Ark. Econ. Developers. Republican. Methodist. Avocations: reading, electric trains. Office: Magnolia Econ Devel Corp PO Box 2262 Magnolia AR 71754-2262 Office Phone: 870-234-0800. Business E-Mail: mjuniker@medc.cc.

JUNKER, BOBBY RAY, research and development company executive, physicist; b. San Antonio, Tex., Aug. 29, 1943; s. Richard Eugene and Alice Emma (Gruetzmacher) J.; m. Judith Lynne Combs, Sept. 12, 1968 (div. Aug. 1974); 1 child, Bryce Allyn; m. Sheryl Ann Watson, Oct. 8, 1976 (div. July 1995); children: Melissa Sheryl, Evan Ryan; m. Virginia C. Katt, July 13, 1996. BS, U. Southwestern La., 1965; MA, U. Tex., 1967, PhD in Chemistry, 1969. Instr. chemistry U. Tex., Austin, 1969-70; rsch. assoc. physics U. Pitts., 1970-72; asst. prof. physics U. Ga., Athens, 1972-76; sci. officer Office Naval Rsch., Arlington, Va., 1977-84, dir. physic. divsn., 1983-86, dir. math. and phys. scis. dept., 1986-93, head electronics, info. and surveillance dept., 1993—. Contbr. chpts. to books. Treas. PTA, Fairfax, Va., 1988-89, county rep., 1990-92; treas. Fairfax Christian Ch., 1982-87, 92-95. Recipient Presdl. Meritorious Rank award U.S. Govt., 1989, 99, Presdl. Disting Rank award U.S. Govt., 2003. Mem. AAAS, Am. Phys. Soc., Sigma Xi. Achievements include rsch. theoretical atomic physics, including electron-atom and ion-atom collisions. Office: Office Naval Rsch Info Electronics and Surveillance Dept 800 N Quincy St Arlington VA 22203-1906

JUNZ, HELEN B., economist; d. Samson and Dobra Bachner. BA, PhD, U. Amsterdam; MA, New Sch. Social Rsch. Acting chief consumer price sect. Nat. Indsl. Conf. Bd., N.Y.C., 1953-58; research officer Nat. Inst. Econ. and Social Research, London, 1958-60; economist Bur. Econ. Analysis, Dept. Commerce, Washington, 1960-62; adviser div. internat. fin. bd. govs. Fed. Res. System, Washington, 1962-77; dep. asst. sec. Office of Asst. Sec. for Internat. Affairs, Dept. Treasury, Washington, 1977-79; v.p., sr. advisor 1st Nat. Bank Chgo., 1979-80; v.p. Townsend Greenspan & Co., Inc., N.Y.C., 1980-82; sr. advisor European dept. IMF, 1982-87, dep. dir. exch. and trade rels. dept., 1987-89, spl. trade rep., dir. Geneva office, 1989-94; dir. gold econs. svc. World Gold Coun., Geneva, Switzerland, 1994-96; pres. HBJ Internat., London, 1996—. Adviser OECD, Paris, 1967-69; sr. internat. economist Council of Econ. Advisers, The White House, Washington, 1975-77. Author: Where did all the money go?, 2002; contbr. articles to profl. jours. Mem. Am. Econ. Assn., Coun. Fgn. Rels., Cosmos Club, Reform Club. Office: HBJ Intnat 39 Chalcot Sq London NW1 8YP England E-mail: hbjunz@planet.nl.

JURA, JAMES J., electric utility executive; b. Creston, Nebr., Dec. 9, 1942; s. Joseph James and Edna Helena (Mackenstadt) J.; m. Sylvia; children: Joseph, James, John, Fredericka. BA, U. Wash., Seattle, 1967; MBA, Seattle U., 1971; postgrad., Harvard U., 1985. With indsl. rels. staff Boeing Co., Seattle, 1968-71; with policy devel. staff OSHA, Washington, 1971-73; legis. and budget analyst Office Mgmt. and Budget, Washington, 1973-78; asst. adminstr. Bonneville Power Adminstrn., U.S. Dept. Energy, Washington, 1978-80, from exec. asst. adminstr. to adminstr. Portland, Oreg., 1980-91; CEO, gen. mgr. Assoc. Electric Coop. Inc., Springfield, Mo., 1991—. Bd. dirs. Assn. Mo. Elec. Coops., Mo. Employers Mut. Ins. Co., Hawthorne Found. With U.S. Army, 1963-65. Republican. Office: Associated Electric Coop PO Box 754 Springfield MO 65801-0754 Office Phone: 417-881-1204. E-mail: jjura@aeci.org.

JURAFSKY, DANIEL, linguist; b. Yonkers, NY, 1962; BA in Linguistics, U. Calif., Berkeley, 1983, PhD in Computer Sci., 1992. Software engr.; postdoc. rschr. Internat. Computer Sci. Inst., 1992—96; assoc. prof. U. Colo., 1996—; assoc. prof. linguistics Stanford U. Drummer Too Many Notes. Mem. editl. bd.: Computer Speech Lang.; co-author: Speech and Language Processing. Recipient CAREER award, NSF; fellow MacArthur Found. fellow, 2002. Office: Stanford Univ Dept Linguistics Bldg 460 Stanford CA 94305-2150 Office Phone: 650-723-4284. E-mail: jurafsky@stanford.edu.*

JURAN, SYLVIA LOUISE, editor; b. Chgo. d. Joseph Moses and Sadie (Shapiro) J. BA, U. Minn.; MA, Columbia U., 1960; PhD, Harvard U., 1975. Project editor Macmillan Pub. Co., N.Y.C., 1981-91; editor Ralph Appelbaum Assocs. Inc., N.Y.C., 1991—. Faculty The New Sch., N.Y.C., 1980-82. Project editor: Ency. of the Holocaust, 1990 (Dartmouth medal ALA, 1990), Ency. of the Third Reich, 1991; editor scripts for mus. exhbns.; contbr. articles to profl. jours. Nat. Def. fgn. lang. fellow, 1960-61, 62-63. Mem. Harvard Club of N.Y.C., Harvard Grad. Sch. Alumni Assn. (N.Y. exec. com. 1984—). Office: Ralph Appelbaum Assocs Inc 88 Pine St New York NY 10005-1801 Office Phone: 212-334-8200. Business E-Mail: sylviajuran@raany.com.

JURCH, GEORGE R., JR., retired science educator; b. New Britain, Conn., Feb. 1, 1934; s. George and Alice Jurch; m. Molly Irene Brown; children: George III, Steven, Carol. BS in Chemistry, U. Fla., 1957; MS in Chemistry, U. Ky., 1961; PhD, U. Calif., San Diego, 1965. Technician Thorton Chem. Lab., Tampa, Fla., 1952—56; rsch. chemist IBM, Lexington, Ky., 1961; rsch. assoc. Yale U., New Haven, 1965—66; prof. U. South Fla., Tampa,

1966—99; ret., 1999. Cons. USDA, Fla., 1975—99. Author: (book) Lab Manual General Chemistry, 1969, Lab Manual Organic, 5 edits., 1975—99. Sgt. U.S. Army, 1957—59. Democrat. Roman Catholic. Achievements include patents in field. Avocation: wine consultant. Home: 1215 E Brandon Blvd Brandon FL 33511

JURGENS, DORIS V., special education educator; b. Salem, Ohio, Mar. 12, 1945; d. Forrest Lee and Florence Olive Vincent; m. Kenneth Wayne Jurgens, Nov. 24, 1966; children: Eric, Elizabeth. BA, Lincoln Christian Coll., 1967. Tchr. 1st and 3d grades Grayville Cmty. Schs., Ill., 1968—69, 1971—72; tchr. learning disabled Ripley Union Lewis Sch., Ripley, Ohio, 1974—75, Wooster City Schs., 1983—89, Washington City Schs., Ind., 1990—2001, Seymour Cmty. Schs., 2001—. Mem.: Coun. Exceptional Children. Independent. Avocations: reading, crocheting, gardening. Office: Seymore High Sch 1350 W 2d St Seymour IN 47274

JURGENS, JULIE GRAHAM, mathematics professor; b. Washta, Iowa, Mar. 8, 1950; d. Albert Harm and Thelma Ann (Johnson) Haenfler; m. Dennis Dean Graham, Mar. 16, 1969 (div. Oct. 17, 1988); children: Tracy Ann Graham-Lester, Tricia Jean Graham-Banta; m. David Dallas Jurgens, Apr. 17, 1998. Undergrad., Morningside Coll., Sioux City, Iowa, 1968—69; BA in Math. Edn./Phys. Edn., Wayne State Coll., 1969—72; MS, Marycrest Coll., Davenport, Iowa, 1985; PhD, U. Iowa, 1997. Prof. math. and computer sci. Marycrest U., 1985—97; dept. chair math., sci., and tech. Flagler Coll., St. Augustine, Fla., 1997—. Mem.: AAUP, Fla. Coun. Tchrs. Math., Fla. Assn. Computer in Edn., Nat. Coun. Tchrs. Math., Math. Assn. Am., Phi Delta Kappa. Home: 138 Creekside Rd Satsuma FL 32189 Office: Flagler Coll Saint Augustine FL 32085 Office Phone: 904-819-6267.

JURGENSEN, W.G., insurance company executive; BS in Fin., MBA, Creighton U., Omaha, Nebr. Exec. v.p. Norwest Corp.; corp. banking officer Norwest Investment Svcs., pres., CEO; mgmt. First Chicago NBD Corp.; exec. v.p. Bank One Corp.; CEO Nationwide Ins., 2000—, Nationwide Fin. Svcs., 2000—. Fin. Svcs. Roundtable; Ohio Bus. Roundtable; Columbus Downtown Develop. Corp.; Columbus Partnership; vice chmn., trustee Loyola U., Chgo.; trustee Newberry Libr.; bd. dir. Greater Columbus C. of C., Law Enforcement Found. Ohio, Columbus Children's Hosp.; chair Governor's Commn. on Teaching Success, 2001—03. Office: Nationwide Ins 1 Nationwide Plz Columbus OH 43215

JURICIC, DAVOR, mechanical engineering educator; b. Split, Croatia, Aug. 2, 1928; arrived in U.S., 1968; s. Mate and Slavka (Franceschi) J.; m. Milesa L. Harris, Mar. 10, 1984; 1 child, Ivanna Albertin. Dipl.Ing., U. Belgrade, Yugoslavia, 1952, DSc, 1964. Stress analyst Icarus Aircraft Industries, Zemun, Yugoslavia, 1953-58; rsch. engr. Inst. Aeronautics, Belgrade, 1958-63; asst. prof. U. Belgrade, 1963-65, assoc. prof., 1965-68, S.D. State U., Brookings, 1968-73, prof., 1973-75; vis. prof. Stanford (Calif.) U., 1975-78; prof. mech. engrng. U. Tex., Austin, 1978-98, prof. emeritus, 1998—. Contbr. numerous articles to profl. jours. Rsch. grantee various agencies, 1962—. Mem. ASME, Am. Soc. Engrng. Edn. (Chester F. Carlson award 1993), Sigma Xi. Achievements include research in suspension system for railway vehicles (patent). Business E-Mail: juricic@mail.utexas.edu.

JURKA, EDITH MILA, psychiatrist, researcher; b. NYC, Dec. 4, 1915; d. Charles Anton and Edith Dorothy (Schevcik) J. BA, Smith Coll., 1936; postgrad., Charles U., Prague, Czechoslovakia, 1936-38; MD, Yale U., 1944. Diplomate Am. Bd. Psychiatry and Neurology. Intern in children's med. svc. Bellevue Hosp., N.Y.C., 1944-45, asst. alienist, 1947-49; rotating intern Gallinger Hosp., Washington, 1945-46; intern N.Y. State Psychiat. Inst., N.Y.C., 1946-47; asst. psychiatrist Mt. Sinai Hosp., N.Y.C., 1949-51; pvt. practice N.Y.C., 1949—; asst. psychiatrist Roosevelt Hosp., N.Y.C., 1954-57; chief psychiatrist Pleasantville (N.Y.) Cottage Sch., 1961-74. Bd. dirs. intuition network Inst. Noetic Scis.; founder Wind Song Inst. Sec. Jane Coffin Childs Fund, 1938-41. Fellow Am. Orthopsychiat. Assn.; mem. Am. Psychiat. Assn., N.Y. Coun. Child and Adolescent Psychiatry, N.Y. County Med. Soc., N.Y. State Med. Soc. (psychiat. medicine com.), Westchester Psychiat. Soc. Avocations: architecture, parapsychology, travel, gardening, theater. Home: 16 Apple Bee Farm Ln Croton On Hudson NY 10520-3612 Office: 116 E 66th St New York NY 10021-6547 Office Phone: 212-737-0591.

JURKAT, MARTIN PETER, mathematician, statistician, management educator; b. Berlin, July 23, 1935; came to U.S., 1946, naturalized, 1951; s. Ernest Herman and Dorothy (Bergas) J.; m. Mayme Porter, May 31, 1958; children: Martin Alexander, Susanna, Maria. BA in Math. and Stats. with honors, Swarthmore (Pa.) Coll., 1957; MA, U. N.C., 1961; PhD, Stevens Inst. Tech., Hoboken, N.J., 1972. Programmer Burroughs Corp. Research Lab., Paoli, Pa., 1960-61; sr. program analyst ITT Corp., Paramus, N.J., 1961-64; dir. Center Mcpl. Studies and Services Stevens Inst. Tech., 1975-77, chief transp. analysis div. Davidson Lab., 1964-75, Alexander Crombie Humphreys prof. mgmt. sci., 1979—2001. Cons. Tank-Automotive Devel. Command, U.S. Army, 1975-88, AT&T, 1995-2001, Lucent, 1996-2001; dir. Cause project NSF, 1978-81. Co-author: The NATO Reference Mobility Model, 1980; author studies, reports on mobility, transp., human factors, math. edn. Mem. Assn. Computing Machinery. Democrat. Mem. Soc. Of Friends. Home and Office: 2822 Don Quixote Santa Fe NM 87505 Office Phone: 201-888-8934. E-mail: mpeterj@comcast.net.

JURKEVICH, GAYANA, Spanish language educator, consultant; b. Montreal, Que., Can., Apr. 24, 1953; came to U.S., 1953; d. Igor and Marianna (Pospielovsky) J. AB, Mt. Holyoke Coll., 1974; MA, U. Minn., 1977; PhD, NYU, 1987. With pers. mgmt. U.S. Dept. of State, Washington, 1977-81; rsch. fellow NYU, 1983-86; asst. prof. Baruch Coll./CUNY, 1987-92, assoc. prof., 1993—97, prof., 1998—. Actress, dir., voice-over artist; mem. exec. com. PSC, campus grievance officer Baruch Coll., 1999—, mem. presdl. search com., 2004. Author: The Elusive Self: Archetypal Approaches to the Novels of Miguel de Unamuno, 1991, In Pursuit of the Natural Sign: Azorín and the Poetics of Ekphrasis, 1999; contbr. articles in Hispanic Rev., Comparative Lit., MLN, Hispania, ALEC, Revista Hispánica Moderna, Can. Rev. of Comparative Lit., Symposium, Bulletin of Hispanic Studies; mem. editorial bd. Jour. of Inter-disciplinary Lit. Studies. Recipient Publ. award Program for Cultural Cooperation Spanish Ministry of Culture and U.S.'s Univs., 1990, 99, Sabbatical grantee, 1995, PSC/CUNY Rsch. award, 1993, 94, Sabbatical Leave grantee, 1995-96. Mem. MLA, Am. Assn. Tchrs. Spanish and Portugese, Am. Soc. for Hispanic Art Hist. Studies, Phi Kappa Phi. Office: Baruch Coll Dept Modern Langs One Bernard Baruch Way Box B 6-280 New York NY 10010-5518 Office Phone: 646-312-4221. Business E-Mail: gayana_jurkevich@baruch.cuny.edu.

JURKIEWICZ, MAURICE JOHN, surgeon, educator; b. Claremont, NH, Sept. 24, 1923; s. Charles B. and Mary (Ostrowska) J.; m. Mary de Forest Freeman, July 7, 1951; children— Elizabeth de Forest, John Christopher. D.D.S. magna cum laude, U. Md., 1946; MD, Harvard U., 1952. Diplomate: Am. Bd. Surgery, Am. Bd. Plastic Surgery (mem. bd. 1971-77, chmn. 1977-78). Intern Barnes Hosp., Washington U., St. Louis, 1952-53, resident, 1953-58, clin. fellow, 1958-59, instr. surgery, 1957-59; mem. staff U. Fla. Hosp., Gainesville; asst. prof. surgery U. Fla., 1959-64, assoc. prof., 1964-67, prof., 1967-71, chief div. plastic and reconstructive surgery, 1959-71; chief of surgery VA Hosp., Gainesville, 1968-71; prof. surgery, chief of plastic and reconstructive surgery Emory Affiliated Hosps., Atlanta, 1971-92; chief surg. services Grady Meml. Hosp., Atlanta, 1972-77; chief of surgery VAMC, Atlanta, 1989-93. Cons. in plastic surgery Walter Reed Gen. Hosp., Washington, 1971-91; sci. counselor Nat. Inst. Dental Rsch., 1966-71; chmn. com. on study of evaluation procedures Am. Bd. Med. Spltys., 1979-81; mem. at large Nat. Bd. Med. Exams., 1985-93; commr. Joint Commn. on Accreditation of Health Care Orgns., 1985-94 (sec. 1989-90, treas. 1990-91, vice chmn. 1991-92), Nat. Cons. in Plastic Surgery to the Shriners Hosp., 1995—. Editor: Operative Techniques in Plastic Surgery, 1994-99; assoc. editor: Plastic and Reconstructive Surgery, 1972-78, 79-83, co-editor, 1985-89; assoc. editor Am. Surgeon, 1977-87. Served to lt. (j.g.) USNR, 1946-48. Fellow Royal Australasian Coll. Surgeons (hon.); mem. AMA, Am. Cancer Soc., Am. Cleft Palate Assn., ACS (bd. regents 1979-88, vice chmn. 1985-88, pres.-elect 1988, pres. 1989-90), Am. Soc. Plastic and Reconstructive Surgeons, Southeastern Soc. Plastic and Reconstructive Surgeons, Ga. Soc. Plastic and Reconstructive Surgeons, Southeastern Surg. Congress (hon. fellow), Am. Soc. Head and NEck Surgeons (pres. 1989), Ednl. Founds. Plastic Surgery Coun., Am. Assn. Plastic Surgeons (pres. 1989-81, dist. fellow), Am. So. Surg Assns. (1st v.p. 1993-94, hon. fellow), Med. Assn. Ga Home: 715 Old Post Rd NW Atlanta GA 30328-4758 Office: Emory U Clinic 550 Peachtree St 8th Fl Ste 4300 Atlanta GA 30308 Office Phone: 404-686-8143.

JURKOWITZ, DANIEL S., lawyer, prosecutor, judge; b. Tucson; s. Harvey and Chaya Jurkowitz; m. Lisa A. Klein. BA, U. Ariz., 1994, JD, 1997. Bar: Ariz. 1997, U.S. Dist. Ct. Ariz. 1998, U.S. Ct. Appeals (9th cir.) 1998, U.S. Supreme Ct. 2000. Intern Ariz. Atty. Gens. Office, Dept. Econ. Security, Tucson, 1994; appeals clk. criminal divsn. Pima County Attys. Office, Tucson, 1995—96, student prosecutor criminal divsn., 1996; Westlaw student rep. West Pub. Corp., Tucson, 1996—97; law clk. civil divsn. Pima County Attys. Office, Tucson, 1997, dep. county atty. criminal divsn., 1997—98, dep. county atty. civil divsn., law clk. supr., 1998—2001; adminstrv. law judge Ariz. Dept. Transp., Tucson, 2001—; judge pro tempore Ariz. Superior Ct., 2003—; arbitrator State Bar of Ariz. Fee Arbitration Pgm, 2003—; hearing officer Sunnyside Unified Sch. Dist., 2002—04; faculty U. Phoenix, 2003—; hearing officer Ariz. Supreme Ct., 2004—; justice of the peace pro tempore Pinal County, 2004—. Legal columnist: Daily Jour. Corp., 2000—01; co-author: Arizona Employment Law Handbook, Vol. 1, 2d edit., 2004; co-editor: Arizona DUI Trial Notebook, 2d edit., 2005. Teen ct. judge Pima County Teen Ct., 2001—02; treas. Fountain Park Homeowners Assn., 2002—03; mem. City of Tucson Citizens' Transp. Adv. Com., 2001—03; co-chair NCALJ Judicial Tech. Com., 2004—; state and precinct committeeman Ariz. Rep. Party, Tucson, 1994—2001; vice chmn., sec. exec. com. Pima County Rep. Party, 1999—2001; v.p, pres. Sienna Homeowners Assn., Tucson, 1998—2000. Nat. merit scholar. Mem.: ABA (co-chair NCALJ jud. tech. com.), Pima County Bar Assn. (co-chair, sch. coord., tutor Lawyers for Literacy, Young Lawyers div. 1997—2002, bd. dirs. Young Lawyers divsn. 1999—2003, bd. dirs. 2002—), Mensa, Phi Beta Kappa. Jewish. Avocations: guitar, tennis, reading. Office: Arizona Dept Trans Motor Vehicle Exec Hearing Office 3565 S Broadmont Dr Second Fl Tucson AZ 85713-5240

JURKOWITZ, LISA AMY, language educator; b. N.Y.C., 1972; d. A. and J. Klein; m. Dan Jurkowitz, 1996; 2 children. BA in French, U. Ariz., 1995, MA in French Pedagogy, postgrad. in second lang., aquisition and tchg., U. Ariz., 1997—. Cert. French and ESL. Grad. tchg. assoc. in French U. Ariz., Tucson, 1995—2000; mem. faculty ESL Pima C.C., Tucson, 2001—, chmn. dept. ESL, 2003—, adj. faculty in French, 2000—01. Adj. faculty in French Am. Grad. Sch. Internat. Mgmt., Glendale, Ariz., 2000; asst. coord. French dept. basic lang. program U. Ariz., Tucson, 1998—99, co-chmn. French dept. So. Ariz. lang. fair, 1998—99, editor pedagogy and program adminstrn., 1999—2000, rsch. asst. collaborative computerized lang. classroom, 2000—01, mem. hiring com., 2002, coord. ESL orientations, 2004—, mem. hiring com., 2005, mem. faculty senate, 2005—; presenter in field. Contbr. articles to profl. jours. (prize, 97). Recipient award, French Alliance, 1993, Best of Ariz. award, Ariz. Lang. Assn., 1999; fellow, U. Ariz. Dept. French and Italian, 1996; travel grantee, Computer Assisted Lang. Instrn. Consortium, 2001. Mem.: Coll. Discipline Area Com. (faculty senate 2005—), Am. Assn. Tchrs. French (sec.-treas. 2000—01), Ariz. Lang. Assn., Partnership Across Langs., Tchg. English to Speakers of Other Langs., Second Lang. Acquisition and Tchg. Student Assn. (sec. 1998—2000), Computer Assisted Lang. Instruction Consortium, French Forum, Phi Beta Kappa. Office: 1255 N Stone Ave Tucson AZ 85709 Office Phone: 520-206-7218. Business E-Mail: lisa.jurkowitz@pima.edu.

JURNEY, NANCY JANNETTE, school librarian; d. Cecil McLean and Mignonnette Norwood Hardison; m. Larry Louis Jurney, Aug. 27, 1965; children: David Louis, Nancy-Susan. BA, David Lipscomb U., 1965; MLS, U. Mich., 1976. Social sci. libr. Okla. State U., Stillwater, 1988—95; serials and reference libr. Langston (Okla.) U., 1996—. Sunday sch. tchr. Wilshire Ch. Christ, Oklahoma City, 1997—2005. Mem.: Okla. Libr. Assn. Mem. Church Of Christ. Avocations: watercolor, reading. Office: G Lamar Harrison Libr Langston Univ PO Box 1600 Langston OK 73050 Office Phone: 405-466-3457. Office Fax: 405-466-3459. E-mail: nhjurney@lunet.edu.

JURTSHUK, PETER, JR., microbiologist, educator; b. N.Y.C., July 28, 1929; s. Peter and Mary (Ferens) J.; m. Rebecca Jones, Jan. 2, 1971; children: Peter, Larissa. AB, NYU, 1951; MS, Creighton U., 1953; PhD, U. Md., 1957. Asst. prof. pharmacology Bklyn. Coll. Pharmacy, L.I. U., 1957-59; asst. prof. enzyme chemistry U. Wis.-Madison, 1962-63; asst. prof. microbiology U. Tex., Austin, 1963-69; assoc. prof. biology and biochemistry U. Houston, 1970-76, prof., 1976—, undergrad. chmn., 1976—80, dir. program in microbiology, 1990—. Mem. vis. biol. program Am. Inst. Biol. Scis., 1969-72. Contbr. chpts. to books. Recipient Disting. Svc. award Tex. br. Am. Soc. Microbiology, 1982; NIH grantee, 1964-75; NSF grantee, 1986-89. Fellow Am. Acad. Microbiology; mem. Am. Soc. Microbiology (pres. Tex. br. 1972-74), N.Y. Acad. Scis., Am. Soc. Biochemistry and Molecular Biology, Am. Chem. Soc., Sigma Xi (pres. U. Houston chpt. 1979-80). Russian Orthodox. Home: 879 Ramada Dr Houston TX 77062-5607 Office: U Houston Biology and Biochemistry Dept Houston TX 77204-5001 Office Phone: 713-743-2668. Business E-Mail: jurtshuk@uh.edu.

JUSKOWIAK, TERRY EUGENE, career military officer; b. Danville, Pa., May 29, 1951; s. Joseph Leon and Betty Lorraine (Dilliplane) J.; m. Susan Kay Renn, Sept. 15, 1974; children: John, Christopher, Jennifer. BA, The Citadel, Charleston, S.C., 1973; MS, Fla. Inst. Technology, Melbourne, 1981. Commd. 2d lt. U.S. Army, 1973, advanced through ranks to major gen., 1999, contract cost mgmt. analyst Army Mat. Ctr. Alexandria, Va., 1980-84, aide-de-camp Sec. Army Washington, 1984-85, dep. V Corps logistics officer Frankfurt, Germany, 1986-88, exec. officer 122 Main 3d Armored Divsn. Hanau, Germany, 1988-89, from divsn. staff to battalion cmdr. 82d Airborne Divsn. Ft. Bragg, NC, 1989-92, spl. asst. to chief of Staff Washington, 1992-94, brigade cmdr. 10th Mtn. Divsn. Ft. Drum, NY, 1994-96, asst. divsn. cmdr. support 10th Mtn. Divsn., 1996—; dep. comdg. gen. NATO SFOR Spt Cmd, 1996-98; dir. logistics I4 U.S. Atlantic comd. Norfolk, Va., 1997-98; comdr. 1st Corps Support Command (Airborne), Ft. Bragg, NC, 1998-2000; dir. logistics U.S. Forces Command, Ft. McPherson, Ga., 2000-01; quartermaster gen., comdt. Quartermaster Sch., 2001—02; comdr. Combined Arms Support Command, 2002—04; exec. IBM, 2004—. Decorated DSM, Def. Superior Svc. medal, Legion of Merit, Bronze Star, Def. Meritorious Svc. medal. Mem. Assn. Citadel Men, Assn. U.S. Army, Quartermaster Assn., 82d Airborne Assn., 10th Mtn. Divsn. Assn. Presbyterian. Avocations: reading, running, skiing. Personal E-mail: tjuskowiak@aol.com. Business E-Mail: tjuskowiak@us.ibm.com.

JUST, GEMMA RIVOLI, retired advertising executive; b. N.Y.C., Nov. 29, 1921; d. Philip and Brigida (Consolo) Rivoli; m. Victor Just, Jan. 29, 1955. BA, Hunter Coll., N.Y.C., 1943. Copy group head McCann Erickson, N.Y.C., 1958-62; copy supr. Morse Internat., N.Y.C., 1962-67; v.p., dir. creative svcs. Deltakos divsn. J. Walter Thompson, N.Y.C., 1967-75; v.p., copy dir. Sudler & Hennessey divsn. Young & Rubicam, N.Y.C., 1980-87, sr. v.p., assoc. creative dir. copy, 1987-88, ret., 1989. Mem. Episcopal Ch. Women of Ch. of Incarnation, N.Y.C., also ch. altar guild pres. and acolyte. Recipient Aesculapius awards Modern Medicine mag., 1980-88; named Best Writer, Art Dirs. Club N.Y., 1979, Best Writer Young & Rubicam, 1981. Mem. Coun. Comms. Soc., Pharm. Advt. Coun., Am. Med. Writers Assn. (exec. com. 1973). Home: 155 E 38th St Apt 5D New York NY 10016-2663

JUST, RICHARD EUGENE, economist, consultant, agriculturist, educator; b. Tulsa, Feb. 18, 1948; s. William and Leah (Flaming) J.; m. Janet Lee Humphries, Aug. 26, 1989; children: Angela K. Eisinger, David R., Ronald L. Mower. BS, Okla. State U., 1969; MA, U. Calif., Berkeley, 1971, PhD, 1972. Prof. agrl. econs. and stats. Okla. State U., Stillwater, 1972-75; prof. agrl. and resource econs. U. Calif., Berkeley, 1975-85, U. Md., College Park, 1985-92, chmn. dept., 1992-95, U Md., College Park, 2003—04; disting. univ. prof. U. Md., College Park, 1995—. Cons. The World Bank, Washington, 1976-93, Oak Ridge Nat. Lab., 1976-81, Winrock Internat., 1979-81, Electric Power Rsch. Inst., 1981-83, Stanford Rsch. Inst., 1981, Safeway Stores, Inc., Oakland, Calif., 1983-86, Price Waterhouse, 1987-91, The Pillsbury Co., Mpls., 1988-89, U.S. Gen. Acctg. Office, Washington, 1978-79, 90-95, U.S. Dept. Justice, 1999, others; prin. Law and Econs. Consulting Group, 1993-2000; vis. prof. Ben Gurion U. Negev, 1977, Brigham Young U., 1977, 79-80, 94; sr. rsch. fellow The Inst. for Policy Reform, 1991—; sr. cons. Charles River Assocs., 2001—. Author: A Comprehensive Assessment of the Role of Risk in U.S. Agriculture, 2002, Applied Welfare Economics and Public Policy, 1982, Commodity and Resource Policies in Agricultural Systems, 1991, Conflict and Cooperation on Trans-Boundary Water Resources, 1998, (monographs) Econometric Analysis of Production Decisions, 1975, Econometric Analysis of Processing Tomatoes, 1978, The Welfare Economics of Public Policy: A Practical Approach to Project and Policy Evaluation, 2004, Economics ofRegulation of Agricultural Biotechnologies, 2005; editor Am. Jour. Agrl. Econs., 1984-86, mem. editl. com., 1978-80; mem. editl. bd. Jour. Devel. Planning Lit., 1985—, Springer-Verlag, 1989—; mem. editl. coun. We. Jour. Agrl. Econs., 1982-84; also articles to jours. Mem. task force on economy Calif. Dem. Com., 1981-83; mem. agrl. policy task force for speaker Calif. Assembly, 1983-84; bishop LDS Ch., 1993-97, stake pres., 1997—. Internat. Inst. Ecol. Econs. fellow, 1991—. Fellow Am. Agrl. Econs. Assn. (dissertation awards com. 1976-78, selected papers com. 1981-93, com. on jour. pub. 1986, fellows election com. 1991-96, 2005—, mem. pub. enduring quality com. 1998—02, Quality of Rsch. Discovery award 1977, 80, 83, 89, 90, 96, 2002, Outstanding Jour. Article award 1981, 93, Enduring Quality award 1992, 94, 98, 2003, 05); mem. Western Agrl. Econs. Assn. (editl. coun. 1982-84, Outstanding Pub. Rsch. award 1974, 83, 96, 2003, 05), Am. Econ. Assn., Royal Econ. Soc., Econometric Soc., Atlantic Econ. Soc., Alpha Zeta. Office: Agrl/Resource Econs U Md College Park MD 20742-0001

JUST, WARD SWIFT, author; b. Michigan City, Ind., Sept. 5, 1935; s. F. Ward and Elizabeth (Swift) J. Student, Lake Forest (Ill.) Acad., 1949-51, Cranbrook (Mich.) Sch., 1951-53, Trinity Coll., Hartford, Conn., 1953-57. Reporter Waukegan (Ill.) News-Sun, 1957-59, Newsweek, 1959-61, Reporter mag., 1962-63; corr. Newsweek, 1963-65, Washington Post, 1965-70; writer Vineyard Haven, Mass., 1970—. Author: To What End, 1968, A Soldier of the Revolution, 1970, Military Men, 1970, The Congressman Who Loved Flaubert and Other Washington Stories, 1973, Stringer, 1974, Nicholson at Large, 1975, A Family Trust, 1978, Honor, Power, Riches, Fame, and the Love of Women, 1979, In the City of Fear, 1982, The American Blues, 1984, The American Ambassador, 1987, Jack Gance, 1989 (Heartland prize for Fiction, Chgo. Tribune, 1989), Twenty-One Selected Stories, 1990, The Translator, 1991, Ambition & Love, 1994, Echo House, 1997, A Dangerous Friend, 1999 (Cooper prize for Fiction, Soc. Am. Historians, 1999); (play) Lowell Limpett, 2000, The Weather in Berlin, 2002, An Unfinished Season, 2004 (Heartland prize for Fiction, 2004); contbr. Best Am. Short Stories, 1972-73, 76. Recipient O. Henry award, 1985, 86, 93.

JUSTER, KENNETH IAN, lawyer, sales executive; b. New York City, Nov. 24, 1954; s. Howard H. and Muriel (Uchitelle) J. BA, Harvard U., 1976, MA in Pub. Policy, JD, Harvard U., 1980. Bar: D.C.and U.S. Dist. Ct. D.C. 1981, U.S. Ct. Appeals (D.C. cir.) 1982, U.S. Ct. Internat. Trade 1984, U.S. Ct. Appeals (Fed. cir.) 1985, U.S. Supreme Ct. 1985. Staff Nat. Security Coun., 1978; law clk. to judge U.S. Ct. Appeals (2d cir.), Brattleboro, Vt., 1980—81; assoc. Arnold and Porter, Washington, 1981—87, ptnr., 1988—89; dep., sr. adviser to the dep. Sec. of State, Washington, 1989—92; acting counselor U.S. Dept. State, Washington, 1992—93; ptnr. Arnold and Porter, Washington, 1993—97, sr. ptnr., 1998—2001; under sec. export admin. U.S. Dept. Commerce, Washington, 2001—02, under sec. industry & security, 2002—05; exec. v.p. legal affairs and corp. devel. Salesforce.com, San Francisco, 2005—. U.S. Dept. of Commerce, Washington mem. faculty Internat. Law Inst., 1987-89, 93-95; vis. fellow Coun. Fgn. Rels., Washington, 1993. Editor Harvard U. Internat. Law Jour., 1979-80; contbg. articles to profl. journals. Mem. ABA (internat. law sect., chair internat. investment and devel. com. 1994-96, coun. mem. 1996-99, chair tech. legal assistance bd. 2000-01, coun. mem. 2003-04), D.C. Bar Assn. (internat. law sect., mem. faculty continuing legal edn. program 1987-89), Am. Coun. on Germany, Coun. on Fgn. Rels., U.S., Panama Bus. Coun. (bd. mem.), Phi Beta Kappa. Office: Salesforce.com Ste 300 One Market Plaza San Francisco CA 94105 Office Phone: 415-536-8004. Business E-Mail: kjuster@salesforce.com.

JUSTICE, BLAIR (DAVID BLAIR JUSTICE), psychology educator, writer; b. Dallas, July 2, 1927; s. Sam Hugh and Lou-Reine (Hunter) J.; m. Rita Norwood, July 26, 1972; children: Cynthia, David, Elizabeth (dec.). BA, U. Tex., Austin, 1948; MS, Columbia U., 1949; MA, Tex. Christian U., 1963; PhD, Rice U., 1966. Diplomate Am. Bd. Med. Psychotherapists; cert. expert in traumatic stress. Reporter Ft. Worth Star-Telegram, 1952-55; sci. writer N.Y. Daily News, 1955-56, Ft. Worth Star-Telegram, 1956-64; sci. editor, columnist Houston Post, 1964-73; exec. asst. to Mayor Houston, 1966-72; prof. psychology Sch. Pub. Health, U. Tex., Houston, 1968—2001, prof. emeritus, 2001—; assoc. dean for acad. affairs U. Tex., Sch. Pub. Health, Houston, 1994-2000; dir. Project Support, Imagery & Immune Function in Breast Cancer, 1993-99; co-investigator Alt. Medicine Ctr. for Cancer Rsch. U. Tex. Sch. Pub. Health, Houston, 1995-98; patient advocate M.D. Anderson Cancer Ctr., Houston, 2000—. Co-investigator U. Tex. Ctr. for Alternative Med. Cancer Rsch.; sr. psychologist, group therapist, psychiat. residency faculty Tex. Rsch. Inst. Mental Scis., 1973-85; cmty. assoc. Rice U., Lovett Coll.; cons. child abuse Tex. Dept. Human Resources; faculty assoc. Ctr. for Health Promotion, R & D, U. Tex. Health Sci. Ctr., mem. inter-faculty coun., 1991-92; dir. Ctr. for Prevention of Violence and Injury, 1987-89, chmn. faculty Sch. of Pub. Health, 1990-91, chmn. faculty policy com., 1989-90, faculty marshal, 1990, mem. exec. com., 1991-93, vice chair interfaculty coun., 1992-93; vis. scholar U. Colo., 1990—; founding assoc. Blaffer Gallery U. Houston. Author: Violence in the City, 1969, Detection of Potential Community Violence, 1967, (with Rita Justice) The Abusing Family, 1976, The Broken Taboo: Sex in the Family, 1979, Perspectives in Public Mental Health, 1982, Who Gets Sick: Thinking and Health, 1987, Who Gets Sick: How Beliefs, Moods and Thoughts Affect Your Health, 1988, revised edit., 2000, The Abusing Family, rev. edit., 1990, A Different Kind of Health: Finding Well-Being Despite Illness, 1998; Visits with Violet: Lessons on How to Be Happy 100 Years, 1999; editor: Your Child's Behavior, 1972; editorial bd.: Internat. Jour Mental Health, 1980—. Gen. chmn. Houston Job Fair, 1967-73; chmn. Houston Manpower Area Planning Council, 1972-74; mem. Tex. Urban Devel. Commn., 1970-72; bd. dirs. Houston Housing Devel. Corp., Tex. Citizens Human Devel., 1979-84, Greater Houston Com. Prevention of Child Abuse, 1982-88; sec. bd. mgrs. Tarrant County Hosp., Dist., 1961-64; pres. Greater Houston Youth Council, 1978-79, Houston Area Council on Sudden Infant Death Syndrome, 1977-78; mem. nat. adv. com. Marine Biomed. Inst., U. Tex. Med. Br., 1971-84; mem. Office of Minority Affairs, Resource Persons Network, HHS, 1988—; mem. community bd. Tex. Youth Council; vestry, chmn. adult edn. St. John The Divine Episc. Ch., 1984-88. Served with USNR, 1945-46. Recipient most outstanding book award Tex. Writers Roundup, 1970, award of recognition City of Houston, 1973, Benjamin Franklin Book award Pubs. Mktg. Assn. Am., 1988, Excellence in Media award APA, 1988, Friends of Fondren Libr. book award Rice U., 1989, 91, Heritage award for child abuse rsch. Child Abuse Prevention Coun., 1989, award for outstanding contbn. to sci. Tex. Psychol. Assn., 2001, Living Principles award Internat. Assn. Transactional Analysis, 1999; named One of Five Outstanding Young Men of Tex., 1962; recipient numerous awards for sci. writing; grantee NIH. Fellow Am. Coll. Psychology, Am. Inst. Stress, Phi Beta Kappa (dir. Houston chpt. 1979-89, pres. Houston chpt. 1982-83); mem. APHA (chmn. mental health sect. 1980-81, governing coun. 1983-85, action bd. 1985-87, mental health sect. award 1989), Nat. Assn. Sci. Writers (life; exec. com. 1965-67), Houston Psychol. Assn. (pres.

1975, Lifetime Achievement award for contbn. to psychology 2002)), Knights of the Vine. Home: 6416 Sewanee St Houston TX 77005-3760 Office: 1200 Hermann Pressler Dr Houston TX 77030-3900 Office Phone: 713-500-9157. E-mail: bjustice@sph.uth.tmc.edu.

JUSTICE, FRANKLIN PIERCE, JR., oil industry executive; b. Wanego, W.Va., May 5, 1938; s. Franklin Pierce and Jeneta Ruth (Cooley) J.; m. Eva Mae Hartley, June 8, 1960; children: Kerry, Kelly, Kevin. BSBA, W.Va. State Coll., 1967; MBA in Fin., Marshall U., 1977; postgrad., U. Louisville, 1971—72. Reporter Dun & Bradstreet, Inc., Charleston, W.Va., 1960-63, reporting mgr., 1963-65, office mgr., Huntington, W.Va., 1966-68; domestic trade specialist U.S. Dept. Commerce, Charleston, 1968-70; pres., investment mgr. Equal Opportunity Fin., Inc., Ashland, Ky., 1970-93; adminstrv. asst. to v.p. personnel Ashland Oil, Inc., 1973-74, adminstrv. asst. to v.p. external affairs, 1974-75, mgr. spl. projects, 1975-76, dir. pub. affairs, 1976-78, v.p. pub. rels., 1978-82, v.p., 1985-93; v.p. ops. support Ashland Services Co., 1982-85; pres. Marshall U. Rsch. Corp., 1993-98; exec. dir. Rsch. and Econ. Devel. Ctr. Marshall U., Huntington, W.Va., 1993-95, v.p. devel., 1995-99, dir. major gifts, 2002—03; assoc. dean Southeastern CC, 1999—2000. Pres. Roundtable Venture Fund; cons. in field. Vice chmn. Ky. Ctr. for Arts, Louisville, 1982-92; bd. dirs. Ky. Coun. Econ. Edn., 1978-90, chmn. bd., 1980-83; dir. Marshall U. Bus. Adv. Bd., 1982—; exec. com. bd. dirs. W.Va. State Coll. Found., Inc., 1988-95; bd. dirs. Delta Dental of Ky. Mem. W.Va. C. of C. (life; chmn. bd. dirs. 1992-94, exec. com.), Ashland Area C. of C. (1st v.p. 1978-79, pres. 1980, bd. dirs. 1978-98), Ky. C. of C. (chmn. bd. dirs. 1983, life). Republican. Home: 4401 Hitching Post Ln Murrells Inlet SC 29576-6804 Personal E-mail: fpjemj@sc.rr.com.

JUSTICE, JACK BURTON, retired lawyer, writer; b. Hardy, Ky., Aug. 2, 1931; s. George Edward and Goldia (Alley) J.; m. Martha Monser, Dec. 28, 1957 (dec. Feb. 1974); m. Judith Farquhar Lang, Apr. 26, 1975; children—Jonathan Burton, George Lewis, Paul Williamson. AB in Polit. Sci, W.Va. U., 1952, postgrad. in law, 1954-55; BA in Jurisprudence, Oxford (Eng.) U., 1954, MA, 1960. Bar: Pa. 1956. Assoc. firm Drinker Biddle & Reath, Phila., 1956-62, ptnr., 1962-82, White & Williams, Phila., 1982-96. Bus. mgr. Am. Oxonian, 1967-86; lectr. in field. Contbr. articles to profl. and lit. jours. Pres. Youth Svc., Phila., 1962-65; chmn. Phila. Com. on City Policy, 1966-67, Southeastern Pa. chpt. Ams. for Democratic Action, 1968-70; bd. overseers William Penn Charter Sch., Phila., 1978-91, clk., 1986-89. Rhodes scholar, 1952-54. Mem. Assn. Am. Rhodes Scholars (sec. 1967-86, pres. 1986-94), Rancho Viejo North Cmty. Assn. (pres. 2003-04). Democrat. Home: 10 Coyote Pass Rd Santa Fe NM 87508

JUSTICE, RICHARD, computer company executive; married; 3 children. BSME, U. Santa Clara, 1971; MBA, Stanford U., 1974. Former mem. sales orgn. Hewlett Packard; sr. v.p. Ams. Cisco Systems, Inc., San Jose, Calif., 1996—2000, sr. v.p. worldwide field ops., 2000—. Bd. regents U. Santa Clara. Avocation: golf. Office: Cisco Systems Inc 170 W Tasman Dr San Jose CA 95134

JUSTINIANO, JOSE M., mechanical engineer; BME, Poly. U. PR, San Juan; A in Prodn. Engring., U. PR, Bayamon. Lic. profl. engr., Dept. of State P.R. Project engr. Schering Plough Products LLC, Manatí, PR, 2000—02; project and process engr. Lilly del Caribe, Carolina, PR, 2002—. Product applications engr. Honeywell, Guaynabo, PR, 1999—2000. Mem.: Coll. Engrs. and Land Surveyors P.R. (assoc.).

JUSZCZYK, JAMES JOSEPH, artist; b. Chgo., Jan. 30, 1943; s. Joseph Peter and Pauline (Polak) J.; m. Phyllis Ann Pozar, May 30, 1965 (dec. Jan. 1992). BFA, Cleve. Inst. of Art, 1966; MFA, U. Pa., 1969. Artist pvt. practice, Zurich, 1986-92; lectr., cons. Binney & Smith Liquitex Paints, Easton, Pa., 1992-94, Lascaux Colours & Restauro, Alois Diethelm AG, Zürich, Switzerland, 1995-98; lectr. Daler-Rowney USA, Cranbury, N.J., 1998—. Adj. prof. art CCNY, 1996—; presented master class workshops in acrylic techniques in the Benelux countries (Amsterdam, DeHaag, Antwerp, Brussels), 1996-99; presenter in field. One-man shows include Phila. Coll. Textiles and Sci., 1970, Rosa Esman Gallery, NYC, 1974, 76, 1978-79, Gimpel-Hanover Galerie, Zurich, 1975, 82, Galerie Christel, Stockholm, 1980, Jan Cicero Gallery, Chgo., 1980, 83, 92, Galerie S65, Aalst, Belgium, 1981, Andre Emmerich Galerie, Zurich, 1982, Galerie Konstructiv Tendens, Stockholm, 1982, Galerie Storrer, Zurich, 1987, Galerie Meissner Edition, Hamburg, 1987, Merril Lynch Internat., Zurich, 1987, ACP Viviane Ehrli Galerie, Zurich, 1988, 93-94, 97, 2000, Galerie Bruno Bucher, Poitiers, France, 1992, Galerie Vromans, Amsterdam, 1995, Fine Arts Gallery L.I. U., Southampton, 1997, Found. for Concrete and Constructivist Art, Zurich, 1991, Galerie Albergo Giardino, Ascona, Switzerland, Ann Reid Art Gallery, Princeton, NJ, 1998, Pearl Conard Gallery, Ohio State U., Mansfield, Ohio, 1999, Bohem Press Galerie Moderne Kunst, Zurich, 2001, Bohem Press, 2003, Galerie Stuker, Zurich, 2004, Look Gallery, Chgo., 2004; group exhbns. include Mondrian House Gallery, Amersfoort, Netherlands, 1999, 16 Young Artists, Inst. Contemporary Art, Phila., 1969, Eight Abstract Painters, 1978, Andre Zarre Gallery, NY, Geometry of Color, 1977, Cleve. Mus. Art, 1982, Bronx Mus. of the Arts, Editions Fanal, Basel, Paris, Saga 93, 96-2003, ACP Viviane Ehrli Gallerie Art-Frankfurt, 1994-96, Noyes Mus., Oceanville, NJ, 1994, Mus. Coopmanhus, Franeker, Netherlands, 1995, DePaul U. Art Gallery, Chgo., 1997; Forum Konkrete Kunst, Erfurt, Germany, 1998, Mus. for Moderne Kunst, Hiebuell, Germany, 1999, Hunter Coll. Times Sq. Gallery, NYC, 2001, 03, Nat. Mus. Szezecin, Poland, 2002; represented in corp. and pub. collections, AT&T, NYC, Arco. Internat.-Anaconda Aluminum, Chgo., Art Inst. Chgo., Chase Manhattan Bank, NYC, Citicorp, NYC, Lehman Bros, NYC, Madison (Wis.) Art Ctr., Merrill Lynch Internat., Zurich, Prudential Life Ins., Newark, Shearson Am. Express, NYC, Svenska Handelsbanken, Stockholm, Swiss Bank Corp., NYC, NJ State Mus., Whitney Mus. Am. Art., Mondrian House Found., Amersfoort, Netherlands, Nat. Mus. Szezecin, Poland. Student Work scholar Cleve. Inst. Art, Angel Fund award U. Pa.; Ford Found. Undergrad. grantee Cleve. Inst. Art, 1965, Pollock-Krasner Found., 1995; 50th Aniversary Print Portfolio, Am. Abstract Artist, 1987, 60th, 1997. Mem. Am. Abstract Artists. Home: 6601 Broadway #6-L Bronx NY 10471-2075 Personal E-mail: james4j@earthlink.net.

JUTTON, ROBERT FREDERICK, educational association administrator; b. Schenectady, NY, Sept. 22, 1948; s. Robert Charles and Annette Marie Jutton; m. Suzanne Janice Kraft, Aug. 21, 1973; 1 child, Allison L. BS in music edn., SUNY, Crowe Sch. of Music, 1970; MEd, Boston U., 1974; cert. of advanced study, SUNY New Paltz, 1983. Cert. sch. dist. adminstr. and supr., tchg. K-6, music K-12 NY. Music, choral tchr. Wappingers Ctrl. Sch. Dist., Wappingers Falls, NY, 1970—88; dir. music New Hackensack Reformed Ch., Wappingers Falls, 1974—2000; coord. for fine and performing arts Wappingers Ctrl. Sch. Dist., Wappingers Falls, 1988—. With U.S. Army, 1970—73, Germany. Recipient Excellence Adminstrn. award, Mid-Hudson Sch. Study Coun., 2000, Spl. Citation for Adminstr. award, NY State Arts Tchrs' Assn., 2002. Mem.: NY State ARt Tchr's Assn., Music Educators Nat. Conf., NY State Sch. Music Trchrs. Assn., Dutchess County Music Educator's Assn. Office: John Jay HS 2012 Rt 52 PO Box 38 Hopewell Junction NY 12533 Office Phone: 845-897-6729. Office Fax: 845-897-6775. E-mail: robert.jutton@wappingersschools.org.

JUVAN, DENNIS PAUL, securities trader; b. Ravenna, Ohio, Nov. 2, 1950; s. Henry William and Geraldine Ann J.; m. Vicki Ann Kline, June 10, 1995; children: Andrew, Jayne, John, Lori, David, Lisa, Danny. BS, Ashland (Ohio) U., 1973. Registered securities rep.; lic. health and life ins. V.p. Juvan Mfg., Ravenna, 1974-89, Butler Wick & Co., Kent, Ohio, 1989—. Mem. Sales and Mktg. Execs., Akron, 1998—. Bd. dirs. Leadership Portage County, Kent, Ohio, 1999—; mem. Saint Joseph's Ch., Suffield, Ohio, 1988—; 1st Dan Black belt World Black Belt Bur., 2000—, Mus. of Am. Fin. History, N.Y., 1999—. With Army N.G., 1971-77. Mem. Mfrs. Circle of Distinction, Am. Funds All Am. Team, Akron Toastmasters (treas. 1996—, sponsor Hudson chpt. 1996-2000. Roman Catholic. Avocations: tae kwon doe, running, public speaking, golf, reading. Home: 1282 Congress Lake Rd Mogadore OH 44260 Office: Butler Wick & Co PO Box 990 149 N Water St Kent OH 44240 Fax: 330-678-6515.

JUVET, RICHARD SPALDING, JR., chemistry professor; b. LA, Aug. 8, 1930; s. Richard Spalding and Marion Elizabeth (Dalton) J.; m. Martha Joy Myers, Jan. 29, 1955 (div. Nov. 1978); children: Victoria, David, Stephen, Richard P.; m. Evelyn Raeburn Elthon, July 1, 1984. BS, UCLA, 1952, PhD, 1955. Rsch. chemist Dupont, 1955; instr. U. Ill., 1955-57, asst. prof., 1957-61, assoc. prof., 1961-70; prof. analytical chemistry Ariz. State U., Tempe, 1970-95, prof. emeritus, 1995—; founding mem. Emeritus Coll., Ariz. State U., Tempe, 2005—. Vis. prof. UCLA, 1960, U. Cambridge, Eng., 1964-65, Nat. Taiwan U., 1968, Ecole Polytechnique, France, 1976-77, U. Vienna, Austria, 1989-90; air pollution chemistry and physics adv. com. EPA, HEW, 1969-72; adv. panel on advanced chem. alarm tech., devel. and engring. directorate, def. sys. divsn. Edgewood Arsenal, 1975; adv. panel on postdoctoral associateships NAS-NRC, 1991-94; mem. George C. Marshall Inst., 1998—. Author: Gas-Liquid Chromatography, Theory and Practice, 1962, Russian edit., 1966; editl. advisor Jour. Chromatographic Sci., 1969-85, Jour. Gas Chromatography, 1963-68, Analytica Chimica Acta, 1972-74, Analytical Chemistry, 1974-77; biennial reviewer for gas chromatography lit. Analytical Chemistry, 1962-76. Deacon Presbyn. Ch., 1960—, ruling elder, 1972—, commr. Grand Canyon Presbytery, 1974-76; moderator, communion com. Valley Presbyn. Ch., Scottsdale, Ariz., 1999-2001. NSF sr. postdoctoral fellow, 1964-65; recipient Sci. Exch. Agreement award to Czechoslovakia, Hungary, Romania and Yugoslavia, 1977. Fellow Am. Inst. Chemists; mem. AAAS, Am. Chem. Soc. (nat. chmn. divsn. analytical chemistry 1972-73, nat. sec.-treas. 1969-71, divsn. com. on chem. edn., subcom. on grad. edn. 1988—, councilor 1978-89, coun. com. analytical reagents 1985-95, coauthor Reagent Chemicals, 7th edit. 1986, 8th edit. 1993, 9th edit. 2000, chmn. U. Ill. sect. 1968-69, sec. 1962-63, directorate divsn. officers' caucus 1987-90), Internat. Union Pure and Applied Chemistry, Internat. Platform Assn., Am. Radio Relay League (Amateur-Extra lic.), Sigma Xi, Phi Lambda Upsilon, Alpha Chi Sigma (faculty adv. U. Ill. 1958-64, Ariz. State U. 1975-95, profl. rep.-at-large 1989-94, chmn. expansion com. 1990-92, nat. v.p. grand collegiate alchemist 1994-96, trustee ednl. found. 1994-2004). Achievements include research on gas and liquid chromatography, instrumental analysis, computer interfacing, plasma desorption mass spectroscopy. Home: 4821 E Calle Tuberia Phoenix AZ 85018-2932 Office: Ariz State U Dept Chem and Biochem Tempe AZ 85287-1604 Personal E-mail: rsjuvet@juno.com.

JUVILER, PETER HENRY, political scientist, educator; b. London, Mar. 26, 1926; s. Adolphe Adam and Katie (Henry) J.; m. Anne C. Stephens, June 20, 1982; children: Gregory, Geoffry. BE, Yale U., 1948, ME, 1949; PhD, Columbia U., 1960. Project engr. Sperry Gyroscope Co., 1949-52; tchr. polit. sci. Princeton U., 1957-58, Columbia U., 1959-60, Hunter Coll., CUNY, 1960-64; prof. Barnard Coll., 1974—, prof. emeritus, 2001—, dir. human rights studies, 2001—04. Co-dir. Columbia U. Ctr. for Study Human Rights, 1986—. Author: Revolutionary Law and Order, 1976, Freedom's Ordeal: The Struggle for Human Rights and Democracy in Post-Soviet States, 1998; co-editor, contbr. Gorbachev's Reforms: U.S. and Japanese Assessments, 1988, Human Rights for the 21st Century, 1993, Religion and Human Rights: Competing Claims?, 1999; contbr. numerous articles. With USN, 1944-46. Business E-Mail: pjuvilver@barnard.edu.

JUYAL, SHREESH C., political science professor, director; s. Ravi Datt and Kushleswari Devi Juyal; m. Zillah Amelia Muttoo, Feb. 22, 1949; children: Anshumala, Malini. Cert., Can. Inst. of Internat. Affairs, 1996; LittD, V.K.S. U., 1997. Prof. mil. Grad. Sch. Am. Mil. U., Charles Town, W.Va., 1997—; prof. polit. sci. U. Regina, Canada. Recipient Global Citizen award, Gov. Gen. Can. for UNA Can., 1995. Master: Can. Peace Rsch. Assn. (pres. 200—0); mem.: World Fedn. Sci. Workers (v.p. 1995—2005). Home: 2639 McCallum Avenue Saskatchewan Regina Canada S4S 0P6 Office: University of Regina 3737 Wascana Parkway Saskatchewan Regina Canada S4S 0A2 Office Phone: (306) 585-4202. Home Fax: (306) 585-2057; Office Fax: (306) 585-4815. Personal E-mail: shreesh.juyal@uregina.ca.

KAAKAJI, WAYEL, neurosurgeon, educator; b. Aleppo, Syria, May 19, 1967; s. Mohamed Kaakaji and Souna Nasri. BS, McGill U., 1989; MD, U. Tex., San Antonio, 1993. Surg. intern Cleve. Clinic Found., 1993—94, neurosurg. resident, 1994—99; staff neurosurgeon Neurol. and Spinal Surgery, Inc., Merrillville, Ind., 1999—2002, St. John Hosp., Detroit, 2002—. Adv. cons. EPS Pharms., Detroit. Contbr. articles to profl. jours., chapters to books. Mem.: Nat. Assn. Spine Specialists (congl. liaison), Congress of Neurol. Surgeons, Am. Assn. Neurol. Surgeons (Dewey Penehouse award 1999), Alpha Omega Alpha. Avocations: tennis, rowing, hiking. Office Phone: 219-947-6852. Personal E-mail: wkaakaj@yahoo.com.

KAATZ, LYNN ROBERT, artist, graphics designer; b. Elyria, Ohio, Apr. 28, 1945; s. Herbert and Mildred K.; m. Linda Lee Sarnovsky. Aug. 8, 1945; children: Stephanie Lyn Lugo, Tiffaney Lyn Lambert. Student, Ohio State U., 1964-65, Cooper Sch. Art, Cleve., 1965-68. Designer, art dir. Evans Type Art, Elyria, 1964-68; designer, art dir. photography, packaging, advt. Buzza Cardosa Greeting Cards, Anaheim, Calif., 1968-71; artist/prin. Calif. Graphics, Anaheim, 1972-74, Great Lakes Graphics, Elyria, 1974-81, Sportsman's Collection, Inc., Lagrange, Ohio, 1978—. Spkr. Elyria Art Coun., 1994—. Designer Ducks Unltd. 50th-yr. logo, 1985, Ohio wetlands habitat stamp/print, 1986, 89, 99, Ky. duck stamp/print, 1987; illustrations in book The Labrador Retriever; designer various corp. logs; participant in many fine art shows and exhibits. Recipient award of merit for packaging design Soc. Illustrators, 1969, Nat. Paper Box, 1971, Pacific Paper Box, 1971, Best of Show award for waterfowl Ducks Unltd., 1979, Advt. Excellence award Graphex Art Dir. Club, 1980, Plate of Yr. award Bradford Exch., 1991; named Artist of Yr. Genesse du Artist of Yr., 1994. Mem. Ohio Watercolor Soc. (bronze medal 1987), Watercolor U.S.A. (hon., Purchase award 1994), Fretted Instrument Guild Am., Ducks Unltd. (sponsor, Pallet and Chisel award 1987, Nat. Artist Yr. 1999), St. Augustine Art Assn. Republican.

KABACK, MICHAEL, medical educator; b. Phila., Sept. 1, 1938; MD, U. Pa., 1963. Diplomate Am. Bd. Med. Genetics, Am. Bd. Pediatrics. Intern Johns Hopkins Hosp., Balt., 1963—64, resident pediatrics, 1966—68; fellow molecular biology and genetics NIH, Bethesda, Md., 1964—66; mem. staff Children's Hosp., San Diego; prof. pediatrics and reproductive medicine U. Calif., San Diego. Recipient William Allan Meml. award, Am. Soc. Human Genetics, 1993, Harland Sanders award, March of Dimes, 2000. Fellow: AAAS; mem.: NAS, AMA, Soc. for Pediatric Rsch., Am. Soc. Human Genetics, Am. Coll. Med. Genetics, Am. Pediatric Soc., Am. Acad. Pediatrics. Office: Univ Calif San Diego Sch Medicine 9500 Gilman Dr La Jolla CA 92093-0930 Office Phone: 858-822-6400. Business E-Mail: mkaback@ucsd.edu.

KABAKOV, ILYA, artist; b. Dnepropetrovsk, Russia, Sept. 30, 1933; arrived in US, 1988; s. Joseph and Bertha Kabakov; m. Emilia Kabakov. Attended, Leningrad Inst. of Painting, Sculpture & Architecture; grad., Moscow Art Sch., 1951, Surikov Art Inst., 1957. Illustrator Children's Literature, 1956—, Little One, 1956—. Created 155 installations from 1983 to 2005 including Ten Characters, 1988, The Red Wagon, 1991, The Bridge, 1991, We Are Leaving Here Forever, 1991, The Life of Flies, 1992, The Boat 1993, We Live Here, 1995, One the Roof, 1996, Golden Apples, 1997, The Antenna, 1997, The Palace of Projects, 1998; public projects include The Toilet, 1992, The Blue Dish, 1992, Life With an Idiot, 1992, An Extraordinary Incident, 1995, The Fallen Sky, 1995, Wings, 1996, The Fallen Chandelier, 1997, The Old Bridge, 1998, We Are Free!, 1998, They Are Looking Down, 1999, The Fountain, 2000, The Rice Fields, 2000, The Egg, 2001, Drinking Fountain, 2003, Pianist and Musa, 2003, The Shining Circus and its Spectators, 2004; solo exhbns. include 10 Characters, 2003, House of Photography, 2003, Center of Cosmic Energy, 2003, The Empty Mus., 2004, others. Recipient Best Show award, Internat. Art Critic Assn., 1997.

KABALIN, JOHN NICHOLAS, urologist; b. L.A., Dec. 23, 1958; s. Nicholas Augustin and Mary Jane (Engleman) Kabalin; m. Pamela Grace White, July 11, 1981. BS, Stanford U., 1980; MD, Johns Hopkins U., 1984. Diplomate Am. Bd. Urology. Intern in surgery Stanford U. Med. Ctr., 1984-85, resident in surgery, 1985-86, resident in urology, 1986-90, chief resident in urology, 1989-90; chief urology sect. Va Med. Ctr., Palo Alto, Calif., 1990-97; asst. prof. urology Stanford (Calif.) U., 1990-97; asst. prof. surgery U. Nebr. Coll. Medicine, 1999—. Contbr. over 100 articles to profl. jours., over 20 chpts. in books. Fellow: ACS, Sexual Medicine Soc. of N. Am., Am. Soc. for Laser Medicine and Surgery, Internat. Coll. Surgeons; mem.: AAAS, AMA, Am. Bd. Forensic Medicine, N.Y. Acad. Scis., Internat. Soc. Urology, Biomed. Optics Soc., Am. Lithotripsy Soc., Endourol. Soc., Soc. Univ. Urologists, Soc. Urol. Oncology, Am. Soc. Clin. Oncology, Am. Urol. Assn., Am. Assn. Clin. Urologists, Alpha Omega Alpha, Phi Beta Kappa. Roman Catholic. Achievements include adaptation and clinical development of Holmium laser sources for soft tissue and prostatic surgery. Office: Ste 2200 3911 Ave B Scottsbluff NE 69361-4669 Office Phone: 308-632-5315.

KABANOVA-BARNETT, TATIANA VALENTINOVNA, journalist, critic; b. Tumen, Russia, June 8, 1956; arrived in U.S., 2001; d. Valentine A. Kabanov and Nadezda A. Gotina; m. John Francis Barnett, July 19, 2001. BA, Kyrgyz State U., Frunze, Kyrgyzstan, 1973, MA, 1978; PhD in Lit., Moscow State U., 1983; prof. (hon.), Kygyz Conservatory of Music, Bishkek, Kyrgyz Republic, 1991. Asst. prof. fgn. lit. Kyrgyz State U., Frunze, Kyrgyzstan, 1984—95; chair dept. world culture Kyrgyz State Conservatory of Music, Bishkek, 1992—97; journalist Meerim mag., 1998—2000; ind. scholar, lectr. ILR, Hamden, Conn. Author essays. Grantee Münster U., Germany, 1992, Beinecke Libr., Yale U., 1995; Fulbright fellow, 1994—95. Mem.: MLA, Internat. Soc. for the Studies in Romanticism, Am. Lit. Assn., Thornton Wilder Soc.

KABBES, DOUGLAS JOHN, physician; b. Effingham, Ill., Oct. 27, 1959; s. John Robert and Jane Claire K.; m. Cheryl Ann Gennaro, Oct. 27, 1990; children: Courtney, Connor, Christa. BA with honors, So. Ill. U., 1981, MD, 1985. Diplomate Am. Bd. Family Practice. Dir., chmn. dept. emer. medicine St. Anthony's Hosp., Effingham, Ill., 1997—. Founder, CEO Emergency Cons., Effingham, 1999—; founding ptnr. Effingham Ptnrs. progress, 1999—; founder KKG Devel. Corp., 1995—, pres., 1995-97; founding ptnr. Kabbes Properties, Inc., Effingham, 1994—; founder, pres. Effingham State Bank Land Trust 1951, 1997—; ptnr. Nat. Trail LLC, Effingham. Chmn. ch. picnic St. Anthony's Ch., Effingham, 1994; mem. adv. bd. St. Anthony's Hosp., Effingham, 1996-2001; tech. planning com. St. Anthony's Sch., Effingham, 1996, mem. sch. bd.; v.p. Effingham chpt. Am. Cancer Soc. So. Ill. U. Pres. scholar, 1977-81. Mem. Am. Coll. Emergency Physicians, Am. Acad. Family Physicians, Am. Coll. Physicians Execs., KC, Phi Eta Sigma. Republican. Roman Catholic. Avocations: golf, travel, real estate development. Home: 903 Park Hills Dr Effingham IL 62401 Office: St Anthony's Meml Hosp 503 N Maple Effingham IL 62401 E-mail: DougKabbes@hotmail.com.

KABEL, ROBERT JAMES, lawyer; b. Burbank, Calif., Nov. 30, 1946; s. Herman James and Margaret Elizabeth (Doyle) K. BA, Denison U., 1969; JD, Vanderbilt U., 1972; LL.M. in Taxation, Georgetown U., 1979. Bar: D.C., Tenn., Ohio, U.S. Supreme Ct. Adminstrv. asst. to Gov. Winfield Dunn of Tenn., Nashville, 1972-75; legis. asst. to Senator Paul Fannin, Washington, 1975-77; legis. dir. Senator Richard G. Lugar of Ind., Washington, 1977-82; spl. asst. to pres. White House, Washington, 1982-84; ptnr. Manatt, Phelps & Phillips and precedessor firm, Washington, 1985—2002; of counsel Baker & Daniels, Washington, 2002—; sr. cons. B & D Sagamore, Washington, 2002—. Part-time mem. Fgn. Claims Settlement Commn., 1987-91. Mem. Bretton Woods Commn.; Vanderbilt Law Sch. Alumni Bd., 1997-2000; bd. trustees Denison U., 1999—; chmn. bd. dirs. Log Cabin Reps., 1994-99; chmn. Liberty Edn., 1999—2005; mem. D.C. Rep. Com.; chmn. AIDS Responsibility Project 2004-; mem. Rep. Nat. Com. Recipient citation Denison U. Alumni. Mem. ABA, Rep. Lawyers Assn., Denison U. Alumni Soc. (pres. 1994-96), Met. Club Washington, The Federalist Soc. Republican. Presbyterian. Office: Baker & Daniels 805 15th St NW Ste 700 Washington DC 20005 Office Phone: 202-312-7408. E-mail: Robert.Kabel@bakerd.com.

KABEL, ROBERT LYNN, chemical engineering professor; b. Champaign, Ill., Apr. 3, 1932; s. Myron Charles and Marietta Louise (Lynn) K.; m. Barbara Jean Robb, June 8, 1958; children: Joseph Robb, Douglas Alan. BS, U. Ill., 1955; PhD, U. Wash., 1961. Registered profl. engr., Pa. Engr. Conoco, Ponca City, Okla., 1954, Sun Oil Co., Marcus Hook, Pa., 1955, Chevron Rsch. Co., LaHabra and Richmond, Calif., 1967, 68; rsch. scientist NASA Ames Rsch. Ctr., Palo Alto, Calif., 1969; engr. Exxon, Linden, N.J., 1976-78; prof. chem. engring. Pa. State U., University Park, 1963—. Invitational prof. chem. and bioengring. Ariz. State U., Tempe, 1984-85; vis. prof. Tech. U. Norway, Trondheim, 1971-72, Pahlavi U., Shiraz, Iran, 1978, U. N.S.W., Sydney, Australia, 1988, 89, U. Canterbury, Christchurch, New Zealand, 1989, Chulalongkorn U., Bangkok, 1989; co-editor/author: Scaleup of Chemical Processes, 1985; cons. in field. Co-author: Sources and Control of Air Pollution, 1998. Bd. dirs. Oreg.-Calif. Trails Assn., 1999-2002. With USAF, 1961-63. Decorated Air Force Commendation medal; recipient Outstanding Tchg. award Amoco Found., 1983, award for Excellence in Instrn., Western Electric, 1983, Nat. Catalyst award for Excellence in Chem. Tchg., Chem. Mfrs. Assn., 1984, Disting. Achievement award Ariz. State U., 1985, Corcoran award ASEE, 1989, Disting. Vol. award Oreg.-Calif. Trials Assn., 2003; ASEE fellow, 1969, Royal Norwegian Coun. for Sci. and Indsl. Rsch. fellow, 1971-72, NATO fellow, 1974, Erskine fellow, 1989. Fellow AIChE (editl. bd. 1980-85); mem. Am. Chem. Soc., Sigma Xi, Phi Lambda Upsilon, Alpha Chi Sigma, Tau Beta Pi, Phi Eta Sigma. Republican. Presbyterian. Office: 130 Fenske Lab University Park PA 16802-4400 Business E-Mail: r8k@psu.edu.

KABEL, STEVE, construction executive; m. Kathleen Kabel; 2 children. Grad., Ca. Polytechnic U., U. So. Ca. Lic. building contractor, Ca. Regional pres. WL Homes, Inc., 1998—. Office: WL Homes 895 Dove St Ste 200 Newport Beach CA 92660-2979

KAC, VICTOR G., mathematician, educator; b. Buguruslan, USSR, Dec. 19, 1943; came to U.S., 1977; s. Gersh and Clara (Landman) K.; m. Elena Bourdenko; children: Luba, Marianne. Diploma, Moscow State U., 1965, cand. of sci., 1968. Asst. Moscow Inst. Electronic Machine Bldg., 1968-71; sr. tchr. MIEM, Moscow, 1971-76; assoc. prof. MIT, Cambridge, Mass., 1977-81, prof., 1981—. Author two books on infinite-dimensional Lie algebras, a book on vertex algebra and a book on quantum calculus; contbr. numerous articles to profl. jours. Recipient Medal Coll. de France, 1981, Wigner medal Group Theory Found., 1994; Guggenheim fellow, 1985, Sloan fellow, 1981. Mem. Am. Math. Soc., Moscow Math. Soc. (hon.). Achievements include structure and representation theory of infinite-dimensional groups and algebras that arise in mathematics and physics. Home: 273 Mason Ter Brookline MA 02446 Office: MIT Math Dept 77 Massachusetts Ave Cambridge MA 02139-4307 Office Phone: 617-253-2945. Business E-Mail: kac@math.mit.edu.

KACHERGIS, JOYCE W., book designer; b. Omaha, Feb. 9, 1925; d. Lawrence Benjamin Webster and Olga Agnes Olsen; m. George J. Kachergis, July 6, 1946 (dec. Aug. 1974); children: Peter W., Karl George, Anne Olga; m. Jess G. Bell, 1986 (dec. Apr. 2001). AA, Stephens Coll., 1945; BFA, Sch. of the Art Inst., Chgo., 1947. Prodn. design mgr. U. N.C. Press, Chapel Hill, 1963-77; prodn. and design mgr. Stanford U. Press, Palo Alto, Calif., 1977-80; founder, pres., designer Kachergis Book Design, Pittsboro, N.C., 1980—. Vis. prof. Radcliffe Sch. Pub., Cambridge, Mass., 1979-82. Mem. Am. Assn. Univ. Presses (bd. dirs. 1978-80). Office: Kachergis Book Design 14 Small St N Pittsboro NC 27312-5453 Personal E-mail: jwkb@mindspring.com.

KACULI, XHEMAL T., oil industry analysis engineer; B in Mech. Engring., Poly. U. Albania, Tirana, 1995; M in Engring. Sci., Lamar U., 1999, D in Engring., 2002. Lic. profl. engr., Tex. Rschr. Lamar U., Beaumont, Tex., 1997—2003; engring. analysis and design, product devel. dept. Dril-Quip, Inc., Houston, 2001. Contbr. articles to profl. jours. Pres. Albanian Am. Assn., Houston, 2002—04. Fellow, Lamar U., 2001—02; scholar, 1998, 1999, 2000. Mem.: ASME, Nanotechnology Inst., Am. Soc. Metals, Am. Soc. Petroleum Engrs. Achievements include research in effect of mechanical alloying and bulk shear processing on the quality of Tungsten Carbide Tool products; microstructure and properties of mechanical alloyed and equal channel angular extruded Tungsten Carbide; integration of mechanical alloying and equal channel angular extrusion for production of nanostructured materials; application of mechanical alloying and bulk shear processing to produce superior quality oil field tool products; use of mechanical alloying and ECAE for production of nanostructured titanium silicide; patents for ball valve assembly. Office Phone: 281-216-7644. Personal E-mail: kaculi@hotmail.com.

KACZANOWSKI, WITOLD, painter, sculptor; b. Warsaw, May 15, 1932; arrived in US, 1968; s. Feliks and Zofia Kaczanowski; divorced; children: Paul, Paulina, Wit. Grad., Fine Art Acad., Warsaw, 1956. Exhibitions include Otis Inst., LA, 1973, Represented in permanent collections Conoco Oil Co., Houston, United Calif. Bank, Beverly Hills. Achievements include Co-designer Auschwitz Cultural Ctr. Home: 329 Detroit St Denver CO 80206

KACZKA, JEFF, trucking/relocation services executive; CFO I-Net, 1995—96, Wang, 1996—98, Allied Worldwide, Naperville, Ill., 1999—2001; sr. v.p., CFO Owens & Minor, Inc., Richmond, Va., 2001—. Office: Owens-Minor Inc 4800 Cox Rd Richmond VA 23261-7626

KACZMARCZYK, JEFFREY ALLEN, journalist, music critic; b. Patuxent River Naval Air Base, Md., Jan. 7, 1963; s. Frank Joseph and Diane Catherine Kaczmarczyk; m. Cynthia L. Shimmel, Aug. 13, 1988; children: Jessica, Michael, David. BA, Western Mich. U., 1986; postgrad., Calif. State U. Editor-in-chief Western Herald, Kalamazoo, Mich., 1986-87; staff writer, acting editor Albion (Mich.) Recorder, 1987; staff writer, columnist Hastings (Mich.) Banner, 1987-92; arts writer, classical music critic The Grand Rapids (Mich.) Press, 1992—. Freelance arts writer, critic Kalamazoo (Mich.) Gazette, 1990-93; editor The Weekender, Hastings, 1991-93. Dir., sec. Thornapple Arts Coun., Hastings, 1992-97; dir. Grand Rapids Area Coun. for Humanities, 1995-2001; vestryman Emmanuel Episcopal Ch., Hastings, 1997-99, sr. warden, 1999. Episcopalian. Office: The Grand Rapids Press 155 Michigan St NW Grand Rapids MI 49503-2353 Home: 819 E Grant St Hastings MI 49058-1323 Office Phone: 616-222-5585. Business E-Mail: jkaczmarczyk@grpress.com.

KACZMAREK, JANE, actress; b. Dec. 21, 1955; d. Edward and Evelyn Kaczmarek; m. Bradley Whitford; 3 children. BFA in Theatre, U. Wis.; MFA, Yale Sch. Drama, 1982. Actor: (TV series) Malcolm in the Middle (nominated for 3 Golden Globe awards for best performance actress tv series, nominated for 4 Emmy awards for outstanding lead actress comedy series, Am. Comedy award, Family Friendly award, 2 Individual Achievement in a Comedy awards, TV Critics Assn., nominated best actress quality comedy, Viewers for Quality TV), St. Elsewhere, Felicity, American Playhouse, The Paper Chase-The Second Year (ACE nomination), Hometown, Equal Justice, Big Wave Dave's, Party of Five, Frasier, The Practice, Cybill, (guest appearances) Touched by an Angel, Picket Fences, L.A. Law, Hollywood Division,; (TV films) All's Fair, 1989, Apollo 11, 1996, Educating Mom, 1996, Jenifer, 2001, The Deception, Boys Will Be Boys, I'll Take Manhattan, Something About Amelia, The Christmas Story, The Three Kings; (films) The Chamber, 1996, The Spittin' Image, 1997, Pleasantville, 1998, Wildly Available, 1999, Vice Versa, Uncommon Valor, D.O.A., The Heavenly Kid, Falling in Love; (plays, Broadway) Lost in Yonkers; (plays) Kindertransport, Raised in Captivity, Wasp, Escape from Happiness, Eve's Diary, Pride and Prejudice, The Legends of Oedipus, Loose Ends, Ice Cream/Hot Fudge, Better Living, Hands of Its Enemy.

KACZMAREK, JORUNN SIGRI, music educator; b. LaCrosse, Wis., May 14, 1972; d. Dale A. and Judith A. Anderson; m. Maciej Kaczmarek, Jan. 2, 1994. BA in Music Edn., Boston U., 1994. Lic. music educator Mass., 1994. Music dir. Lafayette Sch., Everett (Mass.) Pub. Schs.; owner Kaczmarek Music Studio, Bradford, Mass., 1994—. Violin instr. Foxboro (Mass.) Pub. Schs., 1994—96, Needham (Mass.) Pub. Schs., 1997—2000; Meml. Day show musical dir. Everett Music Dept., 2002—02; co-dir. Everett All-City Orch.; all-city choral dir. Everett Pub. Schs., Everett. Composer: (musical compositions for strings) Various String Ensemble Works. Recipient Golden Apple award, Everett Pub. Schools, 1999, 2001; grantee, Everett Bus. Coop., 2003, 2004. Mem.: Music Educators Nat. Conf., Am. String Tchrs. Assn. Home: 43 Valley View Farm Rd Bradford MA 01835 Office: Everett Public Schools 117 Edith St Everett MA 02149 Personal E-mail: kaczmarekstudio@hotmail.com.

KACZOROWSKI, GREGORY JOHN, biochemist, researcher, science administrator; b. South Bend, Ind., Nov. 20, 1949; s. John Walter and Jean (Bankowski) K.; m. Maria L. Garcia, June 21, 1982. BS in Chemistry summa cum laude, U. Notre Dame, 1972; PhD in Biochemistry, MIT, 1977. Helen Hay Whitney postdoctoral rsch. fellow Roche Inst. Molecular Biology, 1977-80; sr. rsch. biochemist Merck Inst. for Therapeutic Rsch., Rahway, N.J., 1980-84, assoc. dir. dept. membrane biochemistry and biophysics, 1986-88, dir., 1988-96, sr. dir., 1996—; rsch. fellow Biochemistry, Fundamental and Exploratory Rsch., Rahway, 1984-86. Reviewer NIH, NSF, U.S.-Israel Binational Sci. Found.; invited speaker, presenter papers at various profl. meetings; adj. prof. dept. pharmacology and physiology Robert Wood Johnson Med. Sch., UMDNJ, 2005—. Contbr. numerous articles, revs. to profl. jours.; patentee in field. Hoosier scholar, 1968-72, Notre Dame scholar, 1968-72. Mem. AAAS, Am. Chem. Soc., Am. Soc. Biol. Chemists, Am. Physiol. Soc., Biophys. Soc., N.Y. Acad. Sci., Phi Beta Kappa. Home: 5 Ashbrook Dr Edison NJ 08820-4318 Office: Merck Sharp & Dohme Rsch Labs PO Box 2000 Rahway NJ 07065-0900 Office Phone: 732-594-7565. Business E-Mail: gregory_kaczorowski@merck.com.

KADAKIA, SHIRISH, information technology manager; BS in Mech. Engring. with distinction, MS U., India; MS in Indsl./Systems Engring., U. Houston; MBA degree equivalent courses, AT&T Bus. Edn. Ctr. Mem. tech. staff Bell Labs, 1977—82; bus. svcs. mgr. AT&T Packet/E-Mail/Video/SDN Svcs., 1982—91; program mgr. AT&T Global ATM/Frame Relay Networks Operations, 1991—99; dist. mgr. transport, telemetry and data networks engring. AT&T, NJ, 2000—. Recipient Global Product Mgmt. Appreciation for Outstanding Effort award, 1993, Global BMS Way to Go award, 1995, 1997, 1998, Govt. Market Commitment to Excellence award, 1996, Global BMS Five Star Team award, 1996, V.P. Culture in Action award, 2002.

KADANOFF, LEO PHILIP, physicist, educator; b. NYC, Jan. 14, 1937; s. Abraham and Celia (Kibrick) Kadanoff; children: Marcia, Felice, Betsy. AB, Harvard U., 1957, MA, 1958, PhD, 1960. Fellow Neils Bohr Inst., Copenhagen, 1960—61; from asst. prof. to prof. physics U. Ill., Urbana, 1961—69; prof. physics and engring., univ. prof. Brown U., Providence, 1969—78; prof. physics U. Chgo., 1978—82, John D. MacArthur Disting. Service prof., 1982—. Mem. tech. com. R.I. Planning Program, 1972—78, mem. human svcs. rev. com., 1977—78; pres. Urban Obs. R.I., 1972—78. Author: Electricity Magnetism and Heat, 1967; co-author: Quantum Statistical Mechanics, 1963; adv. bd. Sci. Year, 1975—79, editl. bd. Statis. Physics, 1972—79, Nuc. Physics, 1980—. Recipient Wolf Found. prize, 1980, Boltzmann medal, Internat. Union Pure and Applied Physics, 1990, Grande Medaille d'Or, Acad. Scis. Inst. France, 1998, Nat. med. Sci., 1999; fellow NSF, 1957—61, Sloan Found., 1963—67. Fellow: Am. Acad. Arts and Scis., Am. Phys. Soc. (Buckley prize 1977, Onsager prize 1998); mem.: NAS. Home: 5421 S Cornell Ave Apt 15 Chicago IL 60615-5678 Office: U Chgo James Franck Inst 5640 S Ellis Ave Chicago IL 60637-1433

KADAR, AVRAHAM, immunologist; b. Rishon Le Zion, Israel, Nov. 13, 1950; s. Yosef and Amalia (Hayon) K.; m. Naomi Carol Prawer, Sept. 2, 1976; children: Maya, Nadav, Einat. BS in Physics, Hebrew U., Jerusalem, 1972; MD, Sackler Sch. Medicine, Tel Aviv, Israel, 1983. Diplomate Am. Bd. Pediatrics, Am. Bd. Diagnostic Lab. Immunology, Am. B. Allergy and Immunology, Am. Bd. Medicine. Intern Tel-Hashomer, Ramat Gan, Israel, 1982, Albert Einstein Coll. of Medicine, N.Y.C., 1983, resident, 1984-86, asst. prof., 1989-92, asst. clin. prof., 1992—; fellow NIH, Bethesda, Md., 1986-89. Immunology cons. Pediatric HIV Primary Care, N.Y.C., 1989—. Mem. AAAS, N.Y. Acad. Scis. Avocations: classical music, literature. Home: 5 Woodland Ct Bedford NY 10506-2034 Office: 530 Park Ave New York NY 10021-8015 also: 666 Lexington Ave Mount Kisco NY 10549-3632

KADAR, KARIN PATRICIA, librarian; b. Oil City, Pa., May 30, 1951; d. Michael Joseph and Bette Lee (Painter) Kadar; divorced; 1 child, Michael L. BS, Clarion U., 1973; MLS, U. Pitts., 1975; postgrad., U. S.C. Lic. instrnl. II in libr. sci. and elem. edn., pub. libr. lic. Substitute tchr. McKeesport (Pa.) Area Schs., 1973, elem. sch. libr., 1973-75, 3d grade tchr., 1975-78, elem. sch. libr., 1978-81; adj. prof. Pa. State U., McKeesport, 1988; periodicals libr. Seton Hill Coll., Greensburg, Pa., 1986-89; dir. Penn Twp. Pub. Libr., Level Green, Pa., 1989-90; grade sch. libr. substitute St. Agnes Sch., North Huntington, Pa., 1992; mid. sch. libr. substitute Belle Vernon (Pa.) Area Sch. Dist., 1993-95; dir. West Newton (Pa.) Pub. Libr., 1993-95, Highland Cmty. Libr., Richland, Pa., 1996; libr. Ridgeland (S.C.) Elem. Sch., 1996-98; spl. orders coord. Barnes and Noble, Hilton Head Island, SC, 1998-99; mgr. Bluffton (S.C.) Cmty. Libr., 1998-99; media specialist Jasper (S.C.) County H.S., 1999—2001, dist. libr./ media specialist coord., 1999—; sch. tech. coord. West Hardeeville Sch., 2001—, media specialist, 2002—. Mem. consumer appeals bd. Ford Motor Co., 1989-92, coord. Sch. Dist. Libr. Media Svcs., 2000—; staff writer Current Diversions. Author: (booklet) Sammy the Smokeless Dragon, 1976. Panelist Scan Trak Shoppers, 1984—, Nat. Family Opinion, 1984—; vol. Am. Cancer Soc., 1969-94, pub. edn. chmn., 1974-80, cancer prevention study II chmn., 1982-88, pub. affairs chmn., 1984-86, residential area crusade chmn., 1984-85. Named Vol. of Yr. Am. Cancer Soc. Mon Youch Unit, 1983-84; recipient Crusade award Am. Cancer Soc., Mon Yough unit, 1985-86. Mem. ALA, Pa. Libr. Assn., Parent-Tchr. Guild, Pa. State Edn. Assn., Low Country Reading Assn. (pres-elect), S.C. Assn. Sch. Librs. (regional rep. Jasper County, writer and mem. editl. bd. Messenger), Westmoreland County Hist. Soc., McKeesport Coll. Club, Heritage Hist. Assn. (Hilton Head, S.C.). Avocations: freelance writing, collecting books, genealogical research. Office: West Hardeeville Sch Hwy 46 Hardeeville SC 29927 Office Phone: 843-717-1251. Personal E-mail: kkadar@jcsd.net.

KADEL, PAULA RUTH RITCHIE, public relations executive; b. Salisbury, NC, July 12, 1946; d. Paul Wilson and Mary Ruth (Ketner) Ritchie; m. Thomas Edward Kadel, Aug. 23, 1969 (div. May 1994). BA, Lenoir-Rhyne Coll., 1968; MEd, N.C. State U., 1969; MA, La Salle U., Phila., 1985. Psychiat. caseworker S.C. State Hosp., Columbia, 1969-71; copy editor Luth. Ch. in Am., Phila., 1971-72, 73-75, asst. editor, 1975-76, assoc. editor, 1976; planning analyst S.C. Office Econ. Opportunity, Columbia, 1972-73; coord. promotion and interpretation Luth. Ch. Women, Phila., 1976-87; v.p. for project mgmt. Genesis Communications, Inc., Plymouth Meeting, Pa., 1988-92; dir. found. and corp. rels. Luth. home, Germantown, 1992-95; mgr. mktg. and comm. Ken-Crest Svcs., Plymouth Meeting, 1995—. Mem. comm. unit Nat. Ch. of Chs., N.Y.C., 1984—92; mem. planning com. Religious Comm. Congress, Nashville, 1986—. Mem. Evang. Luth. Ch. Am. Recipient Neo-Graphics award, Graphics Arts Soc., 1985. Mem.: LWV, Assn. Fundraising Profls., Religious Pub. Rels. Coun. (nat. pres. 1986—88, DeRosa-Hinkhouse award 1983, 1984, 1986), Pub. Rels. Soc. Am., Assn. Luth. Devel. Democrat. Lutheran. Office: Ken-Crest Svcs 502 W Germantown Pike Plymouth Meeting PA 19462 Office Phone: 610-825-9360. E-mail: pkadel@kencrest.org.

KADEMANI, DEEPAK, oral surgeon; DMD, U. Pa., 1997, MD, 2000. Asst. prof. surgery Mayo Clinic Coll. Medicine, Rochester, Minn., 2003—. Dir. maxillofacial oncologic surgery, co-dir. rsch. Mayo Clinic Coll. Medicine, 2004. Scholar, Mayo Clinic, 2003; fellow Head and Neck Surgery, Legacy Emanuel Hosp., Portland, 2003—04. Mem.: Am. Head And Neck Soc., Internat. Assn. Oral And Maxillofacial Surgeons, Brit. Assn. Oral And Maxillofacial Surgeons, Am. Assn. Oral And Maxillofacial Surgeons (Faculty Edn. award 2004, Faculty Devel. award). Office: Mayo Clinic 200 First St Rochester MN 55905 Office Phone: 507-538-1943.

KADEN, ELLEN ORAN, lawyer, consumer products company executive; b. N.Y.C., Oct. 1, 1951; m. Lewis Kaden; 2 children. AB, Cornell U., 1972; MA, U. Chgo., 1973; JD, Columbia U., 1977. Bar: N.Y., 1978. Law clerk U.S. Dist. Ct. (so. dist.) N.Y., 1977-78; asst. prof. Columbia U. Sch. Law, 1978-82, assoc. prof., 1982-84; exec. v.p., gen. counsel, sec. CBS Inc., NYC, 1991-98; sr. v.p. law and govt. affairs Campbell Soup Co., Camden, NJ, 1988—. Reporter jud. coun. 2nd Cir. Adv. Comm. on Planning for Dist. Cts., 1979-81; assoc. Cravath, Swaine & Moore, 1981-86. Trustee Columbia U. Office: Campbell Soup Co One Campbell Pl Camden NJ 08103

KADEN, LEWIS B., lawyer, educator; b. 1942; AB, Harvard U., 1963, LLB, 1967. Bar: NY 1970, NJ 1974. Harvard scholar Emmanuel Coll., Cambridge U., 1963-64; law clk. U.S. Ct. Appeals, 1967; legis. asst. Senator Robert F. Kennedy, 1968; ptnr. Battle, Fowler, Stokes & Kheel, 1969-73; chief counsel to gov. State of N.J., 1974-76; assoc. prof. Columbia U., 1976-79, prof., 1979-84, adj. prof., 1984—, dir. Ctr. for Law and Econ. Studies, 1979-83; ptnr. Davis, Polk & Wardwell, N.Y.C., 1984—2005; vice chmn., chief adminstrv. officer Citigroup, Inc., 2005—. Chmn. U.S. Govt. Overseas Presence Adv. Panel, 1999. Chmn. NY State Indsl. Coop. Coun., 1986—92. Office: Citigroup Inc 399 Park Ave 2nd Fl New York NY 10022 Business E-Mail: kaden@citigroup.com.

KADER, NANCY STOWE, nursing consultant, consultant, philosopher; b. Ogden, Utah, May 29, 1945; d. William Hessel and Mildred (Madsen) Stowe; m. Omar Kader, Jan. 25, 1967; children: Tarik, Gabriel, Aron, Jacob. BSN, Brigham Young U., 1967; Ph.D., U. Md., 2005. RN. Nurse ICU Glendale (Calif.) Adventist Hosp., 1970-75, Utah Valley Hosp., Provo, 1975-83; campaign coord. Matheson for Gov., Salt Lake City, 1976-85, Wilson for Senate, Salt Lake City, 1980; nurse cons. MESA Corp., Reston, Va., 1984—85; mgr. cost containment Health Mgmt. Strategies, Washington, 1985-88; nurse cons. Birch & Davis, Washington, 1988-90; cons. Inst. Medicine NAS, Washington, 1990-92; cons. Pal-Tech Inc., Arlington, Va., 1992—. Vice chmn. Utah State Bd. Nursing, Salt Lake City, 1977—83; adj. prof. Hood Coll., Md., 2000; ethics cons. to Healthcare Systems, Washington; cons. in field. Dem. county chmn., Utah, 1977-79; del. Dem. Nat. Conv., 1980; del. Va. State Dem. Conv., 1984-95; vice chmn. Gov.'s Commn. on Status of Women, Salt Lake City, 1975-78; bd. dirs. Health Systems Agy. of No. Va., 2000—. Democrat. Home: 10301 Dunfries Rd Vienna VA 22181

KADING, KEVIN HENRY, brokerage house executive, securities trader; b. Sharon, Conn., Sept. 21, 1957; s. Henry Herbert and Anne Ruth (Phillips) K.; m. Laurette Margaret Quirk, Oct. 22, 1983; 1 child, Kaitlin Margaret. Student, Bennett Coll., 1977. Br. mgr. First Jersey, N.Y.C., 1979-87; regional v.p. Sherwood Group, N.Y.C., 1987-88; mgr. Hibbard Brown, N.Y.C., 1988; v.p. J.T. Moran, N.Y.C., 1988-90; assoc. Baird Patrick, N.Y.C., 1990-94; pres. Consol. Holdings. Corp., N.Y.C., 1990-93, also pres. bd. dirs.; pres., sole shareholder The Wellington Group, N.Y.C., 1994—95; pres., dir. Avery Comms., 1993-94; pres. bd. dirs. Kading Cos., S.A., 1995—. Treas. dir. QMT Restaurant and Catering, N.Y.C., 1988-90; chmn. Advanced Reconnaissance Corp., 2002-; cofounder Syringex Med., Inc., 1998-; pres. CKL Assoc., 1997-. Republican. Methodist. Office: Kading Companies SA 48 Wall St Staten Island NY 10005-4556 Business E-Mail: kkading@kadvrecom.com.

KADIR, DJELAL, literature educator; b. St. Theodoros, Larnaca, Cyprus, Jan. 21, 1946; m. Juana Celia Cohen, May 24, 1969; 1 child, Aixé. BA, Yale U., 1969; PhD, U. N.M., 1972. Prof., chair comparative lit. Purdue U., West Lafayette, Ind., 1973-91; Disting. prof. lit. U. Okla., Norman, 1991-95, Neustadt prof. comparative lit., 1995-97; E.E. Sparks prof. of comparative lit. Pa. State U., 1998—; dir. Internat. Sch. Theory in Humanities, 1999—2001; founding pres. Internat. Am. Studies Assn., 2000. Editor World Literature Today, U. Okla., Norman, 1991-96; cons. Libr. Congress, Washington, 1975—; vis. scholar Russian Acad. Scis., Moscow, 1992; lectr. in field; sr. rsch. assoc. U. Leipzig, 1994—, Borges Ctr., Aarhus U. Denmark; bd. dirs. Coun. on Nat. Lits., Internat. Writers Ctr.; sr. rsch. fellow, mem. exec. bd. Internat. Sch. of Theory in the Humanities, Santiago, Spain, 1997-99; sr. fellow, mem. internat. bd. Synapsis: European Sch. Comparative Studies, 2000—. Author: Juan Carlos Onetti, 1977, Questing Fictions, 1986, Columbus and the Ends of the Earth, 1992, The Other Writing, 1993; editor, translator selected poetry of Joao Cabral de Melo Neto, 1994; editor: Longman Anthology of World Literature, 2003, Oxford History of Latin American Literature, 2004; mem. editl. bd. PMLA 1998-2002. Mem. State Arts Coun. Okla., Oklahoma City, 1991-96; cons. Indpls. Mus. Art.; v.p. UNESCO Commn. for Ency. Life Support Sys., 2005-. Resident fellow Rockefeller Found., Bellagio, Italy, 1993, 2000. Mem. MLA (chmn. Del. Assembly 1999-2000), Internat. Comparative Lit. Assn. (exec. bd. com. Lit. Histories, 1992—, chmn. com. on theory 1998—), Am. Comparative Lit. Assn., Internat. Found. Global Studies (sec. 1998-2000), Internat. Coll. Global Studies (v.p. 1998-2000). Avocations: music (cello), hiking, horseback riding, polo. Office: Dept Comparative Lit PA State U 311 Burrowes Bldg University Park PA 16802-6203 Business E-Mail: dxk50@psu.edu.

KADISH, RICHARD L., lawyer; b. Newark, Dec. 1, 1943; s. Irving Jerome and Henrietta (Appleblatt) K.; m. Bethany Tortis, Aug. 6, 1972; children: Jennifer, Andrew, Jill. BA, U. Pa., 1965; MA, Rutgers U., 1968, JD, 1970. Deputy atty. gen. N.J. Atty Gen., Trenton, N.J., 1971-74; deputy exec. dir. N.J. Housing Fin. Agy., Trenton, N.J., 1974-77; sr. v.p. CRI Inc., Rockville, Md., 1978-87, exec. v.p., 1987-94; pres. Capital Apt. Properties, Inc., Rockville, Md., 1994-97, CAPREIT, Inc., Rockville, Md., 1998—. Dir. Nat. Multifamily Housing Coun. Mem. ABA, N.J. Bar Assn. Office: CAPREIT Ste 100 11200 Rockville Pike Rockville MD 20852-3154 Business E-Mail: dkadish@capreit.com.

KADISH, RONALD T., retired career military officer; BS in Chemistry, St. Joseph's U., 1970; MBA, U. Utah, 1975; Diploma, Squadron Officer Sch., 1975; Grad., Air Command and Staff Coll., 1981; Diploma, Indsl. Coll. of Armed Forces, 1988, Def. Systems Mgmt. Coll., 1990. Commd. 2d lt. USAF, 1970, advanced through ranks to lt. gen., 1996, ret., 2004; various assignments to program dir. for C-17 System Program Aeronautical Systems Ctr., Wright-Patterson AFB, Ohio, 1993-96; comdr. Electronic Systems Ctr., Hanscom AFB, Mass., 1996-99; dir. Ballistic Missile Def. Orgn., Pentagon, 1999—2004. Decorated Meritorious Svc. medal with three oak leaf clusters, Air medal, Air Force Commendation medal with two oak leaf clusters, Nat. Def. Svc. medal with svc. star, others.

KADISH, SANFORD HAROLD, law educator; b. N.Y.C., Sept. 7, 1921; s. Samuel J. and Frances R. (Klein) K.; m. June Kurtin, Sept. 29, 1942; children: Joshua, Peter. B Social Scis, CCNY, 1942; LLB, Columbia U., 1948; JD (hon.), U. Cologne, 1983; LLD (hon.), CUNY, 1985, Southwestern U., 1993. Bar: N.Y. 1948, Utah 1954. Pvt. practice law, N.Y.C., 1948-51; prof. law U. Utah, 1951-60, U. Mich., 1961-64, U. Calif., Berkeley, 1964-91, dean Law Sch., 1975-82, Morrison prof., 1973-91, prof. emeritus, 1991—. Fulbright lectr. Melbourne (Australia) U., 1956; vis. prof. Harvard U., 1960-61, Freiburg U., 1967; lectr. Salzburg Seminar Am. Studies, 1965; Fulbright vis. lectr. Kyoto (Japan) U., 1975; vis. fellow Inst. Criminology, Cambridge (Eng.) U., 1968. Author: (with M.R. Kadish) Discretion to Disobey—A Study of Lawful Departures from Legal Rules, 1973, (with Schulhofer) Criminal Law and Its Processes, 6th edit., 1995, Blame and Punishment—Essays in the Criminal Law, 1987; editor-in-chief Ency. Crime and Justice, 1983; contbr. articles to profl. jours. Reporter Calif. Legis. Penal Code Project, 1964-68; pub. mem. Wage Stblzn. Bd., region XII, 1951-53; cons. Pres.'s Commn. Adminstrn. of Justice, 1966; mem. Calif. Coun. Criminal Justice, 1968-69. Lt. USNR, 1943-46. Fellow, Ctr. Advanced Study Behavioral Scis., 1967—68, Guggenheim fellow, Oxford U., 1974—75, vis. fellow, All Souls Coll. Oxford U., 1983. Fellow AAAS (v.p. 1984-86), Brit. Acad. (corr.); mem. AAUP (nat. pres. 1970-72), Am. Assn. Law Schs. (exec. com. 1960, pres. 1982), Order of Coif (exec. com. 1966-67, 74-75), Phi Beta Kappa. Home: 774 Hilldale Ave Berkeley CA 94708-1318 E-mail: shk@law.berkeley.edu.

KADISON, RICHARD VINCENT, mathematician, educator; b. N.Y.C., July 25, 1925; married, 1956; 1 child. MS, U. Chgo., 1947, PhD, 1950; hon. doctorate, U. d'Aix-Marseille, 1986, U. Copenhagen, 1987. NRC fellow math. Inst. Advanced Study, 1950-52; from asst. prof. to prof. Columbia U., 1952-64; Kuemmerle prof. math. U. Pa., 1964—. Fulbright rsch. grantee, Denmark, 1954-55; Sloan fellow, 1958-62; Guggenheim fellow, 1969-70. Mem. NAS (chmn. math. sect. 2003—), Am. Math. Soc. (Steele prize for lifetime achievement 1999), Royal Danish Acad. Sci. and Letters (fgn. mem.), Norwegian Acad. Sci. and Letters (fgn. mem.), Sigma Xi. Office: U Pa Dept Math Philadelphia PA 19104-6395

KADOHATA, CYNTHIA, writer; b. Chgo. 1 adopted child. BA in Journalism, Univ. So. Calif. Author: (books) The Floating World, 1989, In the Heart of the Valley of Love, 1992, The Glass Mountains, 2002, (children's books) Kira Kira, 2004 (John Newbery Medal, 2005). Avocation: travel. Mailing: Antheneum Simon & Schuster 1230 Ave Of The Americas New York NY 10020 E-mail: cynthia@kira-kira.us.*

KADOHIRO, JANE K., nurse, educator, consultant; b. Lima, Ohio, July 20, 1947; d. Howard M. and Betty J. (Johoske) Keller; m. Howard M. Kadohiro, Dec. 27, 1969; children: Christopher, Jennifer. BA in Sociology and Edn., U. Hawaii, Manoa, 1969; BS in Nursing, U. Hawaii, Honolulu, 1977, MPH, 1990; MS, U. Hawaii, 1994, DrPH, 1999; postgrad., Yale U., 2001. Staff nurse Children's Hosp., Honolulu, 1977-78; staff pub. health nurse Hawaii State Dept. Health, Honolulu, 1978-80, coord. hypertension and diabetes, 1980-85, projects adminstr., 1985-89, chief chronic diseases, 1989-91; office mgr. Hanalei Trends, Honolulu, 1985-89; clin. nurse specialist Queen's Med. Ctr., Honolulu, 1991-94; cons. Aiea, Hawaii, 1991—; nurse investigator Honolulu Heart Program, 1991-95; asst. prof. U. Hawaii at Manoa, Honolulu, 1991—; dep. dir. health State of Hawaii, 2003—04. Leader, advisor, life mem. Girl Scouts U.S., Honolulu, 1978—; mem. diabetes project Office of Hawaiian Affairs, 1993-95. Named Disting. Alumni U. Hawaii Sch. Nursing, 1987; one of Hawaii's Unsung Heroes, Honolulu Star Bull., 1993. Mem. ANA (polit. action com. 1994—), APHA, Hawaii Nurses Assn. (Excellence in Clin. Practice award 1995), Am. Diabetes Assn. (nat. del. yearly, nat. programs com. nat. youth congress 1993-95, nat. youth task force and design team 1996-97, nat. profl. edn. com. 1997-98, nat. sci. sessions planning com 2004—, Pacific N.W. regional pres.-elect 1998-99, pres. health care and edn. 1999-2000, Reaching People award 2002, outstanding contbns. to diabetes and camping nat. award 1994, Hawaii affiliate founding bd. dirs. 1978—, leadership coun., camp nurse and camp dir. 1982-2004, pres. 1986-87, bd. dirs. 2003—, Lifetime Achievement award 2005), Hawaii Pub. Health Assn. (pres. 1985, chair advocacy com. 2004—, chair Safe 4 Schs. Project 2005—, lifetime achievement award 2005), Am. Assn. Diabetes Educators (bd. dirs. 1997-2004, chair 1999-2001, rsch. com. 2001-03, awards com. 2001-02, pub. affairs com. 2002-03, 1st v.p. 2000-01, pres.-elect 2001-02, nat. pres. 2002-03, continuing edn. com.), Hawaii Assn. Diabetes Educators (founding mem., bd. dirs. 1989—, pres. 1996-97, state legis. coord. 1996-2001, 2004—, treas. 1994-95, pub. affairs chair 1996-2001, Diabetes Camp Edn. Nat. award 1995, Disting. Svc. award 2003), Diabetes Advocacy Alliance Hawaii (convener and chair 1997-2000), Assn. Asian and Pacific Health Orgns. (adv. bd. 2002—), Internat. Diabetes Fedn., Internat. Soc. Pediat. and Adolescent Diabetes (steering com. Internat. Diabetes camping program 1989—), Am. Heart Assn. (cardiovasc. nursing coun. 1985-97), Sigma Theta Tau (founding mem., chair nominating com. 1995-97 Gamma Psi chpt. and chpt.-at-large, chmn. recognition com. 1986-89, Leadership award 2003). Avocations: travel, people, community and organization work, lifelong learning. Home: 1629 Wilder Ave Apt 504 Honolulu HI 96822-4652 Office Phone: 808-956-6841. Business E-Mail: kadohiro@hawaii.edu.

KADONAGA, JAMES TAKURO, biochemist; b. Ft. Bragg, N.C., Aug. 24, 1958; s. Tadashi and Alice Ayako K.; m. Anne Kadonaga, Sept. 15, 1984; children: William, Natalie. SB, MIT, 1980; AM, Harvard U., 1982, PhD, 1984. Fellow U. Calif., Berkeley, 1984-88, asst. prof. molecular biology San Diego, 1988-92, assoc. prof., 1992-94, prof., 1994—, vice chmn., 2000—03, chmn. Molecular Biology, 2003—. Mem. editl. bd. Molecular Cell Jour., 1997—, Genes and Devel. Jour., 1994—, Molecular and Cellular Biology, 1993-2001, Protein Expression and Purification, 1990—, Pub. Libr. of Sci., 2005—; contbr. articles to profl. jours. Recipient Biochemistry grant award Eli Lilly, 1989-91, Am. Inst. of Chemists/MIT award, 1980, prize Alpha Chi Sigma/MIT, 1980; named to Hall of Fame, East Side Union H.S. Dist., San Jose, Calif., 1991; DuPont fellow Harvard U., 1983-84, Miller fellow, 1984-86, sr. fellow Am. Cancer Soc. (Calif. divsn.), 1986-87, Presdl. Faculty fellow Pres. George Bush, 1992-97; Lucille P. Markey scholar, 1987-93. Fellow AAAS, Am. Acad. Microbiology; mem. Am. Chem. Soc., Am. Soc. Microbiology. Office: U Calif San Diego 2212B Pacific Hall 9500 Gilman Dr La Jolla CA 92093-0347 Office Phone: 858-534-4608.

KADOTA, TAKASHI THEODORE, mathematician, electrical engineer; b. Omogo, Ehime-Ken, Japan, Nov. 14, 1930; s. Shigeru and Kikuko (Tominaga) K.; m. Helena Littau, Dec. 21, 1956 (div.); children: Mari, Amy, Kimberley; m. Charlie Frances Hampton. BSEE, Yokohama (Japan) Nat. U., 1953; MSEE, U. Calif., Berkeley, 1956, PhDEE, 1960. Mem. tech. staff AT&T Bell Labs., Whippany, N.J., 1960-66, Murray Hill, N.J., 1966-94; ret., 1994. Vis. prof. U. Hawaii, Honolulu, 1978, U. Calif., Berkeley, 1975, Stanford U., 1974. Fellow IEEE (assoc. editor 1977-80).

KADOUS, TAMER ADEL, research scientist; b. Al-Mahal Al-Koubra, Gharbia, Egypt, Sept. 19, 1970; arrived in U.S., 1998; s. Adel Abd El-Ghany Kadous and Rawia Abd El-Hamid El-Ghanam; m. Nermeen Ahmed Bassiouny; children: Sarah children: Mariam. MSc, Alexandria (Egypt) U., 1997, U. Wis., 1999, PhD, 2001. Registered engr. Sys. engr. Thorn Security, Alexandria, 1994—97; rsch. asst. U. Wis., Madison, 1998—2001; rsch. intern NOKIA INC., Dallas, 1999—2000; rsch. engr. QUALCOMM INC., San Diego, 2001—. Tchg. asst. Alexandria U., 1994—97, U. Wis., Madison, 1998—2000. Contbr. articles to profl. jours. Mem., pres. Muslim Student Assn., Madison, 1998—2001. Soldier Egyptian Air Force, 1995—96. Mem.: IEEE. Office: QUALCOMM INC 5775 Morehouse Dr San Diego CA 92121

KADYK, CHARLES C., music educator, director, musician; b. Bryn Mawr, Pa., Apr. 21, 1961; s. Folkert Herpel and Jean Frickson Kadyk; m. Diane Leslie Berstler, Sept. 28, 1991. B in Music Edn., Temple U., Phila., 1983, M in Music Performance, 1985. Cert. profl. tchr. Maine, Pa. String quartet coach Haverford Twp. Schs., Pa., 1985—87; music tchr. Villa Maria Acad., Paoli, Pa., 1985—87, Owen J. Roberts Sch. Dist., Pottstown, Pa., 1987—92, M.S.A.D. 54, Skowhegan, Maine, 1992—2001; dir. orchs. sch. dist. Bangor HS, Maine, 2001—. Music dir. youth orch. Muse Inc., Bangor, 1994—2002; music dir. Augusta Symphony, Maine, 1997; dir. Bangor Fiddlers, 2001—. Mem.: NEA, Meetinghouse Strings (mem. bd. 1985—90), Music Educators Nat. Conf., Maine Music Educators Assn. (v.p. 2000—02), Am. String Tchrs. Assn. (pres. Maine chpt. 1983—, 1998—2000), Tri-Music (hon.). Republican. Avocations: model railroading, listening to ham radio, bicycling, hiking. Home: 9 Waverly Ave Pittsfield ME 04967 Office: Bangor HS Bangor Sch Dist 885 Broadway Bangor ME 04401 Office Phone: 207-941-6200 ext. 154. Office Fax: 207-941-6212. Personal E-mail: fiddler4967@verizon.net.

KADZ, ROGER DEAN, banker; s. Robert Harald and Betty Jane Kadz; m. Leslie G. Kadz, Aug. 7, 1971; children: Allison, Lisa, John, Christina. BA, U. Redlands, 1970. Mortgage banker First Interstate Mortgage, Pasadena, Calif., 1984—87; banker First Interstate Bank Nev., Las Vegas, 1987—95; banker, sr. v.p., mgr. 1st Nat. Bank Nev., Reno, 1995—. With USAR, 1970—76. Mem.: Am. Guild Organists (No. Nev. chpt. bd. dirs. 2004—05, No. Nev. chpt. treas 1998—).

KAEGI, WALTER EMIL, history professor; b. New Albany, Ind., Nov. 8, 1937; s. Walter Emil and Ruth Ann (Mergell) K.; m. Louise Polk Mullikin, June 9, 1969; children: Frederick George, Christian Emil. AB, Haverford Coll., 1959; AM, Harvard U., 1960, PhD, 1965. Tchg. fellow Harvard U., Cambridge, Mass., 1961-63; fellow Ctr. for Byzantine Studies Dumberton Oaks Rsch. Libr., Washington, 1963-65; asst. prof. history U. Chgo., 1965-69, assoc. prof. history, 1969-74, prof. history, 1974—, voting mem. Oriental Inst., 1997—. Co-founder Byzantine Studies Conf., 1975; co-editor Byzantinische Forschungen, Amsterdam, Las Palmas, 1981—. Author: (book) Byzantium and the Decline of Rome, 1968, Byzantine Military Unrest, 1981, Army, Society and Religion in Byzantium, 1982, Byzantium and the Early Islamic Conquests, 1992, Heraclius Emperor of Byzantium, 2003; editor: The Southern Star, 1947-50; mem. editl. bd. The Shenandoah, 1955-56; co-editor: Byzantinische Forschungen, 1980—; contbr. articles to numerous profl. jours. Recipient Highest Hons. in History, Haverford Coll., 1959, fellow Inst. for Advanced Study, Princeton U., 1971, 85, Am. Coun. Learned Socs., 1978-79, Am. Rsch. Ctr. in Egypt, 1979, Dumbarton Oaks, 1980, Fulbright fellow in Islamic Civilization, Syria, Jordan, 1984, to Iraq, 1988, NEH, 1988-89, 90-91, John Simon Guggenheim Found., 1996-97, Nat. Humanities Ctr. Rsch., Triangle Pk., N.C., 1996-97, Social Sci. Rsch. Coun., N.Y.C., 1996-97; recipient travel grants to Internat. Byzantine Congresses, 1977, 91, travel grant to Southeastern European Studies Internat. Congress, Athens, 1970, U. Jordan grant to participate in Fourth Internat. Conf. on History of Bilad al-Sham, 1983, 85, 87, IREX grant to visit USSR, 1991; Fulbright-Hays fellow Tunisia, Moroccco, Algeria, 2004. Mem. Byzantine Studies Conf. (governing bd. mem. 1994-98), U.S. Nat. Com. for Byzantine Studies, Medieval Acad. of Am., Swiss-Am. Hist. Soc., Mid. East Medievalists, Phi Beta Kappa. Avocations: gardening, travel, walking. Office: Univ of Chicago Dept of History 1126 E 59th St Dept Of Chicago IL 60637-1580 Business E-Mail: kwal@uchicago.edu.

KAEHELE, BETTIE LOUISE, accountant; b. Sherwood, Tenn., Oct. 29, 1950; d. James Henry and Ruby Katherine (Clark) Shetters; divorced; children: Josiah Dean, Dana Marie. AAS, Albuquerque Tech. Vocat. Inst., 1990; BSBA, Nat. Coll., Albuquerque, 1991. Acctg. clk. Am. Auto Assn., Albuquerque, 1980—81, Ryder Truck Rental, Inc., Albuquerque, 1981—82; owner Sherwood Svcs., 1982—86; bookkeeper, sec. Grants Steel Sash & Hardware, Albuquerque, 1986—87; acctg. specialist Burton & Co., Albuquerque, 1987, Neff & Co., Albuquerque, 1987—91; acctg. tech. U. N.Mex. Found., Albuquerque, 1991—92; acct. II biology dept. U. N.Mex., Albuquerque, 1992—97, acct. II dept. family and cmty. medicine, 1997—2002, acct. III dept. family and cmty. medicine, 2002—. Mem.: Bible Study Bernalillo Metro. Detention Ctr. Republican. Avocations: reading, dance, theater, poetry, writing. Home: 7408 Desert Canyon Pl SW Albuquerque NM 87121-6424 Personal E-mail: bkaehele@yahoo.com.

KAELIN, EUGENE FRANCIS, philosophy educator; b. St. Louis, Oct. 14, 1926; s. Albert Aloysius and Bertha (Earni) K.; m. Pierrette Nicole Demartini, Dec. 30, 1952; children: Valérie Chantal, Carolyne Pascale, Martine Laurence. BA with distinction, U. Mo., 1949, MA, 1950; diploma of higher studies, U. Bordeaux, France, 1951; PhD, U. Ill., 1954. Instr. philosophy U. Mo., 1952-53; fellow philosophy U. Ill., 1953-54, post-doctoral fellow, 1954-55; instr. philosophy U. Wis., 1955-57, asst. prof., 1957-61, assoc. prof., 1961-65, Fla. State U., 1965-67, prof., 1967-96, ret., 1996. Mem. nat. adv. bd. aesthetic edn. program Central Midwestern Regional Ednl. Lab., 1968-76 Author: An Existentialist Aesthetic, 1962, Art and Existence, 1970, The Unhappy Consciousness, 1981, Heidegger's Being and Time: A Reading for Readers, 1988, An Aesthetics for Art Educators, 1989, Texts on Texts and Textuality, 1999. With USMC, 1945-46. Recipient William Henry Kiekhofer Meml. Teaching award U. Wis., 1959 Mem. Am. Philos. Assn., Am. Soc. Aesthetics, Am. Soc. Phenomenology and Existential Philosophy, Fla. Philos. Assn. (pres. 1977-78) Home: 1910 Atapha Nene Tallahassee FL 32301-5851 E-mail: eugkael@aol.com.

KAEN, NAIDA, state representative; b. Frankenmuth, Mich., May 12, 1946; m. Fred R. Kaen; two children. BEd, U. Mich., 1968; MBA, U. N.H., 1977. Realtor; state rep. N.H. Ho. of Reps., 1995—. Mem. sci., tech. and energy com. N.H. Ho. Reps. Office: NH State Legis State House Concord NH 03301 Address: 22 Toon Ln Lee NH 03824-6507 E-mail: naidakaen@hotmail.com.

KAENEL, ROSEMARY THERESE, writer; b. Chgo., Apr. 26, 1928; d. Martin Joseph Murphy and Rose Helen O'Connell; m. John Joseph Kaenel, Oct. 11, 1952; adopted children: James, Judy foster children: Glen Bywater, Grace Bywater, Bonnie Bywater 1 child, Joseph. BS in home econs., Rosary Coll., Ill., 1950; AA in nursing, Elgin (Ill.) Cmty., 1982. Lic. practical nurse, Ill., 1979. Home econs. tchr. various HS, Burlington, Ill., 1950—52; grades 4, 5, 6 tchr. Winfield (Ill.) Sch., 1952—53; grades 2, 4-6 and jr. high tchr. Longfellow Sch., Wheaton, Ill., 1954—76; grades 4, 5, 6 and jr. high tchr. Glendale Heights (Ill.), 1965—72; jr. high home econ. Glendale Heights (Ill.) Dist., 1972—75; grades 4, 5 and 6 tchr. Winnebago Sch., Glendale Heights, Ill., 1976—81; staff nurse Ctrl. DuPage Hosp., Winfield, Ill., 1981—2001. Mem. treas. Coun. of Cath. Nurses, Wheaton, Ill., 1985—88. Election judge Ill. Citizens for Life, 1975—; bd. dirs. Project Love. Republican. Roman Catholic. Avocations: writing, reading, cooking, travel. Home: 831 Warrenville Rd Wheaton IL 60187 E-mail: trumpitter@aol.com.

KAESBERG, PAUL JOSEPH, virology researcher; b. Engers, Germany, Sept. 26, 1923; came to U.S., 1926, naturalized, 1933; s. Peter Ernst and Gertrude (Mueller) K.; m. Marian Lavon Hanneman, June 13, 1953; children— Paul Richard, James Kevin, Peter Roy. BS in Engring, U. Wis., Madison, 1945, PhD in Physics, 1949; D. Natural Scis. (hon.), U. Leiden, The Netherlands, 1975. Instr. biometry and physics U. Wis., 1949-51, asst. prof. biochemistry, 1956-58, assoc. prof., 1958-60, prof., 1960-63, prof. biophysics and biochemistry, 1963—, Beeman prof. biophysics and biochemistry, 1983-87, chmn. Biophysics Lab., 1970-88, Wis. Alumni Research Found. prof., 1981—, Beeman prof. molecular virology and biochemistry, 1987-90, prof. emeritus, 1990. Cons. in field. Contbr. chapts. to books and articles to profl. jours. Mem. NAS, Am. Soc. Virology (pres. 1987-88). Home: 5002 Bayfield Ter Madison WI 53705-4811 Office: U Wis Inst Molecular Virology 1525 Linden Dr Madison WI 53706-1534 Office Phone: 608-262-2205. Personal E-mail: pjkaes@aol.com.

KAESS, JOHN PHILIP, music educator, director; b. St. Paul, Jan. 9, 1942; s. Romen Albert and Lucy Belle (Houle) Kaess. MusB, U. St. Thomas, 1965; MusM, U. Minn., 1967, postgrad., 1968—73; PhD music performance, Pacific We. U., 1999. Cert. tchr. K-12 Minn. Music coord. and tchr. Guardian Angels Ch. & Sch., Chaska, Minn., 1971—73; tchr., choir dir., organist St. Paul; tchr. music St. Mary's Acad. and Coll., Kans., 2000—. Music dir. Regina Coeli Youth Choir, St. Paul, 1973—79; organist, accompanist Twin Cities Schola Cantorum, St. Paul & Mpls., Minn., 1973—99; curriculum comm. Archdiocese St. Paul & Mpls., 1978—88. Author articles (Catholic publs.). Organist music dir. St. Ambrose Ch., St. Paul, 1979—89. Mem.: Ch. Music Assoc. of Am. (assoc.), Minn. Music Tchr. Assoc. (assoc.), The Evergreen Club (assoc.). Republican. Roman Catholic. Achievements include known in Catholic cir. around the country and locally as a ch. musician, choir dir., music tchr., and organist. Avocations: collecting cars, travel. Home: 3622 Cleveland St NE Minneapolis MN 55418

KAESS, KEN, advertising executive; married; 2 children. BA in Psychology, Vassar Coll., 1976. Acct. exec. Doyle Dane Bernbach (DDB), 1977; mgmt. supervisor job Jordan, Case & McGrath, 1981—83, v.p., 1984—86; sr. v.p., mgmt. supervisor DDB, LA, 1986—88; v.p. children's programming New World Entertainment, LA, 1986—90; exec. v.p., pres. entertainment div. DDB, LA, 1990—93; mng. ptnr. DDB New York, 1994; pres. US operations DDB Worldwide, 1997, pres. N. Am. operations, 1998, pres. NYC, 1999—, CEO, 2001—. Mem.: Ad Coun. (bd. dirs.), Am. Assn. Advt. Agys. (chmn.). Office: DDB Worldwide Omnicom Group Inc 437 Madison Ave New York NY 10022*

KAFARSKI, MITCHELL I., chemical processing company executive; b. Detroit, Dec. 15, 1917; s. Ignacy A. and Anastasia (Drzazgowski) Kafarski; m. Zofia Drozdowska, July 11, 1967; children: Erik Michael, Konrad Christian. Student, U. Detroit, 1939-41, Shrivenham (Eng.) Am. U., 1946. Process engr. Packard Motor Car Co., Detroit, 1941-44; organizer, dir. Artist and Craftsman Sch., Esslingen, Germany, 1945-46; with Nat. Bank of Detroit, 1946-50; founder, pres. Chem. Processing Inc., Detroit, 1950-65, also bd. dirs.; chmn. bd., pres., treas. Aactron Inc., Madison Heights, Mich., 1965—; chmn. bd., pres. Imtech of Mich., Inc., 1988-92. Treas. Detroit Magnetic Insp. Co., 1960-65; also dir.; v.p. KMH Inc., Detroit, 1960-64; also dir.; treas. Packard Plating Inc., Detroit, 1962-67, also dir. Commr. Mich. State Fair, 1965-72; mem. com. devel. and planning to build Municipal Stadium State of Mich., 1965-88; benefactor, mem. Founders Soc., Detroit Inst. Arts, 1965—; trustee Founders' Soc., Detroit Inst. Arts, 1982-90; sponsor, host world celebrity for World Preview Mich., 1965-66; mem. dist. adv. council SBA, 1971-73; del. White House Conf. on Aging, 1971; organizer, treas. Mich. Reagan for Pres. Com., 1980; treas. Straith Meml. Hosp., Southfield, Mich., 1972—, chmn. bd., 1976; trustee Mich. Opera Theater, 1982—; bd. dirs. Gilbert and Sullivan Light Opera Soc., Palm Beach, Fla., 1985—; White House rep. to opening of first U.S. Trade Center, Warsaw, Poland, 1972; chmn. fund-raising Bloomfield Arts Assn., Birmingham, Mich., 1973-74; mem. Space Theatre Consortium, Inc., Seattle, 1981-83; bd. regents Orchard Lake (Mich.) Schs., 1981-83; Vice chmn. Republican State Nationalities Council Mich., 1969-73; bd. dirs. Bloomfield Arts Assn., 1973-84, Friends of Kresge Library, Oakland U., 1973-86; presdl. appointee bd. dirs. U.S.A. Pennsylvania Ave. Devel. Corp., Washington, 1973-81; chmn. bd. Straith Meml. Hosp., Detroit, 1971—, Detroit Sci. Center, 1972—, corp. dir.; mem. Internat. Soc. Palm Beach; trustee Greater Palm Beach Symphony, 1986; mem. Citizen's Commn. to Improve Mich. Cts., 1986-88; contbr. Kravis Ctr. for Performing Arts, West Palm Beach, 1989; mem. Bus. Com. for the Arts, Palm Beacvh, 1991—. Served with AUS, 1944-46, ETO. Recipient Nat. award for war prodn. invention War Prodn. Bd., 1943; decorated knight's Cross Order of Poland's Rebirth Restituta, 1975, chevalier Chaine des Rotisseurs, 1982, Knight of Malta Order of St. John. Mem. Nat. Assn. Metal Finishers, Mich. Assn. Metal Finishers (dir., chmn. bd. 1976), N.A.M., Am. Electroplaters Soc., Cranbrook Acad. Arts, Am.-Polish Action Coun. (chmn. 1971-76), Am. Assn. Mus. (treas. Detroit), Poinciana Club, Village Club. Clubs: Capitol Hill (Washington); Detroit Athletic. Home: 21 Kingsley Manor Ct Bloomfield Hills MI 48304-3520 Office: Aactron Inc 29306 Stephenson Hwy Madison Heights MI 48071-2394 Office Phone: 248-642-2730. *A basic ingredient to success usually is determined by special events in one's life. In the course of my experiences, a sprinkling of tribulations were a must. From these were gleaned the principles, goals and conduct in attaining success. During the course of my life's pursuit, the ability to help others ensured a complete fulfillment of my goals.*

KAFENTZIS, JOHN CHARLES, journalist, educator; b. Butte, Mont., Aug. 18, 1953; s. Christian and Betty Ann (Gaston) K.; m. Teresa Marie Nokleby, June 5, 1976; children: Kathryn Anne, Christian John. BA in Journalism, U. Mont., 1975. Reporter The Missoulian, Missoula, Mont., 1974-76, The Hardin (Mont.) Herald, 1976, The Spokesman-Rev., Spokane, Wash., 1976-80, copy editor, 1980-83, chief copy desk, 1983-89, news editor, 1989-94, news designer, 1994—2003, design editor, 2003—. Adj. faculty Ea. Wash. U., Cheney, 1982—, Whitworth Coll., 1998, Gonzaga U. 2004-. Greek Orthodox. Avocation: competitive swimming. Office: The Spokesman Rev 999 W Riverside Ave Spokane WA 99201-1098

KAFF, ALBERT ERNEST, reporter, writer; b. Atchison, Kans., June 14, 1920; s. John and Ethel Mae (Worley) K.; m. Lee Chuan Diana Fong, Oct. 15, 1960; children: Arthur Fong, Alban Fong. BA in Econs., U. Colo., 1942. Reporter Atchison Globe, summers 1939-41, Ponca City (Okla.) News, 1946-48, Daily Oklahoman, Oklahoma City, 1948-50; fgn. corr. U.P.I., Korea and Japan, 1952-56, bur. mgr. Saigon Vietnam, 1956—58, bur. mgr. Taipei, Taiwan, 1958—61, Manila, Philippines, 1961—63, news editor Tokyo, 1963-72, dir. Asian svcs. Hong Kong, 1972-75, asst. dir., dir. pers. rels. N.Y.C., 1975-78, v.p., gen. mgr. Asia-Pacific Hong Kong, 1978-84, v.p., mgr. N.Y., 1984-85; media cons., 1985; bus. internat. editor Cornell U. News Svc., 1986-93. Freelance journalist Stamford, Conn., Alexandria, Va., Fairfield, Conn., 1993—; columnist Overseas Press Club Bull. Contbg. author: How I Got That Story, 1967, Eyewitness on Asia, 1997, Foreign Correspondents in Japan: Covering a Half Century of Upheavals from 1945 to the Present, 1998; author: (with Avner Arbel) Crash: Ten Days in October... Will It Strike Again?, 1989. Served with AUS, 1943-46, 50-52. Decorated Bronze Star Mem. Fgn. Corrs. Club Japan (pres. 1967-68), Fgn. Corrs. Club Hong Kong (pres. 1974-75), Overseas Press Club Am. (v.p. 1984-86, bd. dirs. 1988-92, trustee Found. 1992—), Ithaca Press Club (vice chmn. 1987-88) Sigma Chi. Episcopalian. Home and Office: 393 Unquowa Rd Fairfield CT 06824-5028 Office Phone: 203-259-3324. *During 52 years of reporting, writing and editing the news, I missed several opportunities because I ignored a basic rule: If you can accomplish the assignment today or tomorrow, do it today. Tomorrow will bring new demands.*

KAFFER, ROGER LOUIS, bishop; b. Joliet, Ill., Aug. 14, 1927; s. Earl Louis and Helen Ruth (McManus) K. BA, St. Mary of the Lake, Mundelein, Ill., 1950, STB, 1952, MA, 1953, licentiate in sacred theology, 1954; licentiate of canon law, Pontifical Gregorian U., Rome, 1958; D of Pastoral Ministry, St. Mary of the Lake, Mundelein, Ill., 1983; MEd, DePaul U., 1965; LHD (hon.), Felician Coll., 1986; DHL (hon.), Coll. St. Francis, 1990; doctorate (hon.), Lewis U., 1990. Ordained priest Roman Cath. Ch., 1954; cert. K-14 supr. Ill. Eccles. notary Roman Cath. Diocese of Joliet, 1954—56; asst. chancellor Roman Cath. Diocese Joliet, 1958—65; aux. bishop Roman Cath. Diocese of Joliet, 1985—, vicar gen., vicar for clergy, 1985—2004; rector St. Charles Borromeo Sem., Lockport, Ill., 1965—70; prin. Providence High Sch., New Lenox, Ill., 1970—85; rector Cathedral of St. Raymond, Joliet, 1985; consecrated bishop, 1985; ret., 2002. Past. mem. Marriage Tribunal, Diocesan Sem. Bd., Diocesan Bd. Religious Edn. Named Cleric of Yr., KC, 1973, Citizen of Yr., New Lenox Assn. Commerce, 1976, Man of Yr., Joliet Cath. High Alumni Assn., 1978, Citizen of Yr., UNICO, Joliet, 1996; recipient DeLa Salle medallion, Lewis U., 1984, Lifetime Achievement award, Joliet C. of C., 1999, award, Paluch Family Found., 2002. Mem.: Nat. Conf. Cath. Bishops Conf. Ill., KC (Ill. state chaplain 1993—). Roman Catholic. Avocations: youth work, retreat work. Address: 425 Summit St Joliet IL 60435-7155

KAFIN, ROBERT JOSEPH, lawyer; b. Phila., Jan. 1, 1942; s. Jacob A. and Anna C. (Cohen) K.; m. Carol A. Friedman, June 20, 1965; children: Tammy Ellen, Peter Douglas. AB magna cum laude, Franklin & Marshall Coll., 1963; JD magna cum laude, Harvard U., 1966. Bar: N.Y. 1967, U.S. Dist. Ct. (so. dist.) N.Y. 1968, U.S. Dist. Ct. (no. dist.) N.Y. 1971, U.S. Dist. Ct. (we. dist.) N.Y. 1974, U.S. Ct. Appeals (2d cir.) 1971, U.S. Supreme Ct. 1972, D.C. 1997. Ptnr. Kafin and Needleman, Glens Falls, NY, 1971-78; prin. Miller, Mannix, Lemery & Kafin, Glens Falls, NY, 1978-87; assoc. Proskauer Rose LLP, NYC, 1967-71, ptnr., 1987-91, chief operating ptnr., 1991—. Trustee Adirondack Conservancy Com., Elizabethtown, N.Y., 1980-87; judge Glens Falls City Ct., 1976; counsel N.Y. State Senate, Albany, N.Y., 1973-87. Editor: N.Y. Environmental Law Handbook, 1988, 92. Bd. dirs. Environ. Planning Lobby, Albany, 1977-88; active Manhattan Solid Waste Adv. Bd., N.Y.C., 1987—; dir. Park & Trails NY, 1995—, chmn., 1999; trustee Preservation League N.Y. State, 1997—; dir. Times Square Alliance, 2004—; dir. Adirondack Coun., 2004—. Mem. N.Y. Bar Assn. (sec. environ. law sect. 1988, treas. 1989, 1st vice chmn. 1991, chair 1992-93), Assn. Bar City N.Y. (environ. law com. 1987-89). Democrat. Jewish. Home: 340 E 72d St Apt 3-SE New York NY 10021 Office: Proskauer Rose LLP 1585 Broadway Fl 27 New York NY 10036-8299

KAFKA, GERALD ANDREW, lawyer; b. Martins Ferry, Ohio, Sept. 9, 1951; s. Andrew and Mary (Spustek) K.; m. Rita A. Cavanagh; children: Andrea, Sarah, Justin. BA, Wheeling Jesuit Coll., 1972; JD, U. Cin., 1975; LLM in Taxation, Georgetown U., 1979. Bar: Ohio 1975, D.C. 1982, Md. 1984, U.S. Tax Ct. 1977, U.S. Claims Ct. 1978, U.S. Supreme Ct. 1979, D.C. 1982, U.S. Dist. Ct. (D.C. dist.) 1983, U.S. Ct. Appeals (D.C., fed., 3d, 4th, 5th, 6th, 7th 8th and 9th cirs.). Trial atty. honors program tax div. U.S. Dept. Justice, Washington, 1975-79; ptnr. Scribner, Hall & Thompson, Washington, 1979-84, Steptoe & Johnson, Washington, 1984-92, Dewey Ballantine, Washington, 1992-2000, Mokee Nelson, LLP, Washington, 2000—03, Latham & Watkins, 2003—. Mem. adj. faculty Georgetown U. Law Ctr., Washington, 1979—; master J. Edgar Murdoch Am. Inn of Ct., U.S. Tax Ct., 1989—. Author: Litigation of Federal Tax Civil Controversies, 1996; editor procedure dept. Jour. Taxation; contbr. articles to profl. jours. Named Outstanding Atty., Tax Divsn. US Dept. Justice, 1977. Fellow Am. Coll. Tax Counsel; mem. ABA (chair ct. procedure com. tax sect. 1993-95, chmn. task force civil tax litigation process 1989-90, task force on large case audits and litigation 1990-91, ad hoc joint com. tax ct. jurisdiction 1987, task force on taxpayer bill of rights legis 1987-88, chair tax ct. appts. com. 2003-05), D.C. Bar Assn. (steering com. tax sect. 1986-91, chmn. com. audits and litigation tax sect. 1987). Office: 555 Eleventh St NW Washington DC 20004 Office Phone: 202-637-2198. E-mail: jerry.kafka@lw.com.

KAGAN, DONALD, historian, educator; b. Kurshan, Lithuania, May 1, 1932; arrived in US, 1934, naturalized, 1940; s. Max and Leah (Benjamin) K.; m. Myrna Dabrusky, Jan. 13, 1955; children: Robert William, Frederick Walter. AB, Bklyn. Coll., 1954; MA, Brown U., 1955; PhD, Ohio State U., 1958. Instr. history Pa. State U., University Park, 1959-60; asst. prof. ancient history Cornell U., 1960-64, assoc. prof., 1964-67, prof., 1967; sterling prof. classics and history Yale U., 1969—2002, master Timothy Dwight Coll., 1976-78, acting dir. athletics, 1987-88, dean Yale Coll., 1989-92. Jefferson lectr. NEH, Washington, 2005. Author: The Great Dialogue, 1965, The Outbreak of the Peloponnesian War, 1969, The Archidamian War, 1974, The Western Heritage, 1979, (with Frank Turner and Steven Ozment) The Peace of Nicias and the Sicilian Expedition, 1981, The Fall of the Athenian Empire, 1987, Pericles of Athens and the Birth of Democracy, 1991, On the Origins of War and the Perservation of Peace, 1995, (with Frederick W. Kagan) While America Sleeps, 2000; The Peloponnesian War, 2003. Named Jefferson lectr., 2005; recipient Nat. Humanity medal, 2002. Home: 37 Woodstock Rd Hamden CT 06517-2949 Office: Yale Univ Hall of Grad Studies 215 New Haven CT 06502 E-mail: donald.kagan@yale.edu.

KAGAN, ELENA, dean, law educator; b. 1960; BA summa cum laude, Princeton, 1981; MPhil, Worchester Coll., Oxford, 1983; JD magna cum laude, Harvard Law School, 1986. Law clk. US Ct. of Appeals for Judge Abner Mikva of the US Supreme Ct. for the DC Circuit, 1986—87, US Ct. of Appeals for Justice Thurgood Marshall of the US Supreme Ct., 1987—88; assoc. Williams & Connolly, Wash., DC, 1989—91; faculty mem. Univ. of Chgo. Law Sch., Chgo., 1991—99; nominated to serve as judge US Supreme Ct. of Appeals, Wash., DC, 1999; asst. prof. Univ. of Chgo. Law Sch., 1991, prof. of law tenure Chgo., 1995; assoc. counsel to the Pres. White House, Wash., DC, 1995—96, dep. asst. to the Pres. for Domestic Policy, 1997—99, dep. dir. of the Domestic Policy Coun., 1997—99; vis. prof. Harvard Law Sch., Cambridge, Mass., 1999, prof., 2001—, dean, 2003—, Charles Hamilton Houston prof. of law, 2003—. Author: (article) Harvard Law Rev. Article, Pres. Admin., 2001 (honored as the year's top scholarly article by the Am. Bar Assoc. Section on Admin. Law and Reg. Pract., 2001). Kagan has also written on a range of First Amendment issues, including the role of governmental motive in different facets of First Amendment doctrine, and the interplay of libel law and the First Amendment. Mem.: Harvard Law Sch. faculty appt. comm., Harvard Law Sch. Locational options comm. (chair 2001—02). Kagan is a prof. of law at Harvard fLaw Sch. where she teaches admin. law, constitutional law, and civil procedure. Her recent sholarship focuses primarily on the role of the Pres. of the US in formulating and influencing fed. admin. and regulatory law. Office: Harvard Law Sch Griswold 200 1563 Mass Ave Cambridge MA 02138

KAGAN, ILSE ECHT, librarian, researcher, historian; b. Free City of Danzig, Sept. 23, 1927; d. Samuel and Hella Echt; m. Robert A. Kagan, Aug. 26, 1951 (dec. Oct. 1994); children: Jonathan, Miki. BA (hon.), Oxford U., MA, 1954; MLS, Columbia U., 1960. With Pira Energy, N.Y.C., 1987—; village historian Village of Gt. Neck (N.Y.) Estates, 1996—. Past pres. Gt. Neck Estates Civic Assn., sec., 2000—; past pres. Gt. Neck chpt. Hadassah; bd. dirs. Am. Jewish Com. Mem.: Oxford U. Club, Brit. Schs. Univ. Club, Harvard Club. Avocations: tennis, theater, music. Home: 25 Elm St Great Neck NY 11021 Office: Pira Energy 3 Park Ave New York NY 10016 Office Phone: 212-686-6808. E-mail: piraiek@concentric.net.

KAGAN, JEROME, psychologist, educator; b. Newark, Feb. 25, 1929; s. Joseph and Myrtle (Liebermann) K. BS, Rutgers U., 1950; PhD, Yale, 1954. Instr. psychology Ohio State U., 1954-55; research assoc. Fels Research Inst., Yellow Springs, Ohio, 1957-59, chmn. dept. psychology, 1959-64; assoc. prof. psychology Antioch Coll., 1959-64; rsch. prof. psychology Harvard U., 1964-2000, dir. Mind Brain Behavior Initiative, 1996-2000, rsch. prof., 2000—. Adv. com. Nat. Inst. Child Health and Devel. Author (with G.S. Lesser): Contemporary Issues in Thematic Apperceptive Methods, 1961; author: (with Moss) Birth to Maturity, 1962; author: (with Mussen, Conger and Huston) Child Development and Personality, 7th edit., 1990; author: (with Segal) Psychology, 7th edit., 1991; author: (with Janis, Mahl and Holt) Personality, 1969, Understanding Children, 1971, Change and Continuity in Infancy, 1971; author: (with Kearsley and Zelazo) Infancy, 1978; author: (with Brim) Constancy and Change, 1980, The Second Year, 1981, The Nature of the Child, 1984; author: Unstable Ideas, 1989, Galen's Prophecy, 1994, Three Seductive Ideas, 1998, Surprise, Uncertainty and Mental Structures, 2002; author: (with Snidman) The Long Shadow of Temperament, 2004; author: (with Norbert Herschkovitz) A Young Mind in a Growing Brain, 2005. Served with AUS, 1955-57. Recipient Lucius Cross medal Yale U., 1981; Phi Beta Kappa scholar, 1988-89. Fellow AAAS, APA (Disting. Sci. Contbn. award 1987, G. Stanley Hall award 1995), Am. Acad. Arts and Scis., Soc. Rsch. Child Devel. (Disting. Sci. Contbn. award 1989); mem. NAS, Inst. Medicine, Ea. Psychol. Assn. Home: 210 Clifton St Belmont MA 02478-2605 Office: Harvard U Dept Psychology William James Hall 33 Kirkland Hl Cambridge MA 02138 Business E-Mail: jk@wjh.harvard.edu. *My success has been aided by a combination of hard work, openess to new ideas, a readiness to discard beliefs that are proven invalid; a desire to nurture the growth of others; and belief in the beauty of ideas and the perfectibility of man.*

KAGAN, JULIA LEE, magazine editor; b. Nurnberg, Fed. Republic Germany, Nov. 25, 1948; d. Saul and Elizabeth J. Kagan. AB, Bryn Mawr Coll., 1970. Rschr. Look Mag., N.Y.C., 1970-71; editl. asst., asst. editor McCall's mag., N.Y.C., 1971-74, assoc. editor, 1974-78, sr. editor, 1978-79; articles editor Working Woman mag., N.Y.C., 1979-85, exec. editor, 1985-88; editor Psychology Today, 1988-90; sr. editor McCalls, 1990-91; contbg. editor Working Woman, 1991-93; editor-in-chief Lamaze Parents' Mag., 1992-93, Lamaze Baby Mag., 1993; spl. projects dir. Child Mag., 1993-94; sr. v.p. EDK Assocs., N.Y.C., 1994; psychology/health dir. Fitness Mag., N.Y.C., 1995-96; dep. editor Consumer Reports Mag., Yonkers, NY, 1996, editor, 1996-2000; v.p. and editl. dir. Consumers Union, 2000—03; v.p. content Zagat Survey, 2003—04; nat. editor-in-chief Back Stage, 2005—. Vis. J. Stewart Riley prof. journalism Ind. U., 1991-93. Co-author: Manworks: A Guide to Style, 1980; contbg. author: The Working Woman Success Book, 1981, The Working Woman Report, 1984. Pres. Appleby Found., N.Y.C., 1982-84; trustee Bryn Mawr Coll., 2000—. Recipient 2d Ann. Advt. Journalism award Compton Advt., 1983 Mem. Am. Soc. Mag. Editors, Womens Media Group (bd. dirs.), Journalism and Women Symposium (treas. 1993-94, pres. 1995-96). Clubs: Princeton (N.Y.C.). Office: Consumer Reports 101 Truman Ave Yonkers NY 10703-1044

KAGAN, MARILYN D., retired architect; b. Providence, Nov. 13, 1930; d. Jacob L. and Emma Kenner Kagan. BS in Arch., Drexel U., 1972; student in Cert. Program, R.I. Sch. Design, 2005—. Cartographer U.S. Army Map Svc., Providence, 1952-53, Redevel. Authority, Phila., 1958-68; arch. George Ewing Inc., Phila., 1969-70, City of Phila. Water Dept., 1971-91; ret., 1991. Designer jewelry. Bd. dirs. Philly Walks-Pedestrian Safety Coalition, 1996-98; chair Soviet Jewry Com. of Society Hill Synagogue, Phila., 1980-90. Recipient Cert. of Appreciation, Jewish Family Svc., 1993-96. Mem.: Na'Amat/Pioneer Women (pres. R.I. chpt. 2002—). Democrat. Jewish. Avocations: jewelry design, painting, photography, gardening, travel. Home: 311 Rochambeau Ave Providence RI 02906-3507 Personal E-mail: busybeaderkagan@aol.com.

KAGAN, ROBERT ALLEN, law educator; b. Newark, N.J., June 13, 1938; s. George and Sylvia K. AB, Harvard U., 1959; LLB, Columbia U., 1962; PhD, Yale U., 1974. Now prof. polit. sci. and law U. Calif., Berkeley. Office: U Calif Sch Law Boalt Hall Berkeley CA 94720

KAGAN, STEPHEN BRUCE (SANDY KAGAN), corporate financial executive; b. Elizabeth, NJ, Apr. 27, 1944; s. Herman and Ida (Nadel) K.; m. Susan D. Kaltman, July 3, 1966; children: Sheryl, Rachel BS in Econs., U. Pa., 1966; MBA in Fin., Bernard Baruch Coll., 1969. Chartered fin. analyst. CPA security analyst Merrill Lynch Pierce Fenner & Smith, N.Y.C., 1966-68; dir. rsch. Deutschmann & Co., N.Y.C., 1968-70; v.p. Equity Sponsors, Inc., N.Y.C., 1970-72; v.p., investment counselor Daniel H. Renberg & Assocs., Inc., LA, 1972—78; CFO, COO Carlson Travel Network, Van Nuys, Calif., 1978—95; rep. Excel Telecomms., Van Nuys, Calif., 1995—2000; CFO, ptnr. Tatum Ptnrs., LLP, 2000—; CFO Calif. Tan, Inc., 2005—. Vice pres. bd. Temple Beth Hillel, North Hollywood, Calif., 1976-83 Mem. Inst. Cert. Fin. Analysts, Beta Gamma Sigma Avocations: golf, skiing, poker, travel. Home and Office: 18119 Calvert St Tarzana CA 91335

KÅGE, JONAS, performing company executive; b. Stockholm; m. Deborah Dobson; 1 child, Isabelle. Student, Royal Swedish Ballet Sch. Mem. Royal Swedish Ballet, Am. Ballet Theatre, 1971-75, soloist, 1972-75, prin. dancer, 1973-75, Stuttgart (Germany) Ballet, 1975-76, Geneva (Switzerland) Ballet, 1976-78, Zürich (Switzerland) Ballet, 1978-88; artistic dir. Malmo (Sweden) Opera Ballet, 1988-95; freelance guest artist, master tchr., 1995-97; artistic dir. Ballet West, Salt Lake City, 1997—. Quest artist Am. Ballet Theatre, 1977—, Frankfort Ballet, Germany, Basel Ballet, Switzerland, Royal Swedish Ballet, 1980—81, Deutsche Opera Berlin, 1982, Pitts. Ballet, 1984—85, Nat. Ballet of Can., 1984—86, Milw. Ballet, 1984—85, NAPAC Dance Co., 1985—86, Munich Opera Ballet, 1985—86, Nat. Ballet of Portugal, 1986—87, Ariz. Ballet, 1987—88. Dancer prin. (ballets) Swan Lake, Coppélia, La Bayadere, Tales of Hoffmann, Lander's Etudes, Shadowplay, Leaves are Fading, Balanchine's Theme and Variations, Am. Ballet Theatre, 1971—75, Gemini, Some Times, Intermezzo, Les Noces, 1971—75, Swan Lake, Don Quixote, Sphinx, Voluntaries, 1977, The Taming of the Shrew, Romeo & Juliet, Onegin, Gemini, La Sacre de Printemps, Greening, Stuttgart Ballet, 1975—76, Apollo, The Four Temperaments, Agon Symphony in C, Who Cares?, Geneva Ballet, 1976—77, Romeo & Juliet, The Sleeping Beauty, Sphinx, Rosalinda, London Festival Ballet (now English Nat. Ballet), 1977, Cinderella, Swan Lake, Giselle, Romeo & Juliet, 1982—83, Swan Lake, Frankfort Ballet, 1980—81, Giselle, Basel Ballet, 1980—81, Don Quixote, Vienna Ballet, 1980—81, The Taming of the Shrew, Manon, Royal Swedish Ballet, 1980—81, La Sylphide, Deutsche Opera Berlin, 1982, Coppélia, Giselle, Greening, Apollo, Spoleto and Naples, 1982, Swan Lake, Pitts. Ballet Theatre, 1984—85, Romeo & Juliet, Nat. Ballet of Can., 1984—85, Swan Lake, 1985—86, The Merry Widow, Milw. Ballet, 1984—85, Apollo, NAPAC Dance Co., 1985—86, Romeo & Juliet, Munich Opera Ballet, 1985—86, Apollo, Nat. Ballet of Portugal, 1986—87, The Nutcracker, Ariz. Ballet, 1987—88; creator prin. role (ballets) Chopin Pas de Deux, Malmo Opera Ballet, 1993—94; choreographer (ballets) Swedish TV, 1983, Simple Symphony, Zurich Ballet, 1984, Baroque Variations, Malmo Opera Ballet, 1988, Swan Lake, 1992—93 (Thalia prize, 1993); master of ceremonies dance competition, Swedish TV, 1997. Bd. dirs. Swedish Dance U., Stockholm, Dalhalla amphitheater, Rattvik, Sweden. Recipient Dance medal, Carina Ari Found., 1994. Avocations: photography, skiing, mountain climbing, horseback riding, wilderness guide training.

KAGGEN, LOIS SHEILA, non-profit organization executive, advocate; b. N.Y.C., Jan. 2, 1944; d. Elias and Sylvia (Muntner) K.; m. Harold Jay Burns, June 29, 1969 (dec. June 1975); 1 child, David Henry (dec.); m. Michael Francis McCann, Sept. 26, 1984. BS in Fine Arts, Skidmore Coll., 1964; postgrad., Cooper Union, 1967-70; MA in Art Edn., CCNY, 1973; PhD in Art Edn., NYU, 1997. Tchr. fine arts grades 7-9 Jr. H.S. 149, Bronx, N.Y., 1967-74; founder, pres. Resources for Artists With Disabilities, N.Y.C., 1987—. Traumatic Brain Injury Consumer Adv., 1977—; mem. adv. bd. com. Art in Edn. Project, N.Y. State Coun. on the Arts, Ctr. for Safety in the Arts, N.Y.C., 1987; cons. Ea. Paralyzed Vets. Assn., Guggenheim Mus. Art, N.Y.C., 1990; mem. bd. advisors Ind. Arts Gallery, Queens Ind. Living Ctr., Jamaica, N.Y., 1987-97, 98; mem. steering com. Ann. Disability Independence Day March, 1992-93, mem. Media Outreach, 1992; provider written and oral testimony in field to orgns.; bd. dirs. Ctr. for Independence of the Disabled of N.Y., Inc., N.Y.C., 1996—, Gov.'s appt. to Traumatic Brain Injury Svcs. Coordinating Coun., Albany, 1997-2001, others; presenter NIH Consensus Devel. Conf. on Rehab. of Persons with Traumatic Brain Injury, Bethesda, Md., 1998, 5th Ann. Conf., Traumatic Brain Injury Program, N.Y. State Dept. Health, Albany, 1998, Info. and Comm. Com. TBISEC (TBI Coun.) NYS-DOH, Delmar, N.Y., 2001, N.Y. State Assembly task force on people with disabilites: pub. hearing City U. N.Y. Grad. Ctr., N.Y., 2001, Am. Coun. Edn. conf. The Student with a Brain Injury: Achieving Goals for Higher Edn., DC, 2001; originator, conf. com. co-organizer, consumer panelist NYU Moses Ctr. for Students with Disabilities and Ctr. for Independence of Disabled of N.Y., Loeb Student Ctr., NYU, N.Y.C., 1998; panel organizer, moderator, presenter Inst. for Rsch. on Women's 16th Ann. Celebration of Our Work Conf., Douglass Coll., Rutgers U., New Brunswick, N.J., 1998; mem. search com. for dir. Tang Tchg. Mus. and Art Gallery, Skidmore Coll., Saratoga Springs, N.Y., 2004; gave testimony Taxi and Limousine Commn., 2004; art presenter in field. Photography exhbns. include 80 Washington Sq. East Galleries, N.Y.C., 1977, Soho Photo Gallery, N.Y.C., 1978, 4th St. Photo Gallery, N.Y.C., 1979, Womanart Gallery, N.Y.C., 1979, Leslie-Lohman Gallery, N.Y.C., 1980, 81, Window Gallery, Met. Savs. Bank, N.Y.C., 1980, Cathedral St. John-the-Devine Gallery, N.Y.C., 1980, Donnell Libr. Gallery, 1981; originator, organizer various exhbns. African-Am. Artists with Disabilities, Artists with Phys. Disabilities; contbr. articles, photographs to profl. jours. Mem. Nat. Inst. Disability and Rehab. Rsch.; mem. Office Spl. Edn. and Rehab. Svcs. U.S. Dept. Edn., Washington, mem. per rev. registry, 1995—; active Disabled in Action of Greater N.Y., 1989—, Manhattan Borough Pres. Disability Adv. Coun., 1988—98, 1999—; access subcom. 504 Dem. Club for Persons with Disabilities, 2000—; mem. Mayor's Adv. Com. on People with Disabilities, N.Y.C., 1991—93, Citywide Coalition on Disability, N.Y.C., 1994—95; active in assistive signage needs Planning Meeting NYC Coun./Dept. Disabled, 2000; mem. info. subcom. NYC Coun. Planning Com. Dept. Disabled, 2000—; mem. Disabilities Network of NYC, 2000—; mem. disability rights steering com. 504 Dem. Club for Persons with Disabilities, 1987—88, mem. exec. com., 1990—2002; mem. N.Y. County Dem. Com. 102ED, 1995—; exec. com. The Village Independence Democrats, NYC, 2003—. Grantee Whitney Mus. Am. Art and the Smithsonian Instn., summer 1967, summer film inst. Stanford U., 1968; Cooper Union scholar, 1967-70; recipient Appreciation cert. Manhattan Borough Pres., 1991, Dean's Disting. Alumni Achievement award NYU, N.Y.C., 1998. Mem. Coll. Art Assn. (com. mems. with disabilities for accessible programs and places 1990—), N.Y.C. Coun. dept. for disabled. Office: Resources for Artists with Disabilities 77 7th Ave Ste PH-H New York NY 10011-6645 Personal E-mail: loiskaggen@att.net.

KAGIWADA, REYNOLD SHIGERU, electronics executive; b. LA, July 8, 1938; s. Harry Yoshifusa and Helen Kinue (Imura) K.; children: Julia, Conan. BS in Physics, UCLA, 1960, MS in Physics, 1962, PhD in Physics, 1966. Asst. prof. in residence physics UCLA, 1966-69; asst. prof. physics U. So. Calif., 1969-72; mem. tech. staff TRW (now NGST), Redondo Beach, Calif., 1972-75; scientist, sect. head TRW (now NGST), 1975-77, sr. scientist, dept. mgr., 1977-83, lab. mgr., 1984-87, project mgr., 1987-88, MIMIC chief scientist, 1988-89, asst. program mgr., 1989-90, advanced technology mgr., 1990—2001, dir. advanced electronics, 2002—. Presenter in field. Contbr. articles to profl. jours. Recipient Gold Medal award TRW, 1985, Ramo Tech. award, 1985, Transfer award, IEEE MTT-S N. Walter Cox award, 1997. Fellow IEEE (v.p. IEEE MTT-S adminstrn. com. 1991, pres. 1992, Disting. Svc. award 2001); mem. Assn. Old Crows, Sigma Xi, Sigma Pi Sigma. Achievements include patents for in solid state devices. Home: 3117 Malcolm Ave Los Angeles CA 90034-3406 Office: NGST Bldg M5 Rm 1492 One Space Park Bldg Redondo Beach CA 90278 Personal E-mail: reynold.kagiwada@ngc.com.

KAGLE, JOSEPH LOUIS, JR., artist, arts administrator, art historian, educator; b. Pitts., May 2, 1932; s. Joseph Louis and Edith (Marcellus) K.; m. Anne Cornelia Schiller, Jan. 19, 1957; children: Samantha Anne, Christopher Yung Wook. Student, Carnegie Mus. Sch. Art, 1938-51; BA in English, Dartmouth Coll., 1955; MFA in Art and Art History, U. Colo., 1958; MEd in Gifted and Talented Edn., U. Ark., Little Rock, 1984. Instr. Wis. State U., Whitewater, 1958-60; head dept. art, asst. prof. Washington and Jefferson Coll., Pa., 1960-64; head dept. art, assoc. prof. Keuka Coll., 1964-68; artist in residence Chapman Coll., World Campus Afloat, 1968-69; prof., head dept. fine arts, visual arts, dance, music and theatre U. Guam, 1970-76; prof. art Community Coll. Finger Lakes, 1976-78; exec. dir. S.E. Ark. Arts and Sci. Center, Pine Bluff, 1978-84; dir. Brockton (Mass.) Art Mus., 1984-86, The Art Ctr., Waco, Tex., 1987—2000, Bridgewater State Coll., 1986-87. Artist in residence Wash. State U., Spokane, 1965—66, Naples Mill Sch., 1976—2001, Internat. Plentary of Artists, Kutaisi, Georgia, 2001; bd. contbrs. Waco Tribune-Herald Opinion Editls.; lectr. USIS, Taiwan, 1970—76; critic Pine Bluff (Ark.) News; prof. McLennan C.C., 1987—. Work exhibited in over 500 nat. and internat. exhbns. including Nat. Gallery, Washington, Nat. Mus., Tiblisi, Georgia; dir. 50 TV shows on art; muralist, Hafa Adai Theatre, Bank of Guam, Fine Arts Bldg. U. Guam; author: Death Is All the Time, 1976. Mem. planning bd. Pine Bluff Com. Gifted and Talented, 1979-80; mem. adv. bd. Sta. KCTF, 1989-92; bd. dirs. Greater Waco Coun. on the Arts, 1989—; bd. dirs. Assn. for Retarded Citizens., chmn., 1990-92, 93-94. Named Fulbright scholar, Taiwan, 1965, Georgia, 2001—02, Fulbright specialist, Mongolia, 2004, Smithsonian Instn. Kellog Found. Project scholar, 1983, artist of yr., Pacific chpt. AIA, 1976—77; recipient Fulbright specialist, Mongolia, 2003. Mem. Am. Mus. Assn., Coll. Art Assn., Tex. Assn. Mus., Coll. Art Assn., Am. Assn. Mus., Waco Assn. Mus. (chmn. bd. dirs. 1995-97), Waco C. of C. (bd. dirs. 1994-97). Home: 3758 Glade Forest Dr Houston TX 77339-1739 Office Phone: 254-751-9651. E-mail: joe_kagle@hotmail.com.

KAHAN, BARRY DONALD, surgeon, educator; b. Cleve., July 25, 1939; s. Jacob Marvin and Pearl (Schultz) Kahan; m. Rochelle Liebling, Sept. 22, 1963 (dec.); 1 child, Kara. BS, U. Chgo., 1960, PhD, 1964, MD, 1965. Intern Mass. Gen. Hosp., Boston, 1965-66, resident in surgery, 1968-72; staff asso. in immunology NIH, 1966-68; asst. prof. surgery and physiology Northwestern U. Sch. Medicine, Chgo., 1972-74, asso. prof., 1975-76; prof. surgery U. Tex. Med. Sch., Houston, 1977—, also dir. divs. organ transplantation dept. surgery, dir. program immunology, grad. sch. Bd. dirs. Ill. Kidney Found., 1974—76. Mem. ACS, AAAS, Soc. Univ. Surgeons, Am. Soc. Clin. Investigation, Am. Soc. Transplant Surgeons (pres. 1989—), Am. Surg. Assn., Internat. Transplantation Soc. (charter, treas. 1990—), Am. Surg. Assn., Am. Assn. Immunologists, Am. Assn. Cancer Rsch., Am. Physiol. Soc. Office: U Tex Houston MSB 6-240 6431 Fannin St Houston TX 77030

KAHAN, DAN M., law educator; BA, Middlebury Coll., 1986; JD, Harvard U., 1989. Bar: Md., US Ct. Appeals (4th cir.). Law clk. for Judge Harry T. Edwards US Ct. Appeals, DC Cir.; law clk. for Justice Thurgood Marshall US Supreme Ct., 1990—91; atty. Mayer, Brown & Platt, 1991—93; asst. prof. U. Chgo., 1993—97, prof., 1997—99; vis. prof. Yale U., New Haven, 1998, prof. law, 1999—2003, Dollard prof., 2003—; vis. prof. Harvard U., Cambridge, 1999. Author: Urgent Times: Policing and Rights in Inner-City Communities, 1999. Office: Yale Law Sch PO Box 208215 New Haven CT 06520 E-mail: dan.kahan@yale.edu.

KAHAN, DAVID MICHAEL, education educator; b. Los Angeles, Sept. 21, 1967; s. Osher and Bernice Golden Kahan; m. Amy Laura Waldman, Sept. 5, 1993; children: Jeremy Aaron, Rachel Lyn. BS, UCLA, 1990, MEd in Tchr. Edn., 1991; PhD in Phys. Edn., Ohio State U., 1995. Asst. prof. U. Texas, Odessa, 1995—98, U. N. Mex., Albuquerque, 1998—2000; assoc. prof. in phys. edn. San Diego State U., 2000. Author: (articles) various profl. jours., 1995—. Soccer coach Am. Youth Soccer Orgn., San Diego, 2002. Recipient Friend of Edn., Ector County Ind. Sch. Dist., 1998, Outstanding Tchrs. of Am., 2000, Faculty Award, Rho Lambda Honor Soc. of SDSU, 2003; fellow Rsch. Consortium, 2004. Mem.: Am. Alliance for Health Phys. Edn., Recreation & Dance, Nat. Assn. for Phys. Edn. in Higher Edn., Calif. Assn. for Health Phys. Edn., Recreation & Dance, Phi Kappa Phi (hon.). Democrat. Office: San Diego State U 5500 Campanile Dr San Diego CA 92182-7251 Business E-Mail: dkahan@mail.sdsu.edu.

KAHAN, JONATHAN SETH, lawyer; b. N.Y.C., Apr. 5, 1948; s. Paul Herbert and Henrietta Kahan; m. Barbara Kahan, Apr. 28, 1984; children: Rachel, Paul, David, Adam. BA, George Washington U., 1970, JD, 1973. Bar: D.C. 1974, U.S. Dist. Ct. D.C. 1974, U.S. Ct. Appeals (D.C. cir.) 1974. Law clk. to hon. judge Oliver Gasch U.S. Dist. Ct. D.C., Washington, 1973-74; assoc. Hogan & Hartson LLP, Washington, 1974-82, ptnr., 1982—. Contbg. editor Med. Devices and Diagnostics indsl. mag., 1987—, mem. bd. editors, 1989—; mem. bd. editors Food Drug Cosmetic Law Jour., 1989-92. Mem. Fed. Bar Assn. (chmn. fed. bar assn. sect. on health and human svcs. Washington chpt. 1985-90, co-chmn. D.C. Bar sect. on adminstrv. law and agy. practice 1988-93). Office: Hogan & Hartson LLP 555 13th St NW Ste 800E Washington DC 20004-1161 Office Phone: 202-637-5794. Office Fax: 202-637-5910. Business E-Mail: jskahan@hhlaw.com.

KAHAN, MARCEL, law educator; b. 1962; BA, Brandeis U., 1984; MS, Sloan Sch. of Mgmt., MIT, 1988; JD, Harvard Law Sch., 1988. Bar: NY 1989. Assoc. Kramer, Levin, Nessen, Kamin & Frankel, NYC, 1989—90; asst. prof. law NYU Sch. Law, 1990—93, assoc. prof., 1993—95, prof., 1995—, George T. Lowy prof. law. Past vis. prof. Harvard Law Sch., Columbia Law Sch., Hebrew U.; bd. dirs. Ctr. for Law and Bus. NYU, 1997—. Office: NYU Sch Law Vanderbilt Hall Rm 314C 40 Washington Sq S New York NY 10012-1099 Office Phone: 212-998-6268. Office Fax: 212-995-4341. E-mail: kahanm@juris.law.nyu.edu.

KAHAN, MITCHELL DOUGLAS, museum director; BA, U. Va., 1973; MA, Columbia U., 1975; M of Philosophy, CUNY, 1978, PhD, 1983. Mus. aide Nat. Mus. Am. Art, Washington, 1978; curator Montgomery Mus. Fine Art, Ala., 1978-82, N.C. Mus. Art, Raleigh, 1982-86; dir. Akron Art Mus., Ohio, 1986—. Cons. La. World's Exposition, New Orleans, 1983-84. Author: Art Inc.: American Paintings in Corporate Collections, 1979, Roger Brown, 1981, Minnie Evans, 1986, Art Since 1850-Akron Art Museum, 2001. Columbia U. fellow, 1973, Smithsonian Inst. fellow, 1976-78, CUNY grad. research fellow, 1978, Nat. Endowment for Arts fellow, 1987. Mem. Coll. Art Assn., Intermus Conservation Assn. (trustee 1986-95, pres. 1990-92, 95), Assn. Art Mus. Dirs., Akron Area Arts Alliance (pres. 2003—), Akron Roundtable (pres. 2001). Office: Akron Art Mus 70 E Market St Akron OH 44308-2084*

KAHANA, EVA FROST, sociology educator; b. Budapest, Hungary, Mar. 21, 1941; came to U.S., 1957; d. Jacob and Sari Frost; m. Boaz Kahana, Apr. 15, 1962; children: Jeffrey, Michael. BA, Stern Coll., Yeshiva U., 1962; MA, CCNY, CUNY, 1965; PhD, U. Chgo., 1968; HLD (hon.), Yeshiva U., 1991. Nat. Inst. on Aging predoctoral fellow U. Chgo. Com. on Human Devel., 1963-66; postdoctoral fellow Midwest Council Social Research, 1968; with dept. sociology Washington U., St. Louis, 1967-71, successively research asst., research assoc., asst. prof.; with dept. sociology Wayne State U., Detroit, 1971-84, from assoc. prof. to prof., dir. Elderly Care Research Ctr., 1971-84; prof. Case Western Res. U., Cleve., 1984—, Armington Prof., 1989-90, chmn. dept. sociology, 1985—, dir. Elderly Care Research Ctr., 1984—, Pierce and Elizabeth Robson prof. humanities, 1990—. Cons. Nat. Inst. on Aging, Washington, 1976-80, NIMH, Washington, 1971-75. Author: (with E. Midlarsky) Altruism in Later Life, 1994; editor: (with others) Family Caregiving Across the Lifespan, 1994; mem. editl. bd. Gerontologist, 1975-79, Psychology of Aging, 1984-90, Jour. Gerontology, 1990-94, Applied Behavioral Sci. Rev., 1992—; contbr. articles to profl. jours., chpts. to books (recipient Pub.'s prize 1969). Bd. dirs. com. on aging Jewish Community Fedn., Cleve.; vol. cons. Alzheimer's Disease and Related Disorders Assn., Cleve. NIMH Career Devel. grantee, 1974-79, Nat. Inst. Aging Merit award grantee, 1989—; Mary E. Switzer Disting. fellow Nat. Inst. Rehab., 1992-93; recipient Arnold Heller award excellence in geriatrics and gerontology Menorah Park Ctr. for Aged, 1992, Diekhoff awrd for disting. grad. tchg., 2002; named Outstanding Geontological Rschr. in Ohio, 1993, 04. Fellow Gerontol. Soc. Am. (chair behavioral social sci. com. 1984-85, chair 2000—, Disting. Mentorship award 1987, Polisher award 1997); mem. Am. Sociol. Assn. (coun. sect. on aging 1985-87, Disting. Scholar award sect. on aging and life course 1997, chair sect. on aging and life course, 2000-2001), Am. Psychol. Assn., Soc. for Traumatic Stress, Wayne State U. Acad. Scholars (life), Sigma Xi. Avocations: reading, antiques, travel.

KAHANE, JEFFREY, conductor, pianist; b. L.A., Sept. 12, 1956; BMus, San Francisco Conservatory, 1977. Prof. piano Eastman Sch. Music, 1988-95; music dir. Santa Rosa (Calif.) Symphony, 1995—2005, LA Chamber Orch., 1996—, Green Music Festival, 2001, Colo. Symphony Orch., 2005—. Office: IMG Artists 825 7th Ave New York NY 10019-6014 E-mail: artistsny@imgworld.com.

KAHKONEN, DOROTHY M., endocrinologist; b. Detroit, Jan. 23, 1941; d. William Walter Kahkonen and Dorthay May Estes. BS, U. Mich., 1963, MD, 1965. Cert. Am. Bd. Internal Medicine. Intern Los Angeles County Hosp., L.A., 1965—66; resident in internal medicine Henry Ford Hosp., Detroit, 1966—69, fellow in metabolic diseases, 1969—70, sr. staff in metabolic diseases, 1970—95; divsn. head, endocrinology Henry Ford Health Sys., Detroit, 1995. Fellow: Detroit Acad. Medicine (pres. 1999—2000); mem.: Mich. State Med. Soc. (pres. 2002—03, spkr. ho. of dels. 1997—2001, bd. dirs. 1993—), Am. Heart Assn. (fellow Coun. on Arteriosclerosis), Am. Diabetes Assn., Assn. Lipid and Atherosclerosis Rsch. (pres. 2001—02). Office: Henry Ford Health Sys 3031 West Grand Blvd Ste 800 Detroit MI 48202 Office Phone: 313-916-2141.

KAHL, JASON J., music educator; b. Indpls., June 9, 1978; s. Bernard J. Kahl and Misty A. Slentz; m. Kristin L Woodling, June 30, 2001. MusB, Butler U., Indpls., 2000. Tchg. cert. Ind., 2000. Dir. of bands Tri-Central Mid. and High Schools, Sharpsville, Ind., 2000—. Office: Tri-Central Middle and High School 2115 W 500 N Sharpsville IN 46068 Office Phone: 765-963-2560.

KAHL, WILLIAM FREDERICK, retired academic administrator; b. May 23, 1922; s. William Frederick and Bessie (Glading) K.; m. Mary Carson, Jan. 25, 1964; children: Frederick Glading, Sarah Hartwell. BA, Brown U., 1945; MA, Harvard U., 1947, PhD, 1955, LHD, 1993. Lectr. history Boston U., 1947-48, 50; from instr. to prof. Simmons Coll., Boston, 1948-76, provost, 1965-76; pres. Russell Sage Coll., Troy, N.Y., 1976-88. Bd. dir. Norstar. Author: The London Livery Companies: An essay and bibliography, 1960; contbr. articles to profl. jours. Vice-chmn. Hudson River Valley Assn.; bd. dirs. Albany Symphony Orch., Lower East Side Conservancy; chmn. bd. Tenement Mus., N.Y. State Nature Conservancy, Albany Inst. History and Art, Friends of the Hudson River Valley, Hudson River Valley Coordinating Coun., Russell Sage Pres. Adv. Coun.; pres., trustee, Albany Acad. for Girls,

Wildwood Sch., Albany C. of C. Found. Social Sci. Coun. rsch. grantee, 1957-58. Mem. Am. Hist. Assn., Anglo-Am. Hist. Conf. Episcopalian. Home: 29 Old Niskayuna Rd Albany NY 12211-1349 Office: Russell Sage Coll Troy NY 12180

KAHLENBECK, HOWARD, JR., retired lawyer; b. Ft. Wayne, Ind., Dec. 7, 1929; s. Howard and Clara Elizabeth (Wegman) K.; m. Sally A. Horrell, Aug. 14, 1954; children: Kathryn Sue, Douglas H. BS with distinction, Ind. U., 1952; LLB, U. Mich., 1957. Bar: Ind. 1957. Ptnr. Krieg DeVault, LLP, Indpls., 1957—2005; ret. Sec., bd. dirs. Maul Tech. Corp. (formerly Buehler Corp.), Indpls., 1971-81, Am. Monitor Corp., Indpls., 1971-86, Am. Interstate Ins. Corp. Wis., Milw., 1973-84, Am. Interstate Ins. Co. Ga., Am. Underwriters Group, Inc., Indpls., 1973-86, Pafco Gen. Ins. Co., 1987-88. With USAF, 1952-54. Mem. ABA, Ind. Bar Assn., Indpls. Bar Assn., Alpha Kappa Psi, Delta Theta Phi, Beta Gamma Sigma, Delta Upsilon Internat. (sec., bd. dirs. 1971-83, chmn. 1983-86, trustee found. 1983-98). Lutheran. Home: 6320 Old Orchard Rd Indianapolis IN 46226-1041 Office: Krieg DeVault LLP One Indiana Sq Ste 2800 Indianapolis IN 46204 Business E-Mail: hk@kdlegal.com.

KAHLER, HERBERT FREDERICK, manufacturing executive; b. St. Augustine, Fla., Sept. 20, 1936; s. Herbert E. and Marie (Strieter) K.; m. Erika Rozsypal, May 16, 1964; children: Erik, Stephen, Christopher, Michael, Craig. AB, Johns Hopkins, 1958; LLB, Harvard U., 1961. Bar: N.Y. bar 1962. With Simpson, Thacher & Bartlett, N.Y.C., 1961-65; sec., gen. counsel Insilco Corp., Meriden, Conn., 1965-70; pres., CEO W.H. Hutchinson & Son, Inc., Chgo., 1970-73, Miles Homes Co., Mpls., 1973-86; v.p., dir. Insilco Corp., 1979-88; pres. Kahler & Assocs., 1988—; pres., CEO Crown Fixtures, Inc., Plymouth, Minn., 1990—, Power Generation Svc., Inc., 1990—97, chmn., 1997—; pres., CEO Crown Tonka Calif., Inc., 2000—. Hon. consul Republic of Austria, 1998—. Bd. corporators Meriden Hosp., 1965-70, Harvard, 1970; bd. govs. Meriden/Wallingford Hosp., 1987; bd. dirs. St. Paul Chamber Orch., 1974-87, St. Paul Opera Assn., 1975-77, Minn. Opera Co., 1977-87. Lt., arty. AUS, 1962-64. Mem. ABA, Mpls. Club, Phi Beta Kappa. Office: Crown Fixtures Inc 10700 Highway 55 Ste 300 Plymouth MN 55441-6134 Office Phone: 763-541-1410.

KAHLER, NANCY J., music educator, director; d. Frederick Charles and Grace Miriam (Moyer) Knerr; children: Denise Marie, Timothy Charles, Debra Joan Bucklin, Allan Curtis, Donald James. B in Music Edn., Esther Boyer Coll. Music, Phila., 1983. Music tchr. Camden Bd. Edn., NJ, 1984—. Organist, choir dir. Karmel UCC, Phila., 1982—2000; organist St. Hedwig's, Phila., 1983; singer Mendelssohn Club Phila., 1987—; dir. music Temple Lutheran, Pennsauken, NJ, 2000—; elections' chair Camden Edn. Assn., NJ, 2000. Contbr. articles to profl. jours. Mem.: Music Tchrs. Nat. Assn., Music Educators Nat. Convention, Am. Guild Organists, Delta Mu. Avocations: baking, gardening, composing. Home: 7703 West Chester Pike Upper Darby PA 19082-1418 E-mail: studiok@snip.net.

KAHLES, CHERYL MARY, elementary school educator; b. Bklyn., Aug. 5, 1950; d. Thomas and Cornelia Mary Dickson; m. B. Antonio Cherot (div.); children: Nicole Marie Cherot, Jason Anthony Cherot; m. James Francis Kahles, June 6, 1998. BS in Edn., U. Ill., 1973; MEd, Coll. Mt. St. Joseph, 1987. Tchr. Oakwood (Ill.) Elem. Sch., 1972—74, Diamond Elem. Sch., Danville, Ill., 1974—78, Monee (Ill.) Elem. Sch., 1978—79, Amelia (Ohio) Elem. Sch., 1979—2005. Mem. The St. John Passion Play, Cinn., 1999—2005, Immaculate Heart of Mary Roman Cath. Ch., Cinn., 1979—2005. Mem.: NEA, Nat. PTA, Ohio Edn. Assn. Roman Catholic. Avocations: travel, sailing, celtic and renaissance festivals. Office: Amelia Elem Sch 5 E Main St Amelia OH 45102 Business E-Mail: kahles_c@westcler.org.

KAHMANN, CHESLEY, composer, music educator, pianist; b. N.Y.C., Aug. 12, 1930; d. George Ames Kahmann and Mable Grace Chesley; m. Judson A. Parsons Jr.; children: Ames, Brookett. BA in Music, U. Rochester, 1952; postgrad., Eastman Sch. of Music, Rochester, 1954, Peabody Conservatory/Johns Hopkins U., 1954—58, Chautauqua (N.Y.) Instn., 1957. Dir. music Oldfields Sch., Glencoe, Md., 1952—58, Bklyn. Friends Sch., 1958—60; founder, dir., composer The Interludes, Summit, NJ, 1971—; pvt. tchr. piano and theory, 1971—; founder Orbiting Clef Prodns., Summit, 1971—. Recs. include Patterns, 1995, An American Mass, 2003, Chamber Music by Chesley Kahmann, 2003, The Village Store Expanded, 2004, Chamber Music by Chesley Kahmann, Vol. II, 2004, The Kahmann Touch, Vol. I, 2005; composer: Bells in B Major, 1937, Prayer at Nightfall, 1944, Bird Song, 1943, Hay, Hay, What's Say?, 1944, Passacaglia for Strings, 1952, The Show Must Go On, 1953, Ankles Away, 1954, Sonata for Violin & Piano, 1954, Song Cycle No. 1 for High Voice, 1954, Sonata-Allegro for Piano, 1955, Theme & Variations for Orchestra, 1955, Fugue for Orchestra, 1955, Cricket Kingdom, 1956, Suite for Orchestra, 1956—57, Twenty-Six Minus X, 1957, For Everything There is a Season, 1962, Songs for Flute and Strings, 1962, Suite for Strings & Timpani, 1962, Sonata for Violincello & Piano, 1963, Sonata for Piano, 1963, Five Short Pieces for Piano, 1963, String Quartet, 1963, Symphony, 1963—64, Dance for Flute, Oboe and Piano, 1964, Song Cycle No. 2 for High Voice and Orch., 1964, Without the Mercy, 1965, We Will Give Thanks for Thee, 1965, The Voice of My Beloved, 1965, Little Piano Piece, 1965, Trio for Flute, Oboe, Bassoon, 1965, I Have a Bird in Spring, 1965, Concerto for Piano & Orch., 1955—66, Trio for Flute, Violin & Piano, 1966, Trumpet I for Ames, 1971, Adagio for Organ, Violin and Viola, 1973, Amen for Mixed Choir, 1976, Trumpet II for Ames, 1976, Exercise for High Voice, 1977, Call for Two Trumpets and Two Trombones, 1979, The American Suite for flute, oboe & piano, 1983, Angels We Have Heard on High, 1983, Patterns for Trumpet and Keyboard, 1993, Second Patterns for Trumpet and Keyboard, 1994, Dances for Piano, 2001, The Summit Songs (90), 1971—, Gypsy Summer, 1958, An America Mass, 1980—2000. Mem.: ASCAP, Am. Music Ctr. Methodist. Avocations: gardening, reading, pets. Home and Office: Orbiting Clef Prodns 36 Baltusrol Rd Summit NJ 07901 Office Phone: 908-277-3881. E-mail: chesleykahmann@comcast.net.

KAHMANN, SARAH STUBER, retired foundation administrator; b. Clay, Pa., Jan. 18, 1928; d. Harry Miles and Mamie (Stauffer) Stuber; children from previous marriage: Lynne Einhaus, Ed III, Susan Hasty, Barbara Amato. V.p. Nat. Coalition Protection Children and Families, Cin., 1989-93; ret., 1993. Bd. mem. St. Luke Found.; founder Enough is Enough Bd., 1996—2002; apptd. by gov. Ky. Commn. Women, 1998—; grad. Leadership Ky., 2000; bd. dirs. Women's Crisis Ctr., 2003—; apptd. rev. bd. Historic Preservation, 2005—. Named Woman of the Yr., Cin. Enquirer, 1997. Avocations: community service, politics, art, travel. *My experience has been a willingness to risk, along with the belief that set-backs are not failures but an opportunity to learn and grow--these principles have led me to risk much, and thus accomplish much and enriched my life tremendously.*

KAHN, ALAN EDWIN, lawyer; b. N.Y.C., Aug. 9, 1929; s. Joseph and Harriet Rose (Rubel) K.; m. Regina Wolf, Aug. 7, 1960 (div. Jan. 1978); 1 child, Jolie Galen; m. Patricia Ann Dugan, June 4, 1978. BBA, CCNY, 1950; JD, Bklyn. Law Sch., 1956. Bar: N.Y. 1956, U.S. Dist. Ct. (so. and ea. dists.) N.Y. 1978, U.S. Tax Ct. 1978; CPA, N.Y. Staff asst.-acct. Feinberg, Jacobs & Furman, N.Y.C., 1956-57; pvt. practice N.Y.C., 1957-96, 98—; prin. Law Office of Alan E. Kahn, N.Y.C., 1957—; sr. ptnr. Kahn, Boyd, Levychin CPAs, N.Y.C., 1993—2003; pvt. practice, 2003—. Tax cons. to various nonprofit orgns., N.Y.C., 1977—. Cons. Vol. Lawyers for the Arts, N.Y.C., 1978—. Sgt. U.S. Army, 1951-52. Mem. ATLA (mem. com. 1990—), N.Y. State Bar Assn. (elder law com.), N.Y. State Trial Lawyers Assn. (chmn. subcom. on legis. estate and trusts 1979, spkr. bd. 1990—, mem. com. 1991—, chair 2000—), N.Y. County Lawyers Assn. (taxation com. 1988—, sec. com. on taxation 1996-2000, chair com. on taxation 2000—), Spkr.'s Bur., Assn. Trial Lawyers City N.Y., Jewish Lawyers Guild, N.Y. State Soc. CPAs, Nat. Sculpture Soc. (patron mem.), Odd Fellows (grand adv. bd. N.Y. chpt. 1979-80, gen. counsel grand lodge 1989—), Mchts. Club (bd. govs., asst. treas., treas. and gov. 1992—, award chmn. legal com. 1995—), Democrat. Avocations: collecting prints, paintings and oriental ceramics. Home: 370 1st Ave New York NY 10010-4923 Office: 17 Battery Pl New York NY 10004 Office Phone: 212-271-4345. E-mail: aekwacs@aol.com.

KAHN, ALFRED EDWARD, economist, educator, government official; b. Paterson, N.J., Oct. 17, 1917; s. Jacob and Bertha (Orlean) K.; m. Mary Simmons, Oct. 10, 1943; children: Joel, Rachel, Hannah. AB, NYU, 1936, MA, 1937; postgrad., U. Mo., 1937-38; PhD, Yale U., 1942; LLD (hon.), Colby Coll., 1978, U. Mass., 1979, Ripon Coll., 1980, Northwestern U., 1982, Colgate U., 1983; DHL (hon.), SUNY, Albany, 1985. Mem. staff Brookings Inst., 1940, 51-52; with anti-trust div. Dept. Justice, 1941-42, Dept. Commerce, 1942, WPB, 1943; economist on Palestine surveys, 1943-44, Twentieth Century Fund, 1944-45; asst. prof., chmn. dept. econs. Ripon Coll., 1945-47; asst. prof. Cornell U., 1947-50, asso. prof., 1950-55, prof., 1955-89, chmn. dept. econs., 1958-63, Robert Julius Thorne prof. econs., 1967-89, emeritus, 1989—, dean Coll. Arts and Scis., 1969-74; chmn. N.Y. State Pub. Service Commn., 1974-77, CAB, 1977-78, Council on Wage and Price Stability (adviser to Pres. on inflation), 1978-80. Mem. atty. gen's nat. com. to study anti-trust laws, 1953-55; sr. staff U.S. Coun. Econ. Advisers, 1955-57; spl. cons. Boni, Watkins, Jason & Co., N.Y.C., 1957-61, Nat. Econ. Rsch. Assocs., 1961-74, 80—, U.S. Fgn. Agrl. Svc., Israel, 1960-61, Dept. Justice, 1963-64, FTC, 1965, Ford Found., 1967; econ. adv. coun. AT&T, 1968-74; econ. adv. com. U.S. C. of C., 1964-66; mem. environ. adv. com. Fed. Energy Adminstrn., 1974-77; mem. rev. com. sulfur emissions from power plants Nat. Acad. Scis., 1974-75; adv. bd. Electric Power Rsch. Inst., 1974-77; mem. Nat. Antitrust Law Rev. Com., 1978-79; adv. to N.Y. gov. on comm. regulation, 1980-81; mem. usage panel Am. Heritage Dictionary, 1982—; mem. N.Y. Gov.'s Adv. Com. on Pub. Power for L.I., 1986, N.Y. Gov.'s Fact-Finding Panel on Shoreham Nuclear Plant, 1983, N.Y. State Coun. on Fiscal and Econ. Priorities, 1983-89; chmn. adv. com. on price reform and competition in the USSR Internat. Inst. for Applied Systems Analysis, 1990-92; econ. commentator Nightly Bus. Report (pub. TV), 1981-97; mem. Ohio Blue Ribbon Panel Telecomm. Regulation, 1992-93; mem. N.Y. State Telecomm. Exch., 1992-94; Ct.-apptd. expert U.S. Dist. Ct., 1993-94; com. study of competition U.S. airline industry Nat. Rsch. Coun., 1999—; mem. adv. com. Digital Age Comms. Act Project, 2005—. Author: Great Britain in the World Economy, 1946; co-author (with J.B. Diriam): Fair Competition, The Law and Economics of Anti-Trust Policy, 1954; co-author: (with M.G. de Chazeau) Integration and Competition in the Petroleum Industry, 1959; author: The Economics of Regulation, 2 vols., 1970, 71, reprinted/new intro., 1988, Letting Go: Deregulating The Process of Deregulation, 1998, Whom the Gods Would Destroy, Or How Not to Deregulate, 2001, Lessons From Deregulation: Telecommunications and Airlines After the Crunch, 2004. Trustee Cornell U., 1964-69; mem. nat. governing bd. Common Cause, 1982-85; chmn. Blue Ribbon Panel to Investigate Pricing of Electricity in Calif., 2000. Fulbright Rsch. fellow Italy, 1954-55; recipient Wilbur Cross medal for outstanding achievement Yale U., 1995, L. Welch Pogue award for Lifetime Contbn. to Aviation, 1997, Soverign Fund award 1997, J. Rhoads Foster award, 1999. Mem. Am. Econ. Assn. (v.p. 1981-82), Nat. Assn. Regulatory Utility Commrs. (exec. com., chmn. com. on electricity 1975-77), Am. Acad. Arts and Scis., Phi Beta Kappa. Office: 221 Savage Farm DR Ithaca NY 14850-6501 Office Phone: 607-277-3007.

KAHN, ALFRED JOSEPH, social services researcher, educator; b. N.Y.C., Feb. 8, 1919; s. Meyer and Sophie (Levine) K.; m. Miriam Kadin, Sept. 3, 1949 (div. 1980); 1 child, Nancy Valerie. B in Social Sci., CCNY, 1939; B in Hebrew Lit., Sem. Coll. Jewish Studies, N.Y.C., 1940; MS, Columbia U., 1946, D in Social Welfare, 1952; DHL (hon.), Adelphi U., 1984; DSc (hon.), U Md., 1989; Dr. (hon.), York U., Eng., 1998. Psychiat. social worker Jewish Bd. Guardians, N.Y.C., 1946-47; mem. faculty Sch. Social Work Columbia U., 1947-89, prof. Sch. Social Work, 1954-89, prof. emeritus, 1989; co-dir. Cross Nat. Studies Rsch. Program, 1973—; Disting. vis. prof. Grad. Sch. Social Svc., Fordham U., 1990-2001. Staff cons. Citizens Com. for Children, N.Y.C., 1948-72; mem. summer faculty Smith Coll. Sch. Social Work, 1949-54; cons. govts., founds., vol. agys., 1949-2004; mem. numerous adv. coms.; mem. adv. com. child devel. NRC-Nat. Acad. Scis., 1971-76, mem. com. child devel. rsch. and pub. policy, Acad. Scis., 1977-83, chmn., 1980-83; mem. adv. bd. Inst. Rsch. Poverty, U. Wis., 1967-2002. Author: A Court for Children, 1953, Planning Community Services for Children in Trouble, 1963, Neighborhood Information Centers, 1966, (with Anna Mayer) Day Care as a Social Instrument, 1966, Theory and Practice of Social Planning, 1969, Studies in Social Policy and Planning, 1969, Social Policy and Social Services, 1973; co-author: Not for the Poor Alone, 1975, Social Service in the U.S., 1976, Social Services in International Perspective, 1977, Child Care, Family Benefits and Working Parents, 1981, Helping America's Families, 1982, Maternity Policies and Working Women, 1983, Income Transfers for Families With Children, 1983, Child Care: Facing the Hard Choices, 1987, The Responsive Workplace, 1987, Mothers Alone, 1988, Social Services for Children, Youth and Families in the United States, 1989, Social Services for Children, Youth and Families: The New York City Study, 1990, A Welcome for Every Child, 1994, Social Policy and the Under 3s, 1994, Starting Right, 1995, Big Cities in the Welfare Transition, 1998, Contracting for Child and Family Services, 2000; contbr. monographs, articles to profl. jours., chpts. to books; editor: Issues in American Social Work, 1959, Shaping The New Social Work, 1973; co-editor: Family Policy: Government and Famlies in Fourteen Countries, 1978, Child Support, From Debt Collection to Social Policy, 1988, Privatization and the Welfare State, 1989, Child Care, Parental Leaves and The Under 3s: Policy Innovation in Europe, 1991, Children and Their Families in Big Cities, 1996, Family Change and Family Policies in Great Britain, Canada, New Zealand, and the United States, 1997, Beyond Child Poverty: The Social Exclusion of Children, 2002. With USAAF, 1942-46. Mem. AAUP, Nat. Assn. Social Workers (chmn. div. practice and knowledge 1963-66, bd. dirs. 1967-70), Council Social Work Edn., Assn. for Policy Analysis and Mgmt. Home: 250 Gorge Rd Apt 17B Cliffside Park NJ 07010-1309 Office: Columbia U Sch Social Work New York NY 10027 Office Phone: 212-851-2271. Business E-Mail: ajk7@columbia.edu.

KAHN, ANTHONY F., lawyer; b. Washington, Apr. 29, 1954; s. Henry and Claudia F.; m. Cynthia Marie Farhart, Aug. 11, 1979; children: Brian, Andrew, Stephen. BA, Wake Forest U., 1976; MBA summa cum laude, JD magna cum laude, U. Notre Dame, 1980. Bar: N.Y. 1981. Ptnr. White & Case LLP, N.Y.C., 1980—. Office: White & Case LLP 1155 Avenue of the Americas New York NY 10036-2711 Office Phone: 212-819-8338. E-mail: akahn@whitecase.com.

KAHN, BERND, radiochemist, educator; b. Pforzheim, Baden, Germany, Aug. 16, 1928; US1938; s. Eric Herman and Alice Dora (Meyer) K.; m. Gail Pressman, Aug. 6, 1961; children: Jennifer, Elizabeth. BSChemE, N.J. Inst. Tech., 1950; MS in Physics, Vanderbilt U., 1952; PhD in Chemistry, MIT, 1960. Commd. officer USPHS, 1954, advanced through grades to capt., 1970, health physicist, radiochemist, Oak Ridge (Tenn.) Nat. Lab., 1951-54, engr. various facilities, 1954-74, ret., 1974; prof. nuc. engrng. and health physics Ga. Inst. Tech., Atlanta, 1974-96, prof. emeritus, 1996—, dir. Environ. Resources Ctr., 1974—. Co-editor: Management of Low-Level Radioactive Waste, 1979; co-inventor recovery of magnesium salts from sea water. Mem. Nat. Coun. Radiation Protection and Measurments (hon.), Am. Chem. Soc., Am. Phys. Soc., Health Physics Soc. Achievements include research in radiochemistry and environmental radioactivity. Office: Ga Tech Rsch Inst Atlanta GA 30332-0841 Business E-Mail: bernd.kahn@me.gatech.edu.

KAHN, C. RONALD, research laboratory administrator; b. Louisville, Jan. 14, 1944; s. David L. and Reva W. (Waldman) K.; m. Susan Becker; children: Stacy, Jeffrey. BA, U. Louisville, 1964, MD, 1968, MS, 1984; MA (hon.), Harvard U., 1984; DSc (honoris causa), U. Louisville, 1984, U. Paris-Pierre and Marie Curie, 1990, U. Geneva, 2000. Diplomate Am. Bd. Internal Medicine, Am. Bd. Endocrinology and Metabolism. Intern and resident in ward medicine Barnes Hosp., St. Louis, 1968-70; clin. assoc., sr. clin. assoc., clin. endocrinology br. Nat. Inst. Arthritis, Metabolism and Digestive Diseases, NIH, Bethesda, Md., 1970-73; sr. investigator Diabetes Br. NIH, Bethesda, Md., 1973-78, chief diabetes br., 1979-81; rsch. dir Joslin Diabetes Ctr., Boston, 1981-2000, dir., 1997-99, exec. v.p., dir., 1997-99; assoc. prof. Harvard Med. Sch., Boston, 1981-84, prof. medicine, 1984—, Mary K. Iacocca prof. medicine, 1986—; pres. Joslin Diabetes Ctr., 2000—. Lectr. symposia, meetings, thesis supr., course dir. and devel. numerous med. instns.; admitting and attending physician NIH Clin. Ctr., 1972-81; physician Brigham and Women's Hosp., Boston, 1981, chief div. Diabetes and Metabolism, 1981-92; assoc. staff Endocrinology/Internal Medicine, New Eng. Deaconess Hospital, Boston, 1982, active staff, 1986; clin. assoc. prof. medicine, Uniformed Svcs. U. Health Scis, Bethesda, Md., 1979-81; vis. scientist Centre de Moleculaire, Centre National de la Recherche Scientifique, Gif-sur-Yvette, France, 1979-80; adj. prof. genetics George Washington U., 1980-81; overseas vis. prof. Royal Melbourne Hosp., Australia, 1985; vis. prof. Royal Postgrad. Hosp., London, 1985; Rosemary Sarver vis. prof. in endocrinology and metabolism, The Hosp. of the Good Samaritan, L.A., 1985. Author or co-author over 430 publs. in field; mem. editl. bds. Jour. Clin. Endocrinology and Metabolism, 1977-80, Diabetes, 1977-84, Am. Jour. Medicine, 1979-84, Jour. Clin. Investigation, 1979-84, Jour. Receptor Rsch., 1980-83, Hormone and Metabolic Rsch., 1980-83, Endocrinology, 1981-85, Jour. Biol. Chemistry, 1983-88, Diabetes and Metabolism Revs., 1984, Receptor, 1989—; exec. editor Trends in Endocrinology and Metabolism, 1989-90; cons. editor Jour. Clin. Investigation; assoc. editor Diabetes, 1996-2001. Mem. Nat. Diabetes Adv. Bd., 1981-85, co-chmn. rsch. com., 1982-85. Recipient David Rumbough Meml award for Sci. Achievement Juvenile Diabetes Found., 1977, CIBA-Geigy Drew award for biochem. rsch., 1981, Mary Jane Kugel award Juvenile Diabetes Found., 1982, AFCR award for Outstanding Clin. Rsch. under Age 40, 1983, Sol Berson Meml. lectureship NIH, 1983, Hehnemann Lectr. in Pharmacology U. Calif.,1984, Pfizer Biomed. Rsch. award, Pfizer inc., 1986, Cristobal Diaz award Internat. Diabetes Fedn., 1988, Banting award Am. Diabetes Assn., 1993, Nat. Acad. Scis. award, 1999, Inst. Medicine, 1999, Hamden award U.A.E., 2000, Lawson-Wilkins Lectr. Pediatric Endocrine Soc., 2001, Freedom to Discover Achievement Award for Metabolic Disease, Bristol-Myers Squibb, 2004, others. Fellow AAAS; mem. Nat. Acad. Scis., Am. Acad. Arts & Scis., Am. Fedn. Clin. Rsch., The Endocrine Soc. (Edwin B. Astwood lectr. 1987, Kocl award 2000), Am. Diabetes Assn. (Eli Lilly award for rsch. 1980, Otto Brandman award N.J. affiliate 1989, Elliott P. Joslin medal Mass. affiliate, Albert Renold award 1998), Am. Soc. Clin. Investigation (nat. coun. 1986—, pres. elect 1987-88, pres. 1988-89), Am. Soc. Biol. Chemistry, Assn. Am. Physicians, Sigma Xi, Alpha Epsilon Delta, Phi Kappa Phi, Alpha Omega Alpha. Achievements include rsch. in insulin receptors and insulin action, insulin-like growth factors, diabetes mellitus, hypoglycemia, immunity, autoimmunity and viruses in endocrine disorders. Office: Joslin Diabetes Ctr One Joslin Pl Boston MA 02215 E-mail: c.ronald.kahn@joslin.harvard.edu.

KAHN, CHARLES N., III, (CHIP KAHN), medical association administrator; BA, Johns Hopkins U.; MPH, Tulane U., 1980. Adminstrv. resident with Tchg. Hosp. Dept. Assn. Am. Med. Colls.; former dir. Office Fin. Mgmt. Edn. Assn. Univ. Programs in Health Adminstrn.; former sr. health policy advisor Sen. David Durenberger; former legis. asst. of health Sen. Dan Quayle; minority health counsel Ho. Ways and Means Health Subcom., Washington, 1986—93; exec. v.p. Health Ins. Assn. Am., Washington, 1993—94; pres., 1998—2001; staff dir. health subcom. Ho. Ways and Means Com.; pres. Fedn. Am. Hosps., Washington, 2001—. Chmn. Econ. Rsch. Initiative on the Uninsured U. Mich.; bd. dirs. Partnership for Prevention; mem. adv. com. Ctr. for Studying Health Sys. Change; mem. program adv. bd. Robert Wood Johnson Health Fellowships Program; mem. Medicare Competetive Pricing Adv. Com.; instr. health policy Johns Hopkins U., George Washington U., Tulane U.; adj. clin. prof. Tulane U. Sch. Pub. Health and Tropical Medicine. Contbr. articles to profl. jours. Mem.: Delta Omega. Office: Fedn Am Hosps Ste 245 801 Pennsylvania Ave NW Washington DC 20004-2604 Business E-Mail: ckahn@americashospitals.com.

KAHN, DANIEL, physician; Nuc. medicine Univ. Iowa and VAMC, Iowa City, 1986—2005. Office: Univ Iowa and Iowa City VAMC Hihgway 6 Iowa City IA 52246 Office Phone: 319-338-0581.

KAHN, DAVID, editor, author; b. N.Y.C., Feb. 7, 1930; s. Jesse and Florence (Abraham) K.; m. Susanne Monika Fiedler, Oct. 22, 1969 (div. Jan. 1995); children: Oliver, Michael. AB, Bucknell U., 1951; DPhil, Oxford (Eng.) U., 1974. Reporter Jersey Jour., Jersey City, 1952-53; copyboy N.Y. Daily News, 1953-55; reporter Newsday, Garden City, N.Y., 1955-63; freelance writer, 1963-65, 67-74; news desk editor Internat. Herald Tribune, Paris, 1965-67; prof. journalism NYU, 1974-79; asst. viewpoints editor Newsday, Melville, N.Y., 1979-94, mem. editorial bd., 1988-94; scholar in residence Nat. Security Agy., 1995; asst. editor features Newsday, Melville, N.Y., 1996-98; ret., 1999; freelance author, 1999—. Adj. prof. modern polit. and mil. intelligence Yale U., New Haven, 1985, Columbia U., N.Y.C., 1986-88; founding co-editor Cryptologia mag., 1977—; mem. editorial bd. Intelligence and Nat. Security, 1986—, Internat. Jour. Intelligence and Counterintelligence, 1986—, Jour. Cryptology, 1991-2001, Jour. Intelligence History, 2001-; witness Congl. coms.; adj. prof. journalism SUNY, Stony Brook, 1991-94. Author: Two Soviet Spy Ciphers, 1960, Plaintext in the New Unabridged, 1963; The Codebreakers, 1967, Hitler's Spies, 1978, Seizing the Enigma, 1991 (named Notable Naval Book of 1991 U.S. Naval Inst.), The Reader of Gentlemen's Mail, 2004; editor: Kahn on Codes, 1983; editor, translator: Clandestine Operations, 1983; cons. on cryptology to Oxford English Dictionary; contbr. articles to profl. jours. and encys. Bd. trustees St. Antony's Coll. Trust, ret., 2000; bd. dirs. Nat. Cryptologic Mus. Found.; sr. assoc. mem. St. Antony's Coll., Oxford U., 1972-74; bd. dirs. Great Neck Libr., 2002-; patron Bletchley Park (U.K.) Trust. Recipient spl. award, Nat. Security Agy., 1991, 2004, Nat. Intelligence Study Ctr., 1992. Mem. Am. Cryptogram Assn. (pres. 1965-67), World War II Studies Assn. (bd. dirs. 1987—), Internat. Intelligence Study Group, Internat. Spy Mus. (mem. adv. bd. dirs.), Internat. Assn. for Cryptologic Rsch. (bd. dirs. 1980-90), Century Assn., Phi Beta Kappa. Democrat. Jewish. Avocation: tennis. Home and Office: 120 Wooleys Ln Great Neck NY 11023-2301 Office Phone: 516-487-7181. Personal E-mail: davidkahn1@aol.com.

KAHN, DEBORAH, artist, educator; BFA, Kansas City Art Inst.; NFA, Yale U. Asst. prof. Am. U., Washington, DC, 1989—. Guest artist Dartmouth Coll., Swathmore Coll., RI Sch. Design, Chautauqua Sch. Art, Nat. Women's Mus., U. Iowa Sch. Art, Vt. Studio Ctr. Exhibitions include Bowery Gallery, Les Yeux du Monde, Hood Mus., Dartmouth Coll., Swarthmore Coll., Pierogi 2000, Ruth Siegal Gallery, George Hemphill and David Adamson Galleries, Albright-Knox Mus. Fellow Guggenheim Meml. Found., 2004. Office: Am U Dept Art Watkins Bldg 116 4400 Massachusetts Ave, NW Washington DC 20016*

KAHN, DOUGLAS ALLEN, legal educator; b. Spartanburg, SC, Nov. 7, 1934; s. Max Leonard and Julia (Rich) K.; m. Judith Bleich, Sept. 24, 1959; m. Mary Briscoe, June 12, 1970; children— Margery Ellen, Jeffrey Hodges. BA, U. N.C., 1955; JD with honors, George Washington U., 1958. Bar: D.C. 1958, Mich. 1965, U.S. Ct. Appeals (D.C. cir.) 1958, U.S. Ct. Appeals (5th and 9th cirs.) 1959, U.S. Ct. Appeals (3d, 4th and 6th cirs.) 1960, U.S. Supreme Ct. 1963. Atty. Civil and Tax div. U.S. Dept. Justice, 1958-62; assoc. Sachs and Jacobs, Washington, 1962-64; prof. law U. Mich., Ann Arbor, 1964—, Paul G. Kauper Disting. prof., 1984—. Vis. prof. Stanford Law Sch., 1973, Duke Law Sch., 1977, Fordham Law Sch., 1980-81, U. Cambridge, 1996. Author: (with Gann) Corporate Taxation, 1989, (with Waggoner and Pennell) Federal Taxation of Gifts, Trusts and Estates, 1997, (with Lehman) Corporate Income Taxation, 2001, (with J. Kahn) Federal Income Tax, 2005; comment editor George Washington U. Law Rev., 1956-58; contbr. articles to profl. jours. Recipient Emil Brown Found. prize, 1969 Mem. ABA, Order of Coif. Republican. Jewish. Office: U Mich Law Sch 625 S State St Ann Arbor MI 48109-1215 Office Phone: 734-764-9341. Business E-Mail: dougkahn@umich.edu.

KAHN, EDWIN LEONARD, lawyer; b. N.Y.C., Aug. 1, 1918; s. Max L. and Julia (Rich) K.; m. Myra J. Green, Oct. 20, 1946 (dec. 1994); children: Martha L., Deborah K. Spiliotopoulos. AB, U. N.C., 1937; LLB cum laude,

Harvard U., 1940. Bar: N.C. 1940, D.C. 1949. Atty., asst. head legislation and regulations div. Office Chief Counsel IRS, 1940-52, dir. tech. planning div., 1952-55; ptnr. Arent, Fox, Kintner, Plotkin & Kahn (now Arent Fox LLC), Washington, 1955—86, of counsel, ret., 1986—. Lectr. NYU Tax Inst., mem. adv. bd., 1959-70; lectr. tax insts. Coll. William and Mary, U. Chgo., U. Tex. Editor: Harvard Law Rev, 1939-40; editorial adv. bd. Tax Advisor of Am. Inst. CPA's, 1974-86. Bd. dirs. Jewish Community Ctr. Greater Washington, 1972-78; trustee Cosmos Club Found., 1989-93, chmn., 1989-91. With U.S. Army, 1943-46, ETO. Decorated Bronze Star. Fellow Am. Bar Found. (life); mem. ABA (coun. 1963-66, vice chmn. sect. taxation 1965-66), Fed. Bar Assn. (chmn. taxation com. 1967-68), D.C. Bar Assn., Nat. Tax Assn.-Tax Inst. Am. (adv. coun. 1967-69, bd. dirs. 1969-73), Am. Law Inst. (life), Am. Coll. Tax Counsel, J. Edgar Murdock Am. Inn Ct. (master bencher 1988-91), Phi Beta Kappa (life mem. fellows). Jewish. Home: 4104 40th St N Arlington VA 22207-4805 Office: 1050 Connecticut Ave NW Washington DC 20036-5303

KAHN, EDWIN SAM, lawyer; b. N.Y.C., Jan. 22, 1938; m. Cynthia Chutter, May 30, 1966; children: David, Jonathan, Jennifer. BA, U. Colo., 1958; JD, Harvard U., 1965. Bar: Colo. 1965, U.S. Dist. Ct. (Colo.) 1965, U.S. Ct. Appeals (10th cir.) 1965, U.S. Supreme Ct. 1968. Assoc. Holland & Hart, Denver, 1965-70, ptnr., 1970-77; ptnr., shareholder Kelly, Haglund, Garnsey & Kahn, LLC, Denver, 1978—. Spl. coun. Colo. Ctr. Law and Policies, 2004—. 1st lt. USAF, 1959-62. Fellow Am. Coll. Trial Lawyers; mem. Denver Bar Assn. (pres. 1984-85). Home: 2345 Leyden St Denver CO 80207-3441 Office: Kelly Haglund Garnsey & Kahn LLC 1441 18th St Ste 300 Denver CO 80202-1255 E-mail: edkahn@4dv.net.

KAHN, EIKO TANIGUCHI, artist; b. Fukuoka, Kyushu, Japan, Jan. 24, 1929; arrived in US, 1955, naturalized, 1958; d. Tosuke Yamashita and Masano Taniguchi; m. Frederick Joseph Kahn, Sept. 28, 1954; children: Karen, Miho Kahn Wiedis. Gen., Sumiyoshi Women's Sch., Osaka, Japan, 1944. Solo exhbns. include Gregg Gallery, N.Y.C., 1982, Nat. Arts Club, Celadon Gallery, N.Y.C., 1988, The Korby Gallery, Cedar Grove, N.J., 1995, AWS Salmagundi Club, N.Y.C., 1995, The Koh Gallery, Union City, N.J., 1996, AT&T Bell Lab. Gallery, Hopewell, N.J., 1996, Ocean County Artists Guild Gallery, N.J., 1996, Gratella Gallery, Princeton, N.J., 1997, Ellarslie Trenton City Mus., 2000. Recipient Pres.'s award Nat. Arts Club, 1981, Ablert Baldwin prize Nat. Acad. Design, 1983, Award for Excellence Middlesex County Mus., 1985. Mem. N.J. Water Color Soc. (award 1990), Audubon Artists (Medal of Honor 1981), Artists Fellowship. Avocations: golf, gardening. Address: 217 Cleveland Ln RD 4 Princeton NJ 08540-9517 Office Phone: 732-329-6242.

KAHN, ELLIS IRVIN, lawyer; b. Charleston, S.C., Jan. 18, 1936; s. Robert and Estelle Harriet (Kaminski) Kahn; m. Janice Weinstein, Aug. 11, 1963; children: Justin Simon, David Israel, Cynthia Kahn Nirenblatt. AB in Polit. Sci., Citadel, 1958; JD, U. S.C., 1961. Bar: S.C. 1961, U.S. Ct. Appeals (5th cir.) 1963, U.S. Ct. Appeals (4th cir.) 1964, U.S. Supreme Ct. 1970, DC 1978, U.S. Claims Ct. 1988, diplomate: Nat. Bd. Trial Advocacy, Am. Bd. Profl. Liability Attys. (trustee 1989-), cert.: (civil ct. mediator). Law clk. U.S. Dist. Ct. S.C., 1964—66; prin. Kahn Law Firm, Charleston. Adj. prof. med.-legal jurisprudence Med. U. S.C., 1978—87; mem. rules com. U.S. Dist. Ct., 1984—96. Mem. nat. coun. Am. Israel Pub. Affairs Com., 1982—88, Hebrew Benevolent Soc., pres., 1994—96; mem. Hebrew Orphan Soc., S.C. Organ Procurement Agy., 1989—94; chmn. campaign Charleston Jewish Fedn., 1986—87, pres., 1988—90. Capt. USAF, 1961—64. Fellow: Internat. Soc. Barristers; mem.: ATLA (state committeeman 1970—74), ABA, S.C. Trial Lawyers Assn. (pres. 1976—77), 4th Cir. Jud. Conf. (life), S.C. Bar. Home: 316 Confederate Cir Charleston SC 29407-7431 Office: PO Box 31397 Charleston SC 29417-1397 Office Phone: 843-577-2128.

KAHN, HERMAN L. (BUD KAHN), financial advisor; b. Pitts., Dec. 14, 1954; s. Joseph Carl and Sylvia (Herman) K.; m. Jane Beth Resnick, June 10, 1984; children: Aaron H., Elliot C. BA cum laude, U. Pitts., 1975, MBA, 1976; MS in Taxation, Robert Morris Coll., 1985. CPA, Pa., CFP. Staff acct. Coopers & Lybrand, Pitts., 1976-77, sr. acct., 1977-79; tax mgr. Horovitz, Rudoy and Roteman, Pitts., 1979-85, Arthur Young, Pitts., 1985-88; sr. v.p. Mid Atlantic Capital Group, Pitts., 1988-91; pres. Wealth Mgmt. Strategics, Inc., Pitts., 1991—. Bd. dirs. Jewish Chronicle, Pitts.; mem. Leadership Pitts. XIV. Mem. AICPA (accredited pers. fin. specialist), IMCA, Estate Planning Coun. of Pitts., Allegheny Tax Soc., Inst. Cert. Fin. Planners. Democrat. Jewish. Office: Wealth Mgmt Strategies Inc 147 Delta Dr Ste 200 Pittsburgh PA 15238-2805

KAHN, HERTA HESS (MRS. HOWARD KAHN), retired investment company executive; b. Wuerzburg, Germany; naturalized, U.S. d. Ferdinand and Lilly (Suesser) Hess; m. Herbert Levy (dec.); 1 child, Linda Levy; m. Howard Kahn (dec.). Student, Northwestern U. Sch. Commerce. Joined Paine, Webber, Jackson & Curtis, Inc., Chgo., 1941; registered rep. Paine, Webber Inc. (now UBS Fin. Svcs. Inc.), acct. v.p., v.p. investments; mktg. cons., 1995—. Author: (book) What Every Woman Should Know About Investing Her Money, 1968. Hon. life mem. nat. commn., hon. life. mem. Chgo. exec. com. Anti-Defamation League B;nai B'rith; bd. dirs. Found. Hearing and Speech Rehab., Chgo. Mem.: Chgo. Crime Commn., Chgo. Fin. Exch., CFA Inst., Investment Analysts Soc. Chgo., N.Y. Soc. Security Analysts, Tamarisk Country Club (Rancho Mirage, Calif.), Execs. Club (Chgo.), Econ. Club, Std. Club, Northmoor Country Club (Highland Park, Ill.).

KAHN, JACK MERRILL, television producer; b. Boston, Nov. 25, 1952; s. David Lowell and Shirley Florence Kahn; m. Diana Burlant; 2 children. B of Hebrew Lit., Hebrew Coll., 1974; BS, Boston U., 1974; MA, Am. U., 1975. Reporter James Srodes News Svc., Washington, 1975-76, WCIX-TV, Miami, Fla., 1976-78, exec. prodr., 1978-79; prodr. Nightly Bus. Report WPBT-TV, Miami, 1979-90; sr. prodr. spl. projects NBR Enterprises/WPBT, Miami, 1990-95, dir. program devel., 1996—. Prodr.: (videotapes) How Wall Street Works, 1991 (AFVA 1991), NBR Guides to Retirement Planning, Buying Insurance, 1992 (AFVA 1992), Stock Market Strategies (WorldFest Houston Platinum award 2003), How to Find the Right College, 1992, 2001 (N.Y. Festivals award 1992, WorldFest Houston Gold award 2001), How to Plan Your Estate, 1993 (N.Y. Festivals award 1993, Silver Gavel award ABA 1994), How to Invest in Mutual Funds (N.Y. Festivals award 1994), How to Find The Right Franchise (Silver Cindy award 1997), Making Your Company a Better Place for Employees (Silver Cindy award 1999), Careers for the 21st Century (Bronze Cindy award 1999), NBR Guide to Buying Bonds (World-Fest Houston Platinum award 2002), (CD-Rom) Encyclopedia of Personal Finance, NBR Edition (Dalton Comms. award, Multi-media 2005). Bd. dirs. Beth David Congregation, Miami, 1980-2002. Recipient Excellence in Fin. Writing award Pannell Kerr Forster, 1989, Excellence in Fin. Journalism award N.Y. State Soc. CPA's, 1991, 2002, Journalism award for excellence in personal fin. reporting Investment Co. Inst. Edn. Found., The Am. U., 1992, Gracie Allen award Am. Women Radio TV, 1998, Silver award, Platinum, Gold Remi awards, World Fest, Houston, 2005. Mem. Soc. Am. Bus. Editors and Writers Inc. Jewish. Office: NBR Enterprises/WPBT 14901 NE 20th Ave Miami FL 33181-1121 Personal E-mail: jsharjoel@aol.com. Business E-Mail: jack_kahn@nbr.com.

KAHN, JAMES ROBERT, lawyer; b. Indpls., Apr. 11, 1953; s. Robert D. and Rose Doris (Hyman) K.; m. Debra Amper, Oct. 21, 1984; children: Adam Joshua, Aliza Toby. BA, U. Pa., 1974; JD, Harvard U., 1978. Bar: Pa. 1978, U.S. Dist. Ct. (ea. dist.) Pa. 1978, U.S. Ct. Appeals (3d cir.) 1982, N.J. 1985, U.S. Dist. Ct. N.J. 1985, U.S. Dist. Ct. (ea. and so. dists.) N.Y. 1988. Jud. clk. U.S. Dist. Ct. Dist. N.J., Camden, 1978-79; assoc. Blank, Rome, Comisky & McCauley, Phila., 1979-88, ptnr., 1988-95, Margolis Edelstein, 1995—. Chair Phila. Bar state civil cts. com., 1994; mem. Gov.'s Task Force on Med. Malpractice, 2002-2003. Bd. dirs., chair, v.p., sec. Jewish Family and Children's Svcs., Phila., 1988—; bd. dirs. Phila. Pride, Inc., 1994-97; bd. dirs., sec. Schylkill River Devel. Coun., Inc., 1993-2002; trustee Jewish Fedn. Greater Phila., 1993—; mem. United Jewish Appeal Young Leadership Cabinet, 1992-96. Recipient Young Leadership award Jewish Fedn. of Greater Phila., 1993, Stella Moore award for contbns. to dance in Phila., 1994. Mem. Pa. Bar Assn., Phila. Bar Assn., Assn. Trial Lawyers Am., Pa. Trial Lawyers Assn., Phila. Trial Lawyers Assn., Phila. Bicycle Club. Avocation: biking. Home: 2420 Fitlers Walk Philadelphia PA 19103-5562 Office: Margolis Edelstein Curtis Ctr 4th Fl Independence Sq W Philadelphia PA 19106-3304 Office Phone: 215-931-5887. Business E-Mail: jkahn@mangolisedelstein.com.

KAHN, JAMES STEVEN, retired museum director; b. N.Y.C., Oct. 14, 1931; 3 children. BS in Geology, CCNY, 1952; MS in Mineralogy, Pa. State U., 1954; PhD in Geol. Sci., U. Chgo., 1956. Instr. U. R.I., Kingston, 1957, asst. prof., 1958-60, research assoc. Narragansett Marine Lab., 1957-60; group leader U. Calif., Livermore, 1960-70; dept. head Physics Internat. Co., San Leandro, Calif., 1970-71; div. head geophysics U. Calif., Livermore, 1972—74, dep. assoc. dir. human resources, 1975-78, assoc. dir. nuclear testing, 1978-80, dep. dir. lab., 1980-87; pres., chief exec. officer, dir. Mus. Sci. and Industry, Chgo., 1987-97; retired, emeritus. Trustee Mus. Sci. and Industry; mem. math. scis. edn. bd. NAS, 1991-94; chmn. sci. adv. com. Gov. Ill., 1994-98; IMAX Corp. Co-author: Statistical Analysis in Geological Sciences, 1962; contbg. author: Microstructure, 1968; mem. adv. bd. Reno Jour. Gazette, 2004—; contbr. articles to sci. jours. Trustee Geol. Soc. Am. Found., 1997—, fellow Geol. Soc. Am.; bd. dirs. Franklin and Eleanor Roosevelt Inst., 1994-2001, Dubuque (Iowa) Art Inst., 1999-02, emeritus trustee Dubuque Mus. Art; rector sci. and medicine Lincoln Acad. Ill., 1994-2002; mem., vice-chmn. Bd. Natural Resources and Conservation, State of Ill. Centennial fellow Pa. State U. Coll. Earth and Mineral Scis., 1996. Mem.: Sigma Xi. Personal E-mail: jbkahn@mac.com.

KAHN, JAN EDWARD, manufacturing executive; b. Dayton, Ohio, Aug. 29, 1948; s. Sigmond Lawrence and Betty Jane K.; m. Deborah Ann Deckinga, Nov. 28, 1975; children: Jason Edward, Justin Allen, Julie Ann. BS in Metall. Engring., U. Cin., 1971. Mgmt. trainee U.S. Steel Corp., Gary, Ind., 1971-72; plant metallurgist Regal Tube Co., Chgo., 1972-74, gen. foreman, 1974-76, supt., 1976-77, mgr. tech. svc., 1978-80, materials mgr., 1980-81; mgr. quality contrl Std. Tube Co., Detroit, 1977-78; dir. ops. Boye Needle Co., Chgo., 1981-82, v.p. ops., 1982-83, v.p., gen. mgr., 1984-85, pres., 1985-88; v.p. sales and mktg. Caron Internat., Washington, N.C., 1988—. Bd. dirs. Warm Up Am., Craft Yarn Coun., pres., 2002—04; bd. dirs. Helping Hands Found., 2004—. Mem. Am. Soc. Metals, AIME, ASTM, Ravenswood Indsl. Coun. (bd. dirs. 1983-84, pres. 1985), Hand Knitting Assn. (chmn. 1986-88). Republican. Mem. Christian Reformed Ch. Home: 13909 Teakwood Dr Homer Glen IL 60491 Office: Caron Internat PO Box 3000 Orland Park IL 60462-1099 Business E-Mail: jankahn@caron.com.

KAHN, JEFFRY, mathematics professor; Prof. math. dept. Rutgers U., New Brunswick, N.J. Recipient George Polya prize Soc. Indsl. & Applied Math., 1996. Office: Math Dept-Hill Ctr-Busch Campus Rutgers U New Brunswick NJ 08903

KAHN, JIM, former magazine publisher; m. Cyd Kahn; 1 child, Miranda. BS in Bus. mgmt., State U. N.Y., Binghamton, 1980. Jr. acct. exec. Vanguard Advt., N.Y.C., NY, 1980—82; account exec. Golf Mag. Properties, N.Y.C., 1986, west coast mgr. L.A., assoc. pub. N.Y.C., 1990-96, group pub., sr. v.p., 1996—2000; sr. v.p. group pub. Entrepreneur Media, Inc., NY, 2000—02; exec. v.p. sales and mktg. Profile Pursuit, Inc., NY, 2002; v.p. nat. equipment sales Advanced Mag. Pub., Inc., Staten Island, NY, 2002. Office: Advance Publ, Inc 950 W Fingerboard Rd Staten Island NY 10305-1453

KAHN, KATHLEEN PICA, photojournalist, arbitrator, mediator; b. Houston, Feb. 21, 1951; d. Adrien and Sarah Retha (McGuffey) K.; 1 child, Adrien Yuri Mathieu. A, Delgado Coll., New Orleans, 1985; cert., U. De L'Etat A Mons, Belgium, 1986, U. Cath. de L'Ouest, Angers, France, 1987; BA, Nichols State U., 1988; MH, U. Houston, 1989, postgrad., 1997—. Video editor Cox Cable TV, New Orleans, 1984-85; film editor French Consulate, New Orleans, 1984-87; journalist, corr. Daily Shipping Guide, New Orleans, 1990; journalist, corr. spl. sects. Houston Chronicle, 1990—. Pres. Bay Area Mediators Assn., Houston, 1996; interviewer Steven Spielberg's Shoah Found., L.A., 1996—. Bd. dirs. Congregation B'Nai Israel, 1996. Grantee City New Orleans, 1985; scholar Coun. Devel. French Lang., Quebec, Can., 1986, Mons, Belgium, 1987, Angers, France, 1988. Mem. Nat. Fedn. Press Women, Nat. Coun. Jewish Women, Soc. Profl. Journalists, Tex. Accts. Arts, Hadassah. Avocations: sculpting, jewelry design. Home: 1119 Chase Park Dr Bacliff TX 77518-2486

KAHN, MARC LESLIE, orthopedic surgeon; b. Phila., Mar. 12, 1956; s. Sigmund and Joanne (Pokras) K.; m. Cynthia Petrowsky; 5 children. AB, Lafayette Coll., 1978; MD, Hahnemann Med. Coll., 1982. Resident in orthopedics Monmouth Med. Ctr., Long Branch, N.J., 1987; surgeon, maj. U.S. Army, Ft. Dix, N.J., 1987-91; orthopedic surgeon Garden State Orthopedics, Cherry Hill, NJ, 1991—. Clin. instr. N.J. Sch. Osteo. Medicine. Contbr. articles to profl. jours. Decorated Army Achievement medal with 2 oak leaf clusters, Meritorious Svc. medal. Fellow: Arthroscopy Assn. N.Am., Am. Acad. Orthop. Surgeons; mem.: AMA, N.J. Med. Soc., Camden County Med. Soc, Orthop. Surgeons of N.J. (bd. dirs., vice chmn.), N.J. Orthop. Soc. (pres.-elect, bd. dirs.), N.J. Med. Soc. Home: 455 Rte 70 West Cherry Hill NJ 08002 Office: Garden Hill Orthopedics 455 Rte 70 W Cherry Hill NJ 08002

KAHN, MARK LEO, arbitrator, educator; b. NYC, Dec. 16, 1921; s. Augustus and Manya (Fertig) K.; m. Ruth Elizabeth Wecker, Dec. 21, 1947 (div. Jan. 1972); children: Ann Mariam, Peter David, James Allan, Jean Sarah; m. Elaine Johnson Morris, Feb. 12, 1988 (dec. July 2004). BA, Columbia U., 1942; MA, Harvard U., 1948, PhD in Econs., 1950. Asst. economist U.S. OSS, Washington, 1942-43; tchg. fellow Harvard U., 1947-49; dir. case analysis U.S. WSB, Region 6-B Mich., 1952-53; mem. faculty Wayne State U., Detroit, 1949-85, prof. econs., 1960-85, prof. emeritus, 1985—, dept. chmn., 1961-68, dir. indsl. rels. M.A. program, 1978-85. Co-author: Collective Bargaining and Technological Change in American Transportation, 1971; mem. editl. bd. Employee Responsibilities and Rights Jour., 1988-96; contbr. articles to profl. jours. Bd. govs. Jewish Welfare Fedn. Detroit, 1976-82; bd. dirs. Jewish Home for Aged, Detroit, 1978-93, Lyric Chamber Ensemble, Southfield, Mich., 1995-97, Detroit Empowerment Zone Devel. Corp., 1996-99. Pvt. to Capt. AUS, 1943-46. Decorated Bronze Star; recipient Disting. Svc. award U.S. Nat. Mediation Bd., 1987, Am. Arbitration Assn., 1992. Mem. AAUP (past chpt. pres.), Nat. Acad. Arbitrators (hon. life mem., bd. govs. 1960-62, v.p. 1976-78, chmn. membership com. 1979-82, pres. 1983-84, chmn. nominating com. 1995-96), Indsl. Rels. Rsch. Assn. (pres. Detroit chpt. 1956, exec. sec. 1979-89, nat. exec. bd. 1985-88), Soc. Profls. in Dispute Resolution (v.p. 1982-83, pres. 1986-87). Home and Office: 15151 Ford Rd Apt 321 Dearborn MI 48126-5027 Office Phone: 313-584-0007. Personal E-mail: mleokahn@aol.com.

KAHN, MICHAEL, stage director; b. NYC; s. Frederick J. and Adele (Gaberman) K. BA, Columbia U.; DHL (hon.), U. S.C., 1994, Kean Coll., 1974. Artistic dir. Am. Shakespeare Theatre, Stratford, Conn., 1969-77, The Acting Co., 1978-88, Chautauqua Conservatory Theatre Co., 1985-88, Shakespeare Theatre, Washington, 1986—; dir. Chautauqua Inst. Theatre Sch., 1983-88; dir. drama divsn. Juilliard Sch., N.Y.C., 1992—; acad. chmn. Brit. Am. Drama Acad., Oxford, Eng., 1992-96; artistic dir. The Shakespeare Theatre Acad. for Classical Acting George Washington U., Washington, 2000—. Mem. faculty Circle in the Square, N.Y.C., Princeton U.; mem. faculty grad. program Sch. Arts, NYU; mem. panel League of Profl. Theatre Tng. Programs; bd. dirs. Theatre Comm. Group, Theatre Panel, N.Y. State Coun. of Arts; mem. theatre panel Nat. Endowment for Arts; panel mem. D.C. Commn. on Humanities and the Arts; artistic dir. Shakespeare Theater, 2000—. Dir. Romeo and Juliet (Helen Hayes nomination), The Winter's Tale, Macbeth (Helen Hayes nomination), All's Well that Ends Well (Helen Hayes nomination), Anthony and Cleopatra, As You Like It, Twelfth Night (Helen Hayes award 1989), Merry Wives of Windsor (Helen Hayes nomination), Richard III, 1990 (Helen Hayes nomination), King Lear, 1991, Much Ado About Nothing, 1992, Measure for Measure, 1992, Hamlet, 1993 (Helen Hayes award 1993), Mother Courage (Helen Hayes award), 1993, Richard II, 1993, The Doctor's Dilemma, 1994, Henry IV, 1994 (Helen Hayes award), Henry V (Helen Hayes nomination), Volpone, 1996, Henry VI (Helen Hayes award), 1996, Mourning Becomes Electra, (Helen Hayes Award) 1997; Peer Gynt (1997), Sweet Bird of Youth, 1998, A Woman of No Importance, 1998, King John, 1999, The Merchant of Venice, 1999, King Lear, 1999, Coriolanus, 1999, Camino Real, 2000, Timon of Athena, 2000, Don Carlos, 2001 (Helen Hayes nomination), The Oedipus Playe, 2001, The Duchess of Malfi, 2002, Hedda Gabler, 2001, The Winters' Tale, 2002, The Silent Woman, 2003, Five by Tenn at the Kennedy Ctr., 2004, Manhattan Theatre Club, 2004, Cyrano de Bergerac, 2004 (Helen Hayes award, Outstanding Dir., 2005), Macbeth, 2004, Lorenzaccio, 2005; producing dir. McCarter Theater, Princeton, N.J.; plays including Beyond The Horizon, Mother Courage, Grave Undertaking, The Heiress, Angel City, The Torchbearers, A Month in the Country, Put Them All Together, 1974—; dir. Broadway prodns. The Death of Bessie Smith, 1967, Here's Where I Belong, 1968, Cat On A Hot Tin Roof, 1974, Night of the Tribades, 1977, Whodunnit, 1983, Showboat, 1983 (Tony nomination); off-Broadway prodns. Funnyhouse of A Negro, 1966, Rimers of Eldritch, 1967, Thorton Wilder plays, 1967, N.Y. Shakespeare Festival's Measure for Measure, 1966, Grand Magic, Manhattan Theatre Club, 1978, A Month in the Country, Roundabout, 1980, Hedda Gabler, Roundabout, 1981, Flux, 1982, Something Different, 1983, Ten By Tennessee, 1986, Sleep Deprivation Chamber, 1996, Goodman Theatre, Chgo., Old Times, 1972, Tooth of Crime, 1973, Tis Pity She's a Whore, 1974, Showboat, Cairo, Egypt, 1987, Five By Tennessee, 1989, Moscow, Leningrad, Vilmius Warsaw, Belgrade, 1990, Signature Theatre Otabenga, Va., 1994, The Oedipus Plays, Athens Festival, 2003, Five by Tenn, Manhattan Theater Club, 2005; TV prodn. Beyond the Horizon, WNET, 1975; San Francisco Opera Julio Cesare, 1978, The Acting Co., 1978—, A New Way to Pay Old Debts, 1984, The White Devil, 1979, Carmen, Houston Grand Opera, 1981, Carmen, Washington Opera, 1982, The Glass Menagerie, Chautauqua Conservatory Theatre, 1985, Tis Pity She's a Whore (Am. Repertory Theatre), 1988, Much Ado About Nothing, McCarter Theatre, 1993, Vanessa, Dallas Opera, 1994, Washington Opera, 1995, Lysistrata (world premiere) Houston Grand Opera, 2005. Recipient Best Dir. Revival award Saturday Rev., 1966; Charles MacArthur award for best dir. Old Times, 1973, Joseph Jefferson award, 1974, Washington Post award, 1989; named Best Dir. N.J. Drama Critics, 1974, 76, Washingtonian of Yr. Washingtonian mag., 1989; nominated for 4 Vernon Rice awards, 1967, John Houseman award, Globe Theater award, Bravo award Opera Music Theatre Internat., 1997, D.C. Mayor's Art award, 1997, Champs Cmty. award, 2000, William Shakespeare award for Classical Theatre, 2002, Univ. Club Cultural award of the Yr., 2002, GLAAD Capitol Area award, 2002, Lifetime Achievement award SETC, 2003, Arts Founder award D.C. Cultural Alliance, 2005. Home: 1 W 72nd St New York NY 10023-3486 Office: The Shakespeare Theatre 301 E Capitol St SE Washington DC 20003-3808 E-mail: mkahn@shakespearedc.org.

KAHN, NORMAN, dental educator, pharmacologist; b. N.Y.C., Dec. 28, 1932; s. Louis Meyer and Dorothy (Simon) Kohn; m. Dale Krasnow, Mar. 30, 1958 AB, Columbia U., 1954, D.D.S., 1958, PhD, 1964. Lic. dentist, N.Y. State. Dental intern Montefiore Hosp., Bronx, N.Y., 1958-59; instr. Coll. Physicians and Surgeons, Columbia U., N.Y.C., 1962-65, asst. prof., 1965-72, assoc. prof., 1972-80, prof. pharmacology, 1980-99, prof. dentistry, 1980-92, Edwin S. Robinson prof. dentistry, 1992-99; assoc. dean acad. affairs Sch. Dental and Oral Surgery, Columbia U., 1989-94, acting dean, 1994-95; attending dentist Presbyn. Hosp., N.Y.C., 1985-99, Robinson prof. dentistry & pharm. emeritus, spl. lectr., 1999—, cons. dentist, 1999—. Vis. assoc. prof. UCLA, 1978; chair instl. rev. bd. Columbia-Presbyn. Med. Ctr., N.Y.C., 1981-91; cons. pharmcologist Harlem Hosp., N.Y.C., 1966-80; vis. scientist U. Pisa, Italy, 1965-66. Contbr. chpts. to books, articles to profl. jours. NIH grantee, 1969-75, Nat. Fund Med. Edn. grantee, 1973; recipient Outstanding Contbn. to Teaching award Columbia U. Coll. Physicians and Surgeons, 1980, Physicians & surgeons Disting. Svc. award in Pre-Clinical Yrs., 2001; hon. research fellow Univ. Coll., London, 1986. Mem. Am. Physiol. Soc., ADA, Am. Assn. Dental Schs., Confrerie des Chevaliers du Tastevin, Alpha Omega Alpha, Omicron Kappa Upsilon Jewish. Avocation: oenology. Office: Columbia U 630 W 168th St New York NY 10032-3795

KAHN, PAUL FREDERICK, executive search company executive; b. Indpls., Oct. 10, 1935; s. Paul L. and Florence (Copeland) K.; m. Helen Gail Bass, Dec. 27, 1961; children— Hartley, Meredith. BS, Purdue U., 1957; MBA, Harvard U., 1963. Brand mgr. Procter and Gamble, Cin., 1963-69; v.p. Foote, Cone & Belding, N.Y.C., 1969-70; sr. v.p. Wilson Sporting Goods, Chgo., 1970-78, Sara Lee Corp., Chgo., 1978-87; pres., chief exec. officer Kayser-Roth Hosiery Co., 1988; mng. ptnr. Heidrick & Struggles, Chgo., 1989—2002. With USMC, 1957—60. Mem.: Sharon Country Club, Hillsboro Club, Harvard Club (N.Y. chpt.), Univ. Club, Indian Hill Country Club. Presbyterian. Home: 177 Scott Ave Winnetka IL 60093-1529 also: 100 Low Rd Sharon CT 06069-2015

KAHN, PAUL W., law educator; BA, U. Chgo., 1973; PhD in Philosophy, Yale U., 1977, JD, 1980. Bar: DC 1982. Law clk. for Justice Byron White US Supreme Ct., 1980—82; assoc. Powell, Goldstein, Frazier & Murphy, Washington, DC, 1982—85; legal cons. Constl. Commn. of Liberia, 1982—83; assoc. prof. Yale U., New Haven, 1985—90, prof. law, 1990—93, Nicholas deB. Katzenbach prof., 1993—99, Robert W. Winner prof., 1999—, dir. Orville H. Schell, Jr. Ctr. for Internat. Human Rights, 1999—. Author: Legitimacy and History: Self-Government in American Constitutional Theory, 1993, The Reign of Law: Marbury v. Madison and the Construction of America, 1997, The Cultural Study of Law: Reconstructing Legal Scholarship, 1999, Law and Love: The Trials of King Lear, 2000, 2004; contbr. articles to law jours. Coker Fellow, 1979—80. Office: Yale Law Sch PO Box 208215 New Haven CT 06520 E-mail: paul.kahn@yale.edu.

KAHN, PETER B., physics professor; b. N.Y.C., Mar. 18, 1935; s. Morton E. and Lillian E. (Miller) K.; m. Lois Gibbs, Sept. 16, 1956 (div. 1986); children: Miriam, David, Jeffrey; m. Victoria McLane, Jan. 8, 1989. BS, Union Coll., 1956; PhD, Northwestern U., 1960. Research assoc. U. Iowa, Iowa City, 1960-61; from asst. to assoc. prof. physics SUNY, Stony Brook, 1961-71, prof. physics, 1971—2003, emeritus prof., 2003—, chmn. dept. physics, 1974-85. Fellow Am. Physics Soc. Office: SUNY Dept Physics Stony Brook NY 11794-3800

KAHN, RICHARD DREYFUS, lawyer; b. N.Y.C., Apr. 25, 1931; s. David Effrian and Lucille (Kahn) K.; m. Judith Raff, Sept. 10, 1961 (div. 1977); children— Jason, Adam, Alexander; m. Elaine H. Peterson, July 21, 1983 AB, Harvard U., 1952, JD, 1955. Bar: NY 1955. Assoc. Debevoise & Plimpton, N.Y.C., 1955-62, ptnr., 1963-90, of counsel, 1991-93. Editor: Harvard Law Rev., 1953—55. Trustee Am. Soc. Psychical Rsch., N.Y.C., 1966-73; bd. dirs. The Emerson Sch., N.Y.C., 1968-71, J. M.R. Barker Found., N.Y.C., 1968—, C. G. Jung Found. Analytical Psychology, 1984-90, Concerned Citizens of Montauk, 1991—, Group for the South Fork, 1993—; bd. dirs. Found. Child Devel, N.Y.C., 1970-88, coun. vice chmn., 1996-2000; mem. Montauk Citizens Adv. Com., 1992—. Mem. Assn. of Bar of City N.Y. (chmn. com. atomic energy 1965-68), Harvard Club N.Y.C. (bd. mgrs. 1991-93), Phi Beta Kappa. Home: 224 W Lake Dr Montauk NY 11954-5235 Personal E-mail: arcon@optonline.net.

KAHN, ROBERT E., electrical engineer; b. Dec. 23, 1938; BEE, CCNY, 1960; MA, Princeton U., 1962, PhD in Elec. Engring., 1964. Mem. tech. staff Bell Telephone Labs.; asst. prof. elec. engring. MIT, Cambridge; sr. scientist Bolt, Beranek & Newman; dir. info. processing techniques U.S. Defense Advanced Rsch. Projects Agy. (DARPA), 1972—85; founder, pres. Corp. Nat. Research Initiatives, Reston, Va., 1986—. Recipient Nat. medal of Tech., U.S. Dept. of Commerce, 1997. Fellow: ACM (Software Systems award, SIGCOMM award, Pres.'s award), AAAI, IEEE (Koji Kobayashi Computer and

Communications award, Alexander Graham Bell medal, Third Millennium medal); mem.: NAE. Office: Corp for Nat Rsch Initiatives 1895 Preston White Dr Ste 100 Reston VA 20191-5434*

KAHN, SANDRA S., psychotherapist; b. Chgo., June 24, 1942; d. Chester and Ruth Sutker; m. Jack Murry Kahn, June 1, 1965; children: Erick, Jennifer. BA, U. Miami, 1964; MA, Roosevelt U., 1976. Tchr. Chgo. Pub. Schs., 1965-67; pvt. practice psychotherapy, Northbrook, Ill., 1976—. Host Shared Feelings, Sta. WEEF-AM, Highland Park, Ill., 1983—; author: The Kahn Report on Sexual Preferences, 1981, The Ex Wife Syndrome Cutting The Cord and Breaking Free After The Marriage Is Over, 1990; columnist Single Again mag. Mem. Ill. Psychol. Assn., Chgo. Psychol. Assn. (past pres. 1990). Jewish. Office: 801 Skokie Blvd Northbrook IL 60062-4039 Office Phone: 847-272-2228.

KAHN, SIGMUND BENHAM, retired internist, dean; b. Phila., May 18, 1933; s. Maxwell Louis and Clara (Parris) K.; m. Joanne Pokras, June 11, 1955; children: Marc L., Elissa Kahn Petrosky, Hillary Kahn Roth, Lauren B. Westlake. BA, U. Pa., 1954, MD, 1958. Diplomate Am. Bd. Internal Medicine; cert. hematology and med. oncology. Rotating intern Albert Einstein Med. Ctr., Phila., 1958-59; resident in internal medicine Hosp. of U. Pa., Phila., 1959-61, fellow in hematology, 1961-62, USPHS rsch. fellow dept. hematology, 1962-63; assoc. in hematology medicine Hahnemann U. Hosp., Phila., 1963-66, asst., assoc., then prof. medicine, 1966-99; prof. dept. neoplastic disease Hahnemann Univ. Hosp., Phila., 1978-99, dir. edn., vice chmn. dept., 1978-94; assoc. dean Hahnemann U., Phila., 1986-94; prof. emeritus, 1999—2002; prof. dept. medicine divsn. hematology/ med. oncology Med. Coll. Pa./Hahnemann U., Phila., 1992-94, assoc. dean edn., 1992-94, prof. emeritus, 1999—2002, Drexel U. Coll. of Med., 2002—. Cons., chmn. dean's com. Wilkes-Barre (Pa.) VA Hosp., 1987-92. Mem. editl. bd. Jour. Cancer Edn., 1985-95, Am. Jour. Clin. Oncology; contbr. articles to profl. jours. Instl. rep. Boy Scouts Am., 1970-75; pres. Temple Beth Sholom, Cherry Hill, N.J., 1977-80; mem. med. bd. Lupus Found., Delaware Valley, 1977-79. Mem. AMA, ACP, Phila. County Med. Soc., Phila. Hematology Soc., Pa. Med. Soc., Am. Fedn. Clin. Rsch., Am. Hematology Soc., Am. Assn. Cancer Rsch., Am. Soc. Clin. Oncology, Am. Assn. Cancer Edn., Am. Cancer Soc. (chmn. patient svc. com. Phila. divsn. 1981-83, chmn. med. subcom. profl. edn. com. 1979-81, fin. com. 1981), Phi beta Kappa, Alpha Omega Alpha. Jewish. Home: 2307 Sagemore Dr Marlton NJ 08053-4315

KAHN, STEVEN EMANUEL, medical educator; b. Durban, South Africa, July 28, 1955; m. Stephanie Berk Kahn; 2 children. MB, ChB, U. Cape Town, South Africa, 1978. Diplomate Am. Bd. Internal Medicine. Intern depts. ob./gyn. and medicine Somerset Hosp., Cape Town, South Africa, 1979; resident dept. ob./gyn. 2 Mil. Hosp., Wynberg, South Africa, 1980, resident and coord. dept. ob./gyn., 1981; resident dept. medicine divsn. endocrinology Groote Schuur Hosp., Cape Town, 1982; rsch. fellow diabetes and endocrine rsch. group U. Cape Town, 1983; resident dept. medicine Albert Einstein Med. Ctr., Phila., 1983—86; sr. rsch. fellow divsn. metabolism, endocrinology and nutrition Dept. Medicine U. Wash. Sch. of Medicine, VA Med. Ctr., Seattle, 1986—88; assoc. investigator, staff physician divsn. endocrinology and metabolism Dept. Medicine VA Med. Ctr., Seattle, 1988—91, rsch. assoc., staff physician divsn. endocrinology and metabolism Dept. Medicine, 1991—95; acting instr. divsn. metabolism, endocrinology and nutrition Dept. Medicine U. Wash. Sch. of Medicine, Seattle, 1988—92, asst. prof. divsn. metabolism, endocrinology and nutrition Dept. Medicine, 1992—95, assoc. prof. divsn. metabolism, endocrinology and nutrition Dept. Medicine, 1995—2001, prof. divsn. metabolism, endocrinology and nutrition, 2001—; dir. R&D VA Puget Sound Health Care Sys., 2001—. Prizer vis. prof. Case Western Res. U., 1999. Mem. editl. bd.: Jour. Clin. Endocrinology and Metabolism, 1995—98, Diabetes Care, 1997—99; contbr. articles to profl. jours. Named Assoc. Investigator, Dept. VA, 1988, Rsch. Assoc., 1991; recipient Career Devel. award, Juvenile Diabetes Found., 1988, NIH, 1999, Feasibility award, Dana Found., 1989, Clin. Investigator award, NIH, 1991, New Investigator award, Diabetes Rsch. Coun., 1992—94, rsch. award, NIH, 1997, Novartis Young Investigator award in diabetes rsch., 2001; scholar Amelia Schenkman, 1973—75. Mem.: ACP, Gen. Med. Coun. (U.K.), Western Soc. Clin. Investigation (councillor 1998—), Endocrine Soc., Am. Soc. for Clin. Investigation, Am. Fedn. Clin. Rsch. (chair program com. for metabolism 1994, 1996, councillor western sect. 1994—96, pres.-elect western sect. 1996, pres. western sect. 1997, nat. councillor 1996), Am. Diabetes Assn. (bd. dirs. Wash. affiliate 1993—94, exec. bd. dirs. 1994—98, rsch. grant rev. panel 1994—97, rsch. award 1996, mentor award 1999). Office: VA Puget Sound Health Cr Dept Medicine 151 1660 S Columbian Way Seattle WA 98108-1532*

KAHN, SUSAN, artist; b. N.Y.C., Aug. 26, 1924; d. Jesse B. and Jenny Carol (Peshkin) Cohen; m. Joseph Kahn, Sept. 15, 1946 (dec.); m. Richard Rosenkranz, Feb. 1, 1981. Grad., Parsons Sch. Design, 1945; student, Moses Soyer, 1950-57. Subject of: book Susan Kahn, with an essay by Lincoln Rothschild, 1980; One-woman shows include Sagittarius Gallery, 1960, A.C.A., Galleries, 1964, 68, 71, 76, 80, Charles B. Goddard Art Center, Ardmore, Okla., 1973, Albrecht Gallery Mus. Art, St. Joseph, Mo., 1974, N.Y. Cultural Center, N.Y.C., 1974, St. Peter's Coll., Jersey City, 1978, Heidi Neuhoff Gallery, N.Y.C., 1989, Sindin Galleries, 1996; exhibited in group shows Audubon Artists, N.Y.C., Nat. Acad., N.Y.C., Springfield (Mass.) Mus., City Center, N.Y.C., A.C.A., Galleries, N.Y.C., Nat. Arts Club, N.Y.C., Butler Inst., Youngstown, Ohio, Islip Art Mus., East Islip. N.Y., 1989, Fine Arts Mus. of S., Mobile, Ala., 1989, Chatanooga Regional History Mus, 1989, Longview (Tex.) Mus. Art, 1990; represented in permanent collections, Tyler (Tex.) Mus., St. Lawrence U. Mus., Canton, N.Y., Fairleigh Dickinson U. Mus., Rutherford, N.J., Syracuse U. Mus., Sheldon Swope Gallery, Terre Haute, Ind., Montclair (N.J.) Mus. Fine Arts, Butler Inst. Am. Art, Youngstown, Ohio, Reading (Pa.) Mus., Albrecht Gallery Mus. Art, St. Joseph(Mo.), Cedar Rapids (Iowa) Art Center, N.Y. Cultural Center, N.Y.C., Edwin A. Ulrich Mus., Wichita, Kans., Wichita State U., Johns Hopkins Sch. Advanced Internat. Studies, Washington, Joslyn Mus., Omaha, U. Wyo., Laramie. Recipient Knickerbocker prize for best religious painting, 1956; Edith Lehman award Nat. Assn. Women Artists, 1958; Simmons award, 1961; Knickerbocker Artists award, 1961; Nat. Arts Club award, 1967; Knickerbocker Medal of Honor, 1964; Famous Artists Sch. award, 1967 Mem. Nat. Assn. Women Artists (Anne Barnett Meml. prize 1981, Solveig Stromsoe Palmer Meml. award 1987, Dorothy Schweitzer award 1990), Artists Equity, Met. Mus., Mus. Modern Art, Nat. Assn. Women Artists. *I choose to be a realist and humanist in my work. The most important objects of my concern are people, their lives and times. I believe that art is a way of communicating, subject matter translated into color, form and line, so that the work will express the idea convincingly.*

KAHN, THOMAS, medical educator; b. Offenburg, Germany, June 23, 1938; s. Ludwig and Ellen (Kaufman) K.; m. Si Mi Pak, Nov. 7, 1968; children: Diana, David, Philip. BA, NYU, 1958, MD, 1962. Intern medicine Balt. City Hosps., 1962-63, U. Pitts. Hosps., 1963-64, Mt. Sinai, N.Y.C., 1964-65, resident in nephrology, 1965-67; chief renal sect. Bronx VA Med. Ctr., 1979-96; prof. medicine Mt. Sinai Sch. Medicine, N.Y.C., 1988—. Maj. U.S. Army, 1967—69. Office: VA Med Ctr 130 W Kingsbridge Rd Bronx NY 10468-3904 Office Phone: 718-584-9000.

KAHN, VICTORIA ELAINE HOPKINS, special education educator; b. Grand Junction, Colo., Dec. 11, 1953; d. William Stanley Hopkins, Jr. and Bernice Irene (Porter) Hopkins; m. James Michael Humphrey, Sept. 17, 1982 (div. June 1986); m. Jerome Isidor Kahn, May 1, 1988 (div. June 2004). *Father, William Stanley Hopkins, Jr., was a World War II veteran, Technical Sergeant, awarded the Good Conduct medal and the Bronze Star, and a long time employee of American Telephone and Telegraph. After his death in 1969, mother, Bernice Irene, moved her family to California, where she originated and operated a dress design shop, Fabric Sculpture. She married a retired Marine Sergeant Major George Albert Dawson, who was a veteran of World War II, the Korean War, the Vietnam War and was awarded the Air medal, the Good Conduct medal, and many others. They celebrate their 32nd wedding anniversary in 2006.* AA in Theatre Arts, Santa Ana Coll., 1974; BA with distinction in psychology, San Diego State U., 1985. Cert. edn. specialist Calif. State U., 2001. Owner, freelance photographer Victoria Vincent Photography, San Diego and Vista, Calif., 1984—94, Glendale, Ariz., 1993—94; enrichment instr. Felicita Found. for the Arts, Escondido, Calif., 1990—91; photographer, artist Vista (Calif.) Initiative for the Visual Arts, 1990—93; sub. tchr. and aide spl. edn. grades K-14 Orange County Dept. Edn., Costa Mesa, Calif., 1996—98; sub. tchr. spl. edn. grades K-6 Garden Grove (Calif.) Unified Sch. Dist., 1997—2002; resource specialist tchr. grades 1-5 Long Beach (Calif.) Unified Sch. Dist., 2002—03; sub. spl. edn. tchr. grades K-6 Encinitas (Calif.) Union Sch. Dist., 2003—04; owner, designer Curriculum Creations, San Diego, 2003—; cmty. trainer United Cerebral Palsy Network, Escondido, Calif., 2005—. Charter mem., artist Gallery Vista (Calif.) Artists' Assn., 1989—91; artist, photographer Holman Gallery, Scottsdale, Ariz., 1993—94. Editor: (book of poetry) Autumn Meditations, 1994, The Complete Poems of James L.O. Porter, 2002, (novella) The Chance, 2002. Vol. genealogy rsch. rm. Nat. Archives and Records Adminstrn., Laguna Niguel, Calif., 1998—2001; vol. South Coast Repertory Theatre, Costa Mesa, Calif., 1978—79; vol. summer stock The Magic Theatre, Berkeley, Calif., 1972. Recipient Achievement award, Nat. Archives and Records Adminstrn., 2000, 2001. Mem.: DAR (chmn. conservation com. Cerritos chpt. 2002—04, vol. lineage rsch. look up com. 2004—, mem. lineage rsch. com. Calif. state chtp.), Know Thyself as Soul Found. S.W., Nat. Campaign for Tolerance, Dubois Family Assn., Tchrs. Assn. Long Beach, Coun. for Exceptional Children, Humane Farming Assn., Phi Kappa Phi, Pi Lambda Theta. Achievements include patents pending for a scenario method of teaching multiplication and division concepts (Cowboy Tim); a multi-sensory method of motivating students to read and write (The Reading Drum). Avocations: historial and geneaological research, writing, art, educational manipulatives and methods design, bird and nature watching. E-mail: kahnv@msn.com.

KAHN, WOLF, artist; b. Stuttgart, Germany, Oct. 4, 1927; came to U.S., 1940, naturalized, 1946; s. Emil and Nellie (Budge) K.; m. Emily Mason, Mar. 2, 1957; children: Cecily, Melany. Student, Hans Hofmann Sch., 1948-49; BA, U. Chgo., 1951; degree (hon.), Wheaton Coll., 2002, Union Coll., Schenectady, 2004. Vis. prof. painting U. Calif., Berkeley, 1960; adj. assoc. prof. Cooper Union Art Sch., 1961-77; jury mem. numerous regional art shows; artist-in-residence Dartmouth Coll., 1984. One-man shows include Borgenicht Gallery, N.Y.C., 1957-95, Beadleston Gallery, N.Y.C., 1998, 2000, Thomas Segal Gallery, Balt., 2000, Jerald Melberg Gallery, Charlotte, N.C., 1993-2000, Ft. Lauderdale Mus. Art, 1991, Boca Raton Mus. of Art, 1997, NAD, 2004, Addison Ripley Gallery, Wash. DC, 2005; group shows include Whitney Mus., N.Y.C., 1960, 77, Met. Mus., N.Y.C., 1975-76, Ameringer/Yohe Gallery, N.Y.C., Provincetown Art Assn., Mass., 2005, Melberg Gallery, Charlotte, NC, 2005; represented in permanent collections Mus. Modern Art, N.Y.C., Whitney Mus., Houston Mus. Fine Arts, Chase Manhattan Coll., Va. Mus., Met. Mus., N.Y.C., L.A. County Mus., Hirschhorn Mus., Washington; author: Pastel Light, 1983, Wolf Kahn pastels, 2000; contbr. articles to profl. jours. Trustee Brattleboro Mus. Vt., 1979—, Vt. Studio Sch.,1988—; apptd. N.Y.C. Art Commn., 1993-95. With USNR, 1945-46. Recipient award for art Am. Acad. Arts and Letters, 1979; Fulbright fellow Italy, 1964-65; Guggenheim fellow, 1967-68; Ford Found. grantee, 1969 Mem. Nat. Acad. Design (academician, 1980-, coun. mem. 1982-96), Am. Acad. Arts and Letters (treas. 2005—). Democrat. Jewish. Office: c/o Ameringer Yohe Gallery 20 W 57th St New York NY 10019

KAHNE, STEPHEN JAMES, systems engineering educator, engineering company executive, academic administrator; b. N.Y.C., Apr. 5, 1937; s. Arnold W. and Janet (Weatherlow) Kahne; m. Irena Nowacka, Dec. 11, 1970; children: Christopher, Kasia. BEE, Cornell U., 1960; MS, U. Ill., 1961, PhD, 1963. Asst. prof. elec. engring. U. Minn., Mpls., 1966-69, assoc. prof., 1969-76; dir. Hybrid Computer Lab., 1968-76; founder, dir., cons. InterDesign Inc., Mpls., 1968-76; prof. dept. sys. engring. Case Western Res. U., Cleve., 1976-83, chmn. dept., 1976-80; dir. divsn. elec., computer and sys. engring. NSF, Washington, 1980-82; prof. Poly Inst. N.Y., 1983-85, dean engring., 1983-84; pres. Oreg. Grad. Ctr., Beaverton, 1985-86, prof. dept. applied physics and elec. engring., 1985-89; chief engr. civil systems divsn. MITRE Corp., McLean, Va., 1989-90, chief scientist Washington Group, 1990-91, cons. engr. Ctr. for Advanced Aviation Sys. Devel., 1991-94; exec. dir., CEO Triangle Coalition for Sci. and Tech. Edn., 1994; chancellor, v.p. Embry-Riddle Aeronautical U., Prescott, Ariz., 1995-97, prof. engring., 1995—. Bd. dirs. West Yavapai Guidance Clinic; spl. advocate, U.S. Ct., 2005—; cons. in field; exchange scientist NAS, 1968, 75 Contbr. articles to sci. jours. Active Mpls. Citizens League, 1968-75; regent L.I. Coll. Hosp., Bklyn., 1984-85; trustee Yavapi Regional Med. Ctr., 1999-2004; chmn. Beaverton Sister Cities Found., 1986-89; ct. appointed spl. adv., Ariz., 2005—; dir. West Yavapai Guidance Clinic, 2005-. Served with USAF, 1963-66. Recipient Amicus Poloniae award POLAND Mag., 1975, John A. Curtis award Am. Soc. Engring. Edn., Outstanding Svc. award Internat. Fedn. Automatic Control, 1990; Case Centennial scholar, 1980 Fellow: AAAS, IEEE (life; editor Transactions on Automatic Control 1975—79, pres. Control Sys. Soc. 1981, bd. dirs. 1982—86, v.p. tech. activities 1984—85, mem. editl. bd. Spectrum 1979—82, Centennial medal 1984, Disting Mem. award 1983, Richard Emberson award 1991, Disting. Lectr. 1998—2000), Internat. Fedn. of Automatic Control (life; hon. editor 1975—81, dep. chmn. mng. bd. publs. 1976—87, chmn. 1999—, v.p. 1987—90, pres.-elect 1990—93, pres. 1993—96, adv. 1999—); mem.: Air Traffic Control Assn., Am. Soc. Engring. Edn., Eta Kappa Nu. Office: Embry Riddle Aero U 3700 Willow Creek Rd Prescott AZ 86301-3721 Office Phone: 928-777-3779. Personal E-mail: s.kahne@ieee.org.

KAHNEMAN, DANIEL, psychology professor; b. Tel Aviv, 1934; BA in Psychology and Math., The Hebrew U., Jerusalem, Israel, 1954; PhD in Psychology, U. Calif., 1961; DSc (hon.), U. Pa., 2001; degree (hon.), U. Trento, 2002, Ben-Gurion U., 2003, New Sch., 2003, Univ. Brit. Columbia, 2004, Harvard Univ., 2004, Univ. East Anglia, 2004, Univ. Wurzburg, 2004. Lectr. in psychology The Hebrew U., Jerusalem, 1961—66, sr. lectr. in psychology, 1966—70, assoc. prof., 1970—73, prof., 1973—78, fellow Ctr. for Rationality, 2000—; prof. psychology U. B.C., Canada, 1978—86, U. Calif., Berkeley, 1986—94; Eugene Higgins prof. psychology, prof. pub. affairs in Woodrow Wilson Sch. Princeton U., NJ, 1993—. Vis. scientist dept. psychology U. Mich., 1965—66; fellow, Ctr. for Cognitive Studies, lectr. in psychology Harvard U., 1966—67; vis. scientist Applied Psychol. Rsch. Unit, Cambridge, England, 1968—69; fellow Ctr. for Advanced Studies in the Behavioral Scis., 1977—78; assoc. fellow Canadian Inst. Advanced Rsch., 1984—86; vis. scholar Russell Sage Found., 1991—92; fellow, Ctr. for Rationality Hebrew Univ., Jerusalem, 2000—. Mem. editl. bd. Jour. Risk and Uncertainty, Thinking and Reasoning, Econs. and Philosophy. Named Katz-Newcomb lectr. in social psychology, 1979; recipient Fitts Lectures, U. Mich., 1987, Disting. Scientific Contbn. award, Soc. Consumer Psychology, 1992, Tanner Lecture on Human Values, U. Mich., 1994, Bartlett Lecture, Exptl. Psychology Soc., Eng., 1995, Hilgard award lifetime contbn. to gen. psychology, 1995, Nobel Prize in econ. scis., 2002, Grawemeyer Prize in Psychology, 2002, Career Achievement Award, Soc. Med. Decision Making, 2002. Fellow: Econometric Soc., Canadian Psychol. Assn., Am. Psychol. Assn., Am. Psychol. Soc. (William James Fellow, Disting. Scientific Contbn. award 1982), Am. Acad. Arts and Scis.; mem.: NAS, Soc. Judgment and Decision Making (pres. 1992—93), Soc. Econ. Sci., Psychonomic Soc., Soc. Exptl. Psychologists (pres. 1992—93, Warren medal 1995). Office: Princeton U 3-S-3 Green Hall Dept Psychology Princeton NJ 08544-1010*

KAHOL, KANAV, researcher; b. Jammu, Kashmir, India, June 26, 1979; s. Ashok and Renu Kahol. B in Tech. Elec. and Comm. Engring., Guru Nanak Dev Engring. Coll., Ludhiana, India; MS in Computer Sci., Ariz. State U.; PhD in Computer Sci., Ariz. State U., Tempe, 2005. Rsch. assoc. CUbiC (Ctr. Cognitive Ubiquitous Computing), Ariz. State U., Tempe, 2001—. Scholar Ariz. Regents Scholarship, Ariz. State U., 2001-2005. Mem.: IEEE (assoc.). Achievements include research in haptic user interfaces for individuals who are blind; multimodal systems for stroke rehabilitation; human motion analysis for complex motion sequences; psychological basis for haptic perception. Office: CUbiC Ariz State Univ 699 S Mill Ave #370AB Tempe AZ 85287 Office Phone: 480-727-3612. Home Fax: 480-965-3190; Office Fax: 480-965-3190. Business E-Mail: kanav@asu.edu.

KAHOLOKULA, JOSEPH KEAWEAIMOKU, mental health services professional, researcher; b. Honolulu, Nov. 11, 1969; s. Lawrence Pauahi and Beverly Leilani Lyons Kaholokula. BA in Psychology, U. Hawaii, 1996, MA in Psychology, 2001, PhD in Psychology, 2003. Rsch. specialist Native Hawaiian Health Rsch. Project, Honolulu, 1994—2001; psychology resident Tripler Army Med. Ctr., Dept. Psychology, 2002—03; asst. rschr., faculty John A. Burns Sch. Medicine, Dept. Native Hawaiian Health, 2004—. Instl. rev. bd. mem. Native Hawaiian Health Care Sys., Honolulu, 2005—. Sr. mem. and protocol com. mem. Halemua o Kuali'i, Honolulu, 1999—2005, Halemua o Mauiloa, Kahului, 1999—2005. Named Outstanding New Program Vol., Am. Diabetes Assn., Hawaii, 2002; recipient Student Rsch. award, Hawaii Psychol. Assn., 2001; fellow, APA Minority Fellowship Program, 1998—2001, Tripler Army Med. Ctr., Dept. Psychology, Honolulu, 2003—04; scholar, Kamehameha Schools/Bishop Estate, 1994—2001, U.S. Achievement Acad., 1995, Honolulu Hawaiian Civic Club, 1996, NIMH, 1996, Native Hawaiian Leadership Program, U. of Hawaii, 2000—03; J. Watumull scholar, Sch. Social Scis., U. Hawaii at Manoa, 1996, Pacific-Asian scholar, U. Hawaii, Dept. Psychology, Manoa, 1998—2001, Dr. Hans & Clara Zimmerman Found. scholar, Hawaii Cmty. Found., 1999—2003, Na Liko Noelo scholar, 'Imi Hale, Native Hawaiian Cancer Network, 2002—05. Mem.: APA, Soc. Behavioral Medicine, Am. Diabetes Assn., Golden Key Nat. Honor Soc. (life). Achievements include research in biological and psychosocial models in predicting depression in people with type 2 diabetes; ethnic-by-gender interactions in cigarette smoking behavior among Asian and Pacific Islanders; the relationship between acculturation and depression among Native Hawaiians; the relationship between cigarette smoking and depression among Native Hawaiians; ethnic differences in the relationship between health-related quality of life and depression in people with type 2 diabetes; diabetes care issues in a state psychiatric hospital. Avocations: native hawaiian cultural activities, travel, volleyball, wood carving. Office: Department Native Hawaiian Health 677 Ala Moana Blvd Ste 1016B Honolulu HI 96813 Office Phone: 808-692-1047. Office Fax: 808-587-8565. E-mail: kaholoku@hawaii.edu.

KAHRILAS, PETER JAMES, medical educator, researcher; b. Culver City, Calif., June 9, 1953; s. Peter Jerome and Leticia (Llorett) K.; m. Elyse Anne Lambiase, Mar. 30, 1984; children: Genevieve Anne, Ian James, Miranda Elyse. Student, Yale U., 1971-75, U. Rochester, N.Y., 1975-79. Resident in medicine U. Hosp. of Cleve., 1979-82; fellow in gastroenterology Northwestern U., Chgo., 1982-84; rsch. fellow Med. Coll. of Wis., Milw., 1984-86, asst. prof. medicine, 1986-90, assoc. prof. medicine, 1990-95, prof. medicine, 1995-99; chief gastroenterology Northwestrn U. Feinberg Sch. Medicine, Chgo., 1999—. Contbr. articles to profl. jours. NIH grantee, 1990—. Fellow ACP, Ctrl. Soc. for Clin. Rsch., Am. Coll. Gastroenterology; mem. Am. Gastroenterol. Assn., Am. Fedn. for Clin. Rsch., Am. Soc. for Clin. Investigation, Am. Motility Soc. Democrat. Home: 203 Columbia Ave Park Ridge IL 60068-4923 Office: Northwestern U 676 N St Clair Ste 1400 Chicago IL 60611 Office Phone: 312-695-4016. Business E-Mail: p-kahrilas@northwestern.edu.

KAHRL, ROBERT CONLEY, lawyer; b. Mt. Vernon, Ohio, June 2, 1946; s. K. Allin and Evelyn Sperry (Conley) K.; m. LaVonne Elaine Rutherford, July 12, 1969; children: Kurt Freeland, Eric Allin, Heidi Elizabeth. AB, Princeton U., 1968; MBA, JD, Ohio State U., 1975. Bar: Ohio 1975, U.S. Ct. Appeals (6th cir.) 1976, U.S. Dist. Ct. (no. dist.) Ohio 1977, U.S. Ct. Appeals (9th cir.) 1979, U.S. Ct. Appeals (fed. cir.) 1984, U.S. Ct. Appeals (D.C. cir.) 1986. Law clk. to presiding judge US Ct. Appeals (6th cir.), Cleve., 1975-76; assoc. Jones, Day, Reavis & Pogue, Cleve., 1976-84, ptnr., 1985—; ptnr., chair intellectual property practice area Jones Day (formerly Jones, Day, Reavis & Pogue), Cleve., 1991—. Author: Patent Claim Construction. With USN, 1968—72. Mem. Ohio State Bar Assn. (chmn. emeritus intellectual property sect.), Am. Intellectual Property Law Assn., Order of Coif, Am. Guild Organists. Republican. Presbyterian. Achievements include patents for Claim Construction (NY, 2001, 05). Home: 7624 Red Fox Trl Hudson OH 44236-1926 Office: Jones Day North Point 901 Lakeside Ave E Cleveland OH 44114-1190 Office Phone: 216-586-3939. E-mail: rckahrl@jonesday.com.

KAID, LYNDA LEE, communications educator; b. Harrisburg, Ill., Aug. 22, 1948; d. Billy Cameron and Leona Elizabeth (Oglesby) K.; m. Clifford Alan Jones. BA, So. Ill. U., 1970, MS, 1972, PhD, 1974. Prof. dept. comm. U. Okla., Norman, 1974—2001, dir. Polit. Comm. Ctr., 1984—2001; sr. assoc. dean Coll. Journalism. and Comm. U. Fla., Gainesville, 2001—. Mem. adv. bd. Mus. of Broadcast Comm., Chgo., 1990—. Co-author: Political Campaign Communication: A Bibliography and Guide to the Literature, 1974 (Outstanding Reference Book of 1974, Choice mag.); co-editor Political Communication Yearbook 1984, 1985, Political Campaign Communication: A Bibliography and Guide to the Literature, Vol. 2, 1973-1982, 1985, New Perspectives on Political Advertising, 1986, The Political Commercial Archive: A Catalog and Guide to the Collection, 1991, Mediated Politics in Two Cultures: Presidential Campaigning in the United States and France, 1991, Die Massenmedien im Wahlkampf, 1993, The Lynching of Language: Gender, Politics and Power in the Hill-Thomas Hearings, 1996, Political Advertising in Western Democracies: Parties and Candidates on Television, 1995, The Electronic Election, 1999; contbr. numerous articles to profl. jours. Recipient Rsch. award on Polit. Advt., NSF & Nat. Endowment for Humanities, 1992—; Fulbright scholar USIA-Fulbright Commn., Western Europe, 1987-88, 1997. Mem. Am. Film Inst., League of Women Voters, Internat. Comm. Assn. (pres. polit. comm. divsn. 1979-81). Avocation: travel. Office: U Fla Weimer Hall Gainesville FL 32611 Office Phone: 352-392-7922. Business E-Mail: lkaid@jou.ufl.edu. E-mail: llkaid@att.biz.

KAIDY, MITCHELL, retired journalist, legislative staff member; b. Bklyn., Mar. 23, 1925; s. Murad Abdallah and Asma Araman Kaldy; m. Jean Harris Kaldy; children: Kristen, Mark. Student, U. Miss., 1943—44, Clemson (S.C.) A&M Coll., 1944; BS in Journalism, NYU, 1948. Reporter, editor Monticello (N.Y.) Evening News, 1948—49, Middletown (N.Y.) Times Herald, 1949—50, Rochester (N.Y.) Dem. Chronicle, 1950—65; legis. aide and speech writer N.Y. State Legis., Albany, 1966—83; freelance TV comml. prodr. Rochester, 1983—90; freelance writer, 1983—. Dir. rsch. N.Y. State Joint Legis. Com. on Conservation, 1967; legis. aide NY State Senate Com. on Labor, Albany, 1966; pres., sec. Rochester (N.Y.) Newspaper Guild, 1953—60, N.Y. State Newspaper Guild. Manuscript editor Becoming American: The Early Arab Immigrant Experience, by Alixa Naff, 1985; contbr. columns in newspapers, articles to profl. jours. (Project Censored award, 1993), articles to series (Pulitzer Prize citation, 1963). Founder Peace and Justice Edn. Ctr., Rochester, 1962; founder Genesee Valley chpt. Vets. of Battle of the Bulge; candidate Monroe County, 1963, N.Y. Legis., 1963, Congress, 1982—84; founder Genesee Valley chpt. N.Y. Civil Liberties Union. Cpl. U.S. Army, 1943—45, ETO. Decorated Bronze Star medal, 3 Battle Stars, Combat Infantry Badge with three battle stars, Army of Occupation medal European Theater; named Journalist of Yr., Utica, N.Y., 1966; recipient Project Censored award, 1993;, Am. Newspaper Guild fellow, 1963. Mem.: Amnesty Internat. (founder group 89), Vets. of the Battle of the Bulge (founder, pres.). Democrat. Achievements include design of and writing of four plaques in Belgium, commemorating 87th Infantry Divsn. engagements during Battle of the Bulge; plaque in Oswego, N.Y. honoring S/Sgt. Curtis F. Shoup, Medal of Honor winner, Battle of the Bulge, 1995. Avocations: travel, journalism, writing. Home: 921 Crittenden Rd Rochester NY 14623-1157 Office Phone: 585-424-4746. Personal E-mail: mkaldy@rochester.rr.com.

KAIER, EDWARD JOHN, lawyer; b. Sewickley, Pa, Sept. 23, 1945; s. Edward Anthony and Mary Patricia (Crimmins) K.; m. Annette Thomas, July 31, 1976; children: Elizabeth Anne, Charles Crimmins, Thomas Edward. AB,

Harvard U., 1967; JD, U. Pa., 1970. Bar: DC 1970, Pa. 1970, US Dist. Ct. (ea. dist.) Pa. 1971, US Ct. Appeals (3rd and DC cir.) 1971, US Dist. Ct. DC, 1971. Law clk. to presiding justice US Dist. Ct. for DC, Washington, 1970-71; assoc. Dechert Price & Rhoads, Phila., 1971-74; ptnr. Kaier and Kaier, Phila., 1974-77, Hepburn Willcox Hamilton & Putnam, Phila., 1977—. Pres. Savoy Co., Phila., 1978-80; bd. dir. Mgr. Funds, Norwalk, Conn., Mgr. AMG Funds, Boston, Third Avenue Funds, NY Vice chmn. Rosemont (Pa.) Sch. of Holy Child, 1981-90. Mem.: ABA, Phila. Bar Assn. (chmn. office practice com. probate sect. 1987—90, exec. com. 1990—92, 2002—04), Harvard-Radcliffe Club (Phila.) (sec. 1989—2004), Avalon Yacht Club (trustee 1987—90, 1992—93, treas. 1990—92), Phila. Country Club, Phila. Club, Merion Cricket Club. Republican. Roman Catholic. Avocations: sailing, golf. Home: 111 N Lowrys Ln Bryn Mawr PA 19010-1408 Office: Hepburn Willcox Hamilton & Putnam 1100 One Penn Ctr Philadelphia PA 19103 Personal E-mail: macoejk@aol.com. Business E-Mail: ejkaier@hepburnlaw.com.

KAIGE, ALICE TUBB, retired librarian; b. Obion, Tenn., Jan. 27, 1922; d. George Easley and Lucile (Merryman) Tubb; m. Richard H. Kaige, Aug. 1952; children: Robert H., Richard C. (dec.), John S. (dec.) BA, Vanderbilt U., 1944; BS in Libr. Sci., Geo. Peabody Coll., 1947. Libr. Martin (Tenn.) High Sch., 1946-47, Demonstration Sch. Geo. Peabody Coll. Joint U. Librs., Nashville, Tenn., 1947-52; acquisitions libr. Lincoln Libr., Springfield, Ill., 1967-70; office coord. Springfield (Ill.) Chpt. ACLU, 1974; staff rep. Am. Fed. State, County & Mcpl. Employees, Springfield, 1975; libr. Ill. Dept. of Commerce and Community Affairs, Springfield, 1976-89. Vice chmn. Women's Internat. League for Peace and Freedom, 1969-70, various coms., 1970—; treas. Cen. Ill. Women's Lobby, 1971-72; com. on local govt. League of Women Voters, 1973-76; career day com. Urban League Guild, 1970-71; co-founder West Side Neighborhood Assn., Springfield, 1977. Recipient Elizabeth Cady Stanton award, Springfield Women's Political Caucus, 1982. Mem. Sangamon County Hist. Soc., Women's Internat. League for Peace and Freedom, War Resisters League. Avocations: reading, walking. Home: 1912 Turnberry Ct Springfield IL 62704-6211

KAIL, FLOYD MICHAEL, lawyer; b. Boston, June 19, 1945; s. Nathan and Harriett (Lenox) Kail; m. Wendy Green, June 23, 1968; children: Nicole, Thomas, Kathryn. BA magna cum laude, Yale U., 1967, LLB, 1970; cert. in edn., Oxford (Eng.) U., 1971. Bar: Conn. 1972, DC 1973, US Ct. Appeals (DC Cir.). From assoc. to ptnr. Steptoe & Johnson LLP, Washington, 1972—, various mgmt positions on exec. & compensation & partnership com., co-chmn. hiring com., chmn. associates com., vice chmn. Author: What Washington Said, Administration, Rhetoric, and the Vietnam War, 1949-69, 1973. Campaign ofcl. Tsongas Presdl. Campaign, Washington, 1992-93. Mem. Yale Club (bd. dirs. Washington, program chair, pres.). Avocations: carpentry, racquetball, reading. Office: Steptoe & Johnson LLP 1330 Connecticut Ave NW Washington DC 20036-1704 Office Phone: 202-429-6327. Office Fax: 202-429-3902. Business E-Mail: mkail@steptoe.com.

KAILAS, LEO GEORGE, lawyer; b. N.Y.C., May 28, 1949; s. George and Evanthia (Skoulikas) K.; m. Merle S. Duskin; children: Arianne, George, Shirley. AB, Columbia U., 1970, JD, 1973. Bar: N.Y. 1974. Assoc. Olwine, Connelly, Chase, O'Donnell and Weyher, N.Y.C., 1973-77; ptnr. specializing in internat., comml.-admiralty litigation Milgrim Thomajan Jacobs & Lee, PC (now Piper Rudnick LLP), N.Y.C., 1977-2000, mem. internat. trade and litigation group, until 2000; ptnr. Reitler Brown & Rosenblatt LLC, N.Y.C., 2000—. Mem. ABA, Assn. Bar City N.Y. (mem. admiralty com. 1985-88). Office: Reitler Brown Rosenblatt LLC 800 3d Ave 21st Fl New York NY 10022 Office Phone: 212-209-3012. E-mail: lkailas@reitlerbrown.com.

KAILATH, THOMAS, electrical engineer, educator; b. Poona, India, June 7, 1935; arrived in U.S., 1957, naturalized, 1976; s. Mamman and Kunjamma (George) K.; m. Sarah Jacob, June 11, 1962; children: Ann, Paul, Priya, Ryan. BE, U. Poona, 1956; SM, MIT, 1959, ScD, 1961; Dr. Tek (hon.), Linkoping U., Sweden, 1990; Doctorate (hon.), U. Carlos III, Madrid, 1999; D honoris causa, Strathclyde U., Scotland, 1992; D honoris causa (hon.), U. Bordeaux, France, 2003. Comm. rschr. Jet Propulsion Labs., Pasadena, Calif., 1961-62; faculty Stanford (Calif.) U., 1963—, prof. elec. engring., 1968—, Hitachi Am. prof. engring., 1988—2001, Hitachi Am. prof. emeritus, 2001—; dir. Info. Systems Lab., 1971-81, assoc. chmn. dept., 1981-87. Vis. prof., cons. univs., industry, govt. Author: Linear Systems, 1980, Least-Squares Estimation, 2d edit, 1981, Linear Estimation, 2000; mem. editl. bd. various jours.; contbr. articles to profl. jours. Recipient Edn. award Am. Control Coun., 1986, Tech. Achievement and Soc. awards Signal Processing Soc. IEEE, 1989, 91, Donald G. Fink Prize award, 1996, Shannon award, 2000; Sr. Vinton Hayes fellow MIT, 1992, Guggenheim fellow, 1970, Churchill fellow, 1977, Michael fellow Weizmann Inst., Israel, 1984, Royal Soc. guest rsch. fellow, 1989; Alexander Humboldt fellow, 2003. Fellow: IEEE (Edn. medal 1995), Am. Acad. Arts and Scis., Inst. Math. Stats.; mem.: NAS, Royal Spanish Acad. Engring., Third World Acad. Scis., Soc. Indsl. and Applied Math., Am. Math. Soc., Nat. Acad. Engring., Indian Nat. Acad. Engring., Sigma Xi. Home: 1024 Cathcart Way Palo Alto CA 94305-1047 Office: Stanford U Dept Elec Engring Stanford CA 94305-9510 Business E-Mail: kailath@stanford.edu. E-mail: profkailath@yahoo.com.

KAIMOWITZ, JEFFREY HUGH, librarian; b. N.Y.C., Nov. 3, 1942; AB, Johns Hopkins U., 1964; PhD in Classics, U. Cin., 1970; MS in Libr. Svc., Columbia U., 1976. Asst. prof. Miami U. Ohio, Oxford, 1969—73; libr. trainee N.Y. Pub. Libr., N.Y.C., 1973—77; curator Watkinson Libr. Trinity Coll., Hartford, Conn., 1977—2001, curator Enders Ornithology Collection, 1994—, head libr., 2001—. Home: 27 Stoneham Dr West Hartford CT 06117 Office: Trinity College Watkinson Library 300 Summit St Hartford CT 06106-3186 Office Phone: 860-297-2266.

KAIMSTHORN, LORD RENFREW OF See RENFREW, ANDREW

KAIN, ROBERT J., architectural firm executive; BArch, Calif. State Poly. U. Joined HMC Group, Ontario, Calif., 1978—, pres., CEO, 1995—2000, prin., v.p. design, chmn., dir. healthcare, 2000—. Post chair San Bernardino County Children's Fund; chmn. Cal Poly Pomona; bd. dirs. ednl. trust Cal Poly Pomona U. Mem.: AIA (nat. com. on arch. for health), Am. Coll. Healthcare Archs. (founder), Healthcare Execs. So. Calif., Arch. for Health Com., AIA Acad. Arch. for Health, Archtl. Alumni Assn., Old Baldy Coun. Explorer Post (dir.). Office: HMC Group 3270 Inland Empire Blvd Ontario CA 91764-4854

KAIN, ZEEV, anesthesiologist, educator; m. Tatiana Kain, July 4, 1985; 1 child, Danielle. MD, Ben Gurion U. Sch. Medicine, 1985; MBA, Columbia Bus. Sch., 2002; MA (hon.), Yale U. Bd. cert. anesthesiologist Am. Bd. Anesthesiology, 1993, bd. cert. pediatrician Am. Bd. Pediat., 2002. Resident in pediat. Schnider Children's Hosp., Albert Einstein Coll. Medicine, New Hyde Park, NY, 1986—89; resident in anesthesiology Yale-New Haven Hosp., 1989—91; fellow in pediatirc anesthesiology Boston Children's Hosp., Harvard Med. Sch., Boston, 1991—92; Robert Wood Johson fellow Yale U. Sch. Medicine, 1992—92, asst. prof. anesthesiology and pediat. and child psychiatry, 1993—97, assoc. prof. anesthesiology and pediat. and child psychiatry, 1997—2001, prof. anesthesiology and pediat. and child psychiatry, 2001—, exec. vice-chair, dept. anesthesiology, 2004—; anesthesiologist-in-chief Yale-New Children's Hosp., 1997—. Co-editor: Handbook Pediat. Anesthesia; editl. bd. Jour. Anesthesiology, Pediat., Jour. Pediat. Psychology; contbr. scientific papers. Bd. governers Yale Med. Group, 2000. Grantee Med. Rsch., NIH, 1998-2003, Nat. Inst. Child and Health Diseases, 2003-2008; Career Grant, Donghue Found., 1998-2003. Mem.: AMA (assoc.), Am. Soc. Anesthesiology (assoc.; mem. numerous com.), Conn. State Soc. Anesthesiology (assoc.; sec. 2002—04), Am. Acad. Pediat. (assoc.; mem. exec. com. 2002—, chair anesthesiology QA com. 1999—2003). Achievements include discovery of described the adverse postoperative behavioral changes and dissaminated the data world wide. Office: Yale Univ Sch Medicine Anesthesiology/ Tompkin 3 333 Cedar St New Haven CT 06510 E-mail: zeev.kain@yale.edu.

KAINE, TIMOTHY M., lieutenant governor; m. Anne Holton; children: Annella, Woody, Nat. AB summa cum laude, U. Mo., 1979; JD cum laude, Harvard U., 1983. Law clk. to judge R. Lanier Anderson III U.S. Ct. Appeals (11th cir.); mem. law firm; mem. City Council, Richmond; mayor City of Richmond, 1998—2001; lt. gov. State of Virginia, 2002—. Mem. local and state govt. adv. com. FCC. Contbr. articles to profl. jours. Bd. dirs. Historic Jackson Ward Found. Mem. ABA, Va. Bar Assn., Richmond Bar Assn. Democrat. Office: Office Lt Gov 900 E Main St Ste 1400 Richmond VA 23219*

KAINEN, MICHAEL ROLAND, lawyer, state representative; b. Simsbury, Conn., Dec. 25, 1965; m. Michelle M. Newman; 2 children. BA, U. Conn., 1988; JD, MSL, U. Vt., 1992. Bar: Vt. 1993, NH. Atty.; ranking mem., House Judiciary vice-chair, judicial rules and judicial retention coms. Vt. State Ho. Reps., 1999—. Mem. Hartford Housing Authority. Mem.: ABA, Vt. Bar Assn., N.H. Bar Assn., Am. Inns of Ct. Republican. Episcopalian. Home: PO Box 919 51 Marsh Family Rd White River Junction VT 05001 Office Phone: 802-296-2100.

KAINTHLA, RAMESH CHAND, manufacturing executive; b. Shimla, India, Feb. 18, 1954; came to U.S., 1983; s. Hira Nand and Belku (Devi) K.; m. Neetu Dua, Aug. 9, 1981; children: Priyanka, Radhika. BS, HP Univ., Shimla, 1973, MS in Physics, 1975; PhD in Physics, IIT Delhi, India, 1980. Rsch. assoc. IIT Delhi, 1980-81, U. NSW, Sydney, Australia, 1981-83, Tex. A&M U., College Station, 1984-86, sr. rsch. assoc., 1986-88, rsch. scientist, 1988-89; v.p. Rechargeable Battery Corp., College Station, 1989—. Dir. Rechargeable Battery Corp., 1990—. Contbr. articles to profl. jours.; patentee in field. Mem. Electrochem. Soc. Avocations: music, movies, gardening, web creation. Office: Rechargeable Battery Corp 809 University Dr # 100E College Station TX 77840-1431 Office Phone: 979-260-1120. Personal E-mail: kainthla@hotmail.com.

KAISCH, KENNETH BURTON, psychologist, priest; b. Detroit, Aug. 29, 1948; s. Kenneth R. Kaisch and Marjorie F. (Howe) Bourke; m. Suzanne Carol LePrevost, Aug. 31, 1969 (div. May 21, 2004); 1 child, Samuel. BA, San Francisco State U., 1972; MDiv, Ch. Divinity Sch. Pacific, 1976; MS, Utah State U., 1983, PhD in Clin. Psychology, 1986. Ordained deacon Episcopal Ch., 1976, priest, 1977; lic. clin. psychologist, Calif.; diplomate Nat. Inst. Sports Psychologists. Intern local parish, 1973-76; ordinand tng. program Ch. of the Good Shepherd, Ogden, Utah, 1976-77; pastor St. Francis' Episc. Ch., Moab, Utah, 1977-80, St. John's Episc. Ch., Logan, Utah, 1980-84; psychol. asst. Peter Ebersole, Ph.D., Fullerton, Calif., 1984-86; intern in clin. psychology Patton State Hosp., Calif., 1985-86; psychol. asst. Ronald Wong Jue, Ph.D., Fullerton and Newport Beach, Calif., 1986-88; pvt. practice clin. psychologist Calif., 1988—; clin. dir. Anxiety Clinic, Fullerton, 1993—, Consultants for Change, 1994—. Exec. dir. Contemplative Congress, Fullerton, 1988-91, Inner Peace Conf., 1995-97; founder, pres. OneHeart, 1986-98, Contemplative Visions, Fullerton, 1990-2000; supply priest Episc. Diocese of L.A.; invited lectr. Acad. Sch. Profl. Psychology, Moscow, 1992, 93, Moscow Med. Acad., 1998; sports psychologist UCLA Men's and Women's Golf Teams, 2004-2005. Co-author: Fundamentals of Psychotherapy, 1984, Developing Your Feel for Golf, 1998; author: Finding God: A Handbook of Christian Meditation, 1994, The Mental Golf Inventory, 1998, Hit it With Your Best Shot: How to Play Golf in the Zone, 2000; co-editor: God in Russia: The Challenge of Freedom, 1999, Turning the Heart to God, 2001; contbr. articles to profl. jours. Active St. Andrew's Episc. Ch., Fullerton. Mem. APA, Calif. Psychol. Assn., Anxiety Disorders Assn. Am., Nat. Register of Health Svc. Providers in Psychology, Phi Kappa Phi, Rotary (past bd. dirs., past officer). Episcopalian. Office: 2555 E Chapman Ave Ste 617 Fullerton CA 92831-3621 Office Phone: 714-992-4656. Personal E-mail: kenkaisch@yahoo.com.

KAISER, ALBERT FARR, manufacturing executive; b. N.Y.C., May 14, 1933; s. Albert Louis and Lucille (Daggett) K.; m. Joy E. White, Sept. 16, 1961; children— Elizabeth Ann, Albert Farr. BA, Hamilton Coll., Clinton, N.Y., 1955; MBA, Harvard U., 1960. With acquisitons dept. AMF Inc., 1960-61; with data processing div. IBM Corp., 1961-84; with Sperry and Hutchinson Co., 1974-82; pres. The Gunlocke Co., Inc., 1977-79, pres. promotional services div., also chmn. motivation and travel div., 1979-80; corp. exec. v.p. Sperry and Hutchinson, Inc., N.Y.C., 1980-82; investment banker J.J. Lowrey & Co., N.Y.C., 1983-84; pres. ABB Power Distbn. Inc., 1984-92; ret., 1992—. Served to lt. (j.g.) USNR, 1955-58. Mem.: Hamilton Coll. Alumni Assn. (former pres. Westchester County chpt.), Key Royale Club (Holmes Beach, Fla.), Champlain Country Club (St. Albans, Vt.), Bradenton Country Club, Fox Meadow Tennis Club (Scarsdale). Republican. Mem. Reformed Ch. Am. Home: PO Box 2205 105 Sunset Ln Anna Maria FL 34216 Home (Summer): 25 Camp Rich Rd Milton VT 05468 E-mail: alkaiser@sprintmail.com.

KAISER, ALLEN BERNARD, health facility administrator; b. Columbia, S.C., 1942; BA, MD, Vanderbilt U., 1967. Intern Johns Hopkins Hosp., Balt., 1967—68, resident internal medicine, 1968—69, Vanderbilt U. Hosp., 1971—72, fellow, 1972—74; (former) hosp. epidemiologist St. Thomas Hosp., chief divsn. infectious diseases, chief dept. medicine; vice-chmn. clin. affairs Vanderbilt U. Hosp., prof. medicine, chief of staff, 2004—; chief med. officer Vanderbilt U. Med. Ctr., 2004—. Mem.: Soc. Healthcare Epidemiology Am. (past pres.). Office: Vanderbilt Med Ctr D 3100 Med Ctr N Nashville TN 37232

KAISER, ANN CHRISTINE, magazine editor; b. Milw., Apr. 7, 1947; d. Herbert Walter and Annette G. (Werych) Gohlke; m. Louis Dan Kaiser; children: Richard L., Michael D. BS in Journalism, Northwestern U., 1969. Reporter Waco (Tex.) Tribune-Herald, 1969-71; editor Country Woman, Greendale, Wis., 1971—; mng. editor Taste of Home, Greendale, 1993—. Named among People of the Yr., Milw. Mag., 1998. Lutheran. Avocations: sailing, tennis, golf, travel. Office: Reiman Publs 5400 S 60th St Greendale WI 53129-1404

KAISER, ANTON J., lawyer; b. College Point, N.Y., May 6, 1929; s. Anton and Anna (Schaudenecker) K.; m. Mildred Mary Muldoon, Aug. 12, 1950; children— Eric, John, David. LL.B., St. John's U., 1951. Bar: N.Y. 1951. Atty., mortgage officer Franklin Nat. Bank, L.I., N.Y., 1954-74; atty., mortgage officer European Am. Bank, L.I., 1974-79, outside counsel to real estate dept., 1979—1997, ret. Republican. Roman Catholic. Club: Garden City Country (N.Y.). Lodge: Kiwanis Internat. (pres. 1987-88). Home: 37 Acme Ave Bethpage NY 11714-4628

KAISER, DANIEL HUGH, historian, educator; b. Phila., July 20, 1945; s. Walter Christian and Estelle Evelyn (Jaworsky) K.; m. Jonelle Marie Marwin, Aug. 10, 1968; children: Nina Marie, Andrew Eliot. AB, Wheaton Coll., 1967; AM, U. Chgo., 1970, PhD, 1977. Asst. prof. history U. Chgo., 1977-78, Grinnell (Iowa) Coll., 1979-84, assoc. prof., 1984-86, prof. history, 1986—, Joseph F. Rosenfield prof. social studies, 1984—, chair dept. history, 1988-90, 96-98. Mem. adv. bd. Soviet Studies in History, 1979-85; rsch. assoc. dept. Slavonic studies, vis. mem. Darwin Coll., Cambridge (Eng.) U., 1992-93; vis. prof. dept. Slavic langs. and lits. Ctr. for Medieval and Renaissance Studies, UCLA, 1996. Author: The Growth of the Law in Medieval Russia, 1980; editor: The Workers' Revolution in Russia, 1917, 1987; translator, editor: The Laws of Rus' Tenth to Fifteenth Centuries, 1992; co-editor: (with Gary Marker) Reinterpreting Russian History 860-1860s, 1994; editl. bd. Slavic Rev., 1996-2001. Elder 1st Presbyn. Ch., Grinnell, 1985, 87-89. Fellow Nat. Endowment Humanities, 1979, 92-93, 2000, John Simon Guggenheim Meml. Found., 1986, Fulbright-Hays Faculty Rsch. Abroad Found., 1986, Woodrow Wilson Internat. Ctr. Scholars, 1986, Internat. Rsch. Exchs. Bd. fellow to USSR/Russia, 1974-75, 78-79, 86, 93. Mem. Am. Assn. for Advancement Slavic Studies, Am. Hist. Assn., Early Slavic Studies Assn. (v.p. 1995-97, pres. 1997-99), Slavonic and East European Medieval Studies Group (U.K.), Study Group on 18th Century Russia (U.K.), 18th Century Russian Studies Assn. Office: Grinnell Coll Dept History Grinnell IA 50112-1670 E-mail: kaiser@grinnell.edu.

KAISER, FRAN ELIZABETH, endocrinologist, gerontologist; b. N.Y.C., Dec. 6, 1949; d. Philip Francis and Bronia (Weiss) K. BS, CCNY, 1970; MD, N.Y. Med. Coll., N.Y.C., 1974. Diplomate Am. Bd. Internal Medicine, Am. Bd. Geriat. Intern Beth Israel Med. Ctr., N.Y.C., 1974-75, resident to chief resident, 1975-78; fellow in endocrinology and metabolism U. Minn., Mpls., 1978-81, instr. dept. medicine, 1980-81, asst. prof., 1981-86; asst. prof. in residence UCLA Sch. Medicine, 1986-89; assoc. prof. medicine St. Louis U., 1989-94, prof., 1994-97, assoc. dir. divsn. geriatric medicine, 1989-97, prof., 1994-97; sr. regional med. dir. Merck & Co., Inc., Irving, Tex., 1997—2003, exec. med. dir., 2003, 2005—, 2005—; CEO, Kaiser and Assocs. Cons., 2004—05. Adj. prof. medicine St. Louis U, 1997-; chief sect. endocrinology and metabolism Dept. Internal Medicine, St. Paul Ramsey Med. Ctr./U. Minn. Hosps., St. Paul, 1981-86; John A. Hartford Geriatric Faculty Devel. award scholar Hartford Found., NYC/UCLA Sch. Medicine, 1986-87; chief geriatric medicine Olive View Med. Ctr./UCLA San Fernando Valley Program, Sylmar, Calif., 1987-89; med. dir. Hosp. Based Home Care, VA Med. Ctr., Sepulveda, 1987-89; clin. prof. medicine U. Tex. Southwestern Med. Sch., Dallas, 1999-. Mem. editl. bd.: Jour. Clin. Endocrinology and Metabolism, ad hoc reviewer: Endocrinology, Jour. AMA, Jour. Am. Geriatrics Soc., past mem. editl. bd.: Am. Geriatric Soc., Internat. Medicine Bull., cons. editor: Am. Health Mag.; contbr. articles to profl. jours. Grantee NIH, 1980-81, 97, Genetech, 1987-89, Syntex Corp. 1990-92, Hoechst-Roussel, 1992-94, Bur. Health Professions, 1991-97, VIVUS, 1993-97, Merck, 1994-97, Upjohn, 1995-97. Fellow: Am. Geriat. Soc.; mem.: Am. Assn. Home Care Physicians, Am. Geriatrics Soc. (past mem. editl. bd. Internal Medicine Bull., Jour. Geriatric Nephrology & Urology), Gerontol. Soc. Am., N.Y. Acad. Sci., Am. Fedn.Clin. Rsch., Endocrine Soc. (mem. women in endocrinology group), Am. Diabetes Assn., AAAS. Achievements include research in hormonal changes with aging, studies of therapy of erectile dysfunction, testosterone, estrogen and frailty and women's health and sexuality. Office: 3510 Edgewater Dr Dallas TX 75205 Office Phone: 214-686-6008. E-mail: Kaiserf@sbcglobal.net.

KAISER, GEORGE B., corporate financial executive; b. 1943; s. Herman George Kaiser; m. Betty Eudene, 1965 (dec. 2002); 3 children. BS, MS, Harvard U. Chmn. BOK Fin., Tulsa; prin. owner Kaiser-Francis Oil Co., Fountains Continuum of Care, Inc. Founder Tulsa Cmty. Found., 1998. Achievements include being listed as one of the world's richest people and among the 400 richest Americans by Forbes Mag. Office: Bok Fin Bank of Okla Tower PO Box 2300 Tulsa OK 74192

KAISER, GERARD A., hospital administrator; Postgrad, Columbia U. Sr. v.p. med. affairs Jackson Meml. Hosp., prof. of cardiothoracic surgery; deputy dean clinical affairs U. Miami Sch. of Medicine; residency U. Hosp. Thoracic Surgery. Mem.: Am. Bd. Thoracic Surgery, Am. Bd. Surgery, Am. Assn. Thoracic Surgery. Office: Jackson Meml Hosp 118 W Wing Miami FL 33136

KAISER, JUDITH ARLENE, retired elementary education educator; b. Newark, Ohio, Apr. 8, 1940; d. Ernest and Eunice (Griffith) K. BS, Ohio State U., 1962; MEd, Ohio U., 1973. Tchg. cert. Ohio. Tchr. Newark City Schs., 1962-99. Vol. Ctr. Alt. Resources, Newark, 1972-98. Mem. Newark Bus. & Profl. Women. Home: 35 W National Dr Newark OH 43055-5325

KAISER, KAREN SUE, elementary school educator; d. Reuben and Dorothy Ruth Miller; m. Richard Eugene Kaiser, Dec. 11, 1971; 1 child, Bryan Patrick. AA, Northeastern Jr. Coll., Sterling, Colo., 1969; EdB, U. No. Colo., 1972. K-2 tchr. Atwood (Colo.) Elem., 1972—73; kindergarten tchr. Sexson and Padroni Elems., Sterling, Colo., 1974—75, Sexson Elem., Sterling, 1976—84, Campbell Elem., Sterling, 1985—89, 4th grade tchr., 1990—. Art instr. Colo. Christian U., Denver, 2003; mem. achievement coun. RE-1 Valley Sch. Dist., Sterling, 1990—. Mem.: Colo. Edn. Assn., Alpha Delta Kappa (Silver Sister award 2002).

KAISER, LARRY ROBERT, thoracic surgeon; b. St. Louis, Aug. 31, 1952; s. Patricia Glaser; m. Lindy Snider; children: Jonathan, Jeffrey. BS, Tulane U., 1973, MD, 1977. Diplomate Am. Bd. Thoracic Surgery. Resident in surgery UCLA, 1977—83, fellow in surg. oncology, 1979—81; resident in thoracic and cardiovasc. surgery U. Toronto, Canada, 1983—85; asst. attending surgeon Meml. Sloan-Kettering Cancer Ctr., 1985—88; asst. and assoc. prof. surgery Washington U. Sch. Medicine, 1988—91; prof. and chief thoracic surgery U. Pa. Sch. Medicine, Phila., 1991—2001, John Rhea Barton prof. and chmn. dept. surgery, 2001—. Home: 408 Barbara Lane Bryn Mawr PA 19010 Office: Univ Pa Hosp 3400 Spruce St 4 Silverstein Philadelphia PA 19104 Office Phone: 215-662-7539. Business E-Mail: larry.kaiser@uphs.upenn.edu.

KAISER, MARY AGNES, chemist, chemical company executive; b. Pittston, Pa., June 11, 1948; d. Fredolin Anthony and Agnes Regina (Searfoss) K.; m. Cecil Dybowski, May 11, 1979; 1 child, Marta. BS, Wilkes Coll., 1970; MS, St. Joseph's U., Phila., 1972; PhD in Chemistry, Villanova (Pa.) U., 1976. Postdoctorate U. Ga., Athens, 1976-77; research chemist E.I Du Pont De Nemours & Co., Wilmington, Del., 1977-79, supr. research, 1979-86, sr. supr., 1986—2002, rsch. fellow, 2002—. Co-Author: Environmental Problem Solving Using Gas and Liquid Chromatography, 1982; contbr. articles to profl. jours. Recipient Alumni award, Villanova U., 1997. Mem. Am. Chem. Soc. (chmn. div. analytical chemistry, Analytic Divsn. Disting. Svc. award 2004), Fedn. Analytical Chemistry and Spectros Copy Soc. (chmn. governing bd.), Ea. Analytical Symposium (pres.), Chromatography Forum (chmn.), Sigma Xi (research recognition award 1970), Phi Kappa Phi. Avocation: swimming. Office: DuPont PO Box 80402 Wilmington DE 19880-0402

KAISER, MICHAEL M., performing company executive; b. NYC, 1953; s. Harold and Marion Kaiser. B magna cum laude, Brandeis U.; M in Mgmt., MIT. Rsch. economist for Wassily Leontief; past. owner Kaiser Assoc.; past gen. mgr. Kansas City Ballet, 1985; past. exec. dir. Ailvin Ailey Dance Theater Found.; past assoc. dir. Pierpont Morgan Libr.; past exec. dir. Am. Ballet Theatre, Royal Opera House, 1999—2001; pres. John F. Kennedy Ctr. for Performing Arts, Washington, 2001—. Cons. arts orgn.; adj. prof. arts adminstrn. N.Y. U.; lectr. U. Witwatersrand, Johannesburg. Author: Understanding the Competition: A Practical Guide of Competitive Analysis, 1981, Developing Industry Strategies: A Practical Guide of Industry Analysis, 1983, Strategic Planning in the Arts: A Practical Guide, 1995. Achievements include arranged, in conjunction with the U.S. State Dept., the historic concert of the Iraqi Natl. Symphony Orch. with the Nat. Symphony Orch., Kennedy Ctr., Dec. 2003. Office: John F Kennedy Ctr Performing Arts 2700 F St NW Washington DC 20566*

KAISER, NINA IRENE, health care consultant; b. San Diego, Nov. 29, 1953; d. Louis Frederick and Mary Elizabeth (Wright) K.; children: Kellen Anne Kaiser, Ethan Andrew Kaiser-Klimist. BSN, BA in Women Studies, San Francisco State U., 1980; MBA, U. Phoenix, 2001. RN, Calif. RN Calif. Pacific Med. Ctr., San Francisco, 1980-81, Ralph K. Davies Med. Ctr., San Francisco, 1982-85, Planned Parenthood, San Francisco, 1985-86, Visiting Nurses and Hospice, San Francisco, 1986-88; RN supr. St. Mary's Home Care, San Francisco, 1991-93; RN dir. St. Vincent's Homecare and Hospice, Fremont, Calif., 1993-94; aux. dir. Home Health Link, San Leandro, Calif., 1994-99; mgmt. cons. Kaiser Home Health, Oakland, Calif., 1999—2002, mgr., 2003—. Regional coun. chair San Francisco Bay Area, 1999. Pres. Daus. of Bilitis, San Francisco, 1977-78; founding mem. Buena Vista Lesbian and Gay Parents Assn., San Francisco, 1985; treas., bd. dirs. Holladay Ave. Homeowners Assn., San Francisco, 1984-96; bd. dirs. Midrasha High Sch., Berkeley, Calif., 1996. With USN, 1971-74. Personal E-mail: missnynak@aol.com.

KAISER, PETER K., physician, researcher; s. Peter and Anafu Kaiser; m. Maureen O. Oyola, Sept. 4, 1994; children: Peter M., Stephanie M. MD, Harvard Med. Sch., Boston, Mass., 1992. Lic. MD Ohio, 1997. Staff physician Cole Eye Inst., 1997—. Recipient Sr. Achievement Award, Am. Soc. of Retina Specialists, 2003. Mem.: Am. Acad. of Ophthalmology. Achievements include research in Am. Acad. of Ophthalmology Honor Award. Home: Shaker Heights OH Office: Cole Eye Inst 9500 Euclid Ave Desk i3 Cleveland OH 44195 Office Phone: 216-444-6702. Office Fax: 216-445-2226. Personal E-mail: pkkaiser@aol.com.

KAISER, PHILIP MAYER, retired diplomat; b. Bklyn., July 12, 1913; s. Morris and Temma (Sloven) K.; m. Hannah Greeley, June 16, 1939; children: Robert Greeley, David Elmore, Charles Roger. AB, U. Wis., 1935; BA, MA (Rhodes scholar), Balliol Coll., Oxford (Eng.) U., 1939. Economist, bd. govs. Fed. Res. System, 1939-42; chief project ops. staff, also chief planning staff enemy br. Bd. Econ. Warfare and Fgn. Econ. Adminstrn., 1942-46; expert on internat. orgn. affairs State Dept., 1946; exec. asst. to asst. sec. labor in charge internat. labor affairs, 1946-47; dir. Office Internat. Affairs, Dept. Labor, 1947-49, asst. sec. labor for internat. affairs, 1949-53; labor adviser to Com. for Free Europe, 1954; spl. asst. to Gov. W. Averell Harriman of N.Y., 1955-58; prof. internat. rels. Sch. Internat. Svc. Am. U., 1958-61; U.S. ambassador to Republic Senegal, Islamic Republic Mauritania, 1961-64; minister Am. Embassy, London, Eng., 1964-69; chmn. Ency. Brit. Internat. Ltd., London, 1969-75; dir. Guinness Mahon Holdings, Ltd., 1975-77; amb. to People's Republic of Hungary, 1977-80, Austria, 1980-81; professorial lectr. Johns Hopkins Sch. Advanced Internat. Studies, 1981—83, Woodrow Wilson vis. fellow, 1984; sr. cons. SRI Internat., 1981-97. Mem. interdept. com. to develop programs under Marshall Plan, 1947—48, interdept. com. to develop programs for Greek-Turkish aid and Point 4 Tech. Assistance, 1947—49, Internat. del. to Hungary's Parliamentary elections, 1990; spl. amb. for Pres. Kennedy to Rwanda for its ind. day, 62. Author: Journeying Far and Wide: A Political and Diplomatic Memoir, 1993. Bd. dirs. Am. Ditchley Found., Ptnrs. for Dem. Change, Coun. Am. Ambs., Assn. Diplomatic Studies, Am. Acad. Diplomacy. Decorated knight comdr. Austrian Govt., Cross of Order of Merit of Republic of Hungary. Mem. Am. Assn. Rhodes Scholars, Coun. Fgn. Rels., Washington Inst. for Fgn. Affairs, Phi Beta Kappa. Home: 2101 Connecticut Ave NW Washington DC 20008-1728 Fax: 202-332-6124.

KAISER, ROBERT A., telecommunications industry executive; CFO Mobile Sys. Southwestern Bell, 1987—96; CFO SkyTel, 1996—99, CEO, CFO, 2000; CEO WorldCom Broadband Solutions Group, 2000—01, MobileStar Network Corp., 2001; sr. v.p. CellStar Corp, Carrollton, Tex., 2001—, CFO, 2001—, treas., 2001—, pres., 2003, CEO, 2004—. Office: Cellstar Corp 1730 Briercroft Ct Carrollton TX 75006

KAISER, ROY, artistic director; b. Perth Amboy, NJ; Studied ballet with Karen Irvin; student, San Francisco Ballet Sch., Sch. Pa. Ballet. With Pa. Ballet, 1979, prin. dancer, 1980-92, asst. ballet master, 1987-92, ballet master, 1992, assoc. artistic dir., 1993, interim artistic dir., 1994-95, Ruth and A. Morris Williams, Jr. artistic dir., 1995—. Featured artists (with brothers) N.Y. World's Fair and throughout the U.S.; performer on TV with Wayne Newton Music Carnival, Cleve.; performer on TV NBC-TV's Kraft Music Hall. Leading classical roles include Siegfried in Swan Lake, Franz in Coppelia, the Cavalier in The Nutcracker, Bolero, Symphonic Etudes, A Musical Offering, other prin. roles include George Balanchine's Symphony in C, Western Symphony, Symphony in Three Movements, Iago in The Moor's Pavane, Franklin Ct. Office: Pennsylvania Ballet 1101 S Broad St Philadelphia PA 19147-4410 E-mail: rkaiser@paballet.org.*

KAISER, WALTER, language educator; b. Bellevue, Ohio, May 31, 1931; AB magna cum laude, Harvard Coll., 1954; PhD, Harvard U., 1960. Allston Burr sr. tutor Eliot House Harvard U., 1957-58, from instr. to assoc. prof. English, comparative lit. Cambridge, Mass., 1960-62, prof. English, comparative lit., 1969—, chmn. dept., 1969-75, 82-85. Mem. coms. degrees in history and lit. Harvard U., 1960—, Faculty coun., 1971-74, libr. com., 1971-74; dep. dir. Villa I Tatti, Florence, 1971-86, dir. 1988-2002. Author: Praisers of Folly: Erasmus, Rabelais, Shakespeare, 1964, Essays of Montaigne, 1964; co-author Program in Literature and the Arts for the Core Curriculum, 1977; transl.: (with intro.) Three Secret Poems, (George Seferis), 1969, Alexis (Marguerite Yourcenar), 1984, Two Lives and a Dream (Marguerite Yourcenar), That Mighty Sculptor, Time (Marguerite Yourcenar), 1992; edit. bd. Studies in English Lit., 1977-88; editor-in-chief I Tatti Studies: Essays in the Renaissance, 1988-2002; editor (with M. Mallon) On Artists and Art Historians: Selected Book Reviews of John Pope Hennessy, 1994; contbr. numerous articles, reviews, poems to profl. jours. Chair ad hoc vis. com. to Addison Gallery Am. Art, 1978; trustee Michael Rockefeller Meml. Fellowship, 1965-68, 69-70, Rockefeller Family Fund, 1973-79, Mus. Fine Arts, Boston, 1978-88, Bogliasco Found., 2001—; bd. dirs. Philip H. Rosenbach Found., 1974-78. Fulbright fellow U. Paris, 1954-55; Tower fellow Ecole Normale Supérieure Paris, 1955-56; fellow to Rome Am. Coun. Learned Socs., 1964-65; Walter Channing Cabot fellow Fac. Arts. and Scis., 1977-78. Mem. PEN, Boston Athenaeum, Am. Comparative Lit. Assn., Renaissance Soc. Am., Signet Soc. (assoc.), Modern Greek Studies Assn., Shakespeare Assn. Am., Coun. Fgn. Rels., Knickerbocker Club, Somerset Club, Harvard Club, Old Salopian, Boston Libr. Soc., Century Assn., Phi Beta Kappa. Home and Office: 25 Sutton Pl S Apt 20M New York NY 10022 E-mail: walter_kaiser@harvard.edu.

KAISERLIAN, PENELOPE JANE, publishing company executive; b. Paisley, Scotland, Oct. 19, 1943; came to U.S., 1956; d. W. Norman and Magdalene Jeanette (Houlder) Hewson; m. Arthur Kaiserlian, June 29, 1968; 1 child, Christian. BA, U. Exeter, Eng., 1965. Copywriter, sales rep. Pergamon Press, Elmsford, N.Y., 1965-68; exhibits mgr. Plenum Pub., N.Y.C., 1968-69; asst. mktg. mgr. U. Chgo. Press, 1969-76, mktg. mgr., 1976-83, assoc. dir., 1983-2001; dir. U. Va. Press, 2001—. Mem. Soc. for Scholarly Pub., Assn. for Documentary Editing, Am. Assn. Geog., Colonnade Club. Office: Univ Va Press PO Box 400318 Charlottesville VA 22904-4318

KAISH, LUISE CLAYBORN, sculptor, educator; b. Atlanta, Sept. 8, 1925; d. Harry and Elsa (Brown) Meyers; m. Morton Kaish, Aug. 15, 1948; 1 child, Melissa. BFA magna cum laude, Syracuse U., 1946, MFA, 1951; student, Escuela de Pintura y Escultura, Escuela de las Artes del Libro, Taller Grafico, Mexico, 1946-47. Artist-in-residence Dartmouth Coll., 1974; prof. sculpture and painting, 1980-93, chmn. div. painting and sculpture Columbia U., 1980-86, prof. emerita, 1993; vis. artist U. Wash., Seattle, Battelle seminars and study program, Seattle, 1979; artist-in-residence U. Haifa, Israel, 1985. One-man shows Meml. Art Gallery, Rochester, N.Y., 1954, Sculpture Ctr., N.Y.C., 1955, 58, Staempfli Gallery, N.Y.C., 1968, 81, 84, 87, 88, Minn. Mus. Art, St. Paul, 1969, Jewish Mus., N.Y.C., 1973, U. Ark., 1990, The Century Assn., 1998; exhibited (with Morton Kaish), Rochester Meml. Art Gallery, 1958, USIS, Rome, 1973, Dartmouth Coll., 1974, Oxford Gallery, Rochester, 1988; represented in permanent collections Whitney Mus. Am. Art, N.Y.C., Met. Mus. Art, N.Y.C., Jewish Mus., N.Y.C., Export Khleb, Moscow, Minn. Mus. Art, Gen. Mills Corp., Minn., Rochester Meml. Art Gallery, Smithsonian Instn., Nat. Mus. Am. Art, Washington, also numerous pvt. collections, commns., Syracuse U., Temple B'rith Kodesh, Rochester, Temple Israel, Westport, Conn., Holy Trinity Mission Sem., Silver Springs, Md., Temple Beth Shalom, Wilmington, Del., Beth-El Synagogue Ctr., New Rochelle, N.Y., Temple B'nai Abraham, Essex City, N.J., Continental Grain Co., N.Y. Trustee Am. Acad. in Rome, 1973-81, mem. exec. com., 1975-81, trustee emerita, 1994; trustee St. Gaudens Found., 1978-90, mem. exec. com., 1980-90. Recipient awards Everson Mus., Syracuse, 1947, awards Rochester Meml. Art Gallery, 1951, awards Ball State U., 1963, awards Ch. World Service, 1960, awards Council for Arts in Westchester, 1974, Emily Lowe award, 1956, Audubon Artists gold medal, 1963, Honor award AIA, 1975, Arents Pioneer medal, Syracuse U., 1989; Louis Comfort Tiffany grantee, 1951; Guggenheim fellow, 1959; Rome prize fellow Am. Acad. in Rome, 1970-72 Mem. Nat. Acad. Design, The Century Assn., Eta Pi Upsilon. Home and Office: 610 W End Ave # 9-a New York NY 10024-1605 Office Phone: 212-595-6815. Business E-Mail: lk4@columbia.edu.

KAISH, MORTON, artist, educator; b. Newark, Jan. 8, 1927; s. Morris and Sophie K.; m. Luise H. Meyers, Aug. 15, 1948; 1 dau., Melissa. BFA, Syracuse U., 1949; postgrad., Academie de la Grande Chaumiere, Paris, 1951, Istituto d' Arte, Florence, Italy, 1952, Accademia delle Belle Arti, Rome, 1957. Vis. critic Parsons Sch. Design, N.Y.C., 1966-70, Phila. Coll. Art, 1983; mem. faculty Art Students League, N.Y.C., 1974—; guest critic Sch. Visual Arts, N.Y.C., 1967; vis. prof. Queens Coll., Flushing, N.Y., 1979; vis. artist U. Wash., Seattle, 1979; fellow MacDowell Colony, 1976; artist-in-residence Dartmouth Coll., 1974, U. Haifa, Israel, 1985; prof. Fashion Inst. Tech., SUNY, N.Y.C., 1973—; vis. artist Susquehanna U., 1985; dir. Carl Fischer Mus. Instrument Co., 1964-70. Vis. artist Columbia U., N.Y.C., 1986, Boston U., 1987. One-man shows include Manhattanville Coll., Purchase, N.Y., 1955, Rochester (N.Y.) Meml. Art Gallery, 1955, Guild Hall, Easthampton, L.I., 1969, U.S. Info. Service, Rome, 1973, Dartmouth Coll., Hanover, N.H., 1974, Staempfli Gallery, N.Y.C., 1964, 67, 71, 73, 79, 83, 86, 89, Oxford Gallery, Rochester, N.Y., 1989, Century Assn., N.Y., 1989, Hollis Taggart Galleries, Washington, 1993, N.Y.C., 1996; group shows Mus. Galleria 11 Torcoliere, Rome, 1957, Barone Gallery, N.Y.C., 1959, Art Inst. Chgo., 1964, Sheldon Meml. Art Gallery, Lincoln, Nebr., 1964, U. Nebr., Lincoln, 1964, Krannert Art Mus., U. Ill., Urbana, 1965, 68, Herron Mus. Art, Indpls., 1965, Mary Washington Coll., Fredericksburg, Va., 1965, Am. Acad. Arts and Letters, N.Y.C., 1966, Pa. Acad. Fine Arts, Phila., 1966, Ark. Art Ctr., Little Rock, 1966, Whitney Mus. Am. Art, N.Y.C., 1966, Finch Coll. Mus. Art, N.Y.C., 1966, N.J. State Mus., Trenton, 1966, Krannert Art Mus., 1968, Kent (Ohio) State U., 1970, U.S. Info. Service, Rome, 1972, New Sch. Social Research, N.Y.C., 1973, Child Hassam Purchase Fund Exhbn., N.Y.C., 1973; invitational exhbns. Child Hassam Purchase Fund, 1975, Am. Acad. Arts and Letters, 1975, Drawings U.S.A., 1975, Minn. Mus. Art, St. Paul, 1975, Springfield Art Mus., 1975, Springfield Mus. Art, Mo., 1975, Galerie Brusberg, Berlin, W.Ger., 1980, Taft Mus., Cin., 1981, NAD, N.Y.C., 1983, 85, 89, 91; represented in permanent collections Met. Mus. Art, N.Y.C., Whitney Mus. Am. Art, N.Y.C., Bklyn. Mus., Nat. Mus. Art, Smithsonian Instn., Washington, Brit. Mus., London, The Fitzwilliam Mus., Cambridge, Guild Hall, Easthampton, N.Y., Williams Coll., Williamstown. Mass., Syracuse U., N.Y., Swarthmore Coll., Indpls. Mus. Art, U. Mich. Mus. Art., Guilford Coll., Greensboro, N.C., Rochester (N.Y.) Meml. Art Gallery, Bates Coll., Lewiston, Maine, New Britain (Conn.) Mus. Am. Art, Newark Mus., N.J., Butler Inst. Am. Art, Youngstown, Ohio. Recipient SUNY Rsch. Found. award, 1983; Gervasi award, 1985, William Ward Ranger Fund purchase award, 1983, 85, Benjamin Altman prize, 1989, Andrew Carnegie prize, 1992, Adolph and Clara Obrig prize, 2003, Disting. Alumni award for Achievement in the Visual Arts Syracuse U., 1989; faculty exch. scholar SUNY, 1987. Mem. NAD (corr. sec., William A. Paton prize 1983), Century Assn., Artists' Choice Mus. (bd. artists), Artists' Fellowship (trustee, v.p.). Address: 610 W End Ave New York NY 10024-1605 Office Phone: 212-217-8058.

KAJI, AKIRA, microbiology scientist, educator; b. Tokyo, Jan. 13, 1930; arrived in U.S., 1954; s. Kiichi and Chiyo (Hanai) K.; m. Hideko Katayama, Aug. 22, 1958; children: Kenneth, Eugene, Naomi, Amy. BS, Tokyo U., 1953; PhD, Johns Hopkins U., 1958; MS (hon.), U. Pa., 1973. Rsch. fellow Johns Hopkins Hosp., Balt., 1958-59; guest investigator Rockefeller U., NYC, 1959; rsch. assoc. microbiology Vanderbilt Med. Sch., Nashville, 1959-62; vis. scientist Oak Ridge (Tenn.) Nat. Lab., 1962-63; assoc. U. Pa. Med. Sch., Phila., 1963-64, asst. prof. microbiology, 1964-67, assoc. prof., 1967-72, prof., 1972—. Permanent mem. bd. sci. councilors Nat. Eye Inst., Bethesda, Md., 1987-92; prof., chair Tokyo U. Faculty Pharm. Scis., 1972-73; vis. prof. Kyoto U. Virus Rsch. Inst., 1985. Contbr. over 200 articles to profl. jours. Recipient Fulbright-Smith-Mundt award, 1954, Helen Hay Whitney award, 1964-69, John Simmon Guggenheim award, 1972-73, Fogarty Internat. Sr. award, 1985-86. Mem. Am. Soc. Biol. Chemistry and Molecular Biology, Am. Soc. Cell Biology, Am. Soc. Microbiology, Am. Soc. Chemistry. Avocations: ice dancing, swimming. Office: U Pa Sch Medicine Dept Microbiology Johnson Pavilion Philadelphia PA 19104 Business E-Mail: kaji@mail.med.upenn.edu.

KAJITANI, MOTOHISA, sociology educator; b. Kamioka, Gifu, Japan, May 8, 1937; s. Miyokichi and Nui (Taguchi) K.; m. Yoko Shimizu, Nov. 1969; 1 child, Kuri BA, Tokyo U. & Sch. of Journalism; Diploma in Social Sci., U. Tokyo, 1961; MA, Kyoto (Japan) U., 1964. Lectr. Meijo U., Nagoya, Japan, 1964-69, prof., 1976—, chmn. libr., 1991-2001, univ. prof. grad. sch., 2002—; joint lectr. Tokyo U. Fgn. Studies, 1965—72, 1975—82. Vis. prof. dept. sociology UCLA, 1990; non-resident mem. Queen Elizabeth House, Oxford, 1972-74; guest prof. U. Klagenfurt, Austria, 1996; guest lectr. Nagoya City U., 1997—. Assoc. editor History of Sociology, 1981-87; author: Kokusai Shakaigaku to Nippon, A Step to International Sociology, 2005; Press and Empire, 1981; author, editor: Shakaigaku no Rekishi: A History of Sociology, 1982, 89; editor: (with Hisao Naka) Sociologie Globale, 1987; editor: (with J. Langer) Shakaigatu to Europa, 1994; contbr. articles to Global, 1984-87. Recipient prize of social thought Akegarasu Fund, Tokyo and Kanazawa Univs., 1964, Outstanding Achievement award in edn., Cambridge, Eng., 1999; over 10 grants in Japan. Mem.: others, Japanese Sociol. Assn., Internat. Sociol. Assn. (life). Avocations: opera, concerts. Office: Meijo U 1-501 Shiogamaguchi Nagoya 468 Japan Fax: (52) 838-7249. Office Phone: (52) 838-2197. E-mail: kajitani@meijo-u.ac.jp.

KAJOSEVIC, INDIRA, cultural organization administrator; b. Podgorica, Serbia-Monteneg (former Yugoslavia), June 7, 1966; d. Pranvera and Serif Kajosevic; m. Ivo Ninoslav Skoric, Nov. 12, 1998. MA in Polit. sci., Belgrade, Yugoslavia, 1999; MA in Internat. Rels., CUNY, 2000; postgrad., The Fielding Grad. Inst., Santa Barbara, Calif., 2002—. Exec. dir. Reconciliation and Culture Coop. Network (RACCOON, Inc.), New York, 1997—; coord. NGO Working Group on Women, Peace and Security, New York, 2002—03. Journalist various broadcast and TV media, Belgrade, Serbia-Monteneg (Yugoslavia), 1987—94; confict resolution cons. Am. Friends Svc. Com., New York, 1994—99; cons. Women's Commn. for Refugee Women and Children, New York, 2000—01; tchr. New Sch. U., New York. Founding mem. Women in Black Against the War, Belgrade, 1991. Recipient Spl. prize, Belgrade Documentary Film Festival, 1994; Internat. fellow, AAWU, 2003.

KAKADIARIS, IOANNIS, computer science educator; b. Athens, Greece, May 16, 1966; m. Maria Gasi, Jan. 13, 1996; children: Eugenia, Alexandra. PhD in Computer Sci., U. Pa., 1997. Tchg. asst. Northeastern U., Boston, 1990—90, rsch. asst., 1990—91; rsch. fellow U. Pa., Phila., 1991—96, post-doctoral fellow, 1996—97; asst. prof. U. Houston, 1997—, dir. visual computing lab, 1997—2002, coord. external rels. Virtual Environments Rsch. Inst., 1998—2000, mem. Tex. Learning and Computation Ctr., 1999—, thrust leader bioimaging and biocomputation Virtual Environments Rsch. Inst, 2000—02, interim dir. Virtual Environments Rsch. Inst, 2000—02, co-dir. Visual Computing Lab., 2002—, dir. divsn. bioimaging and biocomputation Inst. for Digital Informatics and Analysis, 2002—. Adj. asst. prof. dept. health informatics Health Info. Scis. U. Tex., Houston, 1999—; adj. asst. prof. dept. plastic surgery U. Tex. M.D. Anderson Cancer Ctr., Houston, 2000—; mem. The W.M. Keck Ctr. for Computational and Structural Biology, 2002—. Editor: Proceedings of the IEEE Human motion analysis and synthesis workshop; contbr. chapters to books, articles to profl. jours. Recipient award, Schlumberger Tech. Found., 1998—99, SHELL Interdisciplinary award, 1999; fellow, Bodosakis Found., 1989—91, Gerondelis Found., 1991—92; grantee, SGI Inc., 1998, NSF, 1998, U. Houston Internat. Space Systems Ops., 2000—02, NSF, 2000—, Tex. Higher Edn. Coordinating Bd., 2000—03, Am. Honda R&D, Inc., 2000—01, MD Anderson Cancer Ctr., 2000—, NSF, 2001—02, Sun Microsystems, 2001—, Tex. Higher Edn. Coordinating Bd., 2001, Keck Ctr. for Computational Biology, 2002—03, Juvenile Diabetes Rsch. Found., 2002—, U. of Houston Faculty Devel. Initiative Program, 2002—03, U. Houston, 2002, Real Time Innovations Inc., 2002. Mem.: IEEE (Disting. Visitor 2002—), Brit. Machine Vision Assn., Internat. Soc. for Computer Aided Surgery, Hellenic Soc. Scientists in Computer and Info. Sci., Assn. for Computing Machinery, Am. Heart Assn., Sigma Xi (pres. 2002—03). Achievements include research in understanding diagrams in technical documents; data interrogation in visual computing; adaptive fuzzy connectedness-based medical image segementation; automatic hybrid segmentation of dual contrast cardiac MR data; g-HDAF multiresolution deformable models for shape modeling and reconstruction; teleoperating robonaut; m-HDAF multiresolution deformable models; automatic computation of the ejection fraction using dual contrast short-axis cardia MR images; estimating the motion of the LAD; tracking methods for medical augemented reality; multi-sensory investigation of geoscientific data; application of virtual reality in surgery; improvement of anthropometry and pose estimation from a single uncalibrated image; numerous others. Office: Univ Houston 4800 Calhoun MS CSC 3010 Houston TX 77204-3010 E-mail: ioannisk@uh.edu.

KAKU, MICHIO, theoretical nuclear physicist, educator; b. San Jose, Calif., Jan. 24, 1947; s. Toshio and Hideko (Maruyama) K. BA, Harvard U., 1968; PhD, U. Calif., Berkeley, 1972; PhD (hon.) Hofstra U., 1997, SUNY, Old Westbury, 1997. Rsch. assoc. Princeton U., N.J., 1972-73; assoc. prof. CCNY and Grad. Ctr., 1973-83, prof., 1983—; vis. prof. NYU, 1988, Inst. for Advanced Studies at Princeton U., 1990. Author: Nuclear Power: Both Sides, 1983; Beyond Einstein, the Cosmic Quest for the Theory of the Universe, 1986, Introduction to Superstrings, 1988, Strings, Conformal Fields, and Topology, 1991, Quarks, Symmetries, and Strings, 1991, Quantum Field Theory: A Modern Introduction, 1993, Hyperspace: A Scientific Odyssey Through Parallel Universes, Time Warps, and the 10th Dimension, 1994, Frontiers in Quantum Field Theory, 1996, Visions: How Science Will Revolutionize the 21st Century, 1997, Einstein's Cosmos, 2004, Parallel Worlds, 2005; contbr. 70 articles to profl. jours. Fellow Am. Phys. Soc. Avocations: nuclear arms control, nuclear power. Office: CCNY Physics Dept 138th St at Convent Ave New York NY 10031 Personal E-mail: mkaku@aol.com.

KAKUTANI, MICHIKO, critic; b. New Haven, Conn., Jan. 9, 1955; BA in English, Yale Univ., 1976. Reporter Washington Post, 1976—77; staff writer Time mag., 1977—79; reporter, cultural news NY Times, NYC, 1979—83, book critic, 1983—, now chief book critic. Recipient Pulitzer prize for criticism, 1998. Office: c/o NY Times Culture News 229 W 43d St New York NY 10036*

KALABZA-BALSAMO, DEBRA ALYCE, music educator; b. Astoria, N.Y., Apr. 26, 1963; d. John Francis Kalabza and Frances Adele Gualtieri-Kalabza; m. Edward Richard Balsamo, Aug. 11, 1996. AS music performance, Suffolk County C.C., Selden, N.Y., 1983; BS in Edn. and performance, Hofstra U., 1985; MS in Edn. and Performance, L.I. U., Greenvale, N.Y., 1989, profl. diploma in Ednl. Admin., 1996; doctral studies, St. John's U., 2004—. Choral and band substitute tchr. Half Hollow Hills Ctrl. Sch. Dist., Melville, NY, 1986; elem. band and orch. substitute dir. Sachem (N.Y.) Ctrl. Sch. Dist., 1986; h.s. and elem. band dir. Island Trees Ctrl .Sch. Dist., Levittown, NY, 1987—88; elem. band dir. Smithtown (N.Y.) Ctrl. Sch. Dist., 1988—91; elem. band dir. and gen. music tchr. Harborfields Ctrl. Sch. Dist., Greenlawn, NY, 1991—93; mid. sch. band dir., lead tchr. Smithtown Ctrl. Sch. Dist., 1993—, h.s. symphonic band dir., head tchr., 2001—. Mem.: NY Statw Band Dirs. Assn., Nat. Flute Assn., L.I. Flute Club, N.Y. Flute Club, N.Y. State Coun. Adminstrs. for Music Educators, Suffolk County Music Edn. Assn., Music Educators Nat. Conf., Phi Delta Kappa. Avocations: music, golf, basketball, softball, travel. Home: 6 Angela Ct Saint James NY 11780 Office: Smithtown High Sch School East 10 School St Saint James NY 11780

KALAFUT, GEORGE WENDELL, distribution company executive, retired naval officer; b. Chgo., Feb. 21, 1934; s. George Andrew and Ann Catherine (Panak) K.; m. Alice Quinn, Nov. 9, 1957; children: Katherine, Tracy. AB in Econs., St. Joseph's Coll., Rensselaer, Ind., 1955; MBA, Harvard U., 1969. Commd. USN, 1956, advanced through grades to capt., 1976; asst dir. air equipment purchasing divsn. Naval Air Systems Command, Washington, 1969-71, dep. dir. F14/Grumman rev. team Washington and Bethpage, N.Y., 1971, dir. airframes purchasing div. Washington, 1972-73; supply officer USS Ranger CV61, San Francisco, 1973-75; dir. plans and budget Naval Supply Systems Command, Washington, 1976-78; retired USN, 1978; dir. inventories Motion Industries, Birmingham, Ala., 1979, v.p., 1980-83, v.p. fin., chief fin. officer, 1983-85, sr. v.p., 1985-89, also bd. dirs.; sr. v.p. fin. and adminstrn. Genuine Parts Co., Atlanta, 1989-91, exec. v.p. fin. and adminstrn., chief fin. officer, 1991—2001, exec. v.p., 2001—04; ret., 2004. Baker scholar Harvard Bus. Sch., 1969. Home: 1755 Spalding Dr Atlanta GA 30350-4321

KALAI, EHUD, economist, researcher, educator; b. Tel Aviv, Dec. 7, 1942; arrived in U.S., 1963; s. Meir and Elisheva (Rabinovitch) Kalai; m. Marilyn Lott, Aug. 24, 1967; children: Kerren, Adam. AB with distinction, U. Calif. at Berkeley, 1967; MS, Cornell U., 1971, PhD in Applied Math., 1972. Asst. prof. dept. stats. Tel Aviv U., 1972-75; vis. asst. prof. decision scis. J. L. Kellogg Grad. Sch. Mgmt. Northwestern U., Evanston, Ill., 1975-76, assoc. prof., 1976-78, prof. managerial econs. and decision scis., 1978-82, Charles E. Morrison Chair prof. decision scis., 1982-2001, prof. math., 1990—, James J. O'Connor disting. prof. decision and game scis., 2001—, IBM rsch. chair managerial econs., 1980-81, J. L. Kellogg rsch. chair in decision theory, 1981-82, chmn. meds. dept., 1983-85, dir. Ctr. Strategic Decision-Making, 1995—. Expert testimony in ct. cases, 1982—; Oskar Morgenstern rsch. prof. game theory NYU, N.Y.C., 1991; cons. Israeli Def. Forces, 1974—75, 1st Nat. Bank, Chgo., 1987, Arthur Anderson, 1990, Kaiser Permanente, 1995, Nath Sonnenschein and Rosenthal, 1999, Baxter Healthcare Corp., 1999—. Founder, editor Games and Econ. Behavior Jour., 1988—, mem. editl. bd. Math. Social Scis., 1980—90, Jour. Econ. Theory, 1980—88, Internat. Jour. Game Theory, 1984—; contbr. articles to profl. jours. Sgt. Israeli Def. Forces, 1960—63. Grantee, NSF, 1979—; Sherman Fairchild Disting. scholar, Calif. Inst. Tech., 1994—95. Fellow: Econometric Soc.; mem.: Game Theory Soc. (founder, exec. v.p. 1998—2003, pres. 2003—), Pub. Choice Soc., Am. Math. Soc., Beta Gamma Sigma. Home: 1110 N Lake Shore Dr Apt 23S Chicago IL 60611-1023 Office: Kellogg Grad Sch of Mgmt Northwestern Univ Evanston IL 60208-0001 Office Phone: 847-491-7017. Business E-Mail: kalai@kellogg.northwestern.edu.

KALAINOV, SAM CHARLES, insurance company executive; b. Steele, N.D., May 11, 1930; s. George and Celia Mae (Makedonsky) K.; m. Delores L. Holm., Aug. 10, 1957; children: John Charles, David Mark. BS, N.D. State U., 1956. CLU. Life ins. agt. Am. Mut. Life Ins. Co., Fargo, N.D., 1956-60, supt. agys. Des Moines, 1960-70, sr. v.p. mktg., 1972-80, pres., chmn., CEO, 1980-95; v.p. agy. Western States Life Ins. Co., Fargo, 1970-72; chmn. bd. dirs. Am. Mut. Holding Corp., Amerus Life, 1995-2000. Bd. dirs. Am. Coun. Life Ins., Washington, Bankers Trust, Des Moines; past chmn. Des Moines Devel. Corp. Bd. dirs. Luth. Health Sys., Fargo, 1974-91, City Corp., Des Moines, 1981-95, Civic Ctr. Ct., 1981-95, Iowa Luth. Hosp., 1982-91; trustee Drake U.; past chmn. Des Moines Conv. and Visitors Bur.; civilian aide to Sec. Army at Large, 1991; past state dir. Selective Svc. Sys.; bd. mem. N.D. State U. Devel. Found. With inf. AUS, 1947-49, lt., 1952-55. Decorated Bronze Star; recipient Alumni Achievement award N.D. State U., 1983, Patrick Henry award Army Nat. Guard, 1998. Mem. Nat. Assn. Life Underwriters, Greater Des Moines C. of C. (past chmn., Nat. Leadership award 1978), Corp. for Internat. Trade (chmn.), Alexis de Tocqueville Soc., Am. Legion, Rotary (past pres. Des Moines chpt.), Grand Lodge Iowa, Royal Order of Jesters, Za-Ga-Zig Temple. Office: AmerUs Group 699 Walnut St Des Moines IA 50309-3929

KALAJIAN-LAGANI, DONNA, publishing executive; b. Mountainside, NJ, Feb. 8, 1955; d. Jack and Analid Kalajian; m. Ron Galotti, Oct. 14, 1981. BS, Penn State U., 1975. Internat. credit analyst Irving Trust Co., N.Y.C., 1976—77; ad sales rep. BMT Pub., N.Y.C., 1977—79, Woman's Day Mag., N.Y.C., 1979—81, cosmetics mgr., 1981—83, ea. mgr., 1984—87; v.p., advt. dir. Ladies' Home Jour., N.Y.C., 1987—89, v.p., pub., 1989—95; pub./sr. v.p. Cosmopolitan Mag., 1996—99; publ. dir. Cosmopolitan Group, N.Y.C.,

1999—, sr. v.p., 1999—. Home: 100 Park Ave New York NY 10017-5516 Office: Cosmopolitan Hearst Magazines 224 W 57th St New York NY 10019-3299 Office Phone: 212-649-3282. Office Fax: 212-397-7581.*

KALAMOTOUSAKIS, GEORGE JOHN, economist, merchant banker, educator; b. Chios, Greece, July 26, 1936; came to U.S., 1953; s. John S. and Marika (Nikolaides) K.; 1 child, Yannis. BA, CUNY, 1956, MA, 1958; PhD, NYU, 1966. Instr. Fairleigh Dickinson, U., Teaneck, N.J., 1958-59; asst. prof. Ithaca (N.Y.) Coll., 1959-62; chief economist Brown Engr., N.Y.C., 1963-64; instr. Washington Sq. Coll., NYU, 1963-65; econ. cons. N.Y. State Office Regional Devel., Albany, 1964-66; adv. economist IBM, Armonk, N.Y., 1969-73; internat. economist Am. Standard, Inc., N.Y.C., 1973-76; prof. finance Grad. Sch. Bus., NYU, 1971-77. External dir. Rank-Xerox, Hellas, Greece, Atlantic Union Ins. Co., Athens, Greece; vis. prof. U. Md. European divsn. USAF, 1960, 67-68; head dept. pub. fin. Ctr. of Planning and Econ. Rsch., Athens, Greece; dir. econ. rsch. Bank of Greece, 1977-79; chief exec. officer, vice-chmn. bd. Bank of Crete, Athens, 1979-84; exec. dir., country head, gen. mgr. Greece, head Middle Ea. region Am. Express Bank Ltd., N.Y.C., 1985-94, fin. svcs. cons., 1995—; mem. William J. Fulbright Scholarship com., 1990-95, Athens; bd. dirs. Egyptian Am. Bank, Cairo, 1989-94. Contbr. articles to profl. jours.; Author books on internat. fin., Cyprus and self determination, common market and econ. devel. Greece. Bd. dirs., trustee Hellenic Theatre Found., bd. dirs. Aegian U., Greece, 1982-94 Am. Ford Found. Faculty Research fellow, 1962 Mem. Am. Econ. Assn., AAUP (v.p. chpt. 1961), Omicron Delta Epsilon. Home: 124 Lakeview Ave Lynbrook NY 11563-1755 Office: 43 Diamantidou Ave Paleo Psychico 15452 Athens Greece Business E-Mail: gkalr@pr-davazi-group.gr.

KALAPACS, ILDIKO, visual artist, dancer; b. Szeged, Hungary, June 13, 1965; came to U.S., 1987; d. János and Mária (Molnar) K.; m. Miklós Frech, Mar. 31, 1984 (div. Oct. 1988); m. Wayne Kraft, Dec. 28, 1988. BA in Studio Art, Ea. Wash. U., Spokane, 1992. Stone carver Városgazdálkodási Vállalat, Szeged, 1984-85, Maróti Lajos, Budapest, Hungary, 1986; instr. art Corbin Art Ctr., Spokane, 1993—. Bd. dirs. mem. coms. Corbin Art Ctr., 1993-94; mem. Davenport Arts Dist., 1993-94; dir., choreographer Erdély Dance Ensemble, 1988-94. Executed mural Raw Energy of Spokane, 1992; choreographer numerous Hungarian folk dance suites, 1988—; designer modern dance choregoraphy backgrounds Namaste Modern Dance Group, 1991. Ea. Wash. U. scholar, 1989-91; Am. Bus. Women's Assn. scholar, 1990-91. Avocation: folk culture research. Home and Office: 804 W 12th Ave Spokane WA 99204-3712

KALAUOKALANI, DONNA A.K., anesthesiologist, researcher; d. Haig Kalauokalani and Darlene Cundiff. BA, Hawaii Loa Coll., 1986; MD, U. Hawaii, 1991; MPH, U. Wash., 1999. Diplomate Nat. Bd. Med. Examiners, bd. cert. pain mgmt. Am. Bd. Anesthesiology, bd. cert. anesthesiology Am. Bd. Anesthesiology. Intern internal medicine Jewish Hosp. Washington U. Sch. Medicine, St. Louis, 1991—92, resident anesthesiology Barnes Hosp., 1992—95; fellow in pain mgmt. Multidisciplinary Pain Ctr. U. Wash., Seattle, 1995—96, postdoctoral rsch. fellow Agy. for Health Care Policy and Rsch., 1996—97, resident preventive medicine, 1996—99, fellow Robert Wood Johnson Clin. Scholars Program, 1997—99; staff physician U. Wash. Med. Ctr., 1995—99, Harborview Med. Ctr., 1996—99, Barnes Jewish Hosp. & Washington U. Pain Mgmt. Ctr., 1999—. Acting instr. dept. anesthesiology U. Wash., Seattle, 1995—96, clin. instr. dept. anesthesiology, 1996—99, affiliate instr. dept. health svcs. Sch. Pub. Health and Cmty. Medicine, 1999—2002; asst. prof. dept. anesthesiology Washington U. Sch. Medicine, St. Louis, 1999—, asst. prof. dept. internal medicine, 1999—, asst. prof. dept. psychiatry, 2000—; rsch. assoc. mem. Alvin J. Siteman Cancer Ctr., St. Louis, 2002—; pain mgmt. cons. Washington Corrections Ctr. for Women, State Wash. Dept. Corrections, 1999—2002; reviewer NIH Consortial Ctr. for Chiropractic Rsch., 1999—; expert reviewer Oreg. Ctr. for Complementary and Alternative Medicine, 2001—; mem. BJC Med. Staff Coun., 2000—, mem. exec. com., 2003; co-chair Mo. Pain Initiative, 2002—; mem. organizing com. Pain Disparities Spl. Interest Group, 2003; lectr. in field. Reviewer: Spine, 1999—, Clin. Jour. Pain, 2000—, Jour. Clin. Anesthesia, 2000—; contbr. chapters to books, articles to profl. jours. Scholar, Am. Bus. Women's Assn., 1986; Straub Hosp. Aux. scholar, 1986—90, Robert Wood Johnson Clin. scholar, U. Wash., 1997—99. Mem.: AMA, Am. Alliance Cancer Pain Initiatives (Mo. Pain Initiative), St. Louis Acad. Sci., So. Med. Assn., Mo. State Soc. Anesthesiologists, Internat. Assn. for the Study of Pain, Assn. Tchrs. Preventive Medicine, Assn. Native Hawaiian Physicians, Assn. for Health Svcs. Rsch., Am. Soc. Regional Anesthesia, Am. Soc. Anesthesiologists, Am. Pain Soc., Am. Coll. Preventive Medicine. Achievements include research in systolic pressure variation during open heart surgery; botulinum toxin for the treatment of chronic low back muscle spasm; acupuncture for chronic low back pain; malpractice claims associated with non-operative pain management; psychiatric comorbid features of chronic low back pain. Office: Washington Univ Sch Medicine Dept Anesthesiology 660 S Euclid Ave Campus Box 8054 Saint Louis MO 63110-1093 Home: 2756 E Bidwell St 300-112 Folsom CA 95630-6414

KALAVAR, JYOTSNA MIRLE, education educator; b. Bangalore, India, May 17, 1963; d. Mirle Subbarao and Sharadamba Krishnaswamy; m. Gopinath Shankar Kalavar, May 29, 1988; children: Abhinav Rao, Samir Rao. PhD, U. of Md., College Park, 1990; postgrad., U. of Mich., Ann Arbor, 1993. Lic. psychologist Mich. Asst. prof. Fayette campus Pa. State U., Uniontown, 1997—2000, assoc. prof. New Kensington campus Upper Burrell, 2000—. Grantee, Ctr. for Rural Pa., 2000, Nat. Inst. on Aging, 2000—02. Mem.: AASTHA Found. (life) (hon.), Assn. Gerontology (v.p. psychosocial 2002—), Gerontol. Soc. of Am. Achievements include research on homebound elderly; institutionalized elderly; immigrant elderly. Office: Pa State U New Kensington campus 3550 7th Street Rd New Kensington PA 15068 E-mail: jmk18@psu.edu.

KALAYCIOGLU, SERDAR, aerospace engineer, researcher; b. Luleburgaz, Kirklareli, Turkey, Aug. 8, 1963; arrived in Can., 1984; s. Vedat and Aynur (Vural) K.; m. Banu Ayse Kunas, June 28, 1985; children: Dennis Serkan, Isabel Selin. BSc with honors, Mid. East Tech. U., Ankara, Turkey, 1984; PhD, McGill U., Montreal, Que., Can., 1988. Registered profl. engr. Teaching asst., dept. mech. engring. McGill U., Montreal, 1984-88, rsch. asst., dept. mech. engring., 1984-88, rsch. assoc. dept. mech. engring., 1985-86, aux. prof., dept. mech. engring., 1987-88; systems engr. Thomson-CSF Systems Can. Inc., Ottawa, Ont., 1988-89, project mgr., 1989-90, mgr. space robotics and automation, 1990-92; mgr. REACH, Can. Space Agency, St. Hubert, Canada, 1992-96, mgr. dynamics group, mgr. space technologies, 1996—2001. Cons. Comm. Rsch. Ctr., Ottawa, 1985—86; referee Natural Scis. and Engring. Rsch. Coun. Can., Ottawa, 1989—90; invited spkr. Rensselaer Poly. inst., Troy, NY, 1990, Mfg. Rsch. Corp. Ont., Toronto, 1991, U. Waterloo, 1991; organized and chaird sessions Internat. Conf. on Intelligent Teleopration, 1991—; adj. prof. U. Ottawa, 1989—92, McGill U., Montreal, 1994—; adj. assoc. prof. elec. and computer engring. Concordia U., Montreal, 1994—; gen. mgr. Glengo, Istanbul, Turkey, 1998—99; pres. Bensa Sys. Can. Inc., 1999—. Reviewer IEEE, AAIA, AAS, Jour. Can. Aeros. and Space Inst., 1989; contbr. more than 85 articles to profl. jours. Recipient Math. award, Turkish Sci. and Rsch. Coun., 1980, Chemistry award, 1980, Achievement awards ASME, 1994, 96. Mem. IEEE, ASME, AIAA, Am. Astronautical Soc. (sr.), Am. Inst. Aeros. and Space Instrn., Can. Soc. Elec. and Computer Engrs., Can. Astronautics and Space Inst., Assn. Profl. Engrs. Ont., Can. Soc. Mech. Engrs. Achievements include development of a supervised autonomous robots system for Space Station; optimal deployment schemes for space appendages; found analytical solution for deployment of flexible space appendages, dynamics and control techniques for spacecraft and its appendages; special expertise in international financing and bank instruments including letter of credits and bank guarantees; coordinated over $300M USD international loans and bank instruments; introduced international banking and financing in Canada for project funding. Home: 1775 Socrate Brossard PQ Canada J4X 1L6 Office: 1 Wood Ave Ste 602 Westmount PQ Canada H3Z 3C5

KALB, CHESTER H., mathematics professor; b. Cin., Nov. 12, 1945; s. Chester H. and Marie Elizabeth Kalb; m. Gerda C. Rodriguez, Oct. 6, 2000; m. Gale Partee, July 31, 1983 (div. Jan. 30, 1997); children: Cynthia Denise, Deanna Renay. BS in Math. with honors, BS, U. Cin., 1963—68; MS in Math., Xavier U., Cin., 1972—74. Tchr. math. Cin. Pub. Schs., 1967—83; math. tchr. Cleve. Pub. Schs., 1983—98; tchr. math. upward bound Case Western Res. U., Cleve., 1984—98; prof., math. Fla. Keys C.C., Key West, 1998—; tchr. math. Key West H.S., Fla., 1999—. Math. dept. chmn. Woodward H.S., Cin., 1976—83, Lincoln West H.S., Cleve., 1995—98. Recipient Disting. Tchr. Svc. Award, Cin. Pub. Schs., 1979. Mem.: Math. Assn. Am., Nat. Coun. Tchr. Math. Avocations: competitive race walking, fishing, photography, travel. Home: 3930 S Roosevelt Blvd E-105 Key West FL 33040 Office: Florida Keys CC 5901 College Rd Key West FL 33040 Office Phone: 305-296-9081 221. Personal E-mail: chester-h-kalbii@msn.com. E-mail: kalb_c@firn.edu.

KALB, MARVIN, public policy and government educator; Diploma, CCNY; MA, postgrad. in Russian History, Harvard U. Prof. press and pub. policy John F. Kennedy Sch. Govt. Harvard U., dir. Joan Shorenstein Ctr. on Press, Politics, and Pub. Policy, 1987—99; Edward R. Murrow prof. press and pub. policy JFK Sch. Govt., 1987-99; sr. fellow/lectr. in pub. policy Shorenstein Ctr., Washington, 1999—; faculty chair Washington Programs KSG., Wahington, 1999—. Host PBS series: Candidates '88; chief diplomatic corrs. CBS News, NBC News; moderator Meet The Press; sr. rsch. assoc. Ctr. for Sci. and Internat. Affairs; exec. com. Harvard's Russian Rsch. Ctr. Co-author: (with Hendrik Hertzberg) Candidates '88; co-editor: (with Stephen Hess) The Media and the War on Terrorism, 2003; author or co-author 7 non-fiction books, including: One Scandalous Story, The Nixon Memo, Kissinger, Roots of Involvement: The U.S. and Asia, and 2 best-selling novels. Recipient numerous awards for excellence in diplomatic reporting including two Peabody prizes, U. Ga., DuPont prize, Columbia U., and numerous Overseas Press Club awards. Mem. Coun. on Fgn. Rels., Am. Acad. Arts and Scis. Avocations: football, research on political/legacy of Ten Commandments. Office: Harvard U Joan Shorenstein Ctr Kennedy Sch Govt 1779 Massachusetts Ave WW Ste 810 Washington DC 20036

KALBA, KAS, international telecommunications consultant; b. Wangen, Germany, Apr. 13, 1945; came to U.S., 1950; s. Simon J. and Sophia Kalba; m. Patricia A. Carvalho, June 18, 1966; children: Simon Michael, Sontine. BA, Yale U., 1966; MA in Communications, U. Pa., 1967, PhD, 1974. Staff asst. Sloan Commn. on Cable Communications, N.Y.C., 1970-71; lectr., instr. communications planning Harvard U., Cambridge, Mass., 1971-76; vis. lectr. mass media MIT, Cambridge, 1976-77; pres. Kalba Internat. Inc., Lincoln, Mass., 1973—. Mem. adv. com. Cable World (China). Trustee Cambridge Ctr. for Adult Edn., 1984-85, Pacific Telecomms. Coun., trustee, 1997-2001; mem. satellite comms. adv. com. U.S. Info. Agy., 1989-93; mem. cable TV adv. com., Town of Lincoln, 2002—. Mem. Internat. Inst. Comms., Internat. House of Japan.

KALBACKEN, JOAN MURIEL, foreign language educator, author; b. Chgo., June 30, 1925; d. Leslie Edwin and Bertha Esther (Andreen) Formell; m. Norman Merrill, June 19, 1948 (dec.); children: Teryl Engel, Scott. BS in French, Chemistry and Math., U. Wis., 1947; Nat. Def. Edn. Act, Inst. Coe Coll., Iowa and Toulouse, France, 1965; MA in French, Ill. State U., 1968, fgn. lang. supervisory cert., 1971. Tchr. math. Lincoln Jr. H.S., Beloit, Wis., 1947-48; tchr. algebra Pekin (Ill.) Cmty. H.S., 1958-60; French and math. tchr. Chiddix Jr. H.S., Normal, Ill., 1960-86; fgn. lang. supr. McLean County Unit 5 Schs., 1976-86. Cons. Young Authors in Local Schs., 1990-97. Author: Recycling, Wetlands, Foxes, Whitetailed Deer, The Menominee, Peacocks and Peahens, Badgers, Isle Royale National Park, Food Safety, The Food Pryamid, Vitamins and Minerals, 1991-98; author poetry. Chmn. Delta Kappa Gamma Internat. Ednl. Found., 1996-98, state pres., 1987-89; v.p. Local Women of Evang. Luth. Ch., 1993-97, 2002—; worker McLean County Unit 5 Schs. Referendum, 1991; woman lay preacher St. John's Luth. Ch.; vol. Ret. Sr. Vol. Program, Heritage Manor, El Paso, Ill. Recipient Those Who Excel tchg. award, Ill. State, 1980. Mem. AAUW (fin. auditor), NEA (life), Am. Assn. Tchrs. French, PTA (hon. life), Ill. Edn. Assn. (life), McLean County Ret. Tchrs., Phi Delta Kappa (membership v.p., vice-chmn. 1990-97, historian 1997-99), Kappa Delta Pi, Pi Delta Phi. Lutheran. Avocations: rose gardening, crocheting, reading, writing, speaking at schools. E-mail: jokalb@earthlink.net.

KALBFLEISCH, JOHN DAVID, statistics educator; b. Grand Valley, Ont., Can., July 16, 1943; s. Claude Elwyn and Janet Marjorie (Agnew) Kalbfleisch; m. Catherine Sharon Allen; children: Michael Allen, Heidi Kathryn, Kirby Ann. BSc in Math. and Physics, U. Waterloo, 1966, M of Math in Stats., 1967, PhD in Stats., 1969. Rsch. assoc. dept. stats. Univ. Coll., London, 1969-70; asst. prof. dept. stats. SUNY, Buffalo, 1970-73; assoc. prof. dept. stats. U. Waterloo, 1973-79, prof. dept. stats. and actuarial sci., 1979—2002, chmn. dept. stats. and actuarial sci., 1984-90, dean faculty of math., 1990-98; prof., chair dept. biostats. U. Mich., Ann Arbor, 2002—. Vis. prof. dept. biostats. U. Wash., 1979-80, dept. biostats. U. Mich., 1987, dept. epidemiology U. Calif., San Francisco, 1988, dept. statistics U. Auckland, 1998, Nat. U. Singapore, 1999. Author: (with R.L. Prentice) The Statistical Analysis of Failure Time Data, 1980, 2d edit., 2002; assoc. editor Can. Jour. Stats., 1981-89, 1998-2004, Annals of Stats., 1980-83, Biometrics, 2003—; contbr. articles to profl. jours. Recipient Gold medal, Statis. Soc. Can., 1994, COPSS Fisher award, 1999; fellow, Royal Soc. Can., 1994, Am. Statis. Assn., Inst. Math. Stats. Mem.: Internat. Statis. Inst., Royal Statis. Soc., Inst. Biomedical Soc., Statis. Soc. Canada, Internat. Statis. Inst. Office: U Mich Dept Biostatistics Ann Arbor MI 48109 Office Phone: 734-615-7067. E-mail: jdkalbfl@umich.edu.

KALBFLEISCH, JOHN MCDOWELL, cardiologist, educator; b. Lawton, Okla., Nov. 15, 1930; s. George and Etta Lillian (McDowell) K.; m. Jolie Harper, Dec. 30, 1961. AS, Cameron A&M U., Lawton, 1950; BS, U. Okla., 1952, MD, 1957. Diplomate Am. Bd. Internal Medicine, Am. Bd. Cardiovascular Disease. Intern U. Va. Hosp., 1957-58; resident and fellow U. Okla. Med. Ctr., 1958-62, instr. medicine, 1964-66, asst. prof., 1966-69, assoc. clin. prof., 1970-78, clin. prof. Tulsa br., 1978—; pvt. practice Tulsa, 1969—; founder, chmn. bd., CEO Cardiology of Tulsa, Inc., 1969—; dir. cardiovascular svcs. St. Francis Hosp., Tulsa, 1975—. Physician adv. bd. City of Tulsa, 1978-81; bd. dirs. St. Francis Hosp., exec. com., 1987-97, 2001—; exec. v.p., chief med. officer St. Francis Health Sys., 1998-99; treas. Tulsa Med. Edn. Found., 1988-89, v.p., 1990-92, pres., 1992-94; med. dir., chmn. bd. Warren Clinics, 1990-97; mem. Okla. Ctr. for Advancement of Sci. and Tech., 1989-95; mem. adv. com. Ctr. for Lasser Devel. and Applications, Okla. State U. Contbr. articles to profl. jours. With USPHS, 1962-64. Named to, St. Francis Health Sys. Hall of Fame, 2003; recipient Lifelong Svc. award, Tulsa Med. Edn. Found./U. Okla. Coll. Medicine, 2002. Fellow ACP (gov.-elect Okla. 1990-91, gov. 1991-95, Okla. Laureate award 1995), Am. Coll. Cardiology (gov. Okla. 1978-81); mem. AMA, AAAS, Tulsa County Med. Soc., Okla. State Med. Assn., Am. Heart Assn. (Fellow coun. on clin. cardiology), tchg. scholar 1967-69), Okla. Soc. Internal Medicine v.p., pres.-elect 1983-84, pres. 1985-86), Am. Soc. Internal Medicine, Am. Fedn. Clin. Rsch., Am. Inst. Nutrition, U. Okla. Med. Alumni Assn. (Physician of Yr. in Pvt. Practice 1999), Delta Upsilon. Republican. Presbyterian. Office: 6151 S Yale Ave Ste 400 Tulsa OK 74136-1933 Business E-Mail: jmkalbfleisch@cardiologytulsa.com.

KALCZYNSKI, PAWEL JAN, information systems educator; b. Bydgoszcz, Poland, Mar. 8, 1977; arrived in U.S., 2002; s. Jerzy Jozef Kalczynski and Elzbieta Maria Kalczynska; m. Malgorzata Maria Miklas-Kalczynska, June 17, 2000; children: Melita Joanna Kalczynska, Olivia Maria. MSc, Poznan (Poland) U. Econ., 2000, PhD, 2002. Instr. and rschr. Poznan U. Econ., 2000—02, asst. prof., 2002—02; asst. prof. info. systems U. Toledo, 2002—. Author: Filtering the Web to Feed Data Warehouses; contbr. articles to profl. publs. Grantee, Army Rsch. Office and U. Toledo, 2003. Roman Catholic. Achievements include research in temporal document retrieval model; new approach to clickstream analysis for e-commerce; simulation methods for operations management. Avocations: hiking, sailing, camping. Office: U Toledo 2801 W Bancroft St Toledo OH 43606 Office Phone: 419-530-2258. Office Fax: +1 (419) 530-2290. E-mail: pawel.kalczynski@utoledo.edu.

KALDAWY, ROGER M., ophthalmologist; s. Maurice N. Kaldawy and Leila I. Berberi; m. Marie G. Lebbos, Sept. 28, 1996; children: Remy, Nataly. MD, St. Joseph U., Beirut, 1992. Diplomate Am. Bd. Internal Medicine. Attending physician SUNY, N.Y.C., 1996—97; resident in ophthalmology U. Rochester, NY, 1997—2000; fellow in cornea and refractive surgery U. Iowa, Iowa City, 2000—01; asst. prof. Boston U., 2001—02; attending physician Milford-Franklin Eye Ctr., Mass., 2002—. Contbr. articles to profl. jours. Recipient Best Rsch. award, Acad. Medicine Richmond, 2000; Rsch. grantee, Rsch. to Prevent Blindness, 2001. Mem.: Am. Acad. Ophthalmology, Assn. Rsch. in Vision and Ophthalmology, Am. Soc. Cataract and Refractive Surgery. Roman Catholic. Avocations: swimming, music, piano. Office: Milford-Franklin Eye Ctr 391 East Central St Franklin MA 02038 Office Phone: 508-473-7939.

KALDY, CHRISTOPHER LOUIS, music educator, musician; s. Louis and Susan Kaldy; 1 child, Nicholas. BA, San Jose (Calif.) State U., 1998. Lic. tchr. Calif., 2003. Band dir. City Milpitas, Calif., 1996—; dir. instrumental music Milpitas (Calif.) Unified Sch. Dist., 1998—. Music dir. Milpitas (Calif.) Youth Theatre, 1998—; regional coord. Festivals of Music, San Francisco, 1999—. Dir.: (plays, music director/set designer) Chicago (Commendation award Mayor of Milpitas, 04). Recipient Excellence in Tchg. award, UC San Diego Outstanding Teacher Recognition Program, 2004; grantee, Wells Fargo Bank - McCarthy Ranch, Milpitas, 2004. Mem.: Santa Clara (Calif.) County Band Dirs. Assn. (treas. 2003—05), No. Calif. Band Assn., Calif. Tchrs. Assn., Internat. Assn. Jazz Educators, Calif. Band Dirs. Assn., Calif. Music Educators Assn. Office Phone: 408-945-5543. E-mail: ckaldy@musd.org.

KALE, AMIT ANAND, mechanical engineer, reliability engineer; b. Bhopal, Madhya Pradesh, India, Oct. 25, 1978; s. Anand Narayan and Shirish Kale. Bachelor or Tech. in Aerospace Engring., Indian Inst. Tech., India, 2000; MS in Mech. Engring., PhD in Mech. Engring., U. Fla., 2005. Software programmer Delmia Solutions India, Banglore, India, 2000—01; intern SW Rsch. Inst., San Antonio, 2003; rsch. asst. U. Fla., Gainesville, Fla., 2001—. Contbr. scientific papers to profl. jours. Scholar Rsch. Assistantship, Structural and Multidisciplinary Optimization Group, 2001-Current. Mem.: AIAA. Home: 2701 SW 13th St Apt G16 Gainesville FL 32608 Office: Dept Mech and Aerospace 333 MAE A PO Box 116250 Gainesville FL 32611 Office Phone: 352-392-6780. Office Fax: 352-392-7303. Personal E-mail: akale@ufl.edu.

KALECH, MARC, newspaper editor; Mng. editor New York Post, N.Y.C., 1993—. Office: NY Post 10th Fl 1211 Avenue Of The Americas New York NY 10036 E-mail: mkalech@nypost.com.

KALECHOFSKY, ROBERTA, writer; b. N.Y.C., May 11, 1931; d. Julius Kirchik and Naomi Jacobs; m. Robert Kalechofsky; children: Hal, Neal. BA, Bklyn. Coll., 1952; MA, NYU, 1956, PhD, 1970. Pub. Micah Pub., Marblehead, Mass., 1975—; writer Marblehead, 1960—. Author: Bodmin 1349, 1982, Stephen's Passion, 1999, Solomon's Wisdom, 2001. Fellow Literacy fellow, NEA, 1982; grantee Literary fellow in fiction, Nat. Coun. on Arts, 1987, grantee for pub., NEA, 1980. Mem.: Nat. Writers' Union, Authors Guild. Jewish. Avocations: vegetarianism, animal rights. Home: 255 Humphrey St Marblehead MA 01945-1645 E-mail: micah@micahbooks.com.

KALEDIN, EUGENIA OSTER, American studies educator; b. Phila., Sept. 11, 1929; d. Samuel B. and Catherine Sarah (Greenwood) Oster; m. Arthur Daniel Kaledin, Jan. 23, 1953 (div. Mar. 1997); children: Nicholas, Jonathan, Elizabeth. AB, Radcliffe/Harvard Coll., 1951; AM, Harvard U., 1953; PhD, Boston U., 1977. Sr. lectr. Northeastern U., 1964-81; Fulbright lectr. Palacky U., Czech Republic, 1990-92, Beijing U., 1985-86; Am. studies organizer Showa Woman's U., Tokyo, 1988-89. Lectr. Yale U., New Haven, 1985, MIT, 1982-83; scholarly advisor Goddard Coll., Plainfield, Vt., 1978-82; founding mem., dir. Alliance of Ind. Scholars, 1979-90; discussion leader Am. culture Mass. Found. for Humanities, 1983-97, Harvard Inst. for Learning, in ret. 1997-2005. Author: The Education of Mrs. Henry Adams, 1982, reissued, 1996, Mothers and More: American Women in the 1950's, Daily Life in the United States: 1940-1959: Shifting Worlds. Organizer Lexington Oral History Projects, 1980—2004; v.p. Fulbright Assn. for Ea. Mass., 1995—97. Mellon grantee U. Pa., 1983. Mem. Nat. Writers Union, Nat. Coalition Ind. Scholars, Phi Beta Kappa. Avocations: movies, walking. Home: 33 Forest St Apt 312 Lexington MA 02421-4991 Office Phone: 781-862-0614. Personal E-mail: Eugie@theworld.com.

KALEMKERIAN, GREGORY PETER, oncologist, educator; b. Bronx, N.Y., Feb. 9, 1961; MD, Northwestern U., 1985. Diplomate Am. Bd. Oncology. Clin. fellow oncology Johns Hopkins U., Balt., 1989-93; asst. prof. Wayne State U., Detroit, 1993-99; assoc. prof. U. Mich., 1999—2005, prof., 2005—, dir. thoracic oncology. Mem. ACP, Am. Assn. Cancer Rsch., Am. Soc. Clin. Oncology. Office: 1366 Cancer Ctr-0922 1500 E Med Ctr Dr Ann Arbor MI 48109-0922 Office Phone: 734-936-5281. Office Fax: 734-647-8792. Business E-Mail: kalemker@umich.edu.

KALENIK, PETER A., mathematics educator; s. Thomas M. Kalenik and Linda M Shepard. BS in Math. Edn. summa cum laude, SUNY, 2001. Cert. secondary math. tchr. NY, 2002. Tchr. math. Letchworth Ctrl. Sch. Dist., Castile, NY, 2002—02, Orchard Pk. H.S., 2002—. Instr. marching band brass Quaker Marching Band, Orchard Park, 2002—. Mem.: Nat. Coun. Tchr. Math., Kappa Kappa Psi (life). Avocations: travel, college basketball, music. Home: 47 Michael's Walk Lancaster NY 14086-9325 Personal E-mail: petekkpsi@hotmail.com.

KALER, ERIC WILLIAM, chemical engineer, educator; b. Burlington, Vt., Sept. 23, 1956; s. Ronald Maurice and Mary Elizabeth (Kindred) K.; m. Karen Fults, Dec. 30, 1979. BS, Calif. Inst. Tech., 1978; PhD, U. Minn., 1982. Asst. prof. chem. engring. U. Wash., Seattle, 1982-87, assoc. prof., 1987-89; assoc. prof. chem. engring. U. Del., Newark, 1989-91, prof., 1991-98, chair dept. chem. engring., 1996-2000, Elizabeth Inez Kelley prof., 1998—, dean Coll. Engring., 2000—. Vis. prof. U. Graz, Austria; cons. Shell Devel. Co., DuPont P&G, numerous other cos. Conbr. numerous articles to profl. jours. Elder Andrew Riverside Presbyn. Ch., Mpls., 1980-82, Northminster Presbyn. Ch., Seattle, 1984-88. Named Presdl. Young Investigator, NSF, Washington, 1984; Presdl. scholar Dept. Edn., Washington, 1978. Fellow AAAS; mem. AIChE (Chilton award, 2002), Am. Chem. Soc. (Award in Colloid or Surface Chemistry, 1998, Del. Sect. Award, 1998), Am. Soc. Engring. Edn. (Gordon W. McGraw Rsch. Award, 1995), Am. Crystallographic Assn. Lodges: Masons. Republican.

KALES, PAUL ALBERT, engineering educator, cartoonist; b. Boston, Dec. 8, 1937; s. Maurice H. and Eleanor (Kopp) K.; m. Judith Freund, Feb. 27, 1977. BS, Northeastern U., Boston, 1960, MS, 1965. Registered profl. engr., Mass. Engr. GE Co., Lynn, Mass., 1960-64; sr. engr. Avco Corp., Wilmington, Mass., 1964-68, Raytheon Co., Wayland, Mass., 1968-82, C.S. Draper Lab., Cambridge, Mass., 1982-85; assoc. prof. engring. tech. U. Mass., Lowell, 1985-99. Cons., trainer Statis. Process Control and Reliability/Maintainability Engring.; lectr. engring. Northeastern U. Boston, 1979-84. Author: Reliability for Technology, Engineering and Management, 1998, Betty and Jenn, 2002; cartoons published in Moment, Parkhurst Exchange, Union Communications Services, Boston Globe, Eat and Run, others; contbr. articles to profl. jours. Originator, awards com. Mass. Coun. for Quality, Lowell, 1990-91. Mem. NSPE, Profl. Engrs. in Edn., Mass. Soc. Profl. Engrs., Nat. Asst. Indsl. Tech., Am. Soc. Quality Control (founding mem., sec. edn. divsn. 1994). Democrat. Jewish. Office: PO Box 179 Nantucket MA 02554 E-mail: pkales@comcast.net.

KALETSKY, DONALD, art educator, magician; b. New Haven, Conn., June 16, 1943; s. Louis and Minnie Kaletsky; m. Susan Wallnau, Sept. 4, 1966; children: Rebecca, Louis. BS in graphic design, U. Bridgeport, Conn., 1968; MS in art edn., So. Conn. State U., New Haven, 1973. Cert. profl. educator State of Conn. Adj. assoc. prof. art U. Bridgeport, Conn., 1971—91; photography tchr. New Haven Pub. Schs., 1967—. Exhibitions include serigraphy So. Conn. State Coll., 1973. Asst. scoutmaster troop 41 Boy Scouts of Am., Woodbridge, 1984—, dist. commr., 2005. Recipient TAPS award, New Haven Bd. Edn., 2005, Shofar award, Jewish Com. on Scouting, 2005, New Magicians Assn. award. Mem.: New Magicians Assn. (Best Original Magic Effect 1993, Magical Originality 1995, Parlour Magic 3rd 2000, Stage Magic 2nd 2001, Most Improved Magician 2003), Camp Sequassen Alumni Assn., Order of Arrow.

KALFIN, ROBERT Z., theater director; b. Bronx, N.Y., Apr. 22, 1933; s. Alfred A. Kalfin and Hilda Kalfin Epstein. BA, Alfred U., 1954; MFA, Yale Sch. Drama, 1957. Founder, artistic dir. Chelsea Theatre Ctr., NYC, 1965—86; artistic dir. Cin. Playhouse in the Park, Ohio, Pirate Playhouse, Sanibel, Fla., 1997—98; guest dir. various theatres. Prodr.: (plays) Slaveship, Saved, AC/DC, Genet's The Screens, Alan Ginsburg's Kaddish, The Beffars' Opera, Polly, Vanities, The Contractor, Chelsea Theater Ctr., Consuelo Beahr's Thinner Thighs in Twenty Years, Cynthia Adler's Downloaded, and in Denial, Joel Gross's The Color of Flesh (nominated for Best Play and Best Dir. awards, NJ Press), Yentl, Joe Pintauro's What I Did For Love, (London Premiere) Hyam Maccoby's The Disputation, Arthur Miller's The Price; (Broadway plays) Strider, Happy End, Yentl (original prodn.), Truly Blessed, Harold Prince's Candide, Rashomon, The Mistress of the Inn; (TV films) The Prince of Homburg, PBS Great Performances, Theatre in Am. Recipient 5 Tony Awards, 21 off-Broadway Obie Awards, Margo Jones Award, New England Theater Conf. Award, Outer Critics Circle Award, Vernon Rice Award, Audelco Award. Mem.: Dramatists Guild, Soc. Stage Dirs. & Choreographers. Home: 312 W 20th St #2D New York NY 10011 E-mail: robzangwill@juno.com.

KALICH, RICHARD BARRY, writer; b. N.Y.C., Mar. 18, 1947; s. Kalmen and Beatrice Kalich. BA, CCNY, 1969. Prin., owner Kalich Org., N.Y.C., 1970—. Author: The Nihilesthete, 1987 (selected as one of twenty four most noteworthy novels Phila. Enquirer, 1987), The Zoo, 2003. Home and Office: 65 Central Park West New York NY 10023

KALICKI, JAN H., economist, political scientist, energy executive; b. London, Aug. 5, 1948; s. Jan and Mireya (Jaimes-Freyre) Kalicki; m. Jean Ellen Engelmayer, Oct. 22, 1989; children: Jan Harlan, Alexander Van, Peter Daniel. AB with honors, Columbia Coll., 1968; PhD, London Sch. Econ., 1971. Rsch. assoc., lectr. Princeton U., NJ, 1971—72, Harvard U., Cambridge, Mass., 1972; Fgn. Svc. officer U.S. Dept. State, Washington, 1972—75, mem. policy planning staff, 1974—77; chief fgn. policy advisor to Senator Edward Kennedy U.S. Senate, Washington, 1977—84; adj. prof. Georgetown U., Washington, 1983—85; adj. asst. to pres. Brown U., Providence, 1985—88, exec. dir. Ctr. Fgn. Policy Devel., 1985—88, sr. advisor, 1988—94; sr. fellow Watson Inst. Internat. Studies, 1994—99; v.p. Lehman Bros., 1984—88, sr. v.p., 1988—93; U.S. ombudsman for energy and comml. coop. NIS, Washington, 1994—2001; counselor U.S. Dept. Commerce, 1994—2001; pub. policy scholar Woodrow Wilson Internat. Ctr., Smithsonian Instn., 2001—; internat. policy scholar EastWest Inst., 2002—03. Counselor internat. strategy Chevron Corp., San Francisco, 2001—; mem. Coun. Fgn. Rels. Internat. Inst. Strategic Studies, Royal Inst. Internat. Affairs, London; trustee World Affairs Coun. No. Calif. Author: The Pattern of Sino-American Crises, 1975; editor: Russian-Eurasian Renaissance?, 2003, Energy and Security: Towards a New Foreign Policy Strategy, 2005; contbr. numerous chpts. to books and articles to profl. jours. Office: Chevron Corp 6001 Bollinger Canyon Rd San Ramon CA 94583

KALIHER, MICHAEL DENNIS, historian, librarian; b. Santa Monica, Calif., Nov. 7, 1947; s. Eugene Charles and Phyllis Joan (McCrary) K. Student, Calif. State Coll., Hayward, 1969—70; BA, U. Ariz., 1990. Bookseller B. Dalton Bookseller, Newport Beach, Calif., 1991—94; correctional officer Ariz. Dept. Corrections, Winslow, 1994—97, libr., 1997—2001; eligibility specialist Ariz. Long-Term Care Sys., Flagstaff, Ariz., 2001—02; libr. II State of Ariz., 2002—. Pres. Klamath County (Oreg.) Hist. Soc., 1985; founder Native Am. History Week, Klamath County Mus., 1985-86. *Presently manages for Grant Library in Graham County, Arizona. Wrote, "Oregan and the Asian Legend of Fusang," Northwest Review XXXIV (1): 62-74, Winter 1986, University of Oregon; "The Applegate Trail, 1846-1853," Journal of the Shaw Historical Library I (1): 6-23, Fall 1986, Oregon Institute of Technology; "Early Sails on the Oregon Coast: Ferrel, Drake, and Vizcaino," Curry County Echoes, March-August 1986, various pages, Curry County Historical Society; and "Old Bill Williams and Bill Hamilton, Free Trappers," and others by Klamath Country History: 5-7, 9-13, 15-17, 171, and 271-2, Taylor Publishing Co., Dallas, 1984.* Contbr. articles to profl. jours. Mem. Ariz. Libr. Assn., Flagstaff Friends of Traditional Music, Pi Lambda Theta, Phi Alpha Theta. Avocations: backpacking, trout fishing. Home: 2807 S 12th Ave #501 Safford AZ 85546-3838

KALIK, MILDRED, lawyer; b. N.Y.C., Dec. 4, 1947; BA, U. Wis., 1969; JD, George Washington U. Law Ctr., 1972; LLM in taxation, NYU, 1982. Bar: N.Y. 1973, registered: U.S. Tax Ct. 1973, U.S. Dist. Ct., so. dist. N.Y. 1974, U.S. Ct. Appeals, second cir. 1975. Ptnr. Simpson Thacher & Bartlett LLP, N.Y.C. Mem.: New York State Bar Assn., Internat. Acad. Estate & Trust law, Assn. Bar City N.Y. (surrogates ct. 1999—2003), Am. coll. Trust & Estate Counsel, ABA (chmn. generation skipping tax planning 1981—88, asst. sec., probate & trust law sect. 1988—90, coun. 1990—97, co-chmn. task force transfer tax reform). Office: Simpson Thacher & Bartlett LLP 425 Lexington Ave New York NY 10017-3954 Office Phone: 212-455-2778. Office Fax: 212-455-2502. Business E-Mail: mkalik@stblaw.com.

KALIKOW, PETER STEPHEN, real estate developer, former newspaper owner, publisher; b. N.Y.C., Dec. 1, 1942; s. Harold J. and Juliet K.; m. Mary T. Jacobatos; children: Nicholas, Kathryn. BSBA, Hofstra U., 1965, LLD (hon.), 1986. With H.J. Kalikow & Co., N.Y.C., 1966—, pres., 1973—; owner N.Y. Post, 1988-93. Chmn. ins. com. N.Y. State Mortgage Agy., 1981-86. Gov. N.Y. Presbyn. Hosp.; trustee Hofstra U., Mus. Jewish Heritage; gen. chmn. real estate and constrn. divsn. Israel Bonds; apptd. to Met. Transp. Authority, 1994, chmn., 2001--; mem. Port Authority of N.Y. and N.J., 1995. Recipient Israel Peace medal, Israeli Govt. 1982; named Alumnus of Yr., Hofstra U., 1988. Mem. N.Y. Athletic Club, Palm Beach Country Club, Fenway Club (Scarsdale, N.Y.), Royal Automobile Club (London). Office: H J Kalikow & Co LLC 101 Park Ave Fl 25 New York NY 10178-0002

KALIKOW, THEODORA JUNE, academic administrator; b. Lynn, Mass., June 6, 1941; d. Irving and Rose Kalikow. AB, Wellesley Coll., 1962; ScM, MIT, 1970; PhD, Boston U., 1974. From instr. to prof. Southeastern Mass. U., North Dartmouth, 1968-84; dean Coll. Arts and Scis., U. No. Colo., Greeley, 1984-87; dean of the coll. Plymouth (N.H.) State Coll., 1987-94, interim pres., 1992-93; pres. U. Maine, Farmington, 1994—. Contbr. articles to profl. jours. Chair steering com. Maine ACE/NIP, 1995—; chair Coun. Pub. Liberal Arts Colls., 1997-99; bd. dirs. Maine Humanities Coun., 1999—, Fin. Authority Maine, 2000—, Ctr. for the Prevention of Hate Violence, 2004—, Maine Econ. Growth CouN., 2005—. Named to, Maine Women's Hall of Fame, 2002; recipient Mary Ann Hartman award, 2000;, NSF grantee, 1978, Am. Coun. on Edn. fellow, Brown U., 1983—84. Mem.: Assn. Am. Colls. and Univs. (bd. dirs. 2000—03), Western Mountains Alliance (chmn. 2000—03), Am. Coun. on Edn. (commn. on women 1994—97, 2000—03), Soc. Values in Higher Edn. (bd. dirs. 1991—94). Office: U Maine at Farmington Office of the Pres 224 Main St Farmington ME 04938-1911 Office Phone: 207-778-7256.

KALIL, CHARLES JAMES, lawyer, chemicals executive; b. 1951; BA, Mich. State U.; JD, Georgetown U. Law Ctr. Asst. U.S. atty. U.S. Dept. of Justice (ea. dist. Mich.), 1976—80; atty., environ. law Dow Chem., Midland, Mich., 1980—82; gen. counsel Petrokemyia (joint venture of Dow and SABIC), Rotterdam, Netherlands, 1982—83, regional counsel, Middle East/Africa Geneva, 1983—86; various litigation and fin. roles Dow Chem., Midland, Mich., 1986—92; gen. counsel and area dir. of govt. and public affairs Dow Latin Am., Coral Gables, Fla. and Sao Paolo, Brazil, 1992—97; asst. gen. counsel for corp. financial law Dow Chem., Midland, Mich., 2000—03, assoc. gen. counsel and dir., corp. financial law, mergers, and acquisitions, 2003—04, corp. v.p., gen. counsel, 2004—. Office: VP & Gen Counsel Dow Chem 2030 Dow Center Midland MI

KALIL, JAMES, SR., investment executive; b. Buffalo, Oct. 22, 1919; s. Harry and Nazira (Owens) Rossi; m. Claire Homsey, May 5, 1947; children: Donald, Janice, Laura, James Jr. BSChemE, CCNY, 1941; M in ChemE, Poly. U., Bklyn., 1947, PhDChemE, 1951. Rsch. engr. DuPont Co., Wilmington, Del., 1951-80; investment mgr., chmn. bd. dirs. Affinity Wealth Mgmt., Inc., Wilmington, 1974—. Contbr. articles to newspapers; patentee chem products and processes. Fellow Poly. U., 1989. Avocations: reading, travel, writing. Office: Affinity Wealth Mgmt Inc 1702 Lovering Ave Wilmington DE 19806-2120

KALIN, LATIF, civil engineer, researcher; b. Kayseri, Turkey, Mar. 25, 1972; arrived in US, 1997; s. Duran and Sala Kalin; m. Sengul Kalin, July 9, 1995; children: Harun Ibrahim, Haluk Said. BS in Civil Engring., Mid. East Tech. U., Ankara, Turkey, 1995; MS in Civil Engring., Purdue U., 1998, PhD in Civil Engring., 2002. EIT Mich., 2001. Project engr., Ankara, Turkey, 1995—97; Turkish govt. fellowship, 1997—98; teaching asst. Purdue U., 1998—99, rsch. asst., 1999—2002; post doctoral rschr. Nat. Risk Mgmt. Rsch. Lab. U.S. EPA, Cin., 2002—. Contbr. articles to profl. jours. Fellow, Turkish Govt., 1990; scholar, 1997—2001. Office: US EPA 26 W Martin Luther King Drive Cincinnati OH 45268 Office Phone: 513-569-7127. Business E-Mail: kalin.latif@epa.gov.

KALIN, ROBERT, retired mathematics professor; b. Everett, Mass., Dec. 11, 1921; s. Benjamin and Celia (Kraff) K.; m. Shirley Sharney, Oct. 22, 1944; children: Susan Leslie, John Benjamin; m. 2d Madelyn Pildish, Aug. 17, 1962; 1 child, Richard Dean. Student, Northeastern U., 1940-43; BS, U. Chgo., 1947; MAT, Harvard U., 1948; PhD, Fla. State U., 1961. Tchr. math. Holten H.S., Danvers, Mass., 1948-49, Beaumont H.S., Hadley Tech. Sch., Soldan-Blewitt H.S., St. Louis, 1949-52; ednl. statistician Naval Air Tech. Tng. Ctr., Norman, Okla., 1952-53; test specialist, assoc. in research Ednl. Testing Svc., Princeton, N.J., 1953-55; exec. asst. Commn. on Math. of Coll. Entrance Exam. Bd., 1955-56; instr. dept. math. edn. Fla. State U., Tallahassee, 1956-61, asst. prof., 1961-63, assoc. prof., 1963-65, prof., 1965-90, prof. emeritus Tallahassee, 1990, assoc. dept. head, 1968-73, program chmn., 1975-78. Co-author: Elementary Mathematics, Patterns and Structure, 11 vols., 1966, (with George Green) Modern Mathematics for the Elementary School Teacher, 1966, (with E.D. Nichols) Analytic Geometry, 1973, Holt School Mathematics, 9 vols., 1974, rev. 1978, Holt Mathematics, 9 vols., 1981, rev., 1985, (with M.K. Corbitt) Prentice Hall Geometry, 1990, rev. edit., 1993. Mem., treas. Brownsville-Haywood County Libr. Bd., 1991-95, chmn., 1995-97; bd. dirs. Friends of Tenn. Librs., 1995-2002, sec., 1996-97, pres.-elect, 1997-99, pres., 1999-2000, past pres., 2000-02; pres. Temple Adas Israel, 1992-94, treas., 1994-2000; bd. dirs. Jewish Hist. Soc. of Memphis and the Mid-South, 1998-2001, sec., 2000-01. Mem. Math. Assn. Am. (sec.-treas. Fla. sect. 1985-91, Svc. award Fla. sect. 1991), Fla. Coun. Tchrs. Math. (pres. 1960-61), Fla. Assn. Math. Educators (pres. 1984-86), Nat. Coun. Tchrs. Math. (chmn. external affairs com. 1972-73), Nat. High Sch. and Jr. Coll. Math. Clubs (gov. 1972-75, pres. 1978-80). Home: 7 Stoneleigh Pl Brownsville TN 38012-2463

KALINA, JOHN, auto parts company executive; Chief info. officer Walbro Corp., 1995—96; exec. info. tech. cons. IBM, 1997—99; c.p., chief info. officer BorgWarner Inc., Chgo., 1999—. Office: BorgWarner Inc 200 S Michigan Ave Chicago IL 60604

KALINA, RICHARD, artist; b. N.Y.C., May 21, 1946; s. Jacob Wilbert and Helen Ruth (Weinberg) K.; m. Valerie Jaudon, Oct. 23, 1979. BA, U. Pa., 1966. Prof. studio art, art history Fordham U., N.Y.C., 1990—. Chair dept. theatre and visual arts Fordham U.; sr. critic Yale U. One-man shows include Jack Glenn Gallery, L.A., 1970, Okla. Harris Gallery, 1970, Tibor de Nagy Gallery, N.Y.C., 1979, 80, 82, 84, Piezo Electric Gallery, N.Y.C., 1986, 87, L.A., 1986, Elizabeth McDonald Gallery, 1988, 89, Diane Brown Gallery, N.Y.C., 1992, Ledisflam Gallery, N.Y.C., 1992, Lennon, Weinberg Gallery, N.Y.C., 1993, 95, 98, 2001, 2003; group shows include Morris Gallery, Toronto, 1970, Lunn Gallery, Washington, 1970, Inst. Contemporary Arts, Boston, 1970, U. Ala. 1971, Jack Glenn Gallery, 1970, 71, NYU, 1972, Indpls. Mus. Art, 1971, 74, Walker Art Ctr., Mpls., 1974, Cas Thomas Jefferson, Brasilia, Brazil, 1975, Lehigh U., 1975, Norton Gallery, Palm Beach, Fla., 1975, Mus. Am. Found. Arts, Miami, 1977, Sewall Gallery, 1978, 80, Nobe Gallery, 1978, Rutgers U., 1978, Weatherspoon Art Gallery, Greensboro, N.C., 1978, Ill. Wesleyan U., 1980, Aldrich Mus., Ridgefield, Conn., 1970, 80, Sidney Janis Gallery, N.Y.C., 1981, McIntosh-Drysdale Gallery, Washington, 1981, Ericson Gallery, N.Y.C., 1982, Mus. Fine Art, Ft. Lauderdale, Fla., 1982, Okla. Mus. Art, Oklahoma City, 1982, Santa Barbara Mus. Art, Calif., 1982, Grand Rapids Art Mus., Mich., 1982, Hudson River Mus., Yonkers, N.Y., 1983, U. Tex., Austin, 1983, Kalamazoo Inst. Art, 1983, Madison (Wis.) Art Ctr., U. Chgo., 1983, Loch Haven Art Ctr., Fla., 1983, Jacksonville (Fla.) Art Mus., 1983, Haber-Theodore Gallery, N.Y.C., 1983, Tibor de Nagy Gallery, 1984, Monmouth Mus., N.J., 1984, Steinbaum Gallery, N.Y.C., 1985, Bass Mus., Miami Beach, Fla., 1985, New Orleans Mus., Contemporary Art, 1985, Anchorage Mus. Fine Arts, 1985, Piezo Electric Gallery, L.A., N.Y.C., 1987, Barbara Mathes Gallery, 1987, R.C. ERPF Gallery, N.Y.C., 1987, Elizabeth McDonald Gallery, 1987, 89, Tower Gallery, N.Y.C., 1988, White Columns, N.Y., 1988, Hunter Coll. Gallery, 1988, John Good Gallery, N.Y.C., 1988, 91, John Davis Gallery, N.Y.C., 1988, Gallerie Rahmel, Cologne, Germany, 1989, J.B. Speed Art Mus., Louisville, 1989, Shea Beker Gallery, N.Y.C., 1989, Scott Hanson Gallery, N.Y.C., 1990, Fay Gold Gallery, Atlanta, 1991, Trenkman Gallery, N.Y.C., Bennington Coll., Vt., 1991, Pamela Auchincloss Gallery, N.Y.C., 1991, Diane Brown Gallery, 1982, Lennon, Weinberg Gallery, N.Y., 1992, 93, 95, 2004, 2005, Max Protetch Gallery, N.Y.C., 1992, Sergio Tossi Arte Contemporaneo, Prato, Italy, 1992, Stark Gallery, N.Y., 1993, 95, Addison Ripley Fine Art Mus.,Washington, D.C., 1993, Guild Hall Mus., East Hampton, N.Y., 1993, Arco Gallery, Turin, Italy, 1994, U. South Ffla. Contemporary Art Mus., Tampa, 1995, The Century Assn., N.Y., 1996, McNay Art Mus., San Antonio, Lennon Weinberg, Inc., 1998, Lennon Weinberg, N.Y., 1998, 99, 2001, Katonah Mus., N.Y., 1998, U. N.H., Durham, 1999, N.Y. Studio Sch. Hofstra U., 2000, Wadsworth Atheneum, Hartford, Conn., 2000, U. Fla., Gainesville, 2003, Miss. Mus. Art, Jackson, 2003, Ark. Mus. Art, Little Rock, 2003, U. N.Mex. Art Mus., 2004; represented in permanent colelctions Indpls. Mus. Art, Norton Gallery Art, Palm Beach, NYU Aldrich Mus., Nat. Mus. Am. Art, Washington, Ind. U. Mus., Rutgers U. Mus.; numerous pvt. collections; contbg. editor Art in Am. Nat. Endowment for Arts grantee. Mem. Internat. Assn. of Art Critics (bd. dirs., v.p.).

KALINA, ROBERT EDWARD, ophthalmologist, educator; b. New Prague, Minn., Nov. 13, 1936; s. Edward Robert and Grace Susan (Hess) K.; m. Janet Jessie Larsen, July 18, 1959; children: Paul Edward, Lynne Janet. BA magna cum laude, U. Minn., 1957, BS, MD, U. Minn., 1960. Diplomate Am. Bd. Ophthalmology (dir. 1981-89). Intern U. Oreg. Med. Sch. Hosp., Portland, 1960-61, resident in ophthalmology, 1961-62, 63-66; asst. in retina surgery Children's Hosp., San Francisco, 1966-67; Nat. Inst. Neurol. Diseases and Blindness Spl. fellow Mass. Eye and Ear Infirmary, Boston, 1967; instr. ophthalmology U. Wash., 1967-69, asst. prof., 1969-71, acting chmn. dept. ophthalmology, 1970-71, assoc. prof., 1971-72, chmn. dept. ophthalmology, 1971-96, prof., 1972—. Mem. staffs Univ. Hosp., Harborview Hosp., Children's Hosp., Seattle; cons. VA Hosp., Seattle, Madigan Hosp., Tacoma; assoc. head divsn. ophthalmology dept. surgery Children's Hosp., Seattle, 1975-86; pres. U. Wash. Physicians, 1990-93. Contbg. author: Introduction to Clinical Pediatrics, 1972, Ophthalmology Study Guide for Medical Students, 1975; contbr. numerous articles to profl. publs. Served to capt., M.C. USAF, 1962-63. Recipient Outstanding Achievement award, Nat. Eye Inst., 2003. Fellow ACS, Am. Acad. Ophthalmology (Sr. Honor award 1989); mem., Assn. Univ. Profs. Ophthalmology (pres. 1983-84, exec. v.p. 1989-94), Assn. Rsch. in Vision and Ophthalmology, Pacific Coast Oto-Ophthalmol. Soc. (councilor 1972-74), King County Med. Soc., Wash. State Acad. Ophthalmology, Phi Beta Kappa. Office: U Wash Dept Ophthalmology Box 356485 1959 NE Pacific St Seattle WA 98195-0001

KALIS, PETER JOHN, lawyer; b. Detroit, Feb. 20, 1950; s. Michael P. and Helen (Karageorge) K.; m. Beverly A. Poling, Feb. 1, 1976. BA, W.Va. U., 1972; PhD, Oxford U., 1976; JD, Yale U., 1978. Bar: Pa. 1980, U.S. Dist. Ct. (we. dist.) Pa. 1980, U.S. Ct. Appeals (3d cir.) 1983, U.S. Supreme Ct. 1985. Law clk. to presiding justice U.S. Ct. Appeals (D.C. cir.), Washington, 1978-79; law clk. to Justice Byron R. White U.S. Supreme Ct., Washington, 1979-80; assoc. Kirkpatrick & Lockhart, Pitts., 1980-85, ptnr., 1985—2004; ptnr. & chmn. mgmt. com. Kirkpatrick & Lockhart Nicholson Graham LLP, Pitts., 2005—. Adj. prof. law U. Pitts., 1981—. Editor-in-chief Yale Law Jour., 1978; contbr. articles to profl. jours. Bd. dir., mem. exec. com., & chmn. fin. & investment com. Blanchette Rockefeller Neurosciences Inst.; bd. dir. Nat. Pancreas Found. Rhodes scholar, Oxford, Eng., 1973. Mem. ABA, Am. Law Inst., Pa. Bar Assn., Allegheny County Bar Assn. Clubs: Rivers (Pitts.), Shannupin Country. Avocations: theater, literature, sports. Office: Kirkpatrick & Lockhart Nicholson Graham LLP Henry W Oliver Bldg 535 Smithfield St Pittsburgh PA 15222-2312 Office Phone: 412-355-6562. Office Fax: 412-355-6501. Business E-Mail: pkalis@klng.com.

KALISCHER, ALAN LESTER, cardiologist; b. N.Y.C., Mar. 14, 1950; BA, NYU, 1973; MD, N.Y. Med. Coll., 1977; spl. competency exam., Nat. Bd. Echocardiography, 2000. Diplomate in internal medicine, cardiology and nuc. cardiology Am. Bd. Internal Medicine, adult echocardiography Nat. Bd. Echocardiography. Intern Kings County-Downstate Med. Ctr., Bklyn., 1977-78, resident in internal medicine, 1978-80; fellow in cardiology Columbia-Presbyn. Med. Ctr., N.Y.C., 1980-84; cardiologist Muhlenberg Hosp., Plainfield, N.J., 1984—, Overlook Hosp., Summit, N.J., 1984—, Morristown (N.J.) Meml. Hosp., 1987—, John F. Kennedy Med. Ctr., Edison, N.J., 1998—; asst. prof. clin. medicine R.W. Johnson Med. Sch., 1984—. Fellow: AMA; mem.: Med. Soc. N.J. Union County, Am. Soc. Nuc. Cardiology, Am. Coll. Cardiology. Office: Semer-Kalischer Cardiol Assocs Pa 2253 South Ave Scotch Plains NJ 07076 Office Phone: 908-654-3080. Personal E-mail: s/kcardiology@comcast.net.

KALISH, ARTHUR, lawyer; b. Bklyn., Mar. 6, 1930; s. Jack and Rebecca (Biniamofsky) K.; m. Janet J. Wiener, Mar. 7, 1953; children: Philip, Pamela. BA, Cornell U., 1951; JD, Columbia U., 1956. Bar: N.Y. 1956, D.C. 1970. Assoc. Paul, Weiss, Rifkind, Wharton & Garrison, N.Y.C., 1956-64, ptnr., 1965-95, of counsel, 1996—. Lectr. NYU Inst. Fed. Taxation, Hawaii Tax Inst., Law Jour. Seminars Contbr. articles to legal jours. Assoc. trustee L.I. Jewish Med. Ctr., New Hyde Park, N.Y., 1978-82, trustee, 1982-95, hon. trustee, 1995-97; trustee emeritus North Shore - L.I. Jewish Health Sys., 1997-98, life trustee, 1998-2003, trustee, 2003—; trustee S.I. U. Hosp., 2004—; bd. dirs. Cmty. Health Program of Queens Nassau Inc., New Hyde Park, 1978-94, pres., 1981-89, chmn. emeritus, 1994-97; bd. dirs. Managed Health, Inc., New Hyde Park, 1990-98, chmn., 1994-95. Fellow Am. Coll. Tax Counsel; mem. ABA, N.Y. State Bar Assn., Assn. Bar City N.Y., Columbia Law Sch. Assn. (bd. dirs. 1990-94). Home: 2 Bass Pond Dr Old Westbury NY 11568-1307 Office: Paul Weiss Rifkind Wharton & Garrison 1285 Avenue Of The Americas New York NY 10019-6064 Office Phone: 212-373-3095. Personal E-mail: arthurk767@aol.com. Business E-Mail: akalish@paulweiss.com.

KALISH, MYRON, lawyer; b. N.Y.C., Dec. 3, 1919; s. Louis and Bertha (Nacht) K.; m. Evelyn J. Zobler, Apr. 1, 1944; children— Nita Jane, Pamela Sue. BS in Social Sci., CCNY, 1940; LLB cum laude, Harvard U., 1943. Bar: N.Y. bar 1944. Since practiced in, N.Y.C.; sr. ptnr. Arthur, Dry & Kalish and predecessor firms, 1961-84; gen. counsel UNIROYAL, Inc., 1961-84; spl. ptnr. Shea & Gould, N.Y.C., 1985-91, of counsel, 1992-94, Parker Duryee Rosoff & Haft, N.Y.C., 1994—2002; sole practice, 2002—. Editor: Harvard Law Rev, 1942-43. Adv. bd. Southwestern Legal Found. Lt. USNR, 1943-46. Mem. ABA, N.Y. State Bar Assn., Assn. Bar City N.Y., NAM (mem. lawyers adv. com. to gen. cousnel), Harvard Club, Bellport Country Club, Rockefeller Ctr. Luncheon Club, Westhampton Yacht Squadron. Home: 4C Halsey Rd Remsenburg NY 11960 Office: 50 E 79th St New York NY 10021-0232 Office Phone: 212-737-8142. Home Fax: 212-288-6102. Personal E-mail: mikekalish@hotmail.com.

KALISKI, STEPHAN FELIX, economics professor; b. Warsaw, Nov. 4, 1928; emigrated to Can., 1941, naturalized, 1947; s. Jacob and Ludwika (Romanus) K.; m. Marian Ieleen Nelson, Oct. 6, 1960; 1 dau., Susan Maria. BA, U. B.C., 1951; MA, U. Toronto, 1953, postgrad., 1953-54; PhD, U. Cambridge, Eng., 1959. Statistician I Dominion Bur. Statistics, 1951-52; Alexander Mackenzie Research fellow U. Toronto, 1953-54; lectr. Queen's U., Kingston, Ont., 1954-56, prof. econs., 1969-94; chmn. div II Queen's U. (Grad. Sch.), 1971-73; prof. emeritus, 1994—; research fellow in econ. statistics Manchester (Eng.) U., 1958-59; asst. prof. Carleton U., Ottawa, Ont., 1959-62, asso. prof., 1962-65, prof., 1965-69, cmn. dept. econs., 1962-63, 64-66; research supr. Royal Commn. Taxation, 1963-64; Can. Council Sr. fellow, Dept. Labour-Univs. Research Com. research grantee, research asso. U. Calif., Berkeley, 1966-67; Can. Council leave fellow, 1973-74; hon. research asso. in econs. Harvard U., 1973-74. Social Sci. and Humanities Research Council Can. leave fellow, 1980-81, research grantee, 1978, 81; bd. dirs. Nat. Bur. Econ. Research, 1978-84; cons. Royal Commn. on Econ. Union, 1984-85, Commn. of Inquiry on Unemployment Ins., 1985-86. Author: Adjustment Assistance under the U.S. Trade Expansion Act, 1963, The Tradeoff Between Inflation and Unemployment, Some Explorations of Recent Evidence for Canada, 1972; editor, author: Canadian Economic Policy since the War, a Series of Six Public Lectures in Commemoration of the Twentieth Anniversary of the White Paper on Employment and Income of 1945, 1966; mng. editor: Can. Jour. Econs, 1976-79; contbr. articles to profl. publs. Can. Council research grantee, 1969, 77-81; Social Sci. Research Council research fellow, 1956-57 Fellow Royal Soc. Can.; mem. Can. Econs. Assn. (v.p. 1984-85, pres.-elect 1985-86, pres. 1986-87, past pres. 1987-88), Queen's Univ. Club. Home: 649 Fernmoor Dr Kingston ON Canada K7M 8K5 Office: Queen's U Dept Econs Kingston ON Canada K7L 3N6 Office Phone: 613-533-2282. E-mail: kaliskis@qed.econ.queensu.ca.

KALISON, MICHAEL JAY, lawyer; b. New Haven, Conn., Dec. 2, 1945; s. Seymour Lincoln K. and Norma (Jacobson) Link; m. Deborah Lampf, May 20, 1979; children: Jeffrey, Scott. BS in Econs., U. Pa., Wharton, 1967, JD, 1972. U. Pa law clk. N.J. Supreme Ct.; Divsn. Rate Counsel; ptnr. Kalison, McBride, Jackson & Murphy, P.A., Warren, NJ. Headed devel. of hosp. payment by the case (DRG), capital payment system for hosps.; hosp. physician performance bd. incentives. Contbr. articles to profl. jours. Office: Kalison McBride Jackson & Murphy PA 25 Independence Blvd Warren NJ 07059

KALKHOFF, WILLIAM WEBSTER, sociologist, educator; b. Milw., May 26, 1971; s. Rhea Lynn Kalkhoff. BA summa cum laude, Marquette U., 1994; MA, U. Iowa, 1997. Contbr. articles to profl. jours. Rsch. grantee NSF, 2000-2001; Disting. honor scholar Ripon Coll., 1989-92, acad. scholar Marquette U., 1991-94. Mem. Am. Sociol. Assn. (nominations com. 1999-2000, Rsch. Paper award social psychology sect. 1998), Phi Beta Kappa. Avocations: blues and jazz saxophone, long-distance running, camping. Home: 4926 Spring Run Ct Apt E Stow OH 44224-5337

KALKSTEIN, JOSHUA ADAM, lawyer; b. Phila., Oct. 1, 1943; s. Abraham and Helen (Ponemone) K.; children: Aleta K., Trevor W., Maxim J. AB, Brown U., 1965; JD, U. Pa., 1968. Bar: N.Y. 1968, N.J. 1971, Mass. 1978, U.S. Dist. Ct. N.Y. 1968, U.S. Dist. Ct., N.J. 1971, U.S. Dist. Ct., Mass. 1978, U.S. Ct. of Appeals (3d cir.) 1973, U.S. Ct. Mil. Appeals 1969. Asst. gen. counsel Pfizer Inc., Groton, Conn., 1978—2004; assoc. Hellring, Lindeman & Landau, Newark, 1972-75; corp. counsel Hooper Holmes Inc., Basking Ridge, NJ, 1975-78; counsel Hanify & King, Boston, 2004—. Vis. counsel Harvard U., MIT Ctr. for Exptl. Pharmacology and Therapeutics, Cambridge, 1995—. Bd. dirs. Howland Art Ctr., Beacon, N.Y., 1987-91, Congregation Beth El, New London, Conn., 1995-96, Main Street New London, 2000—03; mem. Waterfront Redevel. Commn., Beacon, 1990-91. Lt. USNR, 1969-72. Mem. N.Y. State Bar Assn., N.J. Bar Assn., Mass. Bar Assn. Jewish. Avocations: art collecting, book collecting, golf. Home: 76 Library St Mystic CT 06355-2420 Office: Hanify & King PC One Beacon St 21st Fl Boston MA 02108-2497 Office Phone: 617-226-3497. E-mail: jak@hanify.com.

KALKUS, STANLEY, librarian, administrator, consultant; b. Prague, Czechoslovakia, Apr. 27, 1931; came to U.S., 1952; s. Frank and Zdenka (Hynkova) K.; m. Marta J. Pokorna, Jan. 12, 1952; children: Michaela Z., Olen A., Hynek P. Abitur, Classical Gymnasium, Prague, 1950; Cert. in Germanistics, Charles U., Prague, 1951; MA, U. Chgo., 1959. Librarian, audio-visual coordinator Chgo. Bd. Edn., 1960-62; base librarian U.S. Air Force, Sidi Slimane, Morocco, 1962-63, Hahn AFB, Fed. Republic Germany, 1963-68; slavic bibliographer U. N.C., Chapel Hill, 1968-69; head library dept. Naval Underwater Systems Ctr., Newport, R.I., 1969-77; dir. U.S. Dept. Navy Library, Washington, 1977-86, coord., 1986-89, libr. of Navy, 1990-92; asst. prof. Charles U., Prague, Czech Republic, 1992—. Lectr. U. N.C., Chapel Hill, 1968-69; participant tech. info. panel AGARD (NATO), Brussels, 1974, Copenhagen, 1975, Washington, 1976, Oslo, 1977; adv. com. Intergovtl. Libr. Cooperation, 1981-82; exec. adv. com. Fedlink, 1986-88; rep. Dept. of Navy on Fed. Libr. and Info. Ctrs. com., 1991-92; chmn. libr. com. Ctrl. European Rsch. and Grad. Edn., 1998-2003, Econ. Inst., Acad. Scis., Prague, 1994-2000; mem. libr. com. Parliament of Czech Republic, 1997-99; adv. bd. U. Koblenz (Germany) Exernal LS Studies, 1998-2000. Editor Navy Libraries in 1980s, 1976; contbr. articles to profl. jours. Mem. core com. R.I. Gov.'s Conf. on Libraries, 1976-77. Served with U.S. Army, 1953-55 Fellow U. Chgo., 1957-58 Mem. ALA (pres. Armed Forces sect. 1974), Spl. Libr. Assn. (chmn. mil. librs. div. 1978-79, rep. for Czech Republic), Internat. Fedn. Libr. Assns. (mem. standing com. on social librs. 1986-96, mem. standing com. edn. and tng. 1996-2000), Am. Translators Assn., Czech Libr. and Info. Profl. Assn. (mem. exec. bd. 1999—), Assn. Americans Residing Overseas, Newport Ski Club, Czech-Am. Club (pres. 2003—), Friends of Newport Pub. Libr., Lions Internat. (pres. 2003-04). Roman Catholic. Avocations: skiing, tennis. Office: Charles U Prague FF UISL U Krize 8 150 00 Prague Czech Republic also: 7009 Dreams Way Ct Alexandria VA 22315-4245 Office Phone: +420 2 51 080 368. Fax: +420 2 510 80 413. E-mail: skalkus@yahoo.com, kalkus@cuni.cz.

KALKWARF, KENNETH LEE, dean, dental educator; b. Lincoln, Nebr., Apr. 12, 1946; s. Robert G. and Grace L. (Beck) K.; m. Sharon R. Moore, July 6, 1974; children: Kyle J., Kevin J. Student, U. Nebr., 1964-66, DDS, 1970, MS, 1973. Diplomate Am. Bd. Periodontology. Asst. prof. U. Nebr., Lincoln, 1973-78, prof., 1980-87; assoc. prof. U. Okla., Oklahoma City, 1978-80; prof., assoc. dean U. Tex. Health Sci. Ctr. Dental Sch., San Antonio, 1987-88, prof., dean, 1988—. Cons. Cen. Regional Dental Testing, Topeka, Kans., 1980-87, VA, Nebr., 1981-87, ADA, Chgo., 1982—; vis. prof. Svc. U. Autonoma de Guadalajara/Mexico, 1980-82. Contbg. author textbooks, 1978—; contbr. articles to profl. jours., rsch. abstracts. Bd. dirs. McAllister Park Little League, San Antonio, 1990-94, mem. Leadership San Antonio, 1989-90. Recipient Alumni Achievement award U. Nebr., 1990, Outstanding Tchr. award U. Okla., 1980. Fellow Internat. Coll. Dentists, Am. Coll. Dentists; mem. ADA (chmn. Commn. Dental Accreditation, 2003-04), San Antonio Dist. Dental Soc. (bd. dirs. 1988-93), Am. Acad. Periodontology, S.W. Soc. Periodontology (bd. dirs. 1984-97, pres. 1993-94), Tex. Soc. Periodontists (bd. dirs. 1988-95), Internat. Assn. for Dental Rsch. Republican. Methodist. Avocations: spectator sports, jogging, reading. Office: Univ Tex Health Sci Ctr 7703 Floyd Curl Dr San Antonio TX 78284-6200

KALKWARF, LEONARD V., minister; b. Parkersburg, Iowa, Mar. 17, 1928; s. John Jr. and Helen Kalkwarf; m. Beverly Jane Hardy, May 22, 1954; children— Deborah Joy, Cynthia Sue, Scott Craig. BA, Central Coll., Pella, Iowa, 1950; BD, New Brunswick Sem., 1953; MA, NYU, 1957; STM, Luth. Sem., Phila., 1973; DMin, Princeton Sem., 1980; DD (hon.), Central Coll., 1983. Ordained to ministry Ref. Ch. in Am., 1953. Assoc. pastor Bellevue Ref. Ch., Schenectady, N.Y., 1953-55; assoc. pastor Levittown (N.Y.) Community Ch., 1955-57; pastor Ref. Ch., Willow Grove, Pa., 1957-64, 65-91, Nat. Evang. Ch., Kuwait, Kuwait, 1964-65. Pres. Particular Synod of N.J., 1969-70, 70-71, Gen. Synod of Ref. Ch. in Am., 1983-84 Author: History, 1st Reformed Church of Philadelphia, 1960, God Loves His World, Book I, 1963, Book II, 1964; contbr. articles to religious jours. Pastoral asst. Abington, Pa. Presbyn. Ch., 1998-2004. Served as Chaplain CAP, 1960-62 Mem. Canterbury Cleric Club. Lodges: Rotary. Democrat. Home: 7450 Spring Villiage DR Apt 509 Springfield VA 22150-4944 Office Phone: 703-451-4129. Business E-Mail: kalkway@aeiti.net.

KALLAHER, MICHAEL JOSEPH, mathematics professor; b. Cin., Sept. 4, 1940; s. Martin Henry and Lou Will (Huff) K.; m. Donalyn May Laraway, Aug. 17, 1963; children: Jay, Michael, Christopher, Daniel, Raymond. BS, Xavier U., 1961; MS, Syracuse U., 1963, PhD, 1967. Postdoctoral fellow U. Man., Winnipeg, Can., 1967-69; from asst. prof. prof. math. Wash. State U., Pullman, 1969—, assoc. dean scis., 1979-84, acting dean scis., 1982, chmn. math dept., 1984-92; vis. prof. Auckland U., New Zealand, 1988. Author: Affine Planes with Transitive Collineation Groups; contbg. editor Finite Geometries, 1982; contbr. articles to profl. jours. Grantee NSF; Fulbright Research scholar, Kaiserslautern, Fed. Republic Germany, 1975-76. Fellow Inst. Combinatories and Its Application (founding); mem. Am. Math. Soc., Math. Assn. Am., N.Y. Acad. of Scis., Assn. of Research Profs. (pres. 1986-87), Sigma Xi. Home: 235 NW Joe St Pullman WA 99163-3410 Office: Wash State U Dept Of Math Pullman WA 99163 Business E-Mail: mkallaher@wsu.edu.

KALLAKIS, ACHILLEAS MICHALIS S., transportation executive, real estate company executive; b. London, Sept. 3, 1968; s. Michalis and Erinoula (Angelinakis) K.; m. Pamela Anne Stachowsky, Sept. 1995; children: Erinoula, Michalis and Aristotelis (twins), Dionysios. BSc in Econs. with honors, 1989. Dir. Global Transport, Del., N.Y., 1989—91; chmn., CEO Pacific Group of Cos., London, N.Y.C., 1991—, Pacific Risk Corp., 2000—. Dir. U.S. C. of C., London, 1997—, Ocean Group USA, 1989—, Pacific Maritime, N.Y., 1991—, Bernouli Trust Corp., NY, 1994—, South Pacific Adv. Bd., Sydney, Australia, 1994—2000, Brit. Am. Bus., Inc.; chmn., CEO Pacific Coffee Corp., Hellenic Capital Mgmt., Pacific Real Estate Corp., 2000—, Atlas Alliance Group, 2000—, Atlas E-Risk, 2000—01; chmn. Pacific Vending Group; mem. devel. bd. Nat. Portrait Gallery, London, 2000—. Author: Maritime Registers of the World, 1994, Transport Economics, 1996; co-editor: The Wonders of Italy, 1996. Pres. Youth Anglo-Hellenic Soc. U.K., London, 1986-88; dir. Friends of Florence, Italy, 1997—; mem. com. Youth Enterprise Initiative, London, 1989-92; mem. Royal Opera, London, Navy League. Recipient Churchill award for Excellence Churchill Enterprise Found., 1993, Pres.'s Golden Honor award South Pacific Action, Foru, 1995, Prime Min.'s award South Pacific Action Forum, 1996, Outstanding Emerging Leader award Office of Maritime Affairs, 1997; fellow Duke of Edinburgh Internat., 2003-. Fellow Inst. Dirs., Inst. Transport and Tourism; mem. Friends of Conservation, Queen's Club, Met. Opera Guild (N.Y.C.), Met. Club (N.Y.C.), Nat. Trust (London), Soc. for Protection of Ancient Bldgs. (London), Landmark Trust (Eng.). Greek Orthodox. Avocations: travel, italian studies, back-gammon, fencing, tennis, antiques, poker. Office: Pacific Group Cos 8 Carlos Pl Mayfair London W1K 3AS England

KALLAY, MICHAEL FRANK, II, medical products executive; b. Painesville, Ohio, Aug. 24, 1944; s. Michael Frank and Marie Francis (Sage) K.; m. Irma Yolanda Corona, Aug. 30, 1975; 1 son, William Albert. BBA, Ohio U., 1967. Salesman Howmedica, Inc., Rutherford, N.J., 1972-75, Biochem Procedures/Metpath, North Hollywood, Calif., 1975-76; surg. specialist USCI divsn. C.R. Bard, Inc., Billerica, Mass., 1976-78; western and ctrl. regional mgr. ARCO Med. Products Co., Phila., 1978-80; midwest reigonal mgr. Intermedics, Inc., Freeport, Tex., 1980-82; western U.S. rep. Minntech Renal Systems, Mpls., 1982—. Pres. Kall-Med, Inc., Anaheim Hills, Calif., 1982—. Mem. Am. Mgmt. Assn., Phi Kappa Sigma. Home and Office: 7539 E Bridgewood Dr Anaheim CA 92808-1407 Office Phone: 714-397-3617. Personal E-mail: mfkii@att.net.

KALLEN, LAUREL LYNN, prosecutor; b. Newark, Mar. 26, 1953; d. Arnold Milton and Jessica Yvonne Kallen; m. Michael Piazza, June 28, 1992; children: Maia, Chloe. BA, San Francisco State U., 1982; MA, U. Calif. at Berkeley, 1982—86; JD, Cardozo Sch. Law, 1999—2001. Freelance writer and editor Permanent Mission of Israel to the U.N., NYC, 1986—87, Scholastic Macmillan, NYC, 1988—90; speechwriter Office of the Mayor, NYC, 1990—93; freelance writer and editor Scholastic and McGraw Hill, NYC, 1993—98; assoc. atty. DiJoseph and Portegello, PC, 2002—. Contbr. articles. Pro bono rep. of Sept. 11 victims Trial Lawyers Care, 2003—. Mem.: ABA, NY County Lawyers Assn., NY State Trial Lawyers Assn., NY State Bar Assn. Democrat. Jewish. Avocations: singing, running, writing. Office: DiJoseph and Portegello, PC 50 Broadway Ste 806 New York NY 10004 Office Fax: 212-344-7878. Personal E-mail: elaurel100@yahoo.com.

KALLENBERG, JOHN KENNETH, retired librarian; b. Anderson, Ind., June 10, 1942; s. Herbert A. and Helen S. K.; m. Ruth Barrett, Aug. 19, 1965; children: Jennifer Anne, Gregory John. AB, Ind. U., 1964, M.L.S., 1969. With Fresno County Library, Fresno, Calif., 1965-70, dir., 1976—2003; librarian Fig Garden Pub. Library br., 1968-70; asst. dir. Santa Barbara (Calif.) Pub. Library, 1970-76. Mem. Calif. Libr. Svcs. bd., 1990—99, v.p., 1992—95, pres., 1996—98; mem. libr. of Calif. Bd., 1999—2003, pres., 2003; Beth Ann Harnish lectr. com., 1988—91; mem. adv. bd. Pacific S.W. Regional Med. Libr., 1999—; mem. Heartland Regional Libr. Network Bd., 2000—04. Mem. editl. bd.: Past and Present, Fresno City and County Hist. Soc., 1980—. Mem.: ALA, William Saroyan Soc. (bd. dirs. 1984—, chmn. 2004—), Am. Soc. Pub. Adminstrn., Libr. Adminstrn. and Mgmt. Assn., Calif. Libr. Authority for Sys. and Svcs. (chmn. authority adv. coun. 1978—80), Calif. County Librs. Assn. (pres. 1977), Calif. Libr. Assn. (councilor 1976—77, v.p., pres. 1987), Pub. Libr. Assn., Kiwanis (pres. Fresno 1981—82, lt. gov. divsn. 5 1991—92, co-editor Cal-Nev-Ha News 1993—94, 1995—96, bd. dirs. 1999—2001, 2002—04, editor Kiwaniscape 2004—05). Presbyterian. E-mail: jkk59@cvip.net.

KALLENBERGER, KREG, art gallery owner; b. Austin, Tex., Oct. 1, 1950; s. Ralph Hubert and Martha Francis Kallenberger; m. Mary Christine Knop, Oct. 5, 1984. BFA, U. Tulsa, 1972, MA, 1975. Adj. prof. art U. Tulsa, Tulsa, Okla., 1979—84; owner, artist Kallenberger Studio, Tulsa, Okla., 1984—; tech. Pilchuck Glass Ctr., Stanwood, Wash., 1983; vis. artist Cleve. Inst. of Art, 1985; guest lectr., instr. British Art Glass Soc., Edinburgh, Scotland, 1987; juror Mid-Am. Arts Alliance Fellowship Awards, Kans. City, Mo., 1987; juror, keynote spkr. Olka. Scholastic Art Awards, Tulsa, Okla., 1995. Artist in residence Rocky Mt. Nat. Park, Estes Park, Colo., 1995. Represented in permanent collections Los Angeles County Mus. of Art, Calif., Mus. of Arts and Design, N.Y.C., Victoria and Albert Mus., London, Represented in permanent collections Mus. of Fine Arts, Boston, Musee des Arts Decoratifs, Paris, Hokkaido Mus. of Modern Art, Japan, Hsinchu Cultural Ctr. Mus., Taiwan, Corning Mus. of Glass, NY, Pilkington Glass Mus., England, Prudential Ins. Co., Steelcase Corp., Grand Rapids, Mich., U. Iowa Hosp., Iowa, one-man shows include Glass Art Gallery, Canada, 1989, Habatat Galleries, Mich., 1990, Fla., 1989, 1991, Mich., 1992, 1994, 1999, Fla., 1993, Kurland, Summers Gallery, Calif., 1992, Bentley, Tomlinson Gallery, Ariz., 1992, Leo Kaplan Modern, N.Y.C., 1993, 1994, 1997, 1999, 2003, Decorative Arts Mus., Ark. Art Ctr., Little Rock, 2002, Maine Site Gallery, Okla., 2003, exhibitions include Morris Mus., NJ, 1992, Am. Craft Mus., N.Y.C., 1994, Internat. Exhibit. of Glass Kanazawa, Japan, 1995, Scottsdale Ctr. for the Arts, Ariz., 1996, Cleve. Mus. of Art, Ohio, 1998, Tucson Mus. of Art, Ariz., 1997, Kreft Ctr. Gallery, Concorida Coll., Mich., 2000, Shanghai Fine Arts Mus., China, 2000, Millenium Mus., 2001, Ark. Arts Ctr. Decorative Arts Mus., Ark., 2002, William S. Fairfield Art Mus., Wis., 2003. Recipient Bronze medal, 1984 Olympics, Internat. Art Competition, 1984, Silver prize, Internat. Exhibit. of Brass, Japan, 1995, Fragile Art, first place, Glass Mag., 1982, Judges' award, Marietta Nat., 1982, Artist award for Excellence, Okla. Visual Arts Coalition, 2000; Artist's Fellowship grant, NEA, 1984. Office: Kallenberger Studio Rt 1 Box 1226 Barnsdall OK 74002 E-mail: infor@kregkallenberger.com.

KALLFELZ, FRANCIS A., veterinary medicine educator; b. Syracuse, NY, July 17, 1938; s. Alois Joseph and Josephine Marie (Honold) K.; m. Leonie Heidi Gantner, June 26, 1965; children: Andrew F., Susan E., Douglas P. Student, Lemoyne Coll., 1956-58; DVM, Cornell U., 1962, PhD, 1966. Diplomate Am. Coll. Vet. Nutrition (charter). Asst. prof. vet. medicine Cornell U., Ithaca, N.Y., 1966-73, assoc. prof., 1973-80, prof., 1980—; dir. Vet. Med. Tchg. Hosp., 1990-98, James Law prof. medicine (nutrition), 1997—. Sr. Fulbright lectr., Zagreb, Yugoslavia, 1978; cons. FAO/IAEA, Vienna, 1977-78, Indonesia, 1980-83; vis. prof. Johns Hopkins U. Sch. Medicine, 1999; mem. NAS NRC subcom. Nutrient Requirements of Dogs and Cats, 2000-04. Contbr. articles to profl. jours. Mem. Am. Soc. Nutrition Sci., Soc. Nuclear Medicine, AVMA (coun. on rsch. 1983-89, Am. Bd. Vet. Specialties 1988-2000, chmn. 1999-2000, coun. on edn. 2004—), Soc. Exptl. Biology and Medicine, NY State Vet. Med. Soc. (pres. 2001), NY State Comm. on Animal Health Issues, NY State Bd. for Vet. Medicine. Republican. Roman Catholic. Avocations: handball, stamp collecting/philately, camping. Home: 11 Bean Hill Ln Ithaca NY 14850-9775 Office: Cornell Univ Coll Vet Medicine Dept Clin Sci Ithaca NY 14853 Office Phone: 607-253-3031. Business E-Mail: fak1@cornell.edu.

KALLIAINEN, LOREE K., surgeon, educator; m. Kevin Clemens. BS, Mich. Technol. U., 1987; MD, U. Mich., 1991. Diplomate Am. Bd. Plastic Surgery. Asst. prof. Ohio State U., Columbus, Ohio, 2000—04; clin. asst. prof. U. Minn., Mpls., 2004—; attending surgeon HealthPtnrs., St. Paul, 2004—. Chair Biomed. Instl. Rev. Bd. Ohio State U., Columbus, 2003—04; ethics com. Regions Hosp., St. Paul, 2004—. Contbr. sci. pubs. Former mem. Chassell Schs. Found., Mich. Mem.: ACS, Assn. Women Surgeons, Assn. Surg. Edn., Plastic Surgery Rsch. Coun., Am. Assn. Hand Surgery, Am. Soc. Peripheral Nerve, Am. Soc. Plastic Surgeons, Am. Soc. Surgery Hand (young leader's program 2004—), PEO (v.p. 2002—04). Office: Plastic & Hand Surgery Regions Hosp Mail Stop 11503B 640 Jackson St Saint Paul MN 55101-2595 Office Phone: 651-254-4870.

KALLICK, DAVID A., lawyer; b. Chgo., Nov. 7, 1945; s. Joseph N. and Elizabeth A. (Just) K.; m. Arline E. Chizewer, Nov. 26, 1972; children: Michelle, Robert. AB in History, Princeton U., 1967; JD, Northwestern U., 1971. Bar: Ill. 1971, Calif. 1972. Law clk. to presiding justice Ill. Appellate Ct., Chgo., 1971-72; assoc. McCutchen, Doyle, Brown & Enersen, San Francisco, 1972-74; asst. dean U. So. Calif. Law Ctr., L.A., 1974-76, Ill. Inst. Tech.-Kent Coll. Law, Chgo., 1976-79; ptnr. Hurley Kallick & Schiller, Ltd., Deerfield, Ill., 1979-92, Tishler & Wald, Ltd., Chgo., 1992—. Past bd. dirs. Congregation Solel, Highland Park, Ill., Birchwood Club, Highland Park; past bd. mem., pres. Sch. Dist. 107, Highland Park; former trustee Legacy 107 Edn. Found., Highland Park. With USAR, 1968-74. Mem. ABA, Calif. Bar Assn., Ill. Bar Assn., Chgo. Bar Assn., Princeton Univ. Club. Home: 1887 Spruce Ave Highland Park IL 60035-2150 Office: 200 S Wacker Dr Ste 3000 Chicago IL 60606-5807 Office Phone: 312-876-3800. Business E-Mail: dkallick@tishlerandwald.com.

KALLIN, BRITTA, language educator; b. Badsegeberg, Germany, Feb. 13, 1969; d. Klaus and Edelgard Kallin; m. Protip Biswas, May 10, 2002. MA, U. Cin., 1994, U. Hamburg, 1995; PhD, U. Cin., 2000. Asst. prof. German Ga. Inst. Tech., Atlanta, 2000—. Mem.: Internat. Brecht Soc. (assoc. editor 2001—). Office: Ga Tech Sch Modern Lang 613 Cherry St Atlanta GA 30332-0375

KALLIOKOSKI, SYLVIA MAE, music educator; b. Fargo, N.D., May 16, 1954; d. Aarnold and Myrtle Eleanor Elton; m. Steven Lee Kalliokoski, June 11, 1988; children: Alex Arnold, Anna Mae. EdB, Mayville (N.D.) State U., 1976. Tchr. music and english Border Ctrl. Pub. Sch., Calvin, ND, 1976—79; tchr. instrumental music Twin Valley (Minn.) Pub. Sch., 1979—80; tchr. music North Border Pub. Sch., Neche, ND, 1980—. Pres. Neche-Ettes, Neche, ND, 1984—85. Mem.: ACDA (assoc.). Democrat. Lutheran. Avocation: travel. Office Phone: 701-886-7604.

KALLIR, JANE KATHERINE, art gallery director, author; b. NYC; d. John Otto and Joyce (Ruben) Kallir. BA, Brown U., 1976. Asst. to dir. Lefebre Gallery, NYC, 1977, Galerie St. Etienne, NYC, 1977-78, co-dir., 1979—. Guest lectr. NYU, 1982—85, 1999, Mus. Am. Folk Art, NYC, 1982—85, Nat. Gallery Art, 1994, guest curator, 94; guest lectr. Ft. Lauderdale Mus. Art, 1996, guest curator, Fla., 96; guest lectr. Mus. Modern Art, 1997, Internat. Found. for Art Rsch., 1998, Wexner Ctr., Columbus, Ohio, 1999, San Diego Mus., 2001, Columbus Mus. of Art, 2002, Clark Art Inst., 2002, Van Gogh Mus., 2005; guest curator NY State Mus., Albany, 1983, Internat. Exhbn. Found., Washington, 1984—85, Mus. of City of Vienna, 1986, Austrian Nat. Gallery, 1990, Indpls. Mus. Art, 1994, San Diego Mus. Art, 1994, Nat. Mus. of Women in the Arts, 2001, Orlando Mus. of Art, Fla., 2001, Museo del Vittoriano, Rome, 2001, San Diego Mus. Art, 2001, Van Gogh Mus., 2005. Author: Gustav Klimt-Egon Schiele, 1980, Austria's Expressionism, 1981, The Folk Art Tradition, 1981, Grandma Moses, The Artist Behind the Myth, 1982, Arnold Schoenberg's Vienna, 1984, Viennese Design and the Wiener Werkstaette, 1986, Gustav Klimt: 25 Masterworks, 1989, Egon Schiele: The Complete Works, 1990, rev., 1998, Richard Gerstl/Oskar Kokoschka, 1992, Egon Schiele, 1994, Egon Schiele: 27 Masterworks, 1996, Grandma Moses, 25 Masterworks, 1997, Grandma Moses in the 21st Century, 2001, The Essential Grandma Moses, 2001, Egon Schiele, Watercolors and Drawings, 2003, Egon Schiele: Love and Death, 2005. Mem.: Art Dealers Assn. Am. (bd. dir. 1994—97, chmn. pub. rels. com. 2001—, v.p. 2003—). Democrat. Office: Galerie St Etienne 24 W 57th St New York NY 10019-3918 Office Phone: 212-245-6734. E-mail: gallery@gse.art.com.

KALLMANN, HELMUT MAX, musicologist, retired librarian; b. Berlin, Aug. 7, 1922; emigrated to Can., 1940, naturalized, 1946; s. Arthur and Fanny (Paradies) K.; m. Ruth Singer, Dec. 31, 1955 (dec. July 1993); 1 stepdaughter, Lynn Liora Salter. MusB, U. Toronto, Ont., Can., 1949, LLD, 1971. With CBC Music Libr., Toronto, 1950-70, supr., 1962-70; chief music divsn. Nat. Libr. Can., Ottawa, Ont., 1970-87, ret., 1987. Can. del. Internat. Assn. Music Librs., 1959-71. Author: A History of Music in Canada, 1534-1914, 1960; editor; Catalogue of Canadian Composers, 1952, Music for Orchestra I, Vol. 8, 1990, (with Gilles Potvin and Kenneth Winters) Ency. of Music in Canada, 1981, French edit., 1983, (with Potvin) 2nd edit., 1992, French 2nd edit., 1993, Music for Piano III, vol. 22, 1998; contbr. articles to profl. pubLs. Chmn. Can. Music Heritage Soc., 1982—2000. Decorated Order of Can., 1986; dedicatee Musical Can., Words and Music Honouring Helmut Kallmann, 1988; recipient medal Can. Music Coun., 1977, Award of Merit Assn. for Can. Studies, 1998. Mem. Can. Assn. Music Librs. (co-founder 1956, past chmn.), Faculty Music Alumni Assn. U. Toronto (pres. 1963-64), Order of Can. Home: 38 Foothills Dr Nepean ON Canada K2H 6K3 Personal E-mail: hkallmann@rogers.com.

KALMAN, ANDREW, manufacturing executive, director; b. Hungary, Aug. 14, 1919; came to U.S., 1922, naturalized, 1935; s. Louis and Julia (Bognar) K.; m. Violet Margaret Kish, June 11, 1949; children: Andrew Joseph, Richard Louis, Laurie Ann. With Detroit Engring. & Machine Co., 1947-66, exec. v.p., gen. mgr., 1952-66; exec. v.p. and dir. Indian Head, Inc., 1966-75, also dir. Dir. Acme Precision Products, 1959-80, Reef Energy Corp., 1980-84. Trustee emeritus Alma (Mich.) Coll.; bd. dirs. Am. Hungarian Found., New Brunswick, N.J.; mem. adv. coun., mem. exec. com., U. Mich. Ctr. for Communication Disorders. Home: 708 S Military St Dearborn MI 48124-2108 Office: The Buhl Bldg 535 Griswold Ste 1900 Detroit MI 48226 Office Phone: 313-965-4182.

KALMAN, BERNADETTE, neurologist, researcher; d. Ilona Nemeth and Janos E. Kalman. MD summa cum laude, Med. U. Pecs, 1982; PhD, Thomas Jefferson U., 1995, Hungarian Acad. Scis. Med. diploma Med. Licensing, 1982. Resident in neurology County Hosp., Hungary, 1982—86; neuroimmunology fellow Neurology, Huddinge Hosp., Karolinska Inst., Stockholm, 1987—88. Immunogenetics fellow Nat. Inst. Hematology and Immunology, Budapest, 1988—89; jr. faculty Nat. Inst. Neurology, Budapest, 1990, visting neurology fellow, London, 1998—99; neuroimmunology fellow Neurology, Thomas Jefferson U., Philadelphia, 1990—93, rsch. asst. prof., 1993—96; asst. prof., dir. of neuroimmunology Neurology, Hahnemann U., Philadelphia, 1996—2002; dir. of MS rsch., assoc. prof. Neurology, SLRHC, Columbia U., New York, 2002—; vis. scientist Wellcome Trust Ctr. for Human Genetics, Oxford, 2000—01. Contbr. articles to profl. jours. Mem. internal rev. bd. Hahnemann U., Phila., 1997—2001. Recipient Recognition outstanding accomplishments Med. U., Hungarian Republic, 1978, 1980, 1981; grantee NMSS, 2003—; grant, Nat. MS Soc., 1992, 1994—95, 1996—97, 1996—2000, Celgene, 1996, Nat. MS Soc., 2000—02, 2002—, Traveling grant, Buuroughs Wellcome Fund, 2000—01, grant, Wadsworth Found., 2002—. Mem.: Am. Acad. of Neurology. Achievements include research in immunological, immunogenetic and genetic characterization of multiple sclerosis; screening for mutations in genes of Complex I; screening for pathogenic mutations in mitochondrial DNA; genetic studies on chromosome 17g 11. Avocations: art, running, hiking, literature, classical music. Office: Neurology SLRHC Columbia Univ 432W 58th St New York NY 10019 Business E-Mail: bkalman@chpnet.org.

KALMAN, MARC, radio station executive; b. Appleton, Wis. m. Gail Thoen; children: Robert, Todd, Stacie. Student, Am. U. Disc jockey Sta. WJPD, Ishpeming, Mich., 1967, Sta. WMBD, Peoria, Ill., 1967; account exec. Sta. WMIN, 1968, Sta. KRSI, 1968-69, Sta. WDGY, 1969-74, gen. sales mgr., 1974-81; v.p./gen. mgr. Blair Radio, 1981-88; gen. sales mgr. Sta. WCCO, 1988-92; v.p./gen. mgr. Sta. WLOL, Mpls. Bd. dirs. Variety Children's Hosp. Mem. Minn. Broadcasters Assn. (bd. dirs.). Avocation: spectator sports. Office: Clear Channel Radio 1600 Utica Ave S Ste 400 Saint Louis Park MN 55416-1480

KALMAR, CARLOS, music director; b. 1958; m. Britta Kalmar; children: Svenja, Katja. Condr. Vienna Volksoper, Vienna, 1987; music dir. Hamburg Symphony, 1987—91, Stuttgart Philharmonic, 1991—95, Anhaltisches Theater Dessau and Philharmonie Dessau, 1996—2000, Vienna Niederosterreichisches Tonkunstlerorchester, Vienna, 2000—03, Oreg. Symphony, 2003—. Prin. condr. Grant Park Music Festival, Chgo.; guest condr. numerous symphonies and orch., guest appearance. Avocations: hiking, cooking. Office: Ste 200 921 SW Washington Portland Austria*

KALNICKI, SHALOM, radiologist, educator; b. Tel Aviv, July 18, 1951; s. Samuel and Dina K.; m. Rachel Leia Cukier, May 20, 1975; children: Miriam, Michael, Dina Eva. MD, U. Sao Paulo, 1974. Resident Montefiore Hosp. Med. Ctr., Bronx, 1975-78, chief resident, 1978-79; med. instr. U. Sao Paulo Med. Sch., Brazil, 1979-83; asst. prof., dir. radiotherapy dept. Hosp. of Albert Einstein Coll. Medicine, Bronx, 1983-84; asst. prof. clin. radiotherapy Mt. Sinai Med. Ctr., N.Y.C., 1984-88; assoc. prof. Magee Women's Hosp., oncologist dept. radiation oncology, U. Pitts., 1988—; chmn. dept. radiation oncology Allegheny Gen. Hosp., Pitts., 1993-2000; vice chmn. for clin. affairs, dept. radiation oncology U. Pitts. Med. Ctr., 2000—; vice chmn. clin.

affairs U. Pitts. Cancer Inst., 2000—; prof. radiation oncology U. Pitts., 2000—. Contbr. articles to profl. jours. Named Outstanding House Officer, Montefiore Hosp. Med. Ctr. Alumni Assn., 1979; Sao Paulo Rsch. Found. grantee, 1972. Mem. Am. Soc. Therapeutic Radiologists, Am. Soc. Clin. Oncology, N.Y. Acad. Sci., N.Y. Cancer Soc., N.Y. Roentgen Ray Soc. Home: 5520 Northumberland St Pittsburgh PA 15217-1131 Office: UPMC Cancer Ctr 5th Fl 544 5150 Center Ave Pittsburgh PA 15232

KALO, DOLORES ANN, elementary school educator; b. Lorain, Ohio, Sept. 3, 1941; d. Charles and Susie (Tkacs) K. BS in Edn., Bowling Green State U., 1965. Tchr. Immaculate Conception Sch., Bellevue, Ohio, 1961-65, Maryvale Elem. Sch., Rockville, Md., 1965-75, Coll. Gardens Elem. Sch., Rockville, 1975—98. Instr. computer skills Coll. Gardens Elem. Sch., calligraphy Coll. Gardens Elem. Sch., photography TAPESTRY Program Coll. Gardens Elem. Sch. Exhibited photography in group shows at State of the Art Exhibit, Capitol Hill Cannon Rotunda, 1990, Children's Hosp. Nat. Med. Ctr., 1990, McGrillis Gardens Gallery, 1990, Gallaudet U., 1989 (3rd place award), Martin Luther King Libr. Gallery, 1992. Mem. Coun. Fine Art Photography, Latent Image Workshop. Mem. Delta Kappa Gamma (chpt. pres. 1982-84, dist. pres. 1983-84, state communication chmn. 1983-85, state rec. sec. 1987-89), Friends of Washington Zoo, CFAP/LIW. Democrat. Roman Catholic. Avocations: biking, tennis, photography, sewing, gardening. Office: Montgomery Pub Schs PO Box 1893 Rockville MD 20849-1893

KALODNER, HOWARD ISAIAH, legal educator; b. Dec. 16, 1933; BA, Haverford Coll., 1954; LLB, Harvard U., 1957. Bar: Pa. 1958. Law clk. U.S. Supreme Ct., 1958-59; assoc. Schnader, Harrison, Segal & Lewis, Phila., 1960; legal adviser U.S. Dept. State, Washington, 1961-62; spl. asst. to solicitor U.S. Dept. Labor, Washington, 1962-64; prof. law NYU, 1964-77; dean Western New Eng. Coll. Law, Springfield, Mass., 1977-94, prof. law, 1977—. Bd. dirs. Inst. Jud. Adminstrn., 1976-78. Home: 55 Riverview Ter Springfield MA 01108-1603 Office: Western New Eng Sch Law 1215 Wilbraham Rd Springfield MA 01119-2689 E-mail: hkalodner@law.wnec.edu.

KALRA, MANNUDEEP K., radiologist, researcher; b. Oct. 17, 1972; s. Karanvir Singh and Namarta Kalra; m. Harpreet Sodhi, June 12, 2002. MB, BChir, Govt. Med. Coll., Nagpur, India, 1996; MD in Radiology, Govt. Med. Coll., 1999. Diplomate Nat. Bd. Radiology. Clin. asst. Hinduja Hosp., Mumbai, India, 1999—2001; rsch. fellow Mass. Gen. Hosp., Boston, 2001—03, rsch. asst., 2003—05; physician CT rsch. Emory U. Hosp., Atlanta, 2005—. Presenter, lectr. in field. Contbr. articles to profl. jours. Mentor Home for Little Wanderer, Boston, 2001—03. Recipient Cert. of Merit award, Radiol. Soc. N.Am., 2001, 2003—04, Excellence in Design award, 2002, 2004, Bronze medal, Am. Roentgen Ray Soc., 2002, Exec. Coun. Resident Rsch. award, 2004; grantee, NIH, Siemens Med. Solution, GE Med. Sys., Ptnrs. Healthcare Info. Sys.; Rsch. grant, Radiol. Soc. N.Am., 2004. Achievements include research in CT radiation. Avocations: poetry, writing, reading. Office: Mass Gen Hosp 55 Fruit St Boston MA 02114 Personal E-mail: mannudeep.k.kalra@yahoo.com.

KALSNER, STANLEY, pharmacologist, physiologist, educator; b. N.Y.C., Aug. 21, 1936; s. William Louis and Sadie (Feldman) K.; m. Jenny Book, Aug. 4, 1963; children— Lydia, Pamela, Louisa. AB, NYU, 1958; postgrad., SUNY Downstate Med. Ctr., 1959—62; PhD, U. Man., Can., 1966; postgrad., Cambridge (Eng.) U., 1966—67. Asst. prof. pharmacology U. Ottawa, Ont., Can., 1967-72, assoc. prof., 1972-77, prof., 1977-85; prof. joint dept. physiology and pharmacology CUNY, 1985—. Med. rsch. scientist on heart disease and blood vessel function; sci. referee Med. Rsch. Coun. Can., Can. Heart Found. Editor, contbr. chpts. to books, articles to jours.; asso. editor Can. Jour. Physiology and Pharmacology, until 1985; mem. editorial bd.: Jour. Autonomic Pharmacology, Blood Vessels. USPHS fellow, 1960-67; Med. Rsch. Coun.-NRC and Ont. Heart Found. grantee; Am. Heart Assn. grantee, 1987—. Mem. AAAS, AAUP, Can. Pharmacology Soc., Am. Soc. Pharmacology and Therapeutics. Home: 21 Hillcrest Rd Suffern NY 10901-6834 Office: CUNY Med Sch 138th St and Convent Ave New York NY 10031 Personal E-mail: jskalsner@optonline.net. *I believe that the greatest mystery of all is life and that it is worth devoting oneself to its solution.*

KALSNER-SILVER, LYDIA, psychologist; b. Winnipeg, Can., May 26, 1964; d. Stanley and Jenny Kalsner; m. Jay Silver, Aug. 20, 1994; children: Dylan, Chloe. BS in Psychology, U. Toronto, 1987; MA, EdM, Columbia U., 1992; EdD in Counseling Psychology, Rutgers U., 2000. Dir. clin. assessment dept. psychiatry SUNY, Bklyn., 1992—97; psychology resident Jackson Meml. Hosp., Miami, 1997—98, post-doctoral fellow Juvenile Gun Offender Program, 2000—01; sch. psychologist Temple Beth Am Day Sch., Miami, 2001—02; psychologist Divsn. Alternative Outreach Miami (Fla.) Dade Country Pub. Schs., 2002—; pvt. practice psychotherapist Miami, 2002—. Grant reviewer crime prevention com. Miami (Fla.) Dade Criminal Justice Counsel, Miami, 1997; adj. faculty U. Miami, 1997—98; rsch. writer Higher Edn. Ext. Svc. Columbia U., N.Y., 1991—92; instr. Rutgers U., New Brunswick, NJ. Contbr. articles to profl. jours. Scholar, Tchrs. Coll. Columbia U., 1990. Mem.: APA, Soc. Personal Assessment, Fla. Psychol. Assn. Avocations: cooking, travel. Home: 5151 Collins Ave Miami Beach FL 33140 Office: 5151 Collins Ave Ste 223 Miami Beach FL 33140 Office Phone: 305-301-4264. Personal E-mail: kalsner@aol.com.

KALT, HOWARD MICHAEL, public relations executive; b. Racine, Wis., June 11, 1943; s. Nat and Fay (Schwartz) K.; m. Barbara Lee Schowalter, Feb. 2, 1963; children: Jennifer, Jeffrey. BS in Journalism, U. Wis., 1964. Writer Wis. State Jour., Madison, 1963-64; v.p. Gardner, Jones & Co. (now Hill & Knowlton), Chgo., 1964-74; v.p. comm. Fred S. James & Co., Chgo., 1974-75; dir. comm. The Marmon Group, Chgo., 1975-76; v.p. Ruder & Finn, San Francisco, 1976-77, Hoefer Amidei Assocs., San Francisco, 1977-79; v.p. comm. ISU Cos., Inc., San Francisco, 1979-82; ptnr., co-owner Kalt & Hamlin Pub. Rels., San Francisco, 1984—. Life mem. Cmty. Renewal Soc. Chgo. Mem. Pub. Rels. Soc. Am. (former bd. dirs., past pres. San Francisco chpt., former dist. chmn.; Best Pub. Rels. Program No. Calif. chpt. 1980), Nat. Invester Rels. Inst., San Francisco Pub. Rels. Round Table, The Family Club. Jewish. Office: Kalt Rosen & Assocs 220 Montgomery St Fl 19 San Francisco CA 94104-3402

KALTCHEV, IVO, musician, educator; b. Vladimirovo, Bulgaria, Jan. 12, 1961; arrived in U.S., 1990; s. Lyubomir Kaltchev and Vera Kaltcheva. MusB in Piano Performance, Sofia (Bulgaria) State Acad. Music, 1987; MusM in Piano Performance, Yale U., 1992; Mus D, Rutgers U., 1996. Asst. prof. piano Sofia State Acad. of Music, Sofia, 1988—90; asst. prof. Sofia State U., 1987—90; artist piano faculty Westminster Choir Coll./Conservatory, Princeton, NJ, 1996—2000; asst. prof. Cath. U. Am., Washington, 2000—. Faculty World Piano Pedagogy Conf., 1996—; competition adjudicator U. Md., College Park, 2001; competiton adjudicator Wash. Music Teachers Assn., Washington, 2001—; competition adjudicator 15th Concurso Juvenil de Piano, Toledo, 2002, Broad Creek Music Festival, Washington, 2001—02. Musician: (CD recordings) Piano Works by Soler, Chopin, Debussy, Rachmaninov and B'Racz, 1995, Concertos for Marimba and Piano by Creston and Kurka (with G. Giannascoli), 1997, Piano Works of Charles T. Griffes, 1998, Concerto for Marimba and Piano by J. Basta (with G. Giannascoli), 1999, World Premiere Recording of Piano Works of Florent Schmitt, 2002; musician: (solo pianist) Complete Solo Piano Music of Claude Debussy, 1994; musician: (pianist) Complete Songs for Voice and Piano by Henry Duparc, 2002; musician: (concerts) World, Europe and US Premieres of works by Schmitt, Antheil, Copland, Samonov, Griffes, Spassov, Miki, B'Racz, Basta, Creston, Kurka, Zorman, D.Chavez., solo, concerto, chamber music performances, 2002. Recipient 2nd prize, Obretenov Nat. Competition, Bulgaria, 1979, 1978, 6th Citta di Salerno Internat. Piano Competition, Italy, 1979, 4th prize and prize Musicians' Assn. Bulgaria, 1st P. Vladigerov Internat. Piano Competition, 1986, Disting. Performer prize, 7th Palm Beach Invitational Internat. Piano Competition, 1993, Genia Robinor Pedagogy award, Piano Tchrs. Soc. Am., 2000, 1999, award for Tchg. Excellence, Princeton Steinway Soc., 2000, Bosendorfer Artist, 2003. Mem.: Musicians Assn. Bulgaria, Coll. Music Soc., Music Teachers Nat. Assn. Office: Cath U Am Benjamin T Rome Sch Music Washington DC 20064 Office Phone: 202-319-5861. Business E-Mail: kaltchev@cua.edu.

KALTCHEVA, NADEJDA J., astronomer, researcher; b. Sofia, Bulgaria, Aug. 19, 1961; d. Todor S. Todorov and Magda H. Todorova; m. Matey G. Kaltchev, Aug. 27, 1983; 1 child, Maria. MS in Optics and Spectroscopy, U. Sofia, 1984, PhD in Astronomy, 1991. Asst. prof. astronomy U. Sofia, 1993—2000; advanced rsch. fellow astronomy U. St. Andrews, Scotland, 1997—98; asst. rsch. prof. Niels Bohr Inst. Astronomy, Physics and Geophysics, Copenhagen, 2000; asst. prof. physics and astronomy U. Wis., Oshkosh, 2001—. Contbr. more than 70 articles to sci. publs. Recipient Internat. award, Vander Putten Internat. Fund, 2003, German Acad. Exch. Svc. award, DAAD, 1996; grantee, NATO, 1997, 1999; Royal Soc. Advanced fellow, 1998, rsch. grantee, Bulgarian Nat. Sci. Found., 1993, 1996. Mem.: Internat. Astron. Union.

KALTENBACH, C(ARL) COLIN, dean, educator; b. Buffalo, Wyo., Mar. 22, 1939; s. Carl H. and Mary Colleen (McKeag) K.; m. Ruth Helene Johnson, Aug. 22, 1964; children: James Earl, John Edward. BSc, U. Wyo., 1961; MSc, U. Nebr., 1963; PhD, U. Ill., 1967. Postdoctoral fellow U. Melbourne, Australia, 1967-69; from asst. prof. to prof. U. Wyo., Laramie, 1969-89, assoc. dean, dir. Agrl. Expt. Sta., 1980-89; vice dean, dir. Agrl. Expt. Sta. U. Ariz., Tucson, 1989—. Contbr. 200 articles to profl. publs. Named Outstanding Alumnus Coll. Agriculture U. Wyo., 1991. Mem. Nat. Assn. State Univs. and Land Grant Colls. (mem. policy bd. dirs. 2002—), Soc. for Study Reprodn. (treas. 1979-82), Am. Soc. Animal Sci., Civitan (officer 1972-85), Agrl. Experiment State Dirs. (chair 1996-97). Office: U Ariz Coll Agr and Life Scis Tucson AZ 85721-0001 E-mail: kltnbch@ag.arizona.edu.

KALTER, ALAN, advertising agency executive; m. Chris Lezotte. With W.B. Doner & Co., Southfield, Mich., 1967—, exec. v.p., dir. retail divsn., 1990, vice chmn. account mgmt., 1990-92, pres., COO, 1992-95; CEO, chmn. W. B. Doner & Co. (now Doner), Southfield, Mich., 1995—. Office: W B Doner & Co 25900 Northwestern Hwy Southfield MI 48075-1067*

KALTHOFF, THEODORE JOSEPH, academic administrator; b. Independence, Mo., Oct. 1, 1949; s. Theodore John and Flossie May Kalthoff; m. Sharon Louise Fuller, Sept. 4, 1982; children: Theodore Jay, Lisanne Marie. BA, U. Mo., 1972, MA, 1974; PhD, So. Ill. U., 1980. Cert. tchr. Mo. Asst. dean Park Coll., Parkville, Mo., 1980—82; dean acad. affairs Cleve. Chiropractic, Kansas City, Mo., 1982—88; dean of instrn. Waldorf Coll., Forest City, Iowa, 1988—94; v.p. acad. affairs Cloud County C.C., Concordia, Kans., 1994—. Pres. Kans. Coun. Inst. Adminstrn., 1996; Kans. rep. Nat. Coun. Inst. Ad., 1997—. Active Boy Scouts Am.; chmn. Cloud County Rep. Party, Concordia, 2000—; state del. Kans. Rep. Party, 2002—. Mem.: NCK Rural Devel. Coun. (treas. 1996—), Southtown Bus. Coun. (pres. 1986), Rotary (pres. Forest City chpt. 1992—93). Republican. Lutheran. Avocations: bowling, fishing. Office: Cloud County CC PO Box 1002 2221 Campus Dr Concordia KS 66901 Office Phone: 785-243-1435. Business E-Mail: kalthoff@dustdevil.com.

KALTSOS, ANGELO JOHN, electronics executive, educator, photographer; b. Boston, Aug. 19, 1930; s. John Angelo and Rita Thomas (Goudas) K.; m. Verna Kay Wilson, June 30, 1952 (dec. Jan. 1973); children: Pamela, Elaine, Gregory, Stephanie, Lenora, Demetra, Dana. Student, Mass. Radio and TV Sch., Boston, 1955—57, Harvard Coll. Extension, 1964, Boston State Coll., 1965—67, U. N.M., 1976, Fitchburg State Coll., 1977. Clk. U.S. Postal Svc., Boston, 1954-57; electronic rsch. technician Crosley div. Avco, Cin., 1957; electronic rsch. production technician Raytheon Mfg. Co., Waltham, Mass., 1957-63; educator Cambridge (Mass.) Sch. Dept., 1961-81; ind. ethnology rsch. N.Mex., 1969—; mgr. Pampas, Inc., Boston, 1987-90. Bd. dirs. Expansion Dance Co., Boston; cons. 5 P.I.E., Albuquerque, 1976—, Indian Tribal Group, N.Mex.; lectr. S.W. Indian Culture in Boston, Cambridge area, 1990—; pres., treas. Spartan Enterprises, Inc., 1965-69. Author: Southwest Indian, 1986, (non-fiction) Music You Will Never Hear, 2005, (poetry) Unfurling Leaves of the Mind, 2005; one-man shows include Christmas Tree Gallery, Manteo, N.C., 1977, 4th St. Photo Gallery, N.Y.C., 1980, Cambride Rindge and Latin Sch., Mass., 1981, Jay's, Cambridge, Mass., 1983, Here Today Gallery, Boston, 1984, Andover (Maine) Town Hall, 1984, 86, Piedmont Art Assn., Martinsville, Va., 1985-86, Cambalache Gallery, Boston, 1986-87, The 4th St. Gallery, N.Y.C., 1990, Andover (Maine) Pub. Libr., 1997-98; contbg. journalist in field Chmn. No Thank Q Hydro Quebec, Andover, Maine, 1988-91, coord., Dryden, Maine, 1991-2001; regional and media coord. N.E. Alliance to Protect James Bay, 1990-91, exec. bd., adv. bd., treas., 1991-2001, project dir., 1995-2001; project dir., treas. Hydro Electric Watch, 2001—; senate faculty Cambridge Sch. Dept., 1980-81; sec. New Eng. Model Car Assn. of Raceways, 1966-69; educator Cambridge Adult Ctr., 1990-97, Paulist Ctr., Boston, 1991-92; judge Andover amateur photo contest, 1996-99, coord., judge, 2001—. Recipient Robert Sweeney award Rindge Alumni Assn., 1996. Mem. Appalachian Mountain Club (life). Greek Orthodox. Avocations: ethnography, entomology, cooking, gardening, hiking. Home: PO Box 33 Andover ME 04216-0033

KALTVED, DARREN STANLEY, academic administrator; b. Denver, Feb. 10, 1977; s. James Howard and Kathleen Louise Kaltved. BSc, U. Minn., Duluth, Minn., 2000; MEd, Springfield (Mass.) Coll., 2002. Counselor Office Admissions Springfield (Mass.) Coll., 2000—02; asst. dir. career svcs. St. Mary's Coll. Md., St. Mary's City, 2002—. Intern career svcs. Springfield (Mass) Coll., 2001—02, academic coach, 2001—02; intern Career Devel. Ctr. Mt. Holyoke Coll., South Hadley, Mass., 2000—01; orientation specialist U. Minn., Duluth, 1998—2000, tchg. asst. psychology, 1998—2000. Recipient Disting. Grad. Student award, Office Grad. Studies, Springfield (Mass.) Coll., 2002; fellow, 2000—02. Mem.: Mid. Atlantic Career Counseling Assn. (assoc.; vol. coord. 2003—04), Nat. Assn. Colls. and Employers (assoc.), Md. Coll. Pers. Assn. (assoc.), Coll. Student Educators Internat. (assoc.; conv. planning team 2005—), Psi Chi (life). Luth. Avocations: hiking, kayaking, travel, wrestling, hockey. Office: St Marys College of Maryland 18952 E Fisher Road Saint Marys City MD 20686 Office Phone: 240-895-4203.

KALU, KALU NDUKWE, political scientist, educator; s. Ndukwe Kalu Ndukwe and Ogbenyalu Ndukwe Kalu; children: Rose Chinyere, Renee Aluba N. BSc, Rutgers State U., 1977—79; MBA, Atlanta U., 1980—82; PhD, Tex. Tech U., 1988—94; Post-Doctoral Fellow, Yale U., Sch. of Medicine, 1996—2000. Lectr. polit. sci., pub. adminstrn., health polit. and policy Lamar U., Beaumont, Tex., 1994—96, U. of Conn., 1997—2001; prof., dir. pub. affairs program Emporia State U., Kans., 2000—; rsch. fellow Yale Ctr. for Internat. and Area Studies (Yale U.), 2001—. Mem., bd. of directors ASPA (Am. Soc. for Pub. Adminstrn.) Kans. Chpt., Topeka, 2002—. Schedule programs, policy input to nat. office ASPA , 2002. Mem.: Acad. Mgmt., Am. Polit. Sci. Assn., Am. Soc. Pub. Adminstrn. (pres. Kans. chpt. 2005—), Pi Sigma Alpha (hon.), Pi Alpha Alpha (hon.). Office Phone: 620-341-5573. E-mail: kalukaly@emporia.edu.

KALUARACHCHI, JAGATH JANAPRIYA, environmental engineer, educator; arrived in US, 1984; s. Somapala and Nancy Kaluarachchi; m. Indira Perera, Aug. 25, 1957; children: Rumal J, Malinka I. BS in Engring., U. Moratuwa, Sri Lanka, 1980; PhD, Va. Poly. Inst. and State U., 1989. Registered profl. engr., Utah, 1992. Prof. Utah State U., Logan, Utah, 1990—. Vis. rschr. Swiss Inst. Tech., Zurich, Switzerland, 1989—90; vis. prof. Royal Inst. Tech., Stockholm, 1997—98. Vice chmn. watershed coun. Environment and Water Resources Inst., Reston, Va., 2003—04. Grantee, US State Dept., 2002. Mem.: ASCE (life; vice chmn. com. 1995—2004), Am. Geophys. Union (life). Office: Utah State Univ 1600 Canyon Rd Logan UT 84321 Office Phone: 435-797-3918. Business E-Mail: jkalu@cc.usu.edu.

KALUDIS, GEORGE, management consultant, publishing executive, educator; b. Balt., Oct. 7, 1938; s. Steven George and Theresa (Topal) K.; m. Eugenia Leone Mihalakis, July 21, 1962; children: Stephen George, Michele Maria, William Michael, Kirk Jamie. BA, U. Md., 1960, MEd, 1965; PhD, Fla. State U., 1968. Asst. dean student life U. Md., 1960-65; resident instr. U. S. Fla., 1965-66; dir. divsn. planning and evaluation State Univ. Sys. Fla., 1966-70; vice chancellor ops. and fin. planning, assoc. prof. mgmt. Vanderbilt U., Nashville, 1970-76, adj. assoc. prof. mgmt., 1976-78; exec. v.p. Ingram Book Co., 1976-78; chmn., pres. Kaludis Consulting, Washington, 1978—. Mem. tech. coun. Nat. Ctr. Higher Edn. Mgmt. Sys., 1970—72, bd. dirs., 1972—76, chmn. bd., 1975—76; pres., bd. dirs. Frat. Advisors Group, Inc., Tallahassee, 1968—70; mem. com. chmn. Nat. Com. on Financing Postsecondary Edn., 1972—74. Editor: Strategies for Budgeting, New Directions in Higher Education, 1973; mem. editl. bd.: On the Horizon, 1996—2001, contbg. author: Mission Management a New Synthesis, vol. 1, Dollars, Distance and Online Education, The University and It's Academic Health Center: New Strategic Contexts, 2005. Bd. dirs. NCCJ, Nashville, St. Photios Nat. Shrine, 1986-87; 1st v.p. Family and Children's Svcs., Inc., 1978-80; chmn. Spl. Com. on Cable TV, Nashville, 1982-95; parish coun. Holy Trinity Greek Orthodox Ch., 1971-94, pres., 1972-78, 81-83, 92-94; stewardship commn. Greek Orthodox Archdiocese, 1993-95, archdiocesan coun., 1994-98, 2000—, co-chmn. com. on strategic and long range planning, 1994-97, metropolis coun., NJ, 1999—, v.p.; parish coun. St. George Greek Orthodox Ch., Bethesda, 1998, sec., chair stewardship com., 2000, pres.; del. World Clergy-Laity Congress, Greek Orthodox Ch., Istanbul, 2000, mem. Leadership 100, 2001; nat. xapital campaign com. Fla. State U., 2001; trustee Internat. Orthodox Christian Charities, 2003—; arena seating planning com. U. Md.; chair strategic planning com. Nat. Coun., 2005—. With U.S. Army, 1962-64 Recipient Medal of St. Paul award Greek Orthodox Archdiocese, 1992, Disting. Alumnus award U. Md. Coll. Edn., 1995, Order of St. Andrew of Ecumenical Patriarch, 2003— Mem. Am. Assn. Higher Edn., Assn. Instnl. Rsch., Nat. Assn. Coll. and Univ. Bus. Officers, Fin. Execs. Inst. (pres. Nashville chpt. 1975), Nashville Area C. of C. (gov.), Am. Hellenic Ednl. Progressive Assn., U. Md. Alumni Ctr. (cabinet), Omicron Delta Kappa, Pi Sigma Alpha, Sigma Phi Epsilon (chmn. commn. on univ. rels. 1992-93). Office: 1710 Rhode Island Ave N Ste 400 Washington DC 20036 Office Phone: 202-331-3650. Business E-Mail: gkaludis@kaludisconsulting.com.

KALVEN, JANET, humanities educator, writer, consultant; b. Chgo., May 21, 1913; BS, U. Chgo., 1934; MEd, Boston U., 1971. Instr. great books program U. Chgo., 1937-42; lectr., adminstr. ednl. program for women U.S. Grail Movement, Libertyville, Ill., 1942-43, Loveland, Ohio, 1944-64; coord. internat. meetings Internat. Grail Movement, Paris, 1964-67; coord. academic program Grailville Conf. Ctr., Loveland, 1967-78, conf. coord., lectr., 1978—90; assoc. dir. self directed learning program U. Dayton, Ohio, 1972-86. Founder, trainer Women into Tomorrow, Cin., 1971—76. Co-author, editor: Your Daughters Shall Prophesy, 1980, Value Development, 1982, Women's Spirit Bonding, 1984, With Both Eyes Open, 1988, Women Breaking Boundaries, 1999; contbr. articles to profl. jours. Founder, bd. dirs. Women Inst. Religion and Soc., Cin., 1985—93; co-founder, bd. dirs. Women's Rsch. Devel. Ctr., Cin., 1988—; mem. nat. commn. Ch. Women United, NY, 1970—71; bd. dirs. Met. Area Religious Coalition, Cin., 1969—72, Cin. Indsl. Mission, 1971—74, Women Ch. Convergence, Balt., 1984—. Named to Ohio Women's Hall of Fame, 1990. Mem.: NOW, Nat. Women's Studies Assn., Women's Ordination Conf. (mem. program com.), Phi Beta Kappa. Home: 1615 Chase Ave # 3D Cincinnati OH 45223 Office Phone: 513-683-2340. Personal E-mail: kalven@fuse.net.

KALVIN-STIEFEL, JUDY, public relations executive; b. Valley Stream, Long Island; m. Lewis Stiefel; 1 child, Amy. BA in lit. and journalism, SUNY, Oneonta. Writer, editor Corp. Design mag., 1985—87; account supr. Howard J. Rubenstein Assoc.; dir. pub. rels. Gerstman+Meyers, 1989—93; v.p. pub. rels. Gerstman+Meyers (now Interbrand), 1993—97, Addison, NYC, 1997—99; v.p., dir. comm. Sterling Group, NYC, 1999—2001; founder, pres. Kalvin Pub. Rels., Forest Hills, NY, 2001. Author: Defining Woman: Natural Workout for Body and Mind, 1993. Recipient Women Achievement Pacesetter award, NYC Coun., 2002, NEAL award bus. writing, championship title, World Natural Bodybuilding Fedn., 1990. Mem.: NY Women in Comm. Avocation: bodybuilding. Office: 114 Ogden Ave Dobbs Ferry NY 10522-3312 Office Phone: 718-520-1660. Business E-Mail: jkalvin@kalvinpr.com.

KALYANARAMAN, RAMKI, education educator, researcher; b. Bareilly, UP, India, Apr. 23, 1968; arrived in U.S., 1995; s. Sivaramakrishnan and Uma Kalyanaraman; m. Veena Gopal, Dec. 24, 1998. BA, IIT, Kharagpur, India, 1991; MA, IIT, Kanpur, India, 1994; PhD, N.C. State Univ., Raleigh, N.C., 1998. Postdoctoral rsch. fellow Oak Ridge Nat. Lab and Lucent Tech., Murray Hill, NJ, 1999—2001; asst. prof. Wash. Univ., St. Louis, 2001—. Contbr. chapters to books, articles to profl. jour. Mem.: IEEE, Materials Rsch. Soc., Sierra, Phi Kappa Phi. Achievements include patents for A processs to fabricate a semiconductor device; discovery of Sci. findings publ. in leading internat. sci. jour. Avocations: squash, music, travel. Office: Wash Univ St Louis One Brookings Dr Saint Louis MO 63130 Home: 2 Green Oaks DR Saint Louis MO 63132-3426

KALYANPUR, ARJUN, radiologist; b. Beijing, June 27, 1965; s. Bhaskar Ramkrishna and Leela Rao Kalyanpurkar; m. Sunita Maheshwari, Sept. 24, 1994; children: Alisha, Adil Bharat. MBBS, All India Inst. Med. Scis., New Delhi, 1983—88, MD, 1989—92. Diplomate Am. Bd. Radiology, 1998. Asst. clin. prof. Yale U. Sch. Medicine, New Haven, 1998—. Contbr. articles to profl. jours. Trustee People for People, Bangalore, India, 2003—04. Mem.: Radiologic Soc. N.Am. Avocations: travel, reading, music, theater. Home: Villa 19 Regent Pl Whitefield Mn Rd Bangalore 560066 India Office: Teleradiology Solutions 205 Church St 3rd Fl New Haven CT 06510 Office Phone: 877-295-1705. Home Fax: 91-80-28525479; Office Fax: 775-860-2508. E-mail: arjun.kalyanpur@telradsol.com.

KAM, ANTHONY WING-YUI, physicist, radiologist; b. Hong Kong, Sept. 23, 1961; s. Sung Yeung and Celia (Chang) K. AB in Physics/Chemistry summa cum laude, Cornell U., 1983; AM in Physics, Harvard U., 1985, PhD in Physics, 1992; MD with honors, U. Ill., Urbana, 1996. Rsch. assoc. dept. elec. and computer engring. Beckman Inst., U. Ill., Champaign-Urbana, 1992-96; intern U. Pitts. Dept. Medicine, 1996-97. Contbr. articles to profl. jours. Fellow Shell Found., 1987-88, NSF, 1983-87; recipient: award Am. Inst. Chemists, 1983. Mem. AMA, IEEE, Am. Phys. Soc., Optical Soc. Am. Achievements include first measurement of the lifetime of the metastable state of molecular nitrogen; measurements on electron stimulated desportion of hydrogen and deuterium from silicon. Home: 233 N Craig St Apt 401 Pittsburgh PA 15213-1538 Office: U Pitts Med Ctr 200 Lothrop St Pittsburgh PA 15213-2546

KAM, JAMES TING, engineer, consultant, scientist; b. Hong Kong, July 29, 1945; s. Nai Fai and Big Chun (Au) Kam; m. Winna M. Wong, June 9, 1974; children: Kelvin K., Theresa P. PhD, U. Calif., Berkeley, 1974. Registered profl. engr., Calif., Utah, Colo., N.Mex. Project engr. Internat. Engring. Co., San Francisco, 1975-79; sr. hydrologist Sci. Applications Inc., San Leandro, Calif., 1979-81; chief hydrologist Davy McKee Corp., San Ramon, Calif., 1981-85; prin. engr. MK Environ. Svcs., San Francisco, 1985-97, Yucca Mountain Project, Las Vegas, 1997-2000; sr. engring. specialist Bechtel SAI, 2001—. Scholar, U. Calif., 1972—74. Mem.: Groundwater Scientists and Engrs., Lions Club (bd. dirs. San Francisco chpt. 1984—86), Sigma Xi. Avocations: golf, tennis, marathons and triathlons, singing. Home: 10516 Angel Dreams Ave Las Vegas NV 89144-5437 Office: 1180 N Town Center Dr Las Vegas NV 89144-6363 Office Phone: 702-295-4550. Business E-Mail: jim_kam@ymp.gov.

KAMADA-COLE, MIKA M., allergist, immunologist, medical educator; b. Denver, Dec. 9, 1957; m. Joe Lyn Cole, Dec. 7, 1991. BA in Biology, BA in Chemistry, U. Mo., 1980, MD, 1982. Diplomate: Am. Bd. Allergy and Immunology, Am. Bd. Internal Medicine, Nat. Bd. Med. Examiners. Intern in medicine Barnes Hosp., St. Louis, 1982-83, jr. resident in medicine, 1983-84; rsch./clin. fellow in allergy and immunology Dept of Rheumatology and Immunology Brigham and Women's Hosp., Boston, 1985-88; assoc. in medicine Washington U., 1982-85; rsch. fellow in medicine Harvard Med.

Sch., 1985-88, instr. in pediatrics, 1988-90; instr. Southwestern Med. Sch., 1991-92, U. Tex. Health Sci., 1992—; staff Santa Rosa Healthcare, San Antonio, 1992—, Southwest Gen. Hosp., San Antonio, 1992—, Methodist Hosp., San Antonio, 1992—. Contbr. munerous articles to med. jours. Recipient Vice Chancellor for Student Affairs Honor, 1982, Honor Grad. award Am. Med. Women's Assn., Schering Rsch. award. Fellow Am. Coll. Allergy; mem. Am. Acad. Allergy and Immunology (mem. com. asthma mortality 1987—), Tex. Med. Assn., Bexar County Med. Soc. Office: 5323 Broadway St San Antonio TX 78209-5713 E-mail: mkcole@dnamail.com.

KAMAL, ABU HENA M., electrical engineer, researcher; s. Abdul Hannan and Golenoor Begum; m. Shamima M. Shimu, Sept. 14, 1989; 1 child, Ishmam A. Nawar. BS in Elec. and Electronic Engring., Bangladesh U. of Engring. and Tech., Dhaka, Bangladesh, 1988; MS in Elec. and Electronic Engring., Muroran Inst. of Tech., Japan, 1993; PhD in Elec. Engring., Ariz. State U., 1997. Lectr. Bangladesh U. of Engring. and Tech., Dhaka, 1988—90; sr. process engr. Nat. Semiconductor Corp., Santa Clara, Calif., 1997—99, sr. circuit design rschr., 1999—2001, staff circuit design engr., 2001—. Team leader of cobalt silicide group Nat. Semiconductor Corp., Santa Clara, Calif., 1997—99, leader design team; mng. dir. Imdad-Sitara Khan Kidney Ctrs., Bangladesh, India. Author: (jour. paper) IEEE Trans. of Semiconductor Mfg.; author: (and speaker) (conf.) Silicon Nanoelectronics Workshops; reviewer IEEE, 2000—; dir.(and wrote): (4 bengali dramas), 1995—2003; bur. chief: Exec. Times; contbr. articles to profl. publs. Dir., founder drama group BiNa, Santa Clara; co-founder ORCA-USA, Santa Clara, Calif.; founding mem. SpaandanB, Sunnyvale, Calif., 1998—. Monboshu scholar, Ministry of Edn., Japan, 1990—93. Mem.: Inst. of Electrochem. Soc. (assoc.), Inst. of Elec. and Electronic Engring. (assoc.). Achievements include patents for Low power analog equalizer with current mode digital to analog converter; Method for the formation of a boron-doped silicon gate layer underlying a cobalt silicide layer; Process for the formation of cobalt salicide layers employing a sputter etch surface preparation step; Method for the formation of a poly silicon layer with a controlled, small silicon grain size during semiconductor device fabrication; Apparatus and method for employing gain dependent biasing to reduce offset and noise in a current conveyer type amplifier; Low power analog equalizer with current mode digital to analog converter; Operational amplifier circuit with improved feedback factor. Avocations: writing mag. articles, novels, travel, reading history, music. Home: 3351 Tracy Dr Santa Clara CA 95051 Office: Nat Semiconductor Corp 2900 Semiconductor Dr M/S-E-170 Santa Clara CA 95052 Personal E-mail: ShimaKamal@aol.com. Business E-Mail: abu.kamal@nsc.com.

KAMANGAR, NADER, pulmonologist, educator; b. Tehran, Iran, June 20, 1970; s. Fereidoun and Fari Kamangar; m. Goli Khodadad, Dec. 22, 2001; 1 child, Maya. MD, St.George's U., Grenada, 1997. Diplomate Am. Bd. of Internal Medicine, 2001, Am. Bd. Internal Medicine-Pulmonary Disease, Am. Bd. Internal Medicine-Critical Care, Am. Bd. Sleep Medicine. Resident in internal medicine Highland Gen. Hosp., Oakalnd, Calif., 1997—2000; pulmonary, critical care and sleep medicine fellow Cedars-Sinai Med. Ctr., L.A., 2000—03; asst. clin. prof. UCLA Sch. of Medicine, 2003—. Edn. coord. pulmonary/critical care medicine Olive View-UCLA Med. Ctr., Sylmar, 2003—. Recipient Golden Apple award Best Sub-Specialist, UCLA, 2004, 2005. Fellow: Am. Acad. Sleep Medicine, Am. Coll. Physicians, Am. Coll. of Chest Physicians; mem.: Golden Key Nat. Honor Soc. Home: 15506 Moorpark St #323 Encino CA 91436 Office: Olive View-UCLA Med Ctr 14445 Olive View Dr 2B-182 Sylmar CA 91342-1495 Office Phone: 818-364-3205. Office Fax: 818-364-4573. Business E-Mail: kamangar@ucla.edu.

KAMANU, UCHEMADU CHEE, chemist; b. Umunteke, Asa, Abia, Nigeria, Aug. 8, 1946; s. Lazarus Kamanu Wokaru and Victoria Obiakwa Ogibe Okpor; m. Mgbechi Philomena Nwagboso, Apr. 19, 1984; children: Chihurum Anyatoha, Omumeoma Nneoma, Sowechi Chizuruoke. BS, U. Lagos, Nigeria, 1979; MBA, U. Nigeria, Enugu, Nigeria, 1983. Lectr. Oyo State Coll. Arts & Sci., Ile-Ife, Nigeria, 1979—80; sci. tchr. Anambra State Ministry of Edn., Enugu, Nigeria, 1981—82; bus. ops. and mktg. rsch. exec., dep. circulation mgr. Guardian Newspapers Ltd., Lagos, Nigeria, 1983—88; circulation mgr. Prime Publs. Ltd., Lagos, Nigeria, 1988—91; sales mgr. mag. The Daily Times of Nigeria PLC, Lagos, 1992—94; contr. bus. ops. Sentinel Pub. Ltd, Kaduna, Nigeria, 1994—95; substitute tchr. Balt. City Pub. Schs., 1996—97; chemist Balt. City Wastewater Lab., Patapsco, Md., 1997—. Mktg. cons. Kache Cons., Lagos, 1995—96. Author: (poem) Symphonies Of Words (Editor's award, 2001), The Best Poems & Poets Of 2001 (Editor's award, 2002), Poetry.com, The Colors of Life, 2003 (Editor's award, 2003), The Best Poems and Poets of 2003, 2003, Theatre of the Mind. Dir. personal ministries Pikesville S.D.A. Ch., Balt., 2004—. Mem.: Internat. Soc. Poets (hon.), Acad. Am. Poets (assoc.). Avocations: writing, preaching, bible teaching. E-mail: kamanu3@juno.com, tkflash1@hotmail.com.

KAMAT, ASHISH M, surgeon, oncologist; b. Livingston, NJ, Mar. 28, 1970; s. Madhav and Sukanti Kamat; m. Aparna A Kamat, Feb. 6, 1996; children: Ishan, Rhea. HSC, U. of Bombay, 1986—88. Diplomate U. of Bombay, 1994. Clin. specialist MD Anderson Cancer Ctr., Houston, 2002—03, asst. prof., 2003—. Program dir., urologic oncology fellowship MD Anderson Cancer Ctr., 2004—. Contbr. articles to profl. jours. Chemoprevention of Bladder Cancer, NIH, 2003. Achievements include research in chemoprevention of bladder cancer. Office: MD Anderson Cancer Ctr 1515 Holcombe Blvd Unit 1373 Houston TX 77030 Office Phone: 713-792-3250. Office Fax: 713-794-4824.

KAMAT, DEEPAK M., pediatrician; s. Madhusudan and Sumati Kamat; m. Ambika Mathur, Sept. 20, 1985; children: Amol D, Aarti D. MD, Bombay U., India, 1978; PhD, Bombay U., 1988. Diplomate Am. Bd. of Pediat., 1991. Dir. of med. edn. Regions Hosp., St. Paul, 1985—2002; dir., medicine/pediat. residency program U. of Minn., Mpls., 1997—2002; prof. of pediat. W.Va. U., Morgantown, 2002—03; prof. of pediat., vice chair of edn., dir., inst. of med. edn. Children's Hosp. of Mich., Detroit, 2003—. Recipient Best Tchr. Award, W.Va. U., 2001—02, Clinician of the Yr., 2002. Mem.: Am. Acad. of Pediat. (life). Office: Children's Hospital of Michigan 3910 Beaubien Blvd Detroit MI 48201 Office Phone: 313-966-2810. Office Fax: 313-993-0390. Personal E-mail: dkamat@med.wayne.edu.

KAMAT, PRASHANT V., chemistry educator; b. Binaga, India, July 6, 1953; BS, Karnatak U., Dharwad, India, 1972; MS, Bombay U., 1974, PhD, 1979. Rsch. assoc. Boston U., 1979-81, U. Tex., Austin, 1981-83; jr. scientist Notre Dame (Ind.) Radiation Lab., 1983-88, scientist, 1988-93, prin. scientist, 1993—. Editor: Semiconductor Nanoclusters, 1997, Rsch. in Chem. Intermediates, 2001—; mem. editl. adv bd. Langmuir, Jour. Advanced Oxidation Tech., Jour. Phys. Chemistry; contbr. more than 225 articles to profl. jours. Japan Soc. for Promotion of Sci. fellow, 1997. Mem. The Electrochem. Soc. (chmn. Fullerene group 2000—). Achievements include expertise in nanoparticle research, solar energy conversion and environmental remediation. Office: U Notre Dame Radiation Lab Notre Dame IN 46556

KAMBEITZ, MICHAEL (GUS) AUGUST, music educator; s. Michael Herman Albert Kambeitz and Jan DeShera. BA in Jazz Performance, San Jose (Calif.) State U., 1989; MusM, Wash. State U., 2001. Probation counselor (pt) Santa Clara County Juvenile Hall, San Jose, Calif., 1989—98; tchg. asst. Wash. State U., Pullman, Wash., 1999—2001, music instr., 2001—02; dir. of jazz studies West Valley Coll., Saratoga, Calif., 2001—. Musician Princess Cruise Lines, L.A., Calif., 1985—89, Power Plant, Balt., 1986, Beach Blanket Babylon, San Francisco, 1992—94, Theaterworks, Mt. View, Calif., 1997—99; musical dir. Gt. Am., Santa Clara, Calif., 1990; dir. bands Santa Teresa HS, San Jose, Calif., 1995—99; condr. World U. Games, Beijing, 2001—01. Composer: (songs) Island Dance, 2000, Fall, 2001. Named Best Composition - Vocal Ensemble, Lionel Hampton Jazz Festival, 2000, Best Male Vocalist - Tenor, 2001, Best composition -Big Band, 2001, Best Composition - Vocal Ensemble, 2001. Mem.: IAJE. Avocations: travel, working out. Office: West Valley College 14000 Fruitvale Ave Saratoga CA 95070 Office Phone: 408-741-2460.

KAMBER, VICTOR SAMUEL, political consultant; b. Chgo., May 7, 1943; s. Samuel J. and Cordelia A. Kamber. BA, U. Ill., 1965; MA, U. N.Mex., 1966; JD, Am. U., 1969; LLM, George Washington U., 1971. Adminstrv. asst. Congressman Seymour Halpern, Washington, 1969-72; asst. to pres. Bldg. & Constrn. Trades Dept., Washington, 1974-78; dir. AFL-CIO Labor Law Reform Task Force, Washington, 1978-80; pres., chief exec. officer The Kamber Group, Washington, 1980—. Nat. v.p. Ams. for Dem. Action, Washington; bd. dirs. BB&T Bank, Washington; sr. adv. bd. Am. League Lobbyists, Washington; bd. trustees The Nat. Theatre. Mem. Nat. Dem. Club. With U.S. Army, 1972-74. Mem. ACLU, NOW, Internat. Assn. Polit. Cons., Am. Assn. Polit. Cons. (bd. dirs. 1987-92, treas. 1991-92), Coalition Labor Union Women, Indsl. Rels. Rsch. Assn., Nat. Press Club, Local 35 Newspaper Guild, Phi Gamma Delta. Democrat. Presbyterian. Office: Carmen Group Comms 1301 K St NW Washington DC 20005 Home: 4527 29th St NW Washington DC 20008 Office Phone: 202-218-4156. Business E-Mail: kamberv@carmengroup.com.

KAMBOUR, ANNALIESE SPOFFORD, lawyer, media company executive; b. Schenectady, N.Y., Nov. 19, 1961; d. Roger Peabody and Virginia Louise (Dyer) K. BA, Harvard U., 1983, JD, 1986. Bar: Mass. 1986, N.Y. 1987, U.S. Tax Ct. 1987. Assoc. Paul, Weiss, Rifkind, Wharton & Garrison, N.Y.C., 1986—96, ptnr., 1996—2001; sr. v.p. tax Time Warner Inc., N.Y.C., 2001—. Mem. NOW, N.Y. State Bar Assn. Office: Paul Weiss Rifkind Wharton & Garrison Ste 4A 1285 Avenue Of The Americas Fl 21 New York NY 10019-6028

KAMBOUR, ROGER PEABODY, retired polymer physical chemist, researcher; b. Wilmington, Mass., Apr. 1, 1932; s. George Constantine and Ada Grace (Mattraw) K.; m. Virginia L. Dyer, Oct. 4, 1958 (div. Dec. 1982); children— Annaliese S., Christian R.; m. Barbara Jean Vivier, June 23, 1984; 1 child, Joshua V. BA cum laude, Amherst Coll., 1954; PhD in Chemistry, U. N.H., 1960. Rschr. GE R & D Ctr., Schenectady, N.Y., 1960-94, U. Mass. rsch. prof., 1994-99. Vis. prof. MIT, 1991; vis. scientist Nat. Inst. Standards & Tech., Washington, 1993. Mem. editl. bd. Polymer Engring. and Sci., 1968-87, Ann. Revs. of Materials Sci., 1985-89; contbr. articles on polymer physics and phys. chemistry to profl. publs.; patentee in field Supr. 1st ward Schenectady County Bd. Suprs., N.Y., 1964-65; mem. Schenectady County Charter Commn., 1964-65; mem. Schenectady City Hist. Dist. Commn., 1975-81; mem. art com. Schenectady Mus., 1975-82; mem. Nat. Ski Patrol, 1988-93; chmn. Freedom Forum, 1975-76. Fellow Am. Phys. Soc. (Ford High Polymer Physics prize 1985); mem. NAE, Am. Chem. Soc. (Union Carbide Chems. award 1968) Democrat. Unitarian Universalist. Avocations: choral singing, skiing, sailing. Home: 2572 Rosendale Rd Niskayuna NY 12309-1312 E-mail: kamviv@nycap.rr.com.

KAMEMOTO, FRED ISAMU, retired zoologist; b. Honolulu, Mar. 8, 1928; s. Shuichi and Matsu (Murase) K.; m. Alice Takeyo Asayama, July 20, 1963; children: Kenneth, Garett, Janice. Student, U. Hawaii, 1946-48; AB, George Washington U., 1950, MS, 1951; PhD, Purdue U., 1954. Research assoc., acting instr. Wash. State U., 1957-59; asst. prof. zoology U. Mo., 1959-62; asst. prof. U. Hawaii, Honolulu, 1962-64, assoc. prof., 1964-69, prof. zoology, 1969-94, prof. emeritus, 1995—, chmn. dept., 1964-65, 71-80, 81-90, dir. biology program, 1992-94. Vis. rsch. scholar Ocean Rsch. Inst., U. Tokyo, Biol. Lab., Fukuoka U., 1968-69; vis. prof. Coll. Agr. and Vet. Medicine, Nihon U., Tokyo, summer 1973, 1979; vis. scholar dept. biology Conn. Wesleyan U., 1975-76; sr. scientist dept. fisheries Nihon U., Tokyo, 1986; vis. fgn. rschr. Tropical Biosphere Rsch. Ctr. U. of Ryukyus Okinawa, Japan, 1994. Contbr. articles to profl. jours. Chmn. Hawaii State Natural Areas Reserve System Commn., 1985-88. Served with AUS, 1954-57. NSF grantee, 1960-79; National Oceanic and Atmospheric Administration grantee, 1985-89. Fellow AAAS; mem. Sigma Xi. Buddhist. Home: 3664 Waaloa Way Honolulu HI 96822-1151 Office: U Hawaii Dept Zoology Honolulu HI 96822

KAMEN, D. JONATHAN, film producer; b. N.Y.C., July 26, 1953; s. Saul and Helen K.; m. Angela Wessel, Aug. 21, 1977; children: Lisa Caitlin, Zachary. Student, Sch. Visual Arts, N.Y.C., 1970-71. Asst. to Jerry Abramowitz, Tony Petrocelli; asst. producer Horn/Griner, NYC, 1973-76; pres. Prodn. Analysis, Mt. Kisco, NY, 1981; exec. producer, ptnr. Sandbank Kamen & Ptnrs. (formerly Sandbank & Ptnrs.), NYC, 1976—94; exec. producer, founder @radical.media, NYC, 1994—. Exec. com. The Quills, NYC. Developer bidform computer program, 1981. Pres., Crow Hill Rd. Assn., Mt. Kisco, 1985. Recipient Gold Leo award, Cannes Film Festival, France, 1979, 88, Silver Leo award, 1981, Bronze Leo award, 1982, 88, 89; recipient Clio award for comml. prodn., 1980, Crystal Apple award, Palme D'Or award at Cannes (twice), Jay B. Eisenstat award from AICP, 2004. Mem. Dirs. Guild Am., Assn. Ind. Comml. Producers (v.p. 1982-84, bd. dirs. 1984-89, nat. pres. 1990—). Office: Radical Media Fl 6 435 Hudson St New York NY 10014 Office Phone: 212-462-1500.*

KAMEN, DEAN, biomedical engineer; BS, Worcester Poly. Inst. Founder AutoSyringe, Inc., 1976; biomed. engr. DEKA R&D Corp., Manchester, NH, 1988—92, pres., 1992—. Founder Sci. Enrichment Encounters, 1985, FIRST (For Inspiration & Recognition of Sci. & Tech.), 1989. Named N.H. Bus. Leader of the Year, 1996; recipient Engineer of the Year award, Design News Magazine, 1994, Hoover Medal, 1995, Edwin Church medal, ASME, 1997, Heinz Award, 1998. Mem.: NAE. Achievements include developer of the first portable insulin pump, 1978; developer portable dialysis machine (awarded 'medical product of the year' by Design News Magazine), 1993; holder of more than 100 US patents. Office: DEKA R&D 340 Commercial St Manchester NH 03101-1121

KAMEN, MICHAEL ANDREW, lawyer; b. N.Y.C., May 13, 1952; s. Milton and Renée (Weiss) K. AB, Columbia Coll., 1974; JD, U. Miami, Fla., 1978. Bar: Fla. 1978, U.S. Dist. Ct. (so. dist.) Fla. 1979, U.S. Ct. Appeals (11th cir.) 1987, U.S. Supreme Ct. 1988. Assoc. Fine & Burton, P.A., Ft. Lauderdale, Fla., 1979-84; of counsel Tworoger & Sader, P.A., Ft. Lauderdale, 1984-88; founding ptnr. Kamen & Orlovsky, P.A., West Palm Beach, Fla., 1988—. Author: (with others) Civil Trial Practice, 1994. Recipient Probate Law award Palm Beach County Bar Assn., 1993. Mem. ABA, Assn. Trial Lawyers Am., Acad. Fla. Trial Lawyers. Office: Kamen & Orlovsky PA 1601 Belvedere Rd West Palm Beach FL 33406-1541

KAMEN, PAULA, journalist, playwright; b. Chgo., 1967; B in Journalism, Univ. Ill., 1989. Former reporter Kenosha (Wis.) News. Vis. rsch. scholar, gender studies program Northwestern Univ., Chgo., 1994—. Author: (books) Feminist Fatale: Voices from the Twentysomething Generation Explore the Future of the Women's Movement, 1991, Her Way: The Report on Young Women's Evolving Sexual Choices, 1999, All in My Head, 2005; contributor: books Shiny Adidas Track Suits and the Death of Camp: The Best of Might Magazine, 1998; playwright: Seven Dates with Seven Writers; (plays) Jane: Abortion and the Underground; commentaries, book reviews: in NY Times, Washington Post, Salon, Ms. Chicago Tribune, In These Times. Named one of Chicago's 100 Most Influential Women, Crain's Chicago Business mag., 2004.*

KAMENTSKY, LOUIS AARON, biophysicist; b. Newark, July 28, 1930; s. Harry and Etta (Brodsky) K.; m. Marcia Alpern, Aug. 28, 1955; children: Lee, Howard, Ellen. BSEE, N.J. Inst. Tech., 1952; PhD, Cornell U., 1956. Mem. staff Columbia U. ERL, N.Y.C., 1954-55, Bell Telephone Labs., Murray Hill, N.J., 1956-60, IBM Research, N.Y.C., 1960-68; pres. Biophysics Systems, Mahopac, N.Y., 1968-76; v.p. rsch. Ortho Diagnostics Systems, Cambridge, Mass., 1976-88; chmn. CompuCyte Corp., Cambridge, Mass., 1988—. Vis. scientist Karolinska Inst., Stockholm, 1966; sr. rsch. scientist MIT, Cambridge, 1981-88. Patentee in field; contbr. articles to profl. jours. Home: 180 Beacon St Boston MA 02116-1408 Office: Compucyte Corp 12 Emily St Cambridge MA 02139-4507 E-mail: lakam@verizon.net.

KAMERICK, EILEEN ANN, corporate financial executive, lawyer; b. Ravenna, Ohio, July 22, 1958; d. John Joseph and Elaine Elizabeth (Lenney) K.; m. Victor J. Heckler, Sept. 1, 1990; 1 child, Connor Joseph Heckler. AB in English summa cum laude, Boston Coll., 1980; postgrad., Exeter Coll., Oxford, Eng., 1981; JD, U. Chgo., 1984, MBA in Finance and Internat. Bus. with honors, 1993. Bar: Ill. 1984, U.S. Dist. Ct. (no. dist.) Ill. 1985, Mass. 1986, U.S. Ct. Appeals (7th cir.) 1988, U.S. Supreme Ct. 1993. Assoc. Reuben & Proctor, Chgo., 1984—86, Skadden, Arps et al, Chgo., 1986—89; atty. internat. Amoco Corp., Chgo., 1989—93, sr. fin. mgr. corp. fin., 1993—96, dir. banking and fin. svcs., 1996—97, v.p., treas., 1998—99, Whirlpool Corp., Benton Harbor, Mich., 1997; v.p., gen. counsel GE Capital Auto Fin. Svcs., Barrington, Ill., 1997—98; v.p., CFO BP Am., 1998—2000; exec. v.p. & CFO United Stationers Inc., Des Plaines, Ill., 2000—01; exec. v.p., CFO Bcom3, Chgo., 2001—03; CFO Heidrick & Struggles, 2004—. Advisor fin. com. Am. Petroleum Inst., 1992; bd. dirs. Heartland Alliance, ServiceMaster, Westell Tech. Vol. adv. 7th Cir. Bar Assn., Chgo., 1987—; bd. dirs. Boys & Girls Clubs of Chicago. Mem. Phi Beta Kappa. Roman Catholic. Home: 2627 N Greenview Ave Chicago IL 60614 Office: 233 S Wacker Dr Ste 4200 Chicago IL 60660 Office Phone: 312-496-1557. Personal E-mail: eakesq@aol.com.

KAMERIN, KIM K., music educator; b. Las Vegas, Sept. 1, 1967; s. Kris Kim Kamerin and Mary Louise Browder; m. Elizabeth A. Emmett, May 28, 1993; children: Benjamin Sebastian, Christopher Jameson. MusB, U. Nev., 1993, MusM, 1998. Cert. tchr. K-12 music Calif., 2001, Nev., 1994. Organist St. Joan Arc Cath. Ch., Las Vegas, 1989—96; instr. piano Las Vegas Acad. Performing Arts H.S., 1993—95, choir dir., instr. music, 1996—2001; choir dir. Swainston Mid. Sch., 1994—96; choir dir. varsity men's glee club U. Nev., 1998—2000; instr. music Coll. Sequoias, Visalia, Calif., 2001—, Bakersfield C.C., 2001—02, Reedley Coll., 2003—. Rec. engr. Coll. Sequoias, 2001—; propr. Monsterfingers Studios, Dinuba, Calif., 2003—; pianist The Emerton Club, Tulare, Spiritual Awareness Ctr., Visalia; accompanist, asst. choir dir. children's choir Nev. Sch. Arts, Las Vegas. Composer: Go, Lovely Rose, The Children's Hair Turned White (Regional U. Theater Competition Hon. Mention, 1991), Gloria (Am. Choral Director's Assn. Composer's of the Future, 1994). Music ministry Spiritual Awareness Ctr., Visalia, 2004. Named Concerto Contest Winner, U. Musical Soc., 1987, Mid. Sch. Tchr. of Yr., Clark County, Alexis Pk. Hotel and Gov. Bob Miller, 1996; recipient Presser award Acad. Excellence, U. Nev., Music Dept., 1990; grantee, Coll. Sequoias Found., 2004; Devos scholar, U. Nev., Music Dept., 1987. Mem.: Music Educators Nat. Conv., Am. Soc. Composers and Pubs., Calif. Music Educators Assn., Calif. Edn. Assn., Am. Choral Dirs. Assn. (nev. state repertoire and std. chmn., women's choir 1997—2001, conv. steering com. 2003—04), Phi Kappa Phi. Office Phone: 559-730-3754. Personal E-mail: kimk@cos.edu.

KAMERMAN, SHEILA BRODY, social worker, educator; b. Jan. 7, 1928; d. S. Lawrence and Helen (Golding) Brody; m. Morton Kamerman, Sept. 11, 1947; children: Nathan Brody, Elliot Herbert, Laura Kamerman-Katz. BA, NYU, 1946; MSW, Hunter Coll., 1966; D in Social Welfare, Columbia U., 1973; PhD (hon.), York U., Eng., 1998. Social worker N.Y.C. Dept. Social Svcs., 1966-68; social work supr. Bellevue Psychiat. Hosp., 1968-69; assoc. prof. social work Hunter Coll., 1977-79; from rsch. assoc. to sr. rsch. assoc. Columbia U. Sch. Social Work, 1971-79, assoc. prof. social policy and planning, 1979-81; prof. Sch. Social Work Columbia U., 1981—, Compton Found. Centennial prof., 1996—, interim dean Sch. Social Work, 2001—02. Dir. Columbia U. Inst. for Child and Family Policy, 1998—; chair NAS-NRC panel on work, family and community, 1980-82; mem. Com. Child Devel. Rsch. and Pub. Policy, 1983-88; mem. com. on prenatal care Inst. Medicine, 1986-88; cons. in field; mem. numerous social welfare coms. and adv. bds.; mem. Gov. Cuomo's Task Force on Poverty and Welfare Reform, 1986-87, adv. com. on Work and Family, 1987-88, UN Expert groups on social welfare and family policies; mem. Inst. Medicine/Nat. Rsch. Coun. bd. on children and families, 1998—. Author: (with Alfred J. Kahn) Not for the Poor Alone, 1975, Social Services in the United States, 1976, Social Services in International Perspective, 1977, Family Policy: Government and Families in Fourteen Countries, 1978, Child Care, Family Benefits and Working Parents, 1981, Parenting in an Unresponsive Society, 1980, Maternity and Parental Benefits and Leaves, 1980, Helping America's Families, 1982, Maternity Policies and Working Women, 1983, Income Transfers for Families with Children, 1983, Child Care: Facing the Hard Choices, 1987, The Responsive Work Place, 1987, Child Support: From Debt Collection to Social Policy, 1988, Mothers Alone: Strategies for a Time of Change, 1988, Privatization and the Welfare State, 1989, Social Services for Children, Youth and Families in the United States, 1990, Child Care, Parental Leave, and the Under 3's, 1991, A Welcome for Every Child, 1994, Starting Right: How America Neglects Its Youngest Children and What We Can Do About It, 1995, Children in big Cities, 1996, Confronting the New Politics of Child and Family Policies, (series of 6 reports), 1997, Family Change and Family Policies in Britain, Canada, New Zealand and the United States, 1998, Big Cities in the Welfare Transition, 1998, Contracting for Child and Family Services, 2000; editor: Early Childhood Education and Care, 2001; co-editor: (with Ronald A. Feldman) The Columbia University School of Social Work, 2001; (with Alfred J. Kahn) Beyond Child Poverty, the Social Exclusion of Children, 2002; contbr. articles to profl. jours. Fellow Ctr. Advanced Study in Behavioral Scis., 1983-84; recipient Hexter award Hunter Coll. Sch. Social Work, 1977, Nat. Leadership award in Social Policy, Heller Sch. Brandeis U., 1989, Lifetime Achievement award Social Welfare Policy and Practice, 2002, Significant Lifetime Achievement award Coun. on Social Work Edn., 2005, Significant Lifetime Achieve. award Coun. on Social Work Edn.; named to Hunter Coll. Hall of Fame, 1981, Columbia U Sch. Social Work Hall of Fame, 2003. Mem. NASW, Am. Pub. Human Svcs. Assn., Assn. Policy Analysis and Mgmt., Nat. Acad. Social Ins., Phi Beta Kappa. Home: 1125 Park Ave New York NY 10128-1243 Office: Columbia U Sch Social Work Mail Code 4600 1255 Amsterdam Ave New York NY 10027 Office Phone: 212-851-2270. Business E-Mail: sbk2@columbia.edu.

KAMEROW, MARTIN LAURENCE, accountant; b. Washington, Aug. 25, 1931; s. Jacob and Anne (Adler) K.; m. Corinne Perlmeter, Mar. 24, 1951; children: Deborah, Jacqueline, Haskell. BCS, Benjamin Franklin U., 1951, MCS, 1952. CPA D.C., Md. Staff acct. various CPA firms, Washington, 1949-52; pvt. practice acctg., 1952-59; ptnr. Kamerow & Serber, Washington, 1959-63; sr. ptnr. Harab, Kamerow & Serber, Washington, 1963-74; pres. Harab, Kamerow & Assocs., P.C., Washington, 1974-94, Snyder, Kamerow & Assocs., P.C., Rockville, Md., 1994—96; ptnr. Kamerow, Weintraub & Swain, 1996—. Con. to editor U.S. News and World Report, 1972-84; expert witness on legal and tax matters, D.C., Md., 1975—; lectr. Am. U., 1956-65, tax seminars N.Y. U. Law Inst. and others; mem. faculty 39th NYU Inst. on Fed. Taxation, 1980; comml. arbitrator Am. Arbitration Assn.; mem. Ginat Food Adv. Bd., 1997-98. Author: (with S.A. Kaufman) Consolidated Financial Statements, 1958), (with S. Green) U.S. News and World Reports Book on Income Taxes, 1971, 4th edit., 1974, (with Margaret Daly) Teach Your Wife to Be a Widow, How to Save on Taxes and Stay Out of Trouble, (with others) Statements on Responsibility in Tax Practice, 1988, (with others) Matthew Bender's Tax Service, 1988; contbr. articles to profl. jours. Bd. dirs. World Coun. Synagogues, Suburban Hosp. Inc., Suburban Hosp. Health Care Sys. Inc., Suburban Hosp. Found.; chmn. Jewish Chaplaincy Svcs.; pres. Brandeis Dist. Zionist Orgn. Am., Shma V'Ezer Sch., Hebrew Free Burial Soc.Wolfson Cardiac Surgery Found., 1993-95, Save A Child's Heart Found., 1996—; mem. fin. com., bd. dirs. Suburban Hosp., Bethesda, Md.; active United Jewish Appeal Fedn. Greater Washington, advance gifts chmn., treas., trustee endowment fund. Recipient Nat. Svc. award Kidney Found., 1972, Disting. Alumni award Benjamin Franklin U. Alumni Assn., 1977, Louis D. Brandeis award, 1982, Pub. Svc. award D.C. Inst. CPAs, 1990, Joseph Ottenstein award for Pub. Svc., Jewish Social Svc. Agy., 1993. Mem. AICPA (fed. tax civ. subcom. on responsibilities, Pub. Svc. award 1990), Assn. Practicing CPAs (pres. 1972-73), Greater Washington Soc. CPA's (Profl.

Achievement award 2002), Cosmos Club. Home: 7420 Westlake Ter Bethesda MD 20817 Office: Kamerow Weintraub & Swain LLP 11400 Rockville Pike Ste 800 Rockville MD 20852-3004 E-mail: MKamerow@KWSCPA.com.

KAMERSCHEN, DAVID ROY, economist, educator; b. Chgo., Dec. 8, 1937; s. Robert R. and Elsie Barkell Kamerschen; m. Gena Faye Hampton, Apr. 27, 1985; children: Christine, Steven, Laura, Robert, David, Caroline. Student, Ind. U., 1959-60; BS in Econs., Miami U., Oxford, Ohio, 1959, MA, 1960; PhD in Econs., Mich. State U., 1964. Instr. dept. econs. Miami U., Oxford, Ohio, 1960-61; asst. instr. Mich. State U., summer 1962, 64; asst. prof. econs. U. Washington, St. Louis, 1964-65 65-66; assoc. prof. econs. U. Mo.-Columbia, 1966-68, prof., 1968-74; prof., head dept. econs. U. Ga., Athens, 1974-80, Disting. prof., Jasper N. Dorsey chair, 1980—. Cons. in field; guest appearance Mac Neil-Lehrer Report; host TV show Kamerschen Report Author: Readings in Microeconomics, 1969, (with Walter L. Johnson) Macroeconomics: Selected Readings, 1970, Readings in Economic Development, 1972, (with George M. Vredeveld) Economics, 1975, (with Lloyd Valentine) Intermediate Microeconomic Theory, 1981, (with Albert L. Danielsen) Current Issues in Public-Utility Economics, 1983, (with Albert L. Danielsen) Telecommunications in the Post-Divestiture Era, 1986, (with James C. Bonbright and Albert L. Danielsen) Principles of Public Utility Rates, 2nd edit., 1988, (with Richard McKenzie and Clark Nardinelli) Economics, 1989, Money and Banking, 10th edit., 1992; editor Rev. Social Theory, 1973-74; mem. editorial bds.: Bus. and Govt. Rev., 1968-72, Internat. Behavioral Scientist, 1970—, Indsl. Orgn. Rev., 1974-80, Rev. Indsl. Orgn., 1982-91, Rev. Fin. Econ., So. Econ. Jour., 1978-82, Mgmt. and Decision Econs., 1980-94; contbr. over 200 articles to profl. jours. Recipient Outstanding Grad. Tchr. award U. Ga., 1978; Swift Outstanding Tchr. of Yr. award, 1985; Amy Hayden scholar, 1959; Mich. State U. fellow, 1964; Disting. Research award U. Ga. Coll. Bus. Adminstrn., 1984; Swift Outstanding Teaching award, 1985. Mem. Am. Econ. Assn., So. Econ. Assn., Nat. Assn. Forensic Economists, ABA, (assoc), Phi Kappa Phi, Delta Sigma Pi, Beta Gamma Sigma, Omicron Delta Kappa, Sigma Alpha Epsilon Home: 3818 Sweet Bottom Dr Duluth GA 30096-1416 Office: Department of Economics Terry Coll Bus 536 Brooks Hall Athens GA 30602-6254 Office Phone: 706-542-3681. Office Fax: 706-542-8774. Personal E-mail: davidrkamerschen@bellsouth.net. Business E-Mail: davidk@terry.uga.edu.

KAMERSCHEN, ROBERT JEROME, retired investment company executive; b. Laurium, Mich., Feb. 16, 1936; s. Robert Raymond and Elsie D (Barsanti) Kamerschen; m. Judith A Campbell, July 26, 1958; children: Kathryn, Carol, Jean. BS, Miami U., Oxford, Ohio, 1957, MBA, 1958. Exec. sales trainee Nat. Cash Register, Gary, Ind., 1958—59; mgmt. trainee Foote Cone & Belding, Chgo., 1959—60; dir. consumer mktg. Scott Paper Co., Phila., 1960—71; v.p. mktg. Revlon Inc., N.Y.C., 1971—73; sr. v.p. mktg. ops. Dunkin Donuts Inc., Randolph, Mass., 1973—77; pres., COO Chanel Inc. and Christian Dior Parfums Inc., N.Y.C., 1977—79; pres., CEO Max Factor & Co., Hollywood, Calif., 1979—83; sr. v.p. Norton Simon Inc., N.Y.C., 1980—83; pres., CEO Max Factor & Co., Hollywood, Calif., 1979—83; exec. v.p., office of chmn. sector exec. Norton Simon Inc., 1981—83; pres., COO Mktg. Corp. of Am., 1984-87; pres., CEO RKO Six Flags Entertainment, Inc. div. Wesray Capital Corp., N.Y.C., 1987—88; chmn., CEO ADVO Inc., Windsor, Conn., 1988—99; CEO Dimac Mktg. Corp, Windsor, 1999—2002, pvt. investor, strategic adv., 2002—; chmn. Survey Sampling Internat., 2005—. Disting. practitioner, lectr. U. Ga. Coll. Bus. Adminstrn., 1979—81; guest lectr. various univs. and trade assns.; bd. dirs. Radio Shack Corp., IMS Health Inc., R.H. Donnelley Corp., Vertrue, Inc., Linens 'n Things, Inc., MDC Ptnrs. Inc.; mem. bus. adv. coun., exec.-in-residence Miami U., 1979—82. Trustee, 1st vice chmn. Emerson Coll., 1984—89; trustee Columbia Coll., 1993—96, trustee Bushnell Hall, 1995—2002; trustee Wadsworth Atheneum, 1990—; regent U. Hartford, 1998—2005. Mem.: Metropolitan Club, NY Athletic Club, Sigma Alpha Epsilon, Delta Sigma Pi, Beta Gamma Sigma. Home: 204 Parade Hill Rd New Canaan CT 06840-4132 E-mail: RKamerschen@msn.com.

KAMIL, ALAN C., biology professor; s. Frank and Henrietta Kamil; m. Ellen A. Gorenstein, June 16, 1963; children: Seth I., Melissa E. Gamage. BA cum laude, Hofstra U., 1963; PhD, U. of Wis., Madison, 1967. From asst. to assoc. to full prof. U. of Mass., Amherst, 1967—91; prof. biol. scis. and psychology U. of Nebr., Lincoln, 1991—, George Holmes Univ. prof., 2001—. Dir. Cedar Point Biol. Sta., Ogallala, Nebr., 1999—; vis. fellow Macquarie U., Sydney, Australia, 1998—99. Editor: (book) Foraging Behavior: Ecological, Ethological and Psychological Approaches, Foraging Behavior, Evolutionary Psychology and Motivation, Animal Cognition in the Field; editor, author: textbook Patterns of Psychology; contbr. sci. papers to profl. jours. Mem., chair sch. com. Gateway Regional Schs., Huntington, Mass., 1982—90. Recipient rsch. grants, NSF, 1971—, NIMH, 1988—, Evans fellowship, Otago U., Dunedin, New Zealand, 1989. Fellow: APA, Am. Ornithologists' Union, Animal Behaviour Soc.; mem.: Internat. Soc. for Behavioural Ecology. Office: U Nebr Bio Scis Manter Hall Lincoln NE 68588-0118 E-mail: akamil@unl.edu.

KAMIL, ELAINE SCHEINER, pediatric nephrologist, educator; b. Cleve., Jan. 26, 1947; d. James Frank and Maud Lily (Severn) Scheiner; m. Ivan Jeffery Kamil, Aug. 29, 1970; children: Jeremy, Adam, Megan. BS magna cum laude, U. Pitts., 1969, MD, 1973. Diplomate Am. Bd. Pediat., Am. Bd. Pediatric Nephrology. Intern in pediat. Children's Hosp. Pitts., 1973-74, resident in pediat., 1974-76; clin. fellow in pediatric nephrology Sch. Medicine, UCLA, 1976-79, acting asst. prof. pediat., 1979-80, asst. clin. prof. pediat., 1988-91, assoc. clin. prof. pediat., 1991-97, clin. prof. pediat., 1997—; rsch. fellow in nephrology Harbor-UCLA Med. Ctr., Torrance, Calif., 1980-82; med. dir. The Children's Clinic of Long Beach, Calif., 1984-87; med. dir. pediat. nurse practitioner program Calif. State U., Long Beach, 1984-87; assoc. dir. pediatric nephrology and transplant immunology Cedars-Sinai Med. Ctr., LA, 1990—2001, clin. dir. pediatric nephrology, 2001—. Adj. asst. prof. pediat. Harbor-UCLA, Torrance, Calif., 1983-87, UCLA, 1987-88; cons. in pediatric nephrology Hawthorne (Calif.) Cmty. Med. Group, 1981-2000. Author chpts. to books; contbr. articles to profl. jours. Pres.-elect med. adv. bd. Nat. Kidney Found. So. Calif., 2000-02, pres. med. adv. bd., 2002-04. Recipient Vol. Svc. award Nat. Kidney Found., 1998. Mem. AAUW, Am. Soc. Nephrology, Am. Soc. Pediatric Nephrology, Am. Fedn. Clin. Rsch., Internat. Soc. Nephrology, Internat. Soc. Pediatric Nephrology, Internat. Soc. Peritoneal Dialysis, Renal Pathology Soc., So. Calif. Pediatric Nephrology Assn. (chair steering com. 1998—), Nat. Kidney Found. So. Calif. (med. adv. bd. 1987-96, rsch. com. 1987-90, chmn. pub. info. med. adv. bd. 1988-92, handbook com. 1988, co-chair med. adv. bd. cmty. svcs. com. 1992-93, chair-elect patient svcs. and cmty. edn. com. 1993-94, chair patients svcs. and cmty. edn. com. 1994-95, kidney camp summer vol. physician 1988-91, 93, 94, 97, 99-2003, Arthur Gordon award 1991, Exceptional Svc. award 1992, Exceptional Leadership and Support award 1995, bd. dirs. 1995-96, 2002—), Alpha Omega Alpha, Phi Beta Kappa. Office: Cedars Sinai Med Ctr 1165 WT 8700 Beverly Blvd Los Angeles CA 90048-1865 Office Phone: 310-423-4747.

KAMIL, MICHAEL, education educator; BA, Tulane U., 1964; MA, U. Wis., 1967, PhD, 1969. Faculty assoc. U. Tex., 1969—71; faculty assoc., dir. Reading Clini Ariz. State U., 1971—72; asst. prof. psychology U. Minn., Duluth, 1972—74; asst. prof. edn., dir. Reading Clinic Purdue U., West Lafayette, Ind., 1978—80; asst. prof. edn. U. Ill., Chgo., 1980—89; assoc. prof. ednl. theory and practice Ohio State U., 1990—92, prof. ednl. theory and practice, 1992—96; prof. edn. Stanford (Calif.) U., 1997—. Vis. prof. ednl. theory and practice Ohio State U., 1989—90; mem. Rand Reading Study Group, 2000—, Nat. Inst. Child Health and Devel. Nat. Reading Panel, 1998—; chair tech. com. Nat. Reading Conf., 1998—2001. Mem. editl. adv. bd.: Jour. Literacy Rsch., 1996—. Office: Stanford U Sch Edn 485 Lasuen Mall Stanford CA 94305-3096*

KAMIN, BLAIR DOUGLASS, architecture critic; b. Red Bank, N.J., Aug. 6, 1957; s. Arthur Z. and Virginia P. Kamin. BA, Amherst Coll., 1979; M in Environ. Design, Yale U., 1984; HHD (hon.), Monmouth U., 2003. Reporter Des Moines Register, 1984-87; suburban reporter Chgo. Tribune, 1987—91; culture news reporter, 1992; architecture critic, 1992—. Nominating juror Pulitzer Prize, 2000, 02. Author Why Architecture Matters: Lessons from Chicago, 2001, contbr. articles to profl. jours. Recipient Nat. Edn. Reporting award Edn. Writers Assn., 1985, Edward Scott Beck award Chgo. Tribune, 1990, George Polk award for Criticism, 1996, Pulitzer Prize for Criticism, 1999, Inst. Honor for Collaborative Achievement, AIA, 1999, Peter Lisagor award for Exemplary Journalism, 1993, 94, 95, 96, 97, 98, 2001, 03, Engring. Journalism award Am. Assn. Engring. Socs. and Engring. Found., 1996, Richard Driehaus Found. Preservation award Landmarks Preservation Coun. Ill., 1997, Wright Spirit award Frank Lloyd Wright Bldg. Conservancy, 2001, Presdl. citation AIA, 2004; named to Chgo. Media Elite, Crains Chgo. (Ill.) Bus., 2005. Jewish. Office Phone: 312-222-4138. Business E-Mail: bkamin@tribune.com.

KAMIN, SHERWIN, lawyer; b. NYC, Feb. 5, 1927; s. Theodore and Esther K.; children: Lawrence O., Samuel N., Janet C., David W., Julia E.; m. S. Jeanne Hall, Oct. 1, 1993. BBA, CCNY, 1948; LLB, Harvard U., 1951: Bar: NY 1953. Asst. reporter Fed. Income Tax Project, Am. Law Inst., Cambridge, Mass., 1951—52; assoc. Botein, Hays, Sklar & Herzberg, NYC, 1952—62, ptnr., 1962—68, Kramer, Levin, Naftalis & Frankel, NYC, 1968—93, of counsel, 1993—2001, Fulton, Rowe & Hart and predecessors, NYC, 2002—. Served with USN, 1945-46. Mem. ABA, Assn. Bar City NY, NY State Bar Assn., Am. Law Inst., Am. Coll. Tax Counsel. Home: 163 W 76th St New York NY 10023-8325 Office: Fulton Rowe & Hart One Rockefeller Plz New York NY 10020-2002 Office Phone: 212-586-0700. E-mail: sherwink@aol.com.

KAMIN, WILLIAM STEPHEN, food products executive, photographer; b. Chgo., Feb. 3, 1930; s. Emil Zola and Berta Magid; m. Adrienne Bloomberg, Aug. 28, 1955 (dec. June 15, 2001); children: Steven B., Andrew G. PhB, U. Chgo., 1947; BS, U. Ill., 1952. CPA, Ill. Staff acct. D. Himmelblau & Co., Chgo., 1955-57; budget analyst Westinghouse Electric Co., West Mifflin, Pa., 1957-63; contr. Std. Fruit Co., La Ceiba, Honduras, 1963-68, gen. mgr. Guayaquil, Ecuador, 1968-70; v.p. fin. Dole Fruit Co., Honolulu, 1970-72; v.p. ops. Castle & Cooke, Inc., San Francisco, 1972-78, v.p. strategic planning, 1978-82; pvt. practice photography Menlo Park, Calif., 1985—. Cons. William S. Kamin Cons., Atherton, Calif., 1982-85; adj. prof. Coll. Notre Dame, Belmont, Calif., 1984-85, U. Santa Clara, Calif., 1986, Golden Gate U., San Francisco, 1987. Author, photographer: Tenderloin, 1989. Bd. dirs., fin. cons. Valley Inst. of Theatre Arts, Saratoga, Calif., 1986-87; docent Coyote Point Mus., San Mateo, 1992-95, Fitzgerald Marine Res., Pacifica, Calif., 1995-97. Mem. Sons in Retirement. Avocations: tennis, travel. Home and Office: 169 Stone Pine Ln Menlo Park CA 94025-3050 Office Phone: 650-322-4300. E-mail: billkamin@comcast.net.

KAMINE, BERNARD S., lawyer; b. Dec. 5, 1943; m. Marcia Phyllis Haber; children: Jorge H., Benjamin H., Tovy H. BA, U. Denver, 1965; JD, Harvard U., 1968. Bar: Calif. 1969, Colo. 1969. Dep. atty. gen. Calif. Dept. Justice, L.A., 1969-72; asst. atty. gen. Colo. Dept. Law, Denver, 1972-74; assoc. Shapiro & Maguire, Beverly Hills, Calif., 1974-76; ptnr. Kamine Ungerer LLP and predecessors, L.A., 1976—. Bd. dirs., sec. Pub. Works Stds., Inc., 1996—; mem. adv. com. legal forms Calif. Jud. Coun., 1978—82; bd. dirs. Constrn. Industry Rsch. Bd., 2000—02. Author: Public Works Construction Manual: A Legal Guide for California, 1996; contbr. chpts. to legal texts and articles to profl. jours. Mem. L.A. County Dem. Ctrl. Com., 1982-85; mem. Pacific S.W. regional bd. Anti-Defamation League, 1982—, pres. bd., 1998-00, assoc. nat. commr., 1995—. Col. USAR, 1969-2002. Decorated Meritorious Svc. medal, Joint Svcs. Commendation medal, Army Commendation medal, Expert Infantryman badge. Mem. ABA, Calif. State Bar (chair conf. dels. calendar coordinating com. 1991-92), L.A. County Bar Assn. (chair Superior Cts. com. 1977-79, chair constrn. law subsect. of real property sect. 1981-83), Engring. Contractors' Assn. (bd. dirs. 1985—, affiliate chair 1992-93, affiliate DIG award 1996, Polit Action Com. Disting. Svc. Medal 2004), Assoc. Gen. Contractors Calif. (L.A. dist. bd. dirs. 1995-00), Am. Constrn. Insps. Assn. (bd. registered constrn. inspectors 1990-97), Beavers, Res. Officers Assn. (pres. chpt. 1977-78), Omicron Delta Kappa. Office: 350 S Figueroa St Ste 250 Los Angeles CA 90071-1201 Office Phone: 213-972-0119.

KAMINS, BARRY MICHAEL, lawyer; b. Oct. 3, 1943; s. Abe and Evelyn Bertha (Goffen) K.; m. Fern Louise Kamins, Mar. 30, 1968; 1 child, Allyson. BA, Columbia U., 1965; JD, Rutgers U., 1968. Bar: NY 1969, US Dist. Ct. (ea. and so. dists.) NY 1973, US Supreme Ct. 1974. Asst. dist. atty., 1969-73; dep. chief Criminal Ct. Bur., 1971-73; ptnr. Flamhaft, Levy, Kamins & Hirsch, 1973—. Chmn. grievance com. 2d and 11th Jud. Dist., 1994-98; adj. prof. Fordham Law Sch., Bklyn. Law Sch., Bklyn. Law Sch.; adj. prof. criminal law NY Tech. Coll.; apptd. spl. prosecutor, Kings County, 1990-92; chmn. oversight com. Criminal Def. Orgn. 2d Appellate Divsn., 1997—. Author: The Social Studies Student Investigates the Criminal Justice System, 1978, New York Search and Seizure, 1991; contbr. numerous articles on criminal law to profl. jours. Mem. ABA, NY State Bar Assn. (v.p., chair com. prof. discipline 1999-2004), Bklyn. Bar Assn. (past pres., chair jud. com. 1994-98, v.p.), Kings County Criminal Bar Assn. (past pres.), Assn. Bar City NY (chair jud. com. 1998-2001, exec. com. 2001-2005, chair exec. commn., 2004-2005, v.p. 2005—, mem. continuing legal edn. bd., bd. editors NY Law Jour.). Office: 16 Court St Brooklyn NY 11241-0102 Office Phone: 718-237-1900. Business E-Mail: b.kamins@flkhlaw.com.

KAMINS, EDWARD, information technology executive; 2 children. BS in Elec. Engring., Stevens Inst. Tech.; MBA in Mktg., C.W. Post Ctr., L.I. U. Various positions Digital Equip. Corp.; sr. v.p., bus. devel. for Avnet Computer Mktg. Avnet, Inc., 1996—99, sr. v.p., 1999—, pres., Avnet Applied Computing, 1999—2003, chief info. officer, 2003—. Bd. dirs. Lupus Found. of Am. Named named one of top tech. innovators, Info. Week mag., 2004; recipient Altruism Award, Lupus Found. of Am., 2002. Office: Avnet Inc 2211 S 47th St Phoenix AZ 85034

KAMINS, JOHN MARK, lawyer; b. Chgo., Feb. 7, 1947; s. David and Beulah (Block) K.; m. Judith Joan Sperling, May 5, 1968; children: Robert, Heather. AB with high honors and distinction, U. Mich., 1968, JD, 1970. Bar: Mich. 1971, Fla. 1991. Assoc., Honigman Miller Schwartz and Cohn, Detroit, 1971-75, ptnr., 1976—; lectr. Inst. on Continuing Legal Edn. Pres. Mich. chpt. Leukemia and Lymphoma Soc., 1991-92, 93-96, nat. trustee, 1996—, nat. exec. com., 1997—, chmn. nat. bd. trustees, 2004—; pres. Goodwill Industries of Greater Detroit Found., 2001-03; pres. Temple Beth El, Bloomfield Hills, Mich., 1994-96. Mem. Nat. Assn. Bond Lawyers (vice chmn. com. on opinions 1985-86), Mich. Bar Assn. (chairperson, pub. corp. law sect. 1992-93). Jewish. Home: 1315 Stuyvessant Rd Bloomfield Hills MI 48301-2144 Office: Honigman Miller Schwartz & Cohn llp 2290 First National Bldg Detroit MI 48226

KAMINSHINE, STEVEN J., dean, law educator; BA summa cum laude, NYU; JD, DePaul U. Sch. Law. Ptnr. labor and employment law practice, N.Y.C.; atty. Nat. Labor Rels. Bd., Washington, DC; mem. law faculty Ga. State U., Coll. Law, 1985—, assoc. prof., assoc. dean academic affairs, interim dean, 2004—. Contbr. articles to law jours. Mem.: Atlanta Bar Assn. (chair Labor and Employment Sec.), Ga. Bar Assn. Office: Ga State U College of Law 140 Decatur St Rm 422 Atlanta GA 30303 Office Phone: 404-651-2035. Office Fax: 404-651-2570. E-mail: skaminshine@gsu.edu.

KAMINSKI, DONALD LEON, surgeon, gastroenterologist, educator; b. Elba, Nebr., Nov. 9, 1940; s. Edwin and Irene (Syntek) K.; m. Maureen M. Cudmore, Nov. 28, 1964; children: Christian, Julie, Jane, Kathryn. BS, Creighton U., 1962, MD, 1966. Diplomate: Am. Bd. Surgery. Intern. St. Louis U., 1966-67, resident in surgery, 1967-71; attending surgeon St. Louis U. Hosp., 1972—, dir. gen. surgery, 1982—. Mem. Soc. Univ. Surgeons, Am. Surg. Assn., Central Surg. Soc., Alpha Omega Alpha Republican. Roman Catholic. Home: 1025 Joanna Ave Saint Louis MO 63122-1821 Office: St Louis U 3635 Vista at Grand PO Box 15250 Saint Louis MO 63110-0250

KAMINSKI, LEON R., lawyer; b. LaPorte, Ind., Nov. 21, 1924; s. Stanley A. and Stephanie L. Kaminski; m. Norma Jean Lynn Kaminski, Oct. 28, 1950; children: Daniel, Anne, Lynn, Paul, James, William. AB, Ind. U., 1946; JD, Ind. U., Indpls., 1950. Bar: Ind. 1950, U.S. Dist. Ct. (no. and so. dists.) Ind. 1950, U.S. Ct. Appeals (7th cir.) 1967, U.S. Supreme Ct. 1980. Pvt. practice, LaPorte, 1950—57; dep. pros. atty. Prosecutor's Office, LaPorte, 1953—58; ptnr. Newby, Lewis, Kaminski & Jones, LaPorte, 1958—94, sr. counsel, 1995—. Pres. LaPorte City Bar Assn., 1967, LaPorte County Bar Assn., 1972, Ind. State Bar Assn., 1982—83; mem. Ind. Supreme Ct. Bd. Bar Examiners, 1971—75, Ind. Supreme Ct. Character and Fitness Com., 1991—. Charter mem. LaPorte County Sheriff's Merit Bd., 1970—81; chmn. LaPorte City March of Dimes Dr., 1960; v.p. men's coun. Roman Cath. Diocese Gary, Ind., 1968—76. Named diplomat, Def. Trial Counsel Ind., 1982; recipient Disting. Alumni Svc. award, Ind. U. Sch. Law, Indpls., 1988, Sagamore of the Wabash, 1999. Fellow: Ind. Bar Found. (fellows chair 1991—92, 50 Yr. award 2000), Am. Bar Found., Internat. Soc. Barristers (state chair 1985), Am. Coll. Trial Lawyers (state chair 1981—82). Roman Catholic. Avocations: golf, tennis, travel. Office: Newby Lewis Kaminski & Jones 916 Lincolnway La Porte IN 46350 Office Phone: 219-362-1577.

KAMINSKI, MARGARET, retired librarian; b. Detroit, Mar. 16, 1944; d. John Joseph and Gertrude (Malak) K. BFA, Wayne State U., 1966, MSLS, 1969. Artist Henry Ford Hosp., Detroit; reference librarian Detroit Pub. Libr., 1969-74, 76-85, pub. rels. librarian, 1974-76, asst. mgr., 1985—99. Presenter in field. Author: Martinis, 1972, La Vida de la Mujer, 1979, Guatemalan Diary, 1982; editor: Moving to Antarctica, 1975; editor (jour.) Moving Out: A Feminist Lit. & Arts Jour., 1970—. Sec. Friends of Polish Art, Detroit, 1984-91. Mini-grantee Mich. Coun. for Arts, 1975, 80—. Mem.: AAUW, UAW, NOW (pres. Macomb County chpt. 1993—97, exec. bd. 1997—, mem. clean water action com.), Sierra Club, Audubon Soc., Mich. Archeol. Soc., Detroit Pub. Libr Staff Assn. (newsletter editor 1970—73). Democrat. Avocations: hiking, camping, backpacking, photography, printing and publishing. Home: 22333 Hanson Ct Saint Clair Shores MI 48080-1411

KAMINSKI, PATRICIA JOYCE, lab administrator; d. Lucile Anne Roberts and Tadeusz Kaminski; children: Grant Matthew, Joshua Alan. Cert. dental tech., So. Calif. Coll. Med. and Dental Careers, 1975. Cert. advanced dental implant lab. Germany, spl. jaw reconstruction Calif., prosthetic tng. ITI Straumann, Mass. Implant specialist Haupt Dental Lab., Brea, Calif., 1992—2002; tech. services mgr. Dentsply Friadent Ceramed, Lakewood, Colo., 2002—03; implant dept. mgr. Dynotech Dental Lab., Corona, Calif., 2003—04; owner Kaminski Dental Lab., Orange, Calif., 2004—. Tech. cons. Home Bus., Orange, 2000—. Avocations: travel, boating, 10K races, yoga, gardening. Personal E-mail: pkaminski4043@sbcglobal.net.

KAMINSKY, ALAN, lawyer; b. Jersey City, Feb. 2, 1958; BA, NYU, 1980; JD, Hofstra U., 1983. Bar: NY 1983, NJ 1983, US Dist. Ct. Ea. Dist. NY, US Dist. Ct. So. Dist. NY. Ptnr. Wilson, Elser, Moskowitz, Edelman & Dicker LLP, NYC, chmn. gen. liability/toxic tort practice team. Author: A Complete Guide to Premises Security Litigation, 1995, A Complete Guide to Lead Paint Poisoning Litigation, 1998. Mem.: ABA, Am. Trial Lawyers Assn., Def. Rsch. Inst., NY State Bar Assn., Bronx County Bar Assn. (mem. judiciary com.), NY State Trial Lawyers Assn. Office: Wilson Elser Moskowitz Edelman & Dicker LLP 23rd Fl 150 E 42nd St New York NY 10017-5639 Office Phone: 212-490-3000 ext. 2370. Office Fax: 212-490-3038. Business E-Mail: kaminskya@wemed.com.

KAMINSKY, ALICE RICHKIN, retired literature educator; b. N.Y.C. d. Morris and Ida (Spivak) Richkin; m. Jack Kaminsky (dec.); 1 son, Eric (dec.). BA, NYU, 1946, MA, 1947, PhD, 1952. Mem. faculty dept. English NYU, 1947-49, Hunter Coll., 1952-53, Cornell U., 1954-57, Broome Community Coll., 1958-59, Cornell U., 1959-63, SUNY, Cortland, 1963—, prof., 1968-91, prof. emerita, 1991—; faculty exch. scholar State U. NY. Author: George Henry Lewes as Critic, 1968, Logic: A Philosophical Introduction, 1974; editor: Literary Criticism of George Henry Lewes, 1964, Chaucer's Troilus and Criseyde and the Critics, 1980, The Victim's Song, 1985; contbr. more than 75 articles and revs. to numerous jours. Mem.: MLA, Chaucer Soc. *At a very early age I learned that life is fragile, that many loved and lovely things die or disappear. My way of coping with that knowledge was to latch on to the work ethic. This meant working to achieve some end.*

KAMINSKY, ANATOL, political science professor, writer; b. Ukraine, May 17, 1925; came to U.S., 1960; s. Gregory and Eudokia Kaminsky; m. Tatjana Kripacky; 1 son, Taras. PhD, Ukrainian Free U., Munich, 1990; cert. in internat. rels., London Sch. Econs./Polit. Sci., 1958. Editor Ukrainian Ind., Munich, 1953-58; v.p. rsch. Prolog Assocs., N.Y.C., 1960-81; sr. editor Suchasnist, N.Y.C., 1962-83; dir., chief editor Ukrainian svc. Radio Free Europe/Radio Liberty, Munich, 1983-89; prof. internat. rels. Ukrainian Free U., 1993—, dean faculty of law and socio-econ. scis., 1996-98. Guest prof. Lviv (Ukraine) State U., 1993— Author: 13 books in Ukrainian. Chmn. polit. coun. Rep. of Ukrainian Supreme Liberation Coun., N.Y.C. and Munich, 1996—; assoc. mem. nat. coun. Dem. Party of Ukraine, 1996—. Recipient Internat. Orlyk prize Dem. Party of Ukraine, 1994. Mem. Orgn. Ukrainian Nationalists (chmn. 1991—). Home: 68 The Rise Warwick NY 10990-4234

KAMINSKY, ARTHUR CHARLES, lawyer; b. Bronx, N.Y., Dec. 29, 1946; s. Daniel and Claire (Sternberg) K.; m. Andrea Lynn Polin, Dec. 28, 1969; children: Alexis Kate, Thomas Suradet, Eric Vorapong. BA cum laude with distinction, Cornell U., 1968; JD, Yale U., 1971. Bar: N.Y. 1974, U.S. Dist. Ct. (so. dist.) N.Y. 1975, U.S. Tax Ct. 1977, U.S. Supreme Ct. 1984. Assoc. Paul Weiss Rifkind Wharton & Garrison, 1973-74; ptnr. Taft & Kaminsky, N.Y.C., 1974-81; pres. A.C.K. Sports, Inc., N.Y.C., 1977-95, Profl. Sports Investors, Inc., N.Y.C., 1982-89; exec. v.p. Tha Marquee Group, Inc. 1995-2000; pres. Athletes and Artists, 2002—; mem. selection com. U.S. Olympic Hockey Team, Mpls., 1980. Co-author: One Goal; A Chronicle of the 1980 U.S. Olympic Hockey Team, 1984; weekly columnist N.Y. Times, 1973-77; analyst H.S. and coll. sports broadcasts Telecare TV, 2001—. Intern for 3d congl. dist. N.Y. Adlai E. Stevenson Meml., 1967. Dep. campaign mgr. Lindsay for Pres., N.Y.C., 1972; del. credentials com. Dem. Nat. Conv., Miami, 1972; adminstrv. asst. Rep. Michael Harrington, Washington, 1972-73; pres. Plandome Civic Assn., 1981-82; trustee African-Am. Athletic Assn., 1992-99. Recipient Outstanding Sr. award Cornell U., 1968, Friends of Edn. award N.Y. State Teachers Union, 1988; named one of the 100 Most Powerful Poeple in Sports, The Sporting News, 1991-92; finalist Thurman Arnold Moot Ct. competition, 1970; inducted charter mem. Jericho H.S. Hall of Fame, 1991. Mem. N.Y. State Bar Assn., Assn. of Bar of City of N.Y., Com. Entertainment and Sports, ABA, New Sch. Soc. Research (lectr.), Sports Lawyers Assn. (lectr.), Quill and Dagger, Friars Club (bd. govs. 2000-05), Plandome Country Club, Phi Beta Kappa (hon.). Democrat. Jewish. Home: 157 Colonial Pky Manhasset NY 11030-1414

KAMINSKY, MANFRED STEPHAN, physicist; b. Koenigsberg, Germany, June 4, 1929; came to U.S., 1958; s. Stephan and Kaethe (Gieger) K.; m. Elisabeth Moellering, May 1, 1957; children: Cornelia K.B., Mark-Peter. First diploma in physics, U. Rostock, Germany, 1951; PhD in Physics magna cum laude, U. Marburg, Germany, 1957. German Research Soc. fellow and grad. asst. in physics U. Rostock, 1950-52; lectr. Rostock Med. Tech. Sch., 1952; German Research Soc. fellow and research asst. Phys. Inst., U. Marburg, 1953-57, sr. asst., 1957-58; research asso. Argonne (Ill.) Nat. Lab., 1958-59, asst. physicist, 1959-62, assoc., 1962-70, sr. physicist, 1970-86, dir. Surface Sci. Center-CTR Program, 1974-80, dir. Tribology Program, 1984-86; sole propr. Surface Treatment Sci. Internat., Hinsdale, Ill., 1986—. Cons. Office Tech. Assessment U.S. Congress, 1986, NRC com. on tribology, 1986-88; guest prof. Inst. Energy, U. Que., Montreal-Varennes, 1976-82;

E.W. Mueller lectr. U. Wis., Milw., 1978; symposium chmn. Internat. Conf. Metall. Coatings, 1985-93. Author: Atomic and Ionic Impact Phenomena on Metal Surfaces, 1965; contbr. articles to profl. jours.; editor: Radiation Effects on Solid Surfaces, 1976; co-editor: Surface Effects on Controlled Fusion, 1974, Surface Effects in Controlled Fusion Devices, 1976, Dictionary of Terms for Vacuum Science and Technology, 1980; patentee in field. Bd. dirs. Com. 100, Hinsdale, 1970-75, 90-92, pres., 1973-74; pres. St. Vincent de Paul Soc., Hinsdale, 1972-73. Named Outstanding New Citizen of Year Citizenship Council Chgo., 1968; Japanese Soc. Promotion of Sci. fellow, 1982. Fellow Am. Phys. Soc.; mem. Am. Chem. Soc., Scientific Research Soc., Research Soc. Am., AAAS, Union German Phys. Socs., Am. Vacuum Soc. (sr., trustee 1982-84, chmn. Midwest sect. 1967-68, co-founder Gt. Lakes chpt., dir. 1968-70, chmn. fusion tech. div. 1980-81, editorial bd. jour. 1978-83, hon. 1986), Internat. Union Vacuum Sci., Techs. and Applications (chmn. fusion div. 1984-86), Sigma Xi. also: 300 Galen Dr Apt 506 Key Biscayne FL 33149-2177 Office: 906 S Park Ave Hinsdale IL 60521-4519

KAMINSKY, PHYLLIS, international consulting executive; b. Montreal, Que., Can., Dec. 1, 1936; came to U.S., 1945, naturalized, 1958; d. Julius and Betty (Shapiro) Levitt; m. Samuel Kaminsky, June 24, 1971; children: David, Glenn. BA in Polit. Sci., U. Mich., 1957; postgrad., Columbia U., 1957-58. Sec. spkrs. bur. Fgn. Policy Assn., N.Y.C., 1957-58; editor disarmament procs. UN, Geneva, 1958; secretarial supr. McKinsey and Co., Geneva, 1963-64; adminstrv. asst. Chrysler Internat. S.A., also Internat. Rsch. Cons. S.A., Geneva, 1959-63, Grey Advt. Internat., N.Y.C., 1965-67; exec. asst. Lee Burdick Advt., Inc., N.Y.C., 1967-68; bilingual press attache S.B.M. Resort Complex, Monte Carlo, 1968-69; pub. rels. asst. Mayor's Com. for 25th Anniversary of UN, N.Y.C., 1970-71; consular corps liaison officer N.Y.C. Dept. Pub. Events, 1967-68; media cons., pub. rels. adv. United Jewish Appeal, N.Y.C., 1971-80; media cons. Bush for Pres. Campaign, Pa., Ill., 1980; dep. dir. comm. Coalition for Reagan-Bush, 1980; press sec. to sr. fgn. policy adv. Office of Pres.-Elect, 1980-81; press liaison White House, Nat. Security Coun., 1981; dir. Office of Pub. Liaison, USIA, 1981-83; corp. dir. select appts. PLC (NASDAQ), 1997-99; corp. dir. Leica Geosystems, LLC, 2001—, Vedior N.V., 2001—, Kaba Mas Corp., 2002—; dir. Pegasus Homeland Security, LLC, 2004—. Dir. UN Info. Ctr., Washington, 1983-88; pres. Kaminsky Assocs., 1989—; mem. U.S. ofcl. del. 29th session UN Commn. on Status of Women, 1982. Co-founder Jerusalem Women's Seminar, 1979—; mem. adv. com. trade policy Dept. Commerce and U.S. Trade Rep., 1989-93; mem. bd. visitors Nat. Def. Univ., 2002—. Recipient Gold Key award PR News, 1984. Mem. AAUW, Pub. Rels. Soc. Am., Internat. Pub. Rels. Soc., Women in Comm. (chmn. pub. affairs adv. bd. 1984-85), Exec. Women in Govt., Internat. Women's Forum (bd. dirs. 1986-89), Internat. Women's Media Found. (pres. 1989), Internat. Inst. Women's Polit. Leadership (bd. dirs. 1989-94), The European Inst. (exec. com. 1989), Internat. Rep. Inst. (bd. dirs. 1989-94), USAF Acad. (presdl. appointee bd. visitors 1990-92), Assn. Univs. for Rsch. in Astronomy (bd. dirs. 1992-96), U.S. Commn. for Preservation Ams. Heritage Abroad (presdl. appointee), Nat. Def. U. Found. (bd. dirs. 1995-98), Kids Votings USA (bd. dirs. 1995-98); mem. ofcl. delegation, 59th Session, UN Human Rights Comn.

KAMISAR, YALE, lawyer, educator; b. N.Y.C., Aug. 29, 1929; s. Samuel and Mollie (Levine) K.; m. Esther Englander, Sept. 7, 1953 (div. Oct. 1973); children: David Graham, Gordon, Jonathan; m. Christine Keller, May 10, 1974 (dec. 1997); m. Joan Russell, Feb. 28, 1999. AB, NYU, 1950; LLB, Columbia U., 1954; LLD, CUNY, 1978. Bar: D.C. 1955. Rsch. assoc. Am. Law Inst., N.Y.C., 1953; assoc. Covington & Burling, Washington, 1955-57; assoc. prof., then prof. law U. Minn., Mpls., 1957-64; prof. law U. Mich., Ann Arbor, 1965-92, Clarence Darrow disting. univ. prof., 1992—2004; prof. San Diego U., 2004—. Vis. prof. law Harvard U., 1964-65, San Diego U., 2000-02; disting. vis. prof. law Coll. William and Mary, 1988; cons. Nat. Adv. Commn. Civil Disorders, 1967-68, Nat. Commn. Causes and Prevention Violence, 1968-69; mem. adv. com. model code pre-arraignment procedure Am. Law Inst., 1965-75. Reporter-draftsman: Uniform Rules of Criminal Procedure, 1971-73; author: (with J.H. Choper, S. Shiffrin and R.H. Fallon), Constitutional Law: Cases, Comments and Questions, 9th edit., 2001; (with W. LaFave, J. Israel and N. King) Modern Criminal Procedure: Cases and Commentaries, 11th edit., 2005, Criminal Procedure and the Constitution: Leading Cases and Introductory Text, 2002; (with F. Inbau and T. Arnold) Criminal Justice in Our Time, 1965; (with J. Grano and J. Haddad) Sum and Substance of Criminal Procedure, 1977, Police Interrogation and Confessions: Essays in Law and Policy, 1980; contbr. articles to profl. jours. Served to 1st lt. AUS, 1951-52. Recipient Am. Bar Found. Rsch. award, 1996. Office: U Mich Law Sch 625 S State St Ann Arbor MI 48109-1215

KAMLET, MARK, provost; B in Math., Stanford U.; M in Econs. and Stats., PhD in Econs., U. Calif., Berkeley. Former assoc. dean Coll. Humanities and Social Scis. Carnegie Mellon U., Pitts., former head dept. social and decision scis., former dean H. John Heinz III Sch. Pub. Policy and Mgmt., provost, H. John Heinz III prof. econs. and pub. policy. Past mem. U.S. Panel on Cost Effectiveness in Health and Medicine; past mem. NIH panels; courtesy faculty appointment dept. psychiatry U. Pitts. Sch. Medicine. Contbr. articles to profl. jours. Mem. exec. com. Ford Found. Pub. Policy and Internat. Affairs Fellowship Program; 1st vice chair Pitts. Partnership for Neighborhood Devel.; sec. Pitts. Parks Conservancy; chair Allegheny County Coun. Econ. Devel. Advisors, Pitts. Recipient Vernon prize for outstanding article of yr., Jour. Policy Analysis and Mgmt., 1992. Mem.: Nat. Assn. Schs. Pub. Affairs and Adminstrn. (exec. com.), Assn. Pub. Policy Analysis and Mgmt. (exec. com.). Office: Carnegie Mellon U Office of Provost 5000 Forbes Ave Pittsburgh PA 15213

KAMLOT, ROBERT, performing arts executive; b. Vienna, Nov. 28, 1926; came to U.S., 1938, naturalized, 1943; s. Paul and Elsa (Wilhelm) K.; m. Jayne Bullard, Sept. 18, 1948. Student, CCNY, Syracuse U., Hunter Coll., N.Y.C. Freelance mgr. Broadway prodns., 1964-71; prodn. exec. Zev Bufman Prodns., N.Y.C., 1969-71; co.-mgr. Much Ado About Nothing, N.Y.C., 1972, Two Gentlemen From Verona (nat. co.), Los Angeles, 1973. Gen. mgr. N.Y. Shakespeare Festival, 1973-83; gen. mgr. The Real Thing, Sunday in the Park With George, Biloxi Blues, The Odd Couple, Moon for the Misbegotten, Whoopi Goldberg, Social Security, Long Day's Journey Into Night, 1983-86, (nat. tour) Catskills on Broadway, Fool Moon, Wrong Turn at Lungfish; prodr. Hayfever, 1986; gen. mgr. Carole Shorenstein Hays Enterprises; prodr. Fences, 1987; gen. mgr. Martin Starger/The Really Useful Co. Lend Me a Tenor, 1988, Cates Films-Elmer Gantry, 1991-92, Martin Starger The Red Shoes, 1992, Fool Moon (European prodn.), 1994, BIG The Musical, 1995. Served with AUS, 1944. Mem. Assn. Theatrical Press Agts. and Mgrs., Tony Nominating Commn. Home: 175 W 93rd St New York NY 10025-9313 Office Phone: 212-840-8400. Personal E-mail: jaybob175@aol.com.

KAMM, CHARLES WILLIAM, conductor, music educator, singer; b. Belleville, Ill., Jan. 18, 1969; s. Charles William and Lynne Kamm. BA, Earlham Coll., 1991; MusM, Mich. State U., 1992; M Mus. Arts, Yale U., 2004. Dir. choirs, lectr. in music U. Mass., Boston, 1993—96; dir. choirs, vis. asst. prof. music Vassar Coll., Poughkeepsie, NY, 1996—2002; dir. choirs, asst. prof. music Scripps Coll., Claremont, Calif., 2005—. Chorus master: concert preparation Finnish Radio Chamber Choir, tenor soloist: concerts and radio broadcasts, chorusmaster: Classical Music Festival, Eisenstadt, Austria, prin. asst. conductor: Yale Camerata, music dir.: Reredos Male Vocal Ensemble, Amare Cantare, Durham, New Hampshire, acting assoc. conductor: Harvard U., asst. conductor: Harvard Radcliffe Collegium Musicum, tenor: Robert Shaw/Carnegie Hall Chorus. Pres. Reredos Male Vocal Ensemble, Boston, 1999—2002. Conducting fellow, Harvard U., 1993—96, Conductors Inst., Hartford, 1998, Fulbright fellow, J. William Fulbright Fgn. Scholarship Bd., 2004—05. Fellow: Phi Beta Kappa; mem.: Am. Guild Organists, Am. Musicological Soc., Chorus Am., Conductors Guild, Am. Choral Dirs. Assn. (quarterfinalist conducting awards 2003). Office: Scripps Coll Music Dept 1030 Columbia Ave Claremont CA 91711 Office Phone: 909-607-3266. Personal E-mail: charles@ckamm.com.

KAMM, JOHN, non-profit organization administrator, human rights activist; BA, Princeton U., 1972; MA, Harvard U., 1975. Founded chem. co., Hong Kong and China, 1979; Hong Kong rep. Nat. Coun. U.S.-China Trade, 1976—81; pres. Am. C. of C., Hong Kong, 1990; dir. Nat. Com. U.S.-China Rels.; founder, chmn., exec. dir. Dui Hua Found., San Francisco, 1999—. Dir. rsch. project in human rights diplomacy Stanford U. Named MacArthur Fellow, 2004; recipient Best Global Practices award, U.S. Govt., 1997, Eleanor Roosevelt Human Rights award, 2001. Office: Dui Hua Found 450 Sutter St Ste 900 San Francisco CA 94108 Office Phone: 415-986-0536. Office Fax: 415-986-0579. E-mail: duihua@duihua.org.

KAMM, LINDA HELLER, lawyer; b. NYC, Aug. 25, 1939; d. Seymour A. and Mary Heller; children: Lisa, Oliver. BA in History, Brandeis U., 1961; LLB, Boston Coll., 1967. Bar: Mass. 1967, D.C. 1978, U.S. Supreme Ct. 1985. Counsel Dem. Study Group, Washington, 1968-71; counsel select com. on coms. U.S. Ho. of Reps., Washington, 1973-75, gen. counsel budget com., 1975-77; gen. counsel U.S. Dept. Transp., Washington, 1977-80; ptnr. Foley and Lardner, Washington, 1980-84, of counsel, 1984-95; pvt. practice, 1995—; of counsel Boies, Schiller & Flexner, 2001—. Address: 188 E 70th St Apt 24C New York NY 10021-5170

KAMMAN, ALAN BERTRAM, communications consulting company executive; b. Phila., Jan. 25, 1931; s. Daniel Lawrence and Sara Belle K.; m. Madeleine Marguerite Pin, Feb. 15, 1960; children: Alan Daniel, Neil Charles. BCE, Swarthmore Coll., 1952. With Bell Tel. Co. Pa., Phila., 1952-69, Arthur D. Little, Inc., Cambridge, Mass., 1969-85, v.p. telecommunications scis., 1977-81, v.p. corp. staff, 1981-86; nat. dir. telecommunications markets KPMG Peat Marwick, Lexington, Mass., 1987-91; mng. dir. Global Consulting Group, St. Helena, Calif., 1991—; dir. Cambridge (Mass.) Strategic Mgmt. Group, 1992—; v.p. Symmetrix, Lexington, Mass., 1994-96; exec. dir. Vt. Telecomm. Application Ctr., 1998—. Chmn. adv. bd. grad. program telecommunications U. San Francisco, Intelevent, Europe, Telecom 75, Telecom 79, Telecom 83, Telecom 91, Telecommunications Mag.; world rep. KPMG Peat Marwick to Internat. Telecommunications Union, UN. Contbr. articles to jours. in field. Bd. dirs. U.S. Coun. World Comms. Yr.; dir., sec. Vt. Coun. World Affairs, 2005—; dir., chmn. Vt. Symphony Orch., 1999—, bd. region one. Mem. Appalachian Club (v.p. ops., bd. dirs.).

KAMMAN, CURTIS WARREN, retired ambassador; b. Chgo., Jan. 15, 1939; s. Glenn Forrest and Mildred Isabel (Merry) Kamman; m. Mary Glasgow Curtis, Feb. 10, 1962; children: Edward, John, W Stephen. BA, Yale U., 1959; postgrad., U. Washington, 1964-65. Joined Fgn. Service, U.S. Dept. State, 1960-2000; various diplomatic positions Am. embassies, Washington, Mexico City, Hong Kong, Moscow, Nairobi, 1960-80; dir. East African Affairs, Washington, 1980-82; polit. counselor Am. embassy, Moscow, 1982-84, minister, counselor, 1984-85; prin. officer U.S. Interests sect. Swiss embassy, Havana, Cuba, 1985-87; dep. asst. sec. U.S. Dept. State, Washington, 1987-91; amb. to Chile Santiago, 1991-94; amb. to Bolivia, 1994-97; amb. to Colombia, 1997-2000; ret., 2000. Vis. instr. Univ. Notre Dame, 2001—04, adj. instr., 2004—. Mem. vestry All Saints Ch., Saugatuck, Mich., 2002—05; bd. dirs. Fgn. Students Sch., Havana, 1985—87. Mem.: Am. Acad. Diplomacy, Phi Beta Kappa. Episcopalian. Avocation: choral singing. Address: 2236 Lakeshore Dr Fennville MI 49408-9715 E-mail: ckamman@nd.edu.

KAMMAN, WILLIAM, historian, educator; b. Geneva, Ind., Mar. 23, 1930; s. Harry August and Ruth Lois (Shoemaker) K.; m. Nancy Ellen Prichard, Apr. 19, 1957; children: Frederick William, Elizabeth Ellen, David Paul. AB, Ind. U., 1952, PhD, 1962; MA, Yale U., 1958. Tchr. pub. schs., Bloomington, Ind., 1955-57, 58-59; asst. prof. history U. North Tex. (formerly North Tex. State U.), Denton, 1962-66, assoc. prof., 1966-69, prof., 1969—, chmn. dept. history, 1977-89, 93-94, assoc. dean arts and scis., 1996—2002, interim dean arts and scis., 1997-98. Author: A Search for Stability: United States Diplomacy Toward Nicaragua, 1968; contbg. author: Makers of American Diplomacy, 1974, Ency. World Biography, 1973, 87—, Ency. Am. Fgn. Policy, 1978, 2002, The War of 1898 and U.S. Interventions, 1898-34: An Ency., 1994. Mem. Denton Planning and Zoning Commn., 1976-79, 86-92. Served with U.S. Army, 1952-54. Mem. Am. Hist. Assn., Orgn. Am. Historians, Soc. Historians Am. Fgn. Relations (exec. sec.-treas. 1985-89), Phi Alpha Theta Methodist. Home: 2225 Scripture St Denton TX 76201-3707 Office: U North Tex History Dept Denton TX 76203

KAMMASH, TERRY, nuclear engineering educator; b. Sult, Jordan, Jan. 27, 1927; came to U.S., 1946; m. Sophie C. Kammash, Dec. 31, 1956; 1 child, Dean. BS, Pa. State U., 1952, MS, 1954; PhD, U. Mich., 1958. Instr. engring. mechs. Pa. State U., University Park, 1952-54, U. Mich., Ann Arbor, 1954-58, from asst. prof. to assoc. prof. nuclear engring., 1958-67, prof. nuclear engring., 1967—. Physicist Lawrence Livermore Lab., Livermore, Calif., 1961-62; rsch. scientist Los Alamos (N.Mex.) Nat. Lab., summer 1958; cons. Battelle N.W. Labs., Richland, Wash., 1975-78, Argonne (Ill.) Nat. Lab., 1972-77. Author: Fusion Reactor Physics, 1975; editor/author: Fusion Energy in Space Propulsion, 1995. Fellow AIAA (assoc., nuclear propulsion com. 1993)), Am. Nuclear Soc. (fusion tech. com. 1979), Arthur Holly Compton award 1977, Outstanding Achievement award 1977), Am. Phys. Soc. (plasma physics com. 1977). Office: U Mich Dept Nuclear Engring and Radiol Scis Ann Arbor MI 48109

KAMMEN, MICHAEL, historian, educator; b. Rochester, N.Y., Oct. 25, 1936; s. Jacob M. and Blanche (Lazerow) K.; m. Carol Koyen, Feb. 26, 1961; children: Daniel Merson, Douglas Anton. AB, George Washington U., 1958, LHD (hon.), 1991; MA, Harvard U., 1959, PhD (Bowdoin prize), 1964. Mem. faculty Cornell U., 1965—, Newton C. Farr prof. Am. history and culture, 1973—, chmn. dept. history, 1974—76, dir. ctr. for humanities, 1977—80. Vis. prof. history Yale U., 2005-06; 1st holder chair in Am. history Ecole des Hautes Etudes en Sciences Sociales, Paris, France, 1980-81; Commonwealth Fund lectr. in Am. history U. London, 1976. Author: A Rope of Sand: The Colonial Agents, British Politics and the American Revolution, 1968, Deputyes and Libertyes: The Origins of Representative Government in Colonial America, 1969, People of Paradox: An Inquiry Concerning the Origins of American Civilization, 1972 (Pulitzer Prize for history, 73), Colonial New York: A History, 1975, A Season of Youth: The American Revolution and the Historical Imagination, 1978, Spheres of Liberty: Changing Perceptions of Liberty in American Culture, 1986, A Machine That Would Go of Itself: The Constitution in American Culture, 1986 (Francis Parkman and Henry Adams prizes, 87), Selvages & Biases: The Fabric of History in American Culture, 1987, Sovereignty and Liberty: Constitutional Discourse in American Culture, 1988, Mystic Chords of Memory: The Transformation of Tradition in American Culture, 1991, Meadows of Memory: Images of Time and Tradition in American Art and Culture, 1992, The Lively Arts: Gilbert Seldes and the Transformation of Cultural Criticism in the United States, 1996, In the Past Lane: Historical Perspectives on American Culture, 1997, American Culture, American Tastes: Social Change and the 20th Century, 1999, Robert Gwathmey: The Life and Art of a Passionate Observer, 1999, A Time to Every Purpose: The Four Seasons in Am. Culture, 2004; editor: What is the Good of History?: Selected Letters of Carl L. Becker, 1900-1945, 1973, The Origins of the American Constitution: A Documentary History, 1986, Contested Values: Democracy and Diversity in American Culture, 1994; editor-in-chief: The Past Before Us: Contemporary Historical Writing in the United States, 1980. Bd. dirs. Social Sci. Rsch. Coun., 1980-83. Fellow NEH, 1967, 72-73, 84-85, 97-98, Humanities Ctr. Johns Hopkins U., 1968-69, Ctr. for Advanced Study in Behavioral Scis., Stanford, 1976-77; Guggenheim fellow 1980-81, Regents fellow Smithsonian Instn. 1990, Times-Mirror Found. Rsch. Prof. Am. Studies, The Huntington Libr., San Marino, Calif., 1993-94; guest scholar Woodrow Wilson Ctr., Washington, 1997-98. Mem.: AAAS, Soc. Am. Historians, Mass. Hist. Soc., Am. Antiquarian Soc., Orgn. Am. Historians (exec. bd. 1989—92, pres. 1995—96), Am. Hist. Assn. (coun. 1976—79), Phi Beta Kappa. Office: Cornell U Dept History McGraw Hall Ithaca NY 14853 Home: 110 Iroquois Rd Ithaca NY 14850

KAMMERER, KELLY CHRISTIAN, lawyer; b. N.Y.C., Nov. 29, 1941; s. William Henry and Edith (Langley) K.; m. Nancy Davis Frame, Oct. 2, 1999. BA, U. Notre Dame, 1963; LLB, U. Va., 1968. Bar: Va. 1968, N.Y. 1969, D.C. 1969, Fla. 1969. Peace Corps vol., Colombia, 1963-65; Reginald Heber Smith atty./fellow U. Pa., Washington, 1968-70; atty.-advisor, dep. gen. counsel Peace Corps, Washington, 1970-74; atty.-advisor AID, Dept. State, Washington, 1975-76, asst. gen. counsel, 1976-78, sr. dep. gen. counsel, 1978-82, legal counselor, 1981-82, dir. congl. rels., 1983-89; mission dir. Kathmandu, Nepal, 1989-93, counselor to the agy., 1994-99; vice chmn., U.S. rep. OECD/DAC, Paris, 1999—. Recipient Disting. Honor award AID, 1979, 83, Equal Opportunity award, 1982; presdl. rank of Disting. Sr. Exec., 1984, 89, Meritorious Sr. Exec., 1997. Mem. Inter-Am. Bar Assn., Soc. Internat. Law. Address: Psc 116 Box Oecd/aid APO AE 09777-5000 also: 11 bis Blvd Jules Sandeau 75016 Paris France

KAMP, BARBARA ANN, designer, poet, photographer, educator, artist; b. Beckley, W.Va., Sept. 15, 1945; d. Robert Long and Virginia Ruth Greene; m. Larry Emanuel McRary (div.); 1 child, Robert Arnold McRary; m. Douglas Brian Kamp, May 24, 1997. Grad., Happy Valley HS. Pvt. practice, Lenoir, NC, 1976—85, Statesville, NC, 1986—89, Davidson, NC, 1990—. Cons. in field. One-woman shows include 1st Union Bank, Statesville, NC, 1995, Mooresville Arts Guild, 1996; author: Reflections & Reflections I, 2000, numerous poems; voice (audiotape) Sounds of Poetry, 1999—2004, workshops and seminars. Pres. ways and means West Lenoir (NC) Elem. Sch., 1976; v.p. Mooresville (NC) Art Guild, 1998; active YMCA, NC; bd. dirs. Lake Norman Christian Women, Cornelius, NC, 2000. Named Internat. Poet of Merit, Internat. Library of Poets, 1999; recipient Editor's Choice award, 1999. Master: Christian Women's Club (project chair 1980, spl. features artist 1998—2004); mem.: Lake Norman C. of C. (photography judge 2002—04). Democrat. Presbyterian. Achievements include patents for trash art; guest on Top of the Day Show, giving advice on interior design, 1977; featured on That's My neighbor on Adelphia Cable, talking on turning trash art into art, 2002, 2003; design of 2002 Chamber of Commerce calendar and post card. Avocations: sailing, tennis, cooking, bicycling, movies. Home and Office: PO Box 4357 Davidson NC 28036 Fax: 704-987-0315. Office Phone: 704-987-0315.

KAMP, DAVID PAUL, lawyer; b. Cin., Aug. 10, 1952; s. Robert P. and Dolores O. (Koop) K.; m. Eileen J. McDermott, Oct. 24, 1981; children: Jennifer Kathleen, Jeffrey Michael, Evan William. BA, Thomas More Coll., 1978; JD, U. Cin., 1981. Bar: Ohio 1981, U.S. Dist. Ct. (we. and no. dists.) Ohio, U.S. Dist. Ct. Tenn., U.S. Dist. Ct. Kans., U.S. Dist. Ct. Nev., U.S. Ct. Appeals (6th cir.). Assoc. Dinsmore & Shohl, Cin., 1981-87; mng. ptnr. White, Getgey & Meyer, Cin., 1987—. Arbitrator N.Y. Stock Exch., Am. Stock Exch. Assoc. mem. U. Cin. Law Sch. Alumni Bd. Trustees, 1994; trustee Ohio Supreme Ct. Client Security Fund, Columbus, 1992—. Mem. ABA, ATLA, Ohio State Bar Assn., Cin. Bar Assn. (com. on ins. and tort practice, joint com. with Acad. of Medicine, com. on ins. law), Ohio State Trial Lawyers Assn., Hamilton County Trial Lawyers Assn. (pres.), Am. Arbitration Assn. (arbitrator), Nat. Assn. Securities Dealers (arbitrator). Home: 9942 Indian Springs Dr Cincinnati OH 45241-3629 Office: White Getgey & Meyer Co LPA 1 W 4th St Ste 1700 Cincinnati OH 45202-3698

KAMP, RANDALL WILLIAM, lawyer, accountant; b. Charlotte, N.C., July 5, 1960; s. John F. and Gayla S. (Roberts) K.; m. Linda K. Koster, June 8, 1985; children: Lauren, Jessica, Rebecca. BS, Okla. State U., 1982; JD, U. Okla., 1987. CPA, Okla.; bar: Okla. 1987, U.S. Ct. Appeals (10th cir.) 1992. Acct. Arthur Andersen & Co., Oklahoma City, Okla., 1982-83, Englebach Roberts & Co., Oklahoma City, Okla., 1983-84; assoc. Lytle Soule & Curlee, Oklahoma City, Okla., 1985-89, McKinney Stringer & Webster, Oklahoma City, Okla., 1989-91, Lee M. Holmes & Assocs., Oklahoma City, Okla., 1991-97; pvt. practice Oklahoma City, 1997—. Mem. ABA, Nat. Acad. Elder Law Attys., Okla. Bar Assn. Republican. Avocation: bicycling. Office: 1900 E 15th St Ste 700D Edmond OK 73013-6692 E-mail: kamp@telepath.com.

KAMPHEFNER, PIUS, minister; b. Platte City, Mo., Dec. 22, 1929; s. Ray J. Kamphefner and Ileen Sewell. BS, St. Mary U. of Minn., 1950, MA, 1960. Joined Christian Bros. H.S. tchr. Christian Bros., Ill., 1950—63, H.S. prin. Ill. and Mo., 1963—70; program dir. St. Louis County Juvenile Ct., Mo., 1970—79; resident pastor, min. St. Gabriel Parish, Mound Bayou, Miss., 1991—. Democrat. Roman Catholic. Home: 501 M L King St Mound Bayou MS 38762 Office: St Gabriel Parish 501 M L King St Mound Bayou MS 38762

KAMPINE, JOHN P., anesthesiology and physiology educator; MD, Marquette U. Med. Sch., Milwaukee, WI, 1961, PhD in Physiology, 1965. Intern Med. Coll. of Wis., Milwaukee, 1961—62, Milw. Cty. Gen. Hosp.; fellow, neurosciences NIH, Bethesda, Md., 1965—67; US Pub. Health Svc. postdoctoral rsch. fellow Marquette Sch. Medicine; rsch. assoc. Nat. Inst. Neurological Diseases and Blindness Lab. of Neurochemistry; instr. physiology Med. Coll. of Wis., Milw., 1962—67, asst. prof. physiology and anesthesiology, 1967—71, assoc. prof., 1971—74, prof., chair dept. anesthesiology, 1979—2005, prof. physiology, 1979—2005, prof. anesthesiology and physiology, 1974—. Pres. Assn. for U. Anesthesiologists; mem., surgery, anesthesia, and trauma study sect. NIH. Mem.: Am. Physiological Soc. (chmn., circulation group), Soc. Academic Anesthesia (pres., chmn.), Inst. Medicine-NAS. Office: Froedtert Meml Hosp PO Box 26099 9200 W Wisconsin Ave Milwaukee WI 53226-3596*

KAMPMAN, KEVIN DAVID, music educator; b. Jeanette, Pa., Nov. 25, 1974; s. Carl Edward and Kathleen M. Kampman. BA, Azusa Pacific U., 1997. Cert. tchr. Ariz. Tchr. music Bethany Christian Sch., Tempe, Ariz. Singer: (CD) God Alone Exalted, 1995, Christmas Joy, 1995, All Creation Sings, 1996, Our God Is With Us, 1997, (recording) Crown Him, 1994. Recipient Superior Rating for Beginning Band, ACSI, 2000. Mem.: Music Educators Nat. Conf. Conservative. Home: 1287 N Alma School Rd Unit 246 Chandler AZ 85224-5914 Personal E-mail: SCBKev@hotmail.com.

KAMPMANN, MARTIN, cell biologist; b. Bochum, Germany, Mar. 3, 1978; s. Bernhard and Irmgard Kampmann. BA, Cambridge U., Eng., 2000—03. Grad. fellow, cell biology The Rockefeller U., N.Y.C., 2003—. Fellow, Howard Hughes Med. Inst., 2003—; scholar, German Nat. Academic Found., 1999—2003, Trinity Coll., Cambridge, 2001. Achievements include research in Two-dimensional diffusion in DNA-protein interaction; Protection of DNA in hyperthermophilic organisms. Office: The Rockefeller Univ 1230 York Ave New York NY 10021 Office Phone: 212-327-8101. Office Fax: 212-327-7880. E-mail: martin.kampmann@rockefeller.edu.

KAMPMANN, STEVEN W., literature educator, writer; s. Robert and Lillian Kampmann; m. Judith Ellen Kohan, Aug. 17, 1981; children: Robert, William, Michael; 1 child, Christopher. BA, U. Pa., 1969; MA in Psychology, St. Michaels Coll., 1973. Tchr. English Blair Acad., Bairstown, NJ, 1999—. Actor: (TV series) Newhart, 1981—82, (writer): (plays) Second City Theater, 1975—78; dir.(writer): (films) Stealing Home, 1987. Mem.: Winter Harbor Yacht Club, Sunnybrook Ball Club.

KAMPMEIER, JACK AUGUST CARLOS, chemist, educator; b. Cedar Rapids, Iowa, June 11, 1935; s. Carlos and Nevalou (Brown) K.; m. Anne Margaret Derk, June 14, 1958; children— Scott, Margaret, Stephen. AB, Amherst Coll., 1957; PhD (NSF fellow), U. Ill., 1960. From instr. to prof. chemistry U. Rochester, N.Y., 1960-71, prof., 1971—2005, chmn. dept. chemistry, 1975-79, assoc. dean grad. studies Coll. Arts and Sci., 1982-88, dean Coll. Arts and Sci., 1988-91, prof. emeritus, 2005—. Co-author: Peer-Led Team Learning, A Guidebook, 2001, Peer-Led Team Learning, Organic Chemistry, 2001; contbr. sci. and pedagogical articles to profl. jours. Recipient Nat. Catalyst award Chem. Mfrs. Assn., 1999; NSF sci. faculty fellow U. Calif., Berkeley, 1971-72; Fulbright Hays sr. rsch. scholar U. Freiburg, Germany, 1979-80; NATO sr. scientist, 1979-80. Mem. Am. Chem.

Soc., Sigma Xi. Home: 86 Reservoir Ave Rochester NY 14620-2754 Office: U Rochester Dept Chemistry Rochester NY 14627 Office Phone: 585-275-4441. Business E-Mail: kamp@chem.rochester.edu.

KAMPOURIS, EMMANUEL ANDREW, retired corporate executive; b. Alexandria, Egypt, Dec. 14, 1934; arrived in US, 1979; s. Andrew George and Euridice Ann (Caralli) Kampouris; m. Myrto Stellatos, July 4, 1959 (dec.); children: Andrew, Alexander. Student, King's Sch., Bruton, Somerset, U.K., 1953; MA in Law, Oxford U., 1957; cert. in ceramic tech., North Staffordshire Coll. of Tech., U.K., 1962. Plant mgr., dir. "KEREM", Athens, Greece, 1962-64; dir. "HELLENIT", Athens, Greece, 1962-65; mng. dir. Ideal Standard, Athens, 1966-79; v.p., group exec. internat. and export Am. Standard Inc., New Brunswick, NJ, 1979-84, sr. v.p. bldg. products, 1984-89; pres., chief exec. officer Am. Standard Inc., Am. Standard Cos. Inc., N.Y.C., 1989-99, now chmn.; bd. dirs. Click Commerce Inc, Chgo., Horizon Blue Cross Blue Shields, Stanley Works, Alticor Inc. Bd. dirs. Ideal Refractories SAI, Athens; bd. dirs. Ideal Standard Mexico, Am. Standard Sanitaryware (Thailand) Ltd., INCESA, San Jose, Costa Rica, Hoxan Corp., Sapporo, Japan. Bd. dirs. Greek Mgmt. Assn., Athens, 1975—77, Fedn. of Greek Industries, Athens. Mem.: Young Pres. Orgn., Chief Execs. Orgn., Econ. Club of N.Y., Oxford Union, Oxford Law Soc., Am. Hellenic C. of C. (gen. sec. 1975—79), Spring Brook Country (Morristown, N.J.); Quogue Field, Quogue Beach (L.I., N.Y.)., Chemists Club, Laurel Valley Golf Club. Greek Orthodox. Avocations: golf, tennis, classical music. Office: Click Commerce Inc 200 E Randolph Dr Ste 4900 Chicago IL 60601*

KAMPS, CHARLES Q., retired lawyer; b. Milw., Mar. 21, 1932; s. John G. and Mary (Quarles) K.; m. Mary B. Stehling, Sept. 28, 1963; children: Charles Jr., Louisa. LLB, Marquette U., 1959. Bar: Wis. 1959. Ptnr. Quarles & Brady, Milw., 1959—99. Mem. Preserve Our Parks. Mem. U.S. Sailing Assn; Milwaukee Yacht Club (past commodore, 1971-72). Office: Quarles & Brady 411 E Wisconsin Ave Ste 2040 Milwaukee WI 53202-4497

KAMRAS, JASON, mathematics educator; BS, Princeton U., 1995; MA in Edn., Harvard U., 2000. With Israel Democracy Inst., Jerusalem; mem. Teach For Am., 1996; tchr. math. & social studies John Philip Sousa Middle Sch., Washington, DC, 1996—99, 2000—, co-founder, dir. EXPOSE Program, 1999—; nat. and internat. spokesperson for edn., 2005—. Named Exemplary After School for All Instr., DC Pub. Schs., 2003, Exemplary Resident Mentor Tchr., 2003, Ward 7 Tchr. of Yr., 2003, Tchr. Yr., 2005, Agnes Meyer Outstanding Tchr., Washington Post, 2003, Nat. Tchr. of Yr., Coun. of Chief State Sch. Officers, 2005; recipient Mayor's Art Award, 2001. Mailing: Coun Chief State Sch Officers Ste 700 One Massachusetts Ave, NW Washington DC 20001-1431 Office: John Philip Sousa Middle Sch 3650 Ely Pl, SE Washington DC 20019

KAMRIN, MICHAEL ARNOLD, toxicology educator; b. Bklyn., Aug. 5, 1940; s. Benjamin Barnett and Bessie (Bloom) K.; m. Ritva Anneli Nieminen, July 19, 1964 (dec. Oct. 2002); children: Kari and Edward (twins); m. Katherine O'Sullivan See, Nov 6, 2004. BA in Chemistry, Cornell U., 1960; MS in Biophys. Chemistry, Yale, 1962, PhD in Biophys. Chemistry, 1965. Teaching asst. then rsch. asst. dept. chemistry Yale U., New Haven, 1960-63; rsch. assoc. biology div. Oak Ridge (Tenn.) Nat. Lab., 1963-66; NIH postdoctoral trainee Hopkins Marine Sta. Stanford (Calif.) U., 1966-67; asst. prof. natural sci. Mich. State U., East Lansing, 1967-72, assoc. prof., 1972-79, prof., 1979-89, prof. Inst. for Environ. Toxicology, 1982-2000, prof. resource devel., 1990-2000, prof. emeritus, 2000—. Vis. lectr. dept. zoology U. Turku, Finland, 1973-74, docent, 1996—; vis. scientist Legis. Office Sci. Advisor, State of Mich., 1980-81; participant numerous confs. and workshops, 1965—; mem. internat. evaluation team on environ. toxicology Acad. Finland, Helsinki, 1988; expert Media Resource Ctr., Scientists' Inst. for Pub. Info.; mem. risk comm. project planning group, grant reviewer USDA; peer reviewer for agy.-sponsored rsch. projects Agy. for Toxic Substances and Disease Registry, HHS; numerous others. Author: Toxicology: A Primer on Toxicology Principles and Applications, 1988, (with D.J. Katz and M.L. Walter) Reporting on Risk: A Journalist's Handbook, 1995; also other; editor: (with F.M. D'Itri) PCBs: Human and Environmental Hazards, 1983, (with P. Rodgers) Dioxins inthe Environment, 1985; editor: Pesticide Profiles, 1997, Environmental Risk Harmonization, 1997; contbr. numerous articles and abstracts to sci. jours. Numerous presentations to Rotary, Consumers Coun., LWV, county commrs., Ch. Women United, sch. dists., Mich. Med. Soc.; participant in news broadcasts, radio call-in shows and interview programs. Recipient Meml. medal U. Turku, 1974; grantee USDA, 1983-84, 86-87, 88-89, 91-98, All-Univ. Rsch. Initation grantee, 1989, All-Univ. Outreach grantee, 1995-96, EPA, 1992-95, Agy. for Toxic Substances and Disease Registry, 1992-2000, Nat. Food Safety and Toxicology Ctr., 1993-94, grantee Nat. Inst. Environ. Health Scis., 1995-2000. Fellow AAAS; mem. Am. Chem. Soc., Soc. Toxicology (editor newsletter Mich. chpt. 1984-87, chmn. nominating com. 1986, pres.-elect 1992-93, pres. 1993-94; nat. pub. comm. com. 1987-90, Nat. Pub. Comm. award 1994), Soc. Environ. Toxicology and Chemistry (bd. dirs. Ctrl. Gt. Lakes chpt. 1985-87, v.p. 1988, pres. 1989-90, Disting. Svc. award 1993; nat. govt. affairs com. 1986-2000), Soc. for Risk Analysis. Office Phone: 517-655-1896. Business E-Mail: kamrin@msu.edu.

KAMSO-PRATT, JIMMY MICHAEL, physician, administrator; b. Freetown, Sierra Leone, Feb. 15, 1951; came to U.S., 1972; s. Josiah Pratt and Namina Kargbo; 1 child, Santigi. BS magna cum laude, Cumberland Coll., 1975; MS in Microbiology, McNeese State U., 1982; PhD in Microbiology, Plant Pathology, La. State U., 1985; MD, U. Tenn., 1993. Rsch. assoc. Ministry Health, Sierra Leone, 1969-72, 75-80; lab. technician Patrick's Hosp., Lake Charles, La., 1980-82; grad. rsch. asst. McNeese State U., Lake Charles, 1980-82; grad. rsch. fellow plant pathology/molecular biology La. State U., Baton Rouge, 1982-85; postdoctoral rsch. fellow Dept. Microbiology Meharry Med. Coll., Nashville, 1985-86; postdoctoral rsch. fellow Dept. Pathology Vanderbilt U. Med. Ctr., Nashville, 1987-89; internat. health cons. U. Tenn., Memphis, 1993-94; resident family medicine U. Tenn. Med. Ctr., Knoxville, 1993-96; emergency physician Southeastern Emergency Physicians, Knoxville, 1994-95; med. dir. East Jackson Family Med. Ctr., Jackson, Tenn., 1996—. Contbr. articles to profl. jours. Mem. AMA, Nat. Med. Assn., Am. Acad. Family Physicians, Am. Med. Student Assn., Tenn. Acad. Family Physicians, Tenn. Med. Assn., Sigma Xi. Avocations: soccer, reading. Office: East Jackson Family Med Ctr 655 Lexington Ave Jackson TN 38301-5075

KAMYSZEW, CHRISTOPHER D., film executive, educator, curator; b. Warsaw, May 7, 1958; came to U.S., 1982; s. Mieczyslaw and Zofia (Kubik) K.; children: Oliver G., Samuel. BA, U. Warsaw, 1982, MA in Polish Lit. and Lang., 1984. Freelance writer and translator, Poland, 1977-81; freelance theatre dir. Dearborn Theatre Co., Chgo., 1982-83, Ossetynski Actors Lab., L.A., 1982-83; head lit. sect. Krag-Underground Publishers, Warsaw, 1980-83; head archives dept. Polish Mus. Am., Chgo., 1985-88, dir., curator, 1988-93; pres. Soc. for the Arts, Chgo., 1993—. Bd. dirs. Gallery 58, Chgo.; pres. Inst. Symbological Rsch., Chgo., 1986-95, Internat. Ind. Theatre Found., Washington, 1985-86; exec. dir. Polish TV-USA, 1994-97. Co-author, editor: Collective Works of L.-F Celine, 1983, Literary Essays by L. Tyrmand, 1983; curated more than 120 exhbns. in U.S. Dir., chmn., CEO Polish Film Festival, 1988—, Europe Film Festival, 1996—; founder, pres. Chgo. Internat. Documentary Festival, 2003-. Recipient Zycie Warszawy award, 1977, Audience award Edinburgh Theatre Festival, 1980, award for disting. translation Assn. Polish Translators, 1990, award Found. of Friends of Polish Mus., 1991, award Ministry Fgn. Affairs of Poland, 1993, Laterna Magica award disting. achievements in film, 1994, Copernican award, 2002, Warsaw Gold medal Acad. Fine Arts, 2004; Wiehmann Found. scholar, 1982, Golden Cross of Merit, 2001. Avocations: reading, classical music, map collecting, cross country skiing. Office: Society for Arts 1112 N Milwaukee Ave Chicago IL 60622-4017 Office Phone: 773-486-9612. Personal E-mail: christopherkamyszew@msn.com.

KAN, DIANA ARTEMIS MANN SHU, painter, art educator, writer; b. Hong Kong, Mar. 3, 1926; came to U.S., 1949, naturalized, 1964; d. Kam Shek and Sing-Ying (Hong) K.; m. Paul Schwartz, May 24, 1952; 1 son, Kan Martin Meyer Sing-Si. Student, Art Students League, 1949-51, Beaux Arts, Paris, 1951-52, Grande Chaumiere, 1951-52, Ecole Beau Arts, 1952—54. Instr. watercolor Phila. Mus. Art, 1972, Sumi-e Soc., 1974—2003, Art Students League of NY, 1985, The Nat. Acad. Design, 2001, The Smithsonian Inst., Wash., DC. Fgn. corr., city editor Cosmorama Pictorial Mag., Hong Kong, 1968; art reviewer Villager, N.Y.C., 1960-69; lectr. Birmingham So. U., N.Y. U., Mills Coll., St. Joseph's Coll., Phila. Mus., Smithsonian Instn; keynote spkr. Wellsley's Coll. Asia Week, MA, 1993. Author: White Cloud, 1938, The How and Why of Chinese Painting, 1974, Am. Artist Magazine, 1974, 86; One-man shows, London, 1949, 63, 64, Paris, 1949, Hong Kong, 1937, 39, 41, 47, 48, 52, Shanghai, 1935, 37, 39, Nanking, 1936, 38, Macao, 1947, 48, Bankok, 1947, Casablanca, 1951, 52, San Francisco, 1950, 67, N.Y.C., 1950, 54, 59, 67, 71, 72, 74, 78, Naples, 1971, Elliot Mus., Stuart, Fla., 1967, 73, Bruce Mus., Greenwich, Conn., 1969, Nat. Hist. Mus., Taipei, Taiwan, 1971, N.Y. Cultural Center Mus., 1972, Galerie Barbarella, Palm Beach, Fla., 1972, Hobe Sound (Fla.) Galleries, 1976, 81, Nat. Arts Club, 1979, Dyansen Galleries, 1987-Shenchen Mus., China, 1996, Hong Kong Art Ctr., 1996, 90 others; exhibited in group shows Allied Artists of Am., 1957-90, Royal Acad. Fine Arts, London, 1963-64, Royal Soc. Painters, London, 1964, Nat. Arts Club, N.Y.C., 1964-90, Am. Water Color Soc., N.Y.C., 1966-90, Nat. Acad. Design, N.Y.C., 1967-2003, Charles and Emma Frye Mus., Seattle, 1968, Willamette U., Salem, Oreg., 1968, Columbia (S.C.) Mus. Art, 1969, Audubon Artist, 1974-90, Evansville (Ind.) Mus., 1991, Dyansen Gallery, Boston, 1991; represented permanent collections, Met. Mus. Art, Phila. Mus. Art, Nelson Gallery, Elliot Mus., Fla., Bruce Mus., Dalhousie U., Atkin Mus., Kansas City, Nat. Hist. Mus., Taipei, The Government House, Vancouver, BC, Can., Midtown Payson Galleries, China 2000 Fine Art Gallery; subject of film Eastern Spirit, Western World—A Profile of Diana Kan; paintings were published by UNICEF (christmas cards): Four Children Going Fishing, 1996, Lantern Festival, 1999, Flower Drum Song, 2002, Snow Mountain, 2002. Recipient Summer Festival award N.Y.C., 1959, 1st Prize Nat. Art Club, 1982; named most Outstanding Profl. Woman of the Yr., Washington Sq. chpt. N.Y. League Bus. and Profl. Women's Club, 1971, 79, Gold medal of honor Knickerbocker Artists, 1990, Gold medal of honor Audubon Artists, 1991, 2000, Salmagundi Club, Pres. Gold medal of honor, 1998, Audobon Artists Gold Medal of Honor; Diana Kan Appreciation Day proclaimed by Mayor of Boston, 1991, Diana Kan Day proclaimed by Mayor of NY, 2000; offl. citation proclaimed by Pres. Senate of Mass., 1991. Fellow Royal Soc. Arts; mem. Pen and Brush Club (dir. 1968, Brush Fund award 1968, Alice S. Buell Meml. award 1969, Margaret Sussman award 1991), Nat. Acad. Design (assoc., John Pike Meml. award 1987, cert. of merit 1991), Am. Watercolor Soc. (traveling award 1968, Marthe T. McKinnon award 1978, dir. 1975-77), Art Students League, Nat. League Pen Women, Audubon Artists (v.p. 1983), Allied Artists Am. (Barbara Vassilieff Meml. award 1969, Ralph Fabri Meml. award 1975, corr. sec. 1975-78), Catharine Lorillard Wolf Art Club (Anna Hyatt Huntington bronze medal 1970, 74, Gold medal of honor 1982), NYC Cultural Affairs Adv. Commn., 1999. Clubs: Overseas Press Am., Lotos, The Nat. Arts (NYC), The Salamagundi. Mailing: The Nat Arts Club 15 Gramercy Park S New York NY 10003-1705 E-mail: dianakan@dianakan.com. *Failure is the mother of success.*

KAN, YUET WAI, hematologist, educator; b. Hong Kong, China, June 11, 1936; arrived in U.S., 1960; s. Tong-Po and Lai-Wan (Li) Kan; m. Alvera Lorraine Limauro, May 10, 1964; children: Susan Jennifer, Deborah Ann. BS, MB, U. Hong Kong, China, 1958, DSc, 1980, DSc (hon.), 1987, Chinese U., Hong Kong, 1981; MD (hon.), U. Cagliari, Sardinia, Italy, 1981. Investigator Howard Hughes Med. Inst., San Francisco, 1976—2003; prof. lab. medicine U. Calif., San Francisco, 1977—, Louis K. Diamond prof. hematology, 1991—. Mem. NIDDK adv. coun. NIH, 1991—95; trustee Croucher Found., Hong Kong, 1992—, chmn., 1997—. Contbr. chapters to books, over 250 articles to med. jours. Recipient Dameshek award, Am. Soc. Hematology, 1980, George Thorn award, Howard Hughes Med. Inst., 1980, Gairdner Found. Internat. award, 1984, Allan award, Am. Soc. Human Genetics, 1984, Lita Annenberg Hazen award for Excellence in Clin. Rsch., 1984, Waterford award, 1987, ACP's award, 1988, Genetic Rsch. award, Sanremo Internat., 1989, Warren Alpert Found. prize, 1989, Albert Lasker Clin. Med. Rsch. award, 1991, Christopher Columbus Discovery award, 1992, City of Medicine award, 1992, Excellence 200 award, 1993, Helmut Horten Rsch. award, 1995, Shaw prize, Shaw Found., Hong Kong, 2004. Fellow: AAAS, Am. Acad. Arts and Scis., Third World Acad. Scis., Royal Soc. (London), Royal Coll. Physicians (London); mem.: NAS, Soc. Chinese Bioscientists in Am. (pres. 1998—99), Am. Soc. Hematology (pres. 1990), Assn. Am. Physicians, Chinese Acad. Scis. (fgn. mem.), Acad. Sinica (Taiwan). Office: U Calif 513 Parnassus Ave HSW 901 San Francisco CA 94143-0793 Office Phone: 415-476-5841. Business E-Mail: kanyuet@labmed2.ucsf.edu.

KANADE, TAKEO, science educator, director; b. Hyogo, Japan, Oct. 24, 1945; came to U.S., 1980; s. Kumaichi and Harue (Yamauchi) K.; m. Yukiko Kubo, Mar. 23, 1974; children: Shinichi, Sayaka. BE, Kyoto (Japan) U., 1968, ME, 1970, PhD in Elec. Engring., 1973. Asst. prof. Kyoto U., 1973-76, assoc. prof., 1976-80; sr. rsch. scientist Carnegie Mellon U., Pitts., 1980-82, assoc. prof., 1982-85, prof. computer sci. and robotics, 1985-94, dir. robotics inst., 1992—2001, U.A. & Helen Whitaker prof. computer sci. and robotics, 1994—. Cons. NASA Advanced Tech. Adv. Com., Washington, 1988-90, Martin Marietta, Denver, 1991—. Author: Computer Recognition of Human Faces, 1977; editor: Three-Dimensional Machine Vision, 1987; founding editor Internat. Jour. Computer Vision, 1987—; contbr. articles to profl. jours.; patentee in field. Pres. Japan-Am. Soc. Greater Pitts., 1991-92. Recipient Best Presentation award Audio Visual Info. Rsch. Group, 1980, C&C award, Joseph Engelberger award, FIT award, Allen Newell Rsch. Excellence award, JARA award, Otto Franc award. Fellow IEEE (Marr award 1988), Am. Assn. Artificial Intelligence, Am. Acad. Arts & Sciences; mem. Aeronautics and Space Engring. Bd. of NRC. Office: Carnegie Mellon U Robotics Inst 5000 Forbes Ave Pittsburgh PA 15213-3890

KANAK, DONALD PERRY, JR., insurance company executive, lawyer, diversified financial services company executive; b. Spokane, Wash., Dec. 20, 1952; s. Donald Perry Sr. and Laura Margaret (Trono) K.; m. Kumi Sato, May 28, 1983; children: Daniel, Mia, Saiji. BA in Econs. summa cum laude, U. N.C., 1975; JD cum laude, Harvard U., 1980; MLitt, Oxford (Eng.) U., 1989. Bar: N.Y., Mass. Assoc. Strategic Planning Assocs., Washington, 1980-81, mgr., 1982-84, v.p., 1984-85; dep. pres., COO Equitable Life Assurance Ltd., Tokyo, 1986—89, v.p., 1986—88, pres., CEO, 1990—91; sr. v.p. Equitable Life Ins. Soc. USA, 1988—89; regional v.p. life. ins. ops. AIG Companies Japan & Korea, 1992—95, regional pres., COO, 1995—2000, pres., CEO, 2001—03; v.p. Am. Internat. Group, Inc., 1998—2002, exec. v.p., 2002—03, vice chmn., co-COO, 2004—05, exec. vice chmn., COO, 2005—. Mem., bd. dirs., Amer. Internat. Group, Inc., 2004-; mem. adv. coun. Ed. O. Reischauer Ctr., Johns Hopkins U., Tokyo, 1990-95; mem. Coun. Fgn. Rels., adv. com. Harvard Law Sch. Program on Internat. Fin. Systems Mem. bd. visitors U. N. C., Chapel Hill. Mem. Coun. on Fgn. Rels., Internat. Ins. Soc., Am. Soc. Fin. Svc. Profls., Coun. on Foreign Relations, Internat. Ins .Soc., Am. Soc. of Fin. Svc. Profl., UNC Bd. visitors of U. NC, Am. C. of C. Japan (pres. 2002, chmn. 2003), Tokyo Lawn and Tennis Club. Office: Am Internat Companies AIA Bldg 1 Stubbs Rd Hong Kong Hong Kong

KANAKANUI, LINDON-PATRICK, music educator; b. Dededo, Guam, Jan. 24, 1979; s. Francis Kalani Kanakanui and Patricia Kay Lindon. B in Music Edn., U. Ky., 2002, M in Sacred Music, 2004, M in Music Edn., 2005. Student libr. U. Ky., Lexington, 2000—04; asst. prof. music Trinity Bible Coll., Ellendale, ND, 2004—, cross country coach, 2004—. Interim min. music Real Life Assembly of God, Lexington, 2000—01; asst. min. music Edgewood Bapt. Ch., Nicholasville, Ky., 2003, Trinity Assembly of God, Georgetown, Ky., 2004; acting extra Paramount Studios, Burbank, Calif., 2004. Mem. constrn. team Mission Am. Placement Svc., Cuenca, Ecuador, 2003, mem. med. team Amazon Jungle, Oriente, Ecuador, 2004; mem. New Life Assembly of God, 2005—. Mem.: ND Orff-Schulwerk Assn., Music Educators Nat. Conf. Republican. Mem. Assembly Of God Ch. Avocations: triathlons, fishing, gardening, camping, music. Home: 221 Southwest 2d Ave Ellendale ND 58436 Office: Trinity Bible Coll 50 S 6th Ave 162 Ellendale ND 58436 Office Phone: 701-349-5436.

KANARKOWSKI, EDWARD JOSEPH, data processing company executive; b. Jersey City, May 5, 1947; s. Joseph Anthony and Lillian Dorothy (Pietrowicz) K.; m. Carol Ann Miller, Sept. 14, 1969; children: Edward, Kelly, Paul, Karen, Kevin, Casey Michael. BA, St. Peter Coll., 1969; grad., U.S. Army Command and Gen. Staff Coll., 1985. Cons. corp. comm., NJ, 1973—75; staff writer Daily and Sunday Register, Shrewsbury, NJ, 1975—77; corp. staff writer ADP, Roseland, NJ, 1977, dir. corp. comm., 1983—88, v.p. corp. comm., 1988—93; cons. comm., 1993—. Adj. vis. prof. comm. St. Peter's Coll., 1985—; corp. career adv. grad. sch. bus. Rutgers U., N.J. Author: The ADP Story, 1999. Capt. U.S. Army, 1971—73, maj. N.J. Nat. Guard. Decorated Army Commendation medal (3); named Hon. Ky. Col. Commonwealth Ky., 1988. Mem. Internat. Assn. Bus. Communicators, Meeting Planners Internat., 3d U.S. Inf. Divsn. Assn., N.J. Mil. Acad. (assoc.), VFW (life), U.S. Golf Assn., U.S.O. Orgn. (contbr.), 114th Inf. Regiment Assn. Roman Catholic. Home: 132 Yellowbank Rd Toms River NJ 08753-3167

KANAS, JOHN ADAM, banker; b. Southampton, NY, Nov. 16, 1946; s. George and Barbara K.; m. Elaine; children: Melissa, Allison, Adam, John. BA in History, Southampton Coll., 1968; postgrad., C.W. Post Coll. L.I., U., 1970, Rutgers U., 1976. Mgmt. trainee North Fork Bank & Trust Co., Mattituck, NY, 1971—, various sr. mgmt. positions, 1971—77, pres., CEO, 1977—; chmn. North Fork Bancorporation, Inc., Melville, NY, 1987—. Recipient Tree of Life award, Jewish Nat. Fund, 2003. Mem. N.Y. State Ind. Bankers Assn. (chmn., pres. 1980-81), L.I. Bankers Assn. (pres., dir. 1980), N.Y. State Bankers Assn. (pres.). Office: N Fork Bancorp Inc 275 Broadhollow Rd Melville NY 11747*

KANATSIZ, SUZANNE L., artist, educator; b. Detroit, May 11, 1959; d. Necati Kanatsiz and Marcella Springer; m. Jake Gilson; 1 child, Jacob. AA, Grossmont Coll., Calif., 1979; post grad. in painting, Calif. State U., Long Beach, 1979—80; BA in Painting, San Diego State u., Calif., 1982; MFA in Pictorial Arts and Sculpture, San Jose State U., 1988. Lectr. and drawing instr. San Jose State U., Calif., 1986—88; painting instr. Creativity Unlinited, Calif., 1987—89; assoc. dir. Eye Gallery, San Francisco, 1989—91; sculture instr. Creativity Explored of San Francisco, 1989—95; asst. prof. and gallery dir. U. Nev., Reno, 1995—99; lectr. and drawing instr. Weber State U., Odgen, Utah, 1999—. Artist-in-residence Calif. Arts Coun., 1991—94; art and sculpture instr. Calif. Correctional Sys., 1992—96; exhibit curator and mem. jury panels; guest lectr. and artist. Represented in permanent collections Nev. Mus. Art, Reno, Island Inst., Sitka, Alaska, Capp St. Project, San Francisco, Sun Gallery, Hayward, Calif., San Diego State U., one-woman shows include San Jose State U., 1986, 1988, Sun Gallery, Hayward, Calif., 1987, Lab Gallery, San Francisco, 1989, Studio ZOK, 1989, 1078 Gallery, Chico, Calif., 1994, Site Gallery, L.A., 1995, So. Nev. C.C., Las Vegas, 1996, So. Oreg. State U., Ashland, 1997, San Jose City Coll., 1998, Sheppard Gallery, U. Nev., Reno, 1998, Boise State U., 1999, Nev. Mus. Art, Reno, 2000, Charleston Heights Gallery, Las Vegas, 2002, Nicolaysen Art Mus., Casper, Wyo., 2002, Finch Ln. Gallery, Salt Lake City, 2003, Rio Grande Gallery, 2003, Bush Barn Art Mus., Salem, Oreg., 2003. Nominee SECA award, San Francisco Mus. Modern Art, 1991; recipient Purchase award, Hayward Forum Arts, 1986; grantee, Valley Found. Santa Clara County, 1989, Exptl. Projects award, Capp St. Project, San Francisco, 1992, Ucross Found., Wyo., 1993, Sierra Arts Found., 1996, 1999, Nev. Arts Coun., 1997—99, Connemara Conservancy Found., 1998, Weber State U., 2000—04, Utah Arts Coun., 2002; scholar, Banff Ctr. Arts, Alberta, Can., 1987. Office: Weber State U 2001 Univ Cir Ogden UT 84401

KANDEL, ALAN HAROLD, lawyer; b. St. Louis, Mar. 8, 1955; AB universali cum honore, Washington U., St. Louis, 1983; JD cum laude, St. Louis U., 1986. Bar: Mo. 1986. Assoc. Popkin & Stern, St. Louis, 1986-91, Lewis, Rice & Fingersh, St. Louis, 1991-95; of counsel Farnam Law Firm, St. Louis, 1995-96; sr. atty. Peper, Martin, Jensen, Maichel & Hetlage, St. Louis, 1996-97; ptnr. Blackwell Sanders Peper Martin LLP, St. Louis, 1998—; instr. Fontbonne U., 2000—. Sr. v.p. H.F. Epstein Hebrew Acad., St. Louis, 1999-2001, pres. 2001-2003; pres. Tpheris Israel Chevra Kadisha Congregation, Chesterfield, Mo., 1997-98, Vaad Hoeir of St. Louis, 1998-2000. Mem. Mo. Bar (chmn. employee benefits com. 1991-93), Bar Assn. Met. St. Louis (chmn. employee benefits law com. 1995-96). Office: Blackwell Sanders Peper Martin LLP 720 Olive St Fl 24 Saint Louis MO 63101-2338 E-mail: akandel@blackwellsanders.com.

KANDEL, DENISE BYSTRYN, sociologist; b. Paris, Feb. 27, 1933; came to U.S. 1949; d. Iser and Sara (Wolsky) Bystryn; m. Eric R. Kandel, June 10, 1956; children: Paul, Minouche. BA in French, Acad. Paris, 1950; BA, Bryn Mawr (Pa.) Coll., 1952; MA, Columbia U., 1953, PhD, 1960. Social scientist NIMH, Bethesda, Md., 1959-60; postdoctoral rsch. fellow Harvard Med. Sch., Boston, 1960-62; rsch. assoc. Harvard Sch. Edn., Cambridge, Mass., 1964-69; rsch. scientist VII N.Y. State Psychiatric Inst., N.Y.C., 1969—; from asst. prof. to prof. dept. psychiatry, dept. sociomed. scis. Columbia U. Sch. of Pub. Health, NYC, 1973—. Cons. Nat. Inst. on Drug Abuse, Rockville, 1973—; editl. bd. Jour. Rsch. on Adolescence, 1990—, extramural sci. adv. bd., 1990—93; etiology sci. adv. panel Am. Legacy Found., Ont., Canada, 2000—04. Author (with G. Lesser): (Book) Youth in Two Worlds., 1972; contbg. author: Parental Influences on Adolescent Marijuana Use and the Baby Boom Generation: Findings from the 1979-1996 National Household Surveys on Drug Abuse, 2001; editor: Longitudinal Research on Drug Use, 1978, Stages and Pathways of Drug Involvement: Examining the Gateway Hypothesis, 2002; assoc. editor: Jour. Health and Social Behavior, 1975—78, consulting editor: Am. Jour. Sociology, 1981—83; contbr. articles to profl. jours. Active Nat. Adv. Coun. on Drug Abuse, 1986—90; etiology sci. adv. panel Am. Legacy Found., 2000—04; H. David Archibald lectr. Addiction Rsch. Found., Ctr. for Addiction and Mental Health, Ont., Canada, 2002. Recipient Pacesetter award, Nat. Inst. on Drug Abuse, 1979, Rsch. Scientist award, 1981—, Ann. Norman E. Zinberg Meml. Lectr. award, Cambridge Hosp./ Harvard Med. Sch., 1993, R. Brinkley Smithers Disting. Scientist award, Am. Soc. Addiction Medicine, 2002, Prevention Sci. award, Soc. for Prevention Rsch., 2003; grantee, Addiction Rsch. Found. Ctr. for Addiction and Mental Health, 2002. Mem.: Soc. for Life History Rsch., Internat. Sociol. Assn., Am. Sociol. Assn., Sociol. Rsch. Assn., Soc. for Rsch. on Adolescence (chmn. pubs. 1990—92). Democrat. Jewish. Avocation: collecting art nouveau furniture and glass. Office: Columbia Univ Dept of Psychiatry 1051 Riverside Dr Unit 20 New York NY 10032 Office Phone: 212-304-7080. Business E-Mail: dbk2@columbia.edu.

KANDEL, ERIC RICHARD, neuroscience educator; b. Vienna, Nov. 7, 1929; arrived in U.S., 1939; married, 1956; 2 children. BA, Harvard Coll., 1952; MD, NYU, 1956. Intern Montefiore Hosp., NYC, 1956—57; rsch. assoc. neurophysiology lab. NIH, Washington, 1957—60; psychiatrist Mass Mental Health Ctr. Harvard Med. Sch., 1960-62, 1963—64; dir. Mass. Mental Health Ctr., Boston, 1960—65; from assoc. to prof. physiology and psychiatry NYU Sch. Medicine, 1965—74; prof. physiology, biochemistry and psychiatry, dir. ctr. neurology and behavior Columbia U. Coll. Physicians and Surgeons, NYC, 1974—83, univ. prof., physiology and cell biophysics, psychiatry, biochemistry and molecular biophysics, 1983—; and sr. investigator Howard Hughes Med. Inst. Recipient Lasker award, 1983, Harvey prize, Technion, 1993, Wolf prize, Israel, 1999, Nobel prize in physiology or medicine, 2000, Heineken prize, 2000. Fellow: AAAS; mem.: NAS, N.Y. Acad. of Scis. (Mayor award excellence in sci. and tech. 1994), Internat. Brain Rsch. Orgn., Soc. Neuroscis. (pres. 1980—81), Am. Acad. Arts and Scis. Office: Howard Hughes Med Inst 4000 Jones Bridge Rd Chevy Chase MD 20815-6789 also: Physiology & Biophysics Nyspi-Unit 25 Columbia U 1051 Riverside Dr New York NY 10032*

KANDEL, JESSICA J., pediatric surgeon; b. L.A., June 21, 1959; d. Stephen David and Anne Oakes Kandel; m. Alexander Cassel Dill, June 7, 1997; 1 child, James Kandel Dill. BA, Yale U., 1981; MD, Columbia U., 1985. Surg. resident Mass. Gen. Hosp., Boston, 1986-93; pediatric surg. fellow Johns Hopkins U., Balt., 1993-95; asst. prof. surgery and pediatrics Columbia U., N.Y.C., 1995—. Surg. prin. investigator Children's Oncology Group Columbia U., 1995—; dir. pediatric surg. rsch., 1998—. Recipient Peter Paul Rickham prize British Assn. of Paediatric Surgeons, 1999. Fellow ACS, Am. Pediatric Surg. Assn., Am. Acad. Pediatrics. Avocations: reading, shopping. Office: Babies Hosp/Columbia U 214 North 3959 Broadway New York NY 10032-1551

KANDEL, MYRON, newscaster, columnist; m. Thelma Esan. Bachelor's Degree, Bklyn. Coll., 1952; Master's Degree, Columbia U., 1953. From copy boy to fin. reporter The N.Y. Times, 1951-63; bus. editor Washington Star; fgn. corr. N.Y. Herald Tribune, Bonn, Germany; fin. editor Herald Tribune; editor, pres. The N.Y. Law Jour.; founder, fin. editor, anchor CNN, 1980—2005. Journalism educator Columbia U., CCNY. Author: How to Cash in on the Coming Stock Market Boom, 1982; co-author (syndicated fin. column) The Greer/Kandel Report, 1976-82; fin. editor N.Y. Post, 1977-79; founding editor, pub. (newsletters) The Wall Street Letter, Rev. of the Fin. Press, The Corp. Shareholder; contbr. articles to profl. jours. Recipient Columbia Journalism Alumni award, 1985, Presdl. medal Bklyn. Coll., 2002. Mem. Soc. Am. Bus. Editors and Writers (past pres., Disting. Achievement award 1994), Soc. Profl. Journalists (past pres. N.Y. chpt.), N.Y. Fin. Writers' Assn. (past pres., Elliot V. Bell award 1988), Deadline Club (past pres.), Alumni Assn. Columbia Grad. Sch. Journalism (past pres.). Office: 1 Time Warner Ctr New York NY 10019 E-mail: myron.kandel@turner.com.

KANDEL, NELSON ROBERT, lawyer; b. Balt., Sept. 15, 1929; m. Brigitte Kleemaier, Feb. 28, 1957; children: Katrin, Christopher, Peter. BA, U. Md., 1951, LLB, 1954. Bar: Md. 1954, U.S. Supreme Ct. 1964, DC 1980. Pres. Kandel & Assocs. P.A., Balt., 1957—. With U.S. Army. Mem. Md. Bar Assn., Balt. Bar Assn. Democrat. Lutheran. Office: The World Trade Ctr Ste 1252 401 E Pratt St Baltimore MD 21202 Office Phone: 410-837-0646.

KANDEL, WILLIAM LLOYD, lawyer, arbitrator, educator, mediator, writer; b. N.Y.C., Apr. 25, 1939; s. Morton H. and Lottie S. (Smith) K.; m. Joyce Roland, Jan. 27, 1974; 1 child, Aron Daniel (Ari). AB cum laude, Dartmouth Coll., 1961; JD, Yale U., 1964; LLM in Labor Law, NYU, 1967. Bar: N.Y. 1965, U.S. Dist. Ct. (ea. dist.) N.Y. 1978, U.S. Dist. Ct. (so. dist) N.Y. 1980, U.S. Dist. Ct. (no. dist.) N.Y. 1988, U.S. Ct. Appeals (2d cir.) 1982, U.S. Ct. Appeals (3d cir.) 1997, U.S. Ct. Appeals (5th cir.) 2000. Assoc. Lorenz, Finn & Giardino, N.Y.C., 1964-66; labor atty. NAM, N.Y.C., 1966-68; with Singer Co., N.Y.C., 1968-79, asst. v.p. pers. dept., 1973-76, mng. counsel pers. office of gen. counsel, 1976-79; assoc. Skadden, Arps, Slate, Meagher & Flom, N.Y.C., 1979-85; ptnr. Finley, Kumble, Wagner, Heine, Underberg, Manley, Myerson & Casey, N.Y.C., 1985-87, Myerson & Kuhn, N.Y.C., 1987-89, McDermott Will & Emery, 1989-97, Orrick, Herrington & Sutcliffe, 1997-2000; full-time mediator and arbitrator, 2000—; mediator U.S. Dist. Ct. (so. and ea. dists.), Supreme Ct. N.Y., 2001—; pvt. mediator and arbitrator, 2000—. Adj. prof. employment law Fordham U., 1983-86; lectr. Practising Law Inst.'s Ann. Inst. on Employment Law, 1980—, co-chair, 1995, chair, 1996-2002; vol. mediator U.S. EEO Commn., 2000—, NYU Lawyering Program, 2003—, U.S. Ct. Appeals (2d cir.), 2004—; spl. master Appellate Divsn. of Supreme Ct., N.Y., 2002—; panelist comml. and employment, Am. Arbitration Assn., 2002—; arbitrator, mediator Nat. Assn. Securities Dealers, 2002—. Contbg. editor: Employee Rels. Law Jour., 1975—; contbr. over 100 articles to profl. jours. V.p., bd. dirs. Assn. for Integration Mgmt., 1979-85; bd. dirs. NY chpt. Am. Jewish Com., 1980-82; human resources com. NY YMCA, 1994—. Recipient award of Merit, Nat. Urban Coalition, 1979. Mem.: Assn. Conflict Resolution Greater N.Y., Am. Arbitration Assn. (comml. and employment panels 2001—), Bar Assn. of City of N.Y. (arbitration com. 2005—), University Club. Democrat. Jewish. Home and Office: Mediator/Arbitrator 880 Fifth Ave New York NY 10021 Office Phone: 212-570-9064. Personal E-mail: wlkandel@hotmail.com.

KANDRAVY, JOHN, lawyer; b. Passaic, N.J., May 9, 1935; s. Frank and Anna (Chan) K.; m. Alice E. Sullivan, Feb. 17, 1962; children: Elizabeth Ann (Mrs. Joseph P. Cassidy), Katherine Ann. BA, Wesleyan U., Middletown, Conn., 1957; JD, Columbia U., 1960. Bar: N.J. 1960, D.C. 1969, U.S. Supreme Ct. 1973, N.Y. 1982. From assoc. to ptnr. Shanley & Fisher, Newark, 1961-80, ptnr. Morristown, NJ, 1980-99, mng. ptnr., 1983-85, 89-99; ptnr. Drinker Biddle & Reath LLP, Florham Park, NJ, 1999—. Bd. dirs. Tingue, Brown & Co., VHS Ins. Co., Ltd.; mem. adv. bd. Ridgewood Savs. Bank of N.J. (divsn. Boiling Springs Savs. Bank), 2001—04. Mem. Gov.'s Mgmt. Commn., State of N.J., 1970; chmn. Planning Bd., Ridgewood, N.J., 1981-85, Zoning Bd. Adjustment, 1979-81; mem. bd. advisors Coll. Bus. Adminstrn., Fairleigh Dickinson U., 1983-87, chmn. bd. advisors, 1985-86; mem. Soc. of Valley Hosp., Ridgewood, 1971—, chmn. bd. trustees Ctrl. Bergen Cmty. Mental Health Ctr., N.J., 1970-73; trustee Palisades Counseling Ctr., Rutherford, 1968-81, The Forum Sch., Waldwick, N.J., 1987—, The Forum Sch. Found., Waldwick, 1978—; trustee The Valley Hosp., Ridgewood, 1992-2004, chmn. 2001-04, hon. trusteee, 2004—; trustee Valley Hosp. Found., Ridgewood, 2001-04, Valley Home Care, 2004-, chmn., 2005—; trustee Peer Found. for Plastic Surgery and Rehab., Florham Park, 1996—, Valley Health Sys., Inc., Paramus, 1997—, Children's Aid and Family Svcs., Inc., Paramus, N.J., 1998—; lawyers' adv. coun. Rutgers Law Sch., Newark, 1994-98, vis. com., 1994-98. Edward John Noble Found. grant, 1957-60. Mem. ABA, N.J. Bar Assn., Essex County Bar Assn., D.C. Bar Assn., Morris County Bar Assn., Essex Club (gov. 1976-85), Wesleyan U. Alumni Assn. (chmn. 1981-83), Ridgewood Country Club, Park Ave. Club (gov. 1992-97). Republican. Presbyterian. Home: 56 Monte Vista Ave Ridgewood NJ 07450-2428 Office: Drinker Biddle & Reath LLP 500 Campus Dr Fl 4 Florham Park NJ 07932-1047 Office Phone: 973-360-1100. Business E-Mail: john.kandravy@dbr.com.

KANDRIS, MICHAEL, trucking executive; Former exec. v.p., CFO Transport Corp. of Am.; former pres. North Star Transport; pres. Ruan Transp. Mgmt. Systems, Inc., Des Moines, 2001—. Office: Ruan Transp Mgmt Systems inc 666 Grand Ave Des Moines IA 50309

KANDT, RAYMOND S., neurologist; b. Rochester, N.Y., July 8, 1950; m. Irene Kandt; children: Melanie, Lauren. AB cum laude, U. Va., 1972; MD, U. Va. Sch. Medicine, 1976. Diplomate Am. Bd. Med. Examiners, Am. Bd. Pediatrics, Am. Bd. Psychiatry & Neurology with spl. competence in child neurology and with added qualifications in clin. neurophysiology; cert. neurovascular & pediat. neurosonologist; cert. MRI/CT. Intern, resident in pediatrics Johns Hopkins Hosp., Balt., 1976-78, resident in pediatric neurology, fellow in devel. pediatrics, 1978-81; instr. depts. neurology, pediatrics U. Mich., Ann Arbor, 1981-82, asst. prof. depts. neurology & pediatrics, 1982-84; asst. prof. pediatrics div. pediatric neurology Duke U. Med. Ctr., Durham, N.C., 1984-89, assoc. prof. pediatrics div. pediatric neurology, 1989-92, asst. prof. medicine div. neurology, 1990-92; assoc. prof. neurology, pediatrics Bowman Gray Sch. Medicine, Winston-Salem, N.C., 1992-97; clin. assoc. prof. pediatrics Wake Forest U./Bapt. Med. Ctr., Winston-Salem, 1997—. Chief sect. child neurology Bowman Gray Sch. Medicine, 1992-97, grad. med. edn. com. 1993-97, clin. faculty adv. coun., 1993-97; faculty advisor pediatric house staff U. Mich., 1981-84, faculty advisor med. students, 1983-84, com. on edn., 1982-84; pediatric rep. continuing med. edn. com. Duke U. Med. Ctr., 1985-92; mem. gen. clin. rsch. ctrs. com. nat. ctr. for rsch. resources NIH, 1991-95; cons. in field. Reviewer: Am. Jour. Human Genetics, 1995, Jour. Neurol. Scis., 1993—97, Nature Genetics, 1993, Annals of Neurology, 1998—2002; contbg. editor: Annals of Behavioral Medicine, 1991—93. Adv. bd. My Father's House Group Homes, 1993; med. adv. com. Children's Ctr. for the Physically Handicapped, Winston-Salem, N.C., 1993—. Grantee NIH, 1986-91, 89-92, Nat. Tuberous Sclerosis Assn., 1992-93, grantee Glaxo, 1995-96; recipient Merck award, 1976. Mem.: Profs. Child Neurology, Tuberous Sclerosis Alliance (mem. profl. adv. bd. 1990—, scientific adv. bd. 1995—, chmn. clin. care adv. bd. 1995—97, scientific grant rev. com. 1995—, chmn. med. adv. com. N.C. chpt. 1988—), Child Neurology Soc., N.C. Med. Soc., Am. Neurol. Assn., Phi Sigma, Alpha Omega Alpha. Home: 3428 Jameson Ln Winston Salem NC 27106-4771 Office: Johnson Neurologic Clinic 606 N Elm St High Point NC 27262-4336 Office Phone: 336-889-8877.

KANDUKURI, SUNIL, systems engineer; s. Prasad and Manorama Kandukuri. B of Engring., Andhra U., 1995; MSEE, Stanford U., 1998, PhD, 2001. Intern DSC Comm., Petaluma, Calif., 1997, Extreme Networks, Cupertino, 1998, AT&T Rsch. Labs., Florham Park, NJ, 1999; sr. sys. engr. Qualcomm, Inc., San Diego, 2001—. Avocations: marathons, tennis, hang-gliding, volleyball. Office: Qualcomm Inc 5775 Morehouse Dr San Diego CA 92121 Office Phone: 858-845-7865.

KANE, AGNES BREZAK, pathologist, educator; b. Danbury, Conn., Nov. 3, 1946; d. John Edward and Mary Elizabeth (Hatfield) Brezak; m. David E. Kane, June 22, 1970. BA, Swarthmore Coll., 1968; MD, Temple U., 1974, PhD, 1976. Diplomate Am. Bd. Pathology. Resident Temple U. Hosp., Phila., 1975-76, 77-78; postdoctoral fellow Karolinska Inst., Stockholm, 1976-77; asst. prof. Temple U. Sch. Medicine, Phila., 1977-82, Brown U., Providence, 1982-87, assoc. prof. pathology, 1987-95, prof. pathology, 1995-96, chair dept. pathology and lab. medicine, 1996—. Mem. merit rev. bd. for basic scis. VA, Washington, 1984-86; cons. R.I. Commn. for Safety and Occupational Health, Providence, 1986—; commr. Commn. to Identify Occupational Diseases, Providence, 1987-88; mem. rev. com. Nat. Inst. Environ. Health Scis., Research Triangle Park, N.C., 1988—. Assoc. editor Am. Jour. of Pathology, 1992—; contbr. articles on exptl. pathology to sci. publs. Lucretia Mott fellow Swarthmore Coll., 1969-71; recipient Rsch. Career Devel. award NIH, 1981-86. Mem. Am. Assn. Pathologists (women's com. 1987—, program com. 1990—), Assn. Women Med. Faculty Brown U. (founder, coord.), Women in Medicine (faculty advisor Brown U. chpt.; Mary Putnam Jacobi award 1986), Phi Kappa, Sigma Xi. Avocation: gardening. Office: Brown Univ Box G Providence RI 02912

KANE, ALAN HENRY, lawyer; b. Seattle, Nov. 7, 1940; s. Henry and Alice (Harbak) K.; m. Martha Dressler, June 25, 1966; children: Karen, Graham, Amy. BA in Law, U. Wash., 1963, JD, 1965. Bar: Wash. 1965. Ptnr. Sax & Maciver, Seattle, 1966-84, Preston Gales & Ellis, LLP, Seattle, 1985—. Fellow Am. Coll. Trusts and Estates Counsel (Wash. State chair 1985-88). Avocations: boating, water and snow skiing, fishing. Office: 925 Fourth Ave Ste 2900 Seattle WA 98104-1158 Office Phone: 206-623-7580. Business E-Mail: alank@prestongates.com.

KANE, ALICE THERESA, lawyer; b. N.Y.C., Jan. 16, 1948; AB, Manhattanville Coll., 1969; JD, NYU, 1972; grad., Harvard U. Sch. Bus. Program Mgmt. Devel., 1986. Bar: N.Y. 1973, U.S. Dist. Ct. (so. dist.) N.Y. 1974. Atty. N.Y. Life Ins. Co., N.Y.C., 1972-83, v.p., assoc. gen. counsel, 1983-85, v.p. dept. pers., 1986, sr. v.p., gen. counsel, 1986-89, corp. sec., 1989-94, exec. v.p., gen. counsel, sec., 1992-95, exec. v.p. asset mgmt., 1995-98; exec. v.p. Am. Gen. Investment Mgmt. Corp., N.Y.C., 1998—. Mem. ABA (chmn. employee benefits com., tort and ins. practice sect. 1984-85, mem. corp., banking and bus. law sects., tort and ins. practice sects.), NASD, Assn. Life Ins. Counsel (deps. solvency com.). E-mail: alice_kane@agfg.com.

KANE, CAROL, actress; b. Cleve., June 18, 1952; Stage debut in The Prime of Miss Jean Brodie, 1966; other N.Y.C. theatre appearances include Ring 'Round the Bath Tub, 1972, The Tempest, 1974, 80, The Effect of Gamma Ray on Man-in-the-Moon Marigolds, 1978, Are You Now or Have You Ever Been?, 1978, Benefit of a Doubt, 1978, Tales from Vienna Woods, 1979, Sunday Runners in the Rain, 1980, Macbeth, 1980, The Fairy Garden, 1984, The Debutante Ball, 1988, Frankie and Johnny in the Clair de Lune, 1988; film appearances include Carnal Knowledge, 1971, Desperate Characters, 1971, Wedding in White, 1972, The Last Detail, 1974, Dog Day Afternoon, 1975, Hester Street, 1975 (Acad. award nomination for Best Actress), Harry and Walter Go to New York, 1976, Annie Hall, 1977, Valentino, 1977, The World's Greatest Lover, 1977, The Mafu Cage, 1978, When a Stranger Calls, 1979, The Muppet Movie, 1979, The Sabiana, 1979, Les Jeux, 1980, Pandemonium, 1982, Norman Loves Rose, 1982, Can She Bake A Cherry Pie?, 1983, Over the Brooklyn Bridge, 1984, Racing With the Moon, 1984, The Secret Diary of Sigmund Freud, 1984, Transylvania 6-5000, 1985, Jumpin' Jack Flash, 1986, The Princess Bride, 1987, Ishtar, 1987, License to Drive, 1988, Scrooged, 1988, Sticky Fingers, 1988, Flashback, 1990, Joe Versus the Volcano, 1990, The Lemon Sisters, 1990, My Blue Heaven, 1990, Ted and Venus, 1991, In the Soup, 1992, When a Stranger Calls Back, 1993, Even Cowgirls Get the Blues, 1993, Baby on Board, 1993, Addams Family Values, 1993, The Crazysitter, 1995, Trees Lounge, 1996, Sunset Park, 1996, The Pallbearer, 1996, Big Bully, 1996, American Strays, 1996, Office Killer, 1997, Gone Fishin', 1997, The Tic Code, 1998, Jawbreaker, 1999, Man on the Moon, 1999, The Tic Code, The Office Party, 2000, D.C. Smalls, 2001, My First Mister, 2001, The Shrink is In, 2001, Love In the Time of Money, 2002, Confessions of a Teenage Drama Queen, 2004, The Pacifier, 2005; TV series Taxi, 1981-83, All is Forgiven, 1986, American Dreamer, 1990, Brooklyn Bridge, 1992, Pearl, 1996, Beggars and Choosers, 1999; TV films An Invasion of Privacy, 1983, Burning Rage, 1984, Drop Out Mother, 1988, When a Stranger Calls Back, 1993, Dad, the Angel & Me, 1995, Freaky Friday, 1995, Merry Christmas, George Bailey, 1997, The First Seven Years, 1998, Noah's Ark, 1999, Cosmopolitan, 2003, Audrey's Rain, 2003; TV appearances include Laverne & Shirley, 1982, Faerie Tale Theatre, 1983, Cheers, 1984, Tales from the Darkside, 1985, Crazy Like a Fox, 1985, Tales from the Crypt, 1990, (voice) Tiny Toon Adventures, 1990, Seinfeld, 1994, Empty Nest, 1994, Chicago Hope, 1995, Ellen, 1996, Homicide: Life on the Street, 1997, (voice) As Told by Ginger, (voice) Family Guy, 2001, Hope & Faith, 2004. Recipient Emmy award for outstanding supporting actress in a comedy series, 1981. Office: Krost/Chapin Mgmt 9465 Wilshire Blvd Ste 430 Beverly Hills CA 90212-2613*

KANE, CYNTHIA M., editor, writer; b. Waltham, Mass., June 30, 1957; s. Edwin Julian and Nanette Spillane Kane; m. Harry A. Trumbore, June 26, 1982; children: Dale Trumbore, Douglas Trumbore. BA with distinction, Cornell U., 1978. Editor New Am. Libr., N.Y.C., 1979—84; sr. editor Bantam Books for Young Readers, N.Y.C., 1985—87; editor-in-chief Four Winds Press, N.Y.C., 1987—99; editl. dir., exec. editor Dial Books for Young Readers, N.Y.C., 1991—99; supervising editor Pearson Edn., Parsippany, NJ, 1999—. Chmn. conf. Coun. on Children's Lit. Rutgers U., New Brunswick, NJ, 1990—91. Author (as Cindy Trumbore): (children's book) Discovering the Titanic, 1999, New Year's Around the World, 1999; author: The Genie in the Book, 2004; editor: (by Richard Peck) A Year Down Yonder, 2000 (Newbery medal, 2001). Mem. vestry St. Paul's Episcopal Ch., Chatham, NJ, 2005—. Mem.: Soc. Cildren's Book Writers and Illustrators. Home: 174 Weston Ave Chatham NJ 07928

KANE, DANIEL E., nurse; s. Suzanne Gillis; m. Jennifer Johnson, June 9, 2002; 1 child, Benjamin. BSN, U. NH, 1997; MEd, Cambridge Coll., 1996. Cert. Paramedic Tech. 1990; RN Mass., 1997, cert. emergency nurse, Bd. Certification for Emergency Nursing, 1998, flight RN, Bd. Certification for Emergency Nursing, 2000; EMT-Paramedic Mass., 1990. Paramedic North Suburban EMS, Armstrong Ambulance, Arlington, Mass., 1990—92, Cataldo EMS, Somerville, Mass., 1992—98, MetroWest Med. Ctr., Natick, Mass., 1996—2002; RN Lahey Clinic, Burlington, Mass., 1997—99, Brigham and Women's Hosp., Boston, 1999—2000, clin. nurse educator, 2002—04; flight nurse Hartford Hosp., Conn., 2000—02; rapid reponse nurse Lahey Clinic, Burlington, Mass., 2004—. Director-at-large Mass. Emergency Nurses Assn., 2004—; evaluator Commn. Coll. Nursing Edn., Washington, 2003—; primary stroke adv. com. mem. Mass. Dept. Pub. Health, Boston, 2005—. Contbr. articles to profl. jours. Mem.: Emergency Nurses Assn. (work group mem. 2004—, clin. expert 2004—), Golden Key, Sigma Theta Tau. Personal E-mail: dankanern@aol.com.

KANE, DEAN PHILIP, plastic surgeon; b. Miami, Fla., Sept. 11, 1954; s. Terry and Janet Kane; m. Lauri Jill Parnes; children: Erica, Alex. BS, U. Fla., 1976; MD, U. PR, 1980. Diplomate Am. Bd. Anti-Aging Medicine, Am. Bd. Plastic Surgery, Am. Acad. Wound Mgmt., Nat. Bd. Med. Examiners. Surg. intern Sinai Hosp., Balt., 1980—81, gen. surgery resident, 1981—85; resident in plastic surgery U. Fla., Gainesville, 1985—87; pvt. practice plastic surgery Balt., 1987—; mem. staff, assoc. clin. prof. divsn. plastic and reconstructive surgery Johns Hopkins Hosp., Balt., 1987—; mem. staff N.W. Hosp. Ctr., Balt., 1987—, dir. Wound Care Ctr., 1994—2001; med. dir., cosmetic surgery specialist Mercy Med. Ctr., Balt., 1995—99. Cons. in field; active attending Homewood South Hosp., Balt., 1987—91; cons., mem. staff Carroll County Hosp., Westminster, Md., 1987—96, Union Meml. Hosp., Balt., 1987—97. Author: Wound Healing and Wound Management; Surgical Repair; Chronic Wound Care, 2d edit., 1997, Chronic Wound Healing and Chronic Wound Management; Surgical Wound Repair in Advanced Wound Caring; Chronic Wound Care, 3d edit., 2001; contbr. articles to profl. jours. Fellow: ACS, Lipoplasty Soc. N.Am.; mem.: Baltimore County Med. Assn., Northeastern Soc. Plastic Surgeons, Am. Acad. Aesthetic and Restorative Surgery, Am. Assn. Wound Care, Am. Soc. Aesthetic Plastic Surgery, Am. Acad. Anti-Aging Medicine, John Staige Davis Md. Plastic Surgery Soc. (pres. 1998, membership chmn. 1992—96). Avocations: art, travel, skiing, hiking. Office: Ctr Antiaging Medicine and Cosmetic Surgery 1 Reservoir Cir # 201 Baltimore MD 21208 E-mail: deankane@DrDeanKane.com.

KANE, DIANE GRINKEVICH, urban planner, educator, architectural historian; b. Cleve., Mar. 9, 1947; d. Alex Grinkevich and Helen Magdalene Miko; m. John Jasper Kane, Sept. 3, 1972. BA, UCLA, 1969; MA, U. Calif., Berkeley, 1973; PhD, U. Calif., Santa Barbara, 1996. Tchr. Carondelet H.S., Concord, Calif., 1973-76; archtl. historian Louisville Landmarks Commn., 1978-79; exec. dir. Downtown Fullerton (Calif.) Assn., 1983; program rep. UCLA Ext., L.A., 1984-85, instr., 1986-89; archtl. historian Caltrans, L.A., 1989—2003; prof. New Sch. Architecture, San Diego, 1999—; sr. planner City San Diego, 2003—. Chair 1st Nat. Historic Rds. Conf., 1998. Contbg. author: Saving Historic Roads, 1998. Trustee Calif. Preservation Found., Oakland, 1996-2002, program chair conf., 2001; planning commr. City of La Habra Heights, Calif., 1983-90, mem. coun., 1990-92, mayor, mayor pro-tem, 1993-94. Scenic Byways Corridor Mgmt. Plan grantee Fed. Hwy. Adminstrn., 2000, Transp. Enhancement Activity grantee, 2000, Critical Issues Tng. grantee Nat. Pks. Svc., 1998; recipient Tranny award Calif. Trans. Found., 1997, 2002, 2003, Strive for Excellence Team award Fed. Hwy. Adminstrn., 1999, Caltrans Excellence Transp. award, 1999, 2000, 2002, 2003, Calif. Preservation Found. Design award, 2002, 2003, L.A. Conservancy Preservation award, 2002. Mem. Am. Inst. Cert. Planners, Am. Planning Assn. (award 2005), Soc. Archtl. Historians (treas., v.p., pres. 1989-93), Soc. Comml. Archaeology (bd. dirs. 1996-98, conf. chmn. 1996). Democrat. Avocations: swimming, scuba, hiking, bicycling, travel.

KANE, JACQUELINE, human resources specialist; Various positions in fin. svcs. industry; sr. v.p. human resources capital raising and global capial markets group Bank of Am.; dir. exec. leadership devel., dir. strategic change Hewlett-Packard, 2000—03; v.p. human resources Clorox. Co., Oakland, Calif., 2004—05, sr. v.p., 2005—. Bd. trustees Oakland Mus. Calif. Office: Clorox Co 1221 Broadway Oakland CA 94612-1888 Office Phone: 510-271-7000. Office Fax: 510-832-1463.*

KANE, JAY BRASSLER, banker; b. Bklyn., June 4, 1931; s. Arthur Ferris and Margaret (Brassler) K.; m. Marian Albertson, Oct. 15, 1960 (dec. 1993); children: Lisa Kane Brown, James Brassler. Grad., Poly. Prep. Sch., 1949; AB, Columbia, 1953; MBA, NYU, 1961. With Met. Life Ins. Co., N.Y.C., 1954-55, Bankers Trust Co., N.Y.C., 1955—, asst. v.p., 1965-68, v.p., 1968-88, BT Brokerage Corp., 1988-90; regional dir. Frank Russell Trust. Co., N.Y.C., 1990-97; assoc. P.P.I. Internat., 1997—. Co-pres. Cotton Club, 1999—2000, mgr. corp. pension funds, mktg. dir. trust svcs.; spkr. Am. Bankers Assn.; lectr New Sch. Social Rsch.; Attach bd. dirs.; bd. dirs. Pickwick Soc. Contbr. articles to profl. jours. Mem. N.Y. Soc. Security Analysts, Fin. Analysts Fedn., Am. Pension Conf., Riverside (Conn.) Yacht Club, N.Y. Yacht Club. Home and Office: Hilton Heath Cos Cob CT 06807 Office Phone: 203-661-9478. E-mail: jbkane1@aol.com.

KANE, JOHN LAWRENCE, JR., judge; b. Tucumcari, N.Mex., Feb. 14, 1937; s. John Lawrence and Dorothy Helen (Bottler) K.; m. Stephanie Jane Shafer, Oct. 5, 1993; children: Molly Francis, Meghan, Sally, John Pattison. BA, U. Colo., 1958; JD, U. Denver, 1961, LL.D. (hon), 1997. Bar: Colo. 1961. Dep. dist. atty., Adams County, Colo., 1961-62; assoc. firm Gaunt, Byrne & Dirrim, 1961-63; ptnr. firm Andrews and Kane, Denver, 1964; pub. defender Adams County, 1965-67; dep. dir. eastern region of India Peace Corps, 1967-69; with firm Holme Roberts & Owen, 1970-77, ptnr., 1972-77; judge U.S. Dist. Ct. Colo., Denver, 1978-88, U.S. sr. dist. judge, 1988—. Adj. prof. law U. Denver, U. Colo., 1996—; vis. lectr. Trinity Coll., Dublin, Ireland, winter 1989; adj. prof. U. Colo., 1996, philosophy, 2003. Contbr. articles to profl. jours. Recipient St. Thomas More award Cath. Lawyers Guild, 1983, U.S. Info. Agy. Outstanding Svc. award, 1985, Outstanding Alumnus award U. Denver, 1987, Lifetime Jud. Achievement award Nat. Assn. Criminal Def. Lawyers, 1987, Civil Rights award B'nai B'rith, 1988, Justice Gerald Le Dain award Drug Policy Found., 2000. Fellow Internat. Acad. Trial Lawyers, Am. Bd. Trial Advs. (hon.). Roman Catholic. Office: US Dist Ct US Courthouse 901 19th St Denver CO 80294-1929 Office Phone: 303-844-6118. Business E-Mail: John_L_Kane@cod.uscourts.gov. *There is a tendency to gild the past with uncritical generosity but an even more pronounced one to forget Santayana's dictum that one who forgets history is bound to repeat it. Law is that indispensable mechanism by which we may survive as a free people if we use it to apply a critical understanding of history to a confusing and dynamic present.*

KANE, JOHN MICHAEL, III, oncologist, surgeon, educator; BS, Allegheny Coll., 1987; MD, Johns Hopkins U., 1991. Diplomate Am. Bd. Surgery, 1999. Asst. prof. surgery Sch. Medicine U. Pitts., 2000—02; asst. prof. of surgery Sch. Medicine U. Buffalo, 2002—; surg. oncologist Roswell Pk. Cancer Inst., Buffalo, 2002—. Maj. U.S. Army, 2003—04. Fellow: ACS, Am. Soc. Clin. Oncology; mem.: Connective Tissue Oncology Soc., Radiation Therapy Oncology Group (sarcoma com. 2003). Republican. Roman Catholic. Avocations: travel, reading. Office: Roswell Park Cancer Institute Elm and Carlton Streets Buffalo NY 14263 Office Phone: 716-845-3284. Office Fax: 716-845-2320.

KANE, JONATHAN, art educator; b. Elwood, Ind., Aug. 25, 1957; s. Donald Edward Kane and Nancy Ann (Heflin) Kane; m. Barbara Ann Booker, Aug. 9, 1986; children: Nathan Booker, Julia Ann. BS in Art Edn., Ball State U., 1982, MA in Art Edn., 1987. Art instr. Lakeland Jr. H.S., LaGrange, Ind., 1982—87, Lakeland H.S., LaGrange, Ind., 1987—88, Carmel H.S., Carmel, Ind., 1988—; adj. faculty mem. Marian Coll., Indpls., 2000—03. Art counselor Indian Acres Summer Camp, Fryeburg, Maine, 1984; coord. Japanese Exch. Program, Carmel, Ind., 1990—95; asst. track coach Lakeland Jr. H.S., Carmel, Ind., 1982—87. Pastel drawing, Minnesota Landscape, (hon. mention Ind. State Fair, 2004), The Gardener (design selected for brochure/Carmel Parks and Recreation Dept., 2004), colored pencil drawing, Monarchs (hon. mention Ft. Wayne Mus. Art, 1988). Art instr. Carmel Clay Parks Dept., 1997—99; webelos den leader Cub Scouts, Indpls., 2003—04; soccer coach YMCA, Indpls., 1998; art judge Indpls. Art Ctr. Student Show, 1999; art show judge World Pork Expo. Pigasso Art Show, Indpls., 2000, Auburn Art Festival, 1988; lay dir. Christ Renews His Parish, St. Pius Cath. Ch., Indpls., 2001—03. Named one of Top 25 Sr. Scholastic Awards Influential Tchr. Recognition, Carmel H.S., 2000, 2004, 2005; recipient Best of Show, Purchase Award, Two First Places, Tri-Kappa Regional Exhbn., 1987, Most Influential Tchr. Recognition award, Indpls. Star Newspaper, 2004—05, Outstanding Tchr. Recognition Program, U. of San Diego, 1998, Master Tchr. Cert., Carmel/Clay Schools, 2003—04. Mem.: NEA, Ind. State Teacher's Assn. Roman Catholic. Avocations: running, biking, landscaping. Office: Carmel High School 520 East Main Carmel IN 46032 Office Phone: 846-7721. E-mail: jkane@ccs.k12.in.us.

KANE, LORIE, professional golfer; b. Prince Edward Island, Can., Dec. 19, 1964; d. Jack Kane. Student, Acadia U. Mem. Can. Internat. Team, 1989-92, Can. World Amateur Team, 1992; golfer LPGA, 1993—; du Maurier Ltd. Series champion, 1994, 95; series event winner, 1993-95; 2d place Toray Japan Queens Cup, 1997. Recipient Heather Farr Player Award, 1998, William and Mousie Powell Award, 2000. 1 LPGA career hole-in-one. Office: c/o LPGA 100 International Golf Dr Daytona Beach FL 32124-1082

KANE, MARGARET BRASSLER, sculptor; b. East Orange, NJ, May 25, 1909; d. Hans and Mathilde (Trumpler) Brassler; m. Arthur Ferris Kane, June 11, 1930; children: Jay Brassler, Gregory Ferris. Student, Packer Collegiate Inst., 1920—26, Syracuse U., 1927, Art Students League, 1927—29, N.Y. Coll. Music, 1928—29, John Hovannes Studio, 1932—34; PhD (hon.), Colo. State Christian Coll., 1973. Head craftsman sculpture, arts and skills unit ARC, Halloran Gen. Hosp., NY, 1942—43; jury mem. Bklyn. Mus., 1948, Am. Machine & Foundry Co., 1957; com. mem. An Am. Group, Inc. Exhibitions include, Phila. Mus., Chgo. Art Inst., Am. Fedn. Arts, N.Y. Bot. Garden, 1981, 60th Anniversary Exhbn. Lever House, 1987—98, Sculptors Guild 50th Anniversary Exhbn., Lever House, 1987—96, 1st Bi-Coastal exhibits San Francisco, Collection Donald Trump, 1988, Collection Rene Anselmo, 1991, Shidoni Galleries, Santa Fe, N.Mex., 1989, Am. Sculpture, Hofstra Mus., 1990, exhibitions include nat. tour Am. sculpture by EducArt Projects Inc., 1992, exhibitions include, Stamford Mus. and Nature Ctr., 1996, Zimmerli Art Mus. Historical Exhibit, 1999—2000, Treasures from the Smithsonian Am. Art Mus., 2000—02, numerous others, Represented in permanent collections, Zimmerli Art Mus., Rutgers U., N.J., 1992, Nat. Mus. Am. Art, Smithsonian Instn., Washington, 1993, 2000, Bruce Mus., Greenwich, Conn., 1996, Packer Collegiate Inst., Bklyn., 2003, one-woman shows include sculpture, Friends Greenwich (Conn.) Library, 1962, prin. works include 18 foot carving in limewood, 2002, prin. works include six foot carving Reaching the Galaxies, 2002—, prin. works include sculpture Packer Collegiate Inst., Bklyn., 2003, prin. works include plaque Burro Monument, Fair Play, Colo., prin. works include bronze panels Earthbound, cast by Tallix Art Foundry Beacon, NY, 2005, Symbols, 2005, Micro-macrocosm, 2005; reprodns. Contemporary Stone Sculpture, 1970, Contemporary Am. Sculptures, Am. References, Chgo.; CD-ROM, Smithsonian Nat. Mus. Am. Art, Washington, 1995; contbr. articles to mags. Recipient Hyatt Huntington award, 1942, Am. Artist Profl. League and Monclair Art Assn. awards, 1943, 1st Henry O. Avery prize, 1944, Sculpture prize, Bklyn. Soc. Artists, Bklyn. Mus., 1946, John Rogers award, 1951, Lawrence Hyder prize, 1952, 1954, David H. Zell Meml. award, 1954, 1963, Hon. Mention, U.S. Maritime Commn., 1941, A.C.A. Gallery Competition, 1944, medal of Honor for Sculpture, Nat. Acad. Galleries, N.Y., prize for carved sculpture, 1955, prize for animal sculpture, 1956, 1st award for sculpture, Ann. New Eng. Exhbns., Silvermine, Conn. Fellow: Internat. Inst. Arts and Letters (life); mem.: Nat. Trust Hist. Preservation, silvermine Guild Artists, Internat. Soc. Artists (charter), Internat. Sculpture Ctr., Greenwich Soc. Artists (mem. coun.), Bklyn. Soc. Artists, Artists Coun. U.S.A., Pen and Brush (emeritus 1992), Nat. League Am. Pen Women, Inc. (OWL award for the Arts 1991), Nat. Assn. Women Artists (2d v.p. 1943—44), Sculptors Guild, Inc. (life; sec. to exec. bd. 1942—45, chmn. exhbn. com. 1942, 1944). Home and Studio: 30 Strickland Rd Cos Cob CT 06807-2729 *It is not possible to overestimate the deep satisfaction experienced in having created countless direct carvings in marble, stone, wood and models for bronze. I strongly believe mankind needs to express itself in some meaningful way. My recent mahogany woodcarvings are dedicated to Peace, Love and an end to Violence. If these goals should inspire the many thousands of viewers of my art form, then I am content that my sculpture is a worthwhile contribution to American culture.*

KANE, MARILYN, real estate company executive; m. Jeffrey Nichols (div.); children: Joshua, Julie, Joseph; m. David Kane, 1990. Co-pres. Butler Kane, Inc., N.Y.C. Founder N.Y. chpt. Nat. Coalition for Family Justice. Office: Butler Kane Inc 171 Madison Ave #1000 New York NY 10016

KANE, MARY KAY, dean; b. Detroit, Nov. 14, 1946; d. John Francis and Frances (Roberts) K.; m. Ronan Eugene Degnan, Feb. 3, 1987 (dec. Oct. 1987). BA cum laude, U. Mich., 1968, JD cum laude, 1971. Bar: Mich. 1971. Rsch. assoc., co-dir. NSF project on privacy, confidentiality and social sci. rsch. data sch. law U. Mich., 1971-72, Harvard U., 1972-74; asst. prof. law SUNY, Buffalo, 1974-77; mem. faculty Hastings Coll. Law U. Calif., San Francisco, 1977—, prof. law, 1979—, assoc. acad. dean, 1981-83, acting acad. dean, 1987-88, acad. dean., 1990-93, dean, 1993—; chancellor U. Calif., San Francisco, 2001—. Vis. prof. law U. Mich., 1981, U. Utah, 1983, U. Calif., Berkeley, 1983-84, sch. law U. Tex., 1989; cons. Mead Data Control, Inc., 1971, 74, Inst. on Consumer Justice, U. Mich. Sch. Law, 1972, U.S. Privacy Protection Study Commn., 1975-76; lectr. pretrial mgmt. devices U.S. magistrates for 6th and 11th cirs. Fed. Jud. Ctr., 1983; Siebenthaler lectr. Samuel P. Chase Coll. Law, U. North Ky., 1987; reporter ad hoc com. on asbestos litigation U.S. Jud. Conf., 1990-91, mem. standing com. on practice and procedure, 2001—; mem. 9th Cir. Adv. Com. on Rules Practice and Internal Oper. Procedures, 1993-96; spkr. in field. Author: Civil Procedure in a Nutshell, 1979, 5th edit., 2003, Sum and Substance on Remedies, 1981; co-prodr.(with C. Wright and A. Miller): Pocket Supplements to Federal Practice and Procedure, 1975—; co-author (with C. Wright and A. Miller): Federal Practice and Procedure, vol. 7, 3d edit., 2001, 10, 10A and 10B, 3d edit., 1998, vols. 7-7C, 2d edit., 1986, vols. 6-6A, 2d edit., 1990, vols. 11-11A, 2d edit., 1995, vols. 7A-B, 3d edit., 2005; co-author: (with J. Friedenthal and A. Miller) Hornbook on Civil Procedure, 4th edit., 2005; co-author: (with C. Wright) Hornbook on the Law of Federal Courts, 2002, Federal Practice Deskbook, 2002; mem. law sch. divsn. West. Adv. Editl. Bd., 1986—; contbr. articles to profl. jours. Mem. standing com. on rules of practice and procedure U.S. Jud. Conf., 2000—. Mem. ABA (mem. bar admissions com. 1995-2000, mem. coun. sect. legal edn. and admission to bar 2004—), Assn. Am. Law Schs. (com. on prelegal edn. statement 1982, chair sect. remedies 1982, panelist sect. on prelegal edn. 1983, exec. com. sect. on civil procedure 1983, 86, panelist sect. on tchg. methods 1984, spkr. new tchrs. conf. 1986, 89, 90, chair sect. on civil procedure 1987, spkr. sects. civil procedure and conflicts 1987, 91, chair planning com. for 1988 Tchg. Conf. in Civil Procedure 1987-88, nominating com. 1988, profl. devel. com. 1988-91, planning com. for workshop in conflicts 1988, planning com. for 1990 Conf. on Clin. Legal Edn. 1989, chair profl. devel. com. 1989-91, exec. com. 1991-93, 2000-02, pres.-elect 2000, pres. 2001), Am. Law Inst. (co-reporter complex litigation project 1988-93, coun. 1998—), ABA/Assn. Am. Law Schs. Commn. on Financing Legal Edn., State Bar Mich. Home: 8 Admiral Dr Ste 421 Emeryville CA 94608-1567 Office: U Calif Hastings Coll Law 200 McAllister St San Francisco CA 94102-4707

KANE, RAVI, biomedical engineer; BS, Stanford U., 1993; MS, MIT, 1995, PhD, 1998; postdoctoral rsch., Harvard U., 1998—2001. Merck asst. prof. Isermann Dept. Chemical and Biol. Engring. Rensselaer Polytechnic Inst., 2001—. Contbr. articles to profl. jour. Named one of Top 100 Young Innovators, MIT Tech. Review, 2004; grad. fellow, NSF, 1993. Mem.: Phi Beta Kappa, Sigma Xi. Office: Ricketts Bldg Rm 131 110 8th St Troy NY 12180 Business E-Mail: kaner@rpi.edu.

KANE, RICHARD JOSEPH, lawyer; b. NYC, Feb. 12, 1941; s. Joseph Thomas and Helen Elizabeth (Ward) K.; m. Lorraine Catherine Heckelmann, Nov. 21, 1964; children: Kevin Joseph, Robert Keith, Carol Aileen. BA, St. John's Coll., N.Y., 1962; JD, St. John's U., N.Y., 1965. Bar: NY 1965, Fla. 1967, US Dist. Ct. (So. Dist.) NY 1967, US Dist. Ct. (Ea. Dist.) NY 1967, US Ct. Appeals (2nd and 11th Cirs.) 1967, US Supreme Ct. 1969. Ptnr. Golenbock & Barell, N.Y.; ptnr., real estate dept. Thelen Reid & Priest LLP, NYC. Faculty mem. real estate financing and mortgage instruments NYU, Real Estate Inst. NYU., 1982; adv. bd., mem. First Am. Title Ins. Co., NY; lectr. in field. Contbr. articles to profl. jours. Jud. arbitrator Civil Ct. City of NY 1974—; active NYC Jud. Screening Com. 1982-84; chmn. law sch. homecoming program, 1983; vice-chmn. bldg. com. for the constrn. of Fromkes Hall; moderator TV series on real estate financing. Mem. ABA, Am. Judges Assn., Fla. Bar Assn. (real property law com.), NY State Bar Assn. (real property law sect., chmn. constrn. contracts 1980, lectr. real estate financing 1978), NY Assn. Arbitrators (pres. 1984, sec. 1982, v.p. 1982, bd. dirs. 1977—), St. John's U. Sch. Law Am. Alumni Assn. (bd. dirs. 1968—, pres. 1994-2000), Internat. Legal Frat., Phi Delta Phi Assn. of City of NY (pres. 1968-71, exec. com. 1971—, bd. govs. 1968). Office: Thelen Reid & Priest LLP 875 Third Ave New York NY 10022-6225 Office Phone: 212-603-2032. Office Fax: 212-603-2001. Business E-Mail: rkane@thelenreid.com.

KANE, ROBERT LEWIS, public health service officer, educator; b. N.Y.C., Jan. 18, 1940; m. Rosalie Smolkin, June 17, 1962; children: Miranda, Ingrid, Kate AB, Columbia Coll., N.Y.C., 1961; MD, Harvard U., 1965. Acting coordinator sr. clerkship program dept. community medicine U. Ky., Lexington, 1968-69; svc. unit dir. USPHS Indian Hosp., Shiprock, N.Mex., 1969-70; spl. asst. to regional health dir. USPHS HEW Region VIII, Denver, 1970-71; from asst. to assoc. prof. family and community medicine U. Utah Sch. Medicine, Salt Lake City, 1970-77; sr. researcher The Rand Corp., Santa Monica, Calif., 1977-85; from assoc. prof. to prof. medicine UCLA Sch. Medicine, 1978-85; prof. Sch. Pub. Health UCLA, 1980-85, U. Minn., 1985—, dean, 1985-90; intern U. Ky. Med. Ctr., Lexington, 1965-66, resident in community medicine, 1966-69. Adj. prof. Leonard Davis Sch. Gerontology, U. So. Calif., 1982-85; mem. expert com. on aging WHO, 1986-2002; Minn. endowed chair in long-term care and aging, 1989—; mem. adv. com. on Alzheimer's Disease, Washington, 1988-96; mem. com. on quality Inst. Medicine, 1988-90. Co-author: A Will and A Way, 1985, Long-term Care: Principles, Programs, and Policies, 1987, Essentials of Clinical Geriatrics, 5th edit., 2004, Understanding Health Care Outcomes Research, 1997, The Heart of Long Term Care, 1998, Assessing Older Persons, 2000, It Shouldn't Be This Way, 2005, Meeting the Challenge of Chronic Illness, 2005. With USPHS, 1969-70. Home: 2715 E Lake Of The Isles Pky Minneapolis MN 55408-1053 Office Phone: 612-624-1185.

KANE, SAM, meat company executive; b. Spisske Pohrdie, Czechoslovakia, June 23, 1919; came to U.S., 1948, naturalized, 1953. s. Leopold and Bertha (Narcisenfeld) Kannengiesser; m. Aranka Feldbrand, Jan. 15, 1946; children: Jerry, Harold Ira, Esther Barbara. Grad., Rabbinical Coll. Galanta, 1939. Pres. Sam Kane Wholesale Meat, Inc., Corpus Christi, 1956—, Sam Kane Meat, Inc., Corpus Christi, 1956—, Sam Kane Packing co., Corpus Christi, 1962—, Kane Enterprises, Inc., Corpus Christi, 1956—; pres., chmn. bd., CEO Sam Kane Beef Processors, Inc., 1956—. Pres., Jewish Welfare Appeal, 1962—; pres. Combined Jewish Appeal, 1962—, chmn. bd., 1962-65; mem. nat. cabinet United Jewish Appeal; bd. dirs. Tex. Coun. on Econ. Edn.; mem. Gov. Tex. 2000 Commn. Recipient award chmn. bd edn. B'nai Israel Synagogue, 1965, Israel Service award, 1966, Koach award State of Israel, 2976, Prime Minister of Israel Peace medal, 1980, Brotherhood award Corpus Christi chpt. NCCJ, 1984, Torch of Liberty award Anti Defamation League, 1984; named Outstanding Jewish Citizen of Corpus Christi, 1969. Mem. Tex. Coun. on Econ. Edn. (bd. dirs.), Tex. Taxpayers Assn., B'nai B'rith. Jewish (pres. synagogue 1964-65). Home: 27 Hewitt Dr Corpus Christi TX 78404-1662 Office: San Kane Beef Processors 9001 Leopard St Corpus Christi TX 78409-2502

KANE, THOMAS JAY, III, surgeon, educator; b. Merced, Calif., Sept. 2, 1951; s. Thomas J., Jr. and Kathryn (Hassler) Kane; m. Marle Rose Van Emmerik, Oct. 10, 1987; children: Thomas Keola, Travis Reid, Samantha Marie. BA in History, U. Santa Clara, 1973; MD, U. Calif., Davis, 1977. Diplomate Am. Bd. Orthopaedic Surgery. Intern U. Calif. Davis Sacramento Med. Ctr., 1977-78, resident in surgery, 1978-81; resident in orthopaedic surgery U. Hawaii, 1987-91; fellowship adult joint reconstruction Rancho Los Amigos Med. Ctr., 1991-92; ptnr. Orthop. Assocs. Hawaii, Inc., Honolulu, 1992—; asst. prof. surgery U. Hawaii, Honolulu, 1993—, chief divsn. implant surgery, 1993—, asst. chief orthopedics, 2003—04. Contbr. articles to profl. jours. Mem.: AMA, Western Orthop. Assn., Am. Acad. Orthop. Surgery, Hawaii Orthop. Assn. (v.p. 2003—04, pres. 2004—), Hawaii Med. Assn., Am. Assn. Hip and Knee Surgeons, Phi Kappa Phi, Alpha Omega Alpha. Avocations: tennis, golf, skiing, music, surfing. Office: Orthopaedic Svcs Co LLP 1380 Lusitana St Ste 608 Honolulu HI 96813-2442 Office Phone: 808-521-8124. Personal E-mail: tkaneiii@yahoo.com.

KANE, YVETTE, lawyer, judge; b. Donaldsonville, La., Oct. 11, 1953; d. Thomas R. Pregeant and Julia Tucker; children: Kathleen, Madeline. BA, Nicholls State U., Thibodeaux, La., 1973; JD, Tulane U., 1976. Bar: Pa. Trial atty. U.S. Equal Employment Opportunity Commn., 1977-78; asst. atty. gen. Colo. Atty. Gen.'s Office, 1978-80; dep. dist. atty. Denver Dist. Atty.'s Office, 1980-86; dep. atty. gen. rev. and advice sect. Pa. Office Atty. Gen., 1986-91; chief counsel Pa. Ind. Regulatory Rev. Commn., 1991-92; sr. assoc. Wolf, Block, Schorr & Solis-Cohen, Harrisburg, Pa., 1993-95; sec. state Commonwealth of Pa., 1995-98; U.S. dist. judge U.S. Dist. Ct. (mid. dist.) Pa., Harrisburg, 1998—. Office: US Dist Ct Box 11817 228 Walnut St 8th Fl Harrisburg PA 17108 Office Phone: 717-221-3920.

KANEB, JOHN A., oil industry executive; m. Virginia Kaneb; 6 children. B., Harvard, 1956; LLD (hon.), St. Anslem Coll., 1984; PhD (hon.), U. Notre Dame, 1996. CEO Northeast Petroleum, 1959—83; pres. Catamount Cos.; co-founder, CEO Catamount Petroleum (acquired gen. partnership interest Gulf Oil L.P), 1986—94; chmn. Gulf Oil L.P., 1994—; CEO, pres., chmn. HP Hood, Chelsea, Mass., 1995—. Commr. Nat. Prison Rape Elimination Commn., 2004—; ptnr. Boston Red Sox. Trustee U. Notre Dame; trustee, fin. chmn. Partners Healthcare Sys.; trustee McLean Hosp. Jr. officer USN, 1957—59. Office: HP Hood 90 Everett Ave Chelsea MA 02150-2301*

KANEDA, MASAYOSHI, mathematics professor, researcher; b. Kashiwazaki-shi, Niigata, Japan, Nov. 7, 1971; s. Ichiro and Mutsuko Kaneda. BS in Physics, Kyoto U., Japan, 1995; MS in Physics, U. Tokyo, 1997, MS in Math. Scis., 2001; MS in Math., U. Houston, 2002, PhD in Math., 2003. Tchg. asst. U. Tokyo, Meguro-ku, 1998—98; tchg. fellow, rsch. asst. dept. math. U. Houston, 1998—2003; lectr. U. Calif., Irvine, 2003—. Contbr. articles to profl. jours. Mem.: Math. Soc. Japan, Math. Assn. Am., Am. Math. Soc., Gakushikai U. Alumni Assn. Home: 989 Victoria St Apt C4 Costa Mesa CA 92627-4055 Office: U Calif Irvine 103 Multipurpose Sci and Tech Bldg Irvine CA 92697-3875 E-mail: kaneda@math.uh.edu.

KANE-GILL, SANDRA LUCILLE, medical educator; d. Robert Thomas and Lucille Marie Kane; m. Michael Malloy Gill, May 31, 2003; 1 child, Michael Malloy Jr. BS in Pharmacy, Wayne State U., Detroit, Mich., 1989—94; D in Pharmacy, U. of Toledo, Toledo, Ohio, 1996—98; MS, The Ohio State U., Columbus, Ohio, 1999—2001. Lic. Pharmacist Mich., 1994, Pa., 2003. Asst. prof. U. Pitts., Pitts., 2001—. Residency pharmacy practice W.Va. U. Hosp., Morgantown, W.Va., 1995—96; critical care fellowship Ohio State U., Columbus, Ohio, 1998—2001. Author: (publ.) Intensive Care Medicine, Annals of Pharmacotherapy, Pharmacotherapy, Critical Care Medicine, Hosp. Pharmacy, Annals of Pharmacotherapy. Not applicable. Grantee Medication Safety Grant, Am. Soc. of Health Sys. Pharmacists, 2002, Amgen Biotechnology Rsch. Award, Am. Coll. of Clin. Pharmacy Rsch. Inst., 2002. Mem.: Internat. Soc. of Pharmacoeconomics and Outcomes Rsch., Am. Coll. of Clin. Pharmacy, Soc. of Critical Care Medicine (chair for the clin. pharmacy sect.). Achievements include research in grants to study adverse drug events, patient safety, and the pharmacoeconomics and outcomes of different disease states and drug therapies. Office: Univ of Pitts 904 Salk Hall 3501 Terrace St Pittsburgh PA 15261

KANEHIRO, KENNETH KENJI, insurance educator, risk analyst, consultant; b. Honolulu, May 10, 1934; s. Charles Yutaka and Betty Misako (Hoshino) K.; m. Eiko Asari, June 23, 1962; 1 child, Everett Peter. BA in Counseling Psychology, U. Hawaii, 1956, grad. cert. in Counseling Psychology, 1957; grad. cert. in ins., The Am. Inst., 1971; cert., Nat. Leadership Inst. CPCU; cert. continuing profl. devel. Claims adjustor Cooke Trust Co., Honolulu, 1959-62, underwriter, 1962-66; account supr. Alexander & Baldwin, Honolulu, 1966-68; spl. risk exec. Hawaiian Ins. & Guaranty, Honolulu, 1968-71, br. mgr. Hilo, Hawaii, 1971-72; chief of office Marsh & McLennan, Inc., Hilo, 1972-78; sr. mktg. rep. Occidental Underwriters, Honolulu, 1978-87; pvt. practice Honolulu, 1987—. Coord. Ins. Sch. of Pacific, Honolulu, 1978—; lectr. ins. Hawaii State Cts., 1986—; adv. bd. Ins. Commn., 2000—; mem. adv. bd. Real Estate Commn., 2003—; cons. Dai Tokyo Royal State Ins. Co., 1992—; mem. arbitration panel, ct. observer panel Hawaii State Cts., 1993-96, Hawaii Criminal Ct., 1994—; proctor Hawaii State Bar Exam., 1994—; ins. expert witness, 1995—; instr. ins. agt.'s lic. course, 1995—; dir. edn. Profl. Ins. Agts. Hawaii, 2001—; bd. dirs. Royal Ins. Agy.; mem. bd. ethical inquiry Am. Inst. for Chartered Property Casualty Underwriters, 2002—. Adult leader Boy Scouts Am., Hilo and Honolulu, 1956—, risk mgr. Aloha coun., Honolulu, 1980—; edn. chmn. Gen. Ins. Assn., Hawaii, Hilo, 1971-77; ins. cons. Arcadia Retirement Residence, Honolulu, 1987—; cons. Waikiki Banyan Assn.; bd. govs. U. Hawaii Founders Alumni Assn., Honolulu, 1993—, scholarship chmn., 1993—. With U.S. Army, 1957-59. Recipient First Lady's Outstanding Vol. award, First Lady/State of Hawaii, 1990, Pres.'s award, Boy Scouts Aloha Coun., 1997, Excellence award, Chartered Property and Casualty Underwriters, 2000. Mem.: Profl. Ins. Agts. of Hawaii, Soc. Ins. Trainers and Educators, Soc. Chartered Property and Casualty Underwriters (pres. 1986—87, nat. publs. com. 1996—2000, nat. ethics com. 2000—, contbr. to jour., Excellence award 2000). Avocations: art, photography, music. Home: 1128 Ala Napunani St Apt 705 Honolulu HI 96818-1606

KANE HITTNER, MARCIA SUSAN, bank executive; b. N.Y.C. d. Howard Eugene and Sydell (Friedman) Kane; m. Ellis Hittner. cert. fin. planning, BA in Comm., NYU. Cert. Nat. Ret. Plans Tng. Ctr., software capability maturity model cert. interim profile adminstr. Carnegie Mellon U. Pension specialist Union Dime Savs. Bank, N.Y.C., 1978—81; money market specialist Goldome (formerly Union Dime Savs. Bank), N.Y.C., 1981—82; mgr. customer svc. Citibank, N.A., N.Y.C., 1982—85, mgr. mktg. product, 1986—87, mgr. shareholder comm., 1988—89, asst. v.p., tax shelter conversions, 1990—93, asst. v.p. tech. client interface, 1993—95, asst. v.p. U.S., Europe consumer bank, 1995—99; with product design and devel. Software Engring. Process Group, 1995—99; v.p. mktg. strategy EAB subs. ABN-AMRO, 1999—2001, cons. bus. and mktg. strategy, 2001—. Author: (with others) Critical Reading-Level G, 1980. Bd. dirs. Forest Hills Owners Corp., N.Y.C.

KANEKO, ISAO, air transportation executive; b. Mar. 1, 1938; married; 1 child. Grad. law dept., Tokyo U. Joined Japan Airlines, Tokyo, 1960, internat. cargo dept., indsl. rels. dept., with NYC, 1968—72, dep. v.p. indsl. rels. Tokyo, 1980, v.p. internat. rels., 1985, mng. dir., 1995—97, sr. v.p. human resources, 1995—98, sr. mng. dir., 1997—98, pres., 1998—2002; pres., CEO Japan Airlines System Co., Tokyo, 2002—04; chmn., group CEO Japan Airlines Corp. (formerly Japan Airlines System Co.), Tokyo, 2004—; chmn. Japan Airlines Internat. Co. Ltd., 2004—, Japan Airlines Domestic Co. Ltd., 2004—. Co-chaired 28th ASEAN-Japan Bus. Meeting; chmn. Internat. Air Transport Assn., 2002—04. Avocations: basketball, reading.

KANEKO, MANABU, materials engineer; MS, Tokyo Inst. Tech., 1992. Chief rschr. Mitsubishi Rayon Co., Ltd., Tokyo, 1992—. Vis. rschr. U. Del., Newark, 2002—. Patentee in field. Office: U Del 209 Composites Mfg Sci Lab Newark DE 19716 Office Phone: 302-831-8511. E-mail: hzu02034@nifty.com.

KANELLOS, NICOLAS, language educator, liberal studies educator; b. NYC, Jan. 31, 1945; s. Constantino and Inés (de Choudens) K.; m. Cristelia Pérez, May 12, 1984; 1 child, Miguel José. BA in Spanish, Fairleigh Dickinson U., 1966; MA in Romance Langs., U. Tex., 1968, PhD in Spanish and Portuguese, 1974; postgrad. in Mexican Lit. and Culture, U. Autónoma Mex., Mexico City, 1964-65; postgrad. in Portuguese Lit. and Culture, U. Lisboa, Portugal, 1969-70; LHD (hon.), U. Ariz., 2001. From asst. to assoc. prof. Ind. U. N.W., Gary, 1970-79; assoc. prof. U. Houston, 1979-85, prof., 1985—, Brown Found. prof., endowed chair, 1996—. Founder, dir. Teatro Desengano del Pueblo, Gary, 1972-79; founder, pub. Arte Publico Press/U. Houston, 1979—; pub. The Americas Rev.; apptd. Lit. Policy Panel NEA, 1987-90; apptd. to Arts Adv. Com., Ednl. Testing Svc./The Coll. Bd., 1987; apptd. Pres. Clinton Nat. Coun. on the Humanities, 1994; presenter papers in field assns., confs., univs., symposia U.S., Europe, Mex.; disting. vis. scholar Ctr. Humanities and Arts U. Ga., 2003; lectr. Cuba, France, Germany, italy, Spain, Mex., Venezuela, US, PR, Bellagio, The Sorbonne, AATSP, Pen Internat., Am. Writers Congress, Libr. of Congress, Folger Shakespeare Libr., NEH, and more than 40 univs. Author: Mexican American Theatre: Legacy and Reality, 1987, Hispanic Bibliography, 1988, Biographical Dictionary of Hispanic Literature in the United States up to World War II, 1990, The History of Hispanic Theatre in the United States up to World War II, 1990 (SW Conf. Lat. Am. Studies Book award, 1991, Tex. Inst. Letters award, 1991, San Antonio Conservation Soc. Book award, 1990), A History of Hispanic Theatre in the United States: Origins to 1940, 1990, (chpts.) The Hispanic American Almanac: A Reference Work on Hispanics in the United States, 1993 (ALA award best reference work, 1990), 2004, Hispanic Almanac, 1994, Chronology of Hispanic American History, 1995; author: (edited with Bryan Ryan) Hispanic American Chronology, 1995; author: Hispanic Firsts: Three Hundred Years of Outstanding Achievement, 1997, Thirty Million Strong: Reclaiming the Hispanic Image in U.S. History, 1998, The Adventures of Don Chipote: When Parrots Breast Feed, 1999, Hispanic Periodicals in the United States: A Brief History and Comprehensive Bibliography, 2000, Los aventuras de Don Chipote, o Cuando los pericos mamen, 1985, 2000, Lucas Guevara, Spanish edit., 2001, English edit., 2003, Hispanic Literature of the United States: A Comprehensive Reference, 2004; author, prodr. Lalo Astol: El teatro en mi vida, 1982, author, rschr. The Bilingual Education Controversy: A Houston Perspective, 1982, author, cons. (brochure) Two Centuries of Hispanic Theater in the United States, 1984—85, Our Journeys/Our Stories: Portraits of Latino Cambios/Nuestras Historias: Restratos del Logro Latino, 2004; editor (with Jorge Huerta): Nuevos Pasos: Chicano and Puerto Rican Drama, 1979, 2d edit., 1989; editor: (with Luis Dávila) Latino Short Fiction, 1980; editor: (with Robert E. Beck, Sharon L. Belshaw, others) (textbook series) Introduction to Literature, 1981, Exploring Literature, 1981, Understanding Literature, 1981, Types of Literature, 1981, American Literature, 1981, English Literature, 1981; editor: Mexican American Theater: Then and Now, 1983, Las aventuras de Don Chipote, 1984, English transl., 2000, Spanish transl., 2001, Hispanic Theater in the United States, 1985, Biographical Dictionary of Hispanic Literature in the United States, 1989, Short Fiction by U.S. Hispanic Authors, 1993, The Hispanic American Almanac: A Reference Work on Hispanics in the United States, 1993, 2004; editor: (with Claudio Esteva Fabregat) Handbook of Hispanic Cultures in the United States, 1994; editor: Hispanic American Literature, 1995; co-editor: (textbooks for high sch. English) Ginn Literature Series, 2nd edit., 1989; mem. editl. bd. Latin Am. Theatre Rev., 1982—, Critica, 1983—, Confluencia, 1984—, SW Rev., 1990—, Latino Studies Jour., 1990—, MELUS, 1999—, Theater in the Ams. series; contbr. articles to profl. jours., chapters to books; editor, compiler The Hispanic Literary Companion, 1996, Noche Buena: Hispanic American Christmas Stories, 2000;: Noche Buena: Hispanic American Christmas Stories, 2000; gen. editor: Herencia: The Anthology of Hispanic Literature of the United States, 2002; dir. gen. En otra vez: antología de la literatura hispana de los Estados Unidos, 2002, pub. The Ams. Rev. (formerly known as Revista Chicano-Riqueña), 1973—99, Arte Público Press Books. Member Ind. Civil Rights Commn., Gary, 1974-75; mem. arts adv. com. NY Coll. Bd., 1989—; lit. cons. NEA, Washington, 1985-90; pres. Bishop's Com. Spanish Speaking, Gary, 1974-76; dir. nat. project. Named in honor of achievement as scholar, critic and educator, Soc. Study Multiethnic Lit. Modern Lang. Assn., 1980, 100 Most Influential Hispanic in US, Hispanic Bus. mag., 1989, 1993, 1997, 1998, Disting. Vis. Scholar, Ctr. Humanities and Arts, U. Ga., 2003; named to Tex. Inst. Letters, 1984, 1st Brown Found. Endowed Chair, U. Houston, 1996, Wall of Tolerance, Nat. Campaign Tolerance, 2003; recipient $5,000 award outstanding editor, Coord. Coun. Lit. Mags., 1979, Hispanic Heritage award, Pres. Reagan, 1988, award, Tex. Assn. Chicanos Higher Edn., 1989, Commendation Gov. Tex. high stds. acad. excellence, 1989, Am. Book award pub., editor category, 1989, Best Reference Work of 1993 award, ALA (reference and adult sect.), 1994, Denali Press award, ALA, 1996, 10th Ann. PREMIO award outstanding contbns. in pub. industry, Hispanic Pub. Rels. Assn., LA, 1995, Esther Farfel award, U. Houston, 1995, 1st Ann. Hispanic Publ. award, Hispanic Caucus Am. Assn. Higher Edn., 1996, award for best article in MELUS, 1999, Estrella award contbn. edn., Assn. Hispanic Sch. Adminstrs., Houston, 2001, U. Houston award excellence in rsch. and scholarship, 2001, Cert. of Recognition, Tex. Inst. Letters, 2003, Houston Lit. Achievement award, Barnes and Noble and Bookstop, 2003; Summer fellow, Ind. U., 1974, 1976, Eli Lilli Faculty Open fellow, 1976—77, Calouste Gulbenkian fellow rsch. in Portugal, 1976—90, fellow, NEH, 1979, Ford Found./NRC, 1986—87. Mem.: MLA (NYC chpt., lectr.), Tex. Com. Humanities, Coll. Bd. Task Force Arts in Edn., Nat. Coun. Humanities, Nat. Assn. Puerto Rican Studies, Nat. Assn. Chicano Studies, Hispanic Forum Houston, Inst. Hispanic Culture of Houston, Hispanic Soc. Am. (assoc.; hon. assoc., hon.), Am. Antiquarian Soc. Avocations: jogging, tennis, guitar, singing. Office: U Houston Arte Publico Press Houston TX 77204-0001 also: U Houston Dept Modern and Classical Langs 413 Agnes Arnold Hall Houston TX 77204-3006 Office Phone: 713-743-3128. Business E-Mail: artrec@mail.uh.edu.

KANER, HARVEY SHELDON, lawyer; b. June 26, 1930; s. Rueben and Lillian Kaner; m. Caren Lee Gross, June 5, 1960; children: Amy B., Daniel E., Jason M. (dec.), Joshua A. BBA, U. Minn., 1952, LL.B., 1955. Bar: Minn. Sole practice, Mpls., 1956-58; asst. corp. counsel Farmers Union GTA (now Harvest States Cooperatives), St. Paul, 1958-59, corp. counsel, 1959-77, v.p. law, 1977-82, sr. v.p., corp. counsel, 1982-93; sr. v.p. and exec. counsel Harvest States Cooperatives, St. Paul, 1993-94; ret., 1994. Past sec. St. Louis Grain Corp.; lectr. extension program U. Wis., Madison; past dir. Farmers Export Co.; trustee Corp. Pension Funds Author publs. Products Liability, 1977 Served with USNG, 1947-49 Mem. ABA, Minn. State Bar Assn., Hennepin County Bar Assn., Nat. Council Farmer Coops. (mem. legal, tax and acctg. com.) Jewish. Home: 4000 Royal Marco Way Apt 622 Marco Island FL 34145-7812

KANET, ROGER EDWARD, political science professor; b. Cin., Sept. 1, 1936; s. Robert George and Edith Mary (Weaver) K.; m. Joan Alice Edwards, Feb. 16, 1963; children: Suzanne Elise Zelle, Laurie Alice Burhart. PhB, Berchmanskolleg, Pullach-bei-Muenchen, Ger., 1960; AB, Xavier U., Cin., 1961; MA, Lehigh U., 1963; AM, Princeton U., 1965, PhD, 1966. Asst. prof. polit. sci. U. Kans., Lawrence, 1966-69, assoc. prof., 1969-74; joint sr. fellow Russian Inst. and Rsch. Inst. Communist Affairs, Columbia U., N.Y.C., 1972-73; from vis. assoc. prof. to assoc. prof. to prof. U. Ill., Champaign-Urbana, 1973—97, prof. emeritus, 1997—, head dept. polit. sci., 1984—87, assoc. vice chancellor for acad. affairs, dir. internat. programs and studies, 1989—97; prof. dept. internat. studies U. Miami, Fla., 1997—, dean Sch. Internat. Studies, 1997—2000. Partipant exch. with Hungary and Poland, Internat. Rsch. and Exchs. Bd., 1976; cons. Inst. Pub. Policy Devel., Washington, 1977-79; assoc. Ctr. Advanced Study, U. Ill., 1981-82; mem. Coun. on Fgn. Rels., N.Y., 1991—; mem. Chgo. Coun. on Fgn. Rels., 1993-97; chair internat. edn. panel Com. Instl. Coop. Big 10 & Chgo., 1993-96; co-founder Ill. Consortium for Internat. Edn. Editor: The Behavioral Revolution and Communist Studies, 1971, On the Road to Communism, 1972, The Soviet Union and the Developing Countries, 1974, Soviet and East European Policy, 1974, Soviet Economic and Political Relations with the Developing World, 1975, Background to Crisis: Policy and Politics in Gierek's Poland, 1981, Soviet Foreign Policy and East-West Relations, 1982, Soviet Foreign Policy in the 1980s, 1982, The Soviet Union, Eastern Europe and the Third World, 1987, Asia in Soviet Global Strategy, 1987, The Limits of Soviet Power in the Developing World: Thermidor in the Revolutionary Struggle, 1989, The Cold War as Cooperation: Superpower Cooperation in Regional Conflict Management, 1991, Soviet Foreign Policy in Transition, 1992, Regional Conflicts and Conflict Resolution, 1995, Coping with Conflict After the Cold War, 1996, Foreign Policy of the Russian Fed., 1997, Resolving Regional Conflicts, 1998, The New Security Environment. The Impact on Russian, Ctrl. and Ea. Europe, 2005; contbr. more than 320 articles to scholarly jours. and books. Co-founder, pres. Kans. Parents Assn. Hearing-Handicapped Children, 1968-70. Recipient U.S. Dept. State Rsch. award, 1976, Excellence in Undergrad. Teaching award U. Ill., 1981, 84, Faculty Achievement award Burlington No. Found., 1989,U.S. Inst. Peace award, 1991; fellow NDEA, 1963-66, NATO, 1976, Internat. fellow Fed. Inst. for East European and Internat. Studies, Cologne, Fed. Republic of Germany, 1988; Am. Coun. Learned Socs. grantee, 1972-73, 78. Mem. Am. Assn. Advancement of Slavic Studies, Am. Polit. Sci. Assn., Assn. Internat. Edn. Adminstrs. (bd. dirs. 1994-99), Internat. Polit. Sci. Assn., Internat. Studies Assn. (chmn. Am.-Soviet rels. sect. 1990-92), Midwest Slavic Conf. (program chmn. 1980-81), Internat. Coun. for Ctrl. and Ea. European Studies (program chmn. 1st World Congress 1974, mem. program com. and gen. editor conf. publs. 7th World Congress 2005), Ctrl. Slavic Conf. (pres., program chmn. 1966-67), Midwest Polit. Sci. Assn., Assn. Internat. Edn. Adminstrs., Midwest Univ. Consortium Internat. Activities (bd. dirs. 1989-97), Nat. Assn. State Univ. and Land Grant Colls. (internat. commn. 1992-97). Roman Catholic. Home: 9225 SW 142d St Miami FL 33176 Office Phone: 305-284-3407. Business E-Mail: rkanet@miami.edu.

KANEYOSHI, TAKAHITO, physicist, educator; b. Otaru, Hokkaido, Japan, Aug. 24, 1940; s. Chukichi and Ine (Yoshikawa) K.; m. Yoshiko Yamashina, Mar. 24, 1968; children: Yoshitaka, Akihiro, Yukako. B Tech., Waseda U., Tokyo, 1963; MS, Kyoto (Japan) U., 1965, DSc, 1969. Rsch. assoc. Nagoya (Japan) U., 1968-92, assoc. prof., 1992-93, prof. physics, 1993—2004, prof. emeritus, 2004—. Author: Amorphous Magnetism, 1984, Introduction to Surface Magnetism, 1991, Introduction to Amorphous Magnets, 1992. Mem. Phys. Soc. Japan, Applied Magnetic Soc. Japan, Am. Phys. Soc., Inst. Physics E-mail: kaneyosi@is.nagoya-u.ac.up.

KANFER, JULIAN NORMAN, biochemist, educator; b. Bklyn., May 23, 1930; s. Benjamin N. and Clara (Lichtenberger) K.; m. Beverly Kanfer; children— Brian, Rachel, Addison Slaeton Cressa. BSc, Bklyn. Coll., 1954; MSc, George Washington U., 1958, PhD, 1961. Biochemist Mass. Gen. Hosp., Boston, 1969-75; dir. biochem. research E.K. Shriver Center, Waltham, Mass.; also dir. research W.E. Fernald State Sch., Waltham, 1969-75; adj. asso. prof. biochemistry Brandeis U., Waltham, 1969-75; asso. prof. neuropathology Harvard, 1969-75, prin. research assoc., 1974-75; prof. U. Man., Winnipeg, Can., 1975—, head dept. biochemistry, 1975—. Cons. Health Scis. Centre, Winnipeg, 1976—; mem. med. adv. bd. Nat. Tay-Sachs Found., N.Y.C., 1970—; mem. study sect. on pathobiol. chemistry NIH, 1974—; postdoctoral fellowship com. NRC, 1983—; mem. Grant Commn. Nutrition and Metabolism Med. Rsch. Coun., Can., 1992—; vis. prof. dept. psychiatry U. Pitts. Med. Ctr., 1993-94; vis. prof. Stetson U., Deland, Fla., 1998—; adj. Daytona Beach C.C. Contbr. articles to profl. jours. Bd. dirs. Winnipeg chpt. Multiple Sclerosis Soc. Can., 1976. Named Hon. Citizen of New Orleans, 1997, Fellow Inst. de la Sante et de la Recherche Medicale (France); mem. Am. Soc. Biol. Chemistry, Am., Internat. neurochemistry socs., Am. Chem. Soc., AAAS, Soc. for Complex Carbohydrates, Fedn. Am. Socs. for Exptl. Biology, Can. Fedn. Biol. Socs., Canadian Biochem. Soc. Office: 1415 Ocean Shore Blvd Ormond Beach FL 32176-3673

KANG, BENJAMIN TOYEONG, journalist, minister; b. Republic of Korea, Mar. 30, 1931; came to U.S., 1963, naturalized, 1979; s. Tae-Un and Kumjoo (Lee) K.; m. Katherine Chungcha Chung, Apr. 29, 1955; children: Jennifer, Mira, Gregory. BA, Yonsei U., Republic of Korea, 1954; MA, Kyungbuk U., Republic of Korea, 1959; BD, Temple U., 1967; ThD, Internat. Sem., 1981. Ordained to ministry Christian Ch., 1970. Instr. Yonsei U., 1956-58; exec. dir. Kyungju YMCA, Republic of Korea, 1958-59; asst. prof. Keimyoung U., Republic of Korea, 1959-61; pastor Korean Ch. of Lower Bucks, Levittown, Pa., 1974-84; pres. Korean Sch. of Lower Bucks, 1980-82; pastor Korean Gloria Ch., Phila., 1981-89; parish assoc. First Presbyn. Ch., Levittown, 1990—. Freelance writer, 1992—; columnist Dong-A Daily News, 1992-94, 99—, Christian Post, 2004-. Author: (hymn) In a Strange Land, 1992. Trustee Presbytery of Phila., Presbyn. Ch. USA, 1982-88, Met. Christian Coun. Phila., 1984-88, Coun. Korean Chs. in Phila., 1985-89; comdr. Vol. Student Army Kyungju, Republic of Korea, 1950-51. Home: 3128 Benjamin Rush Ct Bensalem PA 19020-1903

KANG, JAMES D., orthopedist, surgeon; s. Samual Sung-Ik and Soon-Ju Kang; m. Ruby K. Lee, Sept. 1, 1990; children: Robert B., Jennifer L., Thomas B. BS, Wash. U., St Louis, 1982; MD, U. Okla., 1986. Cert. Am. Bd. Surgery (cert. in orthop. surgery). Vice chmn. dept. orthopedic surgery U. Pitts. Sch. Medicine, 2003—. Office: U Pittsburgh 3471 Fifth Ave Ste 1010 Pittsburgh PA 15213 Office Phone: 412-605-3241.

KANG, JINA, management educator; BS, Korea Advanced Inst. Sci. and Tech., 1989; MBA, Wharton Sch., 1995; PhD, UCLA, 2002. Asst. prof. strategic mgmt. Calif. State U., Fullerton, 2002—05, Seoul (Republic of Korea) Nat. U., 2005—. Contbr. articles to profl. jours. Recipient Judge Richard A. Goodman Strategic Planning award, Assn. Strategic Planning, 2002; scholarship, Korea Advanced Inst. Sci. and Tech., 1986—89, Anderson fellowship, Anderson Sch., UCLA, 1995—2002, Jr. Faculty Rsch. grant, Calif. State U., 2002—. Mem.: Acad. Mgmt., Ivy League So. Calif. (assoc.). Avocations: travel, music, art, painting, opera. Personal E-mail: JinaMaria@msn.com.

KANG, KYUNGIN, electronics engineer, researcher; b. Taejon, Korea, July 1, 1967; s. Shinbong and Taebool (Chung) K.; m. Eunhee Cha, June 11, 1994; children: Sohyun, Jeehyun. BS, Kyungpook Nat. U., Taegu, Korea, 1991; MS in Info. and Comms., U. Taejon, 2001. Pres. Fuzzy Tech. Co., Taejon, 1991-94; rschr. SaTReC, KAIST, Taejon, 1995—; rsch. UN ESA-ESTEC, Noordwijk, Holland, The Netherlands, 1999-2000; team leader, head sect. sys. engring. SaTReC, KAIST, 2000—03; designer, developer STSAT2 satellite, KAIST, 2003—. Designer, developer MEIS payload contr. and solid state recorder of KITSAT3 satellite, 1995-99; design and devel. high data rate receiving sys. of ground sta. for remote sensing satellite, 1998, KAISTSAT4 satellite, 2000—; systems engr. KAISTAT4 Satellite, 2000-2003; designer, develper STAT2 Satellite, 2003—. Contbr. articles to profl. jours. Recipient fellowship UN and European Space Agy., 1998, Presdl. citation Republic of Korea, 2004. Avocations: swimming, skiing. Home: Narae Apt 101-105 Chonmin-dong Yusung Taejon 305-729 Republic of Korea Office: SaTReC KAIST 373-1 Kusung-Dong Taejon 305-701 Republic of Korea Fax: 82 42 861 0064. Office Phone: 82 42 869 8640. E-mail: Kyunginkang@paran.com, kikang@kaist.ac.kr, kikang@sem.or.kr.

KANG, SHEON YOUNG, mathematics professor; b. Kimcheon-Si, Republic of Korea, Mar. 22, 1964; s. Hee Yeol Kang and Gyo Hee Ahn; m. Seong Hae Kim. PhD, U. Conn., Storrs, 1994—2000. Full time instr. U. New Orleans, 2000—01; asst. prof., math. Purdue U. N. Ctrl., Westville, Ind., 2001—. Grantee, Purdue U. Rsch. Found., 2001—04. Mem.: Am. Math. Soc., Am. Math. Assn. (corr.). Home: 2206 Normandy Apt 3d Michigan City IN 46360 Office: Mathematics Dept Purdue Univ N Ctrl Michigan City IN 46391 Office Phone: 219-785-5650. Office Fax: 219-785-5507. E-mail: skang@pnc.edu.

KANG, SOON-YI, mathematician, educator; b. YangSan, KyungNam, Republic of Korea, Oct. 12, 1967; arrived in U.S., 1992; d. Boo-Ho Kang and Yoon-Kil Joo; m. Hong Seo Ryoo, Apr. 27, 1967; children: Rachel Hejung Ryoo, Helen E-Jung Ryoo. BS in Math., Pusan (Republic of Korea) Nat. U., 1990, M in Math. Edn., 1992; PhD in Math., U. Ill., 1999. Tchrs. cert. in secondary education Korea Bd. Edn., 1990. Ross asst. prof. dept. math. Ohio State U., Columbus, 2000—. Contbr. articles to profl. jours. Achievements include research in some theorems on the Rogers-Ramanujan Continued Fraction and Associated Theta Function Identities in Ramanujan's Lost Notebook; Ramanujan's formula for the explicit evaluation of the Rogers-Ramanujan continued fraction and theta functions; new proof of Winquist's identity. E-mail: kang@math.ohio-state.edu.

KANG, SUNG-MO (STEVE KANG), electrical engineering educator; b. Seoul, Korea, Feb. 25, 1945; came to U.S., 1969; s. Chang-Shik and Kyung-Ja (Lee) K.; m. Myoung-A Cha, June 10, 1972; children: Jennifer, Jeffrey. BSEE, Fairleigh Dickinson U., 1970; MSEE, SUNY, Buffalo, 1972; PhD in Elec. Engring., U. Calif., Berkeley, 1975. Asst. prof. Rutgers U., Piscataway, N.J., 1975-77; mem. tech. staff AT&T Bell Labs., Murray Hill, N.J., 1977-82, supr., 1982-85; prof. U. Ill., Urbana, 1985-2000, head dept. electrical and computer engring., 1995-2000, assoc. Ctr. for Advanced Study, 1991-92, assoc. dir. microelectronics lab., 1988-95; univ. scholar U. Ill., Urbana, 1995-96. Dir. Ctr. for ASIC R&D, dean sch. engring. U. Calif., Santa Cruz, 2001—; pres. Silicon Valley Engring. Coun., 2002-03. Author 9 books; contbr. over 350 papers to internat. jours. and confs.; 12 patents. Recipient Meritorious Svc. award Cirs. and Sys. Soc., 1994, Humboldt Rsch. award for Sr. U.S. Scientists, 1996, Grad. Teaching award IEEE, 1996, IEEE CAS Soc. Tech. Achievement award, 1997, KBS award in Sci. and Tech., 1998, SRC Tech. Excellence award, 1999, Alumnus award U. Calif., Berkeley, 2001. Fellow AAAS, ACM, IEEE (various offices in Circuits and Systems Soc. including pres. 1991, founding editor-in-chief Trans. on VSLI systems, Disting. lectr. 1994-97, 2003-, Darlington award, SRC Inventor Recognition award 1993, 96, 99, 2001, 02, Meritorious Svc. award Compuer Soc. 1990, CAS Soc. Golden Jubilee medal 1999, Millennium medal 2000, Mac Van Valkenburg award, 2005), Nat. Acad. Engring. of Korea (fgn. mem.). Presbyterian. Avocations: tennis, travel. Office: U Calif Baskin Sch Engring Santa Cruz CA 95064 Office Phone: 831-459-2158. E-mail: kang@soe.ucsc.edu.

KANGAS, EDWARD A., healthcare company executive, former diversified financial services company executive; b. 1944; m. Catherine Elizabeth Stephens, Sept. 17, 1994. Student, Univ. of Kansas, 1967. CPA, staff acct. Touche Ross & Co., Kansas City, 1967-74, ptnr., 1975-76, dir. mgmt. consulting ops., 1976-81, nat. dir. mgmt. consulting, 1981-85, mng. ptnr., CEO N.Y.C., 1985-89; also CEO Touche Ross Internat.; mng. ptnr. Deloitte and Touche, N.Y.C., 1989-94; chmn, chief exec. Deloitte Touche Tohmatsu Internat., 1989—2000; cons. Deloitte Touche, Wilton, Conn., 2000—; chmn. Tenet Healthcare Corp., Dallas, 2003—. Bd. dirs., mem. fin. com., mem. and chmn. fund raising com. Nat. Multiple Sclerosis Soc.; trustee Com. Econ. Devel.; bd. overseers The Wharton Sch.; bd. advisors U. Kans. Sch. of Bus. Office: Tenet Healthcare Corp 13737 Noel Rd Dallas TX 75240*

KANICK, VIRGINIA, retired radiologist; b. Coaldale, Pa., Nov. 10, 1925; d. Martin and Anna (Pisklak) K. BA, Barnard Coll., 1947; MD, Columbia U., 1951. Diplomate Am. Bd. Radiology. Intern Western Reserve U. Hosps., Cleve., 1951-52; resident in radiology St. Luke's Hosp., N.Y.C., 1952-55, attending radiologist, 1955-74; acting dir. radiology St. Luke's Roosevelt Hosp., N.Y.C., 1981-84, dep. dir. of radiology, 1984-89; ptnr. West Side Radiology, N.Y.C., 1989—2003; ret., 2003. Clin. prof. radiology Coll. Physicians and Surgeons Columbia U., N.Y.C., 1975—; pres. Med. Bd. St. Luke's Roosevelt Hosp., 1980-82. Contbr. articles to profl. jours. Bd. dirs. Health System Agy. of N.Y.C., 1978-81. Fellow Am. Cancer Soc., 1955. Fellow Am. Coll. Radiology; mem. Am. Roentgen Ray Soc., Radiol. Soc. N.Am., N.Y. County Med. Soc. (sec., dir. 1978—), N.Y. State Radiol. Soc. (bd. dirs. 1975—). Independent. Avocations: skiing, travel, archeology. Home: 560 Riverside Dr Apt 17B New York NY 10027-3215 Office Phone: 212-666-7258. Business E-Mail: vk3@columbia.edu.

KANIKKANNAN, NARAYANASAMY, chemist, researcher; b. Subramaniapuram, Tamil Nadu, India, Apr. 13, 1964; arrived in U.S., 1998; s. Narayanasamy Venkatasamy and Koppammal Narayanasamy; m. Geetha Krishnasamy, Feb. 22, 1996; children: Lakshmi Subraja, Vishnudev. BPharm, Madurai (India) Med. Coll., 1986; MPharm, Banaras Hindu U., Varanasi, India, 1992, PhD, 1995. Registered pharmacist Pharmacy Coun. India, 1986. Lectr. Tirupur (India) Kalaimagal Coll. Pharmacy, 1986—88, Sankaralingam Bhuvaneswari Coll. of Pharmacy, Thiruthangal, India, 1988—89; tutor in pharmacy Tirunelveli (India) Med. Coll., 1989—90; sr. rsch. fellow Banaras Hindu U., Varanasi, 1992—95; rsch. scientist Ranbaxy Eli Lilly Co., Gurgaon, India, 1995—98; rsch. assoc. Fla. A & M U., Tallahassee, 1998—2001; sr. formulation chemist Paddock Labs., Inc, Mpls., 2001—. Manuscript reviewer Jour. Controlled Release, 2001—, Internat. Jour. Pharmaceutics, 2001—, BMC Dermatology, 2001—; grant applications reviewer The Wellcome Trust, 2001; judge on the panel for the evaluation of posters presented at the Minority Biomed. Rsch. Support symposium Fla. A & M U., Tallahassee, 2001—01. Contbr. articles to profl. jours. Recipient Travel award, Pharm. Congress of Americas, 2001; grantee, Nat. Inst. Arthritis and Musculoskeletal and Skin Diseases, NIH, 2001—04, Dept. Def., 2001—03, Air Force Office of Sci. Rsch., Dept. Def., 2001; Sr. Rsch. fellow, Govt. India, 1992—95. Mem.: Indian Pharm. Assn., Am. Chem. Soc., Controlled Release Soc., Am. Assn. Pharm. Scientists. Achievements include development of several pharmaceutical dosage forms (Tablets, Capsules, Suspensions, Creams, etc) of prescription drugs for global market; research in new drug delivery systems including Transdermal delivery systems, Inhalation delivery systems and Liposomes. Office: Paddock Laboratories Inc 3940 Quebec Ave North Minneapolis MN 55427 Personal E-mail: kanikkannan@hotmail.com. E-mail: nkanikkannan@paddocklabs.com.

KANIN, DENNIS ROY, lawyer; b. Boston, Feb. 22, 1946; s. Irving Lynwood and Doris May (Small) K.; m. Carol Ann Licht, July 9, 1978; children: Zachary Joshua, Jonah Louis, Franklin Jacob. AB, Harvard U., 1968, JD, 1971. Bar: Mass. 1971, D.C. 1978. Assoc. Mahoney Atwood & Goldings, Boston, 1971-73; legis. asst. to congressman Frank Evans U.S. Ho. Reps., Washington, 1973-74, adminstrn. asst. to congressman Paul Tsongas, 1975-78; adminstrv. asst. to senator Paul Tsongas U.S. Senate, Washington, 1979-84; ptnr. Foley, Hoag & Eliot, Boston, 1985—; prin. New Boston Ventures. Mgr. campaign Tsongas for U.S. Senate, Boston, 1978; mem. Nat. Dem. Charter Commn., Washington, 1973-74, Nat. Commn. Dem. Platform Accountability, Washington, 1983-84; mem. exec. com. Mass. Ams. for Dem. Action, Boston, 1985-87; campaign mgr. Tsongas for pres.; vice chmn. Kerry Nat. Fin. Com., 2004; nat. commr., regional vice chair New Eng. bd. Anti-Defamation League, 1985—, chair- elect, 2003-04, regional chair, 2004—; mem. bd. dirs. New Eng. Coun., 1993-98; bd. dirs. Concord Coalition Citizens Coun., 1995—; trustee, v.p. bd. dirs. Epiphany Sch., 1999—, Roxbury Latin Sch., 2000—; bd. overseers cmty. health bd. com. Children's Hosp., Boston, 1996—. Jewish. Home: 65 Stuart Rd Newton MA 02459-1210 Office: 155 Seaport Blvd #1600 Boston MA 02210-2600 Office Phone: 617-542-3500. E-mail: dkanin.nbv@verizon.net.

KANIN, FAY, screenwriter; b. NYC; d. David and Bessie Mitchell; m. Michael Kanin (dec.); children: Joel (dec.), Josh. Student, Elmira Coll., LHD (hon.), 1981; BA, U. So. Calif. Mem. Western regional exec. bd., judge Am. Coll. Theatre Festival, 1975-76. Writer: (with Michael Kanin) screenplays including The Opposite Sex, Teacher's Pet; Broadway plays including Goodbye My Fancy, His and Hers, Rashomon, Grind (Tony nomination 1985); writer, co-prodr. TV spls. including Friendly Fire, ABC-TV (Emmy award for best TV film, San Francisco Film Festival award, Peabody award), Hustling (Writers Guild award for best original drama), Tell Me Where It Hurts (Emmy award, Christopher award); Heartsounds (Peabody award). Recipient Humanitas prize prestigious Kieser award, 2003. Mem. Writers Guild Am. West (pres. screen br. 1971-73, Val Davies award 1975, Morgan Cox award 1976, Edmund H. North award 2005), Am. Film Inst. (trustee), Acad. Motion Picture Arts and Scis. (pres. 1979-82), Nat. Ctr. Film and Video Preservation (co-chmn.), Am. Film Preservation Bd. (chmn.).

KANIPE, BARBARA ELLEN, middle school educator; b. Harlingen, Tex., Dec. 14, 1940; d. Daniel Webster and Ruth Ellen (DeWitt) Beachum; m. K. Keith Kanipe, Apr. 11, 1959; children: Cynthia Lynn Crow, Deborah Ellen. B in Music, Tex. Tech. U., 1964. 4th grade tchr. Carroll Lane Elem. Sch., Corpus Christi, Tex., 1964-65; orch. dir. Miller H.S., Corpus Christi, Tex., 1966-68, Coles H.S., Corpus Christi, Tex., 1968-69, Coles Jr. H.S., Corpus Christi, Tex., 1969-73, Barnes Jr. H.S., Corpus Christi, Tex., 1974-76, Cunningham Jr. H.S., Corpus Christi, Tex., 1976-93, Cunningham Mid. Sch., Corpus Christi, Tex., 1993-2000. Orch. dir. All City Honor Orch., Corpus Christi, 1967, 74, 82; judge Solo and Ensemble Contest, Corpus Christi, 1976-98; chairperson Corpus Christi String Festival, 1982-83. Cahirperson Corpus Christi String Festival, 1982—83; sec. Corpus Christi Antique Car Club, 1972; choir mem. Parkway Presbyn. Ch. Choir, 1970—76, handbell ringer, 1995—2003. Mem. Am. Fedn. Tchrs., Tex. Mus. Educators Assn., M.I. Hummel Club, Hallmark Ornament Collector's Club (charter). Democrat. Avocations: antique cars, doll collector, glass collector. Home: 3420 Santa Fe St Corpus Christi TX 78411-1442

KANJORSKI, PAUL EDMUND, congressman, lawyer; b. Nanticoke, Pa., Apr. 2, 1937; s. A. Peter and Wanda (Nedbalski) K.; m. Nancy Marie Hickerson, Nov. 22, 1962; 1 child, Nancy Marie Student, Temple U., 1957—62, Dickinson Sch. Law, 1962—65. Bar: Pa. Ptnr. Kanjorski & Kanjorski, Wilkes-Barre, Pa., 1966-84; mem. U.S. Congress from 11th Pa. dist., Washington, 1985—; mem. banking and fin. svcs., govt. reform coms. Acting solicitor City of Nanticoke, 1969-81; Pa. Workmen's Compensation referee, 1972-80; bd. dirs. Wyoming Valley Sanitary Authority, Wilkes-Barre, 1972-84; former trustee Wilkes U. Mem.: Wilkes-Barre Law Library Assn. Democrat. Roman Catholic. Avocation: fishing. Office: 2353 Rayburn Ho Office Bldg Washington DC 20515-0001*

KANKEY, ROLAND DOYLE, finance educator; b. Batesville, Ark., Nov. 17, 1946; s. William Jasper Jr. and Verline Violet (Dockins) K.; m. Linda Grace Johnson, July 6, 1974; children: Jason, Andrew, Adam. BS in Math, Wichita State U., 1968; MS in Math, Okla. State U., 1970; MA in Bus. Adminstrn., Ohio State U., 1985, PhD in Bus. Adminstrn., 1988. Tech. mgr. Rome Air Devel. Ctr., NY, 1970—72; chief, mgmt. analysis 51st Air Base Wing, Osan, Republic of Korea, 1972—73; mgmt./cost analysis Headquarters USAF, Pentagon, 1973—77; faculty mem. AFIT, Wright-Patterson, 1977—2000, dir. grad. cost analysis program, 1988—90, head dept. quantitative mgmt., 1990—93; sr. IMA to the commdr. Aerospace Guidance & Metrology Ctr., Newark AFB, 1995—96; sr. IMA to the comptr. Aero. Sys. Ctr., Wright Patterson, 1996—99; head grad. acquisition mgmt. dept. AFIT, Wright Patterson, 1993—98; head dept. contract pricing Midwest region Def. Acq. U., 2000—01, chair Dept. Bus. Analysis, 2004—. Mem. nat. bd. dirs. Soc. Cost Estimating & Analysis, Alexandria, Va., 1993-97, chmn. 1994 nat. conf., 1990-94, editor Jour. Cost Analysis, 1992-98; editor National Estimator Nat. Estimating Soc., Alexandria, 1989-92. Editor: (book) Cost Analysis & Estimating, 1991; contbr. articles to profl. jours. Mem. Greenon H.S. Band Boosters, Enon, 1995-2002, sec. 1995-97, pres. 2000-02. Capt. USAF, 1968-80. Mem. Am. Soc. Military Comptrollers (chpt. pres. 1997-98), Soc. Cost Estimating & Analysis, Beta Gamma Sigma Honor Soc., Phi Kappa Phi. Avocations: genealogy, golf, moderate running, military and air force memorabilia, family history. Home: 115 Cimmaron Trl Enon OH 45323-1653 Office: DAUMW BA 3100 Research Blvd Kettering OH 45420 E-mail: rkankey@woh.rr.com.

KANKIRAWATANA, PONGKIAT, pediatrician, neurologist, educator; s. Yang; m. Suthida Kankirawatana; children: Pongbhud Ake, Arisa Claire. MD, Mahidol U., Bangkok, 1984. Diplomate Am. Bd. Pediat., 1989, Am. Bd. Psychiatry And Neurology, 1994, cert. Cleve. Clinic Found., 1993. Intern Nakorn Pathom Gen. Hosp., Thailand, 1984—85; physician Takuapa Hosp., Pang-Nga, Thailand, 1985—86; resident pediat. Jersey City (N.J.) Med. Ctr., 1986—89; fellow child neurology U. N.C., Chapel Hill, NC, 1989—92; fellow epilepsy The Cleve. (Ohio) Clinic Found., 1992—93; instr. Faculty Medicine Siriraj Hosp. Mahidol U., Bangkok, 1993—95, asst. prof. Faculty Medicine Siriraj Hosp., 1995—97, assoc. prof. Faculty Medicine Siriraj Hosp., 1997—2001; med. dir. Pediatric Epilepsy Program Children's Hosp. U. Ala., 2001—. Dir. Clin. Neurophysiology Lab Children's Hosp. U. Ala., Birmingham, Ala., 2001—. Contbr. articles to profl. jours. Mem.: Epilepsy Soc. Thailand (founder 1996), Am. Clin. Neurophysiology Soc., Am. Acad. Neurology, Am. Soc. Epilepsy.

KANN, PETER ROBERT, publishing executive, journalist; b. NYC, Dec. 13, 1942; s. Robert A. and Marie K. (Breuer); m. Francesca Mayer, Apr. 12, 1969 (dec. 1983); m. Karen Elliot House, 1984; children: Hillary Francesca, Petra Elliot, Jason Elliot, Jade Elliott. BA, Harvard U., 1964. Newspaper fund intern The Wall St. Jour., San Francisco, 1963, staff reporter Pittsburgh, Los Angeles, 1964, resident reporter Vietnam, 1967, roving reporter Hong Kong,

1969—75; pub. The Asian Wall Street Jour., Hong Kong, 1976-79; assoc. pub. The Wall St. Jour., NYC, 1979-88, pub., 1989—2002; v.p. Dow Jones & Co., NYC, 1979—85, exec. v.p., 1985—89, pres., COO, 1989-91, mem. bd. dirs., 1987—, chmn., CEO, 1991—; editl. dir. Dow Jones Publications, NYC, 1989—. Chmn. bd. Far Ea. Econ. Rev., 1987—89; mem. Pulitzer Prize Bd., 1987—96. Trustee Asia Soc., 1989—94, Aspen Inst., 1994—98, Spelman Coll., 1994—97, Inst. for Advanced Study, Princeton, N.J., 1990—. Recipient Pulitzer prize for internat. reporting, 1972. Mem.: Spee Club (Cambridge, Mass.). Office: Wall Street Journal Dow Jones & Co Inc 200 Liberty St New York NY 10281-1003

KANNAN, RAJGOPAL, computer scientist, educator; b. Kumbakonam, Tamil Nadu, India, Mar. 17, 1970; s. Appadurai and Chellammal Kannan; m. Subhashini Krishnaswamy, July 9, 1997; children: Shreya Rajgopal, Narayanan Srinivasan. B of Tech., Indian Inst. Tech., 1991; PhD, U. Denver, 1996. Asst. prof. U. Mich., Dearborn, 1996—2000, La. State U., Baton Rouge, 2000—. Asst. dir. SLAB: Sensor Networking Lab., Baton Rouge, 2004—. Contbr. articles to profl. jours., chpts. to books. Fellow, Office Naval Rsch., 2002; grantee, NSF, 1997, Coop. Assn. Internet Data Analysis, 2000, Def. Advanced Rsch. Projects Agy., 2001, 2002, NSF, 2003. Mem.: IEEE, Sigma Xi. Independent. Hindu. Achievements include patents pending for Fast Web Page Allocation on a Server using Self-Organizing Neural Nets. Avocations: chess, writing. Office: La State U Dept Computer Sci Baton Rouge LA 70803 Office Phone: 225-578-2225. Home Fax: 225-578-1465; Office Fax: 225-578-1465. Personal E-mail: rkannan@csc.lsu.edu.

KANNE, MICHAEL STEPHEN, federal judge; b. Rensselaer, Ind., Dec. 21, 1938; s. Allen Raymond and Jane (Robinson) Kanne; m. Judith Ann Stevens, June 22, 1963; children: Anne, Katherine. Student, St. Joseph's Coll., Rensselaer, 1957—58; BS, Ind. U., 1962, JD, 1968; postgrad., Boston U., 1963, U. Birmingham, Eng., 1975. Bar: Ind. 1968. Assoc. Nesbitt and Fisher, Rensselaer, 1968—71; sole practice Rensselaer, 1971—72; atty. City of Rensselaer, 1972; judge 30th Jud. Cir. of Ind., 1972—82, US Dist. Ct. (no. dist.) Ind., Hammond, 1982—87, US Ct. Appeals (7th cir.), Chgo., 1987—, Moot Ct. Competitions, 1998—; chmn. US Cts. Design Guide, 1988—95. Lectr. law St. Joseph's Coll., 1976—89, St. Frances Coll., 1990—91; faculty Nat. Inst. for Trial Advocacy, South Bend, Ind., 1978—88; mem. Ad Hoc Com. on Law Clerk Hiring, 2004. Bd. visitors Ind. U. Sch. Law, 1987—, Ind. U. Sch. Pub. and Environ. Affairs, 1991—; trustee St. Joseph's Coll., 1984—. 1st lt. USAF, 1962—65. Named Outstanding Alumnus, Today's Cath. Tchr., 1991; recipient Disting. Svc. award, St. Joseph's Coll., 1973, Disting. Grad. award, Nat. Cath. Ednl. Assn. Mem.: FBA, Tippecanoe County Bar Assn., Jasper County Bar Assn. (pres. 1972—76), Ind. State Bar Assn. (bd. dirs. 1977—79, Presdl. citation 1979), Law Alumni Assn. Ind. U. (pres. 1980). Roman Catholic. Avocations: horseback riding, weightlifting. Office: Charles A Halleck Federal Building 234 N Fourth Street PO Box 1340 Lafayette IN 47902-1340 also: US Ct Appeals 219 S Dearborn St Chicago IL 60604*

KANNENBERG, LLOYD CHAMBERS, physicist, researcher; b. Sarasota, Fla., Mar. 23, 1939; s. Werner Frederick Ludwig Kannenberg and Nettie Louise Chambers; m. Susan Lippman, Aug. 10, 1963; 1 child, Susanna. SB, MIT, 1961; MS, U. Fla., 1963; PhD, Northeastern U., 1967. Elec. engr. Electro-Mech. Rsch., Inc., Sarasota, 1961-63; instr. physics Lowell (Mass.) Tech. Inst. (merged with Lowell State Coll.), 1966-67; from instr. to prof. physics U. Mass. (formerly U. Lowell), 1968—; instr. physics Northeastern U., Boston, 1967-68. Translator: (by H. Grassmann) A New Branch of Mathematics, 1994, Extension Theory, 2000; (by G. Peano) Geometric Calculus, 2000; contbr. articles to profl. jours. Mem. Am. Phys. Soc. (life), Am. Math. Soc., Am. Assn. Physics Tchrs., Math. Assn. Am, Sigma Xi, Sigma Pi Sigma, Phi Kappa Phi. Democrat. Office: U Mass-Lowell 1 University Ave Lowell MA 01854 Business E-Mail: lloyd_kannenberg@uml.edu.

KANNER, BERNICE, columnist; b. N.Y.C. d. Al and Lillian Kanner; m. David B. Cuming, Oct. 10, 1982; children: Elisabeth, Andrew. BA, Harpur Coll., Binghamton, N.Y., 1969; MA in English Lit., SUNY, Binghamton, 1972. Account exec. J. Walter Thompson, N.Y.C., 1974-77; sr. editor, reporter Advt. Age Mag., N.Y.C., 1977-81; columnist Daily News, N.Y.C., 1980-81; sr. editor, columnist N.Y. Mag., 1981-94; columnist Bloomberg Bus. News, N.Y.C., 1994—, ScreamingMedia, N.Y.C.; editor-in-chief WomensBiz.US, N.Y.C., 2002—. Author: Are You Normal?, 1995, Lies My Parents Told Me, 1996, The 100 Best TV Commercials And Why They Worked, 1999, Are You Normal About Money, 2001, The Super Bowl of Advertising: How the Commercials Won the Game, 2003, Are You Normal About Sex, Love and Relationships, 2004, Pocketbook Power: Marketing to Women in the 21st Century, 2004. Mem.: exec. com., Women's Bus. Coun. for Peace. Office: WomensBiz US 155 E 55th St Ste 6H New York NY 10022

KANNER, FREDERICK W., lawyer; b. N.Y.C., Apr. 25, 1943; BA, U. Va., 1965; JD, Georgetown U., 1968. Bar: N.Y. 1969. Ptnr. Dewey Ballantine LLP, N.Y.C., 1976—, chmn. corp. fin. group & mem. mgmt. com. Editor: Georgetown Law Jour., 1967-68. Dir. Lawyers Alliance for N.Y.; trustee Lawyers Com. for Civil Rights under Law. Mem. ABA, N.Y. State Bar Assn., Assn. Bar City N.Y. (former mem. securities regulation com.). Office: Dewey Ballantine LLP 1301 Avenue Of The Americas New York NY 10019-6092 Office Phone: 212-259-7300. Office Fax: 212-259-6333. Business E-Mail: fkanner@dbllp.com.

KANNER, RICHARD ELLIOT, medical educator, consultant; b. Bklyn., N.Y. s. Willliam W. and Elsie Alice (Karpf) Kanner; life ptnr. Suzanne Sperling Stensaas. AB, U. Mich., 1958; MD, U. State N.Y. Downstate Med. Ctr., 1962. Cert. internal medicine 1971, pulmonary diseases 1972. Prof. internal medicine U. Utah Health Sci. Ctr., Salt Lake City, 1991—. Cons. tuberculosis Utah State Dept. Health, Salt Lake City, 1970—. Chmn. Utah Air Quality Bd., Salt Lake City, 1995—97; vice chmn. Instnl. Rev. Bd., 1999—, 2004—; rsch. subjects advocate Gen. Clin. Rsch. Ctr., 2004—. Comdr. USNR, 1966—77, Vietnam. Mem.: Am. Thoracic Soc., Am. Coll. Chest Physicians, Am. Coll. Physicians. Office: Univ Utah Health Scis Ctr 26 N 1900 East Salt Lake City UT 84132 Office Phone: 801-581-7806. Office Fax: 801-585-3355. Business E-Mail: richard.kanner@hsc.utah.edu.

KANOF, NORMAN B., dermatologist; b. N.Y.C., May 31, 1920; AB, MD, George Washington U., 1941; D in Med. Sci., Columbia U., 1949. Diplomate Am. Bd. Dermatology. Clin. prof. dermatology NYU Sch. of Medicine, N.Y.C. Home: 737 Park Ave New York NY 10021-4256 Office: 10 E 70th St New York NY 10021-4913 Office Phone: 212-288-2600.

KANOFF, MARY ELLEN, lawyer; m. Chris Kanoff. BA in Econs., U. Calif., Berkeley, 1978, JD, 1984. Large systems mktg. rep. IBM, 1978—81; with Latham & Watkins, L.A., 1984—, ptnr., 1991—. Bd. trustees St. Matthews Sch., Pacific Palisades, Calif., St. John's Hosp., Santa Monica, Calif.; bd. dirs. Chrysalis. Named one of Top 25 Lawyers in Calif. under 45, Calif. Law Bus., 1993, Up and Coming Bus. Persons in So. Calif., L.A. Bus. Jour., 1997; recipient Founders Spirit of Chrysalis award. Mem.: ABA (bus. law and entertainment law sects.), L.A. County Bar Assn., Calif. Bar Assn. Office: Latham and Watkins LLP 633 W Fifth St Ste 4000 Los Angeles CA 90071 Office Phone: 213-485-1234.

KANOFSKY, JACOB DANIEL, psychiatrist, educator; b. Phila., Apr. 16, 1948; s. Philip and Mollie (Edelstein) K. BA in Physics, Temple U., 1965-69; MD, Thomas Jefferson Med. Coll., Phila., 1974; MPH in Epidemiology, Johns Hopkins U., 1978. Diplomate Am. Bd. Psychiatry and Neurology. Intern Met. Hosp., N.Y.C., 1974-75; resident in psychiatry St. Luke's-Roosevelt Hosp. Ctr., Columbia U., N.Y.C., 1978-80, fellow in psychiat. epidemiology, 1980-82; asst. editor-in-chief Med. Tribune, N.Y.C., 1984-85; ward chief rsch. unit Bronx (N.Y.) Psychiat. Ctr., 1986, assoc. clin. dir., 1986-87, acting clin. dir., 1987, pres. med. staff orgn., 1987-89; assoc. dir. schizophrenia rsch. Albert Einstein Coll. Med./Bronx Psychiat. Ctr., 1989-90, sr. rsch. psychiatrist, 1989—, asst. prof. psychiatry, 1986—; asst. prof. epidemiology and social medicine Albert Einstein Coll. Med., 1993—. Lectr. in psychiatry Columbia U., N.Y.C., 1980—; attending psychiatrist St. Luke's-Roosevelt Hosp. Ctr., 1980—; contbg. editor Med. Tribune, 1986—; nutrition cons. Office of Alternative Medicine, NIH, 1992, Time Life Books, 1994—. Consulting editor Jour. of the Am. Coll. of Nutrition, 1990—; contbr. over 50 articles to profl. jours. Fellow Am. Coll. Nutrition; mem. Am. Psychiat. Assn. Jewish. Avocations: swimming, hiking, piano. Office: Bronx Psychiat Ctr 1500 Waters Pl Bronx NY 10461-2723

KANOFSKY, MYRON ROSS, physician; b. Waterloo, Iowa, Sept. 14, 1952; s. Herbert Bernard and Sylvia Reva (Widerschein) K.; m. Carol Susan Brody, June 16, 1974; children: Sarah Joanne (dec.), Megan Ann. BS, U. Wis., 1974; MD, U. Iowa, 1977. Diplomate Am. Bd. Ob-Gyn. Intern U. Wis. Hosps., Madison, 1977-79; resident in ob-gyn Hershey (Pa.) Med. Ctr., 1979-81; physician Arcadia (Calif.) Ob.-Gyn. Med. Group, 1981-82, Cigna Healthplans, Orange, Calif., 1982-87, Irvine, Calif., 1987-88; pvt. practice ob-gyn Orange, Calif., 1988—. Fellow Am. Coll. Ob-Gyn; mem. Orange County Med. Assn., Orange County Ob-Gyn Soc. Avocations: golf, biking, swimming, reading, computers. Office: Ste 560 1140 W La Veta Ave Orange CA 92868-4214 Office Phone: 714-835-0101. Business E-Mail: mkanofsky@pol.net.

KANOUSE, PATRICK, poet, editor; b. Richmond, Ky., Mar. 18, 1971; s. Ronald and Diane Kanouse; m. Gina Brown. BS, Ball State U., Muncie, Ind., 1989—93. Editor Pearson Edn., Indpls., 1993—97, prodn. mgr., 1998—. Author: (poetry) Ten Poems. Liberal. Personal E-mail: webmaster@patrickkanouse.com.

KANOVITZ, HOWARD, artist, educator; b. Fall River, Mass., Feb. 9, 1929; s. Meyer Julius and Dora (Rems) K. BS, Providence Coll., 1949; postgrad., R.I. Sch. Design, 1949-51, NYU, 1959-61. Instr. Bklyn. Coll., 1962-64, Pratt Inst., 1964-66; prof. Southhampton Coll., 1977-78, Sch. Visual Arts, N.Y.C., 1981-85. Artist, painter exhibited Tibor de Nagy Gallery, 1956, Stable Gallery, 1962, Jewish Mus., 1966, Waddell Gallery, 1969; one-man shows include U.S. and Europe, Stefanotty Gallery, N.Y.C., 1975, Galerie Jöllenbeck, Cologne, 1977, Benson Gallery, Bridgehampton, L.I., N.Y., 1977, Akademie der Kunste, Berlin, 1979, Kestner Gesellschaft, Hannover, 1979, Alex Rosenberg Gallery, 1982, Inge Baecker Gallery, 1987, 88, 91, Cologne, 1987, Marlborough Gallery, 1988, 90, Hokin-Kaufman Gallery, Chgo., 1989, Gana Art Gallery, Seoul, 1990, Ulrich Gering Gallery, Frankfurt, 1997, Nabi Gallery, Sag Harbor, L.I., 1998; group exhibits include Whitney Mus., N.Y.C., 1972, Dokumenta 5, Kassel, 1972, Berlin Nat. Gallery, 1976, Guild Hall, East Hampton, L.I., 1976, Dokumenta 6, Kassel, 1977, Alex Rosenberg Gallery, 1978, Louise Himmelfarb Gallery, Watermill, L.I., 1979, L.A. Mus. Contemporary Art, 1984, Indpls. Mus. Art, 1985, Ludwig Mus., Cologne, 1988, Parrish Art Mus., Southampton, L.I., 1988, Fla. Internat. U., Miami, 1989, Met. Mus., N.Y.C., 1991, Weatherspoon Art Gallery, Greensboro, N.C., 1991; represented in permanent collections Met. Mus., N.Y., Whitney Mus. Am. Art, N.Y., Hirshhorn Mus. and Sculpture Garden, Washington, L.A. County Mus. Modern Art, Guild Hall Mus., East Hampton, N.Y, Folkwang Mus., Essen, Germany. Studio: 361 N Sea Mecox Rd Southampton NY 11968-2829 Personal E-mail: nero@optonline.net.

KANSAL, SMRITI KRISHAN KUMAR, electrical engineer, researcher; b. Muzzafarnagar, Uttar Pradesh, India, Sept. 10, 1976; arrived in U.S., 2001; d. Krishan Kumar and Lata Kansal; m. Abhijit Shriniwas Patwardhan, Aug. 6, 2000. BS in Elecs., Vishwakarma Inst.Tech., 1998; MS, George Mason U., 2004. Engr., mgr. TATA Motors, India, 1998—2000; asst. rsch. scientist George Mason U., Fairfax, Va., 2004—. Contbr. articles to profl. jours. Fellow, Sch. of Info. Tech. and Engring. George Mason U., 2002—03. Mem.: Phi Beta Delta (activity coord. 2003—04). Office: George Mason University 4400 University Drive MS 1G5 Fairfax VA 22030

KANSFIELD, NORMAN J., former seminary president; b. East Chicago, Ind., Mar. 24, 1940; s. Orval Russell and Margaret Jeannette (Norman) K.; m. Mary L. Klein, June 25, 1965; children: Ann Margaret, John Livingston. BA, Hope Coll., 1962; BD, Western Theol. Sem., 1965; M Sacred Theology, Union Theol. Sem., 1967; MA, U. Chgo., 1970, PhD, 1981. Pastor Second Reformed Ch., Astoria, Queens, 1965-68; interim pastor First Reformed Ch., Berwin, Ill., 1968-69; assoc. pastor Ivanhoe Reformed Ch., Riverdale, Ill., 1969-70; libr., prof. theology Western Theol. Seminary, Holland, Mich., 1970-83; dir. libr. svcs., assoc. prof. ch. history Colgate Rochester Divinty Sch., NY, 1983-92; dir. libr. svcs. St. Bernard's Inst., Rochester, 1983-92; pres. New Brunswick Theol. Seminary, NJ, 1993—2005. Commn. on history, mem. Reformed Ch. in Am., 1969-74; Rabbi Nathan Kellerman Meml. lectr. Temple Anshe Emmeth, New Brunswick, 1995; lectr. A.J. Muste Meml. lectr. Hope Coll., Holland, Mich., 2000; St. Columba lectr. Oxford U., 2002; 50th Anniversary lectr. Seoul Jang Sin U, 2004; sem. lectr. Near East Sch. Theology, Beirut, 2004; lectr. in field. Co-author: Evangelism: The Church's Proclamation, 1988; editor, contbr. (hymnbook) Rejoice in the Lord, 1985; mem. editl. bd. Perspectives, 1997—2004; contbr. articles to profl. jours. Chair Hist. Adv. Com., Holland, 1970—83; dir. New Brunswick Tomorrow, 1994—2005; pres. Mercersberg Soc., 2002—. Sealantic fellow Rockefeller Bros. Found., 1968-70, Conant fellow Episc. Ch. in USA, 1989-90, Pride Interfaith Coalition award, Boston, 2005; Rabbi Nathan Keller Meml. lectr. Temple Anshe Emeth, New Brunswick, 1995. Democrat. Avocations: book collecting, carpentry, fishing, gardening. Home: 28 3 Point Garden Rd East Stroudsburg PA 18301 Office Phone: 570-421-8151. Personal E-mail: nkansfield@verizon.net.

KANSTOROOM, DAVID ARNOLD, real estate developer, entrepreneur; b. Washington, Oct. 20, 1964; s. Allen Roy and Sara Eta Kanstoroom; m. Cynthia Marie Martinez, May 19, 1996; children: Summer, Jared. BSBA, U. Fla., Gainesville, 1987, MBA, 1991. V.p. network svcs. W2COM LLC, Dayton, Ohio, 1999-2000; CEO, pres., chmn. bd. dirs. Intelicom Holding Corp., Tampa, Fla., 1991—2000, chief devel. officer U.S. local holdings, 2001—02; pres., chmn. Oasis Custom Homes, Tampa, 2002—. Actor, stuntman live we. shows, 1978-84. Vol. Muscular Dystrophy Assn., Gainesville, Fla., 1984-89; pres. Bayport Colony Home Owners Assn., Tampa, 1999—; mem. Tampa Bay Performing Arts Ctr. Mem. Telecom Agent Assn., Ascent Assn. Comm. Enterprises, Tampa Bay C. of C., Sigma Chi (chmn. fundraising 1986-87, scholar 1987). Republican. Jewish. Avocations: football, basketball, boating, travel, skiing. Home: 10404 Double Bayou Way Tampa FL 33615 Fax: 813-854-4350. Office Phone: 813-855-0070. E-mail: dak1@tampabay.rr.com.

KANT, GLORIA JEAN, retired neuroscientist; b. Chgo., June 6, 1944; d. Hans Georg and Jo Sefa Kant; m. Philip Herbert Balcom, July 1, 1967 (div. 1976). BS in Chemistry, Mich. State U., 1965; PhD in Physiol. Chemistry, U. Wis., 1969. Chemist dept. psychiatry Walter Reed Army Inst. Rsch., Washington, 1970-71, neurochemist dept. microwave rsch., 1971-77, neurochemist dept. med. neuroscis., 1977-87, chief dept. med. neuroscis., 1987-95, dir. divsn. neuroscis., 1995—2001; ret. Mem. editl. bd. Pharmacology, Biochemistry and Behavior, 1991—; contbr. over 80 articles to sci. jours. Mem. AAAS, Soc. for Neurosci., Internat. Behavioral Neurosci. Soc., Women in Neurosci. Avocation: golf. Home: 1124 Dennis Ave Silver Spring MD 20901-2171

KANT, ROBERT S., lawyer; b. Little Rock, Ark., Sept. 25, 1944; BA, Univ. Pa., 1966; JD, Villanova Univ., 1970. Bar: Pa. 1970, Ariz. 1978. Shareholder, corporate and securities, bd. dir. Greenberg Traurig LLP, Phoenix. Named one of Best of the Bar in Corp. Law, Phoenix Bus. Jour., 2003, Best of Bar in Securities Law, 2004. Mem.: State Bar Ariz. (small bus. capital formation, chmn., securities sect. 1987—88). Office: Greenberg Traurig LLP Ste 700 2375 E Camelback Rd Phoenix AZ 85016 Office Phone: 602-445-8302. Office Fax: 602-445-8100. Business E-Mail: kantr@gtlaw.com.

KANTARCI, KEJAL, radiologist, researcher; b. Istanbul, Turkey, Dec. 1, 1969; arrived in U.S., 1998; d. Vehbi and Gulesren Aydin; m. Orhun H. Kantarci, Nov. 25, 1994. MS, Marmara U., Istanbul, 1993. Resident Istanbul U., 1993—97; radiologist pvt. practice, 1997—98; asst. prof., assoc. cons. Mayo Clinic, Rochester, Minn., 2004—. Contbr. chapters to books; mem. editl. bd.: Neurosci. Imaging, 2004—. Fellow, Mayo Clinic, 1998—2004; scholar, NIH, 2005—. Mem.: Internat. Soc. Magnetic Resonance Medicine, Radiol. Soc. N.Am. Avocations: mountain climbing, scuba diving, bicycling. Office: Mayo Clinic 200 First St Rochester MN 55905 Office Phone: 507-284-9770. E-mail: kantarci.kejal@mayo.edu.

KANTER, CARL IRWIN, retired lawyer; b. Jersey City, Feb. 17, 1932; s. Morris and Beatrice (Wilson) K.; m. Gail Herman, Nov. 27, 1963; children—Deborah, David, Andrew, Aaron AB, Harvard U., 1953, LL.B., 1956. Bar: Calif. 1956, N.Y. 1959. Assoc. Stroock & Stroock & Lavan, N.Y.C., 1959-67, ptnr., 1967-92; sr. v.p., co-gen. counsel Merck-Medco Managed Care L.L.C., Montvale, N.J., 1992-97, spl. counsel, 1997-99; ret. Served with U.S. Army, 1957-58 Home: 993 Park Ave New York NY 10028 Personal E-mail: kanterart@yahoo.com.

KANTER, DONALD RICHARD, pharmaceutical executive; b. Detroit, Jan. 22, 1951; s. Harry Richard and Dorothy May (Kelch) K.; m. Diane Lynn Fickert, July 9, 1971 (div. Sept. 1993); children: Sean Richard, Donald Mathew, Lauren Marie. BA, Oakland U., Rochester, Mich., 1976; MS, Eastern Mich. U., 1979; PhD, U. Cin., 1983. Instr., lectr. U. Cin., 1978-84; health scis. officer VA med. Ctr., Cin., 1980-85; supr. med. affairs Genetic Systems, Seattle, 1985-88; dir. stats. and clin. rsch. Solvay Pharm.; pres., CEO PharmData, Inc. Cons. in field. Author: (with Karoly et al) Child Health Psychology, 1982; (with Daniel B. Berch) Sustained Attention in Human Performance, 1983; contbr. med. articles to profl. jours. Oakland U. grantee, 1976, NIMH grantee, 1984, VA merit grantee, 1984, Outstanding Contbn. award, 1985. Mem. AAAS, Sigma Xi. Roman Catholic. Home: 2440 Sandy Plains Rd NE Bldg 9 Marietta GA 30066-5702 Office: Bldg E 205 1000 Johnson Ferry Rd Ste E205 Marietta GA 30068-2175 Personal E-mail: dkanter@pharmdata.com.

KANTER, SANDRA MAY, lawyer; b. L.A., Aug. 11, 1956; m. Michael Howard Kanter, May 15, 1983; children: Melanie Robin, Robert Joseph. BA magna cum laude, Brandeis U., 1978; JD cum laude, Harvard U., 1981. Bar: Calif. 1981. Assoc. Cox, Castle, & Nicholson, L.A., 1981—86; prin. Law Offices of Sandra Kanter, Inglewood, Calif., 1986—88; assoc. Fine, Perzik & Singman, L.A., 1989—90; contract ptnr. Nossaman, Guthner, Knox & Elliott, L.A., 1991—. Mem.: ABA, Women's Transp. Seminar, L.A. County Bar Assn., Calif. Bar Assn. Office: Nossaman Guthner Knox & Elliott Ste 3100 445 South Figueroa St Los Angeles CA 90071 Office Phone: 213-612-7851. Office Fax: 213-612-7801. Business E-Mail: skanter@nossaman.com.

KANTER, STACY J., lawyer; b. NYC, 1958; d. Ronald I. and Elaine Kanter; m. Eric Martin Kornblau. BS magna cum laude, SUNY, Albany, 1979; JD cum laude, Bklyn. Law Sch., 1984. Bar: NY 1985. Law clk. to Hon. Raymond J. Dearie US Dist. Ct. Ea. Dist. NY, 1986—87; ptnr. Skadden, Arps, Slate, Meagher & Flom LLP, NYC, 1993—. Mng. editor Bklyn. Law Rev., 1983-84. Named one of NY's rising stars in bus. Crain's mag., 1997. Office: Skadden Arps Slate Meagher & Flom LLP 4 Times Sq New York NY 10036 Office Phone: 212-735-3497. Office Fax: 917-777-3497. E-mail: skanter@skadden.com.*

KANTER, STEPHEN, lawyer, educator, dean; b. Cin., June 30, 1946; s. Aaron J. and Edythe (Kasfir) K.; m. Dory Jean Poduska, June 24, 1972; children: Jordan Alexander, Laura Elizabeth. BS in Math., MIT, 1968; JD, Yale U., 1971. Spl. asst. Portland (Oreg.) City Commr., 1971-72; from staff atty. to asst. dir. Met. Pub. Defender, Portland, 1972-77; prof. law Lewis and Clark Law Sch., Portland, 1977—, assoc. dean, 1980-81, acting dean, 1981-82, dean, 1986-94. Fulbright prof. law Nanjing (China) U., 1984-85, U. Athens (Greece) Faculty of Law, 1993; bd. dirs. Northwest Regional China Coun., 1996-00, pres.- elect, 1997-98, pres., 1998-99; exec. com. Owen M. Panner Am. Inns of Ct., pres., 1994-95; mem. judicial selection com. U.S. Dist. Ct. Oreg., 1993; cons. on drafting and implementation of Kazakhstan Constn., 1992, 94, cons. on Sch. Police funciton, Portland Sch. Dist. Author: The Bear and the Blackberry, 1999; contbr. articles to profl. jours. Mem. bd. overseers World Affairs Coun. Oreg., Portland, 1986-89; mem. Oreg. Criminal Justice Coun., Salem, 1987-92, Oreg. Bicentennial Commn., Portland, 1986-89; pres. Portland Baseball Group, 2000—. Named One of 10 Gt. Portlanders, Willamette Week newspaper, 1980; recipient E.B. MacNaughton Civil Liberties award, 1991. Fellow Am. Bar Found.; mem. ACLU (bd. dirs. Oreg. chpt. 1976-82, pres. 1979-81, lawyers com. 1976-2003), Oreg. State Bar Assn., Am. Law Inst. (ex-officio 1986-94), Fulbright Assn. (bd. dirs. 1987-93, exec. com. 1989-93). Home: 3142 SW Fairview Blvd Portland OR 97205-1831 Office: Lewis & Clark Law Sch 10015 SW Terwilliger Blvd Portland OR 97219-7768 Office Phone: 503-768-6757. Business E-Mail: kanter@lclark.edu.

KANTOR, HARVEY SHERWIN, retired medical educator; b. N.Y.C., Apr. 30, 1938; s. Jack and Henrietta (Feingold) K.; m. Elvia Frostick, Nov. 8, 1992; stepchildren: Harold, Eric Frostick. Student, U. Miami, 1955-58; MD, Washington U., 1962; postgrad., MIT, 1967-69. Diplomate Am. Bd. Internal Medicine, Am. Bd. Pathology certification in Medical Microbiology, Am. Bd. Infectious Diseases. Instr. U. Miami Sch. Medicine, 1969-71; asst. prof. medicine and microbiology U. Ill. Sch. Medicine, Chgo., 1971-75; assoc. prof. medicine and pathology Chgo. Med. Sch., North Chgo., Ill., 1975—93; dir. divsn. infectious diseases VA Med. Ctr., North Chicago, 1975-85, chief med. microbiology, 1985-92; prof. internal medicine Tex. Tech. U. Health Sci. Ctr., Odessa, 1993—2002, dir. divsn. infectious diseases, 1993—2002, interim chmn. dept. internal medicine, 2000—02; ret., 2002. Contbr. chpts. to textbooks, articles to profl. jours. Capt. U.S. Army, 1964-66. Recipient NIH postdoctoral fellowship in infectious diseases New Eng. Med. Ctr. Hosp., Boston, 1966-69, U. Health Scis./Chgo. Med. Sch. Bd. Trustees Rsch. award, 1977. Fellow ACP, Infectious Diseases Soc. Am.; mem. Am. Soc. Microbiology, Soc. Hosp. Epidemiology in Am. Avocations: cooking, photography, computers. E-mail: hkantormd@yahoo.com.

KANTOR, JAMES GRAHAM, music educator, composer; b. Norwalk, Conn., Nov. 22, 1967; s. Geza and Barbara Kantor. MusB in Music Edn., Westminster Choir Coll., 1989, MusM in Conducting, 1990; MusD in Conducting, U. Ariz., 1997. Cert. Prekindergarten-12 tchr. Conn. Dir. of music French Am. Sch. of NY, Larchmont, 1993—95; head of fine arts Ridgefield (Conn.) Acad., 2000—. Condr. Norwalk Chorale, 1993—94. Composer: (composition for orchestra, chorus and ch) Venite Adoramus, 1997 (Commd. by the Reading Choral Soc.). Sponsor Interfaith Hospitality Network, Stamford, Conn., 1993—95. Mem.: Conn. Music Educator's Assn., Am. Choral Director's Assn., Pi Lambda Theta. Home: 3 Spruce Mountain Trail Danbury CT 06810 Office: Ridgefield Acad 223A West Mountain Rd Ridgefield CT 06877 Personal E-mail: jkantor@aol.com. E-mail: jkantor@ridgefieldacademy.com.

KANTOR, MARK ALAN, lawyer, arbitrator; b. LA, Mar. 10, 1955; s. William Victor and Minerva (Wainess) K.; m. Lawranne Stewart. AB in Polit. Sci. and Internat. Relations, U. So. Calif., 1975; M in Pub. Policy, U. M in Pub. Policy, JD, U. Mich., 1979. Bar: N.Y. 1980, D.C. 1992. Assoc. Milbank, Tweed, Hadley & McCloy, N.Y.C., 1979-81, 84-87, Hong Kong, 1981-84, ptnr. N.Y.C. and Washington, 1987-89, 90-99; gen. counsel Resolution Trust Corp. Oversight Bd., 1990. Adj. prof. Georgetown U. Law Ctr., 2000—; patron councillor Atlantic Coun. U.S. Contbr. articles to profl. jours. Mem. ABA, Internat. Law Assn., Mid. East Inst. (sustaining mem.), Am. C. of C. Hong Kong (bd. govs. 1983-84, co-chair legal and fin. com. 1982-84), Phi Beta Kappa. Office Phone: 202-544-4953. Personal E-mail: mkantor@abanet.org.

KANTOR, MARY LOUISE, music educator; d. Randall None and Jean Elizabeth Phillips; m. Michael Bruce Kantor, Feb. 15, 1974; children: Michael David, Jennifer Anne. BA in Music, U. Wash., 1980; Artist's Diploma, Acad. of Music and Performing Arts, Vienna, Austria, 1974.

Applied music instr. Seattle U., 1986—92; clarinet instr. Northshore Sch. Dist., Kenmore, Wash., 1987—97; clarinet coach Seattle Youth Symphony, Seattle, Cascade Youth Symphony, Lynnwood, Wash.; adj. prof. of clarinet Seattle Pacific U., Seattle. Prin. clarinet Seattle Choral Co., Seattle, 1982—; clarinetist The Mazeltones, Seattle, 1983—87, Ensemble Vindobona, Seattle, 1996—, Shalom Ensemble, Seattle, 1996—; prin. clarinet Bellevue Philharm., Bellevue, Wash. Musician: (soloist) Clarinet Concerto by W.A. Mozart, Duet-Concertino for Clarinet and Bassoon by Richard Strauss; contbr. articles various profl. jours. Recipient Honors in Clarinet Performance, Acad. of Music in Vienna, 1974. Mem.: Music Educator's Nat. Conf., Internat. Clarinet Assn. Democrat-Npl. Christian. Avocations: cooking, yoga, mycology.

KANTOR, SIMON WILLIAM, chemistry professor; b. Brussels, Mar. 23, 1925; came to U.S., 1939, naturalized, 1946; s. Joseph Uszer and Josephine (Perez) K.; m. Karen Christine Duncan, 1989; children from previous marriage: Michael Bruce, Sharon Inez; stepchildren: Michael John Eisenbeiser, Jason James Eisenbeiser, Justin Ryan Eisenbeiser. BS, City Coll. N.Y., 1945; PhD, Duke U., 1949. Postdoctoral fellow Duke U., 1949-51; research asso. GE R & D Ctr., Schenectady, 1951-60, sect. mgr., 1960-65, br. mgr., 1965-72; v.p. R & D. GAF Corp., Wayne, N.J., 1972-82; prof. chemistry U. Mass., Amherst, 1982-2000, prof. emeritus, 2000—. Contbr. articles to chem. jours.; patentee in field. Mem. Am. Chem. Soc., AAAS, Soc. Chem. Industry, Indsl. Research Inst., Phi Beta Kappa, Phi Lambda Upsilon. Home: 153 Silver Lake Dr Agawam MA 01001-2351 Business E-Mail: swkantor@polysci.umass.edu.

KANTOR, STEPHEN RICHARD, orthopedic surgeon; b. Montreal, Que., Canada, Dec. 10, 1969; s. Jonathan Kantor and Joyce Kramer, Beatrice Kantor (Stepmother); m. Kimberly Jagodnik, May 30, 1999; 1 child, Avery Brooke. BSc, McGill U., Montreal, 1992, Master of Surgery, MD, McGill U., Montreal, 1996. Cert. physician and surgeon NH. Med. Bd. Orthop. surgery resident McGill U., Montreal, 1996—2002; clin. instr. U. So. Calif., LA, 2002—03; vol. faculty U. Calif., San Diego, 2003—04; assoc. physician Orthop. Med. Group San Diego, 2003—04; asst. prof. orthop. surgery Dartmouth Med. Sch., Hanover, NH, 2004—; attending orthop. surgeron Dartmouth-Hitchcock Med. Ctr., Lebanon, NH, 2004—. Contbr. articles to profl. jours. Mem. univ. senate McGill U., Montreal, 1992—94. Recipient Joseph Sugar award for orthop., McGill U. Faculty Medicine, 1996, Eugene Rogala prize in orthop., 2000, 2001, 2002; Arthritis and Jt. Reconstrn. fellow, U. So. Calif., Keck Sch. Medicine, 2003, U. Calif., San Diego and San Diego Arthritis Surgery Ctr., 2004. Mem.: NH. Med. Soc., Calif. Orthop. Assn., Internat. Soc. for Tech. in Arthroplasty, Med. Coun. Can. (licentiate), Am. Acad. Orthop. Surgeons (assoc.), Can. Orthop. Assn. (assoc.). Achievements include multiple published research projects relating to the design and function of orthopaedic joint replacement implants. Office: Dartmouth-Hitchcock Med Ctr One Medical Ctr Dr Lebanon NH 03756 Office Phone: 603-650-6626. Office Fax: 603-650-2097. E-mail: stephen.r.kantor@hitchcock.org.

KANTROW, JOSH MARK, lawyer; b. Baton Rouge, Feb. 22, 1965; s. Byron R. and Marcia Gail (Kaplan) K.; m. Barbara Ellen March, Sept. 13, 1992; children: Marcia, Eli. BS in Fin., La. State U., 1987, JD, 1990; postgrad., U. Aix-Marseille, Aix-En-Provence, France, 1988. Bar: La. 1991, Ill. 1996, N.Y. 2000, US Dist. Ct. (ea., mid., we. dist.) La. 1996, US Ct. Appeals (5th cir.) 1996, US Dist. Ct. (no. dist.) Ill. 1996, US Ct. Appleals (7th cir.) 1996. Intern U.S. Claims Ct., Washington, 1988; assoc. Nesser, King & LeBlanc, New Orleans, 1990-95, Blatt, Hammesfahr & Eaton, Chgo., 1995-97, ptnr., 1998—; mem. Cozen & O'Connor, Chgo., 2000—. Liaison Lloyd's APEX Study Tour, Bloomington/Normal, Ill., 1996—; lectr. in field Contbr. articles to profl. jours. Intern U.S. Dist. Judge Randall Rader, Washington, 1989; del. to nat. conv. Am. Israel Pub. Affairs Com., Washington, 1998; bd. dirs. Jewish Comty. Ctr., New Orleans, 1994-95; mem. Lemann-Stern Young Leadership Program, New Orleans, 1994-95; intern. U.S. Rep. W. Henson Moore, Washington, 1984; co-chmn. Am. Israel Pub. Affairs Com., Chgo., 1999—, also mem. young leadership bd. Mem. ABA, Ill. State Bar Assn., Maritime Law Assn. of U.S., La. State Bar Assn., Chgo. Maritime Soc. (contbg. columnist 1997-98), Assn. Transp. Law, Logistics, and Policy, Propeller Club of Port of Chgo. Republican. Jewish. Avocations: travel, jogging, rollerblading, skiing. Office: Cozen & O'Connor 222 S Riverside Plz # 1500 Chicago IL 60606-6000 Office Phone: 312-382-3149. Home Fax: 312-382-8910. Personal E-mail: jkantrow@cozen.com.

KANTROWITZ, ADRIAN, surgeon, educator; b. NYC, Oct. 4, 1918; s. Bernard Abraham and Rose (Esserman) K.; m. Jean Rosensaft, Nov. 25, 1948; children: Niki, Lisa, Allen. AB, NYU, 1940; MD, L.I. Coll. Medicine, 1943; postgrad. physiology, Western Res. U., 1950. Diplomate: Am. Bd. Surgery, Am. Bd. Thoracic Surgery. Gen. rotating intern Jewish Hosp. Bklyn., 1944; asst. resident, then resident surgery Mt. Sinai Hosp., N.Y.C., 1947; asst. resident Montefiore Hosp., N.Y.C., 1948, asst. resident pathology, 1949, fellow cardiovascular rsch. group, 1949, chief resident surgery, 1950, adj. surg. svc., 1951-55; USPHS fellow cardiovascular rsch., dept. physiology Western Res. U., 1951-52; asst. prof. surgery SUNY Coll. Medicine, 1955-56, assoc. prof. surgery, 1957-64, prof., 1964-70; dir. cardiovascular surgery Maimonides Med. Ctr., Bklyn., 1955-64, dir. surgery, 1964-70; chmn. dept. surgery Sinai Hosp. Detroit, 1970-75, chmn. dept. cardiovascular surgery, 1975-85; prof. surgery Wayne State U. Sch. Medicine, 1970—. Contbr. articles profl. jours. 1st lt. to major M.C. AUS, 1944—46. Recipient H.L. Moses prize to Montefiore Alumnus for outstanding rsch. accomplishment, 1949; 1st prize sci. exhibit Conv. N.Y. State Med. Soc., 1952; Gold Plate award Am. Acad. Achievement, 1966; Max Berg award for outstanding achievement in prolonging human life, 1966; Theodore and Susan B. Cummings humanitarian award Am. Coll. Cardiology, 1967 Fellow ACS, N.Y. Acad. Sci.; mem. Internat. Soc. Angiology, Am. Soc. Artificial Internal Organs (pres. 1968-69, Barney Clark award 1993), N.Y. County Med. Soc., Harvey Soc., N.Y. Soc. Thoracic Surgery, N.Y. Soc. Cardiovascular Surgery, Am. Heart Assn., Am. Physiol. Soc., Am. Coll. Cardiology, Am. Coll. Chest Physicians, Bklyn. Thoracic Surgery Soc. (pres. 1967-68), Pan Am. Med. Assn., Soaring Soc. Am., Am. Ski Assn. Achievements include being pub. pioneer motion pictures taken inside living heart, 1950; contbr. to devel. pump- oxygenators for human heart surgey; pioneer devel. mech., artificial hearts; performed 1st permanent partial mech. heart surgery in humans, 1966; 1st use phase-shift intra-aortic balloon pump in patient in cardiogenic shock; 1st human heart transplant in U.S., Dec. 1967. Home: 70 Gallogly Rd Auburn Hills MI 48326-1227 Office: 300 River Place Dr Detroit MI 48207-4233 E-mail: adriank3ak@aol.com.

KANTROWITZ, ARTHUR, physicist, researcher, educator; b. NYC, Oct. 20, 1913; s. Bernard A. and Rose (Esserman) K.; m. Rosalind Joseph, Sept. 12, 1943 (div.); children: Barbara, Lore, Andrea; m. Lee Stuart, Dec. 25, 1980. BS, Columbia U., 1934, MA, 1936, PhD, 1947; DEng (hon.), Mont. Coll. Mineral Sci. and Tech., 1975; D.Sc. (hon.), N.J. Inst. Tech., 1981. Physicist NACA, 1935-46; prof. aero. engring. and engring. physics Cornell U., 1946-56; founder, dir., chmn., chief exec. officer Avco-Everett Research Lab., Everett, Mass., 1955-78; sr. v.p., dir. Avco Corp., 1956-79; prof. Thayer Sch. Engring., Dartmouth Coll., 1978—. Vis. lectr. Harvard U., 1952; Fulbright and Guggenheim fellow Cambridge and Manchester univs., 1954; fellow Sch. Advanced Study, MIT, 1957, vis. inst. prof., 1957—; Joseph Wunsch lectr. Technion, Haifa, Israel, 1968; mem., fellow lectr. Am. Inst. Chemists, 1977; Messenger lectr. Cornell U., 1978; 1st Hastings lectr. NIH, 1977; hon. prof. Huazhong Inst. Tech., Wuhan, China, 1980; mem. Presdl. Adv. Group on Anticipated Advances in Sci. and Tech., head task force on sci. ct., 1975-76; mem. tech. adv. bd. U.S. Dept. Commerce, 1974-77; mem. adv. panel NOVA, Sta. WGBH-TV, 1975—; bd. overseers Center for Naval Analyses, 1973-83; mem. adv. council Israel-U.S. Binational Indsl. Research and Devel. Found., 1978-81; bd. govs. The Technion (hon. life); mem. adv. council NASA, 1979, 80; life trustee U. Rochester; past mem. sci. and engring. adv. com. U. Rochester, Princeton U., Stanford U. and Rensselaer Poly Inst.; vis. prof. U. Calif., Berkeley, 1983. Contbr. articles to profl. jours.; patentee in field. Bd. dirs. Hertz Found., 1972—. Recipient award Am. Acad. Achievement, 1966, Theodore Roosevelt medal, 1967, Kayan medal Columbia U., 1973, MHD Faraday Meml. medal UNESCO, 1983, Beamed Energy Propulsion award First Internat. Symposium, 2002-. Fellow AAAS, AIAA (1st Von Kármán lectr. 1964, Fluid and Plasmadynamics medal 1981, Aerospace Contbn. to Soc. award 1990, hon. fellow 1998), Am. Acad. Arts and Scis., Am. Phys. Soc., Am. Astronautical Soc., Am. Inst. for Med. and Biol. Engring.; mem. NAS, NAE, Internat. Acad. Astronautics, Am. Inst. Physics, Sigma Xi. Achievements include scientific collaboration on MHD energy conversion US-USSR, 1968-78; high-energy lasers, interplanetary shock waves, heart assist devices, MHD generators, re-entry from space; early work in fusion, molecular beams and the total energy variometer noteable. Home: 4 Downing Rd Hanover NH 03755-1902 E-mail: arthur.kantrowitz@dartmouth.edu.

KANTROWITZ, JEAN, health products executive; b. Passaic, N.J., May 27, 1922; d. Nathan and Yetta (Applebaum) Rosensaft; m. Adrian Kantrowitz, Nov. 25, 1948; children: Niki, Lisa, Allen. BS, Rider Coll., 1942; MS, U. N.C., 1945; MPH, U. Mich., 1975. Adminstrv. asst. Maimonides Med. Ctr., Bklyn., 1961-70, Sinai Hosp., Detroit, 1970-78, '80-83; program coord., sr. clin. instr. child psyciatry divsn. Case Western Res. U. Sch. Medicine, Cleve., 1978-80; v.p. adminstrn. and bus. devel. L.VAD Tech., Inc., Detroit, 1983—. Mgmt. cons. NIH, Washington, 1974— Mem. Am. Soc. Artificial Internal Organs (co-chairperson project bionics, history work group). Home: 70 Gallogly Rd Auburn Hills MI 48326-1227 Office: LVAD Tech Inc 300 River Place Dr Ste 6850 Detroit MI 48207-5095 Office Phone: 313-446-2800.

KANTROWITZ, JONATHAN DANIEL, publishing executive, educator, lawyer; b. Bridgeport, Conn., Apr. 14, 1945; s. Ralph Samson and Beatrice (Schine) K.; m. Monica Victoria Fractenberg, Dec. 26, 1970; children: Bethany Eve, Ralph Richard. BA, Brown U., 1966; JD, Harvard U., 1969. Bar: Conn. 1969, N.Y. 1980. Ptnr. Kantrowitz & Kantrowitz, Bridgeport, 1969-74; atty. So. New Eng. Tel. Co., New Haven, 1975-76; asst. gen. counsel Touche Ross & Co., N.Y.C., 1977-81; founder, CEO Queue, Inc., Shelton, Conn., 1981. Adj. prof. Sch. Law Bridgeport, 1978-82. Author ednl. software Algebra Word Problems, 1984, How a Bill Becomes a Law, 1985. Vice chmn. Fairfield County Dem. Town Com., 1991-93, 96-2000; Dem. candidate for State Senate, 1972, 88, for U.S. Congress, 1994, 98; coach, mem. adv. bd. Fairfield Youth Soccer, 1985-90; coach Fairfield Little League, 1987, Joel Barlow H.S. Girls Varsity Soccer, 1991; mem. Fairfield Bd. Edn., 1991-93; chmn. bd. trustees Jewish Family Svcs., 1995-99; pres. bd. dirs. The Bridge Acad., 1997-99; mem. Fairfield Bd. Parks and Recreation, 1997-98; founder, pres. bd. Brooklawn Acad., 1998-99. Jewish. Avocations: soccer, tennis, biking, kayaking, books. Office: Queue Inc 1 Controls Dr Shelton CT 06484 Office Phone: 800-232-2224. E-mail: jdk@queueinc.com.

KANTROWITZ, SUSAN LEE, lawyer; b. Queens, N.Y., Jan. 15, 1955; d. Theodore and Dinah (Kotick) Kantrowitz; m. Mark R. Halperin; 1 child, Jacob Joseph Kantrowitz-Sirotkin. BS summa cum laude, Boston U., 1977; JD, Boston Coll., 1980. Bar: Mass. 1982. Assoc. producer Sta. KOCE-TV, Huntington Beach, Calif., 1980-81; acct. exec. Bozell & Jacobs, Newport Beach, Calif., 1981; atty. WGBH Ednl. Found., Boston, 1981-84, dir. legal affairs, 1984-86, gen. counsel, dir. legal affairs, 1986—, v.p., gen. counsel, 1993. Co-author: Legal and Business Aspects of the Entertainment, Publishing and Sports Industries, 1984. Mem. ABA, Mass. Bar Assn., Boston Bar Assn.

KANUK, LESLIE LAZAR, management consultant, educator; b. NYC; d. Charles and Sylvia Lazar; m. Jack Lawrence Kanuk; children: Randi Kanuk Dauler, Alan Robert. MBA, Baruch Coll., 1964; PhD, CUNY, 1974; PhD (hon.), Mass. Maritime Acad., 1981, Maine Maritime Acad., 1988. Pres. Leslie Kanuk Assocs., NYC, 1965—78, 1981—; Lippert Disting. chair Baruch Coll., NYC, 1981-84; prof. CUNY, 1974—99, prof. emeritus, 1999—. Mem. maritime transp. rsch. bd. NAS, 1975—78; commr., vice chmn., chmn. Fed. Maritime Commn., 1978—81; chmn., pres., dir. Containerization and Intermodal Inst., 1981—93; panelist NRC-NAS, 1975—78, 1991; vis. prof. grad. program Maine Maritime Acad., 1984—93. Author: Mail Questionnaire Response Behavior, 1974, Toward an Expanding U.S.M.M., 1976, Consumer Behavior, Prentice Hall, 1978, rev. edits., 1983, 87, 89, 94, 97, 2000, 04, India, 1988, Australia, 1997, 2001, Brazil, 2000, Japan, 2001, China, 2002, Czech Republic, 2004, Croatia, 2004, Internat. Edit., 1997, 2004; mem. editl. bd. Intermodal Forum, 1984-92 Bd. visitors Maine Maritime Acad., 1989—97; trustee United Seaman's Svc., 1988—. Recipient Connie award Containerization and Intermodal Inst., 1980, Diamond Superwoman award Harpers Bazaar mag., 1980, Person of Yr. award NY Fgn. Freight Forwarders and Brokers Assn., 1981, Person of Yr. award Baruch Fgn. Trade Soc., 1981, Disting. Alumnus award CCNY, 1984, Disting. PhD Alumni award CUNY, 1988, Townsend Harris medal, 1986. Mem. Beta Gamma Sigma.

KANUTH, JAMES GORDAN, chemical engineer; b. Lexington, Ohio, June 18, 1953; s. John Gordon and Helena Jane K.; m. Michelle Susan Cronk, Nov. 10, 2000; 1 child, Robert Gordon. BSChemE, U. Cin., 1976. Project engr. Joseph E. Seagram and Sons, Inc., Lawrenceburg, Ind., 1976-80; prodn. engr. Monsanto (name changed to Conoco), Alvin, Tex., 1980-81; sr. area engr. utilities Conoco (name changed to Oxy Chem), Alvin, 1981-89; regional mgr. Puckorius and Assocs., Inc. indsl. water treatment cons., League City, Tex., 1989-95; indsl. water treatment cons. Chemtreat, Inc., Nassau Bay, Tex., 1995—. Pres. Gulf Coast Energy Conservation Soc., Houston, 1988-89, Galveston County Mcpl. Utility Dist. 3, League City, 1983-88; city councilman City of League city, 1988-94; bd. dirs. Houston Galveston Area Coun., 1991; treas. Clear Lake Area Coun. of Cities, Webster, Tex., 1990-94. Mem. Nat. Assn. Corrosion Engrs. (com. mem. 1989—), Am. Inst. Chem. Engrs., Cooling Tech. Inst. (bd. dirs. 2005-), Cooling Tower Inst. (water treatment com. 1981—). Communist. Presbyterian. Avocations: boating, reading, sports cars. Home: 18124 Bal Harbour Dr Houston TX 77058 Office: Chemtreat Inc PO Box 412 League City TX 77574-0412 Office Phone: 800-521-2395. E-mail: jimk@chemtreat.com.

KANWAR, RAMESHWAR SINGH, agricultural engineer, researcher, educator; b. Daulatpur, India, Feb. 11, 1949; came to U.S., 1976; s. Jaswant Singh and Lila (Devi) K.; m. Anjana S. Kanwar, Apr. 20, 1975; children: Bittoo, Pooja. MS, G. B. Pant U. Agrl. and Tech., Pantnagar, India, 1975; PhD, Iowa State U., 1981; Doctorate (hon.), Georgian Nat. Agrarian U., Tbilisi, 2000. Lectr. Punjab Agrl. U., Ludhiana, India, 1969-73, asst. prof., 1973-76; teaching/rsch. asst. Iowa State U., Ames, 1976-81, instr., 1981-82, asst. prof., 1983-86, assoc. prof., 1986-91, prof., 1997—, asst. dir. Experiment Sta., 1997—2002, dept. chmn., 2001—; dir. Iowa State Water Resources Rsch. Inst., 1999—2002. Vis. prof. Cath. U., Leuven, Belgium, 1991, Tech. U. Lisbon, Portugal, 1992-95, Tashkent Inst. of Irrigation and Agr. Mech. Engrs., Uzbekistan, 1995, 96, 97, 98, U. Vienna, 2003; cons. FAO, World Bank, NATO, 1992-2004, USAID, Romania, 2001-04, UN Devel. Program, China, 2001-04, European Commn., 2003. Contbr. numerous articles to profl. jours. Recipient Disting. Faculty award Coll. Agrl. Engring., Punjab Agrl. U., 1990, Disting. Internat. Agr. award Iowa State U., 2002, Internat. Svc. award Iowa State U., 2004. Fellow Nat. Acad. Agrl. Scis., India; mem. Asian Agrl. Engring. Assn. (found. mem., Disting. Svc. award 2000), Am. Soc. Agronomy, Am. Soc. Soil Sci., Am. Soc. Agrl. Engrs. (Achievement award 1991, Engr. of Yr. 1995, mem. of yr. 1995), Am. Water Resource Assn., Internat. Commn. on Irrigation and Drainage. Achievements include development of design criterion for drainage design on the basis of crop stress factors; new mathematical solution to determine aquifer properties; major findings in area of water quality and environment; development of systems to minimize impacts of swine and poultry manure on surface and groundwater quality. Office: Iowa State Univ Dept Agrl & Biosystems Engring 104 Davidson Hall Ames IA 50011-0001 Office Phone: 515-294-1434. Business E-Mail: rskanwar@iastate.edu.

KANY, JUDY C(ASPERSON), retired state senator; b. Ill., June 29, 1937; d. Helmer C. and Florence P. Casperson; m. Robert Kany, Aug. 16, 1958; children: Kristin, Geoffrey, Daniel. BBA, U. Mich., 1959; MPA, U. Maine, Orono, 1976. Mem. Maine Ho. of Reps., 1975-82, Maine Senate, 1982-92; project dir. for health professions regulation Med. Care Devel., Augusta, Maine, 1993—; mem. task force on health workforce regulation Pew Health Professions Commn., 1994-97; mayor Waterville, Maine, 1988-89; mem. issues and policy adv. com. Citizens Advocacy Ctr., Washington, 1994—2000; cmty. liaison Amity Circle Tree Ranch, Tucson, 2003—. Chmn. Maine's Adv. Commn. on Radioactive Waste, 1981-87, Joint Standing Com. Legal Affairs, 1987-88, Joint Standing Com. on State Govt., 1979-82, Joint Standing Com. Energy and Natural Resources, 1983-84, 89-90, Joint Standing Com. Banking and Ins., 1991-92, com. Maine Lakes, 1990-92, adv. com. on accountability to the Maine Health Care Reform Commn., 1994-95; mem. Commn. on Maine's Future, 1976, 87-89; project coord. Amity Found.'s Ariz Gov.'s Innovative Domestic Violence Prevention Grant, Amity, 2004-06. Democrat. Home: PO Box 508 81 Lakeshore Dr Belgrade Lakes ME 04918 also: 36832 S Stoney Flower Dr Tucson AZ 85739 Office Phone: 520-749-5980. Business E-Mail: jkany@amityfdn.org.

KANZEG, DAVID GEORGE, radio station executive; b. Cleve., Apr. 9, 1948; s. George and Ida Marie Ada (Hienz) K. BA, Coll. Wooster (Ohio), 1970; MS, Syracuse (N.Y.) U., 1971; postgrad., SUNY, 1972. Cert. ESL lang. instr. Instr. English Meyer Lang. Ctr., Bogota, Colombia, 1969; grad. teaching asst. Syracuse U., 1971; instr. speech State U. Coll. at Buffalo, N.Y., 1971-73; exec. producer Sta. WCMU-FM Cen. Mich. U., Mt. Pleasant, 1973-76; radio program mgr. Sta. WLRH/Madison County Pub. Libr., Huntsville, Ala., 1976-77; radio program dir. Sta. WOUB-AM-FM Ohio U. Telecommunications, Athens, 1977-83; mgr. programming Radio Sta. WNYC, NYC, 1983—86; sta. advisor Corp. for Pub. Broadcasting, Cleve., 1978-87; dir. programming Radio Sta. WCPN, Cleve., 1987—99, v.p. programming divsn., 1999—2002; cons. Corp. for Pub. Broadcasting Mgmt. Consulting Svc., 1993—; dir. programing for TV, radio and web Sta. WCPN, 2002—, Sta. WVIZ, 2002—. Participant seminars on future pub. radio, San Francisco and Washington, 1984-85; panel mem. Airlie IV Seminar on Art of Radio, N.Y.C., 1983; radio organizer Nat. Assn. Ednl. Broadcasters, Washington, 1976-78; exec. producer Future Forward Nat. Radio Series, 1985. Author: Transit Revisions, 1988, Ever Young: Douglas Moore and the Persistence of Legend, 1993; contbr. articles to publs; author, co-creator website. Mem. Isabella County sub-com. on transp., Mt. Pleasant, Mich., 1975; incorporator Mid-Mich. Opera Assn., Mt. Pleasant, 1975, Tenn. Valley Opera Assn., Hunstville, 1976; mem. media panel Ohio Arts Coun., Columbus, Ohio, 1979-80; active Airlie II Seminar on Art of Radio, 1979. Recipient Tech. Prodn. award Ohio Ednl. Broadcasting, 1980, Ohio State award, 1986. Mem. Ohio Pub. Radio Programming (group chmn. 1978-80), Assn. Inds. in Radio, Sigma Delta Pi. Avocations: roller coasters, opera, traction, bicycling, travel. Home: 16253 Shurmer Rd Cleveland OH 44136-6115 Office: Sta WCPN/Cleve Pub Radio 3100 Chester Ave Ste 300 Cleveland OH 44114-4604

KANZER, ALAN, lawyer; b. NYC, June 28, 1944; BA magna cum laude, Columbia U., 1965; LLB, Yale U., 1968. Bar: NY 1969, US Tax Ct. 1971. Ptnr. Walter, Conston, Alexander & Green P.C. (now Alston Bird LLP), NYC; ptnr., mem. antitrust and investigations group Alston & Bird LLP, NYC, 2001—. Bd. editors Yale Law Jour., 1968. Mem. Assn. of Bar of City of NY, Phi Beta Kappa. Office: Alston & Bird LLP 90 Park Ave Fl 14 New York NY 10016-1301 Office Phone: 212-210-9480. Office Fax: 212-210-9444. Business E-Mail: akanzer@alston.com.

KANZER, LARRY, small business owner, food service director; b. Albany, NY, June 13, 1942; s. Sanford and Beatrice Helen (Strick) K.; m. Ginger Sherman, July 13, 1966 (div. 1983); 1 child, Glen Harris; m. Lynn Karen Trost, June 2, 1985. AAS in Culinary Arts, NYC Community Coll., 1962; Cert. Food Svc. Supr., Auburn U., 1982-83; Master Locksmith, Foley Belsaw Inst., 1985. Food beverage controller Longchamps Restaurants, NYC, 1962-65; dir. food svc. Laurelcrest Prep. Sch., Bristol, Conn., 1965-69; owner, operator Anze's Place Restaurant, Nashua, NH, 1969-73; dir. food svc. Servend-Seilers, Waltham, Mass., 1973-76, Svc. Sys., Cambridge, Mass., 1976-78, ARA Svcs., White Plains, NY, 1978-88; owner Lots of Lock, Etc., 1988—. Com. chmn. Cub Scouts Am., Nashua, 1977-80; umpire Little League, Nashua, 1978-81; bd. dirs. Pike County C. of C., 2002. Served to sgt. USMCR, 1963-69. Recipient Otto Klitgord Meml. award NYC Cmty. Coll., Bklyn., 1962, Student Govt. Svc. award, 1962, Cert. Merit Jewish War Vets. US, Bronx, NY, 1982, Cert. Publ. Locksmith Ledger, Nat. Locksmith, Cert. Cmty. Svc., Pike County Sheriff's Office. Mem.: Rte. 739 Bus. Coun. (treas. 1999, 2000), Pike County C. of C. (bd. dirs. 2002—04). Democrat. Avocations: gunsmithing, clock repair, woodworking, antiques, gardening. Office: Lots of Lock Etc Locksmith Shop Hemlock Plz Rt 739 Hawley PA 18428 Office Phone: 570-775-6790. Business E-Mail: lotslock@ptdprolog.net.

KANZLER, GEORGE, journalist, music critic; b. Elizabeth, N.J., Mar. 30, 1939; s. George and Helen (Yorkunas) K.; m. Margaret A. Dudas, Dec. 31, 1978; children; Sarah Ella Dudas-Kanzler. BA, Seton Hall U., 1960; postgrad. Bread Loaf Sch. of English, Middlebury Coll., 1960; MA, NYU, 1969; postgrad., U. Wis., 1972. Reporter, editor Linden (N.J.) Leader, 1961-63; instr., asst. prof. Ibadan (Nigeria) Polytech., 1966-68; writer, pop and jazz critic Star Ledger, Newark, 1968-90, writer, jazz critic, 1990—2002, Newhouse News Svc., Washington, 1975—2002; contbg. editor Hot House Jazz mag., 2002—. Jazz disc jockey We. Nigeria Radio, Ibadan, 1966-68; instr. Essex C.C., Newark, 1970-73; elector Am. Jazz Hall of Fame, 1989—. Author: (TV show) One Way to Heaven, 1967; contbr. writer All About Jazz--New York. Vice pres. bd. dirs. Newark Jazz Festival, 1991-93; vol. U.S. Peace Corps., 1966-68. With U.S. Army, 1963-65, Congo. Fellow Newspaper Fund, 1972, Music Critics Assn./Smithsonian Inst., 1974. Mem. Nat. Acad. Recording Arts and Scis., Friends of Nigeria, Mbari Artists and Writers Club (sec. pro-tem. 1966-68), Jazz Journalists Assn., N.Y. Jazz Critics Cir. Avocations: hiking, unicycling. Home: 406 Marseille Dr Simpsonville SC 29680 Office Phone: 201-306-6570. E-mail: gkjazz@usa.net, gkjazz@gmail.com.

KAO, CHARLES KUEN, electrical engineer, educator; b. Shanghai, Nov. 4, 1933; s. Chun-Hsien and Tisung Fong K.; m. May Wan Wong, Sept. 19, 1959; children: Simon M.T., Amanda M.C. B.Sc. in Elec. Engring., U. London, 1957, PhD in Elec. Engring., 1965. Devel. engr. Standard Telephones & Cables Ltd., London, 1957—60; prin. rsch. engr. Std. Telecomm. Lab. Ltd., Harlow, England, 1960—70; prof. electronics, chmn. dept. Chinese U. Hong Kong, 1970—74, 1987—96; chief scientist Electro Optical Products div./ITT, Roanoke, Va., 1974—81, v.p., dir. engring., 1981—83; exec. scientist, dir. research ITT Advanced Tech. Ctr., Shelton, Conn., 1983—87; chmn., CEO ITX Svcs. Ltd., Hong Kong, 2000—. Author: Optical Fiber Technology II, 1981, Optical Fibers Systems: Technology, Design and Applications, 1982, Optical Fibre, 1988, A Choice Fulfilled--The Business of High Technology, 1991; contbr. articles to profl. jours.; patentee in field. Decorated comdr. Brit. Empire, 1993; recipient Morey award Am. Ceramic Soc., 1976, Stewart Ballantine medal Franklin Inst., 1977, Rank prize Rank Trust Funds, 1978, LM Ericsson Internat. prize, 1979, gold medal Armed Forces Comm. and Electronics Assn., 1980, Internat. C & C prize Found. for C & C Promotion, Japan, 1987, New Materials prize Am. Phys. Soc., 1989, Gold medal Internat. Soc. for Optical Engring., 1992, Japan prize The Sci. and Tech. Found. Japan, 1996, Morris Liebmann Meml. awrd, 1978, Alexander Graham Bell medal, 1985, Faraday medal, 1989, charles Stark Draper prize, 1999; Marconi Internat. fellow, 1985. Fellow: IEEE, Royal Acad. Engring. (U.K.), Royal Soc. (U.K.), Chinese Acad. Scis.; mem.: NAE, Academia Sinica (Taiwan), Royal Swedish Acad. Engring. Scis. Office: Unit 1708 Office Tower 1 Harbor Rd Wan Chai Hong Kong Hong Kong

KAO, JOHN STERLING, mathematician, educator; b. Salt Lake City, Aug. 30, 1967; s. Shih Kung and Yasuko Watanabe Kao. BS, U. Utah, 1985; MA, Princeton U., 1987, PhD, 1991. Asst. prof. U. San Francisco, 1991—97, assoc. prof., 1997—. Vis. assoc. prof. Princeton (N.J.) U., 1998—99. Assoc. editor: Advances and Applications in Statistics, 2002—; contbr. articles to profl. jours. Grad. fellow, NSF, 1985—91. Mem.: Math. Assn. Am., Inst. for

Ops. Rsch. and the Mgmt. Scis., Soc. for Indsl. and Applied Math., Am. Math. Soc., Phi Beta Kappa, Golden Key. Office: Univ San Francisco 2130 Fulton St San Francisco CA 94117-1080 Office Phone: 415-422-6760.

KAO, PAI CHIH, clinical chemist; b. Nanking, China, June 20, 1934; came to U.S., 1965, naturalized, 1976; s. Gung and Chuu Hui (Chang) K.; m. Joyce Kao; 1 child, Wayne LeRoy. PhD in Biochemistry, U. Louisville, 1971. Diplomate Am. Bd. Clin. Chemistry, Am. Bd. Clin. Biochemistry. Instr. dept. social medicine Nat. Def. Med. Ctr., Taipei, Taiwan, 1958-65; postdoctoral investigator Oak Ridge (Tenn.) Nat. Lab., 1971-73; head dept. new methods devel. and radioimmunoassay CBL Lab., Columbus, Ohio, 1973-75; prof. emeritus clin. chemistry, dept. lab. medicine and pathology Mayo Clinic, Rochester, Minn., 1975—. Cons. clin. chemistry sect., clin. chemistry and hematology devices panel FDA. Contbr. articles to profl. jours. Fellow Nat. Acad. Clin. Biochemistry, N.Y. Acad. Scis.; mem. Am. Bd. Clin. Chemistry, Assn. Clin. Scientists. Home: 1432 Ridge Cliff Ln NE Rochester MN 55906-8705 Office: Mayo Clinic 1014 Plummer Rochester MN 55905-0001 Office Phone: 507-284-2691. Business E-Mail: kao.pai@mayo.edu.

KAO, RACE LI-CHAN, medical educator; b. Chungking, China, Dec. 1, 1943; s. Yu-Ho and Tsing (Tsou) K.; m. Lidia Wei Liu, Aug. 18, 1969; children: Elizabeth, Grace. BS, Nat. Tawian U., 1965; MS, U. Ill., 1971, PhD, 1972. Rsch. assoc. U. Ill., Urbana, 1972, Pa. State U., Hershey, 1972-75, asst. prof. physiology, 1976-77; asst. prof. surgery, psysiology, biophys. U. Tex. Med. Br., Galveston, 1977-82, dir. cardiothoracic rsch., 1977-82; assoc. prof. surgery Washington U., St. Louis, 1982-83; dir. surg. rsch. Allegheny-Singer Rsch. Inst., Pitts., 1983-92; prof. surgery Med. Coll. Pa., Phila., 1988-92; prof., Carroll H. Long chair of excellence surg. rsch. East Tenn. State U., Johnson City, 1992—. Reviewer, cons. Nat. Heart, Blood and Lung Inst., NIH, 1984—. Contbr. numerous articles to profl. jours. Pres. U. Tex. Chinese Assn., 1980. With ROTC, China, 1965-66. Nat. Taiwan U. scholar, 1962-65; grantee NIH, 1979—, Tex. Heart Assn., 1982-83, VA Merit Rev., 1995—. Mem. AAAS, Coun. Circulation, Coun. Basic Sci., Internat. Soc. Heart Rsch., Am. Soc. Artificial Internal Organs, Am. Inst. Biol. Sci., Nat. Soc. Med. Rsch., N.Y. Acad. Scis., Nutrition Today Soc. Home: 4 Blackberry Ct Johnson City TN 37604-1466 Office: East Tenn State U Dept Surgery JH Quillen Coll Medicine PO Box 70575 Johnson City TN 37614-0575 Office Phone: 423-439-8803. E-mail: kao@etsu.edu.

KAO, TIMOTHY WU, civil engineering educator; b. Shanghai, July 20, 1937; came to U.S., 1959; m. May Lee, July 24, 1965; children: Michelle, Erika. BS in Engring., U. Hong Kong, 1959; MS in Engring., U. Mich., 1960, PhD, 1963. Lic. profl. engr., D.C. Rsch. fellow W.M. Keck Lab. Hydraulics and Water Resources Calif. Inst. Tech., Pasadena, 1963-64; from asst. prof. to prof. Sch. Engring. Cath. U. Am., Washington, 1964-70, prof., 1970—2003, chmn. dept. civil engring., 1981—2003, assoc. dean, 1981-94, prof. emeritus, 2003—. Vis. oceanographer Goddard Space Flight Ctr., NASA, Greenbelt, Md., 1978-79. Contbr. over 70 articles to sci. jours. Rsch. grantee NSF, Office of Naval Rsch., D.C. Water Resources Ctr.; named Eminent Engr., Tau Beta Pi, 1985. Fellow ASCE. Achievements include research in selective withdrawal in water quality management of lakes and reservoirs, in solitary waves in coastal oceans and oceanic fronts. Office: Cath Univ Am Dept Civil Engring Cardinal Sta Washington DC 20064-0001

KAOUK, JIHAD, urologist; m. Rula Hajj-Ali; children: Sahar, Reem, Reda. BS, Am. U. Beirut, 1989, MD, 1993. Resident in urology Am. U. Beirut, 1993—99; fellowship in advanced laparoscopic surgery Urol. Inst., Cleve. Clinic Found., 1999—2002, co-dir., robotic surgery, sect. minimally invasive surgery, 2002—. Contbr. articles to profl. jours. Mem.: So. Endourology, Am. Urol. Assn. (assoc.). Achievements include research in surgical techniques in urology such as Laparoscopic and minimally invasive surgery for bladder cancer, prostate cancer, and kidney diseases; development of new robotic urologic surgery techniques. Office: Cleve Clinic Found 9500 Euclid Ave Cleveland OH 44195 Office Phone: 216-444-2976.

KAPCSANDY, LOUIS ENDRE, building construction and manufacturing executive, chemical engineering consultant; b. Budapest, Hungary, June 5, 1936; came to U.S., 1957; s. Lajos Endre and Margit (Toth) K.; m. Roberta Marie Henson, Jan. 25, 1964; 1 son, Louis. BS in Chem. Engring., Tech. U. Hungary, 1956; postgrad. in law, U. San Francisco, 1963-64; MS in Petroleum Tech., U. Calif.-Berkeley, 1969. Freedom fighter Hungarian Revolution, Budapest, 1956; profl. football player San Diego Chargers, 1963-65; western regional mgr. Norton Co., San Francisco, 1965-72; product mgr. Koch Industries, Wichita, Kans., 1972-74; v.p., gen. mgr. Flow Systems, Inc., Seattle, 1974-78; pres. Fentron Bldg. Products, Inc., Seattle, 1978-85; CEO Baugh Enterprises Inc., Seattle, 1985—. Chem. engring. cons. HK Assocs., Seattle, 1974— Contbr. articles to profl. jours.; patentee vacuum fraction of crude oil, purification of hydrogen. Bd. dirs. Boy Scouts Chief Seattle, Seattle C. of C., Virginia Mason Med. Ctr.; active United for Wash., Seattle, 1982. With U.S. Army, 1959-62. Fellow AIChE; mem. Constrn. Specifications Inst., TAPPI, Columbia Tower Club, Rainier Club, Newcastle Golf Club, Seattle Rotary Lodge, PGA West. Republican. Roman Catholic.

KAPEL, DAVID EDWARD, academic administrator, researcher, education educator, educator; b. Wilmington, Del., July 11, 1932; s. Edward M. and Adele (M.) K.; m. Marilyn Brown, Aug. 27, 1955; children: Michael, Larry, Amy. BS in Edn., Temple U., 1955, MEd, 1957, EdD, 1964. Cert. tchr. of history, math., adminstr./prin., Pa. Tchr. of history, math. Phila. Sayre Jr. High Sch. Dist., 1955-57; tchr. of math. Elkins Park Jr. High, Cheltenham, Pa., 1957-59; tchr. of history, math. Cen. High Sch., Phila., 1959-64; prof. edn. Glassboro (N.J.) State Coll., 1964-69, Temple U., Phila., 1969-76; assoc. dean U. Nebr., Omaha, 1976-80, U. Louisville, 1980-85; dean U. New Orleans, 1985-88, Rowan U., Glassboro, NJ, 1988-98, prof. edn., 1998—2002; ret., 2002. Cons. various sch. dists. and colls. nationwide. Co-author: Metric Measure Simpl. 1974, Am. Educator's Encyclopedia, 1982 (ALA award 1982), 2d edit., 1991; contbr. articles to profl. jours. Staff sgt. USAF, 1951-52. Post-doctoral rsch. fellow U.S. Office Edn., Pitts.-AIR, 1966-67. Mem. ASCD, Am. Ednl. Rsch. Assn., Assn. Tchr. Educators (diplomate, dist. tchr. educator 1990—, honored as one of 70 Leaders in Edn. 1990), Am. Assn. Polit. and Social Sci. Democrat. Jewish. Avocations: reading, walking, fishing. Home: 217 Uxbridge Dr Cherry Hill NJ 08034-3731 Personal E-mail: dmkapel@aol.com.

KAPELMAN, BARBARA ANN, internist, hepatologist, gastroenterologist, educator; b. N.Y.C., Apr. 30, 1949; d. Leonard A. and Helen (Hass) K.; m. Lawrence William Koblenz, Mar. 24, 1979; 1 child, Adam. BA, Barnard Coll., 1970; MS in Microbiology, Yale U., 1972; MD, Albert Einstein Coll. Medicine, 1975. Diplomate Am. Bd. Internal Medicine, Am. Bd. Gastroenterology. Clin. asst. prof. hepatology and gastroenterology Mt. Sinai Sch. Medicine Mt. Sinai Hosp., 1981—82; intern Roosevelt Hosp.-Columbia U., N.Y.C., 1975-76, resident, 1976-78, fellow gastroenterology, 1978-80; fellow liver diseases Mt. Sinai Sch. Medicine-CUNY, N.Y.C., 1980-81; attending physician liver diseases Mt. Sinai Hosp., N.Y.C., 1981—82; asst. attending physician in gastroenterology Beth Israel Hosp., N.Y.C., 1982-88, assoc. attending physician in medicine and gastroenterology, 1988-96, attending physician in medicine and gastroenterology, 1996—; clin. instr. in medicine Mt. Sinai Sch. of Medicine, N.Y.C., 1981-87, asst. clin. prof. medicine, 1987-94; bd. dirs. Beth Israel Med. Ctr., N.Y.C., 1984—, trustee, med. liaison, 1996-97; asst. clin. prof. medicine Albert Einstein Coll. Medicine, N.Y.C., 1994—. Trustee Med. Bd. Liaison, 1996-97; attending physician Beth Israel North, Beth Israel Med. Ctr., N.Y.C., 1982—, Hosp. for Joint Diseases-Orthopedic Inst., N.Y.C., 1982—; vis. clin. fellow Columbia U. Coll. Physicians and Surgeons, N.Y.C., 1975-80; cons. gastroenterology and liver disease. Co-author: Gastroenterology for the House Officer, 1989; contbr. articles to profl. jours. Fellow ACP, Am. Coll. Gastroenterology; mem. AMA, Am. Women's Med. Assn., Women's Med. Assn. NYC (officer), Am. Gastroent. Assn., Am. Assn. for Study of Liver Diseases, Am. Soc. for Gastrointestinal Endoscopy, Am. Med. Informatics Assn., NY Acad. Gastroenterology, NY Soc. for Gastrointestinal Endoscopy. Avocations: medical computer software, culinary arts, medical informatics, educational activities. Home: 201 E 87th St New York NY 10128-3215 Business E-Mail: bkapelman@pol.net.

KAPETANAKOS, CHRISTOS ANASTASIOS, science administrator, physics educator; b. Xirokabi, Lakonia, Greece, Jan. 2, 1936; s. Anastasios and Alexandra (Doukas) K.; m. Ioanna Plafoutzi, June 23, 1962 (div. 1993); children: Anastasios, Yula. Diploma, Nat. U. Greece, Athens, 1960; M in Nuclear Engring., MIT, 1964; PhD, U. Md., 1970. Rschr. U. Tex., Austin, 1970-71; br. head, sect. head, rschr. Naval Rsch. Lab., Washington, 1971-92; acting dir. Inst. Plasma Physics, U. Crete, Iraklion, Crete, Greece, 1993-95; prof. of physics U. Crete, Iraklion, 1993-96; pres. Leading Egde Tech. Corp., Washington, 1995—. Cons. Fuel and Mineral Resources, Reston, Va., Icarus Rsch. Inc. Bethesa MD., Naval Rsch. Lab., Washington, SFA. Inc., Largo, Md., FERMI Nat. Accelerator Lab. Patentee in field; contbr. over 110 articles and more than 50 tech. reports to profl. publs. 2d lt. Artillery, 1960-62, Greece. Grantee Dept. Def., Washington, Dept. Energy, Washington, Office of Naval Rsch. Def. Advanced Project Agy., Washington, ELINOIL, Athens, Naval System Command, Fermi Lab. Fellow Am. Phys. Soc., Washington Soc. Scis. Home: 4431 Macarthur Blvd NW Washington DC 20007-2564 Personal E-mail: let-kapetanakos@starpower.net.

KAPIKIAN, ALBERT ZAVEN, physician, epidemiologist; b. N.Y.C., May 9, 1930; s. Zareh Kaloust and Baizar (Bazikian) K.; m. Catherine Firth Andrews, Feb. 27, 1960; children: Albert Kaloust, Thomas Firth, Gregory Baird. BS cum laude, Queens Coll., 1952; MD, Cornell U., 1956; postgrad., Johns Hopkins U. Sch. Hygiene and Pub. Health, 1961-62, Royal Postgrad. Med. Sch. U. London, 1970; DSc (hon.), CUNY, Queens, 1999. Intern Meadowbrook Hosp., Hempstead, N.Y., 1956-57; commd. med. officer USPHS, 1957, advanced through grades to capt., ret., 1988; with USPHS Civil Svc., 1988-90, USPHS Sr. Exec. Svc., 1990-2000; with epidemiology sect. Lab. Infectious Diseases, Nat. Inst. Allergy and Infectious Diseases, NIH, Bethesda, Md., 1957—, asst. chief, head epidemiology sect., 1967—; rsch. prof. child health and devel. George Washington U. Sch. Medicine and Health Svcs., 1977—; with Sr. Biomed. Rsch. Svc., 2000—01, sr. investigator, 2001—. Temporary advisor WHO, 1980-88, 91. Contbr. articles to profl. jours. Recipient Meritorious Svc. medal USPHS, 1970, 74, Disting. Svc. medal USPHS, 1983, Disting. Alumnus award Queens Coll., 1974, Stitt award Assn. Mil. Surgeons, 1974, Kabakjian award Armenian Students Assn. Am., 1974, Diagnostic Virology award (Murex) Pan Am. Soc. for Clin. Virology, 1993, joint recipient Pasteur award Children's Vaccine Initiative, 1998; invited to deliver Theobold Smith Lectr., 1995, Kinyoun Lectr., 1999, NIH Dirs. Lectr., 2000, Wyeth-Ayerst Rhesus Rotavirus Project Team award, 1995, Queens Coll Alumni Star award, 1998, Presdl. Disting. Exec. Rank award, 2000, Butanton medal, Sao Paulo, Brazil, 2005, Albert B. Sabin Gold medal, Sabin Vaccine Inst., 2005. Fellow AAAS, Infectious Disease Soc.; mem. APHA, Am. Epidemiol. Soc. (pres. 1996-97), Am. Soc. Microbiology (Behring Diagnostics award 1987), Am. Soc. Virology, Phi Beta Kappa. Mem. Armenian Apostolic Ch. Home: 11201 Marcliff Rd Rockville MD 20852-3631 Office: NIH Lab Infectious Diseases Bethesda MD 20892-0001

KAPIKIAN, CATHERINE ANDREWS, artist; b. Cleve., Oct. 18, 1939; d. John Robert and Anne Alva (Cosgrove) Andrews; m. Albert Zaven Kapikian, Feb. 27, 1960; children: Albert, Thomas, Gregory. Student, Carnegie Mellon U., 1957—59; BA, U. Md., 1963; MTS summa cum laude, Wesley Theol. Sem., Washington, 1979. Gen. illustrator NIH, Bethesda, Md., 1959—61; artist-in-residence Wesley Theol. Sem., 1979—, mem. faculty, 1980—, founder, dir. Ctr. Arts and Religion, 1984—2001, dir. Henry Luce III Ctr. for the Arts and Religion, 2001—. Designer, fabricator liturgical tapestries, banners, paraments and vestments; mem. commn. on worship and the arts Nat. Coun. Chs., 1991-97. Works exhibited in group shows including Interfaith Forum on Religion, Art and Architecture, Phoenix, 1979, Chgo., 1981, Phila., 1987, Houston, 1989, Boston, 1990, St. Thomas More Newman Ctr. Liturg. Arts Exhibit, Bowling Green (Ohio) U., 1981, Archdiocese of Chgo., 1984, Biennial Exhbns. Liturgical Art Guild of Ohio, Columbus, 1985, 91, 93, 95, 97, 2001; author: Through the Christian Year: An Illustrated Guide, 1983; contbr. forward to (book) Full Circle, 1988; contbr. articles and images to profl. jours. Bd. dirs. Episcopal Ch. Visual Arts, 2002—. Fellow, Coll. Preachers, Washington Nat. Cathedral, 1992. Mem. Arts and Religion Forum of Washington Theol. Consortium (founder, mem. steering com.), Interfaith Forum on Religion, Art and Architecture (bd. dirs. 1983-85, 87-90), Schuyler Inst. Worship and the Arts (bd. dirs. 1987-90). Democrat. Avocations: opera, remote control airplanes. Office: Wesley Theol Seminary Henry Luce III Ctr for Arts and Religion 4500 Massachusetts Ave NW Washington DC 20016-5632

KAPITO, ROBERT S., diversified financial services company executive; BS in Econs., U. Pa., 1979; MBA, Harvard U., 1983. With Mortgage Products Group The First Boston (Mass.) Corp., 1979—88; strategic cons. Bain & Co., 1982; vice chmn. BlackRock Inc., N.Y., 1988—. Bd. dir. Smith Barney Adjustable Rate Govt. Income Fund, BlackRock Closed-End Funds, BlackRock Inc. Office: BlackRock Inc 40 East 52nd St New York NY 10022

KAPLAN, ABNER J., social worker, public relations executive; b. Williamsport, Md., Dec. 27, 1910; s. Harry George and Annie Kaplan; m. Katharine Kirkpatrick Bowser; children: David, George, Douglas. B in Lit., Columbia U., 1932; MSW, U. Pa., 1942. Corr. Washington Times-Herald, 1933—36; caseworker, supr. exec. Washington County Social Svcs., Hagerstown, Md., 1936—46; chief divsn. stats. State Dept. Social Svcs., Balt., 1946—53, chief divsn. child welfare, 1953—70; dir. pub. rels. State Employees Credit Union, Balt., 1971—89, Towson, Md., 1971—89. Dir. pub. rels., bd. mem. Regional Mental Health Ctr., Balt., 1973—2001, Md. Rehab. Ctr., Balt., 1983—89. Contbr. articles to profl. jours. Active Childrens Def. Fund, Pub. Citizen, Common Cause; bd. mem., officer Md. Conf. Social Concern, Balt., 1961—98. Recipient award for svcs. to children, Nat. Foster Parents Assn., 1984, Humanitarian award, Md. State Employees Credit Union, 1986. Mem.: Soc. Profl. Journalists (life), Masons (life), Sigma Delta Chi (life). Democrat. Jewish. Avocations: computers, crossword puzzles, swimming, bowling, exercise. Home: 2402 E Strathmore Ave Baltimore MD 21214-2153

KAPLAN, ALEXANDER EFIMOVICH, physics educator, engineering educator; b. Kiev, Ukraine, USSR, June 9, 1938; came to U.S., 1979; s. Efim S. and Anna A. K. MS in Physics, Moscow Phys. Tech. Inst., 1961; postgrad., USSR Acad. Scis., Moscow, 1963-66; PhD in Physics and Math., Gorkii State U., USSR, 1967. Rsch. scientist Radio R & D Lab., Moscow, 1961-63; rsch. staff mem. USSR Acad. Scis., 1963-79, MIT, Cambridge, 1979-82; prof. elec. engring. sch. Purdue U., West Lafayette, Ind., 1982-87; prof. elec. and computer engring. dept. Johns Hopkins U., Balt., 1987—. Cons. Bell Labs, Homdell, N.J., 1980-81, Los Alamos (N.Mex.) Nat. Lab., 1981, Honeywell Rsch. Ctr., Mpls., 1982; guest scientist Max-Planck-Inst. Quantenoptik, Garching, Fed. Republic Germany, 1981; Alexander-von-Humboldt prof. quantum physics dept. U. Ulm, Germany, 1996. Contbr. more than 110 articles to profl. jours. and 3 books. Recipient Alexander von Humboldt award for sr. U.S. scientists Alexander von Humboldt Found. Germany, 1996. Fellow Optical Soc. Am.; mem. Am. Phys. Soc., Laser & Electro-Optic Soc. Achievements include patent in field. Office: Johns Hopkins U Elec and Comp Engring Dept 34th & Charles Sts Baltimore MD 21218 E-mail: sasha@striky.ece.jhu.edu.

KAPLAN, ALICE, humanities educator, writer; b. Mpls., June 22, 1954; d. Leonore Yaeger and Sidney Joseph Kaplan. BA, U. Calif., Berkeley, 1975; PhD, Yale U., 1981. Asst. prof. N.C. State U., Raleigh, 1981—83, Columbia U., N.Y.C., 1983—86; assoc. prof. Romance studies Duke U., Durham, NC, 1986—94, prof. Romance studies and lit., 1994—, Lehrman prof. Romance studies, 2003—; founding dir. Duke Ctr. French and Francophone Studies, 1999—2002. Author: Reproductions of Banality: Fascism, Literature and French Intellectual Life, 1986, Sources et citations dans "Bagatelles pour un massacre", 1988, French Lessons: A Memoir, 1993 (finalist Nat. Book Critics Cir. award in autobiography/biography, 1993), The Collaborator: The Trial and Execution of Robert Brasillach, 2000 (Book prize in history L.A. Times, 2001, finalist Nat. Book award, finalist Nat. Book Critics Cir. award, 2001), The Interpreter, 2005; translator: (novels) Le Pierrot Noir , 1998, Partita , 2001, OK Joe, 2003. Named Officier dans l'Ordre des Palmes Academiques, French Ministry of Edn., 2001; fellow, Nat. Humanities Ctr., 1989—90, Guggenheim Found., 1994, Stanford Humanities Ctr., 1994—95. Mem.: PEN, MLA, Am. Lit. Translators Assn., Assn. Pour l'Autobiographie et le Patrimoine Autobiographique. Office: Duke U Lit Program 109 Art Mus Durham NC 27708

KAPLAN, ARLINE RAY, editor, writer; b. South Gate, Calif., Oct. 13, 1942; d. Bernard and Annette Kaplan; children: Alysha Taylor, Robert Polgar. AB Journalism, U. So. Calif., Los Angeles, CA, 1964. Reporter Press Telegram, Long Beach, Calif., 1966—72; editor Kern Valley Sun, Kernville, Calif., 1973—74, World Dredging and Marine Constrn. Mag., San Pedro, Calif., 1974—76; pub. rels. specialist Am. Medicorp, Marina del Rey, Calif., 1976—77; med. editor Am. Assn. Gynecologic Laparoscopists, Downey, Calif., 1977—79; pub. affairs cons. Comprehensive Care Corp., Irvine, Calif., 1979—85; mng. editor Psychiat. Times, Irvine, Calif., 1992—95; sr. contbg editor Psychiat. Times / Geriatric Times, Irvine, Calif., 1996—; pres. ARK Comm., Huntington Beach, Calif., 1986—. Author: Thank You for My Life; editor: Endoscopy in Gynecology; contbr. Selling to a Segmented Market - A Lifestyle Approach. Recipient Press Club Awards, Pacific Coast Press Club, 1970, Most Improved Publ., Mag. Publishers Assn., 1994. Mem.: Am. Med. Writers Assn., Long Beach - Sochi Sister City, Phi Beta Kappa. Avocations: travel, singing, lay counseling. Office: Psychiatric Times 2801 McGaw Ave Irvine CA 92614-5835 Personal E-mail: arlinerkaplan@aol.com.

KAPLAN, BARBARA JANE, retired city planner; b. NYC, Sept. 8, 1943; d. Richard S. and Fannie I. (Schutz) Benson; m. Jerry Martin Kaplan, May 29, 1966. BA, Barnard Coll., 1965; MS, U. Southern Calif., 1969. Asst. planner L.A. Regional Planning Commn., 1968-69; from asst. planner to assoc. planner San Diego Comprehensive Planning Orgn., 1969-71; asst. dir. of regional planning North Ctrl. Tex. Coun. of Govts., Arlington, 1971-73; dir. Pennsport Civic Assn., Phila., 1974; city planner III Phila. City Planning Commn., 1974-76, city planner V, 1976-80, dep. exec. dir., 1980-83, exec. dir., 1983-2000, ret., 2000. Trustee U. of the Arts, Phila., 1987—2001; pres. Ctr. for Literacy, Phila., 1991—96, bd. dirs., 1984—, Neighborhood Gardens Assn., Phila., 1987—. Mem.: Pa. Hort. Soc. (bd. dirs. 1993—, v.p. 2000—01, mem. coun.), Nat. Trust for Hist. Preservation, Am. Planning Assn. Avocations: reading, tennis. Home: 2421 Fairmount Ave Philadelphia PA 19130-2517 Personal E-mail: barbarajkaplan@msn.com.

KAPLAN, BARRY HUBERT, physician; b. Bklyn., Nov. 16, 1938; s. Samuel and Mildred (Rabiner) K.; m. Rosalind Perlow Kaplan, June 23, 1962; children: Andrew, Scott. BA summa cum laude, NYU, 1958; MD, Johns Hopkins U., 1962, PhD, 1967. Diplomate Am. Bd. Internal Medicine, Am. Bd. Hematology, Am. Bd. Med. Oncology. Intern in medicine Johns Hopkins Hosp., 1962-63; fellow dept. physiol. chem. Johns Hopkins Sch. of Medicine, 1963-64; rsch. assoc. NIH, 1964-66; resident in medicine Bronx Mcpl. Hosp. Ctr., 1966-67; assoc. in medicine Albert Einstein Coll. Medicine, 1967-70, asst. prof. medicine, 1970-75, asst. prof. biochemistry, 1973-82, acting dir., divsn. med. oncology, 1974-81, acting assoc. dir. clin. rsch., Cancer Ctr. to assoc. dir., 1975-82, assoc. prof. medicine, 1975-82, assoc. clin. prof. medicine, 1982-93, vis. clin. assoc. prof. of medicine, 1993-95; clin. assoc. prof. of medicine Cornell Med. Coll., 1995—. Dir. divsn. med. oncology Albert Einstein Coll. Medicine, 1981-82, vis. asst. prof. biochemistry, 1982-87; physician in charge med. oncology Booth Meml. Med. Ctr., 1985-91, physician in charge med. oncology/hematology N.Y. Hosp. Med. Ctr. of Queens, 1991—; pres. Queens Med. Assocs., 2001—; asst. attending physician Bronx Mcpl. Hosp. Ctr., 1967-71; attending physician The Weiler Hosp. of the Albert Einstein Coll. of Medicine, 1972-93, Bronx Mcpl. Hosp. Ctr., 1972-93, Westchester Square Hosp., Bronx, 1982-93, Union Hosp., 1983-91, N.Y. Hosp. Med. Ctr. of Queens, 1983—. Contbr. articles to profl. jours. Mem. Am. Assn. for Cancer Rsch., Am. Soc. for Clin. Oncology, Am. Soc. Hematology, N.Y. Cancer Soc. (pres. 1981-82), Am. Cancer Soc. (N.Y.C. divsn. bd. dirs. 1981-84, steering com. profl. ednl. and grants com. 1981-83), Queens County Med. Soc., Phi Beta Kappa (Edward J. Noble Found. fellowship student leadership 1958-62). Home: 190 @ 72d St Apt 15D New York NY 10021 Office: 59-16 174th St Fresh Meadows NY 11365 Office Phone: 718-460-2300. Personal E-mail: bhkaplan@aol.com.

KAPLAN, BARRY MARTIN, lawyer; b. NYC, Nov. 9, 1950; s. Stanley Seymour and Lillian (Schner) K.; m. Erica Green, July 26, 1981; children: Matthew Aaron, Elizabeth Rose, Andrew Nathan. BA, Colgate U., 1973; JD cum laude, U. Mich., 1976. Bar: Mich. 1976, Wash., 1978, U.S. Dist. (ea. dist.) Mich. 1976, U.S. Dist. Ct. (we. dist.) Wash. 1978, U.S. Dist. Ct. (ea. dist.) Wash. 1986, U.S. Tax Ct. 1983, U.S. Ct. Appeals (9th cir.) 1990. Law clk. to Hon. Charles W. Joiner U.S. Dist. Ct. (ea. dist.) Mich., Detroit, 1976-78; assoc. Perkins Coie, Seattle, 1978-85, ptnr., 1985—2005, Wilson Sonsini Goodrich & Rosati, Seattle, 2005—. Adj. prof. securities regulation U. Wash. Sch. Law; spkr. in field. Author: Washington Corporate Law, Corporations and LLCs, 2000; contbr. articles to legal jours. and procs. Mem. ABA (litigation sect., securities litigation com., bus. law sect., bus. and corp. litigation com., subcom. chmn. on control transactions 1993), Wash. State Bar Assn. (CLE spkr., bus. law sect., securities com., subcom. chair on dir.'s liability 1993), Wash. Athletic Club, Rainier Club. Office: Wilson Sonsini Goodrich & Rosati 701 5th Ave Seattle WA 98104-7036 Office Phone: 206-883-2500. Business E-Mail: bkaplan@wsgr.com.

KAPLAN, BENJAMIN, judge; b. N.Y.C., Apr. 9, 1911; s. Morris and Mary (Berman) K.; m. Felicia Lamport, Apr. 16, 1942; children: James L., Nancy L. Mansbach. AB, CCNY, 1929; LL.B., Columbia, 1933; LL.D., Suffolk U., 1974, Harvard U., 1981, Northeastern U., 1981. Bar: N.Y. 1934, Mass. 1950. Assoc., then mem. firm Greenbaum, Wolff & Ernst, N.Y.C., 1933-42, 46; vis. prof. law Harvard, 1947, prof. law, 1948—, Royall prof. law, 1961-72, emeritus, 1972—; assoc. justice Supreme Jud. Ct. Mass., 1972-81; recalled to serve as judge Appeals Ct. Mass., 1983—. Reporter to adv. com. on civil rules Jud. Conf. U.S., 1960-66, mem., 1966-70; co-reporter restatement (2d) of judgments to Am. Law Inst., 1970-73 Served to lt. col. AUS, 1942-46. Mem. Am. Law Inst., Assn. Bar City of N.Y., Phi Beta Kappa. Achievements include assisting Justice Jackson on Nuremberg Trial, 1945. Home: 2 Bond St Cambridge MA 02138-2308 Office: Harvard Law Sch Cambridge MA 02138

KAPLAN, BETSY HESS, retired school board member; b. Bridgeton, N.J., Aug. 12, 1926; d. Alfred N. and Betsy (Bolton) Hess; m. Robert Leon Kaplan, June 11, 1953; children: Bruce Alfred, James Edward, Joan Ann. AB, Wesleyan Coll., Macon, Ga., 1947; BFA, Wesleyan Conservatory, 1948. Cert. tchr., Fla. Tchr. 4th grade Miami (Fla.)-Dade County Pub. Schs., 1950-53; edn. and cultural arts adv., 1961—88; instr. Miami Dade Cmty. Coll., 1979-81; admintrv. asst. to Ethel K. Beckham Miami-Dade County Sch. Bd., 1980-82, mem. sch. bd., 1988—2004, chair, 1993-95. Chair fed. rels. network Fla. Sch. Bds., Tallahassee, 1996-98; bd. dirs. New World Sch. Arts, Miami, 1996-2004, found. bd., 2005—; mem. Performing Arts Ctr. Trust, Miami, 1993-2005, student mentor; mem. Human Svcs. Coalition, 1995—. Mem. Emily's List, Washington, 1990—, Women's Emergency Network, Miami, 1990—, Women's Polit. Caucus, 1988—; cultural amb. Heart of the City cultural series Miami-Dade Parks and Recreation Dept., 2002; bd. mem. Lesbian and Straight Edn. Network, 1989—2001, co-chair, 2001—. Named Woman Worth Knowing, Miami Beach Commn. on Status of Women, 1994, Woman of Yr., King of Clubs, 2000; named to Miami-Dade County Women's Park Wall of Honor, 2005; recipient Alumnae Disting. Achievement award, Wesleyan Coll., 1987, French Acad. Palms award, French Min. of Edn. of Youth and Sports, 1991, Ruth Wolkowsky Greenfield award, Am. Jewish Congress, 1993, Trailblazer award, Women's Com. of 100, 1993, Woman of Impact award, Cmty. Coalition for Women's History, 1995, Co. of Women, Pioneer award, Miami-Dade County Pks. Dept., 1997, Red Cross Spectrum award, Women in Edn., 1997, Lifetime Svc. to Music Edn. in Fla. and U.S., Fla. Music Educators Assn., 2000, Branches of Learning award, Women's Divsn. Greater Miami State of Israel Bonds Orgn., 2001, Heart of the Arts award, New World Sch. of the Arts, 2004, Pillar award, Black Heritage Planning Com., Miami-Dade County, 2004, Joseph R. Narot award, Temple Israel of Miami, 2004, Cervantes award, Nova U., 2004, Serving the Arts, Arts and Edn. award, Children's Cultural Coalition and Arts and Bus. Coun., 2004. Mem.: AAUW (Phoenix award 1999), LWV (Margery Rankin award 2004), M. Athalie Range Cultural Found. (bd. dirs. 1995—2002, exec. com. 2002—), Jewish Mus. Fla. (bd. dirs. 1999—2003, adv. bd. 2003—04, exec. bd. 2003), Alliance for Aging (mem. adv. bd. 1996—2004), Fla. Sch. Bds. Assn. (bd. dirs. 1990—99, Pres.'s award 2001), Phi Kappa Phi, Delta Kappa Gamma, Phi Delta Kappa. Democrat. Jewish. Avocations: studying art history, reading and interpreting poetry, studying and practicing French language, cooking. Home: 200 SW 21st Rd Miami FL 33129 Personal E-mail: bakaplan60@aol.com.

KAPLAN, CARL ELIOT, lawyer; b. N.Y.C., Apr. 17, 1939; s. Lawrence S. and Pearl (Eisenberg) K.; m. Diane L. Garvin, Dec. 16, 1965; children: Lynn, Jonathan. BA, Columbia Coll., 1959; LLB, 1962. Bar: U.S. Dist. Ct. (so. and ea. dists.) N.Y. 1964, U.S. Ct. Appeals (2nd cir.) 1966, U.S. Supreme Ct. 1970. Assoc. Fulbright & Jaworski L.L.P., N.Y.C., 1963-69; ptnr., 1969—. Bd. dirs. Savient Pharms., Inc., East Brunswick, NJ. Bd. editors: Columbia Law Rev., 1961-62. Mem. ABA, N.Y. Bar Assn., Assn. of Bar City of N.Y., Am. Soc. Corp. Secs., Univ. Club (N.Y.C.), Phi Beta Kappa. Avocations: biking, jogging. Office: Fulbright & Jaworski LLP 666 5th Ave Fl 31 New York NY 10103-3198 Office Phone: 212-318-3224. Business E-Mail: ckaplan@fulbright.com.

KAPLAN, CATHY M., lawyer; b. NYC, Jan. 22, 1953; BA, Yale U., 1974; JD, Columbia U., 1977. Bar: N.Y. 1978. Ptnr. Brown & Wood, NYC; now ptnr. and co-head securitization practice Sidley Austin Brown & Wood LLP, NYC, and mem. exec. com. Contbr. articles to profl. journals. Mem.: ABA. Office: Sidley Austin Brown & Wood 787 Seventh Ave New York NY 10019 Office Phone: 212-839-5531. Office Fax: 212-839-5599. Business E-Mail: ckaplan@sidley.com.

KAPLAN, CLAUDETTE S. (CLAUDIA KAPLAN), volunteer; b. Chgo., June 4, 1931; d. Jacob and Celia (Lopaty) Mirotsnic; m. Saul M. Kaplan, Nov. 28, 1953 (div. Mar. 1980); children: Allan, Laurie K., David. Grad., Chgo. City Coll., 1951; student, Coll. Jewish Studies, 1951-53. Pres. Hadassah, Memphis, 1970-72, So. region, 1978-81, nat. svc. com., 1981-83, mem. nat. pres.'s coun., 1984—, founder major and big gifts event, 1974, area founders chair nat. major gifts dept. Nat. Israel Edn. Svcs. Com., chpt. cons., 1999; bd. dirs. NCCJ, Memphis Jewish Cmty. Rels. Coun., Memphis Jewish Fedn./Unite Jewish Appeal, 1972-80; mem. So. Poverty Law Ctr. Recipient 25th Anniversary award State of Israel Bonds, 1973, Guardian of the Dream Founder award Hadassah, 1995. Mem. Am. Israel Pub. Affairs Com. (exec. com. Memphis coun.), Nat. Coun. Jewish Women, World Jewish Congress, Am. Soc. for Yad Vashem Simon Wiesenthal Ctr., Hadassah Women's Zionist Orgn. of Am. (life), City Hope (life), Memphis and Mid-South Jewish Hist. Soc., B'nai B'rith. Home: 408 River Oaks Pl Memphis TN 38120-2538

KAPLAN, DAVID L., retired communications educator, actor, artist, sculptor; b. Chgo., Apr. 6, 1918; s. Maurice I and Emily (Seilin) Kaplan; m. Tea Stefancic, June 11, 1977. BS, Northwestern U., 1940, MA, 1941; postgrad., Stanford U., 1952-54. Actor, stage mgr. comml. Chicagoland theatre, Chgo. and Highland Park, 1953-76. Radio speech and theatre instr. Temple U., Phila., 1947—50; from instr. to prof. City Coll. Chgo., 1956—86; stage dir. Peninsula Players, Fish Creek, Wis., 1963—64; cmty. theatre dir., Wilmette, Lincolnwood, Wheaton, Winnetka, Ill., St. Joseph, Mich., 1965—70. Sculpture. Mem Equity Libr. Theatre, Chgo., 1953—99, pres., v.p., sec.-treas.; mem Skokie Art Guild, Ill., 1986—, Evanston Art Ctr, Ill. Recipient numerous artistic awards including Best Dir Award, Ill Community Theater Asn, 1970, Marge Dare Lifetime Achievment Award, Equity Library Theatre Chicago, 1999. Mem.: Actors Equity Assn., Chgo. Artists Coalition, Nat. Sculpture Soc. (assoc.).

KAPLAN, DONNA ELAINE, artist, educator; b. South Amboy, N.J., Dec. 30, 1942; d. Oscar Ivan and Otta Theora (Hamilton) Olsen; m. Barnett Morris Kaplan, Sept. 20, 1975; children: William, Ivan, Benjamin. Diploma in profl. nursing, Chaffey Coll., Alta Loma, Calif., 1964; BS in Occupl. Therapy, U. Puget Sound, Tacoma, 1972; student, Factory of Visual Arts, Seattle, 1977-79. RN, Wash.; cert. psychiat. nurse, Calif.; registered occupl. therapist. Shift charge nurse rsch. unit Langley Porter Neuropsychiat. Inst., San Francisco, 1967-70; supr. nursing Western State Hosp., Steilacoom, Wash., 1972-73; instr. in-svc. edn. Inst. Pa. Hosp., Phila., 1974-75; owner DK Design Studio, North Bend, Wash., 1984—. Juror No. Calif. Reg. Fiber Show, Sacramento, Calif., 1993; guest curator Northwest Gallery, 1994; nat. touring guest arts instr. 1987—. Co-author: Beads as Warp and Weft, 1996; contbr. articles to art jours.; exhibitions include: Tacoma Art Mus., Wash., 1980, Window Gallery of Fine Art, Alaska, 1989, Craft Alliance Gallery, St. Louis, 1989, Tohomo Chul Park Gallery, Ariz., 1995, Whatcom Mus. History and Art, Wash., 1995, Bellevue Art Mus., Wash., 1982, 89, 96, Contemporary Crafts Ctr., Seattle, 1996, Raindance Gallery, Oreg., 1996, La. State U., Baton Rouge, 1997. Recipient Best Creative Use of Materials award Absolutely Beads Show/Beads and Beyond, Bellevue, Wash., 1994, Mus. Purchase award Edmonds (Wash.) Art Festival Mus., 1994, 1st pl. award Art Splash, City of Redmond, Wash., 1995. Mem. Seattle Weavers' Guild (corr. sec. 1982-83, Peoples Choice award 1986, Art 3D award 1995), N.W. Designer Craftsmen, N.W. Craft Alliance (v.p., bd. dirs. 1994-96), N.W. Bead Soc., Fiber Art Profls., Friends of Fiber Art Internat. Studio: DK Design Studio 43406 SE 88th St North Bend WA 98045-9455

KAPLAN, EDWARD L., electronics executive; BSME, Ill. Inst. Tech., 1965; MBA, U. Chgo., 1971. Project engr. Seeburg Corp.; mech. engr. R&D Printer Divsn. Teletype Corp.; from co-founder to CEO, chmn. bd. Data Specialties, Inc. (now Zebra Technologies Corp.), Vernon Hills, Ill., 1969—91; CEO Zebra Technologies Corp., 1991—, chmn. bd. Bd. trustees Ill. Inst. Tech., exec. com.; mem. coun. Grad. Sch. Bus. U. Chgo. Bd. dir. Anti-Defamation League. Named to Entrepreneurship Hall of Fame; recipient High Tech Entrepreneur award, Peat Marwick, 1988, Entrepreneur of Yr. award, Inc. Mag. and Ernst & Young, 1990, Disting. Entrepreneurial Alumnus award, U. Chgo., 1996. Fellow: NDEA; mem.: ASME, Chief Execs. Orgn., World Pres. Orgn., Soc. Advancement Mgmt., Tau Beta Pi. Office: Zebra Technologies Corp 33 Corporate Woods Pkwy Vernon Hills IL 60061

KAPLAN, ELAINE D., lawyer; b. Bklyn., Dec. 18, 1955; BA, SUNY, Binghamton, 1976; JD, Georgetown U., 1979. Atty. Office of the Solicitor U.S. Dept. Labor, 1979-83; atty. State and Local Legal Ctr., Washington, 1983-84; asst. dir. litigation, asst. counsel Nat. Treas. Employees Union, 1984—88, dep. gen. counsel, 1988-97; spl. counsel Office of Spl. Counsel, Washington, 1998—2003; of counsel Bernabei & Katz PLLC, Washington, 2003—. Mem., editorial bd. Journal of Pub. Inquiry, 2000—02. Office: Bernabei & Katz PLLC 1773 T St NW Washington DC 20009-7139

KAPLAN, EUGENE ALKEN, psychiatry professor, department chairman; b. Syracuse, N.Y., Dec. 24, 1933; s. David S. and Florence F. Kaplan; m. Sandra Ecker Kaplan, May 14, 1961; children: Susan Beth Kaplan Lue, Karen Lynn. BA magna cum laude, Syracuse U., 1954; MD, SUNY, Syracuse, 1957. Diplomate Nat. Bd. Med. Examiners, cert. Am. Bd. Psychiatry and Neurology. Med. intern Albert Einstein Med. Ctr., N.Y.C., 1957—58; psychiatry resident, chief resident SUNY Upstate Med. U., Syracuse, 1958—61, from instr. to prof., 1961—, prof., chair dept. psychiatry, 1987—99, prof., chair emeritus dept. psychiatry, 1999—. Cons. Peace Corps tng. programs Syracuse U., 1962—66; vis. prof. Sloan Sch. Cornell U., Ithaca, NY, 1967—82; lectr. Washington Sch. Psychiatry, 1967—69; vis. scientist The Tavistock Psychiat. Ctr., London, 1981; cons. psychiatrist Syracuse U. Health Svc., 1982—87. Co-editor: International Psychiatric Clinics, vol. 2 & 3, 1965; contbr. articles to profl. jours. Bd. dirs. Transitional Living Svc., Syracuse, 1975—82, Syracuse Opera, Syracuse, 1990—98, Syracuse Symphony, Syracuse, 1999—. Comdr. Med. Corps USN, 1967—69. Fellow: Am. Psychiat. Assn. (Disting. Life fellow); mem.: Am. Bd. Psychiatry and Neurology (sr. examiner 1974—98), Phi Kappa Alpha, Phi Beta Kappa. Avocations: sailing, piano. Home: 4804 West Lake Rd Cazenovia NY 13035 Office: SUNY Upstate Med Univ Dept Psychiatry 750 E Adams St Syracuse NY 13210 Office Phone: 315-464-3105.

KAPLAN, GABRIELA DIANA, radiologist; b. Quito, Ecuador, Apr. 28, 1947; arrived in U.S., 1963; d. Isidor and Rosa Ortiz Kaplan. MD, U. Autonoma Guadalajara, 1972; BA, Whittier Coll. Diplomate Am. Bd. Radiology. Fellow in body imaging Johns Hopkins U., Balt., 1980, fellow in neuroradiology, 1982; fellow in whole body magnetic resonance U. Mich., Ann Arbor, 1989, asst. prof. radiology Med. Ctr., 1988—89; asst. prof. Columbia U./Presbyn. Hosp., N.Y.C., 1979; lectr. diagnostic radiology Johns Hopkins Hosp., Balt., 1980—82; pres. Lifewatch Group Ltd., Cleve. Author: Wealth, Hunger and Peace, 1989. Recipient Presdl. Rep. award of merit, Ptnrs. in Conservation award, World Wildlife Fund, 1999, Internat. award of Merit, Internat. Soc. Poetry, 2001. Mem.: Am. Coll. Radiology, P.I.B. Yacht Club (fleet surgeon). Republican. Roman Catholic. Achievements include invention of device to aid women in family planning. Avocations: environmental concerns, poetry, gardening.

KAPLAN, GARY, executive recruiter; b. Phila., Aug. 14, 1939; s. Morris and Minnie (Leve) K.; m. Linda Ann Wilson, May 30, 1968; children: Michael Warren, Marc Jonathan, Jeffrey Russell Wilson. BA in Polit. Sci., Pa. State U., 1961. Tchr. biology N.E. High Sch., Phila., 1962-63; coll. employment rep. Bell Telephone Labs., Murray Hill, N.J., 1966-67; supr. recruitment and placement Unisys, Blue Bell, Pa., 1967-69; pres. Electronic Systems Personnel, Phila., 1969-70; staff selection rep. Booz, Allen & Hamilton, N.Y.C., 1970-72; mgr. exec. recruitment M&T Chems., Rahway, N.J., 1972-74; dir. exec. recruitment IU Internat. Mgmt. Corp., Phila., 1974-78; v.p. personnel Crocker Bank, Los Angeles, 1978-79; mng. v.p. ptnr. western region Korn-Ferry Internat., Los Angeles, 1979-85; pres. Gary Kaplan & Assocs., Pasadena, Calif., 1985—. Bd. dirs. Ptnrs. in Care, Greater L.A. Zoo Assn., Coll. Liberal Arts, Pa. State U. Alumni Assn. Mgmt. columnist, Radio and Records newspaper, 1984-85. Mem. alumni coun. Pa. State U.; former bd. dirs. The Wellness Cmty., Pa. State U. Indsl./Orgn. Psychology Adv. Bd., Vis. Nurs Assn. L.A., Hme Pharmacy of Calif., Calif. Exec. Recruiters Assn. Alumni fellow Pa. State U., 1998. Mem. World at Work, Soc. Human Resources Mgmt., Mount Nittany Soc. Pa. State U., Pa. State U. Alumni Soc., Big Ten Club So. Calif Office: Gary Kaplan & Assocs 201 S Lake Ave Ste 600 Pasadena CA 91101-3018 Office Phone: 626-796-8100.

KAPLAN, GEORGE WILLARD, urologist; b. Brownsville, Tex., Aug. 24, 1935; s. Hyman J. and Lillian (Bennett) K.; m. Susan Gail Solof, Dec. 17, 1961; children: Paula, Elizabeth, Julie, Alan. BA, U. Tex., 1955; MD, Northwestern U., 1959, MS, 1966. Diplomate Am. Bd. Urology. Intern Charity Hosp. of La. at New Orleans, 1959-60; resident Northwestern U., 1963-68, instr. Med. Sch. Chgo., 1968-69; clin. prof. U. Calif., San Diego, 1970—, chief pediatric urology, 1970—98. Trustee Children's Hosp. and Health Ctr., San Diego, 1978-90, Am. Bd. Urology, Bingham Farms, Mich., 1991-96; del. Am. Bd. Med. Specialties, Evanston, Ill., 1992-96. Author: Genitourinary Problems in Pediatrics; asst. editor Jour. Urology, Balt., 1982-89, 98-2002; assoc. editor Child Nephrology and Urology, Milan, Italy, 1988-94; contbr. articles to profl. publs. Pres. med. staff Children's Hosp., San Diego, 1980-82. Lt. USN, 1960-63. Recipient Joseph Capps prize Inst. of Medicine, 1967. Fellow ACS (pres. San Diego chpt. 1980-82), Am. Acad. Pediat. (chmn. sect. on urology 1986); mem. AMA, Soc. for Pediatric Urology (pres. 1993), Am. Urol. Assn., Soc. Internat. Urologie, Soc. Univ. Urologists, Am. Assn. Genito-Urin. Surgeons. Republican. Jewish. Avocations: history of medicine, rare books. Office: Childrens Specialists San Diego Divsn Urology 7930 Frost St Ste 407 San Diego CA 92123-4286 Office Phone: 858-279-8527. Business E-Mail: gkaplan@chsd.org.

KAPLAN, GILBERT B., lawyer; b. Endicott, N.Y., July 9, 1951; s. Marek and Helene Christine (Freund) K.; m. Elizabeth Ann Piserchia, June 26, 1983; children: Katharine, Nicholas. Grad., Phillips Exeter Acad., 1969; AB, Harvard U., 1974, JD, 1977. Bar. Mass. 1977, D.C. 1989. Dir. office of investigations U.S. Dept. Commerce, Washington, 1983-85, dep. asst. sec. import adminstrn., 1985-87, acting asst. sec., 1987-88; sr. ptnr., head internat. trade practice Hale and Dorr, Washington, 1990—2004, chmn. govt. and regulatory affairs dept., 2001—04; ptnr., internat. trade King & Spalding, Washington, 2004—. Sec. Washington Exeter Alumni Assn., 1989-92; Rep. nominee and candidate state rep. BackBay-Beacon Hill Sect., Boston, 1982. Mem. ABA (co-chmn. com. on China, internat. law sect. 1989-91). Republican. Office: King & Spalding 1700 Pennsylvania Ave NW Washington DC 20006 Office Phone: 202-661-7981. Business E-Mail: gkaplan@kslaw.com.

KAPLAN, HARRIET SMITH, psychiatrist, educator; b. Milw., Apr. 17, 1929; d. Manuel J. and Esther Ruth (Erlien) Smith; m. Melvin Raymond Kaplan, Feb. 23, 1958; children: Robert Alan, Martin Russell, Roger Jay. BA, UCLA, 1951; MD, Washington U., St. Louis, 1956. Diplomate Am. Bd. Psychiatry and Neurology. Rotating intern San Francisco Gen. Hosp., 1956-57; resident in internal medicine Wadsworth VA Hosp., L.A., 1957-59; asst. rsch. physician dept. nuc. medicine UCLA Sch. Medicine, 1962-64; resident in psychiatry Harbor/UCLA Med. Ctr., Torrance, 1970-73, mem. faculty dept. psychiatry, 1973—; clin. prof. dept. psychiatry and biobehavioral scis. UCLA Sch. of Medicine, 1996—. Treas. Los Angeles Biomedical Rsch. Inst. at Harbor - UCLA Med. Ctr., Torrance, 1991-94, chair, 1994-97. Distinguished life fellow Am. Psychiat. Assn.; mem. L.A. Acad. Medicine (v.p. 1997, pres. 1998).

KAPLAN, HARVEY L., lawyer; b. Kansas City, Mo., Nov. 11, 1942; BS in Pharmacy, U. Mich., 1965; JD, U. Mo., 1968. Bar: Mo. 1968, U.S. Tax Ct. 1971, U.S. Supreme Ct. 1971. Ptnr. Shook, Hardy & Bacon LLP, Kansas City, chair Pharm. and Med. Device Litig. Div. Faculty mem. NITA Advanced Advocacy Program, 1988-89; mem. Kansas City-St. Louis Panel, CPR Inst. Dispute Resolution, 1989—. Mem. bd. editors Mo. Law Rev., 1967-68. Fellow Internat. Acad. Trial Lawyers (bd. dirs. 1991-97, 98—, sec.-treas. 2001-02), Internat. Soc. Barristers, Am. Bar Found.; mem. Am. Soc. Pharmacy Law, Mo. Orgn. Def. Lawyers (bd. dirs. 1985-93), Internat. Assn. Def. Counsel (exec. com. 1991-94, def. counsel trial acad. 1989, dir.-elect 1992, dir. 1993, v.p., found. bd. dirs. 2001-03), Def. Rsch. Inst. (chmn. drug and med. device litigation com. 1991-94, bd. dirs. 1995-98, Law Inst. 1998-2001), Phi Delta Phi. Office: Shook Hardy & Bacon LLP 2555 Grand Blvd 19th fl Kansas City MO 64108-2613 Office Phone: 816-474-6550. Business E-Mail: hkaplan@shb.com.

KAPLAN, HELENE LOIS, lawyer; b. N.Y.C., June 19, 1933; d. Jack and Shirley (Jacobs) Finkelstein; m. Mark N. Kaplan, Sept. 7, 1952; children: Marjorie Ellen, Sue Anne. AB cum laude, Barnard Coll., 1953; JD, NYU, 1967; LLD (hon.), Columbia U., 1990. Bar: N.Y. 1967. Pvt. practice, N.Y.C., 1967-78; ptnr. Webster & Sheffield, N.Y.C., 1978-86, counsel, 1986-90; of counsel Skadden, Arps, Slate, Meagher & Flom, N.Y.C., 1990—. Bd. dirs. The May Dept. Stores Co., Met. Life Inc. and Met. Life Ins. Co., JP Morgan Chase & Co., Exxon Mobil Corp. Trustee N.Y. Coun. for Humanities, 1976-82, chmn., 1978-82; trustee Barnard Coll., 1973-99, chair bd. trustees, 1984-94, trustee and chair emerita, 1999—; trustee Columbia U. Press, 1977-80, MITRE Corp., 1978-95, N.Y. Found., 1976-86, John Simon Guggenheim Meml. Found., 1981-98, NYU Law Ctr. Found., 1985-87, Neuroscis. Rsch. Found., 1986-92, Am. Mus. Natural History, 1989—, vice chair, 1993—; trustee Am. Trust for Brit. Libr., 1991-93, Com. for Econ. Devel., 1993-96, Commonwealth Fund, 1990-2003, vice chair, 1996-2003; trustee and chair emerita Inst. for Advanced Study, 1986-2002, trustee emerita, 2002—; trustee J. Paul Getty Trust, 1992—, vice chair 1997—; trustee Olive Free Libr.; trustee Carnegie Corp. N.Y., 1979—, vice-chair bd. trustees, 1981-84, 98-2002, chair, 1984-91, 2002—; chair, trustee Mt. Sinai Sch. Medicine, 1999-01, Mt. Sinai NYU Health, 1998-2001, vice-chair bd. trustees, 1993-99; trustee N.Y.C. Pub. Devel. Corp., 1978-83, vice-chair bd. trustees, 1978-82; mem. Adv. Com. on South Africa, U.S. Sec. of State, 1986-88; mem. N.Y. State Gov.'s Task Force on Life and the Law, 1985-90, Women's Forum, Inc., 1982—, Rockefeller U. Coun., 1984-94, Bretton Woods Com., 1985-96, Carnegie Coun. on Adolescent Devel., 1986-96; chair task force on sci. and tech. and jud. decision making Carnegie Commn. on Sci., Tech. and Govt., 1988-93; ptnr. N.Y.C. Partnership, 1987-92; bd. dirs. Am. Arbitration Assn., 1978-82. Mem.: N.Y.C. Bar Assn. (treas. 1991—93, mem. com. on philanthropic orgns. 1975—81, mem. com. on recruitment of lawyers 1978—82, mem. com. on profl. responsibility 1980—83), Am. Philos. Soc., Am. Acad. Arts and Scis., Century Assn., Cosmopolitan Club.

KAPLAN, HENRY JERROLD, ophthalmologist, educator; b. NYC, Dec. 29, 1942; s. Ralph and Henrietta (Davis) K.; m. Adele Lotner, June 26, 1966; children: Wendi Suzanne, Todd Daniel, Ariane Dev. AB, Columbia U., 1964; MD, Cornell U., 1968. Diplomate Am. Bd. Ophthalmology. Intern in medicine Lakeside Hosp., Univ. Hosps. Cleve., Case-Western Res. U., 1968-69; surg. resident Bellevue Hosp., NYU Med. Ctr., 1969-70; NIH rsch. fellow in immunology U. Tex. (Southwestern) Med. Sch., Dallas, 1972-74, asst. prof. dept. cell biology, 1974-75; resident in ophthalmology U. Iowa Hosps. and Clinics, Iowa City, 1975-78; retina-vitreous fellow dept. ophthalmology Med. Coll. Wis., Milw., 1978-79; assoc. prof. dept. ophthalmology Emory U. Sch. Medicine, Atlanta, 1979-84, prof., dir. rsch., 1984-88, assoc. prof. dept. microbiology, 1985-88; prof. dept. ophthalmology and visual scis. Washington U. Sch. Medicine, St. Louis, 1988-2000, chmn. dept. ophthalmology and visual scis., 1988-98; prof., chmn. dept. opthalmology and visual scis. U. Louisville (Ky.) Sch. Medicine, 2000—, William H. and Blondina F. Evans Prof. Ophthalmology, 2000—. Ophthalmologist in chief Barnes-Jewish Hosp., Washington U. Med. Ctr., 1988-98; affiliate scientist in pathology and immunology Yerkes Regional Primate Rsch. Ctr., Atlanta, 1981—; adj. prof. dept. small animal medicine U. Ga., Athens, 1985—; assoc. chief ophthalmology Emory U. Hosp., 1985-88; mem. visual scis. study sect. A-1 NIH, Bethesda, Md., 1985-89, chmn., 1987-89; pres. Barnes Eye Care Network, 1994-98; dir. Ky. Lions Eye Ctr., Louisville, 2000—; pres. Eye Specialists Louisville, Ky.,2000—; chmn. U. Physician Assocs., 2004—. Author, co-author or editor, co-editor more than 200 med. textbooks, chpts. and articles on uveitis and macular degeneration and retinal degeneration pub. in refereed sci. and med. jours., 1974—; mem. sci. jour. rev. bds. Archives Ophthalmology, 1978—, Retina, 1982—, Am. Jour. Ophthalmology, 1983—, Ophthalmology, 1983—, Current Eye Rsch., 1986—, Exptl. Eye Rsch., 1986—; mem. sci. rev. bd. Investigative Ophthalmology and Visual Sci., 1983—, mem. editorial bd., 1990-92; co-editor Ocular Immunology and Inflammation, 1994-98; editor: Ocular Immunology and Inflammation, 1999—. Maj. M.C., USAF, 1970-72. Recipient sci. award Alcon Rsch. Inst., 1987; Olga Keith Weiss rsch. scholar to Prevent Blindness, Inc., N.Y.C., 1984. Fellow ACS, Am. Acad. Ophthalmology (Honor award 1984, Sr. Honor award 1994); mem. AMA, Assn. for Rsch. in Vision and Ophthalmology, Am. Assn. Immunologists, Macula Soc., Am. Uveitis Soc. (pres. 1997-99), Retina Soc., Louisville Ophthal. Soc., Ky. Acad. Eye Physicians and Surgeons. Jewish. Office: U Louisville Sch Medicine Dept Opthalmol & Visual Sci 301 E Muhammad Ali Blvd Louisville KY 40202-1511 Office Phone: 502-852-3716. Business E-Mail: hank.kaplan@louisville.edu. *Faith in pursuit of one's own ideas and persistence in the face of adversity will bring success, but more importantly - personal satisfaction.*

KAPLAN, ISAAC RAYMOND, chemistry professor; b. Baranowicze, Poland, July 10, 1929; came to U.S., 1957; s. Morris and Anny (Chait) K.; m. Helen Fagot, Sept. 4, 1955; children: Debora, David Joel. BS, Canterbury U., Christchurch, New Zealand, 1951, MS, 1953; PhD, U. So. Calif., 1961. Rsch. scientist Commonwealth Sci. and Indsl. Rsch. Orgn., Sydney, Australia, 1953-57; postdoctoral fellow Calif. Inst. Tech., Pasadena, 1961-62; guest lectr. Hebrew U., Jerusalem, 1962-65; assoc. prof. UCLA, 1965-69, prof., 1969-93, prof. emeritus, 1993—. Contbr. over 300 articles to profl. jours. Guggenheim Found. fellow, Sydney, 1970-71. Fellow: AAAS, Geol. Soc. Am., Am. Inst. Chemists; mem.: Am. Assn. Petroleum Geologists (Pres. award 2002), Geochem. Soc. (Alfred Treibs medal 1993), Geophys. Union, Am. Chem. Soc., Russian Acad. Natural Sci. (fgn.) (Kapitsa medal 1998). Office: U Calif ESS Dept Plaza Circle Dr Los Angeles CA 90024

KAPLAN, JARED, lawyer; b. Chgo., Dec. 28, 1938; s. Jerome and Phyllis Enid (Rieber) K.; m. Rosellen Engstrom, Dec. 28, 1964 (div. 1978); children: Brian F., Philip B.; m. Maridee Quanbeck, June 2, 1990. AB, UCLA, 1960; LLB, Harvard, 1963. Bar: Ill. 1963, U.S. Dist. Ct. (no. dist.) Ill. 1969, U.S. Tax Ct. 1978. Assoc. Ross & Hardies, Chgo., 1963-69, ptnr., 1970, Roan & Grossman, Chgo., 1970-83, Keck, Mahin & Cate, Chgo., 1983-94, McDermott, Will & Emery, Chgo., 1994—. Bd. dirs. ESOP (Employee Stock Ownership Plan) Assn., Washington, 1987-90, Family Firm Inst., Boston, 1996-99, gen. counsel, 2003--; adv. coun. Ill. Employee-Owned Enterprise, Chgo., 1984-98; chmn. Ill. Adv. Task Force on Ownership Succession and Employee Ownership, 1994-95. Editor in chief: Callaghan's Fed. Tax Guide, 1988; author: Employee Stock Ownership Plans, 2005. Nat. pres. Ripon Soc., Washington, 1975-76; adv. coun. mem. Rep. Nat. Com., Washington, 1978-80; alt. delegate Rep. Nat. Conv., Detroit, 1980. Fellow Am. Coll. Employee Benefits Counsel; mem. ABA (chmn. section of taxation, administrv. practice com. 1978-80), City Club, Chgo. (bd. govs. 1982-92), Univ. Club, Met. Club. Republican. Jewish. Home: 105 W Delaware Pl Chicago IL 60610-3200 Office: McDermott Will & Emery 227 W Monroe St 47th Fl Chicago IL 60606-5018 Office Phone: 312-984-6955. E-mail: jkaplan@mwe.com, jared.kaplan@att.net.

KAPLAN, JERRY (S. JERROLD KAPLAN), former electronics company executive; B in History and Philosophy of Sci., U. Chgo.; D in Computer and Info. Sci., U. Pa. Prin. technologist Lotus Devel. Corp.; co-founder, chmn. GO Corp.; co-founder, CEO ONSALE, Inc., Menlo Park, Calif., 1994—2000; CEO Egghead.com (merged with ONSALE, Inc.), Menlo Park, 2000. Author: Startup-A Silicon Valley Adventure, 1995. Office: Egghead Com Inc 180 Montgomery St Ste 2340 San Francisco CA 94104-4228

KAPLAN, JOEL A., academic administrator; Sr. v.p. clin. affairs Mt. Sinai Med. Ctr., NY; dean, v.p. health affairs Sch. Medicine U. Louisville, 1998—2003, exec. v.p. and chancellor Health Scis. Ctr., 2003—04, dean emeritus, 2004—. Office: Abell Adminstrn Ctr U Louisville Louisville KY 40202

KAPLAN, JOEL H., lawyer; b. Bklyn., Jan. 10, 1946; BS, Cornell U., 1966; JD, U. Chgo., 1969. Bar: Ill. 1969, US Supreme Ct. 1978. Ptnr. Seyfarth Shaw LLP, Chgo., 1975—, chmn. Labor & Employment Practice Group, 1992—94, mem. exec. com. Bigelow teaching fellow, instr. criminal law & legal writing U. Chgo. Law Sch., 1969—70. Mem.: ABA (railway & airline labor law com.). Office: Seyfarth Shaw LLP 55 E Monroe St Ste 4200 Chicago IL 60603 Office Phone: 312-269-8821. Office Fax: 312-269-8869. Business E-Mail: jkaplan@seyfarth.com.

KAPLAN, JOEL STUART, lawyer; b. Bklyn., Feb. 1, 1937; s. Abraham Larry and Phayne (Moses) K.; m. Joan Ruth Katz, June 19, 1960; children: Andrea Beth, Pamela Jill. BA, Bklyn. Coll., 1958; LLB, NYU, 1961. Bar: N.Y. 1962, U.S. Dist. Cts. (ea. and so. dists.) N.Y. 1964, U.S. Ct. Appeals (2d cir.) 1966, U.S. Supreme Ct. 1979, Fla. 1982, D.C. 1987. Asst. town atty. Town of Hempstead, Nassau County, N.Y., 1962-67; ptnr. Jaspan, Kaplan, Levin & Daniels and predecessors, Garden City, N.Y., 1970-83; sole practice Garden City, 1983-95; counsel Levin Belsky Ross and Daniels, Garden City, 1995—; ptnr. Kaplan Belsky Ross LLP, 2004—. Chmn. Hempstead Town Pub. Employment Rels. Bd., 1973-81; Rep. candidate for N.Y. State Senate, 1974. Mem. ABA, N.Y. State Bar Assn., Nassau County Bar Assn., B'nai B'rith Internat.(pres. 2002—). Office: 666 Old Country Rd Ste 602 Garden City NY 11530-2006 Office Phone: 516-745-1100.

KAPLAN, JOHN, photojournalist, educator, consultant; b. Wilmington, Del., Aug. 21, 1959; s. Ralph Benjamin and Ruth Jillya (Denkin) Kaplan. BJ cum laude, Ohio U., Athens, 1982; MS in Journalism, Ohio U., 1998. Photojournalist, designer Spokesman Rev./Chronicle, Spokane, Wash., 1983—84; photojournalist, picture editor Pitts. Press, 1984—90; photojournalist Pitts. Post-Gazette, 1990—92; spl. corr. Block Newspapers, 1992—94. Tchr., lectr. numerous univs., seminars, profl. groups U.S., Can., 1984—; vis. lectr. Bradley U., Peoria, Ill., 1989; adj. prof. Syracuse U., London campus, 1993; assoc. prof. U. Fla., Gainesville, 1999—; dir. Media Alliance, cons., Pitts., 1990—2000; mem. Pulitizer Prize jury, 1994, 95; photojournalism mem. Ball State U., Muncie, 1998—99. Author: Mom and Me, 1996; contbr. to book series The Best of Photojournalism, Vols. 6, 7, 9, 10, 11, 14, 18, 1981-93; work in permanent collection Carnegie Mus. Art, Pitts.; author: Photo Portfolio Success, 2003. Named Pitts. Photographer of Yr., News Photographers Assn. Greater Pitts., 1986, 1989, 1992, Photographer of Yr., Pa. Photographers Assn., 1989, No. Photographer of Yr., 1992; named to, Ohio U. Coll. Comm. Hall of Fame, 1993; recipient Golden Quill Journalism award, Pitts. Press Club, 1986, 1989, Robert F. Kennedy Journalism award, Kennedy Found., 1989, 2003, Pulitzer prize for feature photography, 1992, 2003, Matrix Mag. award, Women in Comm., 1992, Ohio U. Disting. Grad. award, 1993, award for feature photography, Overseas Press Club, 2003, Harry Chapin award, 2003; Knight fellow, Ohio U., 1997—98. Mem.: Soc. Newspaper Design (Gold award 1989), Nat. Press Photographers Assn. (contest chmn. Region 3 1987—89, Regional Photographer of Yr. award 1985, 1986, 1987, 1989, Nat. Newspaper Photographer of Yr. award 1989, Nikon Documentary Sabbatical award 1990, Harry Chapin award 2023, others), Amnesty Internat. Avocations: racquet sports, furniture design, wines. Address: 3067 Weimer Hall Gainesville FL 32611-8400*

KAPLAN, JOSEPH, pediatrician; b. Boston, Mar. 7, 1941; Student, Dartmouth U., 1958-60; BA, NYU, 1962; MD, Johns Hopkins U., 1966. Intern, resident in pediatrics Johns Hopkins Hosp., Balt., 1969-72; mem. staff Children's Hosp. Mich., Detroit, 1972—; prof. pediat., medicine and immunology-microbiology Wayne State U. Sch. Medicine, Detroit, 1972—. Contbr. article to profl. publ. Maj. U.S. Army, 1969-72. Recipient Rsch. Career Devel. award NIH, 1975-80. Office: Children's Hosp 3901 Beaubien St Detroit MI 48201-2196 Home: 23551 Sutton Dr Apt 816 Southfield MI 48034-3348 E-mail: jkaplan@med.wayne.edu.

KAPLAN, JOSEPH SOLTE, lawyer; b. Paterson, N.J., Mar. 14, 1935; s. Sidney C. and Estelle (Solte) K.; m. Lily Chariton, Dec. 28, 1958; children: Michele Kaplan Green, Andrew Ezra, David Baruch. BA, Yeshiva U., 1956; LLB, Harvard U., 1959. Bar: N.J. 1960, N.Y. 1966, U.S. Dist. Ct. N.J. 1960, U.S. Dist. Ct. (ea. and so. dists.) N.Y. 1967, U.S. Ct. Internat. Trade 1966, U.S. Ct. Appeals (fed. cir.) 1975, U.S. Supreme Ct., 1971. Assoc. Baker, Garber & Chazen, Hoboken, NJ, 1960—65; gen. atty. U.S. Dept. Treasury, N.Y.C., 1965—66; assoc. Siegel Mandel & Davidson, N.Y.C., 1966—70, Busby, Rivkin, Sherman, Levy & Rehm, N.Y.C., 1970—71, ptnr., 1971—77, Rivkin, Sherman & Levy, N.Y.C., 1977—81, Kaplan & Pellegrini, N.Y.C., 1981—83, Baskin & Steingut, N.Y.C., 1984—85, Ross & Hardies, N.Y.C., 1985—2003, exec. com., 1992—95; of counsel McGuire Woods, LLP, N.Y.C., 2003—. Mem. U.S. Ct. Internat. Trade Adv. Com., N.Y.C., 1989-97, chair 9th jud. conf. planning com. Articles editor Internat. Law Practicum, 1995-2003; contbr. articles to profl. jours. and publs. Bd. dirs. Jewish Bd. Family and Children's Svcs., N.Y.C., 1985-93, v.p., 1996-97, pres.-elect, 1996-97, pres., 1998-2001, chmn. bd., 2002—, chmn. ct. and legal svc. com., 1976-84, chmn. cmty. edn. divsn. com., 1985-92, chmn. human resources com. 1989-97, chmn. exec. com., 1993-97. With U.S. Army N.G., 1959-65. Mem. ABA (standing com. on customs law 1979-85), Am. Assn. Importers and Exporters (chmn. harmonized sys. com. 1980-90, bd. dirs. 1993-2003), Customs and Internat. Trade Bar Assn. (chmn. trial and appellate practice com. 1988-92, sec. 1992-94, bd. dirs. 1988-94), N.Y. State Bar Assn. (editor Internat. Trade Newsletter 1986-87) Office: McGuire Woods LLP 1345 Ave of Americas 7 New York NY 10105-0302 E-mail: jskaplan@mcguirewoods.com.

KAPLAN, JUSTIN, author; b. N.Y.C., Sept. 5, 1925; s. Tobias D. and Anna (Rudman) K.; m. Anne F. Bernays, July 29, 1954; children: Susanna Bernays, Hester Margaret, Polly Anne. BS, Harvard U., 1944, postgrad., 1944-46; D Humane Letters (hon.), Marlboro Coll., 1984. Free-lance editing, writing, N.Y.C., 1946-54; sr. editor Simon & Schuster, Inc., N.Y.C., 1954-59; lectr. English Harvard U., 1969, 73, 76, 78; prose writer in residence Emerson Coll., Boston, 1977-78. Vis. lectr. Griffith U., Brisbane, Australia, 1983; lectr. in field; judge Nat. Book Awards, 1968, 73, 78, 87, 93, Pulitzer prizes, 1989, 94, 97, 2003; resident Bellagio Study and Conf. Ctr., Italy, spring, 1990; Jenks prof. contemporary letters Coll. of Holy Cross, Worcester, Mass., 1992-95. Author: Mr. Clemens and Mark Twain, 1966, Lincoln Steffens, A Biography, 1974, Mark Twain and His World, 1974, Walt Whitman: A Life, 1980, (with Anne Bernays) The Language of Names, 1997, (with Bernays) Back Then, 2002; editor: Dialogues of Plato, 1948, With Malice Toward Women, 1949, The Pocket Aristotle, 1956, The Gilded Age, 1964, Great Short Works of Mark Twain, 1967, Mark Twain, A Profile, 1967, Walt Whitman: Complete Poetry and Collected Prose, 1982, The Harper American Literature, 1987, 94, Best American Essays, 1990; gen. editor: Bartlett's Familiar Quotations, 17th edit., 2002; contbr. to N.Y. Times, New Republic, Am. Scholar, Newsweek, Ploughshares, Yale Rev., others. Participant cultural programs USIA, Israel, Dominican Republic, Mex., 1985. Recipient Pulitzer prize for biography, 1967, Nat. Book award for arts and letters, 1967, Nat. Book award for biography, 1981, Guggenheim fellowship, 1975—76. Fellow: Mass. Hist. Soc., Soc. Am. Historians, Am. Acad. Arts and Scis.; mem.: Am. Acad. Arts and Letters, Harvard Club (NY), Phi Beta Kappa. Home: 16 Francis Ave Cambridge MA 02138-2010 Personal E-mail: jknames@aol.com.

KAPLAN, KEITH EUGENE, insurance company executive, lawyer; b. Rahway, N.J., Apr. 6, 1960; s. Eugene Aloysius and Barbara Ann (Dempski) Kaplan; m. Rita Marie Baker, Aug. 8, 1987; children: Matthew Joseph, William Alexander(dec.). BS, U. Pa., 1982; JD, Temple U., 1992. Bar: Pa. 1992. Underwriter Home Ins. Co., Phila., 1982—85, underwriting supr., 1985—86, product line mgr. N.Y.C., 1987; underwriting dir. Reliance Ins. Co., Phila., 1987—88; asst. v.p. Reliance Nat., Phila., 1988—90, N.Y.C., 1990—92, v.p., 1992—96, mng. v.p., 1996—2000, exec. v.p., 2000—. Bd. dirs. Assn. Ins. and Reins. Runoff Cos. Mem.: ABA, Assn. of Ins. and Reinsurance Run-off Cos. (bd. dirs.), Excess and Surplus Lines Claim Assn., Reinsurance and Ins. Arbitration Soc., Pa. Bar Assn. Home: 1240 Pickering Ln Chester Springs PA 19425-1423 Office: Reliance National 5 Hanover Sq New York NY 10004 also: Reliance Ins Co Three Parkway Philadelphia PA 19102

KAPLAN, LAWRENCE JAY, economist, educator; b. Oct. 28, 1915; s. Harris and Estelle (Wilner) Kaplan; m. Jeanne Leon, June 9, 1946; children: Harriet, Sanford S., Marcia. BA, Bklyn. Coll., 1937; MA, Columbia U., 1938, PhD, 1958. Chief info. officer Bur. Labor Stats., Dept. of Labor, N.Y.C., 1949—57; dir. planning and rsch. N.Y.C. Dept. City Planning, Dept. Relocation, 1957—65; prof. econs. John Jay Coll. Criminal Justice, N.Y.C., 1965—86, prof. emeritus, 1986—; now lectr. and cons. Author: Elementary Statistics for Economics and Business, 1966, Ins and Outs of On-Track and Off-Track Betting, 1970, Retiring Right: Planning for A Successful Retirement, 2003; editor: An Economic Analysis of Crime, 1976. Vice-chmn., mem. profl. staff Congress-CUNY Welfare Fund, 1969—86, emeritus, 1986—; chmn. profl. staff Congress-CUNY Retirees chpt., 1991—2001, emeritus, 2001—; chmn. Coun. Mcpl. Retiree Organizations N.Y.C., 1995—2003, emeritus, 2003—. With mil. intelligence U.S. Army, 1942—45. Decorated NY State Conspcuous Svc. Cross, 5 Battle Stars; recipient citation, Republic of France. Mem.: Am. Statis. Assn., Am. Econ. Assn. Democrat. Jewish. Office: John Jay Coll Criminal Justice 899 10th Ave New York NY 10019-1104 E-mail: ljkjj@aol.com.

KAPLAN, LEE LANDA, lawyer; b. Houston, Jan. 26, 1952; s. Charles Irving and Ara Celine (Seligman) K.; m. Diana Morton Hudson, Feb. 6, 1982. AB, Princeton U., 1973; JD, U. Tex., 1976. Bar: Tex., U.S. Dist. Ct. (no., we., ea. and so. dists.) Tex., U.S. Ct. Appeals (5th, 11th and Fed. cirs.), U.S Supreme Ct. Law clk. to sr. cir. judge U.S. Ct. Appeals (5th cir.), Houston, 1976-77; assoc. Baker & Botts, L.L.P., Houston, 1977-84, ptnr., 1985-94, Smyser Kaplan & Veselka, L.L.P., Houston, 1995—. Mem. Tex. Aerospace Commn., 1994-99. Mem. ABA, State Bar Tex., Houston Bar Assn., Am. Bd. Trial Advs. (assoc.), Am. Intellectual Property Law Assn., Houston Intellectual Property Law Assn. Democrat. Jewish. Avocation: history. Office: Smyser Kaplan & Veselka LLP 700 Louisiana St Ste 2300 Houston TX 77002-2728 Office Phone: 713-221-2323. Business E-Mail: lkaplan@skv.com.

KAPLAN, LEONARD EUGENE, accountant; b. Chgo., Mar. 3, 1940; s. David Solomon and Faye Gertrude (Grossman) K.; m. Myrna Dee Shellist, Dec. 20, 1959; children: Sheri Kaplan Mayes, Jodi Kaplan Hoffman, Jeffrey. Student, U. Ill., Chgo., 1958-59; BSc in Acctg., De Paul U., 1961. CPA, Tex., Ill.; cert. ins. counselor. Staff acct. Goldstein, Engerman & Shane, Chgo., 1960-63, BDO Seidman, Chgo., 1963-72, ptnr., 1972-79, Houston, 1979-95, regional tech. dir. region III, 1982-84, mng. ptnr., 1984-89, nat. dir. industry specialization, 1990-92; also bd. dirs.; exec. v.p., sec., CFO Delta Ins. Group Corp., Houston, 1995—. Mem. adv. coun. dept. acctg. U. Tex., 1989-95. Contbr. articles to various publs. Bd. dirs. Chocolate Bayou Theater Co.; mem. WYO standards com. FEMA, 2003—. Ill. State scholar, 1958-61, Jack Claitor Meml. scholar Tex. Surplus Lines Assn., 1998. Mem.: AICPA, Property Casualty Insurers Assn. Am., Tex. Surplus Lines Assn. (sec., treas.), Bus. and Profl. Soc. of Jewish Fedn., Am. Assn. Mng. Gen. Agts., Soc. of Cert. Ins. Counselors, Ill. CPA Soc., Tex. Soc. CPAs (vice chmn. com. on rels. with attys. Houston chpt. 1984—85), B'nai B'rith (newsletter editor 1971—72), Royal Oaks Country Club. Jewish. Avocations: golf, tennis, crossword puzzles. Business E-Mail: lenk@deltains.com. E-mail: lenk@houston.rr.com. *Concern for what might have been is never productive. Yesterday is what it is. Today and the rest of your life are what you make them. Focus on the future and never look back.*

KAPLAN, LEWIS A., federal judge; b. S.I., Dec. 23, 1944; s. Alfred H. and Dorothy A. Kaplan; widowed; 1 child, Merrill; m. Lesley Oelsner, Feb. 29, 2004. AB, U. Rochester, 1966; JD, Harvard U., 1969. Bar: N.Y. 1970, U.S. Ct. Appeals (1st and 2d cirs.) 1970, U.S. Dist. Ct. (so. and ea. dists.) N.Y. 1971, U.S. Ct. Appeals (3d cir.) 1973, U.S. Supreme Ct. 1973, U.S. Dist. Ct. (we. dist.) N.Y. 1975, U.S. Ct. Appeals (DC cir.) 1976, U.S. Dist. Ct. (no. dist.) Calif. 1980, U.S. Ct. Appeals (9th cir.) 1980, U.S. Dist. Ct. (ea. dist.) Mich. 1983, U.S. Ct. Appeals (6th cir.) 1983, DC 1985, U.S. Ct. Appeals (Fed. cir.) 1987, U.S. Dist. Ct. DC 1988. Law clk. to judge U.S. Ct. Appeals (1st cir.), 1969-70; assoc. Paul, Weiss, Rifkind, Wharton & Garrison, N.Y.C., 1970-77, ptnr., 1977-94; judge U.S. Dist. Ct. (so. dist.) N.Y., N.Y.C., 1994—, spl. master Westway litig., 1982. Trustee Lawyers Com. Civil Rights Under Law, 1992—94; mem. com. info. tech. Jud. Conf. U.S., 1997—2003; Brace Meml. lectr. Copyright Soc. U.S.A., 2001. Mem. U.S. Delegation U.S .- Italian Judicial Workshop (sponsored by U.S. Embassy in Haley, 2003, 2005; mem. trustees' coun. U. Rochester, 1982—88, mem. trustees' vis. com. William E. Simon Grad. Sch. Bus. Adminstrn., 1986—88; village trustee NY, 1988—91. Fellow: Am. Coll. Trial Lawyers; mem.: ABA, Fed. Judges Assn. (dir. 1995—2001, exec. com. 1999—2001), Am. Law Inst., Fed. Bar Coun., N.Y. State Bar Assn. Office: US Courthouse 500 Pearl St New York NY 10007-1316

KAPLAN, MANUEL E., physician, educator; b. N.Y.C., Nov. 6, 1928; s. Morris Jacob and Sylvia (Schiff) K.; m. Rita Goldman, May 22, 1955; children— Anne J., Eve D., Joshua M. BSc. Diplomate Am. Bd. Internal Medicine, Am. Bd. Hematology. Intern Boston City Hosp., 1954-55, resident, 1955-56, 58-59; fellow in hematology Thorndike Lab., 1959-62; attending hematologist Mt. Sinai Hosp., N.Y.C., 1962-65, asst. chief hematology, 1963-65; asst. prof. medicine Washington U. Sch. Medicine, St. Louis, 1965-69; asso. prof. medicine U. Minn. Sch. Medicine, Mpls., 1969-72, prof. medicine, 1972-97, prof. emeritus, 1997—. Chief hematology and oncology Mpls. VA Med Ctr., 1969-93; med. dir. physician asst. program Augsburg Coll., Mpls., 1995-2000. Contbr. numerous articles to profl. jours. Served with USPHS, 1956-58. Mem. Am. Fedn. Clin. Research, Am. Soc. Clin. Investigation, Am. Soc. Hematology, Am. Assn. Immunology, AAAS, others Jewish. Home: 2950 Dean Pky Apt 1201 Minneapolis MN 55416-4427 E-mail: mannykaplan@aol.com.

KAPLAN, MARJORIE, broadcast executive; married; 2 children. B in Semiotics, Brown U. Dir. advt. Kraft Gen. Foods; v.p. Ogilvy & Mather; exec. v.p. Lancit Media Entertainment; sr. v.p. children's programming and products Discovery Networks, U.S., 1997—. Cons. Warner Amex Satellite Entertainment; developer Discovery Kids. Office: Discovery Comm 7700 Wisconsin Ave Bethesda MD 20814

KAPLAN, MARK NORMAN, lawyer; b. NYC, Mar. 7, 1930; s. Louis and Ruth (Hertzberg) K.; m. Helene L. Finkelstein, Sept. 7, 1952; children: Marjorie Ellen, Sue Anne. AB, Columbia, 1951, JD, 1953. Bar: N.Y. 1953. Assoc. Garey & Garey, N.Y.C., 1953; law clk. to Hon. William Bondy U.S. Dist. Ct. for So. Dist. N.Y., 1953-54; assoc. Columbia Law Sch., 1954-55, Wickes, Riddell, Bloomer, Jacobi & McGuire, N.Y.C., 1955-59; from assoc. to sr. ptnr. Marshall, Bratter, Greene, Allison & Tucker, N.Y.C., 1959-70; sr. ptnr. Burnham & Co., N.Y.C., 1970-71; pres. Drexel Burnham Lambert Inc., N.Y.C., 1972-77, also CEO, 1976-77; pres. Engelhard Minerals & Chem. Corp., N.Y.C., 1977-79; mem. firm Skadden, Arps, Slate, Meager & Flom, N.Y.C., 1979—. Bd. dirs. Am. Biltrite, Inc., Autobytel, Inc., REFAC Tech. Devel. Corp., DRS Techs. Inc., Volt Info. Sci., Inc., Jim Pattison, Ltd., Internat. Creative Mgmt., Inc., Congoleum Corp., World Wide Spl. Fund N.V.; vice-chmn. Am. Stock Exch., N.Y.C., 1974, bd. govs., 1975, vice-chmn. bd. govs., 1975-76; trustee Bard Coll.; chmn. audit com. City of N.Y. Co-chmn. audit adv. com. Bd. Edn. of City of N.Y.; chmn. Early Edn. Leadership Group; bd. dirs. New Alternatives for Children. Mem. Coun. Fgn. Rels., Century Assn., Econ. Club N.Y. Home: 146 Central Park W New York NY 10023-2005 Office: Skadden Arps 4 Times Sq Fl 24 New York NY 10036-6595 Office Phone: 212-735-3800. Business E-Mail: mkaplan@skadden.com.

KAPLAN, MARSHALL MYLES, medical educator, researcher, gastroenterologist; b. Boston, Feb. 20, 1935; s. Harold and Ginda (Braverman) K.; m. Nancy Proger, June 5, 1960; children: Ginda, William, Thomas, Deborah. BS summa cum laude, Yale U., 1956; MD cum laude, Harvard U., 1960. Intern, resident Columbia-Presbyn., N.Y.C., 1960-62; clin. assoc. NIH, Bethesda, Md., 1962-65; trainee liver disease Yale U., New Haven, 1965-66; asst. prof. medicine Tufts-New England Med. Ctr., Boston, 1966-69, assoc. prof. medicine, 1969-75, prof. medicine, 1975—, chief divsn. gastroenterology, 1972—2002. Chmn. merit rev. com. VA Hosps., Washington, 1975-77; mem. gastroenterology bd. Am. Bd. Internal Medicine, 1983-89, chmn., 1987-89, bd. govs., 1987-89, trustee, Tufts-New England Med. Ctr., 201-05; manuscript reviewer Annals Internal Medicine, Am. Jour. Medicine, Archives of Internal Medicine, Gastroenterology, Hepatology, Digestive Diseases and Sci., Am. Jour. Gastroenterology, Jour. Hepatology Assoc. editor New Eng. Jour. Medicine, 1993-2001; editor Tufts Family Health Guides, 1979-82; mem. editl. bd. Hepatology, 1988-92; contbr. over 290 articles to med. jours., chpts. to books. Lt. comdr. USPHS, 1962-65. Recipient Mentor Rsch. Scholar award, AGA Found., 2005. Master ACP (chair sci. program com. 1990-93, gastroenterology med. knowledge self-assessment program); mem. Assn. Am. Physicians, Am. Soc. Clin. Investigation, Am. Gastroenterology Assn., Am. Assn. for Study of Liver Disease (com. chair 1984-86), Am. Gastroenterology Assn. (Mentors award Am. Gastroenterology Assn. Found. 2005), Phi Beta Kappa, Alpha Omega Alpha (dir. 1983-89). Democrat. Jewish. Avocations: tennis, bridge, golf, gardening, music. Home: 30 Oakridge Rd Wellesley MA 02481-2504 Office: New England Med Ctr 750 Washington St Boston MA 02111-1526 Office Phone: 617-636-5877. Business E-Mail: mkaplan@tufts-nemc.org.

KAPLAN, MARTIN P., allergist, immunologist, pediatrician; b. Bklyn., Oct. 28, 1928; MD, SUNY Downstate. Diplomate Am. Bd. Allergy & Immunology, Am. Bd. Pediatrics. Resident Jewish Hosp., Bklyn., 1954-55, SUNY Upstate Med. Ctr., Syracuse, 1957-58; fellow Children's Hosp., Washington, 1958-59; active staff mem. dept. medicine St. Joseph Hosp., Lexington, Ky., 1959—; clin. assoc. prof. pediatrics and medicine U. Ky. Coll. Medicine, 1982-97. Mem. Am. Acad. Allergy and Clin. Immuniology, Am. Coll. Allergy, Asthma, and Immunology, AMA, Ky. Med. Assn. Office: 166 Pasadena Ste 150 Lexington KY 40503-3014 Office Phone: 859-276-1452. E-mail: omkaplan@aol.com.

KAPLAN, MARTIN PAUL, pediatrician, educator; b. N.Y.C., Sept. 30, 1946; s. Abraham I. and Shirley (Bercovici) K.; m. Cynthia Gordon, June 21, 1970; children: Benjamin Mark, Dara Beth, Rachel Eve. BA, U. Pa., 1968; MD, NYU, 1972. Intern NYU Bellevue, N.Y.C., 1972-73, resident, 1973-74; sr. resident pediatrics Duke Hosp., Durham, N.C., 1974-75; practice medicine specializing in pediatrics Port Jefferson, N.Y., 1978—. Mem. staff St. Charles Hosp.; chief pediatrics, 1994-2000, John T. Mather Hosp., (both Port Jefferson); bd. dirs. L.I. Physicians Holding Corp; clin. asst. prof. SUNY Stony Brook, 1981—. Mem. Brookhaven Youth Bd., Patchogue, N.Y., 1981-88. Lt. comdr. USNR, 1975-78. Fellow Am. Acad. Pediatrics; mem. AMA, N.Y. State Med. Soc., Sufolk Pediatric Soc. (treas. 1984, sec. 1985, v.p. 1986, pres. 1987), Suffolk County Med. Soc. Democrat. Jewish. Office: 12 Medical Dr Port Jefferson Station NY 11776-1588

KAPLAN, MORTON A., political science professor; b. Phila., May 9, 1921; s. Lewis J. and Anthea (Ginsberg) K.; m. Azie Mortimer, 1967. BS, Temple U., 1943; PhD, Columbia, 1951. Instr. Ohio State U., 1951-52; asst. prof. polit. sci. Haverford Coll., 1953-54; mem. staff Brookings Instn., Washington, 1954-55; asst. prof. polit. sci. U. Chgo., 1956-61, asso. prof., 1961-65, chmn. com. internat. relations, 1959-85, prof. polit. sci., 1965-89, Disting. Svc. prof., 1989-91, Disting. Svc. prof. emeritus, 1991—; editor, pub. The World & I, 1985—2004. Dir. Ford. workshop program in internat. relations, 1961-76, dir. faculty arms control and fgn. policy seminar, 1970-75; dir. Ctr. for Strategic and Fgn. Policy Studies, 1976-85; cons. Japan War Coll. and Defense Agy., 1979; rsch. assoc. Ctr. of Internat. Studies, Princeton, 1958-62; vis. assoc. prof. polit. sci. Yale U., 1961-62; mem. staff Hudson Inst., 1961-78, cons., 1978-80; lectr. Command and Gen. Staff Sch., 1965-67, Fgn. Svc. Inst., 1967, Air War Coll., 1967-69, NAt. Def. Coll. Can., 1970-72; bd. assocs. Fgn. Policy Rsch. Inst., 1967-90; Gabrielson Disting. lectr. Bowdoin Coll., 1968; Nulton Disting. lectr. Goucher Coll., 1969; cons. NEH, 1972-74; pres. Cetra Music Corp., 1962—, Moraz Prodns., Inc., 1963—; cons. Com. Econ. Devel., 1965, Braddock, Dunn and McDonald, 1969, 72; cons. USIA, 1972; sect. chmn. Internat. Confs. in Unity Scis., 1975, 76, 78, 79, chmn., 1980-83; bd. dirs. Univ. Ctrs. for Rational Alternatives, 1969-96; bd. govs., rsch. com. Stratis, Israeli Inst. Strategic Studies and Policy Analysis, 1974-79; trustee U. Bridgeport, 1992-2004. Author: System and Process in International Politics, 1957, Some Problems in the Strategic Analysis of International Politics, 1959, The Communist Coup in Czechoslovakia, 1960, (with Nicholas de B. Katzenbach) The Political Foundations of International Law, 1961, (with Reitzel and Coblenz) United States Foreign Policy, 1945-55, 1956, Macropolitics: Essays on the Philosophy and Science of Politics, 1969, On Historical and Political Knowing: An Inquiry into Some Problems of Universal Law and Human Freedom, 1971, Dissent and the State in Peace and War: An Essai on the Grounds of Public Morality, 1970, On Freedom and Human Dignity: The Importance of the Sacred in Politics, 1973, The Rationale for NATO; Past and Future, 1973, (with others) Vietnam Settlement: Why 1973, Not 1969?, 1973, Alienation and Identification, 1976, The Life and Death of the Cold War: Selected Studies in Post-War Statecraft, 1976, Towards Professionalism in International Theory: Macrosystem Analysis, 1979, Science, Language and the Human Condition, 1984, rev. edit., 1989, Law in A Democratic Society, 1993; editor: The Revolution in World Politics, 1962, The New Approaches to International Relations, 1968, SALT: Problems and Prospects, 1973, Strategic Thinking and Its Moral Implications, 1973; editor, contbg. author: Great Issues of International Politics, 1970, 74, Isolation or Interdependence? - Today's Choices for Tomorrow's World, 1975, NATO and Dissuasion, 1974, Global Policy: Challenge of the 80s, 1983, Character and Identity vol. 1: Philosophical Foundations of Political and Sociological Perspectives, 1998, vol 2: Historical and Literary Perspectives, 2000; editor, co-author: Character and Identity: The Philosophical Foundations of Political and Sociological Perspectives, 1998, Character and Identity: The Sociological Foundation of Literary and Historical PErspectives, 2000; co-editor, contbg. author: Japan, America, and the Future World Order, 1976, Justice, Human Nature, and Political Obligation, 1976; co-editor: The Soviet Union and the Challenge of the Future, 4 vols., 1988-89; editor, pub. The World and I, 1986-2004; mem. editl. bd. Jour. Conflict Resolution, 1961-79; mem. editl. bd. World Politics, 1961-71, ORBIS, 1967-90; editor, contbr. The Many Faces of Communism, 1978; editor, Consolidating Piece in Europe, 1987; co-editor: Morality and Religion, 1992, The World of 2044: Technological Development and The Future of Society, 1994. Bd. trustees U. Bridgeport, 1994-2004; pres. Profs. World Peace Acad., 1983—. With AUS, 1943-46. Fellow Center Internat. Studies Princeton, 1952-53; Center Advanced Study in Behavioral Scis., 1955-56; Carnegie fellow, 1959-60 Mem. Am. Polit. Sci. Assn., Instituto Mexicano de Cultura (corr.), Internat. Cultural Soc. Korea (hon.), Profs. World Peace Acad. Internat. (pres. 1983—). Address: 5446 S Ridgewood Ct Chicago IL 60615-5315 *Constantly to seek new ideas, not for their newness, but for their ability to illuminate the condition of man.*

KAPLAN, NADIA, writer; b. Chgo., Feb. 28, 1921; d. Peter and Aniela (Buchynska) Charydchak; m. Norman Kaplan, July 25, 1942 (dec. July 1989); children: Fawn Marie Stom, Norma Jean Martinez. BEd, Pestalozzi Froebel Tchrs. Coll, Chgo., 1948; postgrad., UCLA, 1947, L.A. City Coll., U. Hawaii, Pepperdine U., 1970, Santa Monica Coll., 1981-87. Cert. tchr., Calif. Photographer, mgr. Great Lakes (Ill.) Naval Tng. Sta., 1942-45; primary/kindergarten tchr. L.A. Unified Sch. Dist., 1946-81. Contbr. articles to profl. jours.; creator puzzles various mags. Vol. recreational tchr. Found. for Jr. Blind, L.A., 1956-75, vol. camp counselor Camp Bloomfield, Calif., camp dir., 1956-61, leader cross-country study tour for blind teenagers, 1962; mem. dem. Nat. Com., 1985—. Pestalozzi Froebel Tchrs. Coll. scholar, 1938-41; recipient Norman Kaplan Life Achievement award, 2003. UK Blind, 2003. Mem. AAUW, Women Writers West (membership chair 1982-84), United Tchrs. L.A., Calif. Ret. Tchrs. Assn., Assn. Ret. Tchrs. Ukrainian Orthodox. Avocations: writing, bonsai cultivation, doll collecting, travel, golf. Home: 1827 Fanning St Los Angeles CA 90026-1439

KAPLAN, PAUL A., lawyer; b. Jersey City, Nov. 28, 1951; BA magna cum laude, Boston U., 1973; JD cum laude, U. Pa., 1976. Bar: DC 1976, Md. 1982, admitted to practice: US Ct. Appeals (4th Cir. and DC Cir.), US Dist. Ct, DC, US Dist. Ct., Md. Summer assoc. Wolf, Block, Schorr & Solis-Cohen, Phila., 1975; assoc. Arent, Fox, Kinter, Plotkin & Kahn, Washington, 1976—79, Shaw, Pittman, Potts & Trowbridge, Washington, 1979—82; prin., assoc. David, Hagner, Kuney & Davison, Washington, 1982—98; co-managing mem. Womble Carlyle Sandridge & Rice PLLC, Washington, mem. ethics com., mem. alternative dispute resolution com. Adj. faculty mem. Am. U. Washington Coll. Law. Mem. U. Pa. Law Review, 1974—76. Mem.: Bar Assn. Montgomery County, Md., ABA, Order of the Coif. Office: Womble Carlyle Sandridge & Rice PLLC 1401 Eye St NW 7th Fl Washington DC 20005 Office Phone: 202-857-4458. Office Fax: 202-261-0058. Business E-Mail: pkaplan@wscr.com.

KAPLAN, PAUL MICHAEL, lawyer, educator; b. Lowell, Mass., Sept. 15, 1951; s. Samuel G. and Gladys G. Kaplan; 1 child, Karen D. AB with distinction, Boston U., 1973; JD, Northeastern U. Law Sch., 1974; LLM, London Sch. Econs., 1978. Bar: Mass. 1978, NY 1991, US Dist. Ct. (so. and ea. dist.) NY 1999, US Ct. Appeals (1st cir.) 1981, US Ct. Appeals (10th cir.) 2004, US Ct. Appeals (2nd cir.) 2005, US Supreme Ct. 2005. Law clk. to Judge R. Ammi Cutter Mass. Supreme Judicial Ct., 1980—81; v.p., sr. counsel Citbank (Citigroup), NYC, 1983—86; v.p., divsn. counsel Chem. Bank, 1986—90; ptnr. Shea and Gould, 1991—93, Baer Marks and Upham, 1993—98, Epstein Becker and Green, PC, 1998—. Adj. prof. law Fordham Law Sch., NYC, 1991—. Contbr. articles to profl. jours. Legal counsel domestic and foreign corps. & fin. insts., NYC, 1998. Scholar, Northeastern U. Law Sch., 1974—77; Trustee scholar, Boston U. Coll. Arts and Sci., 1970—73. Mem.: ABA, Clayton Act Com., Banking Law and Antitrust and Trade Regulation Coms., Assn. Bar City NY. Jewish. Avocation: marathon running. Home: 220 Riverside Blvd Apt 28A New York NY 10069 Office: Epstein Becker & Green PC 250 Park Ave New York NY 10177 Office Phone: 212-351-4656. Home Fax: 212-878-8656. Business E-Mail: pkaplan@ebglaw.com.

KAPLAN, PHYLLIS, artist, composer; b. Bklyn. d. Abraham and Ida (Heller) Kaplan. BFA, Cooper Union, 1972; postgrad., Domus Acad., Milan, 1985. Curator art exhibit Orgn. Ind. Artists, NYC, 1995—96, Westside Arts Coalition, NYC, 1997; artist in residence Hungarian Multicultural Ctr., Lake Balaton, Hungary, 2002, F. J. Music Sch., Balatonfured, 2002. Lectr., presenter in field. Exhibitions include Lever House, NYC, 1969, Berkshire Mus., Pittsfield, Mass., 1970, L.I. U., NYC, 1975, Internat. Female Artists Biennial, Stockholm, 1994, Nat. Mus. Women in the Arts, Beijing, 1995, Three Rivers Arts Festival, Carnegie Mus., Pitts., 1995—96, 2001, Fine Arts Mus. L.I., Hempstead, 1996—97, Cork Gallery, Lincoln Ctr., NYC, 1997, Blue Mountain Gallery Invitationals, 1996—98, Trevi Flash Art Mus., Italy, 1998, World Artists for Tibet at Blue Mountain, 1998, Halpert Biennial, Boone, NC, 1999, Blue Mountain Gallery Invitationals, NYC, 2000, 2001, Montgomery Coll. Gallery of Art, Rockville, Md., 2002, Canajoharie Libr. and Art Gallery Invitational, 2002 (Honorable Mention, 2002), City Hall, Balatonfured, 2002, Canajoharie Libr. and Art Gallery Invitational, 2003; contbr. paintings to various publs. including Kings Courier, 1974, The Villager N.Y.C., 1994, Vizivarosi Gallery, Budapest, 2004, ann. calendar Orgn. Ind. Artists; exhibitions include Biola U., La Miranda, Calif. Recipient award for patriotism, U.S. Savs. Bond Dr., 1987, Sharjah Art Mus., United Arab Emirates, 2000, hon. mention award, Open Space Gallery, 2000, Mayfair, Allentown, Pa., 2000, Art Environ. Advocacy U. Oreg., Eugene, 2000, Virtue Coll. Visual Arts Gallery, St. Paul, Minn., 2000, Snapshot Contemporary Mus., Balt., 2000, 35th Internat. Exhbn., San Bernardino County Mus., Redlands, Calif., 2000—01, U. South Fla. Coll. Marine Sci., St. Petersburg, 2001, Sharjah Internat. Arts Biennial, United Arab Emirates, 2001, Univ. Place Gallery, Cambridge Art Assn. Nat. Prize Show, Mass., 2001, pub. project, bear sculpture painting project for Black Bear Film Festival, Milford, Pa., 2001, Artists Studio Tour, Hoboken, NJ, 2001; grantee Artists Space, Ind. Project, 1999. Mem.: Monroe County Arts Coun. (instr. 2001). Avocations: travel, classical music. Personal E-mail: phylliskaplan@mymailstation.com.

KAPLAN, RICHARD JAMES, film producer, educator, film director, consultant, scriptwriter; b. N.Y.C., Jan. 3, 1925; s. Benjamin David and Nathalie (Blaustein) K.; m. Blanche Beatrice Aanesen, Nov. 15, 1957 (div. 1981); children: Kjeld, Kirsti, Eve, Erica. BA in Polit. Sci., Antioch Coll., 1949; Diploma Cinema, U. So. Calif., 1951. Pres. Richard Kaplan Prodns., N.Y.C., 1957—; dir., promotional films Am. Film Theater, N.Y.C., 1973; media dir. Alternative Conf. on Environ., Stockholm, 1972; media cons. CUNY, 1974-75; dir. pub. programing Astoria Motion Picture and TV Studios, N.Y.C., 1979-80; assoc. dean Pratt Inst. Sch Art and Design, N.Y.C., 1984-85; producer ABC News, N.Y.C., 1986; pres., exec. producer The Exiles Project, Inc., N.Y.C., 1987-90. Cons. Harvard U., Cambridge, Mass., 1986-90; instr. NYU, CUNY, Parsons, Hunter Coll., U. Soc. Calif., U. Md., 1970-87; lectr., workshop dir. U.S. Info Svc., Arts Am., 1980, Israel, Egypt, India, Pakistan, Sri Lanka, Bangladesh, 1985; prof. Columbia U. Sch. of the Arts, 1991—; founder, dep. dir. Documentary Ctr. at Columbia U.; panelist NEH Pub. Media Program. Dir. documentary The Eleanor Roosevelt Story, 1965 (oscar 1966); producer documentary King: Montgomery to Memphis, 1970 (numerous awards 1970-71); writer, dir., producer TV film A Look at Liv, 1976, and others; dir., producer The Exiles, 1989 (Emmy award 1991), Assignment Rescue...The Story of Varian Fry and the Emergency Rescue Committee, 1997; exec. prodr./dir.: Varian and Putzi: A 20th Century Tale, 2001. Trustee Antioch Coll., Yellow Springs, Ohio, 1975-78; vice chmn. Rockland County Human Rights Commn., Rockland County, N.Y., 1968-71, Town of Ramapo (N.Y.) Housing Authority, 1972-76. Cpl. U.S. Army, 1943-46, ETO. Grantee NEH, Washington, 1987. Mem. Acad. Motion Picture Arts and Sci., Writers Guild of Am., Assn. Ind. Film and Video, N.Y. Film Video Council (bd. dirs.).

KAPLAN, RICHARD N., broadcast executive; m. Priscilla Kaplan; 2 children. Grad., U. Ill., LittD (hon.), 1999. Assoc. prodr. The CBS Evening News with Walter Cronkite, NYC, 1974—79; sr. prodr. World News Tonight, ABC, 1979; exec. prodr. World News This Morning, Good Morning Am., Nightline, ABC, 1984-89, Viewpoint, The Koppel Report; creator, exec. prodr. Capitol to Capitol; coord. ABC News; exec. prodr. PrimeTime Live, 1989-94, World News Tonight with Peter Jennings, 1994-96; exec. prodr. spl. projects ABC Television Network, 1996-97; pres. Cable News Network, Atlanta, 1997—2000; teaching fellow Shorenstein Ctr. John F. Kennedy Sch. of Govt. Harvard U.; sr. v.p. news ABC News, NYC, 2003—04; pres. MSNBC, Seacaucus, NJ, 2004—. Taught and lectured Duke U., Columbia U., Cornell U., Wellesley, U. Penn., Boston Coll., Columbia Coll., USC, Berkeley; adj. prof. U. Ill. Recipient 34 Emmy awards, 4 Overseas Press Club awards, 3 George Foster Peabody awards, 2 George Polk awards, 4 Alfred I. du Pont-Columbia U. awards, 2 Gold Batons, 12 Headliner awards.

KAPLAN, ROBERT B., linguistics educator, consultant, researcher; b. N.Y.C., Sept. 20, 1929; s. Emanuel B. and Natalie K.; m. Audrey A. Lien, Apr. 21, 1951; children— Robin Ann Kaplan Gibson, Lisa Kaplan Morris, Robert Allen. Student, Champlain Coll., 1947-48, Syracuse U., 1948-49; BA, Willamette U., 1952; MA, U. So. Calif., 1957, PhD, 1962. Teaching asst. U. So. Calif., Los Angeles, 1955-57, instr. coordinator, asst. prof. English communication program for fgn. students, 1965-72, assoc. prof., dir. English communication program for fgn. students, 1972-76, assoc. dean continuing edn., 1973-76, prof. applied linguistics, 1976-95, prof. emeritus, 1995—, dir. Am. Lang. Inst., 1986-91; instr. U. Oreg., 1957-60. Cons. field svc. program Nat. Assn. Fgn. Student Affairs, 1964-84; pres.-elect faculty senate U. So. Calif., 1988-89, pres., 1989-90; adv. bd. internat. comparability study of standardized lang. exams. U. Cambridge Local Exams. Syndicate; vis. sr. prof. grad. sch. applied lang. studies Meikai U., Urayasu City, Chiba, Japan, 1998-2000. Author: Reading and Rhetoric: A Reader, 1963; (with V. Tufte, P. Cook and J. Aurbach) Transformational Grammar: A Guide for Teachers, 1968; (with R.D. Schoesler) Learning English Through Typewriting, 1969; The Anatomy of Rhetoric: Prolegomena to a Functional Theory of Rhetoric, 1971; On the Scope of Applied Linguistics, 1980; The Language Needs of Migrant Workers, 1980; (with P. Shaw) Exploring Academic English, 1984; (with U. Connor) Writing Across Languages: Analysis of L2 Text, 1987; (with W. Grabe) Introduction To Applied Linguistics, 1991, Writing Around the Pacific Rim, 1995, (with W. Grabe) Theory and Practice of Writing: An Applied Linguistics Perspective, 1996—, (with R.B. Baldauf) Language Policy from Practice to Theory, 1997, (with R.B. Baldauf) Language and Language-in-Education Planning in the Pacific Basin, 2003; co-editor: (with R.B. Baldauf) series The Language Situation in Malawi, Mozambique, The Philippines, 1998, Nepal, Taiwan, Sweden, 1999, Botswana, Côte d Ivoir, Hungary, Vanuatu, 2000, Paraguay, Tunisia, South Africa, European Union, 2001, Finland, 2002, Ecuador, 2002, No. Ireland, 2002, The Czech Republic, Fiji, 2004, Africa I: Botswana, Malawi, Mozambique and South Africa, 2004, Europe I: Finland, Hungary, Sweden, 2005; editl. adv.: Oxford Internat. Ency. of Linguistics, 1992, consulting editor 2d edit., 2003; editor: The Oxford Handbook of Applied Linguistics, 2002; editl. bd. Jour. Asian Pacific Comm., Internat. Educator, BBC English Dictionary, Second Lang. Instruction/Acquisition Abstracts, Jour. of Second Lang. Writing, Forensic Linguistics, Jour. Multilingual and Multicultural Devels., Asian Jour. of English Lang. Tchg., Current Issues in Lang. Planning. Bd. dirs. Internat. Bilingual Sch. L.A., 1986-91, Internat. Edn. Rsch. Found., 1986-94. Served with inf. U.S. Army, Korea. Recipient U. So. Calif. Faculty Lifetime Achievement award, 2005; Fulbright sr. scholar, Australia, 1978, Hong Kong, 1986, New Zealand, 1992. Mem. AAAS, AAUP, Am. Anthrop. Assn., Am. Assn. Applied Linguistics (v.p., pres. 1992-94, award for disting. scholarship and svc. 1998), Assn. Internationale de Linguistique Applique, Assn. Internationale Pour La Researche et La Diffusion Des Methodes Audio-Visuelles et Structuro-Globales, Assn. Tchrs. ESL (chmn. 1968-69), Calif. Assn. Tchrs. English to Spkrs. Other Langs. (pres. 1970-71), Can. Coun. Tchrs. English, Nat. Assn. Fgn. Student Affairs (nat. pres. 1983-84), Linguistics Soc. Am., Tchrs. English to Spkrs. of Other Langs. (1st v.p., pres. 1989-91). E-mail: rkaplan@olypen.com.

KAPLAN, ROBERT DAVID, lawyer; b. Ossining, N.Y., July 9, 1939; s. Bernard I. and Helen Rosemarie (Gardner) K. AB, Brown U., 1961; LLM, JD, U. Wash., 1969. Bar: Wash. 1969, U.S. Dist. Ct. (we. dist.) Wash. 1969, U.S. Ct. Appeals (9th cir.) 1969. Ptnr. Bogle & Gates, Seattle, 1969—99; ptnr., chmn., Iraq practice Dorsey & Whitney LLP, Seattle, 1999—. Contbr. articles to law rev. Lt. USN, 1961-66. Named a Wash. Super Lawyer, Wash. Law & Politics Mag. Mem. ABA, Wash. State Bar Assn., U. Wash. Sch. Law Alumni Assn. (bd. dirs. 1975-85). Office: Dorsey & Whitney LLP Ste 3400 US Bank Ctr 1420 Fifth Ave Seattle WA 98101-4010 Office Phone: 206-903-8810. Office Fax: 206-903-8820. Business E-Mail: kaplan.robert@dorsey.com.

KAPLAN, ROBERT DAVID, journalist; b. NYC, June 23, 1952; s. Philip and Phylis (Quasha) K.; m. Maria Cabral, Aug. 26, 1983; 1 child, Michael. BA, U. Conn., 1973. Author: Surrender or Starve, 1988, Soldiers of God, 1990, The Arabists, 1993 (Notable Book of Yr., NY Times Book Rev. 1993), Balkan Ghosts, 1993 (Best Book of Yr., NY Times Book Rev. 1993, Notable Book of Yr., ALA 1993), The Ends of the Earth, 1996 (Notable Book of Yr. ALA 1993), An Empire Wilderness, 1999, Eastward to Tartary, 2000, The Coming Anarchy: Shattering the Dreams of the Post Cold War, 2000, Warrior Politics: Why Leadership Demands a Pagan Ethos, 2001, Soldiers of God: With Islamic Warriors in Afghanistan and Pakistan, 2001, The Ends of the Earth: From Togo to Turkmenistan, from Iran to Cambodia, a Journey to the Frontiers of Anarchy, 2001, Surrender or Starve: Travels in Ethiopia, Sudan, Somalia, and Eritrea, 2003, Mediterranean Winter: The Pleasures of History and Landscape in Tunisia, Sicily, Dalmatia, and Greece, 2004, Imperial Grunts: The American Military on the Ground, 2005; contbg. editor Atlantic Monthly, Boston, 1993—; contbr. articles to profl. jours. Fellow World Econ. Forum. Office: Atlantic Monthly 711 3rd Ave New York NY 10017 Office Phone: 646-695-8500.*

KAPLAN, ROBERT S., investment banker; Head Asia-Pacific investment banking The Goldman Sachs Group, N.Y.C., 1990—93, head Ams. corp. fin. dept., 1994—98, co-chief oper. officer global investment banking, 1998—99, global co-head investment banking divsn., 1999—2001, vice chmn., 2002—. Bd. dirs. Bed Bath & Beyond, Inc. Co-chmn. bd. The TEAK Fellowship, Project A.L.S.; dir. The Jewish Theol. Sem., Everybody Wins, Inc., The Jewish Mus. Office: The Goldman Sachs Group 85 Broad St New York NY 10004

KAPLAN, SAMUEL, psychotherapist; b. Newark; d. Nathan Kaplan and Kaplan Hinde; m. Sara Kaplan; children: Alice, Robert, Diane. BS, Columbia U.; MD, Downstate Med. Sch. Psychoanalyst Boston Psychan Inst., 1950—. Capt. U.S. Army, 1942—46, St. Cloud. Mem.: Am. Psychiatric Assn. Avocations: reading, gardening, music. Home: 38 Hyde St Newton Highlands MA 02461

KAPLAN, SELNA L., medical educator; BA in Zoology cum laude, Bklyn. Coll., 1948; MA in Anatomy, Washington U., St. Louis, 1950, PhD in Anatomy, 1953, MD, 1955. Intern Bellevue Hosp., N.Y.C., 1955—56; sr. resident Kings County Hosp., Bklyn., 1956—58; fellow in pediat. endocrinolgy, 1958—61; instr. Columbia U., N.Y.C., 1961—66; asst. prof. pediatrics U. Calif., San Francisco, 1966—68, assoc. prof. pediatrics, 1968—74, prof. pediatrics, 1974—2001, dir. divsn. of pediatric endocrinology, 1966—2001, assoc. prof. pediatric clin. rsch. ctr., 1985—96, ret., 2001, recalled pediatric clin. rsch. ctr., 2002—. Med. dir. Bay Area chpt. Human Growth Found., 1967—98. Contbr. articles to profl. jours. Recipient Rsch. Career Devel. award, NIH, 1961—71, Myrtle Wreath award, Hadassah, San Francisco, 1972. Fellow: Am. Acad. Pediatrics, N.Y. Acad. Scis.; mem.: Women in Endocrinology, Am. Assn. Physicians, Internat. Neuroendocrine Soc., Lawson Wilkins Pediatric Endocrine Soc., European Soc. Pediatric Endocrinology, Soc. Study Reprodn., Am. Pediatric Soc., Western Soc. Pediatric Rsch., Soc. Pediatric Rsch., Endocrine Soc. (Ayerst award 1987, award 1992), Sigma Xi. Office Phone: 415-476-0518. Office Fax: 415-476-8214.

KAPLAN, SHELDON, lawyer, director; b. Mpls., Feb. 16, 1915; s. Max Julius and Harriet (Wolfson) K.; m. Helene Bamberger, Dec. 7, 1941; children— Jay Michael, Mary Jo, Jean Burton, Jeffrey Lee. BA summa cum laude, U. Minn., 1935; LLB, Columbia U., 1939. Bar: N.Y. 1940, Minn. 1946. Pvt. practice, N.Y.C., 1940-42, Mpls., 1946—; mem. firm Lauterstein, Spiller, Bergerman & Dannett, N.Y.C., 1939-42; ptnr. Maslon, Kaplan, Edelman, Borman, Brand & McNulty, Mpls., 1946-80. Chmn. Kaplan, Strangis and Kaplan, Mpls., 1980—; bd. dirs. Stewart Enterprises Inc., Creative Ventures Inc. Decisions editor Columbia Law Review, 1939. Served to capt. AUS, 1942-46. Mem. Minn. Bar Assn., Hazeltime Nat. Golf Club, Mpls. Club, Phi Beta Kappa. Home: 2950 Dean Pkwy Minneapolis MN 55416-4446 Office: Kaplan Strangis & Kaplan 5500 Wells Fargo Ctr Minneapolis MN 55402 Office Phone: 612-375-1138. Business E-Mail: sk@kskpa.com.

KAPLAN, STANLEY, artist, printmaker, educator; b. Brooklyn, Sept. 4, 1925; s. Morris and Fannie Speller; m. Loretta Starer Kaplan (dec.); children: Robert, Rheva. BS, NYU, 1952; MS, Pratt Inst. Sch. Art, 1978. Cert. of Fine Art Cooper Union Sch. Art, 1949. Art tchr. Nassau County Pub. Sch., NY, 1954—59, Nassau Cmty. Coll., Garden City, NY, 1965—95; freelance artist pvt. practice, Levittown, NY, 1959—65. Muralist ITT Cmty. Develop., Fla., 1975; pub. Tortoise Press, Levittown, NY, 1978—. Author: (books) Images: Between the Lines, 1995, Witness 9/11, 2003, Loretta: A Celebration, 2004; contbr. 63 articles on art; Represented in permanent collections Met. Mus. Art, Phila. Mus. Art, Brooklyn Mus. Art, over 170 group exhibitions, over 45 one-man shows. Sgt. Infantry, 1944—46. Mem.: Mid. Am. Print Coun., Southern Graphic Coun., Soc. Am. Graphic Artists (pres. 1976—78). Avocations: travel, graphology. Home: 47 Trapper Ln Levittown NY 11756 Personal E-mail: tpskaplan@earthlink.net.

KAPLAN, STEVEN, lawyer; b. Washington, Sept. 20, 1953; s. Harry E. and Blanche G. (Friedman) K. BA, New Coll., 1975; JD magna cum laude, Georgetown U., 1978. Bar: D.C. 1978, U.S. Dist. Ct. D.C. 1979, U.S. Ct. Appeals (D.C. cir.) 1979. Assoc. Arnold & Porter, Washington, 1978-85, ptnr., Corp. Securities Practice Group, 1986—. Mem. faculty Bank Merger Tech. Conf., Washington, 1987, SEC Acctg. & Fin. Reporting, Washington, 1986, Bank Merger Seminar, Washington, 1985; speaker Va. Securities Assn., Virginia Beach, 1987. Editor, Georgetown Law Journal; contbr. articles to profl. jours. Mem bd. Washington Trustees Federal City Council; bd. dir. Washington Performing Arts Soc. Mem. ABA (sect. bus. law), Econ. Club of Washington, Japan Commerce Assn., Cosmos Club. Office: Arnold & Porter Thurman Arnold Bldg 555 12th St NW Washington DC 20004-1206 Office Phone: 202-942-5998. Office Fax: 202-942-5999. Business E-Mail: steven.kaplan@aporter.com.

KAPLAN, SUSAN, lawyer; BA summa cum laude, Hofstra U., 1971; JD, Columbia U., 1974. Bar: N.Y. 1975, U.S. Dist. Ct. (so. and ea. dists.) N.Y. 1975. Assoc. Patterson Belknap & Webb, N.Y.C., 1974-76; asst. dist. atty. Nassau County, N.Y., 1976-81; asst. chief prosecution Office Profl. Discipline, State of N.Y., 1981-83; dep. dir. prosecution Office Profl. Discipline State of N.Y., 1983-85; pvt. practice N.Y.C., 1985—. Mem. adv. bd. Employee Assistance Program Health Care Network, 1988-2002; lectr. in field. Contbr. articles to profl. jours. Mem. adminstrv. bd. Soc. Meml. Sloan-Kettering Cancer Ctr., 1975-78; mem. adv. coun. Nassau County Boy Scouts Am., 1977-87, v.p., 1981-84; sec., bd. dirs. Harkness Ballet Found., 1980-86. Assoc. fellow N.Y. Acad. Medicine 1990-91, fellow 1992-2004. Fellow N.Y. Bar Found.; mem. N.Y. State Bar Assn. (com. on pub. health 1975-78, com. on profl. discipline 1983-90, com. on health law 1985-88, 92-96, com. to confer with state med. soc. 1985-96, vice chair 1986-87, chair 1987-92, mem. health law sect. 1996—). Office: 165 W End Ave Ste 27P New York NY 10023-5515 Office Phone: 212-877-5998.

KAPLAN, THOMAS ABRAHAM, physicist, educator; b. Phila., Feb. 24, 1926; s. Michael Jay and Nellie (Cohan) K.; m. Patricia Ruth Roe, Nov. 24, 1956; children: Melissa Ann, Andrea Jean, Laurie Michelle. BSME, U. Pa., 1948, PhD in Physics, 1954. Rsch. assoc. Engring. Rsch. Inst., U. Mich., Willow Run, 1954-56; rsch. assoc. Brookhaven Nat. Lab., Upton, N.Y., 1956-58; staff mem. Lincoln Lab., MIT, Lexington, Mass., 1959-70; prof. physics Mich. State U., East Lansing, 1970-95, prof. emeritus, 1995—. Cons. Naval Rsch. Lab., Washington, summer 1979-80; vis. scientist Max-Planck Inst. für Festkörperforschung, Stuttgart, Fed. Republic Germany, 1981-82, 88-89, summer 1983-84, Inst. für Festkörperforschung der Nuclear Physics Rsch. Inst. Jülich, Fed. Republic Germany, 1982; disting. vis. prof. U. Tsukuba, Ibaraki, Japan, 1989. Contbr. numerous articles on theoretical condensed matter physics to profl. jours. Petty officer 2nd class USN, 1944-46. Recipient Sr. Scientist award Alexander von Humboldt Stiftung, 1981. Fellow Am. Phys. Soc.; mem. Sigma Xi. Democrat. Jewish. Avocations: singing, playing piano and trumpet. Office: Mich State U Dept Physics Astronomy East Lansing MI 48824 Business E-Mail: kaplan@pa.msu.edu.

KAPLOW, HERBERT ELIAS, journalist; b. NYC, Feb. 2, 1927; s. Solomon and Belle (Bernstein) K.; m. Betty Koplow, Aug. 10, 1952; children— Steven, Robert, Lawrence. BA, Queens Coll., N.Y.C., 1948; MS, Northwestern U., 1951. News corr. NBC, Washington, 1951-72, ABC, Washington, 1972-94. Served with AUS, 1945-46. Recipient Alumni awards Queens Coll., 1963, Alumni awards Northwestern U., 1959 Mem. Sigma Delta Chi. Jewish. Home: 211 N Van Buren St Falls Church VA 22046-3654 E-mail: HerbKap@worldnet.att.net. *Curiosity and an open, receptive mind are essential characteristics of good journalism. So too is a certain humility growing from the realization that peoples' lives can be affected by a journalist's work. It is a sobering responsibility.*

KAPLOW, LOUIS, law educator; b. Chgo., June 17, 1956; s. Mortimer and Irene (Horwich) K.; m. Jody Ellen Forchheimer, July 11, 1982; children: Irene Miriam, Leah Rayna. BA, Northwestern U., 1977; AM, JD, Harvard U., 1981, PhD, 1987. Bar: Mass. 1983. Prof. law Harvard U., Cambridge, Mass., 1982—, assoc. dean for rsch. and spl. programs, 1989-91, Finn M.W. Caspersen and Household Internat. prof. law and econs., 2004—. Co-author: Antitrust Analysis, 1997, Fairness Versus Welfare, 2002; contbr. articles to profl. jours.; mem. editl. bd. Jour. of Law, Econs. and Orgn., 1989—, Nat. Tax Jour., 1995—, Legal Theory, 1995—, Jour. Pub. Econs., 2001—. Faculty rsch. assoc. Nat. Bur. Economic Rsch., Cambridge, Mass., 1985—. Mem. AAAS, Am. Acad. Arts and Scis., Am. Econ. Assn., Nat. Tax Assn., Am. Law and Econs. Assn. Jewish. Office: Harvard U 1575 Mass Ave Rm 322 Cambridge MA 02138-2801

KAPLOWITZ, KAREN (JILL), lawyer, consultant; b. New Haven, Nov. 27, 1946; d. Charles Cohen and Estelle (Gerber) K.; m. Alan George Cohen, Aug. 17, 1980; children: Benjamin, Elizabeth. BA cum laude, Barnard Coll., 1968; JD, U. Chgo., 1971. Bar: Calif. 1971, U.S. Dist. Ct. (Cen. Dist.) Calif. 1971. Assoc. O'Melveny & Myers, L.A., 1971-74; ptnr. Bardeen, Bersch & Kaplowitz, L.A., 1974-80, Alschuler, Grossman & Pines, L.A., 1980-96, of counsel, 1997—. Contbr. articles to profl. jours. Mem. vis. com. U. Chgo. Law Sch., 1990-93. Mem. ABA (chmn. employer-employee rels. com. of tors and ins. practice sect.), Assn. Bus. Trial Lawyers (pres.), Calif. Women Lawyers (Fay Stender award 1982), Women Lawyers Assn. L.A. Home: 1 Woodside Ln New Hope PA 18938-9281 Office: 100 Overlook Dr 2d Fl Princeton NJ 08540 Office Phone: 888-890-4240. Business E-Mail: kkaplowitz@newellis.com.

KAPLOWITZ, NEIL, gastroenterologist, educator; b. N.Y.C., Mar. 16, 1943; s. Louis and Henrietta (Schall) K.; m. Fattaneh E. Enayat; children: Hillary C., Gregory D., Daria. BS, NYU, 1964, MD, 1967. Diplomate Nat. Bd. Med. Examiners; diplomate in internal medicine and gatroenterology Am. Bd. Internal Medicine. Intern, resident Bellevue Hosp., 1967-69; resident Albert Einstein Med. Ctr., 1969-70; asst. res. phys. Rockefeller Univ. Hosp., 1970-71; fellowship Cornell U. Coll. Medicine, 1970-72; guest investigator Rockefeller U., N.Y.C., 1970-71; instr. in med. Cornell Univ. Med. Coll., 1971-72; asst. prof. Cornell U. Med. Coll., N.Y.C., 1972-73, UCLA Sch. Medicine, 1975-77; chief hepatology Wadsworth VA Hosp., Los Angeles, 1975-79; dir. UCLA Wadsworth Gastroenterology/Hepatology Fellshp. Tng. Prog., 1980-84; chief gastroenterology/hepatology section Wadsworth VA Hosp., Los Angeles, 1980-89; assoc. prof. UCLA Sch. Medicine, 1977-82, prof., 1982-90, U. So. Calif. Sch. Medicine, L.A., 1990—, chief div. gastrointestinal and liver diseases, 1990—; chief gastroenterology Wadsworth VA Hosp., L.A., 1980-90; prof. molecular pharmacology & toxicology USC Sch. of Pharmacy, 1992—; prof. physiology USC Sch. Med., 1993—; dir. USC Liver Diseases Rsch. Ctr. (NIDDK Digestive Disease Core Ctr. Grant), 1994—. Affiliated investigator Ctr. for Ulcer Rsch., 1978-89, coord. for liver disease UCLA Affiliated Hosps., 1975-89, coord. gastroenterology/hepatology, UCLA Sch. Medicine, 1981-84; vice chair for rsch., bd. dirs., chmn. sci. adv. coun. Am. Liver Found., 1994-96. Editor: Liver and Biliary Diseases, 1992, Drug Induced Liver Dieseases, 2002; assoc. editor: Hepatology, 1985-90, Am. Jour. Physiology, 1991—; contbr. over 150 articles to profl. publs. Lt. comdr. USN, 1973-75. Recipient Western Gastroenterology Rsch. prize Western Gut Club, 1986, Tchr. of Yr., Wadsworth VA, 1977-78, NIH Merit awd. 1992, William S. Middleton awd., 1993, Solomon A. Berson Med. Alumni Achievement awd. in clin. sci., NYU Sch. Med., 1994. Fellow Am. Coll. Gastroenterology; mem. Assn. Am. Physicians, Am. Soc. Clin. Investigation, Western Soc. Clin. Investigation (pres. 1985-86), Am. Fedn. for Clin. Rsch., Am. Assn. for Study of Liver Disease, So. Calif. Gastroenterology Soc., So. Calif. Liver Rsch. Forum (founder), Am. Gastroenterology Soc., Am. Soc. for Pharmacology and Experimental Therapeutics, Internat. Biliary Assn., Internat. Assn. for Study of Liver Disease, Soc. for Exptl. Biology and Medicine, Am. Physiol. Soc., Western Assn. Physicians, Rsch. Soc. on Alcoholism, European Assn. for Study of Liver, Phi Beta Kappa, Alpha Omega Alpha. Achievements include research in regulation and role of hepatic glutathione in detoxification; transport of glutathione and organic anions; identification and characterization of cytosol proteins in liver which bind and transport bile acids, organic anions and tocopherol; mechanisms of cell death due to drugs and toxins; redox regulation of suceptibility to hepatotoxicity; role of endoplasmic stress in alcohol liver injury; role of the innate immune system in drug hepatotoxicity. Office Phone: 323-442-5576. E-mail: kaplowit@usc.edu.

KAPLUN, PAUL T., lawyer; b. Glen Cove, NY, Jan. 20, 1956; BSBA magna cum laude, Georgetown Univ., 1978, JD, 1984. CPA Va., 1980; bar: Md. 1985, DC 1986. Atty. Tucker Flyer (merged into Venable); ptnr.-in-charge, Greater Washington bus. practices group Venable LLP. Adj. faculty Georgetown Univ. Law Ctr., 1992—. Adv. bd. Entrepreneurship Inst.; bd. dir. Children's Chorus of Washington. Mem.: ABA, Am. Inst. CPAs, Md. State Bar Assn., DC Bar. Office: Venable LLP 575 7th St NW Washington DC 20004 Office Phone: 202-344-8535. Office Fax: 202-344-8300. Business E-Mail: ptkaplun@venable.com.

KAPNER, LORI, marketing professional; d. Joseph and Marion Kapner; m. Walter David Hosp, Oct. 7, 2001. BA in journalism, U. Md. Asst. editor Am. Machinst mag.; assoc. mng. editor Success mag., 1984; mgr. bus. devel. Lippincott & Marguiles Inc., NYC, v.p., 1992; sr. v.p. Addison, NYC, 1995—98, prin., 1998—99; founder, pres. Kapner Consulting Inc., NYC, 1999—. Adv. bd. Make-a-Wish Found. Mem.: NY Women in Comm.

KAPNICK, RICHARD BRADSHAW, lawyer; b. Chgo., Aug. 21, 1955; s. Harvey E. and Jean (Bradshaw) Kapnick; m. Claudia Norris, Dec. 30, 1978; children: Sarah Bancroft, John Norris. BA with distinction, Stanford U., 1977; MPhil in Internat. Rels., U. Oxford, 1980; JD with honors, U. Chgo., 1982. Bar: Ill. 1982, N.Y. 1993. Law clk. to justice Seymour Simon Ill. Supreme Ct.,

Chgo., 1982—84; law clk. to Justice John Paul Stevens U.S. Supreme Ct., Washington, 1984—85; assoc. Sidley, Austin, Brown & Wood, Chgo., 1985—89, ptnr., 1989—. Mng. editor: U. Chgo. Law Rev., 1981—82. Vestryman Christ Ch., Winnetka, Ill., 2000—03; trustee Chgo. Symphony Orch., 1995—, vice chmn., 2001—05; bd. dirs., chmn. Civic Orch. Chgo., 1999—2001; bd. dirs. Cabrini Green Legal Aid Clinic, 1990—94, chmn. bd., 1991—93; mem., advisor, bd. dirs. Stanford Inst. Econ. Policy Rsch., 1999—. Fellow, Leadership Greater Chgo., 1989—90; Marshall scholar, 1978—80. Mem.: Chgo. Club, Phi Beta Kappa, Order Coif. Republican. Episcopalian. Fluent in Spanish. Business E-Mail: rkapnick@sidley.com.

KAPNICK, S. JASON, oncologist; b. Providence, Mar. 28, 1949; s. I.H. and Martha (Shaulson) K.; children: Senta Marie-Rose, Isrel Berndt-Stefan, Sesselja Edda, Finn MacComaill. BLS summa cum laude, boston U., 1974; MD, Harvard Med. Sch., 1981. Surg. rsch. assoc. Harvard Med. Sch., Boston, 1976-77, assoc. in ob/gyn., lectr., 1981-85, instr. in gynecology, 1985-87; cons. in gynecologic oncology Dana Farber Cancer Inst., Boston, 1985-87; clin. fellow Am. Cancer Soc., Boston, 1985-87; attending gynecologic oncologist West Palm Beach, Fla., 1989—; cert. gynecologic oncologist, 1991—. Asst. cons. prof. gynecol. oncology Duke U. Med. Ctr., Durham, N.C., 1994—; reviewer of rsch. submissions Cancer med. jour., Bethesda, Md., 1995—; invited lectr., 1995, Palm Beach County Hosps., 1990—. Am. Cancer Soc., Bethesda, 1995, also Switzerland, Germany, France and Eng., 1990—. Contbr. articles on colon, breast, and female pelvic cancers to profl. jours. Vol., contbr. Ctr. for Family Svcs., West Palm Beach, 1992—; mem., donor Bullfinch Soc., Mass. Gen. Hosp.; trustee, founder Helga Helgason BSRN Meml. Fund; mem., dean's coun. Med. Sch., Harvard U.; active Cath. Diocese children's programs, 1998—; mem., donor First Unitarian Ch., North Palm Beach, Fla.; bd. dirs. Palm Beach Opera, 1992—. Henry Merritt Wriston scholarship Brown U. Mem. Harvard Club of Palm Beach. Avocations: philosophy, music. Office: Farris Bldg Gynecol Oncology 1411 N Flagler Dr Ste 5000 West Palm Beach FL 33401-3410 Address: PO Box 30053 Palm Beach Gardens FL 33420-0053 Office Phone: 561-655-9119.

KAPNICK, STEWART, investment banker; b. N.Y.C., Mar. 10, 1956; s. Charles and Ruth Kapnick; m. Alison Sue Cherry, 1988; children: Jordan Leigh, Michael Taylor. BA with honors, George Washington U., 1978; MBA, Baruch Coll., 1986. Summer internship IBM Corp., White Plains, NY, 1977—78; acct. exec. L & C Pub. Inc., LA, 1979—82, 3M Corp., N.Y.C., 1982—83; pres., fin. ops. prin. Ulysses Capital, N.Y.C., 1983—87; lease fin. cons. SK Capital, N.Y.C., 1987—; assoc. dir. product devel. and lease fin. Continental Info. Systems Corp., N.Y.C., 1987-89; dir. equity fin. Info. Processing Systems Inc. subs. USF&G Fin. Svcs. Corp., Hackensack, NJ, 1989—92; v.p. lease acquisitions The CIT Group, Livingston, NJ, 1992—94; sr. v.p. corp. banking-lease fin. HSBC Bank USA (formerly Republic Nat. Bank of N.Y.), N.Y.C., 1994—. Mem. Equipment Lessors Assn., Computer Dealers and Lessors Assn. Avocations: basketball, tennis, golf, playing options and foreign currency.

KAPOOR, NEERA, optometrist, research scientist; b. Melfort, Sask., Can., June 25, 1966; arrived in U.S., 1990; d. Ajit and Prem Kapoor. BSc, U. Toronto, 1989; MS, SUNY, 1993, OD, 1994. Asst. clin. prof. SUNY-Optometry, NYC, 1995—2002, assoc. clin. prof., 2002—, dir. head trauma vision rehab. unit., 1996—2002, dir. Raymond J. Greenwald Rehab. Ctr., 2002—. Cons. neuro-optometry JFK Med. Ctr., NJ Neuro Sci. Inst., Edison, 2001—05. Co-author, co-editor: Visual & Vestibular Consequences of Acquired Brain Injury, 2001. Recipient Founder's award, Brain Injury Assn. N.Y. State, 2002, Disting. Achievement award, N.Y. State Optometric Assn., 2003, Chancellor's award for excellence in faculty svc., SUNY, 2005. Fellow: Am. Acad. Optometry; mem.: Assn. Rsch. in Vision and Ophthalmology, Coll. Optometrists in Vision Devel. (assoc.). Office: SUNY 5th Fl 33 W 42nd St New York NY 10036 Business E-Mail: nkapoor@sunyopt.edu.

KAPOOR, NISCHAL, information technology manager; B in Engring., JN Engring. Coll., Aurangabad, 1997; post grad. diploma in Bus. Adminstrn.-Mktg., Symbiosis U., Pune, India, 2004. Asst. bus. devel. mgr. CVV Pvt. Ltd., Kanpur, India, 1998—2000; asst. mktg. mgr. Open Tech. India Pvt. Ltd., Noida, 2000—02; mktg. mgr. ITIL Internat. Pvt. Ltd., New Delhi, 2002—03; mgr. bus. devel. group Perot Systems TSI Ltd., Noida, India, 2003—04; account mgr. Perot Systems GmbH, Frankfurt, Germany, 2005—05, Perot Systems Corp., USA, 2005—.

KAPOR, MITCHELL DAVID, application developer, foundation administrator; b. Bklyn., Nov. 1, 1950; s. Jesse and Phoebe L. (Wagner) K.; m. Judith M. Vecchione, June 4, 1972 (div. 1979); m. Ellen M. Poss, Aug. 7, 1983 (div. 1998); m. Freada Klein, June 19, 1999. BA, Yale U., 1971; MA, Beacon Coll., 1978; postgrad., Sloan Sch. Mgmt., MIT, 1979; DHL (hon.), Boston U., 1985, Mass. Sch. Profl. Psychology, 1990; DSc (hon.), Suffolk U., 1988, U. Mass., 1996. Freelance cons., Cambridge, Mass., 1978-80; product mgr. Personal Software, Sunnyvale, Calif., 1980; founder Lotus Devel. Corp., Cambridge, Mass., 1982, pres., 1982-84, chmn., 1984-86, ON Tech. Inc., Cambridge, Mass., 1987-90, Electronic Frontier Found., Inc., Cambridge, 1990-94, chmn., pres., 1994-99; ptnr. ACCEL Ptnrs., Palo Alto, Calif., 1999—2001; pres. Kapor Enterprises Inc., 1985—. Chmn. Mass. Commn. Computer Tech. and Law, 1992, 93, 2003—. Designer (with others) Lotus 1-2-3, 1983. Trustee Kapor Family Found., 1984—98, Level Playing Field Inst., San Francisco; founder, dir. Mitchell Kapor Found., 1997—. Jewish. Office: Mitchell Kapor Found 543 Howard St 5th Fl San Francisco CA 94105 Office Phone: 415-946-3016. Business E-Mail: mitch@kapor.com.

KAPP, C. TERRENCE, lawyer; b. Pine Bluff, Ark., Oct. 1, 1944; s. Robert Amos and Guenevere Patricia (DeVinne) Kapp; m. Betsy Langer, May 2, 1987. BA, Colgate U., 1966; JD, Cleve. State U., 1971; MA summa cum laude, Holy Apostles Coll., 1984. Bar: Ohio 1971, U.S. Dist. Ct. (no. dist.) Ohio 1973, U.S. Supreme Ct. 1980, U.S. Tax Ct. 1996. Ptnr. Kapp & Kapp, East Liverpool, Ohio, 1971-84; pvt. practice Cleve., 1984—; ptnr. Marshman, Snyder & Kapp, Cleve., 1991-93, Kapp Law Offices, Cleve., 1994—. Contbr. articles to profl. jours. Chair St. John's Cathedral Endowment Trust, Cleve., 1992—94; pres., bd. dirs. Lake Erie Nature and Sci. Ctr., Bay Village, Ohio, 1991—92. Mem.: ABA (judge finals nat. appellate adv. competition 1987, taxation com. exec. 1988—, nat. chmn. divorce laws and procedures com. family law sect. 1989—93, vice-chmn. step families com. 1991—93, task force client edn. 1991—, commr. presdl. commn. non-lawyer practice 1992—96, chmn. alternative funding com. 1992—, chair nat. symposium image family law atty-fact or myth 1993, domestic rels. taxatoin problems com. exec. tax sect., lit. sect., cert. Outstanding Svc. 1988, 1989, 1993, 1995), Cuyahoga County Bar Assn. (bar admissions com. exec. 1986—, cert. grievance com. 1990—, chair family law sect. 1991—92, jud. selection com. 1991—, unauthorized practice law com. 1992—, cert. Outstanding Leadership 1992), Ohio State Bar Assn. (family law com. exec. 1987—, family law curriculum com. Ohio CLE Inst. 1992—), Bay Men's Club, Cleve. Athletic Club (pres., bd.dirs.). Roman Catholic. Avocations: sailing, handball, racquet sports, dog training. Office: Kapp Law Offices PO Box 40447 Bay Village OH 44140-0447 Business E-Mail: kapplawoffices@ameritech.net.

KAPP, MICHAEL KEITH, lawyer; b. Winston-Salem, N.C., Nov. 28, 1953; s. William Henry and Betty Jean (Minton) K.; m. Mary Jo Chancy McLean, Aug. 13, 1977; 1 child, Mary Katherine. AB with honors, U. N.C., 1976, JD with honors, 1979. Bar: N.C. 1979, U.S. Dist. Ct. (ea. dist.) N.C. 1980, U.S. Ct. Appeals (4th cir.) 1982, U.S. Dist. Ct. (mid. dist.) N.C. 1986, U.S. Supreme Ct. 1988. Law clk. to presiding justice N.C. Ct. Appeals, Raleigh, NC, 1979-80, N.C. Supreme Ct., 1980-81; assoc. Maupin, Taylor & Ellis, 1981-85; ptnr. Maupin, Taylor P.A. (formerly Maupin, Taylor & Ellis, P.A.), 1985—, mng. dir., 2002—. Research editor U. N.C. Jour. Internat. Law and Comml. Regulation, 1978-79; editor Survey of Significant Decisions of North Carolina Court of Appeals and North Carolina Supreme Court, 1979-81, 2d vol., 1981-82. NC teen Dem. advisor, 1983-85; mem. exec. council NC Dem. Party, 1983-85; founding dir. NC Vol. Lawyers for Arts, Raleigh, 1982-85; counsel Moravian Music Found., Winston-Salem, 1982-85, trustee, 1985-90, pres., 1990-92; counsel Raleigh Little Theatre, 1996-98, bd. dir., 1998—, pres., 2003; bd. dir. Moravian Ch. Archives, Winston-Salem, 1984-89, Carolina Charter Corp., 1990—, dir. 1995—; chmn. Raleigh (N.C.) First Night, 2000—, dir.; chmn. Soc. for Preservation of Historic Oakwood, Raleigh, 1981-83. Morehead scholar U. N.C., 1972. Mem. ABA, N.C. Bar Assn. (chmn. young lawyer div. continuing legal edn. 1980-82, membership 1984-86, bd. govs. 1983-86), N.C. State Bar (ethics com. 1981-91, com. on professionalism 1986-87, jud. dist. councilor 2001-), Wake County Bar Assn. (bd. dirs. 1988-90, pres.-elect 1995, pres. 1996), Raleigh Execs. Club (pres. 1998), Kiwanis (Raleigh Kiwanis Found. dir., 1996-98), Phi Beta Kappa, Phi Delta Phi, Pi Lambda Phi. Avocations: historic preservation, hiking, gardening. Home: 1615 Craig St Raleigh NC 27608-2201 Office: Maupin Taylor PA Highwoods Tower One 3200 Beechleaf Ct Ste 500 Raleigh NC 27604-1670 Office Phone: 919-981-4000. Business E-Mail: KKapp@maupintaylor.com.

KAPP, ROBERT HARRIS, lawyer; b. Chgo., Mar. 9, 1934; s. Ben and Gladys (Harris) K.; m. Jean Schlusberg, June 22, 1958; children: Stephen, Lisa, Jonathan, Diana. BS in Econs., U. Pa., 1955; JD, U. Mich., 1958. Bar: Ill. 1958, D.C. 1961. Trial atty. U.S. Dept. Justice, Washington, 1958-61; ptnr. Hogan & Hartson, Washington, 1961—. Mem. adv. bd. Transnational Arbitration Assn., 1994-97. Bd. dirs. Internat. Human Rights Law Group, 1978—, chmn., 1986-89; bd. dirs. Lawyers' Com. for Civil Rights Under Law, 1976—, chmn., 1983-85; bd. dirs. Washington Lawyers' Com. for Civil Rights and Urban Affairs, 1974-96, chmn., 1980-82; bd. dirs. ACLU of Nat. Capitol Area, 1983-95, chmn., 1992-94; bd. dirs. Washington Sch. Psychiatry, 1980-86, Higher Achievement Program, 1991-94; mem. area I planning com. Montgomery County Pub. Schs., 1970; mem. adv. bd. Internat. Legal Studies Program, Am. U. Law Sch.; mem. bd. visitors U. Mich. Law Sch.; commr. Commn. on Independence for Nambia; co-founder, co-pres. Internat. Sr. Lawyers Project; sr. advisor Ethical Globalization Initiative; bd. dirs. Enterprise Works Worldwide. Fellow Am. Bar Found. (Wiley A. Branton Sr. award Wash. Lawyers Com. for Civil Rights and Urban Affairs, Alan Barth Svc. award ACLU of Nat. Capitol Area, C. Anthony Friedrich Meml. award Internat. Human Rights Law Group). Office: Hogan & Hartson 555 13th St NW Ste 800E Washington DC 20004-1161 Office Fax: 202-637-5910. Business E-Mail: RHKapp@hhlaw.com.

KAPPAS, ATTALLAH, physician; b. Union City, N.J., Nov. 4, 1926; s. Attie and Sofia (Kozam) K.; m. Oct. 26, 1963; children: Peter, Michael, Nicholas. AB, Columbia U., 1947; MD with honors, U. Chgo., 1950; ScD, N.Y. Med. Coll., 1978. Diplomate: Am. Bd. Internal Medicine. Med. intern Univ. Service, Kings County Hosp., N.Y.C., 1950-51; ACS rsch. fellow Sloan Kettering Inst., N.Y.C., 1951-54; asst. resident physician and sr. asst. resident physician Peter Bent Brigham Hosp. Harvard Med. Sch., Boston, 1954-56; assoc. div. steroid biochemistry and metabolism Sloan Kettering Inst., 1956-57; from asst. prof. to assoc. prof. dept. medicine, head div. metabolism and arthritis U. Chgo. Med. Sch., 1957-67; Guggenheim fellow, guest investigator Rockefeller U., N.Y.C., 1966-67, assoc. prof., physician, 1967-71, sr. physician, 1971-74, prof., 1971-81, Sherman Fairchild prof., 1981—2004, emeritus, 2004—, v.p., 1983-91, physician-in-chief, 1974-91, physician-in-chief emeritus, 1991—; prof. medicine Cornell U., 1972—2002; Vincent Astor prof. clin. sci. Cornell U. Meml. Sloan Kettering Inst., 1979—81; prof. medicine emeritus Weill Cornell Med. Coll., 2002. Contbr. articles to profl. jours. Bd. dirs. Vis. Nurse Service N.Y., 1982-86, 98—, Scenic Hudson, Inc., 2002—; dir. Theresa and Eugene Lane Ctr. for Rsch. and Edn. NY Hosp. Queens Med. Ctr., Weill-Cornell Med. Coll., 1998-2002, dir. emeritus, 2002; mem. gov.'s com. on rev. sci. studies and devel. pub. policy on problems resulting from hazardous wastes N.Y. State, 1980; mem. vis. com. divsn. biol. sci. and the Pritzker Sch. of Medicine, U. Chgo., 2003—; bd. dirs. Beatrice Renfield Found., N.Y.C., 2003—; mem. dean's coun. U. Vt. Coll. Medicine, 2000-04; mem. coun. SUNY Health Scis. Ctr., 1998-2004. Served with U.S. Army, 1945-46. Named named Sr. Henry Hallet Dale Meml. lectr. and vis. prof., Johns Hopkins Hosp., 1975, Pfizer lectr. clin. pharmacology, Peter Bent Brigham Hosp., Harvard Med. Sch., 1977, Pfizer lectr., Pa. State U., 1980, first Rolf Blomstrand lectr., Karolinska Inst., 1988, first Glaxo lectr., Cornell U. Med. Sch., Gunner and Lillian Nicholson Found. exch. prof., Karolinska Inst., Stockholm, 1985—86, Barowsky Meml. lectr., N.Y. Med. Coll., 1986, First Annual Lang Rsch. lectr., N.Y. Hosp. Med. Ctr., Queens, 2000; recipient Spl. award in clin. pharmacology, Burroghs Wellcome Fund, 1973, Disting. Svc. award in med. scis., U. Chgo. Sch. Medicine, 1975, Citation for profl. achievement, U. Chgo. Alumni Assn., 1995, 1st Ann. award for excellence in clin. rsch., NIH, 1989; fellow Commonwealth Fund, 1961—62, Guggenheim fellow, 1966—67. Fellow ACP; mem. Assn. Am. Physicians, Am. Soc. Clin. Investigation, Am. Clin. and Climatol. Assn., Am. Soc. Pharmacology and Exptl. Therapeutics (pub. affairs com., award for exptl. therapeutics 1978), Practitioners Soc. N.Y., Harvey Soc., Endocrine Soc., Interurban Clin. Club, Cosmos Club (Washington), N.Y. Athletic Club, Lotos Club, Univ. Club. Office: Rockefeller U Hosp 1230 York Ave New York NY 10021-6307 Office Phone: 212-327-8494. Office Fax: 212-327-8690.

KAPPAZ, MICHAEL H., engineering and energy executive; b. Cartagena, Colombia, May 14, 1942; came to the U.S., 1963; s. George and Elena (Hegel) K.; m. Chafica Maria Dau; children: George, Nur-Helene, Christine, Karen, William, Patricia. BS in Indsl. Engring. and Ops. Rsch., Poly. Inst. N.Y., 1970; MBA in Fin. Mgmt., Golden Gate U., 1976; cert. in Global Strategic Mgmt., U. Pa., 1984; cert. in exec. mgmt., Stanford U., 1986. Indsl. engr. for iron and steel Ramseyer and Miller, Inc., N.Y., 1964-71; v.p., gen. mgr. internat. ops. Bechtel Power Corp., Bechtel Group, Gaithersburg, Md. and San Francisco, 1971-86; v.p., mgr. Overseas Bechtel, Inc., Cairo, 1982-84; v.p., project mgr. Internat. Bechtel Corp., Inc., Venezuela, 1979-82; chmn., CEO K&M Engring. and Consulting Corp., Washington, 1987—; chmn. bd. dirs. KMR Power Corp., Arlington, Va., 1993-2000; chmn. K&M Interamerican Investment Corp., Arlington, 1993—2002, K&M Interamerican Energy Leasing, Arlington, 1993—2000, K&M Ventures, L.P., Arlington, 1993—2000, KMtel LLC, 1995—2000, K&M Global Constrn. LLC, 1995—, K&M Panam., LLC. Contbr. articles to various publs., papers to confs. and seminars. Mem. adv. bd. Rep. Nat. Com., 1993—; mem. Am. Rsch. Ctr. (Egyptology and Archeology), 1982-86; mem. engring. adv. com. Am. U., Cairo, 1982-86; co-chmn. coun. Latin Am. studies Johns Hopkins U., 1987-89, mem. adv. coun. 1987-97, mem. devel. com. 1993-98; bd. dirs. Washington Opera, Bus. Coun. for Internat. Understanding; chmn. U.S.-Colombia Bus. Partnership; trustee Latino Student Fund; vice chmn. US-Korea Com. Bus. Cooperation. Recipient Deal of Yr. award Project Fin. Internat. Yearbook, 1993, Infrastructure Fin. Mag., 1993, Blue Chip Enterprise award, 1995, Fast Track award, 1995, Inc 500 award, Nat. Tech. Fast 500 award, 1995, Fast 50 award 1996, Project Fin. Inter. 2000, Top 50 Hispanic High Tech Co. 2000. Mem. U.S. Energy Assn., Am. C. of C. (charter, Cairo), Am. Assn. Cost Engrs. (past v.p., dir. Capital chpt.), D.C. C. of C., Univ. Club, Georgetown Club, Avenel Country Club, Damascus Lodge, Group of 50, Bretton Woods Com., Cambridge Energy Rsch. Assoc. Republican. Roman Catholic. Avocations: opera, baseball, golf, bridge. Office: K & M Engring & Consulting Corp 1300 Wilson Blvd Ste 500 Arlington VA 22209-

KAPPEL, STEPHEN R., retired orthopedist; b. St. Louis, Apr. 14, 1949; s. Louis C. and Helen Elizabeth Kappel; m. Mary Theresa Hutchison, June 17, 1972; children: Jacqueline, Kathleen, Stephen Jr. MD, St. Louis U., 1974. Diplomate Am. Bd. Ortho. Surgery, lic. physician Ill., Mo. Intern St. Louis U. Group Hosp., 1974—75; resident U. Mo., Kans. City, 1975—78; physician Associated Ortho. Surgeons Ltd, Belleville, Ill., 1979—99, Ortho. and Sports Med. Assocs., Belleville, 1999—2004, ret., 2004. Active Boy Scouts Am. Fellow: Am. Acad. Ortho. Surgeons; mem.: ACS, St. Clair County Med. Soc. (pres. 1988), St. Louis Ortho. Soc. (pres. 2002). Office: Ortho and Sports Med Assocs 4600 Memorial Dr Belleville IL 62226

KAPPENBERG, MARILYN KASCIUS, library director; b. Hicksville, NY, July 19, 1948; d. Adolf A. and Mary T. Kascius; m. Richard L. Kappenberg, Apr. 5, 1975; children: Neal, Glenn. BA, Molloy Coll., 1970; MLS, L.I. U., 1972. Children's libr. Hicksville (N.Y.) Pub. Libr., 1972-90; head ref. Hicksville Pub. Libr., 1990-95, asst. libr. dir., 1992-95; libr. dir. Wantagh (N.Y.) Pub. Libr., 1992—, Plainedge Pub. Libr., Massapequa, NY, 2001—. Sec. Hicksville Lions Club, 1990-95. Mem. ALA, Nassau County Libr. Assn., Wantagh C. of C. (mem.-at-large 1995—). Avocations: writing, volunteering. Home: 2873 Janet Ave North Bellmore NY 11710-2026 Office: Plainedge Pub Libr 1060 Hicksville Rd Massapequa NY 11758

KAPPES, PHILIP SPANGLER, lawyer; b. Detroit, Dec. 24, 1925; s. Philip Alexander and Wilma Fern (Spangler) K.; m. Glendora Galena Miles, Nov. 27, 1948; children: Susan Lea, Philip Miles, Mark William. Bar: Ind. 1948. Assoc. Armstrong and Gause, 1948—49, C.B. Dutton, 1950—51; ptnr. Dutton, Kappes & Overman, 1952—85, of counsel, 1983—85; ptnr. Lewis Kappes Fuller & Eads, Indpls., 1985—89, Lewis & Kappes, Indpls., 1989—92, Lewis & Kappes PC, Indpls., 1993—, Creston Group, Indpls.; mgr. Labeco Properties, LLC, Indpls.; pres., dir. K&K Realty, Inc., Indpls. Past sec., dir., mem. Ind. Machine Works, Inc.(formerly named Laboratory Equipment Corp.), Mooresville, Ind.; instr. bus. law Butler U., 1948-49, chmn. bd. govs., 1965-66, bd. trustees, 1987-90; chmn. Ovid Butler Soc., 1982-83. Life bd. dirs. Crossroads Am. coun. Boy Scouts Am., 1965—, v.p. fin., mem. exec. com., pres., 1977-79, chmn. trustees endowment fund, 1987-92, trustee, 1987—, chmn. Gathering of Eagles dinner, 2000; bd. dirs. Fairbanks Hosp., Indpls., 1986-94, chmn. bd., 1988-91, exec. com., 1987-94, mem. audit and fin. com., 1992-94, life dir. emeritus, 1994—, chmn. nominating com., 1991; trustee Butler U., 1987-90, Children's Mus., Indpls., 1969-88, pres. bd. trustees, 1984-85, bd. disting. advisors, 1990-01, hon. trustee, 2001—; mem. First Meridian Heights Presbyn. Ch., 1933—, chmn. bd. trustees, 1958-61, 69-72, 1996— ruling elder 1982-85, 94-99, deacon, 1950-58; mem. planning com. and dir. Indpls. 32-Degree Masonic Learning Ctr. for Children, 1997-98, dir., 1998—, chmn. bd., 2002-2002, vice chmn., 2002—; chmn. Dyslexia Tutor Tng. Inst., 2000—; chmn. Lawyers Title Guaranty Fund Com., 1971-73; dir. Iknd. Citizens for Modern Ct. Sys., 1970; vice chmn., mem. faculty Law in Am. Soc., 1971-73. Recipient Paul H. Buchanan award of excellence Indpls. Bar Found., Disting. Eagle award Boy Scouts Am., 2004, Disting. Alumnus award, Mortar award Butler U. Alumni Assn. Mem. ABA (ho. of dels. 1970-71), Ind. State Bar Assn. (ho. dels. 1959—; chmn. pub. rels. exec. com. 1966-69, sec. 1973-74, bd. mgrs. 1975-77, chmn. law practice mgmt. com. 1991-92), Indpls. Bar Assn. (treas., 1st v.p. 1965, pres. 1970, bd. mgrs. 1968-71, 75-77, chmn. law day com. 1991-92, settlement week com. 1989-95, co-chair Family Law Study Commn., co-chmn. ct. liaison com. 1992-93, family law implementation com. 1993-97, exec. com. bd. mgrs. 1994-96, counsel bd. mgrs. 1994, chmn. sr. lawyers divsn. 1999-2000, Bd. Mgrs. award for jud. sys. improvement 1995), Am. Judicature Soc., Indpls. Legal Aid Soc., Indpls. Jr. C. of C. (past 1st v.p., dir. ct. unification implementation com., chmn. 1995-98), Butler U. Alumni Assn. (past pres., Disting. Alumnus award, Mortar award), Mich. Alumni Assn., Meridian Hills Country Club, Lawyers Club, Gyro Club (pres. 1966), Masons (worshipful master 1975), Indpls. Valley Scottish Rite (33d degree, most wise master 1982-84, trustee 1996—, chmn. bd. trustees 1998-99, 2001—, pres. Indpls. Scottish Rite Cathedral Found., dir., chmn. 2001—, dir. Indpls. Scottish Rite Found.), Shriners, Phi Delta Theta (chpt. advisor 1950-82), Tau Kappa Alpha. Republican. Presbyterian. Home: 624 Somerset Dr W Indianapolis IN 46260-2924 Office: 1 American Square PO Box 82053 Indianapolis IN 46282-0003 Office Phone: 317-639-1210. E-mail: pkappes@lewis-kappes.com.

KAPPLER, ANN M., lawyer, finance company executive; b. New Brunswick, N.J., Dec. 24, 1957; AB magna cum laude, Darmouth Coll., 1979; JD, NYU, 1986. Bar: N.Y. 1988, DC 1989. Law clk. to Hon. Abner J. Mikva U.S. Ct. Appeals (DC cir.), Washington, 1986—87; law clk. to Hon. Harry Blackmun U.S. Supreme Ct., 1987—88; assoc. Jenner & Block, 1989—93, ptnr., 1994—98; sr. v.p., dep. gen. counsel Fannie Mae, Washington, 1999—2000, sr. v.p., gen. counsel, 2000—. Editor-in-chief: NYU Law Rev., 1985—86. Mem.: ABA, Order of Coif, DC Bar Assn., Internat. Human Rights Law Group (bd. dirs. 1999—2001), Coun. Ct. Excellence (bd. dirs. 1999—2001), Wash. Lawyers Com. Civil Rights and Urban Affairs (bd. dirs. 1999—2001). Office: Fannie Mae Legal Dept 3900 Wisconsin Ave NW Washington DC 20016

KAPPLER, KAREN L., music educator, musician; b. Maud, Okla., July 19, 1938; d. Raymond Maxwell and Verdena Mary (Caywood) Edwards; m. Samuel Houston Clifton, June 27, 1959 (div. Apr. 1, 1977); children: Mary Louise Clifton, Catherine Helen Sehorn; m. Karl Heinrich Kappler, Aug. 27, 1989. *Mother, Verdena Mary Caywood, descends from Johannes de Kawode of York, King John's reign. John Cawood (English kings' hereditary forester), Peter Cawode (armiger), John Cawood (Queen Mary's printer), produced future abbots, vicars, musicians, professors, and scientists. An influential teacher, Verdena earned a BA in History at Sterling College in Kansas. Her actions/writings spoke ethics, religion, and equality. Father, Raymond Maxwell Edwards, a business owner, was known for honesty, compassion, and responsibility. Sister Ramona Farthing is a retired French professor and received the Outstanding Teacher award from Oklahoma Baptist University. Her daughters are Mary Clifton (of Seattle) and Catherine Sehorn (of Oklahoma).* BA in Edn. and Music, U. Denver, 1965; postgrad., U. Colo., 1967, MMus in Piano performance, 1980; postgrad., U. No. Colo., 1970, U. Utah, 1971, Columbia U., 1976. Cert. tchr. Colo. Piano and remedial reading tchr. John Marshall H.S., Oklahoma City, 1954—56; pvt. music tchr., 1955—; tchr. Jefferson County Pub. Schs., Lakewood, Colo., 1965—73; tchr., tutor Colo. Dept. Social Svcs., Denver, 1973—75; instr. continuing edn. U. Colo., Boulder, 1977—78; tchr. Met. State Coll., Denver, 1978—80. Pianist, organist, vocalist, primary tchr. Classen Blvd. Bapt. Ch., Oklahoma City, 1948—55; organist, choir soloist, dir. children's choirs Edgewater Meth. Ch., Denver, 1962—65; curriculum writer, nat. tchr. Jefferson County Pub. Schs., 1965—73, percussion ensemble coach, Colo., 2005; nat. coord., tchr. Robert Pace Piano Found., 1970—82; dir. pilot program Colo. State Social Svcs., 1973—75; piano and voice coach dinner theaters, children's auditions, Denver, 1978—; pvt. tchr. piano, organ, voice, theory, composition, improvisation Skinner Cmty. Sch., Denver Pub. Schs., 1980—93; weddings organist First Bapt. Ch., Denver, 1981—84; dir. music and choir, organist Highland Christian Ch., Denver, 1983—87; prin. organist St. Thomas Moore Cath. Ch., Littleton, Colo., 1987—88; dir. music and choirs, organist First Ave. Presbyn. Ch., Denver, 1988—; pvt. tchr., coach to piano and voice students Denver Sch. Performing Arts, 1998—2004. Numerous recitals, concerts. Mem. exec. bd., officer, mem. coms. Jefferson Symphony Orch., Golden, Colo., 1980—90; musician, spkr. Gideons Internat., Nashville and Denver, 1990—; music stock advisor Jefferson County Libr., Lakewood, 1986; cmty. capt. March of Dimes, Northglenn, Colo., 1992—; tchr. historic needlework design. Grantee NDEA, 1963—65; NDEA Inst. fellow, 1968. Mem.: Nat. Fedn. Music Clubs (judge coll. voice competition 1975, judge piano and organ 1998, 1999, 2003, 2004), Am. Guild Organists (com. chair Young Artists' Competition 1988, com. chair Denver Study Groups 1990), Colo. Music Tchrs. Assn. (tchr. state conv. 1981, jr. artists festival piano divisn. judge 2000, 2002, judge local panels, Denver chair State Theory JExaqm 1979—80, group class tchr. state conv. workshop 1979—80, judge local panels), Music Tchrs. Nat. Assn., Hist. Needlework Guild, Steinway Performance Club, Kappa Delta Pi, Sigma Alpha Iota (coll. chpt. pres. 1958—59, chair scholarship com. 1975, rec. sec. 1976—77, chair audit com. 1983, v.p. ritual 1996—97, v.p. music programs and ritual 1996—2001, del. Denver Alumnae chpt. to internat. conv. 1997, pres. state chpt. 1997—2000, chair scholarships com. 1998—2001, honors chair 2000, ex-officio treas. 2000—01, co-chair benefit concert 2000—02, chair bylaws com. 2004—05, chair meml. svc., chair accompanists, Alumnae Chpt. Nat. Achievement award 1998, Rose of Honor 2000, chpt. cert. recognition 2001, 2003). Republican. Presbyterian. Avocations: reading, travel, needlework design. Home and Office: 10449 Lafayette St Northglenn CO 80233-4249

KAPPNER, AUGUSTA SOUZA, academic administrator; b. Bronx, NY, June 25, 1944; d. Augusto and Monica Thomasina (Fraser) Souza; m. Thomas Kappner, Aug. 14, 1965; children: Tania, Diana. AB, Barnard Coll., 1966; MSW, Hunter Coll., N.Y.C., 1968; DSW, Columbia U., 1984. Cert. social worker, N.Y. Lectr., community affairs specialist Dept. Urban Affairs, Grad. Div., Hunter Coll., 1968-70; adj. instr., field supr. N.Y.C.C., 1970-71; instr., coord. urban leadership unit Columbia U. Sch. Social Wk., 1970-72; asst.

prof., dir. admissions and student svcs. SUNY, Stony Brook, 1973-74; assoc. prof., chmn. human svcs. divsn. LaGuardia C.C., 1974-78, prof., dean continuing edn., 1978-84; dean acad. affairs Adult & Continuing Edn., CUNY, 1984, dean acad. affairs, instructional rsch., adult learning, 1984-86; pres. Borough of Manhattan C.C./CUNY, 1986-92; asst. sec. of vocat. and adult edn. Dept. of Edn., Washington, 1993-95; pres. Bank Street Coll., N.Y.C., 1995—. Cons. in field; lectr. in field; former chair Adult Literacy Media Alliance; mem. adv. panel Nat. Ctr. Innovation in Governing Am. Edn., Nat. Writing Project; mem. panel Edn. Policy NYC Dept. Edn, Am. Coun. on Edn. Commn. for Advancement of Racial and Ethnic Equity; former mem. Commn. Nation Lifelong Learners; commr., Commn. Higher Edn., Middle States Assn.; former mem. adv. bd. Fund for the Improvement Post Secondary Edn., US Dept. Edn. Trustees Marymount Manhattan Coll.; mem. N.Y. State Edn. Commr.'s Task Force for the Edn. of Children and Youth at Risk, N.Y. State Gov.'s Coun. on Literacy, N.Y.C. Bd. Edn. Chancellor's U./Schs. Collaborative steering com.; appointed by Mayor of City of N.Y. to Joint Commn. on Integrity in Pub. Schs.; bd. dirs. N.Y. Urban Coalition; mem. N.Y.C. Coun. on Econ. Edn. Whitney M. Young Jr. fellow, 1982, USPHS awardee, 1981, Ford Found. fellow, 1973, Silverman Fund awardee, 1968, NIMH fellow, 1967, others; recipient Harlem Sch. Arts Humanitarian award, 1990, Am. Assn. Women in Community and Jr. Colls. Presdl. award, 1989, Asian Ams. for Equality Community Svc. award, 1989, Columbia U. Medal of Excellence, 1988, Barnard Coll. medal of distinction, 1988, Found. for Child Devel. Centennial award, 1999, Morris T. Keeton award Coun. for Adult and Exptl. Learning, others. Mem. Am. Coun. on Edn.

KAPRAL, FRANK ALBERT, microbiologist, educator, immunologist, educator; b. Phila., Mar. 12, 1928; s. John and Erna Louise (Melching) K.; m. Marina Garay, Nov. 22, 1951; children: Frederick, Gloria, Robert; m. Esther McKenzie, May 10, 2003. BS, U. of the Scis. in Phila., 1952; PhD, U. Pa., 1956. With U. Pa., Phila., 1952-66, assoc. in microbiology, 1958-66; assoc. microbiologist Phila Gen. Hosp., 1962-64, chief microbiology research, 1964-66, chief microbiology, 1965-66; asst. chief microbiol. research VA Hosp., Phila, 1962-66; assoc. prof. med. microbiology Ohio State U., Columbus, 1966-69, prof. med. virology, immunology and med. genetics, 1969—95, prof. emeritus dept. molecular virology, immunology and med. genetics, 1995—. Cons. Ctr. Disease Control, Atlanta, 1980, Proctor and Gamble Co., 1981-87. Contbr. articles to profl. jours. Active Ctrl. Ohio Diabetes Assn., 1992-93. With AUS, 1946-47. Grantee, Ctrl. Ohio Diabetes Assn., 1992—93; Rsch. grant, NIH, 1959—95. Fellow Am. Acad. Microbiology, Infectious Diseases Soc. Am.; mem. AAAS, Am. Soc. for Microbiology, Am. Assn. for Immunologists, Sigma Xi. Democrat. Roman Catholic. Achievements include patents for implant chamber. Home: 873 Clubview Blvd S Columbus OH 43235-1771 Office: 2166B Graves Hall Columbus OH 43223-3226 Personal E-mail: elaureo2@yahoo.com.

KAPRANOS, ALEXANDER (FRANZ FERDINAND), singer, musician; b. Almondsbury, Gloucestershire, England, Mar. 20; Studied English Lit., Glasgow. Singer, guitarist The Blisters (changed name to The Karelia); played bass The Yummy Fur; lead singer and guitarist Franz Ferdinand, 2001—. Performer: 9 Songs, 2004; notable guest appearences Musikprogrammet-programmet om musik, 2004, Friday Night with Jonathan Ross, 2004, Paskvil, 2004, lead singer, guitarist (albums) Darts of Pleasure, 2003, Franz Ferdinand, 2004, (song-single) Take Me Out, 2004 (Best Video, Q Awards, 2004), Matinee, 2004, Micheal, 2004; performer: (DVD Single) Take Me Out, 2004, Matinee, 2004. Co-recipient Mercury Music prize, Britain, 2004, Award for GQ Internat. Band of Yr.; nominee Best Alternative Act, Best New Act, Best UK and Ireland Act, MTV Europe Music Awards, 2004. Address: Domino Recording Co PO Box 47039 London SW18 1WD England Office: Epic Records Inc Sony Music Entertainment Inc 550 Madison Ave New York NY 10022

KAPRIELIAN, WALTER, advertising executive; b. N.Y.C., June 2, 1934; s. Vartan and Shoushan (DerBargamian) K.; m. Julia Hachigian, July 7, 1957 (dec. Nov. 1983); children: Victoria Susan, Siran Marion, John Vartan; m. Dinaz Boga, May 20, 1988. AAS, SUNY, 1953. Licensed charterboat capt. Art dir. BBD&O, N.Y.C., 1953-64; group head, art dir. Grey Advt., N.Y.C., 1964-65; sr. art dir. Ketchum MacLeod & Grove, N.Y.C., 1965-66; v.p., head art dir., 1966-67; v.p., assoc. creative dir., 1967-71; sr. v.p., creative dir., 1971-77; exec. v.p., asst. gen. mgr., 1977-80; gen. mgr., 1980-81; pres., chief exec. officer Ketchum New York, 1981-82; ptnr., co-creative dir., vice chmn. Fearon O'Leary Kaprielian, Inc., 1983-84; chmn., creative dir. Kaprielian O'Leary Advt., 1984-95; pres. Walter Kaprielian & Co., East Hampton, N.Y., 1995—. Instr. N.Y.C. Tech. Coll., 1971-79, Sch. Visual Arts, 1982-88; mem. adv. bd. N.Y.C. Tech. Coll., 1980—; lectr. Graphic Arts Tech. Found., 1970-81; v.p. ADC Pub. Co., N.Y.C., 1986-88. Author/illustrator: The Captain's Cookbook, 1976, rev. edit., 1979; designer: Bliss in Chrysalis, 1968; designer/editor: The Consecration of a Cathedral, 1968; contbr. articles to profl. jours. V.p. Visual Communicators Scholarship Fund, 1986-88, pres., 1988-90; chmn. parish coun. Holy Cross Ch. of Armenia, 1965-66, Armenian Ch. of Holy Martyrs, 1968-69; bd. dirs. N.Y.C. Tech. Coll. Found., 1985-99, Fish Unlimited, 1994-2000. Recipient awards Art Dirs. Club N.Y., awards Art Dirs. Club N.J., awards Soc. Illustrators, awards Am. Inst. Graphic Arts, awards Type Dirs. Club, awards Clio, awards Graphis, awards Advt. Club N.Y., awards Am. Advt. Fedn.; Theodore Rossevelt Meml. medal; St. Gauden's medal. Mem. Am. Inst. Graphic Arts, Art Dirs. Club (bd. dirs. 1974-76, 78-81, 91-93, pres. 1981-83, chmn. adv. bd. 1983-85, mem. adv. bd. 1984—, 1st v.p. 1993, pres. visual communicators scholarship fund 1988-90), U.S. Power Squadron, Nat. Party Boat Owners Alliance, Internat. Game Fish Assn., Maidstone Gun Club, Knights of Vartan. Republican. Avocations: seafood cooking, fishing. Personal E-mail: wkapriel@optonline.net.

KAPS, WARREN JOSEPH, lawyer; b. Bklyn., June 4, 1930; m. Sydelle Tanenbaum, June 29, 1958; children: Lowell, Andrew. AB in Math. and Econs., Rutgers U., 1952, LLB, 1954; LLM, Yale U., 1955. Bar: N.J. 1955, D.C. 1955, U.S. Dist. Ct. N.J. 1955, U.S. Ct. Mil. Appeals 1957, U.S. Tax Ct. 1962, U.S. Ct. Appeals 1962, N.Y. 1964, U.S. Dist. Ct. N.Y. 1965. Law clk. to presiding justice N.J. Supreme Ct., 1954; asst. prof. law U. Ark., 1955-56, U. Md., 1959-60; assoc. Stein & Rosen, N.Y.C., 1960-64, ptnr. N.Y.C. and Ft. Lee, N.J., 1964-75; sole practice Hackensack, N.J., and N.Y.C., 1975-88; ptnr. Kaps & Barto, Hackensack, 1988—. Contbr. articles to profl. jours. Served to capt. JAGC, USAR, 1956-59. Recipient Nathan Burkan Copyright award, Fidelity Union Trust Co. Prize; Bacon scholar, N.J. State scholar; Sterling Grad. fellow. Mem. ABA, N.J. State Bar Assn. (cert. civil trial atty.), Bergen County Bar Assn., Assn. of Bar of City of New York, N.Y. State Bar Assn., Soc. of Am. Magicians (pres. 2001-02). Home: 34 Clover St Tenafly NJ 07670-2804 Office: Kaps & Barto 15 Warren St Hackensack NJ 07601-5436 Office Phone: 201-489-5277. E-mail: warren@kapsbarto.com, kapsbarto@earthlink.net.

KAPSCH, ROBERT JAMES, engineering and architectural historian; b. Elizabeth, N.J., July 25, 1942; s. Joseph Michael and Mary Elizabeth Kapsch; m. Elizabeth Perry Kephart, Nov. 11, 2000. BS in Engring., Rutgers U., 1964; MS in Mgmt., George Washington U., 1974, MA in Am. Studies, 1978; PhD in Engring. and Arch., Cath. U. Am., 1983; PhD in Am. Studies, U. Md., 1993. Chief HABS/HAER, 1980—95; spl. asst. to dir. Nat. Park Svc., Washington, 1996-2000, sr. scholar in hist. arch. and hist. engring., 2001—05. Author: Canals, 2004, Monocacy Aqueduct, 2005; mem. editl. bd. Bldgs. U.S. Publs. Series, 1991-94 Participant various hist. preservation activities, Washington, 1975—. Capt. USAR, 1964—68, Vietnam. Recipient Disting. Svc. medal, U.S. Dept. Interior, 2002. Mem.: AIA, ASCE (history and heritage com. 2000—03), Constrn. History Soc., Nat. R.R. Hist. Assn., Nat. Bldg. Mus., Hist. Medley Dist., Nat. Trust for Hist. Preservation, Nat. Preservation Inst. (bd. dirs. 2001—04), Am. Canal Soc., Soc. Archtl. Historians, Soc. for Indsl. Archeology (bd. dirs. 2001—04), Newcomen Soc., Cosmo Club. Avocations: antique toy trains, travel. Home: 15220 DuFief Dr North Potomac MD 20878-2411 Office: Ctr for Historic Engring and Architecture PO Box 38 Poolesville MD 20837 Office Phone: 301-349-0062. E-mail: robertkapsch@aol.com.

KAPSNER, CAROL RONNING, state supreme court justice; b. Bismarck, ND, Nov. 25, 1947; m. John Kapsner; children: Mical, Caithlin. BA in English lit., Coll. of St. Catherine; postgrad., Oxford U.; MA in English lit., Ind. U.; JD, U. Colo., 1977. Atty. Kapsner and Kapsner, Bismarck, 1977-98; justice ND Supreme Ct., 1198—. Mem. N.D. Bar Assn. (past bd. govs.), N.D. Trial Lawyers Assn. (past bd. govs.), Burleigh County Bar Assn. (pres. 1980, mem. Jud. Conference 1988-96). Office: Supreme Ct State Capitol 600 E Boulevard Ave Dept 180 Bismarck ND 58505-0530 Fax: 701-328-4480. E-mail: ckapsner@ndcourts.com.

KAPTEYN, HENRY CORNELIUS, physics professor, engineering educator; b. Oak Lawn, Ill., Jan. 21, 1963; m. Margaret Mary Murnane, 1988. BS, Harvey Mudd Coll., 1982; MA, Princeton U., 1984; PhD, U. Calif., Berkeley, 1989. Postdoctoral rschr. U. Calif., 1989-90; asst. prof. physics Wash. State U., Pullman, 1990-95, assoc. prof., 1995, U. Mich., Ann Arbor, 1996-99; prof. JILA, U. Colo., Boulder, 1999—. Contbr. articles to profl. jours. Regents fellow U. Calif., 1985, Sloan rsch. fellow, 1995. Fellow Optical Soc. Am. (Adolph Lomb medal 1993), Am. Phys. Soc.; mem. IEEE, Soc. Photo-Optical Instrumentation Engrs. (scholar 1988). Office: JILA Univ Colo Boulder CO 80309-0440 E-mail: kapteyn@jila.colorado.edu.

KAPTUR, MARCIA CAROLYN, congresswoman; b. Toledo, Ohio, June 17, 1946; BA, U. Wis., 1968; M. Urban Planning, U. Mich., 1974; postgrad., U. Manchester, (Eng.), 1974, MIT; LLD (hon.), U. Toledo. Urban planner; asst. dir. urban affairs domestic policy staff White House, 1977-79; mem. U.S. Congress from 9th Ohio dist., Washington, 1983—; mem. appropriations com., Agr. subcom., D.C. subcom., VA, HUD, and indep. agys. subcom. Bd. dirs. Nat. Ctr. Urban Ethnic Affairs; adv. com. Gund Found.; exec. com. Lucas County Democratic Com.; mem. Dem. Women's Campaign Assn. Mem. Am. Planning Assn., Am. Inst. Cert. Planners, NAACP, Urban League, Polish Mus., U. Mich. Urban Planning Alumni Assn. (bd. dirs.), Polish Am. Hist. Assn. Clubs: Lucas County Dem. Bus. and Profl. Women's, Fulton County Dem. Women's. Democrat. Roman Catholic. Office: US House of Reps 2366 Rayburn Washington DC 20515-0001 also: One Maritime Pla 6th Fl Toledo OH 43604*

KAPUR, KAILASH CHANDER, industrial engineering educator; b. Rawalpindi, Pakistan, Aug. 17, 1941; s. Gobind Ram and Vidya Vanti (Khanna) K.; m. Geraldine Palmer, May 15, 1969; children: Anjali Joy, Jay Palmer. BS, Delhi U., India, 1963; M of Tech., Indian Inst. Tech., Kharagpur, 1965; MS, U. Calif., Berkeley, 1968, PhD, 1969. Registered profl. engr., Mich. Sr. rsch. engr. Gen. Motors Rsch. Labs., Mich., 1969-70; sr. reliability engr. TACOM, U.S. Army, Mich., 1978-79; mem. faculty Wayne State U., Detroit, 1970-89, assoc. prof. indsl. engring. and ops., 1973-79, prof., 1979-89; prof., dir. Sch. Indsl. Engring. U. Okla., Norman, 1989-92; dir., indsl. engring. U. Wash., Seattle, 1992—. Vis. prof. U. Waterloo, Can., 1977-78; vis. scholar Ford Motor Co., Mich., summer 1973. Author: Reliability in Engineering Design, 1977; contbr. articles to profl. jours. Grantee GM, 1974-77, U.S. Army, 1978-79, U.S. Dept. Transp., 1980-82. Fellow Am. Soc. Quality Control; mem. Ops. Rsch. Soc. Am. (sr.), Inst. Indsl. Engrs. (assoc. editor 1980—). Home: 4484 E Mercer Way Mercer Island WA 98040-3828 Office: U Wash PO Box 352650 Seattle WA 98195-2650 Office Phone: 206-543-4604. Personal E-mail: kalkapur@hotmail.com. Business E-Mail: kkapur@u.washington.edu.

KAPURAL, LEONARDO, pain management specialist; s. Mile, MD and Zlata Kapural; m. Miranda Bajamic, MD, May 25, 1996; 1 child, Daniella. MD, U. Zagreb, Croatia, 1990, PhD, 1996. Diplomate Am. Bd. Anesthesiology, 2003, pain medicine Am. Bd. Anesthesiology, 2004. Postdoctoral fellow anesthesia rsch. McGill U., Montreal, Canada, 1991—92; postdoctoral fellow dept. physiology U. Conn., Farmington, 1992—96; resident dr. divsn. anesthesiology Cleve. Clinic, 1998—2001; chief fellow, pain mgmt. Cleve. Clinic Found., 2001—02, staff, pain mgmt., 2002—. Reviewer Anesthesia and Analgesia Jour., Cleve., 2001—. Author: approximately 30 articles and 27 abstracts. Mem.: North Am. Spine Soc. (assoc.), Am. Soc. Regional Anesthesia and Pain Mgmt. (assoc.), Am. Soc. Anesthesiology (assoc.), Internat. Assn. Study of Pain (assoc.), Am. Pain Soc. (assoc.). Achievements include research in discogenic lower back pain. Avocations: piano, basketball, travel. Office: The Cleveland Clinic Found 9500 Euclid Cleveland OH 44195 Home Fax: 216-444-9890; Office Fax: 216-444-8980.

KAPUT, JIM L., lawyer; b. Toms River, NJ, May 28, 1960; BS, U Pa., 1982; JD, Cornell U., 1986. Bar: Ill. 1987. Assoc. Sidley & Austin (now Sidley Austin Brown & Wood), Chgo., ptnr., 1994—2000; sr. v.p., gen. counsel The ServiceMaster Co., Downers Grove, Ill., 2000—. Avocation: running. Office: The ServiceMaster Co 3250 Lacey Rd Ste 600 Downers Grove IL 60515-1700

KARAAGAC, JOHN RAPHAEL, political writer; b. Boston, Oct. 2, 1963; s. Ihsan A. Karaagac and Edith Fay McDowell. BA, U. Calif., Berkeley, 1986; MPhil, Cambridge (Eng.) U., 1987; PhD with distinction, Johns Hopkins U., 1997. Polit. writer, 1997—. Author: Between Promise and Policy: Ronald Reagan and Conservative Reformism, 2000, John McCain: An Essay in Military and Political History, 2000. Mem. Phi Beta Kappa, Psi Upsilon.

KARABATSOS, ELIZABETH ANN, career counseling services executive; b. Geneva, Nebr., Oct. 25, 1932; d. Karl Christian and Margaret Maurine (Emrich) Brinkman; m. Kimon Tom Karabatsos, Apr. 21, 1957 (div. Feb. 1981); children: Tom Kimon, Maurine Elizabeth, Karl Kimon. BS, U. Nebr., 1954; postgrad., Ariz. State U., 1980; Cert. contemporary exec. devel., George Washington U., 1985; M Orgnl. Mgmt., U. Phoenix, 1994; student, Scottsdale (Ariz.) C.C., 1999. Cert. tchr. Ariz. Instr. bus. Fairbury (Nebr.) H.S., 1954—55; staff asst. U.S. Congress, Washington, 1955—60; with Karabatsos & Co. Pub. Rels., Washington, 1960—73; conf. asst. to asst. adminstr. and dep. adminstr. Gen. Services Adminstrn., Washington, 1973—76; dir. corr. Office Pres.-Elect, Washington, 1980; assoc. dir. adminstrv. svcs. Pres. Pers.-White House, Washington, 1981; dept. asst. to Sec. and Dep. Sec. Def., Washington, 1981—86, asst. to, 1987—89; dir. govt. and civic affairs McDonnell Douglas Helicopter Co., Mesa, Ariz., 1989—90, gen. mgr. gen. svcs., 1990—92, co. ombudsman, community rels. exec., 1992—95; exec. asst. to dir. adminstrn. State of Ariz., 1995—96; prin., owner Karabatsos & Assocs., bus. consulting and mediation svcs., Scottsdale, 1995—. Bur. chief Office Prevention and Health Promotion Ariz. Dept. Health Svcs., 1997-98; adj. prof. Met. Coll. Phoenix, 2004, Maricopa C.C., 2005, So. Mountain C.C., 2005 Mem. Nat. Mus. Women in Art, Washington; bd. dirs. U.S. C. of C. Com. on Labor & Tng.; mem. Gov.'s Sci. and Tech. Com.; mem. Ariz. Com. Employer Support the Guard and Res., 1991; active Gov. Com. for Ariz. Clean and Beautiful, World Affairs Coun. Ariz. Mem.: ASTD, AAUW, Ariz. Dispute Resolution Assn. (bd. dirs.), Assn. Conflict Resolution, Am. Arbitration Assn., Women in Def., U. Nebr. Cather Group, Internat. Friends Transformative Art, Order Ea. Star, Pi Beta Phi, Pi Omega Pi. Episcopalian. Home and Office: 4446 E Camelback Rd # 110 Phoenix AZ 85018 Office Phone: 602-956-3317. Office Fax: 602-954-0225. Personal E-mail: ebkarabats@aol.com.

KARADY, GEORGE GYÖRGY, electrical engineering educator, consultant; b. Budapest, Hungary, Aug. 17, 1930; arrived in U.S., 1976; s. Gyozo and Anna (Szamek) K.; 1 child, Gyuri. MSEE, Tech. U. Budapest, 1952, DEng, 1960, D (hon.), 1996. Registered profl. engr., NY, NJ, Que. From instr. to assoc. prof., docent Tech. U. Budapest, Hungary, 1952—66; lectr. U. Baghdad, Iraq, 1966—68, U. Salford, England, 1968—69; program mgr. Hydro Quebec Inst. of Rsch., Canada, 1969—76; chief elec. cons. engr. Ebasco Svcs., N.Y.C., 1976—86; prof. Salt River Project Chair Ariz. State U., Tempe, 1986—. Adj. prof. McGill U., Montreal, 1972—76, Poly. Inst. NY, 1980—86; lectr. U. Montreal, 1970—76. Author: Operation of Electric Appliances and Network (in Hungarian), 1964; (with others) Advances in Electronics and Electron Physics, 1976; co-author: Electric Power Systems, Vol. V (in Hungarian), 1963, Electrical Power Systems and Networks (in Hungarian), 1964, Electrical Energy Conversion and Transport, 2005; contbr. articles to profl. jours. Fellow IEEE (paper award 1982, working group achievement award 1986); mem. U.S. Nat. Com. of Internat. Conf. of Large Elec. Network (sec.-treas. 1978-94), Princeton Ski Club (bd. dirs. 1977-86). Avocations: skiing, sailing, tennis, opera. Home: 11836 N 134th Way Scottsdale AZ 85259-3642 Office: Ariz State U Ira Fulton Sch Engring Dept Elec Engring Tempe AZ 85287-5706 Office Phone: 480-965-6569. Business E-Mail: karady@asu.edu.

KARAGULLE KENDI, AYSE TUBA, radiologist, researcher; b. Ankara, Turkey, May 16, 1973; d. Mehmet and Ulku Karagulle; m. Mustafa Kendi, Oct. 1, 2001. Medicine, Hacettepe U., Ankara-Turkey, 1997. Radiology Specialist Turkey. Asst. prof. Kirikkale U. Sch. Of Medicine Radiology Dept., Kirikkale, Turkey, 2002—03; resident Ankara U. Sch. Of Medicine Radiology Dept., Ankara, Turkey, 1997—2001. Postdoctoral assoc. Cmrr U. Minn., Mpls., 2003. Office: Cmrr Univ Minn 2021 6th St SE Minneapolis MN 55455 Personal E-mail: drtubakendi@yahoo.com.

KARAIM, BETTY JUNE, retired librarian; b. Devils Lake, N.D., May 27, 1936; d. Erick Henry and Anna Caroline (Steen) Keck; m. William James Karaim, Dec. 7, 1955 (dec. 1983); children: Reed, Lisa, Ryan, Lynn, Rachel, Lee, Lara. BS in Edn., Mayville (N.D.) State U., 1958; postgrad., U. N.D., summer 1961; MLS, U. Okla., 1972; postgrad., No. Mont. Coll., 1979, 81. Libr. Cando (N.D.) High Sch., 1960-62; asst. libr., tchr. Mayville State Coll., 1962-79; libr. Havre (Mont.) Pub. Schs., 1979-82; libr. dir. Mayville State U., 1982-99, ret., prof. emerita, 1999. Bd. dirs. Mayville (N.D.) Pub. Libr., 1991-97, 2000—, pres., 1994-97, v.p., 2002-05, pres., 2005—; bd. dirs. Goose River Heritage Ctr., Mayville, 2000—, pres., 2002—; bd. dirs. M300 Assn. (arm of Mayville State U. Found.), 2000—, sec., 2002—05. Recipient Orville Johnson Meritorious Svc. award, 1992, Disting. Alumni award Mayville State U. Alumni Found., 1997. Democrat. Avocations: reading, travel. Home: 320 1st St NW Mayville ND 58257-1107 Personal E-mail: bjkaraim@polarcomm.com.

KARAKASHIAN, ARAM SIMON, physics professor; b. Phila., Nov. 16, 1939; s. Aram and Dickranoohi (Bobikian) K.; m. Barbara Mary Burke, July 20, 1975; children: John, Elizabeth. BA, Temple U., Phila., 1961, MA, 1963; PhD, U. Md., 1970. Asst. prof. U. Mass., Lowell, 1970-77, assoc. prof., 1977-82, prof. physics, 1982—, chmn. dept., 1987-93, assoc. chmn. dept., 1993—. Contbr. articles to profl. jours. Bd. dirs. Nat. Assn. Armenian Studies and Rsch., Belmont, Mass. Recipient NSF fellowship, 1964; grantee NSF, 1979-81. Mem. Am. Phys. Soc. (chmn. New Eng. sect. 1993-94), Sigma Xi, Sigma Pi Sigma. Avocation: armenian history and culture. Office: U Mass Lowell 1 University Ave Lowell MA 01854-5009

KARALEKAS, ANNE, marketing executive; b. Boston, Nov. 6, 1946; d. Christus and Helen (Vogiantzis) K. AB, Wheaton Coll., Norton, Mass., 1968; AM, Harvard U., 1969, PhD, 1974. Chief project mgr. def. and arms control project Commn. on Orgn. of Govt. for Conduct of Fgn. Policy, Washington, 1974-75; sr. staff mem. Senate Select Com. on Intelligence, Washington, 1975-78; sr. assoc. McKinsey & Co., Washington, 1978-85; mktg. mgr. The Washington Post, 1985-87, dir. mktg., 1987-89; pub. Washington Post Mag., 1989-96, dir. specialty products group, 1993-96; gen. mgr. Washington Sidewalk, Microsoft Corp., Washington, 1996-99; bd. dirs. Digital Globe, Longmont, 1999—. Author: History of the CIA, 1976; contbr. articles and book revs. to profl. jours. Advisor fgn. policy Mondale-Ferraro Presdl. Campaign, Washington, 1984; trustee Wheaton Coll., Norton, 1985-88. Mem. Council on Fgn. Relations, Phi Beta Kappa. Greek Orthodox. Avocation: twentieth century art and lit.

KARALEKAS, GEORGE STEVEN, advertising agency executive, political consultant; b. Boston, Nov. 26, 1939; s. Steven George and Sotiria (Sarris) K. BS, Boston U., 1962. Vice pres., assoc. media dir. Grey Advt., Inc., N.Y.C., 1962-70; dir. advt. services Can. Dry Corp., N.Y.C., 1970-72, dir. mktg. N.Y. ops., 1972-74; exec. v.p., dir. media and mktg., mgmt. account dir. deGarmo Advt., Inc., N.Y.C., 1974-80; sr. v.p., exec. dir. media, mgmt. dir. D'Arcy-MacManus & Masius, N.Y.C., 1980-85; pres. Karalekas & Co., N.Y.C. and Washington, 1985—. Sr. v.p., exec. dir. media November Group, Pres. Nixon, N.Y.C., Washington, 1971-72; sr. v.p., spl. advt. cons. Campaign 76, Pres. Ford, N.Y.C., Washington, 1975-76; sr. v.p., exec. dir. media Campaign 80, Pres. Reagan, N.Y.C., Washington, 1979-80; spl. advt. cons. Nov. Co., President Bush, N.Y.C., Washington, 1992. Mem. Republican Nat. Com., 1970— . Mem. Internat. Radio and TV Soc., Am. Mgmt. Assn. Republican. Greek Orthodox. Home: Holiday Point 8 Circle Dr Sherman CT 06784-1643 Office: Karalekas & Co 360 E 72nd St New York NY 10021-4753 also: 1211 Connecticut Ave NW Washington DC 20036-2701

KARALIS, JOHN PETER, computer company executive, lawyer; b. Mpls., July 6, 1938; s. Peter John and Vivian Karalis; m. Mary Curtis, Sept. 7, 1963; children: Amy Curtis, Theodore Curtis. BA, U. Minn., 1960, JD, 1963. Bar: Minn. 1963, Mass. 1972, Ariz. 1983, N.Y. 1986, Pa. 1986. Pvt. practice, Mpls., 1963-70; assoc. gen. counsel Honeywell Inc., Mpls., 1970-83, v.p., 1982-83; pvt. practice Phoenix, 1983-85; sr. v.p., gen. counsel Sperry Corp., N.Y.C., 1985-87; v.p. gen. counsel Apple Computer Inc., Cupertino, Calif., 1987-89; of counsel Brown and Bain, Phoenix, 1989-92; sr. v.p. corp. devel. Tektronix, Inc., Portland, 1992-98; ret. Mem. bd. advisors Ctr. for Study of Law, Sci. and Tech., Ariz. State U. Coll. Law, Tempe, 1983-89, 2000—, adj. prof., 1990-91. Author: International Joint Ventures, A Practical Guide, 1992. Recipient Disting. Achievement award Ariz. State U., Tempe, 1985. Mem. Met. Club (N.Y.C.).

KARAMAS, JOYCE EFTHEMIA, art educator, consultant, artist; b. Chgo., July 27, 1926; d. Nicholas Ernest Karamesoutis and Anastasia Asemake Vaselopoulos. BA in Art Edn., Sch. Art Inst., Chgo., 1951; MLS, Chgo. State U., 1961. Cert. art tchr. K-12 Ill., sch. libr. Ill. Tchr. Chgo. Pub. Schs., 1951—62, art supr., 1962—72, tchr., libr., 1972—80, art. coord. curriculum dept., 1980—85. Coord. sch. art at local mus., Chgo., 1962—72, Chgo., 1980—84; coord. organized children's exhibits at pub. places, Chgo., 1980—84. Exhibited in group shows at Mus. Contemporary Crafts, N.Y.C., 1966, Ill. State Traveling Exhbn., 1968, one-woman shows include Chgo. Pub. Libr., 1972. Recipient Merit award, Am. Craftsmen Coun., 1966, Invitational award, Ill. Craftsmen coun., 1968. Avocations: photography, travel. Home: PO Box 174 3057 Peach St Douglas MI 49406-0174

KARAN, DONNA (DONNA FASKE), fashion designer; b. Forest Hills, N.Y., Oct. 2, 1948; m. Mark Karan, 1971 (div.); 1 child, Gabrielle; m. Stephan Weiss, 1983 (dec. June 2001) BFA, Parsons Sch. Design, 1987. Intern Liz Claiborne; With Addenda Co., to 1968; with Anne Klein & Co., NYC, 1968-84, assoc. designer, 1971-74, designer, 1974-84; owner, designer, ptnr. Donna Karan Co., NYC, 1984-96, created DKNY clothing line, 1988, chmn. bd., chief designer, 1996—2001; (Donna Karan merges with Louis Vuitton Moet Hennessy (LVMH), 2001); chief designer Donna Karan Co., NYC, 2001—. Launched fragrance Donna Karan for Women, 1992, Cashmere Mist, DKNY, 1994, Chaos, Donna Karan, 1996, Black Cashmere, 2002. Showed first complete collection for Anne Klein & Co. in 1974; collaborator on Anne Klein collections with Louis dell'Olio; author: DKNY: NYC, 1994. Bd. dirs. Design Industries Found. for AIDS; co-chair Kids for Kids, 1993, Ovarian Cancer Rsch. Super Saturday, East Hampton, N.Y, summers 1998, 99. Recipient Coty award, 1977, Awards Coun. of Fashion Designers of Am., 1985, 86, 92, Frontrunner award Sara Lee Corp., 1992, "Night of the Stars" Award The Fashion Group; co-recipient (with Louis dell'Olio) Coty Return award, 1981, Coty Hall of Fame citation, 1982, Coty award, 1984; named Menswear Designer of Yr. Coun. Fashion Designers Am., 1992. Mem. Fashion Designers Am. (bd. dirs.) Office: Donna Karan Co 550 Seventh Ave New York NY 10018 also: Donna Karan Inc West 40th St New York NY 10018 Office Phone: 212-789-1500.

KARAN, HIROKO ITO, chemistry professor; b. Osaka City, Japan, Jan. 7, 1942; arrived in US, 1965; d. Seito and Haruko Ito; m. Jeffrey David Karan, Dec. 28, 1972; 1 child, Elizabeth Mika. MS, Wilkes Coll., Wilkes-Barre, Pa.,

1967; PhD, Brown U., 1972. Rsch. asst. Hoshi Coll. Pharmacy, Tokyo, 1964-65; rsch. assoc. Fels Rsch. Inst., Temple U., Phila., 1971-72; rsch. scientist NYU, N.Y.C., 1972-73, 76-77; vis. instr. Hoshi Coll. Pharmacy, Tokyo, 1973-74; asst. prof. organic chemistry Medgar Evers Coll. CUNY, Bklyn., 1977-85, assoc. prof. Medgar Evers Coll., 1985-90, prof. Medgar Evers Coll., 1990—; asst. dean Medgar Evers Coll., 1993-98, dean, 1998—. Contbr. articles to profl. jours. Recipient svc. award Medgar Evers Coll., 1984, 90; grantee NIH, 1979—. Mem. Am. Chem. Soc. (chmn., bd. dirs. Bklyn. subsect. 1982-88, chmn. metrowomen chemists com. 1989, bd. dirs. N.Y. sect. 1985, 89-90, sec. 1989-90, Outstanding Svc. award 1993), Sigma Xi. Office: CUNY Medgar Evers Coll 1150 Carroll St Brooklyn NY 11225-2201 E-mail: hiroko@mec.cuny.edu.

KARANIKAS, ALEXANDER, language educator; b. Manchester, N.H., Oct. 5, 1916; s. Stephen and Vaia (Olgas) K.; m. Helen J. Karagianes, Jan. 2, 1949; children: Marianthe Vaia, Diana Christine, Cynthia Maria. Student, U. N.H., 1934-36; AB cum laude, Harvard, 1939; MA, Northwestern U., 1950, PhD in English, 1953. With N.H. Writers Project, 1940-41; editor Allegheny-Kiski Valley Edit. The CIO News, 1941-42; radio news commentator Sta. WMUR, Manchester, 1946; grad. asst. Northwestern U., Evanston, Ill., 1950-52; instr. Kendall Coll., Evanston, Ill., 1952-53, Northwestern U., Evanston, 1953-54, 57-58; mem. faculty U. Ill. at Chgo., 1954—, prof. English, 1974-82, prof. emeritus, 1982—; owner Deerhaven Orchard, 1974-96. Cons. in field. Author: When a Youth Gets Poetic, 1934, In Praise of Heroes, 1945, Tillers of a Myth: The Southern Agrarians as Social and Literary Critics, 1966 (Friends of Lit. award 1967), (with Helen Karanikas) Elias Venezis, 1969, Hellenes and Hellions: Modern Greek Characters in American Literature, 1981; (musical) Nashville Dreams, 1991; (screenplay) Marika (Neptune award Moondance Film Festival 2003); (poetry) Stepping Stones, 1994. Mem. nat. cabinet Am. Youth Congress, 1937-39; exec. sec. Mass. Youth Coun., 1939-40; co-chmn. Nat. Bicentennial Symposium on the Greek Experience in Am., 1976; Publicity dir. N.H. Ind. Voters, 1946; sec. Manchester Vets. Council, 1946; Candidate for Congress, 1948; exec. com. United Hellenic Am. Congress, 1983—; exec. sec. Am. Coun. for Dem. Greece, 1947. With USAAF, 1942-45, Alaska corr. YANK, 1943-45. Named to Goffstown (NH) H.S. Hall of Fame, 2004. Mem. Hellenic Profl. Soc. Ill., Modern Greek Studies Assn., Screen Actors Guild, Friends of Lit., Harvard Club Chgo., Phi Eta Sigma, Order Ahepa (dist. sec. 1946). Mem. Greek Orthodox Ch. Home: 618 N Harvey Ave Oak Park IL 60302-1740 Office: Univ of Ill at Chicago English Dept Chicago IL 60680

KARAS, JAMES, public relations executive, engineering executive; b. New Brunswick, NJ, May 23, 1958; s. James Panayagelos and Angeliki (Karavi-otis) Karas; m. Nancy Ann Davino, June 7, 1986; children: Jimmy Carl Panayagelos, Kristy Daniel, Nikki Ann. Degree in mech. engring., NY Inst. Tech., 1978, Rutgers U., 1979; degree, Middlesex Coll., 1999. Cert. instr. NJ Defensive Driving, 2004. Promotor, sponsor Nat. Physique Com., NJ, 1986—91, Internat. Fedn. Body Builders, 1986—92; dir. devel. Internat. Ctr. for Ednl. Advancement, Newark, 1990—; CEO Savage Promotions, Somerset, NJ, 1990—; steward NJ Turnpike Authority, Newark, 2004—; exec. officer Internat. Peace Angles Project, N.Y.C., 2002—. V.p. product devel. Xelat, East Brunswick, NJ, 1996—98; adv. Maxum Wireless, Ft. Lee, NJ, 1996—2000; cons. in field; bail bondsman/bounty hunter Tri-State area. *In 1988, based upon its expanding reputation and revenue base, the Company opteded Sponsorship of Mr. Olympia-Ms. Olympia-The Arnold Schwarzenegger Classic. Continuing growth in 1989, the Company moved itself into actual participation. Jim, hand picked and headed "Team Savage", a Powerlifting team that included two World Record-holding bench press champions. The team headed by Jim Karas went on taking 1st place honors in three major powerlifting events, which led the team to be recognized in the national magazine Powerlifting U.S.A. Expansion continued in 1990-1991, with events being showcased on ESPN Network, Muscle Sport U.S.A., WWF (World Wrestling Federation-Vincent McMahon), and the Taj Mahal in Atlantic City, New Jersey.* Author: Sponsorship & Promotional Manual, 1985, 3d edit., 1987. Mem.: AFL-CIO (steward), Internat. Fedn. Profl. and Tech. Engrs. (steward). Greek Orthodox. Avocations: weightlifting, football, baseball, reading. Office: Savage Promotions 36 S Dover Ave Somerset NJ 08873 Business E-Mail: savagepromotions@aol.com.

KARAS, KENNETH M., federal judge; b. Colorado Springs, Colo., Apr. 18, 1964; BA magna cum laude, Georgetown U., 1986; JD, Columbia U. Sch. Law, 1991. Bar: NY 1992. Law clerk to the Honorable Reena Raggi US Dist. Ct. (Ea. Dist. NY), 1991—92; asst. US atty. US Dist. Ct. (So. Dist. NY), 1992—2004, organized crime and terrorism chief, criminal div., judge, 2004—. Office: Daniel Patrick Moynihan US Courthouse 500 Pearl St Room 920 New York NY 10007-1312*

KARASA, NORMAN LUKAS, home builder, developer, geologist; b. Balt., June 10, 1951; s. Norman and Ona K.; m. Lois J. Hansen, Jan. 4, 1974; children: Andrew, Jane. AB in Geology, Rutgers Coll., 1973; MS in Geophysics, U. Wyo., 1976; MBA in Fin., U. Colo., Colorado Springs, 1990. Systems mgr. Brit. Petroleum, N.Y.C., 1973-74; seismic processing leader Phillips Petroleum, Bartlesville, Okla., 1976-79, geophysicist Houston, 1979-80; internat. spl. project geophysicist Marathon Oil, Findlay, Ohio, 1980-82, internat. exploration geophysicist Houston, 1982-85, internat. reservoir geologist/geophysicist, 1985-86; home builder, designer, owner D'signer Inc., Monument Homes, Colo., 1986—, developer, hydrologist, 1992—; owner Tri-Lakes Montessori Sch.; ind. broker (realtor), 1997—. Mem. Home Builder Assocs., Nat. Audubon Soc. Office: Monument Homes PO Box 1423 Monument CO 80132-1423

KARASS, ALAN MICHAEL, school librarian, educator; b. Norwalk, Conn., Oct. 10, 1965; s. Morris Irving and Beatrice (Berger) Karass. BA, Clark U., Worcester, Mass., 1987; MS, Simmons Coll., Boston, 1994; MA, U. Conn., 2004. Music libr. Coll. Holy Cross, Worcester, 1992—, lectr., 2004—. Editor: Music Reference Svcs. Quar., 2001—. Mem.: Am. Recorder Soc. (pres. 2002—). Office: Coll Holy Cross 1 College St Worcester MA 01610

KARASU, T(OKSOZ) BYRAM, psychiatrist, educator, writer; b. Feb. 11, 1935; MD, U. Istanbul, Turkey, 1959. Jr. intern St. Jeanne D'Arc Hosp., Montreal, Can., 1963-64; sr. intern St. John Gen. Hosp., New Brunswick, Can., 1964-65; resident in psychiatry Yale-New Haven Med. Ctr., 1967-68, Conn. Mental Health Ctr., 1968-69; fellow in psychiatry Yale U., New Haven, 1969; dir. dept. psychiatry Jacobi Med. Ctr., N.Y., 1975-93; prof. psychiatry Albert Einstein Coll. Medicine, Bronx, NY, 1981—, Silverman prof., chmn. psychiatry, 1993—, univ. chmn., 1998—. Chmn. Albert Einstein Coll. Medicine, 1993—; psychiatrist-in-chief Montefiore Med. Ctr., 1993—. Author: Wisdom in the Practice of Psychotherapy, 1992, Deconstruction of Psychotherapy, 1996, The Psychotherapists's Interventions, 1998, The Psychotherapist as Healer, 2001, The Art of Serenity, 2003; editor: Psychotherapy Research, 1982, The Psychiatric Therapies, 1984, Treatments of Psychiatric Disorders, 1989, others; editor-in-chief: Am. Jour. Psychotherapy, 1994—; contbr. articles to profl. jours.; author: The Art of Marriage Maintenance, 2005. Recipient Sigmund Freud award, 1997. Mem.: Am. Psychiat. Assn. (chmn. commn. 1979—83, task force 1981—90, practice guidelines in major depression 1993, revised 2000, Disting. Svc. award 1993, Spl. Presdl. award 1988, Disting. Life fellow). Office: 2 E 88th St New York NY 10128-0555 Also: Albert Einstein Coll Medicine 1300 Morris Park Ave Bronx NY 10461-1975

KARATZ, BRUCE E., construction executive; b. Chgo., Oct. 10, 1945; s. Robert Harry and Naomi Rae (Goldstein) K.; children: Elizabeth, Matthew, Theodore. BA, Boston U., 1967; JD, U. So. Calif., 1970. Bar: Calif. 1971. Assoc. Keatinge & Sterling, Los Angeles, 1970-72; assoc. corp. counsel Kaufman and Broad, Inc., Los Angeles, 1972-73, dir. forward planning Irvine, Calif., 1973-74; pres. Kaufman and Broad Provence, Aix-en-Provence, France, 1974-76, Kaufman and Broad France, Paris, 1976-80, Kaufman and Broad Devel. Group, Los Angeles, 1980-86; chmn., pres., CEO KB Home (formerly Kaufman and Broad Home Corp.), Los Angeles, 1985—, also bd. dirs.; also chmn. bd. dirs. Kaufman and Broad Home Corp., Los Angeles, 1993. Bd. dirs. Avery Dennison, Edison Internat., Nat. Golf Properties, Inc., Honeywell Internat., Inc., Kroger Co.; trustee RAND Corp. Founder Mus. Contemporary Art, L.A., 1981; bd. councilors U. So. Calif. Law Ctr. Mem. Calif. Bus. Roundtable (chmn.), Coun. on Fgn. Rels., Pacific Coun. on Internat. Policy, L.A. World Affairs Coun. (chmn.). Democrat. Avocations: modern art, skiing, travel, golf. Office: KB Home 10990 Wilshire Blvd Fl 7 Los Angeles CA 90024-3913*

KARATZ, WILLIAM WARREN, lawyer; b. Benton Harbor, Mich., Aug. 9, 1926; s. Harry E. and Grace M. (Campbell) K.; m. Barbara Lansburgh Low, May 25, 1989. Ph.B. (La Verne Noyes scholar), U. Chgo., 1948; postgrad., Sch. Pol. Sci., 1949; LL.B. (Harlan Fiske Stone scholar), Columbia U., 1952. Bar: N.Y. State 1953, U.S. Supreme Ct. 1960. Assoc. in law Columbia U. Sch. Law, N.Y.C., 1952-53; assoc. firm Winthrop, Stimson, Putnam & Roberts, N.Y.C., 1953-62, ptnr., 1963-86, sr. counsel, 1987-2000; retired ptnr. Pillsbury Winthrop, 2001—. Bd. editors: Columbia Law Rev, 1950-52. Served with USN, 1944-46. Fellow Am. Bar Found. (life); mem. ABA, Am. Law Inst. (life), Bar Assn. City of N.Y. (mem. exec. com. 1969-73, chmn. 1972-73, v.p. 1973-74), N.Y. State Bar Assn., (mem. ho. of dels. 1972-77), Am. Coll. Trial Lawyers, Am. Judicature Soc., Century Assn., Confrerie des Chevaliers du Tastevin (grand officer). Home: 100 E 50th St New York NY 10022-6805 Office: Pillsbury Winthrop 1540 Broadway New York NY 10036

KARAVITES, PETER, retired historian; b. Patras, Greece, Apr. 5, 1932; came to U.S. Apr. 14, 1953; s. Themistocles and Kalliope (Aravanis) K.; m. Christine Sophie; children: Kalliope, Themistocles. MA, U. Chgo., 1959; PhD, Loyola U., Chgo., 1971. Teaching asst. Loyola U., Chgo., 1963-68, Rome, 1968-69; asst. prof. Appalachian State U., Boone, N.C., 1971-77, Bridgewater (Mass.) State Coll., 1978-84, assoc. prof., 1984-87, prof., 1987—2005, ret., 2005. Author: Capitulation Treaties, 1982, Promise-Giving & Treaty-Making, Homer & the Near East, 1992, Evil, Freedom, and the Road to Perfection in Clement of Alexandria, 1998; contbg. editor Greek-Am. Review mag.; contbr. numerous articles on modern Greek politics to Greek-Am. newspapers and mags., articles to sci. jours. Recipient: Am. Council of Learned Socs. fellowship, Inst. Advanced Studies Fellowship, Distinguished Svc. Award, Bridgewater State Coll.; named Archon of Ecumenical Patriarchate. Mem. Am. Philological Assn., Friends of Ancient History, Am. Hellenic Ednl. Profl. Assn., Assn. of Ancient Historians. Greek Orthodox. Avocations: cantor, byzantine music. Office: Bridgewater State Coll Dept History Bridgewater MA 02325-0001 Home: 95 Village Dr Quincy MA 02169-0946 Personal E-mail: pk470@gis.net.

KARAYANIS, PLATO STEVEN, opera company executive; b. Pitts., Dec. 26, 1928; BFA, Carnegie Mellon U., 1952; artist's diploma in performance, Curtis Inst. Singer, stage dir., Luzern and Zürich, Switzerland, 1958-65, Met. Opera Nat. Co., 1965-67; exec. v.p., treas. Affiliate Artists Inc., 1967-77; mgr. rehearsal dept. San Francisco Opera, 1965; gen. dir. The Dallas Opera, 1977-2000; artistic cons. Palm Beach Opera, 2002—04. Chmn. Opera Am.; co-developer Affiliation Artist Opera Program, San Francisco; dir. opera, Fed. Republic of Germany and Switzerland. Vice chmn. alumni coun. Curtis Inst. Music, 2004—; bd. dirs. Santa Fe Opera. Grantee Martha Baird Rockefeller Fund Music; recipient Excellence in the Creative Arts, Dallas Hist. Soc., 1993. Mem.: Dallas Assembly, Opera Am. (chmn. bd. dirs. 1993—97), Sigma Alpha Iota.

KARAYANNIS, MARIOS NICHOLAS, lawyer; b. Athens, Greece, Mar. 11, 1961; came to U.S., 1965; s. Nicholas Marios and Alexandra N. Karayannis; m. Kathryn Mary Diamond, Oct. 1, 1988; children: Kathleen A., Nicholas M. BS in Psychology, U. Ill., 1983; JD, John Marshall Law Sch., Chgo., 1986. Bar: Ill. 1986, U.S. Dist. Ct. (no. dist.) Ill. 1986, U.S. Supreme Ct. 1996, U.S. Tax Ct. 1997, U.S. Ct. Appeals (7th cir.) 1997. Asst. state's atty. Kane County State's Atty.'s Office, Geneva, Ill., 1986-90; assoc. Brady & Jensen, Elgin, Ill., 1991—. Mem. Law Rev. John Marshall Law Sch., 1984-86. Coach Youth Soccer League, Elgin, 1998. Mem. ATLA, Ill. Bar Assn., Ill. Trial Lawyers Assn., Kane County Bar Assn., Kiwanis. Greek Orthodox. Avocations: golf, travel, fishing. Office: Brady & Jensen 2425 Royal Blvd Elgin IL 60123-2579 Office Phone: 847-695-2000. Business E-Mail: karayannis@bradylaw.com.

KARBHARI, VISTASP M., engineering educator, researcher; b. Dec. 21, 1961; BCE, U. Poona, India, 1984, M in Structural Engring., 1985; PhD, U. Del., 1991. Rsch. asst. prof., scientist U. Del., Newark, 1991-95; asst. prof. U. Calif., San Diego, 1995-97, assoc. prof., 1997—2001, prof., 2001—. Contbr. over 300 articles to profl. jours. Recipient Best Paper award Am. Soc. Metals/Engring. Soc. Detroit, 1992, CIICE, 1999, ASC, 2000, Charles Pankow award for innovation in design Civil Engring. Rsch. Found., 1996, Career award NSF, 1997; Powell Faculty fellow, 1997—. Mem. ASCE, ASM, ACI, Internat. Soc. for Structural Health Monitoring of Intelligent Infrastructures, Internat. Inst. for FRP in Constrn., Soc. Materials and Process Engring. Office: Univ Calif San Diego Bldg 409 University Ctr 9500 Gilman Dr # Mc0085 La Jolla CA 92093-5004 Office Phone: 858-534-6470. Business E-Mail: vkarbhari@ucsd.edu.

KARCH, JACQUELINE, artist; b. Newark, Jan. 17, 1946; d. Samuel Arthur and Miriam Francis K.; m. William Clinton Keach, June 27, 1991. Student, Art Students League, 1962—66; BFA, Syracuse U., 1968; MAT, R.I. Sch. of Design, 1971. Art tchr. Providence Pub. Schs., 1972-2000; artist, ceramic tile Ceramic Tiles, Providence, 1983-2000, LeLand, N.C., 2000—; tchr. art for trainable mentally disabled New Hanover H.S., Wilmington, NC, 2001—. Judge Spring Art Show Franklin Sq. Gallery, Southport, NC, 2005. One-woman shows include Gallery 401, Providence, RI, 1980, 1987, WHQR Gallery, Wilmington, N.C., 2003, exhibited in group shows at San Regret Gallery, Boston, 1980, Am. Soc. on Aging, San Diego, 1988, Gallery 401, Providence, 1986, Bell St. Gallery, 1991—92, visual documentary, Trinity Square Repertory Theatre Productions, 1983—85, Jewish Home for the Aged, 1988; costume designer: (plays) The Charlatans, 1972; The Red Hat; author: Recipes Remembered, 1996. Mem. The Arts Students League (life). Avocations: animal rescue, calligraphy, costume design, cooking, gardening. Office: Ceramic Tiles-Jacqueline Karch 904 Woodridge Ct SE Leland NC 28451 Office Phone: 910-383-6108.

KARCHER, JOHN DRAKE, textile and apparel company executive; b. Washington, Sept. 10, 1939; s. Raymond Edward and Mary Frances (Drake) K.; B.B.A., Wake Forest U., 1961; M.B.A., Wharton Sch., U. Pa., 1964; m. Lois Allison Lynch, Apr. 3, 1965; children: Kimberly P. Karcher-Nelson, John Drake, II, Christopher Brett. Pres. Wamsutta Decorative Fabrics, N.Y.C., 1972-77, Baxter/Kelly, Inc., N.Y.C., 1977-80; pres., dir. Scorpio Ventures, Inc., cons. and investment firm, Darien Conn., 1981-83; v.p. mktg. home fashions div. Dan River Inc., N.Y.C., 1983-84; pres., mktg. dir. Soc. Brand Industries, Inc., N.Y.C., 1985-87; chmn. bd., pres., chief exec. officer, dir. P.L. Industries, Inc., N.Y.C., 1987—, P.L. Mex., LLC, N.Y.C., 1995—. Co-chmn. Ox Ridge Sch. PTA, Darien, 1977-78; mem. bldg. fund drive Darian YMCA, 1977; head coach Darien Youth Hockey, 1977-79, Darien Little League, 1977-79, Darien Babe Ruth League, 1981-83; active fund raising Wake Forest U., New Canaan Country Sch.; bd. dirs. Bucknell U. Parents Assn., 1990-93, chmn. devel. com., mem. exec. com., 1991-93, chairperson fund raising com., 1992-93. Named Darien Little League Coach of Yr., 1977. Office: PL Industries Inc 500 5th Ave Ste 5530 New York NY 10110-5521

KARCHIN, LOUIS SAMUEL, composer, educator; b. Sept. 8, 1951; s. Isadore David and Ida (Kessler) K. MusB, U. Rochester, 1973; MA, Harvard U., 1975, PhD, 1978. Asst. prof. music NYU, N.Y.C., 1979-85, assoc. prof. music, 1985-99, prof., 2000—. Pres. U.S. sect. Internat. Soc. for Contemporary Music, 1981-83, chmn., 1983-85; pub. C. F. Peters Corp. Composer: Capriccio for Violin and Seven Instruments, 1978, Duo for Violin and Cello, 1981, Viola Variations, 1982, Songs of John Keats, 1985, Songs of Distance and Light, 1988, Sonata for Cello and Piano, 1989, Romulus, an Opera in One Act, 1990, String Quartet, 1991, A Way Separate, 1992, Ricercare, 1992, Galactic Folds for chamber ensemble, 1993, Sonata da Camera, 1994, Summer Song, 1994, Rustic Dances, 1995, String Quartet No. 2, 1995, Rhapsody for Orchestra, 1996, Cascades, 1997, American Visions: Two Songs on Poems of Yevgeny Yevtushenko, 1998, Quartet for Percussion, 2000, Deux Poèmes de Mallarmé, 2001, Voyages for alto sax and piano, 2001, Carmen de Boheme, 2002, Orpheus, a Masque for baritone, instruments, and dance, 2003, Roethke Songs, 2004; commd. by Fromm Found., 1994, 2003, Koussevitzky Found., 1998, Barlow Found., 2001. Recipient Koussevitsky Composition prize Tanglewood, 1971, Joseph H. Bearns prize Columbia U., 1972, Composer award NEA, 1982, 83, Walter N. Hinrichsen award, AAAL, 1985, Heckscher Found. prize, 1999, Goddard Lieberson prize AAAL, 2001, Maurice Abravanel Disting. vis. composer U. Utah, 2002, Composition award Nat. Tchrs. Singing, 2004, Recording award Aaron Copland Fund, 2004. Office: NYU 24 Waverly Pl Rm 268 New York NY 10003-6757 Office Phone: 212-998-8303.

KARCZ, ANDRZEJ, literature educator; b. Radom, Poland, Oct. 17, 1961; arrived in U.S., 1988; s. Jan and Ewa Karcz; m. Anna Karcz, July 20, 1996; 1 child, Agatha. MA, Cath. U. of Lublin, Poland, 1986; PhD, U. Chgo., 1999. Instr./rschr. Cath. U. of Lublin, 1986—88; asst. prof. U. Kans., Lawrence, 1999—. Author: (book) The Polish Formalist School and Russian Formalism, 2002, Texts From Far and Near: Essays on Literature and Other Matters, 2003; contbr. articles and revs. to profl. jours., encys.; editor: Czeslaw Milosz "Moj Wilenski Opiekun" Listy Czeslawa Milosza Do Manfreda Kridla, 2005. Scholar, Stefan Batory Found., 1996. Mem.: Am. Assn. Advancement Slavic Studies, Am. Assn. Tchrs. Slavic and East European Langs., Polish Inst. Arts and Scis. of Am. Office: U Kans Slavic Dept 1445 Jayhawk Blvd Rm 2133 Lawrence KS 66045

KARCZEWSKI, LISA A., lawyer; b. Toledo, Ohio, Sept. 1, 1970; d. Thomas and Gloria Karczewski. BSc, Mich. State Univ., 1997; JD, Univ. of the Pacific, Sacramento, Calif., 2000. Bar: Calif. 2000, registered: U.S. PTO (patent atty.) 2002. Med. rsch. asst. Tulane Univ. Sch. of Medicine, New Orleans, 1993—94; rsch. asst. William Beumont Hosp., Royal Oak, Mich., 1994—97; law clerk Calif. Inst. of Tech., Pasadena, Calif., 1999; assoc. atty. Fulwider Patton et al, L.A., 2000—03, Chan Law Group LC, L.A., 2004—. Contbr. articles pub. to profl. jour. Nat. resource defense counsel NRDC, N.Y., 2002—; mem. L.A. County Mus. of Art, L.A., 2000—, Met. Mus. of Art, N.Y., 2004—. Mem.: Am. Intellectual Property Law Assn., Beverly Hills Bar Assn. Avocations: exercise, art, reading, writing, travel.

KARDON, JANET, museum director; b. Phila. d. Robert and Shirley (Drasin) Stolker; m. Robert Kardon, Nov. 19, 1955; children: Ross, Nina, Roy. BS in Edn., Temple U.; MA in Art History, U. Pa. Lectr. Phila. Coll. Art, 1968-75, dir. exhbns., 1975-78; dir. Inst. Contemporary Art, Phila., 1978-89, Am. Craft Mus., N.Y.C., 1989-95; ind. curator, 1996—. Adj. prof. Fashion Inst. of Tech., N.Y.C., Pratt Inst., Bklyn., Cooper Hewit; cons., panel mem. Nat. Endowment for Arts, 1975—; mus. panel mem. Pa. Coun. on Arts, Phila., 1988—; U.S. commr. Venice Biennale, Venice, 1980. Exhibitions include Labyrinths, Time, Artists SEts and Costumes, Laurie Anderson, Robert Mapplethorpe, David Salle, Gertrude and Otto Natzler; editor: Twentieth Century American Craft: A Centenary Project, The Ideal Home, 1900-1920, Revivals/Diverse Traditions, 1920-1945, Craft in the Machine Age, 1920-1945. Grantee Nat. Endowment for Arts, 1978. Home and Office: 150 E 69th St Apt 12G New York NY 10021-5704 Office Phone: 212-439-1803. Personal E-mail: jakardon@aol.com.

KARDON, ROBERT, mortgage company executive; b. Phila., Mar. 8, 1922; s. Morris and Sophie (Winkleman) K.; m. Janet Stolker, Nov. 19, 1949; children— Roy, Nina, Ross. Student, U. Miami (Fla.), 1940-42, Shriveham Am. U., Swindon, Eng., 1945-46. Chmn. bd. B.T. Babbitt Co., Inc., 1964-66, Pitts. Mortgage Corp., 1964-72, Murphree Mortgage Co., Nashville, 1966-72, Kardon Investment Co., 1945-75, Peoples Bond & Mortgage Co., Phila., 1950-72. Chmn. bd., v.p. United Container Co., Phila., 1938-75; pres., chief exec. officer Kardon Industries, Inc., 1974—, also chmn. Trustee Phila. Mus. Art. Served with AUS, 1942-46. Mem. Young Pres. Orgn., World Bus. Council. Home: 150 E 69th St # 12G New York NY 10021-5704 Office: Kardon Industries Inc 150 E 69th St Apt 12G New York NY 10021-5704

KARDOS, MEL D., lawyer, educator; b. Phila., Feb. 6, 1947; s. Julius S. and Rose (Klein) K.; children: Lindsay Dara, Matthew Daniel. BS, Temple U., 1970; MEd, Trenton State Coll., 1972; JD, U. Balt., 1975. Bar: Pa. 1975, N.J. 1975, U.S. Dist. Ct. (ea. dist.) Pa. 1975, U.S. Dist. Ct. N.J. 1975, U.S. Supreme Ct. 1984. Asst. pub. defender Bucks County, Doylestown, Pa., 1975-80; ptnr. Kardos & Lynch, Newtown, Pa., 1980, Kardos & Heley, Newtown, 1980-87, Kardos, Rickles, Sellers & Hand, Newtown, 1988—. Adj. prof. Temple U., Phila., 1987, Bucks County C.C., 1995. Sec., bd. dirs. Lower Bucks County Pa. chpt. ARC; mem. exec. bd. Bucks chpt. ARC; supr. Middletown Twp., Bucks County, 1998-2003, chmn. Mem. ABA, Assn. Trial Lawyers Am., Soc. for Am. Baseball Research. Democrat. Avocations: sports broadcasting, sports, history, politics. Office: Kardos Rickles Sellers & Hand 626 S State St Newtown PA 18940-1509 also: 28 West Lafayette Ave Trenton NJ 08608-2405 Office Phone: 215-968-6602, 609-989-7995. Business E-Mail: mkardos@krshlaw.com.

KAREEM, A'ISHA, educational consultant, counselor; b. Dallas, Jan. 11, 1947; d. James and Henrietta Payton; m. Thomas Abdul-Salaam; 1 child, Dawn Ali. BEd, U. of Pacific, 1971, MEd, 1976; PhD, Universal Life, Modesto, Calif., 1985, U. Santa Barbara, 2002. Cert. counselor, ednl. adminstr., in behavioral edn. Gen. edn. instr. Stockton (Calif.) Unified Sch. Dist., 1971—85; ednl. rschr. for behaviorally-challenged students Acad. Human Devel., Stockton, 1985—97; ednl. rschr. Clara Mohammed Schs., Stockton, 1998—2002; counselor, field advisor Calif. Dept. Corrections, Stockton, 1998—2002. Ednl. cons. U. of Pacific, Stockton, 1996—2002, adj. prof., 1998—2002; advisor San Joaquin County A+, Stockton, Calif.; mem. MAS Edn. Monitoring Team, Chgo., 1998—2002; bd. dirs. San Joaquin County Mental Health, Stockton, U. Calif. Affirmative Action, Oakland, 1990—95; program devel. Bush's New Am. Schools, Stockton, 1989—90; facilitator Rotary Read In, Stockton, 1994—2002; participant Black Pedagogy Group, San Francisco, 1982, Pacific Sociology of Edn., Monterey, Calif., 1984; rschr. U. Santa Barbara, 2000. Contbr. (book of poetry) Save Our Children: An Appeal to American Families, 1998; dir.: (ednl. video) Thriller Time, 1985 (Cable Showcase, 1986); composer, dir. Youth Excellence Showcase, 1990 ("Save Our Children" Proclamation, 1995), contbr. (performance theater) Children's Vision Theater, 1994; editor: (newsletter) PEACE, 1999. Mem. Haggin Mus., Stockton, 1996—2002; facilitator Am. Muslim Alliance, Fremont, Calif., 1994—2002, Drug Task Force, Stockton, 1987—92, We Are Family, Stockton, 1995—2002; state rep. Miller Family Genealogy, Dallas, 1972—2002; mem. Good Govt., Chgo., 1996—2002; elected area rep. Rep. Ctrl. Com., Stockton, 1996—98; mem. Profl. Bus. Women, Stockton, 1989—92, NAACP, Stockton, 1988—98. Nominee Stocktonian Of Yr., Am. Friends Assn., 1989, Jefferson award, 1990; named Valley Woman In History, Commn. On Status Of Women, 1989—2002; named to Hall of Fame, Stockton Unified Sch. Dist., 1994. Fellow: Am. Muslim Assn. (scholar 1985); mem.: Black Educators Assn., U. Pacific Alumni Assn., Muslim Am. Soc. (life), Stockton Metro Ministry. Achievements include research in significance of culture in education especially among student of African descent; the significance of rewards in behavior modification program. Home: 1242 W Rose St Stockton CA 95203 Office: Calif Dept Corrections 7150 E Arch Rd Stockton CA 95213-9006 Business E-Mail: habi@gotnet.com.

KAREL, STEVEN, lawyer; b. 1950; BS, Stanford U.; JD, Harvard U. V.p., gen. counsel Robert Half Internat. Inc., Menlo Pk., Calif., 1989—, sec., 1993—. Office: Robert Half International Inc 2884 Sand Hill Rd Menlo Park CA 94025*

KARELITZ, RICHARD ALAN, treasurer, lawyer; b. Elizabeth, N.J., Nov. 1, 1949; s. David Karelitz and Doris Frances (Tuck) Kahn; m. Virginia Lee Harris, Aug. 18, 1974; children: David Benjamin, Daniel Seth. AB, Coll.

William and Mary, 1971; JD, Boston U., 1974, LLM, 1977. Bar: Mass. 1974, U.S. Supreme Ct. 1979; notary pub., Mass. Tax atty. Coopers & Lybrand, Boston, 1974-75; comptr. Internat. Forest Products Corp., Boston, 1975-79, treas., 1979-91, sr. v.p., 1991—. Treas. New Eng. TV Corp., 1987-91, Sta. WHDH-TV, Inc., 1987-91; gen. coun., New Eng. Patriots (NFL) Football Club, 1994—, Foxboro Stadium Assocs. L.P., Foxboro, Mass., 1989-2000, New England Revolution (Major League Soccer Team), Foxboro, 1996—, NPS LLC, Foxboro, 2000—; dir. Carmel Container System, Ltd., Tel Aviv, 1988—, chmn. audit com., 1992—; treas. Chestnut Hill Mgmt. Corp., Boston, 1991—; exec. com. Sch. Law Boston (Mass.) U., 2005— Trustee Kraft Found., Boston, 1979-2002; bd. dirs. Temple Sinai, Sharon, Mass., 1995-99, Caritas Norwood (Mass.) Hosp., 2002—; mem. exec. com. Boston (Mass.) U. Sch. Law, 2005— Mem. ABA, Mass. Bar Assn. Jewish. Avocations: travel, family activities. Home: 31 Sunset Dr Sharon MA 02067-1738 Office: Gillette Stadium One Patriot Pl Foxboro MA 02035

KAREN, LINDA TRICARICO, interior designer; b. Bklyn., June 8, 1961; d. John William and Phyllis Jean (D'Addario) T. Student, Bucks County Community Coll., 1978-79; AAS, Fashion Inst. Tech., 1992. Retail mgr. Canadians, Brooks, Casual Corner, 1980—83; coord. sales and design Sure Snap Corp., NYC, 1983—84; asst. designer E.S. Sutton Inc., NYC, 1984—86; designer Good 'N Plenty Inc., NYC, 1986—90; sr. designer, merchandiser Leonard A. Feinberg, Inc., NYC, 1991—98; freelance designer, 1998—; mem. retail sales staff Oilily, 1999—; children's interior design cons. BOCES N.Y. Interior Decorating, 2000—, Sheffield Sch. Interior Design, 2001—; sales and design cons. Furniture Options, Goshen, NY, 2001—; interior designer Suffern (N.Y.) Furniture, 2002—; decorating cons. Gervic Paint & Decorating Ctr., Monroe, NY, 2002—04, Model Room Interior Design and Decorating, 2004—. Free-lance illustrator, designer; children's designer, party planner, 1999—; seminar spkr. in field. Contbr. fashion trend reports, Milan, Italy, 1984, Rome, 1985, Milan and Florence, Italy, 1986, London and Paris, 1987, Montreal, 1988, 94, 95, L.A., 1993, 95, 96 Mem. Fashion Soc., Women of the Monroe Area, Warsick Valley C. of C. Republican. Roman Catholic. Avocations: fashion design, illustration, travel. Home: 124 Dug Rd Chester NY 10918-2620 Office Phone: 845-782-3361. E-mail: lkdesign@frontiernet.net.

KARENTTE, BETTY, state legislator; b. Paducah, Ky., Sept. 13, 1931; m. Richard; 1 child, Mary. BA, MA, Calif. State U., Long Beach. Tchr. L.A. Unified Sch. Dist., 1961-92, cons., substitute tchr., 1994-96; mem. Calif. State Assembly, Sacramento, 1993—94, 2005—, Calif. State Senate, 1996—2004. Office: 3711 Long Beach Blvd Ste 801 Long Beach CA 90807 Office Fax: 562-997-0799. Business E-Mail: assemblymember.karnette@asm.ca.gov.

KARETZKY, STEPHEN, library director, educator, researcher; b. Bklyn., Aug. 29, 1946; s. Harry and Lillian Dorothy (Abrams) K.; m. Deborah Ann Shaw, Apr. 12, 1970 (div. July 1972); Joanne Louise Ballestrasse, Mar. 17, 1985. BA, CUNY, Flushing, 1967; MLS, Columbia U., 1969, DLS, 1978; MA, Calif. State U., Dominguez Hills, 1991. Libr. Bklyn. Pub. Libr., 1969-70; asst. prof. SUNY, Buffalo, 1974-76, Geneseo, 1977-78; assoc. prof. U. Haifa, Israel, 1978-81, San Jose (Calif.) State U., 1982-85; researcher, editor Shapolsky/Steimatzky Pub., N.Y.C., 1981-82; sr. editor Shapolsky Pubs., N.Y.C., 1985-86; libr. dir. Felician Coll., Lodi, N.J., 1986—. Author: Reading Research and Librarianship: A History and Analysis, 1982 (2d place award for Best Book of Yr. Am. Soc. Info. Sci 1983), The "Cannons" of Journalism, 1984; editor: The Media's War Against Israel, 1985, The Media's Coverage of the Arab-Israeli Conflict, 1989, Not Seeing Red: American Librarianship and the Soviet Union, 2002; bd. advisors Directory of American Scholars, 1999-2001; contbr. articles to profl. jours. Exec. dir. Ams. for a Safe Israel, N.Y.C., 1985-86. Mem.: Author's Guild, Am. Hist. Assn., Am. Soc. Info. Sci. and Tech. Jewish. Avocation: book collecting. Office: Felician Coll Libr 262 S Main St Lodi NJ 07644-2117 Business E-Mail: karetzkys@felician.edu.

KARFF, SAMUEL EGAL, rabbi; b. Phila., Sept. 19, 1931; s. Louis and Reba (Margalit) K.; m. Joan Mag, June 29, 1959; children: Rachel Karff Weissenstein, Amy Karff Halevy, Elizabeth Karff Kampf. AB magna cum laude, Harvard U., 1953; MAHL, DHL, Hebrew Union Coll., 1956. Rabbi Congregation Beth Israel, Hartford, Conn., 1958-60, Temple Beth El, Flint, Mich., 1960-62, Chgo. Sinai Congregation, 1962-74; sr. rabbi Congregation Beth Israel, Houston, 1975-99, rabbi emeritus, 1999—; vis. prof. soc. and health U. Tex. Health Sci. Ctr., Houston, 1999—. Lectr. U. Chgo. Divinity Sch., 1968-75; vis. assoc. prof. U. Notre Dame, 1966-67; adj. prof. religious studies Rice U., Houston, 1976—; assoc. dir. McGovern Ctr. for Health, Humanities, and Human Spirit, U. Tex. Med. Sch., Houston, 2004-, vis. prof. family medicine, 2004-. Author: Agada: The Language of Jewish Faith, 1970, Permissions to Believe Finding Faith in Troubled Times, 2005; editor Centennial Vol. Hebrew Union Coll.-Jewish Inst. of Religion, 1981-84; contbr. chpts. Judaism Religions of the World, 1982. Bd. dirs. United Way, Houston, 1991—, Inst. Religion, Houston, 1990—. Recipient Homiletics award HUC-JIR, Cin., 1956; John Harvard scholar Harvard U., 1951-52. Mem. Cen. Conf. Am. Rabbis (pres. 1989-91), Houston Philos. Soc., Phi Beta Kappa, Kiwanis. Jewish. Avocations: tennis, walking, movies, reading. Office: Congregation Beth Israel 5600 N Braeswood Blvd Houston TX 77096-2901 E-mail: skarff@sph.uth.tmc.edu.

KARG, THELMA AILEEN, writer, retired educator; b. Crawfordsville, Ind., June 30, 1918; d. Fred and Orpha Fern (Stewart) Crow; m. Henry Herbert Karg, Aug. 18, 1944 (dec. June 1982); children: Susan Marie Trissell, Karen Ann Weiss. MS, Ind. State U., 1937; BS, Taylor U., 1952. Sec. Harry N. Fine Atty. at Law, Crawfordsville, Ind., 1937—42; office control clerk R.R. Donnellys & Sons Co., 1942—43, Allisons GM, Indpls., 1943—46; accts. receivable Mid States Steel and Wire Co., 1943-46; tchr. Ind. State Tchrs. Assn.-Nat. Edn. Assn., Milw., Oreg., 1952-55, ISTA-NEA, Crawfordsville, Ind., 1955-62, Evang. United Brethren Ch., Terre Haute, Ind., 1962-65, Harrison, Ohio, 1968-70, Perrysville Highland Elem. Sch., Perrysville, Ind., 1970-74, various schs., Danville, Ill., 1975-76, Shelbyville, Ind., 1976-82, Waldron, Ind., 1983-95. Contbr. article to profl. jours. and newspapers. Mem. Nat. Rep. Congrl. Com., 1993—, senatorial com.; spkr. ladies groups United Meth.; nurse's aid ARC WWII. Recipient Editor's Choice award Nat. Soc. Poets, 1992-95. Mem. Christian Writers' (leader 1983-95), Ind. State Tchrs. United Methodist. Avocations: symphonies, plays, reading, entertaining, flowers. Home: 1004 Cottage Ave Crawfordsville IN 47933-1506

KARGER, WALTER, mechanical engineer; b. Berlin, June 7, 1926; came to U.S., 1949; s. Alfred and Anna Karger; m. Ruth Susskind, Oct. 9, 1965; 1 child, Allen J. BME magna cum laude, NYU, 1954; MS, Purdue U., 1955. Registered profl. engr., Tex., N.Y. Internat. engring. supr. indsl. equipment Carrier Corp., N.Y.C., 1955-67; asst. to v.p. Elliott Overseas Corp., N.Y.C., 1967-69, European engring. mgr. London, 1969-74; regional mgr. application engring. Elliott Co., Jeannette, Pa., 1974-83, Elliott Co. divsn. United Techs., Houston, 1983-87; sr. power engr. Falcon Seaboard Oil Co., Houston, 1987-89; sr. prin. engr. Stone & Webster Engring. Corp., Houston, 1989—. Author: Modern International Units of Measurement, 1974, 77; designer metrication slide rule. Cpl. U.S. Army, 1950-52. Mem. ASME, ASHRAE, Sigma Xi, Tau Beta Pi, Pi Tau Sigma. Office: Stone & Webster Engring Corp A Shaw Group Co 1430 Enclave Pkwy Houston TX 77077-2023

KARGLEDER, CHARLES LEONARD, language educator; b. Milbank, SD, July 19, 1939; s. George Leonard Kargleder and Ruby Teresa Gulck. BA, U. SD, 1960; MA, U. Ala., 1962, PhD, 1968; MS, U. South Ala., 1986. From instr. to prof. Spring Hill Coll., Mobile, Ala., 1963—83, prof., 1983—, chair dept. fgn. lang., 1971—, chair divsn. lang. and lit., 1992—99. Grad. asst. U. Ala., Tuscaloosa, 1965—67. Grantee Nat. Def. Edn. grant, US Govt., 1960—63. Mem.: South Ea. Coun. Latin Am. Studies, Am. Assn. Tchrs. Spanish and Portuguese, Kappa Delta Pi. Roman Catholic. Avocations: travel, reading, music, sports. Home: 1251 Henckley Ave # 207 Mobile AL 36609 Office: Spring Hill Coll 4000 Dauphin St Mobile AL 36608

KARGMAN (WITKIN), MARIE, marriage and family therapist; b. Chgo., Aug. 28, 1914; d. Joseph and Clara (Zucker) Witkin; m. Max Kargman, 1935; children: Donna, William, Robert. JD, DePaul U., 1936; MA, Radcliffe Coll., 1951. Pub. defender Boys' Court, Chgo., 1936-37; ptnr. Kargman & Kargman, 1937-44, Boston, 1953-54, pvt. practice marriage counselor, family mediator, 1953—. Chmn. gov.'s council on home and family, Commonwealth of Mass., Boston, 1966-76. Author: How to Manage a Marriage, 1985; contbr. articles to profl. jours. Mem. Assn. of Practicing Sociologists (cited outstanding contbr.), Nat. Council on Family Relations, DePaul U. Law Sch. Alumni Assn. Avocations: tennis, tv appearances, golf. Home: 115 Rutledge Rd Belmont MA 02478-2631 E-mail: mariekargman@aol.com.

KARI, DAVEN MICHAEL, religious studies educator; b. Hot Springs, S.D., Sept. 24, 1953; s. John Nelson and Corinna Nicolls (Morse) K.; m. Priya Perianayakam, Apr. 4, 1988; children: David Prem, Daniel Michael, Dante Gabriel. BA in English, Bibl. Studies, History, Fresno Pacific Coll., 1975, BA in Music, 1977; MA in English, Baylor U., 1983; MA, PhD in English, Purdue U., 1985, 86; MDiv, PhD, So. Bapt. Theol. Sem., 1988, 91. Lic. to ministry So. Bapt. Ch., 1971, ordained to ministry, 1996. Photography studio technician Johnson's Studio, Manteca, Calif., 1975-77; grad. teaching asst. Baylor U., Waco, Tex., 1978-79; minister of music Calvary Bapt. Ch., West Lafayette, Ind., 1984-85; grad. teaching asst. Purdue U., West Lafayette, Ind., 1979-85; lectr. in English Jefferson C.C., Louisville, 1987-90, Spalding U., Louisville, 1986-90, U. Louisville, 1986-90; asst. prof. English Mo. Bapt. Coll., St. Louis, 1991; assoc. prof. English Calif. Bapt. Coll., Riverside, 1991-93, assoc. prof. English, dir., Christian Ministry and Fine Arts, 1993-98; prof. Christian Studies and English Calif. Baptist U., 1998; acad. dean Washington Bible Coll., Lanham, Md., 1998-2000; adminstr., min. Bapt. Christian Sch., Hemet, Calif., 2000—01; freelance writer, 2001—02; assoc. prof. English Vanguard U. So. Calif., 2002—. Author: T. S. Eliot's Dramatic Pilgrimage, 1990, Bibliography of Sources in Christianity and the Arts, 1995; co-editor: Baptist Reflections on Christianity and the Arts: Learning from Beauty, 1997, Contemporary Authors, 1997. Founder, co-dir. local Boys Brigade, Linden, Calif., 1969-71; asst. pastor Linden (Calif.) First Bapt. Ch., 1971; chair transp. com. Calvary Bapt. Ch., West Lafayette, 1982-83, dir. singles ministry, 1983-85; moderator Scholar's Bowl Quiz Contest, Riverside, 1993-94; min. First Bapt. Ch. Hemet, 2000-01. Recipient Lit. Criticism award Purdue U., 1983; named to Outstanding Young Men Am., 1985; named Faculty Mem. of Yr., Calif. Bapt. Coll., 1993; named to Contemporary Authors, 1997. Mem. Am. Acad. Religion, Conf. on Christianity and Lit., Evang. Theol. Soc. Democrat. Baptist. Avocations: poetry, stained glass windows, sculpture, photography, painting, music. Office Phone: 714-556-3610. Personal E-mail: davenmkari@aol.com.

KARI, DONALD G., lawyer; b. Hood River, Oreg., Jan. 25, 1946; BS in Engring., with great distinction, Stanford U., 1967, MBA, JD, 1972. Bar: Wash. 1972, US Ct. Appeals (9th Cir.), US Dist. Ct. (We. Dist.) Wash. Ptnr., Energy & Utilities Practice Area Perkins Coie LLP, Bellevue, Wash. Mem.: Tau Beta Pi. Office: Perkins Coie LLP The PSE Bldg 10885 NE Fourth St Ste 700 Bellevue WA 98004-5579 Office Phone: 425-635-1406. Office Fax: 425-635-2400. Business E-Mail: dkari@perkinscoie.com.

KARIM, MOHAMMAD ATAUL, electrical engineering educator, researcher; b. Sylhet, Bangladesh, June 1, 1953; came to U.S., 1976; s. Muhammad Abdus and Anwara (Nuri) Shukur; m. Setara Karim, Dec. 20, 1977; children: Lutfi, Lamya, Aliya. BS in Physics with honors, U. Dacca, Bangladesh, 1976; MS in Physics, U. Ala., 1978, MS in Elec. Engring., 1979, PhD in Elec. Engring., 1981. Asst. prof. elec. engring. U. Ark., Little Rock, 1981-83, Wichita (Kans.) State U., 1983-86; dir. electro-optics program U. Dayton, Ohio, 1990-98, chair elect. and computer engring. dept., 1994-98; head Elec. Engring. Dept. U. Tenn., Knoxville, 1998—2000; dean, engring. City Coll. of NY, NYC, 2000—04; v.p. rsch. Old Dominion U., Norfolk, Va., 2004—. Author: Digital Design, 1987, EO Devices and Systems, 1990, Optical Computing, 1992, Electro-Optical Displays, 1992; N.Am. editor Jour. Oprics and Laser Tech.; contbr. over 325 articles to profl. jours. and conf. procs.; editor 15 jour. spl. issues; holder 2 patents. Recipient Outstanding Scientist award Engring. and Sci. Found. (Dayton), 1994, Outstanding Engring. Scholarship award, 1998, Alumni award U. Dayton, 1991, NASA Tech Brief award 1990, Up-Comers award Muse-Machine, Dayton, 1990. Fellow Optical Soc. Am., Soc. Photo-Instrumentation Engrs.; mem. IEEE (sr. mem.), Am. Soc. Engring. Edn. Muslim. Office: Old Dominion U Off Rsch 4807 Hampton Blvd Norfolk VA 23508 Office Phone: 757-683-3460. E-mail: mkarim@odu.edu.

KARIM, MOHAMMED REZAUL, mathematics professor; b. Tangail, Bangladesh, July 6, 1960; arrived in U.S., 1997; s. Mohammed Mozaffar Hossain and Hajera Khatun; m. Natisa Khandakher Karim, Feb. 20, 1987; 1 child, Oishy Reza. BS with honors, Dhaka U., 1982, MS, 1986, Concordia U., 1991, PhD, 1997. Asst. prof. Fisk U., Nashville, 1997—2000, Ala. A&M U., Normal, 2000—04, assoc. prof., 2004—. Cons. Tenn. State U., Nashville, 1997—2000. Co-author: Coherent States, Wavelets and Their Generalization, 2000. Fellow, Concordia U., Monteral, 1994; scholar, Dhaka U., 1982. Mem.: Ala. Edn. Assn., Math. Assn. Am., Am. Math. Soc. Avocations: gardening, music, fishing, travel.

KARIM, MUHAMMAD BAZLUL, political scientist, educator; b. Mymensingh, Bangladesh, Dec. 26, 1949; arrived in U.S., 1975; s. Abdul and Akika Khatoon Bari; m. Jean Ellickson, July 26, 1975. BA with honors, Dhaka U., Bangladesh, 1972, MA in Geography, 1973, Western Ill. U., 1978; cert. in computer programming, Strayer Coll., Washington, 1981; MA in Internat. Studies, U. Denver, 1984, cert. in devel. studies, 1985, PhD in Internat. Studies, 1991. Asst. dir. Integrated Rural Devel. Program, Dhaka, 1973-74; rsch. asst. Rajshahi (Bangladesh), 1974-75; rsch. assoc. Ethikos Rsch., Inc., Silver Spring, Md., 1980-81; rsch. asst. Internat. Food Policy Rsch. Inst., Washington, 1981; owner Asian Am. Net., 1996—; instr. Spoon River Coll., Macomb, 1991-95; asst. prof. Western Ill. U., Macomb, 1994—98; now with Mayer, Brown, Rowe & Maw LLP, Chgo., 2000—. Cons., Ind. U. dept. human rights, 1998-99; presenter in field. Author: A Farmer's Market in America, 1981, The Green Revolution: An International Bibliography, 1986, Structural Constraints to Participatory Development: An Examination of Social Stratification System in Rural Bangladesh, 1992, Participation, Development and Social Structure: An Empirical Study in a Developing Country, 1994; editor Who's Who of Asian Ams., 1998-; contbr. articles and rsch. reports to profl. jours. Vol. flood victims, Kampsville, Ill., 1993; election judge primary and gen. election Macomb City Precinct 7, McDonough County, Ill., 1990. Rsch. fellow Shell Cos. Found., 1987; grad. rsch. assistantship U. Denver, 1984-85, stipend and tuition scholar, 1983-84. Mem. Internat. Studies Assn., Am. Polit. Sci. Assn., Assn. Asian Studies, Assn. Am. Geographers, Assn. Third World Studies (life, web master 1996—). Office Phone: 312-782-0600. Office Fax: 312-701-7711. Business E-Mail: info@asianamerican.net.

KARIN, SIDNEY, computer science engineering educator; b. Balt., July 8, 1943; BEME, CCNY, 1966; MSE in Nuc. Engring., U. Mich., 1967, PhD in Nuc. Engring., 1973. Registered profl. engr., Mich.; lic. comml. pilot FAA, cert. flight instr. FAA. Computer programmer, nuc. engr. ESZ Assocs., Inc., Ann Arbor, Mich., 1968—72; sr. engr., sect. leader Gen. Atomics (formerly GA Techs., Inc.), San Diego, 1973—75, mgr. fusion divsn. Computer Ctr., 1975—82, dir. info. sys. divsn., 1982—85, v.p., 1987—2001; founding dir. San Diego Supercomputer Ctr., 1985—95, dir., 1997—2001; prof. computer sci. and engring. U. Calif., San Diego, 1997—; dir. Nat. Partnership for Advanced Computational Infrastructure, 1997—2001. Adj. prof. computer sci. and engring. U. Calif., San Diego, 1986—97; mem. sci. and tech. adv. bd. Telecordia (Bellcore), 1998—; mem. Coll. Computing adv. bd. Ga. Inst. Tech., 1999—2003; mem. panel on transforming practice of healthcare Pres.'s Info. Tech. Adv. Com., 2000; mem. Deep Computing Inst. Adv. Bd., 2000—02; chair program rev. com. Inst. Def. Analyses Ctr. for Computing Scis., 2000—; mem. divsn. rev. com. U. Chgo., Argonne Nat. Lab., 2001; mem. adv. com. US Nat. Virtual Obs., 2002—; vis. disting. scientist Lawrence Livermore Lab., 2004, Oak Ridge Nat. Lab., 2004; spkr. in field. Contbr. numerous articles to profl. jours.; co-author (with Norris Parker Smith): The Supercomputer Era, 1987; contbg. author Supercomputers: A Key to US Scientific Technological and Industrial Preeminence, 1987, mem. rev. bd. Jour. Supercomputing, 1987, mem. editl. adv. bd. Computing Sys. in Engring., 1990. Named Outstanding Alumnus, U. Mich. Nuc. Engring. Dept., 1989, Entrepreneurial Supporter of Yr., Starcom, 2001; fellow, Nat. Def. Edn. Act., 1966—69, Atomic Energy Commn., 1969—71; grantee, NSF, 1985—89, 1990—95, 1995, 1997—2002, 1998—99, 1999, NIH, 1994—99, 1995, NSA, 1997—99, Dept. of Def., Northrop Grumman, 1997—99, NSF/NASA, 1998—99, 1999, Orincon Corp., 2002—03; NY State Regents scholar. Fellow: AAAS (chair info., computing and comm. sect. 2000—01), Assn. for Computing Machinery (conf. chair San Jose 2001, chair Alan Newell award com. 2001—03); mem.: Am. Nuc. Soc., Computing Rsch. Assn. (bd. dirs. 1998—2001, govt. affairs com. 2002—), IEEE Computer Soc. (Seymour Cray computer engring. award com. 1998—2000), Sigma Xi. Avocations: flying, technical rock climbing, motorcycle riding, alpine skiing, reading. Home: 748 Avocado Ct Del Mar CA 92014-3911 Office: U Calif San Diego Supercomputer Ctr 9500 Gilman Dr La Jolla CA 92093-5003 E-mail: skarin@ucsd.edu.

KARIYA, PAUL, professional hockey player; b. Vancouver, Oct. 16, 1974; Forward/hockey player Anaheim Mighty Ducks, 1994—2003; hockey player Colorado Avalanche, Denver, 2003—. Mem. Can. Olympic Hockey Team, 1994. Named to NHL All-Rookie Team, 1995, NHL All-Star Game, 1996, 1997, 1999—2003, NHL First All-Star Team, 1996, 1997, 1999; recipient Lady Byng Meml. Trophy for Sportsmanship and Gentlemanly Conduct, 1996—97, Silver medal, Olympic Games, 1994, Gold medal, 2002. Office: Colorado Avalanche Hockey Club 1000 Chopper Cir Denver CO 80204

KARJALA, E. DANIEL, human resources specialist, consultant; b. Buenos Aires, Sept. 7, 1955; s. A. Le Roy and Edel Casas (Marin) K.; m. Kathleen Marie Kayser, June 25, 1978 (div. July 1999); children: Maria, Rebekah; m. Missy J. Morris, Dec. 15, 2000. BS, U. Minn., 1980. Computer ops. lead Kodak, Greeley, Colo., 1982-84; supr. AT&T, Denver, 1984; mgr. Ford Aerospace, Colorado Springs, Colo., 1984-91; mgmt. developer Intergraph Corp., Huntsville, Ala., 1991-94; dir. Townsends, Inc., Millsboro, Del., 1994-96; cons. Williams Cos., Houston, 1996-98; regional practice mgr. Shell Svcs. Internat., Houston, 1998—2000; pres., owner EDK Cons., Dallas, 1999—. Vol. fund raiser Senator R. Armstrong, Denver, 1984. Mem. ASTD (dir. fund raising 1990), Orgn. Devel. Network, Greater Dallas C. of C. Avocations: drawing, architecture, art. Home: 4921 Harvest Hill Rd Dallas TX 75244-6520 Office Phone: 214-529-3325. Personal E-mail: e.d.karjala@earthlink.net.

KARKANIAS, GEORGE B., neurologist, educator; BS in Biology, Rutgers U., 1987; MS with honors, Albert Einstein Coll. Medicine, 1991, PhD, 1993. Postdoctoral fellow dept. neurosci. Albert Einstein Coll. Medicine, 1993—94, instr., 1994—95, asst. prof. neurosci., 1995—. Contbr. articles to profl. jours. Grantee rsch. grantee, Juvenile Diabetes Found. Mem.: AAAS, Soc. Neurosci., Internat. Brain Rsch. Orgn., N.Y. Acad. Scis., Am. Diabetes Assn. (rsch. grantee 1995—). Office: Albert Einstein Coll Medicine 1300 Morris Park Ave U103A Bronx NY 10461-1926

KARKHANIS, SHARAD, librarian, political science educator; b. Khopoli, India, Mar. 8, 1935; came to U.S., 1959; s. Dwarkanath D. and Indira (D.) K. BA in Econs., U. Bombay, 1958; MLS, Rutgers U., 1962; MA in Polit. Sci., CUNY, 1967; PhD in Polit. Sci., NYU, 1978. Libr. U.S. Info. Svc., Bombay, 1955-58; libr. trainee Leyton Pub. Libr., Layton, Eng., 1958-59, Montclair (N.J.) Pub. Libr., 1959-60; libr. East Orange (N.J.) Pub. Libr., 1960-63, CUNY, Bklyn., 1963-64; prof. libr. and polit. sci. depts. Kingsborough C.C., Bklyn., 1964—. Author: Indian Politics and the Role of the Press,1981, Jewish Heritage in America, 1988; editor How to Avoid Dead End in Your Career, 1988; Educational Excellence of Asian Americans, 1989. Mem. Ethnic Task Force borough pres., Bklyn., 1987-2000. Mem. ALA, Asian/Pacific Am. Librs. Assn. (pres. 1980-82), Libr. Assn. CUNY pres. 1967-69). Republican. Hindu. Avocations: political biographies, movies. Office: Kingsborough CC Oriental Blvd Brooklyn NY 11235 Personal E-mail: sharad@patriotreturns.com.

KARKOSCHKA, ERICH, planetary science researcher, writer; b. Stuttgart, Federal Republic of Germany, Nov. 6, 1955; came to U.S., 1983; s. Erhard Karkoschka and Rothraut Leiter. Diploma in math., U. Stuttgart, 1981; PhD, U. Ariz., 1990. Wissenschaftlicher Mitarbeiter U. Stuttgart, 1982; rsch. assoc. U. Ariz., Tucson, 1992—2003, sr. staff scientist, 2003—. Group leader Internat. Workshop Astronomy, Europe, 1981-89. Author: The Observer's Sky Atlas, 1990, German edit., 1988, Japanese edit., 1991, Czech edit., 1995, Drehbare Welt-Sternkarte, 1990; co-author: Das Himmelsjahr, 1982—. Recipient 2d European prize European Philips Contest for Young Scientists and Inventors, 1973. Avocations: playing violin in symphony orchestra, playing organ, amateur astronomy, worldwide travel. Office: Univ Ariz Lunar & Planetary Lab Tucson AZ 85721-0001 Business E-Mail: erich@lpl.arizona.edu.

KARL, GEORGE, professional basketball coach; b. Penn Hills, Pa., May 12, 1951; children: Kaci Ryanne, Coby Joseph. Grad., U. N.C., 1973. Guard San Antonio Spurs, NBA, 1973-78, asst. coach, head scout, 1978-80; coach Mont. Golden Nuggets, Continental Basketball Assn., 1980-83; dir. player acquisition Cleve. Cavaliers, 1983-84, coach, 1984-86; head coach Golden State Warriors, Oakland, Calif., from 1986, Albany (N.Y.) Patrons, 1988-89, 90-91, Real Madrid, Spain, 1991-92, Seattle Supersonics, 1992-98, Milwaukee Bucks, 1998—2003, Denver Nuggets, 2005—. Named Coach of Yr., Continental Basketball Assn., 1981, 83. Mem. Continental Basketball Assn. Office: c/o Denver Nuggets 1000 Chopper Circle Denver CO 80204

KARL, HELEN WEIST, pediatric anesthesia and pain management educator, researcher; b. NYC, Oct. 28, 1948; d. Edward C. and Louise (Stursberg) Weist; m. Stephen R. Karl, June 1, 1974 (div. 1990); children: Katherine L., Thomas R., John W.; m. David Munch, 2004. BA in Philosophy, Smith Coll., 1970; MD, U. Va., 1976. Diplomate Am. Bd. Anesthesiology, Nat. Bd. Med. Examiners. Intern Hartford (Conn.) Hosp., 1976-77, resident in anesthesia, 1977-79; fellow pediat. anesthesiology Children's Hosp. of Phila., 1979-81; staff anesthesiologist St. Christopher's Hosp. for Children, Phila., 1981; asst. prof. anesthesiology and pediatrics Pa. State U., Hershey, 1981-90; asst. prof. anesthesiology U. Washington, 1990-97, assoc. prof. anesthesiology, 1997—; Parker B. Francis fellow in pulmonary rsch. Pa. State U., Hershey, 1986-88; dir. pain mgmt. Children's Hosp., Seattle, 1994-99. Adj. assoc. prof. dental pub. health scis., U. Wash., 1997-2000. Contbr. articles to profl. jours. Mem.: AAUW, Wash. Soc. Anesthesiologists, Am. Med. Women's Assn., Am. Soc. Anesthesiologists. Avocations: swimming, trumpet. Office: Children's Hosp & Med Ctr 4800 Sand Point Way NE Seattle WA 98105-3901 Business E-Mail: ekarl@u.washington.edu.

KARL, KURT ERSKINE, economist; b. Eugene, Oreg., Jan. 23, 1952; s. Emil William and Margaret Ann (McClymonds) K.; m. Ida Louise Green, May 27, 1988; children: Zoe Thandiwe, Julia Louise. BA with honors, U. Oreg., 1974; MSc, London Sch. Econs., 1975; PhD, Princeton U., 1992. Rsch. assoc. Birkbeck Coll., London, 1975-77; statistician Cen. Stats. Office, Mbabane, Swaziland, 1977-80; dir. long term svc. Wharton Econometrics, Phila., 1981-86; cons. WEFA Group, Bala Cynwyd, Pa., 1986-90, v.p. U.S. ops., 1990-94, sr. v.p. U.S. macroeconomic svcs., 1994—2000; head econ. rsch. and cons. Swiss Re, N.Y.C., 2000—. Author: two papers on Thailand, 1992, (with others) Third Five Year Development Plan-Swaziland, 1976, Report on Population Development-Swaziland, Analysis of the Treasury's Tax Reform Proposal, 1983. Mem. Am. Econ. Assn., Nat. Assn. Bus. Economists, Phi Beta Kappa. Avocations: carpentry, swimming. Office: Swiss Re 55 E 52d St New York NY 10055

KARLAN, PAMELA SUSAN, law educator; b. 1959; BA in History, magna cum laude, Yale U., 1980, MA in History, JD, Yale U., 1984. Bar: US Supreme Ct., US Dist. Ct. So. Dist. NY, US Ct. Appeals 4th, 5th, 8th, 9th, and 11th Circuits. Law clk. to Judge Abraham D. Sofaer US Dist. Ct. So. Dist. NY, 1984—85; law clk. to Justice Harry A. Blackman US Supreme Ct., 1985—86; asst. counsel NAACP Legal Def. and Ednl. Fund, Inc., 1986—88; assoc. prof. law U. Va. Sch. Law, 1988—93, prof., 1993—98, Roy L. and Rosamond Woodruff Morgan rsch. prof., 1994—98; prof. law Stanford Law Sch., 1998—99, Kenneth and Harle Montgomery prof. pub. interest law, 1999—, academic assoc. dean, 1999—2000. Lectr. FBI Nat. Acad., 1990—2001; commr. Calif. Fair Polit. Practice Commn., 2003; vis. prof. Yale Law Sch., 1992, NYU Sch. Law, 1993, Harvard Law Sch., 1994—95, Stanford Law Sch., 1996, U. Va. Law Sch., 2002. Mem.: Am. Law Inst. Office: Stanford Law Sch Crown Quadrangle 559 Nathan Abbott Way Stanford CA 94305-8610 Office Phone: 650-725-4851. Office Fax: 650-725-0253. Business E-Mail: karlan@stanford.edu.*

KARLAWISH, JASON, geriatrician; MD, Northwestern U., Chgo., 1991. Internal medicine and geriatric medicine Am. Bd. of Internal Medicine, 2005. Asst. prof. of medicine U. Pa., Phila., 1997—. Assoc. dir. Memory Disorders Clinic U. Pa., Phila., 2000—, sr. fellow Ctr. for Bioethics, 2001—, sr. fellow Leonard Davis Inst. Health Econs., 2002—. Recipient Wakley Prize, Lancet, 1997; fellow Paul Beeson Physician Faculty Scholars award, Am. Fedn. for Aging Rsch., 2000—04, Greenwall Faculty Scholar in Bioethics, Greenwall Found., 2002—05, Brookdale Found., 1998—2000. Mem.: Am. Geriatrics Soc. Office: Univ Pa 3615 Chestnut St Philadelphia PA 19104 Office Phone: 215-662-7810.

KARLE, ISABELLA L., chemist; b. Detroit, Dec. 2, 1921; d. Zygmunt Apolonaris and Elizabeth (Graczyk) Lugoski; m. Jerome Karle, June 4, 1942; children: Louise Hanson, Jean Marianne, Madeleine Tawney. BS in Chemistry, U. Mich., 1941, MS in Chemistry, 1942, PhD, 1944, DSc (hon.), 1976; DSc (hon.), Wayne State U., 1979, U. Md., 1986, Athens (Greece) U., 1997, U. Pa., 1999; LHD (hon.), Georgetown U., 1984; DSc (hon.), Harvard U., 2001; Doctor honoris causa, Jagiellonian U., Cracow, Poland, 2002. Assoc. chemist U. Chgo., 1944; instr. chemistry U. Mich., Ann Arbor, 1944—46; physicist Naval Rsch. Lab., Washington, 1946—. Paul Ehrlich lectr. NIH, 1991; exec. com. Am. Peptide Symposium, 1975—81; adv. bd. Chem. and Engring. News, 1986—89. Mem. editl. bd.: Biopolymers Jour., 1975—, Internat. Jour. Peptide Rsch., 1981—; contbr. articles to profl. jours. Named to Mich. Women's Hall of Fame, 1989; recipient Superior Civilian Svc. award, USN, 1965, Fed. Women's award, U.S. Govt., 1973, Annual Achievement award, Soc. Women Engrs., 1968, U. Mich., 1987, Dexter Conrad award, Office Naval Rsch., 1980, WISE Lifetime Achievement award, Women in Sci. and Engring., 1986, award for disting. achievement in sci., Sec. of Navy, 1987, Gregori Aminoff prize, Swedish Royal Acad. Scis., 1988, Adm. Parsons award, Navy League U.S., 1988, Ann. Achievement award, CCNY, 1989, Bijvoet medal, U. Utrecht, The Netherlands, 1990, Vincent du Vigneaud award, Gordon Conf. (Peptides), 1992, Bower Sci. award, Franklin Inst., 1993, Nat. medal of sci., Pres. of the U.S., 1995. Fellow: Am. Inst. Chemists (Chem. Pioneer award 1984), Am. Acad. Arts Scis.; mem.: NAS (Chem. Scis. award 1995), Biophys. Soc., Am. Philos. Soc., Am. Phys. Soc., Am. Chem. Soc. (Garvan award 1976, Hillebrand award 1970, Ralph Hirschmann award in peptide chemistry 1998), Am. Crystallographic Assn. (pres. 1976). Home: 6304 Lakeview Dr Falls Church VA 22041-1309 Office: Naval Rsch Lab Code 6030 Washington DC 20375-5341 Office Phone: 202-767-2624. Business E-Mail: williams@harker.nrl.navy.mil.

KARLE, JEROME, physicist, researcher; b. NYC, June 18, 1918; married, 1942; 3 children. BS, CCNY, 1937; AM, Harvard U., 1938; MS, U. Mich., 1942, PhD in Phys. Chemistry, 1943. Rsch. assoc. Manhattan project, Chgo., 1943—44, U.S. Navy Project, Mich., 1944—46; head electron diffraction sect. Naval Rsch. Lab., Washington, 1946—58, head diffraction br., 1958—68, now head lab. for structure matter, 1968—. Mem. NRC, 1954—56, 1967—75, 1978—87; chmn. U.S. Nat. Com. for Crystallography, 1973—75. Recipient Nobel prize in Chemistry, 1985. Fellow: Am. Phys. Soc.; mem.: NAS (chair chemistry sect. 1988—91), Internat. Union Crystallography (mem. exec. com. 1978—87, pres. 1981—84), Am. Crystallograph Assn. (treas. 1950—52, pres. 1971—73), Am. Math. Soc., Am. Chem. Soc. Office: US Naval Rsch Lab Lab for Structure of Matter Code # 6030 Washington DC 20375-5341 *There is too much administration of everything creative. It distorts our society and its character. The solution is to select competent, well-qualified people and give them freedom and support to pursue their creative gifts.**

KARLEN, DOUGLAS LAWRENCE, soil scientist; b. Monroe, Wis., Aug. 28, 1951; s. Lawrence Herman and Marian Bertha (Trumpy) K.; m. Linda Sue Bender, June 9, 1973; children: Sarah Jean, Steven Douglas, Holly Lin. BS, U. Wis., 1973; MS, Mich. State U., 1975; PhD, Kans. State U., 1978. Rsch. soil scientist Coastal Plains Soil, Water Conservation Rsch. Ctr., USDA-ARS, Florence, S.C., 1978-88, Nat. Soil Tilth Lab. USDA-ARS, Ames, Iowa, 1988—. Team leader Leopold Ctr. for Sustainable Agr., Ames, 1989—94. Asst. scoutmaster, com. chmn. Boy Scouts Am., Ankeny, Iowa, 1991—2005. Fellow Am. Soc. Agronomy (bd. rep. Ag sys. 1997-99, Agronomic Rsch. award 2001, Werner L. Nelson award for diagnosis of Yeild limiting factors 2001), Crop Sci. Soc. Am. (assoc. editor 1988-93, tech. editor 1994-99), Soil Sci. Soc. Am. (bd. rep. divsn. S6, 2002-05, Agronomic Achievement award 1996), Applied Soil Sci. Rsch. award 2002); mem. Coun. Agrl. Sci. and Tech., Soil and Water Conservation Soc. Am., Internat. Soil Tillage Rsch. Orgn. (asst. sec. gen. 2003—). Episcopalian. Office: USDA-ARS-MWA-NSTL 2150 Pammel Ct Ames IA 50011-4420 Office Phone: 515-294-3336. Business E-Mail: karlen@nstl.gov.

KARLEN, PETER HURD, lawyer, writer; b. N.Y.C., Feb. 22, 1949; s. S. H. and Jean Karlen; m. Lynette Ann Thwaites, Dec. 22, 1978. BA in History, U. Calif., Berkeley, 1971; JD, U. Calif., Hastings, 1974; MS in Law and Soc., U. Denver, 1976. Bar: Calif. 1974, Hawaii 1989, Colo. 1991, U.S. Dist. Ct. (so. dist.) Calif. 1976, U.S. Dist. Ct. (no. dist.) Calif. 1983, U.S. Dist. Ct. (Hawaii) 1989, U.S. Supreme Ct. 1990. Assoc. Sankary & Sankary, San Diego, 1976; teaching fellow Coll. of Law U. Denver, 1974-75; lectr. Sch. of Law U. Warwick, United Kingdom, 1976-78; pvt. practice La Jolla, Calif., 1979-86; prin. Peter H. Karlen, P.C., La Jolla, 1986—. Adj. prof. U. San Diego Sch. of Law, 1979-84; mem. adj. faculty Western State U. Coll. of Law, San Diego, 1976, 79-80, 88, 92. Contbg. editor Artweek, 1979-95, Art Calendar, 1989-96, Art Cellar Exch. mag., 1989—92; mem. editl. bd. Copyright World, 1988—, IP World, 1997—; contbr. numerous articles to profl. jours. Mem. Am. Soc. for Aesthetics, Brit. Soc. Aesthetics. Office: 1205 Prospect St Ste 400 La Jolla CA 92037-3613

KARLGAARD, RICH, publishing executive; b. Bismarck, ND; married; 2 children. Co-founder Upside, 1989—92, editor, 1989—92; co-founder, editor Forbes ASAP, 1992—98; pub. Forbes Mag., NYC, 1998—. Co-founder, bd. dir. garage.com, 1977—; co-founder Churchill (public affairs) Club. Recipient Entrepreneur of Yr.-No. Calif. (for Churchill Club), Ernst & Young, 1997. Office: Forbes 60 5th Ave New York NY 10011-8882 also: Forbes 555 Airport Blvd 5th Fl Burlingame CA 94010 Office Phone: 650-558-4810. Office Fax: 212-620-2245. E-mail: publisher@forbes.com.*

KARLIN, EDWARD J., lawyer; b. Chgo., Mar. 10, 1952; BA with distinction, Ind. U., 1974; JD cum laude, Northwestern U., 1977. Bar: Ill. 1977, US Ct. Appeals (7th cir.), US Dist. Ct. (no. dist.) Ill. Mem. Seyfarth, Shaw, Fairweather & Geraldson, Chgo.; ptnr. Seyfarth LLP, Chgo., mem. exec. com., head, Corp. Practice Area. Bd. mem. Physician Insurers Assn. Am. Mem.: Chgo. Bar Assn. (banking law sect.), ABA (bus. law sect.), Phi Beta Kappa. Office: Seyfarth Shaw LLP 55 E Monroe St Ste 4200 Chicago IL 60603 Office Phone: 312-269-8875. Office Fax: 312-269-8869. Business E-Mail: ekarlin@seyfarth.com.

KARLIN, MICHAEL JONATHAN ABRAHAM, lawyer; b. London, Eng., Aug. 27, 1952; came to U.S., 1980; s. Eli Karlin and Miriam (Stahl) Henderson; m. Fiona Jane Wilson, July 20, 1973; children: Laura, Toby. BA with Hons., Cambridge (Eng.) U., 1973, MA, 1977. Bar: Calif. 1980, U.S. Dist. Ct. (cen. dist.) Calif. 1980, U.S. Tax. Ct. 1981; solicitor, Eng. and Wales 1977. Asst. solicitor D.J. Freeman & Co., London, 1975-80; assoc. Gelles, Singer & Johnson, L.A., 1980-83, Morgan, Lewis & Bockius LLP, L.A., 1983-88, ptnr., 1988—97, KPMG LLP, 1998—2000. Contbr. articles to profl jours., 1980—. Mem. ABA (tax sect. com. on U.S. Activities of Foreigners and Tax Treaties 2004, chmn. task force new and temporary immigrants 2004), Calif. State Bar Assn., L.A. County Bar Assn. (chmn. fgn. tax law com. taxation sect. 1989-90). Office: Karlin & Co 150 S Rodeo Dr # 220 Beverly Hills CA 90211-2408 Office Phone: 310-274-5275. Personal E-mail: mjkarlin@karlinks.com.

KARLIN, SAMUEL, mathematics professor, researcher; b. Yonova, Poland, June 8, 1924; s. Morris Karlin; m. Elsie Karlin (div.); children: Kenneth, Manuel, Anna. BS in Math., Ill. Inst. Tech., 1944; PhD in Math., Princeton U., 1947; DSc (hon.), Technion-Israel Inst. Tech., Haifa, 1985. Instr. math. Calif. Inst. Tech., Pasadena, 1948—49, asst. prof., 1949—52, assoc. prof., 1952—55, prof., 1955—56; vis. asst. prof. Princeton U., 1950—51; prof. Stanford U., Calif., 1956—. Wald lectr., 1957; Andrew D. White prof.-at-large Cornell U., 1975—81; Wilks lectr. Princeton U., 1977; pres. Inst. Math. Stats., 1978—79; Commonwealth lectr. U. Mass., 1980; 1st Mahalanobis meml. lectr. Indian Statis. Inst., 1983; prin. invited spkr. XII Internat. Biometrics Meeting, Japan; prin. lectr. Que. Math. Soc., 1984; adv. dean math. dept. Weizmann Inst. Sci., Israel, 1970—77; Britton lectr. McMaster U., Hamilton, Ont., Canada, 1990; Cockerham lectr. N.C. State U., 1996; Elisha Netanyahu Meml. lectr. Technion-Israel Inst. Tech., 2005. Author: Mathematical Methods and Theory in Games, Programming, Economics, Vol. I: Matrix Games, Programming and Mathematical Economics, 1959, Mathematical Methods and Theory in Games, Programming, Economics, Vol. II: The Theory of Infinite Games, 1959, A First Course in Stochastic Processes, 1966, Total Positivity Vol. I, 1968; author: (with K. Arrow and H. Scarf) Studies in the Mathematical Theory of Inventory and Production, 1958; author: (with W.J. Sudden) Tchebycheff Systems: With Applications in Analysis and Statistics, 1966; author: (with H.Taylor) A First Course in Stochastic Processes, 2d edit., 1975; author: A Second Course in Stochastic Processes, 1980, An Introduction to Stochastic Modeling, 1984; author: (with C.a. Michelli, A. Pinkus, I.I. Schoenberg) Studies in Spline Functions and Approximation Theory, 1976. Recipient Lester R. Ford award, Am. Math. Monthly, 1973, Robert Grimmett Chair Math., Stanford U., 1978, The John Von Neumann Theory prize, 1987, award, U.S. Nat. Medal Sci., 1989, The Karlin prize in Math. Biology named in honor, Stanford U. Dept. Biol. Scis., 1992; fellow Proctor, 1945, Bateman Rsch., 1947—48, Guggenheim Found., 1959—60, NSF, 1960—61. Fellow: AAAS, Inst. Math. Statis., Internat. Statis. Inst.; mem.: NAS (award in applied math. 1973), Am. Philos. Soc., Human Genome Orgn., Am. Naturalist Soc., London Math. Soc. (hon.), Genetics Soc. Am., Am. Soc. Human Genetics, Am. Acad. Arts and Scis., Am. Math. Soc. Office: Stanford U Bldg 380 Stanford CA 94305-2125 E-mail: karlin@math.stanford.edu.

KARLIN, SUSAN, design company executive; 1 adopted child, Mia Baixue. BA in comm., MA in spl. edn. Various positions including ptnr. AKM Assoc., 1985—92; founder, pres. Suka Design Inc, NYC, 1992—. Mem.: Fin. Women's Assn., Internat. Assn. Bus. Communicators, Am. Inst. Graphic Arts, NY Advt. and Comm. Network, NY Women in Comm. Achievements include conceived and her firm designed the World Trade Ctr. tribute poster, Americans Side By Side, after 9/11. Office: Suka Design Inc 560 Broadway Ste 107 New York NY 10012 Office Phone: 212-219-0082.

KARLINSKY, SIMON, language educator, writer; b. Harbin, Manchuria, Sept. 22, 1924; arrived in U.S., 1938, naturalized, 1944; s. Aron and Sophie (Levitin) Karlinsky. BA, U. Calif., Berkeley, 1960, PhD, 1964; MA, Harvard U., 1961. Conf. interpreter, music student Europe, 1947-57; tchg. fellow Harvard U., Cambridge, Mass., 1960-61; asst. prof. Slavic langs. and lits. U. Calif., Berkeley, 1963-65, prof., 1967-91, prof. emeritus, 1991—, chmn. dept., 1967-69. Vis. assoc. prof. Harvard U., 1966. Author: Marina Cvetaeva: Her Life and Her Art, 1966, The Sexual Labyrinth of Nikolai Gogol, 1976, 2d edit., 1992, Russian Drama from Its Beginnings to the Age of Pushkin, 1985, Marina Tsvetaeva: The Woman, Her World and Her Poetry, 1986, 2d edit., 1988, Italian edit., 1989, Spanish edit., 1990, Japanese edit., 1991; editor: The Bitter Air of Exile, 1977; editor, annotator: Anton Chekhov's Life and Thought, 1974, 2d edit., 1997, The Nabokov-Wilson Letters, 1979, 2d edit., 2001, French edit., 1988, German edit., 1995, Japanese edit., 2002; co-editor: Language, Literature, Linguistics, 1987, O RUS! Studia literaria slavica in honorem Hugh McLean, 1995; contbr. articles to profl. jours. Guggenheim fellow, 1969—70, 1977—78. Mem.: Phi Beta Kappa. Office: U Calif Dept Slavic Lang & Lit Berkeley CA 94720-0001

KARLL, JO ANN, retired judge, lawyer; b. St. Louis, Nov. 16, 1948; d. Joseph H. and Dorothy Olga (Pyle) K.; m. William Austin Hernlund, Sept. 9, 1990. BS magna cum laude, Maryville U.; JD, St. Louis U. Bar: Mo. 1993. Ins. claims adjuster, 1967-88; mem. Mo. Gen. Assembly dists. 104 and 105, 1991-93; dir. Mo. State Divsn. Workers' Compensation, Jefferson City, 1993-2000, adminstrv. law judge, 2000—03; pvt. practice High Ridge, Mo., 2003—. Founder, 1st pres. scholarship fund Mo. Kids' Chance, Inc., 1995-96, bd. dirs., 1995—; bd. dirs. North Jefferson Ambulance Bd., 2004—. Internat. Assn. of Indsl. Accident Bds. and Commns. (past pres.). Office: Karll Law Ctr LLC 1682 Old Gravois Rd High Ridge MO 63049 Office Phone: 636-677-7000. E-mail: karll.law@sbcglobal.net.

KARLS, JOHN SPENCER, lawyer, accountant; b. Saginaw, Mich., Feb. 26, 1942; s. Harold M. and Mary Ellen (Spencer) K.; div.; children: Michael Berens, Hilary Marie. BA in Econs., U. Mich., 1964; JD, Harvard U., 1967; LLM in Taxation, NYU, 1973; MS in Acctg., Northwestern U., 1971. Bar: N.Y. 1967, Conn. 1978. Acct. Arthur Young & Co., N.Y.C., 1969-74; sr. tax atty., dir. tax planning Texaco Inc., White Plains, N.Y., 1974-87; tax ptnr. Ernst and Young, N.Y.C., 1987—. Prof. taxation Fordham U. MBA program, N.Y.C., 1988—; lectr. NYU Law Sch. Tax Inst., 1994—. Editor: Effective Tax Strategies for International Corporate Acquisitions: assoc. editor Federal Income Taxation of Oil and Gas; adv. bd. Jour. Internat. Taxation; editl. asst. Oil and Gas: Federal Income Taxation (CCH), 1971-74. Deacon First Congregational Ch., Greenwich, Conn.; pres. I Have A Dream Found. of Stamford, Inc., 1991—; treas. Nat. I Have a Dream Found., 1995—; co-founder first homeless shelter in Fairfield County, Conn., 1983; dir. Kids to Coll. Found., 1997—. Lt. USN, 1967-69. Recipient Elijah Watt Sells Silver medal AICPA, 1971; named Citizen of Yr., Fairfield County, Conn., 1998. Mem. ABA (tax sec. fgn. tax com., chmn.), Tax Execs. Inst., Westchester-Fairfield County Corp. Counsel Assn., YMCA, Harvard (N.Y.C.). Home: Harvard Club Box 126 27 W 44th St New York NY 10036-6613 Office: 75 Wall St New York NY 10005-2833

KARLSSON, MAGNUS, science administrator; m. Jurate Karlsson. PhD, Linkoping U., Sweden. Dir. ericsson foresight Ericsson, Stockholm, 1998—2002; counselor sci. and tech. Embassy Sweden, Washington, 2002—. Office: Embassy of Sweden 1501 M St NW Washington DC 20005 Office Phone: 202-467-2654.

KARLTON, LAWRENCE K., federal judge; b. Bklyn., May 28, 1935; s. Aaron Katz and Sylvia (Meltzer) K.; m. Mychelle Stiebel, Sept. 7, 1958 (dec.); m. Sue Gouge, May 22, 1999. Student, Washington Sq. Coll., 1952-54; LL.B., Columbia U., 1958. Bar: Fla. 1958, Calif. 1962. Acting legal officer Sacramento Army Depot, Dept. Army, Sacramento, 1958-60, civilian legal officer, 1960-62; individual practice law Sacramento, 1962-64; mem. firm Abbott, Karlton & White, 1964, Karlton & Blease, 1964-71, Karlton, Blease & Vanderlaan, 1971-76; judge Calif. Superior Ct. for Sacramento County, 1976-79, U.S. Dist. Ct. (ea. dist.) Calif., Sacramento, 1979-83; formerly chief judge U.S. Dist. Ct., Sacramento, 1983-90, chief judge emeritus, 1990-2000, sr. judge, 2000—. Co-chmn. Central Calif. council B'nai B'rith Anti-Defamation League Commn., 1964-65; treas. Sacramento Jewish Community Relations Council, chmn., 1967-68; chmn. Vol. Lawyers Commn. Sacramento Valley ACLU, 1964-76. Mem. Am. Bar Assn., Sacramento County Bar Assn., Calif. Bar Assn., Fed. Bar Assn., Fed. Judges Assn., 9th Cir. Judges Assn. Clubs: B'nai B'rith (past pres.). Office: US Dist Ct 501 I St Sacramento CA 95814-7300*

KARMAN, JAMES ANTHONY, manufacturing executive; b. Grand Rapids, Mich., May 26, 1937; s. Anthony and Katherine D. Karman; m. Carolyn L. Hoehn, Aug. 29, 1959; children: Robb Thomas, Janet Ellen, Edward John, Christopher James. BS cum laude, Miami U., Oxford, Ohio, 1959; MBA, U. Wis., 1960. Instr. corp. fin. U. Wis., Madison, 1960-61; asst. mgr. investment dept. Union Bank & Trust Co., Grand Rapids, 1961-63; treas. RPM, Inc., Medina, Ohio, 1963-69, v.p., treas., 1969-72, v.p., sec.-treas., 1972-73, exec. v.p., sec.-treas., 1973-78, pres., 1978—, also bd. dirs., CFO, 1982-93, vice chmn., 1999—. Instr. Am. Inst. Banking, 1962; bd. dirs. Metro. Fin. Corp., Shiloh Industries, Inc., A. Schulman, Inc. Trustee Trinity Cathedral, Cleve., Western Res. Hist. Soc., Boys & Girls Club, Cleve., The Leelanau Sch., Glen Arbor, Mich.; past bd. trustees Cleve. Orch., Boys Hope, Cleve., Cleve. Playhouse; mem. adv. coun. Miami U. Sch. Bus. Adminstrn.; mem. bd. visitors U. Wis.; mem. corp. coun., fin. com. Cleve. Mus. Art.; mem. Bluecoats, Inc., Cleve. Mem. U.S. Power Squadron, Gt. Lakes Hist. Soc., Mayfield Country Club, Cleve. Playhouse Club, Pine Lake Trout Club, Union Club (Cleve.), St. Louis Club, Order of Artus, Phi Beta Kappa. Home: 110 Seaspray Ave Palm Beach FL 33480-4227

KARMANOS, PETER, JR., computer software company executive, professional sports team executive; m. Debra Karmanos; children: Peter III, Nick, Jason. Grad., Wayne State U. CEO, gov. Hartford Whalers, 1994—96; corp. chmn., CEO Compuware, Detroit, 1973—; CEO, gov. Carolina Hurricanes, 1996—. Sponsor youth hockey Detroit Jr. Whalers; Sponsor youth hockey programs New Eng. Jr. Whalers, Conn. Named Named Entrepreneur of Yr., Inst. Am. Entrepreneurs, 1989. Office: Carolina Hurricanes 1400 Edwards Mill Rd Raleigh NC 27607-3624 also: Compuware Corporation 1 Campus Martius Detroit MI 48226-5099

KARMAZIN, MEL, broadcast executive; b. 1944; Grad., Pace U. Past sta. mgr. CBS radio, NYC, 1960—70; v.p., gen. mgr. Metromedia Inc., NYC, 1970—81; pres. Infinity Broadcasting Corp., NYC, 1981—2001, CEO, 1988—2001; chmn., CEO CBS Station Group, NYC, 1997; pres, COO CBS Corp., NYC, 1998—99; pres., COO Viacom Inc., NYC, 2000—04, ret., 2004, cons., 2004; CEO SIRIUS Satellite Radio Inc., NYC, 2004—. Bd. dir. Westwood One, Blockbuster, New York Stock Exchange. Named to Radio Hall of Fame, 2003; recipient Nat. Assoc. Broadcasters Nat. Radio award, IRTS Gold Medal award. Office: SIRIUS Satellite Radio Inc 1221 Ave Americas 36th Fl New York NY 10020

KARMEIER, DELBERT FRED, engineer, consultant, realtor; b. Okawville, Ill., Apr. 2, 1935; s. Wilbert and Ida (Harre) K.; m. Naomi Firnhaber, Oct. 18, 1958; children: Kenton Howard, Dianne Jill. BSCE, U. Ill., 1957, MS in Transp. Engring., 1959. Rsch. assoc. U. Ill., 1958-59; traffic engr. St. Louis County, Mo., 1959-65, traffic commr., 1965-69; dir. transp. City of Kansas City, Mo., 1969-74, dir. aviation and transp., 1974-90; dir. pub. works City of Hartford, Conn., 1990-92; assoc. exec. dir. Am. Pub. Works Assn., Chgo., 1992-94; cons. Torres Cons. Engrs., Kansas City, Mo., 1994-95; assoc. J.D. Reece, Leawood, Kans., 1995—. Mem. Nat. Com. on Uniform Traffic Control Devices, 1971-85 Automotive Safety Found. fellow U. Ill., 1959. Mem. Inst. Transp. Engrs. (pres. Missouri Valley sect. 1965-66), Airport Operator's Coun. Internat., Am. Rd. and Transp. Builder's Assn. (dir. 1973-83, chmn. pub. transit adv. coun. 1980-83), Transp. Rsch. Bd., Am. Pub. Works Assn., U. Ill. Alumni Club Kansas City (pres. 1996—), Thrivent Fin. for Lutherans (v.p. West Jackson County chpt. 2003—), Beta Sigma Psi (nat. editor 1963-69, pres. Kansas City alumni 1981-82, Disting. Alumnus award 1971, nat pres. 1986-88, nat. treas. 1996-2004). Lutheran. Home: 12206 Avila Dr Kansas City MO 64145-1750 Office: Reece & Nichols 13002 State Line Rd Leawood KS 66209-1756 Office Phone: 816-942-4666. Personal E-mail: delkarm@aol.com.

KARMEIER, LLOYD A., state supreme court justice; b. Washington County, Ill., Jan. 12, 1940; m. Mary Karmeier; 2 children. BS, JD, Univ. Ill. Bar: Ill. 1964, US Dist. Ct. (so. dist. Ill.), US Supreme Ct. Law clk. Justice Byron O. House, Ill. Supreme Ct., 1964—68; state's atty. Washington County, Ill., 1968—72; law clk. Judge James L. Forman, US Dist Ct., Ill., 1972—73; atty. Hohlt, House, DeMoss & Johnson, 1964—86; resident cir. judge Washington County, Ill., 1986—2004; assoc. justice Ill. Supreme Ct., 2004—. Chmn. Com. on Pattern Jury Instructions Ill. Supreme Ct., 2003—04. Mem.: Ill. Judges Assn., Ill. State Bar Assn. (assembly mem. 1996—2002), Ea. St. Louis Bar Assn., St. Clair County Bar Assn., Washington County Bar Assn., So. Ill. Am. Inn of Ct. (pres. exec. com. 2003). Office: Illinois Supreme Court Supreme Court Bldg Springfield IL 62701*

KARMEL, ROBERTA SEGAL, lawyer, educator; b. Chgo., May 4, 1937; d. J. Herzl and Eva E. (Elin) Segal; m. Paul R. Karmel, June 9, 1957 (dec. Aug. 1994); children: Philip, Solomon, Jonathan, Miriam; m. S. David Harrison, Oct. 29, 1995. BA, Radcliffe Coll.; LLB, NYU, 1962; HHD (hon.), King's Coll., 1998. Bar: N.Y. 1962, U.S. Dist. Ct. (so. and ea. dists.) N.Y. 1964, U.S. Ct. Appeals (2d cir.) 1968, U.S. Supreme Ct. 1968, U.S. Ct. Appeals (3d cir.) 1987. Asst. regional adminstr. SEC, Washington, 1962-69, commr., 1977-80; assoc. Willkie Farr & Gallagher, N.Y.C., 1969-72; ptnr. Rogers & Wells, N.Y.C., 1972-77, of counsel, 1980-85; ptnr. Kelley Drye & Warren, N.Y.C., 1987-94, of counsel, 1995—2002. Adj. prof. law Bklyn. Law Sch., 1973-77, 82-85, prof., 1985—, co-dir. Ctr. for Study of Internat. Bus. Law; bd. dirs. Kemper Ins Cos.; trustee Practicing Law Inst. Author: Regulation by Prosecution, 1982; contbr. articles to profl. jours. Fellow Am. Bar Found.; mem. ABA, Assn. Bar City N.Y., Am. Law Inst., Fin. Women's Assn. Home: 66 Summit Dr Hastings On Hudson NY 10706-1215 Office: Bklyn Law Sch 250 Joralemon St Brooklyn NY 11201-3700 Office Phone: 718-780-7946. Business E-Mail: roberta.karmel@brooklaw.edu.

KARMELIN, MICHAEL ALLEN, financial executive; b. Bronx, N.Y., Feb. 26, 1947; s. Samuel and Fannie (Levine) K.; m. Risa G. Kaplan, Apr. 2, 1966. BBA, Baruch Coll. CUNY, 1972; MBA, NYU, 1979. CPA, N.Y. Staff acct. Allied Chem. Corp., N.Y.C., 1965-69; dir. of financial mgmt. analysis Avco Corp., Greenwich, Conn., 1969—85; CFO of various sub divsn. and bus. divsn. Merrill Lynch & Co., N.Y.C., 1985—98; v.p., treas. Ocwen Fin. Corp., West Palm Beach, Fla., 1998-99; CFO, CEO, dir. Touch Tone Techs., Inc., Boca Raton, Fla., 1999—2000; CFO BarPoint.com, Inc., Deerfield Beach, Fla., 2000—02; fin. adv. AXA Advisors, Boca Raton, Fla., 2002—. CFO, Jewish Fedn. of Palm Beach County, 2004—. Mem.: Strategic Leadership Forum, Inst. Mgmt. Accts., Assn. of Financial Profl. Office: Jewish Fedn Palm Beach County 4601 Community Dr West Palm Beach FL 33417 Home: 8270 Muirhead Cir Boynton Beach FL 33437-5063 E-mail: mkarmelin@yahoo.com.

KARNAS, FRED G., JR., urban policy advisor; b. Olean, N.Y., Sept. 9, 1948; BCP, U. Va., 1971; MSW, Va. Commonwealth U., 1980; PhD, Va. Tech. U., 1984. Gen. program dir. Cmty. Coun., Phoenix, 1983-87; exec. dir. Cmty. Housing Partnership, Phoenix, 1987-89, Ctrl. Fla. Coalition for the Homeless, Orlando, Fla., 1989-91, Nat. Coalition for the Homeless, Washington, 1991-95; with HUD, Washington, 1995-2000, dep. asst. sec., 1997-2000; cons. on homelessness, AIDS, housing policies, 2000—; pres. Ariz. Family Housing Fund, Phoenix, 2002—03; policy adv. Gov. of Ariz., 2003—. Office: 5 E Loma Ln Phoenix AZ 85020 Office Phone: 602-542-7011. E-mail: karnas@cox.net.

KARNAUGH, MAURICE, computer scientist, educator; b. N.Y.C., Oct. 4, 1924; s. George Victor and Fannie (Weinstein) K.; m. Linn Blank; children: Robert Victor, Paul Joseph. BS, CCNY, 1948; MS, Yale U., 1950, PhD, 1952. Mem. tech. staff Bell Telephone Labs., Murray Hill, N.J., 1952-56, mgr. digital techs., 1956-66; chief scientist exploratory systems ctr., fed. system ctr.

IBM, Gaithersberg, Md., 1966-70; mem. rsch. staff IBM Watson Rsch. Ctr., Yorktown Heights, N.Y., 1970-93. Disting. adj. prof. Poly. U., Bklyn., 1981-99. Contbr. articles on digital switching and artificial intelligence to profl. jours.; patentee in field. With U.S. Army, 1943-46, ETO. Fellow IEEE; mem. Internat. Coun. Computer Communications (gov. emeritus 1988—).

KARNAZES, ELIZABETH MARIE BARNSON, lawyer, photojournalist; d. Paul Knudsen and Elizabeth Cardon Barnson; children: Shayne Peter Andrew, Alexander John Peter, Zachary Thomas Peter. BA, U. S.C., 1975; JD, Pace U., 1979. Bar: N.Y. 1981, Calif. Owner Law Offices of Elizabeth Karnazes, Foster City, Calif., 1985—, Insight Photography, Foster City, 1988—. Sporting News (Best Sports Photos of the Yr., 1990), Yes! (Finalist Maj. League Baseball Photo of the Yr., 1989, Finalist UPI Sports Photo of the Yr., 1989), Karpov Wins! (Chess Journalists of Am. Photo of the Yr., 1998), Body Of Work (Chess Journalists of Am. Photographer of the Yr., 1998); contbr. photographs and articles to books. Calif. state del. U.S. Chess Fedn., Calif., 1998—2000; chmn. U.S. Chess Fedn. Women in Chess, 1998—2000; v.p. Foster City Little League, 1984—86; mem. internat. women's com. Fedn. Internationale des Echecs, Switzerland, 1997—99. Fellow: Redwings Horse Sanctuary (life); mem.: Omicron Delta Kappa (life), Delta Theta Phi (life). Avocations: sailboat racing, service dog training, travel, coaching, snowboarding. Office: Law Offices of Elizabeth Karnazes PO Box 4747 Foster City CA 94404 Office Phone: 650-345-9200.

KARNER, STEPHEN LESLIE, geophysicist; s. Garry David and Lois Gwenda Karner; m. Karen Ann Davies, Jan. 18, 1992. BS, Flinders U. of South Australia, 1986, BS with honors, 1987; MA, CUNY, Flushing, 1993; PhD, MIT, Cambridge, Mass., 1999. Intern Delhi Petroleum Inc., Adelaide, Australia, 1986—87; geologist South Australian Oil and Gas, Adelaide, Australia, 1987—88; geophysicist Wiltshire Geol. Svcs. Inc., Adelaide, Australia, 1988—89; tchg. and rsch. asst. Queens Coll. of the CUNY, Flushing, NY, 1989—93; rsch. asst. Lamont-Doherty Earth Obs. of Columbia U., Palisades, NY, 1993; tchg. and rsch. asst. MIT, Cambridge, 1993—99, post-doctoral rsch. scientist, 1999—2000; post-doctoral rschr. / rsch. scientist Tex. A&M U., College Station, Tex., 2000—04, adj. rsch. scientist, 2004—; post-doctoral rsch. scientist Wash. State U., Pullman, 2004—; geomechanicist - geothermal energy Idaho Nat. Lab., Idaho Falls, Idaho, 2004—. Cons. Quantitative Basin Analysis Inc., Ramsey, NJ, 2004; steering com. Phys. Properties of Earth Materials, 2004—; attendee and spkr. UN Internat. Decade on Natural Disaster Reduction, Beijing, 1997—97. Author: (family history website) Blackadder - The Whole Damn Dynasty, (family history articles) 1804 First Settlers Association Newsletter; contbr. articles to profl. jours. County coord. FreeCen UK Census Project (freecen.rootsweb.com), 2001—04; dancer George Tomov Folkdance Ensemble, N.Y.C., 1981—93; choreographer and dancer Adelaide Traditional Dancers, Adelaide, Australia, 1984—89, Jedinstvo Folkdance Ensemble, Adelaide, 1986—89, KUD Biljana Folkdance Ensemble, Adelaide, 1984—86, Queanbeyan Folkdance Ensemble, Queanbeyan, Australia, 1983—83, Canberra Internat. Folkdance Assn., Canberra, Australia. Fellow David B. Harris Post-Doctoral fellow, Tex. A&M U., Coll. Sta., TX USA, 2003—04; grantee Keith Runcorn Travel award, European Geophys. Soc., 1997, Rsch. grantee, NSF, 2004—05. Mem.: Seismol. Soc. of Am, Am. Geophys. Union, Am. Assn. of Petroleum Geologists, 1804 First Settlers Assn., Borders Family History Soc., Herefordshire Family History Soc. Avocations: folklore, cultural heritage, dance, family history. Office: Idaho National Laboratory 2525 North Fremont Ave Idaho Falls ID 83415-2107 Office Phone: 208-526-6292. E-mail: karnsl@inel.gov.

KARNES, EVAN BURTON, II, lawyer; b. Chgo. s. Evan Burton and Mary Alice (Brosnahan) K.; m. Bridget Anne Clerkin, Oct. 9, 1976 (dec. June 1994); children: Kathleen Anne, Evan Burton III, Molly Aileen, Lauren Jean; m. Janet Ann Pioli, Nov. 2, 1996. AB, Loyola U., Chgo., 1975; JD, DePaul U., 1978; grad. civil trial advocacy program, U. Calif., 1979. Bar: Ill. 1978, U.S. Dist. Ct. (no. dist.) Ill. 1978, U.S. Ct. Appeals (7th cir.) 1978, U.S. Dist. Ct. (no. dist.) Ind. 1995, U.S. Supreme Ct. 1983. Trial atty. Chgo. Milw. St. Paul & Pacific R.R., Chgo., 1978-81; litigation dept. Baker & McKenzie, Chgo., 1981-87; sr. litigation counsel Levin & Ginsburg Ltd., Chgo., 1987-89; of counsel Oppenheimer, Wolff & Donnelly, 1989-91; prin. Law Offices of Evan B. Karnes II & Assocs., 1992-99; mng. ptnr. O'Connor & Karnes, Chgo., 2000—. Bd. dirs. Triad Communications Inc, Albuquerque, chmn. bd., 1988. Trustee Village of Northfield, Ill., 1999—, mem. fin. com., mem. planning and zoning commn., 1990-99, vice chmn., 1994-99. Mem. ABA, ATLA, Ill. Bar Assn., Fed. Bar Assn. (bd. dirs. Chgo. chpt. 1995-99), Def. Rsch. Inst., Nat. Assn. R.R. Counsel (chmn. sci. evidence com. 1995-2002, nat. exec. com. 1995—, v.p. Midwest region 2000-05), Ill. Trial Lawyers Assn., Blue Key (sec. Loyola U. chpt. 1974-75), Pi Sigma Alpha, Phi Alpha Delta. Office: 2 First Nat Plz 20 S Clark St 20th Flr Chicago IL 60603 Office Phone: 312-629-8900. Business E-Mail: karneslaw@att.net.

KARNES, KEITH DALE, portfolio manager; b. Tyler, Tex., Aug. 20, 1953; s. Ralph Dale and Gloria Anne Karnes; m. Mary Ellis, 1999; children: Kathryn, Kristoffer stepchildren: Will, Stephen, Emily. BBA, Tex. Christian U., Ft. Worth; diploma of grad., Stonier Grad. Sch. of Banking of Am. Banking Assn., 1987. Dir., cashier Royal Nat. Bank, Palestine, Tex., 1984—93; fin. advisor Merrill Lynch, Ft. Worth, 1993—97; v.p., investment officer, portfolio mgr. Wachovia Securities (formerly First Union Securities), Ft. Worth, 1997—. Mem. Jewels Charity Ball; mem. dirs. coun. Modern Art Mus. Mem.: Houston Tex. Angel Group, Ft. Worth Angels Group, Rivercrest Club, Ridglea Country Club, Ft. Worth Rotary. Episcopalian. Office: Wachovia Securities 777 Taylor St Ste 850 Fort Worth TX 76102-4915

KARNES, LUCIA ROONEY, psychologist; b. Moncton, N.B., Can., Mar. 9, 1921; d. Charles William and Jean Waring (Robson) Rooney; m. Thomas Campbell Karnes, June 7, 1946; children: Eleanore, Campbell, Timothy, Charles. BS, Ga. State Coll., 1942; MA, Emory U., 1946; PhD, U. N.C., 1967. Tchr. Decatur Girls High, Decatur, Ga., 1942-46; tchr. Summit Sch., Winston-Salem, N.C., 1947; prof. Salem Coll., Winston-Salem, 1949-54, 60-77; lang. therapist Bowman Grey Sch. Medicine, Winston-Salem, 1950-57, Orton Reading Ctr., Winston-Salem, 1957-72; dir. Ctr. for Spl. Edn., Salem Coll., Winston-Salem, 1972-77; pvt. practice psychology Winston-Salem, 1977—. Dyslexic cons. Jefferson Acad., Winston-Salem, 1980—, Greenfield Sch., Wilson, 1986—, Wingate (N.C.) U., 1988—. Creator Using Computers in Psychology courses, 1972; author (video) Teaching Dyslexics, 1975. Founder, pres. state bd. LWV, Winston-Salem, 1953; pres. state bd. AAUW, Winston-Salem, 1950-54; bd. dirs. YWCA, Winston-Salem, 1950-54; v.p. bd. dirs. Arts Coun., Winston-Salem, 1954-60. Named Outstanding Reading Tchr., Reading Assn., Winston-Salem, 1982; fellow Orton-Gillingham Acad. Mem. APA, Orton Dyslexia Soc. (v.p. bd. dirs. 1960-77), N.C. Psychol. Assn., Assn. for Children with Learning Disabilities (v.p. bd. dirs. 1972—, Orton-Gillingham Acad. fellow), Sorosis Club, Delta Kappa Gamma. Democrat. Presbyterian. Avocation: travel. Home: 131 Lamplighter Cir Winston Salem NC 27104-3419 Office Phone: 336-768-8323.

KARNETTE, BETTY, state assembly member; b. Paduch, Ky., Sept. 13, 1931; m. Richard Karnette; 1 child, Mary. BA, MA, Calif. State U. Sec. office mgr. Terminal Island; tchr. L.A. Unified Sch. Dist., 1961—92; mem. Calif. State Assembly, 1992—94, dist. 27, Calif. State Senate, 1996—2004. Subs. tchr.; mem. Appropriations Com., Ins. Com., Rules Com., Transp. Com., Arts & Entertainment Com.; chair Select Com. on Ports. Mem. Long Beach Meml. Hosp. Children's Clinic; mem. assoc. bd. Sage House in San Pedro; bd. dirs. Young Horizon. Democrat. Mailing: State Capitol Rm 2176 Sacramento CA 95814 Office: 3711 Long Beach Blvd Ste 801 Long Beach CA 90807

KARNI, EDI, economics professor; b. Tel Aviv, Mar. 20, 1944; s. Eliezer and Sara (Vitis) K.; m. Barbara Shapiro, Mar. 16, 1980; children: Anat, Anna. BA in Econs., Hebrew U., 1965, MA in Econs., 1970, U. Chgo., 1970, PhD in Econs., 1971. Asst. prof. Ohio State U., Columbus, 1971-72; fellow Inst. for Advanced Studies/Hebrew U., Jerusalem, Israel, 1976-77; vis. prof. U. Chgo., 1977-79; assoc. prof. Tel Aviv U., 1972-81; prof. econs. Johns Hopkins U., Balt., 1981—. Disting. vis. prof. Vanderbilt U., 1987. Author: Decision Making Under Uncertainty, 1985; contbr. articles to profl. jours. Fellow: Econometric Soc.; mem.: Am. Econ. Assn. Jewish. Home: 6208 Sareva Dr Baltimore MD 21209-3530 Office: Johns Hopkins U Dept Econs Baltimore MD 21218

KARNOVSKY, MORRIS JOHN, pathologist, biologist; b. Johannesburg, June 28, 1926; arrived in U.S., 1955; s. Herman Louis and Florence (Rosenberg) Karnovsky; m. Shirley Esther Katz, Aug. 26, 1952; children: David Mark, Nina Jane. BS, U. Witwatersrand, Johannesburg, 1946, MB, BCh, 1950, DSc, 1984; diploma clin. pathology, U. London, 1954; MA (hon.), Harvard U., 1965. Prof. pathology Harvard U. Med. Sch., Boston, 1968—72, Shattuck prof., 1972—, chmn. program in cell and devel. biology, 1975—90, chmn. pathology dept., 1991—93. Recipient E.B. Wilson award, Am. Soc. Cell Biology. Fellow: Royal Microscopic Soc.; mem.: U.S. and Can. Acad. Pathology (Maude-Abbott award 1994), Am. Soc. for Investigative Pathology (Gold-Headed Cane award 1994), Am. Assn. Pathologists (co-pres. 1978—79, Rous-Whipple award), German Soc. for Cell Biology (hon.), Am. Soc. Cell Biology (pres. 1983—84), Inst. Medicine of NAS. Office: Harvard Med Sch 200 Longwood Ave Boston MA 02115-5701*

KARNOW, STANLEY, journalist, writer; b. NYC, Feb. 4, 1925; s. Harry and Henriette (Koeppel) Karnow; m. Claude Sarraute, July 15, 1948 (div. 1955); m. Annette Kline, Apr. 21, 1959; children: Curtis Edward, Catherine Anne, Michael Franklin. BA, Harvard U., 1947; student, U. Paris, France, 1948—49; postgrad., Inst. d'Etudes Politiques, U. Paris, Paris, 1949—50. Corr. Time mag., Paris, 1950—57; bur. chief North Africa Time-Life, 1958—59, Hong Kong, 1959—62; spl. corr. London Observer, 1961—65, Time, Inc., 1962—63; Far East corr. Sat. Eve. Post, 1963—65, Washington Post, 1965—71, diplomatic corr., 1971—72; spl. corr. NBC News, 1973—75; assoc. editor The New Republic, 1973—75; columnist King Features, 1975—88, Le Point, Paris, 1976—83, Newsweek Internat., 1977—81; editor Internat. Writers Service, 1976—86; chief corr. PBS series Vietnam: A TV History, 1983; chief corr., narrator PBS Series The U.S. and the Philippines: In Our Image, 1989. Author: Southeast Asia, 1963, Mao and China: From Revolution to Revolution, 1972, Vietnam: A History, 1983 (Emmy award, 1984, DuPont award, 1984, Polk award, 1984, Peabody award, 1984), In Our Image: America's Empire in the Philippines, 1989 (Pulitzer Prize for history, 1990), Paris in the Fifties, 1997; co-author: Asian Americans in transition, 1992; contbg. author Passage to Vietnam, 1994, Mekong, 1995, Historical Atlas of the Vietnam War, 1995, Past Imperfect: History According to the Movies, 1995. Bd. advisors Vietnam Vets. Meml. Wall. With USAF, 1943—46. Recipient citation, Overseas Press Club, 1966, Ann. award for best newspaper interpretation of fgn. affairs, 1968, Lifetime Achievement award for coverage of Asia, Shorenstein Ctr. for Press and Politics, Harvard and Stanford Univs., 2002; fellow Neiman fellow, Harvard U., 1957—58; Inst. Politics John F. Kennedy Sch. Govt. fellow, East Asian Rsch. Ctr. fellow, 1970—71. Mem.: Soc. Am. Historians, Asia Soc., Coun. Fgn. Rels., PEN Am. Ctr., Signet Soc., Century Assn., Shek-O Club (Hong Kong). Home: 10850 Spring Knoll Dr Potomac MD 20854-1550

KARNS, ELIZABETH (LIBBY) A., retired daycare administrator; b. Lafayette, Ind., Aug. 26, 1946; d. Harris Lester III and Elizabeth Louise Karns. *Both grandfathers were Methodist ministers. On father's side, lineage was traced to President James Buchanan. Maternal grandmother traced her genealogy back to Revolutionary days and was a member of Daughters of the American Revolution. Father was a navigator for a B-24 bomber during WWII, having a career in the Air Force and retiring as a captain only to become a teacher and then a meteorologist. Mother was a teacher. Brother Les Karns earned his BS and MS from the University of Houston in Social Work. He taught and researched statistics, and is presently a social worker for Hospice.* BA in Elem. Edn., Bethel Coll., 1970; MS in Elem. Edn., Ind. U., South Bend, 1975; MLS, Ind. U., 1989. Cert. tchr. K-6 Ind. Tchr. day care Calvary Temple, South Bend, Ind., 1991—94, resource dir., 1994—95. Contbr. poetry to anthology (Editor's Choice award Internat. Libr. Poetry, 1999, 2000, 2001, 2002, 2004). Recipient Hon. Mention, Writer's Digest, 1998. Mem.: Uplifters, Calvary Temples Women's Ministries, Worship and Creative Arts Leaders (choir libr. 1994—2004). Republican. Avocations: reading, writing. Home: 1215 Fairington Cir Apt 118 South Bend IN 46614-3306

KARNS, PHYLLIS J. SPEAR, dean; BSN, Baylor U., 1960; MSN in Parent-Child Nursing, U. Colo., 1977; PhD in Psychol. Founds. Edn., U. Wyo., 1985. From instr. to asst. prof. U. Wyo., Laramie, 1977-87; dean Sch. Nursing, prof. Baylor U., Dallas-Waco, 1987—. Cons. U. Tulsa, 1993. Contbr. articles to profl. jours. Recipient Baylor U. Rsch. award, 1990; Grantee Wyo. Coun. Humanities, 1986, 80, 86. Mem. ANA, Am. Assn. Colls. Nursing., Christian Nurse Educators (chair 1992—), Nat. League Nursing (cons. 1990—), So. Collegiate Coun. Edn. Nursing (Tex. rep. 1989-90, mem. nominating com. 1988, 89), Tex. Nurses Assn. (bd. dirs. dist. 4 1991-93, mem. sch. adv. com. 1991-92), Sigma Theta Tau. Office: Baylor U Sch Nursing 3700 Worth St Dallas TX 75246-2091

KAROFSKY, PETER STUART, pediatrician, medical educator; b. Boston, Nov. 11, 1939; s. Sydney Bernard Karofsky, Sylvia Ruth Karofsky; divorced; children: Jill, Amy, Andrew; m. Kathryn Jean Anderson, 2000. AB, Bowdoin Coll., 1962; MD, Tufts U., 1966. Pediatrician Jackson Clinic, Madison, Wis., 1971—79; chief pediat. Meth. Hosp., Madison, 1975—76; dir. Gen. Pediat. and Adolescent Clinic U. Hosp., Madison, 1979—86; prof. U. Wis. Med. Sch., Madison, 1979—. Cons. to the Gov. on health care issues State of Wis., Madison, 1975—76; pres. Dane County Pediat. Assn., Madison, 1976—77; med. cons. to Nicaragua U. Wis., Pearl Lagoon, Nicaragua, 1976; cons. on health care issues Bowdoin Coll., Brunswick, Maine, 1979. Radio broadcaster Second Opinion, 1975 (Wis. Outstanding Pub. Svc. Radio Program, 1976); contbr. articles to profl. jours. Team physician Middleton H.S., 1980—91; baseball and softball coach Middleton Youth Baseball and Softball Leagues, 1976—85; founding bd. mem. Emergency Med. Svcs., Middleton, 1975—77. Capt. USAF, 1968—70. Named a Winner, USTA Midwest Sectional 55-year-old Doubles Tournament, United States Tennis Association, 1994, Winner, USTA Midwest Sectional 60-year-old, 2002, Winner, Badger State Games Doubles Tournament, 55-year-old division, 1994, Winner Badger State Games 60-year-old doubles, 2002, Finalist, Badger State Games Singles Tournament, 55-year-old division, 1994, Finalist Badger State Games 60-year-old singles, 2001, Finalist, USTA Midwest Sectional 60-year-old doubles division, 2001, Ranked second in the State of Wisconsin 50-year-old doubles, 1990 and 1993; named Olympian of Yr., Svc. Clubs of Dane County, 1992, Best Doctors in America; Midwest Region, Best Doctors in America, 1995; recipient Disting. Svc. to Youth award, Middleton-Cross-Plains Sch. Dist., 1992, Ann. Mason's award, 1993, award, Wis. Assn. Athletic Dirs., 1994. Fellow: Am. Acad. Pediat. Jewish. Avocations: travel, tennis, bicycling, golf. Home: 1406 Shady Oak Cir Middleton WI 53562 Office: U Wis Health-Westside Clinic 451 Junction Rd Madison WI 53717

KAROL, FREDERICK JOHN, retired industrial chemist; b. Norton, Mass., Feb. 28, 1933; s. John and Valeria (Bzdula) K.; m. Ruth Helen Lindbom, May 31, 1958; children: Mark, Donald, Cynthia. BA, Boston U., 1954; PhD in Chemistry, MIT, 1962. With Union Carbide Corp., Bound Brook, N.J., 1956—, chemist, 1956-59, 62-65, project scientist, 1965-67, rsch. scientist, 1967-72, sr. rsch. scientist, 1972-76, rsch. assoc., 1976-80, corp. fellow, 1980-84, sr. corp. fellow, 1984-2000; ret., 2000. Contbr. numerous articles to profl. jours. With U.S. Army, 1954-56. Recipient Thomas Edison award R&D Coun. N.J., 1982, 99, Excellence in Catalysis award Met. N.Y. Catalysis Soc., 1987, Perkin Medal Soc. Chem. Industry, N.Y., 1989, ACS award for Creative Invention, 1991; named to Nat. Plastics Hall of Fame, 1997. Fellow: Soc. Plastic Engrs. (S.P.E. Conley award 1989, Internat. Gold medal 1990); mem.: Am. Chem. Soc., Nat. Assn. Engrs., Am. Inst. Chemists (Chem. Pioneer award 1988). Achievements include patents for 106 U.S. Home: 157 Skyline Dr Lakewood NJ 08701-5739 E-mail: fkarol@optonline.net.

KAROL, JOHN J., JR., producer, filmmaker; b. Mt. Kisco, NY, Apr. 1, 1935; s. John J. and Ann (Hale) K.; m. Georgina P. Forbes, Oct. 1963 (div. 1977); children: Angelisse F., Christopher H.; m. Portia L. Fitzhugh, June 21, 1980; 1 child, Fitzhugh B. BA, Williams Coll., 1958; LLB, Yale U., 1962. Assoc. Lord, Day & Lord, NYC, 1962-64; parliamentary draftsman Atty. Gens. Chambers, Zomba, Malawi, 1964-67; dep. commr., gen. counsel State Vt. Dept. Taxes, Montpelier, Vt., 1967-69; prodr., filmmaker Apertura, Orford, NH, 1969—. Prodns. include (films) Brush Dance, 1985, Ben's Mill, 1982 (Acad. award nomination 1982, Golden Eagle award 1982), Main Street, 1979, A Place in Time, 1977 (Golden Eagle award 1977), Settling In, 1974, (video) Photographing with Fred Picker, 1991 (Telly award 1992), Printing with Fred Picker, 1990 (Golden Eagle award 1990, Telly award 1990), Ben's Water Tub, 1990. Dir. Inherit NH, Concord, 1984-90; trustee Upper Valley Land Trust, Norwich, Vt., 1987-90, mem. exec. bd. St. Martin's Ch., Fairlee, Vt., 1976-79, jr. warden, 1978. Mem. Soc. Motion Picture TV Engrs., Century Assn. (NYC), Tavern Club (Boston). Home and Office: Apertura Main St Orford NH 03777 Office Phone: 603-353-9067. E-mail: karol@apertura.org.

KAROL, MICHAEL ALAN, editor; b. New Brunswick, NJ, Mar. 1, 1953; s. Reuben Hirsch and Sylvia (Gross) K. BA in Sociology and Comm., U. Pa., 1975; MS in Comm./TV Broadcasting, Boston U., 1977. Rhythm and blues editor Pop Top Mag. Little Face, Inc., Boston, 1976-78; staff photographer, prodn. editor Nat. Jewel Mag., N.Y.C., 1978-79; assoc. editor Gift and Stationery Bus. Gralla Publs., N.Y.C., 1979; mng. editor Modern Floor Coverings Charleson Pub. Co., N.Y.C., 1979-82; editor-in-chief Floor Covering Bus. Thomson Retail Press, N.Y.C., 1982-89; mng. editor Graphic Arts Monthly Cahners Pub.Co., N.Y.C., 1990-96; copy chief Computer Shopper, Ziff-Davis, Inc., N.Y.C., 1996-98; copy flow mgr. CMP, Inc., N.Y.C., 1998-2000; spl. projects editor CNET Networks, 2001—; editl. cons. Martha Stewart Living Omnimedia, 2002—03. Author: Lucy A to Z, 2001, Kiss Me, Kill Me, 2003, Lucy in Print, 2003, Funny Ladies, 2004, The Lucille Ball Quiz Book, 2004; copy chief Soap Opera Weekly, 2003—. Recipient Silver awards for graphic excellence Modern Floor Coverings, MFC Mkt. Report, 1981, 84, Regional Design awards for Modern Floor Coverings covers Print Mag., 1985, 88, 65th Ann. Exhbn. Merit award Art Dirs. Club, 1986, Cert. of Distinction in editl. design for Elvis Lives!, Art Direction mag., 1992, Cert. of Merit, Cmty. Action Network, 1992, Bronze Editl. Medal of Excellence for How'd They Print That?, Cahners Pub. Co., 1995. Democrat. Avocations: travel, biking, reading, writing. E-mail: mkarol@nyc.rr.com.

KAROL, NATHANIEL H., lawyer, consultant; b. N.Y.C., Feb. 16, 1929; s. Isidore and Lillian (Orlow) K.; m. Liliane Leser, July 20, 1967; children: David, Jordan. BS in Social Sci, CCNY, 1949; MA (fellow), Yale U., 1950; LL.B., N.Y. U., 1957, LL.M., 1959, JD, 1966. Bar: N.Y. 1957. Mgmt. trainee Curtiss Wright Corp., Wood-Ridge, N.J., 1956-57; practiced in N.Y.C., 1957-58; contracting officer USAF, N.Y.C., 1958-62; chief contract mgmt. survey and cost adminstrn. Office of Procurement, NASA, Washington, 1962-64; asst. dir. cost reduction, 1964-66; dep. asst. sec. Grants Adminstrn., HEW, Washington, 1966-69; univ. dean CUNY; exec. dir. Research Found., 1969-73; v.p. Hebrew Union Coll., Cin., 1973-75; partner, nat. chmn. cons. services for edn. Coopers & Lybrand (C.P.A.s), Chgo., 1975-81; pres. Nathaniel H. Karol & Assocs. Ltd., 1981—. Cons. to govt. agys. and edn. instns. Author: Managing the Higher Education Enterprise. Served with U.S. Army, 1953-56. Recipient Outstanding Performance award HEW, 1968, Superior Performance award, 1969 Mem. N.Y. Bar, Nat. Assn. Coll. and Univ. Bus. Officers, Nat. Assn. Coll. and Univ. Attys. Home and Office: 1228 Cambridge Ct Highland Park IL 60035-1014 *What one is, is as important as what one does. I regard as successful the man who is able to establish a set of values and to observe them consistently. If there is a single thing for which I would wish to be remembered, it is that I was a man whose word was his bond.*

KARON, BERTRAM PAUL, psychologist, educator; b. Taunton, Mass., Apr. 29, 1930; s. Harold Banny and Celia (Silverman) K.; m. Mary Kathryn Mossop, Oct. 17, 1957; 1 son, Jonathan Alexander. AB, Harvard U., 1952; MA, Princeton U., 1954, PhD (USPHS fellow), 1957; grad. Social Sci. Research Council Inst. Maths. for Social Scientists, Dartmouth, summer 1953. Diplomate in clin. psychology and psychoanalysis Am. Bd. Profl. Psychology. Rsch. fellow psychometrics Ednl. Testing Svc. and Princeton, 1952-55; intern in direct analysis John N. Rosen, M.D., Gardenville, Pa., 1955-56; sr. clin. psychologist Annandale (N.J.) Reformatory, 1958; psychologist, dir. rsch. Akron (Ohio) Psychol. Cons. Ctr., 1958-59; rsch. psychologist Phila. Psychiat. Hosp., 1959, USPHS fellow, 1959-61; practice clin. psychology Phila., 1961-62; asst. prof. psychology Mich. State U., 1962-63, assoc. prof., 1963-68, prof., 1968—. Vis. lectr. Calif. Sch. Profl. Psychology, L.A., 1972; vis. scholar Wright Inst., L.A., 1979; rsch. cons. U.S. Naval Hosp., Phila., 1962, U. Pa., 1962; lectr. psychiatry Ypsilanti (Mich.) State Hosp., 1964-65; cons. VA Hosp., Allen Park, Mich., 1966-75, Ann Arbor, Mich., 1971-72 Author: The Negro Personality: A Rigorous Investigation of the Effects of Culture, 1958, rev. edit., Black Scars, 1975, (with others) Psychotherapy of Schizophrenia: The Treatment of Choice, 1981; contbg. author: Projective Techniques in Personality Assessment, 1968, Techniques for Behavior Change, 1971, The Schizophrenic Syndrome: An Annual Review, 1971, The Construction of Madness, 1976, Assessment with Projective Techniques: A Concise Introduction, 1981, Comprehensive Textbook of Psychotherapy, 1994, Dynamic Therapies for Psychiatric Disorders (Axis I), 1995; editor: Affects, Imagery, and Consciousness (Silvan S. Tomkins), vols. 1 and 2, 1962, 63; contbr. articles to profl. jours. Recipent Fowler award for disting. grad. tchg. APA Grad. Students, 1990; named disting. psychoanalyst Soc. for Psychoanalytic Tng., N.Y., 1988; NIMH grantee, 1966-71 Fellow APA (divsn. psychotherapy, clin. psychology, divsn. psychoanalysis, pres. 1990-91); mem. Soc. Psychotherapy Rsch., Am. Statis. Assn., Psychologists Interested in Study Psychoanalysis (pres. 1987-89), Mich. Psychoanalytic Coun. (pres. 1993-95). Home: 420 Wayland Ave East Lansing MI 48823 Office: 108 Psychology Rsch East Lansing MI 48824-1117 Office Phone: 517-332-3083. Business E-Mail: karon@msu.edu.

KARON, JAN (JANICE MEREDITH WILSON), writer; b. NC; Author (novels): At Home in Mitford, 1996, These High, Green Hills, 1996, Out to Canaan, 1997, A Light in the Window, 1998, A New Song, 1999, A Common Life, 2001, In This Mountain, 2002, Shepherds Abiding, 2003; (children's books) Miss Fannie's Hat, 2001, Jeremy: The Tale of an Honest Bunny, 2003; (cookbooks) Mitford Cookbook and Kitchen Reader, 2004, A Continual Feast, 2005. Mailing: c/o Viking Books Penguin USA 375 Hudson St New York NY 10014*

KARON, SHELDON, lawyer; b. Superior, Wis., Mar. 1, 1930; s. Bert and Betty Karon; m. Lee Goldwasser, Aug. 6, 1950; children: Maureen Byron, Laurie Feig, Peggy Pattis. BS, Northwestern U., 1952; JD, Harvard U., 1955. Bar: Ill. 1955. Assoc. Jenner & Block, Chgo., 1955-61; ptnr. Friedman & Koven, Chgo., 1962-75; ptnr., chmn. Karon, Morrison & Savikas, Chgo., 1975-88, Keck, Mahin & Cate, Chgo., 1988-97; of counsel Foley & Lardner, Chgo., 1997—. Arbitrator CPR Inst. Dispute Resolution, N.Y.C.; mem. Ill. Supreme Ct. Commn. for Jud. Reform, 1993-95. Bd. dirs. Kohl CHildren's Mus., Wilmette, Ill., 1988—, Highland Park (Ill.) Cmty. Edn., 1995—. Fellow Am. Coll. Trial Lawyers; mem. ABA, Ill. State Bar Assn., Chgo. Bar Assn., Fed. Cir. Bar Assn., Am. Arbitration Assn. (chair large complex case panel), Law Club, Legal Club. Office: Foley & Lardner 321 N Clark St Chicago IL 60610 E-mail: skaron@foley.com.

KAROTKIN, ROSE A., marketing professional; d. Robert Edwin and Evelyn Rose (Carver) MacInnis; m. Mark Maynard Karotkin, Sr., Aug. 23, 2002; children: Mark Maynard Karotkin, Jr., Matthew Richard Lewis, Lisa Marie. BS in Bus. Mgmt. (hon.), Albertus Magnus Coll., New Haven, Conn., 2000—03. Mixology and bar mgmt. Boston Bartenders Sch., 2001. Mktg. Yankee Gas Services Co., Berlin, Conn., 2002—; cons. Expressions by Rose, West Hartford, Conn., 2001—; mktg. coord. Phoenix Home Life, Hartford, 1997—2001; asst. to the dir. The Donaghue Found., Hartford, 1995—97; pres. M&R Auto Transport, 2004. Promotional assistance and hon. crew mem. for 2001 season Amistad Am., Mystic, Conn., 1999—2001; mktg. asst. Women's Am. Basketball League, Hartford, 1998—99. Co-author (environmental) R. Karotkin, K. Rook, S. Toelle (2002). Natural Gas Vehicle Marketing Plan 2002-2006. Yankee Gas Services Company, a Northeast Utilities System. Approved by the Connecticut Department of Utility Control August 8, 2002; contbr. criminology. Adv. Interval Ho., Hartford, 1998—2003; little league baseball coach Town of West Hartford, 1996—98; musician, singer, drama team Faith Living Ch., Plantsville, Conn.; co-chair representing Conn. Nat. Rep. Bus. Adv. Coun., Washington, 2003—03; sec. Spl. Friends Charities, Inc., East Hartford, 2002—04. Recipient Nat. Leadership Award as Hon. Co-Chair of the Bus. Adv. Coun. representing Conn. small businesses, Nat. Rep. Congl. Com., 2003, 2003 Businesswoman of the Yr. Award, Nat. Rep. Congl. Committee's Bus. Adv. Coun., 2003. Mem.: Am. Assn. of Home-Based Bus. (assoc.), Nat. Assn. for the Self-Employed (assoc.), NAFE (assoc.), Am. Mktg. Assn. (assoc.), Kappa Gamma Pi. Independent-Republican. Christian. Achievements include designing, developing and publishing website for Special Friends Charities, Inc. Avocations: riding, hiking, travel, volleyball. Office: Expressions by Rose 95 Wilfred Street West Hartford CT 06110 Personal E-mail: karotkin@comcast.net.

KARP, BARRIE, artist; b. Laredo, Tex., Feb. 10, 1945; d. Leonard and Ethel (Weiss) K. BS, Columbia U., 1967; MPhil, CUNY, 1978, MA, 1979, PhD, 1980. Lectr. philosophy CCNY, Bklyn. Coll., Hunter Coll., Manhattan C.C., 1970—94; instr. humanities Sch. Visual Arts, N.Y.C., 1982—; instr. liberal studies Parsons Sch. of Design, New Sch. for Social Rsch., N.Y.C., 1982—2002; instr. Eugene Lang. Coll./New Sch. for Social Rsch., N.Y.C., 1988—. Participant Sexuality, Gender and Consumer Soc. and Sexual Difference and Psychoanalysis Seminars, N.Y. Inst. for Humanities at NYU, 1988-97; lectr. in field. Group exhibits include Bklyn. Mus., Provincetown Art Assn. Mus., Kunstlerhaus, Vienna, Vassar Coll., Bard Coll., Parsons Sch. of Design, Gasworks, London, The Corner House, Manchester, Eng., Pierogi 2000, A.I.R. Gallery, N.Y.C., 1984-98, Provincetown Mus., 1984, Women's Studio Workshop, Rosendale, N.Y., 1986, Jus de Pomme Gallery, N.Y.C., Civilian Warfare Gallery, N.Y.C., 1984; one-person shows include Everhart Mus., Scranton, Pa., 1987, Rastovski Gallery, N.Y.C., 1986, 87; two-person shows include A.I.R. Gallery, 1988, Rastovski Gallery, N.Y.C., 1987, Women's Studio Workshop, Rosendale, N.Y., 1986; represented in permanent collections at Lawrence Markey Gallery, Exit Art, Libr. of Congress, Chatham Coll., also personal collections. Recipient Ford Found. Diversity grant, Eugene Lang. Coll., 1991, 92; grantee New Sch. Faculty Devel., 1989, 92, 94, 95, Artists Space, Ind. Artist grant, 1986, 88. Jewish. Avocation: jazz. Office: New Sch for Social Rsch Eugene Lang Coll 66 W 12th St New York NY 10011-8603

KARP, BRAD S., lawyer; b. N.Y.C., July 25, 1959; BA summa cum laude, Union Coll., 1981; JD cum laude, Harvard U., 1984. Bar: NY 1986, U.S. Dist. Ct. (so. and ea. dist.), NY 1987, Fed. Cir. Ct. Appeals 1987, U.S. Claims Ct. 1988, U.S. Ct. Appeals (2d cir.) 1991. Law clk. to Hon. Irving R. Kaufman U.S. Ct. Appeals, 2d Cir., 1984—85; ptnr. litig. dept., co-chmn. Securities Futures & Derivatives practice, mem. mgmt. com. Paul, Weiss, Rifkind, Wharton & Garrison LLP, 1985—. Bd. dirs. Practicing Attys. for Law Students Program, Inc., 1993—, Legal Action Ctr., 1998—. Contbr. monthly column to NY Law Jour. Named one of 45 Under Forty-Five Leading Lawyers in U.S., Am. Lawyer Mag., 2003. Mem.: ABA, Assn. Bar City of NY, Phi Beta Kappa. Office: Paul Weiss Rifkind Wharton & Garrison LLP 1285 Ave of the Americas New York NY 10019-6064 Office Phone: 212-373-3316. Office Fax: 212-373-2384. Business E-Mail: bkarp@paulweiss.com.

KARP, CATHERINE, writer, publishing executive; b. Lynwood, Calif., Sept. 11, 1971; m. Adam Karp; 1 child, Meggie. BA in Drama, BA in Eng., U. Calif., Irvine, 1993. Pub. svc. editor Harcourt Brace, Acad. Press Divsn., San Diego, 1994—99; freelance writer San Diego, 1999—. Co-owner Coachlight Press, 2001—. Author: (book) Gilded, 2000 (1st pl. Authorlink New Author award, 1999, Hollywood Book award, 1999), 2002. Mem.: Pub. Mktg. Assn., Small Pub. Assn. N.Am. Avocations: history, reading, travel, theater, films. Home: 15 Deer Crk Irvine CA 92604-3070 Personal E-mail: ckarp@catherinekarp.com.

KARP, DIANE R., art educator; b. 1948; PhD in art hist., U. Pa. Prof. 20th century art hist. Temple U.; curator-Ars Medica Phil. Mus. Art; dir. New Observations Mag., Santa Fe Art Inst., 2001—. Exhibitions include with Dan Fox In Time of Plague, Am. Mus. Nat. Hist., N.Y., exhibitions include Art, Med. & the Human Condition, Phila. Mus. Art, 1985; author: (exhibition catalogue) Ars Medica, 1985. Office: Santa Fe Art Institute 1600 St Michaels Dr Santa Fe NM 87505 E-mail: dkarp@sfai.org.*

KARP, DONALD MATHEW, lawyer, banker; b. Newark, N.J., Jan. 15, 1937; s. Michael N. and Beatrice (Laufer) K.; m. Margery Paula Lesnik, June 28, 1962; children: Jonathan David, Kathryn Jill. BA, U. Vt., 1958; JD, Cornell U., 1961. Bar: N.J. 1961, N.Y. 1981. With Broad Nat. Bank and Broad Nat. Bancorp., Newark, N.J., chmn. bd., 1985—, CEO, 1991; regional counsel SBA, N.J., 1966. Vice chmn., dir. Independence Cmty. Bank, 1999. Mem. coun. trustees NJ Performing Arts Ctr.; mem. adv. com. Greater Newark Conservancy; bd. dirs. Ind. Cmty. Found., Newark Hist. Soc., Friends of Newark Pub Libr., Newark Preservation and Landmarks Commn., Local Initiatives Support Corp., Newark Mus.; mem. adv. bd. NJ Coll. Medicine and Dentistry; bd. dirs. Friends of Thirteen, Inc. Recipient CEO of the Yr. Bronze award Fin. World mag., 1994, Businessman of the Yr. award City of Newark, 1999; named City News 100 Most Influential, Newark, Rotary Club Person of the Yr., St. Philip's Acad. Role Model, 1998. Mem. ABA, N.J. Bar Assn., N.Y. State Bar Assn., Fed. Bar Assn., Assn. Bar City of N.Y., Essex County Bar Assn. Clubs: Mountain Ridge Country (West Caldwell). Office: Independence Community Bank 905 Broad St Ste 2 Newark NJ 07102-2695 E-mail: dkarp@icbny.com.

KARP, GARY, marketing and public relations executive; V.p. mktg. and pub. rels. Alliant Foodsvc., Deerfield, Ill., 1992-96, v.p. catagory mgmt., 1996—. Office: Alliant Food Service 9933 Woods Dr Skokie IL 60077-1057

KARP, GERALD CHARLES, biologist, educator, writer; b. LA, Dec. 24, 1942; s. Harry and Sally Karp; m. Patrice Marie Patrick, Nov. 21, 1973; 1 child, Jennifer. BS, UCLA, 1964; PhD, U. Wash., 1970. Postdoctoral rschr. U. Colo. Med. Ctr., Denver, 1970—71; prof. biology U. Fla., Gainesville, 1971—84; vis. scientist U. Iowa, Iowa City, 1984, U. Calif., San Francisco, 1988—89; freelance writer Cin., 1990—. Ad hoc com. med. grants rsch. NIH, Bethesda, Md., 1976; cons. Morrison and Foerster, San Francisco, 1988, Wiley and Sons Publs., NYC, 1990— Author: Development, 1976, 2d edit., 1981, Cell Biology, 1979, 2d edit., 1984, Cell and Molecular Biology, 1996, 4th edit., 2005. Predoctoral fellow NSF, 1964-69, Postdoctoral fellow NIH, 1970-71. Mem. AAAS, Phi Beta Kappa. Personal E-mail: gkarpcell4@netscape.com.

KARP, HARVEY LAWRENCE, metal products executive; b. N.Y.C., Nov. 26, 1927; s. Harry and Sadie (Zimmerman) K.; children: David, Nicholas. BA, Coll. City N.Y., 1949; LLB, Yale U., 1952. Bar: N.Y. 1952, Calif. 1954. Lawyer Chesapeake Industries, Inc., N.Y.C., 1952-54; gen. counsel, v.p. Houston Fearless Corp., Los Angeles, 1955-60; founder, vice-chmn. bd. dirs., pres. Monogram Industries, N.Y.C., 1960-83; chmn. bd. Mueller Industries, Inc., 1991—. With USNR, 1945. Mem. Atlantic Golf Club, Bel Air Country Club. Home: PO Box 30 East Hampton NY 11937-0030 Office Phone: 631-324-2144. E-mail: harvey@karp.com.

KARP, HERBERT RUBIN, neurologist, educator; b. Atlanta, Apr. 13, 1921; s. Louis and Sadie (Fischer) K.; m. Hazel Berman, June 16, 1948; children: Eleanor Beth, Miriam Sarah, Benjamin Chaim. BA, Emory U., 1943, MD, 1951. Diplomate Am. Bd. Psychiatry and Neurology. Intern then resident in internal medicine Grady Meml. Hosp., 1951-54; resident in neurology Duke U. Med. Ctr., 1954-56; clin. and rsch. fellow in neurology and neuropathology Harvard U.-Mass. Gen. Hosp., 1956-58; asst. prof. neurology Emory U., Atlanta, 1958-63, prof., 1963-91, prof. emeritus, 1991—, prof. medicine, 1983-91, chmn. dept. neurology, 1974-83, dir. geriat. program dept. medicine, 1983-90; dir. med. svcs. Wesley Woods Geriatric Ctr., 1983-91, med. dir. emeritus, 1991—. Assoc. med. dir., prin. clin. coord. Ga. Med. Care Found.; trustee Atlanta Symphony Orch., 1975-95, bd. counselors 1996—, sec., 1979-80; pres. Ahavath Achim Synagogue, 1980-82; trustee Nat. Found. Jewish Culture, 1976-84, mem. bd. overseers, 1984-90. With USNR, 1943—46, with U.S. Public Health Svc. Reserve, 1946—. Recipient Thomas Jefferson award Emory U., 1984, Outstanding Med. Alumnus award, 1986, Disting. Med. Achievement award, 2001; Eternal Light award Jewish Theol. Sem. Am., 1985, Civic Endeavor award Med. Assn. Ga., 1989, Myrtle Wreath award Hadassah, 1990, Wakeman award Duke U., 1990; spl. fellow Nat. Inst. Neurol. Diseases, 1956-58; Herbert R. Karp Leadership award established in his name Dept. of Neurology, Emory U., 1999. Fellow Am. Acad. Neurology; mem. Am. Neurol. Assn. (mem. coun.), Assn. Univ. Profs. Neurology, Atlanta Interfaith Broadcasters (bd. dirs. 1991—, sec. 1997-2005, chair 2005—), Alpha Omega Alpha. Democrat. Jewish. Home: 880 Somerset Dr NW Atlanta GA 30327-3732 Office: Ga Med Care Found 1455 Lincoln Pkwy E Ste 800 Atlanta GA 30346 Office Phone: 678-527-3428. Business E-Mail: hkarp02@emory.edu.

KARP, JONATHAN DAVID, editor; b. N.Y.C., Apr. 2, 1964; s. Donald and Margery Karp. BA, Brown U., 1986; MA, NYU, 1992. Reporter Providence Jour., 1987, Miami (Fla.) Herald, 1988; editorial asst. Random House, NYC, 1989-92, assoc. editor, 1992-93, editor, 1993-95, sr. editor, 1995—2003, editorial dir., 2003—04, sr. v.p., editor-in-chief, 2004—05; pub., editor-in-chief, Warner Twelve Warner Books, NYC, 2005—. Office: Warner Twelve Warner Books 1271 Ave of the Americas New York NY 10020*

KARP, MARTIN EVERETT, management consultant; b. N.Y.C., Apr. 30, 1922; s. Albert and Bessie (Ornstein) K.; m. Naomi Joslyn Kaplan, Mar. 14, 1948; children: Betsy, Leslie Karp Goldenberg, Jonathan. B.M.E., CCNY, 1942; student, Harvard U., 1944, MIT, 1945, Northeastern U., 1951-52. Lab. engr. Gen. Electric Co., Lynn, Mass., 1942-44; mgr. research and devel. Nat. Pneumatic Co., Boston, 1946-52; dir. product planning, engring. Remington Office Machine div. Sperry Rand Co., 1953-66, dir. mfg., 1966-68; staff asst. to office of pres. ITT, 1968-69, v.p., group gen. mgr., 1969-82, group exec., 1977-82, dir. product and mktg. strategy, 1980-82; mgmt. cons. Adj. prof. Stevens Inst. Grad. Sch. Mgmt., 1984—87. Contbr. articles to tech. jours.; patentee control systems. Dir. Coun. N.Y. Coops. Served as lt. (j.g.) USNR, 1944-46. Mem. ASME, Tau Beta Pi. Jewish (pres. congregation 1961-63). Home and Office: 250 E 87th St New York NY 10128-3115 Business E-Mail: nitram1@ix.netcom.com.

KARP, MARVIN LOUIS, lawyer; b. Milo, Maine, June 12, 1934; s. Harry and Rose Helen (Kiersh) K.; m. Lesley M. Ulevitch, Aug. 11, 1963; children: Harlan, Elissa, Douglas. BA, Yale Coll., 1955, JD, 1958. Bar: Ohio 1958, U.S. Dist. Ct. (no. dist.) Ohio 1960, U.S. Ct. Appeals (6th cir.) 1963, U.S. Supreme Ct. 1974. Ptnr. Ulmer & Berne, Cleve., 1958—, head litigation dept., 1968—. Pres. Park Synagogue. Fellow Internat. Acad. Trial Lawyers, Am. Coll. Trial Lawyers; mem. ABA (chmn. torts and ins. practice sects., chmn. standing com. on ethics), Cleve. Bar Assn. (trustee 1981-84, pres. 1988-89, professionalism award 2001), Fedn. Ins. and Corp. Counsel (pres.), Am. Judicature Soc., Def. Rsch. Inst. Home: 3180 Lander Rd Cleveland OH 44124 Office: 1300 E 9th St Ste 900 Cleveland OH 44114 Office Phone: 216-931-6014. Business E-Mail: mkarp@ulmer.com.

KARP, NAOMI KATHERINE, United States government administrator; b. Tucson, Mar. 6, 1942; d. James Jacob and Rose (Sosnowsky) Silver; m. Eugene Robert Karp, Oct. 23, 1965; children: Gail, Kevin. Student, Mills Coll., 1960-62; BA in Psychology, U. Ariz., 1964, M in Edn., 1965. Spl. edn. tchr. Tucson Pub. Schs., 1965-77, Fairfax (Va.) County Schs., 1978-80; program specialist U.S. Dept. Edn. OSERS, Washington, 1980-90; cons. Family & Integration Resources, Arlington, Va., 1990-92; pvt. practice Arlington, Va., 1992-93; spl. advisor to asst. sec. & acting dir. of early childhood learning U.S. Dept. Edn. Office Ednl. Rsch. and Improvement, Washington, 1993-95; dir., Nat. Inst. of Early Childhood Devel. and Edn. Dept. of Edn., Washington, 1995—. Cons. to universities, advocacy orgns. and profl. groups, 1990-93. Author: Advocacy for Families, 1991; author, editor: Inclusion: A Right not a Privilege, 1994. Mem. Am. Assn. on Mental Retardation (nat. bd. 1991-92); mem., co-founder Fed. of Families for Children's Mental Health (nat. sec., nat. bd. 1989-92, achievement award 1992).

KARP, NOLAN S., plastic surgeon; b. N.Y.C. BS, Northwestern U., Evanston, Ill., 1979; MD, Northwestern U., 1983. Lic. physician N.Y., diplomate Am. Bd. Surgery, Am. Bd. Plastic Surgery. Resident in gen. surgery NYU Med. Ctr., 1983—88; resident in plastic surgery Inst. Reconstructive Plastic Surgery, NYU Med. Ctr., 1989—91, exec. chief resident, 1990—91, fellow in microsurgery, 1991—92, craniofacial rsch. fellow, 1988—89; asst. prof. plastic surgery NYU Sch. Medicine, 1992—99, assoc. prof. clin. plastic surgery, 1999—; attending physician Tisch Hosp., 1992—, N.Y. VA Hosp., N.Y.C., 1992—; asst. attending physician Bellevue Hosp. Ctr., N.Y.C., 1992—; attending physician Manhattan Eye, Ear, Throat Hosp., N.Y.C., 1992—. Contbr. articles to profl. jours. Recipient Award for best clin. paper, Am. Soc. Maxilofacial Surgery, 1990, 1st place for outstanding paper, N.Y. Acad. Medicine, 1990. Mem.: Am. Soc. Breast Disease, Tissue Engring. Soc., Am. Soc. for Laser Medicine and Surgery, Am. Soc. Plastic and Reconstructive Surgery, Plastic Surgery Rsch. Coun., N.Y. County Med. Soc., Med. Soc. State N.Y. Office: New York Univ Med Ctr 530 First Ave Ste 8Y New York NY 10016

KARP, PETER SIMON, marketing executive; b. New City, N.Y., Dec. 9, 1935; s. Joseph Bernard and Esther (Wexler) K.; m. Mona Leea Pecheux; children: Matthew Henry, Mark Andrew. BA, Hobart Coll., 1954; MFA, Columbia U., 1957. Rschr. Bur. Advt., Am. Newspaper Pubs. Assn., N.Y.C., 1954-56; media dir. Smith, Hagl & Knudsen, Inc., N.Y.C., 1957-59; media and rsch. dir. CAG Advt., Inc., N.Y.C., 1960-62; exec. v.p. Bennett-Chaiken, Inc., N.Y.C., 1963-66; founder, CEO BSI Global Rsch. Inc., N.Y.C., 1967—; mng. dir. The Concept Testing Inst., N.Y.C., 1972—; chairperson, CEO Pimi. Inc., N.Y.C., 1986—. Dir. Office of the Future Panel, N.Y.C., 1976—; co-dir. The Genesis Group, N.Y.C., 1983—; Trendsetter Barometer and Global Mgmt. Barometer, Pricewaterhouse Cooper, 1991—. Co-author: Customer Satisfaction: How to Maximize, Measure and Market your Company's Ultimate Product, 1989, Competing on Value, 1991; creator BSI Tech. Value Assessments, 1989-90; editor BSI Newsletter, 1976—. Pollster Ken Keating Campaign, State of New York, 1964; vol. Grand Cen. YMCA, N.Y.C., 1964-82. Fellow Inst. Dirs. (London); mem. Am. Mktg. Assn., Advt. Rsch. Found., Artificial Intelligence Assn., N.Y. Acad. Scis., Palisades Tennis Club. Jewish. Avocations: art, sculpture, travel, music. Home: 159 Tweed Blvd Nyack NY 10960-4913 Office Phone: 845-359-8200.

KARP, RICHARD M., advertising and communication executive; b. N.Y.C., Aug. 17, 1929; s. Harry and Jo Golden (Bosk) K.; m. Jane Hausman, Nov. 26, 1978; 1 son, David. BS, BA, N.Y. U., 1950; postgrad., Boston U. Publicist 20th Century Fox Film Corp., 1954-56; sr. writer Donahue & Coe Advt., N.Y.C., 1956-58; asso. creative dir., account supr. Reach, McClinton Advt., N.Y.C., 1958-63; exec. v.p., creative dir. Grey Advt. Inc., N.Y.C., 1963-93, ret., 1993—; v.p. Karp Devel. Co., 1993—; guest lectr. Baruch U., 1977-79; chmn. bd. L.A. Weekly, 1993-95. Author: monograph The Films of Buster Keaton, 1949. Mem. coun. of trustees Am. Friends of the Hebrew U., 1998; bd. dirs. Israel Cancer Assn. With AUS, 1950-51, USAF, 1951-54. Recipient Clio award, Internat. Advt. award, Screen Advt. award, Copywriters Club award. Mem. Brit. Inst. Practitioners in Advt. Office: 44 Cocoanut Row Ste 118B Palm Beach FL 33480-4069 Personal E-mail: Janekarp1@juno.com.

KARP, RICHARD MANNING, computer sciences educator; b. Boston, Jan. 3, 1935; s. Abraham Louis and Rose (Nanes) Karp; m. Diana Leigh Grand; 1 child, Jeremy Alexander. AB, Harvard U., 1955, SM, 1956, PhD in Applied Math., 1959; DSc (hon.), U. Pa., 1986, Technion, 1989, U. Mass., 1990, Georgetown U., 1992, U. Ctrl. Fla., 2000. Rsch. staff mem. IBM Watson Rsch. Ctr., Yorktown Heights, NY, 1959—68; visiting assoc. prof. elec. engring. U. Mich., Ann Arbor, 1964—65; prof. computer sci., indsl. engring., ops. rsch. U. Calif., Berkeley, 1968—96, assoc. chmn. elec. engring., computer sci., 1973—75, prof. math., 1980—95; co-chmn. program in computational complexity Math. Sci. Rsch. Inst., Berkeley, 1985—86; rsch. scientist Internat. Computer Sci. Inst., Berkeley, 1988—96; prof. computer sci. U. Wash., Seattle, 1995—99, adj. prof. molecular biotech., 1996—2000; univ. prof. U. Calif., Berkeley, 1999—; Hewlett-Packard vis. prof. Math Sci. Rsch. Inst., Berkeley, 1999—2000. Bd. govs. Weizmann Inst. Soc.; adv. bd. Computer Profns. for Social Responsibility; faculty rsch. lectr., Berkeley, 1981—82; Miller rsch. prof., Berkeley, 1980—81. Contbr. articles to profl. jours. Recipient Fulkerson prize in Discrete Math., 1979, Lanchester prize in Ops. Rsch., 1977, ORSA/TIS von Neumann Theory prize, 1990, ACM Turing award, 1985, Babbage prize, 1995, Nat. medal of Sci. award, NSF, 1996, Harvey prize, 1998; fellow Einstein, Technion, 1983, Lady Davis, 1983. Fellow: ACM; mem.: NAS, NAE, Am. Philos. Soc., Am. Acad. Arts and Scis., Inst. Combinatorics and Applications. Office: U Calif Computer Sci Divsn 387 Soda Hall # 1776 Berkeley CA 94720 E-mail: karp@icsi.berkeley.edu.*

KARP, ROBERTA SCHUHALTER, retail executive, lawyer; b. Livingston, NY, 1958; m. Brad Karp; children: Meredith, David. BA in environ. studies, SUNY, Binghamton; JD, Hofstra U., 1983. Bar: NY 1984. Atty. Kramer, Levin, Naftalis & Frankel, NYC, 1983—86; from legal counsel to v.p., gen. coun. Liz Claiborne Inc., NYC, 1986—96, v.p. corp affairs, gen. counsel, 1996—2000, sr. v.p. corp. affairs, gen. coun., 2000—. Co-chair White House Apparel Industry Partnership, 1996—99; bd. dirs. Bus. for Social Responsibility, Volunteers of Legal Svc., NY. David Rockefeller Fellow, 2000—01. Office: Liz Claiborne Inc 1441 Broadway New York NY 10018*

KARP, RONALD ALVIN, lawyer; b. Bklyn., Feb. 12, 1945; BA, U. Md., 1967; JD, Washington Coll. Law, 1971. Bar: D.C. 1972, Md. 1972, U.S. Dist. Ct. Md. 1972, U.S. Dist. Ct. D.C. 1972, U.S. Ct. Appeals (D.C. cir.) 1972, U.S. Supreme Ct. 1975. Ptnr. Chalkin & Karp, P.C., Washington, 1971-96; mng. ptnr. Karp, Frosh, Lapidus, Wigodsky & Norwind, P.A., Washington, 1996—. Faculty Nat. Coll. Advocacy, Georgetown U., Washington, 1983. Producer, moderator legal programs for NBC Radio, 1974-79, pub. TV programs, 1986—. Trustee McLean Sch. Md., 1985-88; bd. govs. Washington Regional Bd., ADL, 1988—, co-chair, 1996-2000; chair representing victims of terrorism, Am. Adv. Law Sch., 2003. Mem.: ATLA (del. D.C. 1986—88), ABA (litigation sect.), George Washington Am. Inn. Ct. (pres. 1994—95), Am. Bd. Trial Advocates (pres. Washington chpt. 2002—03), Trial Lawyers Assn. Met. Washington D.C. (bd. govs. 1980—82, pres. 1985, named Trial Lawyer Yr. 1988, Best Lawyers in Washington 2004—05), Montgomery County Bar Assn. (chair personal injury sect. 1997—99), Md. Bar Assn., D.C. Bar Assn. Office: Karp Frosh et al 1370 Piccard Dr Rockville MD 20850-4304 also: 1133 Connecticut Ave NW Washington DC 20036-4104 Business E-Mail: rkarp@karpfrosh.com.

KARP, ROSANNE, oncology and women's health nurse; b. Lynn, Mass., Oct. 8, 1946; d. Max and Dorothy (Cohen) Sidman; children: Stacy, Matthew. ADN, Northeastern U., 1967; postgrad., Lesley Coll., 1990—2002. RN, Mass. Staff nurse Holy Family Hosp., Methuen, Mass., 1969-90; staff nurse Mass. Gen. Hosp., Boston, 1990-96, case mgr. gynecology/oncology svc., 1996—. Chair, prof. edn. Greater Lawrence unit Am. Cancer Soc., bd. dirs. Mass. div., 1990-92. Recipient Excellence in Med./Surg. Nursing award Merrimack Valley Area Health Edn. Ctr., 1988, Award for Disting. Vol. Leadership Greater Lawrence unit ACS, 1995, nat. leadership award Hadassah, 1997, Ptnrs. award Ptnrs. Healthcare Sys., Inc., 1999, Jeanette Ives Erickson award for Invaluable Contbns. to Resident Life and Tchg. Vincent Meml. Obstetrics and Gynecology Svc., 2005.

KARP, STEVE, agent; b. Mt. Vernon, N.Y., Apr. 5, 1943; s. Mortimer Lester and Pearl Marion (Radding) K. BA, Tufts U., 1965; postgrad., Boston U., 1965-66, Am. Acad. Dramatic Arts, 1968. Actor Light Opera Manhattan, N.Y.C., 1969-70, Am. Shakespeare Festival, Stratford, Conn., 1972, Long Wharf Theatre, New Haven, Conn., 1972-74, N.Y. Shakespeare Festival, N.Y.C., 1974-75; founder, pres. Perk Prodns. Ltd., N.Y.C., 1974-88; artistic dir. Maxwell Anderson Playwrights Series, Stamford, Conn., 1986-87; founder, producing dir. Stamford Theatre Works, 1988—. Tchr. playwriting Westport (Conn.) Playhouse Theatre Sch., 1986-87; tchr. screenwriting Fairfield (Conn.) U., 1986-87; cons. Perk Prodns. Ltd., N.Y.C., 1988—. Appeared in Broadway plays The Changing Room, 1973, Hertzl, 1975-76; writer, dir., prodr. (dramatic short films) The Tennis Lesson, 1976 (Silver medallion V.I. Film Festival 1976-77, Achievement award Am. Film Festival 1976-77, Achievement award Chgo. Film Festival 1976-77), Inside The Jogger, 1977 (Nat. Film Collection Libr. Congress 1979, Gold medallion V.I. Film Festival 1977-78, Excellent Achievement award Melbourne Film Festival 1977-78), The Tennis Match, 1978 (Nat. Film Collection Libr. Congress 1979, Achievement award Am. Film Festival 1978); playwright, dir. The Warehouse, 1991, Fraternity, 2005. Recipient Best Dir. Theatre award Conn. Critics Cir., 1991-92, Outstanding Contribution to Conn. Theatre award, 1996-97; Film Prodn. grantee Am. Film Inst.-Nat. Endowment, 1976. Avocations: jogging, tennis. Office: Stamford Theatre Works 95 Atlantic St Stamford CT 06901-2403 Office Phone: 203-359-4414. E-mail: stevekarp@aol.com.

KARPA, JAY NORMAN, surgeon; b. Feb. 6, 1935; s. Isador and Dora (Wiener) K.; m. Elizabeth Jane Karpa, Nov. 24, 1960; children: Debra Lynn, Michael David, Lisa Michelle, Jonathan Saul. AB, Johns Hopkins U., 1955; MD, U. Md., 1958. Diplomate Am. Bd. Surgery. Intern Sinai Hosp., Balt., 1958-59, resident, 1959-64; pvt. practice gen. surgery Balt., 1964—; mem. active staff gen. surgery N.W. Hosp. Ctr., Randallstown, Md., 1965—, Sinai Hosp., Balt., 1964—; chief surgery North Charles Gen. Hosp., Balt., 1983-85. Cons. disability determination Social Security Adminstrn., Balt., 1980-82. Fellow ACS; mem. Balt. Acad. Surgery. Office: 1700 Reisterstown Rd Ste 217 Baltimore MD 21208-2920 Office Phone: 410-484-2888.

KARPEL, CRAIG S., journalist, editor; b. Midland, Tex., 1944; married. AB, Columbia U., 1965. Contbg. editor Harper's mag., N.Y.C., 1985-92. Author: The Rite of Exorcism, 1974, The Retirement Myth, 1995; contbr. numerous articles to mags. and newspapers, U.S., S.Am., Europe, Africa, Asia. Office: c/o Don Congdon Assocs 156 5th Ave Ste 625 New York NY 10010-7002 E-mail: karpel@aol.com.

KARPELES, DAVID, museum director; b. Santa Barbara, Calif., Jan. 26, 1936; s. Leon and Betty (Friedman) Karpeles; m. Marsha Mirsky, June 29, 1958; children: Mark, Leslie, Cheryl, Jason. BS, U. Minn., 1956, postgrad., 1956-59; MA, San Diego State U., 1962; postgrad., U. Calif., Santa Barbara, 1965-69; PhD, Atlantic Internat. U., 2003. Founder Karpeles Manuscript Libr. Mus., Montecito, Calif., 1983—, dir., founder Santa Barbara, Calif., 1988—, N.Y.C., 1990—, Tacoma, 1991—, Jacksonville, Fla., 1992—, Duluth, Minn., 1993—, Charleston, SC, 1995—, Buffalo, 1995—, Newburgh, NY, 1999—, Shreveport, 2004—. Dir. 202 mini-museums throughout U.S. and Can.; established the 1st cultural literacy program, presented to schs. by respective mus. staffs, 1993—; tchg. fellow Buffalo State U., 2001—. Creator program to provide ownership of homes to low-income families, 1981. Named commencement spkr. to graduating class, U. Minn., 1996, hon. inductee, Acad. Sci. and Engring., U. Minn., 2002; recipient Affordable Housing Competition award, Gov. Edmund G. Brown Jr., State of Calif. Dept. Housing and Cmty. Devel., 1981, Disting. Alumni award, U. Minn., 1996. Jewish. Home: 465 Hot Springs Rd Santa Barbara CA 93108-2029 Personal E-mail: kmuseumsb@aol.com.

KARPEN, MARIAN JOAN, financial executive; b. June 16, 1944; d. Cass John and Mary (Jagiello) Karpen. BA, Vassar Coll.; postgrad., Sorbonne, Paris, NYU, 1974—77. New England corr. Women's Wear Daily, 1966—68; Paris fashion editor Capital Cities Network, 1966—69; syndicated newspaper columnist, photojournalist Queen Features Syndicate, N.Y.C., 1971—73; acct. exec. Blyth Eastman Dillon (merged into Paine Webber), 1973—75, Oppenheimer, N.Y.C., 1975—76; v.p. mcpl. bond coord. Faulkner Dawkins & Sullivan (merged into Shearson Hayden Stone Smith Barney et al), 1976—77; mgr. retail mcpl. bond dept. Warburg Paribas Becker-A.G. Becker (merged into Merrill Lynch), sr. v.p., prin., 1977—84; sr. v.p., ltg. ptnr. Bear Stearns & Co., 1984—87, assoc. dir., 1987—90; pres., prin., CEO EuroEast® Group, Inc., N.Y.C., 1990—92; writer, creator newsletter Ea. European News; founder, pres., CEO WorkTalk®, Forum WorkTalk®, Inc., N.Y.C., 1992—; website creator, writer newsletter WorkTalk® Times; pres., founder, CEO, counselor Career Renewal Ctr.®, Inc. Past bus. adv. coun. U.S. Senate; lectr., presenter in field. Contbr. articles and photographs to newspapers and mags.; author: Career Crossroads: Ideas and Inspiration for Your Work/Life Journey. Mem. benefit com. March of Dimes, 1983; mem. Torchlight Ball com. Internat. Games for Disabled, 1984; vol. Whitney Mus. Am. Art. Named New Yorker of Week, Channel One, 1996. Mem.: Vassar Club NY (bd. dirs., exec. com., ex-officio chmn. corp. devel. com., chmn. benefit holiday open house 1989, chmn. major scholarship benefit 1991, chmn. scholarship fundraising raffle benefit 1992). Office: WorkTalk® 180 E 76th St at Lexington Ave New York NY 10021 Home: 233 E 69th St New York NY 10021-5414 Office Phone: 212-949-9300. E-mail: mjkarpen@aol.com.

KARPF, MICHAEL, medical administrator; b. Poland; BA, U. Pa., 1967, MD, 1971. Intern Johns Hopkins Hosp., 1972; rsch. assoc., immunology lab. Inst. of Infectious Disease, NIH, 1972—74; resident U. Pa. Hosp., 1974—77, fellowship hematology/oncology; chief resident U. Pa. and VA Hosp., 1976—77; asst. prof., internal medicine dept. U. Pa., 1976—78; asst. prof. U. Miami Med. Sch., 1978—79; with divsn. gen. internal medicine U. Pitts., 1979-1985, Falk Chair in gen. medicine, vice chair dept. medicine, 1985-94; sr. v.p. clin. affairs Allegheny Gen. Hosp. Allegheny Health Systems, 1994-95; sr. v.p. clin. affairs Allegheny Integrated Health Group, 1994-95; dir., vice provost hosp. systems UCLA Med. Ctr., 1995—2003; exec. v.p. for health affairs U. Ky., Lexington, 2003—. Bd. dirs. So. Calif. Organ Procurement Ctr. Contbr., reviewer numerous jours. in field. Chmn. Statewide Healthcare Coord. Com., Pa., 1993; mem. gov.'s task force evaluating managed care, Calif., 1997-98. Mem. Hosp. Assn. So. Calif. (bd. dirs.), AMA (bd. dirs.). Office: U Ky 317 Charles T Wethington Bldg, 323-5126 Lexington KY 40506 Office Phone: 859-323-5767. E-mail: mkarpf@email.uky.edu.

KARPINSKI, ANDREW, psychology professor; PhD, U. Mich., 2001. Asst. prof. Temple U., Phila., 2001—. Office: Temple U Dept Psychology Philadelphia PA 19122 Office Phone: 215-204-3102. E-mail: andrew.karpinski@temple.edu.

KARPINSKI, GENE BRIEN, not-for-profit developer, think-tank executive; b. Bridgeport, Conn., Jan. 14, 1952; s. Eugene Daniel and Madlyn Ann (Capasso) K.; m. Elizabeth Collaton, Sept. 28, 1991; children: Andrew Hunter., Lauren Gail. BA, Brown U., 1974; JD, Georgetown U., 1977. Field dir. Pub. Citizen's Congress Watch, Washington, 1977-81; exec. dir. Colo. Pub. Interest Rsch. Group, Boulder, 1981; field dir. People for the Am. Way, Washington, 1982-84; exec. dir. U.S. Pub. Interest Rsch. Group, Washington, 1984—. Bd. dirs. League of Conservation Voters, Washington, 1993—, Beldon Fund, 1999—, Nat. Assn. for Pub. Interest Law, Washington, 1987-99, Earthshare, Washington, 1992-95. Contbr. chpts. to books, articles to profl. jours.; appeared on four maj. TV news networks. Home: 807 N Irving St Arlington VA 22201-2007 Office: US Pub Interest Rsch Group 218 D St SE Washington DC 20003-1900 Office Phone: 202-546-9707. Business E-Mail: genek@pirg.org.

KARPINSKI, HUBERTA, library trustee; b. Cato, NY, Jan. 4, 1925; d. Alfred Raymond and Lena Margaret (Fuller) Tuxill; m. Edward Karpinski, Nov. 17, 1956; children: Susan Tanielian, Rebecca Hitch, Amy Jaward. Student, U. Mich., 1943—45, Wayne U., 1949—50; grad., NY Art Acad. Design, 1972. Operator to svc. observer supr. Mich. Bell Telephone Co., Detroit, 1946—57; tchr. art Birmingham (Mich.) Pub. Sch., 1977—87; libr. trustee Redford (Mich.) Twp. Dist. Libr., 1971—. Chmn. Lola Valley Civic Assn., Redford, 1960-70; vice chmn. Redford Twp. Coun. Civic Assn., 1967-71; bd. dirs. 17th Dist. Mich. Dem. Party, Redford, 1968-71. Mem. Nat. Mus. Women in arts (charter), Mich. Porcelain Artists, Internat. Porcelain Art Tchrs. Avocations: portrait painting in colored pencil, pastel, oil or on porcelain. Home: 17418 Macarthur Redford MI 48240-2241

KARPLUS, PAUL ANDREW, biochemistry educator; b. Oakland, Calif., Sept. 25, 1957; s. Robert and Elizabeth Jane (Frazier) K.; m. Karen Elisabeth Andersen, July 26, 1980; children: Elisabeth Marie, Christina Jane, Timothy Robert. Student, U. Calif., Berkeley, 1974-76; BS in Biochemistry with highest honors, U. Calif., Davis, 1978. Postdoctoral rsch. assoc. Inst. Organic Chemistry and Biochemistry, U. Freiburg, Federal Republic of Germany, 1984-88; asst. prof. biochemistry, molecular and cell biology Cornell U., Ithaca, N.Y., 1988-93; assoc. prof. biochemistry, molecular and cell biology, 1993-98. Assoc. prof. dept. biochemistry and biophysics Oreg. State U., Corvallis, 1998-99, prof., 1999—. Recipient Nat. Rsch. Svc. award NIH-NIGMS, 1979, Pfizer award in enzyme chemistry Am. Chem. Soc., 1996, Milton Harris award for basic rsch., 2001; Alexander von Humboldt fellow, 1984-85, 90, Guggenheim fellow, 1996-97. Mem. Phi Kappa Phi. Office Phone: 541-737-3200. E-mail: karplus@science.oregonstate.edu.

KARPMAN, HAROLD LEW, cardiologist, educator, writer; b. Belvedere, Calif., Aug. 23, 1927; s. Samuel and Dora (Kastleman) K.; m. Molinda Karpman. Student, UCLA, 1945-46; BA, U. Calif., Berkeley, 1950; MD, U. Calif., San Francisco, 1954. Diplomate Am. Bd. Internal Medicine. Rotating intern L.A. County Gen. Hosp., L.A., 1954-55; cardiovascular trainee Nat. Heart Inst., L.A., 1957-58; asst. resident Beth Israel Hosp., Boston, 1955-57; fellow Wyley Winsor Rsch. Found., L.A., 1958-59; pvt. practice Beverly Hills, Calif., 1958—; clin. instr. medicine U. So. Calif., L.A., 1958-64, asst. clin. prof., 1964-71, assoc. clin. prof., 1971-72; assoc. clin. prof. medicine UCLA Sch. Medicine, 1972-92, clin. prof. medicine, 1992—. Attending physician, bd. govs. Cedars-Sinai Med. Ctr., L.A.; attending physician UCLA Med. Ctr., Brotman Med. Ctr., Culver City, Calif.; examiner in cardiovascular diseases Calif. Indsl. Accident Commn., Calif. Dept. Vocat. Rehab.; founder, bd. dirs., chmn. bd. Cardio-Dynamics Labs., Inc., 1969-82; gen. ptnr. Camden Med. Bldg., L.A., 1970-86; bd. dirs. Mcht. Bank Calif.; bd. dirs. med. rsch. Faberge, Inc., N.Y.C., 1980-84; cardiovascular cons. Delta Air Lines, 1992-94; founder, bd. dirs., chmn. bd., chief med. officer CORDA Med. Care, Inc., 1995-2000; chmn., founder, dir. Integrated Diagnostic Ctrs., Inc., 2000—. Author: Your Second Life, 1979, Preventing Silent Heart Disease, 1989; assoc. editor Internat. Medicine Alert, 1992—; contbr. numerous articles to med. jours. Fellow ACP, Am. Coll. Cardiology, Am. Coll. Chest Physicians, Internat. Cardiovascular Soc., Am. Coll. Angiology, Internat. Coll. Angiology, Am. Thermographic Soc. (charter, pres. 1971-72), Am. Acad. Thermology; mem. AMA, Calif. Med. Assn., L.A. Med. Assn., Nat. Cardiovascular Network (exec. com., bd. dirs. 1994-98), Western Cardiovascular Network (chmn., med. dir. 1993-96), Am. Soc. Internal Medicine, Am. Heart Assn., Calif. Heart Assn., L.A. County Heart Assn. Office: 414 N Camden Dr #1100 Beverly Hills CA 90210-4532 Office Phone: 310-278-3400.

KARR, BEVERLY ANN, counselor; b. Birmingham, Ala., Jan. 24, 1967; d. Ollis Graham and Betty Lou (Simmons) Karr; m. Judson Barber. BS in English/Spanish/Secondary Edn., U. Ala., Birmingham, 1990, MA in Agy. Counseling, 1993, MA in Sch. Counseling, 1994, Ednl. Specialist in Sch. Counseling, 1999. Cert. secondary edn. tchr., sch. counselor. Tchr. Birmingham Bd. Edn., 1990-91; acad. counselor Bradford Adolescent, Pelham, Ala., 1991-93; counselor Jefferson County Bd. Edn., 1994—. Mem. ACA, U. Ala. Birmingham Alumni Assn. (bd. dirs.), Sigma Delta Pi, Chi Sigma Iota, Kappa Delta Pi, Delta Kappa Gamma. Democrat. Office: 225 16th St S Irondale AL 35210-1647 Home: 4455 Preserve Dr Hoover AL 35226-4160

KARR, JAMES RICHARD, ecologist, educator, research director; b. Shelby, Ohio, Dec. 26, 1943; s. Rodney Joll and Marjorie Ladonna (Copeland) K.; m. Kathleen Ann Reynolds, Mar. 23, 1963 (div. Nov. 1982); children: Elizabeth Ann, Eric Leigh; m. Helen Marie Herbst Serrano, Dec. 22, 1984. BS, Iowa State U., 1965; MS, U. Ill., 1967, PhD, 1970. Fellow in biology Princeton (NJ) U., 1970-71, Smithsonian Tropical Rsch. Inst., Balboa, Panama, 1971-72, dep. dir., 1984-87, acting dir., 1987-88; asst. prof. biology Purdue U., Lafayette, Ind., 1972-75; assoc. prof. U. Ill., Urbana, 1975-80, prof., 1980-84; Harold H. Bailey prof. biology Va. Poly. Inst. and State U., Blacksburg, 1988-91; prof. zoology, fisheries, environ. health, civil engring. and pub. affairs U. Wash., Seattle, 1991—, dir. Inst. Environ. Studies, 1991-95. Cons. on water resources EPA, 1978-, OAS, Washington, 1980, South Fla. Water Mgmt. Dist., West Palm Beach, 1989-2002; cons., gen. counsel Fla. Dept. Environ. Protection, 2002-03, 2004—. Recipient Carl R. Sullivan Fishery Conservation award, Am. Fisheries Soc., 2004; grantee, EPA, 1972—85, 1993—2000, U.S. Forest Svc., 1980—81, 1990—91, U.S. Fish and Wildlife Svc., 1979—82, NSF, 1982—84, 1997—2000, TVA, 1990—93, Dept. Energy, 1995—2002. Fellow: AAAS, Am. Ornithologists Union. Achievements include development of Index of Biotic Integrity, now used in North and South America, Asia, Australia, and Europe to assess directly the quality of water resources. Office: U Wash PO Box 355020 Seattle WA 98195-5020 Office Phone: 206-685-4784. Business E-Mail: jrkarr@u.washington.edu.

KARR, KATHLEEN, writer; b. Allentown, Pa., Apr. 21, 1946; d. Stephen and Elizabeth (Szoka) Csere; m. Lawrence F. Karr, July 13, 1968; children: Suzanne, Daniel. BA, Cath. U. of Am., 1968; MA, Providence Coll., 1971; postgrad, Corcoran Sch. Art, 1972. Tchr. English and speech Barrington (R.I.) H.S., 1968-69; curator R.I. Hist. Soc. Film Archives, 1970-71; archives asst. Am. Film Inst., Washington, 1971-72, mem. catalog staff, 1972; gen. mgr. Washington Circle Theatre Corp., Washington, 1973-78; advt. dir. Circle/Showcase Theatres, Washington, 1979-83, dir. pub. rels., 1984-88; mem. pub. rels. staff Circle Mgmt. Co./Circle Releasing, Washington, 1988-93. Asst. prof. George Washington U., 1979, 80-81; lectr., instr. in film and comms. at various instns.; lectr. at film and writing confs.; juror Am. Film Fest., 1971, Rosebud Awards, 1991; mem. adv. bd. Children's Literature, 1994—. Author: It Ain't Always Easy, 1990 ("100 Books for Reading and Sharing" citation N.Y. Public Libr., 1990), Oh, Those Harper Girls!; or, Young and Dangerous, 1992 (Parents' Choice Story Book citation, 1992), Gideon and the Mummy Professor, 1993, The Cave, 1994, In the Kaiser's Clutch, 1995, Light of My Heart, 1984, From This Day Forward, 1985 (Golden Medallion award for best inspirational novel Romance Writers of Am., 1986), Chessie's King, 1986, Destiny's Dreamers Book I: Gone West, 1993, Destiny's Dreamers Book II: The Promised Land, 1993, Go West, Young Women!, 1996, Phoebe's Folly, 1996, Spy in the Sky, 1997, The Great Turkey Walk, 1998, The Lighthouse Mermaid, 1998, Oregon, Sweet Oregon, 1998, Gold-Rush Phoebe, 1998, Man of the Family, 1999 (notable book for 2000 award ALA), Skullduggery, 2000, The Boxer, 2000 (Best Books for Young Adults award ALA, The Golden Kite award 2000), It Happened in the White House, 2000, Playing with Fire, 2001, Bone Dry, 2002, Gilbert and Sullivan Set Me Free, 2003, The 7th Knot, 2002 (Agatha award for Best Children's/Young Adult Novel 2003), Exiled: Memoirs of a Camel, 2004; editor: The American Film Heritage: Views from the American Film Insitute Collection, 1972; author of various short films; contbr. to numerous jours. Mem. Washington Romance Writers (bd. dirs. 1985-86, pres. 1986-87), Children's Book Guild (pres. 2000-01). Office: Adams Literary 295 Greenwich St #260 New York NY 10017

KARR, ROBERT A., financier; Grad., Stanford U.; MBA, Harvard Bus. Sch. Fund mgr. New Japan Securities, NYC, Mitchell Hutchins Asset Mgmt., NYC; analyst Tiger Mgmt. Corp., 1993—96; founder Joho Capital, NY, 1996—. Office: Joho Capital LLC 55 E 59th St New York NY 10022

KARRAKER, LOUIS RENDLEMAN, retired corporate executive; b. Jonesboro, Ill., Aug. 2, 1927; s. Ira Oliver and Helen Elsie (Rendleman) K.; m. Patricia Grace Stahlheber, June 20, 1952; children: Alan Louis, Sharon Elaine Cohen. BA, So. Ill. U., 1949, MA, 1952; postgrad., U. Wis., 1951-52, Washington U., St. Louis, 1954-56. V.p. personnel Am. Appraisal Assocs., Inc., Milw., 1969-73, v.p. adminstrn., 1973-74, group v.p., dir., 1974-77, exec. v.p., dir., 1977-79, pres., dir., 1979-82; bus. mgr. Concordia Coll., Ann Arbor, Mich., 1986-91. Cons. in field, 1982-86; asst. to chmn. Parker Pen Co., Janesville, Wis., 1967-69, personnel mgr., 1964-67; asst. to pres. Augustana Coll., Sioux Falls, S.D., 1962-64, acting chmn., dept. social scis., 1960-61, asst. prof. history, 1956-60. Columnist The Jour. Times, Racine, Wis., 1993-99; speaker Rep. and civic groups, Wis., 1993—. Trustee Better Bus. Bur., Milw., 1979-82, Citizens Govtl. Rsch. Bur., Milw., 1979-82; speaker, canvasser Rep. Party, S.D., 1956-60. With USNR, 1952-53, Korea. Mem. The Heritage Found., Hoover Presdl. Libr. Assn., Am. Legion. Luth. Avocations: church activities, travel, family activities, fishing. Home: 217 S 7th St Apt 11 Waterford WI 53185-4500 Personal E-mail: karr@webtv.net.

KARRAS, ALEX, actor, retired professional football player; b. Gary, Ind., July 15, 1935; m. Susan Clark Player Detroit Lions, 1958-71; host NFL Monday Night Football Preview WLS-TV, Chgo. Former commentator Monday Night Football, ABC-TV; numerous TV appearances including Tonight Show, TV movies: Paper Lion, The 500 lb. Jerk, Mad Bull, Mighty Moose & The Quarterback Kid, Babe, 1975, Mulligan's Stew, 1977, Centennial, 1978, Jimmy B. and Andre, 1979, Alcatraz: The Whole Shocking Story, When Fame Ran Out, 1980, Maid in America, 1982, Fudge-A-Mania, 1994; star TV series Webster, ABC-TV, 1983-86; films include: Blazing Saddles, 1974, Win, Place or Steal, 1977, FM, 1978, Nobody's Perfect, 1981, Victor, Victoria, 1982, Porky's, 1982, Against All Odds, 1984; author: (with Herb Gluck) Even Big Guys Cry, 1977, Alex Karras: My Life in Football, 1979, Tuesday Night Football, 1991. Named All-Pro, 1960, 61, 63, 65; recipient Outland Trophy, 1957, 79. Office: Ste 308 13400 Riverside Dr Sherman Oaks CA 91423-2541

KARRAS, RUTH MAZO, history professor; b. Chgo., Feb. 23, 1957; d. Robert Marc and Joan (Spector) Mazo; m. Christopher George Karras, Dec. 31, 1984; children: Nicola, Elena. BA in History, Yale Coll., New Haven, Conn., 1979; MPhil in European Archeology, Oxford U., Eng., 1981; MPhil in History, Yale U., New Haven, Conn., 1983, PhD in History, 1985. Asst. prof. U. Pa., Phila., 1985—93; assoc. prof. Temple U., Phila., 1993—96, prof., 1996—2000, assoc. dean, 1999—2000; prof. U. Minn., Mpls., 2000—. Gen. editor U. Pa. Press, Phila., 1994—. Author: (book) Slavery and Society in Medieval Scandinavia, 1988, Common Women: Prostitution and Sexuality in Medieval Europe, 1996, From Boys to Men: Formations of Masculinity in Later Medieval Europe, 2003, Sexuality in Medieval Europe: Doing Unto Others, 2005. Fellow, NEH, 1993—94; Rhodes Scholar, Oxford U., 1979—81. Fellow: Am. Philos. Soc. Avocation: knitting. Office: Univ Minn Dept HIstory - Social Sci Bldg 267 19th Ave S Minneapolis MN 55455

KARRAS NEBOYSKEY, ANGELA ROSE, lawyer; b. Oak Park, Ill., Feb. 10, 1975; d. Ernest Christ and Marion Rose Karras; m. David A.P. Neboyskey, Dec. 30, 2001. BS in Journalism, Northwestern U., 1997; JD, Ind. U., 2000. Bar: Ill. 2000, Ind. 2001. Atty. Swanson, Martin & Bell L.L.P., Chgo., 2003—. Notes editor: Fed. Comm. Law Jour., 1999—2000. Mem.: ABA (young lawyer liaison 2000—03), Hellenic Bar Assn., Ill. State Bar Assn., Ind. State Bar Assn. Avocations: piano, creative writing, travel, philanthropic work. Office: Swanson Martin & Bell One IBM Plz Ste 3300 330 N Wabash Chicago IL 60611

KARRICK, BRANT GILMORE, music educator; b. Bowling Green, Ky., Aug. 14, 1960; s. Cecil and Shirley Hewitt Karrick; m. Amy Laura Lindsey, Aug. 3, 1991; children: Connor, Ross, Molly, Natalie. B Music Edn., U. Louisville, 1982; MA in Edn., Western Ky. U., 1984; PhD in Music Edn., La. State U., 1994. Tchr., band dir. Beechwood Ind. Sch., Ft. Mitchell, Ky., 1984—86; dir. instrumental music Bowling Green City Schs., 1986—91; dir. bands U. Toledo, 1994—2003, No. Ky. U., Highland Heights, 2003—. Freelance musician, composer. Composer: (for band) The Dragon's Farewell, 1998, Mambo Furioso, 2001, Bayou Breakdown, 2004. Mem.: Ky. Music Educators Assn., Coll. Band Dirs. Assn., Music Educator's Nat. Conf. Avocations: golf, bicycling, skiing, fishing. Home: 141 Carriage Park Dr Alexandria KY 41001 Office: No Ky U Nunn Dr Highland Heights KY 41099

KARRIEM, FATIMA, real estate broker; b. Houston, Tex., Feb. 12, 1955; d. Hara Lee Washington and Eudora Robbie Hannah; m. Timothy Carlsbeth Moon, July 5, 1972 (div. Aug. 2, 1987); children: Taurus Cornelius Moon, Onica Monique Moon, Tamathy Cee Moon. Degree in Acctg., Upper Iowa U., Fayette, 1991. Lic. Real Estate Broker Tex. Real Estate Commn., 1995, Mortgage Broker Tex. Savs. and Loan, 2003. Cable splicing techician Southwestern Bell Tel. Co., Houston, 1977—92, installation techician Dallas, 1992—95; acctg. rep. We Wholesale, Dallas, 1991—95; reservationist SW Airline, Dallas, 1995—98; real estate agt. Henry S Miller Realtors, Duncanville, Tex., 1993—97, Century 21 Galloway-Herron, Dallas, 1997—2000; real estate agt. / broker ORG Realty, Dallas, 2000—01; broker Meirrak Realty / URA / Mortgage, Desoto, Tex., 2001—. Techician tng. Southwestern Bell Tel. Co., Houston, 1990—92; broker, adminstrn., tng. Meirrak Realty / URA, Desoto, Tex., 2001—. Vol. Paint the Town of Oak Cliff, 1995—2002; adminstr. Dallas Islamic Mosque, Dallas. Recipient Appreciation, Dallas Islamic Acad., 1997—2000, Volunteerism award, Greater Dallas Assn. Realtors, 1996—2002, Relocation Specialists award, Henry S Miller, Realtors, 1997. Mem.: Women's Coun. of Realtors (assoc.), Tex. Assn. Real Estare Brokers (assoc.), Nat. Assn. Real Estate Brokers (assoc.), Greater Dallas Assn. Realtors (assoc.; mem affiliate team, Volunteerism award 1996—2002), Grievance and Profl. Std. Com. (assoc.; com. mem., bd. dirs. 2001—03), Dallas Assn. Real Estate Brokers (assoc.), Paint the Town Oak Cliff (assoc.), Oak Cliff C. of C. (assoc.), Cedar Hill C. of C. (assoc.). Independent. Moslem. Avocations: martial arts, bicycling, body building, golf, creative advertising. Office: Meirrak Realty / URA P O Box 0931 Desoto TX 75123 Office Phone: 214-734-1125. E-mail: fkarriem@sbcglobal.net.

KARSEN, SONJA PETRA, retired literature educator; b. Berlin, Apr. 11, 1919; arrived in U.S., 1938, naturalized, 1945; d. Fritz and Erna (Heidermann) K. Titulo de Bachiller, Ministerio de Educacion Nacional, 1937; BA, Carleton Coll., 1939; MA, Bryn Mawr Coll., 1941; PhD, Columbia U., 1950. Instr. Spanish Lake Erie Coll., Painesville, Ohio, 1943-45; instr. modern langs. U. PR, 1945-46; instr. Spanish Syracuse (NY) U., 1947-50, Bklyn. Coll., 1950-51; asst. to dep. dir. gen. UNESCO, 1951-52, L.Am. Desk, tech. assistance dept., 1952-53, mem. tech. assistance mission Costa Rica, 1954; asst. prof. Spanish Sweet Briar Coll., Va., 1955-57; assoc. prof., chmn. dept. Romance langs. Skidmore Coll., Saratoga Springs, NY, 1957-61, chmn. dept. modern langs. and lits., 1961-79, prof. Spanish, 1961-87, prof. emerita, 1987; cons. Hudson-Mohawk Assn. Colls. and Univs., 1990. Faculty rsch. lectr. Skidmore Coll., 1963; mem. adv. and nominating com. Books Abroad, 1965-67; Fulbright lectr. Free U. Berlin, 1968; lectr. U. Gesamthochschule, Paderborn, Germany, 1995, 99. Author: Guillermo Valencia, Colombian Poet, 1951, Educational Development in Costa Rica with UNESCO's Technical Assistance, 1951-54, 1954, Jaime Torres Bodet: A Poet in a Changing World, 1963, Selected Poems of Jaime Torres Bodet, 1964, Versos y prosas de Jaime Torres Bodet, 1966, Jaime Torres Bodet, 1971, Ensayos de Literatura E Historia Iberoamericana/Essays on Iberoamerican Literature and History, 1988, Papers on Foreign Languages, Literature and Culture, 1982-87, 88, Bericht Über Den Vater: Fritz Karsen 1885-1951, 1993; translator: The Role of the Americas in History (Leopoldo Zea), 1992; editor Lang. Assn. Bull., 1980-83; mem. editl. adv. bd. Modern Lang. Studies, 1977-93; contbr. articles to profl. jours. Decorated Chevalier dans l'Ordre des Palmes Académiques, 1964; recipient Leadership award NY State Assn. Fgn. Lang. Tchrs., 1973, 76, 78, Nat. Disting. Leadership award, 1979, Disting. Svc. award, 1983, 86, Capital Dist. Fgn. Lang. Disting. Svc. award, 1987; recipient Spanish Heritage award, 1981, Alumni Achievement award Carleton Coll., 1982; exch. student auspices Inst. Internat. Ednl. at Carleton Coll., 1938-39; Buenos Aires Conv. grantee for rsch. in Colombia, 1946-47; faculty rsch. grantee Skidmore Coll., summer 1959, 61, 63, 64, 67, 69, 70, 73, ad hoc faculty grantee, 71, 78, 85; scholar in French, Bryn Mawr Coll., 1939-41 Mem. Am. Assn. Tchrs. Spanish and Portuguese (life; emeritus), Nat. Assn. Self-Instrnl. Lang. Programs (v.p. 1981-82, pres. 1982-83), AAUW (life), AAUP (life), MLA (del. assembly 1976-78, Mildenberger medal selection com 1984-86), El Ateneo Doctor Jaime Torres Bodet (founding mem.), Nat. Geog. Soc., Asociación Internacional de Hispanistas, UN Assn. U.S.A., Am. Soc. French Acad. Palms, Fulbright Alumni, Phi Sigma Iota, Sigma Delta Pi. Home: 1755 York Ave Apt 37A New York NY 10128-6875 *Perseverance, hard work and high ethical standards coupled with the opportunities for fulfilling one's potential, available in the United States to a greater extent than anywhere else in the world, have made my life what it is today.*

KARSH, PHILIP HOWARD, advertising executive; b. Salt Lake City, Sept. 19, 1935; s. Sol and Ruth (Marks) K.; m. Carol Hyman, July 3, 1962 (div. Sept. 1973); children: Michael David, Jill Ann; m. Linda Love, Sept. 7, 1984. BA, U. Colo., 1957. Account exec. Ted Levy/Richard Lane & Co., Denver, 1957-59; v.p. Jerome/Philip Advt., Denver, 1959—65, pres., 1962-65; v.p. Frye Sills Advt., Denver, 1965—77; pres. Karsh & Hagan Advt. Inc., Denver, 1977-85, chmn., 1985-97; ret., 1998. Trustee Nat. Jewish Med. and Rsch. Ctr., Denver, 1963—, chmn. 1991-95, Kern Rsch. Found., Denver, 1984—, Mile High United Way, Denver, 1986-92; mem. Denver Metro Conv. and Visitors Bur., 1994—, chmn., 1997. Named to Colo. Tourism Hall of Fame, 2004. Mem. Worldwide Ptnrs. (internat. chmn. 1986-87), Denver Advt. Fedn. (bd. dirs. 1968-69, 87-88), Colo. Hist. Soc. (trustee 1998—, chair 2003—). Democrat. Jewish. Avocations: skiing, travel, golf. Home: 11704 W Auburn Dr Denver CO 80228-4758 Office: 2399 Blake St # 160 Denver CO 80205-2108 Office Phone: 720-596-4664. Personal E-mail: philkarsh@comcast.net.

KARSON, EMILE, lawyer; b. Berlin, Sept. 10, 1921; came to U.S., 1948, naturalized, 1955; s. Bogdan and Zorka (Natowa) Karastoyanoff; m. Lilia Usunowa, Dec. 31, 1944; 1 child, Danielle (dec.). LLB, U. Sofia, 1946, U. PAris, 1946; Docteur-en-Droit, U. Paris, 1948; LLM, Yale U., 1951, JSD, 1953; postgrad., U. So. Calif., 1953-54, U. Pa., 1978, Harvard U., 1978, Cornell U., 1991. Internat. atty. World Bank, Washington, 1951—53; gen. counsel Coast Fed. Savs., Great We. Savs., L.A., 1954—58; F-104 exec. Lockheed Aircraft Internat., L.A., 1959—63; treas. Europe, Zurich, Switzerland Litton Industries, Inc., 1964-69; corp. treas. Continental Grain Co., N.Y.C., 1969-72; v.p. fin. & adminstrn. Loctite Corp., Newington, Conn., 1972-81; founder, CEO, INTECH (internat. high tech. venture capital), Washington, 1981-85; internat. atty., 1998—. Vis. prof. law U. P.R., 1957; organizer 1st symposium on atomic energy and law for L.Am.; lectr. Naval War Coll., Fgn. Svc. Inst., U. So. Calif., Ind. U., U. Pitts.; mem. Rep. Assocs., 1954-56; Bus. Internat. Round Table, 1960-65; cons. Dept. State, 1983, U.S. Dept. Labor internat. programs, 1991, 92. Dir.: (documentaries, 2 films) shown at Cannes and Venice Film Festivals, 1947; (documentaries) Peace Treaty in Paris. Mem. adv. bd. Genetics Unique Fund, 1985-87; broadcaster Voice of Am., 1949-51; pres. Ea. European Orphans, Washington; steering com. Am. U. in Bulgaria, 1992-96; chmn., pres. Bulgarian-Am. Charitable and Ednl. Ctr., 1989-98. Fellow French Govt., 1946-48; recipient Ambrase Gherimi prze Yale U., EE prize Lockheed Aircraft Internat. Mem. State Bar Calif., Bar U.S. Supreme Ct., World Affairs Coun., Yale Club (Calif.), Yale Law Sch. Club (Calif.). Home: 9125 Seven Locks Rd Bethesda MD 20817-2059

KARSON, SAMUEL, psychologist, educator; b. Baltimore, Md., Jan. 3, 1924; s. Norman Jacobson and Annie (Raskin) K.; m. Dorothy Faye Libert, Sept. 6, 1946; children: Linda Catherine, Michael Craig. BS, L.I. U., 1948; PhD, Washington U., St. Louis, 1952. Diplomate Clin. Psychology Am. Bd. Profl. Psychology. With psychiatric unit U.S. Naval Tng. Ctr., San Diego, 1952-55; asst. prof. dept. psychology U. N.H., 1957-58; chief psychologist, dir. rsch. Dade County Child Guidance Clinic, Miami, Fla., 1958-62; rsch. asst. prof. dept. nursing U. Miami, Fla., 1959-62; chief clin. psychologist, office aviation medicine FAA, Washington, 1962-66; prof., head dept. psychology Ea. Mich. U., Ypsilanti, 1966-77; chief psychologist, adminstr. overseas mental health program Dept. State, Washington, 1977-81; regional psychologist Southeast Asia Am. Embassy, Bangkok, Thailand, 1981-83; prof. clin. psychology Sch. Psychology Fla. Inst. Tech., Melbourne, 1983-85, prof., dir. grad. clin. tng., 1985-89; prin. investigator Second Genesis, Inc., Bethesda, Md., 1990-95. Cons. clin. psychology to office aviation medicine FAA, Washington, 1966-75. Author: (with J. O'Dell and M. Karson) 16PF Interpretation in Clinical Practice, 1997, The Karson Clinical Report, A Psychologist's Odyssey (Have PhD Will Travel), 1992, Pioneers in Personality Science: Autobiographical Perspectives. Served with USAAF, 1942-45, with USAF, 1955-57. Recipient Appreciation certificate Sec. State Alexander Haig, 1981, Personality Assessment award Thai Psychol. Assn., 1983, Disting. Profl. Contbns. award Md. Psychol. Assn., 1987. Fellow APA, Soc. Personality Assessment (life); mem. Soc. Multivariate Exptl. Psychology, Assn. Aviation Psychologists (pres. 1973-74).

KARST, GARY GENE, retired architect; b. Barton County, Kans., Sept. 2, 1936; s. Emil and Clara (Nuss) K.; m. Loretta Marie Staub, Nov. 30, 1957; children: Kevin Gene, Sheri Lynn, Stacey Marie. BArch, Kans. State U., 1960. Registered profl. arch., Kans.; Nat. NCARB cert. Staff architect Horst & Terrill Architects, Topeka, 1960—64; ptnr. Horst, Terrill & Karst Architects, Topeka, 1965—2001, dir. design, 1965—2001, sec., 1973—78, v.p., treas., 1978—92, v.p., 1992—99; pres., 1999—2001; ret., 2001; design architect Ruhnau, Evans, Brown & Steinman Architects, Riverside, Calif., 1964—65. Mem. Capital City Redevel. Agy., Topeka, 1978-86; mem. adv. bd. dept. architecture Kans. State U., Manhattan, 1986-87. Prin. works include Emporia (Kans.) H.S., 1972, (Kans. Soc. Architects award 1975), S.W. Bell Telephone Co. Equipment Bldg., 1974 (Bell Sys. award 1976), Durland Hall-Univ. Engring. Bldg., 1981 (Kans. Soc. Architects award 1983), Kans. State Prison Medium Security Facility, 1983 (Kans. Soc. Architects award 1985), Lansing H.S., 1988 (William W. Caudill citation Am. Sch. and Univ. Mag.), Leavenworth H.S., 1990 (citation Am. Sch. and Univ. Mag.), Plant Scis. Bldg., Kans. State U., 1994, Tomanek Hall, Ft. Hays State U., 1995; featured in publs. including Archtl. Record. Mem. Future Heritage Topeka, Capitol City Redevelopment Agy., Topeka, 1978—86. Recipient citation Am. Sch. and Univ. Mag.; Bales Organ Recital Hall, U. Kans., 1995, Weigel scholar Kans. State U., 1958-60; over 80 recognitions for design excellence. Mem. AIA (Henry W. Schirmer Disting. Svc. award 2001), Kans. Soc. Architects (pres. 1981-82), Optimists Internat. (pres. Topeka breakfast club 1970-71, lt. gov. Kans. dist. 1981-82). Republican. Lutheran. Avocations: woodworking, photography, sculpting. Home: 3535 SW Macvicar Ave Topeka KS 66611-1841 E-mail: gkarst@cox.net.

KARST, KENNETH LESLIE, law educator; b. Los Angeles, June 26, 1929; s. Harry Everett and Sydnie Pauline (Bush) K.; m. Smiley Cook, Aug. 12, 1950; children— Kenneth Robert, Richard Eugene, Leslie Jeanne, Laura Smiley AB, UCLA, 1950; LL.B., Harvard U., 1953. Bar: Calif. 1954, U.S. Dist. Ct. (cen. dist.) Calif. 1954, U.S. Ct. Appeals (9th cir.) 1954, U.S. Supreme Ct. 1970. Assoc. Latham & Watkins, Los Angeles, 1954, 56-57; teaching fellow law Harvard U. Law Sch., 1957-58; asst. prof. Ohio State U. Coll. Law, Columbus, 1958-60, assoc. prof., 1960-62, prof., 1962-65; prof. law UCLA, 1965-90, David G. Price and Dallas P. Price prof. law, 1990—. Author: (with Harold W. Horowitz) Law, Lawyers and Social Change, 1969, (with Keith S. Rosenn) Law and Development in Latin America, 1975, Belonging to America: Equal Citizenship and the Constitution, 1989, Law's Promise, Law's Expression: Visions of Power in the Politics of Gender, Race, and Religion, 1993; assoc. editor Ency. of Am. Constn., 1986, co-editor-in-chief, 2d edit., 2000; contbr. articles to profl. jours. Served to 1st lt. JAGC, USAF, 1954-56. Law faculty fellow Ford Found., 1962-63. Fellow Am. Acad. Arts and Scis.; mem. State Bar Calif. Office: UCLA Law Sch PO Box 951476 Los Angeles CA 90095-1476 Business E-Mail: karst@law.ucla.edu.

KARST, WILLIAM B., architectural firm executive; BArch, MArch, Clemson U. CEO Callison Arch., Inc., Seattle, 1995—. Spkr. in field. Trustee Seattle C. of C.; mem. archtl. bd. Clemson U.; active Cmty. Devel. Roundtable, Seattle; founder Puget Sound Developer Forum; bd. dirs. Insight Alliance. Mem.: AIA, China Trade Devel. Coun., Seattle Downtown Assn. Office: Callison Arch Inc Ste 2400 1420 Fifth Ave Seattle WA 98101-2343

KARSTAEDT, ARTHUR R., III, lawyer; b. Madison, Wis., Sept. 15, 1951; BA, U. Wis., 1972; JD, U. Denver, 1975. Bar: Colo. 1976. Formerly lawyer Hall & Evans, Denver; ptnr. Harris, Karstaedt, Jamison & Powers, P.C., Englewood, Colo., 1995—. Office: Harris Karstaedt Jamison & Powers PC 383 Inverness Pkwy S Ste 400 Englewood CO 80112-5816

KARTH, TIMOTHY JAMES, music educator, musician; b. Waukesha, Wis., Aug. 28, 1970; s. David Jerome Karth and Kathryn Marie Becker-Karth; m. Joelle Marie Beutin, Aug. 6, 1994; children: Sean, Rory, Kari, Devin. BS in Music Edn., Carroll Coll., 1996. Dir. jazz studies Wauwatosa (Wis.) West H.S., 1995—96; assoc. dir. bands Pius XI H.S., Milw., 1996—2000; dir. bands North Lake (Wis.) Sch. Dist., 2000—03, Lake Country Sch. Dist., Hartland, Wis., 2003—. Mem. sch. improvement team North Lake Sch. Dist., 2001—03; mem. Arrowhead H.S. Dist. Transition Com., Hartland, Wis., 2003—; mem. comm. com. Lake Country Sch. Dist., 2004—; jazz improvisation coach Pius XI H.S., Milw., 2004—. Composer: (symphonic band) Visions, (concert band) The Great Ape Chase, (handbells) Agony in the Garden, (music for tv) The Protector Fanfare, (music for tvV) The Megabucks Fanfare. Vol. Habitat for Humanity, Milw., 2003—04; asst. cub master Cub Scouts of Am., West Allis, Wis., 2004—; active alumnus Kids From Wis., West Allis, 1989—2004. Recipient Ron Cuzner Raspberry award, Marquette U., 1984, Grad. of the Last Decade award, Carroll Coll., 2004; Chamber Music scholar, 1992—95. Mem.: Civic Music Assn. (assoc. conductor 1998—2002), Wis. Music Educators Assn., Wis. Sch. Music Assn., Music Educators Nat. Conf. R-Consevative. Methodist. Avocations: model railroading, video games, music performance and composition. Office: Lake Country Sch Dist 1800 Vettleson Rd Hartland WI 53029 Office Phone: 262-367-3606. Office Fax: 262-367-3205. Personal E-mail: dizzynmiles@wi.rr.com. E-mail: tim.karth@lcs.k12.wi.us.

KARTHA, KUTTY KRISHNAN, plant pathologist; b. Shertallai, India, Aug. 9, 1941; married, 1972; 2 children. BSc, Saugar U., India, 1962; MSc, Jawaharal Nehru Agrl. U., India, 1965; PhD in Plant Pathology, India Agrl. Rsch. Inst., 1969. Fellow Nat. Inst. Agrl. Rsch., France, 1970-72; vis. scientist Prairie Regional Lab., NRC, Saskatoon, Canada, 1973-74; asst. rsch. officer Plant Biotech. Inst., Saskatoon, 1974-76, assoc. rsch. officer, 1976-81, head cell tech. sect., 1985-87; sr. rsch. officer Plant Biotech. Inst., NRC, Saskatoon, 1981, group leader cereal biotech., 1985-93, acting rsch. dir., 1993-95, dir. gen., 1995—. Adj. prof. U. Sask., Saskatoon, 1987—; mem. Can. Agrl. Rsch. Coun., 1990-94. Editor Jour. Plant Physiology, 1987, Cyropreservation Plant Cells and Organs, 1985. Recipient George M. Darrow award Am. Soc. Hort. Sci., 1981, C.J. Bishop award Can. Soc. Hort. Sci., 1992, Excellence in Rsch. award Treasury Bd. Can., 1992, Commemorative medal for 125th anniversary of Confedn. Can., 1992, Queen Elizabeth II Golden Jubilee medal, 2002, Gold Medal award Profl. Inst. Pub. Svc. Can., 2004. Mem. Internat. Assn. Plant Tissue Culture (nat. corr. 1982-86), Can. Soc. Plant Physiologists, Can. Phytopath. Soc. Achievements include research in plant biotechnology, cryopreservation of plant cells and organs, plant tissue culture. Office: Plant Biotech Inst 110 Gymnasium Pl Saskatoon SK Canada S7N OW9 E-mail: kutty.kartha@nrc-cnrc.gc.ca.

KARTIGANER, JOSEPH, retired lawyer; b. Berlin, June 5, 1935; came to U.S., 1939; s. Harold and Lilly (Wolkowitz) K.; m. Audrey Gertsman Amdursky; children: Deborah Lynn, Alison Beth. AB, CCNY, 1955; LL.B., Columbia U., 1958. Bar: N.Y. 1960, Fla. 1978, D.C. 1979. Assoc. White & Case, N.Y.C., 1960-69, ptnr., 1969-88, Simpson Thacher & Bartlett, N.Y.C., 1988-99; ret., 1999. Lectr. law Columbia Law Sch., N.Y.C., 1973-80; vis. lectr. Sch. Law Yale U., 1997-2000; mem adv. com. N.Y. Estates, Powers and Trust Law-Surrogate's Ct. Procedure Act, 1997—. Mem.: Columbia Law Rev. Fellow Am. Bar Found., Am. Coll. Trust and Estate Counsel (regent 1978-84), Am. Coll. Tax Counsel, N.Y. State Bar Found.; mem. ABA (chmn. real property, probate and trust law sect. 1986-87, co-chair sect. standing com. on govt. submissions 1995—), N.Y. State Bar Assn., Assn. of Bar of City of N.Y. (chmn. com. on trusts, estates and surrogate's cts. 1990-92), Nat. Conf. Lawyers and Corp. Fiduciaries (co-chair 1991-93), Am. Law Inst., Internat. Acad. Estate and Trust Law (exec. coun. 1980-94, 98-2002), Scarsdale Golf Club (Hartsdale, N.Y.). Home: 812 5th Ave # 5B New York NY 10021-7253 Office: Simpson Thacher & Bartlett 425 Lexington Ave Fl 15 New York NY 10017-3954 Personal E-mail: joekart@yahoo.com.

KARWAN, MARK HENRY, engineering educator, dean; b. Cleve., Nov. 16, 1951; B in Engring. Scis. with full honors, MS in Engring., Johns Hopkins U., 1974; PhD, Ga. Inst. Tech., 1976. From asst. prof. to assoc. prof. dept. indsl. engring. Univ. at Buffalo, SUNY, 1976-86, prof. dept. indsl. engring., 1986—, prof., chair dept. indsl. engring., 1987-92, prof., assoc. dean grad. edn. Sch. Engring. & Applied Scis., 1992-94, prof., acting dean Sch. Engring. & Applied Scis., 1994-95, dean Sch. Engring. & Applied Scis., 1996—. Chair U. at Buffalo Bus. Alliance, 1998-2001; cons. Mgmt. Adv. Svcs., Inc., Columbia, Md., 1974, Health Care Plan, Inc., Buffalo, 1984-87, Praxair, Inc., Tonawanda, N.Y., 1987—; faculty advisor student chpt. Inst. Indsl. Engrs. 849, 1977-83; proposal reviewer NSF-Sys. Theory and Ops. Rsch., NSF-Applied Math.; cluster chmn. ORSA/TIMS joint nat. meeting, 1986, chmn. numerous sessions, 1977—; mem. grad. sch. fellowship com. SUNY, Buffalo, 1980-82, grad. sch. exec. com., 1982-85, 92-94, grad. sch. polyc rev. com., 1984-91, chmn., 1984-88, honors coun., 1992-98, mem. Sch. Engring. and Applied Scis. divisional com. of grad. sch., 1976-79, Sch. Engring. and Applied Scis. acad. programs com., 1981-87, chmn. Sch. Engring. and Applied Scis. acad. programs com., 1982-85, 89-90, 93-95, dir. Ctr. for Indsl. Effectiveness, 1993-98, undergrad. affairs com., 1976-78, grad. affairs com., 1979-87, dir. grad. studies, 1982-87. Assoc. editor: Naval Research Logistics, 1987—2003, IIE Transactions, 1991-93; co-editor spl. issue Naval Rsch. Logistics, 1988; mem. editl. adv. bd. Computers & Ops. Rsch., 1984-2004; contbr. more than 70 refereed papers to profl. jours. including Annals of Discrete Math., European Jour. Operational Rsch., IEEE Transactions on Automatic Control, Jour. Mechanics Design, Mgmt. Sci., Math. Programming, Networks, Ops. Rsch., Water Resources Rsch.; patentee two-phase method for real time process control. Pres.'s fellow Ga. Tech. U., 1974-75. Mem. Alpha Pi Mu, Omega Rho (regional dir. N.E. U.S. chpt. 1982-84). Office: Univ at Buffalo Sch Engring And Appld Scis Buffalo NY 14260-1900 Office Phone: 716-645-2771 x 1101. E-mail: mkarwan@buffalo.edu.

KARWEICK, JUNE KLEES, education educator; d. John Robert and Roseann Diane Klees; m. Mark Robert Karweick, June 12, 1999; 1 child, Jane Klees. BS, East Stroudsburg U., 1987—90, MA, 1990—91; PhD, Kent State U., 1991—99. Cert. in Distance Edn. U. of Wis., Madison, 2003. Grad. fellow East Stroudsburg U., Pa., 1990—91, Kent State U., Ohio, 1993—95, tchg. fellow, 1995—97; history prof. Bay Coll., Escanaba, Mich., 1997—. Distance edn. trainer Bay Coll.; history adv. com. Delta-Schoolcraft ISD, Escanaba, Mich.; continuous improvement committees Bay Coll. Reviewer (textbook) Social Fabric Rev. for Publishers, (book rev.) Rev. of 'The Am. Years'; author: (policy document) Gen. Edn. Governance Model. Bd. mem. Delta County Hist. Soc., Escanaba, Mich., 1998—2000. Mem.: Mich. Teachers Assn., Mich. Hist. Soc., Delta Rocks Curling Club, Phi Alpha Theta (life). Office: Bay Coll 2001 N Lincoln Rd Escanaba MI 49829

KASAMI, TADAO, information science educator; b. Kobe, Hyogo, Japan, Apr. 12, 1930; m. Fumiko Okada, May 9, 1964; children: Yuuko, Ryuichi. B in Engring., Osaka (Japan) U., 1958, M in Engring., 1960, D in Engring., 1963. Assoc. prof. engring. Osaka (Japan) U., 1963-66, prof. engring. sci., 1966-94, dean engring. sci., 1990-92, prof. emeritus, 1994—; prof., Grad. Sch. Info. Sci. Nara (Japan) Inst. Sci. and Tech., 1992-98, dean, Grad. Sch. Info. Sci., 1992-94, dir. libr., 1994-98, prof. emeritus, 1998—; prof. Hiroshima (Japan) City U. Sch. Info. Sci., 1998—2003, prof. emeritus, 2003—. Adj. prof. U. Hawaii Grad. Sch., Honolulu, 1992—97; guest prof. Nara Inst. Sci. and Tech., 2003—. Author: Coding Theory, 1978, Discrete Structure II, 1983, Formal Language Theory, 1988, Introduction to Information and Coding Theory, 1989, Trellises and Trellis-based Decoding Algorithms for Linear Block Codes, 1998. Recipient Okawa prize, 2003, Takajanagi Meml. prize, 2003. Fellow IEEE (life), Inst. Electronics, Info. and Comm. Engrs. (hon., Achievement award 1987, Disting. Svc. award 2001); mem. Soc. Info. and Its Applications (hon., pres. 1993), IEEE Info. Theory Soc. (Claude E. Shannon award 1999). Personal E-mail: kasami@empirical.jp.

KASANIN, MARK OWEN, lawyer; b. Boston, June 28, 1929; s. Jacob Sergei and Elizabeth Owen (Knight) K.; m. Anne Camilla Wimbish, Dec. 18, 1960; children: Marc S., James W. BA, Stanford U., 1951; LL.B., Yale U., 1954. Bar: Calif. Assoc. McCutchen, San Francisco, 1957-62, 63-67; ptnr. Brigham McCutchen, San Francisco, 1967—. Mem. planning commn. City of Belvedere, Calif., 1974-76; chair tech. adv. com. San Francisco Bay Area Water Transit Authority, 2001-. Served with USNR, 1955-2005. Named one of Best Lawyers in Am., 1995—2005. Fellow Am. Coll. Trial Lawyers; mem. Maritime Law Assn. U.S. (exec. com. 1984-87), Jud. Conf. U.S. (mem. fed. civil rules adv. com. 1992-2002). Home: PO Box 698 Belvedere Tiburon CA 94920-0698 Office: Bingham McCutchen 3 Embarcadero Ctr San Francisco CA 94111-4003 Fax: 415-393-2286.

KASCH, MARY COURTEOL, occupational therapist; b. Chgo., Feb. 15, 1947; d. Paul and Bernice Zimmerman Courteol; children: Elizabeth Kasch Peter, David Michael. BS, Tufts U., 1970. Registered occupl. therapist, lic., cert. hand therapist. Pres. Hand Therapy Certification Commn., Rancho Cordova, Calif., 1989—2000, exec. dir., 2000—03; hand therapist Campus Commons Phys. Therapy, Sacramento, 1997—2001. Author: Rehabilitation of the Hand, 1979, 1985, 1991, 1996, 2001, Occupational Therapy: Practice Skills for Physical Dysfunction; mem. editl. rev. bd.: Jour. Hand Therapy, 1998—2003. Sec. Sacramento Choral Soc. Orch., Sacramento, 1998—2003. Recipient Award of Excellence, Occupl. Therapy Assn. Calif., 1986, Lillian Terris award, Profl. Exam. Svc., 1997, Nat. Svc. award, Arthritis Found., 1985, Pres.'s Gold award, Am. Soc. Hand Therapists, 1992. Fellow: Am. Occupl. Therapy Assn. Achievements include development of Certified Hand Therapist Credential. Office: Hand Therapy Certification Commission 11160 Sun Ctr Dr Rancho Cordova CA 95670 E-mail: mkasch@htcc.org.

KASCUS, MARIE ANNETTE, librarian; b. Boston, June 2, 1943; d. Anthony Joseph and Mildred (Lochiatto) Martucci; m. Joseph Edward Kascus, July 3, 1966. BA, Northeastern U., Boston, 1966; MSLS, U. Ill., 1969; ArtsD, Simmons Coll., 2004. Libr. asst. Boston Pub. Libr. Br., East Boston, Mass., 1961-66; rsch. asst. Hanscom AFB/Decision Scis. Lab., Bedford, Mass., 1964-66; asst. binding libr. Univ. Ill., Champaign-Urbana, 1970-72; head serials dept. Ctrl. Conn. State U., New Britain, 1972-99, collection mgmt. coord., 1984-86, libr. emerita, 1999; dir. library svcs. Newbury Coll., Brookline, Mass., 1999—2001; interim dir. acad. resources & lab. Champlain Coll., 2002—03, asst. dir., 2003—. Abstracter ABC-CLIO, Santa Barbara, Calif., 1979—2002; indexer Productivity, Inc., Stamford, Conn., Cambridge, Mass., 1981-86; mem. editl. bd. Cataloging and Classification Quar., 1984—; cons. Post Coll., Waterbury, Conn., 1986, State of Conn. Pers. Divsn., Hartford, Conn., 1987-88, Choice Mag., Middletown, Conn., 1990—; mem. program adv. bd. Sixth Off-Campus Libr. Svcs. Conf., 1992-93; mem. adv. bd. ASIS Thesaurus of Info. Sci. and Librarianship, 1993. Referee and contbr. articles to profl. jours.; presenter at profl. confs.; co-author: Library Services for Off-Campus and Distance Education: The Second Annotated Bibliography, 1996. Cons. New England Assn. Schs. and Colls., Newton, Mass., 1990, 92, CCSU Found./George R. Muirhead Scholarship Fund, New Britain, 1991, Harriet Kiser Opera Fund, Hartford, 1991—; apptd. to Mass. State Adv. Com. Librs., 2000-02. Recipient Sears B. Condit award for excellent scholarship Sears Roebuck, Inc., Boston, 1966, Alumni award for profl. promise Northea. U., Boston, 1966; AAUP Faculty Rsch. grantee Ctrl. Conn. State U., 1991; Higher Edn. Act fellow U.S. Govt. U. Ill., Champaign, 1969-70; honoree Women in Leadership YWCA, New Britain, Conn., 1997. Mem. AAUP, ALA, Assn. Coll. and Rsch. Librs. (extended campus libr. svcs. sect., chmn. stats. com., chmn. rsch. com., mem. nominations com., del. at large), Assn. Coll. and Rsch. Librs. (mem. K.G. Saur award com. 1995-98, chair 1999-2000), Am. Soc. Indexers (Conn. chpt. pres. 1988-95, organizer, voting rep. Nat. Info. Stds. Orgn. 1995-98), Phi Delta Kappa, Phi Kappa Phi, Pi Sigma Alpha, Beta Phi Mu. Avocations: opera, reading, cooking, miniature books, walking/hiking. Office: Champlain Coll 83 Summit St Burlington VT 05401 Business E-Mail: kascus@champlain.edu.

KASDAN, LAWRENCE EDWARD, film director, screenwriter; b. Miami Beach, Fla., Jan. 14, 1949; s. Clarence Norman and Sylvia Sarah (Landau) K.; m. Meg Goldman, Nov. 28, 1971; children: Jacob, Jonathan. BA, U. Mich., 1970, MA in Edn., 1972. Copywriter W.B. Doner & Co. (Advt.), Detroit, 1972-75, Doyle, Dane Bernbach, Los Angeles, 1975-77; freelance screenwriter, 1977-80; motion picture dir., screenwriter Los Angeles, 1980—. Co-screenwriter: The Empire Strikes Back, 1980, Return of the Jedi, 1982; screenwriter: Continental Divide, 1981, Raiders of the Lost Ark, 1981; writer, dir.: Body Heat, 1981, Grand Canyon, 1992; co-screenwriter, dir., exec. prodr.: The Big Chill, 1983; co-screenwriter, dir., prodr.: Silverado, 1985, The Accidental Tourist, 1988, Dreamcatcher, 2003; prodr. Cross My Heart, 1987; dir. I Love You to Death, 1989; co-screenwriter, dir. Wyatt Earp, 1994; screenwriter, co-prodr. The Bodyguard, 1992; exec. prodr. Jumpin at the Boneyard, 1992; dir. French Kiss, 1995, Mumford, 1999. Recipient Clio awards for advt., Writers Guild Am. award for the Big Chill, 1983, New York Film Critics Circle award for The Accidental Tourist, 1988; nominated 4 Acad. Awards. Mem. Writers Guild Am. West, Dirs. Guild Am. West.

KASE, NATHAN GINDEN, dean; b. NYC, Apr. 6, 1930; s. Joseph and Flora (Ginden) Kosovsky; m. Judith Caryl Glass, July 8, 1956; children: Deborah Lillian, James, Nancy Kase O'Brasky. AB, Columbia U., 1951, MD, 1955; MA (hon.), Yale U., 1969; LHD honoris causa, Mt. Sinai Sch. Medicine, 2004. Instr. dept. ob-gyn. Yale U. Med. Sch., New Haven, 1962-63, asst. prof., 1963-66, assoc. prof., 1966-69, prof., chmn., 1969-78, prof., 1978-81, Mt. Sinai Med. Ctr., N.Y.C., 1981—; chmn. dept. ob-gyn. Mt. Sinai Sch. Medicine, N.Y.C., 1981-84; acting chief exec. officer Mt. Sinai Med. Ctr., N.Y.C., 1986-88; dean Mt. Sinai Sch. Medicine, N.Y.C., 1984-98, emeritus dean, 1998—, interim dean, 2001—03, interim pres., CEO, 2001—02. Chmn. adv. bd. Gateway Inst. Pre-Coll. Edn., NYC, 2002—05. Co-author: Clinical Gynecologic Endocrinology and Infertility, Advances in Obstetrics/Gynecology, Principles and Practice of Gynecology, Medical Surgical and Obstetrical Complications of Pregnancy, Diagnosis and Management of Ovarian Disorders. Served to capt. USAF, 1957-59. Recipient Francis Gilman Blake award Yale U. Sch. Medicine, 1967. Fellow Am. Coll. Obstetricians and Gynecologists; mem. Am. Fertility Soc., Endocrine Soc., Associated Med. Schs. N.Y. (pres. 1989-91). Office: Mt Sinai Med Ctr Box 1025 One Gustave Levy Pl New York NY 10029 Office Phone: 212-659-9760. Business E-Mail: nathan.kase@mssm.edu.

KASEM, KASEM KAMEL, chemistry professor; PhD, Assiut (Egypt) U., 1978. Lectr. Assiut (Egypt) U., 1978—81; assoc. prof. Ind. U., Kokomo, Ind., 1997—2003, prof., 2003—. Contbr. articles to profl. jours. Achievements include research in electrochemical field. Office: Indiana University Kokomo 2300 S Washington Street Kokomo IN 46904 Office Phone: 765-455-9245. Business E-Mail: kkasem@iuk.edu.

KASER, DAVID, retired librarian, educator, consultant; b. Mishawaka, Ind., Mar. 12, 1924; s. Arthur Leroy and Loah (Steele) K.; m. Jane Jewell, Sept. 1, 1950; children: John Andrew, Kathleen Jewell. AB, Houghton Coll., 1949; MA, U. Notre Dame, 1950; A.M. in L.S, U. Mich., 1952, PhD, 1956. Serials librarian, instr. library sci. Ball State U., 1952-54; asst. in exchanges U. Mich. Library, 1954-56; chief acquisitions Washington U. Libraries, St. Louis, 1956-59, asst. dir., 1959-60; prof. library sci. Peabody Coll. and dir. libraries Vanderbilt U., 1960-68; dir. libraries Cornell U., 1968-73; prof. library sci. Ind. U., Bloomington, 1973-86, Disting. prof., 1986-91, Disting. prof. emeritus, 1991—; pres. Kaser Assocs., Inc., libr. bldg. cons., Bloomington, 1988-95. Fgn. assignments in Ireland, 1960, Korea, 1965, 81, 93, Laos, 1966, Taiwan, 1967, 79, 81, 88, 89, 93, S.E. Asia, 1969, Eng., 1971, France, 1972, Saudi Arabia, 1975-76, 83, Nigeria, 1978, Indonesia, 1978, Malaysia, 1992. Author: Messrs. Carey & Lea of Philadelphia, 1957, Washington University Manuscripts, 1958, Cost Book of Carey & Lea, 1825-1838, 1963, Joseph Charless, Printer in the Western Country, 1963, Books in America's Past, 1966, Book Pirating in Taiwan, 1969, Library Development in Eight Asian Countries, 1969, Book for a Sixpence, 1980, Books and Libraries in Camp and Battle, 1984, The Evolution of the American Academic Library Building, 1997, Just Lucky I Guess, 2000; editor Mo. Libr. Assn. Quar., 1958-60, Coll. and Rsch. Librs., 1963-69. Guggenheim fellow, 1967 Mem. ALA (councilor 1965-69, 75-79), Assn. Coll. and Research Libraries (pres. 1968-69), Assn. Southeastern Research Libraries (chmn. 1966-68), Tenn. Library Assn. (pres. 1968-69), Am. Antiquarian Soc., Phi Beta Kappa, Beta Phi Mu (internat. pres. 1975) E-mail: kaserd@indiana.edu.

KASER, RICHARD TODD, communications executive; b. Dover, Ohio, Aug. 29, 1952; s. Richard I. and Mary (Miller) K.; m. Victoria Cox, June 29, 1974; 1 child, Adaline. BS in Journalism summa cum laude, Ohio U., 1974; MA in Internat. Communications, Ohio State U., 1976. Public info. officer State of Ohio, Columbus, 1974-75; mgr. sales promotion Columbia Nat. Corp., Columbus, 1976-77; sales promotional specialist Chem. Abstracts Svc., Columbus, 1977-79, advt. mgr., 1979-83, corp. communications mgr., 1983-87, planning and communications mgr., 1987-90; group v.p., spl. asst. planning and communication Maxwell Macmillan, McLean, Va., 1990-94; exec. dir. The Nat. Fedn. Abstracting and Info. Svcs., Phila., 1994—2001; v.p. content Info. Today, Inc., Medford, NJ, 2001—. Mem. citizens adv. coun. Ohio Council Internat. Visitors, Columbus, 1985-86. Mem.: Nat. Fedn. Abstracting and Info. Svcs. (chmn., newsletter editor adv. bd. 1985—2001), Phi Kappa Phi. Democrat. Episcopalian. Avocations: jogging, swimming, antiques, books, writing. Office: Info Today Inc 143 Old Marlton Pike Medford NJ 08055-8750

KASERMAN, RANDALL LEE, music educator; b. Massillon, Ohio, Feb. 18, 1975; s. Richard James and Susan Marie Kaserman. B in music edn., Mt. Union Coll., 1997. Music tchr. Canton Ctrl. Cath. H.S., Canton, Ohio, 1997—2000, Dalton Local Schools, Ohio, 2000—. Mem.: Ohio Music Edn. Assn. Office: Dalton HS 177 N Mill St Dalton OH 44618 Business E-Mail: dltn_faserma@tccsa.net.

KASEY, ARTHUR R., III, secondary school educator; b. Louisville, Ky., Jan. 22, 1940; s. Arthur R. Kasey, Jr. and Ruth Prinz. BA, Vanderbilt U., 1962; MS in Geology, U. Tenn., 1965. Life cert. in teaching, Mo. Asst. instr. U. Mo., Columbia, 1965-71; tchr. Fox C-6 Sch. Dist., Arnold, Mo., 1971—. Tchr. Meth. Ch., Arnold, 1972—. Recipient Excellence in Teaching award Emerson Electric St. Louis, V.P. Fair, 1989; named Educator of Yr., Arnold, Mo., 1992, Arnold Walmart Tchr. of Yr., 2004 Mem. NEA, NSTA, Nat. Assn. Geology Tchrs.(Outstanding Earth Sci. Tchr., ctrl. states sect.), Nat. Speleological. Soc., Geol. Soc. Am. (Outstanding Tchr. Earth Sci. 1991), Sigma X. Avocations: travel, videography, photography, pack rat. Home: 2631 Georgia Arnold MO 63010-1615 Office: Fox Sr High Sch 751 Jeffco Blvd Arnold MO 63010-1432 Personal E-mail: artkasey@westv.net.

KASH, DON ELDON, political science professor; b. Macedonia, Iowa, May 29, 1934; s. Albert W. and Blanche Opal (Smith) K.; m. Elizabeth Gunn; children: Kelli Denise, Jeffrey Paul. BA, U. Iowa, 1959, MA, 1960, PhD, 1963. Instr. Tex. Tech. U., 1960-61; asst. prof. Ariz. State U., 1963-65, U. Mo., Kansas City, 1965-66; assoc. prof. Purdue U., West Lafayette, Ind., 1966-70; prof. polit. sci. U. Okla., Norman, 1970-91, George Lynn Cross rsch. prof. polit. sci., 1975-91, dir. Sci. and Pub. Policy Program, 1970-78; John T. Hazel Sr. and Ruth D. Hazel chair in pub. policy George Mason U., Fairfax, Va., 1991—. Vis. assoc. prof. Ind. U., 1969-70; chief conservation div. U.S. Geol. Survey, 1978-81; mem. Assembly Engring., Marine Bd. NRC; prof. Tsinghua U., Beijing. Author: The Politics of Space Cooperation, 1967, Energy Under the Oceans: A Technology Assessment of Outer Continental Shelf Oil and Gas Operations, 1973, North Sea Oil and Gas: Implication for Future U.S. Development, 1973, Energy Alternatives: A Comparative Analysis, 1975, Our Energy Future, 1976, U.S. Energy Policy: Crisis and Complacency, 1983, Perpetual Innovation: The New World of Competition, 1989, The Complexity Challenge: Technological Innovation in the 21st Century, 1999; contbr. articles to profl. jours. With AUS, 1952-54. Recipient Disting. Alumni award, U. Iowa, 1988. Fellow AAAS. Office: George Mason U Sch Public Policy 4400 University Dr Fairfax VA 22030-4444 Business E-Mail: dkash@gmu.edu.

KASHA, KENNETH JOHN, agriculturist, educator; b. Lacombe, Alta., Can., May 6, 1933; s. John Clarence and Mary Jennette (Proudfoot) K.; m. Marion Eileen Lenz, Aug. 14, 1958, children: Lorelei Marion, David John. BSc in Agr., U. Alta., Edmonton, 1957, MSc, 1958; PhD, U. Minn., 1962; LLD (hon.), U. Calgary, Alta., 1986. Rsch. asst. U. Minn., Mpls., 1958-61, fellow rsch. agronomy and plant genetics, 1961-62; rsch. scientist forages Agr. Can. Rsch. Sta., Ottawa, Ont., 1962-66; asst. prof. crop sci. dept. U. Guelph, Ont., 1966-69, assoc. prof. crop sci. dept., 1969-74, prof. crop sci. dept., 1974-98—, Univ. prof. emeritus, 1998—. Cons. Ciba Geigy Seeds Ltd., Ailsa Craig, Ont., 1974-81, Monsanto Co., St. Louis, 1997-2002; organizing chair and editor 1st Internat. Symposium on Haploids in Plants, Guelph, 1974; dir. Plant Biotech Centre, Guelph Waterloo Biotech, 1984-87; program chmn. XVI Internat. Congress Genetics, Toronto, 1988; fgn. corr. Acad. d'Agriculture de France, 2003. Editor: Haploids in Higher Plants, 1974, Plant Cell Culture in Agriculture and Forestry, 1980, Mutation, In Vitro and Molecular Techniques for Environmentally Sustainable Crop Improvement, 2002, Doubled Haploid Production in Crop Plants, A Manual, 2003, Haploids in Crop Production II, 2005; contbr. articles to profl. jours.; mem. numerous jour. editl. bds. Decorated officer Order of Can., 1994; recipient Agrl. Inst. Can. Grindley medal, 1970; Can. Award of Excellence EC Manning Found., 1983, Disting. Rsch. award Ont. Agr. Coll. Alumni, 1984, Outstanding Achievement award U. Minn., 1999, Queen Elizabeth Golden Jubilee medal, 2002. Fellow Royal Soc. Can. (fellow selection com., life scis. 2000-02); mem. Sigma Xi (Disting. Researcher award Guelph chpt. 1974), Genetics Soc. Can. (pres. 1976-77, sec. 1966-69, award of Excellence 1994), Internat. Assn. Plant Tissue Culture (nat. corr. 1990-94), Can. Soc. Plant Molecular Biology (founding mem.), Genetics Soc. Am., Am. Soc. Agronomy, Sigma Xi. Home: 28 Halesmanor Ct Guelph ON Canada N1G 4E2 Office: U Guelph Dept Plant Agr Guelph ON Canada N1G 2W1 E-mail: kkasha@uoguelph.ca.

KASHANI, HAMID REZA, lawyer, computer consultant; b. Tehran, Iran, May 1, 1955; came to U.S., 1976; s. Javad K. BSEE with highest distinction, Purdue U., 1978, MSEE, 1979; JD, Ind. U., 1986. Bar: Ind. 1986, U.S. Dist. Ct. (so. and no. dists.) 1986, U.S. Ct. Appeals (7th cir.) 1986, U.S. Supreme Ct. 1994, U.S. Ct. Appeals (9th cir.) 1996. Rsch. asst. Purdue U., West Lafayette, Ind., 1978-79, 80-81; engr. Cummins Engine Co., Columbus, Ind., 1981-82; assoc. faculty Ind. U.-Purdue U., Indpls., 1983-84; sr. software engr. Engineered System Devel., Indpls., 1985-87; computer cons. Hamid R. Kashani, Indpls., 1986—; pvt. practice law Indpls., 1986—; cons. Good Techs., Indpls., 1987-90; pres. Virtual Media Techs., Inc., 1998—. Cons. Prism Imaging, Denver, 1990-93, Ind. Bar Assn., 1989-95. Editor: Computer Law Desktop Guide, 1995. Mem., bd. dirs. ACLU, 1997—, Ind. Civil Liberties Union, Indpls., 1987—, mem. legis. com., 1987—, mem. screening com., 1985—, del., 1989, 91, 93, 95, 97, 99, 2001, acting v.p. fundraising, 1995-96, v.p. edn., 1996—, chair long-range planning com., 1991-92, 96—, chmn. nominating com., 1997—, pres., 1999—; bd. dirs. ACLU, 1997—. Fellow Ind. U. Sch. Law, 1984; recipient Cert. of Appreciation Ind. Correctional Assn., 1988; named Cooperating Atty. of Yr. Ind. Civil Liberties Union, 1990, 95, 98. Mem. ABA (vice chmn. YLD computer law com. 1990-91, chmn. computer law exec. com. 1991-93, litigation exec. com. 1987-89, 90-93, YLD liaison standing com. on jud. selection, tenure and compensation 1992-94, 95-96, sci. and tech. co-chair first amendment rights in the digital age com. 1997—, vice chair com. on opportunities for minorities and women 1997-99, YLD liaison to ABA tech. coun. 1992-93, vice chmn. nat. info. infrastructure com. sect. sci. and tech. 1993-97, chair privacy info. and civil liberties ABA sect. of individual rights and responsibilities 1998-2002, co-chair technology com., mem. standing com. on jud. selection, tenure and compensation 1995-96, chair privacy info. and civil liberties sect. of individual rights and responsibilities 1998-2002), IEEE (Outstanding Contbns. award 1983), Indpls. Bar Assn. (chmn. articles and bylaws coms. 1994-95), Ind. State Bar Assn. (vice chair computer comms. com. 1995-98, chair computer comms. com. 1998—, chair computer comm. com. 1998—), Eta Kappa Nu, Tau Beta Pi, Phi Kappa Phi, Phi Eta Sigma. Office: 445 N Pennsylvania St Ste 600 Indianapolis IN 46204-1818 Office Phone: 317-632-1000. E-mail: hkashani@kashanilaw.com.

KASHGARIAN, MICHAEL, pathologist, educator; b. N.Y.C., Sept. 20, 1933; s. Toros and Arax K.; m. Jean Gaylor Caldwell, July 2, 1960; children: Michaele, Thea. AB, N.Y. U., 1954; MD, Yale U., 1958. Diplomate: Am. Bd. Pathology. Intern Barnes Hosp., St. Louis, 1958-59; asst. in medicine Washington U., St. Louis, 1958-59; asst. resident in pathology Yale New Haven Med. Center, 1959-61, resident in pathology, 1962-63; rsch. fellow in renal physiology U. Goettingen, Germany, 1961-62; practice medicine specializing in pathology New Haven, 1962—. Instr. Yale U., 1962-64, asst. prof., 1964-67, asso. prof., 1967-74, prof., 1974—, vice chmn. dept., 1976-89, chmn., 1990— assoc. pathologist Yale New Haven Hosp., 1964-66, asst. attending pathologist, 1966-69, attending pathologist, 1969—, pres. med. staff, 1983-84; cons. in pathology, 1962—. Author: (with J.P. Hayslett, B.H. Spargo) Renal Disease, 1974, (with G.N. Burrow) The Endocrine Glands; co-author (with A. Fogo) Diagnostic Atlas of Renal Pathology, 2005; editor: Yearbook of Nephrology, Yale Medicine, Current Opinion in Nephrology; mem. editorial bd. Nephron, 1970—, Am. Jour. Pathology, 1975—, Am. Jour. Kidney Diseases; contbr. articles to med. jours. Chmn. ednl. adv. council North Haven Bd. Edn., 1971; chmn. Christian edn. com. Ch. of Christ, Yale, 1970; bd. dirs. New Haven Symphony Orch.; v.p. Conn. Fund for Environ. 1st lt., M.C. USAR, 1954-65, USPHS fellow, 1963-65; research career devel. awardee, 1965-75. Fellow AAAS, Am. Soc. Clin. Pathologists, Coll. Am. Pathologists, Am. Soc. Nephrology, Am. Heart Assn.; mem. AMA, Internat. Acad. Pathology, Conn. State Med. Soc. (chmn. com. on organ and tissue transfer), New Haven County Med. Assn. (pres. bd. govs.), Am. Soc. Investigative Pathologists, Conn. Soc. Pathologists (pres. 1975), Am. Physiol. Soc., Gesellshaft Nephrologie (hon.), Renal Pathology Soc. (Jacob Churg award), Nat. Kidney Found. (Disting. Achievement award), Sigma Xi, Alpha Omega Alpha, Alpha Kappa Kappa. Home: 22 Old Orchard Rd North Haven CT 06473-3022 Office: 310 Cedar St PO Box 208023 New Haven CT 06520-8023 Office Phone: 203-785-2750. Business E-Mail: michael.kashgarian@yale.edu.

KASHNOW, RICHARD A., electronics executive; m. Marcia, 2 children. B of Physics, Worcester polytech Inst., 1963; D, Tufts U., 1968. Physicist GE Co., 1970-83, gen. mgr. quartz & chem. products bus., 1983; v.p., gen. mgr. Manville Corp., until 1991; pres. Schuller, Denver, 1991-95; CEO, pres. Raychem Corp, Menlo Park, Calif., 1995-99; pres. Tyco Ventures, Menlo Park, 2000—. With U.S. Army. NASA fellow, 1968.

KASHTANOV, VALERIAN, security specialist; b. Moscow; arrived in U.S., 1991; s. Vladimir A. Kashtanov and Vera A. Kashtanova; m. Yevgeniya Ustinova-Kashtanova, Jan. 28, 1978; children: Sergey, Irina, Vladimir. Technician, Tech. Sch., Moscow, 1961; lawyer, Law Corr. Sch., Moscow, 1967; lawyer-investigator, KGB Higher Sch., Moscow, 1969; grad., Oakland C.C., Mich., 2000. Technician of Kadet, investigator Nuclear Industry Rsch. Inst., Moscow, 1965—69; operative, chief of counterintelligence dept. KGB, Moscow, 1969—85; chief security dept. Cold Mainig Concern, 1985—95; chief legal dept., security specialist Pinkerton Securities Corp., Mich., 1997—. Author: And Then God Created America, 2000. Republican. Avocation: writing. Home: 6496 Aspen Ridge Blvd West Bloomfield MI 48322 Office: Guardian Security Svc 1800 8 Mile Southfield MI 48034 Office Phone: 248-740-2331.

KASICH, JOHN R., former congressman; b. McKees Rocks, Pa., May 13, 1952; BA, Ohio State U., 1974. Administrv. asst. Ohio State Senate, 1975-77; mem. Ohio Legislature, 1979-82, 98th-106th Congressses from 12th Ohio dist., Washington, 1983-2001; mem. nat. security com., armed svc. com.; mem. house budget com., chmn.; chmn. New Century Project, Columbus, 2001—.

KASINATH, BALAKUNTALAM S., medical researcher; b. Nov. 9, 1951; m. Uma Kasinath; children: Manasa, Vivek. MBBS in Medicine, Bangalore Med. Coll., India, 1975. With internal medicine Ill. Masonic Med. Ctr., Chgo., 1977-80; with nephrology U. Chgo. Hosps. and Clinics, 1980-83; asst prof. Rush-Presbyn.-St. Luke's Med. Ctr., Chgo., 1983-90; assoc. prof. dept. medicine divsn. nephrology U. Tex. Health Sci. Ctr., San Antonio, 1990-98; chief renal sect., staff physician Audie Murphy Meml. VA Hosp., San Antonio, 1991—. Prof. dept. medicine U. Tex. Health Sci. Ctr., San Antonio, 1998—. Contbr. articles to profl. jours., chpts in books; lectr. in field. Recipient Henry Christian award for excellence in rsch. Am. Fedn. for Clin. Rsch., 1994, Rsch. award Am. Diabetes Assn., 1995, 99, 2002, Rsch. award VA, 1993, 97, 2002, Rsch. award NIH, 1986, 90, 2003. Mem. AAAS, Am. Soc. Nephrology, Internat. Soc. Nephrology, Indian Soc. Nephrology. Achievements include research in metabolic regulation of extracellular matrix molecules in diabetic renal disease. Office: U Tex Health Sci Ctr Dept Medicine-Nephrology Mail Code 7882 7703 Floyd Curl Dr San Antonio TX 78229-3900 Office Phone: 210-567-4707. Business E-Mail: kasinath@uthscsa.edu.

KASISCHKE, LOUIS WALTER, lawyer; b. Bay City, Mich., July 18, 1942; s. Emil Ernst and Gladys Ann (Stuady) K.; m. Sandra Ann Colosimo, Sept. 30, 1967; children: Douglas, Gregg. BA, Mich. State U., 1964, JD, 1967; LLM, Wayne State U., 1971. Bar: Mich. 1968, U.S. Dist. Ct. (southeastern dist.) Mich. 1968; CPA. Acct. Touche Ross & Co., Detroit, 1967-71; atty. Dykema Gossett, Detroit, 1971—; pres. Pella Window and Door Co., West Bloomfield, Mich., 1990-98. Bd. dirs. Barton Malow Co., Southfield. Author: Michigan Closely Held Corporations, 1986; contbr. articles to profl. jours. Mem. ABA, AICPA, State Bar Mich. (editor column Mich. Bar Jour. 1971-83), Mich. Assn. CPAs, Am. Coll. Tax Counsel Republican. Lutheran. Avocations: mountain climbing, skiing, running, squash, golf. Home: 3491 N Lakeshore Harbor Springs MI 49740 Office: Dykema Gossett 39577 Woodward Ave Ste 300 Bloomfield Hills MI 48304-5086

KASKELL, PETER HOWARD, professional society administrator, lawyer; b. Berlin, Mar. 29, 1924; s. Joseph and Lilo (Schaeffer) K.; m. Joan Folsom Macy, Nov. 30, 1968; stepchildren: Bryn, Alison. Grad., Horace Mann Sch., N.Y.C., 1940; BA, Columbia U., 1943, LLB, 1948. Bar: N.Y. 1948. Assoc. White & Case, N.Y.C., 1948-51; atty. Nat. Prodn. Authority, Washington, 1951-52, W.R. Grace & Co., N.Y.C., 1952-54; div. counsel Curtiss-Wright Corp., Buffalo, 1954-56; with Olin Corp., Stamford, Conn., 1956-83, v.p. legal affairs, 1971-83; sr. v.p. CPR Inst. for Dispute Resolution, N.Y.C., 1983-99, sr. fellow, 2000—. Former dir. CARE; former mem. adv. com. U.S. Dist. Ct. (ea. dist.) N.Y. Former trustee Aldrich Mus. Contemporary Art, Ridgefield, Conn., Boys' Athletic League, N.Y.C.; vice chmn. Conn. Humanities Coun.; organizer, chmn. Lawyers Com. for U.N. Conv. on Contracts for Internat. Sale of Goods. With Intelligence Svc., AUS, 1943-45, ETO. Decorated Bronze Star. Mem. Assn. of Bar of City of N.Y., Wilton Riding Club (past gov.), Century Assn. Home: 226 Nod Hill Rd Wilton CT 06897-1717 Office: 366 Madison Ave New York NY 10017-3122

KASKEY, RAYMOND JOHN, sculptor; b. Pitts., Feb. 22, 1943; s. Raymond John and Katherine (Stupak) K.; m. Sherrell Lewis. BArch, Carnegie-Mellon U., 1967; M Environ. Design, Yale U., 1969. Registered architect, Md., Va., D.C. Asst. prof. design Sch. Architecture, U. Md., College Park, 1969-76; architect Robert Bell Assoc., Washington, 1976-81; owner, sculptor Raymond Kaskey Studios, Brentwood, Md., 1981—. Vis. critic Sch. Architecture, Yale U., New Haven, 1977, Kans. State U., Manhattan, 1978; mem. adv. bd. James Wilbur Johnston Sculpture Competition, Washington, 1981—. Prin. works include civic sculpture Portland, Oreg., 1985, Nat. Law Enforcement Memorial, 1993, Nat. World War II Memorial, 2004. Fellow Nat. Sculpture Soc. (Mrs. Louis Bennett award 1981, Henry Hering Meml. medal 1986, 93); mem. AIA (Excellence award 1985). Office: Raymond Kaskey Studios 3804 38th St Brentwood MD 20722-1707

KASKOWITZ, EDWIN, social services executive; b. St. Louis, May 15, 1936; s. Nathan and Fannie K.; children: Joy, Sara, Naomi. BA, Washington U., St. Louis, 1958, MSW. (grad. scholar), 1961. Lic. clin. social worker. Sr. social worker St. Louis County Health Dept., 1965-67; exec. dir. Gerontol. Soc. Am., 1967-80; pres. Business Radio Corp., Atlanta, 1981-82; pres., chief exec. officer The Association Mgmt. Group, Chevy Chase, Md., 1982-86; dir. JCCA Sr. Adult Services, Creve Coeur, Mo., 1986-89, The Forum on Aging Consumers and Employees, St. Louis U., 1989-90; pres. Gerontology Svcs. of Mo., 1991—; CEO, pres. People Sculptures Inc., 2002—. Pres. B'nai-Brith-Habirah, Washington, 1974-75; adv. bd. Over Easy program Sta. KQED-TV, 1977-81. With USAR, 1954-62. Fellow Royal Soc. Health; mem. Gerontol. Soc. Am., Am. Soc. Assn. Execs. (cert. assn. exec.), Nat. Assn. Social Workers, Acad. Cert. Social Workers. Office Phone: 314-434-4905.

KASLICK, RALPH SIDNEY, dentist, educator; b. Bklyn., Oct. 17, 1935; s. John J. and Dorothy K.; m. Jessica Hellinger, Oct. 24, 1976; 1 child, Andrew AB, Columbia U., 1956, D.D.S., 1959, cert. in periodontology, 1962. Instr. Fairleigh Dickinson U., Coll. Dental Medicine, Hackensack, N.J., 1965-67, asst. prof., 1967-70, assoc. prof., 1970-74, prof., 1974-88, asst. dean for acad. affairs, 1973-75, acting dean, 1975-76, dean, 1976-88, acting provost, Teaneck-Hackensack campus, 1983-85, sr. dean Teaneck-Hackensack campus, 1985-88; chief dentistry Coler-Goldwater Splty. Hosp., Roosevelt Island, NY, 1988—; pres. med. staff Coler-Goldwater Meml. Hosp., Roosevelt Island, N.Y., 1992-94, 97-99, dir. consultative svcs., 1995—. Clin. prof. periodontics Coll. Dentistry, NYU, 1988—; cons. in field. Contbr. chpts. to textbooks, articles to profl. jours. Served to capt. U.S. Army, 1962-64. Recipient Journalism award of the Internat. Coll. of Dentists, 1972, medal of Japan Stomatological Soc., 1977, Stanley S. Bergen award for contbn. to dental edn. Seton Hall U., 1982, Disting. Alumnus award Columbia U. Periodontal Alumni Assn., 1984, Achievement award Fairleigh Dickinson U. Periodontal Alumni Assn., 1984, Hirschfeld Meml. medal and cert. Northeastern Soc. Periodontists, 1987, Disting. Practitioner medallion Nat. Acad. Practice, 1999 Fellow Am. Coll. Dentists, N.Y. Acad. Dentistry; mem. ADA, Am. Assn. Dental Schs., Internat. Assn. Dental Rsch. (past pres. N.J. sect.), Am. Acad. Periodontology, Fedn. Spl. Care Orgns. in Dentistry, Sigma Xi, Omicron Kappa Upsilon. Office: Roosevelt Island Coler-Goldwater Splty Hosp New York NY 10044

KASLOW, FLORENCE WHITEMAN, psychologist, educator, family business consultant; b. Phila., Jan. 06; d. Irving and Rose (Tarin) Whiteman; m. Solis Kaslow; children: Nadine Joy, Howard Ian. AB in Sociology with distinction, Temple U., 1952; MA, Ohio State U., 1954; PhD, Bryn Mawr Coll., 1969. Lic. psychologist, marriage and family therapist, Fla.; bd. cert. psychologist Am. Bd. Clin. Psychology, Am. Bd. Forensic Psychology, Am. Bd. Family Psychology. Pvt. practice, Palm Beach Gardens, Fla., 1964—; dir. Fla. Couples and Family Inst., 1982—; adj. prof. med. psychology Duke U. Med. Ctr., Durham, N.C., 1982—; vis. prof. psychology Fla. Inst. Tech., Melbourne, 1985—; disting. vis. prof. Calif. Grad. Sch. Family Psychology, 1989-92. Cons. USN Dept. Psychiatry Residency Tng. Programs, San Diego, Portsmouth, Va., Phila., 1976-88, Palm Beach Inst., 1983-90; weekly radio guest Voice of Am., Focus on Families, 1993-2003; pres. Am. Bd. Forensic Psychology, 1977-80, Am. Bd. Family Psychology, 1996-2000; trustee Am. Bd. Profl. Psychology, 2002-05. Editor: Voices in Family Psychology, 1990; author (with L.L. Schwartz): Dynamics of Divorce: A Life Cycle Perspective, 1987; author: The Military Family in Peace and War, 1993, Handbook of Relational Diagnoses and Dysfunctional Family Patterns, 1996, Painful Partings: Divorce and Its Aftermath, 1997, Handbook of Couple and Family Forensics, 2000, Comprehensive Handbook of Psychotherapy, 4 vols., 2002; author: (with L.L. Schwartz) Welcome Home: an International and Non Traditional Adoption Reader, 2004; mem. editl. bd. Jour. Marital and Family Therapy, 1976—, Jour. Family Psychology, 1987—, Jour. Sex and Marital Therapy, 1984—2002, Jour. Clin. Child Psychology, 1986—, Jour. Psychotherapy, 1988—, Profl. Psychology, 2002—, assoc. editor Jour. Family Psychotherapy, 1990—; contbr. articles to profl. jours., chapters to books. Recipient Outstanding Family Therapy Contbn. award, Am. Assn. Marriage and Family Therapy, 1991, NIMH trainee, 1969. Mem. APA (divsn. family psychology pres. 1987, sec. 1983-85, com. mem. 1987—, pres. divsn. media psychology 1993, coun. rep. 2002-04, Disting. Contbn. Applied Psychology award 2000, Outstanding Conbtn. Internat. Advancement Psychology, 2002), Internat. Acad. Family Psychology (pres. 1998-2002), Am. Assn. Marital and Family Therapy, Am. Bd. Profl. Psychologists (bd. trustees, 2002-2005, Disting. Psychology Contbn. award, 1994), Am. Family Therapy Acad., Coalition Family Diagnosis (chmn. 1989-93), Am. Assn. Sex Educators, Counselors and Therapists, Internat. Family Therapy Assn. (founding pres. 1987-90), Acad. Family Mediators (bd. dir. 1982-88, treas. 1985-87). Office Phone: 561-625-0288. E-mail: drfkaslow@bellsouth.net.

KASMAI, HAMID SALEH, chemistry professor, researcher; b. Tabriz, Azarbaijan, Iran, May 28, 1939; came to U.S., 1962; s. Hoseinguli Saleh-Kasmai and Aameneh Aalemrajabi; m. Roselyn Mae Senior, July 18, 1971; children: Armon, Nikoo. BSc in Chemistry, Tchrs. Coll., Tehran, Iran, 1961; PhD in Chemistry, U. Wis., 1969; postdoctoral, Syracuse U., 1973-74, 78-79. Asst. prof. Pahlavi U., Shiraz, Iran, 1968-74, assoc. prof., 1974-80; adj. prof. Syracuse U., 1980-82; asst. prof. Hamilton Coll., Clinton, N.Y., 1982-87, East Tenn. State U., Johnson City, 1987-91, assoc. prof., 1991-99, prof., 1999—. Cons. chem. industries, 1987—; spkr. in field. Author: (with others) Advances in Heterocyclic Chemistry, 1978, Trends in Organic Chemistry, 1993; contbr. articles to profl. jours. Fulbright-Hays travel grant Fulbright Found., 1973; Cottrell Coll. Sci. grant Rsch. Corp., 1982-84, type B grants Am. Chem. Soc., 1986-88, 89-91, various grants Hamilton Coll. and East Tenn. State U., 1982-94. Mem. AAAS, AAUP, Am. Chem. Soc. (Spkr. of Yr. N.E. sect. 1994), Internat. Soc. Heterocyclic Chemistry, Tenn. Acad. Scis., Sigma Xi. Avocations: woodworking, swimming, hiking, music, stamp and coin collecting. Office: East Tenn State U PO Box 70695 Johnson City TN 37614-1710

KASNOWSKI, CHESTER NELSON, artist, educator; b. Perth Amboy, N.J., Jan. 23, 1944; BFA, Dayton Art Inst., 1971; MFA, Tulane U., 1973. Curator New Orleans Mus. Art, 1971-74; tchr. So. Vt. Art Ctr., Manchester, 1981—2002. One-man show includes Bertha Undang Gallery, N.Y.C., 1984, 85, 87, 91, 93, Carmen Llewellyn Gallery, New Orleans, 1996; group exhbns. at Dartmouth Coll., 1978, Robert Hall Fleming Mus., 1981, Franklin Furnace, 1982, 84, Bertha Undang Gallery, 1983, Hand Gallery, 1985; permanent collections include Bklyn. Mus., Franklin Furnace, Solomon R. Guggenheim Mus., Stedelijk Mus., Tate Gallery, Mus. Modern Art. Grantee Nat. Endowment Arts, 1974, 78. Home: PO Box 1 Weston VT 05161-0001

KASOUF, JOSEPH CHICKERY, lawyer, consultant; b. Syracuse, N.Y., July 3, 1954; s. Herbert Chickery and Helen (Hawa) K.; m. Nancy A. Middleton, Sept. 10, 1977; children: Jennifer C., Lauren E., Joseph P. A. Onondaga C.C., 1976; BA, Syracuse U., 1987, MS, JD, Syracuse U., 1990. Police officer, detective Syracuse Polic Dept., 1977-87; asst. gen. counsel The Pyramid Co., 1988-91; mgr. claims counsel Nationwide Mutual Ins. Co., 1991—2001, asst. gen. counsel Office Gen. Counsel, 2001—. Adj. prof. Syracuse U., 1991-2001. Contbr. articles to profl. jour. Mem. Civic Action Program, Syracuse, 1991—. Mem. N.Y. State Bar Assn. sect. torts, ins. and compensation law), Def. Assn. N.Y., Onondaga County Bar Assn., Def. Rsch. Inst., Am. Corp. Counsel Assn. Avocations: golf, skiing. Office: Nationwide Mutual Ins Co 7th Fl Office Gen Coun 1 Nationwide Plz Columbus OH 43215 Home: 4228 Hertford Ln Dublin OH 43017 Office Phone: 614-249-8953.

KASOWITZ, MARC ELLIOT, lawyer; b. New Haven, June 28, 1952; s. Robert and Felice Beverly (Molaver) K. BA, Yale U., 1974; JD, Cornell U., 1977. Bar: N.Y. 1978, U.S. Dist. Ct. (so. and ea. dists.) N.Y. 1978; U.S. Ct. Appeals (2d cir.), 1989, U.S. Ct. Appeals (3rd cir.), 1993, U.S. Dist. Ct. Colo., 2001. Assoc. Rosenman & Colin, N.Y.C., 1977-86, ptnr., 1986-88, Mayer, Brown & Platt, N.Y.C., 1988-93, Kasowitz, Benson, Torres & Friedman LLP, N.Y.C., 1993—. Editor: Cornell Law Review, 1975—77. Home: 1160 Park Ave Apt 4B New York NY 10128-1212 Office: Kasowitz Benson Torres & Friedman LLP 1633 Broadway New York NY 10019-6022 Office Phone: 212-506-1710. Office Fax: 212-506-1800. E-mail: mkasowitz@kasowitz.com.

KASPAR, FRANCES WOLF, music educator; b. Rome, N.Y., Jan. 10, 1944; d. E. Mark Wolf and Christine Wilma Smith Wolf; m. Frederick Rudolph Kaspar, Feb. 15, 1969; children: Christina Marie Lemaire, Michael Todd. BS, SUNY, Potsdam, 1968; MM, Ariz. State U., 2004—. Gen. music tchr. Chandler (Ariz.) Pub. Sch. Dist., 1968—69; choral and gen. music tchr. Dysart Unified Sch. Dist., El Mirage, Ariz., 1969—72; piano instr. Kaspar Piano Studio, Glendale, Ariz., 1970—74, Mesa, Ariz., 1974—; profl. accompanist Cassilons Choral Soc., Avondale, Ariz., 1971—74; instr. Yamaha Music Sch., Mesa, 1975—78; music coord. Christ the King Cath. Ch., Mesa, 1976—81. Chmn. Ariz. study program Ariz. State Music Tchrs. Assn., 1991—99. Recipient Honored Tchr. award, Ariz. State Music Tchrs. Assn., 1991; scholar, Piano Technicians Guild Found., 2000; Janice McCurnin Tchr. Enrichment grantee, Ariz. Study Program, 2000, 2001, 2004. Mem.: Music Tchrs. Nat. Assn. (nat. cert. tchr. of music), Sigma Alpha Iota. Roman Catholic. Achievements include development of series of 12 workbooks for Ariz. State Music Tchrs. Assn., now used statewide by approximately 3000 students each year. Personal E-mail: frfwkaspar@aol.com.

KASPAR, HANNA G., pathologist, educator; s. George Kaspar and Zahia Haykal; m. Maria C. Kaspar, Sept. 11, 1987; 1 child, Christina. MD, MS, Am. U. Beirut, 1984. Lic. physician Tex. State Bd. Med. Examiner, 1992, diplomate Am. Bd. Pathology, 1993, Am. Bd. Ob-gyn. Resident Am. U. Beirut, N.Y., 1987—93, prof., 1993—. Cons. Am. U. Beirut, 1993—. Contbr. articles to prof. jours. (Best Rsch. in Pathology award U. Tex., 1992). Fellow, St. John's Mercy Med. Ctr., 1993. Fellow: Am. Soc. Clin. Pathology (licentiate), Coll. Am. Pathologists (licentiate); mem.: AMA (assoc.). Office: American University of Beirut 305 E 47th St Fl 8 New York NY 10017-2324 Office Phone: 810-653-4690. E-mail: hannakas@aub.edu.lb.

KASPAR, VICTORIA ANN, school administrator; d. Rudolph Hans and Rose Marie Boysen; m. Ronald Michael Kaspar; children: Ron Jr., John, Jim. BS in Secondary Edn., U. Nebr., 1974, MS in Secondary Adminstrn., 1995, EdD, 2003. Tchr. English Bellevue Pub. Schs., Nebr., 1974—75; dir. daycare pvt. practice, Omaha, 1978—88; tchr. English Millard South H.S., Omaha, 1988—98, chair dept. English, 1995—98, asst. prin., 1998—. Author of poems. Mem. Friends of Omaha Pub. Libr. Mem.: LWV, Met. Reading Assn., Nat. Coun. Staff Devel., Nebr. Assn. Secondary Sch. Adminstrn. (Region II), Nat. Assn. Secondary Sch. Prins., Nat. Coun. Sch. Adminstrs., Internat. Reading Coun., Internat. Soc. Tech. in Edn., Alpha Xi Delta, Phi Delta Kappa. Avocations: reading, gardening, writing.

KASPAREK, GALYIA JOAN, gifted and talented educator; b. Altus, Okla., June 11, 1954; d. James Donald and Freda Marie Beals; m. Jimmie Tim Kasparek Jr., July 21, 1972; children: Gregory Joseph, Lori Dawn. BS in Edn., Midwestern State U., 1986, M of Edn., 2004. Tchr. 5th grade lang. arts Iowa Park Ind. Sch. Dist., Iowa, 2001, tchr. gifted/talented, coord. Mem.: PTA, ASCD, TEPSA, Kappa Delta Pi. Avocations: cooking, golf. Office: WR Bradford Elem Sch 800 Texowa Rd Iowa Park TX 76367

KASPER, EVELYN HARRIET, music educator; b. N.Y.C., June 23, 1952; d. Harry and Helen Stoll; m. Kenneth Alexander Kasper, Dec. 9, 1984; 1 child, Jeremy. BA, Adelphi U., 1974; MA, LI U., 1977. Tchr. Sachem Ctrl. Sch. Dist., Holbrook, NY, 1974—. Singer LI Choral Soc., Selda, NY, 1998—;

dir. musicals in sch. and cmty., 1980—. Mem.: N.Y. State Sch. Music Assn., Suffolk County Music Edn. Jewish. Home: 39 White Birch Cir Miller Place NY 11764 Office: Sachem Sch Dist 245 Union Ave Holbrook NY 11741

KASPER, HORST MANFRED, lawyer; b. Dusseldorf, Germany, June 3, 1939; s. Rudolf Ferdinand and Lilli Helene (Krieger) K.; 1 child, Olaf Jan. Diploma in chemistry, U. Bonn, 1963, D. in Natural Scis., 1965; JD, Seton Hall U., 1978. Bar: N.J. 1978, U.S. Patent Office 1977. Mem. staff Lincoln Lab., MIT, Lexington, 1967-69; mem. tech. staff Bell Tel. Labs., Murray Hill, N.J., 1970-76; assoc. Kirschstein, Kirschstein, Ottinger & Frank, N.Y.C., 1976-77; patent atty. Allied Chem. Corp., Morristown, N.J., 1977-79; pvt. practice Warren, N.J., 1980-83; with Kasper and Weick, Warren, 1983-85, Kasper and Laughlin, 1985—. Contbr. numerous articles to profl. jours.; patentee semicondr. field. Mem. ABA, AAAS, N.J. Bar Assn., Internat. Patent and Trademark Assn., Am. Patent Law Assn., N.J. Patent Law Assn., Am. Chem. Soc., Electrochem. Soc., Am. Phys. Soc., N.Y. Acad. Scis. Home and Office: 13 Forest Dr Warren NJ 07059-5832 Office: ul Na Grzgdkach 9 30421 Krakow Poland

KASPERBAUER, MICHAEL JOHN, plant physiology educator, researcher; b. Manning, Iowa, Oct. 8, 1929; s. John Sixtus and Clara Mary (Balk) K.; m. Isabel Maria Giles, June 3, 1962; children: Maria, John, Paul, Sandra. BS, Iowa State Coll., 1954; PhD, Iowa State U., 1961. NSF postdoctoral fellow botany dept. U. Md., College Park, 1961-62; NRC/NAS rsch. assoc, rsch. plant physiologist USDA Pioneering Rsch. Lab., Beltsville, Md., 1962-63; rsch. plant physiologist USDA-Agrl. Rsch. Svc., Lexington, Ky., 1963-83, Florence, S.C., 1983—. Mem. grad. faculty U. Ky., Lexington, 1965-83, adj. prof., 1965-83, Clemson (S.C.) U., 1983—. Editor, author: Biotechnology in Fescue Improvement, 1990; assoc. editor Agronomy Jour., 1975-83; contbr. over 200 articles to profl. jours. Bd. dirs. Gardenside Little League Baseball, Lexington, 1975-78; v.p. Turfland Babe Ruth Baseball League, Lexington, 1979-82. 1st lt. U.S. Army, 1954-56. Recipient L.M. Ware Rsch. award Am. Soc. Hort. Sci., 1990, Superior Svc. award U.S. Sec. Agrl., 2000. Fellow Am. Soc. Agronomy (Agronomic Rsch. award 1994, So. Branch Career Rsch award, 2002), Crop Sci. Soc. Am. (Crop Sci. Rsch. award 1990, Fed. Lab. Consortium award 1998, Seed Sci. award 1999); mem. Am. Soc. Plant Physiologists, Am. Soc. Photobiology, Scandinavian Soc. Plant Physiology, Sigma Xi, Phi Delta Kappa, Gamma Sigma Delta, Phi Kappa Phi. Achievements include research in botany, photobiology, plant biochemistry, forage grasses, tissue and cell culture and molecular biology. Home: 1717 Williamsburg Ct Lexington KY 40504-2010 E-mail: michaeljkasper@aol.com. *Awards and professional recognitions are nice, but family is the only thing that is really important to me.*

KASPEROWICZ, TANNA BURNS, publishing executive, writer; d. Carolyn Sarba and Robert Samuel Burns; m. Raymond Kasperowicz, Sept. 10, 1965; children: Peter Ilych, Thaddeus. Student, Cedar Crest Coll., Allentown, Pa., 1962—64. Reporter Patriot Ledger, Quincy, Mass., 1976—79; pub. rels. mgr. Office Specialists, Boston, 1981—82; pub. Tinytown Gazette, 1993—, adaytrip.com, 1994—. Editor Mariner Newspaper Group, Marshfield, Mass., 1979—92. Pub. rels. Cohasset C of C, Mass., 1998—2003. R-Liberal. Methodist. Office Phone: 781-383-9115. Business E-Mail: tinytown@comcast.net.

KASPERSON, ROGER, geographer, educator; PhD, U. Chgo., 1966. Faculty U. Conn., Storrs, Mich. State U., East Lansing; geographer, exec. dir. Stockholm Environment Inst., 1999—. Cons. in field; mem. com. NRC, adv. bd. radioactive waste mgmt.; chair Internat. Geog. Union Commn. on Critical Situations/Regions in Global Environ. Change, 1992—96; sci. adv. bd. EPA. Fellow: AAAS, Am. Acad. Arts & Sciences, Soc. for Risk Analysis; mem.: NAS. Office: Stockholm Environment Inst Box 2142 S-103 14 Stockholm Sweden

KASPRZAK, LUCIAN ALEXANDER, physicist, researcher, materials scientist; b. Scranton, Pa., July 22, 1943; s. Alexander Lucian and Helen Frances (Skubic) K.; m. Carole Anne Nowakowski, July 22, 1967; children: Brian, Dawn. BS in Physics, Stevens Inst. Tech., 1965, PhD in Materials, 1972; MS in Physics, Syracuse U., 1970. Engr. failure analysis IBM East Fishkill, Hopewell Junction, NY, 1965—69, engr. reliability Large Scale Integration, 1972—77, mgr. Very Large Scale Integration devel., 1977—81; mgr. vendor memory IBM Gen. Tech. Divsn. Assurance, Poughkeepsie, NY, 1981—82; tech. asst. to corp. v.p. IBM Corp. Hdqrs., White Plains, NY, 1982—83, mgr. memory tech., Gen. Tech. Divsn., 1983—84; program mgr., tech. support IBM Data Systems Divsn. Assurance, Poughkeepsie, 1984—85; program mgr. tech. profl. rels. IBM Corp. Hdqrs., Thornwood, NY, 1985—92; assoc. prof. physics and engrng. sci. Franciscan U. Steubenville, Ohio, 1992—96; reliability mgr. direct radiography Sterling Diagnostic Imaging, Newark, Del., 1996—97; dir. reliability Direct Radiography Corp., Newark, 1997—2001; reliability cons., 2001—03; staff reliability group Dade Behring Corp., 2004—. Bd. dirs. Internat. Reliability Physics Symposium, 1985—, chmn. 1986-87. Contbr. articles to profl. jours.; co-discoverer hot electron effect in Metal Oxide Semiconductor Field Effect Transistor; patentee in field. Mem. Environ. Bd., Wappingers Falls, N.Y., 1973; coach East Fishkill Youth Soccer League, 1974-82; coun. mem. St. Columba Parish, Hopewell Junction, 1985-91. Recipient Benefactors award Franciscan U. of Steubenville, 1989; IBM resident fellow, Yorktown and Hoboken, N.J., 1969-72 Fellow IEEE (chmn. adv. bd. transactions on device and materials reliability); mem. Electron Devices Soc. of IEEE (adminstrv. com. 1986-, treas. 1988-99, adv. bd. Circuits and Devices mag. 1987-98, treas. trans. semiconductor mfg. 1992-, chmn. device reliability com. 1983-97, treas. Device Rsch. Conf. 1989-92, chmn. device reliability physics com. 1997-), Am. Phys. Soc. Roman Catholic. Avocations: music, astronomy, philosophy, theology, art. E-mail: l.kasprzak@ieee.org.

KASPUTYS, JOSEPH EDWARD, corporate financial executive, economist; b. Jamaica, N.Y., Aug. 12, 1936; s. Joseph John and Henrietta Viola (Derenthall) K.; m. Marilyn Patricia Kennedy, Oct. 29, 1953; children: Clare Victoria, Patricia Jeanne, Jacqueline Ann, Veronica Joy. BA magna cum laude, Bklyn. Coll., 1959; MBA with high distinction, Harvard U., 1967, DBA, 1972. U.S. Dept. Def., Washington, 1967-70; asst. adminstr. U.S. Maritime Adminstrn., Washington, 1972-75; asst. sec. U.S. Dept. Commerce, Washington, 1975-77; exec. v.p., COO Data Resources, Inc., Lexington, Mass., 1977-81, pres., CEO, 1981-84; exec. v.p. McGraw-Hill, Inc., N.Y.C., 1984-87; pres., COO Primark Corp. Inc., Waltham, Mass., 1987-88, chmn., CEO, 1988-2000; chmn. Thomson Fin., 2000-01; chmn., CEO, pres. Global Insight, Inc., Waltham, 2001—. Lectr. Am. U., Washington, 1967-68, Bentley Coll., Boston, 1971-72; assoc. prof., lectr. George Washington U., Washington, 1967-77; bd. dirs. Lifeline Systems, Inc., Boston, Logistics Mgmt. Inst., Washington. Chmn. Hitachi Found., Washington, Coun. for Excellence in Govt., Washington; mem. Com. for Econ. Devel., Washington. Comdr. USN, 1956-76. Decorated Legion of Merit; Warren G. Harding Aerospace fellow, 1971 Mem. Phi Beta Kappa. Clubs: Harvard Bus. Sch. (Boston); Capitol Hill (Washington). Republican. Roman Catholic. Home: 398 Simon Willard Rd Concord MA 01742-1624 Office: Global Insight Inc 1000 Winter St Waltham MA 02451 Business E-Mail: joseph.kasputys@globalinsight.com.

KASS, BENNY LEE, lawyer; b. Chgo., Aug. 20, 1936; s. Herman and Ethel (Lome) Kass; m. Salme Lundstrom, Aug. 30, 1963; children: Gale, Brian. BS, Northwestern U., 1957; LLB, U. Mich., 1960; LLM, George Washington U., 1967. Bar: DC 1960. Atty. Maritime Adminstrn., 1960-61; counsel House Info. Subcom., 1962-65; asst. counsel Senate Adminstrv. Practice Subcom., Washington, 1965-69; pvt. practice law Washington, 1969—; mem. Kass, Mitek & Kass, PLLC, 2001; prof. communication law Am. U.; pub. mem. Nat. Advt. Rev. Bd., 1971-74. Life mem. Conf. Uniform State Laws. Columnist: Washington Post, L.A. Times; contbr. articles to profl. jours. Chmn. Ad Hoc Com. Consumer Protection, 1965—; chmn. consumer affairs subcom. Mayor's Econ. Devel. Com., 1968—70. With USAF, 1961—62. Mem.: FBA, ABA, Am. Polit. Sci. Assn. (Congl. fellow 1966), Sigma Delta Chi. Office: Kass Mitek & Kass PLLC 1050 17th St NW Ste 1100 Washington DC 20036-5596 Business E-Mail: bkass@kmklawyers.com.

KASS, DAVID NORMAN, accountant, lawyer; b. N.Y.C., Mar. 8, 1951; s. Joseph Zane and Rosalind (Sperber) K.; m. Esta Gail Millman, Nov. 26, 1977; children: Sean N., Joshua A. BS in Acctg., SUNY, Albany, 1973; JD, St. John's U., Jamaica, N.Y., 1982. Bar: N.Y. 1983. Staff acct. Touche Ross & Co., N.Y.C., 1972-74; sr. acct. Reich Weiner & Co., N.Y.C., 1974-76; ptnr. Brandt, Pollack, Kass & Wilkins, N.Y.C., 1976-79, Kass & Kass CPAs PC, Roslyn, N.Y., 1979—; pvt. practice Roslyn, 1983—. Seminar leader Nassau Acad. Law, Mineola, N.Y., 1993, seminar leader/lectr., 1995. Contbr. articles to The Nassau Lawyer. Baseball coach Roslyn Little League, 1990-95; active in alumni fund campaign SUNY, Albany, 1994. Mem. Am. Arbitration Assn. (comml. law arbitrator), N.Y. State Bar Assn., Nassau County Bar Assn. (mentor), Nat. Assn. CPA Practitioners, N.Y. State Soc. CPAs. Office Phone: 516-627-3136. Personal E-mail: dkass@direcway.com.

KASS, JEROME ALLAN, writer; b. Chgo., Apr. 21, 1937; s. Sidney J. and Celia (Gorman) K.; children from previous marriage: Julie, Adam; m. Delia Ephron, May 21, 1982. BA, NYU, 1958, MA, 1959. Adj. prof. Film Sch. Colulmbia U. Playwright: Monopoly, 1965, Saturday Night, 1968, (mus.) Ballroom, 1978 (Tony nomination), (mus.) Norman's Ark, Montclair U., 2002, (TV) A Brand New Life, 1973, Queen of the Stardust Ballroom, 1975 (Writers Guild Am. award, Emmy nomination), My Old Man, 1979, The Fighter, 1982, Scorned and Swindled, 1984, Crossing to Freedom (aka Pied Piper), 1989, Last Wish, 1991, The Only Way Out, 1993, Secrets, 1995; screenwriter: The Black Stallion Returns, 1981, (miniseries) Evergreen, 1985; author: Four Short Plays by Jerome Kass, 1966, Saturday Night, 1969; adapted to concert form Finian's Rainbow, L.A., 1997, Pajama Game, L.A., 1998, Fiorello, L.A., 1999; musical version Queen of the Stardust Ballroom, Chgo., 1998. Mem. Dramatists Guild, Writers Guild Am., Actors Studio, Phi Beta Kappa. E-mail: kasscade@aol.com.

KASS, LAWRENCE, hematologist, oncologist, educator; b. Toledo, Ohio, Sept. 30, 1938; AB magna cum laude, U. Mich., 1960; MD with hons., MS Anatomy, U. Chgo., 1964. Diplomate Nat. Bd. Med. Examiners, Am. Bd. Internal Medicine/Internal Medicine and Hematology, Med. Oncology, Am. Bd. Pathology/Hematology. Intern Peter Bent Brigham Hosp., Boston, 1964-65, asst. resident internal medicine, 1965-66; sr. asst. resident internal medicine U. Hosps. of Cleve., 1966-68; Elliott Hoyt fellow in hematology Univ. Hosps. of Cleve., 1967-68; various to rsch. assoc. U. Chgo., 1968-70; asst. prof. internal medicine U. Mich. Med. Sch., Ann Arbor, 1970-73, assoc. prof. internal medicine, 1973-78; prof. path., medicine Case Western Res. U. Sch. Medicine, Cleve., 1978—; head hematopathology MetroHealth Med. Ctr., Cleve., 1978—. Cons. in medicine, VA Hosp., Ann Arbor; editorial cons. Williams and Wilkins Pubs., Balt., 1974—, Archives of Pathology and Lab. Medicine Blood, The Jour. of Hematology, The Jour. of Histochemistry and Cytochemistry, Western Jour. of Medicine, Am. Jour. of Hematology, Biotechnic & Histochemistry, 1975—, Rsch. Career Selection Rev. Com., VA, Washington, 1976—; active numerous coms. in field. Contbr. articles to profl. jours. Maj. med corps. U.S. Army, 1968-70. Recipient Internat. Giovanni DiGuglielmo prize, Giovanni DiGuglielmo Found., Accademia Nazionale Die Lincei, Rome, 1976, Diamond Cover award Nat. Soc. Histotechnologists and Jour. of Histotechnology, 1988, C.V. Mosby award, 1964, Merck award 1964. Fellow Am. Coll. Phys., Coll. Am. Pathologists; mem. AAAS, Am. Soc. Hematology, Am. Fedn. Clin. Rsch., Am. Soc. Clin. Oncology, Soc. Exptl. Biology and Medicine, Cen. Soc. Clin. Rsch., Histochem. Soc., Biol. Stain Commn., Am. Soc. Clin. Path., Phi Eta Sigma, Phi Beta Kappa, Alpha Omega Alpha. Office: MetroHealth Med Ctr 2500 Metrohealth Dr Cleveland OH 44109-1900 Office Phone: 216-778-4945. Office Fax: 216-778-5701. Business E-Mail: lkass@metrohealth.org.

KASS, LEON RICHARD, social sciences educator; b. Chgo., Feb. 12, 1939; s. Samuel and Anna (Shoichet) K.; m. Amy Judith Apfel, June 22, 1961; children: Sarah, Miriam. BS, U. Chgo., 1958, MD, 1962; PhD in Biochemistry, Harvard U., 1967. Intern Beth Israel Hosp., Boston, 1962-63; staff assoc. Lab. Molecular Biology, Nat. Inst. Arthritis and Metabolic Diseases, NIH, Bethesda, Md., 1967-69, staff fellow, 1969-70, sr. staff fellow, 1970; exec. sec. com. on life scis. and social policy NRC-NAS, Washington, 1970-72; tutor St. John's Coll., Annapolis, Md., 1972-76; Joseph P. Kennedy Sr. rsch. prof. in bioethics Kennedy Inst., Georgetown U., 1974-76; Henry R. Luce prof. liberal arts of human biology in coll. U. Chgo., 1976-84, prof. com. on social thought, 1984-90, Addie Clark Harding prof. in coll. and com. on social thought, 1990—; Hertog fellow Am. Enterprise Inst., Washington, 2002—. Founding fellow, bd. dirs. Hastings Ctr., 1969-96; bd. govs. U.S.-Israel Binat. Sci. Found., 1982-88; mem. coun. Nat. Humanities Coun., 1984-91, vice chmn. 1987-89; chmn. Pres.'s Coun. Bioethics, 2001-. Author: Toward a More Natural Science: Biology and Human Affairs, 1985, The Hungry Soul: Eating and the Perfecting of Our Nature, 1994, (James Q. Wilson) The Ethics of Human Cloning, 1998, (Amy A. Kass) Wing to Wing, Oar to Oar: Readings on Courting and Marrying, 2000, Life, Liberty, and The Defense of Dignity: The Challenge for Bioethics, 2002, The Beginning of Wisdom: Reading Genesis, 2003; contbr. articles to profl. jours. Served with USPHS, 1967-69. NIH postdoctoral fellow, 1963-67, John Simon Guggenheim Meml. Found. fellow, 1972-73, Nat. Humanities Ctr. fellow, 1984-85, W.H. Brady, Jr. Disting. fellow Am. Enterprise Inst., 1991-92, 98-99; NEH grantee, 1973-74; recipient Bradley prize The Lynde and Harry Bradley Found., 2003. Mem. Phi Beta Kappa, Alpha Omega Alpha. Jewish. Office: American Enterprise Inst 1150 17th St NW Washington DC 20036-4603

KASS, MICHAEL ALLEN, ophthalmologist, educator; b. Chgo., Dec. 24, 1941; MD, Northwestern U., Evanston, Ill., 1966. Diplomate Am. Bd. Ophthalmology. Intern Passavant Meml. Hosp., Chgo., 1966-67; asst. prof. ophthalmology Sch. Medicine Yale U., New Haven, 1973-75; resident Sch. Medicine Washington U., St. Louis, 1969-71, asst. ophthalmologist, 1972-73, asst. prof., 1975-77, assoc. prof., 1977-83, prof., 1983—, chmn., 1999—. Mem. AMA, Am. Acad. Ophthalmology, Assn. for Rsch. in Vision Ophthalmology. Office: Washington U Sch Medicine 660 S Euclid Ave # 8096 Saint Louis MO 63110-1010

KASS, ROBERT EBEN, statistician, educator; b. Boston, Sept. 7, 1952; s. Edward Harrold and Fae Ann (Golden) Kass; m. Loreta Myra Matheo, Sept. 12, 1992; children: Nicholas Matheo, Gabriel Lorenzo. BA in Math., Antioch Coll., 1975; postgrad., U. Wis., Madison, 1975—76; PhD, U. Chgo., 1980. NSF postdoctoral rsch. fellow Princeton (N.J.) U., 1980—81; asst. prof. stats. Carnegie Mellon U., Pitts., 1981—86, assoc. prof. stats., 1986—92, prof. stats., 1992—, head dept. stats., 1995—, mem. faculty, Ctr. Neural Basis of Cognition, 1997—. Bd. math. scis. NRC, 2002—; bd. mem. Nat. Inst. Statis. Scis., 2004—; exec. editor Statis. Sci., 1992—94. Author (with Paul W. Vos): Geometrical Foundations of Asymptotic Inference, 1997; contbr. articles to profl. jours. Named one of 10 Most Cited Rschrs. in Math., Inst. Scientific Info., 1993—2003. Fellow: Inst. Math. Stats. (Medallion lectr. 2002), Am. Statis. Assn.; mem.: AAAS (chair-elect sect. on statis. 2003—04). Office: Carnegie Mellon U Dept Stats 132 Baker Hall Pittsburgh PA 15213 Office Phone: 412-268-8723. Business E-Mail: kass@stat.cmu.edu.

KASSABIAN, GAGUIK SERGEYEVICH, history educator; b. Madrassa, USSR, May 14, 1978; arrived in U.S., 1999; s. Sergey Akopovich Kassabian and Tatiana Arkadierna Shakhverdian. BA in Journalism, Pyatigorsk (Russia) State U., 1996, BA in Gen. studies Mgmt., 1999; BA in English and Psychology, Pyatigorsk Linguistic U., 1999; MBA, Calif. Coast U., 2001; PhD in History and Philosophy, U. Devon, Eng., 2004. Store mgr. Mcpl. Enterprise KSiD, Park Zretnik, Russia, 1993—94; asst. adminstr. Pansionat Teploseriy, KSiD, Pyatigorsk, 1994—95; newspaper corr. Karkazyiy Kray, Pyatigorsk, 1994—96, Kavrazkaja Zebranitra, Pyatigorsk, 1994—96; interpreter, translator Rosario Productive BV, Novoalenadrovsk, Russia, 1999, Sparex Internat. Concern Glass Factory, Novoalenadrovsk, 1999; pres., owner Vostok Internat. Corp., St. Petersburg, Fla., 2000—. Recruiting mgr. Inst. Econs., Pyatigorsk, 1999. Author: Karun the Way to Freedom, 2002, Destruction of the United States or to the New Lands, 2004. Recipient BBC Radio contest award, Radio Russia, Moscow, 1996. Mem.: Union Entrepreneurs. Home: 7771 43d St N A Pinellas Park FL 33781 Office: Vostok Internat Corp 2711 Centerville Rd Ste 400 Wilmington DE 19808 E-mail: vostok@usa.com.

KASSAN, STUART S., rheumatologist; b. White Plains, N.Y., Nov. 19, 1946; s. Robert Jacob and Rosalind (Suchin) K.; m. Gail Karesh, Apr. 4, 1971; children: Michael Andrew, Merrill Alissa. BA, Case Western Res., 1968; MD, George Washington U., 1972. Diplomate Am. Bd. Internal Medicine, Am. Bd. Rheumatology, Am. Bd. Geriatrics. Intern and resident Grady Meml. Hosp., Altanta, 1972-74; clin. fellow NIH, Bethesda, Md., 1974-76; fellow Hosp. for Spl. Surgery, Cornell Med. Ctr., N.Y.C., 1976-78; head rheumatology clinic VA Med. Ctr., Denver, 1978-80; asst. clin. prof. medicine U. Colo. Health Scis. Ctr., Denver, 1978-84, assoc. clin. prof. medicine, 1984-94, clin. prof. medicine, 1994—; med. dir. rehab unit. Luth. Med. Ctr., Wheatridge, Colo., 1983-87; med. dir. rehab. unit St. Anthony Hosp., Denver, 1987-93. Cons. Annals Internal Medicine, Phila., 1986—, Arthritis and Rheumatism, Atlanta, 1995—, Jour. of Rheumatology, 1996—; vis. alumni scholar George Washington U. Sch. Medicine, 1986; chmn. med. adv. bd. Sjögren's Syndrome Found., Bethesda, 1997—, bd. dirs., 1996—. Co-editor: Sjögren's Syndrome, 1987; contbr. over 30 articles to profl. jours. Bd. dirs. Rocky Mountain chpt. Arthritis Found., Denver, 1978-80, 2002--, Polachek fellow, 1976-77; bd. dirs. Lupus Found. Colo., v.p., 1995-96, pres., 1996-2002; bd. dirs. Lupus Rsch. Inst., N.Y.C., 2002—; pres. Metrowest IPA, Lakewood, Colo., 1997-2003. With USPHS, 1974-76. Fellow ACP, Am. Coll. Rheumatology (network physician 1989), Colo. Rheumatology Assn. (pres. 2004—), George Washington U. Sch. Medicine Alumni Assn.(pres. 2004-); mem. Harvey Soc., Rocky Mountain Rheumatism Soc. (pres. 1997-), Cosmos Club. Jewish. Office: Colo Arthritis Assoc 4200 W Conejos Pl Ste 314 Denver CO 80204-1311 Office Phone: 303-892-6033. E-mail: s.kassan@juno.com.

KASSEBAUM, JOHN PHILIP, lawyer; b. Oct. 24, 1932; s. Leonard Charles and Helen Nancy (Horn) K.: m. Nancy Josephine Landon, June 8, 1955; children: John Philip, Richard L., William A., Linda J. Johnson; m. Llewellyn Hood Sinkler, Aug. 4, 1979; stepchildren: G. Dana, J. Marshall, Huger II, Llewellyn H. Sinkler. AB, U. Kans., 1953; JD, U. Mich., 1956. Bar: Kans. 1956, U.S. Supreme Ct. 1971, U.S. Ct. Appeals (2d, 4th, 10th, D.C. cirs.), U.S. Tax Ct. 1976, N.Y., 1979. Ptnr. Kassebaum & Johnson, N.Y.C. Bd. dirs. Wichita Eagle-Beacon Pub. Co. pres. Wyoming-Paris, Ltd. Author: Kassebaum Collection Vol I, 1981. Spl. asst. atty. gen., Kansas, 1970; chmn. Gov.'s Adv. Commn. Kansas Instl. Mgmt., 1961-69, bd. dirs., pres. Wichita Art Mus. Members; chmn. Kans. Assn. for Mental Health; trustee Price R. and Flora A. Reid Charitable Trust; chmn., bd. dirs. Skowhegan (Maine) Sch. Painting and Sculpture; bd. dirs., pres. Carolina Art Assn. and Gibbes Art Gallery, Charleston S.C.; pres. Spoleta Festival U.S. A., Chaleston; treas. Am. Arts Alliance, Washington; bd. dirs. Nat. Inst. for Music Theater; mem. endowment art com. Ulrich Mus. Art, Wichita; chmn. adv. com Spencer Mus. Art, U. Kans. Hon. curator of ceramics Spencer Mus. Art. Mem. ABA (sect. dispute resolution), ATLA, Am. Arbitration Assn., Nat. Inst. Dispute Resolution, Conflict Resolution Edn. Network, Assn. of Bar of City of New York, Kans. Trial Lawyers Assn., Kans. Assn. Def. Counsel, Fedn. Ins. Counsel, Union Club, (NYC), Met Club (Washington), Phi Delta Theta, Omicron Delta Kappa, Phi Delta Phi. Republican. Episcopalian. Home: 2065 Pettigrew St Sullivans Island SC 29482-8760 Office: 652 Hudson St Fl 5 New York NY 10014-1619 also: Ste 585 River Park Pl 727 N Waco St Wichita KS 67203-3951

KASSEL, CATHERINE M., community, maternal, and women's health nurse, consultant; b. Bklyn., Dec. 18, 1953; d. Christopher Frank and Ana Rosa (Sousa) Pannone; m. David L. Kassel, Dec. 27, 1979. Diploma in nursing, Kings County Hosp., Bklyn., 1974; BA in Cmty. Health, CUNY, 1979; BSN with honors, Columbia U., 1989. RN, N.Y. V.p. Kassel Mgmt. Co., N.Y.C., 1985—; pres. Kassel & Co., LLC, N.Y.C. Bd. dirs., co-chair legis. com. N.Y. Counties of RNs, Dist. 13, trustee, treas. polit. action com.; past bd. dirs. Nat. Abortion Rights Action League; bd. dirs., treas., chmn. fundraising, nominating com., adv. coun., Global Kids Inc.; mem. Women's Leadership Forum of Dem. Nat. Com. Mem. ANA (polit. action com.), ANA Found. (founding mem.), N.Y. State Nurses Assn., PAC. Home: 145 W 67th St Apt 7H New York NY 10023

KASSEL, DANIEL BRIAN, biotechnologist, researcher; b. Midland, Mich., July 30, 1961; s. Fred L. and Dorothy L. Kassel; m. Nancy N. Kassel, Sept. 11, 1993; 1 child, Andrew Evan. BA in Chemistry, Ohio State U., 1983; PhD in Chemistry, Mich. State U., 1988. Postdoctoral fellow MIT, Cambridge, Mass., 1988—89; NIH NRSA fellow Harvard U., Boston, 1989—91; rsch. investigator, various projects Glaxo, Inc., Research Triangle Park, NC, 1991—95; dir., analytical chemistry Combichem, Inc., San Diego, 1995—99; sr. dir., analytical tech. DuPont Pharms., San Diego, 1998—2002; sr. dir., drug discovery Syrrx, Inc., San Diego, 2002—. Scientific adv. bd. Syagen Techs., Tustin, Calif., 1999—, Sepiatec, Inc., Berlin, 2002—. Contbr. articles to profl. jours. Recipient honor, Am. Registry Profls., 2002; grantee NIH, 1989—91. Mem.: Am. Soc. Mass Spectrometry (short course coord. 1985—, invited plenary lectr. 1997—), Am. Chem. Soc. (invited plenary lectr. 1997—), Am. Assn. Pharm. Scis. Achievements include patents in field of parallel spray mass spectrometry; on-line quantitation; first to fast protein analysis using perfusion chromatography coupled with a mass spectrometer; concept and application of "mass-directed" purification of compound libraries. Avocations: golf, musical theater, international travel, skiing. Office: Syrrx Inc 10410 Science Ctr Dr San Diego CA 92121 E-mail: daniel.kassel@syrrx.com.

KASSEL, TERRY, human resources specialist; BA, NYU; JD, Seton Hall U. Pvt. practice, NY and NJ; various leadership positions including asst. gen. counsel and v.p. Office of Gen. Counsel; v.p. human resources U.S. private client group Merrill Lynch, NYC, 1985—2000; sr. v.p. human resources, 2001—. Mem. bd. mgrs. Merrill Lynch Cmty. Devel. Co.; trustee Winthrop H. Smith Meml. Found., Merrill Lynch & Co. Found. Mem. adv. bd. NOW Legal Def. and Edn. Fund. Office: Merrill Lynch 4 World Financial Ctr New York NY 10080*

KASSEL, VIRGINIA WELTMER, television producer, scriptwriter; b. Omaha; d. Tyler and Inez (Willard) Weltmer. BA, Bryn Mawr Coll. Producer Sta. WGBH-TV, Boston; producer NET, N.Y.C., coordinator nat. programs; mgr. spl. projects, exec. prodr. humanities programs WNET, N.Y.C.; sr. producer CBS Cable, N.Y.C., 1981-83; dir. devel. and prodn. East Coast Primetime Entertainment, Inc., 1983-87; v.p. East Coast Primetime Entertainment, Inc., 1987-89; assoc. dir. performance programs, prodn. exec. Great Performances Sta. WNET-TV, N.Y.C., 1989-91; producer, dir., writer Potter Prodns., 1991-92; dir. devel. Internat. Cultural Programming, 1992-94. Creator, prodr.: The Adams Chronicles; prodr.: The Soong Connection, 1995; contbr. articles to profl. jours. Recipient George Foster Peabody award, 1977, 2 Ohio State awards, 1977, Spl. Achievement award Nat. Assn. Ednl. Broadcasters, 1977, Triangle award, 1986; grantee NEH, Mellon Found Mem.: NATAS, N.Y. Women in Film and TV, Brit. Acad. Film and TV Arts (N.Y. and London), Am. Acad. TV Arts and Scis., Writers Guild Am. East, Nat. Com. on U.S. China Rels., Bryn Mawr Club N.Y. (bd. dirs.), Women's City Club N.Y. (bd. dirs.), Princeton Club (N.Y.). Home: 4 E 89th St New York NY 10128-0636 Office Phone: 212-860-4025.

KASSELL, NEAL FREDERIC, neurosurgery educator; b. Phila., Mar. 17, 1946; s. Martin Buddy and Evelyn Abigail (Block) K.; m. Nancy Coffin, Dec. 14, 1967 (div.); children: Natasha Lynn, Lauren Tamara, Nicole Tristan; m. Denise Etheridge, Aug. 30, 1986 (div. 1987); m. Lynn Haire, Mar. 12, 1994 (div. 2000). MD, U. Pa., 1972. Diplomate Am. Bd. Neurol. Surgery. Intern Pa. Hosp., Phila., 1972-73, resident in neurology, 1973-74, resident in neurosurgery, 1974-75, U. Western Ont., London, 1975-77; asst. prof. neurosurgery U. Iowa, Iowa City, 1977-81, assoc. prof. neurosurgery, 1981-82, prof. neurosurgery, 1982-84; prof. and vice chmn. neurosurgery U. Va. Sch. Medicine, Charlottesville, 1984-97, prof., co-chmn. neurosurgery, 1997—; pres. Va. Neurol. Inst., 1993—2000; mem. staff U. Va. Hosp., Charlottesville. Chmn. bd., founder Multimedia Med. Sys., Inc., 1995-2000—; chmn., founder Med.

Specialists, 1999; bd. dirs. Va. Nat. Bank; dir. NIH-Nat. Inst. Neurol. Disorders and Stroke study sects., 1984—. Reviewer Neurosurgery, Jour. Cerebral Blood Flow and Metabolism, 1977—; mem. editl. bd. Stroke, Surg. Neurology; contbr. over 450 papers to profl. jours. Recipient numerous rsch. grants and contracts; recipient McKenzie Meml. award, 1977, Grass award. Republican. Avocations: riding, classical music, hiking. Home: Wingate 2154 Garth Rd Charlottesville VA 22901-5412 Office: U Va Health Sys PO Box 800212 Charlottesville VA 22908-0212 E-mail: neal@virginia.edu.

KASSELL, PAULA SALLY, editor, publisher; b. N.Y.C., Dec. 5, 1917; d. Daniel Herman and Bertha Blanche (Jaret) K.; m. Gerson Gustav Friedman, Aug. 16, 1941 (dec.); children: Daniel Kassell, Claire Florence Friedman. BA, Barnard Coll., 1939. Tech. editor Bell Labs., Whippany, N.J., 1955-65, methods analyst Murray Hill, N.J., 1965-70; founder, editor, pub. New Directions for Women, Dover, N.J., 1971-77, assoc. editor Englewood, N.J., 1977-87, sr. editor, 1987-93, index editor Dover, 1993-98. V.p., UN rep. Women's Inst. for Freedom of Press, Washington, 1990—; convenor, mem. media task force Com. on Status of Women, UN, 1990-98. Contbr. chapters to books. Co-convenor Lakeland chpt. NOW, Dover, 1970; v.p. Dover (N.J.) Child Care Ctr., 1979-91; bd. dirs. Nat. Woman's Party, Washington, 1991-98; mem. media com. Forum 95, UN, N.Y.C., 1994-95; mem. adv. bd. Vet. Feminists Am., Lafayette, La., 1995—; mem. TV task force Morris County NOW, Morristown, N.J., 1995—; trustee Women's Media Initiative, 1997. Recipient First Feminist Action award NOW NJ, 1985, Women Making Herstory award, 1995, Elizabeth Cady Stanton award Women's Rights Info. Ctr., 1993, Woman of Achievement award Douglass Coll., 1994, Medal of Honor, Vet. Feminists Am., 1998, Millicent Carey McIntosh Feminism Award Barnard Coll., 2004. Featured in exhibit on NJ feminists by Morris County (NJ) Hist. Soc., September 17, 2000 to March 18, 2001, Journalist of Month, on women's e-news, www.womensenews.org, 2002. Mem. Am. Journalism Historians Assn., Internat. Women's Media Found., Journalism & Women Symposium. Avocations: attending opera, concerts, ballet performances, visiting museums, travel. Home: 25 W Fairview Ave Dover NJ 07801-3417

KASSEM, AHMED A., engineer, consultant; b. Damas, Dakahlia, Egypt, May 22, 1964; s. Abdel-Rahman A. Kassem and Aziza E. Nabarawy; m. Halima S. Elsheikh, June 22, 1971; 1 child, Heba A. BS, Mansoura U., 1986; MS, Cairo U., 1991; PhD, Wash. State U., 1996. Registered prof. engr., S.C., 2002. Lectr. asst. Helwan U., Cairo, 1988—93; part-time cons. Misr Consult, Giza, 1988—93; rsch., tchg. asst. Wash. State U., Pullman, 1993—96; asst. prof. Helwan U., Cairo, 1996—2000; rsch. assoc. U. S.C., Columbia, 2000—02, rsch. asst. prof., 2002—. Part-time cons. Misr Cons., Giza, 1996—2000. Grantee, Wash. State U., 1996; scholar, Govt. of Egypt, 1993. Mem.: ASCE (task com. numerical modeling sediemnt transport). Achievements include research in River Mecahnics, Turbidity Currents, Bridge Scour, Mathematical Modeling. Office: U SC 300 S Main St Columbia SC 29208

KASSIMIR, JOEL JACK, dermatologist; married. MD, Mt. Sinai Sch. Med. of NYU. Residency tng. in general surgery Mt. Sinai Med. Ctr.; residency tng. in dermatology NYU Hospitals Ctr.; pvt. practice NYC. Contbr. Reversing Hair Loss, 1985. Office: 10 East 88th St New York NY 10128 Office Phone: 212-876-3319.*

KASSIN, SAUL, psychology professor; b. N.Y.C., Apr. 25, 1953; s. Mordy and Betty (Ashear) K.; m. Carol Beth Goldner, Sept. 19, 1952; children: Briana Rachel, Marc Joseph. BS, Bklyn. Coll., 1974; MA, U. Conn., 1976, PhD, 1978. NIH postdoctoral fellow U. Kans., Lawrence, 1978-79; asst. prof. Purdue U., West Lafayette, Ind., 1979-81, Williams Coll., Williamstown, Mass., 1981-84; rsch. assoc. Fed. Jud. Ctr., Washington, 1984-85; NIH postdoctoral fellow Stanford (Calif.) U., 1985-86; from assoc. to full prof. Williams Coll., Williamstown, 1986—. Jury cons., expert witness. Author: Psychology, 1995, 4th edit., 2004, Essentials of Psychology, 2004; co-author: The American Jury on Trial, 1988, Confessions in the Courtroom, 1993, Social Psychology, 1990, 6th edit., 2005; co-editor: Developmental Social Psychology: Theory and Research, 1981, The Psychology of Evidence and Trial Procedure, 1985, On The Witness Stand: Controversies in the Courtroom, 1987, In the Jury Box: Controversies in the Courtroom, 1987, Readings in Social Psychology, 2002, Current Directions in Psychology, 2005, Psychology in Modules, 2006; cons. editor Jour. Exptl. Social Psychology, 1982-87, Jour. Personality and Social Psychology: Attitudes and Social Cognition, 1992-94; editl. cons. Law and Human Behavior, 1986—; ad hoc reviewer in field; contbr. articles to profl. jours. Recipient MacArthur Found. Rsch. Network, 2003—; rsch. grantee Found. Child Devel., 1984—85, Jud. fellow U.S. Supreme Ct., Washington, 1984—85. Fellow APA, Am. Psychol. Soc.; mem. Am. Psychology-Law Soc., Soc. for Exptl. Social Psychology, Phi Beta Kappa. Office: Williams Coll Bronfman Sci Ctr Williamstown MA 01267 E-mail: skassin@williams.edu.

KASSINGER, THEODORE WILLIAM, former federal agency administrator; b. Atlanta, Jan. 26, 1953; s. Edward Theodore and Sarah Mell (Laurent) K.; m. Ruth Lynn Good, Oct. 13, 1984; children: Anna Laurent, Austen Elizabeth, Alice Caroline. BLA, U. Ga., 1975, JD, 1978. Bar: Ga. 1978, D.C. 1986. Atty.-advisor U.S. Internat. Trade Commn., Washington, 1978-80; atty., advisor U.S. Dept. State, Washington, 1980-81; internat. trade counsel com. on fin. U.S. Senate, Washington, 1981-85, assoc., 1985-89; ptnr. Vinson & Elkins L.L.P., Washington, 1990—2001; gen. counsel U.S. Dept. Commerce, Washington, 2001—04, dep. sec., 2004—05. Co-author: U.S. Regulation of International Trade, 1987, Basic Documents in International Economic Law, 1989. Mem. ABA. Republican. Roman Catholic.

KASSIRER, JEROME PAUL, medical educator; b. Buffalo, Dec. 19, 1932; Grad., U. Buffalo, 1953, MD magna cum laude, 1957; DS (hon.), U. Mass., 1992; D honoris causa, L'Universite Rene Descartes, Paris, 1992; DS (hon.), Thomas Jefferson U., 1994, SUNY, 1995. Diplomate Am. Bd. Internal Medicine (mem. certifying examination com. 1987-89, bd. dirs. 1989-96, mem. exec. com. 1993-96, chmn. 1995-96). Intern, asst. resident in medicine Buffalo Gen. Hosp., Buffalo, 1957—59; fellow in nephrology New Eng. Med. Ctr., Boston, 1959—61, sr. resident in medicine, 1961—62, asst. physician, 1961—65, physician renal svc., 1969-74, assoc. physician-in-chief, 1971—91, acting physician-in-chief, 1976—77; instr. medicine Sch. Medicine, Tufts U., Medford, Mass., 1961-65, asst. prof. medicine, 1965—69, assoc. prof., 1969—74, vice chmn. dept. medicine, 1971—91, acting chmn. dept. medicine, 1974—75, prof. medicine, 1974—, Sara Murray Jordan Prof. Medicine, 1987—91; editor-in-chief New Eng. Jour. Medicine, Boston, 1991—99. Lectr. in medicine Harvard U., 1991—; bd. dirs. Postgrad. Med. Inst. Mass. Med. Soc., 1988—91. Editor in chief: Current Therapy in Internal Medicine, 1990; co-editor: Clin. Problem Solving, Hosp. Practice, 1985—91; cons. editor: Am. Jour. Medicine, 1976—86, mem. editl. bd.: New Eng. Jour. Medicine, 1972—75; co-editor: Nephrology Forum, Kidney Internat, 1978—91, ed. Decision Making, 1987—89; author: On the Take: How Medicine's Complicity with Big Business Can Endanger Your Health, 2004; editl. advisor: Outline of Knowledge, Part 4: Human Life, The New Encyclopaedia Britannica, 1989. Recipient Ednl. Rsch. Found. award, AMA, 1993. Master: ACP (chmn. 1985—88, gov. Mass. 1985—89, mem. exec. com. bd. govs. 1988—89, mem. health and pub. policy com. 1989—91, bd. regents 1990—91, chmn. sci.); fellow: AAAS; mem.: Soc. Clin. Decision Making (charter mem.), Buffalo Acad. Medicine, Mass. Med. Soc. (hon. life), Nat. Libr. Medicine (chmn. bd. sci. counselors 1989—90, mem. biomed. journalism award com. 1992—), Assn of Am. Physicians, Inst. Medicine NAS, Am. Fedn. Clin. Rsch., Am. Soc. Nephrology. Jewish. Avocation: photography. Office: Tufts Univ Sch Med Sackler Ctr 145 Harrison Ave Boston MA 02111*

KASSLER, DAVID, music educator; b. Mt. Pleasant, Iowa, Dec. 4, 1960; s. John P. and Leota M. Kassler. MusB with honors in instrumental music edn., U. Iowa, 1983; MusM in music edn., U. Minn., 1995; PhD in music edn., U. Utah Sch. Music, 1999; MusD in euphonium performance, U. Miami, 2004. Grad. tchg. asst. U. Minn., Duluth, Minn., 1985—87; trombonist Duluth Superior Symphony, Duluth, Minn., 1985—2004, Lake Superior Chamber Orch., Duluth, Minn., 1988—, Northland Opera Theatre Experience Orch., Duluth, Minn., 1995—2000, Utah Symphony Orch., Salt Lake City, 1998; grad. tchg. asst. U. Utah, Salt Lake City, 1998—99; conductor chancel choir, children's choir, women's choir Cmty. Presbyn. Ch., Grand Rapids, Minn., 2001—02; prin. euphonium U. Miami Wind Ensemble, Coral Gables, Fla., 2002—04; grad. tchg. asst. U. Miami, Coral Gables, Fla., 2002—04; prof. music Fort Hays State U., Hays, Kans., 2004—. Composer: Choral Prelude and Fugue on Puer Nobis, 2002; contbr. articles various profl. jours. Scholarship, Keystone Brass Inst., Activities scholarship, U. Iowa. Mem.: Internat. Tuba and Euphonium Assn., Internat. Trombone Assn., Music Educators Nat. Conf., Kans. Music Educators Assn., Am. Choral Dirs. Assn. Office Phone: 785-628-5353. E-mail: tedok2@yahoo.com.

KASSLER, HASKELL A., lawyer; b. Boston, Feb. 8, 1936; s. Harry and Natalie (Steinberg) K.; m. Mary Elizabeth Kelligrew, May 30, 1965; children: Marion Adelaide, Sarah Elizabeth. BA, Tufts U., 1957; JD, Boston U., 1960. Bar: Mass. 1960, U.S. Dist. Ct. Mass. 1961, U.S. Dist. Ct. (no. dist.) Miss. 1964, U.S. Dist. Ct. (so. dist.) La. 1965, U.S. Ct. Appeals (5th cir.) 1965, U.S. Ct. Appeals (1st cir.) 1969, U.S. Supreme Ct. 1967. Assoc. Poster, Wilinsky & Goldstein, Boston, 1960—64; pvt. practice Boston, 1964—66, 1969—71; asst. dir. Vol. Defenders Com., Inc., Boston, 1967—68; ptnr. Kassler & Feuer (formerly Richmond, Kassler, Feinberg & Feuer), Boston, 1971—99, Casner & Edwards, LLP, Boston, 1999—. Regional counsel New Eng. Region, Am. Jewish Congress, 1965-67; counsel Civil Liberties Union Mass., 1968-70; asst. prof. criminal justice Northeastern U., Boston, 1969-76; chmn. Mass. Jud. Nominating Coun., 1987-90; mem. Lawyers Constl. Def. Commn., 1964-65. Trustee U. Mass., 1977-81, U. Mass. Bldg. Authority, 1980-81, Mus. Transp., 1981—; selectman Town of Brookline, 1971-74, elected town meeting mem., 1959-84; mem. Local Redistricting Rev. Commn., 1976-78. Fellow Am. Acad. Matrimonial Lawyers (chpt. bd. mgrs. 1980-90, v.p. 1981-82, pres. 1984-86, Judge Haskell Freedman award Mass. chpt. 1984, Mass. Jurisprudence award 1999, cert. matrimonial arbitrator), Mass. Family and Probate Amm. Inn Ct.; mem. ABA, Mass. Bar Assn., Norfolk County Bar Assn., Tufts U. Alumni Coun. Office: Casner & Edwards LLP 303 Congress St Boston MA 02210 Office Phone: 617-426-5900. E-mail: kassler@casneredwards.com.

KASSMAN, ANDREW LANCE, orthodontist; b. N.Y.C., Nov. 14, 1950; s. David and Phyllis Ivy (Einhorn) K.; children: Stacey Arielle, Alexandria Devin; m. Laurie Ann Kassman, July 7, 1997; 1 child, Dylan Nathaniel BS in Engring., Tulane U., 1972; DMD, Tufts U., 1975; cert. orthodontics, Columbia U., 1978. Lab. technician Tufts Med. Ctr., Boston, 1973-75; resident VA Hosp., Northport, N.Y., 1975-76; pvt. practice Astoria, NY, 1976-78, Phila., 1978—79, East Patchogue, NY, 1979-80; pvt. practice dentistry specializing in orthodontics Tucson, 1980—. Chief orthodontia Crippled Children's Ctr., Tucson, 1980—; assoc. staff Tucson Med. Ctr., 1980—. Bd. dirs. Comstock Found., Tucson, 1980—; active Congregation Or Chadash, Tucson, 1996—, Alta Vista Assn., 1996—, Tucson Boys Club, 1988—, Jewish Cmty. Ctr., Tucson, 1988—. Mem. ADA, Am. Assn. Orthodontists, Pacific Coast Soc. Orthodontists, Tucson Orthodontist Soc., Tucson C. of C. Avocations: baseball, football, tennis, travel. Home: 6501 N Placita Alta Reposa Tucson AZ 85750-4204 Office: 6700 N Oracle Rd Ste 327 Tucson AZ 85704-7740 E-mail: drkaz@mindspring.com.

KASSNER, ANDREW CHARLES, lawyer; b. N.Y.C., Dec. 12, 1959; s. Herbert Seymour Kassner and Sheilah Helen (Goodwin) Keat; m. Maureen Cummins, Mar. 25, 1984; children: Ethan, Gillian, Adam, Joshua, Claudia. BA in History, U. Pa., 1980; JD cum laude, N.Y. Law Sch., 1983. Bar: N.Y. 1984, U.S. Dist. Ct. (so. and ea. dists.) N.Y. 1984, Pa. 1985, Del. 2004, U.S. Dist. Ct. (ea. dist.) Pa. 1985, U.S. Dist. Ct. (no. dist.) Pa. 1990, U.S. Dist. Ct. (ctrl. dist.) Pa. 1995, U.S. Ct. Appeals (4th cir.) 2002. Bankruptcy atty., NYC; assoc. Arott, Nachamie, Benjamin et al, N.Y.C., 1983-85, Fox, Rothschild, O'Brien & Frankel, Phila., 1985-86; from assoc. to mng. ptnr. Drinker, Biddle & Reath, Phila., 1986—2002, asst. to chmn., 1996—2005, ptnr.-in-charge, Wilmington and mem., mgmt. com., exec. ptnr., 2005—. Adj. prof. Rutgers U. Sch. of Law, Camden, N.J., 1989-2000; bd. trustees Consumer Bankruptcy Assistance Project, Phila., 1994—; bd. dirs. Farmers Mkt. Trust, Phila., 1994—. Mem. ABA, N.Y. Bar Assn., Pa. Bar Assn., Phila. Bar Assn., Am. Bankruptcy Inst., Ea. Dist. of Pa. Bankruptcy Conf., Mask and Whig Club (bd. dirs.), fellow, Am. Coll. Bankruptcy. Avocations: photography, travel, golf. Office: Drinker Biddle & Reath One Logan Sq 18th and Cherry Sts Philadelphia PA 19103 also: Drinker Biddle & Reath Ste 1000 1100 N Market St Wilmington DE 19801-1243 Office Phone: 215-988-2700, 302-467-4212. Office Fax: 215-988-2757, 302-467-4201. E-mail: andrew.kassner@dbr.com.

KASSNER, HERBERT SEYMORE, lawyer; b. N.Y.C., Dec. 3, 1931; s. Abraham and Rose (Rosenblatt) K.; m. Sheilah Goodwin, 1957 (div. 1965); children: Andrew, Kenneth; m. Marjorie Fern Golding, 1974 (div. 1992); children: Robin, Jeffrey; m. Linda Rubinstein Finder, 1993. BA (hon.), Franklin and Marshall U., 1952; cert., Hague (Netherlands) Acad. of Internat. Law, 1953; MA, NYU, 1955; LLB (hon.), Harvard U., 1955. Bar: N.Y. 1955, Conn. 1986. Atty. Gallap, Climenko & Gould, N.Y.C., 1955, Otterbourg, Steindler, Huston & Rosen, N.Y.C., 1956; pvt. practice law N.Y.C., 1957-65, 1969; atty. Dryer & Traub, N.Y.C., 1966-68, Kassner & Detsky, N.Y.C., 1970-80, Kassner & Haigney, N.Y.C., 1981-90. Instr. Ohio State U., Columbus, 1956-57; asst. prof. Ark. State U., Pine Bluff, 1965. Contbr. articles to profl. jours. on 1st amendment law. Mem. Phi Beta Kappa. Home: 7221 Montrico Dr Boca Raton FL 33433-6931 Personal E-mail: Sonnykas123@aol.com.

KASSNER, MICHAEL ERNEST, materials science educator, researcher; b. Osaka, Japan, Nov. 22, 1950; (parents Am. citizens); s. Ernest and Clara (Christa) K.; m. Marcia J. Wright, Aug. 19, 1972 (div. Dec. 1976). BS, Northwestern U., 1972; MS, Stanford U., 1979, PhD, 1981. Metallurgist Sargent and Lundy Engrs., Chgo., 1977, Lawrence Livermore (Calif.) Nat. Lab., 1981-90, head phys. metallurgy and joining sect., 1988-90; lectr. San Francisco State U., 1983; prof. Naval Postgrad. Sch., Monterey, Calif., 1984-86; prof., dir. grad. program in materials sci. Oreg. State U., Corvallis, 1990—2003, Chevron endowed prof., 1996, Northwest Aluminium prof., 1997—2003; prof., chmn. dept. aero. and mech. engring. U. So. Calif., L.A., 2003—. Temporary assignment as project mgr. Office Basic Energy Scis., U.S. Dept. Energy, 1991-96, 2000-03; vis. scholar dept. physics U. Groningen, Netherlands, 1985-87; vis. scholar dept. materials, sci. and engring. Stanford U., 1981-83; adj. prof. dept. mech. and aerospace engring. U. Calif., San Diego, 1999—. Author over 160 articles, book on binary phase diagrams, book on creep fundamentals, editor various sci. jours. Lt. USN, 1972-76; lt. comdr. USNR, 1976-81. Fulbright scholar, The Netherlands; fellow ASM Internat., 1998. Mem. ASME, Am. Soc. Metals, The Metall. Soc., Materials Research Soc., Sigma Xi. Home: 987 W 30th St Los Angeles CA 90007 Office Phone: 213-740-7213.

KASSOF, ALLEN H., foundation administrator; b. NYC, Dec. 17, 1930; s. Morris and Sophia B. Kassof; m. Arianne Scholz, 1953; children: Andrea, Arlen, Anita. BA, Rutgers U., 1952; AM, Harvard U., 1954, PhD, 1960. Asst. prof. Smith Coll., Northampton, Mass., 1957-60, Princeton (N.J.) U., 1961-65, assoc. prof., asst. dean coll., 1965-68; founder, exec. dir. Internat. Rsch. and Exchs. Bd., N.Y.C. and Princeton, 1968-92; pres. Project on Ethnic Rels. in Ea. Europe, Carnegie Corp. N.Y., Princeton, 1991—2005, pres. emeritus and sr. advisor, 2005—. Cons. conf. security and cooperation Europe, Hamburg, Germany, Budapest, Hungary, 1980, 85, Warsaw, Poland, 1993; mem. pres. com. fgn. lang., Washington, 1978-79; mem. U.S. task force Romania, Bucharest, 1990-92; prin. mediator between Govt. of Romania and Dem. Union Hungarians in Romania, 1993—; mem. Coun. for Ethnic Accord, 1992—; chair roundtable talks between Slovak and Ethnic Hungarian parliamentary parties of Slovakia, 1995—2001, Serb-Albanian Roundtable on Future of Kosovo, NYC, 1997; chmn. Regional Roundtable of Polit. Leaders from Southeast Europe on Rels. between Albanians and their Neighbors, Budapest and Athens, 2000, Lucerne, 2002, 04; co-chmn. Euro-Atlantic group on interethnic conflicts NATO, Brussels, 1998; chmn. Roundtable for Macedonian Parliamentary Parties on Fulfillment of the Ohrid Agreement, Mavroro, Macedonia, 2003-05. Decorated Grand Officer Nat. Order of Faithful Svc., Pres. of Romania. Mem.: Coun. Fgn. Rels., Am. Assn. Advancement Slavic Studies. Avocation: photography. Home: 949 Mercer Rd Princeton NJ 08540-4823 Office: Project on Ethnic Rels 15 Chambers St Princeton NJ 08542-3707 Personal E-mail: aakassof@cs.com. Business E-Mail: allen.kassof@per-usa.org. E-mail: allenkassof@patmedia.net.

KASSOFF, MITCHELL JAY, lawyer, educator; b. N.Y.C., June 11, 1953; s. Justice Edwin and Phyllis (Brafman) K.; m. Gwendolyn Jones, Mar. 3, 1979; children: Sarah, Jonathan. BS in Pub. Acctg. magna cum laude, SUNY Albany, 1975; JD, U. Va., 1978. Bar: N.Y. 1979, N.J. 1983, U.S. Supreme Ct. 1982, U.S. Ct. Appeals (2d cir.) 1996, U.S. Ct. Appeals (D.C. cir.) 1979, U.S. Ct. Appeals (3d cir.), U.S. Ct. Appeals (3d cir.) 2001, U.S. Tax Ct. 1979, U.S. Ct. Internat. Trade 1981, U.S. Ct. Customs and Patent Appeals 1979, U.S. Dist. Ct. (so., ea., no. and we. dists.) N.Y. 1979, U.S. Dist. Ct. N.J. 1983. Assoc. Herzfeld & Rubin, P.C., N.Y.C., 1978-82; pvt. practice N.Y.C. and N.J., 1982—. Prof. law and taxation Pace U., N.Y.C., 1979—. Contbr. articles to profl. jours. Mem. N.Y. State Bar Assn. Home: 2 Foster Ct South Orange NJ 07079-1002 E-mail: franatty@concentric.net.

KASSON, JAMES MATTHEWS, electronics executive; b. Muncie, Ind., Mar. 19, 1943; s. Robert Edwin and Mary Louise K.; m. Betty Roseman, Aug. 14, 1976. BSE.E., Stanford U., 1964; MSE.E., U. Ill., 1965. Engring. mgr. Santa Rita Tech., Santa Clara, Calif., 1963-69; engring. sect. mgr. Hewlett-Packard, Palo Alto, Calif., 1969-73; v.p. research and devel. ROLM Corp., Santa Clara, 1973-88; fellow IBM Corp., San Jose, Calif., 1988-95; v.p. engring. Echelon Corp., Palo Alto, Calif., 1995-98, CIO, 1998-2000. Patentee in field. Trustee Choate Rosemary Hall, Wallingford, Conn., 1990-96, Ctr. Photog. Art, Carmel, Calif., 2001-03, Monterey (Calif.) Mus. Art, 2005—. Mem. IEEE (citation for contbn. 1981). Home: 33732 E Carmel Valley Rd Carmel Valley CA 93924 E-mail: jim@kasson.com.

KASSOY, HORTENSE (HONEY KASSOY), artist, sculptor, painter; b. N.Y.C., Feb. 14, 1917; d. Adolph and Mary (Apfel) Blumenkranz; m. Bernard Kassoy, June 30, 1946; children: Meredith, Sheila. Diploma, Pratt Inst., 1936; BS, Columbia U., 1938, MA, 1939; student, Parsons Sch. Design, Paris, U. Colo., 1966, NYU, 1966-67; studied sculpture with Sahl Swarz, Chaim Gross & Oronzio Maldarelli. Solo exhbns. include Caravan House Gallery, 1974, Women in the Arts Gallery, 1978, Ward-Nasse Gallery, 1986, Pioneer Gallery, Cooperstown, N.Y., 1987, 91, 97, 80th Birthday Retrospective Solo of Wood Sculpture Prints and Watercolors, Vladeck Hall Gallery, N.Y., 1997, 2002, Pioneer Gallery, Cooperstown, 1997, 2002; group exhbns. include Bronx (N.Y.) Mus., 1971, 75, 85-86, Toledo Mus. Art, Toronto Mus. Art, Hudson River Mus., Bklyn. Mus., New Age Gallery, Lever House, Bklyn. Coll., Fordham U., Lehman Coll., Cork Gallery, Nat. Acad. Design; permanent collections include Slater Meml. Mus. Co-chair visual arts Bronx (N.Y.) Coun. on Arts, 1973-76. Fellow Va. Ctr. for Creative Arts, 1986, 88, 89, 92, 95, 97; recipient 1st prize in watercolor Painters Day at N.Y. World's Fair, 1940, Walker prize for sculpture, Oneonta, NY, 2002. Mem. Am. Soc. Contemporary Artists (v.p. 1989-94, 99-2003, awards in sculpture 1979, 80, 83, 90, 92, 96, 2000, 02), N.Y. Artists Equity Assn. (v.p., bd. dirs. 1971-83), Internation Assn. Art (corr. sec. 1979-93), del. to 10th Congress 1983), Contemporary Arts Guild (rec. sec. 1981-89), Fedn. Modern Painters and Sculptors. Home: 130 Gale Pl Apt 6B Bronx NY 10463-2853 also: Butternut Hill Studio 1577 County Route 16 Burlington Flats NY 13315-3211

KASSULKE, TIMOTHY JAMES, principal; s. Richard George and Jeanette Louise Kassulke; m. Tammie Marie Kassulke, June 14, 1986; children: Aaron Michael, Benjamin David, Emily Kathryn, Alexander James, Olivia Marie. B, Dr. Martin Luther Coll., 1985; EdM, Doane Coll., 2004. Educator St. Paul Luth. Sch., Norfolk, Nebr., 1985—2005, prin., 1993—2005. Mem.: ASCD. Home: 1106 Georgia Ave Norfolk NE 68701 Office: St Paul Luth Sch 1010 Georgia Ave Norfolk NE 68701

KASTAN, DAVID SCOTT, literature educator, writer; b. N.Y.C., Jan. 4, 1946; s. Peter Lewis and Audrey Brown (Kastan); 1 child, Marina Claire; m. Jane Ezersky, Nov. 26, 2004. AB, Princeton U., 1967; MA, U. Chgo., 1968, PhD, 1974. Asst. prof. Dartmouth Coll., 1973-79, 1973-79, assoc. prof., 1979-86; prof. Columbia U., 1987—. Disting. vis. prof. Am. U., Cairo, 1995, Copenhagen U., 1998; vis. prof., hon. rsch. prof. Univ. Coll. London, 1999—. Gen. editor: Arden Shakespeare, 1995; co-editor: Bantam Shakespeare, 2004; author: Shakespeare and the Shapes of Time, 1982, Shakespeare after Theory, 1999, Shakespeare and the Book, 2001; editor (with Marina Kastan): Poetry for Young People: William Shakespeare, 2000; editor: Staging the Renaissance, 1991, Critical Essays on Shakespeare's Hamlet, 1995, New History of Early English Drama, 1997, A Companion to Shakespeare, 1999, 1 Henry IV (Arden Shakespeare), 2002, Norton Critical Doctor Faustus, 2005, Paradise Lost, 2005. Woodrow Wilson fellow, 1968, Folger Libr. fellow, 1994, Huntington Libr. Mellon fellow, 1995, Burke Libr. fellow, 2003, Guggenheim fellow, 2004. Mem. MLA (divisional exec. com.), Renaissance English Text Soc. (coun. mem.), Shakespeare Assn. Am., Renaissance Soc. Am., Phi Beta Kappa. Office: Columbia Univ Dept English 116th St & Broadway New York NY 10027 E-mail: dsk1@columbia.edu.

KASTELIC, DAVID ALLEN, lawyer; b. Ely, Minn., Apr. 19, 1955; m. Janice E Kastelic. BS cum laude, St. John's U., 1977; JD magna cum laude, U. Minn., 1980. Sr. v.p. CHS Inc, Inver Heights, Minn., gen. counsel, 2003—. Office: CHS 5500 Cenex Dr Inver Grove Heights MN 55077 Home: 945 Brooks Ave W Roseville MN 55113-3312

KASTELIC, ROBERT FRANK, aerospace transportation executive; b. Granite City, Ill., July 17, 1934; s. Joseph and Anna Marie (Kries) K.; m. Patricia Ann Dalton, Apr. 8, 1961; children: Michael J., Constance A., Robert J., Kirsten S. BS in Acctg., U. Ill., 1956. Sr. acct. Price Waterhouse & Co., St. Louis, 1956-63; v.p., CFO, comptroller Merc. Bancorp., St. Louis, 1963-72; exec. v.p., CFO Equimark Corp. and Equibank, Pitts., 1972-83, vice-chmn. bd., 1983-84; pres., COO Astrotech Internat. Corp., Pitts., 1986—; chmn., CEO X-Mark Industries, Washington, Pa., 1988—. Bd. dirs. Glenshaw (Pa.) Glass Co., Quasitronics, Inc., X-Mark Industries, Astrotech Internat., Pitts., Fidelity Savs. Bank; chmn. St. Francis Fin. Corp. Mem. rev. com. United Way, Pitts., 1977-78; bd. dirs. St. Francis Hosp., Civic Light Opera. Served with U.S. Army, 1956-58. Mem. AICPA, Am. Mgmt. Assn., Am. Soc. Corp. Secs., Mo., Pa. insts. CPAs, Bank Adminstrn. Inst., Fin. Execs. Inst., Nat. Investor Relations Inst. Clubs: Duquesne. Home: 313 Fox Hunt Rd Pittsburgh PA 15238 Office: X-Mark Industries 2001 N Main St Washington PA 15301-6180 Personal E-mail: rfkastelic@netscape.net.

KASTEN, KARL ALBERT, artist, educator, printmaker; b. San Francisco, Mar. 5, 1916; s. Ferdin and Barbara Anna Kasten; m. Georgette Gautier, Mar. 29, 1958; children: Ross, Lee, Beatrix, Joell, Cho-An. MA, U. Calif., 1939; postgrad., U. Iowa, 1949; student, Hans Hofmann Sch. Fine Arts, 1951. Instr. Calif. Sch. Fine Arts, 1941, U. Mich., 1946-47; asst. prof. art San Francisco State U., 1947-50; prof. U. Calif., Berkeley, 1950-83. Bibliography appears in Etching (Edmondson), 1973, Collage and Assemblage (Meilach and Ten Hoor), 1973, Modern Woodcut Techniques (Kuroski), 1977, California Style (McClelland and Last), 1985, Art in the San Francisco Bay Area (Albright), 1985, Breaking Type: The Art of Karl Kasten (Landauer), 1999, The Stamp of Impulse, Abstract Expressionist Prints (David Acton), 2001; group shows include San Francisco Mus. Art, 1939, Chgo. Art Inst., 1946, Whitney Mus., 1952, Sao Paolo Internat. Biennials, 1955, 61, Achenbach Found., 1976, World Print III Traveling Exhbn., 1980-83, Gallery Sho, Tokyo, 1994, Inst. Franco-Americain, Rennes, 1995, Calif. Heritage Gallery, 1999, Robert Green Fine Arts Gallery, 2002; patentee etching press. Capt. U.S. Army, 1942-46. Decorated 4 battle stars; fellow Creative Arts Inst., 1964, 71, Tamarind Lithography Artist Fellowship, 1968, Regents Humanities, 1977. Mem. Berkeley Art Ctr. Assn. (bd. dirs. 1987-92), Calif. Soc. Printmakers (Disting. Artist award 1997), Univ. Faculty Club, Univ. Arts Club. Home: 1884 San Lorenzo Ave Berkeley CA 94707-1841 Office: Univ Calif Berkeley Art Dept Berkeley CA 94707

KASTEN, ROBERT W., JR., former senator; b. Milw., June 19, 1942; s. Robert W. and Mary (Ogden) K. BA, U. Ariz., 1964; MBA, Columbia U., 1966. With Genesco, Inc., Nashville, 1966-68; dir., v.p. Gilbert Shoe Co., Thiensville, Wis., 1968-75; mem. Wis. Senate, Madison, 1972-75; mem. joint fin. com., 1973-75; chmn. joint survey com. on tax exemptions, 1973-75; mem. 94th-95th congresses from 9th Wis. Dist.; U.S. Senator from Wis., 1980-93; founder Kasten & Co., Thiensville, Wis., 1993—; sr. assoc. Strategic and Internat. Studies Ctr., Washington, 1993—. Mem. 100th Congress Com., appropriations com., budget com., commerce, sci. and transp. com., small bus. com. Regional dir. Milw. Coalition for Clean Water; active Milw. Soc. for Prevention of Blindness; founder Legis. Studies Inst. 1st lt. Wis. Air N.G., 1967-72. Named Jaycee of Yr., 1972; named Legis. Conservationist of Yr. Wis. Wildlife Fedn., 1973, 86; One of Best Legislators Senate Rep. Class of 1980 Nat. Jour., 1985. Mem. Nat. Audubon Soc., Ducks Unltd., Sigma Nu, Alpha Kappa Psi Office: Kasten & Co # 500 1629 K St NW Washington DC 20006-4107

KASTENBERG, WILLIAM EDWARD, engineering educator, science educator; b. N.Y.C., June 25, 1939; s. Murray and Lillian Kastenberg; m. Berna R. Miller, Aug. 18, 1963; children: Andrew, Joshua, Lillian; m. Gloria Hauser, May 3, 1992. BS, UCLA, 1962, MS, 1963; PhD, U. Calif., Berkeley, 1966. Asst. prof. Sch. Engring. and Applied Sci. UCLA, 1966-71, assoc. prof., 1971-75, assoc. dean Sch. Engring. and Applied Sci., 1981-85, chmn. mech. aerospace and nuc. engring., 1985-88, prof. mech., aerospace and nuc. engring. dept., 1975-94; sr. fellow U.S. NRC, Washington, 1979-80; prof. nuc. engring. dept. U. Calif., Berkeley, 1995—, chmn. nuc. engring. dept., 1995-2000, Chancellor's prof., 1996—99, Daniel Tellep disting. prof. engring., 1999—. Guest scientist Karlsruhe (Fed. Republic Germany) Nuc. Rsch., 1972—73; mem. Nat. Rsch. Com. Reactor Safety, 1985—86; chmn. peer rev. com. U.S. NRC, Washington, 1987—88; mem. adv. com. nuc. facility safety Dept. of Energy, 1988—92; mem. adv. com. Diablo Canyon Nuc. Power Plant, 1999—2000; dir. risk and sys. analysis control toxics program UCLA, 1989—95, chmn. Ctr. Clean Tech., 1992—94; project dir. Ctr. Nuc. and Toxic Waste Mgmt. U. Calif., Berkley, 1995—2000. Contbr. articles to profl. jours. Recipient Disting. Tchg. award, Am. Soc. Engring. Edn., 1973. Fellow: AAAS, Am. Nuc. Soc. (chmn. nuc. safety 1984—85, Arthur Holly Compton award); mem.: NAE. Office: Univ Calif Nuc Engring Dept 4155 Etcheverry Hall Berkeley CA 94720-1731 Office Phone: 510-643-0574. Business E-Mail: kastenbe@nuc.berkeley.edu.

KASTENHOLZ, MARY ELLEN CONNELLY, freelance writer; b. Chgo., June 17, 1958; d. Joseph Matthew and Lorraine Patricia (Kissane) Connelly; m. Robert Francis Kastenholz, Oct. 1, 1983; children: Kevin Robert, Brian Joseph, Kathleen Connelly. BA, St. Mary's Coll., Notre Dame, Ind., 1980; MBA, Loyola U. Chgo., 1982. Communications specialist Blvd. Nat. Bank Assn., Chgo., 1982-83, tng. specialist, 1984-85, facility mgr., 1984-86, banking sales and tng. mgr. retail svcs., 1985-86, banking officer, 1985-86; freelance writer, 1986—. Mem. mktg. and mgmt. faculty Am. Inst. Banking; bd. dirs. WestBrook Bank, Westchester, Ill., 1980-82; instr. children's enrichment programs; tchrs. asst., faculty advisor for sch. newspaper, 2000— Editor Monthly Employee News, coll. recruiting brochures, employee handbooks, sales tng. and mgmt. newsletters. Various offices Hinsdale (Ill.) Jr. Women's Club, 1986, com. chmn., 1990-91; active Western Springs (Ill.) Neighborhood Civic Assn., 1990—; den leader Cub Scouts Am., 1995—; ch. and sch. vol. various philanthropic and charity orgns. Avocations: creative writing, calligraphy, fashion and interior design.

KASTER, LAURA A., lawyer; b. N.Y.C., May 24, 1948; BA, Tufts U., 1970; JD magna cum laude, Boston U., 1973. Bar: Mass. 1973, Ill. 1975. Law clk. to Hon. Frank M. Coffin, U.S. Ct. Appeals for 1st circuit, Boston, 1973-75; assoc. Jenner & Block, Chgo., 1975-81, ptnr., 1981-97; gen. atty. law and govt. affairs AT&T Corp., Bedminster, NJ, 1997—. Co-author: Sanctions in Federal Litigation, 1991; co-editor: The Attorneys' Guide to the Seventh Circuit Court of Appeals, 2005, 3rd edit.; note editor Law Rev. Boston U., 1973-72; contbr. chpt. to book and articles to profl. jours. Trustee Lawyers Com. for Civil Rights, 2005—. Fellow Am. Bar Found. (life); mem. ABA, Ill. Bar Assn., 7th Circuit Bar Assn., Fed. Cir. Bar Assn. Office Phone: 908-532-1888. Personal E-mail: lkaster@att.com.

KASTIN, ABBA JEREMIAH, endocrinologist, researcher; b. Cleve., Dec. 24, 1934; s. Isadore I. and Ruth (Urdang) K. AB, Harvard U., 1956, MD, 1960; hon. Dr., U. Nacional Federico Villerarreal, Lima, Peru, 1980; D.Sc. (hon.), U. New Orleans, 1984. Intern Vanderbilt U. Hosp., Nashville, 1960-61, resident in internal medicine, 1961-62; clin. assoc. USPHS, NIH, 1962-64; clin. investigator VA Hosp., New Orleans, 1965-68; chief endocrinology sect. VA Med. Ctr., 1968—2004; prof. dept. medicine Tulane U. Sch. Medicine, New Orleans, 1974—2004; grad. faculty U. New Orleans, 1976—; prof. and endowed chair Pennington Biomed. Rsch. Ctr., Baton Rouge, 2004—. Cons. prof. dept. psychology U. New Orleans, 1986—, FDA, 1979; mem. med. adv. bd. Nat. Pituitary Agy., 1974-77; Wellcome vis. prof., 1990; pre-reviewer in endocrinology, mem. residency com. for internal medicine Accreditation Coun. for Grad. Med. Edn., 1984-95; spkr. in field; lectr. in field. Editor-in-chief: Peptides, an Internat. Jour., 1980—; mem. editl. bd. Jour. Clin. Endocrinology and Metabolism, 1976-80, Brain Rsch. Bull., 1986-95, Neurosci. and Biobehaviorial Rev., 1977-95, New Trends Exptl. Clin. Psychiatry, 1985-2001, Progress in Neuroendocrinimmunology, 1988-90, Pharmacology, Biochemistry and Behavior, 1989-1995, Molecular and Cellular Neuroscis., 1990-95, Physiology and Behavior, 1993-95, Endocrine Practice, 1994-2004, Neuroimmunomodulation, 1995-2000, Current pharm. Design, 2003—, Medicinal Chemistry, 2004—; contbr. more than 800 articles to profl. jours. Advisory bd. La. Philharmonic Orch., 1997—. Recipient Edward T. Tyler Fertility award Internat. Fertility Soc., 1975, Eagle award Fed. Bus. Assn., 1975, Copernicus medal Med. Faculty Krakow, Poland, 1979, William S. Middletown award VA, 1982, Strand award 2001; named in top 100 Most Cited Scientist List, Inst. for Scientific Info. Fellow Am. Coll. Endocrinology; mem. Am. Physiol. Soc., Am. Peptide Soc., Endocrine Soc., Soc. Exptl. Biol. Medicine, Soc. Neurosci., Internat. Soc. Psychoneuroendocrinology (introductory hon. scientific lectr. XVth Congress), Internat. Soc. Neuroendocrinology, Internat. Behavioral Neuroscience Soc. (keynote speaker first meeting, mem. adv. coun.), Internat. Neuropeptide Soc. (pres. 1993—); hon. mem. La Soc. de Dermo-Chimie, Chilean Soc. Endocrinology, Phillippine Soc. Endocrinology and Metabolism, Peruvian Ob-Gyn Soc., Peruvian Endocrine Soc., Polish Endocrine Soc., Hungarian Endocrine Soc., Harvard Club La. (pres. 1991-95), Green Wave Masters Swim Club (pres. 1978-84). Jewish. Office: Pennington Biomed Rsch Ctr 6400 Perkins Rd Baton Rouge LA 70808-4124 Office Phone: 225-763-0266. Business E-Mail: peptides@pbrc.edu.

KASTNER, MARC AARON, physics professor; b. Toronto, Ont., Can., Nov. 20, 1945; came to U.S., 1952; s. Jacob and Ida Pearl (Shidlowsky) K.; m. Marcia Jill Paul, Aug. 27, 1967; 2 children. BS in Chemistry, U. Chgo., 1967, MS, 1969, PhD in Physics, 1972. Rsch. fellow Harvard U., Cambridge, Mass., 1972-73; asst. prof. physics MIT, Cambridge, 1973-77, assoc. prof., 1977-83, prof., 1983-89, Donner prof. of physics, 1989—. Dir. Consortium for Superconducting Electronics, 1989-91, Ctr. for Materials Sci. and Engring, 1993-98; head MIT Dept. Physics, 1998—. Recipient David Adler Lectureship award Am. Physical Society, 1995 Fellow AAAS, Am. Phys. Soc. (councillor at large 1991-94, Oliver E. Buckley prize 2000). Achievements include discovery of single electron effects in nanostructures and research in electronic, optical and magnetic properties of condensed matter, including semiconductors and high temperature superconductors.

KASTNER, MICHAEL JAMES, dentist; b. Huntington, Ind., Oct. 20, 1954; s. James H. and Barbara A. (Bartrom) K.; m. Kimberly A. Ricke, June 18, 1983; children: Kevin Michael, Ryan James, Derek Edward. BS in Biology and Chemistry, Manchester Coll., 1977; DDS, Ind. U., Indpls., 1981; postgrad., Armed Forces Inst. Pathology, 1989. Gen. practice dentistry, Toledo, 1981—. Asst. dentist Toledo Zoo, 1991—; mem. Ohio Mass Disaster Team, 1995—, team capt., 2001—; asst. Lucas County Coroner's Office, 1987—; asst. to N.Y. Med. Examiners Office in dental forensic identification of World Trade Ctr. victims, 2001. Bd. trustees Dental Ctr. Northwest Ohio, 1994-2000, nominating com., 1995-2001, long range planning com., 1999-2001, dental com., 1995-98, 2000; mem. Lucas County Oral Health Coalition. Recipient Alumni Honor award Manchester Coll., 1997, Recognition for Honor award Ohio State Senate Resolution, 1997, Honoring Am. Spirit award Gov. Ohio, 2002, cert. of recognition City of NY Office of Chief Med. Examiner, 2003, Congressman Vito Fosella, 13th Dist. NY, 2003. Fellow Pierre Fauchard Acad., Am. Coll. Dentists; mem. ADA (chmn. local chpt., chmn. area grassroots membership initiative, Recognition for Vol. Svc. Fgn. Country award in Dominican Republic 1984, 87, in Costa Rica 1990, in Nepal 1994, Nicaragua 2000, 01), Ohio Dental Assn. (state del. 2002, 03, 04, 05, alt. del. 1999, 2000, 01, statewide subcom. on peer rev. 2000—, chmn. 2004—, dental OPTIONS program, 1999—, Humanitarian of Yr. 1995, 2002), Toledo Dental Soc. (bd. dirs. 1996-99, peer rev. com. 1998—, nominating com. 1999-2003, chmn. 2003, program and continuing edn. com. 1999—, relief fund subcom. 1999, fin. com. 2000, long range planning com. 2000, exec. office com. 2000-03, exec. bd. sec./treas. 2000, v.p. 2001, pres. 2002, constitution by-laws com., 2002—), Am. Acad. Cosmetic Dentistry, Am. Soc. Forensic Odontology, Am. Coll. Oral Implantology, Am. Soc. Osseointegration Internat. Congress Oral Implantologists, Mensa. Roman Catholic. Avocations: photography, basketball, travel, outdoor activities, oenology. Home: 6944 Hickory Ridge Rd Sylvania OH 43560

KASTNER, MICHAEL PAUL, music educator; b. Tiffin, Ohio, May 8, 1961; s. Paul Richard and Merilyn Audrey (Hamilton) Kastner; m. Mary Elizabeth Gierak, Aug. 3, 1960; children: Michelle Marie, Melissa Christine, Matthew Paul. BA, Siena Heights Coll., 1983; postgrad., Haildelberg Coll., 1985—2004, Kent State U., 1987, Bowling Green State U., 1988. Tchr. St. Joseph Sch., Tiffin, Ohio, 1983—88; tchr. vocal music WRHS, Collins, 1987—88; with Cleve. Playhouse, 1988; tchr. music Gesu Sch., Toledo, 1988—; dir. music St. Francis de Sales High Sch., 1988—. Bd. dirs. Bellevue Soc. Arts, Ohio. Mem.: Ohio Music Educators Assn., Nat. Cath. Ednl. Assn., Nat. Assn. Music Educators. Avocation: theater. Home: 206 Arion St Bellevue OH 44811 Office: St Francis de Sales High Sch 2323 W Bancroft St Toledo OH 43607

KASTNER, RYAN, engineering educator; b. Greensburg, Pa., Aug. 17, 1977; s. Charles and Janet Kastner. BSEE, BS in Computer Engring., Northwestern U., Evanston, Ill., 1999, MS in Engring., 2000; PhD in Computer Sci., UCLA, 2002. Grad. student rschr. UCLA, 2000—02; asst. prof. U. Calif., Santa Barbara, 2002—. Author: Synthesis Techniques and Optimizations of Reconfigurable Systems; contbr. articles to profl. jours. Walter P. Murphy fellow, Northwestern U., 1999-2000. Mem.: IEEE. Achievements include patents pending for system and method for optimizing polynomial expresssions. Office: U Calif Electrical and Computer Engring Santa Barbara CA 93106 Office Phone: 805-893-3985. Office Fax: 805-893-3262. Business E-Mail: kastner@ece.ucsb.edu.

KASTON, LISA MARSHA, social services administrator; b. N.Y.C., Apr. 1, 1955; d. Seymour Albert Kaston and Susan Zuckerman Kaston; children: Adam Louis Garcia, Emily Beth Garcia. MPS, New Sch. U., N.Y.C., 1987. Mgr. grants and cmty. initiatives Devereux Fla., Orlando, 1995—2002; dir. program devel. and contract mgmt. Hope and Help Ctr. of Ctrl. Fla., Winter Park, 2002—. Mem. steering com. coun. agy. execs. Heart of Fla. United Way, Orlando, 1998—2002; mem. Leadership Orlando, 1999—2000; mem. funding rev. panel Victims of Crime Assistance Program, 18th Jud. Cir., Brevard and Seminole Counties, Fla., 1999—2001. Mem.: Grant Profls. Network Ctrl. Fla. (pres. 2000—01, Excellence in Grant Professionalism and Advocacy Award 2000). Avocations: travel, reading, arts. Office: Hope and Help Ctr of Ctrl Fla 1935 Woodcrest Dr Winter Park FL 32792 E-mail: lkaston@hopeandhelp.org.

KASTOR, FRANK SULLIVAN, language educator; b. Evanston, Ill., Aug. 19, 1933; s. Herman Walker and Rebecca (Sullivan) K.; m. Tina Bennett, Oct. 28, 1979; children: Jeffrey, Mark, Harlan, Kristina, Patrick, Liam, Mary Elisabeth, Caroline. BA, U. Ill., 1955, MA, 1956; PhD, U. Calif., Berkeley, 1963. Teaching asst. U. Ill., 1955-56, U. Calif., Berkeley, 1960-63; asst. prof. English U. So. Calif., 1964-66, 67-68; assoc. prof. English No. Ill. U., 1968-69; prof. English, Wichita State U., 1969—, chmn. dept., 1969-75, prof. emeritus, 1998, ret., 1998. Contbr. to: The Milton Ency., The Dictionary of Literary Biography; author books, articles, revs., TV documentaries, C.S. Lewis study guides. Served with USAF, 1956-59. Rsch. grantee U. Calif., Berkeley, 1962, U. So. Calif., 1964, No. Ill. U., 1969, Wichita State U., 1970, 72, 73, 74, 84, 86, 92; Fulbright lectr., Spain, 1966-67; Kans. Com. for Humanities grantee, 1973, 74, 94; recipient NEH award, 1971, 84. Mem. MLA, AAUP, Milton Soc. Am., N.Y. C.S. Lewis Soc., C.S. Lewis Soc. of Kans. (founder), Phi Kappa Phi. Christian Ch. E-mail: fskdr3@cox.net.

KASTOR, JOHN ALFRED, cardiologist, educator; b. N.Y.C., Sept. 15, 1931; s. Alfred Bernard and Ellen Voigt Bentley; m. Mae Belle Eisenberg, July 4, 1954; children: Elizabeth Mae, Anne Sarah, Peter John. BA, U. Pa., 1953; MD, NYU, 1962. With NBC, N.Y.C., 1956-58; intern, asst. resident in medicine Bellevue Hosp., N.Y.C., 1962-64; chief resident physician N.Y. U. Hosp., N.Y.C., 1964-65; clin. and research fellow in medicine Mass. Gen. Hosp., Boston, 1965-68, clin. asst. and asst. in medicine, 1968-69; instr. in medicine Harvard Med. Sch., 1968-69; dir. med. intensive care unit Hosp. U. Pa., Phila., 1969-72, assoc. chief cardiovascular sect., 1972-77, chief, 1977-81; physician-in-chief U. Md. Hosp., 1984-97; prof. medicine U. Pa. Sch. Medicine, Phila., 1976-83; Theodore E. Woodward prof. medicine U. Md. Sch. Medicine, 1984-97, chmn. dept. medicine, 1984-97, prof. medicine, 1997—. Vis. prin. fellow Nat. Heart and Lung Inst., London, 1995. Author: Arrhythmias, 1994, 2nd edit. 2000, Mergers of Teaching Hospitals in Boston, New York and Northern California, 2001, Governance of Teaching Hospitals: Turmoil at Penn and Hopkins, 2003; founding editor Internat. Jour. Cardiology, 1981-84; contbr. numerous articles on cardiac electrophysiology and gen. cardiology to med. jours. Served with U.S. Army, 1953-55. Fellow ACP, Am. Coll. Cardiology, Coun. Clin. Cardiology Am. Heart Assn.; mem. Am. Fedn. Clin. Rsch., Am. Heart Assn. (bd. govs. Southeastern Pa. chpt. 1975-81, bd. govs. Md. affiliate 1990-93), Assn. Am. Physicians, Assn. Univ. Cardiologists, Venezuelan Soc. Internal Medicine, Paul Dudley White Soc. (dir. 1977-86), Alpha Omega Alpha. Home: 2415 Boston St Baltimore MD 21224-4733 Office: U Md Hosp 22 S Greene St Baltimore MD 21201-1544

KASULIS, THOMAS PATRICK, humanities educator; b. Bridgeport, Conn., Mar. 5, 1948; s. Joseph John and Albina Anna (Checkanouskas) K.; m. Ellen Elizabeth Sponheimer, June 5, 1970; children: Telemachus, Matthias, Benedict. BA, Yale U., 1970, MPh, 1972, PhD, 1975; MA, U. Hawaii, 1973. Asst. prof. philosophy U. Hawaii, Honolulu, 1975-80; from asst. prof. to prof. philosophy and religion Northland Coll., Ashland, Wis., 1981-91; prof. comparative studies The Ohio State U., Columbus, 1991—, chair East Asian langs. and lit., 1993-95, chair comparative studies, 1995-98. Mellon faculty fellow in humanities Harvard U., Cambridge, Mass., 1979-80; vis. facility rschr. Osaka (Japan) U., 1982-83; Numata vis. prof. U. Chgo., Ill., 1988. Author: Zen Action/Zen Person, 1981, Intimacy or Integrity: Philosophy and Cultural Difference, 2002, Shinto: The Way Home, 2004; editor, co-translator: The Body: Toward an Eastern Mind-Body Theory, 1987; co-editor: Self as Body in Asian Theory and Practice, 1993, Self as Person in Asian Theory and Practice, 1994; contbr. chpts. to books and articles to profl. jours. Fellow Japan Found., 1982-83, 2004; NEH fellow, 1986-87, 2000; Sr. Rsch. fellow East West Ctr., Honolulu, 1988. Mem. Soc. for Asian and Comparative Philosophy (pres. 1988-91), Am. Soc. for the Study of Religion (pres. 1999-2002). Home: 1465 Montcalm Rd Upper Arlington OH 43221-3450 Office: Ohio State Univ Comparative Studies 451 Hagerty Hall 1775 College Rd Columbus OH 43210-1340 Office Phone: 614-292-7892. Business E-Mail: kasulis.1@osu.edu.

KASUM, MICHAEL, humanities educator, writer; b. Milw., Oct. 22, 1934; s. Anton Kasum and Olive Sarah Elmer; m. Patricia W. Kasum, June 17, 1994. BA, U. State NY, Albany, 1998; MFA, Vt. Coll. Norwich U., 1998; PhD, U. Wis., Milw., 2001. Pub. Ouray (Colo.) County Herald, 1966—68; co. exec. Kas-Com Inc., Boise, Idaho, 1969—78; internat. currency cons. Assn.: Amb. Eusebio A. Morales, Harry D. Schultz, PhD, PaulEinzig, PhD, Robert Z. Aliber, PhD, 1974—83; newspaper co. exec. Metro-News Features Inc., Portland, Maine, 1978—94; prof. English Cardinal Stritch U., Milw., 2000—01, U. Wis., Milw., 2000—01, U. South Fla., Tampa, 2001—. Author: Coney Island of the Mind, (novels) The Last Truth, Islands Below the Wind; contbr. articles to profl. jours. Pres. Phoenix Found., Carson City, Nev., 1964—66. Mem.: MLA, Associated Writing Programs, Valdimir Nabokov Soc., Samuel Beckett Soc. Achievements include experimental work in hyperfiction. Avocations: sailing, racquetball, scuba diving, skydiving. Home: 19046 Bruce B Downs Boulevard 145 Tampa FL 33647

KASUNIC, ROBERT, lawyer, educator; b. N.Y.C., Feb. 5, 1959; s. R. J. Sr. and Mary Ann Kasunic; m. Carol Schultze, Sept. 7, 1991; children: Katherine Lang, Elizabeth Joyce. BA, Columbia U., 1985; JD, U. Balt., 1992. Bar: Md. 1992, U.S. Dist. Ct. Md. 1993, D.C. 1995, U.S. Supreme Ct. 1998, U.S. Ct. Appeals (4th cir.) 1999. Pvt. practice, Darnestown, Md., 1992-2000; sr. atty., prin. legal adviser OGC, U.S. Copyright Office, Washington, 2000—. Adj. prof. U. Balt. Law Sch., 1995—, Washington Coll. Law, 2003—. Mem. ABA, FBA, Am. Intellectual Property Law Assn., Md. State Bar, Montgomery County Bar Assn., D.C. Bar Assn., Copyright Soc. U.S.A. Office: PO Box 70400 Washington DC 20024 E-mail: rkasunic@kasunic.com.

KASZAS, WILLIAM JOSEPH, technology educator; b. N.Y.C., Aug. 14, 1944; s. Thomas and Ruth (Trub) Kaszas; m. Ann M. Budnik, Aug. 12, 1966 (div. Dec. 14, 1987). BS, NYU, 1966, MA, 1970. Tchr. indsl. arts Eldred (N.Y.) Cen. Sch., 1966—68, Monticello (N.Y.) Cen. Sch., 1968—81, tchr. tech. edn., 1981—2000. Exhibit designer Lower Hudson Interactive Mus., Middletown, NY, 2000—; presenter in field. Contbr. articles to profl. publs. Scholar NYU scholar, Hebrew Tech. Inst., 1970—2000. Achievements include invention of magnetic levitation track; design of knee brace. Avocations: playing harmonica, reading, Karate. Home: 374 Glen Wild Rd Glen Wild NY 12738

KATA, MARIE L., securities dealer, brokerage house executive; b. Redwood Falls, Minn. m. M. T. Kata, 1984; children: Namue, Karwehn. BS in Bus., U. Minn., 1979. Lic. Series 24, cert. Series 65, Series 7. Stockbroker R.J. Steichen, 1992, Montano Securities, 1993—95, Res. Fin., 1996—97, Eisner Securities, 1997—2001, br. mgr., 1997—2001; stockbroker LaSalle St. Securities, Edina, Minn., 2001—, br. mgr., 2001—. Recipient Hon. Advisor award, Fidelity Investments, 2001. Avocations: skiing, reading, spirituality. Office: LaSalle St Securities LLC 7701 France Ave S #200 Edina MN 55435

KATAI, ANDREW ANDRAS, chemical company executive; b. Gyor, Hungary, Sept. 17, 1937; came to U.S., 1956; s. Ivan and Clara (Szel) K.; m. Debbie Judwin, May 12, 1963 (div. 1970); children: Alisa, Gregory; m. Joan Eleanor Klein, July 30, 1972; children: Peter, Daniel. BS, Juniata Coll., 1960; MS, PhD, Syracuse U., 1965; MS, PhD in Chemistry, SUNY, Syracuse, 1965. Internat. mktg. asst. Esso chem. Co., N.Y.C., 1965-66; asst. prof. Hunter-Lehman Coll. N.Y.C., 1965-70; research chemist Union Carbide Corp., Tarrytown, NY, 1966-67, internat. assoc. prodn. mgr. N.Y.C., 1967-69, internat. product mgr., 1969-71; new bus. devel. mgr. W.R. Grace Constrn. Co., Cambridge, Mass., 1971-73; bus. mgr. internat. div. Inolex Corp., Chgo., 1973-77; Far East devel mgr. Eschem (Swift) Inc., Chgo., 1977, gen. mgr. internat. div., 1977-81, dir. internat. div., 1981-82, v.p. internat. div., 1982-83; pres. Swift Adhesives subs. Reichhold Chem. Co., Downers Grove, Ill., 1983-93; sr. Corridor fellow, assoc. prof. internat. bus. North Ctrl. Coll., Naperville, Ill., 1994-2000; adj. prof. Stuart Sch. Bus. Ill. Inst. Tech., 1997—2005. Contbr. articles to profl. jours. Chmn. coll. fundraising dr., Westchester County, N.Y., 1969; co-chmn. Homeowners' Assn., Flossmoor, Ill., 1981-82. Mem. Adhesive Mfrs. Assn. (treas. 1986-88, pres.-elect 1988, pres. 1990), East West Corp. Corridor Assn. (v.p. 1992-94), Am. Chem. Soc., Sigma Xi, Phi Lambda Upsilon. Avocations: bridge, classical music, kayaking, photography, travel. Home: 1105 E Johnson Dr Naperville IL 60540-8245 Office Phone: 630-983-7591. Personal E-mail: aakatai@sbcglobal.net.

KATAPODI, MARIA C., nursing researcher; d. Chryssanthos J. Katapodis and Eleni G. Karacosta-Katapodi; m. David J. Galgoczy, May 7, 2005. B, Nat. and Kapodistrian U. Athens, 1998; MSc, degree in adult edn., U. Calif., San Francisco, 2000, PhD in Oncology Genomics, 2004. RN Calif., 1999, Govt. of Greece, 1994. RN "LAIKO" Gen. U. Hosp., Tertiary Care, Athens, 1995—96, "VOSTANEIO" Gen. County Hosp. Secondary Care, Mytilini, Greece, 1996—98; clin. nurse rschr. III U. Calif. San Francisco, 2002—. Prin. investigator, rschr., project mgr. U. Calif. San Francisco, 2002—; co-instr. 3 master's level courses (cancer prevention/early detection, topics in genetics/genomics, rsch. utilization) U. Calif. San Francisco, Sch. Nursing, 2003—04; invited spkr., genetic counseling Hellenic Cancer Soc., Athens, 2004—; invited lectr. master's level seminars current issues nursing rsch. Nat. and Kapodistrian U. Athens Faculty of Nursing, Athens, 2004—; rschr. in field. Contbr. to profl. jours. Fellow, U. Calif. Regents, 2001 - 2002; grantee, Fulbright Found., 1998, clin. nurse rschr. congressionally directed rsch., US Dept. Def., 2003 - 2005; scholar, U. Calif. San Francisco, Sch. Nursing, 1998 - 2003, Gerontellis Found., 1999;, Found. Govtl. scholarships Greece, 1992, 1993. Mem.: Internat. Soc. Judgment and Decision Making, Hellenic Nat. Grad. Nurses Assn., Oncology Nursing Soc., Rotary. Greek Orthodox. Achievements include research in data analysis: identification of heuristic thinking and logical shortcuts in narrative data; data analysis and identification of level of knowledge of sporadic and genetic breast cancer risk factors among women in the community; meta-analysis of research data and identification of predictors of perceived breast cancer risk and breast cancer screening; data analysis for the influence of social support on breast cancer screening in a multicultural community sample; critical examination of scientific literature for the influences of culture on breast cancer screening behavior. Avocations: travel, swimming, yoga, reading, hiking. Personal E-mail: maria.katapodi@nursing.ucsf.edu.

KATAVOLOS, WILLIAM, architecture educator, furniture designer; b. N.Y.C., Mar. 14, 1924; s. Peter and Sophia Katavolos; m. Terenia Lombard Katavolos, Dec. 13, 1960. B in Indsl. Design, Pratt Inst., 1949. Fine arts painter John Nichols Residency, Woodstock, NY, 1940—42; designer furniture line Frankel/Robert John, N.Y.C., 1946—; designer Luss Design Office, N.Y.C., 1954—59; designer furniture line Geo. Nelson Office, N.Y.C., 1955—57; tchr. design, chair indsl. design Parson Sch., N.Y.C., 1955—71; tchr. design Pratt Inst., Bklyn., 1957—. Co-dir. Ctr. Exptl. Structures, 1985—; lectr. USIS-USIA. Author: Organics, 1960, Manifestos of Twentieth Century, 1970, Chemical City, 1990. Sgt. USAF, 1942—46. Recipient 1st prize furniture design, Mus. Modern Art, N.Y.C., 1952, 1953, 1st prize furniture, Am. Inst. Design, N.Y.C., 1953—54. Mem.: N.Y. Acad. Sci. Achievements include patents for hydronic and building systems; development of theory of quantum numerodynamics. Avocation: golf. Office: Pratt Inst Ctr Exptl Structures N Higgins Hall 200 Willoughby Ave Brooklyn NY 11205

KATAYAMA, ROBERT NOBUICHI, retired lawyer; b. Honolulu, Oct. 11, 1924; s. Sanji Katayama; married; children: Alice A. Katayama Jenkins, Robert Nobuichi Jenkins, Kent J. Jenkins, Susan H. Ono, Carole Y. Kaneshiro, Wendy L. Lee. BA, U. Hawaii, 1950; LLB, Yale U., 1955; grad., Command and Gen. Staff Coll., 1964; LLM, George Washington U., 1967; grad., Indsl. Coll. Armed Forces, 1971. Commd. 1st lt. JAGC U.S. Army, 1958, advanced through grades to col., 1973, ret., 1973; gen. counsel Overseas Mdse. Inspection Co., San Francisco, 1956-58, Army Contract Adjustment Bd., Washington, 1964-68; prof. law JAG Sch. U. Va., 1968-70; from assoc. to ptnr. Baker & McKenzie, Chgo., Tokyo and San Francisco, 1973-85; ptnr. Seki & Jarvis, San Francisco and San Jose, 1985-86, Nutter, McClennen & Fish, San Francisco, 1986-88; spl. counsel, sr. advisor Crosby, Heafey, Roach & May, Oakland, Calif., 1988; ptnr. Carlsmith Ball, Honolulu, 1988-95, counsel, 1994—2004, ret., 2004. Chmn., CEO Kapolei People's Inc. dba Kapolei Golf Course, Honolulu, 1996—99; pres. Kapolei Holding Corp., 1998—. Trustee Nat. Japanese Am. Meml. Found., 1995—97, gov., 1997—; mem. Hawaii Adv. Coun. to Japanese Am. Nat. Mus., 2001—03; bd. dirs. Japanese Cultural Ctr. Hawaii, 1997—98, bd. govs., 1998—. Named Real

Dean, U. Hawaii, Honolulu, 1950; recipient Disting. Alumni award, 2001. Mem.: ABA, Ill. Bar Assn., 442d Regimental Combat Team Found. (trustee 1993—2004, pres. 1999—2002), Hawaii Army Mus. Soc. (trustee 2001—), Military Officers Assn. Am., Japanese Am. Soc. Legal Studies, Nat. Japanese Am. Hist. Soc. (legal officer 1984—89), Japan Am. Soc. Hawaii, Hawaii Bar Assn., Calif. Bar Assn., Oahu AJA Vets. Coun. (pres. 1997), Japanese C. of C. of No. Calif. (bd. dirs. 1987—89), 442d Vets. Club (legal advisor 1994—95, pres.-elect 1996, pres. 1997—98, legal advisor 2000—). Democrat. Buddhist. Home: 4389 Malia St Apt 553 Honolulu HI 96821 Personal E-mail: bobkata@earthlink.net.

KATCHER, JONATHON A., lawyer; b. Detroit, Oct. 2, 1954; BGS with distinction, Univ. Mich., 1976; student, Northwestern Sch. of Law, Chgo.; JD, Lewis & Clark Coll., Portland, 1981. Asst. public defender State of Alaska, Anchorage, 1981—84; Supervising atty. Protection and Advocacy for Developmentally Disabled (PADD), Anchorage, 1984—85; Barrister I Alaska Inns of Court, Anchorage, 1993—2003; spec. edn. hearing officer State of Alaska, Dept. of Edn., 1990—. Mem.: ABA, Alaska Bar Assn. (pres.-elect 2004—05). Office: Pope & Katcher Ste 220 421 W First Ave Anchorage AK 99501

KATCHER, RICHARD, lawyer; b. N.Y.C., Dec. 17, 1918; s. Samuel and Gussie (Appelbaum) K.; m. Shirley Ruth Rifkin, Sept. 24, 1944; children: Douglas P., Robert A., Patti L. BA, U. Mich., 1941, JD, 1943. Bar: Mich. 1943, N.Y. 1944, Ohio 1946. Assoc. Noonan, Kaufman & Eagan, N.Y.C., 1943-46; from assoc. to ptnr. Ulmer, Berne & Laronge, Cleve., 1946-72; ptnr. Baker & Hostetler, Cleve., 1972-95. Lectr. in fed. income taxation Case Western Res. U. Sch. Law, Cleve., 1953-69, 71-72; mem. adv. bd. on intercollegiate athletics, U. Mich., 2001-2004; chmn. Nat. Conf. Lawyers and CPAs, 1982-. Contbr. articles on fed. tax to profl. jours. Recipient Disting. Alumni Service award U. Mich., 1987, Leadership medal Pres.' Soc. of U. Mich., 1991. Fellow ABA (coun. sect. taxation 1973-76), Am. Coll. Tax Counsel (regent); mem. Am. Bar Retirement Assn. (bd. dirs., v.p. 1986-87, pres. 1987-88), U. Mich. Pres. Soc. (chmn. exec. com. 1987-90), Nat. Conf. Lawyers and CPAs (chmn. 1982-83), U. Mich. Cleve. Club (pres. 1959, Outstanding Alumnus award 1987), U. Mich. Alumni Assn. (dir. 1994-98, sec. 1997-98). Avocation: tennis. Home: 26150 Village Ln Apt 104 Beachwood OH 44122-7527 Office: Baker & Hostetler 3200 National City Ctr 1900 E 9th St Ste 3200 Cleveland OH 44114-3475 Office Phone: 216-861-7476. E-mail: RKatcher@bakerlaw.com.

KATCHER, RICHARD DAVID, lawyer; b. Newark, N.J., May 26, 1941; s. Henry Edward and Eve M. (Kreiger) K.; m. Susan M. Scherer, June 28, 1964; children: Daniel, Andrew. AB, Lafayette Coll., 1963; LLB, N.Y. Univ., 1966. Assoc. Simpson Thacher & Bartlett, N.Y., 1966-68, Wachtell, Lipton, Rosent Katz, N.Y., 1968-71, pntr., 1971—. Office: Wachtell Lipton Rosen & Katz 51 W 52nd St Fl 29 New York NY 10019-6150 E-mail: rdkatcher@wlrk.com.

KATCOFF, DEBRA BIGMAN, art educator; b. McKeesport, Pa., Apr. 13, 1952; d. Bernard and Ruth Halpern Bigman; m. I. Gary Katcoff, July 20, 1975; children: Jason Paul, Steven Ryan. BS in Edn., U. Md., 1974; MEd in counselor Edn., Augusta State U., 2000. Art tchr. Forest Hills Elem. Sch., Augusta, Ga., 1986—93, Westside H.S., Augusta, 1993—. Mem. tchr. adv. panel Morris Mus. Art, Augusta, 1996—99. Campaign v.p. Augusta Jewish Fedn., 2004, chmn. com. Jewish cmty. resources, 2003; edn. v.p. Adas Yeshurun Sisterhood, Augusta, 2004; vol. Atlanta Com. for Olympic Games, 1996; organizer Empty Bowl benefit luncheon; chmn. gala com. Augusta Jewish Cmty. Ctr., 2003. Named Vol. of Yr., Augusta Jewish Cmty. Ctr., 1992, 2003, Woman of Yr., Adas Yeshurun Sisterhood, 1994, Humanitarian of Yr., Augusta Jewish Cmty. Ctr., 2003, Star Tchr., 2001. Mem.: Ga. Art Edn. Assn. (dir. secondary divsn. 2001—, dist. pres. 1999—2001). Avocations: reading, crafts, skiing, exercise, Israeli dance. Office: Westside HS 1002 Patriots Way Augusta GA 30907 Business E-Mail: katcode@boe.richmond.k12.ga.us.

KATEB, GEORGE ANTHONY, political science professor; b. Bklyn., Feb. 27, 1931; s. Anthony Francis and Victoria Anna (Mesnooh) K. AB, Columbia U., 1952, A.M., 1953, PhD, 1960; D.H.L. (hon.), Amherst, 1989. Mem. faculty Amherst Coll., 1957, prof., 1967-87, Kenan prof. polit. sci., 1974-78, Joseph B. Eastman prof. polit. sci., 1980-87; prof. politics Princeton U., 1987—, William Nelson Cromwell prof. politics, 1999—2002, William Nelson Cromwell prof. politics emeritus, 2002—. Vis. lectr. Mt. Holyoke Coll., 1958, Yale U., 1973, Harvard U., 1986. Author: Utopia and Its Enemies, 2d edit., 1972, Political Theory: Its Nature and Uses, 1968, Utopia, 1971, Hannah Arendt: Politics, Conscience, Evil, 1984, The Inner Ocean: Individualism and Democratic Culture, 1992 (Spitz prize Conf. for Study Polit. Thought 1994), Emerson and Self-Reliance, 1994; co-editor: (with David Bromwich) John Stuart Mill, On Liberty; mem. editl. bd. Mass. Rev., 1961-70, Polit. Theory, 1972—, Am. Polit. Sci. Rev., 1976-81, Jour. History Ideas, 1976—, Jour. Utopian Studies, 1977-80, Raritan, 1980-2002; cons. editor: Polit. Theory, 1983-2000. Univ. fellow Columbia U., 1953-54; fellow Soc. Fellows, Harvard U., 1954-57; Guggenheim fellow, 1971-72 Mem. AAUP, Am. Acad. Arts and Scis., New Eng. Polit. Sci. Assn. (exec. com. 1965-66, pres. 1978-79), Am. Soc. Polit. and Legal Philosophy (v.p. 1972-74), Conf. for Study of Polit. Thought, ACLU, Phi Beta Kappa. Office: Princeton U Dept Politics Princeton NJ 08544-0001 Business E-Mail: kateb@princeton.edu.

KATEHI, LINDA P.B., engineering educator; b. Athens, Greece, Jan. 30, 1954; arrived in US, 1979; d. Vasilios and Georgia (Begni) K.; m. Spyros Tseregounis, July 10, 1980; children: Erik Tseregounis, Helena Tseregounis. BSEE, Nat. Tech. U., Athens, 1977; MSEE, UCLA, 1981, PhD in elec. engring., 1984. Teaching asst. Nat. Tech. U. of Athens Greece, 1977—78; rsch. engr. Dept. Def. Naval Rsch. Lab, GETEN, Athens, Greece, 1978—79; rsch. asst. UCLA, 1979-84; asst. prof. elec. engring. U. Mich., Ann Arbor, 1984—89, assoc. prof. elec. engring. and computer sci., 1989—94, prof. electrical engring. and computer sci., 1994—2001, coll. engring. assoc. dir. grad. program, 1994—95, mem. coll. engring. exec. com., 1995—98, assoc. dean grad. edn., 1998—99, sr. assoc. dean academic affairs, 1999—2001; John A. Edwardson Dean of Engring. Purdue U., West Lafayette, Ind., 2001—, prof. of computer and elec. engring., 2002—. Reviewer Army Rsch. Office, 1984—, NSF, 1984—; mem. fgn. admissions U. Mich., 1989—90, undergraduate advisor, 1990—91, graduate advisor for electromagnetics, 1991—94, mem., Coll. Engring. Faculty Advisory Com. on Excellence, 1991—92, mem., univ. senate assembly, 1991—94, mem. tenure com., 1992—95, EECS dept. exec. com., 1992—94, mem., Coll. Engring. Discipline Com., 1992—95, mem. domestic admissions EECS, 1994—97, mem. Coll. Engring., dean search com., 1995, bd. dir., Ctr. for Rsch. Learning and Teaching, 1996—97, mem., provost search com., 1997, chair, grad. chair com., 1998—99, chair, Task Force on MEng programs com., 1998—99, ex-officio, task force on masters programs com., 1998—99, chair, faculty search com. for electromagnetics, 1998—99, mem. com. on internat. inst., 1998, mem. strategic directions com., 1999—, mem., assoc. dean and assoc. provosts academic programs group, 1999—, chair, provost com. on faculty mentoring, 1999—; mem. adv. com. on electron devices Dept. Defense, 1999—; chair Pioneer Revolutionary Technologies Subcom., Aerospace Enterprise NASA, 2002—, mem. Aerospace Tech. Adv. Com. (ATAC), 2002—; chair. adv. com. to Engring. Directorate NSF, 2005—, mem. adv. com. to Directorate for Computer and Info. Sci. and Engring., 2002—; mem. Army Rsch. Lab. adv com. on Sensors and Electrons Divsn. AUS, 2003—; mem. engring. adv. com. Iowa State U., 2003—; provost com. on New Facilities Purdue U., search com. for v.p. research, 2004—05, search com. for the sr. v.p. for fin. affairs, 2003—04. Contbr. articles to profl. jours. Recipient Rsch. Excellence Award, Elec. Engring. and Computer Sci. Dept., U. Mich. Ann Arbor, 1993, Humboldt Rsch. Award, 1994, Faculty Recognition Award, U. Mich. Ann Arbor, 1994. Fellow: IEEE (Antennas and Propagation Soc., Microwave Theory and Techniques Soc., Microwave Theory and Techniques Soc. 3d Millenium Medal 2000); mem.: Advanced Computational Electromagnetics Soc., Internat. Soc. Hybrid Microelectronics, Internat. Union Radio Sci. (Booker Young Scientist Award 1987), Union Radio Sci. Internat., Sigma Xi. Achievements include patents in field. Avocations: skiing, tennis, gardening. Office: Purdue U 400 Centennial Mall Dr West Lafayette IN 47907-2016 Business E-Mail: katehi@purdue.edu.

KATEN, KAREN L., pharmaceutical executive; BA polit. sci. and economics, U. Chgo., 1970, MBA mktg. and fin., 1974. Mktg. assoc. pharms. Pfizer, 1974, various positions Roerig divsn. product mgmt. group, 1975—78, group product mgr. Pfizer Labs., 1980, dir. product mgr. Pfizer Labs., v.p. mktg. Roerig divsn., 1983—86, v.p., dir. ops. Roerig divsn., 1986—91, v.p., gen. mgr. Roerig divsn., 1991—93, exec. v.p. Pfizer US Pharms. Group, 1993—95, pres. Pfizer U.S. Pharms. Group N.Y.C., 1995—2002, v.p., 1992—99; exec. v.p. Pfizer Global Pharmaceuticals (formerly Pfizer Pharmaceuticals Group), 1997—2001; sr. v.p. Pfizer, 1999—2001; pres. Pfizer Global Pharmaceuticals, 2001—; exec. v.p. Pfizer, Inc., 2001—. Bd. dirs. GM, Harris Corp., Catalyst, Nat. Alliance Hispanic Health; mem. internat. coun. J.P. Morgan Chase & Co.; mem. coun. U.S. and Italy, U. Chgo. Grad. Sch. Bus.; trustee U. Chgo.; nat. bd. trustees Am. Cancer Soc. Rsch. Found.; health bd. advisors RAND Corp.; bd. corp. advisors Am. Diabetes Assn.; appointee US-Japan Private Sector/Govt. Commn., 2003, Nat. Infrastructure Adv. Com., 2003. Recipient Salute to Women Achievers award, YMCA, Women Yr. award, Boy Scout Am. Greater N.Y. Coun., NY Women's Agenda Star award, Bus. Leadership award, Burden Ctr. Aging, Iphigene Ochs Sulzburger award, Barnard Coll., Am. Fedn. Aging Rsch. Distinction award, Woman of Yr. award, N.Y.C. Police Athletic League, 2001. Mem.: Am. Diabetes Assn. (mem. bd. corp. advisors, Women of Valor award), Am. Cancer Soc. Rsch. Found. (mem. nat. bd. trustees), Nat. Alliance Hispanic Health, European Fedn. Pharm. Industry Assns. (bd. mem.), Health Leadership Coun., Pharm. Rsch. and Mfrs. Assn. Am. Office: Pfizer Inc 235 E 42nd St New York NY 10017-5755

KATEN-BAHENSKY, DONNA, health facility administrator; BA in Anthropology, U. Mo., Columbia, 1980, MS in Pub. Health Adminstrn., 1982. COO, assoc. hosp. dir., acting hosp. dir. U. Nebr. Hosp., Omaha, 1991—98; vice chancellor bus. and fin. U. Nebr. Med. Ctr., Omaha, 1996—97; v.p. ambulatory care Nebr. Health Sys., Omaha, 1997—98; COO Med. Coll. Va. Hosps., Richmond, 1998—2000, exec. v.p., COO, 2000—02, Clinics of Va. Commonwealth U. Health Sys., Richmond, 2000—02; dir. CEO U. Iowa Hosps. and Cilinics, Iowa City, 2002—. Adj. faculty, preceptor grad. program in health adminstrn. Med. Coll. Va. Hosps.; mem. U. Health Sys. Consortium, Am. Coll. Healthcare Execs.; mem. adv. bd. Pfizer Health Solutions. Office: Univ Iowa Hosps and Clinics 200 Hawkins Dr Iowa City IA 52242

KATERNDAHL, DAVID ARTHUR, medical educator; s. Dean Richard and Ardelle Katerndahl; m. Mitzie Katerndahl, Jan. 3, 2000; children: Tiffany Anne, Tarah Marie, Jennifer Farar. BS in Biology, U. Ill., 1973; MA in Edn., Ohio State U., 1981; MD, U. Ill., 1977. Lic. Family Medicine Am. Bd. Of Family Medicine, 1980. Dir. rsch. and edn. Dept. Family Medicine, San Antonio, 1984—99; prof. Dept. Family And Cmty. Medicine, San Antonio, 1999—. Adult christian edn. Covenant Presbyn. Ch., San Antonio, Tex., 2000—04. Recipient President's award, North Am. Primary Care Rsch. Group, 2002. Mem.: North Am. Primary Care Rsch. Group. Achievements include research in panic disorder and primary care. Office: U Texas Health Sci Ctr 7703 Floyd Curl Dr San Antonio TX 78229 Office Phone: 210-358-3885. Office Fax: 210-223-6940. E-mail: katerndahl@uthscsa.edu.

KATERNDAHL, PAUL DAVID, financial consultant; b. Pontiac, Mich., Feb. 18, 1964; s. Richard Hanley Katerndahl and Estella Marie Rivera-Katerndahl; m. Piezhi Wu-Katerndahl, Sept. 13, 1999. BA, U. of the Pacific, 1986; JD, Golden Gate U., 1989; LLM, Nottingham U., 1990. Bar: Calif., 1989; registered investment advisor. Assoc. Leach, McGreevy & Ellassen, San Francisco, 1989-92; investment advisor Dean Witter Reynolds, Corte Madera, Calif., 1992-94; sr. portfolio mgr. Brindenberg Securities, Copenhagen, 1994-96; fin. cons. Salomon, Smith, Barney, San Francisco, 1996—. Arbitration judge NASD, San Francisco, 1998—. Mem. ABA, Calif. Bar Assn., Internat. C. of C. - San Francisco. Republican. Roman Catholic. Avocations: lacrosse, paintball. Office: Salomon Smith Barney One Sansome St 38th Flr San Francisco CA 94104 E-mail: paul.d.katerndahl@rssmb.com.

KATES, GARY, academic administrator; m. Lynne Diamond; 2 children. Grad., Pitzer Coll., 1974; PhD, U. Chgo., 1978. Mem. faculty dept. history Pitzer Coll., 1978—79; mem. faculty Trinity U., San Antonio, 1980—2001, interim dean arts and humanities, prof. history; v.p. acad. affairs, dean Pomona Coll., Claremont, Calif., 2001—. Author: The Cercle Social, the Girondins, and the French Revolution, 1985, Monsieur d'Eon is a Woman: A Tale of Political Intrigue and Sexual Masquerade, 1995. Recipient Nancy Lyman Roelker Mentor award, Am. Hist. Assn., 1999. Office: Pomona Coll 333 N College Way Claremont CA 91711

KATES, MORRIS, biochemist, educator; b. Galati, Romania, Sept. 30, 1923; arrived in Can., 1924, naturalized, 1944; s. Samuel and Toby (Cohen) K.; m. Pirkko Helena Sofia Makinen, June 14, 1957; children: Anna-Lisa, Marja Helena, Ilona Sylvia. Student, Parkdale Coll., 1936-41; BA, U. Toronto, Ont., Can., 1945, MA, 1946, PhD, 1948. Research asst. Banting Inst., U. Toronto, 1948-49; postdoctoral fellow Nat. Research Council Can., Ottawa, Ont., 1949-51, research officer bioscis. div., 1951-68; prof. chemistry U. Ottawa, 1968-69, prof. biochemistry, 1969-89, prof. emeritus, 1989—, vice-dean research Faculty Sci. and Engring., 1978-82, staff research lectr., 1981, chmn. dept. biochemistry, 1982-85. Author: Techniques of Lipidology, 1972, 2d edit., 1986; co-editor: Metabolic Inhibitors vols. II and IV, 1972, 73, Biomembranes vol. 12, 1984, Handbook of Lipid Rsch., vol. 6, 1990, Biochemistry of Archaea (Archaebacteria), 1993; co-editor: Can. Jour. Biochemistry, 1974-84; contbr. numerous articles on lipid rsch. to profl. jours. Fellow Chem. Inst. Can., Royal Soc. Can.; mem. Can. Biochem. Soc. (pres. 1987-88), Am. Chem. Soc., Am. Soc. Biol. Chemists, Biochem. Soc. (London, Morton lectr. 1995), Am. Oil Chemists Soc. (Supelco rsch. award 1984), Ottawa Biol. and Biochem. Soc. (Sci. prize 1977, pres. 1974-75). Achievements include rsch. on lipid biochemistry. Home: 1723 Rhodes Crescent Ottawa ON Canada K1H 5T1 Office: U Ottawa Dept Biochemistry adn Mibrobiology and Immunology MacDonald Hall 323 150 Louis Pasteur St Ottawa ON Canada KIN 6N5 Business E-Mail: mkates@science.uottawa.ca.

KATH, RUTH ROBERT, foreign language educator; b. New Britain, Conn., Apr. 17, 1948; d. Randolph B. and Ruth (Carlisle) Robert; children: Eleanor, Jessica. BA, Syracuse U., 1970; MA, U. Conn., 1974; PhD, U. Iowa, 1982, MA in Theology, 1998. Instr. Luther Coll., Decorah, Iowa, 1979-82, asst. prof., 1982-87, assoc. prof., 1987-93, prof., 1993—, dept. head modern langs., 1987-92, 95-97, 2003, ch. vocations coord., 2001—, dir. Sense of Vocation program, 2003—. Charter mem. Gov. Commn. on Fgn. Langs., State of Iowa, 1988-91. Author: Bertolt Brecht's Children's Poetry, 1982, The Correspondence of Gerhard Marcks and Marguerite Wildenhain 1970-81, 1991; contbr. articles to profl. jours. Bd. dirs. nat. network Lilly Fellows Program in Humanities and Arts, 2001—. Recipient Deutscher Akademischer Austauschdienst Exch. award German Edn. Exch., Emmendingen, Germany, 1972, Sr. award Germany Summer Sem., Fulbright Commn., Bonn, Germany, 1985; Travel to Collections grantee NEH, Frankfurt, Germany, 1985, Visitors grantee Smithsonian Instn., Washington, 1987. Mem. Am. Assn. Tchrs. German (pres. Iowa chpt. 1984-85), Am. Literary Translators Assn., Iowa Fgn. Lang. Assn. Home: 502 John St Decorah IA 52101-2235 Office: Luther College 700 College Dr Decorah IA 52101-1045

KATHERINE, ROBERT ANDREW, chemical company executive; b. Phila., May 26, 1941; s. John and Winifred Irene (Smith) K.; m. Lynda Ann Ketchell, Dec. 27, 1988. BSCh.E., Drexel Inst. Tech., 1964, MBA, 1968; P.MD, Harvard U. Grad. Sch. Bus., 1977. Plant mgr. synthetic phenol plastics div. Allied Chem. Corp., 1964-66; asst. to dir. Far East sales Air Products & Chems., Phila., 1966-70; product group mgr. corp. devel. P.Q. Corp., 1970-72, div. sales mgr. splty. chems., 1972-74; bus. dir. polymers Hooker Chem. & Plastics div. Occidental Petroleum Corp., Burlington, N.J., 1974-78, v.p., gen. mgr. Ruco div., 1978-80, v.p., gen. mgr. fabricated products div., 1980-81; pres. The McCloskey Corp., 1981-83, chmn. bd., pres., CEO, 1983—89. Chmn. bd. McCloskey Corp. (Calif.), 1981-89, McCloskey Corp. (Oreg.), 1981-89; instr. Villanova U., 1973-75; asst. prof. Phila. Coll. Textiles and Sci., 1969-75 Mem. adv. bd. Modern Paint & Coatings Mag.; contbr. numerous articles to profl. jours. and newspapers. Bd. dirs. Inter-Sci. Found., UCLA Med. Sch., 1983-86; bd. dirs., chmn. fin. com., exec. compensation com., mem. exec. com. Hahnemann U.; corp. adv. bd. Huntington's Disease of Am. Mem. Soc. Plastics Industry (chmn. vinyl film group, exec. com. plastic bottle inst.), Nat. Paint and Coatings Assn. (bd. dirs., indsl. coatings steering com.), Young Pres. Orgn., Am. Chem. Soc., Am. Mgmt. Assn. (pres.' assn.), Pa. Soc. Clubs: Harvard Bus. Sch. (Phila., N.Y.C.); Union League (Phila.); Aronimink. Republican. Baptist. Home: 4102 Battles Ln Newtown Square PA 19073-1602 Office: 7600 State Rd Philadelphia PA 19136-3404 E-mail: rkatherine@webtv.net, rakkat@comcast.net.

KATHREN, RONALD LAURENCE, health physicist; b. Windsor, Ont., Can., June 6, 1937; s. Ben and Sally (Forman) K.; m. Susan Ruth Krafft, Dec. 24, 1964; children: SallyBeth, Daniel, Elana (dec.). BS, UCLA, 1957; MSc, U. Pitts., 1962. Diplomate Am. Bd. Health Physics (bd. dirs. 1982-84, sec.-treas. 1984); Am. Acad. Environ. Engrs., Am Bd. Med. Physics; registered profl. engr., Calif. Health physicist Lawrence Radiation Lab. U. Calif., Livermore, 1962-67; mgr. external dose evaluation, Battelle Pacific N.W. Labs., Richland, Wash., 1967-70, sr. rsch. scientist, 1970-72, staff scientist, program mgr., 1978-89; dir. U.S. Transuranium and Uranium Registries Hanford Environ. Health Found., 1989-92, prof., dir. U.S. Transuranium and Uranium Registries, Wash. State U., 1992-99, prof. emeritus, 1999-; U.S. expert Internat. Atomic Energy Agy., Caracas, Venezuela, 1977; affiliate assoc. prof. U. Wash., 1978-94, prof., 1994, program coordinator in radiol. scis., 1980-82, 86-88; cons. Adv. Com. Reactor Safeguards, Washington, 1979-89; cons. adv. com. Nuc. Waste, 1988-94; mem. adv. com. Richland City Schs., 1985-87; bd. dirs. Mid-Columbia Symphony, 1987-92; chmn. Nat. Coun. Radiation Protection and Measurements Sci. Com. on Collective Dose, 1991-95; mem. Nat. Coun. of Examiners for Engring. and Surveying Com. on Examinations for Profl. Engrs., 1993—; trustee, Richland Public Libr. Found, 2002-, Herbert M. Parker Found, 1989-, Master Gardner Found, 2004-. Author: Ionizing Radiation: Tumorigenic and Tumoricidal Effects, 1983; Radioactivity in the Environment, 1984; Radiation Protection, 1985, The Plutonium Story, 1994. Editor: (with others) Health Physics: A Backward Glance, 1980; Computer Applications in Health Physics, 1984, Environmental Health Physics, 1993. Contbr. numerous articles to profl. jours., tech. reports, and chpts. in books. Trustee Herbert M. Parker Found., 1987—, Richland Pub. Libr. Found., 2002, Berton Franklin Master Garndener Found., 2004—. USPHS fellow, 1961-62; recipient Arthur Humm award Nat. Registry Radiation Protection Technologists, 1988, Hartman medallist and Orator Radiology Centennial, 1995. Mem. NAS (subcom. health effect depleted uranium 2005—), Health Physics Soc. (life fellow, pres. 1989-90, pres. Columbia chpt. 1971, dir. 1973-76, Elda E. Anderson award 1977, founders award 1985, Disting. Sci. Achievement award 2003), Am. Assn. Physicists in Medicine, Am. Acad. Health Physics (bd. dirs. 1984-86, 93—), Soc. Radiol. Protection (cert. in applied health physics).401360 Home: 137 Spring St Richland WA 99354-1651 Office: Wash State Univ 2710 University Dr Richland WA 99354-1641 Personal E-mail: kathren@bmi.net. Business E-Mail: rkathren@tricity.wsu.edu.

KATIN, PETER ROY, pianist; b. Nov. 14, 1930; m. Eva Zweig, 1954;2 children. Ed., Royal Acad. Music.; DMus (hon.), De Montfort U., 1994. Prof. Royal Acad. Music, 1956-60; prof. piano U. Western Ont., Can., 1978-84; prof. Royal Coll. Music, 1992—2001, Thames Valley Univ., 2001—04. Made 1st London appearance Wigmore Hall, 1948; leading interpreter of Chopin; concerts include Europe, Africa, Japan, Can., U.S., Hong Kong, India, New Zealand, Singapore, Malaysia; rec. artist for Athene, Decca, Everest, Unicorn, HMV, Philips, Lyrita, MFP, Carlton, Simax, Claudio, Olympia; formed The Katin Piano Trio, 1997. Pres. Camerata of London; v.p. Bridgwater Arts Centre. Recipient Chopin Arts award, NYC, 1977. Fellow Royal Acad. Music; assoc. Royal Coll. Music; mem. Inc. Soc. Musicians, Royal Soc. Musicians. Avocations: reading, writing, theater, tape recording, photography. Office: 41 First Ave Bexhill-on-Sea East Sussex TN40 2PL England Office Phone: +44 (0)1424 211167. E-mail: peter.katin@btinternet.com.

KATINA, ELENA SERGEJEVNA, singer; b. Moscow; Attended, Moscow State U., Faculty of Psychology. Singer T.A.T.U., 1999—. Rep. for Russia Eurovision Song Contest, 2003. Recipient 3rd Place for song "Ne ver', ne bojsia", Eurovision Song Contest, 2003. Mailing: T A T U Interscope Records 2220 Colorado Ave Santa Monica CA 90404

KATINSKY, STEVEN, communications company executive; b. Phila., Feb. 6, 1959; BA, Rutgers Coll., 1981. CEO, pres. Supertuner.com, Santa Monica, Calif.; co-founder, former CEO Hollywood Online, Santa Monica.

KATIS, JAMES GEORGE, psychiatrist; b. Westchester, N.Y., Apr. 3, 1933; s. George D. and Sophia (Christos) K; m. Lauma Upelnieks, Dec. 12, 1964; children: Peter D., Thomas E., James A. BA, Wesleyan U., 1956; MD, McGill U., 1960. Diplomate Am. Bd. Psychiatry and Neurology. Clin. dir. Silver Hill Found., New Canaan, Conn., 1971-81; dir. in-patient psychiatry St. Luke's Hosp., N.Y.C., 1983-88; assoc. chief Smithers, St. Luke's-Roosevelt Hosp., N.Y.C., 1988-94; cons. staff Greenwich Hosp., Conn., 1989—; clin. asst. prof. Coll. Physicans and Surgeons/Columbia U., N.Y.C., 1983—94. Fellow Am. Psychiat. Assn., N.Y. Acad. Medicine; mem. Am. Physicians. Greek Orthodox. Office: 1215 5th Ave New York NY 10029-5209 Office Phone: 212-427-6300.

KATIYAR, SANTOSH KUMAR, education educator; b. Farrukhabad, India, July 6, 1948; s. Lajja Ram and Roopwati Katiyar; children: Suchitra, Nandan. PhD, Bundelkhand U., 1976—79. Scientist Regional Rsch. Lab., Jammu, India, 1984—91; sr. rsch. assoc. Case Western Res. U., Cleve., 1991—2000; asst. prof. U. of Ala. at Birmingham, 2001—. Author: (scientific) Prevention of cancer. Mem.: Am. Assn. for Cancer Rsch. Achievements include research in role of dietary supplements in prevention of skin, breast and prostate cancer. Home: 2808 Seven Oaks Cir Vestavia Hills AL 35216 Office: Univ Ala 1670 University Blvd Birmingham AL 35294 Office Phone: 205-975-2608. Office Fax: 205-934-5745. Business E-Mail: skatiyar@uab.edu.

KATKIN, EDWARD SAMUEL, psychologist, educator; b. N.Y.C., Aug. 15, 1937; s. Nathan and Rosalind (Davis) K.; m. Felice Lapin, Aug. 10, 1958 (dec. 1961); m. 2d Wendy Sue Freedman, Feb. 3, 1963; children: Kenneth, Elizabeth. BA, CCNY, 1958; PhD, Duke U., 1963. Asst. prof. SUNY, Buffalo, 1963-66, assoc. prof., 1966-70, prof. dept. psychology, 1970-86 (chmn. 1980-86), Stony Brook, 1986—, chmn. dept. psychology, 1986-92, dean divsn. social and behavioral scis., 1993—96, prof. emer., 2000—. Fellow Am. Psychol. Soc.; mem. Soc. Psychophysiol. Rsch. (pres. 1983-84), Am. Psychosomatic Soc. Home: 11 Bayview Ave East Setauket NY 11733-3903 Office: SUNY Dept Psychology Stony Brook NY 11794-2500 Business E-Mail: edward.katkin@sunysb.edu.

KATLIC, JOHN EDWARD, management consultant; b. Washington, Pa., Nov. 3, 1928; s. Frederick John and Dorothy Ann (Gideon) K.; m. Nancy Jean Nicely, Aug. 26, 1950; children: Mark Richard, Kerry Leigh, Kevin Edward, Kathleen Diane, Nancy Ellen. BS in Engring. of Mines, W.Va. U., 1955, MS in Engring. of Mines, 1961. Mine surveyor Rochester & Pittsburgh Coal Co., Indiana, Pa., 1948-49; mine supt. Consolidation Coal Co., Morgantown, W.Va., 1959-62, gen. supt., 1962-66, v.p. Pitts., 1973-75; sr. mining engr. Ea. Assn. Coal, Pitts., 1967-68, divsn. mgr., 1969, v.p. pers. safety and indsl. rels., 1970, v.p., gen. mgr. Semet-Solvay divsn. Allied Chem., 1970-73; exec.v.p. adminstrn. engring. and govt. rels. Island Creek Coal Co., Lexington, Ky., 1975-83; sr. v.p. fuel supply Am. Electric Power Svc. Corp., 1983-93; pres. So. Ohio Coal, Cen. Ohio Coal, Windsor Coal, Conesville Coal (all subs.),

1983-93. Mem. negotiating team Nat. Bituminous Coal Wage Agreement, Joint Industry Devel. Com., 1978; cons. projects in Russia, Siberia, Kazakhstan, S. Africa. Patentee mining machine indicator, dust control in longwall mining. Mem. Morgantown City Coun., 1964-66, Marshall U. Found., 1979; bd. dirs. W.Va. Edn. Found., 1983-90, Inland Waterways Users Bd., 1992-93, Decorative Arts Ctr. Ohio, 1998-2001, Fairfield County Found.; mem. Steering com. W.Va. U.; chmn. bd. trustees Lancaster Fairfield Community Hosp., 1990-91; bd. dirs. Ohio Glass Mus. With inf. U.S. Army, 1946-47, C.E., 1950-52. Named Man of Yr., Coal Age Mag., 1987, Ohio Mining and Reclamation Assn., 1988; recipient Erskine Ramsay medal AIME, 1995, Kingery Safety award Pa. Coal Mining Inst. Am., 1995; named to W.Va. Coal Hall of Fame, 2000. Mem. AIME, VFW, Soc. Mining Engrs., Nat. Mine Rescue Assn., Nat. Mining Assn. (chmn. 1990-92), Mine Rescue Vets. of Pitts. Dist., Lancaster Fairfield C. of C. (pres. 1989), Symposiarchs, Ky. Cols., Cherry River Navy Club, Masons, Shriners. Republican. Presbyterian. Home: 1233 Ridgewood Way Lancaster OH 43130-1154 Office Phone: 740-654-2191. Personal E-mail: minerjack@aol.com.

KATO, RYOZO, ambassador; b. Saitama Prefecture, Japan, Sept. 13, 1941; m. Hanayo Kato; 3 children. Law degree, Tokyo U., 1965. Employee Ministry of Fgn. Affairs, Japan, 1965—81, dir., Security Affairs Divsn., N. Am. Affairs Bur., 1981—84, dir., Treaties Divsn., Treaties Bur., 1984—87, dir., Gen. Affairs Divsn., Minister's Secretariat, 1990—92, dep. dir.-gen., N. Am. Affairs Bur., 1992—94, dir.-gen., Asian Affairs Bur., 1995—97, dep. min. of Fgn. Affairs, 1999—2001; min. Embassy of Japan, 1987—90; consul-gen. of Japan San Francisco, 1994—95; amb. Extraordinary and Plenipotentiary of Japan to U.S. Washington, 2001—. Office: Embassy of Japan 2520 Mass Ave NW Washington DC 20008-2869 Office Phone: 202-238-6700.

KATO, SHUICHI, information scientist, educator; b. Agematsu, Nagano, Japan, Sept. 4, 1943; BSEE, Nagoya (Japan) Inst. Tech., 1969; MS, Chiba (Japan) U., 1976; DMS, Tokyo U., 1981. Cert. in biomed. engring., neurophysiology. Staff Devel. Ctr. of Abilities, Seiko Co. Ltd., Tokyo, 1971-73; vis. rschr. Physiol. Lab., Cambridge (Eng.) U., 1981-82; vis. rschr. dept. electronics and computer sci. U. Calif., Berkeley, 1982-83; prof. faculty informatics Teikyo Heisei U. (formerly Teikyo U. Tech.), 1988—, prof. Grad. Sch. Informatics, 1999—. Lectr. dept. materials sci. Chiba U., 1989—2005; pre-reviewer New Energy and Indsl. Tech. Develop. Orgn. Japan, 2001—; chmn. bd. dirs. NPO Inst. Intelligent Comm., 2003—. Author: Physiological Base of Creativity, 1988, Application of Microprocessor to Monitor and Conditioning during Sleep, 1979, Design of a Life Support Computer Network System for Aged People, 1998, Nonlinearity of the ABR frequency characteristic, 1998; cons. editor Contemporary WHO'S WHO, 2002—. Mem. IEEE, N.Y. Acad. Sci., Physiol. Soc. Japan (nominated Internat. Educator of Yr., Internat. Biographical Centre Cambridge, 2003, Japan Soc. Med. Electronics and Biol. Engring., Japan Soc. EEG and EMG, Inst. Electronics, Info. and Comm. Engrs., Welfare and Med. Soc. Chiba (vice-chmn. 2002—). Home: 3-12-11-206 Yamadabashi Ichihara 290-0021 Japan Office: Tokyo Met Ctrl Libr 5-7-13 Minami-Azabu Minato-ku Tokyo 106 Japan Fax: 0436-42-1496. Office Phone: 0436-74-5783. E-mail: kato@grape.plala.or.jp, kato@ieee.org.

KATO, TOMIKO, artist; b. Tokyo, Nov. 16, 1936; d. Seiji and Yae Suzuki; m. Yasuo Kato, Mar. 7, 1958; 1 child, Yuka. BFA, Tokyo Nat. U. Fine Arts/Music, 1959. Cert. secondary and univ. tchr. Artist in Nihon-ga (Japanese style painting). Solo exhbns. of works at Shiseido Ginza Gallery, Tokyo, Matsuya Ginza Gallery, Tokyo, 1983, 86, 90, 93, Bill Hodges Gallery, N.Y.C., 1996-98, 2002, Takashimaya Art Gallery, Tokyo, 1997, Hammond Mus. and Japanese Stroll Garden, N.Y.C., 2000; group exhbns. at Yamatane Art Mus., Tokyo, 1977, 79, 81, Saitama Prefectural Modern Art Mus., 1988, Takashimaya Gallery, Tokyo, 1981-98, Mitsukoshi Gallery, Tokyo, 1992-96, numerous others; author: Sakura no mori no mankai no shita (Beneath Blossoming Cherry Trees), 1993; dancer, choreographer Performance Art: Dances of My Paintings in Real Space, 1986; guest on TV program; subject of numerous revs. Recipient honorable mention Yamatane Art Mus. Award, 1981. Avocations: japanese dance, shamisen, theater, music.

KATO, WALTER YONEO, physicist; b. Chgo., Aug. 19, 1924; s. Naotaro and Hideko (Kondo) K.; m. Anna Chieko Kurata, June 26, 1953; children: Norman, Cathryn, Barbara. BS, Haverford (Pa.) Coll., 1946; MS, U. Ill., 1949; PhD, Pa. State U., University Park, 1954. Rsch. assoc. Ordnance Research Lab., Pa. State U., 1949-52, Brookhaven Nat. Lab., Upton, N.Y., 1952-53, sr. nuclear engr., asso. chmn. dept. applied sci., 1975-77, assoc. chmn. dept. nuclear energy, 1977-80, dep. chmn., 1980-88, chmn., 1988-91, sr. nuclear engr., 1991-97, cons., 1997—; rsch. affiliate dept. nuclear engring. MIT, Cambridge, 1999—2005, rsch. affiliate dept. nuclear sci. & engring., 2005—. Sr. physicist Argonne (Ill.) Nat. Lab., 1953-75; vis. prof. dept. nuclear engring. U. Mich., Ann Arbor, 1974-75; cons. Office Nuc. Regulatory Rsch., U.S. NRC, 1974-76. Contbr. articles to profl. jours. Bd. dirs. Naperville (Ill.) YMCA, 1966-74; mem. Order of Sacred Treasure 3d class Japanese Govt., 1992. Served with Ordnance Corps AUS, 1946-47. Fulbright rsch. fellow, 1958-59, Sci. and Tech. Agy. Japan fellow, 1998. Fellow AAAS, Am. Nuclear Soc. (dir.), Argonne Univ. Assn. (Disting. Appt. award 1974); mem. Am. Phys. Soc., Sigma Xi. Methodist. Home: 65 Grove St Unit 342 Wellesley MA 02482 E-mail: wykato@mit.edu, walter.kato@worldnet.att.net.

KATOK, ANATOLE, mathematics professor; b. Wash., D.C., Aug. 9, 1944; married; 3 children. MA, Moscow State U., 1965, PhD, 1968. Junior scientific rsch. worker central economics USSR Acad. of Sci. Mathematics Inst., 1968—73, sr. scientific rsch. worker central economics, 1973—78; prof., chair in analysis U. Maryland, 1978—84; prof. Calif. Inst. Tech., 1984—90, Penn State U., 1990—, Raymond N. Shibley prof., 1996—. Vis. lectr. Federal U., Mexico City, 1986, Stanford U., 1979, Federal U., Mexico City, 1988; vis. prof. U. Rome, 1978, U. Paris, 1993, U. Rome, 1997, Tsin Hua U., Taiwan, 1999, Cambridge U., 2000, Independent U. Moscow, 2001—03, U. Paris, 2002; vis. fellow Japan Soc. for Promotion of Sci., 2003; mem. editorial bd. Mathematical Rsch. Letters Jour., 1994—, Discrete & Continuous Dynamical Systems, 1995—, Moscow Mathematical Jour., 2000—. Editor: (books) Cambridge Tracts in Mathematics, Cambridge Studies in Advanced Mathematics, Proceedings, Progress in Mathematics. Fellow: Am. Acad. Arts & Sciences; mem.: Inst. Math. and Applications (bd. govs. 1993—96). Office: Penn State U Mathematics Dept U Park State College PA 16802

KATONA, PETER GEZA, biomedical engineer, educator; b. Budapest, Hungary, June 25, 1937; came to U.S., 1956, naturalized, 1962; s. Stephan and Irene (Renner) K.; m. Jaroslava Blanar, Aug. 27, 1966; children—Catherine Iris, Andrew George. BS in Elec. Engring. U. Mich., 1960; S.M. in Elec. Engring. (Sloan fellow, 1960-62), M.I.T., 1962, Sc.D. in Elec. Engring. 1965. Asst. prof. elec. engring. M.I.T., 1965-69; assoc. prof. biomed. engring. Case Western Res. U., Cleve., 1969-78, prof., 1978-92, chmn. dept., 1980-87. Program dir. biomed. engring. and aiding the disabled NSF, 1989—91; v.p. biomed. engring. The Whitaker Found., 1991—95, exec. v.p. biomed engring., 1995—98, pres. biomed. engring., 1998—2000, pres., CEO, 2000—. Mem. editl. bd. Am. Jour. Physiology, 1975-81; contbr. articles on cardio-respiratory control and automated drug delivery to profl. jours. Recipient Alexander von Humboldt award, 1987-88. Fellow AAAS, Am. Inst. Med. & Biol. Engring. (founding); sr. mem. IEEE, Am. Physiol. Soc., Biomed. Engring. Soc. (bd. dirs. 1977-80, pres. 1984-85), Am. Soc. Engring. Edn. Office: The Whitaker Found 1700 N Moore St Ste 2200 Arlington VA 22209-1923 Office Phone: 703-528-2430. E-mail: katona@whitaker.org.

KATOPIS, GEORGE A., electrical engineer; b. Athens, Greece, Apr. 30, 1944; came to U.S., 1970; s. Alexander G. and Emilia A. K.; m. Angela G. Economopoulou, May 31, 1977; 1 child, Alexander. M in Elect. Engring. and Mech. Engring., Poly. U., Athens, 1967; MS in Elec. Engring., Columbia U., 1972, MPH in Elec. Engring., 1980. From sr. assoc. engr. to sr. engring. mgr. IBM Semiconductor Devel. Lab., East Fishkill, N.Y., 1974-92; sr. engr. IBM S/390 Devel. Lab., Poughkeepsie, N.Y., 1992-98, sr. tech. staff, 1997-2000; disting. engr. IBM ESG Devel. Lab., Poughkeepsie, N.Y., 2000—. Indsl. mentor SRC, Ariz., 1984-94; lectr. U. Ga., 1997; instr. CEI-Europe/Elsevier, Germany, Italy, 1988-90. Co-author: Microelectronic Packaging Handbook, 1989; patentee in field; contbr. articles to profl. jours. Bd. dirs. Kimisis Greek Orthodox Ch., Poughkeepsie, 1988, v.p. bd. dirs., 1989; Greek rep. YMCA, Holland, 1964. Mem. IEEE (sr.). Avocations: sailing, chess, bridge, ping pong/table tennis, photography. Home: 11 Fair Oaks Dr Poughkeepsie NY 12603 Office: IBM 2455 South Rd Poughkeepsie NY 12601 E-mail: katopis@us.ibm.com.

KATOPODIS, LOUIS, supermarket chain executive; Grad., U. Houston, 1971. Joined Fiesta Mart, Houston, 1975—, various positions including non foods buyer, gen. mgr., pres., CEO. Bd. mem. Food Marketing Inst. Treas. bd. dirs. Chronic Lymphocytic Leukemia Global Rsch. Found. Office: Fiesta Mart 5235 Katy Fwy Houston TX 77007-2210

KATRITZKY, ALAN ROY, chemistry professor; b. London, Eng., Aug. 18, 1928; s. Frederick Charles and Emily Gertrude (Lane) K.; m. Agnes Juliane Dietlinde Kilian, Aug. 5, 1952; children: Margaret, Erika, Rupert, Freda. BA, Oxford U., 1951, BSc, 1952, MA, DPhil, Oxford U., 1954; PhD, Cambridge U., 1958, ScD, 1963; ScD (hon.), U. Nac. Madrid, 1986, U. Poznan, Poland, 1990, U. Gdansk, 1994, U. East Anglia, U.K., 1995, U. Toulouse, France, 1996; Prof. (hon.), Xian Modern U., 1995, Beijing Inst. Tech., 1995; ScD (hon.), U. St. Petersburg, Russia, 1997, U. Bucharest, Romania, 1998, U. Rostov, Russia, 2000, U. Ghent, Belgium, 2001, Bundelkhand U., India, 2001, U. Timisoara, Romania, 2003, U. Wroclaw, Poland, 2005. ICI fellow U. Oxford, 1956-58; lectr. chemistry U. Cambridge, 1958-63; fellow Churchill Coll.; prof. chemistry U. East Anglia, 1963-80; dean U. East Anglia (Sch. Chem. Scis.), 1963-70, 76-80; Kenan prof. organic chemistry U. Fla., Gainesville, 1980—. Dir. Fla. Inst. Het. Cpds., 1986—. Editor: Advances in Heterocyclic Chemistry, vols. 1-85, 1963—; regional editor: Tetrahedron, 1980-98; chmn. editl. bd. Comprehensive Heterocyclic Chemistry, 1st edit., 9 vols., 1985, 2d edit., 10 vols., 1996, Comprehensive Organic Functional Group Transformations, 7 vols., 1995, 2d edit., 2004. Decorated Cavaliere Ufficiale. Fellow Royal Soc.; mem. Am., Brit., Italian (hon. mem.), Polish (hon. mem.) Chem. Socs., Internat. Soc. Het. Chem., Polish Acad. Sci. (fgn. mem.), Real Catalan Acad., Slovenian Acad., Russian Acad. Sci. (fgn. mem. Siberian br.), Indian Nat. Acad. Sci. (fgn. mem.). Home: 1221 SW 21st Ave Gainesville FL 32601-8417 Office: U Fla Dept Chemistry Gainesville FL 32611 E-mail: katritzky@chem.ufl.edu.

KATSAKIORES, GEORGE NICHOLAS, state legislator, retired food service executive; b. Derry, N.H., Dec. 11, 1924; s. Nicholas G. and Agorista (Siatravinos) K.; m. Lucille Brunelle, Nov. 11, 1963 (div. July 1980); children: Sheila, Glen, Greg, Karen, Gary; m. Phyllis M. Harrie, Oct. 9, 1983. Student, U. N.H., 1946—48. Owner White's Restaurant, Derry, 1948-88, ret.; mem. N.H. Ho. of Reps., 1982—, chair transp. com., chmn. emeritus, 1991—. Dir. Derry Devel. and Preservation Corp.; vice chmn. Airport Access Hwy. Task Force, Manchester, N.H.; mem. transp. task force Am. Legis. Exch. Coun., Washington, 1984—; appointed to N.H. Integrated Trans. and R.R. Coun., 1985—, Internat. Hellenic Union, 2004-. Dir. Northeast Corridor Initiative, Boston, Greater Derry/Saleit Transp. Coun., 1987—. Nutfield Sr. Devel. Corp., 2000-; mem. Rockingham County Com., 1998—, Brentwood, N.H.; chmn. Rock City Del., 1999-2004, Rep. Nat. Party, N.H. Rep. Com., 1982-. Cpl. Med. Corps U.S. Army, 1943-45, ETO. Inducted into Pinkerton Acad. Hall of Fame, 1999. Mem. VFW (Post 1617), AARP, Nat. Conf. State Legislators, N.H. Transp. and Hwy. Users Coalition, N.H. R.R. Revitalization Assn., Internat. Hellenic Union, Am. Legion, Hoodkroft County Club (Derry) Greek Orthodox. Avocations: golf, politics. Home: 1 Bradford St Derry NH 03038-4258 E-mail: p.katsakiores@comcast.net.

KATSAROS, THOMAS, history educator; b. N.Y.C., Feb. 21, 1926; s. John and Helen (Drivas) K.; B.A., N.Y. U., 1953, M.A., 1956, M.B.A., 1958, Ph.D., 1963, advanced profl. cert., 1975; m. Nancy Louise Massa, June 26, 1971. With Gerdau Export-Import Co. and Argos Import Co., N.Y.C., 1955-63; asst. prof. SUNY, Potsdam, 1963-65; faculty U. New Haven, 1965—, prof. dept. history, 1968-80, prof. history and econs., 1980—, chmn. dept. history, 1968-78, dir. bus. research editor Am. Bus. Rev., 1983—; editor U. New Haven Press. Served with U.S. Army, 1944-47. Decorated Bronze Star. Mem. Am. Hist. Assn., Am. Econs. Assn., Eastern Econs. Assn., Am. Mgmt. Assn., AAUP. Author: (with Nathaniel Kaplan) The Western Mystical Tradition, 1969, The Origins of American Transcendentalism, 1975; (with George Schiro) A Brief History of the Western World, 1978; (with John Teluk) Capitalism: A Cooperative Venture, 1981; (with Sohiro) America and Europe: A Modern History, 1984; The Development of the Welfare State in the Western World, 1995. Home: 11 Carriage Dr North Haven CT 06473-1506

KATSH, SALEM MICHAEL, lawyer; b. NYC, May 5, 1948; s. Abraham Isaac and Estelle (Wachtell) K.; m. Jennette Williams, Sept. 4, 1983; children: Halley Rachel, Emmet Walker. BA, NYU, 1970, JD cum laude, 1972. Bar: N.Y. 1973, U.S. Dist. Ct. (so., ea., no. dists. N.Y.) 1975, U.S. Ct. of Appeals (2d cir.) 1975, U.S. Ct. of Appeals (9th cir.) 1977, U.S. Supreme Ct. 1983, U.S. Ct. Appeals (fed. cir.) 1990, U.S. Dist. Ct. (no. dist.) Calif. 1993. Assoc. Weil, Gotshal & Manges, N.Y.C., 1972-80, ptnr., 1980-97, Shearman & Sterling, N.Y.C., 1997—. Adj. prof. New York Law Sch., 1980-84. Author: Industrial Power and the Law, 1980, (with others) The Limits of Corporate Power, 1981; founder Jour. Proprietary Rights; contbr. articles to profl. jours. Mem.: ABA, NY State Bar Assn., Order of Coif. Office: 599 Lexington Ave New York NY 10022-6030

KATSIFF, BRUCE, artist; b. Phila., Dec. 10, 1945; s. Myer and Rose (August) K.; m. Joane Mitnick, Dec. 30, 1965; 1 child, Timothy. BFA, Rochester Inst. Tech., 1968; MFA, Pratt Inst., 1973; postgrad., Oxford (Eng.) U., 1987. Film producer Eastman Kodak Co., Rochester, N.Y., 1968; adj. prof. Thomas Edison Coll., Trenton, N.J., 1970-74; chmn. fine art Bucks County Coll., Newtown, Pa., 1973-84, prof., 1984-88; chmn. art and music Bucks Coll., Newtown, 1988-89; dir. James A. Michener Art Mus., 1990—. Mng. bd. dirs. Photography Sesquicentennial, Phila., 1988-90. Exhibited at Mus. Modern Art, N.Y.C., 1968, Internat. Mus. Photography, Rochester, N.Y., 1969, Phila. Art Mus., 1970, Am. Arts Ctr., Exeter, Eng., 1970, Tainjan Inst., China, 1987, Pa. Acad. Fine Arts, 1990, Washington Photography Ctr., 1993. Grantee NEA, 1973; fellowship Pa. Arts Coun., 1990. Fellow Soc. Photographic Educators; mem. Pa. Coun. on Arts (mus. panel 1982-85, visual arts panel 1987-90). Home: PO Box 28 Lumberville PA 18933-0028 E-mail: bkatsiff@comcast.net.

KATSOULOMITIS, GEORGIA, foundation administrator, lawyer; Graduate, Tufts Univ.; JD, Catholic Univ., Washington. Spl. asst. US Labor Secy., Robert Reich, Washington; spl. asst. and counsel, oversight and investigations Dept. Labor, Washington; v.p. Robinson Lerer & Montgomery, NYC; now asst. exec. dir. Boston Bar Found. Class of 2004 LeadBoston leadership devel. program; past. exec. dir. Mass. Women's Polit. Caucus. Mem.: Women's Bar Assn. (legis. policy com.), Hellenic Bar Assn. (vice pres. 2005), Mass. Bar. Office: Boston Bar Found 16 Beacon St Boston MA 02108 Office Phone: 617-778-1948. Office Fax: 617-523-0127. Business E-Mail: gkatsoulomitis@bostonbar.org.

KATTAH, JORGE, neurologist, educator; b. Bogota, Colombia, Jan. 12, 1948; s. Jorge Y. and Beatriz (Calderon) K.; m. Janet Marie. MD, Coll. Mayor Ntra Sra Rosario, Bogota, 1972. Intern in neurology Georgetown U. Med., 1976; intern in neurophthalmology Pitts. Eye and Ear Hosp., 1977; assoc. prof. Georgetown U., Washington, 1977-97; prof. neurology, chmn. dept. U. Ill., Peoria, 1997—. Mem. Am. Neurol. Assn. Office: U Ill 1 Illini Dr Peoria IL 61605-2576

KATTI, KATTESH V., biochemist, educator, research scientist; s. Varihanumanthacharya K. Katti; m. Kavita Kattesh Katti; children: Sumidha Kattesh, Nahush Kattesh. PhD, Indian Inst. Sci., Bangalore, 1985. Rsch. assoc. U. Alta., Edmonton, Canada, 1987—90; prof. radiology U. Mo., Columbia, 1990—. Rsch. fellow U. Gottingen, Germany, 1985—87. Contbr. articles, revs. to profl. publs., chpts. to books. Alexander von Humboldt fellow, Alexander von Humboldt Found., 1985, rsch. grantee, NIH, 2003. Fellow: Royal Soc. Chemistry (assoc.); mem.: Soc. Nuc. Medicine, Am. Chem. Soc. (assoc.). Achievements include 12 patents on pharmaceuticals discovery. Office: U Mo Dept Radiology 1 Hospital Dr Columbia MO 65211 Personal E-mail: kattik@health.missouri.edu.

KATTWINKEL, JOHN, pediatrician, educator; b. Newton, Mass., June 24, 1941; s. Egon Emil and Dorothy Lucile (Fish) K.; m. Phyllis Ann Denton, Sept. 14, 1963; children: Susan, Linda. BS, Rensselaer Poly. Inst., 1964; B in Med. Sci., Dartmouth Coll., 1966; MD, Harvard U., 1968. Diplomate Am. Bd. Pediatrics, Am. Bd. Neonatology (bd. dirs. 1981-86). Resident in pediatrics Duke Med. Ctr., Durham, N.C., 1968-70; clin. assoc. NIH, Bethesda, Md., 1970-72; neonatology fellow Case Western Res. U., Cleve., 1972-74; asst. prof. pediatrics U. Va., Charlottesville, 1974-78, assoc. prof., 1978-84, prof., 1984—, dir. neonatology, 1974—, Charles Fuller chair in neonatology, 1998—. Founder Perinatal Edn. Ctr., Charlottesville, 1976—; Poland and China cons. Project HOPE, Milwood, Va., 1979-92; hon. prof. Zhejiang Med. U., Hangzhou, People's Republic of China, 1985. Mem. editl. bd. Pediatrics, 1999—; contbr. articles on newborn respiration and med. edn. to profl. jours.; inventor device for nasal ventilation of infants. Lt. comdr. USPHS, 1970-72. Recipient Discovery Health Channel Med. Honor, 2004. Fellow: Am. Acad. Pediat. (fetus and newborn com. 1983—89, neonatal resuscitation program steering com. 1989—98, chair SIDS task force 1992—, chair 1994—98, editor 1999—, Ross Profl. Edn. award 1989); mem.: Soc. Pediat. Rsch., Am. Pediat. Soc. Avocation: tennis. Home: 920 Charter Oaks Dr Charlottesville VA 22901-0629 Office: U Va Dept Pediatrics Charlottesville VA 22908-0001 Office Phone: 434-924-5428. Business E-Mail: jk3f@virginia.edu.

KATYAL, NEAL K., law educator; AB, Dartmouth U.; JD, Yale U. Law clk. to Justice Stephen G. Breyer U.S. Supreme Ct.; law clk. to Judge Guido Calabresi U.S. Ct. Appeals (2nd cir.); nat. sec. advisor to dep. atty. gen. U.S. Dept. Justice, Washington, 1998—99; assoc. prof. Georgetown U., 1997—2004, John Carroll rsch. prof. law, 2004—. Vis. prof. Yale U., 2001—02, Harvard U., 2002. Contbr. articles to profl. jours. Named one of Top 40 Lawyers Under 40, Nat. Law Jour., 2005. Office: Georgetown U Law Ctr 600 New Jersey Ave NW Washington DC 20001 Office Phone: 202-262-9000.*

KATZ, ABRAHAM, retired foreign service officer; b. Bklyn., Dec. 4, 1926; s. Alexander and Zina (Rabinowitz) K.; children: Tamar, Jonathan, Naomi; m. Marion Scheinberger, July 29, 1996. BA cum laude, Bklyn. Coll., 1948; M.I.A., Columbia U., 1950; PhD, Harvard U., 1968. Commd. fgn. service officer Dept. State, 1951; vice-consul, prin. officer Am. Consulate, Merida, Mexico, 1951—53; 2d sec. Am. Embassy, Mexico, 1953—56; chief Soviet fgn. econ. Bur. Intelligence Rsch., Washington, 1957—59; 1st sec. U.S. missions to NATO, OECD, Paris, 1959-64; counselor Am. Embassy, Moscow, 1964-66; dir. office of OECD European Communities and Atlantic Polit. Econ. Affairs, Washington, 1967-74; dep. chief of mission OECD, Paris, 1974-78; dep. asst. sec. for internat. econ. policy and research Dept. Commerce, Washington, 1978-80, asst. sec. internat. econ. policy, 1980-81; U.S. rep., ambassador OECD, Paris, 1981-84; pres. U.S. Coun. Internat. Bus., 1984-99, pres. emeritus, 1999—. Employer mem. gov. body Internat. Labor Orgn., 1984-99; v.p. Internat. Orgn. Employers, 1984-99. Author: The Politics of Economic Reform in the Soviet Union, 1972. Decorated grand officier Ordre National du Merite (France); recipient U.S. Coun. Internat. Bus. Internat. Leadership award. Mem. Am. Polit. Sci. Assn., Assn. Advancement Slavic Studies, Am. Fgn. Svc. Assn., Am. Assn. Comparative Econ. Studies, Coun. of Fgn. Rels., Cosmos Club, Harvard Club, B'nai Brith, Century Assn. Office: US Coun Internat Bus 1212 Avenue Of The Americas New York NY 10036-1602 Business E-Mail: akatz@uscib.org.

KATZ, ADRIAN IZHACK, medical educator; b. Bucharest, Romania, Aug. 3, 1932; came to U.S., 1965, naturalized, 1976; s. Ferdinand and Helen (Lustig) K.; m. Miriam Lesser, Mar. 31, 1965; children— Ron, Iris. MD, Hebrew U., 1961. Research fellow Yale U., 1965-67, Harvard U., 1967-68; intern Belinson Med. Center, Israel, 1961, resident, 1962-65; practice medicine specializing in internal medicine and nephrology New Haven, 1966-67, Boston, 1967-68, Chgo., 1968—; attending physician U. Chgo. Hosps., 1968—2002, head nephrology sect., 1973-82; asst. prof. medicine U. Chgo., 1968-71, assoc. prof., 1971-74, prof., 1975—2002, prof. emeritus, 2002—. Fogarty sr. internat. fellow, vis. scientist Lab Cell Physiology, Coll. de France, Paris, 1977-78; vis. prof. cellular and molecular physiology Yale U., 1988; vis. scientist dept. molecular medicine Karolinska Inst., Stockholm, 1994—. Co-author: Kidney Function and Disease in Pregnancy; contbr. chpts. to books, articles to profl. jours. Fellow A.C.P.; mem. Am. Physiol. Soc., Am. Soc. Clin. Investigation, Assn. Am. Physicians, Am. Soc. Nephrology, Internat. Soc. Nephrology, Central Soc. Clin. Research, N.Y. Acad. Scis. Home: 1125 E 53rd St Chicago IL 60615-4410 Office: U Chgo 5841 S Maryland Ave Chicago IL 60637-1463 Business E-Mail: akatz@medicine.bsd.uchicago.edu.

KATZ, ALAN, publishing executive; married; 3 children. BA in Comm., William Patterson Univ. Sales rep. NY mag., 1989—91, retail mgr., 1991—92, advt. mgr., 1992—94, advt. dir., 1994—95, assoc. pub., 1995—99, pub., 1999—2003; founding pub. Cargo mag., Conde Nast pubs., 2003—05; v.p., pub. Vanity Fair mag., 2005—. Office: Vanity Fair 4 Times Square New York NY 10036*

KATZ, ALAN CHARLES, toxicologist; b. Kearny, NJ, Nov. 10, 1946; s. Edward Myron and Margaret Ellen Katz; m. Marcia Anne Ellenwood, July 26, 1974; children: Bryan Jeffrey, Jeffrey Alan. BS in Biology, Fairleigh Dickinson U., 1970, MS in Human Physiology, 1977; Cert. in Mgmt., Ctrl. Conn. State U., 1981. Diplomate Am. Bd. Toxicology, Am. Bd. Forensic Examiners. Chemist Union Carbide Corp., Bound Brook, N.J., 1965-70; toxicologist Ortho Pharm. Corp., Raritan, N.J., 1971-74; sr. ophthalmic pharmacologist Cooper Labs., Cedar Knolls, N.J., 1974-76; sr. assoc. toxicologist J&J Rsch. Found., North Brunswick, N.J., 1976-79; study dir. Stauffer Chem. Co., Farmington, Conn., 1979-84; sr. toxicologist EPA, Washington, 1984-87; exec. dir. TAS, Inc., Washington, 1987-97; mgr. tech. affairs Sanachem USA, Inc., 1997-98; prin. Katz Assocs., 1985—, TOXCEL, LLC, 1999—; dir. TOXCEL Internat., Ltd., 2000—. Contbg. editor Acute Toxicity, 1991-97; editl. bd. Jour. Applied Toxicology. Fellow Am. Coll. Forensic Examiners; mem. N.Y. Acad. Scis., Soc. Comparative Ophthalmology (past pres.), Soc. Toxicology, Am. Coll. Toxicology, Am. Chem. Soc., Soc. Toxicologie du Can., Roundtable Toxicology Cons., Food & Drug Law Inst. Home: 16090 Simon Kenton Rd Haymarket VA 20169-2109

KATZ, ALEX, artist; b. Bklyn., July 24, 1927; s. Isaac and Ella (Marion) K.; m. Ada Del Moro, Feb. 1, 1958; 1 child, Vincent. Degree in fine arts, Cooper Union, 1949; DFA (hon.), Colby Coll., 1984; PhD (hon.), 1986. One-man exhbns. include Roko Gallery, N.Y.C., 1954, 57, Fischbach Gallery, N.Y.C., 1964, 65, 67, 68, 70, 71, Stable Gallery, N.Y.C., 1960-61, Tanager Gallery, N.Y.C., 1959, 62, Martha Jackson Gallery, N.Y.C., 1962, Grinnell Gallery, Detroit, 1964, Sun Gallery, Provincetown, Mass., 1958, 59, Pa. State Coll., 1957, David Stuart Gallery, L.A., 1966, Bertha Eccles Art Center, Ogden, Utah, 1968, Towson State Coll., Balt., 1968, Phyllis Kind Gallery, Chgo., 1969, 71, W.Va. U., 1969, Galerie Dieter Brusberg, Hanover, Germany, 1971, Thelen Galerie, Cologne, Germany, 1971, Reed Coll., Portland, 1972, Sloan-O'Sickey Gallery, Cleve., 1972, Carlton Gallery, N.Y.C., 1973, Marlborough Gallery, N.Y.C., 1973, 75, 76, Whitney Mus. Am. Art, N.Y.C., 1974-75, Va. Mus. Fine Arts, Richmond, 1974-75, Santa Barbara Mus. Art, 1974-75, U. Minn., 1974-75, Indpls. Mus. Art, 1975, Marlborough Fine Art, London, 1975, Galerie Marguerite Lamy, Paris, 1975, Galerie Roger d'Amé court, Paris, 1977, traveling show Fresno Arts Center, Art Galleries Calif. State U., Seattle Art Mus., Vancouver Art Gallery, 1977-78, Marlborough Galerie, A.G., Zurich, 1977, Rose Art Mus., Brandeis U., Waltham, Mass., Balt. Art Mus., 1978, Brooke Alexander Gallery, N.Y.C., 1979, Robert Miller Gallery, N.Y.C., 1987, Inge Baecker Galerie, Cologne, Germany, 1987, Hokin Gallery, Chgo., 1987, Bklyn. Mus., 1988, Galerie Daniel Templon, Paris

Marlborough Gallery, N.Y., 1988, Seibu Mus., Tokyo and Osaka, 1988, Cleve. Mus. Art, 1988, Bernd Kluser, Munich, 1989, Mario Diacono, Boston, 1989, Michael Kohn, L.A., Moscow-USSR CAT, 1989, Palma de Malorca, Spain, 1989, I.C.A., London, 1991, Turin, Italy, 1992, Marlborough Gallery N.Y. CAT, 1992, Munson-Williams-Proctor Inst., 1992, Colby Coll. Art Mus., 1992, Robert Miller Gallery, N.Y.C., 1993, Betsy Senior Gallery, N.Y.C., 1993, Rubenstein/Diacono Gallery, 1993, Marlborough Gallery, N.Y.C., 1993, 95, Ark. Art Mus., 1993, 94, Robert Mullen Gallery, 1994, Staatliche Kunsthalle, Baden-Baden, Germany, 1995, Peter Blum, N.Y.C., 1996, Balt. Mus. Fine Arts, 1996, Inst. Valencia de Arte Moderna Mus., Valencia, Spain, 1996, Fred Hoffman, L.A., 1996, Galerie Jablonka, Cologne, Germany, 1997, Saatchi Gallery, London, 1998, The Cultural Found., Germany, 1998, Galerie Thaddaeus Ropac, Paris, 1998, Galerie Barbara Thumm, Berlin, 1998, P.S.I. Contemporary Art Ctr., N.Y., 1998, Centro Cultural Recoleta, Buenos Aires, 1998, Arts Club Chgo., 2000, Carnegie Mes. Art, Pitt., Pa., 2000, Pace Wildenstein Gallery, N.Y.C., 2001, Timothy Tyler Gallery, London, 2002, Peter Blum Gallery, N.Y.C., 2001-2002, Addison Gallery of Am. Art, Andover, Mass., 2001, Whitney Mus. Am. Art, N.Y.C., 2001, Kemper Mus. Contemporary Art, Kansas City, Mo., 2002, Galeria Mario Sequeira, Braga, Portugal, 2002, Utah Mus. Fine Arts, Salt Lake City, U. Calif. at San Diego, Mpls. Mus. Art, Wadsworth Atheneum, Hartford, Conn., 1971, Am. Found. Arts, Miami, Fla., 1976, Whitney Mus. Am. Art, N.Y.C., 1986 (paintings), Bklyn. Mus., 1980 (prints), 1986, 88, Galerie Templon, Paris (paintings), Marlborough Gallery, N.Y.C., Massimo Audiello, N.Y.C., Seibu Mus. at Tokyo, Osaka, Japan, 1988 (paintings, cutouts), Galleria D'Arte Contemporanea Emilio Muzzoli, Modena, Italy, 2003, Deichtovhallen, Hamburg, Germany, 2003, Museum Moderner Kunst Karten, Klagenfurt, Austria, 2003, Galerie Thaddaeus Ropac, Paris, 2003, Jablouka Galerie, 2004, Timothy Taylor Gallery, London, 2004, Stella Gallery, Moscow, 2004, Albertina Mus, Vienna, 2004, Colby Coll. Mus., 2004, numerous others; group shows include Pa. Acad. Fine Arts, 1960, Va. Mus., Richmond, 1960, Whitney Mus. Am. Art, N.Y.C., 1960, 67-68, 72 (Ann.), 73 (Biennial), 79, 86 (traveling show), 88 (Philip Morris), 91 (Biennial), Art Inst. Chgo., 1961, 62, 64, 72, Yale Mus., 1962, Colby Coll., 1961, 63, 64, 70, 85, Am. Fedn. Art., 1964-65, Mus. Modern Art, N.Y.C., 1964, 65, 66, 68, 69, 91, 93 (Pfizer), Milw. Arts Center, 1966, 69, 75, R.I. Sch. Design, 1966, Cin. Art Mus., 1968, Am. Acad. Design, 1968, U. Calif. at LaJolla, 1969, N.Y. Acad. Design, N.Y.C., 1973, Marlborough Gallery, N.Y.C., 1976, Cleve. Mus. Art, 1974, DeCordova Mus., Mass., 1975, Mus. Fine Arts, St. Petersburg, 1975-76, U. Mo., 1979, Bowdoin Coll., Maine, 1985, Wichita State Mus., Kans., 1985, Found. Daniel Templon, 1989, France Madison (Wis.) Art Ctr., 1989, Walker Art Ctr, Mpls., 1989, Whitney Mus. at Equitable Ctr., N.Y.C., P.S. 1 Mus., Kuznetsky Most Exhibition, Moscow, 1990, Nassau County Art Mus., 1991, Art Contemporaire, Lyon, France, 1993, Mus. Contemporary Art, São Paulo, Brazil, 1993, Nat. Gallery Art, Washington, 1993, Nat. Portrait Gallery, Washington, 1993, Whitney Mus., N.Y.C., 1994, Mus. Modern Art, N.Y.C., 1994, 1995, Mus. fur Moderne Kuust, Frankfurt, Germany, 1996, Deichtorhallen, Hamburg, Germany, 1996, Kunsthaus, Zurich, Switzerland, 1997, Am. Acad. in Rome, 2001, Pompidou Ctr., Paris, 2002, Schinn Kunsthalle, Frankfurt, Germany, 2002, travelling exhibitions solo, 1996—; Krusthalle, Baden-Baden, Germany; Alex Katz, American Landscape, 1996; N.Y. Inst. Contemporary Art, 1998, Galleria Civica di Arte Contemporanea Trento, 1999, Whitechapel Gallery, London, 2004-05, numerous others; represented in permanent collections Whitney Mus., Mus. Modern Art, Met. Mus. Art, Brandeis U., N.Y.U., Bowdoin Coll., Detroit Mus., Allentown (Pa.) Art Mus., Weatherspoon Gallery of Art, Greensboro, N.C., Tokyo Gallery, Allen Meml. Art Mus., Oberlin, Ohio, Houston Mus., Tate Gallery, London, The Israel Mus., Jerusalem, Iwaki City Mus., Japan, Nat.Gallery of Scotland, Hiroshima Mus., Museo Rufino Tamayo, Mex., Honolulu Acad. Art, Reina Sofia, Madrid, Valencia Mus., numerous others; vis. critic Yale U., 1960-63; Marshall Crogan vis. artist Harvard U., 1991-92. Subject of books: Alex Katz (Irving Sandler), 1979, Alex Katz: The Complete Prints (Nick Maravell), 1983, Alex Katz (Marshall and Rosenblum), 1986; also contbr. prints to Give Me Tomorrow (Ratcliff), 1984, A Tremor in the Morning (Vincent Katz), 1986, Alex Katz (Ann Beattie); Alex Katz Night Paintings (Donald Kuspit), Alex Katz (Sam Hunter), 1992, Alex Katz Under the Stars American Landscape (Dave Hickey, Simon Shama), 1995-1995, Alex Katz: American Landscape (Margrit Brehm, Jochen Poetter, Robert Starr), 1995, Alex Katz (Juan Manuel Bonet, Kevin Power), 1996, Invented Symbols, 1997, Edges (Robert Creeley and Alex Katz), 1998, Alex Katz 25 Years of Painting (Merlin James, David Sylvester), 1998, Alex Katz (Victorie Coen), 2000, Alex Katz Cutouts (Zdinck Felix, Carta Ratcliff) 2003, others; represented in permanent wing for Alex Katz Colby (Me.) Coll. Mus. Art. Recipient award New Eng. Art, Provincetown, Mass., 1971, Art in Pub. Places award, Harlem Station, Chgo., 1985, Profl. Achievement citation Cooper Union, 1974, alumni medal for achievement, 1980, Augustus St. Gaudens award for professionalism in art, 1980, medal for achievement in painting Skowhegan Sch., 1980; Guggenheim fellow, 1972; U.S.-USSR cultural exch. gurantee 1978; resident Am. Acad. in Rome, 1983; inducted into Am. Acad. and Inst. of Arts and Letters; opening of Paul J. Schupf wing for the Alex Katz collection Colby Coll. Mus., 1996. Address: 211 W 9th St New York NY 10011 E-mail: info@alexkotz.com.

KATZ, ARNOLD MARTIN, medical educator; b. Chgo., July 30, 1932; s. Louis Nelson and Aline (Grossner) K.; m. Phyllis Beck, Apr. 18, 1959; children: Paul, Sarah, Amy, Laura. BA with honors, U. Chgo., 1952; MD cum laude, Harvard U., 1956; D.Med. (hon.), Carol Davila U., 1994. Diplomate Nat. Bd. Med. Examiners. Intern Mass. Gen. Hosp., Boston, 1956-57, asst. resident, 1959-60; rsch. assoc. NIH, Bethesda, Md., 1957-59; asst. registrar Inst. Cardiology, London, 1960-61; rsch. fellow dept. medicine UCLA, 1961-64; asst. prof. physiology Columbia U., N.Y.C., 1963-67; assoc. prof. medicine and physiology U. Chgo., 1967-69; Philip J. and Harriet L. Goodhart prof. cardiology Mt. Sinai Sch. Medicine, N.Y.C., 1969-77; prof. medicine U. Conn., Farmington, 1977—2000, prof. medicine emeritus, 2000—, head cardiology divsn., 1977—95; vis. prof. medicine Dartmouth Med. Sch., 1990—2001, vis. prof. medicine and physiology, 2001—. Cons. VA, 1970; coord. Problem Area #3, US-USSR Collaboration in Cardiovasc. Rsch., 1983—86; mem. adv. com. Chinese Acad. Med. Sci., 1982—89; R.T. Hall lectr. Cardiac Soc., Australia, 1991, New Zealand, 91; chair sci. bd. Stanley J. Sarnoff Endowment Cardiovasc. Sci. Inc., 1992—93; chair, sci. adv. bd. Patrick, Catherine, Weldon, Donaghue Med. Rsch. Found., 1994—97; mem. bd. sci. counsellors Nat. Heart Lung Inst., 1989—92. Author: Physiology of the Heart, 1977, Physiology of the Heart, 3rd edit., 2001, Heart Failure: Pathophysiology, Molecular Biology and Clinical Management, 2000; editor: The Heart and Cardiovascular System, 1986, 1991; Am. Jour. Physiology, 1966—72, mem. editl. bd.: Jour. Molecular and Cellular Cardiology, 1970—92, editor-in-chief:, 1986—92, mem. editl. bd.: Am. Jour. Cardiology, 1970—75, Jour. Mechanochemistry and Cell Motility, 1970—72, Am. Jour. Medicine, 1971—77, Jour. Clin. Investigation, 1971—76, Circulation Rsch., 1974—80, Physiol. Rev., 1976—80, Cardiovasc. Pharmacol., 1979—88, Life Scis., 1979—88, Cardiology, 1980—85, Jour. Am. Coll. Cardiology, 1983—87, Can. Jour. Cardiology, 1988—91, Cardioscience, 1988—95, Circulation, 1992—, reviewer: several profl. jours.; contbr. articles to profl. jours. Served with USPHS, 1957-59. Humboldt fellow Alexander von Humboldt Found., 1975-76, Moseley traveling fellow Harvard U., 1960-61. Fellow ACP, Am. Coll. Cardiology (gov. Conn. 1984-87), Coun. on Basic Cardvasc. Sci. (charter); mem. Am. Heart assn. (advanced rsch. fellow 1961-63, established investigator 1963-68, v.p. couns. 1992-94, bd. dirs. 1992-94, chmn. coun. affairs com. 1992-94, chmn. exec. com. basic sci. coun. 1990-92, Conn. affiliate bd. dirs. 1986-94, Greater Hartford chpt. bd. dirs. 1977-84, sec. 1982-84, v.p. 1984-86, pres. 1986-88, Rsch. Achievement award 1989, Disting. Achievement award Basic Sci. Coun. 1991, award of Meritorious Achievement 1995, Honoree Louis N. and Arnold M. Katz prize Basic Sci. Coun. 1995), N.Y. Heart Assn. (bd. dirs. 1971-74, 75-77), Am. Physiol. Soc., Cardiac Muscle Soc. (pres. 1969-71), Assn. Am. Physicians, Internat. Soc. Heart Rsch. (pres. Am. sect. 1985, founding fellow 2000, Peter Harris Disting. Scientist award 2004), Assn. Univ. Cardiologists, Alpha Omega Alpha. Home: PO Box 1048 1592 New Boston Rd Norwich VT 05055-1048 E-mail: arnold.m.katz@dartmouth.edu.

KATZ, AVERY W., law educator; BA summa cum laude, U. Mich., 1980; MA in Econs., Harvard U., 1983, JD magna cum laude, 1985, PhD in Econs., 1986. Adj. asst. prof. law U. Mich., 1986—87, asst. prof. econs., 1986—93, asst. prof. law, 1987—93, prof. law, adj. assoc. prof. econs., 1993—94; vis. prof. Georgetown U. Law Ctr., 1992, 1994, prof. law, 1995—99, dir. John M. Olin Prog. in Law and Econs., 1998—99; vis. prof. law Columbia U., NYC, 1998, prof. law, 2000—04, Milton Handler prof. law, 2004—. Scholar in residence NYU Sch. Law, 2004. Author: Foundations of the Economic Approach to Law, 1998. Chair adv. bd. Tompkins Hall Nursery Sch. and Child Care Ctr., 2003—. Mem.: Am. Assn. of Law Schs. (chair, Sect. on Law and Econs.), Am. Law and Econs. Assn. (mem. bd. dirs.). Office: Columbia Law Sch 638 Jerome Greene Hall 435 W 116th St New York NY 10027 Office Phone: 212-854-0066. E-mail: avkatz@law.columbia.edu.

KATZ, AVI, lawyer; b. Boston, Jan. 15, 1959; s. I. Norman and Judith (Batt) K.; m. Rivi Kanarek, Aug. 25, 1982; children: Dena, Tamar, Yehoshua. BA, Yeshiva U., 1981; MA, Columbia U., 1984, JD, 1986. Bar: N.Y. 1987. Law clk. to Hon. Lawrence W. Pierce, U.S. Ct. Appeals for 2d Cir., N.Y.C., 1986-87; assoc. Willkie Farr & Gallagher, N.Y.C., 1987-96; assoc. gen. counsel Loral Space & Comm. Ltd., N.Y.C., 1996-97, dep. gen. counsel, 1997-98, v.p., dep. gen. counsel, 1998-99, v.p., gen. counsel, sec., 1999—. Mem. ABA, N.Y. State Bar Assn., New York County Lawyers Assn., Assn. Bar City N.Y. Home: 1460 Hudson Rd Teaneck NJ 07666-2914 Office: Loral Space & Comm Ltd 600 3rd Ave New York NY 10016-1901 Office Phone: 212-338-5340. Business E-Mail: avi.katz@hq.loral.com.

KATZ, AVRUM SIDNEY, lawyer; b. Melrose Park, Ill., Oct. 10, 1939; s. Joseph George and Bessie Goldie (Ancel) K.; m. Sheela Cara Cooperman, Sept. 1, 1963; children: Julie Anne, Aaron Richard, Michele Sharon. BSEE, Ill. Inst. Tech., 1962; JD, George Washington U., 1966. Bar: Ill. 1966, U.S. Dist. Ct. (no. dist.) Ill. 1967, U.S. Patent Office 1967, U.S. Supreme Ct. 1977, U.S. Ct. Appeals (7th cir.) 1978, D.C. 1991, cert.: U.S. Patent Office (examiner). Assoc. Leonard G. Nierman, Chgo., 1966—67, Fitch, Even, Tabin, Flannery & Welsh and predecessor firms, Chgo., 1967—70, ptnr., 1971—82, Welsh & Katz, Chgo., 1983—. Author (with others): Effective Litigation Against Knockoffs, 1984; author: Chip, Mask and Program Protection, 1985, Electronics and Computer Patent and Copyright Practice, 1988, 2d edit., 1990; mem. editl. bd. Mealey's Litig. Report on Intellectual Property, 1992—, mem. adv. bd. Licensing Jour., 1987—, The IP Litigator, 2000—. Mem. ad hoc com. Lake Forest (Ill.) City Coun., 1970; mem. intellectual property adv. bd. George Washington U. Law Sch., 2000—; bd. dirs., mem. exec. com. Midwest region Am. Friends of Hebrew U., 1999—. Recipient award of distinction, Patent Resources Group, 1983. Mem.: ABA, IEEE, Assn. Patent Law Firms (pres. 1998—99), Licensing Exec. Soc., Internat. Trademark Assn., Intellectual Property Law Assn. Chgo., Chgo. Bar Assn., Ill. Bar Assn., Std. Club Chgo., Union League Club Chgo., Sigma Iota Epsilon, Eta Kappa Nu, Tau Beta Pi, Delta Theta Phi. Home: 475 Turicum Rd Lake Forest IL 60045-3363 Office: Welsh & Katz Ltd 120 S Riverside Plz Fl 22 Chicago IL 60606-3913 Office Phone: 312-655-1500. Business E-Mail: askatz@welshkatz.com.

KATZ, BABETTE, artist; b. Roanoke, Va., Aug. 21, 1932; d. William and Dorothy (Kanter) Schneer; m. Robert B. Katz, Oct. 17, 1954; children: Dina Katz Ingersole, Lee Katz Maxwell. BA, Wellesley Coll., 1954. Author: (artist's books in over 60 pub. collections) At the Beach, 1988, Things for People to Do, 1988, Yarn, 1992, Getting There, 1992, My Flag, 1995; spl. collections libr., Met. Mus., N.Y., Mus. Modern Art, Harvard U. Libr., Yale U., UCLA, Victoria and Albert Mus., London, one-woman shows include Sarah Lawrence Coll., Esther Raushenbush Libr., 1998, N.Y. Pub. Libr., Donnell Libr. Ctr., 2001. Recipient Purchase prize, Bradley U. Nat. Print Show, Peoria, Ill., 1983, Roslyn Stern Meml. award, Audubon Artists, N.Y.C., 1984, 2d place, Phoenix Small Fine Art Internat., 1984, Pen and Brush Inc. prize, Salmagundi Club, 2005. Mem.: Ctr. Book Arts N.Y., Soc. Am. Graphic Artists. Home and Studio: 706 Fairway Ave Mamaroneck NY 10543 Office Phone: 914-698-4977.

KATZ, BARBARA STEIN, special education educator; b. Springfield, Mass., July 22, 1933; d. Harry and Pearl (Black) Stein; m. Charles Murry Katz, July 14, 1957; children: Helen Lee, Robert Alan. BS, Am. Internat. Coll., Springfield, 1956, MA in Edn1. Psychology in Learning Disabilities, 1979. Cert. in elem. edn., moderate spl. needs, Mass. Elem. tchr. Springfield Pub. Schs., 1956-60; Jr. Great Books discussion leader, 1968-69; Gillingham remedial tchr. Pub. Schs., Longmeadow, Mass., 1975-78, spl. edn. tchr. Chicopee, Mass., 1978-98, reader, 1998—2002, Pioneer Valley Collaborative, East Longmeadow, Mass., 1998—2002; ret., 2002. Pres. Kodimoh Synagogue Women's Group, Springfield, 1972-74; troop leader Girl Scouts U.S., Longmeadow, 1967-70. Horace Mann grantee, 1988. Mem. NEA, Mass. Tchrs. Assn. Avocations: painting, reading, walking, swimming. Home: 407 Bliss Rd Longmeadow MA 01106-1538 E-mail: lyncam5@aol.com.

KATZ, BRUCE ELLIOT, dermatologist; b. NYC, Apr. 12, 1951; s. Solomon and Rita (Holtz) K.; m. Carol Katz. BS, McGill U., 1973, MD, 1977. Diplomate Am. Bd. Dermatology, 1983. Intern Royal Victoria Hosp., Montreal, Canada, 1977-78; resident in internal medicine Columbia-Presbyn. Med. Ctr., NYC, 1978-79, chief resident dermatology, resident dermatology, 1979-82, dir. Dermatologic Cosmetic Surgery Clinic, assoc. attending dermatologist, Dermatology Svc.; assoc. clin. prof. Coll. of Physicians and Surgeons Columbia U.; courtesy staff St. Luke's Roosevelt Hosp. Ctr. State vice chmn. Dermatology Found., NYC, 1991; presenter in field. Editl. bd. Cosmetic Dermatology Jour.; contbr. numerous articles to profl. jours. Fellow Am. Acad. of Dermatology (public comms. com. 1994—, co-chmn. skin cancer screening NY State 1991-96), Am. Soc. for Dermatologic Surgery (minimum benefits package task force 1995—), Am. Acad. of Cosmetic Surgery, Am. Soc. for Laser Medicine and Surgery; mem. Assn. of Acad. Dermatol. Surgeons, NY State Soc. of Dermatology, Dermatol. Soc. of Greater NY (pres. 1993-94, v.p. 1992-93, scientific program chmn. 1990-93), NY Facial Plastic Surgery Soc., Dermatology Found., Skin Cancer Found., NY State Med. Soc., NY County Med. Soc.

KATZ, COLLEEN, publisher; b. Newark; BA in Math., Montclair (N.J.) Coll.; cert., Ctr. Linguistique Etrangers, Tours, France. Assoc. editor Fawcett Publs., N.Y.C., 1972-73, editor, 1973-76; editorial dir. Butterick Fashion Mktg. Co., N.Y.C., 1976-77; editor Ency. of Textiles, N.Y.C., 1979; editor in chief N.J. Monthly, Morristown, 1982-85; dir. publs. Ins. Info. Inst., N.Y.C., 1985-88; pub., editor-in-chief Journal of Accountancy, N.Y.C., 1988—. Adj. prof. Audrey Cohen Coll., 2000. Editor Ins. Rev., 1985-88; pub. mags. and newsletters AICPA, 1997—; editor Huguenot Heritage, 1999. Vol. tchr. Elizabeth (N.J.) Sch. System; vol. editor Nat. Council Jewish Women, NJ, 1967—71; vol. pub. relations worker Essex County Mental Health Assn., NJ, 1980—81. Named Woman of Yr., Cen. N.J. March of Dimes, 1984, Outstanding Alumnus, Montclair Coll., 1984; recipient Gold Cir. award Am. Soc. Assn. Execs., 1989, award for pub. excellence Comm. Concepts, 1990, Pub. Excellence award Mag. Week, 1990, Gen. Excellence award Soc. Nat. Assn. Publs., 1991, Golden Page award, 2000-01, 0102. Mem.: Conf. des Vins du Cahors, Soc. Nat. Assn. Publs. (Silver medal for gen. excellence 1997), Am. Soc. Mag. Editors, Soc. Profl. Journalists, Nat. Arts Club. Avocation: foreign languages. Office: Jour of Accountancy Harborside III Jersey City NJ 07311 E-mail: ckatz@aicpa.org.

KATZ, DAVID, gastroenterologist, educator; b. Harrisburg, Pa., Nov. 28, 1928; s. William Meyer and Fanny (Zwick) Katz; m. Shirley Eileen Love, Sept. 17, 1987; children: Jonathan, Peter, Jeremy. BS, Tulane U., 1946, MD, 1950. Intern Kings County Hosp., Bklyn., 1950-52; resident in internal medicine VA Hosp., Newington, Conn., 1952-53, West Haven, Conn., 1955, fellow in gastroenterology, 1955-56; asst. prof N.Y. Med., N.Y.C., 1958-62, assoc. prof., 1962-68, prof., 1968—, Valhalla, 1974—. Home: 100 E Hartsdale Ave Apt 6jw Hartsdale NY 10530-3846

KATZ, DAVID, lawyer; b. Freeport, NY, Oct. 1, 1963; BA magna cum laude, Brandeis U., 1985; JD cum laude, NYU Sch. Law, 1988. Bar: NY 1988. Ptnr. corp. dept. Wachtell, Lipton, Rosen, & Katz. Sr. profl. fellow NYU Ctr. Law and Bus.; prof. mgmt. Owen Grad. Sch. Mgmt., Vanderbilt U.; adj. asst. prof. NYU Sch. Law, 1992—96, adj. prof., 1996—. Mem. editl. staff: NYU Law Rev., 1986—87, note and comment editor:, 1987—88. Named Dealmaker of Yr., Am. Lawyer Mag., 2005; named one of 45 Under Forty-Five, 2003; recipient Am. Jurisprudence awards. Mem.: ABA (chmn. com. on negotiated acquisitions, mem. Fed. securities laws com.), Nat. Assn. Corp. Dirs., Am. Soc. Corp. Secretaries, NY State Bar Assn., Assn. Bar City of New York, Order of the Coif, Phi Alpha Delta. Office: Wachtell Lipton Rosen & Katz 51 W 52nd St New York NY 10019-6150 Office Phone: 212-403-1309. Office Fax: 212-403-2309. Business E-Mail: dakatz@wlrk.com.

KATZ, DAVID ALLAN, federal judge; b. Nov. 1, 1933; s. Samuel and Ruth (Adelman) K.; m. Joan G. Siegel, Sept. 4, 1955; children: Linda, Michael S., Debra. BBA, Ohio State U., 1955, JD summa cum laude, 1957. Bar: Ohio 1957. Ptnr. Spengler Nathanson, Attys., Toledo, 1957-86, mng. ptnr., 1986-93; judge U.S. Dist. Ct. (no. dist.) Ohio, Toledo, 1994—. Dir., corp. sec. Seaway Food Town, Inc., Maumee, Ohio, 1980-94; trustee St. Vincent Med. Ctr., 1987-96, sec., 1988-90, vice chmn.-treas., 1990-94, chmn., 1994-96, St. Vincent Med. Ctr. Found., chmn., 1990-92; trustee The Toledo Symphony; v.p. Jewish Edn. Service N.Am., 1985-91; trustee Mercy Health Sys. NW Ohio, 1996—. Pres. Temple B'nai Israel, Toledo, 1970-73, Jewish Welfare Fedn., Toledo, 1977-79, Toledo Bar Assn. Found., 1983-94; trustee Advocates for Victims and Justice, Inc.; bd. dirs. Toledo Zoo Found. Fellow Ohio Bar Found., Toledo Bar Found.; mem. ABA, Toledo Bar Assn. (sec., trustee 1972-78), Ohio State Bar Assn. Office: US Court House 1716 Spielbusch Ave Ste 210 Toledo OH 43624-1347 Office Phone: 419-259-7488. Business E-Mail: david.a.katz@ohnd.uscourts.gov.

KATZ, DAVID LAWRENCE, preventive medicine physician, researcher; b. L.A., Feb. 20, 1963; s. Donald I. and Susan Gail Katz; m. Catherine Sananes; children: Rebecca Wortman, Corinda, Valerie, Natalia, Gabriel. MD, Albert Einstein Coll. Medicine, 1988; MPH, Yale U., 1993; BA in French, Dartmouth Coll., 1984. Diplomate Am. Bd. Internal Medicine, Am. Bd. Preventive Medicine. Assoc. clin. prof. pub. health and medicine Yale U. Sch. of Medicine, New Haven, 1998—; dir. Yale Prevention Rsch. Ctr. Yale U. Sch. Pub. Health, Derby, Conn., 1998—. Mem. editl. bd. Am. Jour. Preventive Medicine; chmn. edn. com. Assn. Tchrs. Preventive Medicine. Author: Preventive Medicine, Epidemiology and Biostatistics, 1996 (Rising Star, American College of Preventive Medicine, 2001), Nutrition in Clinical Practice, 2000, Clinical Epidemiology and Evidence-based Medicine, 2001, The Way to Eat, 2002. Recipient numerous clin. rsch. grants, CDC, NIH, DHHS, USDA, AHA, 1996—. Fellow: Am. Coll. Preventive Medicine (bd. dirs. 2002, chmn. ann. meeting 2002, chmn. prevention practice com., N.W. regent); mem.: ACP, American College of Nutrition. Avocations: skiing, hiking, creative writing. Office: Yale Prevention Rsch Ctr 130 Division St Derby CT 06518 Office Phone: 203-732-1265. Office Fax: 203-732-1264.

KATZ, EDWARD MORRIS, banker; b. Passaic, N.J., Apr. 18, 1921; s. David and Badane (Gubersky) K.; m. Phyllis Kushner, June 20, 1948; children— David, Alan, Michael. BA, Bklyn. Coll., 1947; MA, NYU, 1948. Auditor Amalgamated Bank N.Y., N.Y.C., 1951-55, cashier, 1955-73, v.p., 1957-61, sr. v.p., 1961-71, exec. v.p., 1971-78, pres., chief exec. officer, 1978-89, dir., 1966-89, ret., 1989. Home: 48 Windsor Rd Great Neck NY 11021-2740 E-mail: phyllisedkat@aol.com.

KATZ, ELLEN D., law educator; BA summa cum laude, JD, Yale U. Judicial clk. for Justice David H. Souter US Supreme Ct.; for Judge Judith W. Rogers US Ct. Appeals, DC Cir.; dep. atty. gen. appellate div. Environment and Natural Resources Div., US Dept. Justice; asst. prof. U. Mich. Law Sch., Ann Arbor, 1999, prof. law. Contbr. articles to law jours. Mem.: Phi Beta Kappa. Office: U Mich Law Sch 909 Legal Research 625 S State St Ann Arbor MI 48109 Office Phone: 734-647-6241. Office Fax: 734-764-8309. E-mail: ekatz@umich.edu.*

KATZ, ESTHER, historian, educator; b. Aug. 14, 1948; came to U.S., 1951; d. Harry and Rose (Katz) K. AB, Hunter Coll., 1969; MA, NYU, 1973, PhD, 1980. Instr. SUNY, Brockport, 1976, NYU, 1976, Coll. New Rochelle, N.Y.C., 1981; adj. asst. prof. NYU, 1983-90, rsch. scientist, 1989—, adj. assoc. prof., 1991—. Dir., editor Margaret Sanger Papers Project, 1987—; dep. dir. Inst. for Rsch. in History, N.Y.C., 1983-87; chair bd. dirs. Ctr. Lesbian and Gay Studies CUNY, 1991-94; mem. exec. bd., Nat. History Coalition, 2003—; cons., Ford Found., 1997-98; acting dir. program in archival mgmt. and hist. editing, 1993-94. Editor: The Selected Papers of Margaret Sanger, Vol. I: The Women Rebel, 1900-1928, 2003, The Margaret Sanger Microfilm Edition, 1996, 97; co-editor: Woman's Experience in American, 1980, Procs. of Conf. on Women Surviving Holocaust, 1983; contbr. articles on history of edn., birth control, and Margaret Sanger to profl. jours. Moses Coit Taylor fellow NYU, 1976; ACLS grant-in-aid, 1989. Mem.: Am. Hist. Assn., Orgn. Am. Historians (com. on rsch. and access to hist. documents 2003—05), Assn. for Documentary Editors (exec. coun. 2001—03, pres. 2003—04, exec. coun. 2005). Office: NYU Dept History 53 Washington Sq S New York NY 10012-1098 Business E-Mail: esther.katz@nyu.edu.

KATZ, GEORGE GERSHON, psychologist; b. Aug. 3, 1927; s. Abraham Michael and Dora K.; 1 child, Esti Goodman. BA, Brooklyn Coll., 1950; JD with honors, Calif. Coll. Law, 1978; PhD with honors, N.Y. U., 1956. Diplomate Am. Bd. Clinical Psychology, Am. Bd. Forensic Psychology, Am. Bd. Profl. Psychology. Clin. assoc. U. So. Calif., Los Angeles, 1971-89; instr. Northwestern U., Evanston, Ill., 1960-64; assoc. prof. Calif. State U., Los Angeles, 1969-72; adj. prof. Fuller Inst., Pasadena, Calif., 1982-86; clin. prof. U. Calif., Los Angeles, 1974-94; dir. clin. tng. VAMC, Los Angeles, 1984-93, asst. chief psychology, 1984-94. Mem. pres.'s com. mental health edn., White House, Washington, 1972; cons. senate com. on Vets. Affairs, Washington, 1972-74, Hathaway Sch. for Children:, Calif., 1969-74; co-dir./cons. Project NOVA, L.A., 1971-72; author/presenter papers in field. Co-initiator of the unit system within VA; introduced the first ombudsman program in the VA. Oral commr. Bd. of Psychology, State of Calif., 1992—. With USCG, 1944-46. Grantee NIMH, Va., 1971-75; patient advocate VISTA program, 1973. Fellow: APA, Am. Acad. Forensic Psychology, Am. Psychol. Soc.; mem.: State Bar Calif. (chair, legal profl. com. 1998—), Am. Bd. Profl. Psychology (treas. 1992—2001, v.p. 2001—), Acad. Clin. Psychology, Am. OrthoPsychiatric Assn. Office: Forensic Psych Assocs 17337 Tramonto Dr Pacific Palisades CA 90272-3121 E-mail: bb283@lafh.org.

KATZ, GREGORY, lawyer; b. Suresnes, Seine, France, Sept. 4, 1950; came to U.S., 1960; s. Joseph and Ida (Stein) K.; m. Evelyn Katz, 1972; children: Daniel, Philip. AB, U. Pa., 1970; JD, Harvard U., 1973. Bar: N.Y. 1974, U.S. Dist. Ct. (so. dist.) N.Y. 1974. Assoc. Roth, Carlson & Spengler, N.Y.C., 1973-80; ptnr. Spengler, Carlson & Gubar, N.Y.C., 1980-92, Reid & Priest, N.Y.C., 1992-97, Thelen, Reid & Priest, N.Y.C., 1997—. Mem. Internat. ABA, Am. Arbitration Assn. (arbitrator), N.Y. Bar Assn. (com. fgn. investment in U.S.). Home: 60 East End Ave New York NY 10028-7907 Office: Thelen Reid & Priest 40 W 57th St New York NY 10019-4097

KATZ, HAROLD AMBROSE, lawyer, retired state legislator; b. Shelbyville, Tenn., Nov. 2, 1921; s. Maurice W. and Gertrude Evelyn (Cohen) K.; m. Ethel Mae Lewison, July 21, 1945; children: Alan, Barbara, Julia, Joel. AB, Vanderbilt U., 1943; JD, U. Chgo., 1948, MA, 1958. Bar: Ill. 1948. Ptnr. Katz, Friedman, Eagle Eisenstein & Johnson, Chgo., 1948—; spl. legal cons. to Gov. of Ill., 1961-63; master-in-chancery, circuit ct. Cook County, Ill., 1963-67; mem. Ill. Ho. of Reps., 1965-83, chmn. judiciary com., co-chmn. rules com. Lectr. U. Coll., U. Chgo., 1959-64; Chmn. Ill. Commn. on Orgn. of Gen. Assembly, 1966-82; del. nat. Democratic conv., 1972 Author: Liability of Auto Manufacturers for Unsafe Design of Passenger Cars, 1956; (with Charles O. Gregory) Labor Law: Cases, Materials and Comments,

1948, Labor and the Law, 1979, Harold A. Katz Memoirs, 1988; editor: Improving the State Legislature, 1967; contbr. articles to mags. Recipient Jurisprudence award, Chgo. Am. Orgn. for Rehab. through Tng., 2000, Laureate, Ill. Acad. Lawyers, 2001. Fellow Coll. Labor and Employment Lawyers; mem. ABA, Ill. Bar Assn. (chmn. labor law sect. 1979-80), Internat. Soc. for Labor Law and Social Legislation (U.S. chmn. 1961-67), Am. Trial Lawyers Assn. (chmn. workmen's compensation sect. 1963-64. Jewish. Home: 1180 Terrace Ct Glencoe IL 60022-1241 Office: Katz Friedman Eagle Eisenstein & Johnson 77 W Washington St Fl 20 Chicago IL 60602-2904 Office Phone: 312-263-6330.

KATZ, JAMES E., communications educator; PhD, Rutgers U., 1974. Post doctoral fellow Kennedy Sch. Govt. Harvard U.; post doctoral fellow Ctr. for Policy Alternatives MIT; assoc. prof. Clarkson U.; asst. prof. Lyndon B. Johnson Sch. Pub. Affairs U. Tex., Austin; disting. mem. staff Bell. Comms. Rsch.; prof. comm. Rutgers U., New Brunswick, NJ, 1997—. Editl. bd. Info: An Internat. Jour. Policy and Rsch., 1998—, Info., Comm. & Soc. (jour.), 1997—, Internet Rsch. Jour.: Tech., Policy and Applications, 1996—2001, Personal and Ubiquitous Computing, 1996—2001, Personal Tech., 2001—. Assoc. editor The Information Society, 1996—2001; author: Social Science and Public Policy in the United States, 1975, Presidential Politics and Science Policy, 1978, Congress and National Energy Policy, 1984, Sowing the Serpents' Teeth: The Implications of Third World Military Industrialization, 1986, Connections: Social and Cultural Studies of the Telephone in American Life, 1999; editor: Arms Production in Developing Countries, 1984, People in Space: Policy Perspectives for a Star Wars Century, 1985, Machines that Become Us: The Social Context of Personal Communication Technology, 2002; co-editor: Internet and Health Communication: Experience and Expectations, 2000, Perpetual Contact: Mobile Communication, Private Talk, Public Performance, 2002, Corpo Futuro: Il Corpo Umano Tra Tecnologie, Communicazione e moda, 2002; co-author: Social Consequences of Internet Use: Access, Involvement and Expression, 2002. Office: Rutgers U 4 Huntington Street New Brunswick NJ 08910

KATZ, JASON LAWRENCE, lawyer, insurance executive; b. Chgo., Sept. 28, 1947; s. Irving and Goldie (Medress) K.; 2 children. B.A., Northeastern Ill. U., 1969; J.D., DePaul U., 1973. Bar: Calif. 1976, Ariz. 1973, U.S. Ct. Appeals (9th cir.) 1976. pvt. practice, Scottsdale, Ariz., 1973-76; v.p., corp. counsel Mission Ins. Group, Inc., Los Angeles, 1976-84; exec. v.p., gen. counsel Farmers Group, Inc., Los Angeles, 1984—, bd. dirs., 1986—; v.p., bd. dirs. Calif. Def. Counsel, 1986-88. Mem. Calif. Bar Assn. (exec. bd. ins. law subcom. 1991-94), Los Angeles County Bar Assn. (mem. exec. bd. corp. law sect. 1993-94), Conf. Ins. Counsel (v.p., pres. L.A. chpt. 1981-82), Assn. Calif. Tort Reform (bd. dirs. 1990-94), The Ins. Coun. So. Calif. (City of Hope chpt. 1991-94). Office: Farmers Group Inc 4680 Wilshire Blvd Los Angeles CA 90010-3807

KATZ, JEFF, television personality; s. Harold and Doris Katz; m. Heidi Jaillet, Aug. 15, 1999; children: Harrison Tabor Jaillet, Julia Jaillet, Joseph Jaillet. Grad., Labour Coll. Can., 1993. Cert. mcpls. police officer Commonwealth of Pa. Talk show host WRKO-AM, Boston, 1996—2000, KXNT-AM, Las Vegas, 2000—01, WPHT-AM, Phila., 2001—03, Liberty Broadcasting Network, Washington, 2004, KNEW-AM, San Francisco, 2004—. Profl. pub. spkr., San Francisco, 1992—. TV host (nat. TV show) Mass Madness (Best TV Host, Nat. Wrestling Alliance, 1999). Hon. mem. bd. dirs. Media Partners for Pets, Las Vegas, 2000—01; media rels. dir. Rep. Liberty Caucus, L.A., 2004; chmn. radio & tv com. Conn. State Rep. Party, Hartford, Conn., 1993—94; rep. town committeeman South Windsor Rep. Town Com., Conn., 1993—94; nat. bd. advisors Jews Against Anti-Christian Defamation, 2005; mem. bd. chpt. leaders Rep. Jewish Coalition, Phila., 2004—05. Named Best Talk Show Host In Phila., Achievement In Radio, 2003, Man of the Yr., Shomrim Soc. Phila. and the Del. Valley, 2004; recipient Minuteman award, Conn. Taxpayers' Com., 1992, Rainbow medal, USMC League, 1995, Jack Anderson award Excellence Journalism, Calif. CCPOA, 1996, Quill and Badge award, Internat. Union of Police Associations, AFL-CIO, 1998, Best Radio Program award, Electronic Media Awards, 2001; Abraham Lincoln fellow, The Claremont Inst., 2005. Mem.: Nat. Speakers Assn., Masons (Master Mason 2004), Internat. Brotherhood Knights of Vine (Knight of the Vine 2002), Ancient and Accepted Scottish Rite (Thirty-Second Degree Mason 2004). Jewish. Avocations: wine appreciation, sailing, travel. Office: KNEW Radio 340 Townsend St San Francisco CA 94107 Personal E-mail: radiokatz@aol.com.

KATZ, JEFFREY STEVEN, education educator; b. Boston, Mass., Oct. 31, 1967; s. Alan and Deborah Katz; m. Laura Bell. BA, Ithaca Coll., 1985—89; MS, Tufts U., 1993—96, PhD, 1996—98. Assoc. prof. Auburn U., Ala., 2000—; postdoctoral fellow U. of Tex. Med. Sch. at Houston, 1998—2000; asst. prof. Auburn U., Ala., 2000—05, assoc. prof., 2005—. Recipient Young Investigator award Winner, APA Divsn. 3 (Exptl. Psychology), 2001, Early Career Tchg. award, Auburn U., Coll. Liberal Arts, 2004—05; Mechanisms of Same/Different Concept Learning by Pigeons, NSF, 2003—, Learning Processes in Matching-to-Sample by Pigeons, Nat. Inst. of Mental Health, 2001—. Mem.: APA, Am. Psychol. Soc., Psychonomics (assoc.). Office: Auburn University 226 Thach Hall Auburn AL 36849 Office Phone: 334-844-6490. Business E-Mail: katzjef@auburn.edu.

KATZ, JERI BETH, lawyer; b. Washington, Nov. 6, 1964; d. Stanley J. and Paula (Goldberg) K. BA, U. Md., 1987; JD, Cath. U., Washington, 1990. Bar: Md. 1990, D.C. 1991, U.S. Ct. Appeals (6th cir.) 1991, U.S. Ct. Internat. Trade 1992, Colo. 1994. Assoc. Winston & Strawn, Washington, 1990; ptnr. Law Offices Royal Daniel, Washington, 1990-94, Daniel & Katz, L.L.C., Breckenridge, Colo., 1994-98; pvt. practice, Breckenridge, 1998—. Mem. jud. performance commn. 5th Jud. Dist., 1998—. Mem. Breckenridge Town Coun., 1998—99; chairperson Summit County Transfer of Devel. Rights Commn., 1998—2001; mem. Breckenridge Planning Commn., 1999—2000, Breckenridge Open Space Commn., 2002; bd. dirs. Snowmass Ski Acad., 1995—98, Breckenridge Resort Chamber, 1998—. Mem. Continental Divide Bar Assn. (v.p. 1997-98), Colo. Criminal Def. Bar (rap sheet com. 1998). Home: PO Box 6602 Breckenridge CO 80424-5200 Office: PO Box 5200 101 N Main St Ste 5 Breckenridge CO 80424-6602 Office Phone: 970-453-5533. E-mail: jbkatz@earthlink.net, breckjb@gmail.com.

KATZ, JEROME CHARLES, lawyer; b. Boston, Sept. 25, 1950; s. Ralph and Thelma M. (Clark) K.; m. Nancy M. Green, Aug. 29, 1976; children: Jonathan Green, Elizabeth Rachel. AB magna cum laude, Duke U., 1972; JD, Columbia U., 1975. Bar: N.Y. 1976, U.S. Dist. Ct. (so. and ea. dists.) N.Y. 1976, U.S. Supreme Ct. 1979, U.S. Ct. Appeals (2d cir.) 1981, U.S. Dist. Ct. (we. dist.) N.Y. 1990. Assoc. Chadbourne & Parke, N.Y.C., 1975-83, ptnr., 1983—. Ct.-apptd. neutral mediator U.S. Dist. Ct. (so. dist.) N.Y., 2001—; bd. dirs. The Legal Aid Soc., 2002—; bd. trustees Citizens Budget Commn., 2003—. Assoc. editor Columbia Jour. Transnat. Law, 1974-75. Harlan Fiske Stone scholar Columbia U., 1974. Mem. ABA, Assn. of the Bar of the City of N.Y., Phi Beta Kappa. Home: 77 E 12th St New York NY 10003-5002 Office: Chadbourne & Parke 30 Rockefeller Plz Fl 31 New York NY 10112-0129 Office Phone: 212-408-5100. Business E-Mail: jkatz@chadbourne.com.

KATZ, JOEL ABRAHAM, lawyer; b. Bronx, NY, May 27, 1944; s. Harry and Hilda (Wiesenthal) K.; Kane Swims, 1994; children from previous marriage: Leslie Helaine, Jeni Michelle. BA in Econs., Hunter Coll., 1966; JD, U. Tenn., 1969. Bar: Tenn. 1969, Ga. 1971, U.S. Dist. Ct. (ea. dist.) Tenn. 1970, U.S. Dist. Ct. Appeals (11th cir.) 1971. Co-mng. shareholder, chair internat. entertainment and sports practice Greenberg Traurig LLP, Atlanta. Gen. counsel, bd. dirs. Farm Aid Inc.; spl. counsel Country Music Assn.; vice chmn. Gibson Found., Gibson Guitar Corp., Baldwin Piano Corp.; state music industry rep. State of Ga. Mem. exec. coun. T.J. Martell Found. for Leukemia Rsch., NYC, bd. dirs. Very Spl. Arts. Mem. NARAS (gen. counsel, past v.p., past nat. trustee, dir. found. bd., nat. chmn. bd. trustees, trustee Atlanta chpt., chmn. emeritus), ABA, Fed. Bar Assn., Ga. Bar Assn., Tenn. Bar Assn., Atlanta C. of C. (bd. advisors). Office: Greenberg Traurig LLP The Forum 3290 Northside Pkwy Ste 400 Atlanta GA 30327 Office Phone: 678-553-2100. Office Fax: 678-553-2212. E-mail: katzj@gtlaw.com.

KATZ, JOETTE, state supreme court justice; b. Bklyn., Feb. 3, 1953; BA, Brandeis U., 1974; JD, U. Conn., 1977; LLD (hon.), Quinnipiac U. Bar: Conn. 1977. Pvt. practice, 1977-78; asst. pub. defender Office Chief Pub. Defender, 1978-83; chief legal svcs. Pub. Defender Svcs., 1983-89; judge Superior Ct., 1989-92; assoc. justice Conn. Supreme Ct., Hartford, 1992—; adminstrv. judge Appellate Sys., Hartford, 1994-2000. Instr. U. Conn. Sch. Law, 1981-84; instr. ethics and criminal law Quinnipiac Coll. Sch. Law, 1999—; chair Evidence Code Drafting Com., Chair Adv. Com. Appellate Rules, Client Security Fund; Am. Inns Ct. (past pres. Fairfield County br.), Assn. Reproductive Tech. (mem. com.). Co-author: (book) Connecticut Criminal Caselaw Handbook: A Practitioner's Guide, 1989. Mem. Justice Edn. Ctr. Recipient Maria Miller Stewart award, Conn. Women's Education & Legal Fund, 1993, Harriet Tubman award, Nat. Orgn. for Women, 1993, Women of Distinction award, Nat. Council of Jewish Women, 2001. Mem. Am. Law Inst., Conn. Bar Assn. (Henry J. Naruk Judiciary award 2004). Office: Conn Supreme Ct 231 Capital Ave Hartford CT 06106

KATZ, JOHN, investment banker; b. Washington, Aug. 2, 1938; s. Milton and Vivian (Greenberg) K.; divorced; children: Ellen, Allison; m. Laura Cherkis, May 29, 1988; stepchildren: Ann Cherkis, Nancy Gernstetter. AB, Harvard U., 1960, JD, 1963. Bar: N.Y. 1964. With Hall, Casey, Dickler & Howley, 1963-67; asst. corp. counsel City of N.Y., 1967-69; spl. asst. to Congressman Richard L. Ottinger, 1969; with Poletti, Freidin, Prashker, Feldman & Gartner, 1969-75; atty. Equitable Life Assurance Soc. of U.S., 1975-79, v.p., counsel, 1979-82, v.p. Office of Chief Investment Officer, 1982-86; sr. v.p. Equitable Investment Corp., 1986-88, exec. v.p., 1989-91; chmn., CEO Sam's Restaurant Group, Inc., N.Y.C., 1991-92, investment banker, 1992-2000; mng. ptnr. Associated Mezzanine Investors, LLC, 2000—05, Boo Ventures, LLC, 2005—. Mem. Greater N.Y.C. Com. of Harvard Law Sch. Fund; chmn. admissions com. Harvard Club N.Y.C., 1988-89; bd. dirs. Resources for Children with Spl. Needs, Inc., 1985-98; bd. dirs. My Sisters' Place, 1995-2004, co-chmn., 1996-99, chmn., 1999-2000. Home and Office: 10 Hemlock Rd Hartsdale NY 10530-2951 E-mail: johnkatz@cloud9.net.

KATZ, JOHN W., lawyer, state official; b. Balt., June 3, 1943; s. Leonard Wallach and Jean W. (Kane) Katz; m. Joan Katz, June 11, 1969 (div. 1982); 1 child, Kimberly Erin. BA, Johns Hopkins U., 1965; JD, U. Calif., Berkeley, 1969; DDL (hon.), U. Alaska, 1994. Bar: Alaska 1971, Pa. 1971, U.S. Dist. Ct. D.C. 1971, U.S. Ct. Appeals (D.C. cir.), U.S. Tax Ct., U.S. Ct. Claims, U.S. Ct. Mil. Justice, U.S. Supreme Ct. Legis. and adminstrv. asst. to Congressman Howard W. Pollock of AK, Wash., 1969—70; legis. asst. US Sen. Ted Stevens of Alaska, Washington, 1971; assoc. McGrath and Flint, Anchorage, 1972; gen. counsel Joint Fed. State Land Use Planning Commn. for AK, Anchorage, 1972—79; spl. counsel Gov. Jay S. Hammond of Alaska, Anchorage and Washington, 1979—81; commr. Alaska Dept. Natural Resources, Juneau, 1981—83; dir. state fed. rels. and spl. counsel Gov. Bill Sheffield of Alaska, Washington and Juneau, 1983—86; dir. state-fed. rels., spl. counsel to Gov. Steve Cowper of Alaska, Washington, 1986—90, Gov. Walter J. Hickel of Alaska, Washington, 1990—94, Gov. Tony Knowles, 1994—2002, Gov. Frank Murkowski, 2002—. Mem. Alaska Power Survey Exec. Adv. Com. of FPC, Anchorage, 1972—74; com. hard rock minerals Gov.'s Coun. of Sci. and Tech., Anchorage, 1979—80; guest lectr. on natural resources U. Alaska, U. Denver. Contbr. articles to profl. jours.; columnist (Anchorage Times), 1991. Acad. supr. Alaska Externship Program, U. Denver Coll. Law, 1976—79; mem. Reagan-Bush transition team, U.S. Dept. Justice, 1980. Recipient Superior Sustained Performance award, Joint Fed. State Land Use Planning Commn. for Alaska, 1978, Resolution of Commendation award, Alaska Legis., 1988, Citation for svc. to people of Alaska, 2003, Cert. of Appreciation, Gov. of Alaska, 2004. Republican. Office: State of Alaska Office of Gov 444 N Capitol St NW Ste 336 Washington DC 20001-1529

KATZ, JON, writer, critic; b. Providence, Aug. 8, 1947; s. George and Eve Katz; m. Paula Span, Oct. 1, 1972; 1 child, Emma Katz Span. Student, George Washington U., 1965-67, The New Sch., 1967-68. Reporter, editor Phila. Inquirer, 1973-76; editor Boston Globe, 1976-78; mng. editor, editor-in-chief Balt. News Am., 1978-81; exec. prodr. CBS News, N.Y.C., 1982-86; assoc. prof. NYU, 1986-88; contbg. editor pubs. including Rolling Stone, Wired, HotWired, 1993-99; columnist, critic Slashdot.org, Andover, Mass., 1998—2002. Author: Sign Off, 1991, The Suburban Detective series Death by Station Wagon, the Family Stalker, The Last Housewife, The Fathers' Club, Death Row, Running to the Mountain, 1999, Geeks: How Two Lost Boys Rode the Internet out of Idaho, 2000, A Dog Year: Twelve Months, Four Dogs and Me, 2002. Poynter fellow Yale U., 1997, First Amendment fellow First Amendment Ctr. The Freedom Forum, 1998-2000. Address: care ICM 40 W 57th St New York NY 10019

KATZ, JOSE, cardiologist, theoretical physicist, educator; b. Havana, Cuba, June 6, 1944; s. Lipa and Victoria (Masson) K.; m. Anke Ebsen; children: Susan, David, Rachel, Hannah. BS, U. Ill., 1963, MS, 1964, PhD, 1967; MD, Free U. Berlin, 1980. Rsch. assoc. physicist U. Hamburg, Germany, 1967—69; instr. physics Purdue U., West Lafayette, Ind., 1969—71; asst. prof. physics Free U., West Berlin, Germany, 1971—74, prof. physics, 1974—82; resident in internal medicine Cleve. Met. Gen. Hosp., Mt. Sinai Med. Ctr., Cleve., 1982—85; cardiology fellow Southwestern Med. Sch., Dallas, 1985—88; asst. prof. medicine and radiology Columbia U. Coll. Physicians and Surgeons, NYC, 1988—94, assoc. prof. medicine and radiology, 1994—2003; dir. cardiovasc. MRI and spectroscopy Columbia-Presbyn. Med. Ctr., NYC, 1988—2003, co-dir. EKG lab., 1999—2003; pres., CEO, med. dir. Cardio-Med. Svcs., LLC, NJ, 2004—; pres., CEO Comprehensive Healthcare and Med. Svc. PLLC, N.Y.C., 2004—. Staff attending Columbia-Presbyn. Med. Ctr., NYC, 1988-2004 Contbr. articles to profl. jours., chpts. to books. Fellow ACP, Am. Coll. Physicians, Am. Coll. Cardiology, Am. Coll. Chest Physicians, Am. Coll. Angiology, Am. Heart Assn. (coun. clin. cardiology, coun. on cardiovasc. radiology, coun. on basic scis.), Internat. Soc. Magnetic Resonance in Medicine; mem. AMA, Radiol. Soc. N.Am., Soc. Nuc. Medicine, N.Am. Soc. Cardiac Imaging, Sigma Xi, Phi Kappa Phi, Sigma Tau, Pi Mu Epsilon, Tau Beta Pi. Office: 595 Madison Ave 27th Fl New York NY 10022 Personal E-mail: jkatz@mdadvice.com.

KATZ, JOSEPH LOUIS, chemical engineer, educator; b. Colon, Panama, Aug. 4, 1938; naturalized, 1970; s. Adolfo and Margarita (Eisen) K.; m. Liliane Capelluto, Apr. 10, 1965; children: Daniel P., Alan R. BS, U. Chgo., 1960, PhD, 1963. Amanuensis U. Copenhagen Chem. Lab. III, 1963-64; mem. tech. staff N.Am. Aviation Sci. Ctr., Thousand Oaks, Calif., 1964-70; assoc. prof. chem. engring. Clarkson Coll. Tech., Potsdam, N.Y., 1970-75, prof., 1975-79, Johns Hopkins U., Balt., 1979—, chmn. dept. chem. engring., 1981-84; dir. Energy Rsch. Inst., 1981-83. Prof. U. Aix-Marseille, France, 1976; vis. prof. MIT, Cambridge, 1977. Recipient John W. Graham Rsch. prize, Clarkson U., 1975; John Simon Guggenheim Meml. Found. fellow, 1976-77. Fellow AAAS, Am. Phys. Soc.; mem. AIChE, Am. Chem. Soc. (Md. sect. Chemist of Yr. 1982), Sigma Xi. Home: 5600 Greenspring Ave Baltimore MD 21209-4308 Office: Johns Hopkins U Dept Chem & Biomolecular Engring Baltimore MD 21218 Office Phone: 410-516-8484. Business E-Mail: jlk@sigmaxi.org.

KATZ, JULIAN, gastroenterologist, educator; b. N.Y.C., Apr. 3, 1937; s. Abraham M. and Fay (Sher) K.; m. Sheila Moriber, Aug. 18, 1963; children: Jonathan Peter, Sara Katherine. AB, Columbia U., 1958; MD, U. Chgo., 1962. Diplomate Am. Bd. Internal Medicine. Intern U. Chgo. Hosps., 1962-63; resident in medicine Duke U., 1963-65; fellow in gastroenterology Yale U., 1965—67; practice medicine specializing in gastroenterology, internal medicine and geriatrics Phila., 1969—; prof. medicine and lectr. physiology and biochemistry Med. Coll. Pa., 1970—. Prof. medicine Jefferson Med. Coll., Phila., 1988—2001; chief clin. gastroenterology Med. Coll. Pa.; lectr. in field. Editor profl. jours. and books; contbr. articles to profl. jours. and books. Mem. Bd. Health, City of Phila. With USN, 1967-69. Fellow ACP, Am. Coll. Gastroenterology; mem. Am. Soc. Gastrointestinal Endoscopy, Am. Soc. Study Liver Disease, Am. Gastroent. Assn., Phila. County Med. Soc. (pres. 1997-98), Pa. Soc. Gastroent. (pres. 1999-2001), Del. Valley Geeriatrics Soc. (pres. 2004), Digestive Disease Nat. Coalition (exec. com.) Home and Office: 701 Dodds Ln Gladwyne PA 19035-1516 Business E-Mail: jkatz@icdc.com.

KATZ, LAWRENCE SHELDON, lawyer; b. Newark, N.J., Jan. 30, 1943; s. Edward and Pearl (Weiss) K.; divorced; 1 child, Scott. BBA in Govt., U. Miami, 1965, JD, 1968. Cert.: Fla. Supreme Ct. (mediator). Assoc. Hoffman & St. Jean, Miami Beach, Fla., 1968-70, Jack R. Nageley Law Office, Miami Beach, Fla., 1970-72, Swickle, Katz & Brotman, Miami Beach, Fla., 1972-77; pvt. practice Miami Beach, Fla., 1977—90, Coconut Grove, Fla., 1990—2001, Miami, 2001—. Gen. counsel Fraternal Order of Police, Hialeah, Fla., 1972-89; gen. counsel U.S. Shooting Team Found., Colorado Springs, 1978-95, chmn., 1978-83; mem. U.S. Olympic Com. Ho. Dels., 1978-83. 2d lt. U.S. Army, 1965-69. Recipient Pres.'s award Nat. Assn. Criminal Def. Attys., 1977, 11th Cir. Pro Bono award. Mem. ABA (com. on internat. criminal law 1971-94, criminal def. function com. 1989-98, family law sect. com. on internat. law and procedure, 1996-, internat. child abduction atty. network 1997-, internat. law sect. com. on family law), NRA (bd. dirs. 1977-83), First Family Law Inn of Ct., Internat. Soc. Family Law, Fla. Sportshooting Assn. (pres. 1985), The Fla. Bar (narcotics practice com. 1988-92, mental health profl. in litigation com. 1994-96, domestic violence com. 1994-98, legislation com. 1998-2004), Acad. Fla. Trial Lawyers (vice chmn. criminal law sect.), Fla. Assn. Criminal Def. Attys. (sec. 1978-79, v.p. 1979-80), Fla. Smallbore Rifle Assn. (pres. 1968-70), Safari Club Internat. (v.p. 1992-98, sec. 1997-98, pres.-elect 1998-99, pres. 1999-2000, pres. Miami chpt. 2001-03, pres. So. Fla. chpt. 1988-90, Mem. of Yr. award 1999-2000, Presdl. award 1996, 98), Phi Epsilon Pi (pres. 1964), Phi Alpha Delta, World Forum for Future of Sportshooting (v.p. 2000-01). Jewish. Avocations: flying, photography, scuba, skiing, hunting. Office: 1 Datran Ctr Penthouse 1-Ste 1702 9100 S Dadeland Blvd Miami FL 33156-7814 Office Phone: 305-670-8656. Business E-Mail: katzlaw@bellsouth.net.

KATZ, LEANDRO, artist, filmmaker; b. Buenos Aires, June 6, 1938; came to U.S., 1965; s. Mauricio and Elisa K. BFA, U. Nacional, Buenos Aires, 1961; student, Pratt Graphic Arts Inst., N.Y.C., 1967. Faculty Sch. Visual Arts, N.Y.C., 1971—; asst. prof. Brown U., Providence, 1980-84; prof. William Paterson U., Wayne, N.J., 1987—. One person shows include Museum of Modern Art, Buenos Aires, 2003Museo del Barrio, 1996, Betty Rymer Gallery/Sch. Art Inst. Chgo., 1998, Museo de Arte Moderno, Buenos Aires, 2003; exhibited in group shows Whitney Mus. Am. Art, 1982, R.I. Sch. Design Mus., 1984, Bronx Mus. Art, 1988, New Mus. Contemporary Art, 1990; author: Es Una Ola, 1965, others; filmmaker numerous titles. Recipient Coral prize for The Day You'll Love Me, Havana L.Am. Film Festival, 1997; Meml. fellow Guggenheim Found., 1979-80, fellow NEA, 1979, 91, 94, N.Y. State Coun. on Arts, 1990, 98, Rockefeller Found., 1993; grantee Jerome Found., 1982, 90, N.Y. Found. for Arts, 1989. Home: 25 E 4th St New York NY 10003-7061 Office: William Paterson Univ Wayne NJ 07470 Office Phone: 973-720-3285. E-mail: leandrok@rcn.com.

KATZ, LEO, law educator; BA, U. Chgo., 1979, MA in Econs., JD with honors, U. Chgo., 1982. Law clk. to Hon. Anthony M. Kennedy Ninth Cir. Ct. Appeals, 1982—83; assoc. Mayer, Brown and Platt, 1984—87; asst. prof. law U. Mich. Law Sch., 1987—91; prof. law U. Pa. Law Sch., Phila., 1991—. Vis. prof. Goethe U., Frankfurt, 1995. Author: Bad Acts and Guilty Minds: Conundrums of the Criminal Law, 1987, Ill-Gotten Gains: Evasion, Blackmail, Fraud, and Kindred Puzzles of the Law, 1996, Foundations of Criminal Law, 1999; contbr. articles to law jours. Vis. scholar U. Calif, Berkeley, 1999, Australian Nat. U., 2000. Office: U Pa Law Sch 3400 Chestnut St Philadelphia PA 19104 Office Phone: 215-898-9334. Office Fax: 215-573-2025. E-mail: lkatz@law.upenn.edu.*

KATZ, LEONARD, psychology professor, researcher; b. Boston, Mar. 6, 1938; s. William and Ruth K.; m. Barbara A. Mahoney, May 28, 1962; children: Nicholas, Stephen, Alexis. BS, U. Mass., 1959, PhD, 1963. Postdoctoral fellow Stanford (Calif.) U., 1963-65; prof. psychology U. Conn., Storrs, 1965—; researcher Haskins Labs., New Haven, 1974—. Contbr. articles to profl. jours. Fulbright fellow, Yugoslavia, 1986. Fellow Am. Psychol. Soc., Am. Assn. Advancement of Sci. Office: U Conn Dept Psychology Wab U 20 Storrs Mansfield CT 06269-1020 Business E-Mail: leonard.katz@uconn.edu.

KATZ, LEWIS ROBERT, law educator; b. NYC, Nov. 15, 1938; s. Samuel and Rose (Turoff) K.; m. Jan Karen Daugherty, Jan. 14, 1964; children: Brett Elizabeth, Adam Kenneth, Tyler Jessica. AB, Queens Coll., 1959; JD, Ind. U., 1963. Bar: Ind 1963, Ohio 1971. Assoc. Snyder, Bunger, Cotner & Harrell, Bloomington, Ind., 1963-65; instr. U. Mich. Law Sch., Ann Arbor, 1965-66; asst. prof. Case Western Res. U. Law Sch., Cleve., 1966-68, assoc. prof., 1968-71, prof., 1971—, John C. Hutchins prof. law, 1973—. Dir. Ctr. for Criminal Justice, Case Western Res. U., 1973-91, dir. fgn. grad. studies, 1992—; cons. criminal justice agys. Author: Justice is the Crime, 1972, The Justice Imperative: Introduction to Criminal Justice, 1979, Ohio Arrest Search and Seizure, 2005; (with J. Shapiro) New York Suppression Manual, 1991, Know Your Rights, 1994; (with P.C. Giannelli, B. Blair, J. Lipton) Ohio Criminal Law, 2d edit., 2003; (with P.C. Giannelli) Ohio Criminal Justice, 2005; (with B.W. Griffin) Ohio Felony Sentencing Law, 2004, (with N.P. Cohen) Questions and Answers: Criminal Procedure, 2003. Mem. regional bd. Anti-Defamation League; trustee Women's Law Fund. Recipient Disting. Tchr. award Case West Res. U. Law Alumni Assn., Tchr. of Yr. award Case Western Res. U., 1999; Nat. Defender Project of Nat. Legal Aid and Defender Assn. fellow, 1968 Mem. ABA. Home: 29550 S Woodland Rd Pepper Pike OH 44124-5743 Office: Case Western Res U Law Sch Law Sch Cleveland OH 44106 Office Phone: 216-368-3287. Business E-Mail: lewis.katz@case.edu.

KATZ, LOIS ANNE, internist, nephrologist; b. Rockville Centre, N.Y., Dec. 1, 1941; d. Irvin Martin and Frances (Berenstein) Fradkin; m. Arthur A. Katz, Aug. 18, 1962; children: David, Brian. BA, Wellesley Coll., 1962; MD, NYU, 1966. Diplomate Am. Bd. Internal Medicine, Am. Bd. Nephrology. Intern medicine Bellevue Hosp., NYU, N.Y.C., 1966-67, resident medicine, 1967-68; sr. resident medicine N.Y. Hosp., N.Y.C., 1968-69; from chief resident medicine to assoc. chief staff N.Y. VA Med. Ctr., N.Y.C., 1969—2000, assoc. chief of staff spl. emphasis programs and quality mgmt., 2000—; asst. prof. clin. medicine NYU Sch. Medicine, N.Y.C., 1974-79, assoc. prof., 1979-94, prof. clin. medicine, 1994—2002, prof. medicine, 2002—. Fellow: ACP; mem.: Am. Soc. Hypertension, Women in Nephrology (treas. 1985—89), Soc. Gen. Internal Medicine, Am. Med. Women's Assn., Am. Soc. Nephrology, Wellesley Coll. Alumnae Assn. (region 2 admission rep. 1997—2001), Sigma Xi, Alpha Omega Alpha. Jewish. Avocations: reading, swimming, cooking, music. Office: Dept Vets Affairs NY Harbor Healthcare System 423 E 23rd St New York NY 10010-5013 Office Phone: 212-951-6875.

KATZ, MARC D., apparel executive; Fin. analyst Contel Svc. Corp.; various fin. positions May Dept. Stores Co., 1989—97; retail contr. Foot Locker Inc., 1997—99, contr., 1999—2001, v.p., contr., 2001—02, v.p. CIO, 2002—03, sr. v.p., CIO, 2003—. Office: 112 W 34th St New York NY 10120*

KATZ, MARTHA LESSMAN, lawyer; b. Chgo., Oct. 28, 1952; d. Julius Abraham and Ida (Oiring) Lessman; m. Richard M. Katz, June 27, 1976; children: Julia Erin, Meredith Evin. AB, Washington U., St. Louis, 1974; JD, Loyola U., Chgo., 1977. Bar: Ill. 1977, U.S. Dist. Ct. (no. dist.) Ill. 1977, Calif. 1981, U.S. Dist. Ct. (so. dist.) Calif. 1981, U.S. Dist. Ct. (no. dist.) Calif. 1982, Md. 1993, U.S. Supreme Ct. 1993, D.C. 1994. Assoc. Fein & Hanfling, Chgo., 1977-80, Rudick, Platt & Victor, San Diego, 1981-82, 84-91; asst. sec., counsel Itel Corp., San Francisco, 1982-84; ptnr. Katz & Mann, 1991—95; with legal dept. U.S. Fidelity and Guaranty Co., 1995-99; prin. intellectual property and tech., life scis., biotech. and pharm. Miles &

Stockbridge PC, Balt., 1999—. Mem. Greater Balt. com. Tech. Coun.; mem. High Tech. Md. Mem. Calif. State Bar Assn., Md. Bar Assn. (spl. com. on tech.), Ill. State Bar Assn., Bar Assn. Balt. City (tech. com.), Bar Assn. D.C., Phi Beta Kappa. Jewish. Office: 10 Light St Baltimore MD 21202-1435 Office Phone: 410-385-3570. Office Fax: 410-385-3700. Business E-Mail: mkatz@milesstockbridge.com.

KATZ, MICHAEL, pediatrician, educator; b. Lwow, Poland, Feb. 13, 1928; arrived in U.S., 1946, naturalized, 1951; s. Edward and Rita (Gluzman) Katz; m. Robin J. Roy, July 19, 1986; 1 child, Edward Alexander. AB, U. Pa., 1949, postgrad. (Harrison fellow), 1950—51; MD, SUNY, Bklyn., 1956; MS, Columbia U. Sch. Public Health, 1968. Intern UCLA Med. Ctr., 1956—57; resident Presbyn. Hosp. (Babies Hosp.), N.Y.C., 1960—62, dir. pediatric svc., 1977—92, cons., 1992—; hon. lectr. pediat. Makerere U. Coll., Kampala, Uganda, 1963—64; instr. in pediat. Columbia U., 1964—65, prof. tropical medicine Sch. Pub. Health, 1971—92, prof. pub. health emeritus, 1992—, prof. pediat. Coll. Physicians and Surgeons, 1972—77, prof. pub. health, 1977—92, Reuben S. Carpentier prof., 1977—92, Reuben S. Carpentier prof. emeritus, 1992—; sr. v.p. for rsch. and global programs March of Dimes Birth Defects Found., White Plains, NY, 1992—. Assoc. mem. Wistar Inst., Phila., 1965—71; asst. prof. pediat. U. Pa., 1966—77; cons. WHO, Guatemala, Venezuela, Egypt, Yemen; mem. U.S. del. 32d World Health Assembly, Geneva, 1979; cons. UNICEF, N.Y.C., Tokyo, USAID, Egypt, 1982, Poland, 87; mem. bd. sci. councillors Nat. Inst. Dental Rsch., 1986—90, chmn., 1990—92; vis. prof. U. Würzburg, Germany, 1988; vis. prof. pediat. U. Negev, Beer Sheva, Israel, 1996. Author (with others): Parasitic Diseases, 1982, 2d edit., 1989; editor (with Volker ter Meulen): Slow Virus Infections of the Central Nervous System, 1977; mem. editl. bd.: Med. Microbiology and Immunology, 1975—90, Pediatric Infectious Diseases Jour., 1981—92, Vaccines, 1983—94; co-editor: Manuals in Pediatrics; contbr. articles to profl. jours. Pres. World Allaince of Orgns. for the Prevention of Birth Defects, Inc., 1995—. Lt. M.C. USNR, 1957—59. Recipient Jurzykowski Found. award in Medicine, 1983, Alexander von Humboldt Sr. U.S. Scientist award, 1988; grantee, NIH, 1968—76, WHO, 1972—76. Fellow: AAAS, Am. Acad. Pediat., Infectious Diseases Soc. Am.; mem.: Eastern Soc. for Pediatric Rsch., Inst. Medicine of NAS, World Alliance of Orgns. for the Prevention of Birth Defects (pres. 1995—), Pediatric Infectious Disease Soc., Royal Soc. Tropical Medicine and Hygiene (London), Deutsche Gesellschaft für Neuropathologie und Neuroanatomie E.V. (corr.), N.Y. Soc. Tropical Medicine (pres. 1976—77), Am. Soc. Tropical Medicine and Hygiene, Am. Soc. Microbiology, Harvey Soc., Am. Pediatric Soc., Soc. Pediatric Rsch., Sigma Xi. Home: 1 Griggs Ln Chappaqua NY 10514-1404 Office: March of Dimes Birth Defects Fdn 1275 Mamaroneck Ave White Plains NY 10605-5298 Office Phone: 914-997-4555. Personal E-mail: robinroy@optonline.net. Business E-Mail: mkatz@marchofdimes.com.

KATZ, MICHAEL JEFFERY, lawyer; b. Detroit, May 11, 1950; s. Wilfred Lester and Bernice (Ackerman) K. BE with honors, U. Mich., 1972; JD, U. Colo., 1976; cert. mgmt., U. Denver, 1985, cert. fin. mgmt., 1990. Bar: Colo. 1978. Rsch. atty., immigration specialist Colo. Rural Legal Svcs., Denver, 1976-77, supervising atty. migrant farm lab., 1977-78; ind. contractor Colo. Sch. Fin., Denver, 1978-79; sole practice Denver, 1978-86; assoc. Levine and Pitler, P.C., Denver, 1986-88; gen. counsel, sec. Grease Monkey Internat., Inc., Denver, 1988-92; prin. Katz & Co., Denver, 1992—; ptnr. Corprorn, Eyler & Katz LLC, Denver, 1999—. Lectr. on incorporating small bus. and real estate purchase agreements Front Range Coll., 1986—, condr. various seminars on real estate and landlord/tenant law, 1980—; lectr. on real estate Lorman Ednl. Svcs., Inc., 2001--; of counsel Levine and Pitler, P.C., Englewood, Colo., 1985—. Contbr. Action Line column Rocky Mountain News; contbr. articles to profl. jours. Mem. ATLA, Am. Arbitration Assn. (mem. panel of arbitrators 1989), Denver Bar Assn. (mem. law day com. 1985—, mem. real estate com. 1980—, mem. pro bono svcs. com. 1984—), Colo. Assn. Bus. Intermediaries, U.S. Yacht Racing Assn., Dillon Yacht Club. Avocations: sailing, bicycling, swimming, art collecting, reading. Office: 13710 E Rice Pl Aurora CO 80015-1058 Office Phone: 303-768-8004. Business E-Mail: bizlaw@ix.netcom.com.

KATZ, MICHAEL RAY, Slavic languages educator; b. NYC, Dec. 9, 1944; s. Louis M. and Alice (Gordon) K.; m. Mary K. Dodge, Nov. 19, 1978; 1 child, Rebecca Marie Dodge-Katz BA, Williams Coll., 1966; MA, Oxford U., 1968, PhD, 1972. From asst. to assoc. prof. Williams Coll., Williamstown, Mass., 1972-83; prof., chmn. dept. Slavic langs. U. Tex., Austin, 1984-97, dir. Russian, East European and Eurasian studies; dean lang. schs. and schs. abroad Middlebury (Vt.) Coll., 1998—2004, C.V. Starr prof. Russian studies, 2005—. Author: The Literary Ballad in Early 19th Century Russian Literature, 1976, Dreams and the Unconscious in Russian Literature, 1984; translator: Who Is To Blame? (A. Herzen), 1984, Notes from Underground (Dostoevsky), 1989, What Is To Be Done: (Chernyshevsky), 1989, Tolstoy's Short Fiction, 1991, Devils (Dostoevsky), 1992, Polina Saks (Druzhinin), 1992, Fathers and Sons (Turgenev), 1994, Antonina (Turgenev), 1997, Prologue (Chernyshevsky), 1995, Antonina (Tur), 1997, Sanin (Artsybashev), 2001, The Five (Jabotinsky), 2005. NEH grant, 1981-82; recipient Max Haywood Translation prize, 1982. Mem. Am. Assn. Advancement Slavic Studies, Am. Assn. Tchrs. Slavic and East European Langs. (v.p. 1989-92, pres.-elect 1995-96, pres. 1997-98, past pres. 1999-2000), Am. Coun. Tchrs. of Russian (bd. dirs. 1984-2001), Assn. Dept. of Fgn. Langs. (exec. com. 2000-02). Avocations: flute, jogging. Home: 1712 Sperry Rd Middlebury VT 05753-9442 Office: Middlebury Coll FIC 6 Middlebury VT 05753 Office Phone: 802-443-5122. Business E-Mail: mkatz@middlebury.edu.

KATZ, MITCHELL H., city health department administrator; b. 1959; BS, Yale U., New Haven, Conn.; MD, Harvard U. Med. Sch., Cambridge, Mass., 1986. Attending physician San Francisco Gen. Hosp., AIDS Clinic; chief, rsch., AIDS office San Francisco Dept. Pub. Health, dir., AIDS Office, 1992—97, interim dir., health, 1997—98, dir., health, 1998—.

KATZ, NICHOLAS M., mathematician; b. Balt., Dec. 7, 1943; BA, John Hopkins U., 1964; MA, Princeton U., 1965, PhD, 1966. Instr. Math. Dept., Princeton U., 1966—67, lectr., 1967—68, asst. prof., 1968—71, assoc. prof., 1971—74, prof., 1974—, dept. chair, 2002—. Author: Exponential Sums and Differential Equations, 1990, numerous other math. works. Recipient Conant prize, AMS, 2003; fellow, Sloan, 1971, JSPS, 1983, Guggenheim, 1975, 1987; postdoctoral fellowship, NATO, 1968. Mem.: Am. Acad. Arts and Scis., Nat. Acad. Scis. Office: Princeton U Math Dept Fine Hall Washington Rd Princeton NJ 08544-1000

KATZ, REUVEN J., lawyer; b. Cin., 1924; m. Catherine S. Katz; children: Stewart, Sharon. BA, U. Cin., 1988, LHD (hon.), 2001; JD, Harvard Law Sch., 1950. Bar: Ohio 1950. Assoc. and ptnr. Paxton & Seasongood; pvt. practice Reuven J. Katz Co., L.P.A.; ptnr. Katz, Teller, Brant & Hild, 1980—. Pres. Big Brothers Assn. Cin., Coun. Aging Cmty. Chest; bd. mem. Johnny Bench Scholarship Fund, Greater Cin. Found., Jewish Vocat. Svc., Shetlering Oaks Hosp.; past chmn. bd. U. Cin. Found. Officer USAAF, World War II. Named one of Top 50 Lawyers Cin., Law and Politics Media, Inc., Top 100 Lawyers Ohio; recipient Lifetime Achievement award in Law, Cin. Bar Found., 1999, Chairman's award, U. Cin. Found., 1999. Mem.: Sports Lawyers Assn. (bd. mem.), Tournament Players Club Rivers Bend (bd. gov.), Palm Beach Polo and Country Club, Cin. Country Club, U. Club Cin. Avocations: golf, tennis, theater. Office: Katz Teller Brant & Hild 255 E Fifth St Ste 2400 Cincinnati OH 45202-4787 Office Phone: 513-721-4532. Business E-Mail: rkatz@katzteller.com.

KATZ, RICHARD JON, marketing and advertising company executive; b. Bklyn., Feb. 26, 1932; s. Irving Paul and Lillian Katz; m. Helene Borow, June 7, 1953; children: Robin Lee, Juli Beth, Jennifer Sue. AAS, Bklyn. Coll., 1960. Pres., creative dir. Katz, Jacobs & Douglas Advt., NYC, 1960—75, KLN Advt., NYC, 1975—78, Ric Katz & Assocs. Inc., NYC, 1978—, Pres., chief exec. officer Rams Mktg. Inc., N.Y.C., 1978-90; pres., creative dir. The Ramstar Group Advt., 1986-95; cons. Pinnacle Mktg. & Resources, Inc., 1990; COB Fitness Clinic for Ageless Dynamics; CEO World Digital Deliverance Techs., LLC, 1997; lectr. Fashion Inst. Tech., NYU; bd. dirs. Palletnet. Co-author: Professional Guidelines for Effective Advertising, 1960. Trustee inst. geriatric care New Sch. for Rsch., Hunter, N.Y., The Parker Jewish Inst. Geriatric Care; bd. dirs. Palletnet. Served with USAF, 1951-55. Recipient awards for creativity, graphics, design and mktg. Mem. Am. Mgmt. Assn., Presidents Club. Home: 7227 Montrico Dr Boca Raton FL 33433-6931 Personal E-mail: richardktz@aol.com.

KATZ, ROBERT JAMES, lawyer; b. N.Y.C., Nov. 24, 1947; s. Seymour Milton and Naomi Bernice (Norek) K.; m. Jane Nan Lisman, Aug, 12, 1970; children: James Nicholas, Emily Austen. BA, Cornell U., 1969; JD magna cum laude, Harvard U., 1972; postdoctoral, London Sch. Econs., 1972-73. Bar: N.Y. 1973, U.S. Dist. Ct. (ea. and so. dists.) N.Y. 1973, U.S. Ct. Appeals (2d cir.) 1973, U.S. Supreme Ct. 1981. Law clk. to chief judge U.S. Ct. Appeals (2d cir.), N.Y.C., 1973; assoc. Sullivan & Cromwell, N.Y.C., 1974-80, ptnr., 1980-88; ptnr., gen. counsel Goldman, Sachs and Co., N.Y.C., 1988—2000, sr. counsel, 2000—01, spl. counsel, adv. dir., 2001—04, sr. dir., 2004—. Trustee Cornell U., Ithaca, N.Y., Shoah Visual History Found.; chair Horace Mann Sch.; trustee emeritus Allen-Stevenson Sch.; bd. dirs. Achilles Track Charity. Knox fellow Harvard U., 1972. Mem. ABA, N.Y. State Bar Assn., Assn. Bar City N.Y., Fed. Bar Coun., Cornell Club, Harvard Club (N.Y.C.). Office: Goldman Sachs & Co One NY Plaza New York NY 10004-2456

KATZ, ROBERT NATHAN, ceramics engineer, educator; b. Williamsport, Pa., Sept. 2, 1939; s. Louis and Rose Bernice (Golbitz) K.; m. Barbara Kurn Rubin, June 15, 1986; children: Pamela Lynn, Jonathan Adam. SB, MIT, 1961, PHD, 1969; MS, U. Mich., 1963. Rsch. asst. U. Mich., 1961-62; metallurgist Army Materials Rsch. Agy., Watertown, Mass., 1962-65; ceramic engr. Army Materials Tech. Lab., Watertown, 1965-70, chief ceramics rsch. divsn., 1970-87, chief materials technologist, 1987-95; prin. R. Nathan Katz Assocs., 1995—. Norton assoc. prof. mech. engring. Worcester (Mass.) Poly. Inst., 1990—91, Norton rsch. prof., 1991—2003, rsch. prof., 2004—; apptd. spl. mem. grad. faculty U. Md., 2000—02; liaison mem. various coms. Nat. Materials Adv. Bd.; participant Nat. Rsch. Coun., Bd. of Army Sci. and Tech., Star-21, Strategic Techs. for the Army of the 21st Century study, 1988—92, Nat. Acad. Sci. Naval Studies Bd., Future Carrier Tech. Study, 1990—91, Nat. Acad. Sci., Nat. Materials Adv. Bd., Materials Rsch. for Def.-After-Next study, 2001—02; external examiner Bd. Grad. Studies, U. Cambridge, England, 1979; cons. Dept. Def., Dept. Energy, Congl. Office of Tech. Assessment; mem. U.S. del. NATO Com. on Challenges of Modern Soc., 1974; mem. organizing com., lectr. NATO Advanced Study Inst. Nitrogen Ceramics, 1976, 81. Editor: Ceramics for High Performance Applications, 1974, Vol. II, 1978, Vol. III, 1983; mem. editl. bd. Internat. Jour. High Tech. Ceramics, 1984-89, Jour. European Ceramic Soc., 1989-; columnist Ceramic Industry Mag., 1999-2001; contbr. articles to tech. publs. Trustee Temple Israel of Natick, 1979-80, Temple Beth Zion, Brookline, 1998-, chmn., 1999-2003; Eagle Scout, BSA, Troop 65, Scranton, Pa., 1956. Recipient Tech. Writing award, Dept. Army, 1981, Mass. Rep. of Yr. award, Nat. Rep. Congl. Com., 2002. Fellow Am. Ceramic Soc.; mem. Nat. Inst. Ceramic Engrs., New Eng. Ceramic Soc. (F.H. Norton award 1978), Am. Soc. Metals, Sigma Xi. Home: 1731 Beacon St Apt 1403 Brookline MA 02445-5329 Office: Dept Mech Engring Worcester Polytechnic Inst Worcester MA 01609 Business E-Mail: katz@wpi.edu.

KATZ, ROGER, pediatrician, educator, allergist, immunologist; b. Menominee, Mich., Feb. 23, 1938; s. Peter W. and Mae C. (Chudacoff) Katz; children: Carl, Gary, Robyn. BS, U. Wis., 1960; MD, U. Louisville, 1965. Diplomate Am. Bd. Allergy and Immunology, Am. Bd. Pediatric Allergy, Am. Bd. Pediat. Clin. prof. pediat. UCLA, 1978—. Spkr. in field; expert legal evaluator. Author and editor sci. books and manuscripts. Maj. U.S. Army, 1970-72. Named One of Best Drs. in Am., 1996, 97, 2001, 02. Fellow Am. Acad. Allergy, Asthma and Immunology, Am. Coll. Allergy, Asthma and Immunology (bd. regents 1990-93), Am. Acad. Pediat., Am. Coll. Chest Physicians, Joint Coun. Allergy, Asthma and Immunology (pres. 1986-90). Office: UCLA Med Ctr 1304 15th St # 102 Santa Monica CA 90404-1810 Office Phone: 310-393-1550.

KATZ, RONALD ALAN, dermatologist; b. St. Joseph, Mo., July 13, 1942; s. Walter and Mildred (Talman) K.; m. Jane Ellen Markin, Dec. 26, 1968; children: Jennifer Lynn, Hilary Beth. BS, U. Cin., 1964; MD, U. Md., 1969. Diplomate Am. Bd. Dermatology. Intern Childrens Nat. Med. Ctr., Washington, 1969-70; resident Yale U., New Haven, Conn., 1972-75, chief resident in dermatology, 1974-75; pvt. practice College Park, Md., 1975—. Clin. prof. dermatology and pediats. George Washington U., 1975—. Contbr. articles to profl. jours. Founding vol. U.S. Meml. Holocaust Mus., Washington, 1993-96. Lt. comdr. USPHS, 1970-72. Named Outstanding Physician Specialist, Consumer Checkbook, 1998, 2002; named one of Top Doctors, Washingtonian, 1993, 1995, 1999, 2002, Best Doctors in Am., 2001, 2002, 2005. Mem. AMA, Md. State Med. Soc., Prince George's County Med. Soc., Washington Dermatol. Soc. pres. 1990-91), Am. Acad. Dermatology, Soc. for Pediatric Dermatology, Soc. for Investigative Dermatology, Alpha Omega Alpha. Democrat. Jewish. Avocations: photography, running marathons. Home: 9304 Sprinklewood Ln Potomac MD 20854-2257 Office: 6201 Greenbelt Rd College Park MD 20740-2354 E-mail: ronaldk204@aol.com.

KATZ, RONALD LEWIS, physician, educator; b. Bklyn., Apr. 22, 1932; s. Joseph and Belle (Charnis) K.; children: Richard Ian, Laura Susan, Margaret Karen. BA, U. Wis.-Madison, 1952; MD, Boston U., 1956; postgrad. in Pharmacology (NIH fellow), Coll. Physicians and Surgeons, Columbia U., 1959-60; postgrad. (John Simon Guggenheim fellow), Royal Postgrad. Med. Sch., U. London, 1968-69. Intern USPHS Hosp., S.I., 1956-57; resident Columbia-Presbyn. Med. Center, 1957-60; asst. prof. anesthesiology Coll. Physicians and Surgeons, Columbia U., 1960-66, assoc. prof., 1966-70, prof., 1970-73; prof., chmn. dept. anesthesiology UCLA, 1973-90, prof. anesthesiology, 1990-94, chief staff Med. Ctr., 1984-86; prof., chmn. dept. anesthesiology U. So. Calif., L.A., 1995—2000, prof., 1995—. Cons. NIH, FDA, numerous state agys. Author, editor: Muscle Relaxants, 1975; Contbr. numerous articles to profl. jours.; Mem. editorial bd.: Handbook of Anesthesiology, 1972—, Progress in Anesthesiology, 1973—; editor in chief Seminars in Anesthesia, 1982—. Mem. Am. Soc. Anesthesiologists, Am. Physiol. Soc., Am. Soc. Pharmacology and Exptl. Therapeutics, N.Y. Acad. Medicine; Faculty Anaesthetists of Royal Coll. Surgeons of Eng. Achievements include inventor peripheral nerve stimulator. Home: 2910 Neilson Way Apt 407 Santa Monica CA 90405-5323 Office: U So Calif Dept Anesthesiology Health Sci Campus 1200 N State St Rm 14901 Los Angeles CA 90033-1029 Office Phone: 310-222-3471.

KATZ, RONALD SCOTT, lawyer; b. Norwich, Conn., Dec. 14, 1946; s. Irving David and Joan (Lebovitz) K.; m. Ann Lisa Mark, Dec. 27, 1969; children: Benjamin, Cynthia. BA, Johns Hopkins U., 1968; JD, Columbia U., 1972. Bar: N.Y. 1972, U.S. Ct. Appeals (2d cir.) 1974, U.S. Ct. Appeals (4th cir.) 1993. Assoc. Golenbock & Barell, N.Y.C., 1972—80, ptnr., 1981—89, Whitman & Ransom, N.Y.C., 1990—93, Blank Rome LLP, N.Y.C., NY, 2005—; shareholder, dir. Shack Siegel Katz & Flaherty PC, N.Y.C., 1993—2005. Mem. ABA, N.Y. State Bar Assn. Home: 16 Paxford Ln Scarsdale NY 10583-3318 Office: Blank Rome LLP 405 Lexington Ave New York NY 10174 Office Phone: 212-885-5170. Business E-Mail: rkatz@blankrome.com.

KATZ, SAMUEL, retired geophysics educator; b. Berlin, Feb. 13, 1923; came to U.S., 1934, naturalized, 1940; s. Herman and Bertha (Low) K.; m. Jean Barbara Parker, July 10, 1953; children— David R., Daniel M., Miriam E. BS, U. Mich., 1943; A.M., Columbia, 1947, PhD, 1955. With radiation lab. Mass. Inst. Tech., 1943-46; mem. sci. staff Lamont Geol. Obs., Columbia, 1948-53; sr. physicist Stanford Research Inst., 1953-57; mem. faculty Rensselaer Poly Inst., 1957—, prof. geophysics, 1962-86, prof. emeritus, 1986—, chmn. dept. geology, 1964-69; ret., 1986. Contbr. articles in field to profl. jours. Mem. Am. Geophys. Union, AAAS, Sigma Xi. Home: 908 Karenwald Ln Schenectady NY 12309-6416

KATZ, SAMUEL LAWRENCE, pediatrician, researcher; b. Manchester, N.H., May 29, 1927; s. Morris and Ethel (Lawrence) Katz; m. Betsy Jane Cohan, June 27, 1950; children: Samuel Lawrence Jr.(dec.), John S.L., David L., Deborah Susan, William L., Susan Johanna, Penelope Jennifer; m. Catherine Minock Wilfert, July 23, 1971; stepchildren: Rachel Ann, Katie Claiborne. AB magna cum laude, Dartmouth Coll., 1948; MD cum laude, Harvard U., 1952; DSc (hon.), Georgetown U., 1996, Dartmouth Coll., 1998. Intern Beth Israel Hosp., Boston, 1952—53; resident Children's Hosp., Boston, 1953—54, 1955—56, Mass. Gen. Hosp., 1954—55; from rsch. fellow to asst. prof. Harvard Med. Sch., 1956—68; prof., chmn. dept. pediat. Duke Med. Sch., 1968—90, Wilburt C. Davison prof., 1972—97. Mem. sci. adv. bd. Hasbro Children's Found., St. Jude's Children's Rsch. Hosp.; rschr. on virology, virus vaccines and immunization NIH couns. and study sects. WHO; chmn. India-U.S. Vaccine Action Program (VAP), 1999—2004; chmn. adv. com. immunization practice Ctrs. for Disease Control, Atlanta, 1985—93. Developer (with John F. Enders) attenuated live measles-virus vaccine; contbr. chapters to books, articles to profl. jours. Chmn. bd. trustees Internat. Vaccine Inst., Seoul, Republic of Korea, 2003—. With USNR, 1945—46. Recipient Rsch. Career Devel. award, NIH, 1965—68, Presdl. medal of achievement, Dartmouth Coll., 1991, Sabin Gold medal, Albert Sabin Vaccine Inst., 2003, Duke U. Founder's medal, 2004; fellow, Nat. Found., 1956—58. Mem.: APHA (Needleman medal and award 1997), Inst. Medicine of NAS, Pediat. Infectious Diseases Soc. (Disting. Physician award 1991), Assn. Med. Sch. Pediat. Dept. Chmn. (pres. 1977—79), Am. Acad. Pediat. (Grulee award 1975, Jacobi award 1986), Am. Assn. Immunologists, Infectious Diseases Soc. Am. (co-chmn. vaccine initiative 1998—99, co-chmn. nat. network for immunization info. 1999—2003, Bristol award 1988, Soc. citation 1993), New Eng. Pediat. Soc., Am. Pediat. Soc. (pres. 1986—87, St. Geme award 1988, Howland award 2000), Soc. Pediat. Rsch., Am. Soc. Clin. Investigation, Am. Fedn. Clin. Rsch. Home: 1917 Wildcat Creek Rd Chapel Hill NC 27516-9786 Office: Duke U Med Ctr PO Box 2925 Durham NC 27710-0001 Office Phone: 919-668-4852, 919-684-3734. Office Fax: 919-681-8934. Business E-Mail: katz0004@mc.duke.edu.

KATZ, SANFORD NOAH, lawyer, educator; b. Holyoke, Mass., Dec. 23, 1933; m. Joan Raphael; children: Daniel, Andrew. BA in History with distinction, Boston U., 1955; JD, U. Chgo., 1958; postgrad., Yale U., 1963-64. Bar: D.C. 1959, U.S. Supreme Ct. 1963, Mass. 1970. Law clk. to chief judge U.S Ct. Claims, Washington, 1958-59; from instr. to assoc. prof. Cath. U. Sch. Law, 1959—64; assoc. prof. U. Fla., 1964-66, prof., 1966-68, Boston Coll., 1968-2000, Libby prof. law, 2000—. Vis. prof. U. Mich., summer 1967; lectr. in law and social work Smith Coll., summers 1965-69; assoc. Clare Hall, Cambridge (Eng.) U., 1973; mem. Faculty of Laws, 1973; vis. fellow Hampstead Child Therapy Clinic, London, 1973, All Souls Coll., Oxford U., 1997, Pembroke Coll., Oxford U., 2000; del. White House Conf. on Children, 1970; mem. Spl. Adv. Com. Atty. Gen. Mass., 1974; Joint Mass. House and Senate Commn. on Family, 1977, Mass. Jud. Nominating Commn., 1977-79; chief drafter HEW model acts; research on child abuse and neglect, marriage, child custody in divorce, model legislation, contract law. Author: When Parents Fail, 1971, Adoptions Without Agencies: A Study of Independent Adoptions, 1978, Child Snatching-The Legal Response to the Abduction of Children, 1981; (with Weyrauch) American Family Law in Transition, 1983; (with Weyrauch and Olsen) Cases and Materials on Family Law-Legal Concepts and Changing Human Relationships, 1994; (with Eekelaar and Maclean) Cross Currents, 2000, Family Law in America, 2003, others; also book introductions; editor: The Youngest Minority: Lawyers in Defense of Children, vols. I and II, 1974; (with John Eekelaar) Family Violence: An International and Interdisciplinary Study, 1978, Marriage and Cohabitation in Contemporary Societies, 1980; editor-in-chief Family Law Quar., 1970-83; contbr. articles to profl. jours. Chmn. Lydia Rapoport Endowment Fund Smith Coll. Grantee Field Found., 1968-69, Grant Found., 1971-75, HEW, 1973-78. Mem. ABA (chmn. family law sect. 1980-81), Internat. Soc. Family Law (pres. 1981-84, exec. coun. 1985—).

KATZ, SHERMAN E., lawyer; b. Pitts., July 13, 1943; s. Saul H. Katz and Ann (Sklov) Cohen; m. Maureen Murphy, Jan. 26, 1980; 1 child, Barnaby Simon. Student, U. Stockholm, 1963-64; BA cum laude, Amherst Coll., 1965; JD, MA in Internat. Affairs, Columbia U., 1969; diploma in European Law, Oxford U., 1992. Bar: N.Y. 1969, D.C. 1969, U.S. Ct. Appeals D.C. 1970, U.S. Supreme Ct. 1973, U.S. Ct. Internat. Trade 1984. Ptnr. Coudert Bros., Washington, 1977-94, Squire, Sanders & Dempsey, Washington, 1994-98, Kelley, Drye & Warren, Washington, 1998—, of counsel; William Scholl chair internat. bus. Ctr. For Strategic and Internat. Studies, Washington. Adj. prof. internat. trade Johns Hopkins Sch. Advanced Internat. Studies, 2001—. Contbr. articles to profl. jours. Commr. D.C. Commn. on Arts & Humanities, Washington, 1987—; chmn. exec. com., hon. dir. Washington Performing Arts Soc., 1981—; bd. dirs. The Washington Opera, 1988—, The Source Theatre, Folger Poetry Series. Decorated Knight of the Royal Polar Star by King of Sweden. Mem. ABA (chmn. svcs. trade com. 1987-89, vice-chair internat. bus. transactions com. 1999), N.Y. State Bar Assn., Assn. of Bar of City of N.Y., D.C. Bar Assn., Am. Soc. Internat. Law (chmn. publs. com. 1984-87), Nat. Fgn. Trade Coun. (chmn. internat. trade com. 1986), Coun. Fgn. Rels., Washington Fgn. Law Soc., Cosmos Club. Office: Ctr for Strategic & Internat Studies 1800 K St NW Washington DC 20006-2202 Office Phone: 202-775-3140. E-mail: skatz@csis.org.

KATZ, STANLEY NIDER, law history educator; b. Chgo., Apr. 23, 1934; s. William Stephen and Florence (Nider) K.; m. Adria Holmes, Jan. 16, 1960; children: Derek Holmes, Marion Holmes. AB, Harvard U., 1955, MA, 1959, PhD, 1961; LLD (hon.), Stockton State Coll., 1981, U. Hartford, 1998, Ohio State U., 1998; DHL (hon.), U. Puget Sound, 1994, C.W. Post/L.I. U., 1997, Sacred Heart U., 1997, Roosevelt U., 2003, Ursinus Coll., 2003; DLA (hon.), Dickinson Coll., 2003. Asst. prof. history Harvard U., 1961-65, U. Wis., Madison, 1965-71; prof. legal history Law Sch. U. Chgo., 1971-78; Class of 1921 Bicentennial prof. history Am. law and liberty Princeton U., 1978-86, sr. fellow Woodrow Wilson Sch., 1986-97, lectr. with rank of prof. Woodrow Wilson Sch., 1997—, dir. Ctr. for Arts and Cultural Policy Rsch., Woodrow Wilson Sch., 1998—, acting dir. law and pub. affairs Woodrow Wilson Sch., 2005—; pres. Am. Council Learned Socs., N.Y.C., 1986-97. Vis. prof. law U. Pa., 1978-86, 2003; mem. Oliver Wendell Holmes Devise, Washington, 1976-84; bd. govs. Inst. European Studies, Chgo., 1976—2002; chmn. Coun. on Internat. Exchange Scholars, Washington, 1981-85; adj. prof. Cardozo Law Sch., 1999-2000. Author: Newcastle's New York, 1968; editor: The Case and Tryal of John Peter Zenger, 1963, rev. edit., 1972, Oliver Wendell Holmes Devise History of U.S. Supreme Court, 1984—, Colonial America, 1971, 76, 83, 92, 2000, American History: Promise and Progress, 1983, Constitutionalism and Democracy, 1993, The Life of Learning, 1994, Philanthropy in the World's Traditions, 1998, Mobilizing for Peace, 2002. Active N.J. Com. for Humanities, 1978—84, 1996—; trustee Nat. History Ctr., 2003—, So. Meth. U., 1988—2000, Nat. Cultural Alliance, 1990—97, chmn., 1997—98; trustee Rsch. Librs. Group, 1991—93, 1997—99, Brit.-Am. Arts Assn. CCC, 1991—, Newberry Libr., Chgo., ind. sector, 1989—92, Toynbee Prize Found., 1994—97, pres., 1995—97, Nat. Faculty, 1995—2001, Fulbright Internat. Ctr., 1995—, Copyright Clearance Ctr., 1997—, civic edn. project, 1997—; bd. dirs. Social Sci. Rsch. Coun., N.Y.C., 2002—; v.p. Friends of the Law Libr., Libr. of Congress, 1991—2003, Surpeme Ct. N.J., disciplinary oversight com., 1994—2000, N.J. Ethics Commn., 1991—94, com. model rules of profl. conduct, 1982—83, com. sale of law practices, 1983—84, 1989. Fellow Am. Soc. Legal History (pres. 1978-81); mem. AAAS, Papers of the Founding Fathers, Inc. (chair 1985—), Internat. Soc. Cultural Property (treas. 2005—), Inst. Early Am. History and Culture (coun. 1974-76, 90-93, 97-98), Am. Hist. Assn. (v.p. rsch. 1997-2000), Orgn. Am. Historians (exec. com. 1976-79, pres. elect 1986-87, pres. 1987-88), Am. Antiquarian Soc., Mass. Hist. Soc., Am. Philos. Soc., Soc. Am. Historians, Coun. Fgn. Rels., Phi Beta Kappa. Clubs: Princeton (N.Y.C.). Democrat. Jewish. Office: Princeton U Woodrow Wilson Sch Princeton NJ 08544-0001 Office Phone: 609-258-5637. E-mail: snkatz@princeton.edu.

KATZ, STEPHEN IRA, federal agency administrator, dermatologist, immunologist; b. Bklyn., Jan. 26, 1941; BA with honors, U. Md., 1962; MD with honors, Tulane U., 1966; PhD in Immunology, U. London, 1974. Diplomate Am. Bd. Dermatology. Asst. dermatology Walter Reed Gen. Hosp., Washington, 1970-72; rsch. fellow dept. pathology Royal Coll. Surgeons Eng., London, 1972-74; sr. investigator dermatology Nat. Cancer Inst./NIH, Bethesda, Md., 1974-77, acting chief dermatology br., 1977-80, chief dermatology br., 1980—2001; dir. Nat. Inst. Arthritis and Musculoskeletal and Skin Diseases, 1995—. Marion B. Sulzberger prof. dermatology Uniformed Svcs. U. Health Scis., Bethesda, 1989-95, acting chmn. dermatology dept., 1993-95; dir. Nat. Inst. Arthritis and Musculoskelatal and Skin Diseases; cons. Georgetown U., 1970-72, Walter Reed Army Hosp., 1975-79, Nat. Naval Med. Ctr., 1976-95, Washington Dermatol. Soc., 1980-81. Editl. bd. Internat. Jour. Dermatology, 1977-81, Jour. Investigative Dermatology, 1979-82, Jour. Am. Acad. Dermatology, 1979-83, Jour. Immunology, 1981-85, Am. Jour. Dermatopathology, Epithelia, 1986-88, Regional Immunology, 1988-95, Medicine, 1992—, Am. Jour. Contact Dermatitis, 1992—, Dermatology Internat., 1992—, Proceedings Assn. Am. Physicians, 1995—, others; contbr. over 180 sci. articles and 50 book chpts. Goldberger Summer fellow AMA, 1965, Advanced Tng. fellow Dermatology Found., 1972-74; recipient Presdl. Exec. Meritorious Rank award, PHS Superior Svc. award, Sulzberger Lecture award Am. Acad. Dermatology, D. Martin Carer Mentor award Am. Skin Assn., Stephen Rothman Meml. award Soc. Investigative Dermatology, Messenger of Hope award Scleroderma Found., Inflamatory Skin Disorders Rsch. award. Mem. Inst. Med.-Nat. Acad. Sci. Achievements include research in Langerhans cells and epidermally derived cytokines, demonstrating that skin is a critical component of the immune system; the field of inherited and acquired blistering skin diseases. Office: NIH Bldg 31 Rm 4C32D 31 Center Dr Bethesda MD 20892-2350

KATZ, STEVEN MARTIN, lawyer, accountant; b. Washington, Feb. 8, 1941; s. Joseph and Pauline (Weinberg) K.; m. Lauri Gail Berman, Aug. 23, 1964; children: Benjamin, Aaron, Rebecca, Joshua. BS, U. Md., College Park, 1962; JD, George Washington U., 1965. Bar: D.C. 1966, Md. 1971; CPA, Md. Ptnr. Euzent, Katz & Katz, Washington, 1969-72; sr. ptnr. Katz, Frome & Bleecker, P.A., and predecessors, Rockville, Md., 1972-95; pvt. practice Rockville, 1995—. Mem. Md. State Grievance Commn., 1991—. Mem. Md. Bar Assn., Md. Assn. CPAs, D.C. Bar, Montgomery County Bar Assn., Md. State Bar Found. Jewish. Office: 401 E Jefferson St Ste 208 Rockville MD 20850-2613 Fax: 301-294-9484. Office Phone: 301-738-8441. E-mail: smkatz7@verizon.net.

KATZ, STUART CHARLES, lawyer, musician; b. Chgo., June 9, 1937; s. Jerome H. and Sylvia L. (Singer) K.; m. Penny Schatz, Jan. 23, 1959; children: Steven, Lauren. BA, Roosevelt U., Chgo., 1959; JD with distinction, John Marshall Law Sch., 1964. Bar: Ill. 1964, U.S. Dist. Ct. (no. dist.) Ill. 1965, U.S. Supreme Ct. 1967. Exec. v.p., gen. counsel Heitman LLC, Chgo., 1972—. Jazz pianist and vibraphonist, appeared in concerts with Benny Goodman, Gene Krupa, Bud Freeman. Mem.: ABA, Chgo. Bar Assn., Ill. Bar Assn. Office: 191 N Wacker Dr Ste 2500 Chicago IL 60606-1885 E-mail: skatz@heitman.com.

KATZ, STUART Z., lawyer; b. N.Y.C., July 14, 1942; BA, CCNY, 1964; JD, NYU, 1968. Bar: N.Y. 1968. Ptnr. Fried, Frank, Harris, Shriver & Jacobson, N.Y.C., 1968—. Lectr. Practicing Law Inst., Prentice Hall, N.Y.C. and Mile, Minn. Mem.: ABA. Office: Fried Frank Harris Shriver & Jacobson 1 New York Plz Fl 27 New York NY 10004-1980

KATZ, TONNIE, newspaper editor; BA, Barnard Coll., 1966; MSc, Columbia U., 1967. Editor, reporter newspapers including The Quincy Patriot Ledger, Boston Herald Am., Boston Globe; Sunday/projects editor Newsday; mng. editor Balt. News Am., 1983-86, The Sun, San Bernardino, Calif., 1986-88; asst. mng. editor for news The Orange County Register, Santa Ana, Calif., 1988-89, mng. editor, 1989-92, editor, v.p., 1992-98, editor, sr. v.p., 1998—. Office: Orange County Register 625 N Grand Ave Santa Ana CA 92701-4347

KATZ, TREUMAN P., health facility administrator; b. 1942; m. Sue Ellen Katz. Pres., CEO Children's Hosp. and Regional Med. Ctr., Seattle, 1979—. Office: Children's Hosp and Regional Med Ctr 4800 Sand Point Way NE Seattle WA 98106

KATZ, VERA, former mayor, former college administrator, state legislator; b. Dusseldorf, Germany, Aug. 3, 1933; came to U.S., 1940; d. Lazar Pistrak and Raissa Goodman; m. Mel Katz (div. 1985); 1 child, Jesse. BA, Bklyn. Coll., 1955, postgrad., 1955-57; PhD (hon.), Lewis & Clark Coll., Portland (Oreg.) State U. Market research analyst TIMEX, B.T. Babbitt, N.Y.C., 1957-62; mem. Oreg. Ho. of Reps., Salem, 1985—91; former dir. devel. Portland Community Coll.; mayor City of Portland, Oreg., 1992—2004. Mem. Gov.'s Council on Alcohol and Drug Abuse Programs, Oreg. Legis., Salem, 1985—; mem. adv. com. Gov.'s Council on Health, Fitness and Sports, Oreg. Legis., 1985—; mem. Gov.'s Commn. on Sch. Funding Reform; mem. Carnegie task Force on Teaching as Profession, Washington, 1985-87; vice-chair assembly Nat. Conf. State Legis., Denver, 1986—2003. Recipient Abigail Scott Duniway award Women in Communications, Inc., Portland, 1985, Jeanette Rankin First Woman award Oreg. Women's Polit. Caucus, Portland, 1985, Leadership award The Neighborhood newspaper Portland, 1985, Woman of Achievement award Commn. for Women, 1985, Outstanding Legis. Advocacy award Oreg. Primary Care Assn., 1985, Service to Portland Pub. Sch. Children award Portland Pub. Schs., 1985, Visionary Leadership award, 1998, Legal Citizen of Yr. award, 2002. Fellow Am. Leadership Forum (founder Oreg. chpt.); mem. Dem. Legis. Leaders Assn., Nat. Bd. for Profl. Teaching Standards. Democrat. Jewish. Avocations: camping, jogging, dance. Office: Office of the Mayor City Hall 1221 SW 4th Ave Rm 340 Portland OR 97204-1995*

KATZ, WILLIAM EMANUEL, retired chemical engineer; b. Honesdale, Pa., June 12, 1924; s. Edward David and Aimee Helen (Rosenfelder) K.; m. Martha Elizabeth Legg, Feb. 13, 1960; children: Susan Katz Miller, Martha Katz Laserson, E. David II, James A.L. BSChE, MIT, 1948, MSChE, 1949. Chem. engr. Ionics Inc., Watertown, Mass., 1949-51, asst. treas., 1951-53, treas., 1953-58, v.p. and dir., 1958-81, exec. v.p. and dir., 1981—2003; ret., 2003. Author chapter in AWWA Manual of Water Quality and Treatment, 1964, and 30 articles on water and waste treatment; patentee in field. With U.S. Army, 1942-46, PTO. Recipient Life Achievement award Internat. Desalination Assn., 1999. Mem. Am. Inst. Chem. Engrs., Am. Water Works Assn., Am. Desalting Assn. (Water Quality Person of Yr. 1992), Internat. Desalination Assn. Avocations: piano, composing. Home: 11 Sunset Rd Weston MA 02493-1623

KATZ, WILLIAM LOREN, author; b. Bklyn., June 2, 1927; s. Bernard and Madeline (Simon) K.; m. Laurie Lehman, Sept. 10, 1994. BA, Syracuse U., 1950; MA, NYU, 1952. Tchr. Am. history, N.Y.C., 1954-60, Hartsdale, N.Y., 1960-67; author, 1967—. Cons. N.Y. State Edn. Dept., 1967-68, 83-84, USAF Sch. in Eng., Belgium and Holland, 1974-75; scholar in residence Tchrs. Coll. Columbia, 1971-73, NYU, 1987-91; tchr. Black history Tombs Prison, N.Y.C., 1973, N.Y. U. Afro-Am. Inst., 1973; faculty Inst. Urban and Minority Edn., Gen. Assistance Ctr., Tchrs. Coll. Columbia U., 1976; tchr. Am. history New Sch. for Social Rsch., N.Y.C., 1977-83; pres. Ethrac Publs., 1971—. Author: Eyewitness: The Negro in American History, 1967 (Gold medal for nonfition NCCJ), 5th edit., 2005, Teachers' Guide to American Negro History, 1968; author: (with Warren J. Halliburton) American Majorities and Minorities: A Syllabus of United States History for Secondary Schools, 1970, A History of Black Americans, 1973; author: The Black West: A Documentary and Pictorial History, 1971 (Mark Twain award for non-fiction), 4th edit., 1996, Teaching Approaches to Black History in the Classroom, 1973, The Constitutional Amendments, 1974, An Album of Reconstruction, 1974, An Album of the Civil War, 1974, Minorities in American History, Vols. I-VI, 1974—75, Making Our Way, 1975, Black People Who Made the Old West, 1977, 2d edit., 1994, An Album of the Great Depression, 1978, An Album of Nazism, 1979, Black Indians: A Hidden Heritage, 1986, 2d edit., 1997, The Invisible Empire: The Ku Klux Klan Impact on History, 1986, A History of Multicultural America, Vols I-VIII, 1993—94; author: (with Marc Crawford) The Lincoln Brigade: A Picture History, 1989, 2d edit., 2002, Proudly Red and Black, 1993, Black Women of the Old West, 1995, Flight From the Devil: Six Slave Narratives, 1996, Black Legacy: A History of New York's African Americans, 1997, Black Pioneers: An Untold Story, 1999, The Cruel Years: American Voices at the Dawn of the 20th Century, 2002; author: (with Laurie R. Lehman) 2d edit., 2003; editor: The American Negro: History and Literature., 1968—71; editor: (with James M. McPherson) The Anti-Slavery Crusade in America, 1969; editor: (with Henry Steele Commager and Arthur Schlesinger Jr.) Vital Sources in American History for High School Students, 1980; columnist: NY Daily Challenge, 1986—; contbr. articles to profl. jours. Exec. bd. Art Against Apartheid, 1984; nat. coun. Nat. Emergency Civil Liberties Com., 1983-85; curator Black West Exhibit, Schomburg Ctr. for Rsch. in Black Culture, NYC, 1985-86. With USNR, 1945-46. Recipient Imani White Dove Peace award, 2000. E-mail: wlkatz@aol.com. *If you believe that people have no history worth mentioning, it's easy to assume they have no humanity worth defending.*

KATZBERG, ROBERT F., lawyer; b. Bklyn., Mar. 12, 1946; BA with honors, CUNY Brooklyn Coll., 1967; JD cum laude, George Washington U., 1971. Bar: NY 1972, US Dist. Ct., NY (Ea. Dist.) 1974, US Ct. of Appeals, Second Circuit 1974, US Supreme Ct. 1975, US Dist. Ct., NY (So. Dist.) 1976, US Ct. of Appeals, Eleventh Circuit 1981, US Tax Ct. 1985, US Ct. of Appeals, Third Circuit 1991. Law clerk to Judge Oliver Gasch US Dist. Ct., Washington, 1971—72; asst. US atty. Ea. Dist. of NY, 1972—77; now ptnr. Kaplan & Katzberg, NYC. Prof. Nat. Inst. of Trial Advocacy, Benjamin N. Cardozo Law Sch., 1983—; mem. bd. dirs. NY Council of Defense Lawyers, 1989—91, Ea. Dist. Assn., 1989—; prof. Legal Aid Soc. Trial Advocacy Program, 1990—93. Mem.: ABA (co-chmn, white collar crime com. 1993—97), NY County Lawyers Assn., NY State Bar Assn. Office: Kaplan & Katzberg 767 Third Ave New York NY 10017 Office Phone: 212-750-3100. Office Fax: 212-750-8628.

KATZEN, DEBBY JOY BACHER, elementary school educator; b. Balt., Oct. 18, 1970; d. Norman Myron and Selma Ann Bacher; m. Jeffrey Jon Katzen, Aug. 4, 2002. BS in Elem. Edn., U. Del., 1992; MS in Edn.-Tech. for Educators, Johns Hopkins U., 1998. Advanced profl. cert. Md. State Dept. Edn., 2002, profl. cert. sch. improvement leadership Goucher Coll., Towson, Md., 2003. Long term sub. Owings Mills Elem. Sch., Md., 1992; first grade tchr. Freedom Elem. Sch., Sykesville, Md., 1992—97; staff devel. facilitator Carroll County Pub. Schs., Westminster, Md., 1997—98, coord. instrnl. tech., 1998—99; fifth grade tchr. Cranberry Sta. Elem. Sch., Westminster, 1999—. Presenter at confs. in field. Recipient Computer Educator of Yr. Carroll County, Md. Instrnl. Computer Coord.'s Assn., 1997, East Regional Student Pub. award, Time for Kids and Assn. Ednl. Pubs., 2004; Tech. Initiative grant, Md. State Dept. Edn., 1996-1997, 2001-2002. Mem.: ASCD, Md. Instrnl. Computer Coords. Assn. Avocations: dance, reading. Home: 11 Columbine Ct Baltimore MD 21209 Office: Cranberry Sta Elem Sch 505 N Center St Westminster MD 21157 Office Phone: 410-386-4440. Personal E-mail: dbacher@bcpl.net.

KATZEN, JAY KENNETH, retired diplomat, state legislator, government agency administrator; b. N.Y.C., Aug. 23, 1936; s. Perry and Minerva (Rich) K.; m. Patricia Anne Morse, May 30, 1963; children: John Timothy Rich, David Mark Nicholas, James Alexander Scott. BA magna cum laude, Princeton U., 1958; MA, Yale U., 1959. Joined U.S. Fgn. Svc., 1959; fgn. svc. officer Dept. State, Washington, 1959-60, 62-63, 66-69; consular-comml. officer Am. consulate gen. Sydney, Australia, 1960-62; econ. officer Am. embassy Bujumbura, Burundi, 1963-64; labor attaché Am. Embassy, Kinshasa, Zaire, 1964-66, polit. officer Bucharest, Rumania, 1969-71, counselor of embassy Bamako, Mali, 1971—73; adviser U.S. Mission to UN, N.Y.C., 1973-77; with Office of Vice Pres., Washington, 1977, Nat. War Coll., 1977; chargé d'affaires Am. Embassy, Brazzaville, Congo, 1977-78; polit. adv. to U.S. del. World Adminstrv. Radio Conf., 1979; pres., CEO Victims of Communism Meml. Found., Washington, 2003—04; regional dir. Peace Corps., 2004—. Vis. prof. Boston Coll. Grad. Sch. Mgmt., 1978-79; vice-chmn. bd. dirs. African Devel. Found., 1988-90; bd. advisers Patterson Sch. Diplomacy and Internat. Commerce, U. Ky., 1989—, Duke U. Primate Ctr., 1986—. Chmn. Fauquier County (Va.) Rep. Com., 1992-94; elected to Ho. of Dels. of Va. Gen. Assembly, 1993, 95, 97, 99; Republican candidate lt. gov., Va., 2001; Republican candidate U.S. Congress, 2002. Mem. Princeton Quadrangle Club, Army and Navy Club, Dacor House Club, Lions Internat. Address: PO Box 9917 Arlington VA 22219

KATZEN, MOLLIE, writer; b. Rochester, N.Y., Oct. 13, 1950; d. Leon and Betty (Heller) K.; m. Jeffrey David Black, June 26, 1983 (div. Oct. 1985); 1 child, Samuel Katzen Black; m. Carl Shames, Dec. 12, 1986. BFA, San Francisco Art Inst., 1972. Author, illustrator: Mossewood Cookbook, 1977, Enchanted Broccoli Forest, 1982, Still Life with Menu, 1988, Molly Katzen's Still Life Sampler, 1993, Pretend Soup & Other Real Recipes: A Cookbook for Preschoolers & Up, 1994, Enchanted Broccoli Forest, 1995, Moosewood Cookbook Classics: Miniature Edition, 1996. Recipient Graphic Arts award Arnot Art Gallery, 1976, Cert. of Commendation, Calif. State Assembly, 1989. Jewish. Avocations: classical pianist, painter. Office: care Ten Speed Press PO Box 7123 Berkeley CA 94707-0123

KATZEN, RAPHAEL, consulting chemical engineer; b. Balt., July 28, 1915; s. Isidor and Esther (Stein) K.; m. Selma M. Siegel, June 19, 1938; 1 child, Nancy Katzen Riedel. B.Chem. Engring., Poly. U. Bklyn., 1936, M.Chem. Engring., 1938, D.Chem. Engring., 1942. Registered profl. engr. in 16 states. Tech. dir. Northwood Chem. Co., Phelps, Wis., 1938-42; project mgr. Diamond Alkali Co., Painesville, Ohio, 1942-44; mgr. engring. divsn. Vulcan, Cin., 1944-53; mng. partner Raphael Katzen Assos., Cin., 1953-80; chmn. Raphael Katzen Assos. Internat., Inc., 1956—97. Contbr. articles to profl. jours; patentee in field. Mem. Cin. Air Pollution Bd., 1972-75. Recipient Disting. Alumnus award Poly. Inst. Bklyn., 1970, Dedicated Alumnus award, 1977; Disting. cons. award Ohio Assn. Cons. Engrs., 1978; Profl. Accomplishment, Disting. Engr. award Tech. and Sci. Socs. Coun., 1978, 79, Personal Achievement in Chem. Engring. award Chem. Engring., McGraw Hill, 1988, Renewable Fuels Assn. Lifetime Achievement award, 1999, 16th Ann. Fuel Ethanol Workshop award of excellence, 2000, others; Poly. U. fellow, 1981. Fellow AIChE (Chem. Engring. Practice award 1986, Robert L. Jacks Meml. award 1990, Founders award 2001), Am. Inst. Chemists; mem. NAE (elected), TAPPI, PAPTAC, Am. Chem. Soc. (Spl. Lifetime Achievement award 2000), Am. Arbitration Assn., Am. Club Miami, Fla., Sigma Xi, Tau Beta Pi, Phi Lambda Upsilon. Home: 27901 Riverwalk Way Bonita Springs FL 34134-8692 Office: 9220 Bonita Beach Rd Ste 200 Bonita Springs FL 34135-4231 Office Phone: 239-498-2552. E-mail: rkatzenpe@aol.com. *We are put on this earth to produce to the best of our ability to improve the lot of mankind, and our talents should not be wasted through lack of effort or misguided direction.*

KATZEN, SALLY, lawyer, educator; b. Pitts., Nov. 22, 1942; d. Nathan and Hilda (Schwartz) K.; m. Timothy B. Dyk, Oct. 31, 1981; 1 child, Abraham Benjamin. BA magna cum laude, Smith Coll., 1964; JD magna cum laude, U. Mich., 1967. Bar: D.C. 1968, U.S. Supreme Ct. 1971. Congl. intern Senate Subcom. on Constl. Rights, Washington, 1963; legal rsch. asst. civil rights divsn. Dept. Justice, Washington, 1965; law clk. to Judge J. Skelly Wright U.S. Ct. Appeals (D.C. cir.), 1967-68; assoc. Wilmer, Cutler & Pickering, Washington, 1968-75, ptnr., 1975-79, 81-93; gen. counsel Coun. on Wage and Price Stability, 1979-80, dep. dir. for policy, 1980-81; adminstr. Office of Info. and Regulatory Affairs Office of Mgmt. and Budget, Washington, 1993-98, counselor to the dir., 1999-2000, dep. dir. mgmt., 2000-2001; dep. dir. Nat. Econ. Coun., The White House, Washington, 1998-99. Adj. prof. Georgetown U. Law Ctr., 1988, 1990—92, U. Pa. Law Sch., 2003; resident scholar and lectr. Smith Coll., 2001—04; vis. lectr., fellow Johns Hopkins U., 2002—04; vis. prof. U. Mich. Law Sch., 2004—05; pub. mem. Adminstrv. Conf. U.S., 1988, govt. mem. and vice chair, 1993—95; mem. exec. com. Prettyman-Leventhal Inn of Ct., 1988—90, counselor, 1990—91; mem. Jud. Conf. for D.C. Cir., 1972—91; sr. policy advisor Joe Lieberman for Pres., 2003—04. Editor-in-chief U. Mich. Law Rev., 1966-67. Mem. com. visitors U. Mich. Law Sch., 1972—; cons., sr. policy advisor Joe Lieberman for Pres., 2003-04. Fellow ABA (ho. of dels. 1978-80, 89-91, coun. adminstrv. law sect. 1979-82, chmn. adminstrv. law and regulatory practice sect. 1988-89, governing com. forum com. comm. law 1979-82, chmn. standing com. Nat. Conf. Groups 1989-92); mem. D.C. Bar Assn., Women's Bar Assn., FCC Bar Assn. (exec. com. 1984-87, pres. 1990-91), Women's Legal Def. Fund (pres. 1977, v.p. 1978), Order of Coif. Home: 4638 30th St NW Washington DC 20008-2127 Personal E-mail: dykatzen@earthlink.net.

KATZENBACH, NICHOLAS DEBELLEVILLE, former United States attorney general; b. Phila., Jan. 17, 1922; s. Edward Lawrence and Marie Louise (Hilson) K.; m. Lydia King Phelps Stokes, June 8, 1946; children—Christopher Wolcott, John Strong Minor, Maria Louise Hiltson, Anne deBelleville. BA, Princeton U., 1945; LL.B., Yale U., 1947; Rhodes scholar, Balliol Coll., Oxford (Eng.) U., 1947-49. Bar: NJ 1950, Conn. 1955, NY 1972. With firm Katzenbach, Gildea & Rudner, Trenton, N.J., 1950; atty.-adviser Office Gen. Counsel Air Force, 1950-52, part-time cons., 1952-56; assoc. prof. law Yale Law Sch., 1952-56; prof. law U. Chgo. Law Sch., 1956-60; asst. atty. gen. US Dept. Justice, 1961-62, dep. atty. gen., 1962-64, acting atty. gen., 1964, atty. gen., 1965-66, under sec. state, 1966-69; sr. v.p., gen. counsel IBM Corp., 1969-84, sr. v.p. law and external relations, 1984-86, also bd. dirs.; ptnr. Riker, Danzig, Scherer, Hyland & Perretti, Morristown, NJ, 1986-91; non-exec. chmn. MCI, 2004—. Author: (with Morton A. Kaplan) The Political Foundations of International Law, 1961; editor-in-chief: Yale Law Jour, 1947; contbr. articles to profl. jours. Served to 1st lt. USAAF, 1941-45. Decorated Air medal with three clusters; Ford Found. fellow, 1960-61 Mem. AAAS, ABA, Am. Law Inst. (mem. coun.), Am. Judicature Soc., Am. Philos. Soc. Democrat. Episcopalian.

KATZENBERG, JEFFREY, motion picture studio executive; b. NYC, Dec. 21, 1950; m. Marilyn Siegel; children: Laura, David. Asst. to chmn., chief exec. officer Paramount Pictures, N.Y.C, 1975-77, exec. dir. mktg., 1977; then v.p. programming Paramount TV, Calif., 1977-78; v.p., feature prodn. Paramount Pictures, 1978-80, sr. v.p., prodn. motion picture divsn., 1980—82, pres. prodn., motion pictures & TV, 1982-94; chmn. Walt Disney Studios, Burbank, Calif., 1994; chmn., founding ptnr. DreamWorks SKG, 1994—. Co-prodr.: Nightmare Before Christmas, 1993, exec. prodr.: Prince of Egypt, 1998, Road to El Dorado, 2000, Chicken Run, 2000, Joseph: King of Dreams, 2000, Shrek 2, 2004, Shark Take, 2004; prodr.: (films) Shrek, 2001, Spirit: Stallion of the Cimarron, 2002, Sinbad: Legend of the Seven Seas, 2003; exec. prodr.: TV series Father of the Pride, 2003. Named one of 50 Most Powerful People in Hollywood, Premiere mag., 2005. Office: Dreamworks SKG 1000 Flower St Glendale CA 91201-7500*

KATZEN-GUTHRIE, JOY, performance artist, engineering executive; b. Memphis, Nov. 11, 1958; d. Eli and Bess (Bloomfield) Katzen; m. Mark C. Guthrie, Aug. 7, 1983. BFA in Music cum laude, BA in Comms. magna cum laude, Stephens Coll., Columbia, Mo., 1980. Traffic dir. WPLP News/Talk Radio, Pinellas Park, Fla., 1981-83, ops. mgr., 1982-83; traffic reporter WUSA-FM and WDAE-AM, Tampa, Fla., 1985-86; announcer, programmer, pub. rels. mgr. WXCR-FM Classics 92, Safety Harbor, Fla., 1983-87; v.p., dir. Katzen and Guthrie Assocs., Inc., Palm Harbor, Fla., 1987—; pres. Tune-of-the-Century Music, 1989—. Creator, designer, owner website www.JoyfulNoise.net, 1998—. Co-author, composer musical comedy Once Around Manhattan, 1985; author: (one-act play) A Murder in Pine County, 1987; composer, lyricist some 600 songs; performance artist CD/Cassette albums Seasons of Joy, 1989, Heart of Ancient Promise, 1993, New State of Mind, 1993, How Good and Pleasant, 1996, Passages, 1998; studio vocalist Jeff Arthur Prodns., St. Petersburg, Fla., 1985, 86, Studio C. Prodns., Tampa, 1991-92; studio vocalist, jingle writer West End Rec., Tampa, 1989, 90; session musician Hurricane Pass Studios, Clearwater, Fla., 1993—. Music dir. religious sch. Temple B'nai Israel, Clearwater, 1988-89; music dir. Perry-Mansfield Performing Arts Camp, Steamboat Springs, Colo., 1987; cantorial soloist B'nai B'rith Hillel Found., Tampa, 1990-93, Temple Shir Shalom, Gainesville, 1994-99, Congregation B'nai Emmunah, Tarpon Springs, 1996-99, Congregation Aliyah, Clearwater, 1999-2000, Temple B'nai Israel, Clearwater, 2000—. Recipient 1st and 3d place awards Memphis Songwriters Assn. Competition, 1988, others; Pinellas County Arts Coun. grantee, 1997. Mem. AAUW (dir. pub. rels. 1985-97), ASCAP, Songwriters Guild Am., Dramatists Guild, Nat. Acad. Songwriters, Nashville Songwriters Assn. Internat., Guild of Temple Musicians, Fla. Music Assn., Women's Musicians' Alliance (bd. dirs. 1998—), Hadassah (life). Democrat. Jewish. Avocations: photography, travel, music, theater, film, books. Home and Office: 2487 Indian Trl E Palm Harbor FL 34683-2806 Office Phone: 727-785-4568, 800-354-1302. Personal E-mail: joyfulnoise@earthlink.net.

KATZENSTEIN, ANDREW M., lawyer; b. Oct. 13, 1957; BA magna cum laude, U. Mich., 1979, JD cum laude, 1982; LLM in Taxation, U. San Diego, 1985. Bar: Calif. 1982, NY 1990. Ptnr. Katten Muchin Zavis Rosenman, LA. Tchr. estate tax UCLA Law Sch.; tchr. estate planning Golden Gate U., Grad. Tax Prog. Mem.: Am. Com. for Weizmann Inst. of Sci., LA County Bar Assn., Beverly Hills Bar Assn., Cure Diabetes Now. Office: Katten Muchin Zavis Rosenman Ste 2600 2029 Century Park E Los Angeles CA 90067 also: Ste 450 260 Sheridan Ave Palo Alto CA 94306 Office Phone: 310-788-4540. Office Fax: 310-712-8420. E-mail: andrew.katzenstein@kmzr.com.

KATZMAN, RICHARD ALAN, lawyer, arbitrator; b. NYC, Sept. 3, 1953; s. George and Ellen Delyse (Shure) K.; 1 child, Braden Michael Harris Katzman. AA, Miami-Dade Jr. Coll., 1972; BA, Fla. Internat. U., 1973; JD, U. Miami, 1976; MA, U. So. Calif., 1981. Bar: Fla. 1976, N.J. 1977, Calif. 1980, U.S. Dist. Ct. (so. dist.) Fla. 1976, U.S. Dist. Ct. N.J. 1977, U.S. Dist. Ct. (cent. dist.) Calif. 1980, U.S. Ct. Appeals (9th cir.) 1980, U.S. Ct. Appeals (5th and 11th cirs.) 1981, U.S. Supreme Ct. 1979, U.S. Dist. Ct. (no. dist.) Calif. 1996. Of counsel Black and Denaro, Miami, 1976-78; rsch. atty. 3d Dist. Ct. Appeal, Miami, 1978; labor atty. Pomona (Calif.) divsn. Gen. Dynamics, 1980-82; assoc. atty. Balowitz & Wolf, Santa Ana, Calif., 1982-84; sr. assoc. Petersen & Ferguson, Santa Ana, Calif., 1984-86; sr. litig. L.A. County Met. Transp. Authority, L.A., 1986-94; prin. dep. county counsel County of L.A., L.A., 1994-96; asst. gen. counsel Santa Clara Valley Transp. Authority, 1996—. Jud. arbitrator L.A. County Superior Ct., 1986-96, Orange County Superior Ct., Santa Ana, Calif., 1988-96. Judge Pro Tempore West Orange County Mun. Ct., Westminster, Calif., 1985-96. Mem. Amer. Coll. of Legal Medicine (assoc.-in-law). Avocations: boating, skiing, rv. Home: 310 N 1st St Apt 2 Campbell CA 95008-1341 Office: 3331 N 1st St Fl 2 San Jose CA 95134-1906 Office Phone: 408-321-7561. E-mail: richard.katzman@vta.org.

KATZMAN, ROBERT, neurologist, medical educator; b. Denver, Nov. 29, 1925; s. Maurice and Leah K. (Schnitt) K.; m. Nancy Bernstein, Sept. 2, 1947; children: David Jonathan, Daniel Mark. BS, U. Chgo., 1949, MS, 1951; MD cum laude, Harvard U., 1953. Diplomate Am. Bd. Psychiatry and Neurology. Intern Boston City Hosp., 1953-54; chief resident Neurol. Inst. Columbia Presbyn. Hosp., N.Y.C., 1956-57; faculty mem. Albert Einstein Coll. Medicine, N.Y.C., 1957-84, prof., chmn. neurology dept., 1964-84, dir. Resnick Gerontology Ctr., 1979-84; chmn. dept. neurosci. U. Calif., San Diego, 1984-90, Florence Riford prof. neurosci. and rsch. in Alzheimer's disease, 1984-94, rsch. prof. neurosci., 1994—2002, prof. emeritus neurosci., 2003—. Mem. clin. rsch. adv. com. Nat. Found. March of Dimes, 1975-76; mem. adv. coun. Nat. Inst. on Aging, 1982-85; chmn. med. and sci. bd. Alzheimer Disease and Related Disorders Assn., Chgo., 1979-85; mem. adv. panel on Alzheimer's disease HHS, 1987-93. Co-author: Brain Electrolytes and Fluid Metabolism, 1973, Neurology of Aging, 1983, Alzheimer Disease: The Changing View, 2000; co-editor: Basic Neurochemistry, 1972-81, Principles of Geriatric Neurology, 1992, Alzheimer Disease, 1994, Alzheimers Disease, 2d edit., 1999; mem. editl. bd. Clin. Neuroscience Rsch. Jour., ARNMD, 2001—. With USN, 1944-46, PTO. Recipient Humanitarian Award Alzheimer's Disease and Related Disorders Assn., 1985, Disting. Svc.

award, 1989, Allied Achievement in Aging award Allied Signal Corp., 1985, Henderson Meml. award Am. Geriatric Soc., 1986, 7th Ann. Chgo. Rita Hayworth Gala award Alzheimer's Assn., 1994, Crystal Tower award Alzheimer's Assn., 1998, IPA Luigi Amaducci Meml. award Internat. Psychogeriatric Assn., 2003. Fellow Am. Acad. Neurology (S. Weir Mitchell award 1960, George W. Jacoby award 1989, co-recipient Potamkin prize for Alzheimer's disease rsch. 1992); mem. Assn. for Rsch. in Nervous and Mental Disorders (pres. 1977), Am. Physiol. Soc., Inst. Medicine NAS, Am. Neurol. Assn. (pres. 1985-86), Internat. Soc. for Alzheimer's Disease Rsch., Alpha Omega Alpha. Office: U Calif San Diego Sch Medicine 9500 Gilman Dr Dept 0949 La Jolla CA 92093-0949 Office Phone: 858-622-5850. Business E-Mail: rkatzman@ucsd.edu.

KATZMANN, GARY STEPHEN, judge; b. NYC; AB summa cum laude, Columbia U., 1973; MLitt, Oxford U., 1976; MPPM, JD, Yale U., 1979. Bar: Mass. 1982, U.S. Dist. Ct. Mass. 1983, U.S. Ct. Appeals (1st cir.) 1983, D.C. 1984, U.S. Ct. Appeals (2d cir.) 1987, N.Y. 1990, U.S. Ct. Appeals (fed. cir.) 1991. Law clk. to judge U.S. Dist. Ct. (so. dist.) N.Y., N.Y.C., 1979-80; law clk. to Hon. Stephen Breyer U.S. Ct. Appeals (1st cir.), Boston, 1980-81; rsch. assoc. ctr. criminal justice Law Sch. Harvard U., Cambridge, Mass., 1981-83; asst. U.S. atty., chief appellate atty., dep. chief criminal div., chief legal counsel U.S. Atty.'s Office, Mass., 1983—2004; assoc. dep. atty. gen. U.S. Dept. Justice, Washington, 1993-94; assoc. justice Mass. Appeals Ct., 2004—. Lectr. Harvard U. Law Sch., 1989-97; project dir. J.F. Kennedy Sch. Govt., Harvard U., 1997-2000; participant Yale Law Sch. Sentencing Seminar, 1999; mem. bd. visitors Discovering Justice. Author: Inside the Criminal Process, 1991, Securing Our Children's Future: New Approaches to Juvenile Justice and Youth Violence, 2002. Recipient Dir's. Superior Performance awards U.S. Dept. Justice, 1993, 2003; fellow Harvard U., 1997-2003, Governance Inst. Mem. ABA, Gov.'s Juvenile Justice Adv. Com., Phi Beta Kappa. Office: Mass Appeals Ct John Adams Courtho One Pemberton Sq Ste 3500 Boston MA 02108-1767

KATZMANN, ROBERT ALLEN, federal judge; b. NYC, 1953; AB summa cum laude, Columbia U., 1973; MA in Govt., Harvard U., 1975, PhD in Govt., 1978; JD, Yale U., 1980. Bar: Mass. 1982, NY, U.S. Ct. Appeals (1st cir.) 1983, D.C. 1984, U.S. Dist. Ct. Mass. 1984. Law clk. to judge U.S. Ct. Appeals (1st cir.), Concord, N.H., 1980-81; rsch. assoc. Brookings Instn., Washington, 1981-85, fellow, 1985-99; adj. prof. law, pub. policy Georgetown U., Washington, 1984-92, William J. Walsh prof. govt., prof. law, 1992-99; pres. Governance Inst., Washington, 1986-99; acting dir. govt. studies Brookings Instn., Washington, 1998; judge U.S. Ct. Appeals (2nd cir.), 1999—; adjunct prof. of Law New York University, New York, 2001—. Vis. prof. polit. sci. UCLA, Washington program, 1990-92; vis. chair, Wayne Morse prof. law and politics U. Oreg., 1992; cons. Fed. Cts. Study Com., 1990; adj. prof. law NYU, 2001— Author: Regulatory Bureaucracy: The Federal Trade Commission and Antitrust Policy, 1980, Institutional Disability: The Saga of Transportation Policy for the Disabled, 1986, Courts and Congress, 1997; co-editor: Managing Appeals in Federal Courts, 1988; editor: Judges and Legislators, 1988, The Law Firm and the Public Good, 1995; editor, co-author, Daniel Patrick Moynihan: The Intellectual in Public Life, 1998, 2d edit, 2004; article and book editor Yale U. Law Jour., 1979-80. Recipient Chas. E. Merriam award, Am. Political Sci. Assn., 2001. Fellow: Am. Acad. Arts and Scis.; mem.: ABA (vice chair com. on govt. ops. and separation of powers 1991—94, pub. mem. adminstrn. conf. 1992—95, adminstrv. law sect.), Am. Assn. Law Schs. (chmn. legis. sect. 1999—2000), Am. Polit. Sci. Assn. (Charles E. Merriam award 2001), Am. Judicature Soc. (bd. dirs. 1992—98), Phi Beta Kappa. Office: US Ct Appeals 2d Cir 40 Foley Sq New York NY 10007-1502

KATZNELSON, IRA ISAAC, social sciences educator, writer; b. NYC, July 3, 1944; s. Ephraim and Sylvia (Rosenbaum) K.; m. Deborah Ruth Socolow, Jan. 14, 1967; children: Jessica, Zachary, Emma, Leah. BA summa cum laude, Columbia U., 1966; PhD, Cambridge U., 1969. Asst. prof. Polit. Sci. Columbia U., N.Y.C., 1969-73, assoc. prof., 1973-74, Ruggles prof. Polit. Sci., History, 1994—; assoc. prof., prof. Polit. Sci. U. Chgo., 1974-82; dean grad. faculty New Sch. for Social Rsch., N.Y.C., 1983-89, Loeb prof. Polit. and Social Sci., 1983-94, co-dir. Ctr. for Politics, Theory and Policy, 1989-94. Trustee Russell Sage Found., N.Y.C., 1992—; mem. acad. adv. bd. Inst. for Human Scis., Vienna, 1997—, chair selection com. Rsch. and Policy Reform Program on the Social Costs of Economic Transformation in Central Europe, 1996—. Author: Liberalism's Crooked Circle: Letters to Adam Michnik, 1996 (Lionel Trilling book award, 1997, Michael Harrington award, 1997), Paths of Emancipation: Jews, States and Citizenship, 1995, Marxism and the City, 1993, Working Class Formation: Nineteenth Century Patterns in Western Europe and North America, 1986 (Socialist Rev. book award, 1986), Schooling for All: Class, Race and the Decline of the Democratic Ideal, 1985, City Trenches: Urban Politics and the Patterning of Class in the United States, 1983, The Politics of Power: A Critical Introduction to American Government, 1987, The Politics and Society Reader, 1974, Black Men, White Cities: Race, Politics, and Migration in the United States, 1900-1930, and Britain, 1948-1968, 1973, rev. edit., 1976, When Affirmative Action was White, 2005; editl. bd. Jour. Policy History, 1993—, U. Chgo. Wilder House Series in Politics, History, and Culture, 1988-94, Politics and Soc., 1969— (founding editor 1969-75); co-editor: (with Martin Shefter and Theda Skocpol) (book series) Princeton Studies in American Politics: Historical, International, and Comparative Perspectives, 1991—; adv. bd. Social Policy, 1989—; editl. adv. bd. Polit. Sci. Quarterly, 1977—. Recipient German Marshall Fund fellowship, 1978, 79, Danforth Found. fellowship, 1966-69, Euretta J. Kellett fellowship, 1966-68; Phi Beta Kappa vis. scholar, 1990-91; Disting. Polit. Scientist U. Vermont, 1989-90. Mem. Social Sci. History Assn. (pres. 1997-98), Am. Polit. Sci. Assn. (pres. politics and history sect. 1992-93), Phi Beta Kappa.

KATZOWITZ SHENFIELD, LAUREN, philanthropy consultant; m. Marc Shenfield. BS in Comparative Lit. with honors, Brandeis U., 1970; MS with honors, Columbia U., 1971. With Newsweek mag.; then with Phila. Bull.; freelance writer, editor, cons., until 1975; cons. Ford Found., 1972-75; mgr. PBS programs Exxon Corp., 1978-81; mgr. Exxon Rsch. and Engring. Co., 1981-84; regional liaison for Europe and Africa, Exxon Corp., 1984-86; exec. dir. Philanthropy Advisors - A Svc. of UJA-Fedn. of N.Y., 1986—; pres. Lauren Katzowitz Cons., Croton on Hudson, N.Y., 1986—. Mem. profl. adv. coun. Met. Mus. of Art, 2000—, Central Park Conservancy, 2001—; bd. dirs. N.Y. Regional Assn. of Grantmakers, 2000—, Women and Philanthropy, 2003—. Named one of 12 Women to Watch in the Eighties, Ladies' Home Jour., 1979. Office: Philanthropy Advisors 130 E 59th St New York NY 10022 Office Phone: 212-836-1358. Personal E-mail: katzowitzl@philanthropyadvisorsny.org.

KATZUNG, BERTRAM GEORGE, pharmacologist; b. Mineola, N.Y., June 11, 1932; m. Alice V. Camp; children: Katharine Blanche, Brian Lee. BA, Syracuse U., 1953; MD, SUNY, Syracuse, 1957; PhD, U. Calif., San Francisco, 1962. Prof. U. Calif., San Francisco, 1958—. Author: Drug Therapy, 1991, Pharmacology, Examination and Board Review, 2004, Basic and Clinical Pharmacology, 2005; contbr. to profl. jours Markle scholar. Mem. AAAS, AAUP, Am. Soc. Pharmacology and Exptl. Therapeutics, Biophys. Soc., Fed. Am. Scientists, Internat. Soc. Heart Rsch., Soc. Gen. Physiologists, Western Pharmacology Soc., N.Y. Acad. Sci., Astron. Soc. of Pacific, Internat. Dark-Sky Assn., Nat. Deep Sky Observers Soc., Planetary Soc., Royal Astron. Soc. Canada, San Francisco Amateur Astronomers Soc., Sonoma County Astron. Soc., Profl. Photographers Am., Golden Gate Computer Soc., Phi Beta Kappa, Alpha Omega Alpha. Office: U Calif San Francisco Dept Cellular/Molec Pharm PO Box 450 San Francisco CA 94143-0450

KAUDERER, BERNARD MARVIN, retired naval officer, consultant; b. Phila., July 21, 1931; s. Harry Thau and Anne Mae (Mandell) K.; m. Myra Frances Weissman, Mar. 21, 1954; children: Howard Todd, Heidi Susanne, Robin Beth. BS, U.S. Naval Acad., 1953. Commd. ensign U.S. Navy, 1953, advanced through grades to vice adm., 1983; comdr. Submarine Group Five, 1977-79; dep. dir. research, devel., test and evaluation Office Chief Naval Ops., Navy Dept., Washington, 1979-81; comdr. submarine forces U.S. Pacific Fleet, 1981-83; comdr. submarine force U.S. Atlantic Fleet, 1983-86; ret. U.S. Navy, 1986. Cons. to industry and govt. Decorated D.S.M., Legion of Merit, Meritorious Service medal, Navy Commendation medal, Navy Expeditionary medal. Mem. Naval Submarine League (dir.), Masons, Shriners. Home: 7025 Ibis Pl Carlsbad CA 92011-5011

KAUFER, CONNIE TENORIO, special education educator, researcher; b. Saipan, No. Mariana Islands, June 12, 1945; d. Lino Pangelinan and Magdalena Faosto (Arriola) Tenorio; m. Leonard James Kaufer, Jan. 20, 1974; 1 child, Lucile Tenorio. AA in Elem. Edn., Chaffey Coll., 1968; BS in Lang. Arts, Calif. State Poly. U., 1971; MA in Edn., San Jose State U., 1983. Cert. tchr., Calif., Mariana Islands. Elem. tchr. Marianas Dept. Edn., Chalan Kanoa, Saipan, Mariana Islands, 1964-66, 74-76, 80-84, elem. and h.s. tchr., 1970-71, elem. sch. supr. Lower Base, Saipan, 1971-74, elem. sch. prin. Tanapag Village, Saipan, 1979-80; comprehensive lang. arts skills project dir. Pub. Sch. Sys., Lower Base, Saipan, 1984-87, reading specialist, 1984-94, trainer Marianas instrument for obs. of tchr. activities, 1986—94, trainer onward to excellence, 1988—94; ret., 1994. Part-time instr. U. Guam Ext., No. Marianas Coll., Saipan, 1993—; sec. Diocesan Bd. Edn. Saipan, 1985-90; trainer pacific region pacific effective schs. Pacific Region Edn. Lab., Honolulu and Saipan, 1991-93; presenter in field. Mem. Mariana Islands rep. Trust Ter. Curriculum Coun., Saipan, 1970-72; coord. cross cultural Peace Corps, Saipan, 1973, coord. Chamorro lang., 1975; pres. Chalan Kanoa Sch. Saipan Tchrs. Assn., 1981-83. Scholar Marianas Edn. Found., 1966-70, Bilingual Edn. scholar Trust Ter. Dept. Edn., 1975. Mem. ASCD, AAUW, Internat. Reading Assn. (Saipan chpt. pres. 1975-76), Pacific Islands Bilingual/Bicultural Assn., Phi Delta Kappa. Roman Catholic. Avocations: raising orchids, cooking, baking. Home: PO Box 7611 Saipan MP 96950

KAUFER, KAREN EVANS, academic administrator; b. Easton, Pa., Apr. 24, 1954; d. George Richard Evans and Rose Ann Luntz; m. Richard Elliot Kaufer, Oct. 14, 1983; 1 child, Zachary. BA in Art, Wilkes U., 1989; MA in Art History, Bloomsburg (Pa.) U., 1991. Caseworker Luzerne/Wyoming County Mental Health Ctr., Wilkes-Barre, Pa., 1977—84; dir. devel. rsch. Wyoming Sem., Kingston, Pa., 1992—97; bus. mgr. Kingston (Pa.) Vet. Clinic, 1997—2000; interim dir. Sordoni Art Gallery Wilkes U., Wilkes-Barre, 2000—01, assoc. dir. Sordoni Art Gallery, 2001—. V.p. programming Wilkes-Barre (Pa.) Chpt.Hadassah, 1987—89; bd. dirs. Fine Arts Fiesta, 1999—, v.p. bd. dirs., 2003—; bd. dirs. Wyoming Valley Montessori Sch., 1992—98, Luzerne County Hist. Soc., 1990—2000. Mem.: Pa. Fedn. Mus. and Hist. Orgs., Nat. Mus. Women in Arts, Am. Assn. Mus. Avocations: gardening, reading, travel. Office: Sordoni Art Gallery Wilkes Univ 150 S River St Wilkes Barre PA 18766

KAUFFELT, JAMES DAVID, lawyer; b. Glendale, W.Va., May 5, 1952; s. Thaddeus David and Lois Zeigler (McQuade) K. BA, W.Va. U., 1974, JD, 1977. Bar: W.Va. 1977, U.S. Ct. Appeals (4th cir.) 1979, U.S. Ct. Appeals (D.C. cir.) 1982, U.S. Supreme Ct. 1995. Ptnr. Kauffelt & Kauffelt, Charleston, W.Va. Office: Kauffelt & Kauffelt 803 Kanawha Valley Bldg Charleston WV 25301 E-mail: jkauffelt@citynet.net.

KAUFFMAN, ALAN CHARLES, lawyer; b. Atlantic City, Aug. 12, 1939; s. Joseph Bernard and Lilyan (Abraham) K.; children: Julie Beth, Debra Amy, Paige Tyler. AB, Rutgers U., 1961; JD, Villanova U., 1964. Bar: Pa. 1964, U.S. Ct. Appeals (3d cir.) 1965, U.S. Dist. Ct. (ea. dist.) Pa. 1965, U.S. Supreme Ct. 1968, Fla. 1985, U.S. Dist. Ct. (so. dist.) Fla. 1985. Pres. Alan C. Kauffman & Assocs., P.A., Boca Raton, Fla. Mem., bd. dirs. Am. Diabetic Assn., Fla. Philharmonic Orch., Caldwell Theater; vice chmn. Fla. Victory Com.; founding chmn. Gold Coast Forum; bd. mem. Fla. Elections Commn. Cmty. Rels. bd. City of Boca Raton; mem. Greater Boca Raton Senate, Palm Beach County Film & TV Bd.; mem. Jewish Adv. Coun. U.S. Senator Connie Mack; Mem. Internat Bd. Weizmann Inst., Rep. Senatorial Inner Circle. Mem. ABA, ATLA, Pa. Bar Assn. (former mem. bd. govs., former trustee), Palm Beach County Bar Assn., Acad. Fla. Trial Lawyers, Phila. Trial Lawyers Assn., Phila. Bar Assn., Fla. Bar Assn., Palm Beach County Film Bd., Boca Roundtable. Office: 1900 NW Corporate Blvd Ste 200E Boca Raton FL 33431-7367

KAUFFMAN, DAVID LIN, lawyer; b. Mohrsville, Pa., June 13, 1930; s. James L. and A. Catherine (Mengel) Kauffman; m. Nancy Ruth Loose, July 18, 1953; children: Randolf, Eric, Scott. BA in Polit. Sci., Albright Coll., 1958; LLB, U. Md., 1964. CPA Md. Acct. Met. Edison Co., Reading, Pa., 1952—55, Easco Corp., Balt., 1958—71, sec., corp. counsel, 1971—2004; ret. Served with U.S. Army, 1949. Mem.: Am. Assn. Attys.-C.P.A., Md. Soc. C.P.A.s, Md. Bar Assn., ABA. Republican. Meth.

KAUFFMAN, ERLE GALEN, geologist, paleontologist; b. Washington, Feb. 9, 1933; s. Erle Benton and Paula Virginia (Graff) K.; children: Donald Erle, Robin Lyn, Erica Jean; m. Claudia C. Johnson, Sept. 1989. BS, U. Mich., 1955, MS, 1956, PhD, 1961; MSc (hon.), Oxford (Eng.) U., 1970; DHC, U. Göttingen, Germany, 1987. Teaching fellow, instr. U. Mich., Ann Arbor, 1956-60; from asst. to full curator dept. paleobiology Nat. Mus. Natural History Smithsonian Instn., Washington, 1960-80; prof. geology U. Colo., Boulder, 1980-96, chmn. dept. geol. scis., 1980-84, interim dir. Energy, Minerals Applied Rsch. Ctr., 1989-91; prof. geology Ind. U., 1996—2003, prof. emeritus, 2004—. Adj. prof. geology George Washington U., Washington, 1962-80; cons. geologist, Boulder, 1980-96. Author, editor: Cretaceous Facies, Faunas and Paleoenvironments Across the Cretaceous Western Interior Basin, 1977; contbg. editor: Concepts and Methods of Biostratigraphy, 1977, Fine-grained Deposits and Biofacies of The Cretaceous Western Interior Seaway, 1985, High Resolution Event Stratigraphy, 1988, Paleontology and Evolution: Extinction Events, 1988, Extinction Events in Earth History, 1990, Evolution of the Western Interior Basin, 1993; also jour. articles. Recipient U.S. Govt. Spl. Svc. award, 1969, NSF Best Tchr. award U. Colo., 1985 named Disting. Lectr. Am. Geol. Inst., 1963-64, Am. Assn. Petroleum Geologists, 1984, 85, 91, 92; Fulbright fellow Australia, 1986. Fellow Geol. Soc. Am., AAAS; mem. Paleontol. Soc. (councilor under 40, pres. elect 1981, pres. 1982, past pres. 1983, chmn. 5 coms.); mem. NRC (rep.), Palaeontol. Assn., Internat. Paleontol. Assn. (v.p. 1982-88), Paleontol. Research Instn., Soc. Sedimentary Geology (com. mem., Spl. Svc. award 1985, Best Paper award 1985, Raymond C. Moore Paleontology medal 1991, William H. Twenhofel medal 1998), Rocky Mountain Assn. Geologists (project chief) (Scientist of Yr. 1977), Paleontol. Soc. Wash. (pres., sec., treas.), Geol. Soc. Wash. (councilor), Md. Acad. Scis. (hon. Paleontology sect.), Sigma Xi, Phi Kappa Phi, Sigma Gamma Epsilon. Democrat. Avocations: music, fishing, climbing, photography. Office: Dept Geol Sci Ind Univ 1001 E 10th St Bloomington IN 47405-1405 E-mail: kauffman@indiana.edu.

KAUFFMAN, GEORGE BERNARD, chemistry professor; b. Phila., Sept. 4, 1930; s. Philip Joseph and Laura (Fisher) K.; m. Ingeborg Salomon, June 5, 1952 (div. Dec. 1969); children: Ruth Deborah (Mrs. Martin H. Bryskier), Judith Miriam (Mrs. Mario L. Reposo); m. Laurie Marks Papazian, Dec. 21, 1969; stepchildren: Stanley Robert Papazian, Teresa Lynn Papazian Baron, Mary Ellen Papazian. BA with honors, U. Pa., 1951; PhD, U. Fla., 1956. Grad. asst. U. Fla., 1951-55; rsch. participant Oak Ridge Nat. Lab., 1955; instr. U. Tex., Austin, 1955-56; rsch. chemist Humble Oil & Refining Co., Baytown, Tex., 1956, GE, Cin., 1957, 59; asst. prof. chemistry Calif. State U., Fresno, 1956-61, assoc. prof., 1961-66, prof., 1966—. Guest lectr. coop. lecture tours Am. Chem. Soc., 1971; vis. scholar U. Calif., Berkeley, 1976, U. Puget Sound, 1978; dir. undergrad. rsch. participation program NSF, 1972. Author: Alfred Werner— Founder of Coordination Chemistry, 1966, Classics in Coordination Chemistry, Part I, 1968, Part II, 1976, Part III, 1978, Werner Centennial, 1967, Teaching the History of Chemistry, 1971, Coordination Chemistry: Its History through the Time of Werner, 1977, Inorganic Coordination Compounds, 1981, The Central Science: Essays on the Uses of Chemistry, 1984, Frederick Soddy (1877-1956): Early Pioneer in Radiochemistry, 1986, Aleksandr Porfirevich Borodin: A Chemist's Biography, 1988, Coordination Chemistry: A Century of Progress, 1994, Classics in Coordination Chemistry, 1995, Metal and Nonmetal Biguanide Complexes, 1999; contbr. articles to profl. jours.; contbg. editor: Jour. Coll. Sci. Tchg., 1973—, The Hexagon, 1980—, Polyhedron, 1983-85, Industrial Chemist, 1985-88, Jour. Chem. Edn., 1987—, Today's Chemist, 1989-91, The Chemical Intelligencer, 1994-2000, Today's Chemist at Work, 1995—, Chemical Heritage, 1996—, The Chemical Educator, 1998—, Chem. 13 News, 1998—; guest editor: Coodination Chemistry Centennial Symposium (C3S) issue, Polyhedron, 1994; editor tape lecture series: Am. Chem. Soc, 1975-81. Named Outstanding Prof., Calif. State U. and Colls. Sys., 1973; recipient Exceptional Merit Svc. award, 1984, Meritorious Performance and Profl. Promise award, 1986-87, 88-89, Coll. Chemistry Tchr. Excellence award Mfg. Chemists Assn., 1976, Chugaev medal, 1976, Kurnakov medal, 1990, Chernyaev medal, 1991, USSR Acad. Sci., George C. Pimentel award in chem. edn. Am. Chem. Soc., 1993, Dexter award in history of chemistry, 1978, Marc-Auguste Pictet medal Soc. Physique et d'Histoire Naturelle de Genève, 1992, Pres.'s medal of Distinction, Calif. State U., Fresno, 1994, Rsch. award at an Undergraduate Instn., Am. Chem. Soc., 2000, Laudatory Decree Inst. History of Sci. and Tech. Russian Acad. Sci., 2000; Rsch. Corp. grantee, 1956-57, 57-59, 59-61, Am. Chem. Soc. Petroleum Rsch. Fund grantee, 1963-64, 69-70, NSF grantee, 1960-61, 63-64, 67-69, 76-77, NEH grantee, 1982-83; John Simon Guggenheim Meml. Found. fellow, 1972-73, grantee, 1975; Strindberg fellow Swedish Inst., Stockholm, 1983. Fellow: AAAS; mem.: Mensa, Am. Chem. Soc. (chmn. divsn. history of chemistry 1969, mem. exec. com. 1970, councilor 1976—78, George C. Pimentel award in chem. edn. 1993, Helen M. Free Pub. Outreach award 2002, Legis. Action Honor Roll 2004), Soc. History Alchemy and Chemistry, History of Sci. Soc., Assn. Univ. Pa. Chemists, AAUP, Gamma Sigma Epsilon, Alpha Chi Sigma, Phi Kappa Phi, Phi Lambda Upsilon, Sigma Xi. Home: 1609 E Quincy Ave Fresno CA 93720-2309 Office: Calif State U Dept Chemistry Fresno CA 93740-8034 Office Phone: 559-323-9123. Business E-Mail: georgek@csufresno.edu.

KAUFFMAN, GORDON LEE, JR., surgeon, educator; b. Grand Rapids, Mich., Mar. 30, 1946; s. Gordon Lee Sr. and Jeanne (Klunder) K.; m. Christie Lyn VanSweden, June 28, 1969; children: Gordon Lee III, Christian Anthony. BS, Wheaton Coll., 1968; MD, U. Mich., 1972. Diplomate Nat. Bd. Med. Examiners, Am. Bd. Surgery. Resident in surgery U. Mich., Ann Arbor, 1972-77; rsch. assoc. VA Wadsworth, L.A., 1977-80, staff surgeon, 1977-85; asst. prof. surgery UCLA Sch. Medicine, 1979-83, assoc. prof., 1983-85; prof. surgery and physiology, chief div. gen. surgery Pa. State U., Hershey, 1985—, vice chmn. dept. surgery, 1994—. Investigator Ctr. for Ulcer Rsch. and Edn., L.A., 1979-81, key investigator, 1981-85; cons. City of Hope Nat. Med. Ctr., Duarte, Calif., 1982-85, Harbor Gen. Hosp., Torrance, Calif., 1983-85; mem. surgery and bioengring. study sect. NIH, 1990-94, mem. consensus devel. panel on helicobacterpylori, 1994. Mem. editl. bd. Surgery, 1988—, Jour. Gastrointestinal Surg., 1997—, Jour. Surg. Rsch., 1990-97, Am. Jour. Surgery, 1994-97; contbr. chpts. to books, numerous articles to profl. jours. Grantee Coun. Tobacco Rsch., 1969, VA, 1980-85; Galens Fgn. fellow, 1971, Med. Assistance Program Fgn. fellow, 1971, Frederick Coller resident fellow, 1976, James IV fellow, 1991. Mem. ACS (sec.-treas. cen. Pa. chpt. 1990-96), Assn. Acad. Surgery (chmn. edn. com. 1985-87), Am. Fedn. for Clin. Rsch., Soc. for Exptl. Biology and Medicine, Am. Gastroenterol. Assn. (chmn. abstract rev. com. 1986-87, 95-96), Soc. Univ. Surgeons (chmn. com. on publs.), Soc. Surgery of Alimentary Tract (nominating com. 1990, publ. com. 1991-93, chmn. 1994, recorder 1994-97), Frederick A. Coller Surg. Soc., Collegium Internat. Chirurgiae Digestivae, Surg. Biology Club I, Soc. Clin. Surgery (membership com. 1992-95, chmn. 1995-96), Cent. Surg. Soc. (councilman at large 1995-96), Am. Surg. Assn. (membership adv. com. 1993-97). Office: Milton S Hershey Med Ctr H149 500 University Dr Hershey PA 17033-2391 Fax: (717) 531-4335. E-mail: gkauffman@psu.edu.

KAUFFMAN, LEON A., internist, educator; b. Phila., July 26, 1934; s. Isadore and Clara (Kenig) K.; B.A., Temple U., 1957, M.D., 1961; m. Rita A. Young, Apr. 2, 1969; children— Christopher I., Chandler S. Intern, Einstein Med. Center, Phila., 1961-62, resident in pathology, 1962-63; resident in internal medicine Hahnemann U. Hosp., Phila., 1963-65, fellow in pulmonary physiology and chest diseases, 1965-66; sr. instr. medicine Hahnemann U. Med. Sch., 1966-70, asst. prof., 1970-77, assoc. prof., 1977—, dir. pulmonary function lab., 1968-70, dir. respiratory intensive care unit, 1969-73, pulmonary cons. to shock and trauma unit, 1970-80; asst. dir. div. pulmonary medicine, 1970-73; pulmonary cons. U.S. Naval Hosp., 1973-77; med. dir. respiratory therapy St. Agnes Med. Center, Phila., 1973-78, assoc. attending in medicine; chmn. div. pulmonary medicine Met. Hosp., Phila., 1974-83, dir. Sch. Respiratory Therapy Tech., 1978-83; chmn. sub com. on sterilization of respiratory therapy equipment Am. Lung Assn. of Phila., 1975-81. Past mem. adv. com. Sch. Respiratory Therapy, Community Coll. Phila. Diplomate Am. Bd. Internal Medicine, subsplty. Bd. Pulmonary Disease. Fellow Am. Coll. Chest Physicians, Phila. Coll. Physicians; mem. Laennec Soc. Phila. (pres. 1975-76, exec. com. 1972-78), AMA, Pa. Med. Soc., Am. Thoracic Soc., A.C.P., Phila. Drinker Soc. Critical Care Medicine, N.Y. Acad. Scis. Contbr. articles to profl. jours. Office: 1930 Pine St Philadelphia PA 19103-6626

KAUFFMAN, MARTA, producer, writer; m. Michael Skloff. B.A., Brandeis University, 1978. With Bright-Kauffman-Crane Prodns., Burbank, Calif. Creator, prodr., writer Dream On, 1990-96; creator, exec. prodr. Friends, 1994-2004 (Emmy nominee 1995, 96), Veronica's Closet, 1997-2000, Jesse, 1998-2000; lyricist Friends theme I'll Be There for You.

KAUFFMAN, N. LEROY, academic administrator; b. Goshen, Ind., Nov. 6, 1951; s. Norman Daniel and Margaret Annette Kauffman; m. Judy A. Wyse, June 17, 1982; children: Elizabeth A., Norman Daniel Christopher, Rachel K. BS in Acctg. and Mgmt., Ea. Mennonite Coll., Va., 1977; MBA, U. of Mont., 1978; PhD, Ohio State U., 1988. CPA NC, 1995. Dean, coll. of bus. Western Carolina U., Cullowhee, NC, 2002—, prof., acctg., 1994—2002, Va. Tech, Blacksburg, Va., 1988—94. Home: 141 Oak Park Dr Clyde NC 28721 Office: Western Carolina Univ College of Business Cullowhee NC 28723 Office Phone: 828-227-3480. Office Fax: 828-227-7075. Personal E-mail: kauffmanlj@juno.com. E-mail: kauffman@email.wcu.edu.

KAUFFMAN, PETER H., lawyer, energy executive; b. 1946; AB, U. Ill., JD, 1972. Bar: Ill. 1972. Joined Peoples Energy Corp., 1972, asst. gen. counsel, sec., 1998—, Peoples Gas and North Shore Gas (subsidiary of Peoples Energy Corp.), 1998—. Office: Peoples Energy Corp 130 E Randolph Dr Chicago IL 60601

KAUFFMAN, ROBERT A., lawyer; b. Atlantic City, Aug. 5, 1963; BA, U. Pa., 1985, JD, 1988. Bar: Pa. 1989, Fla. 1989. With Reed Smith, LLP, Phila., 1988—92; asst. U.S. atty. criminal and asset forfeiture divsn. Phila., 1992—96; ptnr. Reed Smith, LLP, Phila., 1997—2003; shareholder Berger & Montague, Phila., 2003—04; sr. v.p., gen. counsel Harleysville Group, Inc., Harleysville, Pa., 2004—, chief governace officer, 2004—. Office: Harleysville Group Inc 355 Maple Ave Harleysville PA 19438-2297 Office Phone: 215-256-5173. Office Fax: 215-256-5631.

KAUFFMAN, STEPHEN BLAIR, law librarian, educator; b. St. Louis, Mo., Sept. 25, 1948; s. William Porter and Patricia Mary (Cain) Kauffman; m. Susan Heffernan, Jan. 24, 1971 (dec. Aug. 1972); m. Mary Ann Royle, Aug. 24, 1979 (div. 1997); children: Ashley, Stephanie, Cameron. BS, U. Mo., St. Louis, 1971; JD, U. Mo., Kansas City, 1975, LLM, 1976; MLL, U. Wash., 1977. Bar: Mo. 1975. Law libr. Reiderer Eisberg, Kansas City, Mo., 1973—75; law libr. asst. U. Wash., Seattle, 1976—77; law libr. Nat. Jud. Coll., Reno, 1977—81; asst. prof. of law No. Ill. U., DeKalb, 1981—84, law libr. dir. and assoc. prof., 1984—88; prof. law., law libr. dir. U. Wis., Madison, 1988—94; affiliate faculty Sch. of Library and Info. Studies, 1992—94; prof. law., law libr. Yale U., New Haven, 1994—. Mem. adv. bd. Conn. State Law Libr. Sys., 1994—; bd. dirs. LLMC, 2000—04; bd. academic adv. Oceana Publ., 1999—2000; bd. adv. Assn. of Bar City NY, 1996—98. Contbr. articles to profl. jours.; co-author (with Bonnie Collier): Law in America: An Illustrated Celebration, 2001. Mem.: ABA, New England Consortium of Law

Libraries (pres. 2000—02), Mo. Bar Assn., Spl. Librs. Assn., Am. Assn. Law Librs. Democrat. Office: Yale Law Sch PO Box 208215 New Haven CT 06520 Home: 41 Old Smugglers Rd Branford CT 06405*

KAUFFMAN, WILLIAM JOSEPH, editor, writer; b. Batavia, N.Y., Nov. 15, 1959; s. Edward Joseph and Sandra Jean (Baker) K.; m. Lucine Margaret Andonian, May 22, 1987; 1 child, Gretel. BA, U. Rochester, 1981. Rsch. asst. Senator D.P. Moynihan, Washington, 1981-82, legis. asst., 1982-83; asst. editor Reason, Santa Barbara, Calif., 1985-86, Washington, 1986-87; assoc. editor The Am. Enterprise, 1994—. Author: Every Man a King, 1989, Country Towns of New York, 1994, America First! Its History, Culture and Politics, 1995, With Good Intentions? Reflections on the Myth of Progress in America, 1998, Dispatches from the Muckdog Gazette, 2003. Bd. dirs. Genesee Landmark Soc., 1993—, Holland Purchase Hist. Soc., 1993—, Friends of the Richmond Meml. Libr., 1995—, Genesee County Baseball Club, 2002—. Roman Catholic. Avocations: astronomy, music, collecting coins and political campaign items. Home: 28 Chapel St PO Box 266 Elba NY 14058-0266 Office Phone: 585-757-2455. Personal E-mail: bkauffman@2ki.net.

KAUFFMANN, ELIZABETH LOUISE, art educator; b. Ashland, Ky., Dec. 9, 1951; d. William Edwin and Eva Louise Hoy; m. Alan Jacques Kauffmann, July 5, 1987; children: Zachary Alan, Tyler John. BA, Agnes Scott Coll., 1973; cert. in Tchg., Ga. State U., 1977; MEd, U. Ga., 1982. Cert. tchr. Ga., 1977. Instr. visual arts mid. sch. Clayton County Pub. Schs., Jonesboro, Ga., 1983—85; instr. visual arts H.S. Douglas County Pub. Schs., Lithia Springs, Ga., 1985—86; instr. visual arts elem. sch. Atlanta (Ga.) Pub. Schs., 1986—95, Cobb County Pub. Schs., Marietta, Ga., 1996—. Cons. Binney and Smith, Pa., 2004—. Grantee, Atlanta Jr. League, 1988; scholar, Cortona, Italy, 1982. Mem.: Ga. Art Edn. Assn., Nat. Art Edn. Assn. Office Phone: 678-594-8071.

KAUFFMANN, STANLEY JULES, author; b. N.Y.C., Apr. 24, 1916; s. Joseph H. and Jeannette (Steiner) K.; m. Laura Cohen, Feb. 5, 1943. B.F.A., NYU, 1935. Mem. Washington Sq. Players, 1931-41; asso. editor Bantam Books, 1949-52; editor-in-chief Ballantine Books, 1952-56, consulting editor, 1957-59; editor Alfred A. Knopf, 1959-60; film critic New Republic, N.Y.C., 1958-65, 67—, assoc. lit. editor, 1966-67; theater critic New York Times, 1966, New Republic, N.Y.C., 1969-79, Saturday Rev., 1979-85. Condr. program The Art of Film, Channel 13, N.Y.C., 1963-67; vis. prof. Sch. of Drama, Yale U., 1967-86, 95, 97; vis. prof. CUNY, 1973-76, 77-92, Hunter Coll, 1993—; Disting. vis. prof. Adelphi U., 1992-94, profl. performing arts, 1994-96. Author: The Hidden Hero, 1949, The Tightrope, 1952, A Change of Climate, 1954, Man of the World, 1956, A World on Film, 1966, Figures of Light, 1971; editor: (with Bruce Henstell) American Film Criticism: from the Beginnings to Citizen Kane, 1973, Living Images, 1975, Persons of The Drama, 1976, Before My Eyes, 1980, Albums of Early Life, 1980, Theater Criticisms, 1983, Field of View, 1986, Distinguishing Features, 1994, Regarding Film, 2001. Recipient George Jean Nathan award for dramatic criticism, 1972-73, George Polk award for criticism, 1982, Outstanding Tchr. award Assn. for Theater in Higher Edn., 1995, Telluride Film Festival medal, 1998; Ford Found. fellow for study abroad, 1964, 71, hon. fellow Morse Coll., Yale U., 1964, Guggenheim fellow, 1979-80. Address: 10 W 15th St New York NY 10011-6838

KAUFFOLD, RUTH ELIZABETH, clinical psychologist; b. Decatur, Ill., Sept. 5, 1946; d. James Henry and Elizabeth Opal Kauffold; m. Paul Dwight Entner, Aug. 23, 1968; 1 child, James Paul. BA, Cedarville (Ohio) Coll., 1968; MEd, Wright State U., 1972; MS, U. Dayton, 1986; PhD, The Union Inst., 1997. Tchr. Springfield (Ohio) Pub. Schs., 1968-72, Pomona (Calif.) Unified Sch. Dist., 1973-76, Bethel Sch. Dist., New Carlisle, Ohio, 1977-81; practicum Sycamore Hosp., Miamisburg, Ohio, 1994; intern, resident clin. psychology Agape Counseling Ctr., Centerville, 1995-2000. Co-hostess radio talk show WHIO Radio Sta., Dayton, 1998; lectr. nat. and internat. profl. convs.; spkr. AACC World Conf., 2001. Lectr., missionary Project Ptnr., Lima, Peru, 1986; lectr., tchr. For Hills Bapt. Ch., Dayton, Ohio, 1997; lectr., tchr. Fair Haven Ch., 2000-2004. Jennings scholar Martha Holden Jennings Found., 1972. Mem. APA, AACC, Dayton Area Psychol. Assn. Avocations: interior design, architecture, gardening, reading, walking. Office: Agape Counseling Ctr 175 S Main St Centerville OH 45458-2372

KAUFMAN, ALBERT I., lawyer; b. NYC, Oct. 2, 1936; s. Israel and Pauline (Pardes) K.; m. Ruth Feldman, Jan. 25, 1959; 1 son, Michael Paul. AA, L.A. City Coll., 1957; BA, U. San Fernando Valley, 1964, JD, 1966. Bar: Calif. 1967, U.S. Ct. Appeals (9th cir.) 1968, U.S. Supreme Ct. 1971, U.S. Dist. Ct. (cen. dist.) Calif. 1967, U.S. Tax Ct. 1971, U.S. Ct. Internat. Trade 1981. Pvt. practice, Woodland Hills, Calif., 1967—; judge pro tem L.A. Superior Ct., 1980; family law, personal injury and bus. mediator L.A. Superior Ct., 1980—. Mem. Pacific S.W. regional bd. Anti-Defamation league of B'nai B'rith, 1970-91. With USAF, 1959-65, to col. CAP, 1956—. Recipient Disting. Svc. award B'nai B'rith, 1969; Exceptional Svc. award CAP, 1977, 95. Mem. ABA, L.A. County Bar Assn., San Fernando Valley Bar Assn., Consumer Atty. of Calif., Consumer Atty. Assn. L.A. Republican. Clubs: Toastmasters, Westerners 1117 (pres. 1969), B'nai B'rith (pres. 1971-72), Santa Monica Yacht (rear commodore) Office: 22900 Ventura Blvd Ste 205 Woodland Hills CA 91364 Office Phone: 818-222-4010. Personal E-mail: lawyer4@earthlink.net.

KAUFMAN, ANDREW LEE, law educator; b. Newark, Feb. 1, 1931; s. Samuel and Sylvia (Meltzer) K.; m. Linda P. Sonnenschein, June 14, 1959; children: Anne, David, Elizabeth, Daniel. AB, Harvard U., 1951, LL.B., 1954. Bar: DC 1954, Mass. 1979, US Supreme Ct. 1961. Assoc. Bilder, Bilder & Kaufman, Newark, 1954-55; law clk. to Justice Felix Frankfurter U.S Supreme Ct., 1955-57; ptnr. Kaufman, Kaufman & Kaufman, Newark, 1957-65; lectr. in law Harvard U., Cambridge, Mass., 1965-66, prof., 1966-81, Charles Stebbins Fairchild prof. law, 1981—, assoc. dean, 1986-89, vice dean acad. planning, 2005—. Author: (with others) Commercial Law, 1971, 82, Problems in Professional Responsibility, 1976, 84, 89, 2002, Cardozo, 1998. Treas. Shady Hill Sch., 1969-76; treas. Hillel Found. Cambridge, Inc., 1977-86. Mem. Mass. Bar Assn. (chmn. com. profl. ethics 1982—). Office: Harvard U Law Sch Cambridge MA 02138

KAUFMAN, ANDREW MICHAEL, lawyer; b. Boston, Feb. 19, 1949; s. Earle Bertram and Miriam (Halpern) K.; m. Michele Moselle, Aug. 24, 1975; children: Peter Moselle, Melissa Lanes, Caroline Raney. BA cum laude, Yale U., 1971; JD, Vanderbilt U., 1974. Bar: Tex. 1974, Ga. 1976, Ill. 1993, U.S. Ct. Appeals (5th and 11th cirs.) 1981. Assoc. Vinson & Elkins, Houston, 1974-76, ptnr., 1982-83, Austin, 1983-92, Dallas, 1992; assoc. Sutherland, Asbill & Brennan, Atlanta, 1976-80, ptnr., 1980-81, Kirkland & Ellis LLP, Chgo., 1993—. Editor in chief Vanderbilt U. Law Rev., 1973-74. Mem. nat. alumni bd. Vanderbilt U.Law Sch., 1994—2000; Alumi fund raiser Yale U., 1971—, mem. alumni schs. com., 1986—92, 2003—; mem. med. ethics coun. Seton Hosp., 1988—92; participant Leadership Austin, 1987—88; bd. dirs. KLRU-TV, 1989—93; mem. Austin (Tex.) Entrepreneurs Coun., 1991—92; mem. adv. bd. Dallas Bus. Com. Arts Leadership Inst., 1992—93; governing bd. mem. Chgo. Symphony Orch.; bd. dirs. United Way, Austin, Tex.; pub. TV Ballet Austin, Tex., 1986—92; mem. adv. bd. Austin Tech. Incubator, 1989—93. Mem. ABA (bus. law sect. 1978—, chmn. lease financing and secured transactions subcom. of com. devels. in bus. financing 1993-99, UCC com., legal opinions com., comml. fin. svcs. com.), Tex. Bar Assn., Yale U. Alumni Assn., Order of Coif, Headliners Club, Yale Club, N.Y.C. and Chgo., Knights of the Symphony Austin. Avocation: sailing. Office: Kirkland & Ellis LLP 200 E Randolph St Fl 54 Chicago IL 60601-6636 Office Phone: 312-861-2313. Business E-Mail: Andrew.Kaufman@chicago.kirkland.com.

KAUFMAN, ANTOINETTE D., information technology manager; b. Phila., Mar. 10, 1939; d. Joseph and Maria Falcone; m. John R. Kaufman, Apr. 30, 1988. Ed., St. Joseph's U., 1968. With N.W. Ayer & Son, Inc., NYC, 1956-81; adminstrv. asst. N.W. Ayer ABH Internat., 1960, asst. corp. sec., 1977, corp. sec., 1978-79, stock transfer agt., 1969-79, info. specialist, 1979-81; exec. v.p., sec., creative dir., chief oper. officer Help Bus. Svcs., Inc., Swarthmore, Pa., 1981—. Mem.: Pa. State U. Alumni Assn. (life), Navy League US (life). Avocations: ballroom dancing, cooking, violin, piano, gardening. Office: Help Bus Svcs Inc 110 Park Ave HBS Bldg Swarthmore PA 19081 Office Phone: 610-544-9787.

KAUFMAN, BARTON LOWELL, financial services company executive; b. Shelbyville, Ind., Mar. 28, 1941; s. Nathan and Hortense (Schwartz) K.; m. Judy Dorman, June 17, 1962; children: Grant, Wendy Kaufman Siegel, Emily Kaufman Frank, Hannah. BS, Ind. U., 1962, JD, 1965. Bar: Ind. 1965. Agt. Kaufman Multi-Million Dollar Agy., Indpls., 1965-70; pres., CEO Kaufman Fin. Corp., Indpls., 1970—. Pres. Twenty-Five Million Dollar Internat. Forum, Chgo., 1989. Republican. Jewish. Office: Kaufman Fin Corp 600 East 96th Street, Suite 595 Indianapolis IN 46240 Home: 414 Springwood Dr Carmel IN 46032-7935 Office Phone: 317-581-7000. E-mail: bartk@kaufin.com.

KAUFMAN, BEL, author, educator; b. Berlin; d. Michael J. and Lala (Rabinowitz) K.; divorced; children: Jonathan Goldstine, Thea Goldstine. BA magna cum laude, Hunter Coll., 1934; DHL, Hunter Coll, 2001; MA with highest honors, Columbia U., 1936; LLD honors, Nasson Coll., Maine, 1965. Adj. prof. English CUNY; lectr. throughout country, also appearances on TV and radio. Mem. Commn. Performing Arts. Editorial bd., Phi Delta Kappan.; Author: Up the Down Staircase, 1965, Love, etc, 1979; also short stories, articles, TV play, translations from Russian, lyrics for musicals. Bd. dirs. Shalom Aleichem Found.; adv. council Town Hall Found. Recipient plaque Anti-Defamation League, award and plaque United Jewish Appeal, Paperback of Year award, Ky. Col. award, Bell Movie award, Nat. Treasure awrd Seasoned Citizens Theatre, 2001; also ednl. journalism awards; named to Hall of Fame Hunter Coll., winner short story contest sponsored by NEA and PEN, 1983. Mem. Author's Guild, Dramatists Guild, P.E.N., English Grad. Union, Phi Beta Kappa. Address: 1020 Park Ave New York NY 10028-0913 E-mail: belkau@aol.com.

KAUFMAN, BERNHARD BARKEN, writer, educator; b. N.Y.C., Mar. 19, 1923; s. Wolf and Yetta Barken Kaufman; widowed; children: Harlen, Lisa, Shari; m. Phyllis Rohm Kaufman, Aug. 6, 1966; children: David, Jennifer, Andrea. Studied, NYU, 1940—41; BA, Bklyn. Coll., 1945—48; PhD (hon.), U. Ctrl. de Venezuela, Caracas, 1986. Mgr. Sun Chem. Corp., Caracas, Venezuela, 1959—68; dir. Mobil Oil Corp., Caracas, Venezuela, 1969—86; sales mgr. Radio WEEB, Southern Pines, NC, 1990—. Author: Who Were the Pre-Columbians, 1989. Pharm. Mate 1st Class USN, 1941—43, Guantanamo Bay, Cuba. Recipient Andres Bello Award 1st Class, Pres. of Venezuela, 1976, World Merit Award 1st Class, 1978. Avocation: archaeology. Home: Knollwood Village 810 Village Ct Southern Pines NC 28387 Office: Radio WEEB 1650 Midland Rd Southern Pines NC 28387 E-mail: newworld@connectnc.net.

KAUFMAN, CHARLIE, scriptwriter; b. NY, Nov. 1958; m. Denise Kaufman. Student, Boston U., NYU. With circulation dept. Star Tribune, Mpls.; writer, 1991—. Author: (TV series) Get a Life, 1990, The Trouble with Larry, 1993, Ned and Stacey, 1995, The Dana Carvey Show, 1996, (screenplays) Being John Malkovich, 1999, Human Nature, 2001, Confessions of a Dangerous Mind, 2002, Adaptation, 2002, Eternal Sunshine of the Spotless Mind, 2004 (DC Film Critics award for best picture, 2004, DC Film Critics award for best original screenplay, 2004, Writers Guild of Am. award for best original screenplay, 2005, Academy award for best original screenplay, 2005); prodr.: (TV series) Ned and Stacey, 1995, Misery Loves Company, 1995; (films) Being John Malkovich, 1999, Human Nature, 2001, Adaptation, 2002. Nominee Golden Globe award, 2000, 2003, Acad. award, 2000, 2003; recipient L.A. Film Critics Assn. award, 1999, Boston Soc. Film Critics award, 1999, 2002, Toronto Film Critics Assn. award, 1999, 2002, San Diego Film Critics Soc. award, 1999, 2002, Saturn award, Acad. Sci. Fiction, Fantasy & Horror Films, 2000, BAFTA Film award, 2000, 2003, Chgo. Film Critics Assn. award, 2000, 2003, Ind. Spirit award, 2000, Nat. Soc. Film Critics award, 2000, Sierra award, Las Vegas Film Critics Soc., 2000, Online Film Critics Soc. award, 2000, 2003, ALFS award, London Critics Cir. award, 2001, Santa Fe Film Critics Cir. award, 2000, Nebula award, Sci. Fiction and Fantasy Writers Am., 2001, Nat. Bd. Rev. award, 2002, N.Y. Film Critics Cir. award, 2002, Southeastern Film Critics Assn. award, 2002, High Hopes award, Munich Film Festival, 2002, Fla. Film Critics Cir. award, 2003, Golden Satellite award, 2003, Broadcast Film Critics Assn. award, 2003. Office: 9560 Wilshire Blcd 5th Fl Beverly Hills CA 90212

KAUFMAN, CHARLOTTE KING, artist; b. Balt., Dec. 5, 1920; d. Ben and Belle (Turow) King; m. Albert Kaufman, July 22, 1945; children: Matthew King, Ezra King. AB, Goucher Coll., 1969; MPH, Johns Hopkins U., 1972, MEd, 1976. Dir. pub. rels. Balt. Jewish Cmty. Ctr., 1962-67; rschr., editor Johns Hopkins U. Sch. Hygiene and Pub. Health, Balt., 1969-72, admissions officer, 1972-74, dir. admissions and registrar, 1974-86, dir. study cons. program for undergrads., 1985-89, pub. health acad. adviser, 1989-95; studio artist, Palm Desert, Calif., 1996—. Mem. APHA, Am. Assn. for Higher Edn., Am. Assn. Collegiate Registrars and Admissions Officers, Artists Equity Assn. (v.p. Md. chpt. 1988-90), Md. Printmakers (exec. bd. 1989-94), Palm Springs Desert Mus. Artists Coun. (exec. bd. 1997-2003), Delta Omega. Democrat. Jewish. Home: Monterey Country Club 159 Las Lomas Palm Desert CA 92260-2153 E-mail: kaufmanchar@dc.rr.

KAUFMAN, CHRISTOPHER HENRY, composer; s. F. Wallace Kaufman and Anna Rita Filameno. MusD in Adminstrn., Cornell U., 1991. Co-dir. La Strada Theatrical Prodns., N.Y., 2005—; founder, pres. CHIRON Performing Arts, N.Y., 1990—, artistic dir., 1990—. Composer (prodr.): (plays) Pickles and the Junkman's Daughter; composer: (condr.) (ballets) The Phoenix, Fober of Darkness and Weeping Light, (songs) Initiations wind ensemble; composer: (musician) Fifteen short works for solo piano; composer: (condr.) Island ('Eeslahnd)' for Orchestra, Madrigal in Spring for piano trio, Brass Quintet, Chiron for Orchestra, Symphonic Waves for wind ensemble, Waken for viola and orchestra; composer: (musician) Over seventy works for a wide variety of mediums. Recipient Individual Artists award, Cmty. Arts Partnership, 1997; grantee, 1991—99; Sage fellowship, Cornell U., 1990, Am. Music and Art grantee, Meet the Composer, 1991—99, Visual Art grantee, 1997. Democrat. Home and Office: CHIRON Performing Arts 474 6th Street 2 Brooklyn NY 11215 Office Phone: 718-499-4070. Personal E-mail: ckaufman5@nyc.rr.com.

KAUFMAN, CHRISTOPHER LEE, lawyer; b. Chgo., Mar. 17, 1945; s. Charles R. and Violet-Page (Koteen) K.; m. Carlyn A. Clement, Jan. 25, 1986; children: Charles Alexander, Caroline Clement. BA, Amherst Coll., 1967; JD, Harvard U., 1970. Bar: Ill. 1970, Calif. 1972. Law clk. to judge U.S. Ct. Appeals (2d cir.), N.Y.C., 1970-71; from assoc. to ptnr. Heller, Ehrman, White and McAuliffe, San Francisco, Palo Alto, Calif., 1974-90; ptnr. Latham & Watkins, Menlo Park, Calif., 1990—. Editor: Harvard Law Review., 1968-70. Mem. ABA (com. on negotiated acquisitions, com. on fed. regulation of securities). Office: Latham & Watkins 135 Commonwealth Dr Menlo Park CA 94025-1105 Business E-Mail: christopher.kaufman@lw.com.

KAUFMAN, DANIEL J., lawyer; b. Wilmington, Del., 1959; m. Cathy Kaufman; children: Michael, Matthew, Andrew. BA in Econs., Rutgers U., 1981; JD, U. Va., 1984. With Richard Layton & Finger, Wilmington, Del.; assoc. White & Case, N.Y.C.; with Robinson Silverman Pearce Aronsohn & Berman, N.Y.C., 1988—90; asset mktg. dir. Resolution Trust Corp., Phila., 1990—93; gen. counsel Zelenkofske, Axelrod & Co., Jenkintown, Pa., 1993—94; gen. counse Zany Brainy Inc.; v.p., gen. counsel Electronics Boutique Holdings Corp., 2002—. Office: EB Games Inc 931 S Matlack St West Chester PA 19382

KAUFMAN, DAVID GRAHAM, construction executive; b. North Canton, Ohio, Mar. 20, 1937; s. DeVere and Josephine Grace (Graham) Kaufman; m. Carol Jean Monzione, Oct. 5, 1957 (div. Aug. 1980); children: Gregory Allan, Christopher Patrick. Student, Kent State U., 1956; grad., Internat. Corr. Schs., 1965, N.Y. Inst. Photography, 1983; postgrad., Calif. Coast U. Cert. constrn. insp., constrn. project mgr., asbestos insp., lead insp., lead risk assessor, asbestos project designer, lock-out/tag-out, environ. insp., environ. specialist, environ. mgr., EPA cert. lead insp. and risk assessor. Machinist apprentice Hoover Co., North Canton, Ohio, 1955-57; draftsman-designer Goodyear Aircraft Corp., Akron, Ohio, 1957-60, Boeing Co., Seattle, 1960-61; designer Berger Industries, Seattle, 1961-62, Puget Sound Bridge & Drydock, Seattle, 1963, C.M. Lovsted, Seattle, 1963-64, Tracy, Brunstrom & Dudley, Seattle, 1964, Rubens & Pratt Engrs., Seattle, 1965-66; founder, owner Profl. Drafting Svcs., Seattle, 1965, Profl. Take-Off Svcs., Seattle, 1966, Profl. Representation Svcs., Seattle, 1967; pres. Kaufman Inc., Seattle, 1967-83, Kaufman-Alaska Inc., Juneau, 1975-83, Kaufman-Alaska Constructors, Inc., Juneau, 1975-83; constrn. mgr. U. Alaska, 1979-84; constrn. cons. Alaskan Native and Eskimo Village Corps., 1984—; prin. Kaufman S.W. Assocs., N.Mex., 1984—, Graham Internat., 1992—, Parsons-Brinckernoff, Santa Fe, 2000—. Trustee advisor Kaufman Internat., Kaufman Group, Kaufman Enterprises. Mem.: Am. Concrete Inst., Am. Contractors Inst., Prodrs. Coun. Alaska, Prodrs. Coun. Hawaii, Prodrs. Coun. Idaho, Prodrs. Coun. Wash., Prodrs. Coun. Oreg., Associated Gen. Contractors Seattle Constrn. Coun., Internat. Conf. Bldgs. Ofcls., Assn. Constrn. Insps., Constrn. Specifications Inst., Environ. Assessment Assn., Nat. Eagle Scout Assn., Portland C. of C., Toastmasters (past gov.), Elks, Lions. Republican. Roman Catholic. Office: PO Box 458 Haines AK 99827-0458 also: PO Box 1781 Santa Fe NM 87504 Home: 505 Oppenheimer # 409 Los Alamos NM 87544

KAUFMAN, DAVID JOSEPH, lawyer; b. Harrisburg, Pa., Apr. 7, 1931; s. S. Herbert and Bessie (Claster) K.; m. Virginia Stern, Aug. 30, 1959; children: David J. Jr., James H. BS in Econs. cum laude, Franklin and Marshall Coll., 1952; JD cum laude, U. Pa., 1955. Bar: Pa. 1955. First assoc., to ptnr., then of counsel Wolf, Block, Schorr & Solis-Cohen, Phila., 1957—; chmn., exec. com., 1979, 83. Trustee Abington (Pa.) Meml. Hosp., 1981—, chmn. bd. trustees, 1992-94; pres. Congregation Rodeph Shalom, Phila., 1983-86; mem. adv. com. on decedents estates laws Pa. Joint State Govt. Commn., 1985-. Fellow Am. Coll. Trust and Estate Counsel; mem. ABA, Pa. Bar Assn. (chmn. real property, probate and trust sect. 1986-87), Phila. Bar Assn. (chmn. probate sect. 1977), Order of Coif. Republican.

KAUFMAN, DAVID MARC, pediatric neurologist; b. Bronx, N.Y., July 10, 1945; s. Harold M. and Edna M. (Markowtiz) K.; m. Harriet B. Kaufman, June 30, 1968; 1 child, Jill R. BS, Union Coll., 1967; MD, Boston U. Sch. of Medicine, 1975. Diplomate Am. Bd. Pediatrics. Intern-resident N.Y. Hosp., N.Y.C., 1975-77; resident-fellow Mt. Sinai Med. Ctr., N.Y.C., 1977-80; pvt. practice in pediatric neurology N.Y.C., 1980—; med. dir. Premier Health Care / YAI Nat. Inst. for People with Disabilities, 1997—. Mem. admissions com. Mt. Sinai Sch. of Medicine, N.Y.C., 1992—, ethics com. Child Neurology Soc., Mpls., 1995—; adv. bd. Winston Prep Sch. Spl. Edn. Sch., N.Y.C., 1990, Young Adult Inst., N.Y.C., 1995—. Author: (with others) The Founders of Child Neurology, 1990. Fellow Am. Acad. Pediatrics; mem. Am. Acad. Neurology, Child Neurology Soc. Office: 3 E 83d St New York NY 10028 Office Phone: 212-737-4911. Personal E-mail: davidneuro@aol.com.

KAUFMAN, DONALD LEROY, building products executive; b. Erie, Pa., May 9, 1931; s. Isadore H. and Lena (Sandler) K.; m. Estelle Friedman, Aug. 15, 1954; children: Craig Ivan, Susan Beth, Carrie Ellen. BS in Bus. Adminstrn, Ohio State U., 1953, LL.B., 1955. Bar: Ohio 1955. Pres. Alside, Inc., Akron, Ohio, 1974—, chief exec. officer, 1982—. V.p., bd. dirs. Assoc. Materials Inc. Mem. adv. com. U. Akron; trustee Jewish Welfare Fund, Akron, 1958-65, young leaders div., 1961-65; trustee Akron City Hosp. Found., 1984-91, Menorah Park Home for Aged, Akron Children's Hosp. Found. Mem. Akron Bar Assn., Sigma Alpha Mu, Tau Epsilon Rho. Home: 2825 Roundhill Rd Akron OH 44333-2273 Office: PO Box 2010 Akron OH 44309-2010

KAUFMAN, DONNA S., lawyer; m. Fred Kaufman; 2 children. BCL, McGill U.; LLM, U. Montreal. Bar: Quebec, (Ontario). Former broadcast exec. Sta. CHCH-TV, Hamilton and Toronto, Canada; former chmn., CEO Selkirk Comm. Ltd.; former ptnr. Stikeman Ellliott. Bd. dirs. BCE Inc., Bell Can., TransAlta Corp., 1989—, Hudson's Bay Co.; gov. Baycrest Centre for Geriatric Care. Author: Broadcasting Law in Canada: Fairness in the Administrative Process; contbr. articles to profl. jours. Recipient Award of Distinction, Faculty of Commerce, Concordia U., Montreal, 1995. Office: 2 54 Clair Ave E Toronto ON Canada M4T 2T5 E-mail: bcecomms@bce.co.

KAUFMAN, GEORGE S., real estate company executive; BS, Ohio State U.; MS, NYU. Chmn. Kaufman Astoria Studios; pres., COO Kaufman Realty Corp. Trustee Whitney Mus. Am. Art, NYC, Hall of Sci. Mus., Fashion Inst. Tech., NYC, NY Coun. Motion Pictures & TV, Am. Mus. Moving Image. Mem.: Real Estate Bd. NY, Midtown Real Estate Owners Assn. (pres.). Office: Kaufman Astoria Studios 34-12 36th St Astoria NY 11106*

KAUFMAN, GLEN FRANK, art educator; b. Fort Atkinson, Wis., Oct. 28, 1932; s. Eli J. and Elynor B. (Jensik) K. BS with honors, U. Wis., 1954; MFA, Cranbrook Acad. Art, 1959; cert., State Sch. Arts and Crafts, Copenhagen, 1960. Head fibers dept. Cranbrook Acad. Art, Bloomfield Hills, Mich., 1961-67; assoc. prof. art U. Ga., Athens, 1967-72, prof. art, 1972—, prof. in charge, fabric design, 1967—, grad. faculty, 1969—. Staff designer Dorothy Liebes Design Studio, N.Y.C., 1960-61; designer Regal Rugs, Inc., North Vernon, Ind., 1966-82; vis. artist Sch. Textiles, Royal Coll. Art, London, 1976; juror The Albuquerque (N.Mex.) Mus., 1981, Midland (Mich.) Art Coun., 1985, Itami Craft Ctr., Osaka, Japan, 1991, others; panelist Visual Artists Fellowship/Crafts, Nat. Endowment for the Arts, Washington, 1992—; cons. in field; lectr. and workshop presenter in field. One-man shows include Gallery Maronie, Kyoto, Japan, 1984, Sembikiya Gallery, Tokyo, 1985, Arrowmont Sch. Arts and Crafts, Gatlinburg, Tenn., 1986, Fiberworks, Berkeley, Calif., 1987, Madison (Ga.)-Morgan Cultural Ctr., 1988, Fuji Gallery, Osaka, Japan, 1988, Wacoal Ginza Art Space, Tokyo, 1989, Allrich Gallery, San Francisco, 1990, Azabu Mus. of Arts and Crafts, Tokyo, 1991, Lamar Dodd Art Ctr., LaGrange (Ga.) Coll., 1992, Gallery Gallery, Japan, 1992, Wacoal Ginza Art Space, Tokyo, 1994, Gallery Nouveau, Pusan, Korea, 1994, Ba Tang Gol Arts Ctr., Seoul, Korea, 1994, Wacoal Ginza Art Space, Tokyo, 1996, Gallery Gallery, Kyoto, Japan, 1996, others; exhibited in group shows at Columbia Mus. Art, SC, 1980, No. Ill. U., DeKalb, 1981, Visual Arts Ctr. Alaska, Anchorage, 1982, Robert L. Kidd Gallery, Birmingham, 1983, Am. Craft Mus., NY, 1986, Denki Kaikan Gallery, Nagoya, Japan, 1987, Gayle Wilson Gallery, Southampton, NY, 1988, Sch. Visual Arts, NY, 1989, Itami Craft Ctr., Osaka, 1989 (Silver prize), Farrell Collection, Washington, 1991, Allrich Gallery, San Francisco, 1991, Nagoya Trade and Industry Ctr., 1991, New Visions Gallery Contemporary Art, Atlanta, 1992, Mus. Kyoto, 1992, Smithsonian Instn., Washington, 1992-93, Atlanta (Ga.) Fin. Ctr., 1993, Nat. Mus. Modern Art, Kyoto, Japan, 1993, Art Inst. Chgo., 1993, Brenau U. Gallery, Gainesville, Ga., 1993, Mus. Kyoto, 1994, Asian Arts Ctr. Towson (Md.) State U., 1994, Am. Craft Mus., NY, 1995, Nogaya and Trade Industry Ctr., Japan, 1995, Gallery, Gallery, Kyota, Japan, 1995, Harbourfront Ctr., Toronto Can., 1995, Museé Marsil, Montreal, Can., 1995, Brown/Grotta Gallery, Wilton, Conn., 1995, NJ Ctr. for Visual Arts, Summit, 1997, Georgia State U. Gallery, Atlanta, 1997, Brown/Grotta Gallery, Wilton, Conn. 12997, Vanderbilt U. Sarratt Gallery, Nashville, 1997, Georgia Mus. Art, Athens, 1997, others; represented in permanent collections Am. Craft Mus., NYC, Juraku Mus, Kyoto, Cleve. Mus. Art, Art Inst. Chgo., U. Wis., Madison, Itami City Craft Ctr., Hyogo Prefecture, Japan, Ithaca (NY) Coll. Mus. Art, Long House Found., L.I., NY, Nat. Mus. Modern Art, Kyoto, Smithsonian Instn., Rockford Art Assn., Ill., S.C. Johnson Collection, U.S.A. Collection Contemporary Crafts, SUNY, Oneonta, Wichita Art Assn., Kans., pvt. collections; works illustrated in many books; contbr. articles to jours. Recipient Fulbright grant to Denmark, 1959-60, Grant for rsch. and travel to Europe, U. Ga., Dept. Art, 1973, Nat. Endowment for the Arts Craftsmen's Fellowship grant,

1976, Nat. Endowment for the Arts Svcs. to the Field grant, 1980-81, 81-82, Faculty Rsch. grant U. Ga. Athens Office of V.P. for Rsch., 1983-96, Nat. Endowment for the Arts Visual Artist's Fellowship grant, 1990, Ga. Coun. for the Arts Individual Artist grant, 1991, Sr. Faculty Rsch. grant U. Ga. Athens Rsch. Found., 1992, others. Fellow Am. Craft Coun.; mem. World Craft Coun., Surface Design Assn. (S.E. regional rep. 1977-80, pres. 1980-82, named hon. life mem. 1983), Phi Beta Delta. Office: Sch of Art Univ Ga Athens GA 30602

KAUFMAN, GORDON DESTER, theology educator; b. Newton, Kans., June 22, 1925; s. Edmund George and Hazel (Dester) K.; m. Dorothy Wedel, June 11, 1947; children: David W., Gretchen E., Anne Louisa, Edmund G. II. AB with highest distinction, Bethel (Kans.) Coll., 1947, LHD (hon.), 1973; MA in Sociology, Northwestern U., 1948; BD magna cum laude, Yale U., 1951, PhD in Philos. Theology, 1955. Ordained to ministry Mennonite Ch., 1953. Asst. prof. religion Pomona Coll., 1953-58; asso. prof. theology Vanderbilt U., 1958-63; prof. theology Harvard U. Div. Sch., Cambridge, Mass., 1963-95, Edward MallincKrodt Jr. prof. div., 1969-95, prof. emeritus, 1995—. Vis. prof. United Theol. Coll., Bangalore, India, 1976-77, Doshisha U., Kyoto, Japan, 1983, U. South Africa, Pretoria, 1984; vis. lectr. Oxford U., 1986, Chinese U. Hong Kong, 1991. Author: Relativism, Knowledge and Faith, 1960, The Context of Decision, 1961, Systematic Theology: a Historicist Perspective, 1968, God the Problem, 1972, An Essay on Theological Method, 1975, 3d edit., 1995, Nonresistance and Responsibility and other Mennonite Essays, 1979, The Theological Imagination: Constructing the Concept of God, 1981, Theology for a Nuclear Age, 1985, In Face of Mystery: A Constructive Theology, 1993, God—Mystery—Diversity: Christian Theology in a Pluralistic World, 1996, In the beginning...Creativity, 2004. Mem. Am. Acad. Religion (pres. 1981-82), Am. Theol. Soc. (pres. 1979-80) Democrat. Home: 6 Longfellow Rd Cambridge MA 02138-4736 Office: 45 Francis Ave Cambridge MA 02138-1911

KAUFMAN, HENRY, diversified financial services company executive; b. Wenings, Germany, Oct. 20, 1927; came to US, 1937; s. Gustav and Hilda (Rosenthal) K.; m. Elaine Reinheimer, Sept. 15, 1957; children: Glenn, Craig, Daniel. BA, NYU, 1948; MS, Columbia U., 1949; PhD, NYU, 1958, LLD (hon.), 1982; LHD, Yeshiva U., 1986. Asst. chief economist research dept. Fed. Res. Bank NY, 1957-61; with Salomon Bros., Inc., NYC, 1962-88, gen. partner, 1967-88, mem. exec. com., 1972-88, mng. dir., 1981-88, also chief economist, charge bond market research, industry and stock research and bond portfolio analysis research and corp. bond research depts., also vice-chmn.; founder Henry Kaufman & Co., NYC, 1988—. Pres. Money Marketeers, NYU, 1964-65; bd. dirs. Lehman Brothers Holdings Inc., 1995-. Bd. dirs. Fed. Home Loan Mortgage Corp. Trustee Whitney Mus. of Am. Art, Cambridge Ctr. for Behavioral Studies, Inst. Internat. Studies; pres. Animal Med. Ctr.; bd. govs. Tel-Aviv U.; chmn. bd. overseers Stern Sch. of Bus. NYU; chmn. Inst. Internat. Edn.; bd. dirs. Statue of Liberty - Ellis Island Found., Mem. Am. Econ. Assn., Am. Fin. Assn., Conf. Bus. Economists, Econ. Club NYC (dir.), UN Assn. (bd. dirs., co-chmn. econ. policy council), Council Fgn. Relations. Mailing: c/o Whitney Mus Am Art 945 Madison Ave New York NY 10021*

KAUFMAN, HERBERT MARK, finance educator; b. Bronx, N.Y., Nov. 1, 1946; s. Henry and Betty (Fried) K.; m. Helen Laurie Fox, July 23, 1967; 1 child, Jonathan Hart. BA, SUNY, Binghamton, 1967; PhD, Pa. State U., 1972. Economist Fed. Nat. Mortgage Assn., Washington, 1972-73; asst. prof. Ariz. State U., Tempe, 1973-76, econs. prof., 1980-88, fin. prof. Tempe, 1988—, chair dept. fin., 1991—2004. Exec. dir. Ctr. for Fin. System, 1988-, cons. World Bank, Washington, 1985-86, Gen. Acctg. Office, Washington, 1985, Congl. Budget Office, Washington, 1980, N.Y. Stock Exch., 1995—. Author: Financial Markets, Financial Institutions and Money, 1983, (with others) The Political Economy of Policy Making, 1979, Money and Banking, 1991; contbr. articles to profl. jours. Mem. Am. Econ. Assn., Am. Fin. Assn., Nat. Assn. of Bus. Economists. Avocations: golf, piano. Home: 1847 E Calle De Caballos Tempe AZ 85284-2505 Office: Ariz State U Bin 3906 Dept Fin Tempe AZ 85287 Business E-Mail: herbert.kaufman@asu.edu.

KAUFMAN, IRVING, retired engineering educator; b. Geinsheim, Germany, Jan. 11, 1925; came to US., 1938, naturalized, 1945; s. Albert and Hedwig Kaufmann; m. Ruby Lee Dordek, Sept. 10, 1950; children— Eve Deborah, Sharon Anne, Julie Ellen. BE, Vanderbilt U., 1945; MS, U. Ill., 1949, PhD, 1957. Engr. RCA Victor, Indpls., Ind. and Camden, N.J., 1945-48; instr., research assoc. U. Ill., Urbana, 1949-56; sr. mem. tech. staff Ramo-Wooldridge & Space Tech. Labs., Calif., 1957-64; prof. engring. Ariz. State U., 1965-94, ret., 1994; founder, dir. Solid State Research Lab., 1968-78. Collaborator Los Alamos Nat. Lab., 1989, 91; vis. scientist Consiglio Nazionale delle Ricerche, Italy, 1973-74; vis. prof. U. Auckland, N.Z., 1974; liaison scientist U.S. Office Naval Rsch., London, 1978-80; lectr. and cons. elec. engring. Contbr. articles to profl. jours. and encys.; patentee in field. Recipient Disting. Research award Ariz. State U. Grad. Coll., 1986-87; Sr. Fulbright research fellow Italy, 1964-65, 73-74, Am. Soc. for Engring. Edn./Naval Rsch. Lab. fellow, 1988. Fellow IEEE (life, Phoenix sect. leadership award 1994); mem. Electromagnetics Acad., Gold Key (hon.), Sigma Xi, Tau Beta Pi, Eta Kappa Nu, Pi Mu Epsilon. Jewish. E-mail: rubyirv@earthlink.net.

KAUFMAN, JASON EDWARD, art critic, reporter, editor; Studies in Italian Art and Language, U. Urbino, Urbino, Italy, 1983; BA in Art History, U. Rochester, Rochester, NY, 1984; MA in Art History, Rutgers U., New Brunswick, NJ, 1987. Art critic NYC Tribune, 1987—90; sr. editor Jour. Art, NYC, 1990—91; NY corr. Art Newspaper, NY, 1991—, ARTnewsletter, publ. of ARTnews, 1994—98; journalism fellow U. Mich., Ann Arbor, Mich., 2000—01. Instr., History of Art Franklin Adult Cmty. Edn., Somerset, NJ, 1986; evaluator for the visual arts program Nat. Endowment for the Arts, Washington, 1993; film evaluator panelist Program for Art on Film (joint program of the Metropolitan Mus. Art and J. Paul Getty Trust), NY, 1993; panelist ARCO, Feria Internacional de ARte COntemporaneo, Madrid, 1995; adj. asst. prof. U. Mich., Sch. Art and Design, Ann Arbor, Mich., 2001; lectr. Flint Inst. Art, Mich., 1992, Oglethorpe U., Atlanta, 1995, Tate Modern, London, 2000, Vassar Coll., Poughkeepsie, NY, 2000, Boston U., 2000, U. Mich., Ann Arbor, Mich., 2001. Contbr. articles to profl. jours.; art critic (reviews for exhbns.), contract writer The American Friends of the British Mus., British Mus., London, Eng., 1994—95, (videodisc) Nat. Gallery Art, Washington, DC, 1994, contbr. (freelance articles) AICA Newsletter, American Arts Quarterly, Appraiser, Art & Antiques, Art & Auction, Artnet mag., ARTnews, Artpapers, AP, Atelier, Baltimore Sun, Bergen Record, Ctr. for Exptl. Perceptual Art Jour., Diario 16, Drawing, Everything Art, Insight Magazine, Kalías: revista de arte, Latin American Art, Los Angeles County Museum of Art Graphic Arts Council Newsletter, Los Angeles Times, New Art Examiner, The New York Sun, Review: Latin American Literature and Arts, Saab Magazine, Sculpture, Sculpture Review, Smithsonian Magazine, Spotlight, The Springfield Republican, The Standard-Times, Times Literary Supplement, Ultimas Noticias, The Wall Street Journal, The Washington Post, The Washington Times, The World & I., writer, observer for session on "The arts and social capital in America," Harvard University, John F. Kennedy School of Government, The Saguaro Seminar: Civic Engagement in America, Cambridge, Mass., 1999. Mem.: Association Internationale des Critiques d'Art, Am. Assn. Mus. Office: Art Newspaper 594 Broadway Ste 406 New York NY 10012 Office Phone: 212-343-0727. Office Fax: 212-965-5367. Business E-Mail: j.kaufman@theartnewspaper.com. E-mail: jason_kaufman@hotmail.com.

KAUFMAN, JEFFREY ALLEN, publisher; b. Mpls., May 28, 1952; s. Theodore and Jean Louise (Tiegs) K. Student, Mankato State U., 1970-71, Ariz. State U., 1971-72; BA, U. Minn., 1975. Pres. Creative Resources, Inc., Mpls., 1976-80; sr. v.p. Literary Resources, Inc., Phoenix, 1980-81; pres. Multi-Media, Phoenix, 1981-83, Where To Go, Inc., Excelsior, Minn., 1983-86; v.p. The Old Utica Co., Mpls., 1986-88; chmn. Actif, Inc., Wayzata, Minn., 1988-89; ptnr. S&K Group, Mpls., 1989-90; editor in chief Spl. Events Pub., Inc., Mpls., 1990-92; founder Electronic Claims Processing, Inc., Edina, Minn., 1992-96; co-owner BIO-Works, Inc., 1994—, Kaufman Capital Funding. Cons. Control Data Corp., Mpls., 1978—81; dir. Nexus Inc., Mpls., 1978—81; founder ECP Inc., 1992; chmn. Dr. Zen Diabetic Ctrs., Inc., 2002—. Author: (books) Where To Go in Minneapolis and Saint Paul, 1984, Where To Go in Los Angeles, 1985, (screenplay) Born To Be Chief, 1985. Avocations: golf, flying, equestrian. Home: PO Box 475 Scottsdale AZ 85252-0475 E-mail: jeffrey_kaufman@msn.com.

KAUFMAN, JEROME BENZION, retired neurosurgeon; b. Waterloo, Iowa, July 22, 1934; s. Louis and Dorothy (Rosenbloom) K.; m. Judith Ellen Lasker, June 29, 1967; children: David, Jonathan, Jefferey. BA, Wayne State U., 1955, MD, 1961; postgrad., U. Madrid. Diplomate Am. Bd. Neurol. Surgery 1975. Rotating intern Michael Reese Hosp. and Med. Ctr., Chgo., 1961-62; resident in internal med. Michael Reeese Hosp. and Med. Ctr., Chgo., 1962-63; resident in gen. surgery VA Hosp., Bronx, 1965-66, resident in neurology, 1966, resident in neurosurgery, 1967, from sr. to chief resident neurosurgery, 1969-70; resident neurosurgery Neurol. Inst. N.Y., Columbia Presbyn. Hosp., 1968; resident neuropathology Mt. Sinai Hosp. and Med. Sch., N.Y.C., 1968; chief resident neurosurgery City Hosp., Elmhurst, N.Y., 1969; chmn. dept. neurosurgery Carle Clinic Assn. and Found. Hosp., Urbana, Ill., 1972—96, prof. emeritus, 1997—, U. Ill. Coll. medicine, Champaign-Urbana. Cons. neurosurgery McKinley Hosp., Urbana, Covenant Hosp., Urbana; asst. instr. internal medicine Chgo. Med. Sch., 1963; clin. assoc. prof. neurosurgery U. Ill. Coll. Medicine, Urbana, 1982-96, clin. prof., chmn. neurosurgery. Contbr. chapters to books to profl. jours. Capt. USAF, 1963—65. Named One of Best Drs. in Am.- Midwest, Ill. Fellow ACS, Am. Assn. Neurol. Surgeons (Continuing Edn. award in neurosurgery 1980, 83, 85, 87, 89, 93, 96), Internat. Coll. Surgeons (vice regent) N.Y. Acad. Scis.; mem. AMA (Physicians Recognition award 1980, 82, 85, 89, 93), Ill. Med. Soc., Champaign County Med. Soc., Congress Neurol. Surgeons, Ctrl. Neurosurg. Soc., Assn. Mil. Surgeons U.S., Chgo. Neurol. Soc. (Best Doctors in Am. Midwest). Home: 2104 Zuppke Dr Urbana IL 61801-6706 Personal E-mail: j-kauf@uiuc.edu.

KAUFMAN, JOANNE MELISSA, sociology educator; BS, Cornell U., 1991; PhD, Emory U., 2001. Vis. fellow Ctrs. for Disease Control and Prevention, Atlanta, 1998—2001; asst. prof. dept. sociology U. Miami, Fla., 2001—. Contbr. articles to profl. jours. Com. mem. Temple Judea, Coral Gables, Fla., 2003—. Grantee, Nat. Inst. Drug Abuse, 2002—03, 2004—05. Mem.: Acad. Criminal Justice Scis., So. Sociol. Soc., Am. Sociol. Assn., Am. Soc. Criminology. Office: U Miami Dept Sociology PO Box 248162 Coral Gables FL 33124-2030 Office Phone: 305-284-6762. Office Fax: 305-284-5310. E-mail: jkaufman@miami.edu.

KAUFMAN, JONATHAN ALLAN (JON KAUFMAN), public relations executive; b. N.Y.C., May 31, 1943; s. Stephen Allan (dec.) and Jean (Friedman) (dec.) K.; m. Jill J. Horowitz, July 17, 1983. BA, Carleton Coll., 1966; MA, Syracuse U., 1967. Vol. VISTA, N.Y.C., 1967-69; rsch. dir. Nat. Welfare Rights Orgn., Washington, 1969-71; polit. campaign mgr. various, San Francisco, 1971-77; exec. dir. Calif. Tax Reform Assn., San Francisco, 1972-77; asst. mgr. Household Fin. Corp., San Francisco, 1977-79; account exec. Solem & Assocs., San Francisco, 1979-84, v.p., 1984-86, exec. v.p., 1986—; rsch. dir. SA Opinion Rsch., San Francisco, 2000—. Contbr. articles to profl. jours. Bd. dirs. J. the Jewish news weekly, No. Calif. Bd. Am. Israel Pub. Affairs Commn. Andrew W. Mellon Fellow, Syracuse U., 1966, Max Bondy Citizenship award Windsor Mt. Sch., Lenox, Mass., 1962. Mem. Am. Assn. Polit. Cons., Am. Mktg. Assn. Jewish. Avocations: hiking, bicycling, travel, food. Home: 107 Alvarado Rd Berkeley CA 94705-1510 Office: Solem & Assocs 550 Kearny St Ste 1010 San Francisco CA 94108-2570 Office Phone: 415-788-7788 119. E-mail: jon_kaufman@solem.com.

KAUFMAN, JOSHUA JACOB, lawyer, editor; b. N.Y.C., Oct. 31, 1950; s. Jay Herbert Kaufman and Aviva (Goodman) Kaufman-Penn; m. Nan Ellin, July 12, 1980; children: Jay Laurence, Aaron Michael. BA U. Md., 1972; JD George Washington U., 1975. Bar: Md. 1977, D.C. 1978, Fed. Dist. Ct. 1978, U.S. Tax Ct. 1981, U.S. Ct. Claims 1981, N.Y. 1983, U.S. Supreme Ct. 1989. Ptnr. Lowe, Bressler & Kaufman, Washington, 1978-83; ptnr. Kaufman & Biel, P.C., Washington, 1984-86, Goldfarb, Kaufman & O'Toole, Washington, 1986-90, Kaufman & Silverberg, Washington, 1990, ptnr., head, Copyright, Unfair Trade and Entertainment practice group, Venable LLP, Washington; adj. prof. entertainment law Am. U. Law Sch., Washington, 1989—; exec. dir. Vol. Lawyers for Arts, Washington, 1977—; exec. dir. Soc. To Prevent Trade in Stolen Art, Washington, 1995—. Author: Art of Investing in Art, 1980; columnist Artist Mag., Art Bus. News, Sculpture mag., Outdoors Unltd., Washington Lawyer mag., 1986—; contbr. articles to profl. jours.; segment producer, corr. (TV show) Washington's Business. Co-dir. City Coun. Task Force on Cable Regulation, 1974-75. Mem. ABA (forum on entertainment and sports industries, subcom. on copyright, various other sects.), Computer Law Forum, Computer Law Assn., Copyright Soc. USA (steering com. mem.). Democrat. Jewish. Avocations: sculpture, scuba diving, computers, computer art. Office: Venable LLP 575 7th St NW Washington DC 20004 Office Phone: 202-344-8538. Office Fax: 202-344-8300. Business E-Mail: jjkaufman@venable.com.

KAUFMAN, JOYCE JACOBSON, chemist, educator; b. N.Y.C., June 21, 1929; d. Abraham and Sarah (Seldin) Deutch; m. Stanley Kaufman, Dec. 26, 1948; 1 child, Jan Caryl. B.S. with honors, Johns Hopkins U., 1949, M.A., 1959, Ph.D. in Chemistry, 1960; D.E.S. with honors in Theoretical Physics, Sorbonne, Paris, 1963. Analytical research chemist Army Chem. Ctr., Md., 1949-52; mem. chemistry rsch. staff Johns Hopkins U., Balt., 1952-60; mem. quantum chemistry group Rsch. Inst. Advanced Studies, Balt., 1960-69, staff scientist, 1965-69, head, 1963-69; prin. rsch. scientist dept. chemistry Johns Hopkins U., Balt., assoc. prof. dept. anesthesiology Sch. Medicine, 1969—; mem. sci. adv. com. Dept. Def., 1977; mem. rev. panel for undergrad. chemistry edn. NSF, 1977; Fogarty Internat. Exchange specialist NIH-USSR Ministry of Health, 1978. Mem. editorial adv. bd.: John Wiley and Intersci. Pubs., 1965-80; Molecular Pharmacology, 1970-80; Internat. Jour. Quantum Chemistry, 1967-85; Jour. Computational Chemistry, 1980—; editor Benchmark Book Series in phys. chemistry-chem. physics, 1975-77, overall chemistry editor, 1977-80. Contbr. articles to profl. jours. Recipient Garvan medal as outstanding woman chemist Am. Chem. Soc., 1974; Md. Chemist award Am. Chem. Soc. Md. sect. 1974. Fellow Am. Phys. Soc., Am. Inst. Chemists; mem. Am. Chem. Soc. (chmn. Md. sect. 1972, councilor phys. chemistry div. 1971-94, budget and fin. com. 1981-91, pubs. com. 1992—), Am. Soc. Pharmacology and Exptl. Therapeutics, European Acad. Scis., Arts and Letters (corr. mem.), Internat. Soc. Quantum Biology, Phi Beta Kappa, Sigma Xi. Office: Johns Hopkins U Dept Chemistry Baltimore MD 21218

KAUFMAN, JULIAN MORTIMER, broadcasting company executive, consultant; b. Detroit, Apr. 3, 1918; s. Anton and Fannie (Newman) K.; m. Katherine LaVerne Likins, May 6, 1942; children: Nikki, Keith Anthony. Grad., H.S., Newark. Pub. Elizabeth (N.J.) Sunday Sun, Inc., 1937-39; account exec. Tolle Advt. Agy., San Diego, 1947-49; pub. Tucson Shopper, 1948-50; account exec. ABC, San Francisco, 1949-50; mgr. Sta. KPHO-TV, Phoenix, 1950-52; gen. mgr., v.p. Bay City TV Corp., San Diego, 1952-95; v.p. Jai Alai Films, Inc., San Diego, 1961—; TV cons. Julian Kaufman, Inc., San Diego, 1985—. Dir. Spanish Internat. Broadcasting, Inc., L.A.; chmn. bd. dirs. Bay City TV Inc. Contbr. articles to profl. jours.; prodr. (TV show) Pick a Winner. Mem. Gov.'s adv. bd. Mental Health Assn., 1958—; bd. dirs. Francis Parker Sch., San Diego BBB, 1979-84, San Diego Conv. and Visitors Bur., World Affairs Coun., Pala Indian Mission. Served with USAAF, 1942-46. Recipient Peabody award, 1975, Emmy award, 1980. Mem. San Diego C. of C., Advt. and Sales Club, San Diego Press Club, Univ. Club (San Diego), Sigma Delta Chi. Republican. Home: 3125 Montesano Rd Escondido CA 92029-7302 Office: 7677 Ronson Rd Ste 210 San Diego CA 92111-1538 E-mail: consultingjmk@aol.com, janoskj66@aol.com.

KAUFMAN, KENNETH ROLAND, psychiatrist, educator; s. Jerome and Rebecca Kaufman; m. Christine Hanson Adams; children: Sarah Jennifer, Deborah Anne, Eliot Michael, Noah Shimon, Nathaniel David. BA summa cum laude, Columbia U., 1968; MA in Chemistry, Harvard U., 1970; MD, Washington U., St. Louis, 1974. Cert. Bd. Med. Examiners Mo., 1977, Pa., 1977, N.Y., 1978, Calif., 1978, N.J., 1995; Psychiatry Bd. Am. Bd. of Psychiatry and Neurology, 1981. Rsch. asst. dept. chem. pathology St. George's Hosp. U. of London, 1966; tchg. fellow dept. chemistry Harvard U., Cambridge, 1968—70; tutor in chemistry Quincy Hosp., Harvard U., Cambridge, 1969—70; asst. instr. psychiatry, NIMH trainee in psychiatry Washington U. Med. Ctr. (Barnes and Renard Hosp.), St Louis, 1974—77; psychiatry resident Washington U. Sch. of Medicine, St. Louis, 1974—77; hon. clin. neurophysiologist Maudsley Hosp., London, 1976; rsch. fellow Inst. of Psychiatry, U. London, 1976; advanced rsch. fellow Western Psychiat. Inst. and Clinic, U. Pitts., 1977; asst. prof. of clin. psychiatry Western Psychiat. Inst. and Clinic, U. of Pitts., 1977—79; rsch. fellow Dept. of Child and Adolescent Psychiatry Inst. of Psychiatry U. of London, 1976; asst. prof. psychiatry U. of So. Calif. Sch. of Medicine, LA, 1979—82, asst. prof. neurology, 1980—82, clin. asst. prof. psychiatry, 1982—84, clin. asst. prof. neurology, 1982—99; asst. clin. prof. of psychiatry and biobehavioral scis. UCLA, LA, 1984—96; pvt. practitioner Kenneth R Kaufman, MD Inc., LA, 1982—96; vis. asst. prof. psychiatry Columbia U. Coll. of Physicians and Surgeons, N.Y.C., 1986—86; assoc. prof. clin. psychiatry U. of Medicine and Dentistry of N.J., Robert Wood Johnson Med. Sch., New Brunswick, 1995—98, assoc. prof. clin. neurology, 1996—98, assoc. prof. psychiatry, 1998—2002, prof. neurology, 2003—, assoc. prof. neurology, 1998—2003, prof. psychiatry, 2002—; attending psychiatrist U. Behavioral Health Care U. of Medicine and Dentistry of N.J., Robert Wood Johnson Med. Sch., New Brunswick, 1997—98, Cmty. Mental Health Ctr. at Piscataway U. of Medicine and Dentistry of N.J., Robert Wood Johnson Med. Sch., New Brunswick, 1996—97, Consultation Liaison Svc., Robert Wood Johnson U. Hosp., New Brunswick, NJ, 1997—, Splty. Psychopharmacology Clinics, New Brunswick, NJ, 1998—. Editl. bd. Annals of Clin. Psychiatry, 1988—2003, contr. editor editl. bd. Mt. Sinai Jour. Medicine, 1986—89, reviewer (9 profl. jours.); author: numerous articles, chpts., abstracts and internat. presentations in field. Team psychiatrist Mem. U.S. Med. Team, 16th Maccabiah Games, Tel Aviv, 2001. Recipient Gold medal in Cricket, 13th Maccabiah Games, 1989, Humanitarian award, Women's Am. O.R.T., 1993; fellow The Harvard Fellowship, Harvard U., 1968—69. Fellow: Am. Psychiat. Assn.; mem.: The Am. Epilepsy Soc., Am. Chem. Soc., Am. Psychopathological Assn., Assn. of European Psychiatrists, Am. Acad. of Clin. Psychiatrists (treas. 1997—99, program chair 1999—2001, v.p. 2001—02), Royal Coll. of Psychiatry, AMA. Jewish. Avocations: travel, cricket, golf, theater, reading. Home: 8 Villa Dr Princeton Junction NJ 08550 Office: UMDNJ-Robert Wood Johnson Medical School 125 Paterson St Ste #2200 New Brunswick NJ 08901 Personal E-mail: adamskaufman@comcast.net. E-mail: kaufmakr@umdnj.edu.

KAUFMAN, MARY JANE YELTON, literature educator; b. Cin., Nov. 28, 1942; AB in Edn., U. N.C., 1965; MEd, Xavier U., 1969; PhD in Edn. Curriculum and Methodology, The Union Grad. Sch., 1996. Cert. ednl. adminstrv. specialist, high sch. prin., secondary supr., high sch. English, drama and computer tchr., Ohio. With Milford (Ohio) H.S., 1970-97; adj. instr. English and edn. U. Cin., 1997-99; enrollment coord. doctoral and undergrad. The Union Inst., Cin., 1999—2001; curriculum dir. and adminstr. Columbus Youth Entrepreneurial Acad., 2001—03; ESOL curriculum specialist Fairfield Schs., Ohio, 2003—. Presenter in field, 1995-2003. Edn. rsch. grantee U. Cin., 1996-98. Mem. AAUW, S.W. Ohio Edn. Assn. (bd. dirs.), Milford Edn. Assn. (pres.), Delta Kappa Gamma (pres. Delta Chi 1990-92, state v.p. 2003-), Phi Delta Kappa. Episcopalian. Avocations: boating, skiing. Home: 6604 Quail Lake Mason OH 45040-7001 Office Phone: 513-404-7630. Personal E-mail: mj239@aol.com. E-mail: mj239@cinci.rr.com.

KAUFMAN, NATHAN, retired pathologist, educator; b. Lachine, Que., Can., Aug. 3, 1915; s. Solomon and Anna (Sabesinsky) K.; m. Rita Friendly, Sept. 10, 1946; children: Naomi, Michael, Miriam, Hannah, Judith. B.Sc., McGill U., Montreal, 1937, MD, C.M., 1941. Mem. faculty Western Res. U. Med. Sch., 1948-60, asst. prof., 1952-54, asso. prof., 1954-60; pathologist-in-charge Cleve. Met. Gen. Hosp., 1952-60; prof. pathology Duke Sch. Medicine, 1960-67; prof. dept. pathology Queen's U. Med. Sch., Kingston, Ont., Can., 1967-81, prof. emeritus, 1981—, head dept., 1967-79; clin. prof. office of humanities Med. Coll. Ga., Augusta, 1980-85. Pathologist-in-chief Kingston Gen. Hosp., 1967-79; past cons. Hotel Dieu Hosp., St. Mary's of the Lake Hosp., Kingston Clinic, Ont. Cancer Treatment and Research Found.; asso. editor Lab. Investigation Jour., 1952-66, editor, 1972-75, mem. editorial bd., 1975—; asso. editor Am. Jour. Pathology, 1967, mem. editorial bd., 1967-71; Mem. grants panel Med. Research Council Can., 1970-74, mem. council, 1971-77, exec. com., 1971-74; active coms. Ont. Council Health, 1968-79, chmn. provincial rev. ednl. subcom., 1972-75 Editor: Modern Pathology, 1988; mem. editl. bd. Modern Pathology, 1989—95. Served to capt. M.C., Royal Can. Army, 1942-4., Decorated mem. Order Brit. Empire; recipient Disting. Alumni award Duke U., 1975, Internat. Acad. Pathology Gold medal, 1996. Mem. Internat. Acad. Pathology (v.p. 1972-74, pres. elect 1974, pres. 1976-78, pres. U.S.-Can. div. 1973-75, sec.-treas. 1979-91, F.K. Mostofi Disting. Svc. award U.S.-Can. div. 1990), U.S. and Can. Acad. Pathology, Royal Coll. Physicians and Surgeons Can. (com. on exams. 1972), Cleve. Soc. Pathologists (past pres.), Am. Assn. Pathologists (editor Symposium series 1970-71), Am. Soc. for Investigative Pathology, Am. Soc. Clin. Pathologists, Am. Assn. Cancer Research, Am. Soc. Cytology, Coll. Am. Pathologists, Canadian Med. Assn., Can., Ont. assns. pathologists, Ont. Med. Assn., Can. Soc. Cytology. Home: 185 Ontario St # 704 Kingston ON Canada K7L 2Y7

KAUFMAN, PAULA T., librarian; b. Perth Amboy, N.J., July 26, 1946; d. Harry and Clara (Katz) K.; m. L. Ratner, 1989. AB, Smith Coll., 1968; MS, Columbia U., 1969; MBA, U. New Haven, 1979. Reference libr. Columbia U., N.Y.C., 1969-70, bus. libr., 1979-82, dir. libr. svcs., 1982-86, dir. acad. info. svcs., 1986-87, acting v.p., univ. libr., 1987-88; dean of librs. U. Tenn., Knoxville, 1988-99; univ. libr. U. Ill., Urbana Champaign, 1999—. Reference coord. McKinsey & Co., N.Y.C., 1970—73; founder, ptnr. Info. for Bus., N.Y.C., 1973—76; prin. reference libr. Yale U., New Haven, 1976—79; bd. dir. Ctr. Rsch. Libr., 1994—2000, chmn., 1996—97; bd. dirs. CAUSE, 1996—98; bd. dir. Assn. Rsch. Libr., 1997—2003, v.p., pres.-elect, 2000—01, pres., 2001—02; bd. dir. ILCSO, 2000—04, chair, 2001—02; bd. dirs. Coun. on Libr. and Info. Resources, 2001—, vice chair, 2001—. Contbr. articles to mags., 1983—. Bd. dirs. Cmty. Shares, Knoxville, 1993—97, Lincoln Trails Libr. Sys., Champaign, Ill., 2001—; bd. trustees Champaign (Ill.) Pub. Libr., 2004—. Mem. ALA, Soc. for Scholarly Pub., Solinet (bd. dirs., chmn. 1992-93).

KAUFMAN, PETER BISHOP, biological sciences educator; b. San Francisco, Feb. 25, 1928; s. Earle Francis and Gwendolyn Bishop (Morris) K.; m. Hazel Elizabeth Snyder, Apr. 5, 1958; children— Linda Myrl, Laura Irene BS, Cornell U., 1949; PhD in Botany, U. Calif.-Davis, 1954. Instr. botany U. Mich., Ann Arbor, 1956-58, asst. prof., 1958-62, assoc. prof., 1962-72, prof. botany, cellular and molecular biology and bioengring. program, 1972-97, emeritus prof. dept. biology, 1998—, 1st yr. seminar Residential Coll., 1997—2002, sr. rsch. scientist integrative medicine program. Cons. NASA Space Biology Program; vis. prof. U. Lund, Sweden, 1964-65, U. Colo., Boulder, 1973-74; mem. faculty agr. Nagoya U., Japan, 1981 Author: Laboratory Experiments in Plant Physiology, 1975, Plants, People and Environment, 1979, Botany Illustrated, 1983, 2d edit., 2005, Practical Botany, 1983, Plants: Their Biology and Importance, 1989; co-author: Handbook of Molecular and Cellular Methods in Biology and Medicine, 1995, 2d edit., 2003, Methods in Gene Biotechnology, 1997, 2d edit., 2003, Natural Products from Plants, 1998, 2d edit., 2005, Creating a Sustainable Future Living in Harmony with the Earth, 2002. Mem. Mich. Natural Areas Coun.; mem. exec. com. U. Mich. Program in Scholarly Rsch. for Urban Minority Students. Grantee NIH, NSF, NASA Fellow AAAS; mem. Am. Inst. Biol. Scis., Am. Soc. Plant Biologists, Am. Soc. Gravitational and Space Biology (sec.-treas., 1985-1993), Internat. Soc. Plant Molecular Biologists, Bot. Soc. Am., Mich.

Bot. Club (pres. 1985-89), Sigma Xi. Democrat. Presbyterian. Home: 317 Woodland Dr Chelsea MI 48118-9322 Office: U Mich B570E MSRB II West Medical Dr Ann Arbor MI 48109 E-mail: pbk@umich.edu.

KAUFMAN, RAYMOND HENRY, physician; b. Bklyn., Nov. 24, 1925; s. Morris and Anne (Markewich) K.; m. Patricia Ann Judson, June 23, 1946; children: Susan Jo (Mrs. Edward B. Kahn), Wendy Beth (Mrs. Seth Katzman), Murri Ellen (Mrs. Raymond Simonetti), Elisabeth Ann. Student, Coll. William and Mary, 1942-43, U. N.C., 1943-44; MD, U. Md., 1948. Diplomate: Am. Bd. Obstetrics and Gynecology. Intern Beth Israel Hosp., N.Y.C., 1948-49, resident obstetrics and gynecology, 1949-53; fellow pathology Meth. Hosp., Houston, 1955-58; asst. prof. obstetrics, gynecology, pathology Baylor Coll. Medicine, Houston, 1959-65, assoc. prof., 1965-72, acting chmn. dept., 1968-72, prof., chmn. dept. ob-gyn, 1973-93, prof. pathology, 1973—, prof. dept. ob-gyn., 1973—. Author: (with H.L. Gardner) Benign Diseases of Vulva and Vagina, 1969, 4th edit. (with S. Faro, E. Friedrich and Gardner), 1994; contbr. over 200 articles to profl. jours. Served with USNR, 1943-45; to capt. USAF, 1953-55. Mem. Am. Coll. Obstetrics and Gynecology, ACS, Cen. Assn. Obstetrics and Gynecology (chmn. com. for cons. gynecol. pathology 1968-87, pres. 1976), Tex. Assn. Obstetrics and Gynecology (v.p. 1971, 81, pres. 1983), Am. Gynecol. and Obstet. Soc. (v.p. 1985-86), Houston Obstet. and Gynecol. Soc. (pres. 1971-72), Soc. Gynecol. Oncology (v.p. 1983-84), Am. Cytology Soc., Am. Fertility Soc., Am. Soc. Colposcopy, Internat. Soc. Vulvar Disease (pres. 1978-79), Phi Delta Epsilon (nat. sec. 1970-75). Office: Baylor Coll Med 1 Baylor Plz Houston TX 77030-3411

KAUFMAN, RICHARD STUART, conductor, music director; b. LA, Nov. 20, 1947; s. Walter S. and Margye L. (Whisler) Kaufman; 1 child, Whitney Claire. BA, Calif. State U., Northridge, 1970. Music dir., condr. Sweet Charity, Two Gentlemen of Verona, Company, nat. tours, 1970-74, LA Civic Light Opera, 1975—80; condr. for various performers including Burt Bacharach, Juliet Prowse, Andy Williams, John Denver, nationwide, 1976—; music assoc. 20th Century Fox Studios, LA, 1982—84; music coordinator Metro Goldwyn Mayer/United Artists Communications, Culver City, Calif., 1984-87; dir. music for TV Metro Goldwyn Mayer/United Artists Comm., Culver City, Calif., 1988—; prin. condr. Dallas Symphony Orch., 1997—; condr. Pacific Symphony, 1990—. Composer: Alma Mater for Calif. State U., 1969. Recipient Best Pop Instrumental Performance, Grammy Awards, 1993; fellow, Berkshire Music Festival, 1969, Tanglewood, 1969. Mem.: Phi Mu Alpha. Avocations: baseball, racquetball. Office: MGM/UA Communications Inc 10000 Washington Blvd Suite 2091 Culver City CA 90232 also: Dallas Symphony 2301 Flora St Dallas TX 75201 also: Pacific Symphony Ste 100 3631 S Harbor Blvd Santa Ana CA 92704*

KAUFMAN, ROBERT JULES, communications consultant, lawyer; b. N.Y.C., Jan. 21, 1921; s. Ernst B. and Gertrude S. (Popper) K.; m. Susan H. Sanger, Feb. 22, 1951; children— Peter S., James H. Student, Columbia Coll., 1942, Yale U. Law Sch., 1948. Bar: N.Y. bar 1949. Assoc. Gale, Bernays, Falk & Eisner, N.Y.C., 1948-53; ptnr. Gale & Falk, 1953-55; asst. gen. counsel DuMont TV Network, 1953-55; with ABC, N.Y.C., 1955-86, v.p., gen. atty. network govtl. regulation, 1968-86; comm. cons. Scarsdale, N.Y., 1986—. Mem. internat. copyright panel Dept. State; guest speaker on radio and television matters at Practicing Law Inst. and N.Y. U. Law Sch. Served to lt. USN, 1942-46. Mem. Bar Assn. City N.Y. (communications com.), Copyright Soc. U.S.A., Nat. Acad. TV Arts and Scis. (mem. U.S. Olympic job opportunity program com.), Phi Beta Kappa. Home and Office: 33 Clarendon Rd Scarsdale NY 10583-2452

KAUFMAN, ROBERT MAX, lawyer, director; b. Vienna, Nov. 17, 1929; came to U.S., 1939, naturalized, 1945; s. Paul M. and Bertha (Hirsch) K.; m. Sheila Seymour Kelley. BA with honors, Bklyn. Coll., 1951; MA, NYU, 1954; JD magna cum laude, Bklyn. Law Sch., 1957. Bar: N.Y. 1957, U.S. Supreme Ct. 1961. Successively jr. economist, economist, sr. economist N.Y. State Div. Housing, 1953-57; atty. antitrust div. U.S. Dept. Justice, 1957-58; legis. asst. to U.S. Senator Jacob K. Javits, 1958-61; assoc. Proskauer Rose LLP, N.Y.C., 1961-69, ptnr., 1969—. Past chmn. bd. Pirelli Cables & Systems, LLC, Pirelli Tires LLC; chmn. bd. Old Westbury Funds, Inc.; bd. dirs. Roytex Inc.; mem. N.Y. State Legis. Adv. Com. on Election Law, 1973-74; chmn. adv. com. N.Y. State Bd. Elections, 1974-78; chmn. N.Y. State Bd. Pub. Disclosure, 1981-82, U.S. Army Chief of Staff's Spl. Commn. on Honor System, 1988-89, N.Y. Chief Judge's Com. on Availability of Legal Svcs., 1988-90; referee Commn. on Jud. Conduct; spl. master N.Y. Supreme Ct. Appellate Divsn., 1999—; mem. Adminstrv. Conf. U.S. (chair com. regulations), 1988-95; chmn. Fund for Modern Cts., 1990-95; mem. Def. Adv. Com. on Women in the Svcs., 1997-99, vice chair com. on equality mgmt., mem. exec. com. 1998. Co-author: Congress and the Public Trust, 1970, Disorder in the Court, 1973; co-gen. editor: Matthew Bender Treatise on Health Care Law, 4 vols., 1992—. Bd. dirs. NOW Legal Def. and Edn. Fund; bd. dirs., mem. exec. com. Lawrence M. Gelb Found., Inc., Lawyers in Pub. Interest, 1986—95, Am. Judicature Soc., pres., 1995—97; bd. dirs., chmn. exec. com. Cmty. Action Legal Svcs., Inc., 1976—78; dir., mem. exec. com. Legal Aid Soc., 1985—90; mem. exec. com. Vols. of Legal Svc., 1986—94; mem. platform com. N.Y. Rep. State Com.; mem. jud. selection adv. coms. Senator Javits, 1972—80, Senator Moynihan, 1977—2000; bd. dirs., v.p. Citizen's Union Found., 1993—; bd. dirs. Women's Rsch. and Edn. Inst.; bd. vis. U. S. Mil. Acad., 1976—79; bd. dirs. Citizen's Union NYC, 1986—, N.Y. Cmty. Funds., James Found., Vis. Nurse Svc. of N.Y.C., Med. and Health Rsch. Assn. N.Y.C.; mem. jud. selection adv. coms. N.Y.C. Quadrennial Comm. on compensation of elected officials, 1995, 1999, mem. distbn. com., vice chair, 2001—, N.Y. Cmty. Trust; dir., mem. exec. com., past chmn. bd. Times Sq. Bus. Improvement Dist.; trustee Bklyn. Law Sch. With U.S. Army, 1957—58. Fellow Am. Bar Found., N.Y. State Bar Found.; mem. ABA, Assn. of Bar of City N.Y. (pres. 1986-88, chmn. house com., co-chmn. com. on campaign fin. reform 1997-2001, past chmn. com. on 2d Century; past chmn. exec. com., past chmn. com. profl. responsibility, past chmn. spl. com. on campaign expenditures, past chmn. com. civil rights, past vice chmn. com. grievances, past chmn. delegation to state bar ho. dels.), N.Y. State Bar Assn. (ho. of dels. 1978, 86-90), N.Y. County Lawyers Assn. (past chmn. com. on civil rights), Am. Law Inst. Office: Proskauer Rose LLP 1585 Broadway New York NY 10036-8299 Office Phone: 212-969-3285. Business E-Mail: rkaufman@proskauer.com.

KAUFMAN, RUSSEL EUGENE, hematologist, oncologist; b. Kenton, Ohio, Mar. 7, 1946; s. George W. and Eileen M. (Risner) K.; m. Jane Ann Steinman, Sept. 25, 1948; children: Jonathon R., Emily J. BS, Ohio State U., 1969, MD cum laude, 1973. Diplomate Am. Bd. Internal Medicine. Resident in medicine Duke U. Med. Ctr., Durham, NC, 1973-77, chief resident in medicine, 1977; rsch. hematologist NIH, Bethesda, Md., 1978-80; asst. prof. medicine Duke U. Med. Ctr., Durham, 1980-86, from asst. prof. to assoc. prof. biochemistry, 1985—2001, from assoc. prof. to prof. medicine, 1986—, prof. dept. biochemistry, 2000—02, prof. emeritus, 2002—, chief divsn. hematology and oncology, 1989-96, chief divsn. med. oncology & transplantation, 1996-98, vice chair dept. medicine, 1995-99, assoc. dean Sch. of Medicine, 1998-99, vice dean for edn. and acad. affairs, 1999—2002, assoc. vice chancellor acad. affairs, 2000—02; dir., CEO Wistar Inst., 2002—03, pres., CEO, 2004—; dir. Wistar NCI Cancer Ctr. Mem. sci. adv. com. Am. Cancer Soc., Atlanta, N.Y.C., 1987—; mem. com. NAS, Washington, 1983-86; mem. sci. rev. coms. NIH, Bethesda, Md., 1985—; assoc. chief of staff edn. Durham VA Med. Ctr., 1998-99; Wistar prof. medicine Sch. Medicine U. Pa. Health Sys., 2003-; bd. dirs. U. City Sci. Ctr., 2002-, BioAdvance, 2004-, U. of Arts, 2005-. Contbr. articles to profl. jours., chpts. to books. Bd. dirs., CEO Coun. for Growth Greater Phila. C. of C., 2003—. Searle Found. scholar, 1983-86, Leukemia Soc. scholar, N.Y.C., 1986-90. Fellow ACP; mem. AAAS, ACS, Am. Soc. Biochemistry, Am. Soc. Hematology (head subcom. on red cell 1985-88, chmn. com. on tng. programs 1995-98), Assn. Subsplty. Profs. (exec. coun. 1994, treas. 1997-98, pres.-elect 1998-99, pres. 1999-2000, past pres. 2000-01), Assn. Hematology/Oncology Program Dirs. (chair 1997-98). Presbyterian. Avocations: golf, tennis. Office: The Wistar Inst 3601 Spruce St Philadelphia PA 19104-4268 Office Phone: 215-898-3926. Business E-Mail: kaufman@wistar.org.

KAUFMAN, RUSSELL E., medical researcher; m. Jane Kaufman; children: Jane, Emily. BS, Ohio State U., 1968, MD, 1973. Medical resident Duke U., 1973—2002, prof. medicine and biochemistry, 1973—2002, vice dean sch. medicine, 1973—2002; pres. and CEO Wistar Inst., 2002—. Recipient Searle Scholar, scholar, Leukemia and Lymphoma Soc. Am. Office: Wistar Inst 3601 Spruce St Philadelphia PA 19104 Business E-Mail: kaufman@wistar.upenn.edu.

KAUFMAN, SANFORD PAUL, lawyer; b. NYC, Jan. 4, 1928; s. Max and Rose (Kornitzky) K.; m. Bernice R. Sulkis, June 17, 1956; children: Leslie Keith, Brad Leigh, Rona Sheryl, Jeffrey Scott, Adam Ira. BBA in Acctg., CCNY, 1948; LLB, NYU, 1952, LLM in Taxation, 1957. Bar: NY 1953, Calif. 1962. With firm Garey & Garey, N.Y.C., 1953-55; asst. gen. counsel Olympic Radio & TV, L.I. City, NY, 1961-63; sec., gen. counsel Tel-Autograph Corp., L.A., 1961-63; asst. gen. counsel Nat. Gen. Corp., L.A., 1963-74; sec., gen. counsel Familian Corp., L.A., 1974-77; pvt. practice Torrance, Calif., 1977—. Bd. dirs. Temple Ner Tamid, S. Bay, Calif. Mem. Am. Soc. Corp. Secs., Los Angeles County Bar Assn., Beverly Hills Bus. Men's Assn., K.P. Club (past chancellor). Home: 28412 Golden Meadow Dr Rancho Palos Verdes CA 90275-2926 Office: 23505 Crenshaw Blvd Ste 246 Torrance CA 90505-5223 Office Phone: 310-534-5901. *A person's finest attributes: honesty, integrity, loyalty, dependability and reliability, and the fear of God.*

KAUFMAN, STEPHEN EDWARD, lawyer; b. N.Y.C., Feb. 16, 1932; s. Herbert and Gertrude Kaufman; m. Marina Pinto, June 22, 1967; children: Andrew H. and Douglas P. BA, Williams Coll., 1953; LLB, Columbia U., 1957. Bar: N.Y. 1958, U.S. Ct. Appeals (2d cir.) 1958, U.S. Dist. Ct. (so. and ea. dists.) N.Y. 1960, U.S. Supreme Ct. 1963. Asst. U.S. atty. (So. dist.) NY US Dept. Justice, 1958, chief criminal divsn., 1964-69; pres. Stephen E. Kaufman, P.C., N.Y.C., 1976—. Bd. dirs. Citigroup Mut. Funds. Trustee Mus. Jewish Heritage; dir. Police Athletic League. Fellow Am. Coll. Trial Lawyers; mem. ABA, N.Y. State Bar Assn., Assn. of Bar of City of N.Y. Office: 277 Park Ave New York NY 10172-0003 Office Phone: 212-826-0820. Business E-Mail: skaufman@sekpc.com.

KAUFMAN, STEPHEN HERSCU, lawyer, engineer; b. Bucharest, Romania, Aug. 14, 1945; s. Herscu and Roza Kaufman; m. Aurelia Kaufman, Feb. 14, 1992. BS, Columbia U., 1969, MS, 1974; JD, Fordham U., 1982. Bar: N.Y. 1983, U.S. Dist. Ct. (ea. and so. dists.) N.Y. 1983, U.S. Supreme Ct.; registered profl. engr., N.Y. Civil engr. Dept. Transp., N.Y.C., 1976-84; pvt. practice N.Y.C., 1984—. Mem. Assn. of Bar of City of N.Y. (constrn. law com. 1996-98), N.Y. State Bar Assn. (alt. dispute resolution com. 1998), Columbia Club (assoc.). Jewish. Avocations: investments, ping pong/table tennis.

KAUFMAN, STEPHEN LAWRENCE, radiologist, educator; b. Phila., Nov. 7, 1942; s. Abraham S. and Genevieve (Finestone) K.; m. Linda S. Brier, Feb. 14, 1996. BA, U. Pa., 1963, MD, 1967. Resident in radiology, then fellow cardiovasc. radiology Johns Hopkins Med. Ctr., Balt., 1970-75, asst. prof. radiology, 1975-79, assoc. prof., 1980-88; prof. radiology, dir. cardiovasc. and interventional radiology Emory U., Atlanta, 1988—2003, prof. emeritus radiology, 2003—; attending radiologist Asheville VA Med. Ctr., 2003—, Asheville (Va.) Med. Ctr., 2003—. Author: Techniques in Interventional Radiology, 1982; editor: Biliary Radiology, 1992; contbr. articles to med. jours. Lt. comdr. USPHS, 1968-70. Fellow Soc. Interventional Radiology, Am. Heart Assn.; mem. Radiol. Soc. N.Am., Am. Coll. Radiology. Avocations: hiking, white-water rafting, golf, computers.

KAUFMAN, THOMAS FREDERICK, lawyer, educator; b. Buffalo, Sept. 10, 1949; s. Frederick J. and Edna M. (Kilian) K.; children: Alycia, Thomas, Jonathan. BSEE, SUNY, Buffalo, 1971; JD, Georgetown U., 1976; MBA, U. Pa., 2001. Bar: Va. 1976, U.S. Ct. Appeals (6th cir.) 1976, DC 1977, U.S. Dist. Ct. DC 1981, Md. 1996. Law clk. to chief judge U.S. Ct. Appeals (6th cir.), 1976-77; assoc. Melrod, Redman & Gartlan, Washington, 1977-81, Willkie Farr & Gallagher, Washington, 1981-84, ptnr., 1985-95, Hunton & Williams, Washington, 1995—. Adj. prof. law Georgetown U., Washington, 1986—. Mem. Am. Coll. Real Estate Lawyers. Office: Hunton and Williams 1900 K St NW Washington DC 20006-1110 E-mail: tkaufman@hunton.com.

KAUFMAN, VICTOR A., broadcast executive, retired film company executive; b. 1943; Various sr. positions Columbia, 1974—87; founding chmn., CEO Tri-Star Pictures, 1987—89; pres. CEO Columbia Pictures Entertainment, Inc., 1987—89; chmn. Savoy Pictures Entertainment, N.Y.C., 1990—96; CFO, vice chmn. HSN, Inc., 1996—98; CFO, chmn. USA Networks, Inc., N.Y.C., 1998—, vice chmn. and office chmn., 1999—2003; vice chmn. Interactive Corp., 2003—. Office: USA Networks Inc 42d Fl 152 W 57th St New York NY 10019-3310

KAUFMAN, VICTOR SCOTT, historian, educator; b. Slidell, La., Feb. 22, 1969; s. Burton Ira and Diane Beatrice (Kallison) Kaufman. BA cum laude, Kans. State U., 1991; MA, Ohio U., 1994, PhD, 1998. Instr. Va. Tech. U., Blacksburg, 1997—98, Geo. State U., Atlanta, 1998—99, Kennesaw State U., Ga., 1998—99; lectr. Southwest Mo. State U., Springfield, 1999—2001; asst. prof. Francis Marion U., Florence, SC, 2001—. Sec. faculty support com. Francis Marion U., mem. bookstore adv. com. Author: Confronting Communism, 2001, The Pig War, 2004; contbr. articles to profl. jours.and numerous papers to confs. and workshops. Grantee, Francis Marion U. Found., 2001, 2002, 2003, 2004; Kelce Found. Scholarship, 1990, Golda Crawford Scholarship, 1990, Contemporary History Inst. fellowship, 1992, 1993, Moody grant, Lyndon Baines Johnson Found., 1996, Eisenhower Presdl. Libr. travel grant, 1999. Mem.: AAUP (editor newsletter S.C chpt.), Soc. for Historians of Am. Fgn. Rels., Phi Alpha Theta (faculty advisor Francis Marion U. chpt.), Phi Kappa Phi, Phi Beta Kappa, Golden Key. Office: Dept History Francis Marion Univ Florence SC 29501 E-mail: vkaufman@fmarion.edu.

KAUFMAN, WILLIAM GEORGE, lawyer; b. Nappanee, Ind., June 4, 1949; s. Joseph Edwin and Phyllis (Reeder) K. BS in History, Ind. State U., 1972; JD, Emory U., 1976. Bar: Colo., U.S. Dist. Ct. Colo. 1976. Assoc. Law Offices F. Ray DeGood, Loveland, Colo., 1976-82; prin. Law Office William G. Kaufman, Loveland, 1982-87, William G. Kaufman, P.C., Loveland, 1987—. County mgr. Rep. Bill Armstrong for U.S. Senate, 1978; county chmn. Larimer County Colo. Rep. Com., 1979, 81, 92; chmn. Econ. Devel. Com., 1987; campaign mgr. Hank Brown for Congress, 1988; exec. bd. Long Peak coun. Boy Scouts Am., 1980-86, bd. trustees, 1986—; bd. dirs. Ft. Collins-Loveland Airport Authority, 1985-91; mem. Colo. Ho. of Reps., 1992-2000, spkr. pro tem, 1999-2000; commn. Statx Tansp., 2003—, Colo. Quarter; nominating commn.Colo. Supreme Ct., 2005—; bd. mem. McKee Med. Ctr. Found., 2003—, Loveland/Berthorp Meals on Wheels, 2003—, Nored Front Range MPO, 2003—. Recipient Eagle Scout Silver Beaver award Boy Scouts Am. Memn. ABA, Colo. Bar Assn., Larimer County Bar Assn., Rotary. Methodist. Avocations: skiing, golf, reading. Office: 200 E 7th St Ste 318 Loveland CO 80537-4870 E-mail: thelaw@verinet.com, bkreplep@aol.com.

KAUFMAN, WILLIAM MORRIS, electrical engineer, consultant; b. Pitts., Dec. 31, 1931; s. Nathan and Sarah M. (Paper) K.; m. Iris F. Picovsky, June 21, 1953; children: Nathan E., Marjorie L., Emily M. BSEE, Carnegie Inst. Tech., 1953, MSEE, PhD in EE, Carnegie Inst. Tech. Registered profl. engr. Supr. Westinghouse Electric Corp., Pitts., 1955-62; dir. rsch. Gen. Instrument Corp., Newark, 1962-65; cons. engr. GE, Valley Forge, Pa., 1965-66; mgr. med. engr. dept. Hittman Assocs. Inc., Columbia, Md., 1966-71; v.p. engring. ENSCO, Springfield, Va., 1971-83; v.p. Ocean Data Systems Inc., Rockville, Md., 1984-85; v.p. applied rsch., dir. Carnegie Mellon Rsch. Inst. Carnegie Mellon U., Pitts., 1985-97, mem. tech. transfer bd., 1989-94, mem. employee retirement and welfare benefit plan com., 1988-97. Chmn. tech. adv. group Fostin Capital, Pitts., 1986-95; mem. adv. bd. Pitts. Seed Fund, 1986-97; bd. dirs. Mellon Pitt Carnegie Corp., Maglev, Inc., Tech. Devel. and Edn. Corp. Patentee in field. Mem. adv coun. on regional devel. U. Pitts., 1986; bd. dirs. Ben Franklin Tech. Ctr. of Western Pa., 1988-97, treas., 1997; cons. tech. acquisition. Fellow IEEE (life); mem. Sigma Xi, Tau Beta Pi, Eta Kappa Nu. Home and Office: 38 Sheridan Rd Swampscott MA 01907-2045 Office Phone: 781-595-1434. Business E-Mail: billkaufman@cmu.edu.

KAUFMANN, CHARLES LEONARD, musician, composer; s. Charles Leonard, Sr. and Jane Dilbahner Kaufmann; children: Nicholas David, Mattias Faeroy. MusB in Bassoon, Eastman Sch. Music, Rochester, N.Y., 1977; MusM in Bassoon Performance, Yale U., 1982. 2d bassoon Bergen (Norway) Philharm. Orch., 1985—90; bassoonist Handel and Haydn Soc., Boston, 1998—, Boston Baroque, 1999—, Apollos Fire, Cleve., 2000—04, Trinity Consort, Portland, Oreg., 2001—. Juried mem., maine arts access Maine Arts Commn., Augusta, 2004—. Composer: (choral music) The Peace of Wild Things (a Wendell Berry Poem) (Finalist Ithaca Choral Music Competition Contest, 2004), Azalea Variations (Three Poems by David Ray); musician (bassoonist): (albums) Divertimento for Solo Bassoon, op. 25, Phoenix for Bassoon and Piano. Tour guide Henry Wadsworth Longfellow House, Portland, Maine, 2004—; organist, choir dir. Congl. Ch. Exeter, NH, 1995—99, Unitarian Ch. Portsmouth, NH, 1999—2004; substitute organist, choir dir. 1st Parish Unitarian Ch., Portland, 2004—. Mem.: Am. Music Ctr., Early Music Am., Am. Guild Organists, Internat. Double Reed Soc., Maine Hist. Soc.

KAUFMANN, HENRY MARK, mortgage banker; b. Basel, Switzerland, May 23, 1929; arrived in US, 1940; s. Ferdinand and Carola (Levy) K.; m. Barbara Lurie, Dec. 23, 1961; children: Frederic, Nancy. Student, Univ. Geneva, Switzerland, 1948; BA in Economics, Oberlin Coll., 1951; JD, Harvard U., 1954. Bar: NY 1957, US Ct. Appeals 1960, US Supreme Ct. 1960, US Tax Ct. 1974. V.p. Pearce Mayer & Greer, NYC, 1958—70, I.F.C. Capital Resources, NYC, 1970—75, Smith Barney Real Estate Corp., NYC, 1975—80; pres., chmn. Henry Kaufmann Assocs., Larchmont, NY, 1980—. With Mil. Intelligence Europe 1955-57. Mem. New Rochelle Bar Assn., NY Bar Assn., New York County Lawyers Assn., Harvard Club. Avocations: numismatist, world travel. Home: 64 Greentree Dr Scarsdale NY 10583-7029 Office: Henry Kaufmann Assocs 2 East Ave Larchmont NY 10538-2462

KAUFMANN, JACK, lawyer; b. Davenport, Iowa, May 14, 1942; s. Ed Kaufmann Jr. and Jean Gilchrist (Ploehn) Wernentin; m. Elizabeth Amanda Phillips, Jan. 27, 1973; children: Suzanne Cathryn, John Frederick, Christine Elizabeth, Amanda Jean. AB, Dartmouth Coll., 1964; JD, Columbia U., 1971. Bar: N.Y. 1972. Assoc. Dewey Ballantine, N.Y.C., 1971-79, ptnr., 1980—. Atty. Village of Pelham Manor, N.Y., 1977-83, trustee, 1983-87, mayor, 1987-89; councilman Town of Pelham, N.Y., 1990-91. Lt. (j.g.) USNR, 1964-68. Mem. ABA, N.Y. State Bar Assn., Assn. of Bar of City of N.Y., Delta Kappa Epsilon, Pelham Country Club (pres. 1994-96). Republican. Episcopalian. Home: 649 Ely Ave Pelham NY 10803-2401 Office: Dewey Ballantine 1301 Avenue Of The Americas New York NY 10019-6022

KAUFMANN, JEFFREY BAER, finance educator; b. St. Louis Park, Minn., Aug. 27, 1959; s. Harold Ralph and Nora Jane (Baer) K.; m. Peggy Alicia Rouleau, May 9, 1994. BBA cum laude, James Madison U., 1987; JD, Coll. William and Mary, 1990; PhD, U. N.C., 1999. Bar: Va. 1990, U.S. Ct. Appeals (4th cir.) 1990. Summer assoc. Jeremiah Denton and Assoc., Virginia Beach, Va., 1989; rsch. asst. Coll. of William and Mary, Williamsburg, Va., 1988-90; instr. U. N.C., Chapel Hill, 1990-94; instr. corp. strategy and internat. bus. St. Mary's U., Winona, Minn., 1995—97; vis. asst. prof. mgmt. U. Ill., Urbana-Champaign, 1997—2001; asst. prof. mgmt. Iowa St. U., Ames, 2001—. Mem. Nat. Moot Ct. Team, Coll. William and Mary, Williamsburg, 1989; adj. assoc. prof. Ctrl. Mich. U., Mt. Pleasant, 1995, 1997. Mng. editor Adminstrv. Law Rev., 1989-90; contbr. chpt. to book and articles to profl. jours.; reviewer profl. jours. and assns. With USN, 1978-82. Decorated Expeditionary Forces medals (2); Richard D. Irwin Doctoral Dissertation fellow Richard D. Irwin Co., 1993-94, Nat. Doctoral Bus. Fellow Am. Assn. Colls. and Schs. of Bus, finalist Free Press Doctoral Dissertation award, Acad. Mgmt. Mem. ABA (vice chmn. internat. law com. sect. adminstrv. law and regulatory practice), Va. Bar Assn., Acad. Mgmt. (4 Outstanding Reviewer awards), VFW, Phi Kappa Phi, Beta Gamma Sigma. Avocations: hiking, exercise, reading, history. Office: Iowa St U Coll of Business 3121 Gerdin Bus Bldg Ames IA 50011-1350 Office Phone: 515-294-1201. Business E-Mail: jkaufmnn@iastate.edu.

KAUFMANN, MARK STEINER, banker, director; b. N.Y.C., Dec. 3, 1932; s. Milton L. and Elsa S. (Steiner) K.; m. Carole Richard, June 16, 1957; children: Jon Richard, Susan Helen. BS cum laude in Bus. Adminstrn., Lehigh U., 1953. V.p., dir. mktg. Standard Fin. Corp., N.Y.C., 1958-64; sr. v.p., dir. Milberg Factors, Inc., N.Y.C., 1964-73; dir. corp. devel. Chase Manhattan Bank, N.Y.C., 1973-87, sr. v.p., 1987-96; chmn. Kaufmann & Ptnrs., LLC, N.Y.C., 1996—. Past chmn. banking divsn. UJA/Fedn.; former chmn. bd. dirs. Industry Leaders Fund. Hon. trustee Calhoun Sch., N.Y.C.; hon. dir. Lower Manhattan Cultural Coun.; former chmn. bd. Temple Israel, N.Y.C.; bd. mem. Matindale Inst., Lehigh U. 1st lt. USAF, 1953—55. Recipient human rels. award Anti-Defamation League, 1973, Am. Jewish Com., 1987. Mem. Harmonie Club, Old Oaks Country Club (bd. mem.), Beta Gamma Sigma, Lambda Mu Sigma, Pi Gamma Mu, Omicron Delta Kappa. Home: 124 W 79th St New York NY 10024-6446 Office: Kaufmann and Ptnrs LLC 124 W 79th St New York NY 10024-6446 Office Phone: 212-496-3800. E-mail: mskaufmann@aol.com.

KAUFMANN, URLIN MILO, English literature educator; b. Cleve., Aug. 27, 1934; s. Albert Walter and Alda Winona (Aiken) K.; m. Helen Elizabeth Olson, Sept. 1, 1956; children: Felice, Laurie, Andrew. BA, Greenville (Ill.) Coll., 1956; MA, U. Ill., 1957; PhD, Yale U., 1960. Instr. North Park Coll., Chgo., 1961-62, U. Ill., Urbana, 1962-63, asst. prof., 1963-67, assoc. prof. English, 1967-94, retired, 1994—. Author: The Pilgrim's Progress and Traditions in Puritan Meditation, 1967, Paradise in the Age of Milton, 1978, Heaven: A Future Finer Than Dreams, 1981, Measures of Breath, 2004; co-author: At Ease: Discussing Money and Values in Small Groups, 1998; contbg. author, editor: Households Under God, 1996. I May Be Different, But I'm Part of The Family, 1999. Pres. Light and Life men's aux. Free Meth. Ch. N.Am., Indpls., 1985-95; bd. dirs. Empty Tomb, Inc., Urbana-Champaign, 1980—. Democrat. Home: 1807 N Concord Ln Urbana IL 61802-7725 E-mail: ukaufman@uiuc.edu.

KAUFMANN, VICKI MARIE, social services administrator; b. Lansing, Mich., Nov. 7, 1946; d. Frank Richard and Sophia Mary (Scieszka) Marczynski; m. Felix Kaufmann May 28, 1988. BA, Carlow Coll., Pitts., 1970; MS in Pastoral Studies, St. Paul U., Ottawa, ON., Can., 1976, MA, 1977. Cert. family life educator, fund raising exec. Tchr. Mt. Nazareth Acad., Pitts., 1969—71; family svc. dir. Mt. Nazareth Ctr., Pitts., 1971—75, 1977—78; parish outreach worker St. Casimir Ch., Lansing, 1978—81; parish outreach cons. Diocese of Lansing, 1980—83; family life educator Cath. Social Svcs., Lansing, 1981—84; agy. dir. Cath. Social Svc., Brighton, Mich., 1984—93, Cath. Charities of Archdiocese Miami, Wilton Manors, Fla., 1994—2002, COO, 2002—04, dir. capital devel., 2004—. Chmn. Consortium on Aging, Howell, Mich., 1988-89; cons. (Lansing chpt.) Nat. Stepfamily Assn., 1982-84; facilitator Cath. Coun. on Aging, Livingston County, Mich., 1986-89. Co-author: Welcoming the Seasons, 1977, Parish Social Ministry, 1985. Co-chmn. Livingston County Emergency Shelter, Howell, Mich., 1988—, vice chmn., 1990; bd. dir. Livingston County United Way, Howell, 1988-89, Mich. Coun. of Family Rels., 1990-93; exec. sec. Coun. of Ch. Bd., Lansing, 1982-84; agy. rep. Energy Bank Coalition, Lansing, 1982-84. Mem. NAFE, Nat. Coun. Family Rels., Cath. Charities U.S.A., Mich. Coun. Family Rels. (bd. dir. 1990-93), Assn. Fundraising Profl. (cert.) Roman Catholic. Avocations: classical music, opera, the arts, travel. Office: Cath Charities 1505 NE 26th St Wilton Manors FL 33305-1323 Office Phone: 954-630-9404.

KAUGER, YVONNE, state supreme court justice; b. Cordell, Okla., Aug. 3, 1937; d. John and Alice (Bottom) K.; 1 child, Jonna Kauger Kirschner. BS magna cum laude, Southwestern State U., Weatherford, Okla., 1958; cert. med. technologist, St. Anthony's Hosp., 1959; JD, Oklahoma City U., 1969, LLD (hon.), 1992. Med. technologist Med. Arts Lab., 1959-68; assoc. Rogers, Travis & Jordan, 1970-72; jud. asst. Okla. Supreme Ct., Oklahoma City, 1972-84, justice, 1984-94, 1998—, vice chief justice, 1994-96, chief justice, 1997-98. Mem. appellate div. Ct. on Judiciary; mem. State Capitol Preservation Commn., 1983-84; mem. dean's adv. com. Oklahoma City U. Sch. Law; lectr. William O. Douglas Lecture Series Gonzaga U., 1990. Founder Gallery of Plains Indian, Colony, Okla., Red Earth (Down Towner award 1990), 1987; active Jud. Day, Girl's State, 1976-80; keynote speaker Girl's State Hall of Fame Banquet, 1984; bd. dirs. Lyric Theatre, Inc., 1966—, pres. bd. dirs., 1981; past mem. bd. dirs. Civic Music Soc., Okla. Theatre Ctr., Canterbury Choral Soc.; mem. First Lady of Okla.'s Artisans' Alliance Com. Named Panhellenic Woman of Yr., 1990, Woman of Yr. Red Lands Coun. Girl Scouts, 1990, Washita County Hall of Fame, 1992, Okla. Women's Hall of Fame, 2001. Mem. ABA (law sch. accreditation com.), Okla. Bar Assn. (law schs. com. 1977—), Washita County Bar Assn., Washita County Hist. Soc. (life), St. Paul's Music Soc., Iota Tau Tau, Delta Zeta (Disting. Alumna award 1988, State Delta Zeta of Yr. 1987, Nat. Woman of Yr. 1988). Episcopalian. Office: Okla Supreme Ct State Capitol Building Rm 242 Oklahoma City OK 73105 Office Phone: 405-521-3841. E-mail: yvonne.kauger@oscn.net.

KAUL, MOHAN LAL, retired social worker; arrived in U.S., 1969, naturalized, 1976; s. Mahanand and Tarawati Kaul; m. Jaya Nagari, Aug. 8, 1950; children: Rajiv M., Sanjiv M., Prerna J. BSc, Panjab U., India, 1947; diploma in social work, Delhi (India) Sch. Social Work, 1958; MSW, U. Pitts., 1967; PhD, Case Western Reserve U., Cleve., 1977. Warden Social Edn. Ctr., Delhi, 1950—59; cmty. organizer Dept. Urban Cmty. Devel., Delhi, 1959, chief cmty. organizer, 1959—63, dir., 1963—65; asst. dir. Dept. Cmty. Svcs., Delhi, 1967—69, East Akron (Ohio) Cmty. House, 1969—71; asst. prof. Kent (Ohio) State U., 1971—77, assoc. prof., 1977—94; ret., 1994. Mem. editl. bd. Pediatric Social Work, 1984—88. Author: My Account, Family Edition, 2004, Sheila, 2004; contbr. articles to profl. jours. Pres. Portage County Housing Advs., 1985—86; coord. Citizens Effort to Close Lucky Shoe Cafe, Akron, 1972. Fellow, Ford Found., 1965—67; grantee, Govt. India, 1957—58, NIMH, 1974—75. Mem.: NASW (Gold Card mem., cert.), Assn. Advancement Social Work Groups, Ohio Ret. Tchrs. Assn. (life), Coun. East Akron Block Club Pres. (founder 1972). Hindu. Avocations: gardening, exercise, writing. Home: 1158 Morningview Dr Tallmadge OH 44278

KAULAKIS, ARNOLD FRANCIS, management consultant; b. Lewiston, Maine, Oct. 6, 1916; s. Frank Kaulakis and Amelia (Vilaniskis) K.; m. Marguerite Marie Adams, Oct. 18, 1940; children: Bernadette, Robert, Michael, Marguerite. BS in Chem. Engring., MIT, 1938. V.p., dir. Exxon Research & Engring. co., Linden, N.J., 1961-66; dep. refining coordinator Exxon Corp., N.Y.C., 1966-68; exec. chmn., chief exec. officer BOC-Airco Cryogenic Plant Ltd., London, 1968-71; mng. dir. Cryoplants Ltd., London, 1971-72; v.p. energy devel. The Pittston Co., Greenwich, Conn., 1972-81; chmn. bd., chief exec. officer Pittston Petroleum Inc., Montvale, N.J., 1977-83; mng. ptnr. Kensyntar Project Co., Greenwich, Conn., 1981-83; pres. Afkay Assocs., Rye, N.Y., 1983—. Patentee in field; contbr. articles to profl. jours. Mem. Welding Research Council (vice chmn. exec. com. 1964-68), Jr. Engring. Tech. Soc. (dir. 1962-68), Am. Petroleum Inst., Am. Mining Congress (synthetic fuels com.) Address: 5005 Theall Rd Rye NY 10580-1445 Office Phone: 914-925-0714.

KAUMEYER, LINDA LOUISE, lawyer; b. Niagara Falls, N.Y., Oct. 4, 1950; BA summa cum laude, Canisius Coll., 1975; JD cum laude, SUNY, Buffalo, 1981, CAS, 1997. Bar: N.Y. 1982, U.S. Dist. Ct. (we. dist.) N.Y. 1982, U.S. Bankruptcy Ct. 1982, U.S. Ct. Appeals (2nd cir.) 1983, U.S. Supreme Ct. 2001. Assoc. Moot & Sprague, Buffalo, 1981-90; spl. counsel Phillips, Lytle, Hitchcock Blaine & Huber, Buffalo, 1990-97; gen. counsel Amherst Ctrl. Schs., 1997—2004; supr. of schs. Pine Plains Cert. Sch. Dist., Pine Plains, NY, 2004—. Bd. dirs. Vol. Lawyers Project, Buffalo, 1988--. Bd. dirs. Child and Adolescent Psychiat. Clinic, Buffalo, 1987—. Mem. ABA, N.Y. State Bar Assn. (Pro Bono award 1987), Erie County Bar Assn. (chmn. alternative dispute resolution 1989-92, Svc. award 1996), Mental Health Assn. Erie County (bd. dirs. 1982-91, Svc. award 1987).

KAUNITZ, JONATHAN DAVIDSON, physician; b. NYC, Nov. 6, 1950; s. Paul Ehrlich and Rita (Davidson) K.; m. Christine Lee, July 31, 1983; children: Justin Lee, Genevieve Jung. BA in Molecular Biology, Columbia Coll., 1972, MD, 1976. Diplomate Am. Bd. Internal Medicine, Am. Bd. Gastroenterology. Intern in medicine Presbyn. Hosp., NYC, 1976-77, resident in medicine, 1977-79; gastroenterology fellow U. Calif., San Francisco, 1979-80, gastrointestinal rsch. fellow, 1980-81, LA, 1981-82; asst. prof. medicine U. Calif. LA Sch. Medicine, 1983-91; assoc. investigator VA Career Devel. Series, 1984-85, rsch. assoc., 1985-88, clin. investigator, 1990-95; assoc. dir. UCLA Integrated Tng. Program in Digestive Diseases, 1986-90, co-dir., 1996-98, dir., 1998-2001; assoc. prof. dept. medicine Sch. Medicine UCLA, 1991-97, prof. dept. medicine Sch. Medicine, 1997—. Assoc. chief med. svc. gastrointestinal sect. Wadsworth VA Med. Ctr., 1993—; mem. legis. assembly UCLA, 1991-94, com. on appointments and promotions, 1991—; mem. gastrointestinal bd. Med. Rsch. Svc., Dept. Vet. Affairs, 1993-96, chair, 1995, mem. coun., 1996; mem. NIH study sects.; vis. lectr. Keio U. Med. Soc., Tokyo, 1994, 97, 2000; vis. prof. Asahi (Japan) Gen. Hosp., 2003, Hamamatsu Seirei Med. Ctr., 2003. Mem. editl. bd. Am. Jour. Physiology. Recipient numerous rsch. grants. Fellow Am. Coll. Gastroenterology; mem. Am. Gastroenterol. Assn., Am. Physiol. Soc., Columbia Coll. Physicians and Surgeons (alumni dir. 1976-86), Soc. for Auditory Integration Tng. (bd. dirs., v.p. 1994-95), Cure Autism Now (bd. dirs., mem. sci. adv. group 1995-2004, chair 1996, mem. sci. rsch. coun. 2000—), Brentwood Biomed. Rsch. Inst. (bd. dirs. 2002—, chair, 2003—), West Coast Salt and Water Club (program chmn. 1989, treas. 1989-98, pres. 1998—), Alpha Omega Alpha. Avocations: sailing, soccer, bicycling, travel, collecting books. Office: CURE Wadsworth VA Med Ctr Los Angeles CA 90073 E-mail: jake@ucla.edu.

KAUNZNER, CAROL BOBKIN, information scientist, educator; d. John Anthony and Alyce Barbara Bobkin; m. Dennis Paul Kaunzner, Sept. 29, 2001; children: John Christopher Oxley, James Michael Oxley. BA, U. Ctrl. Fla., 1974; MEd, Ariz. State U., 2001. Tech. dir. Ft. Huachuca (Ariz.) Accommodation Schs., 1996—, tchr., 1974—96. Adv. bd. Scholastic Adminstr. Mag., N.Y., 2002—; participant in workshop: non-technical strategies for protecting children from pornography on the internet NRC, Washington, 2000—00; participant: leadership and the new techs. Grad. Sch. Edn. Harvard U., Cambridge, Mass., 1999; assoc. faculty computer info. sys. Cochise Coll., Sierra Vista, Ariz., 1984—2000. Recipient Spotlight Dist. award, Scholastic Adminstr. Mag., 2002. Mem.: Consortium Sch. Networking (mem. awards com. 2001—05, Outstanding Achievement K-12 Networking award 2000), Phi Kappa Phi. Avocations: travel, home improvement. Office: Ft Huachuca Accommodation Schools PO Box 12954 Fort Huachuca AZ 85670 Office Phone: 520-452-4454.

KAUPINS, GUNDARS EGONS, education educator; b. Mpls., Dec. 29, 1956; s. Alfreds and Skaidrite Kaupins; m. Debra Ann Queen, Mar. 27, 1998; children: Amanda, Kyle. BA, Wartburg Coll., 1979; MBA, U. No. Iowa, 1981; PhD, U. Iowa, 1986. Sr. prof. in human resources. Grad. asst. U. No. Iowa, Cedar Falls, 1979-81; employee rels. asst. Norand Corp., Cedar Rapids, 1983; grad. asst. Univ. Iowa, Iowa City, 1981-86; prof. Boise (Idaho) State U., 1986—. Cons. in field. Contbr. articles to profl. jours. Recipient rsch. grants Boise State U., 1987-2005, Ponder scholarship U. Iowa, 1983-85; named Adv. of the Yr., Boise State U., 1989; John Elorriaga fellow, 2005—. Mem. Soc. for Human Resource Mgmt. (faculty advisor 1986—), Assn. for Advancement of Baltic Studies, Acad. of Mgmt. Avocations: racewalking, golf, racquetball, tennis, skiing. Home: 8475 W Beachside Ct Boise ID 83714 Office: Boise State U Dept Mgmt Boise ID 83725-0001 Office Phone: 208-426-4014. Business E-Mail: gkaupins@boisestate.edu.

KAUR, HARMINDER, language educator; b. Delhi, India, Jan. 12, 1971; d. Rajinder Pal Singh and Charanjit Kaur. BA in English, U. Delhi, India, 1989—92, diploma in Spanish lang., 1992—93, MA in Spanish Studies, 1993—95; MA in Spanish Edn., U. Alcala, Madrid, 1996—98. Cert. tchr. N.Y., 2004. Guest lectr. Indraprastha Coll., Delhi, India, 1995—99; adj. lectr. Medger Evers Coll., CUNY, N.Y.C., 1999, York Coll., CUNY, N.Y.C., 1999—, Pace U., N.Y.C., 2000—. Aux. prof. Spanish Madrid Plus, N.Y.C., 1998; univ. supr. Pace U., N.Y.C., 2002—03; Spanish instr. for health profls. York Coll., N.Y.C., 2003—. Recipient First Prize in Essay Competition, Ministry of Cuba in Delhi, 1995; scholar, Ministry of External Affairs, Madrid, 1996—98; grad. tchg. fellow, City U. Grad. Ctr., N.Y.C., 1999—2002. Mem.: Profl. Staff Congress. Avocations: reading, walking, travel. Office: York Coll 94-20 Guy R Brewer Blvd New York NY 11433 Office Phone: 718-262-2430. Personal E-mail: hkaur12@hotmail.com.

KAURIN, DOUGLAS EDWARD, protective services official; b. Wyandotte, Mich., Feb. 13, 1958; s. Jack Edward and Alice Joyce Kaurin; m. Jacquelyn Michelle Flaim, Sept. 30, 2000. BS, Madonna U., 1981. Cert. fire safety trainer Wyandotte Fire Dept., 1998. Security officer Henry Ford Wyandotte Hosp., Mich., 1981—97, security investigator, 1997—98, fire safety insp., 1998—. Author: (healthcare fire prevention program) Environment of Care, 2002 (Copyright in 2003). Mem.: Internat. Assn. of Health Care Security and Safety (assoc.), Nat. Fire Protection Assn. (assoc.), Lions Club Internat. Roman Catholic. Avocations: golf, racquetball, mens softball, travel. Office: Henry Ford Wyandotte Hosp 2333 Biddle Ave Wyandotte MI 48192 Business E-Mail: dkaurin1@hfhs.org.

KAUSHANSKY, KENNETH, medical educator; b. 1953; m. Lauren Kaushansky; 2 children. BS, UCLA, MD, 1979. Diplomate Am. Bd. Internal Medicine. Fellow in hematology U. Washington; prof. medicine U. Calif., San Diego, chair dept. medicine, 2002—; chief hematology sect. U. Washington Med. Ctr. Adj. prof. biochemistry U. Washington. Recipient Dameshek award, Am. Soc. Hematology, Outstanding Investigator award, Am. Soc. Med. Rsch. Mem.: Assn. Am. Physicians, Am. Soc. Clin. Investigation (v.p.). Office: U Calif San Diego Dept Medicine 402 W Dickinson Ste 380 San Diego CA 92103-8811

KAUSHIK, SURENDRA KUMAR, economist; b. Malsisar, India, June 21, 1944; came to U.S., 1970; naturalized, 1980; s. Lakminarain Sharma and Rathi Chaturvedy; m. Helena Pokornicki, Sept. 12, 1973. BS in Commerce, U. Rajasthan, India, 1965, MA in Econs., 1967; PhD in Econs., Boston U., 1976. Rsch. asst., instr. Inst. Econ. Growth, Delhi, India, 1968-70; tchg. fellow, rsch. asst., then sr. tchg. fellow and lect. Boston U., 1971-75; lectr. Lowell Tech. Inst. Boston State Coll., 1973-74; asst. prof. Babson Coll., Wellesley, Mass., 1976-81; dir. Inst. Internat. Banking Lubin Grad. Sch. Bus., 1981—; prof. Pace U., White Plains, 1984—. Instr. Northeastern U., Bosron, 1972-73; cons. UN, 1976-77; founder Mrs. Helena Kaushik Women's Coll., Malsisar, India, 1999. Condr. rsch. internat. banking and fin.; editor: Banking, Money Markets and Monetary Policy, 1980, International Banking and Global Financing, 1983, Debt Crisis and Financial Stability: The Future, 1985, Internal Banking and World Economic Growth, 1987, The Practical Financial Manager, 1988; co-author: The Practical Financial Manager, 1988, Multinational Financial Management, 1989. Mem. AAUP, Am. Econ. Assn., Am. Fin. Assn., Western Econ. Assn., Ea. Econ. Assn., Atlantic Econ. Soc. Office: Pace U Lubin Grad Sch Bus 1 Martine Ave White Plains NY 10606-1932

KAUTH, STEPHANIE ANN, music educator; b. Mpls., Apr. 11, 1966; d. Leon James and Frances May Kauth. BA in Music Edn., Coll. of the Ozarks, 1991; MS in Edn., William Woods U., Fulton, Mo., 2002. K-12 vocal and instrumental music instr. Wheaton (Mo.) R-III Sch. Dist., 1991—92, Higbee (Mo.) R-VIII Sch. Dist., 1993—. GED instr., head coord. Higbee R-VIII Dist. Moberly (Mo.) Area C.C., 1996—99; lead tchr. End of the Rainbow Devel. Ctr., Columbia, Mo., 1992—93; instr. flute, piano, violin. V.p. Cmty. Tchrs. Assn., 1995—97; mem. Profl. Devel. Com., 1997—; leader jr. and cadette girl scouts, Higbee, 1998—; dir. cmty. ch. choir. Mem.: ASCD, Mo. Music Educators Assn., Mo. State Tchrs. Assn., Nat. Assn. Elem. Prins., Nat. Assn. Secondary Prins. Avocations: sports, outdoor activities, computers, reading, travel. Home: 405 S Le Fevre Ave Salisbury MO 65281-1140

KAUTSKY, LILLI, early childhood educator; b. Vienna, May 10, 1923; came to U.S., 1940; d. William and Grete Unger; m. John H. Kautsky, Oct. 17, 1947; children: Catherine, Peter. BA, U. Chgo., 1943, MA, 1947; MEd, Tuft's U., 1972. Cert. preschool edn. tchr., Mo. Dir. Ethical Soc. Nursery Sch., St. Louis, 1974-83; tchr., trainer St. Louis Community Coll. at Forest Pk., 1973-74, trainer child devel. assocs. program, lectr., 1987; parent educator Neighborhood Svcs., St. Louis, 1984-85; asst. dir. nanny tng. program Child Day Care Assn., St. Louis, 1984; field cons. Greater St. Louis Child Study Project, 1985—. Cons. Parents and Children Together, St. Louis, 1978, 1985—; lectr. Maryville Coll., St. Louis, 1978, St. Louis Psychoanalytic Inst., 1986—88. Mem. Nat. Assn. for Edn. Young Children (Disting. Svc. award Mo. chpt. 1987), Child Day Care Assn., St. Louis Assn. for Edn. Young Children (conf. organizer 1981, resource chair 1975-77). Avocations: reading, gardening, hiking, crafts.

KAUTT, GLENN GREGORY, financial planner, consultant; b. Arlington, Va., Jan. 25, 1948; s. Elmer Curtis and Phyllis Ruth (Schmalz) K.; m. Elizabeth B. Emerson, Aug. 19, 1971 (div. 1975); 1 child, Christopher Curtis; m. Elizabeth M. Dansereau, Dec. 22, 1989. BS, Purdue U., 1973; MBA, Harvard U., 1979. Cert. fin. planner; enrolled agt., admitted to practice before IRS. Commd. lt. USN, 1969, resigned, 1977; sr. assoc. ICF, Inc., Washington, 1979-81; mng. dir. The Challenger Group, Silver Spring, Md., 1981-85; sr. planner Fin. Svc. Group, Vienna, Va., 1985-87; prin., dir. Capitol Fin. Cons., Inc., Vienna, 1987-91; pres. Kautt Fin. Svcs., Inc., Vienna, 1991-99, The Monitor Group, Inc., Fairfax, Va., 1999—, chmn. bd., 2003—. Lectr. ADA, FPA, Am. Mgmt. Assn., US SBA, also maj. corps. Author: Stochastic Modeling: A New Way to Predict Your Financial Future, 2001; co-author: The Invincibility Shield for Investors, 2003; co-author, editor Inside the Real Estate Business, 1981; mem. editl. adv. bd. Jour. Fin. Planning, 1999-2002; contbr. articles to profl. mags. Mem. Registry Fin. Planning Practitioners, Fin. Planning Assn. Nat. Capitol Area (bd. dirs., pres. 1999, co-chair 2000, nat. chpt. leadership resource coun.2000-02). Republican. Avocations: flying, skiing, scuba diving, singing. Office: 1430 Spring Hill Rd Ste 400 Mc Lean VA 22102 Office Phone: 703-288-0500. Business E-Mail: kautt@themonitorgroup.com.

KAUZLARICH, RICHARD DALE, retired ambassador, political scientist, consultant; b. Moline, Ill., Aug. 18, 1944; s. Victor and Eva Marie (Kronfeld) Kauzlarich; m. Anne Elizabeth Bregstone, Aug. 26, 1967; children: Richard Dale, Jr., Terri Lynne. AA, Black Hawk Coll., Moline, Ill., 1964; BA, Valparaiso U., 1966; MA, Ind. U., 1967, U. Mich., 1976. 2d sec. Am. Embassy, Addis Ababa, Ethiopia, 1973-75; fin. economist Office Devel. Fin., Dept. State, Washington, 1976-77, dep. office dir. Office Investment Affairs, 1977-80; counselor for econ. affairs Am. Embassy, Tel Aviv, 1980-83; office dir. ops. ctr. Dept. State, Washington, 1983-84, dep. asst. sec. internat. orgn. affairs, 1984-86, dep. dir. policy planning staff, 1986-89, office dir. regional polit.-econ. affairs, 1989-91, dep. asst. sec. Bur. European Affairs, 1991-93; prin. dep. to the amb.-at-large and spl. adviser S/NIS Dept State, Washington; U.S. amb. to Republic of Azerbaijan, 1994-97, Bosnia and Herzegovina, 1997-99; sr. advisor to undersec. state econ., bus. and agrl. affairs Dept. State, Washington, 1999-2001; pres. Kauzlarich Cons. Inc., Falls Church, Va., 2001—02; dir. spl. initiative on Muslim World U.S. Inst. Peace, Washington, 2002—03; nat. intelligence officer for Europe Nat. Intelligence Coun., Washington, 2003—. Mem. Am. Internat. Sch. Bd., Tel Aviv, 1981—83. Named Internat. Person of the Yr., Dnevi Avaz, 1997; recipient Presdl. Meritorious Svc. award, 1993, Hall of Fame award, Black Hawk Coll. Alumni Assn., 1993, Disting. Alumnus award, Valparaiso U., 1999. Lutheran. Home: 7019 Ted Dr Falls Church VA 22042-3943 Office: Nat Intelligence Coun Washington DC 20505 Business E-Mail: richadk0@ucia.gov. E-mail: rdkauzlarich@yahoo.com.

KAUZMANN, WALTER JOSEPH, chemistry professor; b. Mt. Vernon, N.Y., Aug. 18, 1916; s. Albert and Julia Maria (Kahle) K.; m. Elizabeth Alice Flagler, Apr. 1, 1951; children: Charles Peter, Eric Flagler, Katherine Elizabeth Julia Kauzmann Pacala. BA, Cornell U., 1937; PhD, Princeton U., 1940; PhD (hon.), U. Stockholm, 1992. Westinghouse research fellow Westinghouse Mfg. Co., E. Pittsburgh, Pa., 1940-42; mem. staff Explosives Research Lab., Bruceton, Pa., 1942-44, Los Alamos Lab., 1944-46; asst. prof. Princeton U., 1946-51, asso. prof., 1951-60, prof. chemistry, 1960-82, chmn. dept., 1964-68, David B. Jones prof. chemistry, 1963-82, chmn. biochem. sci. dept., 1980-81; vis. scientist Atlantic Research Lab., NRC Can., 1983. Vis. lectr. Kyoto U., 1974; vis. prof. U. Ibadan, 1975 Author: Quantum Chemistry, 1957, Kinetic Theory of Gases, 1966, Thermal Properties of Matter, 1967, (with D. Eisenberg) Structure and Properties of Water, 1969. Recipient Linderstrom-Lang medal, 1966, Stein and Moore award, 1993; Jr. fellow Soc. Fellows, Harvard U., 1942. Fellow: AAAS, Am. Phys. Soc., Am. Acad. Arts and Scis.; mem.: NAS, Royal Astron. Soc. Can., Fedn. Am. Scientists, Am. Chem. Soc., Am. Geophys. Union, Protein Soc., Am. Soc. Biochemistry and Molecular Biology, Sigma Xi. Home and Office: 301 N Harrison St PMB 152 Princeton NJ 08540-3512

KAVALEK, LUBOMIR, chess expert; b. Prague, Czechoslovakia, Aug. 9, 1943; came to U.S., 1970; s. Lubomir and Stepanka (Kavalkova) K.; m. Irena Koritsanska, Nov. 24, 1971; 1 child, Steven. Student, Faculty of Transp., U. Zilina, 1960-65, Faculty of Journalism, Charles U., Prague, 1967-68, George Washington U., 1970-71. Journalist Voice of Am., USIA, 1971-72; chief editor RHM Chess Pub., Great Neck, N.Y., 1973-89; mem. German chess team, Solingen, 1969-89, U.S. chess team in chess Olympiad, 1972, 74, 76, 78, 82, 84, 86; reporter world chess championship, chess columnist Washington Post, 1986—; exec. dir. Grandmaster Assn., Brussels, 1987-91, key organizer world cup, 1988-89; coach world championship Challenger, N. Short, 1990-93. Author: Wijk aan Zee 1975 - Grandmaster Chess Tournament, 1976, World Cup Chess, 1990, Tilburg 1977, 2002; author: (with Efim Geller, Svetozar Gligovic and Boris Spessky) The Najdovl Varnation - Sicilian Defense, 1976. Recipient Cramer award, 1999, Best Newspaper Chess Column award Chess Journalists Am., 2003; inductee World and U.S. Chess Hall of Fame, 2001. Mem. Internat. Assn. Chess Journalists, U.S. Chess Fedn. Achievements include being the German chess team champion, 1969, 71, 72, 73, 74, 75, 80, 81, 86, SS Dutch Open champion, 1969, Czechoslovakian champion, 1962, 68, Internat. Grandmaster, 1965-, U.S. co-champion, 1972, 73; U.S. champion, 1978, European Cup team champion, 1976, Olympic champion, 1976, German Internat. champion, 1981; winner 30 internat. all-play-all tournaments. E-mail: lkavalek@att.net.

KAVALER, THOMAS J., lawyer; b. NYC, Dec. 10, 1948; BA, CCNY, 1969; JD, Fordham U., 1972; LLM, NYU, 1975. Bar: N.Y., US Dist. Ct. (So., Ea., We. and No. Dists.) NY, US Ct. Appeals (2nd, 3rd, 4th, 5th, 6th, 7th, 8th, 10th, 11th and Fed. Cirs.), US Supreme Ct., US Tax Ct. Law clk. US Dist. Ct. NY, NYC, 1972-74; assoc. Cravath, Swaine & Moore, NYC, 1974-75, Cahill Gordon & Reindel LLP, NYC, 1975-80, ptnr., 1980—, mem. exec. com. Served to capt. USAR, 1969-77. Fellow Am. Bar Found., Internat. Acad. Trial Lawyers, NY Bar Found.; mem. Fordham Law Alumni Assn. (pres. 2000-02), Fed. Bar. Coun. (v.p. 2002-). Office: Cahill Gordon & Reindel LLP 80 Pine St Fl 17 New York NY 10005-1790 Office Phone: 212-701-3406. Office Fax: 212-269-5420. Business E-Mail: tkavaler@cahill.com.

KAVALER-ADLER, SUSAN, clinical psychologist, psychoanalyst; b. N.Y.C., Jan. 31, 1950; d. Solomon and Alice (Zelikow) Weiss; m. Thomas Kavaler, July 12, 1970 (div. 1975); m. Saul Michael Adler, Aug. 14, 1983. PhD in Clin. Psychology, Adelphi U., 1974. Cert. in psychotherapy, psychoanalysis; diplomate in psychoanalysis, 2003. Psychologist Beth Israel Hosp., N.Y.C., 1974-76, Manhattan Psychiat. Children's Ctr., N.Y.C., 1977-80; pvt. practice psychotherapy-psychoanalysis N.Y.C., 1976—; founder, exec. dir. Object Rels. Inst. Psychotherapy and Psychoanalysis, 1991. Condr. writing and mourning groups; founding dir., supr., faculty, founder, exec. dir., tng. analyst Object Rels. Inst. for Psychotherapy and Psychoanalysis, 1991—; mem. faculty Postgrad. Ctr. Mental Health, N.Y.C., 1984-86, 90; mem. faculty, supr. Nat. Inst. Psychotherapies, N.Y.C., 1985-91; bd. dirs., supr. Bklyn. Inst. Psychotherapy and Psychoanalysis; adj. prof. Fordham U.; founding exec. dir. Object Rels. Inst. Psychotherapy and Psychoanalysis, 1991--; spkr pvt. seminars, writing groups. Author: (books) The Compulsion to Create, 1993, 2d edit., 2000, Women Writers and Their Demon Lovers, 1993, rev. edit., 2000, The Creative Mystique: From Red Shoes Frenzy to Love and Creativity, 1996, International Forum of Psychoanalysis, 1999, The Divine, the Deviant and the Diabolical: A Female Artist's Developmental Journey from Self Fragmentation to Self Integration in a Creative Process Group, 2000, Mourning, Spirituality and Psychic Change, 2003 (Nat. Gradiva award Nat. Assn. Advancement Psychoanalysis, 2004), (article) American Jour. Psychanalysis, 2005; contbr. over 45 articles to profl. jours. and books; editor: book chpts. Recipient 10 writing awards, Postgrad. Ctr. for Mental Health. Office: 115 E 9th St Apt 12P New York NY 10003-5420 also: 41 Central Park West New York NY 10023 Office Phone: 212-674-5425, 212-674-8425. Personal E-mail: suska674@aol.com.

KAVALERCHIK, BORIS YAKOVLEVICH, application developer, researcher; b. Luban, Minsk, Belarus, May 26, 1948; came to U.S., 1992; s. Yakov I. Kavalerchik and Liliya S. Rosengaus; m. Bella K. Kavalerchik, Dec. 27, 1979; 1 child, Inna. MS in Applied Mechanics with honors, Moscow Inst. Physics & Tech., 1969, PhD in Applied Math., 1972; DSc in Computer Sci., Glushkov Inst. Cybernetics, Kiev, Ukraine, 1990. Cert. specialist IBM, 2002, database adminstrn. solution expert 2002, application developer 2003. Project leader Belorussian Rsch. Inst. for Mgmt. Info. Systems, Minsk, USSR (Belarus), 1972-77, head system software dept., 1977-79, head systems devel. dept., 1979-90, prin. rschr., 1990-92; tech. specialist, cons., project leader info. tech. Guardian Life Ins. Co. of Am., NYC, 1992—. Assoc. prof. Belorussian Polytech. Inst., Minsk, 1975-78; leader of many nat. computer projects. Contbr. over 60 articles to Russian, Am. and German profl. jours. Recipient Outstanding Sci. and Engring. Rsch. prize USSR Coun. Ministers, Moscow, 1984. Mem. IEEE, Assn. for Computing Machinery. Jewish. Achievements include research in the fields of data and image compression; reliability and performance of data processing; operations research and its business and engineering applications. Home: 1 Grover Ter Fair Lawn NJ 07410-4506 Office: Guardian Life Ins Co 7 Hanover Sq New York NY 10004-2616

KAVAN, JAN, Czech government official, former president UN General Assembly; b. London, Oct. 17, 1946; 4 children. Degree in internat. rels., London Sch. Econs. and Polit. Sch., 1974; postgrad., St. Anthony's Coll., Oxford, England, U. Reading. Polit. writer, asst. editor; head Czechoslovak sect. East European Reporter jour., 1985—90; founder, Policy Centre for the Promotion of Democracy in the Czech Rep., 1993—; member, Czech Social Democratic Party, 1993—; chmn. fgn. affairs comm., 1994—98; v.p. East European Cultural Found.; mem. Civic Forum Coord. Ctr. Coun., Czech Republic; mem. fed. assembly Czech Republic Parliament, 1990—92, mem. senate, 1996—2000; min. fgn. affairs Govt. of Czech Republic, 1998—2002, dep. prime min. for foreign and security policy, 1999—2002; pres. 57th UN Gen. Assembly, New York, 2002—03; mem. Czech Parliament, 2002—, v.p. fgn. affairs com., 2004—; dep. leader Czech Social Dem. Parliamentary Party, 2004—. Vis. prof. Adelphi U., NY, 1992—93; Karl Loewenstein fellow Amherst Coll., Mass., 1993—94. Mem. Helsinki Civic Coun. Presidium; sec. Peace Groups Info. Ctr.; vice chmn. regional com. for Ctrl. and Ea. Europe Socialist Internat. Office: Czech Parliament 118 26 Prague 1 Czech Republic Office Phone: 420-257-172-185. Business E-Mail: kavanj@psp.cz.

KAVANAGH, CORNELIA KUBLER, sculptor; b. New Haven, Apr. 8, 1940; d. George Alexander and Elizabeth Bushnell Kubler; m. James Penniston Kavanagh, Feb. 6, 1971; children: Alexander, Elena. BA, Barnard Coll., 1962; MA, Columbia U., 1970-71. Solo shows include: Cornelia Kubler Kavanagh "The Shape of Time", Kirshenbaum, Bond, N.Y., 2002-03. Cornelia Kubler Kavanagh "bronze, Plaster, Stone", Tucker Robbins, N.Y. 2001. Qualita Fine Art, Las Vegas, Nev., 1999-2000, Artspace, New Haven,

1997, Conn. Art Competition Stamford Mus. and Nature Ctr., 1992, Art Asia, Hong Kong, 1992, The Discovery Mus., Bridgeport, Conn., 1997, Parish-Hadley Assocs., N.Y., 1996, Silvermine Guild Arts Ctr., New Canaan, Conn., 2000, Openasia, Venice, 2004; commd. works include Long Wharf Theater, Lancaster Winery, Sonoma, Calif.; represented in corp. collections at Kirshenbaum, Bond and Ptnrs., N.Y.C., Parish-Hadley Assocs., Inc., N.Y.C., So. Wine and Spirits, Miami, Sunbelt Beverage Corp., N.Y.C.; represented by Blue Mountain Gallery, N.Y., artformedia.com, PMW Gallery, Stamford, CT; group shows: La Biennale di Venezla, Venice, Italy, St. Pauls Sch., Conord, N.H., 2005; subject of articles. Sec. bd. dirs. New Canaan (Conn.) Country Sch., 1984-88; sec. Rowayton (Conn.) Civic Assn., 1984-88; vol. Mid Fairfield Hospice, Conn., 1984-99; mem. parents exec. com. Colby coll., 1990-98.; mem. cmty. outreach bd. Ctr. for Hope, Darien, Conn., 1996—. Recipient Best Sculpture award Discovery Mus. and Nature Ctr., Bridgeport, Conn., 1997, 1st Pl. award for stone sculpture Art of the Northeast Silvermine Sch. Art, Ct., 2000, Amidar Meml. award for stone sculpture, 2000. Mem. Nat. Sculpture Soc., Conn. Women Artists.

KAVANAGH, EILEEN J., librarian; BA, Ladycliff Coll.; MS in Libr. Sci., Columbia U., 1969; MA in Liberal Studies, SUNY, Stonybrook, 1980. Reference libr. Farmingdale (N.Y.) Pub. Libr., 1969-70; from reference libr. to libr. dir. Bay Shore-Brightwaters (N.Y.) Pub. Libr., 1970—. Office: Bay Shore-Brightwaters Pub Libr 1 S Country Rd Brightwaters NY 11718-1513 Office Phone: 631-665-4350. Business E-Mail: ekavanag@suffolk.lib.ny.us.

KAVANAGH, JOHN JOSEPH, medical educator; b. Phila., Aug. 7, 1947; s. John and Christine Kavanagh; m. Teresa Ann Brown. BA, Sch. Internat. Svc., Washington, 1969; MD, Jefferson Med. Coll., 1975. Clin. asst. prof. U. Nebr., Omaha, 1980-81; instr., asst. internist M.D. Anderson Cancer Ctr., Houston, 1981-82, asst. prof., chief sect. gynecologic med. oncology, 1983-85, assoc. gynecologist, 1987—, assoc. prof., chief sect. gynecologic med. oncology, 1987—; assoc. prof. H. Lee Moffitt Cancer Ctr., Tampa, Fla., 1985-87; assoc. prof. ob-gyn. and reproductive scis. U. Tex. Health Sci. Ctr., Houston, 1991—, prof. dept. clin. investigation, 1996—. Cons. S.W. Oncology Group, San Antonio, 1994—; mem. faculty European Sch. Oncology. With USAR, 1969-71. Grantee ASTA Medica, Inc., Hackensack, N.J., 1994, Hoffman-LaRoche, Nutley, N.J., 1994. Fellow ACP, European Soc. Gynecol. Oncology (assoc.); mem. Internat. Gynecologic Cancer soc. (chmn. membership com., exec. com.), So. Oncology Assn. (pres. 1991-92), So. Med. Assn. (Presdl. com. on endowments 1993—), Tex. Soc. Med. Oncology (founding). Avocations: fishing, boating, reading. Office: M D Anderson Cancer Ctr 1515 Holcombe Blvd # 39 Houston TX 77030-4009

KAVANAGH, RALPH WILLIAM, physics professor; b. Seattle, July 15, 1924; s. Ralph W. and Esther (Weken) K.; m. Joyce Eberhart, July 31, 1948; children: Kathleen, Janet, Stephanie, Linda, William Leonard. BA, Reed Coll., 1950; MA, U. Oreg., 1952; PhD, Calif. Inst. Tech., 1956. Mem. faculty Calif. Inst. Tech., Pasadena, 1956—, assoc. prof. physics, 1965-70, prof., 1970—2000, prof. emeritus, 2000—; rsch. assoc. Centre de Recherches Nucleaires, U. Strasbourg, France, 1967-68; rsch. assoc. Sch. Physics U. Melbourne, Australia, 1983. Contbr. articles to profl. jours. Served with USNR, 1942-46. Fellow Am. Phys. Soc. Home: 450 Bonita Ave Pasadena CA 91107-5064 Business E-Mail: kav@caltech.edu.

KAVANAUGH, EVERETT EDWARD, JR., trade association executive; b. New Haven, June 9, 1941; s. Everett Edward and Marion (Gallagher) K.; m. Martha Gamble Murphy, Feb. 23, 1963; 1 son, Brett Michael. AB, Georgetown U., 1963; MBA, George Washington U., 1970; JD, Am. U., 1978. Bar: Md. 1979, D.C. 1990. Sales rep. Northwestern Mut. Ins. Co., Washington, 1963-68; asst. to exec. offices U.S. C. of C., Washington, 1970-72; pres. Cosmetic, Toiletry and Fragrance Assn., Washington, 1972—2005; ret. Mem.: Congressional Country, Burning Tree (Bethesda, Md.). Roman Catholic. Home: # 12 8500 River Rd Bethesda MD 20817

KAVANAUGH, FRANK JAMES, film producer, educator; b. Chgo., Sept. 12, 1934; s. Kenneth James and Carol Mae (Wilkey) K.; m. Barbara Ann Barrett, Nov. 16, 1957; children: Franklin James Jr., Christopher Barrett, Kenneth Wilkey. BA, Lake Forest Coll., 1956; PhD, Union Inst., 1982. Producer, dir., exec. ABC-TV, Chgo., N.Y.C., 1956-67; pres. Ravens Hollow Ltd., Warrenton, Va., 1967-69; exec. producer Airlie Prodns., Warrenton, 1979-89; prof. comm., prof. med. and pub. affairs, comm. chair George Washington U., Washington, 1983-89. V.p. Airlie Found., 1979—; adj. prof. Union Inst. Grad. Sch., 1987—; pres. Kavanaugh Assocs., Inc., 1989—; mentor Capella U.; pres. Internat. Acad. for Preventive Medicine. Asst. dir. TV Kukla, Fran & Ollie, 1958; producer film The Saving of the President, 1982 (Emmy award 1982); producer dir. films A Moveable Scene, 1968 (Emmy award nominee 1969), Flowers of Darkness, 1969 (Emmy award 1969), Bridge From No Place, 1970 (Emmy award 1970), The Possible Dream, 1970 (Emmy award 1970), More Than a Paycheck, 1978 (Emmy award nominee 1978), others; producer, dir., writer film Each Child Loved, 1972 (Emmy award 1972), others. Bd. dirs. Performing Arts Trust. Recipient Cup of Italy Italian Film Festival, Salerno, 1982, highest award Edinburgh Film Festival, Scotland, 1982, Blue Ribbon Am. Film Festival, N.Y.C., 1983, Gold medal Houston Internat. Film Festival, 1983. Mem. Nat. Acad. TV Arts and Scis. (life), C.I.N.E., Inc. (life), Dirs. Guild Am., Radio and TV Dirs. Guild, Mensa, Nat. Assn. TV Program Execs. (Iris award 1983), Broadcast Pioneers. Avocations: photography, scuba, boating, motorcycling.

KAVANDI, JANET LYNN, aerospace power engineer, chemist; b. Springfield, Mo., July 17, 1959; d. William Winfred and Wanda Ruth (Garner) Sellers; m. Farhad John Kavandi, June 5, 1982. BS magna cum laude, Mo. So. State Coll., 1980; MS, U. Mo., Rolla, 1982; PhD, U. Wash., 1990. Project engr. Eagle-Picher Industries, Joplin, Mo., 1982-84; prin. engr. power systems tech. Boeing Def., Seattle, 1984—95; Astronaut NASA, Houston, 1995—. Mem. AIAA, Am. Chem. Soc. Avocations: skiing, horseback riding, windsurfing, sailing, camping. Office: Astronaut Office MIC CB Lyndon B Johnson Space Center Houston TX 77058

KAVARNOS, GEORGE JAMES, research chemist; b. New London, Conn., Feb. 25, 1942; s. James Spiros and Mary Pantelis Kavarnos. BA, Clark U., 1964; PhD, U. R.I., 1968. Postdoctoral fellow Columbia U., N.Y.C., 1968-70; postdoctoral rschr. Albert Einstein Coll. Medicine, N.Y.C., 1971; clin. chemist Cyto-Roche, Norwich, Conn., 1971-89; chemist Naval Undersea Warfare Ctr., Newport, R.I., 1989-97; scientist Analysis and Tech., Stonington, Conn., 1997, EG&G Inc., Groton, Conn., 1998—. Rsch. prof. U. R.I., Kingston, 1978—, Pa. State U., 2000—01; cons. Pfizer, Inc., Groton, 1996—. Address: 121 Riverview Ave New London CT 06320-5440

KAVEESHWAR, ASHOK G., federal agency administrator; b. Indore, India; arrived in U.S., 1961; m. Tuti Kaveeshwar; 1 child, Jaya. BS, Ujjian Univ., India; PhD in physics, SUNY, Buffalo, 1969. Pres. & CEO Hughes STX Corp.; sr. v.p. Raytheon Tech. Svcs. Co., 1998—2002; pres. Orange Technologies, 2002—05; adminstr., rsch. & innovative tech. adminstrn. U.S. Dept. Transp., Washington, 2005—. Mem. dean's adv. council SUNY, Buffalo. Office: US Dept Transp Room 3103 400 Seventh St SW Washington DC 20590 Office Phone: 202-366-7582.*

KAVESH, ROBERT A., economist, educator; b. N.Y.C., Sept. 12, 1927; s. Samuel and Pearl (Berlin) K.; m. Ruth Freidson, 1951 (div. 1980); children: Richard, Laura, Andrew, Joseph; m. Danielle Nisivoccia, July 11, 1990. BS, NYU, 1949; MA, Harvard U., 1950, PhD, 1954. Asst. prof. econs. Dartmouth Coll., 1953-56; bus. economist Chase Manhattan Bank, N.Y.C., 1956-58; prof. econs. and fin. NYU Grad. Sch. Bus. Adminstrn., 1958-74, Marcus Nadler prof. fin. and econs., 1974—, chmn. dept. econs., 1968-83. Bd. dirs. The Caring Cmty. Neuberger Berman Mutual Funds; econ. adv. bd. U.S. Dept. Commerce, 1968-70; investment adv. com. N.Y. State Compt., 1976-86; pres. The Money Marketeers, 1983-84. Author: Businessmen in Fiction, 1955, How Business Economists Forecast, 1966, Methods and Techniques of Business Forecasting, 1974; contbr. articles to profl. jours.; mem. editl. bd. Bus. Economics, 1965-99. Bd. dirs. Thomas A. Edison Coll. N.J., 1973-78. With U.S. Navy, WWII. Recipient Danforth Found. prize disting. teaching, 1968, Madden Meml. award for profl. achievement NYU, 1979, Gt. Tchr. award NYU, 1983, Lifetime Achievement award for mutual fund trustees Institutional Investor, 2004. Fellow Nat. Assn. Bus. Economists (council 1973-76); mem. Am. Fin. Assn. (exec. sec.-treas. 1961-79), Regional Sci. Assn. (past sec.), Am. Econ. Assn. Office: 4 Washington Square Village Apt 10s New York NY 10012-1906 Home: 60 E 8th St Apt 32B New York NY 10003-6501

KAVIS, GEORGE, engineer, photographer; b. Chgo., Feb. 2, 1935; s. Theodore and Margaret Marie Kavis; m. Patricia Marie Hewison, Dec. 17, 1978 (div. 1989); 1 child, Sherri Lynn. Design draftsman Pullman R.R. Car Mfg. Co., Chgo., 1953—55; design engr. adminstr. Fennell Corp., Harvey, Ill., 1957—66, F.H. Ayer Mfg. Co., Chicago Heights, Ill., 1966—. Cons. for design of machinery for mass prodn. Furniture design and mfg. With U.S. Army, 1955—57. Achievements include patents for furniture, automotive, toys. Avocations: invention, art, photography, writing, collecting. Office: FH Ayer Mfg Co Box 247 Chicago Heights IL 60411

KAVLI, FRED, retired manufacturing executive, retired engineering executive; b. Norway, Aug. 20, 1927; came to U.S., 1956; Grad. in physics, Norwegian Inst. Tech., 1955. Founder, CEO, sole shareholder automotive and aerospace sensor engring.-mfg. Kavlico Corp., Moorpark, Calif., 1958—2000; ret. Bd. dirs. The Found. for Santa Barbara City Coll.; trustee Found. for U. Calif., Santa Barbara; founder, chmn. The Kavli Found./The Kavli Operating Inst.; benefactor The Kavli Insts. (in neuroscience) at Columbia U., Yale U., U. Calif. at San Diego, (in nanoscience) at Caltech, Cornell U., Delft U. of Tech., (in astrophysics and cosmology) at Stanford U., U. Chgo., MIT, (in theoretical physics) at U. Calif., Santa Barbara; mem. pres. bd. on sci. and innovation U. Calif. Named Disting. Grand Patron, Alliance of the Arts, 1998, in honor of the Fred Kavli Theatre for Performing Arts at the Thousand Oak Civic Arts Plaza. Address: Ste 250 1801 Solar Dr Oxnard CA 93030 Mailing: Kavli Found 26 W Micheltorena St Santa Barbara CA 93101 Office Phone: 805-560-6500. Office Fax: 805-899-9100.*

KAVNER, JULIE, actress; b. L.A., Sept. 7, 1951; Grad., San Diego U., 1971. Actress: (TV series) Rhoda, 1974-78 (Emmy award 1978), Petrocelli, 1975, Lou Grant, 1977, Taxi, 1980, The Tracey Ullman Show, 1987-90, The Simpsons, (voice of Marge Simpson and others) 1990—, Sibs, 1991, Birdland, 1994, Tracey Takes On, 1996, (TV movies) Katherine, 1975, The Girl Who Couldn't Lose, 1975, No Other Love, 1979, Revenge of the Stepford Wives, 1980, Don't Drink the Water, 1994, Jake's Women, 1996, (feature films) National Lampoon Goes to the Movies, 1981, Bad Medicine, 1985, Hannah and her Sisters, 1985, Radio Days, 1987, Surrender, 1987, New York Stories, 1989, Awakenings, 1990, Alice, 1990, This Is My Life, 1992, Shadows and Fog, 1992, I'll Do Anything, 1994, Forget Paris, 1995, Deconstructing Harry, 1997, Doctor Dolittle (voice), 1998, A Walk on the Moon, 1999, Judy Berlin, 1999, Story of a Bad Boy, 1999, Someone Like You (voice), Barn Red, 2003, The Lion King 1 1/2, 2004.

KAVNER, ROBERT M., communications company executive; b. Franklin Square, N.Y., July 2, 1943; s. Israel and Adeline (Neuman) Kavner; m. Allyson Pastor; children from previous marriage: Brenda, Janine Kavner Reed. BBA, Adelphi U., 1965; grad. Exec. Mgmt. Program, Tuck Sch. Bus., Dartmouth Coll., 1980. Profl. staff Coopers & Lybrand, N.Y.C., 1965, partnership gen. practice, 1975, personnel ptnr., 1976—79, gen. practice ptnr., 1979—84, co-chmn. info. industry practice, 1983—84; sr. v.p., CFO AT&T, N.Y.C., 1984—87, pres. data systems group, 1988, group exec., mem. exec. com., 1989—. Lectr. Sch. Bus. Columbia U.; mem. Bus. Adv. Council to Sch. Bus.; mem. adv. com. mem. FCC for Rewrite of Uniform Systems of Accts. Chmn. Merce Cunningham Dance Found., 1983—86, Manhattan Lab. Mus., 1984—88. Mem.: N.Y. State Soc. CPAs, AICPA. Office: AT&T 32 Avenue Of The Americas New York NY 10013-2473*

KAVOUKJIAN, MICHAEL EDWARD, lawyer; b. Mpls., Apr. 19, 1958; s. Antranik M. and Leikny Dorthea (Oines) K. AB with distinction, Stanford U., 1980; JD cum laude, Harvard U., 1984. Bar: Minn. 1984, N.Y. 1986, U.S. Dist. Ct. Minn. 1985, U.S. Dist. Ct. (so. dist.) N.Y. 1988, Fla. 1999. From assoc. to ptnr. White & Case, N.Y.C. and Miami, Fla., 1985—. Mem.: ABA (chmn. com. estate planning and drafting 1992—94), Coun. on Fgn. Rels., Assn. of the Bar of the City of N.Y., Soc. Trust and Estate Practitioners (UK), The Fla. Bar, Minn. State Bar Assn., Lincoln's Inn Soc. of Harvard Law Sch. (bd. govs. 1982—84), Nat. Press Club (Washington), Harvard Club (N.Y.C., Washington, Boston). Republican. Presbyterian. Office: White & Case 1155 Avenue Of The Americas New York NY 10036-2787 also: White & Case 200 S Biscayne Blvd Miami FL 33131-2352

KAVOVIT, BARBARA, entrepreneur; b. Bronx; 1 child, Zachary. Degree in fin., SUNY, Oswego, 1987. Asst. commodities trader; former founder, chief exec. Anchor Constrn. Inc., N.Y.C.; founder Barabara K Enterprises, 2002—. Mem. pres.'s adv. bd. New Rochelle Coll. Named one of Superstar Entrepreneurs of Small and Large Bus.; recipient N.Y. State Dept. Econ. Devel. award, Gov. Mario Cuomo. Mem.: Profl. Women in Constrn.

KAVRAKI, LYDIA, computer scientist, educator; BS, U. Crete, Greece, 1989; MS, Stanford U., 1992, PhD, 1995. Postdoctoral fellow Stanford U., research assoc.; assoc. prof. computer sci. Rice U., 1996—99, prof. bioengineering, 1999—; assoc. prof. structural & computational biology, molecular biophysics Baylor Coll. of Med., 1999—. Prog. com. mem. IJCAI, 1997—99; co-chair Internat. Workshop on Algorithmic Foundations of Robotics, 1998; prog. com. mem. IEEE Internat. Conference on Robotics Automation, 1999, ACM Annual Symposium on Computational Geometry, 1999; assoc. editor IEEE Transactions on Robotics and Automation, 1999—. Named one of Top 100 Young Innovators, MIT Tech. Review mag., 2002, Brilliant 10, Popular Sci. mag., 2003; recipient Career award, Nat. Sci. Found., Grace Murray Hopper award, Assn. for Computing Machinery, Early Career award, IEEE Robotics and Automation Soc.; grantee Alfred P. Sloan Rsch. Fellowship. Office: Rice U MS132 PO Box 1892 Houston TX 77251-1892

KAWACHIKA, JAMES AKIO, lawyer; b. Honolulu, Dec. 5, 1947; s. Shinichi and Tsuyuko (Murashige) K.; m. Karen Keiko Takahashi, Sept. 1, 1973; 1 child, Robyn Mari. BA, U. Hawaii, Honolulu, 1969; JD, U. Calif., Berkeley, 1973. Bar: Hawaii 1973, U.S. Dist. Ct. Hawaii 1973, U.S. Ct. Appeals (9th cir.) 1974, U.S. Supreme Ct. 1992. Dep. atty. gen. Office of Atty. Gen. State of Hawaii, Honolulu, 1973-74; assoc. Padgett, Greeley & Marumoto, Honolulu, 1974-75, Law Office of Frank D. Padgett, Honolulu, 1975-77, Kobayashi, Watanabe, Sugita & Kawashima, Honolulu, 1977-82; ptnr. Carlsmith, Wichman, Case, Mukai & Ichiki, Honolulu, 1982-86, Bays, Deaver, Hiatt, Kawachika & Lezak, Honolulu, 1986-95; propr. Law Offices of James A. Kawachika, Honolulu, 1996—2002; ptnr. Reinwald, O'Connor & Playdon LLP, Honolulu, 2002—. Mem. Hawaii Bd. of Bar Examiners, Honolulu; arbitrator Cir. Ct. Arbitration Program State of Hawaii, Honolulu, 1986— Chmn. Disciplinary Bd. Hawaii Supreme Ct., 1991-97; adv. com. on the civil justice reform act of 1990 U.S. Dist. Ct., 1991—; bd. dir. Hawaii Justice Found., 2004—, Legal Aid Soc. Hawaii, 2005— Mem. ABA (ho. of dels., standing com. ethics and profl. responsibility), ATLA, Am. Judicature Soc. (bd. dirs. Hawaii chpt. 2003-), Hawaii State Bar Assn. (bd. dirs. 1975-76, young lawyers sect. 1983-84, 92-93, treas. 1987-88, v.p./pres.-elect 1997-98, pres. 1998-99), 9th Cir. Jud. Conf. (lawyer rep. Honolulu chpt. 1988-90). Avocations: running, tennis, skiing. Office: Pacific Guardian Ctr Makai Tower 733 Bishop St 24th Flr Honolulu HI 96813-4070 Office Phone: 808-524-8350. Business E-Mail: jak@roplaw.com.

KAWAHARA, FRED KATSUMI, research chemist; b. Penngrove, Calif., Feb. 26, 1921; s. Kentaro and Kiku (Seo) K.; m. Sumiko Hayami, May 5, 1952; children: Robert Katsumi, Kiku Seo, Richard Hojo; m. Andrea L. Eary, June 29, 1991. BS with honors, U. Tex., 1944; PhD, U. Wis., 1948. Assoc. chemist USDA, Peoria, Ill., 1948-51; fellow U. Chgo., 1951-53; sr. rsch. scientist Amoco Corp. (formerly Standard Oil of Ind.), Whiting, 1953-65; rsch. chemist EPA, Cin., 1965—. Cons., expert witness U.S. Dept. Def., U.S. Dept. Air Force, U.S. Dept. Justice, State of Pa., State of N.J.; mentor EPA, others, 1965—; patent reviewer in field; lectr. in field. Co-author: Fossil Energy Extraction, 1983, Innovative Site Remediation Technology, Chemical Treatment, vol. 2, 1994; contbr. 8 chpts. to books, over 80 articles to profl. jours. Recipient Superior Svc. award Bur. Indsl. and Agrl. Chemistry, Dept. Agr., 1952. Fellow Am. Inst. Chemists. rsch. scientist EPA. Home: 1632 Cumberland St Covington KY 41011-3716 Office: US EPA 26 Martin Luther King Dr W Cincinnati OH 45220-2242

KAWAKAMI, BERTHA C., state representative; b. Honolulu, July 28, 1931; children: Wendall, Lyndall. BA in Edn., U. Hawaii, 1953; MA in Edn., NYU, 1962. Elem., resource tchr. Hawaii Dept. Edn. Eleele, Pearl Harbor Intermediate Sch., Nanaikapono, 1954—61; mem. lang. arts dist. team, 1962—65; prin., elem. intermediate Eleele and Kekaha Schs., 1965—79; ednl. specialist Kauai Dist. Office, 1980—87, dep. dist. supr. dept. edn., 1987; mem. Hawaiii State Ho. of Reps., 1987—, asst. majority fl. leader, 1987—, mem. fin., human svcs, housing and health coms., vice chair fin. com., 1993—, majority whip, 2003—. Trustee Blood Bank of Hawaii, 1992—; mem. adv. com. Cmty. Health Nursing Divsn., 1991—; mem. quality assurance com. Kauai Vets. Meml. Hosp., 1991—; bd. dirs., v.p. Comml. Properties Inc., 1988—; mem. Waimea United Ch. of Christ, 1989—. Mem.: Japanese Am. Nat. Mus. (hon. chairperson), Hawaii State Found. on Culture and Arts, Delta Kappa Gamma Soc. Internat. Democrat. Office: State Capitol Rm 434 415 S Beretania St Honolulu HI 96813 E-mail: repkawakami@capitol.hawaii.gov.

KAWAMOTO, HENRY K., plastic surgeon; b. Long Beach, Calif., 1937; Intern U. Calif. Hosp., L.A., 1965; resident gen. surgery Columbia Presbyn. Med. Ctr., N.Y., 1969-71; resident plastic surgery NYU, 1971-73; fellow crano-facial surgery Dr. Paul Tessier, Paris, 1973-74; clin. prof. plastic surgery U. Calif., L.A. Mem. Am. Assn. Plastic Surgeons, Am. Soc. Plastic Surgeons, ASMS, AOA. Office: 1301 20th St Ste 460 Santa Monica CA 90404-2054 Office Phone: 310-829-0391.

KAWANO, TOSHIAKI, retired economics professor; b. Shintomi-machi, Miyazaki, Japan, Jan. 25, 1933; s. Yoshimatsu and Kesazuru (Hiezima) K.; m. Miho Kanai, Dec. 8, 1967 (dec. May 1979); children: Chiho, Toshihide, Toshifumi. Bachelor, Miyazaki (Japan) U., 1955; M in Agr., U. Tokyo Grad. Sch., 1958, PhD in Agr., 1982. Rsch. fellow Internat. Christian U., Tokyo, 1955-56; rschr. Nat. Inst. of Agrl. Sci., Tokyo, 1960-73, chief mktg. lab., 1974-80; prof. economic geography Hitotsubashi U., Tokyo, 1983-96; prof. agrl. econ. Ryutsu Keizai U., Ryugasaki, Japan, 1996—2003; ret., 2003. Vis. lectr. Chiba U. Sch. Horticulture, Matsudo, Japan, 1980-98, Tokyo U. Agr. and Engring., 1988-91; lectr. fgn. agrl. trainees Japan Internat. Coop. Agy., 1990-2003; cons. Nat. Rural Devel. Assn., others, Tokyo, 1960-1990; del. to internat. congresses Asian Productivity Orgn., Tokyo, 1970-90; sec. gen. Farm Mgmt. Assn. Japan, Tsukuba, 1982-83; lectr. in field. Author, editor books; editor Agrl. Econ. Soc. of Japan, 1976-77; contbr. articles to profl. jours. FAO fellow UN, Mich. State U., 1964-65. Mem. Internat. Soc. Horticultural Sci. (corr. economic newsletter 1970-80). Buddist. Avocations: gardening, folkmusic. Home: 381-13 Myojin Tsukuba Ibaraki 300-1257 Japan E-mail: aozora_domani@yahoo.co.jp.

KAWARSKY, JAY A., music educator, conductor, composer; b. Des Moines, Iowa, Aug. 29, 1959; s. Irvin Kalman and Eloise Ann Kawarsky. DMA, Northwestern U., Evanston, IL, 1983—85, MM, 1981—82; MusB, Iowa State U., Ames, IA, 1978—81. Asst. prof. Ft. Hays State U., Hays, Kans., 1985—86; instr. Univ. of Wis.-Marathon, Wausau, Wis., 1986—87; asst. prof. Moraine Valley Comm. Coll., Palos Hills, Ill., 1987—89; prof. Westminster Choir Coll. of Rider Univ., Princeton, NJ, 1989—. Condr. NJ. Gay Men's Chorus, Princeton, NJ, 1991—97; artistic dir. Lehigh Valley Gay Men's Chorus, Allentown, Pa., 1997—. Composer: (choral/orchestral) Prayers for Bobby, (choral) I Dreamed in a Dream, Magnificat, Ocho Kandelikas, The Final Word, Blessed is the Match, Life Doesn't Frighten Me, Civil War Voices, Freedom, Erev Shel Shoshanim, As a Driven Leaf, (orchestral) Episodes, (instrumental) Observation I, (choral) Al Hanissim, (choral/orchestral) Alec Baldwin Doesn't Love Me; musician: Sing for the Cure; composer: (choral) Adon Olam, Creed, (instrumental) Rejoice, O Young Man, Awake, North Wind, (orchestral) Grace Dances. Recipient ASCAP award, ASCAP, 1998, 1999, 2000, 2001, 2002, 2003; fellow Summer Fellowships, Rider U., 2000, 2002. Mem.: AAUP (hon.; president-rider univ. chpt. 2002—03). D-Liberal. Jewish. Avocations: theater, travel, weightlifting. Home: PO Box 213 New Hope PA 18938 Office: Westminster Choir Coll of Rider Univ 101 Walnut Lane Princeton NJ 08540 Personal E-mail: jaktg@verizon.net. E-mail: jkawarsky@rider.edu.

KAWASHIMA, HOPE NOZOMI, musician; b. Auburn, Calif., Apr. 2, 1937; d. Peter Shinichi and Mary Etsuko Omachi; m. Mas Kawashima, June 14, 1964; children: Mariya Yoshiko Yamamoto, Rebekah Kawashima Wong. BA in Rec. and Music Therapy, Calif. State U., Sacramento, 1959; MA in Sacred Music, San Francisco Theol. Sem., 1964; postgrad., Juilliard Sch. Music, N.Y.C., 1980—81. Ordained as deacon United Meth. Ch., consecrated to ministry United Meth. Ch., 1982; registered music therapist Calif., cert. dir. music. Music therapist State of Calif., Stockton, Napa, 1959—64; dir., organist 1st Presbyn. Ch., Altadena, Calif., 1964—71, Ontario (Oreg.) Cmty. Ch., 1972—80, J A United Ch., N.Y.C., 1980—88, LaTijera United Meth. Ch., LA, 1988—93, Lake Park United Meth. Ch., Oakland, Calif., 1993—2002; min. music St. Paul's United Meth. Ch., Fresno, Calif., 2002—05, United Japanese Christian Ch., Clovis, Calif., 2005—. Dir. Music Mart Acad., Santa Monica, Calif., 1988—91. Musician: (albums) Songs of Faith, Hope & Love, 1967; composer, musician: albums Love Wider than an Ocean, 1977, prodr., composer, musician: albums Reflections of Faith, Hope & Love, 2002 (CLPEP grantee); author: Learning to Play Piano is as Easy as ABC. Gen. conf. del. United Meth. Ch., St. Louis, 1988, mem. hymnal com. Nashville, 1985—88; chairperson Theol. Forum, Berkeley, Calif., 1994—2002. Recipient Famous Diamond Poet award, Famous Poets Soc., 1995; Sears Roebuck & Co. scholar, 1955, Calif. Civil. Liberties grantee, 2002. Mem.: Nat. Guild Piano Tchrs. (local chair 1979—89), Clergywoman Calif., Calif. Scholarship Fedn. (life), Native Daughters Calif. Office: United Japanese Christian Ch 136 N Villa Clovis CA 93612

KAWAZOE, ROBIN INADA, federal official; b. Wilkinsburg, Pa., Jan. 13, 1959; d. George and Hanako (Nishio) Inada; children: Amy, Steven. BA, U. Md., 1982. Program analyst Alcohol, Drug Abuse & Mental Health Adminstrn., Rockville, Md., 1981-85, 85-87, com. mgmt. officer, 1985—86, extramural programs officer, 1987-88; spl. asst. Nat. Inst. on Drug Abuse, Rockville, 1988-90, dep. dir. Office Sci. Policy and Comm., 1990-96; dir. Office of Sci. Policy and Planning, 1997—. Recipient Recognition award, Pub. Health Svc., 1992, Dir.'s award, NIH, 1994, 2004, Dir.'s Group award, 2000, 2004, 2005, Group award for Disting. Svc., HHS Sec., 2004. Office: NIH Office of Sci Policy & Planning 9000 Rockville Pike Bldg 1, rm 218 Bethesda MD 20892-0003

KAWCZAK, JANUSZ, mathematician, educator; b. Gorowo Ilaweckie, Poland, Dec. 2, 1963; arrived in U.S., 1998, permanent resident; s. Grzegorz and Anna Kawczak; m. Pauline To, Sept. 17, 2000. BSc with hons., U.Man., Winnipeg,Can., 1992—92; MSc, U. Man., Winnipeg, Can., 1993; PhD, U Western Ont., London, Ontario, Can., 1998. Lectr. U. Western Ont., London, Canada, 1997—98; prof. of math. U. N.C., Charlotte, 1998—. Cons. Act Stats Consulting, Charlotte, NC, 2001—. Grantee Scholarship, NSERC, 1995-97, rsch. in probability, stats. and finance, NSF, 2002—. Office: Univ NC Math Dept 9201 University City Blvd Charlotte NC 28223 E-mail: jkawczak@math.uncc.edu.

KAWEWE, SALIWE MOYO, social work educator, researcher; children: Godfrey, Kudawashe children: Neo Jomo, Rujeko N. BSW, University Of Zambia, Lusaka, Zambia, 1970—74; MSW, Washington U., St. Louis, Mo.,

1977—79; PhD, St. Louis U., 1981—85. Cert. edn. accreditation reaffirmation Coun. on Social Work, 2001. Adminstrv. asst. University of Zambia, Lusaka, Zambia, 1974—77; social svcs. officer, probation officer Dept. Social Svcs., Bulawayo, Zimbabwe, 1979—81; instr. Bd. Edn. St. Louis Public Schools, Saint Louis, Mo., 1981—83; social service worker II Mo. Div. of Family Services, St. Louis, 1984—85; asst. prof. Southeastern La. U., Hammond, La., 1985—88, Central State U., Wilberforce, Ohio, 1989, James Madison U., Harrisonburg, Va., 1989—91, Wichita State U., Wichita, Kans., 1991—96; assoc. prof. Southern Ill. U., Carbondale, Ill., 1996—2001, grad. program dir., 1996—98, prof., 2002—. Chair Coun. on Social Work Edn. Internat. Commn.'s Internat.l Issues Symposium, Alexandria, 1999—; contract bargaining team mem. Southern Ill. U. Faculty Assn., IEA-NEA, Carbondale, 1998—2003, dept. rep., 1998—99. Contbr. chapters to books; mem. editl. bd.: Social Devel. Issues, 1998—, mem. guest editl. bd.: Nat. Women Studies Jour., 1997—98; contbr. articles to profl. jours. and publs. Mem. Nat. Assn. Social Workers, Bulawayo, Zimbabwe, 1980—82; Africa regional rep. Inter-Univ. Consortium for Internat. Social Devel., Wichita, 1992—94; mem. Tangipohoa Parish Mayor's commn. on Needs of Women, Hammond, La., 1985—88, Inter-Univ. Consortium for Internat. Social Devel., Carbondale, 1995—, Ill. Hunger Coalition, Chgo., 1998—; sec. Kans. Coun. on Social Work Edn., Topeka, 1992—93; mem. Com. to Enhance Minority, Human and Civil Rights, Springfield, 2000—. Recipient Outstanding Scholastic Achievement award, George Warren Brown Sch. of Social Work, Wash. U., 1979, Superior Acad. Achievement award, St. Louis U. Internat. Student Assn., 1984, Appreciation for Continuing Svc. as a Faculty Advisor, Nat. Assn. Black Social Workers, 2001, Appreciation as Faculty Advisor, 2000, certificate of Dedication, African Student Coun. So. Ill. U. at Carbondale, 2001, Internat. Student Coun So. Ill. U. at Carbondale, 2001, Award of Appreciation of Svc., Nat. Assn. Black Social Workers, 2000, Recognition of Dedicated Svc., African Student Coun. So. Ill. U. at Carbondale, 1998, Dedication of Svc., African Student Coun., So. Ill. U. at Carbondale, 1997, Outstanding Leadership and Guidance, Student Orgn. of Social Work, Wichita State U., 1996, Outstanding Multilateral Study Del. award, World Congress on the Family, 1992; grantee Summer Rsch. Travel Grant, Wichita State U., 1994. Mem.: NASW (asst. dist. chair 1997—99), Internat. Coun. on Social Welfare, Internat. Assn. for Schs. of Social Work, Soc. for Study of Social Problems, Peace and Social Justice Ctr. of So. Ctrl. Kans., Inter-U. Consortium for Internat. Social Devel., Coun. on Social Work Edn., Coun. on Social Work Edn. Internat. Commn., Internat. Assn. Feminist Econs., So. Ill. U. Women's Caucus, Nat. Women Studies Assn., So. Ill. HIV Care Consortium (bd. mem. 1997—2001), Internat. Fedn. Social Workers (life), Beta Delta of Phi Alpha (hon.). Office: So Ill U Sch Of Social Work Mailcode 4329 Carbondale IL 62901 Office Phone: 618-453-3359. Business E-Mail: smkawewe@siu.edu.

KAY, ALAN C., computer scientist; b. May 1940; BS in Math., Molecular Biology, U. Colo., 1966; MSEE, U. Utah, PhD in Computer Sci., 1969; PhD (hon.), Kungl Tekniska Hoegskolan, Stockholm. Instr. Stanford Artificial Intelligence Lab., 1970; group leader Xerox Palo Alto Rsch. Ctr., Calif., 1971—81; chief scientist Atari, 1981—84; fellow Apple Computer, Brentwood, Calif., 1984-96; computer tchr. Open School, West Hollywood; fellow Walt Disney Imagineering, 1997—2001, v.p., rsch. & devel., 1996—2001; sr. fellow Hewlett-Packard Labs., 2002—; adj. prof. computer sci. UCLA Henry Samueli Sch. Engring. and Applied Sci., 2002—; vis. prof. Kyoto U., Japan; pres., founder Viewpoints Rsch. Inst., 2001—. Recipient Turing Award, Assoc. for Computing Machinery, 2003, Charles Stark Draper Prize, Nat. Acad. Engring., 2004, Kyoto Prize for Advanced Tech., Inamori Found., 2004, J-D Warnier Prix d'Informatique, C&C Prize, NEC Corp., Funai Prize. Fellow AAAS, NAE, Royal Soc. Arts. Achievements include invention of Dynabook; creator of Smalltalk, the first complete dynamic object-oriented programming (OOP) language; created an early model of the laptop computer and contbd. to the devel. of Ethernet, laser printing, and the "client-server" network model. Office: HP Labs Palo Alto 1501 Page Mill Rd Palo Alto CA 94304

KAY, AMAN B., language educator, translator; s. Baqer B. Bechernia and Akram Faradji; life ptnr. Loretta J. Levi, June 30, 1957; 1 child, Sheila B. D, N.Mex State U., 1988. Cert. tchr. cert. Tex., 1984. Tchr., dept. chair San Antonio Ind. Sch. Dist., San Antonio, 1981—99; asst. prof. Def. Lang. Inst., Monterey, Calif., 1999—. Editl. cons. various cos., 1993—2003. Author: (novel) Augury of Shebana Ashley, (collection of poetry) With the Wings of Time; contbr. articles to profl. jours. and mags. Scholar, Royal Iranian Ministry of Culture and Arts, 1974. Mem.: Am. Transl. Assn. (assoc.). Avocations: tennis, ping pong/table tennis, walking/jogging, travel, reading. Personal E-mail: docabkay@yahoo.com.

KAY, ARTHUR DAVID, neurologist; b. Bklyn., Jan. 22, 1953; s. William V. and Bette Kay; m. Betty H. Gutwein, Sept. 5, 1977; children: Jason, Jeffrey, Tziporah, Joseph, Elisheva. BA, CUNY, 1974; MD, SUNY Downstate Med. Ctr., Bklyn., 1978. Diplomate Am. Bd. Psychiatry and Neurology. Internship Brookdale Hosp. Med. Ctr., Bklyn., 1978—79; residency Mt. Sinai Med. Ctr., N.Y.C., NY, 1979—82; fellow med. staff NIH, Bethesda, Md., 1982—84; asst. prof. neurology and geriatrics Mt. Sinai Med. Ctr., N.Y.C., 1984—87; chmn. neurology Brookdale Hosp. Med. Ctr., 1988—; assoc. prof. neurology SUNY Downstate Med. Ctr., Bklyn., 1988—; acting chief neurology Flushing Hosp., Queens, NY, 2001—, Jamaica Hosp., Queens, 2002—. Mem.: Am. Acad. Neurology. Office: Brookdale Hosp Med Ctr 1 Brookdale Plz Brooklyn NY 11212 Office Phone: 718-240-5622.

KAY, CHRISTOPHER K., retail executive, lawyer; b. Cin., Jan. 5, 1953; s. Robert and Joan Kay; m. Kristine Kenney, 1977; 1 child, Lauren. BA with honors in polit. sci. and history, U. Mo., 1975; JD, Duke U., 1978. Bar: 1978. Atty. Shughart, Thomson and Kilroy, Kans. City, Mo., 1978—84; chmn. litigation dept. Swann & Haddock, Orlando, Fla., 1984—90; ptnr. Foley & Lardner, Orlando, 1990—96; founding ptnr. Kay, Panzl & Latham, Orlando, Fla., 1996—98, Kay, Gronek & Latham, Orlando, Fla., 1998—2000; exec. v.p., gen. counsel, corp. sec. Toys "R" Us, Inc., Wayne, NJ, 2000—02, exec. v.p. ops., gen. counsel, corp. sec., 2002—03, exec. v.p. ops, corp. sec., 2003—. Mem. US-Japan Pvt. Sector/Govt. Commn., 2002. Presbyn. Fellow: Am. Bar Found.; mem.: ABA (vice chmn. antitrust sect. bus. torts and unfair competition com. 2000—), Am. Bd. Trial Advocates, Fla. State Bar. Office: Toys R Us Inc 1 Geoffrey Way Wayne NJ 07470-2030

KAY, CYRIL MAX, biochemist, educator; b. Calgary, Alta., Can., Oct. 3, 1931; s. Louis and Fanny (Pearlmutter) K.; m. Faye Bloomenthal, Dec. 30, 1953; children: Lewis Edward, Lisa Franci. B.Sc. in Biochemistry with honors (J.W. McConnell Meml. scholar), McGill U., 1952; PhD in Biochemistry (Life Ins. Med. Research Fund fellow), Harvard U., 1956; postgrad., Cambridge (Eng.) U., 1956-57. Phys. biochemist Eli Lilly & Co., Indpls., 1957-58; asst. prof. biochemistry U. Alta., Edmonton, 1958-61, assoc. prof., 1961-67, prof., 1967—, co-dir. Med. Rsch. Coun. Group on Protein Structure and Function, 1974-95, mem. protein engring. network Centre of Excellence, 1990—, chmn. internat. rsch. adv. com. to protein engring. network Centre of Excellence, 2000—; v.p. rsch. Alta. Cancer Bd., 1999—. Med. Rsch. Coun. vis. scientist in biophysics Weizmann Inst., Israel, 1969-70, summer vis. prof. biophysics, 1975, summer vis. prof. chem. physics, 1977, 80; mem. biochemistry grants com. Med. Research Council, 1970-73; mem. Med. Rsch. Coun. Can., 1982-88; Can. rep. Pan Am. Assn. Biochem. Socs., 1971-76; mem. exec. planning com. XI Internat. Congress Biochemistry, Toronto, Ont., Can., 1979; mem. med. adv. bd. Gairdner Found. for Internat. awards in Med. Sci., 1980-89; chmn. Internat. Scientific adv. com. on protein engring., 2000—. Contbr. numerous articles to profl. publs.; asso. editor Can. Jour. Biochemistry, 1968-82; editor-in-chief Pan Am. Assn. Biochem. Socs. Revista, 1971-76. Decorated Order of Can.; recipient Ayerst award in biochemistry Can. Biochem. Soc., 1970, Disting. Scientist award U. Alta. Med. Sch., 1988. Fellow N.Y. Acad. Scis., Royal Soc. Can.; mem. Order of Can., Can. Biochem. Soc. (coun, 1971—, v.p. 1976-77, pres. 1978-79). Home: 9408-143d St Edmonton AB Canada T5R 0P7 Office: U Alta Dept Biochemistry Med Scis Bldg Edmonton AB Canada T6G 2H7 Business E-Mail: ckay@ualberta.ca.

KAY, DAVID CYRIL, psychiatrist; b. Sault Ste. Marie, Mich., Sept. 5, 1932; s. James William and Helen Elizabeth (Dixon) K.; m. Carla Kay Kunkel, Dec. 27, 1981; children: David Carl, James Andrew, Rachel Elizabeth Kay McMahon, Thomas Milton. BS magna cum laude, Wheaton (Ill.) Coll., 1954; MD, U. Ill., Chgo., 1958. Diplomate Am. Bd. Psychiatry and Neurology, Am. Bd. Addiction Psychiatry, Nat. Bd. Med. Examiners. Intern Presbyn.-St. Luke's Hosp., Chgo., 1958-59; resident Ill. State Psychiat. Inst., Chgo., 1961-64; commd. officer USPHS, 1959, advanced through grades to med. dir.; fellow NIMH, 1961-66; chief exptl. psychiatry sect. Addiction Rsch. Ctr., Nat. Inst. Drug Abuse, 1964-80; pvt. practice Houston, 1980—; assoc. prof. psychiatry and pharmacology Baylor Coll. Medicine, 1980-92. Fellow Am. Psychiat. Assn. (life). Office: 1313 Campbell Rd Bldg C Houston TX 77055-6458

KAY, DENNIS MATTHEW, retired publishing company official; b. Chgo., Sept. 20, 1936; s. Edward Francis and Rose Anne (Koziel) Kolodzinski; m. Judy R. Kalinsky, Jan. 9, 1965; 1 child, Alan Edward. BBA, Loyola U., 1976. Customer svc. agt. Am. Airlines, Chgo., 1959-69; expeditor Time Inc., Chgo., 1969-73, traffic mgr. People mag., 1973-75, Time mag. traffic mgr., 1975-78, ops. mgr., 1978-81, electronic data mgr., 1981-83, plant mgr. Waterloo, Wis., 1983-88, field ops. mgr., 1988-95, nat. prodn. analyst, 1995-96, field ops. mgr., 1996-99; ret., 2000. With U.S. Army, 1959-61. Recipient MM&D Excellence award Time Inc., 1989, Prodn. Excellence awards, 1993, 94, Pres. award, 1993. Mem. Moose Lodge River Grove 378 (gov. 1982-83). Roman Catholic. Avocations: stamp collecting/philately, piano, model building. Home: 604 Long Cove Dr Lake In The Hills IL 60156 Personal E-mail: denky1@aol.com.

KAY, GEORGE PAUL, environmental engineer; b. McKeesport, Pa., Sept. 25, 1954; s. George and Darlene Ann (Snyder) K.; m. Rosemary Ann Lynam, July 19, 1986; children: Brittany Elaine, Hope Elise, George Prescott. BS in Biology, U. Pitts., 1975, MS in Environ. Health, 1976, MSCE, 1982. Registered profl. engr., Pa., Ohio; cert. sewage treatment plant and waterworks operator, Pa. Rsch. asst. U. Pitts., 1976-79; from asst. aquatic ecologist to sr. environ. engr. Michael Baker Corp., Beaver, Pa., 1979-87, sect. mgr. water and wastewater Coraopolis, Pa., 1987-89; mgr. water quality engring. Michael Baker Jr. Inc., Coraopolis, Pa., 2000—02, mgr. civil and environ. engring., 2002—; sr. engr. water and wastewater AK Steel Corp. (formerly Armco, Inc.), Butler, Pa., 1989-2000. Contbr. articles to profl. jours. Mem. Pa. Water Environ. Assn., Water Environ. Fedn., World Aquaculture Soc., Aquacultural Engring. Soc. Avocations: traditional archery, bonsai, rock guitar, aquarium science. Home: 4596 Bucktail Dr Allison Park PA 15101-2120 Office: Michael Baker Jr Inc 100 Airside Dr Coraopolis PA 15108 Office Phone: 412-269-6028. Business E-Mail: gkay@mbakercorp.com.

KAY, GWEN, history professor, researcher; s. Edwin and Janice Kay; m. Jeffrey Sneider, May 13, 1949. BA, Bowdoin Coll., 1991; PhD, Yale U., 1997. Vis. prof. U. Tennesee, Chattanooga, 1997—98, DePaul U., Chgo., 1998—99; vis. scholar Mershon Inst. Ohio State U., Columbus, Ohio, 1999—2000; asst. prof. SUNY, Oswego, NY, 2000—. Cons. Onondaga County Med. Soc., Syracuse, NY, 2004—. Office Phone: 315-312-3418.

KAY, HERBERT, retired energy executive; b. Johnsonburg, Pa., Mar. 19, 1924; s. Alexander S. and Carla Z. Racusin; m. Rita Inge Schmidt, May 4, 1956; children: Peter, Darcy, Philip. BS in Chem. Engring., Pa. State U., 1944; S.M., MIT, 1947; postgrad., Sloan Sch., 1968. Process engr. Stanolind Oil & Gas Co., Tulsa, 1947-49; group supr. Consolidation Coal Co., Library, Pa., 1949-55; sr. v.p. Climax Molybdenum Co., 1955-77; v.p. Amax Inc., 1977-85; also dir. U.K., Holland, Italy, France, Japan. Patentee in field. Served with USNR, 1944-45. Mem. AIChE, Univ. Club (N.Y.), Madison Beach and Country Clubs (Conn.), Audubon Country Club (Fla.). Home: 111 E Wharf Rd PO Box 687 Madison CT 06443-0687 Business E-Mail: herbkay@alum.mit.edu.

KAY, HERMA HILL, law educator; b. Orangeburg, S.C., Aug. 18, 1934; d. Charles Esdorn and Herma Lee (Crawford) Hill. BA, So. Meth. U., 1956; JD, U. Chgo., 1959. Bar: Calif. 1960, U.S. Supreme Ct. 1978. Law clk. to Hon. Roger Traynor Calif. Supreme Ct., 1959-60; from asst. prof. to assoc. prof. law U. Calif., Berkeley, 1960-62, prof., 1963, dir. family law project, 1964-67, Jennings prof., 1987-96, dean, 1992-2000, Armstrong prof., 1996—; co-reporter uniform marriage and div. act Nat. Conf. Commrs. on Uniform State Laws, 1968-70. Vis. prof. U. Manchester, England, 1972, Harvard U., 1976; mem. Gov.'s Commn. Family, 1966. Author (with Martha S. West): (book) Text Cases and Materials on Sex-Based Discrimination, 6th edit., 2005; author: (with D. Currie and L. Kramer) Conflict of Laws: Cases, Comments, Questions, 6th edit., 2001; contbr. articles to profl. jours. Trustee Russell Sage Found., NY, 1972—87, chmn. bd. trustees, 1980—84; trustee, bd. dirs. Equal Rights Advs., Calif., 1987—88, chmn., 1976—83; pres. bd. dirs. Rosenberg Found., Calif., 1987—88, bd. dirs., 1978—. Recipient Rsch. award, Am. Bar Found., 1990, Margaret Brent award, ABA Commn. Women in Profession, 1992, Marshall-Wythe medal, 1995; fellow, Ctr. Advanced Study Behavioral Sci., Palo Alto, Calif., 1963. Mem.: ABA (sect. legal edn. and admissions to bar coun. 1992—99, sec. 1999—2001), Order of Coif (nat. pres. 1983—85), Am. Philos. Soc., Am. Acad. Arts and Scis., Assn. Am. Law Schs. (exec. com. 1986—87, pres.-elect 1988, pres. 1989, past pres. 1990), Am. Law Inst. (mem. coun. 1985—), Calif. Women Lawyers (bd. govs. 1975—77), Bar U.S. Supreme Ct., Calif. Bar Assn. Democrat. Office: U Calif Law Sch Boalt Hall Berkeley CA 94720-7200 Office Phone: 510-643-2671. E-mail: kayh@law.berkeley.edu.

KAY, JANICE HOPE, psychologist, consultant; b. Miami, Fla., May 1, 1956; d. Melvin and Roslyn Schaffer; m. James Michael Kay, Aug. 6, 1952; children: Jenessa Lea, Chelsea Jean. BA, U. West Fla., 1978, MA, 1983. Cert. behavior analyst, Fla. Tchr. Children's Resource Ctr., Pensacola, Fla., 1978-80, pub. sch., Robertsdale, Ala., 1980-81; psychologist, qualified mentally retarded profl. MACTown, Inc., Miami, 1984-86; caseworker City of Miami Beach, Fla., 1986-88; staff psychologist RHA Health Svcs., Inc., Statesville, N.C., 1988-94; pvt. practice Statesville, N.C., 1994—. Leader Girl Scouts Am. Mem. Nat. Assn. Dual Diagnoises, Am. Psych. Assn., Am. Assn. Mental Retardation. Avocations: sports, reading, physical fitness. Home and Office: 114 Friar Tuck Rd Statesville NC 28625-9057 E-mail: janhkay@hotmail.com.

KAY, JOEL PHILLIP, lawyer; b. Corsicana, Tex., Aug. 27, 1936; m. Marilyn Soltz, July 9, 1961; children: Arthur Hyman, Sarah Anne, Leslie Anette. BS in Econs., Wharton Sch., U. Pa., 1958; LLB, U. Tex., 1961; LL.M., Georgetown U., 1967. Bar: Tex. 1961, U.S. Dist. Ct. (so. and we. dists.) Tex., U.S. Dist. Ct (so. dist.) Ala., U.S. Ct. Appeals (5th cir.), U.S. Supreme Ct. Trial atty. tax div. Dept. Justice, 1963-67; U.S. atty. So. Dist. Tex., 1967-69; ptnr. Sheinfeld, Maley & Kay, P.C., Houston, 1969—2001; of counsel Hughes, Watters & Askanase, LLP, Houston, 2001—. Mem. Tex. Bd. Pub. Accountancy, 1984-85, quality rev. oversight bd., 1992-93; speaker at numerous institutes on comml. and bankruptcy law. With AUS, 1961-63. Fellow Am. Bar Found., Am. Coll. Bankruptcy (5th cir. regent 1998-2003); mem. ABA, Tex. Bar Assn. (dir. 1979-81, chmn. bd. 1981-82), Houston Bar Assn., Tex. Bar Found. (trustee 1983-86), Houston Bar Found. (dir. 1995-98), Tex. Supreme Ct. (grievance oversight com. 1987-94). Office: Three Allen Center 333 Clay 29th Fl Houston TX 77002 Office Phone: 713-759-0818.

KAY, KENNETH JEFFREY, real estate company executive; b. L.A., Apr. 2, 1955; s. Morton M. and Beverly J. Kay. BS in Acctg., U. So. Calif., 1978, MBA in Fin., 1980. CPA, Calif. Staff acct. in charge Price Waterhouse and Co. (now PriceWaterhouse Coopers LLC), Century City, Calif., 1980-82; mgr. acctg. TRW-Fujitsu Co., L.A., 1982-83; corp. controller Ameron Internat., Pasadena, Calif., 1983-88, sr. v.p. fin. and adminstrn., CFO, 1990-92, group v.p., 1992-94; pres., CEO, dir. Bishop, Inc., Westlake Village, Calif., 1988-90; sr. v.p. fin. and adminstrn., CFO Systemed, Inc., Torrance, Calif., 1994-96; sr. v.p., CFO Playmates Inc., Costa Mesa, Calif., 1997; exec. v.p., CFO Universal Studios Consumer Products Group, Universal City, Calif., 1998-99; v.p., CFO, Dole Food Co., Inc., Westlake Village, Calif., 1999—2002; sr. exec. v.p., CFO CB Richard Ellis Group, L.A., 2002—. Chmn. supervisory com. Ameron Fed. Credit Union, South Gate, Calif., 1986. Bd. govs. Cedars-Sinai Med. Ctr.; mem. exec. com. Friends for Life, L.A.; mem. bd. dirs. Paralysis Project Am.; mem. bd. advisors U. So. Calif. Leven Sch. Acctg. Mem. AICPA, Am. Mgmt. Assn., Calif. Soc. CPAs, Assn. for Strategic Planning, Fin. Execs. Inst. Office: CB Richard Ellis Group 865 S Figueroa St Ste 3400 Los Angeles CA 90017 Office Phone: 213-438-4833. Business E-Mail: kenneth.kay@cbre.com.

KAY, LOIS JEANNE, writer, educator; b. Phila., June 13, 1928; d. Maurice Lantz and Lena Barbara (Hoover) Umble; m. William David Kay, Sept. 10, 1949; children: Barbara Ellen, William David. AS cum laude, Dickinson Jr. Coll., Williamsport, Pa., 1948; BA magna cum laude, Syracuse U., 1968; BA, Empire State U., 1984; MA, Goddard Coll., 1986. Tchr. pub. schs., 1965-70; real estate salesperson Utica, N.Y., 1970-74; owner/mgr. Bird-in-Hand Store, Clinton, N.Y., 1974-79; assoc. prof. SUNY, Utica, 1986—; owner/condr. lit. workshops, pub. Greenwood Press, Clinton, 1985—. Lectr. in field. Author: A Sounding Inland, 1986, Some Certainties, 1987, Adirondack Diner, 1988, Letters From Sagamore, 1994, White Garden Night, 1996, Homeland, 1996; contbr. numerous articles to profl. jours. Recipient Award for Writing Fiction, Regioart, 1st prize Comstock Rev., 1997; Ctrl. N.Y. Art grantee, 1994, 95. Home: 54 Kirkland Ave Clinton NY 13323-1414

KAY, MADELEINE H., writer, lifestyle and career coach, consultant, speech professional; d. Harry and Anne Kay; 1 child, Daniel Bar-Sadeh Sage. BA cum laude, Boston U., 1967; MA, U. Miami, Fla., 1975; cert. in French Lang., Sorbonne, Paris, 1968. Cert. Integrated Studies Min. of Edn., Israel, 1970. Advt. creative and project designer, coord. and mgr. Allyn & Bacon Publ. Co., Boston, 1967; instr. English and writing Tel Aviv U., Ramat Aviv, Israel, 1969—71; media dir, Garber & Goodman Advt, Miami, Fla., 1978—81; instr. writing U. Miami, 1972—78; pres., creative dir. and owner Erica Knight Assoc., Inc. Advt./Mktg., Miami, 1981—95; freelance writer, 1997—. Life coach, cons. Eclectic Practical Therapy, Miami, Fla., 1990—97; commentary writer CBS affiliate, Miami, Fla., 1990—92. Author: Living Serendipitously...Keeping the Wonder Alive, 2003 (Best Seller, 2004). Big sister Big Brothers/Big Sisters, Hendersonville, NC, 2002—04. Mem.: Publ. Mkt. Assn. Avocations: nature/outdoors, dance, singing, acting, travel. Office: Chrysalis Publ PO Box 675 Flat Rock NC 28731 E-mail: mkay@livingseredipitously.com.

KAY, STEPHEN WILLIAM, lawyer; b. Omaha, Dec. 27, 1953; s. Harold Wallace and Patricia Lou (Larson) K.; m. Jean Marie Lawse, Aug. 5, 1978; children: Melissa Marie, Stephen William II, Robert Andrew. BS, U. Nebr., 1975; JD, Creighton U., 1978. Bar: Nebr. 1978, U.S. Dist. Ct. Nebr. 1978, U.S. Ct. Claims 1987, U.S. Ct. Appeals (8th cir.) 1978, U.S. Ct. Appeals (Fed. cir.) 1984, U.S. Ct. Appeals (D.C. cir.) 1987, U.S. Supreme Ct. 1984., U.S. Ct. Appeals 1990, U.S. Ct. Internat. Trade 1990. Assoc. Kay & Satterfield, North Platte, Nebr., 1978-80; ptnr. Kay & Kay, North Platte, 1980—. Mem. standing com. Episcopal Diocese of Nebr., 1985-89, mem. com. on legis., 1990-95, exec. com., 1992-95; exec. bd. dirs. Tri Trails coun. Boy Scouts Am., North Platte, 1982-93, Overland Trails coun., Grand Island, 1993—, v.p. adminstrn., 1996-2001; dist. chmn. Buffalo Bill Dist., 1994-96, vice chmn., 1996-98; chmn. Lincoln County Reps., North Platte, 1982-84; cen. committeeman Nebr. Reps., 1984-98, asst. chmn., 1986, mem. exec. com., 1986; bd. dirs. Mid-Nebr. Cmty. Found., 1988-93, 95-97; provisional dep. Gen. Conv., Episcopal Ch., 1991, 94, 97. Recipient Dist. award of Merit Boy Scouts Am., 1996, Silver Beaver award, 1998. Fellow: Nebr. State Bar Found.; mem.: ABA, Assn. Def. Trial Attys., Nat. Assn. R.R. Trial Coun., Am. Judicature Soc., Nebr. Bar Assn., Western Nebr. Bar Assn., Lincoln County Bar Assn. Episcopalian. Home: 1111 Custer Ct North Platte NE 69101-6305 Office: Wells Fargo Bank Bldg 315 N Dewey St Ste 205 North Platte NE 69103 Office Phone: 308-534-7676. Business E-Mail: kaylaw@alltel.net.

KAY, THOMAS OLIVER, agricultural consultant; b. Anderson, S.C., Sept. 29, 1929; s. Thomas Crayton and Gertrude (Whitworth) K.; m. Rebecca Moore, Aug. 29, 1954 (div. 1965); children— Michael (dec.), Mitchell; m. Bette Hutto, Oct. 1, 1966 (dec. Nov. 1991); stepchildren— Dallon Weathers, Bruce Weathers BA, Furman U., 1950; LL.D. (hon.), John Marshall Law Sch., Atlanta, 1960. Adminstrv. asst. U.S. Congress, Washington, 1966-73; legis. officer USDA, Washington, 1973-77; exec. asst. U.S. Senate, Washington, 1977-79; lobbyist Nat. Assn. Realtors, Washington, 1979-80; asst. to adminstr. Fgn. Agrl. Service USDA, Washington, 1981-82, dir. congl. relations, 1982-83, dep. asst. sec. govtl. and pub. affairs, 1983-85, dep. undersec. internat. affairs and commodity programs, 1985-86, adminstr. fgn. agrl. svc., 1986-90; pres. Kay Assoc., 1989-94. Mem. Litchfield Country Club (Pawleys Island, S.C.). Avocations: golf, swimming. Home: 17 Goodson Loop Pawleys Island SC 29585-8037

KAYA, SAVAS, technologist, researcher; b. Istanbul, Turkey, 1971; s. Cemal and Hediye Kaya; m. Perihan Kaya. BSc, Istanbul (Turkey) Tech. U., 1992; MPhil, U. Cambridge, 1994; PhD, Imperial Coll. Sci., Tech. and Medicine, 1998. Rsch. & tchg. asst. Istanbul (Turkey) Tech. U., 1992—93; post-doctoral rschr. U. Glasgow, Scotland, 1998—2001; asst. prof. Ohio U., Athens, Ohio, 2001—. Mem.: IEEE (assoc.). Achievements include patents for COSMOS devices & circuits. Office: Ohio University 361 Stocker Center Athens OH 45701 Office Phone: 740-597-1633. Office Fax: 740-593-0007. Business E-Mail: kaya@ohio.edu.

KAYAFAS, STEPHANIE ANN, special education educator, consultant, supervisor, actress; b. Pitts., Oct. 18, 1957; d. Nicholas and Helen Kayafas. BS, Rutgers U., 1979; MA, Georgian Ct. Coll., Lakewood, N.J., 1996. Cert. tchr. handicapped, elem. tchr., supr., prin., sch. bus. adminstr. N.J. N.J. spl. edn. tchr. Old Farmers Rd. Elem. Sch., Long Valley, NJ, 1979—82; spl. edn. tchr. Tinton Falls (N.J.) Mid. Sch., 1982-83, Rugby Sch., Wall, NJ, 1982—83; owner, operator Charlie's Auto Body Facility, Asbury Park, NJ, 1983—86; computer trainer Dendrite Internat. Inc., Morristown, N.J., 1998-99; actress Actor's Reps, N.Y.C., 1998—; real estate referral cons. Ind. Referral Cons., Woodstown, N.J., 1999—; spl. edn. tchr. Marlboro (NJ) HS, 1987—2001, supr. spl. edn., 2002—. Mem. People to People Internat., 2001—; del. People's Republic of China Amb. Program, 2001. Mem.: ASCD, Am. Coun. Exercise, Rutgers Alumni Assn. Avocations: reading, poetry, weight training, guitar. Home: Riverview Twrs 28 Riverside Ave Unit 10G Red Bank NJ 07701 Office: Marlboro HS 95 N Main St Marlboro NJ 07746 Personal E-mail: stephanieknj@aol.com.

KAYE, BARRY, insurance company executive; b. N.Y.C., May 20, 1928; s. Herbert and Blanche (Sabin) K.; m. Carole Golison, Mar. 16, 1962; children: Fern L., Alan L., Howard S. CLU, Am. Coll. Life Underwriters. Pres. Barry Kaye, Inc., 1960—; owner Barry Kaye Assocs., Century City, Calif., 1970—; founder, chmn. Wealth Creation Ctrs., L.A., 1980; mem. faculty Practicing Law Inst., 1969—; lectr. UCLA, 1970—. Co-owner, Carole & Barry Kaye Museum of Miniatures. Author: How to Save a Fortune on Your Life Insurance, 1980, rev. edit., 1991, Save a Fortune on Your Estate Taxes, 1990, (tape and audio book) Save a Fortune on Your Estate Taxes, (tape) Wealth Creation and Preservation, Die Rich and Tax Free!, 1995, Live Rich, 1996, The Investment Alternative, 1997, Die Rich 2, 2000, All New Investment Alternative, Give Your Estate Away Twice, 2003. Mem. bd. govs. Diamond Cir. of Hope; trustee City of Hope; fellow Ben Gurion Soc., Ben Gurion Soc. of the Negev; chmn. Love and Hope Ball Inst. Diabetic Rsch., U. Miami, 2002. Recipient Founders award Diamond Cir. City of Hope, 1972, Lifetime Achievement award Ben Gurion U. of the Negev, 1987, Man of Yr. award Gen. Agts. and Mgrs. Conf., 1965, 66, 67, Fin. Advisor of Yr. award Fin. Svcs. Advisor Mag., 1999; named Man of Yr. Anti-Defamation League, 2002, named Man or Yr. Jewish Fedn. Palm Beach County, 2002. Mem. NCCJ (trustee, bd. dirs.), Am. Soc. CLUs, B'nai B-rith (Pres. Club), Uncles of Vista del Mar, Internat. Forum. Office: Barry Kaye Assoc 5100 Town Center Tower II #550 Boca Raton FL 33486 E-mail: barrykaye@barrykaye.com.

KAYE, CELIA ILENE, pediatrics educator; b. July 12, 1943; m. Tod B. Sloan. BS, Wayne State U., 1965, MS, 1968, MD, 1969; PhD, Northwestern U., 1975. Diplomate Am. Bd. Pediatrics, Am. Bd. Med. Genetics; lic. physician, Mich., Ill., Tex. Resident in pediat. Bronx (N.Y.) Mcpl. Hosp. Ctr., 1969-71, U. Ill. Hosp., Chgo., 1971-72; fellow in biochem. genetics Children's Meml. Hosp., Chgo., 1972-75; instr. pediat. Northwestern U. Coll. Medicine, Chgo., 1974-75; from asst. prof. to assoc. prof. pediat. U. Ill. Coll. Medicine, Chgo., 1975-89; chmn. divsn. genetics dept. pediat. Cook County Hosp., Chgo., 1975-80, attending physician divsn. genetics dept. pediat., 1980-89; dir. sect. genetics and genetics lab. divsn. pediat. Luth. Gen. Hosp., Park Ridge, Ill., 1980-89, co-med. dir. perinatal ctr., 1986-89; dep. chmn. Santa Rosa Children's Hosp. Activities, co-dir. clin. cytogenics lab. U. Tex. Health Sci. Ctr., San Antonio, 1990-97, prof. depts. pediat. and cellular and structural biology, 1990—, chief sect. metabolism, 1990—99, vice-chmn. dept. pediat., 1993-97, chmn. dept. pediat., 1997—2002, vice dean med. sch., 2001—, co-dir. cytogenetics lab., 1990—98. Mem. quality assurance com. cytogenetics lab. dept. cellular and structural biology U. Tex. Health Sci. Ctr., 1991-97, chair clin. faculty promotions com. dept. pediats., 1991-97, chair com. for devel. plan for selection, evaluation and promotion of clin. faculty dept. pediats., 1990-91, med. perinatal mktg. com. dept. pediats., 1990-91, mem. residency adv. com. dept. pediats., 1990-2002, mem. faculty tenure and promotions com., 1995-97, mem. search com., chmn. dept. pathology, 1995-96, mem. dual degree program com., 1995-98, vice-chmn. bd. dirs. Univ. Physicians Group, 1995-97, 2001—, chmn. fin. com., 2000—, exec. com. mem, 2000—, mem. contract rev. com. 1995-97, bd. dirs.; mem. clin. coord. com., 1990-92, 2000, ad hoc clin. care com., 1990—92, MSRDP adv. bd., 1991-93, 97—, search com. chmn. dept. medicine, 1992-93; chmn. program comm. sect. on genetics and birth defects Am. Acad. Pediat., 1995-99; dir. sect. genetics, Ctr. Craniofacial Anomalies, U. Ill. Coll. Medicine, Chgo., 1975-85; mem. med. adv. bd. Santa Rosa Children's Hosp., 1990-91, mem. exec. com. sect. on genetics and birth defects, Am. Acad. Pediat., 1995-2001, dir. med. edn., 1991-97, exec. com., 1992-2002, medicine policy com., 1992-97, chair med. edn. com., 1992-94; assoc. med. dir. cytogenetics lab. Santa Rosa Med. Ctr., San Antonio, 1991-98; vis. assoc. prof. pediats. Rush-Presbyn.-St. Luke's Med. Ctr., Chgo., 1979-89; mem. Genetics Task Force Ill., 1981-89, sec., 1981-83, pres., 1983-85; mem. genetics svc. com. Tex. Genetics Network, 1989-94, chmn. steering com., 1992-2000, mem. data com., 1995-2002; chmn. sci. adv. com. on birth defects Tex. Dept. Health, 1995-97; del. Nat. Coun. Regional Genetics Networks, 1992-99, mem. exec. com., 1993-97, bd. dirs., 1997-99; mem. Ill. Genetic and Metabolic Diseases Adv. Bd., 1984-89, chmn. lab. subcom., 1985-89; mem. sci. adv. com. Tex. Dept. Health, 1992-2000; sr. advisor Nat. Newborn Screening and Genetics Resource Ctr., 1998—; chmn. exec. com. Pub. Health Spl. Interest Group Am. Coll. Med. Genetics, 2002—; mem. steering com. Children's Regional Health Care Network, San Antonio, 1993-94; mem. mgmt. com. Children's Regional Health Care Sys., San Antonio, 1993-94; mem. instl. rev. bd. Cook County Hosp., Chgo., 1975-80, Luth. Gen. Health Care Sys., Park Ridge, Ill., 1988-89; chmn. pediat. edn. com. Luth. Gen. Hosp., Park Ridge, 1981-86, chmn. pediat. bioethics com., mem. faculty adv. com., 1986-89; mem. faculty com. tenure and promotion com., 1995, mem. search com. chmn. dept. pathology, 1995-96, mem. cons. Med. Ctr. Hosp. Ward and Nursery, Bapt. Hosp. Sys., Santa Rosa Children's Hosp., Meth. Hosp., Humana Women's Hosp.; mem. by laws com. Santa Rosa Healthcare, San Antonio, 1995-97; mem. ad hoc rev. com. for Ctrs. of Excellence in Ethics Rsch., NIH, 2004. Mem. adv. bd. Am. Jour. Med. Genetics; reviewer Am. Jour. Human Genetics, Pediatric Dermatology; mem. ad hoc rev. com. Ctrs. Excellence in Ethics Rsch., NIH, 2004; contbr. articles to profl. jours., chpts. to books. Mem. program planning com. March of Dimes Defects Found., Chgo., 1985-89, mem. health profl. adv. com., 1983-89, chmn., 1981-83; mem. health profl. adv. com. South Ctrl. Tex. chpt., 1989-90; bd. dirs., mem. exec. com. Harkness House for Children, Winnetka, Ill., 1988-89; mem. Ill. Spina Bifida Assn., 1983-89; mem. exec. bd. El Valor Corp. for Handicapped Children, Chgo., 1980-81; mem. med. adv. com. Tex. Sickle Cell Assn., 1990-91; bd. dirs. Boerne Pub. Libr. Found., 2004—. Fellow Am. Coll. Med. Genetics (founding, edn. com. 1993-97, pub. health com., moderator pub. health and delivery of svcs. sect. ann. meeting 1994); mem. AMA, Am. Soc. Human Genetics (info. and edn. com. 1990-94), Am. Acad. Pediats. (genetics sect., com. on genetics, liaison to bone and joint decade 2002, liaison to Nat. Coun. on Folic Acid 2004—, judge sci. awards uniformed svcs. sect. 1992-93, chair program com. sect. on genetics and birth defects 1995—, mem. exec. com. sect. on genetics and birth defects 1995-99), Soc. for Pediat. Rsch., Soc. for Inherited Metabolic Diseases, So. Soc. for Pediat. Rsch. (moderator genetics sect. ann. meeting 1993), Tex. Med. Soc., Tex. Genetics Soc., Tex. Pediat. Soc., Bexar County Med. Soc., San Antonio Pediat. Soc. Office: U Tex Health Sci Ctr Med Dean's Office 7703 Floyd Curl Dr San Antonio TX 78229-3900

KAYE, DONALD, internist, educator; b. NYC, Aug. 12, 1931; s. Morris and Rose (Hirschtritt) K.; m. Janet Miriam Sovitsky, June 26, 1955; children: Kenneth Marc, Karen Lynne, Kendra Beth, Keith Steven. AB, Yale, 1953; MD, NYU, 1957. Diplomate Am. Bd. Internal Medicine, Am. Bd. Infectious Disease. Intern N.Y. Hosp., 1957-58, resident, 1958-60, fellow infectious diseases, 1960—63, asso. attending physician, 1961-69; physician-in-chief Hosp. Med. Coll. Pa., 1969-95; instr. medicine Cornell U. Med. Coll., 1961-63, asst. prof., 1963-66, asso. prof., 1966-69; prof., chmn. dept. medicine Med. Coll. Pa., Phila., 1969-94, Med. Coll. Pa. and Hahnemann U. Sch. Medicine, 1994-95, prof., 1995-96, Allegheny U. of Health Scis., 1996-98, MCP Hahnemann Sch. Medicine, 1998—2002, Drexel U., Coll. Medicine, 2002—. Cons. Phila. VA Hosp., 1969-95; CEO, pres. Med. Coll. Hosp., 1991-94, Med. Coll. Pa. and Hahnemann U. Hosp. Sys., 1994-96, Allegheny U. Hosps., 1996-98, Allegheny Integrated Health Group, 1996-97, Allegheny U. Health Scis., 1998; revision com. U.S. Pharmacopeia, 1975-95; mem. VA Merit Rev. Bd. in Infectious Diseases, 1976-78; com. on infectious diseases Am. Bd. Internal Medicine, 1976-84, cons., 1984-86. Author: Urinary Tract Infection and Its Management, 1972, Infective Endocarditis, 1976, Fundamentals of Internal Medicine, 1983, Internal Medicine for Dentists, 1983, 2d edit., 1990, Endocarditis, 1984, Infective Endocarditis, 1992; mem. editorial bd. Aging: Immunology and Infectious Diseases, Gerontology: Med. Sci., 1987-98, Antimicrobial Agts. Chemotherapy, 1972-98, Clinical Infectious Diseases, 2001-; contbr. articles to med. jours. Recipient Disting. Tchg. award Lindback Found., 1972; NIH grantee, 1967-76, 82-96; Pharm. Industry grantee, 1965-96, Emilio Ribas medal for disting svc. Brazilian Soc. of Infectious Diseases, 1994, Disting. Achievement award N.Y. Hosp.-Cornell Med. Ctr. Alumni Coun., 1994, Solomon A. Berson Alumni Achievement award NYU Sch. Medicine, 1996, Strittmatter award Philadelphia County Med. Soc., 1997. Master ACP (gov. Ea. Pa. region 1983-88, pres. Pa. chpt. 1987); fellow Gerontol. Soc. Am., Infectious Disease Soc. Am.; mem. AMA, Pa. Med. Soc. (alt. del to AMA 1991-92), Phila. County Med. Soc. (pres. 1991-92), Am. Soc. for Microbiology, Am. Fedn. for Clin. Rsch., Am. Soc. for Clin. Investigation, Assn. Am. Physicians, Am. Clin. and Climatol. Assn., Phi Beta Kappa, Alpha Omega Alpha, Sigma Xi. Home: 1535 Sweet Briar Rd Gladwyne PA 19035-1216 E-mail: donjank@aol.com.

KAYE, GORDON ISRAEL, pathologist, anatomist, educator; b. N.Y.C., Aug. 13, 1935; s. Oscar Swarz and Rebecca (Schachman) K.; m. Nancy Elizabeth Weber, June 4, 1956; children: Jacqueline Elizabeth, Vivienne Rebecca. AB, Columbia U., 1955, AM, 1957, PhD, 1961. From rsch. asst. cytology to dir. Columbia U., N.Y.C., 1953—63, dir. F. Higginson Cabot Lab. Electron Microscopy, 1963—76; rsch. and tchg. asst. cytology Rockefeller Inst., N.Y.C., 1957-58; from Alden March prof. to prof. emeritus Albany (N.Y.) Med. Coll., 1976—99, prof. emeritus pathology, 1999—; prof. biomed. sci. SUNY Sch. Pub. Health, 1986-99; pres., CEO Waste Reduction by Waste Reduction, Inc., Troy, NY, 1993-98, chmn., 1998—, exec. v.p., 2002—. Mem. seminar on creative process Wenner-Gren Found., 1964-65; cons. electron microscopy dept. pathology N.Y. VA Hosp., 1965—99; Raymond C. Truex Disting. lectr. Hahnemann U., 1987. Co-author: Key Facts in Histology, 1985, Histology: A Text and Atlas, 1995, 4th edit., 2003; co-author: (in German) Atlas der Histologie, 1995; co-author: Histology, nat. med. series rev. series, 1997; editor: Current Topics in Cellular Anatomy, 1981; assoc. editor The Anat. Reocrd, 1972—98, edit. reviewer Exptl. Eye Rsch., 1964, Cancer, 1972—, Investigative Ophthalmology, 1973—, Gastroenterology, 1969—, Jour. Morphology, 1999—. Trustee Palisades free Libr., 1965-71; mem. Citizens Adv. Com., Sparkill Palisades Fire Dist., 1968-69; pres. Palisades Free Libr., 1969-71; trustee Orangetown Pub. Libr., 1971-73, Friends of Chamber Music, Troy, N.Y., 1988—; mem. citizens adv. com. Title III Program, S. Orangetown Ctrl. Sch. Dist., 1972-75; chmn. N.Y. State Low Level Waste Group, 1986-95; trustee Rockland Country Day Sch., 1974-78. Recipient Charles Huebschman prize in zoology Columbia U., 1954, Career Scientist award Health Rsch. Coun. N.Y.C., 1963-72, Rsch. Career Devel. award Nat. Inst. Arthritis and Metabolic Diseases, NIH, USPHS, 1972-76, Tousimis prize in biology, 1984; Ford Found. scholar, 1951-55; NSF predoctoral fellow, 1955-56, Nat. Inst. Neurol. Diseases and Blindness predoctoral fellow, 1959-61 Mem.: Lab. Animal Mgmt. Assn., Am. Assn. Lab. Animal Scis., Am. Assn. Vet. Lab. Diagnosticians, N.Y. Soc. Electron Microscopists (dir. 1964—67), Internat. Soc. Eye Rsch., Assn. Career Scientists Health Rsch. Coun., Harvey Soc., Am. Soc. Cell Biology, Am. Assn. Anatomists, Assn. Am. Med. Colls. (rep. con. acad. socs. 1979—2002, mem. adminstrn. bd. CAS 1985—86), Assn. Anatomy Chmn. (pres. 1980—81), Arthur Purdy Stout Soc. Surg. Pathologists (hon.), Waquoit Bay Yacht Club, Sigma Xi. Achievements include patents for (with Dr. Peter B. Weber) Method for disposal of radioactively labeled animal carcasses; methods for treatment and disposal of regulated medical waste; in field. Office: Waste Reduction by Waste Reduction 2910-D Fortune Circle W Indianapolis IN 46241-5502 Office Phone: 317-484-2425. Personal E-mail: wr2kaye@aol.com.

KAYE, JHANI, radio station executive, television producer, television director; b. Maywood, Calif., June 18, 1949; s. Jimmie Eccak and Betty Jo (Holland) Kazaroff. BA, UCLA, 1971. Music dir. Sta. KFXM, San Bernardino, Calif., 1969-73; announcer Stas. KUTE-FM/KKDJ-FM, L.A., 1972-74; asst. program dir. Sta. KROQ, L.A., 1973-74, Sta. WCFL, Chgo., 1980-82, Sta. KFI, L.A., 1982; program dir. Sta. KINT-FM, El Paso, Tex., 1975-80; sta. mgr., program dir. Sta. KOST-FM, L.A., 1982-99; program dir. Sta. KBIG-FM, Glendale, Calif., 1999—2003, sta. mgr., 1999—2003. Dir. adult contemporary programming Clear Channel Radio, 1999—; owner Los Feliz Post Prodn. Video Svcs.; on-air host Radio Medium, radio program. Appeared in TV series Falcon Crest, 1985, Drew Carey Show, 1998; dir. TV commls., 1986—; voice-over motion picture The Couch Trip, 1987; dir., video editor Dick Clark TV Commls. Recipient Marconi Radio awards Nat. Assn. Broadcasters, 1990, 91. Office: Sta KBIG-FM 3400 West Olive Ave Ste 550 Burbank CA 91505 Office Phone: 818-566-4722. E-mail: jhanikaye@clearchannel.com.

KAYE, JUDITH SMITH, state appeals court judge; b. Monticello, NY, Aug. 4, 1938; d. Benjamin and Lena (Cohen) Smith; m. Stephen Rackow Kaye, Feb. 11, 1964; children: Luisa Marian, Jonathan Mackey, Gordon Bernard BA, Barnard Coll., 1958; LLB cum laude, NYU, 1962; LLD (hon.), St. Lawrence U., 1985, Union U., 1985, Pace U., 1985, Syracuse U., 1988, L.I. U., 1989. Bar: NY State 1963. Assoc. Sullivan & Cromwell, NYC, 1962-64; staff atty. IBM, Armonk, NY, 1964-65; asst. to dean Sch. Law NYU, 1965-68; ptnr. Connelly Chase O'Donnell & Weyher, NYC, 1969-83; assoc. judge NY State Ct. Appeals, NYC, 1983-93, chief judge Albany, NY, 1993—. Pres., Conf. of Chief Justices; chair bd. dir., Nat. Ctr. for State Cts., 2002-03; bd. dir. Sterling Nat. Bank. Bd. editor, NY State Bar Journal; contbr. articles to profl. jours. Former bd. dirs. Legal Aid Soc.; chair, Permanent Jud. Commn. on Justice for Children; founding mem., hon. chair, Judges and Lawyers Breast Cancer Alert (JALBCA); trustee, William Nelson Cromwell Found. Recipient Vanderbilt medal NYU Sch. of Law, 1983, Medal of Distinction, Barnard Coll, 1987, John Marshall award, ABA, 2005. Fellow Am. Bar Found.; mem. Am. Law Inst., Am. Coll. Trial Lawyers, Am. Judicature Soc. (bd. dirs. 1980-83), ABA (co-chair, Commn. on the Am. Jury, 2004-05). Democrat. Achievements include being the first women to serve on the New York State's highest court when appointed Associate Judge of the Court of Appeals; being the first women to occupy the State Judiciary's highest office, Chief Judge. Office: NY Court of Appeals Court of Appeals Hall 20 Eagle St Albany NY 12207-1009 also: NY Court of Appeals 230 Park Ave Ste 826 New York NY 10169-0007*

KAYE, JUDY, actress; b. Dec. 11, 1948; d. Jerome Joseph and Shirley Edith (Silverman) K. Student, UCLA. Appeared in plays Fiddler on the Roof, Godspell, You're a Good Man Charlie Brown, 1968, Jesus Christ Superstar, 1972, (N.Y. debut) Grease, 1977, On the Twentieth Century, 1978, Moony Shapiro Songbook, 1980, Oh Brother!, 1981, Four to Make Two, 1982, Love, 1984, Side by Side by Sondheim, Paper Mill Playhouse, Millburn, N.J., 1984-85, Windy City, Paper Mill Playhouse, 1985, The Phantom of the Opera (Tony award for featured actress in a mus.), 1988—, The Merry Widow, 1991, Mamma Mia!, 2002, Souvenir, 2004, Candide, 2005; appeared with Santa Fe Opera, 1985, 90, N.Y.C. Opera, 1989, N.Y. Philharm., 1990, Boston Symphony Tanglewood, 1990, Boston Pops, 1990, London Symphony, 1990. Jewish. Office: care Bret Adams LTD 448 W 44th St New York NY 10036-5205*

KAYE, LORI, actress, news reporter, producer; d. Eldin Bert and Katherine Angeline Onsgard. Student, Detroit Inst. Art, 1951, 56, U. N.Mex., 1960. Actress, radio and TV commls., 1951-82, Warner Bros., 1960-64; dir., v.p. John Robert Powers Schs., L.A., 1961-71; v.p. Electron Industries, Torrance, Calif., 1963-65; pres. Lori Kaye Cosmetics, Hollywood, Calif., 1964-70; co-owner, v.p. K and S Employment, Calif. Fashion Mart, 1965-67; dir. Caroline Leonetti Ltd. Sch., Hollywood, 1976-79; pres. Lori Kaye's Internat. Travel Acad., North Hollywood, Calif., 1980-98. Internat. cons. Internat. Career Acad., Van Nuys, 1978—; pres. Molori Publs., Studio City, Calif., 1981—; cons. A&T Inst. Travel and Tourism, 1982; lectr. in field, 1969—. Hostess TV talk show The New You, Sta. KTTV, Hollywood, 1964-65; hostesss TV show Lori Kayes Week-End Escape, Sta. KCBS, 1997—; travel expert, live travel TV show hostess, spl. assignment TV reporter U-Team, Sta. CBS-2, 1997—; instr. travel tourism UCLA, 1997—. Dir. project Camarillo State Hosp., 1963-69; cons. Job Corps; dir., instr., adminstr. Calif. Pvt. Postsecondary Edn. Instns., 1995; instr. travel tourism U. So. Calif., 1997—. Recipient Mental Health Achievement award, 1967. Mem. AAU, SAG, AFTRA, Smithsonian Assocs., Am. Soc. Travel Agts., Internat. Airline Travel Agts. Network, Internat. Air Transport Assn., Soc. Travel Agts. in Govt., Calif. Assn. Pvt. Postsecondary Schs., Nat. Geog. Soc., Internat. Platform Assn., Better Bus. Bur. (arbitrator), L.A. World Affairs Coun., Universal City-No. Hollywood C. of C. Office: Global Image Prodns 12723 Ventura Blvd Studio City CA 91604-2430 Address: Lori Kayes Internat Travel Ctr Studio City CA 91604- Office Phone: 818-623-8448. E-mail: lorikaye1@yahoo.com.

KAYE, PETER FREDERIC, columnist; b. Chgo., Mar. 8, 1928; s. Ralph A. and Sara Corson (Philipson) K.; m. Martha Louise Wood, Mar. 20, 1955; children: Loren, Terry, Adam. BA in Govt., Pomona Coll., 1949. Reporter Alhambra (Calif.) Post-Advocate, 1950-53; reporter, editorial writer, polit. writer The San Diego Union, 1953-68; news and pub. affairs dir. KPBS-TV, San Diego State Coll., 1968-72; corr., producer Nat. Pub. Affairs Ctr. for TV, Washington, 1972-74; comm. dir. So. Calif. First Nat. Bank, San Diego, 1974-75; press sec. The Pres. Ford Com., Washington, 1975-76; mgr. Copley Videotex, San Diego, 1982-84; assoc. editor The San Diego Union, 1976-94; editl. dir. KNSD, San Diego, 1996-99. Freelance TV producer programs KPBS, PBS, BBC; San Diego corr. Newsweek, 1968-71, McGraw-Hill, 1959-67; lectr. comm. U. Calif., San Diego, 1971; copywriter Washburn-Justice Advt., San Diego, 1959-70. Producer 10 TV programs including including Jacob Bronowski: Life and Legacy, Twenty-Five Years of Presidency, The Presidency, The Press and the People. Press asst. Eisenhower-Nixon Campaign, L.A., 1952; asst. press sec. Richard Nixon Presdl. Campaign, Washington, 1960; dir. Pete Wilson for Mayor Campaign, San Diego, 1971; comm. dir. Flournoy for Gov. Campaign, Beverly Hills, Calif., 1974. With U.S. Mcht. Marines, 1945, U.S. Army, 1950-52. Jefferson fellow East-West Ctr., Honolulu, 1987; recipient Golden Mike awards So. Calif. TV News Dirs. Assn., 1969, 70, 71, Best Pub. Affairs Program award Nat. Edni. TV, 1970, Best Local TV Series award Radio-TV Mirror, 1971, Nat. Emmy award Spl. Events Reporter, Watergate Coverage, 1973-74, Best Editorial awards Copley Newspapers Ring of Truth, 1979, Sigma Delta Chi, 1985, Calif. Newspaper Pubs. Assn., 1985; San Diego Emmy awards, 1985, 87, 91. Mem. NATAS, State Bar Calif. (bd. govs. 1991-97, v.p. 1993-94, 96-97), Sigma Delta Chi. Independent. Home: 240 Ocean View Ave Del Mar CA 92014-3322

KAYE, RONALD LEE, physician, educator; b. Toledo, Apr. 15, 1932; s. Philip and Gertrude (Berman) K.; m. Tobye Davidson, June 19, 1955; children: Brian, Todd, Douglas, Jeffrey. BA, U. Mich., 1953, MD, 1957. Diplomate Am. Bd. Rheumatology, Am. Bd. Internal Medicine. Intern Sinai Hosp., Detroit, 1957-58; fellow and staff mem. Mayo Clinic, Rochester, Minn., 1959-63; chmn. dept. rheumatology, dir. med. edn. Palo Alto (Calif.) Med. Clinic, 1963—; clin. prof. medicine Stanford U. Sch. of Medicine, Palo Alto, 1963—. Contbr. articles to profl. jours. Bd. dirs. Am. Mogan David Adom., N.Y.C., 1967—, U.S.-China Ednl. Inst., San Francisco, 1975—, Sino-Judaic Inst., Palo Alto, 1985—. Served to capt. USAF, 1959-61. Fellow ACP; mem. AMA, Am. Soc. Clin. Rheumatology (pres. 1975-80), Arthritis Found. (bd. dirs., Disting. Service award 1974). Jewish. Avocations: stamp collecting/philately, minerals, coin collecting/numismatics, travel, jazz. Office: Palo Alto Med Clinic 795 El Camino Real Palo Alto CA 94301-2726

KAYE, SAMUEL HARVEY, architect, educator; b. Columbia, S.C., Sept. 27, 1940; s. James B. and Mary Louise (Harvey) K.; m. Patsy Cummings, June 27, 1964; children: Kimbelee Cummings, Elizabeth Harvey, Mary Catherine. BArch, Auburn U., 1963. Mem. staff Yeates & Gaskill, Architects, Memphis, 1965-68, Walk Jones & Francis Mah, Inc., Memphis, 1968-70, prin., 1970-74, Samuel H. Kaye, Architect, Columbus, Miss., 1974-91, Luke & Kaye, P.A., Columbus, 1991—. Instr. architecture Miss. State U., Starkville, 1983-84; instr. interior design Miss. U. for Women, Columbus, 1979-84, asst. prof., 1984-91; mem. Miss. Hist. Preservation Rev. Bd. Contbr. articles on urban design, usage study and historic archeol. research. Mem. St. Paul's Episcopal Ch. Vestry, Columbus, 1975-79, 83-85, bd. mgrs. Gray Ctr., Diocese of Miss., Canton, 1981-86, Salvation Army Adv. Bd., Columbus, 1983—; bd. trustees Miss. Heritage Trust, 1991—, pres. 1991-92, 2002-03. Lt. U.S. Army, 1963-65. Recipient preservation honor award Hist. Columbus, 1976, 81, 82, award of merit Miss. Hist. Soc., 1986, 91, 93, 94. Mem. AIA (bd. dirs. Miss. chpt. 1977, v.p. 1978, pres. 1979, state preservation coord. hist. resources com., urban design and planning com., honor award 1976), Nat. Trust Hist. Preservation (bd. advisors 1989-98, emeritus 1998—), Rotary (v.p. Columbus 1985-86, pres. 1986). Avocations: reading, photography. Home: 424 7th St S Columbus MS 39701-5752 Office: Luke & Kaye PA PO Box 48 114 5th St S Columbus MS 39703-0048 Business E-Mail: samkaye@ebicom.net.

KAYE, STEPHEN RACKOW, lawyer; b. Nyack, N.Y., May 4, 1931; s. Edward and Florence (Karp) K.; m. Judith Smith, Feb. 11, 1964; children: Luisa Marian, Jonathan Mackey, Gordon Bernard. AB, Cornell U., 1952, LL.B. with honors, 1956. Bar: N.Y. 1956, U.S. Supreme Ct. 1961. Assoc. Sullivan & Cromwell, N.Y.C., 1956-63, Proskauer Rose Goetz & Mendelsohn, N.Y.C., 1964-68, ptnr., past chair, co-chmn. lit. dept., 1968—. Mem. Judicial Inst. on Professionalism in the Law, 1999—. Author treatise texts on trials and appeals of comml. cases; mng. editor Cornell Law Quar.; contbr. to profl. publs. Served to 1st lt. AUS, 1952-54, Korea. Mem. ABA, N.Y. State Bar Assn., Assn. of Bar of City of N.Y. (past chmn. com. on profl. and jud. ethics, chmn. com. on profl. discipline), N.Y. County Lawyers Assn. (past vice chmn. com. on Supreme Ct.), 1st Dept. Disciplinary Commn. (hearing panel chair, policy com. 1991-96, 1999-2002), Order of Coif, Phi Kappa Phi. Office: Proskauer Rose LLP 1585 Broadway New York NY 10036-8299

KAYE, STUART MARTIN, lawyer; b. Bronx, N.Y., Dec. 2, 1946; s. Jules Krupnikoff and Gussie (Lipchinsky) Kaye; m. Nancy Elaine Carter, Oct. 19, 1967 (div. 1970); m. Christine Marie Heitkam, Sept. 25, 1970 (div. 1983); children: Joshua Brandon, Jeremy Jason; m. Eve C. Farkas, Apr. 2, 1988 (div. 1991); 1 child, Kimberly I. Morlan; m. Patricia S. Cruise, Mar. 9, 1996; 1 child, Trina S. Cruise. AA, Glendale Community Coll., 1971; BS in Polit. Sci., Ariz. State U., 1974; JD, Western State U., 1978. Bar: Calif. 1980, U.S. Dist. Ct. (no. dist.) Calif. 1980, (so. dist.) Calif. 1985, (cen. dist.) Calif. 1987. Assoc. mgmt. analyst State of Calif., Sacramento, 1978-84; pvt. practice Shingle Springs, 1981-84; legal counsel State of Calif., Sacramento, 1984-85, indsl. relations counsel San Diego, 1985-92; legal asst. Ariz. Atty. Gen., Phoenix, 1992-93; indsl. rels. coun. State of Calif., Santa Ana, 1993-95; atty. Don D. Sessions, APLC, Mission Viejo, 1995-98; pvt. practice La Mesa, 1998-2001; indsl. rels. coun. State of Calif., San Diego, 2001—04; judge U.S. Social Security Adminstrn., L.A., 2004—. With U.S. Army, 1964-68. Democrat. Jewish. Avocation: camping. Office Phone: 213-894-3264. Personal E-mail: stuart7@msn.com.

KAYE, WALTER, corporate financial executive; b. Bklyn., Aug. 22, 1927; s. Jack and Ida (Shapiro) K.; m. Bernice Glatzer, May 6, 1952; children: Steven Mark, Russell Stuart. Student, CCNY, 1950-53; postgrad. (fellow), N.Y. Inst. Credit, 1956. Credit mgr., treas. A. Steinam Co., Inc., N.Y.C., 1951-68; v.p. Ambassador Factors Corp., N.Y.C., 1968-74; sr. v.p. Congress Factors Corp., N.Y.C., 1974-84; pres., chief exec. officer Mcht. Factors Corp., N.Y.C., 1985—. Bd. dirs. The Crossing Homeowners Assn., Trump Plaza, N.Y.C. Served with U.S. Army, 1944-46. Recipient Yitzak Rabin award B'nai B'rith, 1982, plaque Manhattan Credit, 1979; named Needlers Man of Yr., 2000; honoree NY Inst. Credit, 2003. Mem. N.Y. Inst. Credit, N.Y. Credit and Fin. Mgmt., Nat. Comml. Fin. Assn., Manhattan Credit (pres. 1978-79) Empire Credit (pres. 1971-74), The Financemen's Group Club, 475 CEO Club USA, Club, N.Y. Friars Club. Home: 18 The Crossing At Blind Brk Purchase NY 10577-2200 Office: Mcht Factors Corp 1430 Broadway New York NY 10018-3308 Office Phone: 212-840-7575. Personal E-mail: wkaye@worldnet.att.net. E-mail: wkaye@merchantfactors.com.

KAYE, WALTER H., psychiatrist; b. N.Y.C., Aug. 25, 1943; AB in Chemistry, Oberlin Coll., 1966; MD, Ohio State U., 1970. Diplomate Am. Bd. Psychiatry and Neurology. Surg. intern L.A. County/U. So. Calif. Gen. Hosp., L.A., 1970-71, neuropathology resident, 1971-72, neurology resident, 1972-74; pscyhiatry resident Neuropsychiat. Inst. UCLA, 1974-77, psychiat. feloow and dir. Neurobehavioral Clinic, 1977-78; clin. fellow Lab. Clin. Sci./NIMH, NIH, Bethesda, Md., 1979-80, staff psychiatrist, 1980-82, Lab. Psychology and Psychopathology/NIMH, NIH, Bethesda, 1982-85; assoc. to prof. psychiatry Western Psychiat. Inst. and Clinic/U. Pitts., 1985—. Emergency dept. physician L.A. County., U. So. Calif. Gen. Hosp., 1971-74, Martin Luther King Hosp., L.A., 1974-77, Olive View County Hosp., L.A., 1976-78; staff physician Rancho Los Amingos Hosp. Drug Detoxification Program, L.A., 1973-75; sr. srugeon Dept. Health and Human Svcs., Rockville, 1978-85; others. Contbr. articles to profl. jours. Grantee in field. Mem. Am. Acad. Neurology, Am. Psychiat. Assn., Am. Neuropsychiat. Assn., Am. Coll. Neuropsychopharmacology, N.Y. Acad. Scis., Pitts. Regional Orgn. of Child and Adolescent Psychiatry, Pitts. Neurosci. Soc., Soc. Rsch. in Child and Adolescent Psychiatry, Prader-Willi Syndrome Assn. Office: U Pitts Sch Medicine West Psychiat Inst and Clin 3811 Ohara St Pittsburgh PA 15213-2593

KAYLAN, HOWARD LAWRENCE, musical entertainer, screenwriter, composer; b. NYC, June 22, 1947; s. Sidney and Sally Joyce (Berlin) Kaylan; m. Mary Melita Pepper, June 10, 1967 (div. Sept. 1971); 1 child, Emily Anne; m. Susan Karen Olsen, Apr. 18, 1982 (div. June 1996); 1 child, Alexandra Leigh. Student, UCLA; PhD in Philosophy, Am. Coll. Metaphys. Theology, St. Paul, Minn., 2000. Lead singer and founder rock group The Turtles, Los Angeles, 1965—; lead singer rock group Mothers of Invention, Los Angeles, 1970-72, Flo and Eddie, 1972-83; radio, TV, recording entertainer various broadcast organizations, Los Angeles, 1972—; screenwriter Larry Gelbart, Carl Gotleib prodns., Los Angeles, 1979-85; prodr. children's records Kidstuff Records, Hollywood, Fla., 1980-83; singer, prodr. rock band Flo and Eddie, Los Angeles, 1976-83; singer, prodr. The Turtles (reunion of original band), Los Angeles, 1980—; actor, TV and film Screen Actors Guild, Los Angeles, 1983—. Background vocalist various albums for numerous performers; syndicated talk show host Unistar Radio Network, 1989—; radio personality Sta. WXRK-FM, N.Y.C., 1990—91, KLOU, St. Louis, 1993, WGRR, Cin., 1995—97. Author: Hi Bob, 1995, The Energy Pals, 1995; contbr. articles to profl. jours.; actor: (films) 200 Motels, 1971, Get Crazy, 1985, General Hospital, Suddenly Susan, 1999, Riding the Bullet, 2004; performer: at White House, 1970; exec. prodr.(radio): Down Eerie Street, 1998; singer: numerous top ten hit songs with Turtles, Bruce Springsteen, The Ramones, Duran Duran, T. Rex, John Lennon and others; singer: (commls.) Chevrolet, Pepsi, Bruger King and NFL, 1970— (awards); singer: (albums) Dust Bunnies, 2005. Recipient 10 Gold and Platinum LP album awards while lead singer, 1995—, Fine Arts award, Bank of Am., 1965, Spl. award, Billboard Mag., 1992, Best Script award, Slam Dunk Film Festival, 2003, Bubblegum award, 2003. Mem.: AGVA, AFTRA, Am. Fedn. Musicians, Screen Actors Guild. Personal E-mail: kaylan@howardkaylan.com. E-mail: hkaylan@theturtles.com.

KAYLE, BRUCE E., lawyer; b. Bklyn., 1958; BA, BSE summa cum laude, Univ. Pa., 1979; JD cum laude, Harvard Univ., 1982. Bar: N.Y. 1983. Staff atty. Joint Com. on Taxation, U.S. Congress, Washington; ptnr. & chmn. Tax Dept. Milbank Tweed Hadley & McCloy, N.Y.C. Contbr. articles to profl. jours. Bd. dir. Low-Income Taxpayer Clinic, Legal Aid Soc. Recipient Pro Bono award, Legal Aid Soc. Mem.: N.Y. State Bar Assn. (co-chmn. Com. Fin. Instruments, mem. exec. com. Tax sect.), Tax Club (pres.), Tax Forum. Office: Milbank Tweed Hadley & McCloy 1 Chase Manhattan Plz New York NY 10005-1413 Office Phone: 212-530-5956. Office Fax: 212-530-5219. Business E-Mail: bkayle@milbank.com.

KAYNAK, ERDENER, marketing educator, consultant editor; b. Sivas, Turkey, July 17, 1947; came to U.S., 1986; s. Kamil and Munire Saadet K.; m. Glynis Collins, Feb. 8, 1975; children: Oyku H., Ovgu I., Elif. S. B of Econs., Istanbul (Turkey) U., 1968; MA, U. Lancaster, Eng., 1972; PhD, Cranfield U., Bedford, Eng., 1975; DSc (hon.), Turku Sch. Econ. and Bus. Adminstrn., Finland. Asst. prof. Hacettepe U., Ankara, Turkey, 1975-78, Acadia U., Wolfville, Can., 1978-79; from assoc. to full prof., chmn. bus. adminstrn. dept. Mount St. Vincent U., Halifax, N.S., Can., 1979-85; prof. mktg. The Chinese U., Hong Kong, 1985-86, Pa. State U., Harrisburg, 1986—. Vis. prof. Helsinki Sch. of Econs. and Norwegian Sch. Mgmt., 1992-93, Curtin U. Tech., Australia, U. Stirling, Scotland, Univs. of Lund and Uppsala, Sweden, U. Hawaii, Manoa. Author: Marketing in the Third World, 1982, Competitive Marketing Systems, 1983, International Marketing Management, 1984, Global Perspectives in Marketing, 1985, Marketing and Economic Development, 1986, Transnational Retailing, 1986, Management of International Advertising, 1989, Socio-Political Aspects of International Marketing, 1991, World Fund Marketing Systems, 1986, International Business in the Middle East, 1988; exec. editor for Internat. Bus. Press; editor-in-chief Jour. Global Mktg., Jour. Internat. Consumer Mktg., Jour. Agribus. and Food Mktg., Jour. Teaching Internat. Bus. Jour. Of East West Bus.; sr. editor internat. bus. The Haworth Press Inc. New York, London, Australia, Jour. of Euromktg.; contbr. numerous articles to profl. jours. Recipient numerous best paper and svc. awards. Home: 1201 Stonegate Rd Hummelstown PA 17036-9789 Office: Pa State U at Harrisburg 230 US Rte Middletown PA 17057 Personal E-mail: ekg@comcast.net.

KAYNAK, HALE, finance educator, researcher; b. Istanbul, Turkey, Apr. 26, 1956; arrived in U.S., 1989; d. Turgut Nevzat and Gulseren Kaynak. BSChemE, Yildiz U., Istanbul, 1979; MBA, Appalachian State U., 1991; PhD in Prodn./Ops. Mgmt., U. North Tex., 1996. Chief chem. engr. of raw and semi-raw materials lab. CBS Paint Corp., Izmit, Turkey, 1980—86; vis. asst. prof. prodn., ops. mgmt. U. Colo., Colorado Springs, 1996—97; assoc. prof. prodn., ops. mgmt. U. Tex.-Pan Am., Edinburg, Tex., 1997—. Presenter in field. Author: Total Quality Management and Just-in-Time Purchasing: Their Effects on Performance of Firms Operating in the U.S., 1997; contbr. articles to profl. jours. Recipient OrderTrust Academic Excellence award, OrderTrust, Inc., 2000; grantee, Nat. Assn. of Purchasing Mgmt. (now Inst. for Supply Mgmt.), 1996; Rsch. fellow, Am. Soc. for Quality, 1995, 1998. Mem.: Prodn. and Ops. Mgmt. Soc., Acad. Mgmt. (program chair ops. mgmt. divsn. 2005—, profl. devel. workshop chair ops. mgmt. divsn. 2004—05), Decision Sciences Inst., Am. Prodn. and Inventory Control Soc., Inst. Supply Mgmt., Am. Soc. Quality (strategic planning chair local sect. 2003—05, mem. chair local sect. 2005—), Beta Gamma Sigma, Phi Kappa Phi. Office: U Tex Pan American 1201 West University Dr Edinburg TX 78539-2999 Office Phone: 956-381-3380. Personal E-mail: hkaynak@panam.edu.

KAYNE, JON BARRY, industrial psychologist; b. Sioux City, Iowa, Oct. 20, 1943; s. Harry Aaron and Barbara Valentine (Daniel) K.; m. Bunee Ellen Price, July 25, 1965; children: Nika Jenine, Abraham; m. Sandra Kay Fossbender, Jan. 5, 1985; 1 child, Shay-Marie Kathryn. BA, U. Colo., 1973; MSW, U. Denver, 1975; PhD, U. No. Colo., 1978. With spl. svcs. Weld County Sch. Dist. 6, Greeley, Colo., 1975-77; forensic diagnostician Jefferson County (Colo.) Diagnostic Unit, 1977-78; assoc., dir. mktg. 1 Dow Ctr., assoc. prof. psychology Hillsdale (Mich.) Coll., 1978-87; pres. Jon B. Kayne, P.C., Hillsdale, 1980-87; pres. bd. dirs. Lang. Learners in Partnership of Omaha, 1989-93; chmn. bd. dirs., CEO Am. Internat. Mgmt. Assocs., Ltd., Denver, 1984-87; prof. bus. adminstrn. and psychology Bellevue (Neb.) U., 1987—, v.p. profl. and continuing edn. studies, 1987-93, v.p. acad. affairs, 1993—. Chmn. bd. dirs. Domestic Harmony, 1979-82; bd. dir. religious sch., Greeley, 1975-77; candidate for sheriff of Boulder County, 1974. With USAR, 1962. Mem. Am. Psychol. Assn., Am. Soc. Clin. Hypnosis, Am. Statis. Assn., Internat. Neuropsychol. Soc., Mich. Soc. Investigative and Forensic Hypnosis (chmn. bd., pres. 1982), N.Y. Acad. Scis., Phi Delta Kappa, Psi Chi, Alpha Gamma Sigma. Office: Bellevue U 1000 Galvin Rd S Bellevue NE 68005-3098

KAYNES, STEPHANIE D., elementary school educator; d. Henry and Janice Kaynes. BS in Child Psychology, U. Minn., 1997; MEd, Tex. State U., San Marcos, 2002. Cert. elem. edn. Tex., 2002. Second grade tchr. Round Rock (Tex.) Ind. Sch. Dist., 2002—. Mem.: Assn. Tex. Profl. Educators, Kappa Delta Pi. Avocation: walking. Office Phone: 512-464-5401.

KAYS, WILLIAM MORROW, academic administrator, mechanical engineer; b. Norfolk, Va., July 29, 1920; s. Herbert Emery and Margaret (Fechteler) K.; m. Alma Campbell, Sept. 14, 1947 (dec. June 1982); children: Nancy, Leslie, Margaret, Elizabeth.; m. Judith Scholtz, July 17, 1983. AB, Stanford U., 1942, MS, 1947, PhD in Mech. Engring., 1951. Asst. prof. mech. engring. Stanford U., 1951-54, assoc. prof., 1954-57, prof., 1957-90, prof. emeritus, 1990—, chmn. dept. mech. engring, 1961-72, dean engring., 1972-84. Dir. Acurex Corp., Alcohol Energy Systems; cons. to numerous firms. Author: Compact Heat Exchangers, 1964, 93, Convective Heat and Mass Transfer, 1966, 80. Hon. editorial adv. bd.: Internat. Jour. Heat and Mass Transfer. Served with U.S. Army, 1942-46. Fulbright fellow, 1959-60; NSF sr. postdoctoral fellow, 1966-67 Fellow ASME (Heat Transfer Divsn. Meml. award 1965, Max Jacob award 1992); mem. Am. Soc. Engring. Edn., Nat. Acad. Engring. Office: Stanford U Dept Mech Engring Stanford CA 94305

KAYSE, KATHLEEN, publishing executive; b. Chgo., 1959; Grad., Univ. of Ill. Media planning Wells, Rich, Greene and J. Walter Thompson, Chgo., 1980—83; sales trainee Time, 1983; midwest advt. mgr. Time Mag., Chgo.; nat. advt. dir. Time for Kids; pub. Fortune Small Bus. (FSB), Time Mag., NYC, 1998—2001, Money mag., 2001—02, People mag., 2002—. Named Most powerful women in the US, Fortune. Mem.: Fin. Comm. Soc., Advertising Women of NY. Office: People Mag 1271 Ave of the Americas New York NY 10020-1393

KAYSEN, CARL, economics professor; b. Phila., Mar. 5, 1920; s. Samuel and Elizabeth (Resnick) K.; m. Annette Neutra, Sept. 13, 1940 (dec. 1990); children: Susanna, Laura; m. Ruth Butler, 1994. AB, U. Pa., 1940; PhD, Harvard U., 1954. Rschr. Nat. Bur. Econ. Rsch., 1940-42; economist OSS, 1942; mem. faculty Harvard U., 1950—66; jr. fellow Harvard U. (Soc. Fellows), 1947-50, asst. prof. econs., 1950-55, asso. prof., 1955-57, prof., 1957-66, Lucius N. Littauer prof. polit. economy, 1964-66; assoc. dean Harvard U. (Grad. Sch. Public Adminstrn.), 1960-66; dir. Inst. Advanced Study, Princeton, N.J., 1966-76, prof., 1966-77; David W. Skinner prof. polit. economy MIT, 1977-90, dir. program in sci., tech. and soc., 1981-87, prof. emeritus, 1990—. Clk. to Judge C. E. Wyzanski, U.S. Dist. C., 1950-52; dep. spl. asst. to Pres. Kennedy for nat. security affairs, 1961-63; mem. Carnegie Commn. on Higher Edn.; vice chmn., dir. research Sloan Commn. on Govt. and Higher Edn.; faculty lectr. London Sch. Econs., 1956; Haynes lectr. Calif. Inst. Tech., 1966; Stafford Little lectr. Princeton U., 1968; Oliver W. Holmes lectr. Harvard Law Sch., 1969; Paley lectr. Hebrew U., Jerusalem, 1970; Godkin lectr. Harvard U., 1976; Bernard Brodie lectr., U.C.L.A., 1994. Hon. Life trustee U. Pa. Served to capt. air intelligence AUS, 1942-45. Fulbright scholar London Sch. Econs., 1955-56; Guggenheim fellow, 1955-56; Ford Found. fellow Greece, 1959-60 Mem. Am. Philos. Soc., Am. Acad. Arts and Scis., Phi Beta Kappa. Clubs: Century (N.Y.C.). Office: MIT Security Studies Program E 38-614 Cambridge MA 02139 Office Phone: 617-253-4054.

KAYTON, MYRON, engineering company executive; b. NYC, Apr. 26, 1934; s. Albert Louis and Rae (Danoff) K.; m. Paula Erde, Sept. 5, 1954; children: Elizabeth Kayton Kerns, Susan Kayton Barclay. BS, The Cooper Union, 1955; MS, Harvard U., 1956; PhD, MIT, 1960. Registered engr., Calif. Sect. head Litton Industries, Woodland Hills, Calif., 1960-65; dep. mgr. NASA, Houston, 1965-69; mem. sr. staff TRW, Inc., Redondo Beach, Calif., 1969-81; pres. Kayton Engring. Co., Inc., Santa Monica, Calif., 1981—. Chmn. bd. dirs. WINCON Conf., L.A., 1985-92; founding dir. Caltech-MIT Enterprise Forum, Pasadena, Calif., 1984—; dir. Electronic Convs., Inc., 2000-01; tchr. tech. courses UCLA Extension, 1969-88. Author: Avionic Navigation Systems, 1966, 2d edit., 1997, Navigation: Land, Sea, Air and Space, 1990; contbr. articles to profl. jours Founding dir. UCLA Friends of Humanities, 1971-75; West coast chmn. Cooper Union Fund Campaign, 1989-93. Fellow NSF, Washington, 1956-57, 58-60; recipient Gano Dunn medal The Cooper Union, N.Y.C., 1975. Fellow IEEE (life; nominating com. 1999-2001, corp. bd. dirs. 1996-97, pres. aerospace 1993-94, exec. v.p. aerospace 1991-92, v.p. tech. ops. 1988-90, nat. bd. govs. 1983—2000, vice-chmn. L.A. coun. 1983-84, avionics editor Aerospace Transactions 2002—, M.B. Carlton award 1988, Disting. lectr., Millennium medal 2000); mem. ASME, Harvard Grad. Soc. (coun. mem. chmn. nominating com. 1988-91, Inst. Navigation, Soc. Automotive Engr., Harvard Club So. Calif. (pres. 1979-80), MIT Club (L.A.). Avocations: tennis, history, languages, flying. Office: Kayton Engring Co PO Box 802 Santa Monica CA 90406-0802 Office Phone: 310-393-1819.

KAYWOOD, SAM K., JR., lawyer; b. New Haven, Conn., June 14, 1957; BS with distinction, Babson Coll., 1979; JD with distinction, Emory Univ., 1986. CPA; bar: Ga. 1987. With Arthur Andersen; ptnr., chmn. fed. income tax group Alston & Bird LLP, Atlanta, 1993. Mem.: ABA (mem. tax sect.), IFA. Office: Alston & Bird LLP One Atlantic Ctr 1201 W Peachtree St NW Atlanta GA 30309-3424 Office Phone: 404-881-7481. Office Fax: 404-881-7777. Business E-Mail: skaywood@alston.com.

KAZ, NATHANIEL, sculptor; b. N.Y.C., Mar. 9, 1917; s. I. Rudolph and Ida (Elkan) K.; m. Delfina Nahrgang, 1986; children: Naomi Della, Eric Justin. Student, Geo. B. Bridgeman, Samuel Cashwan, 1927, William Zorach; attended, Cooper Union. Tchr. Art Students League, N.Y.C. One-man shows include Downtown Gallery, 1939, Assn. Am. Artists, 1946, Grand Central Moderns, 1954, Joan Avnet Gallery, 1965, Art Students League N.Y., 1991; traveling group exhbn. Bethlehem, Pa., Oshkosh, Wis., Annapolis, Md.; exhbns. include Whitney Mus., Met. Mus. Art, Bklyn. Mus., Art Inst. Chgo., U. Nebr., Phila. Mus. Fine Arts, Mus. Modern Art, N.Y. San Francisco world's fairs, and NAD; represented in permanent collections, Bklyn. Mus., Whitney Mus., Met. Mus., Larry Aldrich Mus., N.Y.U., pvt. collections; designed and executed 10 ft. carving in limestone for Vine St. Temple, Nashville, 6 ft. bronze for Pub. Sch. 59, Bklyn.; exhibited 4 ritual works, Grand Central Moderns, 1957, Temple of Beth Emeth, Albany, N.Y., 1965; designed and executed two 7 ft. colored aluminum reliefs of Thespians-Tragedy and Comedy for Jr. High Sch. 164, Queens, NY, 1958. Grantee Nat. Inst. Arts and Letters, 1959; recipient Mich. Sculpture award, 1929, Sect. Fine Arts award, 1940, Artists for Victory award, 1942, Bklyn. Soc. Artists 32d ann. award, 1952, Sculpture prize Bklyn. Mus., 1952, Alfred G. B. Steel prize 148th ann. exhibit Pa. Acad. Fine Arts, 1953; winner nat. competition UN monument design, Nat. Council U.S. Art, 1955; Award for Sculpture Maury Leibovitz Competition, 1986; Nancy Dryfoos Meml. award Allied Artists Ann. Exhbn., N.Y.C., 1991, C. Percival Dietsch Sculpture prize Nat. Sculpture Soc., N.Y.C., 1992. Mem. Sculptors Guild, Nat. Sculpture Soc., NAD (academician, Merit award 1976, Agop Agopoff award 1988, Saltus Gold medal 1989), Audubon Artists (Medals of Honor 1960, 1981, 83, 87, 88), Sculpture Soc. Studio: 160 W 73rd St New York NY 10023-3012 Office Phone: 212-873-9991.*

KAZA, GREG JOHN, economist, educator; b. Wyandotte, Mich., Nov. 11, 1960; s. John J. and Mary A. Kaza. BA in Econs., U. Detroit, 1989; MSF in Internat. Fin., Walsh Coll., Troy, Mich., 1998. V.p. policy rsch. The Mackinac Ctr., Midland, Mich., 1989-91; adj. prof. Northwood Inst. and Walsh Coll., Troy, Mich., 1998—2000; state rep. State of Mich., 1993-98; exec. dir. Citizen Legislators' Caucus Found., Washington, 1999-2000, Ark. Policy Found., Little Rock, 2001—. Author 9 state laws. Contbr. articles to profl. jours. Republican. Roman Catholic. Office: Ark Policy Found Stephens Bldg 111 Center St Ste 1200 Little Rock AR 72201

KAZAN, ALEXANDRA KHAN, photographer, web site designer; m. Edgar Rolf Schneider, June 26, 1999. Web designer Garfield Images and Design, Ft. Lauderdale, Fla., 1998—. Recipient Golden Web award, Internat. Assn. Web Masters and Designers, 2002, 2003, 2004, 2005. Mem.: AARP, Animal Legal Def. Fund, ASPCA, Nat. Humane Edn. Soc., Internat. Fund Animal Welfare, Gabriel Found., Humane Soc., Coun. Brit. Socs., Wildlife Care Ctr., Tiger Haven, Sierra Club. Green Party. Episcopalian. Avocations: photography, painting, writing, reading, animal welfare.

KAZAN, BENJAMIN, electrical engineer, researcher; b. N.Y.C., May 8, 1917; s. Abraham Eli and Esther (Bookbinder) K.; m. Gerda B. Mosse, Nov. 4, 1988; 1 child from previous marriage, David Louis. BS in Physics, Calif. Inst. Tech., 1938; MA in Physics, Columbia U., 1940; PhD in Physics, Tech. U. Munich, 1961. Radio engr. Dept. Def., Ft. Monmouth, N.J., 1940-50; rsch. engr. RCA Labs., Princeton, N.J., 1950-58; head solid state display group Hughes Rsch. Lab., Malibu, Calif., 1958-61; head imaging sect. Electro-Optical Sys., Pasadena, Calif., 1961-68; head exploratory display group T.J. Watson Rsch. Ctr., Yorktown Heights, N.Y., 1968-74; prin. scientist Xerox Rsch. Ctr., Palo Alto, Calif., 1974-85; cons. display and imaging tech., 1985—. Cons. Advisory Group Electron Devices, Dept. Def., 1973-82; adj. prof. U. R.I., Kingston, 1970-74. Author: (with others) Storage Tubes, 1952, Electronic Image Storage, 1968; editor: Advances in Image Storage, 1968, Advances in Image Pickup and Display series, 1972-84; assoc. editor Advances in Imaging and electron Physics series, 1984—; contbr. articles to profl. jours., patentee in field. Recipient silver medal Am. Roentgen Ray Soc., 1957. Fellow IEEE (assoc. editor Jour. Electron Devices 1979-83), Soc. Info. Display (editor jour. 1974-78); mem. Am. Phys. Soc., Sigma Xi, Tau Beta Pi. Home: 800 Blossom Hill Rd Unit P394 Los Gatos CA 95032-3575 E-mail: bkazan@earthlink.net.

KAZANJIAN, JOHN HAROLD, lawyer; b. Newport, R.I., Jan. 25, 1949; s. Powel Harold and Louise T. (Alexander) K.; m. Jane Mitchell Kohlmeyer, Sept. 26, 1981; 1 child, Sara Jane. BA, Providence Coll., 1971; JD, Notre Dame U., 1975. Bar: N.Y. 1976, U.S. Dist. Ct. (so. dist.) N.Y. 1976, U.S. Dist. Ct. (ea. dist.) N.Y. 1977, U.S. Supreme Ct. 1980, U.S. Ct. Appeals (2d crct.) 1986, U.S. Ct. Appeals (fed. crct.) 1991. Assoc. Cadwalader, Wickersham & Taft, N.Y.C., 1975-86; ptnr. Anderson, Kill & Olick, N.Y.C., 1986-98, Beveridge & Diamond, N.Y.C., 1999—. Mem. U.S. Naval War Coll. Found., Newport, 1985—. Mem. ABA (sects. on litigation, tort and ins. practice and internat. law), Assn. Bar City N.Y. (chair com. on product liability), N.Y. County Lawyers Assn. (chair com. on ins. law, tort law sect.), Metro. Club. Episcopalian. Avocations: caricatures, cartoons, long distance running. Office: Beveridge & Diamond 15th Fl 477 Madison Ave New York NY 10022-5802 E-mail: jkazanjian@bd.law.com.

KAZANJIAN, PHILLIP CARL, lawyer, educator; b. Visalia, Calif., May 15, 1945; s. John Casey and Sat-ten Arlene K.; m. Wendy Coffelt, Feb. 5, 1972; 1 child, John. BA with honors, U. So. Calif., 1967; JD with honors, Lincoln U., 1973. Bar: Calif. 1979, U.S. Dist. Ct. (ctrl. dist.) Calif. 1980, U.S. Tax Ct. 1980, U.S. Ct. Appeals (9th cir.) 1980, U.S. Mil. Ct. Appeals 1980, U.S. Supreme ct. 1983. Ptnr. Brakefield & Kazanjian, Glendale, Calif., 1981-87; sr. ptnr. Kazanjian & Martinetti, Glendale, Calif., 1987—. Judge pro tem L.A. County Superior Ct., 1993—; instr. U.S. Naval Acad., Annapolis, Md., 1981; adj. instr. Glendale C.C., 1997-2005, instr., 2005— Author: The Circuit Governor, 1972; editor-in-chief Lincoln Law Rev., 1973. Mem. Calif. Atty. Gen.'s Adv. Commn. on Cmty.-Police Rels., 1973; bd. dirs. L.A. County Naval Meml. Found., Inc., 1981-85, ARC, 1998-2003, Glendale C.C., 1997—; pres., bd. trustees Glendale C.C. Dist., 1981-97, L.A. World Affairs Coun., Town Hall Calif., Rep. Assocs. (dir.), Rep. Lincoln Club; vice chmn. bd. govs. Calif. Maritime Acad., 1986-94; bd. dirs. ARC, 1998-2003, Glendale C.C. Found., 1997—. Capt. USNR, 1969-99. Decorated Navy Commendation medal, Navy Achievement medal, knight Order of Knights Templar, 1990; recipient Patrick Henry medal Am. Legion, 1963, Congl. Record tribute U.S. Ho. of Reps., 1974, Centurion award Chief of Naval Ops., 1978; commendatory resolutions Mayor of L.A., L.A. City Coun., L.A. County Bd. Suprs., Calif. State Assembly and Senate, and Govt. of Calif., 1982, 2003, Justice award Calif. Law Student Assn., 1973. Mem. ABA (Gold Key 1972), Calif. Bar Assn., L.A. County Bar Assn., Am. Judicature Soc., ATLA, Glendale C. of C. (bd. dirs., Patriot Yr. 1986), Res. Officers Assn. (nat. judge adv., award 1981), Naval Res. Assn. (nat. adv. com.), U.S. Naval Inst., Interallied Confedn. Res. Officers (internat. chmn. 1987-94), Explorers Club, Commonwealth of Calif. Club. Republican. Episcopalian. Office: Kazanjian & Martinetti 520 E Wilson Ave Ste 250 Glendale CA 91206-4346 Office Phone: 818-241-1011.

KAZAS, ANGELIKI, mathematician, educator; b. N.Y.C., June 29, 1970; d. Nikolaos and Maria Kazas. BA, Pace U., 1992; PhD, SUNY, Albany, 2002. Lectr. SUNY, Albany, 2001—02, asst. prof. Oneonta, 2002—. Mem.: Math. Assn. Am. (project NEXT fellow 2003—04), Am. Math. Soc. Home: 3 Okara Dr Schenectady NY 12303 Office: SUNY Oneonta Ravine Pky Oneonta NY 13820 Office Phone: 607-436-3657. Business E-Mail: kazasa@oneonta.edu.

KAZAZIAN, HAIG HAGOP, JR., pediatrician, researcher, educator; b. Toledo, July 30, 1937; s. Haig Hagop and Hermine Adriene (Papelian) K.; m. Lillian Agnes Cleaver, Oct. 13, 1962; children: Haig Hagop III, Sonya Elizabeth. AB, Dartmouth Coll., 1959; MD, Johns Hopkins U., 1962. Diplomate Am. Bd. Pediatrics, Am. Bd. Medical Genetics (pres. 2000). Asst. prof. pediatrics Johns Hopkins U., Balt., 1969-74, assoc. prof. pediatrics, 1974-77, prof. pediats., 1977-94, prof. biology, 1979-94, prof. ob-gyn., 1985-94, prof. medicine, 1989-94, dir. Ctr. Med. Genetics, 1989-94, Sutland prof. pediat. genetics, 1991-94; chmn. dept. genetics U. Pa. Sch. Medicine, Phila., 1994—. Mem. mammalian genetics study sect. NIH, Bethesda, Md., 1981-85; pres. bd. dirs. Citizens for Good Govt., Balt., 1973-75; bd. dirs. Am. Bd. Med. Genetics. Author more than 250 sci. papers; editor jour. Human Mutation, 1992. Sr. surgeon USPHS, 1966-68. Grantee NIH, 1968—; recipient Mead Johnson award Am. Acad. Pediatrics, 1976. Mem. Inst. of Medicine, Am. Pediat. Soc., Am. Soc. Human Genetics (bd. dirs. 1982-85), Am. Soc. Clin. Investigation, Assn. Am. Physicians, Alpha Omega Alpha. Democrat. Episcopalian. Avocations: jogging, tennis, classical music. Home: 1015 Winding Way Baltimore MD 21210-1232 Office: U Pa Sch Medicine 475 Clinical Research Bldg 415 Curie Blvd Philadelphia PA 19104-4218

KAZEMI, FARHAD, political scientist, educator; b. Tehran, Iran, Jan. 7, 1943; came to U.S., 1960; s. Parviz and Irandokht (Ehteshami) K.; m. Tina A. Garber, July 9, 1966 (div. 1975); children: Shirin, Sara; m. Jane Opper, Apr. 28, 1977; stepchildren: Lygeia, Maude. BA, Colgate U., 1964; MA, George Washington U., 1966, Harvard U., 1968; PhD, U. Mich., 1973. Teaching fellow U. Mich., Ann Arbor, 1968-70; from instr., asst. prof., assoc. prof. to prof. pol. sci. NYU, 1971-88, acting dean Grad. Sch. Arts and Sci., 1989-91, vice provost, 1999—2003. Vis. lectr. U. Pa., 1979; cons. U.S. Govt., 1980—; dir. Kevorkian Ctr., NYU, 1982—85, 2004—, chmn. dept. polit. sci., 1985—89, 1992—93, 1996—97; vis. prof. Princeton U., 1996; vis. sr. fellow Oxford (Eng.) U., 1997; apptd. mem. U.S. Adv. Group on Pub. Diplomacy for Arab and Muslim World, 2003. Author: Poverty and Revolution in Iran, 1980, Politics and Culture in Iran, 1988; author, editor: Iranian Revolution, 1980, Civil Society in Iran, 1995-96; co-editor: A Way Prepared: Studies on Islamic Culture, 1987, Peasants and Politics in the Modern Middle East, 1991, other books and articles. Grantee NSF, 1973, Social Sci. Rsch. Coun., 1974-75, 84-85, Kervorkian Fund, 1985, Ford Found., 1992-93, 94-95, Rockefeller Found., 1993, 94. Fellow Middle East Studies Assn. (bd. dirs. 1985-88, pres. 1995-96); mem. Am. Polit. Sci. Assn., Internat. Polit. Sci. Assn., Internat. Studies Assn., Middle East Inst., Soc. Iranian Studies (coun., editor 1982-86, pres. 1998-99), Internat. Soc. Polit. Psychology, Coun. Fgn. Rels., Atlantic Coun. Washington (acad. assoc. 1985-98). Democrat. Avocations: tennis, biking, sailing. Office: NYU Dept Politics 726 Broadway New York NY 10003-6860 Office Phone: 212-998-8506.

KAZEMI, HOMAYOUN, internist, educator; b. Teheran, Iran, Sept. 28, 1934; came to U.S., 1953, naturalized, 1970; s. Parviz and Irandokht K.; m. Katheryne McNulty, June 7, 1958; children: Paul, Laili. BA, Lafayette Coll., 1954; MD, Columbia U., 1958; MSc (hon.), Harvard U., 1990. Diplomate: Am. Bd. Internal Medicine. Intern M.I. Bassett Hosp., Cooperstown, N.Y., 1958-59; resident in medicine Mass. Gen. Hosp., Boston, 1963, chief pulmonary unit, 1967-89, chief pulmonary and critical care unit, 1989-98, chief emeritus, 1998—, sr. physician, 2005; assoc. prof. medicine Harvard U., 1971-78, prof., 1979—, prof. medicine Harvard/MIT program in health sci. and tech., 1980—. Hon. cons. in intrenal medicine Shanghai 1st People's Hosp., 1992—; vis. scholar dept. medicine, U. Calif., San Diego, 1998-99; bd. dirs. Boston Tb Assn.; vis. prof. U. Ghent, 1975-76, Peking Union Med. Coll., China, 1992; dir. U.S. Beryllium Case Registry, 1968-78; vis. fellow Hammersmith Hosp., London, 1965; cons. Fed. Aviation Agy., 1987. Author: (book) Poon C-S and Kazemi, H Editors, Frontiers in Modeling and Control of Breathing, 2001, Disorder of the Respiratory System, 1976, (with L.G. Miller) Manual of Pulmonary Medicine, 1982—, Acute Lung Injury, 1986; mem. editl. bd. New Eng. Jour. Medicine, 1981-90, Respiratory Mgmt., 1989-93, Current Opinion in Pulmonary Medicine, 1993-99, Current Opinion in Critical Care, 1993-2000; guest editor Respiration Physiology, 2000. Dir. Am. Lung Assn. Boston; mem. rsch. evaluation subcom. Am. Heart Assn., mem. cardiopulmonary coun., 1979—, v.p. 1985-87, pres. 1987-89, mem. rsch. rev. com.; bd. trustees Dublin (N.H.) Sch., 1987-97. Fellow Am. Heart Assn, 1961-63, Am. Heart Assn. (inaugural 2003); named Dickinson Richards lectr., 1996; recipient Chadwick medal Mass. Thoracic Soc., 1988, Lifetime achievement award AMA, 2000. Fellow ACP; mem. Am. Fedn. Clin. Rsch., Am. Thoracic Soc. (pres. Ea. sect. 1974-75), Mass. Med. Soc., Am. Physiol. Soc, Am. Soc. Clin. Investigation, Soc. Occupl. and Environ. Health, Sigma Xi. Office: Mass Gen Hosp Boston MA 02114 E-mail: Hkazemi@partners.org.

KAZHDAN, DAVID, mathematician, educator; b. Moscow, June 20, 1946; came to U.S., 1975; s. Alexander and Rimma (Ivanskaya) K.; m. Helena Slobodkina, Mar. 22, 1968; children: Eli, Dina, Misha, Daniel. MA, Moscow State U., 1967, PhD, 1969; BA (hon), Harvard U., 1977. Researcher Moscow State U., 1969-75, vis. prof., 1975-77; prof. Harvard U., Cambridge, Mass., 1977—. MacArthur fellow. Mem. NAS. Office: Harvard U 1 Oxford St Cambridge MA 02138-2901 Home: 34 Rushmore St Brighton MA 02135-3900

KAZIMI, MUJID SULIMAN, nuclear engineer, educator; b. Jerusalem, Nov. 20, 1947; came to U.S., 1969; s. Suliman Ishak Kazimi and Fikrat Nuseibeh; m. Nazik D. Denny, Sept. 1, 1973. B. Engring., Alexandria U.,

Arab Republic of Egypt, 1969; MS, MIT, 1971, PhD, 1973. Sr. engr. Westinghouse Electric Corp., Madison, Pa., 1973-74; assoc. scientist Brookhaven Nat. Lab., Upton, N.Y., 1974-76; asst. prof. MIT, Cambridge, 1976-79, assoc. prof., 1979-86, prof., 1986—, head dept. nuclear engring., 1989-97. Tokyo Elec. Power Co. (TEPCO) chair for nuc. engring. at MIT, 2000—; dir. Ctr. Advanced Nuc. Energy Systems, 2000—; chmn. high-level waste tank safety adv. panel U.S. Dept. Energy, Washington, 1990-95, chmn. new prodn. reactor severe accident group, 1990-91. Co-author: (with Neil Todreas) Nuclear Systems: Volume I: Thermal Hydraulic Fundamentals, 1990, Nuclear Systems: Volume II: Elements of Thermal Hydraulic Design, 1990; editor: Perspectives on Technological Development in the Arab World, 1978. Pres. Assn. Arab-Am. Univ. Grads., Belmont, Mass., 1980, 87. Fellow Am. Nuclear Soc. (bd. dirs. N.E. chpt. 1978, 80, exec. com. thermal hydraulics divsn. 1988-90); mem. ASME, AAAS, AIChE (chmn. nuclear heat transfer com. 1980-83), Am. Soc. for Engring. Edn. (exec. com. nuclear engring. divsn. 1995-97). Office: MIT Dept Nuc Engring 77 Massachusetts Ave Rm 24-215 Cambridge MA 02139-4307 Office Phone: 617-253-4206. Business E-Mail: kazimi@mit.edu.

KAZIN, MICHAEL, historian, writer; b. N.Y.C., June 6, 1948; s. Alfred and Carol Bookman (Salvadori) K.; m. Beth Horowitz, Aug. 24, 1980; children: Daniel, Maia. BA, Harvard U., 1972; PhD, Stanford U., 1983. Instr. history San Francisco State U., 1978-82; asst. prof. history Stanford (Calif.) U., 1983-85; prof. history Am. U., Washington, 1986-99, Georgetown U., 1999—. Author: The Populist Persuasion, 1995, 96, revised edit., 1998, Barons of Labor, 1987, 89 (Gutman award 1988), America Divided, 1999, rev. edit. 2003; contbr. articles to profl. hist. jours., popular mags. and newspapers; book editor Tikkun, San Francisco/N.Y.C., 1987-96; assoc. editor Socialist Rev., San Francisco, 1978-84; hist. advisor several documentaries, 1982—. Mem. steering com. Com. for a Teach-In with Labor, N.Y.C., 1996-97; spkr., local leader Nuc. Freeze Campaign, San Francisco, 1982-84. John Adams chair Am. Studies, Fulbright program, Utrecht, The Netherlands, 1996; Fulbright lectr. Ritsumeikan U., Tokyo/Kyoto, 1997; sr. fellow William and Mary Coll. Commonwealth Ctr., Williamsburg, Va., 1990-91; postdoctoral fellow Smithsonian Instn., Washington, 1988-89; NEH fellow, 1998-99; Woodrow Wilson Ctr. fellow, 1998-99, Guggenheim fellow, 2004. Mem. Am. Hist. Assn., Orgn. Am. Historians (chair com. for Ellis Hawley award). Democrat. Jewish. Avocations: baseball, fiction. Office: Georgetown U Dept History Washington DC 20057-0001 Office Phone: 202-687-0007. Business E-Mail: mk8@georgetown.edu.

KAZMERZAK, RICHARD ANTHONY, art educator; b. De Smet, S.D., July 15, 1960; s. Larwence Arnold and Franicis Janice Kazmerzak; m. Deb Lynn Greenlee, June 21, 1086; 1 child, Carly Rae. BFA in Edn., U. No. Iowa, Cedar Falls, 1985. Tchr. art Indianola H.S., Iowa, 1996—; adj. prof. ceramics Simpson Coll., 1999—. Ceramic sculpture, Light at the End of the Tunnel (commd., 2004). Office: Indianola HS Indianola IA 50612 Office Phone: 515-961-9510 335. E-mail: richard.kazmerzak@indianola.k12.ia.us.

KAZRAGYS, LINDA KAYAN BUBLIS, elementary school educator; b. East Chicago, Ind., Nov. 26, 1946; d. Bert Charles and Irma Aldonna (Matuck) Bublis; m. Vitas Joseph Kazragys, June 22, 1968; children: Amanda, Julianna, Adam. BSE, Ball State U., 1968; MSE, Purdue U., 1984. Elem. tchr. East Chicago Pub. Schs., 1968-70, 73-78; dir. nursery sch. St. John the Bapt. Sch., Whiting, Ind., 1978-83, elem. tchr. Dicoese of Gary, 1983—, mem. home and sch. com., chair lang. arts and sci. dept. On-site rev. team performance based accreditation INd. Dept. Edn. Dir. adult edn. Girl Scouts Calumet Council, Highland, Ind., 1982-84. Recipient St. Anne's award Girl Scouts of Calumet Council, Gary, Ind., 1972, Thanks Badge, Highland, Ind., 1978. Mem. Nat. Cath. Educators Assn. Democrat. Avocations: travel, outdoor activities, reading, art, music. Home: 2028 Lake Ave Whiting IN 46394-1832 Office: St John the Bapt Sch 1844 Lincoln Ave Whiting IN 46394-1532

KE, YONG, medical educator, researcher; b. Huang Shi, Hubei, China, Jan. 31, 1956; s. Zheng Dong Ke and You Ru Chen. MS in Physics, Mont. State U., 1988; PhD in Physics, U. of Minn., 1993. Rschr. UCLA, 1997—98; instr. McLean Hosp., Harvard Med. Sch., Belmont, Mass., 1998—. Mem. sci. com. 2nd Internat. Conf. on Biomed. Spectroscopy, London, 2002—. Contbr. scientific papers to profl. publs. (NARSAD Young Investigator award, 1999). Recipient Young Investigator award, NARSAD, 1999, Nat. Rsch. Svc. award, NIH, 1996. Mem.: Am. Psychiat. Assn., Internat. Soc. for Magnetic Resonance in Medicine. Achievements include invention of A new method for quantification of 2D magnetic resonance spectroscopy; discovery of Creatine and phosphocreatine in vivo have different transverse relaxation times in proton MRS. E-mail: yke@mclean.harvard.edu.

KEACH, STACY, JR., actor, theater director, theater producer, musician, composer; b. Savannah, Ga., June 2, 1941; s. Stacy and Mary Cain (Peckham) K.; m. Malgosia Tomassi, 1986; children: Shannon and Karolina. AB in English and Drama, U. Calif. at Berkeley, 1963; student, Yale Drama Sch., 1963-64, London Acad. Dramatic Art, 1964-65. Assoc. prof. drama Yale, 1967-68. Pres. Positron Prodns. Ltd. Contbr. articles to newspapers and mags.; mem. Lincoln Ctr. Repertory Co., Long Wharf Theatre, Washington Shakespeare Theatre, Williamstown Summer Theatre, Oreg. Shakespeare Festival, Tufts Arena Theatre; charter mem. The Yale Theatre Circle, 1986; Broadway debut in Indians, 1969; appeared in Broadway prodn. Deathtrap, 1979, Solitary Confinement, 1992, The Kentucky Circle, 1993 (Helen Hayes award for Best Actor 1993, Outstanding Performance award Drama League); off-Broadway appearances in Macbird, 1966-67, The Niggerlovers, 1967, Peer Gynt, 1969, Henry IV, 1 and 2, 1968, Hamlet, 1972, King Lear, 1968, Long Day's Journey Into Night, 1971, Cyrano de Bergerac, 1978, Hughie, London, 1980; Nat. Touring Co., Barnum, 1981; Kennedy Ctr. Prodn. of Idiot's Delight, 1986, Nat. Touring Co., Sleuth, 1988, The King & I, 1989, Love Letters, 1990-93, Richard III, 1991, Stieglitz Loves O'Keefe, 1995, MacBeth, 1995, The Ten Unknowns, 2003; film appearances include: The Heart is a Lonely Hunter, 1968, End of the Road, 1969, Doc, 1970, The Traveling Executioner, 1970, The New Centurions, 1971, Fat City, 1971, Brewster McCloud, 1970, Luther, 1972, The Dion Brothers, 1973, Conduct Unbecoming, 1974, Jesus of Nazareth, 1967, The Killer Inside Me, 1974, The Squeeze, 1976, Gray Lady Down, 1976, The Greatest Battle, 1977, Two Solitudes, 1977, Cheech & Chong's Up in Smoke, 1977, The Ninth Configuration, 1978, The Long Riders, 1979, Road Games, 1980, Butterfly, 1980, Cheech & Chong's Nice Dreams, 1981, That Championship Season, 1982, Butterfly, 1982, The Class of 1999, 1990, The Forgotten, Milena, 1989, Escape from L.A., 1996, The Sea Wolf, 1996, Die Gang, 1996, American History X, 1998; TV appearances in: Orville and Wilbur, 1971, Particular Men, 1972, Classics For Today, 1972, Man of Destiny, 1973, all PBS, All the Kind Strangers, 1974, Caribe, 1974-75, both ABC, The Michener Dynasty, NBC, 1975, A Rumor of War, CBS, 1979, The Blue and the Gray, 1981, Wait Until Dark, 1982, Murder Me, Murder You, 1983, Princess Daisy, 1983, Mistral's Daughter, 1984, Intimate Strangers, 1986, More Than Murder, 1983, Mickey Spillane's Mike Hammer series, 1983, 86-87, Return of Mickey Spillane's Mike Hammer, 1986, starring role 6 hour mini-series on life of Ernest Hemingway, 1988 (Best Actor award Golden Globes 1988), Murder Takes All, 1989 (Emmy nominee Best Actor in Special or Miniseries), Body Bags, 1992 (Cable Ace Award nominee Best Actor), Against Their Will, 1994, Texas, 1995, Titus, 2000, The Santa Trap, 2002, The Simpsons, 2002-03 Frozen Impact, 2003; host TV programs Missing/Reward, 1988, Arts and Entertainment Stage Series, 1988-89, Circus of Stars, 1991, Case-Closed, 1993-94; dir.: Pullman Car Hiawatha, 1964-65, The Stronger, 1964-65, The Maids, 1964-65, The Repeater, 1971 (Cine Golden Eagle award, London Film Festival outstanding film), Incident at Vichy, 1974, Six Characters in Search of an Author, 1976, A Blinding Fear (episode of The New Mike Hammer), 1987; host PBS July 4th Festivities, 1995; narrator (TV documentary) Nova, Nat. Geographic, Am. Experience, Discover Channel Flight Over the Equator, 1995, Planet of Life, 1995, Stupid Behavior Caught on Tape, 2003; (books on tape) Hardboiled, 1994, Mickey Spillane's Works, 1990, CD-ROM, 1994, Ten Lost Tribes of Israel, Shakespeare's Sonnets; screen writer, producer The Long Riders, 1979. Sponsor Nat. Repertory Theatre Found. (Nat. Play Award Com.), 1986; hon. chair Cleft Palate Assn., 1995; spokesman United Indian Devel. Assn.; mem. Nat. Citizens Comm. Lobby, Entertainment Industries Coun. before House Select Com. on Drug Abuse, 1985; panelist Am. TV, Arts and Scis. Substance Abuse Conf., 1986, Artists Com. Kennedy Ctr. Honors, 1986—; mem. Players Club; charter mem. L.A. Classic Theatre Works, Artists Rights Found.; mem. artistic adv. bd. Nat. Found. for Advancement in Arts; mem. Helen Hayes Honorary Com. Fulbright award, 1964-65; recipient Best Actor award U. Calif., 1963, Best Actor award Oreg. Shakespeare award, 1963, Obie award, 1967, 71, 73, Vernon Rice Drama Desk award, 1967, 71, 72, Saturday Rev. award, 1967, Helen Hayes Best Actor award, 1994, Hon. chmn. Am. Cleft Palate Found., 1995—, Celebrity Outreach honoree, 1995, Master of Ceremonies, Capitol Mall, 1995. Address: c/o Jim Palmer 2423852 Pacific Coast Hwy #950 Malibu CA 90265 *The fundamental virtue of success is making your dreams come true. But without loved ones to share it with it means little or nothing.*

KEADY, GEORGE CREGAN, JR., judge; b. Bklyn., June 16, 1924; s. George Cregan and Marie (Lussier) K.; m. Patricia Drake, Sept. 2, 1950; children: Margaret Keady Goldberg, Marie E., George Cregan, Catherine A. Keady Sharp, Kathleen V. Student, U. Kans., 1943-44; BS, Fordham U., 1949; JD, Columbia U., 1950; LL.D., Western New Eng. Coll., 1973. Bar: Mass. 1950. Since practiced in, Springfield, Mass.; assoc. firm Ganley & Crook, 1950-53; assoc. firm Peter D. Wilson, 1953-57; partner firm Wilson, Keady & Ratner, 1958-79; justice Dist. Ct., Springfield, 1979-82; assoc. justice Superior Ct., Springfield, 1982-93; ret., 1993; freelance mediator and arbitrator, 1993—. Dean Western New Eng. Coll. Law Sch., 1970-73; dir. Western Mass. Bar Rev., 1956-63, Western New Eng. Coll. Bar Rev., 1965-72; chmn. Mass. Continuing Legal Edn., Inc., 1977-80; mem. Mass. Commn. on Jud. Conduct, 1988, chmn., 1990-93. Active United Fund, Springfield, 1950-72, Joint Civic Agys.; chmn. fund drive Am. Cancer Soc., 1962, selectman, Longmeadow, Mass., 1958-68, chmn. selectmen, 1960-61, 63-64, 66-68, moderator, 1968-73; vice chmn. Rep. Town Com., Longmeadow, 1956-60; alt. del. Rep. Nat. Conv., 1960, del., 1964; pres. Hampden Dist. Mental Health Clinic, Inc., 1968-71, Child Guidance Clinic, Springfield, 1962-64; corporator, trustee, chmn. bd. Baystate Med. Center, 1985-87, trustee, 1984-92, 94-99; chmn. bd. Baystate Health System, 1987-90; trustee Western New Eng. Coll., 1978-84, Baypath Jr. Coll., 1972-87, Baystate Health Systems, 1993-98; dir. BHIC, 1993—. Served with AUS, 1943-46. Decorated Bronze star. Mem. Am. Law Inst., Mass. Bar Assn., Hampden County Bar Assn. (exec. com. 1960-79, pres. 1965-67), Supreme Ct. Hist. Soc., Longmeadow Country Club, Phi Delta Phi. Roman Catholic. Home: 16 Meadowbrook Rd Longmeadow MA 01106-1341 Office Phone: 413-567-7412.

KEAGY, DOROTHY (DOTTI KEAGY), copy director; b. Waltham, Mass., Mar. 3, 1945; d. Albert Stanley and Bertha (Bluestein) Rouffa; m. Neil Woolf, 1996; children: Meredith, Brian. Student, U. Ill., 1963-65, Pratt Inst., N.Y.C., 1965-66. Mgr. depts. Neiman-Marcus, Lou Lattimore, Tex., 1970-75; writer, editor Dallas Morning News, Fashion Showcase, 1975-78; bur. chief, regional editor Women's Wear Daily, Dallas, 1978-84; dir. mktg. communications Dallas Apparel Mart, Trammel Crow Co., 1984-85; sr. editor Women's Wear Daily, N.Y.C., 1985-88; editor fitness N.Y. Times Mag. Group, 1988-90, writer, publicist, 1990-95; copy dir., promotion & design Rowland Co., 1995-97; copy dir. Liz Claiborne Inc., N.Y.C., 1998—. Contbr. mag. articles to publs. Mem. Tacassociates, Dallas. Recipient Editorial award Dallas Apparel Mart, Dallas Fashion awards, 1980. Mem. Fashion Group Internat., Sigma Delta Phi. Office: 240 E 35th St Apt 5L New York NY 10016-4215 E-mail: dotti_keagy@liz.com.

KEALA, FRANCIS AHLOY, security executive; b. Honolulu, June 1, 1930; s. Samuel Louis and Rose (Ahloy) K.; m. Betty Ann Lyman, Nov. 28, 1952; children— Frances Ann, John Richard, Robert Mark. BA in Sociology, U. Hawaii, 1953. Patrolman Honolulu Police Dept., 1956-62, detective, 1962-65, lt., 1965-68, capt., 1968-69, chief of police, 1969-83; dir. security Hawaiian Telephone Co., 1983-93. Bd. dirs. Liliuokalani Trust; trustee St. Louis Sch., 1980-87, S. Keala Trust, 1989—, Kamehameha Schs. Bishop Estate, 1999-2001. Bd. dirs. Aloha coun. Boy Scouts Am., 200 Club, Sex Abuse Treatment Center, Am. Automobile Assn. of Hawaii, Hawaii Meml. Park Assn., St. Louis Found., ARC-Hawaii chpt., St. Francis Med. Ctr.-West; bd. govs. Boys and Girls Clubs of Honolulu; mem. Civilian Adv. Group U.S. Army; mem. Commn. on Jud. Discipline; v.p., dir. Hawaiian Music Hall of Fame and Mus.; mem. Honolulu City and County Ethics Commn. Served with U.S. Army, 1953-55. Mem. Internat. Assn. Chiefs of Police, Hawaii State Law Enforcement Ofcls. Assn., FBI Nat. Acad. Assocs. Clubs: Oahu Country, Pacific.

KEALEY, EDWARD J., priest, historian; b. N.Y.C., Aug. 1, 1936; s. John C. and Margaret L. Kealey. BA, Manhattan Coll., 1958; MA, PhD, The John Hopkins U., 1962; MA in Theology, Sem. Immaculate Conception, 1989. Odained to ministry Cath. Ch., 1989. Prof. history Coll. Holy Cross, Worcester, Mass., 1962—86; priest Diocese Rockville Ctr., NY, 1986—. Author: Roger of Salisbury, Viceroy of England, 1972, Medieval Medicus: A Social History of Anglo-Norman Medicine, 1981, Harvesting the Air: Windmill Pioneers in Twelfth Century England, 1987; contbr. articles to profl. jours. Fellow, Danforth Found., 1958—62, NEH, 1976. Office: St Syvesters Ch 68 Ohio Ave Medford NY 11763

KEALEY, ERIN, philosopher; b. Phila., Jan. 15, 1976; d. Elizabeth Kealey. BA, U. Va., 1997; MA in Liberal Studies, Georgetown U., 2002; MA in Philosophy, Boston Coll., 2004; postgrad., Purdue U., 2005—. Hotline vol. & suicide prevention trainer Open Ho. Hotline (currently known as Help Line), Ctrl. Va., 1994—97; paralegal civil litig. Hazel & Thomas, P.C., Falls Church, Va., 1997—99; crisis call listener No. Va. Hotline (currently known as CrisisLink), No. Va., 1999—99; proctor & continuity ops. plan dep. U.S. Senate Page Program, Washington, 1999—2002; libr. asst. John J. Burns Libr. Rare Book and Spl. Collections, Chestnut Hill, Mass., 2002—04. Contbr. articles to profl jours. Mem.: Am. Philos. Assn., Internat. High IQ Soc., Am. Mensa, U. Va. Alumni Assn. (life).

KEAN, HAMILTON FISH, lawyer; b. NYC, Mar. 1, 1925; s. Robert Winthrop and Elizabeth Stuyvesant (Howard) K.; m. Ellen Shaw Garrison, Mar. 25, 1950 (div. 1976); children: Leslie, Elizabeth K. Douglas, Lloyd Garrison, Lewis Morris; m. Alice Newcomer Baker, July 6, 1981 (dec. 1986); m. Edith Williamson Bacon, Sept. 23, 1989. AB cum laude, Princeton U., 1949; JD, Columbia U., 1954. Bar: NY 1954, NJ 1955. Asst. counsel Waterfront Commn. NY Harbor, 1954; law sec. NJ Supreme Ct., 1954-55; asst. U.S. atty. NJ Dist., 1955-57; ptnr. Clapp and Eisenberg and predecessors, Newark, 1957-62; trustee various funds, 1963—; lectr. law Rutgers U. Sch. Law, 1960; lectr. environ. law SUNY at Purchase, Westchester Cmty. Coll., 1974-76. Supervising atty. clin. program environ. law NYU Sch. Law, 1972-76; chmn. Livingston Nat. Bank, 1984; bd. dir. Realty Transfer Co., 1982-. Assoc. editor: NJ Law Jour., 1957—62. Bd. dir. Morris County Urban League, 1956-51; mem. Urban Crisis Task Force, 1976; bd. dir. Youth Counseling League, 1969-93, pres., 1979-83, hon. dir.; bd. dir. Citizens Com. for Children NY, 1971-2002, now hon. dir., pres., 1972-77, Eleanor Roosevelt award, 2001; chmn. Joint Action for Children, 1976; trustee Natural Resources Def. Coun., 1973-2002, hon. trustee, 2002—, treas., 1973-76; bd. dir., sec. Environ. Advocates, 1972-78, hon. bd. dir., 1999--; bd. dir. Fountain House, 1966—, pres., 1975-78; mem. Adv. Coun. to NY State Office Mental Health, 1979-83; mem. Mental Health Svc. Coun., 1983-90; trustee Coro Found., 1979-85; mem. NY State Mental Hygiene Planning Coun., 1981-85; trustee Alice Desmond and Hamilton Fish Libr., 1981-98; trustee Schuyler Ctr. for Analysis and Avocacy, 1982—, pres., 1985-92; mem. adminstrv. bd. Lab. Ornithology Cornell U., 1982-87; trustee Hancock Shaker Village, 1986-92; mem. adv. bd. Panel of Ams., 1986—; bd. dir., sec. Episc. Charities, 1995-2002, Citizens for Global Solutions Edn. Fund, 2004—; trustee World Federalist Assn. Endowment Fund, 1998—, chmn., 2001—. Served to 2d lt. US Army, 1943-46. Decorated Purple Heart. Mem.: ABA, Assn. Bar City NY, NY State Bar Assn. (chmn. conf. on pub. interest law 1975), Columbia Law Sch. Alumni Assn. (treas. 1958—62), New Bedford Yacht Club, Millbrook Golf and Tennis Club, NY Health and Racquet Club, Princeton Club, Knickerbocker Club, Century Assn. Home: 130 East End Ave New York NY 10028-7553 Office: 120 E 56th St New York NY 10022

KEAN, JAMES CAMPBELL, lawyer; b. Colorado Spring, Colo., July 7, 1956; s. James Edward and Maxine Edna (Wolfe) K.; m. Suzanne Lee Bereswill; children: Kathryn Ashley, Jennifer Campbell. BS, U. Tex., Austin, 1978; JD, U. Houston, 1981, LLM in Environ., Energy & Natural Resources Law, 1996. Bar: Tex. 1981, U.S. Ct. Appeals (5th cir.) 1981, U.S. Dist. Ct. (so. dist.) Tex. 1982, U.S. Dist. Ct. (we. dist.) Tex. 1984, U.S. Dist. Ct. (no. dist.) Tex. 1986, U.S. Supreme Ct. 1987; cert. civil trial law. Assoc. Hoover, Cox & Shearer, Houston, 1981-83; ptnr. Dotson, Babcock & Scofield, Houston, 1983-89; litigation counsel Browning-Ferris Industries, Inc., Houston, 1989-93, sr. litigation counsel, 1993-94, asstn. gen. counsel mgr., litigation sect., 1994-95, sr. environ. counsel Houston, 1995—99; ptnr. Benthul & Kern, LLP, 2000—03, Squire, Sanders & Dempsey, LLP, Houston, 2003—. Mem. faculty Trial Advocacy Inst., Houston, 1986-92 Mem. ABA, Tex. Bar Assn., Fed. Bar Assn., Houston Bar Assn. (chmn. litigation sect. 1990-91, bd. dirs. environ. law sect. 2004-05) Roman Catholic. Avocations: bicycling, running, guitar. Home: 4811 Fern St Bellaire TX 77401-5031 Office: Squire Sanders & Dempsey LLP 600 Travis Ste 6250 Houston TX 77002 Office Phone: 713-546-3370. Business E-Mail: jkean@ssd.com.

KEAN, JOHN VAUGHAN, retired lawyer; b. Providence, Mar. 12, 1917; s. Otho Vaughan and Mary (Duell) Kean. AB cum laude, Harvard U., 1938, JD, 1941; grad., U.S. Army War Coll., 1970. Bar: R.I. 1942, U.S. Dist. Ct. R.I. 1946, U.S. Ct. Appeals (1st cir.) 1950, U.S. Ct. Appeals (4th cir.) 1955, U.S. Ct. Claims 1963, U.S. Supreme Ct. 1982. With Edwards & Angell, Providence, 1941—, ptnr., 1954-87, ret. ptnr., 1987—. Bd. dirs. Greater Providence YMCA, 1964—76; chmn. Downtown Providence YMCA, 1964—67, Providence Com. on Fgn. Rels., 1994—2000. Capt. AUS U.S. Army, 1943—46, capt. AUS U.S. Army, 1950—52, brig. gen. R.I. Nat. Guard U.S. Army, 1964—72. Decorated Legion of Merit. Mem.: ABA, R.I. Bar Assn., Res. Officers Assn., N.G. Assn., Soc. Cin. (hon.; R.I.), Assn. U.S. Army, Urban League R.I., Nature Conservancy (hon.), Alexis de Tocqueville Soc. R.I., Soc. Colonial Wars in R.I., Providence Art Club, Harvard Club R.I. (pres. 1964—66), Sakonnet Golf Club (Little Compton, R.I.), Army and Navy Club (Washington), Hope Club (bd. govs. 1996—2000, v.p.), Agawam Hunt Club. Office: c/o Edwards & Angell 2800 Financial Plz Providence RI 02903-2499 Home: 355 Blackstone Blvd Apt 334 Providence RI 02906-4957

KEAN, THOMAS H., former academic administrator, former governor; b. NYC, Apr. 21, 1935; s. Robert W. and Elizabeth Stuyvesant Kean; m. Deborah Bye; children: Thomas, Reed, Alexandra. AB, Princeton; MA, Columbia; LLD (hon.), Dartmouth Coll., 2005. Mem. NJ Assembly, 1967-77, asst. majority leader, 1970—71, majority leader, 1971—72, speaker, 1972, minority leader, 1974; acting gov. State of NJ, Trenton, 1973, gov., 1981-89; pres. Drew U., Madison, NJ, 1990—2005. Chmn., The Nat. Commn. on Terrorist Attacks Upon the US, 2002-04; bd. dirs. Beneficial Corp., Carnegie Corp. of NY, Robert Wood Johnson Found. Bd. dirs. World Wildlife Fund/Conservation Found.

KEANE, BERNADETTE ELIZABETH, health facility administrator; b. Balt., Jan. 30, 1967; d. Marie Agnes Debelius-Berry and Francis Gillan Debelius, Sr.; m. Mark Edward Keane, Sept. 8, 2001. BA in Bus., The Coll. of Notre Dame of Md., 1998. Medicaid and managed care receivable mgr. The Johns Hopkins Health Sys., Balt., 1999—2003, IS tng. mgr., 2003—. HMO/MCO receivable mgr. MedSTAR Health, Balt., 1998—99; receivable mgr. Mt. Wash. Pediatric Hosp., Balt., 1997—98. Vol. Our Lady of Fatima Ch., Balt., 1994—98. Mem.: Am. Assn. of Healthcare Adminstrn. Mgmt. (assoc.). Home: 4330 Penn Ave Nottingham MD 21236-1728 Office: The Johns Hopkins Health System 5300 Alpha Commons Ste 100 Baltimore MD 21224 Office Phone: 410-550-1344. Home Fax: 410-550-8016; Office Fax: 410-550-8016. Personal E-mail: berniekeane@aol.com. E-mail: bdebeli@jhmi.edu.

KEANE, BIL, cartoonist; b. Phila., Oct. 5, 1922; s. Aloysius William and Florence Rita (Bunn) K.; m. Thelma Carne, Oct. 23, 1948; children: Gayle, Neal, Glen, Christopher, Jeff. Student pvt. schs., Phila. Staff artist, Phila. Bull., 1945-58, syndicated cartoonist, Register & Tribune Syndicate, Des Moines, 1954—; creator, cartoonist: Channel Chuckles, 1954-77, Family Circus, 1960—; author numerous books of cartoon collections; cartoonist: Stars and Stripes, 1945. Served with US Army, 1942-45, PTO. Named Cartoonist of the Yr. Nat. Cartoonist Soc., 1982, Reuben award. Mem. Nat. Cartoonists Soc. (Best Syndicated Panel award 1967, 71, 74, Cartoonist of yr. 1982), Newspaper Features Coun., Cartoonists Guild. Office: King Features 888 7th Ave Ph2 New York NY 10106-0003*

KEANE, BRIAN TEAGAN, software development company executive; b. Boston, Feb. 6, 1961; s. John Francis and Marilyn (Teagan) K. BA, Harvard U., l983, MBA, l987. Trader Mitsui & Co. (USA), Inc., Miami, Fla., 1983-85; mktg. rep. Keane, Inc., Boston, 1987-88, nat. account mgr., 1988-89, br. mgr. New Providence, N.J., 1989—. Contbr. articles to yacht racing mag. Fund raiser Harvard U., Boston, l988. Mem. Soc. Info. Mgmt. Republican. Roman Catholic. Avocations: yacht racing, skiing, tennis.

KEANE, JAMES P., manufacturing executive; Joined Steelcase, Grand Rapids, Mo., 1997; sr. v.p. corp. strategy rsch. devel. Steelcase Inc., sr. v.p. fin. CFO, 2001—. Mem.: Microfield (bd. dirs. 1998—). Office: Steelcase Inc 901 44th St Grand Rapids MI 49506

KEANE, JOHN B., lawyer; b. Beverly, Mass., Aug. 25, 1946; m. Katherine Keane; 2 children. BA in economics, Brown U., 1968; JD, Harvard U., 1972. Bar: Mass. 1972, Ohio (corp.) 2004. With Hill & Barlow, Boston, 1972—80, N.E. Utilities, Berlin, Conn., 1980—2002, v.p., sec., gen. counsel corp., 1992—93, v.p., treas., 1993—98, v.p. adminstrn., 1998—2002; pres. Bainbridge Crossing Advisors, West Hartford, Conn., 2003—04; sr. v.p., gen. counsel, sec. Am. Electric Power Co. Inc., Columbus, Ohio, 2004—. Overseer Bushnell Ctr. for the Arts, Hartford, Conn.; corporator St. Francis Hosp. and Med. Ctr., Hartford, Conn. Office: Am Electric Power Co Inc 1 Riverside Plz Columbus OH 43215 Office Phone: 614-716-2929. Business E-Mail: jbkeane@aep.com.

KEANE, JOHN PATRICK, retired secondary education educator; b. NYC, Nov. 28, 1931; s. John and Mary (Walsh) K.; m. Lucille Ann Dunn, Apr. 3, 1976. BA in English, Iona Coll., 1954; JD, Fordham U., 1963, MS in Edn., 1965; EdM, Columbia U., 1973; MA in English, CUNY, 1984. Cert. secondary tchr. (English), adminstr., N.Y.C., N.Y. State. Tchr. area jr. h.s., N.Y.C., 1962-65; tchr. h.s. English N.Y.C. Bd. Edn., Bklyn., 1965-93; dean of boys W.H. Taft H.S., Bronx, 1969-72; reading, writing coord. John F. Kennedy H.S., Bronx, 1985-91; tchr. English advanced placement John F. Kennedy H.S., Manhattan Coll., Bronx, 1991-93, retired, 1993. Editor, compiler: (manual) Handbook for Teachers of Reading and Writing, 1987, Writing Sampler (student's work), 1989-91 biannual. Founder Hamilton Heights Dems., 1965-69; candidate NY State Assembly, 1965; Dem. candidate 1st Selectman, North Stonington, Conn., 1997; active North Stonington Bd. Edn; justice of peace North Stonington; past chmn. North Stonington Dem. Town Com.; music min. St. Mary's Ch., Groton. MA thesis placed on permanent display as model, Lehman Coll., CUNY, Bronx, 1984. Mem. NEA (del. local 2), Am. Fedn. Tchrs. (del. local 2), United Fedn. Tchrs. (del N.Y. State, chpt. leader, unity com.), N.Y. State United Tchrs., Delta Kappa Pi, Phi Delta Kappa. Roman Catholic. Avocations: poetry, drama, environmentalist. Home: 6 Wyassup Lake Rd North Stonington CT 06359-1124 E-mail: jpkwyassup@aol.com.

KEANE, KAREN M., auction house executive; m. Dan Elias. Masters Degree, Boston U. Mng. dir., v.p., exec. v.p. Skinner, Inc., Boston, ptnr., CEO, 1997—. Regular featured appraiser Antique Roadshow, PBS, 1996—. Contbr.

articles to profl. jours. Benefit auctioneer AIDS Action Com., Mass. Coll. Art, Inst. Contemporary Art, Boston; mem. bd. overseers DeCordova Mus., Lincoln, Mass. Office: Skinner INc 357 Main St Bolton MA 01740

KEANE, KEVIN W., federal agency administrator; Grad., U. Wis., Eau Claire, 1987. Reporter Fond du Lac (Wis.) Reporter Newspaper; asst. city editor Waukesha (Wis.) Freeman Newspaper; Washington corr. Thompson Newspapers, 1992—94; dir. comm., exec. asst. Gov. Tommy G. Thompson, 1994—2001; asst. sec. for pub. affairs U.S. Dept. HHS, Washington, 2001—. Fellow Paul Miller fellow, Freedom Forum. Office: Dept HHS Pub Affairs 200 Independence Ave SW Washington DC 20201

KEANE, MICHAEL J., lawyer; b. Boston, Aug. 27, 1953; BA, U. Md., 1974; JD magna cum laude, Stetson U., 1978. Bar: Fla. 1978, U.S. Dist. Ct. (no. and mid. dists.) Fla. 1979, U.S. Dist. Ct. (so. dist.) Fla. 1981; bd. cert. bus. litig and civil trial lawyer, Nat. Bd. Trial Advocacy; cert. mediator, Fla. Law clk. to Hon. Ben F. Overton Fla. Supreme Ct., 1978-79; atty. Keane, Reese & Vesely, P.A., St. Petersburg, 1979—. Adj. prof. Stetson U.; chmn. Fla. Bd. Bar Examiners, 2002—03. Editor-in-chief Stetson Law Rev., 1977—78. Office: 770 2nd Ave S Saint Petersburg FL 33701-4006

KEANE, WILLIAM FRANCIS, nephrology educator, research foundation executive; b. N.Y.C., Sept. 21, 1942; s. William F. and Theresa (Crotty) K.; m. Stephanie M. Gaherin, June 10, 1967; children: Alicia Anne, Elizabeth Gaherin. BS, Fordham U., 1964; MD, Yale U., 1968. Diplomate Am. Bd. Internal Medicine, Am. Bd. Nephrology. Intern Cornell N.Y. Hosp. Med. Ctr., 1968-69, resident, internal medicine, 1969-70, 72-73; fellow nephrology U. Minn. Hosps., Mpls., 1973-75; chmn. dept. Hennepin County Med. Ctr., Mpls., 1991—; asst. prof. medicine U. Minn., Mpls., 1976-82, assoc. prof., 1982-87, prof., 1987-89; pres. Minn. Med. Rsch. Found., Mpls., 1989-95; nephrologist Hennepin County Med. Ctr., Mpls., 1995. Chmn. dept. medicine Hennepin County Med. Ctr., 1992—. Mem. Am. Coll. Physicians, Am. Fedn. Clin. Rsch., Am. Soc. Clin. Pharmacology and Therapeutics, Am. Soc. Nephrology. Office: Hennepin County Med Ctr 701 Park Ave Minneapolis MN 55415-1623 Home: PO Box 665 Spring House PA 19477-0665

KEANEY, THOMAS ADDIS, academic administrator, management consultant, educator, military officer; b. Boston, June 14, 1940; s. James Francis and Anna Catherine (Keefe) K.; m. Mary Beth Martin, June 22, 1963; children: Thomas M., Kathleen P., Maura E., Anna C. BS, USAF Acad., Colo., 1962; MA, U. Mich., 1971, PhD, 1975. Commd. 2d lt. USAF, 1962, advanced through grades to col., 1982; assoc. prof. history USAF Acad., Colo., 1973-77; flight comdr., ops. officer 7th Bomb Wing USAF, Fort Worth, 1977-79, squadron comdr. B-52, 43rd Strategic Wing Andersen AFB, Guam, 1980-81, dep. base comdr., 1981-82, mil. planner air staff Washington, 1983-85, base comdr. Wurtsmith AFB, Mich., 1985-86; chmn. dept. mil. strategy Nat. War Coll., Washington, 1986-91; rschr., author Dept. Air Force, Washington, 1991-92; prof. mil. strategy Nat. War Coll., Washington, 1993-98; exec. dir. Fgn. Policy Inst. Nitze Sch. Advanced Internat. Studies, Johns Hopkins U., Washington, 1998—, exec. dir. Merrill Ctr. Strategic Studies, 2004—. Author: Strategic Bombers and Conventional Weapons, 1984, Gulf War Air Power Survey, 2 vols., 1993, Revolution in Warfare?, 1995, U.S. Allies in a Changing World, 2000, Armed Forces in the Middle East: Politics and Strategy, 2001. Roman Catholic. Home: 3047 Holly St Falls Church VA 22044-2617 Office: Nitze Sch Advanced Intl Studies Fgn Policy Inst 1619 Massachusetts Ave NW Washington DC 20036-2213 E-mail: tkeaney@jhu.edu.

KEANY, SUTTON, lawyer; b. Limon, Costa Rica, Feb. 19, 1943; s. Francis Xavier and Winsome (Scoltock) K.; m. Susanne Elvera Andover, June 12, 1965; children: Damian Winsome, Alison Arwen, Courtney Vanessa, Sutton Andover. AB, Yale U., 1963; JD, Harvard U., 1966. Bar: P.R. 1967, N.Y. 1971, U.S. Supreme Ct. 1977. Assoc. McConnell, Valdes, Kelly & Sifre, San Juan, P.R., 1966-70, Winthrop, Stimson, Putnam & Roberts, N.Y.C., 1970-75, ptnr., 1976—2001, Pillsbury Winthrop LLP, N.Y.C., 2001—. Mediator, early neutral evaluator U.S. Dist. Ct. (ea. dist.) N.Y., 1992—. Author: (with Jay M. Vogelson) Complying with International Antitrust Regulations; contbr. articles to Bklyn. Law Rev. Trustee Aperture Found., N.Y.C., 1988-92; dir. The Fund for Modern Cts., 1992-99, The Legal Aid Soc., 1995-2001. Mem. ABA, Assn. Bar City N.Y., Am. Arbitration Assn. (arbitrator 1990-2000), Yale Club of N.Y. Avocation: squash. Home: 20 Buttonball Ln Weston CT 06883 Office: Pillsbury Winthrop Shaw Pittman LLP 1540 Broadway New York NY 10036 Office Phone: 212-858-1724. E-mail: sutton.keany@pillsburylaw.com.

KEAR, MARIA MARTHA RUSCITELLA, lawyer; b. Phila., May 9, 1954; d. Ulysses Thomas and Joan Marie (Hagner) Ruscitella; m. Daniel John Kear, May 31, 1988; children: Caitlin Joan, Daniel John II. BA, Elmira Coll., 1975; JD, Del. Law Sch., 1978. Bar: Pa. 1979, Md. 1985, Va. 1991. Atty. pvt. practice, Wayne, Pa., 1979-80, Paoli, Pa., 1982-83; gen. counsel Theriault's, Inc., Annapolis, Md., 1983-85; corp. counsel Devel. Resources, Inc., Alexandria, Va., 1985-87; st. atty., asst. corp. sec. People's Drug Stores, Inc., Alexandria, Va., 1987-91; gen. counsel Jenco Group, Alexandria, Va., 1991-92; ptnr. Fullerton & Kear, Alexandria, Va., 1992-93; mng. ptnr. Kear & Gilbert, Fairfax, Va., 1993-97; owner The Kear Law Firm, Fairfax, Va., 1997—. Contbr. monthly newsletter The Dollmasters, 1983; contbr. The Law Forum, 1976—. Mem. Annapolis Law Ctr., 1983—; treas. Women's Law Ctr., Anne Arundel County. Mem. ABA, Pa. Bar Assn., Md. Bar Assn., Va. Bar Assn., Women's Bar Assn. Md., Internat. Conf. Shopping Ctrs., Nat. Retail Tenants Assn., Delta Theta Phi. Republican. Roman Catholic. Home: 6801 Tepper Dr Clifton VA 20124-1639 Office: 10605 Judicial Dr Ste A-2 Fairfax VA 22030-5167

KEARFOTT, JOSEPH CONRAD, lawyer; b. Martinsville, Va., Sept. 24, 1947; s. Clarence P. and Elizabeth (Kelly) K.; m. Mary Jo Veatch, Feb.10, 1969; children: Kelly, David. BA, Davidson Coll., 1969; JD, U. Va., 1972. Bar: Va. 1972, U.S. Dist. Ct. (ea. and we. dists.) Va. 1973, U.S. Ct. Appeals (4th cir.) 1973, U.S. Tax Ct. 1979, U.S. Ct. Appeals (1st cir.) 1981, U.S. Ct. Appeals (5th cir.) 1982. Law clk. to presiding judge U.S. Dist. Ct. (ea. dist.) Va., Richmond, 1972-73; assoc. Hunton & Williams, Richmond, 1973-80, ptnr., 1980—. Lectr. NITA program, Washington and Lee U., 1982-83, Va. Com. on Continuing Legal Edn., 1984—; mem. 4th Cir. Jud. conf. Co-author: Virginia Evidentiary Foundations, 1998. Mem. Richmond Bd. Housing, 1977-85, Richmond Dem. Com., 1978-82; trustee Libr. Va. Found., 1994-, chmn., 2004-, William Byrd Cmty. House, 1978-84, chmn., 1982-84; trustee United Way Svcs., Richmond, 1989-95, treas., 1993-95; trustee Libr. Va., 1989-94, vice chmn., 1990-91, chmn., 1991-92; trustee Trinity Episcopal Sch., 1986-94, treas., 1989-92, chmn., 1993-94; mem. Richmond Regional Bd., Thomas C. Sorensen Inst. Polit. Leadership, chmn., 2004; treas. St. Paul's Episcopal Ch., 2003—; fellow, Va. Law Found. 2005. Fellow: Va. Law Found.; mem.: ABA, Richmond Bar Assn., Va. Bar Assn. (Boyd Graves conf. chmn. 1999—2001), Order of Coif, Country Club Va. Avocations: golf, skiing. Home: 4436 Custis Rd Richmond VA 23225-1012 Office: Hunton & Williams East Tower Riverfront Pla 951 E Byrd St Richmond VA 23219-4074

KEARNEY, ANDREW WILLIAM, music educator, musician; b. Olean, N.Y., Nov. 16, 1972; s. Dennis Joseph and Gwendolyn Kearney. MusB in Music Edn., SUNY, Fredonia, 1994; MusM, Ithaca (N.Y.) Coll., 1998. Cert. tchr. N.Y. Elem. band dir. Owego (N.Y.) Apalachin Ctrl. Sch. Dist., 1994—2002, mid. sch. band dir., 2003—. Tech. crew advisor, asst. pep/marching band dir., soccer coach Owego Apalachin Ctrl. Sch. Dist. Sunday sch. supt. Owego 1st Ch. of the Nazarene, 2002—05. Grantee, Owego Apalachin Found. for Excellence in Edn., 2003—05. Mem.: N.Y. State Sch. Music Assn., Music Educators Nat. Conf. Avocations: hiking, kayaking, skiing. Home: 28 New St Apalachin NY 13732 Office: Owego Apalachin Ctrl Sch Dist 36 Talcott St Owego NY 13827 E-mail: akearney@oagw.stier.org.

KEARNEY, CHRISTOPHER J., manufacturing executive, lawyer; b. Mount Pleasant, Pa., 1955; BA, U. Notre Dame, 1977; JD, DePaul U. Law Sch., 1981. Sr. atty. Borg-Warner Chems.; sr. counsel, global materials bus. GE; sr. v.p., gen. counsel Grimes Aerospace Co., 1995—97; v.p., sec., gen. counsel SPX Corp., Charlotte, NC, 1997—2004, pres., CEO, dir., 2004—. Office: SPX Corp 13515 Ballantyne Corp Pl Charlotte NC 28277*

KEARNEY, JOHN WALTER, sculptor, painter; b. Omaha, Aug. 31, 1924; m. Lynn Haigh, June 2, 1951; children: Daniel Raymond, Jill Ann. Student, Cranbrook Acad. Art, 1946-48. Tchr., 1948—; co-founder, 1949; since pres. Contemporary Art Workshop Chgo. Mem. adv. bd. Art Inst. Chgo., A.R.S.G., Fine Arts Work Ctr., Provincetown, Mass., Chgo. Coun. on Fine Arts; vis. artist Am. Acad. in Rome, 1985, 92, 98, 03—; mem. summer faculty Fine Arts Work Ctr., Provincetown, 1996. Numerous one-man shows including A.C.A. Gallery, N.Y.C., (5 shows) 1964-79, 03-04, Ft. Wayne (Ind.) Mus., 1966, Galleria Schneider, Rome, 1969, Ill. Inst. Tech., 1976, 91, Ulrich Mus. Art, Wichita State U., 1976, Dirksen Fed. Bldg., Chgo., 1979, Cherrystone Gallery, Wellfleet, Mass., 1980, 92, Contemporary Art Workshop, 1981, 84, Goldman-Kraft Gallery, Chgo., 1985, others in N.Y.C., 1964-79, Venice, 1964, Rome, 1964, 68, Chgo., 1966-85, Berta Walker Gallery, Provincetown, Mass., 1992, 93, 95, 97, 2005, Mitchell Mus., Mt. Vernon, Ill., 1994; sculpture show 1998, Thomas McCormick Fine Art, Chicago, 1998. 2-person show, Art Inst. Chgo., A.R.S.G., 1977; represented in permanent collections, Mus. Contemporary Art, Chgo., Standard Oil Bldg., Chgo., Lawrence U., Appleton, Wis., Interfirst Plaza, Dallas, Mundelein Coll., Chgo., Norfolk (Va.) Art Mus., Ulrich Mus. Art of Wichita State U., Canton Art Inst., Capitol Bldg. Complex State Ill., Springfield, 1993, Detroit Children's Mus., Ft. Wayne Art Mus., Minn. Mus., St. Paul, New Sch. Social Rsch., N.Y.C., City of Chgo. Park Dist., Northwestern U., Roosevelt U., Chgo., U. Wyo. Art Mus., St. Lawrence U., Canton, N.Y., Wichita Art Mus., Youth Art Ctr., Fayetteville, Ark., Peace Mus., Chgo., Kans. Coliseum, Wichita, Fourth Fin. Ctr., Wichita, Kresge Collection, Troy, Mich., Ill. State Mus., Ill. Capitol Bldg. Mitchell Mus., Mt. Vernon, Ill., Cranbrook Acad. Art, Bloomfield Hills., Mich., Oakton Coll., Des Plaines, Ill., Oz Park, Chgo., Tin Man, Screcrow and Cowardly Lion, Goudy Sch., Chgo.; also pvt. collections including, John D. Rockefeller IV collection, Robert Mayer collection, spl. sculpture in bronze and silver, Sculpture Park (4 works) Munster Ind., 2000, steel bumpers sculpture, others. Trustee Ill. Com. for Handgun Control. Served with USN, World War II, PTO. Named Man of Year in Arts in Chgo., 1963; Fulbright grantee, 1963-64; Italian Govt. grantee, 1963-64; grantee Nat. Endowment Arts, 1968 Mem. Provincetown Art Assn. (former v.p. and trustee) Home: 830 W Castlewood Ter Chicago IL 60640-4217 Studio: (summer) 638 Commercial St Provincetown MA 02657 Office Phone: 773-472-4004. E-mail: jaklynk830@aol.com.

KEARNEY, JOSEPH D., dean, law educator; b. Dec. 28, 1964; BA summa cum laude, Yale U., 1986; JD cum laude, Harvard U., 1989. Bar: Ill., Wis. Law clerk to Judge Diarmuid F. O'Scannlain U.S. Ct. Appeals, Ninth Cir., Portland, Oreg., 1989—90; to Justice Antonin Scalia U.S. Supreme Ct., Washington, DC, 1995—96; assoc. Sidley & Austin, Chgo., 1990—95, 1996—97; asst. prof. Marquette U. Law Sch., 1997—2001, assoc. prof., 2001—03, dean, prof. law, 2003—. Contbr. articles to law jours. Mem.: Am. Inns Ct. (mem. Thomas Fairchild Chap. 1999—), Federalist Soc., Milwaukee Lawyers' Chap. (mem. bd. dirs. 2000—), Wis. Bd. Bar Examiners, Wis. Bar Assn. (mem. bd. dirs. Ea. Dist. 2002—). Office: Marquette U Law Sch 1103 W Wisconsin Ave PO Box 1881 Milwaukee WI 53201 Office Phone: 414-288-1955. E-mail: joseph.kearney@marquette.edu.

KEARNEY, JOSEPH LAURENCE, retired athletic conference administrator; b. Pitts., Apr. 28, 1927; s. Joseph L. and Iva M. (Nikirk) K.; m. Dorothea Hurst, May 13, 1950; children: Jan Marie, Kevin Robert, Erin Lynn, Shawn Alane, Robin James. BA, Seattle Pacific U., 1952, LLD, 1979; MA, San Jose State U., 1964; EdD, U. Wash., 1970. Tchr., coach Paradise (Calif.) H.S., 1952-53; asst. basketball coach U. Wash., 1953-54, athletic dir., assoc. dir., 1964-76; coach, tchr. Sunnyside (Wash.) H.S., 1954-57; prin., coach Onalaska (Wash.) H.S., 1957-61; prin. Tumwater (Wash.) H.S., 1961-63; asst. dir. Wash. H.S. Activities Assn., 1963-64; athletic dir. intercollegiate athletics Mich. State U., East Lansing, 1976-80, Ariz. State U., Tempe, 1980; commr. Western Athletic Conf., Denver, 1980-95; ret., 1995. Hon. chmn. Holiday Bowl, 1994, commr. emeritus, 1994. Pres. Cmty. Devel. Assn., 1957-61; bd. dirs. U.S. Olympic Com., 1985-94, chmn. games preparation com., 1985-2001. With USN, 1945—47. Recipient Disting. Svc. award Mich. Assn. Professions, 1979, Citation for Disting. Svc. Colo. Sports Hall of Fame, U.S. Olympic Com. Order of Olympic Shield, 1996. Mem. Nat. Football Found. (ct. of honors com., Western Regional Leadership award 1999), NCAA, Nat. Assn. Collegiate Dirs. Athletics (Corbett award 1991, Adminstr. Excellence award), Collegiate Commrs. Assn. (pres., award of Merit 1998), Am. Football Assn. (Commrs. award 1996, Athletic Dir.'s award 1998). Home: 2810 W Magee Rd Tucson AZ 85742-1500 Personal E-mail: josephlkea@msn.com.

KEARNEY, MICHAEL JOHN, banker; b. Clinton, Iowa, Jan. 2, 1940; s. Vincent Joseph and Evelyn Lorraine (Lynch) K.; m. Lisa von Kaenel, Sept. 8, 1973 (divorced); children: Bridget, Andrew, Patrick. BSEE, Washington U., St. Louis, 1962; MBA, U. Pa., 1964. Tech. draftsman Alfred E. Teves K.G., Frankfurt, Fed. Republic of Germany, 1966-67, Hussmann Refrigerator Co., Mexico City, Mex., 1967-68, gen. mgr. Guatamala City, Guatamala, 1968-71, internat. sales mgr. Buenos Ares, Argentina, 1971-72; loan officer 1st Nat. Bank Chgo., Mexico City, 1972-76, asst. v.p. Chgo., 1976-79, v.p., 1979-86, Phila. Nat. Bank, Chgo., 1986-88; regional mgr. Valuation Rsch. Corp., Milw., 1988-90, v.p. internat. ops., 1990-94; v.p., group head credit Deutsche Genossenschaftsbank, N.Y.C., 1995-97; v.p. Bank Hapoalim, Chgo., 1997—; pres. Pan Am. Bank, Chgo., 2001. Author: Midwest Families, 1979. Pres. St. Stephen's Green Property Owners, Northbrook, Ill., 1982-90, treas., 1980-82; mem. Northbrook Caucus, 1986-87, pres., 1987-89, chmn., Sesquicentennial Com., Clinton, Iowa, 2003-, bd. mem. Clinton County Hist. Soc., 2004-, chmn., Historic Preservation Commn., Clinton, 2004-; councilman Clinton City Coun., 2005— 1st lt. U.S. Army, 1964—66. Mem. Beta Theta Pi (dist. chief 1982-90, Dist. Chief of Yr. 1987, asst. gen. treas. 1995—), Omicron Delta Kappa (pres. 1961-62). Republican. Roman Catholic. Avocations: genealogy, running. Office: 12 N Michigan Ave 5th Floor Chicago IL 60603 Home: 200 Fifth Ave S #304 Clinton IA 52732 Office Phone: 847-877-0730. E-mail: Michael.Kearney.WG64@Wharton.UPenn.edu.

KEARNEY, STEPHEN MICHAEL, federal agency administrator; b. Washington, Apr. 8, 1956; s. John James and Helen Joan (Gaffney) K.; m. Julie Elizabeth Mosio, June 30, 1984; children: Justin Samuel, Caitlin Elizabeth. BA, McGill U., 1978; MBA, George Washington U., 1985; AMP, Harvard Bus. Sch., 2000. CFA, cert. Treasury profl. Fin. economist US Treasury Dept., Washington, 1978-80; investment officer US Postal Svc., Washington, 1980-81, investment mgr., 1981-90, treas., 1990-99, v.p., treas., 1999—2000, sr. v.p. corp./bus. devel., 2000—01, v.p. pricing, 2001—. Mem. sch. bd. of advisors, chmn. endowment com. St. Anselm's Abbey. First class honors, Univ. scholar McGill U., 1978; recipient Alexander Hamilton award for Excellence in Treasury Mgmt., 1996, 98, 99, Postmaster Gen. award, 1997, 99. Mem.: Assn. for Fin. Profl., Washington Soc. Investment Analysts, Washington Assn. Money Mgr. (pres. 1985—86), Assn. for Investment Mgmt. and Rsch., Fin. Execs. Internat., Beta Gamma Sigma. Democrat. Roman Catholic. Office: US Postal Svc 475 L Enfant Plaza SW Washington DC 20260-5014 Business E-Mail: skearney@usps.com.

KEARNS, DAVID RICHARD, chemistry professor; b. Urbana, Ill., Mar. 20, 1935; s. Clyde W. and Camille V. (French) K.; m. Alice Chen, July 5, 1958; children: Jennifer, Michael. BS in Chem. Engring., U. Ill., 1956; PhD., U. Calif., Berkeley, 1960. USAF doctoral fellow U. Chgo., 1960-61, MIT, Cambridge, 1961-62; asst. prof. chemistry U. Calif., Riverside, 1962-63, assoc. prof., 1964-67, prof., 1968-75, San Diego, 1975—. Assoc. editor Molecular Photochemistry, 1969-75, Photochemistry and Photobiology, 1971-75, Chem. Revs., 1974; assoc. editor Biopolymers, 1975-78, editorial bd., 1978-95. Sloan Found. fellow, 1965-67; Guggenheim fellow, 1969-70. Mem. Am. Chem. Soc. (Calif. sect. award 1973), Am. Phys. Soc., Am. Soc. Photobiology. Home: 8422 Sugarman Dr La Jolla CA 92037-2225 Office: U Calif San Diego Dept Chemistry La Jolla CA 92093 Office Phone: 858-534-2760. E-mail: drk@chem.ucsd.edu.

KEARNS, ELLEN CECELIA, lawyer; b. Washington, Apr. 15, 1945; d. Lawrence Mark and Mary (Moran) K. AB, Regis Coll., 1967; JD, Boston Coll., 1976. Bar: Mass. 1977, U.S. Supreme Ct. 1989, U.S. Ct. Appeals (1st cir.) 1979, U.S. Dist. Ct. (Mass.) 1980. Ptnr. Kearns & Rubin, Boston, 1992—99, Epstein Becker & Green, Boston, 1999—. Mem. Gov.'s Commn. on Status of Women, 1983-86; del. Mass. Dem. Conv., 1988-90; trustee, Regis Coll.; mem. Reading Mcpl. Light Bd.; founder, bd. dirs. Sister Spirit, Inc., 1990-91; lector St. Agnes Ch. Recipient Cushing-Gavin award for Excellence in Labor-Mgmt. Rels., 1993, Regis Coll. Alumni Achievement award 1993, Boston Coll. Law Sch. Alumnae of Yr., 1992. Mem. ABA (chmn. fed. labor stds. legis. com. 1991-94), Mass. Bar Assn. (labor and employment sect. coun. 1990-93), Nat. Conf. Women's Bar Assns. (pres. 2004-), Women's Bar Assn. (bd. dirs. 1990-92, treas. 1993-95, v.p. 1995-96), Boston Bar Assn. (chmn. labor law sect. 1988-90), Boston Coll. Alumni Assn. (pres.), Reading Jaycees (treas.). Democrat. Roman Catholic. Home: 2 Beaver Rd Reading MA 01867-1103 Office: Epstein Becker & Green 26th Fl 111 Huntington Ave Boston MA 02199

KEARNS, JAMES JOSEPH, artist; b. Scranton, Pa., Aug. 7, 1924; s. David Joseph and Ann Mary (Keller) K.; m. Betty Ione Hough, June 19, 1948; children: David, Diane, Mark, Aaron, Lisa. B.F.A., Sch. Art Inst. Chgo., 1950. Instr. Sch. Visual Arts, N.Y.C., 1960-90, Skowhegan (Maine) Sch. Painting, summers 1961-64. Illustrator: Can These Bones Live (E. Dahlberg), 1962, The Heart of Beethoven (S. Rodman), 1969; One-man shows include, Grippi Gallery, N.Y.C., 1956, 57, 60, 62, 68, Bloomfield (N.J.) Coll., 1967, 72, Sculpture Center, N.Y.C., 1973, Caldwell (N.J.) Coll., 1976, Trenton (N.J.) State Mus., 1984, group shows include, Whitney Mus. Am. Art, 1959, 60, 61, 80, Am. Fedn. Art, Art Inst. Chgo., 1979, traveling exhbns., Pa. Acad. Fine Arts, Phila., 1964, 65, Butler Inst. Am. Art, Youngstown, Ohio, 1964, Monmouth (N.J.) Mus., 1969, Squibb Gallery, Princeton, N.J., 1974, sculpture, Schenectady Mus., 1976, 35th Audubon Artists, N.Y.C., 1977, Whitney Mus. Am. Art, N.Y.C., 1980; represented in permanent collections, Mus. Modern Art, N.Y.C., Whitney Mus. Am. Art, Newark Mus. Art, Montclair (N.J.) Mus., Topeka Pub. Library, Smithsonian Nat. Collection Fine Arts, Washington, Hirshhorn Mus., Washington, also numerous pvt. collections. Served with U.S. Army, 1943-46. Recipient Ann. Disting. Artist-Tchr. award Sch. Visual Arts, 1990; Nat. Inst. Arts and Letters grantee, 1959 E-mail: jbkearns@ix.netcom.com.

KEARNS, KEVIN LAWRENCE, political association executive, lawyer; b. Bklyn., Sept. 5, 1947; s. John C. and Alice C. (Kelleher) K.; children: Kathleen, Christopher, Kevin Michael. BA, Fordham U., 1969; MA, SUNY, Stony Brook, 1970; JD, Bklyn. Law Sch., 1976. Bar: N.Y. 1977, D.C. 1977. Legis. counsel State Senator Sheldon Farber, Queens, N.Y., 1976-77; fgn. svc. officer U.S. Dept. State, Washington, 1977-90; assigned to Am. Consulate Gen., Frankfurt, Germany, 1977-79, Am. Embassy, Bonn, Germany, 1979—80, Seoul, 1981-83, Tokyo, 1986-88; congrl. fellow Senate Fgn. Rels. Com., 1988—89; dir. Office Strategic Trade, 1989—90; sr. rsch. fellow Econ. Strategy Inst., Washington, 1990-92, Mfg. Policy Project, Washington, 1992-93; pres. U.S. Bus. and Industry Coun., Washington, 1993—. Roman Catholic. Office: US Bus & Industry Coun 910 16th St NW Ste 300 Washington DC 20006-2903 Office Phone: 202-728-1980.

KEARNS, MERLE GRACE, state representative; b. Bellefonte, Pa., May 19, 1938; d. Robert John and Mary Katharine (Fitzgerald) Grace; m. Thomas Raymond Kearns, June 27, 1959; children: Thomas, Michael, Timothy, Matthew. BS, Ohio State U., 1960. Tchr. St. Raphael Elem. Sch., Springfield, Ohio, 1960-62; substitute tchr. Mad River Green Dist., Springfield, 1972-78; instr. Clark Tech. Coll., Springfield, 1978-80; commr. Clark County, Ohio, 1981-91; mem. Ohio Senate, Columbus, 1991-2000, majority whip, 1998—2000; mem. Ohio Ho. of Reps., Columbus, 2001—, majority floor leader, 2005—. Mem. fin. and appropriations com. Ohio Ho. of Reps., mem. health com., mem. joint com. agy. rule rev.; pres. Bd. County Commrs., 1982—83, 1987, 90. Sec. County Commrs. Assn. Ohio, 1988, 2d v.p., 1989—90, 1st v.p., 1990; mem. exec. com. Springfield Reps., 1984—2001; chair Ohio Children's Trust Fund, 1995—2000; past chair Legis. Office of Edn. Oversight; active NCSL Welfare Reform Task Force, 2001—05; vice-chair Policy Consensus Initiative Bd., 2002—; chair Head Start Plus Study Coun.; bd. dirs. Springfield Symphony, 1980—86, Arts Coun., 1980—85; bd. dirs., mem. exec. bd. Nat. Conf. State Legislatures, 2000—03. Named Woman of the Yr., Springfield Pilot Club, 1981, Wittenburg Woman of Accomplishment, 1991, Watchdog of Treasury, 1991, 1996, 2000, Legislator of the Yr., Assn. Mental Health and Drug Addition Svcs. Bds., 1996, Pub. Childrens Svcs. Agys. Ohio, 1999, Ohio Cmty. Colls., 1997, Ohio Disting. Nurses, 2000, Advance Practice Nurse Assn., 2002, Legis. Co-Person of the Yr., Assn. Joint Vocat. Sch. Supts., 1996, Mental Health Adv. of the Yr., 2002, Outstanding Head Start Legislator of the Yr., Miami Valley, 2002, Legislator of Yr., Ohio Fedn. Tchrs., 2003, Advocate of Yr., Ohio County Alzheimer Assn., 2004, Alzheimer Legis. Advocate of Yr., 2004; recipient Pub. Policy Leadership award, 1997, Disting. Svc. Pub. Ofcls. award, Assn. Ohio Philanthropic Homes, 1999, 1st Ann. Jane Swart Disting. Svcs. to Nursing, 2000, Citizenship award, Ohio State U. Coll. Human Ecology, 2000, Legislator of Yr., Behavioral Health Authorities Assn., 2003, Ohio Better World award, Ohio Mediation Assn., 2004;, Ohio State U. scholar, 1957—59. Mem.: LWV (bd. dirs. 1964—78, pres. 1975—78), Ohio Nurses Assn. (Legislator of the Yr. 1995, 1999), Rotary, Omicron Nu. Roman Catholic. Avocation: reading. Office: Ohio Ho of Reps 72d Dist 77 S High St Columbus OH 43215 Office Phone: 614-466-2097.

KEARNS, NANCY J., language educator; b. Huntsville, Ala. d. Wiley Thomas and Lillian Estelle Jones; m. William Thomas Kearns (dec.); 1 child, Michael Thomas. BA, Athens Coll., 1966; MA, U. North Ala., 1979, U. Valencia, 1980, Middlesex U., 2000. Tchr. Hartselle H.S., Ala., 1966—68, Decatur H.S., Ala., 1968—82; adj. faculty Okaloosa-Walton C.C., Niceville, Fla., 1983—90, U. Ala.-Huntsville, 1990—93; asst. prof. Ala. A&M U., Normal, 1993—. Contbr. articles to profl. jours. Mem.: Nat. Coun. Tchrs. English, Delta Kappa Gamma Beta chpt. Republican. Avocations: writing, poetry. Home: Box 253 5462 Winchester Rd New Market AL 35761 Office: Ala A&M U PO Box 333 Normal AL 35762

KEARNS, RICHARD P., diversified financial services company executive; Vice chmn. Price Waterhouse L.L.P. - U.S. (now PriceWaterhouse Coopers), N.Y.C., now global ptnr. affairs.

KEARNS, RONALD EDWIN, music educator; b. Raleigh, N.C., May 16, 1952; s. Laura Henderson Kearns; m. Lillie Broughton, Feb. 5, 1950; 1 child, Tiffany. MusM, Cath. U. Of Am., 1980; MusB in Edn., Knoxville Coll., 1974. Tchr. Balt. City Pub. Schools, Baltimore, 1975—84, Montgomery County (Md.) Pub. Schools, 1985—. Record prodr. Ron Kearns Prodns., Columbia, Md., 1980—. Prodr.: (record) Time To Let Go, Terell Stafford, Candid Records, Ltd, 1990, (record sound recording) Centripetal Force, Terell Stafford, Candid Records, Ltd, 1992, (sound recording) Introducing Kenny Reed, 1990, Paul Carr - Pc 10, 1987, Buck Hill-up Hill, 1991, Ronnie Wells Live At Montpelier, 1998, (musician) The Ron Kearns Quintet Live At Blues Alley, 1999; musician: (sound recording) Hand Prints, 1997. Regional pres. Md. Music Educators, Silver Spring, 1990—93; elder Presbyn. Ch., Washington, 1985—2002; hon. bd. mem. Fish Middleton Jazz Scholarship Fund, Silver Spring, Md., 1991—2002. Mem.: Md. Music Educators, Internat. Assn. Of Jazz Educators, Music Educators Nat. Conf., Alpha Phi Alpha Frat., Inc. Presbyterian. Office: Ron Kearns Prodns Po Box 514 Columbia MD 21045-0514 Personal E-mail: ron@ronkearns.com.

KEARNS, TERRANCE BROPHY, English language educator; b. Staten Island, N.Y., July 15, 1946; s. Francis and Geraldine Mae (Brophy) Kearns; m. Jean Theresa Watts, Feb. 23, 1968; children: Sean Brophy Kearns, Gwendolyn Elizabeth Kearns. BA cum laude, Holy Cross Coll., 1968; PhD, Ind. U., 1978. Teaching asst. Ind. U., Bloomington, 1969-74; instr. U. Cen. Ark., Conway, 1974-78, asst. prof., 1978-83, assoc. prof., 1983-89, prof. English, chair English dept., 1990-98. Campus rep. Mellon Fellowships in the Humanities, U. Cen. Ark., Conway, 1982-90. Assoc. editor SLANT: A Jour.

of Poetry, 1986-90; contbr. articles to profl. jours.; cons. (coll. textbooks) About Language, 1988, Discovering Language, 1991. Dist. commr. Boy Scouts Am., Conway, 1983, dist. com., 1984-89, mem. troop 71 com., 1990-91, dist. com., 1992—. Fenwick scholar Holy Cross Coll., 1967; Woodrow Wilson fellow Woodrow Wilson Found., Ind. U., 1968; recipient Dist. Award of Merit, Boy Scouts Am., Little Rock, 1989, Silver Beaver award, 2002. Mem. Assn. Lit. Scholars and Critics, Ark. Philol. Assn. (assoc. editor 1979-90), Mo. Philos. Assn. Office: U Cen Ark Dept English Conway AR 72035-0001

KEARNS, WARREN KENNETH, manufacturing executive, director; b. Wilmington, Ohio, July 15, 1929; s. Roy William and Marie (Kay) K. BS in Civil Engring., Case Western Res. U., 1951. Registered profl. engr., Ohio, Pa. Supr. Pa. R.R. Co., 1951-56; exec. v.p. Pitts. & W.Va. Rwy. Co., 1956-64; mgr. mfg. services Wheeling Steel Corp., W.Va., 1964-67; v.p. L. B. Foster Co., Pitts., 1967-70, pres., 1979-85; v.p. Sharon Steel Co., Pa., 1970-73; pres. Ogden Steel Co., Cleve., 1973-79, Warren Kearns Assocs., 1985—. Bd. dirs. N.W. Pipe & Casing Co., Portland, Oreg., Erie (Pa.) Forge & Steel Co. Mem.: Sigma Xi, Tau Beta Pi. Avocation: music. Home: 2 High St Hudson OH 44236-2912 Office: Warren Kearns Assocs 1507 Guenevere St Streetsboro OH 44241-5025

KEARNS, WILLIAM MICHAEL, JR., investment banker; b. Orange, N.J., June 26, 1935; s. William Michael and Doris Mae (Hodgkinson) K.; m. Patricia Anne Wright, Aug. 17, 1957; children: William Michael III, Susan Elizabeth (Mrs. Eric R. Hubbard), Kathleen Anne, Michael Patrick, Elizabeth Anne (Mrs. James P. Leonard). AB, U. Maine, 1957; AM, NYU, 1960; postgrad., Boston Coll. Law, 1957-58, NYU, 1960-64; LLD (hon.), Gonzaga U., 1988. With Chase Manhattan Bank, 1958-59; security analyst Hayden, Stone & Co., Inc., N.Y.C., 1960-62; assoc. instl. sales and syndicate dept. Kuhn, Loeb & Co., N.Y.C., 1962-64, asst. v.p., 1964-66, v.p., 1966-68, sales mgr., 1968-69, gen. ptnr., 1970-75; mng. dir. Kuhn, Loeb & Co., Inc., 1976-77, Lehman Bros. Kuhn Loeb Inc., 1977-84, Shearson Lehman Bros. Inc., N.Y.C., 1984—93; pres. W. M. Kearns & Co. Inc., Morristown, N.J., 1994—; vice chmn. Keefe Mgrs., LLC, N.Y.C., 1998—2002, chmn., co-CEO, 2002—. Bd. dirs. Selective Ins. Group, Inc., Branchville, N.J., Transistor Devices, Inc., Cedar Knolls, N.J.; trustee EQ Advisors Trust, AXA Fin. N.Y.C., AXA Equitable Life Ins. Co.; AXA Enterprise Funds; dir. U.S. Shipping Ptnrs. LLC, Edison, N.J.; sr. adv. Proudfoot Cons., Plc., London, 1997—; adv. dir. Gridley and Co. LLC, N.Y.C., 2001—, Pvt. Client Resources LLC; investment adv. Young Nichols Gilstrap, Inc., Phoenix, 1982-1992; sr. cons. Ing Baring Furman Selz LLC, N.Y.C., 1994-98; mem. faculty Fairleigh Dickinson U. Coll. Bus. Adminstrn., 1959-68; instr. security analysis N.Y. Inst. Fin. 1961-67; adj. prof. Grad. Sch. Bus. Adminstrn., NYU, 1971-72, chmn. NYU Forum Fin., 1971; lectr. Columbia U., Fairleigh Dickinson U., U. Rochester, NYU. Trustee Drumthwacket Found., Inc., 1985-95, Morristown-Beard Sch., 1982-88, Rider Univ., 1982-88, Morristown Meml. Health Found., 1999—2005; trustee Morris Mus., 1968-86, mem. adv. bd., 1987—; trustee Tri-County Scholarship Fund, 1982—, v.p., 1985-86, pres., 1987-89, pres. emeritus, 1990—; bd. dirs. Greater N.Y. coun. Boy Scouts Am., 1986—, exec. v.p., 1990—; bd. dirs. The Am. Friends of Covent Garden and the Royal Ballet, London, 1989—; mem. N.J. Rep. Fin. Com., 1978-84; adv. bd. Intrnat. Tennis Hall of Fame, 1984-86, bd. dirs., 1986-95, internat. coun., 1995-97; mem. adv. bd. Templeton Prize, Lyford Cay, Nassau, Bahammas, 1990—; exec. com. William E. Simon Grad. Sch., Bus. Adminstrn., U. Rochester, 1986—; devel. com. U. Maine, 1990-96, diocesan investment com., Diocese of Paterson N.J., 1986-2003; mem. Cardinal's Com. of Laity, N.Y.C.; mem. 1910 Soc., Boy Scouts Am., 2000; dir. Malta Human Resources Found., 2004—. Decorated Am. Assn. Master Knights Sovereign Mil. Order Malta; Pontifical Order of St. Gregory The Great; recipient Leadership award Tri-County Scholarship Fund, 1990, Leadership award Morristown Meml. Hosp., 1998, Augusta Stone award Morristown Meml. Health Found., 1999. Mem. Nat. Assn. Security Dealers (corp. fin. com. 1976-80), Securities Industry Assn. (minority capital com. 1978-86, exec. com. N.Y. dist. 1970, vice chmn. 1973, chmn. 1974), New Eng. Soc., Soc. Friendly Sons St. Patrick City of N.Y., Univ. Club (N.Y., trustee 1978-81), Bond Club N.Y., Econ. Club (N.Y.), Morris County Golf Club (Convent, N.J. gov. 1976-82), Green Jacket Club (Homestead, Va., founder 1991—), Morristown (N.J.) Club, Log Cabin Gun Club (Sterling, N.J.), Rolling Rock Club (Ligonier, Pa.), Mid-Ocean Club (Bermuda), Palm Beach (Fla.) Polo and Country Club, Beta Theta Pi, Kappa Phi Kappa. Roman Catholic. Office: W M Kearns & Co Inc 310 South St Morristown NJ 07960-7301 E-mail: wkearnes@wesandsons.com.

KEARSE, AMALYA LYLE, federal judge; b. Vauxhall, NJ, June 11, 1937; d. Robert Freeman and Myra Lyle (Smith) K. BA, Wellesley Coll., 1959; JD cum laude, U. Mich., 1962. Bar: N.Y. 1963, U.S. Supreme Ct. 1967. Assoc. Hughes, Hubbard & Reed, N.Y.C., 1962—69, ptnr., 1969—79; judge U.S. Ct. Appeals (2d cir.), 1979—. Lectr. evidence NYU Law Sch., 1968—69. Author: Bridge Conventions Complete, 1975, Bridge Conventions Complete, 3d edit., 1990, Bridge at Your Fingertips, 1980; transl., editor: Bridge Analysis, 1979; editor: Ofcl. Ency. of Bridge, 3d edit., 1976; mem. editl. bd.: Charles Goren, 1974—. Trustee N.Y.C. YWCA, 1976—79, Am. Contract Bridge League Nat. Laws Commn., 1975—; mem. Pres.'s Com. on Selection of Fed. Jud. Officers, 1977—78; Bd. dirs. NAACP Legal Def. and Endl. Fund, 1977—79, Nat. Urban League, 1978—79. Named Women's Pairs Bridge Champion Nat. div., 1971, 1972, World div., 1986, Nat. Women's Teams Bridge Champion, 1987, 1990, 1991; named to, Bridge Hall of Fame, 2004. Mem.: ABA, Lawyers Com. for Civil Rights Under Law (mem. exec. com. 1970—79), Am. Law Inst., Assn. of Bar of City of N.Y. Office: US Ct Appeals US Courthouse 40 Foley SqRm 2001 New York NY 10007

KEARSE, JEVON, professional football player; b. Ft. Myers, Fla., Sept. 3, 1976; Student, U. Fla. Defensive end Tennessee Titans, Nashville, 1999—2003, Philadelphia Eagles, 2004—. Named All-Pro, AP, Pro Football Weekly, Dr. Z of Sports Illustrated, 1999, Defensive Rookie of Yr., AP, Football News, Football Digest, Pro Football Weekly/Pro Football Writers Assn. of Am., 1999, AFC Defensive Player of Month of Dec., 1999, NFL Rookie of Month of Sept., Nov., Dec., 1999, NFL Pass Rusher of Yr., NFL Alumni group, All-AFC and All-Rookie, Football News, Pro Football Weekly, 1999, All-Pro, All-Rookie, Football News, Coll. and Pro Football Weekly, 1999. Office: c/o Philadelphia Eagles 1 Novacare Way Philadelphia PA 19145

KEATING, CANDICE SUE, elementary school educator; b. Buffalo, Mar. 13, 1972; d. John and Carolyn Sue McCoy; m. Jeff Keating; children: Jeffrey, Kayla. B Sociology, Rollins Coll., 1994; MS in Reading, Canisius Coll., 1996. Cert. reading, lang. arts, early and mid. childhood tchr. 4th grade tchr. J.D. Parker Sch. Sci., Math. and Tech., Stuart, Fla., 1997—. Adj. prof. Fla. Atlantic U., Jupiter, Fla., 1999—; reading first developer Just Read, Fla., No Child Left Behind, Tallahassee, 2003—; tchr., Iwawa, Poland, 1997. Pres. PTO, Stuart, 2004—05; women's advocate for abused women Sitka, Alaska, 1995. Grantee, Martin County, Reading is Fundamental program, 2004; Ednl. Resource Ctr. grantee, Martin County Edn. Found., 2004—05. Mem.: NEA (assoc.), Martin County Edn. Assn. (assoc.), Am. Fedn. Fedn. (assoc.), Internat. Reading Assn. (assoc.). Office: Palm City Elem Sch 1951 SW 34th St Palm City FL 34990 Office Phone: 772-219-1565. Personal E-mail: keatinc@martin.k12.fl.us.

KEATING, CHARLES, actor; b. London, Oct. 22, 1941; married; children: Sean, Jamie. Actor: (films) Funny Money, 1982, The Rocking Horse Winner, 1983, Awakenings, 1990, The Bodyguard, 1992, The Thomas Crown Affair, 1999, Harlem Aria, 1999, Deuce Bigelow: European Gigolo, 2005; (TV series) As the World Turns, 1989-90, Another World, 1983-85, 91-98, 99, All My Children, 1987-88, Going to Extremes, 1992-93, Port Charles, 1997-2003, (TV miniseries) Brideshead Revisited, 1982, Fresno, 1986, (TV films) Richard II, 1978, A Deadly Game, 1979, A Talent for Murder, 1984; (theatre) Loot!, The Doctor's Dilemma, A Man for All Seasons, Light Up the Sky, Pygmalion. Recipient Best Lead Actor in Drama Series Daytime Emmy. Avocations: gardening, painting.*

KEATING, EUGENE KNEELAND, animal scientist, educator; b. Liberal, Kans., Feb. 15, 1928; s. Arthur Hitch and Nilie Charlotte (Kneeland) K.; m. Iris Louise Myers, Aug. 12, 1951; children— Denise Keating Schnagl, Kimberly Alan. BS, Kans. State U., 1953, MS, 1954; PhD, U. Ariz., 1964. Owner, mgr. ranch, Kans., 1954—; instr., farm mgr. Midwestern U., Wichita Falls, Tex., 1957-60; rsch. asst. U. Ariz., Tucson, 1960-64; prof. animal sci. Calif. State Poly. U., Pomona, 1964-98, prof. emeritus, 1998—, chmn. dept., 1971-78. Contbr. articles to profl. jours. Bd. dirs. Los Angeles County Jr. Livestock Fair, 1971-79, chmn., 1975. With USAAF, 1946-49. Recipient Farm Bur. Century award, 2000. Fellow: Am. Inst. Chemists; mem.: NRA Whittington Ctr. Founders Club, NRA (benefactor), Brit. Soc. Animal Prodn., Am. Soc. Lab. Animal Sci., Coun. for Agrl. Sci. and Tech. (life), Am. Soc. Animal Sci. (life), Nat. Intercollegiate Rodeo Assn. (West Coast regional faculty dir. 1972—76), Western Heritage Ctr., Rep. Nat. Com. (life), Calif Rifle and Pistol Assn. (Gold Eagle), Am. Legion, Block and Bridle Club, Santa Fe Trail and Gun Club (life), Ind. Order Foresters, Sigma Xi, Alpha Zeta, Gamma Sigma Delta, Phi Lambda Upsilon. Presbyterian. Home: 149 W Loretto Ct Claremont CA 91711-1739 Office: 3801 W Temple Ave Pomona CA 91768-2557

KEATING, FRANCIS ANTHONY, II, former governor, lawyer; b. St. Louis, Feb. 10, 1944; s. Anthony Francis and Anne (Martin) K.; m. Catherine Dunn Heller, 1972; children: Carissa Herndon, Kelly Martin, Anthony Francis III. AB, Georgetown U., 1966; JD, U. Okla., 1969. Bar: Okla. 1969. Spl. agt. FBI, 1969-71; asst. dist. atty. Tulsa County, 1971-72; mem. Okla. Ho. of Reps., 1972-74, Okla. Senate, 1974-81; U.S. atty. No. Dist. Okla., 1981-84; asst. sec. U.S. Treasury Dept., Washington, 1985-88; assoc. atty. gen. Dept. Justice, 1988-89; gen. counsel, acting dep. sec. Dept. Housing and Urban Devel., Washington, 1989-93; gov. State of Okla., 1995—2003; pres. Am. Coun. Life Insurers, Washington, 2003—. Mem. Okla. Bar Assn. Republican. Office: Am Coun Life Insurers 101 Constitution Ave NW Washington DC 20001*

KEATING, ISABEL, actress; Actor: (regional stage shows) Dinner With Friends, The Rise and Fall of Little Voice, Three Sisters, One Foot on the Floor, Chilean Holiday, Indian Ink, 2000 (Helen Hayes award best actress, 2000); (Broadway plays) Enchanted April, 2003, The Boy From Oz, 2003 (nominated Outer Critics Cir. best actress, 2004, Tony nom. best featured actress in a musical, 2004, Drama Desk award best featured actress in a musical, 2004), (off Broadway shows) Bonnie, Once in a Lifetime, Waiting at the Waters Edge, The Museum of Dreams, On the March to the Sea, 2005, Lady Windermere's Fan, 2005. Office: c/o Blue Ridge Entertainment 41 Union Sq W New York NY 10003*

KEATING, SISTER KEVINA, nun, education educator; arrived in US, 1966; d. Patrick and Deborah Keating. BA cum laude, Dominican Coll., 1974; MA, U. San Francisco, 1985, EdD, 1987; MA, Stanford U., 1988. Joined Sisters of Charity of the Incarnate Word, 1966; cert. tchr. Tex., H.S. math. and English Tex. State Bd. Edn. Nun Sisters of Charity of Incarnate World, Houston, 1966—; English tchr. St. Francis of Assisi, Houston, 1970—71; English and math. tchr. Jesse Jones Sr. HS, Houston, 1973—74, Our Lady of Fatima Sch., Texas City, Tex., 1974, prin., 1984—85; English and math. tchr. St. Ann Sch., Salt Lake City, 1975—81, prin., 1981—83, Immaculate Heart of Mary Sch., Big Spring, Tex., 1983—84; dir. tchr. edn., asst. prof. U. San Francisco, 1987—96; asst. to v.p., assoc. prof. U. Incarnate Word, San Antonio, 1997—98; v.p. on congl. leadership Congregation of Sisters of Charity of the Incarnate Word, Houston, 1998—. Dir. planning Sisters of Charity of the Incarnate Word, Houston, 1991—94, Houston, 1998—; presenter in field. Co-author: Pioneer Mentoring in Teacher Preparation, 2001; contbr. chpt. to book. Chair Intercongregational Literacy Ministry, Houston, 1999—; com. mem. U.S./Mexico border conditions Leadership Conf. Women Religious, Region 12, 2001—; bd. mem. McCauley Housing, Silver Springs, Md., 1999—2001, CHRISTUS Health, Dallas, 1999—. Multicultural Action Plan grantee, U. San Francisco, 1996. Mem.: Am. Assn. Colls. Tchrs. Edn., Assn. Tchr. Educators, Nat. Cath. Ednl. Assn., Phi Delta Kappa. Democrat. Avocations: hiking, dance, reading, concerts. Office: Sisters of Charity of the Incarnate Word 6510 Lawndale Ave Houston TX 77023 Office Phone: 713-928-6053. Business E-Mail: keating@ccvi-vdm.org.

KEATING, MARY TUCKER, retired school system administrator; b. Vienna, Ga., Apr. 6, 1939; d. Julian Ray and Mary Ward Tucker; m. Charles Leonard Keating, July 4, 1981; m. Herschel Arnold Gentry, July 21, 1956 (div. Oct. 12, 1979); children: Georganne Nmn Waters, Julie Ruth Thames, Joy Louisa Woodfin. BA, Tift Coll., Forsyth, Ga., 1972; MEd, Ga. State U., 1976; EdD, Nova Southeastern U., 1996. Cert. social studies tchr. Ga. Profl. Standards Commn., 1972, gifted edn. tchr. Ga. Profl. Standards Commn., 1973, ednl. leadership Ga. Profl. Standards Commn., 1990, tchr. support specialist Ga. Profl. Standards Commn., 1994. Tchr. history Crawford County Schs., Roberta, Ga., 1972—73, tchr. gifted, 1973—77, dir. spl. projects, 1977—79; cons. gifted edn. Ga. Dept. of Edn., Atlanta, 1980—81; tchr. gifted Arbor Sta. Elem. Sch., Douglasville, Ga., 1987—90; asst. prin. Chapel Hill Elem. Sch., Douglasville, Ga., 1990—94, Matilda Harris Elem. Sch., Kingsland, Ga., 1994—96; prin. Woodbine Elem. Sch., Ga., 1996—2000; curriculum dir. Camden County Schs., Kingsland, Ga., 2000—04. Dir. Ga. Partnership for Excellence in Edn., Atlanta, 2000—; mem. Adult Literacy Coun., Kingsland, Ga., 2000—, Ga. PreK-16 Coun., Brunswick, 2000—04; presenter in field. Mem./officer PTA, Macon, Roberta, Ga., 1963—79, NOW, Roberta, Ga., 1975—79; mem. Camden County Libr. Bd., Kingsland, Ga., 2000—05, Coastal Conservation Coun., St. Marys, Ga., 2001—04; bd. dirs. Friends of the Pk., St. Marys, Ga., 2001—03; vol. Hospice of the Golden Isles, Brunswick, Ga., 2005—05, Dem. Party, Roberta, Ga., 1968—70, Habitat for Humanity, St. Marys, Ga., 2004—05; mem. Our Lady Star of the Sea Cath. Ch., St. Marys, Ga., 1994—2005. Recipient Exemplary Sch. Leader award, Ga. Leadership Inst., 2003, Oxford Roundtable participant, Oxford U., 2004. Mem.: ASCD (assoc.), Ga. Compensatory Edn. Leaders (assoc.), Ga. Assn. of Elem. Sch. Prins. (assoc.), Internat. Reading Assn. (assoc.), Nat. Assn. for Gifted Edn. (assoc.), Ga. ASCD (assoc.), Ga. Assn. of Ednl. Leaders (assoc.), Nat. Alliance of Black Sch. Educators (assoc.), PA of Ga. Educators (assoc.), Delta Kappa Gamma. Roman Catholic. Avocations: reading, travel, dancing. Home: 706 Hill St Saint Marys GA 31558 Personal E-mail: cmkeating@tds.net.

KEATING, MICHAEL BURNS, lawyer, educator; b. Cambridge, Mass., May 17, 1940; s. John Stuart and Anne Veronica (Burns) K.; m. Martha Harrison McGuire, OCt. 12, 1974; children: Michael Burns, Andrew Wade, Lucy Harrison. BA, Williams Coll., 1962; LLB, Harvard U., 1965. Bar: Mass. 1965, U.S. District Ct. Mass. 1966. Law clk. to presiding justice Superior Ct. Mass., Boston, 1965-66, U.S. Dist. Ct. Mass., Boston, 1966-67; assoc. Foley Hoag, Boston, 1967-74, ptnr., 1974—. Adj. prof. trial practice Northeastern Law Sch., Boston, 1985—. Trustee Brooks Sch., North Andover, Mas., 1978—, Foley, Hoag & Eliot Found., Boston, 1981-89, Williams Coll., Williamstown, Mass., 1996—; pres. Crime & Justice Found., Boston, 1985-94; bd. dirs. Navy Meml. Found., 1994—. Lt. (j.g.) USNR, 1967-72. Fellow Am. Coll. Trial Lawyers, Harvard Club; mem. Boston Bar Assn. (pres. 2001-02). Democrat. Roman Catholic. Avocations: tennis, squash, skiing, sailing. Home: 3 W Cedar St Boston MA 02108-3535 Office: Foley Hoag 155 Seaport Blvd Boston MA 02210-2600 Office Phone: 617-832-1136. Business E-Mail: mkeatinge@foleyhoag.com.

KEATING, PATRICK J., academic administrator; BA in Econs., D in Higher Edn. Adminstrn., Mich. State U.; MA in Pub. Policy Studies, U. Mich. Budget officer Mich. State U., 1978—83; v.p. univ. planning Carnegie Mellon U., v.p. bus., CFO, 1990; v.p., CFO UNext, Inc.; exec.v .p. Boston Coll., Chestnut Hill, Mass., 2001—. Office: Boston Coll Botolph House Genrl 18 Old Colony Rd Chestnut Hill MA 02467

KEATING, TIM, chef; Studied with. Chief La Reserve Omni Hotel; cook Rancho Mirage, Ritz-Carlton Resort, Le Meridien; owner Catering Co., San Diego; chief DeVille Four Seasons, Houston, 2002—. Serves regional steering com. Chefs Collaborative; mem. Houston chpt. Am. Heart Assn. Com. Office: Deville Restaurant Four Seasons Hotel 1300 Lamar St Houston TX 77001

KEATING, TIMOTHY J., career military officer; b. Dayton, Ohio; m. Wanda Lee Doerkson; children Daniel, Julie. Grad., U.S. Naval Acad., 1971; completed flight tng., 1973. Commd. ensign USN, 1971; advanced through grades to adm., 2004; duty USS Mason (DD-852) We. Pacific; ordered to VA-82 deploying USS Nimitz (CVN-68); reported to VA-122 NAS Lemoore, Calif., 1978; staff LSO with comdr. carrier air wing fifteen USS Kitty Hawk, We. Pacific, Indian Ocean; adminstrv. officer, ops. officer, maint. officer VA-94 USS Enterprise, We. pacific, 1982-84; aide, flat lt. to Comdr. in Chief U.S. Pacific Cmd., 1984-87; comdr. VFA-87, deployed with CVW-8 USS Theodore Roosevelt North Atlantic and Mediterranean, 1987; head aviation LCDR/jr. officer assignments br. naval mil. personnel cmd., Washington; dep.comdr. carrier air wing seventeen combat. ops. Desert Storm USS Saratoga, 1991; CNO fellow strategic studies group Newport, R.I.; temp. duty with joint task force S.W. Asia Riyadh, Saudi Arabia; comdr. Naval Strike Warfare Ctr., 1994—95; dep. comdr. carrier air wing nine USS Nimitz Arabian Gulf; dir. aviation officer distbn. divsn. naval mil. personnel cmd., 1995—96; comdr. Battle Force 7th Fleet (carrier group 5, carrier strike force) USN, 1998—2000; dep. chief naval ops., (plans policy & ops.) US Navy, 2000—02; comdr. US Naval Forces Cent. Command, US Fifth Fleet, 2002—03; dir. The Joint Staff, Washington, 2003—04; comdr. N.Am. Aerospace Defense Command, Peterson AFB, Colo., 2004—, US Northern Command, 2004—. Decorated Legion of Merit with gold star. Office: Northern Command Public Affairs 250 Vandenberg Ste B016 Peterson Afb CO 80914*

KEATING, TIMOTHY JAMES, academic administrator, language educator; b. Elgin, Ill., Oct. 6, 1946; s. John Richard and Doris Anna (Fischer) K.; m. Jayne Annette Stefani, Aug. 17, 1968; children: Ruth Johanna, Jacob Michael. BA, Gonzaga U., 1968; MA, SUNY, Albany, 1971, PhD, 1981. Instr. Spanish Hartwick Coll., Oneonta, N.Y., 1971-75, asst. prof. Spanish, 1975-81, assoc. prof. Spanish, 1981-91, prof. Spanish, 1991-93, asst. dean spl. programs, 1985-87, assoc. dean, 1987-88, acting provost, 1988-89, assoc. dean for acad. affairs, 1987-93; dean Franklin Coll., Lugano, Switzerland, 1993-2001; dean arts and scis. Coll. So. Md., La Plata, 2001—. Evaluator programs abroad Commn. on Higher Edn. Mid. States, Phila., 1983—. Translator: (book, poetry) Six Cuban Poets, 1983. Pres. bd. dirs. Modern Dance Artists, Oneonta, 1990-93; commr. Zoning Bd. Appeals, Oneonta, 1989-93; mem. internat. adv. bd. Batuz Found., Washington, 1991. NDEA Title IV Grad. fellow, SUNY, Albany, 1968-71. Mem. MLA, Am. Assn. Tchrs. Spanish and Portuguese. Avocations: soccer, travel. Office: Coll So Md PO Box 910 La Plata MD 20646-0910 E-mail: timothyk@csm.cc.md.us.

KEATINGE, ROBERT REED, lawyer; b. Berkeley, Calif., Apr. 22, 1948; s. Gerald Robert and Elizabeth Jean (Benedict) K.; m. Katherine Lou Carr, Feb. 1, 1969 (div. Dec. 1981); 1 child, Michael Towne; m. Cornelia Elizabeth Wyma, Aug. 21, 1982; 1 child, Courtney Elizabeth. BA, U. Colo., 1970; JD, U. Denver, 1973, LLM, 1982. Bar: Colo. 1974, U.S. Dist. Ct. Colo. 1974, U.S. Ct. Appeals (10th cir.) 1977, U.S. Tax Ct. 1980. Ptnr. Kubie & Keatinge, Denver, 1974-76; pvt. practice Denver, 1976; assoc. Richard Young, Denver, 1977-86; counsel Durham & Assoc. P.C., Denver, 1986-89, Durham & Baron, Denver, 1989-90; project editor taxation Shepard's/McGraw-Hill, Colorado Springs, Colo., 1990-96; of counsel Holland & Hart, LLP, Denver, 1992—. Lectr. law U. Denver, 1982-92, adj. prof. grad. tax program, 1983-94; spkr. in field. Author, cons. (CD-ROM) Entity Expert, 1996; co-author: Ribstein and Keatinge on Limited Liability Companies, 1992; contbr. articles to profl. jours. and treatises. Recipient Law Week award U. Denver Bur. Nat. Affairs, 1974. Fellow: Am. Coll. of Tax Counsel; mem.: Am. Law Inst., Denver Bar Assn., Colo. Bar Assn. (taxation sect. exec. coun. 1988—94, sec.-treas. 1991—92, chmn. 1993—94, bd. govs. 1996—2004, bus. law sect. sec.-treas. 2001—03, vice chair 2003—, ethics com., corp. code revision com., co-chmn. ltd. liability co. revision com.), ABA (chmn. subcom. ltd. liability cos. of com. on partnerships 1990—95, ABA adviser to Uniform Ltd. Liability Co. Act 1995, chmn. com. on taxation 1995—99, mem. ho. of dels. 1996—2002, ABA/Nat. Conf. Commrs. on Uniform State Laws joint editl. bd. on uninc 1996—, editl. bd. ABA/BNA Lawyer's Manual on Professional Conduct 1998—2002, chmn. com. on partnerships 2000—04, ABA adviser to Revision of Uniform Ltd. Partnership Act 2001). Home: 460 S Marion Pky Apt 1904 Denver CO 80209-2544 Office Phone: 303-295-8595. Business E-Mail: rkeatinge@hollandhart.com.

KEATON, DIANE, actress; b. Santa Ana, Calif., Jan. 5, 1946; Student, Neighborhood Playhouse, N.Y.C., 1968. Appeared on N.Y. stage in Hair, 1968, Play It Again Sam, 1969, The Primary English Class, 1976; appeared in numerous films including Lovers and Other Strangers, 1970, Play It Again Sam, 1972, The Godfather, 1972, Sleeper, 1973, The Godfather Part II, 1974, Love and Death, 1975, I Will, I Will...For Now, 1975, Harry and Walter Go To New York, 1976, Annie Hall, 1977 (Best Actress Acad. award 1978, Brit. Acad. Best Actress award 1978, N.Y. Film Critics Circle award 1978, Nat. Soc. Film Critics award 1978), Looking for Mr. Goodbar, 1977, Interiors, 1978, Manhattan, 1979, Reds, 1981 (Acad. award nominee), Shoot the Moon, 1982, Little Drummer Girl, 1984, Mrs. Soffel, 1984, Crimes of the Heart, 1986, Radio Days, 1987, Baby Boom, 1987, The Good Mother, 1988, The Lemon Sisters, 1990, The Godfather Part III, 1990, Father of the Bride, 1991, Manhattan Murder Mystery, 1993, Look Who's Talking Now, 1993 (voice), Father of the Bride 2, 1995, Marvin's Room, 1996, First Wives Club, 1996, The Only Thrill, 1997, The Other Sister, 1999, Hanging Up, 2000, Town and Country, 2001, Plan B, 2001, Something's Gotta Give, 2003 (Golden Globe for best actress in a musical or comedy, 2004, Acad. Award nomination for best actress, 2004, Screen Actors Guild Award nomination for best actress, 2004); (TV movie) Running Mates, 1992, Amelia Earhart, 1994, Sister Mary Explains It All, 2001, Crossed Over, 2002, On Thin Ice, 2003; dir. film: Heaven, 1987, Wildflower, 1991, Unstrung Heroes, 1995; accomplished artist and singer; author book of photographs: Reservations, 1980; editor: (with Marvin Heiferman) Still Life, 1983, Mr. Salesman, 1994; prodr.: The Lemon Sisters, 1990; exec. prodr.: Northern Lights (TV), 1997. Recipient Golden Globe award, 1978 Office: John Burnham William Morris Agy 151 S El Camino Dr Beverly Hills CA 90212-2704

KEATON, JOHN J., artist; b. Chester, Pa., Jan. 8, 1959; s. John Barnett Keaton and Florence May Moriarity; 1 child, Daniel Jon. B, ILS, Germany, 1985. Cert. graphic design instr. Calif., 2001. Product designer Lava Enterprises, San Diego, 1996—2002; muralist John Keaton Art & Design, San Diego. Muralist John Keaton Art & Design, San Diego. Author: (biography) Leonardo DaVinci: A Legacy of Immortal Genius; paintings, Flower SSeries, Fantascapes. With USAF, 1979—82. Mem.: Artists Rights Soc. Roman Catholic. Personal E-mail: johnkeaton1@comcast.net.

KEATON, MICHAEL, actor, comedian; b. Coraopolis, Pa., Sept. 5, 1951; m. Caroline MacWilliams, 1982 (div. 1990); 1 child, Sean. Student, Kent State U. With comedy group Second City, L.A. Appeared in movies Night Shift, 1982, Mr. Mom, 1983, Johnny Dangerously, 1984, Gung Ho, 1985, The Squeeze, 1987, Touch and Go, 1987, Beetlejuice, 1988 (Nat. Soc. Film Critics Best Actor award 1988), Clean and Sober, 1988 (Nat. Soc. Film Critics Best Actor award), The Dream Team, 1989, Batman, 1989, Pacific Heights, 1990, One Good Cop, 1991, Batman Returns, 1992, Much Ado About Nothing, 1993, My Life, 1993, The Paper, 1994, Speechless, 1994, Multiplicity, 1996, Jackie Brown, 1997, Inventing the Abbotts, 1997, Desperate Measures, 1998, Out of Sight, 1998, Jack Frost, 1998, A Shot at Glory, 2000, Quicksand, 2001, First Daughter, 2004, White Noise, 2005, Game Six, 2005, Herbie: Fully Loaded, 2005; TV series include All's Fair, 1976-77, The Mary Tyler Moore Hour, 1979, Working Stiffs, 1979, Report to Murphy, 1982; Studs Lonigan (mini-series), 1979; TV movies: Live From Baghdad, 2002; TV guest appearances include Mister Roger's Neighborhood, 1968, Maude, 1975, (voice) The Simpsons, 1989, Frasier, 1993, (voice) King of the Hill, 1997, (voice) Gary the Rat, 2003; exec. prodr. Body Shots, 1999. Office: care ICM Management 8942 Wilshire Blvd Beverly Hills CA 90211-1934*

KEATON, MOLLIE M., elementary school educator; d. Lorenzo and Katie Mae (Thomas) K. BS, Kent State U., 1976; MA, Atlanta U., 1980, EdD, 1985. Counselor, asst. prin. DeKalb County Bd. Edn., Decatur, Ga.; rsch. asst. Atlanta U.; tchr. Canton (Ohio) Bd. Edn. Mem. Assn. for Supervision and Curriculum Devel., Phi Delta Kappa. Home: 4076 Chapel Mill Bnd Decatur GA 30034-5335

KEATS, DONALD HOWARD, composer, educator; b. N.Y.C., May 27, 1929; s. Bernard and Lillian K.; m. Eleanor Steinholz, Dec. 13, 1953; children: Jeremy, Jennifer, Jeffrey, Jocelyn. MusB, Yale U., 1949; MA, Columbia U., 1951; PhD, U. Minn., 1962; student, Staatliche Hochschule fur Musik, Hamburg, Germany, 1954-56. Teaching fellow Yale U. Sch. Music, New Haven, Conn., 1948-49; instr. music theory U.S. Naval Sch. Music, Washington, 1953-54; post music dir. Ft. Dix, N.J., 1956-57; faculty Antioch Coll., Yellow Springs, Ohio, 1957-76, prof., 1967-76, chmn. music dept., 1967-71; vis. prof. music U. Wash. Sch. Music, 1969-70, Lamont Sch. Music, U. Denver, 1975-76; composer-in-residence Colo. Music Festival, 1980, Arcosanti, 1986; vis. composer Aspen Music Festival, 1987; prof. music, composer-in-residence Lamont Sch. Music, U. Denver, 1975-99, Phipps Prof. in the humanities, 1982-85, prof. emeritus, 1999—. Concerts devoted solely to his music often with his participation as pianist, London, 1973, Tel Aviv, 1973, Jerusalem, 1973, N.Y.C., 1975, Denver, 1984, 91; Composer: Sonata for Clarinet and Piano, 1948, String Trio, 1948, Divertimento for Winds and Strings, 1949, The Naming of Cats, 1951, The Hollow Men, 1951, String Quartet 1, 1952, Concert Piece for Orchestra, 1952, Variations for Piano, 1955, First Symphony, 1957, Piano Sonata, 1960, An Elegiac Symphony, 1962, Anyone Lived in a Pretty How Town, 1965, String Quartet 2, 1965; ballet New Work, 1966; Polarities for Violin and Piano, 1968-70, A Love Triptych, 1970, Dialogue for Piano, and Winds, 1973, Diptych for Cello and Piano, 1975, Upon the Intimation of Love's Mortality, 1975, Branchings for Orch., 1976, Four Puerto Rican Love Songs: Tierras del Alma for soprano, flute and guitar, 1978, Musica Instrumentalis for chamber group, 1980, Concerto for Piano and Orch., 1990, Revisitations for Violin, Cello and Piano, 1992, Elegy for chamber orch., 1995, Fanfare for Brass, 1996, String Quartet No. 3, 2001. Served with U.S. Army, 1952-54. Recipient ASCAP awards, 1964—; awards from Ford, Danforth and Lilly founds., Nat. Endowment for Arts; winner Rockefeller Found. Symphonic Competitions, 1965, 66; Guggenheim fellow Europe, 1964-65, 72-73; Nat. Endowment for Arts grantee, fellow, 1975; Fulbright Scholar, 1954-56. Mem. ASCAP, Am. Music Ctr., Phi Beta Kappa. Home: 12854 Buckhorn Rd Littleton CO 80127 Business E-Mail: dkeats@du.edu.

KEATS, THEODORE ELIOT, radiologist, educator; b. New Brunswick, N.J., June 26, 1924; m. Margaret E. McNamara, Aug. 27, 1949 (dec.); children: Matthew Mason, Ian Stuart B.; m. Patricia L. Hart, Mar. 30, 1974. BS, Rutgers U., 1945; MD, U. Pa., 1947. Diplomate Am. Bd. Radiology (trustee). Intern U. Pa. Hosp., Phila., 1947-48; resident U. Mich. Hosp., Ann Arbor, 1948-51; instr. U. Calif. Sch. Medicine, San Francisco, 1953-54, asst. prof., 1954-56; assoc. prof. U. Mo. Sch. Medicine, Columbia, 1956-59, prof. radiology, 1959-63, U. Va. Sch. Medicine, Charlottesville, 1963—, chmn. dept. radiology, 1963-92, alumni prof. radiology, 1992—. Vis. prof. Karolinska Hosp., Stockholm, 1963-64. Author: Atlas of Roentgenographic Measurement, 7th edit., 2001 (with Christopher Sistrom), An Atlas of Normal Roentgen Variants That May Simulate Disease, 7th edit., 2001, Self-Assessment of Current Knowledge in Diagnostic Radiology, 2d edit., 1980, An Atlas of Normal Developmental Roentgen Anatomy, 1978, 2d edit., 1988, (with Thomas H. Smith) Radiology of Musculoskeletal Injury, 1990; editor Emergency Radiology, 1984, 2d edit., 1989, editor-in-chief Current Problems in Diagnostic Radiology, 1981, 2001; Am. editor Skeletal Radiology, 1987-97; editor Applied Radiology, 1989-2001, Emergency Radiology, 1993-2001. Served with AUS, 1943-47; to capt., M.C. AUS, 1951-53. Fellow Am. Coll. Radiology (Gold medal 1995); mem. AMA, Am. Roentgen Ray Soc., Radiol. Soc. N.Am., Soc. Pediatric Radiology (hon.), So. Med. Assn., Internat. Skeletal Soc. (medal 1995), Soc. Emergency Radiology (gold medal 1999), Phi Beta Kappa, Sigma Xi, Alpha Omega Alpha. Home: 421 Key West Dr Charlottesville VA 22911-8423 Office: U Va Hosps Lee St Rm 1831 Charlottesville VA 22911 also: U Va Sch Medicine Dept Radiology Charlottesville VA 22908-0001 Office Phone: 434-924-9377. Business E-Mail: tek@virginia.edu.

KEATY, ROBERT BURKE, lawyer, business consultant; b. Baton Rouge, July 7, 1949; s. Thomas St. Paul and Alicia (Armshaw) K.; m. Erin Kenny, July 6, 1973; children: Kellen Elizabeth, Kathryn Ellen, Robert Burke II, Kaneil Erin, Rory Bridgette-Anne. BS, U. La., 1971; JD, Tulane U., 1974. Law clk. to judge U.S. Dist. Ct. for Ea. Dist. La., New Orleans, 1974-76. Mem. pres.'s com. Offshore Tng. and Survival Ctr., U. Lafayette, 1988-89; co-chmn. United Giver Fund Jud. Legal, 1994, Bishops Charity Ball Legal Com., 1995. Member dean's adv. com. Tulane U. Law Sch., New Orleans, 1987; mem. dean's exec. adv. com. Coll. Bus. Adminstrn., U. La., Lafayette, 1991. Sears scholar, 1971, Teagle scholar, 1973; recipient Most Outstanding Alumnus award U. La. Coll. Bus., Lafayette, 1991. Fellow La. Bar Found. (lifetime charter mem.). Avocations: reading, woodworking, tennis, fishing, carpentry.

KEBAUGH, LANCE DAVID, school psychologist; b. Sharon, Pa., Nov. 5, 1950; s. Peter Jacob Kebaugh and Julia Eva Sonowski; m. Betsy Jean Hucker, Oct. 25, 1975; children: Kyle David, Kurt Allen. BA in Psychology, Grove City Coll., 1972; MA in Psychology, Western Caroline U., 1973; PhD in Counseling Psychology, Southwest U., 1989. Cert. sch. psychologist. Sch. psychologist St. Mary's County Pub. Schs., Leonardtown, Md., 1973—. Adj. prof. Embry-Riddle U., Pax River, Md., 1990—; mem. adv. bd. Learning Disabilities Assn., Leonardtown, 1990—2002. Baseball coach St. Mary's Little League, 2000—03, basketball coach, 2001—03. Mem.: Nat. Assn. Sch. Psychologists, Nat. Assn. Sports Ofcls. Presbyterian. Home: 22969 Piney Wood Cir California MD 20619

KECECIOGLU, DIMITRI BASIL, reliability engineering educator, consultant; b. Istanbul, Turkey, Dec. 26, 1922; came to U.S., 1946, naturalized, 1956; s. Basil C. and Mary (Melayios) K.; m. Lorene June Legan, Dec. 22, 1951; children: Zoe Diana Kececioglu Draelos, John Dimitri. BS, Robert Coll., Istanbul, 1942; MS, Purdue U., 1948, PhD, 1953. Asst. instr. Purdue U., Lafayette, Ind., 1943-47, instr., 1947-52; engring. scientist in charge mech. research labs. Allis-Chalmers Mfg. Co., Milw., 1952-57, asst. to dir. mech. engring. industries group, 1957-60, cons. engr. industries group, 1960-63, dir. corp. reliability engring. program, 1960-63; prof. aerospace and mech. engring. U. Ariz., Tucson, 1963—, prof.-in-charge reliability engring. program, 1963—. Reliability and maintainability engring. cons., Tucson, 1963-; dir. Reliability Engring. and Mgmt. Inst., 1963-, Reliability Testing Inst., 1975-; applied reliability engring. and product assurance cons. Northrop Space Labs., Gen. Elec. Co., Center for Mgmt. and Indsl. Devel., Rotterdam, Netherlands, Delco Radio div. Gen. Motors Corp., Aerojet-Gen. Corp., Westinghouse Elec. Co., U.S. Army Mgmt. Engring. Tng. Agy., Allied Signal, Data General, Polaroid, Storage Tek, Motorola, Digital Equipment, ITT, B.F. Goodrich, Gen. Dynamics, Xerox, Ford, JPL, Bendix, Cummins Engine, MOOG, Copeland, Eastman Kodak, Allied Chem., GE, Honeywell, IBM, Ventara Med., Hamilton Sundstraud, and many others; Fulbright scholar Nat. Tech. U., Athens, 1971-72; sr. extension tchr. UCLA, 1983; hon. prof. Shanghai U. Tech., 1984; assoc. prof. Tech. U. Bordeaux, France; vis. prof. reliability engring. UCLA. Author: Bibliography on Plasticity, 1950, Introduction to Probabilistic Design for Reliability, 1975, Manual of Product Assurance Films and Videotapes, 1980, Reliability Engineering Handbook, Vols. 1-2, 1991, revised edit., 2002, 1997, The 1992-94 Reliability Maintainability and Availability Software Handbook, 1992, Reliability and Life Testing Handbook, Vols. 1-2, 1993, revised edit., 2002, Environmental Stress Screening, 1995, revised edit., 2002, Burn-in Testing, 1997, revised edit., 2002, Maintainability, Availability and Operational Readiness Engineering Handbook Vol. 1, 1995, revised edit., 2002, Robust Engineering Design by Reliability, Vol. 1, 2003; contbr. numerous articles to profl. jours.; patentee in field. Founder, fund raiser Dr. Dimitri Basil Kececioglu Reliability Engring. Rsch. Fellowships Endowment Fund, 1987. Recipient Presidency award Milw. Tech. Coun., 1962, Automotive Industries Author award, 1963, Ralph E. Teetor Outstanding Engring. Educator award Soc. Automotive Engrs., 1977, Anderson prize U. Ariz., 1983, U. Ariz. Scholarship Devel. Office award, 1991, Acad. of Achievement award in edn. Am. Hellenic Ednl. Progressive Assn., 1991-92. Fellow Soc. Automotive Engrs. (Disting. Probabilistic Methods Educator award 1997), Am. Soc. for Quality, Soc. Reliability Engrs. (founder, pres. Tucson chpt. 1974-77); mem. ASME (chmn. Milw. sect. 1960), IEEE, Soc. Exptl. Stress Analysis (chmn. Milw. sect. 1957), Am. Hellenic Ednl. Progressive Assn. (Acad. Achievement award in edn. 1992), Am. Soc. Engring. Edn., Am. Soc. Quality Control (Reliability Edn. Advancement award 1980, Allen Chop award for outstanding contbns. to reliability 1981), Hellenic Ops. Rsch. Soc. Greece, Phi Beta Kappa (hon.), Sigma Xi (pres. Univ. chpt. 1990-91), Tau Beta Pi, Phi Kappa Phi (pres. U. Ariz. chpt. 1988-89), Nat. Golden Key Soc. Home: 7340 N La Oesta Ave Tucson AZ 85704-3119 Office Phone: 520-621-6120. Business E-Mail: dimitri@u.arizona.edu.

KECHIJIAN, PAUL, dermatologist, educator; b. Providence, Mar. 17, 1940; s. Harry Maderos and Annette (Rhia) Paré; m. Janice Ann Kechijian, July 31, 1976; children: Douglas Paul, Lisa Ann. AB in Psychology, Brown U., 1961, ScM in Biology, 1964; MD, Albany Med. Coll., 1968. Lic. Nat. Bd. Med. Examiners, N.Y. State Med. Lic.; diplomate Am. Bd. Dermatology, diplomate Dermatopathology Am. Bds. of Dermatology and Pathology. Med. intern, med. resident Barnes Hosp., St. Louis, 1968-69, 69-70; dermatology resident Mass. Gen. Hosp., Boston, 1970, Univ. Miami (Fla.) Sch. of Medicine, 1973-75; dermatopathology fellow NYU Med. Ctr., N.Y.C., 1975-76; instr. clin. dermatology NYU Sch. of Medicine, N.Y.C., 1975-78, clin. asst. prof. dermatology, 1978-84, clin. assoc. prof., 1984—2002; asst. attending physician to assoc. attending physician Bellevue Hosp., 1976-81, 81—, NYU Med. Ctr., 1976-84, 84—; asst. attending dermatologist to sr. asst. North Shore Univ. Hosp., 1978-87, 87—. Chief inpatient dermatology svc. Bellevue Hosp., 1976—86; cons. Holy Martyrs Armenian Day Sch., 1976—; hon. surgeon (dermatology) N.Y.C. Police Dept., 1981—; chief nail sect. NYU Med. Ctr., 1983—2002; presenter and lectr. in field. Contbg. editor: Jour. Dermatologic Surgery and Oncology, 1983-85; contbr. reports and articles to profl. jours. and chpt. to books. Fellow ACP, Am. Acad. Dermatology (com. on evaluation 1980-84, coun. on govtl. liaison key contact program 1986—), Am. Soc. Dermatopathology; mem. AMA, N.Y. Acad. Scis., Dermatology Found., Soc. for Investigative Dermatology, Nassau County Med. Soc., L.I. Dermatol. Soc., Soc. for Dermatol. Surgery, Internat. Soc. Dermatol. Surgery, others. Office: 935 Northern Blvd Great Neck NY 11021-5309 Office Phone: 516-482-0650. Personal E-mail: kech1@optonline.net.

KECK, BEVERLY MORSE, elementary school educator; d. Daryl Scott and Martha (Gadberry) Morse; m. Thomas William Keck; children: Heidi Swan Diegel, Eric Shane. Student, Joliet Jr. Coll., 1963; BS, Ill. State U., 1967; MEd, U. Vt., 1974, CAS, 1988. Tchr. Joliet (Ill.) Pub. Schs., 1964-68; dir., founder Bethel Nursery Sch., Joliet, 1968-71; tchr. Vt. Coll., Norwich U., Montpelier, 1972-76; cons. Inst. Gas Tech., Algeria, 1976-77; tchr., curriculum coord. Montpelier Pub. Schs., 1978—. Mem. adv. bd. Early Sch. Achievement, Montpelier, 1978—; math. cons. Inst. Math Mania, Essex, Vt., 1989—91. Bd. dirs. Montpelier Theater Guild, 1990—; chmn. music com. Vt. Choir. Mem.: Nat. Sci. Tchrs. Assn., Vt. Coun. Tchrs. Math. (directing bd. 1989—91), Nat. Coun. Tchrs. Math. Avocations: opera, theater, horseback riding, choral singing. Office: Park Ave Montpelier VT 05602

KECK, DONALD BRUCE, physicist; b. Lansing, Mich., Jan. 2, 1941; s. William G. and Zelda D. Keck; m. Ruth A. Moilanen, July 10, 1965; children: Lynne Ann Vaia, Brian William. BS, Mich. State U., 1962, MS, 1964, PhD, 1967; DSc (hon.), Rensselaer Poly. Inst., 2004. With Corning (N.Y.) Glass Works, 1968-76, mgr. applied physics, 1976-86; dir. optics and photonics Corning, Inc., 1986-91, v.p., dir. optics and photonics, 1997—2000, v.p., exec. dir. rsch., 2000—02; chief tech. officer Infotonic Tech. Ctr., 2002—04; cons. Big Flats, NY, 2004—. Bd. dirs. PCO, Inc., L.A.; mem. vis. com. Advanced Tech.; lectr. in field. Editor: Jour. Lightwave Tech., 1989—94, co-author (5 books on optical fibers); contbr. more than 150 to profl. jours. Chmn. planning bd. Town of Corning, 1990—; mem. adv. bd. Corning Salvation Army; moderator 1st Congl. Ch., Corning, 1986—87, 1991—92; bd. dirs. ARC-Corning chpt., 1995—, Cmty. Found., 2000—; chmn. troop com. Boy Scouts Am., Corning, 1968—71; pres. Civic Music Assn., Corning, 1971—75; bd. dirs. Nat. Inventors Hall of Fame Found., 1994—, pres., 2001—02; bd. dirs. Nat. Inventors Hall of Fame, 2000—, sec., 2002, vice chair, 2003—. Recipient Tech. Achievement award Internat. Soc. Optical Engring., 1981, IR-100 award Indsl. Rsch., 1981, Engring. Achievement award Am. Soc. Metals, 1983, Am. Innovator award, 1995, John Tyndall award IEEE/Optical Soc. Am., 1992, Disting. Alumni award Mich. State U., 1996, Lauren Publishing, "Distinction in Photonics" award, 2002, Nat. medal of Tech., U.S. Pres., 2000; inductee Nat. Innovators Hall of Fame, 1993; Paul Harris fellow Rotary Internat., 1998. Fellow IEEE, OSA, Optical Soc. Am. (bd. dirs. 1994-96), Nat. Acad. Engring., Opto-Electronics Industry Devel. Assn. (bd. chmn. 1999-2002); mem. Nat. Inst. Stds. and Tech. (vis. com. Advanced Tech. 2004-). Achievements include 36 patents in field. Avocations: water skiing, music, woodworking, snow skiing, piano. Home: 2877 Chequers Cir Big Flats NY 14814-9610 Personal E-mail: dkeck@stny.rr.com.

KECK, VAIL E., conductor; b. Cleve., Mar. 28, 1972; d. James Edward Keck and Mary Ann Molnar; m. Steve Rowland, Aug. 4, 2002. MusB, U. Calif., Santa Cruz, 1998, MA in Choral Conducting, 2000. Condr. Cabrillo Coll., Aptos, Calif., 1999—2003; instr. U. Okla., Norman, 2003—. Dir. music 1st Meth. Ch., Campbell, Calif., 2000—01, Gilroy (Calif.) Presbyn. Ch., 2001—03. Mem.: Coll. Music Soc., Am. Choral Dirs. Assn. Office: U Okla Sch Music 500 W Boyd St Rm 138 Norman OK 73019-3130

KECKLER, WILLIAM BERNARD, writer, survey research analyst; b. Harrisburg, Pa., Jan. 3, 1966; s. Bernard Leroy and Marie Jeanette Keckler. AS, Harrisburg Area C.C., 1992; student, Pa. State U., 1993-94. Editor Logodaedalus Press, Harrisburg. Author: (poetry) Ants Dissolve in Moonlight, 1995, Recombinant Image Day, 1998. Fellow in poetry NEA, 1997-99, Pa. Coun. on the Arts, 1996; recipient Gertrude Stein award in innovative Am. poetry Sun & Moon press, 1995, 96. Avocations: drawing, xeroxial art, internet communities, lexical games, cricket. Home: 420 Luther Rd Harrisburg PA 17111-2052

KEDDERIS, PAMELA JEAN, academic administrator; b. Waterbury, Conn., May 15, 1956; d. Leo George and Evelyn Helen (Fenske) K. Student, U. Nice, 1976—77; BA, Assumption Coll., 1978; MBA, U. New Haven, 1981. Cert. fin. mgr., mgmt. acct. Credit analyst Citytrust Bank, Bridgeport, Conn., 1980-81, sr. credit analyst, 1981-82, fin. analyst, 1982-83, seminar instr., 1981-83; planning analyst Continental Ins. Co., N.Y.C., 1983-84, sr. planning analyst, 1984-85, dir. planning, 1985-87, asst. v.p., 1987-92, v.p., 1992-95; v.p., controller Marine Office of Am., Cranbury, N.J., 1995-97; exec. officer for fin. Conn. State Univ. Sys., Hartford, 1997-98, CFO, 1998—. Mem. State of Conn. Ins. and Risk Mgmt. Bd., 2002—. Mem.: Conn. Coun. Chief Fiscal Officers, Inst. Mgmt. Accts., New Eng. Resource Ctr. for Higher Edn. CFO Think Tank. Democrat. Lutheran. Avocations: music, travel. Office: Conn State Univ Sys 39 Woodland St Hartford CT 06105-2337 Business E-Mail: kedderisp@so.ct.edu.

KEDDIE, ROLAND THOMAS, retired physician, retired health facility administrator, retired lawyer; b. Altoona, Pa., Oct. 21, 1928; s. John Barkeley and Jessie E. (Keddie) Isenberg; m. Suzanne M. Seno, Feb. 6, 1978; 1 child, Dawn Michelle; children by previous marriage: Roland, Thomas, Francis, Robert, Michael, Karen, Andrew, Rosemary. BS cum laude, U. Pitts., 1956, MD, 1957, JD, 1970. Diplomate Am. Bd. Family Practice. Bar: Pa. 1970. Intern St. Josephs Hosp., Pitts., 1958; practice medicine specializing in emergency medicine and family practice, 1958—2003; ret., 2003. Med. dir. Westmoreland Manor, Greensburg, Pa., 1971; dir. emergency dept. Conemaugh Valley Meml. Hosp., Johnston, Pa., 1976-77, Shadyside Hosp., Pitts., 1978-80, chmn. dept. emergency svcs. McKeesport (Pa.) Hosp., 1980-83, dir. emergency medicine residency program; pres. EmergiCenters Inc., 1983-97; chmn. dept. family practice St. Clair Hosp., Pitts., 1990-93; pres. Emergency Med. Svcs. Inst., 1982-85; adj. prof. U. Pitts. Sch. Nursing; cons. in field. Served with USN, 1946-47, 50-52. Mem. Am. Coll. Emergency Physicians (life, bd. dirs. Pa. chpt. 1977-81, 83-86, v.p. 1980-81, pres. 1985-86), Pa. Med. Soc., Hosp. Assn. Pa. (mem. profl. practice com. 1981-82), Allegheny County Bar Assn., AMA (Physicians Recognition award 1974, 77, 80), Allegheny County Med. Soc., Pa. Emergency Health Services Council (dir. 1980), Soc. Tchrs. Emergency Medicine, Beta Beta Beta. Roman Catholic. Home and Office: 45 Meadowcrest Dr Cecil PA 15321-1118 E-mail: RTKeddie@msn.com.

KEDES, LAURENCE H., biochemistry professor, physician, researcher; b. Hartford, Conn., July 19, 1937; s. Sammuel Ely and Rosalyn (Epstein) K.; m. Shirley Beck, June 15, 1958; children: Dean Hamilton, Maureen Jennifer, Todd Russell. Student, Wesleyan U., 1955-58; BS with distinction, Stanford U., 1961, MD, 1962. Intern Presbyn. U. Hosp., Pitts., 1962-63, asst. resident, 1963-64; rsch. assoc. lab. biochemistry Nat. Cancer Inst. Peterson, 1964-66; sr. asst. med. resident Peter Bent Brigham Hosp., Boston, 1966-67; surgeon USPHS, 1964-66; postdoctoral fellow dept. biology MIT, 1967-68; jr. assoc. in medicine and hematology assoc. Peter Bent Brigham Hosp., Boston, 1967-69; rsch. trainee in embryology Marine Biol. Lab., Woods Hole, Mass., 1969; instr. biology MIT, Boston, 1969-70; asst., assoc. then prof. medicine Stanford U., 1970-89, dir. admissions med. sch., 1978-81; William M. Keck prof. biochemistry and medicine, chair biochemistry, dir. Inst. Genetic Medicine U. So. Calif. Keck Sch. Medicine, LA, 1989—2002. Staff physician VA, 1970-92; vis. scientist Lab. Molecular Embryology, Naples, Italy, 1969-70, Dept. Animal Genetics, U. Edinburgh, 1970, Imperial Cancer Rsch. Fund, London, 1976-77; instr. embryology Marine Biol. Lab., Woods Hole, 1976; investigator Howard Hughes Med. Inst., 1974-82; founder, dir. IntelliCorp., Mountain View, Calif., 1980-90, chmn., 1982-86. Mem. editorial bd. Jour. Biol. Chemistry, 1982-88, Molecular and Cellular Biology, 1982-89, Jour. Applied Molecular Biology, 1982-85, Oxford Surveys on Eukaryotic Genes, 1983-94, Trends in Genetics, 1984-88; assoc. editor Jour. Molecular Evolution, 1982-90; cons. editor Circulation Rsch., 1994-99. Mem. fellowship award com. Am. Cancer Soc., 1978-81; co-principle investigator BIONET, 1984-89; mem. rsch. com. Am. Heart Assn., 1987; mem. sci. adv. bd. Muscular Dystrophy Assn., 1988-93. Fellow Med. Found. Boston, 1967-69, John Simon Guggenheim Found. fellow, 1976-77; Leukemia Soc. Am. scholar, 1969-74. Mem. Western Soc. for Clin. Rsch., Am. Soc. Clin. Investigation, Assn. Am. Pysicians, Am. Soc. Microbiology, Am. Soc. Biochemistry and Molecular Biology, Internat. Soc. Devel. Biology, Alpha Omega Alpha. Office: 2250 Alcazar St Ste 240 Los Angeles CA 90089-0107 Office Phone: 323-442-1144. Business E-Mail: kedes@usc.edu.

KEE, HOWARD CLARK, religion educator; b. Beverly, N.J., July 28, 1920; s. Walter Leslie and Regina (Corcoran) K.; m. Janet Burrell, Dec. 15, 1951; children: Howard Clark III, Christopher Andrew, Sarah Leslie. AB, Bryan (Tenn.) Coll., 1940; Th.M., Dallas Theol. Sem., 1944; postgrad., Am. Sch. Oriental Research, Jerusalem, 1949-50; PhD (Two Bros. fellow), Yale, 1951. Instr. religion and classics U. Pa., 1951-53; from asst. prof. to prof. N.T. Drew U., 1953-68; Rufus Jones prof. history of religion, chmn. dept. history of religion Bryn Mawr (Pa.) Coll., 1968-77; William Goodwin Aurelio prof. Biblical studies Boston U., 1977-89, chmn. grad. div. religious studies, 1977-86; sr. rsch. fellow U. Pa., 1987—. Vis. prof. religion Princeton U., 1954-55, Brown U., 1985; vis. lectr. U. of Durham, 1987, Claremont Sch. of Theology, 1991; Rsch. scholar, Miss. state U., 1992, vis. scholar, Princeton Theological Seminary, 1993; mem. archaeol. teams at Roman Jericho, 1950, Shechem, 1957, Mt. Gerizim, 1966, Pella, Jordan, 1967, Ashdod, Israel, 1968; chmn. Coun. on Grad. Studies in Religion; cons. for transls. Am. Bible Soc., 1989—. Author: Understanding the New Testament, 1957, 4th edit., 1983, 5th edit., 1992, Making Ethical Decisions, 1958, The Renewal of Hope, 1959, Jesus and God's New People, 1959, Jesus in History, 1970, 3d edit., 1995, The Origins of Christianity: Sources and Documents, 1973, The Community of the New Age, 1977, Christianity: An Historical Approach, 1979, Christian Origins in Sociological Perspective, 1980, Miracle in the Early Christian World, 1983, The New Testament in Context: Sources and Documents, 1984, Medicine, Miracle and Magic in New Testament Times, 1986, Knowing the Truth: A Sociological Approach to New Testament Interpretation, 1989, What Can We Know About Jesus?, 1990, Good News to the Ends of the Earth: The Theology of Acts, 1990, Christianity: A Social and Cultural History, 1991, 2d edit., 1998, Who Are the People of God? Early Christian Models of Community, 1995, To Every Nation Under Heaven: The Acts of the Apostles, 1997; editor: Biblical Perspectives on Current Issues, 1976-83, Understanding Jesus Today, 1985—; editor Cambridge UP Annotated Study Bible, 1993, Cambridge Annotated Study Apocrypha, 1994, Cambridge Companion to the Bible, 1997, Removing Anti-Judaism From the New Testament, 1996, Removing Anti-Judaism From the Pulpit, 1998, The Evolution of the Synagogue, 1999; librettist: New Land, New Covenant (Howard Hanson), 1976; contbr.: Interpreter's Dictionary of the Bible, 1962, supplement, 1976, Harper's Bible Dictionary, Dictionary of Bible and Religion, The Books of the Bible, Anchor Bible Dictionary. Bd. mgrs. Am. Bible Soc., 1956-89, chmn. transls. com., 1985-89; chmn. transls. com. United Bible Socs., 1985-89; bd. dirs. Mohawk Trail Concerts, Inc., Charlemont, Mass.; mem. adv. bd. Yale U. Inst. Sacred Music; exec. bd. Liberty Mus. Am. Assn. Theol. Schs. fellow Germany, 1960; Guggenheim fellow Israel, 1966-67; Nat. Endowment Humanities grantee Eng., 1984 Mem. Soc. Values in Higher Edn., Phila. Seminar on Christian Origins, Am. Acad. Religion, Soc. Bibl. Lit., Bibl. Theologians, Studiorum Novi Testamenti Societas, New Haven Theol. Discussion Group, Assn. for Sociology of Religion (pres.), Am. Interfaith Inst. (pres.). Presbyterian. Home: 3300 Darby Rd Haverford PA 19041-1061 *Life is a gift from the Creator. It is mediated to us through parents, family, friends, teachers. It is conveyed through love and learning, through challenge and conflict, through accomplishment and disappointment. The gift must be shared, not jealously guarded or proudly prized. By sharing life, we can approach others with candor and honesty, with joy and sympathy, with wonder and understanding. The shared gift brings gratitude and fulfillment.*

KEE, TERRY MICHAEL, lawyer; b. Kansas City, Mar. 12, 1953; s. James Jefferson and Ruth Anne (Brunton) K.; m. Jeanine Jackson, Aug. 17, 1976; children: Lucy Alice, Ruth Mildred, Johanna Grace. BA, U. Tex., Austin, 1975; JD, U. Tex., 1979. Bar: Calif. 1979, U.S. Dist. Ct. (no. dist.) Calif. 1979. Assoc. Pillsbury, Madison & Sutro, San Francisco, 1979-86, ptnr., 1987—; (Pillsbury, Madison & Sutro merged with Winthrop, Stimson, Putnam, 2001); ptnr., corp. & securities dept. Pillsbury Winthrop LLP, San Francisco, 2001—, former chair mergers & acquisitions, former chair, legal opinions com.; (Pillsbury Winthrop LLP merged with Shaw Pittman LLP, 2005); ptnr., corp. & securities dept. Pillsbury Winthrop Shaw Pittman LLP, San Francisco, 2005—. Mem.: ABA, San Francisco Bar Assn. Office: Pillsbury Winthrop Shaw Pittman LLP 50 Fremont St San Francisco CA 94105-2228 Office Phone: 415-983-1724. Office Fax: 415-983-1200. Business E-Mail: terry.kee@pillsburylaw.com.

KEEBLER, LOIS MARIE, elementary school educator; b. Jasper, Ala., Nov. 24, 1955; d. Roosevelt T. and Marie (Smiley) K. Student, Cen. State U., Wilberforce, Ohio; cert., North Ala. Regional Hosps., 1981. Cert. tchr., Ala. Tchr. Mamani Vallied Children Devel. Ctr., Dayton, Ohio. Vol. pub. schs. Democrat. Baptist. Avocation: bowling.

KEECH, ELOWYN ANN, interior designer; b. Berrien County, Mich., Oct. 5, 1937; d. Earl Docker and Elizabeth Hall (Paullin) Stephenson; 1 child, Robert Earl Stephenson. Print designer, 1957-75; freelance interior designer, photoset and video set designer St. Joseph, Mich., 1975—; owner Fog Horn Records & Tapes. Trustee Mich. Maritime Mus., 1994—97; bd. dirs., mem. steering and long-range planning coms. United Way Mich., 1980—87; bd.

dirs. Blossomland United Way, 1981—86. Mem.: Internat. Interior Design Assn., Am. Rottweiler Club, Econ. Club S.W. Mich., Rotary Club (vol. chair 47th Ann. Rotary Track Meet S.W. Mich.).

KEEDY, CHRISTIAN DAVID, lawyer; b. Worcester, Mass., Jan. 9, 1945; BBA, Tulane U., 1967, JD, 1972. Bar: Fla. 1972; bd. cert. in admiralty and maritime law, Fla. Pvt. practice Christian D. Keedy, P.A., Miami, Fla., 1981—. Mem. Maritime Law Assn. U.S., Southeastern Admiralty Law Inst. (dir. 1982-83), The Fla. Bar (chmn. 1981-82, 2003—, admiralty law com.), Miami Maritime Arbitration Coun. Office: Christian D Keedy PA 7931 SW 59th Ave South Miami FL 33143-5513 Office Phone: 305-669-4478. E-mail: ckeedy@bellsouth.net.

KEEFE, ARTHUR THOMAS, III, non-profit fund raising executive; b. N.Y.C., Mar. 1, 1953; s. Arthur Thomas and Marie Lorraine (Bernard) K.; m. Lorene Ann Lion, Aug. 7, 1981; children: Ryan Arthur, Garrett Thomas. BA in Econs., Yale U., 1975. Assoc. dir. The Campaign for Yale U., New Haven, 1976-79; dir. devel. Georgetown Prep., Rockville, Md., 1980-84; dir. resource devel. Greater S.E. Community Hosp., Washington, 1984-86, United Svcs. Orgn., Washington, 1987; dir. devel. Franklin Square Hosp., Balt., 1988-89, The Humane Soc. U.S., Washington, 1990-95; v.p. devel. AOPA Air Safety Found., Frederick, Md., 1995—2004. Bd. dirs., corp. sec. Nat. Catholic Cmty. Found. Named NCAA All-Am., Inter Collegiate Yacht Racing Assn. N. Am., 1973; recipient Gold Maxi, Direct Mktg. Assn. D.C., 1989. Mem. Nat. Soc. Fund Raising Execs. (cert.), The Planned Giving Study Group Washington, D.C. (pres. 1990-94), Nat. Com. on Planned Giving (bd. com. mem.). Republican. Roman Catholic. Avocations: duplicate bridge, numismatics, art collecting. Home: 9017 Willow Valley Dr Potomac MD 20854 E-mail: arthurkeefe3@aol.com.

KEEFE, CAROLYN JOAN, tax accountant; b. Huntington Park, Oct. 11, 1926; d. Paul Dewey and Mary Jane (Parmater) K. AA, Pasadena (Calif.) City Coll., 1947; BA, U. So. Calif., 1950. Tax acct. Shell Oil Co., L.A., 1950-71, Houston, 1971-91, ret., 1991. Advisor Midwest Mus. Am. Art, 1993—; vol. Houston Mus. Fine Arts, 1991—; vol. docent Houston Mus. Natural Sci., 1991—, Theatre Under the Stars, 1991—, Houston Pub. TV Channel 8, Houston, 1989—; donor Paul Dewey and Mary Jane Keefe scholarships. Mem. LWV, Inst. Mgmt. Accts. (emeritus life mem.), Desk and Derrick Club (bd. dir. 1994-95), Houston Alumni Club of Alpha Gamma Delta, USC Houston Alumni Club. Christian Scientist. Avocation: travel. Home: 1814 Auburn Trl Sugar Land TX 77479-6333

KEEFE, EDWARD STEPHEN, lawyer; b. Boynton Beach, Fla., Oct. 12, 1971; s. Charles William, Jr. and Dorothy Louise Keefe; m. Blessed Ngozi Chuksorji, Feb. 26, 2005. BA, Holy Cross Coll., Worcester, Mass., 1993; JD, U. Pa., 2000. Atty. Dept. Justice, Washington, 2000—04, Morgan Lewis & Bockius, Washington, 2004—. Mem.: ABA, DC Bar Assn. Home: 1320 Park Rd NW #1 Washington DC 20001

KEEFE, FRANCIS JOSEPH, psychology educator; b. Framingham, Mass., May 7, 1949; s. Francis Joseph and Jeanne (Landry) K.; m. Delia Ware, Sept. 2, 1972; children: Daniel, Anne, John. BA, Bowdoin Coll., 1971; PhD, Ohio U., 1975. Psychologist Learning Therapies, Inc., Newton, Mass., 1975-76; postdoctoral fellow psychology lab. Med. Sch. Harvard U., Boston, 1976-78; asst. prof. Duke U. Med. Ctr., Durham, N.C., 1978-84, assoc. prof., 1984-95; assoc. prof. social and health scis. Duke U., Durham, 1991—, prof. med. psychology, 1995-98; prof. health psychology program Ohio U., 1998—. Cons. dept. labor Nat. Inst. Occupational Safety and Health, Washington, 1987-91; mem. behavioral medicine study sect. NIH, Washington, 1991—. Author: A Practical Guide to Behavioral Assessment, 1978, Behavioral Medicine in General Medical Practice, 1982, Assessment Strategies in Behavioral Medicine, 1982; editor Annals of Behavioral Medicine, 1990-93. Fellow APA; mem. Internat. Assn. for Study of Pain, Assn. Advancement of Behavior Therapy, Soc. of Behavioral Medicine. Achievements include development of reliable and valid method for recording pain-related behaviors in chronic pain patients; demonstration that coping skills training protocals; co-developer widely used pain coping measure. Office: Health Psychology Program Porter Hall Rm 229 Ohio U Athens OH 45701

KEEFE, JAMES WASHBURN, educational writer, researcher, consultant; b. L.A., Oct. 23, 1931; s. James E. and Leah M. (Washburn) K.; m. Jean Showalter, Dec. 6, 1980. BA maxima cum laude, St. Ambrose Coll., 1953; MusB, Mt. St. Mary's Coll., 1965, MA in Edn., 1966; EdD, U. So. Calif., LA, 1973. Cert. tchr., adminstr., Calif. Dean of studies Pius X H.S., Downey, Calif., 1962-67, prin., 1967-75; instr. U. So. Calif., 1972-75; lectr. Loyola Marymount U., LA, 1975-77, adj. prof. edn., 1977-78; coord. rsch. Nat. Assn. Secondary Sch. Prins., Reston, Va., 1978-80, dir. rsch., 1980-95. Mem. various nat. adv. bds. including Dept. of Edn. Ctr. on Orgn. and Restructuring of Schs., Nat. Study Sch. Evaluation-Evaluative Criteria Com., Sizer Coalition of Essential Schs. Author: Take Five: A Methodolgy for the Humane School, 1979, Student Learning Styles: Diagnosing and Prescribing Programs, 1979, Middle Level Principalship, 1981, 83, Student Learning Styles and Brain Behavior, 1982, High School Leaders and their Schools, 1988, 90, Instructional Leadership Handbook, 1984, 91, Learning Style Profile Handbook, 1989, The CASE-IMS School Improvement Process, 1991, Teaching for Thinking, 1992, Leadership in Middle Level Education, 1993, Instruction and the Learning Environment, 1996, Redesigning Schools for the New Century, 1997, Personalized Instruction: Changing Classroom Practice, 2000, Changing the School Learning Environment, 2004; PDK Fastback: Personalized Instruction, 2005. Recipient Disting. Achievement award City of Downey, 1975, Award for Outstanding Ednl. Rsch. Calif. State U., Fullerton, 1992-93, Disting. Svc. award Nat. Cath. Edn. Assn., 1981. Mem. ASCD, Learning Environs. Consortium (pres., forum coord.), Nat. Assn. Secondary Sch. Prins., Nat. Cath. Honor Soc., Phi Delta Kappa. Office: JK Cons Ltd 1419 Belcastle Ct Reston VA 20194-1245 E-mail: jimkeefe_j@hotmail.com.

KEEFE, MAUREEN RUTH, dean; b. Madison, Wis., Oct. 30, 1947; m. Michael Gaviglio; children: Erin, Ryan. BSN, U. Mich., 1970; MS, U. Colo., 1974, PhD, 1984, postgrad., 1985. Cert. PNP. Pub. health nurse Washtenaw County Health Dept., Ann Arbor, 1971-73; PNP Denver (Colo.) Health and Hosps., 1974-75, Univ. Hosp., Denver, 1978-85; instr. dept. psychology Univ. Colo., Denver, 1985-86; v.p. nursing The Children's Hosp., Denver, 1985—; assoc. dir. Kempe Rsch. Ctr., Denver, 1985—; asst. prof. Univ. Colo., Sch. Nursing, Denver, 1985-90, assoc. prof., 1990—; dean Coll. Nursing Med. U. S.C., Charleston, U. Utah, Salt Lake City. Cons. Emergent Tech. Corp., Boca Raton, Fla., 1985; vis. prof. Children's Hosp., Columbus, Ohio, 1990; mem. Nat. Adv. Bd. for Clin. Trials of the Preterm; mem. adv. bd. Johnson & Johnson Pediat. Inst. Co-author: A Primary Care Process Measure: The Nurse Practitioner Rating Form, 1981. Troop leader Brownies, Denver, 1983-84; bd. mem. Step Families Assn. Denver, 1984-85, pres., 1985. Recipient Book of Yr. award Am. Jour. Nursing, 1981, First award NIH/NCNR, 1987; named People to Watch, Denver Mag., 1988. Mem.: Western Inst. Nursing (exec. com. 1992—), Nat. Assn. Pediatric Nurse Assocs. and Practitioners (co-chair Internat. Yr. of the Child 1979), Sigma Theta Tau (perinatal grant selection com./Mead Johnson 1991, internat. rsch. com. 1992—, Alpha Kappa chpt. rsch. com. 1984—85, 1991—92, v.p. 1985—87, pres. 1988—90, bd. dirs. 2000—, Rsch. Excellence award 1988). Office: U Utah Coll Nursing Deans Office 10 S 2800 E Front Salt Lake City UT 84112-5880

KEEFE, WILLIAM JOSEPH, political science educator; b. Piper City, Ill., Nov. 28, 1925; s. Joseph and Elfreda (Huxtable) K.; m. Martha Maria Schroeder, Dec. 22, 1948; children: Kathryn, Robert, Nancy, Mary Jo, John. BS, Ill. State U., 1948; MA, Wayne State U., 1949; PhD, Northwestern U., 1951. Asst. prof. polit. sci. U. Ala., 1951-52; mem. faculty Chatham Coll., Pitts., 1952-68, asso. prof., 1955-61, prof., 1961-68; prof. dept. polit. sci. U. Pitts., 1968—2002, prof. emeritus, 2002—, chmn. dept., 1968-75. Mem. adv. com. Eagleton Inst. Politics, Rutgers U., 1965— Author: (with Morris Ogul) The American Legislative Process: Congress and the States, 10th edit., 2001, Parties, Politics and Public Policy in America, 1972, 9th edit., 2003, Congress and the American People, 1980, 3d edit., 1988, American Democracy, 3d edit., 1990; contbr. articles to profl. jours. Del. Democratic Nat. Conv., 1976. Served with USNR, 1944-46. Mem. Am. Polit. Sci. Assn. (chmn. program com. 1975—, chmn. Congl. fellowship program 1968-75, chmn. Woodrow Wilson award com. 1977, treas. 1981, trustee trust and devel. bd. 1981-85, 90-93), Pi Sigma Alpha (pres. 1998—, mem. exec. coun. 1992-96, pres.-elect 1996-98). Home: 838 7th St Oakmont PA 15139-1429 Office: U Pitts Dept Polit Sci Pittsburgh PA 15260

KEEFER, ELIZABETH J., lawyer; b. New London, Conn., July 3, 1948; d. Edward Boyd and Elizabeth Keefer; m. Richard A. Brown, May 13, 1978; 1 child, Andrew Boyd Keefer Brown. BA cum laude, Barnard Coll., 1969—71; JD mem. Order of Coif, U. Colo., 1966—67, George Wash. U., 1977. Trial atty. Fed. Trade Commn., Wash., DC, 1977—79; assoc. Bergson Borkland Margolis & Adler, Wash., DC, 1979—82; atty. adv. Dept. State, Wash., DC, 1982—86, asst. legal adv., 1986—89; dep. under sec. Internat. Affairs, U.S. Air Force, Wash., DC, 1989—92; ptnr. Hughes Hubbard & Reed, Wash., DC, 1992; dep. gen. counsel Teledyne, L.A., 1995—97; gen. counsel Columbia U., N.Y.C., 1997—. Bd. trustees Mitre Corp., McLean, Va., 2001—. Mem. bd. dirs. Women's Commn. for Women Refugee and Children, N.Y.C., 2003—. Mem.: Am. Corp. Counsel Assn. (mem. bd. dirs. 2001—). Avocations: hiking, theater, tennis. Office: Columbia U 412 Low Libr 535 W 116th St New York NY 10027 Business E-Mail: ejk27@columbia.edu.

KEEFER, J(AMES) MICHAEL, lawyer; b. Ft. Wayne, Ind., July 16, 1947; s. James Martin and Helen Patricia (Smith) K.; m. Jan Elaine McDonald, June 3, 1972; children: Christopher, Sean, Alison. AB in Hist., U. Notre Dame, 1969, JD, 1972. Bar: Ind. 1972, U.S. Dist. Ct. (no. and so. dists.) Ind. 1972. With legal dept. Lincoln Nat. Corp., Ft. Wayne, Ind., 1972—2002; 2d v.p., assoc. gen. counsel Lincoln Nat. Corp. and Lincoln Nat. Life Ins. Co., 1982-88, v.p., assoc. gen. counsel, 1988—2002; v.p., gen. counsel and dir. Lincoln Investment Mgmt., Inc., Ft. Wayne, 1997-2000; v.p., dep. gen. counsel Lincoln Nat. Reassurance Co., 2001—02; of counsel Barnes & Thornburg, Ft. Wayne, 2002—03; sr. v.p., gen. counsel, sec. Security Benefit Group, Topeka, 2003—. Bd. dirs. Allen County unit Am. Cancer Soc., Ft. Wayne, 1975-82, Embassy Theatre Found., 1998-2003, The Lincoln Mus., 1996-2000, Ft. Wayne-Allen County Hist. Soc., pres., 1993-95, Ft. Wayne Mus. Art, 1999-2003; bd. dirs. Topeka Performing Arts Ctr., 2004—. Fellow: Ind. Bar Found., Am. Coll. Investment Counsel; mem.: Assn. Life Ins. Counsel (sec.-treas. 1994—2000, bd. govs. 2000—, pres.-elect 2003—), Am. Corp. Counsel Assn., Am. Coun. Life Ins. (various task forces), Allen County Bar Assn. (bd. dirs., pres. 1996—97), Ind. Bar Assn. Roman Catholic. Office: Security Benefit Group One Security Benefit Plaza Topeka KS 66636 Home: 5621 SW Urish RD Topeka KS 66610-9158 E-mail: michael.keefer@securitybenefit.com.

KEEFFE, EMMET BRITTON, medical educator; b. San Francisco, Apr. 12, 1942; s. Emmet Britton and Corinne M. (Walsh) K.; m. Melenie M. Laskey, June 18, 1966; children: Emmet III, Brian, Meghan. BS, U. San Francisco, 1964, secondary teaching credential, 1965; MD, Creighton U., 1969. Intern Oreg. Health Sci. U., Portland, 1969-70, resident, 1970-73, fellow gastroenterology, 1973-74, asst. prof. medicine, 1979-83, assoc. prof. medicine, 1983-89, prof. med., 1989-92; fellow gastroenterology U. Calif., San Francisco, 1977-79, clin. prof. medicine, 1992—95; chief divsn. gastroenterology, hepatology Calif. Pacific Med. Ctr., San Francisco, 1992—95, med. dir. liver transplant program, 1992—95; prof. medicine, chief of hepatology, co-dir. liver transplant program Stanford Univ. Med. Ctr., 1995—. Author: Flexible Sigmoidoscopy, 1985, Handbook of Liver Disease, 1998, 2004, Atlas of Gastrointestinal Endoscopy, 1998; editor: Liver Update, 1991—94; mem. editl. bd. Hepatology, 1993—; mem. editl. bd.: Jour. Hepatology, 2000—, Am. Jour. Gastroenterology, 2002—, Ailimentary Pharmcology Therapeutics, 2003—; assoc. editor Liver Transplantation and Surgery, 1995—2000, Digestive and Nutrition, 1999—2004, Reviews in Gastroenterological Disorders, 2000—, sec. editor Current Opion in Organ Transplatation, 2000—; exec. editor: GastroHep.com, 2000—; contbr. chapters to books, articles to profl. jours. Lt. comdr. USN, 1974-77. Fellow: ACP, Am. Coll. Gastroenterology; mem.: AMA, Found. Digestive Health and Nutrition (bd. dirs. 2004—), Am. Digestive Health Found. (bd. dirs. 1994—2001, vice chair pub. health programs 1997—2001), Am. Clin. and Climatology Assn., European Assn. Study of Liver, Western Gut Club (pres. 1991), Internat. Assn. for Study of Liver, Internat. Liver Transplantation Soc., North Pacific Soc. of Internal Medicine, Am. Fedn. Clin. Rsch., Am. Soc. Transplantation, Am. Soc. Gastrointestinal Endoscopy (sec. 1991—94, pres.-elect 1994—95, pres. 1995—96), Am. Assn. Study Liver Diseases, Am. Gastroenterologic Assn. (v.p. 2002—03, pres.-elect 2003—04, pres. 2004—05), Am. Liver Found. (bd. dirs. 1991—95). Home: 22 Weatherly Dr Mill Valley CA 94941-3272 Office: Stanford University Med Ctr 750 Welch Rd Ste 210 Palo Alto CA 94304-1509 Office Phone: 650-498-5691. E-mail: ekeeffe@stanford.edu.

KEEFFE, JOHN ARTHUR, lawyer, director; b. Bklyn., Apr. 5, 1930; s. Arthur John and Mary Catherine (Daly) K.; m. Frances Elizabeth Rippetoe, July 24, 1952; children: Virginia Frances, Cynthia Louise, Amy Marie. AB, Cornell U., 1950; JD, U. Va., 1953. Bar: Va. 1953, NY 1956. Asst. U.S. atty. so. dist. State of N.Y., 1955-57; assoc. Rogers, Hoge & Hills, N.Y., 1957-63; of counsel Havens, Wandless, Stitt & Tighe, N.Y., 1963-65; ptnr. Keeffe & Costikyan, N.Y.C. and Washington, 1965-74, Keeffe Bros., N.Y.C. and Washington, 1974-77; sec., mng. dir. Saud Al-Farhan Inc., N.Y.C., 1979-80; pres., dir. J.A. Keeffe, PC, Eastchester, NY, 1981—2000. Bd. dirs., sec. The Street Theater, White Plains, N.Y., 1973-2002, trustee emeritus, 2002-. 1st lt. USAF, 1953-55. Mem. ABA, ATLA, N.Y. State Bar Assn., Va. Bar Assn., Westchester County Bar Assn. (dir. 1989-90, chmn. com. on fed. courthouse plans and procedures 1994-2000), N.Y. State Trial Lawyers Assn., Eastchester Bar Assn. (v.p. 1988-89, pres. 1989-90, bd. dirs. 1990-2000), Rotary (bd. dirs. 1991-2000, sec. 1991-92, pres.-elect 1992-93, pres. 1993-94, co-chair Eastchester Rotary Gift of Life 1993-94, co-chair dist. 7230 Gift of Life 1995-97). Republican. Congregationalist. Avocations: golf, reading. Home: 315A Heritage Hls Somers NY 10589-1716 Personal E-mail: fkeeffe@msn.com.

KEEGAN, DANIEL T., museum director; BA, U. Wis.; MFA, So. Ill. U. Dir. Kemper Mus. Contemporary Art, Kansas City, Mo., San Jose Mus. Art, 2000—. Tchr. W.Va. Wesleyan Coll., Avila Coll., Kansas City. Office: San Jose Mus Art 110 S Market St San Jose CA 95113-2383 Office Phone: 408-291-5381. E-mail: dkeegan@sjmusart.org.*

KEEGAN, JAMES JOSEPH, financial executive; b. Phila., Sept. 6, 1947; s. George Washington and Kathryn Margaret (Eckels) K.; m. Martha Jana Pettinga, Apr. 27, 1984. BBA in Acctg. cum laude, Tex. Christian U., 1969; MBA in Internat. Fin., U. Mich., 1970. CPA, Colo. Supervising sr. acct. Peat Marwick Mitchell, Denver, 1974-79; pvt. practice acctg. Englewood, Colo., 1979-81; pres. Trinity Securities, Englewood, 1981-83, Keegan Capital Devel., Englewood, 1983-89, Fairway Sys., Inc., Englewood, 1989—. CPA Small Bus. Adv. Coun., 1984-85; mem. rules and course rating coms. Colo. Golf Assn., committeeman, 1986-2002; rules ofcl. World Club Championship, Chdng-do, Korea; mem. sectional affairs com. USGA, 1996-97, Golf Mag. panelist, 2002—; mem. Fellowship Christian Athletes. Capt. USAF, 1971-74. Mem. AICPA, Beta Gamma Sigma, Beta Alpha Psi, Delta Sigma Pi. Achievements include playing top 100 golf courses in U.S. Office: Fairway Systems Inc 6 Inverness Ct E Ste 120 Englewood CO 80112-5517 E-mail: JKeegan@fairway.com.

KEEGAN, JOHN E., lawyer; b. Spokane, Wash., Apr. 29, 1943; BA, Gonzaga U., 1965; LLB, Harvard U., 1968. Bar: Wash. 1968, U.S. Ct. Appeals (9th cir.) 1976, U.S. Supreme Ct. Gen. counsel Dept. Housing and Urban Devel., Washington, 1968-70; instr. in bus. sch. and inst. environ. studies U. Wash., 1973-76, instr. land use and environ. law, 1976-78; now ptnr. Davis, Wright & Tremaine, Seattle. Author: (novels) Clearwater Summer, 1994, Piper, 2001, A Good Divorce, 2003. Office: Davis Wright Tremaine 2600 Century Sq 1501 4th Ave Seattle WA 98101-1688 Office Phone: 206-628-7688. Business E-Mail: johnkeegan@dwt.com.

KEEGAN, ROBERT J., manufacturing executive; b. NY, July 27, 1947; m. Lynn Keegan; 2 children. BS in Math., LeMoyne Coll.; MBA in Fin., U. Rochester, 1972. With Kodak, Rochester, NY, 1972—95; gen. mgr. Kodak New Zealand, 1986—87; dir. fin. photographic products group Kodak, Rochester, NY, 1987—90; gen. mgr. Kodak Spain, 1990—91; gen. mgr. consumer imaging Kodak European Middle Ea. African Region, 1991—93; exec. v.p., global strategy officer Avery Dennison Corp., Pasadena, Calif., 1995—97; pres. Kodak Profl., 1997; corp. v.p. Kodak, Rochester, 1997—2000, pres. consumer imaging, sr. v.p., 1997—2000, exec. v.p., 2000; pres., COO, dir. Goodyear Tire & Rubber Co., 2000—03, chmn., CEO, 2003—. Office: Goodyear Tire & Rubber Co 1144 E Market St Akron OH 44316*

KEEGEL, C. THOMAS, labor union administrator; b. Mpls., Sept. 27, 1941; m. Patricia Keegel; 3 children. AA in History, N. Hennepin Jr. Coll., Mpls., 1969; student, U. Ariz., 1970—73, U. Minn., 1970—73. Joined Teamsters Local 544, Mpls., 1959, various positions including sec.-treas., 1980—99; trustee, rec. sec. Teamsters Joint Coun. 32, 1980—99; gen. sec.-treas. Internat. Brotherhood Teamsters, Washington, 1999—. Office: Internat Brotherhood Teamsters Office Gen Sec-Treas 25 Louisiana Ave NW Washington DC 20001

KEEHN, SILAS, retired bank executive; b. New Rochelle, N.Y., June 30, 1930; s. Grant and Marjorie (Burchard) K.; m. Marcia June Lindquist, Mar. 26, 1955; children: Elisabeth Keehn Lewis, Britta Keehn Scott, Peter. AB in Econs, Hamilton Coll., Clinton, N.Y., 1952; MBA in Fin, Harvard U., 1957. With Mellon Bank N.A., Pitts., 1957-80, v.p., then sr. v.p., 1967-78, exec. v.p., 1978-79, vice-chmn., 1980; v.p. Mellon Nat. Corp., 1979-80, vice-chmn., 1980; chmn. bd. Pullman, Inc., Chgo., 1980; pres. Fed. Res. Bank Chgo., 1981-94; ret., 1994. Bd. dirs. Kewaunee Sci. Corp., Nat. Futures Assn. Trustee Rush U. Med. Ctr., Hamilton Coll., Clinton, N.Y. With USNR, 1953-56. Mem. Chgo. Club, Comml. Club Chgo., Econ. Club Chgo., Fox Chapel Golf Club (Pitts.), U. Club, Links Club (N.Y.C.), Rolling Rock Club (Ligonier, Pa.), Indian Hill Club. Office: 707 Skokie Blvd Ste 600 Northbrook IL 60062-2841 Office Phone: 847-509-2757.

KEEHNER, MICHAEL ARTHUR MILLER, investment company executive; b. Cedar Rapids, Iowa, Nov. 15, 1943; BS in Nuclear Physics, MIT, 1965; MBA in Fin. with high distinction, Harvard U., 1971. Registered securities rep. Engring. mgr. Gen. Dynamics Corp., Quincy, Mass., 1965-69; investment banking mgr. Kidder Peabody & Co., 1971-89, exec. mng. dir. individual investor svcs. N.Y.C., 1991-94; chmn., dir. Kidder Peabody Internat. Corp., N.Y.C., 1989-91; pres., chief exec. officer K P Exploration, Inc., N.Y.C., 1982-88; mng. dir., mem. exec. com., bd. mem. Kidder Peabody Group, Inc., N.Y.C., 1987-94; mng. ptnr. The Keehner Group, N.Y.C., 1994—. Bd. dirs. Cross Border LLC, LDMI Telecom. Inc.; adj. prof. fin. Columbia U. Trustee Bklyn. Mus. Baker scholar Harvard U.; Loeb Rhodes fellow Harvard U. Mem. India House (N.Y.C.), Rembrandt Club (Bklyn.), Long Island Wyandanch Club (N.Y.C.), Lake Waramug Country Club. Address: PO Box 99 South Kent CT 06785-0099

KEEL, ALTON GOLD, JR., ambassador; b. Newport News, Va., Sept. 8, 1943; s. Alton Gold and Ella Clare (Kennedy) K.; 1 child, Kristen Ann; m. Lynn (Matti) K. BS in Aerospace Engring., U. Va., 1966, PhD in Engring. Physics, 1970; postdoctoral scholar, U. Calif., Berkeley, 1971. Staff Naval Surface Weapons Ctr., Silver Springs, Md., 1971-77; congl. sci. fellow Senate Armed Services Com., Washington, 1977-79, staff mem., 1977-81; asst. sec. for research, devel. and logistics USAF, Washington, 1981-82; assoc. dir., nat. sec. internat. affairs Office Mgmt. and Budget, Washington, 1982-86; exec. dir. Pres.' Commn. on Challenger Accident, Washington, 1986; acting asst. to pres. for nat. security affairs The White House, Washington, 1986; U.S. permanent rep. NATO, Brussels, 1987-89; dep. chmn. The Riggs Nat. Bank, Washington, 1989-92; pres., mng. dir. Carlyle Internat. The Carlyle Group, Washington, 1992-94; chmn. Carlyle SEAG, 1994-95; chmn., mng. dir. Atlantic Ptnrs., L.L.C., Washington, 1992—; chmn., CEO Land-5 Corp., 1999—2002; CEO, InoStor Corp., 2002—05. Chmn. F-16 fighter aircraft multinat. steering com.; nat. del., bd. dirs. Adv. Group for Aerospace R&D, 1982; bd. dirs. Tandberg Data, Inc. (InoStor). Bd. dirs. Fondation pour la Promotion de la Recherche Fundamentale en Cancerologie, Belgium, 1988; mem. dean's adv. bd. U. Va., 1996—. Recipient research award NRC, 1970; Nat. Congl. Sci. fellow AIAA, 1976; recipient Young Engr.-Scientist award AIAA, 1978, Air Force Exceptional Civilian Service award, 1982, NASA Group Achievement award, 1986, Disting. Alumni award U. Va., 1988. Fellow AIAA, Sigma Xi; mem. French Am. C. of C. (mem. sr. adv. group 1990-95), Belgian Am. Assn. (bd. dirs. 1990-94), Phi Eta Sigma, Tau Beta Pi. Office: Atlantic Ptnrs 2891 S River Rd Stanardsville VA 22973-2416 E-mail: altonkeel@direcway.com.

KEELER, JAMES LEONARD, food products company executive; b. Richmond, Va., Jan. 31, 1935; s. Joseph McCauley and Nora Elizabeth (Thomas) K.; m. Joan Sandra Barnhart, Aug. 14, 1954; children: Mark Leonard, Tracy Ann, Steven James, Gregory Wayne. BS, Bridgewater Coll., 1957; JD, U. Va., 1983. CPA Va.; bar: Va. 1983. Ptnr., acct. Hueston & Keeler, CPAs, Harrisonburg, Va., 1958-63; mng. ptnr., acct. Keeler, Phibbs & Co., CPAs, Harrisonburg, 1963-80; ptnr., atty. Wharton, Aldhizer & Weaver, Harrisonburg, 1983-88; CEO WLR Foods, Inc., Broadway, Va., 1988—2001, pres., 1990—2001, Wampler Foods, Inc., Broadway, 1997—2001, chmn., 2003—. Vice chmn. bd. Bridgewater (Va.) Coll., 1974-91, mem. exec. com., trustee, 1974—, chmn. com. on bd. affairs, 1999-2003, mem. investment com., 2001-03, chmn. bd., 2003—; exec. adv. coun. James Madison U. Coll. Bus., Harrisonburg, 1989-95; bd. dirs. Valley of Va. Partnership for Edn., James Madison U., Rockingham Meml. Hosp., 1994-98, Va. Econ. Devel. Partnership, 1995-2001, Massanutten Regional Libr.; mem. Va. Bus. Coun., 1995-2001, vice-chmn., 1999-01; mem. Gov.'s Adv. Com. on Va.'s Strategy, 1998. Recipient disting. alumnus award Bridgewater Coll., 1990; named outstanding bus. person award Harrisonburg-Rockingham C. of C., 1995. Fellow Va. Soc. CPAs (pres. 1970-71, hon. chmn., Outstanding Mem. 1977); mem. ABA, AICPA (governing coun. 1969-70, 74-75, 76-77), Va. Bar Assn., Va. C. of C. (vice chmn. 1994-96, chmn. 1997-98, exec. com., bd. dirs. 1994-98). Republican. Mem. Brethren Ch. Avocation: boating. Personal E-mail: jkeeler@shentel.net.

KEELER, ROSS VINCENT, security firm executive; b. Evansville, Ind., Nov. 28, 1948; s. Mark V. and Lola (Saunders) K.; m. Pamela Person, Jan. 24, 1981; children: Margo, Eric. BS with honors, U. Fla., 1970; MBA with honors, U. So. Calif., 1971. Asst. v.p. SE Banks, Miami, Fla., 1972-74; exec. v.p. Barnett Leasing, Ft. Lauderdale, Fla., 1975-78, 1st Capital, Chgo., 1979-84; pres. Berkshire Investment Advisors (formerly Krupp Securities), Boston, 1984-96; ptnr. various Berkshire Cos., Boston, 1997—, also bd. dirs.; mng. gen. ptnr. First Coast Hedge Fund, Ponte Vedra, Fla., 1997—. Contbr. articles on fin. to profl. publs. Mem. Investors Program Assn. (trustee, chmn. 1988-93), Pension Real Estate Assn., Marsh Landing C.C., Ponte Vedra Inn and Club, Phi Kappa Phi, Beta Gamma Sigma. Home: 108 Teal Nest Ct Ponte Vedra Beach FL 32082-1944

KEELER, THEODORE EDWIN, economics professor; b. Enid, Okla., Mar. 25, 1945; s. Clinton Clarence and Lorene Adda Keeler; m. Marjorie Ann Nathanson, Aug. 29, 1982; 1 child, Daniel C. BA, Reed Coll., 1967; S.M., MIT, 1969, PhD, 1971. Asst. prof. econs. U. Calif.-Berkeley, 1971-77, assoc. prof., 1977-83, prof., 1983—. Key faculty Robert Wood Johnson Postdoctoral Fellows Program, 1993-2001. Author: Railroads, Freight, and Public Policy, 1983; co-author: Regulating The Automobile, 1986; also articles; editor: Research in Transportation Economics, vol. I, 1983, vol. II, 1985 Grantee NSF, 1973-75, 80-82, dept. transp. program, 1988-90, 93-94, NIH, 1990-91, Nat. Inst. on Aging, 1995-96; prin. investigator Sloan Found., 1975-80, Robert Wood Johnson Found., 1996-99; sr. fellow, vis. scholar Brookings Instn., Washington, 1980-82; co-prin. investigator Tobacco Tax Project Calif. Tobacco-Related Disease Fund, 1990-94, 99-2000 Mem. Am. Econs. Assn. Democrat. Office: U Calif Dept Econs Berkeley CA 94720-3880

KEELER, WILLIAM CONRAD, III, curator, librarian, archivist; b. Rochester, N.Y. s. William Conrad Jr. and Alice Prosonic Keeler; m. Caroline Van Brunt Beck, June 26, 1976; children: James William, Anna Jane. BA in Sociology, Fredonia (N.Y.) State U., 1974; MA in Libr. sci., U. at Buffalo, 2000. Archivist, libr., curator Perinton Hist. Soc., Fairport, NY, 1989—; curator, libr. Landmark Soc. of Western N.Y., Rochester, 1999—; libr., archivist Rochester Hist. Soc., 2002—. Mem. Ecumenical and Interfaith Archives Mgmt. Team, Rochester, 2003—. Author, editor: Perinton, Fairport and the Erie Canal, 2001, Perinton and Fairport in the 20th Century, 2004; editor: (newsletter) Perinton Historigram, 2001—. Mem.: Assn. State and Local History, Soc. Am. Archivists, Rochester Regional Libr. Coun. (local history com. 1999—, coll. archives com. 2003—). Democrat. Roman Catholic. Avocations: woodworking, growing antique apples. Office: Landmark Soc Western NY 133 S Fitzhugh St Rochester NY 14608

KEELER, WILLIAM HENRY CARDINAL, cardinal; b. San Antonio, Mar. 4, 1931; s. Thomas. Love and Margaret T. (Conway) Keeler. BA, St. Charles Borromeo Sem., 1952; STL, Pontifical Gregorian U., Rome, 1956, JCD, 1961; DD (hon.), Lebanon Valley Coll., 1984, Gettysburg Coll., 1986, Susquehanna U., 1989; LHD (hon.), Mt. St. Mary's Coll., 1985; LLD (hon.), Gannon U., 1993; LHD (hon.), Loyola Coll., 1995, Shippensburg State U., 1995; DD (hon.), St. Mary's U., Winona, Minn., 1995, Elizabeth Coll., 1996, Western Md. Coll., 1996, St. Vincent Sem., 1996, Coll. of Notre Dame of Md., 1997, U. Notre Dame, 1998, Ateneo de Manila U., 1998, Sacred Heart U., 2000, Cath. U., Lublin, Poland, 2000. Ordained priest Roman Catholic Ch., 1955, consecrated bishop, 1979. Asst. pastor Our Lady of Good Counsel Ch., Marysville, Pa., 1956—58; sec. diocesan tribunal Diocese of Harrisburg, Pa., 1956—58, defender of the bond, 1961—66, vice-chancellor, 1965—69, chancellor, 1969—79, aux. bishop and vicar gen., 1979—83, bishop of Harrisburg, 1984—89; archbishop of Balt., 1989—94; elevated to Cardinal Roman Cath. Church, 1994—; chmn. Md. Cath. Conf., 1989—. Newspaper publ. The Cath. Rev.; co-chmn. Pa. Conf. Inter-Ch. Coop., 1981—89; pres. Pa. Cath. Conf., 1983—89; chmn. com. on ecumenical and inter-religious affairs Nat. Conf. Cath. Bishops, 1984—87, mem., 1984—, sec., 1988—89, Episcopal moderator Cath.-Jewish rels., 1988—92, 1995—, v.p., 1989—92, pres., 1992—95; chmn. World Youth Day Celebration, Denver, 1993; cons. Com. Comm., 1995—; past pastor Marysville Parish; chmn. Com. Pro-Life Activities, 1998—2001; past titular bishop Ulcinium (Dulcigno); mem. Internat. Joint Com. for Cath.-Orthodox Theol. Dialogue, 1986—, Internat. Liaison Com. Caths. and Jews, 1987—, Synod of Bishops for Africa, 1994, World Synod of Bishops for the Consecrated Life, 1994, Synod of Bishops for Am., 1996; sec., spl. advisor 2d Vatican Coun., 1962—65; staff Coun. Digest, 1963—65; apptd. mem. Coun. for Assembly of Synod Bishops, 1997—. Active Black and Native Am. Missions Bd.; exec. bd. Keystone Area coun. Boy Scouts Am., 1979—89; trustee Cath. U. Am.; chancellor, chmn. bd. trustees St. Mary's Sem. and Univ., 1989—; chancellor Mt. St. Mary's Sem., 1989—; vice-chair North Am. Coll. Bd. Govs., 1998—; trustee Basilica of Nat. Shrine of Immaculate Conception, Washington, 1989—; active Interreligious Forum Greater Harrisburg, 1968—89; Pontifical coun. Promoting Christian Unity, 1994—; active Congregation for the Oriental Chs., 1994—; chmn. bd. trustees Associated Cath. Charities, 1989—, Basilica of Nat. Shrine of Assumption of the Blessed Virgin Mary, 1989—; v.p. Cath. Near East Welfare Assn. Named papal chamberlain, Pope Paul VI, 1965, prelate of honor, 1970, Marylander of Yr., Md. Colonial Soc., 1986, The Balt. Sun, 1994, Media Person of Yr., Md. Press Assn., 1994; recipient Gold medal, Pope John XXIII, 1961, John Baum Humanitarian award, Dauphin County unit Am. Cancer Soc., 1984, Americanism award, Anti-Defamation League, 1985, De Tocqueville Soc. award, 1988, Nat. award, Boy Scouts of Am., 1990, Disting. Citizen award, 1998, Weil medal, Jewish Chataqua Soc., 1993, Salvation Army award, 1995, Shaw award, Rotary Internat., 1995, Mahmoud Abu Sand Excellence award, Am. Muslim Coun., 1995, Nostra Aetate award, Inst. Christian Jewish Understanding, 1997, Silver St. George medal, Nat. Cath. Com. Scouting, 1998, Lifetime Achievement award, Shaare Zedek Med. Ctr., Jerusalem, 1999, Disting. Citizens award, Balt. coun. Boy Scouts Am., 1999. Mem.: Cath. Extension Soc. Govs., Am. Cath. Hist. Soc., Canon Law Soc. Am. Roman Catholic.*

KEELEY, EDMUND LEROY, literature educator, writer, translator; b. Damascus, Syria, Feb. 5, 1928; came to U.S., 1931; s. James Hugh and Mathilde (Vossler) K.; m. Mary Stathatos-Kyris, Mar. 18, 1951. BA, Princeton U., 1949; D. Phil., Oxford (Eng.) U., 1952; hon. doctorate, Athens U., 1994. Fulbright tchr. English Am. Farm Sch., Salonika, Greece, 1949-50; Woodrow Wilson fellow, 1950-51; instr. English Brown U., 1952-53; Fulbright lectr. Salonika U., 1953-54; instr. English Princeton (N.J.) U., 1954-57, asst. prof., 1957-63, assoc. prof., 1963-70, prof. English and creative writing, 1970-92, Charles Barnwell Straut Class of 1923 prof. English, 1992-94; Straut prof. emeritus, 1994—; prof. creative writing and English emeritus Princeton (N.J.) U., 1994—, co-chmn. program in comparative lit., 1964-65, dir. creative arts program, 1966-71, dir. program creative writing and theatre, 1971-73, dir. creative writing program, 1974-81, mem. Hellenic studies com., 1979-94, chmn., 1985-94, dir. Hellenic studies program, 1985-94. Lectr. dept. Byzantine and Modern Greek Oxford (Eng.) U., 1960; vis. lectr. Writers Workshop, U. Iowa, 1962-63, U. of the Aegean, 1988; vis. prof. New Sch. Social Rsch., 1980, Sch. Arts Columbia U., 1981; writer-in-residence Knox Coll., spring 1963; Fulbright lectr. Athens U., 1985, U. Thessaloniki, 1986; vis. rsch. fellow U. Crete, Rethymnon, 1986; Fulbright rsch. fellow Athens U., 1987; sr. assoc. mem. St. Antony's Coll., Oxford, 1996; vis. prof., King's Coll., London U., 1996. Author: The Libation, 1958, (with Philip Sherrard) Six Poets of Modern Greece, 1960, George Seferis: Collected Poems, 1924-1955, 1967, C.P. Cavafy: Collected Poems, 1975, 92, Angelos Sikelianos: Selected Poems, 1979, 96, George Seferis: Collected Poems, 1979, 81, 95, The Dark Crystal, Voices of Modern Greece, 1981, Odysseus Elytis: Selected Poems, 1981, A Greek Quintet, 1992, The Gold-Hatted Lover, 1961, (with Mary Keeley) The Plant, The Well, The Angel (V. Vassilikos), 1964, The Impostor, 1970, (with George Savidis) C.P. Cavafy: Passions and Ancient Days, 1972, Odysseus Elytis: The Axion Esti, 1974, Voyage to a Dark Island, 1972, Cavafy's Alexandria, 1976, 1995, Ritsos in Parentheses, 1979, A Conversation with Seferis, 1982, Modern Greek Poetry: Voice and Myth, 1982, A Wilderness Called Peace, 1985, Yannis Ritsos, Exile and Return: Selected Poems, 1967-74, 1985, The Salonika Bay Murder: Cold War Politics and The Polk Affair, 1989, Yannis Ritsos: Repetitions, Testimonies, Parentheses, 1991, School for Pagan Lovers, 1993, George Seferis and Edmund Keeley: Correspondence, 1951-1971, 95, 97, Albanian Journal: The Road to Elbasan, 1997, Inventing Paradise: the Greek Journey, 1937-47, 1999, 2d edit., 2002, On Translation: Reflections and Conversations, 2000, Some Wine for Remembrance, 2001, Borderlines: A Memoir, 2005; editor: (with Peter Bien) Modern Greek Writers, 1972, (with Cone and Frank) The Legacy of R.P. Blackmur: Essays, Memoirs, Texts, 1987, The Essential Cavafy, 1995, (with Bien, Constantine, and Van Dyck) A Century of Greek Poetry: 1900-2000, 2004; bd. editl. direction: Princeton Alumni Weekly, 1964-77; adv. bd. Princeton Essays in the Arts, 1974-78; editl. bd. Byzantine and Modern Greek Studies, 1974-83, Translation Rev., 1978—, Jour. Modern Greek Studies, 1983-91; adv. editor Delos, 1988—; mem. Gennadius Libr. Bd. Trustees, 1995—. Mem. scholarship fund com. Am. Farm Sch., Salonika, Greece, 1955-60, trustee, 1978—; chmn. McCarter Theatre Com., 1969, trustee, 1983-86; mem. nat. bd. Translation Ctr., Columbia, 1975-77, mem. governing bd., 1977-94; mem. translation jury Nat. Book Awards, 1977; bd. dirs. internat. program Aegean U., 1989-90. With USNR, 1945-46; with USAF, 1953-56. Jr. fellow Coun. Humanities, 1956-57, Rome prize fellow Am. Acad. Arts and Letters, 1959-60, Guggenheim fellow, 1959-60, 73, McCosh faculty fellow, 1969-70, Ingram Merrill Found. fellow, 1977-78, resident fellow Va. Ctr. for Creative Arts, 1983, 84, 86, 90, NEA fellow, 1981, 88-89; Rockefeller Found. scholar Bellagio Study Ctr., Italy, 1982, 89; vis. fellow Inst. for the Humanities, U. Mich., 1994; NEH grantee, 1977-78, 83; recipient Columbia Transl. Ctr.-PEN award, 1975, Harold Morton Landon Transl. award Acad. Am. Poets, 1980, judge, 92, Howard T. Behrman award for Disting. Achievement in the Humanities, 1982, PEN/NEA fiction syndicate award, 1983, Pushcart Prize Anthology award, 1984, first European Prize for Transl. of Poetry, 1987, Acad. award in lit. Am. Acad. Arts and Letters, 1999, Ralph Manheim medal for translation PEN, 2000, Criticos prize London Hellenic Soc., 2000, Trustees' Annual award Gennadius Libr., 2003, Phiddipides award Hellenic Pub. Radio, 2004; comdr. Order of the Phoenix, Greece, 2002. Fellow Am. Acad. Arts and Scis.; mem. Authors Guild, Soc. Fellows Am. Acad. Rome (exec. com. 1975-77, 83-87), Am. Lit. Translators Assn. (exec. bd. 1983—), PEN (Am. Ctr. membership com. 1978-83, program com. 1979-82, exec. bd. 1980-96, del. internat. congress 1987, 9-93, 95-2000, v.p. 1989-91, pres. 1991-93, bd. trustees 1996-2001, trustee Internat. PEN Found. 2000—, trustee Coll. Yr. in Athens 2001—), Modern Greek Studies Assn. (pres. 1969-73, 80-82, exec. bd. 1995-98), Poetry Soc. Am. (v.p. 1977-78, 81-83), Acad. Athens (corr.), Hellenic Authors' Soc.(hon.), Phi Beta Kappa. Home: 140 Littlebrook Rd Princeton NJ 08540-4041 Also: 17 Loukianou St 10675 Athens Greece Business E-Mail: keeley@princeton.edu.

KEELEY, IRENE PATRICIA MURPHY, federal judge; b. 1944; BA, Coll. Notre Dame, 1965; MA, W.Va. U., 1977, JD, 1980. Bar: W. Va., 1980. Atty. Steptoe & Johnson, Clarksburg, W.Va., 1980-92; dist. judge U.S. Dist. Ct. (no. dist.), W. Va., 1992—. Adj. prof. law W.Va. U., 1990-91; bd. dirs. W.Va. U. Alumni Assn., 1995—, 1st v.p., 1997-98; mem. bd. advisors W.Va. U. Vis. com. W.Va. U. Coll. Law, 1987-91, 94-98; chmn. adv. bd. W.Va. U., 1997-98. Mem. ABA, Nat. Conf. Fed. Trial Judges (exec. com. 1996—,), W.Va. State Bar, W.Va. Bar Assn., Harrison County Bar Assn., Clarksburg Country Club, Oral Lake Fishing Club, Immaculate Conception Roman Cath. Ch. Office: US Courthouse PO Box 2808 500 W Pike St Rm 202 Clarksburg WV 26302-2808 Office Phone: 304-624-5850. Office Fax: 304-622-1928.*

KEELEY, LARRY, innovation strategist; Co-founder, pres. Doblin Inc., Chgo., 1981—. Lectr. in field; adj. prof., graduate design strategy courses Inst. Design, Ill. Inst. Tech., bd. dir.; lectr. in innovation Northwestern U., Kellogg Sch. Mgmt., U. Chgo.; bd. dir. WBEZ-FM, Chgo. Named one of Magnificent Seven Gurus of Innovation, BusinessWeek, 2005. Office: Doblin Inc 300 N Wabash Ave Ste 1300 Chicago IL 60611 Office Phone: 312-443-0800. Office Fax: 312-443-0567.*

KEELEY, ROBERT DENIUS, physician, researcher; b. Boston, Mar. 6, 1965; s. Robert Hunter and Sandra Denius Keeley; m. Margaret Louise Driscoll, Aug. 23, 1997; children: Hunter, Liam. MD, Stanford U., Calif., 2004—04; MS in Pub. Health, U. of Colo., 2004. Primary care rsch. fellow UCHSC, Aurora, Colo., 2001—04. Vis. scholar Stanford U., Calif., 2004—. Author: (research) North American Primary Care Research Group (Disting. Talk, North Am. Primary Care Rsch. Group, 2003). Dir. Cmty. Health Rsch. Initiative, Longmont, Colo., 2000—. Grantee Practice-Based Rsch. Network grantee, Am. Assn. of Family Practice, 2002. Mem.: AMA (none, none none). Avocation: fly fishing. Home: 350 Lincoln St Longmont CO 94304 Office: Stanford University 411 Quarry Rd Palo Alto CA Office Phone: 650-725-5720. Home Fax: 650-323-1239. Personal E-mail: robert.keeley@uchsc.edu. E-mail: robkeeley@pol.net.

KEELEY, ROBERT VOSSLER, retired academic administrator, ambassador; b. Beirut, Sept. 4, 1929; s. James Hugh and Mathilde Julia (Vossler) K.; m. Louise Schoonmaker, June 23, 1951; children: Michal M., Christopher J. AB, Princeton U., 1951, postgrad., 1951-53; postgrad. (Princeton fellow in pub. affairs), 1970-71; postgrad. (Nat. Inst. Pub. Affairs fellow), Stanford U., 1965-66. With Fgn. Service, Dept. State, Washington, 1956-89; officer in charge Congo (Leopoldville) external affairs Washington, 1963-64; officer-in-charge Congo (Brazzaville), Rwanda and Burundi affairs, 1964-65; polit. officer Athens Greece, 1966-70; detailed Woodrow Wilson fellow Princeton U., 1970; dep. chief mission Kampala, Uganda, 1971-73; alt. dir. E. African affairs Washington, 1974; dep. chief mission Phnom Penh, Khmer Republic, 1974-75; dep. dir. Interagency Task Force for Indochina Refugees, 1975-76; ambassador Mauritius, 1976-78; dep. asst. sec. for African Affairs Dept. State, Washington, 1978-80; ambassador to Zimbabwe, 1980-84; sr. fellow Ctr. for Study Fgn. Affairs, Fgn. Service Inst., Washington, 1984-85; ambassador to Greece, 1985-89. Pres. Middle East Inst., Washington, 1990-95; writer, lectr., cons. Pub. Five and Ten Press, 1995—. Lt. (j.g.) USCGR, 1953-55. Mem. Am. Fgn. Svc. Assn., Washington Inst. Fgn. Affairs, Am. Acad. Diplomacy, Cosmos Club. Home: 3814 Livingston St NW Washington DC 20015-2803

KEELING, JOE KEITH, theology studies educator, retired dean; b. Muskogee, Okla., Apr. 21, 1936; s. William Lytle and Anna Madge (Watts) K.; m. Marjorie Ann Brotherton, 1957; children: Kara Kay, William Kent. BA in History, Northeastern State U., 1958; BD in Theology, So. Meth. U., 1962; MA in Theology, U. Chgo., 1967, PhD, 1974. Ordained to ministry United Meth. Ch., 1962. Dir. orientation, acad. advisor U. Chgo., 1964-68; asst. prof. religion Augustana Coll., Sioux Falls, SD, 1968-72; from asst. to assoc. prof. philosophy and religion Rockford (Ill.) Coll., 1972-86, dean of spl. acad. programming, assoc. dean of coll., 1981-86; adj. assoc. prof. dept. medicine U. Ill. Coll of Medicine at Rockford, 1984-86; provost, dean, prof. religion and philosophy Baker U., Baldwin City, Kans., 1986-96; v.p., dean Ctrl. Meth. U., Fayette, Mo., 1996—2002, prof. emeritus philosophy and religion, 2002—. Mem. bd. ordained ministry Kans. Ea. Conf. United Meth. Ch., 1987-96; cons., evaluator, mem. accreditation rev. coun. North Ctrl. Assn. Colls. and Schs., Am. Conf. Acad. Deans, Midwest Bioethics Ctr. Author and lectr. in field. Mem. Kansas City Regional Coun. Higher Edn., 1986-94; mem. instnl. rev. com. Swedish-Am. Hosp., Rockford, 1981-86. Mem. Am. Acad. Religion (v.p., program chmn. Midwest region 1981-82, pres. 1982-83), Rockford C. of C. (bd. dirs. 1983-86), AAUP (Ill. state coun. mem. 1979-81), Archael. Inst. Am. (bd. dirs. Rockford chpt. 1984-86), Rotary. Democrat. Avocations: fishing, camping, canoeing. Home: PO Box 429 878 Highway 5 And 240 Fayette MO 65248-9509 Office: Ctrl Meth U Stedman 313 411 Central Methodist Sq Fayette MO 65248-1129 Office Phone: 660-248-6276. Business E-Mail: kkeeling@centralmethodist.edu.

KEELING, J(OHN) MICHAEL, lawyer, trade association executive; b. Kilgore, Tex., Feb. 24, 1947; s. Frank Marion and Eva Mae (Buse) K.; m. Michaela Eleanora Halik, Aug. 2, 1969; children: Alexandra Halik, J. Michael Jr. BA, Yale U., 1969; JD, U. Tex., 1971. Bar: Tex. 1972, D.C. 1982. Rsch. dir. Tex. Legislature Interim Com. on Ad Valorem Taxation, Austin, 1971; rsch. dir. gubernatorial gov. campaign Frances T. Farenthold, Austin, 1972; legis. dir. office congressman J.J. Pickle 10th Dist. Tex., Washington, 1972-73; chief staff office congressman J.J. Pickle 10th Jud. Dist. Tex., Washington, 1973-81; prin. David P. Stang, P.C., Washington, 1981-88; counsel Zuckert, Scott & Rasenberger, Washington, 1988-91; gen. counsel Employee Stock Ownership Plan Assn., Washington, 1984-91, pres., 1991—. Host Employee Ownership Talk Radio. Recipient Disting. Svc. award Small Bus. Coun. Am., 1993. Mem. ABA, Nat. Assn. Royalty Owners (life), Am. Soc. Assn. Execs. (cert.). Democrat. Baptist. Avocation: civil war history. E-mail: michael@esopassociation.org.

KEELING, KENNETH AUGUSTUS, SR., music educator; b. Norfolk, Va., May 29, 1938; d. Willis Eugene and Helen Ballard Keeling; m. Jean Ellis Keeling, June 10; children: Lorri Jeanne children: Kenneth, Jr. Augustus, Anthony Charles. Mus D Musical Arts, Cath. U., Washington, D.C., 1969—72. Prof. of music Carnegie Mellon Univ., Pitts., 1996—, head, sch. of music, 1996—2001. Musician: (conductor, clarinetist) Performing Musician. Bd. mem. Gateway to the Arts, Pitts., 1997—2003. Lt. comdr. U.S. Naval Res., 1977—87, Columbia, MD. Liberal. Baptist. Achievements include Recording Artist. Avocations: training, travel, reading. Home: 101 Country Club Drive Pittsburgh PA 15235 Office: Carnegie Mellon Univ Sch of Music 5000 Forbes Ave Pittsburgh PA 15213 Personal E-mail: kak@andrew.cmu.edu.

KEELING, LARRY DALE, journalist; b. Anderson County, Ky., May 5, 1947; s. Elmer Pascal and Ida Elizabeth (Gregory) K.; m. Cynthia Maria Taylor, Nov. 28, 1987 (div. Feb. 2001); m. Dorothy Elizabeth Cayce Wilson, Sept. 18, 2002. BA, U. Ky., 1969. Reporter Henry County Jour., Bassett, Va., 1972, Martinsville (Va.) Bull., 1972-74, Bradenton (Fla.) Herald, 1974-75, Lexington (Ky.) Herald, 1975-79; editl. writer Lexington Herald-Leader, 1979—. 1st lt. USAF, 1969-72, Taiwan. Recipient Sigma Delta Chi award for editl. writing, 1993, Nat. Headliner award for editl. writing, 1994, Green Eyeshade award for editl. writing, 1995, 97, spl. citation for opinion Nat. Awards for Edn. Reporting, 1997; fellow Knight Ctr. for Specialized Journalism, 1997. Mem. Soc. Profl. Journalists (Bluegrass chpt.), Nat. Conf. Editorial Writers. Office: Lexington Herald-Leader 100 Midland Ave Lexington KY 40508-1999

KEEM, MICHAEL DENNIS, veterinarian; b. Buffalo, July 29, 1950; s. Sanford Joseph and Clara C. (Chmiel) K.; m. Mary Beth Fix, June 1, 1973 (div. 1993); children: Chelsey, Erin, Daniel, Ryan. BS, Niagara U., 1972; MS, U. Wyo., 1974; DVM, Cornell U., 1979. Assoc. veterinarian Spink Vet. Assn., Attica, N.Y., 1979-80, Cheektowaga (N.Y.) Vet. Hosp., 1980-1984, vet., owner, pres., 1985—, Amclare Vet. Hosp., P.C., Williamsville, N.Y., 1987—; vet., owner Aurora Pet Hosp., 2004—. Ptnr. Greater Buffalo Vet. Emergency Svcs., P.C., 1985—, also bd. dirs. Com. chmn. pack 601 Boy Scouts Am., 1989-91, Webelos den leader, 1991-92, asst. scoutmaster troop 601, 1992-96, com. mem. 1996—. Mem. AVMA, Animal Birth Control Soc. (bd. dirs. 1981-2004), N.Y. State Vet. Med. Soc., Western N.Y. Vet. Med. Assn. (pres.-elect 1988, pres. 1989, past pres. 1990, bd. dirs. 1991-94), Niagara Frontier Vet. Soc. (bd. dirs. 1986-96, 2000-2004), Buffalo Acad. Vet. Medicine (sgt.-at-arms 1995-96, sec./treas. 1996-97, v.p. 1997-98, pres. 1998-99), Phi Kappa Phi, Phi Zeta, Omega Tau Sigma. Republican. Roman Catholic. Office: Cheektowaga Vet Hosp PC 957 Dick Rd Cheektowaga NY 14225-3554 also: Amclare Vet Hosp PC 895 Hopkins Rd Williamsville NY 14221-1728 Office: Aurora Pet Hosp 400 Olean Rd East Aurora NY 14052 Office Phone: 716-655-0305.

KEEN, CONSTANTINE, retired manufacturing company executive; b. N.Y.C., Jan. 1, 1925; s. Andrew and Sophie (Findani) K.; m. Kally Carajikis, Sept. 23, 1951; children: Katherine, Andrew. BA, NYU, 1952. Asst. treas. Sandz Indsl. Corp., N.Y.C., 1951-55; with Fedders Corp., Edison, N.J., 1955—, asst. credit mgr., 1955-57, credit mgr., 1957-60, dir. credit, 1960-68, v.p., dir. credit, 1968-75, v.p., dir. distbr. relations, 1975-77, v.p., treas., 1980-87, v.p. internat., 1984-86; pres. Fedders Internat. Corp., 1987-93, dir., 1996—2004. With USAAF, 1942-45. Decorated D.F.C., Air medal. Mem.: Ahepa, Masons. Greek Orthodox.

KEEN, VICTOR F., lawyer; b. Pueblo, Colo., Oct. 6, 1941; BA, Trinity Coll., 1963; JD, Harvard U., 1966. Bar: DC 1967, NY 1970, Pa. 1994, NJ 1994. Jud. clk. to Hon. John W. Kern US Tax Ct., 1966—68; assoc. Milbank, Tweed, Hadley & McCloy, NYC, 1968—76; ptnr. Whitman & Ransom, NYC, 1976—83, Kronish, Lieb, Weiner & Hellman, NYC, 1983—92, Cohen, Shapiro, Polisher, Shiekman & Cohen, Phila., 1993—95, chair tax dept., 1993—95; ptnr. Duane Morris LLP, 1995—, chair firm tax dept., 1999—. Bd. dirs. Spring Garden Civic Assn. Mem.: ABA (taxation sect.), Phila. Bar Assn. (tax sect.), Pa. Bar Assn. (tax law sect.). Office: Duane Morris LLP One Liberty Pl Philadelphia PA 19103-7396 Office Phone: 215-979-1945. Office Fax: 215-979-1020. Business E-Mail: vfkeen@duanemorris.com.

KEENAN, BARBARA MILANO, state supreme court justice; b. Vienna, 1950; BA, Cornell U., 1971; JD, George Wash. U., 1974; LLM, U. Va., 1992. Asst. commonwealth atty., Fairfax County, Va., 1974—76; pvt. law practice, 1976—80; judge Gen. Dist. Ct., Fairfax County, 1980-82, Circuit Ct., Fairfax County, 1982-85, Ct. Appeals, Va., 1985-91; assoc. justice Va. Supreme Court, Richmond, 1991—. Recipient Am. Jurisprudence award, Fairfax Bar Assn., 1995. Office: Va Supreme Ct PO Box 1315 Richmond VA 23218-1315

KEENAN, EDWARD L., linguist, educator; b. Somerset, Pa., Dec. 10, 1937; m. Carol Archie; 1 child, David. BA in Philosophy and Religion, Swarthmore Coll., 1959; diploma in lit., U. Paris, Sorbonne, 1961, cert. in French lit., 1962; MA in Linguistics, George Washington U., 1966; PhD in Linguistics, U. Pa., 1969. Sr. fellow King's Coll., Cambridge, England, 1970—74; vis. prof. U. Amsterdam, Netherlands, 1977, U. Tel Aviv, 1978—79; fellow Max Planck Inst. for Psycholinguistics, Nijmegen, Netherlands, 1984—85; Fulbright scholar U. Antananarivo, Madagascar, 1995; prof. linguistics UCLA, 1974—. Co-author: Boolean Semantics for Natural Language, 1985, Bare Grammar: A Study of Language Invariants, 2003, Universal Grammar: 15 Essays, 1987; mem. adv. editl. bd.: Lang. Rsch., 1985—, consulting editor: Jour. Semantics, 1987—, Jour. Lang. and Computation, 1997—. Grantee, NSF, 2000—01, Binational Sci. Found., 2000, 2002. Mem.: AAAS, ACLU, Linguistic Soc. Am., Am. Math. Soc. Green Party. Achievements include discovery of accessiblity hierarchy in syntactic typology; conservativity constraint on natural language quantification. Avocation: poetry. Office: UCLA Dept Linguistics 3125 Campbell Hall Box 951543 Los Angeles CA 90095 E-mail: keenan@humnet.ucla.edu.

KEENAN, EDWARD LOUIS, history professor; b. Buffalo, May 13, 1935; s. Edward Louis and Emma (Boudiette) K.; m. Joan Glasser, Nov. 25, 1961 (div. Oct. 1986); children: Edward, Christopher, Nicholas, Matthew (dec.); m. Judith Kapp Davison, Jan. 4, 1987. AB, Harvard U., 1957, MA, 1962, PhD, 1966; postgrad., Leningrad State U., 1959-61. From tchg. fellow to prof. Harvard U., Cambridge, Mass., 1962—91, Mellon prof. humanities, 1991; dir. Dumbarton Oaks Rsch. Libr. and Collections, Washington, 1998—. Lectr. Slavic Workshop, Ind. U., 1962-64; dir. Ctr. for Mid. Ea. Studies, 1981-83, 86-87, 93, 95. Author: The Kurbskii-Groznyi Apocrypha, 1972, Joseph Dobrovsky and the Origins of the Igor Tale, 2003; contbr. articles to profl. jours. Bd. govs. Reza Shah Kabir U., 1975—. Guggenheim fellow, 1970 Mem. Am. Assn. for Advancement Slavic Studies (pres. 1994). Democrat. Office: Dumbarton Oaks 1703 32nd St NW Washington DC 20007 Office Phone: 202-399-6413.

KEENAN, GAIL M., nursing educator; b. Burlington, Iowa, Sept. 7, 1950; d. William and Elizabeth Walters; m. William Keenan, May 11, 1974; children: Erin, Megan, Casey. BSN, Rutgers U., 1977; MS in Nursing Adminstrn., U. Ill., Chgo., 1981, PhD, 1994; postgrad., U. Iowa, 1994—96. RN Ill., Mich. Various positions in staff and adminstrv. in acute care; asst. prof. Loyola U., Chgo., 1993—94, U. Mich., Ann Arbor, 1994—2003, assoc. prof., 2003—. Ednl. specialist Multiple Sclerosis Soc., Dupage County, Ill. Recipient Healthcare Info. Tech. Innovator of Yr. award, Coll. Healthcare Info. Mgmt. Exec., 2003. Mem.: AMA (mentor 1997—), Mich. Nurses Assn. (chair standardized nursing language taskforce 1999—2004), Am. Nurses Assn. (nursing practice com. 2001—). Democrat. Avocations: opera, travel, skiing, basketball. Office: Univ Mich 400 N Ingalls Ann Arbor MI 48109

KEENAN, JAMES GEORGE, classics educator; b. NYC, Jan. 19, 1944; s. George F. and Cecilia Anna (Schmidt) K.; m. Laurie Haight; children: James, Kathleen, Kenneth, Mary, Lisa, Brian, Laura. AB, Holy Cross Coll., 1965; MA, Yale U., 1966, PhD, 1968. Asst. prof. Classics U. Calif., Berkeley, 1968-73; assoc. to full prof. Classics Loyola U. of Chgo., 1973—, chmn. classics, 1978-84, acting chmn., 1987-88. Cons. Petra Scrolls Conservation Project, 1995. Co-editor: edition of Greek papyri: The Tebtunis Papyri, vol. IV, 1976. Fellow Nat. Endowment for Humanities, 1973-74; travel grantee Am. Council Learned Socs., 1974, 83, 86; grant-in-aid Am. Philos. Soc., 1987. Mem. Am. Philol. Assn., Am. Soc. Papyrologists (pres. 1989-93), Chgo. Classical Club (pres. 1999-2001), Classical Assn. Midwest and South, Assn. Internat. des Papyrologues (mem. com. 1995-2004), Egypt Exploration Soc., Internat. Soc. Arabic Papyrology. Roman Catholic. Office: Loyola U Chgo Dept Classical Studies 6525 N Sheridan Rd Chicago IL 60626-5344 Office Phone: 773-508-3665. Business E-Mail: jkeenan@luc.edu.

KEENAN, JOHN FONTAINE, federal judge; b. N.Y.C., Nov. 23, 1929; s. John Joseph and Veronica (Fontaine) K.; m. Diane R. Nicholson, Oct. 6, 1956; 1 child, Marie Patricia BBA, Manhattan Coll., N.Y., 1951; LLD (hon.), Manhattan Coll., 1989; LLB, Fordham U., 1954; LLD (hon.), Mt. St. Vincent Coll., 1989. Bar: N.Y. 1954, U.S. Dist. Ct. (so. dist.) N.Y. 1983. From asst. dist. atty. to chief asst. dist. atty. N.Y. County Dist. Atty.'s Office, 1956-76; spl. prosecutor, dep. atty. gen. City of N.Y., 1976-79; chmn. bd., pres. N.Y.C. Off-Track Betting Corp., 1979-82; criminal justice coord. City of N.Y., 1982-83; judge U.S. Dist. Ct. So. Dist. N.Y., N.Y.C., 1983—; chief asst. dist. atty. Queens County Dist. Atty.'s Office, N.Y., 1973. Adj. prof. John Jay Coll.

Criminal Justice, N.Y.C., 1979-83, Fordham U. Sch. Law, N.Y.C., 1992, 93; mem. Fgn. Intelligence Svc. Ct., 1994-2001, Judicial Panel on Multi-Dist. Litigation, 1998—. Contbr. articles to law jours. Chmn. Daytop Village, Inc., N.Y.C., 1981-83. Served with U.S. Army, 1954-56. Recipient Frank S. Hogan award Citizens Com. Control of Crime in N.Y., 1975, Emory R. Buckner award Federal Bar Coun., 1993; cert. of recognition Patrolmen's Benevolent Assn., 1976; 1st Ann. Hogan-Morgenthau Assocs. award N.Y. County Dist. Atty.'s Office, 1976, Medal of Achievement, N.Y. County Lawyers Assn., 1992; Excellence award N.Y. State Bar Assn., 1978, award N.Y. Criminal Bar Assn., 1979, Disting. Faculty award Nat. Coll. Dist. Attys., 1978, Louis J. Lefkowitz award Fordham U. Law Sch. Urban Law Jour., 1983, Charles Carroll award Guild Cath. Lawyers, 1994, Ellis Island medal of honor, Nat. Ethnic Coalition of Orgns. Found., Inc., 1998. Mem.: Brehon Soc. (award 2002), Skytop Club, Amackassin Club. Republican. Roman Catholic. Office: US Dist Ct Daniel Patrick Moynihan US Courthouse 500 Pearl St Rm 1930 New York NY 10007-1312

KEENAN, JOSEPH MICHAEL, military officer; b. Drexel Hill, Pa., Jan. 12, 1969; s. Joseph Michael and Rose Marie Keenan. BA, Villanova U., 1991; MA, Naval Postgrad. Sch., 1998. Commd. ens. USN, 1991, advanced through grades to lt., 1994; comms. officer USS Boulder, Norfolk, Va., 1992-94; damage control asst. USS Ramage, Norfolk, 1995-96; weapons control officer USS Laboon, Norfolk, 1999—. Mem. Surface Navy Assn.

KEENAN, KATHLEEN, state legislator; b. Burlington, Vt., May 7, 1940; d. Roland and Madelyn M. (Cahill) K.; 8 children. Dipl., Jeanne Mance Sch. Nursing, 1961; postgrad. in nurse practitioner program, U. Vt., 1976. Nurse; mem. Vt. Ho. of Reps., Montpelier, 1989—, chair commerce com. Mem. Hinesburg Dem. Com., 1954-68, chair, 1965-68; mem. St. Albans Dem. Com., 1968—; mem. Vt. Econ. Progress Coun., 1994-98; bd. dirs. Efficiency Vt., Vt. Electric Power Prodrs., State Human Resources Investment Coun. Mem. St. Albans Skating Assn. (charter), Emergency Nurses Assn., Nat. Conf. Ins. Legislators (mem. exec. com., former pres.), Bus. and Profl. Women. Address: 8 Thorpe Ave Saint Albans VT 05478-1834

KEENAN, MICHAEL E., professional hockey team executive; m. Nola Keenan; 1 child, Gayla. Student, St. Lawrence U., N.Y. Player Roanoke Valley Rebels, So. Hockey League, Va., 1973-74; coach Met. Toronto Hockey League, Ont., Can., Peterborough Petes, Ont. Hockey League, 1979-80; head coach Can. Nat. Jr. Team, 1980, Rochester Ams., Am. Hockey League, N.Y., 1980-83, Toronto Hockey Team, Can. Collegiate League, Ont., 1983-84, Phila. Flyers, NHL, 1984-88, Chgo. Blackhawks, NHL, 1988-92, gen. mgr., 1990-92; head coach N.Y. Rangers, NHL, 1993-94; head coach, gen. manager St. Louis Blues, 1994-96; head coach Vancouver Canucks, 1998-99, Florida Panthers, 2001—03, gen. mgr., 2004—. Named Most Valuable Player, Roanoke Valley Rebels, So. Hockey League, 1974; winning coach World Amateur Hockey Championships, 1980, Calder Cup Championship, 1982-83, Can. Collegiate Championship, U. Toronto, 1983-84, Stanley Cup Championship, 1994, Can. Cup Championship, 1987, 91; recipient Jack Adams award as NHL Coach of Yr., 1985; Coach of Yr. award Sporting News, 1985, Hockey News, 1985; Coach, NHL All-Star team 1985-86,1987-88,1992-93; Coach, Canadian national team, 1993. First season as NHL coach led Phila. Flyers to best record in NHL, 1984-85. Office: Florida Panthers One Panther Parkway Sunrise FL 33323 Home: 1075 Duval St #PMB175 Key West FL 33040-3115

KEENAN, MICHAEL EDGAR, marketing professional; b. Columbus, Ohio, Mar. 15, 1934; s. Edgar Charles and Kathryn Ellen (Dowden) K.; divorced; children: Margaret, Matthew, Emily, Jennifer, Andrew, Martha. AB, Duke U., 1955. Media buyer Compton Advt., N.Y.C., 1957-59; assoc. media dir. Foote, Cone & Belding, N.Y.C., 1959-61; media dir. Lennen & Newell, N.Y.C., 1961-63; sr. v.p., dir., cons. products div. Fuller & Smith & Ross, N.Y.C., 1963-70; chmn. Keenan & McLaughlin Inc., N.Y.C., 1970-82, cons., 1982-85; mng. dir. Western International Media Corp., N.Y.C., 1985-98; CEO TELA Interactive, Inc., NYC, 1998—2003; pres. Keenan & Co., Inc., NYC, 1998—; sr. v.p. Internat. Media, NYC, 2004—. Lectr. mktg. NYU, 1960-64; cons. FTC, Washington. Served with CIC, AUS, 1955-57. Mem. Am. Assn. Advt. Agys. (chmn. N.Y. coun. 1978), Nat. Agri-Mktg. Assn. (past pres. 1979), Rear Guard (treas., pres.), Thursday Club (chmn. 1960-2004). Republican. Roman Catholic. Avocation: sailing. Home: 63 Avenue A New York NY 10009-6539 Office: Keenan & Co Inc 666 5th Ave Ste 281 New York NY 10103-0001 Office Phone: 212-673-5314. Personal E-mail: mikekeenan@nyc.rr.com.

KEENAN, NANCY A., foundation administrator; BA in Elem. and Spl. Edn., Mont. State Univ., 1974; MA Edn. Adminstrn., Univ. Mont. Tchr. Yellowstone Boys' Ranch, 1974-75; tchr. spl. edn. Anaconda, Mont., 1975-88; mem. Mont. Ho. of Reps., 1982-88; supt. of pub. instrn. State of Mont., 1988—2000; pres. NARAL Pro-Choice America, Washington, 2004—. Mem. taxation, edn., local govt. and revenue oversight coms., 1982-84; chmn. ho. human svcs. and aging com.; asst. Dem. whip 1989. Active Anaconda Local Devel. Corp.; past pres. A.W.A.R.E.; past nat. pres. & chair legis. com. Council of Chief State Sch. Officers; bd. dirs. Deer Lodge County Hospice; mem. Mont. Coun. for Exceptional Children. Recipient Pub. Svc. award Mont. Coun. for Exceptional Children, 1981. Mem. AAUW. Office: NARAL Pro Choice America 1156 15th St NW Washington DC 20005

KEENAN, TERRY, anchor, correspondent; Degree in math., Johns Hopkins U. Anchor bus. news programs CNBC; from segment prodr. to on-air corr. CNN Fin. News, N.Y.C., co-anchor Street Sweep, sr. corr. The Moneyline News Hour with Lou Dobbs; anchor, Cashin' In FOX News Channel, N.Y.C. Writer, prodr. Wall St. Week with Louis Rukeyser; editor fin. newsletter Going Pub. Recipient Cable Ace award. Office: Fox News Channel 1211 Ave Of Am New York NY 10036 Office Phone: 212-301-3000.

KEENE, DONALD, writer, translator, language educator; b. 1922; BA, Columbia U., 1942, AM, 1947, PhD, 1949; DLitt, U. Cambridge, 1978. Lectr. Cambridge U., 1948-53; guest editor Asahi Shimbun, Tokyo, 1982-92; prof. Columbia U., N.Y.C., 1955-92, prof. emeritus, 1992—. Author: The Battles of Coxinga, 1951, The Japanese Discovery of Europe, 1952, 69, Japanese Literature: An Introduction for Western Readers, 1953, Living Japan, 1957, Bunraku, The Puppet Theatre of Japan, 1965, No: The Classical Theatre of Japan, 1966, Landscapes and Portraits, 1971, Some Japanese Portraits, 1978, World Within Walls, 1978, Meeting with Japan, 1978, Travels in Japan, 1981, Dawn to the West, 1984, The Pleasures of Japanese Literature, 1988, Travelers of a Hundred Ages, 1989, Seeds in the Heart, 1993, On Familiar Terms, 1994, Modern Japanese Diaries, 1995, The Blue-Eyed Tarokaja, 1996, Emperor of Japan, 2002, Five Modern Japanese Novelists, 2003, Yoshimasa and the Silver Pavilion, 2003; editor: Anthology of Japanese Literature, 1955, Modern Japanese Literature, 1956, Twenty Plays of the No Theatre, 1970; translator: The Setting Sun, 1956, Five Modern No Plays, 1957, No Longer Human, 1958, Sources of Japanese Tradition, 1958, Major Plays of Chikamatsu, 1961, The Old Woman, the Wife and the Archer, 1961, After the Banquet, 1965, Essays in Idleness, 1967, Madame de Sade, 1967, Friends, 1969, Chushingura, 1971, The Man Who Turned into a Stick, 1972, Three Plays by Kobo Abe, 1993, The Narrow Road to Oku, 1996, The Tale of the Bamboo Cutter, 1998, The Breaking Jewel, 2003. Office: Columbia Univ 407 Kent Hall New York NY 10027

KEENE, JACK DONALD, molecular genetics and microbiology educator; b. Jacksonville, Fla., June 21, 1947; s. Jack Donald and Stella Collene (Ellis) K.; m. Judy May Keene, Sept. 6, 1969; children: Mike, Lisa. AB, U. Calif., Riverside, 1969; PhD, U. Wash., 1974. Staff fellow NINDS/NIH, Bethesda, Md., 1974-78; asst. prof. microbiology and immunology Duke U. Med. Ctr., Durham, NC, 1979-84, assoc. prof., 1984-88, prof., 1988-92, chmn., 1992—2002, James B. Duke disting. prof., 1997—, dir. Ctr. for RNA Biology, dept. molecular genetics and microbiology, 2002—. Exptl. virology study sect. NIH, 1984—88; mem. nat. sel. and adv. bd. PEW Scholars in the Biomed Scis., 1991—96; mem. molecular biology study sect. NIH, 1991—95, chmn., 1993—95; co-chmn. Diversity Biotech. Consortium, Santa Fe, 1994—; dir. basic sci. rsch. Duke U. Comprehensive Cancer Ctr., 1995—2003; dir. program in genetics, program in molecular and cellular biology Duke U.; dir. combinatorial scis. ctr. Duke U. Med. Ctr., 1994—2000; biotech. cons. LipoGen, Inc., BioWhittaker, Inc., Med. and Biol. Labs., Inc., Nagoya, Japan; co-founder SARCO, Inc., Combinatorial Sci. Systems, Inc., ChemCodes, LLC; founder Ribonomics, Inc., Research Triangle Park, NC. Assoc. editor Virology, 1983—, RNA Biology, 2005-; mem. editl. bd. Jour. of Virology, 1985-95, Molecular and Cellular Biology, 1991—, Alliance Cellular Signaling; editor Microbiology and Molecular Biology Revs., 1992-2000, editor-in-chief, 2000-05; editor Molecular Diversity, 1995-2003, Jour. Biol. Chemistry, 2003—; primary reviewer Jour. Immunology, 1996—. Mem. fellowship com. Arthritis Found., 1990-92, mem. rsch. com., arthritus found, 1990-92. Recipient Faculty Rsch. award Am. Cancer Soc., 1981-86, Devil's Bag award Arthritis Found.; Nanaline Duke Faculty Scholar, 1981-84, PEW Scholar in the Biomed. Scis., 1986-90. Fellow Am. Acad. Microbiology; mem. Am. Soc. Virology, Am. Soc. Biochemistry and Molecular Biology, Am. Soc. Microbiology (mem. pub. bd. 2000-05), Ribonucleic Acid Soc., The Henry Kunkel Soc., Ny Acad. Scis. Office: Duke Univ Med Ctr Box 3020 Mol Gen and Microbiol Dept Research Dr/414 Jones Bldg Durham NC 27710 Office Phone: 919-684-5138.

KEENE, LONNIE, lawyer; BS, U.S. Mil. Acad., 1976; MPA, Harvard U., 1984; JD, NYU, 1998. Bar: N.Y. Asst. prof., instr. U.S. Mil. Acad., West Point, N.Y., 1984-87; asst. army attache U.S. Embassy, Beijing, 1988-90; mem. policy planning staff U.S. Dept. State, Washington, 1990-94; sr. policy analyst, office sci. & tech. policy The White House, Washington, 1994-95; assoc. Linklaters, London, 1998-99, Milbank, Tweed, Hadley & McCloy, London, Hong Kong, 1999—2001, Wollmuth Maher & Deutsch, NYC, 2002; v.p., asst. gen. counsel Goldman, Sachs & Co., N.Y.C., 2002—. Lt. col. U.S. Army, 1976—95, ret. U.S. Army. Decorated Legion of Merit; Olmsted scholar George and Carol Olmsted Found., Beijing, 1981-83. Mem. Coun. Fgn. Rels. (Internat. Affairs fellow 1990-91), Harvard Club N.Y.C. Avocations: golf, art, travel, skiing. Office: One New York Plz New York NY 10004 Business E-Mail: Lonnie.Keene@gs.com.

KEENE, RICHARD BRIAN, school system administrator, educational consultant; b. Falls Church, Va., Sept. 11, 1962; BS, SUNY, 1987; MEd, U. Utah, 1991; EdS, U. Idaho, 1993, PhD, 2003. Behavioral specialist, tchr. math, sci., & phys. edn. Western Inst. Neuropsychiatry, Salt Lake City, 1986—87; instr. algebra & calculus Utah Valley C.C., Orem, 1988—89; tchr. algebra & geometry Payson H.S., 1987—89; tchr. pre-algebra & algebra Lehi Jr. H.S., 1989—90; supr. test ctr. Am. Coll. Testing Svc., Iowa City, 1990—91; dir. counseling & testing, counselor, psychology Delta H.S., Utah, 1990—91; test scorer, reader, supr. test ctr. supr. Ednl. Testing Svc., Princeton, NJ, 1990—2003; dir. counseling & testing dir., counselor Hansen Sch. Dist., Idaho, 1991—92; counselor, adminstr. dist. office level Filer Sch. Dist., 1992—94; h.s. counselor, tchr.careers, ESL, math Minidoka County Sch. Dist., Rupert, 1994—97; dir., asst. dean, counselor Kern H.S. Dist., Bakersfield, Calif., 1997—2001; vice prin. Delano Elem. Sch. Dist., 2001—03; counselor, adminstr. computer sys. Clark County Team Acad., Las Vegas, 2003—04; coord. region data Clark County Sch. Dist., 2004—. Adj. faculty Nev. State Coll., Henderson, Nev., 2003—. Author: (study guide) Advanced Mathematics I (Pre-Calculus). Elected voting mem. Nev. State Dem. Ctrl. Com., Carson City, 2004—, Clark County Dem. Ctrl. Com., Las Vegas, Nev., 2004—. With USN, 1982—84, with USAR, 1984—. Mem.: NEA, ASCD, Am. Assn. Phys. Edn. Health Recreation and Dance, Nat. Coun. Tchrs.Math., Nev. Assn. Sch. Administrators, Optimist Internat., Am. Legion, Lions Internat., Phi Delta Kappa. Democrat. Avocations: scuba diving, travel, swimming. Home: 340 Abbington St Henderson NV 89074 Office Phone: 702-799-1719 5323. Home Fax: 702-799-3841; Office Fax: 702-799-3841. Personal E-mail: rbkeene@cox.net. E-mail: rbkeene@interact.ccsd.net.

KEENE-BURGESS, RUTH FRANCES, military official; b. South Bend, Ind., Oct. 7, 1948; d. Seymour and Sally (Morris) K.; m. Leslie U. Burgess, Jr., Oct. 1, 1983; children: Michael Leslie, David William, Elizabeth Sue, Rachael Lee. BS, Ariz. State U., 1970; MS, Fairleigh Dickinson U., 1978; grad., U.S. Army Command and Gen. Staff Coll., 1986. Inventory mgmt. specialist U.S. Army Electronics Command, Phila., 1970-74, U.S. Army Communications-Electronics Material Readiness Command, Fort Monmouth, N.J., 1974-79; chief inventory mgmt. div. Crane (Ind.) Army Ammunition Activity, 1979-80; supply systems analyst Hdqrs. 60th Ordnance Group, Zweibruecken, Fed. Republic Germany, 1980-83; chief inventory mgmt. div. Crane (Ind.) Army Ammunition Activity, 1983-85, chief control div., 1985; inventory mgmt. specialist 200th Theater Army Material Mgmt. Ctr., Zweibruecken, 1985-88; analyst supply systems U.S. Armament, Munitions and Chem. Command, Rock Island, Ill., 1988-89; specialist logistics mgt. U.S. Army Signal Command, Ft. Huachuca, Ariz., 1989—. Troop leader Girl Scouts Am. Mem. Federally Employed Women (chpt. pres. 1979-80), NAFE, Soc. Logistics Engrs., Assn. Computing Machinery, Am. Soc. Public Adminstrn., Soc. Profl. and Exec. Women, AAAS. Democrat.

KEENER, NANCY ELAINE LAROSE, secondary school educator; b. Independence, Mo., June 16, 1952; d. Ralph Charles LaRose; m. Joel Donald Keener; children: Joshua, Abby, Emily. BS in Art Theater, Ctrl. Mo. State U. Theater tchr. Macon (Mo.) HS; art tchr. Ft. Smith (Ark.) Pub. Sch., Alma (Ark.) HS, 2000—. Midday TV host Channel 40/29 TV, Ft. Smith, Ark. Office: Alma HS PO Box 2139 Alma AR 72921-2139

KEENEY, JOHN C., lawyer; b. Wilkes-Barre, Pa., Feb. 19, 1922; s. James M. and Mae M. (Clark) Keeney; widower; children: John C. Jr., Terence, Jean Marie, Joan, Kathleen. BS, U. Scranton, 1947; LLB, Dickinson Sch. of Law, Carlisle, Pa., 1949; LLM, Geo. Washington Law Sch., Washington, 1953. Chief Smith Act Unit, internal security sect. Dept. Justice, Washington, 1957-60, dep. chief organized crime sect. criminal divsn., 1966-69, chief fraud sect. criminal divsn., 1969-73, dep. asst. atty. gen. criminal divsn., 1973—. 1st lt. U.S. Army Air Force, 1943-45 ETO. Recipient Disting. Career award Pres. Reagan, 1983, Pres. Bush, 2004, Disting. Alumnus in Govt. award U. Scranton, 1997, Atty. Gen.'s Disting. Svc. award, 1987, D.C. Bar award for disting. govt. svc., 1996, Life Time Achievement award Dickinson Sch. Law, 2002. Roman Catholic. Home: 11101 Lund Pl Kensington MD 20895-1624 Office: US Dept Justice 10th And Pennsylvania NW Washington DC 20530-0001 Office Phone: 202-514-2621.

KEENEY, JOHN CHRISTOPHER, JR., lawyer; b. Washington, Aug. 29, 1951; s. John Christopher and Eugenia M. (Brislin) Keeney; m. Kathleen V. Gunning; children: Katherine, Jaclyn. AB summa cum laude, U. Notre Dame, 1973; JD cum laude, Harvard U., 1976. Bar: Md. 1976, DC 1977, US Dist. Ct. DC 1978, US Dist. Ct. Md. 1977, US Ct. Appeals (4th cir.) 1977, US Ct. Appeals (DC cir.) 1978, US Supreme Ct. 1980, US Ct. Appeals (7th cir.) 1984, US Ct. Appeals (10th cir.) 1989, US Ct. Appeals (11th cir.) 1990, US Ct. Appeals (9th cir.) 1997, US Ct. Appeals (6th cir.) 1999. Law clk. presiding judge US Dist. Ct. Md., Balt., 1976-78; assoc. Hogan & Hartson, Washington, 1978-84, ptnr., 1985—, ptnr. charge pro bono cmty. svcs. dept., 1989—93. Adj. instr. legal ethics Am. U. Law Sch., 2000—02. Co-author: (book) Civil and Criminal Remedies for Racially and Religiously Motivated Violence, 1983, 2d edit., 1999. Dir. Pub. Justice Ctr., Balt., 1990—95, 1997—2000; co-chair Dem. Nat. Lawyers Coun., 1999—2003; counsel del. selection Babbitt US Pres. campaign, 1987—88; counsel Dem. credentials com., 1989—91; hearing officer Dem. Nat. Conv., 1992, 1996; chmn. Berlage County Coun. campaign, Montgomery County, Md., 1989—94; bd. dirs. Washington Lawyers Com. Civil Rights Urban Affairs, 1999—. Mem.: ABA (former co-chair adjudication com., ad. law regulatory practice sec. 1999—2002, ho. dels. 2003—), Election Law Adv. Commn., DC Bar (bd. govs. 2000—, pres. elect 2003—04, pres. 2004—05), Phi Beta Kappa. Roman Catholic. Office: Hogan & Hartson 555 13th St NW Ste 10W-206 Washington DC 20004-1109 Office Phone: 202-637-5750. Business E-Mail: jckeeney@hhlaw.com.

KEENEY, STEVEN HARRIS, lawyer; b. Phila., Oct. 1, 1949; s. Arthur Hail and Virginia (Tripp) K.; m. Jean Ashburn, May 10, 1974 (div. Oct. 1986); 1 child, Christian Jeffrey; m. Lorri Caram Carty, Sept. 2, 2003. BA with honors, Trinity Coll., Hartford, Conn., 1971; MA, Hartford Sem. Found., 1973; JD, U. Conn., 1980. Bar: Ky. 1980, U.S. Dist. Ct. (we. dist.) Ky. 1981, U.S. Dist. Ct. (ea. dist.) Ky. 1983, U.S. Ct. Appeals (6th cir.) 2001. Staff reporter/edn. editor The Hartford Courant, 1971-74; asst. to supt. Hartford Pub. Schs., 1974-77; assoc. Igor Sikorsky & Assocs., Hartford, 1979-80, Brown, Todd & Heyburn, Louisville, 1980-82; ptnr. Barnett & Alagia, Louisville, 1982-88, KLO The Keeney Law Office, Louisville, 1988-90; prin. Amerilaw, Louisville, 1990-93; pres. LawTech Svcs. Co., Louisville, 1988—2002; mng. mem. Trautwein & Keeney PLLC, Louisville, 1993—2002, Keeney Law Office, LLC, Louisville, 2002—; city atty. City of Pineville, Ky., 2002—. Chmn., CEO Write2U; chmn. Pro Check Ctrl.; lectr. in field. Co-author/editor: Death Benefit: A Lawyer Uncovers A 20 Year Pattern of Seduction, 1993, 94, Reader's Digest Today's Best Non-Fiction Vol. 24, 1994; featured in Ct. TV's Forensic Files, 2004-2005, Cable TV's Inside Edition, Discovery Channel, others; contbr. articles to profl. jours. Bd. dirs. Hospice of Louisville, Inc., 1984-86; exec. dir. Juvenile Justice Pub. Edn. Project, West Hartford, Conn., 1978-80; pres. bd. dirs. Stage One: Louisville Children's Theatre, 1982-83; founding bd. dirs. Ky. Citizens for Arts, Frankfort, 1983; mem. Lebanon (Conn.) Bd. Edn., 1975-80; campaign mgr. Mazzoli 3d C.D. Ky., Jefferson County, 1982, 84; ruling elder 2d Presbyn. Ch., Louisville, 1984-86, Presbytery, 1990-, commr. counsel Recipient Disting. Contbn. award Nat. Com. for Prevention of Child Abuse, Ky. chpt., 1982, Disting. Svc. award Conn. Assn. Bds. of Edn., 1976, Profl. Achievement for Gen. Reporting Series award Soc. Profl. Journalists, Sigma Delta Chi, Conn. chpt. 1974. Mem. ABA (editl. com. The Tax Lawyer 1984-89), ATLA, Nat. Assn. Criminal Def. Lawyers, Ky. Acad. Trial Attys., Ky. Bar Assn., Louisville Bar Assn., Million Dollar Advocates Forum, Order of Ky. Cols., Sigma Phi Epsilon. Democrat. Presbyterian. Avocations: bibliophile, marksman, golf. Office: Keeney Law Office PO Box 263 Harrods Creek KY 40027 Office Phone: 502-599-1154.

KEENGWE, JARED, education educator; s. Zedekiah and Jerusha Keengwe. MS, Ind. State U., 2000—05. Student tchr. Moi Girls H.S., Eldoret, Kenya, 1994—95; career advisor Study Abroad Ctr., Nairobi, Kenya, 1996—99; h.s. tchr. Karura H.S., Nairobi, Kenya, 1997—99; web instr. Rose-Hulman Inst. Tech., Terre Haute, Ind., 2003; grad. tchg. asst. Ind. State U., Terre Haute, 2002—03, instr., faculty mem., 2004—. V.p. Grad. Student Assn., Ind. State U., Terre Haute, 2003—; libr. com. rep. Coll. Edn., Ind. State U., Terre Haute, 2004—, scholarship com. rep., 2004—, Adams grad. fellow, 2004—; dept. faculty search com., faculty senate grad. student rep. Ind. State U., Terre Haute, 2003—04; grad. programming asst. Office of Ethnic Diversity, Ind. State U., Terre Haute, 2001—02. Mem.: Internat. Soc. for Tech. in Edn. (corr.), Nat. Assn. for Multicultural Edn. (corr.), Am. Ednl. Rsch. Assn. (corr.), Assn. for Ednl. Comm. and Tech. (corr.), Assn. for the Advancement of Computing in Edn. (corr.). Office Phone: 812-237-4497.

KEENY, SPURGEON MILTON, JR., professional society administrator; b. NYC, Oct. 24, 1924; s. Spurgeon Milton and Amelia (Smith) K.; m. Sheila Spear, May 3, 1952; children: Christopher Spear, Christy Virginia, Spurgeon Milton III. BA, Columbia U., 1944, MA in Physics, 1946; postgrad., Sch. Internat. Affairs and Russian Inst., 1946-47; LLD (hon.), U. Notre Dame, 1991. With Directorate of Intelligence, Hdqrs. USAF, 1950-55; mem. staff Panel on Peaceful Uses Atomic Energy, Joint Congl. Com. Atomic Energy, Washington, 1955-56; chief atomic energy div. Office of Asst. Sec. Def. for Research and Engring., Washington, 1956-57; mem. Gaither security resources panel Exec. Office of Pres., 1957; tech. asst. to President's Sci. Adviser, Washington, 1958-69; sr. staff mem. Nat. Security Council, 1963-69; asst. dir. for sci. and tech. U.S. Arms Control and Disarmament Agy., Washington, 1969-73, dep. dir., 1977-81; scholar-in-residence Nat. Acad. Scis., Washington, 1981-85; pres., exec. dir. Arms Control Assn., Washington, 1985—2001; sr. fellow Nat. Acad. Sci., Washington, 2002—. Dir. policy and program devel. Mitre Corp., McLean, Va., 1973-77; mem. U.S. del. to Geneva Conf. Experts on Nuclear Test Detection, 1958; to Geneva Conf. on Discontinuance of Nuclear Weapons Tests, 1958-60; chief U.S. del. U.S./Soviet Talks on Theater Nuclear Forces, 1980; mem. adv. com. Program Sci. and Internat. Affairs, Harvard, 1973-77; dep. chmn. com. environ. decision making Nat. Acad. Scis., 1974-77; chmn. Nuclear Energy Policy Study Ford Found., 1975-77; mem. com. on internat. security and arms control Nat. Acad. Scis., 1981-; mem. com. on Technical Issues Relating to Ratification of the Comprehensive Test Ban Treaty, Nat. Acad. Scis., 2000—03. Co-author: Nuclear Power Issues and Choices, 1977; Nuclear Arms Control Background and Issues, 1985; Management and Disposition of Excess Weapons Plutonium, 1994, The Future of U.S. Nuclear Weapons Policy, 1997, Comprehensive Nuclear Test Ban Treaty, 2002, Monitoring Nuclear Weapons and nuclear Explosive Materials, 2005. Served to 1st lt. USAF, 1948-50. Recipient Rockefeller Pub. Service award, 1970; Disting. Honor award U.S. Arms Control and Disarmament Agy., 1981 Fellow Am. Acad. Arts Scis., Am. Phys. Soc. (mem. study group on light-water reactor safety 1974-75, forum award 1986); mem. Council on Fgn. Relations, Phi Beta Kappa. Home: 3600 Albemarle St NW Washington DC 20008-4216 Office: Nat Acad Scis CISAC 500 5th St NW Washington DC 20001 Personal E-mail: sskeeny@aol.com.

KEEP, MARCUS FLOYD, neurosurgeon; b. N.Y.C., Mar. 15, 1959; s. Charles Russell Keep Jr. and Nancy Garland Stotz. AB in Religion, Dartmouth Coll., 1980; BS in Chemistry, U. SC, 1981; MD, Med. U. SC, 1984; postgrad., Shanxi U., Taiyuan, China, 1981—82, St. George's U., Grenada, W.I., 1984—85. Surgery intern Med. U. S.C., Charleston, 1988-89; neurosurgery resident Montreal Neurol. Inst., McGill U., Que., Can., 1989-94; rsch. fellow Restorative Neurology Unit, Lund (Sweden) U., 1994-96; pres. Restorative Neurosurgery Found., Honolulu, 1996—; CEO, founder Maas BiolAB, LLC, Honolulu, 1997—; asst. prof. div. neurosurgery U. N.Mex., Albuquerque, 2002—. Rsch. fellow INSERM-Neuromorphology Lab.-Salpetriere Hosp., Paris, 1989—90; asst. prof. dept. surgery John A. Burns Sch. Medicine, U. Hawaii, Honolulu, 1997—2002; rschr. Ctr. for Study of Neurol. Disease, Honolulu, 1997—98, Lab. Matrix Pathology, Honolulu, 1999—2002; asst. prof. dept. anatomy John A. Burns Sch. Medicine, U. Hawaii, Honolulu, 2000—02. Patentee in field; contbr. chapters to books, sci. articles to profl. jours. V.p. Nova Arts Found., Honolulu, 1997—2002; mem. instnl. rev. bd. St. Francis Med. Ctr., Honolulu, 1999—2001; mem. sci. adv. com. Clin. Rsch. Ctr., Honolulu, 2000—01; union rep. Montreal Neurol. Inst., Assn. Residents of McGill, Montreal, 1992—94; pres. Fellows' Soc. of Montreal Neurol. Inst., 1993—94. Rsch. grantee Omina-Freundeshilfe Found., 1994, Bradley & Victoria Geist Found., 1998-2000, Ingeborg V.F. McKee Fund, 2001, RCMI-NIH, 2001-02, U. N.Mex. Dept. Surgery, 2004; fellow Phadhar Hosp., India, 1988, Burn Unit, Cali, Colombia, Ptnrs. of the Ams., 1987. Fellow: Royal Coll. Surgeons of Can.-Neurosurgery; mem.: Rocky Mountain Neurosurg. Soc., Soc. Stereotactic and Functional Neurosurgery, Congress Neurol. Surgeons, Cell Transplant Soc., Hawaii Assn. Neurol. Surgeons (treas. 1997—2000, v.p. 2000—02), Soc. for Neurosci., Am. Soc. for Neural Transplantation and Repair, Am. Epilepsy Soc., Am. Assn. Neurol. Surgeons., Internat. Brain Rsch. Orgn., Mass. Soc. Mayflower Descs., Outrigger Canoe Club. Home: 318 Tulane Pl Albuquerque NM 87106 E-mail: mkeep@maasbiolab.com.

KEEPHART, LYDIA FABBRO, lawyer, mediator; b. Trenton, N.J., Apr. 19, 1952; d. Leo Fabbro and Elide Agnes Romano; m. William Joseph Keephart; 1 child, Jonathan Fabbro. BA, Coll. N.J., 1973; MA, Rider U., 1978; JD, Seton Hall U., 1991; diploma in mediation, Rutgers U., Newark, 1998, Harvard U., 2000. Bar: N.J., Pa., Colo. Tchr. East Windsor Bd. Edn., Hightstown, NJ, 1973—81; test developer, program adminstr. Ednl. Testing Svc., Princeton, 1981—87; ptnr. Pellettieri, Rabstein & Altman, Princeton, 1991—. Mem. adv. bd. Fleet Bank Boston, NJ, 1995—2004, St. Lawrence & Morris Hall, NJ, 1999—, Bank Am., 2004—. Mem.: ABA, N.J. Bar Assn., Pa. Bar Assn., Colo. Bar Assn., Green Acres Country Club. Office: Pellettieri Rabstein and Altman 100 Nassau Park Blvd Ste 111 Princeton NJ 08540 Office Phone: 609-520-0900. Business E-Mail: lkeephart@pralaw.com.

KEEPIN, GEORGE ROBERT, JR., physicist; b. Oak Park, Ill., Dec. 5, 1923; s. George Robert and Erlene Marie (Bennett) K.; m. Madge Mary Twomey, June 13, 1948; children: Robert, William, Ardis, Mavis, Denice. PhB, U. Chgo., 1943; BS, MIT, 1946, MS, 1947; PhD in Physics, Northwestern U., 1949. Tchg. fellow dept. physics MIT, Cambridge, 1947; postdoctoral fellow U. Calif., Berkeley, 1950-52; rsch. physicist Los Alamos (N.Mex.) Sci. Lab., 1952-63, group leader nuclear safeguards rsch., 1966-76, dir. nuclear safeguards program, 1976-80; head physics divsn. IAEA, Vienna, Austria, 1963-65, spl. adviser to dep. dir. gen. nuclear safeguards, 1982-85; fellow Los Alamos Nat. Lab., 1985—. Mem. U.S. del. UN Atoms-for-Peace Conf., Geneva, 1955, 71, IAEA tech. adviser, 1964 Author: Progress in Nuclear Energy-Delayed Neutrons, 1956, Physics of Nuclear Kinetics, 1965; Arms Control Verification: The Technologies That Make It Possible, 1986; editor: Nuclear Analysis R and D; patentee in field. Fellow Los Alamos Nat. Lab, Am. Phys. Soc., Am. Nuclear Soc. (exec. com. 1967-69); mem. Inst. Nuclear Materials Mgmt. (nat. chmn. 1978-80, Disting. Service award 1984), N.Y. Acad. Scis., Sigma Xi. Home: 600 La Bajada Los Alamos NM 87544-3805

KEER, LEON MORRIS, engineering educator; b. LA, Sept. 13, 1934; s. William and Sophia (Bookman) Keer; m. Barbara Sara Davis, Aug. 18, 1956; children: Patricia Renee, Jacqueline Saundra, Harold Neal, Michael Derek. BS, Calif. Inst. Tech., 1956, MS, 1958; PhD, U. Minn., 1962. Registered profl. engr., Calif. Mem. tech. staff Hughes Aircraft Co., Culver City, Calif., 1956-59; research fellow, instr. U. Minn., Mpls., 1959-62; asst. prof. Northwestern U., Evanston, Ill., 1964-66, assoc. prof., 1966-70, prof. engring., 1970—, Walter P. Murphy prof. mech. and civil engring., 1994—, assoc. dean research and grad. studies, 1985-92, chmn. dept. civil engring., 1992-97. Preceptor Columbia U., N.Y.C., 1963—64; co-dir. Ctr. for Surface Entring. and Tribology, 1997—2004; dept. acad. advisor civil and structural engring. Hong Kong U., 1998—2002; Chau Wei-Yin meml. lectr. Hong Kong Poly. U., 2000; S.W. Mechanics lecture tour, 2003—04. Co-editor: (monograph) Solid Contact and Lubrication, 1980; contbr. articles to profl. jours. Fellow, NATO, 1962, Guggenheim Found., 1972, Japanese Soc. for the Promotion of Sci., 1986. Fellow: NAE (elected 1997), ASME (life; tech. editor Jour. Applied Mechanics 1988—92, Innovative Rsch. award tribology divsn. 2001, Daniel C. Drucker medal 2003), ASCE (life; chmn. engring. mech. divsn. 1992—93), Acoustical Soc. Am., Am. Acad. Mechanics (sec. 1981—88, pres.-elect 1987—88, pres. 1988—89); mem.: Tau Beta Pi, Sigma Xi. Home: 2601 Marian Ln Wilmette IL 60091-2207 Office: Northwestern U Dept Civil Engring 2145 Sheridan Rd Evanston IL 60208-0834 Business E-Mail: l-keer@northwestern.edu.

KEESLING, KAREN RUTH, lawyer; b. Wichita, Kans., July 9, 1946; d. Paul W. and Ruth (Sharp) Keesling. BA, Ariz. State U., 1968, MA, 1970; JD, Georgetown U., 1981. Bar: Va. 1981, Fla. 1981, Ariz. 2000. Asst. dean of women U. Kans., Lawrence, 1970-72; exec. sec., sec.'s adv. com. on rights and responsibilities of women HEW, Washington, 1972-74; dir. White House Office of Women's Programs, Washington, 1974-77; head civil rights and equal opportunity sect., Gov. Div., Congl. Rsch. Svc. Libr. Congress, Washington, 1977-80; legis. aide Sen. Nancy Kassebaum, Washington, 1979-81; mem. pers. office staff Office of Pres.-elect, Washington, Jan. 1981; pvt. practice Falls Church, Va. and Peoria, Sun City, Ariz., 1981-88, 90—; dept. for equal opportunity dept. Dept. Air Force, Washington, 1981-82, dep. asst. sec. manpower res. affairs and installations, 1982-83, prin. dep. asst. sec. manpower res. affairs, 1983-87, prin. dep. asst. sec. readiness support dept. Washington, 1987-88, prin. dep. asst. sec. manpower and res. affairs, 1988, asst. sec. manpower and res. affairs, 1988-89; acting wage and hour adminstr. U.S. Dept. Labor, Washington, 1992-93; pvt. practice Falls Church, Va., Peoria, Sun City, Ariz. Bd. advisers Outstanding Young Women Am., 1983—90. Mem. Nat. Women's Polit. Caucus, Washington, 1980, Nat. Fedn. Rep. Women's Club, Washington, 1975; pers. com. chair Faith Presbyn. Ch., 2000—04, elder, 2000—05, mission com. chair, 2005—. Named One of Ten Outstanding Young Women of Am., 1975, Kans. Women's Golf Champion, 1966, Wichita Women's Champion, 1968, 1970, Outstanding Woman Golfer in Kans., 1966; recipient Alumni Achievement award, Ariz. State U., 1976, Elizabeth Boyer award, Women's Equity Action League, 1986, Meritorious Civilian award, USAF, 1987, Woman of Distinction award, Nat. Conf. Coll. Women, Student Leaders and Women of Distinction, 1988, Exceptional Civilian Svc. award, USAF, 1988. Mem.: Va. Bus. and Profl. Women's Found. (trustee 1985—93), The Women's Inst. Inc. (adv. coun. 1985—96), No. Va. Women atty.'s Assn. (steering com. 1990—95), Va. Fedn. Bus. and Profl. Women's Clubs (2d v.p. 1987—88, 1st v.p. 1988—89, pres.-elect 1989—90, pres. 1990—91), Fla. Bar Assn., Va. Bar Assn., Ariz. Bar Assn., P.E.O. (treas. 2001—02, v.p. 2002—03, pres. chptr. 2003—), U.S. Com. for UNIFEM (gen. counsel 1983—2002), Pi Beta Phi. Avocation: golf. Home: 9606 W Lindgren Ave Sun City AZ 85373 E-mail: Keeslingkr@aol.com.

KEESLING, RUTH MORRIS, foundation administrator; b. New Brunswick, N.J., Apr. 4, 1930; d. Mark Loren and Louise Weber Morris; m. Thomas Marion Keesling, June 30, 1956; children: Thomas Mark, James H., Frank M. BS in Journalism, U. Colo., 1953. Advt. dept. Burlingame (Calif.) Advance, 1953—54; news dept. Oakland (Calif.) Tribune, 1954; pub. rels. Mark Morris Assoc., Inc., Topeka, 1955; co-owner Pub. Rels., Inc., Denver, 1955—64; pres. Digit Fund, Denver, 1986—88; founder, sponsor Mountain Gorilla Vet. Project, Denver, 1986—2001; founder, pres. Mountain Gorilla Conservation Fund, Denver, 2001—. Founder Morris Animal Found., Denver, 1955—; pres. Dian Fossey Gorilla Fund, Denver, 1988—91, pres. internat., 1991—93; bd. trustees Dian Fossey Gorilla Fund Europe, London, 1989—; trustee Denver Zool. Found., Denver, 1969—; lectr. mountain gorillas; sponsor, founder Mt. Gorillas in Africa, 1987—; founder Wildlife Animal Medicine Dept. Makerene U., Uganda, 1994; head task force Rwandan Govt., 2000. Author: (brochures) Small Animal Clinical Nutrition, 1959; designer (exhibitions) Mus. Display Diane Fossey items, 1992—94. Recipient Outstanding Alumni award, U. Colo., 1976, award for animal welfare, Collier County Humane Soc., 2002, Lifetime Achievement award, Brit. Airways, 2002, award, Collier County Humane Soc., 2002. Mem.: Port Royal Club, Naples Yacht Club, Denver Country Club, Pi Beta Phi (chmn. adv. bd. 1957—60, mem. house bd. 1958—61, Carolyn Lichtenberg Crest award 2000). Home: 3220 Cherryridge Rd Englewood CO 80110 Office: Mountain Gorilla Conservation Fund PO Box 2211 Englewood CO 80150-2211 E-mail: RuthKee@aol.com.

KEETER, LYNN CARPENTER, language educator; b. Charlotte, N.C. d. John Franklin and Georgiana (LaVender) Carpenter; children: John Blair, Eric William. BA in English, Gardner-Webb U., 1980, MA in Edn., 1985, MA in English, 1994; devel. educator specialist, Appalachian State U.; postgrad., The Union Inst., Cin. Instr. Taylor Finishing, Charlotte, 1970-74, Gardner-Webb U., Boiling Springs, N.C., 1980-86, prof. English, 1988—; tchr. self-devel. classes for underprivileged women Robeson County Schs., Lumberton, N.C., 1986-88. Founder, dir. personal devel. program for women; freelance writer for vintage clothing jours.; storyteller Appalachian folklore. Co-author: Fundamentals of Reading and Writing, 1997; writer children's stories. Mem. Internat. Reading Assn. (award 1997), A.C.E.I., pres. local chpt. N.C.R.A., N.C.Reading Assn. (pres. local coun. 1998—), Woman's Club Internat. (v.p., pres., Outstanding Woman 1980), Woman's Prayer Assn. (pres.), Coll. English Assn. (editor newsletter 1993—), Beta Sigma Phi (pres., v.p., sec., Woman of Yr. award 1991, 92, Alpha Omega award 1992), Sigma Tau Delta, Phi Delta Kappa. Avocations: antiques, interior decorating, dance.

KEETON, ROBERT ERNEST, federal judge; b. Clarksville, Tex., Dec. 16, 1919; s. William Robert and Ernestine (Tuten) K.; m. Elizabeth E. Baker, May 28, 1941; children: Katherine, William Robert. BBA, U. Tex., 1940, LLB, 1941; SJD, Harvard U., 1956; LLD (hon.), William Mitchell Coll., 1983, Lewis and Clark Coll., 1988. Bar: Tex. 1941, Mass. 1955. Assoc. firm Baker, Botts, Andrews & Wharton (and successors), Houston, 1941-42, 45-51; assoc. prof. law So. Meth. U., 1951-54; Thayer teaching fellow Harvard U., 1953-54, asst. prof., 1954-56, prof. law, 1956-73, Langdell prof., 1973-79; assoc. dean Harvard, 1975-79; judge Fed. Dist. Ct., Boston, 1979—. Commr. on Uniform State Laws from Mass., 1971-79; trustee Flaschner Jud. Inst., 1979-86; exec. dir. Nat. Inst. Trial Advocacy, 1973-76; ednl. cons., 1976-79; mem. com. on ct. adminstrn. U.S. Jud. Conf., 1985-87, mem. standing com. on rules, 1987-90, chmn., 1990-93. Author: Trial Tactics and Methods, 1954, 2d edit., 1973, Cases and Materials on the Law of Insurance, 1960, 2d edit., 1977, Legal Cause in the Law of Torts, 1963, Venturing To Do Justice, 1969, (with Jeffrey O'Connell) Basic Protection for the Traffic Victim: A Blueprint for Reforming Automobile Insurance, 1965, After Cars Crash: The Need for Legal and Insurance Reform, 1967, (with Page Keeton) Cases and Materials on the Law of Torts, 1971, 2d edit., 1977, Basic Text on Insurance Law, 1971, (with others) Tort and Accident Law, 1983, 2d edit., 1989, (with others) Prosser & Keeton, Torts, 5th edit., 1984, Pocket Part, 1988, (with Alan Widiss) Insurance Law, 1988, Judging, 1990, Judging the American Legal System, 1999, Guidelines for Drafting, Editing, and Interpreting, 2002; also articles. Served to lt. comdr. USNR, 1942-45, PTO, 1945-56. Recipient Wm. B. Jones award Nat. Inst. Trial Advocacy, 1980; recipient Leon Green award U. Tex. Law Rev., 1981, Francis Rawle award Am. Law Inst.-ABA, 1983, Samuel E. Gates litigation award Am. Coll. Trial Lawyers, 1984 Fellow Am. Bar Found., mem., Am. Acad. Arts and Scis., Am. Bar Assn., Mass. Bar Assn., State Bar Tex., Am. Law Inst., Am. Risk and Ins. Assn., Chancellors, Friars, Order of Coif, Beta Gamma Sigma, Beta Alpha Psi, Phi Delta Phi, Phi Eta Sigma. Office: US Dist Ct 1 Courthouse Way Ste 3130 Boston MA 02210-3005

KEETS, JOHN DAVID, JR., insurance company executive; b. Atlantic City, Apr. 1, 1948; s. John D. and Doris F. (Fleiss) Keets; m. Julianne Zellers, Nov. 3, 1973; children: J. David, Brian. BA, High Point Coll., 1970. CLU., cert. fin. planner, chartered fin. cons. Account exec. Mgmt. Recruiters, Phila., 1972-75; sales mgr. Cigna Fin. Svc., Miami (Fla.), Balt., 1975-82; agy. mgr. Fidelty Mut., Balt., 1983-85, Provident Mut. Ins. Co., Phila., 1985-88; regional v.p. Equitable Ins. Co., Mpls., 1988-90; prin. Keets & Assocs., Mpls., 1991—; mgr. Prudential Ins. Co., Mpls., 1993-94; v.p. bus. devel. Carlson Mktg. Group, Mpls., 1994-96; gen. mgr. Mut. of Omaha Cos., Mpls., 1998-2000; regional dir. 10F Foresters, 2000—03; treas., regional v.p. TransAm. Capital, Inc., 2004—. With U.S. Army, 1970-72, Germany. Mem. Mpls. Assn. Life Underwriters, Gen. Agts. and Mgrs. Assn, Internat. Assn. Fin. Planners, Am. Soc. CLU, Chartered Fin. Cons. Avocations: golf, boating. Home: 2420 Comstock Ln N Minneapolis MN 55447-2303 Office Phone: 612-801-1933. Personal E-mail: jkeets@msn.com.

KEEVER, CYNTHIA LUCAS, academic administrator; b. Columbus, Ind., June 30, 1950; d. Sherman Charles and Doris Mae (Brannan) Lucas; m. Matthew L. Keever, Dec. 20, 1970; children: Jared Benjamin, Kristin Suzanne. BA in English and French, Ball State U., Muncie, Ind., 1972; MA in Sch. Adminstrn., 1994. English tchr. Daleville (Ind.) Jr./Sr. H.S., 1972-75; English/French tchr. Wapahani H.S., Selma, Ind., 1976-77; homemaker, ednl. vol. Westfield (Ind.) Schs., 1978-85; teaching position Washington Elem., Westfield, Ind., 1985-86; English tchr. Marion-Adams Jr./Sr/ H.S., Sheridan, Ind., 1986-89; Drug Free-At Risk coord. Westfield (Ind.) Washington Schs., 1989-94, coord. Student Svcs., 1994-95, h.s. English tchr., 1995-97, prin., 1997—. Sec., exec. bd. Hamilton County Coun. Alcohol and Other Drugs, Noblesville, Ind., 1993-94; adult spon. Hamilton County Teen Adv. Coun., Noblesville, Ind., 1993-95; mem. student assistance Adv. Bd. Ind. Dept. Edn., Indpls., 1991-95; participant Gov.'s Commn. for Drug Free Ind., Indpls., 1995—. Recipient Program of Excellence Nat. Orgn. Student Assistance Profls., 1990, Exemplary Leadership Program, Nat. Coun. States on Inservice Edn., 1992, One Person Can Nominee U.S. Drug Enforcement Adminstrn., 1992; named Ind. Acad. All Star Tchr. Ind. Acad. Competitions for Excellence, 1992. Mem. ASCD, Nat. Orgn. Student Assistance Profls., Ind. Assn. for Student Assistance Profls., Hamilton County Student Assistance Coords. Avocations: reading, bicycling. Office: Westfield-Washington Schs 326 W Main St Westfield IN 46074-9384

KEEVEY, RICHARD FRANCIS, federal official, state official, educator; b. Phila., June 20, 1942; s. Richard Patrick and Eileen (Wright) K.; m. Elizabeth Regina Dwyer, Aug. 5, 1967; children: Richard, Michael, John. BA, La Salle Coll., Phila., 1964; M of Govt. Adminstrn., U. Pa., 1967. Various positions Commonwealth of Pa., City of Phila., State of N.J., 1967-70; dir. adminstrn., fiscal officer dept. community affairs N.J. Dept., Trenton, 1971-75, asst. to dir. div. budget and acctg. Treasury Dept., 1975-81, supr. Bur. Budget, Office Mgmt. and Budget, 1981-83, dep. budget dir., dep. conptr., 1983-89, dir. Office Mgmt. and Budget, 1989-94; dep. under sec. for fin. mgmt. Dept. Def., Washington, 1994-95, dir. defense fin. and acctg. agy., 1995-97; CFO U.S. Dept. Housing and Urban Renewal, 1997-99; dir. budget and fin. practice Arthur Andersen, Washington, 1999—2002; dir. adminstrv. and fin. programs Unisys corp., McLean, Va., 2002—03; dir. performance consortium Nat. Acad. Pub. Adminstrn., Washington, 2004—. Instr. Rutgers U., New Brunswick, N.J., 1971-75; adj. prof. fin. Rider Coll., Lawrenceville, N.J., 1979-82, mem. adv. com. grad. program in pub. mgmt., 1983-87; adj. prof. Seton Hall U., South Orange, N.J., 1990-93; adj. prof. budgeting systems George Mason U., Fairfax, Va., 1999-2001; vis. prof. Princeton U., 2002-05. Contbr. articles to profl. jours.; mem. bd. editors Pub. Adminstrn. Rev., 1979-84. Coach Little League Baseball and Soccer, 1975-82; trustee Police Athletic League Sports, Cinnaminson, N.J., 1978-81; mem. counsle president's adv. bd. La Salle U., 1984-87; bd. dirs. Zurbrugg Meml. Hosp., Willingboro, N.J., 1985-88; mem. Leadership N.J. Class of 1990, 1989—; pres. Cinnaminson Twp. Bd. Edn., 1980-90; mem. N.J. Commn. on Capital Budgeting and Planning, N.J. Bldg. Authority, N.J. Commn. on Health Benefits and Pensions, N.J. Transit Corp., N.J. Capital Joint Mgmt. Commn., N.J. Lease Mgmt.-Planning Bd. Recipient: Ken Howard award Career Achievement in Budget and Finance Am. Soc. Pub. Adminstrn., 2000; decorated DSM, medal for outstanding svc. U.S. Dept. Def., 1996. Mem. Nat. Assn. State Budget Officers, Nat. Assn. Comptrs., Am. Soc. for Pub. Adminstrn. (N.J. Pub. Adminstr. of Yr. award 1992), Assn. Govtl. Accts. (Disting. Leadership award N.J. chpt. 1991), Govt. Fin. Officers Assn. (tech. group to rev. budgets for nat. award certs.). Home: 2808 Roesh Way Vienna VA 22181-6165 Office: Nat Acad Pub Adminstrn Washington DC 20005 Office Phone: 202-204-3621. E-mail: RKeevey@napawash.org.

KEEVIL, NORMAN B., mining executive; b. Cambridge, Mass., Feb. 28, 1938; s. Norman Bell and Verna Ruth (Bond) Keevil; m. Joan E. MacDonald, Dec. 1990; children: Scott, Laura, Jill, Norman Bell III. BA in Sci., U. Toronto, Ont., Can., 1959; PhD, U. Calif., Berkeley, 1964; LLD (hon.), U. BC, 1993. V.p. exploration Teck Corp., Vancouver, Canada, 1962-68, exec. v.p., 1968-81, pres., CEO, 1981-89, chmn., pres., CEO, 1989-94, pres., CEO, 1994-2000, CEO, 2000—; chmn. Teck Cominco Ltd., Vancouver, 2001—. Named Mining Man of Yr., No. Miner, 1979; named to Can. Mining Hall of Fame, 2004. Mem.: Soc. Exploration Geophysicists, Prospectors and Developers Assn. (Disting. Svc. award 1990, Viola R. MacMillan Developer's award 1997), Can. Inst. Mining and Metallurgy (Selwyn G. Blaylock medal 1990, Inco medal 1999), Royal & Ancient Golf Club (St. Andrews, Scotland), Shaughnessy Golf and Country Club, Vancouver Club. Office: Teck Cominco Ltd 200 Burrard St # 700 Vancouver BC Canada V6C 3L9 Office Phone: 604-687-1117.

KEEVIL, PHILIP CLEMENT, investment banker; b. London, Oct. 19, 1946; s. Ambrose Clement Arthur and Olwen Marjorie Enid (Gibbins) K.; m. Augusta Day McGrail, June 10, 1972; children: Adrian Ambrose Clement, Augusta Hall, Peter Larimer. BA, Oxford U., Eng., 1968, MA, 1972; MBA, Harvard U., 1975. Mgr. Unilever plc, Eng., 1968-73; assoc. Morgan Stanley & Co., N.Y.C., 1975-78, Lazard Freres & Co., N.Y.C., 1979-80, v.p., 1981-82, gen. ptnr., 1983-87; mng. dir., head mergers and acquisitions S.G. Warburg and Co. Inc., N.Y.C., 1987-91, head investment banking, 1991-95; mng. dir. Salomon Brothers Inc. (now Citigroup Global Markets), 1995—, head internat. mergers and acquisitions N.Y.C., 1995—97; head European mergers and acquisitions Salomon Smith Barney, London, 1997-2000; head mergers and acquisitions Schroder Salomon Smith Barney, London, 2000—02. Bd. dirs. S.G. Warburg & Co., Ltd., London, 1987-95, Am. for Oxford Inc., 1995-02; mem. devel. bd. Said Bus. Sch., Oxford (Eng.) U., 1999—. Freeman of City of London, 1968; liveryman Worshipful Co. of Poulters, London, 1968—; mem. of the Court, 1992—, renter warden, 1998-99, upper warden, 1999-2000, master, 2000-01; vestryman St. John's Ch., Locust Valley, N.Y., 1986-89; trustee St. Bernard's Sch., N.Y., 1991-97, St. Andrew's Sch., Del., 1993-2001; bd. govs. City of London Sch. for Girls, 2002—; mem. adv. coun. London Symphony Orch., 2004—. Baker scholar Harvard Bus. Sch., Boston, 1975. Fellow: Royal Soc. Arts; mem.: Brit.-Am. Bus. Inc. (dir. 1993—2000, dep. chmn. 1999—2001, dir. 2004—), London Rowing Club, Queenwood (Ottershaw, Eng.), Cavalry and Guards (London), Leander Club (Henley, Eng.), Brook Club, Piping Rock Club (Locust Valley) (gov. 1986—96). Episcopalian. Avocations: choral music, field sports, racquet sports. Office: Citigroup Global Markets 33 Canada Sq Canary Wharf London E14 5LB England E-mail: philip.keevil@citigroup.com.

KEFALIDES, NICHOLAS ALEXANDER, physician, educator; b. Alexandroupolis, Greece, Jan. 17, 1927; came to U.S., 1947, naturalized; s. Athanasios and Alexandra (Aematidou) K.; m. Eugenia Georgia Kutsunis, Nov. 24, 1949; children: Alexandra Jane (dec.), Patricia Ann, Paul Thomas. BA, Augustana Coll., Rock Island, Ill., 1951; BS, U. Ill., Chgo., 1953, MS in Biochemisry, MD, U. Ill., Chgo., 1956, PhD in Biochemistry, 1965; MS (hon.), U. Pa., 1971; doctorate (hon.), U. Reims, France, 1987. Resident in internal medicine U. Ill. Coll. Medicine, Chgo., 1960-62, NIH fellow in infectious disease, 1962-64, asst. prof. medicine, 1964-65, U. Chgo., 1965-69, assoc. prof. medicine, 1969-70; assoc. prof. medicine and biochemistry U. Pa., Phila., 1970-74, prof. medicine, 1974—96, prof. medicine emeritus, 1996—, prof. biochemistry and biophysics, 1975—; assoc. dean rsch. U. Pa. Sch. Medicine, 1994-95. Vis. prof. Oxford (England) U., 1977—78, 1984—85; mem., chmn. pathobiochemistry study sect. NIH, 1982—86; dir. project on burns NIH, USPHS, Lima, Peru, 1957—60; dir. Connective Tissue Rsch. Inst., Phila., 1977—2002; chmn. Instn. Rev. Bd. U. Pa., 1995—98, exec. chmn., 1998—2003; initiator, chair Gordon Rsch. Confs. on Basement Membranes, 1982; sci. mentor biotech. cos. Sci. Ctr., Phila., 2002—. Creator lecture series Lunch for Hungry Minds, Phila., 1998-; contbr. chpts. to books, articles to profl. jours. Served as surgeon USPHS, 1957-60. Recipient Borden Rsch. Found. award, 1956, award for pioneering rsch. on connective tissue Collagen Gordon Confs. and Collagen Corp., 1997; Guggenheim fellow, 1977. Fellow AAAS; mem. Am. Assn. Pathologists, Am. Soc. Clin. Investigation, Am. Soc. Biochemistry and Molecular Biology, Am. Soc. Cell Biology. Achievements include discovery of Collagen type IV in basement membranes and its role in suppressing tumor cell growth and angiogenesis. Office: U Pa Univ City Sci Ctr 3701 Market St Rm 468 Philadelphia PA 19104-5502

KEFAUVER, WELDON ADDISON, publishing executive; b. Canal Winchester, Ohio, Apr. 3, 1927; s. Ross Baker and Virginia Marie (Burtner) K. BA, Ohio State U., Columbus, 1950. Mem. faculty Columbus Acad., 1956-58; mng. editor Ohio State U. Press, 1958-64, dir., 1964-84, dir. emeritus, 1984—. Dir. Am. Univ. Press Services, Inc., 1971-72, 76-79; mem. U.S. del. 2d Asian Pacific Conf. Publs., Taiwan, 1978 Author: Scholars and their Publishers, 1977; editorial adv. bd. Scholarly Publishing. Served with AUS, 1945-46. Recipient Centennial Service award Ohio State U., 1970; citation Ohioana Library Assn., 1974; Disting. Service award Ohio State U., 1986; recognized for service to Ohio State U. by Ohio Senate and Ohio Ho. of Reps., 1986. Mem. Assn. Am. Univ. Presses (v.p. 1971-72, dir. 1971-72, 76-79, pres. 1977-78), Soc. Scholarly Pub., Nathaniel Hawthorne Soc., AAUP, Phi Eta Sigma, Phi Kappa Phi Clubs: Torch (Columbus), Crichton (Columbus), Ohio State U. Faculty (Columbus). Home: 675 Eastmoor Blvd Columbus OH 43209-2252 Office: 1050 Carmack Rd Columbus OH 43210-1002

KEGEL, WILLIAM GEORGE, mining company executive; b. Pitts., Mar. 15, 1922; s. William G. and Gertrude (Holl) K.; m. Jacqueline Treacy, Feb. 17, 1942; children: Kathy, Danyele, Janice, Jacqueline, William, Madeline, Colleen, Lisa, Brian. Student elec. engring. U. Pitts., 1940-43; LLD (hon.), Ind. U. of Pa., 1986. Mgr. mech. and elec. depts. Lee Norse Co., 1941-50; with Jones & Laughlin Steel Corp., Pitts., 1950-76, gen. mgr. raw materials and traffic, 1975-76; pres. Cerro Marmon Coal Group, 1976-79; pres., chief exec. officer Rochester & Pitt. Coal Co., Indiana, Pa., 1979-88, chmn. bd., 1988-98. Dir. emeritus Savs. and Trust Co. Pa., Indiana. Mem. Indiana (Pa.) Airport Authority, 1980-2001; bd. dirs. Brownsville Gen. Hosp., 1964-71; mem. Centerville Borough Council, 1952-60. Mem. AIME, Coal Mining Inst. Am., Am. Mining Congress (dir.), Pitts. Coal Mining Inst., Duquesne Club, Ind. Country Club, Laurel Valley Country Club. Republican. Roman Catholic. Home: 61 Duck Woods Dr Southern Shores NC 27949

KEGERREIS, ROBERT JAMES, management consultant, marketing professional, educator; b. Detroit, Apr. 2, 1921; s. I. G. and A. M. (Merry) K.; m. Katherine L. Falknor, Oct. 30, 1943; children: Merry, Duncan, Melissa. BA, BS, Ohio State U., 1943, MBA, 1946, PhD, 1968, U. Dayton, 1982, EdD (hon.), EdD (hon.), U. Dayton; LLD (hon.), U. Akron, Wilberforce U.; ScD (hon.), Cen. State U., Japan, 1992; EconD (hon.), Okayama U., Japan, 1992. Economist Fed. Res. Bank, Cleve., 1946-49; pres. KV Stores, Inc., Woodsfield, Ohio, 1949-69; v.p., sec. KBK Devel. Co., Inc., 1955-62; assoc. prof. Ohio U., Athens, 1967-69; dean Coll. Bus. and Adminstrn. Wright State U., Dayton, Ohio, 1969-71, v.p. adminstrn., 1971-73, pres., 1973-85; cons. RJK Co., Dayton, 1985—. Bd. dirs. Robbins & Myers, Dayton, Miami Valley Rsch. Found., Tait Found. Exec. dir. Arts Ctr. Found., Dayton. Lt. (j.g.) USN, 1943-46. Mem. Moraine Country Club, Bicycle Club, Pelican Bay Country Club. Methodist. Avocations: flying, golf. Office: Kettering Tower Ste 1480 Dayton OH 45423-1000

KEGLEY, CHARLES WILLIAM, JR., political science professor; b. Evanston, Ill., Mar. 5, 1944; s. Charles William and Elizabeth Euphemia (Meck) K.; m. Ann Curry Taylor, Apr. 1, 1966 (div.); 1 child, Mrs. Suzanne, Mitchell Douglas; m. Pamela Ann Holcomb, July 2, 1975 (div.); m. Debra Annette Jump, July 6, 2002. BA, Am. U., 1966; PhD, Syracuse U., 1971. Asst. prof. Sch. Fgn. Svc., Georgetown U., 1971-72, prof., chmn. dept. polit. sci., 1981—85; dir. Byrnes Internat. Ctr. U. SC, 1986—88, holder Pearce endowed chair in internat. rels., 1985—. Vis. prof. U. Tex., 1976; Moses Back Peace prof., Rutgers U., New Brunswick, N.J., 1989, People's U. China, Beijing, 1996, Grad. Inst. Internat. Studies, Geneva, 2004. Author: A General Empirical Typology of Foreign Policy Behavior, 1973; co-author, co-editor (with William Coplin): A Multi-Method Introduction to International Politics: Observation, Explanation and Prescription, 1971, Analyzing International Relations: A Multi-Method Introduction, 1975; co-author: (with Eugene R. Wittkopf) American Foreign Policy: Pattern and Process, 1979, 6th edit., 2003, World Politics: Trend and Transformation, 1981, 10th edit., 2005; (with Gregory A. Raymond) When Trust Breaks Down: Alliance Norms and World Politics, 1990, A Multipolar Peace? Great-Power Politics in the 21st Century, 1994, How Nations Make Peace, 1999, From War to Peace: Fateful Decisions in International Politics, 2002, Exorcising the Ghost of Westphalia: Building World Order in the New Millennium, 2002, The Global Future, 2005; co-editor: (with Robert W. Gregg) After Vietnam: The Future of American Foreign Policy, 1971; (with Gregory A. Raymond, Robert M. Rood, Richard A. Skinner) International Events and the Comparative Analysis of Foreign Policy, 1975; (with Patrick J. McGowan) Challenges to America: U.S. Foreign Policy in the 1980's, 1979, Threats, Weapons, and Foreign Policy, 1980, The Political Economy of Foreign Policy, 1981, Foreign Policy: USA/USSR, 1983; (with Eugene R. Wittkopf) Perspectives on American Foreign Policy, 1983, The Global Agenda: Issues and Perspectives, 1984, 6th edit., 2001 (with Patrick McGowan) Foreign Policy and the Modern World System, 1983; (with Eugene R. Wittkopf) The Nuclear Reader: Strategy, Weapoons, War, 1985, 2d edit., 1989; (with Charles F. Hermann and James N. Rosenau) New Directions in the Study of Foreign Policy, 1987, (with Eugene R. Wittkopf) The Domestic Sources of American Foreign Policy, 1988, (with Kenneth Schwab) After the Cold War: Questioning the Morality of Nuclear Deterrence, 1991, (with Eugene R. Wittkopf) The Future of American Foreign Policy, 1992; editor: The Long Postwar Peace: Contending Explanations and Projections, 1990, International Terrorism: Characteristics, Causes, Controls, 1990, Controversies in International Relations Theory: Realism and the Neoliberal Challenge, 1995, The New Global Terrorism, 2003; contbr. chpts. to books, articles to profl. jours. Trustee Carnegie Coun. for Ethics in Internat.

Affairs, 1992-98, 2000—. Recipient Disting. Alumni award Am. U., 1984; R.M. Davis scholar, 1962-66; Maxwell fellow, 1968-69, 70-71; N.Y. State Regents fellow, 1969-70; Fulbright sr. scholar, 1978, Russell rsch. awardee in humanities and social scis., 1982. Mem. Am. Polit. Sci. Assn., Am. Soc. Internat. Law, Am. Soc. Advancement Sci., Internat. Polit. Sci. Assn., Internat. Studies Assn. (assoc. dir. 1980-84, pres. 1993-94), Peace Sci. Soc., Peace Rsch. Soc., So. Polit. Sci. Assn., Pi Sigma Alpha, Omicron Delta Kappa, Delta Tau Kappa, Alpha Tau Omega. Home: 35 Veranda Ln Blythewood SC 29016-7602 Office: U SC Dept Polit Sci Columbia SC 29208-0001 Office Phone: 803-777-8180. E-mail: jumpkegs@aol.com.

KEGLEY, JACQUELYN ANN, philosophy educator; b. Conneaut, Ohio, July 18, 1938; d. Steven Paul and Gertrude Evelyn (Frank) Kovacevic; m. Charles William Kegley, June 12, 1964; children: Jacquelyn Ann, Stephen Lincoln Luther. BA cum laude, Allegheny Coll., 1960; MA summa cum laude, Rice U., 1964; PhD, Columbia U., 1971. Asst. prof. philosophy Calif. State U., Bakersfield, 1973-77, assoc. prof., 1977-81, prof., 1981—, chair dept. philosophy and religious studies. Vis. prof. U. Philippines, Quezon City, 1966-68; grant project dir. Calif. Coun. Humanities, 1977, project dir. 1980, 82; mem. work group on ethics Am. Colls. of Nursing, Washington, 1984-86; mem. Am. Bd. Forensic Examiners; chair acad. senate Calif. State U., 2000-03, exec. com., 2003-04. Author: Introduction to Logic, 1978, Genuine Individuals and Genuine Communities, 1997; editor: Humanistic Delivery of Services to Families, 1982, Education for the Handicapped, 1982, Genetic Knowledge, 1998; mem. editl. bd. Jour. Philosophy in Lit., 1979-84; contbr. articles to profl. jours. Active CSU Acad. Senate, 1999—; Bd. dirs. Bakersfield Mental Health Assn., 1982—84, Citizens for Betterment of Community. Recipinet Golden Roadrunner award Bakersfield Cmty., 1991, Wang Family Excellence award, 2000. Mem. Philosophy of Sci. Assn., Soc. Advancement Am. Philos. Soc. (chmn. Pacific divsn. 1979-83, nat. exec. com. 1974-79, 2003-), Philosophy Soc., Soc. Interdisciplinary Study of Mind, Am. Philos. Assn. (bd. mem. 1999-2003, chair com. on tchg.), Dorian Soc., Phi Beta Kappa. Democrat. Lutheran. Avocations: music, tennis. Home: 7312 Kroll Way Bakersfield CA 93309-2336 Office: Calif State U Dept Philosophy Bakersfield CA 93311 Office Phone: 661-664-2249. Business E-Mail: jkegley@csub.edu.

KEHELEY, BONNY W., elementary school educator; b. Albany, Ga., Feb. 21, 1956; d. Charles McCuin and Jeanne Helene Ward; m. John Edward Keheley. BS in early childhood edn., Ga. Southwestern Coll., 1974—77, MEd, 1978—79. Tchr. Leesburg Elem., 1977—80, Peachtree Elem., Norcross, Ga., 1981, Cherokee Co., Woodstock, Ga., 1985—. Beginning Educator Support Team, 0199—2003. Named Woodstock Elem. Yearbook Dedication, 2003; recipient Tchr. of the Yr., Little River PTA, 1986, Little River Elem. Sch., 1987, Outstanding Young Educator, Woodstock Jayees, 1987, Cmty. Action Agy. Vol. of the Yr., Canton, Ga., 1994. Mem.: Profl. Assn. Ga. Educators. Home: 630 Mountain Rd Woodstock GA 30188 Office: Woodstock Elem Sch 230 Rope Mill Rd Woodstock GA 30188

KEHL, LARRY BRYAN, lawyer; b. Cheyenne, Wyo., Nov. 5, 1959; s. Lawrence E. and Ruth A. (Deines) K. BS with honors, U. Wyo., 1982, JD with honors, 1985. Bar: Wyo. 1985, U.S. Dist. Ct. Wyo. 1985, U.S. Ct. Appeals (10th cir.) 1985, Colo. 1986. Law clk. Dist. Ct. (7th dist.) Wyo., Casper, 1985-86; atty. Guy, Williams, White & Argeris, Cheyenne, 1986-92; ptnr. Buchhammer & Kehl, Cheyenne, 1992—. Instr. People's Law Sch., Cheyenne, 1997. Contbr. articles to law jours. Mem. Cheyenne L.E.A.D.S., 1989—, Cheyenne Frontier Days, 1995—. Mem. Assn. Wyo. Def. Counsel, Wyo. Trial Lawyers, Def. Rsch. Inst., C. of C. Home: 1518 Pole Mountain Rd Cheyenne WY 82009-8305 Office: Buchhammer & Kehl 1821 Logan Ave Cheyenne WY 82001-5007 E-mail: lbk454@msn.com, obk@wyoming.com.

KEHLBECK, JOSEPH H., software developer, consultant; b. Clifton, NJ, Sept. 14, 1926; s. Joseph John and Elizabeth Harriet (Lockhoff) K.; m. Mary Kathryn Russell, Nov. 15, 1957; 1 child, Keith Alan. BS in Engring., State U. Iowa, 1950; MBA in Fin., Rutgers U., Newark, 1954. Registered profl. engr., Calif. Various positions Gen. Electric, 1952-69, mgr. mfg. engring. Louisville, 1969, mgr. mfg. Trenton, N.J., 1969-72, Louisville, 1972-77, mgr. material resource ops., 1977-85, gen. mgr. internat. purchasing Bridgeport, Conn., 1986; cons., software developer Kehlbeck & Assocs., Prospect, Ky., 1987—. Mem. adv. bd. On Display, San Ramon, Calif., 1998-99; bd. dirs. Philippine Appliance Co., Manila, 1979-85. Author: Production Leveling, 1959. Mem. ch. fin. com., 2005; bd. dirs. Mercer City Hosp., NJ, 1970—71; mem. City of Prospect Ordinance Bd., Ky., 2004. Paratrooper U.S. Army, 1943—45, lt. res. Corps. of Engrs. U.S. Army, 1946—52. Recipient award Order of Engrs., 1977. Fellow Inst. Indsl. Engrs. (pres. 1977), Hunting Creek Country Club (bd. dirs.), Home Owners Assn., Shriners, Tau Beta Pi. Avocations: golf, tennis. Office: Kehlbeck & Assocs 7812 Cedar Ridge Ct Prospect KY 40059-9491 Personal E-mail: kehlbeck@aol.com.

KEHLMANN, ROBERT, artist, critic; b. Bklyn., Mar. 9, 1942; BA, Antioch Coll., 1963; MA, U. Calif., Berkeley, 1966. Instr. glass design Calif. Coll. Arts and Crafts, Oakland, 1978-80, 91, Pilchuck Glass Ctr., Stanwood, Wash., 1978-80; guest curator Mus. Glass, Tacoma, Wash., 2001. One-man shows include Richmond Art Ctr., Calif., 1976, William Sawyer Gallery, San Francisco, 1978, 82, 86, Gallerie M. Kassel, Fed. Republic Germany, 1985, Anne O'Brien Gallery, Washington, 1988, 90, Dorothy Weiss Gallery, San Francisco, 1993, Hearst Art Gallery, Moraga, 1996; group shows include Am. Craft Mus., NYC, 1978, 86, Corning (NY) Mus. Glass, 1979, Tucson Mus. Art, 1983, Kulturhuset, Stockholm, 1985; represented in permanent collections at Corning Mus. Glass, Leigh Yawkey Woodson Art Mus., Hessesches Landes Mus., Germany, Bank of Am. World Hdqrs., San Francisco, Toledo Mus. Art, Hokkaido Mus. Modern Art, Sapporo, Japan, Huntington Mus. Art, W.Va., Am. Craft Mus., NYC, Mus. des Arts décoratifs, Lausanne, Switzerland, Oakland Mus. Author: Twentieth Century Stained Glass: A New Definition, 1992, The Inner Light: Sculpture By Stanislau Libensky and Jaroslava Brychtova, 2002; contbg. editor: New Glass Work mag., 1988-89; editor: Glass Art Soc. Jour., 1981-84. Chmn. Landmarks Preservation Commn., Berkeley, 1995-98. NEA grantee, 1977, 78. Mem. Glass Art Soc. (bd. dirs. 1980-84, 89-92, hon. life). Personal E-mail: rkehlmann@sbcglobal.net.

KEHOE, JOHN P., brokerage house executive; b. NYC, Aug. 5, 1938; s. John M. and Mary K. (Denning) K.; m. Veronica Lally McAuley, Dec. 1, 1984; children: John Michael, Maura Ann, Kevin Denning, Brendan, Allise McAuley Cert. in investment analysis, N.Y. Inst. Fin., 1960; MS in Bus. Policy, Columbia U., 1979; BA in English Lit., Fordham U., 1985. Sr. assoc. Baker Weeks & Co., Inc., N.Y.C., 1957-61; v.p., asst. to pres. McDonnell & Co., Inc., N.Y.C., 1961-65, sr. v.p., chmn. investment policy com., 1965-67; pres. McDonnell Fund, N.Y.C., 1965-67; exec. v.p. Crosby M. Kelly Assocs. Ltd., N.Y.C., 1967-69; pres., founder, chmn. Kehoe, White, Savage & Co. (Kehoe Ptnrs., Inc.), N.Y.C., 1969—98; chmn. Kehoe Ptnrs., Inc., N.Y.C., 1998—; sr. advisor Abernathy MacGregor Group, N.Y.C., 2000—. Lectr. in field Served as sgt. USMCR, 1958-64. Mem.: Nat. Assn. Corp. Dirs., Nat. Investor Rels. Inst. (charter), N.Y. Roadrunners Club, Ea. Yacht Club (Marblehead, Mass.), Racquet and Tennis Club, Princeton Club (N.Y.C., Beta Gamma Sigma, Phi Kappa Phi. Home: 55 E 72nd St New York NY 10021-4149 also: 63 Cleveland Dr Montauk NY 11954-5030 Office: Kehoe Ptnrs Inc 501 Madison Ave Fl 13 New York NY 10022 Office Phone: 212-371-5999. E-mail: jpk@abmac.com.

KEHOE, L. PAUL, state judge; b. Carthage, N.Y., May 21, 1938; s. Leo A. and Mildred (Piddock) K.; m. Elizabeth M. Weber, 1963; children: L. Paul, John Michael, Patrick Lewis. BA, Syracuse U., 1959, JD, 1962. Bar: N.Y. 1962. Dist. atty., Wayne County, N.Y., 1967-71; mem. N.Y. Assembly, 1979-80, N.Y. State Senate, 1981-92; justice N.Y. Supreme Ct., 1993—; adminstrv. judge 7th Jud. Dist., 1996-2000; assoc. Justice Appellate Divsn., 4th Dept., 2000—. With AUS, 1962-63. Mem. ABA, Wayne County Bar Assn., N.Y. State Bar Assn., Elks. Republican. Office: 50 East Ave Ste 627 Rochester NY 14604-2214 Office Phone: 585-530-3205. E-mail: lpkehoe@courts.state.ny.us.

KEHOE, THOMAS J., food products executive; b. N.Y.C., Apr. 9, 1949; s. Thomas J. and Aileen F. Kehoe; m. Carole M. Cassidy, Oct. 1, 1994; m. Doreen A. Hydell, Sept. 1, 1975 (div. June 1, 1990); children: Yvonne, Thomas, Matthew, Veronica, Rebecca, Marrielle. BA, U. Dayton, 1971. Sales and mktg. exec. Xerox Corp., N.Y.C., 1971—75; owner Bayville (N.Y.) Fish, 1976—78; polit. cons. Kehoe Assocs., Strafford, NH, 1978—80; dir. mktg. PG Assco Inc., Syosset, NY, 1980—82; pres., ptnr. Galilee Seafood, N.Y.C., 1982—87; pres. Thomas J. Kehoe Inc., Northport, NY, 1982—90; pres., ptnr. K&B Seafood Inc., East Northport, NY, 1990—. Bd. dirs. Mid Atlantic Fishery Devel. Coun., 1985—88, Nat. Fisheries Inst., 2006—. Coach Eaton's Neck Basketball, 1987—92; coach, v.p. Northport Little League, 1987—94. Mem.: AAU (karate), Pacific Coast Shellfish Growers Assn. (bd. dirs.), East Coast Shellfish Growers Assn. (bd. dirs. 2003—), Juko Kai Internat., East Northport C. of C. (bd. dirs.), Nat. Fisheries Inst., U.S. Fencing Assn., Friends of Raynham Hall, Friends of Sagamore Hill, Nat. Eagle Scout Assn., N.Y. Athletic Club. Avocation: martial arts. Home: 51 Mariners Ln Northport NY 11768 Office: K&B Seafood Inc 176 Laurel Rd East Northport NY 11731 Office Phone: 631-261-8161. E-mail: tjkehoe@verizon.net.

KEHOE, VINCENT JEFFRÉ-ROUX, photographer, cosmetics executive; b. Bklyn., Sept. 12, 1921; s. John James and Bertha Florence (Roux) K.; m. Gena Irene Marino, Nov. 2, 1966. Student, MIT, 1940-41, Lowell Technol. Inst., 1941-42, Boston U., 1942; BFA in Motion Picture and TV Prodn., Columbia U., 1957. Dir. make-up dept. CBS-TV, N.Y.C., 1948-49, NBC Hallmark Hall of Fame series, 1951-53; make-up artist in charge of make-up numerous film, tv and stage prodns., 1942—; dir. make-up Turner Hall Corp., 1959-61, Internat. Beauty Show, 1962-66. Pres., dir. rsch., founder Rsch. Coun. Make-Up Artists, Inc., 1963-; chief press officer Spanish Pavilion N.Y. World's Fair, 1965; free-lance photographer, 1956-; founder 10th Rgt. of Foot, Am. Contingent, 1968, Nat. Assn. Taurino Clubs, 1961, Club Taurino N.Y., 1960. Author: The Technique of Film and Television Make-Up for Color, 1970, The Make-Up Artist in the Beauty Salon, 1969, We Were There: April 19, 1775, 1974, A Military Guide, 1974, 2nd rev. edit., 1993, 3rd rev. edit., 1998-99, The Re-Created Officer's Guide, 5 vols., 1996-98, The Technique of the Professional Make-Up Artist, 1985, 2nd edit., 1995, Special Make-Up Effects, 1991, The British Story of the Battles of Lexington and Concord, 2000, The History of the 10th Regiment of Fort in Am., 3 vols., 2005; co-author The Professional Make-up Artist, Vol. 1 and 2, 2005; author, photographer: (bullfighting book) Aficionado! (N.Y. Art Dirs. Club award 1960), Wine Women and Toros! (N.Y. Art Dirs. award 1962); prodr.: (documentary color film) Matador de Toros, 1959; contbr. photographs to numerous mags. including Time, Life, Sports Illustrated, Argosy, Popular Photography Served with U.S. Army, WWII, ETO. Decorated Purple Heart, Bronze Star, CIB; recipient Torch award Coun. of 13 Original States, 1979. Fellow Co. Mil. Historians; mem. Tenth Foot Royal Lincolnshire Regimental Assn. (life; Hon. Col. 1968), Soc. Motion Picture and TV Engrs. (life), Acad. TV Arts and Scis., Soc. Army Hist. Rsch. (Eng., life), Brit. Officers Club New Eng. (life), Army Hist. Found. (life), 10th Mountain Divsn. Assn. (life), NRA (life), 70th Divsn. (life), Am. Chem. Soc., DAV (life), Eagle Scout Assn. (life), Naval Club (London). Home and Office: PO Box 850 Somis CA 93066-0850 Office Phone: 805-386-4744.

KEHOE, WILLIAM FRANCIS, lawyer; b. Stoneham, Mass., Dec. 3, 1933; s. William Andrew and Josephine Agnes (Crowley) K.; m. Dorothy Landry Kehoe; children by previous marriage: John William, Kathleen Emily. AB summa cum laude, Dartmouth Coll., 1955; MA, Yale U., 1956; LLB, Harvard U., 1963. Bar: Mass. 1963, U.S. Dist. Ct. Mass. 1964. Instr. English Middlebury (Vt.) Coll., 1956-57; ptnr. Gaston & Snow, Boston, 1970-91; counsel Hutchins, Wheeler & Dittmar, Boston, 1991-94, Taylor, Ganson & Perrin, Boston, 1995—. Mng. trustee Katharine L.W. and Winthrop Murray Crane, 3d Charitable Found.; mem. standing adv. com. on rules of civil procedure Supreme Jud. Ct.; lectr., panelist Mass. Continuing Legal Edn. Program and Mass. Jud. Inst. Author: Enjoying Ireland, 1966; contbr. articles and revs. to profl. jours. Served with U.S. Army, 1957-59. Fulbright scholar, Trinity Coll., Dublin, Ireland, 1959-60. Fellow Am. Coll. Trust and Estate Counsel; mem. Boston Bar Assn., Phi Beta Kappa. Office: Taylor Ganson & Perrin 160 Federal St Fl 20 Boston MA 02110-1722 Office Phone: 617-951-2777.

KEHRET, PEG, writer; b. LaCrosse, Wis., Nov. 11, 1936; d. Arthur Robert and Elizabeth (Showers) Schulze; m. Carl Edward Kehret, July 2, 1955; children: Bob. C., Anne M. Kehret Konen. Student, U. Minn., 1954—55. Trustee Pacific Northwest Writers Conf., Seattle, 1983-86. Author: Vows of Love and Marriage, 1979, Refinishing and Restoring Your Piano, 1985, Winning Monologs for Young Actors, 1986, Deadly Stranger, 1987 (Children's Choice award, 1988), The Winner, 1988, ENCORE!-More Winning Monologs for Young Actors, 1988, Nightmare Mountain, 1989 (Young Hoosier Book award, 1992, Golden Sower award Nebr. Libr. Assn., 1993, Iowa Children's Choice award, 1994, Maud Hart Lovelace award, 1995), Wedding Vows, 1989, Sisters, Long Ago, 1990, Cages, 1991 (Maud Hart Lovelace award, 1996), Acting Natural, 1992, Terror at the Zoo, 1992 (Pacific N.W. Young Reader's Choice award, 1995, N.Mex. Land of Enchantment award, 1995, Iowa Children's Choice award, 1996), Horror at the Haunted House, 1992 (Sequoyah Children's Book award, 1995, Young Hoosier award, 1995), Night of Fear, 1994, Richest Kids in Town, 1994, Cat Burglar on the Prowl, 1995, Danger at the Fair, 1995, Bone Breath and the Vandals, 1995, Don't Go Near Mrs. Tallie, 1995, Desert Danger, 1995, The Ghost Followed Us Home, 1996, Earthquake Terror, 1996 (W.Va. Children's Book award, 1998, Children's Crown award Nat. Christian Sch. Assn., 1998, Utah Children's Book award, 1999, Va. Young Readers award, 1999), Race to Disaster, 1996, Screaming Eagles, 1996, Backstage Fright, 1996, Small Steps: The Year I Got Polio, 1996 (Soc. Children's Book Writers and Illustrators Golden Kite award nonfiction, 1997, PEN Ctr. USA West award, 1997, Dorothy Canfield Fisher award, 1998, Mark Twain award, 1999, Young Hoosier award, 2001), Searching for Candlestick Park, 1997, The Volcano Disaster, 1998 (Fla. Sunshine award, 2000), The Blizzard Disaster, 1998, The Flood Disaster, 1999, Shelter Dogs, 1999, I'm Not Who You Think I Am, 1999 (Lamplighter award), The Secret Journey, 1999, My Brother Made Me Do It, 2000, Don't Tell Anyone, 2000, The Hideout, 2001, Saving Lilly, 2001 (Henry Bergh award ASPCA, 2001), The Stranger Next Door, 2002 (Sequoyah award, 2005, Nev. Young Readers award, 2005), Five Pages a Day: A Writer's Journey, 2002, Spy Cat, 2003, Escaping the Giant Wave, 2003, Abduction!, 2004 (Edgar award nominee, 2005), The Ghost's Grave, 2005, (plays) Cemeteries are a Grave Matter, 1977, Let Him Sleep 'Till It's Time for His Funeral, 1978, Spirit!, 1979 (Forest Roberts Playwriting award No. Mich. U., 1979, Best New Play award Pioneer Drama Svc., 1980), Dracula, Darling, 1980, Charming Billy, 1981, (musical) Bicycles Built for Two, 1985; contbr. articles to mags., short stories to mags. Vol. Humane Soc., SPCA, Bellevue, Wash., 1975—. Recipient Achievement award Pacific N.W. Writers, Celebrate Lit. award N.W. Reading Coun. of Internat. Reading Assn., 1993; named Artist of Yr., Redmond Arts Commn., 1998. Mem. Author's Guild, Soc. Children's Book Writers, Mystery Writers Am. Office: Curtis Brown Ltd Ten Astor Pl New York NY 10003

KEHRT, ALLAN WILLIAM, architect; m. Michaele Kehrt; children: Matthew, Emily, Kathleen. BA in Econs., Ohio Wesleyan U., 1967; MArch, Va. Polytechnic Inst. and State U., 1978. Registered architect, N.J., Fla. Asst. prof. design Coll. Architecture and Urban Studies Va. Polytechnic Inst. and State U., Blacksburg, 1977-79; mgr. C.D.P. Assocs., Wilmington, Del.; with Geddes Brecher Qualls Cunningham, Princeton, N.J.; founding and design ptnr. KSS Architects, Princeton, 1983—. Vis. critic, lectr. Va. Polytechnic Inst. and State U., U. Pa.; past treas., bd. dirs. Life Industries Corp.; adj. faculty Coll. Arch., Phila. Univ. Vice chmn. N.J. Planning Bd., Cranbury; active N.J. Environ. Commn., Cranbury; past chmn. N.J. Hist. Preservation Commn., Cranbury. With USN, 1967-71. Recipient awards Interfaith Forum Religion, Art and Architecture, 1993, Franklin award March of Dimes Birth Defect Found., 1999. Fellow AIA; mem. N.J. Soc. Architects (awards 1986, 87, 89, 90, 93, 94, 96, 98, 2000, 2001, 2004), Phi Kappa Phi, Tau Sigma Delta. Office: KSS Architects 337 Witherspoon St Princeton NJ 08542-3470 Office Phone: 609-921-1131. Business E-Mail: akehrt@kssarch.com.

KEICHER, WILLIAM EUGENE, electrical engineer; b. Pitts., Dec. 28, 1947; s. William John and Gina Rina (Magrini) K.; m. Barbara Marie Gurgacz, Aug. 12, 1972; children: Lisa Anne, Kathy Marie, William Michael. BSEE, Carnegie-Mellon U., 1969, MSEE, 1970, PhD in Elec. Engring., 1974. Sr. elec. engr. CBS Labs., Stamford, Conn., 1974-75; mem. tech. staff Lincoln Lab., MIT, Lexington, Mass., 1975-83, asst. group leader, 1983-85, group leader, 1985-93, 2000—, assoc. group leader, 1993-2000. Cons. Sci. and Engring. Support Group for Strategic Def. Initiative, Arlington, Va., 1988; co-chair for numerous confs. in field. Editor: Millimeter Wave Technology, 1982, Applied Laser Radar Technology, 1993, Industrial Applications of Laser Radar, 1994; contbr. articles to profl. publs.; patentee spatial filter sys. Capt. U.S. Army, 1974. Mil. Sensing Symposium fellow, 2003. Fellow Mil. Sensing Symposium; mem. IEEE (sr.), Optical Soc. Am., Nat. Rsch. Coun. (Air Force sci. and tech. com. on rev. of Air Force hypersonic tech. program 1997-98), Assn. Old Crows. Roman Catholic. Avocations: astronomy and astrophotography, history, snorkeling, travel, microcomputers. Home: 6 Winn Valley Dr Burlington MA 01803-4727 Office: MIT Lincoln Lab 244 Wood St Lexington MA 02421-6426 Office Phone: 781-981-7677. Business E-Mail: keicher@ll.mit.edu.

KEIDERLING, TIMOTHY ALLEN, chemistry educator, researcher; b. Waterloo, Iowa, June 22, 1947; s. Glenn Allen and Ethel V. (Kalainoff) K.; m. Candace Ruth Crawford, Sept. 4, 1976; 1 son, Michael Crawford. B.S., Loras Coll., 1969; M.A., Princeton U., 1971, Ph.D., 1974. NSF fellow Princeton U., 1969-72; research assoc. U. So. Calif., L.A., 1973-76; asst. prof. U. Ill., Chgo., 1976-81, assoc. prof. chemistry, 1981-85, prof., 1985-; guest prof. Max Planck Inst., Garching, Germany, 1984, U. Freiburg, 2004, U. Padova, Italy, 2005; sr. vis. Oxford U., 1994. Contbr. chpts. to books, more than 220 articles to profl. jours. Fellow Fulbright Found. 1984, Guggenheim Found. 2004-05; grantee NSF, NIH, Petroleum Research Found., various times; sr. rsch. scholar U. Ill., 1991-94. Mem. Am. Chem. Soc., Am. Phys. Soc., Biophys. Soc., Soc. Applied Spectroscopy. Achievements include the development of technique of vibrational circular dichroism, making of first such measurements of polypeptides, proteins and nucleic acids, and first magnetic applications to small molecules. Office: U Ill Dept Chemistry 845 W Taylor St M/C 111 Chicago IL 60607-7061 Office Phone: 312-996-3156.

KEIL, JOHN MULLAN, advertising agency executive, artist; b. Rochester, N.Y., Dec. 30, 1922; s. Alvin Richard and Elizabeth (Mullan) K.; m. Barbara Louise Miller, Sept. 16, 1950; children: Peter Mullan, Nicholas John, Elizabeth Jane. BA, U. Rochester, 1946. Copywriter advt. dept. Armstrong Cork Co., Lancaster, Pa., 1946-48, Wendell P. Colton Advt., N.Y.C., 1948-51, Needham & Grohmann, Inc., N.Y.C., 1951-55, v.p., account exec., 1955-60; v.p., creative dir. Dancer, Fitzgerald, Sample, Inc., N.Y.C., 1960-64, copy group head, 1964-67, v.p., 1967-70, sr. v.p., creative dir., 1970-75, dir., 1971-87, exec. v.p., 1975-87, chmn. creative planning con., 1973; exec. creative dir. Dancer, Fitzgerald, Sample, 1983-86; dir. creative devel. DFS-Dorland Worldwide, 1986-87; creative cons. Saatchi & Saatchi Adv. Worldwide, 1987—. Lectr. Amos Tuck Sch. Dartmouth Coll., Assn. Nat. Advertisers; Phillips Meml. lectr. U. Fla., 1987; painter acrylic on wood Frank J. Miele Gallery, N.Y.C., Toadhall Gallery, N.Y.C., Reed Gallery, Chester, Vt., So. Vt. Art Ctr., Manchester, Vt., Hartnett Gallery/U. Rochester, Hopper House Gallery, Nyack, NY, Minnebank Gallery, Mt. Vernon, Maine. Author: The Creative Mystique, How To Manage It, Nurture It, Make It Pay, 1985, How to Zig in a Zagging World, 1987; contbr. articles to Jour. Advt., Air and Space, Smithsonian, Time, N.Y. Times. Vice chmn. Zoning Bd. Appeals, Grandview-on-Hudson, N.Y., 1961-71; pres., trustee Rockland Country Day Sch., 1970-75; mem. trustees coun. U. Rochester, 1979-85, trustee, 1986-91 (life trustee, 1991—), U. Rochester Sports Hall of Fame, 2000, N.Y. State Coun. Governing Bds., 1989-94, Nat. Crime Prevention Coun., 1987—; trustee Tappan Zee Preservation Coalition, 1995—; mem. corp. Nyack Hosp., 2001—. Served with USAAF, 1943-45. Decorated D.F.C., Air medal with two oak leaf clusters;, ETO ribbin with four battle starts, recipient Silver Bell award Advt. Coun., 1981, 84, Carl M. Loeb, Jr.-McGruff award Nat. Crime Prevention Coun., 1987. Mem. Alpha Delta Phi. Clubs: Nyack (N.Y.) Field, Upper Nyack Tennis. Home: 251 River Rd Nyack NY 10960-5001 Home (Summer): 7128 Westminster West Rd Putney VT 05346 E-mail: bobo5@optonline.net.

KEIL, KLAUS, geology educator, consultant; b. Hamburg, Germany, Nov. 15, 1934; s. Walter and Elsbeth K.; m. Rosemarie, Mar. 30, 1961; children: Kathrin R., Mark K.; m. Linde, Jan. 28, 1984. MS, Schiller U., Jena, Germany, 1958; PhD, Gutenberg U., Mainz, Fed. Republic Germany, 1961; Doctorate (hon.), Friedrich-Schiller U., Jena, Germany, 2002; DSc (hon.), U. N.Mex., 2003. Rsch. assoc. Mineral. Inst., Jena, 1958-60, Max Planck-Inst. Chemistry, Mainz, 1961, U. Calif., San Diego, 1961-63; rsch. scientist Ames Rsch. Ctr. NASA, Moffett Field, Calif., 1963-68; prof. geology, dir. Inst. Meteoritics, U. N.Mex., Albuquerque, 1968-90; pres., prof. U. N.Mex., 1985-90, chmn. dept. geology Albuquerque, 1986-89; prof. geology U. Hawaii, Honolulu, 1990—, rsch. prof., head planetary geoscis. div., 1990-93, dir. Hawaii Inst. Geophysics and Planetology, 1994—2003, interim dean Sch. Ocean Earth Sci. and Tech., 2003—; cons. Sandia Labs., others. Contbr. over 600 articles to sci. jours. Recipient Apollo Achievement award, NASA, 1970, Exceptional Sci. Achievement medal, 1983, George P. Merrill award, NAS, 1970, Leonard medal, Meteoritical Soc., 1988, Zimmerman award, U. N.Mex., 1988, numerous others, new extraterrestrial mineral Keilite named after him. Fellow Meteoritical Soc., AAAS, Mineral. Soc. Am., Am. Geophys. Union, German Mineral. Soc., Microbeam Analysis Soc. (Pres.'s Sci. award 2002), others. Office: U Hawaii at Manoa Hawaii Inst Geophys & Planetology Honolulu HI 96822 Office Phone: 808-956-8760. E-mail: keil@hawaii.edu.

KEIL, M. DAVID, retired international association executive; b. Hinsdale, Ill., Jan. 22, 1931; s. Milton Derby and Lydia Anne (Landwehr) K.; m. Marilyn Jean Martin, May 15, 1976 BSJ, Northwestern U., 1952. Brand mgr. Armour & Co., Chgo., 1953-60; sr. v.p. Young & Rubicam, Chgo., 1960-74, Sandy Corp., Detroit, 1974-75, D'Arcy-MacManus & Masius, Chgo., 1976-80; pres., mng. dir. Audit Bur. Circulations, Schaumburg, Ill., 1980-96; ret., 1996. Named to Medill Sch. Journalism Hall of Fame, 1997. Mem. Internat. Fedn. Audit Burs., Circulation (sec. gen. 1986-88), Hinsdale Golf Club, Univ. Club Chgo. Lutheran. Avocations: sports, reading, travel, music.

KEIL, MARILYN MARTIN, artist; b. Balt., Nov. 6, 1932; d. Francis and Mary Blanche (Murphy) Martin; m. Herbert Bruce Keil, Dec. 18, 1954; children: Braden, Mary-Beth, Sue-Ann, Nancy, Bryant. Student, Corcoran Sch. Art, Washington, 1991-94, U. Md., 1995. Active art in embassies program U.S. Dept. State; juried Washington area printmakers calendar Balt. Mus. fine Arts, 1995—. One-woman show Ralls Collection, Washington, 1993; exhibited in group shows at Rockville Art League (watercolor award), 1991, Corcoran Sch. Art, 1994, Nat. Cathedral, Washington, 1994, U. Md. Sch. Arts and Sociology, 1995, West Gallery, 1995, Md. Fedn. Art, 1996; contbr. juried Washington Area Printmakers Calendar, Va. Mus. Fine Art, 1997, Calendar Corcoran Gallery, 1998, Nat. Gallery of Art, 1999; represented in permanent collections at Corcoran Gallery Art, Washington, 1996, Nat. Mus. Women in the Arts, 1996, Libr. of Congress, 1996, juried Washington Printmakers Original Print Calendar, 2000, 01. Bd. dirs. Potomac Glen Civic Assn., Potomac, Md., 1988-94. Mem. AAUW, Rockville Art League, Nat. Mus. Women in the Arts (charter), Washington Area Printmakers, Golden Key, Alpha Lambda. Avocations: etching, lithography. Home: 11540 S Glen Rd Potomac MD 20854-1852

KEIL, STEPHEN LESLEY, astrophysicist; b. Billings, Mont., Feb. 21, 1947; s. Nolan F. and Billy Lou (Benjamin) K.; m. Alice Ann Orient, June 18, 1972; children: Pamela Lynn, Wesley Forrester. BS in Physics, Univ. Calif., Berkeley, 1969; PhD in Astronomy, Boston U., 1975. Teaching fellow Boston (Mass.) Univ., 1969-74; postdoctoral fellow Univ. Colo., Sunspot, N.Mex., 1975-76; rsch. fellow, applied math. dept. Univ. Sydney, Australia, 1976-78; NRC fellow Sacramento Peak Obs., Sunspot, 1978-80, rsch. scientist, 1980-83; chief, solar rsch. USAF Solar Rsch. Br., Sunspot, 1983-99; dir. Nat. Solar Observatory, Sunspot, 1999—. Mem. Nat. Solar Obs. adv. com., Tucson, 1983-89; prin. investigator USAF Solar Mass Ejection Imager,

1996-99; project dir. Advanced Tech. Solar Telescope, 2000—. Editor: (workshop proceedings) Small-Scale Dynamical Processes in Quiet Stellar Atmospheres, 1984; co-editor: (workshop proceedings) Solar Drivers of Interplanetary and Terrestial Disturbances, Innovative Telescopes and Instrumentation for Solar Astrophysics, SPIE 4853, 2003. Mayor Sacramento Peak Community, Sunspot, 1990-91, treas., 1981-87. Maj. USAF, 1980-85. Named Company Grade Officer of Yr., USAF, 1984, Officer of the Yr., Geophysics Lab., Boston, 1983. Mem. Internat. Astron. Union, Am. Astron. Soc., Am. Phys. Soc., Calif. Scholarship Fedn. (life). Achievements include first to make an accurate determination of the height variation of convective penetration in the solar atmosphere. Home: 3015 Corona Loop Sunspot NM 88349 Office: National Solar Observatory 1 Corona Loop Sunspot NM 88349 Business E-Mail: skeil@nso.edu.

KEILING, ANDREAS DETLEF, physicist, researcher; b. Berlin, Oct. 13, 1964; m. Beverly Lynn Smith, June 23, 2001. BSc in physics, Imperial Coll., U. London, England, 1994; MSc in computer sci., Tech. U. Berlin, Germany, 1992; PhD, U. Minn., 2001. Cert. tchg. U. Minn., 2001. Lectr. of physics U. Wis., River Falls, Wis., 2001—02; postdoctoral fellow European Space Agy., Toulouse, France, 2002—04; rsch. assoc. Space Scis. Lab., Berkeley, Calif., 2004—. Contbr. articles various profl. jours. Recipient Associateship of the Royal Coll. of Sci., U. London, Imperial Coll., 1994; European Space Agy. Postdoctoral fellowship, European Space Agy., 2002-2004. Mem.: Am. Geophys. Union. Achievements include discovery of one power source for the Aurora. Office: Space Scis Lab 7 Gauss Way Berkeley CA 94720 Business E-Mail: akeiling@belka.space.umn.edu, keiling@ssl.berkeley.edu.

KEILL, STUART LANGDON, psychiatrist; b. Binghamton, N.Y., Oct. 5, 1927; s. Kenneth and Dorothy B. (Langdon) K.; m. Joanne Veness, Sept. 2, 1950; children: Elinor Anne Moran, Patricia J., Brian S., Victoria M. Keill Lo Russo. BA, Princeton U., 1947; MA, Cornell U., 1948; MD, Temple U., 1952. Intern Highland Hosp., Rochester, N.Y.; resident in psychiatry N.Y. State Psychiat. Inst., Presbyn. Hosp., Columbia U., N.Y.C., 1955-58; dir. edn., dir. West Side Community Mental Health Ctr., N.Y.C., 1958-71, Roosevelt Hosp., N.Y.C., 1958-71; regional dir. N.Y. State Dept. Mental Health, 1971-75; prof. clin. psychiatry SUNY, Stony Brook, 1975-80; chmn. dept. psychiatry Nassau County Med. Ctr., East Meadow, N.Y., 1975-80; clin. prof. psychiatry SUNY, Buffalo, 1980-86, emeritus prof. psychiatry, 1993—; chief psychiat. service VA Med. Ctr., Buffalo, 1981-86; prof. of psychiatry Sch. of Medicine U. Md., 1986-94, vice chmn. dept. psychiatry, 1986-93, prof. sch. social work, 1993-94, acting chmn., 1991-92; clin. prof. psychiatry Sch. Medicine NYU, 1994—; counselor Advocates Coalition for Psychiat. Patients, 1980-86; med. dir. Inst. for Psychiatry and Human Behavior, 1986-93. Mem. adv. com. mental health laws Md. Atty. Gen. Office, 1987-93; hon. rsch. fellow Dept. Psychol. Medicine U. Glasgow, 1994. Author: (with others) Textbook on Administrative Psychiatry, 1992; also 52 articles; mem. editl. bd. Social Work and Health Care, 1975—, Social Work in Mental Health Care, 2000—, Hosp. and Community Psychiatry; assoc. editor Gen. Hosp. Psychiatry Jour., 1981-94. Chmn. Nassau coun. Health Systems Agy., 1977-80; mem. adv. com. Dr. Glory's Children's Theatre, N.Y.C., 1980—; mental health laws adv. com. State's Atty. Gen., 1987; warden Christ Ch., Oyster Bay, 2002—. With USN, 1953—55, lt. USN, 1953—55. Recipient Julius T. Marcus award dept. psychiatry SUNY, Stony Brook, 1980, Jour. Social Work in Health Care editl. award, 1985; hon. sr. fellow U. Glasgow, Dept. Psychol. Medicine, Scotland, 1994. Fellow Am. Coll. Psychiatrists, Am. Psychiat. Assn. (Distinction in Adminstrn. award 1990); mem. MEDIPP Psychiatry Coun. (dist. chmn. 1981-86), Am. Assn. Psychiat. Adminstrs. (pres. 1981-82), Am. Hosp. Assn. (chmn. psychiat. svcs. sect. 1985), Am. Assn. Gen. Hosp. Psychiatrists (pres. 1985-87), N.Y. Soc. Clin. Psychiatry (pres. 1974-75, chmn. pub. psychiatry com.), Md. Psychiat. Soc. E-mail: skeill@linds.com.

KEILLER, JAMES BRUCE, clergyman, dean; b. Racine, Wis., Nov. 21, 1938; s. James Allen and Grace (Modder) K.; m. Darsel Lee Bundy, Feb. 8, 1959; 1 dau., Susanne Elizabeth. Diploma, Beulah Heights Bible Coll., 1957; BA, William Carter Coll., 1963, EdD (hon.), 1973; LLB, Blackstone Sch. Law, 1964; MA, Evang. Theol. Sem., 1965, BD, 1966, ThD, 1968; MA in Ednl. Adminstrn., Atlanta U., 1977; degree, Nat. Tax Tng. Sch., Monsey, N.Y., 1986; EdS, Ga. State U., 1987; DD, Heritage Bible Coll., 2001; postgrad., Atlanta Law Sch., Harvard U., 2001—03. Ordained to ministry Internat. Pentecostal Assemblies, 1957. Pastor Maranatha Temple, Boston, 1957-58, Midland (Mich.) Full Gospel Ch., 1958-64; v.p. acad. dean Beulah Heights Bible Coll., Atlanta, 1964—, trustee, 1964-92; nat. dir. youth and Sunday sch. dept. Internat. Pentecostal Assemblies, 1958-64, dir. world missions Atlanta, 1964-76; missionary editor Bridegroom's Messenger, 1964—; dir. global missions Internat. Pentecostal Ch. of Christ, 1976—, mem. exec. com., 1976—; mem. exec. bd. Mt. Paran Christian Sch., 1980-91. Named Alumnus of Yr., William Carter Coll., 1965. Fellow: Coll. of Tchrs.; mem.: Am. Assn. Higher Edn., Assn. Supervision and Curriculum Devel., Am. Conf. Acad. Deans, Nat. Assn. Scholars, Intercollegiate Studies Inst., Nat. Fedn. for Decency (bd. dirs.), Am. Bd. Master Educators (cert.), Am. Inst. Parliamentarians, Soc. for Bibl. Lit., Little Mountain Village Condo Assn. (bd. dirs. 1994—), So. Accrediting Assn. Bible Colls. (exec. sec. 1970—93), Am. Acad. Religion, Evang. Theol. Soc., Ind. Order Foresters, Kiwanis (lt. gov. Ga. dist. 1986—87, chmn. human values state com. Ga. dist. 1989—90). Republican. Home: 21A Little Mountain Vlg Ellenwood GA 30294-3150 Office: Beulah Heights Bible Coll 892 Berne St SE Atlanta GA 30316-1873 Office Phone: 404-627-2681. Business E-Mail: james.keiller@beulah.org.

KEILLOR, GARRISON EDWARD, writer, radio personality; b. Anoka, Minn., Aug. 7, 1942; s. John P. and Grace R. (Denham) K.; m. Jenny Lind Nilsson; children: Jason P., Maia Grace. BA, U. Minn., 1966. Former staff mem. The New Yorker. Author: Happy to be Here, 1982, Lake Wobegon Days, 1985, Leaving Home, 1987, We Are Still Married: Stories and Letters, 1989, WLT: A Radio Romance, 1991, The Book of Guys, 1993, Cat, You Better Come Home, 1995, The Old Man Who Loved Cheese, 1996, (with J. Nilsson) The Sandy Bottom Orchestra, 1996, Wobegon Boy, 1997, Me, by Jimmy (Big Boy) Valente, 1999, Lake Wobegon Summer 1956, 2001, Love Me, 2003; creator, writer and host radio show A Prairie Home Companion; contbr. articles to mags. and newspapers (Harpers, The Atlantic Monthly, The N.Y. Times, others). Recipient Grammy award for best non-mus. recording Lake Wobegon Days, 1987, Ace award, 1988, Best Mus. and Entertainment Host awards, 1988, 89, medal for spoken lang. Am. Acad. and Inst. Arts and Letters, 1990, Nat. Humanities medal, 1999, Pres. Clinton; inducted into Am. Acad. Arts and Scis., 1999. Democrat. Episcopalian. Address: A Prairie Home Companion 45 7th St E Saint Paul MN 55101-2202*

KEIM, BETTY LOU, actress, literary consultant; b. Malden, Mass., Sept. 27, 1938; d. Buster and Dorothy Clair (Tracy) Keim; m. Warren Berlinger, Feb. 18, 1960; children: Lisa, David, Edward, Elizabeth. Grad., Lodge Acad., N.Y.c., 1956. Appeared in films These Wilder Years, 1956, Teenage Rebel, 1956, Wayward Bus, 1957, Some Came Running, 1958; appeared on Broadway in Strange Fruit, Rip Van Winkle, Crime and Punishment, Texas Lil Darlin, The Remarkable Mr. Pennypacker, Roomful of Roses; appeared on TV in Omnibus, Playhouse 90, Alcoa Hour, Philco PlayHouse; appeared in TV series My Son Jeep, The Deputy. Assoc. Aid Project L.A., 1984-97; life mem., vol. Actors Fund of Am. Recipinet Motion Picture award Calif. Women's Club, 1956, Filmdoms Famous Five award Film Daily Critics, 1956, Laurel award, 1956.

KEIM, DONALD BRUCE, finance educator; b. Bethlehem, Pa., Feb. 7, 1953; s. Elwood Benjamin and Doris Mae (Wanamaker) K.; m. Susan Langshaw, July 10, 1976; children: Sarah Elizabeth, Julia Diane. BSBA, Bucknell U., 1975; MBA, U. Chgo., 1980, PhD, 1983; MS (hon.), U. Pa., 1988. Rsch. assoc. Fed. Deposit Ins. Corp., Washington, 1978; lectr. Loyola U. of Chgo., 1981—82; asst. prof., fin. U. Pa., Phila., 1982-88, assoc. prof. fin., 1988-94, prof. fin., 1994—98, John B. Neff prof. fin., 1998—. Vis. prof. INSEAD, Fontainebleau, France, 1994, 96-98, 2004; vis. scholar Dimensional Fund Advisors, Santa Monica, Calif., 1990, 1995-96; mem. acad. adv. bd. Brandywine Asset Mgmt., Wilmington, Del., 1993-2000. Assoc. editor Jour. of Fin. and Quant. Analysis, 1993-2001; co-editor European Fin. Rev., 1998-2003; contbr. articles to profl. jours. Rsch. grantee Inst. for Quantitative Rsch., 1984, 92, 99; recipient Graham and Dodd award Fin. Analysts Fedn., 1987, 99, N.Y. Stock Exch. award, 1996. Mem. Am. Fin. Assn., Western Fin. Assn. (program com. 1992-96, 2000-05), European Fin. Assn. (program com. 1996-2005) Avocations: music, photography, golf, gardening. Office: Univ Pa The Wharton Sch 2300 Steinberg Hall Philadelphia PA 19104

KEIM, MICHAEL RAY, dentist; b. Sabetha, Kans., June 8, 1951; s. Milton Leroy and Dorothy Juanita (Stover) K.; m. Christine Anne Lorenzen, Nov. 20, 1971; children: Michael Scott, Dawn Marie, Erik Alan. Student, U. Utah, 1969-72; DDS, Creighton U., 1976. Pvt. practice, Casper, Wyo., 1976—. Mem. vertical math. com. Natrona County Sch. Dist., 1997-2000; mem. Coll. Nat. Finals Rodeo Com., 2002—. Mem. organizing bd. dirs. Ctrl. Wyo. Soccer Assn., 1976-77; mem. Casper Mountain Ski Patrol, Nat. Ski Patrol Sys., 1980-2000, Big Horn Ski Patrol, 2001—, avalanche and ski mountaineering advisor No. Divsn. Region III, 1992-96, outdoor emergency care instr. trainer, 1996-99, 1st asst. patrol dir., 1996-98, patrol dir., 1998-99; bd. dirs., dep. commr. for fast pitch Wyo. Amateur Softball Assn., 1980-84; bd. dirs. Ctrl. Wyo. Softball Assn., 1980-84; head coach Big Horn Mountain Ski Team, 2002—; pres. Wyo. Spl. Smiles Found., 1995-96; mem. organizing com. Prevent Abuse & Neglect thru Dental Awareness Coalition, Wyo., 1996; mem. adv. com. Natrona County Headstart, 1985—; mem. City of Casper Leisure Svc. Adv. Com., 2002-. Recipient Purple Merit Star for Saving a Life, 1992, Hixon award, 2002. Fellow: Acad. Gen. Dentistry; mem.: ADA, Wyo. Donated Dental Svcs. (organizing bd. dirs. 1994, pres. 1995—96), Wyo. Dental Hist. Assn. (bd. dirs. 1989—95), Ctrl. Wyo. Dental Assn. (sec.-treas. 1981—82, pres. 1982—83, sec.-treas. 2002—03, pres. 2003—04), Wyo. Dental Polit. Action Com. (sec.-treas. 1985—97), Wyo. Dental Assn. (bd. dirs. 1992—97, v.p. 1993—94, ADA alt. del. 1994—95, pres.-elect 1994—95, pres. 1995—96, editor 1997—, chmn. conv. 1999—), Wyo. Acad. Gen. Dentistry (sec.-treas. 1980—82, pres. 1982—87), Pierre Fauchard Acad., Fedn. Dentaire Internat., Am. Acad. Cosmetic Dentistry, Acad. Computerized Dentistry, Creighton Club (pres. 1982—84), Kiwanis (bd. dirs. 1986—96, v.p. Casper club 1988—89, pres.-elect 1989—90, internat. del. 1989—91, pres. 1990—91, chmn. internat. rels. com. 1992—99, Rocky Mountain dist. lt. gov.-elect divsn. 1 1997—98, lt. gov. divsn. 1 1998—99, Hixon award 2002). Methodist. Avocations: hunting, skiing, sports, woodworking, photography. Home: 58 Jonquil St Casper WY 82604-3863 Office: 1749 S Boxelder St Casper WY 82604-3538 Office Phone: 307-234-6358. Personal E-mail: mogul_mike@msn.com.

KEIM, WAYNE FRANKLIN, retired agronomist, geneticist; b. Ithaca, N.Y., May 14, 1923; s. Franklin David and Alice Mary (Voigt) K.; m. Ellen Joyce Neumann, Sept. 6, 1947; children: Kathryn Louise Keim Logsdon, David Wayne, Julie Anne Keim Hughes. BS with distinction, U. Nebr., 1947; MS, Cornell U., 1949, PhD, 1952. Instr., then asst. prof. Iowa State U., Ames, 1952-56; from asst. prof. to prof. Purdue U., West Lafayette, Ind., 1956-75; vis. prof., NSF sci. faculty fellow U. Lund, (Sweden), 1962-63; vis. prof. Colo. State U., Fort Collins, 1971-72, prof. dept. agronomy, 1975-92, chmn. dept., 1975-85. Recipient Best Tchr. award Sch. Agr., Purdue U., 1965, 68. Fellow AAAS, Am. Soc. Agronomy (Agronomic Edn. award 1971, Agronomic Svc. award 1991), Crop Sci. Soc. Am. (pres. 1983-84); mem. Am. Inst. Biol. Sci., Agronomic Sci. Found. (trustee). Home: 1441 Meeker Dr Fort Collins CO 80524-4311 Office: Colo State U Dept Soil Crop Scis Fort Collins CO 80523-0001

KEINER, CHRISTIAN MARK, lawyer; b. Omaha, Mar. 16, 1953; s. John Frederick Keiner and Geraldine Elizabeth (Smith) Eadie; m. Rosemary Monique White, Nov. 21, 1980; 1 child, Colin MacGregor. BA with high honors, U. Calif., Santa Barbara, 1977; JD with distinction, U. of Pacific, 1980. Bar: Calif. 1980, U.S. Ct. Appeals (9th cir.) 1988, U.S. Supreme Ct. 1991. Assoc. Biddle, Walters, Bukey, Sacramento, 1980-82, Biddle and Hamilton, Sacramento, 1982-92; pvt. practice, Sacramento, 1992-98; ptnr. Girard and Vinson, Sacramento, 1998—. Contbr. articles to law jours. Bd. dirs. Calif. Found. for Improvement Employer-Employee Rels., Sacramento, 1994-99, Calif. Coun. Sch. Attys., Sacramento, 1996-98; instr., mem. labor-mgmt. adv. com. U. Calif. Davis Ext., Sacramento, 1986-99. Recipient award for adminstrv. law Am. Jurisprudence, 1979. Mem. ABA (pub. law sect.), Sacramento County Bar, Anthony M. Kennedy Inn of Ct., Harry S. Truman Club (pres. 1992), Order of Coif. Democrat. Roman Catholic. Office: Girard and Vinson 1006 4th St 8th Fl Sacramento CA 95814-3326 E-mail: keiner@gandv.com.

KEINER, R(OBERT) BRUCE, JR., lawyer; b. Washington, July 12, 1942; s. R. Bruce and Alice Miriam (Draeger) K.; m. Suellen Terrill, June 15, 1968; children: Scott, Grant, Terrill. BA, Dickinson Coll., 1964; LLB, U. Va., 1967. Bar: D.C. 1968, U.S. Supreme Ct. 1980. Assoc. to ptnr. Jones, Day, Reavis & Pogue, Washington, 1970-79; ptnr. Crowell & Moring LLP, Washington, 1979—; pres. Internat. Aviation Club of Washington, 1995. Pres., bd. trustees Maret Sch., 2000—04. Capt. U.S. Army, 1968-69. Mem.: Columbia Country Club, Chevy Chase, Md., U. Club Washington, Internat. Aviation Club Washington (pres. 1995). Home: 1730 Crestwood Dr NW Washington DC 20011-5334 Office: Crowell & Moring LLP 1001 Pennsylvania Ave NW Fl 10 Washington DC 20004-2595 Office Phone: 202-624-2615. Business E-Mail: rbkeiner@crowell.com.

KEIPER, JOHN EDWARD, music educator; b. Irvington, N.J., July 24, 1937; s. Joseph Allen and Jean Frances (Misch) K.; m. Frances Durham Lyle, Aug. 10, 1964 (div. Oct. 1976); children: Amanda Merritt, Joseph Allen II; m. Jeanne Marie Hubert, Dec. 29, 1979; children: Kristin Marie, Katherine Jean. B in Music Edn., Stetson U., 1963. Cert. in music edn. K-12, Fla.; cert. in music and phys. edn., N.Mex. Tchr., coach, prin. Encino (N.Mex.) Rural Ind. Schs., 1963-74; tchr., coach New Smyrna Beach (Fla.) High Sch., 1974-84, Mainland Sr. High Sch., Daytona Beach, Fla., 1984-87; tchr. Ormond Beach (Fla.) Elem. Sch., 1987—. Vis. artist Appalachian State U., Boone, N.C., 1982. Composer: (music) Five Favorites for Four Octaves, 1992. Chmn. ofcl. bd. Encino United Meth. Ch., 1967-74; charter v.p. Lions Club, Encino, 1968. Aviation ordnance 3rd class petty officer USN, 1955-58. Named one of Outstanding Secondary Educators of Am., 1973, Tchr. of Yr., 1985. Mem. Music Educators Nat. Conf. Republican. Presbyterian. Avocations: golf, fishing. Office: Ormond Beach Elem Sch 100 Corbin Ave Ormond Beach FL 32174-6301 E-mail: jekeiper@ormonderem.volusia.k12.fl.us.

KEIR, GERALD JANES, banker; b. Ludlow, Mass., Aug. 22, 1943; s. Alexander J. and Evelyn M. (Buckley) K.; m. Karen Mary Devine, July 22, 1972; children: Matthew J., Katherine B., Megan E. BA, Mich. State U., 1964, MA, 1966. Reporter Honolulu Advertiser, 1968-74, city editor, 1974-86, mng. editor, 1986-89, editor, 1989-95; exec. v.p. corp. comms. First Hawaiian Bank, Honolulu, 1995—. Co-author: Advanced Reporting: Beyond News Events, 1985, Advanced Reporting: Discovering Patterns in News Events, 1997. Bd. dirs. First Hawaiian Found., Salvation Army Bd. Hawaii, East-West Ctr. Found. Recipient Nat. Reporting award Am. Polit. Sci. Assn., 1971, Benjamin Fine Nat. award Am. Assn. Secondary Sch. Prins., 1981; John Ben Snow fellow, 1983, NEH fellow, 1973. Mem. Social Sci. Assn., Honolulu Cmty.-Media Coun., Fin. Svcs. Roundtable Pub. Affairs Coun. Office: First Hawaiian Bank PO Box 3200 Honolulu HI 96847-0001 Office Phone: 808-525-7086. Business E-Mail: gerry.keir@fhwn.com.

KEISER, BERNHARD EDWARD, engineering executive, communications engineer, consultant; b. Richmond Heights, Mo., Nov. 14, 1928; s. Bernhard and Helen Barbara Julia (Buerkle) K.; m. Florence Evelyn Keiser, Jan. 22, 1955; children: Sandra, Carol, Nancy, Linda, Paul. BSEE, Washington U., St. Louis, 1950, MSEE, 1951, DScEE, 1953. Registered profl. engr., Va. Mgr. plans and programs RCA, Cape Canaveral, Fla., 1964-67, adminstr. advanced system planning Moorestown, N.J., 1967-69; v.p., tech. dir. Page Communication Engrng., Washington, 1969-70; dir. advanced engring. Atlantic Rsch. Corp., Alexandria, Va., 1971-72; dir. anaylsis Fairchild Space & Electronics Co., Germantown, Md., 1972-75; pres. Keiser Engring., Inc., Vienna, Va., 1975—2003. Author: EMI Control in Aerospace Systems, 1979, Principles of Electromagnetic Compatibility, 1979, rev. edit. 1987, Broad band Coding, Modulation and Transmission Engineering, 1989, rev. edit. 1994; co-author: Digital Telephony and Network Integration, 1985, rev. edit. 1995. Fellow IEEE (chmn. No. Va. sect. 1980-81), Washington Acad. Scis., Radio Club Am. Republican. Lutheran. Home and Office: 2046 Carrhill Rd Vienna VA 22181-2917 *I am neither the master of my fate nor the captain of my soul. I owe everything to the Lord Jesus Christ, who is my Savior, my Redeemer.*

KEISER, CATHERINE ANN, band director; b. Neenah, Wis., Apr. 8, 1958; d. Clinton L. and Dolores Clark; m. John T. Ludgate, Dec. 22, 1979 (div. June 1989); children: Kelly Lynn, Jennifer Ann; m. Richard L. Keiser, July 15, 1995; stepchildren: Ryan, Jennifer, Lindsey. BFA in Music Edn., U. S.Dak., 1980; MusM, U. Nebr., Okla., 2005. Gen. music tchr. St. James Elem., Omaha, 1980—81; band & vocal dir. Roncalli H.S., Omaha, 1981—82; music dir. Father Flanagan's Boys Town, Boys Town, Nebr., 1983—2002; asst. dir. bands Millard North High Sch., Omaha, 2002—. Scholar, Arrow Stage Line, 1992. Mem.: Boys Town Education Assn., Nebr. Education Assn., Nebr. State Bandmaster Assn. (treas. 1986—96, Jack R. Snider Young Band Dir. award 1990), Music Educators Nat. Conf., Nebr. Music Educator Assn., Phi Beta Mu (treas. 1999—). Republican. Avocations: tennis, skiing, motorcycle touring with husband. Home: 13955 Arbor Circle Omaha NE 68144 Office: Millard North High Sch 1010 South 144th St Omaha NE 68154 E-mail: ckeiser@hotmail.com.

KEISER, DAVID WHARTON, pharmaceutical executive; b. East Orange, NJ, July 13, 1951; s. Robert Emil and Jean Gage (Van Buskirk) Keiser; m. Barbara Ann Biecher, Aug. 28, 1976; children: Stephanie, Amanda, Joseph. BA in Psychology, Gettysburg Coll., 1973; postgrad., Med. Sch. U. Basel, 1975-76. Area mgr. Hoffmann-La Roche, Basel, Switzerland, 1981-83; new bus. opportunities mgr. Mundipharma AG, Basel, 1984-85; mgr. licensing G.D. Searle and Co., Skokie, Ill., 1985-86, dir. licensing, Europe, 1987-89, sr. dir. licensing, 1989-90, sr. dir. Asia/Pacific ops., 1990-92; exec. v.p., COO Alexion Pharma, New Haven, 1992—2002, pres., COO, 2002—, also bd. dirs. Bd. dirs. Conn. United Rsch. Excellence. Bd. dirs. A Better Chance, Madison, Conn., 1997—99. With Swiss Army, 1978—85. Mem.: Licensing Execs. Soc. Avocations: travel, languages, golf, hiking, investing. Office: Alexion Pharma Inc 352 Knotter Dr Cheshire CT 06410 Personal E-mail: keiserd@aol.com.

KEISER, EDMUND DAVIS, JR., biologist, educator; b. Appalachia, Va., Feb. 18, 1934; s. Edmund Davis and Ora Elizabeth (Wade) K.; m. Alice Sue Tucker, Sept. l0, l982; children: Mark Edmund, Julie Ann; stepchildren: Louis King III, Jenifer King. BA, So. Ill. U., 1956, MS, 1961; PhD in Zoology, La. State U., 1967. Tchr. sci. Kinmundy High Sch., Ill., 1956-57, Mt. Vernon Twp. Sch. Dist., Ill., 1957-58; dist. sci. coordinator Freeburg Sch. Dist. 70, Freeburg, Ill., 1958-62; instr. biology La Salle-Peru-Oglesby Jr. Coll., La Salle, Ill., 1962-64; teaching asst. La. State U., Baton Rouge, 1964-66; asst. prof. U. Southwestern La., Lafayette, 1966-70, assoc. prof., 1970-75, prof. biology, 1976, mem. coun. grad. coords., 1973-76; prof. biology U. Miss., Lafayette, 1976—, chmn. dept. University, 1976-87. Mem. Atchafalaya River Basin Rsch. Coun., l972-74; exec. coun., state dir. sci. teaching La. Acad. Scis., l972-74; rsch. assoc. Gulf South Rsch. Inst., l972-74; dir. Lafayette Natural History Mus. and Planetarium, 1973, Atchafalaya River Basin herpetofaunal study U.S. Fish and Wildlife Svc., l973-76; exec. coun. Gopher Tortoise Soc., l979-8l; commr. Miss. Dept. Wildlife Conservation, l978-79, 80-84, chmn., 1983-84; cons. Ecolog. Consulting, 1998—, U.S. Fish and Wildlife Svc., 2000—; rsch. assoc. Miss. Mus. Natural Sci., 2001–. Mem. Miss. Wildlife Heritage Com., 1980-84, Miss. Gov.'s Select Com. on Radioactivity and Radioactive Waste Depository, 1979-80; environ. cons. NASA/Lockheed Sci. and Engring., 1990-91, 94-95, NASA/Sverdrup Engring., 1994-95; cons. on aquatic ecosys. U.S. Army C.E., 1992-95, 98-2002; cons. NASA/GBTech, 1998-2000, Miss. Dept. Wildlife, Fisheries and Parks, 1998—, Tetra Tech., Inc. Atlanta, 2000-01; cons. Nat. Park Svc., 2001-02, U.S. Fish and Wildlife Svc., 2002—; field assoc. Miss. Mus. Natural Sci., 2001—. Recipient numerous grants; Disting. Prof. award U. Southwestern La., 1973; Govs. Meritorious Service award State of Miss., 1979; citation for outstanding sci. teaching Nat. Sci. Tchrs. Assn.-Ill. Supt. Public Instrn., 1962 Fellow Explorers Club; mem. Soc. for Study Amphibians and Reptiles, Herpetologists League, Golden Key Honor Soc., Sigma Xi (chpt. pres. 1976, 79-80), Beta Beta Beta, Phi Eta Sigma, Phi Kappa Phi. Home: 211 Saint Andrews Cir Oxford MS 38655-2518 Office: U Miss Dept Biology University MS 38677 Office Phone: 662-816-7800. Business E-Mail: bykeiser@olemiss.edu.

KEISER, HARRY ROBERT, retired physician; b. Chgo., Aug. 9, 1933; s. Harry Rudolph and Anna Mae (Hungerford) Keiser; m. Linda Lee Hallsten, June 11, 1965 (div. 1989); children: Harry Rudolph, Robert Hungerford; m. Phyllis Swain Bentz, May 9, 1992. BA, Northwestern U., 1955, MD, 1958. Diplomate Nat. Bd. Med. Examiners, Am. Bd. Internal Medicine. Intern Phila. Gen. Hosp., 1958-59; resident in internal medicine VA Research Hosp., Chgo., 1959-60; clin. assoc. Nat. Heart Inst., NIH, Bethesda, Md., 1960-63; resident in internal medicine U. Calif. Hosp., San Francisco, 1963-64; sr. investigator, then acting chief exptl. therapeutics br. Nat. Heart Inst., 1964-73; clin. asst. prof. medicine Georgetown U. Med. Sch., 1965-90, clin. prof. medicine, 1990—; dep. chief hypertension-endocrine br. Nat. Heart, Lung and Blood Inst., 1974-85; chief hypertension-endocrine br., 1985-98; clin. dir. inst., 1976-98; commd. officer USPHS, 1960-98, med. dir., 1972-98; scientist emeritus NIH, 1998—2004, ret., 2004. Contbr. articles to profl. jours. Fellow: ACP; mem.: Am. Soc. Hypertension, Am. Soc. Pharmacology and Exptl. Therapeutics, Sierra Club. Home: 2573 SW Bridgeview Ter Palm City FL 34990 Office: Nat Heart Lung & Blood Inst 10 Center Dr MSC 1754 Bldg 10 Bethesda MD 20892-1754 Personal E-mail: keiser2573@adelphia.net.

KEISER, JOHN DOUGHERTY, business educator; b. Bellefonte, Pa., May 7, 1962; s. James Ralph and Josephine Dougherty Keiser; m. Lynn Marie Pelkey, July 1, 2000; 1 child, Alecia Marie Rumpp. BS, Pa. State U., 1984; PhD in Orgnl. Behavior, U. of Ill., Urbana, 1995. Asst. prof. U. of Mass., Amherst, 1995—2001, SUNY, Brockport, NY, 2001—. Recipient Anbar Citation of Excellence, Anbar Electronic Ingelligence, 2000. Mem.: Soc. for Bus. Ethics, Acad. of Mgmt. Achievements include research in changes in the traits of American CEOs between 1960 and 1989, and research in service and nonprofit organizations. Home: 21 Brockway Pl Brockport NY 14420 Office: SUNY 350 New Campus Dr Brockport NY 14420 E-mail: jkeiser@brockport.edu.

KEISER, KENNETH E., food products executive; With Pepsi-Cola Metro. Bottling, 1976—90; sales, oper. Pepsi-Cola Bottling Group; pres. Pepsi-Cola Puerto Rico; pres., COO Delta Beverage Group, 1990—2000, PepsiAmericas (prior to merger with Whitman), 1998—2002; pres., COO worldwide PepsiAmericas, Mpls., 2002—. Office: Pepsi Americas 4000 Dain Rauscher Plaza 60 S Sixth St Minneapolis MN 55402

KEISER, PAUL HAROLD, retired hospital administrator; b. Dalton, Ohio, June 1, 1927; s. Austin R. and Elrena E. (Tschantz) K.; m. Nancy F. Homan, May 27, 1950; children— James William, Martha Ann Lee, Elizabeth Louise Green, Patricia Elrena Bell. BS, Mt. Union Coll., 1948; MS in Hosp. Adminstrn., Northwestern U., 1952. Adminstr. Community Hosp. Evanston, Ill., 1952-54, Burlington Hosp., Iowa, 1954-67; pres. York Hosp., Pa., 1967-88, ret., 1988. Lectr., seminar leader Northwestern U., Chgo., 1952-54, U. Iowa Hosp., Iowa City, 1955-59; lectr. George Washington U., 1969-86. Contbr. articles to profl. jours. Bd. dirs. United Way, York, Pa., 1970-78, York Habitat for Humanity, 1992-98, 99-2005, York County Parks Charitable Trust Bd., 1989-, vice chmn., 1990-; bd. dirs. York County Farm and Natural Land Trust, 1992-98, mem. adv. bd., 1998—; dir. adv. bd. Pa. State U., York, 1979—; sec. North Codorus Twp. Plan Commn., 1994-96; mem. North Codorus Twp. Bd. Suprs., 1995—2005, vice chmn., 1997-99, chmn. 2000-2002, S.E. (York County) Regional Police Bd., chmn. 2002-05; mem. gov. bd. Byrnes Health Edn. Ctr., 1995—. Fellow Am. Coll. Hosp. Adminstrn. (life, regent 1964-67); mem. Iowa Interprofl. Assn. (pres. 1963-64), Iowa Hosp. Assn. (pres. 1961-62), Am. Hosp. Assn. (del. 1975-86), Hosp. Assn. Pa.

(chmn. bd. dirs. 1983, bd. dirs. svcs. corp. 1986-89), Northwestern U. Hosp. Adminstrn. Alumni Assn. (pres. 1957-58), Rotary (bd. dirs. 1979-82), Sigma Alpha Epsilon. Republican. Presbyterian. Avocations: tennis, woodworking. Home: 3053 Markle Rd York PA 17403-9103

KEISER, RICHARD ALLAN, political science professor, consultant; b. Phila., May 23, 1959; s. Sidney Leonard Keiser and Doris Blum; m. Teena Ballard Keiser; 1 child, Alana Ballard. BA, MA, U. Pa., 1980; PhD, U. Calif., Berkeley, Calif., 1989. Asst. prof. U. Denver, 1989—91; prof. polit. sci. Carleton Coll., Northfield, Minn., 1991—, assoc. dir. Am. Studies, 2001—04, dir. Am. Studies, 2004—. Scholar, U. Pa., 1980. Jewish. Office: Carleton College 100 North College St Northfield MN 55057

KEISER, ROBERT LEE, retired gas and oil industry executive; b. 1942; BSEE, U. Mo., 1965. Engrng. trainee Sunray DX, 1965-68; mgr. internat. Sun Co., 1968-87; v.p. planning and devel. Sun Exploration and Prodn. Co., 1987-88, Oryx Energy Co. (now Kerrmcgee Corp.), Dallas, 1988-91, pres., COO, 1991-94, chmn., CEO, pres., 1994-99. Bd. dirs. U. Tex., Dallas. Mem. Soc. Petroleum Engrs., Dallas Petroleum Club. Office: 16666 Northchase DR Houston TX 77060-6014

KEISLER, PETER DOUGLAS, federal agency administrator, lawyer; b. Hempstead, N.Y., Oct. 13, 1960; s. William and Sydelle (Prisand) K.; m. Susan Keisler; children: Sydelle, Alexander, Philip. BA, Yale U., 1981, JD, 1985. Bar: Pa. 1985, D.C. 1989. Law clk. to hon. judge Robert Bork U.S. Ct. Appeals (D.C. cir.), Washington, 1985-86; assoc. counsel to Pres. of U.S. White House, Washington, 1986-88; law clk. to assoc. justice Anthony Kennedy U.S. Supreme Ct., Washington, 1988-89; assoc. Sidley & Austin, Washington, 1989—93; ptnr. Sidley Austin Brown & Wood (formerly Sidley & Austin), 1993—2002; prin. dep. assoc. atty. gen U.S. Dept. Justice, Washington, 2002; acting assoc. atty. gen, 2002—03; asst. atty. gen., civil division, 2003—. Mem. ABA, Pa. Bar Assn., D.C. Bar Assn. Republican. Jewish. Home: 4964 Allan Rd Bethesda MD 20816-2722 Office: Dept Justice Civil Divsn 950 Pennsylvania Ave NW Washington DC 20530-0001

KEISLING, BRUCE LOWELL, librarian; b. Towanda, Pa., Aug. 28, 1964; s. Wayne Warren and Bessie Lorraine Keisling; m. Jennifer Mira Hong, Dec. 12, 1998; children: Jacob Lowell, Elizabeth Graybill, Johannes Christian. BA, Cedarville U., 1986; MLS, Cath. U. Am., 1995. Libr. Va. Theol. Sem., Alexandria, 1995—98; assoc. libr. So. Bapt. Theol. Sem., Louisville, 1998—2001, assoc. v.p. acad. resources and sem. libr., 2002—. Mem.: Am. Theol. Libr. Assn. Office: Southern Bapt Theol Sem 2825 Lexington Rd Louisville KY 40280 Office Phone: 502-897-4807. Office Fax: 502-897-4600. E-mail: bkeisling@sbts.edu.

KEISLING, MAI DINH, art educator; b. Bien Hoa, Vietnam, Apr. 17, 1966; arrived in U.S., 1982; d. Thoai Van Dinh and Buom Thi Do; m. Charles Michael Keisling, Dec. 29, 1986; children: Nicholas Bao-Khanh, Sheridan Khanh-An. At engrng. program, Jacksonville U., Fla., 1986—89, BFA in Studio Art cum laude, 1990, MAT in Art Edn. summa cum laude, 1991. Fin. planner John Hancock Mutual, Jacksonville, Fla., 1990—92; tchr. math Landon Mid. Sch., 1992—93; tchr. art Landon Mid. Sch. Arts, 1993—2003, Paxon Sch. Advanced Studies, 2003—. Exec. bd. Asian-Am. Cultural Coun., 1993—96; presenter Infusion of Art and Academics Asian-Am. Cultural Coun. State Conf., Fla.; participant Internat. Art Educators Forum, Savannah, Ga., 1994, 95, 97, Jax Cultural Coun. Arts, Jacksonville, Fla., 1995—98; presenter in field. Fin. chairperson Christ the King Vietnamese Cath. Ch., Jacksonville, Fla., 1996—; mem. bldg. fund bd. Vietnamese Ctr., 2000—; mem. pastoral coun. Diocese of St. Augustine, 2001—. Whatley scholar, Kappa Pi, 1989—90. Mem.: Duval Art Tchrs. Assn. Democrat. Avocations: reading, travel, cooking, jogging, finance. Home: 4918 Island Club Ct Jacksonville FL 32225 Office: Paxon Sch Advanced Studies 3239 Norman Thagard Blvd Jacksonville FL 32254

KEISTER, BEVERLY JANE, accountant; b. Louisville, Sept. 6, 1955; d. Joe Tivis and Leta Fern Keister; 1 child, Sara. BSBA in Food and Lodging Sys. Mgmt., BA in Acctg., M Accountancy, So. Ill. U., 1983. CPA. Acct. Peat, Marwich & Mitchell, St. Louis, 1984-87; asst. contr. Prime Bank, Decatur, Ga., 1987-91; project mgr. Arthur Andersen, Atlanta, 1991-92; mgr. Hazlett, Lewis & Bieter, Atlanta, 1992-96; CFO Cobb C. of C., Marietta, Ga., 1996-97; fin. acct. Watkins Engrs. & Contractors, Tallahassee, Fla., 1997—. Mem. Ga. Soc. CPA, Golden Key Honor Soc. (pres. 1982-83), Nat. Honor Soc., moose, Beta Alpha Psi. Democrat. Methodist. Avocations: flying, boating, swimming, skating, dance. Office: Watkins Engrs & Constructors 2101 Maryland Cir Tallahassee FL 32303

KEISTER, LISA A., sociology professor; b. Erie, Pa., Jan. 30, 1968; d. James and Barbara Vargo; m. James Wilson Moody, Aug. 21, 1999. PhD, Cornell U., 1997. Asst. prof. U. N.C., Chapel Hill, 1997—99, Ohio State U., Columbus, 1999—2000, assoc. prof., 2000—04, prof., 2004—, assoc. dean Coll. Social and Behavioral Scis., 2005—. Author: Wealth in America, 2000, Chinese Business Groups, 2000, Getting Rich: America's New Rich and How They Got There, 2005. Home: 1066 Neil Ave Columbus OH 43201 Office: 300 Bricker Hall 190 N Oval Mall Columbus OH 43210 E-mail: keister.7@osu.edu.

KEISTER, STEPHEN LEE, artist; b. Lancaster, Pa., Aug. 22, 1949; s. John Shenk and Martha Elizabeth (Heim) K. BFA, Tyler Sch. Art, 1970, MFA, 1972. One-man shows include Nancy Lurie Gallery, Chgo., 1977, 79, Pam Adler Gallery, N.Y.C., 1978, Tex. Gallery, Houston, 1980, Mus. Contemporary Art, Chgo., 1980, Blum Helman Gallery, N.Y.C., 1981, 82, Larry Gagosian Gallery, L.A., 1982, Carol Taylor Gallery, Dallas, 1984, Galerie Rudolf Zwirner, Cologne, Germany, 1984, Blum Helman Warehouse, N.Y.C., 1986, U. Mo., Kansas City, 1987. Pollock-Krasner Found. grantee, 1987.

KEITEL, HARVEY, actor; b. Bklyn., May 13, 1939; m. Lorraine Bracco, 1982 (div. 1983); 1 child, Stella; m. Daphna Kastner, Oct. 7, 2001; 1 child. Studied with Lee Strasberg, Frank Corsaro, Actors Studio. Actor (films) Reflections in a Golden Eye, 1967, Who's That Knocking at My Door?, 1967, Mean Streets, 1973, Alice Doesn't Live Here Anymore, 1974, That's the Way of the World, 1975, Taxi Driver, 1976, Mother Jugs and Speed, 1976, Buffalo Bill and the Indians or Sitting Bull's History Lesson, 1976, Welcome to L.A, 1976, The Duellists, 1977, Blue Collar, 1978, Fingers, 1978, Eagle's Wing, 1979, La Mort en Direct, 1980, Saturn 3, 1980, Bad Timing: A Sensual Obsession, 1980, The Border, 1982, La Nuit de Varennes, 1982, Copkiller, 1983, Exposed, 1983, Une Pierre Dans la Bouche, 1983, Nemo, 1984, Falling in Love, 1984, Knight of the Dragon, 1985, A Complex Plot About Women, Alleys and Crimes, 1986, Off Beat, 1986, Wise Guys, 1986, The Men's Club, 1986, The American Bride, 1986, The Pick-Up Artist, 1987, The Inquiry, 1987, Down Where the Buffalo Go, 1988, The Last Temptation of Christ, 1988, Caro Gorbaciov, 1988, January Man, 1989, The Two Jakes, 1990, The Battle of the Three Kings, 1990, Two Evil Eyes, 1990, Bugsy, 1991 (Acad. award nominee), Mortal Thoughts, 1991, Thelma and Louise, 1991, Sister Act, 1992, Bad Lieutenant, 1992, The Piano, 1993, Point of No Return, 1993, Rising Sun, 1993, Dangerous Game, 1993, The Young Americans, 1993, Monkey Trouble, 1994, Pulp Fiction, 1994, Somebody to Love, 1994, Imaginary Crimes, 1994, Smoke, 1995, Clockers, 1995, Ulysses' Gaze, 1995, From Dusk Till Dawn, 1996, Head Above Water, 1996, City of Industry, 1997, Cop Land, 1997, Fairy Tale: A True Story, 1997, Shadrach, 1998, Lulu on the Bridge, 1998, Finding Graceland, 1998, Il Mio West, 1998, Holy Smoke, 1999, Presence of Minde, 1999, U-571, 2000, Prince of Central Park, 2000, Little Nicky, 2000, Nailed, 2001, Vipera, 2001, Taking Sides, 2001, Nowhere, 2002, Ginostra, 2002, Red Dragon, 2002, Beeper, 2002, Crime Spree, 2003, The Galindez File, 2003, Who Killed the Idea, 2003, Puerto Vallerta Squeeze, 2003, National Treasure, 2004, The Bridge of San Luis Ray, 2004, Be Cool, 2005, Shadows in the Sun, 2005; (TV films) A Memory of Two Mondays, 1974, The Virginia Hill Story, 1974, La Bella Otero, 1983, Baciami strega, 1985; actor, exec. prodr. (films) Blue in the Face, 1995, Three Seasons, 1999, The Grey Zone, 2001; actor, prodr. (films) Dreaming of Julia, 2003; actor, co-prodr. (films) Reservoir Dogs, 1992; TV appearances include Kojak, 1973, The FBI, 1974, Amazing Stories, 1985; stage appearances include A Lie in the Mind, Death of a Salesman, 1975, Hurlyburly, 1984. Recipient Lifetime Achievement award, Istanbul Film Festival, 2005. Office: c/o William Morris Agy 151 S El Camino Dr Beverly Hills CA 90212-2704 also: care Susan Culley Assoc 150 S Rodeo Dr Ste 220 Beverly Hills CA 90212-2409*

KEITEL, WILLIAM E., communications executive; BBA, U. Wis.; MBA, Ariz. State U. With PepsiCo, 1980—83; various sr. fin. positions Nortel, 1983—96; from mgr. corp. fin. to sr. v.p., CFO QUALCOMM Inc., San Diego, 1996—2002, sr. v.p., 2002—, CFO, 2002—. Office: QUALCOMM Inc 5775 Morehouse Drive San Diego CA 92121

KEITH, BRIAN THOMAS, automotive executive; b. Houston, Aug. 2, 1951; s. Thomas Ross and Elsie Ann (Carden) K.; m. Anna Lee Rogers, Nov. 17, 1973; children: Kevin Patrick, Lindsay Rogers. BSBA, Samford U., 1973. Educator installation IBM, Birmingham, Ala., 1971-73; salesman Albeco-Ala. Bus. Equipment Co., Birmingham, 1973-74; pres., owner Walter S. White Auto Parts, Inc., Birmingham, 1974—. Bd. dirs. Ala. Power Co. Vendor Rels. Bd., Birmingham, Automotive Wholesalers Worker Compensation Trust, 2001—; trustee Automotive Wholesalers Ins. Trust, Montgomery, 1985—, treas. investment com., 1992—, chmn. trust, 1996-99; industry spkr. Automotive Market Rsch. Coun., 1995, Automotive Aftermarket Assn. S.E., Automotive Aftermarket Industry Assn. Pub. mag. Auto Svc. and Repair, 1988-98; contbr. articles to publs. and mags. V.p. Park Bd. Patriot Baseball, Homewood, Ala., 1985-89; celebrity fundraiser Am. Cancer Soc., 1993; mem. canvass com. All Sts. Ch., Homewood, 1986-90, youth com., 1992-95; active St. Andrews Soc. of the Middle South. Named Outstanding Young Men in Am., U.S. Jaycees, 1983; recipient Tech. Tng. award Arvvin Industries, 1983-88. Mem. Automotive Aftermarket Assn. S.E. (bd. dirs. 1985—, chmn. 1986-91, treas. 1992-95, 98-2001, polit. action com. 1992-99, exec. com. 1991-2001, Leadership award 1991), Automotive Aftermarket Industry Assn. (bd. dirs. 1992-98, nat. polit. action com. 1993-99, co-chmn. automotive com. 1994-98), Birmingham C. of C., U.S. C. of C., Young Exec. Forum, Assn. Enterprises (pres. 1991-92), Jr. Achievement, Nat. Fedn. Ind. Bus. Episcopalian. Avocations: family, golf, travel.

KEITH, BRUCE EDGAR, political scientist, genealogist; b. Curtis, Nebr., Feb. 17, 1918; s. Edgar L. and Corinne E. (Marsteller) Keith; m. Evelyn E. Johnston, Oct. 29, 1944; children: Mona Louise, Kent Marsteller, Melanie Ann. AB with high distinction, Nebr. Wesleyan U., 1940; MA, Stanford U., 1952; grad, Command and Staff Marine Corps Schs., 1958; sr. resident, Naval War Coll., 1962; PhD, U.Calif., Berkeley, 1982. Commd. 2d lt. U.S. Marine Corps, 1942; advanced through grades to col., 1962; ret., 1971; officer in charge Marine Corps Nat. Media, N.Y.C., 1946—49; support arms coord. 1st Marines, Seoul, Republic of Korea, 1950; cmmdg. officer 3d Bn, 11th Marines, 1958—59; ops. officer Pres. Dwight D. Eisenhower visit to Okinawa, 1960, Fleet Marine Force, Pacific Cuban Missile Crisis, 1962; mem. U.S. del. SEATO Planning Conf., Bangkok, 1964; G-3 Fleet Marine Force, Pacific, 1964—65; head strategic planning study dept. Naval War Coll., 1966—68; genealogist, 1967—; exec. officer Hdqrs. Marine Corps programs, Washington, 1968—71; election analyst inst. govtl. studies U. Calif., Berkeley, 1974—86; polit. analyst, 1986—; tchg. asst. U.Calif., Berkeley, 1973—74. Contbr. Book The Descendants of Daniel and Elizabeth (Disbrow) Keith, 1979—81, Book Hstory of Curtis Nebraska—The First Hundred Years, 1984; author: (Book) A Comparison of the House Armed Services Committees in the 91st and 94th Congresses: How They Differed and Why, 1982, The Johnstons of Morning Sun, 1979, The Marstellers of Arrellton, 1978, The Morris Family of Brookville, 1977, Japan-The Key to America's Future in the Far East, 1962, A United States General Staff, A Must or a Monster?, 1950; co-author: California Votes, 1960—72, 1974, The Myth of the Independent Voter, 1992, Furher Evidence on the Partisan Affinities of Independent Leaners, 1983. Bd. dirs. Bay Area Funeral Soc., 1980—83, v.p., 1981—83. Decorated Bronze Star, Navy Commendation medal, Presdl. Unit Citation with 3 bronze stars.; recipient Phi Kappa Phi Silver medal, Nebr. Weslyan U., 1940, Alumni award, 1964. Mem.: Ret. Officers Assn., Am. Acad. Polit. and Social Sci., Acad. Polit. Sci., Am. Polit. Sci. Assn., No. Calif. Marine Corps Assn., World Affairs Coun., Marines Meml. (San Francisco), Commonwealth of Calif. (San Francisco), Masons, Pi Gamma Mu, Phi Kappa Phi. Republican. Unitarian. Address: PO Box 2368 Walnut Creek CA 94595-0368

KEITH, BRUCE EDWARD, sociologist; b. Decatur, Ill., Dec. 22, 1961; s. Donald and Elizabeth Keith; m. Kate Franklin, Dec. 17, 1988; children: Barbara, Mary. BA, Western Wash. U., Bellingham, Wash., 1984, MA, 1986; PhD, U. Nebr., Lincoln, Nebr., 1990. Asst. prof. sociology W.Va. U., Morgantown, W.Va., 1991—96; asst. dean academic assessment US Mil. Acad., West Point, NY, 1996—2000, assoc. prof. sociology, 1996—2001, assoc. dean academic affairs, 2000—, prof. sociology, 2001—. Pres. North Ctrl. Sociol. Assn., 2003—04; cons. Mid. States Commn. on Higher Edn., Phila., 1999—. Author: Inside West Virginia, 1999, Contexts for Learning, 2004; contbr. scientific papers, articles to profl. jour. Office: US Mil Acad Office of the Dean Academic Affairs West Point NY 10996 Office Phone: 845-938-6321.

KEITH, CAROLYN AUSTIN, secondary school counselor; b. Mobile, Ala., July 15, 1949; d. Lloyd James Jr. and Aletia Delores (Taylor) Austin; m. Carlos Lamar Keith Sr., Aug. 14, 1971; children: Carlos Lamar Jr., Carolyn Bernadette Austin Keith. BA in English and History, Mercer U., 1971; Cert. in Gifted Edn., Valdosta State Coll., 1979, MEd in Counseling, 1982, postgrad., 1987, Nova Southeastern U., 1997—. Tchr. English Crisp County High Sch., Cordele, Ga., 1971-77; tchr. gifted Tift County Jr. High Sch., Tifton, Ga., 1977-81, Dooly County Sch. System, Vienna, Ga., 1981-82; counselor Worth County High Sch., Sylvester, Ga., 1982-86, Monroe Comprehensive High Sch., Albany, Ga., 1986-91, Dougherty County Alternative Sch., Albany, 1991-98, Dougherty County Mid. Sch., Albany, 1998—. Cons. Ga. State U., Atlanta, 1986-89, Dept. Family and Children Svcs., Albany, 1993, 94; presenter Nat. Dropout Prevention Fall conf., 1997. Mem. West Point Parent's Club, U.S. Mil. Acad., 1992-96, Dougherty County Commn. on Children/Youth, Albany, 1991—; mem. adv. bd. Southwest Ga. Prevention Resource Ctr., Teen Plus Clinic, 1998, S.W. Ga. Area Health Edn. Ctr., 1996—; mem. Nat. Family Life Inst., U. N.C., Charlotte, 1997; presenter Nat. Dropout Prevention Fall Conf., 1997. Named Vol. of Yr., Dougherty County Coun. on Child Abuse, 1993, Student Assistance Program Counselor of Yr. for State of Ga., 1994. Mem. Am. Counseling Assn., Ga. Sch. Counselors Assn. (sec. 2d dist. 1985-91, Counselor of Yr. 1993), Am. Sch. Counselors Assn., Nat. Bd. Cert. Counselors (cert. family life instr.), Ga. Lic. Profl. Counselors, South Ga. Regional Assn. Lic. Profl. Counselors, Delta Sigma Theta. Democrat. Roman Catholic. Avocations: reading, classical music. Office: PO Box 50261 Albany GA 31703-0261

KEITH, DALE MARTIN, management consultant; b. Kansas City, Mo., Oct. 22, 1940; s. Floyd LeRoy and Pauline Constance (Brown) K.; m. Judith Ann Reynolds, May 8, 1965; children: Stephanie Deanna, Kirsten Michelle. BSBA in Indsl. Mgmt., U. Mo., 1965. Cert. mgmt. cons. Staff analyst Black & Veatch, Kansas City, Mo., 1965-68, asst. project mgr., 1968-75, adminstrv. coord., 1975-77, project mgr., 1977-88, mktg. dir., 1988-90, project dir., 1990-92; pres. Cert. Mgt. Cons., 1992—, Keith and Assocs., Ltd., Kansas City, 1993—. Internat. speaker, trainer, advisor Coun. of Econ. Regulation, Washington, 1988—. Mem. Eggs & Issues Forum, Kansas City, 1988—. Mem. Assn. Energy Engrs., Inst. Mgmt. Cons. (mem. Coll. Firm Prins., bd. dirs., past chmn., pres. Kansas City chpt., founding bd. mem. LAW Spl. Interest Group, IMC Comms. Com. chmn., 1996 IMC Nat. Conv. chpt. leadership and mgmt. com.), Assn. Mgmt. Cons., Menninger Soc., U.S. Energy Assn. (tech. collaboration com.), Inst. of Ams., Internat. Platform Assn., Internet Soc., Optimists Internat. (bd. dirs. Kans. dist., past pres. Blue Valley chpt., Optimist Youth Homes), Intellect Exchange EC Europe People Force, Digital Strategies Som. Republican. Presbyterian. Avocations: jaguar motor cars, photography, golf, reading, computers. Home: 17101 Canterbury Dr Stilwell KS 66085

KEITH, DAMON JEROME, federal judge; b. Detroit, July 4, 1922; s. Perry A. and Annie L. (Williams) K.; m. Rachel Boone Keith, Oct. 18, 1953; children: Cecile Keith, Debbie, Gilda. BA, W.Va. State Coll., 1943; JD, Howard U., 1949; LLM, Wayne State U., 1956; PhD (hon.) (hon.), U. Mich., Howard U., Wayne State U., Mich. State U., N.Y. Law Sch., Detroit Coll. Law, W.Va. State Coll., U. Detroit, Atlanta U., Lincoln U., Marygrove Coll., Detroit Inst. Tech., Shaw Coll., Ctrl. State U., Yale U., Loyola Law Sch., L.A., Ea. Mich. U., Va. Union U., Ctrl. Mich. U., Morehouse Coll., Western Mich. U., Tuskegee U., Georgetown U., Hofstra U., DePaul U. Bar: Mich. 1949. Atty. Office Friend of Ct., Detroit, 1951—55; sr. ptnr. firm Keith, Conyers Anderson, Brown & Wahls, Detroit, 1964—67; mem. Wayne County Bd. Suprs., 1958—63; dist. judge U.S. Dist. Ct. (ea. dist.) Mich., 1967—77, chief judge, 1975—77; judge U.S. Ct. Appeals (6th cir.), Detroit, 1977—95, sr. judge, 1995—. Mem. Wayne County (Mich.) Bd. Suprs., 1958—63; chmn. Mich. Civil Rights Commn., 1964—67; pres. Detroit Housing Commn., 1958—67; commr. State Bar Mich., 1960—67; mem. Detroit Bar Assn., Mich. Com. Manpower Devel. and Vocat. Tng., 1964, Detroit Mayor's Health Adv. Com., 1969; rep. dist. judges 6th Cir. Jud. Conf., 1975—77; adv. com. on codes of conduct Jud. Conf. U.S., 1979—86; subcom. on supporting pers. Jud. Conf. Com. on Ct. Adminstrn., 1983—87; chmn. Com. on the Bicentennial of Constn. of Sixth Cir., 1985—; nat. chmn. Jud. Conf. Com. on the Bicentennial of Constn., 1987—; mem. Commn. on the Bicentennial of U.S. Constn., 1990; lectr. Howard U., 1972, Ohio State U. Law Sch., 1992, N.Y. Law Sch., 1992; guest lectr. Howard U. Law Sch., 1981; Bicentennial of Constn. lectr. W.Va. State Coll., 1987; keynote speaker Black Law Students Assn., Harvard Law Sch., 1987. Contbr. articles to profl. jours. Trustee Med. Corp. Detroit, Interlochen Arts Acad., Cranbrook Sch., U. Detroit, Mich. chpt. Leukemia Soc. Am.; mem. Citizen's Adv. Com. Equal Ednl. Opportunity Detroit Bd. Edn.; gen. co-chmn. United Negro Coll. Fund Detroit; 1st v.p. emeritus Detroit chpt. NAACP; mem. com. mgmt. Detroit YMCA; mem. Detroit coun. Boy Scouts Am., Detroit Arts Commn.; vice chmn. Detroit Symphony Orch.; vis. com. Wayne State U. Law Sch.; adv. coun. U. Notre Dame Law Sch.; chmn. Citizen's Coun. for Mich. Pub. Univs.; deacon Tabernacle Missionary Bapt. Ch.; Deacon Bapt ch.; bd. dirs. Detroit Bd. Table, NCCJ. U.S. Army, 1943—46. Named 1 of 100 Most Influential Black Ams., Ebony Mag., 1971—92, Damon J. Keith Elementary Sch. named in his honor, Detroit Bd. Edn., 1974, Damon J. Keith Ann. Civic and Humanitarian award established in his honor, Highland Park YMCA, 1984, 15th Mich. Legal Milestone The Uninvited Ear presented in honor of The Keith Decision, 1991; named one of The Century's Finest Michiganders, Mich. Chronicle, 1999; recipient Mich. Chronicle outstanding Citizen award, 1960, 1964, 1974, Alumni citation, Wayne State U., 1968, Ann. Jud. award, 1971, Citizen award, Mich. State U., Disting. Svc. award, Howard U., 1972, Jud. Independence award, 1973, Spingarn medal, NAACP, 1974, Fed. Judge of Yr. award, Black Law Students Assn., 1974, award for Outstanding Contbns. to Black Community, Nat. Assn. Black Social Workers, 1974, Judge of Yr. award, Nat. Conf. Black Lawyers, 1974, Bill of Rights award, Jewish Community Coun., 1977, A. Philip Randolph award, Detroit Coalition Black Trade Unionists, 1981, Human Rights Day award, B'nai B'rith Women's Coun. Met. Detroit, Robert L. Millender award, So. Christian Leadership Conf. Mich. chpt., 1982, Afro-Asian Inst. award, Histadrut in Israel, 1982, civil rights lectr. award, Creighton U. Ahmanson Law Ctr., 1983, Nat. Human Rels. award, Greater Detroit Roundtable of NCCJ, 1984, Knights of Charity award, Pontifical Inst. for Mission Extension, 1986, Disting. Pub. Svc. award, Mich. Anti-Defamation League of B'nai B'rith, 1987, Nat. Chpt. award, 1988, Black Achievement award, Equitable Fin. Cos., 1987, Menorah award, Afro-Asian Inst. Histadrut of Israel, 1988, Dr. George Derry award, Marygrove Coll. Detroit, One Nation award, The Patriots Found./GM, 1989, 1st Ann. Move Detroit Forward award, City of Detroit, 1990, Gov's. Minuteman award, Rotary Club Lansing, 1991, Disting. Warrior award, Detroit Urban League, 1998, Edward J. Devitt award for disting. svc. to justice, 1998, Pinnacle award, Turner Broadcasting Sys., 2000, Spirit of Excellence award, ABA, 2001. Mem.: ABA (coun. sect. legal edn. and admission to bar), Am. Judicature Soc., Nat. Lawyers Guild, Detroit Bar Assn. (pres'. award), Mich. Bar Assn. (champion of justice award), Nat. Bar Assn. (William H. Hastie award Jud. Coun., 8th Ann. equal Justice award), Detroit Cotillion Club, Alpha Phi Alpha. Office: US Ct Appeals US Courthouse 231 W Lafayette Blvd Rm 240 Detroit MI 48226-2779 also: Potter Stewart US Courthouse 100 E 5th St Cincinnati OH 45202-3988*

KEITH, DAVID, symphony orchestra conductor; b. Tacoma, Oct. 9, 1930; s. David and Barbara K.; m. Ginni Paynton, July 5, 1972. *Great grandfather David Keith I immigrated to America via Nova Scotia from Scotland in 1870. Settling in Salt Lake City, he co-founded the famous Silver King mine. The Keith mansion in Salt Lake City is preserved as a Historical Landmark. Great, great grandfather General Isaac Ingalls Stevens was the first Territorial Governor of Washington in 1857. General Stevens was a Civil War hero. Commander of the 70th New York Highlanders, he died in 1862 at the battle of Chantilly, Virginia, leading his men into combat, carrying the Union flag. Great grandfather Elisha P. Ferry was the first Governor of Washington State.* Student, San Francisco Conservatory of Music, 1948-50; studied choral conducting, Rodney Eichenberger, U. Wash., 1968; studied orchestral conducting, Dr. Stanley Chapple and Vilem Sokol, U. Wash., 1968-72; studied piano with, Ira Schwarz, Can., Louise van Ogle, U.S. Assoc. condr. Bellevue (Wash.) Philharm. Orch., 1968-70; condr., music dir. Seattle Concert Orch., 1970-73; founder, music dir. emeritus, condr. laureate L.A. Mozart Orch., 1974-91, also trustee, 1974-91. Avocations: breeding purebred, all-black German shepherds. Office: LA Mozart Orch 1771 Seaview Trl Los Angeles CA 90046 Office Phone: 360-468-3060.

KEITH, DAVID, band director; MusB, Ga. So. U. Dir. of bands Richmond Hill (Ga.) H.S., 2001—. Named Most Influential Tchr., Savannah Morning News, 2005. Mem.: Ga. Music Educator's Assn. (chmn. dist. honor band 2001—05, coord. all-state band 2002).

KEITH, DAVID LEMUEL, actor; b. Knoxville, Tenn., May 8, 1954; s. Lemuel Grady Jr. and Hilda Earle (Coulter) K.; m. Nancy Clark, 2000. BA, U. Tenn., 1985. Actor: (stage prodns.) Red Bluegrass Western Flyer Show, 1977, Harvey, 1985, Greater Tuna, 1986, Bus Stop, 1986, (feature films) The Great Santini, 1979, The Rose, 1980, Brubaker, 1980, Back Roads, 1981, Take This Job and Shove it, 1982, An Officer and a Gentleman, 1982 (Golden Globe award nomination 1982), Independence Day, 1982, The Lords of Discipline, 1983, Firestarter, 1984, Deadly Sins, 1995, Red Blooded American Girl II, 1995, Judge and Jury, 1996, A Family Thing, 1996, Invasion of Privacy, 1996, Secret of the Andes, 1998, Running with Scissors, 1998, Ambushed, 1998, U-571, 1999, If...Dog...Rabbit, 1999, Question of Privilege, 1999, Men of Honor, 2000, Cahoots, 2000, Burning Down the House, 2001, World Traveler, 2001, Anthrax, 2001, Behind Enemy Lines, 2001, The Stickup, 2001, Clover Bend, 2001, Mother Ghost, 2002, Daredevil, 2003, Deep Shock, 2003, The Kings of Brooklyn, 2004, Raise Your Voice, 2004, others; (TV movies) Are You in the House Alone?, 1978, Friendly Fire, 1978, The Golden Moment, 1980, Gulag, 1985, If Tomorrow Comes, 1986, Heartbreak Hotel, 1988, The Two Jakes, 1990, Epoch, 2000, Love and Treason, 2001, Carrie, 2002, Epoch: Evolution, 2003; TV series: Happy Days, 1978, Co-Ed Fever, 1979, Flesh 'N' Blood, 1991, Still Life, 2004; TV guest appearances include Happy Days, 1974, Walker, Texas Ranger, 1993, Law & Order: Special Victims Unit, 1999; dir. (film) The Farm (also rec. artist for soundtrack). Mem. Screen Actors Guild, AFTRA, Dirs. Guild. Methodist. Office: Writers & Artists Agy Ste 550 8383 Wilshire Blvd Beverly Hills CA 90211 also: Peluce Accts 449 S Beverly Dr Beverly Hills CA 90212-4428

KEITH, DELORESE PARKER, elementary school educator; b. Lynchburg, Va., July 21, 1931; d. Charles Edward and Odell Routon Parker; m. Charles Elisha Keith, July 5, 1958; children: Edward, Sharon Keith Brem. BA in Edn. and Psychology, Lynchburg Coll., 1952; student in Theatre, SUNY,

1979—81, MS in Edn., 1983. Cert. tchg. permanent Cert. N.Y., Collegiate Profl. Cert. State of Va. Elem. tchr. Fairfax County Schs., Va., 1952—56, USAF, Japan, 1956—57, Oyster Bay & Greene Pub. Schs., NY, 1958—76; humanities instr. Broome Cmty. Coll., Binghamton, NY, 1979—84; resource tchr. for gifted Fluvanna County Schs., Va., 1985—88; historic intpreter Monticoello Edn. Dept., Charlottesville, Va., 1989—98. Puppeteer & instr. Kids on the Block and Therapeutic Recreation, Charlottesville, Va., 1990—; bd. mem. Girls Scouts of Am., varrious, 1972—96. Trainer Girl Scouts of Am., various, 1972—96. Recipient Jeannie Special Achievement Award in Childrens Theatre, Broome Cmty. Coll., 1980, Thanks Badge award, Girl Scouts USA, 1984, cert. of Appreciation Award, Charlottesville Parks and Recreation, 1994. Episc. Avocations: hiking, oragami, candle making, painting, travel. Home: 1405 Auburn Dr Charlottesville VA 22902

KEITH, JENNIE, anthropology educator, academic administrator, writer; b. Carmel, Calif., Nov. 15, 1942; d. Paul K. and Romayne Louise (Fuller) Hill; m. Marc Howard Ross, Aug. 25, 1968 (div. 1978); 1 child, Aaron Elliot Keith Ross; m. Roy Gerald Fitzgerald, June 21, 1980; 1 child, Kate Romayne Keith-Fitzgerald. BA, Pomona Coll., 1964; MA, Northwestern U., 1966, PhD, 1968; Dr.Letters (hon.), Pomona Coll., 2002. NIMH fellow, Paris, 1968-70; asst. prof. anthropology Swarthmore Coll., 1970-76, assoc. prof., 1976-82, prof., 1982—, Centennial prof. anthropology, 1990—, chmn. sociology and anthropology, 1987-92, provost, 1992-2001; exec. dir. Eugene M. Lang Ctr. for Civic and Social Responsibility, 2002—. Mem. rsch. edn. rev. com. NIMH, Washington, 1979-82; co-dir. workshop on age and anthropology Nat. Inst. Aging, Washington, 1980-81, task group leader nat. rsch. plan on aging, 1981; mem. human devel. rev. bd. NIH, 1985-89; mem. adv. coun. Brookdale Found., 1990-93. Author: Old People, New Lives, 1977, 2d paperback edit., 1982 (Am. Jour. Nursing Book of Yr. 1978), Old People as People, 1982; co-author: The Aging Experience, 1994 (Richard Kalish award Gerontol. Soc. Am. 1994); co-editor: New Methods for Old-Age Research, 1980, 2d edit., 1986, Age in Anthropological Theory, 1984; mem. editorial bd. Gerontologist, 1981-89, Jour. Gerontology, 1987-91, Jour. Aging Studies, 1989-98; assoc. editor Rsch. on Aging, 1981-88. Bd. dirs. Cmty. Svcs., Folsom, Pa., 1980-82, Inst. Outdoor Awareness, Swarthmore, 1980—; bd. dirs. Kendal-Crosslands, 1987-92, chmn., 1989-92, Kendal Corp., 1992-95. Conf. grantee Nat. Inst. Aging, 1980, rsch. grantee, 1982-90. Fellow Am. Anthrop. Assn., Gerontol. Soc. Am. (exec. bd. behavioral and social scis. sect. 1985-87, program chmn. 1989, chair 1989-90, publs. com. 1993-95); mem. Assn. Anthropology and Gerontology (founder, sec. 1980-81). Office: Swarthmore Coll Lang Ctr for Civic and Social Responsibi Swarthmore PA 19081 Business E-Mail: jkeith1@swarthmore.edu.

KEITH, JOHN A(UGUSTINE) C(HILTON), lawyer; b. Washington, Aug. 22, 1946; BA, U. Va., 1968, JD, 1974. Bar: Va. 1975, D.C. 1976. Law clk. Hon. Albert V. Bryan, Jr. U.S. Dist. Ct. (ea. dist.) Va., 1974-75; ptnr. Blankingship & Keith, Fairfax, Va. Fellow Am. Bar Found.; mem. ABA, Am. Counsel Assn., Va. State Bar (10th dist. com. 1983-86, chmn. 1985-86, chmn. standing com. on legal ethics 1996-97, bar coun. 1991—, exec. com. 1993—, pres.-elect 1997-98, pres. 1998—), Fairfax Bar Assn. Office: Blankingship & Keith PC 4020 University Dr Ste 312 Fairfax VA 22030-6802 E-mail: JKeith@blankeith.com.

KEITH, KENT MARSTELLER, academic administrator, writer, lawyer, recreational facility executive; b. N.Y.C., May 22, 1948; s. Bruce Edgar and Evelyn E. (Johnston) K.; m. Elizabeth Misao Carlson, Aug. 22, 1976. BA in Govt., Harvard U., 1970; BA in Politics and Philosophy, Oxford (Eng.) U., 1972, MA, 1977; JD, U. Hawaii, 1977; EdD, U. So. Calif., 1996. Bar: Hawaii 1977, D.C. 1979. Assoc. Cades, Schutte, Fleming & Wright, Honolulu, 1977-79; coord. Hawaii Dept. Planning and Econ. Devel., Honolulu, 1979-81, dep. dir., 1981-83, dir., 1983-86; energy resources coord. State of Hawaii, Honolulu, 1983-86, chmn. State Policy Coun., 1983-86; chmn. Aloha Tower Devel. Corp., 1983-86; project mgr. Mililani Tech. Park Castle and Cooke Properties, Inc., 1986-89, v.p. pub. rels. and bus. devel., 1988-89; pres. Chaminade U., Honolulu, 1989-95; v.p. devel. and comm. YMCA Honolulu, 1998—2001, sr. v.p., 2001—04; pres. Carlson Keith Corp., 2004—. Author: Jobs for Hawaii's People: Fundamental Issues in Economic Development, 1985, The Paradoxical Commandments: Finding Personal Meaning in a Crazy World, 2001, Anyway: The Paradoxical Commandments, 2002, Do It Anyway, 2003; contbr. articles on ocean law to law jours. Trustee Hawaii Loa Coll., 1986—89, vice chmn., 1987—89; bd. dirs. St. Louis Sch., 1990—95, Hanahauoli Sch., 1990—98, Cath. Charities, 1997—2003; chmn. Manoa Neighborhood Bd., 1989—91; mem. platform com. Hawaii Dem. Conv., 1982, 1984, 1986; pres. Manoa Valley Ch., Honolulu, 1976—78; mem. Diocesan Bd. Edn., 1990—95, chmn., 1990—93. Rhodes scholar, 1970; named one of 10 Outstanding Young Men of Am., U.S. Jaycees, 1984; recipient Disting. Alumni award U. Hawaii, 1993. Mem. Am. Assn. Rhodes Scholars, Internat. House of Japan, Nature Conservancy, Pla. Club, Pacific Club, Harvard Club Hawaii (Honolulu, bd. dirs. 1974-78, sec. 1974-76), Rotary (Honolulu Sunrise). Home: 2626 Hillside Ave Honolulu HI 96822-1716 E-mail: kentkeith@hotmail.com.

KEITH, MICHAEL CURTIS, communication educator, writer; b. Albany, N.Y., Mar. 17, 1945; s. Frederick Curtis Keith and Margaret (McKenna) Harney; m. Susanne Riette, Jan. 1, 1986; 1 child, Marlo. MA, U. R.I., 1977, PhD, 1998. Broadcaster various radio stas., 1965-75; dir. radio and TV Dean Coll., Franklin, Mass., 1978-90; prof. George Washington U., Washington, 1990-92; chair edn. Mus. Broadcasting, Chgo., 1992-94; prof. Boston Coll., 1993—. Author: Signals in the Air, 1995, Voices in the Purple Haze, 1997, The Radio Station, 5th edit., 2004; co-author: (with R. Hilliard) The Broadcast Century: A Biography of American Broadcasting, 4th edit., 2004, The Next Better Place, 2003. With U.S. Army, 1962-65. Mem. Broadcast Edn. Assn., Popular Culture Assn., Mus. Broadcast Comm. Office: Boston Coll 3 Howard St South Easton MA 02375-1448

KEITH, PAULINE MARY, artist, illustrator, writer; b. Fairfield, Nebr., July 21, 1924; d. Siebelt Ralph and Pauline Alethia (Garrison) Goldenstein; m. Everett B. Keith, Feb. 14, 1957; 1 child, Nathan Ralph. Student, George Fox Coll., 1947—48, Oreg. State U., 1955. Illustrator Merlin Press, San Jose, Calif., 1980-81; artist, illustrator, watercolorist Corvallis, Oreg., 1980-94. Author 6 chapbooks including Christmas Thoughts, Retelling the Story, 1985, Poems, 1999; editor: Four Generations of Verse, 1979; author numerous poems; contbr. articles to profl. jour; one-woman shows include Roger's Meml. Libr., Forest Grove, Oreg., 1959, Corvallis Art Ctr., 1960, 98-99, Human Resources Bldg., Corvallis, 1959-61, Corvallis Pastoral Counseling Ctr., 1992-94, 96, Hall Gallery, Sr. Ctr., 1993-2003, Consumer Power, Philomath, Oreg., 1994, 2002, 2003, 2004, 2005, Art, Etc., Newburg, Oreg., 1995-2002; exhibited in group shows at Hewlett-Packard Co., 1984-85, Corvallis Art Ctr., 1992, Chintimini Sr. Ctr., 1992, 94, 2001-04. Co-elder First Christian Ch. (Disciples of Christ), Corvallis, 1988-89, co-deacon, 1980-83, elder, 1991-93; sec. Hostess Club of Chintimini Sr. Ctr., Corvallis, 1987, pres., 1988-89, v.p., 1992-94; active Luth. Ch. Coun., 1999-2000. Recipient Watercolor 1st price Benton County Fair, 1982-83, 88-89, 91, 2d prize, 1987, 91, 3d prize, 1984, 90, 92. Mem. Oreg. Assn. Christian Writers, Internat. Assn. Women Mins., Am. Legion Aux. (past pres.), ArtVine (Pres.'s Choice, 1999-2002, honorable mention, 2005) Republican. Avocations: nature walks, singing in church choir. Office: 304 S College St Newberg OR 97132-3114

KEITH, ROBERT GORDON, data processing executive, historian, researcher; b. Phila., Nov. 18, 1940; s. Edward Gordon and Margaret Soutter (Woods) Keith; m. Anne Howard Brown, June 7, 1964; children: Rebecca Keith Matusovich, Robert Ubardo. BA, Amherst Coll., 1962; MA in History, Harvard U., 1965, PhD of History, 1970; MBA in Pub. Mgmt, Boston U., 1987. Asst prof. history Southeastern Mass. U., North Dartmouth, 1969—73; lectr. history (part time) Boston U., 1975—78; Mellon faculty fellow history Harvard U., Cambridge, 1978—79, rsch. assoc, Ctr for Latin Am., 1979—82; project mgr., sr. planner divsn capital planning & ops. State of Mass., Boston, 1983—88, mgr. policy planning & rsch. divsn. capital planning & ops., 1988—93; cons. Yarmouth, Maine, 1992—94; sys. devel. specialist Muskie Sch. Pub. Svc. U. So. Maine, Portland, 1994—98, mgr. data, rsch. analyst Muskie Sch. Pub. Svc., 1998—. Author: (book) Conquest and Agrarian Change: The Emergence of the Hacienda System on the Peruvian Coast, 1976; editor: Haciendas and Plantations in Latin American History, 1977; co-editor (with J.H. Parry): (book (5 volumes) New Iberian World: A Documentary History of the Discovery and Settlement of Latin America to the Early 17th Century, 1984. Pres. Neighborhood Devel. Corp. of Jamaica Plain, Mass., 1979—84. Office: Univ So Maine Muskie Sch Pub Svc 96 Falmouth St PO Box 9300 Portland ME 04104-9300 Office Phone: 207-780-4475. Business E-Mail: bobk@usm.maine.edu.

KEITH, ROBERT WILLIAM, banker; b. Chgo., July 28, 1926; s. Nathan William Keith and Myrtle A. (Bull) Simons; m. Helen L. Weichel, Sept. 4, 1948; children— Melissa, Matthew, Andrew Student, Wentworth Military Acad., 1944; BS, U. Mo., 1947; MBA, Hofstra U., 1956. Employment mgr. Equitable Life Assurance Soc., N.Y.C., 1947-56; asst. treas. Hanover Bank, N.Y.C., 1956-59; asst. v.p. Mfrs. Hanover Trust Co., N.Y.C., 1959-63, v.p., 1963-77, sr. v.p., 1977-83, exec. v.p., 1983-86. Regent Stonier Grad. Sch., Washington, 1981-84. Fellow Life Office Mgmt. Assn.; mem. CLU (chartered), Am. Inst. Banking (life), Am. Bankers Assn. (chmn. pers. divsn., dir. 1980-81), Beta Gamma Sigma, Beta Theta Pi, North Fork Country Club. Republican. Presbyterian.

KEITH, SUSAN S., lawyer; V.p., sec. and corp. counsel Halliburton Co., Dallas, 1990—. Office: Halliburton Company 4100 Clinton Dr Houston TX 77020-6299 E-mail: susan.keith@halliburton.com.

KEITH, TOBY (TOBY KEITH COVEL), country singer, songwriter, producer; b. Clinton, Okla., July 8, 1961; s. H.K. and Joan Covel; m. Tricia Keith, Mar. 24, 1984; children: Shelly Reeve, Krystal, Stelen Keith Covel. Worked in oil industry; former band mem. The Easy Money Band; played defensive end Okla. City Drillers, minor league, semi-pro football team; football player Okla. Outlaws, US Football League (USFL) team; signed with Mercury Records, Nashville, 1984—99, DreamWorks, Nashville, 1999; founder Show Dog Nashville Records, 2005—. Singer: (albums) Toby Keith, 1993, Christmas to Christmas, 1995, Boomtown, 1995, Blue Moon, 1996, Dream Walkin', 1997, Greatest Hits, Vol. 1, 1998, How Do You Like Me Now?, 1999 (Album Yr., Acad. Country Music Awards, 2000), Pull My Chain, 2001, Unleased, 2002 (Favorite Country Album, Am. Music Awards, 2003), 20th Century Masters- The Millennium, 2003, Shock 'n Y'all, 2003 (Album Yr., Acad. Country Music Awards, 2003, Best Country Album, Am. Music Awards, 2004), Greatest Hits 2, 2004, (singles) Should've Been A Cowboy, 1993 (Named Most Played Song of Decade in th 90's, Billboard), He Ain't Worth Missing, 1993, Who's That Man, 1994, Upstairs Downtown, 1994, You Ain't Much Fun, 1995, Does That Blue Moon Ever Shine On You, 1995, Closin' Time at Home, 1996, We Were in Love, 1997, I'm So Happy I Can't Stop Crying, 1997, Getcha Some, 1998, How Do You Like Me Now?, 2000 (Named Most Played Song of 2000, Billboard); singer: (with Chris Le Doux) (songs) "Copenhagen", Rodeo Rock & Roll Collection, 1995; singer: (with Beach Boys) "Be True to Your School", Stars and Stripes, Vol. 1, 1996; singer: (with Lari White) "Only God Could Stop Me Loving You", Stepping Stones, 1998; singer: "I Can't Be A Slave", Prince of Egypt original soundtrack, 1998; prodr.: (song) "I Can't Be A Slave", Prince of Egypt original soundtrack, 1998; singer (guest appearance with Willie Nelson): (video) Beer for My Horses, Willie Nelson and Friends, Live and Kickin', 2003. Named Entertainer Yr., Acad. Country Music Awards, 2002, 2003, Top Male Vocalist, 2000, 2003, Favorite Male Country Artist, Am. Music Awards, 2004; recipient Hottest Video of Yr. for song Whiskey Girl, Country Music Television Music Awards, 2005. Achievements include invited by George W. Bush to addresss at MacDill Air Force Base in Tampa, Fla., site of US Cent. Command and headquarters of Gen. Tommy Franks; "Courtesy of the Red, White and Blue (The Angry American)", a super-patriotic response to Sept. 11th that became one of country's most highly charged political statements; songwriting, 12 of his 16 #1 hits have been self-penned; radio airplay, 8 Billboard country #1's and eight R&R country #1's from his DreamWorks Records alone; sales of more than $13.5 million. Avocations: hunting, fishing, golf, collecting baseball cards and memorabilia. Office: Dreamworks Nashville 1516 16th Ave S Nashville TN 37212 Office Phone: 615-463-4600.*

KEITH, WILLIAM DOUGLAS, lawyer; b. Chgo., Apr. 11, 1950; s. William H. and Mary N. Keith; m. Jill Marie Keith, Nov. 27, 1977; children: William P., Robert D., Lauren M. BA, Rutgers Coll., 1972; JD, Stetson U., 1976. Bar: Fla. 1976; cert. civil trial lawyer, bus. litigation lawyer, civil trial advocate; cert. cir. mediator. Ptnr. Cardillo, Keith & Bonaquist, P.A., Naples, Fla., 1976—. Mem. judicial nominating commn. Twentieth Judicial Circuit, 2003—; mem. Fla. Bar Bus. Litigation Cert. Com., 2004—. Paul Harris fellow Rotary, 1988; bd. dirs. YMCA of Collier County, 1991-94. Mem. Am. Bd. of Trial Advocates (nat. bd. dirs. 2000-03), Am. Inns of Ct. (pres. 2000-01, master bencher), Assn. of Trial Lawyers of Am., Acad. Fla. Trial Lawyers (sustaining mem., bd. dirs. 1993-96), Collier County Bar Assn. (pres. 1983-84, pres. trial lawyers sect. 1986-87). Avocations: reading, golf, fly fishing. Office Phone: 941-774-2229. E-mail: wkeith@ckblaw.com.

KEITHLER, JOHN WILLIAM, investment executive; b. Elizabeth, N.J., Mar. 2, 1947; s. George King and Mary Keithler; m. Karen Dorothy Keithler, Apr. 13, 1996; 1 child, Jennifer Lynn Mirande. BS in Commerce, Rider U., 1970. Cert. cash mgr. Corp. banker Chase Manhattan Bank, N.Y.C., 1970-80; fin. planner Am. Brands, Inc., N.Y.C., 1980-85, cash mgr., 1985-86; investment mgr. Group Health Inc., N.Y.C., 1987—. With USN, 1971. Mem. Treasury Mgmt. Assn., Assn. for Fin. Profls. Avocations: foreign travel, stamp collecting/philately, coin collecting/numismatics.

KEITHLEY, BRADFORD GENE, lawyer; b. Nov. 23, 1951; s. Sanderson Irish and Joan G. (Kenneday) K.; m. Kathy Carrington, Nov. 6, 2004; children: Thomas Ryan Carrington, John Nathaniel Carrington; 1 child from previous marriage Paul Michael. BS, U. Tulsa, 1973; JD, U. Va., 1976. Bar: Va. 1976, Okla. 1978, D.C. 1979. Atty. Office of Gen. Counsel to Sec. USAF, Washington, 1976-78; ptnr. Hall, Estill, Hardwick, Gable, Collingsworth and Nelson, Tulsa, 1978-84; sr. v.p. gen. counsel natural gas divsn. Arkla, Inc. (now CenterPoint Energy, Inc.), Shreveport, La., 1984—90; ptnr. co-head global oil and gas practice team Jones Day, Dallas, 1990—. Mem. ABA, Fed. Energy Bar Assn., Va. State Bar, Okla. Bar Assn., D.C. Bar Assn., Am. Gas Assn. (mem. legal sect.), Dallas Petroleum Club. Office: Jones Day 2727 N Harwood Dallas TX 75201-1515

KEITHLEY, ROGER LEE, judge; b. Macomb, Ill., July 19, 1946; s. Gilbert Lee and Mary Jane (Torrance) K.; m. Karen Sue Metzger, Apr. 1, 1973; children: Roger Livingston, Terrance Christopher, Kathryn Suzanne. BS, U. Ill., 1968; JD, Harvard U., 1973. Bar: Colo. 1973, U.S. Dist. Ct. Colo. 1973, U.S. Ct. Appeals (10th cir.) 1976. Law clk. to justice Colo. Supreme Ct., Denver, 1973—74; trial atty. SEC, Denver, 1974—76; assoc. Morrato, Gueck & Colantuno, Denver, 1976—80; ptnr. Krys, Boyle, Golz & Keithley, Denver, 1980—86, Law, Knous & Keithley, Denver, 1986—90, Law, Keithley & Tuttle, Denver, 1990—93; pvt. practice Roger L. Keithley, P.C., Denver, 1993—98; presiding disciplinary judge Colo. Supreme Ct., 1998—2003. Prof. physics U. Asmara, Eritrea, Ethiopia, 1969-70. With U.S. Army, 1968-70. Mem.: ABA, Am. Law Inst., Denver Bar Assn., Colo. Bar Assn. Home: 5239 E 17th Ave Denver CO 80220-1313 Personal E-mail: rlkeithley@aol.com.

KEITT, ANDREW WANNAMAKER, history professor; b. Boston, July 2, 1962; s. Alan Seaver and Ruth Morris Keitt; m. Aileen Elizabeth Guerrero, Nov. 16, 2001; 1 child, Kurtis Joens. BA cum laude, Duke U., 1985; MA, U. Calif., Berkeley, 1992, PhD, 1998. Assoc. prof. U. of Ala., Birmingham, Ala., 1999—. Office Phone: 205-934-7083.

KEIZS, MARCIA V., academic administrator; BA, U. Manitoba, Winnipeg, Can., 1967; MA, Columbia U., 1971, EdD, 1984. Prof. English Queensborough CC, CUNY, v.p., dean student svcs., 1988—94, acting vice chancellor student affairs; asst. dir. External Edn. Degree Prog. for Homebound Student; asst. dean External Affairs, Labor Rels., and Personnel LaGuardia CC, CUNY, 1984—88; acting pres. Borough of Manhattan CC, 1994—95, York Coll., CUNY, Queens, NY, 1996, pres., 2005—; v.p. academic affairs Bronx CC, 1997—2005. Founding editor New York Carib News. Chair bd. Morris Heights Health Ctr., Bronx. Mem.: Greenburgh Libr. Found. Office: CUNY 94-20 Guy R Brewer Blvd Jamaica NY 11451 Office Phone: 718-262-2000.

KEKER, JOHN WATKINS, lawyer; b. Winston Salem, N.C., Jan. 4, 1944; s. Samuel J. and Lucy Hearn (Spinks) K.; m. Christina Snowden Day, Sept. 11, 1965; children: Adam, Nathan. AB cum laude, Princeton U., 1965; LLB, Yale U., 1970. Bar: Calif. 1971, U.S. Dist. Ct. (so., no., ea., cen. dists.) Calif. 1971, U.S. Ct. Appeals (9th cir.) 1971, U.S. Supreme Ct. 1974. Law clk. to ret. chief justice Earl Warren U.S. Supreme Ct., Washington, 1970-71; staff atty. Nat. Res. Def. Coun., Washington, 1971, Office Fed. Pub. Defender, San Francisco, 1971-73; pvt. practice Keker & Van Nest and predecessor firms, San Francisco, 1973—. Assoc. counsel Iran/Contra Investigation, Washington, 1987—. Co-author: Effective Direct and Cross Examination, 1986; contbr. articles to profl. jours. Chmn. bd. Bay Area Water Quality Control, Oakland, Calif., 1980-82; v.p. San Francisco Fire Commn, 1988; pres. San Francisco Police Commn., 1990-91, 96-97. Served to 1st lt. USMC, 1965-67, Vietnam Named Best Lawyer in Bay Area, San Francisco Chronicle, 2003; named to Litig. Hall of Fame, Calif. State Bar, 2002; recipient Significant Contribution to Criminal Justice Award, Calif. Attys. for Criminal Justice, 1996. Fellow: Am. Bar Found., Am. Bd. Trial Advocates, Internat. Acad. Trial Lawyers, Am. Coll. Trial Lawyers. Office: Keker & Van Nest 710 Sansome St San Francisco CA 94111 Office Phone: 415-391-5400.

KEKES, JOHN, philosopher, educator; b. Budapest, Hungary, Nov. 22, 1936; came to U.S., 1965, naturalized, 1977; s. Eugene and Anna (Borsodi) K.; m. Jean Justilliano, May 20, 1968. BA, Queen's U., Kingston, Ont., Can., 1961, MA, 1962; PhD, Australian Nat. U., 1967. Instr. to assoc. prof. philosophy Calif. State U., Northridge, 1965-71; prof. U. Sask., Regina, Can., 1971-74, SUNY, Albany, 1974—, chmn. dept. philosophy, 1974-77, prof. philosophy and pub. policy, 1981—. Sr. rsch. fellow Ctr. for Philosophy of Sci., U. Pitts., 1984-85; vis. prof. U.S. Mil. Acad., West Point, N.Y., 1985-86, Nat. U. Singapore, 1989, Portuguese Cath. U., Lisbon, 2001. Author: A Justification of Rationality, 1976, The Nature of Philosophy, 1980, Dimensions of Ethical Thought, 1987, The Examined Life, 1988, Moral Tradition and Individuality, 1989, Facing Evil, 1990, The Morality of Pluralism, 1993, Moral Wisdom and Good Lives, 1995, Against Liberalism, 1997, A Case for Conservatism, 1998, Pluralism in Philosophy: Changing the Subject, 2000, The Art of Life, 2002, The Illusion of Egalitarianism, 2004, The Roots of Evil, 2005; gen. editor: Studies in Moral Philosophy, 1986—91; editor: Pub. Affairs Quar., 1999—2001. Recipient Comdrs. Pub. Svc. award U.S. Army, 1986; Rockefeller Found. humanities fellow, 1980-81, fellow Earhart Found., 1983, 88, 89, 98, 2002; resident scholar Rockefeller Found. Study Ctr., Bellagio, Italy, 1982, 89. Mem. Am. Philos. Assn., Royal Inst. Philosophy Home: 2041 Cook Rd Charlton NY 12019-2909

KELAHER, JAMES PEIRCE, lawyer; b. Orlando, Fla., Oct. 28, 1951; s. Philip James and Neva Cecelia (Peirce) K. BA, U. Fla., 1973; JD, Fla. State U., 1981. Bar: Fla. 1981, U.S. Dist. Ct. (mid. dist.) Fla. 1982, U.S. Ct. Appeals (11th cir.) 1983, U.S. Supreme Ct.; cert. civil trial law. Assoc. Law Office of Nolan Carter, P.A., Orlando, 1981-83, Law Office of James Kelaher, P.A., Orlando, 1983-87; ptnr. Kelaher & Wieland, P.A., Orlando, 1987—, Kelaher, Wieland and Hilado, P.A., Orlando, 1996-98, Kelaher Law Offices, P.A., Orlando, 1998—. Contbr. articles to profl. jours. Eagle benefactor Rep. Party. Mem. ABA, ATLA (sustaining), Orange County Bar Assn., Acad. Fla. Trial Lawyers (sec. 1994-95, treas. 1995-96, pres. 1997-98, bd. dirs. coll. diplomates, membership exec. com. bd. trustees Fla. lawyers action group), Ctrl. Fla. Trial Lawyers Assn. (pres. 1992-94). Roman Catholic. Avocations: tennis, golf, skiing, fishing. Office: Kelaher Law Offices 800 N Magnolia Ave Ste 1301 Orlando FL 32803-3255 E-mail: jim@kelaherlaw.com.

KELALIS, BARBARA ANNA LISA, interior designer; b. San Antonio, Mar. 12, 1940; d. William Lewis and Wilma Ann (McClish) Wilson; m. Daniel Steen Fletcher, June 12, 1965 (div. 1968); m. Panayotis Petros Kelalis, Apr. 8, 1970; 1 child, Steven Michael Fetcher. BA, UCLA, 1964; postgrad., Rochester Community Coll., 1972-74. Interior designer Hilton Hotels Office, Beverly Hills, 1975-78, Rochester-Tour-of-Homes, 1978-86; pres. Camelot Designs, Inc., 1986—. Pres. Cmty. Concerts, Rochester, 1972. Recipient Golden Poet awards, 1989, 90. Avocations: tennis, ballet, horseback riding, painting, writing short stories.

KELCH, ROBERT PAUL, former dean, pediatric endocrinologist; b. Detroit, Dec. 3, 1942; s. Paul and Iona Bertha (Schmitt) Kelch; m. Jeri Anne Parker, Aug. 17, 1963; children: Randall Paul, Julie Marie. PhB, Wayne State U., Detroit, 1964; MD, U. Mich., Ann Arbor, 1967. Intern then Wyeth pediatric residency fellow U. Mich. Med. Center, 1967—70, research fellow, 1969—70, mem. faculty, 1972—94, prof. pediatrics, 1977—94, acting chmn. dept., 1979—80, chmn. dept., 1981—94; physician-in-chief C.S. Mott Children's Hosp. U. Mich., 1983—94; chief clin. affairs U. Mich. Hosps., 1989—92; NIH trainee pediatric endocrinology U. Calif. Med. Center, San Francisco, 1970—72; prof. pediat., dean U. Iowa Coll. Medicine, Iowa City, 1994—2003, v.p. statewide health svcs., 2001—02; exec. v.p., med. affairs, prof. pediatrics U. Michigan, Ann Arbor, 2003—. Co-author: A Practical Approach to Pediatric Endocrinology, 1975; contbr. articles to med. jours. With USNR. Fellow: Am. Acad. Pediat.; mem.: Midwest Soc. Pediat. Rsch. (pres. 1983—84), Lawson Wilkins Pediat. Endocrine Soc., Ctrl. Soc. Clin. Rsch., Assn. Med. Sch. Pediat. Dept. Chmn. (pres. 1989), Am. Soc. Clin. Investigation, Am. Fedn. Clin. Rsch., Endocrine Soc., Am. Bd. Pediat. (sec.-treas. 1992, chmn. 1995), Soc. Pediat. Rsch. (pres. 1988), Inst. Medicine NAS. Methodist.

KELCHNER, THOMAS ALLEN, art educator; b. Williamsport, Pa., Apr. 20, 1961; s. Norman Edward Kelchner; m. Lisa Rose Baskin, May 11, 1985; 1 child, Emily Beatrice. BS in Art Edn., Kutztown U., 1983, MEd in Art Edn., 1989. Art educator Williamsport Area Sch. Dist., 1984—96, supr. K-12 art edn., 1996—. Pa. rep. J.F. Kennedy Ctr., Washington, 1995—; presenter workshops in field. Coord. Milken Festival Arts, Williamsport, 2004—05; regional dir. Crayola Dream-Maker. Named Milken Nat. Educator, Milken Family Found., 2001, Disting. Alumni, Kutztown U., 2002. Mem.: ASCD, Nat. Art Edn. Assn. (Pa. del. 2000—), Pa. Art Edn. Assn. (pres. 2002—04, Eduator of Yr. 2000). Lutheran. Avocations: photography, painting, reading, travel. Home: 504 Reynolds St Williamsport PA 17702 Office: Williamsport Area Sch Dist 201 W 3d St Williamsport PA 17701 Office Phone: 570-327-5500. E-mail: TKelchne@wasd.org.

KELEHER, DAVID, electronics executive; b. 1950; BA in econ., U. N.H.; MBA, Cornell U. CPA, N.H. Various sr. mgmt. positions in corp. fin. and ops. Digital Equipment Corp.; various exec. positions Raytheon Co., asst. corp. contr., group contr. comml. electronics div.; v.p., CFO Dynamics Rsch. Corp., Andover, Mass. Office: Dynamics Rsch Corp 60 Frontage Rd Andover MA 01810-5498

KELEHER, JAMES P., bishop; b. July 31, 1931; BA, St. Mary of the Lake Sem., Mundelein, Ill., 1954; DST, St. Mary of the Lake Sem., 1961, Licentiate in Sacred Theology, 1968; MA in Edn. administrn., Loyola U., Chgo., 1967; PhD, Gregorian U., Rome. Ordained priest Roman Cath. Ch., 1958. Rector Quigley Sem. South, Chgo., 1976—78; pres., rector St. Mary of the Lake Sem., Mundelein, Ill., 1978—84; bishop Belleville, Ill., 1984—93; archbishop Archdiocese of Kansas City, 1993—2005, archbishop emeritus, 2005—. Mem. Papal Visitation Com. for Sems.; chmn. bishop's com. on priestly formation; mem. com. migration; mem. com. econ. concerns of the Holy See Nat. Conf. Cath. Bishops. Mem.: Midwest Assn. Theol. Schs., Nat. Cath. Edn. Assn. (sem. dept.). Office: Archdiocese of Kansas City Chancery Office 12615 Parallel Kansas City KS 66109*

KELEHER, MICHAEL LAWRENCE, lawyer; b. Albuquerque, Sept. 21, 1934; s. William A. Keleher and Loretta Barrett; m. Margaret Anne Wills, June 10, 1961; children: Anne Barrett, Elizabeth Katherine, Margaret Mary, Mary Ann, Loretta Wills, Michael Wills. BA, U. N. Mex., 1956; MA, NYU, 1958; JD, U. Miss., 1962. Bar: N.Mex. 1962. Atty. Keleher & McLeod PA, Albuquerque, 1962—2001, of counsel, 2001—. Mem. N.Mex. Old Lincoln County Meml. Commn., 1969—76; chmn. N.Mex. Diamond Jubilee/U.S. constl. Bicentennial Commn., 1986—89; bd. dirs. Bernalillo County unit Am. Cancer Soc., 1966—74, pres., 1969—70; mem. Albuquerque Environ. Planning Commn., 1973—75, chair land controls bd., 1974—75; mem. Shared Vision, Inc., 1994—98; trustee U. Albuquerque, 1970—78, sec., 1974—78; chair N.Mex. State U. Rio Grande Hist. Collectors, 1978—79; chmn. Archdiocese Santa Fe Devel. Coun., 1990—93; trustee Archdiocese Santa Fe Cath. Found., 1991—2003; spiritial affiliate Equestrian Order of the Holy Sepulehre of Jerusalem, 1994—, Order of Friars Minor, 1996—; pres. Archdiocese Santa Fe Cath. Found., 1997—99, Guadalupe Inst.; bd. dirs. Robert O. Anderson Schs. Mgmt. Found., 1995—99. Lt. (j.g.) USNR, 1956—58. Mem.: ABA, N.Mex. Bar Assn., U. N.Mex. Alumni Lettermen's Assn., Phi Theta Phi, Sigma Chi. Democrat. Roman Catholic. Office: Keleher & McLeod PA 201 3rd St NW Albuquerque NM 87102-3370 Office Phone: 505-346-4646. Business E-Mail: mlk@keleher-law.com.

KELEMEN, ARPAD, computer scientist, information scientist; b. Szeged, Hungary, Mar. 31, 1972; s. Belane and Bela Kurilla (Stepfather); m. Yulan Liang, 1998; children: Adam, Erik. BS, U. Szeged, Hungary, 1993, MS, 1995; PhD, U. Memphis, 2002. Asst. prof. U. Miss., Oxford, 2002—03; rsch. asst. prof. U. Buffalo, 2003—; asst. prof. Niagara (N.Y.) U., 2003—. Author: (book) Studies in Fuzziness and Soft Computing, 2002, Recent Advances in Simulation, Computational Methods and Soft Computing, 2002. Mem.: Bolyai Janos Math. Soc., Am. Math. Soc., IEEE (reviewer and tech. com. mem. 2001—04), Phi Kappa Phi, Internat. Mensa, Upsilon Pi Epsilon. Achievements include research in Neural Networks for Microarrays; design of Conscious Software Agents. Office: Univ at Buffalo 249 Farber Hall 3435 Main St Buffalo NY 14214 Office Phone: 716-829-2715. Office Fax: 716-829-2200. E-mail: akelemen@buffalo.edu.

KELEMEN, CHARLES F., computer science educator; b. Mt. Vernon, N.Y., Jan. 7, 1943; s. Frank K. and Eleanor E. K.; m. Sylvia J. Brown, July 26, 1975; children— Rebecca, Colin, Elizabeth. BA, Valparaiso U., 1964; MA, Pa. State U., 1966, PhD, 1969. Asst. then assoc. prof. Ithaca Coll., N.Y., 1969-80; prof. LeMoyne Coll., Syracuse, N.Y., 1980-84, Swarthmore Coll., Pa., 1984—, chmn. divsn. natural scis. and engring. Pa., 2000—03, Edward Hicks Magill prof. math. and natural scis., 2002—. Cons. in field; chair computer sci. dept. Swarthmore Coll., 1984-99, 2001—; vis. assoc. prof. Cornell U., Ithaca, N.Y., 1978, summers 1979-81. Co-author: (with others) Fundamentals of Computing II Abstraction Data Structures, and Large Software Systems, 1995, Fundamentals of Computing II C++ Laboratory Manual, 1995. Grantee NSF, 1977-81 Mem. Assn. Computing Machinery, IEEE, Computer Soc., Math. Assn. Am. Office: Swarthmore Coll Dept Computer Sci Swarthmore PA 19081 Business E-Mail: ckeleme1@swarthmore.edu.

KELER, MARIANNE MARTHA, lawyer; b. Budapest, Hungary, Oct. 2, 1954; d. Tibor and Margaret (Feja) Keler; m. Michael Richmond Kershow, Aug. 21, 1981; children: Stefan, Madeleine. BS Sch. Fgn. Svc., Georgetown U., 1976, JD, 1980. Bar: DC 1980. Law clk. to assoc. judge Hon. Catherine B. Kelly US Ct. Appeals DC cir., Washington, 1980-81; staff atty. office of gen. counsel SEC, Washington, 1981-83, asst. to chmn. John Shad, 1983-84; sr. atty. SLM Corp. (formerly Student Loan Mktg. Assn.), Washington, 1985-86, asst. gen. counsel, 1986-88, sr. asst. gen. counsel, 1988-90, v.p., assoc. gen. counsel, 1990-97, sr. v.p., gen. counsel, 1997—2001, exec. v.p., gen. counsel, 2001—. Sec. bd. trustees Cmty. Found for the Nat. Capital Region. Recipient Alumni Award, Georgetown U. Law Ctr., 2004. Mem. ABA (corp. and securities div.), Am. Corp. Counsel Assn. Office: SLM Holding Corp 12061 Bluemont Way Reston VA 20190*

KELKAR, PRAMOD SHRINIWAS, allergist; s. Shriniwas Vishnu and Mandakini Kelkar; m. Monica Sowden, Mar. 29, 1974. MD, BJ Med., Pune, 1988. Physician Allergy & Asthma Care, PA, Maple Grove, Minn., 2004—. Mem.: AMA (Found. leadership award 2000). Office Phone: 763-420-1010.

KELL, LYLE NICHOLAS, retired minister, retired real estate broker; b. Sedro Woolley, Wash., May 8, 1924; s. Tate Maxville and Nancy Arzelia (Howard) Kell; m. Dorothy Jane Rasar; children: Nicholas Raymond, Brenda Jane. Student, U. Wash., Seattle U., 1960—62, Seattle Pacific Coll., 1960—62, Golden Gate Bapt. Theol. Sem., Federal Way, Wash., 60's—70's. Lic. ins. agt. Wash.; ordained minister Bapt. Ch., 1965; lic. real estate broker Wash. Log truck driver Lyman Timber Co., Sound View Pulp Co., Hamilton, Wash., 1947—51; switchman Gt. No. R.R., Seattle, 1953—59; broker, owner Spring Homes Realty/Kell Lynnwood Properties/Kell Realty Inc., Seattle/Lynnwood/Arlington, 1962—85; pastor Northgate Bapt. Ch., Seattle, 1965—72, First Bapt. Ch. of Martha Lake, Lynnwood, Wash., 1973—80. Author: Personal Biography of World War II, 1997. Mem. exec. bd., co-chmn. Snohomish County Vets. Assistance Fund Bd., Wash., 1995—; nat. chaplain WWII USN Armed Guard Hdqs., Rolesville, NC, 1995—; chaplain U.S. Senate, Washington, 1997; missionary to vets. Puget Sound Bapt. Assn. of Wash. State, 2002; chaplain Post 1561 VFW, Arlington, Wash., 1995. Served with USN, 1943—46. Decorated 5 Bronze Engagement Stars USN, 1 Small Silver Star, China Svc. medal with clasp, Russian medal, World War II Combat Ribbon U.S. Govt.; recipient 2 Spl. Recognition awards, Downtown Seattle Kiwanis Club, 1963. Mem.: VFW (nat. chaplain 1995—96), DAV, SAR. Baptist. Achievements include research in for new major anesthetic. Home: 2821 180th St NE Arlington WA 98223 E-mail: bkell@kell-co.com.

KELL, MICHAEL JON, physician, researcher; b. Dhahran, Saudi Arabia, Nov. 1, 1949; arrived in U.S., 1951; s. Edgar Michael Kell and Elvira Therea Hannevig; children: Alexander Niels, Andrew Halvdan. BSChemE, U. Calif., Santa Barbara, 1971; MSChemE, MIT, 1972; MD cum laude, Emory U., 1985, PhD with highest honors, 1985. Diplomate Am. Bd. Anti-Aging Medicine, Am. Acad. Pain Mgmt., Am. Bd. Clin. Chem., Am. Bd. Froensic Medicine, Am. Bd. Clin. Hypnosis. Rschr. Dow Chem., Wayland, Mass., 1973-74; program mgr. Cordis-Dow, Concord, Calif., 1976—79; med. dir. Michael Jon Kell, PhD & Assoc., P.C., Atlanta, 1987-2000; rsch. dir. Urine Drug Testing, Inc., Marco Island, 1997—; med. dir. Pvt. Clinic Labs., Inc., Atlanta, 1991—2000; editor, author Harrison Publs., Suwanee, Ga., 2000—. Exec. dir. Expert Witness & Cons. Group; radio host Mind Brain Body. Author: (book) My Boyhood, 1965, Journey to Planet Earth, 1967, Electrostatic Fields and Surface Potentials from Individual, 1985, The Song of Solomon: A 3000 Year Postcript, 1985, The Journey of Self, 1987, Determining Disability and Personal Injury Damage, 4th edit., 2000, Medical Practice for Trial Lawyers, 5th edit., 2001; author: (with others) Noise, Impedance and Single Channels, 1983, Charged Membrane Proteins, Vault of Adepti, 1995; contbr. articles to profl. jours. Fellow, NSF, 1982; scholar, European Molecular Biology, 1982; Merit scholar, Brown U., 1967, Pres. Undgrad. Rsch. grantee, U. Calif., 1971, Grass Found. fellow, Marine Biol. Lab., 1982. Fellow: Am. Chem. Soc., Am. Soc. Clinic Hypnosis (approved cons.), Nat. Acad. Clin. Biochemistry, Am. Bd. Forensic Medicine, Am. Bd. Forensic Examiners, Am. Acad. Pain Mgmt. Achievements include invention of; patents for biotechnology; full foreign fillings. Avocations: writing, lecturing, meditating, philosophy, mathematics. Office: The Labyrinth Inst 4715 Atlanta Rd Smyrna GA 30080 Office Phone: 404-362-5621. Business E-Mail: mjkell@alum.mit.edu.

KELLAM, CARAMINE, volunteer; b. Painter, Va., Jan. 23, 1941; d. Emerson Polk and Amine (Cosby) Kellam; m. Isaac Somers White, Nov. 25, 1961 (div. 1975); children: Kellam White Griffin, Caramine White, Somers Farkas White; m. Harry Sherman Holcomb, III, May 12, 1979 (div. Mar. 2001). AA, St. Mary's Coll., Raleigh, 1960; cert., Richmond Bus. Coll., Va., 1961. Bd. dirs. Kellam Energy, Inc. Contbr. articles to profl. jours. Trustee Northampton-Accomack Meml. Hosp., Nassawadox, Va., 1986—98, v.p. aux., 1986—88, pres., 1988—90, sec. bd. trustees, 1989—91, vice chmn., 1991—94, chair, 1994—96; bd. dirs. Eastern Shore CC Found., 1998—, v.p. bd. dirs., 2001—03, pres., 2003—04; sec. E. Pol. Kellam Found., 1991—; mem. session Belle Haven Presbyn. Ch., 1999—2002; bd. dirs. Ea. Shore Hist. Soc., Onancock, Va., 1987—92, Shore Life Svcs., 1998—, pres., 2004—; bd. dirs. Med. Soc. Va. Alliance, Richmond, Va., 1984—94, v.p., 1989—91, pres., 1992—93; trustee Shore Meml., 2003—, sec., 2004—. Mem.: DAR (regent 2004—), Med. Soc. Va. Trust, AMA Alliance Bd. (mem. ERF com. 1994, AMA-ERF com. chmn. 1994—95, field dir. 1995—98, bylaws chmn. 1999—2000), Garden Club Eastern Shore (pres. 1973—75, Garden Week chmn. 2001—02). Avocations: travel, reading, flower arranging. Home: PO Box 38 Franktown VA 23354-0038

KELLAR, CHARLOTTE AVRUTIS, writer; b. N.Y.C., Nov. 15; d. Aaron and Fannie (Kantor) Avrutis; m. Harold Kellar, Feb. 14, 1947 (dec. Mar. 1980); 1 child, Jeffrey Hamilton. BA, NYU, 1951; student, Harrison Lewis Dramatic Sch. Editor Futurific Mag.; contbr. stories and articles to jours. and newspapers; appeared in films and music videos. Recipient 3d Prize Fiction Contest, West Side Spirit, 1988, First Prize Essay Contest, 1989, 4th Prize, W.O.R. Radio, 1988, 2d pl. award N.Y. Daily News, 1989, 3d prize Woman's Day, 1984. Mem. Pen and Brush Club (3d prize poetry 1982, 2d prize fiction 1985, 87, 1st prize poetry 1984, 4th prize prose 1989), West Side Arts Coalition (grantee 1987), Screen Actors Guild. Avocations: theater, music. Home: 645 W End Ave New York NY 10025-7322

KELLEHER, HERBERT DAVID, air transportation executive, lawyer; b. Camden, N.J., Mar. 12, 1931; s. Harry and Ruth (Moore) K.; m. Joan Negley, Sept. 9, 1955; children: Julie, Michael, Ruth, David. BA cum laude, Wesleyan U., 1953; LLB cum laude, NYU, 1956. Bar: N.J. 1957, Tex. 1962. Clk. N.J. Supreme Ct., 1956-59; assoc. Lum, Biunno & Tompkins, Newark, 1959—61; ptnr. Mathews, Nowlin, Macfarlane & Barrett, San Antonio, 1961—69; sr. ptnr. Oppenheimer, Rosenberg, Kelleher & Wheatley, Inc., San Antonio, 1969—81; founder, gen. counsel, dir. Southwest Airlines Co., Dallas, 1967—81, pres., CEO, bd. dir., 1981—2001, exec. chmn., bd. dir., 2001—. Home: 144 Thelma Dr San Antonio TX 78212-2516 Office: SW Airlines Co PO Box 36611 Dallas TX 75235-1611 Office Phone: 214-792-4110. E-mail: vickie.shuler@wnco.com.

KELLEHER, KATHLEEN, financial services retirement income marketing specialist; b. Suffern, NY, May 3, 1951; d. John James and Carol (Re) K. BA, Fairleigh Dickinson U., 1973. CLU, chartered fin. cons., mut. fund counselor, advisor sr. living, advisor for sr. living. Ins. sales adminstr. Blyth Eastman Dillon & Co., 1977-79; product mktg. assoc. Dean Witter Reynolds, N.Y.C., 1980-82; mgr. product mktg. annuities and ins. dept. Kidder, Peabody & Co., 1982-85; v.p. nat. sales mgr. ins. Paine Webber, 1985-88; v.p., dir. mktg. and sales support Landmark Fin. Corp., Oklahoma City, 1988-91; cons. fin. svcs., 1991—; dir. Mktg. Svcs. Protective Life investment product divsn., Cin., 1993-94, mktg. cons. fin. svcs., 1995—; dir. mktg. Prudential Annuity Svcs.; v.p. mut. funds and annuity tng. Prudential Investments, 1996, v.p. edn. strategy and integration, 2000; 1st v.p., dir. ins. mktg. UBS Fin Svcs. Inc., Weehawken, NJ, 2002—. Mem.: Soc. Fin. Svc. Profls. Republican. Office: 1200 Harbor Blvd Weehawken NJ 07086-6761

KELLEHER, ROBERT JOSEPH, judge; b. N.Y.C., Mar. 5, 1913; s. Frank and Mary (Donovan) K.; m. Gracyn W. Wheeler, Aug. 14, 1940; children: R. Jeffrey, Karen Kathleen Kelleher King. AB, Williams Coll., 1935; LL.B., Harvard U., 1938. Bar: N.Y. 1939, Calif. 1942, U.S. Supreme Ct 1954. Atty. War Dept., 1941-42; asst. U.S. atty. So. Dist. Calif., 1948-50; pvt. practice Beverly Hills, 1951-71; U.S. dist. judge, 1971-83; sr. judge U.S. Dist. Ct. 9th Cir., 1983—. Mem. So. Calif. Com. Olympic Games, 1964; capt. U.S. Davis Cup Team, 1962-63; treas. Youth Tennis Found. So. Calif., 1961-64. Served to lt. USNR, 1942-45. Recipient Bicentennial Medal award Williams Coll., 2001; enshrined in Internat. Tennis Hall of Fame, 2000. Mem. So. Calif. Tennis Assn. (v.p. 1958-64, pres. 1983-85), U.S. Lawn Tennis Assn. (pres. 1967-68), Internat. Lawn Tennis Club U.S.A., Gt. Britain, France, Can., Mex., Australia, India, Israel, Japan, All Eng. Lawn Tennis and Croquet (Wimbledon), Harvard Club (N.Y./So. Calif.), Williams Club (N.Y.), L.A. Country Club, Delta Kappa Epsilon. Office: US Dist Ct 255 E Temple St Ste 1434 Los Angeles CA 90012-3334

KELLEHER, TIMOTHY JOHN, retired publishing company executive; b. Massillon, Ohio, Jan. 4, 1940; s. John Joseph and Catherine Isabelle (Quinlan) K.; m. Mary Gray Thornton, Aug. 27, 1966; children— Catherine, Joseph, Sarah BS in Polit. Sci., Xavier U., Cin., 1962; postgrad., Xavier U., 1965, Morehead State U., Ky., 1975-76. Mgr. labor rels. GM, Norwood, Ohio, 1964-73; pers. mgr. Rockwell Internat., Winchester, Ky., 1973-77, dir. labor rels. Troy, Mich., 1977-82; v.p. human resources Detroit Free Press, 1982-89; sr. v.p. labor rels. Detroit Newspaper Agy., 1989—2004; ret. Dir. Detroit Macomb Hosp. Corp. Bd. dirs. Greater Detroit Alliance of Bus., annually 1983-89, Winchester/Clark Hist. Soc., Ky., 1975, pres., 1976-77; bd. dirs. New Detroit Inc., annually 1983-89. Served to sgt. U.S. Army, 1962-64 Mem. Coop. Edn. Assn. Ky. (bd. dirs. 1975-77, Employer of Yr. award 1976), Indsl. Rels. Rsch. Assn., Xavier U. Alumni Assn. (pres. Detroit chpt. 1991-93), Forest Lake Country Club (bd. dirs. 1991-94, 2000-02, pres. 2002). Republican. Roman Catholic. Avocations: golf, fishing. E-mail: TKelleher@cinci.rr.com.

KELLER, AIMEE LYNNE, lawyer; b. Wilmington, Del., Feb. 13, 1966; d. William E. Keller and Martine Davis. BS, Cornell U., 1988, JD, 1993. Bar: Ohio 1993. Assoc. Wagner & Bloch, Cin., 1994—2003, Taft, Stettinius and Hollister LLP, Cin., 1999—2004, ptnr., 2004—. Office: Taft Stettinius Hollister LLP Ste 1800 425 Walnut St Cincinnati OH 45202-3957 E-mail: kellera@taftlaw.com.

KELLER, ARMOR, artist, arts advocate; b. Montgomery, Ala., June 16, 1937; d. Alton Mason and Margaret Elizabeth (Bell) ARmor; m. Ronald Thomas Keller, Nov. 28, 1958; 1 child, Kimberlin Marie. Student, Huntingdon Coll., 1955-56, U. Guam, 1972-74; BA, U. Ala., 1982. Planning bd. Nat. Book Makers Conf., Tuscaloosa, Ala., 1995; panelist grant rev. Ala. State Coun. on Arts, Montgomery, 1995-96, 98; judge HS art exhibn. 6th Congl. Dist. Arts Caucus, Birmingham, 1995-96; cons. Birmingham Mus. Art, 1996. Shows include Meridian (Miss.) Mus. Art, 1986, Vanderbilt U., Nashville, 1987, Birmingham Mus. Art, 1989, Birmingham So. Coll., 1990, Kennedy-Douglas Ctr. for the Arts, Florence, Ala., 1992, Wiregrass Mus. Art, Dothan, Ala., 1993, Ctr. Cultural Arts, Gadsden, Ala., 1994, Kentuck Mus., Northport, Ala., 1994, Ch. of the Nativity, Huntsville, Ala., 1996, Huntsville Mus. Art, 1999, Heritage Hall Mus., Talladega, Ala., 2000, Masur Mus. Art, Monroe, La., 2001, Mercedes-Benz Internat., Mus. and Visitor Ctr., Tuscaloosa, Ala., 2003; spl. commns. for Ala. Symphony Orch. and Children's Aid Soc.; featured in Wild Wheels, 1992-93, Smithsonian, Japan Esquire, Spiegel; illustrator: Haiku: The Travelers of Eternity, 2001. Artist del. Sister City Commn., Japan, 1994; mem. Sister City Japan Com., Birmingham, 2002—; bd. dirs. Birmingham Sister City Commn., 2003—; project dir. Sister City Friendship, 2005. Fellow Escape to Create Seaside (Fla.) Inst., 1993, 94. Mem. Nat. League Am. Pen Women, Watercolor Soc. Ala. (pres. 1988-89), Birmingham Art Assn. (pres. 1982-83), Montgomery Art Guild (pres. 1976-78), Space One Eleven (pres. 1991-93), Bluff Park Art Assn. (project dir. 1997), Japan Am. Soc. Ala. (bd. dirs. 2002—). Avocations: tai chi, ikebana, travel, music. Home: 204 Vestavia Cir Birmingham AL 35216-1328

KELLER, BILL, editor; m. Ann Cooper (div.); 1 adopted child, Tom; m. Emma Gilbey, Apr. 10, 1999; children: Molly, Alice. BA, Pomona Coll., 1970. Reporter The Portland Oregonian, 1970—79, The Congressional Quarterly Weekly Report, 1980—82, Dallas Times Herald, 1982—84; corr. NY Times, Washington, 1984—86, Moscow, 1986—91, bur. chief, 1989—91, Johannesburg, 1992—95, fgn. editor NYC, 1995—97, mng. editor, 1997—2001, exec. editor, 2003—; op-ed columnist & sr. writer NY Times Mag., NYC, 2001—03. Mem. bd. trustees Pomona Coll. Recipient Pulitzer Prize in Journalism for Internat. Reporting, 1989. Office: NY Times 229 W 43rd St New York NY 10036-3959*

KELLER, BRUCE P., lawyer; b. Nov. 28, 1954; BS, Cornell U., 1976; JD, Boston U., 1979. Bar: NY 1980, NJ 1981, Mass. 1981. Assoc. Debevoise & Plimpton LLP, NYC, 1982—88, ptnr., 1988—, head Intellectual Property Litig. practice. Mem.: ABA, Internat. Trademark Assn. Office: Debevoise & Plimpton LLP 919 Third Ave New York NY 10022 Office Phone: 212-909-6118. Office Fax: 212-909-6836. E-mail: bpkeller@debevoise.com.

KELLER, DENNIS JAMES, management educator; b. July 6, 1941; s. Ralph and Dorothy (Barckman) K.; m. Constance Bassett Templeton, May 28, 1966; children: Jeffrey Breckenridge, David McDaniel, John Templeton. AB, Princeton U., 1963; MBA, U. Chgo., 1968. Account exec. Motorola Comm., Chgo., 1964-67; v.p. fin. Bell & Howell Comm., Waltham, Mass., 1968-70; v.p. mktg. Bell & Howell Schs., Chgo., 1970-73; pres. Keller Grad. Sch. Mgmt., Chgo., 1973-81, chmn., CEO, 1981—87. Chmn. bd., CEO DeVry Inc., 1987-2004, chmn. bd. 2004-; cons., evaluator North Central Assn., Chgo., 1979-84; bd. dir., Nicor Inc., 1994-. Trustee Glenwood (Ill.) Sch. for Boys, 1980-2002, Chgo. Zool. Soc., Brookfield, Ill., 1979-, Princeton (N.J.) U., 1994-98, 2000-, Lake Forest Acad.-Ferry Hall, Ill., 1980-87, George M. Pullman Found., Chgo., 1987-2002; bd. trustees U. Chgo., 1998-; bd. dirs. Great Books Found., Chgo., 1986-98; chmn. U. Chgo. Grad. Sch. Bus. Coun., 1994-2002, Princeton U. Sch. Engring. and Applied Scis. Leadership Coun., 1992-; commr. North Cen. Assn.-Commn. on Instns. of Higher Edn., 1985-88. Nat. Merit scholar, 1959-63; U. Chgo. Grad. Sch. Bus. fellow, 1967-68. Mem. Hinsdale Golf Club, Econ. Club, Comml. Club Chgo., Chgo. Club, Nantucket Golf Club, Sankaty Head Golf Club. Republican. Mem. United Ch. of Christ. Office: DeVry Inc 1 Tower Ln Ste 2350 Oakbrook Terrace IL 60181

KELLER, DOROTHY BOSCH, fine arts educator; b. Bristol, Conn., Dec. 30, 1940; d. Joseph John and Catherine Dorothy (Roskosky) Bosch; m. Deane Galloway Keller, July 5, 1969. BS cum laude, U. Hartford, (Conn.), 1962; MEd, U. Hartford, Bloomfield, Conn., 1963; MA in Religious Studies, St. Joseph Coll., West Hartford, Conn., 1985, degree, 1997. Asst. to curator Wallace Nutting Collection Am. Furniture Wadsworth Atheneum, Hartford, 1961, rsch. asst., 1962-69, researcher, catalogue asst., 1965, dir. edn., 1963-64; researcher, catalogue asst. G.M.V. Smith Art Mus., Springfield, Mass., 1960-63; grad. asst. U. Hartford Sch. Edn., 1962-63; instr. fine arts St. Joseph Coll., West Hartford, Conn., 1967-72, asst. prof., 1972-85, assoc. prof., 1986-91, prof., chairperson dept. fine arts and performing arts, 1991—. Rsch. asst. Wadsworth Atheneum, summers, 1965-67, lectr. history of art, 1963-68; juror painting, sculpture, graphic arts Promenade Gallery, Bushnell Meml., 1989, New Brit. Mus. Am. Art, 1982, Guilford (Conn.) Handicrafts Ctr., 1990; mem. edn. com. Lyman Allyn Art Mus., New London, Conn., 1991, Mark Twain Meml., 1987-90; elector Wadsworth Atheneum, 1984—. Author: (audio tape) Credence Cassettes, 1991; one-woman show at The Cragin Meml. Libr., Colchester, Conn., 1989; exhibited in group shows at Edward Hopper House Arts Found., Nyack, N.Y., 1983-91, Essex (Conn.) Art Assn., 1982-91, West Beth Gallery, N.Y.C., 1988, New Brit. Mus. Am. Art, 1982-87, Chinese Liberation Coalition and China Info. Ctr., Hartford, 1989, Lyme Acad. Fine Arts, 1991, 92, Art Students League, N.Y.C., N.Y.; contbr. articles to profl. jours. Mem. Inland, Wetlands, Conservation Commn., Town of Marlborough, 1980-87, Bi-Centennial Commn., 1976, Old Town Hall Study Com; bd. dirs. Hartford Preservation Alliance, 2004-. Recipient Teaching Excellence and Campus Leadership award Sears-Roebuk Found., 1990, Lewis Lecture award in sci. and humanities, 1993, Disting. Alumni award St. Joseph Coll., 1999; travel grantee St. Joseph Coll., West Hartford, 1988-93, Artist Invitational Slater Memorial Mus., Norwich, Conn, 2004. Mem. Internat. Thomas Merton Soc., Coll. Art Sch., Essex Art Assn., Antiquarian and Landmarks Soc., Wethersfield Hist. Soc., Conn. Hist. Soc., Old Lyme Hist. Soc., Florence Griswold Soc., Bibl. Archaeol. Assn. Internat., Conn. Archaeol. Soc., Albert Morgan Archaeol. Soc., Archaeol. Inst. Am., Internat. Ctr. Medieval Art, Nat. Trust for Hist. Preservation, The Hagiography Soc. Democrat. Roman Catholic. Avocations: archaeology, painting, reading. Home: 211 West Rd Marlborough CT 06447-1033 Office: Saint Joseph Coll 1678 Asylum Ave West Hartford CT 06117-2764 Office Phone: 860-231-5236. Business E-Mail: dkeller@sjc.edu.

KELLER, EDWARD LOWELL, electrical engineer, educator; b. Rapid City, S.D., Mar. 6, 1939; s. Earl Lowell and E. Blanche (Oldfield) K.; m. Carole Lynne Craig, Sept. 1, 1963; children: Edward Lowell, Craig, Morgan. BS, U.S. Naval Acad., 1961; PhD, Johns Hopkins U., 1971. Mem. faculty U. Calif., Berkeley, 1971—, assoc. prof. elec. engring., 1977-79, prof., 1979-94, prof. emeritus, 1994—; assoc. dir. Smith Kettlewell Eye Rsch. Inst., San Francisco, 1998—; chmn. bioengring. program U. Calif., Berkeley and San Francisco, 1989, chmn. engring. sci. program Coll. of Engring. U. C., Berkeley, 1991-94. Contbr. articles to sci. jours. Served with USN, 1961-65. Sr. Von Humboldt fellow, 1977-78 Fellow IEEE; mem. AAAS, Assn. for Rsch. in Vision and Ophthalmology, Soc. for Neurosci., Internat. Neural Network Soc. Achievements include rsch. on oculomotor system and math. modelling of nervous system. Office: Smith-Kettlewell Eye Rsch Inst 2318 Fillmore St San Francisco CA 94115-1813 E-mail: elk@ski.org.

KELLER, ELIOT AARON, broadcast executive; b. Davenport, Iowa, June 11, 1947; s. Norman Edward and Millie (Morris) Keller; m. Sandra Kay McGrew, July 3, 1970; 1 child, Nicole. BA, U. Iowa, 1970; MS, San Diego State U., 1976. Corr. Sta. WHO-AM-FM-TV, Des Moines, 1969-70; newsman Sta. WSUI-AM, Iowa City, 1968-70; newsman, corr. Sta. WHBF-AM-FM-TV, Rock Island, Ill., 1969; newsman Sta. WOC-AM-FM-TV, Davenport, 1970; freelance newsman and photographer Iowa City, 1969-77; pres., dir., treas. KZIA, Inc. (formerly KRNA, Inc. and Communicators, Inc.), Cedar Rapids, Iowa, 1971—; gen. mgr. Sta. KRNA FM, Iowa City, 1974-98, Sta. KQCR FM, Cedar Rapids, 1994-95, Sta. KXMX FM, Cedar Rapids, 1995-98, Sta. KZIA-FM, Cedar Rapids, 1998—. Adj. instr. dept. comm. studies U. Iowa, Iowa City, 1983, Iowa City, 84, mem. prof. adv. bd. Sch. Journalism and Mass Comm., 2002—; mem. adv. bd. dept. comm. arts Wartburg Coll., Waverly, Iowa, 2001—; treas. KZIA, Inc., 2003—. Named Broadcaster of Yr., Iowa Broadcasters Assn., 2001; named to Hall of Fame, Advt. Fedn. Cedar Rapids, Iowa, 2004. Mem.: Iowa City Area C. of C., Iowa Assn. R.R. Passengers (chmn. transition subcom. 2000—05, vice chmn. 2004—05, chmn. 2005—, legis. coun., chmn. excursion 1988—), R.R. Passenger Car Alliance, Mid-Continent Rlwy. Hist. Soc. (bd. dirs. 2000—03). Jewish. Home: 1244 Devon Dr NE Iowa City IA 52240-9628 Office: Sta KZIA FM 1110 26th Ave SW Cedar Rapids IA 52404-3430 Office Phone: 319-363-2061. Business E-Mail: eliot@kzia.com. *The chance only comes once.*

KELLER, EVELYN FOX, history professor, philosophy of science professor; b. N.Y.C., Mar. 20, 1936; divorced; children: Jeffrey, Sarah. BA, Brandeis U., 1957; MA, Radcliffe Coll., 1959; PhD, Harvard U., 1963; hon. doctorate, Mt. Holyoke Coll., 1991, U. Amsterdam, 1993; D of Humane Sci. (hon.), Simmons Coll., 1995; LHD (hon.), Rensselaer Polytech. Inst., 1995; D of Tech. (hon.), Tech. U. of Lulea, Sweden, 1996; LHD, New Sch. U., 2000, Alleghany Coll., 2000, Wesleyan U., 2001. Prof. math. and humanities Northeastern U., Boston, 1982-88; prof. U. Calif., Berkeley, 1988-92; prof. history and philosophy of sci. MIT, 1992—. Vis. fellow MIT Program in Sci., Tech. and Soc., 1979-80, vis. scholar, 1980-84, vis. prof., 1985-86; vis. prof. math. and humanities Northeastern U., 1981-82; Kregerb Wolf Disting. vis. prof. Northwestern U., 1985; sr. fellow Soc. for the Humanities, Cornell U., 1987; mem. Inst. for Advanced Study, Princeton, 1987-88; co-chair U. Calif. Systemwide Coun. on Women's Studies. Editor: A Feeling for the Organism: The Life and Work of Barbara McClintock, 1982, 2d edit., 1993, Reflections on Gender and Science, 1985, 10th edit., 1995, Refiguring Life: Metaphors of Twentieth Century Biology, 1995, Secrets of Life, Secrets of Death, 1992, The Century of the Gene, 2000, Making Sense of Life: Explaining Development with Medals, Metaphors and Machines, 2002; co-editor Body/Politics: Women and the Discourses of Science, 1990, Conflicts in Feminism, 1990,

Keywords in Evolutionary Discourse, 1992, Feminism and Science, 1996; Am. editor Fundamenta Scientiae, Internat. Jour. for Critical Analysis of Sci. and the Responsibility of Scientists; editl. bd. Women's Review of Books, Hypatia, Biology and Philosophy, Literature and Sci. Series, Jour. of the History of Biology; contbr. articles to profl. jours. Numerous grants and fellowships. Mem. History of Sci. Soc. Office: MIT E51-171 77 Mass Ave Cambridge MA 02139-4307 E-mail: efkeller@MIT.edu.

KELLER, FRANCES RICHARDSON, history educator; b. Lowville, N.Y., Aug. 14, 1914; d. Stephen Brown and Sarah Eliza (Bell) Richardson; m. Chauncey A.R. Keller, June 20, 1936 (div. 1964); children: Reynolds, Stephen, Julia, William; m. William P. Rhetta, May 10, 1969. BA, Sarah Lawrence Coll.; MA, U. Toledo; PhD, U. Chgo., 1973. Lectr., U. Ind.-Gary, 1966-67, U. Ill.-Chgo., 1967-68, Chgo. City Coll., 1968-70, Centre Inter. Universitaire, Paris, 1970-71, U. Calif.-Berkeley Extension, 1972-74, San Jose (Calif.) State U., 1974-78; adj. prof. history San Francisco State U., 1978—; panelist, reader NEH, 1978, 79, 81. Author: An American Crusade: The Life of Charles Waddell Chesnutt, 1978; editor, contbr.: Women in Western Tradition; translator, editor, author interpretive essay in Slavery and the French Revolutionists (Anna Julia Cooper), 1988. Mem. Nat. Women's Studies Assn. (chair publicity and pub. relations, founding conv. 1976, ofcl. historian 1978), Western Assn. Women Historians (program chair 1979, pres. 1981-83), Am. Hist. Assn. (nominating com. 1983—), Orgn. Am. Historians, Women in Hist. Profession (pres. coordinating com. 1985-88), Western Soc. French History. Office: San Francisco State U Dept History 1900 Holloway San Francisco CA 94132

KELLER, GEORGE CHARLES, higher education consultant, writer; b. NJ, Mar. 14, 1928; s. Charles and Elizabeth K.; m. Gail Faithfull, 1960 (div. 1973); children: Bayard, Elizabeth; m. Jane Eblen, 1975. AB, Columbia U., 1951, MPhil, 1954. Acad. dir. Gt. Books Found., Chgo., 1954-56; instr. polit. sci. Columbia U., NYC, 1957-59, asst. dean, 1959-61, editor, 1962-70; asst. to chancellor SUNY, Albany, 1970-78; asst. to pres. U. Md., College Park, 1979-82; sr. v.p. Barton-Gillett Co., Balt., 1983-88; sr. fellow Grad. Sch. Edn. U. Pa., Phila., 1988-94. Author: Academic Strategy, 1983; co-author: Post-Land Grant University, 1981, The Best of Planning, 1997, Transforming a College, 2004; editor: Planning for Higher Education, 1990-97; contbr. numerous articles, revs. to ednl. publs. With USN, 1946-48. Recipient Sibley award, Coun. for Advancement and Support of Edn., 1963, 64, 65, U.S. Steel Found. award, 1965; named Best U.S. Edn. Writer, Atlantic mag., 1968; James Fisher award CASE, 2003. Mem. Assn. Study Higher Edn., Soc. Coll. and Univ. Planning (Founders award 1988). Office: 4900 Wetheredsville Rd Baltimore MD 21207-6625 Office Phone: 410-448-5930.

KELLER, GLEN ELVEN, JR., lawyer; b. Longmont, Colo., Dec. 21, 1938; s. Glenn Elven and Elsie Mildred (Hogsett) K.; m. Elizabeth Ann Kauffman, Aug. 14, 1960; children: Patricia Carol, Michael Ashby. BS in Bus., U. Colo., 1960; JD, U. Denver, 1964. Bar: Colo. 1964, U.S. Dist. Ct. Colo. 1964, U.S. Ct. Appeals (10th cir.) 1982. Assoc. Phelps, Hall & Keller and predecessor, Denver, 1964-67, ptnr., 1967-73; asst. atty. gen. State of Colo., Denver, 1973-74; judge U.S. Bankruptcy Ct., Dist. Colo., 1974-82; ptnr. Davis, Graham & Stubbs LLP, Denver, 1982—2004, sr. counsel, 2004—. Lectr. law U. Denver, 1977-87; adj. prof., 1987-98, Frank E. Rickston Jr. adj. prof. law, 1998-2003; ct. adminstrn. com. Jud. Conf. US; fin. com. sch. constrn. Colo. Lawyers' Com., 1997-2000, exec. com., 1999-2000, chmn. task force on sch. discipline, 1999-2000; bd. dirs. Western Stock Show Assoc.; adj. instr. law U. Colo., 2003. Mem. Colo. Bd. Health, 1968-74, pres., 1970-74; pres., dir. The Westernaires, Golden, Colo., Jefferson County R-1 Sch. Bd., 1984-89; dir. Jefferson County Sch. Fin. Corp., 1992—. Named Colo. Horse Person of Yr., Colo. Horse Coun., 1999, Best Lawyers in Am., 1995-. Fellow Am. Coll. Bankruptcy; mem ABA, Colo. Bar Assn., Denver Bar Assn., Nat. Conf. Bankruptcy Judges, Law Club. Republican. Office: Davis Graham & Stubbs LLP 1550 17th St Ste 500 Denver CO 80202-1202 Office Phone: 303-985-2537.

KELLER, HERBERT BISHOP, mathematics professor; b. Paterson, N.J., June 19, 1925; BEE, Ga. Inst. Tech., 1945; MA, NYU, 1948, PhD in Math., 1954. Instr. physics & math. Ga. Inst. Tech., 1946-47; rsch. scientist divsn. electromagnetic rsch. Inst. Math Sci., NYU, 1948-53; head dept. math. Sarah Lawrence Coll., 1951-53; lectr. math. Washington Sq. Coll., 1957-59; assoc. prof. NYU, 1959-61; prof. applied math. Courant Inst., 1961-67; assoc. dir. AEC Computer & Appl. Math. Ctr., 1964-67; prof. applied math. Calif. Inst. Tech., 1967—2000, prof. emeritus, 2000—; rsch. scientist U. Calif., San Diego, 2000—. Vis. prof. Calif. Inst. Tech., 1965-66; mem. math. divsn. Nat. Rsch. Coun., 1969-72; mem. coun. Conf. Bd. Math. Sci., 1971-73; dist. vis. fellow Christ's Coll., Cambridge, 1993-94; cons. various industry & govt. concerns. Assoc. editor: (jour.) Jour. Appl. Math., Soc. Indsl. & Appl. Math., 1961-66, Jour. Computer & Systems Science, 1971-74; Japan Jour. Appl. Math., 1984—, Monogr. Ser. Assn. Computing Machinery, 1963-65, Jour. Numerical Analysis, 1964-71, Jour. Numerical Math., 1981—; ed. bd. ActaNumerica, 1992-. Recipient, Theodore von Kármán Prize, Soc. of Industrial and Applied Mathematics, 1994; Guggenheim fellow, 1979-80. Fellow AAAS; mem. Am. Math. Soc., Math. Assn. Am., Soc. Indsl. & Applied Math. (pres. 1975-76), Assn. Computing Machinery. Office: Calif Inst Tech Dept Applied Math 1201 E California Blvd Pasadena CA 91125-0001 Office Phone: 626-395-4557. Business E-Mail: hbk@caltech.edu.

KELLER, JACK, agricultural engineering educator, consultant; b. Roanoke, Va., Jan. 5, 1928; s. Eugene and Clara (Lauber) Keller; m. Sara Altick, June 4, 1954; children: Andrew A., Jeffery S., Judith. BSCE, U. Colo., 1953; MS in Irrigation Engring., Colo. State U., 1955; PhD in Agrl. Engring., Utah State U., 1967. Registered profl. engr., Utah, Calif. Work unit engr. USDA Soil Conservation Svc., Victor, Colo., 1953; sales engr. So. Irrigation Co., Memphis, 1955-56; chief irrigation engr. W.R. Ames Co., San Jose, Calif., 1956-60; prof. Utah State U., Logan, 1960-88, dept. chmn., 1979-85, project mgr., 1978-88; pres., founder Keller-Bliesner Engring. Co., Logan, 1962—, CEO, 1989—. Co-dir. U.S. AID Water Mgmt. Synthesis Project, Logan, 1978—88, team leader tech. assistance teams, worldwide, 1980—98; chmn. Conservation Verification Cons. IID/MWD Conservation Agreement, Imperial, Calif., 1992—; sr. policy advisor to Egyptian Ministry Pub. Works and Water Resources U.S. AID WRSR Activity, 1995—98; sr. rsch. assoc. Internat. Water Mgmt. Inst., 1995—2000; sr. adv. agrl. water use efficiency program CALFED, 1999—; sr. irrigation policy advisor, bd. dirs. Internat. Devel. Enterprises, 2000—; team leader Project Advisor Cons. Navajo Indian Irrigation Project, 2001—; mem. bd. execs. sci. bd. and ind. sci. bd. Calif. Bay-Delta Authority, 2003—. Co-author: Trickle Irrigation Design, 1974, Sprinkle and Trickle Irrigation, 1990; contbr. NRC com. Soil and Water Rsch. Priorities for Devel. Countries, Washington, 1988; chmn. Red River Chloride Control Panel, Tulsa, 1988. With USN, 1945—47, PTO, sgt. USAF, 1951—53. Named Engr. of Yr., Utah Joint Engring. Coun., 1988. Fellow: ASCE, Am. Soc. Agrl. Engrs. (award for advancement of surface irrigation 2002); mem.: NAE, The Irrigation Assn. (Man of Yr. 1972), Internat. Commn. Irrigation and Drainage. Mem. Bahai Ch. Achievements include patents in field. Avocation: Avocations: bicycling, hiking, gardening, fishing. Home: 35 River Park Dr Logan UT 84321-4345 Office: Keller-Bliesner Engring 78 E Center St Logan UT 84321-4619 Office Phone: 435-752-9542.

KELLER, JAMES, retired state supreme court justice; b. Harlan, Ky., 1942; m. Elizabeth Keller; 2 children. Student, Ea. Ky. U.; JD, U. Ky. Pvt. practice, 1966—76; master commr. Fayette Cir. Ct., 1969-76, judge, 1976-99; justice Ky. Supreme Ct., 1999—2005. Former chair Lexington-Fayette Urban County Criminal Justice Commn.; mem. Judicial Advisory Com. to Governor's Office of Child Abuse & Domestice Violence Services; chair Child Support Guidelines Review Commn.; mem. Special Legislative Task Force on Parenting & Child Custody; chair Ky. Civil Filing Fees Com.; mem. Gubernatorial Task Force on Delivery, Funding Quality Public Defendant Services. Co-founder Kid's Time Clinic, Ky., Parents Education Clinic, Ky., Mediation Ctr. of Ky. Recipient 5th Annual Kentuckians Involved in Dependents' Support award, 1990, Mediation Ctr. award, Mediation Ctr. of Ky., 1992, Henry V. Pennington Outstanding Trial Judge award, Ky. Acad. Trial Attorneys, 1994, Bowling Green Bar Assn. award, 1995, Law Day award, 1998. Mem. Ky. Bar Assn., Fayette County Bar Assn. (Henry T. Duncan Memorial award 1987) Office: Supreme Ct Ky 155 E Main St Ste 200 Lexington KY 40507-1332

KELLER, JAMES R., manufacturing executive; BSME, U. Vt., 1972; MBA, Dartmouth Coll., 1974. Investment evaluation analyst Weyerhaeuser Co., 1974—77, with Land and Timber divsn., 1977—81, gen. mgr. shipping container divsn., various mgmt. positions in paper products businesses Lithonia, Ga., 1981—97, v.p., gen. mgr. Containerboard Packaging and Recycling, 1997—2002, sr. v.p. Containerboard Packaging and Recycling, 2002—. Mem. bus. conduct com., PAC adv. bd., IT policy bd., human resources adv. bd. Weyerhaeuser Co.; bd. dirs. Weyerhaeuser Co. Found. Mem.: Fibre Box Assn. (past chmn.), AF&PA Containerboard Com. (past chmn.), Internat. Corrugated Case Assn. (bd. dirs.), Electronic Engring. and Mfg. Inc. (bd. dirs.), Internat. Corrugated Packaging Found. (bd. dirs.), Corrugated Packaging Alliance (co-chair). Office: Weyerhaeuser Co 33663 Weyerhaeuser Way S Federal Way WA 98063-9777

KELLER, J(AMES) WESLEY, credit union executive; b. Jonesboro, Ark., Jan. 6, 1958; s. Norman Grady and Norma Lee (Ridgeway) Patrick; m. Patricia Marie Delavan, July 7, 1979. Student, U. Miss., 1976-78; BS in Bus. and Mgmt., Redlands U., 1991, MBA, 1994. Sr. collector Rodkwell Fed. Credit Union, Downey, Calif., 1978-79; acct. Lucky Fed. Credit Union, Buena Park, Calif., 1979-84; pres., CEO Long Beach (Calif.) State Employees Credit Union, 1984—2000, Ocean Crest Credit Union, 2000—. Mem. Credit Union Exec. Soc., Calif. Credit Union League (bd. govs. Long Beach chpt., treas. 1985-86), So. Calif. Credit Union Mgrs. Assn., U. Redlands Whitehead Leadership Soc., Nat. Assn. State Charted Credit Unions (chmn. 1995-97), Kiwanis. Republican. Baptist. Avocations: photography, skiing, woodworking, biking. Office: Ocean Crest Credit Union 3840 N Long Beach Blvd Long Beach CA 90807-3312

KELLER, JANICE N., lawyer, councilwoman; b. L.A., Nov. 29, 1947; d. Max B. and Ruth (Dobris) Musicer. BA, U. Calif., Santa Barbara, 1969; JD, U. Pacific, 1984. Bar: Calif. 1986; cert. C.C. tchg. Campaign cons. various candidates, Santa Barbara, 1978—88; mng. atty. Legal Aid Found., Lompoc, 1988—91; dep. pub. defender Santa Barbara County, Santa Maria, Calif., 1991—2005; councilwoman City of Lompoc, Calif., 1998—. Instr. Allan Hancock C.C., Lompoc, 1989—98. Environ. rev. commr. City of Santa Barbara, 1985—88; human svcs. commr. City of Lompoc, 1991—92, planning commr., 1992—98. Recipient Cmty. Svc. award, Citizens Planning Found., 2001, Sadie West Pub. Servant award, No. Santa Barbara County Women's Polit. Com., 2001, Cert. Congl. Recognition, U.S. Congress, 2001. Mem.: No. Santa Barbara County Bar Assn. Avocations: photography, travel. Home: PO Box 504 Lompoc CA 93438 E-mail: jkeller2002@msn.com.

KELLER, JENNIFER L., lawyer; b. Ft. Wayne, Ind., Feb. 26, 1953; AB, U. Calif., Berkeley, 1975; JD, U. Calif., Hastings Coll. Law, 1978. Bar: Calif. 1978, U.S. Dist. Ct., Ctrl. and So. Dists., Calif., U.S. Ct. Appeals, Ninth Cir. 1984, U.S Dist. Ct., No. and Ea. Dists., Calif. 1997, U.S. Dist. Ct., Ariz. 1998, U.S. Supreme Ct. 1999, cert.: Specialist in Criminal Law. Sr. rsch. atty. Ct. Appeals, 4th Dist., Div. 3, 1986—89; sr. dep. pub. defender Orange County Pub. Defender's Office; pvt. practice Law Offices of Jennifer L. Keller, 1992—. Bd. dir. Pub. Law Ctr. Orange County, 1995—2000; lawyer rep. 9th Cir. Jud. Conf., 1996—99; lectr. Calif. Pub. Defenders Assn., Continuing Edn. of the Bar, 1996. Mem. Hastings Constl. Law Quarterly, 1976—77. Bd. visitors Chapman U. Sch. Law, 1995—2003, Dean's Coun., 2004—. Named Atty. of Yr., Orange County Women Lawyers, 2003, Pub. Law Ctr. Orange County, 1996; named one of The One Hundred Most Influential Lawyers in Calif., Calif. Law Bus., 2001, California's 30 Top Women Litigators, 2002; recipient Wiley Manuel award for Pro Bono Svc., State Bar Calif., 1998, Lawyer of Yr., Constl. Rights Found. Orange County, 1983, Criminal Defense Trial Lawyer Yr., Orange County Trial Lawyers Assn., 2000, Jurisprudence Award, Anti-Defamation League of Orange County & Long Branch, 2001. Mem.: Orange County Trial Lawyers Assn. (named Criminal Def. Atty. of Yr. 2000), Calif. Attys. for Criminal Justice (bd. govs. 1992—93, lectr.), State Bar Calif. (commr., Bd. Legal Specializtion, Criminal Law Advisory Comn. 1990—92, vice-chair, Bd. Legal Specializtion, Criminal Law Advisory Comn. 1992—93, chair, Bd. Legal Specializtion, Criminal Law Advisory Comn. 1993—94, convention lectr., White Collar Crime 1994, commr. Bd. Legal Specialization 2002—05), Orange County Bar Assn. (bd. dir. 1991—93, officer 1993—97, pres. 1996, lectr., State Bar of Calif. President's Pro Bono Svc. award for Dist. 8), Orange County Women Lawyers (life; bd. dirs. 1984—86, Atty. of Yr. 2003). Office: 18500 Von Karman Ave Ste 560 Irvine CA 92612-1043 Office Phone: 949-476-8700. Office Fax: 949-476-0900. E-mail: jkeller@prodigy.net.

KELLER, JOHANNA BEALE, writer, editor; MusB, U. Colo., 1977; MA in Lit., Antioch U., 1996. Editor Chamber Music mag., N.Y.C., 1997—. Author: The Skull: North Carolina, 1961, 1998; contbr. articles, revs., translations, essays, and poetry to The New York Times, S.W. Rev., Chelsea, Hudson Rev., others. Recipient Arts fellow in poetry N.Y. Found. for the Arts, 1997; grantee Ludwig-Vogelstein Found., 1997; recipient Editor's award in poetry Fla. Rev., 1997.

KELLER, JOHN FRANCIS, retired food products executive, mayor; b. Mt. Horeb, Wis., Feb. 5, 1925; s. Frank S. and Elizabeth K. (Meier) K.; m. Barbara D. Mabbott, Feb. 18, 1950; children: Thomas, Patricia, Daniel, David, John. BBA in Acctg., U. Wis., 1949; MBA, U. Chgo., 1963; grad., Stanford Exec. Program, 1978. CPA, Wis., Ill. Acct. Bank of Am., 1949-51; mgr. statis. control and gen. accounting Miller Brewing Co., Milw., 1951—58; contr. Maremont Corp., 1958-68, Heublein, Inc., 1968-84; v.p. fin. Hamm's Brewing Co., 1968-70; v.p. fin., dir. United Vintners, Inc., San Francisco, 1970-80, chmn. bd., CEO, dir., 1980-84; group v.p. Heublein Wines Group, 1980-84; pres. ISC Wines of Calif., 1983-85; adminstrv. dir. Winegrowers of Calif. (a Calif. state mktg. order for wineries and grape growers), 1985-87; mgmt. cons. J.F. Keller & Assocs., 1985—2000. Lectr., assoc. prof. Calif. State U./Hayward Grad. Sch. Bus. and Econs., 1978-82; adj. prof. Golden Gate U. Grad. Sch. Bus., 1983-86, lectr., instr. Coll. San Mateo, 1990; bd. dirs. Servicor, Inc., Duckhorn Vineyards, Fife and Horn Vineyards. Active Boy Scouts Am., 1952—58; dir. Serra H.S. Bd., 1979—82; bd. dirs. U. Wis. Found., 1986—92, Seton Health Svcs. Found., 1988—2002, chmn., 1994—96; bd. dirs. Seton Med. Ctr., 1989—96; sec.-treas. St. Bartholomew Cath. Ch., 1992—94; bd. dirs. Cath. Health Care West, 1996—2001, fin. and investment com.; pres. bd. dirs. Alemany Scholarship Found., 1983—95; bd. dirs. Peace and Justice Task Force Commn., 1986—92; dir. St. Vincent de Paul-San Meteo County, 1997—; bd. dirs. Big Bros., San Francisco, 1971—75, Hill High St., St. Paul, 1969—70, Lesley Found., 1983—85; vol. Internat. Exec. Svc. Corp., 1995—2000; councilman City of Hillsborough, Calif., 1982—91, mayor, 1988—90; mem. parish coun. St. Lamberts Cath. Ch., 1966—68; pres. parish coun. St. Bartholomew Cath. Ch., 1980; mem. Pastoral Planning Commn., San Francisco, 1994—95; trustee St. Patrick's Sem., 1994—, investment advisor, 1990—. 2d lt. 82d Airborne divsn. AUS, 1944—46, ETO, with USAR, 1946—52. Decorated Knight of Magistral Grace in Obedience, Order of Malta, Knight of Grand Cross, Equestrian Order of the Holy Sepulchre of Jerusalem; recipient Disting. Bus. Alumnus award, U. Wis. Sch. Bus., 1990, St. Louise de Marillas award, Daughters of Charity. Mem.: VFW, AICPA, Nat. Assn. Accts., Calif. Soc. CPAs, Wis. Soc. CPAs, Fin. Execs. Inst., Junipero Serra Internat. (pres. San Mateo chpt. 1992—94, treas. Legatus chpt., San Francisco 1999—2005), Am. Legion, Peninsula Golf and Country Club, World Trade Club, Commonwealth Club, Phi Kappa Alpha (past treas., bd. dirs.). Home and Office: 785 Tournament Dr Hillsborough CA 94010-7423 Personal E-mail: jf.keller@comcast.net.

KELLER, JOHN WARREN, lawyer; b. Niagara Falls, Aug. 6, 1954; s. Joseph and Edith Lilian (Kilvington) K.; m. Sandra D. Hubbard, Dec. 18, 1981; children: Sean, Christopher. BA, Rider U., 1976; JD, Coll. William and Mary, 1979. Bar: Ky. 1980. Staff atty. Appalachian Rsch. & Def. Fund Ky., Inc., Barbourville, 1979-82; assoc. F. Preston Farmer Law Offices, London, Ky., 1982-88; ptnr. Farmer, Keller & Kelley, London, 1988-91, Taylor, Keller, Dunaway & Tooms, London, 1991—, Lexington, Ky., 1991—. Mem. Fla. Adv. Com. on Arson Prevention, 1990—; chmn. bd. dirs. Appalachian Rsch. & Def. Fund Ky., 1994-96; founder, chmn. bd. dirs. Ky. Lawyers for Legal Svcs. to the Poor. Contbg. editor: ABA Annotations to Homeowner's Policy, 3rd edit., 1995, ABA Bad Faith Annotations, 2d edit., 2001. Pres. Access to Justice Found., 1996—; bd. dirs. Christian Ch. in Ky., 1994—98; elder First Christian Ch., London, 1994—97, 2002—, chmn. bd. elders, 2002—03. Recipient Access to Justice award Ky. Legal Svcs. Programs, 1995, Outstanding Svc. award Ky. chpt. Nat. Soc. Profl. Ins. Investigators, 2000. Fellow: Ky. Bar Found. (bd. dirs. 2000—, v.p. 2004); mem.: ABA (vice chair property ins. law com. 1992—97), Nat. Soc. Profl. Ins. Investigators (bd. 2001—, 2d v.p. 2002—03, 1st v.p. 2003, pres. 2004, F. Lee Breninger award 2004), Laurel County Bar Assn. (pres. 1992—93), Ky. Bar Assn. (bd. govs. 1996—2002, Donated Legal Svcs. award 2001), The Honorable Order of Ky. Cols. Office: Taylor Keller & Dunaway 1306 W 5th St London KY 40741-1615 also: Hamburg Place Office Park 1795 Alysheba Way Ste 2102 Lexington KY 40509 Business E-Mail: wkeller@tkdlaw.com.

KELLER, JOSEPH BISHOP, mathematician, educator; b. Paterson, N.J., July 31, 1923; s. Isaac and Sally (Bishop) Keller; m. Evelyn Fox, Aug. 29, 1963 (div. Nov. 17, 1976); children: Jeffrey M., Sarah N. BA, NYU, 1943, MS, 1946, PhD, 1948. Prof. math. Courant Inst. Math. Scis., NYU, 1948—79; chmn. dept. math. Univ. Coll. Arts and Scis. and Grad. Sch. Engring. and Sci., 1967—73; prof. math. and mech. engring. Stanford U., 1979—93, prof. emeritus, 1993—. Hon. prof. math. scis. Cambridge U., 1990—; rsch. assoc. Woods Hole Oceanographic Instn., 1965—; Gibbs lectr. Am. Math. Soc., 1977; von Neumann lectr. Soc. Indsl. and Applied Math., 1983; Rouse Ball lectr. U. Cambridge, Eng., 1993. Contbr. articles to profl. jours. Recipient von Karman prize, Soc. Indsl. and Applied Math., 1979, Eringen medal, Soc. Engring. Scis., 1981, Timoshenko medal, ASME, 1984, U.S. Nat. medal of Sci., 1988, NAS award in Applied Math. and Numerical Analysis, 1995, Frederic Esser Nemmers prize in math., Northwestern U., Evanston, Ill., 1996, Wolf prize, Israel, 1997. Mem.: NAS, Soc. Indsl. and Applied Math., Am. Phys. Soc., Am. Math. Soc., Am. Acad. Arts and Scis., Royal Soc. (fgn.). Home: 820 Sonoma Ter Stanford CA 94305-1072 Office: Stanford U Dept Math Stanford CA 94305-2125

KELLER, JUAN DANE, retired lawyer; b. Cape Girardeau, Mo., Jan. 30, 1943; s. Irvin A. and Mercedes (Crippen) K.; m. Sandra Anne Solomon; children: Mary, John, Katharine, Robert, Michael, Cassandra. AB in History, U. Mo., l965, JD, l967; LLM, Georgetown U., l97l. Bar: Mo. Assoc. Bryan, Cave, St. Louis, 1971-78, ptnr., 1979—2004. Contbg. author: Missouri Bar Taxation Handbook, 1988-95. Capt. JAGC, U.S. Army, 1967-71. Mem. ABA, Mo. Bar (tax com. 1971—), Met. St. Louis Bar Assn., Order of Coif. Methodist. Home: 12512 Glencroft Dr Saint Louis MO 63128-2513 Office Phone: 314-705-3889. Personal E-mail: juandk@aol.com.

KELLER, JULIA, reporter; b. Huntington, WV; BA in English, MA in English, Marshall Univ.; PhD in English, Ohio State Univ. Reporting intern syndicated columnist Jack Anderson, Washington; reporter Ashland Daily Independent, Ky., Columbus Dispatch, Ohio; cultural critic, reporter Chgo. Tribune, 1998—. Recipient Pulitzer Prize for feature writing, 2005; grantee Nieman fellowship, Harvard Univ., 1998. Office: Chicago Tribune 435 N Michigan Ave Chicago IL 60611 Office Phone: 312-222-0245.*

KELLER, KENNETH HARRISON, engineering educator; b. NYC, Oct. 19, 1934; s. Benjamin and Pearl (Pastor) K.; m. Dorothy Robinson, June 2, 1957 (div.); children: Andrew Robinson, Paul Victor; m. Bonita F. Sindelir, June 19, 1981; children: Jesse Daniel, Alexandra Amelie. AB, Columbia U., 1956, BS, 1957; MS in Engring., Johns Hopkins U., 1963, PhD, 1964. Asst. prof. dept. chem. engring. U. Minn., Mpls., 1964-68, assoc. prof., 1968-71, prof., 1971—, prof. Hubert H. Humphrey Inst. Pub. Affairs, 1996—, Charles M. Denny Jr. prof., assoc. dean Grad. Sch., 1973-74, 99—, acting dean Grad. Sch., 1974-75, head dept. chem. engring. and materials sci., 1978-80, v.p. acad. affairs, 1980-85, pres., 1985-88; Philip D. Reed sr. fellow for sci. and tech. Coun. on Fgn. Rels., 1990-96, sr. v.p., 1993-95. Cons. in field; cardiology adv. com. NIH, 1982-86; mem. sci. and tech. adv. panel to dir. CIA, 1995-99; commn. on phys. scis., math. and applications NRC, 1996-2000; bd. dirs. LASPAU: Acad. and Profl. Programs for the Ams., 1996—; trustee Sci. Mus. Minn., 1997-2003; chmn. Med. Technology Leadership Forum, 1998—. Adv. com. program for Soviet emigré scholars, 1974-82; bd. govs. Argonne Nat. Lab., 1982-85; bd. dirs. Walker Art Ctr., 1982-88, Charles Babbage Found., 1991-99. Lt. USNR, 1957-61. NIH Spl. fellow, 1972-73; vis. fellow Woodrow Wilson Sch. of Pub. and Internat. Affairs, Princeton U., 1988-90. Founding fellow Am. Inst. for Med. and Biol. Engring.; fellow AAAS; mem. Am. Soc. Artificial Internal Organs (pres. 1980-81), AIChE (Food and Bioengring. award 1980), Am. Coun. for Emigrés in the Professions (dir. 1972-80), Nat. Acad. Engring., Mpls. C. of C. (bd. dirs. 1985-88), Coun. Fgn. Rels., Phi Beta Kappa, Sigma Xi (nat. lectr. 1978-80). Office: U Minn Chem Engring and Math Sci 151 Amundson Hall 421 Washington Ave SE Minneapolis MN 55455

KELLER, MARTHE, artist, painter; b. N.Y.C., Dec. 8, 1948; d. Charles and Judith (Herman) K.; m. Bradford H. Ensminger, July 12, 1989. Student, Overseas Sch. of Rome, 1961-64, St. Stephen's Sch., Rome, 1964-66, Temple U., 1968, Boston U., 1966-69; BFA, Md. Inst., 1971; postgrad., George Washington U., 1972-73. Vis. artist Whitaker Found., Palermo, Italy, 1982, U. Calif., Santa Barbara, 1987, Sch. of the Art Inst. of Chgo., 1990, R.I. Sch. of Design, Providence, 1993, Sarah Lawrence Coll., Bronxville, N.Y., 1991; instr. multi-level painting Sch. of Art Inst. Chgo., 1991, 95; lectr. in visual arts Princeton U., 1991-92, 98-99; instr. N.Y. Studio Sch. of Painting, 1992; adj. instr. Kingsborough Cmty. Coll., Bklyn., 1993, 94; guest lectr. Temple U., Tyler Sch. of Art, Rome, 1994, Parsons' Sch., 1995, 96, 97, Hunter Coll., CUNY, 96, 97, 98, 99, guest artist Ringling Sch., Fla., 1997; chair Coll. Art Assn. Conf., Toronto, 1997-98. One woman shows include Albuquerque Arts Ctr., U. N.Mex., 1978, Whitaker Found. Mus., Palermo, 1982, Stephen Rosenberg Gallery, N.Y., 1986, 87, 89, Conlon Gallery, Santa Fe, N.Mex., 1990, Galleria Plurima, Udine, Italy, 1991, Halsey Gallery, Coll. of Charleston, 1994, Turchetto Gallery, Milan, 1994, Rosenberg & Kaufman Fine Art, N.Y., 1997, 98, Atrium Gallery, U. Conn., 1999, Fold Color Replay, NY, 2001-02; exhibited in group shows at Stephen Rosenberg Gallery, 1986, 89, 90, 91, McNay Art Mus., San Antonio, 1986, Gallery 53 Cooperstown, N.Y., 1986, Carlo Lamagna Gallery, N.Y., 1988, Genovese Gallery, Boston, 1988, Dart Gallery, Chgo., 1988, Ill. Ctr. Gallery, Chgo., 1989, 55 Mercer Gallery, N.Y., 1990, Galleria Plurima, Udine and Milan, 1992, Edwin A. Ulrich Mus. of Art, Wichita, 1992, Cummings Art Ctr., Conn. Coll., 1992, 55 Ferris St, Bklyn., 1993, Jessica Berwind Gallery, Phila., 1993, Krasdale Foods Gallery and Lehman Coll., Westchester, N.Y., 1993, Lilian Heidenberg Gallery, N.Y., 1993, Werner Kramarsky, N.Y., 1993, Art in Embassies Program, Vienna, Austria, 1994, Noyes Mus., Oceanville, N.J., 1994, Art Initiatives and Bill Bace, 1995, Rosenberg & Kaufman Fine Art, N.Y., 1995, Mishkin Gallery, Baruch Coll., 1996, Bockenheimer Depot Internat. Exhbn., Frankfurt, Germany, 1996, Islip Art Mus., N.Y.,1997, Condeso/Lawler Gallery, 1997, Snug Harbor Cultural Ctr., 1997, Islip Art Museum., N.Y., 1997, Pratt Inst. Gallery, N.Y., 1999, Hillwood Art Mus., N.Y., 2000, Hunter Coll., 2000, 21st Suffragettes, Brooklyn, 2001, Les Fables de la Fontaine, France & U.S.A., 2002-03, Eleven Painters Eleven Views of Abstraction, Santa Fe, 2003, Intersections, Douglas Elliman Tribeca Gallery, N.Y., 2004; represented in permanent collection Met. Mus. Art, N.Y.C., 1996, Fogg Art Mus., Harvard U., Cambridge, Mass., San Jose Mus. Art, Whitney Mus. Art, Mus. Modern Art N.Y.C., others. Recipient fellowships The Mac Dowell Colony, 1990, Nat. Endowment for the Arts, 1989-90, The Mac Dowell Colony, 1989-90; grantee Ludwig Vogelstein Found., 1987, CETA grantee for costume design Albuquerque Dance Theatre, 1978. Home: 39 Walker St New York NY 10013-6001

KELLER, MICHAEL ALAN, librarian, musicologist; b. Sterling, Colo., Apr. 5, 1945; s. Ephraim Richard and Mary Patricia (Warren) K.; m. Constance A. Kyle, Sept. 3, 1967 (div. Aug. 1979); children: Kristen J., Paul B.; m. Carol Lawrence, Oct. 6, 1979; children: Laura W., Martha M. BA, Hamilton Coll., 1967; MA, SUNY, Buffalo, 1970, postgrad., 1970-91; MLS, SUNY, Geneseo, 1972. Asst. libr. for reference and cataloging SUNY Music Libr., Buffalo, 1970-73; acting undergrad. libr. Cornell U., Ithaca, N.Y., 1976, music libr., sr. lectr., 1973-81; head music libr. U. Calif., Berkeley, 1981-86; assoc. univ. libr. for collection devel. Yale U., 1986-93; director Stanford (Calif.) U. Librs., 1993-94, univ. libr., dir. acad. info. resources, 1994—; pub. HighWire Press, Stanford, 1995—, Stanford U. Press, 2000—. Cons. numerous orgns.; mem. Nat. Digital Libr. Fedn., 1993—2005, chair exec. com., 2002—; mem. Bibliog Commn., Repertoire Internat. de la Presse Mus. de XIXve Siecle, 1981—84; chmn. music program com. Rsch. Librs. Group, 1982—86; reviewer NEH, 1982—88, panelist, 1979—95; chmn. Assoc. Music Librs. Group, Joint Com. Retrospective Conversion in Music, 1989—93; mem. collection mgmt. devel. com. Rsch. Librs. Group, 1986—91, chmn., 1989—91, mem. program adv. com., 1991—93; dir. Berkeley Italian Renaissance Project, 1985—95, Digital Libr. Fedn., 1994—; mem. bd. overseers Stanford U. Press, 1997—; mem. gov. com. Stanford-Japan Ctr. Rsch.; mem. adv. bd. Ebrary, Inc., 1999—; bd. dirs. Alibris Inc., 1999—; dir. Long Now Fedn., 1999—; trustee Hamilton Coll., 2001—05; mem. info. tech. adv. group New Libr. of Alexandria, Egypt, 2001—; mem. adv. bd. Groxis, Inc.; trustee Cisco Learning Inst., 2004—; chair adv. bd. rsch. libr. Los Alamos Nat. Lab., 2005—. Author: MSS on Microfilm in Music Libr. at SUNYAB, 1971, (with Duckles) Music Reference and Rsch. Materials; an annotated bibliography, 1988, 94; contbr. articles to profl. jours. Firefighter, rescue squad mem. Cuyuga Heights Vol. Fire Co., N.Y., 1980-81; bd. dirs. Long Now Found., 1998—; bd. trustees, Hamilton Coll., 2001-05 Recipient spl. commendation Nat. Music Clubs, 1978, Berkeley Bronze medal U. Calif.-Berkeley, 1983, Deems Taylor award ASCAP, 1988; NDEA Title IV fellow SUNY-Buffalo, 1967-70, Pierson Coll., Yale U., Stanford U., 1994-95, World Econ. Forum, 2000, 01; Cornell Coll. Arts and Scis. rsch. grantee, 1973-81, U. Calif.-Berkeley humanities rsch. grantee, 1983-84, Coun. on Libr. Resources grantee, 1984, 93-99, Libr. Assn. U. Calif. grantee, 1985-86, NEH grantee, 1986; recipient various grants NSF, 1999—, State Libr. Calif., Mellon Found. Mem. ALA, AAUP, Music Libr. Assn. (bd. dirs. 1975-77, fin. com. 1982-83, editl. com. index and bibliography series 1981-85), Internat. Assn. Music Librs., Am. Musicol. Soc. (com. on automated bibliography 1982-83, coun. 1986-88), Conn. Acad. Arts and Scis. (bd. dirs.), Ctr. Rsch. Librs. (adv. com. 1988-90), Conn. Ctr. for Book (bd. dirs.), Book Club of Calif., Bohemian Club, San Francisco. Home: 809 San Francisco Ter Stanford CA 94305-1070 Office: Stanford U Cecil Green Libr Stanford CA 94305-6004 E-mail: michael.keller@stanford.edu.

KELLER, MICHELLE R., science educator, secondary school educator; b. Rolla, N.D., Aug. 15, 1951; d. Raymond Charles Halone and Yvonne M. (Klier) Edwards; m. Fred F. Keller, June 30, 1973; 1 child, Brent F. BS in Foods and Nutrition, N.D. State U., 1973; cert. sci. edn., Minot State U., 1977; MEd in Secondary Sci. Edn., N.Dak. State U., 2001. Instr. sci. Bisbee (N.D.)-Egeland H.S., 1975—. Judge Seiko Youth Challenge, 1993, 94; ND tchr. portfolio trainer, assessor. Access Excellence fellow Genentech/NSF, 1994; recipient Presdl. award for excellence in sci. tchg., 1993, Edn.'s Unsung Hero award 1998; named Hon. Mention Tchr., Radio Shack/Tandy scholars program, 1998, 99. Mem. Am. Assn. Physics Tchrs. (pres. N.D. sect. 2001—), Nat. Sci. Tchrs. Assn., N.D. Sci. Tchrs. Assn., N.D. Orienteering Alliance, Nat. Edn. Assn., N.D. Edn. Assn. Democrat. Roman Catholic. Avocations: walking, reading, gardening. Home: PO Box 265 201 3rd Ave W Bisbee ND 58317-0265 Office: Bisbee-Egeland H S P O Box 217 204 3rd Ave W Bisbee ND 58317 Office Phone: 701-656-3536. E-mail: mkeller@ndsualumni.net.

KELLER, PAUL, advertising agency executive; b. Mainz, Germany, Sept. 23, 1921; came to U.S., 1937, naturalized, 1942; s. Bernhard and Johanna (Metzger) K.; m. Ruth Ettinghouse, Dec. 25, 1948; children: Steven A., Richard M., Susan F. BA, NYU, 1948; MA, Columbia U., 1949. Research analyst N.W. Ayer, N.Y.C., 1950-55; media research dir. Bryan Houston, N.Y.C., 1955-57; v.p., dir. media and rsch., corp. sec., bd. dirs. Reach McClinton, N.Y.C., 1957-69; v.p., assoc. rsch. dir. Ted Bates Advt., N.Y.C., 1969-80, sr. v.p., rsch. dir., 1980-84; prin. Keller Cons. Co., 1985—. Vol. cons. Nat. Exec. Svc. Corps, 1985—. With U.S. Army, 1942-45, PTO. Decorated Bronze Star, Purple Heart. Mem. Phi Beta Kappa, Pi Mu Epsilon. Personal E-mail: pkelrack@aol.com.

KELLER, RACHAEL See ANDERSON, RACHAEL

KELLER, RANDAL JOSEPH, toxicology educator; b. Salem, Ind., Nov. 22, 1957; s. Frank Joseph and Virginia Francis (Barrett) K.; m. Pamela Marie Stroman, Sept. 17, 1994. BA, Eisenhower Coll., Seneca Falls, N.Y., 1979; MS, Utah State U., 1984, PhD, 1988. Cert. indsl. hygienist; cert. safety profl.; diplomate Am. Bd. Toxicology. Postdoctoral fellow Nat. Ctr. Toxicology Rsch., Jefferson, Ark., 1988-90; instr. U. Ark. for Med. Scis., Little Rock, 1990-91, coord. occupl. and environ. health program, 1991-96; assoc. prof. dept. occupl. safety and health Murray (Ky.) State U., 1996—. Peer reviewer Ctr. for Indoor Air Rsch., 1995—. Contbr. articles to profl. jours. Rsch. grantee U.S. EPA, Washington, 1993-96, NIOSH, Morgantown, W.Va., 1993-95. Fellow Am. Acad. Indsl. Hygiene; mem. Am. Indsl. Hygiene Assn. (pres. elect. Ark. sect. 1993-94, pres. 1994-95), Am. Conf. Govt. Indsl. Hygienists, Am. Soc. Safety Engrs., Am. Soc. Toxicology (1st pl. award metals splty. sect. 1986). Republican. Avocations: racquetball, dog training, running, reading, microbrewing. Home: 411 N 10th St Murray KY 42071-1949 Office: Murray State U Dept Occupl Safety & Health PO Box 9 Murray KY 42071-0009 Office Phone: 270-762-6655. Business E-Mail: randal.keller@murraystate.edu.

KELLER, RIC, congressman, lawyer; b. Orlando, Sept. 5, 1964; m. Cathy; children: Nick, Christy. BA, East Tenn. State U.; JD, Vanderbilt U. Former ptnr. Rumberger, Kirk and Caldwell; mem. U.S. Congress from 8th Fla. dist., 2001—; mem. edn. and workforce com., judiciary com., small bus. com. Mem. Congressional com. House Edn., Judiciary. Chmn. bd. Orlando/Orange County COMPACT program. Republican. Office: 419 Cannon House bldg Washington DC 20515-0908

KELLER, SHARI ANN, small business owner; d. Leslie Allen and Nancy Gail Hampton; m. Charles Arnold Keller, Dec. 23, 1986; 1 child, David J. Hampton; 1 child, Suzanne M. Restaurant mgr. Hardee's Food Sys., Tampa, 1994—2001; owner C & C Auton Salvage, Tampa, 2003—. Author: (book) World Peace Anthologies, 2003. Republican. Roman Catholic. Avocations: writing, mixing techno music, fishing, singing, fixing computers. Home: 12312 Pittsfield Ave Tampa FL 33624 Office Phone: 813-630-9201. E-mail: poetluver39@aol.com.

KELLER, STANLEY, lawyer; b. N.Y.C., Aug. 16, 1938; s. Irving S. and Ceil (Silverstein) K.; m. Sandra Freshman, Dec. 25, 1960; children: Andrew J., Eric L., Matthew A. AB, Columbia U., 1959; LLB, Harvard U., 1962. Bar: Mass. 1962. Assoc. Palmer & Dodge LLP, Boston, 1962-68, ptnr., 1969—. Lectr. Boston U. Law Sch., 1969-79; treas., trustee Mass. Continuing Legal Edn., Inc., Boston, 1985-91; panelist continuing legal edn. programs for profl. orgns. Chmn. legal sect. United Way of Boston, 1982. Fellow Am. Bar Found., Mass. Bar Found.; mem. ABA (chair fed. regulation of securities com. 1999-2003), Mass. Bar Assn. (chmn. bus. law sect. 1983-85), Boston Bar Assn. (chmn. corp. law com. 1988-89, chmn. bus. law sect. 1989-91, co-chair legal opinions com. 1992-95, co-chair com. to revise Mass. Bus. Corp. Law 1992—), Tri Bar Opinion Com. Jewish. Office: Palmer & Dodge LLP 111 Huntington Ave Boston MA 02199-7613 Office Phone: 617-239-0217. Business E-Mail: skeller@palmerdodge.com.

KELLER, SUZANNE, sociologist, psychotherapist; arrived in U.S., 1942; d. Joseph and Martha Infield; m. Charles M. Haar, July 5, 1975. PhD, Columbia U., N.Y.C., 1955; HHD (hon.), Hunter Coll., N.Y.C., 1990. Rsch. assoc. ctr. internat. studies MIT, Cambridge, Mass., 1955—58; asst. prof. of sociology Brandeis U., Waltham, Mass., 1959—62, Vassar Coll., Poughkeepsie, NY, 1963—64; fulbright scholar Athens Ctr. of Ekistics, Greece, 1964—68; prof. of sociology Princeton U., NJ, 1967. Author: (books) Beyond the Ruling Class, 1963, Community: Pursuing the Dream, Living the Reality, 2003; editor: Bldg. for Women. Pres. Ea. Sociol. Soc., 1986, Queenston Common Homeowners Assn., 1992. Recipient Hon. Fellow, AIA, 1974, Malfi prize, 2005. Mem.: AIA (life hon.), Am. Sociol. Assn. (life; v.p. 1984), World Soc. for Ekistics (life; v.p. 1991, pres. 2005), Phi Beta Kappa. Achievements include first woman granted tenure in the 226 year history of Princeton University. Avocations: reading, opera, travel, philanthropy, writing. Office: Princeton U Dept of Sociology 107 Wallace Hall Princeton NJ 08544 Business E-Mail: skeller@princeton.edu.

KELLER, THEODORE G., JR., investment property owner and manager; b. Toledo, Ohio, July 22, 1933; s. Theodore George and Edna Louise (Christen) K.; m. Carolyn Mary Lord, Aug. 25, 1956 (dec. May 1985); children: Bradford W., Matthew C., Theodore G. III, Lathrop L.; m. Gayla Claire Rampel, Sept. 20, 1986. BS, Miami U., Oxford, Ohio, 1955; MBA, U. Pa., 1959. Advt. mgr. Procter & Gamble, Cin., 1959-73; v.p. Eastern Airlines, Miami, Fla., 1973-76, Sara Lee Corp., Chgo., 1976-78; corp. officer, exec. v.p. Pet Inc., St. Louis, 1978-92; v.p., gen. mgr. Right Assocs., St. Louis, 1992-96; owner, mgr. 22 Cottage St., LLC, South Orange, NJ, 1986—. Former pres., bd. govs. Naples Bath and Tennis Club, 2002-2004; dir. Naples Bath and Tennis Club Homeowners Assn. Lt. USNR, 1951-59. Republican. Avocations: tennis, bridge. also: 1031 Oriole Cir Naples FL 34105-7425 Home: 1031 Oriole Cir Naples FL 34105-7425 E-mail: gaylaandted@earthlink.net.

KELLER, THOMAS A., chef; Chef, owner The French Laundry, Yountville, Calif. Spokesperson Calif. Milk Adv. Bd., 1997—98. Named Best Am. Chef: Calif., James Beard Found., 1996, Outstanding Chef Am., 1997, Best Chef, San Francisco Focus, 1997, Chef of Yr., Bon Appétit, 1998, Ams. Best Chef, Time Mag., 2001, Best Wine Dir., San Francisco Mag., 2002, Best Chef, Readers' Digest, 2004; recipient Ivy award, Restaurants & Instns., 1996, Robert Mondavi Culinary award of excellence, 1997, Wedgewood award, World Master Culinary Arts, 2001. Mem.: Relais & Chateaux: Relais Gourmands, Traditions & Qualité. Office: 6640 Washington St Yountville CA 94599

KELLER, WILLIAM FRANCIS, publishing consultant; b. Meyersdale, Pa., May 22, 1922; s. Lloyd Francis and Dorothy Marie (Shultz) K.; m. Frances Jane Core, Mar. 31, 1944. AA, Potomac State Coll. of W.Va. U., 1941; BS, U. Md., 1943, MS, 1945. Ednl. rep. Blakiston Co., 1945-51, assoc. editor, 1951-54; editor coll. div. McGraw Hill Book Co., N.Y.C., 1954-56; editor-in-chief Blakiston divsn. McGraw Hill Book Co., 1956-65, gen. mgr. div., 1965-68; pres. Year Book Med. Publs., Chgo., 1968-81, chmn. bd., 1968-82; pub. cons. Crystal Lake, Ill., 1982-95; adminstrv. sec. Am. Med. Pubs. Assn., 1985-91. Served with U.S. Army, 1945-46. Office: 7916 W Hillside Rd Crystal Lake IL 60012-2939

KELLERMAN, JONATHAN SETH, writer, pediatric psychologist, educator; b. NYC, Aug. 9, 1949; s. David Kellerman and Sylvia Fiacre; m. Faye Marilyn Marder, July 23, 1972; children: Jesse, Rachel, Ilana, Aliza. BA in Psychology, UCLA, 1972; MA in Psychology, U. So. Calif., 1973, PhD in Clin. Psychology, 1974. Lic. psychologist, Calif. Intern in psychology Children's Hosp. of Los Angeles, 1973-74, postdoctoral fellow, 1974-75, U. Southern Calif. Sch. Medicine, Los Angeles, 1974-75, staff psychologist, 1975-78, asst. clin. prof. pediatrics, 1978—79, clin. assoc. prof. pediatrics, 1979-98, clin. prof. pediats., psychology, 1998—. Founding dir. Psychosocial Program Children's Hosp., Los Angeles, 1977-81. Author: (non-fiction) Psychological Aspects of Childhood Cancer, 1980, Helping the Fearful Child, 1981, (fiction) When the Bough Breaks, 1985, Blood Test, 1986, Over the Edge, 1987, The Butcher's Theater, 1988, Silent Partner, 1989, Time Bomb, 1990, Private Eyes, 1991, Devil's Waltz, 1992, Bad Love, 1993, Daddy, Daddy Can You Touch the Sky?, 1994, Self-Defense, 1994, Jonathan Kellerman's ABC of Weird Creatures, 1995, The Web, 1995, The Clinic, 1996, Survival of the Fittest, 1997, Billy Straight, 1998, Savage Spawn, 1999, Monster, 2000, Dr. Death, 2000, Flesh And Blood, 2001, The Murder Book, 2002, A Cold Heart, 2003, Therapy, 2004, Twisted, 2004, Double Homicide, 2005. Recipient Samuel Goldwyn Creative Writing award UCLA, 1972, Edgar Allan Poe award, Mystery Writers of Amer., 1985, Anthony Boucher award, 1986, Disting. Alumnus award dept. psychology UCLA, 1997. Mem. Am. Psychol. Assn. (Media award 1994, Presdl. award 1998), Mystery Writers of Am. (Edgar Allan Poe award 1985, nominated Shamus award 2001). Jewish. Avocations: painting, guitar playing and collecting, book collecting, art collecting. Office: c/o Karpfinger Agcy 357 W 20th St New York NY 10011

KELLERMAN, SALLY CLAIRE, actress; b. Long Beach, Calif., June 2, 1937; d. John Helm and Edith Baine (Vaughn) K.; m. Richard Edelstein, Dec. 19, 1970; 4 step-daughters; m. Jonathan Krane, 1980. Student, Los Angeles City Coll., Actor's Studio, N.Y.C. Stage appearances include Singular Man, N.Y.C., Breakfast at Tiffany's; films include Reform School Girl, 1959, The Third Day, 1965, The Boston Strangler, 1968, The April Fools, 1969, M*A*S*H, 1970 (Acad. award nominee 1970, Golden Globe award 1970), Brewster McCloud, 1970, Last of the Red-Hot Lovers, 1972, Slither, 1973, Reflection of Fear, 1973, Lost Horizon, 1973, Rafferty and the Gold Dust Twins, 1975, The Big Bus, 1976, Welcome to L.A., 1977, The Mouse and His Child, 1977 (voice), Magee and the Lady, 1978, It Rained All Night The Day I Left, 1978, A Little Romance, 1979, Foxes, 1980, Loving Couples, 1980, Serial, 1980, Head On, 1980, September Gun, 1983, Moving Violations, 1985, Lethal, 1985, Back to School, 1986, That's Life, 1986, Meatballs III, 1987, Three for the Road, 1987, Someone to Love, 1987, Paramedics (voice), 1988, You Can't Hurry Love, 1988, All's Fair, 1989, Limit Up, 1989, The Secret of the Ice Cave, 1990, Happily Ever After, 1990 (voice), The Player, 1992, Younger and Younger, 1993, Mirror, Mirror 2: Raven Dance, 1994, Ready to Wear (Prêt-à-Porter), 1994, It's my Party, 1995, She's So Lovely, 1997, The Maze, 1997, The Lay of the Land, 1997, Live Virgin, 1998, Bar Hopping, 1999; also TV roles Chrysler Theatre, Mannix, It Takes a Thief, Columbo: Ashes to Ashes; TV films Verna: USO Girl, 1978, For Lovers Only, 1982, Dempsey, 1983, Secret Weapons, 1985, Elena, 1985, Boris and Natasha, 1992; miniseries Centennial, 1978-79. Recipient nominations Acad. and Golden Globe awards for MASH. Mem. Actor's Equity, AFTRA. also: 7944 Woodrow Wilson Dr Los Angeles CA 90046

KELLERMAN, SHIRLEY ROSE, artist; b. Comyn, Tex., Jan. 9, 1928; d. William Ellis and Rose Bessie (Touchtone) Pulley; m. Robert Eugene Kellerman, Sept. 3, 1949; children: Scott, Shellie. B in Journalism, U. Tex., 1949; postgrad., Tex. Christian U., Ft. Worth, 1965—. Represented by Evelyn Siegel Gallery, Ft. Worth, 1994—, McMahon Fine Arts, Ruidoso, N.Mex., 2000—. One person shows include Dallas Gallery, Ruidoso, N.Mex., 1991, Trinity Arts Guild, Bedford, Tex., 1993, Gallery 10, Ft. Worth, 1994, Fenton's Art Gallery, Ruidoso, 1994, 97, Evelyn Siegel Gallery, Ft. Worth, 1996, 2001, McMahon Fine Arts, Ruidoso, N.Mex., 2000—; exhibited in group shows at Mus. of the Horse, Ruidoso, 1994-2002, Evelyn Siegel Gallery, 1994-97. Mem. Nat. Mus. Women in Arts (charter). Avocations: piano, poetry, golf, mountain home. Studio: 4833 Lafayette Ave Fort Worth TX 76107-3725 also: 103 Spring Canyon Rd Ruidoso NM 88345-7221

KELLERMANN, ARTHUR L., medical educator; MD, Emory U., 1980; MPH, U. WAsh., 1985. Cert. Emergency Medicine. Chief, prof. emergency medicine, chmn., dir. Emory U., 2000—, dir. Ctr. Injury Control, 1996—. Prof. and chmn., dept. of emergency medicine Emory University Sch. Medicine. Contbr. articles to profl. jours. Mem.: Inst. of Medicine. Achievements include research on the epidemiology of firearm related injuries and deaths. Office: Ctr Injury Control Rollins Sch Pub Health 1518 Clifton Rd NE Atlanta GA 30322-4201 Office Phone: 404-778-2600. Office Fax: 404-778-2630. Business E-Mail: akell01@emory.edu.

KELLERT, BONNIE, music educator, concert pianist; b. Washington, Jan. 25, 1947; d. Milton Morris and Edythe Ada (Sugar) K.; m. Allen Jay Goldberg, Sept. 7, 1969; children: Emily Esther, Sarah Rosanne. BMus in Performance, Peabody Conservatory of Music, 1969, MMus in Performance, 1971. Profl. cert. in piano Music Tchrs. Nat. Assn. Pvt. piano instr. Peabody: Preparatory Dept., Balt., 1966-68, Glen Elg Sch. of Music, Ellicott City, Md., 1972-74, Jewish Cmty. Ctr. of Greater Washington, Rockville, Md., 1972-78, chair piano dept., 1974; instr. prof. studies program Levine Sch. Music, Washington, 1994—, pvt. piano instr., 1983—. Lectr. recitals for adult seminars Jr. C. of C. Greater Washington; lectr. resident assoc. program Smithsonian Inst.; guest panelist Nat. Piano Pedagogy Conf., 1996. Editor: (syllabus) Md. State Music Tchrs. Keyboard Musicianship Program, 1995; concerts/recitals held at Nat. Gallery of Art, Phillips Collection, Cosmos Club, Barker Hall, Am. U., Howard U., Western Md. Coll., Textile Mus., Rockville Performing Arts Ctr., 6-Hand Concert in Kils, Sweden, Sumner Sch. Mus., Lyceum Series. Mem. Montgomery County Music Tchrs. Assn. (pres. 1995-97, rec. sec. 1993-95), Friday Morning Music Club Found. (treas. 1972-74), Md. State Music Tchrs. Assn. (co-chair, keyboard musicianship, state cert.), Music Tchrs. Nat. Assn., Nat. Guild of Piano Tchrs., Friday Morning Music Club (corr. 1st v.p.), Mu Phi Epsilon (pres. Washington alumni chpt. 1988-90). Avocations: cooking, embroidery. Home: 9140 Falls Chapel Way Potomac MD 20854-2454

KELLEY, A. BENJAMIN, writer, consultant; b. N.Y.C., May 15, 1936; s. Hubert Williams and Anna Alberta (Davis) K.; children: Sumako Chongyol, Hubert Chongsu. Student, Def. Lang. Inst., 1955, Naganuma Inst., Tokyo, 1957-58, Sophia U., 1957, Harvard U. Bus. Sch., 1972. News editor Shipping and Trade News, Japan, 1957-60; Washington transp. corr. N.Y. Jour. Commerce, 1960-63; policy adviser ICC, 1963-65; mgr. transp. and communications dept. U.S. C. of C., 1966-67; dir. pub. affairs Fed. Hwy. Adminstrn., 1967-69; sr. v.p. Ins. Inst. Hwy. Safety, Washington, 1969-85; pres. A.B. Kelley Corp., Crofton, Md., 1985-96, Inst. for Injury Reduction, Crofton, 1988-95; pvt. auto safety cons., 1996—. Vis. faculty mem. Tufts U. Med. Sch., 2001-; exec. dir. Pub. Health Advocacy Inst., 2001-2003, dir. Hazards Archive project, 2003—; guest lectr. Johns Hopkins Sch. Pub. Hygiene and Pub. Health, 1974-95, U. So. Calif., 1974, U. Fla., 1972, UCLA, 1970, U. Calif., Davis, 1977; bd. dirs. Center Auto Safety, 1975—, Com. on Non-Theatrical Events, 1984—1992 Author: The Pavers and The Paved, 1971; author-narrator: Boobytrap!, 1971, Cars That Crash and Burn, 1973, Crashes That Need Not Kill, 1976, Faces in Crashes, 1984; also articles. Served with AUS, 1954-57. Recipient Golden Eagle award Council Internat. Nontheatrical Events, 1971, 73, 76, 1st prize Zagreb (Yugoslavia) Film Festival, 1973, 75, Bronze Venus Medallion Virgin Islands Internat. Film Festival, 1976 Mem. Internat. Transp. Research Forum (past dir.), Nat. Safety Coun. (past dirs.), Am. Assn. Automotive Medicine, Soc. Automotive Engrs., Ctr. for Auto Safety (bd. dirs.).

KELLEY, ALLEN CHARLES, economist, educator; b. Everett, Wash., Sept. 5, 1937; s. Charles Edward and Velma L. (Allen) K.; m. Patty Ann Cochran, June 20, 1959; children: Brian Allen, Mark Andrew, Michael Charles. Student, Linfield Coll., 1955-57; AB, Stanford U., 1959, PhD, 1964. Vis. research fellow Australian Nat. U., 1962-63; cons. Rand Corp., 1962-67; acting asst. prof. Stanford U., 1963-64; faculty U. Wis., Madison, 1964-72, prof., 1970-72; prof. econs. Duke U., Durham, N.C., 1972-81, James B. Duke prof., 1981—, chmn. dept., 1973-80; asso. dir. Center for Demographic Studies, 1973—. Vis. prof. Monash U., Melbourne, Australia, 1970-71; Esmee Fairbairn research prof. Herriot Watt U., Edinburgh, Scotland, 1978; research scholar Internat. Inst. Applied Systems Analysis, Laxenburg, Austria, 1979 Author: (with J.G. Williamson and R.J. Cheetham) Dualistic Economic Development, 1972, (with B.A. Weisbrod et al.) Disease and Economic Development, (with J.G. Williamson) Lessons from Japanese Development - An Analytical Economic History, 1974, The Professor's Guide to TIPS, 1975, (with R.M. Schmidt) The User's Guide to TIPS, 1975, TIPS Program Manual, 1976, (with J.G. Williamson) Modeling Urbanization and Economic Growth, 1980, (with A. Khalifa and M.E. El-Khorazaty) Population and Development in Rural Egypt, 1982; mem. editorial bd. Jour. Econ. Edn, 1973—; Contbr. articles, revs. to profl. jours. Scholar, fellow Weyerhaeuser Co., 1955-59; Scholar, fellow Ford Found., 1961-62; Scholar, fellow Earhart Found., 1959-61; Scholar, fellow Social Sci. Research Council, 1962-63; Richard I. Downing fellow econs. U. Melbourne, 1987-88; grantee Carnegie Found., 1964-65; grantee Exxon Edn. Found., 1965-67, 68-70, 71-74; grantee Ford Found., 1973-79; grantee Nat. Inst. Edn., 1974-75; grantee NSF, 1966-68; grantee Rockefeller Found., 1967-69; grantee Sloan Found., 1969-73, 79—; co-recipient Arthur Cole prize Econ. History Assn., 1972. Mem. Am. Econ. Assn. (chmn. com. econ. edn. 1978—), So. Econ. Assn. (v.p. 1981-82), Internat. Union for Sci. Study Population, Population Assn. Am., Joint Council on Econ. Edn. (trustee 1978—, exec. com. 1978—), Phi Beta Kappa. Home: 4607 Chicopee Trl Durham NC 27707-5208 Office: Duke U Econs Dept Durham NC 27708

KELLEY, ALOYSIUS PAUL, academic administrator, priest; b. Carlisle, Pa., Oct. 4, 1929; s. Aloysius Paul and Teresa (Barron) K. AB, St. Louis U., 1955, MA, PhL, St. Louis U., 1956; STL, U. Innsbruck, Austria, 1963; PhD, U. Pa., 1968; LLD (hon.), Sacred Heart U., 1985. Joined S.J., 1949; ordained priest Roman Catholic Ch., 1962; chmn. dept. classics Georgetown U., 1969-71, asst. acad. v.p., 1971-72, acting acad. v.p., 1972-74, exec. v.p. for acad. affairs and provost, 1974-79; pres. Fairfield (Conn.) U., 1979—2004. Trustee Georgetown Prep. Sch., 1969-72, Loyola Coll., Balt., 1971-75, Scranton U., 1974-80, Bridgeport Area C. of C., 1979-82, St. Joseph's U., Phila., 1980-86, Georgetown U., 1982-88, 89-95, Conn. Grand Opera, 1980-82, John Carroll U., 1987-93, LeMoyne Coll., 1993-99, 2004—, The Gesu Sch., 1993-97, St. Joseph's Prep. Sch., 1997—2002, St. Peter's Coll., 1998-2004, Nat. Assn. Ind. Colls. and Univs., 1997-2000; mem. D.C. Commn. Postsecondary Edn., 1974-79; vice chmn. Conn. Conf. Ind. Colls., 1980-81, chmn., 1981-83; pres. New Eng. Colls. Fund, 1993-95. Fulbright-Hayes fellow, 1971 Mem. Am. Philol. Assn., Am. Assn. Univ. Adminstrs., Am. Assn. Higher Edn., Patterson Club, Newcomen Soc. Democrat. Home and Office: Fairfield U Jesuit Community 1073 N Benson Rd Fairfield CT 06824-5195

KELLEY, BARBARA BANNIN, physical education educator; b. Far Rockaway, N.Y., Feb. 29, 1952; d. Robert Joseph and Regina (Auspitzer) Bannin; m. Edward L. Kelley, Feb. 14, 1976; children: Ryan Patrick, Timothy Bannin. BS, Longwood Coll., 1974; MEd, U. Maine, 1976. Cert. tchr., Maine. Phys. edn. tchr. Mecklenburg County Schs., South Hill, Va., 1974-75, Bangor (Maine) Sch. Dept., 1975—. Mem. Nat. Bd. Profl. Teaching Standards, Washington, 1992—. Named Coach of Yr., Maine High Sch. Coaches Assn., 1981, Tchr. of Yr., Maine Assn. Health, Phys. Edn., Recreation and Dance. Mem. NEA (bd. dirs. 1991—), Maine Tchrs. Assn. (bd. dirs. 1986—), Bangor Edn. Assn. (chief negotiator 1985-92). Democrat. Avocation: tennis. Office: Vine St Sch Bangor ME 04401 Home: 1105 Ivy Ln Raleigh NC 27609-4733

KELLEY, BRIAN P., transportation executive; b. Cin. BA in Econs., Coll. Holy Cross. With Procter & Gamble; sr. exec. appliance bus. GE, 1983; v.p. Global Consumer Svcs. Ford Motor Co., 2001—02, pres. Lincoln Mercury oper. unit, 2002; CEO SIRVA, Westmont, Ill., 2002—, bd. dirs. Office: SIRVA World Hdqrs 700 Oakmont Ln Westmont IL 60559

KELLEY, BRUCE GUNN, insurance company executive, lawyer; b. Phila., Mar. 17, 1954; s. Robb Beardsley and Winifred Elizabeth Gray (Murray) K.; m. Susan Aldrich Barnes, Oct. 1, 1983; children: Dashle Gunn, Barnes Gunn, Onnalee Kinkaid. AB, Dartmouth Coll., 1976; JD, U. Iowa, 1979. Bar: Iowa 1979; CPCU; CLU. Assoc. Bradshaw, Fowler, Proctor & Fairgrave, Des Moines, 1979-84, ptnr., 1984-85; gen. counsel Employers Mut. Casualty Co., Des Moines, 1985-89, exec. v.p., 1989-91, pres., 1991—, also bd. dirs. Trustee Am. Inst. for Chartered Property Casualty Underwriters/Ins. Inst. Am.;

bd. dirs. Property Casualty Insurers Assn. of Am.; chmn. adv. bd. Iowa Pub. Employees Retirement Sys. Trustee Nat. Com. on Drunk Drivers; bd. dirs. Property Loss Rsch. Bur., Salisbury House Found. Mem. Polk County Bar Assn., Des Moines Club, Rotary, Masons. Republican. Mem. United Church of Christ. Home: 14 Glenview Dr Des Moines IA 50312-2546 Office: EMC Ins Cos PO Box 712 Des Moines IA 50303-0712

KELLEY, CLEOPHUS O., city official; b. Birmingham, Ala., Sept. 17, 1932; s. Gladys Turner Kelley; m. Ann E. Kelley, Mar. 26, 1952 (div.); children: Cleophus O. Jr., Michael, Kelvin, Regina. Student, U. Cin., 1997, Ohio State Employment Relation Sch., 1991, Padgett Thompson Bus. Sch., 1991. With Fleet Svcs., 1057-60, Pub. Works Dept., Cin., 1960-99; asst. supt. Pub. Svc. Dept., Cin., 2000—. U. Cincinnati Leadership Development, 1997. Vice pres. Cin. Middle Mgmt. Bd., 1988-90; leader Boy Scouts Am., Cin., 1951-75. Mem. Solid Waste Assn. N.Am, Am. Public Works Assn. Office: City of Cincinnati 3320 Millcreek Rd Cincinnati OH 45223-2419

KELLEY, COLLEEN M., labor union administrator; b. Pitts., 1944; B Acctg., Drexel U.; MBA, U. Pitts. CPA. Agt. revenue IRS; dir. membership and benefits programs Nat. Treasury Employees Union; pres., chief steward, v.p. chpt. 34 Nat. Treasury Employees Union, Pitts., nat. exec. v.p.; exec. v.p. Nat. Treasury Employees Union; pres. Nat. Treasury Employees Union, 1999—. Avocation: skiing. Office: National Treasury Employees Union 1750 H St NW Washington DC 20006-4600

KELLEY, DARCY B., biology professor; AB, Barnard Coll.; PhD, Rockefeller Univ., 1975. Co-dir., neural sys., behavior Marine Biological Lab, Woods Hole, Mass.; prof., biological sciences Columbia Univ. Forbes lectr. Grass Found., and Marine Biological Lab.; spl. lectr. Soc. Neuroscience; plenary lectr. Soc. Neuroethology; rsch. prof. Howard Hughes Med. Inst., 2002—. Editor: Jour. Neurobiology; contbr. articles to profl. journals. Recipient Jacob Javits Neuroscience Investigator award (twice), Howard Hughes Med. Inst. grant, 2002. Office: Biological Sciences Columbia Univ MC 2432 911 Fairchild Ctr New York NY 10027 Office Phone: 212-854-5108. Business E-Mail: dbk3@columbia.edu.*

KELLEY, DAVID CHRISTOPHER, philosopher; b. Lakewood, Ohio, June 23, 1949; s. Walter Carl and Patricia Kelley; m. Susan McCloskey, Mar 25, 1982. BA, MA, Brown U., 1971; PhD, Princeton U., 1975. Asst. prof. philosophy Vassar Coll., Poughkeepsie, N.Y., 1975-84; freelance writer, lectr., 1984-89; exec. dir. Objectivist Ctr., Poughkeepsie, 1990—2004, sr. fellow DC, 2005—. Vis. lectr. in philosophy Brandeis U., Waltham, Mass., 1989-90 Author: The Evidence of the Senses, 1986, The Art of Reasoning, 1990, Unrugged Individualism, 1996, A Life of One's Own, 1998, Contested Legacy of Ayn Rand, 2000; co-author: Laissez Parler, 1985. Mem. Am. Philos. Assn. Office: Objectivist Ctr 1001 Connecticut Ave NW Ste 425 Washington DC 20036 Office Phone: 202-296-7263. Business E-Mail: dkelley@objectivistcenter.org.

KELLEY, DAVID E., producer, writer; b. Waterville, Maine, Apr. 4, 1956; m. Michelle Pfeiffer, 1993; 2 children. BA, Princeton U., 1979; JD, Boston U., 1983. CEO David E. Kelley Prodns., Inc., L.A. Writer, story editor, exec. story editor, supervising prodr., exec. prodr. L.A. Law (Emmy award for Outstanding Drama Series 1989, 90, Emmy award for outstanding writing in a drama series 1990); writer, exec. prodr. Picket Fences (Emmy award for outstanding drama series 1993, 94), Chicago Hope, 1994-2000, The Practice, 1997—2004 (Golden Globe award for best TV drama 1998, Emmy award for outstanding drama series, 1998, 99), Ally McBeal, 1997-2002 (Golden Globe winner, Emmy award for best TV series-musical or comedy 1997, 98, Emmy award for outstanding comedy series 1999), Snoops, 1999-2000, Boston Public, 2000—04, Girl's Club, 2002, The Brotherhood of Poland, New Hampshire, 2003, Boston Legal, 2004-, The Law Firm, 2005-. Office: David E Kelly Prodns care 20th Century Fox 10201 W Pico Blvd Bldg 80 Los Angeles CA 90064-2606 also: William Morris Agency One William Morris Pl Beverly Hills CA 90212*

KELLEY, DAVID N., lawyer, former prosecutor; b. Dec. 1, 1959; AB, Coll. William & Mary, 1981; JD, N.Y. Law Sch., 1986. Bar: 1986. Police officer East Hampton; co-chief organized crime and terror unit U.S. Dept. Justice, 1993—2003, asst. U.S. atty. to deputy U.S. atty. (So. dist.) NY, 1988—2003, U.S. atty., 2003—05; sr. litig. ptnr. Cahill Gordon & Reindel LLP, NYC, 2005—. Adj. prof. N.Y. Law Sch. Office: Cahill Gordon & Reindel LLP 80 Pine St New York NY 10005

KELLEY, DELORES GOODWIN, state legislator; b. Norfolk, Va., May 1, 1936; d. Stephen Cornelius and Helen Elizabeth (Jefferson) Goodwin; m. Russell Victor Kelley, Jr., Dec. 26, 1956; children: Norma Kelley Johnson, Russell III, Brian. BA, Va. State Coll., 1956; MA, NYU, 1958, Purdue U., 1972; PhD, U. Md., 1977. Dir. religious edn. N.Y.C. Protestant Coun., Bronx, 1959-60; tchr. N.Y.C. Pub. Schs., Bklyn., 1962-64, Ctrl. Sch. Dist., Plainview, N.Y., 1965-66; asst. prof. Morgan State U., Balt., 1966-70; prof. speech comms. and English Coppin State Coll., Balt., 1973—2004; mem. Md. Ho. of Dels., Annapolis, 1991—94; former chmn. Joint Com. on Fed. Rels./Md. Senate, 1995—98; vice-chmn. exec. nomination com. Md. Senate, 1995—. Joint com. legis. policy, joint com. legis. ethics, co-chair joint com. on fair practices Md. State Senate, 1999—, vice chair, joint com. on health care delivery and fin., 2000—, fin. com., 1998—; senate chair Joint Com. on Adminstrv., Exec. and Legis. Rev., 2001—02; vice-chair sen. com. exec. nomination; vice-chair Balt. County Senate Delegation, 2003—; panelist, reviewer NEH, Washington, 1978—82, Nat. Inst. Justice, 1998—; dean Coppin State Coll., Balt., 1979—82; fellow Am. Coun. on Edn., Washington, 1982—83; vice-chair bd. dirs. Harbor Bank Md., 1982—; mem. Gov.'s Commn. on Adoption, 1995, Atty. Gen.'s and Lt. Gov.'s. task force on family violence, 1996—, Md. Commn. on Criminal Sentencing Policy, 1996—, Md. Commn. on Infant Mortality, 1999—2002; mem. strategic planning com. Balt. County Schs., 1999—2000; adv. com. Md. Medicaid, 1998—; commr. Edn. Commn. of States, 2004—. Editor (monograph) Concepts of Race, 1981; moderator (TV series) Teaching Writing: Process Approach, 1982. Sec. Md. Dem. Party, Annapolis, 1986-90; bd. dirs. Balt. Urban League, 1986-89; pres. Black Jewish Forum, Balt., 1990-92; commr. Md. Commn. on Values, Annapolis, 1980-85; bd. dirs. Balt. Mental Health Systems, 1991-95; host Internat. Visitors Ctr., 1976—; commn. mem. Md. Commn. Hereditary and Congenital Disorders, Balt., 1992-95; del. White House conf. on Aging, 1995. Fellow Purdue U., 1970-72; grantee Md. Com. for Humanities, Balt., 1977-78, NEH, Washington, 1988-89; recipient Racial Justice award YWCA of Met. Balt., 1995; named to Md. Top 100 Women, Warfields Bus. Record, 1995, 97, 2004, Cir. of Excellence award The Daily Record, 2004. Mem. Nat. Inst. Justice (panelist, rev. 1997). Inst. for Govtl. Svcs. (bd. dirs. 1993-94), Nat. Polit. Congress Black Women (bd. dirs., Balt. chair 1993-95), Women Legislators Md. (1st v.p. 1995-96, pres. 1998-99), 10th Dist. Dem. Club Md. (founder, pres. 1995—). Baptist. Avocations: travel, public speaking, reading. Office: 302 James Senate Office Bldg Annapolis MD 21401-1991 Office Phone: 410-841-3606. Business E-Mail: delores_kelley@senate.state.md.us.

KELLEY, DONALD REED, historian; b. Elgin, Ill., Feb. 17, 1931; s. Walter Louis and Helen Lenore (Davis) K.; m. Bonnie Gene Smith, June 30, 1979; 1 son, John Reed. BA, Harvard Coll., 1953; MA, Columbia U., 1956, PhD, 1962; postgrad., U. Paris, 1958—59. Instr. Queens (N.Y.) Coll., 1960-63; asst. prof. So. Ill. U., 1963-65, SUNY, 1965-68, assoc. prof., 1968-70, prof., 1970-72; vis. prof. Harvard U., Cambridge, Mass., 1972-73; prof. U. Rochester, NY, 1973, Marie Curran Wilson and Joseph Chamberlain Wilson prof. history, 1984-91; James Westfall Thompson prof. Rutgers U., New Brunswick, NJ, 1991—. Author: Foundations of Modern Historical Scholarship, 1970, François Hotman, 1973, The Beginning of Ideology, 1981, Historians and the Law in Postrevolutionary France, 1984, History, Law, and the Human Sciences, 1984, The Human Measure, 1990, The Writing of History and the Study of Law, 1997, Faces of History, 1998, The Descent of Ideas, 2002, Fortunes of History, 2003; editor: The Monarchy of France (Claude de Seyssel), 1981, History of Ideas, 1990, Versions of History, 1991, The Shapes of Knowledge, 1991, What is Property? (P.-J. Proudhon), 1994, History and the Disciplines, 1997; exec. editor Jour. History of Ideas, 1985—. With U.S. Army, 1953—55. Fulbright fellow, 1958-59, Newberry libr. fellow, 1965, Am. Coun. Learned Socs. fellow, 1967-68, Folger Libr. fellow, 1970, 85; mem. Inst. for Advanced Study, 1969-70, 77-78, 96-97; Guggenheim fellow, 1974-75, 81-82, NEH fellow, 1977-78, Nat. Humanities Ctr. fellow, 1984, Shelby Cullom Davis Ctr. fellow, Princeton U., 1987-88, Wilson Ctr. fellow, 1992-93. Fellow Am. Acad. Arts and Scis.; mem. Am. Philos. Soc., Am. Hist. Assn., Renaissance Soc. Am., Medieval Acad., Internat. Soc. Intellectual History (pres.). Home: 45 Jefferson Ave New Brunswick NJ 08901-1737 Office: Rutgers U Dept History New Brunswick NJ 08901 Business E-Mail: dkelley@rci.rutgers.edu.

KELLEY, EDWARD ALLEN, publisher; b. Clinton, Mass., June 28, 1927; s. Edward Francis Kelley and Lillian Marion (Keigwin) French; m. Margaret Jordan Talbott, Feb. 24, 1962; children: Catherine, Edward, Michael. BA, Trinity Coll., Hartford, Conn., 1950; STM, Gen. Theol. Sem., N.Y.C., 1953. Prodn. asst., customer svc. rep. Colonial Press, Clinton, 1953-57; mgr. bookstore Morehouse-Barlow Co. Inc., N.Y.C., 1957-61, v.p., editorial dir., 1961-74; sr. v.p. Oxford U. Press, N.Y.C., 1974-83; pres. Kelley Assocs., Ridgefield, Conn., 1983-87; pres., pub. Morehouse Pub. Co., Ridgefield, 1988-97; pvt. practice pub. cons. Ridgefield, 1997—. Editor The Episcopal Ch. Ann., 1967-74, 87-97. With USNR, 1945-47, World War II. Democrat. Episcopalian. Avocations: golf, reading.

KELLEY, EUGENE JOHN, retired business educator; b. N.Y.C., July 8, 1922; s. Eugene Lawrence and Agnes Regina (Meskill) K.; m. Dorothy W. Kane, Aug. 3, 1946; 1 child, Sharon A.; m. Linda S. Phillips, Sept. 30, 1992. BS, U. Conn., 1945; MBA, Boston U., 1949, MEd, 1948; PhD, NYU, 1955. Instr. mktg. Babson Inst., 1947-49; dir. divsn. bus. adminstrn. Clark U., 1949-56, asst. prof., 1949-54, assoc. prof., 1954-56; vis. lectr. Harvard U. Bus. Sch., 1956-57; asst. prof. Mich. State U., East Lansing, 1957-58, assoc. prof., 1958-59; prof. mktg., asst. dean Grad. Sch. Bus. Adminstrn. NYU, N.Y.C., 1959-60, prof., assoc. dean, 1960-64; rsch. prof. bus. adminstrn. Coll. Bus. Adminstrn. Pa. State U., 1963-88, dean, 1973-88; dean and rsch. prof. emeritus Pa. State U., 1988; disting. prof. mktg. Fla. Atlantic U., Boca Raton, 1989—, dir. Ctr. for Svcs. Mktg. and Mgmt., Coll. Bus., 1990—. Regional dir. Mellon Bank Central; mem. nat. adv. Council SBA; mem. Commn. on Edn. for Bus. Professions of Nat. Assn. State Univs. and Land Grant Colls.; cons. GAO, N.J. Bd. Higher Edn. Author: Marketing Planning and Competitive Strategy, 1972, Managerial Marketing: Policies, Strategies and Decisions, 1973, Social Marketing: Perspectives and Viewpoints, 1973; Editor: Jour. Mktg, 1967-73. Served with USAAF, 1942-43. Mem. Am. Mktg. Assn. (pres. 1982-83, dir., mem. disting. mktg. educator com.), Acad. Mgmt., Am. Assembly Collegiate Schs. of Bus. Office: Pa State Univ Bus Adminstrn University Park PA 16802 Home: 237 Lions Hill Rd State College PA 16803-1860

KELLEY, FRANK JOSEPH, lawyer, former state attorney general; b. Detroit, Dec. 31, 1924; s. Frank Edward and Grace Margaret (Spears) Kelley; m. Nancy Courtier; children: Karen Ann, Frank Edward II, Jane Francis. Pre-law cert., U. Detroit, 1948, JD, 1951. Bar: Mich. 1952. Pvt. practice law, Detroit, 1952—54, Alpena, 1954—61; atty. gen. State of Mich., Lansing, 1962—98; pvt. practice Lansing, 1998—. Instr. econs. Alpena CC, 1955—56; instr. pub. adminstrn. Alpena County, 1956; atty. city real estate law U. Mich. Extension, 1957—61. Mem. Alpena County Bd. Suprs., 1958—61; pres. Alpena Cmty. Svcs. Coun., 1956; chmn. Gt. Lakes Commn., 1971; founding dir., 1st sec. Alpena United Fund, 1955; founding dir., 1st pres. Northeastern Mich. Child Guidance Clinic, 1958; pres. bd. dirs. Northeastern Mich. Cath. Family Svc., 1959. Mem.: ABA, Nat. Assn. Attys. Gen. (pres. 1967), State Bar Mich., 26th Jud. Cir. Bar Assn. (pres. 1956), Internat. Movement Atlantic Union, KC (4 deg., past legal adv.), Alpha Kappa Psi. Address: 101 S Washington Sq Fl 9 Lansing MI 48933-1731 Office Phone: 517-371-1400.

KELLEY, HEATHER RYAN, artist, educator; b. New Haven, Jan. 19, 1954; d. Charles Peter and Jeanne Therese (Burr) Ryan; m. Frank Whitney Kelley Jr., Dec. 29, 1973 (div. Jan. 1988); 1 child, Matthew Ryan. BFA, So. Meth. U., 1975; MA, Northwestern U., 1984. Vis. lectr. McNeese State U., Lake Charles, La., 1981-83, asst. prof., 1984-89, from assoc. to prof. art, 1990-96, prof., 1996, coord. works in paper exch., 1988—. Exhibited in numerous one-person shows including Irving (Tex.) Arts Ctr., 1992, 94, Evelyn Siegel Gallery, Fort Worth, Tex., 1994, Still Zinsel Contemporary Fine Art, New Orleans, 1993, 96, 97, Hooks-Epstein Gallery, Houston, 1996, 98, James Joyce Ctr., Dublin, Ireland, 1997, North Light Gallery Ariz. State U., Tempe, 1999; group shows include La. State U., Baton Rouge, 1992 (1st Place award), Mainstreet Fine Arts Exhbn., Fort Worth, 1993 (cash award 1993), Cheekwood Nat. Contemporary Painting Exhbn., Nashville, 1993 (Jurors Mention 1993), Masur Mus., Monroe, La., 1994 (Best of Show), 173d Ann. Exhbn. Nat. Acad. Mus., N.Y.C., 1998. Contbr. work to ann. auction S.W. La. AIDS Coun., Lake Charles, 1992, 93, 94, 95, 96, 97. Recipient award Border to Border Drawing Biennial, Shearman Endowed Professorship, 1993-94, 1995-96; named Artist of Yr. Arts Coun. SW La., 1997; grantee Calcasieu Arts and Humanities Coun., 1991, La. Div. Arts, 1995. Mem. Coll. Art Assn., Phi Kappa Phi. Office: McNeese State U Art Dept Ryan And Sale Sts Lake Charles LA 70609-0001

KELLEY, HENRY PAUL, academic administrator, psychology educator; b. Cleburne, Tex., July 4, 1928; s. Henry Rowell and Jane Frances (Wynn) K.; m. Lucerle DeCourcy Scott, Aug. 18, 1949; children: Roger Wynn, Scott Franklin, Gordon Henry. BA in Pure Math., U. Tex., 1949, MA in Ednl. Psychology, 1951; AM, PhD in Psychology, Princeton U., 1954. Cert. and lic. psychologist, Tex. Psychometric fellow Ednl. Testing Svc., Princeton, N.J., 1951-54; pers. mgmt. and evaluation psychologist pers. and tng. rsch. ctr. USAF, San Antonio, 1954; aviation exptl. psychologist U.S. Naval Sch. Aviation Medicine, Pensacola, Fla., 1955-57; coord. measurement svcs., testing and counseling ctr., from asst. to assoc. prof. ednl. psychology U. Tex. Austin, 1958-64, lectr., 1964-67, dir. measurement and evaluation ctr., prof. ednl. psychology, 1967—99, prof. emeritus ednl. psychology, 1999—; regional dir. southwestern office Coll. Entrance Exam. Bd., Austin, 1964-67. Regional coord. Project TALENT, Austin, 1959-61; mem. southwestern regional adv. com. Coll. Entrance Exam. Bd., Austin, 1968-73, vice-chmn. com. rsch. and devel., N.Y.C., 1970-73, chmn., 1973-76, mem. adv. panel econ. implications recognizing prior learning, 1979-80; vis. faculty mem. ann. inst. coll. entrance, acad. placement and student fin. assistance Coll. Entrance Exam. Bd. and U. N.C., Chapel Hill, 1975-94; tech. reviewer, panel mem. rsch. projects br., bur. edn. handicapped, office edn. HEW, Washington, 1977; asst. hearing officer minimum competency study Nat. Inst. Edn., 1980-81; mem. gen. faculty U. Tex. Austin, 1960-64, 67-99, sec., 1981-87, mem. faculty senate, 1972-74, 81-95, sec., 1975-79, adminstrv. adviser ednl. policy com., 1968-99; reviewer comprehensive program fund improvement secondary edn. U.S. Dept. Edn., 1983; mem. rsch. adv. panel, manpower and pers. divsn. Air Force Human Resources Lab., Brooks AFB, San Antonio, 1984-86; mem. com. testing, coordinating bd. Tex. Coll. and Univ. Sys., Austin, 1985-86, mem. adv. com. basic skills testing, coordinating bd., 1987; mem. basic skills test rev. panel Tex. Edn. Agy., Austin, 1987; mem. Tex. acad. skills coun. Tex. Higher Edn. Coord. Bd., 1987-93, chmn. adv. com. tests and measurements Tex. acad. skills coun., 1987-93; mem. planning com. Ann. Tex. Testing Conf., 1987-94; cons., spkr. in field. Author: (with Bruce Walker) Self-Audit of CLEP Policies and Procedures: A Guide to Policy Decisions for Colleges and Universities, 1981; contbr. articles to profl. jours. and publs. Lt. USNR. Recipient Edward S. Noyes award Coll. Bd., 1976, Advanced Placement Spl. Recognition award, 1985; recipient numerous grants in field. Fellow APA, Am. Psychol. Soc.; mem. Am. Assn. Applied and Preventive Psychology, Am. Ednl. Rsch. Assn., Nat. Coun. Measurement Edn., Nat. Soc. Study Edn., Am. Assn. Higher Edn., Am. Evaluation Assn., Measurement Svcs. Assn., Nat. Coll. Testing Assn., Psychometric Soc., Phi Beta Kappa, Phi Delta Kappa, Phi Eta Sigma, Phi Kappa Phi, Sigma Xi. Methodist. Avocations: reading, bridge. Home: 2522 Jarratt Ave Austin TX 78703-2433 Office: U Tex Austin Ednl Psychology Dept 1 Univ Station D5800 Austin TX 78712-0383 Office Phone: 512-471-0526. Business E-Mail: p.kelley@mail.utexas.edu.

KELLEY, JAMES FRANCIS, lawyer; b. Dec. 30, 1941; s. James O'Connor and Marcella Cecilia (Salb) K.; m. Anne H. Morgan; children: Sarah, Leah; AB, Yale U.; JD, U. Chgo. Bar: N.Y. 1967, Tex. 1981. Assoc. Breed, Abbott & Morgan, NYC, 1967-75; dep. gen. counsel United Tech. Corp., Hartford, Conn., 1975-81; sr. v.p., gen. counsel Maxus Energy Corp (formerly Diamond Shamrock Corp.), Dallas, 1981-88; ptnr. Jones, Day, Reavis & Pogue, Dallas and Paris, 1988-93; sr. v.p. law, gen. counsel Georgia-Pacific Corp., 1993-2000; exec. v.p & gen. coun., 2000-; Gov. Dallas Symphony Assn., 1985-89; bd. dir. North Tex. Pub. Broadcasting Found., Dallas, 1983-91, mem. exec. com., 1988-91; bd. dirs. Atlanta Symphony Orch., 1994—, mem. exec. com., 1996—, chair fin. com., 2002—; bd. dirs. Ga. Trust Hist. Preservation, 1994—99, Piedmont Healthcare Inc., 2003-; mem. bd. visitors Emory U., 1999—2001. Mem. ABA, Assn. Gen. Counsel. Office: Georgia-Pacific Corp 133 Peachtree St NE Atlanta GA 30303-1847

KELLEY, JANET GODSEY G., lawyer; b. Ky., May 9, 1953; d. Paul and Christine Godsey; m. Peter Marcum (div.); m. Michael R. Kelley, Sept. 5, 1988; children: Megan Marcum, Christina Kelley. AB, Morehead State U., 1975; JD, U. Ky., 1978. Bar: Ky. 1978. Assoc. Wyatt Tarrant & Combs, Louisville, 1978-83, ptnr., 1983-94; gen. counsel Sunbeam Corp., Ft. Lauderdale, Fla., 1994—99; v.p., sr. counsel The Limited Inc., 1999—2001; exec. v.p., gen. counsel Kmart, Troy, Mich., 2001—03; sr. v.p., sr. counsel Family Dollar Stores, Charlotte, NC, 2004—05, sr. v.p., gen. counsel, 2005—. Notes editor Ky. Law Jour., 1990. Mem. Ky. Sch. Facilities Constrn. Com. Mem. ABA, Ky. Bar Assn. for Women, Women Laywers' Assn., Exec. Inst., Order of the Coif. Democrat. Office: Family Dollar Stores PO Box 1017 Charlotte NC 28201-1017 Office Phone: 704-849-7427. Business E-Mail: jkelley@familydollar.com.

KELLEY, JOHN JOSEPH, JR., lawyer; b. Cleve., June 17, 1936; s. John Joseph and Helen (Meier) K.; m. Gloria Hill, June 20, 1959; children: John Joseph III, Scott MacDonald, Christopher Taft, Megan Meredith. BS cum laude in Commerce, Ohio U., 1958; LL.B., Case Western Res. U., 1960. Bar: Ohio bar 1960. Clk. firm Walter & Haverfield, Cleve., 1957-60; assoc. Walter, Haverfield, Buescher & Chockley, Cleve., 1960-66, partner, 1967-72; chief exec. officer Fleischmann Enterprises, Cin., 1972-77; pvt. practice law Cin., 1977-87; ptnr. Kohnen & Patton, Cin., 1988—. Chmn. bd. Basic Packaging Systems, Inc., 1982-87; dir. Orgamac Leasing Ltd; pres. Naples Devel. Inc., 1974-87, Yankee Leasing Co. Mem. Lakewood (Ohio) City Council, 1965-72, pres., 1972; mem. exec. com. Cuyahoga County (Ohio) Republican Central Com., 1965-72; mem. Hamilton County (Ohio) Rep. Policy Com.; Ohio chmn. Robert Taft, Jr. Senate Campaign Com., 1970, 76; bd. govs. Case Western Res. U., 1961, 84-87. Mem. Assn. Ohio Commodores, ABA, Ohio State Bar Assn., Cin. Bar Assn. Clubs: Cin. Country, Queen City (Cin.); Naples Bath and Tennis. Home: 5 Woodcreek Dr Cincinnati OH 45241-3255 Office: PNC Center 201 E Main St Ste 800 Cincinnati OH 45202 Office Phone: 513-381-0656. Business E-Mail: jkelley@kohnenpatton.com.

KELLEY, JOHN PAUL, communications consultant; b. Columbus, Ohio, May 12, 1919; s. John Adrian and Josephine (Nash) K.; m. Dorothy Rose Peters, July 31, 1942; children: John M., Ann P., Daniel O., Peter D. BS in Journalism, Ohio State U., 1941; MBA, Harvard U., 1946. Mgr. sales promotion Seiberling Rubber Co., Akron, Ohio, 1946-48; account supr. Batten, Barton, Durstine & Osborn, Cleve., 1948-51; mgr. consumer advt. Monsanto Chem. Co., St. Louis, 1951-54; pres. Mumm, Mullay & Nichols, Advt. Agy., Columbus, 1954-59; v.p. Goodyear Tire and Rubber Co., Akron, 1959-84; communications consultant, 1984—. Lt. AUS, 1943-46. Mem. Assn. Nat. Advertisers (past chmn.), Advt. Coun. (past chmn. bd. dirs.). Republican. Roman Catholic. Home: 76240 Fairway Dr Indian Wells CA 92210-8822 E-mail: jpk240@msn.com.

KELLEY, JOHN TIMOTHY, lawyer, animal breeder; b. Tex., June 9, 1963; JD, Tex. Tech U., 1988. Bar: Tex. 1988. Prin. J.T. Kelley, P.C., Lubbock, Tex., 1995—. Office: JT Kelley PC 3823 84th Street Lubbock TX 79423 Office Phone: 806-783-0544.

KELLEY, JOSEPH E., career officer; BS, USAF Acad., 1974; MD, Rush U., 1977; student, Sch. Aerospace Medicine, Brooks AFB, Tex., 1984, Air Command and Staff Coll., 1986, Air War Coll., 1988, George Washington U., 1992; physician in mgmt. I, ACP Execs., Sheppard AFB, Tex., 1992, physician in mgmt. II, 1994, physician in mgmt. III, 1997. Diplomate Am. Bd. Surgery. Commd. capt. USAF, 1977, advanced through grades to brig. gen., 1997; intern then resident in gen. surgery David Grant Med. Ctr., Travis AFB, Calif., 1977-82; gen. surgeon then chief surgery Nellis USAF Hosp., Nellis AFB, Nev., 1982-84; chief hosp. svcs. Misawa USAF Hosp., Misawa Air Base, Japan, 1984-86; comdr. 90th Strategic Hosp., Francis E. Warren AFB, Wyo., 1986-89, 857th Strategic Hosp., Minot AFB, N.D., 1989-91, Fifth Med. Group, Minot AFB, 1991-92, Ehrling Bergquist Hosp., Offutt AFB, Nebr., 1992-93; chief med. resources, directorate med. programs/resources Office Air Force Surgeon Gen., Bolling AFB, D.C., 1993-95; command surgeon Pacific Air Forces, Hickam AFB, Hawaii, 1995-96; comdr. 74th Med. Group, Wright-Patterson AFB, Ohio, 1996—; lead agt. Dept. Def. Health Svc. Region 5, Wright-Patterson AFB, Ohio, 1996—. Air Force state faculty mem. course ATLS. Decorated Legion of Merit. Mem. ACP Execs., Soc. Med. Cons. Armed Forces.

KELLEY, KEVIN H., insurance company executive; b. Boston, Oct. 12, 1950; s. Hugh and Anne Kelley; m. Maryellen Moran; children: Meghan, Maura, Katherine. BS/BA, Boston U., 1972. CPCU. Trainee Fireman's Fund, Boston, 1973-75; exec. underwriter Lexington Ins. Co. (AIG), Boston, 1975-78, casualty mgr., 1979-83, exec. v.p., 1984-86, pres., 1987-97, chmn., CEO, 1997—. Roman Catholic.

KELLEY, KITTY, writer; b. Spokane, Wash., Apr. 4, 1942; d. William V. Kelley; m. Michael Peter Edgley (div.); m. Johnathan Zucker. BA in English, Univ. Wash., Seattle, 1964. Employee Wash. Post, 1969—71. Author: The Glamour Spas, 1975, Jackie Oh!, 1978 (NY Times bestseller list), Elizabeth Taylor: The Last Star, 1981 (NY Times bestseller list), His Way: The Unauthorized Biography of Frank Sinatra, 1986 (#1 NY Times bestseller list, record sales made it best selling biography in publishing history), Nancy Reagan: The Unauthorized Biography, 1991 (NY Times bestseller list), The Royals, 1997 (#1 NY Times bestseller list, Publishers Weekly bestseller list), The Family: The Real Story of the Bush Dynasty, 2004 (Publishers Weekly bestseller list). Named one of The Most Famous, FAscinating and Influential Alumni of the Past 100 Years, Univ. Wash., 1999, the 20 Georgetowners of the Century, Georgetowner newspaper; named to Vanity Fair Hall of Fame; recipient Outstanding Author award, Am. Soc. Journalists and authors, Philip M. Stern award for outstanding svc. to writers and the writing profession, Medal of Merit, Lotos Club, NYC. Office: c/o Doubleday Author Mail Random House Inc 1745 Broadway New York NY 10019*

KELLEY, LARRY DALE, retired army officer; b. Geary, Okla., Sept. 1, 1944; s. Cecil and Myrtle Irene (Burch) K.; m. Ellen Neeley; children: Sara M., Rebecca I., Stacey A. BS, Cameron U.; M in Criminal Justice, Okla. City U.; MBA, U. Okla. Enlisted U.S. Army, 1964, advanced through grades to lt. col., 1990, spl. forces officer, capt., 1964-79; ret., 1992. Bd. dirs. Muskogee Fed. Credit Union. V.p. student senate Cameron U., Lawton, pres. student senate; pres. chpt. 32 Spl Forces Assn., chpt. 95 Res. Officers Assn. Decorated Bronze Star, Vietnamese Cross of Gallantry, Combat Infantryman's badge, Parachutist badge. Mem. VFW (life), DAV (life), NRA, Res. Officers Assn. (life), Ret. Officers Assn. (life), Spl. Forces Assn. Avocations: model railroading, genealogy, travel.

KELLEY, MARK ALBERT, physician, educator, health products executive; b. Boston, Oct. 31, 1947; s. Albert Joseph and Virginia Marie Kelley; m. Gail Riggs Kelley, Aug. 4, 1974; children: Christopher Riggs, Amy Morgan. AB, Harvard U., Cambridge, Mass., 1969; MD, Harvard U., Boston, 1973. Diplomate Am. Bd. Internal Medicine, Am. Bd. Pulmonary Disease, Am. Bd. Critical Care. Intern Hosp. U. Pa., Phila., 1973—74, resident, 1974—76, chief med. resident, 1977—78, fellow in pulmonary diseases, 1976—77; dir. pulmonary fellowship U. Pa., Phila., 1979—82, from asst. to assoc. prof. medicine, 1979—92, prof., 1992-2000; dir. pulmonary fellowship tng. program, 1979—82; vice chmn. med. U. Pa. Sch. Medicine, Phila., 1986—90; dir. pulmonary fellowship tng. program, 1979—82; assoc. chmn. clin. svcs., dir. med. residency tng. program, 1982—86; dir. faculty group practice, 1985—90; vice dean clin. affairs U. Pa. Sch. Medicine, Phila., 1990—99; chief of medicine Phla. VA Med. Ctr., 1999—2000; exec. v.p. Henry Ford Health Sys., Detroit, 2000—; CEO Henry Ford Med. Group, Detroit, 2000—; fellow in pulmonary disease Hosp. U. Pa., Phila., 1978—79. Spkr. in field. Mem. editl. bd. Annals Internal Medicine, 1990—93, Critical Care Medicine, 1992—98. Fellow: ACP, Am. Coll. Chest Physicians; mem.: Am. Bd. Med. Specialties, Soc. Critical Care Medicine, Am. Bd. Internal Medicine (critical care medicine test com. 1988—93, chmn. 1990—93, bd. govs. 1990—98, exec. com. 1993—98, sec.-treas. 1994—96, chmn. 1997—98, sec.-treas. found. bd. 1999—2003, chmn. 2003—), Am. Thoracic Soc. (chmn. nat. manpower study 1996—2000, critical care work force project 2001—04), Alpha Omega Alpha. Office: 1 Ford Pl Detroit MI 48202-3450 Office Phone: 313-876-8701. Business E-Mail: mkelley1@hfhs.org.

KELLEY, MARY ELIZABETH (MARY LAGRONE), information technology specialist; b. Temple, Tex., Feb. 12, 1947; d. Harry John and Mary Erma (Windham) LaGrone; m. Roy Earl Kelley, May 10, 1968; children: Roy John, James Lewis, Joanna Marylu. BS, U. Mary Hardin-Baylor, 1968. Cert. tchr. Tex. Math tchr. Killeen HS, Tex., 1977-78; clk. typist Readiness Region VIII, Aurora, Colo., 1979; statis. clk. Fitzsimons Army Med. Ctr., 1980-81, mgmt. asst., 1981-83; clk. typist Corpus Christi Army Depot, Tex., 1984; mgmt. asst. Health Care Studies and Clin. Investigation Act, Fort Sam Houston, 1984-85; computer programmer, analyst Health Care Systems Support Act, 1985-88, computer systems analyst, 1988-92, computer specialist, 1992-94, data base adminstr., 1994-96, Lotus Notes sys. adminstr., 1996-98; process integrator, asst. comdr. force integration US Army Med. Dept. Ctr. and Sch., 1998-99, computer specialist, 1999—2002, info. tech. specialist, 2002—. Tchr. Fitzsimmons Army Med. Ctr., 1978—79; cons., 1978—79. Author: (database) Health Care Management System, 1988—94. Vol. Parents Encouraging Parents, Denver, 1979—83, Friends of Safe House, Denver, 1980—83, Heidi Search Ctr., San Antonio, 1990; vol. family assistance crisis team San Antonio Police Dept., 1997—99, vol. Vols. in Policing, 1998—99; founder Top of Hill Residents' Alliance, San Antonio, 1997. Recipient achievement medal for civilian svc., Dept. Army, 1991. Mem.: DAR, Gold Star Wives, Soc. Mayflower Descs., Daus. Republic of Tex., United Daus of Confederacy Tex., Alpha Phi, Sigma Tau Delta, Delta Psi Theta, Alpha Chi. Roman Catholic. Avocations: reading, needlecrafts, genealogy, Special Olympics, poetry.

KELLEY, MAURICE LESLIE, JR., gastroenterologist, educator; b. Indpls., June 29, 1924; s. Maurice Leslie and Martha (Daniel) K.; m. Carol J. Povec, Feb. 11, 1967; children: Elizabeth Ann, Mary Sarah. Student, U. Vt., Va. Poly. Inst., Princeton U., 1943-45; MD, U. Rochester, 1949. Intern, resident Strong Meml. Hosp., Rochester, N.Y., 1949-51, Bixby fellow in medicine, 1953-56; fellow in gastroenterology Mayo Clinic, Rochester, Minn., 1957-59; asst. prof. medicine U. Rochester, 1959-64, assoc. prof., 1964-67; practice medicine specializing in gastroenterology Rochester, N.Y., 1959-67; assoc. prof. clin. medicine Dartmouth Med. Sch., 1967-74, prof. clin. medicine, 1974-88; chmn. sect. internal medicine Hitchcock Clinic, 1972-74, chmn. sect. gastroenterology, 1974, 88; prof. medicine emeritus Dartmouth Med. Sch., 1988—; mem. staff Strong Meml. Hosp., Hitchcock Clinic, Mary Hitchcock Meml. Hosp. Cons. Canandaigua VA, Rochester Gen., Genesee hosps., VA. Med. Ctr., White River Junction. Contbr. articles to profl. jours., chpts. to books. Served with AUS, 1942-45; M.C. USAF, 1951-53. Fellow ACP (gov. for N.H. 1974-78, Laureate award 1993), Am. Gastroenterol. Assn.; mem. Am. Soc. Gastrointestinal Endoscopy, AMA (chmn. sect. gastroenterology 1970-71), Am. Physiol. Soc., Alpha Omega Alpha. Avocations: sports cars, cinema. Home: 15 Ledge Rd Hanover NH 03755-1612 Office: Dartmouth-Hitchcock Med Ctr 1 Medical Center Dr Lebanon NH 03756-0002 Office Phone: 607-653-3850.

KELLEY, MICHAEL GARHART ROOSEVELT, historian, educator, writer; b. Cambridge, Mass., July 25, 1943; s. John Joseph Kelley and Elisabeth Ann Garhart. BA in History, Boston U., 1966, MA in History, 1967; PhD in Scottish History, U. Edinburgh, 1973. Prof. history, chair history dept. Blackburn Coll., Carlinville, Ill., 1974—85; vis. prof. U. San Francisco, 1983—84, Calif. Poly. State U., San Luis Obispo, Calif., 1987—88; chmn. dept. history Utah State U., Roosevelt/Vernal, 1989—97. Accreditation team mem. North Ctrl. Coll. Assn., Ill., 1978—79; founding assoc. editor The Outlaw Trail Jour., 1991; apptd. nat. grader to grade SAT Am. history exam. Ednl. Testing Svc., 1996—98. Contbr. numerous articles to profl. jours. Charter mem. Outlaw Trail Assn., Utah, 1991; bd. dirs. Macoupin County Mental Health, Carlinville, 1980—85; bd. advisors Am. Biog. Inst., Raleigh, 1994—; dir. Am. Bicentennial, Carlinville, 1976; bd. dirs. 150th Hist. Anniversary, Macoupin County, 1979. Fellow Postgrad. fellow, U. Edinburgh, 1970—72, Midwest Faculty fellow, U. Chgo., 1979, Summer fellow, NEH, 1980. Fellow: Dutch Settlers Soc. of Albany (life), Internat. Biog. Assn. (life), The Augustan Soc. (life); mem.: We. Ill. Hist. Assn. (charter mem.), Scudder Family Assn. (life), Phi Alpha Theta, Phi Beta Kappa. Roman Catholic. Avocations: local and regional history, environmentalist, politics. Home: Apt 111 1008 Larkin St San Francisco CA 94109 Office Phone: 415-567-0579.

KELLEY, MICHAEL JOHN, newspaper editor; b. Kansas City, Mo., July 5, 1942; s. Robert Francis and Grace Lauretta (Schofield) K.; 1 child, Anne Schofield BA, Rockhurst Coll., 1964. Reporter, polit. writer Kansas City Star & Times, 1960-69; asst. Sen. Thomas F. Eagleton, Washington, 1969-76; pres. Swensen's Midwest, Inc., Kansas City, 1976-80; exec. asst. Ctrl. States Pension Fund, Chgo., 1981-83, 85-87; asst. mng. editor Kansas City Times, 1984; editor The Daily Southtown, Chgo., 1987-97; mng. editor Las Vegas (Nev.) Sun, 1997—. Office: Las Vegas Sun 2275 Corporate Cir Henderson NV 89074

KELLEY, PATRICIA HAGELIN, geology educator; b. Cleve., Dec. 8, 1953; d. Daniel Warn and Virginia Louise (Morgan) Hagelin; m. Jonathan Robert Kelley, June 18, 1977; children: Timothy Daniel, Katherine Louise. BA, Coll. of Wooster, 1975; AM, Harvard U., 1977, PhD, 1979. Instr. New Eng. Coll., Henniker, N.H., 1979; asst. prof. U. Miss., University, 1979-85, assoc. prof., 1985-89, acting assoc. vice chancellor acad. affairs, 1988, prof., 1989-92, assoc. dean, 1989-90; program dir. NSF, Washington, 1990-92; prof., chmn. dept. geology U. N.D., Grand Forks, 1992-97; prof. U. NC, Wilmington, 1997—, chmn. dept. earth scis., 1997—2003. Editor several books; contbr. articles to profl. jours. Deacon Bethel Presbyn. Ch., Olive Branch, Miss., 1985-90. Rsch. grantee NSF, 1986-89, 90-99, 2000-03; NSF fellow, 1976-79. Fellow AAAS, Geol. Soc. Am.; mem. Paleontol. Soc. (coun. 1984-85, 95-96, 98-2004, chair S.E. sect. 1984-85, chair N.C. sect. 1995-96, pres.-elect 1998-2000, pres. 2000-02, past pres. 2002-04), Assn. Women Geosci. (Outstanding Educator award 2003), Paleontol. Rsch. Inst. (trustee 2003-, pres. bd. trustees 2004-), Soc. Econ. Paleontologists and Mineralogists, Sigma Xi, Phi Beta Kappa. Presbyterian. Avocations: writing, music, travel. Office: Dept Earth Scis Univ NC Wilmington NC 28403-5944 Office Phone: 910-962-7406. Business E-Mail: kelleyp@uncw.edu.

KELLEY, PATRICK ALAN, neurologist, educator; b. Hinsdale, Ill., Sept. 24, 1947; s. Joseph John and Carol (Obalil) K.; m. Anne Nancy Trifilo, Feb. 22, 1975 (div. Aug. 1979). BA, Knox Coll., 1969; MD, Loyola U., Maywood, Ill., 1973. Diplomate Am. Bd. Psychiatry and Neurology. Resident in neurology Tufts U., Boston, 1974-77; asst. clin. prof. U. Conn., Farmington, 1977-79, U. Tenn., Chattanooga, 1979-88; staff neurologist Group Health Assn., Washington, 1988-94; chmn. dept. neurology Humana Group Health Plan, Washington, 1994-97; asst. clin. prof. George Washington U., Washington, 1988—; staff neurologist Kaiser Permanent, Kensington, Md., 1997—. Neurol. cons., Washington Hosp. Ctr., 1988—, Meml. Hosp., Chattanooga, 1979-88; clin. instr. neurology, Northeastern U., Boston, 1976-77. Author: Clinical Medicine: Selected Problems with Pathophysiologic Correlations, 1988. Candidate for Ho. of Dels., Gen. Assembly of Commonwealth of Va., 1999; mem. Pres.'s club Rep. Nat. Com., Washington, 1996—. Fellow Am. Acad. Neurology; mem. AMA (Physician Recognition award 1998), Am. Epilepsy Soc., Am. Med. EEG Assn., Med. Soc. Va., Phi Beta Kappa. Republican. Roman Catholic. Avocations: collecting original french impressionist prints, collecting editions of thomas jefferson's work. E-mail: PAKIrishmD@aol.com.

KELLEY, PATRICK MICHAEL, minister, state legislator; b. Maryville, Mo., Oct. 27, 1948; s. Gilbert B. and Wilma M. K.; m. Nancy E. Schroeder, July 30, 1976; children: Ryan, Shane, Kristen. BS, William Jewell, 1970; MDiv, St. Paul, 1985. V.p. Kelley-Rickman Construction Col, 1970-72, pres., 1972-75; salesman Sequoia Supply Co., North Kansas City, Mo., 1975-77; owner, pres. Energy Expositions, North Kansas City, 1977-83; pastor United Meth. Chs., Bates County, Mo., 1983-87, Aldersgate United Meth. Ch., Lee's Summit, Mo., 1987-90, Glenwood Park United Meth. Ch., Independence, Mo., 1990—; Rep. caucus chmn. Mo. State Ho. Reps., 1991, 92, minority floor leader, 1993, 94. Chmn. Lee's Summit D.A.R.E. task force; adv. bd. Community Mental Health Svcs., Lee's Summit; bd. dirs. Community Svcs. League, Lee's Summit. Mem. Lee's Summit Rep. Club (treas., pres.). Home: 3924 SW Windsong Dr Lees Summit MO 64082-4051 Office: Mo Ho Reps Capitol Bldg Jefferson City MO 65101 E-mail: pkelley@services.state.mo.us.

KELLEY, PATRICK W., health science association administrator, preventive medicine physician; MD, U. Va.; PhD, Johns Hopkins Sch. of Hygiene and Public Health. Dir. Global Emerging Infections System US Dept. of Defense, Silver Spring, Md.; dir. Preventive Medicine Walter Reed Army Inst. of Research, Silver Spring, Md. Fellow Am. Coll. of Preventive Med.; dir. Bd. on Global Health, IOM. Office: DoD-GEIS Div of Preventive Med Walter Reed Army Inst of Research Silver Spring MD 20910-7500

KELLEY, RICHARD ROY, hotel executive; b. Honolulu, Dec. 28, 1933; s. Roy Cecil and Estelle Louise (Foote) K.; m. Jane Zieber, June 21, 1955 (dec. 1978); children: Elizabeth, Kathryn, Charles, Linda J., Mary Colleen; m. Linda Van Gilder, June 23, 1979; children: Christopher Van Gilder, Anne Marie. BA, Stanford U., 1955; MD, Harvard U., 1960. Pathologist Queen's Med. Ctr., Honolulu, 1962-70, Kapiolani Maternity Hosp., Honolulu, 1961-70; asst. prof. pathology John A. Burns Med. Sch., U. Hawaii, Honolulu, 1968-70; chmn. bd. Outrigger Enterprises, Honolulu. Bd. dirs. First Hawaiian Bank, Outrigger Internat. Travel, Inc. Former trustee, past chmn. Punahou Sch.; dean's adv. bd. Travel Industry Mgmt. Sch., U. Hawaii; former vice-dean Ednl. Inst. AH & MA Pres.'s Acad. Bd. Regents; former chmn. bd. councilors Hawaii Pacific divsn. Am. Cancer Soc., past chmn. commn. on performance stds. State of Hawaii; trustee Kent-Denver Sch., Craig Hosp., Denver, U. Denver, 2003. Named Marketer of Yr., Am. Mktg. Assn., 1985, Communicator of Yr., Internat. Bus. Communicators, 1987, Salesperson of Yr., Sales & Mktg. Execs. Honolulu, 1995; named to Hawaii Bus. Hall of Fame, 1993; recipient Hope award Multiple Sclerosis Soc., 1995, Ihe award Hawaii Army Mus. Soc., 2000, Lifetime Achievement award Nat. Assn. Indsl. and Office Properties, 2003, Legacy in Tourism award U. Hawaii Sch. Travel Industry Mgmt., 2004. Mem.: World Travel and Tourism Coun., World Pres.'s Orgn., Pacific Asia Travel Assn., Japan Hawaii Econ. Coun., Chief Execs. Orgn., Hawaii Visitors Bur. (bd. dirs., chmn. 1991—92). Office: Outrigger Hotels & Resorts 2375 Kuhio Ave Honolulu HI 96815-2992 Office Phone: 808-921-6610. E-mail: richard.kelley@outrigger.com.

KELLEY, ROBERT OTIS, medical educator, anatomist; b. Santa Monica, Calif., Apr. 30, 1944; s. David Otis and Onetia May (Nettles) K.; m. Marcia Jean Bell; children: Jennifer Leigh, Karin Michelle, Matthew Philip, Sarah Ann. BS, Abilene Christian U., 1965; MA, U. Calif., Berkeley, 1966, PhD, 1969. Asst. prof. U. N.Mex. Sch. of Medicine, Albuquerque, 1969-74, assoc. prof., 1974-79, prof., 1979—; chmn. dept. anatomy U. N.Mex. Sch. Medicine, Albuquerque, 1981-97; assoc. vice chancellor rsch., exec. dean grad. coll. U. Ill., Chgo., 1997-99; dean Coll. Health Scis., U. Wyo., 1999—. Vis. scientist Okazaki (Japan) Nat. Labs., 1984-85; mem. study sect. NIH, Bethesda, Md., 1982-86, U.S. Med. Licensing Exam. Step 1, 1995—; anatomy com. Nat. Bd. mex. Examiners, Phila., 1992—. Author: Basic Histology, 1989; editor Cell and Tissue Rsch., 1970—, Anat. Record, 1970-97; contbr. articles to profl. jours. Patroller Nat. Ski Patrol, 1970—. Recipient Rsch. Career Devel. award NIH, 1972-77, Kaiser award U. Calif., Irvine, 1976; Internat. Exch. Scholar NSF; NIH grantee, 1970— Mem. Fedn. Am. Socs. for Exptl. Biology (pub. affairs exec. com. 1993—), Am. Soc. Cell Biology, Soc. for Devel. Biology, Electron Microscopy Soc. Am. (bd. dirs. 1987—), Am. Assn. Anatomists (exec. com. 1988—), Assn. Am. Med. Colls. (exec. coun. 1995—, chair assembly 1997-99), Nat. Caucus of Basic Biomed. Sci. Chairs, Nat. Bd. Med. Examiners. Democrat. Avocations: sailing, skiing, soaring, scuba diving, backpacking. Address: 1162 Granito Dr Laramie WY 82072-5027 Office: U Wyo PO Box 3432 Laramie WY 82071-3432

KELLEY, ROBERT PAUL, JR., management consultation executive; b. Mansfield, Ohio, Mar. 27, 1942; s. Robert Paul and Rachel Marie Kelley; m. Mimi Grant, June 15, 1975; children: Robert, Laura, Elizabeth. BBA, Notre Dame U., 1964; MBA, Harvard U., 1969. Corp. devel. exec. Holly Sugar Corp., 1969-70; mktg. cons., supr. Laventhol & Horwath, L.A., 1972-73; dir. mktg., entertainment and mdsg. Knott's Berry Farm, Buena Park, Calif., 1974-76; sr. v.p. mktg. Am. Warranty Corp., L.A., 1978-80; co-founder Gen. Group of Cos., 1981; CEO Strategy Network Corp., 1976—. CEO So. Calif. Tech. Exec. Network, 1985—; co-founder, CEO ABL Health Care Exec. Network, 1989-91; chmn. bd. Micro Frame Tech., Inc., 1990-95, chmn. emeritus, 1995-2000; chmn. bd. ABL Orgn., 1991—; chmn., CEO Quickstart Tech., 1993-94; chmn, bd. V-Systems, Inc., 1994-99; mem. adv. bd. Westec Security Group, 1996-99; mem. adv. bd. Impac Tech., Inc., 1998-99; chmn. bd. dir. Upstanding Sys., Inc., 1999-2003; chmn. bd. dir. China Mfg. Network, 2003. Author: The Board of Directors and its Role in Growing Companies, 1984, Break-Through Boards of Directors, 1999; co-author: Better Than Money Resource Capitalism, 1993. Served with USNR, 1964-67. Home: 6004 E West View Dr Orange CA 92869-4314 Office: 930 W Town and Country Rd Orange CA 92868-4714

KELLEY, ROBERT SUMA, network engineer; b. Chgo., July 2, 1961; s. Jerry Dean and Jean (Laine) K.; m. Melissa Ann Beacham, Aug. 15, 1999. BA in Philosophy, Western Md. Coll., 1985; MBA in MIS, Ind. U., 1989. Human resource specialist Marriott Corp., Gaithersburg, Md., 1985-86; mgr. in tng. Courtyard by Marriott, Fairfax, Va., 1986-87; sys. analyst Hewlett-Packard, Palo Alto, Calif., 1989-98, network engr. Sunnyvale, Calif., 1998—. Mem. adv. com. for implementation of Calif. Assembly bill for improving edn. opportunities for learning disabled children, 1991-94. Counselor Camp Allen for the Physically Handicapped, Manchester, N.H., 1977; track coach for disadvantaged youth Rockville (Md.) Recreation, 1980. Avocation: endurance horseback riding. Office: Agilent Techs 5301 Stevens Creek Blvd Santa Clara CA 95051-7201 Mailing: 8 Camellia Ct East Palo Alto CA 94303

KELLEY, SCOTT CHARLES, academic administrator; b. Loma Linda, Calif., May 26, 1958; s. Charles Brenton and Marjorie (Taylor) K.; m. Nancy Elizabeth Serage, Aug. 22, 1981; children: Taylor, Brent, Sarah, Emily, Paul, Kent, Mary, Adam. BS in Econs., Brigham Young U., 1981; MBA in Fin., Okla. City U., 1986; EdM in higher Edn., Harvard U., 1988, EdD in higher Edn., 1995. Supr. receivables Hertz Corp., Oklahoma City, 1982-83, asst. mgr. treasury ops., 1983-85, acct. mgr., 1985-87; mng. auditor Harvard U., Cambridge, Mass., 1989-90; controller The U. Toledo, Toledo, 1990-92, asst. v.p. bus. affairs, 1992-93, assoc. v.p. fin. affairs, 1993-95; v.p. for adminstrn. and fin. W.Va. U., Morgantown, 1995—2004; exec. vice chancellor for bus. affairs U. Tex. System, Austin, Tex., 2004—. Vice chair audit com. Cen. Assn. College & Univs. Bus. Officers, 1993-95; adj. instr. Fitchburg State Coll., Fitchburg, Mass., 1989-90. Bishop Ch. of Jesus Christ of LDS, Bowling Green, Ohio, 1992-95, Morgantown, W.Va., 1999-2004; cmty. svcs. com. mem. Lucas County Mental Health Bd., Toledo, 1991-93; missionary Ch. of Jesus Christ of Latter Day Saints, Cen. Am., 1977-79. Mem. Morgantown C. of C. (bd. dirs.). Republican. Office: U Tex Sys 201 W 7th St Austin TX 78701-2982 Office Phone: 512-499-4560.

KELLEY, SHANA O., biochemist; BS in chemistry, Seton Hall U., 1992; PhD in chemistry, Calif. Inst. Tech., 1999; postdoctoral rsch., Scripps Rsch. Inst., 1999—2000. Asst. prof. dept. chemistry Boston Coll., 2000—. Founding scientist and cons. GeneOhm Scis., La Jolla, Calif., 2001—. Contbr. articles to profl. jour. Named one of Top 100 Young Innovators, MIT Tech. Review, 2004; recipient NSF Career award, 2004; Alfred P. Sloan fellowship, 2004. Office: Merkert Chemistry Ctr 140 Commonwealth Ave Chestnut Hill MA 02467 Business E-Mail: shana.kelley@bc.edu.

KELLEY, SHEILA SEYMOUR, public relations consultant; b. Bronxville, NY; d. William Joseph and Jane (Seymour) K.; m. Robert Max Kaufman, 1959. BA magna cum laude, Syracuse U., 1949. Reporter Yonkers Herald Statesman, N.Y.C., 1950; reporter, editor Close Up column Herald Tribune, N.Y.C., 1950-53; writer, prodr. Sta. WNBC-TV, N.Y.C., 1953-54, asst. to Alfred Gwynne Vanderbilt, 1955; media cons. to Senator Jacobs K. Javits, N.Y.C., 1956-74, press sec. Washington, 1958-61; account supr., v.p. Harshe Rotman Druck, N.Y.C., 1961-76; founder, pres. VOTES, Inc., N.Y.C., 1973-75; v.p. Doremus Pub. Rels., N.Y.C., 1976-86, sr. v.p., 1987-90, exec. v.p., 1990, Gavin Anderson & Co., N.Y.C., 1990-96, sr. counselor, 1996-97; prin. The Dilenschneider Group, N.Y.C., 1997—. Mem.: Women Execs. in Pub. Rels. (pres. 1987—88, dir. found. 1999—, bd. dirs. 2003), Pub. Rels. Soc. Am. (accredited), Hon. Order Ky. Cols., Phi Beta Kappa. Republican. Avocations: skiing, golf, gardening. Office Phone: 212-922-0900. Business E-Mail: skelley@dgi-nyc.com.

KELLEY, STEPHEN MICHAEL, bank executive; s. Charles Francis and Dawn Priscilla Kelley; m. Susan Strong, Aug. 16, 1980; children: Harty Tilton, Benjamin James. BS, SUNY, Geneseo, 1978; MBA, St. John Fisher Coll., Rochester, N.Y., 1988; JD, SUNY, Buffalo, 1998. Adj. instr. Monroe C.C., Rochester, NY, 1988—94; gen. counsel Rulison & Co., Rochester, NY, 1998—2001; v.p. Fleet Nat. Bank, Rochester, NY, 2001—04, Bank of Am., Rochester, NY, 2004—. With U.S. Army, 1972—75. Recipient William E. McKnight Vol. Svc. award, Vol. Legal Svcs. Project, 2003. Mem.: ABA, D.C. Bar Assn., NY State Bar Assn. (assoc.), SUNY Geneseo Alumni Assn. (bd. dirs. 1989—2004, Meritorius Svc. award 2002), Hunt Hollow Ski Club (bd. dirs. 2000—04), Genesee Valley Club (bd. govs. 2003—04). Avocations: tennis, skiing, fox hunting, travel. Home: 371 Allens Creek Rd Rochester NY 14618 Office: Bank of Am One East Ave Rochester NY 14638 Office Phone: 585-546-9557. Office Fax: 585-546-9560. Business E-Mail: stephen.m.kelley@bankofamerica.com.

KELLEY, SYLVIA JOHNSON, financial services firm executive; b. Butte, Mont., Dec. 29, 1929; d. John O. and Hilja W. (Koski) J.; m. Dan H. Kelley, June 1, 1950 (div. Jan. 1973); children: David D., Bruce J., Sheila K. Miller, Kathleen Kelley; m. Richard T. Marshall, June 10, 1979. CLU; ChFC; cert. fin. planner; registered fin. cons.; cert. sr. advisor. Legal sec. various law firms, L.A., 1959-69; registered rep. Met. Life, N.Y.C., 1969-75, SMA Equities, Inc., Worcester, Mass., 1975-89, Multi-Fin. Securities Corp., Denver, 1989—2003; CEO Advance Funding, Inc., El Paso, Tex., 1981—; registered rep. Geneos Wealth Mgmt. Co., Denver, 2003—. Contbr. articles to profl. jours. Bd. dirs., chmn. bus. adv. com. Marina Del Rey C. of C., 1974-75; bd. dirs., pub. rels. chmn. Am. Heart Assn., El Paso, 1972-74; charter pres. El Paso Exec. Women's Coun., 1972-73; mem. fin. adv. com. El Paso C.C., 1992-95; bd. dirs., past pres. El Paso Estate Planning Coun., 1993-2001. Mem. Am. Soc. CLUs and ChFC (past pres. El Paso chpt., bd. dirs. 1981-85), Registry of CFP Practitioners (cert. sr. advisor). Avocations: contract bridge, ballroom dancing, international travel, photography. Office: Advance Funding Inc 5959 Gateway Blvd W Ste 250 El Paso TX 79925-3316 Office Phone: 915-772-2277.

KELLEY, WENDY THUE, fine art advisor, independent curator; b. Santa Monica, Calif., July 4, 1941; d. Horace Wendel and Marjory (Simmons) Thue; children: David Byron Jr., Christopher S., Jennifer M. AA, Stephens Coll., 1960; BA, Phillips U., 1963; postgrad., NYU, 1996, Instituto Allende, San Miguel de Allende, 1993. Cert. tchr., Conn. Prin., owner Wendy Kelley Art Advisor, Old Greenwich, 1985—. Curator exhbns. U. So. Calif. Inst. Genetic Medicine Gallery, LCOR Devels., Home Box Office/Time Warner, N.Y.C., 1990-2002, Hines, Inc.; cons. curator Discovery Mus., Bridgeport, Conn.; cons. Aetna, Cornell Med. Ctr., Time-Warner, Apple Computer, Marriott Corp. Bd. dirs. YMCA, 1987-93 Mem. Nat. Assn. Profl. Art Advisors, N.E. Appraisers Assn., Kappa Alpha Theta. Avocations: printmaking, photography, travel, books. Home: 3132 6th St Santa Monica CA 90405 Office Phone: 310-450-2424. Personal E-mail: wtko@mindspring.com.

KELLEY, WILLIAM NIMMONS, physician, educator, science administrator, dean; b. Atlanta, June 23, 1939; s. Oscar Lee and Willa Nimmons (Allen) Kelley; m. Lois Faville, Aug. 1, 1959; children: Margaret Paige, Virginia Lynn, Lori Ann, William Mark. MD, Emory U., 1963; MA (hon.), U. Pa., 1989. Diplomate Am. Bd. Internal Medicine (chmn. 1985-1986). Intern in medicine Parkland Meml. Hosp., Dallas, 1963—64, resident, 1964—65; sr. resident medicine Mass. Gen. Hosp., Boston, 1967—68; clin. assoc., sect. on human biochem. genetics NIH, 1965—67; tchg. fellow medicine Harvard U. Med. Sch., 1967—68; asst. prof. to prof. medicine, asst. prof. to assoc. prof. biochemistry, chief divsn. rheumatic and genetic diseases Duke U. Sch. Medicine, 1968—75; Macy faculty scholar Oxford U., 1974—75; prof., chmn. dept. internal medicine, prof. dept. biol. chemistry U. Mich. Med. Sch., Ann Arbor, 1975—89; Robert G. Dunlop prof. medicine, biochemistry and biophysics U. Pa., Phila., 1989—2000, dean Sch. Medicine, 1989—2000; CEO U. Pa. Med. Ctr. and Health Sys., Phila., 1989—2000; prof., 2000—. Human gene therapy subcom. NIH, 1986—92, recombinant DNA com., 1988—92, dirs. adv. com., 1992—95; bd. dirs. Merck & Co., Beckman Coulter, Inc., Advanced Biosurfaces, GenVec, Inc. Author (with J.B. Wyngaarden): Gout and Hyperuricemia, 1976; author: (with I.M. Weiner) Uric Acid, 1979; author: (with Harris, Ruddy and Sledge) Textbook of Rheumatology, 1981, 5th edit., 1997, Arthritis Surgery, 1994; author: (with M. Osterweiss and E.R. Rubin) Emerging Policies for Bio-Medical Research (Health Policy Annual III), 1993; editor-in-chief: Textbook of Internal Medicine, 1989, Textbook of Internal Medicine, 3rd edit., 1997, Essentials of Internal Medicine, 1994; contbr. articles to profl. jours. Trustee Emory U., 1992—, Emory U., Woodruff Health Scis. Ctr. Recipient C.V. Mosby award, 1963, John D. Lane award, USPHS, 1969, Rsch. Career Devel. award, 1972—75, Geigy Internat. prize rheumatology, 1969, Heinz Karger Meml. Found. prize, 1973, Disting. Med. Achievement award, Emory U., 1985, John Phillips Meml. award and medal, ACP, 1990, Nat. Med. Rsch. award, Nat. Health Coun., 1993, Robert H. Williams award, Assn. Profs. of Medicine, 1995, David E. Rogers award, Assn. Am. Med. Coll., 1999, Emory medal, 2000; scholar, Mead Johnson, 1967, Josiah Macy Found., 1974—75; Clin. scholar, Am. Rheumatism Assn., 1969—72. Master: AAAS, ACP, Am. Coll. Rheumatology; fellow: Am. Philos. Soc., Am. Acad. Arts and Scis.; mem.: Assn. Profs. Medicine (sec.-treas. 1987—89), Am. Soc. Internal Medicine, Am. Soc. Human Genetics, Ctrl. Rheumatism Soc. (pres. 1978—79), Australian Rheumatism Assn. (hon.), Royal Coll. Physicians Ireland (hon.), Am. Coll. Rheumatology (editl. bd. 1972—77, pres. 1986—87, Gold Medal award 1997), Assn. Am. Physicians (Kober medal 2005), Am. Fedn. Med. Rsch. (pres. 1979—81), Am. Soc. Biochemistry and Molecular Biology (editl. bd. 1976—81), Am. Soc. Clin. Investigation (editl. bd. 1974—79, pres. 1983—84), Inst. Medicine of NAS (chmn. sect. 4 1988—90, chmn. membership com. 1990—94, coun. mem., exec. com. 1996—2001), Ctrl. Soc. for Clin. Rsch. (pres. 1986—87), Alpha Omega Alpha, Sigma Xi. Home: 203 Elgin Ct Wayne PA 19087 Office: Univ Pa Health Sys 757 Biomed Rsch Bldg II/III Philadelphia PA 19104 Office Phone: 215-573-9953. E-mail: kelleywn@hotmail.com.

KELLEY, ZELDA MARY, small business owner, writer; b. Camden, N.J., 1953; d. Anthony James and Jean Helen (Kelley) Waldron; m. Ray Grabinski, June 18, 2002; m. Nick Medosch (div.); 1 child, Chloe. BA, Tulane U., 1979; JD, We. State U., 1981. Asst. editor Gazette Newspapers, Long Beach, Calif., 1987—2002; pres., CEO e m Enterprises, Long Beach, 1990—; city editor Long Beach (Calif.) Bus. Jour., 1992—2002. Bd. dirs. Elizabeth George Found., Huntington Beach, Calif. Author: Coaxing Sculpture, 2003, Autoerotica, 2005; contbr. columns in newspapers. Scholar, Elizabeth George Found., 1999. Avocations: painting, sculpting.

KELLEY-HALL, MARYON HOYLE, retired social worker; b. Anderson, Ind., Aug. 5, 1924; d. Arthur Dent and Mildred Madeline (Hall) Hoyle; m. Dean M. Kelley, June 8, 1946; 1 child, Lenore Wadsworth Hervey; m. Richard A. Hall, Oct. 14, 2000. AB, U. Denver, 1945; MSW, Columbia U., 1967. Psychiat. social worker Rockland State Hosp., Orangeburg, N.Y., 1963-67, psychiat. social work supr., 1967-70; dir. social svcs. Rockland Children's Psychiat. Ctr., Orangeburg, 1970—72, chief child care svc., 1972—73; chief children's habilitation svc. Suffolk Devel. Ctr., Melville, NY, 1974—79; med. social worker Suffolk County Health Svcs., Hauppauge, NY, 1983-89; med. social work supr. Brentwood (N.Y.) Family Health Ctr., 1990—93. Home: 800 S 15th St # I-869 Sebring OH 44672

KELLING, SHERRY LEE, music educator, interior designer, educator; d. Reed LaMar and Marjorie Nadine Whitaker; m. Rodney Dale Kelling, June 11, 1983; children: Kristopher Reed, Kyrie Grace, Deborah Lila. AAS, postgrad., Ricks Coll., Rexburg, Idaho, 1982. Sales, interior desgin Ho. of Decor, Hugoton, Kans., 1982—84; interior design instr. Seward County C.C., Liberal, Kans., 1984—; pvt. practice piano tchr. Hugoton, 1975—; accompanist Rolla H.S., Rolla, Kans., 1993—. Pres. PTA, Hugoton, 1995—96. Conservative. Mem. Lds Ch. Avocations: swimming, horses, crafts. Home: 206 S Van Buren Hugoton KS 67951 Office: Sherry Kelling Studio 206 S Van Buren Hugoton KS 67951 Office Phone: 620-544-1857. Personal E-mail: rkelling@pld.com. E-mail: slkelling@hotmail.com.

KELLISON, JAMES BRUCE, lawyer; b. Richmond, Va., June 18, 1922; s. John Ray and Clara (Cato) K.; m. Audrey Cresswell, May 5, 1962; children: Bruce, Jr., Elizabeth, Julia. BA, U. Richmond, 1943; JD, George Washington U., 1948. Bar: D.C. 1948. Ptnr. Hogan & Hartson, Washington, 1954-73, Altmann Kellison & Siegler, Washington, 1973-83; pvt. practice Washington, 1983—. Mem. adv. com. on rules of probate procedure Superior Ct., 1972-94. Pres., bd. trustees Louise Home, 1971—; trustee, Columbia Lighthouse for the Blind, 1969-76; trustee Audubon Naturalist Soc., 1968-71. Served with USNR, 1943-45. Fellow Am. Coll. Trust and Estate Counsel; mem. Am., D.C. bar assns., Omicron Delta Kappa, Lambda Chi Alpha, Phi Delta Phi. Clubs: Metropolitan (Washington), Barristers (Washington), St. Albans Tennis (Washington); Chevy Chase (Md.); Lawyers (Washington). Republican. Home: 2801 New Mexico Ave NW Apt 1409 Washington DC 20007-3914 Office: 910 17th St NW Washington DC 20006-2601

KELLISON, STEPHEN GEORGE, actuarial consultant; b. Ord, Nebr., Mar. 20, 1942; s. Orin Albian and Sarah Viola (Crouch) K.; m. Chery Le Wagner, June 14, 1963 (div. Jan. 1970); m. Erica Elizabeth Bowers, Jan. 27, 1978 (div. June 1985); m. Maureen Antoinette Gage, Nov. 15, 1986. AB, U. Nebr., Lincoln, 1963, MS, 1967. CFP. Actuarial supr. Occidental Life Ins. Co., L.A., 1963-65; actuary Lincoln Liberty Life Ins. Co., Lincoln, Nebr., 1965-66; prof. U. Nebr., 1966-75; consulting actuary G.V. Stennes & Assocs., Dallas, 1975-76; exec. dir. Am. Acad. Actuaries, Washington, 1976-88; chmn. Dept. Risk Mgmt. and Ins. Ga. State U., Atlanta, 1989-93; sr. v.p. instnl. svcs. Am. Gen. Retirement Svcs., Houston, 1994—2001. Mem. tech. panel Social Security Adv. Bd., 2003—04; chmn. tech. panel Social Security Adv. Coun., 1989—91; pub. trustee Social Security and Medicare, 1995—2000; mem. task force on interest methods Fin. Acctg. Stds. Bd., 1989—95; sec. Actuarial Edn. and Rsch. Fund, 1989—92. Author: The Theory of Interest, 1970, 2d edit., 1991, Fundamentals of Numerical Analysis, 1975. Fellow Soc. Actuaries (bd. dirs. 1973-75, 90-93, v.p. 1999-2001, pres. 2003-05); mem. Nat. Acad. Social Ins., Am. Acad. Actuaries (bd. dirs. 1975-76), Internat. Actuarial Assn., Phi Beta Kappa. Home and Office: 9301 Wickham Way Orlando FL 32836-5518 Office Phone: 407-909-0853. Personal E-mail: sgkellison@aol.com.

KELLMAN, SANDRA Y., lawyer; b. Mar. 21, 1952; BA with high honors, Univ. Ill., Urbana-Champaign, 1973; JD cum laude, Northwestern Univ., 1977. Bar: Ill. 1977. Ptnr. co-chmn. Lodging & Timeshare practice group DLA Piper Rudnick Gray Cary, Chgo. Editor (note & comment): Jour. of Criminal Law & Criminology; contbr. articles to profl. jours. Office: DLA Piper Rudnick Gray Cary Suite 1900 203 N LaSalle St Chicago IL 60601-1293 Office Phone: 312-368-4082. Office Fax: 312-236-7516. Business E-Mail: sandra.kellman@dlapiper.com.

KELLMAN, STEVEN G., literature educator, author; b. Bklyn., Nov. 15, 1947; s. Max and Pearl (Pomerantz) K. BA, SUNY, Binghamton, 1967; MA, U. Calif., Berkeley, 1969, PhD, 1972. Asst. prof. Bemidji (Minn.) State U., 1972-73; lectr. Tel-Aviv U., 1973-75; visiting lectr. U. Calif., Irvine, 1975-76, visiting assoc. prof. Berkeley, 1982; Fulbright sr. lectr. Tbilisi State U., Soviet Georgia, USSR, 1980; asst. prof. U. Tex., San Antonio, 1976-80, assoc. prof., 1980-85, prof. comparative lit., 1985—, Ashbel Smith prof., 1995-2000; Fulbright Disting. chair in Am. Lit., U. Sofia, 2000. Columnist, critic The San Antonio Light, 1983-93; fiction critic Gettysburg Rev., 1991-93; editor lit. scene USA Today mag., Valley Stream, N.Y., 1985—; film critic San Antonio Current, 1986-89, 98—, The Tex. Observer, 1989—; NEH seminar, U. Natal, South Africa, 1996. Author: The Self-Begetting Novel, 1980, Loving Reading: Erotics of the Text, 1985, The Modern American Novel, 1991, The Plague: Fiction and Resistance, 1993, Perspectives on Raging Bull, 1994, The Translingual Imagination, 2000, Redemption: The Life of Henry Roth, 2005; editor: Approaches to Teaching Camus's The Plague, 1985, (lit. mag.) Occident, 1969-70, Switching Languages: Translingual Writers Reflect on their Craft, 2003, Redemption: The Life of Henry Roth, 2005; co-editor: Into the Tunnel, 1998, Leslie Fiedler and American Culture, 1999, Torpid Smoke: Vladimir Nabokov's Short Fiction, 2000, The Translingual Imagination, 2000, Magill's Literary Annual, 2000—, UnderWords: Perspectives on Don DeLillo's Underworld, 2002. Pres. bd. dirs. Gemini Ink. 1998-2002, bd. editors Jewish Jour. San Antonio, 1987—, chmn., 1991-95; bd. dirs. Nat. Book Critics Circle, 1996-2002; adv. humanities Inter-Am. Book Fair, San Antonio, 1987-94; adv., judge Tex. Film Festival, San Antonio, 1986-87, Cine Festival, San Antonio, 1985-90; v.p., bd. dirs. Tex. Humanities Resource Ctr., 1991-92; del. Dem. Nat. Conv., 1992. Recipient H.L. Mencken award The Baltimore Sun, 1986, Fulbright Lectureship to USSR U.S. Govt., 1980, lectureship to Peru Ptnrs. of the Ams., Washington, 1988, 95, Fulbright Disting. professorship, Bulgaria, 2000; Fulbright grantee People's Republic of China, 1995; Sawyer fellow Harvard U., 1997. Mem. MLA, Nat. Book Critics Circle (bd. dirs. 1996—), PEN Am. Ctr., Tex. Inst. Letters Home: 302 Fawn Dr San Antonio TX 78231-1519 Office: U Tex Dept Modern Langs and Lits San Antonio TX 78249 Office Phone: 210-458-5216.

KELLNER, GEORGE, financial analyst; b. Budapest, Hungary, Nov. 28, 1942; came to U.S., 1947; s. Paul J. and Clara Elizabeth Kellner; m. Martha Bicknell, July 22, 1967; children: Peter B., Catherine S. BA, Trinity Coll., 1964; JD, Columbia U., 1967, MBA, 1973. Cert. fin. analyst. Assoc. Carter, Leelyard & Milburn, N.Y.C., 1967-70; v.p. Madison Fund, N.Y.C., 1970-75; ptnr. I. Boesky & Co., N.Y.C., 1975-77; sr. v.p. Donaldson, Lulkins & Jennette, N.Y.C., 1977-81; mng. ptnr. Kellner Dileo & Co., N.Y.C., 1981—. Chmn. bd. dirs. Childtime Children's Ctr., Farmington, Mich., KD Equities. Bd. dirs. Phoenix House, N.Y.C., 1992—; trustee Milton (Mass.) Acad., 1988-, Trinity Coll., Hartford, Conn., 1989—, Bard Coll., Annandale-on-Hudson, 1999—; bd. overseers Leonard Stern Sch. Bus., N.Y.C., 1995—. Mem. Univ. Club, Union Club, Maidstone Club. Avocations: skiing, tennis, mountain climbing, travel, squash. Office: 900 3d Ave New York NY 10022

KELLNER, IRWIN L., economist; b. N.Y.C., Oct. 4, 1938; s. Phillip and Mildred (Isaacson) Kellner; m. Ann Heiman, Jan. 22, 1961; children: Lori, Shari. BA in Econs., Bklyn. Coll., 1960, MA in Econs., 1964; PhD in Econs., New Sch. for Social Rsch., 1973; LHD (hon.), Hofstra U.; LLD (hon.), St. Joseph's Coll. Asst. bus. outlook editor Bus. Week Mag., prior to 1960, 1966-70; rsch. analyst Philip Morris, Inc., 1960-63; sr. rsch. analyst William Esty Co., Inc., 1963-66; assoc. economist Mfrs. Hanover Trust Co., N.Y.C., 1970-72, v.p., 1972-78, dep. chief economist, 1973-78, sr. v.p., 1978—; chief economist The Chase Regional Bank, N.Y.C., 1980-97; Augustus B. Weller Disting. Chair of Econs. Hofstra U., Hempstead, N.Y., 1997—. Chief economist CBS MarketWatch, 1997—, Northfork Bancorp.; adj. full prof. sch. bus. Adelphi U., 1983—91; adj. vis. lectr. colls.; spkr. bus. and cmty. groups; bd. dirs. Internat. Bioimmune Sys., Universal Heights, Claire's Stores, Inc. Author: Econ. Report/Hofstra U.; weekly guest News 12 L.I., Cablevision, CBS Radio and TV; contbr. articles and commentaries to profl. publs. Mem. village planning bd. Port Washington, N.Y., 1972—; commr. Hist. Landmarks, Village of Port Washington North, 1971-74; former bd. dirs. Juv. Diabetes Found., 1986-92, N.Y. Inst. Tech., sch. bus. Adelphi U.; bd. dirs. Children's AIDS Network, 1986—, Don Monti Found., 1992—; assoc. trustee North Shore U. Hosp., 1992—; chmn. adv. bd. Barry Z. Levine Sch. of Health Scis., Touro Coll., 1991—; mem. L.I. Regional Transp. adv. com. N.Y. State Senate Com. on Transp., 1988—; mem. N.Y. Dist. Adv. Coun. of Sml. Bus. Adminstrn. Region II; mem. N.Y. State Comptroller's Econ. Adv. Com., 1995—; past mem. N.Y.C. Economist's Roundtable, 1991-93; mem. numerous pro bono bds. including North Shore Univ. Hosp., Don Monti Meml. Rsch. Found., Epilepsy Found. of L.I., Nassau County Coun. of Boy Scouts of Am.; mem. adv. bd. C.W. Post's Coll. of Mgmt., 1997; numerous other civic activities. Recipient award for tobacco econs. Tobacco Mchts. Assn., 1978; named Number One Prognosticator, Instl. Investor mag., Most Accurate Forecaster (twice), Bus. Week mag., one of Top 5 Interest Rate Forecasters, Wall St. Jour.; recipient Disting. Leadership award for health edn., Barry Z. Levine Sch., Human Rels. award Am. Jewish Com., Humanitarian award Juv. Diabetes Found., Gary Sherman Humanitarian award North Shore Health System. Mem. Conf. Bd. (mem. Econ. Forum), Forecasters Club N.Y. (past pres.), Money Marketeers (past gov.), N.Y. Assn. Bus. Economists (past pres.), Am. Econ. Assn., Am. Statis. Assn., Bus. Economists Council, Downtown Economists Luncheon Group, Nat. Assn. Bus. Economists, N.Y. Acad. Scis., Met. Econ. Assn., Am. Bankers Assn. (adv. com.). Achievements include the innovation of the Mfrs. Hanover (now Chase) Trade-Weighted Dollar and the Mfrs. Hanover (now Chase) Cost-of-Living Index.

KELLNER, JAMIE, broadcast executive; With CBS, 1969; former v.p. first-run programming, devel., sales Viacom Enterprises; pres. Orion Entertainment Group, 1979—86; pres., CEO Fox Broadcasting Co., L.A., 1986—93; CEO, pres. WBTV Network, Burbank, Calif. Office: WBTV Network 4000 Warner Blvd Bldg 34R Burbank CA 91522-0001

KELLNER, LAWRENCE W. (LARRY KELLNER), air and aerospace transportation company executive; m. Susan Kellner; 4 children. BS Bus. Admin. magna cum laude, Univ. SC. CFO, exec. v.p. Am. Savings Bank; CFO, sr. v.p. Continental Airlines, Houston, 1995—96, CFO, exec. v.p., 1996—2001, pres., 2001—04, COO, 2003—04, chmn., CEO, 2004—. Bd. dir. Continental Airlines, Marriot Internat., Belden & Blake Corp., Air Tranp. Assn. Bd. dir. Spring Branch Edn. Found., YMCA Greater Houston Area, Houston Minority Bus. Council, Greater Houston Partnership. Recipient Disting. Alumni award, Univ. SC, 1998. Office: Continental Airlines 1600 Smith St Houston TX 77002*

KELLNER, MARK ALLEN, writer; b. N.Y.C., July 17, 1957; s. Jacques and Arlene Kellner; m. Jean Ann Viechec. Student, Boston U., 1975—77. Editl. dir. Kellner Editl. Svcs., Marina del Rey, Calif., 1998—; editor-in-chief PC Portables Mag./LFP, Inc., Beverly Hills, Calif., 1996—98; sr. editor Govt. Computer News, Silver Spring, Md., 1996; editor, "Report on AT&T" Capitol Pubs., Alexandria, Va., 1988—93; "On Computers" columnist The Washington Times, Washington, 1991—; asst. dir. News & Info., Gen. Conference of Seventh-day Adventists, 2003—. Team mem. USIS Y2K Lecture Team, Nairobi, Kenya, 1999; lectr. World Journalism Inst., L.A., 2002—. Author: WordPerfect 3.5 for Macs For Dummies, 1995, God on the Internet, 1996, Y2K: Apocalypse or Opportunity, 1999; contbr. L.A. Times, 2000-02; editor: Philatelic Communicator, 1995—96. Recipient Cahners Editl. Merit award, Cahners Pub. Inc., 1996, Linn's Lit. award, Linn's Stamp News (Amos Press, Inc.), 1974. Mem.: Am. Philatelic Soc. Avocation: philately. Office: 12501 Old Columbia Pike Room 3K-16 Silver Spring MD 20904-6600 Office Phone: 301-680-6306. Personal E-mail: mark@kellner.us, mkellner98@yahoo.com. Business E-Mail: kellnerm@gc.adventist.org, mkellner@gmail.com.

KELLNER, RICHARD GEORGE, mathematician, computer scientist; b. Cleve, July 10, 1943; s. George Ernst and Wanda Julia (Lapinski) K.; m. Charlene Ann Zajc, June 26, 1965; children: Michael Richard, David George. BS, Case Inst. Tech., 1965; MS, Stanford U., 1968, PhD, 1969. Staff mem. Los Alamos Sci. Lab., N.Mex., 1969—79, Los Alamos Nat. Lab., 1983—88; co-owner, dir. software devel. KMP Computer Systems, Inc., Los Alamos, 1979—84; mgr. spl. projects KMP Computer Systems divsn. 1st Data Resources, Inc., Los Alamos, 1986—87, with microcomputer divsn., 1988. Owner CompuSpeed, 1986—; co-owner Computer-Aided Communications, 1982-84; v.p., COO, bd. dir. Applied Computing Systems Inc., 1988-2003; cons., 1979—; owner Sys. Automation Tech., 2003-4; pres., Autonomous Innovations, Inc., 2004-; CTO Innovative Autonomous Sys., LLC, 2005—. Recipient Commendation award for outstanding support of operation Desert Storm. Mem. IEEE, Assn. Computing Machinery, Math. Assn. Am., Soc. Indsl. and Applied Math., Am. Math. Soc. Home: 8 Lookout Ln Santa Fe NM 87506-8258

KELLOGG, DAVID WAYNE, agricultural studies educator, researcher; b. Seymour, Mo., Aug. 19, 1941; s. Martin David and Lula May (Spurlock) K.; m. Mary Sue Powell, June 7, 1964; children: Kirk David, Susan Joann Franz, Kimberley Annelle Van Vacter, Gregory William. BS, U. Mo., 1963, MS, 1964; PhD, U. Nebr., 1968. Profl. animal scientist. Asst. prof. agriculture N.Mex. State U., Las Cruces, 1967-71, assoc. prof., 1971-78, prof., 1978-81; prof., dept. head U. Ark., Fayetteville, 1981-86, prof., 1986—. Cons. AID-N.Mex. State U. Mission, Asuncion, Paraguay, 1971; spkr. Ark. Farm Bur., Little Rock, 1981-90, ORFFA Seminar, Rennes, France, 1995, Breda, Holland, 1996, San Jose, Costa Rica, 1999; Brenen and Leipsig, Germany, 2002, Bergano and Piedmont, Italy, 2002, Santa Cruz, Bolivia, 2002, 04, Belo Horizonte, Brazil, 2004. mem. adv. com Ark. Livestock and Poultry Commn., 1989-94; reviewer rsch. proposals USDA, Small Bus. Innovation. Mem. editl. bd.: Jour. Dairy Sci., 1978—84, nutrition sect. editor:, 2000—05; contbr. chapters to books, articles to profl. jour. Mem. Fellowship Bible Ch. Mem.: Ark. Nutrition Coun., Ark. Registry Profl. Animal Scientists (sec., treas. 1989—93, charter), So. Assn. Agrl. Sci. (bd. dir. 1993—94), Am. Grassland and Forage Coun., Am. Soc. Animal Sci. (awards com. 1990—92, spkr. symposium on chelated trace minerals 1996), Am. Dairy Sci. Assn. (sec. so. sect. 1991, v.p. 1992, pres. 1993, awards com. 1996—98, spkr. symposium on highest producing dairy herds 2000), Am. Registry Profl. Animal Sci. (bd. dir. 1989—91, pres.-elect 1993—94, pres. 1994—95, nominating com. 1996—98), Rotary Internat., Gideons Internat. (trustee 1975—81), Gamma Sigma Delta. Office: U Ark Dept Animal Sci Fayetteville AR 72701 Business E-Mail: wkellogg@uark.edu.

KELLOGG, FREDERIC RICHARD, religious studies educator; b. San Angelo, Tex., Dec. 16, 1939; s. John Franklin III and Naomi Lucille (Cory) K.; m. Jeannette Villeret Boykin, June 1, 1963; children: Christopher, Mark. BS summa cum laude, La. Tech. U., 1962; ThM with honors, So. Meth. U., 1965; postgrad., U. Goettingen, 1965-66; PhD, Yale U., 1972. Ordained to ministry Meth. Ch., 1969. Asst. prof. religion Emory & Henry Coll., Emory, Va., 1969-75, assoc. prof., 1975-83, Floyd Bunyan Shelton prof., 1984—, acting dean faculty, 1993-94. Mem. Am. Acad. Religion, Soc. Biblical Lit., Mid. East Studies Assn. Democrat. Home: PO Box 24 Emory VA 24327-0024 Office: Emory & Henry Coll Dept Religion PO Box 947 Emory VA 24327 Office Phone: 276-944-6150.

KELLOGG, HERBERT HUMPHREY, metallurgist, educator; b. N.Y.C., Feb. 24, 1920; s. Herbert H. and Gladys (Falding) K.; m. Jeanette Halstead, July 20, 1940; children— Thomas Bartlett, Jane Falding, David Humphrey, Elizabeth Ann. BS, Columbia, 1941, MS, 1943. Asst. prof. mineral preparation Pa. State U., State Coll., 1942-46; faculty Columbia U., N.Y.C., 1946—, Stanley-Thompson prof. chem. metallurgy, 1968-90, prof. emeritus, 1990—. Chmn. titanium adv. com. Office Def. Mblzn., 1954-58 Research; contbr. numerous articles to publs. Recipient Best Paper award extractive metals div. Am. Inst. Mining., Metall. and Petroleum Engrs.; James Douglas Gold medal Am. Inst. Mining, Metall. and Petroleum Engrs., 1973 Fellow AIME (chmn. extractive metallurgy div. 1958), Metall. Soc., Instn. Mining and Metallurgy (London); mem. NAE, Sigma Xi, Tau Beta Pi. Home: Closter Rd Palisades NY 10964

KELLOGG, JOSEPH K., JR., military career officer; b. Dayton, Ohio, May 12, 1944; BA in Polit. Sci., U. Santa Clara; MA in Polit. Sci., U. Kans.; grad., Command and Gen. Staff Coll., US Army War Coll. Advanced through grades to maj. gen. US Army, 1967—96, reconnaissance platoon leader, E Co., 2d Bn. (Airbourne), 506th Inf., 101st Airbourne Divsn., 1967—68, jr. aide-de-Camp to Commdg. Gen., 101st Airbourne Divsn., Vietnam, 1968, pathfinder sect. leader, 160th Combat Avaiation Group, 101st Airbourne Divsn., Vietnam, 1968, exec. officer, Forces Armee Nat. Khmer (Cambodia), army advisory group, Dong Ba Thin Tng. Bn., Vietnam, 1971—72, comdr., spl. forces operational detachment "A", B Co., later S-3 (ops.), 2nd Bn., 10th spl. forces group (Airbourne), 1st spl. forces Fort Devens, Mass., 1972—74, area comdr., US Army Phoenix Dist. Recruiting Command Ariz., 1974—75, ops. staff officer, later chief, ground ops. branch, spl. ops. task force Europe, US European Command, 1976—79, emergency deployment readiness exercises team chiel, XVIII Airbourne Corps, 1979—80, S-3 (Ops.) later exec. officer, 1st brigade, 82d Airbourne Divsn. Fort Bragg, NC, 1980—83, comdr. 1st Bn. (airborne), 504th Inf., 82d Airborne Divsn. Ft. Bragg, NC, 1983-85; ops. officer Office of the Chief of Staff U.S. Army, Washington, 1985-86, G-3 (ops.), 7th Inf. Divsn. (light) Ft. Ord, Calif., 1987-88, comdr. 3d Brigade, 7th Inf. Divsn. (light), 1988-90, chief of staff 82d Airborne Divsn. Saudi Arabia, 1990-91, ops. Desert Shield/Desert Storm Saudia Arabia, 1990—91, asst. divsn. comdr. (ops.) 82d Airborne Divsn. Ft. Bragg, 1991-92; comdr., C Co., 4th Battalion, 2nd Basic Combat Training Brigade US Army Training Ctr., Fort Lewis, Wash., 1968—70; commdg. gen. spl. ops. command Europe U.S. European Command, Germany, 1992-94; asst. dep. chief of staff for combat devel. U.S. Army Tng. and Doctrine Command, Ft. Monroe, Va., 1994-96, dep. chief of staff for combat devel., 1994-96; commdg. gen. 82nd Airborne Divsn. U.S. Army, Ft. Bragg, 1996-98, asst. dep. chief of staff for ops. and plans Washington, 1998—2000; dir., command, control, comm., and computer sys. (J-6) Joint Chiefs of Staff, Washington, 2000—. Decorated Disting. Svc. medal with Oak Leaf Cluster, Silver Star, Legion of Merit with Oak Leaf Clusters; recipient Defense Superior Svc. medal, Bronze Star medal with "V" Device, Bronze Star medal with 3 Oak Leaf Clusters, Defense Meritorious Svc. Medal, Meritorious Svc. medal with Oak Leaf Clusters, Air medal with "V" Device; Air medals, Joint Svc. Commendation medal, Army Commendation medal with 4 Oak Leaf Clusters, Army Achievement medal, Spl. Forces Tab, Combat Infantryman badge, Expert Infantryman badge, Master Parachutist badge, Ranger Tab, Pathfinder badge.

KELLOGG, PAUL, opera company director; b. Hollywood, Calif. BA, U. Tex.; student, Sorbonne, France, U. Nancy, Columbia U.; DFA (hon.), Hartwick Coll., U. Syracuse, Hamilton Coll. Head Lower Sch.; prof., asst. headmaster Allen-Stevenson Sch.; artistic dir. Glimmerglass Opera, Cooperstown, NY, 1979—; gen., artistic dir. N.Y.C. Opera, 1996—. Vice chmn. bd. Opera Am. Chmn. bd. Shen Wei Dance Arts; mem. exec. com. N.Y. State Hist. Assn. Mem.: Nat. Acad. Arts and Scis., OPERA Am. (bd. dirs.). Office: NYC Opera NY State Theater 20 Lincoln Center Plz New York NY 10023-6913

KELLOGG, PETER NEWMAN, biotechnology company executive; b. Bryn Mawr, Pa., Mar. 20, 1956; s. Paul Vincent and Jean (Flynn) K.; m. Carol Anne Curley, Apr. 26, 1986; 1 child, Charlotte. BS in Engring., Princeton U., 1978; MBA, U. Pa., 1982. Sr. cons. Arthur Andersen and Co., Phila., 1978-80; job mgr. Booz Allen and Hamilton, N.Y.C., 1981-87; dir. corp. planning PepsiCo, Inc., Purchase, N.Y., 1987-89, div. fin. dir., Pepsi Cola Internat. Somers, NY, 1989—91, v.p. fin., chief fin. officer, Senior Vice President, Pepsi Cola South to sr. v.p., PepsiCo E-Commerce Dallas, 1991—2000; exec. v.p., CFO Biogen Inc., Cambridge, Mass., 2000—. Mem. Planning Forum, Princeton Club, Merion Golf Club, Cap and Gown Club. Office: Biogen Inc 14 Cambridge Ctr Cambridge MA 02142

KELLOGG, PETER R., securities dealer; b. Sept. 1942; s. James C. Kellogg III; married. Student, Babson Coll., 1963. With Stern Frank Meyer Fox, 1964-67; sr. ptnr. Spear Leeds & Kellogg, N.Y.C., 1967—99; chmn., CEO Spear Leeds & Kellogg Securities Inc. (sold to Goldman Sachs for 5.7 billion in 2000), N.Y.C., 1969—99. Bd. dirs. Nam Tai Electronics, Inc., Ziegler Companies.

KELLOGG, WILLIAM WELCH, meteorologist, researcher; b. New York Mills, NY, Feb. 14, 1917; s. Frederick S. and Elizabeth (Walcott) K.; m. Elizabeth Thorson, Feb. 14, 1942; children: Karl S., Judith K. Liebert, Joseph W., Jane E., Thomas W. BA, Yale U., 1939; MA, UCLA, 1942, PhD, 1949. With Inst. Geophysics UCLA, L.A., 1946-52, asst. prof., 1950-52; scientist Rand Corp., Santa Monica, Calif., 1947-59, head planetary scis. dept., 1959-64; assoc. dir. Nat. Ctr. Atmospheric Research, Boulder, Colo., also dir. lab. atmospheric scis., 1964-73, sr. scientist, 1973-87; sr. rsch. assoc. Nat. Ctr. Atmospheric Rsch., Boulder, Colo., 1994—. Mem. earth satellite panel IGY, 1956-59; mem. space sci. bd. Nat. Acad. Scis., 1959-68, mem. com. meteorol. aspects of effects of atomic radiation, 1956-58, mem. com. atmospheric scis., 1966-72, mem. polar research bd., 1972-77; mem. Rocket and Satellite Research Panel, 1957-62; mem. adv. group supporting tech. for operational meteorol. satellites NASA-NOAA, 1964-72; rapporteur meteorology of high atmosphere, commn. aerology World Meteorol. Orgn., 1965-71; chmn. internat. commn. meteorology upper atmosphere Internat. Union Geodesy and Geophysics, 1960-67, mem., 1967-75; mem. internat. com. climate Internat. Assn. Meteorology and Atmospheric Physics, 1978-87; mem. sci. adv. bd. USAF, 1956-65; chmn. meteorol. satellite com. Advanced Research Projects Agy., 1958-59; mem. panel on environment President's Sci. Adv. Com., 1968-72; mem. space program adv. council NASA, 1976-77; chmn. meteorol. adv. com. EPA, 1970-74, mem. nat. air quality criteria adv. com., 1975-76, air pollution transport and transformation adv. com., 1976-78; mem. council on carbon dioxide environ. assessment Dept. Energy, 1976-78; adv. to sec. gen. on World Climate Program, World Meteorol. Orgn., 1978-79; dir. research Naval Environ. Prediction Research Facility, Monterey, Calif., 1983-84; chmn. adv. com. Div. Polar Programs NSF, 1983-86; researcher on meteorology, dynamics and turbulence of upper atmosphere, prediction radioactive fallout and dispersal, applications of infrared techniques, atmospheres of Mars and Venus, theory of climate and causes of climate change Served as pilot-weather officer USAAF, 1941-46. Co-recipient spl. award pioneering work in planning meteorol. satellite Am. Meteorol. Soc., 1961; recipient Risseca award contbn. human relations in scis. Jewish War Vets. U.S.A., 1962-63, Exceptional Civilian Service award Dept. Air Force, 1966, Spl. award for pioneering meteorol. satellites Dept. Commerce, 1985, Spl. Citation award for atmospheric conservation Garden Club of Am., 1988. Fellow Am. Geophys. Union (pres. meteorol. sect. 1972-74), Am. Meteorol. Soc. (council 1960-63, pres. 1973-74), AAAS (chmn. atmospheric and hydrospheric sect. 1984); mem. Sigma Xi. Home: 445 College Ave Boulder CO 80302-7131 *If there is anything that generally characterizes a gratifying and successful career in science, it is the challenge of diversity. The really important problems of the universe, and especially of society, involve several disciplines, and we are compelled to work at these discipline interfaces. Pigeon holes are for pigeons, not scientists.*

KELLS, ALBERT JOHN, financial consultant; b. Providence, Jan. 20, 1935; s. John S. and Mary M. (Wise) K.; m. Carole P. Coloura, July 6, 1957; children: Karen A., Kathleen M. BS in Fin., Bryant Coll., Providence, 1960; MBA, U. Conn., 1967. Fin. analyst Rexall Drug & Chem., Stamford, Conn., 1960-63; econ. analyst The Fantus Co., N.Y.C., 1963-64; budget mgr. CBS Inc., Stamford, 1964-67; strategic planning mgr. IBM, East Fishkill, N.Y., 1967-90; mergers and acquisitions cons. The Gottesman Co., N.Y.C., 1991, Kells & Co., Stormville, N.Y., 1991—. Chmn. Kells Found., 1981-92; mem. Rep. Nat. Com., 1979. Capt. U.S. Army, 1954-64. Mem. Inst. Indsl. Engrs., Internat. Bus. Brokers Assn. Avocations: tennis, history, computers. Home and Office: 105 Townview Dr Wappingers Falls NY 12590-7017 Office Phone: 845-238-6223. E-mail: kellsaj@aol.com.

KELLS, KARI JOY, indexer, librarian; b. Columbus, Ohio, May 25, 1970; d. Paul Kerry and Myrnella Joy (Barney) McDowell; m. Raymond Lee Bero, Nov. 9, 1992 (div. 1998). BA, U. Ill., 1993, MS, 1994. Owner, indexer Index West (formerly Bero-West Indexing Svcs.), Olympia, Wash., 1994—; libr. U. Wash., Seattle, 1994-95; libr. faculty, internet trainer Pierce Coll., Lakewood, Wash., 1995-97; libr. faculty Highline C.C., Des Moines, Wash., 1997-99, Pierce Coll., Puyallup, Wash., 1999—. Author: Inside Indexing, 2005; contbr. articles to profl. jours. Mem. Am. Soc. Indexers (Web Site com. 1995-98, Webmaster 1995-97, vice chmn. Pacific N.W. chpt. 1997-98, chmn. Pacific N.W. chpt. 1998-99, Webmaster Pacific N.W. chpt. 1996—), Indexing & Abstracting Soc. of Can., 2003-. Office: PO Box 615 Olympia WA 98507 Office Phone: 360-870-4384. E-mail: info@indexw.com.

KELLUM, DONALD ARTHUR, military officer; b. Schofield Barracks, Hawaii, Dec. 13, 1935; s. Harry Snow and Edna Lois (Pickels) Kellum; m. Martha Ann Myers, Mar. 10, 1957; children: Kathryn Ann Kellum Comer, Donald Wainright. B in Gen. Edn., U. Nebr., Omaha, 1962; MS in Pub. Adminstrn., George Washington U., 1966. Commd. officer USAF, 1953, advanced through grades to col., fighter, bomber navigator, 1956—75, numbered Air Force vice comdr., 1975—77, numbered Air Force dir., 1977—86, ret., 1986; def. cons. JAYCOR, 1986—88; co-founder, bd. dirs., sr. mil. scientist Simulation Techs., Inc., 1988—2004; sr. mil. analyst Anteon Corp., 2004—. Decorated Legion of Merit with two oak leaf clusters, DFC, Purple Heart, Air medal with eleven oak leaf clusters, Air Force Commendation medal. Home: 904 Sassafras Dr Sumter SC 29150

KELLUM, NORMAN BRYANT, JR., lawyer; b. Maysville, N.C. BS, JD, Wake Forest U. Bar: N.C., U.S. Dist. Ct. (ea. dist.) N.C., U.S. Dist. Ct. (mid. dist.) N.C., U.S. Ct. Appeals (4th cir.), U.S. Supreme Ct. Salesman, mgr. The Southwestern Co., Nashville, summers 1962-68; research asst. N.C. Supreme Ct., Raleigh, NC; atty. Norman Kellum Jr., New Bern, NC; ptnr. Beaman & Kellum, New Bern; pres., majority shareholder Kellum Law Firm and predecessor law firms, New Bern, Jacksonville, Goldsboro, N.C., 1975—. Trustee Meredith Coll., 1988-92, 94-97, 99—, chmn., 1996, 97; bd. visitors Wake Forest U. Sch. Law, 1992-99; mem. Craven Regional Med. Ctr. Found., 1997-2000, pres., 1998, 99; bd. dirs. Craven Regional Med. Authority, 2001—. 1st lt. U.S. Army. Mem. ATLA, N.C. State Bar, N.C. Acad. Trial Lawyers (bd. govs. 1983-87), N.C. Bar Assn., Ea. N.C. Inn Ct. (pres. 1995), Am. Bd. Trial Advs., Wake Forest U. Law Sch. (Alumni of Yr. award 1993). Avocations: travel, boating, golf. Office: Kellum Law Firm PO Box 866 New Bern NC 28563-0866

KELLY, A. DAVID, lawyer; b. St. Paul, June 8, 1948; s. David and Katherine (Tappins) K.; m. Elizabeth Woehrle, Oct. 25, 1978; children: Charles, George. BA, Carleton Coll., 1970; JD, Harvard U., 1973. Bar: Minn. 1973. Ptnr. Faegre & Benson, Mpls., 1973-90, Oppenheimer, Wolff & Donnelly, Mpls., 1990-95, Kelly, Hannaford & Battles, Mpls., 1995—. Trustee Carleton Coll., Northfield, Minn., 1972-76;, Minn. Mus. Am. Art, 2003—; chmn. Voyageurs Nat. Pk. Assn., Mpls., 1984-90; treas. Messiah Episc. Ch., St. Paul, 1988-96; pres. St. Paul Boys' and Girls' Club, 1992-95. Office: Kelly Hannaford & Battles 3900 Campbell Mithun Tower 222 South Ninth St Minneapolis MN 55402-3309

KELLY, ALFRED F., JR., diversified financial services company executive; married; 4 children. BA, Iona Coll; MBA, Iona Coll. Adj. asst. prof. Iona Coll., New Rochelle, NY, 1980—85; with Am. Express, 1987—, exec. v.p. gen. mgr. U.S. consumer card mktg., exec. v.p., gen. mgr. consumer mktg. TRS, 1997—98, pres. consumer card svcs. group TRS, 1998—2000, group pres. U.S. consumer and small bus. svcs. TRS, 2000—. Chmn. Wall St. Charity Golf Classic; trustee Iona Coll., New Rochelle, NY. Office: Am Express Co World Fin Ctr 200 Vesey St New York NY 10285

KELLY, ANASTASIA DONOVAN, lawyer; b. Boston, Oct. 9, 1949; d. Charles A. and Louise V. Donovan; m. Thomas C. Kelly, Aug. 23, 1980; children: Michael, Brian. BA cum laude, Trinity Coll, 1971; JD magna cum laude, George Washington U., 1981. Bar: D.C. 1982, Tex. 1982. Analyst Air Line Pilots Assn., 1971-74; dir. employee benefits Martin Marietta Corp., Bethesda, Md., 1974-81; assoc. Carrington, Coleman, Sloman & Blumenthal, Dallas, 1981-85, Wilmer, Cutler & Pickering, Washington, 1985-90, ptnr., 1990-95; sr. v.p., gen. counsel, sec. Fannie Mae, Washington, 1995-99, Sears, Roebuck & Co., 1999—2003; exec. v.p., gen. counsel MCI Inc., 2003—, sec., 2003—04. Bd. dirs. Owens-Ill., Toledo. Trustee Trinity Coll., Washington, 2003—; mem. adv. coun. Woodrow Wilson Ctr. for Internat. Scholars, 2001—; bd. dirs. Equal Justice Works, 1999—. Named one of Outstanding Young Women of Am., 1980; recipient Aiing High award Nat. League Def. Fund, 2002, Myra Blackwell award Chgo. Women's Bar, 2002. Mem. Am. Bar Found., Am. Corp. Counsel Assn. (bd. dirs. 2001-), Order of Coif. Republican. Roman Catholic. Office: Gen Counsel MCI Inc 22001 Loudoun County Parkway Ashburn VA 20147

KELLY, ANTHONY ODRIAN, textiles executive; b. Dublin, June 12, 1935; s. John Peter and Delia Mary (Finnegan) K.; m. Sheila Josephine Clancy, Sept. 4, 1963; children— Barbara Anne, Adrienne Elizabeth, Damian Anthony. Grad., Coll. Commerce, Dublin, 1958; MBA, Columbia U., 1965, doctoral degree, 1971. Adj. asst. prof. Columbia U., N.Y.C., 1968-69; dir. econ. studies Sperry & Hutchinson Co., 1969-71, asst. to pres. furnishings divsn., 1975; dir. mktg. Irish Agrl. Devel. Co., 1971-74; sr. v.p. mktg. Bigelow-Sanford, Inc., Greenville, S.C., 1976-79, exec. v.p., COO, 1979-85, pres., CEO, 1985-86; pres., chief ops. officer Mannington Mills Inc., 1992, pres., CEO, 1993-2000, ret., 2000. Ford Found. fellow; Samuel Bronfman fellow. Mem. Inst. Cost and Mgmt. Accts., Kiawah Island Club, Beta Gamma Sigma.

KELLY, ARTHUR LLOYD, investment company executive; b. Chgo., Nov. 15, 1937; s. Thomas Lloyd and Mildred (Wetten) Kelly; m. Diane Rex Cain, Nov. 25, 1978; children: Mary Lucinda, Thomas Lloyd, Alison Williams. BS with honors, Yale U., 1959; MBA, U. Chgo., 1964. With A.T. Kearney, Inc., 1959-75, mng. dir. Dusseldorf, Germany, 1964-70, v.p. for Europe Brussels, 1970-73, internat. v.p. London, 1974-75, ptnr., dir., 1969-75, mem. exec. com., 1972-75; pres., COO, dir. LaSalle Steel Co., Chgo., 1975-81; pres., CEO, dir. Dalta Corp., Chgo., 1982—; mng. ptnr. KEL Enterprises L.P., Chgo., 1983—. Dir. BASF Aktiengesellschaft, Ludwigshafen, Germany, BMW A.G., Munich, DataCard Corp., Minnetonka, Minn., Deere & Co., Moline, Ill., No. Trust Corp., Chgo., Snap-On, Inc., Kenosha, Wis., Robert Bosch G.m.b.H., Stuttgart; trustee U. Chgo.; mem. adv. coun. Ditchley Found., Oxford, England; bd. dirs. Chgo. Coun. Fgn. Rels. Fellow: Royal Geog. Soc. London (life); mem.: Coun. Fgn. Rels. NYC, World Pres.' Orgn., Brook Club (NYC), Yale Club (NYC), Racquet Club, Econ. Club, Comml. Club, Casino Club, Everglades Club (Palm Beach), Chgo. Club, Beta Gamma Sigma. Office: 20 S Clark St Ste 2222 Chicago IL 60603-1805

KELLY, ARTHUR PAUL, physician; b. Asheville, N.C., Nov. 23, 1938; s. Joseph Paul and Amanda Lee (Walker) Kelly; m. Beverly Gayle Baker, June 25, 1966; children: Traci Allyce, Kara Gisele. BA, Brown U., 1960; MD, Howard U., 1965. Intern Harper Hosp., Detroit, 1965-66; resident in dermatology Henry Ford Hosp., Detroit, 1968-71; instr. in dermatology Brown U., Providence, 1971-73; asst. prof. internal medicine Charles R. Drew U. Medicine and Sci., Los Angeles, 1973-77, prof. L.A., 1983; chief div. dermatology King.-Drew Med. Ctr., L.A., 1976—, interim chmn. dept. internal medicine, 1985-86, vice chmn., 1987-91, chmn., 1992-95; assoc. prof. medicine U. So. Calif., L.A., 1977-80; prof. UCLA, 1995—. Contbr. articles to profl jours, chapters to books; editor-in-chief: Jour. Nat. Med. Assn., 1997—2004. Served to capt U.S. Army, 1966—68, Vietnam. Recipient Act-So award, NAACP, 1983. Fellow: Am Acad Dermatology; mem.: Am Dermatology Asn (vpres 1997—98, pres 1998—99), Asn Profs Dermatology (pres-elect 1996—98, pres 1998—2000), Nat Med Asn (chmn sect dermatology 1978—80, Oustanding Minority Dermatology Fellow 1972), Metropolitan LA Dermatology Soc (vpres 1986—87, pres 1987—88). Democrat. Avocations: travel, tennis. Office: King/Drew Med Ctr 12021 S Wilmington Ave Los Angeles CA 90059-3019 Business E-Mail: apkelly@cdrewu.edu.

KELLY, CAROL A., travel company executive; married; 3 children. BS in Computer sci. Engring., Mich. State U.; MBA, U. Chgo. CPA. With COVIA, United Airlines; v.p., CFO Apollo Travel Svcs., Rolling Meadows, Ill.; v.p., corp. svcs. Sabre Holdings, Southlake, Tex., 1998—99, sr. v.p., corp. svcs., 1999, sr. v.p., chief info. officer, 1999—. Recipient Best Marriage of IT and Bus. Processes award, Salomon Smith Barney, 2001. Office: Sabre Holdings 3150 Sabre Dr Southlake TX 76092

KELLY, CAROLYN SUE, newspaper executive; b. Pasco, Wash., Oct. 25, 1952; d. Jerald Davin and Margaret Helen (Nibler) K. BBA, Gonzaga U., 1974; MBA, Seattle U., 1985. CPA, Wash., 1976. Acct. Brajcich & Loeffler, Spokane, Wash., 1972-74; auditor Peat, Marwick, Mitchell & Co., Seattle, 1974-77; fin. analyst Seattle Times, 1977-81, asst. circulation mgr., 1981-83, spl. project advt. mgr., 1983—87, dir. mktg. and new bus., 1987—89, v.p., CFO, 1989—95, sr. v.p., CFO, 1995—97, sr. v.p., gen. mgr., 1997—2001, pres., COO, 2001—. Mem. Fin. Execs. Avocation: running. Office: Seattle Times PO Box 70 Seattle WA 98111-0070

KELLY, CHARLES ARTHUR, lawyer; b. Evanston, Ill., Mar. 2, 1932; s. Charles Scott and Bess (Loftis) K.; m. Frances Kates, Sept. 9, 1961 (div. 1979); children: Timothy, Elizabeth, Mary; m. Patricia Lynn Francis, June 28, 1979 (div. 1995); m. Jean E. Glazier, June 25, 2005. BA with honors, Amherst Coll., 1953; LLB, Harvard U., 1956. Bar: D.C. 1956, Ill. 1956. Assoc. Hubachek & Kelly, Chgo., 1956-64, ptnr., 1964-82, Chapman & Cutler, Chgo., 1982—99, of counsel, 2002—. Sec. Speedfam Internat., Inc., 1992-99, gen. counsel, 1998-99. Bd. dirs. Gads Hill Ctr., Chgo., pres., 1977—82; bd. dirs. Quetico Superior Found., Mpls., v.p., 1964—; bd. dirs. Lakeland Found., Chgo., 1960—96, pres., 1970—85, Ernest C. Oberholtzer Found., Mpls., 1962—2002, v.p., treas., 1998—2002; bd. dirs. Chgo. Hearing Found., 1990—94, Wilderness Rsch. Found., Chgo. Recipient Legion of Merit, USAF, 1982. Fellow Am. Coll. Trust and Estate Counsel; Mem. ABA, Chgo. Bar Assn., Ill. Bar Assn., Fed. Bar Assn., Univ. Club, Mid-Am. Club, Mich. Shores Club (Wilmette, Ill.), Harvard Club (Boston). Republican. Presbyterian. Office: Chapman and Cutler 111 W Monroe St Ste 1800 Chicago IL 60603-4080 Office Phone: 312-845-3009. Business E-Mail: ckelly@chapman.com.

KELLY, CHARLES HAROLD, advertising agency executive; b. Omaha, Mar. 30, 1950; s. Kerwood Michael and Erma Lenore (Johnson) K.; m. Susan Marie Nielsen, Dec. 28, 1971; children: Matthew Michael, Laura Elizabeth. BA, Hastings Coll., 1972; MS, Iowa State U., 1973. Account exec. Kerker & Assocs., Mpls., 1977-80, v.p., dir. client services, 1983—99; account exec. Foote, Cone & Belding, Chgo., 1980-82; account supr. Bozell, Jacobs, Kenyon & Eckhardt, Mpls., 1982-83; chmn, CEO Kerker. Mpls. Bd. dirs. YMCA of Greater Mpls.; bd. of visitors Penn State U., Coll. of Comm. Mem. Advt. Fedn. Mpls. (pres. 1987-88), Am. Assn. Advt. Agys. (past pres. Twin Cities). Republican. Lutheran. Avocations: jogging, golf, photography, music. Office: Kerker 7701 France Ave S Minneapolis MN 55435-5288 Office Phone: 952-897-9420.

KELLY, CHARLES J., JR., investment company executive; b. June 10, 1929; s. Charles J. and Margaret (Grimes) K.; m. Marguerite Stehli, Dec. 23, 1962; children: Karen Grimes (Mrs. B.H. Warner IV), Marguerite Grace (Mrs. James J. Walton), Lisa Stehli Kelly-Wolf. BA, Stanford U., 1951; LL.B., Yale U., 1954. Bar: N.Y., U.S. Supreme Ct. Asso. atty. Chadbourne, Parke, Whiteside & Wolff, N.Y.C., 1957-58; spl. counsel CAB, 1959-60; spl. asst. to Sec. Comm., Washington, 1960-61; with Reynolds & Co., 1961-62; partner Kelly, Grimes & Winston, 1962-69; pres., dir. Meridian Investing and Devel. Co., N.Y.C., 1969-72, pres., chief exec. officer, 1972-74; pres. Capital Strategy, Inc. Bd. dirs., mem. exec. com. Balt. Bancorp, Bank of Balt.; trustee The Hotel Investors, 1970-77; dir. Big Sky Montana, 1971-75, Sta. KTCA-TV, Mpls., 1978-85; mng. dir. Weeden and Co.; assoc. mem. NYSE, 1985-88; chmn. Capital Strategy, 1988—; dir. Caribbean Marine Rsch. Found., 1993—. Author: The Sky's The Limit: The History of the Airlines, 1962; repub. with introduction by Charles A. Lindbergh, 1972. Bd. dirs. Charles A. Lindbergh Fund; founder Citizens for Colin Powell, 1996 Presdl. Draft, 1994—. 1st lt. USAF, 1954-56. Mem. Racquet & Tennis Club (N.Y.C.), Yale Club (N.Y.C.), Met. Club (Washington). Office: 3018 N St NW Washington DC 20007-3404

KELLY, CHERYL ANN, health science association administrator; b. Bay City, Mich., July 28, 1956; d. Frederick Joseph and Julie Frances (Filary) Budzinski; m. Hugh Paul Kelly, Aug. 3, 1979; 1 child, Jenna Ann. BS, U. Mich., 1977; MS, U. Ariz., 1981, MBA, 1988. Cert. rehab. counselor. Tchr. Northview Pub. Schs., Grand Rapids, Mich., 1977-78; rehab. counselor St. Mary's Hosp., Tucson, 1980-81; mgr. Jewish Family Service, Tucson, 1981-82; service coordinator Pima County, Tucson, 1982-86; bus. devel. officer Western Savs. and Loan, Tucson, 1986-88; dir. social services Carondelet Holy Family, Tucson, 1988-89; dir. mktg. Devon Gables Healthcare, 1989-90; asst. adminstr. Desert Life, Valley House, 1990; healthcare adminstr. The Forum, Tucson, 1990-93; adminstr. Manor Care Health & Rehab. Ctr., Tucson, 1993-95; asst. hosp. adminstr. Am. Transitional Hosp., Tucson, 1995-97; adminstr. Vencor Villa Campana, Tucson, 1997-98; exec. dir. Alterra Sterling Ho., Tucson, 1998—. Instr. U. Phoenix, 1991—. Bd. dirs. Tucson Old Pueblo Exch., 1987, U. Mich. Alumni Club, Tucson, 2004—; vol., Make a Wish Found. Mem. NAFE. Republican. Roman Catholic.

KELLY, CHRISTINA, editor; BA in English & history, Colgate U. Contbg. editor US; editor Sassy, 1988—94; dep. editor/founding editor Jane Mag., 1997—2000; exec. editor YM Mag., 2000—01, editor-in-chief, 2001—04; exec. editor ELLEgirl, 2004—05, editor-in-chief, 2005—. Publisher: freelance articles include Rolling Stone, Spin, Premiere, The Rolling Stone Book of Women in Rock. Mem.: ASME. Office: Elle Girl Hachette Filipacchi Media 1633 Broadway New York NY 10019*

KELLY, CHRISTOPHER M., lawyer; b. Buffalo, Apr. 27, 1961; BA summa cum laude, Canisius Coll., 1983; JD with honors, Duke Univ., 1986. Bar: New York 1988, Ohio 2001. Atty. Simpson Thacher & Bartlett, NYC; ptnr., chair, corp. fin. practice Jones Day, Cleve. Office: Jones Day North Point 901 Lakeside Ave Cleveland OH 44114-1190

KELLY, CHRISTOPHER PAT, dean, educator; b. Las Vegas, Nev., July 22, 1947; s. James Albert and Patsy Jean Kelly; m. Wendy Leigh Miller, Nov. 24, 1989; children: Brandon Charles Dimick, Heather Dawn Roberts. BS in Bus. Adminstrn., U. Nev., Las Vegas, 1970, MEd, 1975, MS in Acctg., 1996, EdD, 2002. Acct. Sunrise Hosp., Las Vegas, 1971—72; bus. edn. tchr., coord. Clark County Sch. Dist., Las Vegas, 1973—78; prof., chair acctg. C.C. of So. Nev., North Las Vegas, Nev., 1978—98, dean of bus., industry, and pub. svcs., 1998—. Recipient Burlington Outstanding Tchg. Faculty award, C.C. of So. Nev., 1993, Excellence award, Nat. Inst. for Staff and Orgn. Devel./U. Tex., Austin, 1994. Mem.: Inst. Mgmt. Accts/, UNLV Alumni Assn. (bd. dirs.). Avocation: tennis. Office: CC of So Nevada 3200 E Cheyenne Ave Z2A North Las Vegas NV 89030-4296 Office Phone: 702-651-4148. E-mail: chris_kelly@ccsn.nevada.edu.

KELLY, CURTIS HARTT, retired publishing executive; b. Ft. Atkinson, Wis., May 17, 1935; s. Curtis and Edna (Guenther) K. BA, Yankton Coll., 1957. With fin. divsn. Scott Foresman Co., Glenview, Ill., 1962-86, with info. sys. divsn., 1986-97. Home: 1363 W Estes Ave Apt 2-U Chicago IL 60626-5465

KELLY, DANIEL GRADY, JR., lawyer; b. Yonkers, N.Y., July 15, 1951; s. Daniel Grady and Helene (Coyne) K.; m. Annette Susan Wheeler, May 8, 1976; children— Elizabeth Anne, Brigid Claire, Cynthia Logan. Grad., Choate Sch., Wallingford, Conn., 1969; BA magna cum laude, Yale U., 1973; JD, Columbia U., 1976. Bar: N.Y. 1977, U.S. Dist. Ct. (so. and ea. dists.) N.Y. 1977, Calif. 1986, U.S. Dist. Ct. (cen. dist.) Calif. 1987. Law clk. to judge U.S. Ct. Appeals (2d cir.), N.Y.C., 1976-77; assoc. Davis Polk & Wardwell, N.Y.C., 1977-83; sr. v.p. Lehman Bros., N.Y.C., 1983-85; sr. v.p., gen. counsel Kaufman & Broad, Inc., L.A., 1985-87; ptnr. Manatt, Phelps, Rothenberg & Phillips, L.A., 1987-90, Sidley & Austin, L.A. and N.Y., 1990-99, Davis Polk & Wardwell, N.Y.C. and Menlo Park, Calif., 1999—. Mem. editl. bd. Columbia Law Rev., 1975-76. Office: Davis Polk & Wardwell 1600 El Camino Real Menlo Park CA 94025-4119 Office Phone: 650-752-2001. E-mail: dankelly@dpw.com.

KELLY, DANIEL J., retail executive; CPA. Former contr., CFO Justice Builders, Inc. and JICO; former ptnr. Arthur Andersen LLP; former CFO, exec. v.p. Konover Property Trust, Inc.; CFO The Pantry, Inc., Sanford, NC, 2002—. Office: The Pantry Inc 1801 Douglas Dr Sanford NC 27331-1410

KELLY, DANIEL JOHN, physician; b. Binghamton, NY, June 23, 1940; s. William James and Mary Elizabeth (Schmitt) K.; m. Lois Ann Lanshe, Aug. 21, 1965; children: Britton James, Jeffrey Daniel, Reid William, Piper Ann. AB in History, Yale U., 1962; MD, Jefferson Med. Coll., 1966. Diplomate in Pathology, Nuclear Medicine, Dermatopathology. Intern Naval Hosp., Boston, 1966-67, resident Oakland, Calif., 1966-71, asst. chief lab. Great Lakes, Ill., 1971-73, chief lab. svcs., 1973-75; co-dir. lab. Highland Park (Ill.) Hosp., 1975-97, dir. lab., 1980-89, 96-97; co-dir. lab. Lake Forest (Ill.) Hosp., 1975-97, dir. lab., 1989-91; with Dean, Hoffman & Clark Pathologists S.C., Lake Forest, 1975-97, Associated Lab. Physician Svcs., Wauwatosa, Wis., 1997-99; chief of staff elect Highland Park (Ill.) Hosp., 1992-94, chief of staff, 1994-96, also bd. dirs.; with Consolidated Pathology Cons., S.C., Lake Bluff, Ill., 1999—. Med. exec. com. Highland Park Hosp., 1992-97, Lake Forest Hosp., 1989-91. Bd. dirs. Lake Forest Hist. Preservation Found., 1979-88; mem. bldg. rev. bd. City Govt., Lake Forest, 1989-93; mem. clin. lab. and blood bank adv. bd. Ill. Dept. Pub. Health, 1990-95; mem. Am. Pathology Found. Comdr. USNR, 1966-75. Fellow Coll. Am. Pathology, Am. Soc. Clin. Pathology, Internat. Acad. Pathologists; mem. AMA, Ill. Soc. Pathologists, Am. Soc. Microbiology, Am. Soc. Dermatopathology, Internat. Soc. Dermatopathology, Am. Acad. Dermatology, Assn. Military Surgeons. Roman Catholic. Avocations: reading, art, music, fishing. Home: 499 E Illinois Rd Lake Forest IL 60045-2364 Office: Dept Pathology Lake Forest Hosp 660 N Westmoreland Rd Lake Forest IL 60045-1659 Office Phone: 847-535-6218. Office Fax: 847-535-6237. Personal E-mail: danjkelly@pol.net.

KELLY, DAVID AUSTIN, food products executive; b. Mt. Kisco, N.Y., June 24, 1938; s. William Andrew and Katharine Elizabeth (Barrett) K.; m. Judith Boesel, June 18, 1966; children: Carolyn K. Patten, Douglas Austin. BA, Lafayette Coll., 1962; MBA, U. Chgo., 1964. Chartered fin. analyst. Asst. v.p. investment mgmt. group Citibank, N.Y.C., 1964-69; portfolio mgr., v.p. J.M. Hartwell & Co., Inc., N.Y.C., 1969-72; pres., CEO P/H Mgmt. Corp., Pitts., 1972-74; asst. treas. Gulf Oil Corp., Pitts., 1974-80; v.p., treas. Borden, Inc., N.Y.C., 1980-95, treas., prin. fin. officer, dir. BCP Mgmt., Inc., Borden Chemicals and Plastics Ltd. Partnership, 1987-95; pres. Three Lakes Advisors, Inc., 1996—. Past bd. dirs. Ctr. for Redirection through Edn., Inc., Bedford Hills, N.Y. Past councilor N.Y. Soc., Order of Founders and Patriots Am.; mem. fin. policy com. Lafayette Coll., Easton, Pa., 1976-79; treas. bd. dirs. The Greenwich (Conn.) Land Trust Inc. Served with U.S. Army, 1957-59. Mem. NAM (chmn. auditing com. 1983-92), Assn. for Investment Mgmt. and Rsch., N.Y. Soc. Security Analysts, Stanwich Club (Greenwich, Conn.). Home: 303 Overlook Dr Greenwich CT 06830-6716 Office: Three Lakes Advisors Inc 303 Overlook Dr Greenwich CT 06830-6716 Office Phone: 203-869-4046. E-mail: thrlakeadv@aol.com.

KELLY, DAVID M., lawyer; b. Mt. Pleasant, Pa., Oct. 18, 1957; BCE, U. Pitts., 1979, MCE with highest honors, 1980; JD, Duquesne U., Pa., 1983. Bar: Pa. 1983, La. 1985, DC 1987, registered: US Patent & Trademark Office. Ptnr. Finnegan, Henderson, Farabow, Garrett & Dunner LLP, Washington, chmn., Trademark & Copyright Practice Group. Mem. Duquesne Law Rev., 1981—83. Co-author (with Monica Talley): The High Price of Popularity, 2004 (Burton award, 2005). Mem.: Internat. Trademark Assn., Am. Intellectual Property Law Assn., ABA, DC Bar. Office: Finnegan Henderson Farabow Garrett & Dunner LLP 901 New York Ave NW Washington DC 20001-3315 Office Phone: 202-408-4000. Office Fax: 202-408-4400. Business E-Mail: david.kelly@finnegan.com.

KELLY, DEANNA LYNN, pharmacologist, educator; b. Meadville, Pa., Nov. 15, 1971; d. John B. and Alfreda W. Kurtich; m. Todd E. Kelly, June 29, 1996; children: Jackson A., Jemma E. PharmD, Duquesne U., 1996. Bd. cert. psychiatric pharmacy practice; cert. pharmacy Pa., Md., 1996, in psychiatric pharmacy practice BPS, 1998. Asst. prof., psychiatry U. Md., Md. Psychiat. Rsch. Ctr., Balt., 1997—. Author: (medical book) Pharmacologic Treatment of Schizophrenia, 2000, 2d edit., 2003; contbr. articles to profl. jours. Mem.: Coll. Psychiat. and Neurologic Pharmacists (treas. 2005—), Am. Coll. Clin. Pharmacy, Am. Soc. Health Sys. Pharmacists. Protestant. Avocations: travel, gardening. Home: 2165 Bernays Dr York PA 17404 Office: Md Psychiatric Rsch Ctr Box 21247 Baltimore MD 21228 Office Phone: 717-764-9260. Office Fax: 410-402-6880. Personal E-mail: deanna@thekellyfamily.org. E-mail: dkelly@mprc.umaryland.edu.

KELLY, DEE J., lawyer; b. Bonham, Tex., Mar. 7, 1929; s. Dee C. and Era L. (Jones) K.; m. Janice LeBlanc, Dec. 30, 1954; children: Cynthia Kelly Barnes, Dee J., Craig LeBlanc. BA, Tex. Christian U., 1950; LL.B., George Washington U., 1954. Bar: Tex. 1954. Pvt. practice law, Ft. Worth, 1956-79; founding, sr. ptnr. Kelly, Hart & Hallman, P.C., Ft. Worth, 1979—. Bd. dirs. A.M.R., 1983—2000, Justin Industries, Inc., 1986—2000, The SABRE Group Holdings, Inc., 1996—2000. Trustee Tex. Christian U., 1971—; bd. dirs. Tex. Turnpike Authority, 1967-76, chmn., 1969-76; bd. regents Tex. State U. System, 1969-75; trustee U. Tex. Law Sch. Found., 1983-2002; bd. dirs. Ctr. Am. and Internat. Law, 1986—; trustee Scott and White Meml. Hosp. and Scott, Sherwood and Bridley Found., 1989-98, U. Tex. Southwestern Moncrief Radiation Ctr., 1985-; bd. visitors U. Tex. Cancer Ctr., 1980-87; mem. Joint Select Com. on Judiciary, 1988, Task Force on Jud. Selection, 1995-96, Fed. Jud. Evaluation Com., 1989—; dir. Southwestern Expn. and Livestock Show, 1986—; mem. bd advisors George Washington U. Law Sch., 2001—. 1st lt. USAF, 1951-53. Named Disting. Alumni, Tex. Christian U., 1982, George Washington U., 2001, Ft. Worth's Outstanding Bus. Exec., 1993, Ft. Worth's Outstanding Citizen, 2000; recipient Horatio Alger award Horatio Alger Assn. Disting. Ams., 1995, Blackstone award, 1998, Disting. Citizen award Boy Scouts Am., 2003. Fellow Am. Bar Found.; mem. Tarrant County Bar Assn., Tarrant County Bar Found., Tex. Bar Found. (founding mem.). Avocation: golf. Home: 1315 Hillcrest St Fort Worth TX 76107-1577 Office Phone: 817-332-2500. E-mail: dee_kelly@khh.com.

KELLY, DENNIS MICHAEL, lawyer; b. Cleve., May 6, 1943; s. Thomas Francis and Margaret (Murphy) K.; m. Marilyn Ann Divoky, Dec. 28, 1967; children: Alison, Meredith. BA, John Carroll U., 1961-65; JD, U. Notre Dame, 1968. Bar: Ohio 1968. Law clk. U.S. Ct. Appeals (8th cir.), Cleve., 1968-69; assoc. Jones, Day, Reavis & Pogue, Cleve., 1969-75, ptnr., 1975—. Mem. Ohio Bar Assn., Bar Assn. Greater Cleve. Office: Jones Day Reavis & Pogue North Point 901 Lakeside Ave E Cleveland OH 44114-1190 E-mail: dmkelly@jonesday.com.

KELLY, DIANA KAY, counselor, educator; b. Shaw AFB, S.C., July 31, 1958; d. Donald I. and Georgianna Kelly; life ptnr. Mary L. Baldwin. BA in Sociology, U. N.Mex, Albuquerque, 1979; MA in Rehab. Counseling, Calif. State U., San Bernardino, 1995. Cert. rehab. counselor Commn. Rehab. Counselor Certification, 1995. Prof. City Colls. Chgo., Brunssum, Netherlands, 1979—80; test examiner U.S. Army, Brunssum, Netherlands, 1980—81; supr. FEDCO, Ontario, Calif., 1982—88; asst. mgr./title asst. World Title Co., Colton, Calif., 1989—94; title asst. Stewart Title Co., Riverside, Calif., 1994—95; counselor/asst. prof. Bakersfield (Calif.) Coll., 1996—. Mem. adv. bd. WorkAbility III, Bakersfield Coll., 1996—; counselor coord. Calif. C.Cs., Disabled Student Programs and Svcs., Region V, Fresno, Calif., 2002—03. Advisor, student club Students for the Ethical Treatment of Humanity, Bakersfield Coll., Bakersfield, Calif., 2000—02; presenter Nat. Orgn. for the Mentally Ill (NAMI), Bakersfield, Calif., 2002—02, Kern County Mental Health In-Service, Bakersfield, Calif., 2002—02, Calif. Placement Assn. (CPA) ann. Conf., Fresno, Calif., 2003—03, Multiple Sclerosis Soc., Bakersfield, Calif., 2003—03, Calif. State Dept. of Rehab., Bakersfield, Calif., 1997—2002. Mem.: Calif. Assn. for Counseling and Devel. (assoc.), Calif. Assn. for Postsecondary Edn. and Disability (CAPED) (assoc.), Nat. Rehab. Assn. (assoc.), Nat. Rehab. Counseling Assn. (assoc.), Chi Sigma Iota (assoc.; v.p., student club 1994—95), Phi Kappa Phi (life). Avocations: reading, travel. Office: Bakersfield Coll Support Svcs 1801 Panorama Dr Bakersfield CA 93305

KELLY, SISTER DOROTHY ANN, academic administrator; b. Bronx, NY, July 26, 1929; d. Walter David and Sarah (McCauley) K. BA in History, Coll. New Rochelle, 1951; MA in Am. Ch. History, Cath. U., Washington, 1958; PhD in Am. Intellectual History, U. Notre Dame, 1970; LittD (hon.), Mercy Coll., Dobbs Ferry, N.Y., 1976; LLD (hon.), Nazareth Coll. of Rochester, N.Y., 1979; DHL (hon.), Coll. St. Rose, 1981, Manhattan Coll., 1979, LeMoyne Coll., 1990, St. Thomas Aquinas Coll., 1990, St. Joseph Coll., Conn., 1996, Iona Coll., 1997. Joined Order of St. Ursula, Roman Cath. Ch., 1952. Assoc. prof. history Coll. New Rochelle, N.Y., 1957—, chmn. dept. history, 1965-67, acad. dean, 1967-72, acting pres., 1970-71, pres., 1972-97, chancellor, 1997—. Mem. Interreligious Coun. New Rochelle, 1974—, exec. com., 1974-79, v.p., 1980-84, pres., 1984-88, mem. Commn. Ind. Colls. and Univs. State of N.Y., 1976-78, chmn. bd. trustees, 1978-80, mem. govt. rels. com., 1980-81; chmn. Com. Higher Edn. Opportunity, 1976-78; mem. commr. of edn. Adv. Coun. on Higher Edn. for N.Y. State, 1975-77, subcom. on postsecondary occupational edn., 1975-77; exec. com. Empire State Found. Ind. Liberal Arts Colls., 1975—, vice chmn., 1977-81, chmn., 1981—; trustee, mem. exec. com. Assn. Colls. and Univs. State of N.Y., 1976-80; mem. com. on purpose and identity Assn. Cath. Colls. and Univs., 1975-80; mem. steering com. Neylan Conf., 1978-81, mem. bishops and pres. com., 1979-84; mem. adv. coun. on fin. aid to students Office Edn., HEW, 1978-86; chmn. Women's Coll. Coalition, 1981-83; chmn. govt. rels. adv. com. Nat. Assn. Ind. Colls. and Univs., 1981-82, chair, 1987-88. Chair City-wide Confs., New Rochelle, 1977-79; bd. dirs. United Way Westchester, 1977-84, mem. planning, allocations, evaluation com., 1977-80, nominating and campaign coms., 1990—; bd. dirs. Westchester County Assn., 1980-90, New Rochelle Community Action Program, 1982-83, New Rochelle Cmty. Fund, 1989-91; mem. steering com. Westchester County Women's Hall of Fame, 1984-85; bd. dirs. Vis. Nurse Svcs. in Westchester, Inc., 1983-86, chair nominating com., 1985-86; trustee LeMoyne Coll., 1982-88, vice chairperson, 1984-87; mem. bd. govs. New Rochelle Hosp. Med. Ctr., 1987—; trustee United Student Aid Funds, 1980-90, Ursuline Sch., New Rochelle, 1988—, Cath. U. Am., 1988—, Am. Coun. on Edn., 1990—, Ind. Coll. Fund Am., 1982-85; mem. ofcl. U.S. del. to UN 4th World Conf. on Women in Beijing, 1995; mem. nat. adv. bd. Nat. Mus. Women in the Arts, 1996—. Recipient Medallion award Westchester C.C., 1978, Leadership award Am. Soc. Pub. Adminstrn., 1986, Sch. Svc. award Thornton-Donovan Sch., 1977, Henry D. Paley award, 1994, Father Theodore M. Hesburgh award, 1998, N.Y. State Gov.'s award for excellence, 1997; inducted into Westchester County/Avon Women's Hall of Fame, 1989; Paul Harris fellow, 1997. Mem. AAUP, AAUW, NCCJ (trustee 1989—), Am. Hist. Assn., Nat. Fedn. Bus. and Profl. Women, Am. Assn. Higher Edn., Nat. Assembly Women Religious, Am. Coun. Edn. (bd. dirs. 1990), Assn. Am. Colls. (bd. dirs. 1983-86), Tchrs. Ins. and Annuity Assn. Am. (trustee 1987—, fin. com. 1987-88, exec. com. 1988—, audit com. 1990—, products and svcs. com. 1990-91, nominating and pers. com. 1991), Assn. Colls. Mid-Hudson Area (pres. 1979-81, exec. com. 1982—).

KELLY, DOROTHY ANN, language educator, writer; b. N.Y.C., N.Y., July 5, 1948; BS, SUNY, Buffalo, 1970; MA, Hofstra U, 1974; ArtsD, Adelphi U, 1990. Speech-lang. tchr. pathologist various private and pub. inst., Suffolk County, NY; assoc. prof., dept. chair St. Joseph's Coll., Patchogue, NY, 1991—; editl. cons. Advance for Speech-Lang. Pathologists, King of Prussia, Pa., 1991—. Author: Ctrl. Auditory Processing Disorder: Strategies For Use in Children and Adolecants, 1995, A Winner's Workbook, 1998; author: (asessment pub.) Screening for Ctrl Auditory Processing Difficulties, 2001. Mem.: Am. Psychological Assn. (assoc.), Am. Speech-Lang.-Hearing Assn. (assoc.). Avocations: reading, travel, writing. Office: St Joseph's College 155 W Roe Blvd Patchogue NY 11772 Home: 44 Long Meadow Place S Setauket NY 11720

KELLY, DOROTHY HELEN, pediatrician, educator; b. Fitchburg, Mass., July 29, 1944; BS in Nursing magna cum laude, Fitchburg State Co., 1966; BS with distinction, Wayne State U., 1968, MD with distinction, 1972. Diplomate Am. Bd. Pediatrics, Pediatric Pulmonology. Intern Children's Svc. Mass. Gen. Hosp., Boston, 1972-73, resident in pediatrics, 1973-75, fellow in pediatrics pulmonary medicine, 1976-79, co-dir. pediat. pulmonary lab., 1976—83, assoc. dir. pediatric pulmonary unit, 1983—95; teaching fellow Harvard Med. Sch., Boston, 1973-75, clin. fellow, 1972-75, instr. in pediatrics, 1975-81, asst. prof. pediatrics, 1981-89, assoc. prof. pediatrics, 1989-95, U. Tex., Galveston, 1995-97, Houston, 1995—; assoc. dir. S.W. SIDS Rsch. Inst. Meml. Herman S.W. Hosp., Houston, 1995—. Cons. Bur. Community Health Svcs., NEW, 1979-80, FDA, 1986, 88-92, ECRI, 1987-88, also others; chmn. apnea adv. com. Nat. Sudden Infant Death Syndrome Found., 1979-81; mem. com. anesthesiology and respiratory devices panel Ctr. for Devices and Radiol. Health, FDA, 1990-94; chmn. physicians' com. Nat. Assn. Apnea Profls., 1990-91, also others; reviewer numerous jours. in field. Contbr. numerous articles to profl. jours. Recipient Woman of Vision award Nat. Soc. for Prevention of Blindness, Mass. Affiliate, 1981, First Disting. Alumni award Fitchburg State Coll., 1984, grants in field. Mem. Am. Med. Woman's Assn., Am. Acad. Pediatrics (task force on prolonged apnea 1978), Am. Thoracic Soc., Internat. Pediatric Soc., Assn. for Psychophysiol. Study Sleep, Soc. for Pediatric Rsch., Tex. Thoracic Soc., Tex. Med. Assn., Tex. Pediatric Soc., Am. Autonomic Soc., Am. Assn. SIDS Prevention Physicians (bd. dirs.). Office: North Country Pediatrics Littleton Regional Hosp Littleton NH 03561 Office Phone: 603-484-2803. Personal E-mail: dkellymd@sbcglobal.net. Business E-Mail: dhkelly@aap.net.

KELLY, EAMON MICHAEL, university president emeritus; b. N.Y.C., Apr. 25, 1936; s. Michael Joseph and Kathleen Elizabeth (O'Farrell) K.; m. Margaret Whalen, June 22, 1963; children: Martin (dec.), Paul, Andrew, Peter. BS, Fordham U., 1958; MS, Columbia U., 1960, PhD, 1965. Officer in charge Office of Social Devel., Ford Found., N.Y.C., 1969—74; officer in charge program related investments Ford Found., 1974—79; exec. v.p. Tulane U., New Orleans, 1979—81, pres., 1981—98, pres. emeritus, prof. Payson Ctr. Internat. Devel. and Tech. Transfer, 1998—. Dir. policy formulation div. Econ. Devel. Adminstrn., Dept. Commerce, Washington, 1968; spl. asst. to adminstr. SBA, Washington, 1968-69; spl. cons. to sec. Dept. Labor, 1977; bd. dirs. So. Edn. Found., La. Land and Exploration Co., Nat. Captioning Inst., Assn. Gov. Bds. Colls. and Univ., Econ. Devel. Commn. State of La.; mem. Nat. Sci. Bd., 1996-2002 (chmn. 1998-2002), Nat. Security Edn. Bd., Humphrey Fellows Nat. Adv. Bd., Bus. Higher Edn. Forum, com. econ. devel. Gabelli Enterprises Inc., exec. com. Assn. Am. Univs.; pres. Commission NCAA, Found. for Biomed. Rsch., Nat. Sci. Bd., 1996; former chair Presidential Adv. Bd. Pres. city coun., councilman-at-large City of Englewood, N.J., 1974-77; bd. advocates Planned Parenthood of La. Mem. AAUP, La. Conf. Univs. and Colls., La. Assn. Ind. Colls. and Univs., Bus. Coun. New Orleans, City Club, Inc., Met. Area Com., New Orleans Ednl. Telecom. Consortium. Democrat. Roman Catholic. Office: Tulane U Payson Ctr Bldg 7 Rm 300 6823 Saint Charles Ave New Orleans LA 70118-5698*

KELLY, EDMUND FRANCIS, insurance company executive; b. 1945; With Aetna Life & Casualty Co., 1974-92; pres., COO Liberty Mut. Ins. Co., Boston, 1992-98, pres., CEO, 1998—2001, chmn., 2000—01; chmn., pres., CEO Liberty Mutual Holding Co. Inc., Boston, 2001—. Office: 175 Berkeley St Boston MA 02116-5066

KELLY, EDMUND JOSEPH, lawyer, bank executive, investment banker; b. Mount Vernon, N.Y., May 18, 1937; s. Hugh Joseph and Catherine (Rice) K.; m. Joan Anne Fee, Nov. 18, 1961; children: Kathleen Kelly Broomer, Edmund Murphy, Thomas More, Mary Kelly Mehr, Michael McNaboe. AB cum laude, Coll. of Holy Cross, 1959; JD (James Kent scholar), Columbia U., 1962. Bar: N.Y. 1962. Sec. of Air Force Office of Gen.Counsel, Washington, 1962-65; assoc. White & Case, N.Y.C., 1965-70, ptnr., 1971-84; vice chmn. Dominick & Dominick Co., N.Y.C., 1984-91, Eighteen Seventy Corp., Purchase, N.Y., 1991—. Lectr. Practicing Law Inst., Am. Mgmt. Assn.; bd. dirs. Fed. Paper Bd. Co., Inc., Montvale, N.J., 1981-96; bd. dirs., mem. exec. com. Chgo. Pneumatic Tool Co., N.Y.C., 1980-86. Author: The Takeover Dialogues, A Discussion of Hostile Takeovers, 1987; editor Columbia Law Rev., 1961-62; contbr. articles to legal jours. Air Force mem. Armed Services Procurement Regulation Com., 1964-65. Office: Eighteen Seventy Corp Two Manhattanville Rd Purchase NY 10577-2118

KELLY, EDWARD JOSEPH, lawyer; b. Scranton, Pa., Oct. 31, 1966; s. Edward Joseph and Jane Elizabeth (Lavelle) K. BA, Duke U., 1988; JD, Boston U., 1991; LLM in Internat. Law, Golden Gate U., 2000. Bar: N.Y. 1992, Calif. 2000. Assoc. Blank Rome Comisky & McCauley, Phila., 1990; ptnr. Kelly Rode & Kelly, LLP, Mineola, N.Y., 1991-2000, Harris Corp. Counsel, Redwood Shores, Calif., 2000—. Lectr. in field. Cons. Legal Ctr. for Def. of Life, N.Y.C., 1991—. Emery Worldwide Inc. scholar, 1984-88; Internat. Legal Studies Merit scholar, 2000. Mem. N.Y. State Bar Assn., Bar Assn. San Francisco, Practising Law Inst., Computer Law Assn., Nat. Inst. Trial Advocacy, Guild Cath. Lawyers, N.Y. State Trial Lawyers Inst. Republican. Roman Catholic. Avocations: golf, sailing, weight training. Home: PMB 924 751 Laurel St San Carlos CA 94070-3113 Office: Harris Corp Microwave Comms Divsn 350 Twin Dolphin Dr Redwood City CA 94065-1408 also: 218 Griffing Ave Riverhead NY 11901-3009 E-mail: eKelly01@harris.com.

KELLY, ELLSWORTH, painter, sculptor; b. Newburgh, N.Y., May 31, 1923; Student, Pratt Inst., 1941—43, Boston Mus. Fine Arts Sch., Ecole des Beaux-Arts, Paris, 1946-48; DFA (hon.), Pratt Inst., 1993, Bard Coll., 1996; hon. doctorate, Royal Coll. Art, London, 1997. Works exhibited: Salon de Realities Nouvelles, Paris, 1950, 51, Carnegie Inst., 1958, 61, 64, 67, 85, Sao Paulo Biennial, 1961, Tokyo Internat., 1963, Documenta III, Germany, 1964, Documenta IV, 1968, Documenta IX, 1992, Venice Biennale, 1966, Guggenheim Internat., 1967, Corcoran Ann., Washington, 1979, others; one-man shows include Galerie Arnaud, Paris, 1951, Galerie Maeght, Paris, 1958, 64, 65, Sidney Janis Gallery, N.Y.C., 1965, 67, 68, 71, Betty Parsons Gallery, N.Y.C., 1956, 57, 59, 61, 63, Tooth Gallery, London, 1962, Washington Gallery Modern Art, 1964, Inst. Contemporary Art, Boston, 1964, Dayton's Gallery 12, Mpls., 1971, Albright Art Gallery, 1972, Hans Mayer Gallery, Dusseldorf, Germany, 1972, Leo Castelli Gallery, N.Y.C., 1973, 77, 79, 81, 82, 84, 85, 86, 88, 89, 92, Irving Blum Gallery, Los Angeles, 1965-68, 73, Greenberg Gallery, St. Louis, 1973, 89, Whitney Mus. Am. Art, N.Y.C., 1982, St. Louis Mus. Art, 1983, N.Y. Mus. Modern Art, 1973, Pasadena (Calif.) Mus. Modern Art, 1974, Walker Art Mus., Mpls., 1974, 94, Detroit Inst. Fine Arts, 1974, Ace Gallery, Venice, Calif., 1975, Janie Lee Gallery, Houston, 1975, Blum/Helman Gallery, N.Y.C., 1975, 77, 79, 81, 82, 84, 85, 86, 88, 89, 92, Met. Mus., N.Y.C., 1979, Stedelijk Mus., Amsterdam, 1979, Hayward Gallery, London, 1980, Centre Georges Pompidou, Paris, 1980, Staatliche Kunsthalle, Baden Baden, 1980, Margo Leavin Gallery, L.A., 1984, 91, John Berggruen Gallery, 1991, Castelli Graphics, N.Y., 1988, BlumHelman Gallery, L.A., 1988, Daniel Templon, Paris, 1989, 92, Overholland Mus., Amsterdam, 1989, Susan Sheehan Gallery, N.Y.C., 1990, 92, 95, 96, Gallery Kasahara, Osaka, Japan, 1990, Portikus, Frankfurt, Fed. Rep. Germany, 1990, Matthew Marks Gallery, N.Y.C., 1992, 94, 96, 98, 99, 2001, Anthony D'Offay, London, 1992, 94, Paula Cooper Gallery, N.Y.C., 1992, 94, Modern Art Mus. Ft. Worth, 1987, Mus. Fine Arts, Boston, Art Gallery Ont., Toronto, Balt. Mus. Art, San Francisco Mus. Modern Art, Nelson-Atkins Mus. Art, Kansas City, Detroit Inst. Arts, 1987, Huntsville Mus. Art, Ala., Des Moines Art Ctr., Iowa, Neuberger Art Mus., Purchase, N.Y., Los Angeles County Mus. Art, U. Okla. Mus. Art, Berkshire Mus., Pittsfield, Mass., Univ. Art Mus., Berkeley, Calif., Hood Mus. Art, Hanover, N.H., Ellsworth Kelly, The French Years, 1948-54, Galerie Nationale du Jeu de Paume, Paris, 1992, Westfalishes Landesmus, Munster, Germany, 1992, Nat. Gallery, Washington, 1993, Eli Broad Found., L.A., 1994, Milw. Art Mus., 1994, Gugghenheim Mus., 1996, Mus. Contemporary Art, L.A., 1997, Tate Gallery, 1998, Haus der Kunst, 1998, Met. Mus. Art, 1998, Fogg Art Mus., 1998, 99, Boston U., 1998, New Brit. Mus. Am. Art, 1998, Newcomb Gallery Art, 1998, High Mus. Art, 1999, Art Inst. Chgo., 1999, Kunstmuseum Winterthur, 1999, Stadtische Galerie, 1999, Kunstmuseum Bonn, 1999, Del. Art Mus., 1999, Smithsonian, 2000, Whitney Mus. Am. Art Philip Morris, 2000, San Francisco MOMA, 2002; represented in permanent collections Mus. Modern Art, Met. Mus., Whitney Mus., Carnegie Inst., Albright Art Gallery, Buffalo, Chgo., Art Inst., Worcester Mus., Toronto (Can.) Mus.,Tate Gallery, London, Walker Art Center, Mpls., Guggenheim Mus., N.Y.C., Los Angeles County Mus., Centre Georges Pompidou, Paris,Stedlijk Mus., Amsterdam, Kroller-Mueller Mus., Otterlo, Holland, Munster Mus., Germany, UNESCO, Paris, Centro Reina Sofia, Madrid, Lenbachhaus, Munster, Balt. Mus. Art, Nat. Gallery, Washington, San Francisco Mus. Modern Art. sculpture: lobby, Transp. Bldg., Phila., 1956, Barcelona, Spain, 1985, Balt. Mus. Garden, 1988, Walker Art Ctr. Garden, 1988, Mus. Fine Arts, Houston, 1986, Myerson Symphony Ctr., Dallas, 1989, Nestle S.A., Vevey, Switzerland, 1991, Carre d'Art, Museee d'Art Contemporain, Nimes, France, Holocaust Mus., Washington, 1993. Mem. USAAF, 1943—45. Decorated chevalier Ordre Arts et Lettres, Legion of Honor, comdr. Arts et Lettres (France); recipient Brandeis painting award, 1963, Edn. Min. award Tokyo Internat., 1963, 4th prize Carnegie Inst., 1962, painting prize, 1964; painting prize Art Inst. Chgo., 1964, 74, Showhegan, 1981, medal Pratt Inst., Bklyn., 1993, medal for outstanding achievement Sch. Mus. Fine Arts, Boston, 1996, ann. tribute award Friends Art and Preservation in Embassies, U.S. Dept. State, 1996, Govs. award N.Y. Sate Coun. on Arts, 1998; named Friend of Barcelona and recipient medal Mayor of Barcelona, 1993. Fellow Acad. Arts and Scis.; mem. Nat. Acad. Arts and Letters, NAD (academician, 1994-). Address: Matthew Marks Gallery 523 W 24th St New York NY 10011-1104*

KELLY, ERIC DAMIAN, lawyer, educator; b. Pueblo, Colo., Mar. 16, 1947; s. William Bret and Patricia Ruth (Ducy) K.; children: Damian Charles, Eliza Jane, Valissitie Christina Heeren, Douglas Ray Heeren; m. Sandra Walker, 1996. BA, Williams Coll., 1969; JD, M of City Planning, U. Pa., 1975; PhD, Union Inst., 1992. Bar: Colo. 1975, U.S. Dist. Ct. 1976, U.S. Tax Ct. 1976, U.S. Ct. Appeals (10th cir.) 1986. Chief citizens' participation unit Region III EPA, Phila., 1971-72; project planner Beckett New Town, N.J., 1972-73; v.p., project mgr. Rahenkamp Sachs Wells & Assocs., Inc., Denver and Phila., 1973-76; sole practice Pueblo, 1976-83; pres. Kelly & Potter, P.C., Pueblo, Albuquerque and Santa Fe, 1983-90. Adj. prof. U. Colo. Coll. Architecture and Planning, 1976-90; chmn., prof. Dept. cmty. and regional planning Iowa State U., 1990-95; adj. asst. prof. grad. sch. bus. U. So. Colo., 1986-90; dean coll. architecture and planning Ball State U., 1995-98, prof. urban planning, 1999—; mem. city devel. bd. State of Iowa, 1991-95. Gen. editor Zoning and Land Use Controls, 1995—; author: Enforcing Zoning and Land Use Codes, 1988, Managing Community Growth: Policies, Techniques and Impacts, 1993, Selecting and Retaining Consultants, 1993, Planning, Growth and Public Facilities: A Primer for Public Officials, 1994; editor, prin. author: The Roadtripper, 1969; contbr. articles to profl. planning and legal jours. Mem. adv. bd. Mcpl. Legal Studies Ctr., S.W. Legal Found., 1989—; mem. nat. adv. bd. Rocky Mountain Land Use Inst. Coll. Law U. Denver, 1992—; bd. dirs. Broadway Theatre League, Pueblo, 1976-77, Pueblo Beautiful Assn., 1978-82, Better Bus. Bur., 1988-89; trustee Sangre de Cristo Arts and Conf. Ctr., 1981-87, chmn. 1986; trustee Christ Congl. Ch., 1982-83; mem. Ind. Land Resources Coun., 1999—; bd. dirs., mem. adv. bd. Nature Conservacy Ind. With U.S. Army, 1969-71. Named Outstanding Student, Am. Inst. Planners, 1976; recipient Outstanding Faculty award Order of Omega, 1992. Mem. ABA, Am. Inst. Cert. Planners (charter, elected Coll. of Fellows 1999), Am. Planning Assn. (nat. pres., 1997—, chair planning & law divsn. 1996-97, pres. Iowa chpt. 1994-95, amicus curiae com. 1988-94, 95-97, legis. & policy com. 1993-97, Colo. chpt. excellence award 1989), Williams Coll. Alumni Assn. (class sec. 1969-74, regional sec. 1980-82, class agt. 1985-89), Rotary (local dir. 1988-90, dir., pres. Pueblo Rotary Found. 1988-89, v.p. 1988-89, pres. 1989-90, area rep. for dist. gov. 1991-92), Phi Kappa Phi. Democrat. Home: 2312 W Audubon Dr Muncie IN 47304-2003 Office: Ball State U Coll Architecture Planning Muncie IN 47306-0001

KELLY, EVELYN JUNE, writer, educator; b. Knoxville, Tenn., Oct. 28, 1934; d. Ralph G. and Bonnie L. Bell; m. Charles Lehman Kelly, June 26, 1956; children: Natalie, Marsha, Charlene, Kurt. BA, U. Tenn., 1955; MRE, So. Theol. Sem., Louisville, 1956; PhD, U. Fla., 1985. Instr. Marion County Schs., Ocala, Fla., 1966—95; prof. St. Leo (Fla.) U., 1995—2002; writing inst. Long Ridge Writers Group, West Redding, Conn., 2000—. Mem. spkrs. bur. Phi Delta Kappa, Bloomington, Ind., 1990—; edn. cons., Ocala, 1990—. Author: Legal Basics for Educators Coping with Schizophrenia; contbr. articles to profl. jours. Mem. Marion County C. of C., Ocala, 1990—93; sec. Pilot Club, Ocala, 1995—96; polit. affairs chmn. Woman's Club of Ocala, 1998—2001. Recipient Leadership award, Marion County C. of C., 1991. Mem.: Am. Soc. Journalists and Authors, Nat. Assn. Sci. Writers, Am. Med. Writers Assn. (Fla. pres. 1988—90), Delta Kappa Gamma (chpt. pres. 1986—88). Baptist. Home: 4621 NW 47th Ave Ocala FL 34482 Office Phone: 352-622-8733. Home Fax: 352-622-8733. Personal E-mail: evelykell@aol.com.

KELLY, FRANCIS J., III, global marketing company president and COO; m. Heather Kelly; children: Whitney, Jay (twins). BA, Amherst Coll.; MBA, Harvard. With Young & Rubicam, N.Y.C., 1978-81; from acct. exec. to sr. v.p., group acct. dir. Humphrey Browning MacDougall, 1983-88; prin., dir. client svcs., COO Leonard Monahan, Lubars & Kelly, Providence, 1989-94; chief mktg. officer, dir. planning and client svcs. Volkswagen, Am. Legacy Found., Talbots, Royal Caribbean, Titleist, FootJoy, The Hartford, Citizens Fin. Arnold Comm., 1994—; pres., COO Arnold Worldwide, Boston. Spkr. in field. Author (with Heather Kelly): What They Really Teach You at the Harvard Business School. Mem.: Essex County Club, Harvard Club Boston, Boston Ad Club (past pres.). Avocations: golf, paddle tennis, travel, reading, coaching youth sports. Office: Arnold Worldwide 101 Huntington Ave Boston MA 02199-7603

KELLY, GARY C., air transportation executive; m. Carol Kelly; children: Caroline, Elizabeth. BBA in Acctg., U. Tex., 1977. CPA, Tex. Audit mgr. Arthur Young & Co., Dallas; controller Sys. Ctr. Inc., Irving, Tex., Southwest Airlines Co., Dallas, 1986-89, CFO, 1989—2004, v.p. fin., 1989—2001, exec. v.p., 2001—04, vice chmn., CEO, 2004—. Office: Southwest Airlines Co 2702 Love Field Dr Dallas TX 75235

KELLY, GERALD F, JR., retail executive; BA in econ., U. of Ill. Mng. ptnr. Prof. Computer Resources, Inc., 1980—82; prin. Arthur Young & Co., 1982—84; v.p., mgmt. services Wilson Sporting Goods Co., 1984—86; sr. v.p. info. services Payless Shoesource, Inc., 1986—90, sr. v.p., CFO, 1990—96, sr. v.p. logistics, info. sys. and tech., 1986—2001; sr. v.p, chief info. officer Sears Roebuck and Co, 2002—. Office: Sears Roebuck and Co 3333 Beverly Rd Hoffman Estates IL 60179

KELLY, GRACE DENTINO, secondary school educator; b. Peoria, Ill., Mar. 30, 1934; d. Michael and Arnita Balagna (Barto) Dentino; m. Robert N. Kelly, Aug. 31, 1957; children: Susan, James, Stephen, Patrick. Cert. med. tech., St. Francis Sch. Med. Tech., 1955; BS, Bradley U., 1971, MS, 1973. Tchr. sci. St. Mark Sch., Peoria, asst. prin., 1980-83; prin., chmn. jr. H.S. curriculum com. for drug edn. St. Thomas Sch., Peoria Heights, Ill., 1983-89; tchr. biology and chemistry Woodruff High Sch., Peoria, 1989-90; prin. Blessed Sacrament Sch., Morton, Ill., 1991-92, St. Mark Sch., Peoria, 1992-98, Trewyn Mid. Sch., Peoria, 1998—2002, mem. math. curriculum com.; lead tchr. Glen Oak Primary Sch., Peoria, 2002—. Presenter Ill. Math Tchr. Conv., Peoria, 1992; tchr. Aurora (Ill.) U. Mem. adv. bd. Peoria Jour. Star Newspaper, 1973—. Bd. dirs. Spl. People Encounter Christ, 1997. Recipient Econs. Educator award Joint Coun. on Econ. Edn., N.Y.C., 1982—, dedication to excellence in edn. and to justice and equality award NOW, 1998, Esmark Found. award Ill. Coun. Econ. Edn., 1984, Those Who Excell award Ill. State Bd., 1989, PARC award, 1989, Today's Cath. Tchr.'s Project: Sharing award, 1992, Adminstr. of Yr. award Today's Cath. Tchr. Mag., 1992, Jean Tucker award Ill. Valley Mental Health Assn., 1994, Positive Promotions 1st prize Midwest Exceptional Tchr. award, 2005; named Tchr. of Yr., Positive Promotions, 2004; grantee Nat. City Bank, 2003, 2005. Mem. AAUW (Outstanding Cmty. Svc. award, Justice Edn. award 1998), Nat. Sci. Tchrs. Assn., Am. Soc. Clin. Pathologists, Ill. Sci. Tchrs. Assn. (dir. region III, presenter papers), Ill. Jr. Acad. Sci. (dir. region I), Phi Delta Kappa Roman Catholic. Home: 1815 W High St Peoria IL 61606-1635 Office: Glen Oak Primary Sch 809 Frye St Peoria IL 61603 Office Phone: 309-672-6518.

KELLY, HENRY ANSGAR, language educator; b. Fonda, Iowa, June 6, 1934; s. Harry Francis and Inez Ingeborg (Anderson) K.; m. Marea Tancred, June 18, 1968; children— Sarah Marea, Dominic Tancred. AB, St. Louis U., 1959, A.M., Ph.L., St. Louis U., 1961; PhD, Harvard U., 1965. From asst. prof. English to prof. emeritus U. Calif., L.A., 1967—2004, prof. emeritus, 2004—, dir. Ctr. for Medieval and Renaissance Studies, 1998—2003. Author: The Devil, Demonology and Witchcraft, 1968, 74, Divine Providence in the England of Shakespeare's Histories, 1970, Love and Marriage in the Age of Chaucer, 1975, The Matrimonial Trials of Henry VIII, 1976, Canon Law and the Archpriest of Hita, 1984, The Devil at Baptism, 1985, Chaucer and the Cult of St. Valentine, 1986, Tragedy and Comedy from Dante to Pseudo-Dante, 1989, Ideas and Forms of Tragedy from Aristotle to the Middle Ages, 1993, Chaucerian Tragedy, 1997, Inquisitions and Other Trial Procedures in the Medieval West, 2001; co-editor Viator 1970-90, editor, 2003—. Fellow Guggenheim fellow, 1971—72, Nat. Endowment Humanities, 1980—81, 1996—97. Fellow Medieval Acad. Am.; mem. Medieval Assn. of Pacific (pres. 1988-90). Roman Catholic. Home: 1123 Kagawa St Pacific Palisades CA 90272-3838 Office: UCLA Dept English 405 Hilgard Ave Los Angeles CA 90095-9000 Office Phone: 310-825-7486.

KELLY, HUGH RICE, lawyer, retired energy executive; b. Austin, Tex., Dec. 16, 1942; s. Thomas Philip and Cecilia Elizabeth (Rice) Kelly; m. Marguerite Susan McIntosh, Dec. 27, 1971; children: Susan McIntosh, Cecilia Rice. BA, Rice U., 1965; JD, U. Tex., 1972. Bar: Tex. 1972, U.S. Dist. Ct. (so. dist.) Tex. 1974, U.S. Ct. Appeals (5th cir.) 1975, U.S. Supreme Ct. 1975. Assoc. Baker Botts, Houston, 1972-78, ptnr., 1979-84; exec. v.p., gen. counsel Reliant Energy (formerly Houston Lighting & Power Co.), Houston, 1984—2003; gen. counsel Texans for Lawsuit Reform, 2003—. 1st lt. U.S. Army, 1966—69. Fellow: ABA Found., Houston Bar Found., Tex. Bar Found.; mem.: ABA, Am. Law Inst., Houston Bar Assn., State Bar Tex., Coronado Club. Republican. Home and Office: 1936 Rice Blvd Houston TX 77005-1635

KELLY, J. MICHAEL, lawyer; b. Hattiesburg, Miss., Dec. 5, 1943; BA, Emory U., 1966; LLB, U. Va., 1969. Bar: Ga. 1969, U.S. Supreme Ct. 1978, D.C. 1980, Utah 1982, Calif. 1988. Law clerk to Judge Griffin B. Bell (5th cir.) U.S. Ct. Appeals, Atlanta, 1969-70; ptnr. Alston & Bird (formerly Alston, Miller & Gaines), Atlanta, 1970-77, 81-82; counselor to atty. gen. U.S. Dept. Justice, Washington, 1977-79; counselor to sec. U.S. Dept. Energy, Washington, 1979-81; ptnr., shareholder, dir. Ray, Quinney & Nebeker, Salt Lake City, 1982-87; ptnr. Cooley Godward LLP, San Francisco, 1987—. Mem. Omicron Delta Kappa, Phi Alpha Delta. Office: Cooley Godward LLP 101 California St 5th Fl San Francisco CA 94111-5800 Office Phone: 415-693-2076. Business E-Mail: kellyjm@cooley.com.

KELLY, JAMES, editor; b. Brooklyn, NY, Dec. 15, 1953; m. Lisa Henricksson; 1 child, Luke. Grad. in Pub. and Internat. Affairs, Princeton Univ., 1977. Worked on Bill Bradley senatorial campaign, NJ, 1977; joined Time Mag., NYC, 1978, dep. mng. editor, 1996—2001, mng. editor, 2001—. Office: Time Inc Time Life Bldg 1271 Avenue of the Americas New York NY 10020-1300*

KELLY, JAMES ANDREW, former federal agency administrator, former policy research executive; b. Fond du Lac, Wis., Sept. 15, 1936; s. James Daniel and Clarice K.; m. Audrey Pool, July 30, 1960; children— James, Archer BS, U.S. Naval Acad., 1959; MBA, Harvard U., 1968; postgrad., Nat. War Coll., 1977. Commd. ensign U.S. Navy, 1959, advanced through grades to capt.; staff officer Vietnam Office, Dept. Def., Washington, 1974-75; mil. asst. to U.S. def. rep. Dept. Def., Tehran, Iran, 1975-76, Iran desk officer Washington, 1977-79; comptroller U.S. Pacific Fleet, Pearl Harbor, Hawaii, 1979-82; ret. U.S. Navy, 1982; with Pacific Analysis Corp., Honolulu, 1982-83; dep. asst. sec. Dept. Def., Washington, 1983-86; spl. asst. to pres., sr. dir. Asian affairs NSC, 1986-89; pres. EAP Assocs. Inc., Honolulu, 1989-94, Pacific Forum/CSIS, Honolulu, 1994—2001; asst. sec. for E. Asian & Pacific affairs U.S. Dept. State, Washington, 2001—05. Decorated Legion of Merit with gold star Mem. Japan-Am. Soc., U.S. Naval Inst., U.S. Nat. Com. for Pacific Cooperation, Asia Soc.

KELLY, JAMES ANTHONY, priest; b. Worcester, Mass., Apr. 22, 1949; s. James and Elisabeth (Allen) K. BA in Philosophy and Govt., Harvard Coll., 1971; PhD in Philosophy, CUNY, 1979; postgrad., Pontifical U. of the Holy Cross, Rome. ordained priest Roman Cath. Ch., 1982. Dir. Riverside Study Ctr., N.Y.C., 1977-79; procurator Prelature of Opus Dei, Rome, 1984-88, vicar USA region New Rochelle, N.Y., 1988-98; work with vicar of Opus Dei, 1998—2002; work with Del. Vicar of Opus Dei in Calif., 2002—. Avocations: philosophy, basketball, jazz, literature. Home and Office: 765 14th Ave San Francisco CA 94118-3558 Office Phone: 415-386-0431. Business E-Mail: jakelly@prkvw.com.

KELLY, JAMES M., astronaut, military officer; b. Burlington, Iowa, May 14, 1964; s. William and Mary Ann Kelly; m. Dawn Renee Timmerman; 4 children. BS in Astronautical Engrng. (with honors), USAF Acad., Colo. Springs, Colo., 1986; MS in Aerospace Engrng., U. Ala., Moontgomery, 1996; Disting. grad., Undergraduate Pilot Tng. Euro-NATO Joint Jet Pilot Tng., Sheppard AFB, Wichita Falls, Tex.; Top-Gun at 426th F-15 replacement tng. unit for initial F-15 Eagle tng., Luke AFB, Phoenix, Ariz. Commd. 2d lt. USAF, Colo. Springs, 1986, advanced through grades to lt. col., fighter pilot F-15, 67th Fighter Squadron, 18th Fighter Wing Kadena Air Base, Okinawa, Japan, 1987—92, instr., mission commdr. Otis Air Nat. Guard Base, Cape Cod, Mass., 1992—93; student Test Pilot Sch., Edwards (Calif.) AFB, 1993—94; project test pilot, asst. ops. officer USAF Nellis AFB, Las Vegas, Nev., 1994—96; astronaut Johnson Space Ctr., Houston, 1996—, pilot space shuttle flight crew. Recipient Meritorious Svc. medal, Air Force Commendation medals (2), Outstanding Unit awards (2), Combat Readiness medals (2). Mem.: USAF Acad. Assn. Grads. 2,500 flight hours in 35 different aircrafts; over 370 hours in space; pilot on STS-102 (Discovery), March, 2001; pilot on STS-114(Discovery) Return to Flight mission in which the crew will test and evaluate new procedures for flight safety and shuttle inspection and repair techniques in July, 2005. Office: Astronauts Office Johnson Space Ctr Houston TX 77058*

KELLY, JAMES MICHAEL, plant and soil scientist; b. Knoxville, Feb. 2, 1944; s. Woodrow Wilson and Thelma Lucille (Miller) K.; m. Susan Kay Morris, Aug. 9, 1969; children: John Kip, Christopher Kenneth. BS, E. Tenn. State U., 1966; MS, U. Tenn., 1968, PhD, 1973. Cert. profl. soil scientist. Assoc. ecologist NUS Corp., Pitts., 1973-74; rsch. assoc. Forestry Dept. Purdue U., West Lafayette, Ind., 1975-76; program mgr. Tenn. Valley Authority, Oak Ridge, 1977-88, sr. rschr., 1990-94; sr. tech. specialist, team leader, 1994-95; prof., chair dept. forestry Iowa State U., Ames, 1995—2001, chair dept. natural resource ecology and mgmt., 2002—04; dean Coll. Natural Resources Va. Tech. U., Blacksburg, 2004—. Vis. prof. agronomy Purdue U., 1988-89; adj. prof. U. Tenn., Knoxville, 1980-95, forestry dept. Purdue U., 1985-95. Author: Carbon Forms and Functions in Forest Soils, 1995; assoc. editor Soil Sci. Soc. Am. Jour., 1989-95, Forest Sci., 1998-2001; editl. bd. Forest Ecology and Management, 2001-; contbr. more than 100 articles to profl. jours. Head referee Ayso Youth Soccer, Oak Ridge, 1985-88; troop com. Boy Scouts Am., Oak Ridge, 1989-95. Oak Ridge Assoc. Univ. fellow, 1970-72; Elec. Power Rsch. Inst. grantee, 1978, 82, 89, 91, 95, NSF grantee, 1995; recipient Rsch. Champion award Elec. Power Rsch. Inst., 2002. Fellow Soil Sci. Soc. Am. (chmn. divsn. S7 1986-87, bd. dirs. 1988-89, awards com. 1992-93, fellows com. 1997-99, profl. svc. com. 2000-02); mem. AAAS, Ecol. Soc. Am., Soc. Am. Foresters, Exptl. Aircraft Assn. (chpt. pres. 1991-93), Trees Forever (bd. dirs. 1995—), Sigma Xi, Gamma Sigma Delta, Xi Sigma Pi. Achievements include research and application of environmental science. Office: Va Tech Univ Coll Natural Resources Blacksburg VA 24061

KELLY, JAMES PATRICK, lawyer; b. Twin Falls, Idaho, Mar. 25, 1946; s. James Patrick Sr. and Ynes Mary (Alastra) K.; m. Carol Louise White, June 6, 1968; children: Mary Louise, Christopher John. AB, Harvard U., 1968, JD, 1975. Bar: Ga. 1975, U.S. Dist. Ct. (no. and so. dists.) Ga. 1976, U.S. Ct. Appeals (5th cir. 1976, 6th cir. 1996, 1st cir. 1997, 11th cir.), U.S. Supreme Ct. 1999. Assoc. Kilpatrick & Cody, Atlanta, 1975-80; ptnr. Morris & Manning, Atlanta, 1980-83, Smith, Gambrell & Russell, Atlanta, 1983-85, Asbill, Porter & Churchill, Atlanta, 1985-86; sr. ptnr. Kelly Law Firm, P.C., Atlanta, 1986—. Bd. dirs. Sr. Citizen Services of Met. Atlanta, 1980-83. Served to capt. U.S. Army, 1968-72. Named Ga. Super Lawyer, 2005. Mem. ABA (corp. and banking law sect., health law forum), Ga. Bar Assn., Atlanta Bar Assn., Ga. Acad. Healthcare Attys. (bd. dirs. 1987-89), Am. Health Lawyers Assn. (bd. dirs. 1993-99, arbitrator, mediator, fellow 2005-), Internat. Network Boutique Law Firms, Lawyers Club Atlanta, Harvard Alumni Assn. (bd. dirs. 1983-84), Harvard Law Sch. Assn. Ga. (v.p. 1988-89, pres. 1989-91), Cochise Club, Harvard Club (pres. 1982-83, bd. dirs. 1990—), Georgian Club, Commerce Club, Capital City Club, Kiwanis (pres.). Episcopalian. Avocations: public speaking, marathon running, travel. Office: 200 Galleria Pky NW Ste 1510 Atlanta GA 30339-5946

KELLY, JAMES PATRICK, JR., retired engineering and construction executive; b. Bklyn., July 19, 1933; s. James Patrick and Marion Rita (Gleason) K.; children: Kathryn, Mark, Lisa Angelique, Trevor, Lisa, James (dec.). BSEngrng., U.S. Naval Acad., 1955; postgrad., U. Houston, 1968-69. Registered profl. engr., Calif. Asst. site mgr. Pathfinder reactor Allis Chalmers Mfg. Co., Sioux Falls, S.D., 1963-67; nuclear project mgr. Brown & Root, Houston, 1967-69; from constrn. project mgr. to asst. v.p. Gibbs & Hill, Omaha and N.Y.C., 1969-75; pres. Dravo Lime Co., Pitts., 1975-77; group v.p. natural resources Dravo Corp., Pitts., 1976-81, sr. v.p. engrng. and constrn., domestic and internat., 1982-84; pres., dir. C.F. Braun & Co., Alhambra, Calif., 1984-86; pres., CEO Hadson Power Systems, Inc., Irvine, Calif., 1986-91, ret., 1991. Bd. dirs. Hadson Corp., 1986—91. Bd. dirs. S.D. Mental Health Assn., 1966-67, Western Pa. Sch. Blind Children, 1978-84; mem. Sioux Falls Bd. Edn., 1965-66, Assn. Retarded Citizens Pitts., 1970—; pres. found. bd. Calif. State U., L.A., 1985-95; pres. Santa Ana Com. for Edn1. and Recreational Redevel. Plan, 1992-93, mem. Devel. Disabilities Area Bd., 1995-98; foreman Orange County Grand Jury, 1997-98. Mem. NSPE, Mensa, Sierra Club. Home: 1413 Franzen Ave Santa Ana CA 92705-6926 Personal E-mail: JPK159@webtv.com.

KELLY, JERRY BOB, social services administrator; b. Chgo., Feb. 6, 1942; s. Robert Lee and Mildred Florence (Griffin) K.; m. Diane Joyce Wilburn, Nov. 29, 1969; children: Jerold Robert, Joycelyn Reneé. B.S. in Acctg., Roosevelt U., 1968. Lic. real estate salesman and life ins. prodr., Ill. Acct. Weather Bloc Mfg. Co., Chgo., 1967-68; programmer Morton Salt Co., Chgo., 1968-69; br. mgr. Chgo. Econ. Devel. Corp., 1970-77; ptnr. Smith Distbrs., 1977-79; mgr. fin. and adminstrn. Suburban Cook County Area Agy. on Aging, Chgo., 1979-85; exec. dir. Lawndale Bus. and Local Devel. Corp., Chgo., 1985-88; dir. fin. No. Cook County Pvt. Industry Coun., Chgo., 1988-89; contr. Howard Area Cmty. Ctr., Chgo., 1989—; bd. dirs. Northside Cmty. Fed. Credit Union. Treas. Day Care Crisis Coun. Met. Chgo., 1973-76, appreciation award; 1st v.p. West Side Health Planning Orgn., 1974-76, appreciation award; treas. Met. Chgo. chpt. Nat. Caucus and Ctr. on Black Aged, 1992-94; treas. bd. dirs. St. Leonard's House; Cook County State's atty. African-Am. Adv. Coun., 1995—; vol. Ill. CPA. Soc.; treas. N. Lawndale Small Grants Human Devel. Corp.; adv. coun. John Marshall Metro H.S. Acad. Fin. Served with AUS, 1964-67. Recipient appreciation award Chgo. Black Caucus, Am. Fedn. Tchrs., Chgo. Bd. Election Commrs., Comprehensive Health Planning Orgn. Chgo. Mem. Assoc. Photographers Internat, John Marshall H.S. Alumni Assn. (pres.), Am. Legion (fin. officer Milton Lee Olive Post). Baptist. Club: Elks (2d v.p. Ill.-Wis., past grand exalted ruler). Research on redevel. plans for East Garfield. Home: 1415 N Mayfield Ave Chicago IL 60651-1015 Office: Howard Area Community Ctr 7648 N Paulina St Chicago IL 60626-1018 Office Phone: 773-622-1073. Personal E-mail: jbk59@aol.com. *Personal philosophy: The things that have helped me most in my life is believing in myself, trusting in God and the strength of the Griffin Family.*

KELLY, JOHN BARRY, II, lawyer; b. Washington, Dec. 17, 1942; s. John Barry and Blanche (O'Brien) K.; m. Elizabeth Ann MacDonald, June 26, 1965; children: Christine, John. BA in Am. History, Cath. U. Am., 1965, JD, 1971. Bar: Fla. 1971, Md. 1972, U.S. Dist. Ct. D.C. 1972, U.S. Ct. Appeals (D.C. cir.) 1972, U.S. Dist. Ct. (no. dist.) Fla. 1987. Law clk. U.S. Dist. Ct. D.C., Washington, 1971-72; assoc. Donahue & Ehrmantraut, Rockville, Md., 1972-75; pvt. practice Rockville, 1975-78; atty., project mgr. Westat, Inc., Rockville, 1978-80; trial atty. Tenn. Valley Authority, Knoxville, 1980-85; ptnr. Law Ctr., Pensacola, Fla., 1986-87, Ray, Kievit & Kelly, Pensacola, 1988—96, Kelly & Odom, Pensacola, 1996—2003; founder, mng. ptnr. Kelly & Assoc. Fla., LLC, Pensacola, 2003—. Faculty advanced adv. seminars Fla. Bar, Gainesville, 1990-94, Labor and Employment Trial Seminar, Fla. Bar, Miami, 1995; diplomate advanced advocacy Nat. Inst. Trial Advocacy, 1989-90; spkr. in field. Author: Labor and Employment Seminars, 1990-95; exec. editor Cath. U. Law Rev., 1970. Active Leadership Pensacola, Fla., 1992—. With USMC, 1966-68. Named Gulf Coast's Best Atty., Pensacola (Fla.) News Jour., 1988. Mem. Fla. Bar, D.C. Bar Assn., Escambia/Santa Rosa Bar. Avocations: reading, golf. Office: Kelly & Assoc of Fla LLC 649 Reservoir Rd Burnsville NC 28714-7160

KELLY, JOHN E., III, information technology executive; BS in Physics, Union Coll., 1976; MS in Physics, Rensselaer Poly. Inst., 1978, D in Materials Engrng., 1980. Numerous mgmt. and tech. positions IBM, 1980—90, dir. semiconductor rsch. and devel. ctr., 1990—94, v.p. bus. process reengrng. divsn. microelectronics, 1994—95, v.p. sys., tech. and sci., divsn. rsch., 1995—96, v.p. strategy, tech. and ops., divsn. microelectronics, 1996—97, v.p. server devel., 1997—99, gen. mgr. divsn. microelectronics, 1999—2000, sr. v.p., group exec. tech. group, 2000—. Fellow: IEEE; mem.: Semiconductor Industry Assn. (bd. dirs., former chmn.).

KELLY, JOHN FRANCIS, lawyer, law educator; b. Buffalo, Mar. 14, 1929; s. John James and Catherine McGeever Kelly; m. Louise Mary Heretick; children: Michael J., Catherine E. Cabell, Martin P., Theresa A. Poland, Timothy P., Mary L. Gressens, John F. Jr., Christopher D., Dawn M. Siedlecki. BA, U. Richmond, 1951, LLB, 1956; LLM, William and Mary, 1980. Bar: (Va.) 1956. From assoc. to mng. ptnr. Cohen, Cox & Kelly, Richmond, Va., 1956—70; ptnr., mng. ptnr. Hirschler Fleischer, Richmond, 1970—81; mgr. Kelly & Lewis, PC, Richmond, 1981—98; mgr., mem. Kelly & Kelly, PLC, Richmond, 1998—. Adj. prof. William and Mary Law Sch., Williamsburg, Va., 1986—95, U. Richmond Law Sch., 1996—2001. Cpl. U.S. Army, 1951—53. Fellow: Am. Coll. Tax Counsel. Roman Catholic. Avocations: golf, sports. Home: 4315 Northwich Ct Midlothian VA 23112 Office: Kelly & Kelly PLC Ste 300 7400 Beaufont Springs Dr Richmond VA 23225

KELLY, JOHN HUBERT, diplomat; b. Fond du Lac, Wis., July 20, 1939; s. James Daniel and Clarice L. Kelly; m. Helena Marita Ajo; children: David Snowdon, Maria Louise. BA, Emory U., 1961; advanced studies cert., Georgetown U., 1982. Vice consul Am. Consulate, Adana, Turkey, 1965-66; 3rd sec. Am. Embassy, Ankara, Turkey, 1966-67, 2nd sec. Bangkok, 1968-69; consul Am. Consulate, Songkhla, Thailand, 1969-71; 1st sec. Am. Embassy, Paris, 1976-80; fgn. svc. U.S. Dept. of State, Washington, 1972-76, dep. exec. sec., 1980-81, dep. asst. sec. of state, 1982-85, asst. sec. state for Near East and South Asia, 1989-91; U.S. amb. Am. Embassy, Beirut, 1986-88, amb. Helsinki, Finland, 1991-94; pres. John Kelly Cons., Conyers, 1994—; mng. dir. Internat. Equity Ptnrs., Atlanta, 1995-98. Mem. adv. coun. Una Chapman Cox Found., 1982-86; trustee Lebanese Am. U., 1996-2005. Mem. Coun. on Fgn. Rels., Mid. East Inst. Office: John Kelly Cons 2440 Wall St Ste D Conyers GA 30013-6341

KELLY, JOHN JAMES, lawyer; b. Rockville Centre, NY, July 4, 1949; s. John James Sr. and Eleanor Grace (Vann) K.; m. Clara Sarah Gussin; 1 child, John James III. AB in Govt., Georgetown U., 1971, JD, 1975. Bar: Pa. 1976, D.C. 1979, U.S. Dist. Ct. D.C. 1980, U.S. Claims Ct. 1982, U.S. Ct. Appeals (D.C. cir.) 1980, U.S. Ct. Appeals (fed. cir.) 1982. Law clk. to judge U.S. Dist. Ct., Washington, 1975-77; assoc. Corcoran, Youngman & Rowe, Washington, 1977-80, Capell, Howard, Knabe & Cobbs, Washington, 1980-83, Loomis, Owen, Fellman & Howe, Washington, 1983-86, ptnr., 1986-90; v.p., sec., gen. coun. Electronic Industries Alliance, Arlington, Va., 1990-96, exec. v.p., gen. counsel, 1997—; pres. JEDEC Solid State Tech. Assn., 2000—; counsel Howe, Anderson & Steyer, Washington, 1990—. Mem. Jud. Conf., D.C. Cir., Washington, 1983, Jud. Conf. Fed. Cir., Washington, 1988—. Contbr. articles to legal and profl. publs. Mem. ABA, D.C. Bar, Pa. Bar Assn., Am. Soc. Assn. Execs. (bd. dirs. legal section 1989-94, chmn. 1992-93), Fed. Bar Assn., Met. Club. Democrat. Roman Catholic. Office: Electronic Industries Alliance 2500 Wilson Blvd Arlington VA 22201-3834 Business E-Mail: johnk@jedec.org.

KELLY, JOHN JOSEPH, JR., federal official; b. Paterson, N.J., Dec. 28, 1940; s. John Joseph Sr. and Helen C. (Ebersach) K.; m. Brenda Ruth Miller, July 1, 1966; children: Elizabeth Ann, Kathleen Anne, John J. BS in Chemistry, Seton Hall, 1963; MS, Pa. State U., 1969; MPA, Auburn U., 1976. Commd. 2d lt. USAF, 1963, advanced through grades to brig. gen., 1989, dir. spl. projects, HQ Scott AFB, Ill., 1978-80; comdr. 15 WEA Squadron USAF, McGuire AFB, N.J., 1980-81; dep. dir. programs/policy Air Force info. systems USAF, Washington, 1981-84; vice comdr. 7th Weather Wing Scott AFB, 1984-85; comdr. 5th Weather Wing Langley AFB, Va., 1985-88; comdr. Air Weather Svc. Scott AFB, 1988-91; dir. weather AF/XOW Washington, 1991-94; dir. Nat. Weather Svc., 1998—2003; dep. under sec. oceans and atmosphere DOE, 2003—. Cons. Dept. Commerce, 1991. Fellow Am. Meteorol. Soc., Air Force Assn., Nat. Weather Assn. Roman Catholic. Avocations: golf, reading. Office: DOE 14th and Constitution NW Rm 6811 Washington DC 20230

KELLY, JOHN MARTIN, lawyer; b. Oshkosh, Wis., Dec. 13, 1948; s. Martin Paul and Ivy Cecile (James) Kelly; m. Teresa Jean Wendland, July 24, 1982. BA, U. Wis., Madison, 1971; JD, Georgetown U., 1974; postgrad. in bus., Harvard U., 1976-77. Bar: Wis. 1974, D.C. 1975. Atty. office chief counsel IRS, Washington, 1974—76; assoc. Dempsey, Magnusem, Williamson & Lampe, Oshkosh, 1977—82; ptnr. Dempsey Williamson, Young, Kelly & Hertel, LLP, Oshkosh, 1983—. Mem. ABA, Wis. Bar Assn., D.C. Bar Assn., Winnebago County Bar Assn. Office: Dempsey Williamson Young Kelly & Hertel LLP 1 Pearl Ave Oshkosh WI 54903-0886 Office Phone: 920-235-7300. Business E-Mail: jmkelly@dempseylaw.com.

KELLY, JOHN PATRICK, lawyer; b. Boston, May 9, 1952; s. Patrick and Elizabeth (Glennon) K.; m. Eileen Linda Obuchowski, May 28, 1983; children: John Patrick, Laura Beth, Kevin Sean. AB, Coll. Holy Cross, 1974; JD, Vanderbilt U., 1978. Bar: Mass. 1978, Fla. 1979, US Dist. Ct. (so. dist.) Fla. 1980, US Supreme Ct. 1981; cert. trial lawyer, Fla., bus. litig. specialist, Fla. Law clk. to presiding justice Tenn. Supreme Ct., Nashville, 1978—79; assoc. Fleming, O'Bryan & Fleming, Ft. Lauderdale, Fla., 1979—84, ptnr., 1984—96, Gunster, Yoakley, Valdes-Fauli & Stewart, Ft. Lauderdale, 1996—2000, Lorusso Loud & Kelly LLP, Ft. Lauderdale, 2000—05, The Kelly Law Firm, Ft. Lauderdale, 2005—. Lectr. Ctr. for Internat. Legal Studies, Kitzbuhel, Austria, 1999. Co-author Florida Business Litigation Manual, 1989-2000. Mem. Fla. Bar Assn. (civil rules com., lectr. Continuing Legal Edn. 1988-2000, prof. edn. seminars 1991-2000), Am. Arbitration Assn. (arbitrator), Nat. Futures Assn. (arbitrator), Tower Club, St. Thomas More Soc., Nat. Bd. Trial Advocacy, Phi Beta Kappa. Roman Catholic. Avocations: skiing, scuba diving, photography. Office: The Kelly Law Firm Suite 604 2601 E Oakland Pk Blvd Fort Lauderdale FL 33306 Office Phone: 954-568-5555. E-mail: jkelly@businesslitigation.com.

KELLY, JOHN TERENCE, architect; b. Elyria, Ohio, Jan. 27, 1922; s. Thomas Alo and Coletta Margaret (Conrad) K. BArch, Carnegie Mellon U., 1949; MArch, Harvard U., 1951, M of Landscape Architecture, 1952. Prin. architect John Terence Kelly, Cleve., 1954—. Vis. critic, lectr. U. Mich., U. Cin., Case Western Res. U., McGill U. Bd. dirs. Nova. With inf. AUS, 1943-46. Recipient Cleve. Arts prize in Architecture, 1968, hist. Bldg. award Architects Soc. Ohio, 1986; Charles Eliot Norton fellow, 1952, Fulbright fellow, Munich, Germany, 1953. Mem. AIA (nat. com. design). Home: 2646 N Moreland Blvd Cleveland OH 44120-1461 Office: 2646 N Moreland Blvd Cleveland OH 44120-1461

KELLY, JOHN WILLIAM, JR., academic administrator; b. Greenville, S.C., Jan. 5, 1955; s. John William and Betty (Kelly) K.; children: Christopher, Kimberly. BS, Clemson U., 1977; MS, Ohio State U., 1979, PhD, 1982. Asst. prof. Tex. A&M U., 1982-85, Clemson (S.C.) U., 1985-89, assoc. prof., 1989-91, prof., dept. head, dir. bot. garden, 1991-96, sch. dir., interim v.p. pub. svc. and agr., 1996-97, v.p. pub. svc. and agr., dir. S.C. Bot. Garden, 1997—. Cons. in field. Contbr. more than 50 articles to profl. jours. Bd. govs. S.C. BIO; chmn. bd. dirs. Am. Distance Edn. Corp., Pate Found Recipient Outstanding Contbr. award S.C. Nurseryman's Assn., 1991. Fellow Am. Soc. Hort. Sci. (v.p. 1995-99, pres. 1999, chmn. bd. dirs. 2000, Outstanding Rschr. 1994, Outstanding Adminstr. 1995, So. region Outstanding Educator 1989); mem. So. Assn. Agrl. Scientists (past pres.), S.C. Greenhouse Growers Assn. (life, exec. sec. 1991). Avocations: gardening, nature. Office: Clemson U Pub Svc and Agr 130 Lehotsky Hall Clemson SC 29634-0101

KELLY, KATHLEEN ANN, immunologist; b. Florissant, Mo., Nov. 12, 1960; m. Anthony William Butch. PhD, Ohio State U., 1990, degree in med. technology, 1983. Asst. prof. UCLA, L.A., 1999—. Recipient Young Scientist award, Assn. Clin. Scientists, 2003. Mem.: Am. Soc. Microbiology (assoc.; chmn. divsn. E 2004—05). Office: UCLA 10833 Le Conte Ave Los Angeles CA 90095-1732 Office Phone: 310-206-5562. E-mail: kkelly@mednet.ucla.edu.

KELLY, KEVIN, editor; b. Penn State, Pa., Apr. 27, 1952; s. Joseph John and Patricia Kelly; m. Gia-Minn Fuh, Jan. 2, 1987; children: Kaileen, Ting, Tywen. Freelance photographer, 1971-80; editor, pub. Walking! Jour., Athens, Ga., 1982-84, Whole Earth Rev., Sausalito, Calif., 1984-90; exec. editor Wired Mag., San Francisco, 1992-98; chmn. All Species Found., 2001—. Editor: Signal, 1988; author: Out of Control, 1994, New Rules for the New Economy, 1998, Asia Grace, 2002, Cool Tools, 2003, Tune Films, 2004. Recipient Gen. Excellence Nat. Mag. Award, 1993, 96. Mem.: Long Bets Found. (pres. 2002—). Avocation: beekeeping. Home and Office: 149 Amapola Ave Pacifica CA 94044-3102 Office Phone: 650-355-7676. E-mail: kk@kk.org.

KELLY, LUCIE STIRM YOUNG, nursing educator; b. Stuttgart, Germany, May 2, 1925; came to U.S., 1929; d. Hugo Karl and Emilie Rosa (Engel) Stirm; m. J. Austin Young, Aug. 30, 1946 (div. Feb. 1971); m. Thomas Martin Kelly, 1972 (dec. Aug. 2003); 1 child by previous marriage, Gay Aleta (Mrs. Donald Meyer). BS, U. Pitts., 1947, MLitt, 1957, PhD, 1965; D in Nursing Edn. (hon.), U. RI, 1977; LHD (hon.), Georgetown U., 1983; DSc (hon.), Widener U., 1984; D of Pub. Svc. (hon.), Am. U., 1985; DSc (hon.), U. Mass., 1989; DHL (hon.), SUNY, 1996. Instr. nursing McKeesport (Pa.) Hosp., 1953-57, asst. adminstr. nursing, 1966-69; asst. prof. nursing U. Pitts., 1957-64, asst. dean, 1965; prof., chmn. nursing dept. Calif. State U., LA, 1969-72; co-project dir. curriculum rsch. Nat. League for Nursing, 1973-74; project dir. patient edn., office consumer health edn., also adj. assoc. prof. cmty. medicine Coll. Medicine and Dentistry N.J.-Rutgers Med. Sch., 1974-75; prof. pub. health and nursing Sch. Pub. Health and Sch. Nursing Columbia U., N.Y.C., 1975-90, prof. emeritus Sch Pub. Health, Sch. Nursing, 1990—, assoc. dean acad. affairs Sch. Pub. Health, 1988-90, hon. prof. nursing edn. Tchrs. Coll., 1977-93, acting head divsn. health adminstrn. Sch. Pub. Health, 1980-81, 86-88; on leave as exec. dir. Mid-Atlantic Regional Nursing Assn., 1981-82. Cons. U. Nev., Las Vegas, 1970-72, Ball State U., Ind., 1971, Long Beach (Calif.) Naval Hosp., 1971-72, Travis AFB, Calif., 1972, Brentwood VA Hosp., LA, 1971-72, Ctrl. Nursing Office VA, Washington, 1971-94, N.J. Dept. Higher Edn., 1974-78, John Wiley Pub., 1974-76, Sch. Nursing Am. U. Beirut; mem. spl. med. adv. group VA Dept. Medicine and Surgery, Washington, 1980-84; cons. nursing com. AMA, 1971-74, Citizen's Com. for Children, N.Y.C.; v.p. Pa. Health Coun., 1968-69; mem. adv. com. physicians assts. Calif. Bd. Med. Examiners, adv. com. Cancer Soc. L.A., 1970-72, com. nursing VA, Washington, 1971-74, chair 1975-90, regional med. programs, Pa., 1967-69, Calif. 1970-72; mem. spl. adv. com. on med. licensure and profl. conduct N.Y. State Assembly, 1977-79, mem. nat. adv. com. Encore (nat. YWCA post-mastectomy group rehab. project), 1977-83; assoc. mem. N.Y. Acad. Medicine, 1988-90; mem. ethics com. Palisades Med. Ctr., 1993-05, bd. govs., 1995-05, mem. profl. and quality rev. com., 1995-2005, chair, 1998-05, exec. com., 1998-99; 2d vice chair N.Y. Presbyn. Healthcare Sys., Palisades Med. Ctr., 1999-03, 1st vice chair 2003-; lectr., cons., guest Beijing Med. Coll., China, 1982, Aga Khan U., Pakistan, 1990; bd. visitors U. Pitts. Sch. Nursing, 1986-93; mem. editl. adv. bd. Am. Jour. Pub. Health, 1992, chair, 1993-97; nat. and internat. lectr. in field; chair adv. com. grad. program in pub. health U. Medicine and Dentistry of N.J., 1995-00; vol. cert. mediator for Hudson County mcpl. cts., 2004-05. Author: (textbooks) Dimensions of Profl. Nursing, 9th edit., 2003, The Nursing Experience: Trends, Challenges, Transitions, 4th edit., 2001; contbg. editor: (jour.) Jour. Nursing Adminstrn., 1975—82; columnist: jour. Nursing Outlook, editor-in-chief, 1982—91; mem. bd. advisors (jour.) Nurses Almanac, 1978, Nurse Manager's Handbook, 1979, Nursing Administration Handbook, 1992; editor (editl. bd.): (jour.) Am. Health, 1981—91; editl. bd. (jour.) Nursing and Health Care, 1991—95, Internat. Nursing Index, 1997—2001. Bd. dirs. ARC, LA, 1971-72; bd. dirs. Vis. Nurse Svc. N.Y., 1980-2001, mem. exec. com., chmn. human resources, 1989-2001; bd. dirs. Concern for Dying, 1983-89; trustee Calif. State Coll. LA Found., 1971-72, U. Pitts., 1984-90, mem. exec. com. 1988-90; chair bd. visitors U. Pitts. Sch. Pub. Health, 1988-90; bd. visitors U. Miami Sch. Nursing, 1986—; mem. health svcs. com. Children's Aid Soc., N.Y., 1978-84; v.p. Am. Nurses Found., 1980-82; mem. nat. adv. coun. on nurse tng. HRA, 1981-85; mem. nurses leadership coun. Chlorine Chemistry Coun., 1999-2003; hon. bd. dirs. NOVA Found., 1998—, Health Professions Panel, Am. Legacy Found., 2000—; vol. cert. mediator Hudson County Mcpl. Cts. Named Outstanding Alumna U. Pitts. Sch. Nursing, 1966, Pa. Nurse of Yr., 1967, Roll of Honor N.J. State Nurses Assn., 1990; named to Tchrs. Coll. Columbia U. Nursing Edn. Alumni Hall of Fame, 1999; recipient Disting. Alumna award U. Pitts. Sch. Edn., 1981, Shaw medal Boston Coll., 1985, Bicentennial Medallion of Distinction, U. Pitts., 1987, R. Louise McManus Medallion for Disting. Svc. to Nursing, Tchrs. Coll.

Columbia U., 1987, Dean's Disting. Svc. award Columbia Sch. Pub. Health, 1995, Second Century award in health care, Columbia U. Sch. Nursing, 1996; fellow HEW, 1965. Fellow Am. Acad. Nursing (named Living Legend 2001); mem. ANA (dir. 1978-82, Hon. Recognition award 1992), APHA (Ruth Freeman Pub. Health Nursing award 1993), Pa. Nurses Assn. (pres. 1966-69), Nat. League Nursing (bd. govs. 1991-95), Nurses Ednl. Funds Bd., U . Pitts. Sch. Nursing Alumni (pres. 1959), Vis. Nurse Assn. Ctrl. Jersey (bd. dirs. 1999-2001, mem. bd. trustees), Am. Hosp. Assn. (com. chmn. 1967-68), Assn. Grad. Faculty Cmty. Health/Pub. Health Nursing (v.p. 1980-81), Sigma Theta Tau (sr. editor Image 1978-81, pres.-elect 1981-83, pres. 1983-85, nat. campaign chair Ctr. for Nursing Scholarship 1987-89, chair devel. com. 1989-95, spl. advisor 1995-97, planned giving task force 1998-2001, Mentor award 1985, 93, 97, Spirit of Philanthropy award 1997), Pi Lambda Theta, Alpha Tau Delta (Cert. of Merit 1968). Achievements include collection of papers in Mugar Library, Boston U.

KELLY, MARGUERITE STEHLI, fashion executive, consultant; b. N.Y.C., June 9, 1931; d. Henry E. and Grace (Hays) Stehli; m. Charles J. Kelly, Jr., Dec. 23, 1962; children: Marguerite Grace Kelly Walton, Lisa Stehli Kelly-Wolf. BA, Bryn Mawr Coll., 1953. Exec. trainee Macy's, N.Y.C., 1953-54, asst. buyer, 1954-57; buyer Bloomingdale's, N.Y.C., 1957-63; pres. Maggie, Inc., Wayzata, Minn., 1964-86, also brs. Georgetown, D.C., 1964-70, Locust Valley, N.Y., 1970-75; ret., 1986. Founder Workshop for Learning, 1987—. Mem. com. for spl. fund Foxcroft Sch., Middleburg, Va., 1974-76, trustee, 1978-87; mem. alumnae coun. Brearley Sch., N.Y.C., 1973-75; trustee Abbott Northwestern Hosp., Mpls., 1984-86; co-founder Citizens for Colin Powell Presdl. Draft Movement, 1994—. Episcopalian. Home: 3018 N St NW Washington DC 20007-3404

KELLY, MARILYN, state supreme court justice; b. Apr. 15, 1938; m. Donald Newman. BA, Ea. Mich. U., 1960, JD (hon.); postgrad., U. Paris.; MA, Middlebury Coll., 1961; JD with honors, Wayne State U., 1971. Assoc. Dykema, Gossett, Spencer, Goodnow & Trigg, Detroit, 1973-78; ptnr. Dudley, Patterson, Maxwell, Smith & Kelly, Bloomfield Hills, Mich., 1978-80; owner Marilyn Kelly & Assocs., Bloomfield Hills, Birmingham, Mich., 1980-88; judge Mich. Ct. of Appeals, 1989-96; justice Mich. Supreme Ct., 1997—. Tchr. lang., lit. Grosse Pointe Pub. Schs., Albion Coll., Ea. Mich. U.; past mem. rep. assembly, comms. com., family law coun. Mich. State Bar; co-chair Open Justice Commn., 1999-2003; mem. governing bd. Nat. Consortium for Racial & Ethnic Fairness in Cts. Active Mich. Dem. Party, 1963—; bd. mem. Channel 56-Public Television, Detroit, Women's Survival Ctr., Pontiac; v.p. Detroit Inst. Technology; devel. com. mem. St. Joseph Mercy Hospital, Pontiac; mem. citizens advisory com. Detroit Public Schools, Wayne County Community Coll., Oakland County Community Coll. Recipient Disting Alumni award Ea. Mich. U., Disting. Svc. award Mich. Edn. Assn., Eleanor Roosevelt Humanities award State of Israel Bonds Atty. Div., 2003. Mem. Soc. Irish-Am. Lawyers, Women Lawyers Assn. (past pres.), Oakland County Bar Assn. (past chair family law com.), State Bar Mich. (Michael Franck award 2003); Fellow Mich. State Bar Found. Office: Mich Supreme Ct PO Box 30052 Lansing MI 48909

KELLY, MARY, sculptor; b. Fort Dodge, Iowa, 1941; BA, Coll. St. Teresa, Minn., 1963; MA, Piux XII Inst., Florence, Italy, 1965; post grad. diploma, St. Martins Sch. Art, London, 1968—70. Visiting artist & fellow New Hall Coll., Cambridge U., England, 1985—86; dir. studios-Ind. Study Program Whitney Mus. Am. Art, NYC, 1989—96; prof.-interdisciplinary study UCLA. One-woman shows include Santa Monica Mus. Art, Calif., Generali Found., Vienna, New Mus. Contemporary Art, NY, Power Plant, Toronto, Can., Vancouver Art Gallery, Konstmuseet Malmö, Helsinki City Art Mus., Inst. Contemporary Art, London, Herbert F. Johnson Mus., Cornell U., LA Contemporary Exhbns., Riverside Studios, London, Mus. Modern Art, Oxford, exhibited in group shows at La. Mus. Modern Art, Denmark, UCLA Hammer Mus., Mus. Contemporary Art, LA, Bronx Mus., NYC, Tate Modern, London, Kunsthalle, Vienna, Art Gallery, ON, Carnegie Mus. Art, Whitney Biennial, Whitney Mus. Am. Art, 1991, 2004, Am. Century, 1999, Inst. Contemporary Art, Boston, Yale Ctr. British Art, 4th Biennial, Gallery Sydney New South Wales, Musee d'Art Moderne de la Ville de Paris, The Hague Gemeentemuseum; author: Imaging Desire, 1996, Mary Kelly, 1997, Post-Partum Document, 1998, Rereading Post-Partum Document, 1999. Visual Arts Fellowship, Nat. Endowment Arts, 1987. Mailing: c/o Postmasters Gallery 459 West 19th St New York NY 10011*

KELLY, MARY ELIZABETH WIESE, medical educator; b. Oakland, Nebr., Dec. 29, 1947; d. William A. and Hildred H. (Grabbe) Wiese; m. William Renard Kelly, Sept. 8, 1972. BS in Biology magna cum laude, Wayne State Coll., 1968; MSc, U. S.D., 1996. Cert. med. technologist; cert. point of care testing evaluator; specialist in hematology. Instr. Logan View Jr./Sr. High Sch., Hooper, Nebr., 1969-70; med. technologist St. Vincent Hosp., Sioux City, Iowa, 1971-76, St. Luke's Regional Med. Ctr., Sioux City, Iowa, 1976-84, sr. technologist, 1984—, clin. edn. coord., 1989-98, supr. lab. collection ctr., 1998—2002, point of care testing coord., 1998—2002. Adj. prof. Western Iowa Tech. C.C., Sioux City, 1996—. Active Children's Miracle Network Telethon. Mem.: Clin. Lab. Mgmt. Assn., St. Luke's Regional Med. Ctr. Sch. Med. Tech. (clin. edn. coord. 1989—, guest rels. facilitator 1990—94), Am. Soc. Clin. Pathologists, Siouxland Humane Soc. Avocations: needlecrafts, reading, gardening, writing, golf. Home: 1515 27th St Sioux City IA 51104-3015 Office: St Luke's Med Ctr 2720 Stone Park Blvd Sioux City IA 51104-3734 E-mail: KWllm@aol.com.

KELLY, MARY JOAN, librarian; b. Baton Rouge, Nov. 25, 1947; d. Theodore McKowen Sr. and Patricia Marilyn (Faul) Wilkes; m. Karl Joseph Nix; 1 child, Patricia Lynn Woodworth. BS, La. State U., 1970, MEd, 1973, EdD, 1980. Cert. English and social studies tchr., city/parish materials and/or media ctr. dir., sch. libr., La. Instr. conversation class La. State U., Baton Rouge, 1979—80; writer, prodr. The Video Co., Baton Rouge, 1983—90; freelance writer, pre and post video prodn., storyteller DBA-The BookDoctor, Baton Rouge; tchr. East Baton Rouge Parish Sch. Bd., ret., 1991; prin. St. Isidore Mid. Sch., 1991—95; libr. Holy Family Sch., Port Allen, La., 1995—2001, East Baton Rouge Parish Sch. Bd., 2001—. Presenter in field. Contbr. numerous articles to profl. jours.; sponsor yearbook and lit. mags.; storyteller and spkr. Mem. Non-Pub. Sch. Commn., La. Bd. Elem. and Secondary Edn., 1992-97; mem. adminstrn. commn. St. Aloysius Cath. Ch., 1989—, mem. comms. com., 1987—, chmn., 1989—. Mem. NEA, ASCD, La. Assn. Educators (mem. com. 1978-91), East Baton Rouge Parish Assn. Educators (v.p.), La. Assn. Classroom Tchrs. (mem. com. 1972-81), East Baton Rouge Parish Assn. Classroom Tchrs. (pres.), Assn. Ednl. Comm. and Tech., La. Assn. Ednl. Comm. and Tech., Internat. Platform Assn., La. Libr. Assn., Capital Area Reading Coun., Cath. Diocese of Baton Rouge Librs. Assn. (sec. 1996-97, pres. 99-01), East Baton Rouge Parish Librs. Assn., Gamma Beta Phi, Phi Lambda Pi, Phi Delta Kappa. Home: 2005 Lee Dr Baton Rouge LA 70808-3932 Office: Park Forest Elem 10717 Elain St Baton Rouge LA 70814 Office Phone: 225-272-0814. Business E-Mail: mkelly@ebrpsb.k12.la.us. E-mail: marykelly14@prodigy.net.

KELLY, MICHAEL JOSEPH, academic administrator, consultant; b. NYC, July 2, 1931; s. Hugh and Mary Agnes (Harrison) K.; m. Helen Janet Nee, Oct. 4, 1969; children: Joan T., Jean M. BA, Marist Coll., 1955; BEE, Cath. U., 1960, MEE, 1961; DEng, U. Detroit, 1968. Tchr. U. Detroit, 3 yrs., dir. Computer Ctr.; tchr., adminstr. Marist Coll., 4 yrs.; assoc. prof. electrical and mech. engring., dir. engring. case program Stanford U.; mgr. CAD, litho sys. IBM, East Fishkill, NY, 1969-79, mgr. Mfg. Tech. Ctr. Boca Raton, Fla., 1979-84, dir. Quality Inst., 1984, mgr. quality improvement and profl. devel. programs systems tech. divsn., 1986-87; dir. computer integrated mfg. and tech. transfer NJ Inst. Tech., NJ, 1987-89; dir. def. mfg. office Def. Advanced Rsch. Projects Agy., 1989-91; exec. dir. Nat. Adv. Com. on Semiconductors, 1989-91; dir. Mfg. Rsch. Ctr. Ga. Inst. Tech., Ga., 1991-96, prof. technology mgmt., 1995-96; Northrop-Grumman endowed chair mfg. and design Calif. State U., LA, 1996-99; ind. mgmt. and ednl. cons., 1999—. Adj. prof. Stony Book U., 2003—. Home: 42 Tillotson Ave Saint James NY 11780-1728 Personal E-mail: jkelly931@optonline.net.

KELLY, MICHAEL JOSEPH, II, publishing executive, investment company executive; b. Chicago, May 17, 1957; s. Michael Joseph and Mariann Julia (Williams) K.; m. Martha Joanna (Hall), Oct. 16, 1982; children: Katherine Rose, Mary Elizabeth, Michael Joseph III. Attended, U. Wis., 1975-77; BA, U. Ill., 1979; cert. exec., Columbia U., 1995. Sales rep. Chgo. Tribune, 1980-83, Fortune Mag., Time Inc., Chgo., 1983-84, s.e. mgr. N.Y.C., 1984-87, N.Y. mgr., 1987-89; ea. sales dir. Entertainment Weekly, Time Inc., N.Y.C., 1989-91, v.p. advt. sales, 1991-93, v.p. advt. sales and mktg., 1993-96, pub., 1196—2000; prin. Growth Capital Partners, Greenwich, Conn., 2000—. Bd. mem. Cabin Life, Inc. Piermont, N.Y. Bd. mem., com. chair Youth Lit. Vol., Chgo., 1981-85. Mem. Sleepy Hollow Club, U. Club N.Y.; Alpha Delta Phi (v.p. 1975-79). Avocations: golf, history, yoga.

KELLY, MICHAEL LEROY, JR., music educator; b. Warren, Ohio, Jan. 16, 1971; s. Michael LeRoy and Linda Susan Kelly; m. Diana Lynn Schwartz, June 23, 2000; 1 child, Ethan Michael. B in music edn., Youngstown State U., 1997, MusM, 2003. Music tchr. James A. Garfield Schools, Garretsville, Ohio, 1997—. Mem.: Ohio Music Edn. Assn., Ohio Edn. Assn. (bldg. rep. 2000—02). Democrat. Protestant. Avocations: golf, reading, music. Home: 460 Housel Craft Rd Bristolville OH 44402 Office: James A Garfield HS 10233 SR 88 Garrettsville OH 44231 Personal E-mail: mkellyd23@cs.com.

KELLY, MOIRA, actress; b. Queens, NY, Mar. 6, 1968; Student, Marymount Coll. Appeared in films The Boy Who Cried Bitch, 1991, Billy Bathgate, 1991, The Cutting Edge, 1992, Mr. Saturday Night, 1992, Chaplin, 1992, Twin Peaks: Fire Walk With Me, 1992, With Honors, 1994, Little Odessa, 1994, The Tie That Binds, 1995, (voice) The Lion King, 1994, Unhook the Stars, 1996, Entertaining Angels: The Dorothy Day Story, 1996, Changing Habits, 1997, Drive, She Said, 1997, Love Walked In, 1998, Dangerous Beauty, 1998, Hi-Life, 1998, Henry Hill, 1999, The Safety of Objects, 2001, (voice) The Lion King 1 1/2, 2004; TV movies include Monday After the Miracle, 1998; television appearances include (movies) Love Lies and Murder, 1991, Daybreak, 1993, To Have and To Hold, 1998, (series) The West Wing, 1999-2000. Office: care Gersh Agy 232 N Canon Dr Beverly Hills CA 90210-5302

KELLY, NANCY FOLDEN, art association administrator; b. Fredericksburg, Va., Oct. 28, 1951; d. Virgil Alvis Jr. and Frances Virginia (DeShazo) Folden; m. Frank R. Kelly, Aug. 11, 1973; 1 child, Katherine Elizabeth Kelly. BA in Theatre Arts, Va. Poly. Inst. and State U., 1973; MFA in Theatre Directing, So. Meth. U., 1975. Coord. student programs Lincoln Ctr. Inst., N.Y.C., 1976-79; dir. N.Y.C. Opera Nat. Co. and edn. dept. Lincoln Ctr., 1979-93, mem. coun. on ednl. programs, 1979-93; mng. dir. Broadway Arts Theatre for Young Audiences, N.Y.C., 1994-96; dir. family and cmty. programs Ctrl. Park Conservancy, N.Y.C., 1996-98; fin. mgr., assoc. dir. devel. Film Soc. Lincoln Ctr., N.Y.C., 1999—. Office Phone: 212-875-5208. E-mail: nkelly@filmlinc.com.

KELLY, NANCY FRIEDA WOLICKI, lawyer; b. Chgo., Sept. 8, 1953; d. Samuel and Ingrid (Rappel) W. BA in Journalism and Sociology, U. Ariz., 1974, JD, 1977. Bar: Ariz. 1977. Law clk. Ariz. Ct. Appeals, 1977-78; legis. asst. fgn. policy and armed svcs. health, staff atty. Billy Carter investigation to U.S. Sen. Dennis DeConcini, 1979-81; staff dir. Senate Subcom. on Alcoholism and Drug Abuse, Washington, 1981-84; mem. staff Senator Gordon J. Humphrey, Washington, 1984-87; coord. adv. com. Voluntary Fgn. U.S. Aid, 1987; sr. analyst legal and drug related issues president's Commn. on the HIV Epidemic, 1987-88; sr. policy analyst Commn. Exec. Legis. Jud. Salaries, 1988-89; counselor Sec. Energy, 1989-93; v.p. Kelly, Anderson & Assocs., Alexandria, Va., 1993—. Recipient William Spaid Meml. award U. Ariz. Coll. Law, 1977, Senate commendation for Billy Carter investigation, 1980. Mem. Ariz. Bar Assn., Phi Kappa Phi. Jewish. Office: 424 N Washington St Alexandria VA 22314-2312 Home: 1290 Beresford Ct Mc Lean VA 22101-2426 Office Phone: 703-518-8828. Business E-Mail: nancy.kelly@kapa.net.

KELLY, PAMELA B., lawyer; BA, U. Va., 1981; JD, UCLA, 1986. Bar: Calif. 1986. With Latham & Watkins, L.A., 1986—, ptnr., 1994—. Mem.: ABA (bus. law sect.), L.A. County Bar Assn., Calif. Bar Assn. Office: Latham & Watkins LLP 633 W Fifth St Ste 4000 Los Angeles CA 90071

KELLY, PATRICK JOSEPH, neurosurgeon, educator; b. Lackawanna, NY, Sept. 19, 1941; s. Joseph P. and Mary D. (Conner) K.; m. Carol Huey; children: Patrick D., Michael, Caitlin. BS, U. Mich., 1962; MD, SUNY, Buffalo, 1966. Cert. Am. Bd. Neurol. Surgery 1978. Intern U.S. Naval Hosp., Phila., 1966-67; resident neurosurgery Northwestern U., Chgo., 1970-72; resident neurosurgery med. branch U. Tex., Galveston, 1972—74; from asst. prof. to assoc. prof. U. Tex. Med. Sch., Galveston, 1974—79; assoc. prof. SUNY, Buffalo, 1979-84; prof., cons. Mayo Med. Sch./Mayo Clinic, Rochester, Minn., 1984-93; prof., chmn. neurosurg. dept. NYU Med. Ctr., 1993—. Cons., adv. bd. mem. Jet Propulsion Lab NASA, Pasadena, Calif., 1994—. Author: Tumor Stereotaxis, 1991; co-editor: Computers in Stereotactic Neurosurgery, 1992; mem. editl. bd. Neurosurgery, 1991—, Surg. Neurology, 1990—, Jour. Stereotactic and Functional Neurosurgery, 1986—; contbr. chpts. in books and articles to profl. jours.; profiled Am.'s Top Drs. and Top Drs.: New York Metro Area 2000-2002 of Castle Connolly Guide. Lt. comdr. MC USN, 1968—70. Recipient Scoville award World Fedn. Neurol. Surgery, 1997; named Citizen of Yr. Buffalo Evening News, 1982, Best Doctors in Am. Good Housekeeping, 1993, Town & Country, 1992, Am. Health, 1996, Top 100, Irish Am. mag., 1996, 99, Best Drs. N.Y., New York Mag., 1999, 2000-05, Woodward/White, Inc., 1998, 2000, 01, 02, Obrador medal Spanish Neurol. Soc., 1996, Sir Peter Freyer medal, Irish Surgical Soc., 2001, Invitee d'Honneur French Neurosurg. Soc., 2000, Olivacrona medal Karolinska Inst., Stockholm, 2002, Schneider Lectr. Am. Assn. Neurolog. Surgeons, 1996, 2002; inducted Boys and Girls Clubs Am. Hall of Fame, 2001. Fellow ACS; mem. Am. Soc. Stereotactic Neurosurgery (past pres., bd. dirs.), Am. Assn. Neurol. Surgeons (Van Wagenen fellow 1977, com. chmn.), Acad. Neurol. Surgery, Soc. Neurol. Surgeons (com.), Soc. Neurochurgic de Lange Francaise., Brain Tumor Found. (founder 1997). Roman Catholic. Achievements include development of a computer-assisted image guiding stereotactic neurosurgery for brain tumors. Avocations: sailing, watercolor painting. Home: 7 Gracie Sq New York NY 10028-8001 Office: NYU Med Ctr 530 1st Ave New York NY 10016-6402 Office Phone: 212-263-8002. Business E-Mail: kellyp01@med.nyu.edu. E-mail: kelly@brainscans.com.

KELLY, PAUL J., lab administrator, physician, researcher; b. Australia; MB, BChir, MD, U. New S. Wales. Sr. rsch. physician Garvan Inst. for Med. Rsch., Sydney; co-founder, CEO Gemini Genomics, 1995—2001; CEO Orchid BioScis., Inc., 2003—. Former CEO, exec. dir. OmniViz, Inc.; dir. Nanovis, MedCenter Solutions, AgaMatrix. Contbr. articles to profl. jours. Fellow: Australasian Coll. Physicians. Office: Orchid BioSciences Inc 4390 US Rte 1 Princeton NJ 08540 Office Phone: 609-750-2200. Office Fax: 609-750-6400.*

KELLY, PAUL JOSEPH, JR., federal judge; b. Freeport, N.Y., Dec. 6, 1940; s. Paul J. and Jacqueline M. (Nolan) Kelly; m. Ruth Ellen Dowling, June 27, 1964; children: Johanna, Paul Edwin, Thomas Martin, Christopher Mark, Heather Marie. BBA, U. Notre Dame, 1963; JD, Fordham U., 1967. Bar: N.Mex. 1967. Law clk. Cravath, Swaine & Moore, N.Y.C., 1964—67; assoc. firm Hinkle, Cox, Eaton, Coffield & Hensley, Roswell, N.Mex., 1967—71, ptnr., 1971—92; judge U.S. Ct. Appeals (10th cir.), Santa Fe, 1992—. Mem. N.Mex. Bd. Bar Examiners, 1982—85, N.Mex. Ho. of Reps., 1976—81, chmn. consumer and pub. affairs com., mem. judiciary com.; mem. N.Mex. Pub. Defender Bd., U.S. Jud. Conf. Com. on the Jud. Br., 1994—99, U.S. Jud. Conf. Civil Rules Adv. Com., 2002—; chair 10th Cir. Rules com., 10th Cir. Uniform Criminal Jury Instrn. Com. Bd. visitors Fordham U. Sch. Law, 1992—; pres. Oliver Seth Inn of Ct., 1993—, Roswell Drug Abuse Com, 1970—71; mem. Appellate Judges Nominating Commn., 1989—92, Eastern N.Mex. State Fair Bd., 1978—83; pres. Chaves County Young Reps., 1971—72; vice chmn. N.Mex. Young Reps., 1969—71, treas., 1968—69; pres. parish coun. Roman Cath. Ch., 1971—76; bd. dirs. Zia coun. Girl Scouts Am., Roswell Girls Club, Chaves County Mental Health Assn., 1974—77, Santa Fe Orch., 1992—93, Roswell Symphony Orch. Soc., 1969—82, treas., 1970—73, pres., 1973—75. Mem.: State Bar N.Mex. (v.p. young lawyers sect. 1969, mem. continuing legal edn. com. 1970—73, co-chmn. ins. sub-com. 1972—73, mem. Bench-Bar com. 1994—), Fed. Bar Assn. Office: US Court Appeals 10th Circuit Federal Courthouse PO Box 10113 Santa Fe NM 87504-6113 Office Phone: 505-988-6541.

KELLY, PAUL KNOX, investment banker; b. Boston, Feb. 18, 1940; s. Thomas Joseph and Rita Patricia Kelly; m. Nancy Lee Belden, July 17, 1978; 1 child, 3 stepchildren. AB in English, U. Pa., 1962; MBA in Fin., Wharton Sch., 1964. Investment analyst bond dept. Prudential Ins. Co. Am., 1964-65; asst. treas. Comml. Credit Co., 1965-68; v.p. First Boston Corp., N.Y.C., 1968-75; ptnr., mem. mgmt. com., dir. Prescott, Ball & Turben, Cleve., 1975-77; sr. v.p., dir. Butcher & Singer, Inc., 1977-78; exec. v.p., mem. exec. com., dir. Blyth Eastman Dillon & Co., N.Y.C., 1978-80; mng. dir. Merrill Lynch White Weld Capital Markets Group, N.Y.C., 1980-82; exec. v.p., dir. Dean Witter Reynolds, Inc., 1982-84; pres., dir. Quadrex Securities Corp., 1984-85, Peers & Co., N.Y.C., 1985-90, PH II, Inc., Westport, Conn., 1988—, Knox & Co., N.Y.C., 1992—. Trustee U. Pa.; bd. dirs. Knox Enterprises, Inc. Mem. Union Club (Cleve.), Chagrin Valley Hunt Club, Penn Club N.Y., The LInks, Union League (Phila.), The No. Club (Auckland, New Zealand). Office: Knox & Co 33 Riverside Ave Westport CT 06880-4223

KELLY, PAUL VINCENT, federal agency administrator; BA in Econ., Merimack Coll.; MS in Mgmt. Sci., U. Lowell; diploma in nat. security studies, Indsl. Coll. of Armed Forces. Commd. ensign USMC, 1979, advanced through ranks to Col., various inf. and fin. mgmt. positions, sr. officer Dept. of Navy liaison to House and Senate appropriations com.; sr. officer legis. asst. to chmn. of Jt. Chiefs of Staff U.S. Dept. of State, dir. Marine Corps War Coll.; ret. USMC, 1999; asst. sec. of state for legis. affairs U.S. Dept. of State, Washington, 2001—. Office: US Dept of State Legis Affairs 2201 C St NW Washington DC 20520

KELLY, PETER, communications executive; m. Lorraine Kelly; 2 children. Pres., CEO Continuum Health Ptnrs., Inc., 2000—, exec. v.p., COO. Office: Continuum Health Ptnrs 555 W 57 St New York NY 10019

KELLY, PETER MCCLOREY, II, lawyer; b. Chgo., Mar. 23, 1948; s. John Stephen and Helen (Patterson) K.; m. Susan Barrett, Aug. 17, 1995; children: Peter, Eli, Eamon, Liam. A.B., U. Notre Dame, 1970; J.D. cum laude, Ind. U., 1973. Bar: Ill. 1973. Assoc. McDermott, Will & Emery, Chgo., 1973-78, ptnr., 1979-81; ptnr. Kirkland & Ellis, Chgo., 1981-84, Bell, Boyd & Lloyd, Chgo., 1984-91, Murphy, Smith & Polk, Chgo., 1991-98, Ogletree Deakins (formerly Murphy Smith & Polk), 1999—; adj. prof. Sch. of Law, Loyola U., Chgo., 1976-84, Ind. U. Law Sch., Bloomington, 1985; speaker to various profl. groups and orgns. Mem. U.S. C. of C. (employee benfits council 1981—), ABA (life fellow), charter fellow, bd. govs., Am. Coll. Employee Benefits Counsel Chgo. Bar Assn. (sec. employee benefits com. 1982-83, vice chmn. employee benefits com. 1983-84, chmn. 1984-85), Midwest Pension Conf. (exec. bd. 1984—), Order of Coif. Home: 1316 Davis St Evanston IL 60201-4104 Office: Ogletree Deakins 2 1st Nat Plz Fl 25 Chicago IL 60603 E-mail: kellypm@odnss.com.

KELLY, QUENTIN THORN, water and power company executive, writer; b. New Orleans, La., July 14, 1934; s. Edgar Joseph and Leola (Pilcher) Kelly; m. Peggy R. Richey; children: Lisa Scott Curtis, Carolyn Kelly Colella, Quentin T. Jr. Student, Kenyon Coll., Gambier, Ohio. Asst. to pres. Westinghouse Electric Corp., New York City, NY, 1965—72; chmn. and CEO WorldWater & Power Corp., Pennington, NJ, 1984—. Writer MGM Studios, Hollywood (Culver City), Calif. Named to N.J. Inventors Hall of Fame, 1998. Mem.: Army and Navy Club (Wash., DC), Williams Club (N.Y.C.). Achievements include invention of Solar Water Pumps, 1992. Office: WorldWater & Power Corp 55 Route 31 South Pennington NJ 08534

KELLY, R. JAMES, retail executive; From nat. dir. mid. market and fast growing cos. divsn. to mng. ptnr. Carolinas ops. Price Waterhouse LLP, 1973—97; vice-chmn., CFO, adminstrv. officer Family Dollar Stores, Charlotte, NC, 1997—; also bd. dirs. Past chmn. bd. dirs. Charlotte Symphony Orch. Office: Family Dollar Store PO Box 1017 10401 Old Monroe Rd Charlotte NC 28201

KELLY, RALPH WHITLEY, emergency physician, health facility administrator; b. Hernando, Miss., Oct. 13, 1949; s. Leslie Athrel and Nina Earline (Christopher) K.; m. Janet Sue Evans Burns, May 15, 1971 (div. May 1991); children: Rochelle, Angela, Melanie, Christopher; m. Virginia Markle Alfson, Mar. 13, 1993. BS, U. Tex., Arlington, 1972; DO, Tex. Coll. Osteo. Medicine, Ft. Worth, 1976. Diplomate Am. Bd. Emergency Medicine, Am. Bd. Pediat. Emergency Medicine, Am. Bd. Pediat., Am. Bd. Quality Assurance and Utilization Rev. Physicians, Nat. Bd. Med. Examiners; subsplty. bd. cert. in risk mgmt.; cert. physician exec. Mem. staff pediat. USAF, Wichita Falls, Tex., 1979-82; med. dir. emergency dept. Fischer-Mangold Group, Pleasanton, Calif., 1982-90, EmCare, Inc., Dallas, 1990-91; chmn. emergency dept. Hillcrest Bapt. Med. Ctr., Waco, Tex., 1990-91; dir. EMS tng. programs Vernon Regional Jr. Coll., Wichita Falls, 1991-95; dir. emergency svcs. Wichita Gen. Hosp., Wichita Falls, 1991-95; pres. Texoma Emergency Assn., Wichita Falls, 1991-95; dir. practice mgmt. MEPA, Dallas, 1995-98; chmn. emergency dept. Trinity Med. Ctr., Carrollton, Tex., 1995—, also chmn. QA Ctr.; chmn. emergency dept. RHD Meml. Med. Ctr., 1996—. Bd. dirs. Foster Child Advocacy Svcs., Wichita Falls, 1983-85; mem. faculty Tex. affiliate Am. Heart Assn., Austin, 1985—, course dir. ACLS, 1982—; mem. exec. com. Wichita Gen. Hosp., 1991-95; physician advisor for quality Trinity Med. Ctr., 1996—. Rev. editor Tex. Emergency Bulletin of Tex. Coll. Emergency Physicians, 1987-89. Mem. pre-med. adv. com. Midwestern State U., Wichita Falls, 1987-89; mem. child mortality com. DA's Office, Wichita Falls, 1994-95; EMS med. dir. Lifeline EMS, Wichita Falls, 1992-94, AMT EMS, Waco, 1990-91. Major USAF, 1976-82. Recipient Physician Recognition award AMA, 1985. Fellow Am. Coll. Emergency Physicians, Am. Acad. Pediat.; mem. Tex. Med. Assn., Tex. Osteo. Med. Assn., Group Mgmt. Sect. (charter), Pediat. Emergency Med. Sect. Republican. Avocations: bicycling, downhill skiing, coin collecting/numismatics, hiking, computers. Home: 2405 Winding Hollow Ln Plano TX 75093-4108 Office: Trinity Med Ctr 4343 N Josey Ln Carrollton TX 75010-4603 E-mail: Dr13Kelly@aol.com.

KELLY, RAYMOND ALOYSIUS, JR., lawyer, educator; b. Yuma, Ariz., July 6, 1944; s. Raymond A. and Josephine V. (Schulz) K.; m. Mary Jo Battaglia, Mar. 8, 1980; 1 child, Kyle Patrick. B.A., Providence Coll., 1966; J.D., Albany Law Sch., 1973. Bar: N.Y. 1974, U.S. Dist. Ct. (no. dist.) N.Y. 1974, U.S. Ct. Appeals (2d cir.) 1984. Asst. dist. atty. Albany County, Albany, N.Y., 1974-80; asst. pub. defender Albany County, Albany, 1980—; sole practice, Albany, 1980—; mem. adj. faculty Albany Law School, 1975—; mem. continuing legal edn. faculty N.Y. State Lawyers and Advs., Albany, 1981—. Mem. editorial bd. Albany Law Rev., 1972-73. Contbr. articles to N.Y. State Defender, 1983-84. Active Big Bros.-Big Sisters, Providence, 1962-66. Served to capt. U.S. Army, 1966-70; Vietnam. Decorated D.S.C., Bronze Star, Purple Heart with 3 oak leaf clusters. Mem. Nat. Inst. Trial advocacy, Assn. Trial Lawyers Am., Nat. Coll. Criminal Def., N.Y. State Trial Lawyers Assn., N.Y. State Bar Assn. (Denison Ray award 1998, Outstanding Practitioner of Yr. 2000). Democrat. Roman Catholic. Clubs: Wolferts Roost Country, Steuben Athletic (Albany). Home: 293 Loudonville Rd Albany NY 12211-2015 Office: 112 State St Suite 1005 Albany NY 12207 E-mail: rakelly@albany.net.

KELLY, RAYMOND BOONE, III, lawyer; b. Ft. Worth, Oct. 12, 1947; s. Raymond Boone Jr. and Martha (Morehead) K.; m. Ellen McCarthy; children: Alice Katherine, Anne Rowan. BA, Tulane U., 1970; JD, So. Meth. U., 1974. Bar: Tex. 1974. Ptnr. Decker, McMackin & McClane, Ft. Worth, 1974—. V.p., trustee William E. Scott Found., Ft. Worth, 1978—. Bd. dirs., past pres. Goodwill Industries Ft. Worth, 1975-94; bd. dirs. Arts Coun. Ft. Worth and

Tarrant County, 1980-91, 95-97, Conf. of S.W. Founds., Dallas, 1986-89, 97-2000, Davey O'Brien Found., 2001—, Ft. Worth Mus. Sci. and History, 2003-, Big Bros./Bis Sisters, Ft. Worth, 1987-94, Intercultura, Inc., Ft. Worth, 1989-96, chmn., 1992-94, Funding Info. Ctr., 1993-97, Ft. Worth Dallas Ballet, 1996-97, Cmty. Found. North Tex., 1996-2002, Bishop Davies Ctr, 1999-2005, Baylor All Saints Med. Ctr., 1997—; trustee All Saints Health Found., 1987-, chmn. 1991-2002; trustee Modern Art Mus. Ft. Worth, 1981—, Fort Worth Country Day Sch., 1996-2002, Goodwill Industries Ft. Worth Found., 1997—2003, Ft. Worth Club, 1999-2002. Mem. ABA, State Bar Tex., Tarrant County Bar Assn., Tarrant County Young Lawyers Assn. (v.p., sec. 1976-77), Tex. Bar Found. (life fellow), Tarrant County Bar Found., Ft. Worth Club, Exchange Club, Rivercrest Country Club, Steeplechase Club, Ind. Petroleum Assn. Am., Tex. Oil and Gas Assn. Republican. Episcopalian. Home: 301 Virginia Pl Fort Worth TX 76107-1611 Office: Decker, McMackin & McClane 801 Cherry St Ste 2000 Fort Worth TX 76102-3812

KELLY, RAYMOND W., police commissioner; married; two children. LLM, NYU, St. John's U.; grad., Manhattan Coll.; MPA, Harvard U.; Doctorate (hon.), Marist Coll., 1995, Manhattan Coll., 1996, Coll. St. Rose, 1997, St. John's U., 1998. Various positions ending with commr. N.Y.C. Police Dept., ret., 1994; under sec. for enforcement U.S. Treasury Dept., 1996-98; commr. U.S. Customs Svc., Washington, 1998—2001, N.Y.C. Police Dept., NY, 2001—. V.p. Ams., INTERPOL, 1997. Col. USMCR. Office: NYC Police Dept One Police Plaza New York NY 10038

KELLY, RICHARD C., energy company executive; BS in Acctg., MBA, Regis U.; postgrad., U. Colo., U. Mich. With auditing dept. Pub. Svc. Co. Colo., 1968-74, staff asst. to mgr. acctg., 1974-76, corp. reports mgr., 1976-83, mgr. acctg., asst. contr., 1983-86, treas., 1986-87, v.p. fin. svcs., 1987-90, sr. v.p. fin., 1990—97; exec. v.p., CFO New Century Energies, Denver, 1997—2000; pres. enterprises Xcel Energy Inc., Minneapolis, Minn., 2000—02, v.p., CFO, 2002—03, pres., 2003—, COO, 2003—03, CEO, chmn., 2005—. Past pres. Arvada Optimist Club; past dir. Ronald McDonald House, Denver Metro C. of Colo. Pub. Expenditures Coun., Mercy Housing; bd. dir. Minneapolis Downtown Coun.; mem. Regis Acctg. Adv. Com. Office: Xcel Energy Inc 414 Nicollet Mall Minneapolis MN 55401-1993*

KELLY, RITA MAE, academic administrator, researcher; b. Waseca, Minn., Dec. 10, 1939; d. John Francis and Agnes Mary (Lorentz) Cawley; m. Vincent Peter Kelly, June 2, 1962; children: Patrick, Kathleen. BA, U. Minn., 1961; MA, Ind. U., 1964, PhD, 1967; doctorate (hon.), U. Umeå, Sweden, 1998. Rsch. scientist Ctr. for Rsch. in Social Systems, 1968-70; sr. rsch. scientist Am. Inst. for Rsch., Inc., Kensington, Md., 1970-72; cons. OEO, 1972-73; pres. Rita Mae Kelly & Assocs., 1973-75; tenured prof. Rutgers U., 1977-79, prof., 1979-82; from tenured to full prof. Sch. Justice Studies Ariz. State U., Tempe, 1982-87, tenured prof. justice studies, pub. affairs, polit. sci. and women's study, 1987-96, chair, dir. Sch. Justice Studies, 1990-95; dean social scis. U. Tex., Dallas, 1996—. Mem. credentials com. U.S. Dem. Party, Atlanta, 1988; mem. state com. Ariz. Dem. party, Phoenix, 1988; dist. committeeman Tempe Dist. 27 Dem. Party, 1988; charter mem., hon. bd. dirs. Ariz. Women's Inst., 1988; founding mem. Inst. for Women's Policy Rsch., Washignton, 1988, Ariz. Found. for Women, Inc., 1995—; bd. dirs. Ariz. Leadership 2000 Alumni Assn., 1993—; co-dir. Ariz. Leadership 2000 and Beyond, 1993—; co-chair Arizonians for a Healthy Future, 1994-95. Author: (with others) The Making of Political Women: A Study of Socialization and Role Conflict, 1978, Promoting Productivity in the Public Sector: Problems, Strategies, Prospects, 1988, Comparable Worth, Pay Equity, and Public Policy, 1988, (with Mary M. Hale) Gender, Bureaucracy, and Democracy: Careers and Equal Opportunity in the Public Sector, 1989, The Gendered Economy, 1991, Advances in Policy Studies Since 1950, 1992, Gender Power, Leadership and Governance, 1995, Gender, Globalization and Democratization, 2000; editor book series Women in Politics Series, 1981-88; editor: (with Dennis J. Palumbo) Sage Series in Public Policy, 1989-94; co-editor: Gender, Globalization and Democratization, 2001; editor Women & Politics Jour. Dep. gov. Am. Biog. Inst., 1995—; co-chair Airz. Women's Vote Project, 1996—; coord. scientific rsch. com. engendering globalization democratization internat. Social Sci. Coun., 1998—. Internat. Soroptomists of Phoenix, Inc. grantee, 1987, GTE Found. Rsch. grantee, 1988, Ind. U. Rsch. grantee, 1964-65; Ford Found. fellow, 1962-63; recipient Rutgers U. Outstanding Faculty merit award, 1979, All-Am. Women's award, 1985, YWCA Camden County award, 1980; Fulbright award to Brazil, 1991; recipient Aaron Wildovsky award for best book pub. policy, 1992, 93, Outstanding Mentor award Women's Caucus for Polit. Sci., 1991, 97, Miriam Mills award, 1995; U.S. Dept. Labor Step Out grantee, 1993-95. Mem. Am. Polit. Sci. Assn. (chair roundtable 1985, chair B. William Anderson award com. 1983-84, reviewer 1977-78, 83-84, head policy sect. 1989), APA Soc. for Psychol. Study of Social Issues (chair nat. task force on productivity in the pub. sector 1975-80), Am. Soc. for Pub. Adminstrn. (exec. coun. sect. on mgmt. sci. and policy analysis 1986-89, vice chair planning and evaluation com. 1985-86, Achievement award 1981, Disting. Rsch. award for rsch. on women 1991), Internat. Polit. Sci. Assn. (chair com. on status of women 1986-88), Western Polit. Sci. Assn. (pres. 1988-89), Policy Studies Orgn. (pres. 1988-89, Merriam Mills award 1995, Thomas R. Dye Svc. award 1997). Office: U Tex PO Box 830688 Richardson TX 75083-0688

KELLY, ROBERT A., music educator; s. James J. and Anne W. Kelly. Bachelor, Hartt Coll. of Music, West Hartford, 1969—73; M, Ctrl. Conn. State U., 1978. Music tchr. Catherine M. McGee Mid. Sch., Berlin, Conn., 1973—83; choral dir. music tchr. Berlin H.S., Berlin, Conn., 1973—. Recipient Tchr. of Yr., Berlin Bd. Edn., 1995. Mem.: NEA, Conn. Edn. Assn., Nat. Band Assn., Am. Choral Dirs. Assn., Music Educators Nat. Conf. Office: Berlin High School 139 Patterson Way Berlin CT 06037 E-mail: rkelly@berlinwall.org.

KELLY, ROBERT D, finance company executive; B in commerce, Meml. U. of Newfoundland, 1979; MBA, Dalhousie U., 1980. Various positions Bank of Nova Scotia, 1982—89; v.p. Lloyds Bank PLC, 1989—90; mktg. mgr. Westinghouse Credit Corp., 1990—91; project fin. mgr., 1991—92; dir. Project Fin., 1992—94; v.p. Calpine Fin., 1994—98, sr. v.p., 1998—2002; CFO, exec. v.p., Calpine Corp., San Jose, Calif., 2002—; pres. Calpine Fin. Co., 2001—. Office: Calpine 50 W San Fernando St, 5th Fl San Jose CA 95113

KELLY, ROBERT DONALD, management consultant; b. Chgo., Sept. 14, 1929; s. Donald Francis and Irene Sarah (Gardner) K.; m. Kay R. Black, Apr. 25, 1959; children: Kim Robert, Kris Donald, Candis Elizabeth. BS in Indsl. Engring., Iowa State U., 1951; MS, Purdue U., 1955, PhD, 1957. Cert. mgmt. cons.; lic. inds. psychologist, Ill. Mem. faculty Purdue U., West Lafayette, Ind., 1953—57; from assoc. prin. to ptnr., dir. Kearney Mgmt. Cons., Chgo., 1957—79; mng. ptnr. pers., internat. pers. Arthur Andersen World Hqtrs., Chgo., 1979—90; sr. internat. cons. Watson Wyatt Co., Chgo., 1990—2003; freelance cons. Chgo., 2003—. Bd. dirs. Allied Farm Equip., Duff Truck Line, Smith, U.S. Contbr. articles to profl. jours. Chmn. bd. trustees Clarendon Hills Presbyn. Ch., 1969-72; chmn. bd. deacons, 1966-69; pres. Bd. Edn. Hinsdale Sch. Dist. 1975-83; trustee and chmn. bd. Coll. DuPage, 1985-91; trustee, bd. dirs. Village of Hinsdale, 1995-99; chmn. Hist. Preservation Commn., Village of Hinsdale, 2001-03. With USAF, 1951-53. Mem. Am. Inst. Mgmt. Cons., Am. Compenstion Assn., Am. Psychol. Assn., Univ. Club, Econs. Club Chgo., Sigma Xi. Home: 120 S Elm St Hinsdale IL 60521-4227 Personal E-mail: kelly80369@aol.com.

KELLY, ROBERT EDWARD, engineer, educator; b. Abington, Pa., Oct. 20, 1934; s. Bernard Joseph and Rose Monica (Lautenschlager) K.; m. Karin Elizabeth Lampert, Aug. 15, 1964; children: Nicholas, Jennifer. BA, Franklin & Marshall Coll., 1957; BS, Rensselaer Poly. Inst., 1957; MS in Aero. Engring., MIT, 1959, ScD, 1964. Asst. prof. UCLA, 1967-70, assoc. prof., 1970-75, prof. dept. mech. and aerospace engring., 1975—2003, vice chair grad. affairs, 1976, 1994—99. Sr. vis. fellow Imperial Coll. Sci. and Tech., London, 1974; vis. prof. Northwestern U., Evanston, Ill., 1985, U. Manchester, Eng., 1994; vis. scientist Japan Atomic Energy Rsch. Inst., Tokai-mura, 1991; cons. Hughes Aircraft Co., El Segundo, Calif., 1976-83. Assoc. editor Physics of Fluids, 1981-83, 92-97; mem. editl. bd. Phys. Rev. E, 1990-96; contbr. over 70 articles to profl. jours. Fellow ASME, Am. Phys. Soc. (chmn. divsn. fluid dynamics 1980-81). Avocation: gardening. Office: MAE Dept UCLA Los Angeles CA 90095-1597 E-mail: rekhome@ucla.edu.

KELLY, ROBERT EDWARD, JR., lawyer; b. Pitts., Nov. 28, 1950; s. Robert E. Sr. and Adelaide Cecelia (Harris) K.; m. Noreen Theresa Quinn, Oct. 23, 1976; children: Robert E. III, Christopher Patrick, Andrew Clifford. BA, Siena Coll., 1972; JD, Georgetown U., 1975. Bar: Pa. 1975, U.S. Dist. Ct. (we. dist.) Pa. 1975, U.S. Dist. Ct. (ea. and mid. dist.) Pa. 1978, U.S. Ct. Appeals (3d cir.) 1979, U.S. Supreme Ct. 1980, U.S. Dist. Ct. (no. dist.) N.Y. 1992, U.S. Dist. Ct. (no. dist.) Calif. 1994. Assoc. Houston, Harbaugh, Cohen & Lippard, Pitts., 1975-77; assoc., dep. atty. gen. Commonwealth of Pa., Harrisburg, 1977-80; assoc. Duane, Morris & Heckscher, Harrisburg, 1980-86, ptnr., 1986—2002, Kelly, Hoffman & Goduto, LLP, 2002—. Mem. ABA, FBA, Pa. Bar Assn., Pa. Def. Inst., Dauphin County Bar Assn., Pa. Soc., Am. Inns of Ct., St. Thomas More Soc., West Shore Country Club (Camp Hill, Pa.). Republican. Roman Catholic. Home: 3610 Horsham Dr Mechanicsburg PA 17050-2204 Office: Kelly Hoffman & Goduto LLP Commerce Towers 10th Fl 300 N 2d St Harrisburg PA 17101 Office Phone: 717-920-8200. Business E-Mail: rkelly@khgllp.com.

KELLY, ROBERT EMMETT, physicist, researcher; b. Cape Girardeau, Mo., Nov. 26, 1929; s. Robert Emmett and Gladys (Adams) K.; m. Sarah Grace Combs, June 6, 1962; children: Katelyn, Frank, Tara. BS, S.E. Mo. State U., 1950; MS, U. Mo., 1952; PhD, U. Conn., 1959. Physicist E.I. DuPont de Nemours & Co., Inc., Aiken, S.C.; mem. faculty dept. physics U. Miss., University, 1959-88, prof., 1966-88. Mem. research staff Los Alamos (N.Mex.) Nat. Lab., 1988—, Boeing, Gen. Electric Co., Am. Optical Co., Lawrence Radiation Lab., Woods Hole Oceanographic Inst., Hanford Lab., Marshall Space Flight Center; cons. Los Alamos Sci. Lab., Lawrence Livermore Lab. Contbr. articles to profl. jours.; woodwind performer various civic symphonies, concert bands. Served with AUS, 1954-56. AEC fellow, 1965; NASA fellow, 1970-71 Mem. Am. Radio Relay League, Acoustical Soc. Am., Am. Geophys. Union, Am. Fedn. Musicians, Benton Lit. Soc., Chamber Music Players, Chemistry, German, Amateur Radio clubs, Sigma Xi, Pi Mu Epsilon, Omicron Delta Kappa, Sigma Pi Sigma. Methodist. Home: 75 Tesuque St Los Alamos NM 87544-2638 Office Phone: 505-662-4516.

KELLY, ROBERT F., federal judge; b. 1935; BS, Villanova U., 1957; LLB, Temple U., 1960. Pvt. practice law, Media, Pa., 1961-62, 64-76, Chester, Pa., 1962-64; law clk. to Hon. Francis J. Catania Ct. Common Pleas, Delaware County, Pa., 1964-72; prothonotary Delaware County, 1972-76; former judge Ct. Common Pleas 32d Jud. Dist. Pa.; judge U.S. Dist. Ct. (ea. dist.) Pa., Phila., 1987—, sr. judge, 2001—. Lectr. law Villanova U. Law Sch. Voluntary defender Delaware County, 1962; chmn. Delaware County Rep. Exec. Com., 1972-76, Subcom. on Libr. Programs; mem. Judicial Coun. com. on Automation and Tech., 1989—. Mem. ABA, Am. Judicature Soc., Pa. Bar Assn., Pa. Trial Judges Assn., Delaware County Bar Assn. (judicial counsel's com. automation and tech., 1989—, chmn. subcom. libr. programs). Office: US Dist Ct 11613 US Courthouse 601 Market St Philadelphia PA 19106-1713 Office Phone: 215-597-0736.

KELLY, ROBERT LYNN, advertising agency executive; b. Chgo., Oct. 25, 1939; s. Carl Robert and Annabel Pauline (Lindsay) K.; m. Maria Graciela Gonzalez, Oct. 26, 1963; children: Albert E., Elizabeth A. BA, Gettysburg Coll., 1961. Dir. pub. info. Oxnard AFB, Calif., 1961-64; with Armstrong World Industries, Lancaster, Pa., 1964-67; owner Bob Kelly Advt., Quito, Ecuador, 1967-70; ptnr., writer, acct. exec., mgr. Ibold & Kelly Advt., Lancaster, 1970-72; founder, pres. Kelly Advt., Inc., Lancaster, 1972-84; pres. Kelly Michener, Inc., Lancaster. 1984—2004, chmn., 2005—. Guest lectr. F & M Coll., and Millersville U., 1971—; lectr. Lancaster Community Gallery, 1977. Contbr. articles to profl. jours. Active various civic orgns.; bd. dirs. Lancaster Cmty. Gallery, 1978-89, v.p., 1983-89; mem. campaign coms. Lancaster County Rep. orgns., 1973-75; bd. dirs. Rockford Plantation, 1979-89, v.p., 1988-89; v.p. Let's Lifebelt Lancaster, 1984-85. With USAF, 1961-64. Mem. Nat. Advt. Agy. Network (nat. chmn. 1984), Am. Assn. Advt. Agys. (chmn. regional bd. govs. 1989-90, mem. regional bd. govs. 1998—), Lancaster Advt. Agy Coun. (sec. 1987-61, pres. 1992—2004), N.G. Assn. U.S., Sales and Mktg. Exec., Hamilton Club, Lancaster Tennis and Yacht Club (bd. dirs., v.p. 1986-87, commodore 1988-89), Port Herman Beach Assn. (pres. bd. dirs. 1998-99). Episcopalian. Office: Kelly Michener Inc PO Box 959 Lancaster PA 17608-0959 E-mail: rkelly@kellyadv.com.

KELLY, ROBERT VINCENT, JR., metal products executive; b. Phila., Sept. 29, 1938; s. Robert Vincent and Catherine Mary (Hanley) K.; m. Margaret Cecilia Taylor, Feb. 11, 1961; children: Robert V. III, Christopher T., Michael J., Tasha Marie. BS in Indsl. Mgmt., St. Joseph's U., Phila., 1960; postgrad., Roosevelt U., 1965-66. Gen. foreman prodn. Republic Steel Corp., Chgo., 1963-68; supt. prodn. Phoenix Steel Corp., Phoenixville, Pa., 1969-73; gen. supt. ops. Continental Steel Corp., Kokomo, Ind., 1973-77; gen. mgr. MACSTEEL div. Quanex Corp., Jackson, Mich., 1977-81; corp. v.p. Quanex Corp., Houston, 1979—, pres. MACSTEEL group Jackson, 1982—. Pres. La Salle Steel Co., Hammond, Ind., 1985-87, Arbuckle Corp., Jackson, 1984-88. Leader, com. mem. Boy Scouts Am., Jackson. Lt. USN, 1960-63. Mem. Am. Mgmt. Assn. (pres.), Inst. Indsl. Engrs., Assn. Iron and Steel Engrs., Am. Soc. for Metals, USN Inst., Jackson C. of C. Clubs: Jackson Country. Avocations: hiking, camping, sailing, scouting. Home: 1734 Metzmont Dr Jackson MI 49203-5379 Office: Macsteel, Quanex Corp 1 Jackson Sq Ste 500 Jackson MI 49201-1446

KELLY, ROBERT WILLIAM, economist; b. Washington, June 11, 1939; s. Robert Joseph and Emily Thersa (Markiewicz) K.; BA, U. Wyo., 1963; MA, U. Pitts., 1965; m. Lily Hsui, Dec. 28, 1966. Econ. adviser to undersec. of state Dept. State, Vietnam, Thailand, Cambodia, 1965-72; dir. policy food controls Cost of Living Council, Exec. Office of Pres., 1973-74; policy adviser to dep. adminstr. Fed. Energy Adminstrn., 1974-75; dir. planning and analysis, Office Commercialization ERDA, 1975-76, dir. commercialization studies, 1976-77; dir. policy analysis Office Energy Rsch., Dept. of Energy, 1977-79, adviser to undersec. energy, 1980-81, dir. U.S. /Korea Coop. Energy Assessment, 1979-80; sr. economist Gas Research Inst., 1981-90; dep. asst. adminstr. Dept. of State/AID Mid. East and North Africa, 1990-93; chief economist Internat. Econ. and Energy Analysis SAIC, 1993-99; fgn. policy advisor Dole for Pres. campaign, 1994-96, pvt. cons., 2000_. Served with USMCR, 1958-60. Ford fellow, 1963-64; recipient cert. of achievement Fed. Energy Adminstrn., 1974; cert. of appreciation Energy R & D Adminstrn., 1976; Cash award Dept. Energy, 1979; Letter of Commendation Republic of Korea, 1980. Mem. Am. Econs. Assn., Rep. Nat. Com. Nat. Policy Forum, Internat. Trade Com. (chmn. 1994-97), foreign policy trade adv. to GOP pres. nom. Sen. Robert Dole, 1994-96, Omicron Delta Epsilon. Roman Catholic. Author articles, papers. Home: PO Box 725 Mc Henry MD 21541-0725 Personal E-mail: rwkelly@mindspring.com.

KELLY, SEAN DORRANCE, philosophy educator; BS with honors, MS in Cognitive and Linguistic Scis., Brown U., 1989; PhD in Philosophy, U. Calif., 1992. Tchg. asst. philosophy U. Calif., Berkeley, 1989—97, Ralph K. Church departmental fellow in philosophy, 1997—98, instr. philosophy, 1996; lectr. philosophy Stanford U., Calif., 1998—99; asst. prof. philosophy Princeton (N.J.) U., 1999—, Jonathan Edwards Bicentennial preceptor, 2002—, Old Dominion faculty fellow, 2000—01, chair Old Dominion Faculty Fellows, 2001—02. Vis. scholar U. Calif., Berkeley, 2000; lectr. in field. Author: The Relevance of Phenomenology to the Philosophy of Language and Mind, 2000; contbr. articles. Campbell's Coll. Scholarship, Brown U., 1985—89, Fellowship in Complex Sys., Santa Fe Inst. and Los Alamos Labs., 1989, Howison fellowship in philosophy, U. Calif., 1995—96, fellow, NEH Summer Inst. on Consciousness and Intentionality, 2002, James S. McDonnell sr. fellowship in philosophy and neuroscis., 2000—, fellow, John Simon Guggenheim Meml. Found., 2003—, vice-chancellor's rsch. grant in the humanities, U. Calif., 1995, Humanities Grad. Rsch. grant (2), 1996. Mem.: Am. Philosoph. Assn. Office: Princeton U Dept Philosophy 1879 Hall Princeton NJ 08544-1006

KELLY, SUE W., congresswoman; b. Lima, Ohio, Sept. 26, 1936; m. Edward Kelly; 4 children. BA, Denison U., 1958; MA in Health Advocacy, Sarah Lawrence Coll., 1985. Rschr. New England Inst. Med. Rsch., 1958; tchr. John Jay Jr. H.S., 1962-63, Harvey Sch.; real estate rehabilitator, 1963—; campaign coord. Rep. Hamilton Fish, N.Y., 1971-72; intern Ruth Taylor Home, 1973-74; florist, owner Somerstown Flower Shop, 1978-79; patient advocate St. Luke's Hosp., 1984-87; adj. prof. of health advocacy Sarah Lawrence Coll., 1987-92; mem. 105th to 108th Congress from 19th N.Y. dist. U.S. Ho. of Reps., 1995—. Vice chmn. com. fin. svcs. U.S. Ho. Reps., mem. com. transp. and infrastructure, mem. com. small bus., mem. various subcoms. Republican. Home: 2025 Crompond Rd Yorktown Heights NY 10598 Office: US House Reps 1127 Longworth Bldg Washington DC 20515-3219

KELLY, T. MARK, lawyer; b. Houston, May 5, 1957; BA magna cum laude, Tex. A&M U., 1978; JD, So. Methodist U., 1981. Bar: Tex. 1981. Ptnr., co-chair Corp. Fin. and Securities Practice, mem. Mgmt. Com. Vision & Elkins, LLP, Houston. Fellow: Houston Bar Found., Tex. Bar Found.; mem.: ABA, Houston Bar Assn., Tex. Bar Assn. Office: Vinson & Elkins LLP First City Tower 1001 Fannin St, Ste 2300 Houston TX 77002-6760 Office Phone: 713-758-4592. E-mail: mkelly@velaw.com.

KELLY, THADDEUS ELLIOTT, medical geneticist; b. N.Y.C., 1937; MD, Med. Coll. S.C.; PhD, Johns Hopkins U. Diplomate Am. Bd. Genetics (pres. 1993-94), Am. Bd. Pediat. Prof. pediat. U. Va., Charlottesville, dir. med. genetics. Office: U Va Hosp Div Med Genetics PO Box 800386 Charlottesville VA 22908-0386*

KELLY, THOMAS CAJETAN, archbishop; b. Rochester, N.Y., July 14, 1931; s. Thomas A. Kelly and Katherine Eleanor (Fisher) Conley. AB, Providence Coll., 1953; STL, Dominican House of Studies, Washington, 1959; D in Canon Law, U. St. Thomas, Rome, 1962; STD (hon.), Providence Coll, 1979; DHL (hon.), Spalding Coll., 1983. Ordained priest Roman Cath. Ch. 58, aux. bishop 77. Sec. Dominican Province, N.Y.C., 1962—65; sec. Apostolic Del., Washington, 1965—71; assoc. gen. sec. Nat. Conf. Cath. Bishops-U.S. Cath. Conf., Washington, 1971—77; gen. sec. U.S. Cath. Bishops Conf., Washington, 1977—82; archbishop Archdiocese of Louisville, 1982—. Chmn. Cath. Conf. Ky., Louisville, 1982—. Chancellor Bellarmine Coll.; bd. dirs. St. Luke Inst. Recipient Veritas medal, St. Catharine Coll., 1984. Mem.: Nat. Cath. Edn. Assn. (chmn. bd. dirs. 1991—94), Canon Law Soc. Am. Roman Catholic. Home and Office: 212 E College St Louisville KY 40203-2334

KELLY, THOMAS J., JR., lawyer; b. Williamsport, Pa., July 18, 1953; BS, LaSalle Coll., 1976; JD, Cath. U. Am., 1980. Bar: DC 1981. Law clk. to chief judge H. Carl Moultrie Superior Ct. of D.C., 1980—82; asst. US atty. Washington, 1986—89; with Venable LLP, Washington, 1989—, ptnr., corp. def./white collar, environ., 1992—, pro bono coord., 2003—. Founder Zacchaeus Free Legal Clinic, NW Washington, DC. Named a Top Lawyer, Washingtonian Mag., 2004; named Young Lawyer of the Yr. award, DC Bar Assn., 1991. Mem.: ABA, Assn. Asst. US Attys, Nat. Assn. Criminal Def. Lawyers, Bar Assn. DC, DC Bar. Office: Venable LLP 575 Seventh St NW Washington DC 20004 Office Phone: 202-344-4889. Office Fax: 202-344-8300. Business E-Mail: tjkelly@venable.com.

KELLY, THOMAS JESSE, JR., molecular biologist; b. Birmingham, Ala., Nov. 21, 1941; s. Thomas Jesse and Agnes (Allen) K.; m. Mary Lucinda Schwartz, June 25, 1969; children: Mark Thomas, Andrew Samuel. BA with honors, Johns Hopkins U., 1962, PhD in Biophysics, 1968, MD, 1969. Served with USPHS, 1970-72. Postdoctoral fellow Harvard Med. Sch., Boston, 1968, Johns Hopkins U. Sch. Medicine, Balt., 1969-70; staff assoc. Nat. Inst. Health, Bethesda, Md., 1970-72; asst. prof. microbiology Johns Hopkins U. Sch. Medicine, Balt., 1972-75, assoc. prof., 1976-79, Boury Prof. molecular biology and genetics, 1980—2002, dir. dept., 1982—2002; dir. Sloan-Kettering Inst., NYC, 2002—. Chmn. study sect. virology NIH, 1988-90. Mem. editorial bd. Jour. Biol. Chemistry, 1982-94, Jour. Virology, 1980-90, Virus Rsch., 1983-93, Oncogene Rsch., 1989-94, Seminars in Virology, 1989-95, Am. Soc. Biochem. Molecular Biology, 1989-94. Awards assembly Gen. Motors Cancer Prize; bd. dirs. Passano Found. Recipient Career Devel. award NIH, 1972-77. Fellow Am. Acad. Arts and Sci.; mem. NAS, Am. Soc. Biological Chemists, Am. Soc. Microbiology, Am. Soc. Virology, Phi Beta Kappa, Alpha Omega Alpha, Inst. Medicine. Office: Sloan-Kettering Inst 1275 York Ave New York NY 10021*

KELLY, THOMAS M., headmaster; BA, Fairfield U.; MEd, Columbia's Teachers Coll.; PhD & MPhil, Columbia U. Former principal Hendrick Hudson High Sch.; superintendent Valhalla Union Free Sch. Dist., Westchester, NY, 1999—2005; head of sch. Horace Mann Sch., Riverdale, NY, 2005—. Adjunct prof. Columbia's Teachers Coll., 1994—. Pres. & bd. dirs. Hawthorne Found.; founder Valhalla Schools Found. Mem.: Nat. Psychology Honor Soc., Nat. Education Honor Soc. Office: Horace Mann Sch 231 W 246th St Bronx NY 10471*

KELLY, THOMAS MICHAEL, lawyer; b. Atlanta, Oct. 5, 1958; s. Edward (dec.) and Marie K. AB cum laude, Columbia U., 1979; JD cum laude, Harvard U., 1983. Bar: N.Y. 1985. Law clk. to Hon. Eugene Nickerson U.S. Dist. Ct. (ea. dist.) N.Y., Bklyn., 1983-84; assoc. Debevoise & Plimpton, N.Y.C., 1984-93, ptnr., 1993—. Mem. Assn. of Bar of City of N.Y. Democrat. Office: Debevoise & Plimpton 919 3rd Ave 42d Fl New York NY 10022-6225 Office Phone: 212-909-6907. Business E-Mail: tmkelly@debevoise.com.

KELLY, THOMAS N., JR., telecommunications industry executive; Degree, Wofford Coll. With Howard Bedford Nolan, 1981—93; v.p. mktg. AT&T Wireless, 1993—96; exec. v.p., chief mktg. officer Nextel Commn., 1996—2003, exec. v.p., COO, 2003—. Bd. Radioframe Networks Inc., Bellevue, Wash. Vol. sch. and youth athletic orgn., Va. Office: Nextel Commn Inc 2001 Edmund Halley Dr Reston VA 20191

KELLY, THOMAS PAINE, JR., retired lawyer; b. Tampa, Fla., Aug. 29, 1912; s. Thomas Paine and Beatrice (Gent) K.; m. Jean Baughman, July 25, 1940; children: Carla, Thomas Paine III (dec.), Josie. AB, U. Fla., 1935, JD, 1936. Bar: Fla. 1936, U.S. Dist. Ct. (no. dist.) Fla. 1936, U.S. Ct. Appeals (5th cir.) 1936, U.S. Dist. Ct. (mid. dist.) Fla. 1940, U.S. Dist. Ct. (so. dist.) Fla. 1939, U.S. Ct. Appeals (11th cir.) 1983, U.S. Supreme Ct. 1990. Since practiced in, Tampa; assoc. McKay, Macfarlane, Jackson & Ferguson, 1939-40; ptnr. McKay, MacFarlane, Jackson & Ferguson, 1940-48, Macfarlane, Ferguson, Allison & Kelly, 1948-83, sr. ptnr., 1983-91; of counsel Shear, Newman, Hahn & Rosenkranz, 1992-95; shareholder MacFarlane Ferguson & McMullen, P.A., Tampa, Fla., 1996—, ret., 2005. Chmn. Tampa Com. 100, 1960-61; pres. Tampa Citizens' Safety Coun., 1961-62; Bd. dirs. Tampa chpt. ARC, 1955-62, pres., 1958-59; bd. dirs. Boys Clubs Tampa, 1956-67, pres., 1966-67. Col. F.A. AUS, 1940-45. Decorated Silver Star. Fellow Am. Coll. Trial Lawyers, Internat. Acad. Trial Lawyers; mem. Am. Bar Assn., Bar Assn. Hillsborough County, Fla. Bar (chmn. com. profl. ethics 1953-58, chmn. com. ins. and negligence law 1962-63, chmn. fed. rules com. 1969-70) Republican. Home: 5426 Lykes Ln Tampa FL 33611-4747

KELLY, THOMAS PATRICK, rail transportation executive; b. Galveston, Tex., Dec. 30, 1948; s. Joseph J. and Eileen L. Kelly; m. Kathryn E. Maurer, July 10, 1971; children: Kristen L., Kevin T., Kathleen E. BBA, Baylor U., Waco, Tex., 1971. Ops. mgr. Santa Fe Rlwy., Richmond, Calif., 1972—78, Atchison, Topeka & Santa Fe Rlwy., L.A., 1978—80, terminal mgr. Houston, 1983—89; dir. sys. intermodal ops. Burlington Northern Santa Fe Rlwy., Ft. Worth, 1989—. Author: Stacking Offers Solutions. Dir. fundraising Am.

Diabetes Assn., Ft. Worth, 2000—04; participant / sponsor Spl. Olympic. Recipient Founders award Outstanding Achievement, Atchison, Topeka & Santa Fe/ Burlington Northern Santa Fe Rlwy., 1993, 1995, 2002, 2004. Mem.: Intermodal Assn. N.Am. (chmn. ops. com. 1998—2003), Am. Assn. Rlwys. (chmn. 2004—). Methodist. Achievements include design of equipment and intermodal terminals; development of computer programming; safety and operational processes; patents for design of lift equipment and container design components, now industry standards. Avocations: sports, golf, woodworking, travel, reading. Office: BNSF Rlwy 2650 Lou Menk Dr Fort Worth TX 76131 Office Phone: 817-867-6122. Office Fax: 817-352-7203. E-mail: tom.kelly@bnsf.com.

KELLY, T(HOMAS) ROSS, chemistry educator; BS with honors, Holy Cross Coll., 1964; PhD, U. Calif., Berkeley, 1968. NIH postdoctoral fellow Brandeis U., Waltham, Mass., 1968-69; from asst. prof. to assoc. prof. chemistry Boston Coll., 1969-80, prof., 1980—, chmn. dept. chemistry, 1983-86, Vanderslice prof. chemistry, 1989—. Mem. editl. adv. bd. Jour. Organic Chemistry, 1996—; contbr. articles to profl. jours. Recipient Arthur C. Cope Scholar award, 1996; NIH Career Devel. awardee, 1975-80; NIH grantee, 1971—. Mem. Am. Chem. Soc. Office: Boston Coll Dept Chemistry Eugene F Merkert Chem Ctr Chestnut Hill MA 02467-3860

KELLY, TIMOTHY E., communications executive; B in Mktg., U. Fla. Various pos., including acct. mgr. Procter & Gamble, Burger King, and Arm & Hammer, D'Arcy, Masium Benten & Bowles, Inc., and Lever Bros. Co., N.Y.C.; asst. v.p. corp. brand, media and sponsorship mktg. initiatives, to v.p.-consumer long distance mktg. Consumer Svcs. Group, 1994—99; pres. Tickets.com, 1999—2002; pres.-Sprint Bus., Global Markets Group Sprint Corp., Dallas, 2002—.

KELLY, TIMOTHY MICHAEL, newspaper publisher; b. Ashland, Ky., Nov. 28, 1947; s. Robert John and Pauline Elizabeth (Henneman) K.; m. Carol Ann Knight, Aug. 2, 1969; children: Kimberly, Kevin. BA, U. Miami, Fla., 1970. Sports copy editor, writer The Courier-Jour., Louisville, 1970-71; exec. sports editor The Phila. Inquirer, 1971-75; dep. mng. editor Dallas Times Herald, 1975-81; mng. editor The Denver Post, 1981-84; exec. editor Dallas Times Herald, 1984; editor Daily News, LA, 1984-87; mng. editor The Orange County Register, Santa Ana, Calif., 1987-89; editor, sr. v.p. Lexington (Ky.) Herald-Leader, 1989-96, pub., 1996—. Juror Pulitzer Prize, 1987-88. Bd. dirs. YMCA of U.S.A., 2004—, nat. sec., 2005. Recipient Excellence Cmty. Svc. award Knight Ridder, 1995, Ida B. Wells award, 1999, Ky. Journalism Hall of Fame award, 2000, Byron B. Harless award Knight Ridder, 2003. Roman Catholic. Office: Lexington Herald Leader 100 Midland Ave Lexington KY 40508-1999 Office Phone: 859-231-3257. Business E-Mail: tkelly@herald-leader.com.

KELLY, TODD, music educator; s. Pete and Helen Kelly; m. Kirsten Ellen Gregory, July 8, 1995; children: Connor, Maren. MusB Edn., U. of Mont., Missoula, 1988; MusM in Trumpet Performance, U. of No. Colo., Greeley, 1992; ArtsD, Ball State U., Muncie, Ind., 1998. Asst. dir. of jazz studies Ball State U., Muncie, Ind.; asst. prof. of music Bradley U., Peoria, Ill., 1998—. Artist/clinician Conn/Selmer Musical Instruments, Elkhart, Ind., 2000—. Recipient Parent's Award for Svc. to Students, Bradley U. Parent's Assn., 2004. Mem.: Internat. Assocation for Jazz Edn. (Ill. unit sec. 2001—03). Office: Bradley University 1501 W Bradley Ave Peoria IL 61625 Home Fax: 309-677-3871; Office Fax: 309-677-3871. Personal E-mail: tkelly@bradley.edu.

KELLY, WILLIAM CHARLES, JR., retired lawyer; b. Mpls., June 9, 1946; s. William Charles and Marian Eileen (Moritz) K.; m. Cynthia Ann Churchill, June 28, 1969; children: Patrick, Brian. AB, Harvard U., 1968; JD, Yale U., 1971. Bar: Maine 1972, D.C. 1973, U.S. Supreme Ct. 1973. Law clk. to Judge Coffin U.S. Ct. Appeals (1st cir.), Portland, Maine, 1971-72; law clk. to Justice Powell U.S. Supreme Ct., Washington, 1972-73; exec. asst. to sec. HUD, Washington, 1975-77; ptnr. Latham & Watkins, Washington, 1978—2003, ret., 2003. Bd. dirs. Nat. Low Income Housing Coalition, Washington, 1983-94, The Governance Inst., 1986—, Washington Legal Clinic for the Homeless, 1999—; trustee Sheridan Sch., 1992-98; mem. Ashoka World Coun., 1997—; dir. Ashoka Innovators for the Public, 1999—; pres. Stewards Affordable Housing for Future, 2004—. Lt. USNR, 1973-75. Mem. ABA, D.C. Bar Assn. Office: Latham & Watkins Ste 1000 555 11th St NW Washington DC 20004-1304 Office Phone: 202-637-2233. Business E-Mail: bill.kelly@lw.com.

KELLY, WILLIAM FRANKLIN, JR., lawyer; b. Houston, Feb. 12, 1938; s. William Franklin and Sara (McAshan) K.; m. Ingrid Leach, Sept. 11, 1965; children: Kristin Adams, Sara McAshan. BA, Stanford U., 1960; LLB, U. Tex., 1963. Bar: Tex. 1965. Assoc. Vinson & Elkins, Houston, 1965-72, ptnr., 1972-97. Served to 1st lt. U.S. Army, 1963-65. Fellow Houston Bar Found; mem. ABA, Tex. Bar Assn., Houston Bar Assn. Clubs: Forest (Houston), The Houston. Episcopalian. Avocation: sport diving. Home: 600 E Friar Tuck Ln Houston TX 77024-5707 Office: Vinson & Elkins LLP First City Tower 1001 Fannin St Ste 2300 Houston TX 77002-6706

KELLY, WILLIAM JOHN, lawyer; b. Beaver Falls, Pa., Oct. 17, 1927; s. Leon W. and Margaret Mary (Wyrough) K.; m. Joan P. Kelly, Aug. 25, 1956; children: Anne Kelly Schenkel, Kimberly Ellen Hill, Elizabeth Kerstin Kelly, William J. Kelly Jr. BA, Geneva Coll., 1949; JD, Harvard Law Sch., 1952. Bar: Pa., N.Y., U.S. Dist. Ct. (we. dist.) Pa., U.S. Ct. Appeals (3d cir.). Assoc. atty. Sage Grey Todd & Simms, N.Y.C., 1952-56, Isaac J. Silin, Esquire, Erie, Pa., 1956-58; ptnr. Fischer & Kelly, Erie, 1958-62; sr. atty. Elderkin Martin Kelly & Messina, Erie, 1962—; spl. asst. atty. gen. Commonwealth of Pa., Pa., 1966-76. Active Sisters of Mercy Adv. Bd., Erie Cath. Cemeteries Adv. Bd., bd. trustees Gannon U.; bd. incorporators Hamot Med. Ctr. Col. USAR, 1948-86. Recipient Gen. Pershing award U.S. Army, 1976. Mem. Pa. Bar Assn., Erie County Bar Assn. (pres. 1984), Chancellor of the Bar. Avocations: jogging, skiing, bicycling, spear fishing. Office: Elderkin Martin Kelly & Messina 150 E 8th St Erie PA 16501-1269

KELLY, WILLIAM MICHAEL, investment company executive; b. Pittsfield, Mass., Feb. 3, 1944; children: Alyssa A., Eileen J.; m. Christina E. Houlihan, 2003. BA in Polit. Sci., St. Anselm Coll., 1966; MA in Polit. Sci., Duquesne U., 1968; MBA in Fin., NYU, 1972. Portfolio mngr., v.p. Chase Manhattan Bank, N.Y.C., 1968-77; v.p. Nat. Aviation and Tech., N.Y.C., 1977-80; assoc. Lingold Assocs., N.Y.C., 1980—, pres., 1992—. Trustee 1st Eagle Funds, N.Y.C., 1999—; ind. gen. ptnr. ML Venture Ptnrs. II, N.Y.C., 1991-2001; dir., treas., Black Forest Consortium, Inc., Black Forest Preserve, N.Y., 1989—; trustee N.Y. Found., 1985-2005, chmn., 1992-95; asst. treas. Neuroscis. Rsch. Found., Calif, 1982-99; v.p., treas. Sergei Zlinkoff Fund Med. Edn., 1992—; trustee St. Anselm Coll., N.H., 1998—. Bd. govs. Eugene Lang Coll, 1994-02; trustee Pathways for Youth, 1976—, pres. 1981-84. Mem. AAAS, (investment and fin. com. 1985-99), N.Y. Acad. Scis. (fin. affairs com. 1987-2002), Sleepy Hollow Country Club, The Union League Club. Office: 500 5th Ave Fl 50 New York NY 10110-5099 Office Phone: 212-391-8960.

KELLY, WILLIAM WATKINS, educational association executive; b. Asheville, N.C., Sept. 21, 1928; s. John Jackson and Trula (Watkins) K.; m. Lura Jane Kelly, Feb. 14, 1953 (div. Jan. 14, 1983); children: William Watkins, Robert Jackson, Blair Massey, Gregory Clark.; m. Catherine Messer Penney, Jan. 22, 1983. BA, Va. Mil. Inst., 1950; A.M., Duke U., 1955, PhD, 1957. Commandant cadets, tchr. English John Marshall High Sch., Richmond, Va., 1950-52; instr. English Va. Mil. Inst., 1952-53, English Air Force Acad., 1957-58, asst. prof., 1958-60, English Va. Mil. Inst., 1960-62; asst. prof. Am. thought and language Mich. State U., 1962-65, assoc. prof., 1965-69; assoc. dir. The Honors Coll., 1965-68, dir., 1968-69; pres. Mary Baldwin Coll., 1969-76, Transylvania U., Lexington, Ky., 1976-81; sr. assoc. Univ. Assos., 1981-82; exec. v.p. L.Q.C. Lamar Soc., 1981-82; pres. Ala. Assn. Ind. Colls. and Univs., 1982-88, Ga. Found. for Ind. Colls. Inc., Atlanta, 1988-96; pres. emeritus, 1996—; pres. Assn. Pvt. Colls. and Univs. in Ga., Atlanta, 1990-96; sr. v.p. Jon McRae & Assocs. Inc., Atlanta, 1996—2001; dir. coll. and unv. rels. Connexxia, 2001—05; sr. adv. higher edn. divsn. James Tower, 2005—. Mem. Va. Commn. on Status of Women, 1973-76, Ky. Commn. on Status of Women, 1977-81; chmn. Ky. Rhodes Scholar Selection Com., 1978-79; pres. Coun. Ind. Ky. Colls. and Univs., 1978-80; bd. dirs. Ala. Humanities Found., 1983-88, chmn. bd. dirs., 1985-87; bd. dirs., exec. com. Ga. Humanities Coun., 1989-96, vice chair, 1991-93, chair, 1994-96. Author: Ellen Glasow: A Bibliography, 1964. Bd. dirs. ODK Found., 2002—, Ky. State C. of C., 1980—82; trustee Greensboro Coll., 1993—2000, 2002—. Ellis L. Phillips Found. intern Rutgers U., 1964-65; Ala. recipient IBM Disting. Performance award Ind. Coll. Funds Am., 1986, Outstanding Ala. Fund Raising Exec. award Nat. Soc. Fund Raising Execs., 1986, Leadership award Brunswick Pub. Charitable Found., 1993; Danforth fellow, 1953-57; Duke scholar, 1954-55; William Watkins Kelly Endowed Scholarship in the Humanities established Ga. Found. Ind. Colls., 1996. Fellow Found. Ind. Higher Edn. (nat. presiding officer 1992-94, Disting. Performance award 1996); mem. MLA, Am. Studies Assn., Soc. Values in Higher Edn., Am. Assn. Higher Edn., Ellen Glasgow Soc. (pres. 1973-75), Newcomen Soc. N.Am., Rotary (Paul Harris fellow), Phi Beta Kappa, The Fellows of Phi Beta Kappa (bd. dirs. 2000—), Omicron Delta Kappa (Found. bd. dirs. 2002—), Rotary. Home and Office: 4015 Brockton Close Marietta GA 30068-4931 Office Phone: 770-859-9799. E-mail: bwkelly@jamestower.com.

KELLY, YVAN J., economics professor, professional basketball scout; b. Broadstairs, Eng., Apr. 25, 1957; arrived in U.S., 1958; s. William Edward and Myriam Ardila Kelly; m. Kristine K. Thornton, Aug. 12, 1983; 1 child, Allison Elizabeth. B.S., U. Ctrl. Fla., Orlando, 1979, B.A., 1981; M.A., Auburn U., Ala., 1986. Ch. adminstr. First Presbyn. Ch., Santa Barbara, Calif., 1981—84; asst. prof. of economics Gordon Coll., Barnesville, Ga., 1986—89; assoc. prof. of economics and dept. chair Flagler Coll., St. Augustine, Fla., 1989—. NBA scout Seattle SuperSonics, 1993—. Elder Meml. Presbyn. Ch., St. Augustine, 1995—98; coord. Christmas Internat. Ho., St. Augustine, 2003—05; founder Coll. Fellowship Program, St. Augustine, 1992—2004. Mem.: Western Econ. Assn., So. Econ. Assn., Ancient City Astronomy Club, Omicron Delta Kappa. Republican. Presbyterian. Avocations: astronomy, guitar. Home: 7 Sunfish Dr Saint Augustine FL 32080 Office: Flagler College 74 King St Saint Augustine FL 32084 Office Phone: 904-819-6219. E-mail: kellyyj@flagler.edu.

KELLY-CHALAS, JOSE ANTHONY, mathematician, educator; b. Santa Domingo, Dominican Republic, June 9, 1953; arrived in U.S., 1979; s. Inocencio Kelly and Fidelia Chalas; m. Sandra M. Peguero (div.); m. Juana Cuello, Oct. 1, 1988; 1 child, Nelson Kelly. BA in Edn., U. Destodgo, 1985; MA in Edn., U. Dominican Republic, 1991. Cert. tchr. Tchr. Coll. San Ignacio, PR, 1986—91, Dept. Edn., PR, 1991—94; prof. Interamerican U., PR, 1994—2004; tchr. Dept. Edn., PR, 2004—. Tchr., Phila., 1994; prof. U. P.R., 1994—2004, Turabo (P.R.) U., 1994—99; tchr., Boston, 2000. Contbr. articles to mags. Grantee, Dept. Edn. P.R., 1998. Fellow: Rosacrucian Lodge (aux. mastar 2005); mem.: AMA, Tchr. Assn. P.R. Roman Catholic. Avocations: chess, martial arts. Home: AF 23 Toluca St Venus Gardens San Juan PR 00926 Office: Dept Edn Fordasm and Las Priners San Juan PR 00928

KELM, BONNIE G., art museum director, educator; b. Bklyn., Mar. 29, 1947; d. Julius and Anita (Baron) Steiman; m. William G. Malis; 1 child, Michael Darren. BS in Art Edn., Buffalo State U., 1968; MA in Art History, Bowling Green (Ohio) State U., 1975; PhD in Arts Adminstrn., Ohio State U., 1987. Art tchr. Toledo Pub. Schs., 1968—71; ednl. cons. Columbus (Ohio) Mus. Art, 1976—81; prof. art Franklin U., Columbus, 1976—88; legis. coord. Ohio Ho. of Reps., Columbus, 1977; pres. bd. trustees Columbus Inst. for Contemporary Art, 1977—81; tech. asst. cons. Ohio Arts Coun., Columbus, 1984—88; dir. Bunte Gallery Franklin U., Columbus, 1978—88; dir. art mus. Miami U., Oxford, Ohio, 1988—96, assoc. prof., 1988—96; dir. Muscarelle Mus. of Art Coll. William and Mary, Williamsburg, Va., 1996—2002, assoc. prof. art and art history, 1996—2002; dir. Univ. Art Mus. U. Calif., Santa Barbara, 2002—. Adj. prof. dept. art history U. Art Mus. U. Calif., Santa Barbara; grant panelist Ohio Arts Coun., Columbus, 1985—87, Columbus, 1991—95; art book reviewer William C. Brown Pub., Madison, Wis., 1985—92; mem. acquisitions adv. bd. Martin Luther King Ctr., Columbus, 1987—88; field reviewer Inst. Mus. Svcs., Washington, 1990—; chairperson grant panel Art in Pub. Places, 1992—95; trustee Ohio Mus. Assn., 1993—96; apptd. to mus. com. Coll. Arts Assn.; mem. adv. bd. Women Beyond Borders, 2004—; state apptd. mem. adv. com. Ohio Percent for Art, 1994—96; bd. dirs. Assn. Univ. and Coll. Mus. Galleries, 1998—; guest spkr.; keynote spkr.; presenter in field. Author, editor (mus. catalogues) Connections, 1985, Into the Mainstream: Contemporary Folk Art, 1991, Testimony of Images: PreColumbian Art, 1992, Collecting by Design: The Allen Collection, 1994, Photographs by Barbara Hershey: A Retrospective, 1995, Georgia O'Keeffe in Williamsburg, 2001; contbr. chpt. to book Modernism Gender & Culture, 1997, articles to profl. jours. Founding mem., mem. adv. coun. Columbus Cultural Arts Ctr., 1977-81; coord., curator Cultural Exch. Program, Honolulu-Columbus, 1980; mem. acad. women achievers YWCA, 1991—; mem. adv. bd. Women beyond Borders, 2004—. Recipient Marantz Disting. Scholar award Ohio State U., 1995, Gelpe award YWCA, 1987, Cultural Advancement of City of Columbus award, The Columbus Dispatch, 1984, Disting. Svc. award, Columbus Art League, 1984, Critic's Choice award Found. for Cmty. of Artists, N.Y., 1981; Fulbright scholar USIA, 1988 (The Netherlands); NEH fellow East-West Ctr., Honolulu, 1991. Mem. Am. Assn. Mus. (advocacy task force, surveyor mus. assessment program 1996—, nat. program com. 2001), Assn. Coll. and Univ. Mus. and Galleries, Western Mus. Assn., Fulbright Assn., Coll. Art Assn. (session chair, mem. mus. com. 2004—), Internat. Coun. Mus., Calif. Assn. Mus. Office: Univ Art Mus U Calif Santa Barbara 1626 Arts Bldg Santa Barbara CA 93106 Office Phone: 805-893-4564. Business E-Mail: bgkelm@uam.ucsb.edu. *Pay attention to all of the potentials and resources that others overlook in your every day environment. Never let any one convince you that something you're committed to is impossible. Make an art of putting people and possibilities together.*

KELM, CAROL RANEY, retired librarian; b. Spokane, Wash., Aug. 28, 1929; d. Carl Delano and Ellen Minnesota (Keyes) Raney; m. Raymond Louis Kelm, Oct. 24, 1971 (dec.). Student, Reed Coll., Portland, 1947—48; BA in History, Wash. State U., 1952; BLS, U. Calif., Berkeley, 1953. Libr., cataloger U. Calif., Davis, 1953—56; subject cataloger, head serials divsn. Yale U. Libr., New Haven, 1956—65; asst. catalog libr. Jt. World Bank and IMF, Washington, 1965—66; chief catalog dept. Smithsonian Instn. Libr., Washington, 1966—69; exec. sec. Resources and Tech. Svcs. Divsn. ALA, Chgo., 1969—77; curator, exec. dir. Hist. Soc. Oak Park/River Forest, Ill., 1981—93; ret., 1993. Mem.: ALA, Phi Kappa Phi, Phi Alpha Theta, Phi Beta Kappa. Avocations: travel, hand crafts. Home: 1224 Cornwall Ave Apt 502 Bellingham WA 98225-5043

KELMAN, EDWARD MICHAEL, lawyer; b. NYC, Aug. 29, 1943; s. Jack H. and Evelyn (Karp) K.; children: Matthews S., Joshua K. AB, Cornell U., 1965; JD, NYU, 1968. Bar: N.Y. 1969, Conn. 1972. Asst dist. atty. N.Y. County Dist. Atty.'s Office, 1968-71; assoc. Glazer & Wechsler, Stamford, Conn., 1971-72, Squadron, Gartenberg, Elenoff & Plesent, N.Y., 1972-73; sr. atty. CBS Records, CBS, Inc., N.Y., 1973-76; asst. gen. atty. CBS Pub., CBS, Inc., N.Y., 1976-77; v.p. law Chappell Music Co., N.Y., 1977-80; of counsel Law Offices of Michael Sukin, N.Y., 1980-82; v.p. bus. affairs and acquisitions Thorn EMI Video & TV, N.Y., 1982-83; pvt. practice entertainment and media law N.Y., 1983—. Recipient Spl. award Rec. Ind. Assn. Am., 1975. Mem. NARAS, Assn. Bar City N.Y., Conn. Bar Assn., Nat. Acad. Popular Music, Cornell Club of N.Y. Avocations: sports, movies, theater. Office: 100 Park Ave 20th Fl New York NY 10017 Fax: 212-750-1356. Office Phone: 212-371-9490. E-mail: Emknyc@aol.com.

KELMAN, MARK GREGORY, law educator; b. NYC, Aug. 20, 1951; s. Kurt and Sylvia (Etman) Kelman; m. Ann Barbara Richman, Aug. 26, 1979; 1 child, Nicholas. BA in Social Studies, magna cum laude, Harvard U., 1972, JD magna cum laude, 1976. Bar: NY 1977. Cons., dir. criminal justice projects Fund for the City of NY, 1976—77; mem. faculty Stanford Law Sch., 1977—, prof., 1982—, William Nelson Cromwell prof., 1996—, academic coordinator, 1994—96, academic assoc. dean., 1999—2001, vice dean, 2004—. Author: A Guide to Critical Legal Studies, 1987, Strategy or Principle? The Choice Between Regulation and Taxation, 1999; co-author (with Gillian Lester): Jumping the Queue: An Inquiry into the Legal Treatment of Students with Learning Disabilities, 1997; author: (novels) What Followed Was Pure Lesley, 1973. Office: Stanford Law Sch Crown Quadrangle 559 Nathan Abbott Way Stanford CA 94305-8610 Office Phone: 650-723-4069. E-mail: mkelman@stanford.edu.*

KELMAN, MARYBETH, retired health care consultant, health policy analyst; AS in Nursing, Rutgers U., 1964; BA, Douglas Coll., 1977; MA, Rutgers U., 1988. Program dir. health promotion N.J. Hosp. Assn., Princeton, NJ, 1983-87; policy analyst N.J. Dept. Human Svcs., Trenton, NJ, 1988-89; exec. dir. Eye Screening Coord. Coun. N.J., Inc., Monmouth Junction, NJ, 1989-91; health care cons. N.J. Divsn. Pensions and Benefits, Trenton, 1992—2004; ret., 2004. Chmn. bd. trustees Forums Inst. for Pub. Policy, Princeton, 1998—. Home: 1500 Sawyer Ave Manasquan NJ 08736 Personal E-mail: mbkelman@verizon.net.

KELMAN, STEVEN JAY, education educator; b. N.Y.C., May 1, 1948; s. Kurt and Sylvia (Etman) K.; m. Shelley Metzenbaum, July 5, 1980; children: Jody, Leora. AB summa cum laude, Harvard Coll., 1970; PhD, Harvard U., 1978. Asst. prof. pub. policy Harvard U., 1978-80; with Federal Trade Comm., Washington, 1980-81; assoc. prof. and prof. pub. mgmt. Harvard U., 1982-93, 97—; adminstr. Office of Fed. Procurement Policy, Washington, 1993-97. Editor: Internat. Pub. Managements Jour., 2005—. Democrat. Jewish. Office: Harvard Univ JFK Sch of Government Cambridge MA 02138 Office Phone: 617-496-6302. E-mail: steve_kelman@harvard.edu.

KELMENSON, LEO-ARTHUR, advertising executive; b. N.Y.C., Jan. 3, 1927; s. Joseph A. and Ruth (Rothberg) K.; m. Gayle Frances Abrams, Sept. 1989; children from previous marriage: Todd-Arthur, Joel Adam. BS, Columbia U., 1951; postgrad., Grad. Sch. Bus., 1952. From TV prodn. to sr. v.p., asst. to pres. Lennen & Newell, 1951-65; exec. v.p., mem. exec. com. Norman Craig & Kummel, 1965-66; sr. v.p., dir., mem. exec. com. Kenyon & Eckhardt, 1967-68, chmn., chief exec. officer, 1968-86; chmn. Bozell, Jacobs, Kenyon & Eckhardt, 1986-93, chmn. exec. com.; chmn. Bozell Worldwide; chmn. bd. advisors, chmn. devel. com. Tisch Sch of Arts NYU, 1988—; chmn. Bozell de Mexico, 1992-99, FCB Worldwide, N.Y.C., 1999—. Pres. Kelmenson Funds Ltd.; dir. Lorimar, Locations Unltd., On-Line Software Internat.; bd. trustees Am. Cinematheque; lectr. New Sch. Social Rsch.; Adviser communications office U.S. Atty. Gen., 1960-63; spl. project officer Dept. State, 1952-64; co-founder, v.p., dir. African Med. and Rsch. Found., 1957—. Author: (poetry) Epilogue, 1964; also short stories. Mem. pub. rels. com. Nat. Cancer Found., 1958—; adv. com. Nat. Cultural Center, 1962; pres. Shoes for Little Souls, 1960, Remsenburg Assn., 1968; bd. dirs. ASPCA, Stop Cancer Found., 1990, 91; mem. pres.'s adv. coun. Am. Diabetes Assn., 1977-78. Served with USMCR, World War II. Recipient Theodore Roosevelt Man of Year award, 1955; Silver Quill Poetry award, 1955; Res. Officers Assn. award, 1965; Guggenheim World Peace award, 1951; Am. Jewish Com. Humanitarian award; Humanitarian award St. Frances Cabrini. Mem. U.S. Olympic Com., N.Y. Advt. Club, Soc. Am. Businessmen Club, Sigma Phi Epsilon. Clubs: Sands Point, Ocean Reef, Key Largo, Sands Point Yacht, L.I. Polo, U.S. Yacht Racing Assn. (N.Y.). Office: NYU Tisch Sch Arts New York NY 10003 also: FCB Worldwide 100 W 33rd St #5 New York NY 10001-2921 Fax: 212-885-3399. E-mail: lkelmenson@fcb.com.

KELMENSON, LITA, artist, educator; b. Buffalo, June 30, 1932; d. Albert and Helene (Schniedt) Barback; m. Emanuel Kelmenson, Feb. 19, 1955; children: Gary, Steven. Student, Albright Art Sch., Buffalo, 1953; BA cum laude, SUNY, Buffalo, 1954; postgrad., Columbia U., 1958; MA, CUNY, Queens Coll., 1964. N.Y. State Tchrs. Certification, 1964. Tchr. art Robert Williams Sch., Jericho, N.Y., 1964-68, Jr. High Sch., West Islip, N.Y., 1968-70, East Islip High Sch., N.Y., 1970—. Tchr. sculpture Adelphia U., Garden City, NY, 1974, Hofstra U., Hempstead, NY, 1975-76; adj. prof. Dowling Coll., 1987, SUNY, Farmingdale, 1987, Nassau CC, 1990-2005; adv. bd. Islip Art Mus., 1975-80, guest curator exhibit, 1975-80, dir. HS exhibit program, 1975-80 Contbr. articles to profl. jours.; one-woman shows include Mari Galleries Westchester, Ltd., Mamroneck, N.Y., 1978, 1981, B.J. Spoke Gallery, Port Washington, N.Y., 1981, 1985, Plandome (N.Y.) Gallery, 1997, exhibited in group shows at Firehouse Gallery Nassau C.C., Garden City, NY, 1973, DeAndreis Gallery St. John's U., NY, 1974, Hansen Galleries, SoHo, N.Y., 1977, Hudson River Mus., Yonkers, N.Y., 1977, Elaine Benson Gallery, Bridgehampton, N.Y., 1978, Sculpture Garden, Union-Carbide Bldg., N.Y.C., 1978, Artists Craftsmen of N.Y., 1978, Gallery Odin, Port Washington, 1980, Fed. Bldg. N.Y., 1980, Heckscher Mus., Huntington, N.Y., 1982, Nassau Mus Fine Art, Roslyn, N.Y., 1982, Shadow Box Gallery, Glen Cove, N.Y., 1982, B.J. Spoke Gallery, Port Washington, N.Y., 1983, Nat. Assn. Women Artists, 1984, Nabisco Brands, East Hanover, N.J., 1987, Ednl. Assn., Washington, 1987, The Monmouth Mus. Fine Arts, 1987, Nese Alpan Gallery, N.Y., 2000, Omni Gallery, 2002, Ormond Art Mus., Fla., 2003, Silvermine Guild Arts Ctr., Conn., 2003, Mason Murer Fine Art, Atlanta, 2005, Represented in permanent collections Mari Galleries of Westchester Ltd., Zimmerli Art Mus., others, pvt. collections. Recipient awards including L.I. Craftsmen's Guild award of excellence, Firehouse Gallery, Nassau C.C., Garden City, N.Y., 1973, First award sculpture, Bay Shore Art Exhibit-Nat. N.Y., Islip Town Art Gallery, 1976, Jeffrey Childs Willis Meml. prize, Nat. Assn. Women Artists, 1980, Spl. award, Nassau County Mus. Fine Arts, 1988, medal of honor and Amelia Peabody Meml. award. Mem. Nat. Art Edn. Assn., Nat. Assn. Women Artists. Personal E-mail: litakel@yahoo.com.

KELSAW, GEOFFREY LADORN, musician; b. Fort Wayne, Ind., July 3, 1963; s. Paul Edward and Mary Elizabeth Kelsaw; m. Juanita V Curtis. BS, U. of Indpls., 2000—02. Min. of music Mt. Zion Bapt. Ch., Indpls., 2000—; gospel choir dir. Christian Theol. Sem., Indpls., 2001—05; artist in residence Purdue U., West Lafayette, Ind., 2001—04; adj. faculty Taylor U., Upland, Ind., 1991—2001; min. of music Pilgrim Bapt. Ch., Ft. Wayne, Ind., 1988—2000; choral dir. of boy's choir Oaklandon Elem. Sch., Indpls., 2002—; lectr. on ch. music Martin Luther King State Conv. of Ind., 2003—. Guest dir. and musician Harrison Hill Elem. Sch., Ft. Wayne, Ind., 1997, Snider H.S., Ft. Wayne, Ind., 1986—93, Irwin Elem. Sch., Ft. Wayne, Ind., 1986—89; artist in residence Ft. Wayne Urban League, 1998—2000. Composer: (music composition) Lord, You Showed Me The Way, Over There, To God Be The Glory, The Church Will Stand. Cmty. devel. chair Ft. Wayne Philharm. Orch., 1991—97; bd. mem. Heartland Chamber Chorale, Ft. Wayne, Ind., 1999—2000. Named Outstanding Young Men of Am., 1985 and 1989, 1989; recipient Arts, Ft. Wayne Chpt. The Links, INC, 1999, Gt. Men.Then and Now, Multicultural Services Indiana-Purdue U. Ft. Wayne, 1998, Black Achiever, Ind. Black Expo Ft. Wayne Chpt., 1990, Mark of Excellence, Eta Upsilon Zeta Chpt. Zeta Phi Beta Sorority, Inc., 1990. Office Phone: 317-924-4748. Personal E-mail: g.l.kelsaw@usa.net.

KELSAY, DAVID ROLAND, chemist; b. Clinton, Mo., July 25, 1955; s. Ralph Waldo and Mary Fern K.; m. Joyce Elaine Hopkins, Oct. 22, 1983; children: Rebecca Sue, Rachael Anne. BA in Chemistry, William Jewell Coll., 1977. Lab. tech. Upsher Labs., Kansas City, 1978-80; process attendant Kansas City Power & Light, Clinton, Mo., 1980-86, plant chemist, 1986—. State committeeman Mo. Rep. Party, 1992-2002, congrl. dist. chmn., 1994-98, 2000—, county com. chmn., 1988-98, 2000—, county com. sec., 1998-2000; mem. apportionment com. Mo. Ho. of Reps; del. Mo. Rep. Nat. Convention, 2004. Baptist. Avocations: sports, reading, geneology, civil war studies. Home: 901 Willow St Clinton MO 64735-3057 Office: Kansas City Power & Light 400 SW Hwy P Clinton MO 64735-9093 Office Phone: 660-885-2284. E-mail: jkelsay@iland.net.

KELSEY, ANN LEE, library administrator; b. Kokomo, Ind., June 20, 1946; d. Harry Willard and JoAnn Kelsey. BA in Anthropology and English cum laude, U. Calif., Riverside, 1968; MLS, UCLA, 1969. Adminstrv. libr. U.S.

Army Spl. Svcs., Cam Ranh Bay, Vietnam, 1969-70; children's libr. Elmont (N.Y.) Meml. Libr., 1970-71; libr. Queensborough Pub. Libr., Jamaica, N.Y., 1971-73; children's libr. Upper Saddle River (N.J.) Pub. Libr., 1973-75; prin. libr. Morris County Libr., Whippany, N.J., 1975-83; assoc. dir. Learning Resource Ctr., County Coll. Morris, Randolph, N.J., 1983—. Networked assoc. fellow 60s workgroup Inst. for Advanced Tech. in Humanities, U. Va., 1994—; ptnr., cons. libr. automation and planning DocuMentors, Rockaway, N.J., 1985—; ind. cons. infosys., Whippany, 1978—. Co-author: Planning for Automation: A How-To-Do-It Manual for Librarians, 1993, 2d edit., 1997, Writing and Updating Technology Plans: A Guidebook with Sample plans in CD-ROM, 1999, Planning for Integrated Systems and Technologies, 2001; contbr. chpt. to: Insider's Guide to Library Automation, 1993; editor: Resources for Teaching the Vietnam War: An Annotated Guide, rev. edit., 1996; also articles. V.p. Project: Hearts and Minds, Inc., Greenwich, Conn., 1995; bd. dirs. NJ Vietnam Vets. Oral History Project, Kean U., 1998, NJ Vietnam Vets. Meml. Found., 2001; edn. adv. com. N.J. Vietnam Vets. Meml. Found., Vietnam Era Ednl. Ctr., 1998; active Morris County Dem. com., 1992. Named to honor roll Vietnam Women's Meml. Project, Washington, 1993; recipient award African Am. Cultural Coun. Virginia Beach, 1999. Mem. ALA (travel grantee 1988), Am. Soc. Info. Sci., Spl. Librs. Assn. (pres. N.J. chpt. 1989-90, chairperson cataloging com. 1992-93), N.J. Libr. Assn. (chairperson automated libr. svcs. sect. 1992-93, mem. pers. adminstrn. com. 1986-87, mem. pay equity task force 1985-86), Women's Overseas Svc. League (scholarship com. chair 2003-), UCLA Alumni Club (co-chmn. scholarship com. N.Y. chpt. 2003—), Phi Beta Kappa. Avocations: bicycling, internet, gardening. Office: DocuMentors 7 Valley View Dr Rockaway NJ 07866-1506 Business E-Mail: akelsey@ccm.edu.

KELSEY, CLYDE EASTMAN, JR., philosophy and psychology educator; b. Wadena, Minn., Mar. 30, 1924; s. Clyde Eastman and Lorraine (Lamb) Bagley) K.; m. Betty Jean Williams, Apr. 1, 1949 (dec.); children: Becky Kelsey Marcin, Nancy Kelsey Eargle; m. Jamie Lee Reagan, 1987. BA, U. Tex., El Paso, 1948; MA, U. Tulsa, 1951; PhD, U. Denver, 1960; hon. degree, U. de Oriente, Venezuela, 1969. Dir. counseling bur. U. Tex., El Paso, 1951-61, prof., head dept. philosophy, psychology, 1961-62, vice chmn. dept. philosophy and psychology, 1951-61; dean students, dir. Inter-Am. Inst., 1962-66; program adv. Venezuela, Ford Found., 1966-69; vice chancellor public affairs U. Denver, 1969-72; v.p. devel. and univ. relations Tex. Tech U., Lubbock, 1972-81, prof. edn., 1981-88, prof. emeritus, 1988—; sr. rsch. fellow Nat. Center Higher Edn. Mgmt., 1983-87. Lectr. 4th Army U.S., 1961-65; cons. U.S. Dept. State, Peace Corps, 1961-66; mem. adv. bd. Kans. Wesleyan Coll., 1970-71; vis. scientist NSF, 1962-66; v.p. Colo. Ptnrs. of Alliance, 1971-73; examiner, cons. Tex. State Bd. of Examiners of Psychologists, 1992-98; cons. Agy. for Internat. Devel., Coll. Bd., Civil Svc. Commn., World Bank to India, Saudi Arabia, Turkey, Republic of Mauritius, InterAm. Bank to Guyana, S.A. Contbr. articles to profl. jours. Bd. dirs. El Paso Mental Health Assn., 1951-58, pres. 1953-55; bd. dirs. El Paso Sch. Retarded Children, 1952-57, pres., 1953-55; bd. dirs. Lubbock Goodwill Industries, 1972-85, v.p., 1973-77, pres., 1978-80; bd. dirs. St. Mary's Hosp. Found., 1986-2000, chmn., 1994-96. With USNR, 1942-45. Decorated Order San Carlos Republic Colombia, 1964; recipient Disting. Alumni Svc. award U. Denver, 1972; Fulbright scholar Colombia, 1960-61 Fellow Tex. Acad. Sci.; mem. APA, Tex. Psychol. Assn., Phi Beta Delta. Home: 13413 North Shore Dr Montgomery TX 77356

KELSEY, DAVID, manufacturing executive; Grad. in civil and geol. engring., Princeton U.; MBA, Harvard Bus. Sch. With GE Co.; CFO Oglebay Norton Co.; v.p., CFO Sealed Air Corp., Saddle Brook, NJ, 2001—. Office: Sealed Air Corp Park 80 E Saddle Brook NJ 07663

KELSEY, ROBIN E., art history educator; m. Sara St. Antoine; 1 child, Adelaide Rosa. PhD, Harvard U., 2000. Asst. prof. history of art and archiecture Harvard U. Recipient Arthur Kingsley Porter Prize, Coll. Art Assn. for essay "Viewing the Archive: Timothy O' Sullivan's Photographs for the Wheeler Survey, 1871-74", 2004; fellow, Sterling & Francine Clark Art Inst., Williamstown, Mass., 2004. Office: Harvard U Dept History of Art and Architecture Sackler Mus 485 Broadway Cambridge MA 02138

KELSEY, RONALD GRANT, retired military officer, environmental engineer; b. Town of Orleans, NY, July 22, 1944; s. Lynwood Jerome and Dorothy Mable (Simpkins) K.; m. Linda York, Mar. 24, 1987; 1 child, Grant A.K. BS in Civil Engring., Norwich U., 1965; MS in Sanitary Engring., Va. Poly. Inst. & State U., 1974; MA in Bus. Mgmt., Ctrl. Mich. U., 1981. Commd. 2d lt. U.S. Army Corps of Engrs., 1965, advanced through grades to col., 1988, ret., 1992; sr. environ. engr. Meta, Inc., Gaithersburg, Md., 1992-95; dir. govt. environ. svcs. AWK Cons. Engrs., Turtle Creek, Pa., 1995, Envirohealth Mktg.-An Ind. Rep. of Equinox Internat., Frederick, Md., 1995-96; sr. environ. engr. TRW, FAA Spt, Leesburg, Va., 1997—98; sr. environ. planner URS Greiner Woodward Clyde, Hunt Valley, Md., 1999; sr. environ. engr. Northrop Grumman FAA Spt. Leesburg, 1999—2004; ret., 2004. Decorated Bronze star Dept. of the Army, Vietnam, 1968, Meritorious Svc. medal with two oak leaf clusters Dept. of the ARmy, Washington, 1977, 83, 85, Legion of Merit with two oak leaf clusters Dept. of the Army, 1985, 89, 92. Mem. ASCE, Soc. Am. Mil. Engrs. (pres. 1991-92, Gavel award 1992), Water Environment Fedn., Hiram Lodge (master mason). Republican. Lutheran. Avocations: jogging, reading, travel, enviromental issues. Home: 525 Sage Hen Ct Frederick MD 21703-1302 Personal E-mail: thekelseys@adelphia.net.

KELSO, JOHN HODGSON, retired federal agency administrator; b. Iowa City, June 16, 1925; s. Edward Lewis and Eliza (Hodgson) K.; m. Marian Louise Towers, Aug. 22, 1948; 1 child, John T. BA, State U. Iowa, 1949, MA, 1950. Occupational research analyst Bur. Naval Personnel, Dept. Navy, Washington, 1951-55; orgn. and methods examiner Agr. Research Services, Dept. Agr., Washington, 1955-57; mgmt. analyst mgmt. adv. br. Bur. State Services, USPHS, HEW, Washington, 1957-58, chief survey group, 1958-60, chief mgmt. adv. br., 1960-62, asst. exec. officer, 1962-66; exec. officer USPHS, Bethesda, Md., 1966-68; asso. adminstr. mgmt. Health Services and Mental Health Adminstn., 1968-73; dir. office regional operations USPHS, Office Asst. Sec. for Health, HEW, 1973-76; dep. adminstr. Health Services Adminstrn., 1976-81, acting adminstr., 1981-82; dep. adminstr. Health Resources and Services Adminstrn., 1982-94, acting adminstr., 1985-86, 88-89. Cons. United Network for Organ Sharing, Richmond, Va., 1994—. Served with AUS, 1943-46. Recipient Superior Svc. award USPHS, 1969, Disting. Svc. award HEW, 1972, Presdl. Meritorious Rank award 1983, Disting. Presdl. Rank award 1989, Surgeon Gen.'s medallion, 1989. Mem. Sigma Alpha Epsilon. Methodist.

KELSO, LINDA YAYOI, lawyer; b. Boulder, Colo., 1946; d. Nobutaka and Tai Ike; m. William Alton Kelso, 1968. BA, Stanford U., 1968; MA, U. Wis., 1973; JD, U. Fla., 1979. Bar: Fla. 1980. Assoc. Mahoney, Hadlow & Adams, Jacksonville, Fla., 1979-82, Commander, Legler, Werber, Dawes, Sadler & Howell, Jacksonville, 1982-86, ptnr., 1986-91, Foley & Lardner, L.L.P., Jacksonville, 1992—. Mem. ABA (bus. law sect.), Jacksonville Bar Assn., Phi Beta Kappa, Order of Coif. Avocations: music, gardening, cooking. Office: Foley & Lardner LLP PO Box 240 Jacksonville FL 32201-0240 Office Phone: 904-359-2000. E-mail: lkelso@foley.com.

KELSON, RICHARD B., metal products executive; b. Pitts., Nov. 20, 1946; B in Polit. Sci., U. Pa.; JD, U. Pitts. Atty. Alcoa, Pitts., 1974-77, gen. atty., 1977-83, mng. gen. atty., 1983-84, asst. sec., mng. gen. atty., 1984-89, asst. gen. counsel, 1989-91, sr. v.p. environ. health and safety, 1991-94, exec. v.p. environ., health and safety, gen. counsel, 1994-97, exec. v.p., CFO, 1997—. Bd. dirs. Meadwestvaco. Bd. dirs. Alcoa Found., U. Pitts. Law Sch. Bd. Visitors, Pitts. Civic Light Opera; mem. Fin. Exec. Inst. the Officers Conf. Group, The Pvt. Sector Coun.'s CFPs; mem. bd. trustees Carnegie Mellon. Mem. ABA. Office: Alcoa 390 Park Ave New York NY 10022*

KELTNER, ROBERT EARL, lawyer, researcher, hotel executive; b. Parkersburg, W.Va., Apr. 11, 1940; s. Earl L. and Chloe H. (Hendershot) K.; 1 child, David B. BA, Marietta Coll., 1959; JD, W.Va. U., 1962; PhD, Thomas Edison Coll., 1965. Bar: W.Va. 1962, U.S. Supreme Ct. 1968. Assoc. Redmond, Campbell & Keltner, Parkersburg, 1962-64; sr. ptnr. Keltner & Yankiss, Parkersburg, 1964-80; pres. Americar Inc., 1986—90, Big K Co., 1990—, Palm Tree Tel. Co., 1990—97. Psychotherapist Palm Beach Health Clinic, 1965; U.S. Appeals agt., Parkersburg, 1966-75; cons. Pacific Test Labs., L.A., 1970—; pres. United Innkeepers Am., Fla., 1973—, Americar Inc., Palm Tree Motels Inc. Mem. ABA, W.Va. State Bar Assn., Wood County Bar Assn., Am. Arbitration Assn., Lawyer Pilots Assn., Internat. Platform Assn., Kiwanis (pres. 1968). Methodist. Address: 4415 N Tamiami Trl Sarasota FL 34234-3863 also: 2660 17th St Sarasota FL 34234

KELTON, ELMER STEPHEN, novelist; b. Andrews County, Tex., Apr. 29, 1926; s. Robert William and Neta Beatrice (Parker) K.; m. Anna Lipp, July 3, 1947; children: Gary, Stephen Lee, Kathryn Ann. BA in Journalism, U. Tex., 1948. Agrl. editor San Angelo (Tex.) Standard Times, 1948-63; editor Sheep and Goat Raiser Mag., San Angelo, 1963-68; assoc. editor Livestock Weekly, San Angelo, 1968-90; ret., 1990. Author: (novels) Hot Iron, 1955, Buffalo Wagons, 1956, Barbed Wire, 1957, Shadow of a Star, 1959, The Texas Rifles, 1960, Donovan, 1961, Bitter Trail, 1962, Horsehead Crossing, 1963, Massacre at Goliad, 1965, Llano River, 1966, After the Bugles, 1967, Captain's Rangers, 1968, Hanging Judge, 1969, Shtogun Settlement, 1969, Bowie's Mine, 1971, The Day the Cowboys Quit, 1971, Wagontongue, 1972, The Time it Never Rained, 1973, Manhunters, 1974, Joe Pepper, 1975, Long Way to Texas, 1976, The Good Old Boys, 1978, The Wolf and the Buffalo, 1980, Eyes of the Hawk, 1981, Stand Proud, 1984, Dark Thicket, 1985, The Man Who Rode Midnight, 1987, Sons of Texas, Book One, 1989, Sons of Texas, Book Two, 1989, Sons of Texas, Book Three, 1990, Honor at Daybreak, 1991, Slaughter, 1992, The Far Canyon, 1994, The Pumpkin Rolers, 1996, Cloudy in the West, 1997, Bitter Trail, 1999, Way of the Coyote, 2001, Ranger's Trail, 2002, Lone Star Rising, 2003, Jericho's Road, 2004 Texas Vendetta, 2004, Sons of Texas, 2005, Six Bits a Day, 2005; (non-fiction) Looking Back West, 1972, Frank C. McCarthy: The Old West, 1981, Permian, A Continuing Saga, 1986, Living and Writing in West Texas, 1988, The Art of Howard Terpning, 1992, The Art of Frank McCarthy, 1992, The Art of James Bama, 1993, The Indian in Frontier News, 1993, My Kind of Heroes, 1995 (rev. ed. 2004). Bd. dirs., exec. com. West Tex. Boys Ranch, San Angelo. With U.S. Army, 1944-46. Recipient Western Heritage awards (4); Spur award (7); Nat. Cowboy Hall of Fame, Career award Western Lit. Assn., 1990. Mem. Western Writers Am. (7 Spur awards, pres. 1963-64), Tex. Inst. Letters (Tinkle-McCombs award for excellence 1985), Tex. Folklore Soc., West Tex. Hist. Soc. (pres. 1990-91). Methodist. Avocations: reading, classic films.

KELTZ, AMY LYNN MARSHALL, foundation administrator; b. New Haven, Apr. 11, 1966; d. David Irwin and Sondra Lois (Ofstrock) Marshall; children: Jennifer, Samuel. BA in French Lit., Johns Hopkins U., 1988; student, Am. Coll. Paris, 1986, Gallaudet U., 1988. Dir. devel. Friendship Ho., Washington, 1990-92; sr. devel. assoc. Econ. Policy Inst., Washington, 1993-95; v.p., dir. devel. Inst. Women's Policy Rsch., Washington, 1996-98; exec. dir. Frederick B. Abramson Meml. Found., Washington, 1998-2000; dir. external rels. The Am. Prospect, Washington, 2000—03; v.p. devel. The Washington Monthly, 2003—. Fundraising cons. Ben Lomond Manor Ho., Manassas, Va., 1995—; profl. fundraising spkr. AAUW, Prince William, Va., 1997—98. Columnist: Dialy Jour., 1999—2002. Chair grants panel Prince William County Arts Coun., 1994—98; bd. dirs., pub. rels. Prince William Chorale, Manassas, 1993—99; participant Cmty. Leadership Inst., Prince William County, 1994; bd. dirs., sec. Prince William Com. 100, 1995—2002; bd. dirs., pres. Vpstart Crow, Manassas, 1999—; bd. dirs., sec. Manassas Dance Co., 1999—2005; mem. Prince William County Dem. Com., 2003—; mem. 2d Decade Soc. Johns Hopkins U., 1998—. Mem.: Nat. Ctr. Responsive Philanthropy, Washington Regional Assn. Grantmakers, Ind. Sector, Am. Soc. Assn. Execs., Nat. Soc. Fund Raising Execs. (cert.). Office: Washington Monthly 733 15th St NW #520 Washington DC 20005 Office Phone: 202-393-5155.

KELZ, ROCHELLE SHELLE K., academic administrator; d. Samuel and Florence W. Kanter; m. Theodore Kelz, Dec. 19, 1965 (div.); children: Melissa B. children: Max B.; m. Arnold Abrams, July 28, 1988. BS, Northwestern U., Evanston, IL, 1966, MA, 1968, PhC, 1969, PhD, 1971; I.E.M. Cert., Harvard U., Cambridge, MA, 1998. Cert. K-12 Tchr. Spanish & French Ill., 1966, Bilingual Tchr. Ill., 1982. Tchg. asst., Northwestern U., Evanston, Ill., 1967—69; prof. of Spanish, French & Fnglish as a second lang. North Pk. U., Chgo., 1969—80; vis. prof. of med. Spanish U. of Ill. at Chgo., 1980—84, U. of Ill. at Chgo. Med. Ctr., 1980—87; dir. of ext. programs & evening coll. North Pk. U., Chgo., 1982—90; dir. of ext. programs Roosevelt U., Chgo., 1990—94; dean of liberal arts & sciences C. S. Mott CC, Flint, Mich., 1994—98; dean of arts & sciences Ind. U., Kokomo, 1998—2001; v.p. of academic affairs Cin. State Tech CC, Ohio, 2001—. Cons. mem. Leadership Coun. for Fgn. Languages and Internat. Studies, Ill. State Bd. of Edn., 1986—93; expert Ill. State Bd. of Edn., Springfield, 1986—93, fgn. lang. cons., 1986—94; alumni adv. bd. of directors Coll. of Arts & Sciences, Northwestern U., Evanston, Ill., 1992—94; fgn. lang. adv. bd Truman Coll., Chicago, Ill., 1994—95; alumni admission coun. Northwestern U., Evanston, Ill., 1995—; bd. mem., sch. improvement Mott Mid. Coll. H.S., Flint, Mich., 1995—98; dir. Spanish Speaking Info. Ctr., Flint, Mich., 1995—98; adv. bd. TEAMS, Flint, Mich., 1995—98; chair Riegle Dinner for Russian Resettlement, Flint, Mich., 1997—98; co-chair, gen. programs Rotary Club of Flint, Flint, Mich., 1997—99; pres. Liberal Arts Network for Devel., Mich., 1999; program planning com. Cin. Pub. Schools, 2001—, program implementation com., 2002—; steering com. Greater Cin. Tech Prep Consortium, 2001—. Author: (book) Diego Sanchez de Badajoz and the Old Testiment, 1971, Conversational Spanish for Medical Personnel, 1978 (Nominee for AMWA Med. Book Award, 1978), Conversational Spanish for Medical Personnel, 2nd ed, revised & greatly expanded, 1982, (books, dictionary) Delmar's English/Spanish Pocket Dictionary for Health Professionals, 1997 (Outstanding U. Prof. of Spanish in the US, 1987), (book) Conversational Spanish for Health Professionals, 1999, translator american dental assoc.-spanish & french; editor: (bilingual newsletter) Chicago Area AATSP Chapter Newsletters, 1977-, 1991 (1st Place-Award of Gen. Excellence, 1991). Chair membership com. Network for Youth Svcs., 1990—93; mem. Kokomo/Howard County C.of C., Kokomo, Ind., 1999—2001, Met. Growth Alliance, Cin., 2001; panelist Flint (Mich.) Jour. Citizens' Adv. Panel, 1998; mem. Flint Women's Forum, 1995—98, Urban League of Flint, 1996—98, Chicago-Area Hispanic C. of C., 1982—94, Mexican Mus. & Fine Arts Ctr., Chgo/, Ala., 1985—94, Ctr. for Quality Mgmt., Cin., 2001; local planning team mem. Wellhead Protection Mgmt., Kokomo, Ind., 1999—2000; mem. Mi Raza Fine Arts Coun., Chgo., 1980—90, Altrusa, Kokomo, Ind., 2000—01, Women's Bus. Coun., Kokomo, Ind., 1999—2001, Nat. Alliance for Hispanic Health, National Organization, 1984. Nominee Athena Award, Flint, MI's Women's Organizations, 1997; recipient Outstanding U. Prof. of Spanish in the US, Am. Assn. of Teachers of Spanish & Portuguese, 1987, Pan Hellenic Scholarship Award, Northwestern U., 1966. Mem.: TESOL (hospitality co-chair, nat. conv. 1991), Am. Assn. of Higher Edn., Am. Assn. of Cmty. Colleges, Alumni Assn., Northwestern U. (class rep. 1986—87), Internat. Trade Club of Chgo. (chair, academic liaison com. 1988), Profl. Standards Com., IL State Bd. of Edn. (chair 1986—94), Ill. Fgn. Lang. Leadership Coun. (treas. 1992—94), Network for Youth Services, Am. Coun. on the Tchg. of Fgn. Languages (pub. rels. chair 1990—94), Nat. Coun. of Instrnl. Administrators, Ind. Campus Compact, Chgo. Met. Bd. for Higher Edn. (bd. mem. 1982—94), Coun. of Colleges of Arts & Sciences, Greater Ill. ESL Program Directors' Network (bd. mem. 1985—91), Coalition for Lang. and Internat. Studies (pres. 1990—91), Chgo. Area Chpt. of Am. Assn. of Teachers of Spanish & Portuguese (editor & editor in chief, greater chgo. area newsletter 1978—94), Ill. Coun. on the Tchg. of Fgn. Languages (editor state newsletter 1987—90), Ill. Fgn. Lang. Teachers' Assn. (newsletter -spanish editor 1983—85), Nat. Soc. for Experiential Edn., Nat. Assn. for Bilingual Edn., MLA, Ctrl. States Conf. on the Tchg. of Fgn. Languages (adv. coun. 1988), Ctr. for Quality Mgmt., Academic Quality Improvement Project, Ill. Coun. on the Tchg. of Fgn. Languages (pres. 1990—91). Jewish. Avocations: reading, music. Office: Cincinnati State Tech& CC 3520 Central Plwy Cincinnati OH 45223-2690 E-mail: shelle.kelz@cincinnatistate.edu.

KEM, RICHARD SAMUEL, retired army officer; b. Richmond, Ind., Aug. 9, 1934; s. Charles Edward and Janice Allene (Beard) K.; m. Ann Callahan, May 7, 1960 (dec. June 2003); children: Michelle, John Samuel, Steven Edward; m. Ann Brown, Apr. 17, 2004 BS, U.S. Mil. Acad., 1956; MS in Civil Engring., U. Ill., 1962; MS in Internat. Affairs, George Washington U., 1972; postgrad., Naval War Coll., 1972, Northwestern U., 1979, Harvard U., 1983. Commd. 2d lt. U.S. Army, 1956, advanced through grades to maj. gen., 1984; comdg. officer 577th Engr. Bn. Vietnam, 1968-69; staff, faculty U.S. Mil. Acad., West Point, N.Y., 1969-71; staff officer Mil. Personnel Center, 1972-74, Office Army Chief Staff, 1974-75; chief public affairs Office Chief Engrs., 1975-76; comdg. officer 7th Engr. Brigade, Germany, 1976-78; chief installations and constrn. U.S. Army Europe, 1978-79; dep. asst. chief engrs., 1979-80; dep. dir. civil works Office Chief Engrs., 1980; comdr., div. engr. Ohio River div., 1981-84; bd. engrs. Rivers and Harbors, 1982-84, Mississippi River Commn., 1982-84; comdg. gen. U.S. Army Engr. Sch. and Fort Belvoir, Va., 1984-87; dep. chief of staff, engr. U.S. Army, Europe, 1987-88, chief of staff, 1988-89; dep. chief of engrs. Washington, Washington, 1989-90; ret., 1990; dir. pub. works Arlington (Va.) County, 1990—2004. Decorated DSM with oak leaf cluster, Legion of Merit with oak leaf cluster, Bronze Star, Gold Order of de Fleury medal. Mem. ASCE, Soc. Am. Mil. Engrs., Am. Def. Preparedness Assn., Army Engr. Assn. (bd. dirs. 1992—), Am. Pub. Works Assn. (bd. dirs. 1989-90). Episcopalian. Office: Burde Assoc Ltd 4701 Sangamon Rd Bethesda MD 20816

KEMBLE, PENN, government official; m. Marie-Louise Caravatti. BA, U. Colo., 1962. Program dir. League for Indsl. Democracy, 1963-69; chmn. Frontlash, Inc., 1969-72; spl. asst., speech writer Senator Patrick Moynahan of N.Y., 1978-79; producer, writer WETA-TV, Washington, 1979-81; pres. Prodemca, 1981-88; mem. Bd. for Internat. Broadcasting, 1991-93; dep. dir. USIA, 1993-99, acting dir., 1999-2000; spl. rep. U.S. Dept. State SOS Office, 2000—02; sr. scholar, dir. project on democracy and the global edn. Freedom House, Washington, 2002—. Bd. dirs. Coun. for a Cmty. of Democracies; chair Internat. Eminent Persons Group on Slavery and Forced Servitude in Sudan, U.S. Dept. State, 2003. Contbr. articles to Commentary, The New Republic, N.Y. Times, Washington Post.

KEMELHOR, ROBERT E(LIAS), mechanical engineer; b. N.Y.C., May 19, 1919; m. Shirley P. Tennen; children: Judith Ellen Bielecki, Joel Martin, Barry Alan. Student Pre-Law, Bklyn. Coll., 1936-38; BSME, George Washington U., 1949. Registered profl. engr., Washington. Sr. draftsman Bur. Ships Navy Dept., Washington, 1940-43, design engr. Bur. Ordnance, 1943-46, sr. engr. head weapon launching sect. Bur. Aeros., 1946-53; chief engr. design, devel. prodn. McLean Devel. Labs., Copiague, N.Y., 1953-58; dir. rsch. and devel. Pesco Products div. Borg-Warner Corp., Bedford, Ohio, 1958; with applied physics lab. Johns Hopkins U., Laurel, Md., 1958-91, program mgr., 1982-85, chief engr. tech. svcs. dept., 1986-91; pvt. practice cons. Bethesda, Md., 1991—. Cons. Advanced Tech. and Mfg. Enterprise Programs, Nat. Inst. Stds. and Tech., U.S. Dept. Commerce, Aeronautics Indsl. Tech. Program, NASA/JPL. Contbr. articles to profl. jours. U.S. del. Internat. Standards Orgn. Subcom., Mfg. Automation; mem. western region and inter-county recreation adv. bd. Montgomery County, Md.; bd. dirs. Alumni Assn., George Washington U. Fellow AIAA (assoc.); mem. AAAS (sr. sci. and engr.'s), Soc. Mfg. Engrs. (sr. mem., chmn. Washington chpt. No. 48), Sigma Tau, Tau Beta Pi. Achievements include patents in field. Home: 6211 Redwing Ct Bethesda MD 20817-5914

KEMENY, M. MARGARET, oncologist, surgeon, educator, hospital administrator; b. Elizabeth, NJ, May 7, 1946; d. George Kemeny and Ellen Sagi. BS, Harvard U., 1968; MD, Columbia U., 1972. Dir. cancer ctr. Queens Cancer Ctr., N.Y.C., 2001—; divsn. chief surg. oncology SUNY Stony Brook. Editor: Jour. Clin. Oncology. Fellow: ACS (bd. govs., vice chair bd. govs.); mem.: Assn. Women Surgeons (pres.). Home: 36 Perry St New York NY 10014 Office: Queens Cancer Ctr at Queens Hosp 82-68 164th St Jamaica NY 11432 Office Phone: 718-883-4031. Business E-Mail: kemenym@nychhc.org.

KEMME, DAVID MICHAEL, economics professor; b. Cin., Nov. 12, 1950; s. Raymond J. and Velma Mae (Cushing) K.; m. Jan L. Hess, Dec. 17, 1976; children: Sarah Kathryn, Lindsay Rae. BA in Math., Miami U., Oxford, Ohio, 1973; MA in Econs., Ohio State U., 1975, PhD in Econs., 1980. With Wharton E.F. Assocs., 1979-81, SRI Internat., Washington and Arlington, Va., 1979-81, FAO, Rome, 1984, The Rand Corp., Santa Monica, Calif., 1985; asst. prof. econs. Wichita (Kans.) State U., 1986-88, assoc. prof., 1988-89, prof., 1991-94; dir. econs. program Inst. for East-West Studies, N.Y.C., 1989-91; disting. fellow Mitsui Rsch. Inst., Tokyo, 1991; prof. econs., Morris prof. intrnat. econs. U. Memphis, 1994—, interim chmn., 1996-97, dir. Internat. MBAs, 1994-97. Cons. IBRD, Washington, 1990-91; vis. prof. U. Warsaw, Poland, 1992; scholar-in-residence Pew Charitable Trusts, Pa., 1989-91. Mem. bd. editors Comparative Econ. Studies, 1994-97, Atlantic Econ. Jour., 1998—; contbr. articles to profl. jours., including Jour. Comparative Econs., Soviet Studies, So. Econs. Jour. Rsch. grantee Nat. Coun. for Soviet and Ea. Europe, 1987-88; Fulbright scholar, 1991-92. Mem. Memphis World Affairs Coun. (bd. dirs. 1995-98), Econ. Club Memphis (exec. dir. 1998—), Emerging Markets Finance and Trade (editl. bd. 1998-). Home: 1822 Hartwell Mnr N Collierville TN 38017-0827 Office: U Memphis 405 Fogelman College Bus Memphis TN 38152-0001

KEMMERER, KATHLEEN MARY, language educator; b. Wilkes-Barre, Pa., May 19, 1952; d. S. Edgar and Mary (Sullivan) Nulton; m. Eugene G. Kemmerer, July 19, 1975; children: Mary, Laurie, Timothy, Elizabeth. BA magna cum laude, Coll. Misericordia, Dallas, 1974; MA, U. Scranton, 1988; PhD, Fordham U., 1993. Sec. tchr. Dallas (Pa.) Schs., 1974-78; editor/writer Blue Cross of Northeastern Pa., Wilkes-Barre, Pa., 1978-80; adj. prof. English Coll. Misericordia, Dallas, 1985-88; adj. prof. communications and English U. Scranton, 1989-90; asst. prof. English Wilkes U., Wilkes-Barre, Pa., 1990-92. Lectr. in field. Editor: A History of the Descendants of Benjamin Spaulding, 1988; author poetry. Fordham U. presdl. scholar, 1988-89, Coll. Misericordia scholar, 1970-74. Mem. Nat. Coun. Tchrs. English, Am. Soc. for 18th Century Studies, N.E. Am. Soc. for 18th Cen. Studies (travel grant 1989), E. Cen. Soc. 18th Cen. Studies (Grad. Student prize 1989), MLA, Coll. Lang. Assn., Johnson Soc. of Cen. Region, Kappa Gamma Pi (pres. 1980-88). Avocation: literature. Home: 346 Harris Hill Rd Shavertown PA 18708-9684 Office: Wilkes U Wilkes Barre PA 18766

KEMMERER, KENNETH C., music educator, musician; b. Reading, Pa., Dec. 29, 1959; s. Harold Edwin and Carolyn Myrtle Kemmerer; m. Kristel Pfeil, July 11, 1987; children: Kate Marie, Karl Arthur. BS in Music Edn., Millersville U., Millersville, Pa., 1981; MusM in Music Performance, Rutgers U., New Brunswick, N.J., 1986. Cert. music educator Pa., 1981. Band dir. North Plainfield H.S., North Plainfield, NJ, 1981—84; asst. band dir. Rutgers U., New Brunswick, NJ, 1984—86; band dir. Muhlenberg Elem. Ctr., Reading, Pa., 1986—. Dir. Berks Summer Band Inst., Reading, Pa., 2004—; arranger/musician Basic'ly Brass, Reading, Pa., 1987—, Hesse's Nasty 9, Reading, Pa., 2003—. Musician: (music arranging) Over 70 Arrangments For School And Professional Ensembles. Asst. scout master Troop 569, Boy Scouts Am., Oley, Pa., 2005; den leader Pack 155, Boy Scouts Am., Reading, Pa., 1999—2004. Grantee Meet The Composer grantee, Berks County Intermediate Unit, 1988, Berks Summer Band Inst. grantee, Reading Musical Found., 2004—05. Mem.: Music Educators Nat. Conf., NEA, Internat. Tuba and Euphonium Assn., Internat. Trombone Assn., Am. Fedn. of Musicians. Democrat-Npl. Lutheran. Avocation: motorcycling. Office: Muhlenberg Elementary Center Kutztwon Road & Sharp Ave Reading PA 19605 Office Phone: 610-921-8028. Office Fax: 610-921-7905.

KEMMERER, PETER REAM, financial executive; b. NYC, Dec. 20, 1942; s. Mahlon Sistie and Colette Noel (Fitch) K.; m. Lillian Reilly, Sept. 15, 1990. BS, Georgetown U., 1966; MBA, Am. U., 1970; MA, New Sch., 1975; BS, US Army Fin. Corps, 1968. Analyst corp. planning Otis Elevator Co., N.Y.C., 1971-74; mgr. fin. and adminstrn. bus. equipment div. SCM Corp., N.Y.C., 1975-80; pres. Mesa Verde, Inc., Cranbury, N.J., 1980—, also bd. dirs. Mng. ptnr. Jezel-Bezel Ptnrs., Cranbury, 1980—. Mem.: Princeton (N.Y.C.). Roman Catholic. Avocations: sailing, reading, sports. Office: 37 N Main St Cranbury NJ 08512-3203 Personal E-mail: kem344@aol.com.

KEMMERLY, JACK DALE, retired state official; b. El Dorado, Kans., Sept. 17, 1936; s. Arthur Allen and Eythel Louise (Throckmorton) K.; m. Frances Cecile Gregorio, June 22, 1958; children: Jack Dale Jr., Kathleen Frances, Grant Lee. BA, San Jose State U., 1962; cert. in real estate, UCLA, 1970; MPA, Golden Gate U., 1973; cert. labor-mgmt. rels., U. Calif., Davis, 1978; cert. orgnl. change, Stanford U., 1985. Right of way agt. Calif. Div. Hwys., Marysville, 1962-71; adminstrv. officer Calif. Dept. Transp., Sacramento, 1971-82, dist. dir. Redding, 1982-83, chief aeros. Sacramento, 1984-94; mgmt. cons. U.S. Dept. Transp., Riyadh, Saudi Arabia, 1983-84. Chmn. tech. adv. com. on aeronautics Calif. Transp. Commn. Bd. dirs. Yuba-Sutter Campfire Girls, 1972-73. With USN, 1954-57. Recipient superior accomplishment award Calif. Dept. Transp., 1981. Mem. Nat. Assn. State Aviation Ofcls. (nat. pres. 1989—), Am. Assn. State Hwy. and Transp. Ofcls. (aviation com. 1985-94), Calif. Assn. Aerospace Educators (adv. bd. 1984—), Calif. Assn. Airport Execs., Calif. Aviation Coun., Aircraft Owners and Pilots Assn. (dir. regional reps.), Elks (exalted ruler Marysville, Calif. 1974-75). Republican. Roman Catholic. Avocations: non-partisan political activities, reading, flying. Office: 1285 Charlotte Ave Yuba City CA 95991-2803 Office Phone: 530-674-3694. Personal E-mail: jdkemmerly@sbcglobal.net.

KEMMERLY, JAMES ROBERT, obstetrician, gynecologist; b. Baton Rouge, La., Aug. 15, 1936; s. Carl Edward and Edith May (Wright) Kemmerly; m. Sue L. Martin, June 12, 1960 (div. Jan. 1992); children: David Lee, Kelly Renee, Celeste Danielle; m. Dana Clawson Bell, Sept. 12, 1992 (div. Jan. 1999). BS, La. State U., 1953-56, MD, 1956-60; summer student, Perkins Sch. Theology, So. Meth. U., 1957, 58, 59. Diplomate Am. Bd. Ob-Gyn. Intern So. Bapt. Hosp., New Orleans, 1960-61, resident, 1963-66; practice medicine specializing in ob-gyn. Minden, La., 1966—; founding pres. The Women's Clinic A Med. Corp. Clin. asst. prof. La. State U. Med. Ctr., Shreveport, 1972—82; pres. med. staff Minden Med. Ctr., 1972, 1976—77, 1988—89, med. dir., 2002—; bd. dirs. Peoples Bank & Trust Co., Minden. Lay leader 1st United Meth. Ch., Minden, also past chmn. adminstrv. bd., pastor com., del. to state and nat. confs. With USAF, 1962-63. Fellow Am. Coll. Ob-Gyn.; mem. AMA, La. State Med. Assn., So. Med. Assn., Webster Parish Med. Soc. (pres. 1986-). Office: The Womens Clinic A Med Corp 431 Homer Rd Minden LA 71055-2933

KEMNITZ, JOSEPH WILLIAM, physiologist, researcher; b. Balt., Mar. 15, 1947; s. Harold Clarence Kemnitz and Alice Mae (Ziebarth) Delwiche; m. Amanda Marye Tuttle, Jan. 5, 1991; children: Julia Ellen, Joseph Andrew. BA, U. Wis., 1969, PhD, 1976. Rsch. assoc. Wis. Nat. Primate Rsch. Ctr., Madison, 1976-79, asst. scientist, 1979-84, assoc. scientist, 1984-94, sr. scientist and assoc. dir., 1995-96, dir., 1996—; assoc. scientist dept. medicine U. Wis., Madison, 1991-94, sr. scientist dept. medicine, 1995-97, prof. dept. physiology. Cons. NIH, Bethesda, Md., 1981—; mem. Children's Diabetes Ctr., Madison, Wis., 1990—; steering com. Inst. on Aging, Madison, 1989—. Assoc. editor Hormones and Behavior, 1986-96; contbr. articles to profl. jours. Grantee (various) NIH, 1977—. Mem. Am. Physiol. Soc., Am. Inst. Nutrition, Am. Diabetes Assn., Am. Soc. Primatologists, Gerontol. Soc. Am., N.Am. Assn. Study of Obesity, Internat. Primatol. Soc. Office: Primate Rsch Ctr UW 1220 Capitol Ct Madison WI 53715-1237

KEMNITZ, THOMAS MILTON, publisher; b. Washington; s. Milton Neumann and Esther L. K.; m. Myrna Kaye Glick, Dec. 10, 1982; 1 son, Thomas Milton Jr. BA, U. Mich., 1964; PhD, U. Sussex, Eng., 1969. Prof. U. N.H., Durham, 1969-75; pres. Kemnitz Audio Video, Boston, 1976-78, Trillium Press Inc., Unionville, N.Y., 1978—. Pres. KAV Books, Inc., 1980—, Royal Fireworks Pub., 1989—, Silk Label Books, 1998—; chmn. bd. Royal Fireworks Printing Co., 1989—. Author: Kids Working with Computers (12 vol. series), 1983-85, Brain Booster, 1985, Computer Ethics, 1985, Buck Fang's Logo Challenge, 1985, other books and pieces of software; pub. Our Gifted Children mag. Office: Royal Fireworks Printing Co #1 1st Ave Unionville NY 10988-0399 Business E-Mail: tmk@rfwp.com.

KEMP, ALSON REMINGTON, JR., b. Rossville, Ga., July 3, 1941; s. Alson R. Dorothy (Walters) K.; m. Martha Gudenrath, Aug. 7, 1967; children— Alson Remington, Colin T. BS, U. Tenn., 1962; JD, U. Cin., 1965. Bar: Tenn. 1965, Ohio 1965, Calif. 1970, U.S. Dist. Ct. (no. and cen. dists.) Calif. 1971, U.S. Ct. Appeals (9th cir.) 1971, U.S. Ct. Appeals (D.C. cir.) 1982. Asst. prof. Hancock Coll., Santa Maria, Calif., 1966-68; asst. prof. U. Tenn., Chattanooga, 1969; mem. Morgan & Garner, Chattanooga, 1968-70, Pillsbury, Madison & Sutro, San Francisco, 1970-75, ptnr., 1975-99; pvt. practice Healdsburg, Calif., 1999—. Dir. Green Diamond Reserve Campaign; dir Smith Brothers Holding Campaign, 2001—05, vice chair, 2001—03, chair, 2003—05, chair bd., 2005; chair Northern Sonoma County Healthcare Found. Capt. USAF, 1965—68. Benwood Found. grantee, 1962-65 Fellow Am. Coll. Trial Lawyers; mem. ABA, Calif. Bar Assn. Republican. Home and Office: 22190 Puccioni Rd Healdsburg CA 95448 Office Phone: 707-433-1199. Personal E-mail: arkemp@gmail.com.

KEMP, ANN, retired librarian; b. Providence, Ky., Aug. 2, 1941; d. Charlie and Rubye (Sigler) Kemp Page. BA, Belmont U., 1964; MLS, Vanderbilt U., 1965, postgrad., 1968-79. Cert. tchr. Ky. Libr. Nashville Pub. Libr., 1965, U. Louisville Libr., 1965-67, Dawson Springs (Ky.) Ind. Schs., 1967-93; instr. Murray (Ky.) State U., 1973-78. Author: Poem, The ABC's of Parthenon. Mem.: DAR, Ky. Libr. Assoc., Ky. Edn. Assoc., Nat. Edn. Assoc., The Parthenon Patrons. Baptist. Avocations: studying architecture and folklore, poetry. Home: 113 Woodlawn Dr Madisonville KY 42431-3254

KEMP, BETTY RUTH, retired librarian; b. Tishomingo, Okla., May 5, 1930; d. Raymond Herrell and Mamie Melvina (Hughes) K. BA in Libr. Sci., U. Okla., 1952; MS, Fla. State U., 1965. Extramural loan libr. U. Tex., Austin, 1952-55; libr. lit. and history dept. Dallas Pub. Libr., 1955-56; head Oaklawn Br., 1956-60, Walnut Hill Br., 1960-64; dir. Cherokee Regional Libr., Lafayette, Ga., 1965-74, Lee-Itawamla Libr. Sys., Dupelo, Miss., 1975—92. Bd. libr. commrs. State of Miss., 1979-83, chmn., 1979-80. Chmn. Chickasaw Hist. Soc., 1994-96, bd. dirs., 1994-98; active Native Am. Chickasaw Nation, United Meth. Women. Mem. AAUW, ALA, Nat. Soc. Daus. Am. Colonists, Nat. Soc. U.S. Daus. of 1812, United Daus. of the Confedercy, Nat. Soc. Dames of Ct. of Honor, Am. Indian Cultural Soc., Am. Indian C. of C., First Families Twin Ters, Beta Phi Mu. Democrat. Home: 3313 Winchester Cir Norman OK 73072-2937 Office: Kemp Rsch & Cons Svc PO Box 720531 Norman OK 73070-4388 Personal E-mail: bkrcs@aol.com.

KEMP, EUGENE THOMAS, retired veterinarian; b. McDonough, NY, Mar. 22, 1930; s. Oswald Milton and Almira Dorothy (Allen) K.; m. Ruth Emer Stoll, Sept. 29, 1951 (dec. Sept. 1977); 1 child, William Allen; m. Margaret Atenna Rowland, Dec. 27, 1980. BS, Cornell U., 1951, DVM, 1957. Sr. ptnr. Day Hollow Animal Clinic, Owego, NY, 1957—2000; ret., 2000. Author: Serfs on a Fief, 2002; contbr. articles to profl. jours. Bd. dirs. First Ch. of Nazarene, Owego, 1991-98; v.p. Tioga County Bd. Health, 1988-96, pres., 1996—; mem. Owego-Apalachin Bd. Edn., 1961-71; mem. Broome-Tioga Bd. Coop. Edn. Svcs., Binghamton, 1969-83, pres., 1971-76; founding pres. Broome-Tioga Coun. Sch. Bd. Pres., 1973. Mem. So. Tier Vet. Med. Assn. (pres. 1992). Republican. Avocations: jazz piano, creative writing. Home: 478 Hiawatha Rd Owego NY 13827-5307

KEMP, GEOFFREY THOMAS HOWARD, political scientist, consultant; b. U.K., May 20, 1939; came to U.S., 1967, naturalized, 1974; s. Thomas Howard and Gwendoline (Reeves) K.; m. Vivian Reubens, Sept. 1968 (div. 1979); m. Tamara Levin Weisberg, Nov., 1998. BA, Oxford U., 1963, MA, 1967; PhD, MIT, 1971. Research assoc. Internat. Inst. Strategic Studies, London, 1965-67; research assoc. Ctr. Internat. Studies, MIT, Cambridge, 1967-71; assoc. prof. internat. politics Fletcher Sch. Law and Diplomacy, Tufts U., 1971-80; spl. asst. to Pres. for nat. security affairs White House, Washington, 1981-85; sr. fellow Ctr. for Strategic and Internat. Studies, Georgetown U., Washington, 1985-86; sr. assoc. Carnegie Endowment for Internat. Peace, 1986-95; dir. regional strategic programs Nixon Ctr., Washington, 1995—. Author: The Control of the Middle East Arms Race, 1991, Forever Enemies? American Policy and the Islamic Republic of Iran, 1994; co-author: Strategic Geography and the Changing Middle East, 1997. Served to lt. Army U.K., 1958-60 Mem. Council on Fgn. Relations (internat. affairs fellow 1976), Internat. Inst. Strategic Studies, Oxford Union Soc. Avocations: tennis, evelyn waugh literature, movies, english watercolor paintings. Office: Nixon Ctr 1615 L St NW Washington DC 20036-5610 Office Phone: 202-887-5228. E-mail: gkemp@nixoncenter.org.

KEMP, H. JANE, librarian; b. Davenport, Iowa, Apr. 10, 1944; d. Milton and Henrietta Jane (Bonnell) Zagel; m. Donald R. Kemp, Apr. 25, 1969; 1 child, Anna Mary Amanda. BA, U. Iowa, 1966; MLS, U. Pitts., 1971. Libr. Luther Coll., Decorah, Iowa, 1981—. Supr. fine arts collection Luther Coll. Libr. Bibliographer: (book) Letters of Gerhard Marcks, 1991; co-author: (book) Displays and Exhibits in College Libraries, 1997; contbr. articles to profl. jours. Pres. Am. Assn. Univ. Women, Decorah, 1988. Recipient Frank B. Sessa scholarship, Beta Phi Mu, 1999; grantee, Am. Luth. Ch., 1988, 1992, 1999. Mem. ALA, Art Librs. Assn. N.Am., Am. Assn. Mus., Assn. Coll. and Rsch. Libr. (pres. Iowa chpt. 1989), Iowa Libr. Assn. (exec. bd. 1991-93). Democrat. Lutheran. Avocations: gardening, reading, travel. Office: Luther Coll Preus Libr 700 College Dr Decorah IA 52101-1039 Office Phone: 563-387-1195. Business E-Mail: kempjane@luther.edu.

KEMP, JACK FRENCH, former congressman; b. L.A., July 13, 1935; m. Joanne Main; children: Jeffrey, Jennifer, Judith, James. BA, Occidental Coll., 1957; postgrad., Long Beach State U., Calif. Western U. Spl. asst. to gov., Calif., 1967; spl. asst. to chmn. Republican Nat. Com., 1969; mem. 92d-100th congresses from 31st N.Y. Dist., 1971-89; former sec. Dept. of Housing and Urban Development, 1989-92; co-dir. Empower America, Washington, D.C., 1993—. Profl. football player for 13 years; pub. relations officer Marine Midland Bank, Buffalo; candidate for Rep. Presdl. nomination, 1987-88; Rep. nominee for v.p., 1996. Mem. Pres.'s Council on Phys. Fitness and Sports; mem. exec. com. player pension bd. NFL Recipient Disting. Service award N.Y. State Jaycees; Outstanding Citizen award Buffalo Evening News, 1965, 74 Mem. Nat. Assn. Broadcasters, Engrs. and Technicians, Buffalo Area C. of C., Sierra Club, Am. Football League Players Assn. (co-founder, pres. 1965-70) Republican. Office: Empower America Ste 900 1701 Pennsylvania Ave NW Washington DC 20006-5807*

KEMP, JAMES WILLIAM, graphic artist; b. Alliance, Ohio, Aug. 7, 1950; s. Albert William and Ethel Jean (Bricker) K.; m. Anita Karl, design ptnr., Aug. 20, 1999 BA, U. Pa., Phila., 1972; MLS, CUNY, 2001. Project editor Random House, Inc., N.Y.C., 1972-78; prin. designer, ptnr. Compass Projections Design Studio, Bklyn., 1978—; head libr. Poly Prep. CDS, Bklyn., 1999—. Map, lettering designer Random House, NYC, 1978—, Harcourt Brace, San Diego, 1982—, Franklin Libr., NYC, 1978-85, Doubleday, NYC, 1985—, Simon and Schuster, NYC, 1992—, Rolling Stone Mag., NYC, 1980-81, 89-93, NY Times, 1988—, Kirshenbaum & Bond, NYC, 1997, 98, Romann Group, NYC, 1998, Pub. Affairs Books, 1998—. Exhibited in group shows at Art Dir. Club, NYC, 1981, 90, 91, 95, Master Eagle Gallery, NYC, 1981, 83-84, 87, 90, Donnell Libr., NYC, 1987, ITC Gallery, NYC, 1987, 90-93, Berthold Type Ctr., Toronto, Ont., Can., 1988, 90, Cooper-Hewitt Mus., NYC, 1996, AIGA Gallery, NYC, 1999; contbr. articles to profl. jour.; artwork appearing in books and anns. Co-founder Summer Mus. Theater for Young Adults, Bennington, Vt., 1985—96. Recipient cert. of excellence Am. Inst. Graphic Arts, NYC, 1987, Type Dir. Club, NYC, 1989-94, merit award Art Dir. Club, NYC, 1991, 94; inducted, Beta Phi Mu, libr. hon. soc., 2003 Mem.: Beta Phi Mu. Avocations: writing, drawing. Home and Office: 263 Eastern Pkwy Apt 2I Brooklyn NY 11238 E-mail: jwilliamkemp@aol.com.

KEMP, KARL THOMAS, insurance company executive; b. Petoskey, Mich., Dec. 16, 1940; s. Vernon L. and Dorothy Jean (Olson) K.; m. Mary Ormston Graham, July 21, 1973; children: Karl Thomas Jr., John Walter, James Edward. BA, Harvard U., 1964. V.p. corp. fin. GEICO Corp., Washington, 1966-81; sr. v.p., pres. Resolute Reins. Co., N.Y.C., 1981-90; pres., CEO White Mountains Ins. Group, Ltd., Hanover, N.H., 1997—. Bd. dirs. Folksamerica Holdings, Inc., N.Y.C., chair Human Resources Com., 1996—; bd. dirs. FSA Holdings, N.Y.C., chair human resources com., 1994—; bd. dirs. Eldorado Bancshares, Inc., Calif., chair human resources com., 1996—; bd. dirs. Main St. Am. Holdings, Keane, N.Y., exec. com., 1994—; pres., CEO White Mountain Holdings, Inc., Hanover, 1994—; bd. dirs. Amlin, plc., London. Mem. Am. Bonanza Soc., Aircraft Owners and Pilots Assn., Harvard Club (N.Y.C., Vt., N.H.). Avocation: flying. Home: 6 Goodfellow Rd Hanover NH 03755-4800 Office: White Mountains Ins Group Ltd 80 S Main St Hanover NH 03755-2053

KEMP, MICHAEL EDWARD, music educator, conductor; b. Sellersville, Pa., Feb. 28, 1946; s. John Stanley Couch and Helen (Hubbert) Kemp; m. Janice Brown, Nov. 3, 1950; children: Michael Todd, Bradley Ryan, Erin Michelle. Spl. cert., Royal Conservatory Music, The Hague, The Netherlands, 1963; MusB, Westminster Choir Coll., 1968; MusM, Okla. U., 1972. Dir. music ministries Toms River (N.J.) Presbyn. Ch., 1965—68, 1st Presbyn. Ch., Arlington, Tex., 1972—84, Westminster Presbyn. Ch., Nashville, 1984—91, Abington (Pa.) Presbyn. Ch., 1991—98; choral dir. Montgomery Bell Acad., Nashville, 1985—91; dir. cmty. music and U.S. choral and string orch. Germantown Acad., Ft. Washington, Pa., 1997—. Barness chair disting. tchg., 2003—. Guest condr., lectr. in field, 1972—; lectr. So. Meth. U., Dallas, 1973—84. Author: Well-Kemped Secrets, 2005, composer. Founder, condr. Arlington Choral Soc., 1973—84; founding condr. Acad. Chamber Soc., Acad. Chorale, Ft. Washington, 1997—. With U.S. Army, 1968—70. Fellow: Melodious Accord; mem.: Pa. Acad. Music, Music Educators Nat. Conf., Am. Choral Dirs. Assn. Avocations: reading, landscaping, violin, tennis. Home: 1238 Jericho Rd Abington PA 19001 Office: Germantown Acad 340 Morris Rd Fort Washington PA 19034 Office Phone: 215-646-3300 368. Business E-Mail: mkemp@germantownacademy.org.

KEMP, ROBERT BOWERS, JR., investment manager; b. Balt., July 25, 1941; s. Robert Bowers and Edwina Reid (Rose) K.; 1 child, Amy Nicole. BS, U. Md., 1963; MBA, U. Houston, 1968. Market mgr. Kimberly Clark Corp., Neenah, Wis., 1968-70; dir. rsch., sr. portfolio mgr. Provident Mgmt. Co., Phila., 1970-73; trust investment officer 1st Tenn. Nat. Bank, Chattanooga, 1973-77; v.p., sr. investment officer Mchts. Nat. Bank, Indpls., 1977-83; sr. v.p., chief investment officer 1st Tenn. Investment Mgmt., Chattanooga, 1983-93; prin., pres., investment advisor Trust Investment Mgmt., LLC, Chattanooga, 1993—. Adj. prof. U. Tenn., Chattanooga, 1976. Mem. CFA Assn., Nat. Assn. Bus. Economists, Chattanooga (Tenn.) Soc. Fin. Analysts (chmn.), Atlanta Econs. Club. Home: 1732 Valley Forge Dr Hixson TN 37343-3468

KEMP, STEPHANIE ANN, language educator, special education educator; b. Baytown, Tex., Mar. 24, 1955; d. Robert M. Stefflec and Virginia Dale Smith; m. Donald G. Kemp Jr., Aug. 21, 1976; children: William Robert Rial, Kathryn Anna. BA, U. Tex., Austin, 1976. Youth min. St. Lukes Luth. Ch., 1995—98; dir. childrens ministry Lovers Lane Meth. Ch., 1998—99; tchr. secondary sch. CSID, Cappell, Tex., 2002—. Leader Girl Scouts Am.; sponsor Richardson Symphony Orch. League, 2004—05, bd. dirs., 1984—88, PTA, 1993—98. Mem.: Tex. Assn. Alternative Edn., Tex. Tchrs. English Lang. Arts, Nat. Coun. Social Studies. Republican. Lutheran. Avocations: reading, travel. Home: 706 Westminster Richardson TX 75081 Office: Coppell Edn Assn 1201 Wrangler Cir Coppell TX 75019

KEMP, THOMAS JAY, librarian; b. Nashua, N.H. s. Willard Henry and Eleanor Frances (Huse) K.; m. Vi Lam; children: Andrew Thomas, Sarah Eleanor. BA, Brigham Young U., 1973, MLS, 1974; cert. photographic preservation, Rochester Inst. Tech., 1979. Office supr., history div. Lee Library, Brigham Young U., Provo, Utah, 1971-74; local history and genealogy librarian Ferguson Library System, Stamford, Conn., 1974-86; grant reviewer NEH, Washington, 1978-84; ref. libr. Sacred Heart U., Fairfield, Conn., 1980-82; head libr. Weed Meml. Libr. Ferguson Libr. Sys., 1981-82, head libr. Turn of River Libr., 1982-86; asst. dir. Pequot Library, Southport, Conn., 1986-89; libr. dir. Hist. Soc. Pa., Phila., 1989-91; dir. spl. collections dept. U. So. Fla. Libr., Tampa, Fla., 1991—. Tchr. Office of Continuing Edn., Stamford, 1975-80; lectr. in field; called to testify U.S. Senate hearings on the new archivist of U.S., 1986; called as Bishop The Ch. of Jesus Christ of Latter-day Saints, Temple Terrace, Fla., 1993—; mem. U. So. Fla. Faculty Senate, 1992-96, sec., 1994-95; chair U. So. Fla. Libr. Coun., 1996-98. Author: Office of Patriarch to the Church in The Church of Jesus Christ of Latter-day Saints, 1981, Stamford, Connecticut 1872 City Directory, 1981, Connecticut Periodical Index, 1981-86, Genealogies in the Ferguson Library, 1982, Connecticut Researcher's Handbook, 1982, Connecticut Biography and Portrait Index, 1985-89, Genealogies in Connecticut Libraries and Historical Societies, 1985, Kemp Family of County Cavan, Ireland, 1985, Inexpensive Items for Building Your Genealogical Library, 1977, Home Study Courses of Interest to Genealogists and Local Historians, 1986, Kemp Bibliography, 1986, Kemp Family Records, 1986, Kemp Family Passport Records, 1986, Vital Records Handbook, 1988, Connecticut Divorces Granted by Resolve of the General Assembly of the State of Connecticut, 1988, Connecticut Changes of Name Granted by Resolve of the General Assembly of the State of Connecicut, 1988, Darien Connecticut, 1989 Vital Records: An Index to Birth, Engagement, Marriage and Death Announcements, 1990, Litchfield County, Connecticut Obituary Announcements 1989, 1990, New Canaan, Connecticut 1989 Vital Records: An Index to Birth, Engagement, Marriage and Death Announcements, 1990, International Vital Records Handbook, 1990, 94, Connecticut Historians and Genealogists 1890-1990, 1991, Genealogy Annual, 1995—; editor: Connecticut Ancestry, 1987-89, Richmond Family News Jour., 1971-76, Gradalis Review, 1973-74; local history and genealogy collection Thomas Jay Kemp Genealogy and Local History Collection Darien Libr., 1989; contbr. articles to profl. jours. Missionary to Colo.-N.Mex. Mission, Denver, 1968-70; bd. dirs. Pa. Ctr. for the Book, 1990-91. With USN, 1965-71. Recipient Hattie M. Knight award NYU, 1974, Merit award Conn. League Hist. Socs., 1983. Mem. Assn. for Bibliography of History, New Eng. Libr. Assn. (bibliography com. 1979-80), Conn. Libr. Assn. (hon. mention, Librarian of the Yr, 1987), Orgn. Am. Historians U.S. newspaper project, 1977), Am. Libr. Assn., (ref. svcs. div., chmn. history sect. 1989-90, chmn. nominations com., 1984, chmn. program com. 1983, pre-conf. planning com. 1981, genealogy com. 1978-82, local history com. 1986-91, 1996—), Coun. of Nat. Libr. Info. Assns. (chmn. 1989-90), New Eng. Archivists, N.H. Libr. Assn., N.Y. Geneal. and Biog. Soc., Geneal. Soc. Pa. (pubs. com. 1989—, acquisitions com. 1989—), Libr. Assn. (U.K.), Libr. Assn. of Ireland, Libr. Assn. China, Soc. Am. Archivists, Am. Soc. Indexers (pres. 1987-88), Assn. Profl. Genealogists (exec. v.p. 1988-90, trustee 1990-92), Middlesex Geneal. Soc. (Darien, Conn., bd. dirs. 1984-89, trustee 1989—), Gen. Soc. Mayflower Descendants (bd. assts. Conn. 1983), SAR, Order of Founders and Patriots, Phi Alph Theta. Mem. Lds Ch. Avocation: promotion of bibliography and indexing of local history and genealogy resources. Home: c/o Godfrey Memorial Library 134 Newfield St Middletown CT 06457-2534

KEMP, THOMAS JOSEPH, retired electronics executive; b. Holy Cross, Iowa, Aug. 17, 1943; s. Joseph Peter and Margaret Gertrude (Wilgenbusch) K.; m. Ruth Anne Pfohl, Aug. 22, 1964; children: Geoffrey Joseph, Jennifer Anne, Julie Marie, Jack Thomas. BA in Bus. Acctg., Loras Coll., 1964; MS in Sys. Mgmt., St. Mary's U., San Antonio, 1978. Commd. 2d lt. USAF, 1964, advanced through grades to lt. col., 1980, pilot, mgr., 1964-85; ret., 1985; Instructional systems design mgr., dep. program mgr. United Airlines Svcs. Corp., Irving, Tex., 1985-87; divsn. mgr., project mgr. Flight Safety Svcs. Corp., Irving, 1987-90; program mgr. ElectroCom Automation, Arlington, Tex., 1990—2002; mgr. Integrated Logistics Support Siemens Dematic, Arlington, 1997—2002. Congl. advisor Vets. and Budget Com., Ft. Worth, 1994—; pres. Tarrant County Vets. Coun., Ft. Worth, 1995-96. Mem. VFW (life), Mil. Officers Assn. Am. (life), Air Force Assn. (life, state pres. Tex. 1995-97, nat. v.p. 1998-99, nat. dir. 2000-03, nat. sec. 2003-, exec. com. 2000—, Texoma region pres. 1999-2000, Exceptional Svc. award 1990, 91, 94, Presdl. citation 2000, Mem. of Yr. 2002), Am. Legion, KC (Grand Knight 2003-05, Knight of Month award, Family of Month award). Republican. Roman Catholic. Avocations: fishing, golf, gardening. Home: 3608 Kimberly Ln Fort Worth TX 76133-2147 Office Phone: 817-313-9187. E-mail: tjkafatx@flash.net.

KEMPE, FREDERICK SCHUMANN, newspaper editor, columnist, author; b. Salt Lake City, Sept. 5, 1954; s. Fritz Gustav and Johanna Irmgardt (Schumann) K. BA in Comm. magna cum laude, U. Utah, 1976; MA in journalism, Columbia U., 1977; LLD (hon.), U. Md., 1995; HD (hon.), Queen Coll., 1999; LHD (hon.), Queens Coll., 1999. Frankfurt corr. AP-Dow Jones, Germany, 1978-79; Bonn corr. Newsweek, Germany, 1979-81; London corr. The Wall St. Jour. (USA), 1981-84, Vienna bureau chief, 1984-86, chief diplomatic corr. Washington, 1986-89; founder, mng. editor Cen. European Econ. Rev., 1993-94, editor, 1995-96; mng. editor Wall St. Jour. Europe, Brussels, 1992-96, editor, assoc. publ., 1998—. Author: Divorcing the Dictator: America's Bungled Affair with Noriega, 1990, Siberian Odyssey: A Voyage Into the Russian Soul, 1992, Father/Land: A Personal Search for the New Germany, 1999. Bd. dirs. Aspen Inst. Berlin, Am. Inst. for Contemporary German Studies, Washington, Economia, Prague, Czech Republic. Recipient Quentus Wilson award U. Utah, 1987, Alumni Achievement award Columbia U. Grad. Sch. Journalism, 2002; named Top Young Alumnus of Yr. U. Utah, 1987. Mem. Coun. Fgn. Rels. Office: Wall Street Jour Europe Blvd Brand Whitlock 87 1200 Brussels Belgium Business E-Mail: fred.kempe@wsj.com.

KEMPE, LUDWIG GEORGE, neurosurgeon; b. Prenzlau, Germany, Oct. 16, 1915; came to U.S., 1946; s. George Joseph and Maria Theresa (Koustantin) K.; m. Czenta Groll, Dec. 23, 1955 (dec. March 20, 1996); m. Louise Goin. MA, Konigsberg Coll., Fed. Republic of Germany, 1936; MD, U. Berne, Switzerland, 1942. Diplomate Am. Bd. Neurol. Surgery. Commd. 2d lt. U.S. Army, 1951, advanced through grades to col., 1965, ret., 1974; instr. Neuroanatomy U. Berne, Switzerland, 1940-41; chief surgeon U.S. Air Command, Arctic, 1951-52; asst. surgeon US Army, Ft. Dix, N.J., 1952-64; chief neurosurgery Walter Reed Meml. Hosp., Washington, 1964-73; ret. U.S. Army, 1974; prof. Neurosurgery U. S. C. Med. Sch., Charleston, S.C., 1974-84, Georgetown U., Washington, 1980-84. Assoc. prof. George Washington U., Washington, 1964-73; rsch. prof. Anatomy U.S.C., Charleston, 1974-84; cons. Neurosurgery Sugeon Gen. U.S. Army, Washington, 1965-73, chmn., dir. tng. program Neurosurgery, Neurolog. Rsch., Walter Reed Hosp., 1963-73. Author: Operative Neurosurgery, 1970, 75, 81, 86; editor 3 neurology jours.; contbr. numerous articles to profl. jours. Col. U.S. Army, 1951-74. Decorated with Legion of Merit (2 oak leaf clusters) U.S. Army, Washington, 1965, '69, 74, Order of Dumas, Govt. of Brazil, 1969, Great Cross of Merit, Fed. Republic of Germany, 1975. Fellow Am. Coll. Surgery; mem. (sr.) Am. Assn. of Neurol. Surgeons, Congress of Neurol. Surgeons, Soc. of Neurol. Surgeons, Military Surgeons U.S.A.; (hon.) German Soc. Neurol. Surgeons, Yugoslav Soc. Neurol. Surgeons; Am. Anatomic Soc. Avocations: history, ornithology. Home: 12 Valley View Dr Pisgah Forest NC 28768-9509

KEMPER, CHRISTINA, small business owner, respiratory therapist, elementary school educator; b. St. Louis, Feb. 16, 1952; d. Edward James and Norma Helen (Renner) K.; m. Don Eichholz, Dec. 23, 1972 (div. Apr. 1994); children: Cherie L., Derek V. BS in Edn., U. Mo., St. Louis, 1976, MA in

Polit. Sci., 1980; AAS in Respiratory Therapy, Maryville U., 1983. Registered respiratory therapist. Intensive and critical care specialist various hosps., St. Louis, 1974—. Tchr. Parish Sch. Religion, St. Joseph's Ch., Manchester, Mo.; leader Girl Scouts Am., St. Louis. Mem. NOW (treas.), Am. Assn. for Respiratory Care, Nat. Bd. for Respiratory Care, Kappa Delta Pi. Avocations: floral designing, reading, interior decorating. Home: 12930 Twin Meadow Ct Creve Coeur MO 63146-1803 Personal E-mail: raregem24kt@yahoo.com.

KEMPER, DAVID WOODS, II, banker; b. Kansas City, Mo., Nov. 20, 1950; s. James Madison and Mildred (Lane) K.; m. Dorothy Ann Jannarone, Sept. 6, 1975; children: John W., Elizabeth C., Catherine B., William L. BA cum laude, Harvard U., 1972; MA in English Lit., Oxford, Worcester Coll., 1974; MBA, Stanford U., 1976. With Morgan Guaranty Trust Co., N.Y.C., 1975-78; v.p. Commerce Bank of Kansas City, Mo., 1978-79, sr. v.p., 1980-81; pres. Commerce Bancshares, Inc., 1982-86, pres., ceo, 1986-91, chmn., pres., ceo, 1991—; also dir. Commerce Bancshares, Inc; chmn. Commerce Bank N.A., St. Louis, 1985—. Bd. dirs. Kansas City, Tower Properties, Kansas City, Ralcorp Holdings, Inc. Contbr. articles on banking to profl. jours. Trustee Mo. Bot. Garden, Washington U., Donald Danforth Plant Sci. Ctr. Mem. Acad. Arts and Scis., Fin. Svcs. Roundtable, Kansas City Country Club, River Club (Kansas City), St. Louis Club, St. Louis Country Club, Racquet Club, Old Warson Country Club (St. Louis). Office: Commerce Bancshares Inc 8000 Forsyth Blvd Clayton MO 63105

KEMPER, DORLA DEAN EATON (DORLA DEAN EATON), real estate broker; b. Calhoun, Mo., Sept. 10, 1929; d. Paul McVay and Jesse Lee (McCombs) Eaton; m. Charles K. Kemper, Mar. 1, 1951; children: Kevin Keil, Kara Lee. BS in Edn., Ctrl. Mo. State U., 1952. Tchr. pub. schs., Twin Falls, Idaho, 1950-51, Mission, Kans., 1952-53, Burbank, Calif., 1953-57; real estate sales Minn., 1967-68, 1971-73, Deanie Kemper, Inc. Real Estate Brokerage, Loomis, Calif., 1974-76, pres., 1976-91; sr. couns. Capital holdong Corp., Louisville, 1991-93. Pres. Battle Creek Park Elem. Sch. PTA, St. Paul, 1966-67; mem. Placer County (Calif.) Bicentennial Commn., 1976; mem. Sierra Coll. Adv. Com., 1981—; active Placer County Hist. Soc. Named to Million Dollar Club (lifetime) Sacramento and Placer County bds. Realtors, 1978-94; designated Grad. Realtors Inst., Cert. Residential Specialist. Mem. Nat. Assn. Realtor, Calif. Assn. Realtors, Nat. Assn. Real Estate Appraisers, Placer County (mem. profl. stds. com.), Bds. Realtors, DAR (chpt. regent 1971-73, organizing chpt. regent 1977—, dist. dir. 1978-80, state registrar Calif. 1980-82, state vice regent 1982-84, state regent 1984-86, nat. resolutions com., nat. rec. sec. gen. 1986-89, nat. chmn. units overseas 1983-86, nat. pres. gen. 1995-98, hon. nat. pres. gen. 1998—, nat. chmn. WWII Meml. Campaign 1998-2001), Nat. Gavel Soc., Daus Am. Colonists, Colonial Dames Am., Internat. Platform Assn., Hidden Valley Women's (pres. Loomis club 1970-71), Auburn Travel Study (pres. 1979). Republican. Home: 8165 Morningside Dr Granite Bay CA 95746-8163

KEMPER, EDWARD CRAWFORD, lawyer; b. Seattle, Dec. 7, 1942; s. Edward C. and Sarah (Tolman) K.; m. Joleen Osterling, Sept. 5, 1964; children: Kevin, Kirsten. BA, George Washington U., 1965, JD with honors, 1968. Bar: Hawaii 1969, U.S. Dist. Ct. Hawaii 1969, U.S. Ct. Appeals (9th cir.) 1974, U.S. Supreme Ct. 1974. Assoc. Cades, Schutte, Fleming & Wright, Honolulu, 1968—71; ptnr. Mattoch, Kemper & Brown, Honolulu, 1971—75, Kemper & Watts, Honolulu, 1975—. Editor-in-chief Hawaii Bar Jour., 1972—92; editor: Hawaii Bar Jour., 1992—; author: articles, —. Pres. Kokua Kalihi Valley, Honolulu, 1983, Friends of Kailua (Hawaii) High Sch., 1985-, pres. Hawaii Family Support Ctr. 2001-03, v.p., dir. Epilepsy Found. Hawaii, 2002-; newspaper auto columnist Honolulu Star Bulletin Mem. Hawaii Bar Assn. (bd. dirs. 1974). Clubs: Honolulu. Home: 1307 Onaona Pl Kailua HI 96734-3752 Office: Kemper & Watts Alakea Corp Tower 1100 Alakea St #2400 Honolulu HI 96813 Office Phone: 808-524-0330. E-mail: edracers@aol.com.

KEMPER, JAMES DEE, lawyer; b. Olney, Ill., Feb. 23, 1947; s. Jack O. and Vivian L. Kemper; m. Diana J. Deig, June 1, 1968; children: Judd, Jason. BS, Ind. U., 1969, JD summa cum laude, 1971. Bar: Ind. 1971. Law clk. U.S. Ct. Appeals (7th cir.), Chgo., 1971-72; ptnr. Ice Miller, Indpls., 1972—, mng. ptnr., 1993—98. Note editor Ind. U. Law Rev., 1970-71; contbr. articles to profl. jours. Past officer, bd. dirs. Marion County Assn. for Retarded Citizens, Inc., Indpls.; past bd. dirs. Cen. Ind. Easter Seal Soc., Indpls., Crossroads Rehab. Ctr., Inc, Indpls.; pres., bd. govs. Orchard Country Day Sch., Indpls.; mem. bd. Eiteljorg Mus. Native Americans, Butler U. Fellow Ind. Bar Found.; mem. ABA (employee benefit com.), Ind. Bar Assn., The Group, Inc., Midwest Pension Conf., U.S. C. of C. (employee benefit com.), Stanley K. Lacy Leadership Alumni. Office: Ice Miller 1 American Sq Indianapolis IN 46282-0200

KEMPER, JOHN DUSTIN, mechanical engineering educator; b. Portland, Oreg., May 29, 1924; s. Clay Wallace and Leona Bell (Landis) K.; m. Barbara Jeanne Lane, June 28, 1947; 1 dau., Kathleen Lynne. BS, UCLA, 1949, MS, 1959; PhD, U. Colo., 1969. Chief mech. engr. Telecomputing Corp., North Hollywood, Calif., 1949-55, H.A. Wagner Co., Van Nuys, Calif., 1955-56; v.p. engring. Marchant div. SCM Corp., Oakland, Calif., 1956-62; faculty U. Calif., Davis, 1962-91, prof. engring., 1967-91, dean coll. Engring., 1969-83, ret., 1991. Panel chmn. Engring. Grad. Edn. and Research, NRC, 1985. Author: Engineers and Their Profession, 1967, 5th edit., 2001, Introduction to the Engineering Profession, 1985, 2d edit., 1993, (with G.C. Andrews) Canadian Professional Engineering Practice and Ethics, 1992, Birding Northern California, 1999, Southern Oregon's Bird Life, 2002, Exploring Southern Oregon's Beautiful Places, 2003. Served with USAF, 1944-46. Fellow ASME (chmn. San Francisco sect. 1962-63), AAAS; mem. Am. Soc. Engring. Edn. Achievements include having engineering building on University of California-Davis campus named after him.

KEMPER, ROBERT VAN, anthropologist, educator, minister; b. San Diego, Nov. 21, 1945; s. Ivan L. and Roberta (King) K.; m. Sandra L. Kraft, Sept. 9, 1967; 1 child, John Kraft. BA, U. Calif., Riverside, 1966; MA, U. Calif., Berkeley, 1969, PhD, 1971; MDiv, So. Meth. U., 1999. Ordained to ministry Presbyn. Ch., 1999. Postdoctoral fellow U. Calif., Berkeley, 1971-72; asst. prof. So. Meth. U., Dallas, 1972-77, assoc. prof., 1977-83, prof., 1983—, chmn., 1992-94, 2004—, pres. faculty senate, 2005—. Visiting rsch. scholar U. Iberoamericana, Mexico City, 1970, 79-80, Ctr. U.S.-Mex. Studies, LaJolla, Calif., 1983, U. Nat. Autónoma Mex., Mexico City, 1990-91, El Colegio de Michoacán, Zamora, Mex., 1991; sec. Inst. Study of Earth and Man, Dallas, 1989-92; Coun. Preservation Anthrop. Records; founding chair Com. Anthropology Tourism, Internat. Union Anthrop. and Ethnol. Scis., 1993-96. Author: Migration and Adaptation, 1977; co-author: History of Anthropology, 1977; co-editor: Anthropologists in Cities, 1974, Migration Across Frontiers, 1979, (series) Contemporary Urban Studies, 1990—, Chronicling Cultures, 2002; editor Socio Cultural Anthropology, Am. Anthropologist, 1985-90, Human Orgn., 1995-98; mem. editl. bd. Ency. World Cultures, 1990-96, Ency. Urban Cultures, 1999—2002. Elder North Pk. Presbyn. Ch., Dallas, 1987-89, 95-97; parish assoc. Trinity Presbyn. Ch., 1999—; mem. Mcpl. Libr. Adv. Bd., Dallas, 1975-79; bd. dir. Oasis Housing Corp., 2000-04, Presbyn. Assn. Cmty. Transformation, 2003-04. Fulbright fellow, 1979-80, 91-92, Wenner-Gren fellow, 1974-76, 79-83, Woodrow Wilson fellow, 1966-67. Fellow AAAS, Am. Anthrop. Assn. (bd. dirs. 1990-92), Soc. Applied Anthropology (chmn. Malinowski award com. 1979-80, bd. dirs. 1995-98); mem. Latin Am. Studies Assn. (co-chmn. XI Internat. Congress 1983), Soc. Urban Anthropology (pres. 1988-90), Soc. Latin Am. Anthropology (pres. 1981-82), Phi Beta Kappa (pres. chpt. 1987-88). Home: 10617 Cromwell Dr Dallas TX 75229-5110 Office: So Meth Univ Dept Anthropology 3225 Daniel Ave Dallas TX 75205-1437 Office Phone: 214-768-2928. Business E-Mail: rkemper@smu.edu.

KEMPER, RUFUS CROSBY, JR., retired bank executive; b. Kansas City, Mo., Feb. 22, 1927; s. Rufus Crosby and Enid (Jackson) Kemper; m. Mary Barton Stripp; children: Rufus Crosby III, Pamela Warrick Gabrovsky, Sheila Kemper Dietrich, John Mariner, Mary Barton Wolf, Alexander Charles, Heather Christian. Grad., Phillips Acad., Andover, Mass., 1942; student, U. Mo.; LL.D. (hon.), William Jewel Coll., 1976; DFA (hon.), Westminster Coll., 1983. Joined City Nat. Bank & Trust Co. (now UMB Fin. Corp.), Kansas City, 1950; exec v.p. UMB Fin. Corp., 1957—59, pres., 1959—71, chmn. & CEO, 1971—2000; sr. chmn. UMB Fin. Corp. & UMB Bank, 2000—04; ret., 2004. Hon. trustee Thomas Jefferson Found.; mem. nat. com. Whitney Mus. Am. Art, NYC.; commr. Nat. Mus. Am. Art., Washington; founder, chmn. bd. trustees The Kemper Mus. Contemporary Art, Kansas City, 1994-; trustee Kemper family foundations; founder, mem. bd. dirs. The Agriculture Future of Am., 1996-. Served USNR, WWII. Recipient Key Man Kansas City Jr. C. of C., 1952, Disting. Svc., 1964, Man of Yr. Award Kansas City Press Club, 1974, Outstanding Kansas Citian Award Native Sons Kansas City, 1975, 82, 1st Advocacy Award Mid-Continent Small Bus. Assn., 1980, Banker Adv. of Yr. Award Small Bus. Adminstrn., 1981, Lester Milgram Humanitarian Award, 1982, Man of Yr. Award Downtown, Inc., 1982, Pirouette Award Kansas City Ballet Guild and Kansas City Tomorrow Alumni Assn., 1983, Faculty Alumni Award U. Mo. Columbia Alumni Assn., 1982, Mo. Arts Coun. Award, 1984, Kansas City Chancellor's Medal U. Mo., 1984, Disting. Svc. Award St. Paul Sch. Theology, 1987, Advocacy Award Mo. Citizens for the Arts, 1987, Outstanding Patron of Excellence in the Arts and Architecture Am. Inst. Architects - Kansas City, 1994, VIP Leadership Award Centurions Leadership Program Greater Kansas City C. of C., 1995; named Man of Yr. Kansas City Press Club, 1974, Kansas Citian of Yr., 1997; named one of Top 200 Collectors ARTnews mag., 2004. Mem. Am. Royal Assn. (v.p., bd. dirs.), Man of the Month Fraternity, Beta Theta Pi (Man of Yr. 1974) Clubs: River, Carriage, Kansas City Country, Kansas City, 1021, Mo, Chathan, Mass., Garden of the Gods, Cheyenne Mountain Country (Colorado Springs, Colo.). Republican. Episcopalian. Avocations: Collector Old Masters, modern and contemporary art, farming, tennis, sailing, horseback riding, raising cattle. Office: Kemper Mus Contemporary Art 4220 Warwick Blvd Kansas City MO 64111*

KEMPF, DONALD G., JR., lawyer; b. Chgo., July 4, 1937; s. Donald G. and Verginia (Jahnke) K.; m. Nancy Kempf, June 12, 1965; children: Donald G. III, Charles P., Stephen R. AB, Villanova U., 1959; LLB, Harvard U., 1965; MBA, U. Chgo., 1989. Bar: Ill. 1965, U.S. Supreme Ct. 1972, N.Y. 1986, Colo. 1992. Assoc. Kirkland & Ellis, Chgo., 1965-70, ptnr., 1971-2000; exec. v.p., chief legal officer, sec. Morgan Stanley, NYC, 2000—. Trustee Chgo. Symphony Orch., 1995—, Am. Inns of Ct., 1997-, v.p., 2002—; bd. govs. Chgo. Zool. Soc., 1975—, Art Inst. Chgo., 1984—; bd. dirs. United Charities Chgo., 1985-2003, chmn. bd., 1991-93; trustee N.Y.C. Opera, 2002—. Capt. USMC, 1959-62. Fellow Am. Coll. Trial Lawyers; mem. Am. Econ. Assn., ABA, Chgo. Club, Econ. Club, Univ. Club, Mid-Am. Club, Saddle and Cycle Club (Chgo.), Snowmass (Colo.) Club, Quail Ridge (Fla.) Club, Westmoreland Club. Roman Catholic. Address: Morgan Stanley 1585 Broadway Fl 39 New York NY 10036-8200 Office Phone: 212-761-6321. Business E-Mail: donald.kempf@morganstanley.com.

KEMPNER, JOSEPH, aerospace engineering educator; b. Bklyn., Apr. 25, 1923; s. Arthur and Anna (Richman) K.; m. Carol F. Brown, Jan. 12, 1947; children: Robert M., Marien A. Barker. B.Aero. Engring. summa cum laude, Poly. Inst. Bklyn., 1943, M.Aero. Engring., 1947, PhD in Applied Mechanics, 1950. Registered profl. engr., NY. Research fellow Poly. Inst. Bklyn., 1944, mem. faculty, 1947-90, prof. applied mechanics and aerospace engring., 1957-90, prof. emeritus, 1990—, chmn. undergrad. aerospace studies, asst. dir. research, 1962-63, dir. applied mechanics, 1964-76, head dept., 1966-76; aero. engr. NASA, 1944-47. Cons. indsl. and govt. research labs; former mem. adv. group II, ship structural design procedure and analysis, ship research com. Maritime Transp. Research Bd., Nat. Acad. Scis.-NRC; also former mem. com. basic research, adv. to Army Research Office, 1973-76, 81-85; prin. investigator research contracts Office Naval Research and Air Force Office Sci. Research. Contbr. articles to profl. jours. Recipient citation disting. research Poly. chpt. Sigma Xi, 1973; named Outstanding Educator Am., 1973, 74-75 Fellow N.Y. Acad. Scis. (I.B. Laskowitz Gold medal 1973), Am. Acad. Mechanics; assoc. fellow AIAA; mem. Am. Soc. Engring. Edn., Sigma Xi, Tau Beta Pi, Sigma Gamma Tau. Home: 82 Murray Hill Ter Marlboro NJ 07746-1751 Office: 333 Jay St Brooklyn NY 11201-2907

KEMPNER, MAXIMILIAN WALTER, dean, lawyer; b. Berlin, Feb. 27, 1929; came to U.S., 1939; s. Paul H. and Marga Marie (von Mendelssohn) K.; m. Barbara Paige Mooney, 1952; children: Paul, Daphne, Emily Mayne. BA, Harvard U., 1951, LLB, 1954; LLM, Columbia U., 1957; LLD, Vt. Law Sch., 1997. Bar: N.Y. bar 1954. With Webster & Sheffield, N.Y.C., 1957-91; dean Vt. Law Sch., South Royalton, 1991-96. Chmn. Vt. Legis. Apportionment Bd.; dir. Lawyers Com. for Civil Rights under Law. Trustee Marlboro Sch. Music, Inc., Conservation Law Found.; former dir. Legal Aid Soc., Am. Coun. on Germany, Albert Schweitzer Fellowship, Coun. on Libr. Resources; active Coun. Fgn. Rels., Inc. With U.S. Army, 1954-56. Fellow Am. Bar Found. (life); mem. ABA (past chmn. legal edn. and admissions to bar sect.), Am. Law Inst. (life), Assn. Bar City N.Y., N.Y. State Bar Assn., Harvard Law Sch. Assn. N.Y.C. (past pres.). Office Phone: 802-763-2222. Business E-Mail: mkempner@vermontlaw.edu.

KEMPRECOS, PAUL, writer; Writer The Cape Codder, Cape Cod, Mass.; editor Cape Cod Business Journal, Cape Cod, Mass. Author: (novels) Cool Blue Tomb, 1991, Neptune's Eye, 1991, Death in Deep Water, 1992, Feeding Frenzy, 1993, The Mayflower Murder, 1996, Bluefin Blues, 1997; co-author (with Clive Cussler) Blue Gold, 2000, Serpent, 2001, Lost City, 2003.

KEMPSTER, NORMAN ROY, journalist; b. Sacramento, Jan. 4, 1936; s. Roy Dixon and Viola Alice (Cox) K.; m. Jane Leon, June 30, 1957; children: Jill Suzanne Zemke, David Norman. BA, Calif. State U., 1957. Reporter U.P.I., 1957-73, Washington Star-News, 1973-76; reporter Washington bur. L.A. Times, 1976—80, reporter Jerusalem bur., 1981—84, reporter Washington bur., 1984—2001. Joe Alex Morris meml. lectr. Harvard U., 1983, adj. prof. Lenoir-Rhyne Coll., Hickory, NC, 2003. Served with AUS, 1959-61. Profl. Journalism fellow, 1967; recipient Gerald Loeb award, 1980 Mem. Fgn. Press Assn. in Israel (v.p. 1982-83), White House Corrs. Assn. (dir. 1974-75), State Dept. Corrs. Assn. (treas. 1986, v.p. 1987, pres. 1988), Overseas Writers of Washington (pres. 1989-91). Episcopalian. Home and Office: 321 N Cedar St Lincolnton NC 28092 Personal E-mail: nrkempster@aol.com.

KEMPTHORNE, DIRK ARTHUR, governor; b. San Diego, Oct. 29, 1951; s. James Henry and Maxine Jesse (Gustason) K.; m. Patricia Jean Merrill, Sept. 18, 1977; children: Heather Patricia, Jeffrey Dirk. BS in Polit. Sci., U. Idaho, 1975. Exec. asst. to dir. Idaho Dept. Lands, Boise, 1975-78; exec. v.p. Idaho Home Builders Assn., Boise, 1978-81; campaign mgr. Batt for Gov., Boise, 1981-82; lic. securities rep. Swanson Investments, Boise, 1983; Idaho pub. affairs mgr. FMC Corp., Boise, 1983-86; mayor Boise, 1984—91; mem. U.S. Senate from ID, 1993-98; gov. State of ID, 1999—. 1st v.p. Assn. of Idaho Cities, 1990-93; chmn. U.S. Conf. of Mayors Standing Com. on Energy and Environment, 1991-93, mem. adv. bd., 1991-93; sec. Nat. Conf. of Rep. Mayors and Mcpl. Elected Officials, 1991-93; mem. Senate Armed Svcs. Com., 1993-98, Senate Small Bus. Com., 1993-98, Senate Environ. and Pub. Works Com., 1993-98, Nat. Rep. Senatorial Com., 1993-98; chmn. Senate Drinking Water, Fisheries and Wildlife Subcommittee, 1995-98, mem. advisory commn. on Intergovernmental Rels., 1995-96; chmn. Armed Svcs Personnel Subcommittee, 1996-98. Pres. Associated Students U. Idaho, Moscow, 1975; chmn. bd. dirs. Wesleyan Presch., Boise, 1982-85; mem. magistrate commn. 4th Jud. Dist., Boise, 1986-93; mem. task force Nat. League of Cities Election, 1988; bd. dirs. Parents and Youth Against Drug Abuse, 1987—; mem. bd. vis. USAF Acad., 1994—; chmn. Idaho Working Ptnrs. Ltd., 1993—; hon. chmn. Idaho Congressional Award, 1994—. Named Idaho Citizen of Yr. The Idaho Statesman, 1988, Legislator of the Year Nat. Assn. Counties, 1995, State Legislator of the Year Nat. Assn. of Towns and Townships, 1995; recipient U.S. Conference of Mayor's Nat. Legis. Leadership award, 1994, Disting. Svc. award Nat. Conf. State Legislatures, 1995, Disting. Congressional award Nat. League of Cities, 1995, Guardian of Freedom award Council of State Governments, 1995. Republican. Methodist. Office: Office of Governor PO Box 83720 Boise ID 83720-0034 also: Office of the Governor 700 West Jefferson, 2nd Floor Boise ID 83702

KEMPURAJ, DURAISAMY, research scientist; s. Ramagounder Duraisamy and Rajammal Perumal; m. Bhuvaneshwari Madhappan; 1 child, Deepak. PhD Human Physiology - Brain Tumour Immunology, U. Madras, Chennai, India, 1995. Asst. prof of physiology VMS Med. and Dental coll., Salem, Tamil Nadu, India, 1986—88; sr. rsch. fellow U. Madras, Chennai, Tamil Nadu, India, 1989—95. Post doctoral fellow Nat. Children's Med. Rsch. Ctr., Tokyo, 1996—99, prin. investigator, 1999—99; post doctoral fellow Tufts U. Sch. of Medicine, Boston, 1999—2002, rsch. assoc., 2002—. Mem. editl. bd., sci. manuscript reviewer: Internat. Jour. Immunopathol,. Pharmacology (Indira Vasudevan Award for the best rsch., 1994); contbr. more than 50 articles to profl. jours. Fellow, Ind. Coun. Med. Rsch., Ind. Coun. Agrl. Rsch. Fellow: Internat. Union Against Cancer. Achievements include development of new anti-allergic and anti-inflammatory drug; research in Evaluating new anti-allergic drugs; Mast cells/basophil; Interstitial cystitis, endometriosis. Office: Tufts Univ Sch Medicine Pharmacology 136 Harrison Ave M&V Bldg Rm 320 Boston MA 02111 Office Phone: 617-636-0426. Home Fax: 617-636-6738; Office Fax: 617-636-6738. Personal E-mail: kempuraj@tufts.edu. Business E-Mail: kempuraj@yahoo.com.

KENAGY, CHERI LYNN, nurse; b. Houston, Nov. 12, 1958; d. Kenneth Leigh and Mary Louise Kenagy; m. William J. Balan, July 30, 1982 (dec. Jan. 15, 1991). Student, San Jacinto Coll., 1980. Lic. vocat. nurse, cert. physician asst., pediat. advanced life support. Hosp. staff relief Pulse Staffing, Houston, 1998—. CPR instr. AHA, Houston, 1998—. Conservative. Presbyterian. Avocations: travel, scuba diving. Home: Box 5885 Pasadena TX 77508-5885

KENAGY, ROBERT COFFMAN, planning consulting company executive; b. Hartford, Conn., July 10, 1931; s. Herbert Glenn and Mary Emily (Hardesty) K.; m. Karen Miriam Emanuelson, June 8, 1957; children: Neil S., Lynn S., Gretchen P. BA, Princeton U., 1953; postgrad., U. Pa., 1953—54. Various mktg. mgmt. positions IBM, N.Y.C., White Plains, Armonk, NY, 1957—69; v.p. mktg. Data Dimensions, Inc., Greenwich, Conn., 1969—73; fin. prin. Sidney A. Staunton, Inc., New Canaan, Conn., 1973—78; pres. RCK Mgmt. Co., Ltd., New Canaan, Litchfield, Conn., 1978—. Mem. Larchmont-Mamroneck (N.Y.) Bd. Edn., 1968-72; bd. dirs. YMCA, New Canaan, 1975-81, pres., 1980-81, trustee The Aloha Found., Fairlee, Vt., 1976-91, pres., 1983-84, trustee emeritus, 1991—; trustee First Congl. Ch., Litchfield, 2002—, vice chair, 2002-05, chair, 2005—; bd. dirs. United Way, New Canaan, 1979-82, campaign chmn., 1979-80. 1st lt. U.S. Army, 1954—56. Mem. Ctr. for Positive Thinking, Princeton Club N.Y. Avocations: singing, travel. Home and Office: RCK Mgmt Co Ltd 24 Fox Crossing Ln Litchfield CT 06759-2305 Office Phone: 860-567-0260. E-mail: kenagy@optonline.net.

KENAN, THOMAS STEPHEN, III, philanthropist; b. Durham, NC, Apr. 19, 1937; s. Frank Hawkins Kenan and Harriet Gregg (DuBose) Gray. BA in Econ., U. N.C., 1959. Trustee Sarah G. Kenan Found., Durham, 1968-74, N.C. Mus. Art, Raleigh, 1972-91, Randleigh Found. Trust, 1981-95, N.C. Sch. the Arts, Winston-Salem, 1983-91, W.R. Kenan Charitable Trust, Chapel Hill, N.C., 1986-97, U. N.C. Arts and Sci. Found., Chapel Hill, 1989-91, The Nat. Tropical Bot. Gardens, Hawaii, The Coun. of Nat. Trust for Hist. Preservation, Henry Morrison Flagler Mus.; dir. William R. Kenan Jr. Fund, 1995—. Exec. com. Flagler System, Inc., Palm Beach, Fla., 1968-97; chmn. Kenan Transport Co., Chapel Hill, 1968-97; pres. Westfield Co., Durham, 1971-91. Founder Liberty Hall Restoration Commn., 1966, Duplin Outdoor Drama Soc., 1976; trustee The Duke Endowment; trustee Mary Duke Biddle Found., Durham, 1984-85 Mem. Hope Valley Country Club, Treyburn Golf and Country Club, Breakers Beach and Golf Club, Univ. Club, Landfall Golf and Tennis Club. Episcopalian. Avocations: music, horseback riding, golf, reading, gardening. Address: PO Box 4150 Chapel Hill NC 27515-4150

KENDALL, CHARLES TERRY, librarian; b. Chambersburg, Pa., Aug. 13, 1949; s. Guy William and Virginia Mae (Naugle) K.; m. Alice Marie Bienz, Aug. 21, 1971; children: Terri, Anita, Kendra. BA, Huntington (Ind.) Coll., 1971; MLS, George Peabody Coll., 1972; postgrad., Asbury Theol. Sem., 1982-83; MA in Religion, Anderson (Ind.) U., 1990. Dir. Byrd Meml. Libr. Anderson Sch. Theology, Anderson U., 1983-89; theol. studies libr. Anderson U. Libr., 1989-98, archivist, 1992-98; dir. Mabee Libr. Sterling (Kans.) Coll., 1998—2002; head circulation and tech. svc. Alexandrian Public Library, Mt. Vernon, Ind., 2003—05, head collection svcs., 2005—. Mem. ALA, Public Library Assn.

KENDALL, DAVID E., lawyer; b. Camp Atterbury, Ind., May 2, 1944; BA, Wabash Coll., 1966; MA, Oxford U., England, 1968; JD, Yale U., 1971. Bar: N.Y. 1974, U.S. Ct. Appeals (5th cir.) 1976, D.C. 1978, U.S. Supreme Ct. 1978, Md. 1993. Law clerk to Justice Byron R. White U.S. Supreme Ct., 1971-72; assoc. counsel NAACP Legal Def. & Ednl. Fund, 1973—78; assoc. Williams & Connolly LLP, Washington, 1978—81, ptnr., 1981—. Adj. prof. Columbia U. Law Sch., 1977-78, Georgetown U. Law Ctr., 1985-95. Note and comment editor Yale Law Jour., 1970-71; author (with Leonard Ross) The Lottery and the Draft, 1970; auth Constitutional Vandalism, 30 U. New Mexico Law Review 155, 2000, Opinion Is Protected Expression Under the Constitution, 2 Communications Lawyer 5, 1984, How to Keep Your Client Alive, 3 Criminal Defense 9, 1976, The Affirmative Duty to Integrate in Higher Education, 79 Yale Law Journal 666, 1970. 2nd lt. U.S. Army, 1972—73. Rhodes scholar; named one of 75 Best Lawyers in Washington, Washingtonian survey mag. Mem. N.Y. State Bar Assn., Md. State Bar Assn., Washington, DC Bar Assn., bd. dirs., NAACP Legal Def.& Ednl. Fund Inc. Office: Williams & Connolly 725 12th St NW Washington DC 20005-5901 E-mail: dkendall@wc.com.

KENDALL, FRANK RUSSELL, SR., lawyer; b. Houston, June 14, 1920; s. William E. and Theodora Dudley (Kuker) K.; m. Anne Benson, Sept. 9, 1942; children: Theodora, Bernard, Frank, John, Thomas. Student, Gregorian U., Rome, 1937-40, U. Houston, 1940-42; LLB, South Tex. Coll. Law, 1949. Bar: Tex. 1949, U.S. Dist. Ct. (so. dist.) Tex. 1949, U.S. Ct. Appeals (5th cir.) 1949, U.S. Supreme Ct. 1969, U.S. Ct. Claims 1974. Asst. dist. atty. Harris County State of Tex., Houston, 1948-52; ptnr. Vinson & Elkins, Houston, 1953—. Vice gov. Gen. Equestrian Order of the Holy Sepulchre of Jerusalem, Protection of Holy See. Lt. (s.g.) USNR, 1942-45, PTO. Mem. ABA, Am. Coll. Trial Lawyers, Tex. Bar Assn., Tex. Bar Found., Houston Bar Assn. Roman Catholic.

KENDALL, HARRY WESLEY, playwright, writer; b. Tarentum, Pa., Aug. 10, 1931; s. Wesley Chappell Kendall and Emma Jane Lucas; children: Victor, Michael, Susan(dec.), Harry, Rochelle, Joel, Mitchell. BA, Rutgers U., 1977; MFA, Norwich U., 1988. Sr. writer/editor Boeing Helicopter Co., Ridley Township, Pa., 1980—95; writer/reporter Phila. Bulletin, 1972—80, Trenton Times, Trenton, NJ, 1969—72; elec. tech. Radio Corp. of Am., Camden, NJ, 1963—69; field svc. tech. Jacy Inc. Cons. Engr., Camden, NJ, 1960—63. Author: (historical fiction) Truth Crushed to Earth, 1999, (plays) Resistance in Christiana, 2001. Pres. Willingboro Pub. Libr., Willingboro, NJ, 1989—; co-chair Communications Com., 1987—2004; v.p., bd. dirs. Theater of Seventh Sister, 2002—04; pres. Kinsmen of Willingboro, 1968—70; v.p. Greater Willingboro Assn., 2000—; with Mt. Carmel Baptist Ch., Wash.; judge Optimist Internat., 1987—93, Recipient Cmty. Svc. award, Alpha Kappa Alpha Sorority, 2004, Commitment Youth award, Zion Bapt. Ch., 2004, Cert. of Appreciation, Mt. Carmel Bapt. Ch., Boeing Vertol Toastmasters, Dist. 38. Mem.: South Jersey Regional Libr. Coop. Democrat. Avocations: yoga, jazz. Office Fax: 609-871-8683. E-mail: kentehuti@aol.com.

KENDALL, JASON DANIEL, professional baseball player; b. San Diego, June 26, 1974; s. Fred Kendall. Selected first-round free-agt. draft Pitts. Pirates, 1992; catcher Gulf Coast League Pirates, 1992, Augusta (South Atlantic League), 1993, Salem (Carolina), 1994, Carolina (So. League), 1994-96, Pitts. Pirates, 1996—2004, Oakland A's, 2004—. Named to Nat. League All-Star team, 1996, 1998, 2000. Office: c/o Oakland A's 7000 Coliseum way Oakland CA 94621

KENDALL, JOHN WALKER, JR., internist, researcher, dean; b. Bellingham, Wash., Mar. 19, 1929; s. John Walker and Mathilda (Hansen) K.; m. Elizabeth Helen Meece, Mar. 19, 1954; children: John, Katherine, Victoria. BA, Yale Coll., 1952; MD, U. Wash., 1956. Intern, resident in internal medicine Vanderbilt U. Hosp., Nashville, 1956-59, fellow in endocrinology, 1959-60, U. Oreg. Med. Sch., Portland, 1960-62; asst. prof. medicine Oreg. Health Scis. U., Portland, 1962-66, assoc. prof. medicine, 1966-71, prof. medicine, 1971—, head divsn. metabolism, 1971-80; dean Oreg. Health Scis. U. Sch. Medicine, Portland, 1983—92; assoc. chief staff-rsch. VA Med. Ctr., Portland, 1971-83, dep. chief of staff, 1993, VA disting. physician, 1993-96, acad. affiliates officer, 1997—, grad. med. edn. adv. com., 2001—04. Cons. Med. Rsch. Found. Oreg., Portland, 1975-83; sec. Oreg. Found. Med. Excellence, Portland, 1984-89, pres., 1989-91; grad. med. edn. adv. com. Dept. Vets. Affairs, 2001—; commn. mem. VA Cares, 2003-04. Lt. comdr. M.C., USN, 1962-64 Recipient Outstanding Physician award Found. Med. Excellence, 1995. Mem. AMA (governing coun. med. sch. sect. 1989-93, chair 1991-92, alt. del. 1992-93, Oreg. del. 1994-98, rep. Coun. Grad. Med. Edn. 1993-94), Assn. Am. Physicians, Am. Soc. Clin. Investigation, Am. Fedn. Clin. Rsch., We. Soc. Clin. Rsch. (councillor 1972-75), Endocrine Soc., Multnomah County Med. Soc. (treas. 1989, pres. 1991), Med. Rsch. Found. (Mentor award 1992), Royal Soc. Medicine (endocrinology sect. coun. 1999—2004). Presbyterian. Home: 3131 SW Evergreen Ln Portland OR 97201-1816 Office: Oreg Health Scis U Sch Medicine L-607 3181 SW Sam Jackson Park Rd Portland OR 97239

KENDALL, JULIUS, consulting engineer; b. Boston, May 14, 1919; m. Edythe Tobias; children: Jane, Richard Tobias. BS in Aero Engring., Northeastern U., Boston, 1941; MS, MIT, 1941. Registered Profl. Engr., N.Y., N.J., Mass., Conn., Maine; cert. fluid power engr. V.p. Greer Hydraulics, N.Y.C., 1945-56, Arkwin Industries, Inc., Westbury, N.Y., 1956-58; pres. Kenett Corp., Westboro, Mass., 1958-91; cons. engr. Kendall Cons. Group, Weston, Mass., 1991—; v.p. Kenett Hydraulic Distbn. divsn. Entwistle Co., Hudson, Mass., 1993—. Cons. in field. Patentee in field. Contbr. many articles to profl. jours. With USN, 1941-46. Mem. Am. Soc. Naval Engrs., ASME, Soc. Automotive Engrs., Fluid Power Soc., Aleppo Yacht Club, Shriners, Masons. Avocations: fishing, boating, golf. Home and Office: 200 W Farm Pond Rd Apt 168 Framingham MA 01702-6253 Business E-Mail: jkendall@entwistleco.com.

KENDALL, KATHERINE ANNE, social worker; b. Muir-of-Ord, Scotland, Sept. 8, 1910; came to U.S., 1920, naturalized, 1940; d. Roderick and Annie Scott (Walker) Tuach; m. Willmoore Kendall, June 22, 1935 (div. Apr. 1950). BA, U. Ill., 1933; MA, La. State U., 1939; PhD, U. Chgo., 1950; D Public Service (hon.), Syracuse U., 1981; DSW (hon.), U. Pa., 1985, La. State U., 1987, U. Ill., 1989. Asst. prof. Richmond Sch. Social Work, 1941-42; asst. dir. home service A.R.C., 1942-44; lectr. U. Chgo. Sch. Social Service Adminstrn., 1944-45; asst. dir., tng. supr. Inter-Am. and Internat. Tng. units U.S. Children's Bur., 1945- 47; social affairs officer UN Secretariat, 1947-50; exec. sec. Am. Assn. Schs. Social Work, 1950-52; edn1. sec. Council on Social Work Edn., 1952-58, assoc. dir., 1958-63, exec. dir., 1963-66, dir. internat. edn., 1966-71; Carnegie vis. prof. U. Hawaii, 1960-61; mem. exec. bd. Internat. Assn. Schs. Social Work, 1954-66, sec.-gen., 1966-78, hon. pres., 1978—. Ofcl. non-govtl. rep. UN, 1954-94; Moses prof. Hunter Coll. Social Work, 1983-84; dir. Internat. Conf. on Social Work Edn., Population and Family Planning, East-West Ctr., Hawaii, 1970; exec. sec. Coun. of Advisors to Hunter Coll., Hunter Coll. Sch. Social Work and Lois and Samuel Silberman Fund, 1985-87. Author: Reflections on Social Work Education, 1950-1978, Social Work Education: Its Origins in Europe, 2000, The Council on Social Work Education: Its Antecedents and the First Twenty Years, 2002; UN reports International Exchange of Social Welfare Personnel, 1949, Training for Social Work: First International Survey, 1950; editor: Social Work Values in an Age of Discontent, 1970, Population Dynamics and Family Planning: A New Responsibility for Social Work Education, 1971, World Guide to Social Work Edn., 1984, Eileen Blackey; Pathfinder for the Profession, 1986; co-editor: Gerontological Social Work: International Perspectives, 1988; compiler: Social Casework— Cumulative Index 1920-1979, 1981. Active UN Internat. meeting experts on social work tng., Munich, 1956; faculty UN Seminar, Keeru, Finland, 1952; assignment social work edn., Guatemala, 1949, Brazil, 1952, Paraguay, 1954; dir. 1st seminar Schs. Social Work in Central Am., 1963. Mem. NASW, Mortar Bd., Internat. Assn. Schs. Social Work, Council on Social Work Edn., Internat. Council on Social Welfare, Phi Beta Kappa, Chi Omega. Home: Collington # 2003 10450 Lottsford Rd Mitchellville MD 20721-2734 E-mail: k.kend@erols.com.

KENDALL, KAY LYNN, interior designer, consultant; b. Cadillac, Mich., Aug. 20, 1950; d. Robert Llewellyn and Betty Louise (Powers) K.; 1 child, Anna Renee Easter. BFA, U. Mich., 1973. Draftsman, interior designer store planning dept. Jacobson Stores, Inc., Jackson, Mich., 1974-79, sr. interior designer store planning dept., 1981—98; prin., pres. Kay Kendall Designs LLC, Jackson, 1979—; sr. interior designer Maddalena's Inc., Jackson, 1998—2002; realtor Edward Surovell Realtors, Ann Arbor, Mich., 2000—. Cons. in field. Big sister Big Bros./Big Sisters Jackon County. Mem. Am. Soc. Interior Designers (profl. mem., assoc. Ctrl. Mich. chpt.), Nat. Assn. Realtors, Ann Arbor Area Assn. Realtors, Mich. Assn. Realtors. Avocations: tennis, golf, gardening, skiing. Home: 701 Church St Grass Lake MI 49240-9206 Office: Edward Surovell Realtors 1898 W Stadium Blvd Ann Arbor MI 48103 Office Phone: 517-522-5871. E-mail: kkendall@acd.net.

KENDALL, LEIGH WAKEFIELD, surgeon; b. Brattleboro, Vt., Mar. 8, 1937; s. Irwin Samuel and Laura Eliza (Walbridge) Kendall; m. Grace Eleanor Fullarton, July 1, 1961; children: William Leigh, Bradley Edward. AB, U. Pa., Phila., 1959; D of Medicine, U. Vt., 1963; MS, U. Ill., Chgo., 1965. Diplomate Nat. Bd. Med. Examiners, Am. Bd. Surgery, cert. ACLS. Intern then resident surgery U. Ill. Hosp., Chgo., 1963-69; rsch. fellow Am. Cancer Soc., Chgo., 1964-65, clin. fellow, 1968-69; staff surgeon USN Hosp., Great Lakes, Ill., 1969; surgeon USN Hosp. Ships, Vietnam, 1969-70; pvt. practice Lancaster, Pa., 1971-93; med. dir. Alliance Health Plan, Lancaster, 1995—2005; assoc. med. dir. St. Joseph Regional Health Network, Lancaster and Reading, 1999—; med. dir. St. Joseph Hosp., Lancaster, 2000—, Lancaster Regional Med. Ctr., 2000—. Instr. surgery U. Ill. Hosp., Chgo., 1968—69; active staff St. Joseph Hosp., Lancaster, 1971—, sect. chief gen. surgery, 1981—88, chmn. dept. surgery, 1989—93; mem. courtesy staff Lancaster Gen. Hosp., 1971—; cons. surgery Franklin & Marshall Coll., Lancaster, Pa., Masonic Homes, Elizabethtown, Pa.; staff physician Millersville U., 1993—2004; staff physician cardiac rehab. Lancaster Gen. Hosp. Health Campus, 1995—98. Lt. comdr. M.C. USNR, 1959—71, Vietnam. Decorated 1st Class Mil. Honor medal Republic of Vietnam. Fellow: ACS; mem.: AMA, Am. Coll. Physicians Execs., Royal Soc. Medicine (Eng.), Pa. Med. Soc., Internat. Soc. Surgeons, Warren H. Cole Soc. (pres. 1994—95), Intrepids Club, Sigma Nu. Republican. Episcopalian. Avocations: photography, travel. Home: 1314 Quarry Ln Lancaster PA 17603-2424 Office: Med Affairs Office Lancaster Regional Med Ctr Lancaster PA 17604-3434 Office Phone: 717-291-8167. Fax: 717-291-8205.

KENDALL, PETER LANDIS, television news executive; b. Toledo, Oct. 8, 1936; s. Roy Cline and Edythe Mae (Kindy) K.; m. Beate Margit Fritz, June 11, 1966; children: Adrian Peter, Stefanie Karin. BA, U. Cin., 1959; BS cum laude, U. Ill., Urbana, 1960. News producer-writer Voice of Am., Washington, 1961-64; corr. Deutsche Welle, Bonn, Fed. Republic Germany, 1964-66; morning news producer CBS News, Washington, 1971-74, producer London, 1974-77, bur. chief, 1977-82, sr. producer-asst. bur. mgr. Washington, 1982-86, bur. chief Bonn, 1986-88; pvt. practice internat. TV cons. Washington, 1988-90; exec. producer Washington bur. Cable News Network, 1990—2002, cons., 2002—; exec. producer CNN Washington Coverage of Gulf War, 1991. Producer: Econ. Summits, London, 1977, 84, Bonn, 1978, Versailles, 1982; Iranian Hostages Return, Frankfurt, West Germany, 1980, Moscow Olympics, 1980, London, The Royal Wedding, 1981; numerous presdl. visits to Europe. Recipient Emmy award for Senate and Watergate coverage Nat. Acad. TV Arts and Scis., 1974 Mem. Am. Corrs. Assn. (exec. bd. London 1977-80), Health Vols. Overseas (bd. dirs. 1996-2002), Sigma Delta Chi. Espiscopalian. Club: Tamesis Sailing (London). Home: 4955 Quebec St NW Washington DC 20016-3230 Personal E-mail: pandbkendall@aol.com.

KENDALL, ROBERT IAN, writer, educator; b. Ottawa, Ont., Can., Nov. 21, 1958; arrived in U.S., 1980; s. Lorne Melvin and Mary Elizabeth Kendall; m. Melinda Miles, Aug. 1, 1981; children: Marisa, Chelsea. BMus, U. B.C., Vancouver, Can., 1980; MA, NYU, 1982. Freelance writer, Menlo Park, Calif., 1985—2001, Rahway, NJ, Cranford, NJ; instr. New Sch. On-line U., N.Y.C., 1995—2001; directory supr. Electronic Lit. Orgn., L.A., 1999—2001. Mem. lit. adv. bd. Electronic Lit. Orgn., L.A., 1999—2001; dir. Word Circuits website, Menlo Park, 1997—2001; short-list com. judge $10,000 Electronic Lit. Award, L.A., 2001. Author: A Wandering City, 1992 (CSU Poster Ctr. prize, 1990); contbr. articles to mags. and anthologies; author: (interactive lit.) A Life Set for Two, 1996, The Seasons, 1999—2000. Recipient New Voices award, Gershman Y Poetry Ctr., Phila., 1988; fellow, NJ State Coun. on Arts, 1995; grantee, Painted Bride Art Ctr., Phila., 1992. Mem.: Poetry Soc. Am. Avocation: music. Home and Office: 1800 White Oak Dr Menlo Park CA 94025

KENDALL, ROBERT LOUIS, JR., lawyer; b. Rochester, N.H., Oct. 13, 1930; s. Robert Louis and Marguerite (Thomas) K.; m. Patricia Ann Palmer, Aug. 13, 1955; children: Linda J., Cynthia J., Janet L. AB cum laude, Harvard U., 1952; JD cum laude, U. Pa., 1955; Diploma in Law, Oxford (Eng.) U., 1956. Bar: Pa. 1957, Ga. 1993. Assoc. Schnader, Harrison, Segal & Lewis, Phila., 1956-65, ptnr., 1966-95. Lectr. Temple U. Law Sch., Phila., 1976-77; spl. instr. U. Pa. Law Sch., 1959-62. Contbr. to Antitrust Law Developments, 2d edit. 1984 Bd. dirs. Mann Music Ctr., Inc., Phila., 1971-98, Settlement Music Sch., Phila., Pa., 1984—, Jr. C. of C., Phila., 1962-65; mem. Gladwyne Civic Assn., 1960—, Phila. Orch. Assn., 1983—. Fellow Soc. Values in Higher Edn.; mem. ABA, Pa. Bar Assn., Ga. Bar Assn., Phila. Bar Assn., Atlanta Bar Assn., U. Pa. Law Alumni Assn. (bd. mgrs.), Rotary, Order of Coif (pres. 1979-80), Lawyers Club Atlanta, Harvard Club. Democrat. Episcopalian. Home: 1208 Hartdale Ln Gladwyne PA 19035-1434 Office: Schnader Harrison Segal 1600 Market St Ste 3600 Philadelphia PA 19103-7287

KENDALL, ROBERT STANTON, newspaper editor, journalist, automotive executive; b. Greensburg, Ind., July 30, 1921; s. Wilber Lawrence and Marguerite (Groenier) K.; m. Dorothy Jane Rumbold, Oct. 2, 1943; children: Mark Curtis, Lee Rachel, Amy Robin. BA, Coll. of Wooster, 1946. Asst. pub. Martinsville (Ind.) Daily Reporter, 1946-48, editor, 1948-98; chmn. Reporter-Times Inc., Martinsville, 1983-98, Adkins Inc., Martinsville; editl. columnist Schurz Comms., 1998—. 2d lt. USAAF, 1943-45, ETO. Decorated Air medal; recipient Meritorious Svc. award Am. Legion, Martinsville, 1973, citation Coun. for Def. of Freedom, 1978, Honor medal DAR, 1987. Mem. Kiwanis, Phi Beta Kappa, Phi Alpha Theta. Republican. Lutheran. Home: 53181 Kinglet Ln South Bend IN 46637-5112 Office: Martinsville Daily Reporter 60 S Jefferson St Martinsville IN 46151-1968

KENDALL HULL, MARGARIDA, art educator, painter; b. Lisbon, Portugal; Attended studied history & philosophy, U. Lisbon; BFA, Corcoran Sch. Art, 1973; MFA, Catholic U., 1982. Visiting prof. studio art Towson State U., 1986; asst. prof. studio art George Mason U., 1987, assoc. prof., 1994, 2000—. Represented in permanent collections, Art Inst. Chgo., Gulbenkian Mus. Contemporary Art, Lisbon, Portugal, one-woman shows include, Osuna Gallery, Washington D.C., 1983, Gulbenkian Found., 1984, exhibitions include, Baltimore, Chgo., N.Y., Phila., Gallery K, Dupont Cir. Office: Art Dept George Mason U 4400 University Dr Fairfax VA 22030-4444*

KENDE, ANDREW STEVEN, chemist, educator; b. Budapest, Hungary, July 17, 1932; arrived in U.S., 1941, naturalized, 1951; s. George and Elizabeth Kende; m. Frances Boothe, Sept. 14, 1954; 1 child, Mark. AB, U. Chgo., 1951; MS, Harvard, 1954, PhD, 1957. Sr. rsch. scientist Lederle Labs., Am. Cyanamid Co., Pearl River, NY, 1957-63, rsch. assoc., 1963-66, rsch. fellow, 1966-68, cons., 1968-94; prof. chemistry U. Rochester, NY, 1968—2002, prof. emeritus, 2002—. Charles Frederick Houghton prof. chemistry, 1981-2000, prof. oncology, 1982-2000, chmn., 1979-83, assoc. chmn., 1989-90. Vis. prof. SUNY, Buffalo, 1967, Mich. State U., East Lansing, 1968, U. Genéve, 1974, U. Amsterdam, 1989; cons. study sect. NIH, 1972—76, chmn., 1974—76; vis. scholar Stanford U., 1975; cons. Dow Chem. Co., 1975—2001, Bausch and Lomb Co., 1985—90, Eastman Kodak Co., 1987—94, Procter and Gamble Pharms., 1988—2004, Dow Agrosciences, 1994—2002; Bicentenary lectr. Royal Australian Chem. Inst., 1988; pres. Organic Syntheses Inc., 1992—2002. Mem. bd. editors Organic Reactions, 1968—83; editor-in-chief: Organic Reactions, 1983—88; mem. bd. editors Chem. Revs., 1973—76, Organic Syntheses, 1978—87, Synthetic Comm., 1981—96; assoc. editor: Jour. Organic Chemistry, 1997—2002. Am. Cancer Soc. fellow, Glasgow (Scotland) U., 1956—57, Guggenheim fellow, 1978—79. Fellow: Japan Soc. Promotion Sci.; mem.: Am. Chem. Soc. (mem. exec. bd. Rochester sect. 1970—72, chmn. organic chem. divsn. 1978—79, mem. editl. bd. Jour. Am. Chem. Soc. 1995—2000, Arthur C. Cope Sr. scholar 2003). Home: 19 Larchwood Dr Pittsford NY 14534-2432 Office: U Rochester River Campus Dept Chemistry Rochester NY 14627-0216 Office Phone: 585-275-4236. E-mail: kende@chem.rochester.edu.

KENDE, CHRISTOPHER BURGESS, lawyer, educator; b. NYC, Apr. 28, 1948; s. Herbert Alexander and Helga Henrietta (Wieselthier) K.; m. Barbara Gonzales, May 22, 1976. BA, MA, Brown U., 1970; JD, NYU, 1973. Bar: NY 1974, Mass. 1975, DC 1988, Calif. 1996, US Dist. Ct. (So. and Ea. dists.) NY 1974, US Ct. Appeals (2nd cir.) 1976, US Ct. Appeals (9th cir.) 1996, US Supreme Ct. 1978. Staff atty. Legal Aid Soc., NYC, 1973-76; assoc. Dewey, Ballantine et al., NYC, 1976-78, Hill Betts & Nash, NYC, 1978-82, ptnr., 1982-89, Holtzmann, Wise & Shepard, NYC, 1989-96, Cozen O'Connor, NYC, 1996—. Adj. prof. maritime and admiralty law Bklyn. Law Sch., 2003—. Contbr. articles to profl. jours. Recipient Silver medal, Caisse des Depots, 1984. Mem. ABA, NY County Lawyers Assn. (past chmn. com. on admiralty and maritime law 1998-99), Maritime Law Assn. (marine ecology com., com. on the CMI), French Maritime Law Assn., Union Internat. des Avocats (pres. ins. law commn.), India House, Edgartown Yacht Club, Univ. Club NY, The Travellers (Paris), Yacht Club de France, Order of Coif, Phi Beta Kappa. Democrat. Presbyterian. Avocations: sailing, motorcycling, tennis, exercise, gardening. Home: 545 W End Ave Apt 2B New York NY 10024-2723 Office: Cozen & O'Connor 45 Broadway New York NY 10006-3007 Office Phone: 212-908-1242. Business E-Mail: ckende@cozen.com.

KENDE, STEPHEN JAMES, insurance sales executive; b. N.Y.C., May 28, 1947; s. Stephen and Helene (Donahue) K.; m. Sally McMahon, June 12, 1971; children: Stephen, Alexander. BA, Norwich U., Northfield, Vt., 1970. CLU, 1981. Ins. salesman, Moscow, Vt., 1977—. Capt. U.S. Army, 1970-77. Mem. Million Dollar Round Table, Assn. for Advanced Life Underwriters, Am. Soc. CLUs, Internat. Forum, Internat. Assn. Fin. Planning, Burlington Assn. Life Underwriters, Norwich U. Alumni Assn. (bd. dirs. 1977-80). Home and Office: PO Box 175 Moscow VT 05662-0175

KENDELL, ZINA, nurse, consultant; d. Silas Lewis and Ellestine Johnson Grant; m. Marcellus Thomas Kendall, Nov. 8, 1997; children: Miles Aizac, Marcus Alexander. BS, Towson State U., 1986; MS in Adminstrn., Ctrl. Mich. U., 1990; BSN, Howard U., 1994. Project facilitator U. Md. Shock Trauma Ctr., Balt., 1988—92; clin. nurse Union Meml. Hosp., Balt., 1994—2001; asst. dir. nursing HCR Manor Care, Towson, Md., 1998—2000, Erickson Retirement Cmtys.-Oak Crest Village, Parkville, Md., 2000—. Author (project facilitator): (clin. rsch.) Gut Failure-Predictor of or Contributor to Mortality in Mechanically Ventilated Blunt Trauma Patients?. Mem.: Amer. Assoc. Legal Nurse Cons. Office Phone: 410-882-3248 3417. E-mail: zizi68@hotmail.com.

KENDER, WALTER JOHN, horticulturist, educator; b. Camden, N.J., Dec. 20, 1935; s. Walter and Martha K.; m. Carole Holm, May 26, 1957; children: David, Lily BS, Del. Valley Coll., 1957, DSc (hon.), 1993; MS, Rutgers U., 1959, PhD, 1962. From asst. prof. to assoc. prof. horticulture U. Maine, Orono, 1962-69; mem. faculty Cornell U., N.Y. State Agrl. Expt. Sta., Geneva, 1969-82, prof. pomology, 1975-82, head dept. pomology and viticulture, 1972-82; chmn. dept. pomology Cornell U., Ithaca, 1975-82; dir. citrus rsch. and edn. ctr. U. Fla., Lake Alfred, 1982-96, prof., 1982-2001, prof. emeritus, 2001—. Co-chmn. task force fruit rsch. N.E. USDA State Exptl. Stas., 1973-75; sec. Internat. Working Group Juvenility Woody Plants, 1974-82; cons. Winrock Internat. (USAID) Pakistan, 1989, Indonesia, 1992, P.R. Dept. Agr., 1996; disting. scientist Agrl. U., Wageningen, Netherlands, 1974; mem. adv. bd. Archbold Biol. Sta., 1991-2001. Contbg. author: Blueberry Culture, 1966; contbr. articles to profl. jours. Bd. dirs. Green Horizon Land Trust, 2004. Fellow AAAS, Am. Soc. Hort. Sci. (dir. 1975-85, trustee endowment fund 1982-87); mem. N.Y. State Hort. Soc., Internat. Soc. Hort. Sci., Internat. Citriculture Soc. (corr.), Am. Pomological Soc. (mem. adv. com.), Fla. Inst. Food Tech., Coun. Agrl. Sci. and Tech., Fla. State Hort. Soc. (hon. mem. 2000, pres. 1996, chmn. of bd. 1997), N.Y. State Fruit Testing Assn. (sec.-treas. 1972-82), Farm Bur. Adv. Com., Haines City Citrus Growers Assn. (bd. dirs. 1991-96), Fla. Citrus Showcase (bd. dirs. 1996-2000), Sigma Xi (past chpt. pres.). Office: Citrus Rsch & Edn Ctr 700 Experiment Station Rd Lake Alfred FL 33850-2243 Office Phone: 863-956-1151. E-mail: kender@crec.ifas.ufl.edu.

KENDERIAN, SHANT, engineer, consultant; s. Hagop Kenderian and Janet Janoian; m. Ani Manjikian, Sept. 6, 1997; children: Nairy, Talar. BS in Prodn. Engring. & Metallurgy, U. Tech., 1985; MS in Mfg. Engring. & Tech., Calif. State U., 1996; PhD in Materials Sci. & Engring., MS in Materials Sci. and Engring., The Johns Hopkins U., 2002. Lic. profl. engr., Md., 2000. Mfg. engr. A&H Jewelry Mfg. Co, Glendale, Calif., 1995—96, Weckerle, Santa Monica, 1996—97, Space Systems/Loral, Palo Alto, 1997—98; rsch. scientist The Johns Hopkins U., Balt., 2002—03; sr. engr. Jet Propulsion Lab., Pasadena, Calif., 2003—04; sr. staff mem. The Aerospace Corp., El Segundo, Calif., 2005—. Cons. engr. MM & NDE, West Hills, Calif., 2003—. Exhibitions, Oil Paintings; contbr. scientific papers to profl. jours. Fellow, Am. Soc. Nondestructive Testing, 2001. Mem.: NSPE, Soc. Mfg. Engrs., Acoustical Soc. Am., Am. Soc. Nondestructive Testing. Achievements include patents for Laser-Air Hybrid Ultrasonic Non-Contact And Remote Testing of Railroad Wheels; Laser-Air Hybrid Ultrasonic Non-Contact And Remote Testing of Railroad Tracks. Personal E-mail: kenderian@msn.com.

KENDIG, WILLIAM LAMAR, federal official, accountant; b. York, Pa., Apr. 11, 1938; m. Esther Delores Mostoller, Oct. 14, 1961; 1 child, Marc Daniel. BS, Elizabethtown Coll., 1960; MBA, Am. U., 1965, PhD, 1969. Spl. agt. U.S. Treasury Dept., Washington, 1960—65; staff asst. Procter & Gamble Co., Cin., 1965-66; mgr., cons. Price Waterhouse & Co., Washington, 1968-71; asst. vice chancellor U. Md., College Park, 1971-74, acting vice chancellor, 1974-75; dir., mgmt. cons. U.S. Dept. Interior, Washington, 1975-76, dep. dir. audit and investigations, 1977-78, acting insp. gen., 1978-79, dep. asst. sec., 1979-81, dir. fin. mgmt. and dep. chief fin. officer, 1981-94, chair mgmt. control coordinating com., 1987—92, acting prin. dep. asst. sec., 1988. Mem. Fed. Acctg. Stds. Adv. Bd., 1991-94; ind. cons., 1996—. Contbr. articles to profl. jours. Chmn. ops. com., chmn., mem. steering com. 69 Corridor Concerned Citizens, 2001—02; mem. Mayor's Compensation Com., Prescott, Ariz., 1999; chair sponsorship com. Leukemia and Lymphoma Soc., Yavopai County "Light the Night" Walk, 2004. Named Meritorious Exec., Pres. of U.S., 1986, Disting. Exec., 1988; recipient Donald Scantlebury award Joint Fin. Mgmt. Improvement Program, 1990. Mem. Fed. Fin. Mgrs. Coun. (chmn. 1982-85), Assn. Govt. Accts. (nat. exec. com. 1984-87, Chpt. Outstanding Achievement award 1983, 86, Frank Greathouse Disting. Leadership award 1992, Cornelius E. Tierney/Ernst & Young Lifetime Rsch. Achiever award 1996), Pub. Employees Roundtable (bd. dirs. 1987-89, Dir.'s award 1988), Sr. Execs. Assn. (bd. dirs. 1985-91, Ted Kern award 1984), Worldwide Assurance for Employees Pub. Agys. (bd. dirs. 1993-96), Nat. Assn. Ret. Fed. Employees (1st v.p. Prescott chpt. 2001-02, pres. 2003, chpt. exec. com. 2004-05). Avocations: reading, exercising. E-mail: kendig@commspeed.net.

KENDLE, CANDACE, pharmaceutical executive; m. Christopher C. Bergen; 2 children. BS in Pharmacy, U. Cin., 1970, PhD in Pharmacy, 1972. Resident Cin. Children's Hosp. Med. Ctr., 1972; epidemiology fellow U. N.C. Sch. Pub. Health; dir. pharmacy The Children's Hosp. Phila., 1979—81; clin. asst. prof. Phila. Coll. Pharmacy and Scis., 1979—81; clin. assoc. prof. pediat. U. Pa. Sch. Medicine., 1979—81; co-founder, CEO Kendle Internat., Inc., Cin., 1981—, chmn., 1991—. Adj. assoc. prof. U. Cin. Sch. Pharmacy, 1982—84; bd. dirs. U. Cin., H.J. Heinz Co., Isabella Venture Fund, UMD Inc. Contbr. articles to profl. jours. Named one of Nations Top 25 Female CEO's, Worth Mag., 2001; recipient Entrepreneur of Yr. award, Cin. Mag., 1998, Disting. Alumni award, U. Cin. Dept. Women's STudies, 1999, Arthur C. Glasser Disting. Alumni award, U. Cin., Coll. Pharmacy, 2001, William Howard Taft medal for notable achievement, U. Cin., 2002. Mem.: Com. of 200, Assn. Clin. Rsch. Orgns. (founder). Office: Kendle Internat Inc 1200 Carew Tower 441 Vine St Cincinnati OH 45202

KENDLER, BERNHARD, retired editor; b. Cin., Jan. 28, 1934; s. Harry Harlan and Mildred (Black) K.; m. Jill Ferguson, Dec. 12, 1975. BA in English, NYU, 1955; MA in Comparative Lit, U. Mich., 1956. Research asst. Calif. Tchrs. Assn., 1958-60; editor A.S. Barnes & Co., Inc., N.Y.C., 1960-62; copy editor J.B. Lippincott Co., Phila., 1962-63; mng. editor, editor, exec. editor Cornell U. Press, Ithaca, NY, 1963—2005; ret. Mem. Phi Beta Kappa. Home: 500 Harbison Blvd Apt 1009 Columbia SC 29212 Business E-Mail: bk32@cornell.edu. E-mail: calamity@sc.rr.com.

KENDLER, HOWARD H(ARVARD), psychologist, educator; b. NYC, June 9, 1919; s. Harry H. and Sylvia (Rosenberg) K.; m. Tracy Seedman, Sept. 20, 1941 (dec. July 2001); children: Joel Harlan, Kenneth Seedman. AB, Bklyn. Coll., 1940; MA, U. Iowa, 1941, PhD, 1943. Instr. U. Iowa, 1943; rsch. psychologist OSRD, 1944; asst. prof. U. Colo., 1946-48; assoc. prof. NYU, 1948-51, prof., 1951-63; chmn. dept. Univ. Coll., 1951-61; prof. U. Calif., Santa Barbara, 1963-89, prof. emeritus, 1989—, chmn. dept. psychology, 1965-66. Project dir. Office Naval Rsch., 1950-68; prin. investigator NSF, 1953-65, USAAF, 1951-53; mem. adv. panel psychobiology NSF, 1960-62; tng. com. Nat. Inst. Child Health and Human Devel., 1963-66; cons. Dept. Def., Smithsonian Instn., 1959-60, Human Resources Rsch. Office, George Washington U., 1960; vis. prof. U. Calif., Berkeley, 1960-61, Hebrew U., Jerusalem, 1974-75, Tel Aviv U., 1990; chief clin. psychologist Walter Reed Gen. Hosp., 1945-46. Author: Basic Psychology, 1963, 3d edit., 1974, Basic Psychology: Brief Version, 1977, Psychology: A Science in Conflict, 1981, Historical Foundations of Modern Psychology, 1987, Amoral Thoughts About Morality: The Intersection of Science, Psychology, and Ethics, 2000; co-author: Basic Psychology: Brief Edition, 1970; co-editor: Essays in Neobehaviorism: A Memorial Volume to Kenneth W. Spence; assoc. editor: Jour. Exptl. Psychology, 1963-65; contbr. to profl. jours., chpts. to books. Served as 1st lt. AUS. Fellow Ctr. for Advanced Studies in Behavioral Scis., Stanford, Calif., 1969-70; NSF grantee, 1954-76. Mem. Am. Psychol. Assn. (pres. divsn. exptl. psychology 1964-65, pres. divsn. gen. psychology 1967-68), Western Psychol. Assn. (pres. 1970-71), Soc. Exptl. Psychologists (exec. com. 1971-73), Psychonomic Soc. (governing bd. 1963-69, chmn. 1968-69), Sigma Xi. Home and Office: 300 Hot Springs Rd Santa Barbara CA 93108 E-mail: kendler@psych.ucsb.edu.

KENDLER, KENNETH S., medical educator; b. N.Y.C., July 12, 1950; married; 3 children. BA with hons., U. Calif., Santa Cruz, 1972; MD, Stanford U., 1977; DSc (hon.), U. Birmingham, Eng., 1999. Diplomate Am. Bd. Psychiatry and Neurology. Intern Yale U., 1977-78, resident, 1977-80; fellow biological scientist tng., 1978-80; asst. prof. Mt. Sinai Sch. Medicine, N.Y.C., 1980-83, rsch. assoc., 1981-83; assoc. prof. Med. Coll. Va./Va. Commonwealth U., Richmond, 1983-86, prof., dept. psych., dept. human genetics, 1987—, Rachel Brown Banks Disting. Prof. Psych., 1991—; dir. Va. Inst.

Psychiat. and Behavioral Genetics, 1996—. Thomas William Salmon lectr. N.Y. Acad. Medicine, 2001. Mem. editl. bd. Archives of General Psych., Bipolar Disorders, Current Psychiatry Reports, Neuropsychiat. Genetics, Schizophrenia Research, Social Psychiat. and Psychiat. Epidemiology, British Jour. of Psych.; internat. adv. panel Indian Jourl. of Psychiatry; contbr. articles to profl. jours., chpts. to books. Named 2d most frequently cited author of high-impact papers in psychiatry, 1990—98; recipient First prize, Anna-Monika-Found., 1997, Stanley R. Dean award, Am. Coll. Psychiatrists, 1998, Kurt Schneider Sci. award, 1998, Outstanding Paper award in humility theology, Templeton Found., 1999, Edward Strecker award, 2000, Fundacion Castillo del Pino award, 2001, Edward J. Sachar award for outstanding contbns. to psych. rsch., 2001, Rema Lapouse award, Am. Pub. Health Assn., 2002, Philip R.A. May Meml. award Leadership Disting. Svc. Psychiatry, UCLA, 2002, Erik Stromgren medal and Meml. Lectureship, Stromgren Found., Denmark, 2003. Fellow: Am. Psychiatric Assn.; mem.: Am. Assn. for Advancement of Sci., Behavior Genetics Assn., Genetic Epidemiology Soc., Neuroscience Rsch. Program (assoc.), Am. Soc. Human Genetics, Am. Psychiatric Assn. Office: Va Commonwealth U/Med Coll Va Dept Psychiatry PO Box 980126 Richmond VA 23298-0126 Office Phone: 804-828-8590.

KENDRICK, BUDD LEROY, psychologist; b. Pocatello, Idaho, Apr. 19, 1944; s. Oscar Fredrick Kendrick and Miriam Stuart (Thorn) Stewart; m. Sue Lorraine Allen, Nov. 11, 1966; children: Aaron Matthew and Edgar Seth; m. Beverly Ann Dockter, Dec. 26, 1978; children: Cassandra Rachelle, Angela Priscilla. BA, Idaho State U., 1967, MEd, 1969, EdD, 1974. Lic. psychologist, lic. counselor, Idaho; lic. clin. profl. counselor Mont.; cert. health svc. provider in psychology, nat. cert. counselor; cert. clin. mental health counselor; nat. bd. cert. fellow hypnotherapist; cert. profl. qualification in psychology, critical incident stress mgmt. provider, Red Cross disaster mental health svc. provider; cert. supr. Idaho Profl. Counselors and Marriage and Family Therapists. Tchr. psychology Pocatello H.S., 1967-69; dir. counseling svcs. Midwestern Coll., Denison, Iowa, 1969-70; rehab. counselor Idaho Divsn. of Vocat. Rehab., Pocatello, 1970-73; counselor (doctoral internship) Counseling Ctr., Idaho State U., Pocatello, 1973-74; rehab. counselor Idaho Divsn. of Vocat. Rehab., Pocatello, 1974-75; chief of psychology Mental Health and Devel. Disabilities Program, Boise, Idaho, 1975—; pvt. practice psychology Boise, 1977—. Vice-chmn. Idaho State Counselor Licensing Bd., 1982-84, chmn. 1984-85, sec. 1985-86; sec., treas. Nat. Bd. Cert. Counselors Inc., Alexandria, Va., 1986-93; mem. licensure com. Idaho Pers. and Guidance Assn., 1975-78, chmn. 1977-78, rep. Am. Pers. and Guidance Assn. Licensure Network, 1977-78; allied clin. staff Intermountain Hosp., Boise, 1983-93, Northwest Passages Adolescent Hosp., Boise, 1986-93, Saint Alphonsus Regional Med. Ctr., Boise, 1986-93; designated examiner and dispositioner involuntary commitments, conservatorships and guardianships State of Idaho, 1981—; cons. Idaho Pers. Commn., 1982—; grad. sch. lectr. Idaho State U., 1975; grad. sch. faculty affiliate, Coll. of Idaho, Caldwell, 1981-86; presenter concerning counselor credentialing issues, 1981-86; treas. Idaho Mental Health Assn., 1980-81; mem. Idaho Psychology, Social Work reclassification task force, 1990-91; mem. Idaho Assn. Counseling and Devel. Legis. Task Force for Third Party Benefits for Lic. Profl. Counselors, 1990. Editor: Directory of the Idaho Psychol. Assn., 1983; author numerous articles on hypnosis, counseling and profl. credentialing. Mem. adv. bd. Trio (Upward Bound, Talent Search, Head Start), Idaho State U., 1975-76; mem. Human Rights Com., Idaho State Sch. and Hosp., 1977; mem. adv. com. Nat. Bd. Cert. Counselors and WHO Internat. Global Counseling, Surrey, Eng., 2005 Recipient Disting. Svc. award Idaho Pers. & Guidance Assn., 1978, Profl. Achievement award Idaho State U., 1987, Spl. Recognition award Idaho Assn. for Counseling and Devel., 1989, Lawrence Schumacher Meml. Employee of Yr. award State of Idaho, 1995, Disting. Grad. award Idaho State U., 2001, Friend of Rsch. and Assessment for Counseling, Inc. Fellow Am. Coll. Advanced Practice Psychologists (founding mem. Idaho chpt.), Idaho Psychol. Assn. (sec. 1982-84); mem. Idaho Mental Health Counselors Assn. (charter), Idaho Counseling Assn. (leadership coun. 1977-78), Am. Counseling Assn. (pub. policy and legis. com., mem.-at-large 1992-94, chairperson nat. licensure subcom. 1992-94), Am. Mental Health Counselors Assn., Am. Psychol. Assn. (divsn. 17 counseling psychology, divsn. 30 psychol. hypnosis), Sons of Confederate Vets., Chi Sigma Iota Internat. Profl. Counseling and Acad. Honor Soc., Idaho Hist. Soc. (cert. Idaho pioneer descendant), Stuart-Mosby Hist. Soc., Kappa Delta Pi, Aneora Impara Hon. Soc Avocations: sword collecting, genealogy, history, collecting autographed celebrity photographs. Office Phone: 208-334-0900. Personal E-mail: psy108@cableone.net.

KENDRICK, DAVID ANDREW, economist, educator; b. Gatesville, Tex., Nov. 14, 1937; s. Andrew Green and Nina Alice (Murray) K.; m. Gail Tidd, July 4, 1964; children— Ann, Colin. BA, U. Tex., 1960; PhD (Woodrow Willson fellow 1961-62), MIT, 1965. Asst. prof. Harvard U., Cambridge, Mass., 1966-70; vis. scholar Stanford U., Calif., 1969-70; vis. prof. MIT, Cambridge, 1978-79; prof. econs. U. Tex., Austin, 1970—. Author: (with A. Stoutiesdijk) The Planning of Industrial Investment Programs, 1978, (with P. Dixon and S. Bowles) Notes and Problems in Microeconomic Theory, 1980, Stochastic Control for Economic Models, 1981, Feedback: A New Framework for Macroeconomic Policy, 1988, Models for Analyzing Comparative Advantage, 1990. Served with U.S. Army, 1960-61. Ford faculty fellow, 1969-70 Fellow AAAS; mem. Econometric Soc., Am. Econs. Assn., Soc. Econ. Dynamics and Control. (pres. 1980), Soc. Computational Econs. (pres. 1998). Home: 7209 Lamplight Ln Austin TX 78731-2119 Office: U Tex Dept Econs ECB 3-134E Austin TX 78712

KENDRICK, JOHN WHITEFIELD, economist, educator, consultant; b. N.Y.C., July 27, 1917; s. Benjamin Burks and Elizabeth W.W. (Shields) K.; m. Maxine Fillyaw; children: Bonnie Elizabeth, Karen Johanna, John Burks. AB, U. N.C., 1937, MA, 1939; PhD, George Washington U., 1955. Economist Nat. Resources Planning Bd., Washington, 1941-43, U.S. Dept. Commerce, Washington, 1946-53, chief economist, 1976-77; sr. staff mem. Nat. Bur. Econ. Rsch., N.Y.C., 1953-56, part-time, 56-78; prof. econs. George Washington U., Washington, 1956-88, prof. emeritus, 1988—. Univ. prof. U. Conn., Storrs, 1964-66; vis. prof. Georgetown U., UCLA, Stanford U., U. Hawaii, Simon Fraser U., v.p. for econ. rsch. The Conf. Bd., N.Y.C., 1972-73, part-time, 1973-76; dir., trustee Pioneer Mut. Funds, Boston, 1961-2000; bd. dirs. Am. Productivity and Quality Ctr., Houston, 1977—; cons. AT&T, 1964-83, Office Mgmt. and Budget, NSF, GAO, other cos. and govt. agys.; mem. Conf. on Rsch. in Income and Wealth, chmn. 1963-64; adj. scholar Am. Enterprise Inst., 1980-86. Author: Productivity Trends in the United States, 1961 (Pres. Kennedy Libr. award 1962), (with Daniel Creamer) Measuring Company Productivity: Handbook with Case Studies, 1961, rev. edit., 1965, Economic Accounts and Their Uses, 1972, The Formation and Stocks of Total Capital, 1976 (also Russian trans.), Improving Company Productivity, 1977, (with E. Grossman) Productivity in the United States: Trends and Cycles, 1980, (with John B. Kendrick) Personal Productivity, 1988 (trans. in Korean and Japanese), other books; editor 6 conf. vols.; mem. editl. bds. Rev. of Income and Wealth, Bus. Econs.; contbr. over 150 articles to profl. jours. 1st lt. A.C., U.S. Army, 1943-45; served with U.S. Strategic Bombing Survey, 1945-46, ETO. Recipient Graham Dodd award for article Fin. Analysts Jour., 1962, Abramson award for article in Bus. Econs. jour., 1987. Fellow Am. Statis. Assn., Nat. Assn. Bus. Economists; mem. Am. Econ. Assn., So. Econ. Assn. (pres. 1982-83), Nat. Economists Club (pres. 1975-76, chmn. bd. 1976-77), World Acad. Productivity Sci., Atlantic Econ. Soc. (disting. assoc., pres. 1992-93), George Washington U. Club, Phi Beta Kappa. Unitarian-Universalist. Avocations: swimming, walking, reading, tv talk shows. Office: George Washington U Dept Econ Washington DC 20052-0001 Home: Apt 1228 3440 S Jefferson St Falls Church VA 22041-3131 Office Phone: 202-668-6686.

KENDRICK, KATHERINE, lawyer; b. S.C. BA, U. Calif., Berkeley; JD, Columbia U., 1986. Assoc. Latham & Watkins, Los Angeles; with legal dept. Hollywood Pictures, Walt Disney Studios, 1989—96, v.p. legal affairs in Europe; gen. counsel DreamWorks Animation SKG, Inc., 1996—, bd. dirs. Bd. mem. Next Generation Coun., Motion Picture and Television Fund; adv. bd. LA Sports and Entertainment Commn., Kernochan Ctr. Law, Media and Arts, Columbia U. Sch. Law. Adv. bd. Big Brothers/ Big Sisters of Greater Los Angeles. Office: DreamWorks SKG 1000 Flower St Glendale CA 91201

KENDRICK, KERRY, military officer; b. Southside, Tenn. Degree in polit. sci., Austin Peay State U., 1977; MPA, Jacksonville State U. Commd. 2d. lt. US Army, advanced through grades to col., dept. provost marshal Bamberg, Germany, platoon leader 501st mil. police co., chief enlisted evaluations army mil. polic sch. Ft. McClellan, Ala., co. comdr., recorder promotion bd. Washington, assignment officer mil. police br., personnel policy joint staff Pentagon, force protection officer dept. army, served in Ops. Desert Shield and Desert Storm, exec. officer Protection Officer and Law Enforcement Divsn., staff leader combined arms & svc. staff sch. Ft. Leavenworth, Kans., commdr. 728th mil. police battalion Taegu, Republic of Korea, comdr. 89th mil. police brigade; chief staff Army Rsch. Lab., Adelphi, Md. Recipient Bronze Star medal, U.S. Army, Meritorious Svc. medal with five oak-leaf clusters, Joint Svc. Commendation medal, Army Commendation medal, Army Achievement medal. Office: US Army Rsch Lab Attn AMSRL-CS-EA-PA 2800 Powder Mill Rd Adelphi MD 20783-1197

KENDRICK, NISBET S., III, lawyer; b. Ga., Apr. 04; m. Bambi Kendrick; children: Harris, Merideth. BA in Philosophy, U. Ga., 1974, JD, 1977. Pvt. practice, Marietta, Ga., 1977—82; ptnr. Fishman, Kendrick & Gordon, Atlanta, 1982—88, Parker, Johnson & Montgomery, Atlanta, 1988—96, Womble, Carlyle, Sandridge & Rice, PLLC, Atlanta, 1996—. Bd. dirs. Primier/First Alliance Bankshares. Mem.: ABA (co-chair ADR Inst.), Ga. Bar Assn. (mem. alt. dispute resolution sect.). Republican. Episcopalian. Avocation: iron man triathalon. Office: Womble Carlyle Sandridge and Rice PLLC 1 Atlantic Ctr 1201 W Peachtree St Ste 3500 Atlanta GA 30309 Business E-Mail: kkendrick@wcsr.com.

KENDRICK, PETER MURRAY, communications executive, investor; b. Winchester, Mass., Oct. 8, 1936; s. Wallace Dolloff and Esther (Burke) K.; m. Grace Terry, June 17, 1967; children: Caroline, Timothy. BSBA, Babson Coll., 1962. Office mgr. Am. Hosp. Supply Corp., Chgo. and Charlotte, N.C., 1962-65; registered rep. Hayden, Stone & Co., 1966-69; gen. mgr. Continental Cablevision, Concord, N.H. and Jackson, Mich., 1969-74; pres. New Eng. Cablevision, Portland, Maine, 1974-79, chmn. bd., 1980; pres. Home Theater Network, Portland and N.Y.C., 1977-87; chmn. bd. Envirologic Data Corp., Portland, 1984-86; sr. v.p. Watson Techs., Portland, 1994-96; pres., chmn. Internet Maine, Internet N.E., Inc. (merger Harvard Net, Inc.), Portland, 1997; interim CEO Compass Cablesys., Portland and Marblehead, Mass., 1998—99. Founder, pres. The Travel Channel, 1981-86; founder The Disney Channel, 1981; vice chmn. bd. dirs., pres., treas. Internat. Cablevision, Inc., Bronxville, N.Y., 1987-93; chmn. bd. Kendrick Corp., Portland, Maine, 1986—, Kendrick Tech. Corp., 1992—, Legal Document Systems, Inc., Washington, 1993-94, The Film Channel, Inc., Portland, 1987-90, Yankee Books, Camden, Maine, 1989-91. Trustee North Yarmouth Acad., Yarmouth, Maine, chmn. ann. giving campaign, 1986-87; bus. mgr. Foreside Cmty. Ch., Flamouth & Cumberland Foreside, Maine, 2005—. With USAF, 1956-59. Recipient Highest Programming award Cable TV Nat. Assn., 1973, 86. Mem. New Eng. Cable TV Assn. (v.p. 1972, pres. 1975), Mich. Cable TV Assn. (v.p. 1973), Portland Country Club, Portland Yacht Club, Cable TV Pioneers. Office: 4 Landing Woods Ln Falmouth ME 04105-1948 E-mail: kendrick@maine.rr.com.

KENDRICK, WILLIAM BRYCE, biologist, consultant, editor; b. Liverpool, Lancashire, Eng., Dec. 3, 1933; arrived in Can., 1958; s. William and Lillian Maud (Latham) K.; m. Laureen Anne Carscadden, Dec. 14, 1978; children: Clinton, Kelly. BSc with honors, U. Liverpool, 1955, PhD, 1958, DSc, 1980. Postdoctoral fellow NRC, Ottawa, Canada, 1958-59; rsch. scientist Agr. Can., Ottawa, 1959-65; asst. prof. U. Waterloo, 1965-66, assoc. prof., 1966-71, prof., 1971-94, disting. prof. emeritus, 1994—, assoc. dean, 1985-93. Adj. prof. U. Victoria, B.C., 1994—; propr. Mycologue Pub. and Cons.; tech. adv. Aerobiology Lab. Assocs., Reston, Va.; cons. in field. Author: The Fifth Kingdom, 1985, 2d rev. and enlarged edit., 1991, 3rd edit., 2001, CD Rom version 4.0, 2005, A Young Person's Guide To The Fungi, 1986; co-author: Genera of Hyphomycetes, 1980, An Evolutionary Survey of Fungi, Algae and Plants, 1992; editor: Taxonomy of Fungi Imperfecti, The Whole Fungus, Biology of Conidial Fungi; contbr. articles to profl. jours. Guggenheim fellow, 1979-80. Fellow Royal Soc. Can.; mem. Acad. Sci. (hon. sec. 1984-91), Mycol. Soc. Am. (Disting. Mycologist award 1995), Brit. Mycol. Soc. (centenary fellow 1996), Can. Bot. Assn. (Lawson medal 2001). Mem. Green Party. Avocations: reading, music, walking, photography, rowing. Home and Office: 8727 Lochside Dr Sidney BC Canada V8L 1M8 Office Phone: 250-655-5051. E-mail: bryce@mycolog.com. *Curiosity is the key to a full life. Keep on asking questions-and keep on trying to answer them-until the day you die.*

KENDRICK-HOPGOOD, DEBRA JO, small business owner; b. Mount Vernon, Ill., June 26, 1958; d. L. John and B. Jean (Stovall) K.; m. Joseph Jefferson Hopgood Jr., Jan. 10, 1981; children: Jillian Denise, Ashley Erin. Owner Balloons and Tunes, 1985-90; with Kendrick Paper Stock Co., Mt. Vernon, Ill., 1980—; owner Shenanigans Restaurant, 1990—2004. Com. mem. Mt. Vernon Civic Ctr., 1983-86, Jefferson County Crime Stoppers, Mt. Vernon, 1984-85; chaperone Loiterers Club, Mt. Vernon, 1987; mem. adv. bd. Good Samaritan Hosp., 1988-93; bd. dirs. Mt. Vernon Twp. High Sch. Bd. Edn., 1986—, Mt. Vernon Women's Crisis Ctr., 1988-91, Jefferson County, 1988; bd. suprs. Jefferson County, 1988—; bd. dirs. Bright and Beautiful, 1989—; mem. Mt. Vernon Econ. Devel. Commn., 1997—; mem. adv. bd. Jefferson County Health Dept., 1995-98; asst. leader Girl Scouts USA, 1998—, girl scout leader, 2005—; mem. Mt. Vernon Econ. Devel. Commn., 1997—. Named Woman of Yr. Mt. Vernon Bus. and Profl. Women's Club, 1998, DBE of Yr. Ill. Dept. of Transp. Bus. of Small Bus. Enterprise, 1997, Trucker of the Month, Midwest Truckers Assn. Mem. Nat. Fedn. Female Execs., Bus. and Profl. Womens Club, People Against Violent Environments (bd. dirs.), Jefferson County C. of C. (bd. dirs.). Baptist. Avocations: collecting coins, reading, tennis, old movies. Office: Kendrick Paper Stock Co PO Box 1385 Mount Vernon IL 62864-0028 Office Phone: 800-346-1326. E-mail: kendrickpaper@msn.com.

KENDZIOR, ROBERT JOSEPH, marketing executive; b. Mar. 24, 1952; s. Joseph W. and Josephine R. Kendzior. BArch, Ill. Inst. Tech., 1975. Account supr. Burger King Corp. Rogers Merchandising, Inc., Chgo., 1975-77; account exec. Walgreen Corp. Eisaman, Johns & Laws Advt., Inc., Chgo., 1977-78; v.p. mktg. Dunkin Donuts Am., Inc., Randolph, Mass., 1978-95; v.p., chief mktg. officer Factory Card Outlet Am., Inc., Chgo., 1995-98; v.p. internat. mktg. Allied Domecq Retailing, 1999—2005; v.p. Internat. Mktg. and Retail Concepts, Randolph, 2003—; chief mktg. officer Captain D's Seafood Restaurants, Nashville, 2005—. Bd. dirs. Baskin-Robbins, Japan. Recipient Most Valuable Promotion award PepsiCo, 1984. Mem. Triangle Fraternity. Achievements include guest spkr., Boston U. (Internat. Mktg.), 2004. E-mail: rkendzior@msn.com.

KENEALLY, KATHRYN MARIE, lawyer; b. Dayton, Ohio, Apr. 30, 1958; d. William Henry and Joanna Gertrude K.; m. Thomas Marshall, Oct. 16, 1992. BA, Cornell U., 1979; JD, Fordham U., 1982; LLM in Taxation, NYU, 1993. Bar: N.Y., 1983, U.S. Dist. Ct. (so., ea. dists.) N.Y., 1983, U.S. Ct. Appeal (2d, 3d, 11th cirs.), U.S. Tax Ct. Law clk. to Hon. E. R. Neaher U.S. Dist. Ct. (ea. dist.) N.Y., Bklyn., 1982-83; assoc. Skadden Arps Slate Meagher & Flom, N.Y.C., 1983-85, Kostelanetz Ritholz Tigue & Fink, N.Y.C., 1985-90, ptnr., 1990-93, Kostelanetz & Fink, LLP, N.Y.C., 1993-99; mem. Owen & Davis, PC, N.Y.C., 2000—02; ptnr. Fulbright & Jaworski, L.L.P., N.Y.C., 2002—. Columnist The Champion, 1996—, Jour. Tax Practice and Prodecure, 1999-; co-author: Practice Under Federal Sentencing Guidelines, 1998; contbr. articles to profl. jours. Mem. practitioners adv. group U.S. Sentencing Commn., 1993—. Mem. ABA (chmn. taxation sect., civil and criminal tax penalties com. 2000-02), Nat. Assn. Criminal Def. Lawyers (life). Home: 48 Charlotte Pl Hartsdale NY 10530-2602 Office: Fulbright & Jaworski LLP 660 Fifth Ave New York NY 10103 Office Phone: 212-318-3000. E-mail: kkeneally@fulbright.com.

KENEALLY, THOMAS MICHAEL, author; b. Australia, Oct. 7, 1935; s. Edmund Thomas and Elsie Margaret (Coyle) K.; m. Judith Mary Martin, Aug. 21, 1965; children: Margaret Ann, Jane Rebecca. Ed., St. Patrick's Coll., Strathfield, N.S.W. Writings include (fiction) The Place at Whitton, 1965, The Fear, 1965, Bring Larks and Heroes, 1967, Three Cheers for the Paraclete, 1968, The Survivor, 1969, A Dutiful Daughter, 1971, The Chant of Jimmie Blacksmith, 1972 (Heinemann award for lit. Royal Soc. Lit. 1973), Blood Red, Sister Rose, 1974, Gossip From the Forest, 1975, Moses the Lawgiver, 1975, Season in Purgatory, 1977, A Victim of the Aurora, 1977, (children's book) Ned Kelly and the City of Bees, 1978, Passenger, 1979, Confederates, 1979, The Cut-Rate Kingdom, 1980, Schindler's List, 1982 (Booker McConnell prize for fiction 1982, Fiction prize L.A. Times 1983), Outback, 1983, (play) Bullie's House, 1985, A Family Madness, 1985, The Playmaker, 1987, To Asmara, 1989, Flying Hero Class, 1991, (non-fiction) The Place Where Souls Are Born, 1992, (non-fiction) Now and in Time to Be, 1992, Woman of the Inner Sea, 1992, Jacko: The Great Intruder, 1994, A River Town, 1995, Homebush Boy-A Memoir, 1995; (plays) Halloran's Little Boat, 1966, Childermass, 1968, An Awful Rose, 1972; (non-fiction) The Great Shame, 1999, (fiction) Bettany's Book, 2000, (non-fiction) An American Scoundrel, The Life of the Notorious Civil War General Dan Sickles, 2002, An Angel in Australia, 2002, (non-fiction) Lincoln, 2003, The Tyrant's Novel, 2004. Inaugural mem. Australia-China Coun., 1978-83; mem. adv. panel Australian Constn. Commn., 1985-88; mem. Literary Arts Bd. Australia, 1985-88; chmn. Australian Rep. Movement, 1991-93, dir., 1994—. Decorated Officer Order of Australia; recipient Miles Franklin award, 1967, 68, Captain Cook Bi-Centerary prize, 1970. Fellow Royal Soc. Lit. (London), Am. Acad. Arts and Scis.; mem. PEN, Australian Soc. Authors (chmn. 1987-90), Nat. Book Coun. Australia (pres. 1985-90. Office: Curtis Brown (Australia) P/L PO Box 19 Paddington NSW 2021 Australia

KENEFICK, JOHN STEPHEN, lawyer; b. Chgo., Feb. 27, 1962; s. John Stephen and Josephine K.; m. Angelina Robledo, May 25, 1996. BS, Purdue U., 1984; JD cum laude, No. Ill. U., 1992. Assoc. Landau, Omahana & Kopka Ltd., Chgo., 1994-96, ptnr., 1996-98, mng. ptnr. Dallas, 1998-99; shareholder McCauley, Macdonald, Devin & Huddleston, Dallas, 1999—. Mem. Def. Rsch. Inst., Chgo., 1994—. Musician Johnny Bravo! Recipient Am. Jurisprudence award, 1990. Mem. Dallas Bar Assn., Tex. Bar Assn., Ill. State Bar. Office: McCauley Macdonald Devin & Huddleston 1201 Elm St Ste 3800 Dallas TX 75270-2014 Fax: 972-769-9446. E-mail: john.kene@gte.net, jsk@mmdh.com.

KENEN, PETER BAIN, economist, educator; b. Cleve., Nov. 30, 1932; s. Isaiah Leo and Beatrice (Bain) K.; m. Regina Horowitz, Aug. 21, 1955; children: Joanne Lisa, Marc David, Stephanie Hope, Judith Rebecca. AB, Columbia U., 1954; MA, Harvard U., 1956, PhD, 1958. Mem. faculty Columbia U., 1957-71, prof. econs., 1964-71, chmn. dept., 1967-69, provost univ., 1969-70; prof. econs. and internat. fin. Princeton (N.J.) U., 1971—2004, dir. internat. fin. sect., 1971-99; Ford rsch. prof. U. Calif., Berkeley, 1979-80; sr. fellow internat. econs. Coun. on Fgn. Rels., 2004—. Rschr. on internat. monetary theory and policy; cons. Coun. Econ. Advisors, 1961, U.S. Treasury, 1962-68, 77-80, 95-98, Bur. Budget, 1964-68, IMF, 1990, 92. Author: British Monetary Policy and the Balance of Payments (1951-1957), 1960, Giant Among Nations, 1960; author: (with A.G. Hart and A. Entine) Money, Debt and Economic Activity, 4th edit., 1969; author: (with R. Lubitz) International Economics, 3d edit., 1971; author: A Model of the U.S. Balance of Payments, 1978; author: (with P.R. Allen) Asset Markets, Exchange Rates and Economic Integration, 1980; author: Essays in International Economics, 1980, Managing Exchange Rates, 1988, Exchange Rates and Policy Coordination, 1989, Exchange Rates and the Monetary System, 1994, Economic and Monetary Union in Europe, 1995, International Economy, 4th edit., 2000, The International Financial Architecture: What's New? What's Missing?, 2001; editor: International Trade and Finance, Frontiers for Research, 1975; editor: (with others) The International Monetary System Under Flexible Exchange Rates, 1982; editor: (with R.W. Jones) Handbook of International Economics, 1984; editor: Managing the World Economy, 1994, Understanding Interdependence, 1995; editor: (with A.K. Swoboda) Reforming the International Monetary and Financial System, 2000; contbr. articles to profl. jours. Recipient David A. Wells prize Harvard U., 1958-59, Univ. medal Columbia U., 1977; Ctr. Advanced Study Behavioral Scis. fellow, 1971-72, John Simon Guggenheim Found. fellow, 1975-76, Res. Bank Australia fellow, 1983-84, Royal Inst. Internat. Affairs fellow, 1987-88, German Marshall Fund fellow, 1987-88, Houblon-Norman fellow Bank of Eng., 1991-92, fellow Res. Bank New Zealand, 2002. Mem.: Am. Econ. Assn., Coun. Fgn. Rels., Royal Econ. Soc, Group of Thirty. Home: 176 Western Way Princeton NJ 08540-7208 Office: Princeton U Dept of Econs Fisher Hall Princeton NJ 08544-1021 Office Phone: 609-258-4051. Business E-Mail: pbkenen@princeton.edu.

KENESSON, FRANK GIRAULT, history educator, writer; b. Detroit, Sept. 11, 1942; s. Frank Girault Sr. and Leona Mae (Snider) K.; m. Susan Christopher Nunn, Aug. 3, 1963 (div. Mar. 1967); m. Mary Suzanne Ferguson, Aug. 12, 1967; children: Christian C., Summer S., Alexander A. Diploma in field archaeology, U. Birmingham, Eng., 1963; BA in History and Edn., Am. U., 1969, MA in History and Econs., 1975; PhD in Comparative Lit., U. Md., 1988. Econs. rschr. U.S. Dept. Labor, Washington, 1970-73; tchr. Queen Anne Sch., Upper Marlboro, Md., 1978-83; internat. baccalaureate program adminstr. Glenelg (Md.) H.S., 1983-91; instr. ancient history Howard C.C., Columbia, Md., 1989-95; tchr. sr. integrative seminar Glenelg Country Sch., 1991-94; adj. prof., lectr. Towson (Md.) State U., 1991-94; lectr. ancient medieval, early modern, Asian and intellectual history Shepherd Coll., Shepherdstown, W.Va., 1996—. Contbr. articles to profl. jours.; author poetry, play, lit. criticism; also translator. Mem. MLA, AAUP, Internat. Ctr. Medieval Art, Phi Kappa Phi. Avocations: comparative poetics, zen meditation, preservation of french antiquities.

KENIRY, WILLIAM JOSEPH, lawyer; b. Troy, NY, Oct. 13, 1964; s. William Henry and Marie Domenica (Parente) K. BA in Philosophy, Union Coll., 1986; JD, Western New Eng. Coll., 1989. Bar: Mass. 1989, N.Y. 1990. Pvt. practice Keniry Title Abstract, Clifton Park, NY, 1986-89; assoc. Iannniello Law Firm, Clifton Pk., 1989-90, Tabner & Ryan, Albany, NY, 1990-96, ptnr., 1996-97, Tabner, Ryan & Keniry, Albany, NY, 1997—. Shareholder, officer, dir. Colonie Abstract Corp., Albany, 1996—, Attorney Town Planning Bd., Town of Charlton, 2001-. Pres. Town Halfmoon (N.Y.) Rep. Club, 1993-95; committeeman, mem. N.Y. State Rep. Com. 108th Assembly Dist., 1996—, Saratoga County Rep. Com., Halfmoon, 1991—. Mem. NY State Bar Assn., Trial Lawyers Exec. Comm., 2001-, Albany County Bar Assn., Saratoga County Bar Assn., New York State Trial Lawyers Assoc. Roman Catholic. Avocations: extreme skiing, mountain biking. Office: Tabner Ryan & Keniry 18 Corporate Woods Blvd Albany NY 12211

KENISON, RAYMOND ROBERT, fraternal organization administrator, director; b. Mo., Sept. 23, 1932; s. Raymond Roy and Emma Oleta (Holder) Kenison; m. Marjorie White, Feb. 1, 1955; children: Debra Kenison Brown, Peggy Kenison Crim, Raymond Roger, Robert B. AA, Hannibal LaGrange Coll., 1953; BA, U. Mo., 1961; postgrad., Cen. Bapt. Sem., Kansas City, 1957, Midwestern Bapt. Sem., 1965; DivD, Hannibal LaGrange Coll., 1994. CFP; cert. instr. Pastor 1st Bapt.Ch., Bates City, Mo., 1954-56, Friendship Bapt. Ch., Mexico, Mo., 1956-62, Immanuel Bapt. Ch., Hannibal, Mo., 1962-77; dir. devel. Mo. Bapt. Children's Home, Bridgeton, 1977-80, exec. dir., 1980—; pres., 1992—. Pres. bd. trustees Hannibal-Lagrance Coll.; co-founder, pres. Viability R & D Group; pres. MBCH Found., 2001—; chmn. contract com. Spl. Care Homes of Mo., 2002—; pres. MBCH Properties, 2002—; pres., chmn. bd. MBCH Profl. Devel. Inst., 2003. Mem. Child Welfare League Am., Inc.; pres. Hannibal Coun. Alcohol and Drug Abuse; bd. dirs. Hannibal Cmty. Chest, 1974—79, Alliance Children and Families, Mo. Alliance Children and Families; pres. Hannibal Ministerial

Alliance. Named Kenison Complex in his honor. Mem.: Viability R & D Group (co-founder, pres.), Inst. CFPs, S.W. Assn. Child Care Execs., Mo. Child Care Assn. (bd. dirs., pres. 1994—), So. Bapt. Child Care Execs. (pres.), Nat. Soc. Fund Raising Execs. (sec.), Nat. Assn. Homes Children, Nat. Foster Parents Assn., Hannibal Investment Club (pres. 1976—78, 1982—83). Home: 4 River Hills Hannibal MO 63401-6218 Office: Mo Bapt Children's Home 11300 Saint Charles Rock Rd Bridgeton MO 63044-2793 Office Phone: 314-739-6811.

KENISTON, KENNETH, psychologist, educator; b. Chgo., Jan. 6, 1930; s. Hayward and Roberta (Cannell) K.; m. Ellen Uviller, June 20, 1960 (div. Aug. 1975); children: Ann Rogers, Sarah Hayward; m. Suzanne Berger, Jan. 10, 1976; 1 child, Daniel Eben. BA, Harvard Coll., 1951; DPhil, Oxford U., 1956; LLD (hon.), Notre Dame U., 1971; DSc (hon.), Colgate U., 1972. From rsch. asst. to rsch. assoc. dept. social rels. Harvard U., Cambridge, Mass., 1955-62; from asst. prof. to assoc. prof. psych. Yale Med. Sch., New Haven, 1962-68, prof. psych., 1968-75; Andrew W. Mellon prof. human devel. Mass. Inst. Tech., Cambridge, 1975—. Lectr. on clin. psychology Harvard U., 1958-62, resident fellow, asst. sr. tutor Eliot House, 1953-59; assoc. dir., acting dir., then dir. Behavior Scis. Study Ctr., Yale Med. Sch., 1965-72; fellow Davenport Coll., Yale U., 1962-75; chmn., exec. dir. Carnegie Coun. on Children, New Haven, 1972-78; dir. program in sci., tech. and soc. Mass. Inst. Tech., 1987-92, dir. grad. studies, 1993-96, dir. projects, 1996—; dir. MIT India Program, 1998—; mem. Carnegie Commn. on Higher Edn., 1966-73, bd. dirs. Overseers Harvard Coll., 1969-75,MacArthur Prize Fellows selection com., 1979-85; com. on selection Guggenheim Found., 1992-94; vis. scholar Ecole de Mines, Paris, 1980-81; vis. prof. U. Paris Sorbonne, 1986-87, Centro de Estudios Avanzados de Ciencias Sociales, Madrid, 1990, Nat. Inst. Advanced Studies, Indian Inst. Sci., Bangalore, 1999, 2001. Author: The Uncommitted, 1966, Young Radicals, 1968, All Our Children, 1977, The Fragile Contract, 1994, Earth, Air, Fire, Water, 1999, IT Experience in India, 2004—; contbr. articles to profl. jours., chpts. to books. Rhodes scholar Balliol Coll., Oxford U., 1951-53; jr. fellow Harvard U., 1953-56; Guggenheim fellow, 1980-81. Fellow AAAS; mem. Coun. Fgn. Rels., Phi Beta Kappa, Sigma Xi. Office: Mass Inst Tech E51-163 77 Massachusetts Ave Cambridge MA 02139 Business E-Mail: kken@mit.edu.

KENNA, GEORGE ANTHONY, pharmacist, researcher; s. Merrill Carlton and Esther Ann Kenna; m. Nancy Constantino Kenna, May 17, 1981; 1 child, John. BS in Pharmacy, U. R.I., 1975, MA in Psychology, 2001, PhD in Philosophy, 2003. Registered pharmacist Va. Pharmacist Potomac Hosp., Woodbridge, Va., 1977—80, Liggett Rexall, Middletown, RI, 1980—81, Douglas Drug, RI, 1981—96; grad. asst. U. R.I., 1997, rsch. asst., 1999; pharmacist Walmart Pharmacy, North Kingstown, RI, 1998—2001; clin. pharmacist Kent County Hosp., Warwick, RI, 1999—. Tchg. asst. stats. U. R.I., Kingston, 2001—02; rsch. fellow dept. biomedicine Brown U., Providence, 2003—04; postdoctoral fellow Ctr. for Alcohol and Addiction Studies, Providence, 2004—; cons. Brown U., Providence, 2003—04. Contbr. articles to profl. jours. Recipient Young Investigator award, Rsch. Soc. Alcoholism, 2004, Rsch. Award grant, Ctr. for Alcohol and Addiction Studies, 2004. Mem.: APA, Rsch. Soc. Am., Am. Pharm. Assn. Episcopalian. Avocations: skiing, bicycling, golf, writing. Home: 59 Bedford Ln North Kingstown RI 02852 Office: Brown U Box G-BH Providence RI 02908

KENNADY, EMMETT HUBBARD, III, lawyer; b. Houston, Dec. 13, 1957; s. Emmett Hubbard Jr. and Ruth Gail (Lewis) K.; m. Monta Kennady, Sept. 21, 1985; children: Jennings Randolph, Emmett Hubbard IV. BA in Theology, BA in Polit. Sci., Washington and Lee U., 1980; JD, St. Mary's Sch. Law, San Antonio, 1984. Bar: Tex. 1984, U.S. Army Ct. Criminal Appeals 1994, U.S. Ct. Appeals for Armed Forces 1997. Asst. dist. atty. Brazos County Dist. Atty.'s Office, Bryan, Tex., 1985-87; atty. Lawrence, Thornton, Payne, Bryan, 1987-88; sole practitioner College Station, Tex., 1988—. Mem. staff St. Mary's Sch. Law. Co-author: Medico-Legal Considerations for Dental Practitioner, 1988; contbr. articles to profl. jours. Mem. College Station City Coun., 1992-98, mayor pro tem, 1996-98; mem. Leadership Brazos, Bryan, 1989-90; judge College Station Bd. Adjustment, 1990-91; mem. College Station Capital Improvement Com., 1989-90; bd. dirs. Bryan-College Station Econ. Devel. Bd., 1997-2000, Opera and Performing Arts, College Station, 1997-2001, United Way, Bryan, 1991-96, Arts Coun., College Station, 1990-93. Capt. U.S. Army, 1999. L.B.J. Congl. scholar, 1980. Republican. Baptist. Avocation: flying. Office: 424 Tarrow St College Station TX 77840-7813

KENNAN, ELIZABETH TOPHAM, academic administrator, retired historian; b. Phila., Feb. 25, 1938; AB summa cum laude, Mt. Holyoke Coll., 1960; MA, Oxford (Eng.) U., 1962; PhD, U. Wash., 1966; LHD (hon.), Trinity Coll., 1978, Amherst Coll., 1980, St. Mary's Coll., 1982, Oberlin Coll., 1983; LLD (hon.), Smith Coll., 1984; LittD (hon.), Cath. U. of Am., 1985, U. Mass., Amherst, 1988. Asst. prof. history Cath. U., Washington, 1966-70, assoc. prof. history, dir. medieval and Byzantine studies, 1970-78, dir. program in early Christian humanism, 1970-78; pres. Five Colls. Inc., 1985-94; pres., prof. history Mt. Holyoke Coll., South Hadley, Mass., 1978-95, pres. emeritus, 1996. Bd. dirs. Coun. on Libr. Resources, 1980-95; mem. com. Folger Shakespeare Libr., 1994-2001; lead dir. N.E. Utilities, Hartford, Conn.; bd. dirs. The Putnam Funds, Boston, Talbots, Hingham, Mass. Co-author: (under pseudonym Clare Munnings) Overnight Float, 2000; contbr. articles to profl. jours. including Georgetown Univ. Press, Univ. of Wash. Press, Cath. Univ. of Am., Cath. Univ. Press, Cistercian Publs., Mem. Coun. on Econ. Devel., 1991-95; mem. bd. selectors Jefferson awards Am. Inst. for Pub. Svc., 1991-96; trustee U. Notre Dame, 1985-94, Miss Porter's Sch., 1980-85; mem. higher edn. program com. Dana Found., 1986-90, Indo-U.S. Subcommn. on Edn. and Culture, 1986-91; vice chmn. 1000 Friends of Mass., 1989-91, Mass Gov.'s Nominating Coun., 1990-91; trustee Trustees for the Reservations, 1999—, Centre Coll., Danville, Ky., 2001—, Midway Coll., Midway, Ky., Nat. Trust Hist. Preservation, 2004—. Marshall scholar, 1960; Woodrow Wilson fellow (hon.), 1960. Mem. Coun. Fgn. Rels. Home and Office: Cambus-Kenneth Farm PO Box 1989 Danville KY 40423

KENNARD, JOYCE L., state supreme court justice; b. Bandung, West Java, Indonesia, May 6, 1941; AA, Pasadena City Coll., 1970, U. So. Calif., 1970, BA in German magna cum laude, 1971, MPA, JD, U. So. Calif., 1974; JD (hon.), Pepperdine Sch. Law, 1989; LLD (hon.), Calif. Western Sch. Law, 1990, Southwestern U. Sch. Law, 1991, Whittier Law Sch., 1994, Northwestern Sch. Law, Lewis and Clark Coll., 1997, Lincoln Law Sch., 1997, San Joaquin Coll. Law, 2004. Dep. atty. gen., LA, 1975—79; sr. atty. State Ct. Appeals, LA, 1979—86; judge LA County Mcpl. Ct., 1986—87; assoc. justice pro tempore State Ct. Appeal (divsn. three), LA, 1987; judge LA County Superior Ct., 1987—88; assoc. justice State Ct. Appeals (divsn. five), LA, 1988—89, Calif. Supreme Ct., San Francisco, 1989—. Chair appellate adv. com. Calif. Jud. Coun., 1996—. Recipient Contbg. Progress of Dignity and Self-Esteem Among Amputees award, Sacramento Women Amputees Group, 1990, Lifetime Achievement award, Ind. Living Ctr. So. Calif., 1990, award, Gov.'s Hall of Fame for People with Disabilities, 1990, Ernestine Stahlhut award, Women Lawyers' Assn. of LA, 1990, award, San Fernando Valley Bar, 1990, Asian/Pacific Women's Network, LA, 1991, YWCA award, LA, 1991, Justice of Yr. 1991 award, Calif. Trial Lawyers Assn., 1992 Chinese-Am. Pioneers So. Calif. Judiciary award, Chinese Hist. Soc. of So. Calif., First Ann. Women of 90's award, Robinson's Dep. Store, LA, 1992, First Ann. Netherlands-Am. Heritage award, Netherlands-Am. Arts and Cultural Found., 1992, Atty. Gen. award, Asian and Pacific Islander Employee Adv. Com., Atty. Gen.'s Office, 1992, award, ABA Task Force on Opportunities for Minorities in Jud. Adminstrn. Divsn. and Commn. on Opportunities for Minorities in Profession, 1992, Margaret Brent Women Lawyers of Achievement award, ABA, 1993, Trailblazer award, Nat. Asian Pacific Am. Bar Assn. (NAPABA), 1994, Founders award, Nat. Asian Pacific Am. Law Students Assn. (NAPALSA), 1994, Access award, LA County Commn. Disabilities, 1994, St. Thomas More Medallion award, St. Thomas More Law Honor Soc. and Loyola Law Sch., 1995, 1996 Spirit Excellence award, ABA's Commn. on Opportunities for Minorities in the Profession, award, Marin Women's Hall of Fame, 1997, San Francisco Women Lawyers Alliance, 1997, Asian Pacific Am. Legal Ctr. So. Calif., LA, 1997, Coun. Asian Pacific Islanders Together Active Leadership (C.A.P.I.T.A.L.), 1997, Accompanying award, Asian Bar Assn. Sacramento, Legal Impact award, Asian Law Alliance, San Jose, Calif., 2000, First Justice Rose Bird Meml. award, Calif. Women Lawyers San Francisco, 2001, Pub. Svc. award, Asian Pacific Am. Bar Assn., 2001, Jud. Coun.'s award, San Francisco, 2004. Mem.: Alpha Gamma Sigma Soc., Alpha Mu Gamma, Phi Kappa Phi, Phi Beta Kappa. Office: Calif Supreme Ct 350 McAllister St San Francisco CA 94102-4783

KENNARD, LYDIA H., airport terminal executive; BA, Stanford U.; MS, MIT; JD, Harvard U. Former pres./prin.-in-charge KDG Devel. Constrn. Consulting, L.A.; former mem. L.A. Planning Commn.; dep. exec. dir. design and constrn. L.A. World Airports, 1994-99, interim exec. dir., 1999-2000, exec. dir., 2000—03; chmn. KDG Develop. & Constrn. Cons., LA, 2003—. Mem. Calif. Air Resources Bd., 2004-; bd. dir. IndyMac Bank; lawyer in real estate and constrn. law. Active UniHealth Found. Bd.; past mem. Calif. Med. Ctr. Found. Bd., Equal Opportunity Adv. Coun. So. Calif. Edison. Named Woman of Yr. L.A. chpt. Women's Trans. Seminar, 1995, Civic Leader of Yr. Nat. Assn. Women Bus. Owners-L.A., 2000. Office: KDG Development Construction Ste 1800 1055 W 7th ST Los Angeles CA 90017*

KENNARD, MARY ELIZABETH, lawyer; b. Phila., Dec. 1, 1954; d. Rodman Ramos and Mary Elizabeth Kennard. BAS, Boston U., 1976; JD, Temple U., 1980; LLM, George Washington U., 1982. Bar: Pa. 1980, R.I. 1988, D.C. 1988, U.S. Dist. Ct. (we. dist.) Pa. 1985, U.S. Ct. Appeals (3d cir.) 1985, U.S. Dist. Ct. R.I. 1988, U.S. Ct. Appeals (1st cir.) 1989, U.S. Dist. Ct. D.C. 1989, U.S. Supreme Ct. 1985. Assoc. Obermayer, Rebmannn, Maxwell & Hippel, Phila., 1979-80; asst. exec. dir. Nat. Assn. Coll. and Univ. Attys., Washington, 1981-83; asst. univ. counsel U. Pitts., 1984-85; asst. to v.p. for legal affairs Howard U., Washington, 1985-87; legal counsel U. R.I., R.I. Coll. and C.C. of R.I., Kingston, 1987-94; v.p., gen. counsel Am. U., Washington, 1995—. Bd. dirs. Washington Trust Bank, Washington metro area Am. Corp. Counsels Assn. Mem. Nat. Assns. Coll. and Univ. Attys., R.I. Black Lawyers Assn. Democrat. Avocation: golf. Office: American Univ 4400 Massachusetts Ave NW Washington DC 20016-8165

KENNARD, SHEILA DIANE, consultant to home business entrepreneurs; b. Caribou, Maine, Aug. 20, 1965; d. Melvin and Flora Jane (Michaud) Kennard; children: Daniel Craig, Janelle Marie. Cert. legal asst., Hillcrest Inst., Portland, Maine, 1993; cert med. transcriptionist, At-Home Professions, Ft. Collins, Colo., 1993; cert. in fin. statement analysis, payroll I & collections, Am. Inst. Profl. Bookkeepers, 1995; AS in Bus. Adminstrn., So. Calif. U., 1998. Lic. occupl. sec., Fla.; cert. pvt. investigator; cert. in property mgmt. Sec., data entry processor Aroostook County Courthouse, Caribou, Maine, 1983; typist, adminstrv. asst. Continental Contracting Co., Mascoutah, Ill., Houston, 1986-87; sales assoc. AAFES Main Exch., Torrejon AB, Spain, 1990-91; family daycare provider MWR (USAF), Torrejon AB, Spain, 1991; med. clk., adminstrv. asst. 401st Hosp. (USAF), Torrejon AB, Spain, 1991-92; med. transcriptionist, sec. Bridgeway Ctr., Inc., Ft. Walton Beach, Fla., 1993-94; owner, med. transcriptionist, billing specialist Smith's Bus. Svcs., Eglin AFB, Fla., 1994—2001; office mgr. J.P. Smith's Dental Handpiece Repair, 1996—99, Heppel's Handpiece Repair, Eglin AFB, 2000—01; freelance cons. Tucson, 2002—. Vol. Girl Scouts Am., Eglin AFB, 1994-95; mem. nat. steering com. Clinton/Gore '96 Campaign, Washington, 1995-96. Mem. AAUW, NAFE, Am. Inst. Profl. Bookkeepers, Smithsonian Inst. (assoc.). Roman Catholic. Avocations: snorkeling, travel, reading, cooking, gardening. Office: 553 W Mossman Rd Tucson AZ 85708-3002

KENNEALLY, MICHAEL E., diversified financial services company executive; BS in Econs., MBA, U. Mo. Rsch. analyst Boatmen's Trust Co., 1983—87, instl. portfolio mgr., sr. v.p., dir. rsch., 1993—97; pres.,chief investment officer NationsBank Pvt. Investments, 1997—98; chmn., chief investment officer Banc of Am. Capital Mgmt.; pres., investment mgmt. Bank of Am.; chmn., global CEO Credit Suisse Asset Mgmt, 2003—. Office: Credit Suisse First Boston LLC 11 Madison Ave New York NY 10010-3629 Office Phone: 212-325-2000.

KENNEDAY, ELIZABETH, fine arts educator; b. Orange, Calif., Dec. 7, 1950; m. John Kenneth Corathers II. BA, Calif. State U., Long Beach, 1972, MA, 1980; MFA, The Claremont Grad. U., 1988; PhD, Claremont Grad. U. Lectr. art edn., photography Calif. State U., Long Beach, 2000—. Works in collections of Lydia Pierce, Nathan Pettengill, Thomas Peckenpaugh, Alaska State Mus., Fairbanks, Calif. State U. Spl. Collections, Long Beach. Exhibited in solo and group shows at Angels Gate Cultural Ctr., House of Photographic Art, Goldwyn Hollywood Gallery; rsch. publs. Local Landscapes/Global Issues, 2002, Landscape Into Place, 2003, Beauty, the Subline and Ecological Disaster, The Salton Sea, 2003 Claremont Grad. U. rsch. grantee, 1987, Visual Arts Ctr. of Alaska grantee, 1984, Fulbright grantee, 2003-04. Mem. InSEA, NAEA, CAEA, WIPI, Angels Gate Cultural Ctr. Artist. Roman Catholic. Office: Calif State Univ Art Dept 1250 Bellflower Blvd Long Beach CA 90840

KENNEDY, ADRIENNE LITA, playwright; b. Pitts., Sept. 13, 1931; d. Cornell Wallace and Etta (Haugabook) Hawkins; m. Joseph C. Kennedy, May 15, 1953 (div. 1966); children: Joseph C., Adam. BS, Ohio State U., 1953; student creative writing, Columbia U., 1954-56; student playwrighting, New Sch. Social Research, Am. Theatre Wing, Circle in the Sq. Theatre Sch., 1957-58, 62; doctorate (hon.), Ohio State U., 2003. Mem. playwriting unit Actors Studio, N.Y.C., 1962-65; lectr. Yale U., New Haven, 1972-74; CBS fellow Sch. Drama, N.Y.C., 1973; lectr. Princeton (N.J.) U., 1977; vis. assoc. prof. Brown U., 1979-80. Rep. to conf. Internat. Theatre Inst., Budapest, 1978; vis. lectr. Harvard U., 1990, 91, vis. prof., 1997—. Author: (plays) Funnyhouse of a Negro, 1964, Cities in Bezique, 1965, A Rat's Mass, 1966, A Lesson in Dead Language, 1966, The Lennon Plays, 1968, Sun, Cities of Bezique, 1969; A Movie Star Has To Star in Black and White, 1976, Ohio State Murders, She Talks to Beethoven, 1990, (with Adam Kennedy) Sleep Deprivation Chamber, 1995; (memoirs) People Who Led to My Plays, 1987 (Manhattan Borough Pres.'s award 1988), Letter to My Students, Lancashire Lad; commd. by Empire State Youth Inst., 1979, Onestes, Electra, Juilliard Sch. Music, 1980, Black Children's Day, Rites and Reason, Brown U., 1980; represented in numerous anthologies Norton Anthology of Am. Lit. Recipient Obie award, 1964, 96, Pierre Lecomte du Novy award Lincoln Ctr., 1994, award Am. Acad. Arts and Letters, 1994, Anisfield-Wolf Lifetime Achievement awad, 2003; fellow Guggenheim Found., 1968, Rockefeller Found., 1967-68, NEA, 1993, Lila Wallace Readers Digest, 1994, Yale U., 1974-75; grantee Nat. Endowment Arts, 1973, Rockefeller Found., 1974, Creative Artists Pub. Svc., 1974; Disting. lectr. U. Calif., Berkeley, 1980, 86. Fellow: MLA (hon.); mem.: PEN (bd. dirs. 1976—77). Address: 325 W 89th St New York NY 10024 *I believe in listening to one's inner voices.*

KENNEDY, ANTHONY MCLEOD, United States Supreme Court Justice; b. Sacramento, July 23, 1936; s. Arthur J. and Gladys McLeod Kennedy; m. Mary Davis, June 29, 1963; children: Justin Anthony, Gregory Davis, Kristin Marie. AB, Stanford U., 1958; student, London Sch. Econs., 1957—58; LLB, Harvard U., 1961; JD (hon.), U. Pacific, 1988, U. Santa Clara, 1988. Bar: Calif. 1962, U.S. Tax Ct. 1971. Assoc. Thelen, Martin, Johnson, and Bridges, San Francisco, 1961—63; pvt. practice Sacramento, 1963—67; ptnr. Evans, Jackson & Kennedy, 1967—75; adj. prof. constl. law McGeorge Sch. Law, U. of Pacific, 1965-88; judge U.S. Ct. Appeals (9th cir.), Sacramento, 1975—88; assoc. justice U.S. Supreme Ct., Washington, 1988—. Mem. bd. student advisors Harvard Faculty, 1960-61, Advisory Com. on Codes of Conduct, 1979-87, Com. on Pacific Territories, 1979-88 (chmn., 1982-88), Fed. Jud. Ctr., 1987-88. With Calif. Army Nat. Guard, 1961. Fellow Am. Bar Found. (hon.), Am. Coll. Trial Lawyers (hon.); mem. ABA, Sacramento County Bar Assn., State Bar Calif., Phi Beta Kappa. Office: US Supreme Ct One First St NE Washington DC 20543-0001

KENNEDY, BERNARD JOSEPH, retired utilities executive; b. Niagara Falls, N.Y., Aug. 16, 1931; s. Edward J. and Frances (Coyle) K.; m. Geraldine Drexelius, Sept. 20, 1958; children: Mary Kathleen, Maureen Jean, Patricia, Colleen, Joseph B. BA, Niagara U., 1953; LL.B., U. Mich., 1958. Bar: N.Y. 1960. Legal asst. Nat. Fuel Gas Distbn. Corp., Buffalo, 1958-63, gen. atty., 1963-67, sec., gen. counsel, 1967-75, v.p., gen. counsel, 1975-77, sr. v.p., 1977-87, pres., 1987; chief exec. officer Nat. Fuel Gas Co., Buffalo, 1988—, chmn. bd., 1989—; pres. Nat. Fuel Gas Supply Corp., 1978-89, Penn-York Energy Corp., 1978-89, Seneca Resources Corp., 1983-89, Empire Exploration, 1983-89; chmn. Inst. of Gas Tech., Chgo., 1989—; CEO Nat. Fuel Gas Co., Buffalo, 1989—2002. Chmn. Lloyd's Syndicate 1225; bd. dirs. Associated Electric & Gas Ins. Svc. Ltd. Past chmn. Greater Buffalo Partnership; past chmn., bd. regents, past chmn. coun. Bus. Sch. of Canisius Coll.; past trustee Niagara U.; past chmn. bd. dirs. Erie County chpt. ARC; chmn. Cath. Charities Appeal, 1981; bd. dirs. Nat. Petroleum Coun., 1990-2004. 1st lt. U.S. Army, 1953-55. Mem. ABA (past vice chmn. gas com.), N.Y. State Bar Assn. (chmn. pub. utilities com. 1973), Fed. Energy Bar Assn., Erie County Bar Assn. (past dir.), Am. Gas Assn., Buffalo Club, Buffalo Canoe Club, Country Club of Buffalo, Sitzmarker Ski Club. Home: 6363 Main St Williamsville NY 14221 Office Phone: 716-857-7200. E-mail: kennedy8@natfuel.com.

KENNEDY, BRIAN JAMES, marketing executive; b. N.Y.C., Nov. 7, 1941; s. James and Una K.; m. Donna Lee Rugendorf, Dec. 7, 1968; children: Kerry, Kelly. BS in Fgn. Service, Georgetown U., 1963; grad. Japanese lang., Def. Lang. Inst., 1965; postgrad., NYU, Monterey Inst. Fgn. Studies. Various positions, then v.p. advt. and sales TWA, N.Y.C., 1967-83; sr. v.p. mktg. The Hertz Corp., N.Y.C., 1983-87, exec. v.p. mktg and sales, 1987—. Pres. Duneview Devel. (real estate) Corp., Wainscott, N.Y. Home: 163 Bay Ln Water Mill NY 11976-3103 Office: Hertz Co 225 Brae Blvd Park Ridge NJ 07656-1888

KENNEDY, CAROLINE See SCHLOSSBERG, CAROLINE

KENNEDY, CHARLES, retired neuroscientist, retired medical educator; b. Buffalo, Aug. 27, 1920; m. Eulsum Kennedy, Aug. 27, 1968; 3 children from previous marriage. BA in Chemistry cum laude, Princeton U., 1942; MD, U. Rochester, 1945. Diplomate Am. Bd. Pediats., Am. Bd. Psychiatry and Neurology, lic. N.Y., Pa., DC, Maine, Md. Intern in pathology New Haven Hosp., 1945-46; instr. pathology Sch. Medicine Yale U., New Haven, 1945-46; fellow in child psychiatry Children's Hosp., Buffalo, 1948-49, resident pediatrician, 1949-51; fellow in physiology Grad. Sch. Medicine U. Pa., Phila., 1951-53, assoc. pediats. Sch. Medicine, 1952-55, assoc. in neurology, 1955-58, asst. prof. neurology in pediats., 1958-61, assoc. prof., 1961-67; chief divsn. neurology, dir. child neurology Children's Hosp., Phila., 1959-67; prof. pediats., neurology Sch. Medicine Georgetown U., Washington, 1971-90, prof. emeritus, 1990—. Vis. fellow in neurology Neurol. Inst. Columbia Presbyn. Med. Ctr., 1957—58; mem. Lab. Clin. Sci. Nat. Inst. Mental Health, 1967—68, Lab. Cerebral Metabolism, 1968—95; cons. Pa. Hosp., Phila., 1960—69, Hosp. U. Pa., Phila., 1961—67, Bd. Edn. City of Phila., 1962—64; lectr. U.S. Naval Hosp., Phila., 1962—68; mem. adv. com. dyslexia State of Tex., 1965; guest lectr. Nat. Naval Med. Ctr. Uniformed Svcs. U. Health Scis., 1977—87. Mem. editl. bd. Pediat. Rsch., 1978—84, Brain Rsch., 1980—96, Jour. Cerebral Blood Flow and Metabolism, 1981—88. Lt. (j.g.) USNR, 1946—48. Fellow, Life Ins. Med. Rsch. Fund, 1951—53. Fellow: Coll. Physicians Phila.; mem.: Profs. Child Neurology, Child Neurology Soc., Soc. Neuroscience, Assn. Rsch. Nervous and Mental Disease, Phila. Neurol. Soc. (v.p. 1967), Phila. Pediat. Soc. (pres. 1964), Internat. Soc. Cerebral Blood Flow and Metabolism (dir. 1989—93, chmn. fin. com. 1992—96), Internat. Soc. Neurochemistry, Nat. Bd. Med. Examiners (mem. pediat. com. 1960—64), Am. Soc. Neurochemistry, Am. Acad. Neurology (chmn. sect. child neurology 1964—66, mem. com. problems mental reatardation 1965—67), Am. Neurol. Assn., Am. Acad. Pediats., Am. Pediat. Soc. E-mail: chasken@suscpm-maine.net.

KENNEDY, CHARLES ALLEN, lawyer; b. Maysville, Ky., Dec. 11, 1940; s. Elmer Earl and Mary Frances Kennedy; m. Patricia Ann Louderback, Dec. 9, 1961; 1 child, Mimi Mignon. AB, Morehead State Coll., 1965, MA in Edn., 1968; JD, U. Akron, 1969; LLM, George Washington U., 1974. Bar: Ohio 1969. Asst. cashier Citizens Bank, Felicity, Ohio, 1961-63; tchr Triway Local Sch. Dist., Wooster, Ohio, 1965-67; with office of gen. counsel Fgn. Agr. and Spl. Programs Divsn. USDA, Washington, 1969-71; ptnr. Kauffman, Eberhart, Cicconetti & Kennedy Co., Wooster, 1972-86, Kennedy, Cicconetti, Knowlton & BuyTendyk, LPA, Wooster, 1986—. Mem.: ATLA, ABA, Wayne County Bar Assn., Ohio Acad. Trial Lawyers, Ohio State Bar Assn., Am. Coll. Barristers, Fed. Bar Assn., Lions, Exch. Club, Elks, Phi Delta Kappa, Phi Alpha Delta. Republican. Home: 275 W Henrietta Wooster OH 44691 Office: Kennedy Cicconetti & Know Ken 558 N Market St Wooster OH 44691-3406 Office Phone: 330-262-7555. Personal E-mail: knndy558@netscape.net.

KENNEDY, CHESTER RALPH, JR., retired state official, art director; b. Middleboro, Mass., Apr. 22, 1926; s. Chester Ralph and Mary Carmen (Mello) K.; m. Barbara Ann Partridge, June 27, 1953; children: Karen Brooke, Scott Douglas. BFA, Mass. Coll. Art, 1951; postgrad., New Eng. Adult Edn. Inst., 1959, Boston U., 1966, Brandies U., 1985. Supr. pub. health edn. Mass. Dept. Pub. Health, Boston, 1953-56, coordinator health edn., 1956-74, asst. dir. health edn., 1974-81, dir. health edn., 1981-84, dist. health officer, 1984-89; ret., 1989. Asst. art dir. Barchét Studios, Middleboro, 1949-59, art dir., co-owner, Sherborn, Mass., 1959—; cons. USPHS, Assn. State and Territorial Health Officers; lectr., instr. Harvard, Boston U., Mass. Coll.; mem. Acad. Master Plan Adv. Commn., Mass. State Coll. System; exhibit chmn. 22nd World Health Assembly. Editor: Commonwealth of Mass. Secretarial Reference Manual, 1969; designer blue ribbon exhibit New Eng. Hosp. Assembly, 1969; designer five pvt. homes. Pres. Pub. Health Museum in Mass., 1991-93, mem. exec. bd., 1993-, exec. dir., 2002-; pres. Reach Out, Inc., 1970-74, bd. dirs., 1974-; bd. dirs. Greater Framingham Mental Health Assn., 1974-76; elected to Sherborn Bd. Health, 1974-86; mem. Solid Waste Recovery Tech. Com., 1975-84; co-chair Coalition Organized for Health Edn. in Schs., 1982-89. Served with USN, 1944-46. Recipient Boy Scouts Am. Organizer award, 1941, Commonwealth Mass. Disting. Svc. citation, 1971, Health Edn. citation New Eng. Consortium Health Edn. Assn., 1975, Coalition Organized for Health Edn. in Schs. citation, 1989, hon. award, 2002, Reach Out award, 1977, Southeastern Assn. Health Bds. award, 1989, Michael Dukakis Gov.'s award, 1989, Mass. Dept. Pub. Health award, 1989, Pub. Health Museum Organizer award Mass. Ho. of Reps., 1993, Gov. William Weld Museum Founder award, 1993. Mem. New Eng. Health Edn. Assn. (pres. 1971-72), Mass. Health Coun., New Eng. Health Promotion Coun., Soc. Pub. Health Edn., Mass. Audubon Soc., Mass. Archeol. Soc., Mass. Coll. Art Alumni (pres. 1968-72), Assn. Mass. State Colls. Alumni (pres. 1973-75), Mass. Pub. Health Assn. (health edn. chmn. 1974-76, 25 yr. award 1986, Paul Revere award 1990), Mass. Health Officers Assn. (emeritus, Curtis M. Hillard award 1989, exec. sec. 1992-98), Mass. Assn. Health Bds. (hon., exec. bd. 1990-94), New Eng. Pub. Health Assn. (pres. 1984-85, Ira Hiscock award 1980, 25 yr. award 1989, pres.'s award, 2001). Office: Barchét Studios 178 Washington St Sherborn MA 01770-1022 E-mail: chet.kennedy@att.net.

KENNEDY, CHRISTOPHER P., lawyer; b. Phila., June 25, 1963; s. John and Margaret Kennedy; m. Claudia Piccinini, July 7, 2001. JD, Cath. U. Am., 1989. Judical clk. Ct. Appeals Md., Annapolis, Md., 1989—90; assoc. Smith, Somerville & Case, Balt., 1990—94, Schochor, Federico & Staton, PA, Balt., 1994—99, ptnr., 1999—. Office: Schochor Federico and Staton PA 1211 St Paul Street Baltimore MD 21202 Office Phone: 410-234-1000. Office Fax: 410-234-1010. E-mail: ckennedy@sfspa.com.

KENNEDY, CHRISTOPHER ROBIN, ceramics engineer, director; b. Ottawa, Ont., Can., June 25, 1948; s. Robert Alvin and Ruth Christina (Downie) K.; m. Christine Willa Wayman, Jan. 28, 1978; children: Scott Wayman, Stuart James. BS, Rutgers U., 1969; MS, Pa. State U., 1971, PhD, 1974. Asst. ceramist Argonne Nat. Lab., Ill., 1974-79; ceramist Argonne (Ill.)

Nat. Lab., 1979-82; staff engr. Exxon Rsch. and Engring. Co., Florham Park, N.J., 1982-83, group leader materials devel. group, 1984; mgr. materials rsch. sect. Lanxide Corp., Newark, 1984-87, mgr. def. products devel. sect., 1987-92; mgr. composite devel. and engring. sect., 1992-93; v.p. tech. Lanxide Corp., Newark, 1993-98; dir. R & D Ceramco, Burlington, NJ, 1998—2003; dir. R & D Prosthetics Divsn. Dentsply Internat., 2003—. Contbr. numerous articles to profl. jours. Patentee in field. Mem. Am. Ceramic Soc., Nat. Inst. Ceramic Engrs., Keramos. Office: 550 W College Ave York PA 17405

KENNEDY, CORNELIA GROEFSEMA, federal judge; b. Detroit, Mich., Aug. 4, 1923; d. Elmer H. and Mary Blanche (Gibbons) Groefsema; m. Charles S. Kennedy, Jr. (dec.); 1 son, Charles S. III. BA, U. Mich., 1945, JD with distinction, 1947; LL.D. (hon.), No. Mich. U., 1971, Eastern Mich. U., 1971, Western Mich. U., 1973, Detroit Coll. Law, 1980, U. Detroit, 1987. Bar: Mich. bar 1947. Law clk. to Chief Judge Harold M. Stephens, U.S. Ct. of Appeals, Washington, 1947-48; assoc. Elmer H. Groefsema, Detroit, 1948-52; partner Markle & Markle, Detroit, 1952-66; judge 3d Judicial Circuit Mich., 1967-70; dist. judge U.S. Dist. Ct., Eastern Dist. Mich., Detroit, 1970-79, chief judge, 1977-79; circuit judge U.S. Ct. Appeals, (6th cir.), 1979-99, sr. judge, 1999—. Mem. Commn. on the Bicentennial of the U.S. Constitution (presdl. appointment). Recipient Sesquicentennial award U. Mich. Fellow Am. Bar Found.; mem. ABA, Mich. Bar Assn. (past chmn. negligence law sect.), Detroit Bar Assn. (past dir.), Fed. Bar Assn., Am. Judicature Soc., Nat. Assn. Women Lawyers, Am. Trial Lawyers Assn., Nat. Conf. Fed. Trial Judges (past chmn.), Fed. Jud. Fellows Commn. (bd. dirs.), Fed. Jud. Ctr. (bd. dirs.), Phi Beta Kappa. Office: US Ct of Appeals 6th Circuit 532 Potter Stewart US Courthouse 100 E Fifth St Cincinnati OH 45202*

KENNEDY, CORNELIUS BRYANT, retired lawyer; b. Evanston, Ill., Apr. 13, 1921; s. Millard Bryant and Myrna Estelle (Anderson) K.; m. Anne Martha Reynolds, June 20, 1959; children: Anne Talbot, Lauren K. Mayle. AB, Yale U., 1943; JD, Harvard U., 1948. Bar: Ill. 1949, D.C. 1965. Assoc. Mayer Meyer Austrian & Platt, Chgo., 1949-54, 55-59; asst. to U.S. atty. Dept. Justice, Chgo., 1954-55; counsel to minority leader U.S. Senate, 1959-65; sr. ptnr. Kennedy & Webster, Washington, 1965-82; of counsel Armstrong, Teasdale, Schlafly & Davis, Washington, 1983-88; public mem. Adminstrv. Conf. U.S., 1972-82, sr. conf. fellow, 1982-90, chmn. rulemaking com., 1973-82; ret., 1988. Contbr. articles to law jours. Fin. chmn. Lyric Opera Co., Chgo., 1954; chmn. young adults group Chgo. Coun. Fgn. Rels., 1958-59; pres. English Speaking Union Jrs., Chgo., 1957-59; trustee St. John's Child Devel. Ctr., Washington, 1965-67, 75-87, pres., 1983-85; exec. dir. Supreme Ct. Hist. Soc., 1984-87. 1st lt., AC U.S. Army, 1942-46. Fellow Am. Bar Found.; mem. Am. Law Inst., ABA (coun. sect. adminstrv. law 1967-70, chmn. sect. 1976-77), Fed. Bar Assn. (chmn. com. adminstrv. law 1963-64), Legal Club Chgo., Explorers Club, N.Y.C. Club, Capitol Hill Club, Chevy Chase Club, Sailing Club of Chesapeake, Adventurer's Club. Home: 8462 Brook Rd Mc Lean VA 22102-1703

KENNEDY, CRAIG, rental company executive; b. St. Louis; m. Mary Kennedy; 2 children. Programmer/analyst Enterprise Rent-a-Car, St. Louis, 1989—90, programming supr., 1990, founder Advanced Tech. Group, 1991—92, dir. software devel., 1992—93, asst. v.p., 1993—96, v.p. info. systems, 1996—2002, chief info. officer, 2002—, sr. v.p., 2003—. Office: Enterprise Rent-a-Car 600 Corporate Park Dr Saint Louis MO 63105-4211

KENNEDY, DANE KEITH, history educator; b. Bonne Terre, Mo., May 30, 1951; s. William Joseph Kennedy and Helen Marie Mueller; m. Martha Hoeprich, June 16, 1974; 1 child, Alene Elizabeth. BA, U. Calif., Berkeley, 1973, MA, 1975, PhD, 1981. Asst. prof. U. Nebr., Lincoln, 1981—87, assoc. prof., 1987—94, prof., 1994—2000, chair dept. history, 1997—2000; Elmer L. Kayser prof. George Washington U., Washington, 2000—. Vis. fellow Davis Humanities Ctr. U .Calif., Davis, 1989—90. Author: Islands of White, 1987, The Magic Mountains, 1996, Britain and Empire, 1880-1945, 2002, The Highly Civilized Man: Richard Burton and the Victorian World, 2005. Bd. dirs. German Hist. Inst., Washington, 2000—; chair internat. com. Am. Hist. Assn., Washington, 2000—. Crossing Borders grantee, Ford Found., 1997—2002, Indo-Am. fellow, Coun. for Internat. Exch. of Scholars, 1991, Guggenheim fellow, 2003—. Fellow: Royal Hist. Soc. Office: George Washington U Dept History Phillips T312 2121 Eye St Washington DC 20052*

KENNEDY, DANIEL BOWERS, lawyer, law educator; b. Sewickley, Pa., Sept. 15, 1946; s. George Clark and Charlotte Bowers Kennedy; m. Kim Louise McKenna, June 20, 1981; children: Colin Patrick, Maura Caitlin. BA in English lit., Wash. and Jefferson Coll., 1968; JD cum laude, U. Pitts., 1979. Bar: Ill. 1979, Pa. 1980. Pvt. practice, Champaign, Ill., 1991—; adj. prof. law Coll. Law U. Ill., Champaign, 1998—, adj. prof. law Sch. Social Work Urbana, 1997—, founding editor Ill. Quar. mag. Editor: (magazine) Illinois Quarterly Magazine (Award of Excellence, WICI/PRSA for Magazines; Award f Achievement for Editl. Writing, WICI/PRSA, 1990); mem. law rev.: U. Pitts.; contbr. more than 200 articles to profl. jours. Pres. U. Lab. H.S. Parent Faculty Orgn., Champaign, 1998—2000; packmaster Cub Scouts of Am., Champaign, 1993—96; trainer Champaign County Ct. Apptd. Spl. Advocates, Champaign, 1996—2000; counsel Citizen's Adv. Com. to the Juvenile Ct.; trainer avoiding sex abuse allegations Episcopal Diocese of Springfield, Ill., 1997—2002. Decorated Army Commendation medal U.S. Army; recipient Colin Thorne award for Outstanding Svc., U. Lab. H.S., 1998—2000; scholar, US Army, 1965—69. Republican. Mem. Anglican Ch. Achievements include development of training standards for guardians ad litem in juvenile abuse and neglect cases; first juvenile abuse and neglect law course for the University of Illinois. Avocations: writing, fly fishing. Home: 1307 Belmeade Dr Champaign IL 61821 Office: Attorney at Law One E Main Plaza Ste 217 Champaign IL 61820 Office Phone: 217-355-1458. Home Fax: 217-355-4964; Office Fax: 217-355-4964. Personal E-mail: dbk1946@yahoo.com.

KENNEDY, DAVID BOYD, foundation executive, lawyer; b. Ann Arbor, Mich., Sept. 2, 1933; s. James Alexander and Elizabeth (Earhart) K.; m. Sally Martin Pyne, 1964; children: Jane Elizabeth Mack, Douglas Earhart. Student, McGill U., 1951-52, U. Mich., 1952-54; AB, Ind. U., 1958; LLB, U. Mich., 1963. Bar: Mich. 1964, Wyo. 1965. Pvt. practive law, Sheridan, Wyo., 1964-84; pres. Earhart Found., Ann Arbor, Mich., 1985—2003, trustee, 1979—. Trustee Citizens Rsch. Coun. of Mich.; chmn., bd. dirs. Inst. for Justice, Washington; mem. bd. overseers Hoover Instn./Stanford U. Mem. Wyo. Ho. Reps., 1967-72; chmn. Wyo. Rep. State Ctrl. Com., 1971-73; Rep. nat. committeeman, 1976-80, vice chmn., 1978-80; atty. gen. State of Wyo., 1974-75; mem. Mont Pelerin Soc.; apptd. mem. Pres.'s Com. on Arts and Humanities, Washington, 1990-93; bd. dirs. Philanthropy Roundtable, Washington, 1993-2000; bd. dirs. Univ. Music Soc., 1986-90, pres., 1990; trustee World of Learning, Inc., Brattleboro, Vt., 1993-98. With U.S. Army, 1954-57. Mem. Wyo. Bar Assn., Mich. Bar Assn. Republican. Office: Earhart Found 2200 Green Rd Ste H Ann Arbor MI 48105-1569 Office Phone: 734-761-8592.

KENNEDY, DAVID BURL, physician; b. Indpls., Jan. 26, 1950; s. Robert Dean and Esther Evelyn (Stephani) K.; m. Barbara Anne Ehrgott, Jan. 6, 1973; children: Elizabeth Anne, Jeffrey Townsend, Catherine Patricia, Marissa Rose. B.S., Ind. U., 1972, M.D., 1975. Diplomate Am. Bd. Psychiatry and Neurology. Intern, resident Ind. U. Med. Ctr., Indpls., 1975-78; cons. psychiatrist Psychiat. Clinics of Ind., Anderson, 1977, Four County Mental Health Ctr., Logansport, Ind., 1980-86; staff psychiatrist Regional Mental Health Ctr., Kokomo, Ind., 1978-80; pres. David B. Kennedy, M.D., Inc. and Kennedy Clinics, Indpls. and Kokomo, 1980—; clin. prof. psychiatry Ind. U. Sch. Medicine, Indpls., 1978—; active staff St. Vincent Stress Ctr., Indpls.; assoc. med. dir. Logansport St. Hosp.,1994-2001; med. dir., 2002-.Mem. AMA, Ind. State Med. Assn., Marion County Med. Soc., Am. Psychiat. Assn., Ind. Psychiat. Soc., Phi Beta Kappa. Club: Columbia, Skyline (Indpls.). Avocations: boating, computers. Office Phone: 765-453-6767. Business E-Mail: kennedyclinic@sbcbglobal.net.

KENNEDY, DAVID MICHAEL, historian, educator; b. Seattle, July 22, 1941; s. Albert John and Mary Ellen (Caufield) Kennedy; m. Judith Ann Osborne, Mar. 14, 1970; children: Ben Caufield, Elizabeth Margaret, Thomas Osborne. BA, Stanford U., 1963; MA, Yale U., 1964, PhD, 1968; MA, Oxford U., 1995; D (hon.), LaTrobe U., 2001. From asst. prof. history to prof. Stanford U., Calif., 1967—80, prof., 1980—, chmn. program in internat. relations, 1977—80, assoc. dean Sch. Humanities and Scis., 1981—85, William Robertson Coe prof. history and Am. studies, 1987—93, Donald J. McLachlan prof. history, 1993—, chair, history dept., 1990—94. Vis. prof. U. Florence, Florence, Italy, 1976—77; lectr. Internat. Comms. Agy., 1976—77; vis. prof. Am. history Oxford U., 1995—96, Tanner lectr., 2003; co-dir. Bill Lane Ctr. Study of the North Am. West, 2005. Author: Birth Control in America: The Career of Margaret Sanger, 1970 (Bancroft prize, John Gilmary Shea Prize), Over Here: The First World War and American Society, 1980, Freedom from Fear: The American People in Depression and War, 1929-1945, 1999 (Pulitzer Prize, 2000, Francis Parkman prize, 2000, Ambassador's prize, 2000, Calif. Gold medal for lit., 2000); author: (with Thomas A. Bailey and Lizabeth Cohen) The American Pageant: A History of the Republic, 13th edit., 2005; co-editor: Power and Responsibility: Case Studies in American Leadership, 1986; mem. adv. bd. (TV program) The American Experience, Sta. WGBH, 1986—. Mem. planning group Am. Issues Forum, 1974—75; bd. dirs. CORO Found., 1981—87, Environ. Traveling Companions, 1986—, Stanford U. Bookstore, 1994—2003, The Pulitzer Prizes, 2002—. Recipient Richard W. Lyman award, Stanford U. Alumni Assn., 1989, Francis Parkman prize, 2000, Ambs. Book prize, 2000, Calif. Book award, 2000, Pulitzer prize, 2000; fellow, Am. Coun. Learned Socs., 1971—72, John Simon Guggenheim Meml. Found., 1975—76, Ctr. for Advanced Study in Behavioral Scis., 1986—87, Stanford Humanities Ctr., 1989—90. Fellow: Am. Philos. Soc., Am. Acad. Arts and Scis.; mem.: Soc. Am. Historians, Orgn. Am. Historians, Am. Hist. Assn. Democrat. Roman Catholic. Office: Stanford U Dept History Stanford CA 94305 Office Phone: 650-723-0351. Business E-Mail: dmk@stanford.edu.

KENNEDY, DAVID WILLIAM, law educator; b. Phila., Apr. 5, 1954; AB in History & Internat. Rels., with honors, Brown U., 1976; MALD in Internat. Rels., Fletcher Sch. Law & Diplomacy, Tufts U., 1979, PhD in Internat. Rels., 1984; JD magna cum laude, Harvard U., 1980. Bar: DC 1980. John Harvey Gregory lectr. on world orgn. Harvard Law Sch., Cambridge, Mass., 1981—83, asst. prof. law, 1983—86, prof. law, 1986—, Henry L. Shattuck prof. law, 1994—2003, Manley O. Hudson prof. law, 2003—, dir. European Law Rsch. Ctr., 1991—, faculty dir. grad. & internat. legal studies, 1991—97; of counsel Cleary, Gottlieb, Steen & Hamilton, Brussels, 1989—90. Vis. prof. U. Paris X, Nanterre, 1995—96, 1996—97, 1998, 2001—02, U. Paris II, 1998, U. Toronto, 1998, 99, NYU Law Sch., 1999, Australian Nat. U., 2000, U. Turin, 2001, 02, Paris I Pantheon Sorbonne, 2005; vis. scholar Sch. Oriental and African Studies, U. London, 2000—01. Author: The Dark Sides of Virtue: Reassessing International Humanitarianism, 2004. Fellow, Inst. Internat. Law, Kiel U. & Inst. Internat. Affairs, Hamburg U., Germany, 1980—81; Fulbright Fellow, Belgium, 1984, Alexander von Humboldt Stiftung and Sheldon Fellow, Germany. Mem.: Coun. Fgn. Rels. Office: Harvard Law Sch 1563 Massachusetts Ave Cambridge MA 02138 Office Phone: 617-495-3132. Office Fax: 617-496-4947. Business E-Mail: dkennedy@law.harvard.edu.*

KENNEDY, DAVID WILLIAM, otolaryngologist, medical educator; b. York, Eng., June 27, 1948; s. Michael Leo and Winifred Pearl (Shepherd) K.; m. Edna Mae Schirmer, Apr. 20, 1978; children: Garrett David, Kirin Suzanne. Ed. pre-med. program, Ampleforth Coll., York, 1962-66; MD, Royal Coll. Surgeons, Ireland, 1972. Diplomate Am. Bd. Otolaryngology, Am. Bd. Head and Neck Surgery; lic. physician Pa., Md. Intern St. Laurence's Hosp., Dublin, 1972-73; asst. resident in surgery Johns Hopkins U., Balt., 1973-74, asst. resident in otolaryngology, 1974-77, mem. staff, 1977-91, chief resident in otolaryngology, asst. prof. otolaryngology, 1977-78, asst. prof., 1978-86, assoc. prof. otolaryngology-head and neck surgery, 1986-91, assoc. prof. neurosurgery, 1987-91; mem. staff Loch Raven VA Hosp., Balt., 1980-87, cons. physician, 1987-91; mem. staff Sinai Hosp. Balt., 1981-88; chmn. U. Pa. Med. Ctr., Phila., 1991—2003; mem. staff VA Hosp., Phila., 1991—; vice dean profl. svcs. U. Pa. Sch. of Medicine, 2002—; sr. v.p. U. Pa. Health Sys., 1991—. Dir. Penn Internat. Rhinology Course, Phila., 1991—; spkr. in field; lectr. in field. Contbg. author: Rhinitis, 2d edit., 1991, Diseases of the Nose, Throat, Ear, Head and Neck, 1991, Otolaryngology, 3d edit., 1991, Surgery for Skull Base Tumors, 1991, Sinus Disease: Guide to First Line Management, 1994, Diseases of the Sinuses: Diagnosis and Management, Living with Chronic Sinusitis, 2004, others; mem. editl. bd. Ear, Nose and Throat Jour., 1983—, Am. Jour. Rhinology, 1986—, Laryngoscope, 1988—, Auris Nasus Larynx, 1996—, ACTA Oto-Rhino-Laryngologica Belgica, 1995—; editor-in-chief (otolaryngology) Am. Jour. Rhinology, 1984—, Current Opinion in Otolaryngology and Head and Neck Surgery, 1992—, Jour. Otolaryngology, 1993—; editor Auris Nasus Larynx, 1996—, ACTA Oto-Rhino-Larynngologica Belgica, 1995—; contbr. numerous articles to profl. jours. Recipient Leonard Abrahamson Meml. Gold medal, 1971, Lyons Meml. medal, 1971, gold medal Coombe Lying-In Hosp., 1971, Reuben-Harvey prize, 1972, Coun.'s prize and gold medal, 1972, Sr. William Wilde medal, 1995, Predl. Citation Am. Acad. Otolaryngology - Head and Neck Surgery, 2002; rsch. grantee Schering Corp., 1981, HHS, 1983-88, Norwich-Eaton Corp., 1984-86, Minn. Mining and Mfg. Co., 1984, Healthtek, 1990-91. Fellow Am. Acad. Otolaryngology-Head and Neck Surgery (mem. hearing subcom. 1985-91, mem. rhinology-paranasal sinus com. 1986-93, 97—, mem. CPT com. 1992-97, legis. alt. bd. govs. 1991—, mem. adv. coun. on continuing edn. with TV subcom. 1994, instr. endoscopic sinus surgery 1985, mem. internat. otolaryngology com. 2000)), Royal Coll. Surgeons (anatomy demonstrator/lectr. 1972-73, vis. prof. 1980-81, Sir William Wheeler Meml. medal 1972, Fitzsimmons Gold medal for surgery 1972, Bronze medal), Royal Coll. Surgeons (Ireland); mem. ACS (com. on emerging surg. tech. and edn. 1999), AMA (hon.), NAS-Inst. Medicine, Am. Rhinologic Soc. (bd. dirs. 1988-96, v.p. 1989-90, pres. 1992-93, cons. to bd. dirs. 1987-88), Internat. Rhinologic Soc. (bd. dirs. 1995—, v.p. 2004-), Phila. Laryngol. Soc., Assn. Acad. Depts. Otorhinolaryngology (pres. 1996-98), Soc. Univ. Otolaryngologists (mem. nominating com. 1985-86), Nat. Acad. Scis., Inst. of Medicine, Pa. Acad. Otolaryngology, John Morgan Soc., Johns Hopkins Med. and Surg. Assn., Danish Otolaryngology Soc. (hon.), Johns Hopkins Soc. Scholars. Achievements include introduction of endoscopic sinus surgery to U.S.; development of extended applications of endoscopic surgical techniques; clinical development of surgical localizers. Office: Univ Pa Med Ctr 5 Ravdin 3400 Spruce St Philadelphia PA 19104-4206 Office Phone: 215-662-6971.

KENNEDY, DONALD, editor, environmental scientist, educator; b. NYC, Aug. 18, 1931; s. William Dorsey and Barbara (Bean) Kennedy; children: Laura Page, Julia Hale stepchildren: Cameron Rachel, Jamie Christopher. AB, Harvard U., 1952, AM, 1954, PhD, 1956; DSc (hon.), Columbia U., Williams Coll., U. Mich., U. Ariz., U. Rochester, Reed Coll., Whitman Coll., Coll. William & Mary. Mem. faculty Stanford (Calif.) U., 1960-77, prof. biol. scis., 1965-77, chmn. dept., 1965-72, sr. cons. sci. and tech. policy Exec. Office of Pres., 1976, commr. FDA, 1977-79, provost, 1979-80, pres., 1980-92, prof. emeritus, Bing prof. environ. sci., 1992—. Bd. overseers Harvard U., 1970—76; bd. dirs. Health Effects Inst., Nat. Commn. Pub. Svc., Carnegie Commn. Sci., Tech. and Govt. Author: Academic Duty, 1997; mem. editl. bd. Jour. Neurophysiology, 1969—75, Sci., 1973—77; editor-in-chief: Sci., 2000—; contbr. articles to profl. jours. Bd. dirs. Carnegie Endowment Internat. Peace, David &I Lucile Packard Fedn. Fellow: AAAS, Am. Acad. Arts and Scis.; mem.: NAS, Am. Philos. Soc. Office: Stanford Univ Inst Internat Studies Encina Hall 401 Stanford CA 94305-6055 Office Phone: 650-725-2749. Business E-Mail: kennedyd@stanford.edu.

KENNEDY, DUNCAN MCLEAN, law educator; b. Washington, DC, March 4, 1942. AB in Economics, Harvard U., 1964; LLB, Yale U., 1970. Law clk. to Justice Potter Stewart, US Supreme Ct., 1970-71; asst. prof. law Harvard Law Sch., Cambridge, Mass., 1971-76, prof., 1976-, Carter prof. gen. jurisprudence, 1996-. Vis. prof. law U. Paris I, 1998; disting. vis. prof. Suffolk U. Sch. Law, 2002. Author: Legal Education and the Reproduction of Hierarchy, 1983, Sexy Dressing, etc., 1993, A Critique of Adjudication, 1997, Libertad y restriccion en la decision judicial, 1999, Legal Education and the Reproduction of Hierarchy: A Polemic Against the System, A Critical Edition, 2004. Office: Harvard Law Sch 1563 Massachusetts Ave Cambridge MA 02138 Office Phone: 617-495-4619. Office Fax: 617-496-4863. Business E-Mail: kennedy@law.harvard.edu.*

KENNEDY, EDWARD MOORE (TED KENNEDY), senator; b. Boston, Feb. 22, 1932; s. Joseph Patrick and Rose (Fitzgerald) K.; m. Joan Kennedy (div. 1982); children: Kara Anne, Edward Moore, Patrick Joseph; m. Victoria Anne Reggie, 1992. AB, Harvard U., 1956; postgrad., Internat. Law Sch., The Hague, Netherlands, 1958; LL.B., U. Va., 1959. Bar: Mass. 1959, U.S. Supreme Ct. 1963. Asst. dist. atty., Suffolk County, Mass., 1961-62; U.S. senator from Mass., 1962—; chmn. judiciary com., 1979-81; ranking Dem. mem. labor and human resources com., 1981—; also mem. armed service, joint econ., labor and human resources (chmn. full com., chmn. subcom. on health 1971-80) and judiciary coms.; also mem. Dem. steering & coordination com.; chmn. health, edn., labor and pensions com. Author: Decisions for a Decade, 1968, In Critical Condition: The Crisis in America's Health Care, 1972, Our Day and Generation, 1979, (with Mark O. Hatfield) Freeze: How You Can Help Prevent Nuclear War, 1979. Pres. Joseph P. Kennedy, Jr. Found., from 1961; trustee Children's Hosp. Med. Ctr., Boston, John F. Kennedy Library, Boston Symphony (emeritus), John F. Kennedy Ctr. for Performing Arts, Robert F. Kennedy Meml. Found., Boston Coll., Mass. Gen. Hosp. Served with AUS, 1951-53. Decorated knight comdr. Order of Phoenix (Greece), grande croce Al Merito della Republica Italiana (Italy), Order el Sol (Peru); named One of 10 Outstanding Young Men, U.S. Jaycees, 1967; recipient meritorious svc. citation U.S. Com. for Refugees and Am. Immigration and Citizenship Coun., Solidarity award Nat. Conf. on Soviet Jewry, award Nat. Mil. Family Assn., 1985, Homeric award Chian Fedn., Scopus award Am. Friends Hebrew U., Hubert H. Humphrey award Leadership Conf. on Civil Rights, others. Mem. Tech. Assessment Bd., Congl. Friends of Ireland, Biomed. Ethics Bd., Arms Control Observer Group, Commn. on the Bicentennial of the U.S. Constitution, Martin Luther King Jr. Fed. Holiday Commn., NAACP. Democrat. Office: US Senate 317 Russell Senate Bldg Washington DC 20510-0001*

KENNEDY, ELAINE, religious studies educator, writer; b. York, Pa., Feb. 20, 1949; d. Wilford Leon and Catherine Artella Myers; m. Neil Craig Kennedy, June 10, 1972; children: Justin, Jason, Joyce. B in religious Edn., Bapt. Bible Sem., Clark Summit, Pa., 1971; student in Religious Edn., Asia Bapt. Theol. Sem. Tchr. 1st grade Chester (S.C.) Bapt. Ch., 1971—72; missionary Assn. Bapt. Evangelism, Philippines, 1975—. Author: Christian Education in the Church for Children, 2000, Baptist Centennial History of the Philippines, 2000, Leading and Guiding Youth, 2003. Republican. Avocations: piano, counted cross stitch, sewing, swimming. Home: 5908 Bennetts Rd Camillus NY 13031 Personal E-mail: ncraigkennedy@yahoo.com.

KENNEDY, ELIZABETH CAROL, psychologist, educator; b. Rochester, N.Y., May 5, 1948; d. Carl Elmore and Ruth Frances (Loebs) Riggs; m. James Barry Elvin, July 29, 1967 (div. Jan. 1989); 1 child, Krista Ann; m. William Jerald Kennedy, Aug. 12, 1989 (div. Jan. 1997). AA, Broward C.C., Coconut Creek, Fla., 1986; BA, Fla. Atlantic U., 1989, MA, 1993, PhD, 1998. Paraprofl. gifted edn. Havencroft Elem. Sch., Olathe, Kans., 1980-83; asst. recreational therapist South Fla. State Hosp., Pembroke Pines, 1987-88; asst. mental health therapist Ft. Lauderdale (Fla.) Hosp., 1986-89; instr. psychology Fla. Atlantic U., Boca Raton, 1990-96; rsch. asst., 1993-96; asst. prof. Southeastern Okla. State U., Durant, 1996—. Statis. cons. South Fla., 1994-96. Co-author: (book chpt.) Conflict in Child and Adolescent Development, 1992; contbr. articles to profl. jours. Mem. APA, Am. Psychol. Soc., Soc. for Rsch. in Child Devel., Phi Kappa Phi (scholarship 1989), Psi Chi. Avocations: scuba diving, travel, painting, skiing. Office: Southeastern Okla State U Dept Psychology/Counseling Durant OK 74701-0609 E-mail: ekennedy@sosu.edu.

KENNEDY, ELIZABETH MAE, musician; b. Medford, Mass., Oct. 16, 1949; d. Thomas Power and Anne Cecelia (Coyne) Sullivan; m. William David Kennedy, Oct. 12, 1970 (div. 1984); children: Mary Elizabeth, Jonathan Martin. AS, N.S. C.C., 1969; student, Aquinas Coll., 1991—92. Cert. liturgical musician music and liturgy. Retail sales mgmt. Jordan Marsh Co., Peabody, Mass., 1966—69; retail mgmt. Sears, Roebuck and Co., Lynn, Mass., 1969—70; asst. bookkeeper Henry Leather Co., Peabody, 1970—76; office mgr. Bartlett and Steadman Co. Inc., Marblehead, Mass., 1981—90. Bandleader, performer New England Area, 1983—; music dir., contract organist St. John The Evangelist Ch., Swampscott, Mass., 1985-98; co-founder New Sch. of Music and Performing Arts, Marblehead, Mass., 1994; dir. music St. Charles Borromeo Ch., Waltham, Mass., 1998-99, Incarnation Parish, Melrose, Mass., 1999-2003. Organizer Devereux Neighborhood Assn.; active North Shore Piano Tchrs. Guild, 1988—, v.p., 1998-2000, co-pres., 2000-02; chairperson Marblehead Festival of the Arts, 1998-99. Democrat. Roman Catholic. Avocations: reading, swimming, midi, computers. Home: 46 Ocean Ave Marblehead MA 01945-3616 Fax: 781-631-1519. E-mail: elizmkenn@aol.com.

KENNEDY, EUGENE CULLEN, psychology professor, writer; b. Syracuse, N.Y., Aug. 28, 1928; s. James Donald and Gertrude Veronica (Cullen) K.; m. Sara Connor Charles, Sept. 3, 1977. AB, Maryknoll Coll., 1950; STB, Maryknoll Sem., 1953, MRE, 1954; MA, Cath. U. Am., 1958, PhD, 1962; LHD (hon.), Barat Coll., 1990. Lic. psychologist Ill., 1961. Instr. psychology Maryknoll Sem., Clarks Summit, Pa., 1955-56, Cath. U., Washington, 1959-60; prof. psychology Maryknoll Coll., Glen Ellyn, Ill., 1960-69, Loyola U., Chgo., 1969-95, prof. emeritus, 1995—. Cons. Menninger Found., 1965-67; mem. profl. adv. bd. Chgo. Dept. Mental Health; bd. dirs., cons. King Kullen Grocery Co., 1985—, mem. exec. com., 1994—; ptnr. Associated Growth Investors, 1992—; bd. dirs. Crown Mktg. Group, Inc. Author 40 books, including Himself! The Life and Times of Richard J. Daley, 1978 (Carl Sandburg award 1978), Father's Day, 1981 (Soc. of Midland Authors fiction award 1981, Friends of Lit. award 1981, Carl Sandburg award 1981), Queen Bee, 1982, The Now and Future Church, 1984, (with Sara Charles) Defendant, 1985, Tomorrow's Catholics, Yesterday's Church, 1988, Fixes, 1989, Cardinal Bernardin, 1989, (with Sara Charles) On Becoming a Counselor, 1990, (with Sara Charles) Authority, 1996, This Man Bernadin, 1996, My Brother Joseph, 1997, The Unhealed Wound, 2001, Thou Art That, 2001, Meditations at the Center of the World, 2002, Cardinal Bernardin's Stations of the Cross, 2003; author TV play: I Would Be Called John, PBS, 1987; also articles, book revs.; columnist Religion News Svc., 1991-92, 97—, Chgo. Tribune, 1992-93. Trustee U. Dayton, 1977—86. Recipient Thomas More medal, 1972, 78, Wilbur award Religious Pub. Relations Council. Fellow Am. Psychol. Assn. (div. pres. 1975-76); mem. Authors Guild. Democrat. Roman Catholic. *My principal goal in all my work is to try to understand and to try to help others understand what is so human about all of us.*

KENNEDY, EUGENE RICHARD, microbiologist, university dean; b. Scranton, Pa., July 3, 1919; s. Thomas A. and Margaret (Culkin) K.; m. Marjorie Giblin, July 24, 1945; children— Anne, Michael, Christine. BS, U. Scranton, 1941; MS, Cath. U., 1943; PhD, Brown U., 1949. Diplomate Am. Bd. Microbiology. Serologist Walter Reed Army Med. Center, Washington, 1942; instr. bacteriology and immunology R.I. Hosp. Sch. of Nursing, Providence, 1946-48, Brown U., Providence, 1946-48; instr. Cath. U. Am., Washington, 1949-51, asst. prof., 1951-55, assoc. prof., 1956-66, prof. microbiology, 1966-85, prof. emeritus, 1985—, dean Sch. Arts and Scis., 1973-85. Contbr. articles to profl. jours. Served to capt. Med. Service Corps U.S. Army, 1943-46. Mem. Am. Soc. for Microbiology, AAAS, Sigma Xi, Phi Beta Kappa. Home: 15100 Interlachen Dr Apt 912 Silver Spring MD 20906-5608 Office: Cath U McCort-Ward Bldg Washington DC 20064

KENNEDY, EVELYN SIEFERT, foundation executive, textiles executive; b. Pitts., Nov. 11, 1927; d. Carmine and Assunta (Iacobucci) Rocci; m. George J. Siefert, May 30, 1953 (dec. 2000); children: Paul Kenneth, Carl Joseph,

Ann Marie; m. Lyle H. Kennedy II, Oct. 12, 1974 (dec. 1990); m. Frederick J. Commentucci, Feb. 24, 2001. BS magna cum laude, U. RI, 1969, MS in Textiles and Clothing, 1970. Accredited appraiser of personal property, Internat. Soc. Appraisers. With Pitts. Pub. Schs., 1945-50, Goodyear Aircraft Corp., Akron, Ohio, 1950-54; clothing instr. Groton (Conn.) Dept. Adult Edn., 1958-68; pres. Sewtique, Groton, 1970—, Sewtique II, New London, Conn., 1986; v.p. Kennedy Capital Advisors, Groton, 1973-85, Kennedy Mgmt. Corp., Groton, 1974-85, Kennedy Intervest, Inc., Groton, 1975-85; pres., exec. dir. PRIDE Found., Inc., Groton, 1978—. Clothing cons. Coop. Ext. Svc., Dept. Agr.; internat. lectr. on clothing for disabled and elderly; adj. faculty U. Conn., Ea. Conn. State Coll., St. Joseph Coll.; hon. prof. U. RI, assoc. prof., 1987-2000; fed. expert witness Care Label Law, FTC, 1976; mem. Major Appliance Consumer Action Panel, 1983-89. Author: Dressing With Pride, 1980, Clothing Accessibility: A Lesson Plan to Aid the Disabled and Elderly, 1983, Textiles Speak, 1996. Regional adv. coun. SBA Active Corps Execs., Hartford, 1985—; bd. dirs. Small Bus. Devel. Ctr., 1989—, Easter Seal Rehab. Ctr. Southeastern Conn., Southeastern Conn. Women's Ctr., 1997—, Women's Ctr. New London County, 1997—; bus. adv. coun. U. RI, 1979-89, trustee, 1985—; active LWV; mem. Groton Vocat. Edn. Adv. Coun. Recipient award of distinction U. RI, 1969, Adv. of Yr. SBA, 1984, Outstanding Svc. in Cmty., 1991; named Woman of Yr. Bus. and Profl. Women's Club, 1977, Conn. Home Economist of Yr., 1987; named to Wall of Fame U. RI, 2004. Mem. Internat. Sleep Coun. (consumer affairs rep., SBA award 1991), Internat. Soc. Appraisers (accredited appraiser personal property, panelist FMHA roster, farmer's credit mediator 1989-92), Nat. Assn. Bedding Mfrs., Conn. Home Economists in Bus. (founder 1977, Women of Yr. 1987), Nat. Home Economists in Bus. (chmn. internat. rels., nat. fin. chmn. 1986), Am. Home Econs. Assn., Coll. and Univ. Bus. Instrs. of Conn., Am. Occupl. Therapy Assn. (resource cons. 1986—), Web-Re-Stor Assn. (wedding restoration specialist 1993-2000), Southeastern Women's Network, Textile Soc. Am., Fashion Group, Costume Soc. Am., New London Zonta Club, Bus. and Profl. Women's Club (Outstanding Women of Yr. 1977), Omicron Nu. Office: 391 Long Hill Rd Groton CT 06340-3812 Office Phone: 800-332-9122. Personal E-mail: textileappraisal@aol.com.

KENNEDY, FAYE, retired social worker, author; b. Kansas City, Mo., Apr. 3, 1931; d. Wiley Choice and Zella Rae (Jackman) K.; m. Patrick Joseph Daly, Jan. 7, 1961. AA, Pasadena City Coll., 1951; BA, Hunter Coll., 1955; cert., Alliance Francaise, Paris, 1956. Vocat. counselor N.Y. State Divsn. Employment, N.Y.C., 1957-65; social worker N.Y. State Div. Parole, N.Y.C., 1965-77. Author: Good-bye, Diane, 1976; assoc. editor Afro-Hawaii News, 1990-92. Hawaii adv. com. U.S. Civil Rights Commn., Honolulu, 1990—; active Hawaii State Commn. on Status of Women, Honolulu, 1993-95, Hawaii Civil Rights Commn., Honolulu, 1995-2003, Honolulu County Com. Status of Women, 2004—, Martin Luther King Jr. Commn., Honolulu, 1989-93; del. Hawaii Dem. Party State Cen. Com., 1994—, Dem. Nat. Conv., 1996, 2000, 04; bd. dirs. Hawaii Literacy, Inc., 1987-97, Hawaii Youth at Risk, 1991-94, ACLU of Hawaii, 1999-2002; 1st v.p. NAACP-Hawaii, 2003. Recipient Gov.'s Cert. of Appreciation, State of Hawaii, 1989-93, Making of the King Holiday award Martin Luther King Jr. Commn., 1991, Outstanding Achievement award Hawaii Literacy, Inc., 1988, 92, Outstanding African Ams. citation Mahogany, 1996, Afro-Hawaii News, 1992, Hawaii Personalities Recognition citation RSVP mag., 1989, Lifetime Dedication to Pub. Svc. cert. Honolulu City Coun., 1996. Mem. Hawaii Women's Polit. Caucus (pres. 2003-), Hawaii Yacht Club. Democrat. Avocations: reading, writing, movies, gardening. Home: 3071 Felix St Honolulu HI 96816-1911

KENNEDY, GARY F., air transportation executive, lawyer; b. May 13, 1955; m. Michele Valdez; 4 children. BA magna cum laude, U. Utah, 1977, JD, 1980. Atty. Roe & Fowler, Salt Lake City, 1980—82, Suitter, Axland, Armstrong and Hanson, Salt Lake City, 1982—84; atty. legal dept. Am. Airlines, 1984—87, sr. atty. legal dept., 1987—91, mng. dir.-properties corp. real estate dept., 1991—96, v.p. corp. real estate, 1996—2003, sr. v.p., gen. counsel, 2003—. Mem.: Phi Beta Kappa. Office: AMR Corp 4333 Amon Carter Blvd Fort Worth TX 76155

KENNEDY, GWENDOLYN DEBRA, artist, scriptwriter, playwright; b. Daly City, Calif., Nov. 18, 1960; d. Adolphus Brooks and Ella (Robinson) K.; children: Gwendolyn Fincher, Edward James, Jr. AA in Theater Prodn., City Coll. San Francisco, 1992. Artist Walt Disney Animation Art, 1991; artist animation and fine art www.blackpantherpartypress.tv, 1994—; owner Black Panther Party Press and Pub., 1993—. Owner mail order co. La Chateau D'Gwendolyn Kennedy Co., 1991—. Author: Billie Holliday Collection Book, 1993, Kane Kut Murder Trial, 1993, Poetic Justice, 1994, No Struggle No Progress, 1995, Nyami the Sky God, 1996. Recipient Journalist of Yr. award City News Svc., Mo., 1995. Lutheran. Avocations: guitar, ballet, art, track, piano, computers. Home: 285 Bellevue Ave Daly City CA 94014-1305 Office: PO Box 135 Daly City CA 94016-1305 Personal E-mail: sareenlove@aol.com.

KENNEDY, HAROLD EDWARD, lawyer; b. Pottstown, Pa., Oct. 18, 1927; s. Freeman S. and Alice (Brehm) K.; m. Eleanor Henry, Jan. 9, 1960; children: Kathleen, Nancy, Harold, Robert, Ellen, Anne, Susan. Student, Colgate U., 1945-47; LLB, Syracuse U., 1952. Bar: N.Y. 1952, U.S. Dist. Ct. (no. dist.) N.Y. 1954, U.S. Supreme Ct. 1956, U.S. Dist. Ct. (so. dist.) N.Y. 1962. Ptnr. Taylor & Kennedy, Amsterdam, N.Y., 1952-59; sr. assoc. Kissam & Halpin, N.Y.C., 1959-60; vice chmn., gen. counsel, dir. mergers and acquisitions Foster Wheeler Corp., Clinton, N.J., 1960-94, legal advisor, 1994-97, also bd. dirs. Bd. dirs. W.I. Refining Ltd. Trustee First Presbyn. Ch., Orange, N.J., 1973-76, St. Barnabas Corp., 1996-2003; sec., 1996-2003, St. Barnabas Med. Ctr., 1986-2003, Kessler Inst. for Rehab., 1987-97, vice chmn., 1992-97, Union Hosp., 1994-2003, Beth Israel Hosp., 1996-2003; bd. visitors Syracuse U. Coll. of Law, 1987-2003. Served with USAF, 1945-47. Mem. Order of Coif, Baltusrol Golf Club, Sea Pines Country Club.

KENNEDY, HARVEY EDWARD, science information publishing executive; b. Goldsboro, N.C., Oct. 2, 1928; s. Robert H. and Zilphia E. (Taylor) K.; m. Dorothy Childress, Aug. 18, 1951; children: Connie Grayce, Jeffrey Reynolds. BA, Barton Coll., 1948; MS, N.C. State Univ., 1952; PhD in Microbiology, N.C. State U., 1954. Rsch. scientist U. N.C. Med. Ctr., Chapel Hill, 1954-58; asst. prof. Ohio State U., Columbus, 1958-61; dir. product devel. Vetco div. Johnson & Johnson, New Brunswick, N.J., 1961-67; dir. sci. affairs Biosis, Phila., 1967-75, exec. dir., 1975-80, pres., 1980-93. Editor: (spl. series) International Communication for Biomedical Research, 1980. Mem. Fahrney Medal com. Sci. and Arts com., Franklin Inst., 1985-93. Mem. Internat. Fedn. Sci. Editors (interim bd., v.p. 1980-83, 91—), Internat. Orgn. Plant Info. com. 1991-93), Am. Soc. Info. Sci., Am. Inst. Biol. Scis. (exec. com. 1983-88, pres. 1987), Coun. Biology Editors (pres. 1978-79, award for excellence in sci. communication 1990), Nat. Fedn. Abstracting and Info Svcs. (pres. 1974-75, Miles Conrad award 1986), Am. Soc. Microbiology (chmn. com. info. sci. 1976-79), Soc. for Scholarly Pub. (interim bd. 1978-81), Internat. Coun. for Sci. and Tech. Info. (pres. 1989-92).

KENNEDY, JACK LELAND, lawyer; b. Portland, Oreg., Jan. 30, 1924; s. Ernest E. and Lera M. (Talley) K.; m. Clara C. Hagans, June 5, 1948; children: James M., John C. Student, U.S. Maritime Commn. Acad., Southwestern U., L.A.; JD, Lewis and Clark Coll., 1951. Bar: Oreg. 1951. Pvt. practice, Portland; ptnr. Kennedy & King, Portland, 1971-77, Kennedy, King & McClurg, Portland, 1977-82, Kennedy, King & Zimmer, Portland, 1982-98, Kennedy, Watts, Arellano & Ricks L.L.P., Portland, 1998—. Trustee Northwestern Coll. Law, Portland; dir. Profl. Liability Fund, 1979-82. Contbr. articles to legal jours. Mem. bd. visitors Lewis and Clark Coll. With USNR, 1942-46. Recipient Disting. Grad. award Lewis and Clark Coll., 1983. Fellow Am. Coll. Trial Lawyers, Am. Bar Found. (life), Oreg. Bar Found. (charter); mem. ABA (ho. of dels. 1984-88), Oreg. State Bar (bd. govs. 1976-79, pres. 1978-79), Multnomah Bar Assn., City Club, Columbia River Yacht Club. Republican. Office: Kennedy Watts Arellano & Ricks LLP Ste 2850 1211 SW Fifth Ave Portland OR 97204-3733 Office Phone: 503-228-6191. Business E-Mail: kennedy@kwar.com.

KENNEDY, JACK STANNERS, lawyer; b. Terre Haute, Ind., Apr. 14, 1945; BA magna cum laude, Harvard U., 1967; JD, U. Va., 1972. Bar: Conn. 1972. With Robinson & Cole LLP, Hartford, mng. ptnr., 1994-2000. Mem. editorial bd. Va. Law Review, 1970-72. Mem. ABA (sect. bus. law), Conn. Bar Assn. (past chair sect. bus. law), Order of Coif. Office: Robinson & Cole LLP 280 Trumbull St Hartford CT 06103-3597

KENNEDY, JAMES ANDREW, chemical company executive; b. Millburn, N.J., Dec. 15, 1937; s. James Andrew and Dorothy Frances (Van Cleve) K.; m. Judith Lynne Tunstall, Jan. 26, 1974; children— Brian James, Karen Jeanne, Kevin Van Cleve. BA in Econs., Holy Cross Coll., Worcester, Mass., 1959; MBA in Fin. and Mktg., Columbia U., N.Y.C., 1962. With Nat. Starch and Chem. Co., 1967-77, from v.p. internat. divsn. to exec. v.p., dir., COO Bridgewater, N.J., 1977-90; pres., CEO Nat. Starch and Chem. Corp., Bridgewater, N.J., 1990-99, chmn., 1996-97; bus. group pres. Unilever, 1996-97; exec. v.p., dir. Imperial Chem. Industries, Eng., 1997; chmn. Nat. Starch and Chem. Co., Bridgewater, N.J., 1997-99; ret., 1999. Lectr. Notre Dame U., NYU, Pace U., Am. Mgmt. Assn., Babcock Sch. Mgmt. Wake Forest U.; dir. Guardian Life Ins. Co. Am., 2000—; bd. dirs. Unilever U.S., Inc., Guardian Lif Ins. Co. Am., Freedom House Found. Trustee, chmn. bd. trustees N.J. Inst. Tech., 2000—. Served to lt. (j.g.) USN, 1959-61. Mem. NAM (bd. dirs.), Chem. Mfrs. Assn. (bd. dirs.). Home: 11 Crest Dr Bernardsville NJ 07924-1707 Office: Nat Starch & Chem Co 10 Finderne Ave Bridgewater NJ 08807-3355

KENNEDY, JAMES COX, publishing and media executive; b. Honolulu, 1947; married, two sons, one daughter. BBA, U. Denver, 1970. With Atlanta Newspapers, 1972-79, prodn. asst., 1972-76, exec. v.p., gen. mgr., 1976-79; pres. Grand Junction Newspapers, 1979-80; pub. Grand Junction Daily Sentinel, 1980-85; v.p. Cox newspapers div. Cox Enterprises Inc., Atlanta, 1985-86, exec. v.p., 1986-87, pres., chief oper. officer, exec. v.p., 1986-87, also chmn., 1987—88, now chmn., chief exec. officer, 1988—. Office: Cox Enterprises Inc PO Box 105357 Atlanta GA 30348-5357 also: 1601 W Peachtree St NE Atlanta GA 30309-2641

KENNEDY, JAMES M., editor; b. Watertown, NY; Grad., Amherst Coll. Various positions to mng. editor Ogdensburg Journal and Advance News, NY; bus. editor, bur. chief The Tampa Tribune, Fla.; bus. enterprise editor AP, NYC, 1987—88, bus. news editor, 1988—95, dir. multimedia services, 1995—2000, strategic planning, 2001—04, v.p., dir. strategic planning, 2004—; exec. dir. product planning WSJ.com Wall St. Jour., NYC, 2000—01. Founding mem. Media Ctr. Am. Press Inst. Recipient Oliver S. Gramling Award for Achievement, AP, 1997. Mem.: Online News Assn. (founder). Office: AP 50 Rockefeller Plz New York NY 10020-1605

KENNEDY, JAMES W., aerospace transportation executive; b. Riverdale, Md. m. Bernadette Kennedy; 2 children. B in Mech. Engring., Auburn Univ., Ala., 1972; MBA, Ga. So. Univ., Statesboro, 1977. With Aerospace Engring. Coop. Edn. Program NASA Kennedy Space Ctr., 1968; dep. dir. of sci. and engring. NASA George C. Marshall Space Flight Ctr., 1998—99, dir. engring. Huntsville, Ala., 1999, dep. dir., NASA Kennedy Space Ctr., Fla., 2002—03, dir., 2003—. With USAF. Recipient Astronautics Engr. of Yr. award, Nat. Space Club, 2003. Office: Dir NASA Kennedy Space Ctr Orlando FL 32899

KENNEDY, JAMES WILLIAM, JR., (SARGE KENNEDY), special education administrator, consultant; b. Santa Rosa, Calif., Oct. 6, 1940; s. James William and Kay Jean (Eaton) Kennedy; m. Lorene Adele Dunaway, May 12, 1962 (div. Sept. 1971); children: Sean, Erin, Mark; m. Carolyn Judith Nighsonger, Mar. 30, 1972 (div. Dec. 1979); m. Patricia Carter Crithlow, Nov. 5, 1988; stepchildren: Jennifer, Dayna, Joy. BA, San Francisco State U., 1964, MA, 1970. Tchr., prin., coord. spl. edn., dir. Spl. Edn. Local Plan Area Napa County (Calif.) Schs., 1968-83; spl. edn. compliance cons. overseas dependent schs. Mediterranean region Dept. Def., 1983-84; adminstr. Spl. Edn. Local Plan Area and dir. spl. programs Tehama County Dept. Edn., Red Bluff, Calif., 1985-99, asst. supt. student programs/ Spl. Edn. Local Plan Area Ops., 1999—2004; ret., 2004; pvt. cons., 2004—; fiscal/policy advisor Rural and Sparsely Populated Cosortium of Calif., 2004—. Cons. in field. Editor: (profl. jour.) Calif. Fed. Coun. Exceptional Children Jour., 1971—77, 1981—83. Mem. Wilson Riles Spl. Edn. Task Force, Calif., 1981—82, Spl. Edn. Fiscal Task Force, Calif., 1987—89. Named Outstanding Spl. Edn. Adminstr. Calif., Spl. Edn. Adminstrs. in County Offices of Edn. in Calif., Spl. Edn. Local Plan Area Adminstrs. Calif., and Calif. Fedn. Coun. Exceptional Children, 1998. Mem.: Spl. Edn. Local Plan Area Adminstrs. Assn. Calif. (co-chair fin. com. 1993—), Coun. for Adminstrs. Spl. Edn., Calif. State Coun. Exceptional Children (treas. 1992—), Internat. Coun. for Exceptional Children (sgt. at arms 1980—95), Profl. Football rschers. Assn., San Francisco State Alumni Assn. Democrat. Avocations: sports history, pop music history, Spanish and Portuguese cultures. Office: CS-CEC PO Box 8057 Red Bluff CA 96080-8057 Office Phone: 530-529-1865. Business E-Mail: skennedy@tcde.tehama.k12.ca.us.

KENNEDY, JANEAN LEE, language educator; b. Altoona, Pa., May 4, 1938; d. Walter Sherman and Mary Elizabeth Kennedy; m. Richard M. Flack, May 26, 1956 (div. Oct. 1981); children: Colleen, Denise, Melissa, Leslie, Richard, Julie, Jonathan; m. Hugh J. Kennedy, Jan. 31, 1981. BA in English, N.C. A&T State U., Greensboro, 1987, MA in English and Afro-Am. Lit., 1988. Instr. N.C. A&T State U., 1988—, Guilford C.C., Jamestown, N.C., 1997—. Mem. AAUP, N.c. Conf. English Instrs. Republican. Methodist. Home: 3714 Konnoak Dr Winston Salem NC 27127-6039

KENNEDY, JOAN PACE, school librarian, educator; b. Bogalusa, La., Dec. 1, 1945; d. Winfred Dutch and Betty Duncan Pace; m. Jay Gould Kennedy, Aug. 15, 1964; children: Juanette Ladell, Jacqueline Kennedy Williams, Justin Ben. Master's degree, Southeastern La. U., Hammond, La., 1980. Libr. sci. state cert. La., cert. prin. La. Dept. of Edn., supr. student tchg. La. Dept. of Edn., parish or city sch. supr. of instrn. La. Dept. of Edn. Tchr. grades 1-2 Wesley Ray Elem. Wash. Parish Sch. Bd., Franklinton, La., 1973—94, libr. Wesley Ray Elem., 1994—. Asst. prin. Wesley Ray Elem. Washington Parish Sch. Bd., 1999—2000. Contbr. creative writing/poetry anthology, articles to profl. jours. and newspapers (1st Pl. Poetry Divsn. award, 1992). Dir. vacation Bible sch. Stateline Bapt. Ch., Franklinton, La., 2003—05. Named Washington Parish Elem. Tchr. of the Yr., Wash. Parish Sch. Bd., 1984, Wesley Ray Elem. Tchr. of the Yr., Wesley Ray Elem., 1989, 1994; recipient WST Mini-Grant, Washington-St. Tammany Electric, 1999, 2002; grantee Bell South Mini-Grant, Bell South Tel. Co., 2001. Mem.: Internat. Reading Assn., La. Libr. Assn., Washington Parish Reading Coun. (pres. 2000—01), La. Reading Assn. (pres. 2004—05, mini-grant 2000—01, Libr. of Yr. 2001), Washington Parish Art Assn., Kappa Kappa Iota (pres. 1998—99), Delta Kappa Gamma (sec. 1999—2001). Baptist. Avocations: reading, writing, singing, camping, painting. Home: 57244 Hwy 438 Angie LA 70426 Office: Wesley Ray Elem 30523 Wesley Ray Rd Angie LA 70426 Office Phone: 985-986-3130.

KENNEDY, JOANN, artist, educator; b. Chgo., June 17, 1950; d. Frank Joseph and Therese Katherine (Engelhardt) Mueller; m. John Fluent, Sept. 4, 1971 (div. May 1976); children: Benjamin, Molly; m. Samuel Joseph Kennedy, Oct. 9, 1982. BFA, No. Ill. U., 1988, MA, 1991, MFA, 1994. Typesetter, draftsperson, keyline illustrator Motorola, Schaumburg, Ill., 1976-84; instr. Harper Coll., Palatine, Ill., 1993—98, Coll. Lake County, Ill., 1998—. Avocation: gardening.

KENNEDY, JOE DAVID, JR., (JOEY KENNEDY), editor; b. Dayton, Tex., Mar. 28, 1956; s. Joe David Sr. and Patricia Ann (Harper) K.; m. Veronica Elaine Pike, Feb. 2, 1980. BA, U. Ala., Birmingham, 1988, MA, 2003. Reporter gen. assignments Houma (La.) Daily Courier, 1974-76; dir. news, sports Sta. KJIN-AM/KCIL-FM, Houma, 1976-77; reporter gen. assignments Cullman (Ala.) Times, 1977-78; asst. sports editor Anniston (Ala.) Star, 1978-81; sports copy editor Birmingham News, 1981-83, asst. editor lifestyle, 1983-85, editor photography, 1985-86, Sunday editor, 1986-89, editor book revs., 1986-95, editl. writer, columnist, 1989—. Adj. prof. dept. English, U. Ala., Birmingham, 2001—. Contbr. Redbook mag., 1997, 98, Iron Horse Lit. Rev., 2004, Aura Lit. Rev., 2005. Mem. Houma-Terrebonne Bicentennial Commn., 1975-76; press sec. rep. gubernatorial candidate Guy Hunt, Ala., 1978; tutor literacy Birmingham Pub. Schs. Adult Learning Ctr., 1990-91; judge J.C. Penney Golden Rule Awards for Vols., 1992; lectr. Lee Coll. Springs Art Festival, Baytown, Tex., 1992; mem. adv. bd. Sch. Journalism, U. Miss., 1992-98; bd. dirs. So. Mus. Flight, 1992-93; mem. Leadership Birmingham Class, 1994-95, AIDS Care Team, 1994-00; bd. dirs. A Baby's Place, 1996-97; mem. Ct. Appointed Spl. Advocates for Children, 1996—; bd. dirs. PATH Orgn. for Homeless, 1997-99, Childcare Resources, 2004-; mem. bd. deacons Southside Bapt. Ch.; reading tutor 4th graders Birmingham Pub. Schs., 1999. Nominee for Pulitzer prize, 1994; named Comm. Alumnus of Yr., U. Ala., Birmingham, 1991, One of the Top 20 Grads., 1994; recipient various awards, La. Press Assn., 1974—77, Ala. Press Assn., 1989—2001, Best Commentary award, 1992, 2000, 2004, Ala. Sportswriters Assn., 1978—81, Hector award, Troy State U., 1991, 1992, 1994, 1995, Pulitzer prize for edtl. writing, 1991, Nat. Edn. Writers Assn., 1994, Ed. Press Award, John S. Coley award as Outstanding Graduate Student, U. Ala.-Birmingham, 2003; scholar Howton Scholarship in Creative Writing, 2002—03. Mem. U. Ala. Birmingham Nat. Alumni Soc. (life; bd. dirs. 1999-2004, v.p. 2002-2004), Outstanding Grad. Student Sch. Arts and Humanities 2003. Avocations: civil war history, reading, writing. Home: 1635 11th Pl S Birmingham AL 35205-5907 Office: Birmingham News 2200 4th Ave N Birmingham AL 35203-3840 Office Phone: 205-325-2466. Personal E-mail: joeyjoey@bellsouth.net. Business E-Mail: jkennedy@bhamnews.com.

KENNEDY, JOHN B., lawyer; BA magna cum laude, Carleton Coll., 1970; MA with honors, U. Chgo., 1976; JD, Columbia U., 1985. Bar: N.Y. 1986. Ptnr. Morrison & Foerster LLP, N.Y.C., co-chmn. tech. transactions group. Mem.: Assn. Bar City N.Y. (co-chmn. 1994—96, sec., tech. & practice law 1993—94). Office: Morrison & Foerster LLP 1290 Avenue of Americas New York NY 10104-0185 Office Phone: 212-468-8066. Office Fax: 212-468-7900. Business E-Mail: jkennedy@mofo.com.

KENNEDY, JOHN BAPTIST, civil engineer; BSc with honors, U. Cardiff, 1955; PhD, U. Toronto, 1961; DSc, U. Wales, 1984. Engr. bridge design, 1955—61; asst. prof. U. Sask., Saskatoon, Canada, 1961—63; assoc. prof. U. Windsor, Ont., Canada, 1963—66, prof., head dept. civil engring., 1966—97, prof. emeritus, disting. prof., 1997—. Recipient Galbraith prize Engring. Inst. Can., 1966, Gzowski medal, 1966, Duggan medal, 1978, T.Y. Lin award ASCE, 1982, Arthur Wellington prize, 1995, 99, Prix P.L . Pratley award Can. Soc. Civil Engring., 1995, 97. Office: U Windsor Civil Engring 362 Dillon Hall Windsor ON Canada N9B 3P4 E-mail: cjk@uwindsor.ca.

KENNEDY, JOHN EDWARD, lawyer; b. Mpls., Feb. 18, 1947; s. John Edward and Margaret (Greathouse) K.; m. Linda Bagwell, June 22, 1968; children: John Harlan, Linda Elizabeth. AB cum laude, Harvard U., 1968, JD magna cum laude, 1971. Bar: Tex. 1971, U.S. Dist. Ct. (so. dist.) Tex. 1972, U.S. Ct. Appeals (5th cir.) 1972, U.S. Supreme Ct. 1975, U.S. Ct. Appeals (D.C. cir.) 1984. Assoc. Vinson & Elkins, Houston, 1971-80, ptnr., 1980—. Served to 2d lt. USAR, 1972. Mem. ABA, Houston Bar Assn., Fed. Energy Bar Assn. Clubs: Houston Ctr. Presbyterian. Home: 2617 Pemberton Dr Houston TX 77005-3441 Office: Vinson & Elkins LLP 2300 First City Tower Houston TX 77002-6760 Office Phone: 713-758-2550.

KENNEDY, JOHN HARVEY, chemistry professor; b. Oak Park, Ill., Apr. 24, 1933; s. John Harvey and Margaret Helen (Drenthe) K.; m. Joan Corinne Hipsky, June 9, 1956 (div. Mar. 1969); children: Bruce Laurence, Bryan Donald, Brent Peter, Jill Amy.; m. Victoria Jane Matthew, July 2, 1970; 1 child, Karen Anne. BS, UCLA, 1954; AM, Harvard U., 1956, PhD, 1957. Sr. research chemist E.I. du Pont de Nemours, Wilmington, Del., 1957-61; asst. prof. chemistry U. Calif., Santa Barbara, 1961-63, 67-69, assoc. prof., 1969-76, prof., 1976-93, prof. emeritus, 1993—, chmn. dept., 1982-85; assoc. prof. Boston Coll., Chestnut Hill, 1963-64; head inorganic chemistry Gen. Motors, Santa Barbara, 1964-67. Cons. Eveready Battery Co., Cleve., 1983-2000; vis. prof. U. N.C., Chapel Hill, 1980-81, Japan Soc. Promotion of Sci., Nagoya, 1974-75, Leningrad State U., 1989, China Acad. Scis., 1990. Author: Analytical Chemistry, Principles, 1990, Analytical Chemistry, Practice, 1990; contbr. articles to profl. jours.; patentee in field. Mus. dir. Christ the King Episcopal Ch., Santa Barbara, 1982-98. Mem. Am. Chem. Soc., Electrochem. Soc. Democrat. Avocation: music. Home: 5357 Agana Dr Santa Barbara CA 93111-1601 Office: U Calif Dept Chemistry Santa Barbara CA 93106 Office Phone: 805-893-2429. Personal E-mail: jvkennedy@aol.com.

KENNEDY, JOHN PATRICK, lawyer, corporate financial executive; b. Oct. 2, 1943; s. Arch R. and Kathryn R. (Delahunty) K.; children: Kathleen, Elizabeth, Christina, Patrick, Lindsay. BA in Econs., U. Kans., 1965, JD, 1967; MBA in Fin., U. Mo., 1972, LLM, 1973. Bar: Kans. 1967, Mo. 1968, Ohio 1973, Wis. 1985, U.S. Supreme Ct. 1972, U.S. Dist. Ct. (we. dist.) Mo. 1972, U.S. dist. Ct. Kans. 1967. Trial atty. Kodas, Gingerich & Stites, Kansas City, Mo., 1967-69; sr. atty. Mobay Chem. Co., Kansas City, Mo., 1969-73; v.p., gen. counsel, corp. sec. Johnson Controls, Inc., Milw., 1984—, sr. v.p., gen. counsel, corp. sec. Small bus. advisor, venture capitalist. Contbr. articles to profl. jours. Served with USAR, 1967-73. Recipient Wall St. Jour. award, 1972, A. Jurisprudence awards, 1966-67. Mem. ABA, Ohio Bar Assn., Columbus Bar Assn., Wis. Bar Assn., Am. Corp. Counsel Assn. Democrat. Roman Catholic. Office: Johnson Controls Inc 5757 N Green Bay Ave PO Box 591 Milwaukee WI 53201

KENNEDY, JOHN W., health products executive; b. Montreal, Can. BS in Molecular Biology, U. New Brunswick, Fredericton, Can., 1979; M in Molecular Biology, McMaster U., Hamilton, Ont., 1984. Mgr. Syntex Can., 1979—84; with Am. Cyanamid, 1984—92; dir. global oncology divsn. Lederle Pharm., Wayne, NJ, 1992—94; gen. mgr. to v.p. mktg. endocrinology Serono Can., Inc., Norwell, Mass., 1994—98; pres., CEO Hemosol Inc., Mississagua, Canada, 1998—. Office: Hemosol Inc 2585 Meadowpine Blvd Mississauga ON L5N 8H9 Canada E-mail: sheagelman@hemosol.com.

KENNEDY, JOHN WILLIAM, engineering company executive; b. Summit, N.J., May 20, 1956; s. William John and Jean Mary (Krutisia) Kennedy; m. Cecelia Marie Hamrock, Dec. 26, 1981; 1 child, Sean Michael. BS with honors, North Adams State Coll., 1978; MBA with honors, Columbia Pacific U., 1987, BS in Indsl. Engring., 1988; PhD in Bus. Mgmt., LaSalle U., 1996. Cert. tchr. N.J. Tchr. Mountainside (N.J.) Sch. Dist., 1979—82, Chatham (N.J.) Boro Sch. Dist., 1982—83; plant mgr. The Chatham Club Recreation Ctr., 1982—85; ops. mgr. Coleman Equipment, Inc., Irvington, NJ, 1985—91; project mgr., acct. mgr. automated sorting systems div. Sandvik Process Systems, Totowa, NJ, 1991—95; gen. mgr. sales and engring. Barnett Industries, Irvington, NJ, 1995—96; pres., owner The Multitech Group Inc., South Plainfield, NJ, 1996—. Plant mgr., ops. mgr., cons. Madison Cmty. Pool, NJ, 1971—87. Contbr. tech. articles to tech. publs. Active Denville area Boy Scouts Am., NJ, 1984—, chmn. dist. advancement com., 1990—95, exec. bd., 1995—, dist. oper. com. chmn., 1998—; area com. Spl. Olympics, Flanders, NJ, 1987—, event dir. Morris, Sussex and Warren counties, 1998—; exec. bd. Morris-Sussex Boy Scouts Am., 1996—; active Madison Environ. Commn., Madison Planning Bd. Named Eagle Scout, Boy Scouts Am., 1970, Alumni of Yr., Mass. Coll. Liberal Arts (formerly North Adams State Coll.), 2005, Disting. Alumni Profl., Mass. Coll., 2005; named to Eagle Scout Hall of Fame, Boy Scouts Am., 1999; recipient Lifetime Achievement award, Boy Scouts Am. Patriots' Path Coun., 2001. Mem.: Am. Soc. for Quality Control, Inst. Indsl. Engring., Am. Mgmt. Assn. Republican. Roman Catholic. Achievements include co-pantentee vacuum lifter, air logic weightless circuit. Avocations: camping, biking, racquetball, softball, coins. Home: 198 Kings Rd Madison NJ 07940-2238 Office: Multitech Group Inc 165A Ryan St South Plainfield NJ 07080-4206 Office Phone: 908-753-0400. Business E-Mail: jkennedy@multitechmail.com.

KENNEDY, JOSEPH PATRICK, II, utilities executive, former congressman; b. Brighton, Mass., Sept. 24, 1952; s. Robert F. and Ethel (Skakel) K.; m. Sheila Rauch, 1979 (div.); 2 children: Joseph P. III, Matthew; m. Beth Kelly, Oct. 1993. BA, U. Mass., Boston, 1976. Chmn., pres. Citizens' Energy Corp., 1979-87, 98—; mem. 100th-105th Congress from 8th Mass. dist., 1987—99; ranking minority mem. banking & fin. svcs. subcom. on housing & cmty. devel., mem. com. on vets.' affairs. Active Can. Robert F. Kennedy Meml. Democrat. Office: Citizens Enterprises Corp Ctr Lobby Ste 342 88 Black Falcon Ave Boston MA 02210-2431

KENNEDY, JOSEPH PAUL, chemist, researcher; b. Budapest, Hungary, May 18, 1928; arrived in U.S., 1956; s. Laszlo and Rosa (Farkas) Kennedy; m. Ingeborg G. Hausen, Feb. 10, 1956; children: Katherine, Cynthia, Julie. PhD, U. Vienna, Austria, 1954; MBA, Rutgers U., 1961; D (hon.), Kossuth U., Hungary, 1989. Rsch. fellow Sorbonne, U. Paris, 1955; rsch. assoc. McGill U., Montreal, Canada, 1956; rsch. chemist Celanese Corp., Summit, NJ, 1957-59; sr. rsch. assoc. Esso Rsch. Engring. Co., Linden, NJ, 1959-70; prof. polymer sci. U. Akron, Ohio, 1970-80, disting. prof. polymer sci. and chemistry, 1980—. Cons. Akron Cationic Polymer Devel. Co., 1983—. Author: (book) Cationic Polymerization, 1975, Carbocationic Polymerization, 1982, Designed Polymers by Carbocationic Macromolecular Engineering: Theory and Practice, 1992. Named Outstanding Rschr., Alumni Assn. U. Akron, 1979; recipient Morley award and medal, Cleve. Am. Chem. Soc., 1982, award Disting. Svc. in Sci., Soc. Polymer Sci., Japan, 2000. Mem.: Am. Chem. Soc. (Polymer Chemistry award 1985, 1995, Applied Polymer Sci. award 1995, George Stafford Whitby award 1996), Hungarian Acad. Scis. Avocation: Japanese art of the Meiji. Home: 510 Saint Andrews Dr Akron OH 44303-1228 Office: U Akron Inst Polymer Sci Akron OH 44325-0001 Office Phone: 330-972-7512. Business E-Mail: kennedy@polymer.uakron.edu.

KENNEDY, JOSEPH WINSTON, lawyer; b. Marshalltown, Iowa, June 5, 1932; s. Roy Wesley and Julia Harriet (Plum) K.; m. Barbara B. Bowman, July 11, 1954 (div. June 1982); children: Kimberle Ann, Kamella Lucille; m. Paula Terry Smith, Nov. 24, 1984. BS cum laude, McPherson (Kans.) Coll., 1954; JD with honors, George Washington U., 1958. Bar: Kans. 1958, U.S. Dist Ct. Kans. 1958, U.S. Ct. Appeals (10th cir.) 1976, U.S. Supreme Ct. 1970. Spl. agt. Office of Naval Intelligence, Washington, 1954-58; assoc. Morris, Laing, Evans & Brock, Wichita, Kans., 1958-62; ptnr. Morris, Laing, Evans, Brock & Kennedy, Wichita, 1962—. Chmn. profl. divsn., atty. United Way of the Plains, Wichita, 1990-93. Recipient Best Lawyers in Am. award, 1987, 89-90, 91-92, 93-94, 95-96. Mem. ABA, Kans. Bar Assn. (bd. law examiners 1993-2002), Wichita Bar Assn. (bd. govs. 1964-66). Office: Morris Laing Evans Brock & Kennedy 300 N Mead St #200 Wichita KS 67202-2745 Office Phone: 316-262-2671. E-mail: jkennedy@morrislaing.com.

KENNEDY, KATHLEEN, film producer; m. Frank Marshall. Student, San Diego State U. With KCST, San Diego; pres. Amblin Entertainment, Universal City, Calif. Assoc. prodr.: (films) Poltergeist, 1982, Twilight Zone-The Movie, 1983, Indiana Jones and the Temple of Doom, 1984, Reform School Girls, 1986; prodr.: (films) E.T. The Extra-Terrestrial, 1982 (Academy award nomination for best picture 1982); (with Quincy Jones, Frank Marshall, and Spielberg) The Color Purple, 1985 (Academy award nomination for best picture 1985); (with Marshall and Art Levinson) The Money Pit, 1986; (with Marshall and Spielberg) Empire of the Sun, 1987, Always, 1989; (with Richard Vane) Arachnophobia, 1990; (with Marshall and Gerald R. Molen) Hook, 1991; (with Robert Watts) Alive, 1993; (with Molen) Jurassic Park, 1993, (with Marshall) Milk Money, 1994; (with Clint Eastwood) The Bridges of Madison County, 1995, Twister, 1996; (with Steven Spielberg), The Six Sense, 1999, Snow Falling on Cedars, 1999, A Map of the World, 1999, Artifical Intelligence: AI, 2001, Jurassic Park III, 2001, Seabiscuit, 2003, The Young Black Stallion, 2003, War of the Worlds, 2005; exec. prodr.: (films)Roller Coaster Rabbit, 1990, A Dangerous Woman, 1993, Schindler's List, 1993 (Academy award for best picture 1993), Trail Mix-Up, 1993, A Far Off Place, 1993, Balto, 1995, Congo, 1995, The Indian in the Cupboard, 1995; (with Marshall and Spielberg) Gremlins, 1984, The Goonies, 1985, Back to the Future, 1985, Young Sherlock Holmes, 1985, *batteries not included, 1987, Jurassic Park: The Lost World, 1997, Dad, 1989, Back to the Future Part II, 1990, Gremlins 2: The New Batch, 1990, Back to the Future Part III, 1990, Joe Versus the Volcano, 1990, Cape Fear, 1991, We're Back! A Dinosaur's Story, 1993, (with Marshall) Fandango, 1985; (with Marshall, Spielberg, and David Kirschner) An American Tail, 1986; (with Marshall, Spielberg, Peter Guber, and Jon Peters) Innerspace, 1987; (with Spielberg) Who Framed Roger Rabbit, 1988; (with Marshall, Spielberg, and George Lucas) The Land Before Time, 1988; (with Marshall and Lucas) Indiana Jones and the Last Crusade, 1989; (with Marshall and Kirschner) An American Tail: Fievel Goes West, 1991; (with Peter Bogdanovich) Noises Off, 1992; (with Marshall and Molen); (with Molen, Kirschner, William Hanna, and Joseph Barbera) The Flintstones, 1994, Olympic Glory, 1999, Signs, 2002; exec. prodr. TV Tummy Trouble, 1989, The Sports Pages, 2001*

KENNEDY, KATHY KAY, library director; b. New Kensington, Pa., Oct. 21, 1942; d. Lawrence Michael Kennedy and Vivian Mae Smeltzer. BA in English, Thiel Coll., 1964; MSLS, Drexel Inst. Tech., 1967. Bibliographer Union Libr. Catalog, Phila., 1964-67; sci./tech. librarian Carnegie Libr. of Pitts., 1967-73, adult svcs. specialist, 1973-74; libr. dir. Peoples Libr., New Kensington, pa., 1974-87; adult svcs. librarian Monroeville (Pa.) Pub. Libr., 1987-89, asst. dir., 1989-93, dir., 1993—. Editor: Review of Iron and Steel Literature, 1972. Bd. dirs. Pa. Citizens for Better Librs., Greensburg, 1996—, Monroeville Arts Coun., 1989-91; mem. bd. assocs. Thiel Coll., 2002--. Mem. Pa. Libr. Assn. (pres. 1995, editor jour. 1976-78, Cert. of Merit 1982), Bus. and Profl. Women of Pitts. (pres. 1975-77), McKeesport Bus. and Profl. Women (Woman of Yr. 1999), Pa. Fedn. Bus. and Profl. Women (dist. dir. 1984-85), Allegheny County Libr. Assn. (bd. dirs. 1999-2001). Lutheran. Avocations: music, theater, reading, travel. Office: Monroeville Pub Libr 4000 Gateway Campus Blvd Monroeville PA 15146-3381

KENNEDY, KENNETH ADRIAN RAINE, biological anthropologist, forensic anthropologist; b. Oakland, Calif., June 26, 1930; s. Walter Burkhart and Margaret Miriam (Madge) K.; m. Mary Caroline Marino, Aug. 5, 1961 (div.); m. Margaret Carrick Fairlie, Aug. 10, 1969. BA, U. Calif., Berkeley, 1953, MA, 1954, PhD, 1962. Diplomate Am. Bd. Forensic Anthropology; lic. lay reader. Instr. U. Calif., 1962-63; asst. prof. anthropology Cornell U., Ithaca, NY, 1964-68, assoc. prof., 1968—81, prof. ecology, anthropology and Asian studies, 1981—2005, prof. emeritus, 2005—. Sec. Am. Bd. Forensic Anthropology, 1999—2002; cons. forensic anthropology N.Y. State, 1964—; field rsch. in India, Pakistan, Sri Lanka, 1963—. Author 12 books; mem. editl. bd. Am. Jour. Phys. Anthropology, 1998-2001, acting editor-in-chief, 1985; field editor Am. Anthropologist, 1982-85; contbr. numerous articles to sci. jours. Guest White House state dinner reception for Pres. Sri Lanka, 1984. Sgt. U.S. Army, 1954-57. Grantee NSF, Smithsonian Instn., Howard Found., NEA, Am. Inst. Indian Studies, numerous others. Fellow AAAS (mem. electorate nominating com. in anthropology 2004—), Am. Acad. Forensic Scis. (sec.-treas. forensic anthropology sect. 1993-94, chmn. 1994-95, chmn. phys. anthropology sect. 1994-95, T. Dale Stewart award in forensic anthropology 1987); mem. Am. Anthrop. Assn. (chmn. biol. anthropology sect. 1986-88, mem. long-range planning com. 2002-2004, William W. Howells Book award 2002), Am. Assn. Phys. Anthropologists (exec. bd. 1990-96, v.p. 1994-96), Cornell Rsch. Club (pres. 1978-80, 89-90), Sigma Xi (pres. 1984-85). Episcopalian. Avocations: violin, playing in chamber music groups. Office: Cornell U Ecology & Evolutionary Bio Corson Hall Ithaca NY 14853-2701 Office Phone: 607-254-4214. Business E-Mail: kak10@cornell.edu.

KENNEDY, KEVIN CURTIS, sports commentator, former professional baseball team manager; b. May 26, 1954; Student, San Diego State U.; BA, Cal. State U. Minor league baseball player, 1976-83; minor league mgr. L.A. Dodgers orgn., 1984-91; dir. minor league ops. Montréal Expos, 1991-92, coach, 1992; mgr. Texas Rangers, 1993-94, Boston Red Sox, 1994-97; baseball analyst Fox Sports TV, radio. Author: Twice Around the Bases: The Thinking Fan's Inside Look at Baseball, 2005. Pioneer League Mgr. Yr., 1985, Pacific Coast league Mgr. Yr., 1990. Office: Baseball Analyst Fox Sports Net 1440 S Sepulveda Blvd Los Angeles CA 90025*

KENNEDY, KEVIN W., finance company executive; Grad., Hamilton Coll., 1970; MBA, Harvard Bus. Sch., 1974. Head corp. fin. Goldman Sachs Group Inc., N.Y.C., 1988—94, head Americas Group, 1994—99, mem. exec. office, 1999—2001, exec. v.p. human capital mgmt., 2001—. Life trustee, former chmn. bd. Hamilton Coll.; mng. dir., v.p. bd. dirs. Met. Opera; trustee N.Y. Pub. Libr.; hon. trustee Chewonki Found. Office: Goldman Sachs Group Inc 85 Broad St New York NY 10004

KENNEDY, LAURIE JEAN, music educator, musician; d. George Archibald and Gladys McCain; m. Carl Rickey Kennedy, Aug. 4, 1979. MusM, Kent State U., 1993. Prin., piano instr. LJK Music Studio, Oberlin, Ohio, 1987—; ballet class accompanist Lorain County C.C., Elyria, 1987—97; music cataloger Oberlin Coll., 1997—2000, instr., 2000—; staff accompanist Ashland U., Ashland, Ohio, 2001—02. Adj. instr. Lorain County C.C., Elyria, 1989—2003; free-lance accompanist. Musician (keyboardist): Images band. Master gardener Ohio State U. Ext., Medina, 1996—2002; dog trainer Grafton (Ohio) Correctional Inst., 2000—, Club K-9, Oberlin, Ohio, 2003—; musician Cmty. of Christ Ch., Elyria, 1975—97. Griffiths Talent scholar, Baldwin-Wallae Coll., 1979—83, Wildlife Habitat Incentive Program grantee, USDA, 1998—. Mem.: Coll. Music Soc. (assoc.), Kappa Delta Pi. Avocations: dog trainer, backpacking, gardening. Office: Oberlin Coll 173 W Lorain St Oberlin OH 44074

KENNEDY, LAWRENCE ALLAN, mechanical engineering educator; b. Detroit, May 31, 1937; s. Clifford Earl and Emma Josephine (Muller) K.; m. Valaree J. Lockhart, Aug. 3, 1958; children: Joanne E., Julie A., Janet A., Raymond L., Jill M., Brian G. BS, U. Detroit, 1960; MS, Northwestern U., 1962, PhD, 1964. Registered profl. engr., N.Y. Chmn. dept., prof. mech. and aero. engring. SUNY-Buffalo, 1964-83; chmn. dept. mech. engring., prof. Ohio State U., Columbus, 1983-93, Ralph W. Kurtz disting. prof., 1992-95; prof. mech. engring. and chem. engring. U. Ill., Chgo., 2004—, dean coll. engring., 1994—2004, Standley Kaplan scholar, 2002—. Vis. assoc. prof. mech. and aero. engring. U. Calif.-San Diego, 1968-69, VonKarman Inst., Rhode-St. Genese, Belgium, 1971-72; Goebel vis. prof. mech. and aero. engring. U. Mich., Ann Arbor, 1980-81; vis. prof. mech. & aerospace engring. Princeton U., 1993-94; cons. Cornell Aero. Lab., Buffalo, 1968-72, Tech. Adv. Service, Fort Washington, Pa., 1969—, Ashland Chem. Corp., Dublin, Ohio, 1983-90, Mech. Engring. Sci. and Application, Buffalo, 1972-83, Columbia Gas, 1987-92; vis. faculty fellow mech. and aerospace engring. Princeton U., 1994. Contbr. numerous articles on engring. to profl. jours.; editor: Progress in Astronautics and Aeros., Vol. 58, 1978, Exptl. Thermal and Fluid Scis., 1987-95; editor in chief Jour. Thermal & Fluid Scis., 1997—; assoc. editor Applied Mechanics Revs., 1985-88, Jour. Propulsion & Power, 1992-98. Recipient Ralph R. Teetor award 1984, AT&T Found. award, 1987, Ralph Coats Roe award, 1993; NATO fellow, 1971-72, NSF fellow, 1968-69, W.P. Murphy fellow, 1960-63; Agard lectr., 1971-72. Fellow AIAA, ASME, AAAS, Am. Phys. Soc.; mem. Combustion Inst., Am. Soc. Engring. Edn., Soc. Automotive Engrs. Roman Catholic. Avocations: skiing, squash, hiking, music. Home: 24306 Turnberry Ct Naperville IL 60564-8127 Office: Dept Mech Engring M/C 251 842 W Taylor St Chicago IL 60607 Office Phone: 312-413-7560. Business E-Mail: lkennedy@uic.edu.

KENNEDY, LEO RAYMOND, engineering executive; b. Cleve., Dec. 29, 1942; s. Leo Raymond and Jane (Brady) K.; m. Doris Elaine Jurgens, Feb. 18, 1967; children: James Raymond, Brian Robert, Kristin Lee. BS, U.S. Mil. Acad., 1965; EdM, U. Ill., 1972; MBA, L.I. U., Greenvale, N.Y., 1975; grad., Army War Coll., Carlisle, Pa., 1986. Commd. 2d. lt. U.S. Army, 1965, advanced through grades to col., 1987, adc, 1970; assoc. dir. admissions U.S. Mil. Acad., West Point, N.Y., 1972-75; dir. pers. mgmt. armored divsn. U.S. Army, Killeen, Tex., 1976-78, chief staff divsn. Clay Kaserne, Germany, 1980-82, comdr. battalion Colorado Springs, Colo., 1982-85, inspector gen. inf. divsn., 1985-86, dir. resource mgmt. Pentagon Washington, 1986-92; pres., CEO Kennedy & Assocs., Fairfax, Va., 1993-96; divsn. mgr. Sci. Applications Internat. Corp., McLean, Va., 1996-2000, v.p., 2000—. Acquisition budget com. Army program, Washington, 1987-92; guest spkr. fed. budgeting process, Washington, 1988-92. Decorated Legion of Merit, Bronze Star medal. Mem. AUSA, TROA (life), USAWC (life), Soc. Mil. Comptrs., Non-Commd. Officers Assn. (hon. life), N.Y. Acad. Sci., Kappa Delta Pi. Republican. Roman Catholic. Avocations: squash, racquetball, basketball, railroading.

KENNEDY, LEONARD JERVEY, telecommunications industry executive, lawyer; b. Bklyn., 1951; m. Ellen Mears Kennedy; children: Julia Anne, Emma McMath. BA, Cornell U., 1974, JD, 1977. Bar: Md. 1978. With Venable, Batjer, & Howard, 1977—78; from mem. staff to sr. legal advisor FCC, 1980—88, 1990—91; counsel Dow, Lohnes & Albertson, P.L.L.C., Washington, 1989—90, 1991—93, ptnr., 1993—2001; sr. v.p., gen. counsel Nextel Comm. Inc., 2001—. Bd. dirs. Appleseed Found., Washington, 2002—. Office: Nextel Comm Inc 2001 Edmund Haley Dr Reston VA 20191

KENNEDY, LINDA DALE, music educator, musician; d. William Lawrence and Jessie Merle Dale; m. Kurt Kennedy, June 7, 1969; children: Jennifer Tish, Terra Lee. MusB, Southeastern La. U., Hammond, 1968, MusM, 1975. Cert. profl. music tchr. Music Tchrs. Nat. Assn., Ark. State Music Tchrs. Assn. Instr. Yamaha Music Program, New Orleans, 1968—69; pvt. practice Piano Studio of Linda Kennedy, Maumelle, Ark., 1975—; organist - accompanist F.E. Warren Air Force Base, Cheyenne, Wyo., 1969—71, Woodland Pk. Bapt. Ch., Hammond, La., 1972—75, Goodwood Bapt. Ch., Baton Rouge, 1976—79, Ct. St. United Meth. Ch., Hattiesburg, Miss., 1981—85, Winfield United Meth. Ch., Little Rock, 1987—2001, First United Meth. Ch., North Little Rock, 2001—. Contbr. articles to profl. jours. Sec. Congress of Artists Maumelle Performing Arts Coun., Ark., 2002—. Mem.: Am. Guild of Organists, Nat. Guild Piano Tchrs., Ark. Fedn. Music Clubs (state composition chmn. 2003—), Music Tchrs. Assn. Ctrl. Ark. (pres. 1997—2001, v.p., region III chmn.), Ark. State Music Tchrs. Assn. (chairperson region III 2005), Music Tchrs. Nat. Assn., Nat. Guild of Piano Tchrs., Little Rock Musical Coterie (assoc.). Methodist. E-mail: pianolk@aol.com.

KENNEDY, LINDA MANN, neuroscience educator, researcher; b. Malden, Mass., July 29, 1939; d. Alfred William Mann and Etta May (Maglue) Stenquist; m. Richard Dearman Kennedy, Apr. 15, 1961; children: Pamela Lea, Ruth Alexander. Diploma in nursing, New England Deaconess Hosp., 1959; AB, Simmons Coll., 1975; PhD, Harvard U., 1980. RN, Mass. Staff nurse Lahey Clinic, Boston, 1959-61, various hosps., Mass., Ga., 1962-72; tchg. asst. Simmons Coll., Boston, 1972-75; vis. rsch. fellow Cornell U., Ithaca, NY, 1978-81; rsch. assoc. Worcester (Mass.) Found. Exptl. Biology, 1980-83; rsch. asst. prof. Clark U., Worcester, 1983-84, asst. prof., 1984-91, assoc. prof., 1991—, U. Mass. Med. Sch., 1995—2000. Co-founder, co-dir., dir. interdisciplinary neurosci. program Clark U., Worcester, 1984—97; vis. scientist Weizmann Inst. Sci., Rehovot, Israel, 1991—92; mem. adv. panel various programs NSF, Washington, 1993—, vis. program dir. Sensory Sys. program, 2000—02; mem. study sections various programs NIH, 1988—. Mem. editl. com. Univ. Press New England, 1989-91; contbr. articles to profl. jour. Mem. conservation com. Town of Framingham, Mass., 1973-74. Recipient Grad. fellowship for women Danforth Found., 1975-79, Rsch. Svc. award NIH, 1980-83, multiple Rsch. grants NSF, NIH, 1978—. Mem. New Eng. Psychol. Assn. (hon.), Assn. Chemoreception Sci. (exec. bd. councilor 1986-88), Soc. for Neurosci., Soc. for Values in Higher Edn., European Chemoreception Orgn., Internat. Brain Rsch. Orgn. Unitarian Universalist. Avocations: swimming, classical and jazz concerts, travel, reading mysteries. Home: 98 Waterford Dr Worcester MA 01602-3512 Office: Clark Univ Dept Biology Worcester MA 01610

KENNEDY, MARC J., lawyer; b. Newburgh, N.Y., Mar. 2, 1945; s. Warren G. K. and Frances F. (Levinson) K.; m. Karen Karatsu; children: Kayla R., Shawna D. BA cum laude, Syracuse U., 1967; JD, U. Mich., 1970. Bar: N.Y. 1971. Assoc. Davies, Hardy, Ives & Lawther, N.Y.C., 1971-72, London, Buttenweiser & Chalif, N.Y.C., 1972-73, Silberfeld, Danziger & Bangser, N.Y.C., 1973; counsel Occidental Crude Sales, Inc., N.Y.C., 1974-75; v.p., gen. counsel Internat. Ore & Fertilizer Corp., N.Y.C., 1975-82; asst. gen. counsel Occidental Chem. Corp., Houston, 1982; v.p., gen. counsel Occidental Chem. Agrl. Products Inc., Tampa, Fla., 1982-87; v.p., gen counsel agrl. products group Occidental Chem. Corp., Tampa, 1987-91, assoc. gen. counsel Dallas, 1991—. Faculty mentor Columbia Pacific U., Mill Valley, Calif., 1981—88. Contbr. articles to profl. jours. Mem. governing bd. Ctr. for Brain Health U. Tex. Dallas, 2001—; trustee Bar Harbor Festival Corp., N.Y.C., 1974-87; bd. dirs. Am. Opera Repertory Co., 1982-85; mem. com. planned giving N.Y. Foundling Hosp., 1977-88; Explorer post advisor Boy Scouts Am., 1976-78. Mem. ABA (vice-chmn. com. internat. law liaison young lawyers sect. 1974-75, chmn. sub-com. proposed trade barriers to the importation of products into U.S. 1985-88, vice chmn. corp. counsel com. 1992-93, co-chmn. corp. counsel com. 1993-98), N.Y. State Bar Assn., Assn. Corp. Counsel, Tex. Bar Assn. Office: Occidental Chem Corp PO Box 809050 Dallas TX 75380-9050 Office Phone: 972-404-3800.

KENNEDY, MARJORIE ELLEN, librarian; b. Dauphin, Man., Can., Sept. 14, 1946; d. Stanley Harrison and Ivy Marietta (Stevens) May; m. Michael P.J. Kennedy, Apr. 3, 1980. BA, U. Sask., Regina, 1972; BLS, U. Alta., Edmonton, 1974; BEd, U. Regina, 1981. Profl. A cert. edn., Sask. Elem. sch. tchr. Indian Head (Sask) Pub. Sch., 1965-66, Elgin Sch., Weyburn, Sask., 1967-68; tchr., libr. Ctrl. Sch., Prince Albert, Sask., 1970-71; elem. sch. tchr. Vincent Massey Sch., Prince Albert, 1969-70, 72-73; children's libr. J.S. Wood br. Saskatoon (Sask.) Pub. Libr., 1974-77, asst. coord. children's svcs., 1977-79; programme head, instr. libr. tech. SIAST-Kelsey Campus, Saskatoon, 1979—. Presenter workshops on reference materials for elem. sch. librs., storytelling and libr. programming for children, 1980—; vol. dir. Children's Lit. Workshops, Sask. Libr. Assn., 1979-80; mem. organizing com. Sask. Libr. Week, Saskatoon, 1988. Mem. Vanscoy (Sask.) and Dist. Agr. Soc., 1983-95. Named to Libr. Edn. Honor Roll ALA, 1987. Mem. Can. Libr. Assn. (instl. rep. 1984—), Sask. Libr. Assn. (insl. rep. 1984—, mem. children's sect. 1982-83), Sask. Assn. Libr. Techs. (instl. rep. 1984—), Can. Club (bd. mem. 1981-84). Mem. United Ch. Can. Avocations: antique doll restoration, antiques, gardening. Office: SIAST Kelsey Campus Box 1520 Libr Info Tech Program Saskatoon SK Canada S7K 3R5 E-mail: Kennedy@siast.sk.ca.

KENNEDY, MARK ALAN, secondary school educator; b. Oklahoma City, July 20, 1951; s. Millford Gordon and Lyn (Cheaney) Kennedy. BA with honors, Calif. State U., 1978; postgrad., Western Sem., 1978-79, Fuller Sem., 1980-83; MEd, U. LaVerne, 1997. Cert. tchr., Calif. Sales mgr. Kennedy Investments, Ontario, Calif., 1980-83; regional v.p. A.L. Williams, Rancho Cucamonga, Calif., 1983-89; loan officer Funder's Mortgage Corp., Covina, Calif., 1989-90; math., social sci. tchr., lang. devel. specialist Ontario-Montclair Sch. Dist., 1990-96, San Bernardino County Cmty. Sch., 1996—, lead tchr., 1998—2000, acting prin., 1998-99. Tchg. asst. Western Sem., Portland, Oreg., 1978-79; instr. Cmty. Inst., 1979; adj. prof. tchr. edn. Chapman U., 2001—; soccer coach DeAnza Mid. Sch., Ontario, 1990-93, core team leader, coop tchr., 1992-95, student coun. advisor, 1992-93, bilingual adv. coun., 1992-96, dist. lang. arts/social sci. trainer, 1993-94; advisor U. Calif. Riverside Honors Students' Inner City Literacy Program, 1993-95; mentor tchr. Ontario-Montclair Sch. Dist., 1994-95; cons. Inst. in Local Self Govt., Sacramento, 1994-96, Assn. Calif. Sh. Adminstrs., 1994-2002; learning styles cons., 1994—; mem. sch. attendance rev. bd., 1996-99. Author: Lessons from the Hawk, 2001, Classroom Management: The Dance of the Dolphin, 2004; contbr. articles to profl. jours. With USN, 1971-75. Named Tchr. of Yr., Inland Coun. for Social Studies, 2000, San Bernardino County Alternative Educators, 2003. Mem.: Am. Soc. Journalists and Authors, Calif. Tchrs. Assn., Phi Alpha Theta (mem. chair 1976—78). Episcopalian. Avocations: German and Latin philosophy and literature, exegesis of koine Greek, conversational Spanish, Am. Kenpo, Kung Fu San Soo. Office: Upland Cmty Day Sch 832 9th St Upland CA 91786 Office Phone: 909-931-2542.

KENNEDY, MARK R., congressman; b. Benson, Minn., Apr. 11, 1957; m. Debbie Kennedy; 4 children. BA, St. John's U., Minn.; MBA, U. Mich. CPA. Mem. U.S. Congress from 6th Minn. dist. (formerly 2nd), 2001—. Mem. agriculture com., transportation and infrastructure com.; subcom. gen. farm commodities, risk mngmt., conservation, credit, rural devel. and rsch., aviation, highways and transit (vice ch.). Republican. Office: 1415 Longworth House Office bldg Washington DC 20515-2302*

KENNEDY, MARY SUSSOCK, artist; b. Liverpool, Eng., Oct. 29, 1926; came to U.S., 1951; d. Charles Archibald and Maria (Mullin) Sussock; m. Rogers Jack Kennedy, May 18, 1946 (dec. Jan. 1987); children: Jacollyn Fenny-Maria, Beverley Gillian, Kimberley Tara. AAS with highest honors, Fashion Inst. Tech., N.Y., 1975; BA summa cum laude, Montclair State Coll., 1977; postgrad., Montclair State Univ., 1977-78. Portrait, stage and wedding photographer Wilkinson and Kennedy, Liverpool, 1943-47; freelance artist Montville, Barnegat Light, NJ, 1956-73; freelance artist Key Largo, Fla., 1984—; grad. asst. in sculpture Montclair State Univ., Upper Montclair, NJ, 1977-78; diamond stylii maker Rogers Kennedy Inc., Saddle Brook, N.J., 1978-84. One woman show at Fashion Inst. Tech., N.Y., 1974; exhibited in group shows at Smithsonian Instn., Washington, 1963, Montclair Art Mus., 1964, U.S. Custom House, N.Y.C., 1979, also exhibit opened by Princess Grace in Monaco, 1960; sculpture exhibited in two person show at Montclair State Univ., 1977. Mem. Phi Kappa Phi. Democrat. Episcopalian. Avocations: anthropology, reading, travel, gardening. Home: PO Box 2560 Key Largo FL 33037-7560

KENNEDY, MARY VIRGINIA, diplomat; b. Pocatello, Idaho, Sept. 5, 1946; d. Charles Millard and Martha Lorissa (Evans) K. BA, U. Denver, 1968, MA, 1969; MAT, U. Idaho, 1971, JD, 2001. Tchr. cert. Idaho. Recreation aide ARC, South Vietnam, 1969-70; ops. officer State Dept. Ops. Ctr., Washington, 1977-78; spl. asst. amb. Philip Habib, Washington, 1979-80, Sec. State, Washington, 1980-81; econ. officer U.S. Embassy, Cairo, 1981-84; consul Am. Consulate, Adana, Turkey, 1985-88; Pearson fellow Office Cong. Bereuter Ho. Reps., 1988-89; exec. asst. Dept. Sec. State, Washington, 1989-91; dep. chief mission Dept. State U.S. Embassy, Kuwait, 1991-93; consul gen. Am. Consulate, Karachi, Pakistan, 1994-96; dean Sch. Profl. Area Studies, Fgn. Svc. Inst., 1996-98. Bd. trustees Idaho State Hist. Soc., 1999—2002. Mem. Am. Fgn. Svc. Protective Assn. (bd. dirs. 1988-91), Phi Beta Kappa, Mortar Bd. Home: 5137 Admiral Way SW Seattle WA 98116 Address: PO Box 16634 Seattle WA 98116-0634 Personal E-mail: niact@aol.com.

KENNEDY, MEGAN CATHERINE, music educator; b. Johannesburg, July 16, 1963; arrived in U.S., 1997; d. Vivian Hector and Shirley Margaret Granger; m. David Mark Kennedy, Apr. 1, 1987; children: Diana, Jane, Kimberley. Student, Trinity Coll. Music, Johannesburg, 1975—80, U. South Africa, 1985—87, student, 1988; internat. diploma, CIDESCO, 1984. Instr. St. Clair Coll., Windsor, Canada, 1988—89; piano tchr. Windsor, 1992—94, Maxwell Music, White Lake, Mich., 2002—, Piano Power, West Bloomfield, Mich., 2002—. Mem.: Mich. Fedn. Music Clubs, Mich. Music Tchrs. Assn., Nat. Guild Piano Tchrs., Am. Coll. Musicians. Episcopalian. Avocations: gardening, walking, travel, history, log homes. E-mail: meegieloo@yahoo.com.

KENNEDY, MICHAEL JOHN, lawyer; b. Spokane, Wash., Mar. 23, 1937; s. Thomas Dennis Kennedy and Evelyn Elizabeth (Forbes) Gordon; m. Pamalee Hamilton, June 14, 1959 (div. July 1968); children: Lisa Marie, Scott Hamilton; m. Eleanore Renee Baratelli, July 14, 1968; 1 child, Anna Rosario. AB in Econs., U. Calif., Berkeley, 1959; JD, U. Calif., San Francisco, 1962. Bar: Calif. 1963, N.Y. 1976, U.S. Ct. Appeals (9th cir. 1963), U.S. Supreme

Ct. 1967, U.S. Ct. Appeals (5th cir.) 1975, U.S. Ct. Appeals 2d cir.) 1977, U.S. Ct. Appeals (1st 3d and 4th cirs.) 1979, U.S. Ct. Appeals (3d and D.C. cirs.) 1982. Assoc. Hoberg & Finger, San Francisco, 1962-67; staff counsel Emergency Civil Liberties, N.Y.C., 1967-69; ptnr. Kennedy & Rhine, San Francisco, 1969-76; sole practice N.Y.C., 1976—. Served to 1st lt. U.S. Army, 1963-65. Mem. ABA, N.Y. Criminal Bar Assn., Nat. Assn. Criminal Defenders. Clubs: N.Y. Athletic. Democrat. Roman Catholic. Home: 150 Central Park S New York NY 10019 Office: 419 Park Ave S FL 16 New York NY 10016-8410

KENNEDY, MICHAEL KELLY, lawyer, state official; b. New Hampton, Iowa, Oct. 30, 1939; s. William J. and Eileen (Kelly) K.; m. Linda Weiss, Aug. 14, 1964; 1 child, Cara Kennedy Ode. BA, U. Notre Dame, 1961; JD, U. Iowa, 1968. Bar: Iowa 1968. State rep., Iowa, 1969-73. Pres. Sch. Attys., Iowa, 1985; bd. of govs. Iowa Bar, 1986-90; bd. dirs. Homestead Housing, New Hampton, 1996-99; co-chmn. Build in Faith com., New Hampton, 1996-99. Avocations: reading, golf. Home: 929 Ash Dr New Hampton IA 50659-1074 Office: Kennedy & Kennedy Kennedy Law Bldg PO Box 406 New Hampton IA 50659-0406 E-mail: kenndlaw@rconnect.com.

KENNEDY, MURIEL, psychologist, consultant, educator; b. Bamberg, S.C., Mar. 29, 1965; d. Harold Lee Kennedy (dec.) and Virginia Morgan Kennedy Marion. BS, U. S.C., 1987; MS, Howard U., 1993, PhD, 1995. Lic. psychologist, Va., Md., D.C. Nuc. engr. Charleston Naval Shipyard, Charleston, S.C., 1987-90; psychology assoc. Child Advocacy Network, Balt., 1996-97; clin. psychologist Child and Family Therapy Ctr., Washington, 1997—. Clin. cons. Inst. for Life Enrichment, Washington, 1997—, Baraka Pastoral Counseling Ctr., Largo, Md., 1997—; adj. prof. Howard U., Washington, 1997—; exec. dir. Perico Inst. for Youth Devel. Entrepreneurship, Inc.; co-founder New Life Enrichment Ctr., Inc. Mem. Assn. Black Psychologists (treas. 1996-97, pres.-elect 1998-99, pres. 1999-2000, immediate past pres. 2000-2001), Psi Chi. Democrat. Baptist. Avocations: inspirational writing, listening to music, poetry, the arts, sports. E-mail: murielkenn@yahoo.com.

KENNEDY, P. LYNN, agricultural studies educator; b. Greeley, Colo., Oct. 5, 1963; s. Philip Wylie and Esther Louise (Faris) Kennedy; m. Julie Ann Ritschard, July 2, 1988; children: John, Sean, Eryn. BS in higher edn., Colo. State U., 1987; MS, Oxford U., 1988; PhD, U. Minn., 1994. Asst. prof. to assoc. prof. to prof. to Alexander Regents prof. La. State U., Baton Rouge, 1994—. Chair, dir. Southern Regional Rsch. Project on Internat. Trade, 1994—; co-dir. Ctr. For No. Am. Studies, 1994—. Author: International Trade and Agriculture, 2005; editor: Agricultural Trade Policies in the New Millenium, 2002. Named Outstanding Tchr. in Coll. of Agrl., La. State U., 2002; recipient Dist. Faculty award, 2003, Sedberry award for Outstanding Grad. Instr., 2001. Mem.: Am. Agrl. Econ. Assn. Office: La State U 101 Agrl Adminstrn Bldg Baton Rouge LA 70803 E-mail: lkennedy@agcenter.lsu.edu.

KENNEDY, PARKER S., finance company executive; b. Orange, Calif. m. Sherry Kennedy; children: Donald, Katie. AB in Econs., U. So. Calif., L.A., 1970; JD, U. Calif., Hastings, 1973. Assoc. Levinson & Lieberman, Beverly Hills, Calif.; sr. v.p. First Am. Title Co. of LA; various positions including v.p.-nat. sales dir. First Am., 1977—84; dir. First Am. Title, 1981—, exec. v.p., 1984-89, pres., 1989—99, chmn., 2003—; exec. v.p. First Am. Corp., 1986-93, dir., 1987—, pres., 1993—2003, chmn., CEO, 2003—. Bd. dir. Ellie Mae. Bd. dir. Fletcher Jones Found., Orange County Council, Boy Scouts of Am., Bowers Mus. Named one of Best Performing Bosses, Forbes Mag., 2003. Mem. Calif. Bar Assn., Am. Land Title Assn. (past pres.) Office: First Am Corp One First American Way Santa Ana CA 92707*

KENNEDY, PATRICK F., federal official; b. Chgo., June 22, 1949; m. M. Elizabeth Swope. BA, Georgetown U.; diploma Sr. Seminar in Fgn. Policy. Mem. Fgn. Svc., 1973, regional adminstrv. officer, 1973-74; pers. officer Bur. African Affairs, 1975-76; spl. asst. to under sec. for mgmt. Dept. of State, 1977-81, supervisory gen. svcs. officer Paris, 1981—85, exec. dir., then dep. exec. sec., 1985-90, adminstrv. counselor Cairo, 1991-93, asst. sec. adminstrn. Washington, 1993—2001; amb., U.S. rep. for mgmt. and reform UN. Office: US Mission to the UN 799 UN Plz New York NY 10017

KENNEDY, PATRICK J., congressman; b. Brighton, Mass., July 14, 1967; s. Edward M. and Joan (Bennett) K. Degree in Social Science, Providence Coll., 1991. Mem. R.I. Ho. Repr., 1989—95, U.S. Congress from 1st R.I. dist., 1995—; mem. appropriations com. Chmn. House Rules Com., 1992; del. 1988 Dem. Nat. Conv.; co-founder, co-chmn. Congressional Portuguese-Am. Caucus; mem. New Eng. Caucus, Congressional Caucus on Armenian Issues, Older Americans Caucus, Democratic Task Force on Tax Policy, AIDS PAC Congressional adv. bd., Italian-Am. Congressional Delegation; co-sponsoramendment in Older Americans Act, Higher Edn. Accumulation Program. Bd. dirs. R.I. Spl. Olympics, R.I. March of Dimes, Nat. Com. for Prevention of Child Abuse (R.I. chpt.), Big Brother R.I. Co-recipient Public Service award, Soc. for Neuroscience, 2002. Mem. R.I. Lung Assn. (bd. dirs.), R.I. Mental Health Assn. (bd. dirs.), Friends of Ireland. Democrat. Address: 249 Roosevelt Ave Pawtucket RI 02860-2908 Office: US House Reps 407 Cannon Ho Office Bldg Washington DC 20515-3901 E-mail: patrick.kennedy@mail.house.gov.*

KENNEDY, RANDALL L., law educator; b. Columbia, SC, 1954; BA, Princeton U., 1977; grad. studies in History, Balliol Coll., Oxford U., 1977-79; JD, Yale U., 1982. Bar: DC 1983. Law clk. to Hon. J. Skelly Wright US Ct. Appeals, 1982-83; law clk. to Hon. Thurgood Marshall US Supreme Ct., 1983-84; asst. prof. law Harvard Law Sch., Cambridge, Mass., 1984—89, prof., 1989—. Author: Race, Crime, and the Law, 1997, Nigger: The Strange Career of a Troublesome Word, 2002, Interracial Intimacies: Sex, Marriage, Identity and Adoption, 2003. Office: Harvard Law Sch 1563 Massachusetts Ave Cambridge MA 02138 Office Phone: 617-495-0907. Office Fax: 617-496-4866. Business E-Mail: rkennedy@law.harvard.edu.*

KENNEDY, RAOUL DION, lawyer; b. San Jose, Calif., Feb. 6, 1944; s. Ralph Craig and Maxine Thelma (Schoemake) K.; m. Patricia Ann Bilbrey. BA, U. Pacific, 1964; JD, U. Calif., Berkeley, 1967. Bar: Calif. 1967, U.S. Supreme Ct. 1970. Assoc. Hagar, Crosby Heafey, Roach & May, Oakland, Calif., 1969-96, Morrison & Foerster, San Francisco, 1996-99; ptnr. Skadden, Arps, Slate, Meagher & Flom LLP, San Francisco, Calif., 1999—. Co-author: California Expert Witness Guide, 1983, 2d edit., 1991. Fellow Am. Coll. Trial Lawyers, Internat. Soc. of Barristers; mem. Am. Bd. Trial Advocates, Internat. Acad. of Trial Lawyers, Am. Acad. Appellate Lawyers, Calif. Acad. Appellate Lawyers (pres. 1983-84). Republican. Home: 1701 Gough St San Francisco CA 94109-4419 Office: Skadden Arps Slate Meagher & Flom LLP Four Embarcadero Ctr San Francisco CA 94111

KENNEDY, RENEAU CHARLENE UFFORD, forensic psychologist, consultant; b. Weiser, Idaho, June 18, 1954; d. Eldon Luther and Iris Jean (Hetrick) Ufford; m. Allen Ken Kennedy (div. Apr. 1999). BS in Psychology and Speech, Willamette U., 1975; MS in Psychology, U. Oreg., 1981; EdD in Psychology, Boston U., 1994; postgrad., Harvard U., 1994-98. Lic. psychologist. Tchr., counselor Victorian Dept. Edn., Melbourne, Australia, 1975-78, 80; fellow in clin. and forensic psychology The McLean Hosp., Harvard Med. Sch., Belmont, 1986-87, fellow in neuropsychology dept. neurology, 1987-89; clin. fellow in forensic psychology Harvard Med. Sch./Mass. Gen. Hosp., Boston, 1992-98; cons. Mass. Dept. Youth Svcs., Boston, 1994-95, Ky. Justice Cabinet, Frankfort, 1995; pvt. practice Weston, Mass., 1996—, Honolulu, 1997—. Affiliate clin. tng. supr., course instr. Am. Sch. Profl. Psychology, Honolulu; dir. tng. Forensic and Behavioral Scis. Inst., Honolulu, 1998-2000, Honolulu Family Therapy Ctr., 2000—; clin. fellow MGH Law and Psychiatry Svc., 1992-98; cons., spkr. in field. Mem. Ky. Justice Cabinet Juvenile Task Force, Frankfort, 1994-96, Mass. Child Death Rev. Team, Boston, 1995-97, Mass. Ct. Subcom. on Risk Assessment, Dedham, 1995—; col., aide de camp Commr. of Ky. State Police, Frankfort, 1994, 95, 96. Predoctoral fellow Harvard Med. Sch., Boston, 1992-94; named to Hon. Order of Ky. Cols. Mem. APA, Soc. for Personality Assessment, Hawaii Psychol. Assn., Homicide Rsch. Working Group, Psi Chi, Phi Delta Kappa, Pi Lambda Theta. Avocations: scuba diving, triathlon events, exotic travel. Home and Office: 3001 Diamond Head Rd Honolulu HI 96815-4716 Fax: 808-923-2299. E-mail: rkennedy@lava.net.

KENNEDY, RICHARD JEROME, writer; b. Jefferson City, Mo., Dec. 23, 1932; s. Donald and Mary Louise (O'Keefe) K.; m. Lillian Elsie Nance, Aug. 3, 1960; children: Joseph Troy, Matthew Cook. BS, Portland State U., 1958. Author: (novel) Amy's Eye, 1985 (Internat. Rattenfanger Lit. prize, Fed. Republic Germany 1988), also 18 children's books including Richard Kennedy: Collected Stories, 1988 and 3 musicals, including adaptation of H.C. Andersen's The Snow Queen; inclusion of stories in: The Oxford Book of Modern Fairy Tales, 1993, The Oxford Book of Children's Stories, 1993. With USAF, 1951-54. Home and Office: 415 W Olive St Newport OR 97365-3716

KENNEDY, ROBERT ALAN, educational administrator; b. Benson, Minn., Sept. 29, 1946; s. William Henry and Mary Rose (Pothen) K.; m. Mary Ellen Rumpho, June 9, 1984; children: Caleb, Alex, Bryce, Curran. BS, U. Minn., 1968; PhD, U. Calif., Berkeley, 1974. Asst. prof. U. Iowa, Iowa City, 1974-78; assoc. prof. to prof. Wash. State U., Pullman, 1979-85; prof., chmn. Ohio State U., Columbus, 1987; program dir. NSF, Washington, 1987-89; v.p. res. U. Md., College Park, 1989-92; v.p. rsch., assoc. provost grad. studies Tex. A&M U., College Station, 1992-2000; from exec. v.p. to pres. U. Maine, 2000—04, pres., 2004—. Contbr. articles to profl. jours. Home: Presidents House Orono ME 04469

KENNEDY, ROBERT EMMET, JR., historian, educator; b. N.Y.C., Dec. 19, 1941; s. Robert Emmet and Jean (MacLeod) K.; m. Jane Marie McMahon, June 23, 1968; children: Mara, Gaëlle Marie, Daniel Patrick, Robert Emmet III. BA, Johns Hopkins U., 1963; MA, Boston Coll., 1965; PhD, Brandeis U., 1973. Instr. history Merrimack Coll., 1964-66; instr. history Kent State U., Ohio, 1968-69; asst.-associé U. Toulouse, France, 1969-73; asst. prof. European history George Washington U., Washington, 1973-77, assoc. prof., 1977-82, prof., 1982—. Co-editor: The Shaping of Modern France: Writings on French History since 1715, 1969; author: A Philosopher in the Age of Revolution: Destutt de Tracy and the Origins of "Ideology," 1978, A Cultural History of the French Revolution, 1989; co-author: Theatre, Opera and Audiences in Revolutionary Paris: Analysis and Repertory, 1996. Fellow Am. Council Learned Socs., 1977-78, Woodrow Wilson Internat. Ctr. for Scholars, 1983-84 Mem. Soc. French Hist. Studies, The Hist. Soc. (editl. bd.). Roman Catholic. Office: George Washington Univ Dept History Washington DC 20052-0001 E-mail: ekennedy@gwu.edu.

KENNEDY, R(OBERT) EVAN, engineering executive, consultant, retired structural engineer; b. Worland, Wyo., Mar. 31, 1916; s. Robert Eaker and Addie Miranda (Pritchard) K.; m. Betty Lou Kaser, Feb. 3, 1945; children: Anne Louise, Carter Evan, Robert Gordon. Student, Jamestown (N.D.) Coll., 1934-35; BS in Civil Engring., U. Colo., 1938. Recorder U. S. Geol. Survey, Denver, 1938-39; jr. hydraulic engr. Colo. Water Consv. Bd., Denver, 1939-41; structural draftsman, jr. designer Am. Bridge Co., Trenton, N.J., 1941-42; stress analyst Goodyear Aircraft Corp., Akron, Ohio, 1942-44, liaison engr., group leader, sect. head Phoenix, 1944-46; sales rep. Luby-Sonnen Co., Madison, Wis., 1946; project engr. Rentenbach Engring. Co., Knoxville, Tenn., 1946-47; field mgr. Kaser Constrn. Co., West Des Moines, Iowa, 1947; design engr. Moffatt, Nichol & Taylor, Portland, Oreg., 1947-49, Cooper & Rose, Portland, 1949-51; chief structural engr. Barrett & Logan Architects, Portland, 1951-52, Edmundson, Kochendoerfer & Kennedy A/E, Portland, 1952-53, chief engr., 1954-55, ptnr., 1955-68; mng. ptnr. Edmundson, Kochendoerfer, Kennedy-Daniel, Mann, Johnson, Mendenhall, Portland, 1968-74; v.p. Daniel, Mann, Johnson and Mendenhall, Baltimore, 1974-79; assoc. Tibbets, Abbott, McCarthy and Stratton, Washington, 1980-84; pres. Kennedy Assocs., Inc., Portland, 1984—. Bd. dirs. Terwilliger Plaza, treas. 2003; chmn. Seismic Design Com., Portland, 1948-50, bd. dirs., treas. Portland Bldg. Code Revisions Com., 1950-53; observer, cons. Effects Nuclear Test U.S. Dept. Commerce, Yucca Flats, Nev., 1955; instr. Oreg. Bd. Higher Edn. Architects Registration Exams., Portland, 1954-58, Engrs. Registration Exams., 1960-63; lectr. Oreg. Dental Sch. Disaster Planning, Portland, 1960-64; mem. A/E Selection Bd. U.S. Gen. Svcs. Adminstrn. NW Divsn., Auburn, Wash., 1973, Nat. Def. Exec. res. U. S. Bur. Pub. Rds., Washington, 1964-71; bd. mem. Portland Chess & Success, 1998—; cons. Seismic Structural Design, 2005. Contbr. articles to profl. jours. Vice chmn. Fernwood Grade Sch. PTA, Portland, 1952-53, Portland Traffic Safety Commn., 1964-74; chmn. scholarship Grant H.S. Dad's Club, Portland, 1964-67; chmn. engrs. divsn. Portland United Good Neighbors, 1965, chmn. profl. divsn., 1967, 68; pres. Portland City Club, 1968; chmn. Interfaith Housing Com., Portland, 1969-73; pres. Dulaney Towers Condo Bd., Towson, Md., 1975-78, Dulaney Towers Maintenance Bd., 1976-78, Waterford Condo. Bd., Kensington, Md., 1985-88, Am. Plz. Condo. Bd., 1999, Portland Housing Devel. Corp., Portland, 1970-74, Metrohousing, Inc., Portland, 1971-74;pres. chmn. Balt. Energy Coun., 1978; mem. Portland Symphonic Choir, 1958-64, Multnomah County Bldg. Code Appeals Bd., Portland, 1964, Nat. Mcpl. League, 1968-79, nat. conv. sect. convenor, 1976, 77, Mayor's Adv. Com., Portland, 1968-69, Congressman Wendell Wyatt Re-election Com., Portland, 1968; treas. Am. Plaza Condo Assn. Bd., Portland, 1991-96; mem., elder Towson Presbyn. Ch., 1974-79. Recipient Meritorious Svc. award City Portland, 1952, Nat. Design Honor award HUD, Washington, 1976, Grand Design award Am. Consulting Engrs. Coun., Washington, 1996, Outstanding Vol. award Am. Plz. Condo, 2001. Mem. ASCE (bd. dirs. Oreg. sect. 1953-55, Capital sect. 1980-90, sec. 1983, mem. Md. sect. 1974-90, Oreg. sect. 1990—), ASTM (chmn. NW dist. 1970), Am. Concrete Inst., Soc. Am. Mil. Engrs. (Merit award Portland Post 1973), Structural Engrs. Assn. Oreg. (life; founder, pres. 1949), Profl. Engrs. Oreg. (bd. dirs. 1948-74, chmn. Conv. 100 Yrs. Engring., founder Engr. Yr. award 1952), Prestressed Concrete Inst., Engring. Coun. Rsch. Inst., Consulting Engrs. Coun. Oreg. (treas. Oreg. 1960, Engring. Excellence Project award 1996, nat. 1997; certificate life mem., founding mem. 2004), Toastmasters. Republican. Home and Office: 2545 SW Terwilliger Plz #1121 Portland OR 97201-6312 Address: 2545 SW Terwilliger Blvd No 1121 Portland OR 97201-6312 Office Phone: 503-299-1108. Business E-Mail: revank@tplaza.org.

KENNEDY, ROBERT FRANCIS, JR., lawyer, environmentalist; b. Washington, Jan. 17, 1954; s. Robert F. Kennedy Sr. and Ethel Skakel Kennedy; m. Emily Ruth Black, 1982 (div. 1992); children: Robert, Kathleen; m. Mary Richardson, Apr. 15, 1994; children: Conor, Kyra, William, Aidan. BA, Harvard U., 1977; JD, U. Va., 1982; LLM, Pace U., 1987; studied at, London Sch. Econs., 1978. Former asst. dist. atty. NYC; sr. atty. Nat. Resources Defense Coun., 1991—; chief prosecuting atty. Hudson Riverkeeper, 1993—; pres. Waterkeeper Alliance; clin. prof., supervising atty. Pace U. Sch. Law Environ. Litig. Clinic, White Plains, NY, 1999—; host Ring of Fire, Air Am. Radio, 2005—. Author: Judge Frank M. Johnson, Jr.: A Biography, 1977, Crimes Against Nature: How George Bush and His Corporate PALS Are Plundering the Country and Hijacking Our Democracy, 2004, (children's book) Saint Francis of Assisi: A Life of Joy, 2005; co-author (with David K. Gordon): The Legend of City Water: Recommendations for Rescuing the New York City Water Supply, 1991; (with John Cronin) The Riverkeepers: Two Activists Fight to Reclaim Our Environment as Basic Human Right, 1997. Avocation: white-water paddling. Office: Nat Resources Defense Coun 40 W 20th St New York NY 10011 also: Pace Law Sch 78 N Broadway White Plains NY 10603 Office Phone: 212-727-2700. E-mail: rkennedy@law.pace.edu.

KENNEDY, ROBERT PHILIP, civil engineer; b. Glendale, Calif., Apr. 2, 1939; BS, MS, Stanford U., 1961, PhD of Structural Engring., 1967. Rsch. engr. Northrop Corp., 1963—64; dir. engring. mechs. Holmes & Narver, 1966—76; v.p. engring. decision Analysis Corp., 1976—80; pres. Structural Mechanics Assn., 1980—86, RPK Structrual Mechanics Consulting, Escondido, Calif., 1986—. Mem. ASCE (Stephen Bechtel Energy Engr. award 1992), Nat. Acad. Engrs., Am. Concrete Inst., Earthquake Engring. Rsch. Inst. Home and Office: RPK Structural Mechanics Cons 28625 Mountain Meadow Rd Escondido CA 92026-6912 Office Phone: 760-751-3510.

KENNEDY, ROGER GEORGE, museum program director, parks director; b. St. Paul, Aug. 3, 1926; s. Walter J. and Elisabeth (Dean) K.; m. Frances Hefren, Aug. 23, 1958; 1 dau., Ruth. Grad., St. Paul Acad., 1944; BA, Yale, 1949; LL.B., U. Minn., 1952. Bar: Minn. 1952, D.C. 1953. Atty. Justice Dept., 1953; corr. NBC, 1954-57; dir. Dallas Council World Affairs, 1958; spl. asst. to sec. Dept. Labor, 1959; successively asst. v.p., v.p., chmn. exec. com., dir. Northwestern Nat. Bank St. Paul, 1959-69; v.p. finance, exec. dir. Univ. Found., Minn., 1969-70; v.p. financial affairs Ford Found., N.Y.C., 1970-78, v.p. arts, 1978-79; dir. Nat. Mus. Am. History Smithsonian Instn., Washington, 1979-92, dir. emeritus, 1993—; dir. Nat. Park Svc., Washington, 1993-97. Spl. asst. to sec. HEW, 1957, cons. to sec., 1969 Author: Minnesota Houses, 1967, Men on a Moving Frontier, 1969, American Churches, 1982, Architecture, Men, Women and Money, 1985, Orders from France, 1989, Greek Revival America, 1989; editl. dir.: Smithsonian Guide to Historic America, 12 vols., 1989-90, Rediscovering America, 1990, Mission 1993, Hidden Cities, 1993, Burr, Jefferson, and Hamilton, 1999, Mr. Jefferson's Lost Cause, 2003; appearances on NBC radio and TV Today, also others, 1954-57; contbr. articles to mags. and profl. jours. Served with USNR, 1944-46. Address: 33 Linnaean St #1 Cambridge MA 02138-1511 Personal E-mail: roger@rkennedy.net.

KENNEDY, RUSSELL EDWARD, academic administrator; s. Russell Eugene and Alice Louise Kennedy; m. Karen Sue Janowiak, Mar. 26, 1977 (div. Oct. 18, 1988); children: Colleen June Kennedy Frazer, Matthew David, Brian Daniel, Curtis Russell. BS in Edn., Ind. U., 1973; MS in Adminstrn., U. Notre Dame, 1986. Cert. Am. Soc. for Hosp. Pub. Rels. and Mktg., 1984. News anchor, prodr., reporter Marion (Ind.) Cable TV, Inc., 1973; news reporter, announcer WGOM-AM/WMRI-FM, Marion, 1973—74; news anchor, prodr., reporter WNDU AM-FM-TV, South Bend, Ind., 1974—77, asst. news dir., 1977—80; cmty. rels. mgr. St. Joseph's Med. Ctr., South Bend, 1980—84, dir. cmty. rels., 1984—85, dir. mktg., 1985—86; dir. market comm. St. Joseph's Care Group, South Bend, 1986—89; adj. faculty mem., pub. speaking and radio news Ind. U., South Bend, 1989—91; dir. edn. Oaklawn Cmty. Mental Health Ctr. and Hosp., Elkhart/Goshen, Ind., 1989—93; mktg. dir. CPC Valle Vista Hosp., Greenwood, Ind., 1993—94; pvt. practice mktg. cons. Indpls., 1994—95; dir. edn. and pub. affairs Mental Health Assn. in Marion County, Indpls., 1995—98; media specialist Media Wise, Indpls., 1998—2000; gen. edn. instr. ITT Tech. Inst., Indpls., 2000—01, assoc. dean, 2001—. Chair nat. membership com. Soc. Profl. Journalists, 1979—80; pres. Michiana Chpt., Soc. Profl. Journalists, South Bend, 1979—80, South Bend Press Club, 1982—83, Ind. Soc. for Healthcare Pub. Rels. and Mktg., 1988—89; mem. coun. on pub. rels. Ind. Hosp. Assn., 1988. Contbr. articles to profl. jours. Chair of one of six pilot sites nationally for anxiety disorders edn. program NIMH, Washington, 1996—98; mem., subcommittee on outreach, edn., and communication Ind. Governor's Adv. Panel on Children's Health Ins., 1998; mem., cmty. adv. com., Marion County cmty. health assessment project Marion County Dept. of Pub. Health, Indpls., 1996; selected by u. adminstrn. to serve on 14-mem. student bd. Ind. U. Meml. Union, Bloomington, Ind., 1971—72. Recipient CASPER Award for Campaign on Clin. Depression, United Way Ctrl. Ind., 1998; Hoosier Scholar, State Ind., 1969. Mem.: Alpha Epsilon Rho, Phi Delta Kappa Internat. Office: ITT Tech Inst 9511 Angola Ct Indianapolis IN 46268

KENNEDY, SANDRA ELAINE, small business owner; b. Jacksonville, Fla., Apr. 27, 1948; d. Amos Edward and Janette Majorie Cordell; m. Charles Stephen Phillips, Oct. 19, 1967 (div. July 8, 1991); children: Amber Mechelle Geiger, Laurie Beth Johns; m. James Hilliard Kennedy, Jr.; children: Andrew Jordon, Justin Franklin Hilliard, Nicole. Student, No. Va. Coll., U. S.C. Learning disability asst. Dept. Def., Keflavick, Iceland, dir. spl. svcs. Exmouth, Australia, spl. edn. asst. Quantico, Va.; specialist FBI, Washington; dir., owner Tiny Junction, Inc., Lexington, SC. Cons. Mil. Base, Exmouth, Australia, 1980—82, FBI, Washington, 1984—90, Parkway Acad., Columbia, 1999—2000. Author: Drax Stone, 1999, Rainbow Collection, 2000, The Bartwell Tradegy, 2001. Grantee, Dept. Health and Human Svcs., 1992. Mem.: S.C. Autism Soc. Avocations: painting, writing. Home: 305 St Thomas Ch Rd Chapin SC 29036 Office: Tiny Junction Inc 1106 Old Two Notch Rd Lexington SC 29073 Office Phone: 803-356-8424. E-mail: kennedy875@bellsouth.net.

KENNEDY, STEPHEN DANDRIDGE, economist, researcher; b. N.Y.C., Feb. 25, 1942; s. Joseph Conrad and Frances (Midlam) K.; m. Joanna Court Bartlett, Nov. 27, 1965; children: Julia Paca, Benjamin Bartlett. AB, Harvard U., 1963; PhD, MIT, 1972. Mem. staff com. on banking and currency U.S. Ho. of Reps., Washington, 1964-66; adminstrv. asst. The Fed. Home Loan Bank Bd., Washington, 1966-67; analyst Abt Assocs., Inc., Cambridge, Mass., 1970, v.p., 1975, chief scientist, 1988—. Adj. lectr. John F. Kennedy Sch. Govt., Harvard U., 1995. Bd. trustees The Commonwealth Sch., 1997—2002. Episcopalian. Avocations: gardening, sailing. Office: ABT Assocs Inc 55 Wheeler St Cambridge MA 02138-1192

KENNEDY, THOMAS J., lawyer; b. Milw., July 29, 1947; s. Frank Philip and June Marian (Smith) K.; m. Cathy Ann Cohen, Nov. 24, 1978; children: Abby, Sarah. BA, U. Wis., 1969, JD cum laude, 1972. Bar: Wis. 1972, U.S. Dist. Ct. (ea. and we. dists.) Wis. 1972, Ariz. 1981, U.S. Dist. Ct. Ariz. 1981, U.S. Ct. Appeals (7th cir.) 1980, U.S. Ct. Appeals (9th cir.) 1981, U.S. Ct. Appeals (D.C. cir.) 1983, U.S. Supreme Ct. 1984, U.S. Ct. Appeals (11th cir.) 1986. Assoc. Goldberg, Previant, Milw., 1972-79, Brynelson, Herrick, Madison, Wis., 1979-81; ptnr. Snell & Wilmer, Phoenix, 1981-93, Lewis and Roca, Phoenix, 1993-96, Ryley, Carlock and Applewhite, Phoenix, 1996-99, Gallagher & Kennedy, 1999—2000, Sherman & Howard, 2000—. Contbg. editor The Developing Labor Laws, 2d, 3d edits., The Fair Labor Standards Act. Mem. ABA, Ariz. State Bar, State Bar Wis., Maricopa County Bar Assn. Avocations: tennis, reading, hiking. Office Phone: 602-636-2015. Business E-Mail: tkennedy@sah.com.

KENNEDY, THOMAS PATRICK, financial executive; b. N.Y.C., Oct. 13, 1932; s. Andrew Francis and Marie P. (Scullen) K.; m. Mary P. Drennan, Jan. 14, 1956 (dec.); children: Thomas Patrick, Kevin M. (dec.), Michael J., Mary P. Kennedy Handsman, Deborah A. Kennedy Carter. BS, St. Peter's Coll., 1958; postgrad., Seton Hall U., 1959. Acct. Haskins & Sells CPAs, N.Y.C., 1953-54, 1955—57; staff Emerson Radio & TV, N.Y.C., 1957-58; various exec. positions CBS, N.Y.C., 1958-67; with Ford Found., N.Y.C., 1967; dir. fin. Pub. Broadcasting Lab., N.Y.C., 1967-69; with Children's TV Workshop (Sesame St.), N.Y.C., 1969-80, CFO, v.p. fin. and adminstrn., 1969-78, treas., 1969-78, sr. v.p., 1978-80; exec. dir. Ctr. Non-Broadcast TV, 1980-85; pres. Tomken Mgmt., Ltd., 1980—, chmn. bd., 1983—; chmn. bd., CEO, Effie Techs., Inc., 1984—. V.p., corp. fin. Jersey Capital Mkts Group, Inc., 1987-88; chief exec. officer, chmn. bd. Corp. Strategies Group, Inc., 1988-89; v.p. Vantage Securities, Inc. (co-venture with Whitehall Fin. Group), 1991-94; cons. in field; bd. advisers Franciscan Comm. Ctr.; bd. dirs., exec. dir. Ctr. for Non-Broadcast TV, 1980-85; ptnr. Hunter Village Estates Realty; officer, dir. Hunter Village Country Club Estates, Inc. With C.E., U.S. Army, 1954-55, Korea. Mem. Fin. Execs. Inst., Internat. Radio and TV Soc., Inst. Broadcast Fin. Mgmt., Nat. Assn. Accts., Internat. Broadcast Inst., Internat. Inst. Comm., Internat. Assn. Fin. Execs., Am. Assn. Individual Investors, Am. Legion, Korean War Vets., Brevard Vets. Council, Vets. Fgn. Wars, N.Y. Athletic Club, Knights of Columbus. Republican. Roman Catholic. Home and Office: 420 E 54th St Apt 16A New York NY 10022 Office Phone: 212-980-6845.

KENNEDY, WILBERT KEITH, SR., agronomy educator, retired university official; b. Vancouver, Wash., Jan. 4, 1919; s. Wilbert Parsons and Gracie Evelyn (Woolf) K.; m. Barbara Josephine Barber, Dec. 9, 1941 (dec. Nov. 1999); children: Wilbert Keith, James Clayton. BS, Wash. State U., 1940; MS in Agr., Cornell U., 1941, PhD, 1947. Asst. prof., asst. agronomist Wash. State Coll., 1947-48, assoc. prof., assoc. agronomist, 1948-49; prof. agronomy Cornell U., Ithaca, N.Y., 1949—; assoc. dir. research N.Y. State Coll. Agr.,

Cornell U.; also assoc. dir. Cornell U. Agr. Exptl. Sta., 1959, dir. research and dir. expt. sta., 1959-65; assoc. dean N.Y. State Coll. Agr., 1965-67, vice provost univ., 1967-72, dean, 1972-78, provost univ., 1978-84, provost emeritus, 1984—; with Atlantic Philantropic Svc. Co., Ithaca, 1988—. Cons. Rockefeller Found., Kasetsart U., Thailand, 1968, Ford Found., Malaysia, 1970 Contbr. articles to profl. jours. Mem. sch. bd., Dryden, N.Y., 1953-55; exec. com. Louis Agassiz council Boy Scouts Am., 1955-70; active local Community Chest; bd. dirs. Tompkins Community Hosp., 1984-94, pres., 1986-88. Served to maj. AUS, 1942-46. Guggenheim fellow; Fulbright scholar, 1956-57; recipient N.Y. Farmers award, 1958, Merit Cert. award Am. Grassland Council, 1964 Fellow Am. Soc. Agronomy, AAAS; mem. Sigma Xi, Phi Kappa Phi, Alpha Zeta. Lodges: Rotary. Home: 410 Savage Farm Dr Ithaca NY 14850-6506

KENNEDY, W(ILBERT) KEITH, JR., retired electronics executive, transportation executive; b. Phoenix, Ariz., Sept. 19, 1943; BSEE, MS, Cornell U., 1966, PhD, 1968. Researcher microwave solid-state devices Cornell U. and RCA Rsch. Labs., Princeton, N.J., 1964-68; researcher, leader devel. team thin-film fabrication facility Watkins-Johnson Co., Palo Alto, Calif., 1968-71, head R & D devel. dept., 1971-74, solid state div. mgr., 1974-78, also v.p., 1977, devices group v.p., 1978-86, v.p. shareowner rels. and planning coord., 1986-88, co. pres., chief exec. officer, 1988—2000; vice chmn. CNF Inc., Palo Alto, Calif., 2002—04, chmn., 2004—. Contbr. articles to profl. jours. and procs. Patentee microwave power generator. Bd. dir. & past chmn. Joint Venture: Silicon Valley Network; bd. dir. Lytton Gardens. Mem. IEEE (sr.); mem. Group Electronic Devices of IEEE, Group Microwave Theory and Techs. of IEEE, Calif. C. of C. (bd. dirs.), Phi Eta Sigma, Eta Kappa Nu, Tau Beta Phi, Phi Kappa Phi, Sigma Xi. Office: CNF Inc 3240 Hillview Ave Palo Alto CA 94304*

KENNEDY, WILLIAM F., retired military officer; b. NYC, Mar. 12, 1940; m. Janet Kennedy. BA, U. Mass., 1973; cert., Bentley Coll. Inst. Paralegal Studies. Enlisted U.S. Army, 1977, advanced through grades to chief warrant officer, 1997; ret., 1997. Author: Life and Eternity, 1958, Korea in My Eyes, 1960. With USAF, 1957—63, Korea. Decorated Korea Def. Svc. medal. Mem.: DAV (comdr. chpt. 45 2000—02, treas. chpt. 45 2005—), VFW. Avocations: chess, swimming, travel. Personal E-mail: wfkenn@hotmail.com.

KENNEDY, WILLIAM JOSEPH, novelist, educator; b. Albany, N.Y., Jan. 16, 1928; s. William Joseph and Mary Elizabeth (McDonald) K.; m. Dana Daisy Segarra, Jan. 31, 1957; children: Dana Elizabeth, Katherine Anne, Brendan Christopher. BA, Siena Coll., 1949; LHD (hon.), Russell Sage Coll., 1980; ArtsD (hon.), Rensselaer Poly. Inst., 1987, LHD (hon.), 1987, L.I. U., 1989, Fordham U., 1992, Trinity Coll., 1992, Notre Dame, 2001, DePaul U., 2002, St. Lawrence U., 2005; LittD (hon.), Siena Coll., 1984, Coll. St. Rose, 1985. Asst. sports editor, columnist Glens Falls Post Star, N.Y., 1949-50; reporter Albany Times-Union, N.Y., 1952-56, spl. writer, 1963-70; asst. mng. editor, columnist P.R. World Jour., San Juan, 1956; reporter Miami Herald, Fla., 1957; corr. Time-Life Publs. in P.R., 1957-59; founding mng. editor San Juan Star, 1959-61; lectr. SUNY, Albany, 1974-82, prof. English, 1983—. Vis. prof. Cornell U., Ithaca, N.Y., 1982-83; founder N.Y. State Writers Inst., 1983. Author: (book) The Ink Truck, 1969, Legs, 1975, Billy Phelan's Greatest Game, 1978, O Albany, 1983, Ironweed, 1983 (Pulitzer prize, 1984, Nat. Book Critics Circle award, 1984, film script, 1987), Quinn's Book, 1988, Very Old Bones, 1992, Riding the Yellow Trolley Car, 1993, The Flaming Corsage, 1996, Roscoe, 2002, (film script with Francis Ford Coppola) The Cotton Club, 1984, (children's books with Brendan Christopher Kennedy) Charlie Malarkey and the Belly Button Machine, 1986, Charlie Marlarkey and the Singing Moose, 1994, (play) Grand View, 1996. Served U.S. Army, 1950-52. Recipient Creative Arts award Brandeis U., 1986, Gov. N.Y. Arts award, 1984, Comdr. Order of Arts and Letters, France, 1993; MacArthur Found. fellow, 1983, Nat. Endowment of the Arts fellow, 1981. Mem.: Am. Acad. Arts and Scis., Acad. Motion Picture Arts and Scis., Am. Acad. Arts and Letters. Office: NYS Writers Inst U Albany 1400 Washington Ave Albany NY 12222-0100

KENNEDY, X.J. (JOSEPH KENNEDY), writer; b. Dover, N.J., Aug. 21, 1929; s. Joseph Francis and Agnes (Rauter) K.; m. Dorothy Mintzlaff, 1962; children: Kathleen, David, Matthew, Daniel, Joshua. BSc, Seton Hall U., 1950; MA, Columbia U., 1951; cert., U. Paris, France, 1956; LHD (hon.), Lawrence U., 1988; DFA (hon.), Adelphi U., 1998; DLitt (hon.), Westfield State Coll., 2002. Teaching fellow U. Mich., Ann Arbor, 1956—60, instr. English, 1960-62; lectr. English Woman's Coll., U. N.C., Greensboro, 1962-63; asst. prof. English Tufts U., Medford, Mass., 1963-67, assoc. prof., 1967-73, prof., 1973-79. Vis. lectr. Wellesley Coll., 1964, U. Calif., Irvine, 1966—67. Author: Nude Descending a Staircase, 1961, 2d edit., 1994, Introduction To Poetry, 1966, 11th edit., (with Dana Gioia) 2005, Growing into Love, 1969, Breaking and Entering, 1971, Emily Dickinson in Southern California, 1974, Celebrations After the Death of John Brennan, 1974, (with J.E. Camp, Keith Waldrop) Three Tenors, One Vehicle, 1975, One Winter Night in August, 1975, Introduction to Fiction, 1976, (with Dana Gioia) 9th edit., 2005, Literature, 1976, (with Dana Gioia) 9th edit., 2005, The Phantom Ice Cream Man, 1979, (with Dorothy M. Kennedy) The Bedford Reader, 1982, (with Dorothy M. Kennedy and Jane Aaron) 8th edit., 2003, Did Adam Name the Vinegarroon?, 1982, French Leave: Translations, 1983, Hangover Mass, 1984, (with Dorothy M. Kennedy) Knock at a Star: a Child's Introduction to Poetry, 1982, revised edit., 1999, The Owlstone Crown, 1983, 2nd edit., 2005, The Forgetful Wishing-Well, 1985, Cross Ties: Selected Poems, 1985, Brats, 1986; (with Dorothy M. Kennedy) The Bedford Guide for College Writers, 1987, 7th edit., (with Dorothy M. Kennedy, Sylvia A. Holladay and Marcia F. Muth) 2005, Ghastlies, Goops and Pincushions, 1989, Fresh Brats, 1990, Winter Thunder, 1990, The Kite That Braved Old Orchard Beach., 1991, (with Dorothy M. Kennedy) Talking Like the Rain, 1992, The Beasts of Bethlehem, 1992, Dark Horses: New Poems, 1992, Drat These Brats!, 1993, The Minimus Poems, 1996, Uncle Switch, 1997, The Eagle as Wide as the World, 1997, Elympics, 1999, Elefantina's Dream, 2002, Exploding Gravy, 2002, The Lords of Misrule: Poems, 1992-2001, 2002, (with Dana Gioia and Mark Baverlein) Handbook of Literary Terms, 2005; translator: Lysistrata in Penn Greek Drama Series, 1999; poetry editor: Paris Rev., 1961-64; editor: (with J.E. Camp) Mark Twain's Frontier, 1963, (with J.E. Camp, Keith Waldrop) Pegasus Descending, 1971, 2nd edit. 2003, Messages, 1973, Tygers of Wrath: poems of hate, anger and invective, 1981, (with Dorothy M. Kennedy) Knee-Deep in Blazing Snow: poems by James Hayford, 2005; editor, pub. (with Dorothy M. Kennedy) Counter/Measures mag, 1971-74. Judge Nat. Coun. on Arts poetry book selections, 1969, 70, T.S. Eliot prize Thomas Jefferson Univ. Press, 1998, X.J. Kennedy poetry award Tex. Rev., 1998, 90, 2000. With USN, 1951-55. Recipient Lamont Poetry award Acad. Am. Poets, Bess Hokin prize Poetry mag., 1961; Golden Rose award New Eng. Poetry Club, 1974; Los Angeles Times book award for poetry, 1985, Michael Braude award for light verse Am. Acad. and Inst. Arts and Letters, 1989, Aiken-Taylor award U. of the South, 1999, Excellence of Poetry for Children award, Nat. Coun. Tchrs. of English, 2000, The Poets' prize, 2004; grant Nat. Council Arts and Humanities, 1967-68; Shelley Meml. award, 1970; Bread Loaf fellow in poetry Middlebury Coll., 1960; Guggenheim fellow, 1973-74; Bruern fellow in Am. civilization U. Leeds, 1974-75. Mem. Assn. Lit. Scholars and Critics, John Barton Wolgamot Soc., PEN (mem. coun. New Eng. 1996—), MLA, Poetry Soc. Am., Nat. Coun. Tchrs. English, Authors Guild, Phi Beta Kappa, Sigma Tau Delta (hon.). Home: 22 Revere St Lexington MA 02420-4424

KENNEL, CHARLES FREDERICK, physics professor, academic administrator, government official; b. Cambridge, Mass., Aug. 20, 1939; s. Archie Clarence and Elizabeth Ann (Fitzpatrick) K.; m. Ellen Lehman; children: Matthew Bochner, Sarah Alexandra. AB, Harvard U., 1959; PhD in Astrophys. Scis., Princeton U., 1964; DSc (hon.), U. Ala., Huntsville, 2003. Prin. rsch. scientist Avco-Everett Rsch. Lab., Mass., 1960-61, 64-67; vis. scientist Internat. Ctr. Theoretical Physics, Trieste, Italy, 1965; faculty UCLA, 1967-71, prof. physics, 1971-98, chmn. dept., 1983-86, exec. vice-chancellor, 1996-98; mem. Inst. Geophysics and Planetary Physics, 1972-98, acting assoc. dir. inst., 1976-77; space sci. bd. NRC, 1977-80, chmn. com. space physics, 1977-80; Fairchild prof. Calif. Inst. Tech., 1987; assoc. adminstr. NASA, Washington, 1994-96; vice-chancellor, dir. Scripps Inst. Oceanography U. Calif.-San Diego, La Jolla, 1998—. Space and earth scis. adv. com. NASA, 1986—89, adv. coun., 1998, chmn., 2001—; bd. physics and astronomy NRC, 1987—94, chmn., 1992—94, chmn. fusion sci. adv. com., 1998—2001, chmn. com. on global change rsch., 1999—2002, chmn. plasma sci., 1990; chmn. Partnership for the Observation of the Global Oceans, 1999—2002; fusion policy adv. com. DOE, 1990; Fulbright lectr., Brazil; visitor U.S.-USSR Acads. Exch., 1988—90; disting. vis. prof. U. Alaska, 1988—93; mem. Pew Oceans Commn., 2000—03; cons. in field. Co-author: Matter in Motion, The Spirit and Evolution of Physics, 1977; co-editor: Solar System Plasma Physics, 1978. Bd. dirs. L.A. Jr. Ballet Co., 1977-83, pres., 1979-80; bd. dirs. Inst. for Theoretical Physics, Santa Barbara, Calif., 1986-90, San Diego Nat. History Mus., 1998-2002, Calif. Climate Action Registry, 2002-05, chmn., 2005-; bd. dirs. Calif. Ocean Sci. Trust, 2002-. Nat. scholar Harvard U., 1959, W.C. Peyton Advanced fellow, 1962-63, NSF postdoctoral fellow, 1965-66, Sloan fellow, 1968-70, Fulbright scholar, 1985, Guggenheim fellow, 1987; recipient Aurelio Peccei prize Acad. Lincei, 1995, Hannes Alfven prize European Geophys. Soc., 1998, NASA Disting. Svc. medal, 1996. Fellow: AAAS, Am. Phys. Soc. (pres. divsn. plasma physics 1989, James Clerk Maxwell prize 1997), Am. Geophys. Union; mem.: NAS, Am. Philos. Soc., Calif. Coun. on Sci. and Tech., Internat. Acad. Astronautics, Am. Acad. Arts and Scis. Office: U Calif San Diego SIO/DO 9500 Gilman Dr La Jolla CA 92093-0210 Office Phone: 858-534-2826, 858-534-2827.

KENNELL, ILANA JOY, music educator; b. Milw. m. Richard Kennell, Aug. 3, 1975; children: Jonathan, Aaron. B in Music Edn., Northwestern U., 1974; MusM, U. Wis., Milw., 1975. Coord. class piano and pedagogy U. Toledo, 1990—. Chair, instr. group piano Interlochen (Mich.) Arts Camp, 1995—2004. Named Nat. Cert. Tchr. of the Yr., Ohio Music Tchrs. Assn. N.W. Dist., 2003, 2005. Office Phone: 418-530-4552. Business E-Mail: ilanakennell@utoledo.edu.

KENNELL, RICHARD WAYNE, recording industry executive, consultant; b. Ft. Wayne, Ind., Aug. 11, 1952; s. John Charles and Betty June (Miller) K.; m. Leah Marie Waybright, Aug. 1, 1976. Student, Ind. U., Ft. Wayne, 1970—71, James Madison U., 1974. Rec. artist (bassist) Arista Records/Happy the Man, Reston, Va., 1974-79; rec. studio owner, prodr., bus. mgr. The Inner Circle, White Plains, NY, 1984-96; bus. mgr. Inner Workings, Briarcliff Manor, NY, 1996—; CFO Great No. Arts, 1990—, Invasion Group Ltd., 1990—, July 4th Music, Inc., 1990—, Castle Hill Pub. Ltd., 1990—; co-owner Innertainment, 2000—. Albums include Happy the Man, 1977, reissued, 1999, Crafty Hands, 1978, reissued, 1999, Better Late, 1983, Retrospective, 1989, Beginnings, 1990, Past, Present, Future, 1991, Happy the Man Live, 1994, Death's Crown, 1999, Beauty Gone Wild, 2001, The Muse Awakens, 2004. Served with U.S. Army, 1971-73. Mem. ASCAP, Audio Engrng. Soc., Am. Fedn. Musicians, NARAS. Avocations: travel, computers, reading. Office: 522 N State Rd Ste 102 Briarcliff Manor NY 10510-1540 Home: 48 Seven Hills Lake Dr Kent Cliffs NY 10512 Office Phone: 914-762-2238. E-mail: manohman@innertainment.net.

KENNELLY, BARBARA B., former congresswoman, federal agency administrator; b. Hartford, Conn., July 10, 1936; d. John Moran and Barbara (Leary) Bailey; m. James J. Kennelly, Sept. 26, 1959 (dec. 1995); children: Eleanor Bride, Barbara Leary, Louise Moran, John Bailey. BA in Econs, Trinity Coll., Washington, 1958; grad., Harvard-Radcliffe Sch. Bus. Adminstrn., 1959; MA in Govt, Trinity Coll., Hartford, 1971. Mem. Hartford Ct. of Common Council, 1975-79; sec. of state State of Conn., Hartford, 1979-83; mem. 98th-105th Congresses from 1st Dist. Conn., Hartford, 1982-98; mem. ways and means com.; counselor, assoc. commr. Social Security Adminstrn., 1999-2000; sr. adv. Baker & Hostetler, Washington; currently pres. & CEO Nat. Com. to Preserve Social Sec. & Medicare. Trustee Trinity Coll., Hartford, Conn.; active in numerous polit., civic, and goft. orgns. Greater Hartford, Conn.; co-chair Ctr. for Democracy, Washington. Democrat. Roman Catholic. Office: Natl Com Preserve Social Security & Medicare 10 G St NE Ste 600 Washington DC 20004*

KENNELLY, DENNIS L., lawyer; b. Jersey City, July 23, 1948; s. Lawrence William and Florence (Taylor) Kennelly; m. Anne Marie Gilles, Jan. 14, 1978; children: Margaret Anne, Maureen Elizabeth. AB cum laude, Coll. of Holy Cross, 1970; JD, Duke U., 1973. Bar: Iowa 1973, Hawaii 1974, Calif. 1975. Labor rels. mgr., counsel San Francisco Newspaper Agy. (Chronicle/Examiner), 1976—79; dir. employee rels., labor counsel Peninsula Times Tribune, Palo Alto, 1979—85; prin. Dennis L. Kennelly Law Office, Menlo Park, 1985—. Lt. JAGC USNR, 1973—76. Republican. Roman Catholic. Avocations: golf, sports, basketball. Office: 1030 Curtis St Ste 200 Menlo Park CA 94025-4501 Office Phone: 650-853-1291.

KENNELLY, SISTER KAREN MARGARET, retired academic administrator, church administrator, nun; b. Graceville, Minn., Aug. 4, 1933; d. Walter John Kennelly and Clara Stella Eastman. BA, Coll. St. Catherine, St. Paul, 1956; MA, Cath. U. Am., 1958; PhD, U. Calif., Berkeley, 1962. Joined Sisters of St. Joseph of Carondelet, Roman Cath. Ch., 1954. Prof. history Coll. St. Catherine, 1962-71, acad. dean, 1971-79; exec. dir. Nat. Fedn. Carondelet Colls., 1979-82; province dir. Sisters of St. Joseph of Carondelet, St. Paul, 1982-88; pres. Mt. St. Mary's Coll., L.A., 1989-2000, pres. emerita, 2000—; congl. dir. Sisters of St. Joseph of Carondelet, St. Louis, 2002—. Cons. N. Ctrl. Accreditation Assn., Chgo., 1974—84, Ohio Bd. Regents, Columbus, 1983—89; trustee colls., hosps., Minn., Mo., Wis., Calif., 1972—; chmn. Sisters St. Joseph Coll. Consortium, 1979—82. Editor, co-author: Am. Cath. Women, 1989; author (with others): Women of Minnesota, 1977; author: Women Religious and the Intellectual Life: The North American Achievement, 1996; co-editor: Gender Identities in American Catholicism, 2001;: Cath. Coll. Women in Am., 2002. Bd. dirs. Am. Coun. on Edn., 1997—99, Nat. Assn. Ind. Colls. and Univs., 1997—2000, Assn. Cath. Colls. and Univs., 1996—2000, Western Region Nat. Holocaust Mus., 1997—2000; coord. History Homes Religious Nature, 1988—. Fellow Fulbright, 1964. Mem.: Western Assn. Schs. and Colls. (sr. commn. 1997—2000), Assn. Cath. Colls. and Univs. (exec. bd. 1996—2000), Am. Coun. Edn. (bd. dirs. 1997—99), Nat. Assn. Ind. Colls. and Univs. (bd. dirs. 1997—99), Am. Assn. Rsch. Historians Medieval Spain, Medieval Acad., Am. Cath. Hist. Assn. Avocations: skiing, cuisine. Office: Congl Ctr 2311 Lindbergh Blvd Saint Louis MO 63131 Office Phone: 314-966-4048. E-mail: kkennelly33@hotmail.com.

KENNELLY, LAURA BALLARD, literature educator, writer; b. Denton, Tex., July 28, 1941; d. E. Garrett and Laura L. (Hutchins) Ballard; m. Kevin J. Kennelly, Aug. 26, 1961 (div. 1996); children: Kathryn, Kevin G., Patrick J., Daniel T., Brendan C.; m. Robert Mayerovitch, Sept. 6, 1996. BA, U. North Tex., 1961, MA, 1969, PhD, 1975. Vis. prof. English U. North Tex., Denton, 1975—95, prodn. assoc. Studies in the Novel, 1987—92; bibliographic editor Restoration: Studies in English Literary Culture, 1980—2000. Assoc. editor Bach: Jour. Riemenschneider Bach Inst., Baldwin-Wallace Coll., 2000—. Author: The Passage of Mrs. Jung: Poems, 1990; editor Grasslands Rev., 1987—, A Certain Attitude: Poems, 1995; contbr. scholarly articles to profl. jours., poetry, essays, and fiction to various publs. Dir. Birth Right of Denton, 1983-85. Grantee South Ctrl. MLA, 1990, Michael Kraus rsch. Am. Hist. Assn., 1992; Am. Antiquarian Soc. rsch. assoc., 1990, fellow, 1994-95. Mem. Am. Soc. for 18th Century Studies (affil. socs. coord. 1991-1998), Am. Hist. Assn., South Ctrl. Soc. for 18th Century Studies, East Ctrl. Soc. for 18th Century Studies, Tex. Assn. Creative Writing Tchrs. (pres. 1993-95). Roman Catholic. Avocations: running, biking. Office: Bach Inst Baldwin-Wallace Coll 275 Eastland Rd Berea OH 44017 Business E-Mail: lkennell@bw.edu.

KENNETT, LEE BOONE, JR., historian, educator; b. Greensboro, N.C., Aug. 11, 1931; s. Lee Boone and Dorothy Mary Kennett; m. Julianne Smythe Hudgens, June 24, 1961 (div. July 1977); children: Caroline Allison, John Calvin; m. Anne Marie Lucille Durand, Feb. 17, 1987. Student, Guilford Coll., N.C., 1948—50; BA, U. N.C., 1952; MA, U. Miss., 1956; PhD, U. Va., 1958. Asst. prof. Converse Coll., Spartanburg, SC, 1958—60; lectr. So. Ill. U., Carbondale, 1960—61; asst. prof. U. Ga., Athens, 1962—66, assoc. prof., 1968—78, prof. history, 1978—87, rsch. prof., 1987—93, prof. emeritus, 1993—; assoc. prof. Guilford Coll., NC, 1967—68. Founder, dir. Consortium on Revolutionary Europe, 1969—74; mem. fellowship selection bd. Inst. of Internat. Edn., 1978, 80; organizer Internat. Conf. on Aviation, Nat. Air and Space Mus., Washington, 1990; directeur d'études associé Ecole Pratique des Hautes Etudes, 4th sect., U. Paris, 1978; Lindbergh prof. Nat. Air and Space Mus., Smithsonian Instn., 1989—90; guest lectr. aero. sect. Inst. Phys. Sci. and Tech., Russian Acad. Sci., 1991. Author: (book) The French Armies in the Seven Years' War, 1968, The French Forces in America, 1780-1783, 1977, A History of Strategic Bombing, 1982, G.I.: The American Soldier in WW II, 1987, The First Air War, 1914-1918, 1990, French edit., 2005, Marching Through Georgia, 1995, Gettysburg: le tournant de la guerre de Sécession, 1997, Sherman: A Soldier's Life, 2001; co-author: The Gun in America, 1975; co-editor: French Military Aviation: A Bibliographical Guide, 1989; translator (editor): The Russian Campaign, 1812, 1970, Clement Ader's Aviation Militaire, 2003; contbr. numerous articles to profl. jours., chpts. to anthologies. Decorated Chevalier, Ordre des Palmes Académiques France; recipient Claiborne History prize, U. Miss., 1956, Fulbright Lectureship to France, 1966—67, Bicentennial Lectureship to France, Fulbright Found., 1974—75, Gilbert Chinard prize, Soc. for French Hist. Studies, 1978, Nat. Book prize, Phi Alpha Theta, 1979, Excellence in Rsch. award, U. Ga., 1980, Disting. Svc. award, Inst. Internat. Edn., 1981; fellow James Wilford Garner fellow, U. Miss., 1955—56, Virginia Mason Davidge fellow, U. Va., 1956—57; grantee Advanced Rsch. grantee, U.S. Army Mil. History Inst., 1979, Rsch. grantee, USAF Hist. Rsch. Ctr., 1988; Fulbright fellow, France, 1960—61. Mem.: So. Hist. Assn., Soc. for Mil. History, Orgn. Am. Historians, N.C. Civil War Roundtable, Greensboro Hist. Mus., Centre d'etudes d'histoire de la Défense, Am. Hist. Assn., Phi Beta Kappa. Home: 1840 Neelley Rd Pleasant Garden NC 27313 Office Phone: 336-674-0179. Personal E-mail: amd2ba@aol.com.

KENNEVAN, WALTER JAMES, computer science educator; b. N.Y.C., Aug. 29, 1912; s. David A. and Ellen Kathleen (Grogan) K.; m. Marguerite Roberta Stevens, Oct. 12, 1940; children: Steven David. BS in Commerce, Columbus U. Am., 1938; MS in Commerce, Cath. U. Am., 1940, M Fiscal Adminstrn., 1943. Mgmt. supr. Nat. Capital Housing Authority, Washington, 1942-48; asst. comptroller Bur. Ordnance U.S. Dept. Navy, Washington, 1948-57; dir. computer systems Office of Navy Comptroller Washington, 1957-69; prof. info. sci. Am. U., Washington, 1969-77, prof. emeritus, 1977—. Cons. NIH, Washington, 1964-65, U.S. Dept. State, Washington, 1964-65, U.S. Civil Svc. Commn., Washington, 1964-65. Author: Management and Computer Systems, 1973; contbr. articles to numerous publs. Mem. Cen. Suffrage Com. D.C., 1946-47, Vets. of the Battle of the Bulge. Staff sgt. U.S. Army, 1943-46, ETO. Mem. Am. Legion, Soc. Info. Mgmt. (nat. sec. 1975), Acad. Mgmt., Assn. Systems Mgmt., Ancient Order of Hibernians, Kenwood Country Club. Democrat. Roman Catholic. Avocation: golf. Home: 4928 Sentinel Dr Apt 106 Bethesda MD 20816 Personal E-mail: jowall@comcast.net.

KENNEY, BELINDA JILL FORSEMAN, information technology executive; b. Oak Ridge, Tenn., Dec. 18, 1955; d. Jack Woodrow and Betty Jean Forseman; m. Ronald Gene Kenney, Feb. 23, 1985; 1 child, Brandon. BS, U. Tenn., 1977, postgrad., 1977-78; MBA, Emory U., 2000. Sales rep. Xerox Corp., Nashville, 1978—82, maj. account sales mgr., 1982—83, region sales ops. mgr. St. Louis, 1984—86, dist. sales mgr. Overland Park, Kans., 1987—89, dist. mgr. San Antonio, 1989—95, v.p. Houston, 1995—97, v.p., region gen. mgr. Bus. Svcs. Atlanta, 1998—99, sr. v.p. region mgr. NASG, 2000—01; corp. officer, exec. v.p. sales and mktg. SpectraLink Corp., Boulder, Colo., 2004—. Exec. in residence Leeds Sch. Bus. U. Colo. Patron M.D. Anderson Cancer Ctr.; bd. dirs. Wise Women's Coun., Women's Vision Found., Foothills United Way Boulder. Mem. Rocky Mountain MENSA. Lutheran. Avocations: jogging, reading, tennis, health and fitness. Office: 5755 Central Ave Boulder CO 80301

KENNEY, BRIGID E., lawyer; b. Balt., Feb. 9, 1951; BA, Goucher Coll., 1973; student, U. N.C.; JD with honors, U. Md., 1977. Bar: Md. 1977. Law clk. to Hon. Rita C. Davidson Ct. Spl. Appeals, Md., 1977-78; ptnr. Venable, Baetjer and Howard, Balt.; now ptnr. Venable LLP, Balt. and Washington. Chair-elect Alliance for the Chesapeake Bay, Inc, 2005. Mem. ABA, Md. State Bar Assn., Bar Assn. Balt. City, Order of Coif. Office: Venable LLP 1800 Mercantile Bank 2 Hopkins Plz Baltimore MD 21201-2930 also: Venable LLP 575 Seventh St NW Washington DC 20004 Office Phone: 410-244-7487. Office Fax: 410-244-7742. Business E-Mail: bekenney@venable.com.

KENNEY, COLLEEN M., lawyer; b. 1959; BS, No. Ill. U., 1981, MS, 1982; JD, U. Chgo., 1991. Bar: Ill. 1991. Ptnr. Sidley Austin Brown & Wood, Chgo., 2000—. Office: Sidley Austin Brown and Wood Bank One Plz 10 S Dearborn St Chicago IL 60603

KENNEY, CRANE H., lawyer; b. Quincy, MA, Dec. 31, 1962; BA cum laude, U. Notre Dame, 1985; JD cum laude, U. Mich., 1988. Bar: Ill., 1988. Sr. v.p., gen. counsel and sec. Tribune Co., Chgo., 1996—. Office: Tribune Co 435 N Michigan Ave Ste 600 Chicago IL 60611-4001 Home: 1220 Lindenwood Dr Winnetka IL 60093-3724 Office Fax: 312-222-4206. Business E-Mail: ckenney@tribune.com.

KENNEY, DION PATRICK, information technology executive, entrepreneur; b. Middletown, N.Y., Apr. 26, 1962; s. John Michel Kenney and Joan Elizabeth (Bennett) Klein. BS in Physics, Fla. State U., 1984; MS in Physics, Tex. A&M U., 1989; MBA, U. Pa., 1995. Engr. Navair-Dept. of Navy, Lakehurst, N.J., 1985-86, Stratford, Conn., 1986-87; software engr. Unisys, Houston, 1990-93; mktg. and bus. planning profl. Health Care Devel. Internat., Tarrytown, N.Y., 1993-95; founder, pres. Cybernet Info. Systems, Yorktown Heights, N.Y., 1994—. Dir. bus. planning AHSC Group, LLC, Tarrytown, N.Y., 1995-2002; prin. cons. Y2 Mktg., N.Y.C., 2002—. Office: 777 Old Sawmill River Rd Tarrytown NY 10591 Home: 104 Joes Hill Rd Danbury CT 06811-4237

KENNEY, ESTELLE KOVAL, artist, educator; b. Chgo., Feb. 15, 1928; d. Hyman English and Florence (Browman) Koval; m. Herbert Kenney, Feb. 6, 1948; children: Carla, Robert. BFA, Art Inst. Chgo., 1976, MFA, 1978; postgrad., Yale U., 1980. Art therapist Grove Sch., Lake Forest, Ill., 1973—78, New Trier H.S., Ctrl. H.S., Winnetka, Ill., 1978—79, Mosely Sch., Chgo., 1979, Cove Sch., Evanston, Ill., 1979—82; dir. art therapy concentration, instr. painting and drawing Loyola U., Chgo., 1981—; pres., art dir. Nuts on Clark, Chgo. Pres., art dir. Nuts on Clark Inc., Chgo. One-woman shows include Evanston Libr., 1971, Zaks Gallery, Chgo., 1977, 1979, 1982, Renaissance Soc.-Bergman Gallery, U. Chgo., 1980, exhibited in group shows at Ill. State Mus., 1975, Women Artists, Here and Now, 1976, Chgo. Connections traveling exhbn., 1976—77, Bat, /wineb's Caucus for Art, 1977, Nancy Lurie Gallery, 1978, Marycrest Coll. Gallery, Davenport, Iowa, 1982, Chgo. Internat. Art Expo, 1981, 1982, 1983, Notre Dame U. Gallery, South Bend, Ind., 1982, Represented in permanent collections Ill. State Mus., Springfield, Union League Club. Chgo. Mem.: Coll. Art Assn., Ill. Art Therapy Assn. (pres. 1979—), Am. Art Therapy Assn. Home: 3830 N Clark St Chicago IL 60613-2812 Office: Loyola U of Chgo Dept Fine Arts 6525 N Sheridan Rd Chicago IL 60626 E-mail: estellekenney@nutsonclark.com.

KENNEY, FRANK DEMING, lawyer; b. Chgo., Feb. 20, 1921; s. Joseph Aloysius and Mary Edith (Deming) K.; m. Virginia Stuart Banning, Feb. 12, 1944; children: Claudia Kenney Carpenter, Pamela Kenney Voetberg, Sarah Kenney Swanson, Stuart Deming Kenney AB, U. Chgo., 1948, JD, 1949. Bar: Ill. 1948, U.S. Dist. Ct. (no. dist.) Ill. 1949. Assoc. J.O. Brown, Chgo., 1948-49; assoc., ptnr. Winston & Strawn, and predecessors, Chgo., 1949-92, ret., 1992. 1st lt. AUS, 1942-46, CBI, PTO. Mem. ABA, Ill. Bar Assn., Chgo. Bar Assn. (chmn. real property law com. 1982-83), Lawyers Club Chgo., Fox River Valley Hunt Club, Quadrangle Club, Nat. Beagle Club Am. (bd. dirs.

1981-92), Spring Creek Basset Hunt Club (master 1977-93, chmn. bd., 1993-98, hon. chmn. bd. 1998-2002, hon. master 2002-), Kappa Sigma (nat. housing fin. commr. for U.S. and Can., 1959-91). Republican. Roman Catholic. Home: PO Box 581 333 Old Sutton Rd Barrington IL 60010-9368 Office: Winston & Strawn 35 W Wacker Dr Ste 3800 Chicago IL 60601-1695

KENNEY, H. WESLEY, JR., (HARRY WESLEY KENNEY JR.), television producer, television director; b. Dayton, Ohio, Jan. 3, 1926; s. Harry Wesley and Minnie Ruth (Keeton) K.; m. Kay Ann Snure (div. 1964); children: Nina, Harry Wesley III, Kara; m. Heather North, May 22, 1971; 1 child, Kevin. BFA, Carnegie Inst. Tech., 1950. Dir. Fights at St. Nicks, Rocky King Detective, Night Beat Dumont Network, N.Y.C., 1950-57; producer, dir. TV shows True Story, Modern Romances NBC, N.Y.C., 1957-61; freelance dir. Omnibus, N.Y.C., 1958; dir. theater prodn. My Three Angels Totem Pole Playhouse, 1955; dir. theater prodn. The King and I Melody Fair Summer Theatre, Niagra Falls, 1959; dir. theater prodn. Twelfth Night Antioch, Yellow Springs, Ohio, 1962; dir. TV series The Doctors NBC, N.Y.C., 1964-66, exec. producer, dir. TV series Days of Our Lives Los Angeles, 1967-77; dir. TV series All in the Family CBS, Los Angeles, 1974, dir. pilots The Jeffersons, Filthy Rich, Ladies Man, Rosenthal & Jones, Side By Side, exec. producer, dir. TV series The Young and the Restless, 1981-86; producer, dir. (spl.) Miss Kline, We Love You ABC, 1974, exec. producer, dir. TV series General Hospital Los Angeles, 1987-90; freelance dir., 1990—. Cons. Televisa-Mexico City UCLA Ext. Sch., 1990, guest instr. TV directing, 1975, guest instr. multiple camera directing, 1991, 93; instr. profl. seminar in TV for Televisa, 1990; guest lectr. profl. seminar dor srs. and students in drama Carnegie Mellon U., Pitts., 1990; assoc. prof. TV prodn. UCLA Sch. Theatre, Film and TV, 1993-99, 2001—; assoc. prof. TV prodn. Sch. Cinema and TV U. So. Calif., 1998, 99—, guest prof. Frostburg Mo. State U. summer TV Festival, 2004. Dir. closed cir. med. shows including Dr. Salk Polio Vaccine Report from U. Mich., Ann Arbor, 1956; dir. (theater prodns.) Ten Little Indians, Advent Theatre, L.A., 1991, The Best Christmas Pageant Ever, 1993, Love Letters, W.Va. Pub. Theatre, Morgantown, 1994, Shadowlands, Tracy Roberts Theater, 1995 (Dramalogue award for Directing), Scrooge, W.Va. Pub. Theatre, 1995; dir. Sebiyophrenin: The Relapse, 3-part series; dir. (infomercials) Elements of Beauty-The Merle Norman Experience, 1993, Therapy Without Tears-The EMLA Study, 1993; dir. (series spls.) Soap Break, CBS, 1994-95 (Emmy nomination). Served with USN, 1943-46. Recipient 7 Emmy awards Acad. TV Arts and Scis. 1973, 78, 79, 82, 83, 84, 86, 13 Emmy award nominations Acad. TV Arts and Scis., 1972-88, 95 Mem. Dirs. Guild Am., Producers Guild Am., Actors Equity, Omega Delta Kappa. Avocations: athletics, tennis, travel, bungy jumping. Home: 12996 Galewood St Studio City CA 91604-4045 Personal E-mail: marle333@aol.com. *I recognize myself as an "average guy" with an average intelligence and talent and more than average patience and luck. An awareness of this fact has allowed me to accept the success I have had, always working for something better, but recognizing those shortcomings that have at times made me fail. Also because of this, thank God, I have had more than my share of happiness.*

KENNEY, JOHN ARTHUR, lawyer; b. Oklahoma City, Aug. 3, 1948; s. Jack H. and Betty Jo (Hill) K.; m. Jane Francis, Sept. 4, 1971; children: John Graham, Lauren Elizabeth. BS in Indsl. Engring. with distinction, U. Okla., 1971, JD, 1975. Bar: Tex. 1975, US Dist. Ct. (so. dist.) Tex. 1976, U. Ct. Appeals (5th cir.) 1977, Okla. 1981, US Dist. Ct. Okla. 1981, US Ct. Appeals (10th cir.) 1983, US Supreme Ct. 2003. Assoc. Baker & Botts, Houston, 1975-81; shareholder McAfee & Taft, Oklahoma City, 1982—. Temp. judge Okla. Ct. of Appeals, atty. appointed panels, Leadership Oklahoma City; magistrate judge merit selection com. and civil justice reform act adv. com. U.S. Dist. Ct. (we. dist.) Okla. Bd. advisors dept. indsl. engring., bd. visitors Coll. Engring., Okla. U.; past trustee, deacon Westminster Presbyn. Ch.; dir., past pres. Rebuilding Together with Christmas in April, Oklahoma City. Mem. ABA, Okla. Bar Assn. (adminstrn. of justice com. 1990-2000), Fed. bar Assn. Okla. City (chpt. pres. 2001-03), Okla. County Bar Assn. (dir. 1997-98, pres. 1999-2000), Order of Coif, Tau Beta Pi. Office: McAfee & Taft Two Leadership Sq 10th Fl Oklahoma City OK 73102

KENNEY, JOHN JOSEPH, lawyer; b. NYC, July 13, 1943; s. Joseph Charles and Regina Elizabeth (Hulbert) K.; m. Charlotte O'Brien, May 23, 1971; 1 child, Alexander Hulbert. BA, St. Michael's Coll., 1966; JD, Fordham U., 1969. Bar: N.Y. 1970, U.S. Dist. Ct. (so. dist.) N.Y. 1973, U.S. Ct. Appeals (2d cir.) 1973, U.S. Dist. Ct. (ea. dist.) N.Y. 1980, U.S. Supreme Ct. 1991. Assoc. Dunnington, Bartholow & Miller, N.Y.C., 1969-71; asst. U.S. atty. U.S. Dist. Ct. (so. dist.) N.Y., N.Y.C., 1971-80; assoc. Simpson, Thacher & Bartlett, N.Y.C., 1980-81, ptnr., 1981—. Mem. deptl. disciplinary com. Appellate Divsn. 1st Dept., 2002—. Counsel, Village of Bronxville, 1983-86; mem. Planning Bd. of Bronxville, 1992-98, counsel, 1981-83; trustee Hist. Deerfield Inc., 1992-98, Bennington Coll., 1999—, Bronxville Pub. Libr., 2003-; bd. dirs. Citizens Crime Commn., 1998—, Am. Assn. for Internat. Commn. Jurists, 2000—. Recipient John Marshall award U.S. Dept. Justice, 1980. Fellow Am. Coll. Trial Lawyers (chmn. com. on fed. rules of evidence 2003-05); mem. ABA, Fed. Bar Coun. (pres. 1994-96), Assn. Bar City NY (chmn. criminal law com. 1992-95), New York County Lawyers Assn. (pres. 1996-97), NY State Bar Assn. (exec. com. 1997-2000, chmn. spl. com. bar exam and lawyer competence 2005—), NY State Bar Found. (bd. dirs. 2004—), Wong Sun Soc. San Francisco. Republican. Roman Catholic. Home: 8 The Byway Bronxville NY 10708-4934 Office: Simpson Thacher & Bartlett 425 Lexington Ave 15th Fl New York NY 10017-3954 Office Phone: 212-455-2588. Business E-Mail: jkenney@stblaw.com.

KENNEY, JOHN MICHEL, architect; b. N.Y.C., Oct. 22, 1938; s. John Peter and Madeline Loretta (Fuller) K.; children: John Michel, James Brian, Dion Patrick. AAS, Orange County Community Coll., 1966; student, Columbia U., 1969. Registered arch., N.Y., N.J., Conn., Ill., Pa., Del., Ill., S.C., N.C., Ga. V.p., ptnr., dir. health facilities Perkins & Will Architects, White Plains, N.Y., 1968-81; mng. mem. AHSC Archs. P.C., Tarrytown, N.Y., 1981—, AHSC/Melellan, Copenhagen. Mng. mem. AHSC Group LLC; co-chmn. AHSC/Destefano and Ptnrs., Chgo.; pres. ArquInter-AHSE Europe, Madrid. Vice chmn. Orange County Dem. Coms., N.Y., 1968; chmn. Dem. Com., Middletown, N.Y., 1966-68; co-chmn. Robert Kennedy Presdl. Election Primary, Orange/Sullivan County, 1968; mem. United Hosp. Fund; bd. mem. Aging in Am. Found. Mem. AIA, Nat. Coun. Archtl. Registration Bds., N.Y. Soc. Hosp. Planning, Am. Assn. Hosp. Planners, N.Y. Acad. Scis. Democrat. Avocations: skiing, sailing, travel. Office: AHSC Architects 777 Old Saw Mill River Rd Tarrytown NY 10591-6717

KENNEY, JOHN PATRICK, dentist; b. Joliet, Ill., July 8, 1946; s. John Edward and Nellie Kenney; divorced; 1 child, David J. BS in Mktg., Christian Bros. Coll., 1968; DDS, Loyola U., Maywood, Ill., 1977; MS in Oral Biology, Loyola U., Chgo., 1979. Diplomate Am. Bd. Forensic Odontology. Supr. passenger services Am. Airlines, Chgo., 1968-72; pvt. practice in pediatric dentistry Park Ridge, Ill., 1980—; asst. prof. pediat. dentistry Northwestern U., Chgo., 1983-97, clin. assoc. prof. pediat. dentistry, 1997-2000; chief forensic odontologist Cook County Med. Examiner, 1991-97; assoc. prof. clin. surgery Northwestern U. Med. Sch., 2000—. Forensic odontologist Cook County Med. Examiner, Chgo., 1984-97, Kane County (Ill.) Coroner, Geneva, 1984-97; cons. forensic odontologist Am. Airlines, Chgo., 1979, Midwest Express Airlines, Milw., 1985, Am. Eagle Airlines, Ind., 1995, United Express Airlines, Quincy, Ill., 1996, Comair Airlines, Mich., 1997, U.S. Army Central ID Lab., Honolulu, 1997—, Amtrak, Ill., 1999, NYCME, 2001; mem. Nat. Disaster Med. Sys. D-Mort team USPHS, forensic oversight com., 2001—; dir. Identification Svcs. Dupage County Ill. Coroners Office, 1997—. Mem. editl. bd. Jour. Forensic Scis., 1997—; contbr. articles to profl. jours. Dep. coroner DuPage County, 2001—. Fellow Am. Acad. Pediatric Dentistry, Am. Coll. Dentists, Am. Acad. Forensic Scis., Peirre Fauchard Soc., Royal Soc. Medicine; mem. ADA, Internat. Orgn. for Forensic Odonto-stomatology (v.p. 1984-87), Internat. Assn. for Identification (cert. sr. crime scene analyst 1991—), Am. Acad. Pediatric Dentists, Am. Bd. Forensic Odontology (bd. dirs. 1990-96, 2000-03, treas. 1991-93, v.p. 1994, pres. 1995-96, sec. 2003-04, v.p. 2004-05), Ill. State Dental Soc., Ill. Soc. Pediatric Dentists (bd. dirs. 1987-90), Chgo. Dental Soc., Kiwanis (pres. 1983-84, Disting. Pres. 1984). Office: 101 S Washington Ave Park Ridge IL 60068-4200

KENNEY, MARY R., software engineer; b. Richmond, Va., 1945; d. Thomas W. and Clara G. K.; m. Jeremy M. (div.). BS and MS in Math., Howard U., 1967; MS in Computer Sci., Steven's Inst., 1984. Sr. math. aide Ctr. Naval Analysis, Rosslyn, Va., 1967-77; sr. programmer analyst Control Data Corp., Rockville, Md., 1977-81; software quality engr. AT&T Bell Labs., Piscataway, N.J., 1981-84, Bellcore, Piscataway, 1984-99, Telcordia Techs., Piscataway, 1999—. Chair fundraising Youth in Sports Found., Piscataway, 1995-97; mem. fundraising com. Cmty. League Active Youth, New Brunswick, N.J., 1994, N.J. Rams, Newark, 1992-93. Mem. AAUW, NAFE, ACM, Am. Mgmt. Assn. Avocations: reading, crochet, bowling. Office: Telcordia Techs Inc 3 Corp Pl Piscataway NJ 08854

KENNEY, ROBERT JAMES, JR., lawyer; b. Boston, Jan. 16, 1948; BA, Harvard Coll., 1969, JD, 1972. Bar: Mass. 1972, D.C. 1976. Assoc. Hogan & Hartson LLP, Washington, 1976-81, ptnr., 1981—, dir. gov. contracts practice group. Lt. USNR, 1973-76. Recipient Federal 100 award Fed. Computer Week, 1992. Mem. Fed. Bar Assn. (chmn. govt. contracts sect. 1992-94, chmn. ADP procurement com. 1990-92, Disting. Svc. award 1990, 91, 94). Office: Hogan & Hartson LLP 555 13th St NW Washington DC 20004-1161 Office Phone: 202-637-5707. Office Fax: 202-637-5910. Business E-Mail: rjkenney@hhlaw.com.

KENNEY, THOMAS FREDERICK, broadcast executive; b. Dearborn, Mich., Sept. 25, 1941; s. Charles B. and Grace M. (Wilson) K.; m. Beth H. Rockwood, Aug. 22, 1964; children: Sean, Blair. BS, Mich. State U., 1964. Program mgr. Sta. WMBD-TV, Peoria, Ill., 1969-71; exec. producer Sta. WJZ-TV, Balt., 1971-73; program mgr. Sta. KFMB-TV, San Diego, 1973-75; program mgr., then dir. broadcasting ops. Sta. KHOU-TV, Houston, 1975-79; v.p., gen. mgr. KHOU-TV, 1979-84, Sta. WROC-TV, Rochester, N.Y., 1984-90; owner Santa Fe Wireless, Inc., Gainesville, Fla., 1990—99; dist. mgr. Trader Pub. Co., Phoenix, 1999—. Freelance TV cons., Houston, 1984. Home and Office: 1858 E Campbell Ave Gilbert AZ 85234-8228 Office Phone: 623-869-8888. Personal E-mail: thoskenney@gmail.com.

KENNEY, WES, III, conductor, educator; b. N.Y.C., Apr. 15, 1955; s. Harry Wesley Kenney Jr. and Kathryn Ann (Snure) Sharon; m. Leslie Lucille Stewart, July 22, 1990. BA in Music, U. S.C., 1978; MusM, San Francisco State U., 1992. Music dir. Oakland Youth Orch., Calif., 1991—96; co-prin. condr. Oakland Lyric Opera, 1995—97; assoc. condr. Va. Symphony, Norfolk, 1996—2002; music tchr. Va. Ballet Theatre, 1998—2002; condr. William and Mary Symphony, Williamsburg, 1999—2000, 2001—03; artistic advisor Williamsburg Symphony, 2003—, Ft. Collins Symphony, Colo., 2004—; assoc. prof. Colo. State U., 2003—. Guest condr. L.A. CYSOC Honor Orch., 1987, Spokane Symphony, 1989, Red-Mountain Chamber Orch., Birmingham, 1990, Ala. Symphony, Birmingham, 2000, Buffalo Philharm., 2000—03, Richmond Symphony, 2000, Dubuque Symphony, 2000, San Juan Symphony, 2002, Acadiana Symphony, 2003, Va. All-State Orch., 2004; conducting fellow Condrs. Inst., Columbia, SC, 1988—90; condr. European tour, 1993, China, Hong Kong, Taiwan tour, 1995, Berlin, Leipzig tour, 2004. Music dir. (mus.) Bess, 1975, No, No, Nanette, 1982, Oliver, 1983, Joseph and the Amazing Technicolor Dreamcoat, 1983, Don Giovanni, 1989, TWAIN, 1990, Aida, 1994, Die Kluge, 1996, Gianni Schicei, 1997, Carmen, 2001, Hansel & Gretel, 2003, Albert Herring, 2004, Tenderland, 2005, Fledermaus, 2005. Pres. Choral Condrs. Guild, San Fernando Valley, Calif., 1986—88; music dir. Canoga Park (Calif.) Presbyn. Ch., 1980—88; bd. dirs. L.A. County Youth Symphony Orch. Coun., 1986—88. Recipient Music Dir. of Yr. L.A.W.E.E. award, L.A. Weekly Mag., 1984, Merit award, County of L.A., 1986, B'nai B'rith, 1986, Carmen Dragon prize, Calif. State U. Sys., Long Beach, 1992; State of Calif. scholar, 1976. Mem. Am. Musicol. Soc., Music Tchr.'s Assn., Choral Condr.'s Guild (pres. 1986-88), Condr.'s Guild (pres. 1999-2000), Am. Symphony Orch. League (bd. dirs. Youth Orch. div.). Avocations: golf, hiking, skiing, bicycling, wine, art. Office: Ft Collins Symphony Orch 214 S Coll Ave Fort Collins CO 80523

KENNEY, WILLIAM FITZGERALD, lawyer; b. San Francisco, Nov. 4, 1935; s. Lionel Fitzgerald and Ethel Constance (Brennan) K.; m. Susan Elizabeth Langfitt, May 5, 1962; children: Anne, Carol, James. BA, U. Calif.-Berkeley, 1957, JD, 1960. Bar: Calif. 1961. Assoc. Miller, Osborne Miller & Bartlett, San Mateo, Calif., 1962-64; ptnr. Tormey, Kenney & Cotchett, San Mateo, 1965-67; pres. William F. Kenney, Inc., San Mateo, 1968—; gen. ptnr. All Am. Self Storage, 1985—, Second St. Self Storage, 1990-96, Cochrane Rd. Self Storage, 1996—, Marina Bus. Ctr., 1998—; pres. The Positive Edge, 2000—. Trustee San Mateo City Sch. Dist., 1971-79, pres., 1972-74; pres. March of Dimes, 1972-73; bd. dirs. Boys Club San Mateo, 1972-90, Samaritan House, 1989—, Lesley Found., 1992-2004. With U.S. Army, 1960-62. Mem. State Bar of Calif. (taxation com. 1973-76), San Mateo County Bar Assn. (bd. dirs. 1973-75), Calif. Assn. Realtors (legal affairs com. 1978—), San Mateo C. of C. (bd. dirs. 1987-93), Self Storage Assn. (we. region, pres. 1989-90, nat. bd. dirs. 1990-97, nat. v.p 1994-95, pres. 1996), Rotary (pres. 1978-79), Elks (exalted ruler 1974-75). Republican. Roman Catholic. Home: 221 Clark Dr San Mateo CA 94402-1004 Office: 120 N El Camino Real San Mateo CA 94401-2705 E-mail: bill1135@rcn.com.

KENNEY, WILLIAM JOHN, JR., real estate developer; b. Huntington Park, Calif., Mar. 9, 1949; s. William John Sr. and Dorothy Marie (Smith) K.; m. Susan Louise Wattson, Sept. 26, 1987. BS in Econs., Calif. State U., Fullerton, 1970, BBA, 1971. Lic. real estate broker, Calif., Ariz.; cert. leasing specialist. Leasing agt. John S. Griffith, Irvine, Calif., 1972-78, dir. leasing, 1978-84; v.p. leasing John S. Griffith (now Donahue Schriber), Newport Beach, Calif., 1984-85, sr. v.p., 1986-91, sr. v.p. devel., 1991-95; founder The Kenney Co., 1995—. Spkr. numerous orgns. Bd. dirs. Riverside (Calif.) YMCA, 1989-92, Promontary Bay Cmty. Assn. Recipient Certs. Appreciation Hemet C. of C., Riverside Bd. Realtors, Hemet Valley Kiwanis, Riverside Kiwanis. Mem. Calif. Bus. Properties Assn. (chmn. 1988-89, dir. 1976-96), Internat. Coun. Shopping Ctrs. (assoc., chair govt. affairs com. 1994-98), Newport Harbor Bd. Realtors (cert. appreciation), Frank Miller Club (life), Balboa Yacht Club (sec. 2003, bd. dirs. 2004-). Avocations: surfing, fishing, skiing. Office: The Kenney Co 824 Harbor Island Dr Newport Beach CA 92660-7228 Office Phone: 949-675-7038.

KENNICOTT, JAMES W., lawyer; b. Latrobe, Pa., Feb. 14, 1945; s. W.L. and Alice (Hayes) K.; m. Margot Barnes, Aug. 19, 1975 (div. 1977); m. Lynne Dratler Finney, July 1, 1984 (div. 1989). AB, Syracuse (N.Y.) U., 1967; JD, U. Wyo., 1979. Bar: Utah 1979. Prin. Ski Cons., Park City, Utah, 1969—; pvt. practice Park City, 1979-87, 89—; ptnr. Kennicott & Finney, Park City, 1987-89; pvt. practice Park City, 1989—. Cons. Destination Sports Specialists, Park City, 1984-99; judge pro tem Utah 3d Dist. Ct., Park City, 1988-2000; arbitrator Am. Arbitration Assn., 1989-2000. Chmn. Park City Libr. Bd. 1987; bd. dirs. Park City Libr., 1985-91, Park City Handicapped Sports, 1988-94, The Counseling Inst., 1993-97, chmn., 1994-95, treas. 1995-96, mem. program com. Gov.'s Commn. on Librs. and Info. Svcs., 1990-91. Mem. Utah Bar Assn. Avocations: skiing, sailing, hiking, bicycling, literature. Home and Office: PO Box 683430 Park City UT 84068-3430 Office Phone: 435-649-6623. E-mail: jimkenn@lawyer.com.

KENNICUTT, ROBERT CHARLES, JR., astronomer; b. Balt., Sept. 4, 1951; s. Robert Charles and Joyce Ann K.; m. Norma Graceila Crosa Kennicutt, Feb. 17, 1976 (div. Jan. 18, 1996); 1 child, Laura. BS in Physics, Rensselaer Polytech. Inst., Troy, N.Y., 1973; MS in Astronomy, PhD in Astronomy, U. Wash., Seattle, 1978. Carnegie fellow Hale Observatories, Pasadena, Calif., 1978-80; asst. prof. astronomy U. Minn., Mpls., 1980-85, assoc. prof. astronomy, 1985-88; assoc. prof., astronomer U. Ariz., Tucson, 1988-92, prof., astronomer, 1992—; Beatrice Tinsley Centennial prof. U. Tex., Austin, 1994; Plumian prof. astronomy and natural philosophy U. Cambridge, England, 2005—. V.p. AAS, Washington, 1998-01; com. on Astronomy and Astrophysics Nat. Rsch. Coun., Washington, 1998-2001; Space Telescope Sci. Inst. coun., AURA, Washington, 2000-2004; next generation space telescope interim sci. working group, NASA, Washington, 2000-01, adv. com., chmn. 1996-99; vis. com. chmn. NOAO Observatories, AURA, Washington, 1996-2000; vis. com. European Southern Observatory, Garching bei Munich, Germany, 1997-2003, Gemini Obs., AURA, 2003—. Author: Galaxies: Interactions and Induced Star Formation, 1998; editor-in-chief The Astrophys. Jour., 1999—. Named Alfred P. Aloan fellowship 1983-87, Beatrice M. Tinsley Centennial professorship, U. Tex. at Austin, 1994, Carnegie fellowship Carnegie Instn. Washington, 1978-80, Blaauw Prof. U. Groningen, 2001. Fellow Am. Acad. Arts & Scis.; mem. AAS (v.p. 1998-01), Internat. Astron. Union, Astron. Soc. pf the Pacific. Office: Steward Observatory U Arizona Tucson AZ 85721 Fax: 520-621-1532. E-mail: rkennicutt@as.arizona.edu.

KENNY, CHARLES, counselor; BA in Psychology, Seton Hall U., 1989, MA in Counseling, 1991; MA in Psychology, New Sch. for Social Reseach, 1997. Lic. profl. counselor N.J., 1999. Adjunctive therapist/mental health worker St. Mary's Hosp., Hoboken, 1991—96; coord. counseling svcs., therapist PSI Family Svcs., Edison, NJ, 1997—2001; family support divsn. dir. Multicultural Cmty. Svcs., Edison, 2001—. Named Big East Academic All-Star, Big East Conf. Mem.: ACA, Am. Mental Health Counselors Assn., N.J. Mental Health Counselors Assn., N.J. Counseling Assn., Kappa Delta Pi, Psi Chi. Office: Multicultural Cmty Services Ste 108 1 Ethel Rd Edison NJ 08817

KENNY, DEBORAH, marketing professional, finance educator; b. N.J., Nov. 13, 1962; BA, U. Pa., 1983; MA, PhD, Columbia U., 1994. Publ. Dimension Mag., N.Y.C., 1987-90; pres. N.Am. opers. The Jerusalem Report, N.Y.C., 1994-97; v.p. mktg. Parenting group Time Warner, N.Y.C., 1998-99; pres. publ. divsn. Sesame St., N.Y.C., 1999—. Bd. dirs. Domestic Abuse Prevention Project. Fellow IWF-Harvard Leadership Found., 1997-98; recipient Clarion Advt. award, 1997, Echo Leader award Direct Mktg. Assn., 1989. E-mail: dkenny2222@aol.com.

KENNY, GREGORY B., industrial equipment executive; Exec. v.p. General Cable, 1994—97, bd. dir., 1997—, exec. v.p., COO, 1997—99, pres., COO, 1999—2001, pres., CEO, 2001—. Dir. Corn Products International, Inc. Office: c/o General Cable 4 Tesseneer Dr Highland Heights KY 41076*

KENNY, JAMES CASEY, ambassador, construction company executive; b. Evanston, Ill., June 29, 1953; s. John Edward and Rosalie (Casey) K.; m. Margaret Mackin, Apr. 21, 1979; children: Colleen, Courtney, Casey. BS in Bus., Bradley U., 1976. Safety and field engr. Kenny Constrn. Co., Wheeling, Ill., 1976-79, project supt. Chgo., 1979-82, bus. devel. dir. Wheeling, 1982-89, v.p., 1989—; pres. Kenny Mgmt. Svcs.; U.S. amb. to Ireland U.S. Dept. State, Dublin, 2003—. Bd. dirs. Ill. Rd. Builders Assn., Chgo., Am. Underground Space Assn., St. Paul. Bd. dirs. Met. Pier and Expo Authority, Chgo., 1991-92, Ill. Ambs., Chgo., 1992, Nat. Corp. for Housing Partnerships, Washington, 1991-92; co-fin. chmn. Bush/Quayle 1992 Campaign, Chgo., 1992. Named Contractor of Yr., Am. Pub. Works Assn., 1990, Minorities in Constrn., 1992. Mem. North Shore Country Club, Pinehurst Nat. Club. Tavern Club. Roman Catholic. Avocations: golf, skiing, platform tennis. Office: Kenny Constrn Co 250 Northgate Pkwy Wheeling IL 60090-2684 also: American Embassy Dublin Ireland 5290 Dublin Pl Washington DC 20521-5290

KENNY, JANE M., management consulting executive; b. Jersey City; m. Greg Myer; 3 children. B, Trinity Coll., Washington, 1974; M in English and Am. Lit., Rutgers U., 1982. Chief policy and planning Gov. Whitman, 1994—96; v.p. corp. cmty. affairs Beneficial Mgmt. Corp., Peapack, NJ, 1990—94; cabinet sec. Gov. Tom Kean, 1986—90; commr. NJ Dept. Cmty. Affairs, 1996—2001; regional adminstr. region 2 US EPA, 2001—; sr. v.p. The Whitman Strategy Group, LLC. Recipient Nat. Pub. Svc. award, Women in Govt. award, Good Housekeeping. Fellow: Nat. Acad. Pub. Adminstrs. Office: Whitman Strategy Group LLC 240 Main St Gladstone NJ 07934 Office Phone: 212-637-5000, 908-719-6510. Business E-Mail: jane.kenny@whitmanstrategygroup.com.

KENNY, JOHN EDWARD, computer analyst; b. Buffalo, Oct. 28, 1945; s. Thomas Edmund and Dorothy Elizabeth (Krull) K. AAS, Erie C.C., 1972. Systems analyst Nat. Fuel Gas, Buffalo, 1969-70; programmer Svc. Systems Corp., Clarence, N.Y., 1974-77, Carborundum, Niagra Falls, N.Y., 1973-74; analyst, programmer A. Marine Midland Bank N.A., Buffalo, 1977-83; sr. analyst, programmer, project leader Empire of Am., FSA, Buffalo, 1983-85, applications project supr., 1985-89, asst. v.p. software devel., 1989-91; pres. Can.-Am. Bus. Svcs., 1991—, GPS Sys., 1995—; sr. analyst, programmer Cardinal Health Corp., Amherst, N.Y., 1995—. Data processing cons. First Union Nat. Bank, NC, Elec. Data Sys., Plano, Tex., 1996—, Ernst & Young LLP-Med. Mut. of Ohio, 1997—2000; computer analyst Citicorp Student Loan Corp., Pittsford, NY, 1996—97; tchr. programming langs. Advanced Tng. Ctr., Buffalo; cons. M&T Bank Corp., Buffalo, 2000—01, Tyco Electronics, Harrisburg, Pa., 2001—02, Antares Mgmt. Solutions, Cleve., 2002—03, N.Y.C. Taxation and Fin. Dept., Albany, NY, 2004—; sr. IT cons. Bank of N.Y., Syracuse, 2004—05, Med. Mutual of Ohio, Cleve., 2005—; instr. computer tech. Acad. Med. Arts and Bus., Harrisburg, 2001—02. Mem. Rep. Presdl. Task Force; mem. Town of Tonawanda Conservative Com., 1980-2002, chmn., 1993-96; state committeeman 29th U.S. Congl. Dist., 1996-1999; mem. Erie County Conservative Com., 1980-2002, mem. exec. bd., 1994-97; 911 asst. Erie County Ctrl. Police Svcs., 1995-1997; mem. Erie County Rep. Com., 2004—. Mem. Am. Inst. Banking, Assn. Sys. Mgmt., Kenton C. of C., Greater Fort Erie C. of C. Can., US Golf Assn. (patron), Judges and Police Conf. Erie County (NY), Tonawanda Chmn. Men's Club, KC, Lions, Internat. Order Alhambra, World Future Soc. (profl.). Republican (nat. com.). Roman Catholic. Home and Office: 212 McKinley Ave Kenmore NY 14217-2438 Business E-Mail: cabussrv@aol.com.

KENNY, MAURICE FRANCIS, writer; b. Watertown, N.Y., Aug. 16, 1929; s. Andrew Anthony Kenny and Doris Marie (Herrick) Kenny Welch. Student, Butler U., 1950-55, NYU, 1957; Doctorate (hon.), St. Lawrence U., 1995. Poet-in-residence North Country C.C., Saranac Lake, N.Y.; vis. prof. U. Okla., Norman, En'owkin Ctr., U. Victoria, B.C., Can., Paul Smith's Coll., SUNY, Potsdam; mem. panel N.Y. Found. for the Arts, N.C. Arts Coun., N.Y. State Coun. on the Arts, Arts Recognition and Talent Search for the Ednl. Testing Svc.; bd. dirs. Coord. Coun. Lit. Mags., N.Y. Found. for the Arts, WSLU-FM; coord. Iroquois Arts Festival, Saranac Lake, Writer's Week at Tupper Lake; presenter in field. Author: The Hopeless Kill, 1956, Dead Letters Sent, 1958, With Love to Lesbia, 1959, And Grieve, Lesbia, 1960, I Am The Sun, 1976, North: Poems of Home, 1979, Dancing Back Strong the Nation, 1979, Only As Far As Brooklyn, 1981, Kneading the Blood, 1981, Boston Tea Party, 1982, The Smell of Slaughter, 1982, Blackrobe: Isaac Jogues, 1982, The Mama Poems, 1985, Is Summer This Bear, 1985, Rain & Other Fictions, 1985, Between Two Rivers, 1987, Humors And/Or Not So Humorous, 1987, Selections, 1988, Last Mornings in Brooklyn, 1991, Interpreting the Indian, 1991, On Second Thought, 1991, 93, 95, Tekonwatonti: Molly Brant, 1992, 2002, Backward to Forward, 1997, Greyhounding This America, 1988, Tortured Skins, 2000, In the Time of the Present, 2000, Stories for a Winter's Night, 2000, Carving Hawk: New and Selected Poems, 2002; co-editor Contact/II; editor, pub. Strawberry Press, Native American Fiction, 2000, Stories For A Wintor's Night, 2000; poetry editor Adirondac Mag; contbr. to profl. jours. Past dir. The Little Gallery; art dir. Saranac Lake. Home: PO Box 1029 Saranac Lake NY 12983-1029

KENNY, ROBERT, lawyer; b. Bklyn., June 26, 1947; s. Raymond John and Madeline Catherine (McNally) K.; children: Kaitlin Simon, Brendan William. BBA, Manhattan Coll., 1968; JD, Northeastern U., 1973. Bar: Mass. 1973, Ill. 1975, Mich. 1983, U.S. Dist. Ct. (no. dist.) Ill. 1975, U.S. Tax Ct. 1976, N.J. 1994, U.S. Dist. Ct. N.J. 1997, U.S. Ct. Appeals (3rd cir.) 2004; CPA, N.Y. Dir. taxes and tax counsel Whirlpool Corp., Benton Harbor, Mich., 1981-87;

dir. taxes and asst. sec. Rhone-Poulenc Inc., Princeton, N.J., 1987-93; dir. corp. tax strategy Ricoh Corp., West Caldwell, N.J., 1994-95; pvt. practice Princeton, 1995—. Adj. prof. Seton Hall U. Sch. of Law, 1997, Rider U., Lawrenceville, N.J., 1996—; arbitrator N.J. State Superior Ct., 1996—. Contbr. articles to profl. jours. Counsel, Friends West Windsor Open Space, 1996-. Mem. Rotary Internat. (bd. dirs. 1996-97, Princeton Corridor chpt.), N.J. State Bar Assn. (tax com. 1999—), Princeton Bar Assn., N.J. Soc. CPAs (tax com., bd. Mercer Chpt. 1999—), Mercer County Estate Planning Coun., Tax Execs. Inst. N.J. (pres. 1985, program chair 1984, membership chair 1992, IRS liaison chair 1993). Roman Catholic. Avocations: jogging, theater, volleyball, scuba, tennis. Office: 212 Carnegie Ctr Ste 206 Princeton NJ 08540-6236 Office Phone: 609-844-7604. Business E-Mail: taxdefender@lawyer.com.

KENNY, ROBERT WADE, social sciences educator, writer; arrived in U.S., 1989; BA in Psychology, St. Mary's U., Halifax, 1975, BEd cum laude, 1976, MA in Ednl. Psychology, 1979; PhD in Rhetoric, U. Pitts., 1994, MA in Sociology, 1995. Prof. U. Dayton, Pa., 1996—. Contbr. articles to profl. jours.; author: The Attic, 1985. Office: Univ Dayton 300 College Park Dayton OH 45469 Office Phone: 937-229-2376. Personal E-mail: doctorwadekenny@hotmail.com. E-mail: wade.kenny@notes.udayton.edu.

KENNY, SHIRLEY STRUM, academic administrator; b. Tyler, Tex., Aug. 28, 1934; d. Marcus Leon and Florence (Golenternek) Strum; m. Robert Wayne Kenny, July 22, 1956; children: David Jack, Joel Strum, Daniel Clark, Jonathan Matthew, Sarah Elizabeth. BA, BJ, U. Tex., 1955; MA, U. Minn., 1957; PhD, U. Chgo., 1964; LHD (hon.), U. Rochester, 1988, Chonnam U., 1996, Donguk U., 2000, Ajou U., 2004. Chair English dept. U. Md., College Park, 1973-79, provost Arts and Humanities, 1979-85; pres. CUNY Queens Coll., Flushing, 1985-94, SUNY, Stony Brook, 1994—; chair Brookhaven Sci. Assocs. Author: The Conscious Lovers, 1968, The Plays of Richard Steele, 1971, The Performers and Their Plays, 1982, The Works of George Farquhar, 2 vols., 1988, British Theatre and the Other Arts, 1984, Reinventing Undergraduate Education: A Blueprint for America's Research Universities, 1998; contbr. articles to profl. jours. Bd. dirs. Goodwill Greater N.Y., L.I. Assn. Named Outstanding Woman, U. Md., 1983, Outstanding Alumnus, U. Tex. Coll. Comm., 1989, Disting. Alumna, U. Tex., 1999; recipient Disting. Alumnus award, U. Chgo. Club Washington, 1980, Svc. and Leadership award, N.Y. Urban League, 1988. Mem.: Woodrow Wilson Found., Boyer Comm. Educating Undergrads. (chair), Assn. Am. Colls. and Univs. (bd. dirs. 1988—91, 2005—). Office: SUNY 310 Adminstrn Bldg Stony Brook NY 11794-0701 Business E-Mail: shirley.kenny@stonybrook.edu.

KENO, LEIGH R., antiques dealer, appraiser; b. Mohawk, N.Y., 1957; BA in Art History, Hamilton Coll., 1979. Dir. Am. furniture dept. William Doyle Galleries, 1979—84; v.p. appraisal dept. and specialist in Am. furniture dept. Christie's, 1984—86; owner Leigh Keno Am. Antiques, N.Y.C., 1986—. Vis. scholar Winterthur Mus., Del.; regular featured appraiser PBS' Antiques Roadshow, 1996—; co-host with Leslie Keno Find! on PBS, 2003—. Co-author (with Leslie Keno and Joan Barzilay Freund): Hidden Treasures: Searching for Masterpieces of American Furniture, 2000; co-author: (with Leslie Keno) (column) This Old House mag., 2003—. Fellow, Hist. Deerfield Summer Fellowship Program, 1979. Mem.: Antiques Dealers Assn. Am., Nat. Antique and Art Dealers Assn. Am. Avocations: fly fishing, racing vintage sports cars. Office: Leigh Keno Am Antiques 127 E 69th St New York NY 10021

KENO, LESLIE B., antiques dealer, appraiser; b. Mohawk, N.Y., 1957; s. Ronald and Norma Keno; m. Emily Keno; 2 children. Grad. in Am. art, Williams Coll., 1979. Joined Sotheby's, N.Y.C., 1980, sr. v.p., dir. Am. furniture and decorative arts, 1983—. Regular featured appraiser PBS' Antiques Roadshow, 1996—; co-host with Leigh Keno Find! on PBS, 2003—. Co-author (with Leigh Keno and Joan Barzilay Freund): Hidden Treasures: Searching for Masterpieces of American Furniture, 2000; co-author: (with Leigh Keno) (column) This Old House mag., 2003—. Fellow, Hist. Deerfield Summer Fellowship Program, 1979. Avocations: fly fishing, skiing, racing vintage sports cars. Office: Am Furniture and Decorative Arts Sothebys 1334 York Ave New York NY 10021

KENOFER, DORIS DILLON See DILLON, DORIS

KENRICH, JOHN LEWIS, retired lawyer; b. Lima, Ohio, Oct. 17, 1929; s. Clarence E. and Rowena (Stroh) Katterheinrich; m. Betty Jane Roehll, May 26, 1951; children: John David, Mary Jane, Kathryn Ann, Thomas Roehll, Walter Clarence. BS, Miami U., Oxford, Ohio, 1951; LLB, U. Cin., 1953. Bar: Ohio 1953, Mass. 1969. Asst. counsel B.F. Goodrich Co., Akron, Ohio, 1956-65; asst. sec., counsel W.R. Grace & Co., Cin., 1965-68, v.p. Splty. Products Group divsn., 1970-71; corp. counsel, sec. Standex Internat. Corp., Andover, Mass., 1969-70; v.p., sec. Chemed Corp., Cin., 1971-82, sr. v.p., gen. counsel, 1982-86, exec. v.p., chief adminstrv. officer, 1986-91, ret., 1991. Trustee Better Bus. Bur., Cin., 1981-90; mem. bus. adv. coun. Miami U., 1986-88; mem. City Planning Commn., Akron, 1961-62; mem. bd. visitors Coll. Law U. Cin., 1988-92; mem. area coun. trustees Franciscan Sisters of Poor Found., Cin., 1989-93; bd. govs. Ohio River Valley chpt. Arthritis Found., 1992-95, 2000—04; mem. Com. on Reinvestment City of Cin., 1991-93. 1st lt. JAGC U.S. Army, 1954-56. Mem. Beta Theta Pi, Omicron Delta Kappa, Delta Sigma Pi, Phi Eta Sigma. Republican. Presbyterian. Home and Office: 4691 Pebble Bay Cir Vero Beach FL 32963 E-mail: kenrich1@bellsouth.net.

KENRICK, CHARLES WILLIAM, lawyer; b. Chgo., June 16, 1946; s. Ralph Schwarting and Angela Augusta (Shostrom) K.; m. Patricia June Ogilvie, Dec. 27, 1969; children: Hugh, Alex, Graham, Charlotte, Blair. AB cum laude, Kenyon Coll., 1968; JD, Duquesne U., 1972. Bar: Pa. 1972, U.S. Dist. Ct. (we. dist.) Pa. 1972, U.S. Ct. Appeals (3rd cir.) 1977, U.S. Supreme Ct. 1984, U.S. Ct. Appeals (6th, 7th and 10th cirs.), 1988. From assoc. to ptnr. Dickie, McCamey & Chilcote, Pitts., 1972—98, mng. ptnr., 1993-97; ptnr. Gorr Moser Dell & Loughney, Pitts., 1999-2000, Grogan & Graffam, Pitts., 2000—04, Meyers, Kenrick & Giuffre, LLC, Pitts., 2004—. Articles editor Duquesne U. Law Rev., 1971; editor Pitts. Legal Jour., 1980-84. Fellow: ABA, Allegheny Bar Found. (ho. of dels. 1980—2000), Pa. Bar Found.; mem.: Pa. Bar Assn., Allegheny County Bar Assn. (bd. govs. 1984—, adminstrv. v.p. 1986—, pres.-elect 1990, pres. 1991), Kenyon Coll. Nat. Alumni Coun., Kenyon Coll. Alumni Assn. Pitts. (pres. 1983—84), Duquesne U. Law Alumni Assn. (pres. 1985—86), Duquesne Club, Valley Brook Club, Rivers Club. Democrat. Office: Meyers Kenrick & Giuffre LLC US Steel Tower 600 Grant St Ste 5745 Pittsburgh PA 15219-1000 Office Phone: 412-281-4100. E-mail: ckenrick@meyersmedmal.com.

KENSINGTON, ANDREW JUSTUS, litigation specialist, small business owner; b. Elmhurst, Ill., Oct. 3, 1950; s. Walter Alan Kerr and Esther Elizabeth Blanton. Cert. litigation specialist, Roosevelt U., 1981; BA in Psychology and Sociology, Ill. State U., 1984; grad., Gabriel Richard Inst., 1984. Cert.: (Westlaw specialist). Pres. U.S. Justice Party Americâle, 1976—; owner Orion Inst., Buckingham, Va., 2001—; asst. Niro, Scavone, Haller & Niro, Chgo., 1983—85; with Johnson, Cusack & Bell, Chgo., 1986—87; legal asst. Trexler-Bushnell, et al, Chgo., 1987—88; patent cons. Legal Pers., Northbrook, Ill., 1990; sales rep. Radio Am./APAC Corp., Chgo., 1991—93; litigation cons., asst. Paul Armstrong, Atty. at Law, Chgo., 1993—94; resident property mgr. Joel Kaplan, Herbert G. Dorsey III, Sedona, Ariz., 1994—98; patent cons. Office Tech. Develop. Office Vice Chancellor U. Ill. Asst. project mgr. Amoco Corp., Chgo., Olsten Svcs., Inc., Chgo., 1989—90; lead litig. asst. Niro, Scavone, Chgo.; rschr. in field. Author 300 page report of custom rsch.; contbr. free verse poetry; creator, producer, engr., arranger (personalized audio tapes);, author press releases. Participant anti-war movement Vietnam War, 1968—76; candidate U.S. Presidency U.S. J.P.A., Va., 2003—04; co-founder, advocate N.A.C.G., Va., 1993—. Capt. USAR. Named Excellence in Mil. Sci., U.S. Army, Howe, Ind., 1965; U. Ill. scholarr. Mem.: NACDL, ABA, ATLA (assoc.), Vietnam Vets. Against the War. Episcopalian. Avocations: music, game collecting, walking. Home: 403 10th St NW Charlottesville VA 22901 Office Phone: 434-806-5554.

KENSINGTON, COSTA NICHOLAS, lawyer; b. Bristol, Eng., Feb. 7, 1948; came to U.S., 1954; s. Nicholas K. and Moira Esther Georgiou; m. Cheryl Lee Dees; children: C. Ragan, C. Nicholas. JD, Rutgers U., 1972, BA, 1996. Bar: N.Y. 1973. Assoc. Sullivan & Cromwell, N.Y.C., 1973-77, Skadden, Arps, Slate et. al., N.Y.C., 1977-79; ptnr. Kensington & Ressler, LLC, N.Y.C., 1980—2003, Anderson, Kill & Olick, P.C., N.Y.C., 2003—. Henry Rutgers scholar Rutgers U., 1969. Mem. U.S.-Cyprus C. of C. (bd. dirs. 1998—), The Univ. Club, County Club Darien. Avocations: golf, tennis. Home: 366 Mansfield Ave Darien CT 06820-2112 Office: 1251 Avenue of Americas 42 Floor New York NY 10020-1182 E-mail: ckensington@andersonkill.com.

KENT, ALLEN, library and information sciences professor; b. N.Y.C., Oct. 24, 1921; s. Samuel and Anna (Begun) K.; m. Rosalind Kossoff, Jan. 24, 1943; children: Merryl Frances Kent Samuels, Emily Beth Kent Yeager, Jacqueline Diane Kent Maryak, Carolyn May Kent Hall. BS in Chemistry, CCNY, 1942. Sci. editor Intersci. Pubs., 1946-51; research assoc. Ctr. Internat. Studies, MIT, 1951-53; prin. documentation engr. Battelle Meml. Inst., Columbus, Ohio, 1953-55; asso. dir. Ctr. for Documentation and Communication Research; prof. library sci. Western Res. U., Cleve., 1955-63; dir. office communications programs, chmn. interdisciplinary doctoral program info. sci., prof. info. sci., edn. and computer sci. U. Pitts., 1963-76; Univ. Disting. Service prof. library and info. sci. and assoc. dean U. Pitts. Sch. Library and Info. Sci., 1976-91, interim dean, 1985-86, prof. emeritus, 1992. Mem. mgmt. info. com. Health and Welfare Assn. Allegheny County, Pa., 1972-80; dir. Marcel Dekker, Inc., N.Y., 1978-93. Author (with others): Machine Literature Searching, 1956; author: (with J.W. Perry) Documentation and Information Retrieval, 1957; author: Tools for Machine Literature Searching, 1958, Centralized Information Services, 1958, Mechanized Information Retrieval, 1962, 2d edit., 1966, also fgn. transls. Specialized Information Centers, 1965, Information Analysis and Retrieval, 1971, Resource Sharing in Libraries, 1977, On-Line Revolution in Libraries, 1978, Structure and Governance of Library Networks, 1979, Use of Library Materials, 1979, Information Technology, 1982; editor, co-editor numerous books in field, exec. editor Ency. Libr. and Info. Sci., 1968—2003, Ency. Computer Sci. and Tech., 1972—2002, Ency. Microcomputers, 1984—2001, Ency. of Telecomm., 1988—98. Chmn. bd. Interuniv. Comms. Coun. Inc., 1971-74. Served with USAAF, 1942-46. Recipient Info. Tech. Merit award Eastman Kodak Co., 1968. Fellow AAAS; mem. ALA, Assn. Computing Machinery, Am. Soc. Info. Sci. (award of merit 1977, award for Best Info. Sci. Book of Yr. 1980, Pioneer in Info. Sci. 1987), Acad. Sr. Profls. Eckerd Coll. Home: 5108 Brittany Dr S Apt 601 Saint Petersburg FL 33715-1525 *My goal has been to be useful. This entails service, dedication to my profession and to the institution which supports my work, and absolute standards of honesty.*

KENT, BARTIS MILTON, retired physician; b. Terrell, Tex., June 23, 1925; s. Bartis William and Annie (Smalley) K.; m. Ann L. Kiel, July 6, 1954; children: Susan Ruth, Martha Lucille, Bartis Michael. Student, So. Meth. U., 1942-44; MD, Baylor U., 1948. Diplomate Am. Bd. Internal Medicine. Intern Jefferson Davis Hosp., Houston, 1948-49; resident pathology Mass. Meml. Hosps., Boston, 1951; resident in internal medicine Baylor U., 1953-56; indsl. physician Humble Oil Co., Houston, 1949-51; instr. dept. medicine U. Iowa, 1956-58; staff physician Iowa City VA Hosp., 1956-58; practice medicine specializing in internal medicine Muskogee, Okla., 1958—2002. Cons. Muskogee VA Hosp.; clin. asst. prof. medicine U. Okla. Sch. Medicine, 1975-98. Chmn. Muskogee County chpt. Am. Nat. Red Cross, 1963-65. With USAF, 1951—53. Decorated Air medal. Fellow A.C.P.; mem. Indsl. Med. Assn., Soc. Nuclear Medicine, Am. Fedn. Clin. Research, Am. Heart Assn., Aerospace Medicine Assn., Am., Okla. socs. internal medicine, Muskogee C. of C. Methodist. Mason (Shriner). Avocations: fishing, gardening. Home: 800 N 45th St Muskogee OK 74401-1505 Personal E-mail: bmkent@cox.net.

KENT, CALVIN ALBERT, university administrator; b. Kansas City, Kans., Sept. 8, 1941; m. Nita Sue Davis, Aug. 23, 1963; children: Nita Christine, Anna Elaine. BA, Baylor U., 1963; MA, U. Mo., 1965, PhD, 1967; postgrad., U. Va., 1967, Wichita State U., 1972, U. Chgo., 1975, Rice U., 1987. Instr. econs. U. Mo., Columbia, 1963-64; instr. social scis. Stevens Coll., Columbia, 1964-67; faculty U. S.D., Vermillion, 1967-78, prof. econs., 1973-78, dir. public fin. studies, 1971-78; Herman W. Lay prof. pvt. enterprise, dir. Center Pvt. Enterprise Baylor U., Waco, Tex., 1978-90; adminstr. Energy Info. Adminstrn., Washington, 1990-93; dean, Lewis Disting. chair bus. Coll. Bus. Marshall U., Huntington, W. Va., 1993—, v.p. tech. commercialization, 2003—04, v.p. bus. and econ. rsch., 2004—. Exec. dir. S.D. Council on Econ. Edn., 1969-78; chief economist taxation coms. S.D. Legislature; cons. S.D. Dept. Rev. Alderman, Vermillion, 1969-78; mem. Pres.'s Adv. Com. Entrepreneurship Edn., 1983-85. Author: Indian Poverty, 1969, Taxation of Cooperative Enterprise, 1970, Death Taxes in the American States, 1974, Municipal Regulation and Franchising, 1975, Encyclopedia of Entrepreneurship, 1981, The Environment for Entrepreneurship, 1984, Entrepreneurship and the Privatization of Government, 1987, The Texas Economy, 1989, Entrepreneurship Education: Present Practices Future Direction, 1990, The Public Utilities Holding Company Act: 1935-92, 1993, Agenda for Fair Taxation, 1998; contbr. articles to profl. jours. Pres. City Coun., Vermillion, 1974-78; vice chmn. S.D. Mcpl. League. Dist. 2, 1972-74; councilman City of Huntington, W.Va., 1997—, City of Woodway, Tex., 1985-90, mayor, 1986-90, chmn. City Coun., 2002-03; co-chair Gov.'s Commn. on Tax Fairness, 1997-2000; mem. Tri-State Airport Authority, v.p., 2001—. Outstanding Tchr., U. S.D., 1970-72, Outstanding Prof., Baylor U., 1983; Outstanding Young Religious Leader, 1976, Disting. Prof. Baylor Sch. Bus., 1981, Piper Prof. Piper Found., 1988; recipient Freedoms Found. at Valley Forge award for excellence in pvt. enterprise edn., 1980, Sargent Americanism award, 1986, John Schramm Leadership award Nat. Assn. Econ. Edn. and Joint Coun. on Econ. Edn., NSF award, 1974, Gov.'s citation for disting. achievement, 1996. Mem. Nat. Assn. Econ. Educators (pres. 1978-80), Assn. Pvt. Enterprise Edn. (sec.-treas. 1982-90, Disting. Svc. award 1988, Outstanding Scholar award 1992, bd. dirs. 1994), Soc. Econ. Educators (sec.-treas. 1987-90, v.p. 1993, pres. 1994), Rotary (pres. 1999-2000, Paul Harris fellow), Masons. Republican. Presbyterian. Home: 133 Woodland Dr Huntington WV 25705-1349

KENT, DAVID CHARLES, lawyer; b. Shreveport, La., July 23, 1953; s. Keith C. and Louise (Goode) K.; m. Carol Elizabeth Hittson, July 3, 1976; children: John, Meredith, Robert. BA, Baylor U., 1975, JD, 1978. Bar: Tex. 1978, U.S. Dist. Ct. (no. dist.) Tex. 1980, U.S. Ct. Appeals (5th cir.) 1980, U.S. Dist. Ct. (so. and we. dists.) Tex. 1981, U.S. Ct. Appeals (11th cir.) 1981, U.S. Dist. Ct. (ea. dist.) Tex. 1981; bd. cert. civil trial law, personal injury trial law. Briefing atty. Supreme Ct. Tex., Austin, 1978-79; ptnr. Hughes & Luce L.L.P., Dallas, 1979-2000, Diamond McCarthy Taylor Finley Bryant & Lee, LLP, 2000—03, Sedgwick Detert Moran & Arnold LLP, 2003—. Editor: Managing Scarce World Resources, 1975, Crime and Justice in America, 1976, Medical Care and Health in America, 1977, Meeting America's Energy Needs, 1978; contbr. articles to profl. jours. Coord. employee campaign United Way Dallas, 1981-90; teamwalk March of Dimes, Dallas, 1981-87; nat. exploring com. Boy Scouts Am., Irving, Tex., 1982-92; mem. HOBY Tex. North, bd. dirs., 1999-, sec., 2000-; mem. Baylor Parents League, pres. North Dallas Area chpt., 1999-2001; pres. Twin Bridge Homeowners Assn., 2000-02; bd. dirs. High Adventure Treks for Dads & Daus., Inc., chmn. bd. dirs., 2005—; bd. dirs. Law Focused Edn., Inc., 1997-, pres. 2004-06. Named Outstanding Young Lawyer Dallas, Dallas Assn. Young Lawyers, 1989; recipient Cert. Recognition, United Way, 1983. Fellow: Tex. Bar Found., Dallas Bar Found. (co-chair elect Bench Bar Conf. Com. 2005—); mem.: ABA (life fellow ABA Young Lawyer Divsn.), Coll. of State Bar of Tex., Dallas Bar Assn. (chair Tex. h.s. mock trial program 1994—99, chair Law Day com. 2000—01, chair Speakers Com. 2002, dir. tort and ins. practice sect. 2005—, Outstanding Com. Chair award 1998), Baylor U. Alumni Assn. (scholarship com. 1980—81). Republican. Methodist. Office: Sedgwick Detert Moran & Arnold LLP 1717 Main St Ste 5400 Dallas TX 75201 Office Phone: 469-227-4658. Business E-Mail: david.kent@sdma.com.

KENT, DEBORAH WARREN, hypnotherapist, consultant, lecturer; b. N.Y.C., May 6, 1947; d. Fred Warren and Margo (Lefebre) North. BS in Spl. Edn., U. Cin., 1969; MS in Counseling, CUNY, Hunter Coll., 1973; cert. master level hypnotherapist, Am. Hypnosis Tng. Acad., Silver Spring, Md., 1987; MSW, Columbia U., 1997. Cert. clin. mental health counselor, social worker; nat. cert. counselor; nat. cert. clin. hypnotherapist. Remediation specialist, counselor, psychometrist N.Y.C. Bd. Edn., 1973-79; cons. on assessment and remediation, N.Y.C., 1979-81; prodn. mgr. The Singing Experience, N.Y.C., 1981-83; hypnotherapist Inst. for Hypnotherapy, N.Y.C., 1983-85; pvt. practice hypnotherapy and counseling, N.Y.C., 1985—. Conducted workshops and seminars in clin. hypnosis, comm. skills and tng., stress mgmt.; lectr. to bus. and univs.; vocat. specialist Alternatives for Growth, N.J.; cons. vocat. case mgmt. assessment Ams. with Disabilities Act, 1994-96; social work cons. personal svc. unit Nat. Maritime Union, N.Y.C., chem. dependency coord., 1997-99, clin. svcs. utilization rev. coord., USCG liaison. Author, columnist Ofcl. Map and Guide mag., 1990-91. Action writer Nat. Abortion Rights Action League, Washington, 1987—; co-developer Counselors Legis. Action Support System, 1989; v.p. Joint Coun. for Mental health Svcs., 1989-97. Recipient Profl. Svc. award Am. Mental Health Counselors Assn., 1992. Fellow Am. Acad. Pain Mgmt., Am. Assn. Profl. Hypnotherapists (cert.); mem. ACA, ASCD (N.Y.C. br.), NASW (N.Y.C. chpt., chem. dependency com.), Nat. Certified Counselors, Am. Mental Health Counselors Assn., Nat. Bd. Cert. Clin. Hypnotherapists (diplomate, examining bd., chairperson ethics com. 1993-97), Acad. Clin. Mental Health Counselors, Cert. Clin. Mental Health Counselors (approved clin. supr.), Nat. Soc. Neurolinguistic Programming (cert.), Am. Assn. for Assessment in Counseling (bd. dirs.), Am. Acad. Experts in Traumatic Stress (diplomate), N.Y. Mental Health Counselors Assn. (legis. rep. 1989-95, v.p. 1989-91), N.Y. Counselors Assn. (Legis. Svc. award 1991). Avocations: acting, singing, performing. Home and Office: 245 E 19th St #18K New York NY 10003 E-mail: dk4hypnos@nyc.rr.com.

KENT, DEBRA DIANE, secondary school educator; b. Keosaugua, Iowa, Oct. 2, 1955; d. William Wayne and Margaret Sharlene Luke; children: Bradley Allen, Andrew Jared, Katelyn Jo, Ashley Irene. BA, Westmar Coll., 1977. Tchr. family and consumer scis. Davis County H.S., Bloomfield, Iowa, 1991—99, Ottumwa (Iowa) H.S., 1999—. Mem.: Iowa Cheerleading Coaches Assn., Iowa Family and Consumer Sci. Educators Progress (pres. 2001—02, v.p. 2000—01). Home: 911 N Jefferson St Ottumwa IA 52501 Office: 501 E Second St Ottumwa IA 52501

KENT, DENNIS V., paleomagnetist, educator, researcher; b. Prague, Czech Republic, Nov. 4, 1946; came to U.S., 1953; s. Frank D. and Olga Kent; m. Carolyn Ann Cook, Dec. 18, 1971; 1 child, Amanda Grace. BS, CCNY, 1968; PhD, Columbia U., 1974. Rsch. assoc. Lamont-Doherty Earth Obs., Palisades, N.Y., 1974-79, sr. rsch. assoc., 1979-84, Doherty sr. rsch. scientist, 1984-98, assoc. dir., 1987-89, interim dir., 1989-90, dir. rsch., 1993-94, adj. sr. rsch. scientist, 1998—. Adj. prof. dept. geol. scis. Columbia U., N.Y.C., 1987-98; prof. geol. scis. Rutgers U., Piscataway, N.J., 1998—; Gast prof. Inst. for Geophysik, Swiss Tech. Inst., Zurich, 1982, 97, 2003; vis. scholar Scripps Inst. of Oceanography, 2003; mem. ocean history panel Joint Oceanographic Instns. for Deep Earth Sampling, 1987-90, mem. exec. com., 1989-90, 93-94, 1998-2003; mem. bd. govs. Joint Oceanog. Inst., Washington, 1989-90, 93-94, vice chair, 2002-04, chmn., 2004—; mem. bd. govs. IODP Mgmt. Internat., Inc., Washington, D.C., 2003—; mem. forum organizing com. U.S. Continental Sci. Drilling Program, 1993-95; rev. and adv. com. Inst. Rock Magnetism, U. Minn., 1994-99; mem. U.S. Sci. Adv. Com., Compost II, 1996-97; founding mem. ISI Highly Cited Rschrs. database, 2002. Assoc. editor Jour. Geophys. Rsch., 1981-83, Geophys. Rsch. Letters, 1984-87, Paleoceanography, 1989-96, Terra Nova, 1997-99, G-cubed, 1999—; contbr. more than 200 refereed articles to profl. jours. Recipient VMSG medal Vening Meinesz Sch. Geodynamics, Delft, Holland, 2003; NSF grantee, 1974—; named Conoco Disting. lectr. Woods Hole (Mass.) Oceanog. Inst., 1983, Turner/Conoco Disting. lectr. U. Mich., Ann Arbor, 1985, Cox lectr. Am. Geophys. Union, 1998. Fellow AAAS, Am. Geophys. Union (pres.-elect geomagnetism and paleomagnetism sect. 1992-94, pres. 1994-96), Geol. Soc. Am. (Arthur L. Day gold medal 2003); mem. NAS. Office: Lamont-Doherty Earth Obs 61 Rt 9W Palisades NY 10964 also: Rutgers U Dept Geol Scis Piscataway NJ 08854 Office Phone: 845-365-8544. Business E-Mail: dvk@rci.rutgers.edu.

KENT, DONALD CHARLES, retired physician; b. Bonesteel, S.D., Apr. 26, 1923; s. Charles Alfred and Thelma Marguerite (Wilson) K.; m. Anna I. Marshall, May 2, 1953; children: Martha, Micahel, Sara, Christopher. BS, U. Nebr., 1945; MD, 1947. Diplomate Am. Bd. Internal Medicine, Am. Bd. Pulmonary Diseases. Rotating intern Wayne County Gen. Hosp., Eloise, Mich., 1947-48; staff physician in psychiatry Norfolk (Nebr.) State Hosp., 1947; gen. practice medicine Wahoo, Nebr., 1948-50; physician C. & N.W. R.R., 1948-50; county physician Madison County, Nebr., 1949-50; physician La. Indsl. Health Office, 1950-51; lt. (j.g.) M.C. USN, 1950; advanced through grades to capt., 1963; regtl. surgeon 1st Marine Divsn., 1951-52; resident internal medicine, chief allergy clinic U.S. Naval Hosp., Chelsea, Mass., 1952-54; officer-in-charge Cardiopulmonary Lab. St. Albans, N.Y., 1954-56; fellow Trudeau Sanitorium, Saranac Lake, N.Y., 1954; officer-in-charge U.S. Naval Dispensary Nice, France, 1956-58; post physician U.S. Consulate, Nice, 1956-58, Fgn. Svc. Lang. Sch., Nice, 1957-58; chief of medicine, exec. officer U.S. Naval Hosp., Bainbridge, Md., 1958-60; cons. internal medicine U.S. Army Hosp., Aberdeen, Md., 1958-60; fellow pulmonary disease rsch. Cardiovasc. Rsch. Inst., San Francisco, 1960-61; chief pulmonary diseases and infectious disease svc. and cardiopulmonary lab. U.S. Naval Hosp., San Diego, 1961-63, chief of medicine, 1970-71; dir. Cardiopulmonary Technicians Sch. USN, 1961-63; clin. instr. medicine U. Calif., San Francisco, 1960-61; mem. attending staff San Diego County Hosp., 1963; head chest svc., chief oxygen therapy and cardiopulmonary function lab, asst. chief med. svc. U.S. Naval Hosp., St. Albans, 1963—65, chief med. svc., 1965—67; asst. prof. clin. medicine NYU Med. Sch., N.Y.C., 1971—2002, assoc. prof. clin. medicine, 1973—82, Downstate Med. Sch., Bklyn., 1963—67, clin. prof. internal medicine, 1972—73; dir. medicine Meth. Hosp., Bklyn., 1972—73; assoc. prof. clin. medicine U. Calif., San Diego, 1970—71; staff physician, dir. occupl. and environ. medicine Pfizer Ctrl. Rsch., Groton, Conn., 1999—2004; clin. physician, dir. Free Clinic S.E. Conn., Groton, 2000—04; ret., 2003. Cons. VA Hosp., Castle Point, N.Y., 1963-67, Nassau County tb. Sanatorium, Farmingdale, N.Y., 1963-65, Nat. Lung Assn., 1973-82, IBM, Internat. Paper Co., Continental Can Co., W.T. Grant Co., 1974-82, Reactor Plant Svcs., 1988-92, Occupl Medicine Ctr., Pequot Health Ctr., Lawrence and Meml. Hosp., Groton, Conn., 1995—; assoc. med. dir. Pan Am. World Airways, JFK Internat. Airport, N.Y.C., 1988-91, also numerous other cos. in N.Y.C.; med. dir. Electric Boat divsn. Gen. Dynamics Corp., 1982-88, 92-93, cons., 1988-92; guest lectr. pulmonary physiology U.S. Naval sch. submarine Medicine, Groton, Conn., 1964-67, Haile Selassie I Med. Sch., Addis Ababa, 1967-70, Cairo U., 1967-70, Ein Shams Med. Sch., Cairo, 1967-70, Am. U., Beirut, 1968-70; nat. chmn. Nat. Interagy. Coun. on Smoking and Health, 1973-76; med. dir. Life Extension Inst., N.Y.C., 1973-82, v.p., 1977-78; cons. in field. Editor: Clinical Notes of Respiratory Diseases, 1972; exec. editor: Basics of RD, 1972-77; contbr. articles to med. jours. Decorated Legion of Merit, Bronze Star, Purple Heart; recipient Meritorious award for disting. svc. Am. Acad. Oral Medicine, 1977. Fellow ACP, Am. Coll. Chest Physicians, N.Y. Acad. Medicine, Royal Soc. Tropical Medicine, Royal Soc. Medicine, Explorers Club; mem. Bklyn. Thoracic Soc., Am. Lung Assn., Am. fedn. Clin. Rsch., N.Y. Trudeau Soc. (program chmn. 1966-67), Am. Soc. Tropical Medicine and Hygiene, Tb. and Health Assn., N.Y. State Am. Pub. Health Assn., Undersea Med. Soc., Am. Occupl. and Environ. Medicine Assn., Nat. Tb. Assn., Assn. Mil. Surgeons (life, Stitt award 1971), Soc. Occupl. and Environ. Health, Navy League U.S., Med. Execs. N.Y.C., Alpha Omega Alpha. Democrat. Roman Catholic. E-mail: dkents33@comcast.net.

KENT, EDGAR ROBERT, JR., investment banker; b. Balt., May 28, 1941; s. E. Robert and Marian (Mueller) K.; children: E. Robert, Josephine Townsend, Louise Daniel. BS, Princeton U., 1963; MBA, Columbia U., 1966; JD, U. Md., 1975. CFA. Mng. dir. DeutscheBancAlex.Brown, Balt., 1968-2001; dir. Alex.Brown Realty, Balt., 2001—. Trustee Calvert Sch., Balt., Ctr. Stage, Balt., Endowment Fund of U. Md., Balt. Cmty. Found. Home: 103 Castlewood Rd Baltimore MD 21210-1360 Office: Alex Brown Realty Inc Ste 1200 300 E Lombard St Baltimore MD 21202-6740

KENT, E(VERETT) ALLEN, performing arts association administrator, theater producer; b. Ronan, Mont., Oct. 16, 1938; s. George Douglas Kent and Fern Louise Hickman-Reed; m. Janice Gay Gustafson-Kent, June 2, 1962 (div. Apr. 1969); 1 child, Kyla Kolleen; m. Gloria Madeline Sontag-Kent, Mar. 21, 1969 (div. Apr. 6, 1990); 1 child, Patrick. BA, U. Wash., 1965, MA, 1967; PhD (abd), Wayne State U., 1974. Actor Aqua Theater, 1958, Bellevue Playbarn, 1959; actor-technician Erie Playhouse, 1960; floor mgr. KING-TV, 1965; prodn. stage mgr. sch. drama U. Wash., 1965-66; stage mgr. A Contemporary Theater, 1966; tech. dir., lighting designer Pitts. Playhouse, 1966-67; tech. dir. Lorretto Hilton Rep. Co., 1967, St. Louis Mcpl. Opera; dir., designer, tech. dir., instr. Florissant Valley C.C., St. Louis, 1967-69; tech. dir. Mo. Repertory Theatre, Kansas City, 1969-70; dir., designer Eastern Wash. U., Cheney, 1969-73; arts and crafts specialist Dept. Commerce State of Alaska, 1974—75; CEO Alaska Theatrical Svcs., Inc., Eagle River, 1974-87; dir. Performing Arts Ctr. U. Alaska, Anchorage, 1975-80, assoc. prof., chair dept. theater and dance, 1975-80; CEO KAE Enterprises, Ltd., Eagle River, 1987-90, Kent Artist Svcs., N.Y.C., 1990-96; exec. dir. Jennifer Muller/The Works Dance Co., 1990-91; mng. dir. Denishawn Repertory Dance Co., N.Y., N.J., 1991-93; dir. devel. Repertorio Espanol, 1992; exec. dir. Williams Ctr. for Arts, Rutherford, N.J., 1992-93; producing artistic dir. Music Theatre North, Potsdam, N.Y., 1993-94; gen. mgr. Garth Fagan Dance, Rochester, N.Y., 1995-96; mng. dir. Ballet: The Daring Project, 1996-97; CEO Am. Theatrical Svcs., 1996—. CEO Am. Classic Theater, 1999—; artistic dir. Spokane Civic Theater, 1971, Sky Hook Prodn. Co., 1999—; exec. dir. Magic Cir. Ctr. for the Arts, 2000; founder dept. theatre U. Alaska, Anchorage, 1976; lighting designer Alaska Repertory Theatre, Anchorage, 1977; lobbyist Anchorage Faculty Assn. U. Alaska, 1978—80; arts cons. Actors Studio, Town Hall, N.Y.C., 1991; dance panelist N.J. State Coun. on Arts, 1991—93; exec. dir. Greater Palmer C. of C., Palmer, Alaska, 2002—. With U.S. Army, 1961—67. Recipient Artist award Alaska State Coun. Arts, 1980. Mem. Soc. Stage Dirs. and Choreographers, Actors' Equity Assn. Roman Catholic. Avocations: hunting, fishing. Address: Po Box 6635 Boise ID 83707-0635 E-mail: ev@palmerchamber.org.

KENT, JEFFREY FRANKLIN, professional baseball player; b. Bellflower, Calif., Mar. 7, 1968; Grad., Edison H.S., Calif. 2d baseman Toronto Blue Jays, 1992, N.Y. Mets, 1992-96, San Francisco Giants, 1997—2002, Houston Astros, 2003—04, Los Angeles Dodgers, 2004—. Named Nat. League MVP, 2000; named to Nat. League All-Star Team, 1999—2001, 2004, Nat. league All-Star Team, 2005. Office: LA Dodgers 1000 Elysian Park Ave Los Angeles CA 90012

KENT, JILL, midwife; b. Cottage Grove, Oreg., May 22, 1953; d. Laurence Durward and Laurel Naomi Kent; m. Mark Taylor White, June 15, 1974 (div. Nov. 12, 1987); children: Darcy Michelle Shargo, Kara Naomi White, Cameron St. John White, Brendan Morrison White; m. Stashenko Emil Hempeck, Aug. 26, 1989; children: Duncan Alexandre Kent/Hempeck, Ethan Ambrosius Kent/Hempeck. Student, Ctrl. Mo. State U., 1971—72, Moorhead (Minn.) State U., 1990—91. Lic. midwife Bd. Med. Practice, Minn., 2000, cert. profl. midwife N.Am. Registry Midwives. Midwife, owner, operator The Stork's Nest Birth Ctr., Moorhead, 1981—. Apptd. chair Midwifery Adv. Coun. Minn. Board of Med. Practice, 2000—03. Mem. health adv. coun. for Headstart SENDCAA (SE ND Comm. Action Agy.); vol. first responder rural rescue squad, 1988—2002; vol. Hospice Red River Valley, 2004—. Mem.: Minn. Assn. Midwives (pres. 1985—88), Minn. Midwives Guild (pres. 1988—94), Minn. Coun. Cert. Profl. Midwives (treas. 2000—03), Midwives Alliance N.Am. (midwest regional rep. to bd. 1985—88). Unitarian Universalist. Achievements include first midwife in Minn. to be granted midwife lic. since 1938; opened first and only freestanding birth ctr. in Minn., ND, and SD, 2002; mem. task force that devel. Cert. Profl. Midwife credential, 1993-95. Avocations: antiques, books, travel, gardening, music. Home: 520 32d Ave S #327 Moorhead MN 56560 Office: The Stork's Nest Birth Ctr 312 Hwy 75 N Moorhead MN 56560 E-mail: jk-cpm1@juno.com.

KENT, JILL ELSPETH, entrepreneur, art appraiser, lawyer; b. Detroit, June 1, 1948; d. Seymour and Grace (Edelman) K.; m. Mark Elliott Solomons, Aug. 20, 1978. BA, U. Mich., 1970; JD, George Washington U., 1975, LLM, 1979. Bar: D.C. 1975. Mgmt. intern U.S. Dept. Transp., Washington, 1971-73; staff analyst Office Mgmt. and Budget, Exec. Office of Pres., Washington, 1974-76; legis. counsel U.S. Treasury Dept., Washington, 1976-78, dir. legis. reference divsn. Healthcare Financing Adminstrn., 1978-80; sr. budget examiner Office Mgmt. and Budget, Exec. Office of Pres., Washington, 1980-84; chief Treasury, Gen. Svcs. Office of Mgmt. and Budget, Washington, 1984-85; dep. asst. sec. for departmental fin. and planning U.S. Dept. Treasury, Washington, 1985-86, dep. asst. sec. for dept. fin. and mgmt., 1986-88, asst. sec. of treasury, 1988-89; CFO U.S. Dept. State, Washington, 1989-93, acting under sec. of state for mgmt., 1991; exec. devel. program Office of Mgmt. and Budget, Washington, 1994; CFO George Washington U. Med. Ctr., Washington, 1993-97; v.p. IPAC, 1997-98, The Columbus Group. Pres. CEO Atlantic Threadworks Inc.; gen. mgr. The Frogeye Co., 1995—; adj. prof. pub. policy U. Md., 1993—. Bd. dirs. Mobile Med. Care Inc., 1987-91; Trustee Newport Sch., 1988-91, Washington Civic Symphony, 1994-95; bd. dirs. China Found., 1997—; sr. counselor Atlantic Coun. U.S., 1997—; bd. dirs., sec. Wash. Bach Consort. Recipient Adminstrs. award Healthcare Financing Adminstrn., 1980; named on of Top 40 Performers, Mgmt. mag., 1987, Disting. Svc. award Dept. Treasury, 1989, Am. Assn. Govt. Accts. award, 1992, Disting. Svc. award Dept. State, 1993. Mem. ABA, D.C. Bar Assn., Pres's. Coun. on Mgmt. Improvement, CFO Roundtable Healthcare Forum, Fin. Execs. Inst., Exec. Women in Govt. (treas. 1991-92, pres. 1992-93), Va. Assn. of Female Execs. (adv. coun. 1990), Coun. Excellence in Govt. (prin. 1993—). Republican. Home: 2419 California St NW Washington DC 20008-1615 Office Phone: 202-483-7209. Personal E-mail: jekent@earthlink.net.

KENT, JOHN BRADFORD, lawyer; b. Jacksonville, Fla., Sept. 5, 1939; s. Frederick Heber and Norma Cleveland (Futch) Kent; m. Monett Powers, Dec. 18, 1969; children: Monett, Susan, Sally, Katherine. AB, Yale U., 1961; JD, U. Fla., 1964; LLM in Taxation, NYU, 1965. Bar: Fla. 1964, U.S. Dist. Ct. (mid. dist.) Fla. 1965, U.S. Tax Ct. 1965, U.S. Ct. Appeals (11th cir.) 1973, U.S. Supreme Ct. 1973, U.S. Dist. Ct. (so. dist.) Fla. 1981, Nebr. U.S. Dist. Ct. 1995. Assoc. Ulmer, Murchison, Kent, Ashby & Ball, Jacksonville, 1965-67; ptnr., shareholder Kent, Watts & Durden, P.A. and predecessor firms, Jacksonville, 1967-85; shareholder Carlton, Field, Ward, Emmanuel, Smith, Cutler & Kent, Jacksonville, 1985-88, Kent, Crawford, P.A., Jacksonville, 1988—2003, Marks Gray, P.A., Jacksonville, 2003—. Past pres., trustee Fla. Cmty. Coll. Found.; past. pres., bd. dirs. N.E. divsn. Children's Home Soc. Fla.; past bd. dirs. Jacksonville Legal Aid Soc.; bd. dirs. Children's Home Soc. Fla. Mem.: Nat. Assn. Theatre Owners Fla. (bd. dirs., officer 1969—2000), Rotary (past officer, Paul Harris fellow). Office: Marks Gray PA 1200 Riverplace Blvd Ste 800 Jacksonville FL 32207

KENT, JULIE, dancer, actress, model; b. Bethesda, Md., July 11, 1969; d. Charles Lindbergh and Jennifer Elsie Cox; m. Victor Barbee, 1996. Grad. high sch., Potomac, Md. Apprentice Am. Ballet Theatre, N.Y.C., 1985-86, mem. corps de ballet, 1986-1990, soloist, 1990-93, prin. dancer, 1993—. Starring role (films) Dancers, 1986, Center Stage, 2000; performed as a guest artist nationally and internationally. Recipient Prix de Lausanne Internat. Ballet competition, 1986, 1st prize at Erik Bruhn Competition in Toronto, 1993, Prix Benois de la Danse, Stuttgart, Germany, 2000; named one of 50 Most Beautiful People, People Mag., 1993. Office: Am Ballet Theatre 890 Broadway Fl 3 New York NY 10003

KENT, LINDA GAIL, dancer; b. Buffalo, Sept. 21, 1946; d. Jerol Edward and Dorismae (Kohler) K.; m. Nicholas Wolff Lyndon, June 9, 1996. BS, Juilliard Sch., 1968. Dancer Alvin Ailey Am. Dance Theater, 1968-74, then prin. dancer, 1970-74; prin. dancer Paul Taylor Dance Co., N.Y.C., 1975-89; dir. dance Perry-Mansfield Performing Arts Sch. and Camp, Steamboat Springs, Colo., 2001—. Faculty Juilliard Sch., 1984—; artist-in-residence Union Theological Seminary, N.Y. Mem. Am. Guild Mus. Artists, Actors Equity. Democrat. Unitarian Universalist. Home: 91 Payson Ave New York NY 10034-2722 Office: The Juilliard Sch Dance Divsn 60 Lincoln Center Plz New York NY 10023-6588 Office Phone: 212-799-5000 x 7057. E-mail: lgk921@aol.com.

KENT, M. ELIZABETH, lawyer; b. NYC, Nov. 17, 1943; d. Francis J. and Hannah (Bergman) K. AB, Vassar Coll. magna cum laude, 1964; AM, Harvard U., 1965, PhD, 1974; JD, Georgetown U., 1978. Bar: D.C. 1978, U.S. Dist. Ct. D.C. 1978, U.S. Ct. Appeals (D.C. cir.) 1978, U.S. Supreme Ct. 1983, U.S. Dist. Ct. Md. 1985. From lectr. to asst. prof. history U. Ala., Birmingham, 1972-74; assoc. Santarelli and Gimer, Washington, 1978; sole practice Washington, 1978—. Mem. Ripon Soc., Cambridge and Washington, 1968-93; rsch. dir. Howard M. Miller for Congress, Boston, 1972; vol. campaigns John V. Lindsay for Mayor, 1969, John V. Lindsay for Pres., 1972, John B. Anderson for Pres., 1980. Woodrow Wilson fellow 1964-65; Harvard U. fellow 1968-69. Mem.: ACLU, ABA, Superior Ct. Trial Lawyers Assn., DC Assn. Criminal Def. Lawyers (bd. dirs. 2001—), Women's Bar Assn., DC Bar Assn., Phi Beta Kappa. Republican. Avocations: history, politics. Home: 35 E St NW Apt 810 Washington DC 20001-1520 Office: 717 D St NW Ste 210 Washington DC 20004 Office Phone: 202-347-6952.

KENT, MICHAEL SEAN, veterinarian, educator; b. Hillcrest, N.Y., Dec. 5, 1965; life ptnr. Karl Edward Jandrey, June 23, 1967. DVM, U. Calif. Davis, 1997. Diplomate Am. Coll. of Vet. Radiology, 2003, Am. Coll. of Vet. Internal Medicine. Lectr. radiation oncology U. Calif. Davis, 2001—04, asst. prof., 2004—. Office: U Calif Davis 1 Shields Dr Davis CA 95616 Home Fax: 530-752-9620; Office Fax: 530-752-9620. Personal E-mail: mskent@ucdavis.edu.

KENT, MOLLIE, writer, publishing executive, editor; b. Abilene, Tex., July 21, 1933; d. Henry Lee and Clyde Radia (Free) Summers; m. Paul Raymond Kintzinger, June 15, 1954 (div. July 1982); children: Katrina, Alice, Sarah. Student, Tulsa (Okla.) U., 1962-64, U. N.Mex., 1970-72. Lic. insurance and real estate agt., N.Mex. Owner, pub. Jemez Pub. Co., Jemez Springs, N.Mex., 1976-81, Albuquerque and Bernalillo, N.Mex., 1976-81; pub., editor S.W. Chronicle mag., La Plata, 1999—. Pub., editor Jemez Mountain Views, 1976-80, Sandoval County Rev., 1977-80, Sandia Sun, 1979-81; assoc. editor, advt. mgr. Aztec (N.Mex.) Local News, 1993-98. Republican. Avocations: writing, travel, music, art, family. Home: PO Box 360 La Plata NM 87418-0360

KENT, PAULA, public relations, marketing and management consultant, lecturer; b. N.Y.C.; d. John and Estelle (Frye) Smith; BS, State Tchrs. Coll., Worcester, Mass., 1939; MS, Boston U., 1941; m. Stanley J. Lloyd, Jan. 23, 1943; children: Diane Adrienne Noel, Robin Michele Cheri, Kevin Christopher Kent, Gisele Nicolette Jolie. Methods engr. Internat. Bus. Machines, 1941-42; personnel dir., fashion editor Daily Jour., San Diego, also radio sta. KSDJ, 1946-48; fashion and beauty editor, columnist The San Diego Union, 1949-64; promotion dir. The San Diego Union and the Evening Tribune, 1948-71, also UCLA Extension Div. Faculty, 1961-63; pub. relations, mktg. and mgmt. cons., 1970—; v.p. La Jolla Clin. Labs., Inc., 1970-81. Lectr. mktg. workshop tour, speaker at seminars, Brussels, London, Paris, Madrid, 1972; speaker nat. and regional confs. in maj. U.S. cities; del. Nat. Fedn. Press. Women Touring Russia, 1973. Formerly active ARC, Am. Cancer Soc., Med. Aux. San Diego. Officer USN; lt. (s.g.) USCG, 1942-45. Recipient over 158 awards 1950—, including: 39 nat., 18 western states, over 100 Calif. state awards, 13 Lulus L.A. Advt. Women's Assn., 1 local award, resulting from ann. competitions sponsored by Los Angeles Advt. Women's Club, Nat. Newspaper Publs. Assn., Calif. Press Women, Los Angeles Sales Promotion Execs. Assn., Nat. Fedn. Press Women, Editor and Pub. Mag.; recipient Outstanding Service award Boy Scouts Am., 1962, 65; civic awards City of San Diego, Distinguished Service award Investment Edn. Inst., Detroit, 1969, Golden Spear award Twin Cities Sales Promotion Execs. Assn., Mpls., 1965; Outstanding Service thru Annual Investment Clinics N.Y. Stock Exchange, 1964, L.A. Theta Sigma Phi Walter O'Malley Unique Coverage award, 1968; named Woman of Achievement San Diego, 1958, 59, 64, Woman of Valor, 1958, Woman of Year, San Diego, 1965, Woman of Achievement, Nat. Fedn. Bus. and Profl. Women's Clubs, 1966; Advt. Man of Distinction, San Diego, 1970, Don award, Legion of Portola, 1968.; fellow Boston U. 1940-41. Mem. Advt. and Sales Club San Diego (dir. 1951-71), Sales and Marketing Execs. Club San Diego (pres. 1970-71), Personnel Mgmt. Assn. (hon. mem., plaque 1963), Sales and Mktg. Execs. Internat. (dir. at large 1971-73), Sales Promotion Execs. Assn. Los Angeles (Man of Year 1965), Am. Advt. Fedn. (western region chmn. edn. com., mem. nat. edn. com. 1971-72) Nat. Newspaper Promotion Assn. (pres. Western region 1964, dir. 1968-70, chmn. western regional conv. 1964), Calif. Assn. Press Women, Nat. Fedn. Press Women, Internat. Newspaper Promotion Assn. (bd. dirs. 1971-73), Am. Mgmt. Assn. (San Diego pres's coun. bus., profl. womens' clubs outstanding svc. plaque 1969). Roman Catholic. Editor: Monthly Bull., Personnel Mgmt. Assn., 1955-59, monthly bull., Sales Execs. Club. Chmn. San Diego's Ann. Giant Sales Rally, 1953-55, 70-71, co-chmn., 1964, 65; chmn. Advt. Recognition Week Campaign, 1953-54, Nat. Unltd. Hydroplane Races, San Diego, 1953-54, sponsor rep. Evening Tribune; pub. relations advisor Nat. Mrs. Am. Pageant, honored by London Press Club Members Luncheon, 1970, San Diego 200th Anniversary celebration; producer, emcee ann. Holiday for Housewives, San Diego, 1955-60; producer, co-ordinator U. Calif., Today's World, San Diego, 1962; exec. dir., producer, dir. San Diego Ann. Golden Gloves Boxing Tournament, 1961-68; producer San Diego Ann. Metrotennis Championships, 1952-70; dir. Ann Power Boat Regatta, 1950-62; exec. dir. Ann Jr. Golf Championships; dir. Ann. Hole-in-One Tournament, 1951-70; master ceremonies, producer, emcee Gentlemen of Distinction Awards, 1967, 68, 69; producer/dir. San Diego Advt. Salesrama, 1971; producer, dir. master ceremonies San Diego Ann. Woman of Yr. Awards, 1967, 68, 69; producer/designer 34 exhibits for convs. and fairs; developed and produced A Day in San Diego for European Travel Commn., 1964; produced and emceed Ann. Boy Scout Jamboree Stage Show, 1967. Del. Nat. Fedn Press Women touring Russia. Commd. ensign, Women's Reserve, USNR, 1942, transferred USCG, served from ensign to lt. (s.g.), 1943-46. Avocation: world travel. Office: PO Box 2243 La Jolla CA 92038-2243

KENT, PHILIP, communications executive; With sales team Blair Television, 1975; co-founder subs. Blair Entertaiment John Blair & Co., 1981, v.p. program develop., 1984; packaging agent TV dept. Creative Artist's Agency, 1986—93; pres. Turner Home Entertainment Turner Broadcasting Sys., Atlanta, 1993—96; pres. Turner Broadcasting Systems Internat. Inc., Atlanta, 1996—2000, pres., COO CNN News Group, 2000—01; chmn., CEO Turner Broadcasting System, Inc. Time Warner Corp., 2003—. Bd. dirs. Ad Coun., Atlanta Braves. Bd. dirs. Woodruff Arts Ctr., Atlanta. Mem.: Metro Atlanta C. of C. (bd. dirs.), Nat. Cable and Telecommunications Assn. (bd. dirs.).*

KENT, RICHARD W., mechanical engineer; BS in mech. engring., U. Utah, 1994, MS in mech. engring., 1997; PhD in mech. and aerospace engring., U. Va., 2002. Rsch. asst. prof. Ctr. Applied Biomechanics U. Va. Contbr. articles to profl. jour. Office: U Va Ctr Applied Biomechanics 122 Engineers Way PO Box 400746 Charlottesville VA 22904-4746 Business E-Mail: rwk3c@virginia.edu.

KENT, ROBERT BRYDON, law educator; b. Lowell, Mass., Dec. 2, 1921; s. Silas Stanley and Madeleine (Brydon) K.; m. Barbara Tuttle, Mar. 31, 1951; children: Robert Brydon, Dorothy Clarke, Elizabeth Montgomery, Hugh Clarke. AB, Harvard Coll., 1943; LLB, Boston U., 1949; LLD (hon.), Roger Williams U., 2001. Bar: Mass. 1948. Pvt. practice, Ware, Mass., 1948-50; instr. Boston U. Sch. Law, 1950-52, asst. prof., 1952-54, prof., 1954-81; prof. law, dean U. Zambia Sch. Law, 1970-72; dir. Law Practice Inst., Zambia, 1970-71; Ford fellow in law tchg. Harvard U. Law Sch., 1960-61, part-time vis. prof., 1973-74; vis. prof. Cornell Law Sch., 1980-81, prof., 1981-92, prof. emeritus, 1992—, assoc. dean, 1982-86. Hon. vis. fellow Trinity Coll., Oxford U., 1976; reporter com. on civil rules Supreme Ct. RI, Superior Ct. RI, Dist. Ct. RI; disting. vis. prof. Roger Williams U. Sch. Law, 1997—; vis. prof. Boston U. Sch. Law, 2000-01; cons. in field. Author: (with Austin W. Scott) Cases and Other Materials on Civil Procedure, 1967, Rhode Island Practice: Civil Rules with Commentaries, 1969. Moderator Town of Lexington, Mass., 1965-70, selectman, 1977-81; vice chmn. Civil Liberties Union of Mass., 1966-69; exec. com. Law Assn. of Zambia, 1970-72; trustee Kimball Union Acad., pres., 1973-76. With U.S. Army, 1943-46. Fulbright prof. sch. law U. Zambia, 1988. Mem. Am. Law Inst. Democrat. Unitarian Universalist. Home: 1 Doran Farm Ln Lexington MA 02420-2128 Office: Roger Williams Sch Law Ten Metacom Ave Bristol RI 02809 Office Phone: 401-254-4605.

KENT, ROSE MICHELE, library media specialist; b. Bluefield, W.Va., Oct. 23, 1956; d. Harry and Estelle (Manilow) Finkelman; m. David R. Kent, Dec. 18, 1982 (div. Aug. 6, 1993). BS in Edn., Miami U., Oxford, Ohio, 1977, MEd, 1981. Cert. tchr., libr. media specialist, Ohio. 10th-12th grade English tchr. Finneytown Local Schs., Cin., 1977-79, 9th and 12th grade English tchr., 1980-85, coord. libr. media svcs. grades K-12, 1985—; 9th, 10th and 12th grade English tchr. Wyoming City Schs., Cin., 1979-80. Book reviewer The Book Report, Columbus, Ohio, 1990-92. Contbr. articles, story to profl. publs.; writer Gibson Greeting Cards, 1993—. Trustee, publicity chairperson, newsletter editor Temple Sholom, 1996-97; mem. com. Cinergy Found. Overture Awards, Cin., 1996; vol. Hamilton County SPCA, Cin., 1992; mem. grants evaluation com. Greater Cin. Found. Learning Links, 1997. Ohio writing project fellow, 1981-88; Tchr. Recognition grantee Greater Cin. Found. Mem. NEA, Finneytown Edn. Assn. (pres. 1989-91), Cin. Area Sch. Librs. Assn. (v.p. 1996-97, pres. 1997-98), Ohio Writing Project, Ohio Ednl. Libr. Media Assn., Ohio Edn. Assn. Democrat. Jewish. Avocations: reading, music, theater, travel, writing. Office: Finneytown HS 8916 Fontainebleau Ter Cincinnati OH 45231-4806

KENT, STEVEN, lawyer; b. Port Chester, NY, Feb. 9, 1949; BA, Georgetown U., 1970; JD, St. John's U., 1978; LLM, NYU, 1983. Bar: NY 1978, US Dist. Ct. So. Dist. NY, US Dist. Ct. Ea. Dist. NY, US Ct. Appeals 2nd Cir. Ptnr. Wilson, Elser, Moskowitz, Edelman & Dicker LLP, NYC. Mem.: ABA, NY State Trial Lawyers Assn., NY State Bar Assn. Office: Wilson Elser Moskowitz Edelman & Dicker LLP 23rd Fl 150 E 42nd St New York NY 10017-5639 Office Phone: 212-490-3000 ext. 2268. Office Fax: 212-490-3038. Business E-Mail: kents@wemed.com.

KENT, SUSAN, library director, consultant; b. N.Y.C., Mar. 18, 1944; d. Elias and Minnie (Barnett) Solomon; m. Eric Goldberg, Mar. 27, 1966 (div. Mar. 1991); children: Evan Goldberg, Jessica Goldberg; m. Rolly Kent, Dec. 20, 1991. BA in English Lit. with honors, SUNY, 1965; MS, Columbia U., 1966. Libr., sr. libr. N.Y. Pub. Libr., 1965-67, br. mgr. Donnell Art Libr., 1967-68; reference libr. Paedergaat br. Bklyn. Pub. Libr., 1971-72; reference libr. Finkelstein Meml. Libr., Spring Valley, N.Y., 1974-76; coord. adult and young adult svcs. Tucson Pub. Libr., 1977-80, acting libr. dir., 1982, dep. libr. dir., 1980-87; mng. dir. Ariz. Theatre Co., Tucson, Phoenix, 1987-89; dir. Mpls. Pub. Libr. and Info. Ctr., 1990-95; city libr. L.A. Pub. Libr., 1995—2004, N.Y. Pub. Libr., N.Y.C., 2004—. Tchr. Pima CC, Tucson, 1978; grad. libr. sch. U. Ariz., Tucson, 1995—; panelist Ariz. Commn. Arts., 1981—85; mem. bd. devel. and fundraising Child's Play, Phoenix, 1983; reviewer pub. programs NEH, 1985, panelist challenge grants, 1986—89, panelist state programs, 1988; cons., presenter workshops Young Adult Svcs. divsn. ALA, 1986—88; bd. dirs., mem. organizing devel. and fundraising com. Flagstaff (Ariz.) Symphony Orch., 1988; cons. to librs. and nonprofit instns., 1989—90, 1992—; bd. advisors UCLA Grad. Sch. Edn. and Info. Scis., 1998—2001; presenter in field. Contbr. articles to profl. jours. Chair arts and culture com. Tucson Tomorrow, 1981—85; commr. Ariz. Commn. Arts, 1983—87; bd. dirs., v.p. Ariz. Dance Theatre, 1984—86; bd. dirs. Arizonans Cultural Devel., Ariz., 1987—89, YWCA Mpls., 1991—92; bd. dirs. women's studies adv. coun. U. Ariz., 1985—90; participant Leadership Mpls., 1990—91. Recipient Libr. of the Yr., Libr. Jour., 2002, Info. Assocs. Exec. Leadership award, UCLA Anderson Sch., 2001, Interfaith Leadership award, Archdiocese of L.A., 2004; fellow, Sch. Libr. Sci., Columbia U., 1965—66. Mem.: ALA (mem. membership com. S.W. regional chair 1983—86, mem. com. appts. 1986—87, gov. coun. 1990—98, planning and budget assembly del. 1991—93, chair conf. com. 1996—97, Joseph Lippincott award 2003), Coun. Libr. and Info. Resources (bd. dirs. 2000—), Libr. Adminstrn. and Mgmt. Assn. (mem. John Cotton Dana Award com. 1994—95), Urban Librs. Coun. (mem. exec. bd. 1994—2001, treas. 1996—98, vice chair/chair elect 1998, 1999, chair 1999—2000), Calif. Libr. Assn., Pub. Libr. Assn. (mem. nominating com. 1980—82, v.p. 1986—87, pres. 1987—88, chair publs. assmebly 1988—89, chair nat. conf. 1994, chair legis. com. 1994—95). Office: NYPub Libr Fifth Ave and 42d St New York NY 10018 Office Phone: 212-642-0120. Business E-Mail: skent@nypl.org.

KENTON, EDGAR JACKSON, III, neurologist; b. Phila., Mar. 5, 1940; s. Edgar Jackson Kenton Jr. and Jessie Elizabeth Kenton; m. Geraldine Davis Kenton, Aug. 13, 1994; m. Sandra Payne Kenton, June 24, 1967 (div. Dec. 20, 1991); children: Adrienne Danielle, Brian Michael. BA, Rutgers U., 1961; MD, Cornell Med. Coll., 1965. Diplomate Am. Bd. Psychiatry and Neurology, Nat. Bd. Med. Examiners. Intern in internal medicine Jefferson Med. Coll., Phila., 1965—66, resident in internal medicine, 1966—67, resident in neurology, 1967—70; fellow in cerebral blood flow studies Strok Rsch. Ctr., Phila. Gen. Hosp., Phila., 1970; pvt. practice in neurology, 1972—. Acting cheif dept. neurology Lankenau Hosp., 1972—73, chief dept. neurology, 1973—98; examiner Am. Bd. Psychiatry and Neurology, 1982—92, sr. examiner, 1992—96, dir., 1996—; chief cerebrovascular diseases sect. Main Line Health Sys. Hosps., 1998—; instr. neurology Thomas Jefferson U. Med. Coll., 1972—78, asst. prof. neurology, 1974—78, clin. assoc. prof. neurology, 1978—, prof. clin. neurology, 1999; vis. prof. Morehouse Med. Coll., Atlanta, 1994, Meharry Med. Coll., Nashville, 1998; vis. faculty Marion Merrell Dow Minority Scholars Program, 1994—; cons. Bryn Mawr Child Study Inst., Bryn Mawr Coll., 1975—85; cons. Hill Top Prep. Sch. for the Learning Disabled, 1973—, Lupus Found., 1975—90; presenter in field; bd. dirs. Am. Acad. Neurology, Assn. Black Cardiologists, Am. Heart Assn., stroke task force, 1998—, v.p. Southeastern Pa. Region, 1998—2000, pres. Southeastern Pa. Region, 2000—01; mem. search com. Nat. Inst. Neurologic Diseases and Stroke, 2001; mem. Accreditation Coun. for Continuing Med. Edn., 2001—; mem. med. adv. bd. Lupus Found., Guillian-Barre Found., Inglis House of the Chronically Disabled. Rschr. in field.; musician: Stroke Connection, Am. Heart Assn., 1996—2000; mem. editl. bd. Stroke Jour.; contbr. articles to profl. jours. Mem. adv. com. on stroke prevention and treatment Gen. Assembly, Commonwealth of Pa., 2001; mem. Spkrs. Bur. Alzheimer's Assn. Greater Phila., Lankenau Hosp.; mem. Union League Phila.; bd. trustees Hill Top Prep. Sch., 1973—96, The Shipley Sch., 1984—88. Maj. USAF, 1970—72. Named one of Am.'s Leading Physicians, Black Enterprise Mag., 2001; recipient Recognition award, Nat. Sclerosis Soc., 1983, Humanitarian award, NAACP, 1983, Disting. Svc. award, Hill Top Prep. Sch. for Learning Disabled, 1985, Spl. Recognition award, Am. Heart Assn., 1999, Edn. award, 2000, Heart and Torch award, 2001. Fellow: Am. Stroke Assn. (stroke coun. 1978), Am. Acad. Neurology; mem.: AMA, Phila. Stroke Coun., Montgomery County Med. Soc., Med. Soc. Ea. Pa., Pa. State Med. Soc., Phila. Coll. Physicians, Alpers Soc. Clin. Neurology (sec.-treas. 1980—82, pres. 1982—90), Phila. Neurol. Soc., Sigma Pi Phi. Avocations: volunteering, travel. Office: Mainline/Jefferson Health Sys Lankenau Med Bldg Ste 216 100 E Lancaster Ave Wynnewood PA 19096

KENWORTHY, WILLIAM EUGENE, judge; b. Las Animas, Colo., Apr. 27, 1933; s. William Sydner and Joyce Lovelle (Thedford) K.; m. Lucille Nicoletta Capozzola, July 20, 1963; children: William D., Kathryn J., Randal A. BS, U. Denver, 1955, LLB, 1956. Bar: Colo. 1957, U.S. Dist. Ct. Colo. 1957, U.S. Ct. Appeals (10th cir.) 1962, U.S. Supreme Ct. 1972. Assoc. Fugate & Mitchem, Denver, 1960-63, ptnr., 1964-67; counsel Navajo Freight

Lines, Denver, 1967-69; gen. counsel Rocky Mountain Motor Tariff Bur., Denver, 1970-87; ptnr. Rea, Cross & Auchincloss, Washington, 1988-97; adminstrv. law judge Office of Hearings and Appeals Social Security Adminstrn., Pitts., 1997—. Instr. Coll. Law, U. Denver, 1965-66. Author: Transportation of Hazardous Materials, 2d edit., 1992, Corporate Counsel's Guide to Occupational Safety and Health Law, 1993, with supplements, Transportation Safety and Insurance Law, 2 vols., 1998, with ann. supplements, Killer Roads, 1999; writer columns Electric Light and Power, 1966-84, Heavy Duty Trucking, 1993—; also articles. Served with USNR, 1957-60; comdr. Res. ret. Mem. Assn. Transp. Practitioners (pres. 1985-86), Denver Bar Assn., Colo. Bar Assn., Transp. Lawyers Assn., Fed. Bar Assn., Mil. Officers Assn., Exch. Club, Kiwanis (pres. local club 1965-66). Republican. Roman Catholic. Office Phone: 412-644-2751.

KENWRIGHT, BILL, theatrical producer; Artistic dir. Thorndike Theatre, Eng.; exec. prodr. Theatre Royal, Windsor, Eng.; assoc. prodr. Sir Peter Hall Season Old Vic, Eng. Prodr. plays A Doll's House (Tony, Drama Desk and Outer Critics Circle awards Best Revival 1997), Blood Brothers, Travels With My Aunt (Drama Desk award), Dancing at Lughnasa (Tony award), Medea (Tony award), An Ideal Husband, Lady Windermere's Fan, School For Wives, A Streetcar Named Desire, Cash on Delivery, Shakespeare For My Father, Dial M For Murder, Night Must Fall, Ferry Cross the Mersey, The Aspern Papers, The Odd Couple, Elvis: The Musical, Passion, Company, Present Laughter, Chapter Two, Design For Living, The Roy Orbison Story, Rupert Street Lonely Hearts Club, The Miracle Worker, No Man's Land, Moonlight, Dead Guilty, In Praise of Love, The Deep Blue Sea, The Windslow Boy, On the Piste, Funny Money, My Night With Reg, Jane Eyre, Up 'n' Under, Mind Millie For Me, The Master Builder, Hamlet, An Absolute Turkey, The Gift of the Gorgon, Lysistrata, Separate Tables, She Stoops to Conquer, Piaf, On Approval, Festen, 2005; dir. plays Joseph and the Amazing Technicolor Dreamcoat, West Side Story (London Critics Circle award nomination Best Dir.), Blood Brothers (Tony award nomination Best Dir.); co-prodr. films The Day After the Fair, Stepping Out. Dir. Everton Football Club. Hon. fellow Liverpool John Moores U. Office: Belasco Theatre 111 W 44th St New York NY 10036-4012

KENYHERCZ, THOMAS MICHAEL, pharmaceutical company executive; b. Jan. 6, 1950; s. William Stephen and Goldie Elizabeth (Matica) K.; m. Linda Jane Kostyshak, Mar. 20, 1973; 1 child, Craig Thomas. BS, Youngstown State U., 1971; MS, U. Cin., 1973, PhD in Analytical Chemistry, 1975. Cert. regulatory affairs profl. Postdoctoral fellow in bioanalytical chemistry Purdue U., 1975-77; scientist, sr. scientist, mgr. prodn. support labs. Ortho Pharm. Corp., Raritan, N.J., 1977-80; dir. product devel., quality assurance & regulatory affairs Janssen Pharmaceutica Inc., Piscataway, N.J., 1980-85; pres. KROSS, Inc., Hillsborough, N.J., 1985—. Founder KROSS Coatings, Inc., 1987—, Telluride Pharm. Corp., 1994—; founder, pres. Telluride Analytical Svcs. Corp., 1997—; founder KROSS Devel. Corp., 2001-; participant FDA-approved Orphan Drug Devel. program, IND Treatment of Cachexic AIDS Patients, 1996. Mem. editl. bd.: Jour. Automated Chemistry, 1975—. Coach basketball St. Mary's Sr. H.S., 1979—83; active Ctr. for Creative Living, Religious Sci. Ch. Princeton. Recipient SBIR Rsch. award EPA Phase I and II for studies of marine contamination, 1987, 88, FDA Orphan Drug designation, 1994; Lowenstein Schubert Twitchell fellow U. Cin., 1975, Kissinger fellow Purdue U., 1975-77. Mem. Am. Mgmt. Assn., Am. Assn. Clin. Chemists, Am. Assn. Anti Aging Med., Am. Chem. Soc., Am. Assn. Pharm. Scientists, Am. Soc. for Quality Control, U.S.-N.I.S. C. of C., Electrochem. Soc., Parenteral Drug Assn., Pharm. Mfrs. Assn., Drug Info. Assn., Regulatory Affairs Profl. Soc., Am. Soc. Pharmacognosy, Western Electroanalytical Theoretical Soc., Licensing Execs. Soc., Aquinas Inst., Controlled Release Soc., Soc. for Biomaterials. Byzantine Catholic. Office: Telluride Compound 300 Valley Rd Bldg 278 Hillsborough NJ 08844 Office Phone: 908-369-1900. Personal E-mail: knyhrcz@yahoo.com. Business E-Mail: knyhrcz@ix.netcom.com.

KENYON, ARNOLD OAKLEY, III, lawyer; b. Creston, Iowa, Aug. 15, 1952; s. Arnold O. II and Joy L. (Lawrence) K.; m. Mary Ann Clendenen, Dec. 23, 1972; children: Angela, Joseph, Arnold O. IV. BS, Iowa State U., 1974; JD with honors, U. Iowa, 1977. Bar: Iowa 1977. With Kenyon & Kenyon PC, Creston, 1977-89; ptnr. Steffes Kenyon & Nielsen PC, Creston, 1989-98, Kenyon & Nielsen PC, Creston, 1998—. County atty. Union County Atty.'s Office, Creston, 1979-87, asst. county atty., 1987-89; city atty. City of Creston, 1992—. Chmn. Crestland Betterment Found., 1983-95. Mem. Iowa Trial Attys. Assn. (bd. govs. 1989-91). Avocation: sailing. Home: 1403 Orchard Dr Creston IA 50801-1035 Office: 211 N Maple St Creston IA 50801-2311 E-mail: sklaw@iowatelecom.net.

KENYON, CYNTHIA J., medical researcher; BS in Chemistry and Biochemistry, U. Ga., 1976; PhD, MIT, 1981. Post-doctoral fellow Med. Rsch. Coun. Lab. Molecular Biology, Cambridge, England; prof. U. Calif., San Francisco, 1986—, Herbert Boyer Disting. prof. biochemistry and biophysics. Co-founder Elixir Pharmaceuticals, Inc., Cambridge, Mass. Contbr. articles to profl. jours. Mem.: AAAS, NAS, Inst. Medicine, 2004. Achievements include suppressing a single gene in Caenorhabditis elegans worms-nematodes and doubling their normal life span; in recent research and a few more changes, their lifespan was expanded sixfold. Office: U Calif San Francisco, Genentech Hall 600 16th St Box 2200 San Francisco CA 94143-2200 Office Phone: 415-476-9250, 415-476-9864. Office Fax: 415-514-4147.

KENYON, DAPHNE ANNE, economist; b. Augusta, Ga., Aug. 14, 1952; d. Lawrence Austin and Shirley (Knaus) Kenyon; m. Peter George Kachavos, Oct. 22, 1988. BA, Mich. State U., 1974; MA in Econs., U. Mich., 1976, PhD in Econs., 1980. Asst. prof. Dartmouth Coll., Hanover, NH, 1979—83; sr. analyst US Adv. Commn. on Intergovt. Rels., Washington, 1983—85; fin. economist US Treasury Dept., Washington, 1985—87; sr. rsch. assoc. Urban Inst., Washington, 1987—88; Lincoln fellow Lincoln Inst. of Land Policy, Cambridge, Mass., 1988—89; asst. prof. econs. Simmons Coll., Boston, 1989—90, assoc. prof. econs., 1991—98, chair dept. econs., 1996—99, prof. econs., 1998—2000; pres. The Josiah Bartlett Ctr. for Pub. Policy, 1999—2002; prin. D.A. Kenyon & Assocs., 2002—. Cons. US IRS Adv. Panel, Washington, 1987-99; appt. to Mass. Dept. of Revenue Adv. Group, 1991; bd. dirs. New Eng. Econ. Project, v.p., 1997-98, pres., 1999. Assoc. editor Urban Studies, 1988-93, mem. US editl. adv. com., 1993-2004; co-editor: Coping with Mandates, 1990, Competition Among States and Local Governments, 1991; NH corr. State Tax Notes, 1990-93; mem. editl. bd. Mass. Benchmarks, 1997-99; columnist: State Tax Notes, 2003—; contbr. articles to profl. jours. Mem. gov.'s revenue adv. com., State of N.H., Concord, 1982, 98, consensus revenue estimating panel, 2000-03; bd. dirs. Windham (N.H.) Sch. Bd., 2000-03, vice chmn. 2002-03. Fellow Grad. fellow, NSF, 1974. Mem. Am. Econ. Assn. (com. on the status of women in econs. profession 1995-98), Nat. Tax Assn. (bd. dirs. 1996-99, chair intergovernmental fiscal rels. com. 1996-98, program chair 1999), Nat. Tax Jour. (referee Ea. Econ. Jour.). Episcopalian.

KENYON, EDWARD TIPTON, lawyer; b. Summit, NJ, Jan. 27, 1929; s. Theodore S. and Martha (Tipton) K.; m. Dolores Cetrule, July 11, 1953; children: David S., James N., Jonathan W., Theodore H. AB, Harvard U., 1950; LL.B., Columbia U., 1953. Bar: NY 1956, NJ 1957. Assoc. Thacher, Proffitt, Prizer, Crawley & Wood, NYC, 1955-56; law clk. presiding judge US Dist. Ct. NJ, Newark, 1956-57; assoc. Jeffers, Mountain & Franklin, Morristown, NJ, 1957-59, Bourne, Noll and Kenyon and predecessor firm, Summit, 1959-62, ptnr., 1962-97, of counsel, 1997—. Bd. dirs. Atlantic Mgmt. Corp., 1990-98. Trustee Summit Art Ctr., 1960—72, Trinity-Pawling Sch., Pawling, NY, 1977—2003, Pingry Sch., Martinsville, NJ, 1970—97, Martha's Vineyard Preservation Trust, 1999—, Overlook Hosp., Summit, 1967—75, pres., 1973—75; trustee Overlook Hosp. Found., 1975—84, sec., 1977—80, v.p., 1980—81, pres., 1981—84; trustee Winston Sch., Summit, 1986—93, v.p., 1987—90, pres., 1990—92; mem. planning bd. Town Chilmark, 1998—, chmn., 2000—; deacon Ctrl. Presbyn. Ch., Summit, 1960—65, trustee, 1965—72, 1987—93, pres., 1970—72, 1988—91; deacon First Congl. Ch., West Tisbury, Mass., 2000—05; bd. dirs. Overlook Mgmt. Corp., 1988—97. With M.C. U.S. Army, 1953—55. Mem. ABA, NY State Bar Assn., NJ Bar Assn., Summit Bar Assn. (pres. 1983-84), Union County Bar Assn., Am. Coll. Trust Estate Counsel, Am. Law Inst. Clubs: Beacon Hill (trustee 1977-81, pres. 1979-81), Edgartown Yacht Club, Harvard NYC, Harvard NJ (trustee 1958-69, pres. 1968-69). Home: 49 N Abels Hill Rd Chilmark MA 02535-2026 Office: 382 Springfield Ave Summit NJ 07901-2707 E-mail: kittip@vineyard.net.

KENYON, GARY MICHAEL, gerontologist, educator; b. Montreal, Que., Can., June 12, 1949; s. Raymond George and Frances Evelyn (Duhault) K. B in Commerce cum laude, Loyola U., Montreal, 1970; BA, Concordia U., Montreal, 1977, MA, 1981; PhD, U. B.C., 1985. Postdoctoral fellow Andrew Norman Inst. U. So. Calif., L.A., 1985-86; postdoctoral fellow Swedish Inst. Linkoping U., Sweden, 1986-87; prof., chmn. dept. gerontology St. Thomas U., Fredericton, N.B., Can., 1987—. Adj. prof. McGill U. Ctr. for Studies in Aging, Montreal; hon. rsch. assoc. U. N.B., 1996—. Author: Emergent Theories of Aging, 1988, Metaphors of Aging, 1991, Aging and Biography, 1996, Restorying Our Lives, 1997, Ordinary Wisdom, 2001, Narrative Gerontology, 2001; editor: jour. Gnosis, 1979—81; rev. editor: Can. Jour. on Aging, 1989—90; contbr. articles to profl. jours. Can. Govt. Social Scis. and Humanities fellow, 1983-85. Mem. Gerontology Soc. Am., Can. Assn. Gerontology, N.B. Assn. Gerontology (bd. dirs.). Avocations: skiing, cooking, wine, Tai Chi instructor, language study. Office: St Thomas U Dept Gerontology Fredericton NB Canada E3B 5G3 Office Phone: 506-452-0527. E-mail: kenyon@stu.ca.

KENYON, REGAN CLAIR, educational research executive; b. St. Louis, Jan. 31, 1949; s. Robert Clair and Nina Naoma (Giesler) K.; m. Mary Margaret Quinlan, June 2, 1979; children: Regan Clair Jr., Moriah Quinlan. BA, U. Mo., 1969, MEd, 1973; EdD, Harvard U., 1983. Tchr., Ferguson, Mo., 1971-74; prin. Manor Sch., St. Croix, 1974-77, Country Day Sch., St. Croix, Virgin Islands, 1977-78; exec. asst. U.S. Dept. Edn., Washington, 1978-80; adminstrv. asst. Harvard U., Cambridge, Mass., 1980-81; cons. to pres. MA Higher Edn. Assistance Corp., Boston, 1981-83; pres. Secondary Sch. Admission Test Bd., Princeton, N.J., 1983—. Contbr. articles to profl. jours.; inventor, editor in field. Mem. N.J. State Bd. Edn., Trenton, N.J., 1987-91. Fellow Edn. Policy for George Washington U. Inst. for Ednl. Leadership, Washington, 1978-79; Gustav Harris scholar Harvard U., 1980-83; recipient Horace Mann Prof. Contbr. citation U.S. Dept. Edn., 1980; named Disting Alumni Mo. U., 1996. Mem. Inst. for Ednl. Leadership, Harvard Club, Nassau Club, Phi Delta Kappa. Roman Catholic. Avocations: tennis, golf, ski, fishing, hiking. Home: 5 Cedar Brook Ter Princeton NJ 08540-7407 Office: Secondary Sch Admission Test Bd CN5339 Princeton NJ 08543

KENZLE, LINDA FRY, writer, artist; b. Elkhorn, Wis., May 22, 1950; d. Marvin Delos and Ione Mae (Snyder) Fry; m. Donald Charles Kenzle; 1 child, Joshua Clay. Owner Third Coast, Williams Bay, Wis., 1975-79; artist, 1975—; cartoonist, 1978-79; editor, pub. Stylepages, 1985-88, Dollbeat, 1988-89, Greenleaf Bot. Rev., 1990-93; photographer, 1993—; illustrator, 1996—; abstract outsider artist, 1999—. Author: Embellishments, 1993, Dazzle, 1995, The Irresistible Bead, 1996, Pages, 1997, Gathering, 1998. Avocations: flying, travel, architecture, science, gardening. Office: PO Box 177 Fox River Grove IL 60021-0177 E-mail: lindafrykenzle@hotmail.com.

KEOGH, HEIDI HELEN DAKE, advocate; b. Saratoga, N.Y., July 12, 1950; d. Charles Starks and Phyllis Sylvia (Edmunds) Dake; m. Randall Frank Keogh, Nov. 3, 1973; children: Tyler Cameron, Kelly Dake. Student, U. Colo., 1972. Reception, promotions Sta. KLAK, KJAE, Lakewood, Colo., 1972-73; acct. exec. Mixed Media Advt. Agy., Denver, 1973-75; writer, mktg. Jr. League Cookbook Devel., Denver, 1986-88; chmn., coord. Colorado Cache & Creme de Colorado Cookbooks, 1988-90. Speakers bur. Mile High Transplant Bank, Denver, 1983-84, Writer's Inst., U. Denver, 1988; bd. dir. Stewart's Shops Corp., Jr. League, Denver, The Gathering Pl. (chmn. elect, 2004). Contbr. articles to profl. jours. Fiscal officer, bd. dirs. Mile High Transplant Bank; blockworker Heart Fund and Am. Cancer Soc., Littleton, Colo., 1978—, Littleton Rep. Com., 1980-84; fundraising vol. Littleton Pub. Schs., 1980-98; vol. Gathering Place Assn., bd. dirs., 2003—, pres., 2003—, chmn. Brown Bag benefit, 1996; vol. Hearts for Life, 1991—, Oneday, 1992, Denver Ballet Guild, 1992—, Denver Ctr. Alliance, 1993—, Newborn Hope, 1980—, Girls, Inc., 1995—, Girls Hope, VOA Guild, 1996—, Le Bal de Ballet, 1998—, The Denver Social Register and Record, 1999—. Mem. Jr. League Denver (program rels. bd., v.p. ways and means 1989-90, planning coun./ad hoc 1990-92, sustainer spl. events 1993-94, found. 2002—), Community Emergency Fund (chair 1991-92), Jon D. Williams Cotillion at Columbine (chmn. 1991-93), Columbine Country Club, Gamma Alpha Chi, Pi Beta Phi Alumnae Club (pres. Denver chpt. 1984-85, 93-94, nat. conv. chmn. Denver 2001), Pi Beta Phi Found. (grantee 2000-05). Episcopalian. Avocations: travel, skiing, golf, family activities. Home: 63 Fairway Ln Littleton CO 80123-6648

KEOGH, JAMES, journalist; b. Platte County, Nebr., Oct. 29, 1916; s. David James and Edith (Dwyer) K.; m. Verna Pedersen, May 17, 1940; children— Kevin, Katherine Ann Ph.B., Creighton U., 1938. Reporter Omaha World-Herald, 1938-48, city editor, 1948-51; contbg. editor Time mag., 1951-52, assoc. editor, 1952-56, sr. editor, 1956-61, asst. mng. editor, 1961-68, exec. editor, 1968; spl. asst. Pres. U.S., 1969-70; freelance writer, 1971-72; dir. USIA, 1973-77; exec. dir. The Business Roundtable, 1977-86. Author: This is Nixon, 1956, President Nixon and the Press, 1972, Centennial in Belle Haven, 1989, One of a Kind, 1995, Living By Our Wicks, 1999; editor: Corporate Ethics: A Prime Business Asset, 1988. Bd. dirs. The Phila. Fund, 1987-2003. Recipient Distinguished Nebraskan award, 1972 Mem.: Belle Haven (Greenwich, Conn.) (pres.-commodore 1967-68, 84). Home: 202 W Lyon Farm Dr Greenwich CT 06831-4353

KEOGH, KEVIN, lawyer; b. Omaha, Dec. 24, 1941; s. James Charles and Verna Marion (Pedersen) K.; m. Susan Elizabeth Mary Griffiths, Apr. 26, 1975; children: James, Caroline, Colin, Brendan. AB with honors, Holy Cross Coll., 1963; JD, Harvard U., 1966. Bar: N.Y. 1969, Conn. 1977, U.S. Ct. Appeals (2nd cir.) 1975. Assoc. Breed, Abbott & Morgan, N.Y.C., 1969-75, ptnr., 1975-88, White & Case, N.Y.C., 1988—, exec. ptnr., 1992—. Dir. United Hosp. Fund of N.Y., 1984-88; vol. U.S. Peace Corps., Nicoya, Costa Rica, 1966-68. Mem. Am. Yacht Club (commodore 1985-86, Disting. Svc. award 1989), Assn. Bar City NY (com. on securities regulation 2002—), Yacht Racing Assn. L.I. Sound (Pres. 1983-84, Disting. Svc. award 1985), N.Y. Yacht Club (competitions com. 1990-92). Republican. Episcopalian. Home: 18 Sherwood Farm Ln Greenwich CT 06831-4410 Office: White & Case 1155 Avenue Of The Americas New York NY 10036-2787 E-mail: kkeogh@whitecase.com.

KEOGH, RICHARD JOHN, protective services official, consultant; b. Woonsocket, R.I., Sept. 23, 1932; s. Michael Joseph and Dora Marie (Rumgay) Keogh. BBA, U. Mass., 1958; MA, Pepperdine U., 1974. Lic. explosive disposal technician Mass. Commd. 2d lt. U.S. Army, 1958, advanced through grades to maj., 1967; stationed at various locations including Korea and Vietnam, 1958-73; ret. USAR, 1979; disposal specialist USN, Lualualei, Hawaii, 1973-76; mgmt. analyst Marine Corps Air Sta., Kaneohe Bay, Hawaii, 1976-93. Expert witness explosives and firearms, Hawaii, Mass. Contbr. articles to profl. jours. Pres. Assn. Owners Palms Condominium, Honolulu, 1978—80. Decorated 3 Bronze Stars, 2 Purple Hearts, 2 Air medals, Cross of Gallantry, Commendation medal; recipient Founders award, Order of Arrow Boy Scouts Am., 1989, cert. of Appreciation, FBI, 1991, Silver Beaver award, Boy Scouts Am., 1993. Mem.: Gun Owners Action League, DAV (life), VFW (life), Internat. Assn. Bomb Technicians and Investigators (life; dir. Hawaii chpt. 2000—), Mil. Order Purple Heart (life), Hawaii Rifle Assn. (pres. 1994—96, 2000—02), Bay Colony Weapons Collectors, Ohio Gun Collectors Assn., Nat. Auto Pistol Collectors Assn., Am. Legion (life). Avocations: rifle shooting, ammo reloading, photography. Home: 431 Nahua St Apt 203 Honolulu HI 96815-2915 Office Phone: 808-923-2283.

KEOHANE, NANNERL OVERHOLSER, political scientist, academic administrator; b. Blytheville, Ark., Sept. 18, 1940; d. James Arthur and Grace (McSpadden) Overholser; m. Patrick Henry III, Sept. 16, 1962 (div. May 1969); 1 child, Stephan Henry; m. Robert Owen Keohane, Dec. 18, 1970; children: Sarah, Jonathan, Nathaniel. BA, Wellesley Coll., 1961, Oxford U., Eng., 1963; PhD, Yale U., 1967. Faculty Swarthmore Coll., Pa., 1967—73, Stanford U., Calif., 1973—81; pres., prof. polit. sci. Wellesley (Mass.) Coll., 1981—93, Duke U., Durham, NC, 1993—2004, pres. emerita, 2004—; Laurance Rockefeller disting. vis. prof. Woodrow Wilson Sch., Princeton U., 2005—. Laurance Rockefeller Disting. vis. prof. Woodrow Wilson Sch. Princeton U., Princeton, 2005—. Author: Philosophy and the State in France: The Renaissance to the Enlightenment, 1980; co-editor: Feminist Theory: A Critique of Ideology, 1982. Trustee Colonial Williamsburg Found., 1988—2001, Doris Duke Charitable Found., 1996—; mem. Harvard Corp., 2005—. Named to National Women's Hall of Fame, 1995; recipient Marshall Medal, 2003; fellow, Ctr. for Advanced Study in the Behavioral Scis., 1987—88, 2004—05; Marshall scholar, 1961—63, Dissertation fellow, AAUW. Fellow: Am. Philos. Soc., Am. Acad. Arts and Scis.; mem.: Am. Acad. Achievement, Coun. on Fgn. Rels., Phi Beta Kappa. Democrat. Episcopalian.

KEOHANE, ROBERT OWEN, political scientist, educator; b. Chgo., Oct. 3, 1941; s. Robert Emmet and Mary Irene (Pieters) K.; m. Nannerl Overholser, Dec. 18, 1970; children: Jonathan, Sarah, Stephan, Nathaniel BA, Shimer Coll., 1961; MA, Harvard U., 1964, PhD, 1966; D (hon.), U. Aarhus, Denmark, 1998. From instr. to assoc. prof. Swarthmore Coll., Pa., 1965-73; from assoc. prof. to prof. Stanford U., Calif., 1973-81, chmn. dept. polit. sci., 1980-81; prof. politics Brandeis U., Waltham, Mass., 1981-85; prof. govt. Harvard U., Cambridge, Mass., 1985-96, chmn., 1988-92, Stanfield prof. internat. peace, 1989-96; James B. Duke prof. polit. sci. Duke U., Durham, NC, 1996—2005; prof. internat. affairs Princeton U., 2005—. Author: After Hegemony, 1984, International Institutions and State Power, 1989, Power and Governance in a Partially Globalized World, 2002; co-author: Power and Interdependence, 1977, Designing Social Inquiry, 1994; co-editor: Transnational Relations and World Politics, 1972, The New European Community, 1991, Institutions for the Earth, 1993, After the Cold War, 1993, Ideas and Foreign Policy, 1993, Global Interdependence and Local Communitities, 1994, Internationalization and Domestic Politics, 1996, International Environmental Aid, 1996, Imperfect Unions, 1999, Exploration and Contestation in World Politics, 1999, Legalization and World Politics, 2001, Humanitarian Intervention, 2003; editor: Neorealism and Its Critics, 1986; editor Internat. Orgn., 1974-80; contbr. articles to profl. jours. Chmn. New Democratic Coalition Delaware County, Pa., 1969-71; pres. Triangle Land Conservancy, 2000-02. Recipient Sumner prize Harvard U., 1966, Grawemeyer award, 1989, Skytte prize, 2005; fellow Ctr. Advanced Study in Behavior Scis., 1977-78 87-88, 2004-05; Guggenheim fellow, 1992, Frank Kenan fellow Nat. Humanities Ctr., 1995-96. Mem. Am. Acad. Arts and Scis., Am. Polit. Sci. Assn. (pres. 1999-2000), Am. Econ. Assn., Coun. Fgn. Rels. (Internat. Affairs fellow 1968-69), Internat. Studies Assn. (pres. 1988-89), Nat. Acad. Scis. Home: 179 Prospect Ave Princeton NJ 08540 E-mail: rkeohane@princeton.edu.

KEOUGH, JAMES GILLMAN, JR., minister; b. Reading, Pa., June 2, 1947; s. James Gillman Sr. and Nora (Deturck) K.; m. Dawn Eileen Wiest, Sept. 17, 1976; children: Cynthia Ann, James Michael, Wendy Sue, Danielle Lynn, Erin Mae, Bevin Leigh. BA in History Edn., Messiah Coll., Grantham, Pa., 1970; MDiv, Lancaster (Pa.) Theol. Sem., 1973; D of Ministry, Ashland (Ohio) Theol. Sem., 1980. Ordained to ministry United Ch. Christ, 1973. Minister St. Luke's United Ch. Christ, Kenhorst, Pa., 1972-75, Congl. Ch., Winchester, Va., 1975-78, 1st Congl. Ch., Newton Falls, Ohio, 1978-82, Cen. Congl. Ch., Middleboro, Mass., 1982-85; sr. minister 1st Congl. Ch., Pontiac, Mich., 1985—. Founder Prayer Unlimited, Waterford, Mich., 1997—. Author: Teaching Prayer in the Local Parish, 1980, Prayer Unlimited, 1997. Mem. Oakland County Rep. Club, Mich. Rep. 500 Club; bd. dirs. Clinton Valley coun. Boy Scouts Am.; bd. dirs. Boys Clubs Am., Pontiac; pres. Somebodycares, Pontiac, 1983—. Mem. Nat. Assn. Congl. Christian Chs., S.E. Mich. Congl. Ministerium, Independence Twp. Pastors Assn., Kiwanis. Avocations: reading, hiking, fishing. Home: 3062 St Jude Dr Waterford MI 48329-4359 Office: 1st Congl Church Clarkston Rd at Pine Knob Rd PO Box 221 Clarkston MI 48347-0221

KEOUGH, SHAWN, state legislator; m. Mike Keough; 2 children. Student, North Idaho Coll.; student in bus. mgmt., Lewis Clark State Coll. In pub. rels.; mem. Idaho Senate, Dist. 1, Boise, 1996—, mem. transp. com., mem. health and welfare com., vice chair fin. com. Mem. Idaho Women in Timber, Greater Sandpoint (Idaho) C. of C. Republican. Protestant. Office: State Capitol PO Box 83720 Boise ID 83720-0081 Office Phone: 208-332-1349.

KEOWN, MICHAEL H., food products executive; BA in Econs., Northwestern U. With E&J Gallo Winery and Proctor & Gamble, 1984—97; v.p., gen. mgr. Minute Maid Co., Coca-Cola Co., 1997—2002; pres. Dean Branded Pfoducts Group, Dallas, 2003—. Office: Dean Foods Co 2515 McKinney Ave Ste 1200 Dallas TX 75201-1945 Office Phone: 720-565-2302. E-mail: mkeown@whitewave.com.

KEPCHER, CAROLYN, real estate company executive; b. Westchester, NY, 1968; d. Raymond and Marie Cassidy; m. George Kepcher; children: Connor, Cassidy. Degree in bus. mktg., Mercy Coll., Dobbs Ferry, NY. Dir. sales and mktg. Beck Summit Hotel Mgmt. Group, Boca Raton, Fla.; joined Trump Orgn., 1994, now exec. v.p.; gen. mgr., COO Trump Nat. Golf Club, Briarcliff, NY, Bedminster, NJ. Featured on (TV series) The Apprentice, 2004—; author: Carolyn 101: Business Lessons from The Apprentice's Straight Shooter, 2004—. Mem.: Nat. Golf Course Owners Assn., Profl. Club Mktg. Assn., Met. Club Mgr.'s Assn., Club Mgr.'s Assn. Am. Office: Trump Nat Golf Club 339 Pine Rd Briarcliff Manor NY 10510*

KEPECS, JOSEPH GOODMAN, physician, educator; b. Phila., Oct. 8, 1912; s. Jacob and Mary (Goodman) K.; m. Joan A. Epstein, Oct. 17, 1944 (dec. May 2000); children— Susan, Jonathan. BS, U. Chgo., 1935, MD, 1937; grad., Inst. for Psychoanalysis, Chgo., 1949. Intern Cook County Hosp., Chgo., 1938-39; resident St. Elizabeth's Hosp., Washington, 1940-41; practice medicine, specializing in psychiatry Madison, Wis., 1965—; attending physician dept. psychiatry Michael Reese Hosp., Chgo., 1950-65; prof. psychiatry U. Wis., 1965-84, prof. emeritus, 1984—. Lectr. Chgo. Inst. for Psychoanalysis, 1957-60, mem. faculty, 1974—; professorial lectr. dept. psychiatry U. Chgo., 1960-65 Served with AUS, 1941-46. Mem. Am. Psychoanalytic Assn., Wis. Psychoanalytic Study Group (pres. 1979-80), Am. Psychosomatic Soc., Am. Psychiat. Assn., Chgo. Psychoanalytic Soc. (pres. 1964-65) Home: 3580 Lake Mendota Dr Madison WI 53705-1473

KEPETS, HUGH MICHAEL, artist; b. Cleve., Feb. 6, 1946; s. Nathan and Frances K. B.F.A., Carnegie Mellon U., 1968; M.F.A., Ohio U., 1972. One-man shows include, Fischbach Gallery, N.Y.C., 1974, 75, 78, Vick Gallery, Phila., 1974, 76, 77, Michael Berger Gallery, Pitts., 1975, 82, G.W. Einstein Co., Inc., N.Y.C., 1976, Graphics 1, Graphics 2, Boston, 1976, 79, Rubicon Gallery, Los Altos, Calif., 1977, New Gallery, Cleve., 1978, Women's City Club, Cleve., A.J. Wood Gallery, Phila., Carnegie-Mellon U., Pitts., 1979, Orion Editions, N.Y.C., 1980, Houghton (N.Y.) Coll., 1980, Galerie 99, Bay Harbor Islands, Fla., 1981, Cumberland Gallery, Nashville, 1983, Mattingly Baker, Dallas, 1983, Marcus/Gordon, Pitts., 1981, 85, 90, Roger Ramsay Gallery, 1984, 88, David Adamson Gallery, Washington, 1986, Randall Beck Gallery, Boston, 1986, 89, Ingrid Cusson Gallery, N.Y.C., 1989, Leo Kamen Gallery, Toronto, Can., 1990, Lyman Allyn Mus. Art, New London, Conn., 1992, David Adamson Gallery, Washington, 1992, Brenda Kroos Gallery, Cleve., 1993, 96; exhibited in group shows including, Cleve. Mus. Art, 1968, 71-79, 93—, Bklyn. Mus., 1972, 76, Asso. Am. Artists, N.Y.C., 1972, 74, Butler Inst. Am. Art, 1972, U. Pa., Phila., 1972, Espace Cardin, Paris, Michael Berger Gallery, Yale U. Art Gallery, Tyler Art Gallery, Phila., 1973, New Gallery, 1973, 74, 79, Akron (Ohio) Art Inst., 1974, Virginia Mus. Art, Richmond, Vick Gallery, 1974, Boston Mus. Fine Arts,

1975-77, 82, Phila. Print Club, Westmoreland County Art Mus., Skidmore Coll., 1975, Queens Mus., N.Y.C., Albion Coll., Lehigh U., Indpls. Mus. Art, Grand Palais-Paris, McNay Art Inst. of San Antonio, U. Mo., Kansas City, 1976, Glassboro (N.J.) State Coll., Library of Congress, 1977, Yale U. Art Gallery, 1978, Am. Acad. Arts and Letters, N.Y.C., 1978, 79, 80, Hunt Inst. for Bot. Documentation, Pitts., 1979, Md. Inst. Coll. Art, Balt., 1980, Hudson River Mus., Yonkers, N.Y., 1982, U. Pitts., 1983, Pratt Graphics Ctr., N.Y.C., 1983, Mattingly Baker Gallery, Dallas, 1984, Franklin & Marshall Coll., 1984, U. Calif.-Davis, 1985, Honolulu Acad. Art, 1985, Cleve. Mus. Art, 1985, 86, N.Y. Inst. Tech., 1985, Montgomery Coll., Rockville, Md., 1985, The Del. Art Mus., 1986; represented in permanent collections, Met. Mus. Art, N.Y.C., Cleve. Mus. Art, Phila. Mus. Fine Arts, Library of Congress, Del. Mus. Art, Indpls. Mus. Art, Harvard U. Fogg Mus., N.Y. Public Library, Worcester (Mass.) Art Mus., Yale U. Art Gallery, Minn. Mus. Art, St. Paul, R.I. Sch. Design Mus. Art, Art Inst. Chgo., U. N.C. at Chapel Hill Ackland Art Center, Utah State U., Brandeis U., Middlebury (Vt.) Coll., Kresge Art Gallery, others, also various banks and corps. including, Atlantic-Richfield Corp., N.Y.C., Johns Manville Corp., N.Y.C., FMC Corp., Chgo., AT&T, IBM, Xerox Corp., RCA, Princeton, N.J., Amarada Hess Corp., N.Y.C., Prudential Ins. Co. Am., N.Y.C., Commerce Bancshares, Kansas City, Mo., Bank of Am., San Francisco, Gen. Mills Co., N.Y.C., Westinghouse Electric Corp., Pitts., Oliver Realty, Pitts., Gen. Electric Co., N.Y.C., Chase Manhattan Bank, N.Y.C., Citicorp, N.Y.C., Rockwell Internat., Pitts., Lehman Bros., N.Y.C. Nat. Endowment for Arts grantee, 1976; Creative Artists Public Service grantee, 1975, 79-80; recipient Purchase awards Davidson Nat. Print and Drawing Competition Fashion Inst. Tech., 1976, Purchase awards Davidson Nat. Print and Drawing Competition Phila. Print Club, 1975, Cleve. Arts prize Women's City Club, 1979 Studio: 134 W 26th St #401 New York NY 10001 Office Phone: 917-593-5036.

KEPHART, HELEN JEAN ORR, retired secondary school educator; b. Sioux Falls, S.D., Nov. 23, 1945; d. Joseph S. and Dorothy M. (Kippes) Orr; m. Harold F. Kephart, Dec. 30, 1965 (dec. 1994); children: Jo L., Ann M. BA in Math., U. S.D., 1967, MA in Secondary Edn., 1983. Tchr., math. Vermillion (S.D.) Mid. Sch., 1970-87, Vermillion (S.D.) High Sch., 1987—2002; ret., 2002. Chmn., math. curriculum, Vermillion Pub. Schs., 1986-2002 Recipient NSF Presdl. award Excellence Math. Teaching, 1989. Mem. Nat. Tchrs. Math. (publs. reviewer 1990—), S.D. Coun. Tchrs. Math. (sec.1989-91) Home: 412 W Clark St Vermillion SD 57069-1914

KEPLER, DAVID E., II, chemicals executive; BSChemE, U. Calif. Computer svcs. mgr. Dow USA Ea. Divsn., Strongsville, Ohio, 1984—88; comml. dir. performance products Dow Can., 1989—91; dir. info. sys. pacific area Dow Chem. Co., 1991—93, mgr. info. tech., chems. and plastics, 1993—94, dir. global info. sys. svcs., 1994—95, dir. global info. application, 1995—98, v.p., chief info. officer, 1998—2000, corp. v.p. ebusiness, 2000—04, corp. v.p. advanced electronic materials bus., global purchasing and supply chain, 2002—04, corp. v.p. shared services, 2004—, chief info. officer, 2004—. Bd. dirs. Midland Community Cancer Services, Alden B. Dow Museum of Science and Art; campaign chair United Way Midland County, 2004; bd. dirs. US C. of C. Named a top tech. innovator, Info. Week mag., 2004. Mem.: AIChE, Am. Chem. Soc. Office: The Dow Chem Co 47 Building Midland MI 48067

KEPLINGER, BRUCE (DONALD KEPLINGER), lawyer; b. Kansas City, Kans., Feb. 4, 1952; s. Donald Lee and Janet Adelheit (Viets) K.; children: Mark William, Lisbeth Marie, Kristen Michelle, Kailyn Emily, Courtney Nicole; m. Carol Ann Heinz, Apr. 12, 1991. BA with highest distinction, U. Kans., 1974; JD cum laude, So. Meth. U., 1977. Bar: Kans. 1977, U.S. Dist. Ct. Kans. 1977, Mo. 1980, U.S. Dist. Ct. Mo. 1980, U.S. Ct. Appeals (10th cir.) 1985, U.S. Supreme Ct. 1989. Assoc. Clark, Mize & Linville, Salina, Kans., 1977-79, Blackwell, Sanders et al, Kansas City, Mo., 1979-82; ptnr. Payne & Jones, Overland Park, Kans., 1982-94, Norris & Keplinger LLC, Overland Park, 1994—. Master Kansas Inns of Ct.; chmn. Kans. Lawyer Svcs Corp., 1992—2001. Contbr. articles to profl. jours. V.p. Friends of Libr., Johnson County, Kans., 1980-85; deacon Village Presbyn. Ch., 1982-86; trustee United Meth. Ch. of Resurrection, 2002—. Mem.: Fedn. Def. and Corp. Counsel, Def. Rsch. Inst., Kans. Assn. Def. Counsel (pres.-elect 1992—93, pres. 1993—94), Mo. Bar Assn., Kans. Bar Assn. (chmn. Kans. lawyer svc. corp. 1992—2001), Assn. Def. Trial Attys. (state chmn. 1996—, exec. coun. 1999—2002), Internat. Assn. Def. Counsel, Hallbrook Country Club. Republican. Avocations: reading, golf. Office: Norris & Keplinger LLC 6800 College Blvd Ste 630 Overland Park KS 66211-1556 Office Phone: 913-663-2000. E-mail: bkeplinger@nklaw.net.

KEPNER, JAMES LEE, mathematics educator, researcher, consultant; b. Chgo., May 10, 1943; s. Robert Franklin and Mary E. (Durbin) K.; m. Barbara Ellen Johnson, Aug. 21, 1965; children: Diane Lynn, Jennifer Lynn. BS in Math., Ill. State U., 1965, MS in Math., 1968; MS in Math. Stats., U. Iowa, 1976, PhD, in Math. Stats., 1979. Instr. math. Ill. Central Coll., East Peoria. Ill., 1968-69, Kirkwood Community Coll., Cedar Rapids, Iowa, 1969-75; asst. prof. stats. U. Fla., Gainesville, 1979-83; assoc. prof. math. St. Cloud State U., Minn., 1983-87, prof., 1987—; cons. Nat. Assn. Coll. Admissions Officers, 1983-85, City of Albany, Minn., 1983-87, City of Little Falls, Minn., 1984-85, St. Cloud Orthopedic Assocs., 1987—. Contbr. articles to profl. jours. Mem. council Univ. Luth. Ch., Gainesville, Fla., 1981-83, treas. 1982-83; mem. council Celebration Luth. Ch., Sartell, Minn., 1988—; treas. Salem Luth. Ch., St. Cloud, Minn., 1984-86; treas. Butternut Condominium Assn., Balsam Lake, Wis., 1984-85. Mem. Am. Statis. Assn. (joint com. curriculum in stats. and probability 1985-87, vice chmn. 1987—), Inst. Math. Stats., Nat. Council Tchrs. Math. (joint com. curriculum in stats. and probability 1984-87, vice chmn. 1987—), Minn. Council Tchrs. Math. Avocations: studying stats.; boating; swimming; fishing; ice skating. Home: 4702 NW 18th Pl Gainesville FL 32605-3426 Office: St Cloud State U Dept Math And Statisti Saint Cloud MN 56301

KEPPEL, WILLIAM JAMES, lawyer, educator, writer; b. Sheboygan, Wis., Sept. 25, 1941; s. William Frederick and Anne Elizabeth (Cinealis) K.; m. Polly Holmberg, June 26, 1965; children: Anne Rusert, Timothy, Matthew. BA, Marquette U., 1963; JD, U. Wis., Madison, 1970. Bar: Minn. 1970, U.S. Dist. Minn. 1970, U.s. Ct. Appeals (8th cir.) 1973, U.S. Dist. Ct. (we. dist.) Wis. 1979, U.S. Supreme Ct. 1979, U.S. Ct. Claims 1982. Assoc. Dorsey & Whitney, Mpls., 1970-76, ptnr., 1979-96; assoc. prof. Hamline U. Sch. Law, 1976-79, disting. practitioner in residence, 1996-2000. Instr. U. Minn. Law Sch.; adj. prof. William Mitchell Coll. Law, St. Paul; state adminstrv. law judge, 1977-79, 98-2004; chmn., dir. Legal Advice Clinics, Ltd.; dir. Legal Assistance of Minn., Inc.; head Hennepin County Pub. Defender's Office for Misdemeanors. Author: (with Mc Farland) Minnesota Civil Practice (4 vols.), 1979, 3d edit., 1999, Administrative Practice and Procedure, 1999; co-author, editor: Minnesota Environmental Law Handbook, 2nd edit., 1995; contbr. articles and monographs to legal jours. Lt. USN, 1963-67, Vietnam. Mem. ABA. Roman Catholic. Home: 10 Luverne Ave Minneapolis MN 55419-2612

KEPPLE, LARRY GENE, science educator, anatomist, physiologist, educator; s. Ralph and Irene Kepple; m. Vicky Kepple; 1 child, Kevin. BS in Biol. Scis., So. Ill. U., 1974, MS in Microbiology, 1989; postgrad. in Health Edn., So. Illinois U., 1994. Cert. Health Edn. Specialist Sch. Health Edn. Assn., 1991, Tchg. Credentials Ill. State Bd. of Edn., 1974. Anatomy rschr. So. Ill. U. Sch. Medicine, 1989—93; master sci. tchr. and head track coach North Clay Cmty. H.S., Louisville, IL, Ill., 1981—84; electron microscopy lab instr. So. Ill. U. Coll. of Sci., Carbondale, Ill., 1984—89; coll. anatomy and physiology instr. John A. Logan Coll., Carterville, Ill., 1993—; sci. dept. chair and tchr. Herrin H.S., Ill., 1994—. Polymerase chain reaction cons. So. Ill. U. Sch. of Medicine, Carbondale, 1999; honors genetics instr. Murray State U., Murray, Ky., 2000. Author: (teacher lab manual for biochemistry) Illinois State Bd Edn. Sci. and Vocational Series. Pres. CenterLine South Dressage Orgn., Carbondale, Ill., 1996—97. Fellow Honors Inst. For Master Biology Tchrs., NSF, 1984-1986. Mem.: NSTA (assoc.). Achievements include research in Morphological Effects of Salt Concentration on Halobacterium halobium; Development of a method for a sexually transmitted viral vaccine. Office: Herrin High Sch 700 N 10th St Herrin IL 62948 Office Phone: 618-942-6606.

KEPPLE, THOMAS RAY, JR., college administrator; b. Pitts., Mar. 19, 1948; s. Thomas Ray and Virginia Grace (Hudson) K.; m. Jane Donaldson, Aug. 22, 1971 (dec. 1977); m. Patricia Witcher, May 24, 1994. BA, Westminster Coll., 1970; MBA, Syracuse U., 1973, EdD, 1984. Dir. tech. tng. Morse divsn. Borg-Warner Corp., Ithaca, N.Y., 1970-73; dir. adminstrv. svcs. Rhodes Coll., Memphis, 1975-81, dean adminstrv. svcs., 1981-86, provost, 1986-89; v.p. Univ. South, Sewanee, Tenn., 1989-98; pres. Juniata Coll., Huntingdon, Pa., 1998—. Founding chair bd. dirs. Prepaid Tuition Consortium, The Ind. 529 Plan; chmn. Brethren Coll. Abroad Consortium. Author: Incentive Early Retirement Programs for Faculty. Bd. dirs. Sewanee Housing Inc., 1993-98; mem. exec. com. Vollintine Evergreen Cmty. Assn., Memphis, 1976-85, pres., 1981; mem. Biomed. Rsch. Zone Bd., 1986; sec.-treas. Health and Ednl. Facilities Bd. of Franklin County; bd. dirs. Liberty Bowl Classic; co-chair Gov. Rendell's higher edn. transition com. Mem. Internat. Soc. Planning and Strategic Mgmt. (v.p. coms. 1984-85, pres. 1985-87), Assn. Ind. Colls. and Univs. Pa. (bd. dirs.), Nat. Assn. Coll. and Univ. Bus. Officers, Am. Assn. Higher Assn., Memphis Acad. Forum (pres. 1985-86), Coll. and Univ. Personnel Assn., Assn. Physical Plant Adminstrs., Am. Coun. Edn. (mem. internat. com., adv. bd. Princeton Rev.), Coun. Ind. Colls. (mem. adv. com. N.Y. Times), Univ. Club (N.Y.), Omicron Delta Kappa. Mem. Brethren Ch. Avocations: swimming, painting. Home: 2201 Washington St Huntingdon PA 16652-9762 Office: Juniata Coll Office of the Pres 1700 Moore St Huntingdon PA 16652-2119 Office Phone: 814-641-3101. Business E-Mail: kepplet@juniata.edu.

KEPPLER, HERBERT, publishing company executive; b. N.Y.C., Apr. 21, 1925; s. Victor and Josephine T. (Windmann) K.; m. Louise M. Lyman, July 7, 1956; children— Kathryn Louise, Thomas Victor. BA, Harvard, 1945. Reporter N.Y. Sun, 1948-49; with Modern Photography, N.Y.C., 1950-87, editorial dir., pub., 1967-87; v.p. photog. pub. div. ABC Leisure Mags. Inc. div. ABC, N.Y.C., 1974-78, sr. v.p. photog. pub. div., 1978-87; v.p., pub. dir. photography CBS Mags. Am. Photo and Popular Photography, 1987-88, Diamandis Communications Inc., 1988-90, Hachette Mags. Inc., 1990-93, Hachette Filipacchi Media U.S., Inc., 1993—2004, v.p. sr. counselor, 2004—. Author: Official 35mm Camera Rating Guide, 1957, Keppler on the Eye-Level Reflex, 1960, How to Make Better Pictures in Your Home, 1962, 124 Ways to Test Cameras, Lenses and Equipment, 1962, The Pentax Way, 1966, The Nikon-Nikkormat Way, 1976. Served to ensign USNR, 1945-46. Mem. Rolls-Royce Owners Club. Home: 119 N Highland Pl Croton On Hudson NY 10520-2113 Office: Hachette Filipacchi Media US Inc 1633 Broadway New York NY 10019-6708 Business E-Mail: hkeppler@hfmus.com.

KEPROS, JOHN PAUL, trauma surgeon; b. Cresco, Iowa, Apr. 19, 1964; s. Stanley George and Rita Wilma Kepros; m. Michele Rene Hurrell, Sept. 27, 1997; children: Ethan, Brandon, Madison. BSE in Biomed. Engring., U. Iowa, 1987, MD, 1991; MS, Mich. State U., 1996. Diplomate Am. Bd. Surgery with subspecialty in critical care. Intern LDS Hosp., Salt Lake City, 1991—92; resident Mich. State U., East Lansing, 1992—98; fellow Yale U., New Haven, 1998—99; trauma surgeon Swedish Med. Ctr., Englewood, Colo., 1999—2004, prin. investigator, 2000—, co-med. dir. ICU, 2002—04; pvt. practice Mile High Surg. Specialists, Englewood, 1999—2004; asst. prof. surgery Mich. State U., Lansing, 2004—; physician, med. dir. trauma Sparrow Hosp., Lansing, 2004—. Contbr. articles to profl. jours. Recipient Resident Tchg. award, Mich. State U., 1994, 1996. Mem.: AMA, Eastern Assn. for Surgery of Trauma, Soc. Critical Care Medicine, Western Trauma Assn. Roman Catholic. Achievements include development of evidence based medical practices in the ICU. Avocations: reading, travel. Home: 6478 E Island Lake Dr East Lansing MI 48823 Office: Mich State U Dept Surgery 1200 Michigan Ave Ste 655 Lansing MI 48912 Office Phone: 517-267-2493. E-mail: jkepros@pol.net.

KERA, TIIU, career officer; b. Balingen/Wuerttemberg, Germany; BA in Polit. Sci., Valparaiso U., 1967; M in Polit. Sci., Indiana U., 1969; grad. (disting.), Squadron Officer Sch., Maxwell AFB, Ala., 1976; student, Air Command, Staff Coll., 1982, Air War Coll., 1986; grad., Nat. War Coll., 1988. Commd. 2d. lt. USAF, 1973, advanced through grades to maj. gen., 1998; chief quality control sec. Bolling AFB, Washington, D.C., 1973-75; chief quality control sect., personnel utilization sect. 3245th Air Base Grp., Hanscom AFB, Mass., 1975-78; chief quality progression sect. 51st Combat support Grp., Osan Air Base, South Korea, 1978-79; air staff tng. program officer Hdqs. USAF, Washington, D.C., 1979-80; chief Airmen Base Support Assignments Br., Support Officer Assignments Br. Hdqs. Tactical Air Command, Langly AFB, Va., 1980-83; chief mil. pers. br. 1st. Tactical Command, Langly AFB, Va., 1983-84; chief pers. plans, dir. pers. mgmt. Hdqs. Space Divsn., Los Angeles, 1984-87; strategic planner, then chief Strategic Cconcepts Br., Washington, D.C., 1988-1990; fellow Harvard U., Cambridge, Mass., 1990-91; polit.-mil. affairs officer Hdqs. USAF, Washington, D.C., 1991-92; U.S. def. and air attaché Vilnius, Lithuania, 1993-95; dir. intelligence Hdqs. U.S. Stragetic Command, Offutt AFB, Neb., Lithuania, 1995-98; chief of staff, dep. dir. ops. Nat. Security Agency, Fort George G. Meade, Md., 1998-99, asst. dep. dir. ops., prodn. and strategic issues, 1998—, dep. Ctrl. Security Svc., 1999—. Decorated Def. Superior Svc. medal with oak leaf cluster, D.M.S. medal, Meritorious Svc. medal with three oak leaf clusters, AF Commendation medal with oak leaf cluster. Office: NSA/DCH CSS 9800 Savage Rd Ste 2w118 Fort George G Meade MD 20755-6000

KERBER, FRANK JOHN, diplomat; b. Indpls., June 13, 1947; s. Charles John and Romilda Ida (Molengraft) K.; m. Melanie Alice Niewoehner, July 29, 1989; 1 child, Brandon Eric Kerber. BA in Philosophy cum laude, Athenaeum of Ohio, 1969; MS, Georgetown U., 1976. Faculty coll. prep. sch., Cin., 1970-74; mgmt. cons. USAID, various locations, 1976-80; program officer USAID Mission, Tunis, Tunisia, 1980-84, Dept. of State, 1984; vice consul U.S. Consulate Gen., Winnipeg, Can., 1985-86; econ./comml. affairs officer Jordan, Lebanon and Syria, 1986-88; officer for East-West Affairs European Bur. Office of Regional Polit. and Econ. Affairs, 1988-90; A.I.D. liaison officer Bangui, Ctrl. African Republic, 1991-93; econ. officer Kingston, Jamaica, 1993-96; internat. economist Bur. Internat. Orgn. Affairs, Washington, 1996-98; spl. asst. to Amb. Schifter, 1998-2000, Ireland desk officer, 2000—02; with U.S. Mission to European Union, Brussels, 2002—. Mem. Am. Fgn. Svc. Assn. Home: USEU/NAS PSC 82 Box 002 APO AE 09710 Office: USEU Brussels Belgium Office Phone: 32-2-508-2672. E-mail: kerberf@state.gov.

KERBER, LINDA KAUFMAN, historian, educator; b. N.Y.C., Jan. 23, 1940; d. Harry Hagman and Dorothy (Haber) Kaufman; m. Richard Kerber, June 5, 1960; children: Ross Jeremy, Justin Seth. AB cum laude, Barnard Coll., 1960; MA, NYU, 1961; PhD, Columbia U., 1968; DHL, Grinnell Coll., 1992. Instr., asst. prof. history Stern Coll., Yeshiva U., N.Y.C., 1963-68; asst. prof. history San Jose State Coll., (Calif.), 1969-70; vis. asst. prof. history Stanford U., (Calif.), 1970-71; asst. prof. history U. Iowa, Iowa City, 1971-75, prof., 1975-85, May Brodbeck prof., 1985—. Vis. prof. U. Chgo., 1991-92. Author: Federalists in Dissent: Imagery and Ideology in Jeffersonian America, 1970, paperback edit., 1980, 97, Women of the Republic: Intellect and Ideology in Revolutionary America, 1980, paperback edit., 1986, Toward an Intellectual History of Women, 1997, No Constitutional Right to Be Ladies: Women and the Obligations of Citizenship, 1998, paperback edit., 1999 (Littleton-Griswold prize in legal history Am. Hist. Assn., Joan Kelley prize in womens history Am. Hist. Assn.); co-editor: Women's America: Refocusing the Past, 1982, 6th edit., 2004, U.S. History As Women's History, 1995; mem. editl. bd. Signs: Jour. Women in Culture and Society, Jour. Women's History; contbr. articles and book revs. to profl. jours. Fellow Danforth Found., NEH, 1976, 83-84, 94, Am. Coun. Learned Socs., 1975, Nat. Humanities Ctr., 1990-91, Guggenheim Found., 1990-91, Radcliffe Inst. for Advanced Study, 2003. Mem. Orgn. Am. Historians (pres. 1996-97), Am. Hist. Assn. (pres. elect 2005), Am. Studies Assn. (pres. 1988), Am. Soc. for Legal History, Berkshire Conf. Women Historians, Soc. Am. Historians, Japan U.S. Friendship Commn., PEN/Am. Ctr., Am. Acad. Arts and Scis. Jewish. Office: U Iowa Dept History Iowa City IA 52242

KERBER, LORIANN VALENTINE, music educator; b. Scranton, Pa., May 23, 1970; d. Bruce Charles and Shirley Laverta Valentine; m. Edward Charles Kerber, Aug. 9, 2003. MA in Music Edn., Marywood U., Scranton, Pa., 1997; student, Wilkes U., 2004—. Music tchr. Farmingdale Sch. Dist., Farmingdale, NY, 1993—2001; music dir. Wally Gordon Cmty. Singers, Clarks Summit, Pa., 2002—; music tchr. Wallenpaupock North Intermediate Sch., Hawley, Pa., 2002—. Choir dir. Clarks Summit United Meth. Ch., Clarks Summit, Pa., 2004—. Mem.: Pa. Music Educators Assn., Am. Choral Dirs. Assn., Music Educators Nat. Conf. R-Consevative. United Methodist. Avocations: travel, crafts, scrapbooks. Home: 491 Carnation Dr Clarks Summit PA 18411 Office: Wallenpaupack North Intermediate School HC #6 Box 6070 Hawley PA 18428 Office Phone: 570-226-4557. Personal E-mail: flutie28@juno.com.

KERBER, RICHARD E., cardiologist; b. N.Y.C., May 10, 1939; s. Max and Pauline Kerber; m. Linda K. Kaufman; children: Ross, Justin. AB in Anthropology, Columbia U., 1960; MD, NYU, 1964. Diplomate Am. Bd. Internal Medicine, Am. Bd. Cardiology. Med. intern/resident Bellevue Hosp., N.Y.C., 1964—66; med. resident Stanford (Calif.) U. Hosp., 1968—69, cardiology fellow, 1969—71; asst. prof. internal medicine U. Iowa, Iowa City, 1971—74, assoc. prof. internal medicine, 1974—78, prof. medicine, 1978—. Editor: Echocardiography in Coronary Artery Disease, 1988. Capt. U.S. Army, 1966—68. Grantee RO1 grant, NHLBI, 1995—. Fellow: Am. Coll. Cardiology, Am. Heart Assn., Am. Heart Assn. (chmn. coun. on cardiopulmonary and critical care 1997—99, 1997—99, award of Meritorious Achievement 1996, Scientific Coun. Dist. Achievement award 2001), Am. Coll. Cardiology (gov. for Iowa 1976—79, 1976—79); mem.: Assn. Am. Physicians, Assn. Univ. Cardiologists, Am. Soc. for Clin. Investigation, Am. Soc. Echocardiology (sec. 1978—80, treas. 1993—95, v.p. 1995—97, pres. 1997—99, sec. 1978—80, treas. 1993—95, v.p. 1995—97, pres. 1997—99). Office: U Iowa Dept Medicine 200 Hawkins Dr Iowa City IA 52242-1009

KERBER, ROBERT CHARLES, chemistry educator; b. Hartford, Conn., Nov. 29, 1938; s. Cyril J. and Mildred A. (Taber) K. SB, MIT, 1960; PhD, Purdue U., 1965. Asst. prof. SUNY, Stony Brook, 1965-72, assoc. prof., 1972-87, prof. chemistry, 1987—2002, dist. tchr. prof., 2002—. Vis. scientist Brookhaven Nat. Lab., Upton, N.Y., 1983. Contbr. articles to profl. jours. Recipient Chancellor's award SUNY, 1986; Humboldt fellow Max Planck Institut für Kohlenforschung, 1973-74. Mem.: AAAS, Royal Soc. Chemistry, Am. Chem. Soc. Avocations: informal gardening, topical philately. Office: SUNY at Stony Brook Dept Chemistry Stony Brook NY 11794-3400 E-mail: rkerber@notes.cc.sunysb.edu.

KERBER, RONALD LEE, industrial corporation executive; b. Lafayette, Ind., July 2, 1943; s. John Andrew Kerber and Edith Helen (McMaster) Kerkhoff; children: John, Mark, Stephen, Jacqueline. BS, Purdue U., 1965; MS, Calif Inst. Tech., 1966, PhD, 1970. Registered profl. engr., Mich. Tech. staff Aerospace Corp., Los Angeles, 1971-72; prof. Mich. State U., E. Lansing, 1969-85, assoc. dean, 1984-85; program mgr. Defense Advanced Research Projects Agy., Arlington, Va., 1983-84; dep. undersec. U.S. Dept. Defense, Washington, 1985-88; v.p. advanced systems and tech. McDonnell Douglas Corp., St. Louis, 1988-89, v.p. tech. and bus. devel., 1989-91; exec. v.p., chief tech. officer Whirlpool Corp., Benton Harbor, 1991—2000; pres. SBDC Corp., Charlottesville, Va., 2000—. Contbr. articles to profl. jours. Mem. ASME, IEEE, Am. Phys. Soc.

KERBIS, GERTRUDE LEMPP, architect; m. Walter Peterhans (dec.); m. Donald Kerbis (div. 1972); children: Julian, Lisa, Kim. BS, U. Ill.; MA, Ill. Inst. Tech.; postgrad., Grad. Sch. Design, Harvard U., 1949-50. Archtl. designer Skidmore, Owings & Merrill, Chgo., 1954-59, C.F. Murphy Assocs., Chgo., 1959-62, 65-67; pvt. practice architecture Lempp Kerbis Assocs., Chgo., 1967—; lectr. U. Ill., 1969; prof. William Rainey Harper Coll., 1970—95, Washington U., St. Louis, 1977, 82, Ill. Inst. Tech., 1989-91. Archtl. cons. Dept. Urban Renewal, City of Chgo.; mem. Northeastern Ill. Planning Commn., Open Land Project, Mid-North Community Orgn., Chgo. Met. Housing and Planning Council, Chgo. Mayor's Commn. for Preservation Chgo.'s Hist. Architecture; bd. dirs. Chgo. Sch. Architecture Found., 1972-76; trustee Chgo. Archtl. Assistance Ctr., Glessner House Found., Inland Architect Mag.; lectr. Art Inst. Chgo., U. N.Mex., Ill. Inst. Tech., Washington U., St. Louis, Ball State U., Muncie, Ind., U. Utah, Salt Lake City. Prin. archtl. works include U.S. Air Force Acad. dining hall, Colo., 1957, Skokie (Ill.) Pub. Library, 1959, Meadows Club, Lake Meadows, Chgo., 1959, O'Hare Internat. Airport 7 Continents Bldg, 1963; prin. developer and architect: Tennis Club, Highland Park, Ill., 1968, Watervliet, Mich. Tennis Ranch, 1970, Greenhouse Condominium, Chgo., 1976, Webster-Clark Townhouses, Chgo., 1986, Chappell Sch., 1993; exhibited at Chgo. Hist. Soc., 1984, Chgo. Mus. Sci. and Industry, 1985, Paris Exhbn. Chgo. Architects, 1985, Spertus Mus.; represented in permanent archtl. drawings collection Art Inst. Chgo. Active Art Inst. Chgo. Recipient award for outstanding achievement in professions YWCA Met. Chgo., 1984 Fellow AIA (bd. dirs. Chgo. chpt. 1971-75, chpt. pres. 1980, nat. com. architecture, arts and recreation 1972-75, com. on design 1975-80, head subcom. inst. honors nomination); mem. Chgo. Women in Architecture (founder), Chgo. Network, Internat. Women's Forum, Arts Club Chgo., Cliff Dwellers (bd. dirs. 1987-88, pres. 1988, 89), Lambda Alpha. Office: Lempp Kerbis Assocs 172 W Burton Pl Chicago IL 60610-1310 Personal E-mail: lk172@aol.com.

KERCHER, DAVID MAX, mechanical engineer; b. Goshen, Ind., Nov. 18, 1931; s. Maxwell Mease and Rosemary (Harper) K.; m. Betty Noreen Raycroft, June 7, 1958; children: Kimberly S., Matthew R., Andrew D.R., Steven R., Elizabeth J., Jason R., Amy N. BSME, Purdue U., 1958; MS in Aerospace Engring., U. Cin., 1967. Engr. large jet engine divsn. GE, Cin., 1958-71, sr. engr., 1966-71, unit mgr., 1968, engr. missile and space div. Burlington, Vt., 1959-60, unit mgr. gas turbine dept. Schenectady, 1972-81, sr. engr., 1982, sub-sect. mgr. aircraft engine group Lynn, Mass., 1983-84; sr. engr. GE Aircraft Engines, Lynn, 1985-89, prin. engr., 1989—2001; ret., 2002. V.p. Sunrise Orchards, Inc., Goshen, Ind., 1996—2002, also bd. dirs. Contbr. articles to profl. jours.; 15 patents on gas turbine cooling. Sgt. USAF, 1950-54, USAFR, 1955-58. Fellow ASME (gas turbine heat transfer com. 1980—, vice chmn. com. 1992-94, chmn. 1994-96); mem. AIAA (sr.), ASME Internat. Gas Turbine Inst., Am. Legion (life), Air Force Assn. (life), Tau Beta Pi, Pi Tau Sigma. E-mail: dave@Kercher.org.

KERCHEVAL, ALEC NORTON, mathematician; s. Basyl Hurley Kercheval and Edwina Simi Norton; m. Lilian Garcia-Roig, May 7, 1995; children: Claire Elizabeth Kercheval-Roig, Olivia Anne Kercheval-Roig. BS, Harvey Mudd Coll., 1980; MA, Merton Coll., U. Oxford, 1982; PhD, U. Calif., Berkeley, 1987. Asst. prof. Math., Univ. Tex., Austin, 1989—98; sr. cons. Barra, Inc., Berkeley, 1999—2001; assoc. prof. Math., Fla. State Univ., Tallahassee, 2001—. Marshall scholarship, Marshall Aid Commn., Brit. Govt., 1980-1982, Postdoctoral fellowship math. scis., NSF, 1989-1992. Mem.: Am. Math. Soc. Office: Dept Math Florida State U Tallahassee FL 32306-4510

KERCHEVAL, JOHN WILLIAM, III, aerospace transportation executive, venture capitalist, investment banker; b. Arlington, Va., Aug. 21, 1965; s. John William and Carolyn Ann Booth Kercheval. BS in Chemistry, U. Calif., Berkeley, 1987, MBA in Fin. and Ops. Rsch., 1993. Rsch. assoc. Genentech, Inc., South San Francisco, Calif., 1986—88; assoc. tech. corp. fin. Hambrecht & Quist, LLP, San Francisco, 1988—91, assoc. v.p., corp. fin. dept., 1991—93; v.p. merchant banking Pierce Group, Arlington, 1993—95; dir. fin. planning and analysis Orbital Scis. Corp., Dulles, 1995—97; v.p., treas. Orbital Scis. Corp. / ORBCOMM, Dulles, Va., 1997—2001, European Aeronautic Def. and Space Co., N.V., Amsterdam, Netherlands, 2001—03; exec. v.p., CFO AeroAstro, Inc., Ashburn, Va., 2003—; sr. mng. dir. Mid-Atlantic Vulture Capital Fund, Washington, 2004—. Dir. ORBCOMM

Global, LP, Dulles, 1997—2000, ORBCOMM Internat., LP, London, 1997—2000. Alumni scholar, U. Calif., Berkeley, 1984—87. Mem.: Phi Beta Kappa (sec. Washington chpt. 1999—2002). Conservative. Episcopalian. Office: AeroAstro Inc 20145 Ashbrook Ct Ashburn VA 20147 Office Phone: 703-723-9800. Personal E-mail: johnkercheval@hotmail.com.

KEREIAKES, DEAN JAMES, cardiologist; b. Louisville, Jan. 8, 1953; s. James G. and Helen (Christy) K.; m. Anne Sugar, June 20, 1981; children: Jennifer, David, Andrew, Nicholas. BS, U. Cin., 1974, MD, 1978. Diplomate Am. Bd. Internal Medicine, Am. Bd. Cardiology. Intern, resident U. Calif., San Francisco, 1978-80; sr. resident Mass. Gen. Hosp., Boston, 1980-81; chief med. resident H.C. Moffitt Hosp., San Francisco, 1981-82; adult cardiology fellow U. Calif., San Francisco, 1982-84; coronary angioplasty fellow San Francisco Heart Inst., 1984, Sequoia Hosp., Redwood City, Calif., 1984; attending cardiologist The Christ Hosp., Cin., 1985—; CEO, dir. rsch. Ohio Heart Health Ctr., 2000—. Med. dir. Carl & Edythe Lindner Ctr. Clin. Cardiovasc. Rsch., Cin., 1995—; prof. clin. medicine Ohio State U., 1995—; mem. ACC/AHA task force com on angioplasty and unstable angina guidelines AHA/ACC, 1987—. Mem. editl. bd. Circulation, sect. editor, mem. editl. bd. Jour. Invasive Cardiology, Am. Heart Jour., Am. Jour. Cardiology, Jour. Am. Coll. Cardiology. Fellow Am. Coll. Cardiology; mem. AMA, Am. Heart Assn., Alpha Omega Alpha, Phi Beta Kappa. Republican. Avocation: wine collecting. Office: The Ohio Heart Health Ctr 2123 Auburn Ave Ste 136 Cincinnati OH 45219-2906

KEREN, KINNERET, biophysicist; b. Jerusalem; PhD in physics, Technion Israel Inst. Tech. Postdoctoral rschr. Theriot Lab., Dept. Biochemistry Stanford U. Contbr. articles to profl. jour. Named one of Top 100 Young Innovators, MIT Tech. Review, 2004. Office: Stanford U Dept Biochemistry Stanford CA 94305 Business E-Mail: kinneret@stanford.edu.

KERES, KAREN LYNNE, literature and language professor; b. Evanston, Ill., Oct. 22, 1945; d. Frank and Bette (Pascoe) K.; m. Walter Wilson Berg. BA, St. Marys Coll., 1967; postgrad., U. Notre Dame, 1967-68; MA, U. Iowa, 1969. Assoc. prof. English, humanities and fine arts William Rainey Harper Coll., Palatine, Ill., 1969-95, prof., 1995—, Palomar Coll., San Marcos, Calif., 1990-93. Cons. in field. Mem. MLA, Ill. Assn. Tchrs. English, Am. Fedn. Tchrs., Nature Conservancy, Mensa. Home: 222 Fairfield Dr Island Lake IL 60042-9622 Office: William Rainey Harper Coll Dept Liberal Arts Palatine IL 60067 Personal E-mail: KLK1022@comcast.net. *Experienced consultant in professional organizations: negotiating, multi-cultural and diversity issues. Develop and structure work force team goals for diverse employees. Written and inter-personal communication consultant.*

KERIAN, JON ROBERT, retired judge; b. Grafton, ND, Oct. 23, 1927; s. Cyril Robert and Elizabeth Antoinette (Kadlec) K.; m. Sylvia Ann Larson, Dec. 28, 1959; children: John, Ann. PhB, U. N.D., 1955, LLB, 1957, JD, 1971. Bar: N.D. 1957, U.S. Dist. Ct. N.D. 1958, U.S. Ct. Appeals (8th cir.) 1971, U.S. Supreme Ct. 1963. Pvt. practice law, Grand Forks, N.D., 1958-61; asst. atty. gen. State of N.D., Bismarck, 1961-67; ptnr. Bosard, McCutcheon, Kerian, Schmidt, Minot, N.D., 1967-80; dist. judge State of N.D., Minot, 1980—92, surrogate judge, 1993—, ret. History instr. Bismarck State Coll., 1965-67; asst. city atty. City of Minot, 1968-76; atty. Zoning & Planning Commn., Minot, 1969-76; lectr. in field. Contbr. articles to profl. jours.; editor ABA newsletter, The Judges News, 1990—95. Mem. ABA (bd. editors Judges Jour. 1990-95), Western States Bar Conf. (pres. 1982-83), N.D. Bar Assn. (pres. 1979-80), Nat. Conf. State Trial Judges (exec. com. 1983-89). Home: 1800 8th St SW Minot ND 58701-6410 Office: PO Box 340 Minot ND 58702-0340 Personal E-mail: judex1@srt.com.

KERIK, BERNARD B., former police commissioner; b. Paterson, NJ, Sept. 4, 1955; s. Donald and Patricia Kerik; m. Hala Kerik; 4 children. BS in Pub. Adminstrn., Empire State Coll. (SUNY). Security guard King Faisal Specialist Hosp., Riyadh, Saudi Arabia, 1982—84; comdr. spl. weapons and ops., warden Passaic County Jail, NJ; with NYC Police Dept., 1985—2001; exec. asst. to commr. NYC Dept. Corrections, first dep. commr., 1995—97, commr., 1997—2000; police commr. NYC Police Dept., 2000—01; sr. v.p. Giuliani Ptnrs., NYC, 2001—03; CEO Giuliani-Kerik LLC (name changed to Giuliani Security & Safety), NYC, 2003—04; interim min. interior, sr. policy adv. U.S. Presdl. Envoy to Iraq's Coalition Provisional Authority, 2003. Mem. criminal justice adv. coun. St. John's U., NYC; mem. academe policy rsch. sr. adv. com. U.S. Dept. Homeland Security; prin. mem. Mayor's cabinet overseeing the rescue, recovery, and investigation of the World Trade Center attack; mem. bd. dirs. Taser Internat., Inc., 2002—05. Author: (book) The Lost Son: A Life in Pursuit of Justice, 2002. With Military Police Corps U.S. Army, Korea, with 18th Airborne Corps U.S. Army, Ft. Bragg, NC, various assigments U.S. Army, Middle East.*

KERINS, FRANCIS JOSEPH, college president; b. N.Y.C., Mar. 23, 1927; s. John and Ellen (Mulrooney) K.; m. Mary Elizabeth Costigan, June 2, 1951; children: Mary Ellen Kerins Hayes, Donna (Mrs. Joseph Zelinski), John, Edward, Francis, Joseph, James. AB, St. Francis Coll., 1949; AM, St. Louis U., 1951; EdD, U. Denver, 1959; LHD, Coll. Idaho, 1983; LLD, City U., 1986. Prof., adminstr. Loretto Heights Coll., 1952-68; prof. higher edn. U. Denver, 1968-69; pres. Coll. St. Francis, Joliet, Ill., 1969-74, Carroll. Coll., Helena, Mont., 1974-89, No. Mont. Coll., Havre, 1989-90, St. Mary of the Plains Coll., Dodge City, Kans., 1990-91. Commr. Western Interstate Commn. Higher Edn.; chmn. Western Ind. Colls. Fund, Commn. on Colls. Northwest Assn.; chmn. bd. Bank of Mont.; bd. dirs. Am. Council on Edn., Council Ind. Colls.; active Nat. Commn. on Higher Edn. Issues; cons. in field. Contbr. articles to profl. jours. Chmn. Lewis and Cark County Bicentennial Com., 1975—; trustee Loretto Heights Coll., 1961-67, Coll. St. Francis, 1969-74, Carroll Coll., 1974—; pres. Helena Symphony Soc., 1981—; bd. dirs. Helena YMCA, United Way, Lewis and Clark Libr. Found.; mem. Helena Airport Bd., Coun. on Naturopathic Med. Edn. With AUS, 1950-52. Fellow Am. Council Edn.; mem. Mont. Com. for Humanities (past chmn.), Assn. Cath. Colls. and Univs. (chmn.); mem. Helena C. of C. (bd. dir.), N.W. Assn. of Schs. and Colls. (pres.), Waterton-Glacier Internat. Peace Park Assn. (bd. dirs.), Rotary (past pres.). Roman Catholic.

KERKORIAN, KIRK, investor, former motion picture company executive, consultant; b. Fresno, Calif., June 6, 1917; s. Ahron and Lily K.; m. Hilda Schmidt, Jan. 24, 1942 (div. 1951); m. Jane Maree Hardy, Dec. 5, 1954 (div.); children: Tracy, Linda; m. Lisa Bonder, 1998 (div.) Student pub. schs., L.A. Comml. airline pilot, from 1940; founder L.A. Air Svc. (later Trans Internat. Airlines Corp.), 1948, Internat. Leisure Corp., 1968; co-chmn., pres., CEO Tracinda Corp., 1969—; controlling stockholder Western Airlines, 1970; chief exec. officer Metro-Goldwyn-Mayer, Inc., Culver City, Calif., 1973-74, chmn. exec. com., vice-chmn. bd., 1974-79, dir., 1996—; controlling stockholder MGM/UA Communications Co.; cons., 1979—. Served as capt. Transport Command RAF, 1942-44. Office: Tracinda Corp 150 Rodeo Dr, Ste 250 Beverly Hills CA 90212*

KERMAN, ARTHUR KENT, physicist, researcher; b. Montreal, May 3, 1929; s. Samuel and Ida (Birn) K.; m. Enid Ehrlich, Dec. 21, 1952; children: Ben, Daniel, Elizabeth, Melissa, James. B.Sc., McGill U., 1950; PhD, MIT, 1953. Mem. faculty dept. physics MIT, Cambridge, 1956, prof., 1964—, dir. Ctr. Theoretical Physics, 1976-83, dir. lab. nuclear scis., 1983-92. Vis. prof. SUNY-Stony Brook, 1970-71; adj. prof. Bklyn. Coll., 1971-75; rsch. prof. U. Tenn. and ORNL, 2004—; cons. Argonne Nat. Lab., 1961-83, mem. sci. and tech. adv. com., 1984-90; cons. Brookhaven Nat. Lab., 1965-81, mem. relativistic heavy ion collider policy com., 1985-95, vis. com. 1973-78, chmn. 1977; cons. Lawrence Berkeley Lab., 1975-80, mem. vis. com., 1980-83, chmn. 1981; cons. Lawrence Livermore Lab., 1964—, chmn. phys. sci. advi. com. 1992-96; cons. Nat. Ignition Facility, 1997-99; cons. Los Almos Sci. Lab, 1961—, mem. physics div. adv. com., 1984-96, mem. theol. div. adv. com. 1972, LANSCE divsn. adv. com., 1998-2003; cons. Nat. Bur. Stds., 1980-81, Oak Ridge Nat. Lab., 1979-85, Sandia Nat. Lab., 1998-99; mem. U. Calif. Pres.'s Sci. and Academic Adv. Com. 1981-92; mem. White House Sci. Coun., 1982-85, panel on sci. and tech. in govt., 1985, fed. lab. rev. panel, 1982-83; mem. adv. com. Woods Hole Sub-panel of U.S. Dept. Energy, 1982, com. on sci., engring. and pub. policy rsch. briefing panel on sci. frontiers and superconducting super collider NRC, 1985, nuclear sci. adv. com. Dept. Energy and NSF, 1982-85; mem. U.S. Dept. Energy Fusion Policy Adv. Com., 1990, mem. U.S. Dept. Energy Inertial Confinement Fusion Adv. Com. 1992-96; mem. vis. com. Stanford U. Physics Dept., 1984, Yale U. Physics Dept., 1984, FONDS F.C.A.C. Comite des centres de Recherches pour le Laboratoire de Physique Nucleaire U. Montreal, 1982; mem. NIF Coun., 1997-99, NIF Programs Rev. Com., 2000-02; mem. Physics and Advanced Tech. Adv. Com., 1996—; Nat. Acad. Scis. panel on Inertial Confinement Fusion and Sci. Based Stockpile Stewardship, 1996-97, dirs. adv. com. Lawrence Livermore Nat. Lab., 1994-96; Ligo oversight bd. for MIT and Caltech, 1998-2002; cons. ORNL, 2002—, U. Rochester Lab. for Laser Energetics, 2002—; sci. advisor to asst. dep. adminstr. rsch., devel. and simulation DOE/NNSA, 2000—. Assoc. editor: Rev. Modern Physics, 1968-71. NRC fellow Calif. Inst. Tech., 1953-54, Niels Bohr Inst., Copenhagen, 1954-56; Guggenheim fellow U. Paris, 1961-62. Fellow Am. Phys. Soc. (program com. 1978-79, exec. com. div. nuclear physics 1970-72, pub. com. div. nuclear physics, Tom W. Bonner prize com. 1982-83), Am. Acad. Arts and Scis.; mem. N.Y. Acad. Scis. Office: MIT Dept Physics Rm 6-302A 77 Massachusetts Ave Cambridge MA 02139-4307

KERMAN, BARRY MARTIN, ophthalmologist, educator; b. Chgo., Mar. 31, 1945; BS, U. Ill., 1967, MD with high honors, 1970. Diplomate Am. Bd. Ophthalmology. Intern Harbor Gen. Hosp., Torrance, Calif., 1970-71; resident in ophthalmology Wadsworth VA Hosp., L.A., 1971-74; fellow in diseases of the retina, vitreous and choroid Jules Stein Eye Inst., UCLA, 1974-75; fellow in ophthalmic ultrasonography Edward S. Harkness Eye Inst., Columbia U., N.Y.C., 1975, U. Iowa Hosps., Iowa City, 1975; asst. prof. ophthalmology UCLA/Harbor Gen. Hosp., 1976-78; asst. clin. prof ophthalmology UCLA, 1978-83, assoc. clin. prof., 1983-95, clin. prof., 1995—, dir. ophthalmic ultrasonography lab., 1976—2003; cons. ophthalmologist L.A., 1976—2002, San Francisco, 2002—. Chief ophthalmology Century City Hosp., 1995-98; mem. exec. bd. Am. Registry Diagnostic Med. Sonographers, 1981-87; jour. reviewer in field. Contbr. articles to profl. jours. With USAFR, 1971-77. Fellow Am. Acad. Ophthalmology; mem. Am. Soc. Cataract and Refractive Surgery, L.A. Soc. Ophthalmology (emeritus), Am. Assn. Ophthalmic Standardized Echography, Societas Internat. Pro Diagnostica Ultrasonica in Ophthalmology, Western Retina Study Club. Office: 490 Post St Ste 640 San Francisco CA 94102 Office Phone: 415-982-2020.

KERMAN, PETER F., lawyer; BA, MS, Stanford Univ., 1977; JD, Harvard Univ., 1984. Bar: Calif. 1984. Joined Latham & Watkins, LA, 1984, office mng. ptnr., Silicon Valley Menlo Park, Calif., 1997—2004, now ptnr., and global chair, corp. dept., 2004—. Mem.: ABA. Office: Latham & Watkins Silicon Valley 135 Commonwealth Dr Menlo Park CA 94025

KERMES, CONSTANTINE JOHN, artist, industrial designer; b. Pitts., Dec. 6, 1923; s. John Demetrios and Katina (Katerinis) K.; m. Bessie Saratopoulos, Sept. 14, 1952; children: Harriet Kermes Shuman, Kathy Kermes Dixon. BFA, Carnegie Mellon U. Designer Am.-Std. Co., Pitts., 1952-55; indsl. design cons. New Holland N.A. subs. Fiat, Modena, Italy, 1955-82, indsl. designer, 1982—. One man shows include Grimaldis Gallery, Balt., 1979, 80, Reading (Pa.) Mus., 1980, Jacques Seligmann Gallery, NYC, 1951, 52, 54, 56, 59, 61, 64, 65, 70, 75, 78, 79, Hancock Shaker Mus., Pittsfield, Mass., 1989, Demuth Found., Lancaster, Pa., 1987, Millport Mus., Lancaster, 1989, William Pa. Mus., Harrisburg, 2000, Balt. Watercolor Soc., 2001, Ctrl. Market Art Gallery, 2001, 02, 03, Lancaster Mus. of Art, 2003, 04; exhibited in group shows at Butler Inst. Am. Art, Youngstown, Ohio, 1964, Pa. Watercolor Soc., 1979, 80, 91, Art 81, Washington, 1985, 91, Mus. Art, Lancaster, 1996, Ctrl. Mkt. Art Gallery, Lancaster, 2002, Westmoreland Mus. Art., Greensburg, Pa., 2003, 04; juried exhibitor Okla. Watercolor Soc., 2001, 02, Millersville (Pa.) U., Elizabethtown (Pa.) Coll., Lancaster Mus. Art; represented in permanent collections Storm King Art Ctr., Mountain View, NY, Pa. State U., Hershey (Pa.) Med. Ctr., Case New Holland, Pa., Pa. Hist. Mus., Hancock Shaker Mus., Mus. Art, Lancaster; illustrator Shaker Architecture, 1970; author, illustrator: American Icons, 1975; 24 patents for farm equipment designs. Recipient Am. Design Rev. award Indsl. Design mag., 1962, 64, 68, 72, Design award Am. Iron and Steel Inst., 1963, 69, 73, 75, awards Lancaster CountyArt Assn., award Berks Art Alliance, 2000, Hazleton Art League, 2000, York Art Alliance, 2000, Lancaster County Art Mus., Potomac Soc. award, 2001, prize Mid-Atlantic States Water Color, 2001, award Balt. Watercolor Soc., Art of State award William Penn Mus., Harrisburg, York, Pa. Art Assn. 2000, 01, 02, 03, 04, award Phila. Water Color Soc., 2003, 04, Chester County (Pa.) Art Assn., 2003, 04. Mem. AHEPA (Lancaster), Pa. Watercolor Soc., Hamilton Club (Lancaster). Greek Orthodox. Home and Office: 981 Landis Valley Rd Lancaster PA 17601-4816 Office Phone: 717-569-0780.

KERMODE, FRANK (JOHN KERMODE), literary critic, educator; b. Douglas, Isle of Man, Nov. 29, 1919; s. John Pritchard and Doris (Kennedy) K. BA, Liverpool U., 1940, MA, 1947; DHL (hon.), U. Chgo., 1975; DLitt (hon.), Liverpool U., 1981; PhD (hon.), Amsterdam U., 1988, Newcastle U., 1993, Yale, 1995, U. Wesleyan, 1997, U. London, 1997, U. Sewanee, 1999, Columbia U., 2003, Harvard U., 2004. J.E. Taylor prof. English Manchester U., Eng., 1958-65; Winterstoke prof. English Bristol U., Eng., 1965-67; Lord Northcliffe prof. English U. Coll. London, 1967-74; King Edward VII prof. English Cambridge U., 1974-82; vis. prof. humanities Columbia U., N.Y.C., 1983, 85. Charles E. Norton prof. Harvard U., 1977-78; Henry Luce prof. Yale Y., 1994. Author: Romantic Image, 1957, Wallace Stevens, 1960, The Sense of an Ending, 1967, D.H. Lawrence, 1973, The Classic, 1975, The Genesis of Secrecy, 1979, The Art of Telling, 1983, Forms of Attention, 1985, History and Value, 1988, An Appetite for Poetry, 1989, The Uses of Error, 1991, Not Entitled, 1995, others; (with Anita Kermode) The Oxford Book of Letters, 1995, Shakespeare's Language, 2000, Pleasing Myself, 2001, Pieces of My Mind, 2003, The Age of Shakespeare, 2004; co-editor Encounter, 1965-67; (with Robert Alter) The Literary Guide to the Bible, 1987; editor Modern Masters Series, 1969-91, Oxford Authors, 1984—. Served to lt. Royal Navy, 1940-46. Decorated officier Ordre des Arts et Sciences (France), 1973; named Knight Bachelor granted by the Queen of Eng., 1991; King's Coll. hon. fellow, 1987—. Fellow Brit. Acad., Royal Soc. Lit.; mem. Am. Acad. Arts and Scis. (hon.), Am. Acad. Arts and Letters (hon.), Accademia dei Lincei. Home: 9 The Oast House Pinehurst Grange Rd Cambridge CB3 9AP England Office Phone: 01223 357931. Personal E-mail: frankkermode@lineone.net.

KERN, BERNARD DONALD, retired physicist; b. New Castle, Ind., Oct. 31, 1919; s. William Bernard and Cecile McDonald (Hudson) K.; m. Nedda Wisler Burdsall, Aug. 20, 1946; children: Richard B., Jonathan K., Arthur R. BS, Ind. U., 1942, MS, 1947, PhD, 1949. Physicist Signal Corps and Manhattan Project, Chgo., 1942-43; sr. physicist Oak Ridge Nat. Lab., 1949-50; faculty U. Ky., 1950-85, prof. physics, 1958-85, chmn. dept. physics and astronomy, 1967-69, prof. emeritus, 1985—. Physicist U.S. Naval Radiol. Def. Lab., San Francisco, 1957-58, cons., 1957-69; prof. Inst. Teknologi Bandung (Indonesia), U. Ky., State Dept. Edml. Assistance Program, 1961- 62 Author articles on nuclear physics. Served to lt.(jg) USNR, 1943-46. Fellow Am. Phys. Soc.; mem. Am. Inst. Physics, Am. Assn. Physics Tchrs. Home: 681 Providence Rd Lexington KY 40502-2214 Personal E-mail: slrcamera@aol.com.

KERN, BRAD D., lawyer; s. Frank B. Kern and Donna Jacard. BA, U. Calif., Berkeley, 1995; JD, UCLA, 1999. Extern to Chief Justice Ronald M. George Supreme Ct. Calif., San Francisco, 1997; assoc. Shearman & Sterling, San Francisco, 1999—. Contbr. articles to profl. jours. Mem.: ABA, Calif. Bar Assn. Office: Shearman & Sterling 525 Market St Ste 1500 San Francisco CA 94105 Office Phone: 415-616-1100.

KERN, CHARLES WILLIAM, retired academic administrator, chemist, educator; b. Middletown, Ohio, July 13, 1935; s. Charles Albert and Charme (Bowman) K.; m. Regine Bouchard. BS, Carnegie Inst. Tech., 1957; PhD, U. Minn., 1961; postgrad., Columbia U., 1961-63. Postdoctoral fellow in chem. physics Columbia U., N.Y.C., 1961-63; asst. prof. chemistry SUNY, Stony Brook, 1964-66; adj. assoc. prof. chemistry Ohio State U., Columbus, 1966-71, adj. prof. chemistry, 1971-76, acad. vice chmn., dept. chemistry, 1972-73, prof. chemistry, 1976-80; rsch. scientist Battelle Meml. Inst., Columbus, Ohio, 1966-72, mgr. chem. physics sect., 1972-76, dir. phys. scis. program, 1973-74, inst. scientist, 1973-76, dir. Battelle Inst. program, 1976-84, cons., 1976-84; program dir. theoretical chem. physics, div. chemistry NSF, Washington, 1978-80, sr. staff assoc., computer sci. rsch. network project dir., div. math. and computer scis., 1980-83, program dir. structural chemistry and thermodynamics, acting sect. head phys. chemistry and chem. dynamics, div. chem., 1983-84, acting dir. div. chemistry, 1984-85, dep. dir. div. chemistry, 1985-86; asst. dir. gen. sci., Office of Sci. and Tech. Policy Office of the Pres., Washington, 1986; dean Ohio State U., Columbus, 1986-92; prof. chemistry Coll. Math. and Phys. Scis. Ohio State U., Columbus, 1986-92; v.p. rsch., dean Grad. Sch., Northwestern U., Evanston, Ill., 1992-93, v.p. rsch. and grad. studies, 1993-98, prof. chemistry, 1992-98, prof. emeritus, 1998—. Chmn,. Sch. Many-Body Techniques in Chemistry, Seattle, 1969, Carnegie-Mellon U. Admissions Coun., 1970-72, Summer Rsch. Conf. on Theoretical Chemistry, Boulder, Colo., 1975; co-chmn. Current Biol. Problems, A Sch. for Phys. Scientists, 1977; exec. sec. NSF Dir.'s Task Force on Advanced Sci. Computing Resources, 1983-84. Assoc. editor Chem. Physics Letter, 1967-81; contbr. numerous articles to profl. jours. Mem. Am. Chem. Soc. E-mail: wkern04@comcast.net.

KERN, EDITH, Romance languages and literature educator; b. Dusseldorf, Germany, Feb. 7, 1912; d. L.G. Berg and J. Bison. BA, Bridgewater Coll., 1942; MA, Johns Hopkins U., 1944, PhD in Romance Lang. and Lit, 1946; LHD (hon.), Bridgewater Coll., Va., 2002. Asst. prof. modern langs. U. Md., U. Kans.; dir. Ford Foun. TV project U. Pa., 1946-60; prof. French Grad. Sch., St. Johns U., N.Y.C., 1960-65; prof. Romance lit. and comparative lit. Grad. Sch. U. Wash., Seattle, 1965-72; D. Silbert prof. humanities, chmn. comparative lit. program Smith Coll., Northampton, Mass., 1972-77, prof. emeritus; John Cranford Adams prof. Hofstra U., 1977-81; faculty New Sch. for Social Rsch., N.Y.C., 1986—. Vis. prof. UCLA, 1962, SUNY-Buffalo, 1965, Stanford U., 1970, U. Warwick, Eng., 1978, Brandeis U., fall 1978, SUNY at Binghamton, spring 1979, Colgate U., 1982; disting. prof. Purdue U., 1984; dir. NEH Summer Seminar, 1975; 79, experimental year-long NEH Seminar for Coll. Tchrs., 1977-78; elected. Coun. Scholars for Libr. of Congress, 1983-86; mem. faculty New Sch. Social Rsch., 1985—; docent Met. Mus. Art, 1984-02. Author: French Dramatic Theory, 1949, Sartre, 1962, Existential Thought and Fictional Technique, 1970, The Absolute Comic, 1980; contbg. author: Disciplines of Criticism, 1968, Boccaccio, 1974, Moliere, 1975, Beckett, 1983, Writing in a Modern Temper, 1984, Literary Theory and Criticism, 1985, Waiting For Godot, 1987, Aesthetics and the Literature of Ideas, 1990, Carrefour de Cultures, 1993; mem. editl. bd. Twentieth Century Lit., 1972—; founding editor Dada/Surrealism; contbr. articles to profl. jours. Bollingen Found. fellow, 1967; Nat. Endowment for Humanities fellow, 1972; Guggenheim fellow, 1975-76; Radcliffe-Harvard Fellow, 1975-76; Rockefeller Found. Fellow, 1982 Mem. MLA (v.p. 1975-76, pres. 1977-78), Comparative Lit. Assn. (nat. exec. coun. 1973—), Nat. Soc. Lit. and Arts, Am. Comparative Lit. Assn., Internat. Comparative Lit. Assn., Renaissance Soc. Am., PEN. Home: 1025 5th Ave # 5fs New York NY 10028-0134

KERN, GEORGE CALVIN, JR., lawyer; b. Balt., Apr. 19, 1926; s. George Calvin and Alice (Gaskins) K.; m. Joan Shorell, Dec. 22, 1962; 1 child, Heath. BA, Princeton U., 1947; LLB, Yale U., 1952. Bar: N.Y. 1952. Chief U.S. Info. Ctr., Mannheim, W.Ger., 1947-48; dep. dir. pub. info. Office U.S. Mil. Govt. for Germany, Berlin and Nurnberg, 1948-49; assoc. Sullivan & Cromwell, N.Y.C., 1952-60, ptnr., 1960—. Publ. Cub newspaper, Tehachapi, Calif., 1974—; bd. dirs. McJunkin Corp., Charleston, W.Va. Lt. USN, 1944-46. Home: 830 Park Ave New York NY 10021-2757 Office: Sullivan & Cromwell 125 Broad St Fl 28 New York NY 10004-2489

KERN, HEATH THAYER, television producer; b. N.Y.C., Sept. 19, 1964; s. George C. and Joan Kern. BA, Denison U., 1986; MPA, Harvard U., 2002. Segment prodr. COUR-TV, N.Y.C., 1996-99; assoc. prodr. Fox News Channel, N.Y.C., 1999—2005; dir. pub. diplomacy, pub. liaison U.S. AID, 2005—. Mem. Colony Club. Office: US Agy Internat Devel Washington DC Office Phone: 202-712-5842.

KERN, IRVING JOHN, retired food company executive; b. N.Y.C., Feb. 10, 1914; s. John and Min (Weitzner) Kleinberger; m. Beatrice Rubenfeld, June 22, 1941; children— John A., Arthur H., Robert M. BS, NYU, 1934, student Grad. Sch. Art and Sci., 1960-65; DHL, Mercy Coll., Dobbs Ferry, N.Y., 1980. Asst. buyer Bloomingdale's Dept. Store, N.Y.C., 1934-40; with Dellwood Foods, Inc., Yonkers, N.Y., 1945-82, pres., 1966-77, chmn. and chief exec. officer, 1977-82. Dir. Scarsdale Nat. Bank; adj. prof. polit. sci., San Diego State U., 1989-95. Mem. County Mental Health Svcs. Bd. of Westchester County, 1954-59; mem. bd. dirs., sec. Westchester County Assn., 1950-57, 76-80; exec. bd. Westchester County Better Bus. Bur., 1970-73; bd. dirs. Westchester Coalition, 1972-80, Westchester Minority Bus. Assistance Orgn., 1973-75, Milk Industry Found., 1976-82, Nat. Dairy Coun., 1979-81; bd. dirs., vice chmn. Westchester Pvt. Industry Coun., 1979-82; mil. adv. coun. Ctr. for Def. Info., 1986-97. Lt. col. AUS, 1940-45. Decorated Bronze Star. Mem. N.Y. Milk Bottlers Fedn. (pres., dir.), Met. Dairy Inst. (exec. v.p., dir.), Phi Beta Kappa, Tau Epsilon Phi.

KERN, JOHN MCDOUGALL, lawyer; b. Omaha, Nov. 28, 1946; m. Susan McDougall Kern, Oct. 15, 1977. BA, Creighton U., 1970; JD cum laude, George Washington U., 1973. Bar: DC 1973, Calif. 1980, U.S. Dist. Ct. DC 1974, U.S. Dist Ct. N.D. Calif. 1980, U.S. Dist. Ct. C.D. Calif. 1996, U.S. Ct. Appeals (D.C. Cir.) 1974, U.S. Ct. Appeals (9th Cir.) 1978; bd. cert. specialist in civil trial advocacy, Nat. Bd. Trial Advocacy. Asst. U.S. atty. criminal divsn. Office of U.S. Atty. DC, Washington, 1973-78; asst. U.S. atty. civil divsn. Office U.S. Atty. N. D. Calif., San Francisco, 1978-82; v.p., dir. Crosby, Heafey, Roach & May P.C., San Francisco, Oakland, LA, 1982—2002, Carlson, Calladine & Peterson, LLC, San Francisco, 2003—04. Faculty Nat. Inst. Trial Advocacy, 1987—; spkr., lectr. in field. Contbr. abstracts, book chpt., articles to profl. jours. Fellow: Am. Coll. Trial Lawyers; mem.: Nat. Inst. Trial Advocacy, Am. Inn of Ct., Am. Bd. Trial Advocates (adv.). Address: 80 Maywood Dr San Francisco CA 94127 Office Phone: 415-682-7374. Personal E-mail: jmckern@sbcglobal.net.

KERN, PATRICIA ANN, retired finance company executive; b. Jersey City, N.J., July 9, 1938; d. Wilbur Edwin Kern and Frances Yiona Yinger; m. Louis Frederick Hepburn, July 4, 1983. BS, BA, Pa. State U., 1961. Cert. travel cons. Pan Am. Airlines, N.Y. Sr. mgr. Rosenbluth Travel, King of Prussia, Pa., 1974—82; c.e.o magaha inc. Fin. cons. compnay, Wyncote, Pa., 1982—97; dir. mktg. religious group tours Thomas Garlin Tours, Jenkintown, Pa., 1992—95. Cons. Ocean Reef Travel, Key Largo, Fla., 1982—97. Mem., golf coord. Make-a-Wish Found., 1999—2000; pres. Wyncote (Pa.) Neighbors Assn., 1990—98. Independent. Achievements include patents for PrimATIC. Avocations: golf, swimming, crafts, dog training, photography.

KERN, PAUL JOHN, retired military officer; b. W. Orange, N.J., June 16, 1945; s. Bruno Michael and Marjorie (Bolan) K.; m. Dolores I. Mercaldo, Aug. 28, 1971; children: Paul John Jr., Alexander Matthew. BS, U.S. Mil. Acad., 1967; MS in Mech. and Civil Engring., U. Mich., 1973; fellow nat. security, Harvard U., 1986-87. Registered profl. engr., Va. Commd. 2d lt. U.S. Army, 1967, advanced through grades to gen., 2001, ret., 2004, platoon leader, staff mem., 1967-69; troop comdr. 11th Armored Cavalry Regiment, Republic Vietnam, 1969-70; asst. prof., course dir. dept. engring. U.S. Mil. Acad., West Point, N.Y., 1973-76; ops. officer 2d bn., 33d Armor, 3d Armor Div., Kirch Goens, Fed. Republic Germany, 1976-78; br. chief Bradley Program Mgmt. Office, Warren, Mich., 1979-82; team chief reseach and devel. U.S. Army Staff, Pentagon, Washington, 1982-84; bn. comdr. 5th bn.,

32d Armor, 24th Infantry Div., Ft. Stewart, Ga., 1984-86; mil. asst. to under sec. US Dept. Def., Washington, 1987-89; comdr. 2d brigade, 24th Infantry Divsn. Saudi Arabia/Iraq, 1989-91; dir. requirements Army staff, 1991-92; asst. divsn. comdr.-maneuver, 24 Infantry Divsn. Ft. Stewart, Ga., 1992-93; mil. asst. to sec. US Dept. Def., Washington, 1993-96; comdg. gen. 4th Inf. Divsn., Ft. Hood, Tex., 1996-97; mil. dep. to asst. sec. acquisition, logistics & tech. U.S. Army, Washington, 1997—2001; comdg. gen. U.S. Army Materials Command, Alexandria, Va., 2001—04; sr. counselor The Cohen Group, Washington, 2005—. Head of internal investigation into abuses at Abu Gharaib prison US Army, 2004; mem. bd. dirs. EDO Corp., NYC, 2005—. Co-author: Acquisition Managers - Role and Reality, 1987. Decorated Bronze Star with 3 oak leaf clusters, Silver Star, Purple Heart with 2 oak leaf clusters, Def. Disting. Svd. medal, Army Disting. Svc. medal, Def. Superior Svc. medal, Legion of Merit; Soc. Automotive Engineers Teeter award, Alumni Soc. medal U. Mich, German Cross of Honor Fed. Armed Forces Mem. Soc. Automotive Engrs. (Teetor award 1975), Armor Assn., Assn. U.S. Army, Coun. Fgn. Rels., U.S. Naval Inst., Chi Epsilon. Roman Catholic. Avocations: sailing, woodworking, computers. Office: The Cohen Group 1200 19th St NW Ste 400 Washington DC 20036 E-mail: pkern@cohengroup.net.

KERN, STANLEY ROBERT, physician, forensic psychiatrist; b. Paterson, N.J., Jan. 13, 1928; s. William and Doris (Lunde) K.; m. Allison Kimberg; children: Andrew, Suzanne Gelinas. BA, NYU, 1949; MD, Thomas Jefferson U., 1954. Diplomate Am. Bd. Psychiatry and Neurology, Am. Bd. Forensic Psychiatry. Intern Newark Beth Israel Med. Ctr., 1954-55; resident Phila. Psychiatric Ctr., 1957-60; instr. psychiatry Seton Hall Coll. of Medicine, Jersey City, 1960-61, sr. instr. in psychiatry, 1961-63; clin. asst. prof. psychiatry N.J. Coll. of Medicine, Newark, 1964-71; clin. assoc. prof. psychiatry N.J. Med. Sch., Newark, 1971—. Adj. assoc. prof. law Rutgers U. Sch. Law, Newark, 1984-90; trustee Forensic Psychiat. Hosp., Trenton, N.J., 1988-94; chief sect. of psychiatry The Hosp. Ctr. at Orange, N.J., 1972-92. Editor: Medical-Legal Digest for New Jersey Psychiatrists, 1979. Bd. dirs. Mental Health Assn. of Essex County, East Orange, N.J., 1981-88. Capt. USAF, 1955-57. Fellow Am. Psychiat. Assn. (life), Am. Acad. Forensic Scis.; mem. AMA (Physician's Recognition award 1971—), Am. Acad. Psychiatry and the Law (sec. 1987-91, v.p. 1991-92), N.J. Psychiatry Assn. (pres. 1986-87), N.J. Psychoanalytic Soc. (pres. 1982-84). Avocations: reading, walking. Office Phone: 973-762-0600.

KERN, TERRY C., judge; b. Clinton, Okla., Sept. 25, 1944; s. Elgin L. Kern and Lora Lee (Miller) Renegar; m. Charlene Heinen, Dec. 26, 1970 (dec. Feb. 2002); children: Lauren, Suzanne, Justin Hunter; m. Jeanette Martin, Dec. 31, 2004. BS, Okla. State U., Stillwater, 1966; JD, U. Okla., 1969; LLM, U. Va., 2004. Bar: Okla. 1969, U.S. Dist. Ct. (ea. dist.) Okla. 1974, U.S. Dist. Ct. (we. dist.) Okla. 1979, U.S. Dist. Ct. (no. dist.) Okla. 1993, U. S. Ct. Appeals (10th cir.) 1979. Gen. atty. FTC, Washington, 1969—70; ptnr. Fischl, Culp, McMillin, Kern and Chaffin, Ardmore, Okla., 1971—86; founding ptnr., pres. Kern, Mordy and Sperry, Ardmore, 1986—94; dist. judge U.S. Dist. Ct. (no. dist.) Okla., Tulsa, 1994—, chief judge, 1996—2003. Mem. Jud. Conf. Com. on Security and Facilities, 10th Cir. Jud. coun. Chmn. bd. dirs. Southern Okla. Meml. Hosp., Ardmore, 1982—92, chmn., 1989—91. Served with USAR, 1970—75. Named to, Beta Theta Pi Hall of Fame, 2000; recipient Leadership Legacy award, Okla. State U., 2000, Disting. Alumnus award, 2001. Fellow: Okla. Bar Found. (pres. 1991, Disting. Svc. award 1992), Am. Bar Found.; mem.: ABA, Tulsa City Bar Assn. (bd. dirs.), Fed. Judges Assn., U. Okla. Coll. Law Assn., Okla. Bar Assn., Am. Bd. Trial Advocates (Okla. chpt.), Johnson-Sontag Inns of Ct. (master of bench). Democrat. Episcopalian. Office: US Dist Courthouse 333 W 4th St Tulsa OK 74103-3839

KERN, WILLIAM BLIEM, JR., minister; b. Phila., Nov. 24, 1943; s. William Bliem Sr. and Helen Elizabeth (Kennedy)K.; m. Ellen (Evjen), Dec. 13, 1968 (div. Dec. 1972). BA, Wilmington Coll., 1967; MSc and MST, The New Seminary, 1990. Ordained min. NY State Bd. Regents. Graphic design cons. to chief arch. Gibbs and Hill, N.Y.C., 1976-77; art dir. spl. projects The N.Y. Times Mag. Group, N.Y.C., 1979-80; design dir. Moving House and Home Mag., N.Y.C., 1981; assoc. art dir. Weight Watchers Mag., N.Y.C., 1982-83; market analyst The Comex Commodity Exch., N.Y.C., 1987-89; tv host Satellite Physic, Internat. Satellite Network, N.Y.C., 1991-92; min., pvt. practice spiritual counseling N.Y.C., 1990—. Author: (book of poems) Meditation Meditations Meditations, 1973 (chosen one of top ten books of the yr. by Library Jour., 1973, Distintive Merit in Book Design Award, Art Dir. Club of NY., 1974), (book) Nuc. Prayer, 1978, The Text of Amen, 1981, (CD) The Jewel in the Lotus with Allen Won Quintet, 2003. Mem. masonic edn. com. Mem. Am. Rsch. Ctr. in Egypt, Nat. Coun. for Geosomic Rsch., Soc. for Sci. Exploration, The Rosicsucian Soc. Am. (dir. astrology 1985-92), Chakrasambara Buddhist Ctr., George Washington Lodge # 285(treas. lodge, 1993-98); Lodge Coun. Chpt. Consistory Scottish Rite in the Valley Of N.Y.C. Avocations: watercolor landscape painting, vajrayana buddhist meditation, spiritual astrology. Home: 230 Riverside Dr Apt 15CC New York NY 10025-6172 E-mail: wbkjr3@verizon.net.

KERNAN, BARBARA DESIND, senior government executive; b. N.Y.C., Jan. 11, 1939; d. Philip and Anne (Feuer) Desind; m. Joseph E. Kernan, Feb. 14, 1973. BA cum laude, Smith Coll., 1960; postgrad. Oxford U., 1963; MA, Harvard U., 1963; postgrad. in edn. policy George Washington U., 1980. Editor Harvard Law Sch., 1960-62; tchr. English, Newton (Mass.) H.S., 1962-63; editor Allyn & Bacon Pubs., Boston, 1963-64; edn. assoc. Upward Bound, Edn. Assocs., Inc., Washington, 1965-68; edn. program specialist Title I, Elem. and Secondary Edn. Act, U.S. Office Edn., 1969-73; fellow Am. Polit. Sci. Assn., Senator William Proxmire and Congressman Alphonzo Bell, 1973-74; spl. asst. to dep. commr. for elem. and secondary edn. and dir. dissemination, sch. fin. and analysis, U.S. Office Edn., 1975-77, chief program analysis br. divsn. edn. for disadvantaged, 1977-79; chief grant program coordination staff Office Dep. Commr. for Ednl. Resources, 1979-80; chief priority concerns staff Office Asst. Sec. Mgmt., U.S. Dept. Edn., Washington, 1980-81; dir. divsn. orgnl. devel. and analysis Office of Dep. Undersec. for Mgmt., 1981-86; Sr. Exec. Svc. candidate on spl. project to improve status of women Sec. Transp., Washington, 1983-84; inducted Sr. Exec. Svc., 1986; assoc. adminstr. for adminstrn. Nat. Hwy. Traffic Safety Adminstrn., U.S. Dept. Transp., 1986-94, career devel. leader to presdl. mgmt. interns, 1989-91; trustee Capricorn Galleries, Rockville, Md., 1996-97, pres., 1997—; owner Philip Desind Collection, Am. Realism Fine Arts, 1997—. Recipient awards U.S. Office Edn., 1969, 71, 77, U.S. Dept. Edn., 1981-86, U.S. Dept. Transp., 1991, 94, Small Agy. Coun., 1990; scholarships U. Mich., 1956-58, Smith Coll., 1958-60, Harvard U., 1962-63; Am. Polit. Sci. Assn. fellow, 1973-74; Sr. Exec. fellow John F. Kennedy Sch. Govt. Harvard U., 1983. Office Phone: 301-340-6900. Personal E-mail: bkernan@prodigy.net.

KERNAN, JEROME BERNARD, retired marketing educator, researcher; b. Cin., Nov. 22, 1932; s. E. B. and Alice (Gerver) Kernan; children: Kathleen Kernan Bedree, Brian Michael. BA, U. Cin., 1957; MS, U. Ill., 1959, PhD, 1962; post-doctoral studies in computer simulation, Carnegie Mellon U., Pitts., 1962; post-doctoral studies in math., U.Kans., 1963. Prof. emeritus George Mason U. Consumer rsch. cons., 1965—. Co-author: (book) Perspectives on Marketing Theory, 1968, Comparative Marketing Systems, 1968, Explorations in Consumer Behavior, 1968, Promotion: An Introductory Analysis, 1970, Managerial Analysis in Marketing, 1970, Perspectives in Marketing Management, 1971; contbr. over 120 articles to profl. jours. Pres. Sacred Heart Sch. Bd., Austin, Tex., 1964—67. With USAF, 1951—53. Co-recipient Ferber award, Jour. Consumer Rsch., 1992, Best Article award, Am. Acad. Advt., 1993. Mem.: Soc. for Consumer Psychology, Assn. for Consumer Rsch. (pres. 1978), Am. Mktg. Assn. Avocations: motorsport, golf. Home: 879 Pine Valley Ln Cincinnati OH 45245 Personal E-mail: jkernan@gmu.edu.

KERNAN, JOSEPH EUGENE, III, former governor; b. Chgo., Apr. 8, 1946; s. Joseph E. Kernan II and Marion Kernan; m. Maggie McCullough, 1974. BS, U. Notre Dame, 1968, PhD (hon.), 1998. Product mfg. mgr. Proctor & Gamble Co., 1975—76; sales exec. Schwarz Paper Co., 1976-80; city contr. City of South Bend, Ind., 1980-84, mayor, 1988—96; v.p., treas. MacWilliams Corp., 1984-88; lt. gov. State of Ind., Indpls., 1996—2003, acting gov., 2003, gov., 2003—05. Bd. trustees St. Joseph Med. Ctr. Bd. dirs. St. Joseph County Spl. Olympics, Notre Dame Club, Jr. Baseball Assn., Northside L.L.; campaign cabinet United Way, 1979-82; treas. Studebaker Music Inc. USN, 1969—74. Recipient two Purple Heart medals, Navy Commendation medal, Combat Action Ribbon, Disting. Flying Cross, 2 Air medals, award for Individual Excellence. Democrat.

KERNAN, WILLIAM FRANK, career officer; BA in History, Our Lady of Lake U., 1973; MA in Pers. Adminstrn., Ctrl. Mich. U.; student, Infantry Advanced Course, 1973-74, U.S. Army Command, Gen. Staff, Coll., 1978-79, U.S. Army War Coll., 1986-87. Commd. 2d lt. U.S. Army, 1968, advanced through grades to gen., 2000, platoon leader Co. D. 1-327 Inf. Bn., 101st Airborne Divsn., 1969; reconnaisance platoon leader Tiger Force, liason officer 101st Airborne Divsn. U.S. Army, Vietnam, 1969-70; co. comdr. 2-325 Airborne Inf., 82d Airborne Divsn. Fort Bragg, N.C., 1970-71; comdr. San Antonio Dist. Recruiting Command U.S. Army, Austin, Tex., 1974-76; co.comdr. HHC 2d Bn. (Rangers), 75th Infantry, Fort Lewis, Wash., 1976-77; co. comdr. Co. A., 2d Bn. (Rangers), 75th Infantry, Fort Lewis, 1977-78; recorder secretariat for dept. of army selection bds., later pers. mgmt. officer, Combat Arms Divsn., U.S. Army Pers. Ctr, Alexandria, Va., 1979-81; exchange officer, rifle company comdr. 3d bn. Brit. Parachute Regiment, UK, 1981-83; exec. officer 2d bn. 508th inf. (airborne) to bn. comdr. 2-508th Inf. (Airborne), 82d Airborne Divsn., Fort Bragg, N.C., 1983-85; comdr. 3d bn. 504th inf. (airborne) 82d Airborne Divsn., Fort Bragg, 1985-86; battalion comdr. 1-75th Rangers, 1987-88; from dep. comdr. to comdr. 75th Ranger Regiment, Fort Benning, Ga., 1988-91; asst. divsn. comdr. 7th Infantry Divsn., Ft. Ord, Calif., 1991-93; dir. strategic plans, policies, assessments J-5 U.S. Spl. Ops Command, McDill AFB, Fla., 1993-96; commanding gen. 101st Airborne Divsn. and Fort Campbell, Fort Campbell, Ky., 1996-98, XVIII Airborne Corps & Fort Bragg, 1998-2000; commdr. in chief U.S. joint Forces Commd./Supreme Allied Commdr. Atlantic, 2000—. Decorated Defense Disting. Svc. medal, Disting. Svc. medal with oak leaf cluster, Legion of Merit with 3 oak leaf clusters, Bronze Star medal with V device, Bronze Star medal with oak leaf cluster, Purple heart, Meritorious Svc. medal with 3 oak leaf clusters, Air medals, Army Commednation medal with 4 oak leaf clusters, Army Achievment medal. Office: Supreme Allied Commdr Atlantic and Cinc Joint Forces Command Norfolk VA 28307 Home: PO Box 5006 Pinehurst NC 28374-5006

KERNEN, SANDRA S., school psychologist; d. Douglas E. and Hyja Holestine; m. Scott E. Kernen, Aug. 8, 1992; children: Tyler S., Dale D. BA in Psychology, Wichita State U., 1989. Sch. psychologist Warren City Schs., Ohio, 2002—; bd. edn. legislative liaison Newton Falls Exempted Sch. Dist., 2002—. Mem.: NASP (cert.). Democrat. Avocations: sports, reading, travel. Home: 2525 West River Rd Newton Falls OH 44444 Office: Warren City Schs 202 Loveless Ave Warren OH 44485 Office Phone: 330-307-1739. Personal E-mail: sankernen@aol.com.

KERNER, FRED, book publisher, writer; b. Montreal, Can., Feb. 15, 1921; s. Sam and Vera (Goldman) K.; m. Jean Elizabeth Somerville, July 17, 1945 (div. Apr. 1951); 1 son, Jon Fredrik; m. Sally Dee Stouten, May 18, 1959; children: David, Diane. BA, Sir George Williams U. (now Concordia U.), Montreal, 1942. Mem. editl. staff Saskatoon (Can.) StarPhoenix, 1942; Asst. sports editor Montreal Gazette, 1942-44; news editor Can. Press, Montreal, Toronto, N.Y.C., 1944-50; asst. night city editor A.P., N.Y.C., 1950-57; editor Hawthorn Books, Inc., N.Y.C., 1957-58, pres., 1964-68; exec. editor Crest-Premier Books, Hall House, Fawcett World Libr., N.Y.C., 1958-63; editor-in-chief Crest-Premier Books, Fawcett World Libr., N.Y.C., 1963-64; pres. Centaur House, Inc. (pubs.), 1964-80, Paramount Securities Corp., 1965-67, Veritas Internat. Pubs., 1976—91, Publishing Projects, Inc., 1967—, Communications Unltd., 1968—; editorial dir. book and ednl. divs. Reader's Digest, Can., 1968-75; v.p., pub. dir. Harlequin Enterprises Ltd., 1975-83, sr. cons. editor, 1984-96, editor emeritus, 1983—; v.p. Publitex Internat. Corp. (pubs.), 1968-75; pres. Athabaska House, 1975-77. Dir. Nat. Mint, Inc., others; panelist various profl. confs.; chmn. Internat. Affairs Conf. Coll. Editors, 1965; drama festival adjudicator, 1940-48; Broadway theatrical script cons., 1948-56; speechwriter Adlai Stevenson, 1952, 56; ghostwriter Dr. Joyce Brothers, Anita Colby, Enid Haupt, and others; mem. nat. negotiating com. Am. Newspaper Guild, 1949-54, Wire Svc. Guild, 1954-57, chmn. grievance com., 1955-57; instr. Insider's Guide to Writing and Pub., U. Toronto, 1999—. Author: (with Leonid Kotkin) Eat, Think and Be Slender, 1954, 2d edit., 2000, (with Walter M. Germain) The Magic Power of Your Mind, 1956, (with Joyce Brothers) Ten Days to a Successful Memory, 1957, Stress and Your Heart, 1961, 2d edit., 2000; pseudonym Frederick Kerr: Don't Count Calories!, 1962, 2d edit. (as Fred Kerner), 2000, (with Walter M. Germain) Secrets of Your Supraconscious, 1965, (with David Goodman) What's Best for Your Child and You, 1966, (with Jesse Reid) Buy High, Sell Higher, 1966; (pseudonym M.N. Thaler) It's Fun to Fondue, 1968, (with Ion Grumeza) Nadia, 1977, Careers in Writing, 1985, Mad About Fondue, 1986, (with Andrew Willman) Prospering Through the Coming Depression, 1986, Home Emergency Handbook and First-Aid Guide, 1990, Fabulous Fondues, 2000; contbg. author: Successful Writers and How They Work, 1958, Words on Paper, 1960, Overseas Press Club Cookbook, 1964, The Senior's Guide to Life in the Slow Lane, 1986, The Writer's Essential Desk Reference, 1991, 96, Lifetime: A Treasury of Uncommon Wisdoms, 1992, Chambers's Ency.; books transl. into French, German, Japanese, Portuguese, Spanish and Italian; editor: Love is a Man's Affair, 1958, 2d edit., 2000, Treasury of Lincoln Quotations, 1965, new edit. 1996, The Canadian Writer's Guide, 9th edit., 1985, 10th edit., 1988, 11th edit., 1992, Selling Your Short Fiction, 1992. Mem. local sch. bd., N.Y.C., 1967-68; chmn. sch. com. Westmount H.S., 1970-72; mem. sch. com. Roslyn Sch., 1973; chmn. publs. com. Edward R. Murrow Meml. Fund; judge Dr. William Henry Drummond Nat. Poetry Contest; trustee Gibson Lit. Awards, C.A.A. Lit. Awards, Benson & Hedges Lit. Awards, CA&B Student Creative Writing Awards, Random House Can. Short Story Competition, 2002; bd. govs. Concordia U., 1975-79; hon. life mem. Can. Pubs. Coun.; founding mem. exec. com. Pub. Lending Rights Commn., 1986-89, vice chmn., 1988-89; founding dir. Toronto Book and Mag. Fair, bd. dirs., 1990-94. Recipient Queen's Silver Jubilee medal, 1977, Allan Sangster award, 1982, Internat. Pub. award Air Can., 1982, 2 internat. awards for advertorial writing, 1990, Apex award for newsletter editing, 1992, Fellow Can. Copyright Inst. (vice chmn. 1995, chmn. 2000-02), World Intellectual Property Orgn. (del.), Acad. Can. Writers (vice chmn., bd. govs. 1986—); mem. European Acad. Arts, Scis. and Humanities, Orgn. Can. Authors and Pubs. (founding dir.), Can. Authors Assn. (v.p. 1972-80, founding dir. Lit. Luncheons, pres. Montreal br. 1974-75, nat. pres. 1982-83, hon. nat. pres. 2004—, founding editor Nat. Newsline 1982, pub. Can. Author 1982-95, hon. life, chmn. editl. adv. com. Can. Authors Assn. 1978-94, chmn. grievance com. 1983-93, pub. com. 1986-92), Periodical Writers' Assn. Can. (chmn. grievance com. 1990, contracts com.), Can. Writers' Found. (bd. govs. 1982—), Assn. Am. Pubs. (hon. life), Mystery Writers Am. (editor Third Degree, co-chmn. awards com.), Writers' Union Can. (hon. life, chmn. grievance com. 1990-99, contracts com. 1990-2002), Soc. Profl. Journalists' Pres.'s Club, Book and Periodical Coun. (bd. govs. 1983-94), Authors Guild, Authors League Am., Internat. P.E.N., Nat. Spkrs. Assn., Am. Acad. Polit. and Social Sci., Can. Assn. Restoration of Lost Positives (pres.), Can. Soc. for Preservation of the Natural Bowtie (pres.), Sir George Williams U. Alumni Assn. (founding pres. N.Y.C. br., exec. com. 1970-75, pres. 1971-73), GeorgiAntiques (founding dir.), Avodah Honor Soc., Advt. Club, Deadline Club, Overseas Press Club, Dutch Treat Club (N.Y.C.), Toronto Press Club, Author's Club (London), Sigma Delta Chi. Home: 1405-1555 Finch Ave E Willowdale ON Canada M2J 4X9

KERNER, JOSEPH FRANK, JR., management consultant, educator; b. Cleve., Dec. 29, 1938; s. Joseph Frank Sr. and Magarat Ann (Majoris) K.; m. Marilyn Joy Long, June 14, 1964; children: Joseph, Mark, Michael, Erin. BA, Miami U., Oxford, Ohio, 1961; postgrad., Case Western Res. U., 1963-68. Dir. bus. tech. Marion (Ohio) Tech. Coll., 1969-75; mgr. benefits Cen. Net Bank, Cleve., 1975-78; mgr. compensation L.B. Foster, Pitts., 1978-80; mgr. compensation and benefits Rubbermaid, Wooster, Ohio, 1980-82; dir. compensation and benefits ChemLawn, Columbus, Ohio, 1982-84; v.p. First Nat. Bank of Commerce, New Orleans, 1984-85; instr. Bliss Coll., Columbus, 1985-88; regional v.p. Primerica Fin. Svcs., Columbus, 1985-95; pres. JFK Consultancy & Kerner Connection, Columbus, 1988—; mktg. dir. WMA Securities, 1995-97; v.p. mktg. Environ. Energy Alt. Fuel, 1995-97; mktg. advisor TAASI, 1995-98. Adj. prof. Coll. Fin. Planning, 1988—; co. advisor Ohio Bus. Week, 1994—. Author: National Underwriter: Agent Exposes Himself, 1987, Pension Actuary: My Vision, 1994. Bd. dirs. Environ. Energy, Inc.; mem. Nat. Rep. Glee Club. Mem. Am. Soc. Pension Actuaries (bd. dirs. 1966-69, edn. coord. 1990—, joint bd. enrolled actuary exam. rev. com., editor Pension Actuary 1994, govtl. affairs com. 1993—, cert. fed. tax., cert. data educator), Kiwanis (immediate past pres., club builder New Albany, Ohio), Data Processing Mgmt. Assn. (faculty student chpt. of yr. 1970). Republican. Lutheran. Avocations: snow and water skiing, fishing, photography, travel. Home: 2682 Brianlane Blvd Columbus OH 43231-1642 E-mail: JFKequal@aol.com.

KERNER, MICHAEL BERNARD, gastroenterologist; b. Newark, May 13, 1945; s. Irving and Betty Kerner; m. Cynthia Iris Spitzer, Mar. 24, 1974; children: Jessica, Caroline, David. BA, Rutgers U., 1967; MD, Bowman Gray Sch. Medicine, 1971. Diplomate Am. Bd. Internal Medicine and Gastroenterology. Intern NYU/Manhattan VA Med. Ctr., Manhattan, 1971-72; resident NYU Med. Ctr., Manhattan, 1972-74, gastroenterology fellow, 1974-76; physician, ptnr. Assocs. in Digestive Diseases, Springfield, N.J., 1976—. Asst. clin. prof. medicine Columbia U., N.Y.C., 1989-2002, UMDNJ Med. Sch., 1989—. Named in Top Gastroenterologists in N.J. N.J. Monthly Mag., 1996, named One of Top Doctors in N.Y. Met. Area Castle Connolly Guide, 2001, 02, 03, 04. Fellow ACP, Am. Coll. Gastroenterology; mem. Am. Soc. Gastrointestinal Endoscopy, Am. Gastroenterology Assn., N.J. Soc. for Gastrointestinal Endoscopy (pres. 1985). Home: 21 Hemlock Rd Livingston NJ 07039-1423 Office: 25 Morris Ave Springfield NJ 07081-1404 Office Phone: 973-467-1313. E-mail: associates.dd@verizon.net.

KERNEY, YOLONDA V., music historian; d. James Bell Kerney, Jr. and Nancy McKinney Kerney. MusB, Howard U., 1996, MMus, 2003. Music libr. U.S. Libr. Congress, Washington, 1995—. Chair Daniel Murray African Am. Culture Assn. of the Libr. of Congress, Washington, 1999—. Vol. tutor Met. Delta Adult Literacy Coun., Washington, 1996—2002. Recipient Outstanding Svc. citation, Met. Delta Adult Literacy Coun., 1999; fellow Jr. fellow, Libr. Congress, 1995. Mem.: Black Caucus of the ALA, ALA, Libr. Congress Pa., Music Libr. Assn., TransAfrica Forum. Republican. Episcopalian. Avocation: research of the negro spiritual and historical documents related to slavery in America. E-mail: yker@loc.gov.

KERNFELD, BARRY DEAN, freelance/self-employed writer, musician; b. San Francisco, Aug. 11, 1950; s. Bernard Kernfeld and Elsie Marian Goldstein; m. Sally Ann McMurry, Aug. 15, 1981; children: Paul McMurry, Eric McMurry. BA in Music, U. Calif., Davis, 1975; MA in Musicology, Cornell U., 1978, PhD in Musicology, 1981. Jazz saxophonist Jazza-maphone, State College, Pa., 1998—. Editor: (reference work) The New Grove Dictionary of Jazz, 1988, 2d edit. 2001, The Blackwell Guide to Recorded Jazz, 1991, 2d edit.1995; author: (monograph) What to Listen for in Jazz, 1995. Home: 506 W Foster Ave State College PA 16801-4039 Office: Ste 203 108 W Beaver Ave State College PA 16801 Office Phone: 814-867-4288. Business E-Mail: bdk4@psu.edu.

KERNOCHAN, JOHN MARSHALL, lawyer, educator; b. NYC, Aug. 3, 1919; s. Marshall Rutgers and Caroline (Hatch) K. BA, Harvard U., 1942; JD, Columbia U., 1948. Bar: N.Y. 1949. Asst. dir. Legis. Drafting Research Fund Columbia U., N.Y.C., 1950-51, acting dir., 1951-52, dir., 1952-69, lectr. law, 1951-52, assoc. prof., 1952-55, prof., 1955-77, Nash prof. law, 1977-89, Nash prof. law emeritus, 1990—; spl. lectr., 1991—2000. Cons. Temporary State Commn. to Study Orgnl. Structure of Govt. N.Y.C., 1953; exec. dir. Coun. for Atomic Age Studies, 1956—59, co-chmn., 1960—62; chmn. bd. Galaxy Music Corp., 1956—89; bd. dirs. E.C. Schirmer Music Co., Inc.; pres. Gaudia Music & Arts, Inc., 1987—2004. Author: The Legislative Process, 1980; co-author: Legal Method Cases and Materials, 1980; contbr. articles to profl. jour. Mem. civil and polit. rights com. President's Commn. on Status of Women, 1962-63; dir. emeritus Vol. Lawyers for the Arts; mem. legal and legis. com. Internat. Confedn. Soc. Authors and Composers. Mem. Assn. Bar City of N.Y. Internat. Lit. and Artistic Assn. (mem. d'honneur, internat. exec. com., mem. U.S.A. group), Copyright Soc. U.S.A. (exec. com. 1986-89), Assn. Tchrs. and Rschrs. in Intellectual Property. Office: Columbia Univ Sch Law 435 W 116th St New York NY 10027-7297

KERNS, CHRISTIAN RANDOLPH, chemist; b. Fredicksburg, Va., Apr. 8, 1953; s. Terrill D. and Mary Barbe Kerns. BS in Chemistry, W.Va. Univ., 1978. Chemist Fla. Dept. Agr., Tallahassee, 1986—96, Harbor Br. Oceanographic Instn., Ft. Pierce, Fla., 1997, Aerotek Sci., Ft. Lauderdale, Fla., 1999—2000; engr. Spectro Analytical Instruments, Fitchburg, Mass., 2000—01; chemist Adecco, Leominster, Mass., 2002—. Capt. Colo. State Championship Basketball Team, 1971; chmn. mission com. St. Paul United Meth. Ch., Tallahassee, 1994—96. Named 1st Team All State Colo. Men's Basketball Team, 1971. Mem.: Am. Chem. Soc., Lions Club (past pres.), Phi Theta Kappa (hon.). Methodist. Avocation: stained glass artist. Home: 192 Central St Apt 301 Gardner MA 01440 Office: Adecco 14 Monument Sq #101 Leominster MA 01453 E-mail: crkerns1@juno.com.

KERNS, DAVID VINCENT, lawyer; b. Jan. 29, 1917; s. Clinton Bowen and Ella Mae (Young) K.; m. Dorothea Boyd, Sept. 5, 1942; children: David V., Clinton Boyd. BPh, Emory U., 1937; JD, U. Fla., 1939. Bar: Fla. 1939, U.S. Dist. Ct. (mid. dist.) Fla. 1939, (so. dist.) Fla. 1978, (no. dist.) Fla. 1981, U.S. Ct. Appeals (11th cir.) 1981, U.S. Supreme Ct. 1988. Assoc. Sutton & Reeves, Tampa, Fla., 1939-41, Fowler & White, Tampa, 1945-47; ptnr. Moran & Kerns, Tampa, 1948-49; resident atty. Fla. Road Dept., 1949-53; rsch. asst. Supreme Ct. Fla., 1953-58; dir. Fla. Legis. Reference Bur., 1958-68, Fla. Legis. Svc. Bur., 1968-71, Fla. Legis. Libr. Svcs., 1971-73; gen. counsel Fla. Dept. Adminstrn., 1973-82; mem. Fla. Career Svc. Commn., 1983-86; spl. master Fla. Senate, 1987-96; legal cons. chief inspector gen. Fla. Gov. Office, 1995-98. Contbr. articles to profl. jours. Served with U.S. Army, 1941—45. Mem. Fla. Govt. Bar Assn. (pres. 1966, J. Ernest Webb Meml. award 1982), Fla. Bar (bd. govs. 1978-84), Tallahassee Bar Assn. (spl. dir. 1993-95). Democrat. Methodist. Home: Apt 221 4425 Meandering Way Tallahassee FL 32308-5742

KERNS, JOANNA DE VARONA, actress, writer, director; b. San Francisco, Feb. 12, 1953; d. David Thomas and Martha Louise (Smith) de V.; m. Richard Martin Kerns, Dec. 11, 1976 (div. Dec. 1986); 1 child, Ashley Cooper. Student, NYU, 1970-71. TV series include The Four Seasons, 1984, Growing Pains; TV movies includes A Wedding On Waltons Mountain, 1982, V, 1983, Stormin' Home, 1985, The Return of Marcus Welby, M.D., 1984, The Rape of Richard Beck, 1985, Mother's Day On Waltons Mountain, 1982, A Bunny's Tale, 1985, Robin Cook's Mortal Fear, 1994, Whose Daughter is She?, 1995, No One Could Protect Her, 1995, See Jane Run, 1995, Terror In the Family, 1996; movies include Cross My Heart, 1986, Mother Knows Best, 1997, Sisters and Other Strangers, 1997, Emma's Wish, 1998, Girl Interrupted, 1999. Democrat. Office: Creative Artists Agy 9830 Wilshire Blvd Beverly Hills CA 90212-1804

KERNS, VIRGINIA B., anthropologist, writer; b. San Diego, 1948; d. James T. and Ruth B. Kerns; m. Ronald Adam Hallett. BA in Anthropology, Coll. William and Mary, 1970; PhD in Anthropology, U. Ill., 1977. Vis. asst. prof. Coll. William and Mary, Williamsburg, Va., 1977—78, from asst. prof. to prof., 1985—, chair dept. anthropology, 1988—93; asst. prof. Va. Tech, Blacksburg, Va., 1978—83; vis. asst. prof. U. Iowa, Iowa City, 1981; rsch. anthropologist UN Food and Agr. Orgn., Rome, 1984. Assoc. editor Am. Ethnologist Am. Ethnol. Soc., 1979—84; bd. dirs. U. Press Va., Charlottesville, 1995—98. Author: Scenes from the High Desert, 2003 (Evans Biography award, 2004), Scenes from the High Desert: Julian Steward's Life and Theory, 2003 (William P. Clements award for Best Nonfiction Book on Am. SW, 2004), Women and the Ancestors: Black Carib Kinship and Ritual, 1983, 2d edit., 1997; editor: In Her Prime, 1985, 2d edit., 1992. Named Writer-in-residence, Mesa Refuge, 2005; recipient Faculty award for Advancement of Scholarship, Phi Beta Kappa, Alpha of Va., 1988, Thomas Jefferson Tchg. award, Coll. William and Mary, 1989, Outstanding Faculty award, State Coun. for Higher Edn. in Va., 1991; fellow, Fulbright-Hays Commn., 1974—75, Va. Found. for Humanities, 1989; grantee, Wenner-Gren Found. for Anthrop. Rsch., 1974—75, 1976; Hon. fellow, Woodrow Wilson Found., 1974. Fellow: Am. Anthrop. Assn.; mem.: Phi Beta Kappa. Office: Coll William and Mary Dept Anthropology PO Box 8795 Williamsburg VA 23187-8795 Office Phone: 757-221-1054. E-mail: vbkern@wm.edu.

KERNS, WILMER LEE, researcher; b. Dayton, Va., May 17, 1932; s. Lee Doil and Madeline A. (Grim) K.; m. Marian Iris May, Mar. 21, 1957 (div. 1963); children: Mark Wayne, Susan Kaye Kerns Mitchell; m. Shirley Mitchell Walton, June 19, 1965; children: Robert Todd, Lynelle Madeline, Jacob Scott Walton. AB, Trevecca Nazarene Coll., 1957; AM, U. Mich., 1960; PhD, Ohio State U., 1971. Cert. tchr., counselor, Va. Math. tchr. Norfolk (Va.) Pub. Schs., 1957-59; counselor Washington-Lee High Sch., Arlington, Va., 1960-65; social worker Arlington (Va.) County Pub. Schs., 1965-67; civil rights specialist U.S. Office Edn., Washington, 1967-69; rsch. assoc. Ohio State U., Columbus, 1969-71; assoc. regional commr. Social and Rehab. Svc., Chgo., 1971-74, planning officer Washington, 1974-75, divsn. chief, 1975-77; sr. rsch. analyst Social Security Adminstrn., Washington, 1977-97; ret., 1997. Author: Shanholtzer History and Allied Family Roots, 1980, Historical Records of Old Frederick and Hampshire Counties, Va., 1992, Frederick County, Virginia: Settlement and First Families, 1730-1830, 1995; co-editor Hampshire County West Virginia, 1754-2004, 2004, Waltons of Old Virginia and Sketches of Families in Central Virginia, 2005; columnist The W.Va. Advocate, 1982-92 (Excellence in Journalism award 1992). Lay minister Truro Episcopal Ch., Fairfax, Va., 1988-91. With USN, 1950-53. Decorated Air medal; named Disting. West Virginian, Gov. of W.Va., 1989. Mem. Morgan County Hist. Soc., Winchester-Frederick County Hist. Assn. Republican. Avocations: mountain music, historical and genealogical research. Home: 4715 38th Pl N Arlington VA 22207-2914 Personal E-mail: wkerns4@comcast.net.

KERPA, GARY J., computer science consultant; b. Derby, Conn., Apr. 20, 1958; s. George B. and Marcia J. (Tiano) K. Cert., Tech. Careers Inst., West Haven, Conn., 1978. Auto. tech. Racebrook Auto., Orange, Conn., 1974-77; computer system integration cons. Lawson & Assocs., Ansonia, Conn., 1980—. Regional coord. Ams. for Perot, Dallas, 1992. Mem.: Aircraft Owners and Pilots Assn. Republican. Roman Catholic. Avocation: flying. Home and Office: 18 Fairview St Ansonia CT 06401-2707

KERPER, MEIKE, family violence, sex abuse and addiction educator, consultant; b. Powell, Wyo., Aug. 13, 1929; d. Wesley George and Hazel (Bowman) K.; m. R.R. Milodragovich, Dec. 25, 1963 (div. 1973); children: Dan, John, Teren, Tina, Stana. BS, U. Mont., 1973; MS, U. Ariz., 1975; postgrad., Ariz. State U., 1976-78, Columbia Pacific U., 1990—. Lic. marriage and family therapist, Oreg.; cert. domestic violence counselor, alcoholism and drug abuse counselor, mental health profl. and investigator. Family therapist Cottonwood Hill, Arvada, Colo., 1981; family program developer Turquoise Lodge, Albuquerque, 1982; co-developer abusers program Albuquerque Shelter Domestic Violence, 1984; family therapist Citizens Coun. Alcoholism and Drug Abuse, Albuquerque, 1984-86; pvt. practice cons., trainer family violence and treatment Albuquerque, 1987—. Developer sex offender program Union County, Oreg. Co-author: Court Diversion Program, 1985; author Family Treatment, 1982. Lobbyist CCOPE, Santa Fe, 1983-86; bd. dirs. Union County Task Force on Domestic Violence, 1989-91; developer Choices program treatment of sex offenders and victims union, Wallowa and Baker Counties, Oreg. Recipient commendation Albuquerque Shelter Domestic Violence, 1984. Mem. Assn. for the Treatment Sexual Abusers (Ea. Oreg. rep.), Nat. Assn. Marriage and Family Therapists, PEO Club, Delta Delta Delta. Republican. Episcopalian. Avocations: art history, reading, indian culture, swimming, public speaking. Home: 61002 Love Rd Cove OR 97824-8211

KERR, ALEXANDER DUNCAN, JR., lawyer; b. Pitts., May 6, 1943; s. Alexander Duncan Sr. and Nancy Greenleaf (Martin) K.; m. Judith Kathleen Mottl, May 25, 1969; children: Matthew Jonathan, Joshua Brandon. BS in Bus., Northwestern U., 1965, JD, 1968. Bar: Ill. 1968, Pa. 1969, U.S. Dist. Ct. (ea. dist.) Pa. 1969, U.S. Dist. Ct. (no. dist.) Ill. 1969, U.S. Ct. Appeals (3rd and 7th cirs.) 1969, U.S. Supreme Ct. 1969. Assoc. Clark, Ladner, Fortenbaugh & Young, Phila., 1968-69, 73-74; asst. U.S. atty. U.S. Dept. Justice, Chgo., 1974-79; assoc., ptnr. Keck, Mahin & Cate, Chgo., Oak Brook, Ill., 1979-90; shareholder Tishler & Wald, Ltd., Chgo., 1990—. Staff atty. Park Dist. La Grange, Ill., 1985-2001; active Ill. St. Andrew Soc., North Riverside, 1982—, pres., 1995-97; vestryman, lay reader, chancellor, chalice bearer Emmanuel Episcopal Ch., 1980-99; mem. Pack 177, Troop 19, Order of the Arrow, Boy Scouts Am., La Grange, 1980-2000. With USN, 1969-75. Mem. Am. Legion, DuPage Club, Atlantis Divers. Home: 709 S Stone Ave La Grange IL 60525-2725 Fax: 708-354-1208. Office Phone: 312-876-3800. Business E-Mail: akerr@tishlerandwald.com.

KERR, BAINE PERKINS, oil industry executive; b. Rusk, Tex., Aug. 24, 1919; s. James Herman and Myrta Blake (Perkins) K.; m. Mildred Pickett Caldwell, June 13, 1942; children: Baine Perkins, John Caldwell, James Robinson, Mary Blake Kerr Winters. BA, LL.B., U. Tex. at Austin, 1942. Bar: Tex. 1942. Practiced in, Houston, 1945-77; partner firm Baker & Botts, 1955-77; dir. Pennzoil Co., Houston, 1964-94, chmn. exec. com., 1972-94, pres., 1977-85, dir. emeritus, 1994—. Served with USMCR, 1942-55. Mem. Chancellors, Order of Coif, Phi Beta Kappa. Office: Esperson Bldg 808 Travis St Ste 2200 Houston TX 77002-5704 Office Phone: 713-546-8978.

KERR, CRISTIE, professional golfer; b. Miami, Oct. 12, 1977; Winner Longs Drugs Challenge, 2002, LPGA Takefuji Classic, 2004, ShopRite LPGA Classic, 2004, State Farm Classic, 2004; tied for second U.S. Open, 2000. Winner Fla. State Jr. Girls Championship, 1993, 94, 95; mem. U.S. Curtis Cup Team, 1996, U.S. Solheim Cup Team, 2002, 03. Achievements include low amateur at 1996 U.S. Women's Open; fifth place LPGA money list, 2004; nine top-ten finishes, 2004; winner, Wendy's Championship for Children, 2005. Avocations: fishing, baking. Office: c/o LPGA 100 International Golf Dr Daytona Beach FL 32124-1092

KERR, DARLENE DIXON, electric power company executive; b. Syracuse, N.Y., Nov. 26, 1951; d. James and Mary Dixon; children: E. Kaye, J. Craig. BA, SUNY, Potsdam, 1973; MBA, Syracuse U., 1984. V.p. sys. electric ops. Niagara Mohawk Power Corp., Syracuse, 1988-91, v.p. gas mktg. and rates, 1991-93, v.p. electric customer svc., 1993-94, sr. v.p. electric customer svc., 1994-95, sr. v.p. energy distbn., 1995—98, past mem. steering com. and past chmn. polit. action com., exec. v.p. energy delivery, 1998—99, exec. v.p., chief oper. officer, 1999—2000, pres., chief operating officer, 2000—01; sr. v.p. Nat. Grid U.S.A., 2001—, pres., Nat. Grid U.S.A. Svc. Co., 2001—. Former mem. adv. bd. Rural Metro; former mem. policy coun. Success by 6. Former trustee Onondaga C.C.; former bd. dirs. Cmty.-Gen. Hosp.; mem. Syracuse U. Thursday Morning Roundtable and Corinthian Found.; mem. task force Bus. Alliance for a New N.Y.; past pres. and bd. dirs. Onondaga Citizens League; past v.p. bd. dirs. Regional Learning Svc., Inc.; past mem. policy and planning com. Leadership Grater Syracuse; former mem. Downtown Improvement Task Force; former committeewoman and vice chmn. Onondaga Rep. Com.; former mem. numerous campaign ad. coms. and Onondaga County Rep. task forces; mem. chmn.'s coun. and fin. com. Onondaga County Rep. Com.; bd. dirs. Farmers and Traders Life Ins. Co., Utilites Mutual Ins. Co., Greater Syracuse C.C., M&T Bank, N.Y. State Women in Comm. and Energy, former pres., LeMoyne Coll., Mktg. Execs. conf., Ctrl. N.Y. Regional Compact, Greater Syracuse Econ. Growth Coun., Syracuse 20/20. Named Mover and Shaker for bus. Syracuse Herald Am., 1990, Woman of Achievement for career Post-Std., 1991, Alumni of Distinction, SUNY, 1993, Citizen of Yr. Temple Adath Yeshurun, Syracuse, Woman of Achievement N.Y. State-Gov. Pataki, Extraordinary Woman Nat. Women's Hall of Fame, Seneca Falls, N.Y.; recipient Spirit Am. Women award Girls Inc. Ctrl. N.W., 1993, Multiple Sclerosis Soc. Crusaders for a Cure award, Zonta Crystal award. Office: National Grid USA 300 Erie Blvd W Syracuse NY 13202-4250

KERR, DAVE, state official, marketing professional; m. Patty Kerr; children: Ryan, Dan. Degree in Biol. Sci., Psychology, Kans. State U., 1968; MBA, U. Kans., 1970. Leader com. on Econ. Devel., Edn.; mem. Kans. State Senate, 1984—2004, pres., 2000—04. Bd. dirs. Hutchinson Hosp. Corp., Reno County Mental Health Adv. Com.; with Hutchinson Hosp. Bd. Dirs., Bds. Leadership Hutchinson, Hutchinson C.of C., Healthy Families, Nickerson and Hutchinson HS booster clubs. Mem.: Kans. Tech. Enterprise Corp. (mem. bd. dirs. 1987—98), Republican Ctrl. Com. (sec. 1981—84), Kans. C. of C. and Industry, Kans. Farm Bur., Legis. Post Audit, Joint Pensions, Investments and Benefits (vice chmn.), Legis. Coordinating Coun. (chmn.), Interstate Coop. (chmn.), Ways and Means Com., Commerce Com., Calendar and Rules Com. (chmn.). Republican. Office: State Capitol PO Box 2620 Hutchinson KS 67504

KERR, DAVID WYLIE, utilities executive; b. Montreal, Que., Can., Dec. 14, 1943; s. Dudley Holden and Cecilia (Maguire) K.; m. Sheryl Lee Drysdale, Nov. 1, 1969; children: Ross, Tamara. BSc, McGill U., Can., 1965, chartered acct., 1969. Chartered acct. Touche Ross & Co., Montreal, 1965—72; CFO Edper Investments Ltd., Toronto, Ont., Can., 1972-78; COO Hees Internat. Corp., Toronto, 1978-85; exec. v.p. Brascan Ltd., Toronto, 1985-86; sr. v.p. strategic planning Noranda Inc., Toronto, 1986-87, pres., 1987-90, pres., CEO, 1990—2002, chmn., 2002—, also bd. dirs. Bd. dirs. Brascan Corp., Sun Life Fin. Inc., Shell Can. Ltd., Sustainable Devel. Tech. Can. Found., Can. Spl. Olympics Found; mem. Nat. Roundtable on the Environment, Economy. Mem. Granite Club, Rosedale Golf Club. Mem. United Ch. Can. Avocations: bicycling, farming, golf. Office: Sun Life Fin Inc/BCE PL 181 Bay St Ste 300 Toronto ON Canada M5J 2T3

KERR, DEREK J., transportation executive; BS in Aero. Engring., MBA, U. Mich. Various fin. positions Northwest Airlines; sr. dir., fin. planning Am. West Holdings, 1996—98, v.p., fin. planning and analysis, 1998—2002, sr. v.p., fin. planning and analysis, 2002, sr. v.p., CFO, 2002—. Office: America West Holdings 111 Rio Salado Pkwy Tempe AZ 85281

KERR, DONALD CRAIG, retired minister; b. Pitts., July 29, 1915; s. Hugh Thomson and Olive (Boggs) K.; m. Nora Minetta Lloyd, Sept. 12, 1942; children: Donald Jr., Elizabeth, Douglas. BA, Princeton U., 1937; MDiv, Princeton Theol. Sem., 1940; ThD, U. Toronto, Ont., Can., 1942. Ordained to ministry Presbyn. Ch. (U.S.A.), 1940. Min. East Kiskacoguillas Presbyn. Ch., Reedsville, Pa., 1942-47, 1st Presbyn. Ch., New Haven, 1947-48, Roland Pk. Presbyn. Ch., Balt., 1948-80, pastor emeritus, 1980; pastoral assoc. Presbyn. Ch., Sarasota, Fla., 1980-87; chaplain Plymouth Harbor, Sarasota, 1982-91. Moderator Presbytery of Balt., 1960-61, mem. bd. pensions, exec. com., 1963-66. Author: How the Church Began, 1953, What the Bible Means, 1954, History of Religion in America, 1975; editor: Design for Christian Living, 1952. Bd. advisors Presbyn. Home of Md.; pres. Residents' Assn. Roland Park Pl., Balt. Recipient 50-yrs. in ministry plague Lake Joseph Community Ch., 1989, 50-yr. Ordination Recognition, 1992; honored for being 50 yr. mem. Balt. Presbytery. Mem. St. Andrew's Soc. (trustee, chaplain 1980-91, cert. appreciation 1990), Ivy League Club (v.p. 1991, pres. 1992-93), Princeton Club (pres. 1988-90, class coun. 1937), Univ. Club Sarasota, Sarasota Yacht Club, Sara Bay Club, Gibson Island Club, The Johns Hopkins Club, Shriners, Masons (32 degrees). Home: 700 John Rugling Blvd E202 Sarasota FL 34236

KERR, DONALD MACLEAN, JR., federal agency administrator, physicist; b. Phila., Apr. 8, 1939; s. Donald MacLean and Harriet (Fell) K.; m. Alison Richards Kyle, June 10, 1961; 1 dau., Margot Kyle. B.E.E. (Nat. Merit scholar), Cornell U., 1963, MS, 1964, PhD (Ford Found. fellow, 1964-65, James Clerk Maxwell fellow 1965-66), 1966. Staff Los Alamos Nat. Lab., 1966-76, group leader, 1971-72, asst. div. leader, 1972-73, asst. dir., 1973-75, alt. energy divsn. leader, 1975-76; dep. mgr. Nev. ops. office Dept. Energy, Las Vegas, 1976-77; acting asst. sec. def. programs Dept. Energy, Washington, 1978, dep. asst. sec. def. programs, 1977-79, dep. asst. sec. energy tech., 1979; dir Los Alamos Nat. Lab., 1979-85; sr. v.p. EG&G, Inc., Wellesley, Mass., 1985-88, exec. v.p., 1988-89, pres., bd. dirs., 1989-92; exec. v.p., bd. dirs. Sci. Applications Internat. Corps., San Diego, 1993-96, Info. Sys. Labs., San Diego, 1996-97; asst. dir. FBI, Washington, 1997—2001; dep. dir. sci. & tech. CIA, Washington, 2001—05; dir. Nat. Reconnaissance Office, 2005—. Mem. Navajo Sci. Com., 1974-77, Def. Sci. Bd., 1993-98; mem. sci. adv. panel U.S. Army, 1975-78; mem. engring. adv. bd. U. Nev., Las Vegas, 1976-78, Cornell U., 1985—; chmn. com. R&D Internat. Energy Agy., 1979-85; mem. nat. security adv. coun. SRI Internat., 1980-89; mem. adv. bd. U. Alaska Geophys. Inst., 1980-85; mem. sci. adv. group Joint Strategic Planning Staff, 1981-91; mem. adv. bd. Georgetown U. Ctr. Strategic Internat. Studies, 1981-87; mem. adv. com. Naval Rsch., 1982-85; mem. corp. Draper Lab., 1982-97; mem. DCI Nonproliferation Adv. Panel, 1993-98; mem. bd. San Diego Tech. Coun., 1994-97; bd. dirs. Resources for the Future, Washington. Published research on plasma physics, microwave electronics, ionospheric physics, energy and nat. security. Trustee New Eng. Aquarium, 1989-93. Fellow AAAS, Am. Phys. Soc.; mem. Am. Geophys. Union, Nat. Assn. Mfrs. (bd. dirs. 1986-92), Southwestern Assn. Indian Affairs, World Affairs Coun. Boston (bd. dirs. 1988-92), Atlantic Coun. (bd. dirs. 1991-97), Cosmos Club (Washington), Sigma Xi, Tau Beta Pi, Eta Kappa Nu. Office: Nat Reconnaissance Office 14675 Lee Rd Chantilly VA 20151

KERR, DOROTHY MARIE BURMEISTER, marketing executive, consultant; b. Chgo., Oct. 1, 1935; d. Edwin Charles and Dorothy Gladys (Braithwaite) Burmeister; m. James Robert Kerr, Aug. 27, 1955 (div. Jan. 1970); 1 child, Kathryn Elizabeth; m. James Mullinix, Apr. 20, 1978; 1 son, Mark Edwin Mullinix. BA, Cornell U., 1956. Publicity dir. United chpts. Phi Beta Kappa, Washington, 1957-62; dir. circulation and promotion The Am. Scholar, Washington, 1957-62; pres., creative dir. Dorothy Kerr & Assocs., Inc., Washington, 1962-79, 89-93, Milw., 1995—, sec.-treas., 1979-89; circulation mktg. mgr. U.S. News and World Report, 1979-84, assoc. circulation dir., 1985; circulation dir. Atlantic, 1985; v.p., dir. mktg. Walter Karl Cos., 1986-89; v.p. mktg. GEICO Life Ins. Co., Washington, 1989-90, Equifax Consumer Direct, Washington, 1990-92; v.p. bus. devel. DCI Mktg., Milw., 1993-95; dir. database mktg. and strategic info. Strong Capital Mgmt., Milw., 1995-96; exec. dir. Ctr. for Deaf and Hard of Hearing, Brookfield, Wis., 1999—. Cons. Annenberg Sch. Communication, U. Pa., Phila., 1973-75; lectr. George Washington U., 1974-76, adv. bd. editing and pub. program. Bd. dirs. Florence Crittenton Home, Washington, 1968-71, Better Bus. Bur. Met. Washington, mem. exec. com., 1978-93; bd. dirs. Wis. BBB, mem. exec. com., 1998—, sec., 1998-99, vice chmn., 1999-2002, chmn., 200103; bus. adv. com. Washington Tech. Inst., 1976; Washington adv. coun. SBA, 1976-78. Recipient Man of Year award Mail Advt. Club, 1971; named Woman of Yr. Women's Direct Response Group, 1992. Mem. Am. Mktg. Assn., Direct Mktg. Assn. (chmn. ethics oper. com. 1988-89, judging chmn. Echo awards com. 1994-95), Nat. Soc. Arts and Letters (treas. 1979-83), Assn. Direct Mktg. Agys. (dir., exec. v.p. 1978-79), Wis. Direct Mktg. Assn. (bd. dirs., program chair 1994-95, pres. 1995-96, steering com. 1998-99, Direct Mktg. Profl. of the Yr. 1998), Milw. Advt. Club (v.p. pub. svc. 1995-96, v.p. programs 1996-98), Washington Advt. Club (dir., pres. 1979-80), Capital Spkrs. Club (Washington, v.p. 1971), Direct Mktg. Club (Washington, pres. 1965), Rotary Club Milw., Inc., Kappa Delta. Home and Office: 1509 E Standish Pl Milwaukee WI 53217-1960 E-mail: dkerr@dorothykerrassociates.com. *Much of what must be done in life is neither exciting nor glamorous, but one should be willing to do whatever is needed; any task worth doing is worth doing well.*

KERR, FREDERICK HOHMANN, retired health facility administrator, retired academic administrator; b. Pitts., July 11, 1936; s. Nathan Frederick and Laura Marie (Hohmann) K.; m. Ethyl Nylene Bashline, 1960 (div. 1969); m. Phyllis Jensen, Aug. 21, 1970, 1 child, Linda Jean. BA, Pa. State U., 1958; MPA, U. Pitts., 1961; LLD (hon.), Luth. Coll. Health Professions, Ft. Wayne, Ind., 1996. Exec. sec. Pa. Economy League Fayette County Br., Uniontown, Pa., 1959, Armstrong County Br., Kittanning, Pa., 1959-62; exec. sec. Woodbury Tax Rsch. Conf., Sioux City, Iowa, 1962-65; pub. svc. dir. City of Sioux City, 1965-66; from asst. administr. to assoc. administr. St. Luke's Regional Med. Ctr., Sioux City, 1966-71; administr., CEO, Meml. Hosp. of Michigan City, Inc., Ind., 1971-75; pres., CEO, St. Luke's Hosp., Maumee, Ohio, 1975-86, Luth. Hosp. Ind., Luth. Coll. Health Professions, Ft. Wayne, 1986-95; v.p. for devel. Quorum Health Resources, Inc., Brentwood, Tenn., 1995-2001. Dir. Ohio Hosp. Ins. Co., Columbus, treas. 1981-84. Trustee Ohio Hosp. Assn., Columbus, 1983—85; dir. Siouxland United Way, 1968—71, Ft. Wayne Pub. TV, 1990—94, United Way Allen County, Ft. Wayne, 1990—94; trustee Northwest Med. Ctr., Oro Valley, 2004—; mem. Iowa Intergovtl. Rels. Com., Des Moines, 1964—67; mem. Rancho Vistoso Adv. Bd. N.W. Med. Ctr., Tucson, 2002—05. Mem.: ASPA (life; nat. coun. 1966—69), Am. Protestant Health Assn. (vice chmn. 1988—90). Avocations: wine appreciation, writing. *Being a servant is the most distinguished career of all.*

KERR, GARY ENRICO, lawyer, educator; b. Kewanee, Ill., Feb. 8, 1948; s. Roy Harrison and Marietta (Dani) K.; m. Eileen Elizabeth Straeter, Aug. 18, 1978; 1 child, Victoria Elizabeth. BA, No. Ill. U., 1970; JD, Northwestern U., Chgo., 1973. Bar: Ill. 1974, U.S. Dist. Ct. (cen. dist.) Ill. 1982, U.S. Ct. Appeals (7th cir.) 1983, U.S. Supreme Ct. 1983. Adminstrv. asst. Office Supt. Pub. Instrn. State Ill., Chgo., Springfield, 1971-74; asst. legal advisor Ill. State Bd. Edn., Springfield, 1974-78; spl. counsel Ill. State Comptroller, Springfield, 1978-79; pvt. practice Springfield, 1979—. Adj. faculty Sangamon State U. (now Ill. State U.), Springfield, Ill., 1994; pres., dir. counsel Kerr Products, Inc., Kewanee, Ill., 1980—; instr. paralegal program Robert Morris Coll., Springfield, 1992. Atty. South County Democrats, Sangamon County, Ill.; founder, mgr., Springfield (Ill.) Area Youth Jazz Band; bd. mem. U. Ill., Springfield. Fellow Ednl. Policy program Inst. Ednl. Leadership, George Washington U., 1976-77. Mem. Ill. State Bar Assn. (chmn. sch. law sect. coun. 1983-84), Sangamon County Bar Assn. Avocations: skiing, tennis, fishing. Office: Gary Kerr Ltd 1020 S 7th St Springfield IL 62703-2417 Office Phone: 217-522-2244. E-mail: kerrltd@aol.com.

KERR, GUY HARDIE, lawyer; b. Dallas, Feb. 2, 1953; s. Ben J. Jr. and Marrian (Hardie) K.; m. Cindy Vaughan, May 29, 1976; children: L. Preston, Audrey. BS in Commerce, Washington & Lee U., 1975; JD, So. Meth. U., 1978. Bar: Tex. 1978, U.S. Dist. Ct. (no. dist.) Tex. 1978. Assoc. lawyer Locke Purnell Rain Harrell, Dallas, 1978-84; shareholder Locke, Liddell & Sapp, LLP, Dallas, 1985—2000; sr. v.p., gen. counsel Belo Corp., Dallas, 2000—03, sec., 2000—, sr. v.p. law and govt., 2003—. Office: Belo Corp 400 S Record St PO Box 655237 Dallas TX 75265-5237 Office Phone: 214-977-6692. Office Fax: 214-977-6603. E-mail: gkerr@belo.com.

KERR, JAMES WILSON, engineer; b. Balt., May 21, 1921; s. James W. and Laura Virginia (Wright) Kerr; m. Mary Thomas Montgomery, Feb. 25, 1945 (div.); children: April Kerr Miller, Catherine Kerr Wood(dec.), Wilson, Andrew; m. June Walker, Dec. 27, 1977 (div.); m. Janice White Bain, Jan. 19, 1985. BS with honors, Davidson Coll., 1942; MS, NYU, 1948; postgrad., Freiburg U., 1957—60, Brookings Inst., 1970, postgrad., 1975; PhD, Kennedy Western U., 1989. Registered profl. engr., Calif. Commd. 2d lt. U.S. Army, 1942, advanced through grades to lt. col., 1964, with inf., World War II, Korea, electronics staff Ft. Bragg, N.C., 1948-51, weapons rsch. N.Mex., 1953-57, adviser French Army, 1957-60, staff electronics Ft. Monroe, Va., 1960-62, rsch. mgr., divsn. dir. CD Pentagon, 1962-64, as civilian, 1964-81; asst. assoc. dir. Fed. Emergency Mgmt. Agy. for Rsch., 1981-85; sr. staff Michael Rogers, Inc., Winter Park, Fla., 1986—. V.p. Latherow & Co., Arlington, Va., 1965—86; dr. Mt. St. Helen's Tech. Office, 1980; radiol. officer Talbot County, Md., 1997—. Author: Korean-English Phrase Book, 1951, 19th Century Korea Postal Handbook, 1965, 2d edit., 1990; editor: Korean Philately mag., 1971—80, 1985—95; contbr. articles to profl. jours. Active Boy Scouts Am., 1933—; vol. fireman NY, 1946—48; chmn. libr. bd. Orangeburg, NY, 1946—48; advanced English instr. French Army, 1957—60; cons. Am. Nat. Red Cross Mus., 1968—85, Smithsonian Instn. Dept. Postal History, 1966—85, NSF, 1976—85; vol. fireman, fire commr. Fairfax County, 1975—81, chmn., 1977—81, Orange County, Fla., 1986—, pres., 1987—90, Pike County, Ala., 1994—98, Talbot County, Md., 1997—. Decorated Bronze Star with three oak leaf clusters, Purple Heart; recipient Silver Beaver award, Boy Scouts Am., 1956, James E. West award, 1994; Fulbright fellow, Japan, 1986. Fellow: AAAS (life), Explorers Club (emeritus); mem.: SAR (Fire Safety medal 1995), NAS (mem. various coms. 1962—87), NSPE, IEEE (sr.), Presdl. Nat. Def. Execs., Nat. Fire Protection Assn. (chmn. hosp. disaster com. 1973—86), Fed. Fire Coun., Internat. Assn. Fire Chiefs (chmn. rsch. com. 1969—88, chief sci. adviser 1982—86), Korean War Vets. Assn. (nat. bd. dirs. 1999), Black Forest Mardi Gras (Germany), Marshyhope Rod & Gun, Pentagon Officers Athletic Club, Nat. Comm. Club, Univ. Club Fla., Elks, Phi Beta Kappa, Delta Phi Alpha, Gamma Sigma Epsilon. Presbyterian. Home: PO Box 1537 Easton MD 21601-8929 Office: MR Inc 660 W Fairbanks Ave Winter Park FL 32789-4779

KERR, KIRKLYN M., academic administrator, veterinarian, pathologist; b. Green Bank, W.Va., May 1, 1936; married, 1957; 3 children. BS, U. W.Va., 1961, MS, 1966; DVM, Ohio State U., 1961; PhD in Vet. Pathology, Tex. A&M U., 1970. Diplomate Am. Coll. Vet. Pathology. Vet. practitioner North Side Vet. Clinic, Carlisle, Pa., 1961-62; rsch. assoc. vet. microbiology & pathology W.Va. U., Morgantown, 1962-65; form instr. to assoc. prof. vet. pathology Tex. A&M U. Coll. Vet. Medicine, 1965-72; assoc. prof. vet. pathobiology, dir. divsn. applied pathology Ohio State U. Coll. Vet. Medicine, 1972-78, dir. Ohio Agrl. Rsch. & Devel. Ctr., prof. poultry sci., 1987-91, prof. vet. preventive medicine, mem. faculty dept. preventive medicine, 1991-93; asst. dean rsch. and advanced studies, head vet. sci. La. State U. Sch. Vet. Medicine, La. State U. Agrl. Ctr., 1978-87; dean, dir. Coll. Agr. and Natural Resources U. Conn., Storrs Mansfield, 1993—. Mem. AVMA, Am. Assn. Avian Pathologists, Am. Coll. Vet. Pathologists, Farm Bur., Conn. Vet. Medicine Assn. Achievements include research in veterinary pathology, mycoplasmatacea, cancer research in animals. Office: U Conn Coll Agriculture & Natural Rsch 1376 Storrs Rd U-66 Storrs Mansfield CT 06269-4066 Office Phone: 860-486-2918. Business E-Mail: kirklyn.kerr@uconn.edu.

KERR, LOU C., foundation administrator; b. Oklahoma City, Jan. 24, 1937; d. Lem C. and M. Mae (Beck) Coker; m. Robert S. Kerr, Jr., July, 1972; children: Steven S., Laura Kerr Ogle. BS in Edn. and Health, DHL, Oklahoma City U. V.p. The Kerr Found., Inc., Oklahoma City, 1985-99, pres., 1999—. Dir. UMB Bank, Oklahoma City, Okla. City U.; founder, dir. Red Earth, Inc., Oklahoma City; adv. com. Breast Cancer Prevention and Treatment, 1994—; mem. Commn. on the Status of Women, 1994-99, 2000—; mem. Gov.'s State White House Conf. on Aging; mem. selection com. for Truman Found. Scholars, 1991-2000; mem. Social Security Disability Task Force; chair State Capitol Preservation Commn., 1990—; adv. coun. for gov. Okla. Environ. Concerns Coun., vice chair for gov., others; pres. Ind. Coll. Fund. V.p. fundraising campaign Allied Arts, 1985, v.p. exec. com., 1988—89, sec. exec. com., 1990—; mem. adv. coun. Women's Pres. Orgn.; mem., founder Atty. Gen.'s Consumer Adv. Com.; founder Bizzell Libr. Soc., U. Okla.; exec. com., v.p. Ctr. of the Am. Indian/Red Earth, 1983—; founder, chair Okla. Internat. Women's Forum, 1990—; nat. trustee Nat. Symphony Orch., Washington, 1999—; trustee NPR Found., Washington, 2001—; chair State Capitol Preservation Commn., Oklahoma City, 1990—; women's leadership bd., exec. com. Harvard U., Cambridge, 1999; 3d v.p. Red Lands coun. Girl Scouts U.S., 1993—97; v.p. Global Family Found.; mem. exec. com. Lyric Theatre of Okla., Inc., 1992—; adv. trustee Oklahoma City U.; v.p. Sister Cities, Inc, 1989—, exec. bd.; trustee Okla. Sch. Sci. and Math Found.; adv. dir. Tulsa Ballet Theatre; trustee United Meth. Found. for Christian Higher Edn., 1996—, others; nat. bd. Fund for Am., 1989—; bd. govs. Okla. Ctr. of Sci. and Arts, Inc., 1987—97; mem. adv. bd. U. Okla. Coll. Fine Arts,

1994—2000, U. Okla. Polit. Com., ANSER-Ctr. for Internat. Aerospace Coop., 1995—98, Hazel K. Goddess Fund for Stroke Rsch. in Women, Internat. Gymnastics Hall of Fame, 1997—; adv. bd. dirs. Okla. Breast Inst., 1992—97; bd. dirs., exec. com. Ctrl. Okla. Coun. of World Affairs; bd. dirs. Am. Cancer Soc., Oklahoma County unit, 1995—97, Internat. Women's Forum, Washington, 1992—; exec. bd. Norick Art Mus.; chair, exec. bd. Dulaney-Browne Libr. Soc.; bd. dirs., co-chair Okla. Ind. Colls. Found., 1994—; bd. trustees Totts Gap, 2000—; bd. vis. Okla. U. Health Sci. Ctr. Named to Okla. Commerce and Industry Hall of Honor, Oklahoma City U., 2000, Okla. City Pub. Sch. Found. Wall of Fame, 2001.; knighted into The Byzantine Order of the Holy Sepulchre; recipient Vis A Tergo award Women's Bus. Ctr., 1997, Women Who Make a Difference award Internat. Women's Forum, 1994, Cert. of Merit Vol. Action Com. of Cmty. Coun., Okla. Tourism and Recreation Indsl. Gov.'s award, Nat. Others award Salvation Army, Kirkpatrick Petree award for outstanding cmty. svc. Oklahoma City U. Music Theatre Soc., 1988, Gov.'s Arts award Okla. State Arts Coun., 1988, Woman of Distinction award, Girl Scouts Red Lands Coun., 2002, Leading Lights award Internat. Women's Forum, 2003; named March 2, 2005 as Lou C. Kerr Day, Okla. Gov. Henry. Fellow: Nat. Acad. Pub. Adminstrn. (hon.); mem.: Okla. Med. Rsch. Fdn. (bd. mem. 2000—), League of Hist. Am. Theatres (bd.mem. 2004—), NAPA (hon. fellow 2005). Democrat. Methodist. Office: The Kerr Foundation Inc 12501 N May Ave Oklahoma City OK 73120 Fax: (405) 749-2877. E-mail: lkerr@thekerrfoundation.org.

KERR, NANCY KAROLYN, pastor, mental health services professional; b. July 10, 1934; d. Owen W. and Iris Irene (Israel) K.; m. Richard Clayton Williams, June 28, 1953 (div.); children: Richard Charles, Donna Louise. Student, Boston U., 1953; AA, U. Bridgeport, 1966; BA, Hofstra U., 1967; postgrad. in clin. psychology, Adelphi U. Inst. Advanced Psychol. Studies, 1968-73; MDiv, Associated Mennonite Bibl. Sems., 1986. Ordained pastor Mennonite Ch., 1987; apptd. pastor Kamloops Presbytery Ch., Can., 1992. Pastoral counselor Nat. Coun. Chs., Jackson, Miss., 1964; dir. teen program Waterbury (Conn.) YWCA, 1966-67; intern in psychology N.Y. Med. Coll., 1971-72, rsch. cons., 1972-73; coord. home svcs., psychologist City and County of Denver, 1972-75; cons. Mennonite Mental Health Svcs., Denver, 1975-78; asst. prof. psychology Messiah Coll., 1978-79; mental health cons., 1979-81; called to ministry Mennonite Ch., 1981; pastor Cin. Mennonite Fellowship, 1981-83, mem. Gen. Conf. Peace and Justice Reference Coun., 1983-85; instr. Associated Mennonite Bibl. Sems., 1985; tchg. elder Assembly Mennonite Ch., 1985-86; pastor Pulaski Mennonite Ch., 1986-89; exec. dir., pastoral counselor Bethesda Counseling Svcs., Prince George B.C., 1989-99; pvt. practice, 1999—. Spl. ch. curriculum Nat. Coun. Chs., 1981; mem. Cen. Dist. Conf. Peace and Justice Com., 1981-89; mem. exec. bd. People for Peace, 1981-83. Sec. Ft. George Housing Soc., 2002—; clin. supr. St. Stevens. Sem., Edmonton, Canada; active Prince George Ministerial Assn., chmn. edn. and airport chapel coms., 1990—92; elder St. Giles Presbyn. Ch., 1996—2000; bd. dirs. Tri-County Counselling Clinic, Memphis, Mo., 1980—81, Boulder (Colo.) ARC, 1977—78, PLURA, B.C. Synod, 1995—98, Prince George Neighbor Link, 1995—99, Davis County Mins. Assn., v.p., 1988—89; mem. Waterbury Planned Parenthood Bd., 1964—67, MW Children's Home Bd., 1974—75, Mennonite Disabilities Respite Care Bd., 1981—86, Prince George Children's Svcs. com., 1992—94; adv. com. Prince George Planning Coun., 1997—98; mem. housing Prince George adv. bd. Mennonite Cen. Com., 1998—99. Mem. APA (assoc.), Can. Psychol. Assn., Soc. Psychologists for Study of Social Issues, Christian Assn. Psychol. Studies, Soc. Bibl. Lit. & Exegesis, sec. Ft. Geo. Bd., 2004-. Office: Nancy Kerr Counselling Svcs 110-154 Quebec St Prince George BC Canada V2L 1W2

KERR, REBECCA SPANGLER, science educator; b. Denver, Aug. 28, 1950; d. Richard W. and Caroline W. Spangler; m. Bruce E. Kerr, Oct. 13, 2000; children from previous marriage: Jamie Noah, Alison Tillotson. BS, Colo. State Univ., Ft. Collins, Colo., 1972. Cert. sci. tchg. 7th-12th Univ. No. Colo., 1992. Med. tech. St. Anthony Hosp., Denver, 1970—73; med. tech., microbiologist Colo. Univ. Hosp., Denver, 1973—79; med. tech., microbiologist instr. Weld County Hosp., Greeley, Colo., 1979—84; med. tech., lab. supr. Weld County Health Dept., Greeley, Colo., 1984—88; med. tech., supr. MetWest Regional Lab., Greeley, Colo., 1988—92; sci. educator Farmington Mcpl. Sch., Heights Middle Sch., Farmington, N.Mex., 1992—2004, Aztec (N.Mex.) Mcpl. Sch., 2004—05, Koogler Middle Sch., Aztec, N.Mex., 2004—05, Bloomfield Sch./Bloomfield H.S., N.Mex., 2005—. Bd. mem., pres. Friends of the Nature Ctr., Farmington, N.Mex., 1995—2004; bd. mem., sec. New Mex. Sci. Tchr. Assn., N.Mex., 1999—; bd. mem., commn. sec. Regional Sci. and Engrng. Fair, Farmington, N.Mex., 2000—. Contbr. articles pub. to profl. jour. Recipient Golden Broom award, Farmington Clean and Beautiful, 1995, First Annual Joan an Hy Rosner Environ. Edn. award, New Mex. State Land Office, 1998, Tchr. Yr., Rocky Mountain section, 2002, Honorable Mention for Excellence in Tchg. Nat. Resources in the Earth Sci., Am. Assn. Petroleum Geol. Found., 2002. Mem.: Nat. Edn. Assn. Avocations: painting, cross stitch, walking, ballet, fabric landscapes. Home: PO Box 830 Flora Vista NM 87415-0830 Business E-Mail: bkerr@hubwest.com.

KERR, SANDRIA NEIDUS, mathematics and computer science educator; b. Youngstown, Ohio, Oct. 1, 1940; d. Morris William and Ruth Neidus; m. William Clayton Kerr, June 9, 1963; children: Tamara Jean, Elizabeth Lynne. BA, Coll. Wooster, 1962; MA, Bryn Mawr Coll., 1964; PhD, Cornell U., 1971; postgrad., Inst. Retng. Computer Sci., Potsdam, N.Y., 1983, 84. Instr. math. Coll. Wooster, Ohio, 1963; teaching asst. dept. math. Cornell U., Ithaca, N.Y., 1963-67; vis. lectr. Chalmers U. Tech., Gothenburg, Sweden, 1967; collaborator Los Alamos (N.Mex.) Nat. Lab., 1984-92, cons., 1992-94, long-term vis. staff mem., 1995-96; asst. prof. dept. math. Winston-Salem (N.C.) State U., 1971-74, assoc. prof., 1974-82, prof. dept. math., computer sci., 1982-93, prof. computer sci., 1993—. Author curriculum and course materials, sci. software. Soprano Winston-Salem Symphony Chorale, treas., 1988-90, v.p., 1990-92. Recipient Wachovia Excellence in Teaching award Winston-Salem State U., 1990. Mem. IEEE Computer Soc., Am. Math. Soc., Assn. for Computing Machinery. Democrat. Avocations: reading, hiking. Home: 1938 Faculty Dr Winston Salem NC 27106-5219 Office: Winston Salem State U Dept Computer Sci Winston Salem NC 27110-0001 Office Phone: 336-750-2495.

KERR, STUART H., lawyer, think-tank executive; married; one child. BA, Trinity Coll., Hartford, Conn., 1980; JD, Georgetown U., 1987. Mem. Internat. Law Inst., 1982—, exec. dir., 1988—. Vis. scholar Manchester U., Eng., 1976-77. Office: Internat Law Inst 1055 Thomas Jefferson St NW Washington DC 20007-5259

KERR, THOMAS JEFFERSON, IV, academic official; b. Columbus, Ohio, Oct. 8, 1933; s. Thomas Jefferson and Ruth Glenora (Powell) K.; m. Donna Jean Lawton, June 11, 1955; children: Thomas Jefferson V, Cheryl Lee, Kathleen Anne. BS, Cornell U., 1956; MA, U. Buffalo, 1959; PhD (univ. fellow), Syracuse U., 1965; LHD (hon.), Otterbein Coll., 1984; LLD (hon.), Kendall Coll., 1996. Asst. prof., then prof. history Otterbein Coll., Westerville, Ohio, 1963-71, acting acad. dean, 1969-70, pres., 1971-84, Grant Med. Ctr. Found., Columbus, 1984-89, Kendall Coll., Evanston, Ill., 1990-96, pres. emeritus, 1996—. Chmn. Assn. Ind. Colls. and Univs., Ohio, 1976-78, Ohio Found. Ind. Colls., 1978-80 Mem. Greater Columbus Arts Coun., 1975-78; trustee Nationwide (now Gartmore) Funds, 1971-2005, Blue Cross Ctrl. Ohio, 1978-84, Grant Hosp., 1975-84, Ill. Restaurant Assn. Ednl. Found., 1991-96; mem. exec. com. Ill. Ind. Colls. and Univs., 1993-95; mem. Franklin County Draft Bd., 1969-71. Recipient Cokesbury Grad. Coll. Tchg. award, 1963. Mem. Masons, Rotary, Phi Kappa Phi, Kappa Phi Kappa, Omicron Chi Epsilon, Phi Eta Sigma. Republican. Methodist. Home: 4890 Smoketalk Ln Westerville OH 43081-4431

KERR, THOMAS ROBERT, lawyer; b. Covington, Ky., July 25, 1950; s. Thomas Hoover and Joann (Moffett) K.; m. Janice Duncan, May 26, 1973; children: Julie Ann, Jennifer Suzanne, Jill Mackenzie. BBA, U. Ky., 1972; JD, Chase Coll. Law, 1977. Bar: Ky. 1977, U.S. Dist. Ct. (ea. dist.) Ky. 1977. Sole practice, Covington, 1977—. Mem. pro-bono panel, Covington, 1980—; pub. defender Kenton County Pub. Defender's Office, Covington, 1977—. State rep. Ky. Gen. Assembly, Frankfort, 1985—; dir. Community Coun. on Religious Edn., Covington, 1985—; dir. Victims Assistance Network, Frankfort, 1985—, Calvary Christian Sch., Covington, 1981-87; deacon Calvary Bapt. Ch., Latonia, Ky., 1982; bd. dirs. No. Ky. Area Devel. Dist., 1988-93, Good Will, 1993—. With Air NG, 1971-77. Named One of Outstanding Young Men of Am., 1980, 83. Mem. Ky. Bar Assn., No. Ky. Bar Assn., Am. Trial Lawyers Assn., Ky. Acad. Trial Attys., Covington Christian Businessmans Assn. Clubs: Taylor Mill (Ky.) Swim (bd. dirs. 1983-87). Democrat. Baptist. Avocations: tennis, reading, various sports. Home: 5415 Old Taylor Mill Rd Covington KY 41015-2239 Office: 732 Scott St Covington KY 41011-2418 Office Phone: 606-431-2222. E-mail: thomasrkerr@yahoo.com.

KERR, WALTER BELNAP, retired electrical engineer, language researcher, consultant; b. Salt Lake City, Oct. 14, 1926; s. Walter Affleck and Marion Adeline (Belnap) K.; m. Raida Nebeker, May 2, 1952 (dec. Mar. 1992); children: Valerie Jean Kerr Merritt, Grant Mercer, Janice Arlene Kerr Hahn, Marilyn, m. Lillian Hamilton Nelson Ettinger, Oct. 1, 1992; children: Edgar Nelson Jr., James Nelson, Patricia Nelson Hardwick, Douglas Nelson. BA in French, U. Utah, 1951, BSEE, 1955; MBA in Internat. Bus., U. So. Calif., 1972. Electrical engr. Hughes Aircraft Co., L.A., 1955-61, 67-69; missile instrumentation engr. Hercules Inc., Salt Lake City, 1961-66, 84-89, Rockwell Internat., Anaheim, Calif., 1969-70; investment broker Titan Capital Corp., L.A., Ogden, Utah, 1970-79; electrical engr. White Motor Corp., Ogden, 1979-84; tax examiner IRS, Ogden, 1990-91, ret., 1991. Cons. Soc. for the Advancement of Good English, Pittsford, N.Y., 1985-86. Author: Instrumentation Methods, 1963, Stewart Lives, 2003, (card) Pocket Guide to Good English, 1984; columnist Correct Corner, Cherokee Scout newspaper, 1996-99; inventor. Juggler St. Benedict's Hosp., and various nursing homes, grade schs., h.s., univs., shopping ctrs. and chs., 1947—. With USN, 1945-46, 1st lt. U.S. Army, 1951-53. Mem. IEEE, The Planetary Soc., World Wildlife Fund, Soc. for the Preservation of English Lang. and Lit., Soc. for Alphanumeric Improvement, Sierra Club. Republican. Mem. Lds Ch. Avocations: tennis, juggling, planetoid research, computing, astronomical model building. Home: 395 Messer Rd Murphy NC 28906-9197 E-mail: mtntennispro99@yahoo.com.

KERR, WILLIAM ANDREW, lawyer, educator; b. Harding, W.Va., Nov. 17, 1934; s. William James and Tocie Nyle (Morris) K.; m. Elizabeth Ann McMillin, Aug. 3, 1968 AB, W.Va. U., 1955, JD, 1957; LLM, Harvard U., 1958; BD, Duke U., 1968. Bar: W.Va. 1957, Pa. 1962, Ind. 1980. Assoc. McClintic, James, Wise and Robinson, Charleston, W.Va., 1958; assoc. Schnader, Harrison, Segal and Lewis, Phila., 1961-64; asst. prof. law Cleve. State U., 1966-67, assoc. prof. law, 1967-68, Ind. U., Indpls., 1968-69, 72-74, prof., 1974—98, prof. emeritus, 1998—; contract atty. Indpls. Pub. Defender Agy., 1998—. Asst. U.S. atty. So. Dist. Ind., Indpls., 1969-72; exec. dir. Ind. Jud. Ctr., 1974-86; dir. research Ind. Pros. Attys. Council, 1972-74; mem. Ind. Criminal Law Study Commn., 1973-89, sec., 1973-83; reporter speedy trial com. U.S. Dist. Ct. (so. dist.) Ind., 1975-84; trustee Ind. Criminal Justice Inst., 1983-86; bd. dirs. Indpls. Lawyers Commn., 1975-77, Ind. Lawyers Commn., 1980-83; mem. records mgmt. com. Ind. Supreme Ct., 1983-86. Author: Indiana Criminal Procedure: Pretrial, 1991, Indiana Criminal Procedure: Trial, 2 vols., 1998. Bd. dirs. Ch. Fedn. Greater Indpls., 1979-87. Served to capt. JAGC, USAF, 1958-61. Decorated Air Force Commendation medal; Ford Found. fellow Harvard Law Sch., 1957-58; recipient Outstanding Prof. award Students Ind. U. Sch. Law, 1974, Disting. Service award Ind. Council Juvenile Ct. Judges, 1979, Outstanding Jud. Edn. Program award Nat. Council Juvenile and Family Ct. Judges, 1985. Mem. Ind. State Bar Assn., Indpls. Bar Assn., Phila. Bar Assn., W.Va. Bar Assn., Nat. Dist. Attys. Assn., Am. Judicature Soc., Fed. Bar Assn. (Outstanding Service award Indpls. chpt. 1975), Order of Coif, Phi Beta Kappa. Office: 55 Monument Cir Ste 1017 Indianapolis IN 46204-5901 Office Phone: 317-917-0608.

KERR, WILLIAM T., publishing and broadcasting executive; b. Seattle, Apr. 17, 1941; m. Mary Lang, Oct. 15, 1966; 1 child, Susannah Gaskill Kerr Adler. BA, U. Wash., 1963, Oxford U., Eng., 1965; MA, Harvard U., 1967, MBA, 1969. V.p. Dillon Read & Co., N.Y.C. and London, 1969-73; cons. McKinsey & Co., N.Y.C., 1973-79; v.p. New York Times Co., N.Y.C., 1979-91; pres. New York Times Mag. Group, N.Y.C., 1985-91; exec. v.p., pres. mag. group Meredith Corp., Des Moines, 1991-94, pres., chief oper. officer, bd. dirs., exec. com., 1994-96, pres., CEO, 1997-98, chmn., CEO, 1998—. Bd. dirs. Storage Tek Corp., Prin. Fin. Group, Maytag Corp.; trustee Oxford U. Press. Bd. dirs. Bus. Com. for the Arts; bd. visitors Henry B. Tippie Coll. Bus., U. Iowa. Mem.: Internat. Fedn. Periodical Press (chmn. bd. dirs.), Mag. Pubs. Am. (mem. adv. bd.), Lost Tree Club, Reform Club, Des Moines Club, Wakonda Club, Quogue Field Club, The Brook Club, Union Club, Century Assn. Roman Catholic. Office: Meredith Corp 1716 Locust St Des Moines IA 50309-3023

KERREBROCK, JACK LEO, aeronautics and astronautics engineering educator, department chairman; b. Los Angeles, Feb. 6, 1928; s. Oscar A. and Florence (Hoy) K.; m. Bernice Veverka, Apr. 11, 1953; children: Christopher, Nancy, Peter. Student, U. Oreg., 1946-47; BS, Oreg. State Coll., 1950; MS, Yale, 1951; PhD, Calif. Inst. Tech., 1956. Aero. research scientist Lewis Lab., NASA, Cleve., 1951-53; research fellow Calif. Inst. Tech., 1955-56; engrng. leader Oak Ridge Nat. Lab., 1956-58; sr. research fellow Calif. Inst. Tech., 1958-60; mem. faculty M.I.T., 1960-2001, Richard C. Maclaurin prof. aeros. and astronautics, 1975-96, dir. Gas Turbine and Plasma Dynamics Lab., 1969-78, head div. energy conversion and propulsion, 1970-81, head dept. aeros. and astronautics, 1978-81, 83-85, assoc. dean engrng., 1985-89, acting dean, 1989; assoc. adminstr. Office Aeros. and Space Tech., NASA, Washington, 1981-83. Mem. Air Force Sci. Adv. Bd., 1972-88; mem. NASA Rsch. and Tech. Adv. Com., 1975-77; mem. Aeronautics and Space Engrng. Bd. NRC, 1976-81, 92-95; mem. aero adv. com. NASA, 1978-81, Nat. Commn. on Space, 1984-86; mem. Air Force Studies Bd. NRC, 1990-92, com. on Earth-Orbit Propulsion, 1991-92; mem. adv. com. Space Sta. NASA, 1987-92; chmn. com. Space Sta. NRC, 1992-95; trustee Inst. for Def. Analysis, 1984-2000, Aerospace Corp., 1986-88; bd. dirs. Orbital Scis. Corp., Aerodyne Rsch. Inc. Recipient Gas Turbine Power award ASME, 1971, John Leland Atwood award ASEE and AIAA, 1992; Fairchild Disting. scholar Calif. Inst. Tech., 1990. Fellow AIAA (hon.); mem. Nat. Acad. Engrng., Am. Acad. Arts and Scis. Home: 108 Tower Rd Lincoln MA 01773-4403

KERREY, BOB (J. ROBERT KERREY), academic administrator, former senator; b. Lincoln, Nebr., Aug. 27, 1943; s. James and Elinor Kerrey; m. Sarah Paley; children: Benjamin, Lindsey, Henry. BS in Pharmacy, U. Nebr., 1965. Owner, founder, developer Grandmother's Restaurants, Omaha, 1972—75; owner, founder Prairie Life Ctr., Lincoln and Omaha, Nebr.; gov. State of Nebr., Lincoln, 1983—87; ptnr. Printon, Kane & Co., Lincoln, Nebr., 1987—89; U.S. Sen. from Nebraska, 1989—2001; pres. New Sch. U., N.Y.C., 2001—. Mem. Agrl., Nutrition & Forestry Com.; ranking minority mem. appropriations subcom. Treasury, Postal Svc. & Gen. Govt.; select com. Intelligence, Fin., Prodn. & Price Comptetitiveness Com.; commr. The Nat. Commn. on Terrorist Attacks Upon the U.S. (The 9-11 Commn.), 2002—04; co-chair (with Newt Gingrich) Nat. Com. for Quality Long-Term Care; leader 5 yr. writing challenge Nat. Commn. on Writing in Am.'s Schs. and Colls. Bd. dirs. Lincoln Ctr. Assn., Nebr. Easter Seal Soc. With USN, 1966—69, Vietnam. Decorated medal of Honor, Bronze Star, Purple Heart. Mem.: Lincoln C. of C., DAV, VFW, Am. Legion, Sertoma, Lions, Phi Gamma Delta. Congregationalist. Office: New Sch U Johnson and Kaplan Bldg Rm 800 66 W 12th St New York NY 10011

KERRICK, DAVID ELLSWORTH, lawyer; b. Caldwell, Idaho, Jan. 15, 1951; s. Charles Ellsworth and Patria (Olesen) K.; m. Juneal Casper, May 24, 1980; children: Peter Ellsworth, Beth Anne, George Ellis, Katherine Leigh. Student, Coll. of Idaho, 1969—71; BA, U. Wash., 1972; JD, U. Idaho, 1980. Bar: Idaho 1980, U.S. Dist. Ct. Idaho 1980, U.S. Ct. Appeals (9th cir.) 1981. Mem. Idaho Senate, 1990-96, majority caucus chmn., 1992-94, majority leader, 1994-96. Mem. S.W. Idaho Estate Planning Coun. Mem. ABA, ATLA, Idaho Bar Assn. (3d dist. pres. 1985-86), Idaho Trial Lawyers Assn., Canyon County Lawyers Assn. (pres. 1985), Elks. Republican. Presbyterian. Avocations: skiing, photography. Office: PO Box 44 Caldwell ID 83606-0044 Office Phone: 208-459-4574.

KERRIGAN, NANCY, professional figure skater, retired Olympic athlete; b. Woburn, Mass., Oct. 13, 1969; d. Daniel and Brenda Kerrigan; m. Jerry Solomon, 1995; children: Matthew Eric Solomon, Brian Russell Solomon. Bronze medalist World Championships, 1991, 92; U.S. nat. bronze medalist, 1991; U.S. nat. silver medalist, 1992; bronze medalist Olympic Games, Albertville, France, 1992; U.S. nat. champion, 1993; silver medalist Olympic Games, Lillehammer, Norway, 1994. Numerous commls. and product endorsements including Walt Disney Co., Reebok, Northwest Airlines, Frosted Cheerios, Ray Ban, Revlon, Aetna U.S. Healthcare, Salvino Bammers, AquaTrend, Tostitos, sportsinstruction.com; author: In My Own Words, 1996, (with Mary Spencer) Artistry on Ice, 2002; choreographer Halloween on Ice; performer: (video) Fairy Tales on Ice, Champions on Ice Tour, 1992-04; host Lifetime TV, 2002-04; color commentator, Comcast; TV spls. incl. Dreams on Ice, Breaking the Ice, Nancy Kerrigan and Friends, Holiday Celebration on Ice, One Enchanted Evening, Divas on Ice, Nancy Kerrigan's Winter Wonderland, Colors of Winter, 2003; TV host Nancy Kerrigan's World of Figure Skating (host), 2002, Grand Prix of Figure Skating, ISU Grand Prix Lifetime TV, 2003-04; released Shining Through as part of Reflections Off the Ice CD, 1999, Simply the Best as part of Tina Turner Tribute album, 2004; starred as Sandy in Grease on Ice, 1998-99, Broadway on Ice, Branson, Mo., 2000, Footloose on Ice, 2001; appeared in TV movies and shows including Boy Meets World, 1995, The Journey of Allen Strange, 1998, Ice Angel, Hollywood Squares, 2003, Family Feud, 2003, Lifetime Intimate Portrait, 2004, (voice) The Easter Egg Adventure. Spokesperson Lions Club, 1994, Children's Trust Fund, 1997, Spalding Rehab. Hosp., MADD, Fight for Sight; founder, benefactor Nancy Kerrigan Found.; hon. chair Nancy Kerrigan Golf Classic, 2000—; bd. dirs. Ice Castle Theatre, Myrtle Beach, S.C. Recipient Bronze medal World Figure Skating Championships, 1991, Silver medal, 1992, Bronze medal U.S. Pro Championships, 1997, Bronze medal Goodwill Games, 2000, Outstanding Mother award Mother's Day Found., 2001, Henry Iba Outstanding Citizen-Athlete award Rotary Club, Tulsa, 2002. Office: care of StarGames Bldg 1 40 Salem St Lynnfield MA 01940 Office Phone: 781-224-9655.

KERR-NOWLAN, DONNA COURTNEY, pre-school administrator; b. Wellsboro, Pa., Sept. 25, 1940; d. Sylvan LaRue and Mildred Fowler Kerr; children from previous marriage: Craig Kerr Nowlan, Brent Fowler Nowlan. Cert., Jean Summers Bus. Sch., N.Y., 1956; student, Corning C.C., Mansfield (Pa.) State Tchrs. Coll., 1960. Owner, bridal cons. Bridal Bower, 1960—63; owner Victorian Fingerlakes Tour Guides, 1963—72; dir., owner Building Block Nursery & Pre-K, Elmira, NY, 1969—. Coord. Civil War prison camp Chemung County C. of C., Elmira, 2000—; pres. Hist. Near Westside Bd. Dirs. and Assn., 1985—89; mem. planning commn. City of Elmira; mem. Chemung County Planning Bd.; hostess Orchids and Candlelight Arnot Ogden Hosp., 1991—; dir. Found. for Ctrl. Diocese Episcopal Ch., Syracuse, NY, 1981. Named Woman of Achievement, Chemung County Coun. of Women, 1993; named to Legion of Honor, Chaplin of Four Chaplins, Valley Forge, Pa., 1994; recipient Cmty. Svc. award, Hist. Near Westside Neighborhood Assn., 1982, cert. of appreciation, Elmira Coll., 1985, 1994, Robert Goostrey award, Chemung County C. of C., 1990. Mem.: Twin Tier Jazz Soc. (bd. dirs. 1989—, pres. 2000—), Hal Roach Soc. (bd. dirs. 1987—), Soroptimist Internat. (pres. Elmira chpt. 1989—99, Outstanding Cmty. Svc. award 1994, Outstanding Club Mem. 1995, Outstanding Cmty. Vol. 1996, Outstanding Vol. Svc. award 1986). Republican. Episcopalian. Avocations: walking, gourmet cooking, reading, painting. Home: 715 Winsor Ave Elmira NY 14905 Office: Building Block Pvt Nursery Sch 308 College Ave Elmira NY 14901 Personal E-mail: dnowlan@stny.rr.com.

KERRY, CAMERON F., lawyer; b. Washington, Sept. 6, 1950; s. Richard John and Rosemary (Forbes) K.; m. Kathy B. Weinman, June 28, 1983; children: Jessica Weinman Kerry, Laura Weinman Kerry. BA cum laude, Harvard U., 1972; JD magna cum laude, Boston Coll., 1978. Bar: Mass., D.C. Polit. cons., writer, Cambridge, Mass., 1973-76; law clerk to Hon. Elbert P. Tuttle U.S. Ct. Appeals (5th cir.), Atlanta, 1978-79; assoc. Wilmer, Cutler & Pickering, Washington, 1979-82; mem. Mintz, Levin, Cohn, Ferris, Glovsky & Popeo, P.C., Boston, 1983—. Adj. prof. law Suffolk U. Law Sch. Editor book chpts.; mem. Boston Coll. Law Review, 1977-78; contbr. articles to profl. jours. Campaign mgr. Paul Guzzi for Sec. State, Newton, Mass., 1974; campaign mgr. John Kerry for Lt. Gov., Boston, 1982; advisor and nat. surrogate John Kerry for Pres., 2003-04; trustee Boston Police Found., 1993-98; coop. counsel Civil Liberties Union Mass., Boston, 1985; mem. Brookline (Mass.) Dem. Town Com., 1985—; dir. New Eng. Nordic Skiing Assn., 1999—. Recipient Internat. Security Mgrs. Assn. award, 1993, citation Nat. Press Photographers Assn., 1990. Mem. ABA, Mass. State Bar Assn., Boston Bar Assn., Def. Rsch. Inst. Office: Mintz Levin Cohn Ferris Glovsky and Popeo PC 1 Financial Ctr Fl 38 Boston MA 02111-2621

KERRY, JOHN FORBES, senator; b. Denver, Dec. 11, 1943; s. Richard John and Rosemary (Forbes) K.; m. Julia Stimson Thorne, May 23, 1970 (div. July 25, 1988), children: Alexandra, Vanessa; m. Teresa Heinz, May 25, 1995. BA, Yale U., 1966; MA, JD, Boston Coll., 1976; PhD (hon.), U. Ma., 1988. Bar: Mass. 1976. Nat. coordinator Vietnam Vets. Against The War, 1969-71; asst. dist. atty. Middlesex (Mass.) County, 1976-79; ptnr. firm Kerry & Sragow, Boston, 1979-82; lt. gov. State of Mass., 1983—85; U.S. senator from Mass., 1985—; chmn. Dem. Senatorial campaign com., 1986-88; Democratic candidate for U.S. pres., 2004. Mem. Fgn. Rels. Com., Fgn. Rels. subcom. Internat. Ops., Sen. Dem. Steering & Coordination Com.; mem. Com. Banking, Housing & Urban Affairs, ranking minority mem. Com. Small Bus., Select Com. on Intelligence; ranking minority mem. Commerce, Sci. & Transp. subcom. on Oceans & Fisheries. Author: The New Soldier, 1971, The New War: The Web of Crime That Threatens America's Security, 1997, A Call to Service: My Vision for a Better America, 2003. Democratic candidate for Congress from 5th Mass. Dist., 1972; bd. vistors Walsh Sch. Fgn. Service, Georgetown U. Served to lt. (j.g.) USNR, 1966-69. Decorated Silver Star; decorated Bronze Star with oak leaf cluster, Purple Hearts (3) Mem. Vietnam Veterans Am. (founder). Democrat. Roman Catholic. Achievements include Democratic candidate for Pres. of the US, 2004. Office: US Senate 304 Russell Senate Bldg Washington DC 20510-0001*

KERSAINT, GLADIS, mathematics professor, researcher; BS in Math., U. Miami, Fla., 1990; MS in Math. Edn., U. Miami, 1992; PhD in Math. Edn., Ill. State U., 1998. Mktg. sales asst. IBM, Coral Gables, Fla., 1986—89; math. tchr. Miami-Dade Pub. Schs., 1990—95; instr., rsch. assoc. Ill. State U., Normal, 1995—98; asst. prof. U. South Fla., Tampa, 1998—2004, assoc. prof., 2004—. Author: Meaningful Urban Education Reform: Confronting the Crisis in Education, 2005. Mem.: Nat. Coun. Tchrs. Math., Assn. Math. Tchr. Educators. Home: 1309 Horsemint Ln Zephyrhills FL 33543 Office: U South Fla 4202 E Fowler Ave EDU162 Tampa FL 33620

KERSCHNER, LEE R(ONALD), academic administrator, political scientist, educator; b. May 31, 1931; m. Helga Koller, June 22, 1958; children: David, Gabriel, Riza. BA in Polit. Sci. (Univ. fellow), Rutgers U., 1953; MA in Internat. Relations (Univ. fellow), Johns Hopkins U., 1958; PhD in Polit. Sci. (Univ. fellow), Georgetown U., 1964. From instr. to prof. polit. sci. Calif. State U., Fullerton, 1961-69, prof., 1988—; state univ. dean Calif. State Univs. and Colls. Hdqrs., Long Beach, 1969-71, asst. exec. vice chancellor, 1971-76, vice chancellor for adminstrv. affairs, 1976-77, vice chancellor acad. affairs, 1987-92; exec. dir. Colo. Commn. on Higher Edn., Denver, 1977-83, Nat. Assn. Trade and Tech. Schs., 1983-85, Calif. Commn. on Master Plan for Higher Edn., 1985-87; interim pres. Calif. State U., Stanislaus, 1992-94, spl. asst. to the chancellor, 1994-97; exec. vice chancellor Minn. State Colls. and Univs., St. Paul, 1996-97; vice chancellor emeritus Calif. State U., 1997—. Mem. Calif. Student Aid Commn., 1993-96; cons. in field. Mem. exec. com.

Am. Jewish Com., Denver, 1978-83; internat. bd. dirs. Amigos de las Americas, 1982-88 (chmn. 1985-87). Served with USAF, 1954-58; col. Res., ret. Home: PO Box 748 Weimar CA 95736-0748 Office Phone: 530-878-0312. E-mail: lkconslt@pacbell.net.

KERSEY, TALANA S., mental health counselor; b. Joliet, Ill., May 5, 1947; d. Elgin L. and Virgil D. McMahon; m. Joel Allen Kersey, Dec. 7, 1991; children: Michelle Talana, Eric Charles, Kelly Brooke. BA in Edn., Ariz. State U., 1970; MS in Mental Health Counseling, Nova Southeastern U., 1996. Lic. mental health counselor, real estate salesman, Fla.; cert. tchr., Fla. Secondry tchr. Orange County Schs., Orlando, Fla.; acad. instr. Brevard Start Ctr., Titusville, Fla.; eligibility specialist Ill. Aid to Families and Dependent Children, Apopka; tchr. C.H. Price Mid. Sch., Interlachen, Fla.; instr., job developer displaced homemaker program Santa Fe C.C., Gainesville, Fla.; therapist, mental health counselor Meridian Behavioral Healthcare, Inc., Gainesville, 1996—, Nick Ungson MD, P.A., Leesburg, Fla. Pvt. tutor, Gainesville, 1991-93. Vol. tchr. Head Start, Phoenix, 1970, Sparc, shelter for abused women, Gainesville, 1989; mem. planning bd. Gainesville Area Women's Network, 1990. Mem. ACA, NEA, Real Estate Edn. Assn. Avocations: piano, decorating, sewing. Office: Meridian Behavioral Healthcare 4300 SW 13th St Gainesville FL 32608

KERSNOWSKI, FRANK LOUIS, modern language educator; b. Washington, May 6, 1934; m. Alice Hughes, May 11, 1984; 1 child, Maud Louise. BA, U. Tenn., 1957, MA, 1959; PhD, U. Kans., 1963. Asst. prof. Ohio U., Athens, 1962-64; from asst. prof. to prof. English, Trinity U., San Antonio, 1964—2002. Author: The Outsiders, 1975, John Montague, 1974; editor: (poetry) T. Rivera's Always, 1973; (collection) Robert Graves, 1989, Into the Labyrinth, 1989; co-editor (collection) Conservations with Henry Miller, 1994, (collection) Selected Essays on the Humor of Lawrence Durrell, 1994, The Early Poetry of Robert Graves, 2002. Avocations: classic car restoration, the story of food. Home: 236 W Mandalay Dr San Antonio TX 78212-1503

KERSTETTER, WAYNE ARTHUR, law educator; b. Chgo., Dec. 1, 1939; s. Arthur Edward and Lillian (Asplund) K. BA, U. Chgo., 1964, JD, 1967. Bar: Ill. 1968. Gen. counsel Ill. Drug Abuse Treatement Program, 1968—70; admin. and rsch. assoc. Ctr. for Studies in Crimincal Justice, U. Chgo. Law Sch., 1970—72; asst. commr. N.Y. Police Dept., N.Y.C., 1972-73; supt. Ill. Bur. Investigation, Chgo., 1973-76; assoc. dir. Ctr. for Studies in Criminal Justice, U. Chgo., 1976-78; assoc. prof. criminal justice, dept. criminal justice U. Ill., Chgo., 1978-2000. Sr. rsch. fellow Am. Bar Found., Chgo., 1982-93, fellow, 1993—; cons. U.S. Civil Rights Commn., U. Chgo., ABT Assocs., Univ. Research Assocs., Police Found. Mem. transition team Mayor Washington, Chgo., 1983, Criminal Justice Project of Cook County, 1987. Served with USNR, 1962-64. Rsch. grantee Nat. Inst. Justice, 1976, Chgo. Bar Found., 1979-80, Am. Bar Found., 1983; fellow Ctr. for Studies in Criminal Justice, U. Chgo. Law Sch., 1978-82. Personal E-mail: wkerstett@aol.com.

KERSTIENS, GENE J., mathemagenician, consultant; b. Phoenix, Nov. 7, 1926; s. Joseph Henry and Evangeline Kerstiens; m. Dorothy Louise Bishop, Jan. 27, 1951; children: Rita, Theresa, Mark, Frank, Helen, John, Christopher, Fredryc. BA, U. Portland, 1951; MA, U. Ariz., 1952; EdD, Nova U., Ft. Lauderdale, Fla., 1978. Prof. English El Camino Coll., Torrance, Calif., 1956—71; vis. prof. edn. Western Wash. State U., Bellingham, 1971—72; dean learning assistance El Camino Coll., Torrance, 1972—86; acting dir. Nat. Ctr. for Developmental Edn., Boone, NC, 1987—88; dir. learning assistance Scottsdale C.C., Ariz., 1988—92; dir. Andragogy Assocs., Torrance, 1992—. Cons. adult learning programs Pub. Broadcasting Svc., N.Y.C., 1970—73; developer, pub. English Modular Minicourses, 1972, Academic Skills series, 1977; pub. Study Behavior Inventory, 1994. Author: Study-Reading for College Courses, 1968 (Merit award, 1970); compiler (monograph) Junior-Community College Reading/Study Skills: An Annotated Bibliography, 1970; editor: Educulture, 1971—85; mem. editl. bd. Jour. Developmental Edn., 1980—. Mem. ACLU. With U.S. Army, 1945—47. Fellow: Am. Coun. of Developmental Edn. Assns.; mem.: Coll. Reading and Learning Assn. (pres. 1971, Lifetime Achievement award 1981). Avocations: sailing, travel, hiking, parachuting, motorcycling. Home and Office: Andragogy Associates 3434 W 227 Pl Torrance CA 90505-2632

KERTÉSZ, IMRE, writer; b. Budapest, Hungary, Nov. 9, 1929; With Világosság, Budapest, Romania, 1948—51. Author: Sorstalanság, 1975, A nyomkeresö: Két regény, 1977, A kudarc, 1988, Kaddis a meg nem született gyermekért, 1990, Az angol lobogó, 1991, Gályanapló, 1992, A holocaust mint kultúra: három előadás, 1993, Jegyzőkönyv, 1993, Valaki más: a változás krónikája, 1997, A gondolatnyi csend, amíg a kivégzőosztag újratölt, 1998, A számüzött nyelv, 2001. Active Mil. Svc., 1951—53. Recipient Brandenburger Literaturpreis, 1995, Leipziger Buchpreis zur Europaischen Verstandigung, 1997, Herder-Preis, 2000, WELT-Literaturpreis, 2000, Ehrenpreis der Robert-Bosch-Stiftung, 2001, Hans Sahl-Preis, 2002, Nobel prize in lit., 2002. Office: Northwestern U Press 625 Colfax St Evanston IL 60208-4210

KERTH, LEROY T., physics professor; b. Visalia, Calif., Nov. 23, 1928; s. Lewis John and Frances (Niccolls) K.; m. Ruth Lorraine Littlefield, Nov. 19, 1950; children: Norman Lewis, Randall Thomas, Christine Jane, Bradley Niccolls. AB in Physics, U. Calif., Berkeley, 1950, PhD, 1957. Mem. staff Lawrence Berkeley Lab, U. Calif., Berkeley, 1950-59, sr. scientist, 1959-61; assoc. prof. physics U. Calif., Berkeley, 1961-65, prof., 1965-93, prof. emeritus, 1993—, assoc. dean Coll. Letters and Scis., 1966-70, spl. asst. to chancellor, 1970-71, assoc. dir. for info. and computing scis. div., 1983-87, assoc. lab. dir. for gen. scis., Lawrence Berkeley Lab., 1987-89, assoc. lab. dir. sci. and tech. resources, Lawrence Berkeley Lab., 1990-92. Fellow Am. Phys. Soc. Home: 5 Los Conejos Orinda CA 94563-2214 Office: U Calif Lawrence Berkeley Lab Berkeley CA 94720-0001 Business E-Mail: ltkerth@lbl.gov.

KERTZ, HUBERT LEONARD, telephone company executive; b. San Francisco, July 11, 1910; s. Hubert J. and Laura V. (Seavey) K.; m. Paula Schmoranzer, Mar. 22, 1991; children: Brenda L., Pamela. AB, Stanford, 1934, E.E., 1936. With Pacific Tel. & Tel. Co., 1926-42, 46-61, asst. v.p., 1953-58, v.p., 1958-61; asst. v.p. AT&T, 1961-64, v.p., 1964-75; pres., mng. dir. Am. Bell Internat. Inc., 1975-79; cons., 1980—. Bd. dirs. Teltone Corp., Coasteom Corp. Served from lt. (j.g.) to comdr. USNR, 1942-46, PTO. Decorated Bronze Star. Fellow IEEE; mem. Soc. Calif. Pioneers, Met. Club N.Y.

KERTZER, DAVID ISRAEL, anthropology professor, writer; b. Feb. 20, 1948; m. Susan Dana, May 24, 1970; children: Molly, Seth. BA, Brown U., 1969; PhD, Brandeis U., 1974. From asst. prof. to prof. Bowdoin Coll., Brunswick, Maine, 1973-89, Kenan prof., 1989-92; Dupee prof. Brown U., Providence, 1992—. Author: Ritual, Politics, and Power, 1988, Sacrificed for Honor, 1993, Politics and Symbols, 1996, The Kidnapping of Edgardo Mortara, 1997 (Nat. Jewish Book award, Nat. Book award finalist), The Popes Against the Jews, 2001, Prisoner of the Vatican, 2004. Office: Brown U Dept Anthropology 128 Hope St Box 1921 Providence RI 02912-1921 Business E-Mail: David_Kertzer@brown.edu.

KERTZMAN, MITCHELL E., software company executive; LHD (hon.), U. Mass., Lowell. Founder Computer Solutions, 1974; founder, CEO Powersoft Corp., 1993; chmn. bd. dirs., CEO Sybase, Inc., Emeryville, Calif., 1995-98; pres., CEO Liberate Techs., Redwood Shores, Calif., 1998—2003; ptnr. Hummer Winblad Venture Partners, San Francisco, 2003—. Bd. dirs. Sybase, Inc., Shiva Corp., CNET, Interconnect Syss., Inc., Bridgestream, Sapias, Five9, ActiveGrid, Palamida, Akimbi Sys. Founder, chmn. Mass. Tech. New Commonwealth; mem. N.Y. State Commn. Indsl. Competitiveness, chair task force indsl. policy. Recipient Inc. Mag. and Ernst & Young's New England Entrepreneur of Yr. award, 1993, Disting. Achievement award Tech. Unit New England B'nai B'rith, 1993. Mem.: Mass. Software Coun. (pres. 1994—96), Am. Electronics Assn. (chmn. 1990). Office: Hummer Winblad Venture Partners 2 S Park 2nd Fl San Francisco CA 94107 Office Phone: 415-979-9600. Office Fax: 415-979-9601. E-mail: mkertzman@humwin.com.*

KERWIN, SEAN MICHAEL, biochemist, educator; b. Phila., Aug. 31, 1962; s. James Francis and Anna May Kerwin; m. Wendi David Teter, Dec. 27, 2002; children: Sarah Jane, Zachary Joseph David, Colleen Shea. BS, U. Notre Dame, 1989; PhD, U. Calif. Berkeley, 1989. Postdoctoral rschr. U. Calif., San Francisco, 1989—91; asst. prof. medicinal chemistry U. Tex., Austin, 1991—97, assoc. prof. medicinal chemistry, 1991—. Co-editor-in-chief (journal) Current Medicinal Chemistry-Anti-Cancer Agents. Mem.: Am. Chem. Soc. Roman Catholic. Achievements include discovery of Novel Rearrangements of aza-enediynes; patents for Anti-Cancer and Osteoporosis Drug Design. Avocation: sailing. Office: U Tex 1 University Station A1935 Austin TX 78712 E-mail: skerwin@mail.utexas.edu.

KERWIN, WALTER THOMAS, JR., career officer, consultant; b. West Chester, Pa., June 14, 1917; s. Walter Thomas and Mary Joseph (Farra) K.; m. Barbara Walker Connell, July 10, 1940 (dec. 1980); children: Bruce Richard, Ann Walker; m. Marion Thompson McCutcheon, Oct. 27, 1984. BS, U.S. Mil. Acad., 1939; postgrad., Command and Gen. Staff Coll., 1948, M (hon.) in Mil. Art and Sci., 1978; postgrad., Armed Forces Staff Coll., 1953, U.S. Army War Coll., 1957, Nat. War Coll., 1960; LLD (hon.), U. Akron, 1976. Commd. 2d lt. U.S. Army, 1939, advanced through grades to gen., 1973, chief nuc. activities SHAPE NATO Paris, 1963—65, commdg. gen. 3d armored divsn. Frankfurt, Germany, 1965—66, asst. dep. chief staff ops. gen. staff Washington, 1966—67, chief staff mil. asst. command Saigon, Vietnam, 1967—68, dep. chief staff pers. gen. staff Washington, 1969—72, commdg. gen. continental army command Norfolk, Va., 1973, commdg. gen. forces command Atlanta, 1973—74, vice chief staff Washington, 1974—78. Cons. Martin Marietta Corp., Bethesda, Md., 1978-94, Lockheed-Martin, 1994-97; assoc. dir. ops. Los Alamos (N.Mex.) Sci. Lab., 1953-56; bd. dirs. Gen. Employment Enterprises, Oakbrook, Ill., 1984-2001; mem. bd. mgrs. Army Emergency Relief, 1982—; mem. sci. adv. group Def. Nuc. Agy., 1980-86; mem. tactical tech. adv. group Land Warfare Def. Advance Rsch. Projects, 1983-88; Dept. Def. proxy dir. DKI Electronics-Electro, Tec Corp., Precision Products, Inc., Martin Electronics Fri Corp., Triangle Microwave Inc., 1986-89. Chmn. Army Air Force Mut. Aid Assn., Arlington, Va., 1982-97, chmn. emeritus 1997—; bd. advisors Army Hist. Found., 1995-97, bd. dirs.; mem. coun. trustees Assn. U.S. Army, 1979-82; bd. visitors Nat. Def. U., 1982-90. Recipient Disting. Svc. medal Commonwealth of Pa., 1975, Outstanding Alumnus award U.S. Army War Coll., 1997, Disting Grad. award Assn. Grads. U.S. Mil. Acad., 2003, numerous mil. awards and decorations; named to Henderson Hall of Fame, West Chester, Pa., 1991, Res. Officers Assn. of U.S. Minute Man Hall of Fame, 1978; honored with Papal Benemerenti medal Pope Paul VI, 1977; named in honor of Walter Thomas Kerwin Forces Command Hdqs. Conf. Rm., Ft. McPherson, Ga., 2003. Fellow: Nat. Def. U. Capstone Program (emeritus); mem.: U.S. Field Arty. Assn. (pres. 1980—97), West Point Soc. (Castle-Duty Hon. Country award 1993, Artillery Ctr. Auditorium, Ft. Sill, Okla., dedicated Kerwin Hall 2001), Am. Def. Preparedness Assn. (comdr. Chief award 1984). Avocations: fishing, wilderness hiking.

KERWIN, WILLIAM JAMES, electrical engineering educator, consultant; b. Portage, Wis., Sept. 27, 1922; s. James William and Nina Elizabeth Kerwin; m. Madolyn Lee Lyons, Aug. 31, 1947; children: Dorothy E., Deborah K., David W. BS, U Redlands, 1948; MS, Stanford U., 1954, PhD, 1967. Aero. research scientist NACA, Moffett Field, Calif., 1948-59; chief measurements research br. NASA, Moffett Field, Calif., 1959-62, chief space tech. br., 1962-64, chief electronics research br., 1964-70; head electronics dept. Stanford Linear Accelerator Ctr., 1962; prof. elec. engring. U. Ariz., Tucson, 1969-85, prof. emeritus, 1986—. Cons. Power Electronics, 1980—. Author: (with others) Active Filters, 1970, Handbook Measurement Science, 1982, Instrumentation and Control, 1990, Handbook of Electrical Engineering, 1993, 97; contbr. articles to profl. jours.; patentee in field. Served to capt. USAAF, 1942-46. Recipient Invention NASA, 1969, 70; recipient fellow NASA, 1966-67 Fellow IEEE (Centennial medal 1984) Home: 1981 W Shalimar Way Tucson AZ 85704-1250 Office: U Ariz Dept Elec And Computer Engring Tucson AZ 85721-0001 Office Phone: 520-297-8529. Personal E-mail: wkerwin@theriver.com.

KERXTON, ALAN SMITH, lawyer; b. Balt., Mar. 19, 1938; s. Benjamin and Eva (Smith) Kerxton; m. Leslie Lurie, Aug. 2, 1961; children: Amy Lynn, Susan Deborah, Katherine Diane. BA, Ohio State U., 1960, JD, 1962. Bar: DC 1963, Md. 1965. Atty. corp. reorganization br. SEC, Washington, 1963-66; pvt. practice Washington, Potomac, Md., 1966—; prin. Ezrin, West and Kerxton, Chartered, 1976-84, Dunnells and Duval, Washington, 1990-93, Holland and Knight, Washington, 1994-97; of counsel Stein, Sperling, Rockville, Md., 1998—. Lectr. Cath. U. Am. Law Sch., 1973. With U.S. Army, 1962—63. Mem.: Montgomery County Bar Assn., DC Bar Assn. Home: 11815 Beekman Pl Potomac MD 20854-2177 Office: 25 W Middle Ln Rockville MD 20850-2214 Office Phone: 301-838-3213. E-mail: akerxton@steinsperling.com.

KERZ, LOUISE, historian; b. NYC, Sept. 16, 1936; d. Louis and Catharine Sohn; m. Leo Kerz, Apr., 1965 (dec. 1976); children: Jonathan, Antony; m. Al Hirschfeld, Oct. 1996 (dec. 2003). Student, Queens Coll., 1954-56, Marymount Coll., 1972-74. Theatre producer Leo Kerz Prodns., N.Y.C., 1960-74; theatrical curator N.Y. Cultural Ctr., N.Y.C., 1974, Theatre of Max Reinhardt, 1974, N.Y. Pub. Libr. Lincoln Ctr., N.Y.C., 1984, Calif. Mus. Sci. and Industry, L.A., 1985, The Demille Dynasty, 1984; rsch. cons. CBS: On the Air, 1978, Smith-Hemion TV Prodns., L.A., 1987—, The Phantom of the Opera, 1995. Dir. rsch. Greengage Prodns., Julie Andrews/Greengage Prodns., LA, 1988, Tony Awards Telecast 50th Anniversary Show, 1947—96; rsch. cons. TV Acad. Hall of Fame and Tony Awards telecasts, 1993—96; dir. rights and permissions The Line King (The Al Hirschfeld Story-nominated for Oscar 1996) NY Times, TV documentary; rsch. historian six-part TV series Broadway, 1997; spl. cons. The Demille Family-Documentary Am. Movie Channel, 1997; exec. cons., liaison Hirschfeld Exhbns., catalogs, books and events Mus. of City of NY, cons. Hirschfeld's NY exhibit, 2001; cons. Hirschfeld's Hollywood exhibit Acad. Motion Picture Arts & Scis., Beverly Hills, Calif., 2001; cons. catalogues to exhibits Pub. Harry N. Abrams, 2001; exhibit organizer V&A Theatre Mus., Nat. Theatre Southbank, London, 2005, Al Hirschfeld's Brits on Broadway; organizer London 2005 Hirschfeld Celebration, V&A Theatre Mus. and Royal Nat. Theatre at Southbank; curator book Hirschfeld's British Aisles, 2005. Assoc. prodr. on Broadway: Rhinoceros, 1961; contbg. editor: N.Y.C. Access, 1983; picture editor The DeMilles: An American Family, 1988, Al Hirschfeld: On Line, 1998, curator, dir. Exhibit Broadway, 1995, curator, photographer (exhibitions) Hirschfeld Celebration at Leica Gallery, N.Y.C., 2002; one-woman shows include The Leica Gallery, N.Y.C., 2002; curator, writer Hirschfelds British Aisles, 2005. Vol. Persian Gulf war Am. Jewish Congress, Israel, 1991; elected mem. Tony Awards nominating com. Am. Theatre Wing, 2000-2003; co-chair Al Hirschfeld Centennial, assoc. prodr. Al Hirschfeld 100th Birthday Salute, 2003, dir. Al Hirschfeld Found., 2004-. Mem. Theatre Libr. Assn. Democrat. Address: c/o Al Hirschfeld 122 E 95th St New York NY 10128-1705

KERZNER, ROBERT ALLEN, marketing company executive, former insurance company executive; b. N.Y.C., May 31, 1952; s. Benny and Ann Bd. (Smith) K; m. Sandi D. Delgobbo, June 22, 1975; children: Brian, Benjamin. BS, Cen. Conn. State U., New Britain, 1974. CLU, ChFC. Account exec. Hartford Life Ins. Co., Bridgeport, Conn., 1974-76, sales mgr., 1976-78, regional sales mgr., 1979-91; regional v.p., 1991-94; v.p. individual life-sales office distbn. Hartford Life Ins. Co., Bridgeport, Conn., 1994—98; sr. v.p. Individual Life, The Hartford Fin. Services Group, 1998—2001, exec. v.p., 2001—04; pres. Woodbury Fin. Services, 2001—04; pres., CEO LIMRA Internat. Inc., Windsor, Conn., 2004—. Instr. cert. ins. counselor, 1988—; platform speaker Semi-ann conf. Ind. Ins. Agts. Conn., 1987, 90. Treas. Cong. Beth El, Fairfield, Conn., 1987-88, pres., 1988-90. Mem. Nat. Assn. Life Underwriters, CLUs (mem. bd. 1978-80). Republican. Jewish. Avocations: tennis, woodworking. Office: LIMRA Internat Inc 300 Day Hill Rd Windsor CT 06095

KES, VICKI, museum director; b. Bessemer, Ala., June 2, 1952; d. Gerald Vance and Marjorie Jean (Bush) George; m. Pieter A. Kes, Sr., Nov., 2002; children: Alissa Henson, Rebecca Hubbard. Office worker Mining Corp. of the South, Vance, Ala., 1978-79; artist, sign painter Bob's Sign Shop, Midfield, Ala., 1980—; dir. Iron & Steel Mus. of Ala., McCalla, 1980—. Program completion Office of Mus Programs, Smithsonian, Washington, 1987. Artist (book) Tannehill Crafts, 1982. Events Planner Ala. Reunion State of Ala., Montgomery, 1989. Recipient Top 20 Events in the South East award SE Tourism Soc., Atlanta, 1986-87, 88, 91, Head Start Vol. award, 1994. Mem. Ala. Preservation Alliance, Soc. Indsl. Archaeology, Nat. Trust for Hist. Preservation, Birmingham Area Mus. Assn., Am. Assn. State and Local History (program completion 1980), Am. Assn. Mus., Ala. Mus. Assn. (sec.-treas. 1983-85, chair com. Southeastern Museums Conf. 1999, co-chair com. 2000, Meritorious Svc. award 1983), Ala. State Employees Assn. (pres. Tannehill chpt. 1993-99). Democrat. Baptist. Avocations: pen, ink drawings, painting. Home: 258 Stipes Rd West Blocton AL 35184 Office: Tannehill Historical State Park 12632 Confederate Pkwy Mc Calla AL 35111-2620 Business E-Mail: tannehillmuseum@att.net.

KESARWALA, HEMANT, pediatrician, educator; MD, U. Bombay, India, 1971. Diplomate Am. Bd. Pediatrics, Am. Bd. Allergy/Immunology. Intern in pediat. L.T.M.G. Hosp., Bombay, 1970—71; resident in pediat. Lincoln Hosp., Bronx, NY; fellow in pediatric allergy, immunology Children's Hosp. Med. Ctr. U. Cin., 1978—79, physician dept. pediat., 1992—2004; clin. prof. pediat. Robert Wood Johnson U. Hosp., New Brunswick, NJ; clin. prof. Drexel U. Coll. Medicine, 2005—. Clin. prof. Pediatrics Robert Wood Johnson Univ. Hosp., New Brunswick, NJ, 1992—. Mailing: 3084 Rt 27 6 Kendall Park NJ 08824 Office Phone: 732-821-0595.

KESHVALA, SEELPA H, secondary school educator; b. Milw., June 30, 1975; d. Hamir K and Mani M Keshvala. BS, U. Wis., Milw., 1998, MS, postgrad., U. Wis., Milw., 2000—. Principal and Superintendency Licensure Wis., 2004, Professional Educator Wis. Dept. of Edn., 1998. Tchr. Milw. Pub. Schools, 1998—2002, Milw. Area Tech. Coll., 2002—. Recipient Barbara L. Jackson Scholar, UCEA, 2004, Holmes Scholar, Holmes Partnership Acad., 2005, Lura M. Currithurs Scholarship, Pi Lambda Theta, Beta Epsilon Chpt., 2000, Advanced Opportunity Program (AOP) Fellowship, Grad. Sch., 2002—03, 2003—04, 2004—05. Mem.: Holmes Partnership Acad. (Holmes Scholar 2005), U. Coun. of Ednl. Adminstrn., Am. Edn. Rsch. Assn., Pi Lambda Theta. Hindu. Home: 1100 W Wells St Apt 811 Milwaukee WI 53233 Office: Dept of Administrative Leadership Enderis Hall Room 658 Milwaukee WI 53201 Office Phone: 414-229-2868. Office Fax: 414-229-5300. Personal E-mail: keshvala@uwm.edu.

KESLER, JAY LEWIS, retired academic administrator; b. Barnes, Wis., Sept. 15, 1935; m. H. Jane Smith; children: Laura, Bruce, Terri. Student, Ball State U., 1953-54; BA, Taylor U., 1958, LHD (hon.), 1982; Dr. Divinity (hon.), Barrington Coll., 1977; DD (hon.), Asbury Theol. Sem., 1984, Anderson U., 1999; HHD (hon.), Huntington Coll., 1983; LHD, John Brown U., 1987; LLD (honoris causa), Gordon Coll., 1992; DD (hon.), Union U., 2000, Trinity Internat. U., 2001; LHD (honoris causa), So. Wesleyan U., 2002. Dir. Marion (Ind.) Youth for Christ, 1955-58, crusade staff evangelist, 1959-60, dir. Ill.-Ind. region, 1960-62, dir. coll. recruitment, 1962-63, v.p. pers., 1963-68, v.p. field coordination, 1968-73, pres., 1973-85, also bd. dirs.; pres. Taylor U., Upland, Ind., 1985-2000, chancellor, 2000—03, pres. emeritus, 2003—; tchg. pastor Upland Cmty. Ch., 2002—. Bd. dirs. Star Fin. Group, Christianity Today, Brotherhood Mut. Ins. Co., Nat. Ass. Evangs., Youth for Christ Internat., Youth for Christ U.S.A.; mem. bd. reference Christian Camps Inc.; mem. Council for Christian Colls. and Univs., bd. mem., 2001; chmn. United Christian Coll. Fund; mem. adv. bd. Christian Bible Soc.; co-pastor 1st Bapt. Ch., Geneva, 1972—85; mem. faculty Billy Graham Schs. Evangelism; lectr. Staley Disting. Christian Sch. Lecture Program; past gov.'s appointee Ind. Commn. on Youth. Spkr. on Family Forum (daily radio show and radio program), 1973-98; mem. adv. com. Campus Life mag.; author: Let's Succeed With Our Teenagers, 1973, I Never Promised You a Disneyland, 1975, The Strong Weak People, 1976, Outside Disneyland, 1977, I Want a Home with No Problems, 1977, Growing Places, 1978, Too Big to Spank, 1978, Breakthrough, 1981, Parents & Teenagers, 1984 (Gold Medallion award), Family Forum, 1984, Making Life Make Sense, 1986, Parents and Children, 1986, Being Holy, Being Human, 1988, Ten Mistakes Parents Make With Teenagers (And How to Avoid Them), 1988, Is Your Marriage Really Worth Fighting For?, 1989, Energizing Your Teenagers' Faith, 1990, Raising Responsible Kids, 1991, Grandparenting: The Agony and the Ecstasy, 1993, Challenges for the College Bound, 1994, Emotionally Healthy Teenagers, 1998; contbr. articles to profl. jours. Bd. advisors Prison Fellowship Internat., Christian Camps Inc., Christian Educators Assn. Internat., Evangelicals for Social Action, Love and Action, Venture Middle East, Internat. Com. of Reference for New Life 2000. Named sr. fellow, Coun. Christian Coll., 2000, Sagamore of the Wabash, 2000; recipient Angel award, Religion in Media, 1985, Outstanding Youth Leadership award, Religious Heritage Am., 1989. Office: Taylor U Office Pres 236 W Reade Ave Upland IN 46989-1002

KESLER, STEPHEN EDWARD, economic geology educator; BS with honors, U. N.C., 1962; PhD, Stanford U., 1966. Asst. prof. econ. geology La. State U., Baton Rouge, 1966-70; assoc. prof. U. Toronto, Ont., Can., 1970-77; prof. U. Mich., Ann Arbor, 1977—, assoc. chair, 1998—. Vis. scientist Nat. Inst. Geography, Guatemala, 1966-69, Consejo Recursos Minerales, Mexico City, 1974-75; with Dirección General Minas, Santo Domingo, 1983-84; cons. exploration for metallic and nonmetallic mineral deposits. Author: Our Finite Mineral Resources, 1975; (with others) Economic Geology of Central Dominican Republic, 1984, Mineral Resources: Economics and the Environment, 1994; assoc. editor Econ. Geology, 1981-91, Ore Geology Revs., 1999—; mem. editl. bd. Jour. Geochem. Exploration, 1984-98. Pres. bd. trustees Lord of Light Luth. Ch., 1989-91. Fellow Geol. Soc. Am., Soc. Econ. Geologists (councillor 1983-86, internat. lectr. 1989-90, v.p. 1990-91, Thayer Lindsley lectr. 1994-95, pres. 1998-99); mem. Assn. Exploration Geochemists (councillor 1981-84), Soc. Mining Engrs. of AIME (program chmn. 1977). Lutheran. Office: U Mich Dept Geol Scis Ann Arbor MI 48109 Office Phone: 734-763-5057.

KESLING, WILLARD RAY, JR., music educator; b. Takoma Park, Md., Jan. 2, 1948; s. Willard Ray and Mable Mae (Robertson) K.; m. Janet Elizabeth Sproles, Sept. 6, 1969; 1 child, Shawn Michael. BA, Lynchburg Coll., 1970; MusB in Edn., Peabody Conservatory, 1975; MusM in Edn. with honors, U. Okla., 1976, PhD in Choral Conducting with honors, 1982; postgrad., Cambridge (Eng.) U., 1985. Music therapist Lynchburg (Va.) Tng. Sch. and Hosp., 1970-71; area supr. music Walter State Community Coll., Morristown, Tenn., 1977-80; dir. music, dept. head U. So. Ind., Evansville, 1980-83; dir. Evansville Philharm. Chorus, 1980-83; prof. music, dir. and orchest. activities Utah State U., Logan, 1983—2002; prof. music, dir. choral activities U. Fla., 2002—. Adjudicator, clinician Johnny Mann's Gt. Am. Choral Festival, 1984—, others; assoc. condr. Manhattan Philharm. Orch., N.Y.C., 1989—90; prin. guest condr. St. Petersburg (Russia) State Symphony Orch., 1996—2002; music dir., condr. Mountain West Symphony Orch., Utah, 1990—2002; judge Internat. Youth Music Festival, Vienna; artistic dir. No. Utah Choral Soc. and Orch.; dir. Naval Air Tng. Command Choir; condr. Moscow State Acad. Symphony Orch., Moscow Philharm., Moscow State Symphony Orch., Moscow State Chamber Orch., St. Petersburg State Symphony Orch., Orch. of St. Petersburg Radio & TV, St. Petersburg State Symphony Orch. Classica, St. Petersburg State Symphony Orch. Congress, St. Petersburg Mozarteum Chamber Orch.; condr. 1st professionally produced performance of Handel's Messiah since instn. of Communism Moscow State Chamber Orch. and Bolshoi Opera Chorus, 1992; condr. orchs. in Brazil, Can., Czech Republic, Hungary, Kenya, Korea, Mex.,

Uruguay, Poland, Spain, Nat. Philharm., Seattle Symphony, Utah Symphony, Okla. Symphony, Honolulu Symphony, San Diego Symphony, Atlanta Pops, Conn. Chamber Orch., Mid-Atlantic Chamber Orch., Nat. Chamber Orch.; guest condr. Mormon Tabernacle Choir, 1991. Editor: (choral music series) Will Kesling Choral Editions, 1985—, (books) A Festival of Sacred Music for Male Choirs, 1987, A Festival of Sacred Music for Women's Choirs, 1998; prodr., performer: TV spls. Israel in Egypt by Handel, 1985, Requiem by Brahms, 1987; comml. recs.; condr. feature film scores: The Silence of Speed, The Two Sisters; choirs featured in opening ceremonies Paralympics (NBC-TV); contbr. articles to profl. jours. Served to lt. USNR, 1971-75. Recipient Congl. Order of Merit, 2003, Ronald Reagan Gold medal, 2004. Mem.: Music Educators Nat. Conf., Am. Choral Dirs. Assn., Pi Kappa Lambda, Hon. Order Ky. Cols. Republican. Mem. Lds Ch.

KESMAN, ANTHONY K., medical products executive; BS, U. Iowa; MS, Northwestern U. With Am. Hosp. Supply Corp., 1977—84, v.p., nat. accounts, 1984—86; v.p., gen. mgr., western bus. dist. Baxter Internat. Inc., 1986—89, v.p., gen. mgr., ValueLink Bus. Ctr., 1989—93, pres., critical care divsn., 1993—96; corp. v.p., distribution Allegiance Corp., 1996—99, pres., Care Continuum Products & Svc. Group, 1999—. Bd. dirs. Source Med. Corp., Toronto, Children's Mem. Med. Ctr., Children's Mem. Found., Chgo., Age Wave Impact, Inc., Emeryville, Calif., First Nat. Bank of Brookfield, Ill.; First Brookfield Inc.; Jr. Achievement Chgo. Mem.: Adaptive Bus. Leaders (mem. exec. coun. Tustin, CA)), Multiple Myeloma Rsch. Found. (dir. (New Canaan, CT)). Office: Allegiance Healthcare Corp 1430 Waukegan Rd Mc Gaw Park IL 60085

KESSEL, BRINA, ornithologist, educator, researcher; b. Ithaca, NY, Nov. 20, 1925; d. Marcel and Quinta (Cattell) K.; m. Raymond B. Roof, June 19, 1957 (dec. 1968). BS, Cornell U., 1947, PhD, 1951; MS, U. Wis., Madison, 1949. Student asst. Patuxent Rsch. Refuge, 1946; student tchg. asst. Cornell U., 1945-47, grad. asst., 1947-48, 49-51; asst. Wis. Amumni Rsch. Found., 1948—49; instr. biol. sci. U. Alaska, summer 1951, asst. prof. biol. sci., 1951-54, assoc. prof. zoology, 1954-59, prof. zoology, 1959-96, head dept. biol. scis., 1957-66, dean Coll. Biol. Scis. and Renewable Resources, 1961-72, curator terrestrial vertebrate mus. collections, 1972-90, curator ornithology collection, 1990-95, adminstrv. assoc. for acad. programs, grad. and undergrad., dir. acad. advising, office of chancellor, 1973-80, sr. scientist, 1996-99, prof. emeritus, dean emeritus, curator emeritus, 1999—. Project dir. U. Alaska ecol. investigations for AEC Project Chariot, 1959—63; ornithol. investigations N.W. Alaska pipeline, 1976—81, Susitna Hydroelectric Project, 1980—83. Author books; contbr. articles to profl. jours. Recipient Outstanding Contbn. award Alaska Bird Conf.; U. Alaska with ann. award Brina Kessel Medal for Excellence in Sci. named in her honor; swale pond at Creamer's Field Migratory Waterfowl Refuge in Fairbanks named in her honor. Fellow AAAS, Am. Ornithologists' Union (v.p. 1977, pres.-elect 1990-92, pres. 1992-94), Arctic Inst. N.Am.; mem. Wilson Ornithol. Soc., Cooper Ornithol. Soc., Soc. Northwestern Vertebrate Biology, Pacific Seabird Group, Arctic Audubon Soc. (hon.), Assn. Field Ornithologists, Sigma Xi (pres. U. Alaska 1957), Phi Kappa Phi, Sigma Delta Epsilon. Achievements include research in European Starling in North America; biogeography, seasonality, and the biology of birds in Alaska. Office: U Alaska Mus PO Box 80211 Fairbanks AK 99708-0211 Business E-Mail: ffbxk@uaf.edu.

KESSEL, JAMES MICK, lawyer; b. Phila., Apr. 9, 1977; s. James White Kessel and Nancy Jo Vinson. BA, W.Va. U., 1999; JD, U. Richmond, 2002. Bar: Va. 2003, US Dist. Ct. Ea. Dist. Va. 2003, US Ct. Appeals 4th Circuit 2004. Assoc. Marks & Harrison, PC, Richmond, Va., 2003—. Mem.: Am. Trial Lawyers Assn., Virgina Trial Lawyers Assn., Va. Assn. of Criminal Def. Lawyers. Office: Marks & Harrison PC 215 North Market St Petersburg VA 23803 Office Phone: 804-733-4456. Office Fax: 804-862-1783. E-mail: jkessel@marksandharrison.com.

KESSEL, JOHN HOWARD, political scientist, educator; b. Dayton, Ohio, Oct. 13, 1928; s. Arthur V. and Helen (Hopkins) K.; m. Margaret Sarah Wagner, Aug. 22, 1954; children— Robert Arthur, Thomas John. Student, Purdue U., 1946-48; BA, Ohio State U., 1950; PhD, Columbia U., 1958. Instr. Amherst and Mt. Holyoke colls., 1957-58; instr., asst. prof. Amherst Coll., 1958-61; asst. prof. U. Wash., 1961-65; Arthur E. Braun prof. polit. sci. Allegheny Coll., Meadville, Pa., 1965-70; prof. polit. sci. Ohio State U., Columbus, 1970-94, prof. emeritus, 1994—. Vis. prof. U. Calif., San Diego, 1977, U. Wash., 1980, Am. U., 1980. Author: The Goldwater Coalition: Republican Strategies in 1964, 1968, The Domestic Presidency, 1975, Presidential Campaign Politics: Coalition Strategies and Citizen Response, 1980, 4th edit., 1992, Presidential Parties, 1984, Presidents, the Presidency, and the Political Environment, 2001; co-editor: Micropolitics-Individual and Group Level Concepts, 1970, Theory Building and Data Analysis in the Social Sciences, 1984, Researching the Presidency: Vital Questions, New Approaches, 1993; editor Am. Jour. Polit. Sci, 1974-76; contbr. articles to profl. jours. Mem. exec. council Inter-Univ. Consortium for Polit. Research, 1964-65, 67-68; Exec. dir. Nixon-Lodge Vols. Mass., 1960; dir. arts, scis. div. Republican Nat. Com., 1963-64. Served with USN, 1950-53. Guest scholar, Brookings Inst., 1972, vis. scholar, Am. Enterprise Inst., 1980—82. Mem. Am. Polit. Sci. Assn. (exec. council 1969-71), Midwest Polit. Sci. Assn. (pres. 1978-79) Home: 516 E Schreyer Pl Columbus OH 43214-2273 Business E-Mail: kessel.1@osu.edu.

KESSEL, MARK, lawyer; b. Krasnik, Poland, June 14, 1941; arrived in U.S., 1948; s. Leo and Erna (Friedman) Kessel; m. Elaine Keit, Aug. 29, 1966; children: Greer Kessel Hendricks, Robert W. BA with honors in Econs., CUNY, 1963; JD magna cum laude, Syracuse U., 1966. Bar: N.Y. Assoc. Shearman & Sterling, N.Y.C., 1971-77, ptnr., 1977—2001, mng. ptnr., 1990-94; mng. dir. Symphony Capital LLC, N.Y.C., 2002—. Bd. dirs. Harrods (U.K.) Ltd., 2002—04, Antigenics, Inc. Bd. dirs. San Francisco Psychoanalytic Inst., 1988—90, Mus. City of N.Y., 1993—2003, W.M. Keck Found., L.A., 1985—86; dir. Heller Fin., Inc., 1992—2001; bd. visitors Syracuse U. Coll. Law, 2002—04. Capt. JAGC U.S. Army, 1963—71. Avocations: reading, running. Office: Symphony Capital LLC 875 3d Ave New York NY 10022 Business E-Mail: mark@symphonycapital.com.

KESSEL, RICHARD GLEN, zoology educator; b. Fairfield, Iowa, July 19, 1931; BS in Chemistry summa cum laude, Parsons Coll., 1953; MS in Zoology and Physiology, U. Iowa, 1956, PhD in Zoology and Cytology, 1959; postgrad., Marine Biol. Lab., 1957. Trainee dept. anatomy Wake Forest U. Sch. Medicine, Winston-Salem, NC, 1959-60, Nat. Inst. Gen. Med. Sci. postdoctoral rsch. fellow, 1960-61, instr. anatomy, 1959-61, asst. prof., 1961; asst. prof. biology U. Iowa, Iowa City, 1961—64, assoc. prof., 1964-68, prof., 1968—97, prof. emeritus, 1998—. Vis. investigator Hopkins Marine Sta., Pacific Grove, Calif., 1966; ind. investigator Marine Biol. Lab., Woods Hole, Mass., summers 1960, 62, 64. Author: (with C.Y. Shih) Scanning Electron Microscopy in Biology: A Students' Text-Atlas of Biological Organization, 1974, (with R.H. Kardon) Tissues and Organs: A Text-Atlas of Scanning Electron Microscopy, 1979, (with C.Y. Shih) Living Images, 1982, (with R. Roberts and H. Tung) Freeze Fracture Images of Cells and Tissues, 1991, Basic Medical Histology, 1998; assoc. editor Jour. Exptl. Zoology, 1978-82; mem. editorial bd. Jour. Submicroscopic Cytology, 1980—; mem. internat. bd. editors Scanning Electron Microscopy in Biology and Medicine; contbr. articles to profl. jours., chpts. to books Grantee USPHS, 1961-78, NSF, 1969-71, Whitehall Found., 1982-84; Bodine fellow; George Lincoln Seeley scholar; Nat Inst. Gen. Med. Sci.-USPHS, 1964-69; established endowed med. scholarship U. Iowa Coll. Medicine, established embryology course lecture Marine Biol. Lab., Woods Hole, Mass. Mem. AAAS, Am. Soc. Cell Biology, Am. Assn. Anatomists, Electron Micros. Soc. Am., Am. Physiol. Soc., Soc. for Study of Reprodn., Am. Soc. Zoologists, Am. Inst. Biol. Sci., Soc. Devel. Biology, Sigma Xi, Phi Kappa Phi, Beta Beta Beta. Office: Univ Iowa Dept Biol Scis Iowa City IA 52242

KESSELL, CHARLES ARTHUR, music educator, musician; b. Chgo., Aug. 9, 1955; s. William Arthur and Jane Catherine (Buddemeyer) Kessell; m. Diana Lee Castellanos, Sept. 10, 1983; 1 child, Benjamin. BA in Music Edn., DePaul U., Chgo., 1979. Music dir. St. Sebastian Parish, Chgo., 1974—83, Our Lady of Perpetual Help Parish, Glenview, Ill., 1983—88; mem., archdiocesan music com. Archdiocese of Chgo., Office for Divine Worship, 1985—89; liturgist, music dir. St. Ita Parish, Chgo., 1988—98, St. Isaac Jogues Parish, Chgo., 1998—; music dir., instr. Edgebrook Music Acad., Chgo., 1998—; music dir. One World Choirs, Chgo., Irish Heritage Singers, Chgo., 2000—. Freelance musician, Chgo., 1974—; chgo. area Indiana sales rep. Levsen Organ Co., Buffalo. Composer (arranger): (irish folk music) Tir Na Ceol, 2002. Den leader, asst. cubmaster, cubmaster, asst. scoutmaster, scoutmaster, dist. tng. chair, roundtable commr. dist. commr. BSA., Chgo., 1987—99. Recipient Order of the Arrow, BSA, 1996. Mem.: Pueri Cantores, Percussive Arts Soc., Am. Guild English Handbell Ringers, Nat. Assn. Pastoral Musicians, Irish Am. Heritage Ctr., Am. Guild of Organists. Roman Catholic. Avocations: camping, canoeing, fishing, kayaking. Home: 6042 W Grace Chicago IL 60634 Office: St Isaac Jogues Parish 8149 Golf Road Niles IL 60714 Personal E-mail: perc55@juno.com.

KESSELMAN, JONATHAN RHYS, economics professor, public policy researcher; b. Columbus, Ohio, Mar. 17, 1946; s. Louis C. and Jennie K.; m. Sheila Kaplan, Mar. 12, 1973; 1 child, Maresa. BA with honors, Oberlin Coll., 1968; PhD in Econs., MIT, 1972. Asst. prof. econs. U. B.C., Vancouver, Canada, 1972-76, assoc. prof., 1976-81, prof., 1981—2003, dir. Ctr. for Rsch. on Econ. and Social Policy, 1992—2003; prof. pub. policy Simon Fraser U., Vancouver, 2004—, Can. rsch. chair in pub. fin., 2004—. Rsch. assoc. Inst. for Rsch. on Poverty, Madison, Wis., 1974-75; vis. scholar Delhi Sch. Econs., New Delhi, 1978-79; cons. econs., 1973—; prin. investigator Equality, Security and Cmty. Rsch. Project, 1998-2004. Author: Financing Canadian Unemployment Insurance, 1983, Rate Structure and Personal Taxation, 1990, General Payroll Taxes, 1997; editorial bd.: Can. Pub. Policy, 1997—, Can. Tax Jour., 1999—; contbr. numerous articles on taxation, income security, employment policy to profl. jours. Bd. dirs. Tibetan Refugee Aid Soc., Vancouver, 1980-82; mem. adv. panel Can. Ministry Employment and Immigration, Ottawa, Ont., 1982-83; mem. B.C. Econ. Policy Inst., 1983-86; trustee pension plan U. B.C., 1988-90; chmn. Musqueam Indian Band Taxation Adv. Coun., 1992-96, mem., 1996-98; mem. B.C. Premier's Forum on New Opportunities for Working and Living, 1994-95; mem. compliance adv. com. Revenue Can. Taxation, 1997-99. Sr. scholar Oberlin Coll., 1967-68; NSF fellow, 1968-70; grantee U.S. Dept. Labor, 1971-72; leave fellow Can. Coun., (locat.) New Delhi, 1978-79; grantee Social Sci. and Humanities Rsch. Coun. Can., 1983-84, 90—; vis. fellow Australian Nat. U., Canberra, 1985; professorial fellow in econ. policy Res. Bank of Australia, 1985; recipient Doug Purvis award, Can. Econ. Assn., 1998. Mem. Am. Econ. Assn., Can. Econs. Assn., Can. Tax Found. (Douglas Sherbaniuk award 2002). Office: Simon Fraser U Pub Policy Program 515 W Hastings St Vancouver BC Canada V6B 5K3

KESSELRING, DEBBIE ANNE, systems engineer; b. Durham, N.C., July 21, 1965; d. Henry G. and Maria K.; m. Timothy J. Docey; 1 child, Denise. BS in Aero. Engring., U. Md., 1987; MS in Systems Engring., Va. Tech. Inst., 1995. Engring. cons. VEDA Inc., Arlington, Va., 1988-89; structural engr. Naval Air Sys. Command, Arlington, Va., 1989-93, air-to-air missile program analyst, 1993-95; sys. engr. Ballistic Missile Def. Orgn., Washington, 1995—98, Computer Scis. Corp., 1998—2001, tech. dir., 2003—, Anteon Corp., 2001—03. Mem. AIAA (sr.).

KESSINGER, WILLIAM A., music educator; b. Canton, Ill., Apr. 26, 1951; s. Newell L. and Mary Ellen Kessinger; m. Lee Michele Horner, July 20, 1974. MusB in Edn., Augustana Coll., 1973. Music tchr. Rossville-Alvin Schs., Ill., 1973—75, North Scott Schs., Eldridge, Iowa, 1975—. Mem.: S.E. Iowa Bandmasters Assn. (pres. 1991—92, sec., treas. 1978—91), North Scott Edn. Assn. (pres. 1992—93). Home: 531 26th Avenue Ct East Moline IL 61244 Office: North Scott HS 200 South First St Eldridge IA 52748 Office Phone: 563-285-3316. Personal E-mail: billalan@aol.com.

KESSLER, A. D., business, financial, investment and real estate advisor, consultant, educator, lecturer, author; b. N.Y.C., May 1, 1923; s. Morris William and Belle Miriam (Pastor) K.; m. Ruth Schwartz, Nov. 20, 1944 (div. 1974); children: Brian Lloyd, Judd Stuart, Earl Vaughn; m. Jaclyn Jeanne Sprague. Student U. Newark, 1940-41, Rutgers U., 1941-42, 46, Albright Coll., 1942, Newark Coll. Engring., 1946; PhD in Pub. Adminstrn. U. Fla., 1972; MBA, Kensington U., 1976, PhD in Mgmt. and Behavioral Psychology, 1977. Sr. cert. rev. appraiser; cert. bus. counselor; cert. exchanger; registered mortgage underwriter; registered investment advisor. Pvt. practice real estate, ins. and bus. brokerage, N.J., Pa., Fla., N.Y., Nev., Calif., Hong Kong, 1946—; pres. Armor Corp., 1947-68; pres. Folding Carton Corp., Am., N.Y.C., 1958-68; exec. v.p. Henry Schindall Assocs., N.Y.C., 1966-67; tax rep. Calif. State Bd. Equalization, 1968-69; aviation cons. transp. div. Calif., Dept. Aeros., also pub. info. officer; 1969-71; FAA Gen. Aviation Safety Counselor; broker, mgr. La Costa (Calif.) Sales Corp., 1971-75; chmn. bd. Profl. Ednl. Found., 1975—, Timeshare Resorts Internat., 1975—, Interex, Leucadia, Calif., 1975-82, The Kessler Orgn., Rancho Santa Fe, Calif., 1975—, The Kessler Fin. Group, Fin. Ind. Inst., 1977—; pres. Ednl. Video Inst., 1978—, Fin. Planning Inst., 1975—, Rancho Santa Fe Real Estate & Land, Inc., 1975—; treas., exec. bd. dirs. Nat. Challenge Com. on Disability, 1983-90; dir. Practice Mgmt. Cons. Abacus Data Systems, 1984—; broker mgr. Rancho Sante Fe Acreage & Homes, Inc., 1987-89; mktg. dir. Commercial Real Estate Services, Rancho Santa Fe, 1987—; cons. broker Glenct. Properties Ptnrs., 1989-90; dir. U.S. Advisors, 1989—; founder Creative Real Estate Movement, 1946—; pub., editor in chief Creative Real Estate Mag., 1975—; pub. Creative Real Estate Mag. of Australia and New Zealand; founder, editor Moderator of Tape of the Month Club; founder, producer, chmn. Internat. Real Estate Expo; chmn. bd. The Brain Trust, Rancho Santa Fe, Calif., 1977—; fin. lectr. for Internat. Cruise Ships, Cunard Line, Norwegian Am. Cruises, P&O, Princess, others; lectr. life enrichment and stress mgmt. Internat. Cruise Ships; Calif. adj. faculty, prof. fin. Clayton U., St. Louis; developer, operator Barnegat Baywood Seaplane Base, Barnegat Bay, N.J.; owner, operator Skyline Airport, Hunterdon County, N.J. Scoutmaster Orange Mountain coun. Boy Scouts Am., 1955-62; harbor master N.J. Marine Patrol, 1958-67; dep. sheriff, Essex County, N.J., 1951-65; mem. pres.' adv. bd. Seton Hall U., 1961-64; chmn. Stop Smoking, 1990, Quick Study, 1990; feature broadcaster/producer Kalaidascope Radio Mag., Am. Radio Network, 1990—. Served with USAF, 1942-45. Decorated D.F.C., Air medal, Purple Heart; named to French Legion of Honor, Order of Lafayette; named a flying col, a.d.c., Gov. of Ga., 1957. Mem. Am. Soc. Editors and Pubs., Author's Guild, Internat. Platform Assn., Nat. Speakers Assn., Nat. Press Photographers Assn., Guild Assn. Airport Execs., Aviation and Space Writers Assn., Nat. Assn. of Real Estate Editors, Internat. Exchangors Assn. (founder), Air Force Assn. (dep. comdr. N.J. chpt. 1955-57). Clubs: Nat. Press, Overseas Press, La Costa Country, Cuyamaca, Rancho Santa Fe Country, Passport. Lodges: Masons, Shriners. Author: A Fortune At Your Feet, 1981, How You Can Get Rich, Stay Rich and Enjoy Being Rich, 1981, Financial Independence, 1987, The Profit, 1987, A Fortune at Your Feet in the '90s, 1994, The Midas Touch, Turning Paper Into Gold, 1994; author, instr. Your Key to Success seminar, 1988, Your Key to Creative Real Estate Success tng. program, 1996; The A to Z of Lease Purchase and 11 Other Options Training Prog.; editor: The Real Estate News Observer, 1975—; fin. editor API, 1978—; fin. columnist Money Matters, 1986—; syndicated columnist, radio and TV host of "Money Making Ideas," 1977—; songwriter: Only You, 1939, If I'm Not HomeFor Christmas, 1940, Franny, 1940, Flajaloppa, 1940, They've Nothing More Dear Only They've Got It Here, 1941, The Summer of Life, 1956; producer (movies) The Flight of the Cobra, Rena, We Have Your Daughters, Music Row; speaker for radio and TV as The Real Estate Answerman, 1975—; host (radio and TV show) Ask Mr. Money; conceptualist, exec. prodr. (TV show) The Trading Game, 1994; exec. prodr., moderator (TV show) A.D. Kessler's Real Estate Roundtable, 1993—. Inventor swivel seat, siptop, inflatumbrella. Home: PO Box 1144 Rancho Santa Fe CA 92067-1144

KESSLER, ALAN CRAIG, lawyer; b. Washington, Sept. 16, 1950; s. Alfred Milton and Josephine (Taub) K.; m. Gail Elaine Strauss, June 16, 1974; children: Stacy Ilana, Mark Jay, Daniel Jordan. BA with honors, U. Del., 1972; JD with honors, U. Md., 1975. Bar: Pa. 1975, U.S. Dist. Ct. (ea. dist.) Pa. 1975, U.S. Ct. Appeals (3d and 6th cirs.) 1975. Assoc. Dilworth, Paxson, Kalish, Levy & Kauffman, Phila., 1975-77, Berger & Montague, P.C., Phila., 1977-81; ptnr. Mesirov, Gelman, Jaffe, Cramer & Jamieson, Phila., 1981-91, Buchanan Ingersoll, P.C., Phila., 1991-99, Wolf, Block, Schorr & Solis-Cohen, 1999—. Instr. Inst. for Paralegal Tng., Phila., 1977-96. Mem. Presdl. Transition Team, 1992—93; vice-chmn. Pres.'s Commn. on Risk Assessment and Risk Mgmt., 1993—97; vice-chmn., bd. govs. U.S. Postal Svc., 2000—; chmn. bd. Bldg. Stds. City of Phila., 1983—84, bd. licenses and inspections rev., 1984—91; mem. City Planning Commn., Phila., 1992—97; commr. Lower Merion Twp., Pa., 1988—2000, Mayor's Commn. Homelessness, 1990—, Mayor's Com. on Spl. Svcs. Dist., 1989—; bd. dirs., pres. Randolph Ct. Assn., Phila., 1980—85; bd. dirs., v.p. South St. Neighbors Assn., Phila., 1983—87, Park Towne Pl. Tenants Assn., 1977—79; exec. com. Ctrl. Phila. Devel. Corp., 1989—, Jewish Employment Vocat. Svcs., 1989—, Phila. 2000; chair Supreme Ct. of Pa. Commn. on CLE, 1999—; fin. com. Dem. City Com. Phila., 1981—84, dep. counsel, 1980—84; mng. trustee Dem. Nat. Com., 1992—, fin. vice-chair, 2000—; chair Pa. Dem. Fin., 2003—; bd. dirs. Support Ctr. for Child Advocates, 1983—94, Phila. Indsl. Devel. Corp. Mem. ABA, Pa. Bar Assn., Phila. Bar Assn. (exec. bd. dirs. young lawyers sect., legis. liaison com., officer various coms.), Racquet Club, Radnor Valley Country Club. Democrat. Jewish. Home: 204 Daisy Ln Wynnewood PA 19096-1654 Office: Wolf Block Schorr & Solis-Cohen 1650 Arch St Fl 22 Philadelphia PA 19103-2097 Business E-Mail: akessler@wolfblock.com.

KESSLER, DAVID AARON, dean, medical educator; b. N.Y.C., May 31, 1951; m. Paulette Kessler; children: Elise, Benjamin. BA, Amherst Coll., 1973; JD, U. Chgo., 1978; MD, Harvard U., 1979. Cert. Advanced Profl. Cert. NYU Grad. Sch. Bus. Adminstrn., 1986. Intern in pediatrics Johns Hopkins Hosp., 1979—80, resident in pediatrics, 1980—82; spl. asst. to pres. Montefiore Med. Ctr., NYC, 1982—84; med. dir. Hosp. of Albert Einstein Coll. Medicine, NYC, 1984—90; tchg. appts. dept. pediatrics and dept. epidemiology and social medicine; instr. food and drug law Columbia U., NYC, 1986—90; commr. FDA Dept. Health and Human Svcs., Rockville, Md., 1990—97; dean, prof. pediatrics, internal medicine and pub. health Yale U. Med. Sch., 1997—2003; dean, vice chancellor med. affairs, prof. pediatrics U. Calif. San Francisco Sch. Medicine, 2003—; attending pediatrician Children's Hosp. Cons. US Senate Labor and Human Resources Com., 1981—84; bd. dirs. Doctors of the World; bd. dirs. Nat. Ctr. for Addiction and Substance Abuse Columbia U.; mem. White House Commn. on Presdl. Scholars. Author: A Question of Intent, 2001, numerous articles in med. jours. Chmn. bd. dirs. Elizabeth Glaser Pediatric AIDS Found.; bd. dirs. Henry J. Kaiser Family Found. Recipient Medal of Honor, Am. Cancer Soc., 1996, Pub. Welfare Medal, NAS, 2001, Nat. Pub. Affairs Spl. Recognition Award, Am. Heart Assn., Sheldon W. Andelson Pub. Policy Achievement Award, Am. Fedn. AIDS Rsch., Pub. Svc. Award, Am. Acad. Pediatrics, Franklin Delano Roosevelt Leadership Award, March of Dimes. Fellow: Am. Acad. Arts and Scis.; mem.: Inst. Medicine. Office: U Calif San Francisco Sch Medicine Dean's Office 513 Parnassus Ave San Francisco CA 94143-0410

KESSLER, DIANE COOKSEY, religious organization administrator, minister; b. Jan. 8, 1947; BA in Religion, Oberlin Coll., 1969; MA in Religion and Soc., Andover Newton Theol. Sch., 1971, postgrad., 1979—; DD (hon.), Episcopal Divinity Sch., 2001. Ordained to ministry United Ch. of Christ, 1983. Assoc. dir. for strategy and action Mass. Coun. Chs., Boston, 1975-88, exec. dir., 1988—. Ind. preacher; speaker in field. Author: Parents and the Experts, 1974, God's Simple Gift: Meditations on Friendship and Spirituality, 1988; co-author: Councils of Churches and the Ecumenial Vision, 2000; editor: Together on the Way, 1999, Receive Another..., 2005; co-editor Encounters for Unity, 1995; also articles; mem. editl. adv. bd. Theology and Pub. Policy, 1989, 98, Mid-Stream, 1995-98. Former mem. adv. bd. Mass. Dept. Revenue; active Wellesley Congl. Ch.; mem. coun. for ecumenism United Ch. of Christ, 1984-94, chairperson coun. 1988-89, 90-91; mem. Atty Gen.'s Adv. Com. on Pub. Charities, 1988—, World Coun. of Churches, Joint Working Group, 1998-2005; trustee Hancock Variable Series Trust I, 1999-2005; bd. dirs. Howard Benevolent Soc., 1989-96, New Eng. Holocaust Meml. Com., 1st Ch. Legacy Fund. Recipient Outstanding Woman award Coll. Club, 1990, Focolare award, 1994, Social Action Ministries award, 1995, Patron of Christian Unity award, 1998. Mem. Valiant Woman award 1991), Boston Min.'s Club. Office: Mass Coun Chs 14 Beacon St Ste 416 Boston MA 02108-3704 E-mail: council@masscouncilofchurches.org.

KESSLER, DONALD JOE, research scientist, physicist, consultant; b. Houston, Jan. 30, 1940; s. Joseph Valentine and Mazie Irene (Doegen) Kessler; m. Mary Sue Cain, Dec. 31, 1969 (div. May 1978); m. Lynn Ellen Eddy, Jan. 24, 1990. BS in Physics, U. Houston, 1965. Meteoid scientist NASA, Houston, 1965-70, flight contr., 1970-74, atmospheric scientist, 1974-78, orbital debris rsch. developer, 1978-90, sr. scientist orbital debris, 1990-96; ret., 1996. Orbital debris and meteoroid cons., 1996—. Co-editor: Space Debris Jour., 1998—2002; founding editor:, 2002—04, contbg. author: Orbital Debris: A Technical Assessment, 1995, Interagency Report on Orbital Debris, 1995; contbr. articles to profl. jours. With U.S. Army, 1958—61. Recipient NASA Medal for exceptional Sci. Achievement, 1989. Mem.: AIAA (Losey Atmospheric Sci. award 2000). Avocations: skiing, scuba diving. Home and Office: 25 Gardenwood Ln Asheville NC 28803 Office Phone: 828-277-1948. E-mail: dkessler@vsti.com.

KESSLER, EDWIN, meteorology educator, consultant; b. Bklyn., Dec. 2, 1928; s. Edwin and Marie Rosa (Weil) K.; m. Lottie Catherine Menger; children: Austin Rainier, Thomas Russell. AB, Columbia Coll., 1950; MS in Meteorology, MIT, 1952, ScD in Meteorology, 1957. Chief synoptic meteorology sect. Weather Radar br. Air Force Cambridge Rsch. Lab., Bedford, Mass., 1954-61; sr. rsch. scientist Travelers Rsch. Ctr., Hartford, Conn., 1961-62, dir. atmospheric physics div., 1962-64; dir. Nat. Severe Storms Lab., Norman, Okla., 1964-86; adj. prof. U. Okla., 1964—. Vis. prof. MIT, 1975-76, McGill U., Can., 1980; bd. dirs. LINK, Norman, N.Am. Transp. Inst., Norman Area Land Conservancy, Inc., Norman chpt. LWV. Editor: Thunderstorms, A Social Scientific and Technological Documentary, 3 vols., 1982, 2d edits., 1983-88, paperback edits., vol. 1, 1988, vol. 2, 1992; contbr. over 250 reports, and about 100 peer-reviewed articles to profl. jours. State chair Common Cause, Okla., 1993-99, vice chair, 1999-. With U.S. Army, 1946-47. Recipient award for outstanding authorship NOAA, 1971. Fellow AAAS, Am. Meteorol. Soc. (nat. councilor 1966-69, past mem. coms. on hurricanes, atmospheric electricity, agr. and forestry, cloud and precipitation physics, severe local storms, past chmn. com. on weather radar, cert. cons. meteorologist, Cleveland Abbe award for disting. svc. 1988); mem. AIAA (sr. mem.), LWV, Royal Meteorol. Soc. (fgn.), Am. Geophys. Union, Sigma Xi. Achievements include research in agriculture and energy; manager of 350 acres of pasture, streams and wilderness in central Oklahoma. Office: U Okla 100 E Boyd St Rm 684 Norman OK 73019-1028 Personal E-mail: kess3@swbell.net.

KESSLER, GALE SUZANNE, psychologist, educator; b. Chgo., Sept. 5, 1940; d. George I. Alpert and Celia Larman-Alpert-Shaps; m. Marvin Charles Facktor, June 4, 1960 (dec.); children: Greg Facktor, Charles Facktor, Laura Meehan; m. John W. Kessler, Feb. 20, 1986 (dec. Apr. 4, 2001). BA in Edn., Roosevelt U., Chgo., 1961; MS in Orgnl. Behavior, Adminstrn., George Williams Coll., Aurora, Ill., 1980. Tchr. Chgo. Pub. Schs., 1961; dir. constituency rels. George Williams Coll., 1982—85; dir. alumni rels. Grad. Sch. Bus. U. Chgo., 1986; dir. devel. Nat. MS Soc., Chgo., 1986—87; tchr. Chgo. Pub. Schs., 1987; instr. Columbia Coll., Lake Ozark, Mo., 1993—95; exec. dir. Women's Coun., Mo., 1998—2001. Internat. liaison to human svcs. George Williams Coll., Downers Grove, Ill., 1982—85; advisor Inst. for Women's Policy Rsch., Washington, 2000—01. Columnist: Consultations, 1995—98; author: Male "Mid-Life Crisis In Relation To Job Change", 1980. Chair Elmhurst Citizens for Flood Control, Ill., 1987—90; pres. Arts Coun., Lake Ozark, Mo., 1991—93; candidate state rep. State of Mo., Lake Ozark,

1997—98. Recipient Key to City, City of Elmhurst, Ill., 1990. Fellow: World Affairs Coun. (Seattle); mem.: Women's Univ. Club (co-chair com. 2003, Seattle). Avocations: reading, travel, writing, golf, tennis. Home: 7905 W Mercer Way Mercer Island WA 98040

KESSLER, GLADYS, federal judge; b. 1938; BA, Cornell U., 1959; LLB, Harvard U., 1962. Staff atty. enforcement divsn. Nat. Labor Rels. Bd., 1962-64; legis. asst. to Senator Harrison A. Williams US Senate, 1964-66; legis. asst. to Rep. Jonathan B. Bingham US Ho. Reps., 1966-68; spl. asst. Office Staff Relations N.Y.C. Bd. Edn., 1968-69; ptnr. Berlin, Roisman and Kessler (and successor firms), 1969-77; assoc. judge D.C. Superior Ct., 1977-94; judge U.S. Dist. Ct. D.C., Washington, 1994—. Asst. lectr. law sch. George Washington U., 1971-73; del. to judicial adminstrn. divsn. D.C. Superior Ct., 1985-90; mem. adv. bd. Ctr. for Dispute Settlement Inst. for Judicial Adminstrn., State Justice Inst., mem. adv. com. nat. judicial edn. project on domestic violence; mem BNA adv. bd. Alternative Dispute Resolution Report, 1987-90; mem. family law cirriculum planning com. Georgetown U.; lead judge permanency planning project Nat. Coun. Juvenile and Family Ct. Judges; chair Nat. Conf. on Bioethics, Family and the Law, D.C., 1991; mem. faculty Nat. Inst. Trial Advocacy; exec. com. Nat. ABA Jud. Divsn./Conf. of Federal Trial Judges, 1997-2000; with U.S. Jud. Conf. Com. on Ct. Adminstrn. and Mgmt., 1999. Contbr. articles to legal jours. Recipient Women Lawyer of Yr. award Women's Bar Assn., 1983, Svc. award D.C. Coalition Against Domestic Violence, 1987, Judicial Excellence award Trial Lawyers Assn. Washington, 1987. Fellow Am. Bar Found.; mem. ABA (judicial adminstrn. divsn., com. on bioethics and AIDS, adv. com. on youth, alcohol and drug problems, nat. adv. bd. on child support and criminal justice, individual rights and responsibilities sect.), Am. Judicature Soc. (bd. dirs. 1985-89), Nat. Assn. Women Judges (v.p. 1979-81, pres. 1981-82), Nat. Ctr. for State Cts. (bd. dirs. 1984-87), Women's Legal Def. Fund (founding pres. 1971), Women Judges' Fund. for Justice (bd. dirs. 1980—), Found. for Women Judges (pres. 1980-82). Office: US Courthouse 333 Constitution Ave NW Washington DC 20001-2802

KESSLER, HERBERT LEON, art historian, educator, academic administrator; b. Chgo., July 20, 1941; s. Ben and Bertha K.; m. Johanna Zacharias, Apr. 24, 1976; 1 dau., Morisa. AB, U. Chgo., 1961; MFA, Princeton U., 1963, PhD, 1965. Asst. prof. U. Chgo., 1965-68; assoc. prof., 1968-73; prof., 1973-76; chmn. dept. art, univ. dir. fine arts, 1973-76; prof. Johns Hopkins U., Balt., 1976—, chair dept. art, 1976-89, 95-98. Guest prof. Bibliotheca Hertziana, Rome, 1996-97, dean Sch. Arts and Scis., 1998-99; vis. prof. Harvard U., 2000, Ecole des Hautes Etudes, 2000. Author: French and Flemish Illuminated Manuscripts, 1969, The Illustrated Bibles from Tours, 1977, The Cotton Genesis, 1986, The Dura Synagogue Frescoes and Christian Art, 1990, Studies in Pictorial Narrative, 1994, The Poetry and Paintings in the First Bible of Charles the Bald, 1997, The Holy Face and the paradox of Representation, 1998, Rome 1300: On the Path of the Pilgrim, 2000, Spiritual Seeing: Picturing God's Invisibility in the Middle Ages, 2000, Old St. Peter's and Ch. Decoration in Medieval Italy, 2002, Seeing Medieval Art, 2004. Sr. fellow Dumbarton Oaks, Washington, 1980-86; Woodrow Wilson fellow; Inst. Advanced Study fellow; Am. Council Learned Socs. fellow; Am. Philos. Soc. fellow; Guggenheim fellow; fellow Am. Acad. in Rome Fellow Medieval Acad. Am., Am. Acad. Arts and Scis.; mem. Coll. Art Assn., Phi Beta Kappa. Home: 3601 Greenway Apt 809 Baltimore MD 21218 Office: Johns Hopkins U Baltimore MD 21218 E-mail: hlk@jhu.edu.

KESSLER, IRVING ISAR, epidemiologist, consultant; AB in Math., NYU, 1952; MA in Endocrinology, Harvard U., 1955, PhD in Epidemiology, 1969; MD, Stanford U., 1960; MPH, Columbia U., 1962. Diplomate Nat. Bd. Med. Examiners, Am. Bd. Preventive Medicine; lic. physician Md. Prof. epidemiology Johns Hopkins U., 1972-84; chmn. dept. epidemiology and preventive medicine U. Md. Sch. Medicine, Balt., 1978-88; prof. oncology U. Md. Sch. Medicine Cancer Ctr., Balt., 1984—; prof. medicine U. Md. Sch. Medicine, Balt., 1985—, prof. dermatology, 1995—. Prof. dept. epidemiology & preventive medicine U. Md. Sch. Medicine, 1988-2001; emeritus, 2002-, exec. com. U. Md. Med. Sys., 1984-88; bd. dirs. Md. Med. Rsch. Inst.; v.p. for health scis., bd. dirs. ECRI, Plymouth Meeting, Pa., 1992-93; sci. adv. bd. Ctr. for Indoor Air Rsch., 1988-2001; mem. hazardous and toxic substances study commn., State of Md., 1983-84; cons. and lectr. in field. Bd. dirs. Israel Cancer Rsch. Found.; chmn. advisory panel on toxic shock syndrome AMA, 1984-85. Capt. USPHS res. Recipient Faculty Rsch. award Am. Cancer Soc. Fellow Am. Pub. Health Assn., Am. Coll. Preventive Medicine; mem. AAAS, Am. Epidemiol. Soc., Am. Assn. for Cancer Rsch., Am. Coll. Occupl. Medicine, N.Y. Acad. Sci., Md. Gerontological Assn. (founder, bd. dirs., chmn., program com., pres. 1984-85, Gerontology Recognition award 1989), D.A. Boyes Soc. Gynaecologic Oncology (hon.), Phi Beta Kappa, Soc. Sigma Xi. Office: 9-34 MSTF 10 S Pine St Baltimore MD 21201-1596 Office Phone: 410-706-7866. E-mail: ikessler@epi.umaryland.edu, ikessler@verizon.net. *Epidemiology is the scientific discipline underlying preventive medicine which bridges the gap between medical science and human health. In an era of escalating healthcare costs and diminishing faith in the medical care system, my professional career has been dedicated to the development of preventive medicine as an academic discipline and an instrument of public health policy. Of equal concern to me has been the enhancement of preventive medicine as a rewarding career for the finest of our nation's young physicians. Unfortunately, in recent years, epidemiologists have increasingly emphasized the statistical rather than the biomedical significance of research findings, thereby rendering the field much less attractive to well-trained physicians who are devoted to the aetiology and control of disease.*

KESSLER, JEFFREY L., lawyer; b. NYC, Feb. 19, 1954; s. Milton M. and Edith H. Kessler; m. Regina T. Dessoff, May 21, 1977; children: Andrew Zalman, Leora Miriam. BA, JD summa cum laude, Columbia U., 1977. Bar: N.Y. 1978, U.S. Dist. Ct. (so. dist.) N.Y. 1978, U.S. Ct. Appeals (1st, 2d, 3d, 8th, 11th & Fed. cir.), U.S. Supreme Ct. 1985. Assoc. Weil, Gotshal & Manges, N.Y.C., 1977-85, ptnr., 1985—2003, Dewey Ballantine LLP, N.Y.C., 2003—, co-chair Litigation Dept., 2003—. Adj. assoc. prof. Fordham Law Sch., 1988-98; founder, bd. advisors study pvt. antitrust litig. Georgetown U., 1983-85; adj. prof. Law Sch. Columbia U., 2005—; mem. exec. and mgmt. com. Dewey Ballantine LLP, N.Y.C., N.Y., 2003— Mem. editl. bd.: Columbia U. Law Rev., 1976—77, Competition Laws Outside the U.S., 2001—03, editor-in-chief: State Antitrust Practice Statutes, 1999; co-author: International Trade and U.S. Antitrust Law; contbr. articles to profl. jours. Kent scholar, 1975-76, Stone scholar, 1976-77. Mem. ABA (antitrust law sect., vice-chmn. Sherman Act Sect. 2 com. 1989-90, chmn. internat. law com. 1990-94, co-chmn. pub. com. 1994-96, coun. mem. 1996-99, internat. task force 2001-03), Columbia Coll. Alumni Assn. (bd. dirs. 1996-99), Phi Beta Kappa. Democrat. Jewish. Office: Dewey Ballantine LLP 1301 Avenue of the Americas New York NY 10019-6092 Office Phone: 212-259-8050. Office Fax: 212-259-6333. Business E-Mail: JKessler@DeweyBallantine.com.

KESSLER, JOAN F., judge, lawyer; b. June 25, 1943; m. Frederick P. Kessler, Sept. 1967; 2 children. BA, U. Kans., 1961-65; postgrad., U. Wis., 1965-66; JD cum laude, Marquette U., 1968. Law clk. Hon. John W. Reynolds U.S. Dist. Ct. (ea. dist.) Wis., Milw., 1968-69; assoc. Warschafsky, Rotter & Tarnoff, Milw., 1969-71; pvt. practice Milw., 1971-74; assoc. Cook & Franke, S.C., Milw., 1974-78; U.S. atty. Eastern Dist. Wis., Milw., 1978-81; ptnr. Foley & Lardner, Milw., 1981—2004; judge Ct. Appeals Wisc., Milw., 2004—. Lectr. profl. responsibility U. Wis. Law Sch., Marquette U. Law Sch., Milw., 1994-96; mem. bd. govs. State Bar of Wis., 1985-89, 90-92, 93-95, chair, 1993, bd. dirs. family law sect., 1991-94; mem. Jud. Coun. Wis., Madison, 1989-92; mem. Milw. Bd. Attys. Profl. Responsibility, 1979-85. Bd. dirs. Legal Aid Soc., 1974-78, v.p., 1978, Urban League, 1980-82, Women's Bus. Initiative Corp., 1989-91, Girl Scouts U.S., Milw., 1994-96; bd. dirs., pres. Voters for Choice in Wis., 1989-93. Fellow Am. Matrimonial Lawyers (bd. govs. 1990-96, v.p. 1996-99), Am. Law Inst., Am. Bar Found.; mem. ABA (chair sect. individual rights and responsibilities 2003-04, coun. mem. 1997-2004, editor Human Rights 1997-99), ACLU. Office: Judge Ct Appeals Wis 633 W Wisconsin Milwaukee WI 53203 Office Phone: 414-227-4684. E-mail: joan.kessler@wicourts.gov.

KESSLER, JOHN OTTO, physicist, researcher; b. Vienna, Nov. 26, 1928; arrived in U.S., 1940, naturalized, 1946; s. Jacques and Alice Blanca (Neuhut) K.; m. Eva M. Bondy, Sept. 9, 1950; children: Helen J., Steven J. AB, Columbia U., 1949, PhD, 1953. With RCA Corp., Princeton, NJ, 1952-66, sr. mem. tech. staff, 1964-66, mgr. grad. recruiting, 1964-66; prof. physics U. Ariz., Tucson, 1966-93, prof. emeritus, 1994—. Vis. rsch. assoc. Princeton U., 1962-64; sr. vis. fellow, vis. prof. physics U. Leeds, Eng., 1972-73, sr. vis. fellow, 1990-91; vis. prof. Technische Hogeschool Delft, Netherlands, spring 1979; Fulbright fellow dept. applied math. and theoretical physics Cambridge U., Eng., 1983-84. Contbr. articles to profl. jours. Fellow: AAAS; mem.: Am. Phys. Soc. Achievements include patentee in field; research in low Reynolds number fluid mechanics; mechanisms of bacterial propulsion, interaction and formation of coherent swarms, leading to microturbulence; bioconvection and consumption patterns of micro-organism populations; locomotion, transport of metabolites, and signalling; complementary aspects of mobility of micro-organisms; measurement of probability densities for swimming velocity of algae and bacteria; relationship of interorganism signalling, quorum sensing, and exchange of metabolites to individual and collective motility in Bacillus subtilis and the Volvocales. Home: 2740 E Camino La Zorrela Tucson AZ 85718-3126 Office: U Ariz Physics Dept Bldg 81 Tucson AZ 85721-0001 Office Phone: 520-621-2797. Business E-Mail: kessler@physics.arizona.edu.

KESSLER, JUDD LEWIS, lawyer; b. Newark, Apr. 10, 1938; s. Samuel W. and Ethel S. (Shapiro) K.; m. Marian Osterweis, Jan. 7, 1979 (div. 1986); m. Carol Ann Farris, Oct. 19, 1987; 1 child, Samuel Farris. AB, Oberlin Coll., 1960; LLB, Harvard U., 1963. Bar: N.J. 1963, D.C. 1972, Md. 1989, U.S. Dist. Ct. N.J., U.S. Dist. Ct. D.C., U.S. Dist. Ct. Md., U.S. Ct. Appeals (4th cir.), U.S. Supreme Ct. 1968. Assoc. Toner, Crowley, Woelper and Vanderbilt, Newark, 1963-66; asst. gen. counsel U.S. Agy. for Internat. Devel., Washington, 1966-82; ptnr., chmn. internat. bus. practice group Porter, Wright, Morris & Arthur, Washington, 1982—. Author: (with others) Legal Aspects of Exporting, 1986; contbr. articles to profl. jours. Recipient Outstanding Career Achievement award, U.S. AID, 1982; Presdl. appointee to Sr. Fgn. Svc., 1982. Master: London Court Internat. Arbitration; mem.: ABA, Internat. Ctr. for the Settlement of Investment Disputes (panel of arbitrators 2003—), Fed. Bar Assn. (chmn. internat. sect. 1983—87, nat. coord. Export Legal Assistance Network 1985—, Pres.'s E Excellence Export Svc. award 1997), Am. Soc. Internat. Law, Internat. C. of C. (mem. U.S. arbitration com. 2000), Inter-Am. Bar Found. (pres. 1994—), Inter-Am. Bar Assn. (Internat. Lawyer of Yr. award 2002), Am. Arbitration Assn. (mem. internat. panel arbitrators 1997—), Cosmos Club. Office: Porter Wright Morris & Arthur 1919 Penn Ave NW Washington DC 20006-3434 Office Phone: 202-778-3080.

KESSLER, KEITH, retired computer scientist; s. Jean H. and Carmen E. Kessler; m. Kristine V. Grove, 1978; 1 child, Brian Thomas. BEng in Elec. Engring., The Cooper Union, N.Y.C., 1978; cert. in Artificial Intelligence, NYU, 1988. Owner Keith Kessler Cons., 1976—; rsch. asst. Cooper Union Rsch. Found., N.Y.C., 1974—78; ind. cons. Citibank, N.Y.C., 1975—78; chief analyst Thomas-Reising Assocs., N.Y.C., 1977—78; mem. of the tech. staff Hughes Aircraft Co., Culver City, Calif., 1978—84; prin. engr. LORAL Electronic Systems, Yonkers, NY, 1984—88. Vol. mentor Ednl. Outreach Program, N.Y.C., 1994—95; mem. Maui Peace Action, Maui, Hawaii, 2001, Pax Christi, 1988, Sierra Club, Environ. Action Coalition; supporting mem. Pacific Whale Found., Ma'alaea, Maui, Hawaii, Maui Ocean Ctr., Ma'alaea, Maui, Hawaii. Scholar NY State Regents scholar, State of N.Y., 1974—78. Mem.: NY Acad. of Sci., Assn. of Old Crows, Assn. for Computing Machinery, IEEE, Hawai'i Cultural Found., Mensa. Roman Catholic. Avocations: bodysurfing, hiking, snorkeling, astronomy. Office: Keith Kessler Consulting PO Box 715 Kihei HI 96753-0715 Office Phone: 808-875-7646. E-mail: keith@keith-kessler.us.

KESSLER, KEITH LEON, lawyer; b. Seattle, July 18, 1947; s. Robert Lawrence and Priscilla Ellen (Allbee) K.; m. Lynn Elizabeth Eisen, Dec. 24, 1980; children: William Moore, Christopher Moore, Bradley Moore, Jamie Kessler. BA in Philosophy, U. Wash., 1969, JD, 1972. Bar: Wash. 1972, U.S. Dist. Ct. (we. dist.) Wash. 1973, U.S. Dist. Ct. (ea. dist. 1992); U.S. Ct. Appeals (9th cir.) 1973, U.S. Supreme Ct. 1975. Law clk. to Hon. Robert Finley Wash. Supreme Ct., Olympia, Wash., 1972-73; ptnr. Kessler, Tegland & Urmston, Seattle, 1973-75, Kessler & Urmston, Seattle, 1975-76, Kessler, Urmston & Sever, Seattle, 1976-77, Kessler & Sever, Seattle, 1977-79; assoc. Stritmatter & Stritmatter, Hoquiam, Wash., 1980-83; ptnr. Stritmatter, Kessler & McCauley, Hoquiam, Wash., 1983-93, Stritmatter Kessler, Hoquiam, Wash., 1993-97, Stritmatter, Kessler, Whelan, Withey, Hoquiam, 1997—. Chmn. LAW PAC, Seattle, 1991-93; mem. pattern jury instrns. com. Wash. Supreme Ct., 2000—. Editor: Trial Evidence, 1996, author: (with others) Motor Vehicle Accident Litigation Desk Book, 1988, 1995, 97; contbr. chpt. to book. Pres. Kairos Ctr., Aberdeen, Wash., 1984-86; co-founder Grays Harbor Support Group; bd. dir. Wash. State Head Injury Found., Bellevue, Wash., 1993-96. Recipient Founders award Wash. State Head Injury Found., 1990, Silver award United Way, 1992 Fellow Am. Coll. Trial Lawyers; mem. Am. Bd. Trial Advocates, (pres. Wash. chpt. 1997), Wash. State Trial Lawyers Assn. (pres. 1990-91, named trial lawyer of yr., 1994), Damage Attys. Round Table (pres. 2002-03), Wash. Trial Attys. Political Forum (chmn. 1993-95), Wash. Def. Trial Lawyers (named Outstanding Plaintiff Trial Lawyer 2002), Trial Lawyers for Public Justice (state exec. com. 1994—). Office: Stritmatter Kessler Whelan Withey 413 8th St Hoquiam WA 98550-3607 Office Phone: 800-540-7364. Business E-Mail: keith@skwwc.com.

KESSLER, LYNN ELIZABETH, state legislator; b. Seattle, Feb. 26, 1941; d. John Mathew and Kathryn Eisen; m. Keith L. Kessler, Dec. 24, 1980; children: William John Moore, Christopher Scott Moore, Bradley Jerome Moore, Jamie. Attended, Seattle U., 1958-59. Mem. Wash. Ho. of Reps., 1993—. Majority leader, mem. rules com., mem. appropriations com. Exec. dir. United Way Grays Harbor, 1984-92; mem. adv. coun. Head Start, 1986-89, Cervical Cancer Awareness Task Force, 1990-91, vocat. adv. coun. Hoquiam High Sch., 1991—, strategic planning com. Grays Harbor Community Hosp., 1991-92, Grays Harbor Food Bank Com., 1991-92, Grays Harbor Dem. Ctrl. Com.; vice-chair Grays Harbor County Shorelines Mgmt. Bd., 1989-90; chair Disability Awareness Com., 1988-90, Youth 2000 Com., 1990-91; pres. Teenage Pregnancy, Parenting and Prevention Adv. Coun., 1989-91; v.p. Grays Harbor Econ. Devel. Coun., 1990-; trustee Grays Harbor Coll., 1991-2001, Aberdeen YMCA, 1991— Mem. Aberdeen Rotary (pres. 1993-94). Home: 62 Kessler Ln Hoquiam WA 98550-9742 Office: Wash Ho of Reps Legislative Bldg 3rd Fl Olympia WA 98504-0001

KESSLER, MARTIN ELLIOT, surgeon; b. Bklyn., July 19, 1953; BA, Queens Coll., 1976; MD, Cornell U. Med. Coll., 1980. Diplomate Am. Bd. Plastic and Reconstructive Surgery; cert. in added qualifications surgery of the hand. Intern dept. surgery N.Y. Hosp. Cornell Med. Ctr., N.Y.C., 1980-81, jr. asst. resident dept. of surgery, 1981-82, sr. asst. resident dept. of surgery, 1982-83, resident dept. of surgery, 1983-85; fellow hand surgery The Cleve. Clinic, 1985; fellow reconstructive microsurgery U. Louisville Health Ctr., 1986; plastic and reconstructive surgeon pvt. practice Rockville Ctr., N.Y., 1986—. Clin. instr. plastic surgery Cornell U. Med. Coll., North Shore U. Hosp., Manhasset, N.Y., 1986—. Grantee N.Y. Lung Assn., 1977, March of Dimes, 1978. Fellow Am. Coll. Surgeons; mem. AMA, Am. Soc. Plastic and Reconstructive Surgeons, AmericanBurn Assn., N.Y. County Med. Soc., Med. Soc. State of N.Y., Nassau County Med. Soc., N.Y. Acad. Scis. Office: Martin E Kessler 242 Merrick Rd Rockville Centre NY 11570-5254 Office Phone: 516-536-5858, 516-466-7000.

KESSLER, RALPH KENNETH, lawyer, manufacturing executive; b. N.Y.C., May 23, 1943; s. Ralph G. Kessler and Margaret Gilmore; m. Margaret McQueeney, Oct. 12, 1980; children— Daniel, Anne BA, St. John's U., 1965, JD, 1968; LLM, NYU, 1972. Bar: N.Y., U.S. Dist. Ct. (so. and ea. dists.) N.Y., U.S. SEC. SEC trial atty., N.Y.C., 1968-72; assoc. Mudge, Rose et al., N.Y.C., 1972-76; sec., asst. gen. counsel Singer Co., Stamford, Conn., 1976-86, v.p., dep. gen. counsel, sec., 1986-88; v.p. legal affairs, sec. TI Group Inc., N.Y.C., 1988-98, sr. v.p. legal affairs, sec., 1998-2000; sr. v.p. legal affairs Smiths Group Inc., Whippany, N.J., 2000—. Home: 86 Mountain Ave New Rochelle NY 10804-4708 Office: Smiths Group Inc 110 Algonquin Pky Whippany NJ 07981

KESSLER, RANDALL MARK, lawyer, educator; b. Gainesville, Fla., Nov. 23, 1962; s. Stanley Clifford Kessler and Janet (Miller) Brown. BA, Brandeis U., 1985; JD, Emory U., 1988. Bar: Ga. 1988. Founder, owner Kessler & Schwarz PC, Atlanta, 1991—. Prof. Family Law John Marshall Law Sch., Atlanta, 2004—; judge pro hac vice DeKalb Recorder's Ct., Atlanta, 2000—. Contbr. articles to profl. jours. Mem.: ABA (chair Family Cts. com. 2001—). Jewish. Office: Kessler & Schwarz PC 101 Marietta St Ste 3500 Atlanta GA 30303 Office Phone: 404-688-8810.

KESSLER, RICHARD PAUL, JR., lawyer; b. Latrobe, Pa., July 11, 1945; s. Richard Paul Sr. and Dorothy Henrietta (Comp) K.; m. Kathleen Jane Parker, June 17, 1973 (dec. May 11, 1996); 1 child, Grace Elizabeth; m. Susan Kessler, Oct. 2000. BA, Fairfield (Conn.) U., 1968; JD, Emory U., 1971. Bar: Ga. 1971, U.S. Dist. Ct. (no. dist.) Ga. 1973, U.S. Ct. Appeals (5th cir.) 1974, U.S. Ct. Appeals (11th cir.) 1981, U.S. Supreme Ct. 1995. Law clk. to presiding justice U.S. Dist. Ct. (no. dist.) Ga., 1971-73; ptnr. Macey, Wilensky, Cohen, Wittner & Kessler, LLP, Atlanta, 1973—. Lectr. Practising Law Inst., 1981, 83, Fin. Svc. Corp. Career Conf., Atlanta, 1986, Ga. and Ala. Insts. of Continuing Legal Edn., 1993-95; panelist Credit Union Nat. Assn., Inc. League Attys. Conf., 1980-82, 87, 88-93, ABA, 1990-91; participant Nat. Conf. Commrs. on Uniform State Laws Drafting Com. on U.C.C. Articles, 3, 4, 4A, 1985-90; chair corp. and banking law sect. State Bar Ga., 1995-96. Author: What You Should Know About the New Bankruptcy Code, 1979, Guide to the Bankruptcy Laws: The Bankruptcy Reform Act of 1978, 79, Guide to the Bankruptcy Laws: The Bankruptcy Reform Act of 1978 (Bankruptcy Code) as Amended by the Bankruptcy Amendments and Federal Judgeship Act of 1984, The Bankruptcy Judges, U.S. Trustees and Family Farmer Bankruptcy Act of 1986; contbg. editor Banking and Lending Instn. Forms, 1996-2005; contbr. articles to profl. jours. Mem.: East Lake Golf Club. Office: Ste 600 285 Peachtree Center Ave NE Atlanta GA 30303-1229 Office Phone: 404-584-1200. Business E-Mail: rkessler@maceywilensky.com.

KESSLER, ROBERT W., municipal official; BA in Urban Studies, U. Minn., St. Paul, 1974; MPA in Housing, Comty. Devel., U. So. Calif., Washington, Pub. Affairs Ctr., 1981; postgrad. studies in Project Mgmt., Program Evaluation U. Minn., 1978-94. City planner Office of the Mayor, St. Paul, Minn., 1973-74; devel. grant asst., comty. devel. divsn. City of St. Paul, 1975-80; program analyst HUD, Washington, 1980-81; asst. to chief of staff Mayor's Office City of St. Paul, 1982; comty. devel. specialist City of St. Paul, 1982-83, econ. devel. specialist neighborhood divsn., 1983-86; dir. St. Paul 503 Devel. Co., 1986-87; asst. to mayor City of St. Paul, 1987-88, dir. Mayor's info. and complaint office, 1988-90, license and permit mgr., 1990-92, dir. Office Lic., Inspections and Environ. Protection, 1992—. With U.S. Army Med. Bn., Vietnam, 1969-70. Decorated Bronze Star, U.S. Army, 1970. Mem. Internat. City/County Mgmt. Assn. (affiliate). Home: 2190 Dahl Ave Saint Paul MN 55119-5877 Office: Lics Inspections & Environ Protection 350 Saint Peter St Ste 300 Saint Paul MN 55102-1510

KESSLER, RONALD, author; b. N.Y.C., Dec. 31, 1943; s. Ernest Borek and Minuetta K.; m. Pamela Johnson Whitehead; children: Greg, Rachel Kessler. Student, Clark U., Worcester, Mass., 1962—64. Reporter Worcester Telegram, 1964; reporter, editl. writer Boston Herald, 1964-68; N.Y. bur. reporter Wall Street Jour., 1968-70; investigative reporter Washington Post, 1970-85; journalist/author, 1985—. Author: The Life Insurance Game, 1985, The Richest Man in the World: The Story of Adnan Khashoggi, 1986, Spy vs. Spy: Stalking Soviet Spies in America, 1988, Moscow Station: How the KGB Penetrated the American Embassy, 1989, The Spy in the Russian Club: How Glenn Souther Stole America's Nuclear War Plans and Escaped to Moscow, 1990, Escape from the CIA: How the CIA Won and Lost the Most Important KGB Spy Ever to Defect to the U.S., 1991, Inside the CIA: Revealing the Secrets of the World's Most Powerful Spy Agency, 1992, The FBI: Inside the World's Most Powerful Law Enforcement Agency, 1993, Inside the White House: The Hidden Lives of the Presidents and the Secrets of the World's Most Powerful Institution, 1995, The Sins of the Father: Joseph P. Kennedy and the Dynasty He Founded, 1996, Inside Congress: The Shocking Scandals, Corruption, and Abuse of Power Behind the Scenes on Capitol Hill, 1997, The Season: Inside Palm Beach and America's Richest Society, 1999 (basis for A&E TV prodn.), The Bureau: The Secret History of the FBI, 2002, The CIA at War: Inside the Secret Campaign Against Terror, 2003, A Matter of Character: Inside the White House of George W. Bush, 2004; contbr.: Microsoft Encarta Encyclopedia. Recipient pub. affairs reporting award Am. Polit. Sci. Assn., 1965; citation Freedoms Found., 1966; 1st prize in newswriting UPI, 1967; Sevellon Brown Meml. award AP, 1967; sci. writers award ADA, 1968; 1st place in pub. svc. award Md.-Del.-D.C. Press Assn., 1972; outstanding series award AAUW, 1972; Bill Pryor Meml. Reporting award, 1973; Front Page award Washington-Balt. Newspaper Guild, 1973; George H. Polk Meml. award for cmty. svc., 1973; for nat. reporting, 1979; Washington Dateline award for bus. reporting Sigma Delta Chi-Soc. Profl. Journalists, 1987; 1st pl. in investigative reporting Assn. Area Bus. Publs., 1987; named Washingtonian of Yr. Washington Mag., 1972; Dow Jones Inc. Newspaper Fund intern, 1964. Home and Office: 2516 Stratton Dr Potomac MD 20854-6231 Personal E-mail: KesslerRonald@cs.com.

KESSLER, RONALD N., plastics company executive; b. Youmgstown, Ohio; s. Milton and Justine Kessler; m. Linda Ann Schloss, Aug. 21, 1976; children: Daniel, JamieAnn, Samantha, Seth. Student, Lowell Inst. Tech., Lowell, Mass., 1967—69; BS, Youngstown State Univ., Youngstown, Ohio, 1973. R & D tech. Kessler Products, Youngstown, Ohio, 1973—74; sales Space-Links Inc., Youngstown, Ohio, 1974—75, v.p. mktg., 1975—78; pres., owner Willow Molded Plastics/SLI, Youngstown, Ohio, 1978—84; v.p. fin. Thermal Energy Inc., Youngstown, Ohio, 1980—85; pres. Boardman Molded Products, Youngstown, Ohio, 1986—91, Mr. Charles Shampoo, W. Bloomfield, Mich., 1991—93, Kessler Products, Youngstown, Ohio, 1993—. Bd. dir. Thermal Energy, Youngstown, Ohio, 1980—85, AAMA Am. Archtl. Mfg. Assn., N.Y.C., 1993, N.Y.C., 97. Bd. mem. Jewish Cmty. Ctr., 1977—80, Jewish Cmty. Rels. Coun., Youngstown, Ohio, 2001—, Jewish/Arab Dialeses, Youngstown, Ohio, 2003—. Mem.: Soc. Plastics Industries, Soc. Plastic Engr., Masonic Lodge (32nd degree 2002). Republican. Jewish. Achievements include patents for inventor over 20 domestic and international patents; on board for developing test procedures for weatherstripping. Avocations: golf, tennis, skiing, basketball. Home: 2000 Twin Oaks Girard OH 44420 Office: Boardman Molded Products Inc 1110 Thalia PO Box 1858 Youngstown OH 44501 Office Phone: 330-788-2401. Business E-Mail: rkessler@spacelinks1.com.

KESSLER, STUART, accountant, financial planner; b. Bklyn., May 17, 1929; s. Morris M. and Anne (Blacker) K.; m. Isabel Lois Knecht, Aug. 19, 1956; children: Jeffrey, Glenn, Bradley. BA, Bklyn. Coll., 1950; MBA, CCNY, 1953; JD, Bklyn. Law Sch., 1957; LLM, NYU, 1962. CPA, N.Y.; bar: N.Y. 1957. Staff acct. Klein, Hinds, & Finke, N.Y.C., 1952-60; ptnr. Rothstein, Kessler & Co., N.Y.C., 1960-70; sr. tax ptnr. Goldstein, Golub, Kessler LLP, N.Y.C., 1970—; mng. dir. Am. Express Tax and Bus. Svcs., 1998—. Pres. Found. Acctg. Edn., N.Y.C., 1985-; bd. dirs. Estate Planning Coun. N.Y., N.Y.C., 1990-94. Mem. editorial bd. Fin. Planning Jour., 1985-93; editor estate planning column CPA Jour., 1983; contbr. articles to profl. jours. Trustee Greenburgh Hebrew Ctr., 1974-83. Staff sgt. USAF, 1951-52. Recipient James Kelly Pub. Svc. award Westchester CPA Soc., 1990; named one of 100 Most Influential People in Acctg., Acctg. Today, 1994, 96-2003, One of Am.'s Top Fin. Advisors, Worth Mag., 1994; named to Bkly. Tech. Hall of Fame, 1998. Mem. AICPA (governing coun. 1982-90, 91—, chmn. governing coun. 1997-98, bd. dirs. 1991-99, chmn. pers. fin. planning divsn. 1990-94, chmn. responsibilities in tax practice com. 1988-90, pers. fin. specialist, Gold medal 2003), N.Y. State Soc. CPAs (pres. 1984-85, bd. dirs. 1978-83, Outstanding Svc. award 1990, Hall of Fame 2002), Bklyn. Coll. Acct. Alumni Assn. (pres. 1964-65, Jerome Milgram Svc. award),

Bklyn. Coll. Alumni Assn. (bd. dirs. 1962-85, Alumnus of Yr. 2005). Avocations: running, gardening, collecting headlines, travel, music. Office: Goldstein Golub Kessler LLP 1185 Ave Of The Americas New York NY 10036-2601 Office Phone: 212-372-1304. Personal E-mail: nskessler@aol.com. Business E-Mail: stuart.i.kessler@aexp.com.

KESSLER, WILLIAM EUGENE, healthcare executive; b. St. Louis, Dec. 15, 1944; s. Joseph John and Margaret Mary (Burns) K.; m. Patricia Christine Wilson, Nov. 9, 1968; children: Christina, William, John, Timothy, Jennifer, Catherine, Joseph, Daniel. BS in Commerce, St. Louis U., 1966, MHA, 1968. Various positions St. John's Hosp., St. Louis, 1963-67; adminstrv. resident St. Mary's Hosp., Grand Rapids, Mich., 1967-68; pres. St. Anthony's Health Ctr., Alton, Ill., 1971—. Chmn., prof. and tech. adv. com. Joint Commn. on Accreditation Healthcare Orgn., 1990-94; speaker profl. and community settings, 1972—; preceptor St. Louis U., 1980—, U. Mo., Columbia, 1991; bd. dir. Hosp. Assn. Met. St. Louis, 1975-85. Contbr. articles to profl. jour., 1972—. Admissions advisor US Mil. Acad., 1973-83; treas., bd. dir. Cath. Childrens' Home Alton, 1981-89; v.p. diocesan bd. edn. Diocese of Springfield, Ill., 1981-82, pres. 1982-84, mem. bd. edn. 1986-92; mem. diocesan fin. coun., 1987—; chmn. ARC, Alton, 1983-85; bd. dir. Am. Cancer Soc., Alton, 1984-90; pres. St. Louis Metropolitan Hosp. Coun., 1996. Served to capt. US Army, 1968-71. Decorated Army Commendation medal; recipient Alton Jaycees Disting. Svc. award, Alumni Merit award St. Louis U., 1994; named Knight of the Equestrian Order of the Holy Sepulchre, 1997; recipient Pro Ecclesia et Pontifice Cross Pope John Paul II, 2002, Mercy H.S., Alumni Merit award, 2002. Fellow: Am. Coll. Healthcare Execs. (regent's adv. coun. 1987—93, nominating com. 1991—94, regent 2002, chair ethics com., Regent's award, Sr. Healthcare Exec. of the Yr. award 1993); mem.: Southwestern Ill. Indsl. Assn. (exec. com. 1983—88, bd. dirs. 1989—, chmn. 1997), St. Louis U. Hosp. Administrn. Alumni Assn. (pres. 1978), Cath. Health Assn. U.S.A. (bd. dirs. 1987—, exec. com. 1989—92, chmn.-elect 1990—, chair 1991), Ill. Hosp. Assn. (exec. com. 1981—86, chmn. 1984—85), Am. Hosp. Assn. (Ho. of Dels. 1984—88), Stadium (St. Louis), Stadium Club (St. Louis), Rotary (pres. Alton chpt. 1981-82, Paul Harris fellow 1985), Rotary (pres. Alton chpt. 1981—82, Paul Harris fellow 1979, 1985). Avocations: photography, sports, family travel. Home: 1216 N Hanser Ln Godfrey IL 62035-1840 Office: St Anthony's Health Ctr St Anthony's Way PO Box 340 Alton IL 62002-0340 also: St Clare's Hosp 915 E 5th St Alton IL 62002-6434

KESSLER-HODGSON, LEE GWENDOLYN, actress, corporate executive; b. Wellsville, N.Y., Jan. 16, 1947; d. James Hewitt and Reba Gwendolyn (Adsit) Kessler; m. Bruce Gridley, June 22, 1969 (div. Dec. 1979); m. Jeffrey Craig Hodgson, Oct. 31, 1987. BA, Grove City Coll., 1968; MA, U. Wis., 1969. Prof. Sangamon State U., Springfield, Ill., 1969-70; pers. exec. Bullock's, L.A., 1971-74; owner Brunnen Enterprises, L.A., 1982—. Author: A Child of Arthur, 1981, White King and The Doctor, 2005; prodr., writer play including Anais Nin: The Paris Years, 1986; appeared in TV movies, mini-series including Roots, 1978, Backstairs at The White House, 1979, Blind Ambition, 1980, Hill Street Blues, 1984-87, Murder By Reason of Insanity, 1985, Hoover, 1986, Creator, 1987, Our House, 1988, Favorite Son, 1988, Lou Grant 1983-84, Barney Miller, 1979, L.A. Law, 1990, Hunter, 1991, (screenplay) Settlers Way, 1988; (TV series) Matlock, L.A. Law others. Knapp Prize fellow U. Wis., 1969. Mem. AFTRA, SAG, Actors Equity Assn. Republican. Mem. Ch. Scientology. Avocations: singer, directing, motivational speaking. Mailing: PO Box 1808 Eureka MT 59917 Office Phone: 877-478-0835. Personal E-mail: kesslerl@bww.com.

KESSNER, DOLLY EUGENIO, music educator, concert pianist; b. Hanapepe, Kauai, Hawaii, Nov. 7, 1946; d. Hermogenes Narcissus and Librada Manuel Eugenio; m. Daniel Aaron Kessner, June 29, 1968; children: Darren Eugene, Demian Edward. BA in Music Edn., U. of Calif., L.A., 1968, MA in Composition, 1971; PhD in Music Theory, U. of So. Calif., L.A., 1992; studied piano with, Aube Tzerko; studied composition with, Henri Lazarof, Leon Kirchner, Robert Linn; studied speculative theory with, Robert Moore, William Thomsen. Music prof. Moorpark (Calif.) Coll., 1990—, chair music and dance dept., 2000—. Tchg. assoc. UCLA, 1968—71, 1981—99; asst. prof. U. of So. Calif., L.A., 1978—80, Calif. State U., Northridge, 1975—78; premieres of works by Max Lifchitz, Anthony Vazzana, William Toutant, Frank Campo, Morten Lauridsen, Paul Pisk, Leonard Berkowitz, John Vincent; soloist Orquesta Sinfonica de El Salvador, San Salvador, 1997, Filarmonica Marea Neagra, Constanta, Romania, 1994, Constanta, 94, Constanta, 98. Composer: Five Piano Pieces, Toccata for piano; rec. artist, solo pianist: CD Lyric Piece for piano and orchestra, record Equali II for piano/celeste and 3 percussionists, CD In the Center. Recipient Grad. Merit fellowship in music, U. of So. Calif., 1987—89; grantee Fund for U.S. Artists at Internat. Festivals and Exhbns., NEA, US Info. Agy., Rockefeller Found., Pew Charitable Trusts, Arts Internat., 1996. Mem.: Assn. for Tech. in Music, Coll. Music Soc. Office: Moorpark Coll 7075 Campus Rd Moorpark CA 93021 Personal E-mail: dkessner@vcccd.net.

KESTENBAUM, LAWRENCE, political science educator; b. Chgo., Sept. 13, 1955; s. Justin Louis and Maryhelen (Dietrich) K.; m. M. Janice Gutfreund, Nov. 17, 1990. BA in Econs., Mich. State U., 1979; JD, Wayne State U., 1982; postgrad., Cornell U., 1988-90. Bar: Mich. Atty., cons., East Lansing, Mich., 1983-88, Ithaca, N.Y., 1988-90, Ann Arbor, Mich., 1990—2004; commrs. Ingham County, Mason, Mich., 1983-88; program assoc. Mich. Citizen's Lobby, Lansing, 1983-85; computer lab. dir. Sch. Criminal Justice, Mich. State U., East Lansing, 1992-95, acad. specialist polit. sci. dept., 1995-98; sr. specialist health and retirement study Inst. for Social Rsch., U. Mich., 1998—2004; Washtenaw County clk. and register of deeds Ann Arbor, 2005—; creator, owner Polit. Graveyard web site, 1996—. Adj. faculty Ea. Mich. U., Ypsilanti, 1991-2000. Contbg. author: At the Campus Gate, 1976; contbr. articles to profl. jours. Mem. planning commn. City of E. Lansing, 1977-79; replacement del. Dem. Nat. Mid-term Conv., 1978; county commr. Ingham County, Mason, Mich., 1983-88; mem. hist. dist. commn., City of Ann Arbor, 1992-98, chair hist. dist. commn., 1997-98; bd. dirs. Mich. State U. Student Housing Corp., East Lansing, 1978-79, Ann Arbor Hist. Found., 1992-2000, Arbornet, Inc., Ann Arbor, 1993-95; bd. dirs. Cyberspace Commns. mem. univ. planning com., Wayne State U., Detroit, 1980-82; vice-chmn. Dem. Party, 1994-98; candidate Mich. Ho. of Reps., 1998; county commr. Washtenaw County, Ann Arbor, Mich, 2000-2002. Recipient Arthur F. Lederle scholarship Wayne State U. Law Sch., Detroit, 1979. Mem. State Bar of Mich., Nat. Trust for Historic Preservation, Pittsfield Union Grange. Democrat. Jewish. Avocations: folk dancing, cemeteries, science fiction, local history, given names. Home: 1726 W Stadium Blvd Ann Arbor MI 48103-5225 Office: Washtenaw County Ste 120 200 N Main St Ann Arbor MI 48104 Office Phone: 734-222-6730. Personal E-mail: polygon@potifos.com.

KESTER, CHARLES MELVIN, lawyer; b. Batesville, Ark., Jan. 19, 1968; s. Monty Charles and Phyllis Smith Kester; m. Cheryl Goodwin, June 1, 1991. BA in Philosophy summa cum laude, Liberty U., 1991; JD magna cum laude, Georgetown U., 1994. Bar: Ark. 1994, U.S. Dist. Ct. (ea. and we. dists.) Ark. 1995, U.S. Ct. Appeals (8th cir.) 1995, U.S. Ct. Fed. Claims, 2002, U.S. Supreme Ct. 1998. Law clk. U.S. Ct. Appeals 8th Cir., Fargo, N.D., 1994-95; atty. Lingle Law Firm, Rogers, Ark., 1995-96; pvt. practice law Fayetteville, Ark., 1996—. Assoc. editor Georgetown Law Jour., 1993-94; contbr. articles to profl. jours. Mem. Ark. Bar Assn. (appellate practice com. 1997-2000, young lawyers sect. adv. coun. 1998-99, sec. labor and employment law sect. 2002, chair 2004), Ark. Trial Lawyers Assn. (amicus curiae com. 1997-2003), Phi Alpha Delta. Avocations: camping, rock climbing, spelunking. Home: 13602 White Oak Ln Fayetteville AR 72704-8312 Office: 1160 N College Ave Ste 1 Fayetteville AR 72703-1907 Office Phone: 479-582-4600.

KESTER, HELEN MARY, elementary school educator; b. Three Springs, Pa., Jan. 19, 1953; d. James R. and Phoebe C. (Dalzell) Daniels; m. Hal W. Kester, July 5, 1975; children: Mary Beth, Timothy, William Shondelmyer. BS, Slippery Rock U., 1974, MEd, 1978. Cert. elem. tchr., reading specialist, Pa. 8th grade reading tchr. New Kensington (Pa.)-Arnold Sch. Dist.; chairperson reading dept. Mem. NEA, Pa. State Edn. Assn., Internat. Reading Assn., Phi Delta Kappa, Kappa Delta Pi. E-mail: hkester@comcast.net.

KESTER, RANDALL BLAIR, lawyer; b. Vale, Oreg., Oct. 20, 1916; s. Bruce R. and Mabel M. (Judd) K.; m. Rachael L. Woodhouse, Oct. 20, 1940; children: Laura, Sylvia, Lynne. AB, Willamette U., 1937; JD, Columbia U., 1940. Bar: Oreg. 1940, U.S. Dist. Ct. Oreg. 1940, U.S. Ct. Appeals (9th cir.) 1941, U.S. Supreme Ct. 1960. Assoc., then partner firm Maguire, Shields, Morrison & Bailey, Portland, 1940-57; justice Oreg. Supreme Ct., Salem, 1957-58; partner Maguire, Shields, Morrison, Bailey & Kester, 1958-66, Maguire, Kester & Cosgrave, 1966-71, Cosgrave & Kester, Portland, 1972-78, Cosgrave, Kester, Crowe, Gidley & Lagesen, Portland, 1978-89, Cosgrave, Vergeer & Kester, Portland, 1989—. Instr. Northwestern Coll. Law, 1947-56; gen. solicitor northwestern dist. U.P. R.R., 1958-79; sr. counsel UPRR Co., 1979-81 Co-author: The First Duty: History of the U.S. District Court of Oregon, 1993; contbr. articles to profl. jours. Past v.p. Portland area council Boy Scouts of Am.; past pres. Mountain Rescue and Safety Council Oreg.; past trustee Willamette U.; past bd. dirs. Oreg. Symphony Soc., Oreg. Mus. Sci. and Industry. Recipient Silver Beaver award Boy Scouts Am., 1956, alumni citation Willamette U., 1987. Fellow Am. Acad. Appellate Lawyers; mem. ABA, Am. Bar Found. (life), Multnomah Bar Assn. (past pres. 1956, Professionalism award 1991), Oreg. State Bar (treas. 1965-66, Disting. Svc. award pub. utility sect. 1991), Am. Law Inst. (life), Nat. Ski Patrol, Mt. Hood Ski Patrol (past pres.), Mazamas (past pres., climbing chmn.), Wy'east Climbers, Portland C. of C. (pres. 1973, chmn. bd. 1974), U.S. Dist. Ct. Oreg. Hist. Soc. (past pres, bd. dirs., Lifetime Svc. award) Oreg. Ethics Commons (co-founder, sec.), Phi Delta Phi, Beta Theta Pi, Tau Kappa Alpha. Clubs: Arlington (Portland), City (Portland) (v.p. 1978-80, pres. 1986-87), University (Portland), Multnomah Athletic (Portland). Republican. Unitarian Universalist. Office: Cosgrave Vergeer & Kester LLP 805 SW Broadway 8th Fl Portland OR 97205 Office Phone: 503-323-9000. Business E-Mail: rkester@cvk-law.com.

KESTER, STEWART RANDOLPH, banker; b. Bronxville, N.Y., July 30, 1927; s. Robert Livingston, Jr. and Mae Anna (Jones) K.; m. Marion Fay Syrett, Sept. 23, 1950; children: Cheryl, Stewart Randolph, Valerie, Marcia. BA, Colgate U., 1949. Sales rep. Procter & Gamble Co., N.Y.C., 1949-55; mng. ptnr. Kester Bros., Pompano Beach, Fla., 1955-86, R&S Properties, Pompano Beach, 1956-90, Fla. Coast Banks, Inc., Pompano Beach, 1973-75, vice chmn. bd., 1975-84, chmn. bd., 1984-85, chmn. exec. com., dir.; dir. Barnett Bank So. Fla. N.A., 1985-89, also bd. dirs.; with Kester Bros. Realty Inc., 1991—; pres. Crail Creek Assocs. LC, 1997—. Bd. dirs. Big Sky Western Bank, Mont., chmn. bd., 2000—; pres. Jefferson Valley Ranch, Whitehall, Mont.; sec.-treas. Westfork Devel. Co. Inc., Big Sky, 1991—2000; ptnr. Big Sky Ranch, Inc. LLC. Vice mayor, commr., Pompano Beach, 1964-66, mayor, 1966-67; mem. Broward County Charter Commn., 1974-75; pres. United Way of Broward County, 1978-79; chmn. bd. trustees Pompano Police Edn. Fund, Inc., 1975-86; mem. exec. com. Broward chpt. NCCJ, 1983-86; bd. dirs. Ft. Lauderdale Symphony; founding bd. dirs. Broward Workshop, Inc., 1981-85; founding dir., pres. Pompano Beach Bd. Trade, 1978-86; founding dir., v.p. Broward Cmty. Found., 1985-89; founding bd. dirs. Big Sky Assn. for Arts, 1989-95, Vigilante Theatre Corp., 1992-94. With AUS, 1946-47. Named Outstanding Young Man Pompano Beach Jaycees, 1962; recipient Service award Ft. Lauderdale C. of C., 1975, Silver Medallion award NCCJ, 1984, Community Svc. award Pompano Beach C. of C., 1983, 85. Mem. Pompano Beach Hist. Soc. (founding bd. dirs.), Greater Pompano Beach C. of C. (past dir.), Pompano Beach Exch. Club (past pres., charter mem., Book of Golden Deeds award 1976), Montana Hist. Soc., Custer Battlefield Mus. and Hist. Commn., Custer Battlefield Preservation Commn., Mus. of the Rockies, Buffalo Bill Hist. Ctr., Mus. of Art (Ft. Lauderdale), Sons of the Revolution (N.Y.). Republican. Presbyterian. Office: Kester Bros Realty Inc 619 E Atlantic Blvd PO Box 91 Pompano Beach FL 33061-0091 Office Phone: 954-943-0876. E-mail: srkfsk@aol.com.

KESTERSON, DAVID BERT, language educator, dean; b. Springfield, Mo., Feb. 19, 1938; s. Homer Russell and Dorothy (Mace) K.; m. Cheryl Renee Monk; children: A. Todd, Chad Russell. BSE, S.W. Mo. State U., 1959; MA, U. Ark., 1961, PhD, 1965. NDEA fellow, 1959-62; grad. teaching asst. U. Ark., Fayetteville, 1962-64; asst. prof. English N.C. State U., Raleigh, 1964-68; from asst. prof. to prof. English North Tex. State U. (name now U. North Tex.), Denton, 1968—, disting. Alumni prof., 1979, chmn. dept. English, 1981-86, assoc. dean Coll. Arts and Scis., 1986-92; sr. Fulbright lectr. U. Würzburg (Germany), 1985; interim dean Coll. Arts and Scis. U. North Tex., Denton, 1992-93, vice provost, 1993-98, v.p. for acad. affairs, 1998-2000, provost, v.p. acad. affairs, 2000—03, prof., English and spl. asst. to pres. for humanities, 2003—. Cons. presses on manuscripts in Am. lit Author: Josh Billings, 1973, Bill Nye, 1980; monograph Bill Nye: The Western Writings, 1976; editor: Studies in the Marble Faun, 1971, Critics on Poe, 1973, Critics on Mark Twain, 1973, Critical Essays on Hawthorne's The Scarlet Letter, 1988; founding editor: Hawthorne Soc. Newsletter (now Nathaniel Hawthorne Rev.), 1974-82; assoc. editor: Studies in the Novel, 1970—, Nathaniel Hawthorne Jour., 1980-82. With USAR, 1956-60. Recipient Mortar Bd. Outstanding Educator award, 1980; Outstanding Alumnus award S.W. Mo. State U., 1986, Disting. Grad. Alumnus award Dept. English U. Ark., 1988. Mem. Nathaniel Hawthorne Soc. (co-founder, 1st pres. 1974-76), Am. Humor Studies Assn. (pres. 1980-81), South Ctrl. MLA (exec. com. 1976-77), MLA (del. assembly 1977-80, 84-87), Melville Soc., Soc. Study So. Lit. (pres. 1999-01), Mark Twain Circle, Thoreau Soc., Thomas Wolfe Soc., Fulbright Assn., POE Studies Assn., Phi Kappa Phi, Phi Beta Delta, Golden Key. Office: U North Tex Office PO Box 311307 Denton TX 76203-1307 Office Phone: 940-565-2158. Business E-Mail: kesterson@unt.edu.

KESTERSON, RAY BRENT, dean, retired military officer; b. St. Louis, June 10, 1941; s. Ellis O. and Gladys M. Kesterson; m. Betty J. Wagoner, June 8, 1963; children: Michelyne, Jeff. BA in Edn., Okla. Bapt. U., 1963; MRE, So. Sem., Louisville, 1966. Cert. tchr., Ky. Asst. prin. Parkland Elem. Sch., Louisville, 1965-66; tchr. Parkland Jr. H.S., Louisville, 1966-67; commd. 2d lt. USAF, 1967; assigned to Lowry AFB, Colo., 1967—69; advanced through grades to lt. col. USAF, 1983; assigned to Can. Forces Sta., Val d'Or, Que., 1969-71; Air Force ROTC prof. Grove City (Pa.) Coll., 1971-74; advisor Air Force Assistance Team, Tehran, Iran, 1974-76; asst. tng. dir. Def. Fgn. Lang. Inst., Monterey, Calif., 1976-79; exec. officer Air Tng. Command, San Antonio, 1979—83; tng. liaison officer Hdqs. Pacific Air Forces, Honolulu, 1983-86; chief standardization and evaluation Keesler Tech. Tng. Ctr., Biloxi, Miss., 1986-90; ret., 1990; dean tech. edn. Richland Coll., Dallas, 1991—. Author: Performance Criteria Analysis Manual, 1995 (Tex. Skill Stds. Leadership award 1996). Mem. KC Coun. 807. Mem. Tex. Assn. Coll. Tech. Educators (bd. dirs. 2001-), Richardson C. of C. (edn. com. 1997-2001). Avocation: desktop publishing. Home: 6012 Charleston Dr Frisco TX 75035 Office: Richland Coll 12800 Abrams Rd Dallas TX 75243 E-mail: bkesterson@dcccd.edu, brentkes@aol.com.

KESTIN, HOWARD H., judge; b. Passaic, N.J., July 24, 1937; s. Oscar and Annette K.; m. Joan H. Bard, Aug. 22, 1970: children: Bette Lynn, Anita Louise. BS, St. Louis U., 1959; JD, Rutgers U., 1962; LLM, U. Va., 1995. Bar: N.J. 1962, U.S. Supreme Ct. 1965. Law sec. to assoc. justice N.J. Supreme Ct., 1962—63; dep. atty. gen. N.J., 1963—65; asst. dir. Inst. Continuing Legal Edn., Newark, 1965—66, 1969—70, exec. dir., 1970—78; dir. State N.J. Legal Svcs. to Poor Program, Trenton, 1966—68; pvt. practice law Wayne, NJ, 1968—69; prof. Rutgers U., 1969—78; chief administrv. law judge, dir. Office Administrv. Law State N.J., 1978—83; judge family and civil law divsns. Superior Ct. N.J., Paterson, 1983—91, judge Appellate Divsn., 1992—2002, presiding judge, 2002—. Adj. prof. law Seton Hall U. Sch. Law, Newark, 1972-84. Moderator-host The Blessings of Liberty, Sta. WNBC-TV, 1971, The Right of the People, Sta. WNBC-TV, 1975. Recipient Media awards for TV series on Bill of Rights, N.J. Bar Assn./ABA, 1971. Mem. Am. Law Inst. (life), N.J. Bar Assn. (chmn. administrv. law sect. 1972-74, chmn. young lawyers sect. 1968-69, trustee 1969-70), N.J. Supreme Ct. (chmn. com. on legal edn. and admissions to bar 1976-79, chmn. standing com. on paralegal edn. and regulation 1993-2000), Passaic County Bar Assn., Assn. CLE Adminstrs. (chmn. stds. and accreditation com. 1972-78, v.p. 1978). Office: Superior Ct of NJ Appellate Divsn Ct Plz N 25 Main St Hackensack NJ 07601-7015

KESTIN, RANDI MIRIAM, educational analyst; b. NYC, Nov. 25, 1970; d. Herbert Leonard and Henriette Rita Kestin; m. Ezra Peisach, June 27, 1993; 1 child, Rebecca Hara Kestin Peisach. BA, Barnard Coll. Columbia U., 1992; MA, Tufts U., 1997. Rsch. intern Children's Television Workshop, NYC, 1991—92; student tchr., rschr. Barnard Coll. Toddler Ctr., NYC, 1991—92; rsch. asst., student tchr. Tufts U. Dept. Child Devel., Medford, Mass., 1993—97; project asst. Rsch. Communicators, Ltd., Dedham-Westwood, Mass., 1996—98; asst. project dir. Data Star, Inc., Waltham, Mass., 1998—99; rsch. fellow Mass. Dept. Edn., Malden, Mass., 1999—2000; data analyst Edn. Alliance, Brown U., Providence, 1999—. Rsch. cons. Edn. Devel. Ctr., Newton, Mass., 1999—2000, Jump Start for Young Children, Boston, 1999—2000. Chorus mem., social chair, orch. mem. Sudbury Savoyards, Sudbury, Mass., 1994—2005. Mem.: Am. Edn. Rsch. Assn., Am. Evaluation Assn. (presenter). Democrat. Avocation: musical theatre. Home: 1 Cliff St Apt 3 Attleboro MA 02703 Office: The Edn Alliance Brown U 222 Richmond St Ste 300 Providence RI 02903 Office Phone: 401-274-9548 262. Business E-Mail: Randi_Kestin@brown.edu.

KESTNER, ROBERT STEVEN, lawyer; b. St. Louis, Aug. 6, 1954; s. Robert Steven Sr. and Josephine Ann (LiPuma) K.; m. Denise Marie Dalhart, Apr. 25, 1981; children: Alexander, Jonathan, Joseph. BA in Mathematics & Economics, Ohio Wesleyan U., 1976; JD, Ohio State U., 1979. Bar: Ohio 1979, U.S. Dist. Ct. (no. dist.) Ohio 1979. Assoc. Baker & Hostetler, Cleve., 1979-88, ptnr., gen. bus. practice coord., 1988—2003, exec. ptnr., mem. policy com., 2003—. Mem. ABA, Ohio Bar Assn., Cleve. Bar Assn., Cleve. Mus. of Natural History, Country Club Pepper Pike. Office: Baker & Hostetler 3200 National City Ctr Cleveland OH 44114-3485 Office Phone: 216-861-7558. Office Fax: 216-696-0740. Business E-Mail: skestner@bakerlaw.com.

KETCHAM, BEVERLY LYNN, biologist, educator; b. Norwalk, Conn., Nov. 6, 1949; d. William and Mercedes Mary Ketcham. AA, C.C. Balt., 1969; BS, Frostburg State Coll., 1971; MS, W.Va. U., 1973; EdD, Ball State U., 1978. Instr. biology Ball State U., Muncie, Ind., 1976—78; sales assoc. Ball Stores Collegiene Shop, Muncie, 1978—80; buyer Ball Stores, Inc., Muncie, 1980—81; asst. prof. biology Del Mar Coll., Corpus Christi, Tex., 1982—87; computer sales assoc. CompuSolve, Corpus Christi, 1987—88; sales assoc. J.C. Penney, Corpus Christi, 1988—92; adj. prof. biology Hillsborough C.C., Tampa, Fla., 1992—93, assoc. prof. biology, 1993—98, prof. biology, 1998—. Author: Biological Science I Laboratory Manual, 1996, Microbiology and Human Disease Laboratory Manual, 2003. Mem.: Higher Edn. Consortium for Math. and Sci., Am. Assn. Women in C.C., Fla. Assn. C.C., Am. Inst. Biol. Scis., Nat. Assn. Biology Tchrs. Republican. Roman Catholic. Avocations: horseback riding, reading, movies. Office: Hillsborough CC 2112 N 15th St Tampa FL 33605

KETCHAM, RALPH, history and political science educator; b. Berea, Ohio, Oct. 28, 1927; s. Sherman G. and Laura (Murphy) K.; m. Julia Stillwell, Nov. 30, 1958; children: Benjamin, Laura Lee. AB, Allegheny Coll., 1949, DLitt (hon.), 1985; MA, Colgate U., 1952; PhD, Syracuse U., 1956, D.Litt. (hon.), 1999, McKendree Coll., 1988. Rsch. assoc. U. Chgo., 1956-60; lectr. history Yale U., New Haven, 1961-63; prof. history and polit. sci. Syracuse (N.Y.) U., 1963-97, prof. emeritus, 1997—. Fulbright lectr., Japan, 1965, India, 1974, Netherlands, 1987. Author: James Madison, 1971 (Nat. Book nominee 1972), From Colony to Country, 1974, Presidents Above Party, 1984, Individualism and Public Life, 1987, Participation in Government: Making a Difference, 1988, 4th edit., 2001, Framed for Posterity, 1993, The Idea of Democracy in the Modern Era, 2004. Mem. U.S. framework com. Civitas, 1988-90, Hungarian com., 1992-93, Russian com. 1993-94. With USCG, 1945-47. Named Prof. of Yr., Council for Advancement and Support Edn., 1987. Mem. Orgn. Am. Historians, Am. Studies Assn., Am. Antiquarian Soc., Inst. Early Am. History and Culture (coun. 1986-88). Avocations: skiing, sailing. Home: 1420 Salt Springs Rd Syracuse NY 13214-1434 Office: Syracuse U Maxwell Sch Syracuse NY 13244-0001 Office Phone: 315-443-2210. E-mail: rketcham@syr.edu.

KETCHAM, RICHARD SCOTT, lawyer; b. Columbus, Ohio, Jan. 8, 1948; s. Victor Alvin and Dorothy Eloise (Becher) K.; m. Kim Michelle Halliburton, Apr. 7, 1984 (div. 1989); 1 child, Kate Erin; m. Christy M. Canaday, Sept. 9, 1990 (div. 1994). BS, Bowling Green (Ohio) State U., 1970; JD cum laude, Capital U., Columbus, 1974. Bar: Ohio 1974, U.S. Dist. Ct. (so. dist.) Ohio 1979. Asst. pros. atty. Franklin County (Ohio) Pros., Columbus, 1974-79, sr. asst. pros. atty., 1979-84; ptnr. Ketcham & Ketcham, Columbus, 1984—. Mem. task force Legal Aid Referral Project, Columbus Bar Assn. Homeless Project, 1989—. Mem. Gov.'s Task Force on Family Violence, 1984-86. Mem. Nat. Assn. Criminal Def. Lawyers, Ohio Assn. Criminal Def. Lawyers (bd. dirs. 1989—, v.p. CLE, sec.), Ctrl. Ohio Assn. Criminal Def. Lawyers (pres. 1994-95, bd. dirs. 2001—), Ohio State Bar Assn., Columbus Bar Assn. (chmn. criminal law com. 1994-95, 95-96), Franklin County Trial Lawyers. Avocations: fishing, basketball, model railroads, gardening. Home: 1937 Elmwood Ave Columbus OH 43212-1112 Office: Ketcham & Ketcham 755 S High St Columbus OH 43206-1908 Office Phone: 614-444-3900. Personal E-mail: rsketchz@aol.com.

KETCHAM, WARREN ANDREW, psychologist, educator; b. Manistee, Mich., June 28, 1909; s. Perry Warren and Anna Ella (Ulrich) K.; m. Edna May Wearne, Nov. 23, 1962 (dec. Mar. 1991). BM, U. Mich., 1932, MA, 1947, PhD, 1951. Lic. psychologist Mich., Tex. Tchr. Reed City (Mich.) Pub. Schs., 1934-36, Melvindale (Mich.) Pub. Schs., 1936-38; supr. Dearborn (Mich.) Pub. Schs., 1938-43; sch. psychologist Ferndale (Mich.) Pub. Schs., 1950-53; prof., sch. psychologist U. Mich., Ann Arbor, 1953-77, prof. emeritus, 1978—; pvt. practice clin., indsl., orgnl. psychology Mich. and Tex., 1964—. Cons. Am. Sch., Guatemala City, Guatemala, 1958-80. Sgt. U.S. Army, 1943-45, PTO. Fulbright scholar Leeds U., 1959, Hinsdale scholar U. Mich., 1951. Fellow Am. Psychol. Assn.; mem. Am. Soc. Clin. Hypnotists, Mich. Soc. Clin. Psychologists, Mich. Psychol. Assn., Nat. Registered Health Svc. Providers in Psychology. Address: 2000 Mitchell Road #40 Petoskey MI 49770

KETCHAND, ROBERT LEE, lawyer; b. Shreveport, La., Jan. 30, 1948; s. Woodrow Wilson and Attie Harriet (Chandler) K.; m. Alice Sue Adams, May 31, 1969; children: Peter Leland, Marjory Attie. BA, Baylor U., 1970; JD, Harvard U., 1973. Bar: Tex. 1973, Mass. 1973, D.C. 1981. Assoc., ptnr. Butler & Binion, Houston, 1976-85, Washington, 1981-82; shareholder Brodsky & Ketchand, Houston, 1985-88; ptnr. Webster & Sheffield, Houston, 1988-90; atty. pvt. practice, Houston, 1990-92; ptnr. Short & Ketchand, Houston, 1992-2001; dir. Boyer & Ketchand, P.C., Houston, 2001—. Founder, chmn. bd. dirs. Rolling Waters, d/b/a Houston Legal Clinic. Pres. Prisoner Svcs. Com. Houston, 1986; deacon South Houston Bapt. Ch., 1976—; gen. counsel, dir. Houston Met. Ministries, 1986-88; dir. Interfaith Ministries Greater Houston, 1996-98; gen. counsel Houston Bus. Roundtable, 1988—. Lt. USNR, 1973-76. Mem. ABA, Tex. Bar Assn., Houston Bar Assn. (chmn. dispute com. 1989-90). Avocations: reading, family. Home: 2707 Carolina Way Houston TX 77005-3423 Office: Boyer & Ketchand PC 9 Greenway Plz Ste 3100 Houston TX 77046 Fax: 713-871-2024. E-mail: rketchand@boyerketchand.com.

KETCHERSID, WAYNE LESTER, JR., medical technologist; b. Seattle, Oct. 16, 1946; s. Wayne Lester and Hazel May (Greene) K.; m. Wilette LaVerne Mautz, Oct. 6, 1972; 1 son, William Les. BS in Biology, Pacific Luth. U., 1976, BS in Med. Tech., 1978; MS in Adminstrn., Ctrl. Mich. U., 1990; postgrad., Kennedy Western U., 1996—. Cert. med. technologist; cert. clin. lab. dir. Nat. Cert. Agy. for Med. Lab. Pers. Staff technologist Tacoma Gen. Hosp., 1978-79, chemistry supr., 1979-81, head chemistry, 1981-83,

Multicare Med. Ctr., 1984-86, mgr., 1986-93, clin. lab. scientist, 1993—. Contbr. articles to profl. jours. Mem. Nat. Rep. Com. With U.S. Army, 1966-68. William E. Slaughter Found. scholar, 1975-76. Mem. Am. Soc. Clin. Lab. Sci. (cert., chmn. region IX adminstrn. 1984-94, nat. del. 1984—, vice chmn. govt. affairs com. 1991-92, chmn. 1992-93, vice chair 1993-94, bd. trustees polit. action com. 1991-97, treas. 1994-97, nat. licensure coord. 1996—, sec./treas. bd. dirs. 1996-2001, jud. com. 2001-04, nominee Mem. of Yr. 1992, Bd. Dirs. award 1994, Mendelson award 1994, Pres. award 1996), Wash. State Soc. Clin. Lab. Sci. (chmn. biochemistry sect. 1983-86, dist. pres. 1986-99, co-chair ann. meeting 1996, cert. merit 1983, 84, 86, 88, pres. 1988-89, 89-90, mem. of yr. 1990, chmn. govt. affairs com. 1991-92, chmn. 1992—, Pres.'s award 1996, 97), Am. Soc. Clin. Pathologists (med. technologist), N.w. Med. Lab. Symposium (chmn. 1986-88, 90, 92), Alpha Mu Tau. Lutheran. Office: 2906 S 274th Pl Federal Way WA 98001-1803 Personal E-mail: wayketch@aol.com.

KETCHIAN, SONIA I., literature educator, researcher; b. Lowell, Mass. d. Tzolag "Harry" and Bertha Nakshian Ketchian. AM in Slavic Langs. & Lit., Harvard U., 1968, PhD in Slavic Langs. & Lit., 1975. Tchg. fellow Harvard U., Cambridge, Mass., 1966—70; vis. lectr. Brandeis U., Waltham, Mass., 1971; instr., asst. prof. Dartmouth Coll., Hanover, NH, 1973—76; ctr. assoc. Davis Ctr. for Russian and Eurasian Studies Harvard U., Cambridge, 1974—; asst. prof., Russian Smith Coll., Northampton, Mass., 1978—82; vis. asst. prof. Wheaton Coll., Norton, Mass., 1996; vis. lectr. MIT, Cambridge, 1995—99. Preceptor in Slavic Langs. Harvard U., 1976—77, 1982—83, 1986—92; co-chair, Setchkarev Prize Harvard U. Slavic Dept., Cambridge, Mass., 2001—; organizer Akhmatova Conf., Bellagio Study Conf. Ctr., Rockefeller Found., Am. Coun. Learned Socs., Soros Found., Russian Rsch. Ctr., Italy, 1989; adv. bd. mem. Jour. of Armenian Studies, Belmont, Mass., 1992—. Author: (books) The Poetry of Anna Akhmatova, 1986, The Poetic Craft of Bella Akhmadulina, 1993, Keats and the Russian Poets, 2001; co-editor (with Julian W. Connolly): Studies in Russian Literature in Honor of Vsevolod Setchkarev, 1986; editor: In The Shadow of the Fortress (Bertha Nakshian Ketchian), 1988, Anna Akhmatova, 1889-1989: Papers from the Akhmatova Centennial Conference, Bellagio Study and Conference Center, June 1989, 1993; contbr. articles to profl. jours. Recipient Zirin Prize Award, Assn. of Women in Slavic Studies, Boston, 2001; fellow, NEH, 2001—02; scholar, Internat. Rsch. and Exchange Bd., 1983, 1990. Mem.: Nat. Assn. for Advancement of Armenian Studies and Rsch., N.Am. Pushkin Soc., Am. Assn. of Tchrs. of Slavic & E. European Tchrs., Am. Assn. for Advancement of Slavic Studies. Avocations: reading, birdwatching, opera, ballet. Office: Davis Ctr for Russian and Eurasian Studies Harvard U 1730 Cambridge St Cambridge MA 02138 Business E-Mail: ketchian@fas.harvard.edu.

KETCHUM, JAMES ROE, curator; b. Rochester, N.Y., Mar. 15, 1939; s. George Roe and Mary Louise (Frantz) K.; m. Barbara M. Van Ness, Aug. 18, 1962; children: John Van Ness, Sarah Graham, Timothy Roe, Chester Arthur. AB, Colgate U., 1960; postgrad., Georgetown U., 1960-61, George Washington U., 1961-62. Staff historian Dept. Interior, Washington, 1960-62; registrar The White House, Washington, 1962-63, curator, 1963-70, U.S. Senate, Washington, 1970-95, curator emeritus, 1995—. Editor: The White House: An Historic Guide, 1962-70; contbr. numerous articles to profl. jours. and encys. Mem. Com. Preservation of White House, 1964-70; trustee U.S. Capitol Hist. Soc., 1971-79; alt. mem. Fed. Council Arts and Humanities, 1974-95; trustee Woodrow Wilson Birthplace Found., 1980—. Member Am. Assn. Museums, City Mus. Washington, Nat. Trust Historic Preservation, Theta Chi. Office: US Senate Commn Art Us Capital Bldg Rm S-411 Washington DC 20510-0001

KETCHUM, RICHARD G., stock exchange executive, lawyer; BA, Tufts U., 1972; JD, NYU, 1975. Bar: NY, DC. Assoc. Milbank, Tweed, Hadley and McCloy, NYC, 1975—77; dir. divsn. market regulation Securities and Exch. Commn.; exec. v.p. Nat. Assn. Securities Dealers, 1991—93, COO, 1993—98, pres., 1998—2000; pres., dep. chmn. Nasdaq Stock Market, Inc., 2000—03; gen. counsel global corp. and investment bank Citigroup, Inc., NYC, 2003—04; chief regulator NY Stock Exch., NYC, 2004—.

KETCHUM, WILLIAM CLARENCE, author, educator; b. Columbia, Mo., Mar. 29, 1931; s. William C. and Mildred Ann (Roberts) K.; m. Erica Stoller; children: Aaron, Alison, Ian. BA, Union Coll., 1953; JD, Columbia U., 1956. Bar: N.Y. 1960. Atty. Kriendler & Kriendler, N.Y.C., 1956, Martin, Clearwater & Bell, N.Y.C., 1960-65, R.S. Lane, N.Y.C., 1965-69; law sec. to Judge Lane of Civil Court, New York County N.Y.C., 1969-76; instr. course on Am. antiques New Sch., N.Y.C., 1970-87; instr. antiques course CUNY-Hunter Coll., 1978-79; mem. faculty NYU, 1984—, Folk Art Inst., 1987—, Marymount Coll., Tarrytown, N.Y., 1987-92. Guest curator Mus. Am. Folk Art, N.Y.C., 1974—, curator spl. projects, 1985-90, mem. nat. adv. com., 1992—; guest curator Nassau County Fine Arts Mus., 1980, Boscobel Restoration, 1995; curator Female Folk Artists U.S., Japan, 1988-89, Am. Bd. Games Katonah (N.Y.) Mus. Art, 1992, Scarsdale (N.Y.) Hist. Soc., 1993-94; guest spkr. Seminar on Early Am. Life, Pa. Farm Mus., Lancaster, 1974, Smithsonian Instn., 1976, Mercer Mus., Hancock Shaker Mus., 1977; guest lectr. Flemington Hist. Soc., 1975-76, antiques seminar NYU, 1973-75, 78-79, 81-84, New Haven Hist. Soc., 1975, Shelburne (Vt.) Mus., 1976, 78, St. Mary's of the Woods Coll., Terre Haute, Ind., 1976-78, Cooper-Hewitt Mus., 1978, Nassau County Fine Arts Mus., 1980, Mus. Am. Folk Art, 1978-84, Peale Mus., Balt., 1984, Del. Art Mus., 1985, N.Y. State Mus., 1985, 2000, Seattle Art Mus., 1986-87, Jacksonville (Fla.) Mus. Art, 1987, Marymount Coll., 1987-92, Hiram (Ohio) Coll., 1988, Triton Mus., Santa Clara, Calif., 1988, Chautauqua (N.Y.) Inst., 1989, Art and Culture Ctr. Hollywood, Fla., 1990, Philbrook Mus. Art, Tulsa, 1991, Katonah (N.Y.) Mus. Art, 1993, 99, Scarsdale (N.Y.) Hist. Soc., 1993, Claremont State (N.Y.) Hist. Site, 1994, Edinboro (Pa.) Coll., 1994-2000, Bruce Mus., 1995, 2002, Mus. of City of N.Y., 1995, Canterbury (N.H.) Shaker Village, 1997, N.Y. State Archaeol. Assn., 1997, 2000, N.Y. Hist. Assn., 1999-2001, Conn. Ceramic Cir., 1997, 2002, Am. Soc. Appraisers, 2000, 03, Va. Auctioneers' Assn., 2004; cons. antique series Time-Life, Inc., 1976-78; series cons. Knopf Collectors' Guides to Am. Antiques, 1982-84; spokesperson QVC, 1993; cons. material culture, archaeol. excavations Ft. Edward and Ft. William Henry, N.Y., 1994—, N.Y. State Hist. Assn., 1996—, NJ State Hist. Soc., 2004, Md. Auctioneers' Assn., 2004. Author: Early Potters and Potteries of New York, 1970, second ed. 1987; The Pottery and Porcelain Collectors Handbook, 1971; American Basketry and Woodenware, 1974; American Bottles, 1975; American Hooked Rugs, 1976; A Catalog of American Antiques, 1977, rev., 1990; The Family Treasury of Antiques, 1978; Catalog of American Collectibles, 1979, rev., 1990; Western Memorabilia, 1980; Auction, 1980; Collecting American Craft Antiques, 1980; Toys; Furniture 2, 1981; The Catalog of World Antiques, 1981; The Book of Boxes, 1982; Chests, Cupboards, Desks and Other Pieces, 1982, A Guide to Bottle Collecting, 1985; Am. Folk Art of the Twentieth Century, 1983; Pottery and Porcelain, 1983; Collecting Toys for Fun & Profit, 1985; Collecting 40's and 50's Collectibles for Fun and Profit, 1985; Sports Collectibles for Fun and Profit, 1985; All American, Folk Arts and Crafts, 1986; American Country Pottery, 1987, Making a Living in Antiques, 1990, Holiday Collectables, 1990, American Redware, 1990, Am. Stoneware, 1991, Country Wreaths and Baskets, 1991, Collecting the West, 1992, Western Memorabilia Identification and Price Guide, 1993, American Pottery & Porcelain, Identification and Price Guide, 1994, American Cabinetmakers, 1995, American Folk Art, 1995, The Art of Grandma Moses, 1996, Simple Beauty: The Shakers in America, 1996, The Art of the Golden West, 1996, Remington and Russell, 1997, Native American Art, 1997; contbg. author: The American Sporting Collectibles Handbook, 1982, Is It Genuine, 1986, The Dictionary of Art, 1994, The Encyclopedia of New York, 2000, American Folk Articles: Les Primitife Americains, 2001, The Encyclopedia of Folk Art, 2003; also articles to profl. jours. Lt., USNR, 1956-60. Recipient Amb. of Honor award English Speaking Union, 1984. Mem. Assn. of Bar of City of N.Y. (mem. com. uniform state laws 1972-76, mem. art com. 1976-78), N.Y. State Hist. Soc., N.E. Archeol. Assn., Westchester County Hist. Soc. (bd. trustees 2005—). Home: 241 Grace Church St Rye NY 10580-4217 Office Phone: 914-967-1450. E-mail: esto2@esto.com.

KETEFIAN, SHAKÉ, nursing educator; b. Beirut, Dec. 29, 1939; d. Krikor and Zaghganoush (Soghomonian) K. BSN, Am. U. Beirut, 1963; MEd, Columbia U., 1968, EdD, 1972. From asst. prof. nursing to prof. NYU Sch. Edn., Health, Nursing and Arts Professions, N.Y.C., 1972-84; dir. continuing edn. in nursing NYU, N.Y.C.; with U. Mich., 1984—; prof., assoc. dean for grad. studies, dir. doctoral and postdoctoral studies U. Mich. Sch. Nursing, Ann Arbor, 1984—91, dir. internat. affairs, 1996—, acting dean, 1991-92. Contbr. articles to profl. jours. Fellow AAUW, Am. Acad. Nursing (governing coun.); mem. ANA, Am. Orgn. Nurse Execs., Midwest Nursing Rsch. Soc. (chair sci. integrity task force 1994-96, 2001-03), Mich. Nurses Assn., Internat. Network for Doctoral Edn. in Nursing (co-founder, pres.), Sigma Theta Tau. Office: U Mich Sch Nursing 400 N Ingalls Ann Arbor MI 48109 Office Phone: 734-763-6669. Business E-Mail: ketefian@umich.edu.

KETELS, GERHARD H., lawyer; b. Hackensack, N.J., June 1, 1958; BA, Yale U., 1980; JD, U. Pa., 1983. Bar: N.Y. 1984. Trainee Allianz Ins. Co., Munich, 1983—85; mgr. Munich Re, Germany, 1986—99; sr. v.p. Hannover Re, Germany, 1999—2001; sec., gen. counsel Clarendon Ins. Group, N.Y.C., 2001—. Bd. dirs. Atlantic Capital, Corp., Redland Ins., Co., Clarendon Am. Co., Harbor Splty. Ins. Co. Office: Clarendon Ins Group 1177 6th Ave New York NY 10036

KETHMAN, JERRY DALE, priest, accountant; b. Shrevport, La., May 30, 1946; s. Walter E. Lohman and Beulah Kethman; m. Angela M. Licciardo, June 14, 1982; m. Janet Baker (div.). Assoc., U. Calif., Davis, 1981. Acct. clk. State of Calif., Sacramento, 1979—82; pastor Ch. of God/AM, Pontiac, Mich., 1982—; asst. mgr. Builder Sq., Waterford, Mich., 1992—95. Comdr. Vets. Employment Commn., Sacramento, 1980—85. With USAF, 1966. Mem.: Am. Legion, Disable Am. Vets. (svc. officer 1973—82), Am. Vets. (svc. officer 1972—). Democrat. Home: 59 Monroe #210 Pontiac MI 48341 Office: Church of God/AM 59 Monroe #210 Pontiac MI 48341 Personal E-mail: jkethman@sbcglobal.net.

KETNER, JOSEPH DALE, museum director, art historian; b. Anderson, Ind., Oct. 30, 1955; m. Patricia Ketner; 2 children. BA, Ind. U., 1977, MA, 1980. Curator, registrar Ft. Wayne (Ind.) Mus. Art, 1979-82; curator Washington U. Gallery of Art, St. Louis, 1982-89, dir., 1989—98, adj. lectr. in art history, 1995—98; Henry and Lois Foster dir. Rose Art Mus., Brandeis U., Waltham, Mass., 1998—2005; chief curator Milw. Art Mus., 2005—. Author: Robert S. Duncanson (1921-1972), 1993, A Gallery of Modern Art, 1994; author, curator (exbhn. catalogs) The Beautiful, The Sublime and the Picturesque, 1984, Carl F. Wimar, 1991. Chmn. Mayor's Visual Arts Com., Ft. Wayne, 1982. Office: Milw Art Museum 700 N Art Museum Dr Milwaukee WI 53202 Office Phone: 718-736-3434.*

KETNER, KENNETH LAINE, philosopher, educator; b. Mountain Home, Okla., Mar. 24, 1939; s. Louis Elaine and Johnnie Lucille (Hannah) K.; m. Berti Gabriella Zehetmeier, Aug. 24, 1964 (dec. Oct. 1996); 1 child, Kenneth Laine Jr. BA in Philosophy, Okla. State U., 1961, MA, 1967; MA in Folklore, UCLA, 1968; PhD in Philosophy, U. Calif., Santa Barbara, 1972. Part-time instr. Okla. State U., 1964-67; tchg. asst. U. Calif., Santa Barbara, 1969-70; mem. faculty Tex. Tech U., Lubbock, 1971—, prof. philosophy, 1977-98, chmn. dept., 1979-81; founder, dir. Inst. Studies in Pragmaticism, 1972—, Charles Sanders Peirce prof. philosophy, 1981-98, Charles Sanders Peirce interdisciplinary prof., 1998—, Paul Whitfield Horn prof., 1999—. Asst. prof. philosophy and folklore UCLA, summers, 1972, 74; co-organizer C.S. Peirce Bicentennial Internat. Congress, Amsterdam, Netherlands 1976; Peirce Sesquicentennial Internat. Congress, Harvard U., 1989. Author: A Critical Study of Stephen C. Pepper's Approach to Metaphysics, 1967, An Essay on the Nature of World Views, 1972, An Emendation of R.G. Collingwood's Doctrine of Absolute Presuppositions, 1973; editor, compiler: Charles Sanders Peirce: Contributions to the Nation, 4 parts, 1975, 78, 79, 87, Comprehensive Bibliography of Works of C.S. Peirce, 1977, rev. edit., 1986, Reasoning and the Logic of Things, 1993, A Thief of Peirce, 1995, His Glassy Essence: an Autobiography of C.S. Peirce, 1998; founder, gen. editor Peirce Studies, 1979—, Philosophical Inquiries, 1989—, more. Capt. USAR, 1962-64. Grantee NSF, Nat. Endowment Humanities, Am. Coun. Learned Socs. Fellow Charles S. Peirce Soc. (pres. 1983); mem. Am. Philos. Assn., Freemason, Tau Kappa Epsilon. Democrat. Home: PO Box 65135 Lubbock TX 79464-5135 Office: Texas Tech Univ Library 305 Lubbock TX 79409-0002

KETRON, CARRIE SUE, secondary school educator; b. Clifton, Tex. d. Randolph Allen and Mary (Waggoner) Ogden; m. N.M. Ketron, Aug. 4, 1984; children: John, Robert. B of Applied Arts and Scis., U. North Tex., 1990, MEd, 1993. Tchr. Duncanville H.S., Tex., 1982—. Named Tchr. of Yr., Tex. Vocat. Tech. Assn., 1990, Outstanding Nat. Career & Tech. Tchr. of Yr., 1997. Mem. Golden Key Honor Soc., Am. Vocat. Assn., Cosmetology Instructors' of Pub. Schs. (parliamentarian 1989-90), Vocat. Indsl. Clubs Am. (advisor 1986-93), Iota Lambda Sigma Sigma (pres. 1995-96), Phi Theta Kappa, Alpha Chi. Baptist. Office Phone: 972-708-3782.

KETTEL, EDWARD JOSEPH, retired oil industry executive; b. N.Y.C., Sept. 13, 1925; s. Harold J. and Evelyn M. (Melbourne) K.; m. Janet M. Hinton, Nov. 27, 1952; children: Dorothy A., David A. Student, St. John's U., 1943; BA, St. Francis Coll., 1949; MA, Columbia U., 1953. Ins. mgr. Arabian Am. Oil Co., 1950-56, Ethyl Corp., 1956—63, Sinclair Oil, 1963—65; asst. treas. Atlantic Richfield Co., L.A., 1965-85, Chevron Corp., San Francisco, 1985-94; expert witness, 1994—. Chmn. bd. Oil Ins., Ltd.; pres. Greater Pacific, Ltd.; dir. Am. S.S. Owners Mut. Protection and Indemnity Assn., Inc., Internat. Tanker Indemnity Assn., Ltd. With inf. AUS, 1943-46. Decorated Purple Heart with oak leaf cluster. Mem. Am. Petroleum Inst., Mfrs. Chem. Assn., Nat. Fire Protection Assn., Risk and Ins. Mgmt. Soc., N.Y. Athletic Club, L.A. Athletic Club, Palos Verdes Country Club, Ocean Colony Golf Club, Westhampton Beach Yacht Squadron Ltd. Office Phone: 631-288-2344.

KETTELKAMP, DONALD BENJAMIN, retired orthopedist; b. Anamosa, Iowa, Jan. 21, 1930; s. Enoch George and Elsie (Norden) K.; m. Alice June Mencke, Dec. 30, 1954; children: Karen June, Lisa Marie, Suzanne D., Jonathan B.; m. Clemencia Oliveros Brandon, Apr. 28, 1989. BA, Cornell U., Mt. Vernon, Iowa, 1952; MD, U. Iowa, 1955, MS, 1960. Diplomate Am. Bd. Orthop. Surgery. Intern Thomas D. Dee Meml. Hosp., Ogden, Utah, 1955—56; resident orthopedic surgery U. Iowa, Iowa City, 1958—61; practice medicine specializing in orthopaedic surgery Anchorage, 1961—64; asst. prof. Albany (N.Y.) Med. Coll., 1964—66, assoc. prof., 1966—68, U. Iowa, Iowa City, 1968—71, prof., 1971; prof., chmn. dept. orthopaedic surgery U. Ark., Little Rock, 1971—74, Ind. U., Indpls., 1974—84; assoc. dean Tex. Tech. U., El Paso, 1984—87; exec. dir. Am. Bd. Orthop. Surgery, Chgo., 1986—94. Trustee: Jour. Bone and Joint Surgery, 1991—96. With USPHS, 1956—58. Mem.: ACS, Knee Soc., Assn. Orthopaedic Chairmen (pres. 1981), Am. Orthopaedic Assn. (pres. 1989—90), Am. Soc. Surgery of Hand, Continental Orthopaedic Soc., Russell Hibbs Soc., Am. Acad. Orthopaedic Surgeons.

KETTELL, RUSSELL WILLARD, banker; b. Boston, Feb. 2, 1944; s. Prescott Lowell and Wilhelmina (Schurrman) K.; m. Carol Bailey, Oct. 27, 1973; 1 son, Alexander. BA in Econs., Middlebury Coll.; MBA, U. Chgo. Sr. v.p., treas. World Savs. and Loan Corp., Oakland, Calif. Office: Golden W Fin Corp 1901 Harrison St Fl 6 Oakland CA 94612-3588

KETTER, DAVID LEE, lawyer; b. Portsmouth, Ohio, Jan. 7, 1929; s. William Leslie and Dorothy Aileen (Weidner) K.; m. Beverly Jane Kinker, June 10, 1951; children— Michael David, Sandra Lee, Beth Ann, Richard Douglass AB, Ohio U., 1953; JD, U. Cin., 1955. Bar: Ohio 1955, Pa. 1964. Trial lawyer Dept. Justice, Washington, 1955-56; trial lawyer Chief Counsel's Office, IRS, Pitts., 1956-62; assoc. Kirkpatrick, Pomeroy, Lockhart & Johnson, Pitts., 1962-65; ptnr. Kirkpatrick & Lockhart, LLP, Pitts., 1965-94, of counsel, 1995—. Served as sgt. USMC, 1946-47, 50-52 Mem. ABA (tax sect.), Pa. Bar Assn. (tax sect.), Allegheny County Bar Assn. (chmn. tax sect. 1964-66), Estate Planning Coun. (bd. dirs. 1975-77), Pitts. Tax Club (pres. 1985-86), Order of Coif, Duquesne Club, Rivers Club, Valley Brook Country Club (sec. 1977-78). Clubs: Duquesne, Rivers, Valley Brook Country (McMurray, Pa., sec. 1977-78). Republican. Methodist. Avocations: golf, tennis, shooting. Home: 160 Canterbury Rd Mc Murray PA 15317-2802 Office: Kirkpatrick Lockhart Nicholson Graham LLP Henry W Oliver Bldg 535 Smithfield St Pittsburgh PA 15222-2312 Office Phone: 412-355-6420. Business E-Mail: dketter@klng.com.

KETTERLE, WOLFGANG, physics professor; b. Heidelberg, Germany, Oct. 21, 1957; came to the U.S., 1990; divorced; three children. Physics pre-diploma, U. Heidelberg, 1978; physics diploma, Tech. U., Munich, 1982; PhD in Physics, Ludwig-Maximilians U. Munich, 1986. Rsch. asst. Max-Planck Inst. for Quantum Optics, Garching, Germany, 1982-85, staff scientist, 1985-88; rsch. scientist dept. phys. chemistry U. Heidelberg, 1989-90; rsch. assoc. MIT, Cambridge, Mass., 1990-93, asst. prof. physics, 1993-97, prof., 1997—, John. D. MacArthur prof. physics, 1998—. Officer Order of Legion of Honor, 2002, France. Decorated Medal of Merit Baden-Wurtemberg, Knight Comdr.'s Cross (Badge and Star) Order of Merit Fed. Rep. Germany; recipient Technology Innovation award Discover Magazine, 1998, Fritz London prize in low temperature physics, 1999, Dannie-Heineman prize Acad. Scis., Göttingen, Germany, 1999, Benjamin Franklin medal in physics, 2000, NATO/DAAD Postdoctoral fellow, 1990—91, Michael and Philip Platzman award, 1994, David and Lucile Packard fellow, 1996, The Nobel Prize in Physics, 2001. Fellow Am. Phys. Soc. (Disting. Traveling lectr. 1998, Rabi prize 1997), Am. Acad. Arts and Scis., Inst. of Physics; mem. NAS, German Phys. Soc. (Gustav-Hertz prize 1997), Am. Optical Soc., European Acad. Arts, Scis. and Humanities (titular mem.), Acad. Scis. Heidelberg, Bavarian Acad. Scis. Office: Dept Physics MIT 77 Massachusetts Ave Rm 26-243 Cambridge MA 02139-4307 E-mail: ketterle@mit.edu.*

KETTERSON, ELLEN D., biologist, educator; b. Orange, N.J., Aug. 9, 1945; m. Val Nolan, Jr. BA in Botany, Ind. U., 1966, MA in Botany, 1968, PhD in Zoology, 1974. NIH fellow Wash. State U., 1975-77; asst. prof. biol. scis. Bowling Green State U., 1975-77; from vis. asst. prof. to asst. prof. biology Ind. U., Bloomington, 1977-84, from assoc. prof. to prof. biology, 1984—, co-dir. Ctr. for Integrative Study Animal Behavior, 1990—2002. Vis. scientist Purdue U., Lafayette, Ind., 1991, Rockefeller U., 1985, U. Va., 1984. Mem. editl. bd. Current Ornithology, 1989—, editor, 1994-98; mem. editl. bd. Animal Behaviour, 1997—, assoc. editor, 1991-94; mem. editl. bd. Evolution, 1994, editor, 1994-99; editor: Jour. Avian Biology, 1999—2004. Grantee NSF, 1978—; Guggenheim fellow, 2004. Fellow Am. Ornithologists Union (v.p. 1995-96, coun. 1988-91, Elliot Coues award 1996, Exemplar award); mem. AAAS, Internat. Ornithol. Com., Ecol. Soc. Am., Am. Soc. Naturalists, Animal Behavior Soc., Assn Field Ornithologists, Cooper Ornithol. Soc., Soc. Conservation Biology, Soc. Study of Evolution, Soc. Integrative and Comparative Biology, Soc. Behavioral Neuroendocrinology, Wilson Ornithol. Soc. (Margaret M. Nice award 1998), Sigma Xi. Office: Indiana U Dept Biology Bloomington IN 47405 E-mail: ketterso@indiana.edu.

KETTINGER, DAVID JOHN, broadcast executive; b. Abington, Pa., Feb. 21, 1954; s. Ralph Joseph and Mary Elizabeth (Reilly) K. Student, Villanova U., 1973-75. Disc jockey Radio Sta. WBUX, Doylestown, Pa., 1975-77; disc jockey, rschr. Radio Sta. WPST, Trenton, N.J., 1977-80; disc jockey, pub. rels. dir. Radio Sta. WKHI-FM, Ocean City, Md., 1980-81, ops. dir., program dir., 1981-82; advt. cons. sales dept., producer Agy. Voice Overs, Ocean City, 1983-89, asst. sales mgr., 1989-90; sales mgr. Stas. WWTR and WETT, Ocean City, 1990-91; sales mgr., disk jockey Radio Stas. WWTR and WETT, Ocean City, 1991-94; disc jockey Radio Sta. WQHQ-FM, Salisbury, Md., 1990-91; part-time air announcer, comml. producer, copywriter United Artist Cable TV of Ea. Shore, 1991-92; sta. mgr., with sales dept. Radio Sta. WLVW-FM and WLBW-FM, Salisbury, Md., 1994-2000, Cumulus Broadcasting, Inc.; sales staff Radio Sta. WRXS-FM, Atlantic Radio Broadcasting, LLC, Ocean City, Md., 2000; mktg. dir., customer rels. mgr. Millsboro Ford, Millsboro, Del., 2000—, e-commerce dir., 2004—05; advt. cons WMDT TV and WBD3, Salisbury, Md., 2005—. Vol. fireman Weldon Fire Co. (mem. fire prevention and publicity coms.), 1972-81; active Muscular Dystrophy Assn., Ocean City Power Squadron. Republican. Roman Catholic. Avocations: boating, sketching, autograph collecting, impersonations, golf. Home: 788 Ocean Pkwy Berlin MD 21811-1726 Office: WMDT TV-47 and WBD3 PO Box 4009 Salisbury MD 21803 E-mail: dave_kettinger@wmdt.com.

KETTLER, CARL FREDERICK, airline executive; b. N.Y.C., Dec. 19, 1936; s. William Henry and Martha Maria (Allmendinger) K.; m. Marianne Louis Slagboom, Dec. 19, 1970; 1 child, Patricia Heidi. BS in Aeronautics, St. Louis U., 1965; MBA, U. Calif., Berkeley, 1966. Project mgr. corp. planning Trans World Airlines, 1968-69; dir. internat. market planning Flying Tiger Ln., 1969-71; spl. asst. to U.S. Senator Henry Bellmon, 1971-74; dir. fed. affairs Air Transport Assn. Am., Washington, 1974-78; co-organizer Midway Airlines, Inc., 1974-79; asst. to pres. Airbus Industries No.Am., N.Y.C., 1978-80; vice chmn. bd. govs. Flight Safety Found., 1979-81; prtnr. Sunburst Energy Inc., Enid, Okla., 1980-82; co-founder, exec. v.p., COO Trans-Cen. Airlines, Oklahoma City, 1980—; founder T.H.E. Airline Inc., 1981; chmn., pres. Kettler Korp, Inc., 1981—; founder Kettler Komputer Svcs. Inc., 1987—, Kettler Employee Leasing Inc., 1981—; co-founder Kettler & Kettler Employment Svcs., Inc., Flemington, N.J., 1981; founder, pres. Kettler Airline Planning Svcs., Inc. Advisor to Reagan White House on Nat. Security, 1980-84; lectr. St. Louis U., 1968—; cons. aviation and internat. trade. Founder, pres. Oak Summit Sch. Hist. Soc., Citizens Against Ruining the Environ (CARE), 1985—; del. Rep. Nat. Conv., 1992. With USAF, 1955—61. Recipient Outstanding Svc. award Smithsonian Astrophys. Obs., 1959, Alumni Merit award St. Louis U., 1991. Mem. Nat. Def. Transp. Assn., Am. Inst. Aeronautics and Astronautics (air transport tech. com.), Okla. Heritage Assn., Okla. State Soc., Internat. House (Berkeley), Calif. Alumni Assn., U. Calif. at Berkeley, Ducks Unltd., Grand Nat. Quail Club (exec. com.), Capitol Hill Club, Nat. Aviation Club, Internat. Aviation Club, Wings Club, Aero Club, Alpha Eta Rho, Alpha Sigma Chi, Alpha Sigma Nu (Nat. Jesuit Scholastic Honors award, 1965), Gamma Phi Epsilon. Roman Catholic. Avocations: politics, piloting, boating, travel, writing. Home: 59 Everitts Hill Rd Flemington NJ 08822-4005 E-mail: kettler@blast.net.

KETTLEWOOD, BEA CARD, artist, retired educator; b. Pompton Plains, N.J., June 7, 1929; d. James Whitfield and Florence B. (Payne) Card; m. James Kettlewood, June 28, 1952. BS, Newark State Coll., 1951; MA, NYU, 1955, EdD in Painting, 1972. Cert. tchr., N.J. Tchr. art New Milford (N.J.) Jr.-Sr. High Sch., 1951-84, chmn. art dept., 1960-84, chmn. art, home econs. and lang. depts., 1981-84; part-time instr. in art extension div. William Paterson Coll., Wayne, N.J., 1963-67; freelance painter, 1959—. Free lance illustrator; lectr. in field. Designed stained glass windows for Chapel at Chilton Meml. Hosp., Morristown Meml. Hosp., Rehab. Inst. Morristown, First Reformed Ch., Pompton Plains, Hackettstown Cmty. Hosp.; over 40 solo shows. Elder on consistory 1st Reformed Ch., Pompton Plains, N.J., 1987-90, 92-95; mem. Maine Art Gallery 1962-2003. Mem. AAUW (sec., rep., pres. No. Jersey interbr., co-pres. 1991-92), Arts Coun. Orange County (mem. gallery com. 1985-95), Ringwood Manor Art Assn., Delta Kappa Gamma (chpt. pres. 1978-80). Avocations: writing, architecture history, set design. Home: 45 Wilrue Pky Pompton Plains NJ 07444-1717

KEULEGAN, EMMA PAULINE, special education educator; b. Washington, Jan. 21, 1930; d. Garbis H. and Nellie Virginia (Moore) K. BA, Dumbarton Coll. of Holy Cross, 1954. Cert. tchr. elem. and spl. edn. Tchr. St. Dominic's Elem. Sch., Washington, 1954-56, Sacred Heart Acad., Washington, 1956-59, Our Lady of Victory, Washington, 1959-63, St. Francis Acad., Vicksburg, Miss., 1963-78, Culkin Acad., Vicksburg, 1978-91, substitute tchr. spl. edn., 1991—. Treas. PTA, Vicksburg, 1980; pres. Vicksburg Genealogical Soc., 1999. Mem.: DAR (chpt. regent 1967—69, sec. 1994, chpt. chaplain 1996, chpt. libr. 2002, chpt. membership chmn.), Daus. of United Confederacy (chpt. chaplain), Soc. Descs. of Knights of Most Noble Order of the Garter, Sovereign Colonial Soc. Am. Royal Descent, Soc. Magna Charta

Dames and Barons (state chaplain 2001), Daus. of the War of 1812 (state chaplain 1998, hon. state pres. 2002, state pres. 2002—, hon. state pres. 2003), Daus. Am. Colonists (chaplain 1985—89, state pres. 1992—94, hon. state pres. 1994—), Colonial Dames 17th Century (state v.p. 1987—89, state pres. 1989, hon. state pres. 1991—), Internat. Reading Assn. (pres. Warren County chpt.), Vicksburg Geneal. Soc. (pres. 2003). Republican. Roman Catholic. Avocations: stamp and coin collecting, needlecrafts, reading. Home: 215 Buena Vista Dr Vicksburg MS 39180-5612

KEUNE, RUSSELL VICTOR, retired architect; b. Chgo., Ill., 1938; m. Ingrid Christina Friberg, 1968; 1 child, Eric Richard. BArch, U. Ill., Urbana, 1961, MArch, 1965. Registered arch., Va. Restoration arch. Nat. Park Svc., U.S. Dept. Interior, Washington, 1961-63, from staff arch. of Hist. Am. Bldgs. Survey to asst. keeper of Nat. Register Hist. Places, 1965-68; rsch. and tchg. asst. U. Ill., Urbana, 1963-65; from dir. dept. field svcs. to sr. v.p. preservation programs Nat. Trust for Hist. Preservation, Washington, 1969-83; pvt. practice, 1983-84; sr. project mgr. Geler Brown Renfrow Archs., Washington, 1984-86; v.p. for programs U.S. Com., Internat. Coun. on Monuments and Sites, Washington, 1986-93; dir. internat. rels. AIA, Washington, 1993-99; co-dir. profl. practice commn. Internat. Union Archs., Paris, 2003—; lectr. Goucher Coll., Balt., 2003—. Mem. U.S. delegation 7th Gen. Assembly Internat. Ctr. for Study of Preservation and Restoration of Cultural Property, Rome, 1973, UNESCO Conv. Conf. on Preservation of Hist. Quars., Towns and Sites, Warsaw, Poland, 1975; mem. U.S. exch. delegation Preservation Hist. and Cultural Property, USSR, 1974; mem. task force on tourism and preservation Pacific Area Travel Assn., Macau and The Philippines, 1980, mem. task force on preservation of Chinatown, Singapore, 1985; acad. specialist on hist. preservation to Yemen Arab Republic USIA, 1989; guest lectr., spkr. numerous colls., univs., pub. agys., profl. and preservation orgns. Fellow AIA (mem. hist. resources com. 1968—, chmn. 1988-89), Internat. Coun. Monuments and Sites (bd. dirs. 1977-80, 83-86); mem. Assn. Preservation Tech. (v.p. 1974-77), Ea. Park and Monument Assn., Hist. Am. Bldgs. Survey Found. (vice chmn. 1983-93), Hist. Preservation Roundtable, Cosmos Club, Lamda Alpha. Personal E-mail: rkeune@earthlink.net.

KEUSCH, GERALD TILDEN, academic administrator; b. NYC, Apr. 30, 1938; m. Kathleen Baden, Mar. 23, 1985; 3 children. AB, Columbia Coll., 1958; MD, Harvard U., 1963. Diplomate Am. Bd. of Internal Medicine, Am. Bd. Infectious Diseases. Asst. to prof. Mount Sinai Sch. of Medicine, N.Y., 1970-78; prof. medicine Tufts U. Sch. of Medicine; chief divsn. of geographic medicine and infectious disease New England Med. Ctr., Boston; dir. Fogarty Internat. Ctr. NIH, Dept. Health and Human Svcs., Bethesda, Md., 1998—2003; assist. provost for global health Boston U. Med. Center, Boston, 2003—; assoc. dean for global health Boston U. Sch. of Public Health, Boston, 2003—. Contbr. articles to profl. jours. Recipient Career Scientist award Health Rsch. Coun. of City of N.Y., Inc., 1973-76, Rsch. Career Devel. award Nat. Inst. of Allergy and Infectious Diseases, 1974-79; Heath-Clark award U. London Sch. of Hygiene and Tropical Medicine, 1991. Mem. AAAS, Am. Fedn. Clin. Rsch., NY Acad. of Sci., Infectious Disease Soc. Am. (councillor 1999—, Maxwell Finland lecture award 1997, Squibb award 1981, Bristol award 2002), Am. Soc. Microbiology, Harvey Soc., Am. Soc. Clin. Investigation, MA Infectious Disease Soc. (treas. 1987-91, pres. 1992-95), Assn. Am. Physicians. Avocation: music. Office: Boston U Sch of Public Health 715 Albany St T-4w Boston MA 02215 Office Phone: 617-638-5234. Business E-Mail: keusch@bu.edu.

KEVAN, LARRY, chemistry educator; b. Kansas City, Mo., Dec. 12, 1938; s. Glenn Herman and Myrtle Helena (Johnson) K. BS, U. Kans., 1960; PhD, UCLA, 1963. Research assoc. U. Newcastle, England, 1963; instr. U. Chgo., 1963-65; asst. prof. chemistry U. Kans., Lawrence, 1965-67, assoc. prof., 1967-69; prof. Wayne State U., Detroit, 1969-80; Cullen prof. U. Houston, 1980—. Vis. prof. U. Utah, 1971, Nagoya U., Japan, 1976, U. of Paris, 1977, Armed Forces U., Munich, 1979, Hokkaido U., Japan, 1987, U. Florence, Italy, 1987, 90; chmn. Gordon Conf. Radiation Chemistry, 1975; mem. chemistry rev. com. Brookhaven Nat. Lab., 1974-78, chmn., 1978, chemistry rev. com. Argonne Nat. Lab., 1980-86, chmn., 1982; rev. com. Notre Dame Radiation Lab., 1993, 94, NIH Spl. Study sects., 1982—; users com. mem. Nat. High Field Magnet Lab., 1996-99. Author: Electron Spin Double Resonance Spectroscopy, 1976, Time Domain Electron Spin Resonance, 1979, Advances in Pulsed and Continuous Wave Electron Spin Resonance, 1990; also over 800 articles; editor: Radical Ions, 1968, Electron-Solvent and Anion-Solvent Interactions, 1976; mem. editl. bd. Jour. Chem. Physics, Jour. Phys. Chemistry, Radiation Physics and Chemistry, Concepts in Magnetic Resonance, Jour. Chem. Soc.-Faraday Trans., Applied Magnetic Resonance, Nucleonika, Magnetic Resonance Reviews. Guggenheim fellow, 1970-71; recipient Faculty Rsch. award Wayne State U., 1978, Rsch. award Polish Soc. Radiation Rsch., Warsaw, 1979, Rsch. award Golden Key Nat. Honor Soc., 1986, Rsch. Excellence award U. Houston, 1987, Rsch. award Sigma Xi, 1989, Marie Curie medal, 1995, Silver Medal, Internat. EPR Soc., 2000. Fellow AAAS, Am. Phys. Soc., Royal Soc. Chemistry (London); mem. Am. Chem. Soc. (S.E. Tex. award 1986), S.W. Catalysis Soc. (chmn. 1986-88), Internat. Zeolite Assn., Internat. ESR Soc., Internat. Soc. Magnetic Resonance. Avocations: scuba diving, sailboat racing, skiing, tennis, wine tasting. Office: Univ of Houston Dept Chemistry 136 Fleming Bldg Houston TX 77204-5003 E-mail: Kevan@uh.edu.

KEVICZKY, TAMAS, electrical engineer, researcher; b. Budapest, Hungary, July 2, 1978; s. Laszlo Keviczky and Csilla Banyasz. MSc, Budapest U. of Tech. and Econs., 2001. Rsch. asst. U. Minn., Mpls., 2001—. Fellow Zoltai Grad. fellow, 2001-2002. Office: Univ Minn 110 Union St SE 107 Akerman Hall Minneapolis MN 55455 Office Phone: 612-625-6561. Office Fax: 612-626-1558.

KEVILLE, TERRI DONNA, lawyer; b. Phila., Mar. 5, 1951; d. Bernard Louis and Dora Duchovnay Jacobs; m. Thomas Joseph Keville, Aug. 25, 1974; children: James Thomas, Jordan Brian, Warren Lowell, Owen Stuart. BA, U. Pa., 1972; JD, U. So. Calif., Gould Sch. Law, 1992. Bar: Calif. 1992, US Dist. Ct. (ctrl. dist.) Calif. 1992, US Ct. Appeals (9th cir.) 1992, US Supreme Ct. 2000. Summer assoc. Horvitz & Levy, Encino, Calif., 1990; assoc. Manatt, Phelps & Phillips, LLP, Los Angeles, 1992—97, ptnr., 1998—. Editor: California Health Law News. Cmty. ptnr. mem. LA County Mus. Art, Los Angeles, 2004—. Recipient Order of the Coif, USC Chpt., 1992, Articles Editor, So. Calif. Law Rev., 1991-1992. Mem.: Calif. Soc. Healthcare Attys. (bd. editors 1995—, CFO 2002—03, pres.-elect 2003—04, pres. 2004—05, immediate past pres. 2005—), LA County Bar Assn. (co-chair, bioethics com. 2000—02, LA County Med. Assn./LACBA joint com. on biomedical ethics, co chair), ABA Health Law Sect., Am. Health Lawyers Assn. Jewish. Avocation: classical music. Office: Manatt Phelps & Phillips LLP 11355 W Olympic Blvd Los Angeles CA 90064-1614 Office Phone: 310-312-4183. Office Fax: 310-914-5735. Business E-Mail: tkeville@manatt.com.

KEVLES, DANIEL JEROME, historian, educator, writer; b. Phila., Mar. 2, 1939; s. David and Anne (Rothstein) Kevles; m. Bettyann Holtzmann, May 18, 1961; children: Beth Carolyn, Jonathan David. BA in Physics, Princeton U., 1960; postgrad., Oxford U., 1960-61; PhD in History, Princeton U., 1964. From asst. to prof. history Calif. Inst. Tech., Pasadena, 1964-86, Koepfli prof. humanities, 1986-2001, head program in sci., ethics, and pub. policy, 1987-2001; vis. prof. Yale U., New Haven, 2000-01, Stanley Woodward prof. history, 2001—, dir. grad. studies program in history of sci. and medicine, 2002—05, chair grad. studies program in history of sci. and medicine, 2005—. Vis. rsch. fellow U. Sussex, Brighton, Eng., 1976; vis. prof. U. Pa., Phila., 1979, Princeton U., 1999; dir. studies Ecole des Hautes Etudes en Sciences Sociales, Paris, 1991; chmn. faculty Calif. Inst. Tech., 1995-97. Author: The Physicists, 1978 (Nat. Hist. Soc. prize 1979), In the Name of Eugenics, 1985; (mag. series) Annals of Eugenics (Page One award 1985), The Baltimore Case, 1998 (Watson Davis prize); co-author: Inventing America, 2002; co-editor: The Code of Codes, 1992; contbr. articles to N.Y. Rev. Books, other mags. Charles Warren fellow Harvard U., 1981-82, Ctr. for Advanced Study Behavorial Scis. fellow, 1986-87, Nat. Endowment for Humanities sr. fellow, 1981-82, Guggenheim fellow, 1983. Fellow: AAAS (chmn. sect. L 1983—85), Soc. Am. Historians; mem.: PEN, Am. Philos. Soc., History Sci. Soc. (coun. 1980—82, com. publ. 1984—88, Sarton lectr. 1985, com. honors and prizes 2001—04, George Sarton medal 2001), Am. Hist. Assn., Orgn. Am. Historians, Am. Acad. Arts and Scis., Author's Guild, Century Assn., Yale Club (N.Y.C.), Phi Beta Kappa. Democrat. Office: Yale U Dept History PO Box 208324 New Haven CT 06520-8324 Office Phone: 203-432-1356. E-mail: daniel.kevles@yale.edu.

KEVORKIAN, JIRAIR, aeronautics and astronautics engineering educator; b. Jerusalem, May 14, 1933; came to U.S., 1952; s. Leon and Araxie (Kalemkerian) K.; m. Seta Tabourian, Mar. 8, 1980. BS, Ga. Inst. Tech., 1955, MS, 1956; PhD, Calif. Inst. Tech., 1961. Aerodynamicist Convair, Ft. Worth, 1956-57, Calif. Inst. Tech., Pasadena, 1961-64; asst. prof. U. Wash., Seattle, 1964-66, assoc. prof., 1966-71, prof. applied math., aeros. and astronautics, 1971—2002, prof. emeritus, 2002—, acting chmn. applied math., 1986-87, 88-90. Vis. prof. U. Paris, 1971-72; Fulbright-Hayes vis. lectr., 1975-76. Author: Partial Differential Equations, 1990; co-author: Perturbation Methods in Applied Mathematics, 1981, Multiple Scale and Singular Perturbation Methods, 1996. Home: 3730 W Commodore Way Seattle WA 98199-1104 Office: U Wash Dept Applied Math PO Box 352420 Seattle WA 98195-2420 Business E-Mail: kevork@amath.washington.edu.

KEVORKIAN, RICHARD, artist; b. Dearborn, Mich., Aug. 24, 1937; s. Kay and Stana (Bedeian) K.; m. Salpy Bouroujian; children: Anna, Raffi, Soseh and Ellina (twins), Salpi Serar. BFA, Richmond Profl. Inst., 1961; MFA in Painting, Calif. Coll. Arts and Crafts, 1962. Instr. drawing and painting Richard Bland Coll., Petersburg, Va., 1961-64; instr. dept. fine arts Va. Commonwealth U., Richmond, 1962-66, asst. prof. dept. painting and printmaking, 1967-69, assoc. prof., 1969-77, prof., 1967-93, prof. emeritus, 1993, chmn. dept., 1969-81. One-man exhbns. include Aaron Gallery, Washington, Marita Gilliam Gallery, Raleigh, N.C.; exhbns. include Birmingham Mus. Art, Ala., 1977, Greenville County Mus. Art, S.C., 1977, Southeastern Ctr. Contemporary Art, Winston-Salem, N.C., 1977, 78, Hunter Mus. Art, Chattanooga, 1978, Va. Mus. Fine Art, 1983, U. Tenn., Knoxville, 1983. Mem. selection bd. for visual arts Va. Ctr. for Creative Arts, Sweet Briar. Served with N.G., 1955-63; guest curator Retrospective Exhib. Maurice Bonds Anderson Gallery, 2003. NEA individual sr. artists grantee, 1972, Va. Commonwealth U. Sch. Arts faculty creative research grantee, 1974, Nat. Endowment for Arts, Southeastern Ctr. Contemporary Arts grantee, 1976; Guggenheim fellow, 1978 Home: 7909 Rock Creek Rd Richmond VA 23229-6643 Personal E-mail: rekev@comcast.net.

KEVREKIDIS, PANAYOTIS G., mathematics professor; s. George and Despina Kevrekidis; m. Maria-Eleni Nikolaou, Dec. 28, 2003. MS, MPhil, Rutgers U., PhD, 2000. Asst. prof. U. Mass., Amherst, 2001—. Recipient CAREER award, NSF, 2004—; fellow, Princeton U., N.J., 2000—01, Los Alamos Nat. Lab, N.Mex., 2000—01, Eppley Found. Rsch., 2003—04; grantee, NSF, 2002—05. Mem.: IAMP, SIAM, AMS, APS. Office: U Mass 718 N Pleasant St Lederle GRT Amherst MA 01003 Office Phone: 413-577-1977. Office Fax: 413-545-1801. E-mail: kevrekid@math.umass.edu.

KEWALRAMANI, LAXMAN SUNDERDAS, surgeon, consultant; b. Jaipur, India, Mar. 10, 1943; came to U.S., 1970, U.S. citizen; s. Sunderdas K. and Sugnidevi Kewalramani; m. Dropadi Chellani, May 29, 1970; children: Anupama, Mukul. MB, BS, U. Rajasthn, Jaipur, 1965, M of Surgery, 1969. Diplomate Am. Acad. Pain Mgmt., Am. Bd. Disability Analysts, Am. Bd. Phys. Medicine & Rehab., Am. Bd. Electrodiagnostic Medicine. Fellow neurol. surgery U. Calif. Davis-Sacramento Med. Ctr., 1970-71, resident in phys. medicine and rehab., 1971-73; asst. prof. dept. phys. medicine and rehab. U. Calif., Davis, 1973-76; asst. prof. depts. phys. medicine and rehab. Baylor Coll. Medicine, Houston, 1976-79; assoc. prof. sect. rheumatology and rehab. dept. medicine sch. medicine La. State U., New Orleans, 1979-82; dir. rehab. rsch., coord. patient care La. Rehab. Inst. and Charity Hosp., New Orleans, 1979-82; pvt. practice in phys. medicine and rehab., orthopedic medicine, electrodiagnostic medicine and thermography, 1982—; med. dir. Health South Rehab. Ctr., Harahan, La., 1989-91; med. dir. rehab. unit Chalmette (La.) Med. Ctrs., 1991-92; med. dir. spine and orthopedic inst. Elmwood Med. Ctr., Jefferson, La., 1993-95. Sr. disability analyst Am. Bd. Disability Analysts, 2001; cons. rehab. medicine svc. crippled children svcs. sect. VA Hosp., 1975-76; mem. quality assurance com. Charity Hosp. and La. Rehab. Inst., New Orleans, 1979-82; presenter in field. Reviewer manuscripts, cons. editorial bd. Archives Phys. Medicine and Rehab., 1977-80; contbr. 2 chpts. to books and 96 articles to profl. jours. Cons. Cluster Living and Shared Providers, 1978; trustee New Orleans Pharmacy Mus., 1993—. Fellow: Am. Acad. Pain Mgmt., Am. Acad. Phys. Medicine and Rehab. (subcom. med. practice 1985—86, assessment diagnostic and therapeutic modalities and devices); mem.: Am. Assn. Indian Profls. (pres. New Orleans chpt. 2003), Internat. Med. Soc. Paraplegia, Orleans Parish Med. Soc., La. Phys. Medicine and Rehab. Soc., La. State Med. Soc., Am. Assn. Electromyography and Electrodiagnosis (liaison rep. to profl. stds. com. 1984), Am. Assn. Electrodiagnostic Medicine, Am. Assn. Physicians India (ethics and grievance com. 1992), Am. Spinal Injury Assn. Republican. Hindu. Avocations: reading, music, collecting time pieces and writing instruments, abstract painting. Home: 738 English Turn Ln New Orleans LA 70131-3349 Office: 3301 Saint Charles Ave New Orleans LA 70115-4533 Office Phone: 504-899-3041. Personal E-mail: lexman_kewalramani@yahoo.com.

KEY, HELEN ELAINE, accountant, educator, consulting company executive; b. Cleve., Jan. 16, 1946; d. Maud and Helen (Key) Vance. BS, W.Va. State Coll., 1968; MEd, Cleve. State U., 1977, PhD, 2003. Prin. Cleve. Bd. Edn., 1968—2004; pres. H.E. Key & Assoc., Cleve., 1983—. Instr. Cuyahoga C.C., Cleve., 1969—, Dyke Coll., Cleve., 1979-85; treas. BK4W Inc., Cleve., 1981; sec. Progressive Pioneers, Inc. Mem. AAUW, NAACP, NEA, Am. Assn. Notary Pubs., Women Bus. Owners Assn., Cleve. Area Bus. Tchrs., Toastmistress Club (sec. 1978), Pi Lambda Theta, Alpha Kappa Alpha. Democrat. Baptist. Home: 564 Wilkes Ln Cleveland OH 44143-2622 E-mail: hekey-clev@worldnet.att.net.

KEY, JACK DAYTON, librarian; b. Enid, Okla., Feb. 24, 1934; s. Ernest Dayton and Janie (Haldeman) K.; m. Virgie Ruth Richardson, Aug. 12, 1956; children— Toni, Scot, Todd. BA, Phillips U., Enid, Okla., 1958; MA, U. N.Mex., 1960; MS, U. Ill., 1962. Staff supr. Grad. Library U. Ill., 1960-62; pharmacy librarian U. Iowa, 1962-64; med. librarian Lovelace Found. for Med. Edn. and Research, Albuquerque, 1965-70; dir. Mayo Med. Ctr. Librs., Rochester, Minn., 1970-94, dir. emeritus, 1994—; prof. emeritus biomed. comm. Mayo Med. Sch. Cons. in field; participant Naval War Coll. Conf., 1979; Alberta A. Brown lectr. Western Mich. U., 1979 Author: The Origin of the Vaccine Inoculation by Edward Jenner, 1977, William Alexander Hammond (1828-1900), 1979; editor: Library Automation: The Orient and South Pacific, 1975, Automated Activities in Health Sciences Libraries, 1975-78, Classics and Other Selected Readings in Medical Librarianship, 1980, Journal of a Quest for the Elusive Doctor Arthur Conan Doyle, 1982, Medical Vanities, 1982, William A. Hammond, M.D., 1828-1900: The Publications of an American Neurologist, 1983, Classics in Cardiology, Vol. 3, 1983, Vol. 4, 1989, Medical Casebook of Dr. Arthur Conan Doyle from Practitioner to Sherlock Holmes and Beyond, 1984, Medicine, Literature and Eponyms: An Encyclopedia of Medical Eponyms Derived from Literary Characters, 1989, Conan Doyle's Tales of Medical Humanism and Values, 1992; contbr. articles to profl. jours. Served with USN, 1952-55. U. N.Mex. fellow, 1958-59, N.Mex. Library Assn. Marion Dorroh Meml. scholar, 1960, Rotary Paul Harris fellow, 1979; recipient Outstanding Hist. Writing award Minn. Medicine, 1980, Spl. Svc. award Am. Acad. Dermatology, 1992, Farthing award Baker St. Jour., 1993; decorated knight Icelandic Order of Falcon, 1980; named to Phillips U. Hall Fame, 1988. Mem. Med. Library Assn., Am. Inst. History Pharmacy, Am. Assn. History Medicine, Am. Med. Writers Assn., Am. Osler Soc. (pres. 1990-91), Mystery Writers of Am., Alcuin Soc., Baker St. Irregulars, Ampersand Club, Sigma Xi (cert. of recognition 1982) Mem. Christian Ch. (Disciples Of Christ). Home: PO Box 231 54 Skyline Dr Sandia Park NM 87047-0231 Office: Mayo Clinic Rochester MN 55905-0001

KEY, JAMES EVERETT, ophthalmologist; b. Freeport, Tex., July 19, 1944; s. James Everett and Margaret Ann (Parker) K.; m. Betty Wilson, Dec. 22, 1967; children: Peter Wilson and Courtney Brooke (twins). BA, U. Tex., 1966; MD, Baylor U., 1970. Diplomate Am. Bd. Ophthalmology. Mem. staff Coll. Medicine Baylor U., Houston, 1976-89, clin. assoc. prof. ophthalmology, 1989-93, clin. prof. ophthalmology, 1994—. Chief ophthalmology St. Luke's Episcopal Hosp., Houston, 1987—. Contbr. articles to jours., chpts. to books, editor medical textbooks. Trustee U. of South, Sewanee, Tenn., 1991-96, 98-2000. Lt. USN, 1972-73. Recipient Honor award Am. Acad. of Ophthalmology, 1990. Fellow Am. Acad. Ophthalmology (Hon. award); mem. AMA, Contact Lens Assn. Ophthalmologists (past pres.), Harris County Med. Assn., Tex. Ophthal. Assn. (past bd. dirs.), Houston Ophthal. Soc. (past pres.), Phi Beta Kappa. Episcopalian. Office: 6624 Fannin St Ste 2100 Houston TX 77030-2333 Office Phone: 713-796-0120. E-mail: eyemed1@swbell.net.

KEY, MARCUS M., JR., geologist, educator; b. Cin., July 13, 1961; s. Marcus M. and Dorothy E. Key; m. Maria L. Crowley; children: Dylan J., Lily M., Kevin M., John C., Peter T. BS, U. Tex., Austin, 1981—83; MPhil, Yale U., New Haven, Conn., 1984—86, PhD, 1986—88. Registered profl. geologist Pa., 1993. Asst. geologist Fla. Exploration Co., Houston, 1983; assoc. geologist Exxon Co., U.S.A., Houston, 1984; asst. prof. Dickinson Coll., Carlisle, Pa., 1989—94, assoc. prof., 1994—2005, prof., 2005—. Rsch. assoc. Field Mus. Natural History, Chgo., 1995—; vis. academic Trinity Coll., Dublin, 1999—2000. Sec. Cumberland Valley Habitat for Humanity, Carlisle, Pa., 1992—95. Mem.: Soc. for Sedimentary Geology, Internat. Palaeontological Assn., Harrisburg Area Geol. Soc. (pres. 1992—93), Geol. Soc. Am., Paleontol. Soc., Sigma Xi, The Sci. Rsch. Soc., Internat. Bryozoology Assn. (exec. coun. 1995—2001), Phi Beta Kappa. Roman Catholic. Office: Dickinson Coll Dept of Geology Carlisle PA 17013-2896 Office Phone: 717-245-1448. Office Fax: 717-245-1971. Personal E-mail: key@dickinson.edu.

KEY, RICHARD DUANE, pathologist; b. Jacksonville, Fla., Sept. 1956; s. Herbert Calvin and Mary Elaine Key; m. Laurie Beth Gribas, Oct. 3, 1981; children: Trevor Scott, Amelia Catherine. AA, Northeast Miss. Jr. Coll., 1976; BA, Miss. Coll., 1978; MD, U. Miss., 1982. Diplomate Am. Bd. of Pathology. Intern Eugene Talmadge Meml. Hosp., Augusta, Ga., 1982—83; resident in pathology Med. Coll. Ga., Augusta, 1983—86; med. dir. lab. Flowers Hosp., Dothan, Ala., 2002—. Mem.: AMA, CAP, Ala. Assn. Pathologists, Am. Soc. Clin. Pathology. Home: 102 Fair Oak Dr Dothan AL 36303 Office: Flowers Hosp 4370 W Main St Dothan AL 36305 Business E-Mail: rkey@flowershospital.com. Personal E-mail: ratl_key@juno.com.

KEY, TED, cartoonist; b. Fresno, Calif., Aug. 25, 1912; s. Simon Leon and Fanny (Kahn) K.; m. Anne Elizabeth Wilkinson, Sept. 30, 1937 (dec. July 5, 1984); children: Stephen Lewis, David Edward, Peter Lawrence; m. Bonnie Williams-Cohen, Nov. 17, 1987. BA, U. Calif., Berkeley, 1933. Assoc. editor Judge mag., N.Y.C., 1937-39; radio staff writer J. Walter Thompson Advt. Agy., N.Y.C., 1939-43; cartoonist Hazel Saturday Evening Post, Phila., 1943-70, King Features Syndicate, 1969—. Cartoonist, writer The Econs. Press, Inc., Fairfield, N.J., 1957—; screenwriter Walt Disney Prodns., Burbank, Calif., 1970-77. Writer, cartoonist for CBS, NBC, mags., books, newspapers; playwright (NBC radio prodn.) The Clinic (pub. in anthology Best Broadcasts Of 1939-40); creator (cartoon features) Diz and Liz for Jack and Jill mag., 1961-71, (TV series) Hazel, Peabody and Sherman for Bullwinkle and Rocky Show (TV series), 1959; writer: Hazel, NBC-TV (4 yrs.), CBS-TV (1 yr.), 1946, Here's Hazel, 1949, Many Happy Returns, 1950, If You Like Hazel, 1952, So'm I, 1953, Hazel Rides Again, 1955, Fasten Your Seat Belts, 1956, Phyllis, 1957, All Hazel, 1958, The Hazel Jubilee, 1959, The Biggest Dog in the World, 1960, Hazel Time, 1962, Life With Hazel, 1965, Diz and Liz, 1965, Squirrels in the Feeding Station, 1967, Hazel Power, 1971, Right On Hazel, 1972, Ms. Hazel, 1972, Hazel's Feline Funnies, 1982; story/screenwriter: Million Dollar Duck, The Cat From Outer Space (also wrote novel), Gus; writer: Positive Attitude Posters, 1965-2003, Sales Bullets, 1960-2003; cartoons included in New Yorker, Esquire, Look, Life, Ladies Home Jour., McCall's, Good Housekeeping, Better Homes and Gardens, People, Mademoiselle. Master sgt. Signal Corps AUS, 1943-46. Mem. Nat. Cartoonists Soc. (Best Syndicated Panel award 1977), Writers Guild Am. West.

KEYES, ALAN L., radio and talk show host, former federal government official; b. NYC, Aug. 7, 1950; m. Jocelyn Marcel Keyes; children: Francis, Maya, Andrew. BA, Harvard U., 1972, PhD in govt., 1979. Commd. fgn. service officer Dept. State, 1978, consular officer, 1979-80, desk officer, 1980-81, policy planning staff, 1981-83, asst. sec. for internat. orgn. affairs Washington, 1985—88; US rep. to econ. and social council UN, 1983-85; asst. sec. of state Internat. Organizations, 1985—88; pres. Citizens Against Govt. Waste, 1989—92; interim pres. Ala. A&M Univ., 1991; syndicated columnist Scripps Howard, 1991—92; cand. US Senate Md., 1988, 1992, Illinois, 2004; cand. US Pres., 1996, 2000; natl. talk radio show host The Alan Keyes Show: America's Wake Up Call, 1994—2000; host Alan Keyes: Making Sense, 2002; founder & pres. The Declaration Foundation, 1996. Resident scholar Am. Enterprise Inst., 1987—89. Author: Masters of the Dream: The Strength and Betrayal of Black America, 1995, Our Character, Our Future: Reclaiming America's Moral Destiny, 1996. Republican.*

KEYES, ALLEN E., judge; b. Marlette, Mich., Feb. 22, 1926; s. Elmer James and Myra Blanche Keyes; m. Roma Janice Turner, Feb. 23, 1952; children: Janice, Barbara, Cheryl, David. AB, Wayne State U., 1951, JD, 1956. Bar: Mich. 1956. Claims adjuster Mich. Mut. Liability Co., Detroit, 1953-55, State Farm Ins., Detroit, 1955-57; sole practitioner gen. law practice, Marlette, 1957-58, 68-75; pros. atty. Sanilac County, Sandusky, Mich., 1958-68; cir. ct. judge State of Mich., Sandusky, 1975-90. Mediator St. Clair County, 1990—. Bd. dirs. United Way, Sandusky, 1961-63, Marlette Comty. Hosp., 1968-75. 1st lt. USAF, 1951-53. Recipient Silver Anniversary award Wayne State U., 1981. Avocations: golf, bowling. Home: 3920 Jack Pine Ln Port Huron MI 48060-1578

KEYES, ARTHUR HAWKINS, JR., architect; b. Rutland, Vt., May 26, 1917; s. Arthur Hawkins and Blanche (Emery) K.; m. Lucile Sheppard, Mar. 29, 1941; children: Arthur S., Spencer S., Janet S. AB cum laude, Princeton U., 1939; M.Arch., Harvard U., 1942. Partner Keyes, Lethbridge and Condon, Washington, 1956-75; partner Keyes Condon Florance (Architects), Washington, 1975-80, pres., 1980-85; chmn. Keyes Condon Florance Eich Baum Esocoff King, 1985-92; chmn. emeritus, 1992—; pres. Sea Ridge Devel. Corp., Washington Bldg. Congress, 1964-65; chmn. alumni adv. council Sch. Architecture, Princeton U., 1965-73. Trustee Hist. Soc. Washington D.C. Served with USNR, 1942-46. Fellow AIA (spl. presdl. citation 1982); mem. Nat. Trust Hist. Preservation, Com. of 100 on the Fed. City. Clubs: Cosmos, Chevy Chase. Republican. Home: 2605 31st St NW Washington DC 20008-3519 Office: Smith Group 1825 S St NW Ste 250 Washington DC 20006-5428 Office Phone: 202-842-2100. Personal E-mail: ahkaia@aol.com.

KEYES, DANIEL, author; BA in Psychology, Bklyn. Coll., 1950, MA in English, 1961. Assoc. fiction editor Magazine Mgmt. Co., N.Y.C., 1950-52; v.p. Fenko and Keyes Photography, Inc., 1952-53; tchr. English N.Y.C. Bd. Edn., 1955-62; instr. English Wayne State U., Detroit, 1962-66; mem. faculty Ohio U., Athens, 1966—, prof. English and creative writing, 1972-97, prof. emeritus, 2000—; agt. William Morris Agy., N.Y.C., Calif. Author: (novels) Flowers for Algernon (Hugo award 1959, Nebula award 1966, movie version: Charly, 1968 (Acad. award), The Touch, 1968, The Fifth Sally, 1980, (nonfiction) The Minds of Billy Milligan, 1981 (Spl. award Mystery Writers Am., Kurd Lasswitz award, 1st prize Best Fgn. Book award 1986), Unveiling Claudia, 1986, Daniel Keyes Collected Stories, 1993 (Japan), The Milligan Wars, 1994 (Japan), Daniel Keyes Reader, 1995 (Japan), Until Death Do Us Part: The Sleeping Princess, 1998 (Japan), (TV movie) Flowers for Algernon, 2000, (non-fiction) Algernon, Charlie and I: A Writer's Journey, 2000; (13 episode TV series) flowers for Algernon (Japan), 2002, The Touch, revised 2003; supervising prodr. (TV movie) The Mad Housers, 1990. With U.S. Maritime Svc., 1945—47. Ohio Arts Council Individual Artist fellow,

1986-87; recipient Baker Fund award 1986-87, Disting. Alumnus Honor award Bklyn. Coll. CUNY, 1988. Mem. PEN, Dramatists' Guild, Mystery Writers of Am. (nominated Edgar award), Sci. Fiction Writers Am. (Author Emeritus award 2000). Office: 7491 N Federal Hwy C5-110 Boca Raton FL 33487-1625 E-mail: dankeyes@usa.net.

KEYES, JAMES HENRY, manufacturing executive; b. LaCrosse, Wis., Sept. 2, 1940; s. Donald M. and Mary M. (Nodolf) K.; m. Judith Ann Carney, Nov. 21, 1964; children: James Patrick, Kevin, Timothy. BS, Marquette U., 1962; MBA, Northwestern U., 1963. Instr. Marquette U., Milw., 1963-65; CPA Peat. Marwick & Mitchell, Milw., 1965-66; with Johnson Controls, Inc., Milw., 1967—, mgr. sys. dept., 1967-71, divsn. contr., 1971-73, corp. contr., treas., 1973-77, v.p., CFO, 1977-85, exec. v.p., 1985-86, pres., 1986-99, chief operating officer, 1986-88, chief exec. officer, 1988—2002, chmn. bd. dirs., 1993—. Bd. dirs. Baird Capital Devel. Fund. 1st Wis. Trust Co., LSI Logic, Inc., Universal Foods Corp. Active Milw. Symphony Orch., 1980—. Mem. Fin. Execs. Inst., Am. Inst. CPA's, Wis. Inst. CPA's., Machinery and Allied Products Inst. Office: Johnson Controls Inc 5757 N Green Bay Ave Milwaukee WI 53209-4408

KEYES, JEFFREY J., lawyer; BA magna cum laude, U. Notre Dame, 1968; JD cum laude, U. Mich., 1972. Bar: Minn. 1972. Shareholder Briggs and Morgan, P.A., Mpls.; fellow Am. Coll. Trial Lawyers, Mpls. Mem. Gov.'s Task Force on Tort Reform, 1986; chmn. fed. practice com. U.S. Dist. Ct. Minn., 1990-93, 2002—, chmn. adv. group on civil justice reform act, 1991-93; trainer U.S. Magistrate Judges Tng. Conf. on Settlement, Mpls., 1992; lectr. in field. Contbr. articles to law jours. Chmn. bd. dirs. The Playwright's Ctr. Mem. ABA (chmn. antitrust sect. franchise com. 1989-90, contbg. editor Antitrust Monograph 1987, co-editor Antitrust Sect. State Antitrust Law Handbook, Minn. chpt. 1990), Minn. State Bar Assn. (co-chair Women in the Legal Profn. task force 1996-97, chmn. civil litigation sect. 1985-86), Hennepin County Bar Assn. Office: Briggs & Morgan 80 S 8th St 2200 Minneapolis MN 55402-2157

KEYES, JOAN ROSS RAFTER, education educator, writer; b. Bklyn., Aug. 12, 1924; d. Joseph W. and Hermia (Ross) Rafter; m. William Ambrose, Apr. 26, 1947 (dec.); children: William, Peter, Dion, Kenzie. BA, Adelphi U., Garden City, N.Y., 1945; MS, Long Island U., Greenvale, N.Y., 1973. Prodn. asst. CBS Radio, N.Y., 1943-44; cub news reporter Bklyn. Daily Eagle, 1945-46; advt. copywriter Gimbel's Dept. Store, N.Y., 1946-47; adj. prof. L.I. U., Greenvale, N.Y., 1984—; tchr. Port Wash. Pub. Schs., N.Y., 1970-94. Lectr., cons. pub. sch. dists. nationwide, 1978—; workshop leader Tchrs. English to Speakers Other Langs. convs., 1981—; cons. Kids' Readers, 2005. Author: Beats! Conversations in Rhythm, 1983, (video program) Now You're Talking, 1987, (computer program) Quick Talk, 1990, Oxford Picture Dictionary for Kids Program, 1998; contbr. articles to ednl. mags. Lectr., catechist Our Lady of Fatima Ch., Port Washington, 1987—; vol. Earthwatch, Mallorca, 1988. Australia/New Zealand ednl. grantee Port Washington Pub. Schs., 1992. Mem. Tchrs. of English to Speakers of Other Languages, Am. Fedn. of Tchrs., N.Y. State United Tchrs., Port Wash. Tchrs. Assn. Republican. Roman Catholic. Avocations: music, painting, travel, tennis, photography. Personal E-mail: joanrosskeyes@aol.com.

KEYES, MARION ALVAH, IV, manufacturing executive; b. Bellingham, Wash., May 11, 1938; s. Marion Alvah and Winnefred Agnes (Nolte) K.; m. Loretta Jean Mattson, Nov. 17, 1962; children: Marion A., Zachary Leigh (dec.), Richard. BS in Chem. Engring., Stanford U., 1960; MSEE, U. Ill., 1968; MBA, Baldwin Wallace Coll., 1981. Registered rofl. engr., Calif., Wis., N.Y., Ill., Ohio. Tchg. asst. dept. math. Stanford U., 1958-59; tech. Stanford Aerosol Labs., 1957-59; chem. engr. Ketchikan (Alaska) Pulp Co., 1960-63; dir engring. Control Sys. divsn. Beloit (Wis.) Corp., 1963-70; gen. mgr. digital sys. divsn. Taylor Instrument Co., Rochester, N.Y., 1970-75; v.p. engring. Bailey Controls Co., 1975-80; sr. v.p., group exec. Indsl. Products and Svcs. Group; pres. Bailey COntrols, Ohio, 1980-85; mem. exec. operating bd. McDermott Internat. Inc., 1985-89; pres., CEO Bailey Controls Co., Wickliffe, Ohio, 1989-90; chmn. Dcom Corp., Eastlake, Ohio, 1990-93; sr. v.p. tech. and bus. devel. process group, pres. Rosemount Analytical Inc. divsn. Emerson, St. Louis, 1993—. Bd. dirs. Fibermark Corp. Author: Offshore Platform Automation, 1990; editor: A Glossary of Automatic Control Terminology, 1970; contbr. articles to profl. jours.; holder 54 U.S. and more than 100 fgn. patents. Past bd. advisors Fenn Coll. Engring., Cleve. State U.; bd. dirs. Baldwin Coll., United Cerebral Palsy, Cleve.; past prs., mem. exec. bd. N.E. Ohio coun. Boy Scouts Am.; past pres. Area 5 Boy Scouts Am. Named to, Measurement and Control Hall of Fame. Fellow ISA (hon. life), TAPPI (Pioneer award), IEEE, Am. inst. Chemists, Instrument Soc. Am. (life hon.), Ohio acad. Scis. (life, bd. dirs., Centennial honoree 1991); mem. AIChE, Cleve. Engring. Soc. (bd. dirs.), Soc. Am. Mil. Engrs. (life), Am. Assn. Artificial Intelligence (charter), Am. Mgmt. Assn., U.S. Automation Rsch. Coun., Am. Automatic Control Coun. (past. sec. and bd. dirs., Am. Chem. Soc., Wis. Acad. Arts, Scis. and Letters, Cleve. World Trade Assn. (Man of Yr. 1984), Canterbury Golf Club, Mo. Athletic Club. Republican. Roman Catholic. Home: 8 Washington Terr Saint Louis MO 63112-1914 Office: 8100 W Florissant Ave K-Annex Saint Louis MO 63136 E-mail: bud@keyes.org.

KEYES, ROBERT W., physicist, researcher; b. Chgo., Dec. 2, 1921; s. Lee P. and Katherine K.; m. Sophie Skadorwa, June 4, 1966; children— Andrew, Claire. BS, U. Chgo., 1942, MS, 1949, PhD, 1953. With Argonne Nat. Lab., 1946-50; staff mem. Westinghouse Research Lab., Pitts., 1953-60; mem. research staff IBM Research Lab., Yorktown Heights, N.Y., 1960—. Vis. physicist Am. Phys. Soc. Vis. Indsl. Physicists Program, 1974-75, 77; vice chmn. Gordon Conf. on High Pressure Physics, 1970; chmn. Gordon Conf. on Chemistry and Physics of Microstructure Fabrication, 1976, Nat. Materials Adv. Bd. (ad hoc com. on ion implantation as a new surface treatment tech.), 1978, Internat. Conf. Heavily Doped Semiconductors, 1984; mem. Nat. Acad. Scis.-NAE-NRC evaluation panel Nat. Bur. Standards, 1970-73; cons. physics survey com., mem. statis. data panel Nat. Acad. Sci.-NRC Council Physics Survey Com., 1972; mem. data and info. panel Nat. Acad. Sci.-NRC Com. on Survey of Materials Sci. and Engring., 1974; Girling Watson vis. prof. elec. engring. U. Sydney, Fall 1996. Author: Physics of VLSI Systems, 1987; assoc. editor Revs. Modern Physics, 1976-95; corr.: Comments on Solid State Physics, 1970-85. With USN, 1944—46. Recipient Outstanding Contbn. award IBM, 1963 Fellow Am. Phys. Soc. (chmn. com. applications of physics 1976-78), IEEE (life, chmn. subcom. cultural and sci. relations 1976, mem. del. to USSR 1975, W.R.G. Baker prize 1976, awards bd. 1984, Sigma Xi. Office: IBM PO Box 218 Yorktown Heights NY 10598-0218 Business E-Mail: rwk4@sigmaxi.org.

KEYES, SAUNDRA ELISE, newspaper editor; b. Salt Lake City, June 28, 1945; d. Vernon Harrison and Mildred K.; m. William J. Ivey, June 13, 1969 (div. 1976). BA, U. Utah, 1966; MA, Ind. U., 1969, PhD, 1976. Tchr. Salt Lake City Pub. Schs., 1966-67; asst. prof. Fisk U., Nashville, 1971-76; reporter, city editor The Tennessean, Nashville, 1976-83; staff writer The Courier-Jour., Louisville, 1983-84; dep. mng. editor Orlando (Fla.) Sentinel, 1985-88; mng. editor Phila. Daily News, 1988-90; exec. editor, sr. v.p. Press-Telegram, Long Beach, Calif., 1991-93; mng. editor The Miami Herald, 1993-96, Contra Costa Times, 1996—2000; editor Honolulu Advertiser, 2000—. Ford Found. fellow, 1978. Mem.: Am. Soc. Newspaper Editors (pres. accrediting coun. on edn. in journalism and mass comm. 2004—). Office: Honolulu Advertiser 605 Kapiolani Blvd PO Box 3110 Honolulu HI 96802

KEYFITZ, NATHAN, sociologist, educator, demographer; b. Montreal, Que., Can., June 29, 1913; s. Arthur and Anna (Gerstein) K.; m. Beatrice Orkin, Oct. 8, 1939; children: Barbara Lee, Robert Norman. BS, McGill U., Montreal, 1934; PhD, U. Chgo., 1952; MA (hon.), Harvard U., 1972; LLD (hon.), U. Western Ont., 1973, U. de Montréal, 1984, McGill U., 1984, U. Alta, 1985, U. Siena, Italy, 1991, Carleton U., 1993, U. de Québec, 1993. Census clk., statistician, sr. research statistician Dominion Bur. Statistics, Govt. Can., 1936-59; dir. Colombo Plan Bur., Sri Lanka, 1956-57; prof. sociology U. Toronto, Ont., Can., 1959-63, U. Montreal, 1962-63; prof. U. Chgo., 1963-68, chmn. sociology dept., 1965-68; prof. demography U. Calif., Berkeley, 1968-72; Andelot prof. sociology and demography Harvard U., 1972-82, chmn. dept. sociology, 1978-80, emeritus, 1982—; Robert Lazarus prof. social demography Ohio State U., Columbus, 1980-84, prof. emeritus, 1984—; with Internat. Inst. Applied Systems Analysis, 1984-93; researcher Initiatives on Children, Am. Acad. Arts and Scis., Cambridge, Mass., 1994—. Tech. assistance assignments, Burma, 1951, Indonesia, 1952-53, 64, 79, 85-89, Argentina, 1960, Santiago, Chile, 1963, Moscow, 1977, 85, People's Republic China, 1981; vis. fellow Stanford U., 1986. Author: Introduction to the Mathematics of Population, 1968, 2d edit., 1977, Applied Mathematical Demography, 1977, (with Hal Caswell), 3d edit., 2005, Population Change and Social Policy, 1982, (with Wilhelm Flieger) World Population Growth and Aging, 1990; contbr. articles to profl. jours. Trustee Nat. Opinion Research Ctr., 1966—. Recipient Lazarsfeld award Am. Sociol. Assn., 1990, Common Wealth award, 1991; decorated Cross of Honor for Sci., Austria, 1993; named Laureate, Internat. Union Sci. Study Population, 1997, Norberg award Population Coun. of N.Y. Fellow Royal Soc. Can., Am. Statis. Assn. (chmn. social stats. sect. 1961), Royal Statis. Soc. (hon.), Statis. Soc. of Can. (hon.); mem. NAS, Am. Acad. Arts and Scis., Can. Polit. Sci. Assn. (chmn. sociology and anthropology sect. 1961), Inter-Am. Statis. Inst., Internat. Statis. Inst., Population Assn. Am. (pres. 1969-70), Phi Beta Kappa. Home: 1580 Massachusetts Ave Apt 7C Cambridge MA 02138-2928 E-mail: nathankeyfitz@yahoo.com.

KEYS, ALICIA (ALICIA AUGELLO COOK), vocalist, musician, songwriter; b. N.Y.C., Jan. 25, 1981; d. Craig Cook and Terri Augello. Student, Columbia U. Singer: (albums) Songs in A Minor, 2001 (Video Music Award, two Billboard Awards, two Am. Music Awards, two NAACP Image Awards, three Soul Train awards, two World Music Awards, an ECCHO award, Grammy Award for Best New Artist, Song of Yr., Best R&B Vocal Performance, Best R&B Song and Best R&B Album), The Diary of Alicia Keys, 2003 (MTV Video Music award Best R&B Video for the song "If I Ain't Got You", 2004, R&B/Hip-Hop Singles of Yr.:"If I Ain't Got You", Billboard Music Awards, 2004, R&B/Hip-Hop Airplay Single of Yr.:"If I Ain't Got You", Billboard Music Awards, 2004, Grammy Award for Best R&B Album, 2005); composer: (films) Hollywood Homicide, Dr. Dolittle 2, Ali; actor: (TV guest appearances) The Cosby Show, 1985, Saturday Night Live, 2001, Charmed, 2001, Tonight Show with Jay Leno, 2001, American Dreams, 2003, Oprah Winfrey Show, 2004; author: Tears for Water: Songbook of Poems and Lyrics, 2004. Named Female Artist of Yr., Billboard Music Awards, 2004, Hot 100 Artist of Yr., 2004, Female Hot 100 Artist of Yr., 2004, Hot 100 Songwriter of Yr., 2004; named one of Time Mag. 100 Most Influential People, 2005, 50 Most Influential African-Americans, Ebony Mag., 2004; recipient Favorite Female Artist-Soul/Rhythm & Blues Music, Am. Music Awards, 2004, Female R&B/Hip-Hop Artist of Yr., Billboard Music Awards, 2004, R&B/Hip-Hop Singles Artist of Yr., 2004, Best R&B Video for Karma, MTV Video Music Awards, 2005. Office: BMG Entertainment 1540 Broadway New York NY 10036*

KEYS, JOHN W., III, federal agency administrator; b. Sheffield, Ala. m. Dell Keys. BCE, Ga. Inst. Tech., 1964; Masters Degree, Brigham Young U., 1971. Registered engr., Colo., Wyo., Mont., N.D. Civil and hydraulic engr. Bur. Reclamation, 1964—79, pacific N.W. regional dir.; commr. Bur. Reclamation, dept. Interior, Washington, 2001—. Comml. pilot for Angel Flight, Air LifeLine, County Search & Rescue, Moab, Utah. Coll. football referee, 1970—; H.S. football referee, 1962—. Recipient Disting. Svc. award, 1995. Office: US Dept Interior Bur Reclamation 1849 C St NW Washington DC 20240

KEYS, PAUL ROSS, university provost/academic affairs official, educator; b. St. Louis, Mar. 21, 1940; s. Charles and Josie (Jones) K.; m. Donnielesky Harrington, May 23, 1998; children from a previous marriage, Pamela, Roderick. BS, St. Louis U., 1963, MSW, 1971; PhD, U. Wis., Milw., 1983. Exec. dir. Champaign (Ill.) Urban League, 1969; dep. dir. Concentrated Employment Program, St. Louis, 1971; asst. dir. legis. NASW, Washington, 1971-74; exec. dir. Cmty. Svcs. Coun., Columbia, Mo., 1974-76; dir. Broward County (Fla.) Dept. Human Svcs., 1976-78; dep. adminstr. Comty. Svcs. divsn. State of Wis., 1978-81; prof. Hunter Coll., CUNY, 1983-94; faculty doctoral program CUNY, 1987-94; dean Coll. Health and Human Svcs., S.E. Mo. State U., Cape Girardeau, 1994-2000, also assoc. provost. Fellow Ctr. Social Adminstrn., Hunter Coll., 1985-94. Author: New Management in Human Services, 1988, 2d edit., 1995; founding editor Jour. Multicultural Social Work, 1989—; contbr. articles to profl. jours. Capt. USAF, 1963-69. Recipient Martin Luther King/Woodrow Wilson fellowship, 1970, Commendation Resolution, Mo. Gen. Assembly, 1976, GARIOA/Fulbright Rsch. fellowship, Tokyo, 1990-91, Disting. Alumni Svc. award St. Louis U. Sch. Social Svcs., 1996, Exemplar Mgmt. Excellence award Nat. Network for Social Work Mgrs., 1999; named to Sumner H.S. Hall of Fame, 2001. Mem. Am. Pub. Welfare Assn. (exec. com. 1988), Omega Psi Phi (Cmty. Svc. award 1977). Avocations: travel, computer software, jazz. Office: Provost's Office Governors State Univ 1 University Pkwy University Park IL 60466 Office Phone: 708-534-4980. Personal E-mail: pkeys@prodigy.net. Business E-Mail: p-keys@gaust.edu.

KEYS, ROBERT BARR, JR., lawyer; b. Trenton, N.J. s. Robert B. and Evelyn L. K. BA cum laude, Dickinson Coll., 1975, JD, 1978. Bar: Pa. 1978. Assoc. Edward Miller, Esq., Lebanon, Pa., 1978-81; ptnr. Rowe, Enck & Keys, Lebanon, 1982-85; pvt. practice Lebanon, 1985-91; ptnr. Keys and Burkett, Lebanon, 1992—. Asst. pub. defender Lebanon County, 1981-82; spl. master in divorce Ct. Common Pleas Lebanon County, 1986-2000; child law guardian Ct. Common Pleas Lebanon County, 1987-95 Spl. dep. atty. gen. Commonwealth of Pa., 1993-94; twp. supr. North Cornwall Twp. Lebanon County, 1996-98; bd. dirs. Internat. Assn. Sports Museums & Halls of Fame, 1998—; gen. counsel Pa. Sports Hall of Fame, 1982—. Mem. Lebanon County Bar Assn. (fee dispute chmn. 1990-98, Clarke Seltzer award 1987, 89). Office: Keys and Burkett 250 S 8th St Lebanon PA 17042-6010 E-mail: rbk@lmf.net.

KEYS, RONALD E., career military officer; B in Entomology with disting., Kansas State U., 1967; grad., Squadron Officer Sch., 1971; MBA, Golden Gate U., 1978; student, Air War College, 1988. Commd. 2d. lt. USAF, 1967, advanced through grades to gen., 2005; undergrad. pilot tng. Reese AFB, Ala., 1968; F-4 tng. Davis-Monthan AFB, Ariz., 1968-69; F-4 aircraft comdr. 366th Tactical Fighter Wing, Da Nang Air Base, South Vietnam, 1969-70, 475th Tactical Fighter Wing, Misawa Air Base, Japan, 1970-71; F-4 aircraft commdr., flight examiner, then chief Tactical Fighter Wing, Kadena Air Base, Japan, 1971-74; instr. pilot, flight cmmdr. USAF Fighter Weapons Sch., Nellis AFB, Nev., 1974-79; air ops. officer Directorite Ops. Readiness, Washington, D.C., 1979-81; asst. exec. officer to chief of staff Hdqs. USAF Pentagon, Washington, D.C., 1981-82; chief Ops. tng. divsn., Langley AFB, Va., 1982-84; commdr. 71st Tactical Fither Squadron, Langley AFB, Va., 1984-85; spl. asst. to deputy chief of staff, intelligence Hdqs. Tactical Air Command, Langley AFB, Va., 1985-86; asst. dep. chief of staff for ops. Hdqs. Air Force Res., Robbins AFB, Ga., 1986-87; comdr. USAF Fighter Weapons Sch., Nellis AFB, Nev., 1988-90; vice comdr., then comdr. 36th Fighter Wing, Bitburg Air Base, Germany, 1990-92; sr. mil. asst. to asst. sec. def. for nuclear security and counterproliferation Office Sec. Def., Washington, 1992-94; comdr. 354th Fighter Wing, Eielson AFB, Alaska, 1994-95, 53rd Wing, Eglin AFB, Fla., 1995-97, USAF Doctrine Ctr., Maxwell AFB, Ala., 1997-98; dir. ops. Hdqs. U.S. European Command, Stuttgart, Germany, 1998—2000; comdr. Allied Air Forces So. Europe, Stabilization Forces Air Component & Kosovo Forces Air Component, Comdr. 16th Air Force & 16th Air & Space Expeditionary Task Force, Italy, 2000—02; dep. chief of staff air & space ops. USAF, Washington, 2002—05; comdr. Air Combat Command, Langley AFB, Va., 2005—. Recipient Def. Disting Svc. medal with oak leaf cluster, Disting. Svc. medal, Def. Superior Svc. medal, Legion of Merit with oak leaf cluster, DFC with oak leaf cluster, Def. Meritorious Svc. medal, Air medal with 16 oak leaf clusters, Air Force Commendation medal with oak leaf cluster. Office: Air Combat Command 205 Dodd Blvd Ste 100 Langley Afb VA 23665*

KEYSER, DANIEL, atmospheric scientist, educator; b. Phila., Dec. 21, 1953; s. Gerson and Evelyn (Mokren) K.; m. Wendy Joy Leichter, Oct. 31, 1982; 1 child, Michael Gerson. BS with highest distinction, Pa. State U., 1975, MS, 1977, PhD, 1981. Rsch. meteorologist Naval Postgrad. Sch., Monterey, Calif., 1977-78, Rsch. and Data Systems, Inc., Lanham, Md., 1981-82, NASA/Goddard Space Flight Ctr., Greenbelt, Md., 1982-87; assoc. prof. U. Albany, SUNY, 1987-92, prof., 1992—. Earth and atmospheric scis. evaluation panel for associateship programs NRC, Washington, 1995—2001. Contbr. chpts. to books, articles to profl. jours.; editor Monthly Weather Rev., 1991-93, assoc. editor, 1986-90, 94-97, 2004-. Recipient Disting. Authorship award NOAA/Environ. Rsch. Labs., 1987. Fellow: Am. Meteorol. Soc. (chair com. on mesoscale processes 1987—90, Clarence Leroy Meisinger award 1989, Editor's award 1989); mem.: Royal Meteorol. Soc., Sigma Xi. Office: U Albany SUNY Dept Earth/Atmospheric Scis 1400 Washington Ave Albany NY 12222-0100

KEYSER, LESLIE D., writer; b. Mainville, Pa., June 15, 1923; s. Leslie William and Mabel Bird (Breisch) K.; m. Evelyn Margaret Schramm, Mar. 4, 1955. Student, Bloomsburg Coll., 1946-48, U. Ctr. of Nice, France, 1952-53, Sorbonne U., Paris, 1953-54. Designer Magee Carpet Co., Bloomsburg, Pa., 1955-76; dir. Suncom Industries, Bloomsburg, 1976-86; designer Bloomsburg Carpet, 1986-92; freelance writer Bloomsburg, 1992—. Author: Wild Oats, 1999, The Returning, 1999, (novella) The Golden Tether, 1999, JCT, 2001. With U.S. Coast Guard, 1942-46. Mem. Am. Legion. Avocations: classical music, reading. Home: 2417 John Penn Cir Bloomsburg PA 17815-8900 E-mail: lkeyser@ptd.net.

KEYSER, MATT, transportation engineer; Rschr. Advanced Vehicles and Fuels Rsch. staff, Nat. Renewable Energy Lab US Dept. Energy. Named one of 100 Top Young Innovators, MIT's Tech. Review, 2003. Office: Nat Renewable Energy Lab 1617 Cole Blvd Golden CO 80401

KEYSER, RICHARD LEE, distribution company executive; b. Harrisburg, Pa., Oct. 28, 1942; s. Harold L. and Mary J. K.; m. Mary Ellen Carter, June 20, 1964; children: Jeffrey, Jennifer. BS, U.S. Naval Acad., 1964; MBA, Harvard U., 1971. Commd. ensign USN, 1964, advanced through grades to lt., 1966; resigned, 1969; mktg.-analysis mgr. Fleetguard, Inc., Dallas, 1971-72, dir. logistics Cookeville, Tenn., 1973-77; gen. mgr. parts ops. Cummins Engine Co., Inc., Columbus, Ind., 1977-83, exec. dir. mktg. ops., 1983-84; pres. NL-Hycalog, Houston, 1984-86; v.p. ops. W.W. Grainger, Inc., Chgo., 1986-87, exec. v.p., 1988-90, pres., 1991—, CEO, now chmn., 1995—. Bd. dirs. Morton Internat. County chmn. blood program ARC, Cookeville, 1976-77; bd. dirs. Preserve To Enjoy, Inc., Columbus, 1983-84, Irene Josselyn Clinic, Northfield, Ill., 1989-92, Lake Forest Grad. Sch. Mgmt., 1992—, Evanston Hosp. Corp., 1996—. Former lt. comdr. USNR. Fellow Am. Prodn. and Inventory Control Soc. (cert.); mem. Chgo. Club, Harvard Bus. Sch. Club Chgo. (v.p. 1988-89, pres. 1989-90), Comml. Club Chgo. Office: WW Grainger Inc 100 Grainger Pkwy Lake Forest IL 60045-5201

KEYSER, SAMUEL JAY, linguist, educator; b. July 7, 1935; s. Abraham L. and Sabina (Shaplen) K.; children: Rachel Suzanne, Beth Rebecca, Benjamin Jay Kendall; m. Nancy Kelly, 2001. BA, George Washington U., 1956; BA with honors, Oxford (Eng.) U., 1958, MA, 1962, Yale U., 1960, PhD, 1962. Mem. staff Rsch. Lab. Electronics MIT, Cambridge, 1961-62; mem. faculty Brandeis U., Waltham, Mass., 1965-71, Univ. Coll. London, 1971-72; head dept. linguistics U. Mass., Amherst, 1972-77; head dept. linguistics and philosophy MIT, Cambridge, 1977—84, assoc. provost for inst. life, 1985—94, spl. asst. to the provost, 1994-98, spl. asst. to Chancellor, 1998—, emeritus, 1998—, interim alcohol coord., 1999-2000. Co-author: English Stress: Its Form, Its Growth and Its Role in Verse, 1971, Beginning English Grammar, 1973, CV Phonology, 1983, Rule Generalization and Optionality in Language Change, 1985, Prolegomenon to a Theory of Lexical Argument Structure, 2002; author: (poems) Raising the Dead, 1993, (children's stories) The Pond God and other stories, 2003 (Lee Bennett Hopkins honor book award 2004); editor (with K. Hale): The View From Building 20, 1993; editor: Linguistic Inquiry, 1970—, Current Studies in Linguistics, 1972—, Linguistic Inquiry Monograph Series, 1976—; occasional commentator All Things Considered, NPR, 2004—. Peter de Florez chair MIT, 1989. With USAF, 1962-65. Fulbright scholar, 1956-58, sr. Fulbright scholar, 1971-72; recipient Disting. Alumnus award George Washington U., 1992, Lee Bennett Hopkins Honor Book Poetry award 2004. Mem. Linguistic Soc. Am., MIT Alumni Assn. (hon. mem.), Phi Beta Kappa. Home: 7 Frost St Cambridge MA 02140-1502 Office: Dept Linguistics & Philosophy Rm E32 0770 MIT Cambridge MA 02139-4307 Office Phone: 617-253-1917. Business E-Mail: keyser@mit.edu. *People, like organizations, are very good at starting things and very bad at stopping them. This goes for projects, marriages, and careers. I have found that the best way to stop something is to start something. It makes the stopping much, much easier, at least until the last stop.*

KEYT, DAVID, philosophy and classics educator; b. Indpls., Feb. 22, 1930; s. Herbert Coe and Hazel Marguerite (Sissman) K.; m. Christine Harwood (Mullikin) June 25, 1975; children by previous marriage: Sarah, Aaron. AB, Kenyon Coll., 1951; MA, Cornell U., 1953, PhD, 1955. Instr. dept. philosophy U. Wash., Seattle, 1957—60, asst. prof., 1960—64, assoc. prof., 1964—69, prof., 1969—, chmn. dept. philosophy, 1971-78, acting chmn. dept. philosophy, 1967—68, 1970, 1986, 1994. Vis. asst. prof. dept. philosophy UCLA, 1962-63; vis. assoc. prof. Cornell U., 1968-69; mem. Inst. for Advanced Study, 1983-84; vis. prof. U. Hong Kong, autumn 1987, Princeton U., autumn 1988, U. Calif., Irvine, autumn 1990; vis. scholar Social Philosophy and Policy Ctr., Bowling Green State U., autumn, 2001. Co-editor: (with Fred D. Miller Jr.) A Companion to Aristotle's Politics, 1991; Author: Aristotle Politics, Books V, VI, 1999; contbr. articles in field to profl. jours. Served with U.S. Army, 1955—57. Inst. for Rsch. in the Humanities fellow U. Wis., 1966-67; Ctr. for Hellenic Studies fellow, 1974-75. Mem. Am. Philos. Assn., Soc. Ancient Greek Philosophy. Home: 12032 36th Ave NE Seattle WA 98125-5637 Office: U Wash Box 353350 Dept Philosophy Seattle WA 98195-3350 Business E-Mail: keyt@u.washington.edu.

KEYVAN, SHAHLA, nuclear engineer, educator; arrived in U.S., 1971; d. Mahmood Keyvan and Forough Mortazavi. BS in Engring., U. Wash., 1974; MS in Nuc. Engring., Nuclear Engr. in Nuc. Engring., MIT, 1978; PhD in Nuc. Engring., U. Calif., Berkeley, 1983. Reactor operating license Nuc. Regulatory Commn., Wash., D.C., 1979, U.S. Nuc. Regulatory Commn., Wash., D.C., 1993. Cons. Argonne Nat. Lab., Idaho Falls, 1989; assoc. prof. nuc. engring. dept. U. Mo., Columbia, 1990—2001, rsch. prof., dir. ctr. artificial intelligence engring. and edn., 2001—. Panelist grad. fellowship program NSF, Arlington, Va., 1993—96. Author: (electronic books) Fundamentals Of Nuclear Technology, Introduction to Nuclear Reactor Physics, A Demo Module on Radiation Energy Deposition, A Demo Module on Fundamentals of Radiation Measurement, A Demo Module on Radiation Decay, A Demo Module on Binding Energy; contbr. articles to profl. jours. Grantee, Dept. of Energy Small Bus. Innovation Rsch. Program, 1984—87, Dept. of Energy, 1998—2003, NSF, 1991—93, 1994—97, 1998—2001, Mo. Inst. Instrnl. Devel., 1997—98, Mo. Dept. Econ., 1998—2001. Mem.: Am. Soc. Engring. Edn., Am. Nuc. Soc. (faculty advisor 1990—93, sec. Mo. sect. 1991—94), Phi Kappa Phi, Sigma Xi, Tau Beta Pi. Achievements include patents pending for automated inspection system for nuclear fuel pellet; automated nuclear fuel size measurement; flame image features and their analysis. Office: U Mo E2403D MAE Dept Columbia MO 65211 E-mail: keyvan@missouri.edu.

KEYWORTH, GEORGE ALBERT, II, physicist, consulting company executive; b. Boston, Nov. 30, 1939; s. Robert Allen and Leontine (Briggs) K.; m. Polly Lauterbach, July 28, 1962; children: Deirdre Anne, George Albert III. BS in Physics, Yale U., 1963; PhD in Nuclear Physics, Duke U., 1968; DSc (hon.), Rensselaer Poly. Inst., 1982; D in Engring. (hon.), Mich. Tech. U., 1984; D.Sc. (hon.), U. Ala., 1985. Staff physicist Los Alamos (N.Mex.) Nat. Lab., 1968-74, group leader neutron physics, 1974-78, div. leader, 1978-81; sci. advisor to Pres., dir. Office Sci. and Tech. Policy The

White House, Washington, 1981-85; dir. rsch. Hudson Inst., Indpls., 1988-90, disting. fellow, 1990-95; chmn. The Keyworth Co., Washington, 1986—; chmn. & co-founder Progress and Freedom Found., Washington, 1993—. Hon. prof. Fudan U., Shanghai People's Rep. of China, 1984; mem. V.P.'s Task Force on Regulatory Relief, 1982-85, Presl. Commn. on Indsl. Competitiveness, 1984-85, Alcoa Sci. and Tech. Coun., 1986-; trustee, Santa Fe Inst., 1986-89, chmn. bd. dir. NovaWeb Tech. Inc, 1992-, Encanto Networks Inc., 1997-; bd. dir. Hewlett Packard Co., 1986-, Gen. Atomics, 1995-, Yourtel Telecom, 1998-. Recipient Chmn.'s award Am. Assn. Engring. Sci., 1982, SDI award Am. Def. Preparedness Assn, 1986, Hertz Found. award, 1987, First Internat Sci. and Tech. Cooperation prize People's Rep. of China, 1992. Fellow Am. Phys. Soc, AAAS, mem. Phi Beta Kappa, Sigma Xi. Clubs: Cosmos (Washington). Republican. Office: Progress & Freedom Found 1401 H St NW Washington DC 20005-2110

KEZSBOM, ALLEN, lawyer; b. N.Y.C., July 5, 1941; BA cum laude, Bklyn. Coll., 1962; LLB magna cum laude, Harvard U., 1965. Bar: N.Y. 1966, U.S. Dist. Ct. (so. dist.) N.Y. 1968, U.S. Dist. Ct. (ea. dist.) N.Y. 1972, U.S. Ct. Appeals (1st cir.) 1982, U.S. Ct. Appeals (2d cir.) 1971, U.S. Ct. Appeals (6th cir.) 1986, U.S. Ct. Appeals (8th cir.) 1981, U.S. Ct. Appeals (11th cir.) 1983, U.S. Supreme Ct. 1978. Assoc. Kaye, Scholor, Fierman, Hays & Handler, N.Y.C., 1966-71, ptnr., 1972-86, Fried, Frank, Harris, Shriver & Jacobson, N.Y.C., 1986—. Vis. lectr. Yale Law Sch., New Haven, Conn., 1992-93. Mem. Harvard Law Rev., 1963-65; contbr. articles to profl. jours. Knox fellow Harvard Law Sch., 1965-66. Mem. ABA (antitrust sect., litigation sect., nat. resources, energy & environ. law), N.Y. State Bar Assn. (antitrust sect., litigation, environ.), Assn. Bar City N.Y. Office: Fried Frank Harris Shriver & Jacobson 1 New York Plz Fl 22 New York NY 10004-1980 E-mail: kezsbal@friedfrank.com.

KHABASHESKU, VALERY N., chemist, educator; b. Odessa, Ukraine, Aug. 14, 1950; s. Nikolai F. and Tatyana F. Khabashesku; m. Olga K. Sokolikova, May 30, 1981; 1 child, Dmitry V. MS in Chemistry Cum Laude, Lomonosov Moscow State U., 1973; PhD in Organic Chemistry, Zelinsky Inst. Organic Chemistry, USSR Acad. Scis., 1979; DS in Chemistry, Zelinsky Inst. Organic Chemistry, Russian Acad. Scis., 1998. Prin. scientist Zelinsky Inst. Organic Chemistry, Russian Acad. Scis., Moscow, 1998—. Faculty fellow Rice U., Houston, 2001—. Contbr. articles to profl. jours. Recipient First prize, Coun. Mendeleev Chem. Soc. USSR, 1976, Zelinsky Inst. Organic Chemistry, 1976, award and medal, Pres. USSR Acad. Scis., 1983, First prize, Zelinsky Inst. Organic Chemistry, 1987, Laureate, State Prize of Russia, Russian Govt., 2001. Achievements include patents for solid state synthesis of amorphous carbon nitride, a-C3N4; first to direct spectroscopic characterization of silicon-carbon double bond; prepare sphere-shaped nanoscale carbon nitride of C3N4 stoichiometry; research in direct spectroscopic characterization and theoretical modelling of short-lived molecules with silicon-oxygen, germanium-oxygen and germanium-carbon double bonds; neutralized nitrogen beam assisted cryogenic synthesis of carbon nitride thin films; chemical functionalization and applications of carbon nanotubes, fullerenes and nanodiamonds. Home: 2421B Dorrington St Houston TX 77030 Office: Rice U Dept Chemistry Ctr Nanoscale Sci & Tech 6100 Main St Houston TX 77005 E-mail: khval@rice.edu.

KHABIBULIN, NIKOLAI, professional hockey player; b. Sverdlovsk, Russia, Jan. 13, 1973; Goaltender Winnipeg Jets (now Phoenix Coyotes), 1994—96, Phoenix Coyotes, 1996—99, Long Beach Ice Dogs (IHL), 1999—2000, Tampa Bay Lightning, 2001—05, Chicago Blackhawks, 2005—. Goaltender Team Russia, World Cup of Hockey Tournament, 1996, Team Russia, Olympic Games, Salt Lake City, 2002. Co-recipient James Gatschene Memorial Trophy (MVP), IHL, 2000; named to NHL All-Star Game, 1998, 1999, 2002, 2003. Achievements include mem. Stanley Cup Champion Tampa Bay Lightning, 2004. Office: c/o Chicago Blackhawks 1901 W Madison St Chicago IL 60612*

KHACHADURIAN, AVEDIS, physician; b. Aleppo, Syria, Jan. 6, 1926; s. Khachadur and Aznive (Demirjian) K.; m. Laura Hadidian, July 27, 1961; children: Cynthia, Linda. BA, Am. U. of Beirut, 1949, MD, 1953. Resident in internal medicine Am. U. of Beirut, 1953-56, asst. prof. biochemistry and medicine, 1959-64, assoc. prof., 1964-71, prof., 1971; fellow Postgrad. Sch. Medicine, London, 1956-57, Harvard Med. Sch., 1957-59; prof. pediat., dir. Clin. Rsch. Ctr. Northwestern U. Med. Sch., 1971-73; prof. medicine, head divsn. endocrinology, metabolism and nutrition U. Medicine and Dentistry NJ-R.W. Johnson Med. Sch., Piscataway, 0973—; mem. staff pediat. Children's Meml. Hosp., Chgo. Cons. U. Chgo. Sch. Medicine. Mem. Am. Diabetes Assn., NY Acad. Sci., Am. Fedn. Cin. Rsch., Am. Heart Assn., Am. Inst. Nutrition, Endocrine Soc., NY Lipid Rsch. Club, Sigma Xi, Alpha Omega Alpha. Achievements include research in genetics; natural history, pathogenesis and treatment of hereditary hyperlipidemias; diabetes; studies on various inborn errors of metabolism, osteoporosis. Office: One RW Johnson Place New Brunswick NJ 08901 Office Phone: 732-235-7749. Personal E-mail: khachaav5@yahoo.com.

KHACHATURIAN, ZAVEN SETRAK, neuroscientist; b. Aleppo, Syria, Apr. 15, 1937; s. Setrak N/A and Rahel N/A Khachaturian; m. Alidz Thelma Asadourian; 1 child, Ara. BA, Yale U., New Haven, 1961; PhD, Case Western Res. U., Cleve., 1967; postgrad., Columbia U., NYC, 1967—69. Chief physiology of aging br. Nat. Inst. on Aging/NIH, Bethesda, Md., 1981—86, assoc. dir. neurosci. and neuropsychology of aging, 1987—95, dir., office of Alzheimer's rsch., 1985—95; interim sci. dir. Pitts. Biotech. Ctr., 1986—87; prof. heath svcs. adminstrn. Grad. Sch. Pub. Health U. Pitts., 1986—87; v.p. for rsch. U. Pitts. Heath Ctr., 1986—87; dir. Ronald & Nancy Reagan Rsch. Inst. of the Alzheimer's Assn., Chgo., 1995—99; pres. KRA, Inc. Internat. Cons. on Alzheimer's & Aging, Potmac, Md., 1995—. Sci. - rsch. adminstrn. NIH/Pub. Health Svc./DHHS, Bethesda, 1977—95; brain rschr. - memory & learning U. Pitts. Med. Sch., 1969—77. Editor: (book) Annals NY Acad. Sci., Alzheimer's Disease: A Compendium of Current Theories, 2000, Alzheimer's Disease: Cause(s), Diagnosis, Treatment, & Care, 1996; author: Archives of Neurology, 1985; editor: (book) Calcium, Membranes, Aging & Alzheimer's Disease - NY Acad. Sci, 1989, Alzheimer's Disease: New Treatment Strategies, 1992; contbr. articles to profl. jours. Founder, pres. Armenian-Am. Club of Pitts., 1973—77. Named Scientist of the Yr., Maturity News Svc., 1992, Co-Honoree, with Mrs. Nancy Reagan (Pub. Svc. for Alzheim's Disease), NYC Rita Hayworth Gala Com., 1996; recipient Dir.'s award, NIH, 1983, Sr. Exec. Svc. award, Dept. HHS, 1988, Pres.'s award, Nat. Alzheheimer's Assn., 1993. Mem.: IEEE, AAAS, Soc. for Neurosci., Dana Alliance for Brain Initiatives. Independent. Presbyterian (Armenian). Avocation: woodworking. Office: Khachaturian Radebaugh & Associates Inc 8912 Copenhaver Dr Potomac MD 20854 Office Phone: 301-294-7201. E-mail: zaven_khachaturian@kra.net.

KHACHEMOUNE, AMOR, physician; s. Louiza Khoualed and Mahfoud Khechmoune; m. Faiza Kada, Jan. 3, 1997; 1 child, Nour Leila. MD, Nat. Inst. for Med. Scis., Constantantine, Algeria, 1989. Specialization in Dermatology Universite de Lille II, France, 1993, cert. Advanced Studies of Cosmetic Dermatology Univeriste de Lille II, France, 1993, Wound Specialist Am. Acad. of Wound Mgmt., 2000. Primary care physician pvt. practice, Ain Kechera, Algeria, 1989; cons. dermatologist and primary care team coord. ID formation, Lille, France, 1993—96; sr. rsch. fellow Cardiology Rsch. Found., Washington, 1996—98; med. intern Boston Med. Ctr., Brockton Hosp., 1998—99; wound healing fellow Boston U. Sch. of Medicine, 1999—2001; prodn. mgr., rsch. assoc. Harvard Med. Sch., Brigham and Women's Hosp., Divsn. of Interventional Cardiology, Boston, 2001; sr. dermatology resident Georgetown U. Med. Ctr., Washington, 2001—. Guest spkr. Nat. and Internat. Dermatology and Wound Healing meetings. Editor: (editorial board) The Internet Journal of Dermatology; presenter (peristomal pyoderma gangrenosum successf) Peristomal Pyoderma Gangrenosum Successfully Treated with Graftskin. Kupiec A, Grekin DA, Kauffman CL, Khachemoune A. Wound healing symposium. Baltimore April 27-30, 2002, (world congress of dermatology 2002) Newborn derived skin substitues and their use in chronic wounds. Khachemoune A. 20th World Congress of Dermatology. Paris, France. July 1st- 5th 2002., Factor Leiden mutation associated with leg ulceration. American Academy of Dermatology meeting. Khachemoune A. Oral presentation. AAD meeting, New Orleans, LA. (Feb 2002), White sponge nevus successfully treated with minocycline. Khachemoune A, Bouadjar B. (Poster presentation AAD meeting Feb 2002), Heck's disease. Khachemoune A, Bouadjar B. (Poster presentation AAD meeting Feb 20002), Factors that influence healing in chronic venous ulcers treated with Cryopreserved Cultured Human Epidermal Allografts. Khachemoune A, Bello YM. Phillips TJ. (poster presentation wound healing symposium Las Vegas 2001), Cryofibrinogenemia presenting as leg ulceration. Khachemoune A, Bello YM, Phillips TJ. Oral presentation at the American Academy of Dermatology meeting, Washington DC 03/02/2001, The use of cryopreserved cultured human epidermal allografts in a large recalcitrant venous leg ulcer: A case study. Bello YM, Manzoor J, Rojas AI, Khachemoune A, Green H, Phillips TJ. 2000 symposium on advanced Wound care & medi, Lansky AJ, Mehran R, Popma JJ, Abizaid AS, Saucedo J, Khachemoune A, Ho K, Kuntz RE, Bonan R. Favourable coronary remodelling in patients with non flow limiting dissections after coronary intervention: results from the Internation, Saucedo JF, Abizaid A S, Kennard ED, Curran MJ, Khachemoune A, Kada F, Brahimi A, Baim D. Vessel Size in an independent Predictor of 1 Year Clinical Events After New Device Angioplasty: A NACI Registry Report. Circulation. 1997., Diagnosis and Management of Chronic leg ulcers: A wound specialist approach. Khachemoune A. 20th World Congress of Dermatology. Paris, France. July 1st- 5th 2002., Atypical chronic lower extremity ulcers: Clinical vignette and discussion. Khachemoune A. 20th World Congress of Dermatology. Paris, France. July 1st- 5th 2002., reviewer Jour. of Am. Acad. of Dermatology, (profl. med. jours.) Am. Family Physician; author: (70 scientific papers) Publications in medical journals; contbr. editor (profl. jour.) Skin and Aging. Fellow: Am. Acad. of Wound Mgmt. (licentiate). Achievements include research in Use of skin substitutes in wound healing. Avocation: karate do- shototakan. Office Phone: 617-726-5162. E-mail: amorkh@pol.net.

KHADDURI, MAJID, international studies educator; b. Mosul, Iraq, Sept. 27, 1909; came to U.S., 1947, naturalized, 1954; s. Khadduri Q. and Latifa (Saati) K.; m. Majdia Dawaff, Dec. 9, 1942; children: Farid, Shirin. BA, Am. U., Beirut, 1932; PhD, U. Chgo., 1938; LHD (hon.), Johns Hopkins U., 1985; LLD (hon.), SUNY, Binghamton, 1989. Prof. higher tchrs. and law colls., Baghdad, 1938-47; vis. prof. Ind. U., 1947-48, U. Chgo., 1948-49; prof. Sch. Advanced Internat. Studies, Johns Hopkins, 1949-70, Disting. rsch. prof., 1970. Dir. rsch. and edn., bd. govts. Middle East Inst., Washington, 1950—; lectr. in field. Author: War and Peace in the Law of Islam, 1955, Independent Iraq, 1951, Islamic Jurisprodence, 1961, Arab Contemporaries, 1973, The Islamic Conception of Justice, 1985, The Gulf War, 1988; others. Mem. Iraq del. UN Conf., San Francisco, 1945. Recipient Rockefeller research grant for book on Islamic Law of Nations, 1963; decorated Order of Rafidain (Iraq), Order of Merit (Egypt). Mem. Am. Polit. Sci. Assn., Am. Soc. Internat. Law, Shaybani Soc. Internat. Law of Washington (pres.), P.E.N. (sec. Baghdad Ctr. 1940-47, mem. N.Y. Ctr. 1968—), Acad. of Arabic Lang. (Cairo 1983), The Iraqi Acad. (Baghdad 1986), Cosmos Club (Washington). Home: 4454 Tindall St NW Washington DC 20016-2718 Office: 1740 Massachusetts Ave NW Washington DC 20036-1903

KHAIRALLA, ERIC WILLIAM, plastic surgeon; s. William C. Khairalla and Gaby Koudim; m. Ghislaine Geagea Khairalla, Dec. 30, 1988; children: Thea, William. BSc in Biology, Am. U. Beirut, Lebanon, 1983, MSc in Physiology, 1985, MD, 1988. Bd. cert. Am. Bd. Internal Medicine, 1991, Am. Bd. Plastic Surgery, 2002, diplomate Am. Bd. Plastic Surgery, 2002, cert. Royal Coll. Physicians Surgeons Can. Plastic Surgery, 1997. Resident in intenal medicine Md. Gen. Hosp., Balt., 1988—91; resident in plastic surgery U. Toronto, 1991—97; fellow in plastic suregry Georgetown U. Med. Ctr., DC, 1998; assoc., pvt. practice Bethesda, Md., 1998—2000; pvt. practice Chevy Chase, Md., 2000—. Active staff Suburban Hosp., Bethesda, 1998, Sibley Meml. Hosp., DC, 1999, Inova Fairfax Hosp., Falls Church, Va., 2000. Contbr. articles and papers in field. Vol. reconstructive surgeon Luz del Sol, Dominican Republic, 1998. Fellow: Royal Coll. Surgeons Physicians Can.; mem.: Am. Soc. Plastic Surgeons. Greek Orthodox. Avocations: photography, skiing, windsurfing. Office: Chevy Chase Plastic Surgery 5530 Wisconsin Ave 1235 Chevy Chase MD 20815 Office Phone: 301-657-4744.

KHALID, HUMAYUN, computer scientist, consultant; b. Karachi, Sind, Pakistan, July 9, 1968; s. Khalid Yousuf and Maimoona Khalid; m. Nuzhat Sultana, July 4, 1997; children: Nimra, Nabihah. BSEE magna cum laude, CCNY, 1992, MSEE, 1993; PhD, CUNY, 1996. Rsch. assoc. U.S. Dept. Def., N.Y.C., 1996; staff electronic engr., scientist Motorola, Inc., Austin, 1996-98, sr. staff scientist, 1998—2000; sr. cons. Dell Computer Corp., Austin, 2000—. Mem. program com. Symposium Performance Evaluation Computer and Telecom. Sys., 2000. Contbr. articles to profl. jours. Contbr. N. Austin Muslim Cmty. Ctr., 1996—2000. Univ. fellow, CUNY, 1995, Univ. Tuition scholar, 1995. Mem.: IEEE (editor papers and proceedings), Soc. Computer Simulation Internat., Inst. Elec. and Electronics Engrs. Pakistan (life). Moslem. Home: 1000 Cassat Cove Austin TX 78753 Office: Dell Computer Corp One Dell Way Round Rock TX 78682 Business E-Mail: humayun_khalid@dell.com. E-mail: hkhalid123@aol.com.

KHALID, SYED MUHAMMAD, gastroenterologist, consultant; s. Syed Muhammad and Akhter Tauhid; m. Samiya Ahmed, July 3, 1975; children: Anum, Zeeshan, Faizan. MD, King Edward Med. Coll., Lahore, Pakistan, 1990. Diplomate Am. Bd. Internal Medicine, 1996, Gastroenterology Am. Bd. Internal Medicine, 1999. Gastroenterologist Va. Health Care Sys., Roseburg, Oreg., 1999—2002, Consultants in Gastroenterology, Independence, Mo., 2002—. Fellowship Loyola U. Med. Ctr., Maywood, Ill., 1996—99. Fellow: Am. Coll. Gastroenterology (licentiate); mem.: Am. Gastroenterology Assn. (licentiate). Office: Consultants in Gastroenterology 3800 South Whitney Independence MO 64055 Office Fax: 816-795-0835.

KHALIFAH, RAJA GABRIEL, biochemist, researcher; b. Tripoli, Lebanon, May 5, 1942; s. Gabriel and Mona Khalifeh; m. Lilla Ilona Csonka, July 31, 1971; children: Peter Gabriel, Anthony Paul. BS in Chemistry, Am. U. Beirut, 1962; PhD in Phys. Chemistry, Princeton U., 1969. Asst. prof. chemistry U. Va., Charlottesville, 1973—79; dir. magnetic resonance lab. Kansas City VA Med. Ctr., Mo., 1980—93; rsch. prof. biochemistry U. Kans. Med. Sch., Kansas City, 1993—2000; dir. rsch. BioStratum Inc., Durham, NC, 2000—. Postdoctoral fellow in biochemistry Harvard U., Cambridge, Mass., 1968—70; rsch. assoc. in pharmacology Stanford U. Med. Ctr., Calif., 1970—73. Contbr. over 40 articles to profl. jours. Mem.: Am. Soc. of Biochemistry and Molecular Biology, Am. Chem. Soc. Achievements include 11 U.S. patents in diabetes drug discovery. Home: 109 Bowers Ln Cary NC 27519 Office: BioStratum Inc Ste 200 4620 Creekstone Dr Durham NC 27703 Office Phone: 919-433-1000. Business E-Mail: rkhalifah@biostratum.com.

KHALIL, MOHAMMAD ASLAM KHAN, environmental science and engineering educator, physics educator; b. Jhansi, India, Jan. 7, 1950; came to U.S., 1963; s. M. Ahsan Khan and Aleem-Un-Nisa K.; m. Giti Ara Eshraghi, June 1973; children: Kathayoon Azra, Kaviyaan Aslam. BPhys, BA in Math. and Psychology, U. Minn., 1970; MS in Physics, Va. Polytechnic Inst., 1972; PhD in Physics, U. Tex., 1976; MS in Environ. Sci., Oreg. Grad. Ctr., Beaverton, 1979; PhD in Eviron. Sci., Oreg. Grad. Ctr., 1979. Tchg. asst. dept. physics Va. Polytechnic Inst. and State U., 1970-71; grad. asst. dept. math. and physics U. Tex., Austin, 1971-72, tchg. asst. dept. physics, 1972-73, 76, rsch. scientist asst. Ctr. for Particle Theory, 1972-76; instr. dept. physics Pacific U., Forest Grove, Oreg., 1978; rsch. asst. dept. environ. sci. Oreg. Grad. Ctr., Beaverton, 1977-79, asst. prof. dept. environ. sci., 1980-82, assoc. prof. dept. environ. sci., 1982-84, prof. dept. chem., biol. and environ. sci., 1984-86, prof. Inst. Atmospheric Sci., 1986-90, prof. dept. environ. sci. and engring., dir. Global Change Rsch. Ctr., 1990-95; prof. dept. physics Portland State U., Oreg., 1995—, chmn. dept., 2004—05, dir., environ. sci. and resources program, 2005—. Owner Andarz Co., Portland, 1981—. Editor: Chemosphere: Global Change Science; mem. editl. bd. Handbook of Environ. Chemistry, Environ. Sci. and Pollution Rsch. Internat., Atmospheric Environment; contbr. some 200 articles to profl. jours. Recipient Oustanding Scientist award, Oreg. Acad. Sci., 2004, World's Most Cited Authors award, ICI; grantee, NSF, EPA, Dept. Energy, NASA. Mem. Am. Phys. Soc., Am. Chem. Soc., Am. Geophys. Union, Sigma Xi. Avocation: marathon runner. Office: Portland State U Dept Physics PO Box 751 Portland OR 97207-0751 also: Andarz Co 9961 NW Kaiser Rd Portland OR 97231-2701 Office Phone: 503-725-8396. E-mail: khalilm@pdx.edu.

KHALIL, MOHAMMAD OMER, artist, educator; b. Burri, Khartoum, Sudan, Aug. 1, 1936; came to U.S., 1967; s. Omer Khalil and Sekina Abdeen; divorced; children: Medina, Malik. Student, Sudan Sch. Fine and Applied Arts, Khartoum, 1956-59, Acad. Fine Arts, Florence, Italy, 1963-66, Acad. Fine Arts, Ravenna, Italy, 1966. Tchr. Sch. Fine and Applied Arts, Khartoum, 1959-63, Khartoum Tech. Inst., 1967, Pratt Inst., Bklyn., 1971-83, New Sch. for Social Rsch., NYC, 1971—, Parsons Sch. Design, 1988—, NYU, 1991—. Leader symposia and workshops Asilah, Morocco, summer sessions, 1978-80, 83-84, 94. One-person shows include Grand Hotel, Khartoum, 1960, New Sch. for Social Rsch., N.Y.C., 1981, Ltd. Art Edits., N.Y.C., 1984, Bronx Art Mus., 1987, Galerie Teinturerie, Paris, 1991, Inst. du Monde, Arabe, Paris, 1992, Asilah, Morocco; represented in group exhbns. Ctr. for Foreigners, Florence, 1964, French Cultural Ctr., Florence, 1966, Madison (Wis.) Art Ctr., 1985, Internat. Triennial of Original Graphic Prints, Grenchen, Switzerland, 1985, Baghdad Internat. Festival, Iraq, 1986, Chamalieres Print Triennial, France, 1988, Internat. Monetary Fund Ctr., Washington, 1990, Osaka (Japan) Triennial, 1991, Cleve. Inst. Art, 1992, Hillwood Art Mus., Brookville, N.Y., 1992, 2d Kochi Internat. Triennial, Japan, 1993, Contemporary African Art Gallery, N.Y.C., 1993, Tokyo Small Print, 1995, Poland Small Print, 1996, Mary Ryan Gallery, N.Y.C., 1997, Atelier A/E Gallery, N.Y.C.; represented in corp. collections Con Edison, Am. Express Fin. Advisors, Inc. The McArthur Found., Chgo., in pub. collections Bklyn. Mus., Chamaliers Mus., France, Jordanian Nat. Mus., Amman, Mus. History, Taipei, Taiwan, Mus. Modern Art, Osaka; featured in publs. including Art in Am., Le Matin, Print News: The Internat. Jour. of Contemporary Prints. Recipient 3d prize 2d World Internat. Exhbn., London, 1980, Bronze prize Osaka Triennial, 1991, 1st prize Internat. Biennial of Cairo, 1993; Louis Comforte Tiffany Found. grantee, 1978, Bronx Mus. Coun. on Arts grantee, 1987. Mem.: NAD (academician 1997—). Address: 515 W 29th St New York NY 10001-1319*

KHALIL, MOUNIR A., librarian, educator; b. Ashiwai, Fayuum, Egypt, Nov. 14, 1936; arrived in U.S., 1969; s. Amin Khalil and Mounirah A. Kerolos; m. Sawsan G. Aziz, May 31, 1951; 1 child, Richard. BA in Geography, Cairo U., 1958, BA in Libr. Sci., 1962; MLS in Libr. and Info. Scis., Pratt Inst., 1971, MS in Computer Sci., 1977; adv. cert. in Grad. Sch. Libr. and Info. Scis., U. Pitts., 1977. Cert. med. libr. Med. Libr. Assn. Head libr. Higher Inst. Petroleum, Suez, Egypt, 1962—66, Higher Inst. Social Work, Cairo, 1966—69; reference libr. Queensborough Pub. Libr., Jamaica, NY, 1969—73; br. libr. Bklyn. Pub. Libr., 1974—86; tech. libr. Health Ins. Plan, N.Y.C., 1986—89; chief access series City Coll. CUNY, N.Y.C., 1989—92, reference libr., 1993—; dir. tech. svcs. N.J. Inst., Newark, 1993. Part-time instr. Katharine Gibbs Sch., N.Y.C., 1986—92; adj. asst. prof. GSLIS Queens Coll., 1990; spkr. in field; presenter in field. Contbr. articles to profl. jours. Mem. Coptic Orthodox Ch. Bd., Bklyn., 1995. Bailey scholar, Queens Borough Pub. Libr., 1972, ALA Libr. Automation fellow, Al-Bayyt U., Jordon, 1997, Rsch. award, CUNY Rsch. Found., 2003—. Mem.: ALA, Internat. Fedn. Libr. Assn.s and Instns. (roundtable on bookmobiles 1999—), Spl. Librs. Assn. (moderator conf.). Achievements include development of electronic ILL and document delivery services. Avocations: chess, gardening, soccer, reading, travel. Office: City Coll CUNY West 138th St & Convent Ave New York NY 10031

KHALILZAD, ZALMAY, ambassador; b. Afghanistan, 1951; BA, MA, American U., Beirut, Lebanon; PhD, U. Chgo., 1979. Asst. prof. polit. sci. Columbia U., NYC, 1979—89; spl. advisor to under sec. for polit. affairs US Dept. State, Washington, 1985—89; assoc. prof. U. Calif., San Diego, 1989—91; asst. under sec. for policy planning US Dept. Def., Washington, 1991—92; dir. strategy, doctrine and force structure program Project Air Force RAND Corp., 1993—99; spl. envoy to Afghanistan U.S. Dept. State, 2002—03, U.S. amb. and presdl. envoy to Afghanistan, 2003—05, US amb. to Iraq Baghdad, 2005—. Spl. advisor to under sec. for polit. affairs US Dept. State, 1985—89; sr. polit. scientist RAND, 1989—91; counselor to Sec. Def. Donald Rumsfeld US Dept. Def., head Bush-Cheney Transition Team; spl. asst. to pres. and sr. direct for Middle East and S.W. Asia, 2001—03; spl. presdl. envoy for ambassador for free Iraqis, 2003—04. Office: Am Embassy The Chancery APO AE 09316

KHAMENE, ALI, research scientist; b. Tehran, Iran, Sept. 20, 1971; s. Mohsen Khamene and Akhtar Raofi; m. Farnaz Soltani, Oct. 10, 1996; 1 child, Tara Emily Kamene. BS, Sharif U. Tech., Tehran, Iran, 1990—94, MS, 1994—96; PhD, U. Miami, 1996—2000. Rsch. asst. McKnight Vision Ctr., Bascom Palmer Eye Inst., U. Miami, Miami, Fla., 1996—97, Underwater Vision and Imaging Lab, U. Miami, Coral Gables, Fla., 1997—2000; rsch. scientist 755 Coll. Rad E., Princeton, NJ, 2000—05, sr. rsch. scientist, 2005—. Contbr. articles to profl. jours. Achievements include patents for method and apparatus for spatiotemporal freezing of ultrasound images in augmented reality visualization; method and apparatus for ultrasound guidance of needle biopsies; video assistance for ultrasound guided needle biopsy; thin film measuring device and method. Home: 29 Scarlet Oak Dr Princeton NJ 08540 Office: Siemens Corp Rsch 755 College Rd E Princeton NJ 08540 Office Phone: 609-734-6553. Office Fax: 609-734-6565. E-mail: ali.khamene@siemens.com.

KHAN, AHMED MOHIUDDIN, insurance company executive; b. Hyderabad, Andhra Pradesh, India, Nov. 14, 1955; s. Mohammad Mominuddin and Mehar-Unnisa Begum Hyderabad; m. Marjorie L. Klein-Khan, Mar. 31, 1983; 1 child, Yosef F. MBA, U. Palm Beach, 1975; PhD in Bus. Adminstrn., Northwestern U., 2000; PhD in Fin., Madison U., 2001. Inventory auditor RGIS, Inc., Chgo., 1975-78; staff acct. Sommerset, Inc., Chgo., 1978-85; fin. cons. Provident Mutual Fin. Svc., Inc., Phoenix, 1985-92; pres. Khan and Assocs., Fin./Ins. Svcs., Phoenix, 1992—. Author: Financial-Insurance Services in the New Millenium, 2000. Named Hon. Mem. Exec. Hall of Fame, 2000, named one of Outstanding Scholars of 20th Century; recipient Nat. Sales Achievement award, 2000, Nat. Quality award, 2000. Mem. Assn. MBA Execs., Nat. Assn. Ins. Fin. Advisors, Millon Dollar Round Table. Democrat. Moslem. Avocations: golf, travel, classical music. Office Phone: 602-482-0936. Personal E-mail: amkhan_2001@yahoo.com.

KHAN, ARFA, radiologist, educator; b. Srinagar, Kashmir, India, Dec. 4, 1943; came to U.S., 1966; d. Ghulam Rasool and Ruqia Hayat; m. Faroque A. Khan, Apr. 16, 1966; children: Arif O., Shireen. B of Medicine, B of Surgery, Govt. Med. Coll., Kashmir, 1964. Diplomate Am. Bd. Radiology. Intern Barberton (Ohio) Citizen Hosp., 1966-67; resident in radiology L.I. Jewish Med. Ctr., New Hyde Park, NY, 1967-70, from instr. to assoc. prof. radiology, 1970-93, chief thoracic radiology, 1983—, prof., 1993—, assoc. chmn. radiology, 1994-2000; program dir., 1995. Contbr. 50 articles to radiology jours. Fellow Am. Coll. Radiology; mem. Am. Coll. Radiology, Am. Soc. Neuroradiology, Am. Soc. Head & Neck Radiology, Am. Soc. Thoracic Radiology, Radiol. Soc. N.Am. Democrat. Moslem. Avocations: cooking, tennis, aerobics, gardening, skiing. Fax: 718-343-7463. Office Phone: 718-470-7184. E-mail: khan@lij.edu.

KHAN, AURANGZEB, engineering educator; s. Muhammad Sarwar Khan; m. Shazia Rafique, Dec. 12, 1992; children: Noor-Ul-Hudda, Fiza Firdoos, Danyal Wali. PhD, Toyota Technological Inst., Nagoya, Japan, 2001. Rsch. fellow Quid-i-Azam U., Islamabad, Pakistan, 1992—98; postdoctrol rsch. fellow The Ohio State U., Columbus, 2001—02; asst. prof. U. South Ala., Mobile, 2002—. Student br. counselor IEEE, Mobile, 2003—. Author (reviewer) numerous sci. jours., more than 65 refereed papers on rsch. and devel. of Solar energy. Named Prof. of Yr., Tau Beta Pi, 2004; recipient Gold medal, U. Karachi, 1992; PhD fellow, Japan Soc. for Promotion Sci., 1998—2001. Mem.: IEEE (corr.).

KHAN, AZIM JAHANGIR, dermatologist, surgeon, researcher; arrived in US, 1992; s. Moin Uddin and Surriya Moin Khan; m. Asma Sana Chaudhri, Mar. 30, 1994; 1 child, Lamat-Un-noor Azim. MBBS, Allama Iqbal Med. Coll., Lahore, Pakistan, 1991. Diplomate Am. Bd. Dermatology, 2002, Am. Bd. Internal Medicine, 1996. Resident internal medicine Cook County Hosp., Chgo., 1993—96; rsch. fellow dermatology and wound healing Med. Sch. Northwestern U., Chgo., 1996—97; fellow wound healing SUNY, Stony Brook, NY, 1997—98, resident dermatology, 1998—2000, asst. prof. clin. dermatology, 2000—; fellow cosmetic surgery Affiliated Dermatology Cosmetic Surgery Ctr., Morristown, NJ, 2002—03; dermatologist, cosmetic surgeon Freeport (Ill.) Health Network, 2003—. Assoc. prof. dermatology Fatima Jinnah Med. Coll., Lahore, 2004—. Mem.: AMA, AFL-CIO, Am. Soc. for Dermatolgica Surgery, Internat. Soc. for Hair Restoration Surgery, Am. Soc. for Liosuction Surgery, Am. Acad. Cosmetic Surgery, Am. Acad. Dermatology, Ho. Staff Assn. Cook County Hosp. (pres. 1995—96), Nat. Union Hosp. and Health Care Employees (v.p. 1995—96). Achievements include patents for smart matrix for wound healing. Office Phone: 815-599-7708. Office Fax: 815-599-7666.

KHAN, EJAZ A., chemicals executive, controller; BS, MIT; MBA, U. Pa. With Vulcan Materials Co., Birmingham, Ala., 1979—99, contr., 1992—99, v.p., contr., 1999—, CIO, 2000—. Office: Vulcan Materials Co 1200 Urban Center Dr Birmingham AL 35242

KHAN, HABIB URREHMAN, neurologist; b. Karachi, Sindh, Pakistan, July 6, 1964; came to U.S., 1993; s. Abdul Rehman Khan and Hamida Rehman; m. Marium Habib, Apr. 8, 1992; children: Musaab Bin Habib, Fatimah Habib. MBBS, Dow Med. Coll., Karachi, 1988; MD, Edn. Commn. Fgn. Med. Grads., 1993. Ho. officer surgery Civil Hosp., Karachi, 1988-89, ho. officer medicine, 1989; sr. med. officer Alrahman Med. Ctr., Karachi, 1989-93; intern in neuromedicine U. Medicine Dentistry, Newark, 1994-95, resident in neurology, 1995—98; fellow SUNY, 1998—99; dir. sleep lab., dir. neurophysiology lab., chief neurology Casa Grande (Ariz.) Regional Med. Ctr., 2000—. Scholar, Wyeth Pharm., 1999. Fellow Mini Epilepsy Fellowship Network; mem. AMA, Am. Acad. Neurology, Am. Assn. Sleep Medicine, Pakistan Med. Dental Coun. Avocations: cricket, reading, swimming. Office: Casa Grande Regional Med Ctr 1820 E Florence Blvd Ste D Casa Grande AZ 85222 E-mail: khanhabib@hotmail.com.

KHAN, HALIMUR R., language educator; b. Dhaka, Bangladesh, Dec. 14, 1956; s. Hafizullah Khan and Anjuma Khatoon; m. Nazmun Khan, Jan. 21, 1993; children: Kingshok, Priyana. PhD, U. Mich., 1990. Asst. prof. Wayne State U., Detroit, 1993—98; vis. asst. prof. U. Mich., Ann Arbor, 1998—99; asst. prof. Colgate U., Hamilton, NY, 1999—. Contbr. articles to profl. jours. Mem.: AAASS, AATSEEL. Avocations: chess, tennis, fishing. Home: 32 College St Hamilton NY 13346 Office: Colgate Univ 219C Lawrence Hall Hamilton NY 13346

KHAN, M. WASIULLAH, academic administrator; PhD in Edn. Adminstrn., Ind. U. Chancellor East-West U., Chgo., 1980—. Office: East-West U 816 S Michigan Ave Chicago IL 60605-2185 Office Phone: 312-939-0111. Business E-Mail: chancellor@eastwest.edu.

KHAN, MOHAMMAD ASAD, geophysics educator, retired minister, former senator of Pakistan; b. Aima, Lahore, Pakistan, Aug. 13, 1940; came to U.S., 1964; s. Ghulam Qadir and Hajira (Karim) K.; m. Tahera Pathan, Jan. 4, 1974; 1 dau., Shehzi Samira. BS, U. Punjab, Lahore, Pakistan, 1957, MS, 1963; postgrad., Harvard U., 1964-65; PhD (East West Center scholar), U. Hawaii, 1967. Lectr. in geophysics U. Punjab, India, 1963-64; asst. prof. geophysics and geodesy U. Hawaii, 1967-71, assoc. prof., 1971-74, prof., 1974-96, prof. emeritus, 1996—; chmn. internat. advisors, 1987—. NSF and NASA fellow Summer Inst. Dynamical Astronomy at MIT, Cambridge, Mass., 1968—69; leader Am. Asian Studies and Contemporary Social Problems Seminar Series, Honolulu, 1968—69; sr. vis. scientist geodynamics Goddard Space Flight Ctr. NASA, Greenbelt, Md., 1972—74; sr. resident assoc. NAS, 1972—74; diplomatic minister/adviser Resource Survey and Devel. Pakistan, 1974—76; sr. scientist Computer Scis. Corp., Silver Spring, Md., 1974—76, sr. cons., 1976—77; minister of petroleum and natural resources Govt. of Pakistan, 1983—86; cabinet mem. Econ. Coord. Com. Cabinet Govt. of Pakistan, 1983—86, Nat. Econ. Council Govt. of Pakistan, 1984—86; chmn. Hydrocarbon Devel. Inst., Pakistan, 1984—86, Attock Oil Refinery, 1984—86; senator Govt. of Pakistan, 1984—86. Contbr. articles to profl. publs. Chmn. East and West: A Perspective for the 80's; mem. Hawaii Environ. Council, 1979-83, chmn. exec. com., 1979-83, vice chmn., 1981-83; chmn. Pakistan Relief Fund, Honolulu, 1971. Recipient Gold medal Rawalpindi Union of Journalists, 1985, Pakistan Engring. Coun., 1985, Pakistan Assn. of Minorities, 1984, 85, Disting. Alumnus award for pofl. excellence and leadership U. Hawaii, 1995. Fellow Explorers Club; mem. Geol. Soc. U. Punjab (pres. 1962-63), Am. Geophys. Union, Pakistan Assn. Advancement Sci., Am. Geol. Inst., Am. Geophys. Union, East West Ctr. Alumni Assn. (dir. 1976-80), Internat. Alumni of East West Ctr. (exec. com., chmn. 1977-80, Disting. Alumnus award for Outstanding Career Achievements and Leadership 1984). Achievements include research in geophysics, geodetic and oceanographic applications of satellites, geodynamics, planetary interiors, global tectonics, global correlations, core-mantle boundary problems, equilibrium figures, gravity, isostasy, satellite altimetry, geodesy, earth models, geophysical exploration, ocean dynamics. Office: U Hawaii-Hawaii Inst Geophysics Planetology Post 602 Honolulu HI 96822-2219 *Most men stand the test of adversity quite well, but if you really want to test the character of a man, give him power.*

KHAN, MOHAMMED YOUSUF, physician, consultant; b. Multan, Pakistan, May 1, 1936; arrived in U.S., 1960; s. M.K. and H.K. Durrani; m. Yasmin Yousef Jan, Oct. 31, 1971; children: Irfan, Zeshan. MBBS, Punjab U., Pakistan, 1958; PhD, U. Minn., Mpls., 1969. Diplomate Am. Bd. Internal Medicine, Am. Bd. Infectious Diseases. Resident internal medicine U. Minn., 1962-66, fellow infectious disease, 1966-69; cons. Pakistan Internat. Airlines, Karachi, Pakistan, 1970-72; head infectious diseases Hennepin County Med. Ctr., Mpls., 1972-83; co-dir. Sexually Transmitted Diseases Clinic, 1972-83; asst. prof. Dept. Med., U. Minn., 1972-83; head infectious diseases King Fahad Hosp., Riyadh, Saudi Arabia, 1983-98, King Khalid Hosp., Jeddah, Saudi Arabia, 1998-2000; chief infectious disease Maricopa Med. Ctr., Phoenix, 2000—; assoc. prof. medicine Mayo Med. Sch., Rochester, Minn., 2001—. Keynote speaker Riyadh Med. Forum, Suadi Arabia, 1992. Contbr. articles to jours., chpts. to books. Recipient Physician Recognition award AMA, 1996. Fellow ACP, Infectious Disease Soc. Am., Royal Coll. Physicians. Avocations: fishing, hiking, reading, coin collecting/numismatics. Office: Maricopa Med Ctr Dept Medicine 2601 E Roosevelt Phoenix AZ 85008 Personal E-mail: myousuf_khan@yahoo.com.

KHAN, MUSHFIQUDDIN, neuropharmacologist, researcher; s. Noor Mohammad Khan and Aqila Begum; m. Salma Ansar, June 15, 1966; children: Tooba, Talha, Hamza. BSc with honors, Aligarh Muslim U., India, 1976, MSc, 1978, MPhil, 1980. Postdoctoral rschr. Ehime U., Matsuyama, Japan, 1984—86; rsch. scientist-pool officer Aligarh Muslim U., India, 1986—88; lectr. Shibli Nat. Postgraduate Coll., Azamgarh, India, 1988—90; postdoctoral rschr. Med. U. of S.C., Charleston, 1994—98, asst. prof., 2002—. Scientist Modern Foam Industries, Janupur, 1990—94; sr. scientist Ariz. Inst. for Biomedical Rsch., Scottsdale, 1999—2001; grant reviewer NIH, Washington. Mem. AMU Rsch. Student's Assn., Aligarh, 1980—82. Recipient Mitchell I. Rubin rsch. award, Children's Hosp., MUSC; grantee, NINDS, NIH, Bethesda, MD, 2000—05; Monbusho fellow, Govt. of Japan, jr. rsch. fellow, CSIR, Govt. of India, sr. rsch. fellow. Mem.: AAAS, Indian Soc. for Mass Spectrometry, Am. Soc. for Neurochemistry, Am. Assn. for Biochemistry and Molecular Biology. Avocations: travel, classical music, humor, handball. Home: 3529 Ashwycke St Mount Pleasant SC 29466 Office: Med Univ SC 173 Ashley Ave 508 CRI Charleston SC 29425 Office Phone: 843-792-7991. Personal E-mail: khanm@musc.edu.

KHAN, SAJID A., management consultant, entrepreneur; s. Mohammad Rafiq Khan and Bushra Nasim; m. Aisha Khan, Aug. 25, 1991; children: Dabir, Shanzay, Yasmine, Danial. MBA, Stern Sch. of Bus., N.Y.C., 1997. V.p. Merrill Lynch, N.Y.C., 1998—2002; pres. MicroAgility, Inc., Parlin, NJ, 2003—. Producer. Mem.: OPEN (assoc.), The Exec. Forum. Achievements include development of PMO Methodology. Office: MicroAgility Inc Ste 2 777 Washington Rd Parlin NJ 08859 Personal E-mail: sajid@microagility.com.

KHAN, SHAHNAWAZ, pharmacist, director; b. Nawabshah, Sind, Pakistan, May 22, 1955; arrived in U.S., 1974; s. Abdul Q. Khan and Mehmooda Begum; m. Ghazala Jabeen, June 10, 1988; children: Sidra, Sarah, Shahzaib, Malik. BS in Pharmacy, U. Karachi, Pakistan, 1979. Cert. surg. fitter Phila. Coll., 1989, registered pharmacist NY, NJ, cert. orthotist NY, NJ, lab. technician NY, NJ. Supr. pharmacist Tri-Star Pharmacy, N.Y.C., 1982—84, Empire State Drugs, Bronx, NY, 1984—86; clin. pharmacist Harlem Hosp. Ctr., N.Y.C., 1986—93, clin. coord., 1993—99, dir. pharmacy dept., 2000—. Mem. Franklin Dem. Club, N.Y.C., 2003. Recipient Jim Wright Vulnerable Populations award, 2003. Mem.: Am. Hosp. Pharmacy Assn., Am. Coll. Clin. Pharmacy, Am. Diabetes Assn., Am. Pharmacist Assn., Pakistani Am. Pharm. Assn. (sec.). Democrat. Achievements include development of Once Daily Dosing of Gentamicin: Implementation of Pharmacy on Infectious Diseases; Antibiotic Control Program: Switch from IV to PO dosage of antibiotic and H2 antogonist; Usage of Neuromuscular Blocking Agent. Avocation: reading, driving. Office: Harlem Hosp Ctr 506 Lenox Ave New York NY 10037 Office Phone: 212-939-1761. E-mail: khan2512@aol.com.

KHAN, SURA, film company executive; b. N.Y.C., May 11, 1964; s. Leslie Williamson and Cynthia Richardson Smith; children: Kendell Richardson, Dondre Richardson. Grad. high sch., N.Y., 2000. Cmty. svc. aide N.Y. Housing Authority, Bklyn., 1984—89, dir. cmty. ops. N.Y.C., 2001—03; pres., CEO Kendon Records, Bklyn., 1989—92; exec. prodr. Leslie Richardson Show, Bklyn., 1992—94; TV host Sura Khan Prodn. Co., Bklyn., 1995—97; prodr. STC Comm., Bklyn., 1977—; pres. CEO Vision Surakhan Entertainment, N.Y.C., 2003—. Author: A Filmaker's Journey, 2004; dir.: (films) Brother's Gonna Work It Out, 2003; prodr.: (soundtrack), 2004 (Spirit of Cmty. award, Bklyn. Coun. Pres., 2003, Senate award Senator Montgomery, N.Y., 2003, Congress award Congressman Owens, Bklyn., 2003, Borough Pres. award, 2003); dir.(prodr., host): (documentaries) Life on the Walk of Fame The Virgina Capers Story, 2004; prodr., host Rap Talk, Its Music; prodr., host The Surakhan Report. Avocations: singing, cooking, writing. Office: Vision Surakhan Enterprises Inc 244 5th Ave SteQ254 New York NY 10001

KHAN, TARIQ, marketing professional; b. Karachi, Pakistan, June 25, 1965; arrived in US, 1985; s. N.D. and Shamim Khan; m. Alia, Dec. 24, 1990; children: Shan, Alina. B in Commerce, U. Karachi, 1985; BBA, CUNY, 1988; MBA, U. St. Johns, N.Y.C., 1992. Sales promotion officer Pakistan Internat. Airlines, N.Y.C., 1989-92; mgmt. exec. traniee MetLife, Queens, N.Y., 1993, br. mgr., 1994-95, gen. mgr., 1996-98, nat. dir. mktg. N.Y.C., 1998-2000, v.p. mktg., 2000—04; pres. and CEO Diversity Planning, 2004—05; dir. mktg. Guardian Life Ins. Co. Am., 2005—. Fellow: Life Underwriting Tng. Coun. Home: 63 Parkwood Ave Staten Island NY 10309-2909 Office Phone: 917-679-5811. E-mail: newyorkkhan@aol.com.

KHANDEKAR, JANARDAN DINKAR, oncologist, educator; b. Indore, India, Feb. 1, 1944; came to U.S., 1971; s. Dinker and Sulaochan (Dawlae) K.; m. Amita Oomen, Aug. 28, 1971; children: Manoj, Melin. MD, MBBS, U. Indore, 1969; sabbatical, Northwestern U., Baylor U., 1992. Diplomate Am. Bd. Internal Medicine, Am. Bd. Med. Oncology. Intern M.Y. Hosp., Indore, 1967-70; resident in medicine Allegheny Gen. Hosp., Pitts., 1972-73; head divsn. med. oncology Evanston (Ill.) Hosp., 1975-98, from asst. attending physician to assoc. attending physician, 1975-79, sr. attending physician, 1979—; fellow Med. Rsch. Coun., Montréal, Que., Can., 1970-71, Tufts U., Boston, 1973-75; asst. prof. medicine Northwestern U., Chgo., 1975-80, assoc. prof., 1980-86, prof. medicine, 1986—, Kellogg/Scanlon chair in oncology, 1991-98; dir. cancer control Northwestern U. Cancer Ctr., Chgo., 1991—; assoc. dir. Kellogg Cancer Care Ctr. Evanston Hosp., 1979-87, dir., 1987—; Louise Coon chmn. dept. medicine Evanston Northwestern Healthcare, 1998—. Active NIH Ad Hoc Com. on Nat. Prostate Cancer Program, NIH Team for Audit Clin. Trials at Yale U., Roswell Park Meml. Inst., Mayo Clinic, etc.; chmn. rsch. com. and adv. com. Searle Clin. Pharmacology Unit; sr. investigator Eastern Coop. Oncology Group, 1976-83, Community Clin. Oncology Program, 1983—; lectr. in field. Author (with others): (novels) Radiation-Associated Thyroid Carcinoma, 1977, Adjuvant Therapy of Cancer, 1977; editor: (Archives) of Internal Medicine, 2004; contbr. articles. Recipient cert. of merit Nat. Cancer Inst. Humanitarian award Cancer Wellness Ctr., 2003; grantee Ill. Cancer Coun., 1983-98, Duke U., 1983-90, Nat. Cancer Inst., 1983—, Women's Health Inst., 1993, Evanston Hosp., 1993—, NIH, 1988-91, 93—. Fellow ACP (laureate); mem. AAAS, Am. Soc. Clin. Oncology, Am. Fedn. Clin. Rsch., Am. Assn. Cancer Rsch., Inst. Medicine (Chgo.). Office: Evanston Hosp 2650 Ridge Ave Evanston IL 60201-1781

KHANG, CHULSOON, economics professor; b. Kaesong City, Republic of Korea, May 10, 1935; s. Woon-sung and Ji-chung (Lim) K.; m. Yee Yu Lau, Sept. 15, 1959; children: Kenneth, Maurice. BA in Econs., Mich. State U., 1959; MA in Econs., U. Minn., 1962, PhD in Econs., 1965. Asst. prof. econs. San Diego State U., 1963-66, U. Oreg., Eugene, 1966-69, assoc. prof., 1969-73, prof., 1973-97, prof. emeritus, 1997—. Vis. prof., rsch. grantee U. New South Wales, Australia, 1972-73; vis. prof., Fulbright fellow Hanguk U. Fgn. Studies, Seoul, Korea, 1979; vis. prof. U. Hawaii, Honolulu, 1989. Referee Am. Econ. Rev., Jour. Internat. Econs., Rev. Econ. Studies, Jour. Fin., Jour. Polit. Econs., Jour. Banking and Fin., Jour. Econs. and Bus., Internat. Econ. Rev.; contbr. articles to profl. jours. Mem. Eugene Area Korean Assn. (past pres.), Am. Econ. Assn. Republican. Home: 224 Edgewood Dr Port Ludlow WA 98365-9225 Office: U Oreg Dept Econs Eugene OR 97403 Personal E-mail: chulyeekhang@peoplepc.com.

KHANNA, KANWAL, rheumatologist; b. Larned, Kans., Aug. 25, 1958; s. Jaswant Lal and Prabha Khanna; m. Marcia Gabriel Nino, Dec. 17, 1988; children: Deven Neal, Jacqueline. BS in Biol. Scis. with honors, Stanford U., 1980; MD, U. Calif., San Francisco, 1984. Diplomate Am. Bd. Internal Medicine, Am. Bd. Rheumatology. Resident in internal medicine Cedars-Sinai Med. Ctr., L.A., 1984-87; fellow in rheumatology Harbor-UCLA Med. Ctr., Torrance, Calif., 1987-90; pvt. practice rheumatology Modesto, Calif., 1991—. Contbr. articles to profl. jours.; author abstracts in field. Relevance reviewer Am. Bd. Internal Medicine, 1995; mem. expert witness panel Med. Bd. Calif., 1996. Fellow ACP, Am. Coll. Rheumatology; mem. Calif. Med. Assn., Stanislaus Med. Soc., Mensa Soc., Phi Beta Kappa. Avocations: tennis, exercise, cooking, travel. Office: 1429 College Ave # M Modesto CA 95350-4046 Office Phone: 209-524-2041.

KHANNA, KARUN, mortgage company executive, consultant; BSEE, Birla Inst. Tech. and Sci., India, 1970; MSEE, U. Wash., Seattle, 1972, MBA, 1974. Project mgr. and sys. engr. Weyerhaeuser Co., Tacoma, 1974—84; v.p. Citicorp Mortgage Bank, St. Louis, 1984—86; sr. v.p. Travelers Mortgage, Mt. Laurel, NJ, 1986—88; v.p. Prudential Real Estate, Costa Mesa, Calif., 1989—92; sr. v.p. US Bancorp, Portland, Oreg., 1993—94; mng. dir. and founder Strategic Change Mgmt., 1994—96; exec. v.p. SystemLogic, Inc., Santa Monica, Calif., 1997—98; dir. tech. mktg. and prin. e-bus. devel. Fannie Mae, Washington, 1998—2001; v.p. mortgage lending ALLTELL Info. Svcs., Jacksonville, Fla., 2002—03; cons. Great Falls, Va., 2003—. Address: 10906 Great Point Ct Great Falls VA 22066

KHANNA, KISHANLAL K., lawyer, educator; b. Lahore, Punjab, India, Feb. 18, 1939; s. Kharatiram and Prakashvati Khanna; m. Arun Prabha Bhalla, Apr. 23, 1966; children: Namita, Karunesh. BE, U. Bombay, Bombay, India, 1959; MPA, Kent State U., Kent, OH, 1971, PhD Pub. Admin., 1974; LLB, U. Bombay, Bombay, India, 1994, LLM, 1996; PhD, 2001. Lic.: Bar Assn., New Delhi, India 1995, bar: Colo.; Grad. Brit. Instn. of Radio Engineers, 1960. Sr. class 1 gazetted officer Govt. of India, Various, India, 1961—86; math & sci. tchr. Canton, Ohio Pub. Schools, Canton, Ohio, 1972—73; vis. asst. prof. No. Ill. U., Dekalb, Ill., 1973—74, Kans. State U., Kansas, Kans., 1974—75; sr. prof. & phd guide U. Bombay, Bombay, 1978—95; mng. dir. Unique Integrated Transp. & Mgmt. Consultancies, Bombay, 1986—95; atty. Supreme Ct. India, Bombay, 1995—, Colo. Dir. fin. Mudra Dance Studio. Author: (book) Behavioral Approach to Bureaucratic Development, Bureaucratic Blunder-world, Proactive Bureaucracy, Executive Psychosis, Executive Decision Making, Management of State Enterprises in India, Logistics Management, Judicial Systems of the Third World: The Case of India. Maj. Corps of Engineers, 1963—78, India. Recipient scholarship, U. Bombay, 1954—59, scholarships, Kent State U., 1971—73, Merit Award for top ranking LLM, U. Bombay, 1996. Mem.: Indian Inst. of Public Admin., Inst. of Rail Transp. (life), Indian Soc. Tng. and Devel. (life), Bombay Mgmt. Assn. (life). Avocations: Hindi stage, Hindi music. Home: 16835 E Navarro Drive Aurora CO 80013 Personal E-mail: kishanaruna@aol.com.

KHANNA, MADHU, education educator; b. New Delhi, Feb. 2, 1960; PhD, U. Calif., Berkeley, 1995. Assoc. prof. U. Ill., Urbana-Champaign, Ill., 2001—05, prof., 2005—. Contbr. articles to profl. jours. Office: Univ Ill 1301 W Gregory Dr Champaign IL 61822 Office Phone: 217-333-5176.

KHANNA, RAHUL, engineer; b. New Delhi; m. Sangeeta Kumari; 1 child, Hemen. BS, Birla Inst. Tech., Ranchi, 1986—90; MS, Columbia U., N.Y.C., 1999—2000, PhD, 2000—02, Oreg. State U., Corvallis, 2004. Sr. staff engr. Intel Corp., Hillsboro, Oreg., 1996—. Recipient Intel Achievement Award, Intel Corp., 2000. Mem.: IEEE. Office: Intel Corp 2111 NE 25th Ave Hillsboro OR 97124 Personal E-mail: khanna@ieee.org.

KHANNA, VIKRAMADITYA, law educator; SJD, Harvard U. Faculty mem. Boston U. Sch. Law.; prof. law U. Mich. Law Sch., Ann Arbor, 2004—. Vis. faculty mem. Harvard Law Sch. Grantee John M. Olin Faculty Fellowship, 2002—03; vis. scholar Stanford Law Sch.; sr. rsch. fellow, Columbia Law Sch. Office: U Mich Law Sch 941 Legal Research 625 S State St Ann Arbor MI 48109-1215 Office Phone: 734-615-6959. Office Fax: 734-764-8309. E-mail: vskhanna@umich.edu.*

KHANZADIAN, VAHAN, tenor; b. Syracuse, N.Y., Jan. 23, 1939; s. Avedis Sarkis and Araxey (Youghian) K. BS, SUNY, Buffalo, 1962; post grad., Curtis Inst. Music, Phila., 1961-63. Debut as Ruggero in La Rondine, San Francisco Spring Opera, 1968; leading roles in Wozzeck, Fra Diavolo, Les Troyens, Madama Butterfly, Lucia Di Lammermoor, Tosca; appeared throughout U.S., Can.; appeared in title role in Don Carlo, Basel, Switzerland, 1992; debut as Calaf in Puccini's Turandot with Bavarian State Opera, Munich, Germany, 1995; appeared with all major opera cos., and opera festivals, including San Antonio, Ravinia, Tanglewood, Saratoga, Opera de Colombia; numerous solo recitals throughout N.Am.; appeared with symphony orchs., including Chgo., Boston, Phila., Cleve., Minn., Indpls., St. Louis, Milw., Pitts.; TV appearances include Gherman in Tchaikovsky's Queen of Spades; soloist in world premier of Menotti's Landscapes and Remembrances, PBS, 1976; leading tenor Met. Opera, 1991-99; debut as Gustavo in Un Ballo in Maschera, Met. Opera, 1993, Lyric Opera Chgo., 1993. Appeared in Sondheim's "Follies" at Paperhill Playhouse, 1998, which is recorded on a new CD. Served with U.S. Army, 1964-65. Sullivan Found. grantee, 1971-74; Rockefeller Found. grantee, 1971-73 Address: PO Box 741 Hunter NY 12442-0741 Personal E-mail: vahan@optonline.net. *My ethnic background, Armenian, with its strong Christian influence was instrumental in projecting the importance of family, religion, education, and culture. The strength and knowledge attained in this environment guided me in the arts, where I was fortunate to have had the discipline and the opportunity to pursue my goal of making a contribution in serving music.*

KHANZHINA, HELEN P., language educator, translator; b. Perm, Russia, Aug. 28, 1954; came to U.S., 1995; d. Pavel L. and Dina B. Wexler; m. Yevgenii A. Khanzhin, Dec. 4, 1975 (div. Jan. 1984); 1 child, Dmitri. MA in English Lit., U. Perm, 1976; PhD in World Lit., U. St. Petersburg, 1985; A prof. diploma, USSR State Com. Nat. Edn., Moscow, 1991. Asst. then assoc. prof. dept. world lit. U. Perm, 1976-95; lectr. dept. English div. continuing edn. U. Va., Charlottesville, 1996-98. Interpreter Lang. Learning Enterprises, Washington, 1996—; rsch. analyst joint state govt. commn. gen. assembly Commonwealth Pa., Harrisburg, 1998—; lectr. divsn. comm., arts and social sciences Harrisburg C.C., 1998—; lectr. Sch. of Humanities Pa. State U., Harrisburg, 1999—. Author: The Making of the National Tradition in American Romantic Poetry and William Cullen Bryant's Creative Work, 1987, Genre, Mode and Style in American Romantic Poetry, 1998; editor: Problems of Method and Poetics in World Literature of the Nineteenth and Twentieth Centuries, 1995, 97; contbr. articles to profl. jours. Vis. scholar grantee USIA, 1993-94, Brit. Coun. Beatrice Ward Found., 1990. Mem. MLA, Am. Assn. Tchrs. Slavic and E. European Langs., Pa. Libr. Assn., Spl. Librs. Assn. Avocations: classical music, jazz, ballet, art, travel. Office: Joint State Govt Commn 108 Fin Bldg Harrisburg PA 17120 Business E-Mail: ykhanzhina@legis.state.pa.us.

KHARBANDA, KUSUM K., biologist, educator; d. Duni Chand and Vidya Wati Kharbanda. MSc, U. Delhi, India, 1981, PhD, 1988. Postdoctoral rsch. assoc. All India Inst. Med. Scis., New Delhi, 1988—92; rsch. assoc. U. Nebr. Med. Ctr., Omaha, 1992—96, rschr., 1996—99, asst. prof., 1999—; rsch. biologist Dept. Veterans Affairs Med. Ctr., Omaha, 1999—. Project mgr. Jr. League, Lincoln, Nebr., 1992—96; bd. dirs. Nebr. Polio Survivors Assn., Omaha, 1997—. Recipient Internal Medicine Basic Sci. Rsch. award, U. Nebr. Med. Ctr., Dept. Internal Medicine, 2005; Jr. Rsch. fellow, Coun. Sci. and Indsl. Rsch., 1982—84, Sr. Rsch. fellow, 1984—87. Mem.: Sigma Xi, Rsch. Soc. on Alcoholism, Am. Assn. Study Liver Disease. Achievements include research in prognostic prediction of human brain tumors based on cell culture characteristics; the effect of alcohol consumption on liver lysosomes; acetaldehyde-malondialdehyde-protein adducts on the pro-fibrogenic and pro-inflammatory properties of hepatic stellate cells; betaine administration on alcohol-induced alterations in methionine metabolism.

KHARE, MOHAN, chemist, researcher; b. Varanasi, India, May 15, 1942; arrived in U.S., 1967, naturalized, 1971; s. Dwarka Nath and Rampyari Devi Khare Srivastava; m. Meena K., Nov. 20, 1973; 1 child, Rohit. BSc, Banaras Hindu U., 1961, MSc, 1963, PhD, 1967. Rsch. assoc. U. Md., College Park, 1967-69, Oreg. State U., Corvallis, 1969-70; sr. rsch. assoc. Cornell U., Ithaca, NY, 1970-78; analytical specialist Hydroscience Inc., (subsidiary of Dow Chem. Co.), Knoxville, Tenn., 1978-80; tech. specialist IT Enviroscience subs. IT Corp., Knoxville, 1980-82; rsch. prof. chemistry U. Nev., Las Vegas, 1982-84, mgr. organic divsn. quality assurance lab. under coop. agreement with EPA, 1982-84; mgr. organic analysis lab. Environ. Monitoring Svcs. Rockwell Internat., Thousand Oaks, Calif., 1984-85; dir. environ. analytical lab. EA Engring., Sci., and Tech., Inc., Sparks, Md., 1985-87; sr. v.p. Recra Environ., Inc., Columbia, Md., 1987-89; pres., CEO Envirosystems, Inc., Columbia, 1989—. Cons. to toxic and hazardous waste analytical labs.; mem. panel peer rev. Toxic Organics Lab. Contbr. articles to profl. jours. including protocols and std. oper. procedures for hazardous waste analytical program. Mem. Am. Chem. Soc., Internat. Union Pure and Applied Chemistry, Internat. Assn. of Environ. Testing Lab. Home: 10189 Maxine St Ellicott City MD 21042-6351 Office: Envirosystems Inc 9200 Rumsey Rd Ste 102B Columbia MD 21045-1934 Office Phone: 410-964-0330. Business E-Mail: info@envsystems.com.

KHARGONEKAR, PRAMOD PRABHAKAR, engineering educator; b. Indore, India, Aug. 24, 1956; s. Prabhakar K. and Leela P. K.; m. Seema P. Pai, Apr. 7, 1983; children: Aditya, Shivangi. BTech. in elec. engring., Indian Inst. Tech., Bombay, 1977; MS in math., U. Fla., 1980, PhD in elec. engring., 1981. Asst. prof. elec. engring. U. Fla., Gainesville, 1981-84; assoc. prof. elec. engring. U. Minn., Mpls., 1984-88, prof. elec. engring., 1988-89; prof.

elec. engring. and computer sci. U. Mich., Ann Arbor, 1989—2001, Arthur F. Thurnau Prof., 1995—98, assoc. chair elec. engring. and computer sci., 1995-97, chair elec. engring. and computer sci., 1997—2001, Claude E. Shannon Prof. Engring. Sci., 2000—01; dean Coll. Engring. U. Fla., Gainesville, 2001—, assoc. v.p. Engring. and Indsl. Expt. Sta., 2001—, Eckis Prof. Elec. and Computer Engring., 2001—. Assoc. editor Math. Problems in Engring. Contbr. more than 250 articles to profl. jours. Recipient Sigma Xi award for Outstanding Rsch. on Math. Sys. Theory, U. Fla., 1982, Best Faculty Paper award, Dept. Elec. Engring., 1983, Presdl. Young Investigator award, NSF, 1985, George Taylor award for Rsch., U. Minn. Inst. Tech., 1987, Donald Eckman award, Am. Automatic Control Coun., 1989, O. Hugo Schuck Best Paper award, 1993, Tchg. Excellence award, Elec. Engring. and Computer Sci. Dept., U. Mich., 1992, Rsch. Excellence award, U. Mich. Coll. Engring., 1994, Disting. Alumnus award, Indian Inst. Tech., 1997. Fellow: IEEE (Control Systems Soc. George S. Axelby Best Paper Award 1990, W.R.G. Baker Prize Paper Award 1991). Avocations: reading, music. Office: U Fla Coll Engring 300 Weil Hall PO Box 116550 Gainesville FL 32611-6550 Office Phone: 325-392-6000. Business E-Mail: ppk@ufl.edu.

KHASHU, BUSHAN, urologist; b. Srinagar, Kashmir, India, Jan. 12, 1942; arrived in U.S., 1971; parents Bishambar Nath and Sona Khashu; m. Santosh Khashu, Aug. 13, 1964; children: Anita, Ajay. MD, Nat. Med. Inst., Calcutta, India, 1964. Diplomate Am. Bd. Urology. Chief urology Syosset (NY) Cmty. Hosp., 1984—88, North Shore U. Hosp., Syosset, 1988—97, dir. men's health, 2002—; co-chief urology North Shore U., Forest Hills, NY, 1997—2002. Contbr. articles to profl. jours. Fellow: ACS, Royal Coll. Surgeons Edinburgh; mem.: Am. Urol. Assn. Avocations: running, reading. Office: 69-71 Grand Ave Maspeth NY 11378 Office Phone: 718-507-4400. E-mail: bkhashu200@yahoo.com.

KHATENA, JOE, psychology professor; b. Singapore, Oct. 25, 1925; came to U.S., 1966, naturalized, 1972; s. Jacob J. and Rachel (Rahmin) K.; m. Nelly Joshua, Dec. 17, 1950; children— Annette, Jacob Allan, Moshe, Serena BA with honors, U. Malaya, Singapore, 1960-61; M.Edn., U. Singapore, 1964; PhD, U. Ga., 1969. Tchr. Govt. of Singapore, 1950-57; lectr. English, Singapore Tchrs. Coll., 1961-66; asst. prof. psychology East Carolina U., Greenville, N.C., 1968-69; assoc. prof. Marshall U., Huntington, W.Va., 1969-72, prof., 1972-77; prof., head ednl. psychology Miss. State U., Mississippi State, 1977-91, prof., head emeritus, 1991—. Author: Creatively Gifted Child, 1978, Educational Psychology of the Gifted, 1982, Imagery and Creative Imagination, 1984, Gifted: Challenge and Response for Education, 1992, Creativity of Gifted Children, 1992, others; co-author: Khatena-Torrance Creative Perception Inventory, 1976, Thinking Creatively with Sounds and Words, 1973, Khatena-Morse Multitalent Perception Inventory, 1992; mem. editorial bd. Gifted Child Quar., 1975—, assoc. editor Jour. Mental Imagery, 1981—; contbr. articles to profl. jours. Recipient Book prize U. Malaya, 1957, Rsch. award Marshall U., 1976, Disting. Svc. award Nat. Assn. Gifted Children, 1983, 90, Rsch. award Phi Delta Kappa Miss. State U., 1989; Nat. Assn. Gifted Children Disting. scholar, 1982, Fulbright sr. lectr., 1985. Fellow Am. Psychol. Assn.; mem. Nat. Assn. Gifted Children (pres. 1977-79), Internat. Psychol. Assn., Am. Ednl. Research Assn., N.Y. Acad. Scis., Phi Kappa Phi, Kappa Delta Pi. Office: Miss State U Dept Ednl Psychology PO Drawer EP Mississippi State MS 39762

KHATIB, RUSTOM ATFAT, gynecologist, researcher, endocrinologist, consultant, economist; b. Beirut, Sept. 3, 1962; s. Atfat Rustom and Samia Ibrahim (Jannoun) K.; m. Mona Adnan Tabbara, Feb. 11, 1993; children: Samia Karla, Ryan Atfat. BS with honors, Am. U. Beirut, 1984, MD, 1988; MBA, Hamilton U., Wyoming, 1995; postgrad diploma in econs., U. London, 2000; PhD Business Admin., Hamilton U., Wyoming, 2001. Resident in ob-gyn. Am. U. Beirut, 1992-94; fellow in reproductive endocrinology Mich. State U., Saginaw, 1994, clin. instr., 1992-94; clin. cons. Rizk Hosp., Beirut, 1994—. Clin. cons. European Heart Ctr., Saida, 1994-96; chmn. ob-gyn. United Med. Group, Beirut, 1996—; sci. cons. Beirut Fertility Ctr., 1994-99; dir. fertility unit European Heart Ctr., Saida, 1994-96, United Med. Group, Beirut, 1997--; dir. fertility svc. Jubeily Hosp., Saida, 1996-99; cons. Fertility Unit Kasab Hosp., Saida, 2000—; mem. acad. coun. London Diplomatic Acad.; mem. sci. faculty Internat. Biog. Ctr., Cambridge, England. Contbr. articles to profl. jours. including Gynecologic Oncology, Fertility and Sterility, European Jour. Obstets., Clin. Consultation in Ob-Gyn. Founding cabinet mem. World Peace and Diplomacy Forum, Cambridge; with Green Peace, Beirut, 1996; sec. gen. United Cultural Conv., Raleigh, NC, 2000—. Recipient Physician's Recognition award AMA, 1994, Ob-Gyn. Rsch. award Saginaw Coop. Hosps., 1994. Fellow Am. Coll. Surgeons; mem. Am. Soc. for Reproductive Medicine, N.Y. Acad. Scis., European Soc. for Human Reproduction and Embryology, Am. Soc. for Reproductive Medicine, Greenpeace. Office: United Med Group Abdul Aziz St Al Mabani Ctr 14-5354 Beirut Lebanon Fax: 9611749695. Office Phone: 9611741900 ext. 101. E-mail: 362812@cyberia.net.lb, rustom@cyberia.net.lb.

KHATON, SABRINA ROSLYN, librarian, accountant; b. New Orleans, Mar. 29, 1955; d. Harold Ralph and Edna Eunice (Carstarphen) K; m. Reginald Sanders, Nov. 24, 1979 (div.); children: Adam James, Evan Alan; m. Darryl A. Derbegry, Aug. 26, 1993. BS in Acctg., Xavier U., New Orleans, 1977. Acct. Sub Sea Internat. Inc., New Orleans, 1976-81; grants and projects acct. Xavier U., New Orleans, 1981-85; fiscal officer for office of employment tng. & devel. City of New Orleans, 1986-88; librarian Fisk-Howard Elem. Sch., New Orleans, 1989—90; accountant Christopher Homes Inc., 1990—. Cons. JTPA Grant Proposals, New Orleans, 1988—; tax preparer, cons. Law Office of Darryl A. Derbigny, New Orleans, 1985—. Recording sec. minority task force Xavier U., New Orleans, 1983-85; mem. Mayor of New Orleans' Women Support Group, 1986-88. Recipient Supervisory award Dunn & Brad Street, 1987. Mem. Delta Sigma Theta (amenities chairperson 1973-74). Democrat. Lutheran. Avocations: bicycling, cooking, tennis. Home: 7451 Restgate Rd New Orleans LA 70127-1841 Office: Law Office Darryl Derbigny 2136 N Galvez St New Orleans LA 70119-1631 Office Phone: 504-821-4521. E-mail: sderb.gny@nocoa.org.

KHAVARI, KHALIL AKHTAR, psychology professor; b. Tehran, Iran, Nov. 10, 1932; s. Ardeshir Akhtar and Rouhanghiz Khalili K.; m. Sue Williston, June 6, 1959; children: Paul, Katherine. BS, Bradley U., 1960, MS, 1963; PhD, Ind. U., 1967. Asst., assoc. then prof. psychology U. Wis., Milw., 1967-95, founder, dir. Midwest Inst. on Drug Use, 1974-77, co-founder, coord. peace studies program, 1987-89. Referee, cons. in field. Author: Creating a Successful Family, 1989, Together Forever: A Practical Guide to Successful Marriage, 1993, Introduction to the Baha'i Faith, 1997, Spiritual Intelligence, 2000. Mem. aux. bd. Baha'i Faith, Milw., 1981-86, founding mem. Baha'i Internat. Health Assn., Ft. Lauderdale, Fla., 1984-90; life mem. Tlinget Indian Tribe, Alaska. Avocations: reading, travel, tennis, hiking, gardening. E-mail: Kk1844@aol.com.

KHAVINSON, DMITRY, mathematician, educator; s. Semyon Yakovlevich Khavinson and Valentina Lass; children: Sophie Hannah children: Jack David. PhD, Brown U., 1983. Asst. prof., assoc. prof. U. Ark., Fayetteville, 1983—97, prof. to disting. prof., 1997—. Program officer NSF, Ballston, Va., 1999—2001. Contbr. articles various profl. jours. Recipient Rsch. Grants, NSF, 1983-2003. Mem.: Am. Math. Soc. Office: U Ark Dept Math Fayetteville AR 72701 E-mail: dmitry@uark.edu.

KHAWLI, LESLIE ALBERT, research scientist, educator; s. Albert Antoine and Corinne Khawli; m. Carole Chammas, July 2, 1995; children: Michelle Leila, Joelle Corinne. PhD, U. So. Calif., L.A., 1986. Postdoctoral fellow Harvard Med. Sch., Boston, 1986—88; asst. prof. U. So. Calif., L.A., 1988—94, assoc. prof., 1994—2001, prof., 2001—. Tchg. grad. and med. students U. So. Calif., L.A., 1988—; cons. Peregrine Pharms., Tustin, Calif., 1989—, Cancer Therapeutics, Inc, L.A., Calif., 1995—, NeoTherapeutics, Inc., Irvine, Calif., 1997—2002. Scientist (cancer research) Interface between immunochemistry and nuclear medicine, primarily on the generation of new approaches for the successful immunodiagnosis and therapy of human cancer using genetically engineered monoclonal antibodies. Recipient Rsch. Travel award, NSF, 1983, Rsch. Svc. award, NIH, 1986-1988, Rsch. award, Nat. Cancer Inst., 1992-1995, Contbn. and Excellence in Cancer Rsch. award, Found. for Better Medicine, 2000; Rsch. fellowship, Harvard Med. Sch., 1986-1988, Pilot Rsch. Project grant, Am. Cancer Soc., 1992-1993, Rsch. grant, Nat. Cancer Inst., 1992-1995, Tobacco-Related Disease Rsch. Program, 1994-1996, Cancer Therapeutics, 1994-2003, Perigrine Pharms., 1995-2003, NIH, 2000-2003, Calif. Cancer Rsch. Program, 2000-2003. Mem.: Am. Assn. of Pharm. Scientists, Am. Chem. Soc., Am. Assn. for Cancer Rsch., Soc. of Nuc. Medicine. Achievements include patents for Use Of Promising Immunoregulatory Antibody/Cytokine Fusion Proteins For The Immunotherapy Of Solid Tumors; M-aminophenyltrialkylstannane; Radiohalogenated Half-Antibodies and Maleimide Intermediate Therefor; Modified Antibodies with Controlled Clearance Time; Antibodies Modified at Two Separate Sites; Antibodies with Reduced Net Positive Charge; Vasopermeability Enhancing Peptide of Human Interleukin-2 and; Published many articles and chapters in the fields of cancer research. Office: Univ So Calif 2011 Zonal Ave HMR 304A Los Angeles CA 90033 Business E-Mail: lkhawli@usc.edu.

KHEDOORI, TOBA, artist; b. Sydney, Australia; BFA, San Francisco Art Inst., 1988; MFA, UCLA, 1994. Represented by David Zwirner Gallery, NYC. One-woman shows include Hirshhorn Mus., Mus. Contemporary Art LA, Walker Art Ctr., Whitechapel Art Gallery, London, Mus. Gegenawartskunst, Basel, exhibited in group shows at Mus. Moder Art, NYC, Mus. Contemporary Art, Chgo., Mus. Modern Art, Copenhagen. Fellow MacArthur Found. fellow, 2002. Address: David Zwirner Gallery 525 W 19th St New York NY 10011-2000

KHEEL, ROBERT J., lawyer; b. New Rochelle, N.Y., May 1, 1943; BA, Cornell U., 1965; MSc, London Sch. Econs., 1966; JD cum laude, U. Mich., 1969. Bar: N.Y. 1969, Fla. 1970, D.C. 1983. Mem. Willkie, Farr & Gallagher, N.Y.C. Contbr. articles to profl. jours. Mem. ABA, N.Y. State Bar Assn., Fla. Bar Assn., D.C. Bar, Assn. of Bar of City of N.Y. Office: Willkie Farr & Gallagher 1 Citicorp Ctr 787 7th Ave New York NY 10019-6099

KHEEL, THEODORE WOODROW, lawyer; b. N.Y.C., May 9, 1914; s. Samuel and Kate (Herzenstein) K.; m. Ann Sunstein, July 1, 1937; children: Ellen Jacobs, Robert J., Constance, Martha, Jane Kheel Stanley, Katherine Kheel. AB, Cornell U., 1935, LLB, 1937. Bar: N.Y. 1937. Ptnr. Battle Fowler, 1949-82; of counsel Battle Fowler (now Paul Hastings Janofsky & Walker), 1982—. Pres. Earth Pledge Found., 1991-, Nurture New York's Nature, 2003, Found. for Prevention & Early Resolution of Conflict, 1994-, Carriage House Ctr. on Global Issues, 1991-; mem. presdl. bds. various labor disputes, 1962-66; spl. cons. Pres.'s Com. on EEO, 1962-63. Author: Transit and Arbitration, 1960, Pros and Cons of Compulsory Arbitration, 1961, How Race Relations Affect Your Business, 1963, Guide to Fair Employment Practices, 1964, Kheel on Labor Law, 1974—, Keys to Conflict Resolution, 1999. Pres. Nat. Urban League, 1956-60; mem. Pres.'s Nat. Citizens Com. for Cmty. Rels., 1964-68. Mem. Am. Arbitration Assn. (bd. dirs.). Office: 75 E 55th St New York NY 10022-3205 Home: 800 Fifth Ave New York NY 10021 Office Phone: 212-318-6747.

KHENNER, MIKHAIL, mathematics professor; PhD, U. Aix-Marseille II, France and Perm State U., Russia, 1998. Post doctoral rschr. U. Del., Newark, 2000—02; asst. prof. SUNY at Buffalo, 2002—. Contbr. articles to profl. jours. Mem.: Soc. Indsl. and Applied Math., Am. Phys. Soc. Office: SUNY Buffalo Dept Math Buffalo NY 14260

KHERADPIR, SHAYGAN, information technology executive; B in Elec. Engring., M, PhD, Cornell Univ. Joined GTE, 1987; v.p. GTE Labs, Waltham, Mass., 1994—96; asst. v.p., info. tech. GTE, 1996—98, v.p. info. tech., enterprise sys., 1998—2000; pres., e-bus. group Verizon Comm. (following GTE merger), 2000—02; chief info. officer Verizon Comm., 2002—. Adj. prof., elec. engring. Northeastern Univ., Mass., 1992—94; sr. mem. IEEE; adv. bd. mem. Cornell Univ. Engring. Sch.; mem. tech. adv. coun. Sun Microsystems. Author: more than 20 jour. papers. Named one of nation's 85 outstanding young engineers, Nat. Acad. of Engring., 1996, one of top tech. innovators, Info. Week mag., 2004. Achievements include holding one patent. Office: CIO Verizon Comm 1095 Ave of Americas New York NY 10036

KHERDIAN, DAVID, writer; b. Racine, Wis., Dec. 17, 1931; s. Melkon and Veron (Dumehjian) K.; m. Kato Rozeboom, 1968 (div. 1970); m. Nonny Hogrogian, Mar. 17, 1971. BS in Philosophy, U. Wis., 1960. Lit. cons. Northwestern U., 1965; founder/editor Giligia Press, 1966-72; rarebook cons. Fresno State Coll., Calif., 1968-69, lectr., 1969-70; ofcl. poet-in-the-schs. State of N.H., 1971; editor Ararat mag., 1971-72; dir. Two Rivers Press, Aurora, Oreg., 1978-86. Poetry judge, lectr., reader of own poetry; founder, editor (with Nonny Hogrogian) The Press at Butternut Creek, 1987-88. Author: On The Death of My Father and Other Poems, 1970, Homage to Adana, 1970, Looking Over Hills, 1972, The Nonny Poems, 1974, Any Day of Your Life, 1975, Country, Cat: City, Cat, 1978, I Remember Root River, 1978, The Road From Home: The Story of an Armenian Girl (Lewis Carroll Shelf award, Boston Globe/Horn Book award, Newbery Honor Book award, Jane Addams Peace award, Banta award), 1979, The Farm, 1979, It Started With Old Man Bean, 1980, Finding Home, 1981, Taking the Soundings on Third Avenue, 1981, The Farm: Book Two, 1981, Beyond Two Rivers, 1981 (Friends of Am. Writers award), The Song in the Walnut Grove, 1982, Place of Birth, 1983, Right Now, 1983, The Mystery of the Diamond in the Wood, 1983, Root River Run, 1984, The Animal, 1984, Threads of Light: The Farm Poems Books III and IV, 1985, Bridger: The Story of a Mountain Man, 1987, Poems to an Essence Friend, 1987, A Song for Uncle Harry, 1989, the Cat's Midsummer Jamboree, 1990, The Dividing River/The Meeting Shore, 1990, On a Spaceship with Beelzebub: By a Grandson of Gurdjieff, 1990, The Great Fishing Contest, 1991, Friends: A Memoir, 1993, Juna's Journey, 1993, Asking the River, 1993, By Myself, 1993, My Racine, 1994, Lullaby for Emily, 1995, Seven Poems for Mikey, 1997, The Rose's Smile, 1997, I Called It Home, 1997, The Golden Bracelet, 1998, Chippecotton: Root River Tales of Racine, 1998, The Neighborhood Years, 2000, The Revelations of alvin Tolliver 2001, Seeds of Light: Poems From a Gurdjieff Community, 2002, The Song of the Stork and Other Early and Ancient Armenian Songs, 2004, Letters To My Father, 2004, The Buddha: The Story of an Awakened Life, 2004; also bibliographies.; editor: Visions of America by the Poets of Our Time, 1973, Settling America: The Ethnic Expression of 14 Contemporary Poets, 1974, Poems Here and Now, 1976, Traveling America with Today's Poets, 1976, The Dog Writes on the Window with His Nose and Other Poems, 1977, If Dragon Flies Made Honey, 1977, I Sing the Song of Myself, 1978, Beat Voices: An Anthology of Beat Poetry, 1995; co-editor: Down at the Santa Fe Depot: 20 Fresno Poets, 1970; translator: The Pearl: Hymn of the Robe of Glory, 1979, Pigs Never See the Stars: Armenian Proverbs, 1982, Monkey: A Journey to the West, 1992, Feathers and Tails: Animal Fables From Around the World, 1992; editor: Forkroads: A Journ. of Ethnic-Am. Lit., 1995-97, Stopinder: A Gurdjieff Jour. For Our Time, 2000-2003. Served with AUS, 1952-54. Office: 5082 County Rte 7 Chatham NY 12037-2604 Business E-Mail: tavnon@taconic.net. *The poet understands that everything is connected and all is one. This is all he really knows. But knowing this he is permitted to speak, quietly, disturbing nothing, removing nothing, revealing only the new-old relationships he has been given to see.*

KHIM, JAY WOOK, information technology executive; b. Taegu, Korea, Oct. 22, 1940; came to U.S., 1965; s. Joon Mook and Soon E. (Lee) K. BS in Agrl. Econs., Kyung Pook U., Korea, 1963, MA in Agrl. Econs., 1966; postgrad. PhD program in Econs., U. Md., 1965-69; LLD (hon.), Randolph-Macon Coll., 1988; PhD (hon.), Kyungpook Nat. U., Republic of Korea, 1990. Mem. rsch. staff Brookings Instn., Washington, 1967-69; sr. economist NAB, Dept. of Labor, Washington, 1969-72; sr. assoc. Planning Rsch. Corp., Washington, 1972-74; chmn., CEO JWK Internat. Corp., Washington, 1974—, Internat. Trade and Investment Corp., Washington, 1977—. Bd. dirs. Millennium Bank. Author: The Third Eye, 1998; author, editor more than 100 research reports, articles for fed. govt. in fields of health, energy, def., transp., housing and internat. affairs Bd. dirs. Fulbright Found., 1999—, Asia Soc., Washington, 1999—, George Mason Inst., George Mason U., Fairfax, Va., 1983—, United Bank, 1997—, No. Va. Cmty. Found., 1998—, Worf Trap Found. for Performing Arts, 1998—; mem. World Presidents Orgn., 1992—, chmn. Washington Met. chpt., 1994-2000; bd. govs. U. Md. Alumni Assn.; bd. trustees Fairfax Hosp. Assn., 1986-2001; candidate for U.S. Congress from 11th Va. dist., 1992; chmn. fin. com. Rep. Party, Va.; commr. Small and Minority Bus. Commn., Fairfax County, 1992. Fulbright scholar, 1965, 66; recipient Sam Ill Found. award Korea, 1962, 63 Mem. Young Pres.'s Orgn., Pres. Club of Am. Mgmt. Assn., Nat. Security Assn., Am. Def. Preparedness Assn., Am. Econ. Assn., Fairfax C. of C. (bd. dirs. 1984-87), World Pres.'s Orgn. (chmn. Washington Met. chtp. 1994-95), City Club, Tower Club, Robert Trent Jones Club, Tournament of Players Club, Internat. Club (D.C.), River Bend Country Club, Fairbanks Golf and Country Club (San Diego). Office: JWK Internat Corp Ste 1040 7617 Little River Tpke Annandale VA 22003-2689 also: 10900 Tara Rd Potomac MD 20854-1342

KHINDUKA, SHANTI KUMAR, dean, educator; b. Jaipur, Rajasthan, India, Dec. 22, 1933; came to U.S., 1964; s. Ram C. and Koka D. Khinduka; m. Manorama Khinduka, May 5, 1955; children: Abha, Seema. BA, Rajasthan U., 1953; MSW, Lucknow U., India, 1955, U. So. Calif., 1961; PhD, Brandeis U., 1968. Asst. prof. Lucknow U., 1955-64; assoc. social affairs office UN, N.Y.C., 1965; from assoc. to prof., asst. dean St. Louis U., 1967-74; prof. social work Washington U., St. Louis, 1974—, dean, 1974—2004, George Warren Brown dist. prof., 2004—. Pres. Inter-Univ. Consortium for Internat. Social Devel., 2001-2005; Zellerbach vis. prof. Sch. of Social Welfare, U. Calif., 2005. Editor: Social Work in India, 2d edit., 1965; co-editor: Social Work in Practice, 1976, Profiles in International Social Work, 1992; chmn. edit. bd. Jour. Social Svc. Rsch., 1976-2004; contbr. articles to profl. jours. Bd. dirs. Council on Social Work Edn., 1978-81, commn. accreditation, 1984-88; bd. dirs. United Way of St. Louis, 1982-2004, Mo. Goodwill Industries, 1987-2004, chmn. 2000-2002. Mem. Nat. Assn. Social Workers (chmn. symposium planning com. 1978-79, chmn. publ. com. 1985-89, 97-2001), Nat. Conf. Social Welfare (bd. dirs. 1979-82). Avocations: reading, travel. Home: 6408 Forsyth Blvd Clayton MO 63105-2231 Office: Washington U G Warren Brown Sch Social Work PO Box 1196 Saint Louis MO 63188-1196 Business E-Mail: khinduka@wustl.edu.

KHISTI, RAHUL TRYAMBAK, neuropharmacologist, researcher; s. Tryambak Ambadas and Chhaya Tryambak Khisti; m. Manik Rahul Deshpande, Dec. 17, 2003. BPharm, Nagpur U., India, 1994, MPharm., 1996, PhD, 2001. Lic. pharmacist Maharashtra State Pharmacy Coun., Mumbai. Sr. rsch. fellow dept. pharm. scis. Nagpur U., 1997—2001; rsch. assoc. U. NC, Chapel Hill, 2001—. Sci. jour. reviewer U. NC, Chapel Hill, 2001—. Contbr. articles to sci. jours., chapters to books. Recipient Best Paper Presentation award, Indian Pharm. Assn., 1998, 1999, Achari award, Indian Pharmacol. Soc., 1999; Jr. Rsch. fellow, U. Grants Commn., 1994—96, Sr. Rsch. fellow, Coun. Sci. and Indsl. Rsch., 1997—2001. Fellow: Internat. Brain Rsch. Orgn.; mem.: Soc. for Neurosci., Rsch. Soc. for Alcoholism (Jr. Investigator award 2004). Achievements include discovery of mechanism of ethanol's action to increase neuroactive steroids by increasing expression of adrenal STAR protein; antidepressant-like and antipsychotic action of neuroactive steroids Allopregnanolone; development of Haloperidol-induced catalepsy: a model for depression in Parkinson's disease. Office Phone: 919-966-4977.

KHITERER, VICTORIA M., historian; b. Kiev, Ukraine, Aug. 20, 1968; arrived in U.S., 1999; d. Michael Khiterer and Ludmila Brovarnik; m. James Danaher, Nov. 20, 1999. PhD, Russian State U. of Humanities, Moscow. Vis. lectr. Stanford (Calif.) U., 2002; history instr. Santa Monica (Calif.) Coll., 2003, Quincy (Mass.) Coll., 2004—. Author 2 books; contbr. articles to profl. jours. Shklar fellow, Harvard U., 2002, travel grantee, IREX, Washington, 2002. Mem.: Am. Hist. Assn.

KHO, EUSEBIO, surgeon; b. The Philippines, Dec. 16, 1933; came to U.S., 1964; s. Joaquin and Francisca (Chua) K.; m. Grace Casas Lim, May 24, 1964; children: Michelle Mae, April Tiffany, Bradley Jude, Jaclyn Ashley, Matthew Ryan. AA, Silliman U., The Philippines, 1955; MD, State U. Philippines, 1960. Diplomate Am. Bd. Surgery. Rotating intern Philippine Gen. Hosp., U. Philippines, 1959-60; resident gen. practice Silliman U. Med. Ctr., 1960-63; virology rschr. Van Howelling Lab. Silliman U., 1963-64; intern in surgery Francis Scott Key Med. Ctr., 1964-65, resident in gen. surgery, 1965-67; fellow in surgery Johns Hopkins, 1965-67; rsch. assoc. pediat. surgery U. Chgo. Hosps., 1967-68; resident in gen. surgery then chief resident U. Tex. Hosp., San Antonio, 1968-70; hosp. surgeon St. Anthony Hosp., Louisville, 1970-72; practice medicine specializing in surgery Scottsburg, Ind., 1972—. Chmn. dept. surgery Scott County Meml. Hosp., 1973—; cons. surgeon Washington County Meml. Hosp., Salem, Ind., also Clark County Meml. Hosp., Jeffersonville, Ind., 1973—; courtesy surgeon Suburban Hosp., Louisville, 1973—; gen. surgeon 5010 U.S. Army Hosp., Louisville, 1980—. Bd. dirs. Make-A-Wish Found., Ind., 1992—. Col. M.C., USAR, 1980—, Operation Desert Storm, 1990-91. Named to Chgo. Filipino Am. Hall of Fame in medicine, 1998; recipient Outstanding Svc. Overseas award U. Philippines Med. Alumni Soc., 2002. Fellow: ACS, Am. Coll. Emergency Physicians, Am. Soc. Abdominal Surgeons; mem.: APHA, AMA (Physician's Recognition award 1969, 1972), Phillipine Med. Assn. of Ky. (Disting. Svc. award 2000), Am. Heart Assn., Am. Soc. Law and Medicine, Am. Cancer Soc., Am. Soc. Parenteral and Enteral Nutrition, Soc. Laparoscopic Surgeons, N.Y. Acad. Scis., Surgeons in Am. (life), Assn. Philippine Practicing Physicians in Am. (life), Assn. Mil. Surgeons U.S. (life), Res. Officers Assn. U.S. (life), Soc. Philippine Surgeons in Am. (life), Bradley Aust. Surg. Soc., Mark Ravitch Surg. Assn., Ind. Philippines Med. Assn., Ky. Med. Assn., Soc. of The Philippines, Ind. State Med. Assn., Am. Coll. Internat. Physicians (founding, trustee 1974—), U. Chgo. Med. Alumni Assn., Philippine Heritage Endowment Found., Philippine Ednl. and Cultural Endeavor (life), Silliman U. Alumni Assn. (life), U. Philippines Med. Alumni Soc. Am. (life), Assn. U.S. Army (life), Silliman Alumni Internat., Johns Hopkins Med. Alumni Assn., Optimists, Masons, Hon. Order Ky. Cols. Presbyterian. Home: 14 Carla Ln Scottsburg IN 47170-9707 Office: 137 E Mcclain Ave Scottsburg IN 47170-1846 Office Phone: 812-752-5659.

KHODAREV, NIKOLAI NIKOLAEVICH, biologist, researcher; b. Moscow, June 28, 1952; s. Nikolai Nikolaevich Khodarev and Rema Borisovna Khodareva; m. Irina Anatolievna Sokolova, Mar. 23, 1986; children: Anatoliy Nikolaevich Sokolov, Igor Nikolaevich, Artem Nikolaevich Sokolov, Alexander Nikolaevich. MD, 1st Moscow Med. Sch., 1976, PhD, 1981; DSc, USSR Acad. Med. Sci., Moscow, 1989. Staff scientist Inst. Biomed. Chemistry, Moscow, 1981—83, leading scientist, 1983—89; chief of lab. Ctr. Med. Biotech., Moscow, 1989—92; Fogerty fellow NIH, Bethesda, Md., 1992—95; rsch. asst. prof. Loyola U., Chgo., 1995—98, U. Chgo., 1998—2004, rsch. assoc. prof., 2004—. Mem. sci. bd. Ctr. Med. Genetics, Moscow, 1989—92, Ctr. Med. Biotech., Moscow, 1989—92. Contbr. articles to profl. jours.; patentee in field. Recipient Best Annual Presentation award, Inst. Biomed. Chemistry, 1980, Best Presentation of Yr. award, Dept. Health/Acad. Med. Sci.; fellow Fogerty Internat. Ctr., NIH, 1992—95; grantee travel grantee, USSR Acad. of Med. Sci., 1991;, USSR Acad. Med. Sci., 1982, 1984. Mem.: Internat. Soc. Cellular Oncology, Radiation Rsch. Soc., Am. Assn. Cancer Rsch. Achievements include discovery of supermethylated regions of DNA in chromatin; role of chromatin conformation in DNA methylation; irradiation dose-dependent tumor genes; role of interferon signaling in tumor radioresistance; first to purify apoptic nuclease from human lymphocytes; role of chromatin conformation and repetitive sequences in apoptosis; design of in vitro system of recombination induced by apoptotic nucleases; new methods of DNA array analysis-2003. Avocations: science fiction, bicycling. Office: U Chgo 5841 S Maryland Ave Chicago IL 60637 Office Phone: 773-834-3282. E-mail: nikolai@rover.uchicago.edu.

KHOL, CHAREL L., psychologist; b. Cleve., Apr. 2, 1943; divorced; children: Adrienne Marie, Matthew Philip. BS in Edn., Ohio State U., 1965; MS in Edn., Ohio U., 1969; PhD, Kent State U., 1982. Lic. psychologist, Ohio. Psychologist Kevin Coleman Ctr., Ravenna, Ohio, 1983-87; pvt. practice Ravenna and Kent, 1984—; psychologist Child Guidance Ctr., Akron, Ohio, 1987—. Cons., expert witness. Named Jennings Scholar for

Tchr. Excellence, Jennings Trust, 1967. Mem.: APA, State U. Varsity O, Ohio Psychol. Assn. Avocations: reading, quilting, collecting. Office: 265 W Main St Ste 102 Kent OH 44240 also: Child Guidance Ctr 312 Locust Akron OH 44305-3838 Office Phone: 330-678-9210.

KHONSARI, MICHAEL M., mechanical engineering educator; b. Aug. 17, 1957; m. Karen Sue Troy, Sept. 1, 1990. BS in Mech. Engring. with honors, U. Tex., 1978, MS in Mech. Engring., 1979, PhD in Mech. Engring., 1983. Rsch. and tchg. asst. U. Tex., Austin, 1978-83; asst. prof. Ohio State U., Columbus, 1984-87, U. Pitts., 1988-90, assoc. prof., 1990-96; prof. So. Ill. U., Carbondale, 1996-99, prof., chmn. dept. mech. engring. and energy processes, 1996-99; Dow Chem. endowed chair, prof. mech. engring. La. State U., Baton Rouge, 1999—, Dow Chem. endowed chair in rotating machinery, 1999—. Apptd. project dir. and assoc. commr. Sponsored R&D at La. Bd. Regents, Exptl. Program to Stimulate Competitive Rsch., 2003—; mem. mech. engring. grad. com. U. Pitts., 1988-90, design interest group, 1988-96; mem. faculty ctr. motion control U. Pitts.; reviewer NSF, NASA, Am. Chem. Soc. Books, McGraw Hill Books, Addison Wesley Books, Prentice-Hall Books, Holt Rinehart and Winston Books; lectr. in field. Assoc. editor ASME Jour. Tribology, 1997—, STLE Tribology Transactions, 1990—; mem. editl. bd. Tribological Acta, 1994—; mem. editl. bd., reviewer Jour. Engring. Design Graphics, 1987—; contbr., reviewer, mem. editl. bd. adv. com. CRC Handbook of Lubrication, vol. III, 1991-93; reviewer Lubrication Engring. Jour., Wear Jour., Rheology Jour., Heat Transfer Jour., Tribology Jour., Applied Mechanics Jour.; co-author: Applied Triology, 2001; pub. abstracts and reports; referee various jours.; contbr. articles to profl. jours. Recipient Found. award ALCOA, 1990, 91. Fellow Soc. Tribology Lubrication Engrs. (bearings com. 1985—, chmn. 1988-91, assoc. editor, rev. Tribology Transactions 1990—, assoc. editor Jour. Tribology 1997—, Presdl. Rsch. Coun. award 1993), ASME (conf. planning com. 1989-96, reviewer Jour. Tribology and conf. papers, chmn. ASME/Soc. Tribology and Lubrication Engrs. Internat. Conf. in Tribology 1996, Burt L. Newkirk award 1990). Achievements include research in thermal effects in hydrodynamic bearings, thermal effects in wet clutches, hot spot prediction in mechanical components, Thermoclastic instability, powder lubrication, multi-phase flows in bearings, friction associated with instrument pointing mechanisms operating under ultra low speeds. Office: La State U Dept Mech Engring 2508 Ceba Baton Rouge LA 70803-0001 Office Phone: 225-578-9192. Business E-Mail: Khonsari@me.lsu.edu.

KHORANA, HAR GOBIND, chemist, educator; b. Raipur, India, Jan. 9, 1922; s. Shri Ganpat Rai Khorana and Shrimati Krishna (Devi) Knorana; m. Esther Sibler, 1952; children: Julia, Emilie; 1 child, Dave Roy. BS, Punjab U., 1943, MS, 1945; PhD, Liverpool (Eng.) U., 1948; DSc (hon.), U. Chgo., 1967, Simon Fraser U., Vancouver, Can., 1969, U. Liverpool, Eng., 1971, U. Punjab, India, 1971, U. Miami, 1994; degree (hon.), U. Bergen, Norway, 1996; others (hon.). Head organic chemistry group B.C. Rsch. Coun., 1952—60; vis. prof. Rockefeller Inst., N.Y.C., 1958—; prof., co-dir. Inst. Enzyme Rsch. U. Wis., Madison, 1960—70, prof. dept. biochemistry, 1962—70, Conrad A. Elvehjem prof. life scis., 1964—70; Alfred P. Sloan prof. biology and chemistry MIT, Cambridge, 1970—97, A.P. Sloan prof. emeritus, sr. lectr., 1997—. Vis. prof. Stanford U., 1964; mem. adv. bd. Biopolymers; rschr. chem. methods for synthesis of nucleotides, coenzymes and nucleic acids, elucidation on the genetic code, lab. synthesis of genes, biol. membrane and light-transducing pigments. Author: Some Recent Developments in the Chemistry of Phosphate Esters of Biological Interests, 1961; editl. bd. Jour. Am. Chem. Soc., 1963—, contbr. numerous articles to profl. jours., —. Recipient Merck award, Chem. Inst. Can., 1958, Gold medal, Profl. Inst. Pub. Svc. Can., 1960, Dannie-Heinneman Preiz, Göttingen, Germany, 1967, Remsen award, Johns Hopkins U., 1968, Am. Chem. Soc. award for creative work in synthetic organic chemistry, 1968, Louisa Gross Horwitz prize, 1968, Lasker Found. award for basic med. rsch., 1968, Nobel prize in physiology or medicine, 1968, elected to Deutsche Akademie der Naturforscher Leopoldina, HalleSaale, Germany, 1968; fellow Overseas, Churchill Coll., Cambridge, Eng., 1967. Fellow: AAAS, Am. Acad. Arts and Scis., Chem. Inst. Can.; mem.: NAS, others, Japanese Biochem. Soc. (fgn. hon.), Royal Soc. Edinburgh, Pharm. Soc. Japan (hon.), Royal Soc. (London), Pontifical Acad. Scis. (Rome), Indian Acad. Scis. (fgn. mem.), Am. Philos. Soc. Office: 68-680A Dept Biol MIT 77 Massachusetts Ave Cambridge MA 02139-4307*

KHORSANDI, BEHROOZ, research scientist; b. Tehran, Iran, Mar. 11, 1966; s. Parviz Khorsandi and Parvin Raissi-Fard; m. Bahar Jalali Farahani, Sept. 21, 1973. BS in Materials Sci., Tehran U., 1989; MS in Materials Sci., Iran U. Sci. and Tech., 1995; MS in Nuc. Engring., Ohio State U., 2004. Rsch. dir. Arsenal Industry Group, Tehran, 1989—91, Fuliran, Tehran, 1991—95; dir. hard chromium coating project Hadid Industry, Tehran, 1995—98; quality assurance expert SAPCO, Tehran, 1998—2001; rsch. asst. Ohio State U., Columbus, Ohio, 2002—. Mem.: Am. Soc. Quality (assoc.; quality engr. 2001), Am. Nuc. Soc. (assoc.). Achievements include research in systematic planning to coat tubes with hard chromium. Office: Ohio State U Nuc Engring 650 Ackerman Rd Columbus OH 43202 Personal E-mail: khorsandi.1@osu.edu.

KHOSHABE, STEVEN Y., mortgage company executive; BSc in Mktg., Bradley U.; MBA in Fin., Loyola U. From mem. staff to pres. United Fin. Mortgage Corp., Oak Brook, Ill., 1994—2003, pres., 2003—, CEO, 2003—. Office: United Financial Mortgage Corp 815 Commerce Dr Ste 100 Oak Brook IL 60523

KHOSLA, CHAITAN S., chemical engineer; BTech, Indian Inst. of Tech., Mumbai, 1985; PhD, Calif. Inst. Tech., 1990; postdoctoral work, John Innes Ctr., U.K., 1990—91. Prof. chem. engring, chemistry and biochemistry Stanford Univ., and Wells H. Rauser and Harold M. Petiprin prof., sch. of engring. Recipient Dreyfus new Investigator award, 1991, Young Investigator award, NSF, 1994—99, Allan P. Colburn award, 1997, ACS Lilly award in Biological Chemistry, 1999, Alan T. Waterman award, NSF, 1999, ACS Pure Chemistry award, 2000, Disting. Alumni award, Calif. Inst. Tech., 2000. Achievements include being credited with pathbreaking work on erythromycin biosynthesis and elucidating molecular mechanisms. Office: Stanford Dept Chemical Engring Keck Science Bldg Rm 389 381 North-South Mall Stanford CA 94305-5025 Business E-Mail: ck@chemeng.stanford.edu.

KHOSLA, PRADEEP KUMAR, engineering educator; b. Amritsar, Punjab, India, Mar. 13, 1957; arrived in US, 1982; s. Brijnath and Sharda (Behal) Khosla; m. Thespine Kavoulakis, June 20, 1987; children: Nathan, Alexander. B in tech. with honors, Indian Inst. Tech., Kharagpur, India, 1980; MSEE, Carnegie Mellon U., 1984, PhD, 1986. Asst. engr. Tata Cons. Engineers, India, 1980-81; project engr. Siemens Co., India, 1981-82; asst. prof. elec. and computer engring. and robotics Carnegie Mellon U., Pitts., 1986—90, assoc. prof., 1990—94, prof., 1994—, founding dir. Inst. for Complex Engineered Systems, 1997—99, Philip and Marsha Dowd Professor Coll. Engring. and Sch. Computer Sci., 1998—, head elec. and computer engring. dept., 1999—2004, founding dir. Ctr. for Computer and Comm. Security, 2001—03, founding co-dir. CyLab, 2003—, dean Carnegie Inst. Tech., 2004—; Program Mgr. Software and Intelligent Systems Tech. Office (SISTO), Def. Sciences Office (DSO), and Tactical Tech. Office (TTO) Def. Advanced Rsch. Projects Agy. (DARPA), 1994—96. Mem. bd. on mfg. and enring. design NRC, 2003—; bd. dirs. MPC Corp., Quantapoint Inc., Pitts., co-founder; mem. strategy review bd. Ministry Sci. & Tech., Taiwan; mem. IT adv. com. Commonwealth Sci. & Indsl. Rsch. Orgn. (CSIRO), Australia; mem. coun. deans of aeronautics adv. com. NASA; mem. sr. adv. group Program on Joint Unmanned Combat Air Systems Def. Advanced Projects Rsch. Agy. (DARPA). Bd. dirs. The Children's Inst., Indian Inst. Tech. Found. Recipient Ladd award for excellence in rsch., Carnegie Inst. Tech., 1989, Tech Brief Award, NASA, 1992, 1993, Leadership Award for Excellence in Academics and Tech., siliconindia, 2000, W. Wallace McDowell Award, IEEE Computer Soc., 2001; Inlaks Found. Fellowship, 1982. Fellow: AAAS, Am. Assn. Artificial Intelligence, IEEE (disting. lectr. Robotics and Automation Soc. 1998—2003); mem.: Am. Soc. Engring. Edn. (George Westinghouse Award for Edn. 1999). Avocations: travel, tennis, volleyball. Office: Carnegie Inst Tech Carnegie Mellon U 110 Scaife Hall Pittsburgh PA 15213-3890

KHOSLA, VED MITTER, oral and maxillofacial surgeon, educator; b. Nairobi, Kenya, Jan. 13, 1926; s. Jagdish Rai and Tara V. K.; m. Santosh Ved Chabra, Oct. 11, 1952; children: Ashok M., Siddarth M. Student, U. Cambridge, 1945; L.D.S., Edinburgh Dental Hosp. and Sch., 1950, Coll. Dental Surgeons, Sask., Can., 1962. Prof. emeritus, dir. postdoctoral studies in oral surgery Sch. Dentistry U. Calif., San Francisco, 1968—; chief oral surgery San Francisco Gen. Hosp. Lectr. oral surgery U. of Pacific, VA Hosp.; vis. cons. Fresno County Hosp. Dental Clinic.; Mem. planning com., exec. med. com. San Francisco Gen. Hosp. Contbr. articles to profl. jours. Examiner in photography and gardening Boy Scouts Am., 1971-73, Guatemala Clinic, 1972. Granted personal coat of arms by H.M. Queen Elizabeth II, 1959 Fellow Royal Coll. Surgeons (Edinburgh), Internat. Assn. Oral Surgeons, Internat. Coll. Applied Nutrition, Internat. Coll. Dentists, Royal Soc. Health, AAAS, Am. Coll. Dentists; mem. Brit. Assn. Oral Surgeons, Am. Soc. Oral Surgeons, Am. Dental Soc. Anesthesiology, Am. Acad. Dental Radiology, Omicron Kappa Upsilon. Clubs: Masons. Home: 1525 Lakeview Dr Hillsborough CA 94010-7330 Office: U Calif Sch Dentistry Oral Surgery Div 3D Parnassus Ave San Francisco CA 94117-4342 Office Phone: 650-348-7587. *It is part of the cure to wish to be cured. With God all things are possible.*

KHOSLA, VINOD, investment company executive; b. New Delhi; married; 4 children. MBA, Stanford U.; M in Biomed. Engring., Carnegie Mellon U.; B of Tech. in Elec. Engring., Indian Inst. Tech., New Delhi. Ptnr. Kleiner, Perkins, Canfield and Byers, Menlo Park, Calif.; founding CEO Sun Microsystems; co-founder Daisy Sys. Bd. dirs. Asera, Centrata, Infinera, Juniper Networks, Nanotectonica, Redback, QWEST Comms., Zambeel, Zaplet. Office: Kleiner Perkins Canfield and Byers 2750 Sand Hill Rd Menlo Park CA 94025*

KHOURY, BERNARD V., educational administrator; Asst. dean Grad. Studies and Rsch. U. Md.; assoc. exec. sec. Assn. Am. U.; exec. dir. Grad. Record Examinations Program Ednl. Testing Svc.; assoc. v.p. Academic Affairs U. Md. Sys., assoc. vice chancellor Policy and Planning; exec. officer Am. Assn. Physics Tchrs., 1990—. Office: Am Assn Physics Tchrs One Physics Ellipse College Park MD 20740-3845

KHOURY, COLLEEN A., dean; b. 1943; BA, Colby Coll., 1964; JD, Ill. Inst. Tech., 1975. Dir. info. and devel. pvt. child welfare agy., Chgo.; pub. info. dir. Cook County Dept. Pub. Aid; assoc. Bell, Boyd & Lloyd, 1975—83, ptnr., 1983; gen. counsel Ventrex Labs.; prof. U. Maine Sch. Law, Portland, 1985—, assoc. dean, 1991—93, dean, 1998—. Bd. dirs. Justice Action Group, Banknorth Group, Inc.; chair Commn. on Gender, Justice and Cts., Maine Supreme Jud. Ct., 1993—96. Corporator Boys and Girls Clubs Greater Portland, Maine; trustee Portland Symphony Orch.; vice chair bd. trustees Colby Coll. Recipient Caroline Duby Glassman award, Maine State Bar Assn., 1997, Deborah Morton award, U. New Eng., 2002, Margaret Brent Lawyers Achievement award, ABA, 2003. Mem.: Am. Law Inst., Maine Bar Found. (bd. dirs.). Office: Univ Maine Sch Law 246 Deering Ave Portland ME 04102

KHOURY, GEORGE GILBERT, printing company executive, sports association executive; b. St. Louis, July 30, 1923; s. George Michael and Dorothy (Smith) K.; m. Colleen E. Khoury Czerny, Apr. 3, 1948; children: Colleen Ann, George Gilbert. Grad., St. Louis U., 1946. V.p. Khoury Bros. Printing, St. Louis, 1946—; exec. dir. George Khoury Assn. Baseball Leagues, Inc., St. Louis, 1967—. Author: (novel) Brothers Baseball Bombshells, 2003. Served with U.S. Army, 1943-45, NATOUSA, MTO. Decorated Purple Heart with oak leaf cluster. Roman Catholic. Office: George Khoury Assn Baseball Leagues 5400 Meramec Bottom Rd Saint Louis MO 63128-4624 Office Phone: 314-849-8900. E-mail: czernyce@msn.com.

KHOURY, KENNETH F., lawyer; b. NY, July 17, 1951; BA, Rutgers Coll., 1972; JD, Fordham U., 1977. Bar: NY 1978, NJ 1979. Assoc. White & Case, 1977—82; sr. counsel THE BOC Group Inc., 1982—83; asst. v.p., assoc. counsel The Continental Corp., 1983—88; sr. v.p., assoc. gen. counsel Shearson-Lehman Bros. Inc., 1988—90; from assoc. gen. counsel to v.p., dep. gen. counsel, sec. Georgia-Pacific Corp., Atlanta, 1990—98, v.p., 1998—, dep. gen. counsel, 1998—, sec., 1998—2004. Office: Georgia Pacific Corp 133 Peachtree St NE Atlanta GA 30303*

KHOURY, PHILIP S., academic administrator; b. Washington, Oct. 15, 1949; s. Shukry E. and Angela Mansur (Jurdak) K.; m. Mary Christina Wilson, Aug. 28, 1980. BA with honors, Trinity Coll., 1971; PhD, Harvard U., 1980. Asst. prof. MIT, Cambridge, 1981-84, assoc. prof., 1984-90, prof., 1990—, assoc. dean Sch. Humanities, Arts, and Social Sci., 1987-90, acting dean, 1990-91, dean, 1991—, Kenan Sahin dean, 2002—. Author: Urban Notables and Arab Nationalism, 1983, Syria and the French Mandate, 1987; co-editor Tribes and State Formation in the Middle East, 1990, The Modern Middle East: A Reader, 1993, 2d edit. 2004, Recovering Beirut: Urban Design and Post-war Reconstruction, 1993; mem. editl. bd. Jour. Interdisciplinary History, 1987-, Hist. Abstracts, 1990-, The Beirut Rev., 1991-93. Trustee Am. U. Beirut, 1997—, vice chmn., 2005; vice chmn. Toynbee Prize Found., 1998—, Trinity Coll, 2000—; bd dirs. World Peace Found., 1999—, chmn., 2004; bd. dirs. Harvard Coop. Soc., 1998-2004. Thomas J. Watson fellow Watson Found., 1971-72; Fulbright scholar, 1976-77; Post-Doctoral Social Sci. Rsch. Coun., 1983-84; Mellon fellow Aspen Inst., 1984-85; Class of 1922 Career Devel. Professorship, MIT, 1984-86. Fellow Am. Acad. Arts and Scis.; mem. AAAS, Am. Hist. Assn. (George Louis Beer Prize 1987), Mid. East Studies Assn. (pres. 1998, dir. 1990-92, 97-2000), Brit. Soc. for Mid. East Studies, Pi Gamma Mu. Avocation: tennis. Office: MIT Office Dean Sch Hum/Arts/Social Scis 77 Massachusetts Ave Cambridge MA 02139-4307 Office Phone: 617-253-3450. Business E-Mail: khoury@mit.edu.

KHOYNEZHAD, ALI, cardiothoracic surgeon, researcher; b. Mashad, Khorasan, Iran, Feb. 11, 1970; s. Reza Khoynezhad and Zhaleh Yousefein; m. Ziba Jalali, Mar. 31, 1998. MD, U. Cologne Coll. Medicine, 1996, PhD, 1998. Diplomate Am. Bd. Surgery, 2004. Instr., prosector anatomy U. Cologne Coll. Medicine, Koeln, Germany, 1992—93; instr. surgery Humboldt-University, Berlin, 1996—98, North Shore University-Long Island Jewish Med. Ctr., New Hyde Park, 2002—03, adminstrv. chief resident gen. surgery, 2002—03; instr. urgery Montefiore Med. Ctr. Affiliated Hosp., Bronx, 2004—05, adminstrv. chief resident cardiothoracic surgery, 2004—. Exec. com. mem. Oper. Rm. Quality Assurance Com., New Hyde Park, NY, 2001—02, Grad. Med. Edn. Com., New Hyde Park, 2002—03, Credentials Com., Bronx, 2004—, Thoracic Surgery Resident Assn., NYC, 2004—; rschr. in field. Recipient First Prize, Murry Friedman Competition, Coll. Surgeons, 2002; E. Ferdinand Sauerbruch Grant in Aid, E. Ferdinand Sauerbruch Competition, 1996-1998. Mem.: ACS (licentiate), Am. Coll. Chest Physicians (licentiate Poster of Distinction award 2002), Iranian AMA (licentiate), Soc. Am. Gastrointestinal and Endoscopic Surgeons (licentiate), So. Med. Assn. (licentiate), Mecklenburg County Med. Soc. (licentiate), Internat. Soc. Heart and Lung Transplantation (licentiate), Cardiothoracic Surgery Network (licentiate), Soc. Thoracic Surgeons (licentiate), German Soc. Thoracic & Cardiovasc. Surgery (licentiate). Avocations: photography, travel. Home: 3636 Waldo Ave Bronx NY 10463 Office: Montefiore Medl Ctr 111 Et 210 St Bronx NY 10467 E-mail: akhoy@lycos.com.

KHOZEIMEH, ISSA, electrical engineer, educator; b. Tehran, Iran, Dec. 25, 1939; came to U.S., 1959; s. Ismail and Zohreh (Alam) K.; m. Nahid Khozeimeh; children: Lili, Nini. BSEE, George Washington U., Washington, 1966; MSEE, 1973, D in Engring., 1984, DSc in Engring. Mgmt., 1993. Registered profl. engr. Jr. engr. Potomac Electric Power Co., Washington, 1967-68; substation engr., 1968-73; design standards engr., 1973-79; sr. engr. substation design, 1979-80; dept. head, chief elec. engr. David Volkert and Assocs., Bethesda, Md., 1980-88; mgr. utilities svcs. divsn. Metro Washington Airports Authority Dulles Internat. Airport, 1988—; prof. engring. and mgmt. U. Md., Balt., 1998—; prof. mgmt. U. Balt., 1999—. Pres. Internat. Mktg. and Consulting Corp., Washington, 1980-82; v.p. Horizon Internat., Washington, 1982-88; pres. Forum Internat. Glen Echo, Md., 1988—; prof. U. Md., Balt., 1998—, U. Balt., 1999—. Author: An Automated Maintenance Management System for International Airports, 1993; contbr. articles to profl. jours. Recipient Sch. of Engring Svcs. award, 1976, Gen. Alumni Assn. Svc. award, 1971, George Washington U., 1976, Engr. Coun. Cert. of Appreciation, 1984, 85, Disting. Svc. award 1986, Disting. Alumni Svc. award George Washington U. Alumni Assn., 1998, Tech. Forum Leadership award, 1999, Outstanding Profl Efforts award Met. Washington Airport Authority, 2000. Mem.: NSPE, IEEE (sr.), DC Council Engring. and Archtl. Socs. (bd. mem. 1999—, v.p. 2004—05, pres. 2005—), Washington Soc. Engrs. (bd. dirs. 1975—, pres. 1995), Md. Soc. Prof. Engrs. (pres. 1995—96, 2002—04, Disting. Sr. Engr. award 1997), Instrument Soc. Am. Republican. Moslem. Avocations: water-skiing, snow skiing, hiking, reading, publishing, lecturing, travel. Home: PO Box 557 Glen Echo MD 20812-0557 Office: Metro Washington Airports Authority Dulles Internat Airport PO Box 17045 Washington DC 20041-7045 Office Phone: 703-572-2830. Business E-Mail: issa.khozeimeh@mwaa.com. E-mail: khozeimeh@hotmail.com.

KHUDYAKOV, IGOR VLADIMIR, research chemist; b. Moscow, June 27, 1949; came to U.S., 1990; s. Vladimir Vassily and Valerie Alexander (Matweev) K.; 1 child, Jane. MS, Moscow State U., 1971; PhD, Russian Acad. Scis., Moscow, 1975, DSc, 1984, diploma as prof., 1991. Rsch. officer, head group Inst. Chem. Physics, Russian Acad. Scis., Moscow, 1976-90; rsch. assoc. chemistry dept. Columbia U., N.Y.C., 1990—. Mem. sci. counsel Russian Acad. Scis., 1987-90. Contbr. articles to profl. jours. Recipient awards for young Russian scientists. Mem. Internat. Union Pure and Applied Chemistry. Russian Orthodox. Achievements include discovery of new type of fast bimolecular reactions in the liquid phase, discovery of a new way of uranium enrichment. Office: Columbia U 116th St and Broadway New York NY 10027

KHUNTIA, DEEPAK, oncologist, radiologist; s. Purna C. and Pravat N. Khuntia; m. Sarita R. Ram, Oct. 6, 1969; children: Saila N., Nikhil R. MD, U. Ill., Chgo., 1999. Diplomate Ill., 1999. Clin. asst. prof. U. Wis., Madison, Wis., 2004—; course dir., neopolastic disease U. of Wis. Med. Sch., Madison, Wis., 2004—. Contbr. articles to profl. jours. Achievements include research in Developments in brain tumors, prostate cancer, and head and neck cancers. Office: Univ Wis 600 Highland Avenue K4/B100 Madison WI 53792 Office Phone: 608-263-8500. Home Fax: 608-263-6197; Office Fax: 608-263-6197. Personal E-mail: khuntia@humonc.wisc.edu.

KHUONG, LOC HUU, corporate financial executive; arrived in U.S., 1975; s. Ba Huu and Le Ngoc Tran Khuong; m. Hanh-Phuoc Khuong. BBA, Loyola U., Chgo., 1984; MBA, U. Phoenix, 1994; PhD, Nova Southeastern U., 2002. Pub. acct. Ernest Freier & Assocs., CPA's, Chgo., 1980—82; internal auditor AB Dick Co., Chgo., 1983—84; audit mgr. Cenco, Inc., Oak Brook, Ill., 1984—86; v.p., fin. Indsl. Wastes/ChemLime, Elizabeth, NJ, 1986—89; v.p. fin. Chemstar Lime Corp., Phoenix, 1990—94; dir. bus. analysis Chem. Lime, Ft. Worth, 1995—98; asst. to the CEO Chem. Lime Inc., Ft. Worth, 1998—. Adj. prof. DeVry U., Irving, Tex., 1997—2001; cons. Irvine Biomed., Telcom Netriz, Calif., 1998—99, Chambers Interests, Tex., 2000. Mem.: Nat. Lime Assn., Acad. Mgmt., Am. Mgmt. Assn., Sigma Beta Delta Internat. Avocations: writing, golf, astronomy.

KHURI, FADLO RAJA, oncologist, educator; b. Boston, Sept. 13, 1963; s. Raja Najib and Soumaya Makdisi Khuri; m. Lamya Raja Tannous, June 15, 1991; children: Raja, Layla, Rayya. Student, Am. U. of Beirut, 1982; BS, Yale U., 1985; MD, Columbia U., 1989. Cert. bd. cert. diplomate. Intern in internal medicine Boston City Hosp., Boston U., 1989—90; resident Boston City Hosp., 1990—92; fellow in hematology and med. oncology Tufts-New Eng. Med. Ctr., Boston, 1992—95; instr. medicine U. Tex. M.D. Anderson Cancer Ctr., Houston, 1995—96, asst. prof., 1996—2001, assoc. prof., 2001—02; assoc. dir. clin. and tranlational rsch., prof. hematology, oncology, medicine, pharmacology and otolaryngology, Blomeyer chair translational rsch. Winship Cancer Inst., Emory U., Atlanta, 2002—. 1st author: clin. investigation Nature Medicine, 2000, Journal of the National Cancer Institute, 1997, Journal of Clinical Oncology, 2000. Recipient Career Devel. award, Am. Cancer Soc., 1996; scholar R.G. Haddad scholar, 1985—89; grantee, NIH, Dept. of Def., 1996—. Mem.: Eastern Coop. Oncology Group (chmn. cancer control and prevention com. 2004—), Radiation Therapy Oncology Group (chmn. chemoprevention com. 1998—2002), Am. Soc. Clin. Oncology, Am. Assn. Cancer Rsch. Office: Emory U Winship Cancer Inst Hematology and Oncology 1365 Clifton Rd Bldg C Atlanta GA 30322 Office Phone: 404-778-1900. Business E-Mail: fkhuri@emory.edu.

KHURI, NICOLA NAJIB, physicist, researcher; b. Beirut, May 27, 1933; came to U.S., 1959, naturalized, 1970; s. Najib N. and Odette (Joujou) K.; m. Elizabeth Anne Tyson, Dec. 9, 1955; children: Suzanne Odette, Najib Nicholas. B.A with high distinction, Am. U. Beirut, 1952; PhD, Princeton U., 1957. Asst. prof. Am. U. Beirut, 1957-58, 60-61, assoc. prof., 1961-62; mem. Inst. Advanced Study, Princeton U., 1959-60, 62-63; vis. assoc. prof. Columbia, 1963-64; assoc. prof. Rockefeller U., 1964-68, prof., 1968—. Cons. Brookhaven Nat. Lab., 1963-73; mem. Carnegie Panel on U.S. Security and Arms Control, 1981-83; vis. scientist European Ctr. for Nuclear Research, Geneva, Centre d'Etudes Nucléaires, Saclay, France, Max Planck Inst. für Physik, Munich, Fed. Republic Germany. Contbr. articles to profl. jours. Trustee Am. U. Beirut. Fellow Am. Phys. Soc.; mem. Council on Fgn. Relations. Clubs: Century (N.Y.C.). Office: Rockefeller U New York NY 10021 Home: # 6B 433 E 51st St New York NY 10022-6472

KHUTORYANSKY, NAUM M., mathematician, educator; b. Kiev, Ukraine, Apr. 9, 1946; s. Mark Naumovich Khutoryansky and Genya Davidovna Tsipenyuk; m. Dina G. Baskin, July 19, 1968; 1 child, Natalie. BS, MS in applied math., Gorky State U., Nizhny Novgorod, Russia, 1964—70, PhD in applied math., 1971—74; DSc, Supreme Attestation Commn. of the USSR, Moscow, 1989—89. Jr. scientist Gorky State U., Nizhny Novgorod, Russia, 1975—76, sr. scientist, 1976—84, sci. dir., rsch. dept., 1984—93; rsch. assoc. prof. Drexel U., Phila., 1994—2000; sr. statistician Novo Nordisk Pharmaceuticals, Inc., Princeton, NJ, 2000—01, prin. statistician, 2001—03, assoc. dir., 2003—. Adj. prof. Gorky State U., Nizhny Novgorod, Russia, 1976—92; vis. scientist Linkoping U., Sweden, 1991; adj. assoc. prof. Drexel U., Phila., 1995—2000. Author: (book) Boundary Element Method in Solid Mechanics. Recipient Silver Medal, Exhbn. of Nation's Achievements of the USSR, 1989; grantee, Russian Found. for Basic Rsch., 1992. Mem.: Soc. of Indsl. and Applied Math., Am. Statis. Assn. Achievements include research in new representation formulas and fundamental solutions of piezoelectricity and viscoelasticity; development of new approaches in boundary integral equations of solid and fluid mechanics; nw statistical imputation methods for incomplete longitudinal datan; research in fracture mechanics for piezoelectric bodies. Office: Novo Nordisk Pharmaceuticals Inc 100 College West Rd Princeton NJ 08540 Office Phone: 609-987-5812. Business E-Mail: nakh@novonordask.com.

KHWAJA, SHAMSUDDIN, neurologist, consultant; b. Hyderabad, Pakistan, Mar. 3, 1957; came to U.S., 1991; s. Mianji and Rehmat Bai (Sunesra) K.; m. Farida Khwaja, Apr. 17, 1981; children: Beenish, Misbah, Saqib. MBBS, Liaquat Med. Coll., Jamshoro, Pakistan, 1982. Diplomate Am. Bd. Psychiatry and Neurology, Am. Bd. Electrodiagnostic Medicine. Instr. anatomy Liaquat Med. Coll., 1983-87; registrar in medicine Liaquat Med. Coll. Hosp., 1987-91; intern in internal medicine Wayne State U., Detroit, 1992-93; resident in neurology Henry Ford Hosp., Detroit, 1993-96, fellow in clin. neurophysiology, 1996-98, fellow in movement disorder, 1998, assoc. staff clin. neurophysiology EMG lab., 1997-98; neurologist Mexico (Mo.) Med. Specialists L.C., 1999—2004, Killeen Neurology PA, Tex., 2005—. Mem. AMA, Am. Acad. Neurology (scholar 1995). Office: Killeen Neurology 2105 South Clear Creek Rd Killeen TX 76549 E-mail: khwaja@ktis.net.

KIAMIE, DON ALBERT NAJEEB, accountant; b. Bronx, N.Y., Jan. 23, 1944; s. Samie and Carmen (Torres) K.; m. Olive F. Howell, Sept. 9, 1972; children: Matthew, Marie, Melinda. BS, Fordham U., 1965; MBA, NYU, 1967. CPA, N.Y. Sr. acct. Peat, Marwick, Mitchell & Co., N.Y.C., 1967-70; asst. mgr. stds. acctg. Gen. Foods Corp., N.Y.C., 1970-77; mgr. fin. reporting/planning Qwip Sys. divsn. Exxon Corp., N.Y.C., 1977-79; asst. controller NBC, N.Y.C., 1980-83; exec. v.p., CFO Windsor Mgmt. Corp. and Kiamie Related Properties, 1983—; also bd. dirs.; prof. NYU Grad. Sch., 1998—. Adj. prof. NYU Grad. Sch. Cont. Profl. Studies. Mgr. Lions Babe Ruth Club, 1967-71; soccer and baseball coach Shrub Oak Athletic Club, 1983-87; pres. Pelham Babe RuthLeague,d 1970-71, Pelham Young Rep. Club, 1970-71, v.p. Holy Spirit Parish Coun., 1977-78, chmn. teen group, 1977-78, chmn. fin. com., 1977-78; eucharistic min., dir. youth music group Holy Roary Ch., 1988—; soccer coach AYSO, 1988—; leader GOP 35th Dist. Town of Mt. Pleasant, N.Y., 1991—. Mem. AICPA, N.Y. Soc. CPAs (real estate com. chair 2001—, dir., officer, com. chair Westchester chpt. 1998—, pres.-elect Westchester chpt. 2003-04, pres. 2004—). Roman Catholic. Home: 21 Main St Hawthorne NY 10532-2017 Office Phone: 212-213-2112. Personal E-mail: donalbert@mindspring.com.

KIANG, ASSUMPTA (AMY KIANG), brokerage house executive; b. Beijing, Aug. 15, 1939; came to U.S., 1962; d. Pei-yu and Yu-Jean (Liu) Chao; m. Wan-lin Kiang, Aug. 14, 1965; 1 child, Eliot Y. BA, Nat. Taiwan U., 1960; MS, Marywood Coll., Scranton, Pa., 1964; MBA, Calif. State U., Long Beach, 1977. Cert. fin. mgr. Data programmer IBM World Trade, N.Y.C., 1963; libr. East Cleve. Pub. Libr., 1964-68; lectr. Nat. Taiwan U., Taipei, 1971-73; reference libr. U.S. Info. Svc., Taipei, 1971-74; v.p., sr. fin. advisor Merrill Lynch, Santa Ana, Calif., 1977—, v.p., sr. fin. cons. Costa Mesa, Calif., 1996—. Author numerous rsch. reports in field. Founder Pan Pacific Performing Arts Inc., Orange County, Calif., 1987; pres. women league Calif. State. U., Long Beach, 1980-82. Mem. AAUW (treas. Newport-Costa Mesa br. 1996—), Chinese Bus. Assn. Soc. Calif. (chmn. 1987—, v.p. 1986-87), Chinese Am. Profl. Women's League (treas. 1993, pres. 1997—), Pacific Rim Investment and trade Assn. (vice-chair 1994-96), U.C.I. Chancellor's Club, Old Ranch Country Club, Ctr. Club (bd. dirs. exec. women's coun. Orange County 1998—). Democrat. Roman Catholic. Office: Merrill Lynch 650 Town Center Dr Ste 500 Costa Mesa CA 92626-1905 Office Phone: 714-429-2806. Personal E-mail: amykiang@aol.com. Business E-Mail: AKiang@pclient.ml.com.

KIANG, CHING-HWA, chemical engineering educator; b. Taipei, Taiwan, Jan. 20, 1965; came to U.S., June 24, 1988; d. Song Kiang and Pi-Ying Huang; m. Michael William Deem, Sept. 2, 1995. BSChemE, Nat. Taiwan U., Taipei, 1987; PhD in Chemistry, Calif. Inst. Tech., 1995. Rsch. asst. Inst. Atomic and Molecular Scis. Academia Sinica, Taipei, Taiwan, 1987-88; postdoctoral assoc. dept. Physics MIT, 1995-96; vis. asst. prof. dept. Chemistry and Biochemistry UCLA, 1996—99, cram tchr.-scholar dept. Chemistry and Biochemistry, 1996—99, rsch. asst., physicist Dept. Physics and Astronomy, 2000—02; asst. prof. dept. physics and astronomy Rice U., Houston, 2002—. Grantee NIH, 1998, U. Calif. Energy, 1998. Mem. Am. Phys. Soc., Sigma Xi. Achievements include patent in field. Office: Dept Physics and Astronomy Rice U 6100 Main St MS 61 Houston TX 77005 Office Phone: 713-348-4130. E-mail: chkiang@rice.edu.

KIANG, NELSON YUAN-SHENG, medical educator; b. Wuxi, China, July 6, 1929; came to U.S, 1934; naturalized, 1961; m. 1957, 1976. PhB, U. Chgo., 1947, PhD in biopsychology, 1955; MD (hon.), U. Geneva, 1981; MS (hon.), Harvard U., 1984. Rsch. asst. Eaton-Peabody Lab. Mass. Eye and Ear Infirmary, Boston, 1957-62, dir., 1962—96; staff mem. rsch. lab. electronics MIT, Boston, 1955—96, Eaton-Peabody prof. dept. brain and cognitive scis., 1986—96, Eaton-Peabody prof. health scis. and tech., 1993—96; neurophysiologist, neurology svc. Mass. Gen. Hosp., Boston, 1977—96; prof. physiology, dept. otology and laryngology Harvard Med. Sch., Boston, 1984—96; emeritus on all appts., 1996—. Mem. communicative scis. study sect. NIH, 1968-72, behavior and neurosci. study sect. NIH, 1985-89; mem. Com. Hearing Bioacoustics and Biomechanics NAS/NRC, Collegium Otorhinology-Laryngology Amiticiam Sacrum, Deafness Rsch. Found, Internat. Brain Rsch. Orgn.; hon. prof. Zhejiang U., Hangzhou, China, 1997, Peking Union Med. Coll. of Qinghua U., Beijing, 2001, Sun Yat-sen Med. U., Guangzhou, China, 2001; adv. prof. Fudan U., Shanghai, China, 1997; hon. advisor Chinese Med. Assn. Recipient Beltone award, 1968. Mem. AAAS, Soc. Neurosci., Am. Physiol. Soc., Acoustical Soc. Am., Am. Otology Soc., N.Y. Acad. Sci., Am. Acad. Arts and Scis., Assn. for Rsch. in Otolaryngology, Eastern Psychol. Assn., History of Sci. Soc., Philosophy of Sci. Assn., Royal Soc. Medicine, Psychonomic Soc., Triglav Cir., Sigma Xi. Rsch. in physiology of auditory and other sensory systems; relation of brain to behavior. Office: Eaton Peabody Lab MA Eye & Ear Infirmary 243 Charles St Boston MA 02114 Business E-Mail: bnk@epl.meei.harvard.edu.

KIAT-AMNUAY, SUDARAT, prosthodontist, educator; d. Sompong and Suwanna Kiat-amnuay; m. Kwai Wa Cheng, Feb. 14, 2004; 1 child, Natalie Kiat-amnuay Cheng. DDS with 2d Class Hons., Khon Kaen U., Thailand, 1994; MS in Prosthodontics, U. Louisville, 1999. Cert. in maxillofacial prosthetics and dental oncology U. Tex. M. D. Anderson Cancer Ctr., 2000, diplomate Am. Bd. Prosthodontics. Instr. faculty dentistry Khon Kaen U., Thailand, 1994—2000; adj. asst. prof. Sch. Dentistry U. Louisville, 1999—; vis. investigator Houston Biomaterials Rsch. Ctr., 2000—02; asst. prof. U. Tex. Dental Br., Houston, 2001—; asst. prof. M.D. Anderson Cancer Ctr., U. Tex., 2004—. Contbr. articles to profl. jours., chapters to books. Recipient 3d Pl. winner, poster presentation rsch. competition, Internat. Congress of Maxillofacial Prosthetics, 2000, Kosair Charities award, Kosair Children Hosp., 1997—99; grantee, Khon Kaen U., 1993, U. Louisville, 1998—2002, U. Tex. M. D. Anderson Cancer Ctr., 1999, v.p. rsch., U. Louisville, 2002, Nat. Inst. Dental and Craniofacial Rsch., NIH, 2003—, U. Tex. Health Sci. Ctr., Houston, 2004—05; scholar, U. Louisville, 1998. Fellow: Am. Acad. Maxillofacial Prosthetics (mem. materials and devices com. 2002, mem. rsch. com. 2003, 1st pl. poster presentation rsch. 2001), Internat. Congress Oral Implantologists, Am. Coll. Prosthodontists (diplomate); mem.: Am. Anaplastology Assn., Minority Faculty Assn., Assn. Women Faculty, Acad. Laser Dentistry, Internat. Assn. Dental Rsch., Am. Coll. Oral Implantology, Am. Assn. Dental Rsch., Phi Delta, Sigma Xi. Office: Univ of Tex Dental Br 6516 M D Anderson Blvd Suite # 493 Houston TX 77030 Office Phone: 713-500-4194. Office Fax: 713-500-4108. E-mail: sudarat.kiat-amnuay@uth.tmc.edu.

KIBLER, WILLIAM BENJAMIN, orthopedist, surgeon; b. Kingsport, Tenn., Sept. 29, 1946; s. Jacob B. and Della M. Kibler; m. Elizabeth Fay Mugler, June 20, 1970; children: B. Chase, David. BA, Vanderbilt U., 1968, MD, 1972. Cert. Am. Bd. Orthopedic Surgery, 1978. Intern, surgery Parkland Hosp., Dallas, 1972—73; resident, orthop. surgery Vanderbilt U., Nashville, 1973—77; staff physician Lexington (Ky.) Clinic, 1977—; head of sect. Lexington (Ky.) Clinic Sect. of Orthop. Surgery, 1998—; med. dir. Lexington (Ky.) Clinic Sports Medicine Ctr., 1984—. Bd. dirs. Am. Coll. of Sports medicine, Indpls., 1990—96; pres. Soc. Tennis Medicine and Sci., N.Y.C., 1990—99; lectr. various national and internat. orthop. soc. Author: The Athletic Preparticipation Exam, 1990, Functional Rehabilitation of Sports Injuries, 1998; contbr. articles various profl. jours. Named Best Dr. of Am., N.Y.C., 2004; recipient Citation award, Am. Coll. of Sports Medicine, 1998, Plagenhof Sci. award, Profl. Tennis Registry, 1998. Fellow: Am. Acad. Orthop. Surgeons; mem.: Am. Orthopedic Assn., Am. Coll. Sports Medicine, Am. Shoulder and Elbow Surgeons, Am. Orthop. Soc. for Sports Medicine. Methodist. Avocations: sports, travel, hiking, bible study. Home: 240 Mkt St Lexington KY 40507 Office: Lexington Clinic 1221 S Broadway Lexington KY 40504 Office Phone: 859-258-8575. Office Fax: 859-258-8562. Personal E-mail: wkibler@aol.com. Business E-Mail: bkibl@lexclin.com.

KIBLER, WILLIAM WESTCOTT, French language and literature educator; b. Rochester, N.Y., Jan. 22, 1942; s. Charles J. and Ruth Isabel (Westcott) K.; m. Nancy Irene Schwan, June 29, 1968; children: Mary Alis, Charlotte. AB, Notre Dame U., 1963; MA, U. N.C., 1966, PhD, 1968. Asst. prof. French U. Ark., Fayetteville, 1967-69, U. Tex., Austin, 1969-73, assoc. prof., 1973-81, prof., 1981-83, Superior Oil-Linward Shivers Centennial prof. medieval studies, 1983—. Author: An Introduction to Old French, 1984; author, editor: Chrétien de Troyes' Lancelot, 1981, Chrétien de Troyes' Yvain, 1985; co-author: Lion de Bourges, 1980, Guillaume de Machaut, Judgement du roy de Behaigne and Remede de Fortune, 1988; editor: Eleanor of Aquitaine: Patron and Politician, 1976. Mem. South Cen. MLA (pres. 1986-87), Medieval Acad. Am. (councillor 1993-96), Société Rencesvals (pres. 1978-82, editor-in-chief Am.-Can. br. jour. Olifant 1986-91). Episcopalian. Avocations: squash, stamp collecting/philately, gardening. Office: The Univ of Tex at Austin Dept of French & Italian Austin TX 78712

KIBRICK, ANNE, retired nursing educator, dean; b. Palmer, Mass., June 1, 1919; d. Martin and Christine (Grigas) Karlon; m. Sidney Kibrick, June 16, 1949; children: Joan, John. RN, Worcester (Mass.) Hahnemann Hosp., 1941; BS, Boston U., 1945; MA, Columbia Tchrs. Coll., 1948; EdD, Harvard U., 1958; LHD (hon.), St. Joseph's Coll., Windham, Maine, 1973. Asst. edn. dir. Cushing VA Hosp., Framingham, Mass., 1948—49; asst. prof. nursing Simmons Coll., Boston, 1949—55; dir. grad. div. Boston U. Sch. Nursing, 1958—63, dean, 1963—68, prof., 1968—70; chmn. dept. nursing Boston Coll. Grad. Sch. Arts and Sci., 1970—74; founding chmn. Sch. Nursing Boston State Coll., 1974—82; founding dean Sch. Nursing U. Mass., Boston, 1974—88, prof., 1988—93, prof. emeritus, 1993—. Adv. coun. Coll. Nursing and Health Scis. U. Mass., Boston, 2005—. Mem. editl. bd. Mass. Jour. Cmty. Health. Mem. Brookline Town Meeting, 1995—2000; mem. nat. adv. bd. Hadassah Nurses Coun., 1996—; bd. dirs. Brookline Mental Health Assn., Met. chpt. ARC, Children's Ctr. Brookline and Greater Boston, Inc., 1984—89, Boston Health Care for Homeless, 1988—90, Landy-Kaplan Nurses Coun., 1992—, treas., 1994—96. Named to, Nursing Edn. Alumni Assn. Tchr.'s Coll., Columbia U. Hall of Fame, 1999. Fellow: Am. Acad. Nursing; mem.: Inst. of Medicine of NAS, Mass. Blueprint 2000, Mass. Orgn. Elder Ams. (bd. dirs. 1988—2000), Mass. Med. Soc. (postgrad. med. inst. 1983—96, bd. dirs. 1983—96, exec. com. 1989—96), Nat. Acads. of Practice, Mass. Nurses Found. (v.p. 1983—86), AIDS Internat. Info. Found. (founding mem. 1985), Mass. Nurses Assn. (dir. 1982—86, charter inductee to Hall of Fame 2000), Nat. Mass. League Nursing (pres. 1971—73), ANA, Pi Lambda Theta, Sigma Theta Tau. Home: # 312 130 Seminary Ave Auburndale MA 02466 E-mail: akibrick@lasell.edu.

KICE, JOHN EDWARD, engineer, educator, consultant; b. Wichita, Kans., Sept. 11, 1949; s. Jack and Ruth (Jones) Kice; m. Susan Pappas; children: Adam, Jason. BS in Flour Milling Sci. and Bus. Adminstrn., Kans. State U., 1972; BS in Engring., Wichita State U., 1980; grad. diploma, Glasgow Caladonian U., 2000. Registered profl. engr., Kans. Design engr. Kice Industries, Wichita, 1973-84, v.p. engring., 1984—2003; lectr. Kans. State U., 2003—. Lectr. Wichita State U., 1980-86. Recipient Disting. Svc. award Assn. Operative Millers, 1988, 90, 92, 94, 96. Achievements include patents for Positive Displacement Air Pump, Reciprocating Airlock Valve, Rotary Mixing Damper, Blade Type Mixing Damper, Conveying Air Velocity Control, Pneumatic Conveying Injector, Machinery Access. Office Phone: 785-341-5880.

KICH, MARTIN , education educator; b. Scranton, Pa., Aug. 4, 1955; s. George and Mary Patricia (Poskonski) Kich; m. Sandra Jean Sharkazy, May 11, 1985; 1 child, Michael Vincent. BA in english and history, U. of Scranton, 1973—78; MA, Lehigh U., 1978—89, PhD. Tchg. fellow Lehigh U., Bethlehem, Pa., 1978—83; adj. asst. prof. Cedar Crest Coll., Allentown, Pa., 1983—90, Northampton County Area C.C., Bethlehem, Pa., 1983—90; adj. asst. prof., english Lehigh U., Bethlehem, Pa., 1983—90, e.w. fairchild rsch. fellow in am. studies, 1984—85; asst. prof., english Wright State U.-Lake Campus, Celina, Ohio, 1990—96, assoc. prof., english, 1996—2000; adj. asst. prof. Allentown Coll. of St. Francis De Sales, Pa., 1990; full prof., english Wright State U.-Lake Campus, 2001—. Author: (book) Western American Novelists, (literary reference book) An Encyclopedia of Emerging Writers; contbr. poems to jours., to books. Recipient Distinguished Svc. award, Assn. for the Univ. Regional Campuses of Ohio, 2000. Mem.: MLA, Wallace Stevens Soc., Norman Mailer Soc., James Purdy Soc. (bd. mem., web-page coord.), Western Am. Lit., Two-Year Coll. English Assn., Conf. on Coll. Composition and Commn., Nat. Coun. of Teachers of English, Midwest MLA, Ohio Assn. of Two-Year Colleges, Assn. for the U. Regional Campuses of Ohio (pres., newsletter editor). Office: Wright State University-Lake Campus 7600 State Route 703 Celina OH 45822 Office Phone: 419-586-0374. E-mail: martin.kich@wright.edu.

KICH, ROLF, communications scientist, consultant; b. Panambi, Rio Grande do Sul, Brazil, Sept. 25, 1956; s. Elio and Margarethe K.; m. Catherine Nguyen, May 3, 2003. BSEE, Calif. State U., Fresno, 1981. Sr. scientist (level 7) Boeing Satellite Systems, El Segundo, Calif., 1999—; sr. scientist (level 6) Hughes Space Comm., El Segundo, Calif., 1994—99, scientist, 1989—94, sr. tech. staff, 1987—89; supr. Hughes Aircraft, Space and Comm., El Segundo, Calif., 1984—87. Cons. microwave component design Kich Industries, Redondo Beach, Calif., 2002—. Scoutmaster Boy Scouts Am., Clovis, Calif., 1978—79, leader Irvine, Calif., 2001—03. Republican. Achievements include patents for communication satellite aluminum high power filter, one of the enabling technologies used on Direct TV home broadcast satellite transmission; 22 issued patents in the microwave component field; patents pending for electronically switchable ferrite power divider. Avocations: photography, hiking, backpacking, woodworking. Home: 1624 Harper Ave Redondo Beach CA 90278 Personal E-mail: rolf@kichindustries.com.

KICKISH, MARGARET ELIZABETH, elementary school educator; b. Atlantic City, Nov. 30, 1949; d. James Bernard and Margaret Elizabeth (Egan) Parlett; m. Robert Anthony Kickish, June 30, 1973; children: Eileen, Kathleen, Robert Jr. BS, Franciscan U., 1971; MEd, Coll. NJ, 1977. Cert. elem. tchr., learning disabilities tchr. cons. Tchr. Our Lady Star of the Sea Sch., Atlantic City, 1971-75, Weymouth Twp. Elem. Sch., Dorothy, NJ, 1975-89; curriculum coord. Port Republic (NJ) Sch., 1990-91; tchr. Brigantine (NJ) Bd. Edn., 1991-94, supr. curriculum and instrn., 1995—. Cognetics coord. St. Joseph Sch., Somers Point, NJ, 1989—. Treas. PTA, Somers Point, 1987—89, pres., 1989—90; asst. coach Somers Point Softball Assn., 1991—; rec. sec. Parents Orgn. Mainland Regional HS, 2001—; mem. choir St. Joseph Ch., Somers Point, 1985—. Mem.: ASCD, NEA, AAUW, Assn. Learning Cons., Coun. Exceptional Children, Prins. and Suprs. Assn., NJ Edn. Assn., South Jersey Irish Cultural Soc., Seashore Mother of Twins Club, Phi Delta Kappa (exec. v.p. 2005), Delta Zeta, Kappa Delta Pi. Democrat. Roman Catholic. Avocations: swimming, bicycling, reading, travel, crafts. Home: 526 9th St Somers Point NJ 08244-1458 Office: Brigantine Bd of Edn 301 E Evans Blvd Brigantine NJ 08203-3424 Office Phone: 609-266-2877. E-mail: mskick@aol.com.

KIDD, A. PAUL, health facility administrator, government agency administrator; b. Orange, N.J., Nov. 1, 1939; s. Arthur T. Kidd and Virginia V. McMullen; m. Penelope Kinsey, Mar. 11, 1961; children— Margaret, Lawrence, William, Anne BA, Rutgers U., 1961; MA, George Washington U., 1973. Personnel specialist VA Med. Ctr., Lyons, N.J., 1962-63, personnel specialist Pitts., 1963-66; employee relations specialist VA Central Office, Washington, 1966-71; assoc. hosp. dir. trainee VA Med. Ctr., Washington, 1971-73, assoc. dir. Beckley, W.Va., 1973-75, Temple, Tex., 1975-77, East Orange, N.J., 1977-80, med. ctr. dir. Huntington, W.Va., 1980-83, Lyons, N.J., 1983-96. Bd. dirs. W. Va. Health Systems Agy., Charleston, 1980-82, W. Va. State Health Coordinating Coun., Charleston, 1980-83, Ctrl. Jersey Health Systems Agy., Princeton, N.J., 1983-90. Bd. dirs. Mountaineer Family Health Plan, Beckley, 1973-75; med. ednl. and rehab. coun. Marshall U., Huntington, 1980-83; mem., v.p. No. N.J. Fed. Exec. Bd., Newark, 19873-86, chmn., 1987-89, 92-95; coach mcpl. soccer league. Fellow Am. Coll. Health Care Execs.; mem. Sr. Exec. Service, Phi Beta Kappa Avocations: golf, painting, horticulture. Home: 1110 Veronica St Port Charlotte FL 33952-1147

KIDD, JAMES MARION, III, allergist, immunologist, educator; b. Baton Rouge, Dec. 15, 1950; s. James Marion, Jr. and Germaine Elizabeth (Hunt) Kidd; children: Mackenzie Elizabeth, Katherine Anne. MD, La. State U., 1976. Diplomate Am. Bd. Allergy and Immunology, lic. physician La., Fla., Wis. Resident physician La. State U. Sch. Medicine, New Orleans, 1977—79; rsch. fellow Med. Coll. Wis., Milw., 1980-82; pvt. practice in allergy and immunology Allergy, Asthma, and Immunology Clinic, Baton Rouge, 1982—; clin. asst., prof. medicine La. Sch. Medicine, New Orleans, 1982—; clin. asst., prof. community medicine and pub. health Tulane U. Sch. Medicine, New Orleans, 1992—2003. Dir. Baton Rouge Pollen Counting Sta., Nat. Allergy Bur. Fellow: ACP, Baton Rouge Allergy Soc. (pres. 1990—95), La. Allergy Soc. (pres. 1989—90, exec. sec.-treas. 1992—96), Royal Soc. Medicine (U.K.), Am. Acad. Allergy and Immunology, Rotary (Paul Harris fellow). Office: James M Kidd III MD 8017 Picardy Ave Baton Rouge LA 70809-3538 Fax: 225-768-7642. E-mail: drjmkidd3@aol.com.

KIDD, JASON, professional basketball player; b. San Francisco, Mar. 23, 1973; m. Joumana Kidd; 3 children; 1 child. Student, U. Calif., 1992—94. Guard Dallas Mavericks, 1994—96, Phoenix Suns, 1996—2001; player NJ Nets, 2002—. Mem. men's Olympic Basketball team (Gold medal), 2000. Founder Jason Kidd Found., Jason Kidd Basketball Scholarship Fund. Named Pac-10 Player of Yr., 1993—94, Nat. Freshman of Yr., The Sporting News and USA Today, 1993—94, Co-rookie of the Yr. (with Grant Hill), 1994—95; named to NBA All-star Game, 1996, 1998, 2000—04, All-NBA 1st team, 1999—2002, 1st team All-Defensive, 1999, 2001—02, 2nd team All-Defensive, 2000; recipient Gold medal, U.S. Men's Olympic Basketball team, 2000. Achievements include Led NBA in Assists, 1999-2001, 2003. Avocations: R&B music, movies, basketball. Office: New Jersey Nets 390 Murray Hill Parkway East Rutherford NJ 07073

KIDD, LOVETTA MONZA, music educator; b. Anniston, Ala., Jan. 13, 1943; d. Andrew Jackson and Velma Mildred (Duke) Traywick; m. Everett Wayne Kidd, Dec. 20, 1961 (dec. Dec. 1998); children: Michelle Kidd Belindo, Andy, David. Student, Okla. Coll. for Women, 1961-62, Southwestern Okla. State U., 1982-83. Pvt. piano tchr., Eva, Okla., 1967-69, Sickles, Okla., 1970-71, Dibble, Okla., 1971-78, Anadarko, Okla., 1979—. Pianist First Bapt. Ch., Anadarko, 1980's. Sec. Okla. Conservative Com., Norman, 1994-95; vice chmn. Caddo County (Okla.) Rep. party, 1995-97, chmn., 1997-99; alt. del. Nat. Rep. Convention, San Diego, 1996. Mem. Okla. Fedn. Rep. Women, Concerned Women for Am., Anadarko Eagle Forum (founder, pres. 1994—), Okla.'s First Ladies, Gen. Fedn. Women's Clubs Philomathic Club (sec. 1996-98, v.p. 1998—), Okla. Fedn. Music Clubs (dist. Gold Cup chmn. 1993—), Musical Key Club (founder, pres. 1981—). Avocations: reading, gardening, needlepoint, painting, drawing. Home: 701 W Alabama Ave Anadarko OK 73005-4636

KIDDER, C. ROBERT, food products executive; b. 1943; BSIE, U. Mich., 1966; MS, Iowa State U., 1968. With Ford Motor Co., Detroit, 1968-69, McKinsey & Co., N.Y.C., 1972-78, Dart Industries, 1978-80, Duracell Europe, 1980-81, Duracell Internat. Inc., 1981-95, pres., CEO, 1988-95, past chmn., CEO; chmn., CEO Borden, Inc., Columbus, Ohio, 1995—. Dir. Morgan Stanley. Bd. trustees Ohio U., 2003—. With USN, 1969—72. Office: Borden Inc 180 E Broad St Columbus OH 43215-0003*

KIDDER, CATHY, elementary school educator; b. Little Rock, Feb. 22, 1968; d. Elza Guy and Cathy Lucille Kirkwood; m. Robert A. Kidder, Mar. 19, 1988; children: Matthew Kyle, Justin Michael. BA, La. State U., 1999. Cert. elem. tchr. La. Bd. Elem. and Secondary Edn., 1999. Elem. tchr. Bossier Parish Sch. Bd., La., 2000—. Pres. Meadowview PTA, Bossier City, 2004—. Mem.: NEA. Baptist. Avocations: reading, cross stitch. Home: 1207 Wisteria St Bossier City LA 71111 Office: Meadowview Elem Sch 4315 Shed Rd Bossier City LA 71111

KIDDER, FRED DOCKSTATER, retired lawyer; b. Cleve., May 22, 1922; s. Howard Lorin and Virgina (Milligan) K.; m. Eleanor (Hap) Kidder; children— Fred D. III, Barbara Anne Donelson, Jeanne Louise Haffeman. BS with distinction, U. Akron, 1948; JD, Case Western Res. U., 1950. Bar: Ohio 1950, Tex. 1985, U.S. Dist. Ct. (no. dist.) Ohio 1950, U.S. Dist. Ct. (no. dist.) Tex. 1985. Assoc. Arter & Hadden and predecessors, Cleve., 1950-79, ptnr., 1960-79, Jones Day and predecessors, Cleve., 1980-89, regional mng. ptnr. Tex., 1985-86; gen. counsel Lubrizol Corp., Cleve., 1989-92, spl. counsel, 1993—2003; ret., 2003. Contbr. articles to profl. jours. Trustee Ohio Found. Ind. Colls., 2004—; former mem. Cleve. Growth Assn., Shaker Heights Citizens Com., Citizens League Cleve.; past pres. Estate Planning Coun.; past co-chmn. bd. trustees Lake Erie Coll.; past bd. trustees, v.p., Alzheimer's Assn., Cleve.; trustee, sec. Cleve. Sight Ctr.; trustee Bus. Advisors Cleve.; past alumni coun. U. Akron; past. corp. coun. Dallas Mus. Art; past pres. Case Western Reserve U. Law Sch. Alumni Assn.; past chmn. Shaker Heights Recreation Bd. Mem. ABA, Tex. Bar Assn., Ohio State Bar Assn., Estate Planning Coun. (past pres.), Blue Coats, Soc. Benchers (past chmn.), Country Club, Cleve. Skating Club, Tax Club Cleve. (past pres.), Order of Coif, Ct. of Nisi Prius (former judge), Pepper Pike Club (past sec.), Phi Eta Sigma, Beta Delta Psi, Phi Sigma Alpha, Phi Delta Theta, Phi Delta Phi. Office: Lubrizol Foundation Wickliffe OH 44092-2298

KIDDER, GEORGE HOWELL, lawyer; b. Boston, June 14, 1925; s. Henry Purkitt and Julia Edwards (Howell) K.; m. Ellen Windom Warren, Aug. 17, 1946 (dec. May 1956); children: Susan Warren, George Howell, Stephen Wells; m. Priscilla Peele Hunnewell, Sept. 3, 1958 (dec. Nov. 1993); children: Priscilla Hunnewell, Timothy Hurd, Peter Arnold; m. Nancy D. Kidder, June 3, 1995. Grad., St. Mark's Sch., Southborough, Mass., 1943; student Navy V-12 program, Williams Coll., 1943-44; B in Naval Sci., Tufts Coll., 1945; LLB, Harvard, 1950; DD (hon.), Episcopal Div. Sch., 1987. Bar: Mass. 1951. With Office Gen. Counsel CIA, 1952-54, 1950-52; assoc. Hemenway & Barnes, 1950—52, 1954—55, ptnr., 1956-97, of counsel, 1997—. Mem. panel neutral mediators and arbitrators Jud. Arbitration and Mediation Svc./Endispute, 1997—. Mem. dean's adv bd. Harvard Law Sch., 2001—; chair exec. coun. divsn. sleep medicine Harvard Med. Sch., 1999—; trustee Episcopal Divinity Sch., Cambridge, Mass., 1967—86, 1998—, pres. bd. trustees, 1977—86, hon. trustee, 1986—98; chancellor Episcopal Diocese of Mass., 1988—, dir., Trustees of Donations; trustee St. Mark's Sch., 1959—84, pres. bd. trustees, 1974—84; trustee Fenn Sch., Concord, 1956—77, pres. bd. trustees, 1960—73; trustee Concord Acad., 1963—78, pres. bd. trustees, 1971—78; trustee Boston Symphony Orch., 1977—94, pres. bd. trustees, 1987—94, life trustee, 1994—; trustee Children's Med. Ctr. and Children's Hosp. Corp., 1982—97, chmn. bd. dirs., 1992—97; trustee Wellesley Coll., 1962—80, trustee emeritus, 1980—; bd. dirs. Greater Boston Legal Svcs., 1961—87; dir. Controlled Risk Ins. Co., Ltd., 1988—99, chmn. bd. dirs., 1991—98; dir. Risk Mgmt. Found. Harvard Med. Instns., Inc., 1988—98, chmn. bd. dirs., 1991—98; trustee Harvard Med. Ctr. Inc., 1989—; trustee, mem. exec. com. WGBH Ednl. Found., 1987—2004, vice chmn., 1998—2003, trustee emeritus, 2004—. Mem. Am. Law Inst.(life), Internat. Acad. Estate and Trust Law; Mem. Tau Beta Pi. Home: 110 Spencer Brook Rd Concord MA 01742-5206 Office: 60 State St Boston MA 02109-1800 E-mail: gkidder@hembar.com.

KIDDER, RAY EDWARD, physicist, consultant; b. N.Y.C., Nov. 12, 1923; s. Harry Alvin and Laura Augusta (Wagner) K.; m. Marcia Loring Sprague, June 12, 1947 (div. Aug. 1975); children: Sandra Laura, David Ray, Matthew Sprague. BS, Ohio State U., 1947, MS, 1948, PhD, 1950. Physicist Calif. Rsch. Corp., La Habra, 1950-56, Lawrence Livermore Nat. Lab., Livermore, Calif., 1956—. Mem. adv. bd. Inst. for Quantum Optics, Garching, Germany, 1976-90; bd. editors Nuc. Fusion IAEA, Vienna, 1979-84; cons. Sci. Applications Internat. Corp., San Diego, 1991-94; mem. hon. adv. bd. Inst. for Advanced Physics Studies, La Jolla, Calif., 1991—. Contbr. chpts. to books. With USN, 1944-46. Recipient Humboldt award Alexander von Humboldt Found., 1988. Fellow Am. Phys. Soc. (Szilard award 1993); mem. AAAS, Sigma Xi. Achievements include research in physics of nuclear weapons, inertial confinement fusion, megagauss magnetic fields, laser isotope enrichment, containment of low-yield nuclear explosions. Home: 637 E Angela St Pleasanton CA 94566-7413 Office: Lawrence Livermore Nat Lab PO Box 808 Livermore CA 94551-0808

KIDDER, TRACY (JOHN TRACY KIDDER), writer; b. NYC, Nov. 12, 1945; s. Henry Maynard and Reine Marie (Tracy) K.; m. Frances Toland, Jan. 1971. AB, Harvard U., Cambridge, Mass., 1967; MFA, U. Iowa, Iowa City, 1974. Contbg. editor Atlantic Monthly, Boston, 1982—. Author: The Road to Yuba City, 1974, The Soul of a New Machine, 1981 (Pulitzer prize 1982, Am. Book award 1982), House, 1985, Among Schoolchildren, 1989 (Robert F. Kennedy book award), Old Friends, 1993, Home Town, 1999, Mountains Beyond Mountains, 2003, (non-fiction) My Detachment: A Memoir, 2005; author numerous articles, short stories and book revs. Served to 1st lt. U.S. Army, 1967-69, Vietnam.

KIDDOO, ROBERT JAMES, engineering service company executive; b. Kansas City, Mo., July 8, 1936; s. Robert Leroy and Margaret Ella (Wolford) K.; m. Patricia Anne Wakefield, Apr. 17, 1957; children: Robert Michael, Stacey Margaret Kiddoo-Lee. BSBA, UCLA, 1960; MSBA, Calif. State U., Northridge, 1969; MBA, U. So. Calif., 1972, DBA, 1978. Cert. mgmt. acct. Asst. v.p., nat. divsn. loan officer Crocker-Citizen's Nat. Bank, L.A., 1958—69; v.p., CFO, dir. corp. sec. Kirk-Mayer, Inc., L.A., 1969—87; prof. emeritus acctg. and info. sys. Calif. State U., Northridge, 1970—2005; region adminstr. mgr. CDI Corp.-West, Chatsworth, Calif., 1990; exec. v.p. Kirk-Mayer, Inc., L.A., 1990—92; pres. Creative Software Designs, Inc., Northridge, Calif., 1995—2002. Asst. v.p. financial affairs, univ. contr. Calif. State U., Northridge, 1997-2000. With U.S. Army, 1955-56. Mem. Mensa, Ltd., Beta Gamma Sigma, Beta Alpha Psi. Office: Calif State Univ Acctg And Is Northridge CA 91330-8372

KIDMAN, NICOLE, actress; b. Honolulu, June 20, 1967; m. Tom Cruise, Dec. 24, 1990 (div. Aug. 8, 2001); children: Isabella Jane Kidman, Connor Antony Kidman. Film appearences include BMX Bandits, 1983, Bush Christmas, 1983, Wills & Burke, 1985, Archer's Adventure, 1985, Windrider, 1986, Watch the Shadows Dance (aka Nightmaster), 1986, Bit Part, 1987, Emerald City, 1989, Dead Calm, 1989, Days of Thunder, 1990, Flirting, 1991, Billy Bathgate, 1991 (Golden Globe Award nomination 1992), Far and Away, 1992, Malice, 1993, My Life, 1993, Batman Forever, 1995, Portrait of a Lady, 1996, To Die For, 1995 (Golden Globe award), The Peacemaker, 1997, Practical Magic, 1998, Eyes Wide Shut, 1999, The Others, 2001 (nominee Best Performance by Actress in Motion Picture-Drama Golden Globe award 2002, Best Actress KCFCC award 2001), Birthday Girl, 2001, Moulin Rouge, 2001 (Best Actress in Motion Picture Musical/Comedy Golden Globe award 2001, nominee Best Actress in Leading Role Acad. award 2002, Best Actress London Film Critics Cir. award 2001), The Hours, 2002 (Best Actress Academy award, 2003, Best Actress in Leading Role, British Acad. Film Award (BAFTA), 2003, Best Actress Golden Globe, 2003), Dogville, 2003, The Human Stain, 2003, Cold Mountain, 2003, The Stepford Wives, 2004, Birth, 2004, The Interpreter, 2005, Bewitched, 2005; prodr. (films) In the Cut, 2003; TV appearances include Five Mile Creek, 1983, Chase Through the Night, 1983, Matthew and Son, 1984, Bangkok Hilton, 1989 (Australian Film Inst. Best Actress in Miniseries), Vietnam, 1985 (Australian Film Inst. Best Actress in Miniseries); theatrical prodns. include The Blue Room, London, 1997-98, Broadway, 1998-99. Named one of 50 Most Powerful People in Hollywood, Premiere mag., 2003—05; recipient ShoWest Dist. Decade Achievement award, 2002. Address: Creative Artists Agy 9830 Wilshire Blvd Beverly Hills CA 90212*

KIDWELL, CLARA SUE, education educator; b. Tahlequah, Okla., July 8, 1941; d. Hardin Milton and Martha Evelyn Kidwell. BA, U. of Okla., 1962, MA, 1963, PhD, 1970. Instr. of history Kans. City Art Inst., 1968—70; coord. of publications Exptl. Edn. Unit, U. of Wash., Seattle, 1969—70; instr. of social sci. Haskell Indian Jr. Coll., Lawrence, Kans., 1970—72; asst. prof. Am. Indian Studies Dept., U. of Minn., 1972—74; assoc. prof. to full prof. Native Am. Studies program, U. of Calif., 1974—93; vis. assoc. prof. Native Am. Studies Program, Dartmouth Coll., NH, 1980; asst. dir. for cultural resources Nat. Mus. of the Am. Indian, Washington, 1993—95; dir., native am. studies program U. of Okla., 1995—. Chair, bd. of trustees The Jacobson Found., Norman, Okla., 1998—2003. NDEA fellowship, U.S. Dept. of Edn., 1963—66, Rockefeller Found. Humanities fellowship, Rockefeller Found., 1976—77, Rockefeller Found. fellow, Newberry Libr., 2003—04, grant to direct summer institutes for coll. teachers, Nat. Endowment for the Humanities, 1987, 1990, Rockefeller Found. fellow, Newberry Libr., 2003—04. Mem.: Western History Assn., Am. Soc. for Ethnohistory, Orgn. of Am. Historians. Avocation: baking. Office: University of Oklahoma 633 Elm St Rm 216 Norman OK 73019

KIEC, MICHELLE, music educator, musician; d. MaryAnn and Gerard Kiec. BA in German, SUNY, Buffalo, 1996, MusB in Saxophone performance, 1995; MusM in Clarinet performance, Johns Hopkins U., 1998, Dof Mus. Arts in Clarinet performance, 2004. Clarinet/saxophone tchr. Music & Arts Ctr., Ellicott City, Md., 1997—2000; adj. prof. Clarion U. of Pa., Pa., 1998—2000; student orchestras libr. Aspen Music Festival and Sch., Colo., 1998—2001; asst. prof. music U. of Mary, Bismarck, ND, 2000—; music libr. Nat. Repertory Orch., Breckenridge, Colo., 2002—05. 2d clarinet Mo. Valley Chamber Orch., Bismarck, ND, 2000—; music contest adjudicator N.D. H.S. Activities Assn., Valley City, 2000—; grant rev. panelist N.D. Coun. on the Arts, Bismarck, 2001—; music festival clinician Mandan Band Festival, ND, 2001—; woodwind adjudicator Bismarck Jr. Music Festival, ND, 2001—; music contest adjudiator Mont. Region 13 Music Festival, Glendive, 2002—03; woodwind sectional coach Dakota Youth Symphony, Bismarck, ND, 2003—; clarinetist Trio Apollo, Bismarck, ND, 2003—; woodwind clinician Bismarck-Mandan Invitational Music Festival, ND, 2004—; presenter Marketplace for Kids, Dickinson, ND, 2005—. Musician: (performance) Internat. Clarinet Assn. ClarinetFest, (lecture-recital) N.Am. Saxophone Alliance Biennial Conf., N.Am. Saxophone Alliance Region 3 Conf., (annual) U. of Mary Faculty Recital, (concerto appearance) U. Mary Wind Ensemble Concert, Bismarck-Mandan Wind Ensemble. Bd. dirs. Mo. Valley Chamber Orch., Bismarck, ND. Peabody Career Devel. grant, Peabody Conservatory of Music of Johns Hopkins U., 2004, Profl. Devel. grant, N.D. Coun. on Arts, 2004. Mem.: Bismarck-Mandan Thursday Music Club, Nat. Assn. of Coll. Wind and Percussion Instrs., Nat. Flute Assn., North Am. Saxophone Alliance, Internat. Clarinet Assn. Office: Univ Mary 7500 University Dr Bismarck ND 58504

KIECHEL, WALTER, III, editor; b. Tecumseh, Nebr. BA, Harvard Coll., 1968, MBA, JD, 1977. Reporter, researcher Fortune Mag., 1977-78, assoc. editor, 1978-82, mem. bd. editors, 1982-88, asst. mng. editor, 1988-92, exec. editor, 1992-94, mng. editor, 1994-95; editor for bus. devel. Time, Inc., N.Y.C., 1995; editor Mgmt. Update newsletter Harvard Bus. Sch. Pub. Co. Cons. Bain & Co., 1996; pub. Harvard Bus. Rev., 1997; editl. dir., sr. v.p. H.B.S.P. Co., 1998; editor-at-large H.B.S.P., 2003. With USN. Office: 509 Madison Ave 15th Fl New York NY 10022 Home: 929 Washington St Hoboken NJ 07030 Office Phone: 212-872-9281. Personal E-mail: w.kiechel@gmail.com. Business E-Mail: wkiechel@hbsp.harvard.edu.

KIECHLE, FREDERICK LEONARD, pathologist; b. Indpls., Mar. 26, 1946; s. Frederick Leonard and Bertha Mae (Fackler) K.; m. Terri Lynn Holland, Aug. 15, 1966 (div. 1973); 1 child, Rachel Boerk; m. Janet Beatrice Green, June 21, 1975; children: Elizabeth Heather, Jonothan Edward. BA, Evansville (Ind.) Coll., 1968; PhD, Ind. U., 1973; MD, Ind. U., Indpls., 1975. Diplomate Am. Bd. Pathology. Resident in pathology William Beaumont Hosp., Royal Oak, Mich., 1975-79; fellow clin. chemistry Washington Sch. Medicine, St. Louis, 1979-80; asst. prof. pathology U. Pa., Phila., 1980-83; chief clin. chemistry Wm. Beaumont Hosp., Royal Oak, 1983-88, chmn. dept. clin. pathology, 1988—. Mem. Nat. Com. for Clin. Lab. Stds., Villanova, Pa., 1987-91. Contbr. articles to profl. jours. Wm. Beaumont Hosp. Rsch. Found. award, 1978; Hartford Found. fellow, 1982; named Clin. Scientist of Yr. Assn. Clin. Scientists, 1996, Fellow Am. Soc. Clin. Pathologists, Coll. Am. Pathologists (publs. com.); mem. Acad. Clin. Lab. Physicians and Scientists, Am. Soc. Investigative Pathology, Am. Diabetes Assn., Am. Assn. Clin. Chemistry, Assn. Clin. Scientists, Clin. Ligand Assay Soc., Nat. Acad. Clin. Biochemistry. Avocation: piano. Office: William Beaumont Hospital 3601 W 13 Mile Rd Royal Oak MI 48073-6712 Office Phone: 248-551-8030. Business E-Mail: fkiechle@beaumont.edu.

KIECOLT-GLASER, JANICE KAY, psychologist; b. Oklahoma City, June 30, 1951; d. Edward Harold and Vergie Mae (Lively) Kiecolt; m. Ronald Glaser, Jan. 18, 1980. BA in Psychology with honors, U. Okla., 1972; PhD in Clin. Psychology, U. Miami, 1976. Lic. psychologist, Ohio. Clin. psychology intern Baylor U. Coll. Medicine, Houston, 1974-75; postdoctoral fellow in adult clin. psychology U. Rochester, N.Y., 1976-78; asst. prof. psychiatry Ohio State U. Coll. Medicine, Columbus, 1978-84, assoc. prof. psychiatry and psychology, 1984-89, prof. psychiatry and psychology, 1989—, dir. divsn. health psychology, 1994—, active various coms. Mem. AIDS study sect. NIMH, 1988-91. Editl. bd. Brain, Behavior and Immunity jour., 1986—, Health Psychology jour., 1989—, Brit. Jour. Health Psychology, 1996—, Jour. Behavioral Medicine, 1994—, Psychosomatic Medicine, 1990—, Jour. Cons. and Clin. Psychology, 1992—, Jour. Gerontology, 1992—; reviewer Jour. Personality and Social Psychology, Psychiatry Rsch. jour.; author: Detecting Lies, 1997, Unconscious Truths, 1998, Handbook of Human Stress and Immunity, 1994; contbr. articles to profl. jours., chpts. to books. NIMH grantee, 1985—; recipient Merit award NIMH, 1993; Ohio State Disting. scholar, 1994, Devel. Health Psychology award, Divsn. Health Psychology and Adult Devel. and Aging, Norman Cousins award, Psychoneuroimmunology Rsch. Soc., 1998. Fellow Am. Psychol. Assn. (Outstanding Contbns. award 1988), Acad. Behavioral Medicine Rsch.; mem. Phi Beta Kappa, Inst. Medicine. Avocations: jogging, fiction writing. Office: Ohio State U Coll Medicine Dept Psychiatry 1670 Upham Dr Columbus OH 43210

KIEDIS, ANTHONY, vocalist, recording artist, actor; b. Grand Rapids, Mich., Nov. 1, 1962; Mem. band The Red Hot Chili Peppers, 1983—. Appeared in films The Chase, Point Break, Tough Guys; recordings include The Red Hot Chili Peppers, Blood Sugar Sex Magik, Mother's Milk, One Hot Minute, Various States of Undress; author (autobiography), Scar Tissue, 2004. Office: care Warner Bros Records 3300 Warner Blvd Burbank CA 91505-4632

KIEF, PAUL ALLAN, lawyer; b. Montevideo, Minn., Mar. 22, 1934; s. Paul G. and Minna S. K. BA, LLB, U. Minn., 1957. Bar: Minn. 1957, U.S. Dist. Ct. Minn. 1964, U.S. Ct Appeals (8th cir.) 2004, U.S. Tax Ct. 1968, U.S. Supreme Ct. 1981; cert. criminal trial law specialist Nat. Bd. Trial Advocacy. Gen. practice, Bemidji, Minn., 1959—; ptnr. Kief, Fuller, Baer & Wallner, Ltd., Bemidji, Minn., 1973-97; owner Paul A. Kief Law Firm, Bemidji, Minn., 1998—; pub. defender 9th Jud. Dist. Minn., Bemidji, Minn., 1966-98; panel atty. Fed. Pub. Defender Dist. Minn., 1999—. Chief pub. defender, Bemidji, Minn., 1968—94; vol. atty. Minn. Civil Liberties Union; mem. adv. bd. Innocence Project of Minn.; panel atty Legal Svcs., Northwest, Minn. Vice chmn. Beltrami County Planning Commn., 1964-68; chmn. adv. com. Gov.'s Crime Commn., 1971-77; mem. Minn. Task Force on Standards and Goals in Criminal Justice, 1975-76, Crime Victims Task Force, 1985, Jud. Selection Com., 1987, Com. on Criminal Jury Instrn. Guides, 1988-90; bd. dirs. Legal Svcs. Northwest Minn., 1990-96; capt. CAP, 1969—. Served with USAR, USNG, 1958-64. Mem. ABA, ATLA, NACDL, MACDL, Nat. Bd. Trial Advocacy (cert. crim. law trial specialist 1998), Minn. Bar Assn., Minn. Trial Lawyers Assn., 15th Dist. Bar Assn. (past sec.), Beltrami County Bar Assn. (past pres.), Lawyer-Pilots Bar Assn., Minn. Criminal Def. Lawyers Assn. Clubs: Toastmasters. Democrat. Congregationalist. Home: PO Box 212 Bemidji MN 56619-0212 Office: 514 America Ave NW PO Box 212 Bemidji MN 56619-0212 Office Phone: 218-751-2222. Personal E-mail: paky@paulbunyan.net.

KIEFER, ANSELM KARL ALBERT, artist; b. Donaueschingen, Germany, Mar. 8, 1945; s. Albert and Cacilia (Forster) K.; m. Monika Bornebusch, Feb. 9, 1971 (div.); children: Daniel, Sarah, Julian. Student, State Acad. Arts, Karlsruhe, Fed. Republic Germany, State Acad. Arts, Dusseldorf, Fed. Republic Germany. One-man shows include Galerie am Kaiserplatz Karlsruhe, 1969, Galerie Michael Werner, Cologne, Fed. Republic Germany, 1973, 74, 75, 76, 77, Galerie im Goethe-Institut/Provisorium, Amsterdam, 1973, Galerie Felix Handschine, Basel, Switzerland, 1973, Galerie t'Venster/Rotterdam Arts Found., The Netherlands, 1974, Bonner Kunstverein, Bonn, Fed. Republic Germany, 1977, Galerie Helen van der Meij, Amsterdam, 1977, 80, Galerie Maier-Hahn, Dusseldorf, 1978, Stedelijk Van Abbemuseum, Eindhoven, The Netherlands, 1979, (with George Baselitz) XXXIX Biennale Venedig at German Pavilion, 1980, Mannheimer Kunstverein, Mannheim, Fed. Republic Germany, 1980, Wurttembergischer Kunstverein, Stuttgart, Fed. Republic Germany, 1980, Galerie Paul Maenz, Cologne, 1981, 84, Marian Goodman Gallery, N.Y.C., 1981, 82, 95, 96, Museum Folkwang, Essen, Fed. Republic Germany, 1981, Whitechapel Art Gallery, London, 1982, Mary Boone Gallery, N.Y.C., 1982, Sonja Henie-Niels Onstad Founds., Oslo, 1983, Anthony d'Offay Gallery, London, 1983, Hans-Thoma-Museum, Bernau/Schwarzwald, Fed. Republic Germany, 1983, Mus. Contemporary Art, Los Angeles, 1983-84, Stadtische Kunsthalle, Dusseldorf, and Musee d'Art Moderne de la Ville de Paris, 1983, Israel Mus., Jerusalem, 1983, Kunsthalle Basle, Switzerland, 1986, Edward Tyler Nahem Fine Art, 1996-97, Gagosian Gallery, N.Y.C., 1997-98, Met. Mus. Art, 1999; group shows include Musee d'Art Moderne, Paris, 1977, Teheran Mus. Contemporary Art, Iran, 1978, Badischer Kunstvereine, Karlsruhe, Fed. Republic Germany, 1979, Royal Acad., London, 1981, Palais des Beaux Arts, Brussels, 1981, Kunsthalle, Dusseldorf, 1981, Galeria Stein, Turin, Italy, 1982, Documenta 7, Kassel, Germany, 1982,St. Louis Art Mus., 1983, Inst. for Art and Urban Researches, Long Island City, N.Y., 1983, Inst. Contemporary Art at U. Phila., 1983, Mus. Contemporary Art, Chgo., 1983, New Port Harbour Mus., New Port Beach, Calif., 1983, Cororan Gallery Art, Washington, 1983, Fondacion S. Moragas, Barcelona, Spain, 1983, Biblioteca Nacional, Madrid, 1984, Stedelijk Mus., Amsterdam, 1984-85, Castello di Rivoli, Torino, 1985, La Grande Halle de la Vilette, Paris, 1985, Mus. Art, Carnegie Inst., Pitts., 1985, Nationalgalerie, Berlin, 1985, Royal Acad., London, 1985; represented in permanent collections Art Inst. Chgo., Los Angeles County Mus. Art, Mus. Contemporary Art, Los Angeles, Mus. Modern Art, N.Y.C., Solomon R. Guggenheim Mus., N.Y.C., Mus. Art, Carnegie Inst., Phila. Mus. Art, Va. Mus., Richmond, Hirshhorn Mus., Smithsonian Instn., Washington, Tamayo Mus., Mexico City, Stadtische Galerie mit Sammlung Ludgie, Aachen, Nationalgalerie, Berlin, Kunsthalle, Bielefeld, Folkwang Mus., Essen, Staatsgalerie moderner Kunst im Haus der Kunst, Munich, Staatsgalerie, Stuttgart (all Fed. Republic Germany), Stedelijk Mus., Stedelijk Van Abbemuseum, Eindhoven, Groninger Mus., Groningen, Mus. Boymans-van Beuningen, Rotterdam (all The Netherlands), Kunsthaus Zurich, Switzerland, Tate Gallery, London, Musée Nationale d'Art Moderne Centre Georges Pompidou, Paris; author: A Book by Anselm Kiefer, 1988. Recipient Wolf prize in the arts, 1990, retrospective Nat. Galerie Berlin, 1991. Mem.: Am. Acad. Arts and Sciences (hon. fgn.). Office: Dieselstrabe 2 D-6967 Buchen Germany

KIEFER, J. RICHARD, JR., retired corporate executive; b. Phila., Mar. 3, 1928; m. Gwendolen Clara Watkins, June 20, 1953; children: David Richard, Linda Lauretta, Nancy Ellen, Carol Gwen. BSChemE, Drexel U., 1950; postgrad., Temple U. With McCloskey Corp., Phila., 1947-89, Valspar Corp., 1989-90; with rsch. and devel. McCloskey Corp., Phila., with customer product evaluation dept., v.p. community, industry and regulatory affairs. Mem. Friends of Acad. Vocal Arts, Olney Symphony Assn., Pa. Ballet Assn., Zool. Soc. Phila., Franklin Inst., Friends of Pennypack Park; mem., vol. twilight walking tours guide Friends of Independence Nat. Hist. Park; mem. Funeral Consumers Alliance Greater Phila., past pres., treas., bd. dirs.; vol. tour guide Phila. Soc. Preservation Landmarks, Hist. Power House, Phila. Cultural Coun. Recipient Sr. Statesman award Phila. Paint Industry. Mem. Phila. Paint and Coatings Assn. (past pres., past bd. dirs.), Phila. Soc. Coatings Tech. (past pres., bd. dirs., by-laws com., Liberty Bell, Tech Comm. and Benjamin Franklin awards), Fed. Soc. Coatings Tech. (hon. mem., past coun., bd. dirs., exec. com., Trigg award), Soc. Gallows Birds, N.E. H.S. Alumni Assn. (class reunion treas., Wall of Fame Honor), Masons (32d degree, former chmn. Trustees Charity Funds of Lodge, advisor to trustees, Columbia chpt. Joppa coun., high 12 past pres), Pa. Lodge Rsch., Philalethes Soc., Alpha Phi Omega, Zeta Theta (co-founder). Avocations: travel, classical music, attending ballet performances, opera, theater. Home: 1027 Loney St Philadelphia PA 19111-2624 Personal E-mail: welshamer@juno.com.

KIEFER, RENATA GERTRUD, epidemiologist, pediatrician, economist, management consultant; b. Lorrach, Baden, Germany, July 4, 1946; came to U.S., 1970; d. Friedrich W. and Gertrud Anna (Keller) K.; m. James C. Bridgman. BA, Stanford U., 1963; MA, U. Calif., Berkeley, 1967; MD, U. Geneva, Switzerland, 1982; MPH, U. Calif., Berkeley, 1990. Diplomate Am. Bd. Pediat., Am. Coll. Physician Execs.; cert. physician exec.; cert. in environ. health, Germany. Asst. instr. dissection lab. dept. morphology U. Geneva Sch. of Medicine, Switzerland, 1979-80; interim resident dept. diagnostic radiology Univ. Hosp., Geneva, 1980, intern physician, 1982-83; clin. fellow in pediatrics Harvard Med. Sch., Boston, 1983-85; resident physician Mass. Gen. Hosp., Boston, 1983-85; sr. resident dept. pediatrics U. Calif., San Francisco, 1985-86; attending physician emergency dept. Children's Hosp. Med. Ctr., Oakland, Calif., 1986-94; fellow dept. epidemiology and internat. health U. Calif., San Francisco, 1988-90; German tech. cooperation expert tropical medicine & internat. health Inst. for Health Sci. Rsch., Asuncion, Paraguay, 1990-94, vis. prof. epidemiol. and preventive medicine, 1992—; chief adv. rsch. and human resource devel. Health Strategies Internat.; sci. methods advisor Nat. U. Asuncion, 1994—. Rep. IICS/ Internat. Orgns.; cons. and presenter in field; chief adviser on health projects, dir. internat. teams GTZ/Health Ministry of Colombia, 1997—2000; pres. Winnovations Internat., 2002—. Contbr. numerous articles to profl. jours. Named co-winner nat. sci. prize, Paraguay Parliament, 1994; recipient award, USPHS Nat. Rsch. Svc., 1989—90; fellow internat. fellow in medicine, Floyd Family Trust, 1999, AAUW, 1968; scholar ASSU scholar, Stanford U., 1962—63, Fulbright scholar, 1962—64, Internat. scholar, Swedish Inst., 1968, Internat. Health scholar, U. Calif., 1990. Address: 6 Locksley Ave San Francisco CA 94122-3854 E-mail: jcbkierepaz@msn.com.

KIEFF, ELLIOTT DAN, medical educator; b. Phila., Feb. 2, 1943; s. Irving N. and Florence (Prussel) K.; m. Jacqueline Louise Silverman, June 11, 1944; children: David, Scott, Elizabeth. AB, U. Pa., 1963; MD, Johns Hopkins U., 1966; PhD, U. Chgo., 1971. Intern medicine U. Chgo., 1966-67, resident medicine, 1967-70, asst. prof. medicine, 1971-77, assoc. prof. medicine and molecular genetics, 1977-80, prof. medicine and molecular genetics, 1980-85, L. Block prof. biol. scis., 1985-87, chief infectious disease, 1971-87; Harriet Ryan Albee prof. medicine, microbiology and molecular genetics Harvard U., Boston, 1987—, chief infectious disease Brigham Hosp., 1987, chair virology, 1991—; Meyer hon. vis. prof. U. Calif., San Francisco, 1991—. Assoc. editor Virology, 1980—, Jour. of Virology, 1982—, reviewing editor, Science, 1996—. Recipient Langer award Langer Cancer Rsch., 1983, Finland award, 1987, Ricketts award, 1996. Mem. Nat. Acad. Scis., Am. Acad. Arts and Scis., Am. Soc. Clin. Ivestigation, Assn. Am. Physicians, Inst. Medicine, Inter Urban Club, Quadrangle Club (Chgo.), Harvard Club (N.Y.C.). Avocation: tennis. Home: 269 Lee St Brookline MA 02445-5914 Office: Havard Univ Med Sch 181 Longwood Ave Boston MA 02115-5804

KIEFFER, GEORGE DAVID, lawyer; b. NYC, Nov. 17, 1947; m. Judith Kieffer; 2 children. BA in history, U. Calif., Santa Barbara, 1969; JD, UCLA, 1973. Bar: Calif. 1973. Extern to Hon. David L. Bazelon US Ct. Appeals DC Cir., 1972; joined Manatt, Phelps & Phillips, LA, 1973, ptnr., bd. dirs., co-chair govt. divsn. Mem. transition team Gov. Arnold Schwarzenegger; chair Mayor's Council of Econ. Advisors, Mayor's LA Econ. Impact Task Force, City of LA Charter Reform Commn. Author: (book) The Strategy of Meetings, 1988. Former bd. dirs. Constl. Rights Found.; former chmn. bd. dirs. Ctr. for the Study of Dem. Institutions; former mem., vice chair bd. dirs. LA Urban League, bd. dirs. Automotive Training Ctr.; active Citizens Adv. Coun. on Corporations, 1975—82, Commn. for the Rev. of the Master Plan for Higher Edn. in Calif., 1985—87; trustee, chmn. U. Calif. Santa Barbara Found., 1972—82; bd. regents U. Calif., 1979—80; bd. governors Calif. Cmty. Colleges, 1981—87, pres., 1984—85; mem. exec. com., chair bd. dirs. LA C. of C.; bd. dirs. Calif. C. of C., chair edn. com.; mem. mus. coun. Mus. Contemporary Art, LA; mem bd. dirs., exec. com. Ctrl. City Assn. LA. Named one of 100 Most Influential Lawyers in Calif., Calif. Law Bus., 2000; recipient Social Responsibility Award, LA Urban League, 1999. Mem.: LA County Bar Assn. Avocations: writing and performing music, tennis, golf, basketball. Office: Manatt Phelps & Phillips 11355 W Olympic Blvd Los Angeles CA 90064 Office Phone: 310-312-4146.

KIEFFER, JAROLD ALAN, publishing executive, writer; b. Mpls., May 5, 1923; s. Charles O. and Edith Ida (Feinberg) K.; m. Frances Clarfield, Aug. 13, 1949; children: Edith Charlotte, Charles Edward, Philip William. BA, U. Minn., 1947, PhD, 1950. Tchg. asst. polit. sci. dept. U. Minn., 1949, tchg. asst. social sci. program, 1950-51; rsch. asst., world affairs program Mpls. Star, 1949-50; exec. sec. def. moblzn. manpower coms., staff asst. to exec. sec. Office Def. Moblzn., Exec. Office of Pres., 1951-52, staff sec., 1952, asst. to exec. officer, exec. sec. borrowing authority review bd., 1953, spl. asst. to dir., 1955-56, acting dep. asst. dir. nat. security affairs, 1956-57, cons., 1958; exec. asst. to dir. orgn. and personnel, exec. sec. personnel adv. com. AEC, 1952-53; asst. to Arthur S. Flemming, mem. 2d Hoover Commn., 1953-55; chmn. Herbert Hoover's liaison to Task Force on Pers. and Civil Svc., 1953-55; asst. to Arthur S. Flemming, mem. and asst. to chmn. Pres.'s Adv. Com. on Govt. Orgn., 1953-61, cons., 1958; asst. to Meyer Kestnbaum, spl. asst. to Pres. for Hoover Commn. and intergovtl. rels. commn. matters, The White House, 1955—56; adviser to Meyer Kestnbaum, 1956-57; asst. to Nelson Rockefeller for policy and issues studies, N.Y. gubernatorial campaign, 1957—58. Cons. to sec. HEW, Washington, 1958, asst. to sec., 1958-59, asst. to sec. for program analysis, 1959-61; sec. bd. trustees Nat. Cultural Ctr., 1959-63, exec. dir., 1961-63; renamed John F. Kennedy Ctr. for Performing Arts; assoc. prof. polit. sci. U. Oreg., 1963-67, acting chmn. polit. sci. dept., 1964, asst. to pres., 1963-67; chmn. pub. affairs and adminstrn. programs, prof. pub. policy and adminstrn. Lila Acheson Wallace Sch. Cmty. Svc. and Pub. Affairs, 1967-69; U. Oreg. chmn. Interdisciplinary Masters Program on Pub. Affairs, 1965-69; dir. Macalester Found. for Higher Edn., 1969-70; exec. officer bd. trustees Macalester Coll., 1970-71, also adj. prof. polit. sci., 1969-71; dir. Office Internat. Tng., AID, State Dept., 1971-72, asst. adminstr. for population and humanitarian assistance, 1972-75; adj. prof. internat. rels. Am. U., Washington, 1975, staff dir. pres.' panel on biomed. rsch., 1975-76. Dep. commr. social security U.S. Dept. HHS, 1976-77; staff dir. Task Force on House Adminstrv. Sys., Commn. on Adminstrv. Rev., U.S. Ho. Reps., 1977; dir. Nat. Com. on Careers for Older Ams., Acad. Ednl. Devel., Inc., 1978-80, staff dir., 1981 White Ho. Conf. on Aging, 1980-82; vice chmn. Gov. Planning Coun. Arts and Humanities, State of Oreg., 1965-67; chmn. Project 70's Task Force on State Govt. Reorgn., Oreg. Gov.'s Office, 1968-69; chmn. task force on Strategic Perspectives on Aging, Fairfax, Va., 1986; cons. Office High Speed Ground Transp., U.S. Dept. Transp., 1971; cons. U.S. Office Edn., 1971; officer, mem. exec. com. Lane County Auditorium Assn., Oreg., 1963-69; exec. com. United Way, Fairfax, 1985-88; bd. dirs. World Population Soc., 1983-2002 pres., 1990-92; bd. dirs. Fairfax Vol. Action Ctr., 1967-91, hon. bd. mem., 1991-93; mem. Gov.'s Job Tng. Coordination Coun., Commonwealth Va., 1987-94, chmn. older worker and youth com., 1989-94, mem. exec. com., 1990-94; mem., chmn. transp. com. Fairfax Area Commn. on Aging, 1991-95, exec. com., 1993-95; bd. dirs., sec. No. Va. Coalition of Vol. Interfaith Caregivers, Inc., 1991-94; bd. dirs. Fairfax Alliance for Human Svcs., 1996—, chmn., 2001-2004. With AUS, 1942-46. Mem. ASPA (life), Am. Polit. Sci. Assn., Advanced Transit Assn. (dir. 1976—, chmn. 1983-84, sec.-treas. 1985-95, chmn. 1995-2000), Sr. Employment Resources Inc. (chmn. 1985—, editor SER Publs., 1989-97), Kieffer Publs. (pres., editor 1998—). Home: 9019 Hamilton Dr Fairfax VA 22031-3075 Office Phone: 703-591-8328.

KIEFFER, KATHLEEN CECIL, elementary school educator; b. Hastings, Minn., Sept. 23, 1931; d. William A. and Kathryn (Brummel) Schaffer; m. Ralph W. Kieffer, Aug. 11, 1956 (div. Jan. 1972); 1 child, Joseph W. BS, Coll.

St. Teresa, Winona, Minn., 1953; MA, St. Thomas Coll., St. Paul, 1968. Cert. specific learning disabilities Minn. Elem. tchr. Mpls. Pub. Schs., 1953—68, specific learning disabilities resource tchr., 1968—93, vol. tchr. grade 4 Sheridan Sch., 1996—. Treas., pres. Mpls. Women in Edn., 1982—83, 1992—93. Del. to local, state and dist. convs. DFL Party, State of Minn., 1974—, mem. local, dist. and state ctrl. coms., 1984—; sec. DFL Senate Dist. 52 and 51, Ramsey County, Minn., 1992—; bd. mem. St. John's Ch., New Brighton, 1998—. Mem.: Mpls. Ret. Tchrs., We in Svc. to Edn. (v.p. 1994—), Minn. Assn. for Childhood Edn. Internat. (sec. 1977—80, v.p. 1988—89, pres. 1990—92, com. mem. 1994—, v.p. 2002—, Promoting the Well Being of Children award 2003), St. Vincent DePaul Soc., Delta Kappa Gamma (pres. 1980—82, legis. chmn. Gamma chpt. 1984—, comm. chmn. Tau State chpt. 1983—85, nominations com. Tau State chpt. 1989—90, Woman of Achievement award Gamma chpt. 1988). Roman Catholic. Home: 5180 Bona Rd New Brighton MN 55112

KIEFFER, KEVIN MATTHEW, psychologist, educator; s. Gary Leonard and Laquita Sue Kieffer; m. Kathryn Fleming, May 24, 2003. BS, Ind. U., Bloomington, 1990—94; MS, U. So. Miss., Hattiesburg, 1994—96; PhD, Tex. A&M U., College Station, 1996—2000. Lic. counseling psychologist Fla. Bd. Psychology, 2002. Postdoctoral neuropsychology resident James A. Haley VA Med. Ctr., Tampa, Fla., 2000—02; asst. prof., psychology Saint Leo U., Fla., 2000—. Mem.: ACA, APA, Southeastern Psychol. Assn. Office: Saint Leo Univ PO Box 6665 Saint Leo FL 33574 Office Phone: 352-588-8306.

KIEFFER, MARCIA S., psychotherapist; b. Buffalo, N.Y., Mar. 29, 1951; d. Milford Shepherd and Doris Verna (Nerber) Smith; m. William Charles Kieffer, Nov. 25, 1972; children: Michelle L. Kieffer Kowalski. AA in Applied Sci., Hilbert Coll., 1988; BS, Buffalo State Coll., 1993; MSW, SUNY Buffalo, 1995. LCSW N.Y., cert. alcohol and substance abuse counselor N.Y. Teller, bookeeper Mfrs. & Traders Trust, Buffalo, 1969-71; accounts recieveable Peter J. Schmidt, Buffalo, 1971-72; booking Meyer SFS Niagara, Buffalo, 1972-73; teller Bank of N.Y., Buffalo, 1973-75; headcashier Tops, Markets, Buffalo, 1980-81; teller Evans Nat. Bank, Angola, N.Y., 1981-88; dir. care and devel. Luth. Svc. Soc., Buffalo, 1988; case mgr. Suburban Adult Svcs., Buffalo, 1988-95; clin. social worker, psychotherapist Cmty. Concern, Derby, NY, 1995—2000; clin. dir. Chautauqua County Chem. Dependency Clinic, Dunkirk, NY, 2000—. Student intern supr. St. Bonaventure, Hamburg, N.Y., 2002-03, Sch. Social Work, 2002-03, Hilbert Coll., 1997, Fredonia State Coll., 2000. Vol. Salvation Army, Angola, N.Y., 1989—, Holy Cross Luth. Ch., Farnham, N.Y., 1988—. Recipient Franciscan award, Hilbert Coll., 1988, McGrath award Human Svcs, Hilbert Coll., 1988, Excellency in Social Work, award, Buffalo State Coll., 1993. Mem.: NASW. Avocations: qi gong, walking, reading, gardening, animals. Home: 6786 Wayne Dr Derby NY 14047-9737 E-mail: bkieffer@usadatanet.net.

KIEFFER, SUSAN WERNER, geologist, educator, media consultant; b. Warren, Pa., Nov. 17, 1942; BS in Physics and Math., Allegheny Coll., 1964; MS in Geol. Scis., Calif. Inst. Tech., 1967, PhD in Planetary Scis., 1971; DSc (hon.), Allegheny Coll., 1987. Rsch. physicist UCLA, 1971-73, asst. prof. geology, 1973-79; geologist U.S. Geol. Survey, Flagstaff, Ariz., 1979-90; prof. geology Ariz. State U., Tempe, 1988—, Regents prof., 1991-93; prof., head dept. geol. sci. U. B.C., Vancouver, Canada, 1993-95; co-founder Kieffer & Woo, Inc., Palgrave, Ont., Can., 1996-2000; founder Kieffer Inst. for Devel. of Sci. Based Edn., 1997-99; Walgreen chair, prof. geology U. Ill., Urbana, 2001—. W.H. Mendnhall lectr. U.S. Geol. Survey, 1980. Editor (with A. Navrotsky): Microscopic to Macroscopic: Atomic Environments to Mineral Thermodynamics, 1985. Recipient Disting. Alumnus award, Calif. Inst. Tech., 1982, Meritorious Svc. award, Dept. Interior, 1986, Spendiarov award, Soviet Acad. Scis., 1990; Alfred P. Sloan Found. fellow, 1977—79, MacArthur fellow, 1995—. Fellow: Mineral Soc. Am. (award 1980), Meteoritical Soc., Geol. Soc. Am. (Arthur L. Day medal 1992), Am. Geophys. Union, Am. Acad. Arts and Scis.; mem.: NAS. Avocations: athletics, music. Office: U Ill Dept Geology MC 102 1301 W Green St Urbana IL 61801 Business E-Mail: skieffer@uiuc.edu.

KIEFNER, JOHN ROBERT, JR., lawyer, educator; b. Peoria, Ill., May 31, 1946; s. John Robert and Luna Merle (Froment) K.; m. B.C. Clayton, Feb. 14, 1989; 1 child, John William. BA, Johns Hopkins U., 1968; JD, Stetson U., 1971. Bar: Fla. 1971, U.S. Ct. Appeals (D.C. cir.) 1971, U.S. Ct. Appeals (11th cir.) 1981, U.S. Dist. Ct. (no. dist.) Fla. 1971, U.S. Dist. Ct. (mid. dist.) Fla. 1981, U.S. Ct. Mil. Appeals 1971, U.S. Tax Ct. 1979, U.S. Supreme Ct. 1979. Staff atty. SEC, Washington, 1971-74, br. chief, 1974-77, regional trial counsel, 1977-82; mem. Robbins, Gaynor, Burton, Hampp, Burns, Bronstein & Shasteen, St. Petersburg, Fla., 1982-86; ptnr. Riden, Earle & Kiefner, P.A., St. Petersburg, 1986-99, Harris, Barrett, Mann & Dew, L.L.P., St. Petersburg, 1999—2001, Kiefner & Hunt P.A., St. Petersburg, 2001—. Adj. prof. law Stetson U., St. Petersburg, 1982—. Past chmn. Combined Fed. Campaign, 1976-77. Capt. U.S. Army, 1968-76. Recipient Cert. of Merit, SEC, 1982; Charles A. Dana scholar, 1970-71. Mem. ABA, ATLA, Fla. Bar Assn., St. Petersburg Bar Assn., Fla. Acad. Trial Lawyers, Pinellas County Trial Lawyers Assn., Fed. Bar Assn., Nat. Assn. Colls. and Univs. (recruitment com.), St. Petersburg Area C. of C., Johns Hopkins U. Alumni Assn., Masons, Shriners. Lutheran. Home: 227 126th Ave E Treasure Island FL 33706 Office: Kiefner & Hunt PA Ste 300 146 2nd St N Saint Petersburg FL 33701 Office Phone: 727-894-8000. Business E-Mail: JKiefner@Kiefnerhuntlaw.com.

KIEFT, GERALD NELSON, mechanical engineer; b. Chgo., Dec. 29, 1946; s. Ralph and Alice (Nelson) K.; m. Linda Louise Fank, Oct. 28, 1967; children: Gerald Nelson II, Dawn Michelle. BSME, Midwest Coll. Engring., 1971. Sr. designer Clark Equipment Co., Aurora, Ill., 1971—73; project engr. Elgin Sweeper Co., Ill., 1974—86, GPI Industries, West Chgo., Ill., 1986—. Inventor in field. Company chmn. United Way Campaign, Elgin, 1977. Presbyterian. Home: 42w192 Silver Glen Rd Saint Charles IL 60175-8339 Office: GPI Industries Ste 700 800 E Northwest Hwy Palatine IL 60074-6513

KIEHL, E. ROBERT, manufacturing executive, consultant; b. Phila., Apr. 28, 1920; s. Eugene Phillip and Ida Jean Kiehl; m. Margaret Eleanor Swigart, Oct. 7, 1944; children: Robert Edward, John Marsh, Christine Margaret. *The Kiehl family has an extensive history in engineering. Father Eugene Phillip Kiehl graduated from the University of Pennsylvania in 1912 with a BS degree in Electrical Engineering. He was a professional registered engineer his entire working life. Son Robert received a BS degree in Mechanical Engineering from Drexel University in 1968. After working for Ford Motor Co. and Ford Aerospace for 37 years, he is retired. Grandson Jeffrey graduated from Drexel University in 1994 with a BS in Civil Engineering and is currently employed as a professional engineer. Granddaughter Barbara has a BS degree in Mechanical Engineering from the University of California at Davis and a Masters degree from Santa Clara University. She is an executive at Loral Corp.* BS in chem. engring., Drexel U., 1943; at, Princeton (NJ) U., 1960—65. Chemist, engr. Allied Chem. Corp., Phila., 1940—43, project engr., 1943—44, plant mgr. Bethlahem, Pa., 1944—47, plant and works mgr. Edgewater, NJ, 1947—65; dir. oper. Allied Chem. Corp. Barrett Divsn., NYC, 1965—67; mgr. Gypsum Divsn. Celotex Corp., Tampa, Fla., 1967—84; cons. Internat. Exec. Svc. Corps, Stamford, Conn., 1987—. Chmn. materials handling com. Gypsum Assn., 1971—76; spkr. All Soviet Conf. on Gypsum, Moscow, 1979; chmn. mfg. and mining com. Gypsum Assn., 1979—83; spkr. Bur. of Standards, Washington, 1981; vol. exec. internat. projects Internat. Exec. Svc. Corps, Stamford, Conn., 1987—. Mem. bd. of edn. N. Highland Regional High Sch., Allendale - Saddle River, NJ, 1960—67; com. chmn. Boy Scouts of Am., New Milford, NJ, 1957—59; mem. adv. bd. Comprehensive Zoning Plan, Clearwater, Fla., 1995—96. With U.S. Army, 1938—43. Mem.: Pi Kappa Phi. Republican. Episcopalian. Achievements include expert in fields of prodn. of coal for chemicals and distallation polyurethane foam, microwave cured fiberboard, pvc panels and gypsum products. Avocations: antique car restoration, gardening, bridge, stamp collecting/philately. Home: 3241 San Mateo St Clearwater FL 33759

KIEKEL, JEAN M., secondary school educator; d. Joseph Oscar and Carol Jean Ehalt; m. Darren D Kiekel, Nov. 28, 1981; children: Brandi Nicole, Amber Samantha, Kaitlyn Marie, Austin Rochelle, Madison Janel. BS, Kans. State U., 1991, MBA, 1993. Teaching Certifcation State of Tex., 1999. Tchr. Virtual H.S., 2001—, LaPorte H.S., La Porte, Tex., 1998—2003; doctoral student Kans. State U., 2003—. Leader Girl Scouts South Tex., League City, 1993—2003. Mem.: Phi Delta Kappa.

KIEKHOFER, WILLIAM HENRY, lawyer; b. Madison, Wis., June 19, 1952; s. William and Emily (Graham) K.; m. Leslie A. Cohen., Jan. 27, 1956; children: Allison Laura, Phoebe Leigh, Rachel Elizabeth. BA, U. Wis., 1976; JD, U. So. Calif., 1980. Assoc. Sidley & Austin, L.A., 1980-82, Fried & King, L.A., 1982-83, McKenna Conner & Cuneo, L.A., 1983-90; ptnr. Kelley Drye & Warren LLP, L.A., 1990—2001, Mayer, Brown, Rowe & Maw LLP, L.A., 2001—. Office: Kelly Drye Warren 101 Park Ave New York NY 10178-0062

KIEL, FREDERICK ORIN, lawyer; b. Columbus, Ohio, Feb. 22, 1942; s. Fred and Helen Kiel; m. Vivian Lee Naff, June 2, 1963; 1 child, Aileen Vivian. AB magna cum laude, Wilmington Coll., 1963; JD, Harvard U., 1966. Bar: Ohio 1966, U.S. Supreme Ct. 1972. Assoc. Peck, Shaffer & Williams, Cin., 1966-71, ptnr., 1971-80, Taft, Stettinius & Hollister, Cin., 1980-89; pvt. practice law Cin., 1990—. Co-founder Bond Attys.' Workshop, 1976. Editor: Bond Lawyers and Bond Law: An Oral History, 1993, Bondletter, 1991—, Anderson Insights, 1992—; contbr. articles on mcpl. bond fin. to profl. jours. Arbitrator Mcpl. Securities Rulemaking Bd., 1985-92; mem. Anderson Twp. Govtl. Task Force, 1986—; sec. Anderson Twp. Greenspace Adv. Com., 1990—; rep. precinct exec. Precinct H Anderson Twp., 1991-92, 94-2001, Precinct X Anderson Twp., 2001—; twp. atty. Anderson Twp., 1997-2003; twp. law dir., 2003-, sec. Anderson Twp. Rep. Screening Com., 1999 Mem. Ohio State Bar Assn., Cin. Bar Assn., Nat. Assn. Bond Lawyers (co-founder 1979, dir. 1979-84, pres. 1982-83, hon. dir. 1984—, editor The Quar. Newsletter and The Bond Lawyer 1982—, Bond Attys. Workshop steering com. 1976, 83, 85, scrivener com. stds. of practice 1987-89). Office: 1095 Nimitzview Dr Ste 103 Cincinnati OH 45230-4392

KIEL, STUART, writer; b. N.Y.C. Student, SUNY, New Paltz, 1992—93, SUNY, Stony Brook, 1993—95. Freelance writer, L.I., NY, 1976—; exec. dir. Writers Alliance, Stonybrook, NY, 1982—85; editor Sci. Fiction Writers of America's Forum Mag., Wharton, NJ, 1985—88, Poetry Bone Mag., Lake Grove, NY, 1999—2001. Author: (chapbook) Shivery River, 2001, Multitasking, 2003. Mem.: Horror Writers Assn., Authors Guild, Sci. Fiction Writers of Am. Avocations: anime, Japanese language.

KIELKOPF, WILLIAM (MIKE), language educator, journalist; b. Ottumwa, Iowa, Nov. 23, 1949; s. Bill and Marjorie Kielkopf; m. Mary Guernsey, June 7, 1975; 1 child, Matthew William. BA, U. Iowa, 1972, MA, 1977. Cert. profl. Iowa Dept. Edn., 1981. Editl. page editor, columnist The Argus, Rock Island, Ill., 1978—87; English tchr. King Edward VII H.S., Johannesburg, 1976—76; mng. editor The Daily Std., Excelsior Springs, Mo., 1978—78; English-journalism tchr. North Scott H.S., Eldridge, Iowa, 1987—94, Am. Cmty. Sch., Abu Dhabi, United Arab Emirates, 1994—2003, Kiev Internat. Sch., Ukraine, 2003—04; vis. asst. prof. comm. Jacksonville (Fla.) U., 2004—. Author: (non-fiction books) How 'Bout Them Hawkeye Fans!, 1984, Close Encounters of the South African Kind, 2000, Catalysts for Curious Minds, 2002, (nonfiction book) Imagine That: A Teacher Tells the Truth About Schools, 2003, (non-fiction books) Hobgoblins and Little Minds, 2002; contbr. author: non-fiction book A World of Teaching - Personal Journeys Through the World's English-Speaking Classrooms, 2003. Chaperone Habitat for Humanity, India, 2001, Abu Dhabi, United Arab Emirates, 2003, Hungary, 2003. Recipient William Allen White Editl. Writing 1st pl. in U.S. award, 1984, 1st pl. award, Ill. Assoc. Press, 1984, 4th pl. award, Writers Digest Mag., 2002. Mem.: Soc. Profl. Journalists, Coll. Media Advisers, Sigma Delta Chi. Methodist. Avocations: travel, reading, sports, writing, desktop publishing. Personal E-mail: iowamike21@hotmail.com.

KIELY, DAN RAY, telecommunications industry executive, bank executive, consultant; b. Ft. Sill, Okla., Jan. 2, 1944; s. William Robert and Leona Maxine (Ross) K. BA in Psychology, U. Colo., 1966; JD, Stanford U., 1969. Bar: Colo. 1969, D.C.1970, Va. 1973; cert. property mgr. Assoc. Holme, Roberts and Owen, Denver, 1969—70; pres. DeRand Equity Group, Arlington, Va., 1973-89; pres., chmn. bd. Bankwest Corp and related banks, Denver; pres., dir. United Gibralter Corp. Del., Inc., 1987—92; ptnr. Starlin & Kiely, P.C., 1989-94; trustee DeRand Real Estate Investment Trust, 1974—. Chmn. Pace Holdings, Inc., Washington, 1988—93, Washington Capital Corp., 1989—; pres. Catelyst Comm. Inc., Palm Beach, Fla., 2001—; spkr., lectr. in field. Deacon, McLean (Va.) Bapt. Ch., 1977-80. Officer USAR, 1969-73. Decorated Legion of Merit. Mem. ABA, Nat. Bd. Realtors, Inst. Real Estate Mgmt., Nat. Assn. Rev. Appraisers, Internat. Coun. Shopping Ctrs., Nat. Assn. Real Estate Investment Trusts, Internat. Inst. (cert. valuer), Colo. Indsl. Bankers Assn. (bd. dirs. 1985-87). Office: 3015 Exchange Ct Ste C West Palm Beach FL 33409 Office Phone: 561-547-7870. Personal E-mail: dankiely@aol.com.

KIELY, W. LEO, III, brewery company executive; b. Jan. 16, 1947; AB in Econ. summa cum laude, Harvard U., 1969; MBA, U. Pa., 1971. Brand asst., asst. brand mgr. Procter & Gamble, Cin., 1971—73; from bus. mgr. to v.p. mktg. Wilson Sporting Goods Co., Chgo., 1973—79; pres. Ventura (Calif.) Coastal Corp., 1979—82; v.p. brand mgmt. Frito-Lay, Inc., 1982—83, v.p. mktg., 1983—84, v.p. sales & mktg., 1984—89, sr. v.p. field ops., 1989—90, v.p., gen. mgr. central div., 1990—91, pres., central div., 1991—93; pres., COO Coors Brewing Co., Golden, Colo., 1993—2000, pres., CEO, 2000—, Adolph Coors Co., 2002—. Bd. dirs. SEI Ctr. for Advanced Studies Bd. Wharton Sch. Fin., Phila., Adolph Coors Co and Coors Brewing Co., Golden, Colo., 1998—, Nat. Assn. of Manufacturers, Washington. Trustee Boys & Girls Clubs Am.; bd. dirs. Met. State Coll. Denver Found. Bd., Denver Ctr. for Performing Arts; chmn. Mile High United Way Denver. Mem.: Nat. Assn. Mfrs. (bd. dirs.). Office: Adolph Coors Co & Coors Brewing 311 Tenth St Golden CO 80401

KIENBAUM, THOMAS GERD, lawyer; b. Berlin, Nov. 16, 1942; came to U.S., 1957; s. Gerd Wilhelm Kienbaum and Albertine Brigitte (Kramm) Kettler; m. Karen Smith, June 24, 1966 (div.); 1 child, Ursula; m. Elizabeth Hardy, Jan. 22, 1992. AB, U. Mich., 1965; JD magna cum laude, Wayne State U., 1968. Bar: Mich. 1968, Ill. 1991, U.S. Supreme Ct. 1983. Assoc. Dickinson, Wright, Moon, Van Dusen & Freeman, Detroit, 1968-76, ptnr., 1976-97; ptnr., founder Kienbaum Opperwall Hardy & Pelton, Detroit and Birmingham, 1997—. Contbr. legal articles to profl. publs. Bd. dirs. Wayne County Neighborhood Legal Svc., 1972-76, 87-88. Fellow ABA, State Bar of Mich. Found.; mem. Am. Judicature Soc., Coll. Labor and Employment Lawyers, State Bar Mich. (pres. 1995-96), Detroit Bar Assn. (pres. 1985-86), Barristers Assn. (pres. 1978-79), Oakland County Bar Assn., Order of the Coif. Avocations: reading, skiing, squash, sailing. Office: Kienbaum Opperwall Hardy & Pelton 280 North Old Woodward Ave Ste 400 Birmingham MI 48009-6202 Office Phone: 248-645-0000. Business E-Mail: tkienbaum@kohp.com.

KIENITZ, LADONNA TRAPP, lawyer, librarian, municipal official; b. Bay City, Mich. d. Orlin D. and Mary (Stanford) Trapp; m. John Kienitz, Feb. 9, 1951 (div. Dec. 1974); children: John, Jim, Rebecca, Mary, Timothy, David. BA, Westmar Coll., 1951; MA in Libr. Sci., Dominican U., River Forest, Ill., 1970; M Mgmt., Northwestern U., 1984; JD, Western State U., Fullerton, Calif., 1995; LLM in Taxation, U. San Diego, 2004. Head libr. Woodlands Acad., Lake Forest, Ill., 1973-77; project officer North Suburban Libr. Sys., Wheeling, Ill., 1977-78; libr. dir. Lincolnwood (Ill.) Pub. Libr. Dist., 1978-86; city libr. City of Newport Beach, Calif., 1986—, dir. cmty. svcs., 1994—2002; tax. atty. Chapman U. Sch. Tax Law Clinic, Orange, 2003—. Mem.: ALA, ABA, US Tax Ct. Bar, US Supreme Ct. Bar, Pub. Libr. Assn. (pres. 1995—96), State Bar Calif., Orange County Bar Assn. Office Phone: 949-300-6951. Personal E-mail: ladonnakienitz@sbcglobal.net.

KIENKER, JAMES W., marketing executive; CFO Boatmen's Bancshares Inc.; CFO, sr. exec. v.p. Martiz Inc. Office: Maritz 1375 N Hgwy Dr Fenton MO 63099

KIENTZ, RENEE, newspaper editor; Lifestyle editor Features Desk Houston Chronicle. Adv. bd. Variety Club of Houston. Office: Houston Chronicle Pub Co 801 Texas St Houston TX 77002-2996

KIENZLE, JOHN FRED, history educator; b. Allentown, Pa., Apr. 1, 1945; s. Fred John and Florence Mary K.; m. Patricia Catherine Evertsen, Aug. 22, 1970. BA in history, Albany State U., 1967; MA in History, NYU, 1969; PhD in History, Princeton U., 1972. Libr. aide NYU, N.Y.C., 1967-69, Firestone Libr. Princeton (N.J.) U., 1969-70; tchr. history Maple Hill H.S., Castleton, NY, 1970—. Dir. media svcs. Maple Hill H.S., 1974—; lectr. photography, astronomy,travel and edn. Mem. Met. Mus. Art, 1987—, Lake Chaplain Maritime Mus., 1994—, N.C. Maritime Mus., 1999—, Schodack Faculty Assn., 1970—; trustee Maple Hill H.S. Amateur Radio Club, 1975—; radio officer Rensselaer County (N.Y.) Civil Emergency Svcs., 1980—. Recipient Tchr. of Yr., Schodack Schs., 1996—97, Capital Dist. Coun. Social Studies, 1998—99. Mem. Archaeol. Inst. Am. Republican. Roman Catholic. Avocations: sailing, flying, amateur radio, astronomy, photography. Office: Maple Hill H S 1216 Maple Hill Rd Castleton On Hudson NY 12033-1604 Office Phone: 518-732-7701. E-mail: jkienzle@albany.net.

KIER, CARLOS M., rheumatologist; b. Ft. Worth, Tex., Apr. 28, 1945; s. James M. and Marth A. Kier; children: Catherine A., Kenneth M., Alexandra M. BS in Biology (pre-med.), U. Tex., Arlington, 1966; MD with honors, U. Tex., Galveston, 1970. Diplomate Am. Bd. Rheumatology, Am. Bd. Internal Medicine. Intern medicine, 1966—70; resident, 1971—73; fellow rheumatology, 1973—74, 1976—77; pvt. practice, 1978—; rheumatologist Arlington, Tex., 1980—. Exec. com. and pres. Big Bros.-Big Sisters, Arlington, Tex., 1983—92. Maj. USMC, 1974—76, Ft. Hood, Tex., served in U.S. Army, 1974—76. Named Top Dr., Guide to Top Doctors, 2003. Fellow: ACP, Am. Coll. Rheumatology; mem.: Alpha Omega Alpha. Office: Carlos M Kier MD PA 909-B Medical Centre Drive Arlington TX 76012-4757 Office Phone: 817-274-0996. E-mail: ckier@attglobal.net.

KIEREN, THOMAS HENRY, management consultant; b. Milw., July 23, 1941; s. Henry Lawrence and Hildegard (Luketell) K. BS, Holy Cross Coll., 1963; MBA, U. Chgo., 1968; postgrad., Harvard U., 1963. Mgr. Touche, Ross & Co., 1968-69; asst. v.p. Sunbeam Corp., Chgo., 1969-75; dir. bus. strategy ACF Industries, Inc., N.Y.C., 1975-78; dir. bus. and fin. planning GAF Corp., N.Y.C., 1978-82; dir. bus. planning Engelhard Corp., Edison, N.J., 1982-83; founder, pres., mng. dir. Manhattan Cons. Group, Inc., N.Y.C., 1983—. Bd. dirs. Mothers Stores, Inc.; chmn. mergers and acquisitions, seminar program Exec. Enterprises, Inc., N.Y.C., 1984-87; founder, chmn. Ducks Unltd., Inc., Passaic County; bd. dirs., chmn. Custom Corporate Photography, Inc., 2002--. Author, editor, lectr.: for AMA in corp. strategy, acquisitions and turnaround mgmt., 1980—; contbr. articles to profl. jours. Del. to White House conf. on small bus., Washington, 1986; pres. Bus. Execs. for Bush, 1998; area coord., mem. fin. com. Courter for Gov. of N.J., 1989; mem. fin. com. Whitman for Gov. of N.J. Campaign, 1993, 1997, mem. Inaugural Ball com., 1998; mem. Task Force on Tech. Policy Nat. Assn. Mfrs., Commn. Regulatory Reform and Govt. Waste; bd. dirs. Boy Scouts of Am.; mem. coun. N.Y. Philharm., 1980—; founder Chgo. Symphony Soc., Ctr. for Industry and Corp. Performance, Oak Ridge, NJ; founder, chmn. Greater Wayne Area Young Reps., Inc., 1992—2002; bd. dirs. N.J.-Straight and Narrow, Inc. Mem.: Product Devel. and Mgmt. Assn. (nat. v.p., bd. dirs., founder N.Y. chpt., Leadership award 1993), U. Chgo. Bus. Sch. Alumni Assn. (bd. dirs. 1983—85), Baruch Sch. of Bus. (adj. prof. of bus. strategy), Fordham Grad. Sch. of Bus., Amateur Comedy Club, U. Chgo. Bus. Sch. Club of N.Y. (founder, bd. dirs.), U. Club Chgo., Holy Cross Coll. Club of N.Y., Trout Unltd., Inc. (bd. dirs. N.Y. chpt.). Republican. Roman Catholic. Avocations: fly fishing, tennis, sports car racing, skiing, environmental portrait and architectural photography. Office: The Manhattan Cons Group Inc 150 E 55th St 7th Fl New York NY 10022 E-mail: manconsgroup@earthlink.net.

KIERNAN, EDWIN A., JR., lawyer; b. N.Y.C., Aug. 2, 1926; s. Edwin A. and Helen M. (Clarke) K.; m. Ellen Mary Irving, Feb. 18, 1952; children: Robert Clarke, Katherine Waters. AB, Columbia, 1947, JD, 1950; LL.M., NYU, 1957. Bar: N.Y. 1950. Assoc. Simpson Thacher & Bartlett, N.Y.C., 1950-52, 54-55, Wickes, Riddell, Bloomer, Jacobi & McGuire, N.Y.C., 1956-59; atty. Western Electric Co., Inc., 1959-60, Interpublic Group of Cos., Inc., N.Y.C., 1960-64, mng. atty., 1964-68, asst. sec., asst. gen. counsel, 1968-79, sec. and gen. counsel, 1980-88, v.p., 1973-81, sr. v.p., 1981-88. Sec. McCann-Erickson, Inc., N.Y.C., 1962-79 Lt. (j.g.) USNR, 1944-46, 52-54. Mem. ABA, Phi Beta Kappa. Home: Apt 328 10100 Cypress Cove Dr Fort Myers FL 33908-7662 E-mail: EnEkiernan@aol.com.

KIERNAN, JAMES PATRICK, music educator, fine arts department head; b. NYC, Jan. 15, 1965; s. James Peter and Kathleen Kiernan; m. Chloe Rachel Wheatley, Aug. 5, 1995; 1 child, Julia Louise. BFA in Music Composition, SUNY, Purchase, 1989; Cert. in Edn., Western Ct. St. U., 1993; MS in Music Edn., Ctrl. Ct. St. U., 2005. Cert. music edn. K-12 NY, NJ, Conn., Mass. Music tchr., choir dir. Luis Munoz Marin Sch., Bridgeport, Conn., 1994—96; band and orch. dir. Bergenfield Pub. Schs., NJ, 1996—98, Leonia Pub. Schs., NJ, 1998—99, Great Neck Pub. Schs., NY, 1999—2002; band dir., fine arts dept. head East Longmeadow HS, Mass., 2002—. Marching band percussion arranger, instr. Trumbull (Conn.) H.S., 1991—95. Recipient Presidents award, SUNY, 1989. Mem.: Music Educators Nat. Conf., Mass. Music Educators Assn. Avocations: cooking, fishing, running. Office: E Longmeadow HS 180 Maple St East Longmeadow MA 01028 Office Phone: 413-525-5460.

KIERNAN, JOHN S., lawyer; b. Nov. 22, 1954; BA magna cum laude, Harvard U., 1976, JD magna cum laude, 1980. Assoc. Debevoise & Plimpton LLP, NYC, 1981—88, ptnr., 1988—, co-chair, litig. dept.; law clerk to Hon. Walter R. Mansfield US Ct. Appeals, Second Cir., 1980—81. Village atty. Village of Pelham Manor, NY, 1990—93, village trustee, NY, 1993—99, mayor, NY, 1999—2001; dir. Legal Services for NYC, 1989—, vice-chair, 1993—2003. Office: Debevoise & Plimpton LLP 919 Third Ave New York NY 10022 Office Phone: 212-909-6692. Office Fax: 202-909-6836. E-mail: jskiernan@debevoise.com.

KIERNAN, OWEN BURNS, educational consultant; b. Randolph, Mass., Mar. 9, 1914; s. Thomas Francis and Elizabeth (Burns) K.; m. Esther Harriet Thorley, July 13, 1940; children: Joan Ann, Nancy Elizabeth, John Albert. BS, Bridgewater (Mass.) State Coll., 1935; M.Ed., Boston U., 1940, Sc.D. (hon.), 1968; Ed.D., Harvard U., 1950; L.H.D. (hon.), Lesley Coll., 1956; LL.D., Northeastern U., 1961; Litt.D. (hon.), Stonehill Coll., 1965; Ped.D. (hon.), R.I. Coll., 1966. Prin. Henry T. Wing High Sch., Sandwich, Mass., 1938-44; supt. schs. Wayland and Sudbury, Mass., 1944-51, Milton, 1951-57; commr. edn. State of Mass., 1957-68; exec. dir. Nat. Assn. Secondary Sch. Prins., 1969-79; dir. sch. div. McManis Assos., Inc., 1980-82; cons. Washington, 1983—. Past chmn. Mass. Bd. Edn., Mass. Bd. Vocat. Edn.; corp. mem. MIT Trustee U. Mass.; trustee Lowell Tech. Inst., Mus. Fine Arts, Mus. Sci. Boston, Boston U.; bd. dirs. Atlantic Council U.S.; chmn. edn. com. Atlantic Treaty Assn., 1968-72; gov. bd. Atlantic Info. Centre for Tchrs., London, 1968-76; exec. com. U.S. People-to-People Program. Mem. Am. Assn. Sch. Adminstrs., New Eng., Mass. supts. assns., Council Chief State Sch. Officers (pres. 1967), Phi Delta Kappa. Home: 36 Fernbrook Ln Centerville MA 02632-2908

KIERNAN, RICHARD FRANCIS, publisher; b. N.Y.C., Apr. 17, 1935; s. James J. and Grace (Nolan) K.; m. Jane V. Eickmeyer, Dec. 29, 1962; children: Christopher R., Peter T., Kathy Lynn. BS, U. Conn., 1957. Salesman Med. Econs. Co., Oradell, N.J., 1963-65, sales mgr., 1965-67, gen. mgr. Chgo., 1967-68; pub. Med. Econs. mag., Oradell, 1970-72, sr. v.p., pub., 1990-95; sr. v.p., pub., Redbook, Annual, Med. Econs. mag., Bus. and Health mag., Drug Topics mag., Montvale, N.J., 1991—; pres. Medical Econs. Profl.

Info. Svc. Group, 1995—; pub. RN Mag., Oradell, 1968-70; pres. Cliggott Pub. Co., Greenwich, Conn., 1972-75; exec. v.p. Biomed. Info. Inc., N.Y.C., 1975-79; pres. Hosp. Pubs., Inc., Secaucus, N.J., 1979-89; chmn. R.F. Kiernan Assocs., Ridgewood, N.J., 1989-90; pres., COO PISG, Med. Econs., 1994—. Bd. dirs. Argus Press Holdings, USA; treas. Pharm. Adv. Council, 1979-81, pres., 1981; v.p. Devel. Med. Econs. Co. With U.S. Army, 1957-63. Mem. Pharm. Advt. Coun. (pres.), Assn. Clin. Pubs. (pres.), N.Y. Athletic Club, Ridgewood Country Club, Leland (Mich.) Country Club. Home and Office: 153 Hamilton Rd Ridgewood NJ 07450-1102

KIERSCHT, MARCIA SELLAND, academic administrator, psychologist; b. Rugby, ND; d. Osmund Harold and Cynthia (Thoresen) Selland; m. Charles M. Kierscht, Aug. 19, 1961 (div. 1972); children: Cynthia Ann, Matthew Mason. BA, U. Iowa, 1960, MA, 1962; PhD, Vanderbilt U., 1975. Lic. psychologist, Ill., Minn. Sch. psychologist South Suburban Cook County, Homewood, Ill., 1962-64, Dist. 108, Highland Park, Ill., 1964-65, Spl. Edn. Dist. Lake County Ill., Gurnee, 1966-72; psychol. examiner John F. Kennedy Ctr., George Peabody Coll., 1972-73; instr. in pediatrics Med. Sch. Vanderbilt U., Nashville, 1975-76; assoc. prof. Moorhead (Minn.) State U., 1976-80, asst. to pres., 1980-86; provost, chief exec. officer Tri-Coll. U., Fargo, N.D., 1986-90; dean grad. and profl. sch. Hood Coll., Frederick, Md., 1990-93; v.p. Consortium of Univs. of the Washington Met. Area, 1993-94; pres. Stephens Coll., Columbia, Mo., 1994—2003, pres. emeritus, 2003—. Contbr. articles to profl. jours. V.p. Plains Art Mus., Moorhead, 1986-88; chmn. bd. govs. Fargo-Moorhead Area Found., Fargo, 1983-90; bd. dirs. United Way, Columbia, 1994-2001; mem. mgmt. coun. div. III, NAAA, 2001-03. Recipient Pembina Trail award, Minn. Hist. Soc., 1994. Mem. Am. Coun. on Edn., Coun. of Fellows, Fargo C. of C., Columbia C. of C. (bd. dirs.), Montgomery County High Tech. Coun., Rotary Club (Moorhead, Columbia, Fredericktowne), Cosmos Club, Washington.

KIES, DAVID M., lawyer; b. N.Y.C., Jan. 25, 1944; s. Saul and Lillian (Schultz) K.; m. Emily Bardack, July 6, 1966 (div. 1985); children: Laura, Adam, Abigail; m. Anne Monteith, Oct. 7, 1990 (div. 1998); 1 child, Samuel; m. Kathryn L. Danes, Mar. 11, 2001. AB, Haverford Coll., 1965; JD, NYU, 1968. Bar: N.Y. 1968, U.S. Dist. Ct. (so. dist.) N.Y. 1969, U.S. Ct. Appeals (2d cir.) 1969. Assoc. Sullivan & Cromwell, N.Y.C., 1968-76, ptnr., 1976—, dir. London office, 1992-95; dir. Imclone Systems, Inc. Former trustee Haverford Coll. Root Tilden fellow, NYU Law Sch., 1965. Mem. ABA, N.Y. State Bar Assn., Assn. Bar City of N.Y. Democrat. Jewish. Office: Sullivan & Cromwell 125 Broad St Fl 28 New York NY 10004-2489

KIES, KENNETH J., lawyer; b. Ft. Benning, Ga., Jan. 4, 1952; s. Robert Herman K.; m. Kathleen Barbara Clark, Oct. 11, 1986. BA, Ohio U., 1974; JD, Ohio State U., 1977; LLM in Taxation, Georgetown U., 1986. Bar: Ohio 1977, U.S. Tax Ct. 1978, D.C. 1987, U.S. Supreme Ct. 1992. Assoc. Baker & Hostetler, Cleve., 1977-81; asst. minority tax counsel Com. on Ways & Means U.S. Ho. of Reps., Washington, 1981-82, chief minority tax counsel, 1982-87; ptnr. Baker & Hostetler, Washington, 1987-95; chief of staff joint com. on taxation U.S. Congress, Washington, 1995-98; mng. ptnr. Price Waterhouse Coopers, Washington, 1998—2002; mng. dir. Fed. Policy Group, Clark Cons., Washington, 2002—. Contbr. articles to profl. jours. Mem. Capitol Hill Club, Washington Golf and Country Club, Robert Trent Jones Golf Club, Calusa Pines Club, Currituck Golf Club. Republican. Office: Fed Policy Group 101 Constitution Ave NW 701E Washington DC 20001-2133 Office Phone: 202-772-2480.

KIESBYE, STEFAN, writer, educator; b. Eckernförde, Holstein, Germany, Feb. 20, 1966; arrived in U.S., 1996; s. Hans Uwe and Ruth Helene (Mattern) Kiesbye; m. Sanaz Samimy Kiesbye, Nov. 26, 1999. BA, Free U., Berlin, 1996; MA in Am. Studies, SUNY, Buffalo, 1998; MFA in Creative Writing, U. Mich., 2001. Actor Modernes Theater, Berlin, 1991—93; lectr. U. Mich., Ann Arbor, 2001—02; lectr. creative and argumentative writing Ea. Mich. U., Ypsilanti, 2002—. Author: (story collection) Queen City, 2001 (Chamberlain award, 2001), (chapbook) The End of Some Things, 2003 (Flash Point award, 2002), (novels) Next Door Lived a Girl, 2005. Scholar, German Acad. Exch. Svc., 1996—97; Colby fellow, U. Mich., 1999—2001. Office: Ea Mich Univ 612 Pray Harrold Ypsilanti MI 48197 E-mail: skiesbye@gmail.com.

KIESCHNICK, GERALD B., religious organization administrator; b. Houston, Tex., Jan. 29, 1943; m. Terry Kieschnick; children: Andrew, Angela Keith. BS, Tex. A&M U., 1964; grad., Concordia Theological Seminary, Springfield, Ill., 1970; M.Div., Concordia Theological Seminary, Fort Wayne, In., 1977; LLD (hon.), Concordia U., Austin, Tex., 1996. Pastor Good Shepherd Luth. Ch., Biloxi, Miss., 1970—73, Redeemer Luth. Ch., Beaumont, Tex., 1973—81; dir. public relations, Tex. dist. Luth. Ch. - Mo. Synod, 1976—86, circuit counselor, Tex. dist., 1978—81; pastor Faith Luth. Ch., Georgetown, Tex., 1981—86; pres. Tex. dist. Luth. Ch. - Mo. Synod, 1991—2001, chair, commn. church and theology issues, 1998—2001, pres., 2001—. Office: Luthern Ch Missouri Synod 1333 S Kirkwood Rd Saint Louis MO 63122

KIESLER, CHARLES ADOLPHUS, psychologist, academic administrator; b. St. Louis, Aug. 14, 1934; m. Teru Morton, Feb. 28, 1987; 1 child, Hugo; children from previous marriage: Tina, Thomas, Eric, Kevin. BA, Mich. State U., 1958, MA, 1960; PhD (NIMH fellow), Stanford U., 1963; D (hon.), Lucian Blaga U., Romania, 1995. Asst. prof. psychology Ohio State U., Columbus, 1963-64, Yale U., New Haven, 1964-66, assoc. prof., 1966-70; prof., chmn. psychology U. Kans., Lawrence, 1970-75; exec. officer Am. Psychol. Assn., Washington, 1975-79; Walter Van Dyke Bingham prof. psychology Carnegie Mellon U., Pitts., 1979-85, head psychology, 1980-83, acting dean, 1981-82, dean Coll. Humanities and Social Scis., 1983-85; provost Vanderbilt U., 1985-92; chancellor U. Mo., Columbia, 1992-96, Weil Disting. prof. health svcs. mgmt., 1996-98; prof., sr. advisor San Diego State U., 1998-99. Pres., CEO, Virtual Univ. Internat., 1996-97. Author: (with B.E. Collins and N. Miller) Attitude Change: A Critical Analysis of Theoretical Approaches, 1969, (with S.B. Kiesler) Conformity, 1969, The Psychology of Commitment: Experiments Linking Behavior to Belief, 1971, (with N. Cummings and G. VandenBos) Psychology and National Health Insurance: A Sourcebook, 1979, (with A.E. Sibulkin) Mental Hospitalization: Myths and Facts About a National Crisis, 1987, (with C. Simpkins) The Unnoticed Majority: Psychiatric inpatient care in general hospitals, 1993. Served with Security Service USAF, 1952-56. Recipient Disting. Alumnus award Mich. State U., 1987, Gunnar Myrdal award for Evaluation Practice Am. Evaluation Assn., 1989. Fellow AAAS, APA (Distng. Contbr. to Rsch. in Pub. Policy award 1989), Am. Psychol. Soc. (founding past pres. 1988-90); mem. AAUP, Inst. of Medicine of Nat. Acad. Scis., Sigma Xi, Psi Chi, Phi Kappa Phi. E-mail: ckiesler@san.rr.com.

KIESLING, ERNST WILLIE, civil engineering educator, dean; b. Eola, Tex., Apr. 8, 1934; s. Alfred William and Louise (Kern) K.; m. Juanita Haseloff, Aug. 25, 1956; children: Carol, Chris, Max. BS in Mech. Engring, Tex. Tech. Coll., 1955; MS in Applied Mechanics, Mich. State U., 1959, PhD, 1966. Registered profl. engr. Asst. prof. Tex. Tech. Coll., 1959-63; sr. research engr. S.W. Research Inst., San Antonio, 1966-69; prof. civil engring. Tex. Tech U., Lubbock, 1969—, chmn. dept. civil engring., 1969-88, assoc. dean engring., 1988-93; prof. civil engring. Tex. Tech. U., Lubbock, 1993—2004, sr. assoc. dean, 2004—. NSF faculty fellow, 1963-64 Fellow ASCE; mem. NSPE (life), Am. Soc. Engring. Edn., Nat. Storm Shelter Assn. (exec. dir. 2001—), Sigma Xi, Chi Epsilon, Tau Beta Pi. Achievements include pioneering work in storm shelter research and utilization. Home: 5111 97th St Lubbock TX 79424-4867 Office: Tex Tech U Dept Civil Engring Lubbock TX 79409

KIESSLING, B. ROBBINS, lawyer; b. Atlanta, June 23, 1950; BA, Yale U., 1973; JD, NYU, 1976. Bar: N.Y. 1977. Mem. Cravath, Swaine & Moore LLP, N.Y.C., ptnr., corp. Mem. N.Y. State Bar Assn., Assn. of Bar of City of N.Y. Office: Cravath Swaine & Moore Worldwide Plz 825 8th Ave Fl 38 New York NY 10019-7475 Office Fax: 212-474-3700. Business E-Mail: bkiessling@cravath.com.

KIESSLING, LAURA LEE, chemist, researcher; b. Milw., Sept. 21, 1960; d. William E. and LaVonne V. (Korth) K. SB, MIT, 1983; PhD, Yale U., 1989. Teaching asst. MIT, Cambridge, Mass., 1982-83, Yale U., New Haven, 1983-84, rsch. asst., 1984-89; rsch. fellow Calif. Tech. U., Pasadena, Calif., 1989-91; asst. prof. chemistry U. Wis., Madison, Wis., 1991-97, assoc. prof., 1997-99, prof. chemistry, prof. biochemistry, 1999—. Cons. Ophidian, Inc., 1997-99, Alfred P. Sloan Found. Fellowships, 1997—; mem. bioorganic and natural products study sect. NIH, 1997-2000; Fellow, Am. Assoc. for the Advancement of Sci., 2003; elected Acad. of Arts and Sci., 2003; sci. adv. bd. Promega Corp., 1999—; selection com. for editor Jour. Organic Chemistry, 1999. Mem. editl. bd. Chemistry and Biology, 1997—, Organic Reactions, 2000—; contbr. articles to profl. jour. Recipient Dow Chems. New Faculty award, 1992, Shaw Scientist award, 1992-97, Nat. Young Investigator award NSF, 1993-98, Beckman Young Investigator award, 1994-96, Zeneca Excellence in Chemistry award, 1996, Dreyfus Tchr.-Scholar award Dreyfus Found., 1996; Postdoctoral fellow Am. Cancer Soc., 1989-91, MacArthur fellow John D. and Catherine MacArthur Found., 1999, Alfred P. Sloan Found. fellow, 1997. Mem. AAAS, Am. Chem. Soc. (Cope scholar 1999, Isbell award 2000), Soc. Glycobiology, Am. Soc. for Biochemistry and Molecular Biology, Sigma Xi, Phi Lambda Upsilon. Avocations: canoeing, rowing, running. Office: U Wis Dept Chemistry 1101 University Ave Madison WI 53706-1322 Fax: 608-265-0764.

KIESSLING, LOUISE SADLER, pediatrician, medical educator; b. Utica, N.Y. m. Charles M. Fair. AB in Zoology, Columbia U., 1956; MA in Psychology and Counseling, Cornell U., 1969; MD, Brown U., 1976. Diplomate Am. Bd. Pediat., Nat. Bd. Med. Examiners; lic. M.D. R.I., Mass.; cert. in sch. psychology, N.Y. Intern level I, pediat. to resident level II R.I. Hosp. (Brown U.), Providence, 1976-78; resident level III, ambulatory pediat. Children's Hosp. Med. Ctr., Boston, 1978-79; neurology fellow Children's Hosp. Med. Ctr. (Harvard U.), Boston, 1979-80; dir. pediat. edn., depts. pediat. and family medicine Meml. Hosp. of R.I., Pawtucket, 1980-96; asst. prof. pediat. and family medicine Brown U., 1981-89, assoc. prof. pediat. and family medicine, 1989-96, prof. pediat. and family medicine, 1996—; asst. physician, depts. pediat./family medicine Meml. Hosp. of R.I., 1980-84, assoc. physician, dept. family medicine, 1993—; consulting pediatrician Bradley Hosp., East Providence, R.I., 1994—; assoc. physician, dept. pediat. R.I. Hosp., 1985—; pediatrician-in-chief Meml. Hosp. of R.I., 1984—. Coord. Cerebral Palsy Clinic, Child Devel. Ctr., R.I. Hosp., 1980-87; instr. (part-time) Wheelock Coll., Boston, 1978-80; cons. Project Child Find, R.I. Edn. Dept., 1976-78; mem. various grant rev. bds., state and nat. levels. Contbr. numerous articles and revs. to profl. jours., chpts. to books; presenter and organizer of confs. in field; reviewer Jour. Developmental and Behavioral Pediat., 1987—. Former bd. dirs. R.I. Youth Guidance Ctr.; participant R.I. Med. Soc./R.I. Bar Assn. Partnership Against Drugs Program; mem. R.I. Spl. Edn. Adv. Com., 1993-94. United Cerebral Palsy fellow, Boston, 1978-80. Fellow Am. Acad. Pediat. (co-chmn. Com. on Children with Spl. Health Needs, R.I. chpt., 1991-98), Am. Acad. Cerebral Palsy and Developmental Medicine; mem. AMA, AAUW, Soc. for Developmental and Behavioral Pediat., Ambulatory Pediat. Assn., Nat. Tourette Syndrome Assn. (med. com. 1991—), R.I. Psychol. Assn., R.I. Med. Soc., Pawtucket Med. Soc. Office: Meml Hosp RI Dept Pediatrics 111 Brewster St Dept Pawtucket RI 02860-4499

KIEU, QUYNH DINH, pediatrician, not-for-profit developer; b. Hanoi, Vietnam, Mar. 18, 1950; m. Chan Kieu. MD, U. Saigon, Vietnam, 1975. Intern U. Calif., Irvine, Orange, 1976—77, resident, 1977—78, fellow, 1978—79, asst. clin. prof. pediat., 1985—; pvt. practice, 1979—; founder, pres. Project Vietnam, 1996—. Recipient Woman of Yr. award, Calif. Assembly's 69th Dist., 2004. Mem.: AMA Found. (Pride in Profession award 2004), Healthcare Found. Orange County (bd. dirs.), Vietnamese Med. Assn., Am. Acad. Pediat. Office: Project Vietnam 11100 Warner Ave Ste 116 Fountain Valley CA 92708-7500 Office Phone: 714-641-0850. Business E-Mail: qkieu@aap.org.

KIEWRA, GUSTAVE PAUL, psychologist, educator; b. Garden City Park, N.Y., July 25, 1943; s. Gustave Francis and Alice (Kozyrski) K.; m. Donna Elaine Womack, Nov. 29, 1969; children: Amy Marie, Christopher Paul, Jessica Lauren. BA, Franklin Coll., 1967; MA, Ball State U., 1968, EdD, 1972. Instr. psychology Fla. Jr. Coll., Jacksonville, 1968-70; counselor, asst. prof. counselor edn. Western Ky. U., Bowling Green, 1972-76; prof. psychology Piedmont Va. C.C., Charlottesville, 1976—. Mem. psychology peer group planning com. Va. C.C. Sys., 1996; mem. bldg. com. Piedmont Va. C.C., 1993-98, planning coun., 1996—, mem. info. techs. com., 1996-2000, phys. facilities com., 1999—, coll. diversity com., 1999-2002, exterior signage and way finding com., 1999-2000, safety com., 2002—, chair adminstrv. svcs., 2003-05, bookstore com., 2003-05 Bd. dirs. Western Albemarle Rescue Squad, Crozet, Va., 1987, 88, Am. Lung Assn., Charlottesville; 1986-88; coord. Neighborhood Watch, Crozet, 1985-98; mem. sch. improvement com. Crozet Elem. Sch., 1990-91; mem. Piedmont (Va.) Cmty. Coll. Planning Coun., 1995-96. Recipient svc. award Piedmont Va. C.C., 1981, 86, 91, 96, 2001. Mem. APA, Va. Psychol. Assn., Am. Assn. Marriage and Family Counselors, Va. C.C. Assn. (rep. faculty affairs com. 1990-92), Faculty Profl. Assn., Internat. Platform Assn., Lions (pres. Crozet, Va. 1989-92, Key award 1991, Advancement Key award 1991, Master Key award 1992, 100% Pres. award 1990-92, Dist. Gov. Membership Growth award 1990-92, Va. Multiple Dist. 24 Achievement award 1990-92, Pres. Svc. Appreciation award 1992, Achievement award medal 1992, Melvin Jones fellow Internat. Found.), Phi Delta Kappa, Phi Theta Kappa (hon., faculty advisor 1980-88), Phi Delta Theta. Avocations: volleyball, hiking, gardening, physical conditioning, community service. Office: Piedmont Va CC 501 College Dr Charlottesville VA 22902-7589 Home: 4390 Garth Rd Charlottesville VA 22901-5102 Office Phone: 434-961-5273. Business E-Mail: gkiewra@pvcc.edu.

KIFFMEYER, MARY, state official; b. Balta, N.D., Dec. 29, 1946; m. Ralph Kiffmeyer; children: Christina, Patrick, James, John. RN, St. Gabriel's Sch. Nursing, Little Falls, Minn.; student, Anoka Ramsey C.C. RN, Minn.; cert. election judge. Co-owner RK Anesthesia, Big Lake, Minn.; sec. of state State of Minn., St. Paul, 1999—. Republican. Office: 180 State Office Bldg 100 Dr Martin Luther King Jr Blvd Saint Paul MN 55155-1210

KIGER, JOSEPH CHARLES, history professor; b. Kenton County, Ky., Aug. 19, 1920; s. Carl C. and Genevieve (Hoelscher) K.; m. Jean Myrick Moore, Mar. 27, 1947; children: Carl A., John J. AB, Birmingham-So. Coll., 1943; MA, U. Ala., 1947; PhD, Vanderbilt U., 1950. Teaching fellow Vanderbilt U., 1948-50; instr. history U. Ala., summer 1950, Washington U., St. Louis, 1950-51; dir. research select com. to investigate founds. U.S. Ho. of Reps., 1952; staff asso. Am. Council Edn., Washington, 1953-55; asst. dir. So. Fellowships Fund, Chapel Hill, N.C., 1955-58; asso. prof. history U. Ala., 1958-61; prof. history U. Miss., 1961—, chmn. dept. history, 1969-74, emeritus, 1990—, dir. program on founds. and Comparable orgs., 1993—2002, sr. rsch. assoc. Croft Inst. for Internat. Studies, 2002—. Cons. non-profit orgns., also govt., 1954— Author: Operating Principles of the Larger Foundations, 1954, (with others) Sponsored Research Policy of Colleges and Universities, 1954, American Learned Societies, 1963, (with others) A History of Mississippi, 1973; editor: Research Institutions and Learned Societies, 1982, International Encyclopedia of Foundations, 1990, Internat. Encyclopaedia of Learned Societies and Academies, 1993; co-editor: Foundations, 1984, Historiographic Review of Foundation Literature, Motivations and Perceptions, 1987, Philanthropic Foundations in the Twentieth Century, 2000. Served to capt. USMCR, 1942-46. Recipient Ruth Lilly Archives Rsch. award, 2004; Guggenheim fellow, 1960; grantee Russell Sage Found., 1953; grantee Rockefeller Found., 1961; grantee Am. Philos. Soc., 1964; grantee Am. Coun. Learned Socs., Nat. Acad. Scis., 1980 Mem. Am. Hist. Assn., So. Hist. Assn. (life). Office: U Miss 215 Crost Inst for Internat Studies University MS 38677

KIGER, ROBERT WILLIAM, botanist, researcher, science historian, educator; b. Washington, Oct. 4, 1940; s. William Joseph and Marian (Calvert) K.; m. Suellen Montgomery, June 11, 1968; children: David M., James R. AA with honors, Montgomery Jr. Coll., 1964; BA in Spanish with Social Scis. minor, Tulane U., 1966; MA in History, U. Md., 1971, PhD in Botany, 1972. Tchr. Poolesville Elem. Sch., Md., 1966-67; grad. teaching asst. dept. history U. Md., College Park, 1968-69, grad. teaching asst. dept. botany, 1969-70, grad. rsch. asst. dept. botany, 1969-70; assoc. editor, rsch. botanist Flora N.Am. Program dept. botany Smithsonian Inst., Washington, 1972-73; asst. dir., sr. rsch. scientist Hunt Inst. Bot. Documentation, Carnegie Mellon U., 1974-77, dir., prin. rsch. scientist, 1977—; rsch. assoc. sect. botany Carnegie Mus. Natural History, Pitts., 1978—. Adj. scientist Pitts. Poison Ctr., Children's Hosp., 1990—; distng. svc. prof. botany dept. biol. scis. Carnegie Mellon U., 1984-99, adj. prof. history of sci. dept. history, 1979—, disting. svc. prof. botany dept. biol. scis., 1999—; mem. internat. com. Internat. Congress Systematic and Evolutionary Biology, 1980-90, asst. treas., 1980-90, sec.-gen., 1990-96; mem. adv. com., editorial com. Flora of N.Am. Project, 1983—; cons. Chgo. Botanic Garden, Glencoe, Ill., 1980-83, 87-88, 89, Carnegie Mus. Natural History, Pitts., 1984, European Sci. Found., Stasbourg, France, 1987, Commn. Preservation and Access, Wye, Md., 1991, FBI, Martinsburg, W.Va., 1997. Editor: Memoirs of the Torrey Botanical Club, 1975-88, Huntia, 1978-92, bibliographic editor (all vols.) and taxonomic editor (various families), Flora of North America, 1987—; exec. editor Hunt Inst. publs., 1977—; contbr. articles to profl. jours. Chmn. Lawrence Meml. Award Com., 1979—; steering group Com. Organize a Flora of N.Am. Project, 1982-83; sec. for N.Am. Commn. Taxonomic Database Plant Sci. IUBS, 1986-89, working parties for devel. various standards, 1986—, program com., 1987-90, global plant species info. group, 1990—; mem. adv. com. computer databasing Mo. Botanical Garden, St. Louis, 1988-89, Rocky Mountain Flora Project, 1993—; botanical info. adv. workshop BIOSIS, Washington, 1990; chmn. judges for botany Internat. Sci. and Engring. Fair, Pitts., 1989. With USMC, 1960-61, USMCR, 1960-66. Grantee NSF, 1971-73, 78-80, 90; recipient Full Merit scholarship Montgomery Jr. Coll., 1963-64, Partial Merit scholarship Tulane U., 1964-66, NSF Grad. traineeship U. Md., 1970, Carroll E. Cox award U. Md., 1972-73. Fellow Linnean Soc. London; mem. AAAS, Botanical Soc. Am. (sec./treas. hist. sect. 1979-92, chmn. archives and history com. 1985-86), Am. Assn. Botanical Gardens and Arboreta, Am. Inst. Biol. Scis., Am. Soc. Plant Taxonomists, Internat. Assn. Plant Taxonomy, Internat. Soc. for History and Philosophy Sci., Assn. Tropical Biology, Coun. Botanical and Horticultural Librs., History Sci. Soc., Soc. Econ. Botany, Soc. Study Evolution, Soc. Systematic Biology, Torrey Botanical Club (assoc. editor 1975—), New Eng. Botanical Club. Avocations: music, model aviation, bicycling, motorcycling, photography. Home: 1183 Bucknell Dr Monroeville PA 15146-4319 Office: Carnegie Mellon U Hunt Inst Bot Documentation 5000 Forbes Ave Pittsburgh PA 15213-3890 Office Phone: 412-268-2434. Business E-Mail: rkiger@andrew.cmu.edu.

KIGER, RONALD LEE, retired contract negotiator; b. Pasadena, Calif., Dec. 30, 1940; s. Wallace Lee and Ilo Marie (Smith) K.; m. Carole Ann Bates, Apr. 10, 1965 (div. Dec. 1978); children: Darren Lee, Lorene Elizabeth. Student, U. Calif., Berkeley, 1958-62; BBA, Armstrong Coll., 1964. Auditor GAO, San Francisco, 1964-66; sr. auditor Def. Contract Audit Agy., San Francisco, 1966-84; material price analyst Lockheed Missiles and Space Co., Sunnyvale, Calif., 1984-91, Lockheed Martin Aeronautical Systems, Marietta, Ga., 1991—2002; ret., 2002. State dir. U.S. Jaycees, Castro Valley, Calif., 1968, pres., 1969, dist. lt. gov. Alameda County, Calif., 1970; state credentials chmn. Calif., 1970; vol. Special Olympics, Ga., 1992—, Cobb County Meals on Wheels, 2004—. Mem. Assn. Govt. Accts. (sec. 1968, spl. activities dir. 1982-83, pres. 1983-84, newsletter editor 1984-85, nat. chpt. recognition com. 1985-87, regional v.p. western region, 1988-89, nat. awards com. 1989-91, nat. nominating com. 1990). Democrat. Mem. Christian Ch. Avocations: golf, reading, crossword puzzles. Home: 4523 Savage Dr Marietta GA 30066-1425

KIGGINS, JOANNE DOLORES, writer; d. Robert Joseph and Irma Clara Kiggins; m. Alan L. Markle (div.); children: Angelica Relevant, Stacey Hubbard; m. Stanko (dec.). B in Bus., C.C. Beaver County, Monaca, Pa., 1972, B in Journalism, 1978; M in English, Pa. State U., 1980. Stringer reporter Cleve. Press, Cleve., 1982—84, Maple Heights Press/Bedford Times, Bedford, Ohio, 1982—84, editor, 1984—86; stringer reporter Cleve. Plain Dealer, Cleve., 1983—85; owner, pub., editor Markle Enterprises, Sewickley, Pa., 1986—92; prof. Slippery Rock (Pa.) U., 1988—94; freelance writer Sewickley, Pa., 1992—. Spkr. in field; tchr. numerous writing workshops; instr. Pitts. Bus. Inst. Editor, co-author Taylor Chair Company, 1985, author, editor Who's Who in Bedford Ohio, 1986; author: (monthly column) Absolutewrite.com; contbr. over 2500 articles and essays to mags. and other publs. Former leader Economy 4-H, Pa. Named Woman of Yr., Beaver County, 1970; recipient Times Woman of Yr., 1990. Mem.: NC Writers, Romance Writers Am. Avocations: writing, teaching, camping. Home: 615 Amsler Ridge Rd Sewickley PA 15143 Fax: 724-266-0812. E-mail: joannedkiggins@comcast.net.

KIGGINS, MILDRED L., marketing professional; b. Hempstead, N.Y., Sept. 14, 1927; d. Wolfgang and Hannah Ingeborg (Olsson) Weissman; m. Andrew Edward Kiggins, Jan. 8, 1962 (div. 1982); children: Daniel Mark, David Bruce. Diploma, Donovan Bus. Coll., Hackensack, N.J., 1945, Luther Coll. Acad., 1947. Exec. sec. Greenwich Engring. divsn. Am. Machine & Foundry Inc., Stamford, Conn., 1954-61. Mktg. Dr. Andrew Becker MD, Becker Pharm. Cons., Redwood City, Calif., 2000— Tchr. Sunday sch. St. John's Luth. Ch., Stamford, 1948-50. Republican. Avocations: gardening, music, sports, church activities. Home: 39 Wisteria Ln Tracy CA 95377-8765 Office Phone: 209-836-6064.

KIHLE, DONALD ARTHUR, lawyer; b. Noonan, N.D., Apr. 4, 1934; s. J. Arthur and Linnie W. (Ljunngren) K.; m. Judith Anne, July 18, 1964; children: Kevin, Kirsten, Kathryn, Kurte. BS in Indsl. Engring., U. ND, 1957; JD, U. Okla., 1967. Bar: Okla. 1967, U.S. Dist. Cts. (we. and no. dists.) Okla. 1967, U.S. Ct. Appeals (10th cir.) 1967, U.S. Supreme Ct. 1971. Assoc. Huffman, Arrington, Scheurich & Kincaid, Tulsa, 1967-71, ptnr., 1971-78; shareholder, dir., officer Arrington Kihle Gaberino & Dunn, Tulsa, 1978-97, pres., 1994-97; shareholder, dir. Gable & Gotwals, Tulsa, 1997-99, advisor, dir., 1999-2001, of counsel, 2001—. Dist. chmn. Boy Scouts Am., 1983-85, cubmaster, 1986-88, coun. coms., 1988-96, campiree chmn., 1990; mem. Statewide Law Day Com., 1982-86, chmn., 1983-85; trustee Brandon Hall Sch., Atlanta, 1991—, chmn., 1995-99. Lt. U.S. Army, 1957-59. Recipient Silver Beaver award Boy Scouts Am. Mem.: Okla. Bar Assn. (chmn. constl. bicentennial com. 1986—89), Tulsa Club (bd. govs. 1987—94, pres. 1992), Q Club (scribe 1991—), So. Hills Country Club, Rotary, Order of Arrow (vigil), Order of Coif, Sigma Chi (Tulsa alumni pres. 1995—97), Phi Delta Phi, Sigma Tau. Republican. Home: 4717 S Lewis Ct Tulsa OK 74105-5135 Office: 1100 ONEOK Plz 100 W 5th St Tulsa OK 74103-4240 E-mail: dkihle@gablelaw.com.

KIKAREAS, PANAGIOTIS, retired military officer; BSc with honors, Naval Acad; grad. with honors, Naval War Coll. Commd. ensign Greek Navy, advanced through grades to admiral, ret. Presenter in field. Decorated knight supreme comdr. Cross of the Order of Phoenix, knight comdr. Cross of Phoenix, knight comdr. Cross of Order of Honor. Achievements include first to create war games and crisis mgmt. ctr. Home: 3365 Wedgewood Ln Lady Lake FL 32162

KIKER, BILLY FRAZIER, economics professor; b. Elkin, N.C., Apr. 21, 1936; s. William James and Ruby Lucille K.; m. Martha Jane Parker, Aug. 4, 1962; children: Todd, Jonathan, David. AB, Lenoir-Rhyne Coll., 1961; PhD, Tulane U., 1965. From asst. prof. to prof. Econs. U. S.C., Columbia, 1965—,

Univ. Chr. prof. Dept. Econs., 1973—, chmn. dept., 1973-87, dir. Ctr. for Studies in Human Capital, 1972-75. Vis. prof. U. Edinburgh, Scotland, 1973, U. Minho, Portugal, 1995, 96, Wirtschafts U., Vienna, Austria, 1997; pvt. practice cons. economist, Columbia, 1972. Author: Human Capital in Retrospect, 1968, Macroeconomic Analysis, 1974; editor: Investment in Human Capital, 1971; contbr. numerous articles to profl. jours. Fulbright scholar U. Porto, Portugal, 1988. Mem. Am. Econ. Assn., Nat. Assn. Forensic Econs. Methodist. Avocations: sailing, tennis. Home: 637 Woodland Hills Rd W Columbia SC 29210-5640 Office: U of SC Coll Of Bus Admin Columbia SC 29208-0001

KIKO, PHILIP GEORGE, lawyer; b. Massillon, Ohio, July 16, 1951; s. Willard LeRoy and Stella Jane (Schroeder) K.; m. Colleen Duffy; children: Jamie Lynn, Sarah Elizabeth, Philip George Jr., Michael Ryan. BA, Mount Union Coll., 1973; JD, George Mason Sch. Law, 1977. Bar: Va. 1977, D.C 1978, U.S. Ct. Appeals (D.C. cir.) 1978. Assoc. legal counsel, broadcast asst. Nat. Rep. Congl. Com., Washington, 1973-79; exec. asst., legis. counsel Congressman Sensenbrenner, Washington, 1979-83; assoc. counsel judiciary com. U.S. Ho. Reps., Washington, 1983-86; acting dir. policy and enforcement Office for Civil Rights U.S. Dept. Edn., Washington, 1986-87; officer, bd. dirs. Kiko Heating & Air Conditioning, Canton, Ohio, 1973-89; legis. counsel Dept. Interior, Washington, 1987-89, dir. budget and program resource mgmt., 1989-92, dep. dir. office hearings and appeals, 1992-94; assoc. adminstr. procurement and purchasing U.S. Ho. of Reps., Washington, 1995-96, dep. chief of staff, counsel sci. com., 1997—98; chief of staff, counsel Congressman James Sensenbrenner, 1999-2000; chief of staff, gen. counsel House Com. on the Judiciary, 2001—. Active Arlington Rep. Com., 1978-86, 1995-2001, Fair Housing Bd., Arlington, 1980, St. Charles Parish Coun., 1997—; v.p. Arlington Hts. Citizen Assn., 1991-96, 2002-; pres. St. Charles Sch. PTO, 1994-99, 2001--; scoutmaster Boy Scouts Am., 2000—. Recipient Exceptional Svc. award Sec. Interior, 1988, Presidl. Meritorious Svc. award, 1992. Mem. Va. State Bar Assn., D.C. Bar Assn. Roman Catholic. Avocations: running, hunting, fishing. Office: US Ho of Reps House Judiciary Com 2138 Rayburn House Office Bldg Washington DC 20515-4909

KIKOLER, STEPHEN PHILIP, lawyer; b. N.Y.C., Apr. 24, 1945; s. Sigmund and Dorothy (Javna) K.; m. Ethel Lerner, June 18, 1967; children: Jeffrey Stuart, Shari Elaine. AB, U. Mich., 1966, JD cum laude, 1969. Bar: Ill. 1969, U.S. Dist. Ct. (no. dist.) Ill. 1969, U.S. Ct. Appeals (7th cir.) 1988, U.S. Ct. Appeals (11th cir.) 1994, U.S. Ct. Appeals for the Armed Forces 1970, U.S. Supreme Ct. 1994. Capt. Judge Advocate Gen.'s Corps U.S. Army, 1970-73; with Much, Shelist, Freed, Denenberg, Ament & Rubenstein PC, Chgo. Mem. ABA, Ill. State Bar Assn., Chgo. Bar. Assn. (real property law com., mechanics' liens subcom.), Soc. Ill. Constrn. Attys. Home: 2746 Norma Ct Glenview IL 60025-4661 Office: Much Shelist Freed Denenberg Ament & Rubenstein PC 191 N Wacker Dr Chicago IL 60606-1615 Office Phone: 312-521-2495. Business E-Mail: skikoler@muchshelist.com.

KILAND, LANCE EDWARD, art educator; b. Fargo, ND, Nov. 27, 1947; s. Earl Franklin and Darlene Adeline Kiland; m. Kathleen Ann Kiland, June 14, 1969. BA, Moorhead State U., 1969; MFA, So. Ill. U., 1971. Art dir. Prairie Public TV, Fargo, ND, 1969—70; graphic designer U. Minn., St. Paul, 1971—72; instr. N. Hennepin CC, Bklyn. Park, 1972—. Solo exhibition, Whitney Biennial, 1983, Walker Art Ctr., Mpls., 1985, Represented in permanent collections, Art Inst. Chgo., Walker Art Ctr., Mpls. Inst. Arts, Weisman Art Mus., Milw. Mus. Art, Minn. Mus. Art, exhibitions include represented in numerous pub. and pvt. collections. Block club leader 3200 Club, Mpls., 1990—99. Grantee Fellowship for Artists, The Bush Found., 1984, Fellowship Visual Arts, McKnight Found., 1985, Artist Fellowship grant, Nat. Endowment Arts, 1985, Artist Assistance grant, Minn. State Arts Bd., 1988. Mem.: Am. Inst. Graphic Arts. Democrat. Avocations: gardening, home renovations. Home: 6830 Baker Ave NW Buffalo MN 55313 Office: N Hennepin CC 7411 85th Ave N Brooklyn Park MN 55445

KILBANE, CATHERINE M., lawyer; b. Cleve., Apr. 10, 1963; BA cum laude, Case Western Res. U., 1984, JD cum laude, 1987. Bar: Ohio 1987. Ptnr. Baker & Hostetler, Cleve., 1997—2003; sr. v.p., gen. counsel, sec. Am. Greetings Corp., Cleve., 2003—. Mem. Delta Theta Phi. Office: Am Greetings Corp One American Rd Cleveland OH 44144*

KILBANE, THOMAS STANTON, lawyer; b. Cleve., Mar. 7, 1941; s. Thomas Joseph and Helen (Stanton) K.; m. Sally Conway Kilbane, June 4, 1966; children: Sarah, Thomas, Eamon, James, Carlin. BA magna cum laude, John Carroll U., 1963; JD, Northwestern U., 1966. Bar: Ohio 1966, US Dist. Ct. (no. dist.) Ohio 1969, US Supreme Ct. 1975, US Ct. Claims 1981, US Ct. Appeals (6th cir.) 1982, US Ct. Appeals (3d cir.) 1990, US Ct. Appeals (5th cir.) 1998, US Ct. Appeals (2d, 7th and 9th cirs.) 2002, US Ct. Appeals (4th cir.) 2003, US Ct. Appeals (1st cir.) 2004, US Ct. Appeals (8th cir.) 2005, US Ct. Appeals (10th cir.) 2005, US Ct. Appeals (11th cir.) 2005, US Ct. Appeals (DC cir.). Assoc. Squire, Sanders & Dempsey, Cleve., 1966-76, ptnr., 1976—, adminstrv. com., 1979-80, mgmt. com., 1981-83, 87-90, mng. ptnr. litigation practice area, 1991—. Fed. ct. panelist US Dist. Ct. (no. dist.) Ohio; mem. adv. bd. Inst. Transnat. Arbitration. Mem. editl. bd. Northwestern U. Law Rev., 1965-66. Active Rep. Presdl. Task Force; bd. dirs. United Way Svcs.; chmn. Supreme Ct. Hist. Soc., No. Ohio. Capt. US Army, 1968-69, Vietnam. Decorated Bronze Star; named Greater Cleve. Cath. Man of Yr., 1996. Fellow ABA, Am. Coll. Trial Lawyers, Internat. Acad. Trial Lawyers, Master Bencher of Anthony J. Celebrezze Inns of Ct.; mem. Fed. Bar Assn., Am. Coll. Barristers, Ohio Bar Assn. (AAA corp. counsel com., ctr. for pub. resources constrn. com.), Greater Cleve. Bar Assn., Def. Rsch. Inst., Jud. Conf. 8th Jud. Dist. Ohio (life), Union Club, The 50 Club, The Club, Alpha Sigma Nu. Republican. Roman Catholic. Office: Squire Sanders & Dempsey 4900 Key Tower 127 Public Sq Cleveland OH 44114-1304 Office Phone: 216-479-8564. Office Fax: 216-479-8780. Business E-Mail: tkilbane@ssd.com.

KILBERG, WILLIAM JEFFREY, lawyer, director; b. Bklyn., June 12, 1946; s. Jack and Jeanette Constance (Beck) K.; m. Barbara D. Greene, Sept. 27, 1970. Student, Bklyn. Coll., 1963-64; BS, Cornell U., 1966; JD, Harvard U., 1969. Bar: NY 1970, DC 1972. White House fellow, spl. asst. to sec. Labor, Washington, 1969-70; gen. counsel Fed. Mediation and Conciliation Service, 1970-71; assoc. solicitor U.S. Dept. Labor, 1971-73, solicitor, 1973-77; dep. team leader Dept. Labor, Reagan-Bush transition, 1980-81; ptnr. Breed, Abbott and Morgan, 1977-80, Gibson, Dunn & Crutcher, 1980—, ptnr.-in-charge Washington, 1990—95, now sr. ptnr., 1995—. Mem. exec. and mgmt. committees, Gibson Dunn & Crutcher; pub. mem. Adminstrv. Conf. of US, 1990-95; bd. dirs. Palmer Nat. Bank; prin. Coun. for Excellence in Govt., 1989—. Co-author: Pitfalls for Japanese Employers, 1993; editor-in-chief Employee Relations Law Jour., 1986—2003; co-editor Employers' Rights and Responsibilities, 1988; contbr. articles to profl. jours. Mem. legal affairs adv. com. Rep. Nat. Com., 1977-80, Presdl. Trust, Rep. Nat. Conv., 1988; class rep. Harvard Law Sch. Fund, 1973-74; bd. dirs. Friends of U.S. Dept. of Labor, 1989—. Recipient Man of Yr. award Lafayette High Sch., 1970; League United Latin Am. Citizens award for outstanding service to Spanish-speaking, 1973; Arthur S. Flemming award, 1975; Judge Groat award, 1977; Father William J. Kelly scholar, 1964-66; NY State scholar, 1963-66, named on of Twelve Leading Labor and Employment Litigators in DC Area, Legal Times, 2004. Mem. ABA, Fed. Bar Assn., NY Bar Assn., DC Bar Assn., Cornell Alumni Assn., Harvard Alumni Assn., White House Fellows Assn. (1st v.p. 1981-82, pres. 1982-83), Nat. Jewish Coalition (bd. dirs. 1988—). Jewish. Office: Gibson Dunn & Crutcher 1050 Connecticut Ave NW Ste 900 Washington DC 20036-5306 Office Phone: 202-955-8573. Business E-Mail: wkilberg@gibsondunn.com.

KILBORN, PETER THURSTON, journalist; b. Providence, Apr. 7, 1939; s. John Wiggins and Eleanor Artemesia (McIntire) K.; m. Susan Holly Woodward, Jan. 29, 1966; children: David Thompson, Elizabeth Artemesia Wilhelm. BA, Trinity Coll., 1961; MSJ, Columbia U., 1962. Reporter Providence Jour.-Bulletin, 1963-64; Paris corr. McGraw-Hill World News, N.Y.C., 1966-68; reporter, writer Bus. Week Mag., N.Y.C., 1969-71, L.A. bur. chief, 1971-73; cos. editor Bus. Week, N.Y.C., 1973-74; reporter N.Y. Times, N.Y.C., 1974-75, London corr., 1975-77, editor Sunday bus. sect. N.Y.C., 1979-82, econs. editor Washington bur., 1982-83, sr. econs. corr. Washington bur., 1983-89, nat. corr. Washington bur., 1989—2005; bus. editor Newsweek Mag., N.Y.C., 1977-78. Freelance writer, Wash., DC, 2005—. Trustee Trinity Coll., Hartford, Conn., 1990-96. Profl. journalism fellow Stanford U., 1968-69. Mem.: Sakonnet Yacht Club, Sakonnet Golf Club, R.I. Univ. Club N.Y.C. E-mail: pkborn@aol.com.

KILBOURN, ALDEAN GAE, secondary educator; b. Olympia, Wash., Apr. 27, 1951; d. Alfred Richard and Alda Jane (Gabel) Lewis; m. David Charles Kilbourn, June 24, 1972; children: Benjamin Lee, Adam Richard, Peter David. BA in Polit. Sci., U. Wash., 1972; teaching cert., U. Alaska, 1974. Tchr. fgn. lang. and social studies West Valley H.S., North Star Borough Sch. Dist., Fairbanks, Alaska, 1981-86; tchr. fgn. lang., social studies, reading North Pole Mid. Sch., Fairbanks, 1987-97; tchr. social studies, English, reading Ryan Mid. Sch., Fairbanks, 1997—99, Randy Smith Mid. Sch., Fairbanks, 1999—2003. Mem. social studies curriculum com. Fairbanks North Star Borough Sch. Dist., 1990-2002; presenter dist. and statewide confs./insvc. for sch. dist. on various social studies and computer related topics, 1985—; dist. trainer project CRISS, FNSBSD, 1999— Bd. mem. Cmty. Rsch. Ctr., Fairbanks, 1984-95. Mem. AAUW, Alaska Coun. Social Studies (bd. dirs. 1989-93), Fairbanks Coun. Social Studies (pres. 1992-96), Delta Kappa Gamma (br. pres. 2005—). Republican. Avocations: reading, working with computers, racquetball, gardening. Home: 3217 Riverview Dr Fairbanks AK 99709-4741

KILBOURN, JOSEPH A., lawyer; b. Providence, R.I., June 16, 1926; s. Jonathan Francis Kilbourn and Clara Vivell Kent; m. Elaine Mary Deran, Aug. 1, 1959; children: Mary, Pamela, Kent, Connor, Andrew. BA, Yale U., 1948; LLB, Columbia U., 1952. Bar: N.Y. 1953. Assoc. Bigham, Englar, Jones & Houston, N.Y.C., 1953-63, ptnr., 1963-98, of counsel, 1998—2004; ptnr. Cone & Kilbourn, Mt. Kisco, 2004—. Chmn. excess, surplus lines, reins. com. tort and ins. practice sect. ABA, 1991-92. Pres. Rowayton (Conn.) Hose Co. vol. fire co., 1975-80, 83-84. Staff sgt. U.S. Army, 1944-46. Mem. Comml. Bar Assn. (London, hon.), Order of Founders and Patriots Am. (atty. gen. 1994-96, sec. gen. 1996-98, gov. gen. 1998-2000, Disting. Svc. award 2000), Soc. Colonial Wars in State of Conn. (mem. coun. 1977—), Norwalk Yacht Club. Avocation: sailing. Home: Apt 206 114 Strawberry Hill Ave Stamford CT 06902 Office: Cone & Kilbourn 93 S Bedford Rd Mount Kisco NY 10549 Office Phone: 914-481-6249. Business E-Mail: jkilbourn@conekilbourn.com.

KILBOURN, WILLIAM DOUGLAS, JR., law educator; b. Colorado Springs, Colo., Dec. 9, 1924; s. William Douglas and Clara Howe (Lee) K.; m. Barbara Ruth Neff, Sept. 16, 1950; children: Jonathan VI, Katharine Ann. BA, Yale U., 1949; postgrad., Columbia U., 1949-50, LLB, 1953. Bar: Mass. 1962, Oreg. 1953, Minn. 1974. Acct. Arthur Andersen & Co., 1949-50; assoc. Davies, Biggs, Strayer, Stoel & Boley, Portland, Oreg., 1953-56; asst. prof. law U. Mont., 1956-57; assoc. prof. law U. Mo., 1957-59; prof. law, founding dir. grad. tax program Boston U., 1959-71; prof. law U. Minn., 1971-98, prof. emeritus, 1998—. Dir. U. Mont. Tax Inst., 1956; of counsel Palmer & Dodge, Boston, 1964-75, Oppenheimer, Wolff & Donnelly, St. Paul and Mpls., 1980-94; mem. exec. com. Fed. Tax Inst. New Eng., 1966-72; mem. adv. com. Western New Eng. Coll. Tax Inst; vis. prof. law Duke U., 1974-75, U. Tex., 1977, Washington U., St. Louis, 1977; past ednl. advisor Tax Execs. Inst.; lectr. in 31 states, Mex., The Caribbean, D.C.; expert witness in field. Editor: Estate Planning and Income Taxation, 1957; contbr. articles to profl. jours. Dist. dir. United Fund, Belmont, Mass., chair fair practices com. Recipient numerous tchg. awards; Kent scholar, Stone scholar Columbia U. Law Sch. Mem. ABA (tax sect., corp. stockholder rels. com. 1962-76, chair subcom. inc. 1968-73), Boston Bar Assn. (chair tax sect. 1967-70), Boston Tax Forum, Boston Tax Coun. Avocations: tennis, botany, landscape gardening.

KILBOURNE, EDWIN DENNIS, virologist, educator; b. Buffalo, N.Y., July 10, 1920; s. Edwin I. and Elizabeth (Alward) K.; m. Joy Schmid, Dec. 20, 1952; children: Edwin Michael, Richard Schmid, Christopher Norton, Paul Alward. AB, Cornell U., 1942, MD, 1944; DSc honoris causa, Rockefeller U., 1986. Asst. Rockefeller Inst., 1948-51; mem. faculty Tulane U., 1951-55, Cornell U. Med. Coll., N.Y.C., 1955-68, prof. pub. health, dir. div. virus research, 1961-68; prof., chmn. dept. microbiology Mt. Sinai Sch. Medicine, CUNY, 1968-86, disting. service prof., 1986—; rsch. prof. N.Y. Med. Coll., 1999—2002, emeritus prof., 2002—. Chmn., bd. dirs. Aaron Diamond AIDS Rsch. Ctr. for the City N.Y., 1989-94. Author: (with Wilson G. Smillie) Human Ecology and Public Health, 4th edit, 1968, Influenza, 1987, Strategies of Sex, 2005; Editor: The Influenza Viruses and Influenza, 1975. Mem. Health Rsch. Coun. N.Y.C., 1968-75. Recipient R.E. Dyer Lectureship award NIH, 1973, Borden award Assn. Am. Med. Colls., 1974, Dowling Lectureship award, 1976, Thomas Francis Lectureship award, 1976, Nat. Acad. Scis. 1977, Harvey Lectureship award, 1978, award of distinction Cornell U. Med. Alumni Assn., 1979, acad. medal N.Y. Acad. Medicine, 1982, Jacobi Medallion award Mt. Sinai Alumni Assn., 1991, Fogarty scholar award NIH, 1992. Fellow N.Y. Acad. Scis., Am. Philos. Soc.; mem. Harvey Soc., So. Soc. Clin. Rsch., Ctrl. Soc. Clin. Rsch. (emeritus), AAAS, APHA, Am. Assn. Immunologists, Am. Acad. Microbiology, Soc. Exptl. Biology and Medicine, Am. Soc. Clin. Investigation (emeritus), N.Y. Acad. Medicine, Am. Physicians, Am. Soc. Microbiology, Infectious Diseases Soc. Am., Conn. Acad. Sci. and Engring. Achievements include research in and publications on hormonal influences, genetic studies and exptl. transmission of viruses, and recombinant virus vaccines. Home: 23 Willard Ave Madison CT 06443-3202 Office Phone: 203-245-9349. E-mail: ekilbourne@snet.net.

KILBOURNE, JEAN, adult education educator, media specialist, writer; b. Junction City, Kans., Jan. 4, 1943; d. Willard Wallace and Lillian (Brazier) K.; m. Thomas Lux, June 18, 1983 (div. 1994); 1 child, Claudia Kilbourne Lux. BA, Wellesley Coll., 1964; MEd, Boston U., 1972, EdD, 1980; PhD (hon.), Westfield State Coll., 2004. Tchr. Emerson Coll., Boston, 1972-75; lectr., media analyst Boston, 1977—. Vis. scholar, Wellesley (Mass.) Coll., 1986—; bd. dirs. Dads and Daughters, Teen Talking Circles Project, The Mother's Coun. Author: (books) Deadly Persuasion, 1999, Can't Buy My Love, 2000, (films) Spin the Bottle: Sex, Lies, and Alcohol, 2004, Deadly Persuasion: The Advertising of Alcohol and Tobacco, 2004, (slide shows) The Naked Truth: Advertising's Image of Women, 1970, Under the Influence: The Pushing of Alcohol via Advertising, 1979, others; prodr: (films) Killing Us Softly: Advertising's Image of Women, 1979, Calling the Shots: The Advertising of Alcohol, 1982, Still Killing Us Softly: Advertising's Image of Women, 1987, Advertising Alcohol: Calling the Shots, 2nd edit., 1991, Pack of Lies: The Advertising of Tobacco, 1992, Slim Hopes; Advertising and the Obsession with Thinness, 1995, Killing Us Softly 3, 2000. Bd. dirs. Nat. Coun. on Alcoholism, N.Y.C., 1985-95; Nat. Adv. Coun. to NIAAA, 1993-95, Action Coalition for Media Educators. Recipient Lectr. of Yr. award Nat. Assn. for Campus Activities, 1988, 89, award Acad. Eating Disorders, 2001, Keys to Kans. City, 2004, Myra Sadler Equity award, 2005, Disting. Pub. award Assn. Women in Psychology, 2005; grantee Ednl. Found. Am., 1978. Democrat. Avocations: travel, reading, skiing. Office: Lordly and Dame 51 Church St Boston MA 02116-5417

KILBOURNE, KRYSTAL HEWETT, retired rail transportation executive; b. Sandersville, Ga., Apr. 7, 1940; d. John Ray and Kathleen (Perkins) Hewett; m. Alan Arden Kilbourne, July 1, 1961 (div. May 1972); children: Arden Alan, Keith Ray. A, U. Ga., 1960. Tchr. Massey Bus. Coll., Jacksonville, Fla., 1968-72, editor, reporter, photographer, 1968-72; asst. to pres. Luter Advt. Agy., Jacksonville, Fla., 1973-74; asst. to dir. Leukemia Soc., Jacksonville, Fla., 1975-76; asst. to pres. TeleCheck Corp., Jacksonville, Fla., 1979; mgr. customer svc. railroad ops. CSX Transp., Jacksonville, Fla., 1980—2002; ret., 2002. Chair CSX Equal Employment Opportunity Coun., 1992-94. Tuition scholar U. Ga., 1958; recipient Transp. Workers Leadership award, 1995. Mem. Nat. Assn. Railway Bus. Women, Am. Coun. Railroad Women. Democrat. Presbyterian. Avocations: painting, poetry, snorkeling, travel, reading. Home: 357 Briar Bay Cir Orlando FL 32825

KILBRIDE, THOMAS L., state supreme court justice; b. LaSalle, Ill. married; 3 children. BA magna cum laude, St. Mary's Coll., 1978; JD, Antioch Sch. Law, 1981. Practicioner U.S. Dist. Ct., Ill., U.S. Seventh Cir. Ct. Appeals; justice Ill. Supreme Ct., 2000—. Former mem. bd. dirs., former v.p., former pres. Ill. Twp. Attys. Assn. Vol. legal adv. Cmty. Caring Conf., Quad City Harvest Inc.; charter chmn. Quad Cities Interfaith Sponsoring Com.; former mem. Rock Island Human Rels. Com.; former vol. lawyer, charter mem. Ill. Pro Bono Ctr. Mem.: Rock Island County Bar Assn., Ill. State Bar Assn. Office: Ill Supreme Ct State of Ill Bldg 160 N LaSalle St Chicago IL 60601

KILBY, THEODORE MORGAN, JR., auditor, educator; b. Washington, Mar. 2, 1948; s. Theodore Morgan Sr. and Doris Marie Kilby; m. Valerie Stamps, Aug. 18, 1974 (div. 1989); children: Stephanie Michelle, Eric Hamilton. BS, Columbia Union Coll., 1975; MPA, Southeastern U., 1984, MBA, 1985. Cert. fraud examiner, cert. govt. fin. mgr. Dialysis technician VA Hosp., Washington, 1971-75, sickle cell counselor, 1975-78; staff acct. Dept. Vet. Affairs, Washington, 1978-79; auditor office of inspector gen. Dept. Transp., Washington, 1979-93, audit project mgr. office of inspector gen., 1993—. Chmn. supr. com. Transp. Fed. Credit Union, Washington. Chmn. adv. coun. Childrens Nat. Med. Ctr., 1996, mem., 1997. With U.S. Army, 1970-71. Mem. Nat. Soc. Accts., Assn. Govt. Accts. Avocations: golf, travel, music, arts. Home: 1108 Beatrice Ct Fort Washington MD 20744-3654 Office: Dept Transp OIG/JA-40 400 7th St NW Rm 9201 Washington DC 20590-0001

KILCHER, JEWEL See **JEWEL**

KILCULLEN, AUSTIN, playwright, educator; b. NYC, Apr. 21, 1923; s. Francis Denis and Katherine Kelly Kilcullen. BA, Fordham U., 1943; MA, Columbia U., 1948, diploma, 1951; Marshall McLuhan media study, Fordham U., 1967—68. Instr. LaSalle U., Phila., 1948—50, Villanova U., 1951—53, Sec. Sch. Sys., Westchester, NY, 1953—78. Film assoc. Ezra Baker Short Films, Bronxville, NY, 1963—64, Venice Film Festival, 1966. Author: (drama) Rage Against the Night, 1968 (semi-finalist, Nat. Play Awards, Nat. Repertory Theater, 1980, finalist, nat. playwriting competition, Tenn. Performing Arts Ctr., 1981), The Blind Lions, 1978, The Boudoir, Murmurs on the Wind, 1996; actor: (drama) Lucifer in Starlight, 1993. Trustee J. Acropolis Found., Elmsford, 1975; role of honor Am. Legion, Bronxville, 2003. Sgt. U.S. Army, 1944—46. Recipient Franklin T Baker citation, Columbia U., 1951, Jean Dalrymple's Best Mystery Play award, 1992, Best Mystery Play, Am. Theatre of Actors; Charles Hayden Meml. scholarship, Fordham U., 1940. Mem.: Authors League of Am., Dramatists Guild of Am., Am. Legion.

KILDEE, DALE EDWARD, congressman; b. Flint, Mich., Sept. 16, 1929; s. Timothy Leo and Norma Alicia (Ullmer) K.; m. Gayle Heyn, Feb. 27, 1965; children: David, Laura, Paul. BA, Sacred Heart Sem., 1952; tchr.'s cert., U. Detroit, 1954; MA, U. Mich., 1961; postgrad. (Rotary Found. fellow), U. Peshawar, Pakistan, 1958-59. Tchr. U. Detroit H.S., 1954-56, Flint Central H.S., 1956-64; mem. Mich. Ho. of Reps., 1964-74, Mich. Senate, 1975-76, U.S. Congress from 7th Mich. dist., 1977-93, U.S. Congress from 5th Mich. dist. (formerly 9th), 1993—; sr. mem. edn. and the workforce com., ranking minority mem. subcom. on early childhood, youth, & families; chair Congl. Auto Caucus, 1993—; co-chair Native Am. Caucus, 1997; mem. resources com.; mem. edn. and the workforce com. Mem. NAACP (life), Am. Fedn. Tchrs., Urban League, Phi Delta Kappa. Lodges: K.C; Optimists. Democrat. Office: US Ho of Reps 2107 Rayburn House Bldg Washington DC 20515-2209 also: 432 N Saginaw St Ste 410 Flint MI 48502-2018*

KILEY, KEVIN C., career military officer; BS in biology, U. Scranton, 1972; MD, Georgetown U., 1976; grad., U.S. Army War Coll., 1994. Diplomate Am. Bd. Ob-gyn. Commd. 2d lt. U.S. Army, 1972, advanced through grades to lt. gen., 2004; surg. intern, then resident in ob-gyn. William Beaumont Army Med. Ctr., El Paso, Tex., 1976-80; chief ob-gyn. svcs. 121st Evacuation Hosp., Seoul, South Korea, 1980-82; chief family planning/counseling svc., then asst. chief dept. ob-gyn., William Beaumont Army Med. Ctr., El Paso, 1982-85; divsn. surgeon 10th mountain divsn. Ft. Drum, N.Y., 1985-88; comdr. 10th med. bn., 10th mountain divsn., 1985-88; asst. chief, then chmn. dept. ob-gyn. William Beaumont Army Med. Ctr., El Paso, 1988-90; comdr. 15th evacuation hosp. Ft. Polk, La., 1990-91; dep. comdr. for clin. svcs. Womack Army Med. Ctr., Ft. Bragg, NC, 1991-93; comdr. Landstuhl (Germany) Regional Med. Ctr., 1994-98; command surgeon U.S. Army Europe and 7th U.S. Army, 1995-98; asst. surgeon gen. for force projection U.S. Army Med. Command, dep. chief of staff for ops., health policy and svcs., 1998-2000, comdr. Army Med. Dept. Ctr. & Sch. and Ft. Sam Houston, chief med. corps, 2000—02; comdr. Walter Reed Army Med. Ctr. & North Atlantic Reg. Med. Command & Lead Agent for Region 1, 2002—04, US Army Med. Command, Ft. Sam Houston, Tex., 2004—; surgeon gen. US Army, Ft. Sam Houston, Tex., 2004—. Decorated Disting. Svc. medal, Def. Superior Svc. medal, Legion of merit (with 3 oak leaf clusters), bronze star, Meritorious Svc. medal (with 2 oak leaf clusters), Army Commendation medal, Defense Svc. medal, others. Fellow ACOG. Office: US Army Med Dept Ctr & Sch 2250 Stanley Rd Fort Sam Houston TX 78234-6100*

KILEY, THERESA JANE, education educator, department chairman; b. Aurora, Ill., Oct. 4, 1951; d. John Bernard and Lorene Mae (Hubbard) Kiley; divorced; children: Shauna Shepston, Megan Shepston. BSc, Western Ill. U., 1973, MEd, 1976; EdD, Ill. State U., 1991. Cert. Tchr. Ill. Faculty assoc. Ill. State U., Normal, 1982—90; assoc. prof. Bradley U., Peoria, Ill., 1990—2000, Western Ill. U., Moline, 2004—; chair edn. dept. Hamline U., St. Paul, 2000—04. Cons. VHECEC, Peoria, 2004—. Co-author: (book) Teaching, Leadership & Learning in Pre-K 8 Settings: Strategies for Success, 2005. Bd. mem. Quad Cities Assn. Edn. Young Children, Rock Island, Ill., 2004—. Recipient Tchg. Excellence award, Rsch. Excellence award. Mem.: Am. Edn. Rsch. Assn., Assn. New Am. U. Tchr. Edn. (pres. 2004—05). Roman Catholic. Avocations: running, reading, music. Office: Western Ill Univ 3561 60th St Moline IL 61265

KILEY, THOMAS, rehabilitation counselor; b. Mpls., Aug. 28, 1937; s. Gerald Sidney and Veronica (Roberts) K.; m. Jane Virginia Butler, Aug. 25, 1989; children: Martin, Truman, Tami, Brian. BA in English, UCLA, 1959; MS in Rehab. Counseling, San Francisco State U., 1989. Cert. rehab counselor. Former rsch. profl., businessman various S.E. Asian cos., U.S. Army; sr. social worker Episcopal Sanctuary, San Francisco, 1986-88; dir. social svcs. Hamilton Family Ctr., San Francisco, 1988-89; rehab. specialist Intracorp, Honolulu, 1989-91; v.p. Heritage Counselling Svc., Honolulu, 1991—. Pres. Hunter Employment Svcs., Yuma, Ariz., 1995—, Algo Enterprises, Yuma, 1998—; chief fin. officer Heritage Am., Phoenix, 2004. With U.S. Army. Mem. Am. Counseling Assn., Nat. Assn. Rehab. Profls. in Pvt. Sector, Am. Rehab. Counselors Assn. (profl.), Nat. Rehab. Assn., Rotary, Phi Delta Kappa. Office: Heritage Counselling Svcs PO Box 5945 Yuma AZ 85366-5945

KILGORE, CADA T., III, lawyer; b. Griffin, Ga., Aug. 11, 1952; s. Cada T. Kilgore, Jr. and Margaret Heard Kilgore; m. Nancie Sharon Turner, Sept. 27, 1980; children: Cada T. Kilgore, IV, Christopher T. BBA magna cum laude, Ga. Coll., 1975; JD magna cum laude, MBA, U. Ga., 1979. Bar: Ga. 1979. Assoc. Henkel & Lamon, P.C., Atlanta, 1979—81, Henkel, Hackett, Edge & Fleming, Atlanta, 1981—83; assoc./ptnr. Paul, Hastings, Janofsky & Walker, Atlanta, 1983—93; ptnr. Sutherland Asbill & Brennan LLP, Atlanta, 1993—. Com. mem. Trinity Sch. Ann. Fund, Atlanta, 1998—2000, Westminster Sch. Ann. Fund, Atlanta, 2001—04. Named America's Leading Bus. Lawyers, Chambers and Ptnrs., 2003-2004, Ga. Super Lawyer, Law and Politics, 2004. Mem.: Elec. Coop. Bar Assn., Atlanta Bar Assn., G&T Lawyers' Assn., Ga. Electric Membership Corp. Counsel Assn., Nat. Assn. of Bond Lawyers, G&T Mgrs. Assn. (mem. lawyer's tech. adv. com. 2001—04, bd. dirs.), Capital City Club, Order of the Coif. Home: 2560 Westminster Heath Atlanta GA 30327

Office: Sutherland Asbill & Brennan LLP 999 Peachtree St NE Ste 2700 Atlanta GA 30309-3996 Office Phone: 404-853-8196. Office Fax: 404-853-8806. Personal E-mail: cada.kilgore@sablaw.com.

KILGORE, DONALD GIBSON, JR., pathologist; b. Dallas, Nov. 21, 1927; s. Donald Gibson and Gladys (Watson) K.; m. Jean Upchurch Augur, Aug. 23, 1952; children: Michael Augur, Stephen Bassett, Phillip Arthur, Geoffrey Scott, Sharon Louise. Student, So. Meth. U., 1943-45; MD Southwestern Med. Coll., U. Tex., Dallas, 1949. Diplomate Am. Bd. Pathology, Am. Bd. Dermatopathology, Am. Bd. Blood Banking; notary pub. Intern Parkland Meml. Hosp., Dallas, 1949—50; resident in pathology Charity Hosp. La., New Orleans, 1950—54, asst. pathologist, 1952—54; pathologist Greenville (S.C.) Hosp. Sys., 1956—, dir. labs., 1985—96, Greenville Meml. Hosp., 1972—96. Cons. pathologist St. Francis Hosp., 1963—, Shriners Hosp., Greenville, 1963—, Easley Baptist Hosp.; vis. lectr. Clemson U., 1963—; asst. prof. pathology Med. U. S.C., 1968—; pres. Pathology Assocs. of Greenville, 1983—96. Deacon Westminster Presbyn. Ch., 1961, ruling elder, 1969, trustee, 2001—; mem. bd. govs. S.C. Patient Compensation Fund, 1977—2001; bd. govs. Roper Mountain Sci. Ctr., 2001—. Capt. M.C. USAFR, 1954—56. Recipient Disting. Svc. award S.C. Hosp. Assn., 1976; awarded Order of The Palmetto by S.C. Gov. David M. Beasley, 1996. Fellow: Am. Soc. Dermatopathology, Am. Soc. Clin. Pathologists (councilor S.C. 1959—62), Coll. Am. Pathologists (life; assemblyman S.C. 1968—71); mem.: AMA (life; ho. of dels. 1978—94), Greater Greenville C. of C. (pres. ednl. task force 1965—70, elected trustee sch. dist. of Greenville County 1970—90), S.C. Soc. Pathologists (pres. 1969—72), S.C. Inst. Med. Edn. and Rsch. (pres. 1974—80), Nat. Assn. Med. Examiners, Greenville County Dental Soc. (life), Am. Assn. Blood Banks (life; adv. coun. 1962—67, insp. committeeman Southeast dist. 1965—2001), Am. Numismatic Assn. (life), Am. Coll. Nuc. Medicine, Am. Soc. Cytology, S.C. Med. Assn. (exec. coun. 1969—76, pres. 1974—75, exec. coun. 1978—94, A.H. Robins award for Outstanding Cmty. Svc. 1985), So. Med. Assn., Soc. Med. Friends of Wine, Epicurean Assn. of Am. (selection com.), Confrerie de la Chaine des Rotisseurs (bailli and echanson de l'ordre mondial, Greenville chpt.), Clan Douglas Soc. N.Am., Ltd. (life), Richard III Soc. (co-chmn. Am. 1966—75), Hist. Greenville Found. (exec. com. 1994—2001, pres. 1998—2000), S.W. R.R. Hist. Soc., S.C. Gov.'s Task Force on Hist. Preservation and Heritage Tourism, Roper Mountain Sci. Ctr. Assn. (bd. dirs. 2001—), Brit. Museum Soc., U.S. Power Squadron, Confrerie des Chevaliers du Tastevin (chevalier Atlanta chpt.), S.C. Hist. Soc. (life), Tex. State Hist. Assn. (life), Thomas Wolfe Soc. (life), Medieval Acad. Am. (life), Archeol. Inst. Am. (life), Brookgreen Gardens Found. (life), Friends of Tewkesbury Abbey (life), Canterbury Cathedral Trust in Am. (life), Assn. Friends of Lincoln Cathedral (life), Am. Numis. Soc. (life), Soc. Ancient Numismatics (life), Royal Numis. Soc. (life), S.C. Numis. Assn. (life), Mensa (life), S.C. Congress Parents and Tchrs. (life), Greenville County Hist. Soc. (life), Preservation Soc. of Charleston (life), Wine Acad. Am. (life), Les Amis du Vin (life), Clan MacDuff Soc. Am. (life; exec. coun. 1980—2000), So. Meth. U. Alumni Assn. (life), Highland Park H.S. Alumni Assn. (life), Am. Wine Soc. (life), Blue Ridge Numis. Assn. (life), Am. Numis. Assn. (life), Confrerie de Les Grapilleurs du Beaujolais (chevalier), St. Andrews Soc. Upper S.C. (bd. govs. 1991—93), L'Academie de Gastronomie Brillat-Savarin des Etats-Unis (founding mem.), Soc. Wine Educators, Soc. Med. Friends of Wine, Piedmont Econ. Club, Poinsett Club (life), Commerce Club (life), Greenville Country Club (life), Chandon Club, Thirty-Nine Club (pres. 1981—82), Torch Club (pres. 1964—65), Rotary (Paul Harris fellow 1988), Phi Chi, Phi Eta Sigma. Democrat. Home: 105 Wren Way Greenville SC 29605-5321 Office: 8 Memorial Medical Ct Greenville SC 29605-4400 Office Phone: 864-421-0705.

KILGORE, EDWIN CARROLL, retired federal agency administrator; b. Coeburn, Va., Jan. 24, 1923; s. Cecil Abram and Elizabeth Delle (Horne) K.; m. Ann Hitch, Dec. 30, 1944; children: Ashby Caroline, Elizabeth Cato. BS in Mech. Engring, Va. Inst. Poly., 1944; grad., Fed. Exec. Inst., 1969. With NASA (and predecessor), 1944-81; dep. assoc. adminstr. ops. Langley (Va.) Rsch. Ctr., 1975-76, dir. mgmt. ops., 1976-79, assoc. adminstr. mgmt. ops., 1979-81; cons. to NASA Washington, 1981—. Pres. Old Dominion U. Rsch. Found., Va. Air and Space Ctr. Recipient Outstanding Leadership award NASA, Disting. Svc. medal, Apollo Spl. Achievement award, Solid Propellant Spl. Achievement award, Roger Jones award Am. U. Va., State Sr. Tennis Champion, 1993, 94, 99, Nat. Sr. Olympic Tennis Champion, 2003. Mem. AIAA, Pi Tau Sigma, Omicron Delta Kappa. Clubs: Hampton Kiwanis (pres. 1969). Methodist. Office: Acad Pub Admin Washington DC 20005

KILGORE, GARY LYNN, lawyer; b. Chattanooga, July 17, 1953; s. James Velton Jr. and Frankie Jean (Eggert) K. BA, U. Va., 1975; JD, U. Tex., 1978. Bar: Tex. 1978, U.S. Dist. Ct. (no. dist.) Tex. 1979, U.S. Dist. Ct. (we. dist.) Tex. 1980, U.S. Ct. Appeals (5th cir.) 1979, U.S. Ct. Appeals (11th cir.) 1981, U.S. Dist. Ct. Hawaii 1984, U.S. Supreme Ct. 1985; bd. cert. personal injury tiral lawyer. Assoc. Garcia & Ganne, Austin, 1978-81; pres. Garcia & Kilgore, P.C., Austin, 1981-83, Garcia, Kilgore & Hickman, P.C., Austin, 1983—93; appeals judge Tex. Workers Compensation Commn., 1993—. Pres. Am. Inst. Defensive Driving, Inc. 1981-84. Author, research editor Am. Jour. Criminal Law, 1977-78. Del. Travis County Dem. Conv., Austin, 1980, 84, Tex. State Dem. Conv., Houston, 1984. Mem. ABA, Tex. State Bar Assn. Avocations: tropical fish, computers. Home: 1605A Southgate Cir Austin TX 78704-7747 Office: Tex Workers Compensation Commn 7551 Metro Ctr Dr Ste 100 Austin TX 78744-7551

KILGORE, JEFFREY HARPER, lawyer; b. Prescott, Ariz., Feb. 17, 1948; s. Richard B. Kilgore and Margaret (Poling) Keller; m. Janice Raley, June 7, 1969 (div. June 1980); children: Christopher A., Adam Harper; m. Mary Russell, Jan. 8, 1983; 1 child, Kelsey Love. BA in Banking and Fin., N. Tex. State U., 1970; JD, U. Houston, 1973. Bar: Tex. 1973, U.S. Ct. Appeals (5th cir.) 1975, U.S. Supreme Ct. 1976, U.S. Dist. Ct. (no. dist.) Tex. 1974, U.S. Dist. Ct. (so. dists.) Tex. 1983. Pvt. practice, Dallas, Irving and Galveston, Tex., 1973—. Cons. toxic tort-benzene leukemia cases, 1983—; mediation/arbitration Kilgore Mediation Ctr., 1997—; chmn. Mediation Svcs. Bd. Galveston, 1999-2001. Mem. vestry St. Mark Episcopal Ch., Irving, Tex., 1975-78, Trinity Episcopal Ch., Galveston, 1985-88, 98-2000; bd. dirs., trustee Trinity Episcopal Sch., 1998—. Mem. Assn. Trial Lawyers Am., Tex. State Bar Assn. (mem. litigation and alternate dispute resolution sect.), Galveston County Bar Assn., Lions (bd. dirs. Irving chpt. 1975-83, bd. dirs. Galveston chpt. 1983-87, named Irving chpt. Outstanding Lion 1983), Mediation Assn. of Galceston County (pres. 1998-2000), NASD Regulation Mediator, NASD Regulation Arbitration Bd. Democrat. Avocations: sailing, scuba diving, photography. Office: 2020 Broadway St Galveston TX 77550-4636

KILGORE, JERRY, former state attorney general; b. Aug. 23, 1961; m. Marty Kilgore; children: Klarke, Kelsey. Grad., U. Va.; JD, Coll. William & Mary, 1986. Prin. Richmond law firm Sands Anderson Marks & Miller; asst. Commonwealth atty. Scott County; asst. U.S. atty. (We. dist.) W. Va. US Dept. State; sec. pub. safety State of Va., 1994—97, atty. gen., 2002—05. Republican.

KILGOUR, DAVID, Canadian member parliament; b. Winnipeg, Man., Can., Feb. 18, 1941; s. David Eckford and Mary Sophia (Russell) K.; m. Laura Mae Scott, June 22, 1974; children: Margot, Eileen, David, Hilary. Bar: B.C., 1967, Man. 1970, Alta. 1972. Mem. House of Commons, 1979—; apptd. parliament sec. to pres. of privy coun., 1979; opposition critic for crime prevention, 1981-83; dep. critic external affairs, 1983-84; parliament sec. to min. external rels., 1984—85; parliament sec. to min. Indian affairs and no. devel., 1985—86; parliament sec. to min. transport, 1986—87; asst. city prosecutor Vancouver, B.C., Can., 1967-68; adv. counsel Dept. Justice, Ottawa, 1968-69; chief crown atty. Dauphin Judicial Dist., Man., 1971-72; a sr. agt. Alta. Gen. and Constl. Adv., 1972-79; dep. speaker, chmn. coms. whole house House of Commons, Ottawa, Ont., Can., 1994-97; sec. state Latin America & Africa, 1997—2002, Asia-Pacific, 2002—03. Author: Uneasy Patriots: Western Canadians in Confederation, 1988, Inside Outer Canada, 1990, Betrayal: The Spy Canada Abandoned, 1994. Chair Canadian chpt. Internat. Com. for a Free Vietnam, subcom. Human Rights and Devel., Canadian chpt. PGA. Mem. Can. Bar Assn. Office: House of Commons Rm 163 East Block Ottawa ON Canada K1A 0A6 also: Wellington St Ottawa ON K1A 0A6 Canada E-mail: kilgour@parl.gc.ca.

KILGOUR, FREDERICK GRIDLEY, librarian, educator; b. Springfield, Mass., Jan. 6, 1914; s. Edward Francis and Lillian Bess (Piper) K.; m. Eleanor Margaret Beach, Sept. 3, 1940; children: Martha, Alison, Meredith. AB, Harvard U., 1935; student, Columbia Sch. Library Service, summers 1939-41; LLD (hon.), Marietta Coll., 1980, Coll. of Wooster, 1981; DHL (hon.), Ohio State U., 1980, Denison U., 1983, U. Mo., Kansas City, 1989. Staff Harvard Coll. Library, 1935-42, OSS, 1942-45; dep. dir. office of intelligence collection and dissemination U.S. Dept. State, 1946-48; librarian Yale Med. Library, 1948-65; asso. librarian for research and devel. Yale U. Library, 1965-67; mng. editor Yale Jour. Biology and Medicine, 1949-65; lectr. in history of sci. Yale U., 1950-59, lectr. history of tech., 1961-67; fellow Davenport Coll., 1950-67; pres., exec. dir. Online Computer Library Ctr., OCLC, Inc., 1967-80, vice chmn. bd. trustees Online Computer Library Ctr., 1981-83; founder trustee Online Computer Libr. Ctr., 1984—95; Disting. rsch. prof. U. N.C., Chapel Hill, 1990—2000. Author: Library of the Medical Institution of Yale College and Its Catalogue of 1865, 1960, The Library and Information Science CumIndex, 1975, The Evolution of the Book, 1998; co-author: Engineering in History, 1956, 90; author: Collected Papers, 3 vols., 1984; editor: Book of Bodily Exercises, 1960, Jour. Library Automation, 1968-71; contbr. articles to profl. jours. Served as lt. (j.g.) USNR, 1943-45, overseas duty. Decorated Legion of Merit; recipient Margaret Mann citation in cataloging and classification, 1974, Melvil Dewey medal, 1978; Acad./Research Librarian of Year, 1979, Lifetime Achievement award, Sch. Info. and Libr. Scis., 2004; Library Info. Tech. award, 1979, numerous others Mem. ALA, Am. Soc. Info. Sci. (Merit award 1979), Cosmos Club. Home: 207 Carolina Meadows Villa Chapel Hill NC 27517-8500 Personal E-mail: ekilgour@mindspring.com. Business E-Mail: kilgour@ils.unc.edu.

KILGUS, EDWARD CHIP, singer, actor, writer, poet; b. Flushing, N.Y., Jan. 18, 1947; s. Edward Henry and Dorothy Keefanora (Vita) Kilgus. Student, St. Bonaventure U., 1964—66; BA in English, Adelphi U., 1970. Chief judge Jesters Open Vocal Competition, Ft. Lauderdale, Fla., 2003, Hurricane Lounge, Dania Beach, Fla., 2005, singing contests, 2005; judge Sea Escape Escape to Stardom, Ft. Lauderdale, 2003, Porters Pl. Vocal Competition, Ft. Lauderdale, 2004—05. Author: The School Bus of Our Dreams, 1987, It's a Long Walk to Hollywood, 1991; singer: 13 Sound of Poetry cassettes; actor: (made for TV movie) Black Magic, Miami Vice, 1987, (played a cowboy): Oklahoma, 1962, (played Sammy Fong): Flower Drum Song, 1963, (played Lt. Cable): South Pacific, 1964, (played Slim): Little Mary Sunshine, (played party guest): The Sound of Music, 1988, (played the father): 2x5, 1989; contbr. poems to lit. publs. Vol. hurricane emergency team, Dade County, 1987; Hurricane Andrew shelter vol. ARC, Broward County; mem. Rep. Nat. Com., 1987—, Fla. Rep. Com., 2004; alt. precinct capt. Broward Rep. Exec. Com., Ft. Lauderdale, 1987—92; team leader Bush-Cheney campaign, Ft. Lauderdale, 2003—04, precinct capt., grass roots team leader, 2004; vol. presdl. visits Ft. Lauderdale and Coral Gables, Fla., 2004. Sgt. USAR, 1969—75. Named one of Outstanding Poets, Nat. Libr. Poetry, 1994, Best New Poets, 1995; recipient medal, NY Music Festival Assn., 1959, 22 Hon. Mention awards, World of Poetry, 1985—93, Golden Poet award, 1986—92, Hon. Mention, Iliad Lit. Awards Program, 2001, Editor's Choice award for Outstanding Achievement in Poetry, Internat. Libr. Poetry, 2004. Mem.: ASCAP (assoc.), Am. Numis. Assn., K.C. (#3080 Oakland Park, Fla., 3d degree 2005). Roman Catholic. Avocation: numismatics. Home: 2817 NE 32d St Apt 212 Fort Lauderdale FL 33306

KILIAN, MICHAEL DAVID, journalist, writer, columnist; b. Toledo, July 16, 1939; s. D. Frederick and Laura Casmere (Dulski) K.; m. Pamela H. Reeves, Oct. 17, 1970; children: Eric, Colin. Student, New Sch. for Social Rsch., N.Y.C., 1957-58, U. Md., 1964. Writer Sta. KNTV, San Jose, Calif., 1960-63; reporter City News Bur., Chgo., 1965-66; reporter, asst. polit. editor Chgo. Tribune, 1966-71, editl. writer, 1971-86, editl. page columnist, 1971-86, Washington columnist, corr., cultural commentator, 1986—. Commentator Sta. WBBM, CBS, 1973-82, Sta. WTTW-TV, 1975-78, Nat. Pub. Radio, 1978-79; host. "DC Jour.: CLTV News, 1995-2000; correspondent Roy Leonard Show, WGN, 1996-99. Author: Who Runs Chicago?, 1979, The Valkyrie Project, 1981, Who Runs Washington?, 1982, Northern Exposure, 1983, Blood of the Czars, 1984, Heavy Losses, 1985, By Order of the President, 1986, Dance on a Sinking Ship, 1988, Looker, 1991, The Last Virginia Gentleman, 1992, The Big Score, 1993, Bad Girl Blues, 1994, Postcard from Hell, 1995, Major Washington, 1998, Murder at Manassas, 1999, A Killing at Ball's Bluff, 2000, The Weeping Woman, 2001, The Ironclad Alibi, 2002, The Uninvited Countess, 2002, A Grave at Glorieta, 2003, A Sinful Safari, 2003, The Shiloh Sisters, 2004, Deep Kill, 2005, Antietam Assassins, 2005, (comic strip) Dick Tracy, 1993—. Capt., CAP, 1976—; staff officer USCG Aux., 2002—. With U.S. Army, 1963-65. Recipient Humor Writing award UPI, 1971 Mem. White House Corrs. Assn., English Speaking Union (life), Nat. Press Club. Presbyterian. Office: Chgo Tribune 1325 G St NW Washington DC 20005-3104 Office Phone: 202-824-8222.

KILIAN, PAMELA REEVES, journalist, writer; b. Chgo., July 27, 1946; d. Roy Hester and Marguerite (Shaw) R.; m. Michael D. Kilian, Oct. 17, 1970; children: Eric Shaw Kilian, Colin David Reeves Kilian. B in Journalism, U. Mo., 1969. From reporter to editor United Press Internat., Chgo., Washington, 1970-84; news editor Scripps Howard News Svc., Washington, 1984—2002, asst. mng. editor news, 2002—. Author: (children's book) What Was Watergate?, 1990 (Hon. Mention Va. Coll. Stotes Assn. 1991); (nonfiction) Ellis Island, 1991; (biography) Barbara Bush, 1992, Barbara Bush Matriarch of a Dynasty, 2002. Home: 1003 Heather Hill Ct Mc Lean VA 22101-2024 Office: Scripps Howard New Svc 1090 Vermont Ave NW Ste 1000 Washington DC 20005-4906

KILIK, JON, film producer; b. Milburn, NJ, Dec. 26, 1956; Prodr. films, including: Do the Right Thing, 1989, Mo' Better Blues, 1990, Jungle Fever, 1991, Fathers and Sons, 1992, (with Monty Ross and Preston Holmes) Malcolm X, 1992, (with Robert De Niro and Jane Rosenthal) A Bronx Tale, 1993, Crooklyn, 1994, (with Scott Bushnell) Pret-A-Porter, 1994, (with Martin Scorsese and Spike Lee) Clockers, 1995, (with Tim Robbins and Rudd Simmons) Dead Man Walking, 1995, Basquiat, 1996, Cradle Will Rock, 1999, Pollack, 2000, Bamboozled, 2000, 25th Hour, 2002, Alexander, 2004. Office: 230 Central Park W New York NY 10024-6029

KILKEARY, KEVIN P., hospitality executive; Hotel gen. mgr., resident mgr., dir. sales & marketing Interstate Hotels Corp., regional v.p. ops., Northeast region, corp. v.p. sales & marketing, North Am., pres., COO, Crossroads Hospitality Co., LLC Pitts., 1972—99, pres., COO, pres. Office: Prospera Hospitality Foster Plaza 9 750 Holiday Dr Pittsburgh PA 15220 Office Phone: 412-921-6200. Office Fax: 412-921-5158.

KILKELLY, BRIAN HOLTEN, lighting company executive; b. East Orange, N.J., June 20, 1943; s. Daniel Joeseph and Mary Lorretta (Brown) K.; m. Judith Louise Kroger, May 21, 1966; children: Christopher, James. BS in Mktg., Fairleigh Dickinson U., 1968; MBA, Ga. State U., 1986. Sales rep. Thomas Lighting Div., Northern, N.J., 1965-68; mktg. svcs. Globe Inc., Hazelton, Pa., 1968-70; manpower devel./product mgr. Lithonia Lighting Div., Conyers, Ga., 1970-75; nat. market devel./southeastern mgr. Cooper Lighting Div., Atlanta, 1975-88; prin. Kilkelly Mgmt. Cons. Group, Conyers, 1988-89; partner Landmark Commercial & Investment Real Estate Inc., Conyers, 1988-95; CEO Peachtree Lighting Inc., Covington, Ga., 1988—. Bd. dirs. Tech Able Handicapped Tech. Access.; guest lectr. bus. sch. Ga. State U.; mentor GSU CMBA program; mktg. sponsor Olympic Exec. Vols., 1996. Contbr. articles to profl. jours. Active The Planning Forum, Vision 2020 Region Bd.; vol. Olympics, Atlanta, 1996; mem. permanent diaconate formation program Roman Cath. Diocese of Atlanta; lay witness renewal team, facilitator Renew 2000. With USNR, 1961-67 Mem. Nat. Assn. Realtors (Ga. chpt., comml. coun., strategic planning com.), Nat. Fire Protection Assn. (joint 101/70 com.), Illuminating Engring. Soc. (chmn. tech. com. 1975—), Japan Am. Soc., Ga. Assn. Real Estate Exchangers, KC (grand knight, 1st degree team, chmn. com., Cert. of Merit 1990), EMBA Alumni Assn. (steering com., fund raising). Republican. Roman Catholic. Avocations: walking, teaching, football, working with youths. Home: 2377 Country Club Dr SE Conyers GA 30013-5101

KILLDEER, JOHN See MAYHAR, ARDATH

KILLEA, MICHAEL F., lawyer; b. 1962; BA, Washington & Lee U.; JD, Georgetown U., 1987. Bar: NY, Fla. Assoc. O'Sullivan LLP (now O'Melveny & Myers LLP), NYC, 1987—97, ptnr., 1997—99, Holland & Knight LLP, NYC, Jacksonville, Fla., 1999—2001; exec. v.p., gen. counsel Pacer Internat., Inc., Concord, Calif., 2001—. Office: Pacer Internat 2300 Clayton Rd Ste 1200 Concord CA 94520 Office Phone: 925-887-1400. Office Fax: 925-887-1546.*

KILLEBREW, BETTY RACKLEY, English language educator; b. Pontotoc, Miss., June 26, 1931; d. Aubrey Jesse and Odonnell (Rutledge) R.; m. Willard Wayne Killebrew, Dec. 20, 1974. BS, U. So. Miss., 1953; MA, Miss. State U., 1965, Ednl. Specialist, 1976. Jr. high English tchr. Lambert (Miss.) High Sch., 1953-56; high sch. English tchr. Tunica County (Miss.) High Sch., 1956-59; high sch. English and Spanish tchr. Benoit (Miss.) High Sch., 1959-69; English instr., chair humanities E. Miss. C.C., Scooba, Miss., 1969—. Pres. Scooba (Miss.) Music Club, 1970—. Named Outstanding Young Women of Am., Outstanding Faculty E. Miss. Community Coll., 1989. Mem. Local Faculty Assn., Southeastern Conf. for English Tchrs., Miss. Jr. and Community Coll. Assn., Order of the Eastern Star, Gideon's Aux. Democrat. Baptist. Avocations: reading, gardening. Home: 1151 6th St Scooba MS 39358

KILLEBREW, ELLEN JANE (MRS. EDWARD S. GRAVES), cardiologist, educator; b. Tiffin, Ohio, Oct. 8, 1937; d. Joseph Arthur and Stephanie (Beriont) K.; m. Edward S. Graves, Sept. 12, 1970. BS in Biology, Bucknell U., 1959; MD, N.J. Coll. Medicine, 1965. Diplomate in cardiovasc. disease Am. Bd. Internal Medicine. Intern U. Colo., 1965-66, resident, 1966-68; cardiology fellow Pacific Med. Ctr., San Francisco, 1968-70; dir. coronary care Permanente Med. Group, Richmond, Calif., 1970-83; asst. prof. U. Calif. Med. Ctr., San Francisco, 1970-83, assoc. prof., 1983-93; clin. prof. medicine U. Calif., San Francisco, 1992—, mem. admissions panel, 1998—. Admissions panel joint med. program U. Calif. San Francisco/U. Calif. Berkeley, 1998—; expert med. reviewer Calif. Med. Br., 1999, Bd. of Med. Examiers Calif., 1999—. Contbr. chapters to books. Contbr. Resolution Firm Calif. State Assmebly, 2005. Recipient Physician's Recognition award continuing med. edn., Lowell Beal award Permante Med. Group/House Staff Assn., 1992, Commendation State Assembly of Calif. for Contbr to Women and Heart Disease, 2005; Robert C. Kirkwood Meml. scholar in cardiology, 1970. Fellow ACP, Am. Coll. Cardiology; mem. Fedn. Clin. Rsch., Am. Heart Assn. (rsch. chmn. Contra Costa chpt. 1975—, v.p. 1980, pres. chpt. 1981-82, chmn. CPR com. Alameda chpt. 1984, pres. Oakland Piedmont br. 1995—, bd. dirs. western affiliate). Home: 30 Redding Ct Belvedere Tiburon CA 94920-1318 Office: 280 W Macarthur Blvd Oakland CA 94611-5642 also: 901 Nevin Ave Richmond CA 94801-3143 Business E-Mail: ellen.killebrew@kp.org.

KILLEBREW, FLAVIUS CHARLES, academic administrator, biology professor; b. Canadian, Tex., Apr. 2, 1949; s. Wilbur N. and Nellie M. (Davidson) K.; m. Kathy C. Bartley, Dec. 23, 1981; 1 child, Arian. BS in Biology, West Tex. State Univ., 1971; MS in Biology, West Tex. State U., 1972; PhD in Zoology, U. Ark., 1976. Asst. prof. biology West Tex. A&M U., Canyon, 1976-81, assoc. prof., 1981-88, prof., 1988—, grad. dir., 1988-91, grad. dean, 1991-94, interim provost, v.p. for acad. affairs, 1994—95, provost, v.p. for acad. affairs, 1995—2004; pres. Texas A&M U., Corpus Christi, 2005—. Adj. prof. Tex. A&M U., College Station, 1990—. Sponsor T-Anchor 4-H, Canyon, 1985-90, WT Speakers Bur., Canyon, 1986—. Grantee U.S. Army Corps Engrs, 1978, Killgore Rsch. Ctr., 1989-91 Mem. Herpetologists League, Soc. for Study of Amphibians, Am. Soc. Ichthyologists, Assn. Tex. Grad. Schs. (pres. 1993), Coun. Pub. Univ. Chief Acad. Officers (pres. 1999), Masons, Tri Bet, Alpha Chi. Methodist. Office: Texas A&M U 6300 Ocean Dr Corpus Christi TX 78412-5503 Office Phone: 361-825-2621.*

KILLEEN, MICHAEL F., retail executive; Ptnr. Arthur Andersen LLP, 1978—99; bus. cons., 2000—01; sr. exec. v.p. fin. and corp. strategies OfficeMax, Shaker Heights, Ohio, 2001—02, CFO, 2002—. Office: OfficeMax PO Box 228070 Shaker Heights OH 44122-8070

KILLEEN, MICHAEL JOHN, lawyer; b. Washington, Oct. 5, 1949; s. James Robert and Georgia Winston (Hartwell) K.; m. Therese Ann Goeden, Oct. 6, 1984; children: John Patrick, Katherine Therese, Mary Clare, James Philip. BA, Gonzaga U., 1971, JD magna cum laude, 1977. Bar: Wash. 1977, U.S. Dist. Ct. (we. dist.) Wash. 1979, U.S. Ct. Appeals (9th cir.) 1984, U.S. Supreme Ct. 1990. Jud. clk. Wash. State Ct. Appeals, Tacoma, 1977-79; assoc. Davis Wright Tremaine, Seattle, 1979-85, ptnr., 1985—. Bd. dirs. Seattle Goodwill, 1987—, sec., 1998-2002. Author: Guide to Strike Planning, 1985, Newsroom Legal Guidebook, 1996, Employment in Washington, 1984—. Active Gonzaga Law Bd. Advisors, Spokane, Wash., pres., 1992-96. Recipient Freedom's Light award Wash. Newspaper Pub. Assn., 1999, Disting. Alumni award Gonzaga U., 2002. Mem. ABA, Wash. State Bar Assn., King County Bar Assn. (treas. 1987-89, Pres. award 1989). Republican. Roman Catholic. Office Phone: 206-622-3150. Business E-Mail: mikekilleen@dwt.com.

KILLEEN, TIMOTHY LAURENCE, aerospace scientist, research administrator; b. Cardiff, Wales, Jan. 21, 1952; came to U.S., 1978; married. BSc in Physics (1st class hons.), U. London, Eng., 1972, PhD in Atomic and Molecular Physics, 1975. Rsch. asst. U. Coll. London, 1975—78; postdoctoral scholar U. Mich., Ann Arbor, 1978-79, asst. rsch. scientist, 1979-84, assoc. rsch. scientist, 1984-87, assoc. prof. atmospheric, oceanic and space scis., 1987-90, prof. atmospheric, oceanic and space scis., 1990-2000, dir. Space Physics Rsch. Lab., 1993—98, assoc. v.p. rsch., 1997—2000; dir. Nat. Ctr. Atmospheric Rsch., Boulder, Colo., 2000—, sr. scientist high altitude observatory, 2000—. Vis. scientist Nat. Ctr. for Atmospheric Rsch., 1983, 85, 86, 87 summers, affiliate scientist, 1988-92; adj. prof. U. Mich., 2000-; cons. Rockwell Internat., Westinghouse GE Corp, 1989-92, PRC, Inc., NASA Headqtrs., NSF, Taiwanese Space Program; referee for: Jour. Geophys. Rsch., Geophys. Rsch. Letters, NASA proposals, Applied Optics, Space Sci. Instrumentation, Phys. Scripta, Annales Geophysicae, Planetary and Space Scis, Radio Sci., AFOSR proposals, NSCF proposals, Cambridge U. Press, Am. Meteor. Soc., Nat. Rsch. Coun. Can., and others; co-dir. Rsch. Experiences for Undergrads. Site at U. Mich., 1986—; mem. U.S. Nat. Com. for Solar Terrestrial Energy Program, program rev. com. for NSF CFS and UAF programs, 1989, 90; chm. program review com. for the NSF Aeronomy program, 1986-88, 89; mem. COSPAR Commn. C task force on the CIRA-86 model atmosphere, vice chmn. COSPAR Commn. C.; chm. NSF CEDAR program sci. steering com., 1988-91; prin. investigator on projects for NASA, NSF, Phillip's Lab; presenter in field. Contbr. over 100 articles to profl. jours. including Jour. Geophys. Rsch., Applied Physics, Applied Optics, Space Sci. Instrumentation, Atomic Physics, Planetary and Space Scis., and others; assoc. editor Jour. Geophys. Rsch. (Space Physics), 1987-92; editor-in-chief Jour. Atmopheric and Solar-Terrestrial Physics 1997—; presenter papers at over 200 sci. meetings, confs., symposiums. Mem. U. Mich. Civil Liberties Bd., 1990-93, chmn. 1992-93; mem. U. Mich. faculty grievance bd. Mem. AAAS (sci. program com., 2003-), AAUP, Am. Geophys. Union (solar-planetary rels. exec. com., meetings com., fed. budget rev. com., pub. affairs com., chmn. solar-planetary rels. program com. fall 1987; convenor and presider for spl. sci. sessions at nat. meetings, convenor of Chapman conf. on the lower thermosphere and upper mesosphere 1992, nominations com.,

2002-, pres-elect 2004-), Inst. Physics (Eng.), Am. Meteorological Soc. Office: U Mich Space Physics Rsch 2455 Hayward St Ann Arbor MI 48109-2143 also: Nat Ctr Atmospheric Rsch 1850 Table Mesa Dr Boulder CO 80305-5602 E-mail: kileen@ucar.edu.

KILLEFER, CAMPBELL, lawyer; b. Hermosa Beach, Calif., Mar. 14, 1950; s. Peter and Helen (Campbell) K.; m. Madeline G. Killefer, May 28, 1978; children: Harrison, Dana. BA, Stanford U., Calif., 1972; JD, U. Calif., San Francisco, 1977. Bar: Calif. 1977, D.C. 1979. Adminstrv. asst. Office of Coastal Zone Mgmt., NOAA U.S. Dept. of Commerce, Washington, 1972-73; planner Calif. Coastal Zone Conservation Commn., San Francisco, 1973-74; assoc. Fulbright & Jaworski, Washington, 1977-82; ptnr. Shaw, Pittman, Potts & Trowbridge, Washington, 1982, Venable LLP, Washington. Editor-in-chief, Hastings Constl. Law Quarterly, 1976-77; contbr. numerous articles to profl. jours. Office: Venable LLP 575 Seventh St NW Washington DC 20004 Office Phone: 202-344-8196. Office Fax: 202-344-8300. Business E-Mail: ckillefer@venable.com.

KILLENBERG, GEORGE ANDREW, publishing executive, consultant, retired editor; b. St. Clair County, Ill., Mar. 30, 1917; s. George W. and Lavina (Ruhl) K.; m. Therese Murphy, June 3, 1943; children: George M., Mary K. Riley, John A., Terry M. Hatcher, Susan M. McGinn. BS, St. Louis U., 1954, MA, 1958. Engaged in pub. rels., 1935-41; mem. staff St. Louis Globe-Democrat, 1941—; city editor St. Louis Globe-Dem., 1956-66, mng. editor, 1966-79, exec. editor, 1979-84. Past chmn. Mid-Am. Press Inst. Bd. dirs. Boys Town Mo., 1960-88. With AUS, 1942-46. Mem. Press Club (St. Louis, pres. 1964), Sigma Delta Chi. Roman Catholic. Home: 3042 Hatherly Dr Saint Louis MO 63121-4534 Personal E-mail: gkillenber@aol.com.

KILLGORE, ANDREW IVY, former ambassador; b. Greensboro, Ala., Nov. 7, 1919; s. Robert Morris and Mary Elmae (Wimberly) K.; m. Marjorie Davis Nicholls; children: Elizabeth Nicholls Krieger, Andrew Nicholls, Jane G., Roberta K. McInerney. BS, Livingston U., 1943; JD, U. Ala., 1949. Bar: Ala. bar. Selector-analyst U.S. Displaced Persons Commn., 1949-50, displaced populations officer Frankfurt, Fed. Republic Germany, 1950-51; visa officer Am. Embassy, London, 1951-53; evaluator Dept. State, 1953-55, internat. relations officer, 1961-62; polit. officer Beirut, 1956-57; consul Jerusalem, 1957-59; polit. officer Amman, Jordan, 1959-61; officer-in-charge Iraq-Jordan affairs, 1962-65; pub. affairs officer USIS, Baghdad, Iraq, 1965-67; polit. officer Dacca, East Pakistan (now Bangladesh), 1967-70; polit.-econ. officer Arab Region North Directorate, 1970-72; counselor polit. affairs Tehran, Iran, 1972-74; charge d'affaires Manama, Bahrain, 1974; dep. chief mission Wellington, N.Z., 1974-77; amb. to Qatar Doha, 1977-80; ret., 1980. Pub. Washington Report on Middle East Affairs. Former pres. Am. sect. Musa Al-Alami of Jericho Found.; pres. Am. Ednl. Trust. Lt. (j.g.) USN, 1943-46. Recipient Cert. of Appreciation, Bd. Dirs. of Jerusalem Fund for Edn. and Cmty. Devel., 1995, Fgn. Svc. Cup, 1996. Mem.: Army and Navy, Cosmos. Office: 1904 18th St NW Washington DC 20009-7738 Office Phone: 202-939-6050.

KILLGORE, WILLIAM DALE (SCOTT), JR., neuropsychologist; b. Anchorage, Sept. 2, 1965; s. William Dale and Judith Janine Killgore; m. Desiree Baisden Conrad; children: Siobhan Conrad, Turner Conrad. AA in Liberal Arts, AAS in Radio-TV-Film, San Antonio Coll., 1986; BA summa cum laude, U. N.Mex., 1990; MA in Clin. Psychology, Tex. Tech. U., 1992, PhD in Clin. Psychology, 1996. Lic. clin. psychologist N.H. Predoctoral fellow psychology Yale Sch. Medicine, New Haven, 1995—96; postdoctoral fellow clin. neuropsychology U. Okla. Health Scis. Ctr., Oklahoma City, 1996—97, U. Pa. Med. Ctr., Phila., 1997—99; postdoctoral fellow functional neuroimaging Harvard Med. Sch./McLean Hosp., Belmont, Mass., 1999—2000; instr. psychology Harvard Med. Sch., Belmont, 2000—; asst. rsch. psychologist McLean Hosp./Harvard Med. Sch., Belmont, Mass., 2000—; rsch. psychologist Walter Reed Army Inst. Rsch., Silver Spring, Md., 2002—. Prin. investigator, NICHD Small Grant McLean Hosp./Harvard Med. Sch., Belmont, 2002—; presenter in field. Contbr. articles to profl. jours. Capt. U.S. Army, 2002—03. Grantee, Nat. Inst. Child Health and Human Devel./NIH, 2002—; scholar Maxey Scholarship in Psychology, Tex. Tech. U., 1990—96. Avocations: martial arts, running, reading. Office: Harvard Med Sch/McLean Hosp 115 Mill St Belmont MA 02478 Home: 206 S Summit Ave Gaithersburg MD 20877 Office Phone: 301-319-9391. Business E-Mail: william.d.killgore@us.army.mil.

KILLIAN, EDWARD JAMES, retired pediatrician; b. Bklyn., Nov. 14, 1927; s. Edward James and Helen Marie K.; m. Henriette Marian Killian, 1957; children: Christopher Edward, Bryan Alfred, Paul Matthew. BS, St. John's Coll., 1950; MD, SUNY, 1954. Diplomat Am. Bd. Pediatrics, Nat. Bd. Med. Examiners; lic. physician, N.Y. Intern Bklyn. Hosp., 1954-55, resident, 1955-57, attending pediatrician, 1959-61, Southside Hosp., Bayshore, N.Y., 1961-93, Good Samaritan Hosp., West Islip, N.Y., 1961-93, ret., 1994. Capt. USAF Med. Corps, 1957-59. Fellow Am. Acad. Pediatrics; mem. AMA, Med. Soc. State N.Y. (life), Suffolk County Med. Soc. (life), Suffolk Pediatric Soc. (emeritus). Avocations: swimming, hiking, gardening. Home: PO Box 432 English Mills Way Woodstock VT 05091

KILLIAN, GEORGE ERNEST, retired educational association administrator; b. Valley Stream, N.Y., Apr. 6, 1924; s. George and Reina (Moeller) K.; m. Janice E. Bachert, May 26, 1951 (dec.); children: Susan E., Sandra J.; m. Marilyn R. Killian, Sept. 1, 1984 BS in Edn., Ohio No. U., 1949; EdM, U. Buffalo, 1954; PhD in Phys. Scis., Ohio Northern U., 1989; PhD (hon.), U.S. Sports Acad., 1998, Yeungam U., Korea, 2003. Tchr.-coach Wharton (Ohio) High Sch., 1949-51; insp. USN, Buffalo, 1951-54; dir. athletics Erie County (N.Y.) Tech. Inst., Buffalo, 1954-69, asst. prof. health, phys. edn., recreation, 1954-60, asso. prof., 1960-62, prof., 1962-69; exec. dir. Nat. Jr. Coll. Athletic Assn., Colorado Springs, Colo., 1969—2005; ret. Editor: Juco Rev., 1960— . Served with AUS, 1943-45. Recipient Bd. Trustees award Hudson Valley C. of C., 1969, Erie County Tech. Inst., 1969, Service award Ohio No. U. Alumni, 1972, Service award Lysle Rishel Post, Am. Legion, 1982; named to Ohio No. U. Hall of Fame, 1979, Olympic Order, IOC, 1996, Women's Basketball Hall of Fame, 2000. Mem. U.S. Olympic Com. (dir.), Internat. Olympic Com., Am. Legion, Internat. Basketball Fedn. (pres. 1990-98), Internat. U. Sports Fedn. (1st v.p. 1995, pres. 2000), Phi Delta Kappa, Delta Sigma Phi. Clubs: Masons, Rotary. Home: 325 Rangely Dr Colorado Springs CO 80921-2655 Personal E-mail: gkillian7@adelphia.net.

KILLIAN, LAWRENCE HARDING, II, (LARRY H. KILLIAN), sculptor; b. San Antonio, May 6, 1943; s. Lawrence Harding and Dorothy Louise (Wright) K.; m. Beverly Gayle Schlueder, Dec. 21, 1963 (div. 1979); children: Lawrence Harding III, Michael Ray; m. Janice Kay Nelson, June 18, 1981. Student, Tex. A&M, 1961; BS in Indsl. Arts, Southwest Tex. State, 1971, postgrad., 1971-72, RIT Coll., 1981. Instr., job corps. and trade schs., Tex., 1971-75; owner of metal fabrication and welding bus. Austin, Tex., 1975-81; salesperson Hart Graphics, Austin (Tex.) Times Printing, Random Lake, Wis., 1982-93; freelance metal sculptor Gainesville, Tex., 1991—2002, Lubbock area, 2002—. Exhibitions include World Trade Ctr., Dallas. With Leadership Gainesville, 1999. Southwest Tex. State U. scholar, 1970. Mem.: Rotary, Lions (pres. 1993). Avocations: antiques, real estate, travel, online trading. Home and Office: 355 CR 160 Garza Co Rt 2 Box 147A Post TX 79356-9731 E-mail: killian@poka.com.

KILLIAN, LEWIS MARTIN, sociology educator; b. Darien, Ga., Feb. 15, 1919; s. Lewis Martin and Edith (Robinson) K.; m. Katharine Newbold Goold, Apr. 11, 1942; children: Katharine Newbold, Lewis Martin, John Calhoun. AB, U. Ga., 1940, MA, 1941; PhD, U. Chgo., 1949. Asst. prof. sociology U. Okla., 1949-52; asso. prof. sociology Fla. State U., 1952-57, prof., 1957-68, chmn. dept. sociology, 1966-68; prof., head dept. sociology U. Conn., 1968-69; prof. U. Mass., Amherst, 1969-84, prof. emeritus, 1984—. Vis. prof. UCLA, 1965-66, U. Hawaii, 1972; vis. lectr. Thames Poly., London, 1980-81; adj. prof. U. W. Fla., 1986—; Disting. vis. prof. U. Del., 1986. Author: (with Ralph H. Turner) Collective Behavior, 1957, 3d rev. edit., 1987, (with Charles M. Grigg) Racial Crisis in America, 1963, The Impossible Revolution, 1968, White Southerners, 1970, rev. edit., 1985, The Impossible Revolution: Phase II, 1974, Black and White: Reflections of a White Southern Sociologist, 1994. Cons. com. disaster studies NRC, 1952-57, cons. to atty. gen. of Fla., 1954-55; chmn. human rights advocacy com., dist. 1, State of Fla., 1991-93, 2000-02; mem. Fla. Statewide Human Rights Advocacy Com., 1994-2000; mem. Fla. Local Advocy Coun., 2002-04. Col. USAR, ret. Decorated Legion of Merit; Guggenheim fellow, 1975—76. Mem. Am. Sociol. Assn., So. Sociol. Soc. (pres. 1989-90), Phi Beta Kappa, Omicron Delta Kappa, Kappa Alpha, Phi Kappa Phi. Home: 10100 Hillview Rd Apt 1108 Pensacola FL 32514-5446 E-mail: killiansr@earthlink.net.

KILLIAN, RICHARD M., library director; b. Buffalo, Jan. 13, 1942; m. Nancy Killian; children from previous marriage: Tessa, Lee Ann. BA, SUNY, Buffalo, 1964; MA, Western Mich. U., 1965; grad. advanced mgmt. library adminstrn., Miami U., Oxford, Ohio, 1981; grad. library adminstrn. devel. program, U. Md., 1985. Various positions Buffalo and Erie County Pub. Libraries, 1963-74, asst. dep. dir., personnel officer, 1979-80; dir. Town of Tonawanda (N.Y.) Pub. Library, 1974-78; asst. city librarian, dir. pub. svcs. Denver Pub. Library, 1978-79; exec. dir. Nioga Library System, Buffalo, 1980-87; library dir. Sacramento (Calif.) Pub. Library, 1987—. Mem. ALA, Calif. Library Assn., Rotary. Office: Sacramento Pub Libr Adminstrn Ctr 828 I St Sacramento CA 95814-2589 Home: PO Box 342 The Sea Ranch CA 95497-0342

KILLIAN, WILLIAM PAUL, manufacturing executive; b. Sidney, Ohio, Apr. 26, 1935; s. Ray and Erie K.; m. Beverly Ann Buchanan, Sept.7, 1957; children: William, Katherine, Michael. B in Chem. Engring. with honors, Ga. Inst. Tech., 1957; M in Engring. Adminstrn. with honors, U. Utah, 1968. Chem. engr. Esso, Baton Rouge, 1957—58; mgr. research and devel. mfg. engring., then plant mgr. Thiokol Corp., Brigham City, Utah, 1958—68; mgr. corp. project mgmt. Masonite Corp., Chgo., 1968—70, mgr. new bus. ventures, 1970—73; mgr. strategic planning, chem. and metall. group Gen. Electric Co., Pittsfield, Mass. and Columbus, Ohio, 1973—77; v.p. corp. planning and devel. Hoover Universal Inc., Ann Arbor, Mich., 1977—85; v.p. corp. devel. Johnson Controls Inc., Milw., 1985—87, v.p. corp. devel. and strategy, 1987—2000. Bd. dirs., vice chmn. Aqua-Chem. Inc., Milw.; bd. dirs. RBC Bearing Corp., Oxford, Conn., Premix Inc., North Kingsville, Ohio; chmn., bd. advisors iNUX, Inc., Tampa. Bd. advisors Salvation Army, Sarasota; bd. dirs. All Faiths Food Bank, Sarasota, Fla. Mem.: Coun. Strategy Planning & Devel., Strategic Leadership Forum, Mfrs. Alliance (past chmn.), Coun. Strategic Planning Execs. of Conf. Bd. (past chmn.), Assn. for Corp. Growth Internat. (bd. dirs. Tampa Bay chpt., past nat. pres., past pres. Wis. chpt.), Mensa Soc, Koseme Soc., Tau Beta Pi, Phi Eta Sigma, Pi Delta Epsilon, Phi Kappa Phi, Omicron Delta Kappa. Personal E-mail: wkillian@comcast.net.

KILLINGER, DENNIS KARL, physicist, educator; s. Karl and Evelyn K.; m. Rose Killinger; children: Laura, Robert. BA, U. Iowa, 1967; MA, DePauw U., Greencastle, Ind., 1969; PhD, U. Mich., Ann Arbor, 1978. Physicist Naval Avionics Facility, Indpls., 1969-72; rsch. staff MIT Lincoln Lab, Lexington, Mass., 1979-87; disting. prof. physics U. South Fla., Tampa, 1987—. Tech. dir. Tech. Deployment Ctr.; mem. com. optical sci. & engring. NRC/Nat. Acad., 1995-98. Editor: Optical Remote Sensing, 1984; author: (chpt.) OSA Handbook of Optics, 1994; contbr; editl. advisory bd. Encyclopedia of Optics, 2003; articles to profl. jours. Bd. dirs. USF Rsch. Found. Named Outstanding Researcher State of Fla., 1990. Fellow Optical Soc. Am.; mem. (sr.) IEEE, Am. Phys. Soc. Office: Dept Physics USF 4202 E Fowler Ave Tampa FL 33620-8000

KILLINGER, KERRY KENT, bank executive; b. Des Moines, June 6, 1949; m. Debbie Roush. BBA, U. Iowa, 1970, MBA, 1971. Exec. v.p. Murphey Favre, Inc., Spokane, 1976-82; exec. v.p. fin. mgmt., investor rels., corp. mktg. Wash. Mutual, Seattle, 1983-86; sr. exec. v.p., 1986-88; pres., dir. Wash. Mutual Savs. Bank, Seattle, 1988—, CEO, 1990—, chmn. bd., 1991—. Mem. Thrift Inst. Adv. Coun. to Fed. Res. bd., 1992—94, NY Stock Exch. Listed Co. Adv. Com.; bd. dirs. Wash. Savs. League, Wash. Fin. League, Green Diamond Resource Co., Safeco Corp., 2003—. Bd. dirs. Fed. Home Loan Bank of Seattle, 1995—, Seattle Repertory Theatre, 1990—, Washington Roundtable, 1990—, Downtown Seattle Assn., 1991, Leadership Tomorrow, Seattle Found., 1992—, Com. to Encourage Corp. Philanthropy; mem. Alliance for Edn., 1992—, chair, 1994-96, co-chmn. AIDS Walk-a-thon, Seattle, 1990; chair Partnership for Learning, 1997. Fellow Life Mgmt. Inst.; mem. Soc. Fin. Analysts, Greater Seattle C. of C. (bd. dirs. 1992—), Rotary. Office: Wash Mutual Bank 1201 3rd Ave Seattle WA 98101*

KILLION, REDLEY, government official; b. Weno, Chuuk Stat, Micronesia, Oct. 23, 1951; m. Jacinta Antonio; nine children. BA in Econs., U. Hawaii, 1973; MA in Econs., Vanderbilt U., 1978. With Trust Territory Govt. Hdqtrs./Dept. Resources and Devel., Saipan, Micronesia, 1974-79; dir. Dept. Resources and Devel., Saipan, 1979-86; elected At-Large Four-Yr. Seat FSM Congress, 1987-99; elected 6th v.p. Federated State of Micronesia, 1999—. Vice-chmn. com. on ways and means, mem. com. on resources and devel., health, edn. and social affairs, Congress of Fed. States of Micronesia. Office: Vice Pres FSM National Governemnt Palikir Pohnpei FM 96941

KILLION, VIDA FRAZIER, minister, writer; b. Blue Ridge, Tex., Aug. 28, 1914; d. Charles Jesse Frazier and Mary Albino (Harris) Snow; m. Olen Trueman Killion, Mar. 3, 1933 (dec. June 12, 1996); 1 child, Dou Vena Charlene. *She is the youngest of four children born to Charles Jesse Frazier and Mary Albino (Snow) Harris. Her brother, John (Jack) A. Frazer, was the founder and the president of FRAZIER Inc., in Texas. He built the world's first five-channel stereo system and the talk back feature on sound equipment. He was inducted into the Audio Hall of Fame in 1974. Ola and Erma, her two older sisters, were a school teacher and a minister. Her long-desired milestone in writing was achieved in seeing the article she wrote about her brother, "An Audio Pioneer," published in the January 2005 issue of Good Old Days Special.* Degree, East Tex. State U. (formerly East Tex. State Tchr.'s Coll.), 1931. Lic. min. Assembly God, 1933, ordained min. Assembly God Ch., 1944. Co-pastor Assembly of God, Northridge, Calif., 1948—52, sectional dir. Texarkana, Ark., 1957—63, Abilene, Tex., 1966—75; tchr. Bible Assembly of God Ch., Houston, 1989—. Election clk. Harris County Elections, Houston, 1989, 2000, 2002, 2003, 2004. Recipient Golden Poet award, World of Poetry, 1988, Hon. award 50 Yrs. of Ministry, Assemblies of God, 1933—83. Mem.: Assembly of God Heritage Soc. (life Honor award for 50 yrs. svc. 1983), Cisco Writers Club (life; news reporter 1969—83, 1969—83, cert. achievement 1998). Avocations: reading, writing, music, crocheting, Scrabble. Home: 11919 Bauman Rd Houston TX 77076

KILLIP, THOMAS, cardiologist; AB, Swarthmore Coll., 1948; MD, Cornell U., 1952. Diplomate in internal medicine and cardiovasc. disease Am. Bd. Internal Medicine. Med. intern Strong Meml. Hosp., 1952—53; resident in medicine N.Y. Hosp., N.Y.C., 1953—58, resident in medicine and cardiology, 1954—55, chief divsn. cardiology, 1961—74; rsch. fellow Karolinska Inst., Stockholm, 1960—61; Harriman prof. medicine Cornell U., 1968—74; chmn. dept. medicine Evanston (Ill.) Hosp., 1974—79; assoc. dean Northwestern Med. Sch., Chgo., 1974—79; chmn. dept. medicine Henry Ford Hosp., Detroit, 1979—84; attending physician Beth Israel Med. Ctr., N.Y.C., 1984—86, exec. v.p. med. affairs, 1984—98, interim pres. and CEO, 2002—05; dir. Heart Inst. Continuum Health Ptnrs., Inc., 1998—2002. Prof. medicine Albert Einstein Coll. Medicine. Office: Beth Israel Med Ctr First Ave at 16th St New York NY 10003 Fax: 212-420-2881. Office Phone: 212-420-4010. Business E-Mail: tkillip@bethisraelny.org.

KILLORAN, CYNTHIA LOCKHART, retired educator; b. Collinsville, Ill., June 19, 1918; d. Hugh McLelland and Estelle (Jones) Lockhart; m. Timothy Thomas Killoran, Feb. 9, 1944 (dec. Mar. 1991); children: Margaret, Kathleen, Timothy P., Cynthia, Mary. BS, U. Ill., 1940, postgrad. Home econs. tchr. LaMoille (Ill.) H.S., 1940-41; home supr. Farm Security, Dept. Agr., Pittsfield, Ill., 1941-42; civilian instr. radio operating procedure US-AAC, Sioux Falls, S.D., 1942-44, Batavia, Ill., 1944-69; kindergarten tchr. Batavia Sch. Dist. # 101, 1967-93; ret., 1993. Methodist.

KILLORIN, ROBERT WARE, lawyer; b. Atlanta, Nov. 12, 1959; s. Edward W. and Virgina (Ware) K. AB cum laude, Duke U., 1980; JD, U. Ga., 1983. Bar: Ga. 1984, U.S. Dist. Ct. (no. dist.) Ga. 1984, U.S. Ct. Appeals (11th cir.) 1984. Ptnr. Killorin & Killorin, Atlanta, 1984—. Mem. Atlanta Bar Assn., Ga. Def. Lawyers Assn., State Bar Ga. (chair SCOPE com. 1986, young lawyers sect. legis. affairs com. 1989-91, instr. mock trial program 1989—), Ga. C. of C. (govtl. affairs com.), 11th Cir. Hist. Soc., Assn. Trial Lawyers Am., Nat. Assn. Underwater Instrs., Nat. Speliological Soc., Mil. Order of Carabao, U. Ga. Pres.'s Club, Explorer's Club. Avocations: forestry, scuba diving. Office: Killorin & Killorin 5587 Benton Woods Dr NE Atlanta GA 30342-1308 Office Phone: 404-847-0617. Personal E-mail: rwk@bellsouth.net.

KILLOUGH, DAVID E., lawyer; b. Camp Gordon, Ga., Jan. 30, 1955; BA, North Tex. State U., 1977; JD, Southwestern U., 1983. Bar: Calif. 1983, Tex. 2001. Ptnr., co-head Intellectual Property / Tech. Litig. Sect. Vinson & Elkins LLP, Austin, Tex. Mem.: ABA, Am. Intellectual Property Law Assn. Office: Vinson & Elkins LLP Ste 100 2801 Via Fortuna Austin TX 78746 Office Phone: 512-542-8428. E-mail: dkillough@velaw.com.

KILMAN, JAMES WILLIAM, surgeon, educator; b. Terre Haute, Ind., Jan. 22, 1931; s. Arthur and Irene (Piker) K.; m. Priscilla Margaret Jackson, June 20, 1968; children: James William, Julia Anne, Jennifer Irene. BS, Ind. State U., 1956; MD, Ind. U., 1960. Intern Ind. U. Med. Ctr., Indpls., 1960-61, resident surgery, 1961-66, asst. prof., 1966-69, assoc. prof., 1969-73; prof. surgery Ohio State U. Coll. Medicine, 1973-91, prof. surgery emeritus, 1991—; chmn. dept. thoracic surgery Children's Hosp., 1975-91; attending surgeon Univ. Hosp., Columbus, Ohio; attending staff Children's Hosp., Columbus, pres. staff, 1978; attending staff Grant Hosp., Riverside Hosp. Cons. surgeon VA Hosp., Dayton; pres. Columbus Acad. Medicine, 1977 Contbr. articles to profl. jours. Trustee Central Ohio Heart Assn., Acad. Medicine Edn. Found., Children's Hosp., 1978— . Served with USNR, 1951-55. USPHS Cardiovascular fellow, 1963-64; recipient Alumni Achievement award, Ind. State U., 1989. Fellow ACS, Am. Coll. Cardiology, Am. Acad. Pediats., Coll. Chest Physicians; mem. Columbus Surg. Soc. (hon., pres. 1974), Columbus Acad. Medicine (coun. 1971-73), Am. Surg. Assn., Soc. Univ. Surgeons, Am. Assn. Thoracic Surgery, Cen. Surg. Assn., Western Surg. Assn., Soc. Vascular Surgery, Internat. Cardiovasc. Soc., Internat. Soc. Surgeons, Chest Club, Cardiovasc. Surgery Club, City Club, Palm Aire Country Club, Faculty Club, Capital Club, Columbus Athletic Club, Pickaway County Country Club, Am. Boxer Club (bd. dirs. 2000-03, pres. 2001-03, AKC del. 2002—), Sigma Xi, Alpha Omega Alpha. Achievements include research in infant cardiopulmonary bypass and surgery for congenital heart lesions. Home: 4231 Jackson Pike Grove City OH 43123 Personal E-mail: leoline@aol.com.

KILMANN, RALPH HERMAN, business educator; b. N.Y.C., Oct. 5, 1946; s. Martin Herbert and Lilli (Leob) Kilmann; children: Catherine Mary, Christopher Martin, Arlette Martin. BS, Carnegie Mellon U., 1970; MS, Carnegie-Mellon U., 1970; PhD, UCLA, 1972. Instr. U. Pitts. Katz Grad. Sch. Bus., 1972, asst. prof., 1972-75, assoc. prof., 1975-79, prof., 1979—, George H. Love prof. orgn. and mgmt., 1991—2001, coord. orgnl. studies group, 1981-84, 86-89, dir. program in corp. culture, 1983—; pres. Organizational Design Cons., Pitts., 1975—; vis. scholar Calif. State U. Long Beach Coll. Bus. Adminstrn., 2002—03. Author: Social Systems Design: Normative Theory and the MAPS Design Technology, 1977, Beyond the Quick Fix: Managing Five Tracks to Organizational Success, 1984, 2d edit., 2004, Managing Beyond the Quick Fix: A Completely Integrated Program for Creating and Maintaining Organizational Success, 1989, Escaping the Quick Fix Trap: How to Make Organizational Improvements That Really Last, 1989, Workbook for Implementing the Five Tracks: Vols. I and II, 1991, Logistics Manual for Implementing the Five Tracks: Planning and Organizing Workshop Sessions, 1992, Workbook for Continuous Improvement: Holographic Quality Management, 1993, Quantum Organizations: A New Paradigm for Achieving Organizational Success and Personal Meaning, 2001; co-author: Methodological Approaches to Social Science: Integrating Divergent Concepts and Theories, 1978, Corporate Tragedies: Product Tampering, Sabotage and Other Catastrophes, 1984, The Management of Organization Design: Vols. I and II, 1976, Producing Useful Knowledge for Organizations, 1983, Gaining Control of the Corporate Culture, 1985, Corporate Transformation: Revitalizing Organizations for a Competitive World, 1988, Making Organizations Competitive: Enhancing Networks and Relationships Across Traditional Boundaries, 1991, Managing Ego Energy: The Transformation of Personal Meaning into Organizational Success, 1994; mem. editorial bd. Jour. Mgmt., 1983-86, Acad. Mgmt. Exec., 1987-90, Jour. Organizational Change Mgmt., 1988—; developed Kilmann Insight Test, Learning Climate Questionnaire, Thomas-Kilmann Conflict-Mode Instrument, Organization Courage Assessment, MAPS Design Tech. for Social Systems Design, Kilmann-Saxton Culture-Gap Survey, Kilmann's Organizational Belief Survey; contbr. chpts. to books, articles to profl. jours. Mem. Eastern Acad. Mgmt. (treas. 1975-76, dir. 1983-86), Am. Psychol. Assn., Inst. Mgmt. Scis. (1st prize Nat. Coll. Planning competition 1976), Beta Gamma Sigma, Sigma Xi. *Some live only for themselves, some sacrifice their lives for others. The space between is enjoying one's life while contributing to society. No one should have the full responsibility for saving the world, nor the complete freedom to ignore the future.*

KILMARTIN, DUNCAN FREY, lawyer, state representative; b. Terre Haute, Ind., June 30, 1942; m. Gail Kilmartin; children: Courtney, Tyler. Student, Nyack Coll., 1960—61; Ba cum laude in Polit. Sci., Colgate U., 1964; JD, U. Chgo., 1967. Bar: Vt. 1968. Law clk. Chief U.S. Dist. Judge Ernest Gibson, Jr., 1967—68; trustee Vt. Legal Aid, Inc., 1968—79; del. 2d Cir. Judicial Conf., 1970—71; mem. adv. com. on rules of criminal procedure Vt. Supreme Ct., 1971—80; trial atty. Newport, Vt., 1980—; rep. Vt. State Ho. Reps., Montpelier, Vt., 2001—. Mem. judiciary com. Vt. State Ho. Reps., 2001—, mem. joint judicial rules com., 2001—; gen. counsel The Fold, Inc. Dir. Concerned Parents Vt.; moderator United Ch. Derby, 1975—78, chmn. various coms., 1978—. Mem.: ATLA, Christian Legal Soc. (bd. dirs. 1982—94), Vt. Bar Assn. (bd. mgrs. 1970—73, vice chmn. young lawyers sect. 1970—72, chmn. young lawyers sect. 1972—73), Vt. Farm Bur., Phi Beta Kappa. Republican. Home: 89 Third Street Newport VT 05855 Office: c/o Sergeant at Arms 115 State Street Statehouse Montpelier VT 05633-5201

KILMARTIN, JOSEPH FRANCIS, JR., information technology executive; b. Mar. 11, 1924; s. Joseph Francis and Lauretta M. (Collins) K.; m. Gloria M. Schaffer, June 26, 1954; children: Joanne, Diane. Student, St. Thomas Sem., 1944; BA, Holy Cross Coll., 1947. Prodn. mgr. A.C. Gilbert Co., New Haven, 1947—49; prodr. NBC-TV, N.Y.C., 1950—53; v.p. sales Cellomatic Corp., N.Y.C., 1953—59; sr. v.p. Transfilm Inc., N.Y.C., 1959—62, MPO Videotronics, N.Y.C., 1962—66; pres. Bus. Programs Inc., Larchmont, NY, 1966—75, Greenwich, Conn., 1975—. Pres. Kilarnold Corp.; lectr. in field, cons. Mexican Dept. Agrarian Affairs and Colonization, 1974—. Profl. performer: (Broadway show) Small Wonder, (TV shows) Your Hit Parade, Philco Playhouse, Armstrong Circle Theatre, 1949-50. Active fund-raising Cmty. Chest, 1947-49, ARC, 1947-49, Boy Scouts Am., 1958-66, United Fund, 1970-73; mem. Congl. Adv. Bd., Presdl. Task Force, Atlantic Coun., Conn. Venture Group, Mil. Affairs Coun., Fayetteville, N.C., Harnett County Strategic Planning Commn.; bd. dirs. Lee County Arts Coun.; mem. exec. com., chmn. Lee County Rep. Party Coun.; chmn. Carolina Trace Cmty. Action Com. Recipient medal of excellence Mex. Agrarian Affairs and Colonization Dept., 1976, Golden Medallion award in bus. comm. Miami Internat. Film Festival, 1978, Cmty. Developer of Yr. award Nat. Mfg. Housing Inst., 1998, Cmty. Betterment award N.C. House of Reps., 1998-99, Sovereign Mil. Order of the Temple of Jerusalem, 1998. Mem. Am. Mgmt.

Assn., TV Execs. Soc., Pres.'s Assn., Larchmont Club (N.Y.), Yacht Club, Westchester Country Club, Univ. Club (N.Y.C.), Carolina Trace Country Club, Lambs Club. Home: 4 Classic Circle Mashpee MA 02649 Personal E-mail: jkilma5437@aol.com.

KILMER, NEAL HAROLD, application developer; b. Orange, Tex., Apr. 24, 1943; s. Harold Norval and Luella Alice (Sharp) Kilmer; m. Jody Geary, Oct. 24, 1998. BS in Chemistry and Math., Northwestern Okla. State U., 1964; MS in Chemistry, Okla. State U., 1971; PhD in Chemistry, Mich. State U., 1979. Rsch. assoc. N.Mex. Petroleum Recovery Rsch. Ctr., N.Mex. Inst. Mining & Tech., Socorro, 1979-81, rsch. chemist, 1981-85, lectr. geol. engring., 1984, asst. prof. mining engring., 1985-86; phys. scientist Phys. Sci. Lab., N.Mex. State U., Las Cruces, N.Mex., 1986-96; software engr. Honeywell (formerly AlliedSignal), Las Cruces, 1996—. Contbr. articles to profl. jours. Mem.: Optical Soc. Am., Am. Inst. Physics, Am. Chem. Soc., Sigma Xi, Phi Lambda Upsilon, Pi Mu Epsilon. Presbyterian. Avocation: square and round dancing. Home: 398 No Problem Dr Las Cruces NM 88005-3951 Office: Software Maintenance & Tng Facility PO Box 9000 Las Cruces NM 88004-9000

KILMER, VAL, actor; b. Los Angeles, Dec. 31, 1959; m. Joanne Whalley, 1988 (div. 1996); children: Mercedes, Jack. Educ., Hollywood's Professional Sch., Juillard. Appeared in plays Electra and Orestes, Henry IV, Part One, 1981, As You Like It, 1982, Slab Boys (Broadway Debut), 1983, Hamlet, 1988, 'Tis Pity She's A Whore, 1992, The Postman Always Rings Twice, (Playhouse Theatre, London), 2005; motion pictures include Top Secret!, 1984, Real Genius, 1985, Top Gun, 1986, Willow, 1988, Kill Me Again, 1989, The Doors, 1991, Thunderheart, 1991, True Romance, 1993, The Real McCoy, 1993, Tombstone, 1993, Wings of Courage, 1995, Batman Forever, 1995, Heat, 1995, The Island of Dr. Moreau, 1996, The Ghost and the Darkness, 1996, Dead Girl, 1996, The Saint, 1997, The Prince of Egypt (voice) 1998, Joe the King, 1999, At First Sight, 1999, Pollock, 2000, Red Planet, 2000, Hard Cash (aka Run for the Money), 2002, The Salton Sea, 2002, Masked and Anonymous, 2003, Wonderland, 2003, Mindhunters, 2004, Alexander, 2004, Kiss Kiss, Bang Bang, 2005; TV appearances include The Murders in the Rue Morgue, 1986, The Man Who Broke 1,000 Chains, 1987, Gore Vidal's Billy the Kid, 1989. Office: William Morris Agy One William Morris Pl Beverly Hills CA 90212*

KILNER, URSULA BLANCHE, genealogist, educator, writer; b. Chgo., Feb. 2, 1925; d. Frederic Russell and Blanche (Miller) Gamble; m. Glen Kilner, May 12, 1950 (dec. Feb. 1998). BA cum laude, Mt. Holyoke Coll., 1946; MA, Columbia U., 1947, postgrad., to 1951. Asst. to editor Grolier Pub., N.Y.C., 1947; mgr. Magnamusic Inc., Garrison, N.Y., 1954-55; publicity and fundraising Little Guild of St. Francis Inc., Cornwall, Conn., 1957-68; lectr. U. Conn., Torrington, 1964-66; genealogist Bird Bottom Genealogy, Salisbury, Conn., 1979—. Owner, mgr. The Tenth Muse, phonograph and stereo co., 1958-60; reporter The Comml. Record, 1960-61. Author, editor: A Revolutionary Cook Book, 1985, A Cook Book for All Seasons, 1994; columnist The Voice, 1993—2003, Animal Life, 2004—, book reviewer Heritage Books; contbr. articles to profl. jours. Mem. Planning and Zoning Commn., Salisbury, Conn., 1981-82, N.Y. State Hist. Assn. Mem.: DAR (chpt. registrar Salisbury Arsenal 1982—2004), N.Y. State Hist. Assn., Ill. Geneal. Soc., N.Y. Hist. Assn., Essex (Mass.) Soc. Genealogists, Nat. Geneal. Soc., Soc. Genealogists, Conn. Gravestone Studies, Assn. Gravestone Studies, Vt. Genealogists Soc., Suffolk County Hist. Soc., Conn. Soc. Genealogists, Am. Coll. Genealogists (asst. nat. registrar 1990—91, cert. genealogist), N.H. Genealogy Soc. (life), Nat. Soc. Huguenots (life; adv. bd. 1993—2001, Conn. registrar 1998—2001), N.H. Soc. Genealogists (life), N.Y. Geneal./Biog. Soc. (life), New Eng. Hist./Geneal. Soc. (life), Salisbury Assn., Sons and Daus. First Settlers Newbury, Van Voorhees Family Soc., Greyhound Friends West, Inc., Nat. Soc. Colonial Dames XVII Century (organizing pres. Winthrop Fleet chpt. 1990, Conn. state registrar 1995—99, chpt. pres. 1999—2001, ret.), Sheffield Hist. Soc. (life), Morse Family Soc. (life), Piscataqua Pioneers N.H. (life), Kewanee (Ill.) Hist. Soc. (life), Andover (Mass.) Hist. Soc. (life), Nat. Soc. Daus. Am. Colonists (ret. Conn. registrar), Seeley Family Soc., Whitlock Family Soc., Ea. Star. Avocations: knitting, lecturing, saving greyhounds, greenhouse plants. Home and Office: Bird Bottom Farm RR 1 Salisbury CT 06068-9802

KILPATRICK, CAROLYN CHEEKS, congresswoman; b. Detroit, June 25, 1945; d. Marvell and Willa Mae (Henry) Cheeks; divorced; children: Kwame, Ayanna. AS, Ferris State Coll., Big Rapids, Mich., 1965; BS, Western Mich. U., 1972; MS in Edn., U. Mich., 1977. Tchr. Murray Wright High Sch., Detroit, 1972-78; mem. Mich. Ho. of Reps., Lansing, 1978-96, U.S. Congress from 13th Mich. dist. (formerly 15th), Washington, 1997—; mem. appropriations com. Del. Dem. Convs., 1980, 84, 88. Participant Mich. African Trade Mission, 1984, UN Internat. Women's Conf., 1986; del. participant Mich. Dept. Agr. to Nairobi (Kenya) Internat. Agr. Show, 1986. Recipient Anthony Wayne award Wayne State U., Disting. Legislator award U. Mich., Disting. Alumni award Ferris State U., Woman of Yr. award Gentlemen of Wall St., Inc., Burton-Abercrombie award 15th Dem. Congrl. dist. Mem. Nat. Orgn. 100 Black Women. Democrat. Office: House of Reps 1610 Longworth House Office Bldg Washington DC 20515-2215*

KILPATRICK, CLIFTON WAYNE, book dealer; b. Pontiac, Mich., Nov. 16, 1949; s. Martin Laverne and Shirley Irene (Powell) Ball (dec.). Grad. high sch., Ortonville, Mich. With Royal Castle (restaurant), Miami, Fla., 1969-71, Yankee Clipper (restaurant), Ft. Lauderdale, Fla., 1971-73, Creightons (restaurant), Ft. Lauderdale, Fla., 1973-75; book collector Trivia King, Ft. Lauderdale, Fla., 1975-93. Author: Trivia Professor, 1980. Democrat. Methodist. Home and Office: 2805 NW 30th Ct Oakland Park FL 33311-1331

KILPATRICK, DONALD G., lawyer; b. Orange, NJ, July 11, 1954; BA, Yale Univ., 1977; JD, Columbia Univ., 1981. Bar: NY 1982. Mng. dir. D. George Harris & Assoc., 1993—2001; ptnr., co-chmn. Mergers & Acquisitions practice Pillsbury Winthrop Shaw Pittman, NYC, 2001—. Mem.: Assn. Bar City of NY. Office: Pillsbury Winthrop Shaw Pittman 1540 Broadway New York NY 10036 Office Phone: 212-858-1235. Office Fax: 212-858-1500. Business E-Mail: donald.kilpatrick@pillsburylaw.com.

KILPATRICK, FRANK STANTON, marketing executive; b. San Jose, Calif., Dec. 2, 1950; s. Frank George and Marian (Polk) K. Student, U. Wis., 1968—71; AB in Polit. Sci., U. Calif., Berkeley, 1975, postgrad., 1976. Writer, advt. sales rep., Midwest regional mgr., mktg. mgr. 13-30 Corp. (Whittle Comm.), 1970—74; with Grey Advt., 1977; mktg. mgr. East/West Network, 1978—79; mktg. dir. Calif. Bus. mag., L.A., 1979—81; v.p. mktg. Harlequin Mags., 1981; gen. mgr. new venture devel. Knapp Comm. Corp., 1981—84; gen. ptnr. Pacific Cellular, 1982—86, Calif. Coast Comm., 1981—84; dir., pres. Pasadena Media Inc., 1984—85; mgmt. cons. Kilpatrick & Assocs., L.A., 1984—. Lectr. entrepreneur program U. So. Calif. Sch. Bus. Adminstrn., 1984-85, UCLA Extension, 1989—; pres. Capital Equity Group, 1986-87, HomeTown Television, 1993—, Healthcare Comm. Group, 1998—. Vol. counselor 1736 Teen Crisis Ctr., Hermosa Beach, Calif., 1989-90. Mem. L.A. Advt. Club (Belding award 1980), Direct Mktg. Club So. Calif., Western Publs. Assn., Town Hall Calif., U. Calif. Alumni Assn., Stanford Grad. Bus. Sch. Alumni Assn. (sec. 1985-86, v.p. events 1986-87, dir. 1987-90, pres. 1990-92), Stanford Entrepreneurial Forum (founder), L.A. Venture Assn. (charter mem.) Office: 100 N Sepulveda Blvd 18th fl El Segundo CA 90245 Office Phone: 310-606-5700. E-mail: fkilpatrick@hcg.com.

KILPATRICK, JAMES JACKSON, JR., columnist, writer; b. Oklahoma City, Nov. 1, 1920; s. James Jackson and Alma Mia (Hawley) K.; m. Marie Louise Pietri, Sept. 21, 1942 (dec. May 1997); children: Michael Sean, Christopher Hawley, Kevin Pietri; m. Marianne Means, June 19, 1998. BJ, U. Mo., 1941. Reporter Richmond (Va.) News Leader, 1941-49, chief editorial writer, 1949-51, editor, 1951-67; writer nat. syndicated columns, TV commentator. Author: The Sovereign States, 1957, The Smut Peddlers, 1960, The Southern Case for School Segregation, 1962, The Foxes' Union, 1977, (with Eugene J. McCarthy) A Political Bestiary, 1978, (with William Bake) The American South: Four Seasons of the Land, 1980, The American South: Towns and Cities, 1982, The Writer's Art, 1984, The Ear is Human, 1985, A Bestiary of Bridge, 1986, Fine Print - Reflections on the Writing Art, 1993; editor: We the States, 1964; co-editor: The Lasting South, 1957. Vice chmn. Va. Com. on Constl. Govt., 1962-68; chmn. Va. Magna Carta Com., 1965; trustee Thomas Jefferson Ctr. for Protection of Free Expression, 1990—, Supreme Ct. Hist. Soc., 1987—. Recipient medal of honor for distinguished service in journalism U. Mo., 1953; ann. award for editorial writing Sigma Delta Chi, 1954; William Allen White award U. Kans., 1979; Carr Van Anda award Ohio U., 1987; named to Okla. Hall of Fame, 1978 Fellow Soc. Profl. Journalists; mem. Nat. Conf. Editorial Writers (chmn. 1955-56), Black-Eyed Pea Soc. Am. (No. 1 Pea pro tem 1965—), Gridiron Club. Whig. Episcopalian. Office Phone: 202-793-5301. E-mail: kilpatjj@aol.com.

KILPATRICK, JOHN AARON, construction and development company executive; b. Norfolk, Va., Jan. 7, 1954; s. Marion Calvin and Maude Elaine (Simms) K.; m. Lynnda Christina Peterson, Aug. 19, 1978; children: Lynnda Madonna, Jonathan Simms, Richard Marion, William Valien. B.S., U. S.C., 1976, M.B.A., 1981, PhD, 2002. Bus. mgr. J. Allen Shumaker Builders, Columbia, S.C., 1979-81; stockbroker Dean Witter Reynolds, Columbia, 1981-83; teaching assoc. U. S.C., Columbia, 1982-83; v.p., co-owner Carolina Microsystems, Columbia, 1983; controller Shumaker Bldrs., Columbia, 1985-87; v.p., gen. mgr. Sand Creek Properties, Columbia, 1987-88; pres. The Kilpatrick Co., 1987-90; adj. prof. Webster U., Columbia, 1986-90; asst. sr. v.p. rsch., U.S.C, 1990-94, lectr., Moore Sch. Bus., 1992-98; admin. S.C. Supercomputer Network, 1994-96; exec. dir., Acad. Coalition Intelligent Mfg., 2005-; pres., Greenfield Inst. 2005-. editor: Ctrl. Puget Sound Real Estate Rsch. Report; Author 4 books. fellow Am. Real Estate Soc.; mem. Am. Real Estate Urban Econ. Assn., Am, Econ. Assn., Am. Fin. Assn., ABA (Assoc.), Appraisal Inst, Royal Inst. Chartered Surveyors (U.K.), Real Estate Counseling Group Am., Internat. Code Coun., Wash. Athletic Club, Omicron Delta Kappa, Phi Delta Theta. Republican. Episcopalian. Home: 24024 SE 37th Pl Issaquah WA 98029-6320 Office: Greenfield Adv LLC 1825 Queen Anne Ave N Seattle WA 98109

KILPATRICK, KWAME MALIK, mayor; b. Detroit, June 8, 1970; s. Bernard Kilpatrick and Carolyn (Cheeks) Kikpatrick; m. Carlita Poles; children: Jelani, Jalil, Jonas. BS in Polit. Sci., Fla. A&M Univ.; JD, Detroit Coll. Law, 1999. Cert. teacher Florida A&M U. Mem. Mich. Ho. Reps., 1996—2001; mayor City of Detroit, 2002—. Designer Clean Mich. Initiative, 1998. Democrat. Achievements include youngest elected mayor of any major US city. Office: Coleman A Young Municipal Ctr 2 Woodward Ave Rm 1126 Detroit MI 48226*

KILPATRICK, MAUREEN, food service executive; Grad. cert., Calif. Culinary Acad. Worked with Lydia Shire Pignoli, Boston; worked with Ana Sortun and Moncef Medeb 8 Holyoke, Boston; worked with Rene Becker High-Rise Bread Co., Hi-Rise Pie Co.; with Harvest, Boston; worked with Rene Michelena La Bettola, Boston; pastry chef Oleana, Cambridge, Mass. Office: Oleana 134 Hampshire St Cambridge MA 02139

KILPATRICK, SHERRILL LYNN, elementary school educator; d. Merle Fredrick and Dorothy Evelyn (White) Mooney; m. Roy Alan Kilpatrick, June 12, 1982; children: Matthias Lee, Jason David, Nathan Roy. BA in Elem. Edn., U. of Sioux Fall, S.D., 1977; MA in Edn., Lesley U., Cambridge, Mass., 1992. Cert. profl. tchg. standards bd. cert. tchr. Wyo., 2005. Office worker Zales Jewelry, Cheyenne, Wyo., 1972—74; pre-school tchr. 1st Christian Ch., Cheyenne, 1975—77; tchr. Keith County Schools, Ogallala, Nebr., 1977—81, Converse County Sch. Dist. #1, Douglas, Wyo., 1981—. Chmn. NCA sch. improvement steering com. Converse County Sch. Dist. #1, Douglas, Wyo., 2004—. Ch. pianist Trinity Bapt. Ch., Douglas, Wyo., 1983—, Sunday sch. tchr., 1983—; cmty. edn. tchr. Ea. Wyo. C.C., Douglas, Wyo., 2003—05. Republican. Avocations: quilting, photography, teaching piano lessons, scrapbooks. Office: Converse County School District #1 615 Hamilton Douglas WY 82633 Office Phone: 307-358-2351.

KILRAIN, SUSAN, astronaut; b. Augusta, Ga., Oct. 24, 1961; d. Joe and Sue Still; m. Colin James Kilrain. MS in Aerospace Engring., GA. Inst. Tech., 1985; grad., Test Pilot Sch. Wind tunnel project officer Lockheed Corp., Marietta, Ga.; commd. ensign USN, 1985, advanced through grades to lt. comdr., flight instr. TA-4J Skyhawk; naval aviator EA-6A Electric Intruders for Tactical Electronic Warfare Sq. 33, Key West, Fla.; with NASA Johnson Space Ctr., Houston, 1995—, with Vehicle Sys. and Ops. Br. Astronaut Office, pilot STS-83, 1997, pilot STS-94, 1997, spacecraft communicator in mission control. Decorated Def. Superior Svc. medal, Navy Meritorious Svc. medal, Navy Commendation medal, Navy Achievement medal, (2) NASA Space Flight medals, Nat. Def. Svc. medal; recipient 10 Outstanding Young Ams. award U.S. Jr. C. of C., Good Scout award, 1997. Mem. Assn. Naval Aviation, Assn. Space Explorers, Ga. Tech. Found. Avocations: triathlons, martial arts, playing piano. Office: NASA Lyndon B Johnson Space Ctr Houston TX 77058

KILROY, DAVID P, history professor, writer; b. Dublin, Ireland; arrived in U.S., 1990; s. Michael G and Kathleen Kilroy; m. Jennette Lee Cook, June 15, 1996; children: Ciara, Liam. BA, U. Coll. Dublin, 1987, MA, 1989; PhD, U. Iowa, 1995. Adj. prof. U. Iowa, 1995; asst. prof. Wheeling Jesuit U., Va., 1996—2002, assoc. prof., 2002—; dir. AHA Internat. Summer Program, 2003. Author: (book) For Race and County: The Life and Career of Colonel Charles Young, 2003, Days of Decision: Pivotal Morning 20th Century U.S. Foreign Relations. Rsch. grant, West Va. Humanities Assn., Berger fellowship, Appalachian Coll. Assn., 1998. Mem.: Soc. for Historians of U.S. Fgn. Rels., Org. Am. Historians. Avocations: cycling, soccer, travel, movies, reading. Office: Wheeling Jesuit U 316 Washington Ave Wheeling WV 26003 Business E-Mail: dkilroy@wjm.edu.

KILROY, JOHN MICHAEL, artist, educator; b. Boston, Mar. 20, 1957; BFA, Art Inst. Boston, 1978. Art tchr. Quincy (Mass.) Art Assn., Lynn Art Assn., North River Art Soc., Cape Cod Sch. Art. Exhibited in group shows at Tokyo Designers Gakuin Coll., 1985 (Design award 1985), 1986 (Design award 1986), So. Shore Art Assn., 1985 (award), 90 (award), North Shore Art Assn., Mass., 1987, Colorado Springs Nat. Juried Show, 1989, North River Art Soc., Marshfield, Mass., 1997-2002, Pierce Galleries, Inc., Hingham, Mass., 1998-99, Nantucket, 2002, Attleboro Mus. Art, 1998, Harvard Club, 1999; represented in permanent collections at AT&T, N.Y.C., Boston Globe Collection, Osborne Computer, Calif., He Mingzhang Electronic Computers, Beijing, Alaska Art and Cultural Mus., Skagway, Yankee Mag., N.H. Mem.: North River Art Soc. Office: c/o Pierce Galleries Inc 5 S Water St Nantucket MA 02554 E-mail: piercegalleries@aol.net.

KILROY, JOHN MUIR, lawyer; b. Kansas City, Mo., Apr. 12, 1918; s. James L. and Jane Alice (Scurry) K.; m. Lorraine K. Butler, Jan. 26, 1946; children: John Muir, William Terence. Student, Kansas City Jr. Coll., 1935-37; AB, U. Kansas City, 1940; JD, U. Mo., 1942. Bar: Mo. 1942. Practice in, Kansas City, 1946—; ptnr. Shughart, Thomson & Kilroy, 1948—, pres., 1977-86, chmn. bd. dirs., 1980-88, chmn. emeritus, 1988—. Instr. med. jurisprudence U. Health Scis., 1973-93; panelist numerous med.-legal groups ACS, Mo. Med. Assn., Kans. U. Med. Sch., S.W. Clin. Soc. Contbr. articles to profl. jours. Chmn. bd. dirs. Kansas City Heart Assn.; mem. adv. bd. Midwest Christian Counseling Svc.; bd. dirs., pres. Della Lamb Cmty. Svc., 1991, chmn. bd. dirs., 1993; bd. dirs. Laubach Literacy Coun., 1998-2001, Kingswood Manor, 1992-94, Mo. Meth. Found., 1993-2002. Named Man of Yr., Sigma Chi, 1989. Fellow Am. Coll. Trial Lawyers; mem. ABA, Mo. Bar Assn. (chmn. med. legal com.), Kansas City Bar Assn. (Litigator Emeritus award 1990), Internat. Assn. Barristers, Internat. Assn. Def. Counsel, Am. Coll. Legal Medicine, Am. Bd. Profl. Liability Attys., Fedn. Ins. Counsel, Law Soc. U. Mo., Order Barristers U. Mo., Lawyers Assn., Kansas City (pres. 1968), Kansas City C. of C., Univ. Club (v.p. 1984, pres. 1985), Indian Hills Country Club, Kansas City Club. Home: 6860 Tomahawk Rd Shawnee Mission KS 66208-2176 Office: Shughart Thomson & Kilroy 120 W 12th St Ste 1800 Kansas City MO 64105-1922

KILROY, WILLIAM TERRENCE, lawyer; b. Kansas City, Mo., May 24, 1950; s. John Muir and Katherine Lorraine (Butler) K.; m. Marianne Michelle Maurin, Sept. 8, 1984; children: Kyle E., Katherine A. BS, U. Kans., 1972, MA, 1974; JD, Washburn U., 1977. Bar: Mo. 1977. Assoc. Shughart, Thomson & Kilroy, Kansas City, Mo., 1977-81, mem., dir., 1981—. Contbr. articles to profl. publs. Mem. Kans. City Citizens Assn., 1980—; pres., bd. govs. Sch. Law Washburn, 1992-94; with Civic Coun. of Greater Kansas City, 1999—; legal coun. Heart of Am. Coun. Boy Scouts Am., 1988-92, mem. exec. com., 1988-95, Cmty. adv. Greater Kans. City Cmty. Found. and Affiliated Trusts, 1993-2000; bd. dirs. Kansas City Neighborhood Alliance, 1998—, Greater Kansas City Crime Commn. Mem. Lawyers Assn. Kansas City, Kansas City Bar Assn. (chmn. civil rights com. 1984), Mo. Bar Assn., ABA (subcom. on arbitration, labor law sect. 1977—), Greater Kansas City C. of C., Kansas City Club, Kansas City Country Club. Office: Shughart Thomson & Kilroy 12 Wyandotte Plz 120 W 12th St Ste 1500 Kansas City MO 64105-1929 Office Phone: 816-421-3355. Business E-Mail: tkilroy@stklaw.com.

KILSBY, MARY ELLEN, minister; b. L.A., June 20, 1934; d. Lester Eugene and Mary Anna (Erickson) Green; m. Graham Perry Kilsby, Feb. 11, 1956; children: Mary Kathleen, Richard Perry, Christi Ann, Robin Lynn. BA, Pomona Coll., 1956; MRel, Sch. of Theology, Claremont, Calif., 1971, MDiv, DMin, 1978. Various Christian edn. positions, Claremont, to 1978; assoc. min. Claremont United Ch. of Christ, 1978-83; min., pastor Altadena (Calif.) United Ch. of Christ, 1983-88; sr. min., pastor 1st Congl. United Ch. of Christ, Long Beach, Calif., 1988—2000, ret., 2000—. Speaker in field. Trustee Claremont Unified Sch. Bd., 1971-78. Home: 4647 E 4th St Long Beach CA 90814-3075 Office: 1st Congl Ch 241 Cedar Ave Long Beach CA 90802-3031

KILTS, JAMES M., consumer products company executive; b. 1948; BA, Knox Coll., 1970; MBA in Mktg., U. Chgo., 1974. Pres. Kraft USA Philip Morris Companies Inc., 1989-94, exec. v.p. Kraft Foods Worldwide, 1994-97; pres., CEO Nabisco Inc., 1998—99, Nabisco Holdings Corp., Parsippany, NJ, 1999—2000; pres., CEO, chmn. The Gillette Co., Boston, 2001—. Mem. bd. dirs., The Gillette Co., 2001-, Whirlpool Corp., Mays Dept. Stores, MetLife, Inc., 2005-; mem. internat. adv. bd. Citigroup. Trustee Knox Coll.; chmn. adv. bd. Univ. Chgo. Sch. Bus. Office: Gillette Co Prudential Tower Building Boston MA 02199*

KILTY, JEROME TIMOTHY, playwright, theater director, actor; b. Balt., June 24, 1922; s. Harold Joseph and Irene (Zellinger) K.; m. Cavada Humphrey, May 11, 1956. BA, Harvard U., 1949. Prof. drama U. Okla., Norman, 1971, U. Tex., Austin, 1972, U. Kans., Lawrence, 1973; appointed to O'Conner Chair of Lit., Colgate U., Hamilton, N.Y., 1974-75, 91-92; instr. in drama Harvard U., Cambridge, Mass., 1983-85, 89. Co-founder, dir., actor Brattle Theatre Co., Cambridge, Mass., 1948-52; actor N.Y.C. stage and TV, 1952-57, including Relapse, 1951, Quadrille, 1952, Misalliance, 1953; played: Falstaff, Iago, City Centre, 1954; writer, actor Dear Liar, Chgo. and London, 1957 (Berlin Festival Critics award 1961, Baton Du Brigadier 1962-63, Palma D'Oro 1962-63, Stanislavsky Centenary medal 1963), dir. revival, Paris, 1974, 80, Rome, 1975, 85, for TV, Hallmark Hall of Fame, 1981, dir. Australian Premiere, 1993, Melbourne; writer, dir. for TV Ides of March, London, 1963, Long Live Life, San Francisco, 1967; dir. Marie Bell, Elisabeth Bergner, Maria Casares, Pierre Brasseur in various French, German, Italian prodns., 1962-65; assoc. dir., Am. Conservatory Theatre, San Francisco, 1966-68, Am. Shakespeare Co., Stratford, Conn., 1965-68; dir. Possibilities, N.Y.C., 1968, Sarah Ferrati in Mrs. Warren's Profession (in Italian), Rome, 1976; writer, dir. Don't Shoot Mable, It's Your Husband, 1968; writer, actor Dear Love, Boston, 1969, London, 1973, The Laffing Man, 1975; dir., actor Androcles and the Lion, 1985, Love's Labor's Lost, 1985; writer: The Little Black Book, N.Y.C., 1972, Look Away, N.Y.C.; musicals What the Devil, 1977, Barnum, 1978; play Hey Marie!, 1979; dir. Julius Caesar, San Diego Nat. Shakespeare Festival, 1979, Love's Labor's Lost, 1980, Misalliance, Denver, 1980, I, James McNeill Whistler, Hartford Stage Co., Peter Pan, Kansas City, Mo., 1985; appeared in play A Month in the Country, N.Y.C., 1979-80, Enter a Free Man, N.Y.C., 1984, Foxfire, Kansas City, Mo., 1985; mem., Hartman Theatre Co., 1981-82, 86-87, played the Doctor in Three Sisters and Ernest in Bedroom Farce; dir. Tammy Grimes in The Millionairess; star The Magistrate; mem., Am. Repertory Theatre Co., Cambridge, Mass., 1983-2000, created role: The King in Big River, 1983, directed, played Armado in Love's Labor's Lost, 1985, played Abel Bishop in Right You Are (If You Think So), 1988, played Don Antonio in Saturday, Sunday, Monday, 1988; played title role in King Lear, Col. Treletsky in Platonov, played James Tyrone with Claire Bloom in Long Day's Journey into Night, 1996, played Old Ekdal in Wild Duck, 1997; created role Chairman Bowman in Mastergate by Larry Gelbart, 1989, repeated role on Broadway, Criterion Theater, 1989; co-star: A Moon for the Misbegotten, Cort Theatre, N.Y.C., 1984; repeated role of Phil Hogan, Am. Repertory Theatre (Best Actor award Boston Theatre Critics 1984); mem. Hartford Stage Co., 1985-86, played in The Tempest, Twelfth Night, directed and acted in Androcles and the Lion; played Boss Mangan in Heartbreak House, Yale Repertory Theatre, 1986; dir. The Seagull, Am. Conservatory Theatre, San Francisco, 1987, The Man Who Was Peter Pan, Am. Repertory Theater, Cambridge, 1990, Arms and the Man, Alley Theater, Houston, 1995; co-star The Doctor's Dilemma, N.Y.C., 1990, played Harry Hope in The Iceman Cometh, Chgo., 1990 (Joseph Jefferson award 1991); author plays About to Begin, 1988, Margaret Sanger/Unfinished Business, 1989, The Hermit of Yalta, 1993; starred with Opera Co. of Boston in world premiere of The Balcony, 1990, Bolshoi Theatre, Moscow, 1991, starred in Gigli Concert, Court Theatre, Chgo., Spoleto Festival U.S.A., 1992, The Substance of Fire, Asolo Theatre, Sarasota, Fla., 1992, Stages Repertory Theatre, Houston, 1994, Love Letters, Asolo Theatre, 1993, King Lear, Asolo Theatre, 1993; played Horace Vandergelder in The Matchmaker, McCarter Theater, Princeton, N.J., 1994, Gov. Danforth in The Crucible, Alley Theater, Houston, 1994, King Lear, Nebr. Shakespeare Festival, 1995, Tobias in A Delicate Balance, Stages Repertory Theater, Houston, 1996. Athol Fugard's Valley Song, Arizona Theatre Co., 1997, Michael James in Playboy of the Western World, Steppenwolf Theatre, Chicago, 1998, Long Wharf Theatre, New Haven; guest starred as King Lear, Arizona State Univ., 1998; played Leo Tolstoy in world premiere of The Last Station, Vt. State Co., Burlington, 1999, Scrooge, Va. Stage Co., Norfolk, 1999, 2000, Drummond in Inherit the Wind, Mo. Repertory Co., Kansas City, Ford's Theatre, Washington, 2000; played Sean O'Casey in I Knock at the Door, Westport, Conn., 2001; co-starred in world premiere The Astronaut, Westport, Conn., 2002. Served to capt. USAAF, 1942-46, ETO. Decorated D.F.C., Air Medal with seven clusters. Mem. Signet Soc. Clubs: Players (N.Y.C.). Home: PO Box 1074 Weston CT 06883-0074

KILWAY, KATHLEEN VICTORIA, chemist, educator, researcher; b. Hill AFB, Utah, Mar. 21, 1963; d. James Bernard and Neoma Inez Kilway. BS in Chemistry cum laude, St. Mary's Coll., Notre Dame, Ind., 1985; MS in Chemistry, U. Calif. San Diego, La Jolla, 1987, PhD in Chemistry, 1992. Grad. tchg. asst. U. Calif. San Diego, LaJolla, 1985—91, grad. rsch. asst., 1985—92; postdoctoral rsch. fellow Faculté des Sci. de St. Jerome, Marseilles, France, 1992—93, U. Calif., Berkeley, 1994—96; asst. prof. chemistry U. Mo., Kansas City, 1996—2002, assoc. prof. chemistry, 2002—. Contbr. chapters to books, articles to profl. jours. Recipient Area Rsch. Enhancement award, NIH, 2000, Gov.'s Tchg. award, 2002; grantee Petroleum Rsch. Fund grant, Am. Chem. Soc., 2000; scholar Trustee's Faculty scholar, U. Mo. Kansas City, 2001. Mem.: Am. Chem. Soc., Sigma Xi, Iota Sigma Pi. Avocations: water-skiing, walking, reading. Office: U Mo Kansas City 501 H Foorsheim Hall Dept Chemistry 5100 Rockhill Rd Kansas City MO 64110-2999 E-mail: Kilwayke@umkc.edu.

KIM, BEOMJIN, education educator; m. Youngyeon Kim; children: Jiyeon, Jiwon. BS, Inha U., Incheon, 1988; MS, Ill. Inst. Tech., 1989, PhD, 1998. Asst. prof. Ind. U.-Purdue U., Fort Wayne, 1999—2004, assoc. prof., 2004—. Rschr. Digital Echocardiography Lab., Chgo., 1998—2000. Recipient Disting. Rsch. award, Allied Academies, 2002, Rschr. of the Yr., IPFW Sigma Xi Chpt., 2004; grantee PRF Summer Faculty Grant for Rsch., Purdue Rsch. Found., 2002, 2000, FWCS/IPFW Summer Rsch. Grant, Ft. Wayne Cmty. Sch./GTE, 2000. Mem.: Assn. Computing Machinery. Office: Indiana University-Purdue University 2101 E Coliseum Blvd Fort Wayne IN 46805 Office Fax: 260-481-6880. E-mail: kimb@ipfw.edu.

KIM, CHANG H, medical educator, researcher; PhD, Ind. U. Sch. Medicine, Indpls., 1998. Rsch. scientist Stanford U., Palo Alto, Calif., 1999—2002; asst. prof. Purdue U., West Lafayette, Ind., 2002. Coun. mem. Autumn Immunology Conf., Chicago, 2003—. Guest editor: Current Medicinal Chemistry (Sidney Kimmel Scholar award, 2005); contbr. articles to profl. jours., chapters to books. Grantee, Eli and Edythe Broad Med. Found., 2005. Mem.: Am. Assn. Scientists (corr. Phizer-Showell award 2005). Achievements include patents in field. Office: Purdue Univ VPTH 126 725 Harrison St West Lafayette IN 47907 Office Phone: 765-494-0976. Office Fax: 765-494-9830.

KIM, CHANGICK, researcher; b. Seoul, Republic of Korea, Jan. 18, 1967; m. MiKyoung Lee, Dec. 28, 1991; children: HanKyul, Hanna. PhD, U. Wash., 2000. Sr. rschr. SKC Ltd., Seoul, 1991—97; sr. mem. tech. staff Epson R & D Inc., Palo Alto, Calif., 2001—. Recipient rsch. and devel. excellence award, Seiko-Epson, 2003. Mem.: IEEE. Achievements include research in developing power scalable H.264 codec and MPEG-4 codec; patents pending for for several video-based technological advances. Office Phone: 650-843-8336. Personal E-mail: changickkim@gmail.com.

KIM, CHARLES WESLEY, microbiology educator; b. Nashville, Mar. 20, 1926; s. Herbert Hyungsik and Kyung Sook Kim; m. Soo Johung, June 9, 1956; 1 child, Charles W. Jr. BA, U. Calif., Berkeley, 1949; MS in Pub. Health, U. NC, 1952, PhD in Parasitology and Microbiology, 1956. Instr., asst. prof. NY Med. Coll., NYC, 1956-59, 59-64; assoc. scientist, scientist Brookhaven Nat. Lab., Upton, NY, 1965-68, 68-70; assoc. dean basic health sci. SUNY, Stony Brook, 1972-74, assoc. vice provost, 1974-83, assoc. prof., 1970-87, prof. microbiology and medicine, 1987—, prof. emeritus, 1996—. Author: Microbiology Review, 1962, 11th edit., 1995; editor: Trichinellosis, 1974, 4th edit., 1985; editl. bd. Exptl. Parasitology, 1984—; reviewer Am. Jour. Tropical Medicine and Hygiene, 1990-93. Moderator N.E. Synod Presbyn. Ch., 1997—98; bd. dirs. Mountain Retreat Assn., 2000—; mem. gen. assembly coun. Presbyn. Ch. (USA), 2000—, mem. exec. com. gen. assembly coun., 2003—, chair worldwide ministries com., 2003—04; bd. govs. Friends of Sunwood, Stony Brook, 1973—85, Suffolk Symphonnic Soc., Suffolk County, NY, 1975—77; mem. devel. com. Mus. Stony Brook, 1983—85; bd. govs. L.I. Coun. Chs., 1999—2003; mem. gov. bd. Three Village Hist. Soc., 2000—01; trustee Med. Benevolence Found., 2005—. Tropical medicine fellow La. State U. Sch. Medicine, 1958, USPHS fellow Argonne Nat. Lab., U. Chgo., 1964-65, Royal Soc. Tropical Medicine and Hygiene fellow, London, 1975. Mem. Internat. Commn. Trichinellosis (pres. 1988-93), Am. Soc. Parasitologists (chmn. nominating com. 1987), Am. Soc. Tropical Medicine and Hygiene, NY Soc. Tropical Medicine (pres. 1985-86), Sigma Xi (chpt. pres. 1993-94), Delta Omega. Fax: 631-751-3010.

KIM, CHIN-WOO, linguist, educator; b. Chungju, Korea, Mar. 22, 1936; came to U.S., 1961, naturalized, 1983; s. Hyong-gi and Kyong-ok K.; m. Beverly Jean Kircher, June 14, 1964 (div. June 1982); children: Joseph H., Daniel H; m. Kui-Soon Choe, Oct. 29, 1988. BA in English, Yonsei U., 1958, Wash. State U., 1962; MA, UCLA, 1964, PhD in Linguistics, 1966. Asst. prof. linguistics U. Ill., Urbana, 1967—69, assoc. prof. linguistics, East Asian langs., speech, and English as an internat. language, 1969—72, prof., 1972—, chmn. dept. linguistics, 1979—86, dir. Ill.-Tehran Rsch. Ctr., 1974—78, assoc. dir. Linguistic Inst., 1977, dir. Program in East Asian Studies, 1990—91; assoc. dir. Konan Internat. Exch. Ctr. Konan U., Kobe, Japan, 1993—94, 2004—05; head linguistics U. Ill., 1999—2004. Vis. prof. linguistics U. Hawaii, 1972-73, 86-87, adj. prof. U. Tehran, Irean, 1974-76, vis. prof. English Yonsei U., Korea, 1983-84, Konan U., Kobe, Japan, 1993-94, Korea U., Seoul, 1995-96. Author works in field. Bd. dirs. East Asian Language Inst. Ind. U., 1984-93; pres., bd. trustees Korean Language Sch., Urbana, Ill., 1988-92. Served with Korean Air Force, 1958-61. Am. Council Learned Socs. fellow, 1965-66; postdoctoral fellow MIT, 1966-67; Ctr. Advanced Study Fellow, U. Ill., 1984-85, Overseas Korean of the Year Award, Korean Broadcasting Soc., 2001. Mem. Linguistic Soc. Am., Linguistic Soc. Korea, Internat. Cir. Korean Linguistics (pres. 1978-80), Assn. for Asian Studies, Internat. Soc. Korean Studies (chair lang. and linguistics com. 1990—), Internat. Assn. Humanistic Studies Lang. (pres. 2000—), Korean Assn. Speed Scis. (sr. advisor 1999—) Home: 1401 N Raintree Woods Urbana IL 61802-7749 Office: U Ill Dept Linguistics 707 S Mathews Ave Urbana IL 61801-3625 Office Phone: 217-244-3061. *I grew up in an economically poor and politically oppressive and unstable environment (Japanese colonial rule, World War II, Korean War). The educational system mirrored such a society (books were scarce, pencils were used down to the one-inch length, and classes were often cancelled), but I was determined to learn, as I did not want to let the poor environment be an excuse for ignorance. Now in the States, it saddens me to see many people not realize and make use of excellent opportunities they have, for I believe that in the presence of excellence, mediocrity is a sin.*

KIM, CHONG LIM, political science professor; b. Seoul, Korea, July 17, 1937; arrived in US, 1962; s. Soo Myung and Chung Hwa (Moon) K.; m. Eun Hwa Park, Aug. 21, 1963; children: Bohm S., Lahn S., Lynn S. BA, Seoul Nat. U., 1960; MA, U. Oreg., 1964, PhD, 1968. Instr. U. Oreg., Eugene, 1965-67; asst. prof. U. Iowa, Iowa City, 1968-70, assoc. prof., 1970-75, prof., 1975—. Author: Legislative Connection, 1984, Legislative Process in Korea, 1981, Patterns of Recruitment, 1974; editor: Legislative Systems, 1975, Political Participation in Korea, 1980; contbr. numerous articles to profl. jours. Mem. Am. Polit. Sci. Assn., Midwest Polit. Sci. Assn. Avocations: reading, travel. Office: U Iowa Dept Polit Sci Iowa City IA 52242 Office Phone: 319-335-2344. Business E-Mail: chong-kim@uiowa.edu.

KIM, CHONG SOONG, aerosol science and inhalation dosimetry researcher; b. Inchon, Korea, Dec. 1, 1945; came to U.S., 1971; m. Insook Park, June l0, l972; children: Jeffrey Hosuk, Audrey Wonkyung, Monica Sookyung. BSME, Seoul Nat. U., 1968; MSME, U. Wis., 1973; PhD, U. Minn., 1978. Rsch. engr. Atomic Energy Rsch. Inst., Seoul, 1970-71; aerosol specialist Mt. Sinai Med. Ctr., Miami Beach, Fla., 1978-80, dir. Aerosol Rsch. Lab., 1980-90; chief human dosimetry sect. U.S. EPA Health Effects Rsch. Lab., Chapel Hill, NC, 1993—95; sr. rsch. scientist U.S. EPA Nat. Health and Environ. Effects Rsch. Lab., Research Triangle Park, N.C., 1990—. Vis. scientist GSF Inst. Biophys. and Radiation Rsch., Germany, 1980; vis. scientist divsn. mech. engring. Korea Inst. Sci. and Tech., Seoul, 1985, U. Pisa (Italy) Sch. Medicine, 1987; adj. asst. prof. U. Miami (Fla.) Sch. Medicine, 1983-86, adj. assoc. prof., 1987-90; adj. assoc. prof. U. N.C. Sch. Medicine, Chapel Hill, 1990-2000, adj. prof., 2000—; adj. assoc. prof. dept. mech. engring. N.C. State U., Raleigh, 1997-2000, adj. prof., 2001—; adj. prof. dept. environ. sci. engring. U. N.C. Sch. Pub. Health, Chapel Hill, 2001—i; nvited spkr. U.S.-Germany Environ. Workshop, 1987, Internat. Conf. for Aerosols in Medicine, 1988, Korean Internat. Workshop in Sci. and Engring., 1989, Respiratory Drug Delivery Symposium, 1990, Internat. Symposium on Clean Room Tech. and Contaminations Control, 1990, FDA Sci. Adv. Bd. Mtg., 1993, Fine Particle Soc. ann. meeting, 1994, Am. Respiratory Care Found., 1999, The Royal Soc., London, 2000, European Sci. Found.-NSF Nanoparticle Symposium, Dublin, Ireland, 2000, Am. Assn. Aerosol Rsch. ann. conf., 2000, Asian Aerosol Conf., Busan, Korea, 2001, Internat. Aerosol Conf., Taipei, China, 2002; ad hoc referee NIH, 1988, 91, 99, VA, 1989, 99, 2003, NSF, 1990. Mem. editl. bd. Jour. Aerosol Medicine, l988—; mem. editl. bd. Aerosol Sci. Tech., 1998-2005, editor, 2005—; contbr. articles to profl. jours.; inventor aerosol rebreathing system. Mem. ASME, Am. Assn. Aerosol Rsch. (bd. dirs. 2004—), European Aerosol Assn., Internat. Soc. Aerosols in Medicine. Presbyterian. Home: 109 Brighton Ct Chapel Hill NC 27516-9005 E-mail: kim.chong@epa.gov.

KIM, CHOONG-MAN JOSEPH, radiologist; b. Seoul, Republic of Korea, Sept. 19, 1939; came to U.S., Dec. 1969; s. Chang-Wu Austin and Bok-Nam (Chang) K.; m. Charlyn Young-Hee Oh, Dec. 28, 1969; children: Ronald, Herbert, Daniel, Peter, Timothy. MD, Korea U., Seoul, 1985. Diplomate Am. Bd. Nuclear Medicine. Dir. dept. radiology and nuc. medicine Oteen VA Hosp., Asheville, N.C., 1976-77; staff radiologist S.W. Mich. Radiol. Svcs., Niles, 1977-85, Pawating Hosp., Niles, 1985-92; pres. Michiana Radiology, P.C., Niles, 1992-94, Niles Imaging Physicians, P.C., 1994—. Mem. AMA, Am. Coll. Radiology, Soc. Nuc. Medicine, Coll. Nuc. Physicians. Office: Niles Imaging Physicians PC PO Box 454 31 N Saint Joseph Ave Niles MI 49120-2207 Office Phone: 269-687-1435. E-mail: choongmankim@msn.com.

KIM, CHRISTINA, professional golfer; b. San Jose, Calif., Mar. 15, 1984; Attended, De Anza CC. Winner Longs Drugs Challenge, 2004. Achievements include shot lowest score ever at any USGA event, U.S. Girl's Amateur Championships, 2001; finished second on Futures Tour money list. Avocations: yoga, reading, writing. Office: c/o LPGA 100 International Golf Dr Daytona Beach FL 32124-1092

KIM, DAE RYONG, management information systems educator; b. June 18, 1959; m. Jung Hwa Lee, Apr. 24, 1988; children: Jennifer, Harrison. MS, Iowa State U., 1992; PhD, U. of Miss., 1996. Instr. U. of Miss., Oxford, Miss., 1993—95; asst. prof. U. of Ulsan, 1996—2001; assoc. prof. Del. State U., Dover, 2001—, chmn. dept., 2005—. Dept. chmn. U. of Ulsan, 1998—2001; cons. Electronic Commerce Resource Ctr., Ulsan, 2000—01; web mgr. U. of Ulsan, 1997—2001, computer lab supr., 1997—2001; lab supr. Del. State U., 2001—. Author: The Complete Success II: The Christians Who Succeed at Their Home, 2000, Unemployment, Setting Out a New Life, 2000; translator: Computers, Communications, and Information, 2001; sect. editor Yeungsang Acad. Jour., 2000—; contbr. articles to profl. jours.; editl. bd. The Internat. Jour. Applied Mgmt. and Tech., 2004—, Logos Mgmt. Rev., 2002, reviewer Jour. of Electronic Commerce Rsch., 2002—. Recipient Disting. Rsch. award, DSU, SOM, 2004, Acad. Strategic e-commerce, 2004; grantee Munsu Rsch. grant, U. of Ulsan, 1998, Distance Learning Rsch. grant, Korea Rsch. Found., 2000, Rsch. grant, Del. State U., 2002. Mem.: Korean Mgmt. Scientists in Am. (mng. dir. 2003—), INFORMS (Korean chpt. bd. dir. 2003—), Korean Internet & Electronic Commerce Assn. (dir. 2000—), Korean Assn. Indsl. Bus. Adminstrn. (mng. dir. 2000—01), Korea Soc. of Mgmt., Korea Soc. of MIS, Korea Assn. Info. Sys., Decision Sci. Inst., Inst. Operating Rsch. and Mgmt. Scis., Assn. for Info. Sys. Avocations: tennis, golf, running, travel, reading. Office: Del State U Sch Mgmt Dept Mgmt 1200 N DuPont Hwy Dover DE 19901 Office Phone: 302-857-6946. Personal E-mail: drkim23@hotmail.com. E-mail: dkim@desu.edu.

KIM, DAMIAN BYUNGSUK, psychiatrist, consultant, counselor, writer; b. Seoul, Korea, Mar. 15, 1934; arrived in U.S., 1964; s. Bong-Ju Kim and Sang-Im Park; children: Steven Namgi, Jeanhee, Andrew Wonki. MD, Seoul Nat. Univ., Seoul, Korea, 1959. Diplomate psychiatry Am. Bd. Psychiatry, cert. psychoanalyst Am. Inst. for Psychoanalysis. Chief alcoholism treatment program Coney Island Hosp., Bklyn., 1978—82, dir. psychiatic outpatient divsn., 1982—, assoc. chmn., 1986—. Asst. clin. prof. SUNY Med. Sch., Bklyn., 1979—; faculty Am. Inst. for Psychoanalysis, N.Y., 1982—97. Author: I Still Want to Live (in Korea), 2000, The Road to American Dreams, 2002; editor: (anthology of poems) Mother & Dove. Pres. Soc. for Korean Studies at Stony Brook, N.Y., 1994; founder, pres. Inst. for Korean Am. Culture, 1996—; chmn. bd. dirs. Assn. for Trad. Korean Performing Arts, N.Y., 1986—96. Capt. medicine Korean Air Force, 1959—64, Korea. Named Outstanding Korean -Am., Whomki Kim Found., 1993, Assn. of Korea, 1994. Fellow: Am. Acad. of Psychoanlyas; mem.: Am. Soc. of Clin. Hypnosis, Am. Psychiatry Assn. (life). Buddhist. Avocations: golf, yoga, meditation, writing. Office Phone: 718-460-5190.

KIM, DANIAL, publishing executive; m. Mary Kim; children: Dillon, Marshall. BA, U. Mich., 1984. Atty. Clark, Klein & Beaumont, Detroit; pub. Mich. Lawyers Weekly; editor and pub. ABA Jour., Chgo., 2000—. Mem.: State Bar Mich. (dep. exec. dir., interim exec. dir. 2000). Office: ABA Jour 321 N Clark St 15 Fl Chicago IL 60610*

KIM, DAVID KENNETH, management consultant; b. L.A., Sept. 7, 1977; s. Keun and Sun Sook Kim. BA, U. Pa., 1999; student, U. Hamburg, Germany, 1999—2000. Analyst Mercer Mgmt. Consulting, N.Y., 2000—02; programme cons. UN Devel. Programme, Mbabane, Swaziland, 2002—03, programme mgr. N.Y., NY, 2003—04, programme advisor Addis Ababa, Ethiopia, 2004—. Fellow, Deutscher Akademischer Austauschdienst, 1999—2000. Home: 29039 Woodcreek Ct Agoura Hills CA 91301 Personal E-mail: davidkkimc99@alumni.upenn.edu.

KIM, DAVID SANG CHUL, publishing executive, evangelist, retired academic administrator; b. Seoul, Republic of Korea, Nov. 9, 1915; arrived in U.S., 1959; m. Eui Hong Kang, Jan. 6, 1942; children: Sook Hee, Sung Soo, Hyun Soo, Young Soo, Joon Soo. BA in English Lit., Chosen Christian Coll., Seoul, 1939; postgrad., U. Wales, 1954—55, Western Conservative Bapt. Sem., 1959—61, U. Oreg., 1962—63, MA, 1965; postgrad., Pacific Sch. Religion, Berkeley, Calif., 1965—66; PhD, Pacific Columbia U., 1988. Staff Chosen Rubber Industry Assn., Seoul, 1939-45; fin asst. US Mil. Govt., Kunsan City, Republic of Korea, 1945-48; govt. ofcl. Ministry of Fin., Ministry of Social Affairs and Health, Ministry of Fgn. Affairs Govt. of Republic of Korea, Seoul, Republic of Korea, 1948-59; charter mem. Unification Ch., Seoul, Republic of Korea, 1954—, 1st missionary to Eng., 1954-55, missionary, evangelist, 1959-70; counseling supr. Clearfield Job Corps Ctr., Utah, 1966-70; founder, pres., owner The Cornerstone Press (now Rose of Sharon Press), 1978-85; charter mem., trustee World Relief Friendship Found., Inc. (now Internat. Relief Friendship Found., Inc.), 1974—; pres. Internat. One World Crusade Inc., 1975—. Founder, United Faith, Inc., Portland, Oreg., 1970—, Global Edn. R & D Fund, Inc., 1981-96; pres. Unification Theol. Sem., 1974-94; charter mem., trustee Nat. Coun. Ch. and Social Action, 1976-96; adv. fin. supporter Global Congress of World Religions, Inc., 1978-96; charter mem. Internat. Religious Found., Inc., 1982—; v.p. Unification Thought Inst., 1989-97; founder, pres. Marriage and Family Inst. Am., 1994—; chmn. inauguration The Family Fedn. for Unification and World Peace, Netherlands, 1996—; pres. emeritus Unification Theol. Sem., 2000—. Author: Individual Preparation for His Coming Kingdom: Interpretation of the Principle, 1964, Victory Over Communism and the Role of Religion, 1972; editor: (book series) Day of Hope in Review, Part 1-1972-1974, 1974, Part 2-1974-1975, 1975; exec. prodr.: (radio) The Unification Hour, 1975—2001; editor: (book series) Part 3-1976-1981, 1981; exec. prodr.: (radio) True Love Journey, 1993—2001; contbr. articles to profl. jour. Recipient Byzantine Golden medal Am. Inst. Patristic Byzantine Studies, Inc., 1992, Spl. award for Disting. Svc. Unification Ch., Internat., 1996, Cheon Il Guk Owner award Family Fedn. for World Peace and Unification, Seoul, 2003. Address: PO Box 1755 South Rd Sta Poughkeepsie NY 12601-0755

KIM, DONG WOOK, information technology executive; b. Seoul, Republic of Korea, Aug. 18, 1965; arrived in US, 2000; s. Hyung Young and Young Ja Kim; m. Sook K. Koh, June 26, 1967; children: Minjoo children: Jennifer H. MS, U. Mo., 1991. Cert. Design for Six Simga Green Belt GE, NY, 2001. Asst. engr. Samsung Electronics Co., Ltd, Suwon, 1992—94; sr. rschr. Samsung Biomed. Rsch. Inst., Seoul, Republic of Korea, 1994—97; prin. investigator, project mgr. Samsung Advanced Inst. Tech., Suwon, 1998—2000; sr. profl. GE, Global Rsch. Ctr., Niskayuna, NY, 2001—04; chief tech. officer Novars Tech Inc., Englewood Cliffs, NJ, 2004—05, Btonet Co., Tustin, Calif., 2005—; cons. engr. GE, Energy, Schenectady, NY, 2004—. Advisor and tech. bd. Hearing Aid Forum, Small and Medium Bus. Adminstrn., Korean Ministry Commerce, Industry and Energy, Seoul, 1998—99; tech. bd. Stds. Multimedia and Acoustics, Agy. Tech. and Stds., Korean Ministry Commerce, Industry and Energy, Seoul, 2000—; vis. scientist Johns Hopkins U., Balt., 2000—01. Mem. editl. bd. Korean Acad. Speech Lang. Pathology and Audiology, Seoul, 1998—2000; contbr. articles to more than 35 jours. Mem.: IEEE (tech. program reviewer tech. program com. 2003, contbr. jour.), Sigma Xi, Sci. Rsch. Soc. Achievements include 7 patents in field. Home: 2000 Rachel Ter Apt14 Pine Brook NJ 07058 Office: Bionet Co 2691 Dow Ave Ste B Tustin CA 92780 Office Phone: 888-292-6060. Personal E-mail: dwkim@hearlinx.com. E-mail: dwkim@bto2net.com.

KIM, DONG-JOO, materials scientist; b. Seoul, Korea (South), Sept. 5, 1969; s. Duk-Young Kim and Bok-Soon Park; m. Jounglan Kim, Dec. 10, 1970; children: Albert Minsung, Anna Minkyung. BS, Yonsei U., 1993, MS, 1995; PhD, NC State U., 2001. Rsch. scientist Korea Inst. of Sci. and Tech., Seoul, Republic of Korea, 1995—97; post doctoral assoc. Argonne Nat. Lab., Argonne, Ill., 2001—03; asst. prof. Auburn U., Auburn, Ala., 2003—. Panel reviewer NSF, DC, 2003—, Dept. of Energy, 2004—. Contbr. articles various profl. jours. Grantee, Next Generation Detection Systems for Food Safety, 2003. Mem.: Materials Rsch. Soc. Achievements include patent for electronic material function. Home: 1676 Stone Pointe Dr Auburn AL 36830 Office: Auburn U 201 Ross Hall Auburn AL 36849-5341 Office Phone: 334-844-4864. Home Fax: 334-844-3400; Office Fax: 334-844-3400. Personal E-mail: drdjkim@yahoo.com. Business E-Mail: dkim@eng.auburn.edu.

KIM, DOOHIE, retired public health educator; b. Taegu, Korea, Sept. 17, 1935; s. Dong-Hoon and Hong-Dahl (Chae) K.; m. Keun-Ok Ahn, Mar. 24, 1959; children: Ji-Eoun, Ji-Kwan, Nah-Youn. BA, Kyungpook Nat. U., Daegu, Republic of Korea, 1961, MA, 1963, PhD, 1970. Instr. Sch. Medicine Kyungpook Nat. U., 1968—70, asst. prof., 1970—75, assoc. prof., 1975—78, prof., 1978—95, dir. med. libr., 1978—80, dean Sch. Pub. Health, 1990-92, 94-95, emeritus prof., 1996—; prof. and dean Sch. Medicine Dongguk U., Kyung-ju, Republic of Korea, 1995—2001; ret., 2001. Com. mem. Provincial Com. for Environ. Contamination, Taegu, Korea, 1975-79; adv. mem. Taegu Supervising Corp. for Korean Indsl. Safety, 1985-95. Author: Environmental Sanitation, 1975, Introduction of Health Science, 1989, Practice of School Health, 1979, Making Health for Prolonging Life, 1994. Adv. mem. Provincial Policy Com. of Kyungpook-do Korea, Taegu, 1979-81, Policy Com. Taegu City, 1981-83. Maj. Korean mil., 1964-67. Recipient Letters of Commendation, Prime Ministry Korea, 1963, Minister of Helath and Social Affairs of Korea, Seoul, 1985, Pres. of Kyungpook Nat. U., Taegu, 1987. Mem. APHA, Am. Coll. Preventive Medicine (internat. mem.), Korean Soc. Preventive Medicine (pres. 1987-89, Plaque 1990), Korean Indsl. Health Assn. (leader Kyungpook br. 1974-80), Internat. Commn. Occupl. Health, Korean Soc. Agrl. Medicine and Rural Health (pres. 1994-96). Home: Lombard Mantion 2-101 1-3 Sooseong 2ka Taegu 706-776 Republic of Korea E-mail: doohi@hanmail.net.

KIM, DOW, investment company executive; b. Korea; BSE, Wharton Sch., 1984, MBA, 1990. Credit analyst, comml. banker, derivatives trader Mfrs. Hanover Bank, NY, 1985—91; v.p., head Yen options trading Chem. Bank, Tokyo, 1991—94; mgr. debt derivatives trading desk Merill Lynch & Co., Inc., 1994, mng. dir. and head debt and equity derivatives, mng. dir. and head global enterprise risk mgmt., mgr. integrated fixed income bus., 2000, head global debt markets, 2001—03, exec. v.p., 2003, pres. global markets and investment banking, 2003—. Office: Merrill Lynch & Co Inc Four World Financial Center New York NY 10080

KIM, DUCKSOO, radiologist, inventor and educator; b. Seoul, Korea, Aug. 16, 1948; came to U.S., 1977; s. Changkun and Sunchom (Cho) K.; m. Eunjoo Lee, May 22, 1978; children: LeeAnn, SueAnn, Andrew. BS, Cath. U., Seoul, 1969, MD, 1973; postgrad., Stanford (Calif.) U., 1981-83. Diplomate Am. Bd. Radiology; lic. physician, Mass., N.Y., Calif. Intern St. Mary's Hosp., Seoul, 1976-77, McKeesport (Pa.) Hosp., 1977-78; resident in diagnostic radiology Beth Israel Hosp., Newark, 1978-81; NIH fellow in cardiovascular and interventional radiology Stanford (Calif.) U. Med. Ctr., 1981-83; instr. radiology Harvard Med. Sch., Boston, 1983-86, asst. prof. radiology, 1986-92, assoc. prof. radiology, 1992-98; dir. Divsn. Cardiovascular and Interventl. Radiology Beth Israel Hosp., Boston, 1983-96; co-dir. divsn. cardiovascular and interventional radiology Beth Israel Deaconess Med. Ctr., Boston, 1996-98; prof. radiology and surgery U. Mass. Med. Sch., Worcester, 1999—; dir. divsn. cardiovascular/interventional radiology U. Mass. Med. Ctr., Worcester, 1999—. Vis. prof. radiology U. Zurich, 1987, Nat. Rsch. Ctr. of Surgery, Ministry of Health, Russia, 1992; lectr. in field; rschr. in field. Author: Peripheral Vascular Imaging and Intervention, 1992; reviewer Catheterization and Cardiovascular Diagnosis, 1992-94, Hepatology, 1993; contbr. articles to profl. jours., chpts. in books. Sec. Korean Cath. Community, Boston, 1988-89, v.p., 1989-91, pres., 1991-92. Capt. Korean Army, 1973-76. Cath. U. Med. Coll. scholar, 1969-73; NIH grantee, 1981-83. Fellow Am. Coll. Angiology, Internat. Coll. Angiology, Am. Heart Assn., Soc. of Cardiovascular and Interventional Radiology; mem. AMA, Radiol. Soc. N.Am., Am. Coll. Radiology, New Eng. Soc. for Cardiovascular and Interventional Radiology (pres. 1992-93), New Eng. Korean Med. Soc., Norfolk Dist. Med. Soc., Mass. Med. Soc., Soc. of Magnetic Resonance in Medicine, Soc. of Magnetic Resonance Imaging, New Eng. Alumni Assn. of Cath. U. Med. Coll. (pres. 1991-92). Roman Catholic. Avocations: tennis, golf. Home: 9 Cedar Hill Rd Dover MA 02030-1631 Office: U Mass Med Ctr 9 Cedar Hill Rd Dover MA 02030-1631 Business E-Mail: dicksookim@comcast.net.

KIM, E. HAN, financial analyst, educator; b. Seoul, Korea, May 27, 1946; came to U.S., 1966; s. Chang Yoon and Young Ja (Chung) K.; m. Tack Han, June 14, 1969; children— Juliane H., Elaine H., Deborah H. BS, U. Rochester, 1969; MBA, Cornell U., 1971; PhD, SUNY-Buffalo, 1975. Asst. prof. Ohio State U., Columbus, 1975-77, assoc. prof., 1979-80; assoc. prof., then prof. fin. and bus. adminstrn. U. Mich., Ann Arbor, 1980-84, Fred M. Taylor Disting. prof., 1984—, chmn. dept. fin., 1988-91; dir. Mitsui Life Fin. Rsch. Ctr., 1990—. Vis. assoc. prof. U. Chgo., 1978-79; vis. rsch. fellow Korea Devel. Inst., 1986-87; econ. cons. Govt. of Korea, 1985-87, 98; Cycle and Carriage vis. prof. Nat. U. Singapore, 1989; Yamaichi prof. econs. U. Tokyo, 1990-91; cons. Bank of Korea, 1985, U.S. Dept. Treasury, IRS, 1988-94, World Bank, 1989-91, 93, Posco, 1995-98, Korea Stock Exch., 1997-98; co-chair Citizens for Econ. Freedom, 1997-99; bd. dirs. Posco, Hana Bank, Mut. Savs. Bank. Assoc. editor Jour. Fin., 1979-83, 88-92, Fin. Rev., 1982—2003, Internat. Jour. Fin., 1990—94, Internat. Rev. Fin. Analysis, 1990-92, Rev. No. Am. Jour. of Econs. and Fin., 1990—99, Rev. Quantitative Fin. and Acctg., 1990—, Pacific Basin Fin. Jour., 1991-96; editl. bd. Jour. Bus. Rsch., 1977—; adv. bd. Asia-Pacific Jour. Mgmt., 1990-96, Jour. Asian Bus., 1996—; contbr. articles to profl. jours. Mem. Korea-Am. Econ. Assn. (sec. gen. 1985, v.p. 1986, pres. 1996), Am. Econ. Assn., Am. Fin. Assn., Western Fin. Assn. Avocations: tennis, golf. Office: U Mich Ross Sch Bus Sch Bus Adminstrn Ann Arbor MI 48109

KIM, EARNEST JAE-HYUN, import and export company executive; b. Seoul, Korea, Dec. 9, 1938; s. Chang-Nyun and Gui-Nim (Yun) K.; m. Jung-Ki Eun, Mar. 25, 1967; children: Yoo-Kyoung, Ja-Hong, Yung-Ju, Do-Hyung. Degree, Hanyang U., 1961; postgrad., Sung Kyun Kwan U., 1975. Reporter Daily Econ. News, Seoul, 1966-74; exec. dir. STAP Corp., Seoul, 1975-82; dir. Korea Fedn. Handicrafts Coops., Seoul, 1979-82; pres. Buenos Amigos, Inc., Laredo, Tex., 1982-95, Buenos Hermanos L.L., 1992—, Nueva Moda Mundo, Mexico City, Mex., 1990—, Buenos Amigos de Mex. S.A., 1994—, Amiguitas S.A. de C.V., Mexico City, 1995—. Inventor, patentee Method of Casting, Method of Jewelry Making. Mem. Adv. Coun. on Democratic and Peaceful Unification of Korea, 1999—. Recipient Spl. Congl. Recognition, Congressman Albert Bustamante, 1988, Cert. of Excellence, Senator Judith Zaffirini, 1983, Cert. of Appreciation, Mayor of Laredo, 1988, Cert. of Appreciation, Am. Legion, 1988, recognition award of achievement and contbn. Ministry Commerce, Industry and Energy Korea, 1999. Mem. Laredo C. of C., Korean Assn. Mex. (pres. 1998-99), Korean C. of C. (v.p. nat. chpt. 1999-01), Overseas Korean Trade Assn. (bd. dirs.

1999-01, v.p. 2001-2004), Lions (v.p. Laredo 1991—, pres. award 1989), Laredo Country Club, Coral Golf Resort (Mex.). Buddhist. Avocation: golf. Address: PO Box 6566 Laredo TX 78042-6566 Office: Casa Beauty SA de CV Carmen 58 Col Centro Mexico City 06020 Mexico Home: Apt 201 1555 Vista Club Cir Santa Clara CA 95054-3723 E-mail: happy88@prodigy.net.mx.

KIM, ELLEN YE, music educator; d. Joon Chul and Anne Mija. MusB, Calif. State U., 1995, MusM, 1998. Piano instr. St. John's Conservatory, Orange, Calif., 1998—; prof. piano Golden West Coll., Huntington Beach, Calif., 1999—. Pvt. instr. home studio, Cerritos, Calif., 1992—. Musician: concerts various cities in U.S.A, and Europe, 1999; contbr. articles. Mem.: Coll. Music Soc., Music Tchrs. Assn. Calif., Nat. Guild Piano Tchrs. Avocations: travel, reading, movies, hiking. Personal E-mail: ellenk626@yahoo.com.

KIM, EUGENE, education educator; b. Seoul, Republic of Korea, Dec. 2, 1966; s. Kwang-Soo and Moon-Ja Kim; m. Sungmi Lee, Sept. 30, 1969; 1 child, Je-Hyung Jay. BS in Environ. Engring., Inha U., Republic of Korea, 1992; MS in Civil and Environ. Engring., U. Wash., 1998, PhD, 2000. Postdoctoral fellow EPA NW Rsch. Ctr. for Particulate Air Pollution and Health, Seattle, Wash., 2000—01; rsch. assoc. Clarkson U., Potsdam, NY, 2002—02, asst. rsch. prof., 2003—. Gen. tech. com. Am. Assn. for Aerosol Rsch., Mt. Laurel, NJ, 2004—05. Contbr. scientific papers pub. to profl. jour. Pvt. Republic of Korea Army, 1987—89, Chuncheon, Korea. Grantee Rsch. grant, Calif. Air Resources Bd., 2005, Health Effects Inst., 2004, Lake Mich. Air Dirs. Consortium, 2004. Mem.: Am. Assn. for Aerosol Rsch., Air and Waste Mgmt. Assn. Achievements include research in Separation of ambient particle contbns. from gasoline and diesel emissions using receptor model; development of ambient particle deposition model. Office: Clarkson Univ CARES 8 Clarkson Ave Potsdam NY 13699-5708 Office Phone: 315-268-3949. Business E-Mail: ugene@u.washington.edu.

KIM, GEORGE R., pediatrician, researcher, information scientist; s. Tong Young and Hyun Wha Kim. BS, George Wash. U., Washington, 1980, MD, 1985. Diplomate Am. Bd. Pediat., 1989, lic. physician and surgeon Md. Bd. Physicians, 1988, specialist pediat. Md. Bd. Physicians, 1988. Pediatric resident U. Md. Hosp., Balt., 1985—88; gen. pediatrician and pediatric hospitalist Johns Hopkins Bayview Physicians, 1988—2001; postdoctoral fellow med. informatics Lister Hill Nat. Ctr. Biomedical Comm. Nat. Libr. Medicine, Bethesda, 2001—02; postdoctoral fellow health scis. informatics Johns Hopkins U. Sch. of Medicine, Balt., 2002—04. Mem. credentialing com. Johns Hopkins Bayview Med. Ctr., Balt., 1990—2001, dir. outpatient svcs. children's med. practice, 1990—2001. Contbr. articles to profl. jours. Mem. physician's breakfast com. Our Daily Bread, Balt., 2000—01, vol. friends orgn. Fellow: Am. Bd. Pediat., Am. Acad. Pediat. (editor scocitnews 2001—02, sci. sect. co-chair steering com. on clin. info. tech. 2005—, Leadership award Electronic Networking dist. III Md. chpt. 1996, 2002, 2004); mem.: Am. Med. Informatics Assn. Achievements include development of National Library of Medicine PubMed for handhelds; online proceedings American Medical Informatics Association Annual Symposium.

KIM, HAKYONG, lawyer, accountant; b. Seoul, Republic of Korea; m. Mihe Kim, July 29, 1983; children: Haemin, Phillip Sunghun, Grace H. BS, Seoul Nat. U., 1980; MBA, Pa. State U., 1988; JD, Touro Law Sch., 2002. Bar: NY 2003, DC 2004. Ptnr. Kim, You, & Assocs., N.Y.C., Kim & Kim CPAs, Flushing, Jason Choi CPA, Hyundai Engring. & Constrn. Co., Seoul. Mem.: ABA, AILA. Office: Kim & You Attorneys at Law 350 5th Ave Ste 1232 New York NY 10118 Office Fax: 212-504-8249. Business E-Mail: hk@kimandyou.com.

KIM, HAN PYONG, dentist, researcher; b. Seoul, Korea, May 2, 1945; s. Koe Jin and Jung Bok (Park) K.; m. Young Sook Yoon, Apr. 27, 1974; 1 child, Sung Mo. MA, DDS, Seoul Nat. U., 1975; PhD, Yonsei U., Seoul, 1982; MA, Monterey Inst. Internat. Study, 1996. Prof. Yonsei U., Seoul, 1977-84; vis. scholar UCLA, 1982; project rschr. for health care sys. Korea Dental Assn., Seoul, 1988-92. Mem. bd. health ins. Nat. HIC, Seoul, 1990-92. Mem. Pres.'s Leadership Circle, Washington, 1995. Avocations: golf, fishing, photography. Home: 2800 Keller Dr 11 Tustin CA 92782 Office Phone: 714-724-2580. Personal E-mail: han@diamonda.com.

KIM, HAN-SEOB, pathologist; b. Seoul, South Korea, Sept. 5, 1934; came to U.S., 1969; s. Y.S. and S.Y. (Ahn) K. MD, Seoul Nat. U., 1959, PhD, 1968. Resident Baylor Affiliated Residency Program, Houston, 1965-66, 69-72; from instr. to assoc. prof. Baylor Coll. Medicine, Houston, 1972-93, prof. dept. pathology, 1993—. Office: Baylor Coll Medicine Dept Pathology Houston TX 77030 Office Phone: 713-873-3213. Business E-Mail: hskim@bcm.tmc.edu.

KIM, HONG NACK, political science professor; b. Youngchun, Korea, Aug. 20, 1933; came to U.S., 1956, naturalized, 1973; s. Sang Do and Nam Jo (Sung) K.; m. Boohi Suh, Mar. 26, 1967; children: Michael, Jeffrey, Brian Kim. BA, Seoul Nat. U., Korea, 1956; MA, Georgetown U., 1960, PhD, 1965. Lectr. Georgetown U., Washington, 1965-66; asst. prof. North Tex. State U., Denton, 1966-67, 1967-72, assoc. prof., 1972-77; prof. polit. sci. W.Va. U., Morgantown, 1977—. Author: Scholars Guide to Washington, D.C. for East Asian Studies, 1979; editor-in-chief: Internat. Jour. of Korean Studies, 2000—; editor: Asian Forum, 1972-74, Polit. Studies Rev., 1984-87; co-editor: Essays in Political Science, 1972, Korean Reunification: New Perspectives and Approaches, 1984; contbr. articles to various pubis. Pres. Korean Assn. W.V., 1981-82, Assn. Korean Polit. Scientists N.Am.83-85. Fulbright-Hays Faculty Rsch. Abroad grantee U.S. Dept. Edn., 1979, 82; Fulbright Lecturing/Rsch. grantee U.S. Info. Agy., 1990; recipient Outstanding Rsch. award W.Va. U., 1985. Mem. Am. Polit. Sci. Assn., Assn. Asian Studies. Democrat. Presbyterian. Home: 1270 Braewick Dr Morgantown WV 26505-3339 Office: W Va U Dept Polit Sci Morgantown WV 26505 Business E-Mail: Hongkim@wvu.edu.

KIM, HYONG (NICK) S., physician, researcher; MD, U. Chgo. Pritzker, Chgo., Ill., 1994. Cert. MD Am. Bd. of Internal Medicine, 1994. Asst. prof. medicine UCSD, La Jolla, Calif., 2001—. Achievements include research in Pulmonary Hypertension. Office: UCSD Med Ctr 9300 Campus Point Dr La Jolla CA 92037 Office Phone: 858-657-7100. Business E-Mail: h33kim@ucsd.edu.

KIM, HYUNJOONG, education educator; m. Hyosook Lee, Jan. 8, 1994; children: Seo-Yeon Joanne, Nicole Hee-Yeon. BS, Yonsei U., 1991, MS; PhD, U. Wis., 1998. Prof. stats. Worcester Poly. Inst., Mass., 1998—2001, U. Tenn., Knoxville, 2001—. Office: U Tenn 328 Stokely Mgmt Ctr Knoxville TN 37996

KIM, HYUN-SUNG, information technology educator; b. Damyangup, Cholla, South Korea, Mar. 9, 1971; s. Ok-Soon Jang; m. Hye-Jin Chang, Nov. 23, 2003. PhD, Kyungpook Nat. U., Korea, 2002. Cert. engring. Ministry Info., 1995. Chief rschr. Ditto Tech., Daegu, 2000—02; asst. prof. Kyungil U., Kyungsan, Kyungpuk, 2002—04. Editor Korea Inst. Info. Security & Cryptology, Seoul, South Korea, 2002—. Author: articles in numerous jours. in field. Sgt. 9th Spl. Airforces, 1993—95, Kyungki, Korea. Mem.: Korea Info. Sci. Soc. Roman Catholic. Avocations: tennis, travel, hiking. Office: Kyungil Univ Sch Com Engring Hayangup Kyungsan 712-701 Kyungpuk Republic of Korea Home: 105-301 Seohantown Pookgu 702-701 Daegu Republic of Korea Office Fax: +82-53-850-7609. Business E-Mail: kim@kiu.ac.kr.

KIM, JAE TAIK, adult education educator; b. Seoul, Korea, Oct. 3, 1933; came to the U.S., 1961; s. Hee Joon and Soon Ra Hong Kim; m. Yang Ja Yoon, Aug. 14, 1962; 1 child, Glenn V. BA, Yonsei U., Seoul, 1961; MPA, U. So. Calif., L.A., 1965, PhD, 1971. MPA coord. West Point Off-Campus Program, 1978-94; prof. John Jay Coll., CUNY, N.Y.C., 1991—. Bd. dirs. Cho Hung Bank. Editor: New Reading in Public Administration, 1980; contbr. articles to ency. Chmn. bd. dirs. N.Y. State Adv. Coun. on Ethnic Affairs, 1979-81; rsch. cons., bd. mem. Tri-State Asian Profile, United Way, N.Y., 1979-80; mem. adv. coun. U.S. Commn. on Civil Rights, N.Y., 1980-85; mem. cultural awareness curriculum adv. com. N.Y.C. Police Dept., 1989-90; pres. Korean-Am. Assn. Greater N.Y., 1992-94. Recipient Ellis Island medal of honor Nat. Ethnic Coalition Orgns., N.Y.C., 1994, Spl. award Asian Am. Higher Edn. Coun., N.Y.C., 1994, Pres. Nat. award Republic Korea, Seoul, 1995; named Man of Compassion, Inst. Jewish Humanities, N.Y.C., 1994. Home: 108 Pershing Rd Englewood Cliffs NJ 07632-1917 E-mail: JTYJKim@aol.com.

KIM, JAEGWON, philosophy educator; b. Taegu, Korea, Sept. 12, 1934; came to U.S., 1955, naturalized, 1966; m. Sylvia Hughes, June 18, 1961; 1 child, Justin Lee. AB, Dartmouth Coll., 1958; PhD, Princeton U., 1962. Instr. philosophy Swarthmore Coll., 1961-63; asst. prof. philosophy Brown U., 1963-67, vis. prof., 1975, William Perry Faunce prof. philosophy, 1987—; chair dept. Borwn U., 1990-99; assoc. prof. philosophy U. Mich., 1967-70, prof., 1971-87, chmn. dept., 1979-87, Roy Wood Sellars prof. philosophy, 1986-87. Assoc. prof. Cornell U., 1970-71; prof. Johns Hopkins U., 1977-78; vis. prof. Stanford U., 1967; Fulbright lectr., Republic of Korea, 1984, Seoul Nat. U., 2000; vis. McMahon-Hank prof. U. Notre Dame, 1999, 2001—. Author: Supervenience and Mind, 1993, Philosophy of Mind, 1996, Mind in a Physical World, 1998, Physicalism or Something Near Enough, 2005; editor: (with Alvin I. Goldman) Values and Morals, 1978, (with A. Beckermann and H. Flohr) Emergence or Reduction?, 1992; (with E. Sosa) A Companion to Metaphysics, 1995, Metaphysics: An Anthology, 1999, Epistemology: An Anthology, 2000, Supervenience, 2002; co-editor: Nous, 2005; contbr. numerous articles to profl. publs. Fellow Am. Coun. Learned Soc., 1980-81, NEH, 1985; NSF grantee, 1977-79. Mem. Am. Philos. Assn. (chmn. com. on status and future of profession 1976-81, mem. bd. officers 1976-81, 88-90, v.p. ctrl. divsn. 1987-88, pres. 1988-89), Philosophy of Sci. Assn. (mem. governing bd. 1979-81), Am. Acad. Arts and Scis., Coun. Philos. Studies. Office: Brown U Dept Philosophy Providence RI 02912-0001

KIM, JAI SOO, retired physicist; b. Taegu, Korea, Nov. 1, 1925; came to U.S., 1958, naturalized, 1963; s. Wan Sup and Chanam (Whang) K.; m. Hai Kyou Kim, Nov. 2, 1952; children: Kami, Tomi, Kihyun, Himi. BSc in Physics, Seoul Nat. U., Korea, 1949; MS in Physics, U. Sask., Can., 1957, PhD, 1958. Asst. prof. physics Clarkson U., Potsdam, N.Y., 1958-59, U. Idaho, Moscow, 1959-62, assoc. prof., 1962-65, prof., 1965-67; prof. atmospheric sci. and physics SUNY, Albany, 1967-95, chmn. dept. atmospheric sci., 1969-76; emeritus prof., 1995—; rep. Univ. Corp. for Atmospheric Research SUNY, Albany, 1970-76, cons. Korean Studies Program Stony Brook, 1983-85. Vis. prof. Advanced Inst. Sci. and Tech., Seoul, Korea, 1983; cons. U.S. Army Research Office, 1978-79, Battelle Meml. Inst., 1978-81, Environ. One Corp., 1978-84, N.Y. State Environ. Conservation Dept., 1976-82, Norlite Corp., 1982-84, Korean Antarctic Program, 1988—. Contbr. articles to profl. jours. Mem. Am. Inst. Physics, Am. Geophys. Union, Sigma Xi. Home: 22 Westover Rd Slingerlands NY 12159-3646 Office: 1400 Washington Ave Albany NY 12222-0100 Personal E-mail: kim9664@msn.com.

KIM, JAMES JOO-JIN, electronics company executive; b. Seoul, Korea, Jan. 8, 1936; came to U.S., 1955, naturalized, 1971; s. Hyang-Soo and Seung-Ye (Oh) K.; m. Agnes Chungsook Kil, Dec. 30, 1961; children—Susan, David, John. Student, Seoul Nat. U. Coll. Law, 1954-55; BS, U. Pa., 1959, MA, 1961, postgrad., 1961-63; D in Comml. Sci. (hon.), Villanova U., 1990. Asst. prof. econs. Villanova (Pa.) U., 1964-70; founder, pres. AMKOR Electronics, Inc., West Chester, Pa., 1970-98; chmn., chief exec. officer AMKOR Tech. Inc., chmn., CEO, 1998—. Founder, dir. Electronics Boutique Holding Corp.; bd. dirs. Visalign, LLC, Semiconductor, Inc., CFM Techs. Inc.; dir., chmn. Anam Semiconductor, Inc. (Korea), 1992—. Trustee U. Pa. Recipient Presdl. Commendation award Pres. Park/Chung Hee, Republic of Korea, 1979, Korean Presdl. Order of Indsl. Svc. Merits, 1983, Korean Presdl. Tin-Tower award Pres. Roh/Tae Woo, Republic of Korea, 1990, Grand-Prix, New Industry Mgmt. Acad., 1996, Global Korea award Mich. State U., 1996, Semiconductor award as pioneer in merchant packaging industry, 1998. Mem. Union League Club (Phila.), Beta Gamma Sigma. Office: AMKOR Tech Inc 1345 Enterprise Dr West Chester PA 19380-5964*

KIM, JAY (JIYUB KIM), finance educator; b. Seoul, Republic ofKorea, Nov. 26, 1967; BA, Yonsei U., Seoul, 1991; MBA, U. Mich., 1994; Ph.D, U. Wis., 2000. Rsch. fellow Dartmouth Coll., Hanover, NH, 2000—01; asst. prof. U. So. Calif., LA, 2001—. Office: U So Calif 3670 Trousdale Pkwy Glendale CA 91202

KIM, JINAH, reporter; b. Seoul, S. Korea; BA magna cum laude, UCLA. Intern CBS, NYC; asst. editor KAGRO; weekend desk asst. and newswriter KTLA-TV, Los Angeles, Calif.; prodr. KCCN-TV, Monterey, Calif.; reporter/anchor FOX, Salinas, Calif., KSWB-TV Channel 5, San Diego, KUSA Channel 9, Denver, 2003—. Bd. mem. Project Mercy, Mayor's Asian Pacific Islander Citizens Adv. Bd., San Diego Asian Film Festival, Grossmont High Sch. Dist. Media Adv. Bd., Korean Am. Assn. Recipient Golden Mike award, Radio Television News Assn. Mem.: Asian Am. Journalists Assn. (former pres. San Diego chapter). Office: KUSA Channel 9 500 Speer Blvd Denver CO 80203*

KIM, JOHN Y., insurance company executive; BBA in Fin. and Acctg., U. Mich.; MBA in Fin., U. Conn. Portfolio mgr., investor rels. officer, fin. analyst Aetna Life & Casualty; mng. dir. Mitchell Hutchins; pres., chief investment officer, CEO Aeltus Investment Mgmt., 1995—2000; pres., CEO BondBook LLC, 2001; pres. retirement and investment svcs. Cigna Corp., Phila., 2002—. Mem.: Assn. Investment Mgmt. and Rsch., Hartford Soc. Security Analysts, N.Y. Soc. Security Analysts (chartered fin. analyst). Office: Cigna Corp 1 Liberty Pl Philadelphia PA 19192-1552

KIM, JON-LARK, mathematics educator; b. Gong Ju, Chung Cheong Nam Do, Korea (South), Nov. 15, 1970; s. Hak-Jae Kim and Jong-Bok Lee. BS in Math., Pohang (Republic of Korea) U. Sci. and Tech., 1993; MS in Math., Seoul (Republic of Korea) Nat. U., 1997; PhD, U. Ill., Chgo., 2002. Tchg. asst. U. of Ill., Chgo., 1998—2002; rsch. asst. prof. U. Nebr., Lincoln, 2002—. Fellow U. Ill., Chgo., 2000-2001. Mem.: IEEE, Am. Math. Soc. (assoc.), Inst. Combinatorics and its Applications (assoc.). Office: Univ Nebraska Dept Math 203 Avery Hall Lincoln NE 68588 Office Phone: 402-472-7253. Business E-Mail: jlkim@math.unl.edu.

KIM, JOOCHUL, urban planner, educator; b. Seoul, Korea, June 21, 1948; came to U.S., 1969; s. Kubong and Kumsoon (Song) K.; m. Shinja Rhee Kim, Sept. 16, 1969; 1 child, Matthew. BA in Sociology, U. Calif., Berkeley, 1973; MUP, U. Mich., Ann Arbor, 1977, PhD in Urban and Regional Planning, 1979. Lectr. Boston U., 1977-80; asst. prof. Ariz. State U., Tempe, 1980-85, rsch. assoc., 1980—, assoc. prof., sch. of planning, 1985—. Participant Leadership Acad., Tempe, 1989-90; mgmt. intern Ariz. State U., 1990, dir. spl. project, 1990-2001, acad. program coord., 2001—; vis. prof., Seoul Nat. U., 1987, Hanyang U., 1986-87, vis. chief rsch. assoc., Seoul Devel. Inst., 1995. Editor: Planning Perspectives, 1983—85; author: Seoul: The Making of Metropolis, 1997; contbr. articles to profl. jours. Mem. Ariz. Solar Energy Assn., Phoenix, 1983-84; mem. task force City of Tempe, 1990—; founding bd. dirs. Friends of Internat. Films, Tempe, 1982-86; co-chair City of Phoenix Planning Com., 1982-83. Fulbright scholar Republic of Korea, 1986-87; named one of Outstanding Young Men of Am., U.S. Jaycees, 1982. Mem. Internat. Div. Planners Network, Korean Urban and Regional Planning Assn. Avocations: movies, music, travel, reading. Office: Ariz State U Sch Planning PO Box 872005 Tempe AZ 85287-2005 Office Phone: 480-965-2768.

KIM, JUNG TAEK, electrochemical engineer; b. Chong Ju, Choongbuk, Korea, July 23, 1942; s. Ki chul and Jung Yeul (Yoon) K.; m. En Kyung, Sept. 4, 1970; children: Fredrick, Daniel, Peter. BS in Chemistry, Korea U., Seoul, 1964; MS in Chem. Engring., Wayne State U., 1974, PhD in Chem. Engring., 1978. Rsch. asst. Wayne State U., Detroit, 1972-75, tchg. asst., 1975-78; mem. tech. staff AT&T Bell Labs., Murray Hill, NJ, 1978-81; sr. rsch. engr. Allied Signal, Buffalo, 1981-88; sr. scientist Tritech Co., Buffalo, 1988-93; sr. rsch. engr. Valence Tech., San Jose, Calif., 1993-94; v.p. tech. Tritech, Amherst, NY, 1994-95; invited scientist Korea Inst. Sci. and Tech., 1995-96; v.p. Hanil Valence Co., Ltd., 1996—2002; dir. ATL Battery Co., China, 2002—. Contbr. articles to profl. jours. Recipient Invention of Yr. award Niagara Frontier Assn., 1988. Mem. Electrochem. Soc., Am. Chem. Soc., Korean Scientists and Engrs. in Am., Korean Electrochem. Soc. (vice chmn.). Methodist. Achievements include 4 patents in field. Home: 301 Robin Hill Dr Williamsville NY 14221-1639 Personal E-mail: jtkbattery@yahoo.co.kr.

KIM, K. ALEX, plastic surgeon; s. Sang Ok Kim and Jeong Ja Lee; m. Renee Rauber, May 17, 1996; 1 child, Sophia. MD, Nagasaki (Japan) U., 1984. Diplomate Am. Bd. Surgery, 1998, Am. Bd. Plastic Surgery, 1999, lic. physician Calif., 1990. Intern plastic surgery Med. Ctr. Nagasaki (Japan) U., 1984—86; rsch. fellow plastic surgery U. Pitts., Pitts., 1988—89; intern surgery Nassau County Med. Ctr., East Meadow, NY, 1989—90; resident surgery Cedars-Sinai Med. Ctr., L.A., 1990—91; fellow plastic surgery Med. Ctr. Loma Linda (Calif.) U., 1991—92, resident surgery Med. Ctr., 1992—95; resident plastic surgery U. So. Calif., L.A., 1995—97; pvt. practice Beverly Hills, Calif., 1997—. Office: K Alex Kim MD - Brooks Surgery Center 9001 Wilshire Blvd Suite 202 Beverly Hills CA 90211 Office Phone: 310-860-9502.

KIM, KAI Y., art educator, artist; b. Seoul, Korea, Apr. 6, 1965; d. Nung I. and Chong J. Kim; m. Michael G. Kelley, June 13, 1998. BFA, San Francisco Art Inst., 1989; MFA, U. Mich., Ann Arbor, 1997. Ad. prof. art Coll. Creative Studies, Detroit, 1998—2002, Henry Ford Cmty. Coll., Dearborn, 2000—03, Wayne State U., Detroit, 2000—03; prof. art Mesa Cmty. Coll., Ariz., 2003—. Mem. exhbn. adv. bd. Detroit Contemporary, 1999—2001; galley mgr. Detroit Artist Market, 2002—03. Exhibitions include Body Memory, Zigmond Haz, Budapest, Hungary, 1998, New Generation, Oakland U., Rochester, Mich., 2001, Detroit Now, Urban Inst. Contemporary Art, 2003. Vol. Detroit Empowerment Zone, 1999—2001. Creative artist grant, Detroit Artist Market, 2001. Mem.: Coll. Art Assn., Nat. Campaign for Tolerance. Avocations: culinary arts, music, films. Home: 3017 S Carriage Ln Mesa AZ 85202 Office: Mesa Cmty Coll AC Bldg 1833 W Southern Ave Mesa AZ 85202 Office Phone: 480-461-7133. Personal E-mail: kaikimk@hotmail.com.

KIM, KATHRYN SPITZER, geneticist, consultant, science educator; b. N.Y.C, Mar. 19, 1958; d. Kenneth Henry and Lois Stuber; m. Peter S. Kim, 1985; 3 children. BS, Cornell U., 1979; MS, U Calif., 1985. Cert. genetics counselor Am. Bd. Med. Genetics and Am. Bd. Genetic Counseling. Rsch asst. Stanford U., Palo Alto, Calif., 1980—83; genetic counselor Brigham & Women's Hosp., Boston, 1985—88, Prenatal Diagnostic Ctr., Lexington, Mass., 1988—92; assoc. prof. Brandeis U., Waltham, Mass., 1992—2001; coord. clin. edn. Arcadia U., Glenside, Pa., 2004—. Regional rep. Nat. Soc. Genetic Counselors; diversity co-chair Nat. Soc. of Genetic Counselors, 2001—03. Mem.: Nat. Soc. Genetic Counselors (Leadership award 2002). Office: Arcadia U 450 S Easto Rd Glenside PA 19038 Business E-Mail: spitzerk@arcadia.edu.

KIM, KEEHOON, cybernetic scientist; s. Yong S. and Youngkum Kim; m. Gyeong Sook Kim; children: Somang, Hannah, Samuel. BS, Yonsei U., Korea, 1986; MS Iowa State U., 1992; PhD, Iowa State U., 1994. Postdoctoral rsch. assoc. Adaptive Computing Lab., Ames, Iowa, 1994—95; postdoctorate fellow Korea Atomic Energy Rsch. Inst., Taejon, Republic of Korea, 1995; sr. mem. tech staff Korea Electric Power Rsch. Inst., Taejon, 1996—2001; group leader Physical Optics Corp., Torrance, Calif., 2001—. Session chair Am. Nuclear Soc., 1994—95, Korean Nuclear Soc., Taejon, Republic of Korea, 1996—2001. Contbr. articles various profl. jours. Recipient Author Recognition award, Am. Nuclear Soc., 1993, CEO honor, Korean Electric Power Corp., 1998, Electric Power Tech. Grand award, 2000. Mem.: IEEE, Internat. Neurol Network Soc., Internat. Soc. of Optical Engring. Avocation: carpentry. Office: Physical Optics Corp 20600 Gramercy Pl 100 Torrance CA 90501 Office Fax: 310-320-4667. E-mail: keehoon7@gmail.com.

KIM, KENNY H., secondary school educator; b. Aug. 13, 1975; BA Philosophy, Pomona Coll., Calif., 1997; MA Edn1. Psychology, U. Riverside, Calif., 2003. Cert. Tchr.Math. Calif. Tchr. math. A.B. Miller H.S., Fontana, Calif., 1999—. Recipient Profl. Excellence award, Fontana United Sch. Dist., 1999—2000, Cert. of Appreciation, Team of Parents, 1999—2000. Mem.: Am. Ednl. Rsch. Assn., Am. Psychol. Assn., Calif. Tchrs. Assn., Fontana Tchrs. Assn., Mensa. Avocations: dragon boating, painting, reading, web design. Home: 13154 Pinnacle Ct Chino Hills CA 91709 E-mail: kimken@fusd.net.

KIM, KI HANG, mathematician; b. Moon Duck, Pyongnam, Korea, Aug. 5, 1936; arrived in U.S., 1953; s. Jin Gyong Kim and Mee Lan Hong; m. Myong Ja Kim, Aug. 1, 1963; children: John Churl, Linda Youngmee. BS in Math., U. So. Miss., 1960, MS in Math., 1961; PhD in Math., George Washington U., 1971. Instr. math. U. Hartford, 1961—66; lectr. math. George Washington U., Washington, 1970—72; assoc. prof. math. St. Mary's Coll. Md., St. Mary's City, Md., 1970—72, U. N.C., Pembroke, 1972—74; prof. math. Ala. State U., Montgomery, 1974—, disting. prof. math., 1983—. Vis. prof. U. Lisbon, 1974, Stuttgart (Germany) U., 1978, Chinese Acad. Scis., Beijing, 1983. Editor-in-chief: jour. Math. Social Scis., 1981—94; editor: Jour. Pure and Applied Math., 1987—, (jour.) Future Generations Computer Sys., 1983—; author: 7 advanced math. books. Specialist U.S. Army, 1955—57. Grantee, NSF, 1971—2003. Fellow: Korean Acad. Sci. and Tech. Home: 416 Arrowhead Dr Montgomery AL 36117 Office: Ala State U 915 S Jackson St Montgomery AL 36101 Office Phone: 334-229-4484.

KIM, KWANG WOOK, corporate financial executive; b. Seoul, Korea, Apr. 19, 1970; s. Soo Won and Eun Sook Kim. BA, Loyola Marymount U., 1993; MA, Fletcher Sch. of Law and Diplomacy, 1999. Assoc. project mgr. Interactive Group, Burlington, Mass., 1993—97; cons. The World Bank Group, Wash., DC, 1999—2000, 2002—04; cons. mgr. Monitor Group, Cambridge, Mass., Brazil, 2000—01; mng. dir. INDEX Clusters, San Paolo, Brazil, 2002—. Assoc. Eugene Bell Found (North Korea Bus. Diplomacy), Wash., DC, 1999; cons. US Agy. for Internat. Devel., 2004—05. Contbr. articles to jours. Recipient scholarship, Fletcher Sch. of Law and Diplomacy, 1997—99; fellowship, UNDP/Govt. of Peru, 1998, 1999. Mem.: Korean Econ. Soc., Arnold Air Soc., Fletcher Alumni of Wash. DC and Sao Paulo, Brazil. Home: 44 St Paul St #3 Brookline MA 02446 Office: INDEX Clusters Rua Ribeiro de Lima 2 Ste 707 01122 Sao Paulo Brazil

KIM, KWANG-JEA, research scientist, polymer engineer; arrived in U.S.A., 1990; s. Jun-Girle Kim and Jung-Ja Choi; m. Hyekyong Kim; 1 child, Carol Tongyon. BS, Inha U., Inchon, Republic of Korea, 1984, MS, 1989; PhD, U. Akron, Ohio, 1998. Post doctoral fellow Inst. of Polymer Engring., Akron, Ohio, 1997—99, Inha U., Inchon, Republic of Korea, 1999—2000; mgr. R & D Struktol Co. of Am., Stow, Ohio, 2000—. Lab. mgr. Inst. of Polymer Engring., Akron, Ohio, 1995—97; presenter at nat. and internat. meetings and confs. Contbr. scientific papers to profl. jours. Pres. Korean Student Assn. at The U. of Akron, 1994—95. 1st lt. Republic of Korea Army, 1984—86. Mem.: Am. Chem. Soc. (Rubber divsn.), Polymer Processing Soc., Soc. of Plastic Engrs. Achievements include patents for method for improved mixing of coupled silica filled rubber. Avocations: golf, fishing, tennis. Office: 201 E Steels Corners Rd Stow OH 44224-0649

KIM, KYUNG-SOO, virologist, research scientist; m. Young-Mi Cjoi, Feb. 5, 1965; children: Na-Young, Dong-Hyun. PhD, La Trobe U., Melbourne, 1998. Rsch. fellow La Trobe U., Melbourne, 1991—93; vis. scholar U. Nebr. Med. Ctr., Omaha, 1999—2001, jr. faculty, 2001—. Com. mem. BoyScout Troop 407, Omaha, Nebr., 2004—05. Rsch. fellow, Am. Heart Assn., 2002. Mem.: Am. Soc. Microbiology (corr.), Am. Soc. Virology (corr.). Achievements include discovery of persistence mechanism of viral disease; of unique mechanism of viral persistence; terminally deleted (TD) Entervoirus: Generations of infectious viral clones of mono-cots Potyvirus; research in infectious full-length JGMV clones-monocots potyvirus (1st); terminally deleted RNA virus in myocarditis. Home: 1134 S 96th St Omaha NE 68124 Office: U Nebr Med Ctr 600 S 42nd St Omaha NE 68198-6495 Office Phone: 402-559-7667. Office Fax: 402-559-4077. Business E-Mail: kkim@unmc.edu.

KIM, KYUNG-SUN, library and information scientist, educator; b. Seoul, South Korea, 1964; came to U.S., 1994; d. Jin-Guil and Ha-Woon (Ahn) K. BA, Duksung U., Seoul, 1987; MA, U. Montreal, 1994; PhD, U. Tex., Austin, 1998. Asst. prof. U. Mo., Columbia, 1998-2001, U. Wis., Madison, 2001—. Reviewer Interactive Learning and Info. Sys., 1999—, Jour. Libr. and Info. Sci. Edn., 2000—, Libr. Resources and Tech. Svcs., 2000—; contbr. articles to profl. jours. Mem. ALA, Assn. Computing Machinery, Assn. Libr. and Info. Sci. Edn., Am. Soc. Info. Sci. and Tech. Office: U Wis 4217 HC White Hall 600 North Park St Madison WI 53706

KIM, LEE ANN, reporter, newscaster; b. Seoul, South Korea; arrived in US, 1971; m. Louis Song. BA in Broadcast Journalism, U. Md., Coll. Park. Gen. assignment reporter & anchor, 10News Live KGTV, San Diego, 1996—. Founder, exec. dir. San Diego Asian Film Festival, 2000—. Recipient Emmy award for investigative reporting, Calif. Teacher's Assn. award for best edu. reporting, Calif. Chicano News Media Assn. award. Mem.: Asian Am. Journalists Assn. (former pres., local chapter, Best Reporting awards). Office: KGTV 10News 4600 Air Way San Diego CA 92102*

KIM, LILLIAN G. LEE, retired administrative assistant; b. Toishan, Canton, China, June 17, 1919; came to the U.S., 1921; d. Yick You and Lucy Yu Oy (Louie) Lee; m. Herman Hom Kim, Oct. 12, 1941. Cert., Ea. U., 1941. Stenographer, sec. Peabody Book Shop, Balt., 1937-38; sec. Prisoners Aid Assn., Balt., 1938-41; sec. Civilian Def. Exec. Office Balt. Mcpl. Govt., 1942-44, sec. to safety dir., 1944-48; sec.-stenographer, asst. supr. stenography divsn. Ctrl. Payroll Bur., 1948-64, adminstrv. sec., supr. adminstrv. and stenographic sect., 1946-63, supr. adminstrv. sect., 1964-77; ret., 1977. Ctrl. payroll councilwoman Classified Mcpl. Employee Assn., Balt., 1949-77, columnist Hall Light, 1950-77; chair ret. employee group CHICA-Combined Health/Industry Comb. Appeal and United Way, Balt., 1970-77; bd. dirs. Women's Civic League; pres., bd. dirs. AARP (Rodgers Forge Chpt. 2360), 1996-, publicity and pub. rels. officer, corr. sec., 1997-99; lectr. in field. Author: (with Lee Yick You and Louie Yu Oy) Early Baltimore Chinese Families, 1976, Chinese Americans-A Part of America, 1977; Letters to the Editor: (tribute to Marhsall Sisters) History of Grace & St. Peter's Chinese Ch. Sch., 1975, Tien Nien Poems, Lectures, and Speeches, Gnin-Gnin's China: Our Heritage, 1980, Grace and St. Peter's Chinese Church School (founders Frances L. and Florence M. "Daisy" Marshall), Chinese Traditions, Customs, and Festivals; author short stories, essays, 1960-70; edit. publ. Wah Kue Sim Mon (bilingual news bull.), 1998, Tien Nien Chatter; cmty. news columnist Towson Times, 1978—; freelance writer Senior Digest, 1990—; Gone But Not Forgotten: Nostalgic Maryland Memories, 1993, editor-pub. Tien Nien Chatter, 1946-60; contbg. writer Hall Light, 1950-77. Founder Chinese Young People's Fellowship, sec., mem. pub. rels. sect. 1946-60, pres., 1960-65; mem. Senator Charles McMathias Jr.s' Select. Immigration Com., 1960s; founder, exec. sec. Grace and St. Peter's Bilingual Chinese Lang. Sch., Balt., 1954-73, supr., 1964-85, dir., prin., 1974—, compiler evening prarye svc. and hymn book; vestrywoman Grace and St. Peter's Ch., Balt., mem. parish activity planning, 1969—, compiler bilingual evening prayer svc.; sec. bd. trustees Grace and St. Peter's Sch., Balt., 1980-86, trustee, 1987-90; exec. bd. Boy Scouts Am., 1978-95; bd. dirs. Women's Civic League, 1979-82, exec. bd., 1999; mem. Bishop's Guild, Diocese of Md., 1960-99; mem. Holly Tour Com., Inc. of Balt., 1975-85, sec., 1978-82; sec., pub. rels. Chinese Women's Assn. Balt., 1937-46; Chinese interpreter of Am. laws, social security taxes, federal and state taxes to Chinese; represented Chinese immigrants in cts. as a vol.; advocate Family Reunionifications, Canton, Balt., 1964; participant Testimonial Dinner Tribute to Councilman Leon A. Rubenstein, Senator Charles McMathias Retirement Dinner; spkr. Tribute to Senator Barbara A. Mikulski; del. to Md. Diocesan Conv., selected lay reader Diocesan Conv. Holy Eucharist Svc., St. Anne's Ch., Annapolis, numerous other diocesan activities; cmty. advocate Dept Justice, Immigration and Naturalization Svc., 1997—; initator, coord. Grace and St. Peter's Chinese Lunar New Yr., Balt.; compiler bilingual citizenship study guide; mem. exec. bd. Boy Scouts Am., 1978-1995; organizer Tiger Club program; apptd. to serve on Senator Charles McMathias Jr.'s select immigration com., 1960s. Recipient awards, including Spl. Baltimorean award, 1976, Balt.'s Best Blue and Silver awards, numerous times, award for outstanding svc. in promoting internat. rels., Carnation Volunteerism award, Balt. City Outstanding Woman of Yr. award, Baltimore County Exec. Proclamation, 1985, Balt. County Woman of Yr., 1986, GERI award, 1990, Baltimore County Execs.'s Baltimore County Exec. citation-Humanitarian award honoree, 1993, Gold 13 medal WJZ-TV, Exec. Citation Humanitarian award Baltimore County, Golden Rule award JC Penney's, Best of Towson, 1998, First Place Best Vol. award Readers of Towson Times, 1998; Congratulatory Honors award Club 88 Tchrs. of Lyndhurst Elem. Sch. No. 88), 1999, award for outstanding svc. tchg. and promoting lang., culture, tradition, and history Coordination Coun. for N.Am. Affairs, Dist. Svc. to Balt. Chinese Cmty. award Balt. chpt. Orgn. Chinese Ams., Outstanding Achievement award Dorothy G. Reddick, 1999, Feast of the Dedication cert. of appreciation Grace and St. Peter's Parish, 1999, My Most Significant Memory of 20th Century award Dept. Aging, 2000. Mem. AARP (pub. rels. dir., bd. dirs.), Episcopal Asiamerica Ministry (parish rep. 1975-93, diocesan rep. 1994—), DAR (medal of honr.), Walters Art Mus., Balt. Mus. Art, Md. Hist. Soc., Stars Spangled Banner Assn., Johns Hopkins Alumni Assn., UCLA Alumni Assn., Washington Nat. Episcopal Cathedral Assn., Ellis Island Found.-Statue of Liberty, Chinese Hist. Soc. Am. (life), Chinese Hist. Soc. So. Calif. (life), Assn. Chinese Schs., Chinese Lang. Tchrs. Assn., Crozier Soc., Md. Assn. of Deaf, Historic Towson, Inc., Balto Coun. Fgn. Affairs, Reagan Ranch, WYPR Radio News Sta., Friends of Nat. Parks at Gettysburg, U.S. Capitol Hist. Soc., Nat. Trust for Historic Presevation, Chesapeake Bay Found., Balt. City Hist. Soc., Enoch Pratt Free Libr./State Libr. Resource. Democrat. Episcopalian. Avocations: community service, gardening, bowling, reading. Home: 524 Anneslie Rd Baltimore MD 21212-2009 Office: Grace & St Peters Chinese Lang Sch 707 Park Ave Baltimore MD 21201-4703

KIM, MARIANNE WEISS, humanities educator; b. Herrenberg, Wüerttemberg, Germany, June 24, 1938; arrived in U.S., 1962; d. Karl Bernhard Weiss and Helene Dengler; m. Norman Won Kim, Jan. 24, 1963; children: Christine V. Levy, Bernard C. BA in Speech Pathology, U. Houston, 1985, BA in German Lit., 1986, MA in German Lit., 1989. Instr. U. Houston, 1986—88; lectr. Dillard U., New Orleans, 1990—92. Adj. assoc. prof. Tulane U., New Orleans. Mem. Trinity Ch. Episcopal, New Orleans, 1993—2003. Mem.: AAUP, Tulane Univ. Women's Assn. (treas. 2002—03), Am. Recorder Tchrs. Assn. (bd. dirs. 2001—), Am. Assn. Tchrs. German (bd. dirs. 2001—), Delta Phi Alpha, Golden Key. Avocations: music, gardening, art.

KIM, MICAELA, speech pathology/audiology services professional; b. Seoul, Korea; arrived in US, 1971; BA in Comm., Boston Coll., 1993; MS in Speech-Language Pathology, St. Xavier U., 2001. Documentary rschr. Seoul Broadcast System, Seoul; with ChicagoLand TV, 1994; field prodr. & rschr. WBBM-TV, 1995; gen. assignment reporter then medical anchor/reporter WBTW-TV, Myrtle Beach, 1996—97; freelance reporter WYCC-TV, Chicago, 1997—99; speech-language pathologist Lutheran Gen. Hosp., U. Chicago Hosp., Edward Hosp., Ill. Early Intervention System; now founder Smiling Star Speech & Language, Hinsdale, Ill. Recipient Mark Twain award. Mem.: Ill. Speech-Language-Hearing Assn., Am. Speech-Language-Hearing Assn., Asian Am. Journalists Assn. (treas. Chicago chapter 1995, v.p. Chicago chapter 1996). Office: Smiling Star Speech & Language 112 S Grant St Hinsdale IL 60521*

KIM, MICHAEL CHARLES, lawyer; b. Honolulu, Mar. 9, 1950; s. Harold Dai You and Maria Adrienne K. Student, Gonzaga U., 1967—70; BA, U. Hawaii, 1971; JD, Northwestern U., 1976. Bar: Ill. 1977, U.S. Dist. Ct. (no. dist.) Ill. 1977, U.S. Ct. Appeals (7th cir.) 1981, U.S. Supreme Ct. 1986. Assoc. counsel Nat. Assn. Realtors, Chgo., 1977-78; assoc. Rudnick & Wolfe, Chgo., 1978-83, Rudd & Assocs., Hoffman Estates, Ill., 1983-85; ptnr. Rudd & Kim, Hoffman Estates and Chgo., 1985-87; prin. Michael C. Kim & Assocs., Chgo. and Schaumburg, Ill., 1987-88; ptnr. Martin, Craig, Chester & Sonnenschein, Chgo. and Schaumburg, 1988-91, Arnstein & Lehr LLP, Chgo., 1991—2004; prin. Michael C. Kim & Assocs., Chgo., 2004—. Gen. counsel Assn. Sheridan Condo-Coop Owners, Chgo., 1988—; adj. prof. John Marshall Law Sch., Chgo. Author column Apt. and Condo News, 1984-87; co-author Historical and Practice Notes; contbr. articles to profl. jours. Bd. dirs. Astor Villa Condo Assn., Chgo., 1987-91, 2002—, treas. 1987-89, 2002-03, sec., 2002, treas., 2003, pres., 2003-. Mem. ABA, Chgo. Bar Assn. (chmn condominium law subcom. 1990-92, chmn. real property legis. subcom. 1995-97, vice chmn. real property law com., 1998-99, chmn. real proprty law com. 1999-2000), Ill. State Bar Assn. (real estate law sect. coun. 1999-04, corp. and securities law sect. coun. 1990-92), Asian Am. Bar Assn. Greater Chgo. Area (bd. dirs. 1987-88, 90-91), Cmty. Assns. Inst. Ill. (bd. dirs. 1990-92, pres. 1992), Coll. Cmty. Assn. Lawyers (bd. govs. 1994-98), Univ. Club (Chgo.). Avocations: squash, photography, travel. Office: Michael C Kim & Assocs 19 S LaSalle St Ste 303 Chicago IL 60603 Office Phone: 312-419-4000. Business E-Mail: mck@mkimlaw.com.

KIM, MI-HYUN, professional golfer; b. Inchon, Korea, Jan. 13, 1977; Attended, Sun Gkyun Kwan U. Winner State Farm Rail Classic, 1999, First Union Betsy King Classic, 1999, Safeway LPGA Golf Championship, 2002, Giant Eagle LPGA Classic, 2002, Wendy's Championship for Children. Named Rolex Rookie of Yr., 1999. Avocations: shopping, pool, piano. Office: c/o LPGA 100 International Golf Dr Miami FL 33124-1092

KIM, MIKYONG MINSUN, education educator; b. Shinan, Korea, Jan. 21, 1961; d. Bok-Soo Kim and Young-Soon Choi; m. Jang Wan Ko. BA, Ewha Women's U., Seoul, Republic of Korea, 1984; MEd, U. Nebr., 1988; MA, UCLA, 1992, PhD, 1995. Adj. asst. prof. U. Ariz., Tucson, 1997—98; asst. prof. U. Mo., Columbia, 1998—2004; assoc. prof. George Washington U., Washington, 2004—, dir. doctoral program, 2004—. Cons. NSF, Arlington, Va., 2003—, grant rev. panelist, 2004. Contbr. articles to profl. jours. Mem.: Assn. for Instnl. Rsch. (grantee post-master's cert. program 2001—04), Assn. for Study of Higher Edn., Am. Ednl. Rsch. Assn. Avocations: tennis, painting, travel. Office: George Washington U 2134 G St NW Ste 109 Washington DC 20052 Office Phone: 202-994-3205, 703-726-3771. Office Fax: 202-994-5870. Business E-Mail: kimmi@gwu.edu.

KIM, MOON HYUN, endocrinologist, educator; b. Seoul, Korea, Nov. 30, 1934; s. Jae Hang and Kum Chu (Choi) K.; m. Yong Cha Pak, June 20, 1964; children: Peter, Edward. MD, Yonsei U., 1960. Diplomate: Am. Bd. Ob-Gyn. (examiner 1979-98). Sr. instr. Ob-Gyn Yonsei U., Seoul, 1967-68; intern Md. Gen. Hosp., Balt., 1961-62; resident in Ob-Gyn Cleve. Met. Gen. Hosp., 1962-66; fellow in reproductive endocrinology U. Wash., Seattle, 1966-67, U. Toronto, Ont., Can., 1968-70; asst. prof. Ob-Gyn, also chief endocrinology and infertility U. Chgo., 1970-74; asso. prof. Ob-Gyn Ohio State U., Columbus, 1974-78, prof., 1978-92, chief div. reproductive endocrinology, 1974-92, vice chmn. dept. ob-gyn, 1982-96; prof. U. Calif., Irvine, 1998—2004, prof. emeritus, 2004—. Richard L. Meiling chair in ob-gyn., Ohio State U., 1987-98. Editor: Am. Jour. Ob-Gyn., 1990-2002, editor-in-chief, 2003--; contbg. author books; contbr. articles to profl. jours. Recipient McClintock award U. Chgo., 1975; named Prof. of Yr. Ohio State U., 1976; recipient Clin. Teaching award, 1980 Fellow Am. Coll. Ob-Gyn; mem. Am. Gynecol. and Obstetric Soc., Am. Fertility Soc., Chgo. Gynecol. Soc., Endocrine Soc., Soc. Study Reprodn., Soc. Gynecol. Investigation. Home: 24 Whistler Ct Irvine CA 92612-4069 Office: Univ Calif Irvine Med Ctr 101 The City Dr S Bldg 58 Orange CA 92868-3201 Office Phone: 714-456-7204. Business E-Mail: kimmh@uci.edu.

KIM, NICOLE Y., music educator, pianist; b. Daegu, Republic of Korea, Dec. 23, 1958; arrived in U.S., 1982; d. Kirin Choi and Ock Ryun Um; 1 child, Lowell. MusB, Seoul Nat. U., Korea, 1980; MusM, San Francisco Conservatory of Music, 1984; MusD, U. So. Cal., LA, 1993. Cert. NCTM, Music Tchrs Nat. Assn., 2003. Ch. pianist Korean Meth. Ch. in LA, 1986—87; instr. LA Conservatory, 1987—89; prof. Cerritos Coll., Norwalk, Calif., 1996—98, Sunwon Women's Coll., Republic of Korea, 1999—2000; owner and head tchr. Dr. Kim's Piano Studio, Bellevue, Wash., 2000—. Adjudicator Young Musicians Competition, LA, 1991; soloist Music of City of Bellflower, Bellflower, Calif., 1998; mem. affiliated faculty Bellevue (Wash.) Coll., 2004—; co-chmn. scholarship competition com., Eastside, Wash., 2005—. Performer concerts and recitals. Bd. mem. Federal Way Symphony, Federal Way City, Wash., 2005. Named award winner, Joanna Hodge Internat. Piano Competition, 1985. Mem.: Wash. State Music Tchrs. Assn. (co-chmn. Eastside chpt. scholarship competition 2005). Avocations: painting, carpentry, reading. Office Phone: 425-260-2868.

KIM, PETER SUNGBAI, pharmaceutical research executive, educator, research and development company executive; b. Atlanta, Apr. 27, 1958; s. Mi Heh (Ryu) K.; m. Kathryn H. Spitzer; children: Michael, Jeremy, Alexander. AB magna cum laude with distinction, Cornell U., 1979; PhD, Stanford U., 1985. Whitehead fellow Whitehead Inst., Cambridge, 1985—88, assoc. mem., 1988—92, mem., 1992—2001; asst. prof. biology MIT, Cambridge, 1988—92, assoc. prof., 1992—95, prof. biology, 1995—2001; asst investigator Howard Hughes Med. Inst., Cambridge, 1990—93, assoc. investigator, 1993—97, investigator, 1997—2001; exec. v.p. R&D Merck Rsch. Labs., West Point, Pa., 2001—02, pres., 2003—. Bd. dirs. Fox Chase Cancer Ctr. Recipient Excellence in Chemistry award ICI Pharms., 1989, Walter J. Johnson prize Jour. Molecular Biology, 1989, Nat. Acad. Sci. Molecular Biology award, 1993, Eli Lilly Biol. Chemistry award Am. Chem. Soc., 1994, DuPont Merck Young Investigator award Protein Soc., 1994, Ho-Am. prize for basic sci. Samsung Found., 1998, Hans Neurath award The Protein Soc., 1999, Harvey lectr., The Harvey Soc., 2002. Fellow AAAS, Biophys. Soc., Am. Acad. Microbiology; mem. NAS, Inst. Medicine. Office: Merck Rsch Labs WP14-3500 770 Sumneytown Pike West Point PA 19486

KIM, S. PETER, psychiatrist, educator, health facility administrator, researcher; b. Seoul, Republic of Korea, Oct. 8, 1939; s. Chong Soon Kim and Soon Bok Lim; m. Oksuk Mary Lee, Mar. 30, 1963; children: John, Katherine. CPM, Seoul Nat. U., 1957; MD, Seoul Nat. U. Coll. of Medicine, 1963; PhD, Toho U. Grad. Sch., Japan, 1984; MBA, U. Hawaii Sch. Bus. Adminstrn., 2002. Asst. prof. psychiatry N.Y. U. Sch. of Medicine, N.Y.C., 1976—82, assoc. prof. psychiatry, 1982—88; prof. psychiatry and pediat. U. Ga. Med. Sch., Augusta, 1988—94; prof. psychiatry Sungkyoon Kwan Sch. of Medicine, Seoul, Republic of Korea, 1994—97, U. Hawaii Sch. of Medicine, Honolulu, 1997—. Program dir. child and adolescent psychiatry N.Y. U. and Bellevue Med. Ctrs., N.Y.C., 1979—88, U. Ga. Med. Coll. of Ga., Augusta, 1988—94; dept. chmn. psychiatry Sungkyoon Kwan U. Sch. of Medicine, Seoul, Republic of Korea, 1994—97; dir. Samsung-Johns Hopkins Internat. Clinics, Seoul, 1994—97; program dir. child and adolescent forensic psychiatry U. Hawaii Sch. of Medicine, 1999—. Pres. Hawaii Psychiatric Med. Assn., Korean Am. Med. Assn. of Hawaii, Honolulu, 1999—2001. Fellow: Am. Coll. Psychiatrists; mem.: Pacific Rim Coll. Psychiatrists, Am. Orthopsychiatric Assn., Am. Acad. Child and Adolescent Psychiatry, Am. Psychiatric Assn., Hibiscus Lions Club (pres. 2002—). Office: Dept Psychiatry 4th Fl U Hawaii Sch Medicine 1356 Lusitania St Honolulu HI 96813 Business E-Mail: kimp@dop.hawaii.edu.

KIM, SE JUNG, civil engineer; b. Seoul, Korea, Aug. 29, 1931; came to U.S., 1968, naturalized, 1973; s. Ki Yong and Soon Dong (Cha) K.; m. Yong Ok Son, Mar. 26, 1961; children: Dohi, Ginny. BS, Seoul Nat. U., 1957. Registered profl. engr., N.Y. Civil engr. U.S. Army C.E., Seoul, 1957-65; project mgr. Ghana State Constrn. Corp., Accra, 1965-68; sr. civil engr. Howard, Needles, Tammen & Bergendoff, N.Y.C., 1968-75; ptnr. Solar Engr. and Builders, Spring Valley, N.Y., 1975-79; sr. civil engr. TAMS Consultants, Inc., N.Y.C., 1979—. Mem. NSPE, Am. Water Works Assn., Seoul Nat. U. Coll. Engring. Alumni Assn. (pres. N.Y. chpt. 1984). Home: 68 Minuteman Cir Orangeburg NY 10962-2721 Office: TAMS Consultants Inc 655 3rd Ave Fl 3 New York NY 10017-5627

KIM, SEONG-DONG, engineer; b. Cheonan, Chungnam, Rep. of Korea, Mar. 15, 1967; s. Tae-Young Kim and Bong-Kyun Sin; m. Sookin Cho, July 24, 1971; children: Michelle Boyoung, Matthew Hee. PhD, Seoul Nat. U. Sr. device engr. Hyundai Electronics, Ichon, Republic of Korea, 1996—99; rsch. engr./lectr. UCLA, Los Angeles, Calif., 1999—2003; adv. engr./scientist IBM Sytems& Tech., Essex Junction, Vt., 2003—. Mem.: IEEE Electron Devices Soc. Home: 493 Metcalf Dr Williston VT 05495 Office: IBM Sys Tech 1000 River Rd 972C Essex Junction VT 05452 Office Phone: 802-769-2578.

KIM, SEUNGJIN, nuclear engineer, educator; b. Seoul, South Korea, Feb. 14, 1965; s. Shi-Hwan and Jae-Sook Kim; m. Hyunjong Kim, Dec. 24, 2000; 1 child, Andy Jonghoon. PhD, Purdue U., 1999. Vis. asst. prof. Purdue U., West Lafayette, Ind., 2002—03; asst. prof. nuc. engring. U. Mo., Rolla, 2003—. Postdoctoral rsch. assoc. Purdue U., West Lafayette, Ind., 1999—2002. Mem.: Am. Nuc. Soc. (life). Office: University of Missouri - Rolla 219 Fulton Hall Nuclear Engineering Rolla MO 65409-0170 Office Phone: 573-341-6780. Home Fax: 573-341-6309; Office Fax: 573-341-6309. Personal E-mail: kimsj@umr.edu.

KIM, SOOK CHA, artist; b. Choong-Joo, Korea, Mar. 30, 1940; arrived in U.S., 1973; d. Kyung Nam Chai and Choon Yi Lim; m. Myung Hak Kim, Dec. 5, 1967; 1 child, Young Kyoon. BFA, Hong-Ik U., 1965, MFA, 1967. Owner Morning Star Art Gallery, Washington, 1995—2003. Featured artist Art Addiction Internat. Gallery. Recipient Gold medal--Art Addiction Internat. prize Most Talented Artists Competition, Sweden, 1997, Cert. of Merit 6th Internat. Female Artist Art Exhbn. on Internet Art Mus., 1999. Home: 6540 Braddock Rd Alexandria VA 22312-2206

KIM, SUKHAN, lawyer; b. Seoul, Nov. 20, 1949; BA in Polit. sci., Guilford Coll., 1976; MA in Internat. Politics, Columbia Univ., 1978; JD, Georgetown Univ. Law Ctr., 1981. Bar: DC 1981, US Ct. Internat. Trade 1985, US Supreme Ct. Ptnr., mgr. Korean practice Arnold & Porter, Washington; ptnr., internat. trade and mem. mgmt. com. Akin Gump Strauss Hauer & Feld LLP, Washington. First vice chmn. US-Asia Fgn. Policy Coun.; hon. v.p. Korean War Mem. Mus.; counsel US-Korean Found.; dir. Korea Soc., NYC, Korea Econ. Inst., Washington; adj. prof. internat. trade law Georgetown Univ. Law Ctr., 1994—; disting. vis. prof., Grad. Sch. of Internat. Studies Yonsei Univ., Korea, 2001—. Contbr. numerous articles on US-Korea trade rels. to Korean publications. Recipient Columbia fellowship, 1978. Mem.: Washington Fgn. Law Soc., Am. Soc. of Internat. Law, DC Bar Assn., World Affairs Coun., Asia Soc., Coun. on Fgn. Rels., Phi Beta Kappa. Achievements include being founding pres., Sukhan Kim Found.: Korean-Am.Youth Svc. Orgn. 2001. Office: Akin Gump Strauss Hauer & Feld LLP Robert S Strauss Bldg 1333 New Hampshire Ave NW Washington DC 20036-1564 Office Phone: 202-887-4131. Office Fax: 202-955-7877. Business E-Mail: shkim@akingump.com.

KIM, SUNG WAN, chemistry professor; b. Pusan, South Korea, Aug. 21, 1940; came to U.S., 1966; BS, MS, Seoul U.; PhD, U. Utah. Asst. rsch. prof. U. Utah, Salt Lake City, 1971-73, asst. prof., 1974-76, assoc. prof., 1977-79, prof., 1980—, dir. Ctr. Controlled Chemical Delivery, 1986—. Mem. study section SGYB, NIH, Bethesda, Md., 1985-89, 95—. Editor numerous books; patentee in field; contbr. articles to profl. jours. Recipient Founders award CRS, 1995, Clemson Basic Rsch. award Biomaterials Soc., 1987, Gov.'s medal for sci., State of Utah, 1989, Inst. Soc. Blood Purification award, 1995. Fellow Am. Assn. Pharm. Sci., Am. Inst. Med. Bioengring, Biomaterials Soc. Home: 1711 Devonshire Dr Salt Lake City UT 84108-2562 Office: U Utah Ctr Controlled Chem Delivery 30 52000 E BPRB Rm 201 Salt Lake City UT 84112

KIM, TAESOO, language educator; s. Seok Bong and Ki Hang Kim; m. Myong J. Kim, Oct. 4, 1986; children: Alice, Aron, Ana. BA in Edn. of 2d Lang., Jeon Ju U., Republic of Korea, 1983; BS in Polit. Sci., Han Kuk U. of Fgn. Studies, Seoul, 1987. Instr., Korean U. Anchorage, 1990—; tchr. Korean Lang. Sch., Anchorage, 1990—99; owner Radio Korea Alaska, Anchorage, 1993—99. Master Champ Tae Kwon Do Sch., Anchorage, 1989—; pres. Tae Kwon Do Alaska, Anchorage, 2002—. Editor: The Korea Post, 1999—2000. Exec. dir. Korean Cmty. of Anchorage, 1990—94. Office: Super Com LLC 3101 Penland Pky D-4 Anchorage AK 99508 Office Phone: 907-272-3415. E-mail: tae_soo_kim@hotmail.com.

KIM, VIVIAN, music educator, violinist; arrived in US, 1983; d. Won Pyung Kim and Bang Sik Shim; m. Conrad Cassie, Aug. 18, 2002. MusB, Juilliard Sch., 1996; MusM, De Paul U., 1998; postgrad. in coll. tchg. music, Tchrs. Coll. Columbia U., 2001—. Chamber music instr. Waldorf Sch., Garden City, NY, 2000—03; violin instr. Columbia U., NYC, 2002—03; dir. string program Portledge Sch., Locust Valley, NY, 2003—. Musician: (concert performances) Tedesca String Quartet, Metro Musicians, New York Virtuosi, Prometheus Chamber Orch., New World Symphony, Chgo. Civic Orch. Scholar, De Paul U., 1996-1998. Mem.: Nassau Music Educators Assn., Nat. Assn. Music Edn. Office: Portledge Sch 355 Duck Pond Rd Locust Valley NY 11560 Office Phone: 516-750-3127.

KIM, WAN HEE, engineering educator; b. Osan, Korea, May 24, 1926; came to U.S., 1953, naturalized, 1962; s. Sang Chul and Duck Hyung (Chong) K.; m. Chung Sook Noh, Jan. 23, 1960; children: Millie, Richard K. B.E., Seoul Nat. U., 1950; MS in Elec. Engring, U. Utah, 1954, PhD, 1956. Rsch. asst. U. Ill., Urbana, 1955—56; rsch. staff IBM Rsch. Ctr., Poughkeepsie, NY, 1956—57; asst. prof. Columbia U., N.Y.C., 1957—59, assoc. prof., 1959—63, prof. elec. engring., 1963—78; chmn., CEO Tech. Assessment Corp. Internat., Palo Alto, Calif., 1991—. Chmn. Tech. Cons., Inc., N.Y.C., 1962-69; chmn. KOMKOR Am., Inc., N.Y.C., 1970-72; spl. advisor for the pres. and govt. Republic of Korea, 1967-79; advisor Korea Advanced Inst. Sci., Seoul, 1971-73; chmn. Korea Inst. Electronics Tech., 1977-81; mem. bd. Korea Telecommunication Electric Rsch. Inst., 1977-81; pres. WHK Engring. Corp. Am., 1982-84, WHK Electronics Inc., 1982-84; chmn., chief exec. officer Industries Assn. Electronic Korea, 1978-81; chmn. WHK Industries Inc., 1984-88, AEA Corp., WHK-FJF&M Assocs., 1988-89; pres. Asian Electronics Union, 1979-83; pub. Electronic Times of Korea, 1982-83, Dr. Kim Report on Korea, 1988-2001; cons. The World Bank, Washington, other indsl. orgns.; chmn., CEO Tech. Assessment Corp. Internat. (TACI), 1991—93. Author (with R.T. Chien): Topological Analysis and Synthesis of Communication Networks, 1962; author: (with H.E. Meadows) Modern Network Analysis, 1970; author: (Auto Biography) Embracing Two Suns, 1999, numerous articles, —. U.S. rep. on U.S.-Japan Scientists Coop. Program.; trustee U.S.-Asia Inst., Washington, 1984-88. Served with Korean Army, 1950-53. Decorated Bronze Star; recipient Achievement medal U.S.-Asia Inst., Industry medal Republic of Korea, 1989; Guggenheim grantee, 1964, NSF rsch. grantee, 1958-78. Fellow IEEE, Union Radio Scientifique Internat. (mem. U.S. nat. com. Commn. Band C 1963-78), Sigma Xi, Tau Beta Pi. Achievements include being honorarily named the father of Korean electronics industry for his contbrn. to promotion of industry. Home: PO Box 778 Palo Alto CA 94302-0778 Office Phone: 650-322-1328. E-mail: nhkim@msn.com. *Be prepared five minutes earlier than others.*

KIM, WAN J., lawyer; b. Seoul, South Korea, June 1968; arrived in US, 1973, naturalized, 1978; m. Sarah Whitesell; children: Anna, Abigail. BA in economics, Johns Hopkins U., 1990; JD, U. Chgo., 1993. Law clk. to Hon. James L. Buckley US Ct. Appeals DC Cir., 1993—94; trial atty. criminal divsn. US Dept. Justice, 1994—96; atty. Kellogg, Huber, Hansen, Todd & Evans, 1997—98; asst. US Atty. DC, 1999—2003; dep. asst. atty. gen. civil rights divsn. US Dept. Justice, 2003—. Served USAR, 1985—90. Office: US Dept Justice Civil Rights Divsn 950 Pennsylvania Ave NW Washington DC 20530*

KIM, YONG CHOON, philosopher, theologian, educator; b. Kyongju, Korea, Jan. 1, 1935; came to U.S., 1958, naturalized, 1972; s. Chang Ho and Chung Ja (Choe) K.; m. Joyce Chungja Whang, Dec. 18, 1965; 1 dau., Grace. BA, Belhaven Coll., Jackson, Miss., 1960; Th.M., Westminster Theol. Sem., Phila., 1964; PhD, Temple U., 1969. Asst. prof. Asian studies York Coll., Pa., 1969-70; asst. prof. philosophy and religion Cleve. State U., 1970-71; asst. prof. philosophy U. R.I., Kingston, 1971-74, assoc. prof., 1974-79, prof., 1979—. Founder, dir. Korean-Am. Christian Studies Inst., 1981— Author: Oriental Thought, 1973, The Ch'ondogyo Concept of Man: An Essence of Korean Thought, 1978; cons. editor Dictionary World Philosophy, 2001; author, cons. editor Ency. of Asian Philosophy, 2001. Korean Culture and Arts Found. grantee, 1977; Korea Found. fellow, 1992. Mem. Assn. Asian Studies, Am. Acad. Religion, Soc. for Asian and Comparative Philosophy, AAUP, Korean-Am. Univ. Profs. Assn. (dir. Eastern region 1986-90, 97—, chair law and ethics com. 1990-96). Home: 134 Parkwood Dr Kingston RI 02881-1600 Office: Univ RI Dept Philosophy Kingston RI 02881 Office Phone: 401-874-2208.

KIM, YONG-KYU, behavior geneticist, educator; m. Kyungsun Lee, May 16, 1987; children: Rosemary, Andrew. BS, Sung Kyun Kwan U., Seoul, 1982; MS, Sung Kyun Kwan U., 1984; MS, PhD, CUNY, 1994. Postdoctoral rsch. assoc. SUNY, Purchase, 1994—96; asst. rsch. geneticist U. Ga., Athens, 2000—. Rsch. cons. Nat. Drosophila Species Resource Ctr., Bowling Green, Ohio, 1996—97. Editor: Handbook of Behavior Genetics; assoc. editor Behavior Genetics. Mem.: Behavior Genetics Assn., Animal Behavior Soc., Am. Naturalist. Home: 509 Ashbrook Ct Athens GA 30605 Office: Dept Genetics U Ga Life Scis Bldg Rm C230 Athens GA 30602 Office Phone: 706-542-1448. Office Fax: 706-542-3910. Business E-Mail: yongkyu@uga.edu.

KIM, YONGSEOG, finance educator; PhD, U. Iowa, 2001. Asst. prof. Utah State U., Logan, 2002—. Editl. bd. mem. Jour. Computer Info. Sys., 2004—, Jour. Info. Tech. Cases and Applications, 2004—. Recipient Athlete Recognition award, Utah State U., 2004; fellow, U. Iowa, 1997, 1998, 1999, 2000; grantee, Utah State U., 2003, 2004; Joe E. Whitesides scholar, 2004. Mem.: Am. Assn. Artificial Intelligence (assoc.), Assn. Computing Machinery (assoc.; spl. interest group decision support sys.), Inst. Ops. Rsch. and Mgmt. Scis. (assoc.), Decision Sciences Inst. (assoc.), Assn. Info. Sys. (assoc.). Achievements include development of CRM marketing model based on data mining approach and publish in Management Sciences journal; decision support systems to help decision makers make right decisions at the right time and publish two papers in Decision Support Systems journal; Publish and disseminate findings through journal (7), conference proceedings (14), book chapter (1), and many numerous presentations.

KIM, YOON BERM, immunologist, educator; b. Pyongnam, Republic of Korea, Apr. 25, 1929; arrived in U.S., 1959, naturalized, 1975; s. Sang Sun and Yang Rang (Lee) K.; m. Soon Cha Kim, Feb. 23, 1959; children: John, Jean, Paul. *Son John H. Kim, BA 1982, Yale University; MD 1990, The Chicago Medical School; Internship and Residency in Obstetrics and Gynecology, Women's and Infants' Hospital, Brown University School of Medicine 1990-94; Clinical Instructor OBG, Brown University School of Medicine 1994-95. Fellow, Reproductive Endocrinology and Infertility, Reproductive Endocrinology Center, UCSF School of Medicine 1995-97. Practice OBG, DuKane Obstetrics and Gynecology Ltd., 1997-00; Physician, Reproductive Endocrinology, Kaiser Permanente Hospital, Wallnut Creek, Cali, 2000-present. Daughter Jean M. Kim, BA 1984, Yale University; JD 1987, Boston College Law School; Corporate Attorney 1987— does non-profit work and church ministry. Son Paul J. Kim, BS 1990, Brown University; MD 1995, University of Illinois (Chicago), College of Medicine; Residency in Family Practice, Diplomate Am. Bd. Family Practice, 1998; is currently a physician with Family Med. Group, Turlock, Calif., 1998—.* MD, Seoul Nat. U., 1958; PhD, U. Minn., 1965. Intern Univ. Hosp. Seoul Nat. U., 1958-59; asst. prof. microbiology U. Minn., Mpls., 1965-70, assoc. prof., 1970-73; mem., head lab. ontogeny of immune sys. Sloan Kettering Inst. Cancer Rsch., Rye, NY, 1973-83; prof. immunology Cornell U. Grad. Sch. Med. Scis., NYC, 1973-83, chmn. immunology unit, 1980-82; prof. microbiology, immunology and medicine Rosalind Franklin U. Medicine and Sci., Chgo. Med. Sch., 1983—, chmn. dept. microbiology and immunology, 1983—2004, acting dean Sch. Grad. and Postdoctoral Studies, 1994-95. Mem. Lobund adv. bd. U. Notre Dame, 1977-88. Contbr. numerous articles on immunology to profl. jours. Recipient Rsch. Career Devel. award USPHS, 1968-73, Morris Parker Meritorius Rsch. award U. Health Scis., Chgo. Med. Sch., 1984, Ham Choon Disinction in Med. Rsch. Grand prize Seoul Nat. U. Coll. Medicine Alumni Assn., 2003, Disting. Alumni award Seoul Nat. U., 2004. Fellow Am. Acad. Microbiology; mem. AAAS, Korean Acad. Sci. and Tech., Assn. Gnotobiotics (pres.), Internat. Assn. for Gnotobiology (founding), Am. Assn. Immunologists, Am. Soc. Microbiology, Am. Assn. Pathologists, Korean-Am. Med. Assn., NY Acad. Scis., Soc. for Leucocyte Biology, Internat. Soc. Devel. Comparative Immunology, Harvey Soc., Internat. Soc. Interferon and Cytokine Rsch., Korean Acad. Sci. and Tech., Chgo. Assn. Immunologists (pres.), Assn. Med. Sch. Microbiology and Immunology Chairs, Internat. Endotoxin Soc. (charter), Soc. Natural Immunity (charter), Sigma Xi, Alpha Omega Alpha. Achievements include discovery of the unique germfree dolostrum-deprived immunologically "virgin" piglet model used to investigate ontogenic development and regulation of the immune system including T/B lymphocytes, natural killer/killer cells, and macrophages; research on ontogeny and regulation of immune system, immunochemistry and biology of bacterial toxins, host-parasite relationships and gnotobiology. Home: 313 Weatherford Ct Lake Bluff IL 60044-1905 Office: Rosalind Franklin U Medicine and Sci Chgo Med Sch 3333 Green Bay Rd North Chicago IL 60064-3037 Office Phone: 847-578-8847. Business E-Mail: yoon.kim@rosalindfranklin.edu.

KIM, YOUNG MIN, research engineer; b. Seoul, Republic of Korea, Apr. 1, 1968; s. GapJoon and MalYeon Kim; m. SooHyun Kim, July 17, 1967; children: Sophie, Tony. PhD, Seoul Nat. U., Korea, 1997. Sr. engr. Samsung Electronics Co., Kiheung, Republic of Korea, 1997—99; postdoc U. of Calif., LA, 1999—2000, asst. rsch. engr. Santa Barbara, Calif., 2000—03; rsch. engr. ltd. term employee Sandia Nat. Labs., Albuquerque, 2003—. Contbr. articles and papers to profl. jours. Achievements include development of Successful developments of metamorphic heterjunction bipolar transistors; Successful developments of GaN high power amplifiers. Home: 9023 Lazy Brook Ct NE Albuquerque NM 87113 Office: Sandia Nat Labs PO Box 5800 MS 0603 Albuquerque NM 87185 Office Phone: 505-284-1625. Personal E-mail: kymdow@naver.com. E-mail: ymkim@sandia.gov.

KIM, YOUN-SUK ERNEST, economist, educator; b. Kwangju, Korea, Sept. 15, 1934; arrived in U.S., 1959, naturalized, 1977; m. Y. Hannar, Apr. 24, 1966; children: Y. Herb, Nancy Y., John Y. BA, Seoul Nat. U., 1958; MA, New Sch., 1967, PhD, 1973. Statistician Am. Photog. Corp., 1963—67; econometrician Candeub, Fleissig & Assocs., planning cons. Newark, 1968—70; adj. prof. Fairleigh Dickinson U., Teaneck, NJ, 1971—73; mem. faculty, asst. prof. Kean U., Union, NJ, 1974—78, assoc. prof. econs., 1979—84, prof., 1985—. Vis. prof. Seoul (Republic of Korea) Nat. U., 1987—88; vis. prof. grad. sch. Hankuk U., 1999; pres. Korean-Am. U. Profs. Assn., 1996—98. Author: Political Economics of U.S. Trade, 1988, Postwar Japan's Foreign Trade, 1991, Japanese Foreign Trade, 1992, U.S.-Korea Economic Partnership, 1995, Vision of Korea's Economy in the 21st Century, 1996, Economics of the Triad: Conflicts and Congruence of the U.S.A., Japan and Korea, 1997, New Economics, 1998, The IMF Program and Korean Economy, 2001, The Role of Government in Competitive Economies; mem. editl. bd. Human Sys. Mgmt.; editor: Internat. Jour. Korean Studies, 2001—; contbr. articles to profl. jours., also books. Nat. screening com. mem. (E. Asia) Inst. Internat. Edn. Fellow, Gateway Inst. for Regional Devel., 2001—; grantee, N.E. Asia Coun., Kean U., Korea Econ. Rsch. Inst., 1987. Mem.: Assn. Asian Studies, Korea-Am. Econ. Assn. (pres. 1993—), Japan Econ. Seminar, Atlantic Econ. Soc., Eastern Econ. Assn., Western Econ. Assn., Am. Econ. Assn. Democrat. Office: Kean Univ Morris Ave Union NJ 07083-7117 Home: 3036 N Farwell Ave Milwaukee WI 53211-3306 E-mail: ykim@kean.edu, younkim@aol.com.

KIMBALL, BRUCE ARNOLD, soil scientist; b. Aitkin, Minn., Sept. 27, 1941; s. Robert Clinton and Rica (Barneveld) K.; m. Laurel Sue Hanway, Aug. 20, 1966; children: Britt, Rica, Megan. BS, U. Minn., 1963; MS, Iowa State U., 1965; PhD, Cornell U., 1970. Soil scientist USDA-Agrl. Rsch. Svc. U.S. Water Conservation Lab., Phoenix, 1969—, rsch. leader Environ. and Plant Dynamics Rsch. Group, 1990—. Editor: Impact of Carbon Dioxide, Trace Gases and Climate Change on Global Agriculture, 1990; co-editor: Carbon Dioxide Enrichment of Greenhouse Crops, 1986; assoc. editor Global Change Biology; contbr. articles to profl. jours. Named Highly Cited Rschr. in agr., Ins. for Sci. Info. Fellow: Am. Soc. Agronomy (chmn. program divsn. A3 1988, assoc. editor 1977—83, bd. dirs. 1994—97), Soil Sci. Soc. Am.; mem.: AAAS. Avocations: computers, biking. Office: US Water Conservation Lab 4331 E Broadway Rd Phoenix AZ 85040-8832 Office Phone: 602-437-1702.

KIMBALL, CATHERINE D., state supreme court justice; b. Alexandria, La., Feb. 7, 1945; d. William H. and Jane C. (Kelley) Dick; m. Clyde W. Kimball; 3 children. JD, La. State U., 1970. Law clerk US Dist. Court, Western Dist. La., 1970; spec. coun. La. Attorney Gen. Office, 1971—73; gen coun. La. Commn. Law Enforcement & Admin. Crim. Just., 1973—81; priv. law prac., 1975—82; asst. dist. atty. 18th Jud. Dist., 1978—82; judge La. Dist. Ct. (18th dist.), 1982—92; assoc. justice La. Supreme Ct., 1992—. Adjunct prof. law Tulane Law Sch. Summer Abroad Program; chair La. Supreme Ct. Case Management Information System Task Force, La. Supreme Ct. Technology Com., Alternative Dispute Resolution Com.; ex officio mem. Complex Litigation Com.; chair Jud. Budgetary Control Bd.; mem. La. Data Base Commn.; bd. mem. Juvenile Justice Reform Act Implementation Commn.; mem. US Dept. Justice Nat. Integration Resource Ctr. Task Force; chair Integrated Criminal Justice Information System Policy Bd., Justice Funding Commn. Named one of Top 25 Women of Achievement, Baton Rouge Bus. Report, 1997; recipient Outstanding Jud. award, Victims & Citizens Against Crime, Inc., President's award, La. CASA Assn., 2002, Amb. for Children award., 2003. Mem.: Order of the Coif, Wex Malone Am. Inn of Ct., State-Federal Jud. Council, Am. Judicature Soc., La. State Bar Assn. Office: La Supreme Ct 400 Royal St New Orleans LA 70130*

KIMBALL, CHAD, actor; Grad., The Boston Conservatory, 1999. Actor: (plays, regional) Sweeny Todd, Memphis, Baby, Chess, (Off-Broadway) Godspell, My Life With Albertine, Finian's Ranbow; (Broadway plays) Broadway Spotlight Series (Backstage Bistro award, best cabaret debut), The Civil War, Into the Woods (Named one of 100 most creative people in entertainment, Entertainment Weekly), Good Vibrations, 2004, Lennon, 2005. Office: c/o Blue Ridge Entertainment Tony Cloer 41 Union Square West New York NY 10003*

KIMBALL, CLYDE WILLIAM, physicist, researcher; b. Laurium, Mich., Apr. 20, 1928; s. Clyde D. and Gertrude M. (O'Neil) K. BS in Engring. Physics, Mich. Coll. Mining and Tech., 1950, MS, 1952; PhD in Physics, St. Louis U., 1959. Staff scientist aeronutronic div. Ford Co., 1960-62; assoc. physicist Argonne Nat. Lab., Ill., 1962-64; prof. physics No. Ill. U., De Kalb, 1964—, Presdl. rsch. chair, 1982-86, rsch. prof., 1986-88, disting. prof., 1988—, advisor to pres. sci. and tech., 1982-88, dir. lab. for nanosci., engring. and tech., 2002—. Program dir. low temperature physics Materials Research Div., NSF, Washington, 1978-79; chair, bd. govs. Consortium for Advanced Radiation Sources, 1994—; exec. com. Basic Energy Sci. Synchrotron Rsch. Ctr., 1994—; exec. dir. Inst. for Nanosci., Engring. and Tech., No. Ill. U., 1992—; chair bd. No. Ill. Nanotech, 1994—. Contbr. articles to profl. jours. Served with U.S. Army, 1952-54 Fellow Am. Phys. Soc.; mem. AAAS, Am. Assn. Physics Tchrs., Sigma Xi. Home: PO Box 842 Dekalb IL 60115-0842 Office: No Ill U Dept Physics Faraday West 217 Dekalb IL 60115 E-mail: kimball@physics.niu.edu.

KIMBALL, GEORGE EDWARD, III, sports columnist; b. Grass Valley, Calif., Dec. 20, 1943; s. George Edward and Rita Sue (Laslie) K.; m. Marge Marash; children: Darcy Maeve, George E. IV. Student, Mass. Bay C.C., U. Kans., U. Iowa. Sports editor Boston Phoenix, 1970-79; sports columnist Boston Herald, 1980—. Columnist for Irish Times; featured sports columnist N.Y. Post, 1993; boxing commentator Fox SportsNet, 2002-03. Author: Only Skin Deep, Sunday's Fools; co-host SportsCall, Sta. WRKO, 1986-87, Old Colony Sports Network, 1996-97; appeared numerous TV programs; contbr. articles to mags., author numerous poems. Dem. candidate for sheriff, Douglas County, Kans., 1970. Recipient Best Sports Column award UPI, 1984, 86, Nat Fleischer award Boxing Writers Assn., 1985, First pl. BEst Story, 2002, 03, Best Golf Column award Golf Writers Assn., 1992; named Boston's Best Sports Columnist Boston Mag., 1987. Mem. South Shore Country Club Hingham, Mass. (bd. dirs.), European Club (senate) Brittas Bay, Ireland), St. Andrews Golf Club (Scotland). Office: News Group Boston Inc PO Box 2096 One Herald Sq Boston MA 02106

KIMBALL, HARRY RAYMOND, medical association administrator, medical educator; b. L.A. MD, U. Wash., 1962. Intern King County Hosp., Seattle, 1962—63; resident in internal medicine U. Wash. Hosps., Seattle, 1963—64, 1967—68; fellow infectious diseases NIH Hosps., Bethesda, Md., 1964—67; pres. Am. Bd. Internal Medicine, Phila., 1991—2004; prof. medicine, sr. advisor to dean Sch. Medicine U. Wash., Seattle, 2004—. Office: U Wash Sch Medicine 1325 4th Ave Ste 2000 Seattle WA 98101 Office Phone: 206-221-4743. Office Fax: 206-221-2999. Business E-Mail: hkimball@u.washington.edu.

KIMBALL, JOHN DEVEREUX, lawyer; b. Orange, NJ, Mar. 18, 1949; s. Robert Maxwell and Audrey Josephine (Kerr) K.; m. Astri Jean Baillie; children: Astri, Emily, Elizabeth, Andrew. BA, Duke U., 1971; JD, Georgetown U., 1975. Bar: NY 1976. Assoc. Healy & Baillie LLP, NYC, 1975-80, ptnr., maritime law, 1980—. Adj. prof. law NYU, 1986—. Co-author: Voyage Charters, 2001, Time Charters, 2003; mem. editl. bd. Jour. Maritime Law and Commerce. Mem. ABA, Maritime Law Assn., Assn. of Bar of City of N.Y. Office: Healy & Baillie LLP 61 Broadway New York NY 10006-2701 Office Phone: 212-709-9241. Office Fax: 212-425-0131. Business E-Mail: jkimball@healy.com.

KIMBALL, JULIE ELLIS, small press publisher, humorist, writer; b. Providence, Sept. 30, 1952; d. James Robert and Arlene Barker McDonnell; m. Penn T. Kimball, July 27, 1985; 1 child, Laura J. BA, Brown U., 1974; MS, Columbia U. Grad. Sch. Journalism, 1975. Reporter, copy editor, asst. Sunday editor Daily Register, Red Bank, NJ, 1975—80; headline writer NY Daily News, NYC, 1989—90; pub. Westmeadow Press, Vineyard Haven, Mass., 2001—. Adj. prof. Columbia U. Grad. Sch. Journalism, NYC, 1986—88; media critic The Woman's Reporter, NJ, 1980—87. Author: 45 Minutes to America: Dispatches from Martha's Vineyard, 2001; editor: (poetry anthology) Vineyard Poets, 2003. D-Liberal. Congregationalist. Home: PO Box 4148 Vineyard Haven MA 02568 Office: Westmeadow Press PO Box 4338 Vineyard Haven MA 02568 Office Phone: 508-696-7497.

KIMBALL, LYNN JEROME, historian; b. La Junta, Colo., Sept. 21, 1943; s. Stanley Jerome and Ruth Estelle (Wilson) K.; m. Kathleen May Seker Mitchell, Nov. 13, 1965 (div. Mar. 1974); children: Scott, Lori, Todd; m. Dorothy Jean Bumar, Dec. 15, 1984; children: Donald, Wendy. BS, U.S. Naval Acad., Annapolis, Md., 1965; MS, U.S. Naval Postgrad. Sch., Monterey, Calif., 1971. Commd. USMC, 1965, advanced through grades to lt. col., dir. plans & policies Joint Spl. Ops. Command Ft. Bragg, N.C., 1980-83, ops. officer 3d Marine Divsn. Okinawa, Japan, 1983-84, battalion comdr. Marine Corps Base Camp Lejeune, N.C., 1984-87; def. attache Am. Embassy, Santo Domingo, Dominican Republic, 1988-90; dir. ops. and tng. Marine Corps Base USMC, Camp Lejeune, 1990-91, dir. environ. tng. Marine Corps Base, 1991-92, ret., 1991; writer, historian, 1992—. Vis. lectr. Profl. Mil. Edn., Camp Lejeune, 1990-2001. Columnist Jacksonville Daily News, 1996—, Tideland News, 1996—, Richlands Advertiser, 1996—; author: Battle of New River, 1996, Diary of J.Q.A. Morris, 1997, Camp Lejeune Oral History Project, 2002, Semper Fidelis: A Brief History of Onslow County and MCB Camp Lejeune, 2002; contbr. articles to profl. jours. Adv. bd. Onslow County Bd. Tourism, Jacksonville, N.C., 1995-2002, Onslow County Mus., 1995—. Mem. Marine Corps Assn., U.S. Naval Inst., Co. Mil. Historians, Marine Corps Historical Found., Onslow Hist. Soc., Civil War Roundtable Eastern N.C. Republican. Baptist. Avocations: weightlifting, bicycling, walking, Civil War history. Home: 227 Creedmoor Rd Jacksonville NC 28546-6028 Office Phone: 910-455-9873. E-mail: ljkimbal@onslowonline.net.

KIMBALL, MARY HOLT, retired secondary school educator; b. Janesville, Wis., Oct. 2, 1934; d. Earle Frank and Mildred (Beahm) Holt; m. Robert Parker Kimball, June 30, 1962; children: Emily Beth, Laura Ann, Peter Markham. BA in French, Beloit (Wis.) Coll. Cert. ESL tchr. U. Houston. French/history tchr. Piedmont High Sch., Piedmont, Calif., 1958-60; French tchr. Garfield Jr. High, Madison, Wis., 1960—62; English/social studies tchr. La Vista Jr. High, Hayward, Calif., 1962—64; French tchr. Burlingame Intermediate, Burlingame, Calif., 1964-66; tchr. English-as-second-lang. Klein Forest High Sch., Houston, 1982—94. Author: The Heritage of North Harris County, 1977; editor: SCRAPS, a collection of notes, mementos, and photos left by Mildred Beahm Holt (1903-2002). Mem. AAUW, NEA, Tex. State Tchrs. Assn., Tex. Tchrs. Speakers Other Langs., Phi Beta Kappa. Republican. Presbyterian.

KIMBALL, REID ROBERTS, psychiatrist; b. Draper, Utah, June 29, 1926; s. Crozier and Mary Lenore (Roberts) Kimball; m. Barbara Joy Radmore, Aug. 3, 1962; children: Valery, Michael, Pauline, Karen, Kay. BS, Brigham Young U., 1949; MD, U. Utah, 1951. Intern Thomas D. Dee Hosp., Ogden, Utah, 1951-52; resident Norristown (Pa.) State Hosp., 1952-53, Oreg. State Hosp., Salem, 1953-55, Palo Alto (Calif.) VA Hosp., 1956; practice medicine specializing in psychiatry Eugene, Oreg., 1957-60, Salem, 1960-72, Portland, Oreg., 1972-77; pvt. practice Eugene, 1957-60, Salem, 1960-72, Portland, 1972-77, Eugene, 1977-89; mem. staff Sacred Heart Hosp., Eugene; consultation/liaison psychiatry, 1977-90; locum teneas numerous locations, 1990—. Dir. Out-Patient Clinic Oreg. State Hosp., Salem, 1956—57, dir. med. edn., 1984; asst. prof. psychology U. Oreg., Eugene, 1957—65, prof., 1977—, asst. prof., Portland, 1965, adj. asst. prof., 1982—83, clin. prof., 1983—92. Mem. adv. bd. Lane County Cmty. Mental Health, 1980—81. With USN, 1943—45. Mem.: AMA, Lane County Psychiat. Assn. (pres. 1979—80), N. Pacific Psychiat. Assn. (pres. 1988—89), Am. Psychiat. Assn. (pres. Oreg. dist. br. 1973—74), Lane County Med. Soc., Oreg. Med. Assn. (chmn. psychiatry sect. 1973—74). Home and Office: 4055oyal Ave #99 Eugene OR 97402

KIMBALL, RICHARD ARTHUR, JR., retired lawyer; b. NYC, Feb. 3, 1930; s. Richard Arthur and Josephine (Dodge) K.; m. Hopeton Drake Kneeland, Dec. 22, 1956; children: George J., Samuel W., Sylvia K. Perry. BA, Yale U., 1952, LLB, 1958. Assoc. Debevoise, Plimpton & McLean, N.Y.C., 1958-61; asst. treas. Morgan Guaranty Trust Co., N.Y.C., 1961-63; assoc. Debevoise, Plimpton, Lyons & Gates, N.Y.C., 1963-69; ptnr. Hughes Hubbard & Reed, N.Y.C., 1970-92, counsel NYC, 1993—2001; ret., 2001. Bd. dirs. English-Speaking Union of U.S., N.Y.C., 1985-97, N.Y. br. English-Speaking Union, 1965-89, chmn., 1993-94; pres. Yale Glee Club Assocs., New Haven, 1980-85, Dutchess Land Conservancy, Millbrook, N.Y., 1988—, chmn., 1997—, The Nature Conservancy, Lower Hudson chpt., 1991-94. 1st lt. U.S. Army, 1953-55. Fellow Am. Coll. Trust and Estate Counsel; mem. ABA, N.Y. State Bar Assn., Assn. Bar City N.Y., Century Assn. (N.Y.C., treas. 1983-89), Yale Club (N.Y.C.).

KIMBALL, SYTSKE KAMMINGA, science educator, researcher; d. Kees and Anneke Metha Adriana Kamminga; m. Ronald Charles Kimball, July 10, 1999. Degree in applied math., Delft (The Netherlands) U. Tech., 1988; MS in Applied Math., Monash U., Melbourne, Australia, 1999; PhD, Pa. State U., 1999. Exptl. scientist divsn. atmospheric rsch. Commonwealth Sci. and Indsl. Rsch. Orgn., Melbourne, Australia, 1990—93; asst. prof. U. South Ala., Mobile, 1999—. Recipient Summer Rsch. award, U. South Ala., 2003, Jr. Faculty excellence in scholarship award, Coll. of Arts and Sciences, U. South Ala., 2004; Rsch. Coun. grantee, U. South Ala., 2000, Equipment grantee, Sun Microsystems Inc., 2001, Career grantee, NSF, 2003—. Mem.: Nat. Weather Assn. (pres. and v.p. local chpt. 2003—04), Am. Meteoroloical Soc. (mem. tropical meteorology com. 2003—). Office: U South Ala Dept Earth Scis LSCB 136 Mobile AL 36688 Office Phone: 251-460-7031. E-mail: skimball@usouthal.edu.

KIMBALL, VIRGINIA MARIE, theology studies educator, writer; b. LA, June 28, 1940; d. John Donovan and Bethany June Strong; m. Dean Fiske Kimball, June 3, 1961; children: Cheryl Marie, Laurence Dean, Lucia Marie, Mary Louise, Thomas Justin, Maura Lynn, John Clement, Elizabeth Marie, Katrina Marie. Student, Coll. Notre Dame Md., 1958—59, student, 1960—61; MA, Andover Newton Theol. Sch., 1992; student, Weston Jesuit Sch. Theology, 1992—93; STL, U. Dayton, 2000, STD, 2003. Freelance writer Chelmsford (Mass.) Newsweekly, 1971—75; freelance writer, editor Westford (Mass.) Eagle, 1975—81; tech. writer Vision Machine Rsch., Cambridge, Mass., 1981—82; journalist, reporter, corr. Lowell (Mass.) Sun, 1982—96. Tchr. evening sch. U. Mass., Lowell, 1991—95; tchr. adult edn. Franciscan Ctr., Andover, 1993—95; tchr. grad. religious studies dept. U. Dayton, 1996; adj. tchr. religious studies Merrimack Coll., North Andover, 1995—. Appeared on (TV show) ABC's 20/20 spl. In Search of Mary, 2000, 2002; contbr. articles to profl. jours.; editor: Otros Dies, Memories of "Other Days"...from Mexico in Revolution to a Life of Medicine in Texas, 1984, The Seven Sacraments of the Greek Orthodox CHurch, 1988, On the Sidelines: Decisions, Skills and Training in Youth Sport, 1988, The Loom's Price, 1992; author: (poetry collection) Westford...home blossoms for forever, 1996, (plays) At the Edge, 1980 (2d pl. Lowell Play Competition). Mem. Marian Libr. Nat. Spkrs. Bur., Dayton. Mem.: Women's Orthodox Ministries and Edn. Network, Ecumenical Soc. of Blessed Virgin Mary U.S.A. (v.p., spkrs. bur.), Mariological Soc. Am. (pres.), Orthodox Theol. Soc. Greek Orthodox. Office: Merrimack Coll Turnpike Rd North Andover MA Home: 4 Wayne Rd Westford MA 01886 Office Phone: 978-837-5000 ext. 4189.

KIMBELL, EDITH MARIA, translator, music editor, writer; b. Reinsberg, Austria, May 14, 1945; came to U.S., 1966; d. Herbert V. and Ilse (Rossrucker) Guenther; m. Michael Alexander Kimbell, June 1, 1968; 1 child, Edmund Florian (dec.). Student, Vienna U., 1963-64; BA honours, U. Sask., Saskatoon, Can., 1966; MA, Cornell U., 1969. Translator Cornell U., Ithaca, NY, 1969-71; lectr. Johnson (Vt.) State Coll., 1972-73; freelance writer, editor, translator, 1975—. Woodrow Wilson Found. fellow, 1966. Mem. AAUW. Avocations: reading, hiking, needlecrafts. Home: 314 Clifton Rd Pacifica CA 94044-1429

KIMBERLIN, SAM OWEN, JR., financial consultant; b. Wichita Falls, Tex., Feb. 4, 1928; s. Sam Owen and Mary Ruth (Crowell) K.; m. Alison Gray, Dec. 20, 1955; children: S. Scott, David Winston. BBA, U. Tex., Austin, 1951, LLB, 1953; grad. in banking, Rutgers U., 1972. Bar: Tex. 1953. First asst. Office Dist. Atty., Austin, 1953-54; asst. atty. gen. Office Atty. Gen. State Tex., Austin, 1955; gen. counsel Tex. Dept. Banking, Austin, 1956-62; exec. dir. Assn. State Chartered Banks in Tex., Austin, 1962-64; exec. v.p. Tex. Bankers Assn., Austin, 1964-88; mng. dir. TBA Svcs. Co., Inc., Austin, 1988-90; cons. Austin Trust Co., 1990—, Thornhill Securities, Inc., Austin, 1990—. Chmn. devel. bd. Austin Trust Co., 1991—; mem. Third Age Coun., U. Tex., Austin Author: Banking in Texas, 1972 (honors award 1972);

co-author: Fight Your Texas Tax Appraisal and Win, 1997. Adv. coun. on property tax cons. Tex. Dept. Licensing and Regulation, 1996—; chmn. appraisal rev. bd. Travis Ctrl. Appraisal Dist., 1995-96; trustee S.F. Austin High Continuing Edn. Found. With USMC, 1946-48. Mem. Am. Soc. Assn. Execs., Tex. Assn. Bank Counsel, Adms. Club, Headliners Club, Tarry House Lodge. Methodist. Avocations: tennis, skiing. Home: 3503 Scenic Hills Dr Austin TX 78703-1044 Office: PO Box 5930 Austin TX 78763-5930 E-mail: samkim@austin.rr.com.

KIMBERLING, CLARK HERSHALL, mathematics professor, small business owner; b. Hinsdale, Ill., Nov. 7, 1942; s. Delmer Hershall and Jocelyn Leigh (Babel) K.; m. Margaret Penelope Mitchell, May 30, 1966; children: Amy, David, Brian. BA, North Tex. State U., 1964; MA, La. State U., 1966; PhD, Ill. Inst. Tech., 1970. Instr. N.W. Mo. State Coll., Maryville, 1967-69, Ill. Inst. Tech., Chgo., 1969-70; asst. prof. U. Evansville, Ind., 1970-75, assoc. prof., 1975-81, prof., 1982—; pres. Math. Software Co., Evansville, 1987—. Author: (with others) Emmy Noether: A Tribute to Her Life and Work, 1982; author: (book and software) Triangle Centers and Central Triangles, 1998, Geometry in Action, 2003; author computer software programs including The Geometric Constructor, 1985-90; editor divsn. music U. Evansville Press, 1976-88; editor computer corner Ind. Math. Tchr., Ball State U., 1986-91; contbr. articles to profl. jours.; composer for ch. choirs: This Easter Morn, 1997, The King of Love My Shepherd Is, 1997, Ring Out the Glad Tidings, 2000, O God, Beneath Your Hand, 2002, O God, Who at the Dawn of Time, 2002, The Hills are Hushed This Night of Nights, 2002, Four Anthems for Mixed Voices and Handbells, 2003, others. Choir dir. St. Paul's Episcopal Ch., Henderson, Ky, 1978-84; bd. dirs. Fibonacci Assn., Santa Clara, Calif., 1999—; adv. bd. Forum Geometricorum, Boca Raton, Fla., 2000—. Mem. Nat. Coun. Tchrs. Math., Am. Math. Soc. (spl. session organizer 1999), Math. Assn. Am., Fibonacci Assn. (assoc. editor 1990—, bd. dirs. 2000-), U. Evansville Alumni Assn. (Outstanding Faculty Rsch. and Scholarly Activity award 1987). Achievements include introductions of new notable points in the plane of a triangle: isoperimetric point, Exeter point, other points on the Euler line; interspersions, dispersions and generalized Wythoff arrays. Home: 2316 E Gum St Evansville IN 47714-2338 Office: U Evansville 1800 Lincoln Ave Evansville IN 47714-1506 Business E-Mail: ck6@evansville.edu.

KIMBERLING, JOHN FARRELL, retired lawyer; b. Shelbyville, Ind., Nov. 15, 1926; s. James Farrell and Phyllis (Casady) K. B of Naval Sci. and Tactics, Purdue U., 1946; AB, Ind. U., 1947, JD, 1950. Bar: Ind. 1950, Calif. 1954. Assoc. Bracken, Gray, DeFur & Voran, 1950-51, Lillick McHose & Charles, and predecessor firms, 1953-63, ptnr., 1963-86, Dewey Ballantine, L.A., 1986-89; ret., 1989. Author: What This Country Needs, 2004. Bd. visitors Ind. U. Sch. Law, 1987—; bd. dirs. Ind. U. Found., 1988—. Lt. (j.g.) USNR, 1951-53. Fellow Am. Coll. Trial Lawyers, Acad. Law Alumni Sch. Law Indiana U. (Disting. Alumni Svc. award, 2001); mem. ABA (charter, litigation sect.), State Bar Calif., LA Bar Assn., LA Jr. C. of C. (past pres.), Beta Theta Pi, Phi Delta Phi, Calif. Club, Chancery Club, Lincoln Club. Home: 1180 Los Robles Dr Palm Springs CA 92262-4124 Personal E-mail: jackkim323@aol.com. E-mail: jkimberling@dc.rr.com. *My goal in life is and has been to do the very best of which I am capable in my professional life and in helping to make my community a better place in which to work and live.*

KIMBERLY, JOHN ROBERT, management educator, consultant; b. New Haven, Sept. 16, 1942; s. John T. and Beatrice (Branch) K.; m. Barbara Lenox Christy, June 27, 1970; children: Laura Lenox, John Fowler, Nina-Charlotte Marie. BA, Yale U., 1964; MS, Cornell U., 1967, PhD, 1970. Asst. prof. sociology U. Ill., Champaign/Urbana, 1970—74; vis. fellow Ecole Polytechnique, Paris, 1975-76; from asst. to assoc. prof. Sch. Mgmt. Yale U., New Haven, 1977-82; from assoc. to full prof. Wharton Sch., U. Pa., Phila., 1983—, Henry Bower prof., 1989—. Rsch. prof. Ecole Polytechnique, Paris, 1989-91; cons. OECD, 1975—, Office Tech. Assessment U.S. Congress, 1982-84, Robert Wood Johnson Found., Princeton, N.J., 1984-85; mem. health care tech. study sect. HHS, Washington, 1986-89; Novartis prof. in healthcare mgmt. INSEAD, 1999-2002. Author: The End of an Illusion, 1984, Cases in Health Policy and Management, 1985, The Migration of Managerial Innovation, 1993; editor: The Organization Life Cycle, 1980, Managing Organizational Transitions, 1984; contbr. articles to profl. jours. Bd. dirs. Wissahickon Hospice, Phila., 1985—, Chestnut Hill Hosp. Health Care, 1992—, Bach Festival Phila., 1992—, Community Fin. Bancorp, 1993—. Grantee HCA Found., Nashville, 1984-86, HHS, Washington, 1986—, Commonwealth Found., N.Y.C., 1986-87, Robert Wood Johnson Found., Princeton, 1986-87, Kaiser Family Found., 1994-96; Salmon and Rameau fellow INSEAD, Fountainbleau, France, 1996-99, 2002—. Mem. Am. Sociol. Assn., Acad. of Mgmt., Am. Pub. Health Assn. Avocations: restoration of antique cars and boats, tennis, skiing. Office: U Pa Wharton Sch Philadelphia PA 19104

KIMBERLY, ROBERT PARKER, medical educator; b. New Haven, July 29, 1946; s. John Taylor and Beatrice Eileen (Branch) K.; m. Susan Johnson Alesbury, June 17, 1972; children: Christopher, Taylor, Sarah, Michael, Thomas. AB, Princeton U., 1968; MA, New Coll., Oxford, Eng., 1970; MD, Harvard U., 1973. Diplomate Am. Bd. Internal Medicine. Intern Hosp. of U. Pa., Phila., 1973—74, resident in medicine, 1974—75; fellow in rheumatology Applied Rsch. Br., NIAMDDK, NIH, Bethesda, Md., 1975-77, Hosp. Spl. Surgery-Cornell Med. Ctr., NYC, 1977-79; asst. prof. medicine Cornell U. Med. Coll., NYC, 1979-84, assoc. prof. medicine, 1984-91, prof. medicine, 1991—96; dir. biomedical component and program dir. Cornell Arthritis Ctr., 1988—96; prof. immunology Cornell Grad. Sch. Med. Sciences, 1991—96; Howard L. Holley Prof. Medicine U. Ala. Sch. Medicine, Birmingham, 1996—; program dir. and sr. scientist U. Ala. Arthritis Ctr., 1996—; prof. microbiology and sr. scientist U. Ala. Comprehensive Cancer Ctr., 1996—. Andrew Mellon Found. tchr., scientist, 1980; sci. adv. bd. Alliance for Lupus Rsch.; trustee Arthritis Found. Contbr. numerous articles to profl. jours. Lt. comdr. USPHS, 1975-77. Rhodes Trust scholar, 1968. Fellow ACP, Am. Coll. Rheumatology (pres. N.E. chpt. 1990-91); mem. NY Rheumatism Assn. (pres. NYC chpt. 1992-93), Am. Assn. Immunologists, Am. Soc. Clin. Investigation. Office: U Ala Dept Rheumatology/Immunology 1900 Univ Ave Birmingham AL 35294

KIMBERLY, SUSAN ELIZABETH, city manager, director; b. Tracy, Minn., July 23, 1942; d. Mervin Glen and Blanche Pontius (Lees) Sylvester. BA, U. Minn., Mpls., 1965. Coun. mem. City of St. Paul, Minn., 1974—78; v.p. Piper Jaffray, Mpls., 1978—82; self-employed cons. St. Paul, 1983—86; asst. to mayor City of St. Paul, 1987—88, dep. mayor, chief staff, 1999—2002; commr. Metro Waste Control, St. Paul, 1985—91; exec. dir. Coalition for Cmty. Devel., St. Paul, 1992—97; team leader St. Paul Planning Dept., 1997—98; program adminstr. City of St. Paul, 2002—03; dep. state dir. US Senator Norm Coleman, 2003—04; dir. St. Paul Planning and Environ. Devel. Dept., 2005—. Dir., pres. Minn. Film Bd., Mpls., 1987-98; dir. St. Paul Found., 1998-, Family Housing Fund, 1999—. Republican. Episcopalian. Avocations: running, golf. Office: City of St Paul 25 W 4th St Ste 1300 Saint Paul MN 55102-1621 E-mail: susan.kimberly@usa.net.

KIMBERLY, WILLIAM ESSICK, investment banker; b. Neenah, Wis., Mar. 19, 1933; s. John Robbins and Elizabeth McFarland (Essick) K.; m. Elena Guajardo, Nov. 27, 1965; children: Essicka Amelia, Ariadne Elena, Dagny Maria. Student Williams Coll., 1951-52, U. Wis., 1953-54. Sr v.p. Kimberly-Clark Corp, Neenah, Wis., 1959-83; prin. W.E. Kimberly Investments, Neenah, 1983-85; pres. Kimberly, Brunell, & Lehmann, Inc., Washington, 1986-88; pres. The Manchester Group Ltd., Washington, 1989-92; chmn. NAZTEC Internat. Group, Inc., 1992—; bd. dirs. UOL Pub., Inc., Sytel, Inc., Kimberly Gallery of Art Inc. With USNR, 1956-58. Trustee, Pan Am. Devel. Found., Asheville Sch. Republican. Episcopalian. Club: Met. (Washington). Avocations: auto racing, art, baseball, music. Office: Naztec LLC 4082 Ridgeview Cir Mc Lean VA 22101-5812

KIMBLE, PAMELA KAY, education educator; b. Warren, Ohio, May 5, 1951; d. Williard R. and Vivian Clarice (Wood) Richards; m. James E. Kimble, Jr., May 24; 1 child, Julia Christine stepchildren: Merideth, Elizabeth; m. Larry Bruce Griffith (div.); children: Daniel Richard Griffith, Emily Lynn Griffith. BA, Mt. Union Coll., Alliance, Ohio, 1973; MEd, Kent State U., Ohio, 1981, PhD, 1995. Cert. tchg. State of Ohio, 1973. Elem. tchr. Alliance City Schs., 1973—76, spl. edn. tchr., 1980—88; instr. Kent State U., 1988—92; prof. Mt. Union Coll., 1992—. Pres. Nat. Cabinet Mt. Union Women, Alliance, 1987—89; guest lectr. Africa U., Mutare, Zimbabwe, 1998. Author: Teacher Educators' Curriculum Beliefs, 1995; guest writer Cokesbury Pubs. Campus leader United Way, Mt. Union Coll.; sister P.E.O., Alliance. Mem.: NEA (advisor), Assn. Supervision and Curriculum Development, Nat. Assn. Edn. of Young Children, Nat. Coun. Tchrs. of English, Phi Delta Kappa, Kappa Delta Pi. Avocations: reading, travel, hiking, swimming. Office: Mt Union Coll 1972 Clark Ave Alliance OH 44601

KIMBLE, WILLIAM EARL, lawyer; b. Denver, May 4, 1926; s. George Wilbur and Grace (Fick) K.; m. Jean M. Cayia, Dec. 27, 1950; children: Mark, Cary, Timothy, Stephen, Philip, Peter, Michael. LL.B., U. Ariz., 1951. Bar: Ariz. 1951. Spl. agt. FBI, 1951-52; pvt. practice Bisbee, 1952-60, Tucson, 1962—; judge Superior Ct. Ariz., 1960—62; ptnr. Kimble, Nelson, Audilett & McDonough, 1962—. Commr. Ariz. Oil and Gas Commn., 1958-60; adj. prof. law U. Ariz. Coll. Law, 1962-86. Author: The Consumer Product Safety Act, 1973, Products Liability, 1977; sr. editor Consumer Products Alert newsletter, 1980-81; editor, pub. In Def. of Elec. Accidents newsletter, 1993—. Founder Naval War Coll. Found.; Rep. nominee Ariz. atty. gen., 1956; Rep. nominee Ariz. U.S. Congress, 1964. Served with USNR, 1944-46. Fellow Am. Coll. Trial Lawyers; mem. Sigma Chi, Phi Alpha Delta. Home: 3544 E Placita de Pipo Tucson AZ 85718 Office: Kimble Nelson & Audilett 335 N Wilmot Rd Ste 500 Tucson AZ 85711-2636 Office Phone: 520-748-2440. Personal E-mail: wkimble@comcast.net.

KIMBLER, LARRY BERNARD, real estate executive, accountant; b. Lucasville, Ohio, Sept. 6, 1938; s. Benjamin F. and Elizabeth L. (Kerr) K.; m. Susanna Hayes, June 20, 1964; children: Beth Ann, Carolyn Sue. BBA, U. Cin., 1964. CPA, Ohio; lic. real estate broker, Tex. Acct. Peat, Marwick, Mitchell & Co., Cin., 1964-68; mgr. acctg. and taxes Andrew Jergens & Co., Cin., 1968-70; exec. v.p. Am. Lakes & Land Co., Houston, 1970-74; from group controller real estate and minerals to gen. mgr. land utilization Internat. Paper Co., 1974-81; pres. Internat. Paper Realty Co., N.Y.C., 1977-81; v.p. corp. real estate GTE, Stamford, Conn.; also pres. GTE Realty Corp., 1981-89; prin. Kimbler Assocs., Inc., Stamford, 1989-91; exec. v.p. The Staubach Co., Dallas, 1991—2002, also bd. dirs.; chmn. Washington Staubach Addison Airport Venture, 2002—. Bd. dirs. Stamford Econ. Assistance Corp.; past pres. Westchester So. Conn. chpt., NACORE; trustee, treas. Low-Heywood Thomas Sch., Stamford; lectr., speaker in field; mem. adv. bd. Homer Hoyt Inst.; officer, bd. dirs. Indsl. Devel. Rsch. Coun.; editl. adv. bd. Bldg. Econs. Contbr. articles to profl. jours. With AUS, 1956-59. Mem. Am. Inst. Corp. Asset Mgmt. (bd. govs.), Nat. Assn. Corp. Real Estate Execs. (master corp. real estate designation, chpt. pres.), Am. Inst. CPAs, Indsl. Devel. Research Council (bd. dirs., Officer Disting. Svc. award 1983, 87, Master Profl. designation), Am. Found. for Blind (chmn. bd. dirs. SW Region, nat. trustee), Bent Tree Country Club (bd. dirs., exec. com. 1999-2002). Presbyterian. Republican. Home: 5403 Bent Trail Dallas TX 75248-2034 Office: 15601 Dallas Pkwy Ste 400 Addison TX 75001-6055

KIMBRELL, DEBORAH ANN, geneticist, educator; b. Goodfellow Air Force Base, Tex., July 22, 1950; d. Billy Lee and Dorothy (Babish) K.; m. S. Ingemar C. Olsson, June 15, 1991. BA in Biology and Psychology with honors, Mills Coll., 1972; PhD in Genetics, U. Calif., Berkeley, 1985. Rsch. technician dept. respiration physiology Max Planck Inst. Exptl. Medicine, Göttingen, Germany, 1973-74; NIH predoctoral trainee dept. genetics U. Calif., Berkeley, 1979-85; Am. Cancer Soc. postdoctoral fellow dept. genetics U. Cambridge, Eng., 1985-88; Swedish MRC vis. scientist fellow dept. microbiology U. Stockholm, 1988-90; asst. prof. dept. biology and Inst. Molecular Biology, U. Houston, 1991—97; sr. faculty fellow dept. biochemistry and cell biology Rice U., Houston, 1997—99. Contbr. articles to profl. jours. Pres. Rsch. and Scholarship Fund grantee U. Houston; grantee Am. Cancer Soc. Home: 127 Sunnybrae Ct Martinez CA 94553-5800

KIMBRELL, GRADY NED, writer, educator, retired school system administrator; b. Tallant, Okla., Apr. 6, 1933; s. Virgil Leroy Kimbrell and La Veria Dee Underwood; m. Marilyn Louise King, May 30, 1953 (div.); m. Mary Ellen Cunningham, Apr. 11, 1973; children: Mark Leroy, Lisa Christine, Joni Lynne. BA, Southwestern Coll., Winfield, Kans., 1956; MA, Colo. State Coll., 1958. Cert. tchr. (life), Calif., Colo.; cert. adminstr., Calif. Bus. tchr. Peabody (Kans.) High Sch., 1956-58, Santa Barbara (Calif.) High Sch., 1958-65, coordinator work edn., 1965-75, dir. research and evaluation, 1975-88. Author: Introduction to Business and Office Careers, 1974, The World of Work Career Interest Survey, 1986; co-author: Succeeding in the World of Work, 1970, 7th rev. edit., 2003, Entering the World of Work, 1974, 3rd rev. edit., 1988, The Savvy Consumer, 1984, 4th rev. edit., 2005, Personal and Family Economics, 1996, Marketing Essentials, 1991, 2nd edit., 1997, 3d edit., 2003, 4th edit., 2005, Office Skills, 1998, 3d edit., 2003, Advancing in the World of Work, 1992, Exploring Business and Computer Careers, 1998, Employment Skills for Office Careers, 1998. With U.S. Army, 1953-55. Mem. NEA, Calif. Assn. Work Experience Educators, Nat. Work Experience Edn. Assn., Calif. Tchrs. Assn., Coop. Work Experience Assn. Avocations: breeding and racing quarter horses, photography, travel. E-mail: gradykim@cox.net.

KIMBRELL, ODELL CULP, JR., internist; b. Spartanburg, S.C., May 2, 1927; s. Odell Culp and Leona (Nicholas) K.; m. Etta Lou; children from former marriage: Odell Culp III, Cynthia Anne. AB, Duke U., 1947; MD, U. Pa., 1951. Diplomate: Am. Bd. Internal Medicine, Am. Bd. Life Ins. Medicine. Intern Med. Coll. Va., Richmond, 1951-52, resident in internal medicine, 1954-56; sr. resident in internal medicine VA Hosp., Phila., 1956-57; practice medicine specializing in internal medicine and endocrinology Gallipolis, Ohio, 1957-60, Raleigh, NC, 1960-93; practice ins. medicine, 1967—; mem. hon. staff Wake Med. Ctr.; clin. prof. medicine U.N.C. Med. Sch., 1970-90. Med. dir., cons. Pa. Life Ins. Co., 1998—. Contbr. articles to med. jours. Bd. dirs. Wake County Hosp. System Inc., Raleigh, 1971-81, sec., 1973-74, chmn., 1974-76; bd. dirs. Wake Health Facilities and Service Inc., 1975-81, pres., 1975-76; chmn. Wake County Heart Fund, 1961; deacon Hudson Meml. Presbyn. Ch., Raleigh, 1971-73. Served with USAF, 1952-54. Fellow ACP; mem. AMA, N.C. Med. Soc., Wake County Med Soc., Am. Soc. Internal Medicine, N.C. Soc. Internal Medicine, Am. Acad. Ins. Med., Mid-Atlantic Med. Dirs. Club (pres. 1979-80, 92). Home: 1905 Hunting Ridge Rd Raleigh NC 27615-5515 Office: 201 Shannon Oaks Ste 200 Cary NC 27511 *Serving through devoted application of mind, body and spirit.*

KIMBRELL, WILLARD DUKE, textiles executive; b. Gaston County, N.C., Dec. 28, 1924; s. Curtis C. and Carolyn (Carter) Kimbrell; m. Dorothy Rhyne; 3 children. BS in Textiles, N.C. State Coll., 1949; PhD, U. N.C., Charlotte. Various positions Parkdale Mills, Inc., Gastonia, NC, 1938—, CEO, 1961—2001, chmn. bd. dirs., 2001—. Bd. dirs. Am. Textile Mfg., Inman Mills. Pres. Gaston Cmty. Found.; bd. dirs. YMCA, Gastonia; trustee Bowman Gray Sch. Medicine, U. N.C. With USAF. Mem.: N.C. Textile Mfrs. Assn. (pres.), Am. Yam Spinners Assn. (pres.). Republican. Office: 531 Cotton Blossom Cir Gastonia NC 28054 E-mail: dkimbrell@parkdalemills.com.

KIMBRELL, WILLIAM, marketing professional; Disbr. Richards Med.; clinical rsch. Astra Pharm.; sales mgr. Zimmer-Kloenne Assoc., 1968—77; owner, prin. Zimmer-Kimbrell, Inc., 1977—96; CEO, pres. Zimmer-Health Ptnrs., 1996—. Home: PO Box 24885 Lexington KY 40524

KIMBROUGH, LORELEI, retired elementary school educator, retired secondary school educator; b. Chgo. d. Paul and Lina (Higgs) Bobbett; m. James Kimbrough; children: Denise, Devi, Paul, Jeri Lynn, Sandra, Diane, James III. BS in Edn., Ill. State U., 1947; postgrad., DePaul U., Chgo. U. Cert. tchr., Ill. Tchr. of Latin and English, Greensboro (N.C.) Pub. Schs.; spl. edn. tchr. Chgo. State Hosp./Reed Zone Ctr., Chgo., Jewish Children's Bur., Chgo.; elem. tchr. Chgo. Bd. of Edn., Pasadena (Calif.) H.S.; English tchr. Malala H.S., Madang, 1993-94; tchr. jr. H.S. Cathedral Chapel Cath. Sch., 1995-96, Holy Trinity Sch., L.A., 1998-2000; ret., 2004. Tutor to fgn. students. Missionary worker L.A. Archdiocese, Papua New Guinea; vol. ARC, Solheim Luth. Home, Glendale Meml. Hosp. 4-year scholar State of Ill., Chgo. Musical Coll. award. Mem. Nat. Coun. Tchrs. of English, Ill. Coun. of Social Studies, Nat. Coun. Social Studies.

KIMBROUGH, PATTI WILEY, music educator; b. Russellville, Ala., Oct. 25, 1955; d. Hal Laughuan Wiley, Elsie Ruth Wiley; m. Jerry Glen Kimbrough, June 25, 1976; children: John David, Jennifer Ruth. BS, U. North Ala., 1978, MA in Edn., 1999. Tchr. music K-5 Russellville City Schs., 1976—88, tchr. music 5-8, 1988—90, tchr. music, dir. choir 7-12, 1990—. Interim organist Calvary Bapt. Ch., Russellville, 1978—79, interim youth dir., 1984—86, dir. children and youth choir, 1985—96, min. music, 1983—96; dir. music Russellville Bapt. Assn., 1990—91; tchr. N.W. Jr. Coll., 2002—03. Composer (children's musical): Angel Babies, 1998; composer: (historical song for city) Russellville, Oh Russellville, 1999; composer: (song for cancer drive) Resting Within His Arms, 1999. Chmn. entertainment Sr. Friends Jaycees, Russellville, 1990—, Garden Clubs Cancer Dr, 1990—. Named Min. of Week, WBTG Florence Radio Sta., 1990, Unsung Hero, Franklin County Times, 1985; recipient Disting. Young Woman award, Russellville Jaycees, 1980; grantee Music Edn. grant, Franklin County Arts Coun., 2001. Mem.: NEA, Ala. Choral Dir. Assn., Ala. Mus. Edn. Assn., Music Edn. Nat. Conf. Democrat. Baptist. Avocations: tennis, water-skiing, boating, composing music, writing. Home: 1607 Clay Ave Russellville AL 35653 Office: Russellville High Sch PO Box 740 Waterloo Rd Russellville AL 35653

KIMBROUGH, WALTER MARK, academic administrator; b. Apr. 22, 1967; m. Adria Nobles Kimbrough. BS, U. Ga., 1989; MS, Miami U., Oxford, Ohio, 1991; PhD, Ga. State U., 1996. Coord. Greek life Emory U., Atlanta, 1992-95; dir. new student programs Ga. State U., Atlanta, 1995-96; dir. student activities Old Dominion U., Norfolk, Va., 1997-2000; v.p. Albany (Ga.) State U., Albany, Ga., 2000—04; pres. Philander Smith Coll., Little Rock, 2005—. Spkr. in field. Mem.: Brothers of Acad., Assn. Fraternity Advisors, Nat. Assn. Student Profl. Adminstrs. Office: Philander Smith Coll One Trudie Kibbe Reed Dr Little Rock AR 72202*

KIMERER, ALICE LOUISE, artist, educator; b. Dilley, Tex., Dec. 22; d. William Lee and Effie (Edwards) Crawford; m. Vincent Augustine Braun, Mar. 6, 1944 (div.); children: Vincent Braun Jr., Barbara Ann Braun; m. Perry Eugene Kimerer, Apr. 17, 1976; children: Candance, Toni. BFA in Art Edn., Our Lady of Lake U., 1942; MFA, Art Inst., Mex., 1960. Art tchr. Burbank Jr. H.S., San Antonio, 1943—44, San Antonio Boys Acad., 1950, Mus. Sci. and History, Ft. Worth, 1976; art instr., judge Carswell AFB, Ft. Worth, 1977; artist Left Bank Gallery, St. Simonis, Ga., 1998—99, Upwest Gallery, Ft. Worth, 1999—2001. Regional dir. Tex. Watercolor Soc., San Antonio, 1980. Artist oil paintings; one-woman shows include 6 shows, Represented in permanent collections chs., profl. offices, hosps., banks and homes. Recipient Arts award, USAF, 1972, Purchase prize, Tex. Watercolor Soc., 1975. Mem.: AAUW (art advisor 1999, art show judge 2001), Kimbell Mus. (patron 1974—), Dallas Mus. for Women, Nat. Mus. Women in Arts. Avocations: travel, teaching, sketching, workshops. Home: 6113 Valley View Dr Fort Worth TX 76116

KIMES, DON MARK, artist, educator; b. Oil City, Pa., Nov. 18, 1953; s. Norman Lloyd and Lois Elaine (Toy) K.; m. Lois Ann Jubeck, July 22, 1978; children: Jesse Mark, Jonathan Todd, Elaina Rose. BA, Westminster Coll., 1975; postgrad., U. Pitts., 1975-77; cert., N.Y. Studio Sch., N.Y.C., 1979; MFA, Bklyn. Coll. CUNY, 1980. Founder, dir. Inst. Internat. Art, Corciano, Italy, 1995—. Artistic dir. Chautauqua (N.Y.) Inst. Sch. of Art, 1986—; full prof. Art Am. U., Washington, 1988—; mem. faculty N.Y. Studio Sch., N.Y.C., 1979-89, program dir., 1980-84; vis. prof. art The Am. U. Rome, 1999—; guest artist Acad. Fine Arts, Perugia, Italy, Dartmouth Coll., Georgetown U., Internat. Sch. Art, Umbria, America Haus, Munich, Harvard U., Parsons Sch. Design; artist in residence Monte Malbe, Italy, 1999. One-man shows include Prince St. Gallery, N.Y.C., 1979-80, 82, 84, 86, 88, 90, 92, Villahermosa Exhbn. Ctr., Mex., 1992, NAS, Washington, 1992, Gauman Cicchino Gallery, Fla., 1990, Michael Rockefeller Gallery, Fredonia, N.Y., 1988, Watkins Gallery, Washington, 1989, 97, Galleria ISA, Montecastello, Italy, 1999, Am. Haus, Munich, Germany, 1996, Galleria Rocca Paolina, Perugia, Italy, 1996, Claudia Carr Gallery, N.Y.C., 2000, Stephen Gang, 2001; exhibited in group shows at Balt. Mus. Art, 1986, 99, Nat. Acad. of Design, N.Y.C., 1986, Corcoran Gallery of Am. Art, 1994, 95, Piazza Broletto, Perugia, Italy, 1995, Arte Vivre, Milan, 1995, Kouros Gallery, N.Y.C., 1997, Internat. Visions, Washington, 1999, Kennedy Mus. Art, Athens, Ohio, 1999, Agosto Corcianese, Umbria, 1998, Florence Internat. Bienale, 2001; contbr. articles to profl. mags. Mem. N.Y. Studio Sch. Bd. Govs., N.Y.C., 1980-85. Named Visual Del. to Villahermosa Conferencia de Literatura y Artes, 1992, Soviet Cultural Exch. Eisenhower Found., Chautauqua Inst., 1986; fellow Edna St. Vincent Millay Colony, 1986; recipient artist-in-residence award U.S. Dept. Interior, 1993, Mellon Found. award to live in Italy, 1994-95. Mem. Coll. Art Assn. of Am., Fondo del Sol Mus. of Latino Art. Home: Chautauqua School of Art PO Box 1098 Chautauqua NY 14722-1098 Office: The Am U Dept Art Washington DC 20016 E-mail: dkimes@american.edu.*

KIMES, MARK L., music educator; b. Vancouver, Wash., Apr. 12, 1966; s. Fred and Alice Jane Kimes; m. Kelley Nassict, Aug. 15, 1992; children: Lauren, Katherine. BS, 1991, PSH, 1995. Choral dir. Scappeese HS, Scappeese, Oreg., 1991—95; elem band dir., music tchr. Hartford Sch. Dist., Hartford, Conn., 1996; band dir. Westhampton Beach HS, Westhampton, NY, 1996—2000; choral dir. Kings Pk. HS, Kings Pk., NY, 2000—03, Hauppauge HS, Hauppauge, NY, 2003—. Coord. Westhampton Band Dist., Westhampton Beach, NY, 1997—2000; lead tchr. Kings Pk. HS, Kings Pk., NY, 2000—04. With U.S. Army, 1989—. Recipient 1st place, Oreg. State Choral Competition, 1994, 1995, Gold with Dist., NYSSMA, 2000—04. Mem.: WOA, NYSBDA, NYSSMA, MENC, ACDA. Democrat. Meth. Avocations: running, computers, coin collecting/numismatics. Home: 189 Cranford Blvd Mastic NY 11950

KIMES, SHERYL ELAINE, business educator; b. St. Louis, Apr. 14, 1954; d. John Alfred and Alpha Louise (Johnson) K. AB, U. Mo., 1975; MA in Pub. Adminstrn., U. Va., 1977; MBA, N.Mex. State U., 1983; PhD, U. Tex., 1987. Energy coord. St. Louis County, St. Louis, 1978-79; energy analyst Londe-Parker-Michels, St. Louis, 1979-82; teaching asst. N.Mex. State U., Las Cruces, 1982-83; project mgr. Technol. Innovation Ctr., Las Cruces, 1983-84; asst. instr. bus. U. Tex., Austin, 1984-85, rsch. asst., 1985-86; asst. prof. bus. N.Mex. State U., Las Cruces, 1986-88, Cornell U., Ithaca, N.Y., 1988-93, assoc. prof., 1993-2000, prof., 2000—. U. Tex. fellow, 1984-86. Mem. INFORMS. Avocations: swimming, bridge, wine, puzzles. Office: Cornell U 335 Statler Hall Ithaca NY 14853-6902

KIMETHU, SUSAN WANJA, computer specialist, database manager; b. Nairobi, Kenya, Mar. 13, 1956; d. Samuel Kimama Ngaii and Mary Nyambura Kimama; m. Daniel Mburu Kimethu; children: Hosea Kimethu Mburu, Samuel Kimama Mburu, Esther Njeri Mburu. Diploma, Kenya Tech. Coll., 1983; MBA, Baldwin Wallace Coll., 1992; PhD in Bus. Adminstrn., Kennedy Western U., 2002. Cert. Oracle database adminstr.; h.s. tchr. Sr. acct. Ameritrust Bank, Cleve., 1993—94; sr. fin. analyst Key Bank, Cleve., 1994—98; instr. Sawyer Bus. Coll., Cleve., 1994—98; database mgr. Telesis Of Ohio, Cleve., 1997—99; sr. bus. analyst Emerald Health, Cleve., 1998—99; database mgr. Orbital Computers, Cleve., 2000—01; computer specialist United Labor Agy., Cleve., 2001—; tchr. Life Skills Ctr., Columbus, 2003—04. Tchr. English as second lang. Southwestern City Sch. Dist., Columbus, Ohio, 2004—. Author: Following & Obeying God in Your Youth, 2001, Kids, Let's Follow Christ, 2002, Kids, Let's Follow Christ Workbook, 2002. Mem.: Network Administrs., Oracle User Group. Office: Dansu Pubs LLC PO Box 937 Grove City OH 43123-0937 Office Phone: 216-513-6753. Personal E-mail: skimethu@hotmail.com.

KIM-FARLEY, ROBERT JAMES, epidemiologist, educator; b. Troy, N.Y., Jan. 24, 1948; s. Robert James and Glennie Jean Farley; m. Han Ju Kim-Farley, Sept. 18, 1976; 1 child, Jean. BSEE, U. Calif., Santa Barbara, 1970; MPH, UCLA, 1975; MD, U. Calif., San Francisco, 1980. Cert. preventive medicine and pub. health. Med. epidemiologist Ctrs. Disease Control and Prevention, Atlanta, 1981—2004; dir. communicable disease control and prevention Los Angeles County Dept. Heath Svcs., L.A., 2004—. Regional advisor WHO, New Delhi, 1984—88, dir. expanded programme on immunization, Geneva, 1989—93, rep., Jakarta, Indonesia, 1994—99, New Delhi, 1999—2002; prof. UCLA, 2003—. Recipient Surgeon Gen.'s Exemplary Svc. medal, USPHS, 1993. Mem.: APHA, Baha'i. Baha'I. Avocation: swimming. Office Phone: 213-989-7161. E-mail: rkimfarley@ladhs.org.

KIMM, MICHAEL S., lawyer; b. Seoul, July 12, 1963; came to U.S., 1974; s. Chun Teak and Chong Sim K. BA, Fordham U., 1987; JD, Boston U., 1991. Bar: N.J. 1991, N.Y. 1992, U.S. Dist. Ct. N.J. 1991, U.S. Dist. Ct. (so. and ea. dists.) N.Y. 1993, U.S. Ct. Appeals (2nd, 3rd and Fed cirs.) 1994, U.S. Supreme Ct. 1995. Pvt. practice, Hackensack, NJ. Mng. editor: Boston U. Internat. Law Jour., 1990-91; contbr. articles to profl. jours. Gen. counsel Korean-Am. Assn. for Rehab. of Disabled, Queens, N.Y., 1992-94. Mem. ABA, N.J. State Bar Assn., N.Y. State Bar Assn. Office: 185 Great Neck Rd Great Neck NY 11021 Address: 190 Moore St # 272 Hackensack NJ 07601

KIMMEL, ELLEN BISHOP, psychologist, educator; b. Knoxville, Tenn., Sept. 16, 1939; d. Archer W. and Mary Ellen (Baker) Bishop; divorced; children: Elinor, Ann, Jean, Tracy. BA summa cum laude, U. Tenn., 1961; MA, U. Fla., 1962, PhD, 1965. Asst. prof., rsch. assoc. Ohio U., 1965-68; asst. prof. U. South Fla., Tampa, 1968-72, assoc. prof., dean Univ. Studies Coll., 1972-73, prof. psychology and ednl. psychology, 1975-95, chair, 1992-94, disting. prof., 1996—2003, prof. emerita, 2003—. Disting. vis. prof. psychology Simon Fraser U., Vancouver, B.C., Can., 1980-81; cons. numerous sch. systems, bus. and govt. Author books; contbr. articles to profl. jours., chpts. to books. Mem. Fla. Blue Ribbon Task Force on Juvenile Delinquency, 1976-77; mem. Fla. Gov.'s Commn. on Women, 1979-83; mem. adv. bd. Stop Rape, Good Govt., Inc.; bd. dirs. NCCJ. Recipient Outstanding Svc. award State of Fla., 1975, Outstanding Tchg. award U. South Fla., 1978, Career Achievement award U. Tenn., 1983, Professorial Excellence award Fla. State U. Sys., 1997, Disting. Sr. Scholar Spl. Commendation of Honor, AAUW, 2001; 17 rsch. grants. Fellow: APA (governing coun. 1982—85, pres. divsn. 1986—88, Disting. Leadership award 1993), Am. Assn. Applied and Preventive Psychology (bd. dirs. 1994—97, charter fellow, program chair 1991, Disting. Edn. award 1994), Am. Psychol. Soc. (charter fellow, conf. chair 1990); mem.: Southeastern Psychol. Assn. (pres. 1977—79), Assn. Women in Psychology (Disting. Publ. award 2000), Athena Soc., Omicron Delta Kappa, Delta Kappa Gamma, Sigma Xi. Democrat. Office: U South Fla EDU 162 Tampa FL 33620 Business E-Mail: kimmel@tempest.coedu.usf.edu.

KIMMEL, HERBERT DAVID, psychologist, educator; b. N.Y.C., May 22, 1927; s. Max and Lillian (Neuwirth) K.; m. Barbara B. Kimmel; children: Elinor, Ann Kimmel Ritter, Jean, Tracy. BS, U. Fla., 1948; MA, NYU, 1951; PhD, U. So. Calif., 1958. Lic. psychologist, Fla. Sch. psychometrist William S. Hart Union High Sch., Newhall, Calif., 1950-52; rsch. asst., rsch. assoc., project dir. Mgmt. and Mktg. Rsch. Corp., Human Factors Rsch., 1953-58; asst. prof., then assoc. prof. psychology U. Fla., Gainesville, 1958-65; prof. psychology Ohio U., Athens, 1965-68, U. So. Fla., Tampa, 1968-86, chmn. dept. psychology, 1968-72, disting. rsch. prof., 1986-93, disting. rsch. prof. emeritus, 1993—. Disting. vis. prof. U. Tulsa, fall 1976; vis. prof. psychology U. P.R., summer 1963, Duke U., spring 1961; vis. scientist Human Factors Rsch., Inc., summer 1964; gastprof. U. Giessen, summer, 1982; prof. U. Trier, 1987-94, mem. sci. adv. bd. Ctr. Rsch. in Psychobiology and Psychosomatics, 1994-98; mem. clin. ethics com. M.D. Anderson Cancer Ctr., 1999-2002; mem. pain mgmt. task force, M.D. Anderson Cancer Ctr., 2001-02. Author: Experimental Principles and Design in Psychology, 1970, Experimental Psychopathology, 1971, Biofeedback and Self-Regulation, 1979, The Orienting Reflex in Humans, 1979; author chpts. to books; masthead cons. editor Jour. Exptl. Psychology, 1960-74; mem. editorial bd. Behavior Therapy and Exptl. Psychiatry, 1976—, Jour. Behavioral Assessment, 1979—, Jour. Clin. and Cons. Psychology, 1981-88; mem. editorial bd. Pavlovian Jour. of Biol. Scis., 1976-78, mng. editor, 1978-83; ad hoc editor for various publs. in field; contbr. articles for profl. jours. Recipient A. von Humboldt Sr. Scientist award U. Tuebingen, 1980-81; grantee NIMH, 1959-72, Office Naval Rsch., 1960-61, U.S. Office Edn., 1969-70, Nat. Libr. Medicine, 1973-76, U.S. Army Med. Rsch. and Devel. Command, 1974-83, NSF, 1976-78, German Rsch. Soc., 1983. Fellow APA; mem. N.Y. Acad. Scis., Southeastern Psychol. Assn., Psychonomic Soc., Psychometric Soc., So. Soc. for Philosophy and Psychology (pres. 1977-78), Pavlovian Soc. (2d v.p. 1980, 1st v.p. 1981, pres. 1982, exec. com. 1983—). Home: 20 Menotti St Charleston SC 29401

KIMMEL, JIMMY (JAMES CHRISTIAN KIMMEL), television personality; b. Bklyn., Nov. 13, 1967; m. Gina Kimmel (div. 2003); 2 children. Host/writer (TV series) The Man Show, 1999—2003, Jimmy Kimmel Live, 2003—, host/writer (voice) Crank Yankers, 2002—, co-host Win Ben Stein's Money, 2001—02; actor: (films) Down To You, 2000, Road Trip (voice), 2000, Like Mike, 2002, Garfield (voice), 2004; (TV films) Donner, 2001. Office: c/o Jimmy Kimmel Live 6834 Hollywood Blvd Los Angeles CA 90028

KIMMEL, MARK, author, venture capital company executive; b. Denver, Feb. 15, 1940; s. Earl Henry and Gerry Claire Kimmel; m. Gloria J. Danielewicz, Jan. 29, 1966 (div.); children: Kenton, Kristopher; m. Heidi J. Moller, Sept. 5, 1999. BSEE, BS in Mktg., U. Colo., 1963; MBA in Fin., U. So. Calif., 1966; MA in Psychology, Regis U., 2000. Sales engr., market rsch. analyst 3M Co., Calif. and Minn., 1963-70; mktg. mgr. Am. Computer and Comms., Calif., 1970-71; mgr. new bus. devel. Motorola, Inc., Schaumburg, Ill., 1971-76; v.p. corp. devel. Nat. City Lines, Denver, 1976-77; pres. Enervest, Inc., Denver, 1977-84; gen. ptnr. Columbine Venture Fund Ltd., 1983-91, Columbine Venture Fund II, 1983-91, Columbine Venture Mgmt. I, 1983-91, Columbine Venture Mgmt. II, 1983-91; pres. Columbine Venture Mgmt. Inc., 1983-91, Paradigm Ptnrs., Inc., 1992-96; writer, lectr., 1996. Author: Trillion, 2002, Decimal, 2004, Creating the Cosmic Paradign, 2005. Chmn. Cosmic Paradign Network. Mem. Nat. Assn. Small Bus. Invesetment Cos. (past bd. govs.), Venture Capital Assn. Colo. (past chmn.). E-mail: 77@zqyx.org.

KIMMEL, SANFORD RICHARD, family physician, pediatrician, educator; b. Dennison, Ohio, July 25, 1949; s. Morris Henry and Elaine K.; m. Sharon Lynn Posey, June 15, 1980; children: Isaac David, Katherine Marie. BS, Ohio State U., 1971, MD, 1974. Diplomate Am. Bd. Family Practice, Am. Bd. Pediatrics. Resident in family medicine St. Elizabeth Med. Ctr., Dayton, 1974-77; assoc. residency dir. Grant-Livingston Family Practice Ctr., Columbus, Ohio, 1977-78; resident in pediat. Columbus Children's Hosp., 1978-80; gen. pediatrician Pediat. Assocs. Findlay, Ohio, 1980-82; asst. prof. family medicine Med. Coll. Ohio, Toledo, 1982-90, assoc. prof., 1990—2001, prof., 2001—. Postdoctoral fellow faculty devel. Mich. State U., East Lansing, 1983-84; panel mem., infant expert Bright Futures, Nat. Ctr. for Edn. in Maternal and Child Health, 1992-96; mem. vaccine risk/benefit comm. adv. bd., 1998-2000. Editor: Well Child Care, 1995; guest editor: Pediat./Adolescent Medicine in Primary Care, 1999, Pediatric Medicine in Primary Care, 2000, 2001; contbr. articles to med. jours.; assoc. guest editor: Vaccines Across the Life Span, 2001, 2003, 2005. Mem. Toledo chpt. Safe Kids Coalition, Toledo, 1994-2000, Ptnrs. for Health Kids, Toledo, 1996; bd. dirs. Maumee Valley dhpt. Am. Diabetes Assn., 1989-99, pres. chpt., 1993-94. Co-recipient Soc. Tchrs. of Family Med. Innovative Program award, 2005; recipient Excellence in Tchg. award Med. Coll. Ohio Family Practice Residents, Toledo, 1996, 2004. Fellow Am. Acad. Pediat., Am. Acad. Family Physicians; mem. Soc. Tchrs. of Family Medicine (chair steering com. group on immunization edn. 1998-2002), Ohio Acad. Pediat., Ohio Acad. Family Physicians, Phi Beta Kappa. Avocations: collecting die-cast model cars, bicycling. Office: Med Coll Ohio Family Practice Ctr 1015 Garden Lake Pkwy Toledo OH 43614-2798 Office Phone: 419-383-5500. Business E-Mail: skimmel@mco.edu.

KIMMEL, STACEY ELLEN, librarian; d. Sharon G. and Morton G. Kimmel. BA, Purdue U., West Lafayette, Ind., 1980—84; MLS, U. N.C., Chapel Hill, 1987—89. Collection mgr., edn., bus., and social scis. N.C. State U., Raleigh, 1996—98; team leader, student and gen. svcs. Lehigh U., Bethlehem, Pa., 1998—. Electronic svcs. libr. Miami U., Oxford, Ohio, 1989—96. Office: Lehigh Univ 8A E Packer Ave Bethlehem PA 18015 Office Phone: 610-758-4768.

KIMMELMAN, MICHAEL SIMON, art critic; b. N.Y.C., May 8, 1958; s. David Brown and Edythe Miriam (Weinstock) K.; m. Maria Kathleen Simson, Sept. 10, 1988. BA in History, Yale U., 1980; MA in Art History, Harvard U., 1982. Teaching fellow dept. fine arts, Arthur Kingsley Porter Fellow Harvard U., Cambridge, Mass., 1982-84; music critic Atlanta Journal-Constitution, 1984, Phila. Inquirer, 1985-87; culture editor U.S. News and World Report, Washington, 1987; art critic The N.Y. Times, 1988-90, chief art critic, 1990—. Lectr. in field; sr. fellow, Nat. Arts Journalism Program Columbia U., 2000. Author: Portraits: Talking With Artists at the Met, the Modern, the Louvre and Elsewhere, 1999 (named Notable Book of Yr., Washington Post and The Times, named Best Book of Yr., Publisher's Weekly), The Accidental Masterpiece: On the Art of Life and Vice Versa, 2005; contbr. to the New York Review of Books, articles to other magazines. Named a finalist in criticism for the Pulitzer Prize, 2000. Mem. Phi Beta Kappa. Office: NY Times 229 W 43rd St New York NY 10036-3959

KIMMEY, JAMES RICHARD, JR., foundation administrator; b. Boscobel, Wis., Jan. 26, 1935; s. James Richard and Frances Dale (Parnell) Kimmey; m. Sarah Webster Eastman, June 21, 1958; children: Elisabeth Webster, James Richard III. BS, U. Wis., 1957, MS, 1959, MD, 1961; MPH, U. Calif. at Berkeley, 1967. Diplomate Am. Bd. Preventive Medicine. Intern Univ. Hosps., Cleve., 1961-62; med. resident Univ. Hosps., Madison, 1962-63; served from surgeon to med. dir. USPHS, 1963-68, chief kidney disease br., 1964-66, regional health dir., 1967-68; exec. dir. Cmty. Health Inc., N.Y.C., 1968-70, Am. Pub. Health Assn., 1970-73; sec. Health Policy Coun. Wis., 1973-75; pres. James R. Kimmey Assos., Inc., 1975-85; dir. Midwest Ctr. Health Planning, 1976-79; exec. dir. Inst. Health Planning, 1979-87; prof. pub. health, dir. Ctr. for Health Svcs. Edn. Rsch. St. Louis U. Med. Ctr., 1987-91; dean sch. pub. health St. Louis U., 1991-93, v.p. health scis., 1993-98, exec. v.p., 1998-2000; dir. Inst. Urban Health Policy, 2000-2001; pres. Mo. Found. for Health, 2001—. Adj. prof. NYU, N.Y.C., 1968—70; lectr. Johns Hopkins, 1971—73; clin. instr. U. Wis., 1974—87; pres. Inst. Health Planning, 1979—86; chair Task Force Accreditation Health Professions, 1997—99, St. Louis ConnectCare, 1998—2001; dir. Ctr. Engring. Tech., 1998—2001; vice chair St. Louis Access Health, 1999—2001. Editor: (book) The Nation's Health, 1972—73; mng. editor: Am. Jour. Pub. Health, 1970—73, mem. editl. adv. bd.: Health Cost Mgmt., 1983—87; contbr. articles to profl. jours. Pres. World Fedn. Pub. Health Assns., 1972—73; mem. sci. adv. bd. Gorgas Inst., 1970—73; bd. dirs. Internat. Union Health Edn., 1970—73. Decorated USPHS Commendation medal. Fellow: APHA (governing coun. 1978—81, chmn. cmty. health planning sect. 1979—80, governing coun. 1983—87, 1989—92), Am. Coll. Preventive Medicine; mem.: Prospective Payment Assessment Commn. (commr. 1991—97), Mo. Pub. Health Assn. (Mo. Communicator of the Yr. award 1994), Am. Coll. Health Adminstrs., Am. Health Planning Assn. (dir. 1974—75, 1977—78, corp. sec. 1977—78, pres. 1980—81, Richard H. Schlesinger award 1978, James R. Kimmey award 1994), Alpha Sigma Nu, Delta Omega, Alpha Omega Alpha, Phi Eta Sigma. Democrat. Episcopalian. Home: 1614 S 18th St Saint Louis MO 63104-2504 Office: Grand Ctrl Bldg Ste 400 1000 St Louis Union Sta Saint Louis MO 63103 Office Phone: 314-345-5500. Business E-Mail: jkimmey@mffh.org.

KIMMICH, CHRISTOPH MARTIN, academic administrator, educator; b. Dresden, Jan. 16, 1939; s. Emil and Dora (Dreher) K.; m. Flora Graham Horne, July 10, 1965. BA, Haverford Coll., 1961; DPhil, U. Oxford, Eng., 1964. Asst. then assoc. prof. Columbia U., N.Y.C., 1965-73; assoc. then full prof. Bklyn. Coll., CUNY, 1973—, assoc. provost, 1984-88, provost, v.p. acad. affairs, 1988-97; interim chancellor CUNY, N.Y.C., 1997-99; pres. Bklyn. Coll., 2000—. V.p. bd. dirs. rsch. and devel. fedn. Bklyn. Coll., 1989—; chmn. bd. dirs. rsch. found. of CUNY, 1997-1999, mem., 2000-03; bd. dirs. Bklyn. Philharm. Orch Author: The Free City, 1968, Germany and the League of Nations, 1976, German Foreign Policy: 1918-1945, 1981, 2d edit., 1991. Trustee St. Antony's Coll. Trust, N.Y.C., 1978-2000; bd. dirs. Northeastern Sci. Found., Troy, 1987-98, Coll. Cmty. Svcs., Inc., Bklyn., 1988-95, chmn., 2000—; bd. trustees Cranbury Pub. Libr., 1997-2000, Bklyn. Philharm. Orch., 2003—; mem. adv. bd. Princeton Rev. Admissions Policy Divsn. Fulbright scholar, 1961; Internat. Affairs fellow, 1974; Guggenheim fellow, 1983; decorated Order of Merit Comdr.'s Cross, Republic of Hungary, 2001. Mem. Phi Beta Kappa. Home: 183 Plainsboro Rd Cranbury NJ 08512-2603 Office: Bklyn Coll Office of the Pres 2900 Bedford Ave Brooklyn NY 11210-2889

KIMMICH, HAYDEE JAVIER, orthopedist, consultant; b. Cabo Rojo, P.R., Apr. 25, 1927; d. Bartolome Javier Petrovich and Herminia Deprez Boscio; m. Homer Kimmich (dec. Oct. 7, 1985); children: John Kimmich, Denise Dijkstal. BA, Adelphi U., 1947; MD, Med. Coll. Pa., 1951. Diplomate Am. Bd. Surgery. Med. dir. State Ins. Fund, San Juan, P.R., 1953-57; resident Temple U., Phila., 1958-60; pvt. practive Springfield, Ill., 1961-74; med. dir. Rotary Rehab. Ctr., Mobile, Ala., 1974-76; commd. col. USAF, 1977, chief orthopedic Eglin Air Force Hosp. Ft. Walton Beach, Fla., 1977-80; commd. capt. USN, 1984, chief orthopedic Bethesda Naval Hosp., 1984-95, sr. cons. Naval Hosp. Jacksonville, Fla., 1995-2001. Asst. prof. Uniformed Sensice U. for Health Scis., Bethesda, Md., 1984-2001. Contbr. articles to profl. jours. Vol. physician U.S. AID, Vietnam, 1967, 97, orthopedic overseas, Riua, Peru, 1984. Named Woman of Yr. in Medicine and Military EL-DIA, 1998. Mem. Smithonian Assn., Audubon Soc., Academic Orthopedic Soc., Sierra Club, Ruth Jackson Found. Democrat. Avocations: sailing, travel, cooking. Office: US Navy Naval Hosp Jacksonville FL 32210 Home: 423 W 7th Ave Cheyenne WY 82001-1257

KIMMICH, JON BRADFORD, computer science program executive; b. Lancaster, Pa., Aug. 8, 1964; s. John Howard and Alice (Ingram) K. BS in Computer Sci., Ind. U. Pa., 1986; MS in Computer Sci., Ohio State U., 1988; MBA, Seattle U., 1993. Developer Microsoft, Redmond, Wash., 1988-93, lead program mgr., sr. producer, 1993-97, lead product planner, 1997—. Dir. PKT Found. Contbr. articles to profl. jours. Trustee PKT Found. Mem. IEEE (Computer Soc.), Assn. for Computing Machinery, Acad. Interactive Arts and Scis., Internat. Interactive Comms. Soc., Am. Film Inst. Achievements include 7 patents pending. Home: 1442 W Lake Sammamish Pkwy SE Bellevue WA 98008-5218 Office: Microsoft Corp 1 Microsoft Way Redmond WA 98052-8300

KIMMICH, ROBERT ANDRÉ, psychiatrist; b. Indpls., Nov. 2, 1920; s. John Martin and Renée Marie (Baron) K.; m. Nancy Earle Smith, 1944 (div. 1952); children: Robert, John, Nancy. BS, Ind. U., 1940, MD, 1943. Diplomate Am. Bd. Psychiatry and Neurology; lic. physician, Calif. Intern St. Vincent's Hosp., Indpls., 1943-44; resident in psychiatry Inst. Pa. Hosp., Phila., 1944-45, U.S. Army Hosp., Phoenixville, Pa., 1945-47; chief male psychiat. div. Worcester (Mass.) State Hosp., 1947-48; resident in psychiatry Harvard Advanced Study Mental Health Ctr., Boston, 1948; asst. prof., asst. chief outpatient dept. Yale U. Sch. Medicine, 1949-51; chief psychosomatic svc. VA Hosp., Newington, Conn., 1949-51; med. dir. Territorial Psychiat. Hosp., Kaneohe, Hawaii, 1951-58; clin. dir. Ill. State Psychiat. Inst., Chgo., 1958-59; chief profl. edn. Stockton (Calif.) State Hosp., 1959-60; chief mental health program and svcs. City of San Francisco, 1960-64; dir. dept. mental health State of Mich., 1964-68; chmn. dept. psychiatry Children's Hosp., San Francisco, 1968-76; pvt. practice San Francisco, 1970—. Asst. prof. psychiatry Yale U. Med. Sch., 1948-51; pres. Hosp. Coun. Hawaii, 1956-57.; assoc. prof. Northwestern U. Med. Sch., 1958-59; assoc. clin. prof. U. Calif., San Francisco, 1960-64; assoc. clin. prof. U. Mich. Med. Sch., Ann Arbor, 1964-68, Stanford U. Med. Sch., 1968-80; lectr. U. Hawaii, 1952-58; pres., founder San Francisco Coordinating Coun. on Mental Retardation, 1961-64; com. on psychiat. tng. State of Calif., 1963-64; chair adv. bd. Mich. Mental Health and Mental Retardation, 1964-67; cons. on mental retardation White House, 1965; exec. com. Children's Hosp., San Francisco, 1967-76; pres. Western Inst. for Rsch. in Mental Health, 1962-64, v.p., 1964-67; ind. med. examiner Calif. Bd. Indsl. Accidents, 1984—; bd. dirs. Children's Physicians Assocs. Editor Northern California Psychiatric Physician, 1985-94. Bd. dirs., chmn., fin. com. mem. Nat. Assn. State Mental Health, 1965-66; chmn., managed care com. No. Calif. Psychiat. Soc., 1991-93; bd. dirs. Westside Mental Health Ctr., San Francisco, 1967-77. Capt. M.C., U.S. Army, 1945-47. Fellow Am. Psychiat. Assn. (life, pres. Hawaii dist. br. 1954-55, rep. to nat. assembly 1986-1997, task force on ethics 1989-90, com. on procedures 1990—, commn. psychotherapy 1996—, com. on stds. 1966, spl. com. on prepayment health ins. 1965, com. on mental hosps. 1965), Am. Hosp. Assn. (liaison 1964, nominating com. 1993—); mem. AMA, Mich. State Med. Soc., Calif. Med. Assn., San Francisco Med. Soc., No. Calif. Psychiat. Soc. (pres. elect 1991-93, pres. 1993-95, coun. mem. 1984—, editor 1984-94), San Francisco Psychiat. Soc. (pres. 1984-85), Calif. Pacific Med. Assocs., Inc. (pres. 1997-2005). Office: 341 Spruce St San Francisco CA 94118-1830 Office Phone: 415-752-2331.

KIMMITT, KELLY GENE, specialized cancer research director; b. L.A., Sept. 30, 1953; s. Harry Don and Louise Ann Kimmitt; m. Carol Sue Kimmitt, May 22, 1976; children: Michael, Kristina, Megan, Therese, Ian. BA in Physics, Ill. Wesleyan U., 1975; MS in Computer Sci., No. Ill. I., 1982. Tchr. Somenauk (Ill.) H.S., 1978—81; programmer Caterpillar Tractor Co., Peoria, Ill., 1982; mem. tech. staff AT&T, Naperville, Ill., 1983—97; disting. mem. tech. staff Lucent Italy, Rome, 1997—2002, Lucent, Lisle, Ill., 2002—. Mem. sch. bd. Am. Overseas Sch. Rome, 1999—2002. Recipient Chmn.'s Quality award, AT&T, 1995, Quality Team Gold Corp. award, 1996. Mem.: Am. Soc. for Quality (sr.; cert. quality engr.). Avocation: sports officiating. Home: 1097 Crestwood Ct Bolingbrook IL 60440

KIMMITT, ROBERT MICHAEL, federal agency administrator, former broadcase executive; b. Logan, Utah, Dec. 19, 1947; s. Joseph Stanley and Eunice L. (Wegener) K.; m. Holly Sutherland, May 19, 1979; children: Kathleen, Robert, William, Thomas, Margaret. BS, U.S. Mil. Acad., 1969; JD, Georgetown U., 1977. Bar: D.C. 1977. Commd. 2d lt. U.S. Army, 1969, advanced through grades to maj., 1982, served in Vietnam, 1970-71; maj. gen. USAR, 1999—2005; law clk. U.S. Ct. Appeals, Washington, 1977-78; sr. staff mem. NSC, Washington, 1978-83, dep. asst. to Pres. for nat. security affairs and exec. sec. and gen. counsel, 1983-85; gen. counsel U.S. Dept. Treasury, Washington, 1985-87; ptnr. Sidley & Austin, Washington, 1987-89; undersec. for polit. affairs US Dept. State, Washington, 1989-91, US amb. to Germany Berlin, 1991-93; mng. dir. Lehman Bros., Washington, N.Y.C., 1993-97; sr. ptnr. Wilmer, Cutler & Pickering, Washington, 1997-00; vice-chmn., pres. Commerce One, Pleasanton, Calif., 2000—01; exec. v.p., global pub. policy Time Warner Inc., Washington, 2001—05, chmn. internat. adv. com., 2005; sr. internat. counsel Wilmer, Cutler, Pickering, Hale & Dorr, Washington, 2005; dep. sec. US Dept. Treasury, Washington, 2005—. U.S. mem. panel of arbitrators Ctr. Settlement of Investment Internat. Disputes, 1988—89; bd. dirs. Xign Corp. Bd. dirs. German Marshall Fund, Atlantic Coun., Mike Mansfield Found., Am. Inst. Contemporary German Studies, Am. Coun. on Germany, Internat. Rep. Inst. Decorated Bronze star (3), Purple Heart, Air medal, Vietnamese Cross of Gallantry, German Svc. Cross, German Army Cross in Gold; recipient Arthur Flemming award Downtown Jaycees, 1987, Alexander Hamilton award U.S. Dept. Treasury, 1987, Presdl. Citizens medal, 1991, Def. Disting. Civilian Svc. medal, 1993. Mem. Am. Acad. Diplomacy, Assn. Grads. U.S. Mil. Acad. (trustee 1976-82), Coun. Fgn. Rels. Roman Catholic. Office: US Dept Treasury 1500 Pennsylvania Ave NW Rm 3000 Washington DC 20220

KIMNACH, MYRON WILLIAM, botanist, horticulturist; b. L.A., Dec. 26, 1922; s. Elmer Edward and Ida (Johnson) K.; m. Maria Jaeger, Nov. 17, 1961. Grad. h.s. Asst. mgr. U. Calif. Botanic Garden, Berkeley, 1951-62; dir. Huntington Bot. Gardens, San Marino, 1962—86, dir. emeritus, 1986; book-dealer Monrovia, Calif. Contbr. articles profl. jours. Pres., bd. dir. Palm Soc., 1976-78. With USCG, 1943-46. Fellow Cactus and Succulent Soc. Am. (pres. 1970-71, bd. dir. 1968-74, editor jour. 1993-2003). Home and Office: 509 Bradbury Rd Monrovia CA 91016-3704 Office Phone: 626-358-3043. Personal E-mail: mkimnach@aol.com.

KIMPORT, DAVID LLOYD, lawyer; b. Hot Springs, S.D., Nov. 28, 1945; s. Ralph E. and Ruth N. (Hutchinson) K.; m. Barbara H. Buggert, Apr. 2, 1976; children: Katrina Elizabeth, Rebecca Helen, Susanna Ruth. AB summa cum laude, Bowdoin Coll., 1968; postgrad., Imperial Coll., U. London, 1970-71; JD, Stanford U., 1975. Bar: Calif. 1975, U.S. Supreme Ct. 1978. Assoc. Baker & McKenzie, San Francisco, 1975—82, ptnr., 1982—90, Nossaman, Guthner, Knox & Elliott, 1990—. Active San Francisco Planning and Urban Rsch., 1978—, The Family, 1987—. Served with U.S. Army, 1968-70. Mem. ABA, San Francisco Bar Assn., Commonwealth Club of Calif., Phi Beta Kappa. Democrat. Episcopalian. Office: Nossaman Guthner Knox & Elliott 50 California St Fl 34 San Francisco CA 94111-4624 Office Phone: 415-398-3600. E-mail: dkimport@nossaman.edu.

KIMPTON, JEFFREY S., academic administrator; b. 1950; m. Julie Kimpton; children: Meghan, Adam. Attended polit. sci. & pre-law, Augustana Coll., Rock Island, Ill., 1968—70; BS in music edn., cum laude, U. Ill., 1973, MS in music edn. & sch. adminstr., 1975; cert. in corp. financial mgmt. & acctg., Am. Mgmt. Assn., 1995. Cert. teaching & adminstr. Ill., N.Y., Minn., Kans. Various teaching & adminstr. positions Pub. Sch. Sys., Wichita, Kans., Apple Valley, Minn., Corinth, NY, 1973—88; dir. instl. edn. Yamaha Corp. Am., 1988—96; dir. pub. engagement Annenberg Inst. Brown U., 1996—99; dir. sch. music U. Minn., 1999—2003, prof. music edn., 1999—2003; pres. Interlochen Ctr. for Arts, 2003—. Mem. Rotary Club Traverse City; corp. bd. Munson Healthcare; bd. dir. Traverse Area Arts Coun., ArtServe Mich. Office: Office of the Pres Interlochen Ctr for Arts PO Box 199 Interlochen MI 49643

KIM-ROHRER, HANNAH JOYCE, music educator; b. Quincy, Ill., June 9, 1963; d. Mark S and Helen S Kim; m. Jeffrey L Rohrer, Aug. 31, 1986; children: Mark J Rohrer, Matthew L Rohrer, Melody L Rohrer. BS, U. of Ill., 1981—85; M, Mont. Sate U., 1985—86. Tchr./band dir. South Knox Mid./High Sch., Vincennes, Ind., 1998—; tchr. - band dir. Barr-Reeve Cmty. Schools, Montgomery, Ind., 1987—98; adj. woodwind instr. Vincennes U., Vincennes, Ind. Choir dir. Westminster Presbyn. Ch., Washington. Chmn. Westminster Presbyn. Ch. deacon, Washington, Ind., 2003—05; pres. Barr-Reeve Cmty. Schools PTO, Montgomery, Ind., 2003—04. Mem.: Ind. Music Educators Assn., Ind. Bandmasters Assn. (zone rep. 1992—94, 2005—). Home: R 2 Box 463 G Montgomery IN 47558 Office: South Knox Middle/H S 6136 E State Rd 61 Vincennes IN 47591 Office Phone: 812-726-4450. Office Fax: 812-726-4545. Personal E-mail: jkimrohrer@sknox.k12.in.us.

KIM-RUPNOW, WEOL SOON, education educator; d. Dae-Soo Kim and Ye-Soon Yim; m. Robert James Rupnow; children: Kenneth Rupnow, Hana Rupnow. Degree, Seoul Nat. Tchrs. Coll., 1974; PhD, U. Hawaii, Manoa, 1991. Co-project dir., rschr. U. Hawaii-Manoa Ctr. on Disability Studies, Honolulu, 1997—2001, project dir., 2001—. Contbr. articles to profl. jours. Grantee Dept. Edn., 2001—03. Mem.: Am. Ednl. Rsch. Assn. (corr.). Office: Ctr on Disability Studies 1776 University Ave UA4-6 Honolulu HI 96826 Office Phone: 808-956-5712. Office Fax: 808-956-7878.

KIMURA, DOREEN, psychology professor, researcher; b. Winnipeg, Man., Can. 1 child, Charlotte Vanderwolf. BA, McGill U., Montreal, Que., Can., 1956, MA, 1957, PhD, 1961; LLD (hon.), Simon Fraser U., 1993, Queen's U., 1999. Lectr. Sir George Williams U. (now Concordia U.), Montreal,

1960-61; rsch. assoc. otol. rsch. lab. UCLA Med. Ctr., 1962-63; rsch. assoc. Coll. Medicine, McMaster U., Hamilton, Ont., 1964-67; assoc. prof. psychology U. Western Ont., London, 1967-74, prof., 1974-98, coord. clin. neuropsychology program, 1983-97. Supr. clin. neuropsychology Univ. Hosp., London, 1975-83; vis. prof. psychology Simon Fraser U., 1998—. Author: Neuromotor Mechanisms in Human Communication, 1993, Sex and Cognition, 1999, French, Japanese, Swedish, Spanish, Portuguese edits.; contbr. numerous articles to profl. jours. Recipient Outstanding Sci. Achievement award Can. Assn. Women in Sci., 1986, John Dewan award Ont. Mental Health Found., 1992; fellow Montreal Neurol. Inst., 1960-61, Geigy fellow Kantonsspital, Zürich, Switzerland, 1963-64, D.O. Hebb Disting. Contbn. award, Can. Soc. Brain, Behav. & Cogn. Sciences, 2005. Fellow Royal Soc. Can., Can. Psychol. Assn. (Disting. Contbns. to Sci. award 1985); mem. Soc. Acad. Freedom and Scholarship (founding pres. 1992-93, 98-2000). Office: Simon Fraser U Dept Psychology Burnaby BC Canada V5A 1S6 Office Phone: 604-291-3356. Business E-Mail: dkimura@sfu.ca.

KIN, CAROL JOAN (RAMASKA), elementary school educator; b. Kenosha, Wis., Oct. 25, 1966; d. James Paul and Joan Francis (Chandonais) R. BA in Spanish, U. Wis., 1989, MS in Curriculum and Instrn., 1992. Cert. elem. tchr. 1-8, Spanish 1-9, bilingual 1-8, Wis. Bilingual educator Kenosha Unified Sch. Dist. #1, 1989—. Mem. NEA, Kenosha Edn. Assn., Wis. Edn. Assn. Coun., Tchrs. of English to Speakers of Other Langs., Wis. Assn. Bilingual Educators, Kappa Delta Pi (treas. 1989-92).

KINAHAN, PAUL EUGENE, physicist, researcher; BSc in Enring. Physics, U. BC, 1985, MSc in Engring. Physics, 1988; PhD in Bioengring., U. Pa., 1994. Assoc. prof. radiology U. Pitts., Pitts., 1994—2001; prof. radiology U. Wash., Seattle, 2001—. Cons. in field, 1994—. Mem.: IEEE (program chair conf. 1999—2002, Young Investigator Med. Imaging Sci. Career award 1997). Office: U Wash 1959 NE Pacific St Box 356004 Seattle WA 98195-6004 Office Phone: 206-598-6726. Office Fax: 206-598-4192. Business E-Mail: kinahan@u.washington.edu.

KINARD-WRIGHT, JUDITH LAURETTA, elementary, secondary special education educator; b. Kings County, Aug. 23, 1958; d. Joseph Louis and Shirley M. Kinard; m. Gary K. Wright; children: Amanda Joy, Aleeya Michelle. BS in Spl. Edn., CCNY, 1983, MS in Spl. Edn. with honors, 1988; advanced cert. in adminstrn. and supervi, Brooklyn Coll., 1998. Cert. spl. edn. tchr., adminstrn. and supervision, N.Y.; lic. spl. edn. tchr., asst. prin. elem. sch., asst. prin. spl. edn. sch., N.Y. Pvt. tutor foster care students Faculty Tutoring Svc., Inc., Greenvale, NY, 1985—94; group leader Patchwork Cultural Ctr., Bklyn., 1982-85; tchr. Mini Inst./CCNY after-sch. program, N.Y.C., 1984-93; spl. edn. tchr. P140 N.Y.C. Dept. Edn., also sch. libr P140, coord. SIEVII elem. unit spl. edn. P. 140 Bklyn., 1991—93, spl. edn. tchr. P140 and P.S. 73, 2001—. Pvt. tutor. Vol. play therapist for terminally ill children, Downstate U. Hosp., Bklyn.; cheerleader coach, group leader SIE VII A's, 1990-91; soprano United Voices Mass Concert Choir, Bklyn., 1987-90, asst. unit coord. P.S. 140 1991-93. Office Phone: 718-498-2800.

KINBERG, JUDY, television producer, director; b. Freeport, NY, Sept. 15, 1948; d. Jack H. and Rose M. (Schwartz) K. BA, Hofstra U., 1970. Prodn. asst. various programs including Camera Three CBS TV, N.Y.C., 1970-75; assoc. producer PBS-WNET/Dance in America, N.Y.C., 1975-76, producer, 1977—. NBC co-producer: He Makes Me Feel Like Dancin', 1984 (Acad. award, Emmy award, Chgo. Internat. Film Festival Silver Hugo, CINE Golden Eagle award, Christopher awards); prodr., dir. Who's Dancin' Now? (AFI L.A. Internat. Film Fest. Audience award, Best Documentary, Cine Golden Eagle award, Parents' Choice award), 1999; producer: PBS Dance in America: The Feld Ballet, 1979, The Green Table (with Joffrey Ballet), 1982, The Magic Flute (with N.Y.C. Ballet), 1983, San Francisco Ballet: A Song for Dead Warriors, 1984, A Choreographer's Notebook: Stravinsky Piano Ballets by Peter Martins, 1984, Balanchine, Parts I and II, 1984 (27th Ann. Internat. Film and TV awards of N.Y., gold medal Chgo. Internat. Film Festival Silver Plaque Monitor award, Emmy nomination), San Francisco Ballet in Cinderella, 1985 (Internat. Film and TV Festival of N.Y. gold medal, CINE Golden Eagle award, Parent's Choice award), Mark Morris, 1986 (CINE Golden Eagle award, Am. Film & Video Festival Red Ribbon award), Choreography by Jerome Robbins, 1986 (Chgo. Internat. Film Festival Silver Hugo, CINE Golden Eagle award), Dance Theatre of Harlem in A Streetcar Named Desire, 1986 (Chgo. Internat. Film Festival Silver Hugo), In Memory of...A Ballet by Jerome Robbins, 1987 (Chgo. Internat. Film Festival Silver Hugo, CINE Golden Eagle award), Agnes, the Indomitable de Mille, 1987 (Emmy award, Chgo. Internat. Film Festival Silver Hugo, CINE Golden Eagle award), Paul Taylor: Roses and Last Look, 1988, Balanchine and Cunningham: An Evening at Am. Ballet Theatre, 1988, La Sylphide (with the Pa./Milw. Ballet), 1989, A Night at The Joffrey, 1989, (Emmy nomination, Gold medal Internat. Film and TV Festival of N.Y., Best Video Creation IMZ Video Danse Awards, Gold Hugo award Chgo. Internat. Film Festival), The Search for Nijinsky's Rite of Spring, 1989 (producer/dir., Best Documentary IMZ Video Danse Awards, Internat. Film & TV Festival N.Y. Bronze medal), Baryshnikov Dances Balanchine, 1989 (Emmy nomination, finalist Internat. Film and TV Festival of N.Y.), Paul Taylor's Speaking in Tongues (Gold medal Internat. Film and TV Festival N.Y. Gold Plaque award Chgo. Internat. Film Festival), 1991, The Hard Nut with Mark Morris Dance Group, 1992 (Gold medal Internat. Film and TV Festival of N.Y., Emmy nomination), Balanchine Celebration, 1993 (with N.Y.C. City Ballet, Emmy nomination), The Wrecker's Ball, Three Dances by Paul Taylor, 1996 (Rose d'or de Montreaux Festival finalist); producer, dir. Bob Fosse/Steam Heat, 1990 (Emmy award, Ohio State award, Chgo. Film Festival Silver Plaque, Festival Internat. du Film Sur L'Art, Festival Rose d'Or, Montreux), A Tudor Evening with Am. Ballet Theatre, 1990, Balanchine in Am. with the N.Y.C. Ballet, 1990, Ballerinas: Dances by Peter Martins, 1991, A Renaissance Revisited, 1996 (N.Y. Festivals finalist award), (documentary) Variety and Virtuosity/American Ballet Theatre Now, 1998 (Chris award Columbus Internat. Film & Video Festival), Am. Ballet Theatre in Le Corsaire, (Emmy award 2000)From Broadway: Fosse, 2001 (CINE Golden Eagle award); producer PBS Great Performances: Out of Our Fathers' House, 1978; co-producer PBS Dance in America: Pilobolus Dance Theatre, 1977, Trailblazers of Modern Dance, 1977 (1st pl. 9th Ann. Dance Film and Video Festival), San Francisco Ballet: Romeo and Juliet, 1978, Choreography by Balanchine, Part III, 1978 (Chgo. Internat. Film Festival Silver Plaque, Emmy nomination), Choreography by Balanchine, Part IV, 1979 (Emmy award), The Martha Graham Dance Company: Clytemnestra, 1979 (Chgo. Internat. Film Festival Golden Hugo), Two Duets with Choreography by Jerome Robbins and Peter Martins, 1980, Nureyev and the Joffrey Ballet: In Tribute to Nijinsky, 1981 (Peabody award 1981, Emmy nomination), The Tempest: Live with the San Francisco Ballet, 1981, L'Enfant et Les Sortileges, 1981, Paul Taylor: Three Modern Classics, 1982, Paul Taylor: Two Landmark Dances, 1982, Bournonville Dances (with mems. ofN.Y.C. Ballet), 1982; co-producer PBS Theater in America: When Hell Freezes Over I'll Skate, 1979; prodr., dir. PBS Great Performances: The World of Jim Henson, 1994 (Parents Choice honor, 1995, Emmy award), Born to Be Wild: The Leading Men of American Ballet Theatre, 2002 (Festival Rose d'Or Montreux, N.Y. Festivals Gold World medal, Parents' Choice Silver Honor, Berkeley Video and Film Grand Festival Winner, Chris Statuette 2003, Ojai Film Festival Jury award), 22nd Festival Internat. Du Film Sur L'Art, 4th Constellation Change Screen Dance Festival, London, (with Am. Ballet Theatre) The Dream, 2004, Swan Lake (with Am. Ballet Theatre); prodr. PBS Stage on Screen: The Man Who Came to Dinner, 2000, The Women, 2002. Mem. Dirs.' Guild Am., Acad. TV Arts and Scis. Office: Thirteen/WNET/Dance In America 450 W 33rd St Fl 6 New York NY 10001-2603

KINBERG, ROBERT, lawyer; b. St. Louis, Mo., Feb. 24, 1948; BSEE, Washington Univ., 1970; JD with honors, George Washington Univ., 1975. Bar: Va. 1975, DC 1982. Patent examiner, 1970—72; patent adv., office of JAG Dept. of Navy, 1972—73, Dept. of Air Force, 1973—75; mem., office gen. counsel NASA, 1975—82; ptnr. Spencer & Frank, 1982—87, 1989—98; ptnr., intellectual property litig. Venable LLP, Washington, 1998—; and co-chair, patent prosecution group Power Internat., Inc, Washington, v.p., 1987—89. Instr. Patent Resources Group, 1990—2000. Mem.: Internat. Assn. Protection of Industrial Property, Am. Intellectual Property Law Assn., Va. State Bar, DC Bar, Eta Kappa Nu, Tau Beta Pi. Office: Venable LLP 575 Seventh St NW Washington DC 20004 Office Phone: 202-344-4051. Office Fax: 202-344-8300. Business E-Mail: rkinberg@venable.com.

KINCAID, JAMAICA, writer; b. St. John's, Antigua and Barbuda, May 25, 1949; came to U.S., 1966; d. Annie Richardson; 2 children. Student pub. schs., St. John's; hon. degree, Williams Coll., 1991, L.I. Coll., 1991, Amherst Coll., 1995, Bard Coll., 1997, Middlebury Coll., 1998. Author: At the Bottom of the River, 1983 (Morton Dauwen Zabel award Am. Acad. and Inst. of Arts and Letters 1984), Annie John, 1985, A Small Place, 1988, Lucy, 1990, Autobiography of My Mother, 1996, My Brother, 1997; editor: My Favorite Plant, 1998, My Garden, 1999.

KINCAID, JOHN, political science professor, editor; b. Phila., May 5, 1946; s. John and Louise M. (Berger) K.; children: Karen Louise, Sarah Jeanenne. BA, Temple U., 1967, PhD, 1981; MA, U. Wis., 1968. Instr. St. Peter's Coll., Jersey City, 1969-70; dir. Phoenix Peace Ctr., 1970-72; v.p., treas. Pentagon Papers Fund for Civil Liberties, L.A., 1972-73; instr. Temple U., Phila., 1975-79; asst. prof. North Tex. State U., Denton, 1979-84; assoc. prof. U. North Tex., Denton, 1984-86; dir. rsch. U.S. Adv. Commn. on Intergovtl. Rels., Washington, 1986-87, exec. dir., 1987-94; Robert B. and Helen S. Meyner prof. govt. and pub. svcs. Lafayette Coll., Easton, Pa., 1994—, dir. Meyner Ctr. for Study State and Local Govt., 1994—. Rsch. fellow Ctr. for Study Federalism, Phila., 1982-85. Editor, contbr.: Political Culture, Public Policy and the American States, 1982, Covenant, Polity, and Constitutionalism, 1983, The Covenant Connection: Federal Theology and the Origins of Modern Politics, 2000, Competition among States and Local Governments, 1991, Constitutional Origins, Structure, and Change in Federal Countries, 2005; editor The Covenant Letter, 1979-92, Publius: Jour. Federalism, 1981-, (book series) State Government and Politics, 1983—; contbr. articles to profl. jours. Numerous grants NEH, Earhart Found., Ford Found., Fund for Improvement Postsecondary Edn., North Tex. State U., Nat. Inst. Edn., USIA. Mem. Am. Polit. Sci. Assn., Nat. Acad. Pub. Adminstrn., Acad. Polit. Sci., Southwestern Polit. Sci. Assn. (v.p., program chmn. 1984-86, pres. 1993-94). Episcopalian. Avocation: stamp collecting/philately. Office: Lafayette Coll Meyner Ctr Easton PA 18042-1785 Office Phone: 610-330-5597. Business E-Mail: meynerc@lafayette.edu.

KINCAID, JOHN BRUCE, lawyer; b. Chgo., Aug. 25, 1938; s. Cecil Eldred and Marguerite (Donahue) K.; m. Sharon Louise Middleton, Jan. 8, 1966; children— Stacy, Sarah, Tara. B.S., No. Ill. U., 1960; J.D., Chgo. Kent Coll. Law, 1963. Bar: Ill. 1963, U.S. Dist. Ct. (no. dist.) Ill. 1964, U.S. Ct. Appeals (7th cir.) 1978, U.S. Supreme Ct. 1973. Ptnr. Hinshaw-Culbertson, Chgo., 1963-70, mng. ptnr. Mirabella & Kincaid, Wheaton, Ill., 1970— . Pres. United Way, Wheaton, 1982-84; trustee, elder First Presbyn. Ch., Wheaton, 1981-83. Mem. Assn. Trial Lawyers Am., Ill. Trial Lawyers Assn., Ill. Bar Found. (pres 1996-98), Ill. State Bar (Ill. tort council 1983-85), DuPage Bar Assn. (bd. dirs. 1972-75, chmn. profl. responsibility com. 1980-85, pres. 1991-92). Republican. Office: Mirabella & Kincaid Suite 103A 1776 S Naperville Rd Wheaton IL 60187

KINCAID, JOHN J.P., minister; b. Gastonia, Ga., Dec. 28, 1918; s. Walter F. and Nettie Irene (Harkey) Kincaid; m. Nancy Champion Kincaid, Aug. 16, 1964 (dec. Jan. 6, 2002); children: Sarah Kimberly Ross, James C. Ross, Joel F., Nancy Luzette; m. Mac Geraldine Phillips (div.); children: Rebecca Yvonne, Pricilla Dianne, John Jr., Stephen Ronald. BA Cum Laude, High Point Univ., High Point, N.C., 1950; MDiv, Duke Divinty Sch., Durham, N.C., 1954. Pastor, founder Woodard Meml. Inter Demon. Ch., Greensboro, NC, 1940—46; pastor UMC Ch., Western No., 1947—65; dir. mid south CROP, 1955—59; pastor UMC Ch., Fla., 1965—76; cmty. svc. officer N.C. Dept. Correction, 1977—81, menatl health case mgr., 1982—85; crew leader fedr. funded program H.S. Dropout working on GED, 1987—92. Author: (biography) Love, Life, Living, Cancer, 2002, autobiography; contbr. articles pub. to profl. jour. Participant, contbr. DNC, 1960—2004. Recipient Cert. of Appreciation for Disting. Svcs., Region C Isothernal planning Com., 1991. Democrat. Meth. Avocations: golf, fishing.

KINCAID, JOHN PETER, science educator; b. Pitts., Pa., Sept. 16, 1942; s. John Franklin and Nancy Ange Kincaid; m. Calliopi D Kincaid, Jan. 29, 1966; 1 child, John F. BA, Oberlin Coll., 1964; MS, Roosevelt U., 1966; PhD, Ohio State U., 1971. Modeling and Simulation Professional Cert. Nat. Indsl. Def. Assn.; 2002. Rsch. psychologist Air Force Human Resources Lab, Dayton, Ohio, 1966—69; assoc. prof. Ga. So. U., Statesboro, 1970—77; rsch. engr. Martin-Marietta Aerospace, Orlando, Fla., 1977—78; rsch. psychologist USN, Orlando, 1978—85, US Army, Orlando, 1985—88; grad. rsch. prof. and prin. scientist U. Ctrl. Fla., 1988—. Dir. Internat. Disaster Tng. Inc., Orlando, 1999—. Author (and editor): Computer Based Training School Safety Drills, 2004, (book series) Naval Junior Reserve Officer Training Curriculum, 1989. Chair, edn. com. Nat. Ctr. for Simulation, 2002—. Rsch. grant, State of Fla., 1989. Mem.: Am. Hellenic Ednl. Progressive Assn. Democrat. Greek Orthodox. Avocations: travel, woodworking. Home: 1345 Sawgrass Ct Winter Park FL 32792 Office: Inst for Simulation and Tng U Ctrl Fla 3100 Technology Pkwy Orlando FL 32826 Office Phone: 407-882-1330. Business E-Mail: pkincaid@ist.ucf.edu.

KINCAID, MARILYN COBURN, medical educator; b. Bennington, Vt., July 14, 1947; d. E. Robert and Jean A. (Flagg) Coburn; m. William Louis Kincaid, Dec. 21, 1970. AB, Mt. Holyoke Coll., 1969; MD, St. Louis U., 1975. Cert. Am. Bd. Ophthalmology, Am. Bd. Pathology. Asst. prof. ophthalmology & pathology U. Tex., San Antonio, 1982-86; assoc. prof. ophthalmology & pathology U. Mich. Med. Sch., Ann Arbor, 1986-87, St. Louis U. Sch. Medicine, 1989-94, prof., 1994—. Bd. dirs. Singular Vision Outreach, St. Louis. Author (book) Intraocular Lenses, 1989; contbr. articles to profl. jours. Fellow Am. Acad. Ophthalmology (Honor award 1990), Coll. Am. Pathologists; mem. Am. Assn. Ophthalmic Pathologists (sec.-treas. 1983-86). Avocations: sewing, embroidery.

KINCAID, RICHARD D., bank executive; B, Wichita State U.; MBA, U. Tex. With First Nat. Bank Chgo., Barclays Bank PLC; sr. v.p. finance Equity Group Investments, Inc., 1990—95; exec. v.p., CFO Equity Office Properties Trust, exec. v.p., COO, 1997—2001, pres., CEO, 2001—. Mem.: Real Estate Capitol Adv. Com. Office: Equity Office Properties Trust Two N Riverside Plaza Chicago IL 60606

KINCAID, RODNEY LYLE, construction company executive; b. Orlando, Fla., Feb. 9, 1933; s. Marion Troy and Thelma (Sellers) K.; m. Sue Sims, Dec. 16, 1961; 1 child, James Clay. B of Bldg. Constrn., U. Fla., 1958. Estimator H.J. High Constrn. Co., Orlando, 1958—59; office mgr. Innanen Bros. Constrn. Co., Orlando, 1959—60; estimator R.C. Stevens Constrn. Co., Orlando, 1960—62, Sorensen-Fletcher Constrn. Co., Winter Park, Fla., 1962—63; pres. Kincaid Constrn. Co., Winter Park, 1963—. Pres. Cen. Fla. Builder's Exchange, Orlando, 1978-79. Pres. Assoc. Bd. of Fla. Symphony, 1968; chmn. City of Orlando Bldg. Code Bd., 1973-76, City of Winter Park Code Bd., 1987—; mem. hist. bldg. com. City of Orlando, 1976; mem. econ. devel. task force Greater Orlando Aviation Authority, 1981; 2d v.p. Ctrl. Fla. Fair, Orlando, 1987, pres., 1990-91; bd. dirs. Better Bus. Bur. Ctrl. Fla., Inc., 1989-92, chmn. bd., 1993; pres., founder Oldsmobile Club Fla., 1995-97. With U.S. Army, 1953-55. Mem. Greater Orlando C. of C. (v.p. 1971), Pi Kappa Alpha. Clubs: Country of Orlando (bd. dirs. 1983-86), Econs. of Orlando (pres. 1983-84). Republican. Presbyterian. Avocations: swimming, collecting classic automobiles. Office Phone: 407-647-6178. E-mail: kincaid@kincaidconstruction.com.

KINCAID, STEVEN RANDALL, marketing professional; b. Oklahoma City, July 19, 1953; s. William Calvin Hoover and Mary Elizabeth (Cochran) K. BA, Okla. State U., 1975; MA, U. Ill., 1977, PhD, 1980. Rsch. analyst Gen. Foods Corp., White Plains, N.Y., 1980-82; rsch. assoc. Opinion Rsch. Corp., Princeton, N.J., 1982-85, rsch. dir., 1985-86, rsch. exec., 1986-87, account exec., 1989-91; cons. John Hancock Life Ins. Co., Boston, 1987-88, dir. rsch., 1988-89, Prudential Ins. Co., Newark, 1991-93; sr. assoc. Abt Assocs., Cambridge, Mass., 1993-95; pres. Kincaid Assocs., Boxford, Mass., 1995-98; v.p. Fidelity Investments, Boston, 1998—2003, Bank of Am., 2003—04; pres. Kincaid Assocs., Topsfield, Mass., 2004—. Named Eagle Scout Boy Scouts Am., 1968. Mem. Am. Assn. Pub. Opinion Research, Am. Polit. Sci. Assn., Applied Polit. Sci. Study Group. (charter), Mktg. Sci. Inst. (trustee), Phi Kappa Phi. Republican. Methodist.

KINCANNON, LOUIS, federal agency administrator; b. Waco, Tex., Dec. 1940; m. Lois Claire Green; 2 children. Grad., U. Tex., 1963; postgrad., George Washington U., 1963—65, U. Md., 1966, Georgetown U., 1967. Statistician U.S. Census Bur., Washington, 1963—74, dep. dir., COO, 1982—92, acting dir., 1983—84, 1989; dir. US Census Bur. Dept. Commerce, Washington, 2002—; chief of program rev. staff Social and Econ. Statis. Adminstrn., Dept. Commerce, Washington, 1974; mem. staff Office Mgmt. and Budget, Washington, 1975—77, br. chief, 1978—82; first chief statistician Orgn. for Econ. Cooperation and Devel., Paris, 1992—2000. Spkr. and presenter in field. Mem.: Washington Statis. Soc., Nat. Assn. for Bus. Econs., Am. Statis. Assn., Inter-Am. Statis. Inst., Internat. Statis. Inst. Home: PO Box 66 Paeonian Springs VA 20129 Office: Dept Commerce US Census Bur Federal Center Bldg 3 Washington DC 20233

KINCART, ROBERT OWEN, technological executive; b. Youngstown, Ohio, Feb. 8, 1949; s. Robert E. and Mary Louise (Briach) K.; children: Jeffrey, Jennifer, Michael. Student, Ohio U., 1967-70; BS in Chemistry, U. Fla., 1972. Registered environ. profl., environ. property assessor, environ. lending analyst, Nat. Registry of Environ. Profls.; lic. radon measurement specialist, 1988; cert. hazardous materials mgr.; lic. pollutant storage sys. contr., Fla. Rsch. chemist Roux Labs., Inc., Jacksonville, Fla., 1972-73; sr. control chemist Kerr-McGee Chem. Corp., Jacksonville, 1973-77; ops. mgr. The UpJohn Co./Asgrow, Plant City, 1977-82; pres., founder Resource Recovery Am., Mulberry, 1980-87, Am. Compliance Tech., Lakeland, 1987—. Bd. dirs. Fla. Spillage Com., Jacksonville, Fla. Author: Chemical Handling, 1986, Detection and Measurement of Radon Progeny, 1988, Radon Gas Information, 1988. Judge local sci. fair Little Miss Am. Beauty contest, Fla. State Sci. and Engring. Fair; judge Lakeland Ledger Silver Garland, 1996—2001; bd. dir. Traviss Vo-Tech Inst., Lakeland, Fla., 1984, Goodwill Industries Fla., Lakeland, 1985, Polk County Disaster Com., 1988, Local Emergency Planning Coun., Polk County, Fla., 1989—, Habitat for Humanity. Named to Hon. Order of Ky. Cols., 1994. Mem. Am. Chem. Soc., U. Fla. Alumni Assn., Fla. Physics Soc., Fla. Assn. Water Quality (dir.), Polk County Transp. Soc., Tampa Com. of 100, Fla. Bar Assn., Fla. Petroleum Assn., Inst. Hazardous Material Mgmt., Am. Water Works Assn., Am. Soc. Safety Engrs., So. Environ. Bus. Coun., Fla. Environ. Assesors Assn (bd. dirs.), Propeller Club (bd. dirs.), Rotary (chartered; Paul Harris fellow), Bartow C. of C., Lakeland C. of C., Gator Boosters of U. Fla., U. Fla. Pres.'s Coun. Republican. Methodist. Avocations: family, golf, outdoor activities, community involvement, travel. Office: Am Compliance Techs Inc 1875 W Main St Bartow FL 33830-7718 Office Phone: 863-533-2000. E-mail: rokincart@act-environmental.com.

KINCHELOE, SHARON MORRIS, artist; b. Winston-Salem, N.C., July 31, 1952; d. John J. and Joyce Ann Shetler Morris; m. Alan Bradley Kincheloe, June 7, 1984. Student, Ferrum Coll., 1970-71, Old Dominion U., 1976-77, Tidewater C. C., 1978-82. Prodn. asst. Studio Ctr., Norfolk, Va., 1978-80; graphic artist Tidewater Printing, Norfolk, Va., 1979-82; artist Millboro, Va., 1982—. One woman exhibns. Fern BAnk Sci. Ctr., Stone Mount, Ga., 1986, Calloway Gardens, Pine Mount, Ga., 1987, US Nat. Arboretum, Washington, 1988, Nat. Wildlife Fedn., 1995; featured in Virginia Wildlife mag., 1983, 85, 92, 93. Mem. task force US Forest Svc. Reform, Va. forests, 1986-87. Mem. Nature Conservancy (Va. chpt.), Va. Native Plant Soc. (Blue Ridge chpt.). Home: 1106 N Augusta St Staunton VA 24401-3221

KINCHEN, THOMAS ALEXANDER, college president; b. Thomasville, Ga., Dec. 28, 1946; s. George H. and Annie L. (Castleberry) K.; m. Ruth Ann Hunter, Aug. 27, 1967; children: Alex, Lisa Ann. AB summa cum laude, Ga. So. Coll., 1969; MEd, U. Ga., 1975; MDiv, New Orleans Bapt. Theol. Sem., 1979, PhD, 1982. Pastor several chs., 1972-76; v.p. New Orleans Bapt. Theol. Sem., 1982-86; exec. dir., treas. W.Va. Conv. So. Bapt., Scott Depot, 1986-90; pres. The Bapt. Coll. of Fla., Graceville, 1990—. Editor Laos: All the People of God, 1984; contbr. articles to profl. jours. Bd. dirs. Area Devel. Coun., Graceville, 1991; mem. edn. commn. So. Bapt. Conv., 1992—; pres. bd. dirs. Jackson County Devel. Coun., 1996. Mem. So. Bapt. Adult Edn. Assn. (pres. 1996-98, v.p. 1994-96), Graceville C. of C. (pres. 1993), Kiwanis, Jackson County C. of C. (bd. dirs. 2003—, vice chmn. 2004, chmn. 2005), NOBTS (Outstanding Alumnus 2000), ASBCS (bd. dirs. 2000-03), Phi Kappa Phi, Alpha Psi Omega. Avocations: golf, fishing, woodworking. Office: The Bapt Coll Fla 5400 College Dr Graceville FL 32440-1831 Office Phone: 850-263-3261. E-mail: takinchen@baptistcollege.edu.

KIND, JOSHUA B., art history educator; b. Phila., Nov. 5, 1933; s. Abraham and Sarah Kind. BA, U. Pa., 1955; PhD, Columbia U., 1967. Instr. art history Northwestern U., Evanston, Ill., 1959-62; instr. humanities U. Chgo., 1962-65, Ill. Inst. of Technology, Chgo., 1965-69; prof. art history No. Ill. U., DeKalb, 1969—. Adj. prof. art history Sch. of The Art Inst. of Chgo., 1964-76. Office: No Ill Univ Art Dept 216 Arends Hall Dekalb IL 60115-2294

KIND, PHYLLIS, art gallery owner; BS in Chemistry, U. Pa., 1954, PhD in Phys. Chemistry, 1956; MA in English, U. Chgo., 1965. Mem. staff mdse. control Macy's, New York, N.Y., 1948-53; social worker N.Y.C. Dept. Welfare, 1954; 3d grade tchr. N.Y.C. Bd. Edn., 1956-59; various positions Chgo. Bd. Edn., 1960-67; owner Phyllis Kind Gallery, Chgo., 1967, N.Y.C., 1975—. Office: Phyllis Kind Gallery 136 Greene St New York NY 10012-3202

KIND, RONALD JAMES, congressman, lawyer; b. La Crosse, Wis., Mar. 16, 1963; s. Elroy and Greta Kind; m. Tawni Zappa; 1 child, Johnny. BA with honors, Harvard U., 1985; MA, London Sch. Econs., 1986; JD, U. Minn., 1990. Atty. Quarles and Brady, Milw., 1990—92; district atty. La Crosse County, 1992—96; mem. U.S. Congress from 3d Wis. dist., 1997—; mem. house edn. and workforce com., resources com., agr. com. Active Freshman Bipartisan Campaign Fin. Reform Task Force; co-founder Upper Miss. River Congl. Caucus. Active Boys' and Girls' Club, La Crosse YMCA; bd. dirs. Coulee Coun. Alcohol or Other Drug Abuse. Mem. New Dem. Network, La Crosse Optimists Club. Democrat. Lutheran. Office: 1406 Longworth Bldg Washington DC 20515-4903*

KINDBERG, SHIRLEY JANE, pediatrician; b. Newark, Feb. 4, 1936; d. John Bertil and Mabel Jacoba (deJonge) Kindberg; m. Charles Dale Coln, May 12, 1962; children: Sara Goldstein, Eric Coln, Lois Thompson, Ruth Coln, Mary Mielenz. BS, Wheaton Coll., 1957; MD, Baylor U., 1961. Intern Tex. Children's Hosp., Houston, 1961-62; resident Children's Med. Ctr., Dallas, 1962-63; fellow in pediat. pulmonary disease U. Tex. S.W. Med. Sch., Dallas, 1963-64, fellow in pediat. infectious disease, 1965-67; pvt. practice gen. pediat. Dallas, 1969-81; pvt. practice newborns, 1981—2004. Active N.W. Bible Ch., 1972—; mem. Dallas Symphony Assn. Republican. Avocations: cooking, travel, music, exercise. Personal E-mail: colnoma@sbcglobal.net.

KINDEL, JAMES HORACE, JR., lawyer; b. L.A., Nov. 8, 1913; s. James Horace and Philipina (Butte) K.; children: William, Mary, Robert, John. AB, UCLA, 1934; LLB, Loyola U., Los Angeles, 1940. Bar: Calif. 1941; CPA, Calif., 1942. Pvt. practice Kindel & Anderson, L.A., 1945—96. Former ptnr. Coopers-Lybrand. Mem. ABA, L.A. Bar Assn., Orange County Bar Assn.,

State Bar Calif., AICPA, Chancery Club, Calif. Club, Phi Delta Phi, Theta Xi. Home: 800 W 1st St Apt 2405 Los Angeles CA 90012-2432 Office: 444 S Flower St Fl 7 Los Angeles CA 90071-2901 Personal E-mail: jameskindel@aol.com.

KINDER, PETER D., lieutenant governor, former state legislator; b. Cape Girardeau, Mo., May 12, 1954; s. James A. and Mary Frances (Hunter) K. JD, St. Mary U., 1979; postgrad., U. Mo. Columbia, SE Mo. State U. Spl. asst. to Rep. Bill Emerson US Ho. Reps., Washington, 1981-82; mem. Mo. Senate from 27th dist., Jefferson City, 1992—2005, pres. pro. tempore, 2000—05; lt. gov. State of Mo., 2005—. Staff counsel, real estate rep., 1983-87; assoc. publ., S.E. Missourian Newspaper, 1987, asst. to the pres., 1987-94. Mem. Mo. Bar Assn., Am. Cancer Soc., Mo. Farm Bur., Area Wide United Way, Lions Club. Republican. Office: Office Lt Gov State Capitol Bldg Rm 121 Jefferson City MO 65101*

KINDER, RICHARD DAN, natural gas pipeline, oil and gas company executive; b. Cape Girardeau, Mo., Oct. 19, 1944; s. Luke Frazelle and Edna (Corbin) Kinder; m. Anne Lamkin; 1 child, Kara; m. Nancy McNeil, 1997. BA, U. Mo., 1966, JD, 1968. Sole practice, Cape Girardeau, Mo., 1972—80; sr. atty. Continental Resources/Fla. Gas Cos., Winter Pk., 1981—82, v.p., gen. counsel Winter Park, 1982—84; sr. v.p., gen. counsel Houston Natural Gas Corp., 1985, HNG/InterNorth Inc., Houston, 1985—86; exec. v.p. law and corp. devel. Enron Corp., Houston, 1986—87, exec. v.p., chief of staff, 1987—88, vice chmn. bd., 1988—89, pres., COO, 1989—96; chmn., CEO Kinder Morgan Inc., Houston, 1997—. Bd. dirs. Soc. Performing Arts, Houston, 1986—, Mus. Fine Arts, Houston, 1987—. Capt. U.S. Army, 1968—72. Mem.: Houston Bar Assn., Mo. Bar Assn., ABA, Nat. Bd. of Smithsonian Instn., Petroleum Club, Houston Racquet. Methodist. Office: Kinder Morgan Inc 500 Dallas St, Ste 1000 Houston TX 77002*

KINDER, SUZANNE FONAY WEMPLE, retired historian, retired educator; b. Veszprem, Hungary, Aug. 1, 1927; arrived in U.S., 1948; d. Ernest Fonay and Magda Mihalyfy (Fonay) countess Ernest Szechenyi; m. George Barr Wemple, June 17, 1957 (dec. Apr. 1988); m. Gordon T. Kinder, May 26, 1990. B, English Sisters, Budapest, Hungary, 1945, U. Calif., Berkeley, 1953; MLS, Columbia U., 1955, PhD, 1967. Ref. asst. Columbia U., 1955—58; instr. Stern Coll. Women, N.Y.C., 1962-63; asst. prof. Tchrs. Coll., Columbia U., N.Y.C., 1964-66; from asst. prof. to prof. Barnard Coll., Columbia U., N.Y.C., 1966-92, ret., 1992. Reference asst. Columbia Libr., 1995—98. Author: Atto of Vercelli: Church, State and Christian Society, 1979, Women in Frankish Society, 1981, 1983 (Berkshire prize, 1981); co-editor: Women in Medieval Society, 1985; contbr. chapters to books, articles to ency. and profl. jours. Recipient grant NEH, 1975, 80, 81-85, Spivack summer grant Barnard Coll., 1970, 81, Fulbright grant, 1982. Mem.: NOW, AAUP. Home: 102 Moorings Park Dr Apt E104 Naples FL 34105-2142 E-mail: gtkinder@aol.com.

KINDERWATER, JOSEPH C. (JACK KINDERWATER), publishing company executive; b. Milw., Aug. 5, 1922; s. Joseph Charles and Ida (Noll) K.; m. Jacqueline Shirley Marsh, 1948; children— Mark, Mary Jo, Nancy, Scott, Diane BA, U. Minn., 1948. Advt. copywriter C. Derosier Inc., St. Paul, 1948-50; account exec. David Advt. Agy., St. Paul, 1950-53; advt. rep. The Webb Pub. Co., St. Paul, 1953-63, advt. sales mgr., 1963-68, advt. dir., 1968-78, v.p., pub., 1979-87, exec. v.p., 1987-88, pres., chmn., 1988-89; pub. cons., 1990—; v.p. Midwest Unit Farm Publs., 1979-84, pres., 1985-88. Bd. dirs. Nat. Audit Bur. Circulation, 1985-89, Better Bus. Bur. Minn., St. Paul, 1985-89; fund vol. Am. Heart Assn., St. Paul, 1983-85, Children's Hosp., St. Paul, 1975; instr. Jr. Achievement, St. Paul, 1970-75; bus. exec. rsch. com. U. Minn., 1966. With USAAF, 1943-46; ETO Named one of Top Ten Bus. Execs., City Bus. mags., 1989. Mem. Northwest Farm Equipment Assn. (pres. 1984-87), Nat. Agr. Mktg. Assn. (v.p. 1976-77), State Farm Mag. Pubs. Assn. (dir. 1980-89), Agr. Pub. Assn. (bd. dirs. 1981-89), St. Paul Advt. Club (pres. 1974-76), Am. Advt. Fedn. (Cleo award 1965, dist. gov. 1965-69) Clubs: Minn. Press, Midland Hills Country, St. Paul Athletic, Minn. Advt. Roman Catholic. Office: 13013 N Panorama Dr Unit 101 Fountain Hills AZ 85268

KINDLE, OTIS T., secondary school educator; b. Ullin, Ill., Jan. 28, 1949; s. Odie Clyde and Mary Louise Kindle; m. Marion Kindle (div.); 1 child, Tony; m. Wilma Jean Kindle, Nov. 13, 1980; children: Shawn, Tashika. BS, So. Ill. U., 1988; MS, Ill. State U., 2000. Instr. automotives Dist. 87 Pub. Schs., Bloomington, Ill. With U.S. Army, 1971—73, sgt. Ill. NG, 1985—89. Mem.: N.Am. Coun. Automotive Tchrs., Ill. Tech. Edn. Assn., Ill. Coll. Automotive Instr. Assn. Home: 1205 Eastholme Bloomington IL 61701

KINDLER, JEFFREY B., lawyer; b. Upper Montclair, NJ, May 13, 1955; m. Sharon Sullivan; children: Joshua, Samantha. BA, Tufts Univ., 1977; JD, Harvard Law Sch., 1980. Bar: DC 1980. Law clk. to Hon. William J. Brennan, Jr. US Supreme Ct.; law clk. to Hon. David L. Bazelon U.S. Ct. Appeals (DC cir.); ptnr. Williams and Connolly, Wash., DC; sr. counsel litig. and legal policy GE, Fairfield, Conn., 1990—94, v.p., sr. counsel litig. and legal policy, 1994—96; sr. v.p., gen. counsel McDonald's Corp., Oak Brook, Ill., 1996—97, exec. v.p. corp. rels., gen. counsel, 1997—2001, pres. new brands, 2001; chmn. CEO Boston Market Corp., Oak Brook, Ill., 2000—01; sr. v.p., gen. counsel Pfizer, Inc., NYC, 2002—04, vice-chmn., gen. coun., 2004—, mem. exec. com. Mem. Partnership NYC & Transparency Internat. NY Philharmonic; bd. dirs. Legal Aid Soc., N.Y.C., CorporateProBono.org, Atlantic Legal Found. Mem.: Inst. for Legal Reform, Nat. Ctr. for State Cts., Corp. Counsel Adv. Bd., Civil Justice Reform Group, Assn. of Gen. Coun., U.S. C. of C., Manhattan Theatre Club. Office: Pfizer Office of Vice-chmn & Gen Counsel 235 E 42nd St New York NY 10017

KINDLUND, NEWTON CARLTON, retail executive; b. Detroit, Mich., June 25, 1940; s. Newton K. and Virginia M. Kindlund; children: Anne Kirsten, Erika Page; m. Joanne Weber Kindlund, May 29, 1974; 1 child, Darien F. BA, Mich. State U., 1963; postgrad., Boston Coll., 1969; student, U. Pa., 1977. Nat. sales mgr. Vesely Co., Inc., Lapeer, Mich., 1963-68; v.p. sales and mktg. Midas Internat. Corp., Chgo., 1968-70; pres. Recreation Enterprise Corp., Gainesville, Fla., 1970-73, N.C. Kindlund & Assoc., Glenville, N.C., 1974-75; regional v.p. Recreational Vehicle Industry Assn., Washington, 1976-77; founder, pres. Holiday of Orlando (Fla.), Inc., 1977-85, Holiday RV Rental/Leasing, Orlando, 1985-90; bd. chmn., founder, pres. Holiday RV Superstores, Inc., Orlando, 1987—. Pres. Holiday RV Superstores of N.Mex., Inc., Holiday RV Assurance Svcs., Inc. of Ariz., Holiday RV Superstores of S.C., Inc., Holiday RV Superstores West, Inc.; bd. dirs. Recreational Vehicle Industry Assn., Chgo., 1970-72, Cen. Fla. World Trade Coun., Orlando, 1985-87; adv. bd. Trailer Life Publs., 1985-90; co-founder Kindlund Investments, Inc., Winter Pk., Fla., Gryon, Switzerland. Contbr. articles to profl. jours. Bd. dirs. Fla. Recreational Vehicle Trade Assn., Tampa, 1978; bd. dirs. Ctrl. Fla. Better Bus.Bur., Winter Park, 1994-95, Orlando Festival of Orchestras, 1999, RV Industry Hall Fame; bd. edn. found. Recreational Vehicle Dealer Assn., founder Kindlund family industry scholarship; adv. bd. Crummer Sch. of Bus., Rollins Coll., Winter Park, Fla., 1998, 99; judge Students in Free Enterprise, Clearwater, Fla., 1998, 99; bd. dirs. Recreational Vehicle Found., 1999. Recipient Small Bus. Person of Yr. award Small Bus. Adminstrn., State of Fla., 1982, Entrepreneur of Yr. award Ernst & Young, Inc., Tampa, 1990, 100 award Miami Herald, 1992, 93, semi-finalist Jim Moran Entreprenurial Excellance award Fla. State U., 1996; named one of 500 fastest growing pvt. cos. Inc. Mag., 1983, one of top 150 Fla. pub. corps. Fla. Travel mag., 1993, one of Fla. top 100 cos. Orlando Metro 100, 1993, Industry Exec. of Yr., RV News Mag., 1995; named to RV Industry Hall Fame. Mem. Fla. RV Trade Assn. (founding mem., bd. dirs. 1987-90), Family Motor Coach Assn. (adv. bd. 1990—), Nat. RV Bus. Assn. (adv. bd. 1989-90), Recreational Vehicle Rental Assn. (nat. chmn. 1992, 93), Recreational Vehicle Dealers Assn. (exec. bd. 1992, 93), Orlando C. of C. (bd. dirs., exec. com. 1984-88, Silver 100 award 1992). Republican. Episcopalian. Avocations: skiing, golf, sailing, yachting. Address: 280 Stirling Ave Winter Park FL 32789 Office Phone: 407-628-4211. Personal E-mail: jmkindlund@cfl.rr.com.

KINDREGAN, CHARLES PETER, law educator; b. Phila., June 18, 1935; s. Charles Peter and Catherine (Delaney) K.; m. Patricia Ann. Patterson, Aug. 18, 1962 (dec. 1998); children: Chad, Helen, Tricia, Brian. BA, LaSalle U., 1957, MA, 1958; JD, Chgo.-Kent Coll. Law, 1966; LLM, Northwestrn U., 1967. Bar: Ill. 1966, Mass. 1968, U.S. Dist. Ct. Mass. 1970. Instr. Va. Mil. Inst., 1960-62, Loyola U., Chgo., 1964-67; prof. law Suffolk U., Boston, 1967—, assco. dean, 1990-94. Author: The Quality of Life, 1969, Malpractice and the Lawyer, 1981, Professional Responsibility of the Lawyer, 1995; co-author: Massachusetts Family Law and Practice, 3d edit., 2003; (with M. Inker) Mass. Domestic Relations Rules Annotated, 2005; contbr. articles to profl. jours. Mem. Hull Bd. Zoning Appeals, Mass., 1969; pres. Beacon Hill PTA, Boston, 1974-75. Mem. ABA (academic rep. to publications bd. family law sect.), Mass. Bar Assn. (task force on model rules of profl. conduct 1982-84, co-chair com. on crisis in probate and family ct. 1994-97), Suffolk Ctr. for Advanced Legal Studies (dir. 1982-87). Democrat. Roman Catholic. Home: 150 Staniford St Apt 710 Boston MA 02114-2597 Office: Suffolk U Law Sch 120 Tremont St Boston MA 02108-4977 Office Phone: 617-573-8193.

KINDSCHI, P. DOUGLAS, dean, educator; b. Mitchell, S.D., Feb. 15, 1941; s. Paul Lorenz and Alberta L. (Klatt) Kindschi; m. Barbara Jean Pechuman, Aug. 18, 1962; children: Elizabeth R. Scholze, Paul Aaron, Jennifer Anna, Nicole Andrea. BA, Houghton Coll., 1962; MA, U. Wis.-Madison, 1967; PhD, U. Wis., 1972. Dean ednl. svcs., asst. prof. Sangamon State U., Springfield, Ill., 1970—76; dean Kirkhof Coll. Grand Valley State Colls., Allendale, Mich., 1976—83; dean sci./math., prof. math. Grand Valley State U., 1983—2004. Chmn. adv. bd. Raytheon Polar Svcs. Co., 2000—, Pierce Cedar Creek Inst., 2004—. Contbr. articles to profl. jours. Mem. Med. Benevolence Found., Houston, 2003—, Porter Hills Retirement Comtys. and Svcs., Inc., Grand Rapids, 1995—, Grand Rapids Med. Edn. and Rsch. Ctr., 1999—2003. Fellow: NSF, Danforth Found., Soc. for Values in Higher Edn., Woodrow Wilson; mem.: West Mich. Telecomm. Found. (bd. dirs. 1981), Mich. Acad. Sci., Arts, and Letters (pres. 1993—94), Sigma Xi (chpt. pres. 1984—86), Phi Kappa Phi. Presbyterian. Home: 6761 Shady Oak Ln Hudsonville MI 49426 Office: Grand Valley State U 2350 Mak Allendale MI 49401 Office Phone: 616-331-5878. E-mail: kindschd@gvsu.edu.

KINDSCHY, ERROL ROY, school system administrator; b. Galesville, Wis. s. Roy Clarence and Esther Gustava (Brenengan) Kindschy. BA, Denver U., 1959; MA, U. Wis., LaCrosse, 1972. H.s. tchr. West Salem (Wis.) Schs., 1959—64, tchr. grades 7-8, 1966—93, asst. prin. mid. sch., 1993—96, clk., 2000—03, v.p., 2003—; tchr. grades 7-8 USAF Dependent Schs., Eng. and Germany, 1964—66. Author: History of West Salem, 1963, Leonard's Dream, 1980 (Merit award, 1983). Founder, pres. West Salem Hist. Soc., Coulee Pathways; chmn. Trempealeau County Reps., Wis., 1966—70, LaCrosse County Reps., Wis., 1982—86, Rep. 2d Dist., Wis., 1986—90; bd. dirs. Village People, West Salem. Named Business Person of Yr., West Salem Bus. Assn., 1998, Educator of Yr., Coll. Edn., U. Wis., LaCrosse; recipient George Washington medal of honor, Freedom Found., Valley Forge, Pa., 1973, Bovay award, Wis. State Rep. Party, Madison, 1986, 2000, Excellence in Cmty. Svc. award, DAR, 2000. Mem.: Wis. State Hist. Soc. (bd. dirs. 1987—), Lions (sec. 1972—2004, West Salem Citizen of Yr. 1983, 1996). Lutheran. Avocations: researching local history, collecting elephants, puzzles, travel, reading. Home: 99 E Jefferson West Salem WI 54669

KINDSTEDT, PAUL STEPHEN, food science educator; s. Edward Arvid and Amelia Maria Kindstedt; m. Christina Chunua Ge, May 28, 1994; children: Hans Guoan children: Ingalise Guofan, Annalise Guochang. BS, U. Vt., 1979, MS, 1981; PhD, Cornell U., 1986. Asst. prof. U. Vt., Burlington, 1986—91, assoc. prof., 1991—96, prof., 1996—2003; assoc. dir. New Eng. Dairy Foods Rsch. Ctr., Burlington, 1999—2004; co-dir. Vt. Inst. for Artisan Cheese, 2004—. Contbr. articles to peer-reviewed and tech. publs., 11 chpts. to books, abstracts to profl. publs.; author: Handbook of American Farmstead Cheesemaking, 2004. Recipient R.L. Bickford scholarship, U. Vt., 1999, sr. fellowship, CSIRO Food Sci., Australia, 1996. Mem.: Am. Dairy Sci. Assn. (exec. coun. mem.-at-large dairy foods divsn. 1997—2000, Pfizer award 1993). Evangelical Christian. Avocations: hiking, camping, cross country skiing. Office: U Vt 212 Carrigan Hall 536 Main St Burlington VT 05405-0044 Office Phone: 802-656-2935. Business E-Mail: paul.kindstedt@uvm.edu.

KINDT, JOHN WARREN, lawyer, educator; b. Oak Park, Ill., May 24, 1950; s. Warren Frederick and Lois Jeannette (Woelffer) K.; m. Anne Marie Johnson, Apr. 17, 1982; children: John Warren Jr., James Roy Frederick. AB, Coll. William and Mary, 1972; JD, U. Ga., 1976, MBA, 1977; LLM, U. Va., 1978, SJD, 1981. Bar: D.C. 1976, Ga. 1976, Va. 1977. Advisor to gov. State of Va., Richmond, 1971-72; asst. to Congressman M. Caldwell Butler, U.S. Ho. of Reps., Washington, 1972-73; staff cons. White House, Washington, 1976-77; asst. prof. U. Ill., Champaign, 1978-81, assoc. prof., 1981-85, prof., 1985—. Cons. 3d UN Conf. on Law of Sea; lectr. exec. MBA program U. Ill. Author: Marine Pollution and the Law of the Sea, 4 vols., 1981, 2 vols., 1988, 92, Economic Impacts of Legalized Gambling, 1994; contbr. articles to profl. jours. Caucus chmn., del. White House Conf. on Youth, 1970; co-chmn. Va. Gov.'s Adv. Coun. on Youth, 1971; mem. Athens (Ga.) Legal Aid Soc., 1975-76. Rotary fellow, 1979-80; Smithsonian ABA/ELI scholar, 1981; sr. fellow London Sch. Econs., 1985-86. Mem. Am. Soc. Internat. Law, D.C. Bar Assn., Va. Bar Assn., Ga. Bar Assn. Home: 801 Brookside Ln Mahomet IL 61853-9545 Office: U Ill 350 Wohlers Hall Champaign IL 61820 Office Phone: 217-333-6018.

KINDZRED, DIANA, communications company executive; b. Chgo., Apr. 13, 1946; d. Bernell and Katherine L. (Gee) K. BA in Edn., Northwestern U., 1970—73; cert. in bio-med. scis., U. Chgo. Med. Ctr., 1998; postgrad., DePaul U., 2004. Owner, pres. Kindzred & Co. Comm., Chgo., 1978—. Bd. dirs. WomanMade Gallery. Contbr. articles to profl. jours.; author numerous poems. Bd. dirs. Jewish United Fund/Comm., 1985-95; co-founder mid-west divsn. Am. Sephardi Fedn., Evanston, Ill., 1990; coord. Amnesty Internat., Evanston, 1991; mem. Jewish Coun. Urban Affairs Chgo., 1998, tchr. letcr. on poverty. With U.S. Army, 1964-67. Recipient Award for Poetry Nat. Libr. of Poetry, 1996, Cmty. Svc. award Fred Hampton Scholarship Fund, 1990, Fundraising award Jewish United Fund, 1994. Democrat. Jewish. Avocations: international travel, writing, lecturing, art, art history. Home and Office: 1530 N Sedgwick St Apt 306 Chicago IL 60610-5856 Personal E-mail: berdikind@hotmail.com.

KING, ADELE COCKSHOOT, French language educator; b. Omaha, July 28, 1932; d. Ralph Waldo and Thera Cecil (Brown) Cockshoot; m. Bruce Alvin King, Dec. 28, 1955; 1 child, Nicole Michelle. BA, U. Iowa, 1954; MA, U. Leeds, England, 1960; Doctorate in French Lit., U. Paris, 1970. Lectr. in French U. Ibadan, Nigeria, 1963-65, U. Lagos, Nigeria, 1967-70; reader in French Ahmadu Bello U., Zaria, Nigeria, 1973-76; prof. French Ball State U., Muncie, Ind., 1986—2003, chmn. dept. fgn. langs., 1991-94. Vis. assoc. prof. U. Mo., Columbia, 1976-77, mem. editl. bd. rsch. in African Lit., 2003—. Author: (critical studies) Camus, 1964, 3d edit., 1968, Proust, 1968, Paul Nizan: écrivain, 1976, The Writings of Camara Laye, 1980, French Women Novelists: Defining a Female Style, 1989, Rereading Camara Laye, 2003; (study guides) L'Enfant Noir, L'Etranger, Farewell to Arms, The Power and the Glory, Ghosts, 1980-82; editor: Camus's L'Etranger Fifty Years On, 1992, From Africa: New Francophone Stories, 2003; co-editor Modern Dramatists, 1982—, Women Writers, 1987—; contbr. articles to profl. jours. Summer Rsch. grantee Ball State U., 1987, 90, 95, 2001; postdoctoral fellow AAUW, 1977-78. Mem. MLA, Assn. Drs. of Univs. of France (v.p. 1991-01), Am. Comparative Lit. Assn., Soc. des Etudes Camusiennes, Am. Assn. Tchrs. French, Women in French (sec. 1988-92, v.p. 1996-98, editor Women in French Studies 1996-2000). Avocation: dance. Office: Ball State Univ Dept Modern Langs Muncie IN 47306-0001 Address: 145 Quai de Valmy 75010 Paris France

KING, ALFRED MEEHAN, financial executive; b. Boston, Mass, Oct. 31, 1933; s. Lester S. and Marjorie C. (Meehan) K.; m. Mary Jane Oliver, Dec. 19, 1976; 1 child, Thomas A.; stepchildren: Tina Marie Oliver, Katherine Mary Lefebre. AB magna cum laude, Harvard Coll., 1954, MBA, 1959. Acctg. supr. Gen. Motors Co., LaGrange, Ill., 1959-64; asst. contr. J.I. Case Co., Racine, Wis., 1964-69; v.p. fin. Valuation Rsch. Corp., Milw., Minn., 1978—81, 1991—2005, chmn. bd. dirs., 1996—2005; vice chmn. Marshall Stevens, 2005—. Mng. dir. Nat. Assn. Accts., Montvale, NJ, 1981-91; adj. asst. prof. U. Wis.-Parkside, Kenosha, 1978-81; adj. instr. Fordham U., NYC, 1989-96; vis. com. Fordham Grad. Sch. Bus. Adminstrn. Author: Increasing the Productivity of Company Cash, 1969, Total Cash Management, 1994; Valuation, 2002; mem. editl. adv. bd. Jour. Cost Mgmt. and Strategic Fin. Treas. Village of North Bay, Wis., 1972-76, Racine Symphony Orch., 1979-81; mem. Saddle River (NJ) Sch. Bd., 1992-95. Mem. Inst. Mgmt. Acctg. (regent 1978-81, bd. dir. 1995-98), Fin. Exec. Inst., Valley Club (pres. 1983-84). Republican. Presbyn. Home: 11102 Fawn Lake Pkwy Spotsylvania VA 22553-4667 Office Phone: 540-809-3487. Business E-Mail: alfredking@erols.com.

KING, ALGIN BRADDY, retired marketing educator; b. Latta, SC, Jan. 19, 1927; s. Dewey Algin and Elizabeth (Braddy) K.; m. Barbara I. Kelley, Nov. 29, 1997; children: Drucilla Ratcliff, Martha Louise. BA in Retailing and Polit Sci. cum laude, U. S.C., 1947; MS, NYU, 1953; PhD, Ohio State U., 1966. Exec. trainee Sears, Roebuck & Co., 1948; instr. retailing U. S.C., 1948—51; chief econ. analysis br. dist. OPS, 1951—53; exec. dir. Columbia (S.C.) Mchts. Assn., 1953—54; asst. prof. Tex. A&M U., 1954—55; mem. faculty Coll. William and Mary, 1955—72, prof. bus. adminstrn., 1959—72, dir. Bur. Bus. Research, 1959—63, assoc. dean Sch. Bus. Adminstrn., 1968—72; prof., dean Ctrl. Conn. State U. Sch. Bus., Avon, 1972—73; prof., head dept. bus. and econs. James Madison U., 1973—74; prof., dean Western Carolina U. Sch. Bus., Cullowhee, NC, 1974—76; prof. mktg. and mgmt. Christopher Newport U., Newport News, Va., 1976—87, dean Sch. Bus. Adminstrn. and Econs., 1977—87, head, dept. of mktg., 1987—96; prof. mgmt. and mktg. Towson (Md.) State U. Sch. Bus. and Econs., 1987—2003; ret., 2003—. Pres. Bus. and Adminstrv. Cons. Ltd. (mgmt. and mktg. cons.); teaching asst. Ohio State U., 1963-64; professorial lectr. George Washington U.; mgmt. cons. CSC, U.S. Army. Author: (with others) Hampton Waterfront Economic Study, 1967, The Source Book of Economics, 1973, Management Perceptions, 1976, International Marketing by Dabringer & Muellach Instrn. Manual, 1991; contbr. chpts. to books and articles to profl. jours. Mem. finance resource group Conn. Council Higher Edn., 1972-73; mem. U.S. Senatorial Bus. Adv. Bd. W.T. Grant Retailing scholar, 1947. Mem. Am. Mktg. Assn., Acad. Mgmt., Am. Inst. Decision Scis., Phi Beta Kappa. Episcopalian. E-mail: e-lecturer@comcast.net.

KING, ALLEN B., tobacco company executive; Dir. Universal Corp., 1989—, chmn. exec. com., mem. fin. com., pres., COO Richmond, Va., 1996—2003, pres., CEO, 2003—, chmn. bd., 2003—. Office: Universal Leaf Tobacco Co Inc 1501 N Hamilton St Richmond VA 23230-6003

KING, ALMA JEAN, retired physical education educator, healthcare educator; b. Hamilton, Ohio, Feb. 28, 1939; d. William Lawrence and Esther Mary (Smith) K. BS in Edn., Miami U., Oxford, Ohio, 1961; MEd, Bowling Green State U., 1963; postgrad., Fla. Atlantic U., 1969, '92, Nova U., Ft. Lauderdale, Fla., 1979. Cert. elem. and secondry tchr., Ohio, all levels incl. coll., Fla. Tchr. health, physical edn. Rogers Middle Sch., Broward County Bd. Pub. Instrn., 1963-64; assoc. prof. health, phys edn., recreation, dance Broward C.C., Fort Lauderdale, Fla., 1964-94; ret., 1994. Dir. Intramurals and Extramurals Broward C.C., Fort Lauderdale, Fla., 1964-67, chair person Women's Affairs, 1978, health and safety com., 1975, faculty evaluation com. 1980-85, mem. faculty ins. benefits com. 1993-94. Sponsor Broward County Fire Fighters, Police; active mem. Police Benevolent Assn.; Historical Soc. Grantee Broward C.C. Staff Devel. Fund, 1988. Mem. AAHPERD, NEA, Fla. Edn. Assn., Fla. Assn for Health, Physical Edn., Recreation and Dance, Am. Assn. for Advancement of Health Edn., United Faculty of Fla., Fla. Assn. of C.C., Order of the Eastern Star (past Worthy Matron), Order of Shrine. Avocations: concerts, theater, art, historic museums, recreational activities. Home: 4310 Buchanan St Hollywood FL 33021-5917

KING, ANDRE RICHARDSON, architectural graphic designer; b. Chgo., July 30, 1931; s. Earl James and Margie Verdetta (Doyle) K.; children: Jandra Maria, Andre Etienne; m. Sally M. Ryan, Sept. 19, 1980. Student, Chgo. Tech. Coll., 1956-57, U. Chgo., 1956-59; BAE., Art Inst. Chgo., 1959; grad., Gemological Inst. Am., 1992. ARK, Archtl. & Environ. Graphic Design Firm est., 1982—; With Skidmore, Owings & Merrill, Chgo., 1956-82; ind. designer, cons., 1982—. Mem. alumni bd. Chgo. Art Inst. Served with USAF, 1951-55. Recipient Design award Art Inst. Chgo., 1959, DESI award, 1982; Hon. consul of Barbados, W.I., 1971— Mem. AIA (assoc.), Am. Inst. Graphic Designers, Soc. Environ. Graphic Designers, Soc. Topographic Arts, Chgo. Soc. Communicating Arts, Art Dirs. Club of Chgo. (pres. 1979-80, 80-82), Art Inst. Chgo. Alumni (bd. dirs.), Arts Club of Chgo., Consular Corps of Chgo., Tavern Club of Chgo., Sigma Pi Phi, Beta Boule. Home: 6700 S Oglesby Ave Apt 1603 Chicago IL 60649-1301 Office: 6700 S Oglesby Ave Apt 2406 Chicago IL 60649-1387 *To provide creative excellence for the future through my works.*

KING, ANGUS S., JR., former governor; b. Mar. 31, 1944; m. Mary J. Herman; children: Angus III, Duncan, James, Benjamin, Molly. BA, Dartmouth Coll., 1966; JD, U. Pa., 1969. Bar: Maine 1969. Staff atty. Pine Tree Legal Assistance, Showhegan, Maine, 1969-72; chief counsel Office Senator William D. Hathaway U.S. Senate Subcom. on Alcoholism and Narcotics, Washington, 1972-75; former ptnr. Smith, Lloyd & King, Brunswick, Maine, 1975—83; gov. State of Maine, Augusta, 1995—2003. TV host Maine Watch, Maine Pub. Broadcasting Network, 20 yrs.; v.p., gen. counsel Swift River/Hafslund Co., 1983; founder, pres. N.E. Energy Mgmt. Inc., Brunswick, Maine, 1989-94. Independent. Mailing: PO Box 457 Brunswick ME 04011-0457*

KING, ANN STOCKMAN, retired librarian; b. N.Y.C., Nov. 6, 1931; d. Frank J. and Natalie A. Stockman; m. Albert M. King; 3 children. BS in Edn., So. Conn. State Coll., New Haven, 1959; MLS, So. Conn. U., 1974; postgrad., St. Joseph's U., Hartford, Conn., 1988. Cert. elem. tchr., media specialist Conn. Libr. Fairfield (Conn.) Pub. Schs., 1974—98; ret., 1998. Mem. Mill River Wetlands Com., Fairfield, 1965—; v.p. AAUW, 1975—77, sec., 1982—84. Claire Fulcher Internat. scholar, AAUW, 1988. Mem.: Southwestern Libr. Coun., Fairfield County Sch. Librs., Conn. Edn. Media.

KING, ARTHUR THOMAS, economics professor, retired air force officer; b. Greensboro, Ala., Feb. 10, 1938; s. Harvey James and Elizabeth (Williams) K.; m. Rosa Marie Bryant, June 24, 1962; children: Donald, Kevin. BS in Biology, Tuskegee U., 1962; MS in Econs., S.D. State U., 1971; PhD in Econs., U. Colo., 1977. Comd. 2d lt. U.S. Air Force, 1962, advanced through grades to lt. col., 1979; asst. prof. econs. U.S. Air Force Acad., 1970-74; ops. planner Davis-Monthan AFB, Tuscon, 1975-76; strategic planner, energy economist Wright-Patterson AFB, Ohio, 1977-79; assoc. prof. econs. Air Force Inst. Tech., 1979-82; prof. econs. Baylor U., Waco, Tex., 1982-95; dean bus., econs. Winston-Salem (N.C.) State U., 1995—. Bd. dirs. Goodwill Industries Am. Inc.; bd. regents Wartburg Coll. Contbr. articles to profl. jours. Mem. Am. Econ. Assn., Nat. Econ. Assn. (bd. dirs., pres.), Nat. Assn. Bus. Econs. Baptist. Home: 110 Saddlegate Ct Winston Salem NC 27104-2653 Office: Winston Salem State Univ Sch Bus and Econ PO Box 19308 Winston Salem NC 27110

KING, B. B. (RILEY B. KING), singer, guitarist; b. Itta Bene, Miss., Sept. 16, 1925; LHD (hon.), Tougaloo (Miss.) Coll., 1973; MusD (hon.), Yale U., 1977, Berklee Coll. of Music, 1982; D of Fine Arts, Rhodes Coll. of Memphis, 1990. Began teaching self guitar, 1945, later studied Schillinger System, past disc jockey and singer Memphis radio stas., internat. appearances throughout world, recs. RPM, Crown, Bullet, Kent, ABC Records,

ABC/Dunhill Records, toured Russia, 1979, albums Back in the Alley, B.B. King in London, Do the Boogie!, Completely Well, Electric B.B.-His Best, The Fabulous B.B. King, Guess Who, Heart and Soul, Live at Cook County Jail, Six Silver Strings, 1985, King of the Blues, Indianola Mississippi Seeds, 1989, Live at San Quentin, 1990 (Grammy award), Blues is King, 1990, Live at the Apollo, 1991 (Grammy award), Live at the Regal, 1991, Spotlight on Lucille, There is Always One More Time, 1992, Singin' the Blues, 1993, On the Road with B.B. King: An Interactive Autobiography, 1996, (guest appearance) Six Pack, 1993, Blues on the Bayou, Let the Good Time roll, 1998, guest artist with U2's Rattle and Hum, 1988, Deuces Wild, 1997, subject, collaborator B.B. King, B.B. King Blues Guitar, 1970, B.B. King Songbook, 1971, B.B. King, The World's Greatest Living Blues Artist, Blues Guitar, A Method by B.B. King, 1973, Riding with the King, 2000, Auld Lang Syne, 2002 (Grammy award, 2003), A Christmas Celebration of Hope, 2002 (Grammy award, 2003), Reflections, 2003, The Ultimate Collection, 2005; performer: at closing ceremonies Summer Olympics, 1996; author (autobiography, with David Ritz): Blues All Around Me, 1996 (2d prize 8th Ann. Ralph J. Gleason Music Book awards); appeared (films) When We Were Kings, 1996, Blues Brothers, 1998, 2000. Co-founder Found. Advancement Inmate Rehab. and Recreation, 1972—; founding mem. Kennedy Performing Arts Ctr., 1971. Co-recipient Grammy award for Best Rock Instrumental Performance, 1996; named Best Blues Singer Nat. Assn. TV and Radio Announcers, 1974, Blues Act of Yr., Performance Award Polls, 1985, 1987, 1988, Best Blues Instrumentalist, Ebony Mag., 1974—75, Best Male Blues Singer, 1974—75, Blues Guitarist of Yr., Guitar Player Mag., 1970—74, Most Outstanding Blues Singer, Living Blues Mag., 1993—94, 1996—97, Blues Artist of Yr., 1994; named to Hall of Fame and Best Blues Vocalist and Guitarist, Ebony mag., 1974, Blues Found. Hall of Fame, 1980, Rock and Roll Hall of Fame, 1987, Rock Walk, 1989, Amsterdam Walk of Fame, 1989, Hollywood Walk of Fame, 1989; recipient Humanitarian award, Fed. Bur. Prisons, 1972, B'nai B'rith Music and Performance Lodge, N.Y.C., 1973, Gallery of Greats and Best Blues Guitarist, 1974, Artist of the Decade and Humanitarian award, Record World mag., 1974, Grammy award Best Traditional Blues Rec., 1986, Grammy Lifetime Achievement award, 1987, Grammy award Best Rhythm & Blues Vocal Performance, Male, 1970, Grammy award Best Ethnic of Traditional Recording, 1981, Grammy award Best Traditional Blues Recording1993, 1983, 1985, Grammy award Best Traditional Blues Album for Blues Summit, 1993, Grammy award, 1999, Hall of Fame award Nat. Assn. for Campus Activities, 1986, Presdl. medal of the Arts, 1990, Songwriter's Hall of Fame Lifetime Achievement award, 1991, Orville H. Gibson Lifetime Achievement award, Gibson Guitar Co., Nat. award of distinction, U. Miss., 1992, Kennedy Ctr. Honors, 1995, W.C. Handy award Blues Found., 1983, 1985, 1987, 1988, 1991, Lifetime Achievement award, 1997, MTV Video Music award for Best Video from a Film, 1988—89, Image awards, NAACP, 1975, 1981, 1993, Pioneer in Music award, Nat. Assn. Black Owned Broadcasters, 1997, Living Legend award Trumpet Awards, 1997, Golden Mike award, NATRA, 1969, 1974; Nat. Heritage fellow Nat. Endowment of the Arts, 1991. Office: care Sidney A SeidenbergInc 1414 Avenue Of The Americas New York NY 10019-2514 *I would say to all people, but maybe to young people especially— black and white or whatever color— follow your own feelings and trust them; find out what you want to do and do it, and then practice it and practice it every day of your life and keep becoming what you are, despite any hardships and obstacles you meet.**

KING, BARBARA J, anthropology educator; b. Long Branch, NJ; d. Walter Yule and Elizabeth Dorothy King; m. Charles F Hogg, Mar. 3, 1990; 1 child, Sarah Elizabeth Hogg. BA in anthropology, Douglass Coll., 1978; MA in anthropology, U. Okla., 1980, PhD in anthropology, 1989. Lectr. U. Okla., 1980; rsch. asst. Ctr. Internat. of Medicales, Franceville, French Polynesia, 1983—84; doctoral rschr. Amboseli Nat. Pk., Kenya, 1985—86; vis. asst. prof. Coll. of William-Mary, Williamsburg, Va., 1988—90, asst. prof., 1990—96, assoc. prof., 1996—2003, prof., 2003—. Mem. adv. bd. Anthropological Theory, Family Systems, Sign Language Studies. Author: (book) The Dynamic Dance: Non Vocal Communication in AFrica, 2004, The Origins of Language, 1999, The Information Continuum, 1994. Recipient Thomas Jefferson Tchg. award, State Coun. of Higher Edn.; Guggenheim fellowship, John Simon Guggenheim Found., 2002, Rsch. grant, Wenner Gren Found. for Anthropology, 1999—2002, Nat. Sci. Found. grant, 1985—86. Mem.: Am. Soc. Primatology, Internat. Soc. of Primatologists, Am. Anthropological Assn. Avocations: reading, travel, animal watching. Office: Dept Anthropology Coll of William Mary Williamsburg VA 23187 Business E-Mail: bjking@wm.edu.

KING, BARBARA SACKHEIM, travel company executive; b. Chgo., Apr. 9, 1948; d. Norman Robert and Pauline Huft Sackheim; m. Michael Raymond King, May 24, 1998; children: Lauren Marissa, David Elliott Weiner, Joshua Neal. BS, Northwestern U., 1970. Realtor Prudential Henry and Burrows, Overland Park, Kans., 1990—92; pres. Gt. Getaways, Leawood, 1992—. Life mem. Nat. Coun. Jewish Women, Kansas City, Mo.; v.p. Fine Arts Guild William Jewell, Liberty, Mo., 1986—87; mem. March Dimes, 1992—93. Mem.: Airline Reporting Corp., Internat. Airline Travel Assn., Cruise Line Internat. Assn., Am. Soc. Travel Agents, Virtuoso, Pi Lambda Theta. Home: 4416 W 150th St Leawood KS 66224 Office: Great Getaways 4600 College Blvd Ste 103 Leawood KS 66211 Office Phone: 913-338-2244.

KING, BELINDA CORREA, conductor; d. Zulema Correa; m. William King, Mar. 25, 1978; children: Danielle Mirabelli, Robert. BA in Music Edn., U. South Fla., 1972; MM in Applied Performance, SUNY, Stony Brook, 1974; MS in Adminstrn., No. Ill., 1997. Cert. advanced profl. Md. Band dir. Madeira Beach Mid. Sch., Fla., 1974—84, Seminole H.S., 1984—85, North Chgo. Cmty. Sch. Dist., 1994—2000, Cradlerock Sch., Columbia, Md., 2000—. Avocations: music performance, travel. Home: 2268 Merion Pond Woodstock MD 21163 Personal E-mail: bck-1@comcast.net.

KING, BETSY, professional golfer; b. Reading, Pa., Aug. 13, 1955; Winner U.S. Open-Women, 1989, 1990, LPGA, 1992; 3d ranked woman LPGA Tour, 1992. LPGA tour victories include: Orlando Classic, 1984, Columbia Savings Classic, 1984, Henredon Classic, 1986, Rail Charity Classic, 1986, 88, Tucson Open, 1987, Dinah Shore Invitational, 1987, McDonald's Classic, 1987, Atlantic City Classic, 1987, Kemper Open, 1988, Cellular One-Ping Championship, 1988, Jamaica Classic, 1989, Nabisco Dinah Shore, 1990, U.S. Women's Open, 1989, 1990, Corning Classic, 1991, Mazda Championship, 1992, ShopRite Classic, 1995, Corestates Betsy King Classic, 1997, Solheim Cup, 1998. Inductee LPGA Hall of Fame, 1995. Achievements include LPGA leading money winner, 1984, 89, 93. Office: LPGA 100 International Golf Dr Daytona Beach FL 32124-1092

KING, BILLIE JEAN MOFFITT, retired professional tennis player; b. Long Beach, Calif., Nov. 22, 1943; d. Willard J. and Betty Moffitt; m. Larry King (div. 1987), Sept. 17, 1965. Student, Calif. State U. at Los Angeles, 1961-64; PhD (hon.), Calif. State U., 1997; hon. degree, Trinity Coll., 1998; PhD (hon.), U. Pa, 1999, U. Mass., 2000. Amateur tennis player, 1958-67; profl., 1968—84; mem. Tennis Challenge Series, 1977, 78; dir., ofcl. spokesperson World Team Tennis, Chgo., 1985—; commentator, analyst Wimbledon and other tennis events HBO, N.Y.C. Winner, Singles champion tournaments include: Wimbledon, 1966-68, 72, 73,75, U.S. Open, 1967, 71, 72, 74, Australian Open, 1968, French Open, 1972; Doubles champion Wimbledon, 1961, 62, 65, 67, 68, 70-73, 79 U.S. Open, 1965, 67, 74, 80, French Open, 1972; mixed doubles champion Wimbledon, 1967, 71, 73, 74, U.S. Open, 1967, 71, 73, French, 1967, 70, Australian, 1968; winner 29 Virginia Slims singles titles, 1970-77, 4 Colgate titles, 1977, Fedn. Cup, 1963-67, 76-79, Wightman Cup, 1961-67, 70, 77, 78; World Tennis Team All-Star, 3 times; host Colgate women's sports TV spl. The Lady is a Champ, 1975; sports commentator ABC-TV, 1975-78;founder Women's Tennis Assn., 1973, pres., 1973-75, 80-81; founder, Women's Sports Found, 1974, Profl. World TeamTennis, 1974, World TeamTennis Profl. League, 1981, World TeamTennis Recreational League, 1985, World TeamTennis Charities, 1987; co-founder, pub. WomenSports mag., 1974, Kingdom, Inc., San Mateo, Calif.; founding mem., Women's Sports Legends; first woman commr. (Team Tennis League) profl. sports history, 1984; TV commentator HBO-Sports Wimbeldon coverage; capt. Fed. Cup for USA, 1995; cons. Virginia Slims World Championship Series;mem., Planned Parenthood, US Profl. Tennis Assn., US Profl. Tennis Registry, Chgo. Area Women's Sports Assn., advisory bd, Areta Sports award nomination com., Jim Thorpe Pro sports nomination com. award, sports advisory bd. for the Vic Braden Neurology Rsch. Inst., USTA Player Devel. Com.; bd. dirs. Challenger Ctr., Elton John AIDS Found., S.A.F.E., Nat. AIDS Fund, Altria Group, Inc., Women's Sports Found.; amb. Adventures in Movement Charity; coach Fed. Cup Women's Tennis Team, 1995-96, 98-2003, USA Olympic Women's Tennis Team, 1996, 2000; nat. spokesperson Literary Vols. Am.; tennis tchr. to profls. Author: Tennis to Win, 1970, (with Kim Chapin) Billie Jean, 1974, (with Greg Hoffman) Tennis Love: A Parent's Guide to the Sport, 1978, (with Frank Deford) The Autobiography of Billie Jean King, 1982 (with Cynthia Starr) We Have Come a Long Way, The Story of Women's Tennis, 1988. Named Sportsperson of Yr., 1972, Top 40 Athletes, 1994, Sports Illustrated; Woman Athlete of Yr., A.P., 1967, 73, Top Woman Athlete of Yr., 1972; Woman of Yr., Time mag., 1976, One of 10 Most Powerful Women in Am., Harper's Bazaar, 1977, One of 25 Most Influential Women in Am., World Almanac, 1977, One of 100 Most Important Ams. of 20th Century, Life mag., 1990, woman of the Year, Women in Sports & Events, 2002; named to Internat. Tennis Hall of Fame, 1987, Nat. Women's Hall of Fame, 1990, Chgo. Gay and Lesbian Hall of Fame, 1999, Court of Champions, USTA Nat. Tennis Ctr., 2003; WTA Hon. Membership award, 1986, Female Teaching Pro of the Decade, 1994, Lifetime Achievement award, March of Dimes, 1994, Flo Hymnal award, Women's Sports Found, 1997, "Player Who Makes a Difference award", 1997, US Olympic Com. Nat. Tennis Coach of the Year award, 1997, Nat. Women's Law Ctr. honoree, 1997, Elizabeth Blackwill award for Courage, William & Hobart Smith Colleges, 1998, Arthur Ashe award for Courage, ESPN, 1999, Community Role Model award, LA Gay & Lesbian Ctr., 1999, NFL Players Assn. Lifetime Achievement award, 1999, Sports Illustrated "Athletes Who Changed the Game award, 1999, Capitol award, GLAAD, 2000, Radcliffe medal, Radcliffe Coll., 2002, Internat Olympic Com. Women & Sport World Trophy, 2002, Nat. Assn. Collegiate Women Athletic Administrators award of Honor, 2002, Pillipe Chatrier award, Internat. Tennis Fedn., 2003. Won 71 singles titles, including 12 Grand Slam singles titles; won 20 Wimbledon titles;First woman to win more than $100,000 in a single season in any sport; Highest singles ranking 1(5 times between 1966-72); defeated Bobby Riggs in "The Battle of the Sexes" tennis match, Sept. 20, 1973, Houston, Tex. Office: Billie Jean King Ste 983 960 Harlem Ave Glenview IL 60025

KING, BONNIE BESS WORLINE, writer, educator; b. El Dorado, Kans., Aug. 3, 1914; d. Robert Hite and Grace Lavera (Miller) Worline; m. Irvill King, 1937 (dec. Mar. 1987); children: Courtner, April, Waveland. AB, U. Chgo., 1935; MA, U. Pitts., 1946; PhD, U. Kans., 1961. Cert. in spl. edn., Calif. Writer fiction Chgo. Daily News, from 1933; writer catalog copy and correspondence Montgomery Ward and Co., Chgo., from 1935; continuity editor KCKN, Kansas City, Kans., 1942-44; pub. rels. and publs. dir., instr. journalism and advt. Endicott Coll., Beverly, Mass., 1945; dir. publs. and pub. rels., instr. English Gorham (Maine) State Coll., 1946-51; instr. English, U. Kans., 1951-61; publs. asst. Menninger Psychiat. Clinic, Topeka, 1956-61; tchr. journalism, English and Latin Brawley (Calif.) H.S., 1961-62, dir., instr. spl. edn., 1962-70; asst. prof. humanities Imperial Valley campus San Diego State U., 1963-84; cons. spl. edn. Imperial/San Diego Counties, 1962-84; emeritus asst. prof. humanities San Diego State U., 1984—; tchr. creative writing Calipatria State Prison, 1997—. Spkr. in field. Author: Sod House Adventure, 1956, The Sod Schoolhouse, 1996, Handicap Hut-At Camp Mary Jane, 2005; editor The Imp newsletter San Diego State U., 1965-84. Initiator, Assn. Retarded Citizens, Imperial County, 1964, Woman Haven, Imperial County, 1965, Spl. Olympics, Imperial County, 1967. Named Woman of Yr., Calif. State Legislature, 1988. Mem Calif. State Tchrs. Assn. (past pres.). Democrat. Avocations: gardening, sewing, cooking, swimming. Address: 279 J St Brawley CA 92227-2329

KING, BRIAN MARTIN, music educator; b. Rochester, July 3, 1967; s. Howard Leo and Sharon Lou King; m. Jennifer Lee Pipech, Sept. 17, 1994; children: Amara Darlene, Michael Howard. A in Liberal Arts, Monroe C.C., 1992; B in Edn. and Music, Nazareth Coll., 2001, EdM, 2004. Cert. N.Y. Sales mgr. Marriott Hotels, Rochester, 1994—97; sales assoc. Stereo Shop, Rochester, 1997—2001; music tchr. Hilton (N.Y.) Ctrl. Sch., 2001, Greece Ctrl. Sch., Rochester, 2001—. Percussion instr. Empire Statesmen Drum Corps, Rochester, 1988—99, various local marching bands, 1990—. Avocations: music, softball, martial arts. Home: 84 Seafareus Ln Rochester NY 14612

KING, BRIDGETTE MARCHELLE, management consultant; b. Lawton, Okla., Jan. 20, 1972; d. James Edward III and Dianne Thompson AAS in Liberal Arts, El Centro Coll., 1994; BA in Psychology, U. Tex., 1998; MA in Orgnl. Mgmt., U. Phoenix, 2005. E-commerce element K/Tex. Supr. Luby's Cafeteria's, Inc., Duncanville, Tex., 1990-96; team lead, mgr. Peirson & Patterson, LLP, Dallas, 1998-99; sr. web hosting, e-commerce sales rep. Earthlink Inc., Dallas, 1999-2000; sales mgr. ICOS, Garland, Tex., 2001—02; mgr. HR First Contact, 2002—03; dir. Striking Forward Found., 2004—; owner KSF Unltd., Duncanville, 2005—. Discussion leader John Ben Shephard Leadership Inst., Odessa, Tex.; founder Striving Forward Found Named Most Inspiring Mgr., HR First Contact, 2001. Mem. Psi Chi. Democrat. Avocations: reading, mentoring, volunteering, cooking. Home and Office: 800 Link Dr Apt 707 Duncanville TX 75116-2625 Personal E-mail: breeking@sbcglobal.net.

KING, BRYAN HARRY, neuropsychiatrist, medical educator and researcher; b. Fullerton, Calif., May 18, 1957; s. Raymond Ward and Marian Joan King; m. Jacquelyn G. Lund, June 4, 1983; children: Annalise Louise, Harrison Raymond. BS magna cum laude, U. Calif., Irvine, 1979; MD, Med. Coll. of Wis., 1983. Diplomate Am. Bd. Psychiatry, Am. Bd. Psychiatry and Neurology, Am. Bd. Child and Adolescent Psychiatry. Intern in internal medicine UCLA Ctr. for Health Sci., 1983-84; resident in psychiatry UCLA Neuropsychiat. Inst., 1985-87, fellow in child psychiatry, 1987-90; asst. prof. UCLA Sch. Medicine, 1990-95, assoc. prof., 1996—. Psychiatry cons. Lanterman State Developmental Ctr., Pomona, Calif., 1989— (behavior mgmt. com. 1990—, pharmacy and therapeutics com. 1994—), Fairview State Devel. Ctr., Costa Mesa, Calif., 1993—, People Assisting the Homeless, L.A., 1994-95; psychopharmacology cons. UCLA Neuropsychiat. Hosp., 1991—; psychiatry expert cons. U.S. Dept. Justice, 1993, Calif. Dept. Devel. Svcs. and Office of Atty. Gen., 1995—; profl. adv. bd. Nat. Tuberous Sclerosis Assn., 1993—; bd. mem. Child SHARE, Glendale, Calif., 1994—. Cons. editor Am. Jour. Mental Retardation, 1993—; ad hoc reviewer Archives of Gen. Psychiatry, Brit. Jour. Pharmacology, Gen. Hosp. Psychiatry, Brain Dysfunction, Life Sciences; co-editor: A Curriculum Guide to Psychiatry and Mental Retardation, 1995; contbr. articles to profl. jours., chpts. to books. Laughlin fellow Am. Coll. Psychiatrists, 1988, Gertrude Rogers Greenblatt fellow UCLA Divsn. Child Psychiatry, 1988; recipient NIMH Individual Rsch. Svc. award, 1988-89, NIMH Scientist Development award, 1991-96, George Tarjan award for achievement in mental retardation, Am. Acad. Child and Adolescent Psychiatry, 1995. Mem. Am. Psychiat. Assn. (com. mental retardation and devel. disabilities 1990—, workgroup on rsch. 1992-95), Am. Assn. on Mental Retardation, Acad. on Mental Retardation, Soc. for Rsch. in Child and Adolescent Psychiatry, Soc. for Neurosci., Group for the Advancement of Psychiatry, So. Calif. Psychiat. Soc. Presbyterian. Office: UCLA Neuropsychiatric Inst 760 Westwood Plz Los Angeles CA 90095-8353

KING, CAROLE (CAROLE KLEIN), lyricist, singer; b. Bklyn., Feb. 9, 1942; m. Gerry Goffin; m. Charles Larkey; m. Rick Evers, 1977 (dec., 1978); m. Rick Sorensen, 1982; children: Louise, Sherry, Molly, Levi. Student, Queens Coll. Co-writer (with Gerry Goffin) numerous songs, 1960-68, including Will You Love Me Tomorrow?, Go Away, Little Girl, Up on the Roof, Natural Woman, The Locomotion, Take Good Care of My Baby, It's Too Late; albums include Music, 1971, Tapestry, 1971 (4 Grammy awards), Simple Things, Pearls: Songs of Goffin and King, Rhymes & Reasons, 1972, Fantasy, 1973, Wrap Around Joy, 1974, Really Rosie, 1975, Thoroughbred, 1975, Her Greatest Hits: Songs of Long Ago, 1978, One To One, 1982, Speeding Time, 1983, City Streets, 1989, Colour Of Your Dreams, 1993, In Concert, 1994, A Natural Woman, 1994, The Carnegie Hall Concert, 1996, Pearls/Time Gone By, 1998, Super Hits, 2000, Love Makes the World, 2001; composer music for films Head, 1968, Murphy's Romance, 1985, The Care Bears Movie, 1985; off-Broadway theater appearance in A Minor Incident, 1989; Broadway appearance in Blood Brothers, 1994; appeared in films Murphy's Romance, 1985, Russkies, 1987, TV film Hider in the House, 1989, TV series The Tracy Ullman Show. Inducted in Rock & Roll Hall of Fame, 1990. Office: Carole King Prodns 11684 Ventura Blvd 273 Studio City CA 91604

KING, CAROLYN DINEEN, judge; b. Syracuse, NY, Jan. 30, 1938; d. Robert E. and Carolyn E. (Bareham) Dineen; m. Thomas M. Reavley; children: James Randall, Philip Randall, Stephen Randall. AB summa cum laude, Smith Coll., 1959; LLB, Yale U., 1962. Bar: D.C. 1962, Tex. 1963. Assoc. Fulbright & Jaworski, Houston, 1962—72; ptnr. Childs, Fortenbach, Beck & Guyton, Houston, 1972—78, Sullivan, Bailey, King, Randall & Sabom, Houston, 1978—79; judge U.S. Ct. Appeals (5th cir.), Houston, 1979—, chief judge, 1999—; with U.S. Jud. Conf., 1999—, exec. com., 2000—, chmn. exec. com., 2002—. Trustee, exec. com., treas. Houston Ballet Found., 1967—70; Houston dist. adv. coun. SBA, 1972—76; Dallas regional panel Pres.'s Commn. White House Fellowships, 1972—76, mem. commn., 1977; bd. dirs. Houston chpt. Am. Heart Assn., 1978—79; nat. trustee Palmer Drug Abuse Program, 1978—79; trustee, sec., treas., chmn. audit com., fin. com., mgmt. com. United Way Tex. Gulf Coast, 1979—85; trustee, exec. com., chmn. bd. trustees U. St. Thomas, 1988—98. Recipient Smith Coll. medal, 1997, Outstanding Alumnus award, Phi Beta Kappa Alumni of Greater Houston, 1998, Margaret Brent Women Lawyers of Achievement award, ABA, 2005; rsch. fellow, Ctr. for Am. and Internat. Law, 1989—. Mem.: ABA, Philos. Soc. Tex., Houston Bar Assn., State Bar Tex., Am. Law Inst. (coun. 1991—, chmn. membership com. 1997—99), Fed. Bar Assn. Roman Catholic. Office: US Ct Appeals 11020 US Courthouse 515 Rusk Avenue Houston TX 77002-2694

KING, CHARLES HOMER, manufacturing executive; b. Chgo., July 30, 1938; s. Merle Marine and (Searge) K.; children: Dennis, Denise. BS in Mgmt. and Mktg., Louisville U., 1967; MA in Computer Data Mgmt., Webster U., Jeffersonville,. Ind., 1983. Cert. resource mgmt., prodn. and inventory mgmt. Materials mgr. Navistar Internat. Corp., 1977-99; mfg. cons., APICS trainer in cert., 1999—. Mem. Fraternal Order of Eagles. Republican. Methodist. Home and Office: 1164 Evergreen Dr Greenville OH 45331-3012 Office Phone: 937-547-9229. E-mail: spitzen@wesnet.com.

KING, CHARLES ROSS, physician; b. Nevada, Iowa, Aug. 22, 1925; s. Carl Russell and Dorothy Sarah (Mills) K.; m. Frances Pamela Carter, Jan. 8, 1949; children— Deborah Diane, Carter Ross, Charles Conrad, Corbin Kent Student, Butler U., 1943; BS in Bus., Ind. U., 1948, MD, 1964. Diplomate Am. Bd. Family Practice. Dep. dir. Ind. Pub. Works and Supply, 1949-52; salesman Knox Coal Corp., 1952-59; rotating intern Marion County Gen. Hosp., Indpls., 1964-65; family practice medicine Anderson, Ind., 1965—. Sec.-treas. staff Cmty. Hosp., 1969-72, pres.-elect, dir., chief medicine, 1973—, bd. dirs., 1973-75; sec.-treas. St. John's Hosp., 1968-69, chief medicine, 1972-73, chief pediatrics, 1977—; bd. dirs. Rolling Hills Convalescnet Ctr., 1968-73; pres. Profl. Ctr. Lab., 1965—; vice chmn. Madison County Bd. Health, 1966-69, chmn., 1986—; chmn. bd. dirs. Star Fin. Bank, Anderson. Bd. dirs. Family Svc. Madison County, 1968-69, Madison County Assn. Mentally Retarded, 1972-76, Anderson Fine Arts Ctr., 1996—; trustee St. Johns Health System., 1898—; chmn. bd. dirs. Anderson Downtown Devel. Corp., 1980—; mem. Paramont Restoration Steering Com., 1994—; trustee, sec.-tread. St. John's Med. Ctr., 1989—; mem. exec. com. Madison United Way Fund, vice-chmn., 1995, chmn., 1996; mem. exec. com. Stop Teen Pregnancy Program, 1995—; exec. commr. Health Search Madison County, 1995—. With U.S. Army, 1944-46. Recipient Dr. James Macholtz award, Spl. Olympics, 1986, Sagamore of Wabash award, State of Ind. Gov., 2002. Fellow Royal Soc. Health, Am. Acad. Family Practice (charter); mem. AMA (numerous Physicians Recognition awards), Ind. Med. Assn., Pan Am. Med. Assn., Am. Acad. Gen. Practice, Madison County Med. Soc. (pres. 1970), 9th Dist. Med. Soc. (sec.-treas. 1968), Anderson C. of C. (bd. dirs. 1979-82), Indpls. Mus. Art (corp. mem.), Anderson Country Club (bd. dirs. 1976-79), Phi Delta Theta (pres. Alumni Assn. 1952), Phi Chi. Clubs: Anderson Country (bd. dirs. 1976-79). Methodist. Office: 2015 Jackson St Anderson IN 46016-4337

KING, CHERYL BREA, elementary school educator, secondary school educator, music educator; b. McKeesport, Pa., Apr. 10, 1951; d. Edgar David and Eleanor Coates Brea; m. Richard Wayne King, PhD, June 22, 1974; children: Ashley, Adam, Allyson. B in Music Edn., Grove City Coll., 1973. Cert. instrnl. II grades K-12 music. Elem. music tchr. Grove City (Pa.) City Schs., 1973—74; elem. and middle sch. music tchr. Shaler Area Schs., Pitts., 1974—89; pvt. tchr. piano, dir. ch. choir, 1989—98; middle and sr. high vocal music tchr. East Allegheny Sch. Dist., North Versailles, Pa., 1998—, prodr., dir. H.S. musicals, 1998—. Mem., bd. dirs. McKeesport Little Theatre, 1998—2004; children's choir dir. First United Meth. Ch., East McKeesport, Pa., 1984—95. Mem.: Pa. State Edn. Assn., Pa. Music Edn. Assn., Music Edn. Nat. Coun. Democrat. Methodist. Avocations: reading, crafts, dance, Broadway musicals. Home: 412 Third St North Versailles PA 15137 Office: East Allegheny Sch Dist 1150 Jacks Run Rd North Versailles PA 15137 Office Phone: 412-824-9700. Business E-Mail: cking@eawildcats.net.

KING, CHI-YU, research scientist; b. Nanking, Jian-Su, China, Aug. 14, 1934; came to the U.S., 1958; s. Cheng-Wei and Chan-Ron (Chu) K.; m. Bi-Shia Wang, Sept. 8, 1962; children: Tsu-Jae, Hans Tsi-han, Henry Tsi-heng. BSEE, Nat. Taiwan U., Taipei, 1956; MS, Duke U., 1961; PhD, Cornell U., 1965. Rsch. fellow Calif. Inst. Tech., Pasadena, 1965-66; asst. rsch. geophysicist U. Calif., L.A., 1966-68; geophysicist U.S. Geol. Survey, Menlo Park, Calif., 1968-70, 73-95, Nat. Oceanic and Atmospheric Adminstrn., San Francisco, 1970-73; PNC Internat. fellow, guest rschr. U. Tokyo, 1997-99. Vis. prof. Nat. Ctrl. U., Chung-Li, Taiwan, 1973-74; geophysicist, chmn. Earthquake Prediction Rsch. Inc., Los Altos, Calif., 1995—. Editor: Earthquake Hydrology and Chemistry, 1985, (with R. Scarpa) Modeling of Volcanic Processes, 1988; editor or co-editor (spl. publs.) Jour. Geophys. Rsch., 1980, 86, Geophys. Rsch. Letters, 1981; mem. edit. bd. Jour. Geodesy and Geodynamics, 2003—; contbr. articles to profl. jours. Preacher, Bible tchr. various Christian chs. Calif., Taiwan, Hong Kong, China, Japan, Saipan, Persian Gulf, Europe, 1972—; chmn. bd. Ch. in Palo Alto, 1972-81, House of Christians, Los Altos, 1981-97. Mem. Am. Geophys. Union (assoc. editor Jour. Geophys. Rsch. 1995-97). Home and Office: 381 Hawthorne Ave Los Altos CA 94022-3845 Office Phone: 650-948-4438. E-mail: chiyuking@aol.com.

KING, CHRISTINE ELIZABETH, education educator; b. Birmingham, July 11, 1978; d. Kim William and Carol Sysan Snyder King. BS in Elem. Edn., Auburn U., 1999, PhD in Elem. Edn., 2004; MEd in Elem. Edn., U. Montevallo, 2000. Cert. tchr. Ala., Ga. Presch. tchr. CASA Sch., Birmingham, 1999—2000; tchr. West Point (Ga.) Elem. Sch., 2001—02; instr. Auburn (Ala.) U., 2002—04, adj. prof., 2004; asst. prof. U. W.Ala., Livingston, 2005—. Spkr. in field. Childcare assoc. Asbury Meth. Ch., Birmingham, 1999—. Mem.: APS, NEA, AAUW, Nat. Coun. Tchrs. Math., Nat. Coun. Tchrs. English, Nat. Coun. Social Studies, Nat. Sci. Tchrs. Assn., Assn. Childhood Edn. Internat., Am. Assn. U. Profs., Soc. Info. Tech. and Tchr. Edn., Internat. Soc. Tech. Edn., Ala. Edn. Assn., Soc. Tchg. Psychology, Assn. Tchr. Educators, Phi Delta Kappa, Kappa Delta Pi, Phi Kappa Phi, Alpha Theta Chi. Avocations: scrapbooks, reading, photography, hiking, walking, crafts. Home: 1938 Tahiti Ln Alabaster AL 35007 Office: Univ West Ala UWA Sta #34 Livingston AL 35470

KING, COLBERT ISAIAH, editor; b. Washington, Sept. 20, 1939; s. Isaiah and Amelia (Colbert) K.; m. Gwendolyn Ann Stewart, July 3, 1961; children: Robert, Stephen, Allison. BA, Howard U., 1961, postgrad., 1969. Attache Dept. State, Washington, 1964—70; dir. govt. rels. Potomac Elec. Power Co., Washington, 1976-77; legis. asst. to Md. Senator Charles McMathias Jr. Washington, 1972-76; dep. asst. sec. of treasury Dept. Treasury, Washington, 1977-79; U.S. exec. dir. World Bank, 1979-81; exec. v.p., bd. dirs. Riggs Nat. Bank, Washington, 1984—89; mem. editl. bd. Washington Post, 1990—, dep. editor, 2000—. Mem. Coun. for Excellence in Govt. With U.S. Army, 1961-63. Named one of Outstanding Young Men of Am., U.S. Jaycees, 1974; recipient spl. citation Nat. Rehab. Assn., 1975, Svc. award Ctr. for Sickle Cell Disease, Howard U., 1975, Disting. Svc. award U.S. Treasury, 1979, Outstanding Alumnus award, Howard U., 1984, Pulitzer Prize, 2003. Mem. Kappa Alpha Psi. Democrat. Episcopalian. Office: The Washington Post 1150 15th St Washington DC 20071 Office Phone: 202-334-7475.

KING, CORETTA SCOTT (MRS. MARTIN LUTHER KING JR.), educational association administrator, lecturer, writer, concert singer; b. Heiberger, Ala., Apr. 27, 1927; d. Obidiah and Bernice (McMurray) Scott; m. Martin Luther King, Jr., June 18, 1953 (dec. Apr. 1968); children: Yolanda Denise, Martin Luther III, Dexter Scott, Bernice Albertine. AB, Antioch Coll., 1951; Mus.B., New Eng. Conservatory Music, 1954, Mus.D., 1971; L.H.D., Boston U., 1969, Marymount-Manhattan Coll., 1969, Morehouse Coll., 1970; H.H.D., Brandeis U., 1969, Wilberforce U., 1970, Bethune-Cookman Coll., 1970, Princeton U., 1970; LL.D., Bates Coll., 1971. Voice instr. Morris Brown Coll., Atlanta, 1962; commentator CNN, Atlanta, 1980—; lectr., writer; founding pres., chief exec. officer Martin Luther King Jr. Ctr. for Nonviolent Social Change Inc. Chairwoman Martin Luther King, Jr. Fed. Holiday Commn.; mem. Black Leadership Forum, Black Leadership Roundtable. Author: My Life With Martin Luther King, Jr., 1969, The Words of Martin Luther King, 1983; contbr. articles to mags.; syndicated newspaper columnist N.Y. Times Syndication Sales Corp., 1986-90, United Features Syndicate, 1990-94; concert debut, Springfield, Ohio, 1948; numerous concerts throughout U.S., concerts, India, 1959, performances, Freedom Concert. Del. to White House Conf. Children and Youth, 1960; sponsor Com. for Sane Nuclear Policy, Com. on Responsibility, Moblzn. to End War in Viet Nam, 1966, 67, Margaret Sanger Meml. Found.; mem. So. Rural Action Project, Inc.; pres. Martin Luther King, Jr. Found.; chmn. Commn. on Econ. Justice for Women; mem. exec. com. Nat. Com. Inquiry; co-chmn. Clergy and Laymen Concerned about Vietnam, Nat. Com. for Full Employment, 1974; pres. Martin Luther King Jr. Center for Nonviolent Social Change; co-chairperson Nat. Com. Full Employment; mem. exec. bd. Nat. Health Ins. Com.; active YWCA; bd. dirs. So. Christian Leadership Conf., Martin Luther King, Jr. Found. Gt. Britain; trustee Robert F. Kennedy Meml. Found., Ebenezer Bapt. Ch. Recipient Nat. Coun. Negro Women Ann. Brotherhood award, 1957, Outstanding Citizenship award Montgomery (Ala.) Improvement Assn., 1959, Merit award St. Louis Argus, 1960, Distinguished Achievement award Nat. Orgn. Colored Women's Clubs, 1962, Louise Waterman Wise award Am. Jewish Congress Women's Aux., 1963, Myrtle Wreath award Cleve. Hadassah, 1965, award for excellence in field human relations Soc. Family of May, 1968, Universal Love award Premio San Valentine Com., 1968, Wateler Peace prize, 1968, Dag Hammarskjold award, 1969, Pacem in Terris award Internat. Overseas Service Found., 1969, Leadership for Freedom award Roosevelt U., 1971, Martin Luther King Meml. medal Coll. City N.Y., 1971, Internat. Viareggio award, 1971, Eugene V. Debs award, 1982, numerous others; named Woman of Year Utility Club N.Y.C., 1962, Woman of Year Nat. Assn. Radio and TV Announcers, 1968, UAW Social Justice award, 1980. Mem. Nat. Council Negro Women (Ann. Brotherhood award 1957), Women Strike for Peace (del. disarmament conf. Geneva, Switzerland 1962, citation for work in peace and freedom 1963), Women's Internat. League for Peace and Freedom, NAACP, United Ch. Women (bd. mgrs.), Alpha Kappa Alpha (hon.) Baptist (mem. choir, guild adviser). Club: Links (Human Dignity and Human Rights award Norfolk chpt. 1964). Address: Martin Luther King Jr Ctr 449 Auburn Ave NE Atlanta GA 30312-1503

KING, CURTIS STEEBLE, history professor; b. Atlantic City, N.J., Oct. 1, 1959; s. George Allman and Cecelia Marie King. BS, U.S.Mil. Acad., West Point, N.Y., 1982; MA in History, U. of Pa., Phila., 1992; PhD in History, U. of Pa., 1999. Commissioned U.S. Army, 1982, advanced through grades to maj.; platoon leader, exec. officer, and asst. ops. officer Combat Support Bn., Berlin Brigade, Berlin, 1982—85; adj. and co. comdr. 4-37 Armor Bn., 1st Inf. Divsn., Fort Riley, Kans., 1986—89; asst. divsn. ops. officer 85th Divsn. (Exercise), Arlington Heights, Ill., 1995—98; asst. prof. of history U.S. Mil. Acad., West Point, NY, 1992—95; asst. prof. Combat Studies Inst., Fort Leavenworth, Kans., 1998—99, assoc. prof., 2000—; asisstant historian Stabilizaion Forces, Bosnia, Sarajevo, Bosnia-Herzegovina, 1999—2000. Adj. prof. Kans. State U., Manhattan, 2004—. Contbr. articles to profl. jours., chapters to books. Decorated Joint Svc. Commendation Medal US Dept. of Def., NATO medal, Army Commendation medals (4); recipient Omar N. Bradley Award for Excellence in Writing and Rsch., U.S. Mil. Acad., 1982. Mem.: Army Hist. Found., Nat. Trust for Hist. Preservation, US Armor Assn. (Order of St. George 1995), Soc. for Mil. History, Assn. for the Advancement of Slavic Studies, Am. Hist. Assn., The Soverign Mil. Order of the Temple of Jerusalem (asst. historian for the grand priory of the U.S. 2000—05, Legion of Merit and St. Louis the Crusader Medal 2002 and 2002), Phi Alpha Theta, Phi Kappa Phi. Home: 51 Saint Mary's St Apt D Leavenworth KS 66048 Office: Combat Studies Institute US Army Command and Staff College Fort Leavenworth KS 66027 Office Phone: 913-684-2082. Personal E-mail: kingphillie@aol.com.

KING, CYNTHIA ROSE, literature and language educator, theater arts director; b. Bonne Terre, Mo., Sept. 7, 1948; d. Lourine Frances King. BS in Secondary Edn., S.E. Mo. U., 1971, Cert. in English, 1972. Cert. secondary educator in speech and theatre Mo., secondary educator in English Mo. Educator, dir. theatre arts Notre Dame Regional H.S., Cape Girardeau, Mo., 1972—. Finalist Tchr. of the Yr., Cape Girardeau C. of C., 1998, 1999; named MO-CAPE Educator of Yr., Mo. Coun. for Am. Pvt. Edn., 1997—98; recipient Excellence in Tchg. award, Mo. Scholar's Acad., 2000. Mem.: SE Mo. English Tchrs. Assn., Am. Alliance Theatre in Edn., Speech and Theatre Assn. Mo., Ednl. Theatre Assn., Mo. Assn. English Tchrs. (corr.). Office: Notre Dame Regional HS 265 Notre Dame Dr Cape Girardeau MO 63701 Office Phone: 573-335-6772.

KING, D. KENT, school system administrator; b. Preston, Mo., 1943; m. Sandy King; 3 children. BA, Ctrl. Mo. State U., 1964; MA, Drury Coll., Springfield, 1967; PhD in Ednl. Adminstrn., Okla. State U., 1972. From tchr. to prin. Houston Sch. Dist., Tex. County, Mo., 1964—70; supt. Licking Sch. Dist., Mo., 1971—77, Rolla Sch. Dist., Mo., 1977—96; dir. Mo. Sch. Improvement Program, 1996—99; dep. commr. Mo. Dept. Edn., Jefferson City, Mo., 1999—2000, commr., 2000—. Office: Mo Dept Edn PO Box 480 Jefferson City MO 65102-0480 Office Phone: 573-751-4446. Office Fax: 573-751-1179.

KING, DAVID A., aerospace engineer; m. Lisa King; 2 children. BS in Mech. Engring., U. S.C., 1983; MS in Bus Adminstrn., Fla. Inst. Tech., 1991. Space shuttle main propulsion sys. engr. NASA, 1983—93, flow dir. Space Shuttle Discovery, 1993—95, dep. dir. shuttle processing, 1996—97, shuttle launch dir., 1997—99, dep. dir. Marshall Space Flight Ctr., 2002—03, dir. Marshall Space Flight Ctr., 2004—. Recipient Presdl. Rank award, 2001. Office: DAO1 NASA George C Marshall Space Flight Ctr Huntsville AL 35812 E-mail: david.a.king@nasa.gov.

KING, DAVID A., lawyer; b. LA, Calif., Feb. 26, 1960; married; 2 children. BS, Univ. Tenn., 1982, JD, 1985. Bar: Tenn. 1985. Mem., litigation & healthcare practices Bass Berry & Sims PLC, Nashville. Editor (student materials): Tenn. Law Rev. Named one of Best Lawyers in Nashville, Nashville Post, 2003. Fellow: Nashville Bar Found.; mem.: Am. Health Lawyers Assn., Def. Rsch. Inst., Tenn. Bar Assn., Nashville Bar Assn. Office: Bass Berry & Sims PLC Ste 2700 315 Deaderick St Nashville TN 37239-3001 Office Phone: 615-742-7890. Office Fax: 615-742-2815. Business E-Mail: dking@bassberry.com.

KING, DAVID CARLTON, lawyer; b. Bangor, Maine, May 5, 1947; s. Carlton Edward and Rosemary (Haskell) K.; m. Miriam Jane Jordan, July 19, 1969; children: Andrew, Adam, Michael. BA, Bates Coll., 1969; JD, Boston U., 1973. Bar: Maine 1973, U.S. Dist. Ct. Maine 1973, U.S. Ct. Appeals (1st cir.) 1988. Ptnr. Rudman & Winchell, Bangor, 1980—. Bd. dirs., pres. Opportunity Housing, Inc., Bangor, 1980-92; chmn. Brewer (Maine) Zoning Bd. Appeals, 1978-82. Mem. Am. Bd. Trial Advs., Def. Rsch. Inst., Maine Bar Assn., Maine Trial Lawyers Assn. Office: Rudman & Winchell PO Box 1401 Bangor ME 04402-1401 Office Phone: 207-947-4501. Business E-Mail: dking@rudman-winchell.com.

KING, DAVID PAUL, lawyer, educator; b. Washington, June 20, 1956; s. Ivan Robert and Alice King. AB, Princeton U., 1977; JD, U. Pa., 1982. Bar: Ga. 1984, U.S. Dist. Ct. (no. and so. dists.) Ga. 1984, U.S. Ct. Appeals (11th cir.) 1984, D.C. 1985, U.S. Dist. Ct. Md. 1987, U.S. Ct. Appeals (4th cir.) 1987, Md. 1991, U.S. Dist. Ct. D.C. 1995. Law clk. to Hon. Alvin B. Rubin, U.S. Ct. Appeals for 5th Cir., Baton Rouge, 1982-83; assoc. Rogers & Hardin, Atlanta, 1983-85, Covington & Burling, Washington, 1985-87; asst. U.S. atty. Dept. Justice, Balt., 1987-90; assoc. Hogan & Hartson, L.L.P., Balt., 1990-92, ptnr., 1992—. Adj. prof. U. Md. Law Sch., Balt., 1995—. Mem. ABA, Fed. Bar Assn. (Md. bd. govs.), Md. Bar Assn., D.C. Bar Assn., Ga. Bar Assn., Serjant's Inn. Office: Hogan & Hartson LLP 111 S Calvert St Ste 1600 Baltimore MD 21202-6106 E-mail: dpking@hhlaw.com.

KING, DAVID ROY, lawyer; b. N.Y.C., Jan. 5, 1950; s. Joseph S. and Doris (Kagan) K.; m. Eunice Searles, Aug. 22, 1971; children: Mark B., Anna M. BA, U. Pa., 1971; JD, Harvard U., 1974. Bar: Pa. 1974, U.S. Dist Ct. (ea. dist.) Pa. 1974. Assoc. Morgan, Lewis & Bockius LLP, Phila., 1974-81, ptnr., 1981-2000; CEO Principia Pharms., Inc., 2000; pres. Delsys Pharms., Inc., 2001—; CEO Bio Rexis Pharm. Corp., 2002—.

KING, DAVID T., communications company financial executive; b. Paterson, N.J., Jan. 17, 1952; s. Tunis A. and Loretta (Van Der Well) K.; m. Janet Marie Giordano, Aug. 11, 1973; children: Lori, Debra, Brittany, David. BS in Acctg., Syracuse U., 1974; MBA in Fin., Fairleigh Dickinson U., 1982. CPA, N.J. Acct. Deloitte & Touche, 1974-78; mgr. offshore acctg. controls and procedures Schering-Plough Corp., 1978-82; corp. contr. Childcraft Edn. Corp., 1982-84; v.p. fin. Consol. Laundries, Inc., 1984-87; v.p. fin. and treas. Nat. Telephone Directory Corp., Parsippany, N.J., 1987-93, v.p. sales, 1994—. Athletic scholar Syracuse U., 1970-74. Mem. AICPA, N.J. CPAs, Alpha Beta Psi. Home: 34 Preston Rd Parsippany NJ 07054-4317 Office: Nat Telephone Dir 3 Executive Dr Somerset NJ 08873-4007

KING, DEXTER SCOTT, foundation administrator; b. Atlanta, Jan. 30, 1961; s. Martin Luther King, Jr. and Coretta Scott King. Student, Morehouse Coll., 1979—81. Pres. Visionary Devel. Corp., Atlanta; corrections officer, 1981—83; bus. cons., music prodr., music promoter, 1983—89; bd. dirs. Martin Luther King Jr. Ctr. for Nonviolent Social Change, Inc., Atlanta, 1984—, entertainment coord., 1988—89, pres., 1989, chmn., CEO, 1995—2004. Spkr. in field. Exec. prodr. (record and video project) King Holiday; co-author: Growing Up King: An Intimate Memoir, 2003. Named one of 50 Most Beautiful People, People Mag., 1995. Office: King Ctr Nonviolent Social Change 449 Auburn Ave NE Atlanta GA 30312-1503

KING, DON, boxing promoter; b. Cleve., Aug. 20, 1931; s. Clarence and Hattie K.; m. Henrietta King; children: Deborah, Carl, Eric. D (hon.), Shaw U. Boxing promoter, 1972—; owner Don King Prodns., Inc., Fla., 1974—. Promoter various fighters including Muhammud Ali, Sugar Ray Leonard, Mike Tyson, Ken Norton, Joe Frazier, Larry Holmes, Roberto Duran, George Foreman. Achievements include being featured on the covers of Time, Sports Illustrated, Ebony, Jet and other magazines; appearing in movies, TV shows and on numerous TV and radio talk shows; creating the phrase "Only in America"; establishing the Don King Foundation. Supporter NAACP, United Negro Coll. Fund, Martin Luther King Jr. Found., Simon Wiesenthal Ctr., Nat. Hispanic Scholarship Fund, Nat. Coalition of Title 1/Cptr. 1 Parents, Wheelchair Charities, Our Children's Found.; bd. trustee Shaw U. Named Man of Yr., Black United Fund and Brotherhood Crusade, in his honor "Don King Day", Newark, NJ, Greatest Promoter in History, Internat. Boxing Fedn., World Boxing Assn., World Boxing Coun.; named to Boxing Hall of Fame, 1997, the list of 40 Most Influential Sports Figures of the Past 40 Yrs., Sports Illustrated; recipient Black Achievement award, Martin Luther King Jr. Humanitatian award, So. Christian Leadership, 1987, President's award, NAACP, Lifetime Achievement, Grambling State U. Office: care Don King Prodns Inc 501 Fairway Dr Deerfield Beach FL 33441-1865*

KING, EDWARD JOSEPH, clinical chemist, laboratory administrator; b. Bronx, N.Y., Nov. 17, 1955; s. Edward Paul and May Frances (Kern) K. BS, Manhattan Coll., Riverdale, N.Y., 1978; PhD in Analytical Chemistry, Pacific Western U., 1997. Cert. clin. chemist Nat. Registry Clin. Chemistry. Sr. technologist MetPath, Teterboro, N.J., 1979-91, MetLife Lab., Elmsford, NY, 1991—93; lab. mgr. East Side Physicians P.C., N.Y.C., 1993—2003; clin. chemist ALX Lab c/o Animal Med. Ctr., N.Y.C., 2004—. Contbg. author Procs. of Clinichem -96, Vol. 11, 1996, Procs. of Soc. Forensic Toxicology, 2000. Fellow Nat. Acad. Clin. Biochemists (assoc.); mem. Am. Assn. Clin. Chemistry (Clin. Chemist Recognition award 2000), Am. Soc. Clin. Pathologists (cert.), Am. Chem. Soc. Achievements include research and development of wet chemistry urinalysis methodology. Home: 1173 A Second Ave Box 246 New York NY 10021 Office: ALX Lab c/o Animal Med Ctr 510 E 62d St New York NY 10021 E-mail: eking@optonline.net, edking@nyc.rr.com.

KING, EDWARD LOUIS, retired chemistry professor; b. Grand Forks, N.D., Mar. 15, 1920; s. Edward Louis and Beatrice (Nicholson) K.; m. Joy Kerler, Dec. 20, 1952; children: Paul, Marcia (dec.). Student, Long Beach (Calif.) Jr. Coll., 1938—41; BS, U. Calif., Berkeley, 1942, PhD, 1945. Rsch. chemist Manhattan Project U. Calif., Berkeley, 1942-46; mem. chemistry faculty Harvard U., 1946-48, U. Wis., 1948-62, U. Colo., Boulder, 1963-90, chmn. dept. chemistry, 1970-72; ret., 1990. Author: How Chemical Reactions Occur, 1963, Chemistry, 1979; Editor: Inorganic Chemistry, 1964-68. Guggenheim fellow, 1957-58. Mem. Am. Chem. Soc., Phi Beta Kappa, Sigma Xi. Office: U Colo Dept Chemistry PO Box 215 Boulder CO 80309-0215

KING, EDWARD WILLIAM, retired transportation executive; b. North Fork, W.Va., Jan. 29, 1923; s. Edward Ward and Myrtle (Charlton) K.; m. Mary Elizabeth Preston, Oct. 31, 1947 (dec. 1976); children: Edward William Jr., Elizabeth King Brown, Mary King Sullivan; m. Martha Lee Corns Mather, Apr. 7, 1977. Edn., Va. Poly. Inst., Washington and Lee U., U. Tenn.-Knoxville. Pres., treas. Mason & Dixon Lines, Inc., Kingsport, Tenn., until 1974, chmn. bd., treas., 1974—; pres., treas. Crown Enterprises, Inc.; treas. Mason & Dixon Tank Lines, Inc. Chmn. Regular Common Carrier Conf., 1966-67; dir. Kingsport Nat. Bank, Kingsport Fed. Savs. & Loan Seal sale chmn. Sullivan County TB Assn.; mem. Kingsport Bd. Edn.; dir., sec.-treas. Holston Valley Hosp., 1956-79; trustee East Tenn. State U. Found. Named Young Man of Yr. Kingsport Jaycees, 1958 Mem. Am. Trucking Assn. (Tenn. v.p., trustee ATA Found.), Trucking Employers, Tenn. Motor Transport Assn. (pres. 1957-58), Kingsport C. of C. (v.p.) Clubs: Ridgefields Country (Kingsport); Kingsport Civitan (pres.). Presbyterian.

KING, ELAINE A., curator, art historian, critic; b. Oak Park, Ill., Apr. 12, 1947; d. Casimir Stanley and Catherine Mary (Chmel) Czerwien. BS, No. Ill. U., 1968, MA, 1974; PhD, Northwestern U., 1986. Cert. Fine Arts Appraisal, 2002. Intern George Eastman House, Rochester, NY, 1977; lectr. history of photography Northwestern U., Evanston, Ill., 1977-81; curator Dittmar Meml. Gallery, Evanston, 1978-81; dir. Artemesia Gallery, Chgo., 1976-77; exec. dir., chief curator Carnegie-Mellon Art Gallery, Pitts., 1985—91; prof. critical theory and history of art Carnegie Mellon U., Pitts., 1981—. Bd. dirs. Mountain Lake Criticism Conf., Blacksburg, Va., 1982-91; ind. curator, 1991—; exhbn. rev. panel Pa. Coun. on Arts, 1991; exec. dir., chief curator Contemporary Art Ctr., Cin., 1993-95; guest curator Pitts. Cultural Trust, 1992, 93, 95, 96, Mari de Mater O'Neill med career survey Mus. Arts, P.R.; 10 year Retrospective of Diane Samuels, Mus. of Art, Györ, Hungary, Györ, 1999, bd. dirs. Mid-Am. Coll. Art Assn.; panel chair Midwest CAA Conf., 1997, 2003; co-coord. Wats:ON Festival, 1996-2003; adj. prof. U. Cin., 1994; art critic-in-residence U. Ariz., Tucson; guest curator Hungarian Bienale Exhbn. II, Györ, 1993, Master Graphic Arts Internat. Biennial, 1995, 97, 99, 2001, 03, 05; pres. Internat. Jury, 2003; panelist NEA Visual Arts, 1993; grant reviewer Inst. Mus. Sci., Washington, 1994, Ohio Arts Coun. fellowship and grant evaluator, 1994-95; Internat. Rev. panel AAUW internat. fellowships, Washington, 2000-03; mem. organizing com. Midwest Mus. Con., 1994-95; rep. Inter Arts Spring 1996 Budapest (Hungary) Crossroads; critic rep. Assn. Internat. Critics Art Conf. The Edge, Zagreb, Croatia; chmn. com. disting. exhbn. award Coll. Arts Assn., 1995-98, Assn. Internat. Critics Art XXXIV Congress Internat. Art Critics, Zagreb, Assn. Internat. Critics Art conf. ctrl. European cross-roads, 1996, 97, Assn. Internat. Critics Art Congress 2000, London; juror exhbn. 3rd Prague Internat.; nominator 4th Prague Internat., 2004; art-historian in residence Italian program Am. U., 2005, chair Sch. Visual Arts Plenary Session Conf., 2005, Internat. Popular Culture Assn. Conf., Wales, 2005; spkr. in field Curator, author: Crossing Borders: USA/Europe, Alleghany Coll. Art Galleries, 2000, Marking, 1999, The Figure As Fiction, 1993, Alfred DeCredico: Drawings, 1985-93, Emily Cheng: Monoprints, 1994, (exhbn. catalogues) Barry LeVa: 1966-88, Mel Bochner: 1973-85, Elizabeth Murray: Drawings: 1980-86, Michael Gitlin: Sculpture & Drawings, 1990, New Generations: Chgo., 1990, New Generations: N.Y., 1991, Magdalena Jetalová, 1991, Martin Puryear: Sculpture & Drawings, 1987, Abstraction/Abstraction, Tishan Hsu, Paintings, Drawings & Sculpture, 1987, N.Y. Painting Today, Michel Gerand: Drawings and Site Works, 1989, Drawings and Sculpture, 1990, Art in the Age of Information, 1993, Five Artists at the Airport: Insights into Public Art, 1992, Martha Rosler: In Place of the Public, 1994, Shari Zolla, 1997, Lyzabeth Bayard: 2 Installations, Light Into Art: From Video to Virtual Reality (also booklet), David Humphrey: Paintings and Drawings 1987-95 (also catalogue), others; author: The Misunderstood Patron, The National Endowment for the Arts; critic-in-residence Sch. Art, San Juan, PR; free lance art critic, Washington Post, Grapheion, Tema Celeste, & Sculpture, Cin. Enquirer; Grapheion; Art on Paper, Pitt. Post-Gazette, art critic in residence Delaware Contemporary Ctr. for the Arts, 1992, Mid-Atlantic Arts Fellow, 1991, No. Ill. U., 1997; corr. critic, regional editor Diaglogue, Columbus, Ohio, 1984-89; corr. critic Sculpture; contbr. articles to profl. jours. Active Dem. Party, Evanston, ward judge, 1977-78, precinct capt., 1977. Recipient Hunt Art award, 1977; Art Critics fellow Pa. Coun. on Arts, 1985, 89, 95, 99, 2000; rsch. fellow Smithsonian Inst., 1998, sr. rsch. fellow, 2000—; faculty rsch. grantee, 1985, 87, 89-90, 96-99, 2002, Grant Trust for Mut. Understanding, Rockefeller Found., 1994, Thendora Found., 1995; mem. tech. com., cmty. program scholar Pa. Humanities Coun., 1997; Nat. Mus. Am. Art, 2000, sr. rsch. fellow, short-term rsch. fellow Smithsonian Instn., Nat. Portrait Gallery, 2001; spl. initiatives grantee Pa. Coun. on Arts, 2000; grantee, IREX, 2000; rsch. fellow Inst. for Art History, Acad. Scis., Budapest, Hungary, 2002; fellow Ctrl. European Cultural Inst., 2002. Mem. Coll. Art Assn., Am. Assn. Mus., Assn. Historians Am. Art, Assn. Internat. Critics Art (Am. sect.), Art Table, Midwest Coll. Art Assn. Avocations: cooking, gardening, tennis, swimming, sailing. Office: Carnegie Mellon U Coll Fine Arts Pittsburgh PA 15213 Office Phone: 412-268-1970. Business E-Mail: ek06@andrew.cmu.edu. E-mail: eaking13@yahoo.com.

KING, SISTER ELEACE, special education services professional; b. Greenport, N.Y., Oct. 10, 1946; d. Gerald C. King and Alice Cecelia Ward. BA, Marywood Coll., 1969; MS, Yeshiva U., 1974; EdD, Johns Hopkins U., 1983. First grade tchr. St. John the Evangelist Sch., Scranton, Pa., 1969—70; spl. edn. tchr. Archdiocese of NY, New York, 1970—74; asst. prof. Marywood Coll., Scranton, 1974—86; sr. rsch. assoc. Ctr. Applied Rsch. Apostolate/Georgetown U., Washington, 1988—94; asst. supt. spl. edn. Diocese of Bridgeport, 1994—. Adv. bd. mem. St. Catherine Acad., Bridgeport, 1999—; bd. of trustees Nat. Cath. Partnership Disabilities, Washington, 2003—, treas. bd. trustees. Contbr. chapters to books. Adv. coun. mem. State Dept. Mental Retardation, Southwest Region, Conn., 1999—2000, mem., human rights com., 1998—2003. Scholar, The Inner-City Found. Charity and Edn., 1999—2004, Pitt Found., 2004. Mem.: Coun. Exceptional Children (assoc.), Nat. Cath. Edn. Assn. (assoc.). Roman Catholic. Achievements include Founder, St. Catherine Academy, a special education school for children with intellectual disabilities. Avocations: reading, knitting, walking. Office: Diocese of Bridgeport 238 Jewett Ave Bridgeport CT 06606 Office Phone: 203-372-4301 ext. 330. Office Fax: 203-372-1961. Personal E-mail: sreleace@aol.com. E-mail: srking@diobpt.org.

KING, EMILY WOTKYNS, elementary school educator; b. Denver, Mar. 20, 1952; d. Roger Sherman and Jackie Wotkyns; m. Larry A. King, June 8, 1974; 1 child, Jesse Stocker. PhD, U. Wyo., 2004. Curriculum instr. Natrona County Sch. Dist., Casper, Wyo., 1979—. Home: 1089 Horizon Dr Casper WY 82601 Office: Natrona County Sch Dist 970 N Glenn Rd Casper WY 82601 Office Phone: 307-577-0244. Office Fax: 307-261-6109.

KING, ERNEST WADE, law educator; b. Mobile, Ala., Sept. 20, 1959; s. Robert L. and Esther J. K.; m. Kerri Darlene Ishee, Dec. 17, 1988; children: Jessica Grace, Ernest Wade, Jr. BA, U. S. Fla., 1980; JD, Samford U., 1983; LLM, U. Miami, Fla., 1984. Bar: Fla. 1985, D.C. 1987. Assoc. prof. U. So. Miss., Hattiesburg, 1985—, dir. grad. bus. programs, 1995—99; mng. ptnr. Jude & Jude, PLLC, Hattiesburg. Spkr. in field. Contbr. articles to profl. jours.; reviewer jour. articles and software. Mem. ABA (vice chair eCommerce com., tort, trial and ins. practice sect.), Acad. Legal Studies Bus. (editor procs., newsletter ethics sect.), Southeastern Acad. Legal Studies Bus. (sec.-treas. 1993-94, v.p. 1994-95, pres.-elect, program chair 1995-96, pres. 1996-97). Republican. Baptist. Avocations: reading, writing, sports, music. Office: Jude & Jude Ste 50 6424 US Hwy 98 W Hattiesburg MS 39402

KING, GEORGE G., museum director; Attended, Bennington Coll.; BFA, Md. Inst. Coll. Art. Program dir. Cooper-Hewitt Nat. Design Mus., Smithsonian Instn., NYC; exec. dir. Katonah Mus. Art, NY; dir. Georgia O'Keeffe Mus., Santa Fe, 1998—. Avocations: art, photography. Office: Georgia O'Keeffe Mus 217 Johnson St Santa Fe NM 87501*

KING, GEORGE RALEIGH, retired manufacturing executive; b. Benton Harbor, Mich., May 13, 1931; s. Maurice Peter and Opal Ruth (Hart) King; m. Phyllis Stratton, July 30, 1950; children: Paula King Zang, Angela King Young, Philip. Student, Adrian Coll., 1950-51. Cert. purchasing profl. exec. status. With Kirsch Co., Sturgis, Mich., 1951—, data processing trainee, 1951-53, data processing mgr., 1953-59, asst. purchasing agt., 1959-62, purchasing agt., 1962-68, dir. purchasing, 1968-91, ret., 1991; corp. cons., 1991—. Author: Rods & Rings, 1972. Elder 1st Presbyn. Ch., Sturgis, 1970; pres. Sturgis Civic Players, 1972. Recipient citation Boy Scouts Am., 1966, Jr. Achievement, 1967; nominated candidate for adminstrn. Fed. Procurement Policy, Reagan Adminstrn., Washington, 1980. Mem. Am. Purchasing Soc. (pres. 1979-81), Nat. Assn. Purchasing Mgmt., southwestern Purchasing Assn., Exchange (pres. Sturgis 1959, dis. gov. dist. and nat. clubs 1961), Berrien Hills Country Club, Rotary (Lakeshore), Masons, Elks. Home: 1804 Lakeshore Dr Apt 16 Saint Joseph MI 49085-1616 Office Phone: 269-369-9279. Personal E-mail: kinggeorgemi@aol.com.

KING, GLEN (LENARD GLEN KING), broadcasting educator, composer; b. N.Y.C., Oct. 13, 1935; s. Lawrence Herbert and Marcia Helen (Berger) K.; m. Margaret Elizabeth Gabler, Aug. 26, 1989. BA, Calif. State U., L.A., 1960, MFA, 1964. Prodn. asst. Sta. KABC-TV, L.A., 1963-64; news asst. Sta. KTLA-TV, L.A., 1964-65; disc jockey Sta. KUTE, L.A., 1965-66, Sta. KFOX, L.A., 1966; instr. theater arts Elizabeth Seton Coll., Yonkers, N.Y., 1966-67; assoc. prof. broadcasting West L.A. Coll., Culver City, Calif.,

1977-84; prof. broadcasting Los Angeles Valley Coll., Van Nuys, Calif., 1985—95; founder Silver Kat Music BMI, 1985—. Supr. student cable internships West L.A. Coll., Culver City, Calif., 1980-85; designer broadcasting and TV aesthetics and documentary curriculums area colls.; owner, mgr. Silver Kat Music Pub. affiliate Broadcast Music Inc.; broadcast cons. CBS News, 1991, KMNY, 1992; prodr., dir. Pub. Access TV Adelphia Cable Co., Charlottesville, 1996-2000, dir. M.S. Telethon, 1996-98. Composer popular, country and gospel songs, 1976—. With USN, 1953-56, Republic of Korea. Winner internat. competition Song Writers Hall of Fame and N.Y. Music Pubs. Group, 1985; recipient 1st prize Am. Song Festival, L.A., 1976, Grand prize, 1979. Mem. BMI (affiliate), Nat. Music Pubs. Assn. Avocations: music, antiques, automobiles. E-mail: qualitysongs@yahoo.com.

KING, GREGORY C., petroleum company executive; b. N.Y.C., July 1, 1960; m. Leigh Ann King; children: Gregory Jr., Allison, Andrew, Carolyn. BBA in Finance, U. Tex., Austin, 1982; JD, U. Houston, 1985. Ptnr. Bracewell & Patterson, LLP, Houston, 1985-93; assoc. gen. counsel Valero Energy Corp., Houston, 1993-97, v.p., gen. counsel, 1997-99, sr. v.p., COO, 1999—2003, President, 2003—. Bd. dirs. Mission Rd. Devel. Ctr., San Antonio Zoo; mem. exec. com., trustee United Way of San Antonio and Bexar County. Mem. Tex. State Bar Assn. Office: Valero Energy Corp PO Box 500 San Antonio TX 78292-0500

KING, GUNDAR JULIAN, retired university dean; b. Riga, Latvia, Apr. 19, 1926; came to U.S., 1950, naturalized, 1954; s. Attis K. and Austra (Dale) Kenins: m. Valda K. Andersons, Sept. 18, 1954; children: John T., Marita A. Student, J.W. Goethe U., Frankfurt, Germany, 1946-48; BBA, U. Oreg., 1956; MBA, Stanford U., 1958, PhD, 1964; DSc (hon.), Riga Tech. U., 1991; D Habil. Oecon., Latvian Sci. Coun., 1992. Asst. field supr. Internat. Refugee Orgn., Frankfurt, 1948-50; br. office mfr. Williams Form Engrng. Corp., Portland, Oreg., 1952-54; project mgr. Market Rsch. Assocs., Palo Alto, Calif., 1958-60; asst. prof., assoc. prof. Pacific Luth. U., 1960-66, prof., 1966—, dean Sch. Bus. Adminstrn., 1970-90. Vis. prof. mgmt. U.S. Naval Postgrad. Sch., 1971-72, San Francisco State U., 1980, 1987-88; internat. econ. mem. Latvian Acad. Scis., 1990—; regent Estonian Bus. Sch., 1991-99; vis. prof. Riga Tech. U., 1993-97; dir. Baltic Studies fund, 1995—. Author: Economic Policies in Occupied Latvia, 1965, additional books on business, last five in Latvian, 1999—2004; contbr. articles to profl. publs. Mem. Gov.'s Com. Wash. State Govt., 1965-88; mem. study group on pricing U.S. Commn. Govt. Procurement, 1971-72; pres. N.W. Univs. Bus. Adminstrn. Conf., 1965-66. With AUS, 1950-52. Spidola prize Latvian Culture Found., 1999; Fulbright-Hayes scholar, Thailand, 1988, Fulbright scholar, Latvia, 1993-94. Mem. AAUP (past chpt. pres.), Am. Mktg. Assn. (past chpt. pres.), Assn. Advancement Baltic Studies (pres. 1970), Western Assn. Collegiate Schs. Bus. (pres. 1971), Latvian Acad. Scis., Alpha Kappa Psi, Beta Gamma Sigma. Home: PO Box 44401 Tacoma WA 98444-0401 Office: Pacific Lutheran U Tacoma WA 98447-0003 E-mail: Kingga@plu.edu.

KING, GWENDOLYN BAIR, retired legislative staff member; b. Hartsville, S.C., Oct. 27, 1915; d. William Parlor and Mary Margaret (Scurry) Bair; m. LaBruce Ward King, Dec. 26, 1937; children: John LaBruce King, Margaret Gwendolyn King Farrow. AB, Coker Coll., 1936. With asst. pers. office Libr. Congress, Washington, 1937-39; sec., dir. Libr. Congress, Union Catalog, Washington, 1939-43; asst. to appointments sec. for the President The White House, Washington, 1953-69, dir. correspondence for Pat Nixon, 1969-74; pub. speaker on White House career Calif., 1977—. Contbr. to Presidential Records, The Nat. Archives, Washington, 1988. Dir. Speakers' Bur., Home Hospice, Santa Rosa, Calif., 1985, cert. caregiver, 1982-84; mem. Oakmont Archtl. Com., Santa Rosa Symphony League. Named Paul Harris Fellow, Rotary Internat., 1983, Citizen of the Day, KABL, San Francisco, 1983. Mem. AAUW, Newcomers Club (pres. Santa Rosa chpt. 1977-78), Oakmont Book Club (chmn. 1981-82), Oakmont Golf Club (sec. 1986), Saturday Afternoon Club, Oakmont Classical Music Soc., PEO. Democrat. Avocations: golf, bridge, gardening, travel. Home: 201 White Oak Dr Santa Rosa CA 95409-6346

KING, GWENDOLYN S., retired utility company executive, retired federal official; b. East Orange, N.J. d. Frank M. and Henryne (Walker) Stewart; m. Colbert I. King. BA cum laude, Howard U., 1962; postgrad., George Washington U.; hon. doctorate, U. Md., 1990, U. New Haven, 1992. Legis. asst. to Sen. John Heinz, Washington, 1978-79; dir. Commonwealth of Pa. Office, Washington, 1979-86; dep. asst. to the pres. and dir. Office Intergovtl. Affairs, The White House, Washington, 1986-88; exec. v.p. Gogol & Assocs., 1988-89; commr. Social Security Adminstrn., Balt., 1989-92; sr. v.p. corp. and pub. affairs PECO Energy Corp., Phila., 1992-98; pres. Podium Prose, LLC, Washington. Bd. dirs. Lockheed Martin, Marsh & McLennan Cos., Monsanto Corp. Mem. Pres.'s Commn. to Strengthen Social Security, 2001. Recipient Drum Major for Justice award So. Christian Leadership Conf., 1990, Disting. Alumni award Howard U., 1991, Black Achievement Bus. and Fin. award Ebony Mag., 1992. Mem. Nat. Assn. Corp. Dirs. (bd. dirs.). Office: Podium Prose LLC Ste 1012 1025 Connecticut Ave NW Washington DC 20036

KING, HENRY LAWRENCE, lawyer; b. NYC, Apr. 29, 1928; s. H. Abraham and Henrietta (Prentky) K.; m. Barbara Hope, 1949 (dec. May 1962); children: Elizabeth King Robertson, Patricia King Cantlay (dec.), Matthew Harrison.; m. Alice Mary Sturges, Aug. 1, 1963 (div. 1978); children: Katherine Masury King Baccile, Andrew Lawrence, Eleanor Sturges; m. Margaret Gram, Feb. 14, 1981 AB, Columbia U., 1948; LLB, Yale U., 1951. Bar: N.Y. 1952, U.S. Supreme Ct., other fed. cts. 1952. With Davis Polk & Wardwell, N.Y.C., 1951—, ptnr., 1961—, mng. ptnr., chmn., 1982-96. Mng. editor Yale Law Jour., 1951. Trustee, chmn. bd. Columbia U., 1983-95, chmn. emeritus, 1995—; chmn. bd. Columiba Presbyn. adv. coun.; pres. Assn. Alumni Columbia Coll., 1966-68, Alumni Fedn. Columbia U., 1973-75; chmn. Coll. Fund, 1972-73; pres. Yale Law Sch. Assn., 1984-86, chmn., 1986-88; pres. Cathedral of St. John the Divine, N.Y.C.; bd. dirs. N.Y. Acad. of Medicine, Citizens for N.Y.C., Inc., Am. Skin Assn., Fishers Island Devel. Co.; vestryman Trinity Ch., N.Y.C., 1991-98; trustee Chapin Sch., 1977-89, Columbia U. Press, 1978-92. Recipient Columbia Alumni medal for conspicuous service, 1968, John Jay award, 1992. Fellow Am. Coll. Trial Lawyers; mem. ABA, Coun. on Fgn. Rels., Am. Law Inst., N.Y. State Bar Assn. (pres. 1988-89), Assn. Bar City N.Y., Am. Judicature Soc., Fishers Island Club, Century Assn., Union Club (N.Y.C.), Blind Brook Club, Fishers Island Yacht Club, Pilgrims, Church Club (N.Y.C.), Links Club. Home: 115 E 67th St New York NY 10021-5951 also: Box 657 East End Rd Fishers Island NY 06390 Office: Davis Polk & Wardwell 450 Lexington Ave 27th Fl New York NY 10017-3982 Office Phone: 212-450-4284. Business E-Mail: hking@dpw.com.

KING, HENRY SPENCER, III, lawyer; b. Charlotte, N.C., Feb. 7, 1941; s, Henry Spencer Jr. and Janie Pauline (Jenkins) K.; m. Ellen Frost Hayne, Aug. 31, 1963; children: Cheryl King Hay, Ann Lunsford King. BA with honors, Furman U., 1963; JD cum laude, U. S.C., 1968. Bar: S.C. 1963. Atty. Butler, Means, Evins & Browne, Spartanburg, S.C., 1968-78; ptnr. King and Hray, Spartanburg, 1978-92; shareholder Leatherwood Walker Todd & Mann, P.C., Greenville & Spartanburg, 1992—; city atty. City of Spartanburg, 1987—. Lt. col. U.S. Army, 1963-65. Mem. ABA, S.C. Bar Assn., Spartanburg Bar Assn., Am. Bd. Trial Advocates, Internat. Assn. Def. Counsel, S.C. Def. Trial Attys. (past bd. dirs.), Def. Rsch. Inst., Spartanburg Country Club (bd. dirs. 1982-86), Rotary Club, Sertoma (Sertoman of Yr. 1978). Home: 3 Cateswood Dr Spartanburg SC 29302-3464 Office: Leatherwood lWalker PO Box 3188 Spartanburg SC 29304-3188 E-mail: h.king.@lwtmlaw.com.

KING, IMOGENE M., retired nursing educator; b. West Point, Iowa, Jan. 30, 1923; Diploma, St. John's Hosp., 1945; BSN, St. Louis U., 1948, MSN, 1957; EdD, Columbia U., 1961; PhD (hon.), So. Ill. U., 1990, Loyola U., Chgo., 1998. Instr. med.-surg. nursing, asst. DON St. John's Hosp., St. Louis, 1947-58; from asst. prof. nursing to assoc. prof. Loyola U, Chgo., 1961-66, prof., dir. grad. program in nursing, 1972-80; prof. U. South Fla., Tampa, 1980-90, dir. rsch., 1982-85, prof. emeritus, 1990—. Asst. chief rsch. grants br. div. nursing HEW, Washington, 1966-68; prof., dean sch. nursing Ohio State U., Columbus, 1968-72; def. adv. com. on women in svcs. Dept. Def., 1972-75; adj. prof. U. Miami Sch. Nursing, 1986-89; cons. VA Hosp., health care agencies. Author: Toward a Theory for Nursing, 1971, transl. to Japanese, 1975, A Theory for Nursing: Systems, Concepts, Process, 1981, transl. to Japanese, 1983, transl. to Spanish, 1985, Curriculum and Instruction in Nursing, 1986; mem. editl. bd. Theoria: The Journal of Nursing Theorica, Malmo, Sweden; contbr. articles to profl. jours., chpts. to books. Alderman, chmn. fin. com. Ward 2, Wood Dale, Ill., 1975-79; bd. dirs. operation PAR Inc., Pinellas County, Fla., 1990-92. Recipient Founders award St. Louis U., 1969, Recognition of Contbns. to Nursing Edn. award Columbia U. Tchrs. Coll., 1983, Disting. Scholar award U. So. Fla., 1988-89, Award for Outstanding Cmty. Svc. U. Tampa, 1997, Imogene King Rsch. award U. Tampa, 1997, Fla. Gov.'s medal for contbn. to nursing and health care, 1997, Dirs. award Fla. League Nursing, 1997. Fellow Am. Acad. Nursing (hon., inducted Living Legends 2005); mem. ANA (conv. lectr. 1996, Jessie M. Scott award 1996, ANA Hall of Fame award 2004), Ill. Nurses Assn. (highest recognition award 1975, award 19th dist. 1975), Fla. Nurses Assn. (life, dir. region 2 1981-83, 2d v.p. 1983-85, bd. dirs. 1997-2001, Nurse of Yr. 1984, Nursing Rsch. award 1985, FNA Hall of Fame award 2003), Dist. IV Fla. Nurses Assn. (del. to Fla. Nurses Assn. 1981—, pres.-elect 1982-83, del. to ANA conv. 1982—, pres. 1983-84, Advancing the Nursing Profl. award), Fla. Nurses Found. (sec. 1986-88, pres. 1988-91), Sigma Theta Tau (counselor Delta Beta chpt. 1981-83, pres.-elect 1986-87, pres. 1987-89, disting. lectr. 1990-91, co-chmn. biennial conv. 1991, nominating com. 1993-95, Founders award for excellence in nursing edn. 1989) Sigma Theta Tau (Virginia Henderson fellow 1993), Phi Kappa Phi (scholar award 1988) Personal E-mail: imkn@earthlink.net. *Develop a healthy self-concept and know thyself. Practice the Golden Rule. Be honest and sincere in working with individuals and groups. Live each day to the best of your ability.*

KING, IVAN ROBERT, astronomy educator; b. Far Rockaway, N.Y., June 25, 1927; s. Myram and Anne King; m. Alice Greene, Nov. 21, 1952 (div. 1982); children: David, Lucy, Adam, Jane; m. Judith Schultz, Apr. 20, 2002. AB, Hamilton Coll., 1946; AM, Harvard U., 1947, PhD, 1952; Laurea Honoris Causa (hon.), U. Padua (Italy), 2002. Instr. astronomy Harvard U., 1951—52; mathematician Perkin-Elmer Corp., Norwalk, Conn., 1951—52; methods analyst U.S. Dept. Def., Washington, 1954—56; with U. Ill., 1956—64; assoc. prof. astronomy U. Calif., Berkeley, 1964—66, prof., 1966—93, chmn. astronomy dept., 1967—70, prof. emeritus, 1993—; rsch. prof. U. Wash., Seattle, 2002—. Mem. faint object camera team Hubble Space Telescope. Contbr. numerous articles to sci. jours. Served with USNR, 1952-54. Fellow AAAS (chmn. astronomy sect. 1974), NAS, Am. Acad. Arts & Scis., Am. Astron. Soc. (councillor 1963-66, chmn. divsn. dynamical astronomy 1972-73, pres. 1978-80), Internat. Astron. Union. Achievements include research on study of stellar systems. Office: U Wash Dept Astronomy Seattle WA 98195-1580 Business E-Mail: king@astro.washington.edu.

KING, JAMES C., military officer; b. Mar. 18, 1946; BS in Polit. Sci., Utah State U.; MS in Pub. Adminstrn., U. Mo., Kansas City; grad., Command and Gen. Staff Coll., Army War Coll. Commd. 2d lt. U.S. Army, 1968, advanced through grades to lt. gen., 1998, various assignments, 1968-88; chief mil. intelligence br. U.S. Total Army Personnel Command, Alexandria, Va., 1988-89; chief intelligence, electronic warfare and reconnaissance Office of Dep. Chief of Staff for Ops. and Plans, Washington, 1989-90; comdr. 66th Mil. Intelligence Brigrade, Europe and Germany, 1990-92; exec. officer to dep. chief of staff for intelligence U.S. Army, Washington, 1992; chief of ops. and targeting group Nat. Security Agy., Ft. Meade, Md., 1993-94; dir. intelligence U.S. Ctrl. Command, MacDill AFB, Fla., 1994-96; dir. for intelligence Jt. Staff, Washington, 1996—; dir. Nat. Imagery and Mapping Agy., Bethesda, 1998—2001; ret., 2001.

KING, JAMES CECIL, language educator; b. Uniontown, Pa., Sept. 14, 1924; s. Joseph Herbert and Eliza Ann (Kelley) K.; m. Diana Hanbury, Sept. 5, 1952 (div. Apr. 1958); children— Christopher Hanbury, Sheila Anne. BA, George Washington U., 1949, MA, 1950, PhD, 1954. Master for French, German and Latin St. Albans Sch. for Boys, Washington, 1952-55; asst. prof. German George Washington U., 1955-60, asso. prof., 1960-65, prof., 1965-90, prof. emeritus, 1990—. Rschr. Langs.-of-the-World Archives, 1960-61. Editor (with Petrus W. Tax) of series Die Werke Notkers des Deutschen, 1972—. Served with U.S. Army, 1943—46. German Acad. Exch. Svc. grantee, 1963. Mem. Linguistic Soc. Am., Medieval Acad. Am., Am. Assn. Tchrs. German, MLA, Am. Goethe Soc., Soc. Germanic Linguistics, AAUP, Phi Beta Kappa. Home: 9296 Bailey Ln Fairfax VA 22031-1930

KING, JAMES EDWARD, retired museum director, consultant; b. Escanaba, Mich., July 23, 1940; s. G. Willard and Grace (Magee) K.; m. Frances Bartos, Jan. 15, 1973; 1 child, Scott E. BS, Alma Coll., 1962; MS, U. N.Mex., 1964; PhD, U. Ariz., 1972. Lab asst. in biology Alma Coll., Mich., 1960-62; rsch. asst. dept. biology U. N.Mex., Albuquerque, 1962-64; teaching asst. dept. botany and plant pathology Mich. State U., East Lansing, 1964-66; plant industry inspector Mich. Dept. Agriculture, Lansing, 1966-68; rsch. asst. dept. geochronology U. Ariz., Tucson, 1968-71, rsch. assoc. dept. geoscis., 1971-72; assoc. curator paleobotany Ill. State Mus., Springfield, 1972-78, head sci. sects. and full curator, 1978-85, asst. dir. for sci., 1985-87; adj. assoc. prof. dept. geology U. Ill., Urbana, 1979-88; dir. Carnegie Mus. Natural History, Pitts., 1987-96, Cleve. Mus. Natural History, 1996—2001; mus. cons., 2001—. Adj. prof. biology Sangamon State U., Springfield, Ill., 1983-87; adj. rsch. scientist Hunt Inst. Bot. Documentation, Carnegie Mellon U., Pitts., 1988—; adj. prof. dept. geology and planetary sci., U. Pitts., 1988-96; vis. scientist in residence Alma (Mich.) Coll., 1985. Author sci. papers on topics related to geology and paleobotany; mem. editorial bd. Jour. Archaeol. Sci., 1980-87. Bd. dirs. Western Pa. Conservancy, 1996-97, Allegheny Land Trust, 1995-96; trustee Chagrin River Watershed Ptnrs., 1997—; mem. exec. com. Univ. Cir., Inc., 1996—. Fellow Ill. State Acad. Sci. (pres. 1981-82); mem. Am. Assn. Mus. (bd. dirs. 1994-97), Am. Quaternary Assn., (treas., exec. com. 1976-84), Am. Assn. Stratigraphic Palynologists, Assn. Sci. Mus. Dirs. (v.p. 1992-93, pres. 1993-96), Assn. Systematics Collections (v.p. 1989-91, pres. 1991-93), Sigma Xi (pres. Springfield chpt. 1985-86). Home and Office: Ste 326 6336 N Oracle Rd Tucson AZ 85704

KING, JAMES FORREST, JR., lawyer; b. Salina, Kans., Jan. 9, 1949; s. James Forrest Sr. and Carolyn (Prout) K.; m. Mary Lou A. Goodwin, May 18, 1985; 1 child, James Forrest King III. BA, U. Md., 1970; JD with honors, George Washington U., 1974. Bar: D.C. 1975, U.S. Dist. Ct. D.C. 1976, U.S. Ct. Appeals (D.C. cir.) 1977, U.S. Supreme Ct. 1979, Md. 1982, U.S. Ct. Appeals (4th cir.) 1985. Atty. Law Offices of Washington, 1975-76; ptnr. Reuss, McConville & King, Washington, 1976-80, Reuss, Herndon, McConville & King, Washington, 1980-85; of counsel Herndon, McConville, Brown, Teller & Hessler, Washington, 1986-87; ptnr. Law Offices of James Forrest King, Washington, 1987—. Mem., bd. dirs. Family Ct. Trial Lawyers Assn., Dist. Col. Superior Ct., 2001—. Commr. D.C. Commn. Human Rights, 1984-90. Mem. Am. Arbitration Assn. (panel mem.), ABA (econs. law practice sect.), Superior Ct. Trial Lawyers Assn. (bd. dirs. 1997—), DC Bar Assn. (co-chmn. divsn. 6, 1981-84, arbitration bd. 1981-83, employment discrimination panel, 1977-80). Office Phone: 202-543-1993. E-mail: jkinglaw@msn.com.

KING, JAMES LAWRENCE, federal judge; b. Miami, Fla., Dec. 20, 1927; s. James Lawrence and Viola (Clodfelter) K.; m. Mary Frances Kapa, June 1, 1961; children— Lawrence Daniel, Kathryn Ann, Karen Ann, Mary Virginia BA in Edn., U. Fla., 1949, JD, 1953; LHD (hon.), St. Thomas U., 1992. Bar: Fla. 1953. Assoc. Sibley & Davis, Miami, Fla., 1953-57; ptnr. Sibley Giblin King & Levenson, Miami, 1957-64; judge 11th Jud. Cir. Dade County, Miami, 1964-70; temp. assoc. justice Supreme Ct. Fla., 1965; temp. assoc. judge Fla. Ct. Appeals (2d, 3d and 4th dist.), 1965-68; judge U.S. Dist. Ct. (so. dist.) Fla., Miami, 1970-84, chief judge, 1984-91, sr. judge, 1991—. Temp. judge U.S. Ct. Appeals 5th cir., 1977-78; mem. Jud. Conf. U.S., 1984-87, mem. adv. commn. jud. activities, 1973-76, mem. joint commn. code jud. conduct, 1974-76, mem. commn. to consider stds. for admission to practice in fed. cts., 1976-79, chmn. implementation com. for admission attys. to fed. practice, 1979-85, mem. com. bankruptcy legis., 1977-78; mem. Jud. Conf. U.S., 1984-87; mem. Jud. Coun. 11th Cir., 1989-92; pres. 5th cir. U.S. Dist. Judges Assn., 1977-78; chief judge U.S. Dist. Ct. C.Z., 1977-78; long range planning commn. Fed. Judiciary, 1991-95. Mem. state exec. council U. Fla., 1956-59; mem. Bd. Control Fla. Governing State Univs. and Colls., 1964. Served to 1st lt. USAF, 1953-55 Recipient Outstanding Alumnus award U. Fla. Law Rev., 1980, Lifetime Achievement award Greater Miami Jewish Fedn. Commerce and Professions Attys. Divsn., 1992, 18th Annual Edward J. Devitt Disting. Svc. to Justice award, 2000; The James Lawrence King Fed. Justice Bldg. named in his honor U.S. Congress, 1996. Mem. Fla. Bar Assn. (pres. jr. bar 1963-64, bd. govs. 1958-63, Merit award young lawyer sect. 1967), ABA, Am. Law Inst., Inst. Jud. Adminstrn., Fla. Blue Key, Pi Kappa Tau, Phi Delta Phi Democrat. Home: 11950 SW 67th Ct Miami FL 33156-4756 Office: US Dist Ct James Lawrence King Fed Justice Bldg 99 NE 4th St Rm 1127 Miami FL 33132-2139

KING, JAMES M., lawyer; b. Denver, Colo., July 17, 1948; BSEE with spl. honors, Univ. Colo., 1970, JD, 1976. Bar: Colo. 1976, U.S. Ct. Appeals tenth cir. 1979, U.S. Ct. Appeals ninth cir. 1984. Law clk. Colo. Ct. Appeals, 1976—77; ptnr. Baker & Hostetler, Denver, 1977—. Pres. Rocky Mountain Mineral Law Found. Mem.: ABA, Colo. Bar Assn., Tau Beta Pi, Order of the Coif. Office: Baker & Hostetler Suite 1100 303 E 17 Ave Denver CO 80203-1264

KING, JANE CUDLIP COBLENTZ, volunteer educator; b. Iron Mountain, Mich., May 4, 1922; d. William Stacey and Mary Elva (Martin) Cudlip; m. George Samuel Coblentz, June 8, 1942 (dec. June 1989); children: Bruce Harper, Keith George, Nancy Allison Coblentz Patch; m. James E. King, August 23, 1991 (dec. Jan. 1994). BA, Mills Coll., 1942. Mem. Sch. Resource and Career Guidance Vols., Inc., Atherton, Calif., 1965-69, pres., CEO, 1969—. Exec. asst. to dean of admissions Mills Coll., 1994-99. Proofreader, contbr. Mills Coll. Quarterly mag. Life gov. Royal Children's Hosp., Melbourne, Australia, 1963—; pres. United Menlo Park (Calif.) Homeowner's Assn., 1994—; nat. pres. Mills Coll. Alumnae Assn., 1969-73, bd. trustees, 1975-83; bd. govs. Mills Coll. Alumnae Assn., 1966-73, 75-83, 98-2000, v.p., 2001—. Named Vol. of Yr., Sequoia Union H.S. Dist., 1988, Disting. Woman Mid-Peninsula (forerunner San Mateo County Women's Hall of Fame), 1975; recipient Golden Acorn award for Outstanding Cmty. Svc., Menlo Park C. of C., 1991. Mem. AAUW (Menlo-Atherton br. pres. 1994-96, v.p. programs 1996-97, editor Directory and Acorn, 1994—), Atherlons, Palo Alto (Calif.) Area Mills Coll. Club (pres. 1986), Phi Beta Kappa. Episcopalian. Avocations: reading, gardening.

KING, JANEY HAMPTON, retired music educator, vocalist; b. Port Saint Joe, Fla., Aug. 14, 1941; d. Howell Morton Hampton, Jr. and Mildred Francis Hampton; m. Richard Byron Robbins (div. Feb. 14, 1967); children: Richard Robbins, Michael Robbins; m. Fred Harlan King, Dec. 18, 1971. AA, Pensacola (Fla.) Jr. Coll., 1965—68; BA, U. W. Fla., Penscol, 1970; Master of Arts, University Of West Florida, Pensacola, Florida, 1976—78. Cert. tchr. Fla., 1970. Tchr. choral dir. Pensacola (Fla.) Acad. of Arts and Scis., 1970—75; adjunct voice instr. U. West Fla., Pensacola, 1975—77; teacher/choral dir. Englewood HS, Jacksonville, Fla., 1979—89, Mayport Middle Sch., Atlantic Beach, Fla., 1988—99, LaVilla Sch. of the Arts, Jacksonville, 2000—04; private voice tchr. Home, Various Cities, Fla., 1968—2004; ret. Childrens, youth, and adult ch. choir dir. Fla. Chs., 1960—89; conductor/clinician Duval All County Elem. Chorus, Jacksonville, 1999; asst. conductor North Fla. Women's Chorale, Jacksonville, 1992—98; junior high/middle school coordinator Florida Vocal Association, Fl, 1997—99; conductor/ clinician Pasco County, New Port Richey, Fla., 2000; jr. high/ middle sch. coord, district 4 Fla. Vocal Assn., Jacksonville, 1999—. Singer: (opera) Don Giovanni, 1970; performer (singer): (with) Fla. Women's Chorale Group, 1992—96. Mem. adv. panel Jacksonville (Fla.) Childrens Chorus Edn., 2000—01. Recipient Leadership Award, Pensacola Jr. Coll., 1968, Second Place, Rose Tensie-Palmer Opera Auditions, Mobile, Alabama, 1970, Choral Groups have been Awarded Outstanding Choirs in numerous national competitions, "Music in the Parks", "Music Festivals, USA", "Musicfest, Orlando", 1995,1996, 1997, 2001, Choral Group Invited to Sing in Washington, D.C. (did perform), Music Celebrations, Internat., 1998, Choral Group invited to Sing in England (did perfom), 1999, Current Choral Group invited to perform in Austria, 2001 - 2002. Mem.: Nat. Fellowship of Meth. Musicians (sec./treas. 1965—66), Fla. Vocal Assn., Fla. Music Educators Assn., Music Educators Nat. Conv., Nat. Assn. Tchrs. of Singing, Am. Choral Dirs. Assn. (life), Pensacola Oratorio Soc. (sec. 1965—66), Jacksonville Heritage Singers, Jacksonville Art Singers (pres. 1986—87). Presbyterian. Avocations: interior decorating, singing, travel. Home: 600 Pine Street Jacksonville FL 32266 Office: Lavilla Sch Of The Arts 501 North Davis Street Jacksonville FL 32202 Personal E-mail: soprano@bellsouth.net. Business E-Mail: king_j@firn.edu.

KING, JASON ERIC, medical educator, researcher; b. Ft. Worth, Tex., Aug. 8, 1970; s. James Garfield and Delaine King. BA, Harding U., 1993; PhD, Tex. A&M U., 2000. Rsch. assoc. Office of Continuing Med. Edn. Baylor Coll. Medicine, Houston, 2000—03; adj. prof. dept. tech. and cognition U. North Tex., Denton, 2002—; asst. dir. office of continuing med. edn. Baylor Coll. Medicine, 2003—, asst. prof. dept. family and cmty. medicine, 2003—. Statis. cons., College Station, 1995—2000; dir. ednl. rsch. exch. student conf. Tex. A&M U., 1997—98; mem. web-based evaluation subcom. of info. tech. in edn. com. Baylor Coll. Medicine, 2001—02, mem. tech. in support of curriculum needs of edn. subcom., 2002, mem. longitudinal curriculum evaluation task force, 02, mem. curriculum evaluation com., 2003—, mem. statis. procedure and rev. subcom. of curriculum evaluation com., 2003—, mem. acad. of disting. educators grant rev. com., 2004—; mem., compensation survey subcommittee Tex. Alliance for Continuing Med. Edn., Tex., 2004—; presenter in field. Contbr. articles to profl. jours. Recipient Fox award, Soc. for Acad. Continuing Med. Edn., 2003, William Campbell Felch/Wyeth award, Alliance for Continuing Med. Edn., 2005. Mem.: APA, Nat. Coun. on Measurement in Edn., Am. Ednl. Rsch. Assn., Alliance for Continuing Med. Edn., Phi Kappa Phi, Kappa Delta Pi, Phi Eta Sigma, Psi Chi, Alpha Chi. Ch. Of Christ. Avocations: racquetball, golf, fishing. Office: Baylor Coll Medicine One Baylor Plz MS: BCM155 Houston TX 77030-3411 Office Phone: 713-798-8547. Office Fax: 713-798-6516. E-mail: jasonk@bcm.tmc.edu.

KING, JEFFREY PATTERSON, lawyer; b. Austin, Nov. 8, 1954; BA, Coll. William and Mary, 1976; MBA, JD, Duke U., 1980. Bar: Tex. 1980. Assoc. Haynes and Boone, Dallas, 1980-87, ptnr., health care, 1988—, chair health care sect., 1993—. Mem. campaign cabinet Austin United Way, 2001, 2002, 2003; gen. counsel, exec. com. Greater Austin C. of C., 2005; bd. dir. Eanes Edn. Found., Lifework Inc. Mem.: Am. Health Lawyers Assn., ABA (bus. law sect., health law sect.), State Bar of Texas (bus. law sect., health law sect., administrv. law sect., regulatory practice sect.). Office: Haynes and Boone LLP 600 Congress Ave Ste 1300 Austin TX 78701 Office Phone: 512-867-8413. Office Fax: 512-867-8633. Business E-Mail: jeff.king@haynesboone.com.

KING, JENNIFER JEAN, psychotherapist; d. Lee and Bobbi Jean King. BS, Vanderbilt U., 1999; MA, Mich. State U., 2001—01; PhD, Tex. A&M U., 2005. Spl. edn. tchg. asst. Hawaii Dept. Edn., Honolulu, 1996; resident advisor dept. housing and residential edn. Vanderbilt U., Nashville, 1997—98, head resident, 1998—99; counselor Nashville Crisis Intervention Ctr., Nashville, 1998—99; asst. hall dir. dept. residence life Mich. State U., East Lansing, 1999—2000; career counselor Mich. Dept. Career Devel., Lansing, Mich., 2000—01; counselor Mich. State U. Employee Assistance Program, East Lansing, Mich., 2000—01; tng. dir. asst. dept. counseling psychology Tex. A&M U., College Station, 2001—02, dean's asst., 2002, therapist Student Counseling Svcs., 2003, instr., group counselor dept. ednl. psychology, 2003, counselor dept. ednl. psychology, 2003—04, svc. coord. Counselling and Assessment Clinic Bryan, 2002—04, assessment therapist Counseling and Assessment Clinic, 2002—04; counselor Sherwood Health Care Facility, Bryan, Tex., 2002—03; assessment therapist Navasota (Tex.)

Inpatient Behavioral Health Unit, 2003; psychotherapist U. Fla. Counseling Ctr., Gainesville, 2004—. Cons. Internat. Student Ho. at Weaver Hall U. Fla., Gainesville, 2004—05; cons. U. Fla. Counseling Ctr., Gainesville, 2005; clin. supr. and cons. dept. ednl. psychology Tex. A&M U., College Station, 2003—04; med. residents cons. Tex. A&M U. Med. Sch., College Station, 2003—04. Contbr. articles to profl. jours., papers to conf. exhbns. Amb. APA, Honolulu, 2003—04, Toronto, 2002—03; svc. provider U. Fla. Trauma Response Team, Gainesville, 2004—05; mentor Aggie Women in Leadership, College Station, 2003—04. Scholar, USAF Aid Soc., 1995—99, Hawaii Cmty. Found., 1995—2001, Marion Maccarrell Scott Found., 1995—2005; Hawaii Veterans Meml. Fund scholar, Hawaii Veterans Assn., 1999—2005. Mem.: APA, Tex. Psychol. Assn., Fla. Psychol. Assn., Am. Coll. Pers. Assn., Internat. Honor Soc., Phi Kappa Phi, Psi Chi, Kappa Delta Pi. Avocations: travel, trombone, tennis, hiking, bowling.

KING, JERRY WAYNE, research chemist; b. Indpls., Feb. 19, 1942; s. Ernest E. and Miriam (Sanders) K.; m. Bettie Maria Dunbar, Aug. 8, 1965; children: Ronald Sean, Valerie Raquel, Diana Lynn. BS, Butler U., 1965; PhD, Northeastern U., 1976. Rsch. chemist Union Carbide Corp., Bound Brook, NJ, 1968-70; asst. prof. dept. chemistry Va. Commonwealth U., Richmond, 1974-76; rsch. scientist Arthur D. Little, Inc., Cambridge, Mass., 1976-77; rsch. assoc. Am. Can Co., Barrington, Ill., 1977-79; rsch. scientist CPC Internat., Summit-Argo, Ill., 1979-86; lead scientist NCAUR-ARS divsn. USDA, Peoria, Ill., 1986—2002; program mgr. chem. divsn. Los Alamos Lab., 2002—05; Ansel and Virginia Condray Disting. prof. chem. engrng. U. Ark., Fayetteville, 2005—. Guest lectr. in field; v.p. Supercritical Confs.; adj. prof. depts. food sci. and chem. engrng., U. Ark., 2004. Mem. editl. bd. Jour. Am. Oil Chemists' Soc., Italian Jour. Food Sci., Jour. Supercritical Fluids, Supercritical Fluid Sci. and Tech. Series; contbr. articles to profl. jours. Recipient Scientist of Yr. award Nat. Ctr. Agrl. Utilization Rsch., Agrl. Rsch. Svc., USDA, 1993, Chgo. Chromatography Discussion Group Merit award, 1995, 8th Internat. Symposium on Supercritical Fluid Chromatography and Extraction excellence award, 1998, Merit award Midwest & Tri-State Supercritical Fluid Discussion Group, 1998, Rsch. award for supercritical fluids commercialization Thar Designs, 1998, Underwood Fund award Biotech. and Biol. Scis. Rsch. Coun., U.K., 1998, 1st Pl. award for consumer products Fed. Lab. Consortium for Tech. Transfer-Midwest Area, 2001, honorable mention award for health and medicine, 2001; named v.p. Supercritical Confs.; fellow Georgetown U., 1973-74. Mem. Assn. Ofcl. Analytical Chemists (Harvey W. Wiley award 1997, Keene P. Dimick award Pitts. conf. 2000), Inst. Food Technologists, Am. Oil Chemists Soc. (Herbert J. Dutton award 2003), Am. Chem. Soc., Assn. Advancement of Indsl. Crops, Acad. Georgofili (Italy, corr.), Internat. Soc. for Advancement of Supercritial Fluids, Soc. Chem. Industry (Eng.), Am. Assn. Cereal Chemists European Union Brussels (Marie Curie chair). Home: 1820 W Sunnyview Dr Peoria IL 61614-4662 Office: Univ Ark Dept Chem Engring 3202 Bell Engineering Ctr Fayetteville AR 72701 Office Phone: 479-575-5979. Business E-Mail: jwking1@uark.edu.

KING, J.L., writer; 3 children. National HIV/AIDS prevention activist; CEO Lillie Mae King Found. Consultant several national health orgs. Named one of 50 most Intriguing African Am., Ebony Magazine, 2004. Achievements include citations in over 100 magazines including Jet, Ebony, Sister to Sister Magazine, People, New York Times Magazine, and Essence Magazine; television guest appearances on Oprah Winfrey Show, PBS, BET, The Discovery Network, and CNN. Office: Speakers Etc PO Box 8308 Inglewood CA 90308-8308 Office Phone: 310-671-7136. Office Fax: 310-677-7981.*

KING, JOAN CALUDA, medical educator, neuroscientist; b. New Orleans, Mar. 6, 1938; BS, St. Mary's Dominican Coll., 1961; MS, U. New Orleans, 1970; PhD, Tulane U., 1973. Rsch. assoc. in neuroanatomy U. Iowa Coll. Medicine, Iowa City, 1973-74; NIH postdoctoral fellow (neurosci.) Tulane U., New Orleans, 1974-76, rsch. assoc., vis. asst. prof. neurosci., 1976-79; asst. prof. anatomy Tufts U. Sch. Medicine, Boston, 1979-85, assoc. prof. anatomy and cellular biology, 1985-92, prof., chmn. anatomy and cellular biology, 1992-97, dir. reproductive ctr., 1992-97, prof. emeritus, 1997—. Mem. many nat. rev. coms., NSF, NIH, NICHD, 1979—. Co-author: Exploring the Basic Structures of the Brain, 1991, A Responsive Learning Environment for Medical Neurosciences: Sensory and Motor Pathways in the Spinal Cord, 1991; contbr. articles to profl. jours., chpts. to books; presenter in field; invited participant in numerous rsch. seminars and symposia; editl. bd. Biotechniques; ad hoc reviewer Science, Nature, Biology of Reproduction, Brain Rsch., Brain Rsch. Bull., Endocrinology, Jour. Histochemistry Cytochemistry, Jour. Neurosci., Neuroendocrinology, Neurosci., Peptides. Recipient Career Devel. award USPHS, 1979-84. Mem. Am. Assn. Anatomists, Internat. Soc. Psychoneuroendocrinology, Soc. Neurosci., Endocrine Soc. (animal welfare subcom. 1989), Kappa Delta Pi. Office: 14640 Swanson Ranch Rd Loveland CO 80538-9144

KING, JOHN ALLAN, JR., history professor; b. Miami, July 9, 1972; s. John Allan and Conchita Duca King. BA with high honors, MA, Emory U., 1993; PhD, Vanderbilt U., 1998. Asst. prof. Belmont U., Nashville, 1998—99; Advanced Placement history instr. Ransom Everglades Sch., Miami, 1999—, acad. dean, 2002—; adj. prof. Barry U., 2003—. Cons. AP coll. bd., 1998—. Author: The President's Position, Debating the Issues: The Cold War Presidents, 2005; contbr. chapters to books. Mem.: World History Assn., Orgn. Am. Historians, Am. Hist. Assn. Avocations: music, sports. Home: 555 NE 34th St #703 Miami FL 33137 Office: Ransom Everglades Sch 3575 Main Hwy Miami FL 33133 Office Phone: 305-460-8230. Fax: 305-460-2119. E-mail: jking@ransomeverglades.org.

KING, JOHN CHARLES PETER, editor, writer; b. Vancouver, B.C., Can., Dec. 13, 1949; s. Charles and Pauline K.; m. Jennifer; children: Sheila, James. BA, York U., 1973. Mem. staff The Globe and Mail Ltd., Toronto, 1970—2004, night city editor, 1973-75; bur. chief Ottawa, Can., 1975-78; nat. editor Toronto, 1978-81; bur. chief Washington, 1981-84; assoc. editor Report on Bus., Toronto, 1984-87, exec. editor, 1987-93; dep. mng. editor The Globe and Mail, 1993-99, dir. editl. prodn., 1999—2003, dir. editl. tech., 2003—04. Dir. Can. Mng. Editors Conf., 1997-98, v.p., 1998-99. Akela 65th Toronto Wolf Cub Pack, 2002—04; skipper 65th Toronto Sea Scouts, 2004—. Spanish lang. fellow Nat. Press Found., 1987; Thomson scholar, 1987. Mem. Can. Assn. Newspapers Editors (pres. 1999-2000), Toronto Press Club.

KING, JOHN ETHELBERT, JR., retired academic administrator; b. Oklahoma City, r, July 29, 1913; s. John Ethelbert and Iosa (Koontz) K.; m. Glennie Beanland, Dec. 25, 1936; children: Wynetka Ann King Reynolds, Rebecca Ferriss King Stevens. BA, N. Tex. U., 1932; MS, U. Ark., 1937; PhD, Cornell U., 1941; LLD (hon.), Coll. of Ozarks, 1965; LHD (hon.), No. Mich. U., 1966, U. SC, 1988. Latin tchr., coach Frisco (Tex.) Pub. High Sch., 1933-35; missionary to Native Ams. Presbyn. Ch. U.S.A., Okla., Ariz., 1938-43; asst. prof. N.Y. State Coll. Agr., Cornell U., Ithaca, 1945-47; acad. dean, provost, prof. U. Minn., Duluth, 1947-53; pres., prof. Emporia (Kans.) U., 1953-66; prof., pres. U. Wyo., Laramie, 1966-67; prof., chmn. dept. So. Ill. U., Carbondale, 1967-83; Disting. vis. prof., interim dean U. S.C., Columbia, 1984-90; ret., 1990. Ednl. adviser Civilian Conservation Corps, U.S. Forest Svc., Ozone, Ark., 1935-37; mentor Assn. Governing Bds. Univs. and Coll., Washington, 1977-90. Editor: Work and the College Student, 1967, Money, Marbles and Chalk, 1978. Life trustee U. Ozarks, Clarksville, Ark., 1965—. Officer USN, 1943-45, PTO. Recipient Disting. Alumnus award N. Tex. U., Denton, 1965, U. Ark., Fayetteville, 1983. Mem. NEA (life), Am. Assn. Colls. Tchr. Edn. (pres. 1966-67), Rotary, Blue Key, Omicron Delta Kappa, Lambda Chi Alpha, Sphinx Club, Phi Delta Kappa. Avocations: history, Native American Studies. Personal E-mail: texasglennie@aol.com.

KING, JOHN JOSEPH, manufacturing company executive; b. Toledo, Jan. 12, 1924; s. Walter and Frances (Gwozd) Kawecka; m. Joy G. Mohler, Jan. 28, 1950; children: Catherine M., Carolyn S., David J., Michael R., Mark A.R. BSME magna cum laude, U. Toledo, 1957, MS in Indsl. Engring., 1961. Registered profl. engr., Ohio. Draftsman, Tecumseh Products Co., 1941-42; die designer Bingham Stamping Co., 1942-46; tool designer Spicer Mfg. Co., 1946-47; product designer Am. Floor Surfacing Co., 1947-50; founder, mgr. engr. Kent Industries, 1950-52; mech. engr. Owens Ill. Inc., Toledo, 1953-63; mgr. rsch. and devel. Permaglass Inc., Genoa, Ohio, 1963-69; founder, pres. Ashur Inc., Rossford, Ohio, 1969—, also chmn. bd. dirs. Patentee in field. Mem. Am. Ceramic Soc., Soc. Mfg. Engrs., Phi Kappa Phi, Tau Beta Pi. Republican. Roman Catholic. Clubs: Devils Lake Yacht. Lodges: KC, Eagles. Home: 1111 W Elm Tree Rd Rossford OH 43460-1338 Office: Ashur Inc 28663 Glenwood Rd Perrysburg OH 43551-3011

KING, JOSEPH BERTRAM, architect; b. Greenville, S.C., Sept. 14, 1924; s. Joseph A. and Bertram (Kerns) K.; m. Julia Nelson Hipps, Aug. 2, 1945; children: Allen, David, Thomas. Student, Memphis State Coll., 1943; B in Arch. Engring., N.C. State U., 1949. Prin. J. Bertram King, Asheville, N.C., 1952-94. Chmn. Planning and Zoning Commn., Asheville, 1966—; vice chmn. Met. Planning Bd., 1966-74 Prin. works include Humanities, Social Sci., Art and Mgmt. bldgs., residence hall, student center, U. N.C.-Asheville, occupational edn. bldg, Asheville High Sch., Bank of Asheville, Madison County High Sch, City-County Central Library Bldg, Reynolds High Sch, Sealtest Dairies. Bd. dirs. United Fund; Bd. dirs. N.C. Design Found., mem., 1983-87. Served as pilot USAAF, 1942-45, ETO. Decorated Air medal with 2 oak leaf clusters.; Recipient various archtl. honor awards. Fellow A.I.A. (pres. N.C. chpt. 1973); mem. N.C. Bd. Architecture (past pres.), Asheville C. of C. (past pres. 1972), Tau Beta Pi, Sigma Pi Alpha, Phi Kappa Phi. Home: 222 Country Club Rd Asheville NC 28804-2608

KING, JOSEPH WILLET, child psychiatrist; b. Springfield, Mo., Aug. 26, 1934; m. Doris Ann Toby; children: Pamela Renee, Timothy Wells, Michael Brian, Bradley Christopher. BA, So. Meth. U., 1956; MD, U. Tex. Southwestern, 1962. Diplomate Am. Bd. Psychiatry and Neurology; ordained vocational deacon Episcopal Ch., 96. Intern Baylor U. Med. Ctr., Dallas, 1962-63; clin. instr., asst. clin. prof. U. Tex. Southwestern Med. Sch., Dallas, 1962—78; fellow in child psychiatry Parkland Meml. Hosp. Programs, 1962—67; resident in gen. psychiatry Timberlawn Psychiat. Hosp., 1963-64, Lisbon VA Hosp., 1965; fellow in child psychiatry Hillside Hosp., Glen Oaks, N.Y., 1967; staff child psychiatrist, dir. child and adolescent svcs. Timberlawn Psychiat. Ctr., Inc., Dallas, 1967-78; assoc. attending child psychiatrist dept. psychiatry Baylor U. Med. Ctr., Dallas, 1967-78; active attending child psychiatrist Children's Med. Ctr., Dallas, 1967-78; attenting staff Dallas County Hosp. Dist./Parkland Meml. Hosp., 1967-78; cons. child psychiatry Girls Day Care Rehab. Ctr. Dallas County, Dallas, 1970-73; cons. child psychiatry and adminstrn. Meridell Achievement Ctr., Austin, Tex., 1971-73; dir. adolescent svcs. Portsmouth (Va.) Psychiat. Ctr., 1978-79; active attending child psychiatrist Maryview Hosp., Portsmouth, 1978-80; med. dir., chief exec. officer Psychiat. Inst. Richmond, Va., 1980-86; chief exec. officer, psychiatrist-in-chief Shadow Mountain Inst., Tulsa, 1987-90; v.p. Century Healthcare, Tulsa, 1987-90; med. dir. adolescent svcs. Commanche County Meml. Pavilion, Lawton, Okla., 1997-98; pres., CEO, med. dir. Desert Hills Ctr. for Youth and Families, Tucson, 1998-99; staff psychiatrist Sierra Tucson, Tucson, 1999—2004, Cottonwood de Tucson, Tucson, 2003—. Assoc. clin. prof. Med. Coll. Va., Va. Commonwealth U., 1980-90, Med. Sch. U. Okla., Tulsa, 1987-96; clin. prof. U. Okla., Oklahoma City, 1996-1998. Contbr. articles to profl. jours. Canonical resident Diocese of Ariz.; asst. chaplain Ret. Episcopal Clergy, Diocese of Ariz. Fellow: Am. Othropsychiat. Assn., Am. Psychiat. Assn. (disting. life, Okla. dist. br.), Am. Coll. Psychiatrists (life; emeritus), Am. Soc. Adolescent Psychiatry (life; nat. pres. 1975—76); mem.: AMA, Tucson Psychiat. Soc. (treas.), Ariz. Psychiat. Assn., Tulsa Psychiat. Assn. (bd. dir.), Tulsa County Med. Soc., Okla. Med. Soc., Nat. Assn. Pvt. Psychiat. Hosps. (chmn. adolescent care com. 1971—81, pres. ind. for profit sect. 1991—92, trustee 1992—95, multiple com./task force functions), Am. Acad. Child and Adolescent Psychiatry (ins. com. 1981—86, pres. Okla. coun. 1991—92, state del. to nat. coun.), Dallas County Med. Soc. (various coms.), Alumni Assn. U. Tex. SW Med. Sch. (pres. 1982—85), Blue Key (elected mem.), Beta Theta Pi (pres. Gamma Omega chptr.). Office: Cottonwood de Tucson 4110 West Sweetwater Dr Tucson AZ 85745 Office Phone: 520-743-2150. E-mail: jdking@aol.com.

KING, JOSEPHINE YAGER, law educator; b. Homestead, Pa. d. Charles and Maria Yager; m. Benton Davis King; children: Garrett Davis, Loring Brooke. BA, U. Pa.; MA (fellow), Bryn Mawr Coll., PhD, 1950; JD, SUNY, 1965. Bar: N.Y. 1965, U.S. Dist. Ct. (ea. and so. dists.) N.Y. 1976, U.S. Ct. Appeals (2d cir.) 1976. Prof. SUNY Sch. Law, Buffalo, 1965-69, Hofstra U. Sch. Law, Hempstead, N.Y., 1970-75; dep. chief U.S. atty's office appeals div. Eastern Dist. of N.Y., Bklyn., 1975-76; prof. law Pace U., White Plains, N.Y., 1976—, assoc. dean., 1976-78. Lectr. South African Law Schs., 1997. Contbr. articles to profl. jours. in field of constnl. law. Mem. ABA, Am. Law Inst., Phi Beta Kappa, Delta Phi Alpha, Pi Gamma Mu. Address: 11 Menayas Ct Washingtonville NY 10992-2032

KING, JOY RIEMER, art educator, linguist; d. Bjarne Viggo and Thora Yrsa Xenia (Riemer) Ferdinandsen; m. Charles Banks King, Jr. IV, July 4, 1992; stepchildren: Captain Charles Pat, Dorothy Marie 1 child, Nanette Joy Xenia Riemer. Diploma, Sorbonne, 1959; BA, Principia Coll., 1961; MA, Columbia U., 1968; art specialist diploma, Fla. Internat. U., 1999. Cert. tchr. Ill., 1961, Fla., 1972. Tchrs. aide Columbia U. Team, Kabul, Afghanistan, 1961—62; tchr., curriculum coord. Parents' Coop. Sch., Jeddah, Saudi Arabia, 1967—68; prin., tchr. Latin, French, civics, arts So. Acad., Miami, 1972—77; instr. art Internat. Fine Arts Coll., Miami, 1977—78; instr. French & English Internat. Sch. Langs., Miami Shores, 1978—79; mgr./artist Frances W. Cary Antiques, 1983—89; instr. French & Danish Inlingua, Coral Gables, 1989—90; tchr., art, French, U.S. history Dade County Pub. Schools, 1990—2002; art therapist St. Mary Cathedral Sch., 2002—. Dir. Paul Abrams Found., Miami, Fla., 1998—2001, So. Acad., 1972—77. Exhibitions include Jackie Hinckey Sipes Gallery, Dublin-Kitzen Fine Arts Gallery, Coral Gables, Fairchild Tropical Garden, Bok Tower Gardens, S.E. Pastel Soc., Salmagundi Club, N.Y.C., Hispanic C.C., Miami, Paula Insel Gallery, N.Y., Stern's Gallery, Roselyn Gallery, N.C., Art Works Gallery, Miami, Nat. Art Edn. Assn. Elec. Gallery, Washington; contbr. articles to profl. jours. Pub. rels. dir. Civitan, North Miami, 2000—01. Named in U.S. Congl. Record for art edn. program with at risk students, U.S. Congress, 1992; recipient Marge Pearlson award, Dade Coalition Cmty. Edn., 1997, award of Excellence, Goya Foods, Fla., 1996, cert. of Appreciation, Metro-Dade Police Dept, Northside Sta., 1996. Mem.: ASPCA, Southeastern Pastel Soc., Fla. Watercolor Soc., Nat. Art Edn. Assn., French Teachers Am., Alliance Francaise, Fla. Art Edn. Assn., Nat. Assn. Women Artists, Dade Art Educators Assn., The Nature Conservancy, Friends the Everglades, Nat. Wildlife Fedn., Smithsonian Instn., St. Joseph's Indian Sch., North Shore Animal League, Farm Sanctuary, World Vision, Friends Bok Tower, Internat. Fund for Animal Welfare, Navy League, Nat. Gardening Club (life). Avocations: reading, swimming, painting, sculpting, writing. Office Phone: 305-799-2610. Personal E-mail: joyscapes@bellsouth.net.

KING, KATHY COOPER, music educator; b. Ackerman, Miss., Jan. 12, 1954; d. Bobby Gene and Mary Lou (McGee) Cooper; m. Kenneth A. King, Aug. 1, 1976; children: Matthew Cooper, Katherine Elizabeth. B of Music Edn., 1976, M of Music Edn., 1983, Cert. in Gifted/Talented Music Edn., 1986, ArtsD of Music Edn., Vocal Pedagogy, 1996. Vocal, choral and piano tchr. Weir (Miss.) H.S., 1976—78; dir. of music Ackerman (Miss.) United Meth. Ch., 1978—98; vocal, choral and piano tchr. Ackerman H.S., 1976—96; choral music edn. instr. U. Miss., University, 1996—97; vocal, choral and classroom tchr. Holmes C.C., Goodman, Miss., 1997—. Featured in Making the Grade, WTVA, 1990. Recipient Outstanding Cmty. Leader in Edn., Choctaw County Econ. Devel. Coun., 1991, STAR Tchr. award, Miss. Econ. Devel. Coun., 1995, Tchr. of Yr. award, Choctaw County, 1995. Mem.: Miss. Music Educators Assn., Music Tchrs. Nat. Assn., Nat. Assn. Tchrs. of Singing, Music Educators Nat. Conf., Am. Choral Dirs. Assn., Phi Kappa Phi, Sigma Alpha Iota, Pi Kappa Lambda. Republican. Methodist. Avocations: gourmet cooking, travelling, interior decorating, fitness training. Home: PO Box 413 Ackerman MS 39735 Office: Holmes CC PO Box 369 Goodman MS 39079

KING, KENTON J., lawyer; b. Aberdeen, Maryland, 1954; BA, Stanford Univ., 1977; JD, Univ. Calif., Berkeley, 1987. Bar: Calif. 1987. Law clerk to the Hon. Kenneth W. Starr, US Ct. of Appeals (DC cir.), 1987—88; ptnr. Skadden, Arps, Slate, Meagher & Flom LLP. Editor-in-chief Calif. Law Rev., 1986—87; contbr. articles to profl. journals. Named one of The World's Leading Lawyers, Chambers Global, 2002—03, America's Leading Business Lawyers, Chambers U.S.A., 2003—05. Mem.: Calif. Law Rev. Inc. (pres. 1996—98), Boalt Hall Alumni Assn. (bd. dir.), Order of Coif. Office: Skadden Arps Slate Ste 1100 525 University Ave Palo Alto CA 94301 Office Phone: 650-470-4530. Office Fax: 888-329-2950. Business E-Mail: kking@skadden.com.

KING, LARRY (LARRY ZEIGER), broadcaster, radio personality; b. Bklyn., Nov. 19, 1933; s. Eddie and Jennie Zeiger; m. Alene Akins, 1961 (div. 1963), Mickey Sutphin, 1964 (div. 1966), remarried Alene Akins, 1967 (div. 1971); 1 child, Chaia; m. Sharon Lepore, 1976 (div. 1982); m. Julia Alexander, Oct. 7, 1989 (div. 1992); 1 child, Andy; m. Shawn Southwick, Sept. 5, 1997; 1 child, Chance Armstrong. Disc jockey various radio stas., Miami, Fla., 1957-71; freelance writer, broadcaster, 1972-75; radio personality Sta. WIOD, Miami, 1975-78; writer entertainment sects. Miami Herald, 7 yrs.; radio talk show host The Larry King Show, 1978—; host Larry King Live CNN, 1985—. Columnist USA Today, 1982—2001; host Goodwill Games, 1990. Appeared in films Ghostbusters, 1984, Lost in America, 1985; voice of Ugly Stepsister, Shreck 2, 2004; author: Larry King, Tell It To The King, (with B. D. Colen) Mr. King, You're Having a Heart Attack, 1989, Larry King: Tell Me More, When You're From Brooklyn, Everything Else Is Toyko, 1992, (with Mark Stencel) On the Line: The New Road to the White House, 1993. Chmn. Larry King Cardiac Found.; hon. trustee Am. Women in Radio and TV Com.; mem. Washington Ctr. for Politics and Journalism, The Read-Am. Adv. Bd., Hart Assist Found. Bd. Recipient Radio award Nat. Assn. Broadcasters, 1985, Jack Anderson Investigative Reporting award, 1985, Peabody award for Larry King Show U. Ga. Sch. Journalism, 1987, award for Larry King Live shows Awards for Cablecasting, 1987, 88, 89, also for excellence in cable TV, 1990, Marconi award Nat. Assn. Broadcasters, 1990, Allen H. Neuharth Award for Excellence in Journalism, Gracie Allen Award, Found. Am. Women in Radio and Television, 2003; named Best Radio Talk Show Host Washington Jour. Rev., 1986, Broadcaster of Yr. Internat. Radio and TV Soc., 1989; named to Emerson Hall of Fame, Broadcasters Hall of Fame, 1992, Man Of Yr. Am. Heart Assn., 1992. Mem. Friars Club. Office: CNN Larry King Live 820 1st St NE Washington DC 20002-4243*

KING, LARRY, editor; b. Fonda, Iowa; Degree, U. Nebr. From reporter to exec. editor Omaha World-Herald, 1975—98, exec. editor, 1998—. Office: Omaha World-Herald World-Herald Sq 1334 Dodge St Omaha NE 68102-1138

KING, LARRY J., communications educator; s. Loyd J. and Mary Lou King; m. Malinda Kay Lundsford, Aug. 27, 1962; children: Austin G., Matthew T., Kayla M. AB in Religion and Comm., So. Nazarene U., 1981; MA in Comm., So. Nazarene U., Okla., 1982, MA in Religion, 1983; PhD in Comm., U. Okla., 1990. Assoc. prof. of comm. Lamar U., Beaumont, Tex., 1981—98; asst. prof. of comm. Olivet Nazarene U., Kankakee, Ill., 1988—91; dir. of the basic course in comm. Lamar U., Beaumont, Tex., 1991—98, dir. of broadcasting, 1995—98; speech comm. program coord. Stephen F. Austin State U., Nacogdoches, 1998—2005, prof. of comm., 1998—, dir. of the basic course in communication, 1998—. Other, nat., conv. press rels. com. Nat. Comm. Assn., Washington, 1990—91; pres. Press Club of SE Tex., 1996—97; pres., faculty senate Lamar U., Beaumont, Tex., 1997—98; legislative com. chair Tex. Assn. of Coll. Tchrs., Austin, 1999—2001, state pres., 2001—03; mem., instrn. and ops. com. Tex. Higher Edn. Coord. Bd., 2002—03; chair, faculty senate Stephen F. Austin State U., Nacogdoches, 2002—03; mem., formula funding adv. com. Tex. Higher Edn. Coord. Bd., 2003—; v.p. of confs. Tex. Assn. of Coll. Tchrs., Austin, 2004—. Editor: (book) Speaking Out: A Collection of Activities and Exercises, Public Speaking Workbook. Mem. Risk Mgmt. Planning Comm. Com., Beaumont, 1997—98; bd. mem. First Ch. of the Nazarene, Nacogdoches, Tex., 2003—05. Recipient Regents' Merit award, Lamar U., 1995, Tchg. Excellence award, Coll. of Applied Arts and Scis., Stephen F. Austin State U., 2004, Outstanding Alumni, So. Nazarene U., 2001, Excellence in Tchg., Lamar U., 1994, 1996, 1998; Faculty Scholarship grant, Lilly Endowment, 1990, Faculty Rsch. Enhancement grant, Lamar U., 1992, Dishman grant, Dishman Charitable Trust. Mem.: Tex. Assn. of Coll. Tchrs., Popular Culture Assn. in South, Popular Culture Assn., So. States Comm. Assn., Nat. Comm. Assn., Nat. Mortar Bd. Avocations: hunting, travel.

KING, LARRY L., playwright, actor; b. Putnam, Tex., Jan. 1, 1929; s. Clyde Clayton and Cora Lee (Clark) K.; m. Jeanne Casey, Nov. 25, 1950 (div. Nov. 1964); children: Alexandria, Kerri Lee, Bradley Clayton; m. Rosemarie Courmaris, Feb. 20, 1965 (dec.); m. Barbara Sue Blaine, May 6, 1978; children: Lindsay Allison, Blaine Carlton. Student, Tex. Tech U., 1949-50. Oil field worker El Paso Natural Gas Co., Jal, N.Mex. and Midland, Tex., 1943-45; reporter Hobbs (N.Mex.) Daily Flare, 1949, Midland Reporter-Telegram, 1950-52, Odessa (Tex.) Am., 1952-54; adminstrv. asst. U.S. Congress, Washington, 1954-64; freelance writer Washington, 1964—; pres. Texhouse Corp., Washington, 1979—. Ferris prof. journalism and polit. sci. Princeton (N.J.) U., 1973-75; Disting. Lyndon B. Johnson lectr. Southwest Tex. State University, 1991. Author: (books) The One-Eyed Man, 1966, ... And Other Dirty Stories, 1968, Confessions of a White Racist, 1971, The Old Man and Lesser Mortals, 1974, Wheeling and Dealing, 1978, Of Outlaws, Con Men, Whores, Politicians and Other Artists, 1980, The Whorehouse Papers, 1981, That Terrible Night Santa Got Lost in the Woods, 1981, None But a Blockhead: On Being a Writer, 1986, Warning: Writer At Work, 1986, Because of Lozo Brown, 1988, True Facts, Tall Tales, and Pure Fiction, 1997, Reflections In A Bloodshot Eye: A Writer's Life in Letters, 1999, (plays) The Best Little Whorehouse in Texas, 1978, The Kingfish, 1979, The Night Hank Williams Died, 1986, The Golden Shadows Old West Museum, 1987, Christmas: 1933, 1987, The Best Little Whorehouse Goes Public, 1994, The Dead Presidents' Club, 1995; also numerous articles; starred in: The Best Little Whorehouse in Texas (on Broadway), 1979, The Night Hank Williams Died (off-Broadway), 1989; contbg. editor Harper's, 1967-71, New Times, 1974-77, Tex. Monthly, 1973-78, Tex. Observer, 1964-74. Sgt. AUS, 1946-49. Recipient Stanley Walker Journalism award Tex. Inst. of Letters, 1972, Tony award League of N.Y. Theatres and Producers, 1978-79, Mary Goldwater award Theatre Lobby, 1988, Helen Hayes award, 1989; elected to Tex. Walk of Stars, 1988, Best Non-Fiction Article of Yr. award Tex. Inst. of Letters 2002, Bookends award Tex. Book Festival, 2004; Nieman fellow Harvard U., 1969-70, Duke U. fellow, 1975-76. Mem. Authors Guild, PEN, Writers Guild Am. East, Actors Equity Assn., Nat. Acad. TV Arts and Scis. (Emmy award 1981), Nat. Writers Union, Screenwriters Guild East, Dramatists Guild, Sandhills Club (Monahans, Tex.), Pelican Club (Odessa), Mystic Knights of the Sea. Democrat. Avocations: breeding show dogs, singing opera, ballet dancing. *I have always avoided strong drink and evil companions.*

KING, LEON, investment advisor; b. Phila., 1921; s. Abraham and Ethel (Walton) K.; m. Diane Averbach, Nov. 30, 1946; children: Cheryl, Elliot, Louis. BS in Econs, Wharton Sch., U. Pa., 1945; grad. with honors, Bank Adminstrn. Inst., 1970. CPA, Pa. Pub. acct., 1946-52; contr. hotel divsn. Bankers Securities Corp., 1952-57; contr. Sun-Ray Drug Co., 1957-60, Bellevue Stratford Hotel, 1960-64; with Indsl. Valley Bank and Trust Co., Phila., 1964-83, exec. v.p., 1973-83; with Indsl. Valley Title Ins. Co., Phila., 1964-86, chmn. bd., 1983-86; pres. Bancshares Inc., 1987-97; gen. ptnr. King Assocs. LP, 1996—; pvt. practice, 1987—. Mem. AICPA, Pa. Inst. CPAs, Beta Gamma Sigma. Home: 4030 Woodruff Rd Lafayette Hill PA 19444-1618 *Always be polite and courteous. Treat all people the same regardless of rank, station, or position. We are all human beings and each deserves civility and respect. From a small child to a chief of state, from a beggar to a captain of industry, all should be treated in the same friendly and courteous way.*

KING, LINDA ORR, museum director, consultant; b. Washington, June 21, 1948; d. William Baxter and Jayne (Reiser) Orr; m. James McClain King (dec. Aug. 1997); children: David, Adam, Lindsay. BA, La. State U., 1970, MA in Fine Arts, 1971; postgrad., Ga. State U., 2003—. Fine arts history asst. La. State U., Baton Rouge, 1967-70, grad. asst., 1970-71; assoc. curator La. State Mus., New Orleans, 1971-74; curator Coastal Ga. Hist. Soc./St. Simons Island Lighthouse Mus., St. Simons Island, 1984-87; dir. Coastal Ga. Hist. Soc., St. Simons Island, 1987-2000; dir. exhibitions and collections Atlanta Hist. Ctr., 2000-01; ind. mus. profl., 2001—. Romanian Mus. advisor U.S. State Dept., 2002. Co-editor: (photograph essay) George Francois Mugnier, 1975. Pres. Glynn County Soc. of St. Vincent de Paul, 1990-94; mem. Glynn County Courthouse Renovation Com., 1989-2000; Ga. state dir. S.E. Mus. Conf., 1990-94, also membership chair; mem. adv. coun. Brunswick Downtown Devel. Authority; mem. Leadership Glynn, 1992; mem. Commn. on Preservation of Ga. State Capitol; chmn. adv. coun. on hist. preservation Coastal Regional Devel. Ctr., 1987-98, chmn., 1996-98. Recipient Kellogg Career Enhancement award, Kellogg Found., 1989, Leadership award, Southeastern Mus. Conf., 1995, Nat. Mus. award, 1999, Ga. History Mus. Exhibit of 2002 award, 2002; fellow Internat. Partnership Among Mus. fellow to Sierra Leone, 1992. Mem. Ga. Assn. Mus. and Galleries (treas. 1987-89, Mus. Profl. of Yr. 1993), Coastal Mus. Assn. (treas. 1987-89), Am. Assn. Mus., Low Country Mus. Network (treas. 1993-99). Roman Catholic. Home: 3472 Paces Pl NW Atlanta GA 30327 E-mail: lindaorrking@bellsouth.net.

KING, LISA S., music educator; b. Passaic, N.J., Dec. 3, 1964; d. Guy August and Geraldine Gloria Scognamiglio; m. Michael Christopher King, June 30, 1991; children: Christopher, Victoria, Michael, Nicholas. BMus, William Paterson U., Wayne, N.J., 1988; MA, Montclair (N.J.) State U., 1993; postgrad., U. Siena, Italy, 1994. Cert. tchr. music N.J. Cantor St. Catherine's Ch., Ringwood, NJ, 1986—88; piano tchr. The Music Den, Landing, NJ, 1987—90; vocal music tchr. Ringwood (N.J.) Pub. Schs., 1988—99; cantor St. Anthony ch., Butler, NJ, 1989—; opera singer Amato Opera Theatre, N.Y.C., 1993—; piano and voice tchr. Jefferson Twp., NJ, 1999—. Singer/performer Mozart Opera Project, N.Y.C., 1992, Iron Mountain Stage Co., Ringwood, 1997; concert singer Lyric Opera of Bergen County, Garfield, NJ, 2000, Skylands Chorus & Chamber Soc., Sparta, NJ, 2001. Mem.: N.J. Music Educators Assn., Music Educators Nat. Conf., N.J. Edn. Assn. Avocations: camping, kickboxing, walking, travel. Home: 10 Center Rd Oak Ridge NJ 07438 E-mail: lisasking@optonline.net.

KING, LLEWELLYN WILLINGS, publishing executive, educator, commentator, writer; b. Bulawayo, Zimbabwe, Oct. 6, 1939; came to U.S., 1963; s. Herbert Willings and Dorothy Ann (Hooper) K. Student, Churchill Coll., 1951-55; DSc in Engring. (hon.), Stevens Inst. of Tech., 1995, PhD (hon.). City editor The Citizen, Harare, Zimbabwe, 1958-60; sub-editor Ind. TV News, London, 1960-61, Sunday Mirror, London, 1961-63; copy editor N.Y. Herald Tribune, N.Y.C., 1963-64; pres. Sovereign Assocs., N.Y.C., 1964-66; editor wire desk Washington Daily News, 1966-69; asst. editor Washington Post, 1969-70; reporter McGraw Hill, Washington, 1970-73; chmn. King Pub. Group, Washington, 1973—. Founder Women NOW mag., N.Y.C., 1965; pres. Washington-Balt. Newspaper Guild, 1967-70; host cable TV program The Bull and the Bear; host TV program "White House Chronicle". Colunist: Syndicated by King Pub. Group. Mem. Aircraft Owners and Pilots Assn., Nat. Prss, St. James's Club, London Press Club. Avocations: flying, horseback riding, boating. Office: King Pub Group 1325 G St NW Washington DC 20005 Office Phone: 202-658-4260. E-mail: lking@kingpublishing.com.

KING, LOWELL RESTELL, pediatric urologist; b. Salem, Ohio, Feb. 28, 1932; s. Lowell Waldo and Vesta Ethylwin (Snyder) K.; m. Mary Elizabeth Hill, July 9, 1960; children: Andrew Restell, Erika Lillie. BA, Johns Hopkins U., 1953, MD, 1956. Intern Johns Hopkins Hosp., Balt., 1956-57, resident in urology, 1957-62; asst. prof. urology Johns Hopkins U., 1962-63, Northwestern U., 1963-67, assoc. prof., 1967-70, prof., 1970-81, prof. urology and surgery, 1974-81; prof. urology and pediatrics Duke U., Durham, N.C., 1981-97, prof. emeritus, 1997; prof. surgery/urology U. N.Mex., Albuquerque, 1997—. Prof., chmn. dept. urology Presbyn.-St. Luke's Hosp., 1968-70; surgeon-in-chief Children's Meml. Hosp., Chgo., 1974-80 Author: (with P.P. Kelalis) Clinical Pediatric Urology, 1976, (with A.B. Belman) 4th edit., 2001, Bladder Replacement and Continent Urology Diversion, 1986, 2d edit., 1991, Urologic Surgery in the Neonate and Young Infant, 1992, Reconstructive Urology, 1992, Urologic Surgery in Infants and Children, 1997, Office Guide to Pediatric Urology, 2002; cons. editor Urology; editor profl. jours.; contbr. articles to profl. jours. Vestryman, sr. warden Ch. of Our Savior, 1974-80; bd. dirs. Gads Hill Settlement House, 1969-73. Recipient Gold medal All India Urologic Congress, 1996, Gold medal Mex. Coll. Urology, 1991, Valentine medal N.Y. Acad. Medicine, 2002, Kretchmer medal Chgo. Urol. Soc. Mem. AMA, Am. Urol. Assn. (career achievement award 1996), Am. Acad. Pediats. (chmn. sect. urology 1969-72, sec. 1975-76, pres. 1977-78, Urology medal 1992), Soc. Pediat. Urology (pres. 1983), Soc. Univ. Urologists, Am. Assn. Genitourinary Surgeons, Clin. Soc. Genitourinary Surgeons (pres. 1996). Episcopalian. Home: 2012 Dietz Pl NW Albuquerque NM 87107-3220 Office: U NMex Health Scis Ctr Sch Medicine Dept Surgery Divsn Urology 2211 Lomas Blvd NE Albuquerque NM 87106-2745 Office Phone: 505-272-5504. Home Fax: 505-343-1428. Personal E-mail: octopus@cybermesa.com.

KING, LYNDEL IRENE SAUNDERS, museum director; b. Enid, Okla., June 10, 1943; d. Leslie Jay and Jennie Irene (Duggan) Saunders; m. Blaine Larman King, June 12, 1965. BA, U. Kans., Lawrence, 1965; MA, U. Minn.-Mpls., 1971, PhD, 1982. Dir. Frederick R. Weisman Art Mus., U. Minn., Mpls., 1979—; dir. exhbns. and mus. programs Control Data Corp., 1979, 80-81; exhbn. coord. Nat. Gallery of Art, Washington, 1980. Recipient Cultural Contbn. of Yr. award Mpls. C. of C., 1978; Honor award Minn. Soc. Architects, 1979. Mem. Assn. Art Mus. Dirs. (chair art issues com. 1998-2000, chair tech. comm. com. 2000, bd. trustees 1998—), Art Mus. Assn. Am. (v.p. bd. dirs. 1984-89), Assn. Coll. and Univ. Mus. and Galleries (v.p. 1989-92), Am. Assn. Mus., Internat. Coun. Mus., Upper Midwest Conservation Assn. (pres. bd. dirs. 1980—), Minn. Assn. Mus. (steering com. 1982), Am. Fedn. Arts Bd. Home: 326 W 50th St Minneapolis MN 55419-1247 Office: Weisman Art Mus 333 E River Rd Minneapolis MN 55455-0367 E-mail: wamdir@umn.edu.

KING, MARGARET LEAH, history professor; b. NYC, Oct. 16, 1947; d. Reno C. and Marie (Ackerman) King; m. Robert E. Kessler, Nov. 12, 1976; children: David King Kessler, Jeremy King Kessler. BA, Sarah Lawrence Coll., 1967; MA, Stanford U., 1968, PhD, 1972. Asst. prof. dept. history Calif. State Coll., Fullerton, 1969-70; asst. prof. Bklyn. Coll., CUNY, 1972-76, assoc. prof., 1976-86; prof. Bklyn. Coll. and Grad. Ctr., CUNY, 1987—, Claire and Leonard Tow disting. prof., 2000—02. Disting. guest prof. Centre for Reformation and Renaissance Studies, U. Toronto, 1995. Author: The Renaissance in Europe, 2004, (textbook) Western Civilization: A Social and Cultural History, 2d edit., 2002, Venetian Humanism in an Age of Patrician Dominance, 1986, Women of the Renaissance, 1991, The Death of the Child Valerio Marcello, 1994, The Renaissance in Europe, 2004; editor, translator: (with Diana Robin) Complete Works of Isotta Nogarola, 2004; co-editor series The Other Voice in Early Modern Europe; contbr. articles to profl. jours. Recipient Howard R. Marraro prize, Am. Cath. Hist. Assn., 1986, Tow award for distinction in scholarship, Bklyn. Coll., 1994—95; fellow, Danforth Found., 1967—72, Woodrow Wilson Found., 1967—68, Am. Coun. Learned Socs., 1977—78, NEH, 1986—87, Leonard and Claire Tow Disting. fellow, 2000—; grantee, Am. Coun. Learned Socs., 1976, Gladys Krieble Delmas Found., 1977—78, 1980—81, 1990, Am. Philos. Soc., 1979, 1990, NEH, 1984. Mem. Am. Hist. Assn. (Howard and Helen Mararro prize 1996), Hist. Soc., Renaissance Soc. Am. (exec. dir. 1988-95, editor Renaissance Quar. 1984-88, 97-2002). Home: 324 Beverly Rd Little Neck NY 11363-1125 Office: CUNY Bklyn Coll Dept History 2900 Bedford Ave Brooklyn NY 11210-2814 Office Phone: 718-951-5303. E-mail: mking@nyc.rr.com.

KING, MARIELLE ELISABETH, educational research association administrator, writer, retired secondary school educator; b. Geertruidenberg, The Netherlands, Nov. 20, 1945; arrived in Canada, 1952, arrived in U.S., 1970; d. Andries Willem Schippers and Laurina Jacoba Schippers-Marks; 1 child, Adam Schippers Nichols. AA, St. Petersburg (Fla.) Jr. Coll., 1968; BA, U. South Fla., 1970; M of Trancendental Div., Metaphysical and Unity Sch. Practical Christianity, 1976. Cert. med. tech. Am. Soc. Clin. Pathologists, nutrition cons. Am. Nutrition Consultants Assn.; tchr. sci., math., health, adult edn., dropout prevention, spl. edn. Fla. Dept. Edn. Med. accounts clerk Toronto Gen. Hosp., Canada, 1964—65, vestibular (inner ear) rsch. tech., 1966; tchr., math, health & sci. Pinellas County Sch., 1970—74, sci. dept. chair, 1973—74; tchr., math, health & sci. Pasco County Sch., 1977—79, Hillsborough County Sch., 1979—2000; mng. dir., CEO All Children 'R' Gifted, Inc., Zephyrhills, Fla., 2000—. Med. tech. Bayfront Med. Ctr., St. Petersburg, Fla., 1975—76. Author: All Children 'R' Gifted, 2001, 2d edit., 2005; contbr. poems to books. Creativity grant, U-Save via Hillsborough County Schs., 2000. Mem.: Am. Soc. Ret. Persons, Internat. Soc. Poets (Poet of Merit 2001, nominated Poet of Yr. award 2005). Avocations: reading, poetry, education research, swimming, health, children's rights. Home Fax: 813-782-3094.

KING, MARK, computer company executive; married; 2 children. Grad. summa cum laude, U. Tex. CPA. V.p., asst. contr. MTech Corp.; CFO, ACS Affiliated Computer Svcs., Inc., Dallas, 1988—2001, exec. v.p., CFO, 1995—2001, COO, 2001—, pres., COO, 2002—. Mem.: Dallas Assembly, Econo. Devel. Adv. Coun. Greater Dallas C. of C. Office: Affiliated Computer Svcs Inc 2828 N Haskell Bldg 1 Dallas TX 75204

KING, MARTI FAHNER, music educator; b. Grand Rapids, Mich., Feb. 24, 1953; d. Byron Carl and A. Vivian (Skeoch) Fahner; m. Charles Boardman King III, May 26, 1979; 1 child, Michelle Kristen. BA, Calvin Coll., 1979, MA, 1980; student, Mich. State U., 1992—94, Calvin Coll., 1992—94. Cert. Tchr. Ill., 1979. Music tchr. Forest Hills Pub. Sch., Grand Rapids, Mich., 1975—83, various, Grand Rapids, 1987—90, Forest Hills Pub. Sch., Mich., 1990—. Pvt. instr., Grand Rapids, 1969—88, Grand Rapids, 2002—; music instr. Calvin Coll. Summer Camp, Grand Rapids, 1978—88, Blue Lake Fine Arts Camp, Twin Lake, Mich., 1981—84; course instr. Aquinas Coll., Grand Rapids, 1989—92; adjudicator Mich. State Band and Orch., 1985. Musician: Kenny Roger's Christmas Tour, 1999. Fundraiser co-chmn. DeVos Children's Hosp.; vol. Habitat for Humanity. Named Forest Hills Pub. Schs. Tchr. of Yr., 2000—01; grantee, Forest Hills Found. Mem.: NEA (Mich. chpt.), Music Educator's Nat. Conf., Mich. Music Edn. Assn. (exec. bd. 1975—). Presbyterian. Avocations: reading, piano. Home: 103 Deer Run Ct NE Ada MI 49301 Office: Forest Hills Public Schools 6590 Cascade Rd SE Grand Rapids MI 49546

KING, MARY ELIZABETH, writer, educator; b. N.Y.C., July 30, 1940; d. Luther Waddington and Alba Iregui King; m. Peter Geoffrey Bourne. AB, Ohio Wesleyan U., 1962; PhD, U. Wales, Aberystwyth, 1999. Comm. officer Student Nonviolent Coord. Com., Atlanta, 1963—65; program officer U.S. Office of Econ. Opportunity, Washington, 1968—72; dep. dir. ACTION - a sub-Cabinet fed. agy., Washington, 1977—81; freelance cons., 1981—92; spl. advisor to former Pres. Jimmy Carter Atlanta, 1984—; adviser appointed by Govt. of India, 1998—2003; prof., internat. politics St. George's U., Grenada, 1999—2001; prof., peace and conflict studies U. for Peace of the UN, Costa Rica, 2001—; sr. fellow U. Oxford, Rothermere Am. Inst., 2004—05. Mem. Internat. Comm. on Peace and Food, Madras, India, 1989—94; bd. dirs. AMIDEAST Ednl. and Testing Svc., Washington, 1989—; pres. Global Action, Inc., 1988—. Author: (book) Freedom Song: A Personal Story of the 1960s Civil Rights Movement, 1987 (Robert F. Kennedy Book award, 1988), Mahatma Gandhi and Martin Luther King, Jr.: The Power of Nonviolent Action, 1999; contbr. articles to profl. jours. Pres., co-founder Nat. Assn. Women Bus. Owners, Washington, 1976; bd. dirs. Save the Children Fedn., Westport, Conn., 1980—91, Arca Found., Washington, 1980—; bd. selectors The Jefferson Awards, Wilmington, Del., 1993—; bd. dirs. Albert Einstein Instn., Boston, 2003—. Named to Nat. Women's Hall of Fame, Seneca Falls, N.Y., 1992; recipient Disting. Achievement Award, Ohio Wesleyan U., 1989, Women's Equity Action League, 1977, Jamnalal Bajaj award for internat. promotion of Gandhian values, Mumbai, India, 2003; fellow, Albert Einstein Instn., 1996—98; disting. scholar, Am. U. Ctr. for Global Peace, Washington, DC, 1997—. Mem.: The Author's Guild, Middle East Studies Assn., Women's Fgn. Policy Group. Avocations: British antiques and architecture, farming. Home: 2119 Leroy Pl NW Washington DC 20008-1848

KING, MARY-CLAIRE, geneticist, educator; b. Evanston, Ill., Feb. 27, 1946; m. 1973; 1 child, Emily King Colwell. BA in Math., Carleton Coll., 1966; PhD in Genetics, U. Calif., Berkeley, 1973. Am. Cancer Soc. prof. medicine and genetics U. Wash., Seattle, 1995—. Mem. bd. sci. counselors Nat. Cancer Inst.; cons. Com. for Investigation of Disappearance of Persons, Govt. Argentina, Buenos Aires, 1984—. Contbr. more than 150 articles to profl. jours. Recipient Alumni Achievement award Carleton Coll., Basic Rsch. award Susan G. Komen Breast Cancer Found., 1999. Mem. AAAS, Am. Soc. Human Genetics, Soc. Epidemiologic Research, Inst. Medicine, Phi Beta Kappa, Sigma Xi. Office: U Wash 1959 NE Pacific St # 357720 Seattle WA 98195-0001

KING, MICHAEL HOWARD, lawyer; b. Chgo., Mar. 10, 1943; s. Warren and Betty (Fine) K.; m. Candice M. King, Aug. 18, 1968; children: Andrew, Julie. B.S. Washington U., St. Louis 1967, J.D. 1970. Bar: Ill. 1970, U.S. Dist. Ct. (no. dist.) Ill. 1970, U.S. Dist. Ct. (ea. dist.) Wis. 1972, U.S. Ct. Appeals (7th cir.) 1974, U.S. Ct. Appeals (5th cir.) 1979, U.S. Supreme Ct. 1975, U.S. Ct. Appeals (3d cir.) 1983, U.S. Tax Ct. 1987, U.S. Ct. Appeals (10th cir.) 1987, U.S. Dist. Ct. (no. dist.) Calif. 1987, U.S. Dist. Ct. Nebr. 1988, U.S. Dist. Ct. (ctrl. dist.) Ill. 1992, U.S. Dist. Ct. (no. dist.) N.Y. 1992, U.S. Ct. Appeals (2nd cir.) 1994. Spl. atty. organized crime, racketeering sect. U.S. Dept. Justice, Washington, 1970-73; asst. U.S. atty. No. Dist. Ill., Chgo., 1973-75; assoc. Antonow & Fink, Chgo., 1976, ptnr., 1977-79; ptnr. Ross & Hardies, Chgo., 1979-2005, McGuire Woods LLP, 2005-, Leboeuf, Lamb, Greene and Macrae LLP; chmn. Bd. Commr. Office of State Appellate Defender. Co-author Model Jury Instructions in Criminal Antitrust Cases, 1982, Handbook on Antitrust Grand Jury Investigations, 1988; contbr. articles to profl. jours. Bd. dirs. Chgo. Youth Ctrs., 1977-82; trustee Cove Sch., 1984-88, the Goodman Theatre, 1993—. Mem. ABA (litigation sect., antitrust sect., criminal practice procedure com.), Ill. Bar Assn., Chgo. Bar Assn. (judiciary com., antitrust com.), Am. Judicature Soc., Fed. Bar Assn., Assn. Trial Lawyers Am., Mid-Am. Club (bd. govs.), Econ. Club, Chgo. Inn of Cts., Phi Delta Phi, Alpha Epsilon Pi. Home: 77 W Wacker Ste 4100 Chicago IL 60601 Office: Leboeuf Lamb Greene and Macrae 180 N Stetson Ave Ste 1175 Chicago IL 60601 E-mail: mking@mcguirewoods.com.

KING, NANCY, communications educator; b. Blytheville, Ark., May 10, 1945; d. Willie Lee and Janie (Jones) Garrett; m. Perry King, June 17, 1967; children: Perry Jr., Tiffany, Christopher. BA in Speech Communication, Calif. State U., L.A., 1974, MA in Speech Communication, 1981; MA in Psychology, Chapman U., 1998. Asst. supr. Pacific Telegraph & Telephone, 1968-70; computer operator West Coast Community Exch. Fenton & Lavine, L.A., 1970-71, So. Gas Co., L.A., 1972-81, communication cons., 1982—; devel. lang. specialist Charles Drew Headstart Program, L.A.; prof. speech dept. Marymount Coll., Rancho Palos Verdes, Calif., 1986—. Speechwriter various regional ofcls.; instr. Calif. State U., L.A., 1979-86; mem. Calif. Libr. Svcs. Bd., 1984-94, pres., 1988-89, 90-91; mem. Calif. Libr. Networking Task Force, 1985-2000, Calif. Librs. Adv. Bd., 1984-94, Orange County Friends of Libr. Found., 1988-94, Calif. Alliance for Literacy Task Force, 1988, 92; faculty coord. Webster U., 1996-2--1; intern counselor Am. Inst. Family Counselors, 1999—; Human Options Counseling Ctr., 20002; mem. pastoral parish coun. St. Nicholas Paris, 2000—. Contbr. articles to profl. jours. Co-chmn. black coun. Orange County Hist. and Cultural Found., pres. bd., 1992; campaign mgr. Fran Williams for Santa Ana City Coun.; mem. parish Coun. St. Nicholas Parish, 2004—. Mem. NEA, Nat. Speech Communication Assn., Western Speech Communication Assn., Am. Fedn. Tchrs., AAUW, L.A. Southcentral Planning Coun. (bd. dirs.). Republican. Roman Catholic. Office: Marymount Coll 30800 Palos Verdes Dr E Palos Verdes Peninsula CA 90274 Office Phone: 310-377-5501 239. Business E-Mail: nking@marymountpv.edu.

KING, NICK, newspaper editor; Reporter The Boston Globe, statehouse news editor, focus editor, 1986—91, living editor, 1991—99, editor Globe Mag., 1999—2003, spl. sections editor, 2003—. Office: Boston Globe Globe Newspaper Co PO Box 2378 Boston MA 02107-2378

KING, ORDIE HERBERT, JR., oral pathologist; b. Memphis, Aug. 11, 1933; s. Ordie Herbert and Hazel (Eaton) K.; m. Violette Papagianis, Mar. 21, 1974; children: Catherine Ann, Alexander Carlos; children by previous marriage: Anna LaVelle, Ordie Herbert III. BS, Memphis State U., 1957; DDS, U. Tenn., 1959, PhD, 1965. Diplomate Am. Bd. Oral Pathology. USPHS postdoctoral fellow U. Tenn., 1960-62, rsch. assoc. dept. pathology, 1963-65, asst. prof. pathology, 1965; resident oral pathology U. Tenn., City of Memphis Hosps., 1962-63; asst. prof. pathology Northwestern U., 1966; assoc. prof. oral pathology St. Louis U., 1967-69, prof., 1969-70, chmn. dept., 1967-70, chmn. dept. dentistry univ. hosps., 1967-70; acting chmn., vis. assoc. prof. oral pathology Washington U., St. Louis, 1969-70; prof. oral pathology, assoc. prof. pathology W.Va. U., Morgantown, 1970-74, prof. pathology, 1974, dir. Cytopathology Lab., Med. Ctr., 1971-74; prof. pathology So. Ill. U. Sch. Dental Medicine, Alton, 1974-97; chmn. dept. diagnostic specialties So. Ill. U., Edwardsville, 1979-92; clin. prof. pathology Washington U. Sch. Dental Medicine, St. Louis, 1979-80. Dir. So. Ill. Pathology Lab., Ltd., Godfrey, 1977—; dental cons. to chief med. examiner State of Tenn., 1963-65; mem. exec. com. St. Louis U. Hosps., 1967-70; mem. med. staff West Tenn. Cancer Clinic, 1962-65, W.Va. U. Hosp., 1970-74; mem. med./dental staff dept pathology Alton (Ill.) Meml. Hosp., 1986—; cons. VA Hosp., Clarksville, W.Va., 1973-74; dental cons. St. Louis County Med. Examiner, 1968-70; cons. cancer control program Nat. Ctr. for Chronic Disease Control, USPHS, 1967-70; mem. Mo. Bd. Dental Splty. Examiners, 1982-84. Fellow Am. Acad. Oral Pathology; mem. Am. Soc. Cytopathology, ADA, Am. Cancer Soc. (bd. dirs. W.Va. divsn. 1972-74), Tenn. Walking Horse Breeders and Exhibitors Assn., Spotted Saddle Horse Breeders and Exhibitors Assn., Spotted Saddle Horse Assn. Ill. (pres. 2002-04), Delta Sigma Delta, Kappa Alpha, Phi Rho Sigma, Omicron Kappa Upsilon. Home: 6111 Vollmer Ln Godfrey IL 62035-1062 Office: So Ill Path Lab Ltd Godfrey IL 62035

KING, PAUL FREDERICK, elementary school educator, secondary school educator; b. Urbana, Ill., Sept. 20, 1954; s. Richard Frederick and Mary Jean (Browning) King. BS in Edn., Drake U., 1976, MS in Edn., 1981; postgrad., Kankakee CC, Ill., 2004—. Cert. tchr. Ill. Math. tchr. Keya Paha County HS, Springview, Nebr., 1977—78; HS math. tchr. White River (SD) Sch., 1978—79; math. tchr. grades 7-12 Norwood (Mo.) Sch., 1979—80, Sioux Valley (Minn.) Sch., 1980—81; math. tchr. Crow Creek Reservation HS, Stephen, SD, 1985—86; substitute tchr. Chgo. Pub. Schs., 1987—88, 2004—; HS math. tchr. Sheldon (Ill.) Sch., 1999—2000; elem. music tchr. St. George Sch., Bourbonnais, Ill., 2000—01. Presenter in field. Author: numerous poems. Vacation Bible sch. leader Westchester (Ill.) Bible Ch., 1999—2000; youth leader Oakbrook (Ill.) Cmty. Ch., Ill., 1982—84; Bible study leader LaGrange (Ill.) Bible Ch., 1974, Christ Ch. Oakbrook, 1984, 1994, Sunday sch. tchr., 1989—94; asst. Sunday sch. tchr. First Christian Ch., Watseka, Ill., 2003—04. Mem.: ASCD, Royal Scottish Dance Soc. Republican. Avocations: dance, chess, poetry, art, birdwatching. Home: PO Box 36 Sheldon IL 60966

KING, PETER THOMAS, congressman, lawyer; b. N.Y., Apr. 5, 1944; m. Rosemary King; children: Sean, Erin. Grad., St. Francis Coll., 1965; JD, U. Notre Dame, 1968. Atty.; town councilman Town of Hempstead, N.Y., 1977-81; comptr. Nassau County, N.Y., 1981-93; mem. U.S. Congress from 3rd N.Y. dist., Washington, 1993—; mem. fin. svcs. and internat. rels. coms., homeland sec. com. Spl. asst. to Chief Dep. Nassau County Exec.; gen counsel to Nassau Regional Off-Track Betting Corp.; chief dep. Nassau County Atty.; Acting County Atty. Chmn. Town Bd. Com. on Conservation and Waterways. Recipient cert. of achievement for excellence in fin. reporting (7 yrs) Gov. Fin. Officers Assn., cert. of honor Long Island Com. for Soviet Jewry, Alumni Achievement award St. Francis Coll., Huey award Vets. of Viet Nam War. Mem. Am. Legion, Vets. Corps of 69th Infantry, Knights of Columbus (named Citizen of the Yr.), Sons of Italy. Republican. Roman Catholic. Office: US Ho of Reps 436 Cannon Ho Office Bldg Washington DC 20515-3203*

KING, R. PETER, science professor, director; b. Springs, Transvaal, South Africa, Mar. 12, 1938; came to U.S., 1990; m. July 29, 1961; children: Jeremy P., Andrew J., Janet M. BSc, U. Witwatersrand, Johannesburg, 1958, MSc, 1962; PhD, U. Manchester, Eng., 1963. Lectr. U. Witwatersrand, 1963-65, U. Natal, Durban, South Africa, 1965-73, U. Manchester, 1973-74; prof. U. Witwatersrand, 1974-90, U. Utah, Salt Lake City, 1990—. Dir. comm. ctr. U. Utah, 1990-96; mem. Prime Minister's Sci. Adv. Coun., South Africa, 1979. Author: Modeling and Simulation of Mineral Processing Systems, 2001, Introduction to Practical Fluid Flow, 2002; editor: Principles of Flotation, 1982; editor Internat. Jour. Mineral Processing; contbr. articles to profl. jours. Fellow South African Inst. Mining and Metallurgy (pres. 1983-84); mem. Nat. Acad. Engring., Soc. Mining, Metallurgy and Exploration, Soc. Indsl. and Applied Math. Home: 2055 E 1300 S Salt Lake City UT 84108-2241 Office: U Utah 135 S 1460 E Rm 412 Salt Lake City UT 84112-0114

KING, RAY JOHN, electrical engineering educator, engineering company executive; b. Montrose, Colo., Jan. 1, 1933; s. John Frank and Grace (Rankin) K.; m. Diane M. Henney, June 20, 1964; children: Karl V., Kristin J. BS in Electronic Engring., Ind. Inst. Tech., 1956, BS in Elec. Engring., 1957; MS, U. Colo., 1960, PhD, 1965. Instr. Ind. Inst. Tech., 1956-58, asst. prof., 1960-62, acting chmn. dept. electronics, 1960-62; research asso. U. Colo., 1962-65; research assoc. U. Ill., 1965; assoc. prof. elec. engring. U. Wis., Madison, 1965-69, prof., 1969-82, assoc. dept. chmn. for research and grad. affairs, 1977-79; staff rsch. engr. Lawrence Livermore Nat. Lab. (Calif.), 1982-90, sr. scientist high power microwaves program, 1989-90; co-founder KDC Tech. Corp., 1983, v.p., 1990—, cons. Vis. Erskine fellow U. Canterbury, N.Z., 1977; guest prof., Fulbright scholar Tech. U. Denmark, 1973-74 Author: Microwave Homodyne Systems, 1978; contbr. articles to profl. jours.; patentee in field; guest editor spl. issue Subsurface Sensing Techs. and Applications jour., 2000. NSF Faculty fellow, 1962-65. Fellow IEEE (life); mem. IEEE Soc. on Antennas and Propagation (adminstrv. com. 1989-91, chmn. wave propagation stds. com. 1986-89, gen. chmn. symposium 1989), IEEE Soc. Microwave Theory and Techniques, IEEE Soc. Instrumentation and Measurements, Forest Products Soc. (life), Electromagnetics Acad., Internat. Sci. Radio Union (commns. A, B, F), Sigma Xi, Iota Tau Kappa, Sigma Phi Delta. Home: 2595 Raven Rd Pleasanton CA 94566-4605 Office: KDC Tech Corp 2011 Research Dr Livermore CA 94550-3803 Personal E-mail: rayking@ieee.org.

KING, REBECCA JANE, nursing administrator, educator; b. Warsaw, Ind., Jan. 25, 1970; d. George Allen Chapman and Clematean Hinson Moore; m. Johnny Allen King; 1 child, Nathan John. Student, W.Va. U., Morgantown, 1988—90; BSN, U. Charleston, 1994; MS in Adult Tech. Edn., Marshall U., 2002, MSN, 2004. Cert. BLS instr. W.Va., tchr. W.Va.; RN W.Va. Charge nurse cardiac unit Charleston Area Med. Ctr. Meml., Charleston, W.Va., 1994—96, Eye and Ear Clinic, Charleston, 1996—2001; practical nursing instr. Garnet Career Ctr., Charleston, 1999—2003; HIV/AIDS coord. W. Va. Dept. Edn., 2003—. CPR instr., Charleston, 1993—; vis. nurse Charleston Area Med. Ctr. Home Care, Charleston, 1997—2000. Organizer relay for life team Am. Cancer Soc., Charleston, 2001—; blood drive organizer ARC, Charleston, 2002—; clothing drive Mildred Mitchell Bateman Hosp., Huntington, W.Va., 2002—. Mem.: W.Va. Asthma Coalition, Nat. Assn. State Sch. Nurse Cons., W.Va. Assn. Sch. Nurses, Sigma Theta Tau. Avocations: walking, bicycling. Office: W Va Dept Edn Student Svc and Health Promotions Bldg 6 Rm 309 1900 Kanawha Blvd E Charleston WV 25305 Office Phone: 304-558-8830. E-mail: jking@charter.net.

KING, REGINA, actress; b. L.A., Jan. 15, 1971; m. Ian Alexander, Apr. 23, 1997; 1 child. Actor: (TV series) 227, 1985—90, Leap of Faith, 2002; (TV films) Where the Truth Lies, 1999, If These Walls Could Talk 2, 2000, Damaged Care, 2002; (films) Boyz n the Hood, 1991, Poetic Justice, 1993, Higher Learning, 1995, Friday, 1995, A Thin Line Between Love and Hate, 1996, Jerry Maguire, 1996, Rituals, 1998, How Stella Got Her Groove Back, 1998, Enemy of the State, 1998, Mighty Joe Young, 1998, Down to Earth, 2001, Daddy Day Care, 2003, Legally Blonde 2: Red, White & Blonde, 2003, A Cinderella Story, 2004, Ray, 2004, Miss Congeniality 2: Armed and Fabulous, 2005; actor, prodr.: (films) Final Breakdown, 2002.*

KING, RICHARD ALLEN, lawyer; b. St. Joseph, Mo., July 4, 1944; s. Allen Welden and Lola (Donelson) K.; m. Deedee Gershenson, Apr. 19, 1986; children from previous marriage: Mary, Suzanne, Allen. BA, U. Mo., Columbia, 1966, JD cum laude, 1968. Bar: Mo. 1968. Law clk. Office of Chief Counsel, IRS, 1967; assoc. Reese, Constance, Slayton, Stewart & Stewart, Independence, Mo., 1968-73; ptnr. Constance, Slayton, Stewart & King, Independence, 1973-80, Cochran, Kramer, Kapke, Willerth & King, Independence, 1980-81; exec. asst. to gov. State of Mo., Jefferson City, 1981-82, dir. revenue, 1982-85; ptnr. Smith, Gill, Fisher and Butts, Inc., Kansas City, Mo., 1985-87, Wirken & King, Kansas City, 1988-93; chmn., CEO King Hershey, Kansas City, Mo., 1993—. Asst. city counselor City of Independence, 1968—69, mayor, 1974—78; vice chmn. Nat. Conf. Rep. Mayors, 1975—77; chmn. Mo. Gov.'s Task Force on Cmty. Crime Prevention, 1975—76, Kansas City Pub. Improvements Adv. Com., 1991—96, KC Team Effort, 1991—95; pres. Good Govt. League, Independence, 1972—73; mem. Mo. Commn. Human Rights, 1973—74; bd. dirs. Multistate Tax Commn., 1983—85, Chrisman Sawyer Bank, 1989—95. Contbr. articles to profl. jours. Bd. dirs. Am. Cancer Soc., Independence, 1973-79, chmn. crusade, 1973; bd. dirs. Independence Boys Club, 1972-79, Independence Cmty. Assn. Arts, 1973-76, Independence Sanitarium and Hosp., 1974-78, Jefferson City Meml. Hosp., 1981-85, NE Jackson County Mental Health Ctr., 1978-80, Greater Kansas City Nat. Coun. on Alcoholism, 1978-81, Am. Legion Boys State Mo., 1975—, Jefferson City United Way, 1982-85, Multi-State Tax Commn., 1982-85, Jackson County Hist. Soc., 1999—, Nat. Frontier Trails Mus., 2004—; pres. Friends U. Mo. Truman Campus, 1979-80, Kansas City Consensus, 1989-90; trustee Harry S Truman Scholarship Found., 1975-78, Kansas City U., 1979-80, Andrew Drumm Inst., 1990—, pres. bd. trustees, 1992-94; bd. vis. Park U., 2005-. Capt. U.S. Army, 1969—72. Recipient Outstanding Young Man of Mo. award Mo. Jaycees, 1975, award Mo. Inst. Pub. Adminstrn., 1983 Mem.: ABA, Independence C. of C. (pres. 1980—81), Mo. Econ. Devel. Fin. Assn. (bd. dirs. 1990—, pres. 1999—2001), Kansas City Bar Assn., Internat. Assn. Gaming Attys., Nat. Assn. Bond Lawyers, Kansas City Bar Assn. (chmn. real estate law com. 1988—89), Ea. Jackson County Bar Assn., Mo. Bar Assn., Order of Coif, Beta Theta Pi, Phi Delta Phi. Unitarian Universalist. Home: 206 E 30th St Kansas City MO 64108-3213 Office: King Hershey Ste 2100 2345 Grand Blvd Kansas City MO 64108-2619 Office Phone: 816-842-3636. Business E-Mail: rking@kinghershey.com. *There is nothing in life as important as living. "Success" is an objective which all too often deprives its pursuer of the satisfaction he or she seeks. That satisfaction lies in meaningful personal relationships, spiritual communion with a Higher Power, and appreciation for the meaning and purpose of life.*

KING, RICHARD HOOD, retired newspaper executive; b. Boston, Mass, Jan. 24, 1934; s. Gilbert and Frances (Hood) K.; m. Reta Schoonmaker, July 25, 1959; children: D. Whitney, Richard H. Jr., Nanci A. AB, Harvard U., 1955, MBA, 1961. Mgr. acctg. Hitchiner Mfg. Co., Inc., Milford, NH, 1963-68, div. contr. Wallingford, Conn., 1968-71; sec., treas. Smyth Mfg. Co., Inc., Bloomfield, Conn., 1971-72; v.p. fin. Progressive Trade Corp., Glastonbury, Conn., 1972-73; v.p., treas. Hartford Courant Co., Conn., 1973-85, v.p., asst. to gen. mgr., 1986-90, v.p. adminstrn., 1990-96, ret., 1996. Treas. Hartford Courant Found., 1974—96, trustee, 1993—98; v.p., sec., bd. dirs. Better Bus. Bur., Hartford, 1978; bd. dir. Camp Courant, Inc., 1980—96, treas., 1980—96; bd. dirs. Conn. Prison Assn., 1984—91, treas., 1985, chmn. bd. dir., 1986—89; bd. dir. Hartford Symphony Orch., 1990—98; bd. dir., regional v.p. Conn. Audubon Soc., 1991—92, chmn., 1993—95, chmn. emeritus, 1995—98, bd. overseers, 1988—; bd. dir. Penikese Is. Sch., 1998—, treas., 2001—. Lt. j.g. USNR, 1955—57. Mem.: Conn. Daily Newspapers Assn. (treas. 1992, 1st v.p. 1993—95, pres. 1995, exec. dir. 1996—2004), Fin. Exec. Inst. (treas. Hartford chpt. 1980—81, sec. 1981—82, v.p. 1982—83, pres. 1983—84), Glastonbury C. of C. (treas., exec. bd. dirs. 1991—94), Chapoquoit Yacht Club (West Falmouth, Mass., treas. 1973—74, vice commodore 2002, commodore 2003—04), Harvard-Radcliffe Club No. Conn. (v.p. 1989—90, pres. 1990—92). Home: 11 Snug Harbor Ln PO Box 456 West Falmouth MA 02574-0456

KING, ROBERT ALAN, lawyer; b. Mt. Pleasant, Pa., July 15, 1947; s. Robert O. and D. Juanita (Buskey) King; m. Betsy Reynolds, Aug. 22, 1970; children: Brooke, Blythe, Brice. BA, Colgate U., 1969; JD magna cum laude, U. Pitts., 1972. Bar: Pa., 1972, US Dist. Ct. We. Dist. Pa., 1972, US Supreme Ct., 1979, US Ct. Appeals 3rd Cir., 1975, US Ct. Appeals 2nd Cir., 1988, US Ct. Appeals 11th Cir., 2002, Supreme Ct. Pa., US Dist. Ct. No. Dist. Calif. Assoc. Buchanan Ingersoll, Pitts., 1972-78, ptnr., shareholder, 1979-91, Babst, Calland, Clements & Zomnir, Pitts., 1991—2000; ptnr. Reed Smith LLP, Pitts., 2000—, also practice group leader constrn. group. Spl. master civil cases Ct. of Common Pleas of Allegheny County; arbitrator & mediator US Dist. Ct. We. Dist. Pa. Contbg. author Proving and Pricing Construction Claims, 2nd edit., 1996. Active Govt. Orgn. Com., Hampton Twp., Pa., 1974. Fellow Am. Bar Found; mem. ABA (mem. forum on constrn. industry), Pa. Bar Assn., Allegheny County Bar Assn. (inaugural chair constrn. sect.), Am. Coll. Trial Lawyers, Acad. Trial Lawyers Allegheny County, Am. Arbitration Assn., Master Builders Assn. Avocation: golf. Office: Reed Smith LLP 435 Sixth Ave Pittsburgh PA 15219 Office Phone: 412-288-4128. Office Fax: 412-288-3063. Business E-Mail: rking@reedsmith.com.

KING, ROBERT ALAN, psychiatrist, educator; b. Chgo., Jan. 29, 1943; m. Ruth G. King, 1983; children: Benjamin, Claire, Adam. BA, Oxford U., 1965; MD, Harvard U., 1968; BA, Cornell U., 1963. Cert. psychiatry, child psychiatry. Clin. assoc., staff psychiatrist NIMH, Rockville, Md., 1972—75; dir. for inpatient psychiatry Children's Hosp. Nat. Med. Ctr., Washington, 1976—81; dir. adolescent day svcs. Chestnut Lodge, Rockville, 1981—88; mem. faculty Yale Med. Sch., 1988—; prof. child psychiatry Yale Child Study Ctr., New Haven, 1998—. Mng. editor: Psychoanalytic Study of the Child. Lt. comdr. USPHS, 1972—75. Home: 165 Everit St New Haven CT 06511 Office: 230 S Frontage Rd New Haven CT 06520-7900 Office Phone: 203-785-5880. E-mail: robert.king@yale.edu.

KING, ROBERT BRUCE, federal judge; b. White Sulphur Springs, W.Va., Jan. 29, 1940; m. Julia Kay Doak, Apr. 16, 1965. BA, W.Va. U., 1961; JD, W.Va. Coll. of Law, 1968. Bar: W.Va. 1968, U.S. Dist. Ct. (so. dist.) W.Va. 1968, U.S. Ct. Appeals W.Va. 1968, U.S. Ct. Appeals (4th cir.) 1970, U.S. Dist. Ct. (no. dist.) W.Va. 1972, U.S. Supreme Ct. 1974, U.S. Dist. Ct. (ea. dist.) Ky. 1975, U.S. Claims Ct. 1985, U.S. Tax Ct. 1991. Asst. mgr. Sam Snead All-Am. Golf Course, Sharpes, Fla., 1965; rsch. asst. State and Cmty. Planning Office, Office of R&D, W.Va. U., Morgantown, W.Va., 1966—68; law clk. Chief Judge John A. Field, Jr. U.S. Dist. Ct. (so. dist.) W.Va., Charleston, 1968—69; assoc. Haynes and Ford, Lewisburg, W.Va., 1969—70; asst. US atty. So. Dist. of W.Va., Charleston, 1970—74; assoc. Spilman, Thomas, Battle and Klostermeyer, Charleston, 1975, ptnr., 1976—77, 1981; US atty. So. Dist. of W.Va., Charleston, 1977—81; ptnr. King Allen Guthrie & McHugh, 1981—98; judge US Ct. Appeals (4th cir.), Richmond, Va., 1998—. Mem. Jud. Investigation Commn. of W.Va., 1990—94; vis. com. Coll. of Law of W.Va. U., 1997—; mem. 4th Cir. Jud. Coun. Mem., W.Va. N.G., 1957—59, mem. USAF, 1961—64. Scholar Patrick Duffy Koontz. Fellow: Am. Bar Found., Am. Coll. Trial Lawyers; mem.: ABA, Am. Bd. Trial Advocates (W.Va. chpt. pres. 1986—90), Jud. Conf. of 4th Cir. Ct. Appeals, W.Va. Law Sch. Assn., W.Va. U. Alumni Assn., Greenbrier County Bar Assn., Kanawha County Bar Assn., W.Va. Bar Assn., W.Va. Golf Assn., U.S. Golf Assn., Order of the Coif, Phi Alpha Delta, Pi Sigma Alpha. Presbyterian. Office: Ste 7602 300 Virginia St Charleston WV 25301*

KING, ROBERT CHARLES, biologist, educator; b. N.Y.C., June 3, 1928; s. Charles James and Amanda (McCutchen) King. BS, Yale U., 1948, PhD, 1952. Scientist biology dept. Brookhaven Nat. Lab., 1951-55; mem. faculty Northwestern U., 1956—, prof. biology, 1964-99, prof. emeritus, 2000—. Chmn. 8th Brookhaven Symposium in Biology, 1955; vis. investigator, fellow Rockefeller U., 1959; NSF sr. postdoctoral fellow U. Edinburgh, Scotland, 1958, Commonwealth Sci. and Indsl. Research Orgn. Div. Entomology, Canberra, Australia, 1963, Sericultural Expt. Sta., Tokyo, Japan, 1970 Author: Genetics, 2d edit., 1965, A Dictionary of Genetics, 6th edit., 2002, (with W.D. Stansfield) Ovarian Development in Drosophila melanogaster, 1970, also numerous papers; editor: Handbook of Genetics Series, 5 vols., (with H. Akai) Insect Ultrastructure, 2 vols., 1982. Fellow AAAS; mem. Am. Soc. Zoologists, Histochem. Soc., Am. Soc. Cell Biology (treas. 1972-75), Electron Microscopy Soc. Am., Genetics Soc. Am., Am. Soc. Naturalists, Soc. Devel. Biology, Entomol. Soc. Am., Genetics Soc. Can., Genetics Soc. Korea, Sigma Xi (pres. Northwestern U. chpt. 1966-67) Home: 2890 Fredric Ct Northbrook IL 60062-7504

KING, ROBERT HOWARD, marketing professional; b. Excelsior Springs, Mo., June 28, 1921; s. Howard Churchill King and Nancy (Henry) King Eaton; m. Nancy Brown (dec.); children: John Mcfeeley (dec.), Mary Nan King Murphy, Sarah Ann King Robinson; m. Marjorie Kerr, Feb. 26, 1966 (dec.). Student, Kenyon Coll., 1938-40. V.p. sales Ency. Britannica, Inc., Chgo., 1946-61; pres. Spencer Internat., Inc., Chgo., 1961-66; v.p. Dill-Clitherow & Co., Chgo., 1966-68; pres. Time-Life Librs., Inc., Chgo., 1968-79; chmn., pres., CEO World Book, Inc., Chgo., 1979-83; pres. Consumer Mktg. Internat., Inc., Christiansted, St. Croix, 1983—. Bd. dirs. Good Will, Inc., Charlotte, N.C. Capt. U.S. Army, 1942-46, World War II. Mem. Direct Selling Assn. (chmn., Hall of Fame 1980), World Fedn. Direct Selling Assns. (founder, chmn. 1978-81), Direct Selling Edn. Found. (chmn. Circle of Honor 1992), Direct Mkgt. Assn., Chgo. Club, Lighthouse Point Yacht & Racquet Club. Office: 9375 Swansea Ln West Palm Beach FL 33411-1516 Office Phone: 561-309-0101. Business E-Mail: doorknocker@adelphia.net.

KING, ROBERT L., academic administrator; m. Karen King; 4 children. BA, Trinity Coll.; JD, Vanderbilt U. Prosecutor Monroe County Dist. Atty.'s Office; N.Y. State Assemblyman Rochester, 1987—91; Monroe County exec.; dir. Gov.'s Office of Regulatory Reform, NY, 1995—98; budget dir. N.Y. State, 1998—99; chancellor SUNY, 1999—. Prof. bus. law St. John Fisher Coll., Rochester; appointed mem. U.S. Commn. on Presdl. Scholars, 2001. Avocations: baseball, golf, sailing, reading. Office: SUNY State University Plaza Albany NY 12246*

KING, ROBERT LEROY, business administration educator; b. Decatur, Ga., Jan. 22, 1931; s. John Todd and Charlotte (Stringer) K.; m. Helen Butler Leaptrott, Mar. 25, 1956; children: Robert Todd, Keith Alan, John Christopher. BBA, U. Ga., 1952; MA, Mich. State U., 1953, PhD, 1960; Dr honoris causa, Oskar Lange Acad. Econs., Wroclaw, Poland, 1992. Asst. prof. mktg. U. S.C., Columbia, 1957-61, assoc. prof., 1961-65; prof. mktg. Va. Poly. Inst. and State U., Blacksburg, 1965-82, head dept., 1969-76; prof. bus. adminstrn., head dept. The Citadel, Charleston, S.C., 1982-85, Robert A. Jolley chair bus. adminstrn., 1985-90; dir. internat. bus. studies, prof. mktg. U. Richmond, 1990-96, prof. emeritus, 1996—. Cons. in field; vis. rsch. Warsaw Tech. U., Acad. Econs. in Wroclaw; overseas tchr. in field. Author: An Annotated Index to the Procs. of the Am. Mktg. Assn. Educators Confs., 1973, 90, Procs.: So. Mktg. Assn. 1973 Conf., 1974, Marketing and the New Science of Planning, 1969, Retailing: Theory and Practice for the 21st Century, 1985, Marketing in an Environment of change, 1986, Minority Marketing: Issues and Prospects, 1987, Retailing: Its Present and Future, 1988, Procs. of the 1988 Conf. of the Acad. of Internat. Bus. S.E. U.S. Region, Mktg.: Positioning for the 1990s, 1989, Marketing: Toward the 21st Century, 1991, Retailing: Reflections, Insights and Forecasts, 1991, Developments in Marketing Science, Vol. XIV, 1991, Marketing: Perspectives for the 1990s, 1992, Minority Marketing: Research Perspectives for the 1990s, 1993, Retailing: Theories and Practices for Today and Tomorrow, 1994, Retailing: End of a Century and a Look to the Future, 1997, Internat. Conf. Procs. of Am. Acad. Advt.: 2001 Asia-Pacific Conf., 2001, Internat. Conf. Procs. of Am. Acad. Advt., 2003, Asia-Pacific Conf., 2003; contbr. numerous articles to profl. jours. With AUS, 1953-55, maj. Res., 1955-76. Grantee Ford Found., 1964-65, Va. Poly. Inst. and State U., 1979-82, Citadel Devel. Foun., 1982-90. Mem. Am. Acad. Advt. (exec. sec. 1986-2002, dir. conf. svcs. 2002—, book rev. editor Jour. Advt. 1983-94), Am. Mktg. Assn., Acad. Mktg. Sci. (bd. govs. 1988-94, chmn. bd. govs. 1988-90, v.p. fin., treas. 1986-88), Assn. for Consumer Rsch., Acad. Internat. Bus., Am. Assn. for Advancement of Slavic Studies, Decision Scis. Inst., So. Conf. Slavic Studies, So. Mktg. Assn. (pres. 1972-73), Delta Sigma Pi, Omicron Delta Epsilon, Omicron Delta Kappa, Beta Gamma Sigma. Baptist. Avocations: classical music, history, travel, photography. Home: 2440 Edgeview Ln Midlothian VA 23113-9618 Office: U Richmond Sch Bus Am Acad Advertising Richmond VA 23173 E-mail: rking@richmond.edu.

KING, ROBERT LUCIEN, retired lawyer; b. Petaluma, Calif., Aug. 9, 1936; s. John Joseph and Ramona Margaret (Thorson) K.; m. Suzanne Nanette Parre, May 18, 1956 (div. 1973); children: Renee Michelle, Candyce Lynn, Danielle Louise, Benjamin Robert; m. Linda Diane Carey, Mar. 15, 1974 (div. 1981); 1 child, Debra; m. J'an See, Oct. 27, 1984 (div. 1989); 1 child, Jonathan F.; m. Marilyn Collins, June 15, 1991. AB in Philosophy, Stanford U., 1958, JD, 1960. Bar: Calif., N.Y. 1961. Asst. U.S. atty. U.S. Atty's. Office (so. dist.), N.Y.C., 1964-67; assoc. Debevoise & Plimpton, N.Y.C., 1960-64, 67-70, ptnr. NYC, 1970—2003, mng. ptnr. LA, 1989—95. Lectr. Practicing Law Inst., N.Y.C., ABA, Asia/Pacific Ctr. for Resolution of Internat. Bus. Disputes, CPR Inst. for Dispute Resolution. Fellow: Am. Coll. Trial Lawyers; mem.: Calif. Bar Assn., Assn. Bar City NY. Democrat. Avocation: poetry. Business E-Mail: rlking@debevoise.com.

KING, ROBERT THOMAS, editor, writer; b. Hillside, N.J., Oct. 29, 1930; s. Philip Arthur and Lucy (Davis) K.; m. Fredericka Bredow, 1978 Ed., Emmanuel Coll., Cambridge, Eng., 1948-50; BA, Birmingham (Eng.) U., 1955; postgrad., Shakespeare Inst., Stratford-Upon-Avon, Eng., 1955-56. Trainee Oxford U. Press, N.Y.C., 1957-59; chief copy editor NYU Press, 1959-61, editor, 1961-63, mng. editor, 1963-66; dir. U. S.C. Press, Columbia, 1966-84. Contbr. articles to profl. jours., mags., newspapers. Recipient Lucy Hampton Bostick award, 1978. Mem. Am. Assn. Univ. Presses (bd. dirs. 1972-74, chmn. goals and long-range problems com.), Andiron Club, Grolier Club, Torch Club (Columbia). Episcopalian (dir. The Episcopalian, vestry, lic. lay reader). Home: 3994 Old Douglass Rd Blackstock SC 29014-8539

KING, RONALD AMOS, federal official, retired communications professional; b. Livingston, Mont., July 1, 1942; s. Amos Jefferson and Annie Margaret King; m. Lucinda Ann McIntire, Feb. 20, 1959; 1 child, Kerrilee Boggio. AS, Southwestern Coll., 1973; BA, NYU, 1980; MPA, Golden Gate U., 1983. Enlisted USN, 1960, advanced through grades to sr. chief petty officer, adminstr. USN Comdr. Cruiser-Destroyer Flotilla II San Diego, 1966-67, instr. USN Combined Svc. Support Program Sch. Alameda, Calif., 1967-70, chief adminstrn. Naval Investigative Svc. Taipei, Taiwan, 1970-71, chief adminstrn. Comdr. Task Force 157 Fleet Post Office N.Y.C., 1974-75, adminstrv. officer USS Milwaukee Norfolk, Va., 1975-78, ret. active duty, 1979; mgmt. analyst USN Manpower and Materials Analysis Ctr., Norfolk, 1978-83, U.S. Dept. Energy, Idaho Falls, Idaho, 1983-87, fed. mgr. Butte, Mont., 1987-92, comm. dir. Idaho Falls, 1993—2003; owner King Consulting LLC, Idaho Falls, Idaho, 2003—. Editor (quar. jour.) Survival Today, 1973. Decorated Vietnam Svc. medal USN, 1965, Nat. Def. Svc. medal USN, 1965, Joint Svcs. Commendation medal USN, 1970, Chinese Meritorious Rememberance medal USN, 1971. Mem. Greater Idaho Falls C. of C. (bd. dirs. 1993-2002), Eagle Rock Masonic Lodge, AEC Sportsmens Club. Methodist. Avocations: travel, hiking, photography. Home and Office: 2670 Ridgecrest Dr Idaho Falls ID 83404-8312 E-mail: rking235@msn.com.

KING, RONALD BAKER, federal judge; b. San Antonio, Aug. 16, 1953; s. Donald Dick and Elaine (Baker) K.; m. Cynthia Sauer, June 7, 1975; children: Karen Elizabeth, Ronald Baker Jr., Kelsey Ann. BA with high honors, So. Meth. U., 1974; JD with high honors, U. Tex., 1977. Bar: Tex. 1977, U.S. Dist. Ct. (we. dist.) Tex. 1980, U.S. Ct. Appeals (5th cir.) 1981, U.S. Tax Ct. 1985. Briefing atty. Supreme Ct. Tex., Austin, 1977-78; assoc. Foster, Lewis, Langley, Gardner & Banack Inc., San Antonio, 1978-82, ptnr., 1982-88; judge U.S. Bankruptcy Ct. (we. dist.) Tex., San Antonio, 1988—. Mem. Tex. Bar Assn., Nat. Conf. Bankruptcy Judges. Presbyterian. Avocation: basketball. Office: US Bankruptcy Ct PO Box 1439 San Antonio TX 78295-1439

KING, RONOLD WYETH PERCIVAL, physicist, educator; b. Williamstown, Mass., Sept. 19, 1905; s. James Percival and Edith Marianne Beate (Seyerlen) K.; m. Justine Merrell, June 22, 1937 (dec. Aug. 1990); 1 son, Christopher Merrell; m. Mary M. Govoni, June 1, 1991. AB, U. Rochester, 1927, S.M., 1929; PhD, U. Wis., 1932; student, U. Munich, Germany, 1928-29, Cornell U., 1929-30. Asst. in physics U. Rochester, 1927-28; Am.-German exchange student, 1929-30; White fellow in physics Cornell U., 1929-30; U. fellow in elec. engrng. U. Wis., 1930-32, research asst., 1932-34; instr. physics Lafayette Coll., 1934-36, asst. prof., 1936-37; Guggenheim fellow Berlin, Germany, 1937-38; with Harvard U., 1938—, successively instr., asst. prof., assoc. prof., 1938-46, prof. applied physics, 1946-72, prof. emeritus, 1972—. Cons. electromagnetics and antennas, 1972— Author: Electromagnetic Engineering, Vol. 1, 1945, 2d edit, Fundamental Electromagnetic Theory, 1963, Transmission Lines, Antennas and Wave Guides, (with A.H. Wing and H.R. Mimmo), 1945, 2d edit., 1965, Transmission-Line Theory, 1955, 2d edit., 1965, Theory of Linear Antennas, 1956, (with T.T. Wu) Scattering and Diffraction of Waves, 1959, (with R.B. Mack and S.S. Sandler) Arrays of Cylindrical Dipoles, 1968, (with C.W. Harrison, Jr.) Antennas and Waves: A Modern Approach, 1969, Tables of Antenna Characteristics, 1971, (with G.S. Smith et al) Antennas in Matter, 1981 (with S. Prasad) Fundamental Electromagnetic Theory and Applications, 1986, (with M. Owens and T.T. Wu) Lateral Electromagnetic Waves Theory and Applications to Communications, Geophysical Exploration and Remote Sensing, 1992 (with G. Fikioris and R.B. Mack) Cylindrical Depole Arrays, 2002; also articles in field. Guggenheim fellow Europe, 1937, 58, IBM scholar Northeastern U., 1985; recipient Disting. Service citation U. Wis., 1973, Pender award U. Pa., 1986. Fellow IEEE (Centennial medal 1984, Grad. Edn. award 1997, Disting. Educator award 2001), AAAS, Am. Acad. Arts and Scis., Am. Phys. Soc.; mem. IEEE Antennas and Propagation Soc. (Disting. Achievement award 1991, Chento Tai Disting. Educator award 2001), AAUP, Internat. Sci. Radio Union, Bavarian Acad. Sci. (contbg. mem.), Phi Beta Kappa, Sigma Xi. Home: 92 Hillcrest Pky Winchester MA 01890-1440 Office: Gordon McKay Lab 9 Oxford St Cambridge MA 02138-2901

KING, ROSALYN MERCITA, social sciences educator, researcher, psychologist; b. Jacksonville, Fla., Aug. 16, 1948; d. Morris Charles and Marie (Coleman) K. BS, Howard U., 1970, MA, 1972; EdD, Harvard U., 1979. Dir. police youth project NCCJ, Washington, 1970-73; placement coord. U. North Fla., Jacksonville, 1973-74, instr., student support counselor, 1973-75; career edn. program coord. Roxbury/Harvard Sch. Program, Cambridge, Mass., 1976; rsch. analyst Spl. Commn. on Unequal Ednl. Opportunity Mass. Ho. of Reps., Boston, 1977; program coord. Freedom House, Inc., Roxbury, Mass., 1977-78; sr. program assoc. Expand Assocs., Inc., Silver Spring, Md., 1979; sr. assoc., dir. rsch. Mark Battle Assocs., Inc., Washington, 1980; dir. planning, program devel. and tech. assistance PUSH-Excel Inst. Research and Tng., Washington, 1981; rsch. assoc. So. Ctr. Studies in Pub. Policy Clark Coll., Atlanta, 1981-84; pres. Info. Rsch. Network Svc., Alexandria, Va., 1984—, Bathshua's Greetings, Alexandria, 1988—. Chief racial stats. U.S. Bur. Census, Washington, 1988; vis. prof. psychology Coppin State Coll., Balt., 1989-90; faculty rsch. assoc. U. Md., College Park, 1990-91; adj. lectr. dept. psychology George Mason U., Fairfax, Va., 1991—; adj. prof. psychology Prince George's C.C., Andrews AFB, 1991-94, Mary Washington Coll., Fredericksburg, Va., 1992-93, Catonsville (Md.) C.C., 1991-96, lectr., 1994-96; sr. pub. health analyst Agy. for HIV/AIDS Comm. Pub. Health, Washington, 1992-94; from assoc. prof. to prof. psychology and chair Ctr. for Tchg. Excellence No. Va. Region, No. Va. C.C., Loudoun campus, Sterling, Va., 1996—. Contbr. articles to profl. jours. Mem. APA, Am. Psychol. Soc., Soc. for Tchg. of Psychology, Eastern C.C. Social Scis. Assn. (trustee 2003—, chair bd. trustees 2003—), Psi Chi, Phi Delta Kappa. Office Phone: 703-450-2629. E-mail: rosalynmercita.king@worldnet.att.net, roking@nvcc.edu.

KING, ROY MICHAEL, music educator; b. New Orleans, Nov. 7, 1959; s. Julian L. and Ruth V. King; m. Monya L. King, July 7, 1984; 1 child, Olivia L. B.Mus.Edn., La. State U., 1984, M. Music and Conducting, 1998. Asst. dir. bands East Coweta H.S., Senoia, Ga., 1984—86; dir. bands Fairdale H.S., Louisville, 1986—87; asst. dir. bands Pine Forest H.S., Pensacola, Fla., 1988—93, dir. bands, 1993—96; grad. asst. La. State U., Baton Rouge, 1996—98, asst. dir. bands, 1998—. Mem.: Nat. Band Assn., Coll. Band Dirs. Nat. Assn., La. Music Educators Assn. (bd. dirs. 2002—), Phi Kappa Lambda, Kappa Kappa Psi, Phi Beta Mu. Republican. Episcopalian. Avocation: fishing. Home: 950 S Foster #31 Baton Rouge LA 70806 Office: Louisiana State Univ 292 Band Hall Baton Rouge LA 70803

KING, SHARON LOUISE, lawyer; b. Ft. Wayne, Ind., Jan. 12, 1932; AB, Mt. Holyoke Coll., 1954; JD with distinction, Valparaiso U., 1957; LLM in Taxation, Georgetown U., 1961. Bar: Ind. 1957, D.C. 1958, Ill. 1962. Trial atty. tax divsn. U.S. Dept. Justice, 1958—62; sr. counsel Sidley Austin Brown & Wood, Chgo. Bd. dirs., past pres. Lawyer's Com. for Better Housing, Inc. Fellow Am. Coll. Tax Counsel; mem. ABA (chmn. com. closely-held corps. taxation sect. 1979-81, regulated pub. utilities com. taxation sect. 1982-83, coun. dir. taxation sect. 1983-86), Chgo. Bar Assn. (bd. mgrs. 1973-75, chmn. fed. tax com. 1983-84), Ill. State Bar Assn. (counsel dir. sect. fed. taxation 1989-91), Women's Bar Assn. Ill. Found. (bd. dirs., past pres.). Office: Sidley Austin Brown & Wood Bank One Plaza 10 South Dearborn Street Chicago IL 60603

KING, SHARON MARIE, consulting company executive; b. Clarksville, Ark., Sept. 16, 1946; d. Argie L. and Vida M. K.; m. Robert W. Warnke, Feb. 14, 1983; children: Michael R., Jenna L. AA, Coll. of Ozarks, Clarksville, 1966; BA summa cum laude, Calif. State U., Dominguez Hills, 1979. Sr. exec. asst. Computer Sci. Corp., El Segundo, Calif., 1973-79; office mgr., bookkeeper Internal Charter Brokers, Manhattan Beach, Calif., 1979-80; office mgr. Metal Box Can, Torrance, Calif., 1980-81; sec. to pres. Filtrol, L.A., 1981-82; owner, mgr. Select Secretarial Svc., Manhattan Beach, 1982-89; pres., CEO Chipton-Ross, Inc., El Segundo, Calif., 1989—. Mem. Calif. C. of C. Presbyterian. Office: Chipton-Ross Inc 1756 Manhattan Beach Blvd Manhattan Beach CA 90266-6220 E-mail: sking@chiptonross.com.

KING, SHELDON SELIG, health facility administrator, educator; b. NYC, Aug. 28, 1931; s. Benjamin and Jeanne (Fritz) King; m. Ruth Arden Zeller, June 26, 1955 (div. 1987); children: Tracy Elizabeth, Meredith Ellen, Adam Bradley; m. Xenia Tonesk, 1988. AB, NYU, 1952; MS, Yale U., 1957. Adminstrv. intern Montefiore Hosp., NYC, 1952, 1955; adminstrv. asst. Mt. Sinai Hosp., NYC, 1957—60, asst. dir., 1960—66, dir. planning, 1966—68; exec. dir. Albert Einstein Coll. Medicine-Bronx Mcpl. Hosp. Ctr., Bronx, NY, 1968—72; asst. prof. Albert Einstein Coll. Medicine, NYC, 1968—72; dir. hosps. and clinics Univ. Hosp., assoc. clin. prof. U. Calif., San Diego, 1972—81; acting head div. health care scis., dept. cmty. medicine U. Calif. Sch. Medicine, 1978—81; assoc. v.p. Stanford (Calif.) U., 1981—85, clin. assoc. prof. cmty., family and preventive medicine; exec. v.p. Stanford U. Hosp., 1981—85, pres., 1986—89, Cedars-Sinai Med. Ctr., LA, 1989—94, CEO, 1989—94; exec. v.p. Salick Health Care, Inc., LA, 1994—99, pres. ea. region, 1996—98; interim dir. UCLA Med. Ctr., 1995; interim COO INFOHEALTH Mgmt. Corp., 1999—2000, bd. dirs., 2000—; prin. Creative

Intellectual Commerce, 2001—. Mem. adminstrv. bd. Coun. of Tchg. Hosps., 1981—86, chmn. adminstrv. bd., 1985; preceptor George Washington U., Ithaca Coll., Yale U., U. Mo., CUNY; chmn. health care com. San Diego County Immigration Coun., 1974—77; adv. coun. Calif. Health Facilities Commn., 1977—82; chmn. ad hoc bd. advisors Am. Bd. Internal Medicine, 1985—91; mem. exec. com. St. Joseph Health Sys., 1990—94; acting chmn. Am. Health Properties, 1996—; nat. adv. com. Robert Wood Johnson Exec. Nurse Fellows Program, 1998—; trustee Carondelet Found., Carondelet Health Sys., Tucson, 2003—. Mem. editl. adv. bd. (book) Who's Who in Health Care, 1977, mem. editl. bd. Jour. Med. Edn., 1979—84. Bd. dirs. hosp. coun. San Diego and Imperial Counties, 1974—77, treas., 1976, pres., 1977; bd. dirs. United Way San Diego, 1975—80, Vol. Hosps. Am., 1990—94; mem. Accreditation Coun. for Grad. Med. Edn., 1987—90, Prospective Payment Assessment Commn., 1987—90; bd. dirs. Hosp. Fund, 1987—2000. With U.S. Army, 1952—55. Fellow: APHA, Am. Hosp. Assn. (governing coun. Met. sect. 1983—86, coun. on fin. 1987, ho. of dels. 1987—89), Am. Coll. Health Care Execs.; mem.: Inst. of Medicine, Am. Podiatric Med. Assn. (project coun. 2000 1985—86), Calif. Hosp. Assn. (trustee 1978—81). Office Phone: 520-455-5773. Personal E-mail: xenshel@theriver.com.

KING, SHERYL JAYNE, secondary education educator, counselor; b. East Grand Rapids, Mich., Oct. 29, 1945; d. Thomas Benton III and Bettyann Louise (Mains) K. BS in Family Living, Sociology, Secondary Edn., Cen. Mich. U., 1968, M in Counseling, 1971. Educator Newaygo (Mich.) Pub. Schs., 1968-72; interior decorator Sue King Interiors, Grand Rapids, Mich., 1972-73; dir. girl's unit Dillon Family and Youth Svcs., Tulsa, 1973-74; mgr. Fellowhip Press, Grand Rapids, Minn., 1974-76; educator, counselor Itasca Community Coll., Grand Rapids, 1977-81, Dist. 318, Grand Rapids, 1977—, dept. head, 1977-81, 85-87. Bd. dirs., chair program com. Marriage and Family Devel. Ctr., Grand Rapids, 1985-89. Treas. Cove Whole Foods Coop., 1978-80; chmn. bd. Christian Cmty. Sch., 1977-78; jr. high softball coach, 1983-86; issues com. No. Minn. Citizens League, Grand Rapids, 1984—, Blandin Found. Study, 1985-86; chair Itasca County Women's Consortium, Grand Rapids, 1983-87, Women's Day Conf., Grand Rapids, 1983-87; bd. dirs. audio tech. Fellowship of Believers, Grand Rapids, 1974-87, 90-98, deaconess, 1974—; bd. dir. audio tech Camp Dominion, Cass Lake, Minn., 1976-80; fitness com., chmn. aquatic com., YMCA, Grand Rapids, 1974-87; bd. dirs. Grand Rapids Libr., 2003—. Recipient 6 Outstanding Svc. awards Fellowship of Believers, 1974-79. Mem. Alpha Delta Kappa. Republican. Avocations: photography, tennis, sailing, softball, travel, writing. Home: 1914 Mckinney Lake Rd Grand Rapids MN 55744-4330

KING, STEPHEN EDWIN, novelist, scriptwriter; b. Portland, Maine, Sept. 21, 1947; s. Donald and Nellie Ruth (Pillsbury) K.; m. Tabitha Jane Spruce, Jan. 2, 1971; children: Naomi Rachel, Joseph Hillstrom, Owen Phillip. BS, U. Maine, 1970. Tchr. English, Hampden (Maine) Acad., 1971-73; writer in residence U. Maine at Orono, 1978-79. Novels include Carrie, 1974, 'Salem's Lot, 1975, The Shining, 1976, The Stand, 1978, The Dead Zone, 1979, Firestarter, 1980, Cujo, 1981, Different Seasons, 1982, The Dark Tower I: The Gunslinger, 1982, Christine, 1983, Pet Sematary, 1983, (with Peter Straub) The Talisman, 1984, Cycle of the Werewolf, 1985, Skeleton Crew, 1986, It, 1986, The Eyes of the Dragon, 1987, Misery, 1987, The Dark Tower II: The Drawing of the Three, 1987, The Tommyknockers, 1987, The Dark Half, 1989, The Stand, the Complete and Uncut Edition, 1990, The Dark Tower III: The Waste Lands, 1991, Needful Things, 1991, Gerald's Game, 1992, Dolores Claiborne, 1992, Insomnia, 1994, Rose Madder, 1995, Desperation, 1996, The Green Mile, 1996, The Dark Tower IV: Wizard & Glass, 1997, Bag of Bones, 1998, The Girl Who Loved Tom Gordon, 1999, Storm of the Century, 1999, Dreamcatcher, 2001, (with Peter Straub) Black House, 2001, From A Buick 8, 2002, Dark Tower V: Wolves of the Calla, 2003, Dark Tower VI: Song of Susannah, 2004, The Dark Tower VII: The Dark Tower, 2004; (collections) Night Shift, 1978, Different Seasons, 1982, Skeleton Crew, 1985, Four Past Midnight, 1990, Nightmares and Dreamscapes, 1993, Hearts in Atlantis, 1999, Everything's Eventual: 14 Dark Tales, 2002; (as Richard Bachman) Rage, 1977, The Long Walk, 1979, Roadwork, 1981, The Running Man, 1982, Thinner, 1984, The Bachman Books: Four Early Novels, 1986, The Regulators, 1996; (non-fiction) Danse Macabre, 1981, On Writing: A Memoir of the Craft, 2000, (with Stewart O'Nan) Faithful: Two Diehard Boston Red Sox Fans Chronicle the Historic 2004 Season, 2004; (original screenplays) Creepshow, 1982, Cat's Eye, 1984, Silver Bullet, 1985, Maximum Overdrive, 1986, Golden Years, 1991, Sleepwalkers, 1992; creator, writer (TV mini-series) The Stand, 1994, The Shining, 1997, Storm of the Century, 1999, Kingdom Hospital, 2004; actor (films): Knightriders, 1981, Creepshow, 1982, Maximum Overdrive, 1986, Creepshow II, 1988; dir. (films) Maximum Overdrive, 1986. Recipient Medal for Disting. Contbn. to Am. Letters, The Nat. Book Found., 2003. Mem. Author's Guild Am., Screen Artists Guild, Screen Writers of Am., Writer's Guild. Democrat. Office: 49 Florida Ave Bangor ME 04401-3005

KING, STEVE, congressman; b. Storm Lake, Iowa, May 28, 1949; m. Marilyn King; 3 children. Student, N.W. Mo. State U., 1967-70. Mem. Iowa Senate from 6th dist., Des Moines, 1996—2002; vice chair natural resources and environ. com.; mem. appropriations com., mem. bus. and labor rels. com.; mem. commerce com., mem. state govt. com.; mem. U.S. Ho. of Reps from 5th Iowa dist., 2003—; mem. Ho. Judiciary com. Mem. St. Martin's Cath. Ch.; bd. dirs. Odebolt Cmty. Housing. Mem. Iowa Cattleman's Assn., Land Improvement Contractors Am., U.S. C. of C., Odebolt C. of C., SAC County Farm Bur. Republican. Office: 1432 Longworth House Office Bldg Washington DC 20515-1505*

KING, STEVEN ALAN, pain medicine specialist, physician, educator, journalist; b. N.Y.C., Feb. 20, 1951; s. Meyer and Mildred (Liebstein) K. BA, U. Rochester, 1973; MD, U. Md., 1977; MS in Journalism, Columbia U., 1985; postgrad., Internat. Coll. Acupuncture, 1987-89. Diplomate Am. Bd. Psychiatry and Neurology, Am. Bd. Pain Medicine. Resident U. Md. Hosp., Balt., 1977-80; fellow pain mgmt. Hosp. for Joint Diseases-Orthopaedic Inst., N.Y.C., 1986-87; dir. divsn. pain medicine Temple U. Hosp., Phila., 1994-2000; prof. Temple U. Sch. Medicine, Phila., 1998-2000; co-dir. Pain Ctr. Hosp for Joint Diseases, N.Y.C., 2000—05; clin. prof. NYU Sch. Medicine, N.Y.C., 2000—05; co-dir. pain mgmt. Maimorides Med. Ctr., Bklyn., 2005—. Med. cons. Agy. for Healthcare Policy and Rsch., Clin. Practice Guidelines on Pain Mgmt., 1991—. Mem. editorial bd. Clin. Jour. of Pain, 1992-2000, Pain Medicine, 1999—; columnist Pain Report in Geriatric Times, 2000—; contbr. articles to profl. jours. and chpts. to books; free-lance journalist. Congl. intern U.S. Ho. of Reps., Washington, 1972. Mem. Am. Acad. Pain Medicine, Internat. Assn. for the Study of Pain, Am. Pain Soc., Phi Beta Kappa. Office: Dept of Medicine Mainonides Med Ctr 4802 Tentin Ave Brooklyn NY 11219 E-mail: sak80@columbia.edu.

KING, SUSAN, foundation executive; b. Bklyn., June 29, 1947; d. George Joseph and Mildred Prial Robinson; m. Michael C. King, Apr. 17, 1971; 1 child, Mia. Student, London U., 1968-69; BA in English, Marymount Coll., 1969; M in Comm., Fairfield U., 1973. Reporter ABC-TV News, Washington, 1979-83; anchor, reporter WRC-TV, Washington, 1983-87, WJLA-TV, Washington, 1987-93; freelance journalist Washington, 1994; exec. dir., commr. family leave Dept. Labor, Washington, 1995, asst. sec. pub. affairs, 1995-99; v.p. pub. affairs Carnegie Corp., N.Y.C., 1999—. Trustee Marymount Coll., Tarrytown, N.Y., 1993—2002; mem. adv. bd. Fairfield (Conn.) U., 1994-2005. Recipient Emmy award NATAS, Washington, 1984-85, Matrix award Women in Comm., Washington, 1999. Mem. Internat. Womens Forum, Internat. Women's Media Found. (co-founder). Democrat. Roman Catholic. Avocations: hiking, reading, travel. Office: Carnegie Corp 437 Madison Ave New York NY 10022 Office Phone: 212-207-6273.

KING, SUSAN BENNETT, retired glass company executive; b. Sioux City, Iowa, Apr. 29, 1940; d. Francis Moffatt Bennett and Marjorie (Rittenhouse) Sillin; m. Stephen P. Glantz. AB, Duke U., 1962. Legis. asst. U.S. Senate, Washington, 1963-66; dir. Nat. Com. for Effective Congress, Washington, 1967-71, Ctr. Pub. Financing of Elections, Washington, 1972-75; exec. asst. to chmn. Fed. Election Commn., Washington, 1975-77; chmn. U.S. Consumer Product Safety Commn., Washington, 1978-81; dir. consumer affairs Corning (N.Y.) Glass Works, 1982, v.p. corp. communications, 1983-86; pres. Steuben Glass, N.Y.C., 1987-92; sr. v.p. corp. affairs Corning Inc., 1992-94. Trustee Duke U., Durham, NC, 1987—2001, Nat. Pub. Radio Found.; chmn. bd. Making a Difference in Cmtys., Inc., 1995—, Triangle Cmty. Found., 2002—, trustee; bd. dirs. MPC, Inc., 1995—. Fellow Inst. Politics, Harvard U., 1981.

KING, SUSAN MARIE, special education educator; b. Cambridge, Mass., Feb. 10, 1956; d. V. James and Joan Frances Cannalonga; m. John Charles King, Apr. 27, 1975. Student, Valencia C.C., Kissimmee, Fla., 1996—97; student sign lang., Mid Fla. Tech, Orlando, Fla, 1987—92, Fla. Sch. for the Deaf and Blind, St. Augustine, Fla. Vocat. 7 Teaching Certificate Kissimmee, Fla., 1997, cert. QA Registry of Interpreters for the Deaf, completion Dale Carnegie. Belly dancer, Orlando, Fla., 1980—82; co-owner, mgr. Colonial Motel and Apts., St. Cloud, Fla., 1980—89; tchr. Master's Acad., St. Cloud, Fla., 1989—91, Heartland Christian Acad., Kissimmee, Fla., 1993—94, Kingsway Christian Sch., St. Cloud, Fla., 1994—95, Osceola Assn. for Retarded Citizens and Tech. Edn. Ctr. Osceola (TECO), Kissimmee, Fla., 1995—97; tchr., testing specialist TECO, Kissimmee, Fla., 1995—. Sales rep. Avon, 2000—; mystery shopper, 2003—. Co-dir. (variety shows) Variety Show; translator: (first person to interpret Nat. Anthem performance in sign lang.) Orlando Magic Game, 1990 (cert., 1990). Vol. Spl. Olympics, Kissimmee, Fla., 1994—96, Osceola Ctr.Arts, Kissimmee, Fla., 1995—96, Am. Bible Soc., New York, NY, 1984—89; interpreter Heartland Worship Ctr., Kissimmee, Fla., 1985—95. Recipient Second Pl. Nat. Essay Olympics, Assn. of Christian Sch. Internat., 1994. Mem.: Kissimmee Deaf Club (mem. 1988—91). Republican. Avocations: horseback riding, reading, puzzles and games. Office: Tech Edn Ctr Osceola-TECO 501 Simpson Rd Kissimmee FL 34744-4459

KING, SUZANNE DAMPIER, chemistry educator; b. Chelsea, Mass., Aug. 31, 1953; d. William Edwin Dampier and Geraldine Treadway (Dampier) Miller; children: Christy, Katy. BA in Chemistry, Occidental Coll., 1975; MS in Chemistry, Calif. State U., 1986. Quality assurance worker Curtis Nuclear Labs., LA, 1975—76; rschr. Barter-Travenol Labs., Costa Mesa, Calif., 1976—78; rsch. & development worker Syva Labs., Palo Alto, Calif., 1978—82; chemistry instr. Calif. State U., Haywood, Calif., 1983, Ohlone Coll., Fremont, Calif., 1984—95; chemistry tchr., sci. dept. leader Valley Christian HS, Dublin, Calif., 1995—. Troop leader, event coord. Girl Scouts, Pleasanton, Calif., 1986—2000; elder, session clerk, tchr. John Knox Presbyn. Ch., Dublin, Calif., 1991—. Mem.: Rotary (interact club faculty advisor 1998—). Presbyterian. Avocations: camping, hiking. Home: 7806 Kentwood Way Pleasanton CA 94588 Office: Valley Christian HS 7500 Inspiration Dr Dublin CA 94568

KING, TABITHA, author; b. 1949; m. Stephen King. Author: (novels) Small World, 1981, Caretakers, 1983, The Trap, 1985, Pearl, 1988, One on One, 1993, The Book of Reuben, 1995, Survivor, 1997, (non-fiction) Mid-Life Confidential, 1994, (anthologies) Shadows 4, 1981, The Best of the Best, 1998, (short stories) The Blue Chair, 1981, Djinn and Tonic, 1998; actor: (films) Knightriders, 1981. Trustee The Stephen and Tabitha King Foundation. Office: The Stephen and Tabitha King Found 49 Florida Ave Bangor ME 04401 Office Phone: 207-990-2910. Office Fax: 207-990-2975.

KING, TAMARA C., educational consultant; d. Alonzo and Geraldine King; 1 child, Armani G. EdB summa cum laude, Chgo. State U., 1998; EdM, U. Ill., Chgo., 2001; EdD, Loyola U., Chgo., 2004. Cert. gen. adminstr. Ill., std. elem. tchr. Ill. Tchr. Chgo. Pub. Schs., 1999—2001, adminstr., 2001—04; ednl. cons. Pearson Scott Foresman, Glenview, Ill., 2004—. Fellow Ill. Consortium for Ednl. Opportunity, 2002—04; Cycle scholar for advanced students, Amoco Corp., 1991—93, Jacqueline Vaughn Future Tchrs. scholar, Chgo. State U., 1997. Mem.: ASCD, Ill. Coun. Tchrs. of Math., Benjamin Banneker Assn., Inc., Am. Ednl. Rsch. Assn., Phi Delta Kappa, Delta Sigma Theta (life; v.p. 1994—95). Office Phone: 800-354-6611.

KING, TAMARA POWERS, music educator, musician; b. Spartanburg, S.C., Dec. 29, 1959; d. Douglas Edgar and Patricia Elizabeth Powers; m. Bryan Ray King, June 23, 1985; 1 child, Caroline Dawn. MusB in Edn., So. Missionary Coll., Collegedale, Tenn., 1982; MusM, Converse Coll., 2004. Customer svc. and sales Powers Printing Co., Inc., Spartanburg, 1982—2000; violin tchr. dept. pre-coll. Converse Coll., Spartanburg, 1982—84; violin and viola tchr. Spartanburg, 1996—, Alia Lawson Pre-Coll., Spartanburg, 2001—03; strings and orch. tchr. Spartanburg County Sch. Dist. 1, Inman, SC, 2002—04. Violinist Spartanburg Symphony Orch., 1982—95, Greenville Symphony Orch., SC, 1985—87, Greater Spartanburg Philharm., 1995—97; violinist and violist Converse Symphony Orch., Spartanburg, 2000—04. Mem. music com. Spartanburg Seventh Day Adventist Ch., 1985—2005, asst. choir dir., 2000. Mem.: Am. String Tchrs. Assn., Music Educator's Nat. Conf., Spartanburg Philharm. Music Club. Avocations: reading, birding and nature study, drawing, collecting musical instruments, painting. Home: 1099 Moore-Duncan Hwy Moore SC 29369

KING, TERRY LEE, statistician, mathematician; b. Akron, Iowa, Feb. 24, 1945; s. Stanley W. and Hazel M. (Peck) K.; m. Carol Elizabeth Glass, June 12, 1971; children: Kevin, Shawn, Heather. BA cum laude, Westmar Coll., 1967; MS, U. Iowa, 1969; PhD, Pa. State U., 1980. Instr. Thiel Coll., Greenville, Pa., 1969-71; statistician Desmatics Inc., State College, Pa., 1975-79; instr. Frostburg (Md.) State Coll., 1979-81, assoc. prof. math./stats., 1981-89; chmn. dept. math./stats. N.W. Mo. State U., Maryville, 1988-93, prof. math. and stats., 1989—; dir. acad. programs Mo. Acad. Sci., Math. and Computing, 2000—03. Editl. collaborator Current Index to Statistics, 1980-89. Deacon, active in music program First Bapt. Ch. Mem. Am. Statis. Assn. (membership com. 1982-84, mem. com. on stats. and disability 1995-97, newsletter editor statis. edn. sect. 1997-2003), Nat. Coun. Tchrs. Math., Math. Assn. Am. (vice-chair Mo. sect. 1990-91, chmn. 1991-92, past chair 1992-93), Rotary Internat. (Maryville chpt., program chair 1995-96, sec. 1996-99, 2001-04), Phi Kappa Phi, Kappa Mu Epsilon, Pi Mu Epsilon. Office: NW Mo State U 800 University Dr Maryville MO 64468-6015 E-mail: tlking@mail.nwmissouri.edu.

KING, THOMAS M., theology studies educator, priest; b. Pitts., s. William Martin and Catherine (Mulvihil) K. BA, U. Pitts., 1951; MA, Fordham U., 1959; Doctorat es Sci. Religeuse, U. Strasbourg, 1968. Joined Jesuits, 1951, ordained priest Roman Cath. Ch., 1964. Prof. Theology Georgetown U., Washington, 1968—. Author: Sartre and the Sacred, 1974, Teilhard's Mysticism of Knowing, 1981, Teilhard de Chardin, 1988, Enchantments, 1989, Merton: Mystic at the Center of America, 1992; editor: Teilhard and the Unity of Knowledge, 1983, Letters of Teilhard and Lucile Swan, 1993, Jung's Four and Some Philosophers, 1999, Teilhard's Mass, 2005. Co-founder, bd. dirs. Cosmos & Creation, Loyola Coll., Balt., 1982—. Univ. Faculty for Life, Washington, 1989—. Roman Catholic. Home: Jesuit Community Georgetown U Washington DC 20057-0001 Office: Georgetown U Dept Theology Washington DC 20057-0001 Office Phone: 202-687-6101. Business E-Mail: kingt@georgetown.edu.

KING, TROY, state attorney general; b. Elba, Ala., Aug. 22, 1968; m. Paige Pinson; children: Briggs, Colden, Asher. BS in History and Soc. sci., Troy State U., 1990; JD, U. Ala., 1994. Bar: Ala. Asst. legal advisor to the Gov. State of Ala., Montgomery, 1995, dep. legal advisor to the Gov., 1995—97, acting exec. sec. to Gov., 1997, dep. exec. sec. to Gov., 1997—99, asst. atty. gen., 1999—2003, legal adviser to Gov., 2003—04, atty. gen., 2004—. Mem. Ala. Law Inst., 1994—, Alternative Dispute Resolution Task Force, 1998—99. Office: Office of the Attorney General 11 South Union Street 3rd fl Montgomery AL 36130

KING, VERNON DALE, art educator; b. Houston, Sept. 24, 1948; s. Walter Lee and Lois Louise King; m. Lillie Doris Jamerson (dec.); 1 child, Tahir Kamal. BA, North Tex. State U., 1973; MA, U. Houston, 1981; postgrad., Art Inst. Houston, 1988—89. Tech. illustrator Lockheed Elecs. Corp., Houston, 1973—74; chem. oper. E.I. DuPont de Nemours Co., Inc., La Porte, 1974—99; educator art E.A. Olle Mid. Sch., Houston, 2000—01, R.W. Dowling Mid. Sch., 2001—02, M.B. Smiley High Sch., 2002—04, Crosby Mid. Sch., Crosby, 2004—. Adj. prof. art Cy-Fair Coll., Houston, 2003—; presenter in field. Exhibitions include Adept New Folk Ctr., Houston, 1979, Galerie Triangle, Washington, 1982—83, Pine Tree Gallery, Troy, Ala., 1983, Art League Houston, 1983, Columbia Coll., Mo., 1984, Black Arts Alliance, Austin, Tex., 1984, State Capitol Bldg., 1985, U. Tex. Inst.Texan Cultures, San Antonio, 1985, Coll. Mainland, Texas City, Tex., 1985, City Hall, Houston, 1985, Black Acad. Arts and Letters, Inc., Dallas, 1985, Carver Cmty. Cultural Ctr., San Antonio, 1987, Nat. Conf. Artists, Bahia, Brazil, 1988, U. Houston, 1989, Galeria Mesa, Ariz., 1994, Austin Peay State U., Clarksville, Tenn., 1995, Austin Visual Arts Assn., Tex., 1998, Sharjah Arts Mus., UAE, 2000, 2005, Nat. Art Edn. Assn., 2002—04, All Media, Omaha, Nebr., 2005, Upstream People Gallery, 2005. Recipient award of Excellence, Manhattan Arts Internat. Coun., N.Y.C., 2003; J.O. Patterson Fine Arts scholar, Ch. of God In Christ, Memphis, 1977. Mem.: Houston Art Educators Assn., Tex. Art Edn. Assn., Nat. Art Edn. Assn. Democrat. Home: 7219 Seminole St Baytown TX 77521 Office: Crosby Mid Sch 14705 FM 2100 Crosby TX 77532 Mailing: PO Box 2503 Baytown TX 77522 Office Phone: 281-328-9265. E-mail: vking@crosbyisd.org.

KING, VICKIE RUTH, minister, shop owner; b. Birmingham, Ala., Aug. 19, 1951; d. Oliver Julian and Nellie Ruth Haynes; m. Donald C. King, Aug. 14, 1970; children: Paul C., Angie D. Chappell. Minister Ind. Penticostal Holiness Ch., Birmingham, 1975—; oil painter Hayden, Ala., 1982—; owner/mgr. King's Creations, Hayden, 1985—; oil painter Cullman Art Guild, Ala., 1994—97; pastor New Hope Ch., Springville, Ala., 1995—97; evangelist Gospel Revelation Inc., Ind., 1997—; oil painter Patrons, Artist Council East, Birmingham, 1997—2003. Storyteller Cherokee Tribe of Northeast Ala., 2000—. Recipient The Diamond Hope Trophy, Famous Poets Soc./Calif., 1999, First Prize for oil painting, Cullman Art Guild/Ala., 1997, Shakespeare Trophy of Excellence, Famous Poets Soc., 2003. Mem.: Gospel Revelation Inc. Avocations: writing, porcelain faires. Home: 1091 Jim Thomas Road Hayden AL 35079

KING, VIRGINIA SHATTUCK, painter, retired school nurse, educator; b. Bklyn., Feb. 8, 1921; d. Harold James Shattuck and Lillian Elizabeth Shatluck; m. Stuart G. King, May 26, 1946 (dec. July 1988); children: Richard D.(dec.), Stuart George, Harold James, Douglas Louis. *In May 1992, I visited Plymouth Harbor, England; its dock was worn with the ancient footprints of those who left for the new world and the footprints of tourists who visited the historic sight over the years and centuries. It was from here that an early relative of my father, born in England in 1621, left for Watertown, Massachusetts. He grew up and married Susanna and they began a branch of the Shattuck family in the new world. The whole Shattuck family history is on record. There is no Mayflower in my line; they came on the second or third boat to America.* BS in Nursing, Columbia U. Sch. of Nursing, N.Y.C., 1944; grad. studies, Adelphi U., Garden City, N.J., SUNY, Stonybrook. RN N.Y., 1946; cert. sch. nurse tchr. N.Y., 1960. Head nurse, obstet. fl. Columbia - Presbyn. Hosp., N.Y.C., 1945—46; pub. health nurse Suffolk County, NY, 1953, sch. nurse, 1959—79, tchr. health edn., 1970—79, ret., 1979. *After I retired and moved to Florida in 1980, I decided to start working on art. Much of my training has been self-taught but I have attended many local workshops and classes. The Melbourne area is saturated with artists and I had no trouble finding someone to teach me the techniques of watercolor painting; I have also taken sculpture course. As a writer, I have tried to incorporate my art into my writing. I became involved in the Cape Canaveral Chapter of the National League of American Pen Women. I show my art in local and out of state shows and through the Brigantine Gallery and the Brevard Cultural Alliance.* Author: From Then...To Who Knows When, 1996; one-woman shows include King Center for Performing Arts, 2000, Fla. Revisited, Maxwell C. King Ctr. Performing Arts, 2001—02, exhibitions include Artists Forum Juried Show, King Ctr. Performing Arts, 1993, Fla. State Soc. Nat. Soc. DAR Am. Heritage Art Competition, 1993 (hon. mention), Spacecoast Art League Spring Show, 1996 (hon. mention), Spacecoast Art League Fall Show, 1996 (3d pl.), Spacecoast Art League Spring Show, 1997 (2d pl.), Spacecoast Art League Fall Show, 1997 (2d pl.), Brevard Mus. of Arts and Scis. 19th Juried Show, 1997, Fla. Hist. Soc. - Tebeau Libr., 1998, George Plimpton Zoo-to-Do, Cape Canaveral, 1998, Boundless Expressions, Moffitt Cancer Rsch. Ctr., 1999, Brevard Mus. Arts and Scis., 1999, Fla. Watercolor Soc. Juried Show, 1999, Charlotte Country Art Guild Nat. Exhibit 2000, 2000, Ridge Art League New Mem. Exhibit, 2000, Bayard Ho. Exhibit, 2000, Strawbridge Art League Ann. Juried Show, 2001, 2005, From Grandmother's Brush, Orlando Mus. of Art, 2001, Fla. Watercolor Soc., 2001 (Strathmore award), Patriotic Traveling Show, Strawbridge Art League, 2002, one-woman shows include King Ctr. for Performing Arts, 2001, exhibitions include Southern Watercolor Show, Baton Rouge, La., 2002, So. Watercolor Soc., 2002, 2005, Melbourn Internat. Airport, 2004, Strawbridge Art League, 2004, children's wall mural, Brevard County Libr., 2000. Second v.p. Friends of Eau Gallie Pub. Libr., 1999—. Recipient Strathmore Paper award, Fla. Water Color Soc., 2001. Mem.: DAR, Nat. League Am. Pen Women, NSDAR (vice regent 2005—), Strawbridge Art League (Green Gables Accepted Juried 2005), Ga. Watercolor Soc. (ribbon and prize 2003), So. Watercolor Soc. (Accepted in Juried Show 2005), P-2 Fla. Watercolor Soc., Brevard watercolor Soc., N.Y. State Tchrs. Retired in Fla. Republican. Achievements include the Virginia Shattuck Archives at Health Scis. Divsn. of Columbia U. Avocations: watercolor artist, writing, swimming, tennis, music. Home and Studio: 2419 Apache Dr Melbourne FL 32935 Personal E-mail: hglartiste@aol.com.

KING, W. DAVID, judge; BS, Murray State U., 1967; JD, U. Ky., 1972. Bar: Ky. 1972, U.S. Dist. Ct. (we. dist.) Ky. Pvt. practice, Paducah, Ky., 1972—79; magistrate judge U.S. Dist. Ct. (we. dist.) Ky., Paducah, 1979—. With U.S. Army, 1968-70. Office: US Dist Ct We Dist Ky Fed Bldg Rm 330 501 Broadway St Paducah KY 42001-6856

KING, WARREN R., judge; Grad., Rensselaer Polytech. Inst.; JD, Am. U.; LLM, Yale U. Atty. U.S. Dist. Ct. D.C.; chief grand jury/intake divsn., dep. and acting chief divsn. Superior Ct. Washington; with Office of Improvements in Adminstrn. of Justice U.S. Dept. Justice; assoc. judge Superior Ct. D.C., Washington, 1981—91, U.S. Ct. Appeals (D.C. cir.), Washington, 1991—, D.C. Ct. Appeals, Washington; civil dispute atty. The McCammon Group. Mem. faculty Antioch Sch. Law, 1975—; mem. staff Atty. Gen.'s task force on violent crime; mem. hearing com. Bd. Profl. Responsibility. With USN. Office: Dist of Columbia Court of Appeals 500 Indiana Ave NW Rm 6000 Washington DC 20001-2131*

KING, WAYNE EDGAR, journalist, educator; b. McDowell County, N.C., Mar. 31, 1939; s. Weldon Edgar and Mary King; m. Nina Davis, (div. June 1978); m. Paula Theodore Carroll, July 16, 1984. BA in Journalism, U. N.C., 1964. Reporter, editor The Detroit Free Press, 1964-69; editor, bur. chief, corr. The N.Y. Times, N.Y.C., 1969-93; dir. journalism program Wake Forest U., Winston-Salem, N.C., 1993—. Working group on disability in U.S. Pres. The White House, 1996. Mem. editl. bd. Acad. Mag., Washington, 1996-2002. Recipient Pulitzer prize, 1968. Mem. AAUP Home: 1901 Waycross Dr Winston Salem NC 27106-3416 Office Phone: 336-758-4399. E-mail: kingwe@wfu.edu.

KING, WAYNE T., lawyer; m. Christine; children: Kelly, Justin. BS, Brigham Young U., 1969; JD, Southwestern U., 1976. CPA; Bar: Calif. 1977. Acct. Haskins & Sells, L.A., 1969-72; controller Chazan Constrn., Burbank, Calif., 1972-74; CPA Peat, Marwick, Mitchell, L.A., 1974—81; pvt. practice Burbank, Calif., 1981-86; CFO, dir. Chantal Pharms., Westwood, Calif., 1984-85; ptnr. Thompson, White, King & French, Valencia, Calif., 1987-95, Thompson & King, Valencia, Calif., 1995—. Office: Thompson & King 23929 W Valencia Blvd Ste 304 Valencia CA 91355-5378 Office Phone: 661-253-0222.

KING, WILLIAM, sculptor; b. Jacksonville, Fla., Feb. 25, 1925; Student, U. Fla., 1942-44, Cooper Union Art Sch., 1945-48, Bklyn. Mus. Art Sch., 1949, Acad. dei Belle Arti, Rome, 1949-50, Ctrl. Sch., London, 1952. Art instr. Bklyn. Mus. Art Sch., 1952-55, U. Calif., Berkeley, 1956-66, Art Students' League, 1968-69, U. Pa., Phila., 1972-73. Artist in residence, SUNY at Fredonia, New Paltz, Jamestown, Oswego, Plattsburgh. One person art exhibitions include: Alan Gallery, N.Y.C., 1954, 55, 61, San Francisco Mus. Art, 1970, Santa Barbara Mus. Art, 1970, Ringling Mus., Sarasota, Fla., 1971, Dag Hammerskjold Pla., N.Y.C., 1971, Jacksonville (Fla.) Art Mus., 1972, Worcester (Mass.) Art Mus., 1972, Elvehjom Art Ctr., U. Wis., Eau Claire, 1973, William Benton Mus., U. Conn., 1973, U. Ga., Athens, 1973, Traveling Exhbn. SUNY, 1974, Benson Gallery, Bridgehampton, N.Y., 1976, Louise Himmelfarb Gallery, Water Mill, N.Y., 1980, Wingspread Gallery, N.E. Harbor, Maine, 1981, Alpha Gallery, Boston, 1971, 82, Hunter Mus., Chattanooga, 1987, David Heath Gallery, Atlanta, 1987, Marilyn Pearl Gallery, N.Y.C., 1988, Internat. Sculpture Ctr., Sothebys, 1989, Simmons Visual Arts Ctr., Brenau Coll., Gainesville, Ga., 1992, U. Pitts., 1995, Seacon Sq., Bangkok, Thailand, 1996, Terry Dintenfass Gallery, N.Y.C., 1962, 64-71, 73, 76, 80-84, 86, 89-92, 94, 97. and others: group exhibitions include: Mus. Modern Art, N.Y.C., 1955, Ann. Exhbn. Whitney Mus. Am. Art., 1952, 54, 56, 58, 60, 62, 64, 66, 68, Fogg Art Mus., Dartmouth Coll., Vassar Cool, Bowdoine Coll. (traveling exhbn. 1972-73), Art Gallery Budapest, Hungary, 1973, Weatherspoon Art Gallery, U. N.C., 1974, Galeria Tonay Schubert, Marbella, Spain, 1976, Grand Palais, Paris, 1976, Inst. Contemporary Art, Boston, Dayton Art Inst., 1982, Chgo. Internat. Art Exhbn., 1982, Am. Acad. Arts and Letters, 1995, White House, 1995, many others; collection Met. Mus. Art, N.Y.C., Guggenheim Mus., Whitney Mus., Nelson and John Rockefeller Collections, others; also commissions. Recipient Sculpture prize, Cooper Union Art Sch., 1948, Fulbright grant, 1949-50. Margaret Tiffany Blake fresco award, 1951, Augustus St. Gaudens medal, Cooper Union, 1964, Creative Artist Pub. Svc. award and grant, 1974, Hakone Open-Air Mus., Japan, Distinction prize, 1980, Nat Acad. Design gold medal, 1986, Am. Acad. Arts and Letters, Louise Nevelson award, 1995. Mem.: NAD (academician 1991—, past pres.).*

KING, WILLIAM BRUCE, retired lawyer; b. Boston, June 3, 1932; s. Gilbert and Frances (Hood) K.; m. Sheila Malone, July 9, 1955; children: Stephen Bruce, Rachel Creath, Christopher Bruce. AB, Harvard U., 1954, LL.B., 1959. Bar: Mass. 1959. Assoc. firm Goodwin Procter, Boston, 1959-67, ptnr., 1968-99, of counsel, 2000—; prin. William B. King P.C., 1981-99. Mem. bd. investment Cambridge Savs. Bank, 1973—, trustee, 1969—, corporator, 1965—; sec. Bradley Real Estate, Inc., 1963-99; trustee Cambridge Heritage Trust, 1984—; dir. mem. exec. com. Cambridge Fin. Group, Inc., 1998—, Cambridge Appleton Trust, N.A., 1999—; corp. dir. Cambridge Homes, 2005-. Author: (with others) Real Estate Investment Trusts: Structures, Analysis, and Strategy, 1997. Trustee Buckingham Browne and Nichols Sch., 1970-76, sec., 1970-73, vice chmn., 1974-76; mem. Cambridge (Mass.) Hist. Commn., 1973—, vice chmn., 1973-86, chmn., 1986—; pres Cambridge Civic Assn., 1963-65; bd. govs. Nat. Assn. Real Estate Investment Trusts, 1982-88, chmn. state regulation subcom. of govt. rels. com., 1989-91. Served with USN, 1954-56. Recipient Industry Leadership award Nat. Assn. Real Estate Investment Trusts, 1995. Home: 25 Hurlbut St Cambridge MA 02138-1603 Office: Exchange Pl Boston MA 02109-2803 E-mail: basking@comcast.net.

KING, WILLIAM COLLINS, retired oil industry executive; b. Pitts., Aug. 11, 1921; s. William Raffington and Anne Blatchford (Collins) K.; m. Carolyn Ottilie Thorne, Sept. 1, 1951; children: William R., John Thorne, Louise R., Andrew C. BSChemE, Carnegie-Mellon U., 1943; MSChemE, MIT, 1948. With Gulf Rsch. & Devel. Co. div. Gulf Oil Corp., Pitts., 1948-55, with chems. dept., 1955-57, dir. market rsch. and econ. planning chems. dept., 1957-63, world wide coord. chem. ops., 1963-67, v.p. chem. ops. in Europe and Middle East, 1967-72, dir. corp. policy analysis, 1972-80, v.p. corp. planning, 1980-85, ret., 1985. Bd. dirs. Fertiberia, S.A., Spain, Rio Gulf Petrolquimica, S.A., Spain, Kuwait Chem. Fertilizer Co., Kuwait; spkr., 1975—, participant nat. and local programs, participant local radio programs. Author: Building For Victory, WW-II and The CBI, and 1875 Engr. Av'n Bn., 2004, contbr. articles to profl. publs. Bd. dirs. Hist. Soc. We. Pa., 1977-99, pres., 1986-90, chmn., 1990-98, vice-chmn., 1998-99, trustee emeritus, 1999 (honored with William Collins King Atrium of Senator John Heinz Pitts. Regional History Ctr., 1996); v.p., bd. dirs. Civic Light Opera Co., Pitts., 1978-86 (Golden Hall of Fame, 1996); councillor of the Atlantic Coun. of the U.S., 1985-93. Served with C.E., U.S. Army, 1943-46, CBI. Recipient Alumni Merit award Carnegie Mellon U., 1998. Fellow Am. Chem. Soc.; mem. N.Am. Soc. Corp. Planning (bd. dir. chpt. 1982-85), Strategic Mgmt. Soc., Coun. Planning Execs. (conf. bd.), Am. Inst. Chem. Engrs. Clubs: Duquesne; Fox Chapel Golf (Pitts.). *Do all that you do in that way most likely to enhance the self esteem of others.*

KING, WILLIAM H., JR., lawyer; b. Richmond, Va., Nov. 4, 1940; AB, Dartmouth Coll., 1963; LLB, U. Va., 1967; MA (hon.), Dartmouth Coll., 1992. Bar: Va. 1967, Tex. 1993. Mem. McGuireWoods LLP, Richmond. Fellow Am. Bar Found., Am. Coll. Trial Lawyers; mem. ABA. Office: McGuireWoods One James Ctr Richmond VA 23219-4030 E-mail: wking@mcguirewoods.com.

KING, WILLIAM RICHARD, business educator, consultant; b. McKeesport, Pa., Dec. 24, 1938; s. Dewey Clark and Cambria Edith (Jones) K.; m. Fay Eileen Bickerton, June 20, 1958; children: James David, Suzan Lorain, Cambria H.L. BS with honors, Pa. State U., 1960; MS Case Inst. Tech, 1962, PhD, 1964. Indsl. engr. Pitts. Steel Co., 1960; instr., research fellow, research asst. Case Inst. Tech., 1960-64; asst. prof. ops. research, 1964-65; asst. prof. stats. and ops. research Air Force Inst. Tech., 1965-67; assoc. prof. bus. adminstrn. U. Pitts., 1967-69, prof., 1969-85, univ. prof., 1986—, dir. doctoral program, 1971-74, dir. Strategic Mgmt. Inst., 1980-85. On leave as profl. staff mem. U.S. Senate Budget Com., 1976-77; v.p., dir. Cleland-King, Inc., 1969-85; mgmt. cons.; chmn. Internat. Conf. on Info. Systems profl. corp., 1987-88, 2005—; vis. prof. U. Auckland, New Zealand, 1994, Nat. U. of Singapore, 1997, City U. of Hong Kong, 1997, 98; chair/co-chair Internat. Conf. on Info. Sys., 1987, 2005. Author: Quantitative Analysis for Marketing Management, 1967, Probablilty for Management Decisions, 1968, (with David Cleland) Systems Analysis and Project Management, 1968 (McKinsey Found. award 1969), 3d edit., 1983, Management: a Systems Approach, 1972, Marketing Management Information Systems, 1977, (with David Cleland) Strategic Planning and Policy, 1978, (with John Grant) The Logic of Strategic Planning, 1982; also 300 articles in profl. jours.; editor: (with David Cleland) Systems, Organizations, Analysis, Management, 1969, Project Management Handbook, 1983, 2d edit., 1989 (Inst. Indsl. Engrs. Book of Yr. award 1984); (with Gerald Zaltman) Marketing Scientific and Technical Information, 1979, (with D. I. Cleland) Strategic Planning and Management Handbook, 1987, (with P. Gray, E. McLean and H. Watson) Management of Information Systems, 1989, 2nd edit., 1994, (with V Sethi) Organizational Transformation Through Business Process Reengineering, 1998; assoc. editor: Strategic Mgmt. Jour., 1985-89, Mgmt. Sci., 1971-89, MIS Quar., 1980-82, editor-in-chief, 1983-85; area editor: Internat. Jour. Info. and Mgmt. Scis.; cons. editor Prentice Hall Info. Mgmt. Series, 1989-99; mem. editl. adv. bd. Omega: The Internat. Jour. of Mgmt. Sci., Info. Systems Rsch., Jour. Global Info. Mgmt., Jour. Mgmt. Info. Sys., Jour. Global Info. Tech. Mgmt., Jour. Market-Focused Mgmt., Info. Sys. Mgmt., Acad. Press, Ency. Info. Sys., Idea Group Press Ency. Knowledge Mgmt. Active YMCA; v.p., dir. Pitts. Commerce Inst., 1971-80; bd. dirs. Western Pa. Montessori Sch., 1968-71, pres., 1968-69. Served to 1st lt. USAF, 1965-67. Ford Found. Systems rsch. fellow, 1960-62; Travelers Ins. Co. rsch. fellow, 1963-64, External Examiner City U. of Hong Kong, 1996-99; Alumni Meml. scholar Pa. State U., 1956-60 Fellow AAAS, Decision Sci. Inst., Assn. Info. Sys. (Leo Lifetime Achievement award 2004), Inst. Mgmt. Sci. and Ops. Rsch.; mem. Planning Forum, Ops. Rsch. Soc. Am., Acad. Mgmt., Strategic Mgmt. Soc., Inst. Mgmt. Scis. (v.p. 1986-89, pres. 1989-90), Assn. Info. Sys. (pres. 1995), Assn. Computing Machinery, Am. Mktg. Assn., Soc. Info. Mgmt., World Future Soc., Tau Beta Pi, Beta Gamma Sigma, Alpha Pi Mu, Sigma Tau. Office: Katz Grad Sch Bus U Pitts Pittsburgh PA 15260 Office Phone: 412-648-1587. E-mail: billking@katz.pitt.edu.

KING, WILLIAM TERRY, retired manufacturing company executive; b. Cleve., Dec. 3, 1943; s. William T. and Marion (Rothweiler) K.; m. Judith Ann Cervantes, Oct. 22, 1943; children: Kimberly, Kelly. BSC, St. Louis U., 1968. Contr. for Can. and Latin Am., Monsanto Co., St. Louis, 1977-82, mgr. internat. fin., 1982-84, dir. ops. analysis, 1984-86, asst. contr., 1986-88, asst. controller, 1993-97; ret., 1997; v.p., contr. Fisher Controls Internat. Inc., Clayton, Mo., 1988-92. Mem. Com. to Elect A.J. Cervantes, St. Louis, 1964-65; v.p. adv. bd. dirs., exec. com., chmn. fin. and planning com. St. Mary's Health Ctr. Mem. Inst. Mgmt. Acctg. (cert.). Republican. Roman Catholic. Avocations: golf, fishing, gardening. Home: 16643 Sterling Pointe Ct Chesterfield MO 63005-4509

KINGDON, CASEY DENNIS, secondary school educator; b. Waterloo, Iowa, Nov. 19, 1980; s. Dennis Marvin Kingdon and Diana Lynn Hallberg. B of Music Edn., Morningside Coll., 2003. Tchr. high sch. instrumental music Carroll Cmty. Schs., Iowa, 2003—. Mem.: Music Educators Nat. Conf., Iowa Bandmasters. Avocations: golf, bowling. Home: 802 W 17th St Carroll IA 51401 Office: Carroll HS 2809 N Grant Rd Carroll IA 51401 Business E-Mail: ckingdon@carroll.k12.ia.us.

KINGDON, JOHN WELLS, political science professor; b. Wisconsin Rapids, Wis., Oct. 28, 1940; s. Robert Wells and Catherine (McCune) K.; m. Kirsten Berg, June 16, 1965; children: James, Tor. BA, Oberlin Coll., 1962; MA, U. Wis., 1963, PhD, 1965. Asst. prof. polit. sci. U. Mich., Ann Arbor, 1965-70, assoc. prof., 1970-75, prof., 1975-98, prof. emeritus, 1998—, chmn. dept. polit. sci., 1982-87. Author: Candidates for Office, 1968, Congressmen's Voting Decisions, 1973, 3d rev. edit., 1989, Agendas, Alternatives and Public Policies, 1984, 2d edit., 1995, America the Unusual, 1998. NSF grantee, 1978-82, Soc. Sci. Research Council grantee, 1969-70; Guggenheim fellow, 1979-80, Ctr. for Advanced Study in Behaviorial Scis. fellow, 1987-88. Fellow Am. Acad. Arts and Scis.; mem. Midwest Polit. Sci. Assn. (pres. 1987-88). Office: U Mich Dept Polit Sci Ann Arbor MI 48109

KINGDON, ROBERT MCCUNE, historian, educator; b. Chgo., Dec. 29, 1927; s. Robert W. and Anna Catherine (McCune) K. AB, Oberlin Coll., 1949; MA, Columbia U., 1950, PhD, 1955; postgrad. U. Geneva, 1951—52, PhD (hon.), 1986; HHD, Oberlin Coll., 1999. Instr., asst. prof. history U. Mass., 1952-57; asst. prof., assoc. prof., prof. history State U. Iowa, Iowa City, 1957-65; prof. history U. Wis., Madison, 1965-98, Hilldale prof. history, 1988-98; mem. Inst. Research Humanities, 1974-98, dir., 1975-87. Vis. instr. Amherst (Mass.) Coll., 1953-54; vis. prof. Stanford U., 1964, 80; bd. dirs. Ctr. Reformation Rsch., St. Louis, pres., 1967-2000. Author: Geneva and the Coming of the Wars of Religion in France, 1555-1563, 1956, Geneva and the Consolidation of the French Protestant Movement, 1564-1572, 1967, The Political Thought of Peter Martyr Vermigli, 1980, Church and Society in Reformation Europe, 1985, Myths About the St. Bartholomew's Day Massacres, 1572-1576, 1988, Adultery and Divorce in Calvin's Geneva, 1995; editor: Sixteenth Century Jour., 1973-97; co-editor: Registres de la Compagnie des Pasteurs de Geneve au temps de Calvin, 1962-64, Registres du Consistoire de Geneve au temps de Calvin, t. 1-3, 1996-2004, Bibliography of the Works of Peter Martyr Vermigli, 1990; contbr. articles to profl. jours. Mem. Am. Soc. Reformation Rsch. (v.p. 1970, pres. 1971), Am. Soc. Ch. History (pres. 1980, Disting. Career award 2004), Cen. Renaissance Conf., Renaissance Soc. Am. (exec. bd. 1972-92), Internat. Fedn. Socs. and Insts. for Study of Renaissance (sec.-treas. 1967-89). Home: 4 Rosewood Cir Madison WI 53711-2723 Business E-Mail: rkingdon@wisc.edu.

KINGHAM, RICHARD FRANK, lawyer; b. Lafayette, Ind., Aug. 2, 1946; s. James R. and Loretta C. Kingham; m. Justine Frances McClung, July 6, 1968; 1 child, Richard Patterson. BA, George Washington U., 1968; JD, U. Va., 1973. Bar: DC 1973, U.S. Dist. Ct. DC 1974, U.S. Ct. Appeals (8th cir.) 1977, U.S. Supreme Ct. 1977, U.S. Ct. Appeals (5th cir.) 1980, registered: Law Soc. Eng. and Wales (fgn. lawyer) 1994. Editl. asst. Washington Star, 1964-68, 69-70; assoc. Covington & Burling, Washington, 1973-81, ptnr., 1981—, mng. ptnr. London office, 1996-2000; mem. mgmt. com. Life Scis. Industry Group, 2000—04, co-head, 2000—. Lectr. law U. Va., Charlottesville, 1977—90; mem. com. issues and priorities new vaccine devel. Inst. Medicine, NAS, 1983—86, mem. com. on accelerating biowarfare countermeasures, 2002—04, 2003—04, Nat. Adv. Allergy and Infectious Diseases Coun. NIH, 1988—92; mem. adv. bd. World Pharms. Report, 1990—96; mem. WHO Coun. Internat. Orgns. Med. Scis. Working Party in Pharmacovigilance, 1997—99; lectr. grad. program in pharm. medicine U. Wales, 1999—; adj. prof. Georgetown U., 2003—. Contbr. articles to profl. jours. Pres. Am. Friends of St. Peter's Eaton Sq., 2001—; treas., mem. parochial ch. coun. St. Peter's Ch. Eaton Sq., London, 1998—2001. With U.S. Army, 1968—69. Mem.: ABA, European Forum for Good Clin. Practice, Soc. Vertebrate Paleontology, Food Law Group (U.K.), European Soc. Pharmacovigilance, Food and Drug Law Inst., Drug Info. Assn., Brussels Pharm. Law Group, Reform Club (London), Order of Coif. Republican. Episcopalian. Avocation: vertebrate paleontology. Home: 4821 Dexter St NW Washington DC 20007 Office Phone: 202-662-5268. Business E-Mail: rkingham@cov.com.

KING-NING, TU, materials science and engineering educator; b. Canton, China, Dec. 30, 1937; came to U.S., 1962; s. Ying-Chiang Tu and Sau-Yuk Chen; m. Ching Chiao, Sept. 25, 1964; children: Olivia, Stephen. BSc, Nat. Taiwan U., 1960; MSc, Brown U., 1964; PhD, Harvard U., 1968. Rsch. staff mem. IBM Watson Rsch. Ctr., Yorktown Heights, N.Y., 1968-93, sr. mgr. thin film sci. dept., 1978-85, sr. mgr. materials sci. dept., 1985-87; prof. dept. materials sci. & engring. UCLA, 1993—. Co-author: (textbook) Electronic Thin Film Science, 1992. Recipient Acta/Scripta Metallurgica Lecturer, 1990; grantee Alexander von Humboldt, 1996. Fellow Am. Phys. Soc., The Metall. Soc. (Applications to Practice award 1988), Churchill Coll. (U.K.), Academia Sinica Republic of China. Achievements include 8 patents on thin film technology for microelectronics. Office: UCLA Boelter Hall 6532 B Los Angeles CA 90095-0001 E-mail: kntu@ucla.edu.

KINGSANDERS, NANCY KAY, music educator; b. Plainview, Tex., May 22, 1955; d. John Wesley and Mary Jane King; m. Gregory Lynn Sanders; children: Ashlee Lynn Sanders, Laura Kathryn Sanders. MusM in Clarinet Performance, The U. North Tex., 1983; MusD, U. Ill., 1991. Cert. tchr. Music Tchrs. Nat. Assn., 2002. Clarinetist U.S. Armed Forces Bicentennial Band, Ft. Meade, Md., 1974—76; prin. clarinetist Austin Cmty. Orch., 1977—80; band dir. White Settlement Ind. Sch. Dist., 1980—81; tchg. fellow U. North Tex., 1981—83; prin. clarinetist U. North Tex. Symphonic Orch., 1981—84; pvt. clarinet instr., 1981—87; tchg. fellow U. Ill., Urbana-Champaign, 1988—91; co-prin. clarinet Peoria Symphony Orch., 1987—90; woodwind/theory instr. Bradley U., 1987—90; prin. clarinet Plainview Symphony Orch., 1990—92; asst. prof. music McMurry U., Abilene, Tex., 1990—93; prof. music Tex. A&M U., Kingsville, Tex., 1993—. Grad. coord. music Tex. A&M U., 2000—. Musician: Corpus Christi Symphony Orchestra, Internat. Clarinet Soc. Competition (Finalist and Third Prize winner, 1982), Mozart Clarinet Concerto (Solo Performance with Cath. U. Orch. award, 1975). With U.S. Army, 1974—76. Mem.: Corpus Christi Music Tchrs. Assn. (assoc.; 2nd v.p. 2000), Tex. Music Tchrs. Assn. (assoc.), Music Tchrs. Nat. Assn. (assoc.), Internat. Clarinet Soc. (assoc.), Tex. Music Educators Assn. (assoc.; presenter 1990—), Tex. Fedn. Women's Clubs, A.C.T.I.V.E. Women's Club, Phi Sigma Iota, Pi Kappa Lambda. Presbyn. Avocations: reading, cooking, web design. Office: Texas A&M University-Kingsville Msc 174 Kingsville TX 78363 Office Phone: 361-593-2157. Business E-Mail: kfnks00@tamuk.edu.

KINGSBERY, WALTON WAITS, JR., retired accounting firm executive; b. Evergreen, Ala., 1928; s. Walton Waits and Alpha Lee Kingsbery; m. Helen Elizabeth Clayton, 1953; children: Walton Waits, III, J. Clayton, Peter C. Student Washington and Lee U., 1945—47; BS with honors, U. Ala., 1950. CPA, N.J., N.Y., Calif., Ohio. With Price Waterhouse & Co., 1950, 1953—88, mng. ptnr. Cleve., 1977—82, mng. ptnr. Western area L.A., 1982—87. Mem. bus. adv. bd. Bateman Eichler, Hill Richards, L.A., 1988-90, Employee Office of Atty. Gen. N.J., 1988-95; mem. adv. bd. N.J. Bur. Securities, 1993-98, N.J. Supreme Ct. Com. on Unauthorized Practice of Law, 1990—; commr. N.J. Commn. to Deter Criminal Activity, 1998-01; dir. N.J. Citizens Against Crime, Inc., 1998-01. Author booklets, papers in field. Mem. Shrewsbury (N.J.) Planning Bd., 1972—75; trustee Beech Brook, 1979, Cleve. Playhouse, 1980; clk. Village of Hunting Valley, Ohio; mem. Planning Bd., Spring Lake, NJ, 1997—; trustee Jersey Shore Med. Ctr. Found., 1999—; mem. audit com. Meridian Health Sys., 1999—2005; bd dirs. Greater Cleve. Growth Assn., 1978—82. With U.S. Army, 1950—53. Mem. AICPA, SAR, Nat. Assn. Accts., Ohio Soc. CPAs, N.J. Soc. CPAs, N.Y. Soc. CPAs, Calif. Soc. CPAs, Bluecoats, Newcomen Soc. N.Am., Cleve. Country Club, Union Club, Cleve. Racquet Club, Duquesne Club (Pitts.), Fifty Club, Calif. Club, Jonathan Club, Lincoln Club (L.A.), Univ. Club (N.Y.C.), Spring Lake Golf Club (trustee, exec. com., com. chmn., treas.), 200 Club, Beverly Hills Country Club (bd. govs.). *From a small town in Alabama to partner of Price Waterhouse in New York, then board member, management committee, head of the Cleveland office, then the west coast practice was a long, interesting road made easier by professional mentors, a loving wife and an understanding family. Service to the government and charitable organizations has enriched career and retirement.*

KINGSBURY, BENEDICT, law educator; b. 1961; LLB, U. Canterbury, New Zealand, 1981; MPhil, Oxford U., 1984, DPhil, 1990. Bar: New Zealand 1985. Resident fellow Balliol Coll., Oxford, 1985—88, Exeter Coll., Oxford, 1988—90; univ. lectr. faculty law Oxford U., 1990—93; prof. Duke U. Sch. Law, 1993—98; prof. law NYU Sch. Law, 1998—, Murry and Ida Becker prof. law, 2003—, dir. Inst. Internat. Law and Justice, 2002—. Vis. prof. Cornell U., 1991, Duke U., 1992, Harvard U., 1999, U. Tokyo, 1999; editl. bd. Am. Jour. Internat. Law, 1997—; adv. bd. European Jour. Internat. Law, 2000—, NYU Jour. Internat. Law and Politics, Indigenous Law Jour., Jour. Internat. Law & Internat. Rels., New Zealand Yearbook Internat. Law, Centro Internazionale Studi Gentiliani, Italy, Carnegie Coun. Ethics & Internat. Affairs Human Rights Program. Office: NYU Sch Law Vanderbilt Hall Rm 314D 40 Washington Sq S New York NY 10012-1099 Office Phone: 212-998-6278. E-mail: benedict.kingsbury@nyu.edu.

KINGSBURY, CAROLYN ANN, aerospace engineer, craftsman, writer; b. Newark, Ohio, Aug. 4, 1938; d. Cecil C. Layman and Orpha Edith (Hisey) Layman Dick; m. L.C. James Kingsbury, Apr. 25, 1959; children: Donald Lynn, Kenneth James. BS in Math. and Info. & Computer Scis., U. Calif., Irvine, 1979; postgrad., West Coast U., 1982-84. Systems engr. analyst Rockwell Internat., Downey, Calif., 1979-84; system and software engr. Northrop Corp., Pico Rivera, Calif., 1984-89; systems engr., rsch. engr. Hughes Aircraft Co., Long Beach, Calif., 1989-90, Fullerton, Calif., 1990—91; writer, 2001—. Pres. PTA, Manhattan Beach, Calif., 1971-73; Cub Scout den mother Boy Scouts Am., Manhattan Beach, 1972-73; mem. Fountain Valley Regional Hosp. Guild, 1993-96; radio reader Regional Audio Info. Svc. Enterprises, 1997-98; vol. computer cons. Henderson County Assessor's Office, 1997-98, Head Start program, 1998-99; with Blue Ridge Literacy Coun., 1998, 2002-03, Henderson County Pub. Libr., 2000-02. Recipient Svc. award Calif. Congress Parents and Tchrs., 1973, Leadership Achievement award YWCA, L.A., 1980, 84, NASA Achievement awards, 1983. Mem. NAFE, AAUW, Nat. Mgmt. Assn., Newtowners Club (pres. 1962). Republican. Home: 319 Mockingbird Dr Hendersonville NC 28792-6553 E-mail: kingsburys@bellsouth.net.

KINGSBURY, JOHN MERRIAM, botanist, educator; b. Boston, July 4, 1928; s. Willis Albert and Constance Elizabeth (Merriam) K.; m. Louise Arnold Gerken, June 6, 1956; 1 dau., Joanna Merriam. BS, U. Mass., 1950; A.M., Harvard U., 1952, PhD, 1954; Sc.D. (hon.), Dickinson Coll., 1985. Instr. Brandeis U., Waltham, Mass., 1953-54; mem. faculty N.Y. State Coll. Agr. and Life Scis., Cornell U., Ithaca, NY, 1954—83, prof. botany emeritus, 1983—; prof. clin. scis. Coll. Vet. Medicine, Cornell U., 1978-83, dir. arboretum and bot. garden, 1982-83. Instr. Marine Biol. Lab., Woods Hole, Mass., summers 1958-61; founding dir. Shoals Marine Lab., 1972-79; adj. prof. U. N.H., 1976-78; cons. Upstate Med. Ctr., Syracuse, N.Y., 1977-86; instr. Aquavet course Cornell U. - U. Pa., 1978-01; lectr. Cornell U. Adult U., 1978-2001; propr. Bullbrier Press, 1983—; lectr. Columbus project Sta. WGBH/Pub. Broadcasting Svc., Boston, 1990; mem. endowment com., chmn., 1992-94; vis. faculty U. Tasmania, Australia, 1980. Author: Poisonous Plants of the United States and Canada, 1964, Deadly Harvest-A Guide to Common Poisonous Plants, 1965, Seaweeds of Cape Cod and the Islands, 1969, rev. edit., 1997, The Rocky Shore, 1970, Oil and Water: The New Hampshire Story, 1975, 200 Conspicuous, Unusual, or Economically Important Tropical Plants of the Caribbean, 1988, Here's How We'll Do It-An Informal History of the Construction of the Shoals Marine Laboratory, 1991, Recollections and Reminiscences, 2000; mem. editl. bd. Cornell U. Press, 1985-86; compiler: Catalog of the Library at the Bullard Colonial Farm, 1999. NSF faculty fellow, 1958; Fulbright sr. scholar, 1980; recipient Profile Svc. award U. N.H., 1998; named in his honor: Rsch. Vessel John M. Kingsbury, 1984, John M. Kingsbury Dir., Shoals Marine Lab., Cornell U., 2001, John M. & Louise G. Kingsbury Scholarships, Cornell U., 2001, Kingsbury House, Appledore Island, 2001. Fellow Am. Acad. Vet. and Comparative Toxicology (hon.); mem. Bullard Meml. Farm Assn. (clk. 1978-2003, pres. 1990-94), Sea Edn. Assn. (trustee 1977-92, emeritus, 2002—, pres. 1982-87), Marine Biol. Lab. (life), Nature Conservancy (trustee N.Y. state bd. 1983-90), Audubon Soc. (lectr. Mass. chpt. 1987-89), Mass. Soc. Cin. Office: Cornell U 135A Guterman Lab Ithaca NY 14853-5903 Business E-Mail: jmk11@cornell.edu.

KINGSBURY, MICHAEL BRYANT, organist, retired elementary and secondary education educator; b. Wilmington, N.C., Dec. 25, 1933; s. Walter Russell and Olga Loretta (Lewis) K. BA, Emory U., 1957; MA, Atlanta U., 1978. Cert. mid. sch. sci. tchr., sci. tchr. K-12, social studies tchr., Ga. Tchr. Bouldercrest Elem. Sch., Atlanta, 1958-62; sci. tchr. Northcutt Elem. Sch., College Park, Ga., 1962-66, G.P. Babb Jr. H.S., Forest Park, Ga., 1966-84, Pointe South Mid. Sch., Jonesboro, Ga., 1984-94; organist, choir master Episcopal and Cath. Chs., Atlanta and Decatur, Ga., 1955—; organist, dir. Cath. music Ft. McPherson/U.S. Army, Atlanta, 1994—. Author, editor: Laboratory Manual for Earth Science, 1970. Bd. dirs. Camelot Homeowners Assn., Jonesboro, 1978-84; patron Atlanta Symphony Orch., 1992—; lector St. Luke's Episcopal Ch. Recipient Ritter Music award Atlanta Pub. Schs., 1951, Cmty. Svc. award Clayton County Ret. Tchrs., 1998, Service Playing cert. Am. Guild Organists, Cert. of Appreciation, Clayton County Educators Assn., 1999, others; NSF grant, 1970. Mem. Clayton County Ret. Tchrs. Assn. (pres. 1996—, dirs. dir. 2000-02, Cert. of Appreciation, Plaque 2002), Clayton County Ret. Educators Assn. (pres. 1996-98, dir. 10th dist.), Ga. Ret. Tchrs. Assn. (10th dist. dir. 2000-02), Am. Guild of Organists (membership com. 1958—), Atlanta Music Club (v.p. 2004—), Lake Jodeco Homeowners Assn. (bd. dirs.), Atlanta Music Club (v.p. programs). Democrat. Episcopalian. Avocations: walking, bicycle riding, collecting southern writings and gone with the wind memorabilia. Home: 2669 Lake Jodeco Dr Jonesboro GA 30236-5355 Office: Ft McPherson US Army Lee St Atlanta GA 30330

KINGSLEY, ELLEN, television news reporter; b. N.Y.C., Oct. 1, 1951; d. Theodore Kingsley and Judith Kingsley Fitting; m. Robert M.A. Hirschfeld, Jan. 21, 1984; children: Theodore, Andrew. B.A., Sarah Lawrence Coll., 1973; M.A., N.Y.U., 1977. Speech writer for Elinor Guggenheimer, N.Y.C. Commr. Consumer Affairs, 1974-76, for John Sawhill, Pres. of N.Y.U., 1976-77; consumer affairs reporter, anchor WJZ-TV, Balt., 1977-80; consumer affairs reporter WUSA-TV, Washington, 1980—90; pres., Kingsley Comm., 1990-97, editor, pub., Attitude Mag., 98- . Recipient Six Emmy awards, World Hunger media award, 1983; Best Documentary award UPI, 1984; Consumer Journalism award Nat. Press Club, 1984; Media award Consumer Fedn. Am., 1985. Contbr. articles to newspapers, mags. Office: 1720 Bissonnet Houston TX 77005

KINGSLEY, JEAN-PIERRE, federal official; b. Ottawa, Ont., Can., July 12, 1943; s. Oscar and Françoise (Charette-Bertrand) K.; m. Suzanne Potvin, Aug. 19, 1967; children: Marie-France, Justin, Michèle. B. Comm., U. Ottawa, 1965, MA in Hosp. Adminstrn., 1969. Programmer IBM, Ottawa-Hull, 1965-66; field supr. Travelers Ins., Ottawa-Hull, 1966-67; chief hosps. Dept. Vets.' Affairs Govt. Can., Ottawa-Hull, 1969-71, profl. officer Can. Mortgage & Housing Corp., 1971; assoc. exec. dir. and exec. dir. Charles Camsell Hosp., Edmonton, Alta., Can., 1971-73; prin. exec. officer Office of Dep. Min. Health and Welfare, Dept. Nat. Health and Welfare Govt. of Can., Ottawa-Hull, 1973-74, group chief, Treasury Bd. Secretariat, 1974-76; dir. gen. audit br. Pub. Svc. Commn., Ottawa-Hull, 1976-77; pres., CEO Ottawa Gen. Hosp., 1977-81; dep. sec., Ministry of State for Social Devel. Govt. of Canada, Ottawa-Hull, 1981-84, dep. sec. pers. policy, Treasury Bd. Secretariat, 1984-87, asst. dep. registrar gen. Dept. Consumer and Corp. Affairs, 1987-90; chief electoral officer Parliament of Can., Ottawa, 1990—. Chmn. Monfort Hosp., 1981-90; bd. dirs. Internation Found. for Election Sys., Inst. for Democracy and Electoral Assistance. Avocations: music, community activities, windsurfing, carpentry, swimming. Home: 604-131 Wurtenburg St Ottawa ON Canada K1K 8L9 Office: Elections Canada 257 Slater St Ottawa ON Canada K1A OM6 E-mail: jean-pierrekingsley@elections.ca.

KINGSLEY, JOHN MCCALL, JR., manufacturing executive; b. Berlin, Dec. 1, 1931; s. John McCall and Elizabeth (Curry) K.; m. Ines Hinckeldeyn, 1967; children: John M. III, Kate Lund. BA, Yale U., 1953; MBA, Harvard U., 1955. CPA, N.Y. Sr. staff acct. Price Waterhouse & Co. (CPA's), N.Y.C., 1957-62; assoc. Dillon, Read & Co., Inc., N.Y.C., 1962-65; v.p. fin. Gen. Host Corp., N.Y.C., 1966-69; v.p. corp. fin. F.S. Smithers & Co., Inc., 1970-71; exec. v.p. Sturm, Ruger & Co., Inc., Southport, Conn., 1971-96; pres. Kingsley Cons., LLC, 1997—. Bd. dirs. Sturm, Ruger & Co., Inc., Stamford, Conn., Neuro Inst. N.J., Newark. With AUS, 1955-57. Mem. Round Hill Club, Maidstone Club ((East Hampton, N.Y.). Republican. Episcopalian. Home: 16 Will Merry Ln Greenwich CT 06831-3338 Office: 111 Prospect St Stamford CT 06901-1208 Personal E-mail: johnkingsley@worldnet.att.net.

KINGSLEY, JOHN RAYMOND, surgeon; b. Kansas City, Mo., Oct. 27, 1941; s. James Gordon Kingsley and Blanche Sybil Payne Peak; m. Janet Kay Billings, Apr. 15, 1987; children: Jennifer Nicole, John Randolph, Sarah Ashley. AA, Pensacole (Fla.) Jr. Coll.; BS, U. Fla., 1964, MD, 1970. Diplomate in surgery and gen. vascular surgery Am. Bd. Surgery. Intern U.S. Naval Hosp., Bethesda, Md., 1970-71, resident in gen. surgery, 1971-75; attending surgeon Naval Med. Ctr., Pensacola, 1975-78, Mid-Columbia Med. Ctr., The Dalles, Oreg., 1978-92, Klickitat Valley Hosp., Goldendale, Wash., 1978-92, Russell Hosp., Alexander City, Ala., 1992-97, Carraway Meth. Med. Ctr., Birmingham, Ala., 1997—, Brookwood Med. Ctr., Birmingham, Ala., 2001—; chmn. dept. surgery Norwood Clinic, 2000—02, Carraway Meth. Med. Ctr., 2000—. Contbr. over 50 articles to profl. jours. Recipient Svc. Appreciation award DAV, 1977, Sheard-Sanford award for clin. pathology, 1970, Roger Schnell award for clin. neuorlogy, 1970, others; recognized as one of top surgeons in U.S., Consumers' Rsch. Coun. Am. Fellow ACS, S.E. Surg. Congress, So. Assn. for Vascular Surgery; mem. AMA, Am. Soc. Outpatient Surgeons (pres. 1992-95), Ala. Vascular Soc. (exec. bd. 2001—), Pacific N.W. Vascular Soc. (exec. coun. 1989-92), Am. Coll. Phlebology, Am. Med. Tennis Assn., Beta Beta Beta, Phi Theta Kappa, others. Avocations: tennis, horses, writing. Office: Ala Vascular & Vein Ctr Ste 210 700 Montgomery Hwy Birmingham AL 35216-1869 Office Phone: 205-802-6959. E-mail: johnkingsley@mindspring.com.

KINGSLEY, MARY LEE, marketing professional; d. Thomas Drowne Kingsley and Martha Bush Clark; m. William Charles Johnson, Apr. 23, 1980 (div.); children: Lee Hart Johnson, William Kingsley Johnson. BA in English, Am. U., 1975; MS in Mktg., Johns Hopkins U., 2001, MA in Nonfiction Writing, 2005. Mem.: Washington Ind. Writers, Credit Union Execs. Soc., Nat. Assn. Women Writers, BMW Riders Orgn. (contbg. author and editl. cons. jour. 2001). Episcopalian. Avocations: writing, motorcycling, cooking, gardening, needlepoint. Home: 8204 Old Georgetown Rd Bethesda MD 20814-1452 Office: Bank-Fund Staff Federal Credit Union PO Box 27755 Washington DC 20038-7755 E-mail: mlkingsley@bfsfcu.org.

KINGSMORE, STEPHEN FRANCIS, physician, research scientist; b. Motherwell, Scotland, Sept. 3, 1960; came to U.S., 1988; s. Brian and Rona K. (Ritson) K.; m. Fiona J. McQuaid, Nov. 7, 1987; children: Daniel R., Rebekah F.P., Francesca S. BSc in Med. Microbiology, Queen's U., Belfast, Ireland, 1982; MB, ChB, BAO, Queen's U., Belfast, No. Ireland, 1985. Diplomate Am. Bd. Internal Medicine. Intern Craigavon Hosp., Portadown, No. Ireland, 1985-86; resident Queen's U., Belfast, 1986-88; fellow Duke U., Durham, N.C., 1988-89, intern, 1989-90, resident, 1990-91, fellow, 1991-93, assoc. in medicine, 1993-94; asst. prof. U. Fla., Gainesville, 1994-97; COO Molecular Staging Inc., New Haven; v.p. rsch. CuraGen Corp., New Haven, 1997—2004; pres., CEO Nat. Ctr. for Genome Resources, Santa Fe, 2004—. Contbr. articles to profl. jours. Recipient Sr. Scholar awrd Am. Coll. Rheumatology, 1994, Arthritis Investigator award Arthritis Found., 1995, Jr. Faculty Rsch. award Am. Cancer Soc., 1996. Mem. Am. Fedn. Clin. Rsch. (Trainee Investigator award 1994, Jr. Faculty award 1996), Internat. Mammalian Genome Soc. Office: Pres Nat Ctr for Genome Resources 2935 Rodeo Pk Dr East Santa Fe NM 87505 Office Phone: 505-995-4466. Business E-Mail: sfk@ncgr.org.

KINGSOLVER, BARBARA ELLEN, writer; b. Annapolis, Md., Apr. 8, 1955; d. Wendell and Virginia (Henry) K.; m. Steven Hopp, 1993; 2 children. BA, DePauw U., 1977; MS, U. Ariz., 1981; LittD (hon.), DePauw U., 1994. Sci. writer U. Ariz., Tucson, 1981-85; free-lance journalist Tucson, 1985-87; novelist, 1987—. Book reviewer N.Y. Times, 1988—, L.A. Times, 1989—. Author: The Bean Trees, 1988 (ALA award 1988), Homeland and Other Stories, 1969 (ALA award 1990), Holding the Line: Women in the Great Arizona Mine Strike of 1983, 89, Animal Dreams, 1990 (PEN West Fiction award 1991, Edward Abbey Ecofiction award 1991), Another America, 1992, Pigs in Heaven, 1993 (L.A. Times Fiction prize 1993, Mountains and Plains Fiction award 1993, Western Heritage award 1993, ABBY Honor Book 1994), Essays, High Tide in Tucson, 1995, The Poisonwood Bible, 1998 (ABBY Honor Book 2000, PEN/Faulkner honoree 1999, Pulitzer runner-up 1999, Orange Prize short list 1999), Prodigal Summer, 2001, Small Wonder, 2002; co-author (with Annie Belt) Last Stand: America's Virgin Lands. Recipient Feature-writing award Ariz. Press Club, 1986; citation of accomplishment UN Nat. Coun. of Women, 1989; Woodrow Wilson Found./Lila Wallace fellow, 1992-93; Andrea Egan award Nat. Writers Union, 1998, Nat. Humanities Medal, 2000, Best Am. Sci. and Nature Writing, 2001, Gov.'s Nat. Award in the Arts, Ky., 2002, John P. McGovern award for Family, 2002, Nat. award Physicians for Social Responsibility, 2002. Mem. PEN Ctr. USA West, Nat. Writers Union, Phi Beta Kappa. Avocations: human rights, environmental conservation, gardening, natural history. Office: PO Box 160 Meadowview VA 24361

KINGSOLVER, TONY ROBERT, director; b. Bradenton, Fla., Sept. 30, 1979; s. Judith Susan Kingsolver. BA, postgrad., Ind. U., 2004—. Student activities coord. Ind. U., South Bend, 2002—04; campus activities coord. Sul Ross State U., Alpine, Tex., 2004—. Mem.: Nat. Assn. Campus Activities, Assn. Promotion Campus Activities (bd. dirs. 2004—, Student Promoter of the Yr. 2004), Kiwanis (bd. dirs. 2004—). Democrat. Home: PO Box 1354 Alpine TX 79831 Office: Sul Ross State U PO Box C190 Alpine TX 79832

KINGSTON, ALEX(ANDRA), actress; b. London, Mar. 11, 1963; m. Ralph Fiennes, 1993 (div. 1997); m. Florian Haertel, 1998; 1 child. Student, Royal Acad. Dramatic Arts. T.V. and movie actress. Appeared in T.V. films Foreign Affairs, 1993, The Infiltrator, 1995, Weapons of Mass Distraction, 1997; films include The Cook, The Thief, His Wife & Her Lover, 1989, Carrington, 1995, Virtual Encounters 2, 1998, Croupier, 1998, This Space Between Us, 2000, Moll Flanders, 1999, Essex Boys, 2000, Warrior Queen, 2003; T.V. series include The Knock, 1994, ER, 1997-2004. Recipient SAG award for Outstanding Performance by Ensemble in a Drama Series, 1994. Office: c/o The Gersh Agy 232 N Canon Dr Beverly Hills CA 90210-5302

KINGSTON, JACK, congressman; b. Bryan, Tex., Apr. 24, 1955; m. Libby Kingston; children: Betsy, John, Ann, Jim. BA in Economics, U. Ga.; attended, Mich. State U., 1973—74. Salesman, v.p. Palmer & Cay Carswell Ins. Co., 1979-92; mem. Ga. State Ho. Reps., 1985-93, U.S. Congresses from 1st Ga. Dist., 1993—. Mem. Ways and Means Com., 1985-93, Appropriations Com., Congl. Rural Caucus Exec. Bd., 1993—, chmn. Theme Team (house Rep. comm. team). Vol. Hospice, United Way; mem. Atlantic Coast Conservation Assn., Isle of Hope Community Assn. Recipient Guardian of Small Bus. award Nat. Fed. of Ind. Bus. 103, 104, 105, 106, 1992, Sound Dollar award Free Cong. Found., 1994, Golden Bulldog award mems. 103rd, 104th, 105th, 106th cong., 1994, 96, Golden Eagle award Nat. Security Caucus, 1994, cert. recognition inspector. gen. Criminal Investigator Acad., 1994, plaque of appreciation Camden county bd. realtors, 1995, disting. cit. award Armstrong state coll., 1996, merit award the Seniors Coalition, 1996, comm. police award city of Statesboro, 1997, numerous others. Mem. Am. Legislative Exchange Coun., Soc. Chartered Property and Casualty Underwriters, Solomon's Lodge F&AM, Rotary (Paul Harris fellow). Republican. Episcopalian. Office: US Ho Reps 2242 Rayburn HOB Washington DC 20515-1001

KINGSTON, MAXINE HONG, writer, educator; b. Stockton, Calif., Oct. 27, 1940; d. Tom and Ying Lan (Chew) Hong; m. Earll Kingston, Nov. 23, 1962; 1 child, Joseph Lawrence. BA, U. Calif., Berkeley, 1962; D (hon.), Ea. Mich. U., 1988, Colby Coll., 1990, Brandeis U., 1991, U. Mass., 1991. Tchr. English, Sunset H.S., Hayward, Calif., 1965-66, Kahuku (Hawaii) H.S., 1967, Kahaluu (Hawaii) Drop-In Sch., 1968, Kailua (Hawaii) H.S., 1969, Honolulu Bus. Coll., 1969, Mid-Pacific Inst., Honolulu, 1970-77; prof. English, vis. writer U. Hawaii, Honolulu, 1977; Thelma McCandless Disting. Prof. Eastern Mich. U., Ypsilanti, 1986, sr. lectr. emerita U. Calif., Berkeley, 1990-2003. Author: The Woman Warrior: Memoirs of a Girlhood Among Ghosts, 1976 (Nat. Book Critics Cir. award for non-fiction; cited by Time mag., N.Y. Times Book Rev. and Asian Mail as one of best books of yr. and decade), China Men, 1981 (Nat. Book award; runner-up for Pulitzer prize, Nat. Book Critics Cir. award nominee 1988), Hawai' One Summer, 1987 (Western Books Exhbn. Book award, Book Builders West Book award), Tripmaster Monkey-His Fake Book, 1989 (PEN USA West award in Fiction), Through the Black Curtain, 1988, To Be The Poet, 2002, The Fifth Book of Peace, 2003 (Best Spiritual Book award, Spirituality and Health, 2003); editor: The Literature of California, 2001, (Commonwealth Club Book award 2001); To Be the Poet, 2002; contbr. short stories, articles and poems to mags. and jours., including Iowa Rev., The New Yorker, Am. Heritage, Redbook, Mother Jones, Caliban, Mich. Quarterly, Ms., The Hungry Mind Rev., N.Y. Times, L.A. Times, Zyzzyva; prodr. The Woman Warrior, Berkeley Repertory Co., 1994, The Huntington Theater, Boston, 1994, The Mark Taper Forum, L.A., 1995; host: (TV series) Journey to the West, 1994; subject of documentaries Talking Story, Stories My Country Told Me, Writers and Places; interviews on Dick Cavett, Bill Moyers, Ken Burns' The West, The News Hour with Jim Lehrer; actor Truck Girl, 2004. Guggenheim fellow, 1981; recipient Nat. Endowment for the Arts Writers award, 1980, 82, Mademoiselle mag. award, 1977, Anisfield Wolf Book award, 1978, Calif. Arts Commn. award, 1981, Hawaii award for lit., 1982, Calif. Gov.'s award art, 1989, Major Book Collection award Brandeis U. Nat. Women's Com., 1990, award lit. Am. Acad. & Inst. Arts & Letters, 1990, Lila Wallace Reader's Digest Writing award, 1992, Spl. Achievement Oakland Bus. Arts award, 1994; named Living Treasure Hawaii, 1980, Woman of Yr. Asian Pacific Women's Network, 1981, Cyril Magnin award for Outstanding Achievement in the Arts, 1996, Disting. Artists award The Music Ctr. of L.A. County, 1996, Nat. Humanities medal NEH, 1997, Fred Cody Lifetime Achievement award, 1998, John Dos Passos prize for lit., 1998, Ka Palapola Po'okela award 1999, Profiles of Courage honor Swords to Plowshares, 1999, Alumna of Yr. award U. Calif.-Berkeley, 2000, Gold medal Calif. State Libr., 2002. Mem. Am. Acad. Arts and Scis.

KINIGAKIS, PANAGIOTIS, research scientist, researcher, engineer, writer; b. Chanea, Greece, July 11, 1949; s. John and Evangelia (Vozinakis) K.; m. Kalliopi Pologeos, July 31, 1977 (div. Sept. 2000); children: Evangelia, Maria Anna; m. Tracey Dawn Quart, Jan. 3, 2003. BS, Superior Agrl. Sch., Athens, Greece, 1971, MS, 1973; MS in Food Sci., Rutgers U., 1979. Packaging devel. specialist Am. Cyanamid Co., Clifton, N.J., 1979-81; sr. packaging engr. Warner Lambert Co., Morris Plains, N.J., 1981-83; tech. svcs. supr. M&M Mars Inc., Hackettstown, N.J., 1983-87; sr. tech. prin. Kraft Foods Inc., Glenview, Ill., 1987—, Kraft Food fellow, 2001—. Agrl. engr. Food Agrl. Orgn. div. of UN, Chanea, 1975-77. Patentee pkg. equipment and mfg. systems; contbr. articles to profl. jours. Advisor Greek Orthodox Youth Assn., Randolph, N.J., 1986, Hamilton, N.J., 1990. Mem. ASM, TAPPI, Internat. Materials Info. soc., Inst. Food Tech., Inst. Packaging Profls. (cert.), Soc. Plastics Engrs., N.Y. Acad. Scis. Greek Orthodox. Avocations: golf, volleyball, soccer, tennis, scuba diving. Office: Kraft Foods Inc 801 Waukegan Rd Glenview IL 60025-4391 Office Phone: 847-646-5383. Business E-Mail: pkinigakis@kraft.com.

KINIGSTEIN, JONAH, painter; b. N.Y.C., June 23, 1923; s. Jacob and Yetta (Zelman) Kinigstein; m. Barbara Stein (div.); m. Eileen Muken; children: Noah, Lisa. Degree, Grand Chaumiere, Paris, 1951. Dept. store window designer Tiffany, N.Y.C., Bonwitt Teller, N.Y.C., Bloomingdales, N.Y.C., Austen Display, N.Y.C.; advertising Seagrams Design 375, N.Y.C.; art instr. Nat. Acad. Design, N.Y.C. One-man shows include Les Impressions D'Art, Paris, 1948, Gallerie Breteau, 1950, Alan Gallery, NY, 1954—55, Siembab Gallery, Boston, 1959, Werbin Gallery, Detroit, 1959, Grippi Gallery, NY, 1959, Nordness Gallery, 1961, ACA Gallery, 1968, Rittenhouse Gallery, Phila., 1975—82, Wash. Irving Gallery, NY, 1982, Pindar Gallery, 1988, exhibited in group shows at Nat. Acad. Design, 1978, Denise Cade Gallery, 1986, Nat. Acad. Design, 1990, 2004, Represented in permanent collections Whitney Mus., Mus. Modern Art, Brandeis U., U. Ill., U. Ariz. Mem.: NAD (academician).*

KINIRY, WILLIAM F., JR., lawyer; b. Phila., Dec. 5, 1950; AB, Villanova U., 1972; JD, U. Balt., 1976; student, U.S. Army JAG's Sch. Bar: Pa. 1976, U.S. Dist. Ct. (ea. dist.) Pa. 1978, U.S. Ct. Appeals (3rd cir.) 1978, U.S. Dist. Ct. (mid. dist.) Pa. 1991. Atty. Harvey, Pennington, Herting & Renneisen Ltd., Phila.; mng. ptnr. Phila. off. DLA Piper Rudnick Gray Cary, Phila. Served as co. comdr. US Army spl. ops. forces, USAR. Recipient Dean Joseph Curtis award, Univ. Pres. award. Mem. ABA, Pa. Bar Assn., NY State Bar Assn., Phila. Bar Assn., Product Liability Adv. Council, Def. Rsch. Inst., Soc. Automotive Engineers, Nat. Assn. Railroad Trial Counsel. Office: DLA Piper Rudnick Gray Cary One Liberty Pl Ste 4900 1650 Market St Philadelphia PA 19103-2762 Office Phone: 215-656-3340. Office Fax: 215-656-3301. Business E-Mail: william.kiniry@dlapiper.com.

KINKEL, DOREEN HEATHER, education educator; d. Darrell Laverne and Elaine Dorothy Downer; 1 child, Casey Laine Swakon. BS, U. Ill., 1971—75; MS, U. Fla., 1975—77, PhD, 1977—80. Asst. prof. animal sci. Tex. A&M Univ., Kingsville, 1980—84, assoc. prof., 1984—94, prof. of animal sci., 1994—. Fellow USDA-HSI Program, Wash., DC, 2002; adv. bd. mem. Ctr. for Tchg. Effectiveness, Tex. A&M Univ.-Kingsville, Kingsville, Tex., 2000—04; project dir., USDA-HSI grant Tex. A&M Univ.-Kingsville, 2003—, faculty senate chair. Mem. Young People's Theater Support Assn., Harbor Playhouse, Corpus Christi, 1987—90, Corpus Christi Ballet, Corpus Christi, 1988—93; Nueces County coord. Assn. for Children for Enforcement of Support, Corpus Christi, Tex., 1988—90; mem. Tex. State Aquarium, Corpus Christi, 1990—92. Recipient Hon. Lone Star Sate Farmer, Future Farmers of Am. (FFA), 1983; grantee funding for a Structured Approach to Career Awareness, Career Exploration, and Career Devel., Pioneer Hi-Bred Internat., 2003—05; Grad. Scholarship, Fla. Citrus Processors, 1978. Mem.: Minorities in Agr., Natural Resources, and Related Sciences, Am. Soc. Animal Sci., Profl. and Orgnl. Devel. Network in Higher Edn. Methodist. Avocation: travel. Home: 14514 Cabana E #210 Corpus Christi TX 78418 Office: Texas A&M Univ-Kingsville MSC 228 700 Univ Blvd Kingsville TX 78363-8202 Office Phone: 361-593-3948. Business E-Mail: doreen.kinkel@tamuk.edu.

KINLAW, DENNIS FRANKLIN, clergyman, religious organization administrator; b. Lumberton, N.C., June 26, 1922; s. Wade Hampton and Sally (Burney) K.; m. Elsie Blake, Dec. 31, 1943; children: Elizabeth Kinlaw Coppedge, Dennis Franklin Jr., Katherine Kinlaw Key, Susan Kinlaw Masters, Sally Kinlaw Babcock. BA, Asbury Coll., 1943, LHD (hon.), 1980; MDiv, Asbury Theol. Sem., 1946; MA, Brandeis U., 1961, PhD, 1967; LLD (hon.), Houghton Coll., 1971; DD (hon.), Asbury Coll., 1990. Ordained deacon N.C. Conf. United Meth. Ch., 1949, ordained elder, 1951; transferred to Ky. Conf., 1969, ret., 1984. Pastor Meth. Ch., Faison, 1949-53, Loudenville (N.Y.) Community Ch., 1955-61; assoc. prof., prof. Old Testament langs. and lit. Asbury Theol. Sem., Wilmore, Ky., 1963-68, prof. bibl. theology, 1982-83; pres. Asbury Coll., Wilmore, 1968-81, 86-92; founder, pres. Francis Asbury soc., Wilmore, 1982—. Pres. Francis Asbury Soc., Wilmore, 1982—; vis. prof. Seoul (Republic of Korea) Theol. Coll.; bd. dirs. Christianity Today, Carol Stream, Ill., Ludhiana Christian Med. Bd., N.Y.C.; mem. Lausanne Commn. on World Evangelism, Theol. Commn. of World Evang. Fellowship; chmn. bd. OMS Internat., Greenwood, Ind. Author: Preaching in the Spirit, 1985; contbr. commentaries in bibl. publs. Recipient Alumnus award Asbury Theol. Sem., 1961. Mem. Soc. Bibl. Lit. and Exegesis, Wesley Theol. Soc., Evang. Theol. Soc. Home: 140 Lowry Ln Wilmore KY 40390-1219 Office: Francis Asbury Soc PO Box 7 Wilmore KY 40390-0007 E-mail: kinlawdennis@hotmail.com.

KINLEY, CHRISTINE T., physician assistant; b. Carter County, Tenn. d. Lon Samuel and Mary (Johnson) Turbyfill; children: Amy Nikol, Michael Lon. Diploma, Johnson City Vocat. Tech. Sch., 1977; BSN, East Tenn. State U., 1988; Physician Asst., Trevecca Nazarene U., Nashville, 1997; postgrad., U. Health Scis., St. John's U., St. Lucia Sch. Medicine. LPN, RN, Tenn.; cert. physician asst. Charge nurse Four Oaks Health Care Ctr., Jonesborough, Tenn.; staff nurse VA Med. Ctr., Johnson, Tenn., nurse recruiter; physician asst. Johnson City Emergency Physicians, 1997-1999, emergency care coverage, 2000—; emegency care coverage Olde Towne Gen. Medicine, 2000—. E-mail: CKinley333@aol.com.

KINLIN, DONALD JAMES, lawyer; b. Boston, Nov. 29, 1938; s. Joseph Edward and Ruth Claire (Byrne) K.; m. Donna C. (McGrath), Nov. 29, 1959; children: Karen J., Donald J., Joseph P., and Kevin S. BS in acctg., Syracuse U., 1968, MBA, 1970; JD, U. Nebr., 1975. Bar: Nebr., 1976, Ohio, 1982, U.S. Supreme Ct., 1979, U.S. Claims Ct., 1982, U.S. Tax Ct., 1982, U.S. Ct. Appeals (5th and fed. cir.), 1982. Atty. USAF, Mather AFB, Calif., 1976-78; sr. trial atty. Air Force Contract Law Ctr., Wright Patterson AFB, Ohio, 1978-86, dep. dir., 1986-87; ptnr. Smith and Schnacke, Dayton, Ohio, 1987-89, Thompson and Hine LLP, Dayton, Ohio, 1989—. Mem. adv. bd. Fed. Publ. Inc., Govt. Contract Costs, Pricing & Acctg. Report. Contbr. articles to legal jours. Pres. Forest Ridge Assn., Dayton,Ohio, 1984-96; sec., gen. counsel U.S. Air and Trade Show, 1994-98, chmn., 1998—; bd. dir. Nat. Aviation Hall of Fame, 1998—. Mem. ABA (chmn. sect. pub. contract law 1993-94), sec., budget and fin. officer sect., coun. mem., chmn. fed. procurement divsn., vice chmn. acctg., cost and pricing com., truth in negotiations com., chmn. cost acctg. stas. sub com.), Fed. Bar Assn., Ohio Bar Assn., Nebr. Bar Assn., Contracts Appeals Bar Assn. (bd. govs. 1998-2001). Avocation: travel. Office: Thompson Hine LLP 10 W 2nd St Dayton OH 45402-1758

KINLOCK, TIMOTHY WILLIAM, research scientist, educator; b. Md., Mar. 25, 1953; s. William H. Kinlock, III and Mildred Seiter Kinlock; m. Patricia Elaine Grimes, Oct. 11, 1980. AA, Wesley Coll., 1973; BA, U. Del., 1975; MA, Towson U., 1977; PhD, U. Md., 1993. Tutor, study skills support svcs. ctr. Towson U., Md., 1976—78; rsch. asst. Nat. Ctr. State Courts, Williamsburg, Va., 1978—79; rsch. assoc. Friends Rsch. Inst., Balt., 1979—93; instr. dept. criminal justice and criminology U. Md., College Park, 1994—94; sr. rsch. scientist Friends Rsch. Inst., Balt., 1993—. Cons. Nat. Inst. State Courts, Williamsburg, Va., 1978—79; mem. sci. adv. bd. Balt. Substance Abuse Systems, 1999—; mem. adv. bd. Case-Mix Adjustment Adolescent Treatment Evaluations, Arlington, Va., 2004—; adj. prof. divsn. of criminology, criminal justice, and social policy U. Balt., Balt., 1995—. Contbr. articles to profl. jours., chpt. to book. Grantee, Open Soc. Inst., Balt., 1999, Nat. Inst. Drug Abuse, Rockville, Md., 2001, 2003. Mem.: Am. Soc. Criminology, Phi Kappa Phi. Avocations: raising cats, mentoring exceptional students, civil war history. Office: Friends Rsch Inst 1040 Park Ave Ste 103 Baltimore MD 21201 Office Phone: 410-837-3977 224. Office Fax: 410-752-4218. Personal E-mail: tkinlock@ubalt.edu. E-mail: tkinlock@friendssocialresearch.org.

KINMAN, GARY W., landscape company executive; Owner, CEO Kinman Assocs., Inc., Dublin, Ohio. Conducts seminars in field. Office: Kinman Assoc Inc PO Box 1129 Dublin OH 43017 Office Phone: 614-764-8733. Office Fax: 614-793-0104. E-mail: gary@kinmaninstitute.com.

KINNAIRD, ELEANOR GATES, state legislator, lawyer; b. Rochester, Minn., Nov. 14, 1931; d. E. Vernon and E. Madge (Pollock) Gates; m. Richard W. Kinnaird, July 27, 1954 (div. June 1982); children: Robinson S., Michael G., Paul N. BA, Carleton Coll., 1953; MM, U. N.C., 1973; JD, N.C. Ctrl. U., 1992. Bar: N.C. 1992, U.S. Dist. Ct. (ea. and mid. dists.) N.C. 1992, U.S. Ct. Appeals (4th cir.) 1992. Staff atty. N.C. Prisoner Legal Svcs., Inc., Raleigh, 1993—2003; senator N.C. Gen. Assembly, 1997—; pvt. practice, 2004—. Mayor, Town of Carrboro, 1987-95. Mem.: Phi Alpha Delta. Episcopalian. Avocations: political and civic activities, movies, reading, gardening. Home: 207 W Poplar Ave Carrboro NC 27510-1613 Office: 211 N Columbia St Chapel Hill NC 27514 Office Phone: 919-942-4445. E-mail: elliek@ncleg.net.

KINNAIRD, MARGARET MARY, secondary school educator; b. Apr. 1, 1949; d. Frank Anton and Margaret (Bader) Kinnaird. BA, Coll. of St. Rose, 1971; MS, Russell Sage Coll., 1974; EdD, Boston U., 1982. Tchr. Berne-Knox Westerlo Ctrl. Sch. Dist., NY, 1972; adj. curriculum coord. N.Y. State Dept. Edn., Albany, 1983—95; pres. Berne-Knox Westerlo Tchr.'s Assn., coord. elem. computer, coord. elem. sci., social studies. Co-author: Computers, Utilizing Modern Technology in Adult and Continuing Education Programs, Albany, N.Y.: The State Education Department, 1988. Mem. exec. com. PTA; chairperson NYSUT Regional Edn. Conf. Mem. Pi Lambda Theta, Phi Delta Kappa. Avocations: reading, travel, outdoor sports, music. Home: 193 Cole Rd East Berne NY 12059 Office: Berne-Knox-Westerlo CSD Helderberg Trl Berne NY 12023-9601

KINNAMON, PRISCILLA MOORE, elementary school educator; d. Percy Whitten and Vera Schroeder Moore; m. James Long Kinnamon, June 11, 1966; children: Laura K. Conner, Deborah K. Back, Jeffrey Lee. BA, Roanoke Coll., 1966. Tchr. 2d grade Riverside Elem., Balt., 1966—67, Montpelier Elem., Laurel, Md., 1967—68, Tussing Elem., Colonial Heights, Va., 1980—81, tchr. 3d grade, 1981—82; tchr. 1st grade. Lakeview Elem., Colonial Heights, 1982—. Mem.: Swift Creek Federated Woman's Club (chmn. edn. dept. 2000—02). Republican. Avocations: reading, travel, gardening. Office: Lakeview Elem Sch 401 Taswell Ave Colonial Heights VA 23834

KINNAN, JOEN PRITCHARD, freelance writer, editor, consultant; b. Canton, Ohio, May 21; d. William Davis and Thelma (Gibbs) Pritchard; m. Donald Henry Kinnan, Mar. 8 (div.); children: Glynis Joen, Jason Pritchard. BA, Denison U.; postgrad. Kent State U., Ohio State U. Cert. elem. and secondary tchr., Ohio, Mich. Tchr. English, history, geography and social studies Upper Arlington (Ohio) Schs., later John Norup Jr. High Sch., Berkley, Mich.; sketchwriter, editor Marquis Who's Who, Chgo., 1964-74, asst. dept. head, 1966-68, head sketchwriting dept., 1968-74, freelance writer, editor, 1974-86; sr. assoc., writer, workshop facilitator William M. Young & Assocs., Oak Park, Ill., 1978-83; freelance writer, editor, cons., River Forest, Ill., 1983—; owner Cygnet Comm. Author (4) books; co-author: The Self Health Handbook; contbr. mag. articles in health care and safety. Dem. precinct worker; active Stevenson and Simon senatorial campaigns; past mgr.

River Forest Boys' Little League. Mem. ACLU, Ind. Writers of Chgo. (bd. dirs., past pres.), Chgo. Women in Pub., Greenpeace, Citizens for Better Environment, Nat. Writers Union, Delta Gamma. Avocations: gardening, ethnic cooking, traveling.

KINNE, DAVID WEIR, retired surgeon; b. Amityville, N.Y., July 19, 1936; s. Charles Stanley and Angeline Marian (Simpson) K.; m. Frances Paytas (div. Dec. 1985); children: Lisa Ann, Jonathan Charles, James Andrew; m. Kathleen Liddy. AB, Columbia U., 1957; MD summa cum laude, SUNY Downstate Med. Ctr., N.Y.C., 1964. Diplomate Am. Bd. Surgery. Chief breast svc. Meml. Sloan-Kettering Cancer Ctr., N.Y.C., 1979—93, attending surgeon, 1982—93, dir. surg. edn., 1985—91, mem. Meml. Hosp. in cancer ctr., 1988—93; prof. surgery and chief breast svc. Columbia-Presbyn. Med. Ctr., 1993—2001; ret., 2001. Prof. surgery Cornell U. Med. Coll., N.Y.C., 1978-1993; cons. Rockefeller Hosp. N.Y.C., 1978-1993; co-dir. Breast Exam. Ctr. of Harlem, N.Y.C., 1983-1993. Editor: Breast Diseases, 1987-91. Tour guide Met. Mus. Art, N.Y.C., NY, Carnegie Hall. Fellow ACS; mem. N.Y. Surg. Soc., Soc. Surg. Oncology, Ea. Surg. Soc., N.Y. Met. Breast Cancer Group (pres. 1987-89), N.Y. Athletic Club, St. Andrews Golf Club (Hastings-on-Hudson, N.Y.). Republican. Episcopalian. Avocations: golf, walking. Home: 340 E 64th St Apt 30B New York NY 10021-7507 E-mail: katnkin@aol.com.

KINNE, FRANCES BARTLETT, academic administrator; b. Story City, Iowa; d. Charles Morton and Bertha (Olson) Bartlett; m. Harry L. Kinne, Jr. (dec.); m. M. Worthington Bordley, Jr. (dec.). Student, U. No. Iowa; B of Music Edn., M. of Music Edn., Drake U., DFA (hon.), 1981, hon. degree; PhD cum laude, U. Frankfurt, Fed. Republic of Germany, 1957; LHD (hon.), Wagner Coll., N.Y.; LLD (hon.), Lenoir Rhyne Coll.; DHL (hon.), Jacksonville U., 1995; LLD (hon.), Flagler Coll. Tchr. music Kelley (Iowa) Consol. Sch.; supr. music Boxholm (Iowa) Consol. Sch., Des Moines pub. schs.; sr. hostess Camp Crowder, Mo.; dir. recreation VA, Wadsworth, Kans.; lectr. music, English and Western culture Tsuda Coll., Tokyo; cons. music U.S. Army Gen. Hdqrs., Tokyo; mem. faculty Jacksonville (Fla.) U., 1958—, Disting. Univ. prof., 1961-62, prof. music and humanities, 1963—, dean, founder Coll. Fine Arts, interim pres., 1979, pres., 1979-89, chancellor, 1989-94; chancellor emeritus, 1995—. Past chmn. Ind. Colls. and Univs. Fla.; mem. adv. coun. Nat. Soc. Arts and Letters; hon. mem. staff Mayo Clinic, Jacksonville; corporator Charles Schepens Eye Rsch. Inst. of Harvard U., Cambridge, Mass.; mem. adv. bd. Women's Eye Task Force, Harvard. Author: A Comparative Study of British Traditional and American Indigenous Ballads, 1958, Iowa Girl: The President Wears a Skirt, 2000; contbr. chpt. to book and articles to profl. jours. Trustee Drake U.; bd. dirs., life mem. Jacksonville Symphony Assn., Bert Thomas Scholarship Found., Doug Milne Found.; bd. dirs., exec. com. Eye Rsch. Found.; mem., then chmn. adv. bd. Ronald McDonald House; past mem. bd. govs. Jacksonville C. of C., past v.p.; mem. pres.'s adv. coun. Flagler Coll. Named Eve of Decade, hon. mem., 3d Armored Divsn., U.S. Army, Woman of Achievement, Ponte Vedra Woman's Club, 2005; recipient hon. awards, Bus. and Profl. Women's Clubs, 1962, Disting. Svc. award, Drake U., 1966, 1st Fla. Gov.'s award for achievement in arts, 1972, EVE award in edn., 1973, Arts Assembly Individual award, 1978—79, Roast award, Soc. for Prevention of Blindness, 1980, Brotherhood award, NCCJ, 1981, Top Mgmt. award, Jacksonville Sales and Mktg. Execs., 1981, Alumni Achievement award, U. No. Iowa, Ann. Burton C. Bryan award, Pub. Svc. award, Physicians Edn. Network, Freedom Found. Valley Forge, Disting. Svc. award, Fla. Soc. Ophthalmology, Women of Achievement award, 1st Coast Bus. and Profl. Women's Club Jacksonville, Disting. Educator award, Internat. Longshoremen's Assn., Hope award, Nat. Multiple Sclerosis Soc., Disting. Am. award, Nat. Football Fedn., Fla. State Mus. Tchrs. award, Outstanding Civic Leader award, Civic Roundtable of Jacksonville, Vol. Jacksonville 2d Ann. Bernard Gregory Servant Leader award, Elaine Gordon Lifetime Achievement award, Fla. Fedn. Bus. and Profl. Women, 1996, Order of the South award, So. Acad. Letters, Arts and Scis., Nat. Soc. Arts and Letters, Lifetime Achievement award, Arthritis Found., 2004, Davis award for Lifetime Achievement; inducted into Fla. Women's Hall of Fame, Outstanding Svc. to Theatre Edn. Fla. Assn. for Theatre Edn., day named in her honor, Women's Club of Jacksonville and other orgns., one of six women featured on History Week posters apptd. by Mayor Jacksonville, bldgs. named in honor, Frances Bartlett Kinne Univ. Ctr. Jacksonville U., Frances Bartlett Kinne Alumni and Devel. Ctr. Drake U., Frances Bartlett Kinne Auditorium at Mayo Clinic, Jacksonville. Mem. AAUW, Nat. Music Tchrs. Assn., Fla. Music Tchr. Assn., Music Educators Nat. Conf., Fla. Music Edn. Assn. (past bd. dirs.), Assn. Am. Colls. (past bd. govs., exec. com.), Friday Musicale (life), Fla. Coll. Music Edn. Assn. (past pres., v.p.), Delius Assn. of Fla. (life), Nat. Assn. Schs. Music (past chmn. region 7), Fine Arts Forum (hon.), Ind. Colls. and Univs. of Fla. (past chmn., 1st woman chmn.), So. Acad. Letters, Arts and Scis., Internat. Coun. Fine Arts Deans (past chmn., 1st woman chmn.), Fla. Women's Hall of Fame (Gov.'s First award), Jacksonville Women's Network Inner Wheel, Nat. Soc. Arts and Letters (adv. coun.), P.E.O., Green Key (hon.), Ret. Officers Assn. (hon. mem. Mayport chpt.), St. John's Dinner Club (past pres.), Exch. Club (Golden Deeds award), River Club (1st woman mem.), Rotary (pres. 2000, one of 1st two women elected bd. dirs. Jacksonville chpt., Paul Harris fellow, 1st woman pres. Rotary Club Jacksonville, 2000—), Alpha Xi Delta, Mu Phi Epsilon (Elizabeth Mathias award, judge internat. music edn. award), Alpha Psi Omega (hon.), Alpha Kappa Pi (hon.), Alpha Kappa Psi (hon.), Beta Gamma Sigma, Omicron Delta Kappa (hon.), Alpha Xi Delta (Woman of Distinction award). Home: 4032 Mission Hills Cir W Jacksonville FL 32225-4635 *It has been a delightful challenge to amalgamate my career with happy experience as a U.S. Army wife - as a young bride assigned to China and evacuated to Occupied Japan - in pursuit of my Ph.D. at the University of Frankfurt in Occupied Germany (the lone American student) as a professor, dean, president, chancellor and now Chan. Emer. of Jacksonville University.*

KINNEAR, GREG, actor, film producer; b. Logansport, Ind., June 17, 1963; m. Helen Labdon, May 1, 1999; 1 child. Diploma in Broadcast Journalism, U. Ariz. Wit Armed Forces Radio, Athens, Greece. Appeared on TV series College Mad House, 1989, The Best of the Worst, 1991, Talk Soup, 1991-94, Later with Greg Kinnear, 1994-1996, TV movies What Price Victory, 1988, Murder in Mississippi, 1990, Dillinger, 1991, Based on an Untrue Story, 1993, Dinner with Friends, 2001, films, Blankman, 1994, Sabrina, 1995, Dear God, 1996, A Smile Like Yours, 1997, As Good As It Gets, 1997, You've Got Mail, 1998, Mystery Men, 1999, What Planet Are You From, 2000, Nurse Betty, 2000, Loser, 2000, The Gift, 2000, Someone Like You, 2001, We Were Soldiers, 2002, Auto Focus, 2002, Stuck On You, 2003, Godsend, 2004, The Matador, 2005, (voice) Robots, 2005, Bad News Bears, 2005; co-exec. prodr. TV series The Best of the Worst, 1991; exec. prodr. Talk Soup, 1991-94, Later with Greg Kinnear, 1994-1996, . Mem.: Alpha Tau Omega.*

KINNEARY, JOSEPH PETER, federal judge; b. Cin., Sept. 19, 1905; s. Joseph and Anne (Mulvihill) K.; m. Byrnece Camille Rogers, June 26, 1950. BA, U. Notre Dame, 1928; JD, U. Cin., 1935, JD, 1967, LLD (hon.), 1991. Bar: Ohio 1935, U.S. Supreme Ct 1960. Pvt. practice in, Cin. and Columbus, 1935-61; asst. atty. gen. Ohio, 1937-39; 1st asst. atty. gen., 1949-51; spl. counsel to atty. gen., 1959-61; U.S. atty. So. Dist. Ohio, 1961-66; judge U.S. Dist. Ct. (so. dist.) Ohio, 1966—, chief judge, 1973-75, sr. judge. Lectr. law trusts Coll. Law, U. Cin., 1948 Del. Dem. Nat. Conv., 1952. Served to capt. AUS, World War II. Decorated Army Commendation ribbon. Mem. Phi Delta Phi. Roman Catholic. Office: US Dist Ct 319 US Courthouse 85 Marconi Blvd Columbus OH 43215-2823

KINNEBREW, JACKSON METCALFE, lawyer; b. Oklahoma City, June 29, 1941; s. Jackson A. and Mary Lucille (Metcalfe) K.; m. Carole A. Vadner, Sept. 23, 1967; children: Scott, Sarah. BBA in Acctg., U. Okla., 1963; JD, So. Meth. U., 1967, LLM in Taxation, 1973. Bar: Tex. 1968, U.S. Dist. Ct. (no. dist.) Tex. 1968, U.S. Tax Ct. 1970, U.S. Ct. Appeals (5th cir.) 1971, U.S. Supreme Ct. 1971; CPA, Tex. Assoc. Strasburger & Price, Dallas, 1968-74, ptnr., 1975—. Lectr. Wills and Probate Inst., 1980, 81, 83, 89, Practicing Law Inst., 1983; bd. trustees Ctr. Am. and Internat. Law (formerly Southwestern Legal Found.), 1987-. Contbr. legal articles to profl. jours. Fund raising chmn. Boy Scouts Am., Dallas, 1984—86; chmn. legacy com. Am. Cancer Soc., Dallas, 1978—82; outside gen. counsel Cmtys. Found. of Tex., Dallas, 1987—2005; interim exec. dir. Cmtys. Found. Tex., Dallas, 2001—05; trustee Cmtys. Found. of Tex., Dallas, 2005—. Lt. U.S. Army, 1963—65. Recipient Disting. Alumni award Pub. Interest, So. Meth. U. Sch Law, 2002. Fellow Am. Coll. Trust and Estate Counsel (state chmn. 1984-89, bd. regents 1988-94, membership selection com. 1993-99), Internat. Acad. Estate and Trust Law (academician 1990—); mem. ABA (subcom. chmn. 1979), State Tex. Bar Assn. (lectr. 1981, 82), Dallas Bar Assn. (chmn. probate sect. 1985), Tex. Soc. CPAs, Dallas Estate Planning Coun. (pres. 1985, program v.p. 1984, treas. 1982, sec. 1981), Tex. Bd. Legal Specialization (cert.). Avocations: golf, sports, bridge. Office: Strasburger & Price LLP Bank Am Plz 901 Main St Ste 4300 Dallas TX 75202-3724

KINNEY, ANDERS MICHAEL, history professor, meteorologist; s. Delbert Glenn (Stepfather) and Evelyn Pearl Bartley; m. Michele Anders C. Michele Anders, Dec. 23, 1997; 1 child, Anders Michael Kinney II. BS in Govt. and Politics of the Far East, U. of Md., Yokota, Japan, 1993; AA in Mgmt., U. of Md., 1993; AAS in Weather Tech., C.C. of the Air Force, Maxwell AFB, Ala., 1985; MS in History, MS in Polit. Sci., Ill. State U., Normal, IL, 1995, PhD in Arts in History, 2000. Weather observer USAF, 1973—80, weather forecaster, 1980—91, chief weather sta. ops. Camp Humphrey's, Republic of Korea, 1991—93; archivist State of Ill./Ill. State U., Normal, Ill., 1994—95; grad. tchg. asst. dept. history Ill. State U., Normal, Ill., 1995—96; dept. chair, social sci. Bob Jones H.S., Madison, Ala., 1996—2000; instr. of history and polit. sci. Calhoun C.C., Decatur, Ala., 2000—, divsn. chair: history, polit. sci., geography, and religion, 2004—. Cons. Yancura Polit. Action Com., Madison, Ala., 2004. Author: (book) Joseph Wheeler: Uniting the Blue and the Gray. Traveling lectr. Ala. Found. for the Humanities, Montgomery, 2002—04. Decorated Air Force Commendation Medal, Army Commendation Medal; recipient Pitzenbarger award, US Air Force-Air Weather Svc., 1988. Mem.: Midwest Asian Hist. Assn., Third World Studies, Inc., Ala. Hist. Assn., Am. Hist. Assn., KC. Roman Catholic. Avocations: travel, writing, scuba diving. Office: Calhoun Community College PO Box 2216 Decatur AL 35609-2216 Office Phone: 256-306-2748. Office Fax: 256-306-2908. E-mail: mky@calhoun.edu.

KINNEY, ARTHUR FREDERICK, humanities educator, writer; b. Cortland, N.Y., Sept. 5, 1933; s. Arthur F. and Gladys (Mudge) K. BA magna cum laude, Syracuse U., 1955; MS, Columbia U., 1956; PhD, U. Mich., 1963. Instr. Yale U., New Haven, Conn., 1963-66; asst. prof. U. Mass., Amherst, 1966-69, assoc. prof., 1969-73, prof., 1973-85, Copeland Prof., 1985—. Adj. prof. Clark U., 1973—, NYU, 1990—; dir. Mass. Ctr. for Renaissance Studies, Amherst; spkr. in field. Author: Faulkner's Narrative Poetics, 1978, Resources of Being: Flannery O'Connor's Library, 1984, Humanist Poetics, 1986, John Skelton: Priest as Poet, 1987, Continental Humanist Poetics, 1989, Dorothy Parker Revisited, 1997, Renaissance Drama, 1999, 2nd edit., 2005, Cambridge Companion to English Literature 1500-1600, 2000, Blackwell Companion to Renaissance Drama, 2001, Lies Like Truth: Shakespeare, Macbeth and the Cultural Moment, 2001, New Essays on Hamlet, 2001, Shakespeare by Stages, 2003, Shakespeare's Webs: Networks of Meaning in Renaissance Drama, 2004; editor: Rogues, Vagabonds, and Sturdy Beggars, 1973, 2nd edit., 1990, Elizabethan Backgrounds, 1974, revised edit., 1990, Renaissance Historicism, 1987, English Literary Renaissance jour., (book series) Twayne English Authors Series-Renaissance, Massachusetts Studies in Early Modern Culture; mem. editl. bd. several jours.; editl. cons. in field: With AUS, 1956-58. Recipient Disting. Tchg. award U. Mass., 1990, Chancellor's medal, 1985, Univ. Rsch. fellowship, 1976; named Fulbright fellow, Christ Ch., Oxford U., 1977-78, Sr. Huntington Libr. fellow, 1973-74, 78, 83, Sr. NEH fellow, 1973-74, 87-88, Sr. Folger Shakespeare Libr. fellow, 1974, 90, 92. Mem. MLA (pres. coun. of editors of learned jours. 1971-73, 81-83), Shakespeare Assn. Am. (trustee 1995-1997), Renaissance Soc. Am. (coun. mem.), Renaissance English Text Soc. (pres. 1985—), Sixteenth-Century Studies Conf. Assn, Internat. Sidney Soc. (pres.). Avocations: published photographer, jazz. Home: 25 Hunters Hill Cir Amherst MA 01002-3116 Office: English Dept U Mass Amherst Amherst MA 01003 also: Ctr Renaissance Studies PO Box 2300 Amherst MA 01004-2300 Office Phone: 413-577-3600.

KINNEY, BETTY CAUDILL, elementary school educator; b. Franklin, Ky., Sept. 1, 1939; d. James Donald and Margaret Irene (McReynolds) Chaddock; m. Robert Lee Kinney, Aug. 5, 1961; children: Leanne Michelle Timura, Robert Bryan. BS, Middle Tenn. State U., Murfreesboro, 1961, MEd, 1971. Tchr. 8th grade Murfreesboro City Schs., 1961-62; GED tchr. U.S. Army Edn. Ctr., Frankfurt and Hanau, Germany, 1961-66, USAF Edn. Ctr., Smyrna, Tenn., 1967-68; Title 1 reading tchr. Murfreesboro City Schs., 1968-71; reading tchr. Spartanburg (S.C.) Dist. 7, 1972; cons. Spartanburg Dist. 2, 1972-73; Model Cities project tchr. Charles Lea Ctr., Spartanburg, 1972-73; reading tchr. Sch. Dist. of Greenville County, Greenville, S.C., 1973-76; reading specialist Virginia Beach (Va.) Schs., 1976-82; reading resource tchr. Rush-Henrietta (N.Y.) Ctrl. Schs., 1982—2002; ret., 2002. Part-time test scorer Pearson Ednl. Measurments, Inc. Choir soprano 1st Presbyn. Ch. Choir, Pittsford, N.Y., 1984—; mem. Hendersonville Cmty. Chorus, 2004-05. Named Reading Tchr. of Yr. Monroe County, 1991; recipient Winner's Circle award Henrietta C. of C. Mem. N.Y. State Reading Assn., Rochester Area Reading Coun. (bd. dirs. 1983-85, v.p. 1985-86, pres. 1986-87, historian 1987-92). Democrat. Avocations: gardening, reading, travel, singing. Home: 120 Pembroke Dr Hendersonville TN 37075

KINNEY, CAROLYN, physician; b. Philipsburg, Pa., Feb. 18, 1957; MD, Boston U., 1981. Intern Thomas Jefferson U. Hosp., Phila., 1981, resident, 1982—84; staff Good Samaritan Regional Hosp. Med. Ctr., Phoenix, 1995—; phys. Health South Meridian Point Rehab., Scottsdale, Ariz., 1996—; sec. Am. Bd. Phys. Medicine & Rehab. Office: 9630 E Shea Blvd Scottsdale AZ 85260 also: Health South Meridian Point Rehab Hospital 11250 N 92nd St Scottsdale AZ 85260

KINNEY, CATHERINE R., investment company executive; BS magna cum laude, Iona Coll.; cert. advanced mgmt., Harvard Sch. Bus. Various positions NY Stock Exch., 1974—86, mgr. trading-floor opers. and tech., 1986—95, group exec. v.p., 1995—2002, pres. & co-COO, 2002—. Bd. mem. Depository Trust & Clearing Corp., Met Life Ins. Co. Bd. regents Georgetown U.; bd. dirs. Jr. Achievement NY, NY Stock Exch. Found. Office: attn Ray Pellecchia NY Stock Exch 11 Wall St New York NY 10005

KINNEY, DALE, dean, art history educator; b. NYC, May 10, 1944; d. William Alfred Brabant and Edna Mary Pieper; m. Mark L. Darby, May 10, 1986; m. Peter C. Kinney (div.); 1 child, Aaron C. BA, Syracuse U., 1965; MA, NYU, 1967, PhD, 1975. Asst. prof. Bryn Mawr Coll., Pa., 1975—78, assoc. prof., 1978—87, prof., 1987—, dean arts & sci. grad sch., 2000—. Dir. Internat. Ctr. Medieval Arts, NYC, 1987—2000. Editor: GESTA, 1997—2000. Recipient Lindback award, Bryn Mawr Coll., 1984. Mem.: Coll. Art Assn. (dir. 2003—, Disting. Tchg. of Art History award 2002), Phi Beta Kappa. Office: Bryn Mawr Coll 101 N Merion Ave Bryn Mawr PA 19010

KINNEY, DENNIS K., psychologist, researcher; BA, U. Colo., 1966; PhD, Harvard U., 1972. Asst. prof. psychology UCLA, 1972—77; rsch. psychologist McLean Hosp., Belmont, Mass., 1977—; lectr., assoc. prof., dept. psychiatry Harvard Med. Sch., Boston, 1977—. Dir., genetics lab. McLean Hosp., Belmont, Mass., 1983—. Contbr. articles to profl. jours. Fellow, NSF and Woodrow Wilson Found., 1966—70; grantee, various sponsors including Stanley Med. Rsch. Inst., NIH, 1975—2005. Mem.: APA. Achievements include research in in devel. psychological scales for rating creativity. Office: McLean Hosp 115 Mill St Belmont MA 02478

KINNEY, DONALD JAY, writer, educator; b. Toledo, Ohio, June 7, 1978; s. Donald Jay and Pamela Janette Kinney. BA in English, U. Mont., 2002; MFA in Creative Writing, U. Fla., 2005. Instr. U. Fla., Gainesville, 2003—05. Author: (5 novels including) Red Sky by Morning, 2002 (1st prize for fiction Miscon Sci. Fiction Writers Convention, 2001); contbr. essays and short stories to profl. publs. Nominee Pushcart prize, Vincent Bros. Rev., 2003; recipient 1st prize for fiction, Allegheny Rev., 2002; Marjorie Keenan Rawlings fellow, U. Fla., 2003. Mem.: MLA, Assn. Writing Profls. Avocations: writing, videography, photography, bicycling, hiking. Personal E-mail: djkinney@gmail.com.

KINNEY, DOROTHY JEAN, retired elementary school educator; b. Bklyn., Mar. 25, 1935; d. Joseph Salvatore and Ida (DiCamillo) Longo; m. Robert Frank Masessa, Apr. 3, 1954 (dec. May 1984); children: Robert C., Joseph M., Jeffrey T.; m. Lester Frederick Kinney, Mar. 22, 1986. BA, William Paterson Coll., 1974, MA, 1981. Elem. sch. tchr. West Milford (N.J.) Bd. Edn., 1974-95; ret., 1995. Remedial reading tutor St. Paul's Parochial Sch., Haledon, N.J., 1974. Scout leader Boy Scouts Am., West Milford, N.J., 1964-74; mem. com. Queen of Peace Ch., West Milford, 1960-84. Mem. NEA, N.J. Edn. Assn., West Milford Edn. Assn. Republican. Roman Catholic. also: Apshawa Sch 7867 Gardner Dr Naples FL 34109-0608

KINNEY, EARL ROBERT, mutual funds company executive; b. Burnham, Maine, Apr. 12, 1917; s. Harry E. and Ethel (Vose) K.; m. Margaret Velie Thatcher, Apr. 23, 1977; children: Jeanie Elizabeth, Earl Robert, Isabella Alice. AB, Bates Coll., 1939; postgrad., Harvard U. Grad. Sch., 1940. Founder, North Atlantic Pack Co., Bar Harbor, Maine, 1941, pres., 1941-42, treas., dir., 1941-64; with Gorton Corp. (became subs. Gen. Mills, Inc. 1968), 1954-68, pres., 1958-68; v.p. Gen. Mills, Inc., 1968-69, exec. v.p., 1969-73, chief fin. officer, 1970-73, pres., chief operating officer, 1973-77, chmn. bd., 1977-81; pres., chief exec. officer IDS Mut. Fund Group, Mpls., 1982-87. Bd. dirs. Idexx Labs., Inc. Trustee Bates Coll., also chmn. alumni drives, 1960-64. Office: 4900 IDS Ctr Minneapolis MN 55402 Office Phone: 612-332-1369.

KINNEY, JAMES HOWARD, lawyer; b. Oklahoma City, Mar. 2, 1937; s. William Edgar and Chrissie (Ballingall) K.; m. June Lassick, Mar. 26, 1961; children: Karen Jill, Scott James. BS in Bus. Mgmt., Calif. State U., Long Beach, 1963; JD, UCLA, 1966. Bar: Calif. 1966, U.S. Dist. Ct. (so. dist.) Calif. 1966. Dep. dist. atty. Ventura (Calif.) County, 1966-68; ptnr. Collins, Gleason & Kinney, Torrance, Calif., 1968-85, O'Melveny & Myers, Los Angeles, 1985—2000; sr. v.p. The Macerich Co., Santa Monica, Calif., 2000—. Lectr. Harbor Coll., L.A., 1971-72. Councilman City of Palos Verdes Estates, Calif., 1983-1990, Mayor, 1985-86, 88-89. With USMC, 1955-58. Mem. Los Angeles County Bar Assn., Internat. Council Shopping Ctrs., Sigma Alpha Epsilon. Republican. also: O'Melveny & Myers 400 S Hope St Los Angeles CA 90071-2801 Office: Ste 700 401 Wilshire Blvd Santa Monica CA 90401-1452

KINNEY, JEANNE KAWELOLANI, English studies educator, writer; b. Bayville, N.Y., Nov. 22, 1964; d. Robert Warren Stewart and Genevieve Lehuanani (Okilauea) Kinney. BA, Linfield Coll., 1986; MFA, Bowling Green State U., 1988. Tchr. Hawaii Bus. Coll., Honolulu, 1993-95; ESL tchr. GEOs Lang. Corp., Osaka and Kobe, Japan, 1996-97; English tchr. St. Joseph's H.S., Hilo, Hawaii, 2000. Poet-in-the-schs. Dept. Edn., Honolulu, fall 1994; sub. English tchr. St. Andrew's Priory, Honolulu, 1993; adj. English tchr. Chaminade U., Honolulu, spring 1993, 94; basic skills instr. Kamehameha Schs., Honolulu, 1991-92; English tchr., speech coach Punahou Sch., Honolulu, 1989-91. Contbr. to profl. publs. including Hawaii Rev., Kaimana, Ascent, Seattle Rev., Bamboo Ridge Press. Precinct ops. cood. Office Lt. Gov., Hawaii Elections Divsn., 1991-93, precinct worker trainer, 1989-91; v.p. Hawaii Lit. Arts Coun., Honolulu, 1990; pub. rels. officer Hawaii Speech League, Honolulu, 1991. Avocations: dance, swimming, writing, travel, foreign languages. Home: 10 Ululani St # 10 Hilo HI 96720-2979

KINNEY, JON C., metal products executive; CFO, sr. v.p. Ill. Tool Works, Inc., Glenview, Ill., 1998—. Office: Illinois Tool Works Inc 3600 W Lake Ave Glenview IL 60025-5811

KINNEY, KENNETH PARRISH, retired banker; b. Kansas City, Mo., Aug. 5, 1921; s. Wayne William and Dorothy Fay (Parrish) K.; m. Madeline Shriver Brennan, Aug. 2, 1947 (dec. Sept. 1983); children— Ann, Frank, Catherine, William, Madeline, Ellen, Robert; m. Terese Ann Bargen-Cagney, May 25, 1985. AB, Princeton U., 1943; postgrad., Grad. Sch. Bus. Adminstrn., NYU, 1949-51. Sub-acct. Nat. City Bank N.Y., N.Y.C., 1946-50; asst. mgr. Chem. Bank, N.Y.C., 1950-55; sr. v.p. No. Trust Co., Chgo., 1955-86. Bd. dirs. Hinsdale (Ill.) Libr. Bd., 1985—91, Great Books Found., Chgo., 1997—2002. 1st lt. A.C. U.S. Army, 1943—46, ETO. Mem. Bankers Assn. Fgn. Trade (pres. 1969-70), Chgo. Council Fgn. Rels. (treas. 1967-70), Chgo. Com., Union League Club (Chgo.), Hinsdale Golf Club. Home: 633 S County Line Rd Hinsdale IL 60521-4726

KINNEY, LISA FRANCES, lawyer; b. Laramie, Wyo., Mar. 13, 1951; d. Irvin Wayne and Phyllis (Poe) Kinney; m. Rodney Philip Lang, Feb. 5, 1971; children: Cambria Helen, Shelby Robert, Eli Wayne. BA, U. Wyo., 1973, JD, 1986; MLS, U. Oreg., 1975. Reference libr. U. Wyo. Sci. Libr., Laramie, 1975-76; outreach dir. Albany County Libr., Laramie, 1975-76, dir., 1977-83; mem. Wyo. State Senate, Laramie, 1984-94, minority leader, 1992-94; with documentation office Am. Heritage Ctr. U. Wyo., 1991-94; assoc. Corthell & King, 1994-96, shareholder, 1996-99; owner Summit Bar Rev., 1987—2004; fin. planner VALIC, 2001—. Author: (with Rodney Lang) Civil Rights of the Developmentally Disabled, 1986; (with Rodney Lang and Phyllis Kinney) Manual For Families with Emotionally Disturbed and Mentally Ill Relatives, 1988, rev. 1991, 99, Lobby For Your Library, Know What Works, 1992, Understanding Mental Illnesses: A Family Legal Guide, 2004; contbr. articles to profl. jours.; editor, compiler pub. rels. directory of ALA, 1982. Bd. dirs. Big Bros./Big Sisters, Laramie, 1980-83, Children's Mus., 1993-97; bd. dirs. Am. Heritage Ctr., 1993-97, Citizen of the Century, 1997-99, govt. chmn. 1997-99; pres. Friends Cmty. Recreation Project, 2001—. Named Outstanding Wyo. Libr. Assn., 1977, Young Woman, State of Wyo., 1980; recipient Beginning Young Profl. award, Mt. Plains Libr. Assn., 1980, Arts and Scis. Disting. Alumni award, U. Wyo., 1997, Making Democracy Work award, Wyo. LWV, 2000. Mem.: ABA, Nat. Conf. State Legislatures (various coms. 1985—90), Laramie Area C. of C. (bd. dirs. 1996—2000, mem. 1999, Top Hand award 1997), Zonta, Kiwanis. Democrat. Avocations: photography, dance, reading, travel, languages. Home: 1415 E Baker St Laramie WY 82072 Office: PO Box 1710 Laramie WY 82073-1710 Office Phone: 307-742-6644. Personal E-mail: lfkl@aol.com.

KINNEY, MICHELE A., education educator, lawyer; d. Joe Lee Anders and Reita Lane Ledbetter; m. A. Michael Kinney, Dec. 23, 1997; 1 child, Anders M. III. JD, Samford Univ., Birmingham, Ala., 1994; MEd, Univ. N. Ala., Florence, Ala., 2000; MA in History, U. Ala. Bar: Ala. 1995. Atty. AOC and various firms, Ala.; coll. prof. Columbia Univ., Calhoun C.C., Ala. AP US history reader Edn. Testing Svc., NJ. Recipient Outstanding student Honor Soc., OSHS, 2004. Mem.: Orgn. of Am. Historians (Gilder-Lerman award 2003), Ala. Humanities Found., Phi Alpha Theta. Roman Cath. Avocations: family, reading, travel.

KINNEY, RICHARD GORDON, lawyer, educator; b. Chgo., May 8, 1939; s. Michael James Sr. and Blanche Marie (Gill) K.; m. Katherine Choffen, Dec. 26, 1969; 1 child, Richard Greg. BSEE, U. Ill., 1961; JD, U. Chgo., 1964. Bar: Ill. 1964, U.S. Ct. Customs and Patent Appeals 1975, U.S. Supreme Ct. 1970, U.S. Ct. Appeals (fed. cir.) 1982. With patent dept. Zenith Radio Corp., Chgo., 1963-64, Borg-Warner Corp., Chgo., 1968-73; divsn. patent counsel Baxter Travenol Labs., Inc., Deerfield, Ill., 1973-76; prin. Law Offices of Richard G. Kinney, Chgo. and Merrillville, Ind., 1976-95, 98—; pres. Richard G. Kinney, P.C., 1995-98. Roman Catholic. Office: Richard G Kinney PO Box 11119 Merrillville IN 46411-1119 E-mail: richardgkinney@hotmail.com.

KINNEY, STEPHEN HOYT, JR., lawyer; b. Albuquerque, Feb. 27, 1948; s. Stephen Hoyt and Harriet May (Gadsden) K.; m. Leslie vanLiew, June 10, 1972; 1 child, Erin. BS, MIT, 1970; JD, Harvard U., 1973. Bar: N.Y. 1974, U.S. Dist. Ct. (so. dist.) N.Y. 1974, U.S. Dist. Ct. (ea. dist.) N.Y. 1974, U.S.

Dist. Ct. (no. dist.) N.Y. 1978, U.S. Ct. Appeals (2d cir.) 1975, U.S. Supreme Ct. 1982. Programmer, analyst MIT, 1968-70; law clk. N.J. Organized Crime Unit, Trenton, 1972; assoc. Reid & Priest, N.Y.C., 1973-85, sr. atty., 1985-86, ptnr., 1986-98, Thelen Reid & Priest LLP, N.Y.C., 1998—. Dir. The Friends of Thirteen, Inc. Author, editor: Outline of Arbitration, 1984; contbr. articles to profl. jours.; creator software. Mem.: ABA. Office: Thelen Reid & Priest 875 Third Ave New York NY 10022-6225 Office Phone: 212-603-2168. Business E-Mail: skinney@thelenreid.com.

KINNEY, VIRGINIA LEE, librarian, educator; b. Barnesville, Ohio, Oct. 21, 1934; d. James Jeffrey and Mary Virginia Groves; m. Royce Bentley Kinney, Mar. 11, 1956; children: Charlotte, William, Robert, Margaret, Mary Elizabeth. BS in Home Econ., Ohio State U., 1956; student, Muskingum Coll., 1963, Ohio U., 1965, U. Dayton, 1988, student, 1991, Urbana U., 1968, student, 1970, student, 1975, student, 1997, student, 1998. Instr. County Ext. Agt. Ohio State U., Columbus, Ohio, 1959—60; tchr. Union Local Head Start, Bethesda, Ohio, 1961—62, Barnesville Elem. Sch., Barnesville, Ohio, 1962—62; libr. Miami County Pub. Libr., Troy, Ohio, 1978—. Instr. Newton Local Chpt. I, Pleasant Hill, Ohio, 1979—88; libr. Newton Local, Pleasant Hill, 1984—2002; instr. Adult Basic & Lit. Edn., Piqua, Ohio, 1988—. State pres. Ohio CowBelles, Ohio, 1984—85; historian Epworth Pk., Bethesda, 1997—; mem. Astrobuds Garden Club, 1973—; judge 4-H; mem. Brethren in Christ Ch. Mem.: Miami County Assn. Family and Consumer Sci., Ohio Assn. Adult & Continuing Edn., Ohio Cattlewomen, Miami County Rep. Women, Human Ecology Alumni Soc., Johnny Appleseed Soc., Ohio State U. Alumni Assn., Alpha Delta Pi Alumnae (state pres. 1992—94). Republican. Home: 8055 W State Rt 718 Pleasant Hill OH 45359

KINNEY, WILLIAM LIGHT, JR., editor, publishing executive; b. Bennettsville, SC, Oct. 26, 1933; s. William Light and Annie Laurie (Mayer) K.; m. Margaret Rene Pegues, Mar. 21, 1964; children: Elisabeth Mayer Kinney McNiel, William Light III (dec.). BS, Wofford Coll., 1954, DHL, 1999; BA in Journalism, U. S.C., 1977. Copy editor The State, Columbia, S.C., 1955-58; reporter Marlboro Herald-Advocate, Bennettsville, 1958-59, advt. mgr., 1959-60, bus. mgr., 1960-65, mng. editor, 1965-70, editor, pub., 1970—; pres. Marlboro Pub. Co. Inc., 1970—. Sec. Marlboro Savs. & Loan Assn., Bennettsville, 1970-82, First Nat. Bank of S.C., Bennettsville, 1973-84; mem. adv. bd. S.C. Nat. Bank, Bennettsville, 1984-94, Wachovia Bank, 1994-2000; sec., mem. adv. bd. Security Fed. Savs. & Loan, 1982-90, bd. dirs., 1984-89; pres. Greater Pee Dee Press Inc., 1972-82, Bennettsville Parking and Devel. Co., 1964; v.p. Hamlet (N.C.) News Inc., 1973-82 Editor, pub.: Three Who Dared, 1960, Sherman's March—A Review, 1961, The Story of the Sculpture Light, 2001. Pres. United Fund, Bennettsville, 1963-64; chmn. Marlboro County com. S.C. Tricentennial, 1970, U.S. Bicentennial, 1974—81; councilman, mayor pro tem City of Bennettsville, 1967-69; mem. Marlboro County Devel. Bd., 1958-81; bd. dirs. Kinney Found., 1971-99, chmn. bd. dirs., 1975-99; bd. dirs. Indian Mus. of Carolinas, 1972—; trustee Whipple Found., 1979—2005, chmn., 1981—; trustee S.C. Press Found., 1978-93, 2000—, vice-chmn., 1985-92, chmn., 1992-93; trustee Neil Monroe Trust Fund, 1965-91, chmn., 1977-91; adv. bd. SBA, 1962-64; chmn. fin. com. 1st Meth. Ch., 1985-87, staff parish com. chmn., 1990-92; active Chancel Choir, 1951—; trustee S.C. Meth. Adv., 1968-78, S.C. Hall of Fame, 1980-88, 2005—, v.p., 1980-82; dir. S.C. Confedn. Local Hist. Socs., 1974-75, treas., 1975-78, v.p., 1979, pres., 1980-82; warden St. David's Soc., 1978-80, pres., 1980-81; chmn. Jennings-Brown House Restoration, 1974-76, Bennettsville Downtown Commn., 1977-82; v.p. Bennettsville Downtown Devel. Assn., 1993—; trustee Am. Folklife Ctr., Libr. Congress, Washington, 1982—, chmn. 1987, 92-93, 98-2000, vice-chmn., 1990-92, 94—; mem. S.C. Archives and History Commn., 1987—, vice-chmn., 1988-90, 98—, chmn., 1990-93; SC rev. bd. Nat. Register of Hist. Places, 1988—, chmn., 1990—, S.C. State Devel. Bd., 1993; bd. dirs. Friends Brookgreen Gardens, 1991-97, 2001-, pres., 1993-96, trustee, 1993-96; bd. visitors Coker Coll., 1986-89; bd. dirs. S.C. Com. for Humanities, 1981-85, Pawleys Island Civic Assn., 1979—, dir., 2004—; dir. Palmetto Trails, 1993-97; trustee Scotia Village Retirement Cmty., 1995—; v.p. Marlboro Civic Ctr. Found., 1994—; bd. mgrs. S.C. Hist. Soc., 2005—. Named Bennettsville and S.C. Young Man of Yr., 1961, S.C. Amb. for Econ. Devel., 1990, Knight of Justice of the Order of St. John, Knights of Malta, Sovereign Order of St. John of Jerusalem, 1995—; recipient Jean Laney Harris Folk Heritage award S.C. Gen. Assembly, 2003. Mem. SAR, Nat. Trust for Historic Preservation (bd. advisors So. Region 1997—, chmn., 2000-02, nat. exec. com. 1999-2002), S.C. Press Assn. (pres. 1972-73), Palmetto Conservation Found. (dir. 1997-2001), Palmetto Trust Hist. Preservation (trustee 2002—), Marlboro County Hist. Preservation Com. (chmn. 1986-96), S.C. C. of C. (bd. dirs. 1964-68, 75-78), Bennettsville C. of C. (bd. dirs. 1964-67, 75-78), Bennettsville Jaycees (pres. 1962), S.C. Jaycees (v.p. 1963, nat. dir. 1964), Marlboro Hist. Soc. (bd. dirs. 1967-79, 2000-, pres. 1975-79, Govs. award for Hist. Preservation 1996, Elizabeth O'Neill Verner Gov.'s award for the arts 2002), U. S.C. Soc. (bd. dirs. 1972-82, vice chmn. 1977-82), Wofford Coll. Alumni Assn. (bd. dirs. 1968-72), Marlboro Country Club, Marlboro Cotillion (pres. 1984-86, 2004—), Nat. Debutante Cotillion (sponsor 1987-95), Sans Souci Club (pres. 1980-82), Rotary (bd. dirs. 1968-70, 99-2001, pres. 1970-72), McLeod Med. Ctr. Found. (trustee 1997—), SC Hist. Soc. (bd. mgrs., 2005—), Phi Beta Kappa, Sigma Alpha Epsilon, Sigma Delta Chi. Home: Magnolia 508 E Main St Bennettsville SC 29512-0656 Office: Marlboro Herald-Adv Shiness 100 Fayetteville Ave Bennettsville SC 29512-0656 Office Phone: 843-479-3815. Business E-Mail: wlkinneyjr@mecsc.net. *"Service to humanity is the best work of life" is a tenet of the Jaycee Creed that still drives me to work through my avocations as well as my vocation to help make my community, state and nation better than I found. These efforts have broadened my horizons, enriched my life and heightened my spirit. I recommend active service to one's home community, state and nation to all.*

KINNIBURGH, ALAN JAMES, molecular biologist, educator; b. Elmhurst, Ill., Oct. 3, 1951; s. Theodore and Elizabeth (Pitcarin) K. BS, U. Ill., 1973; PhD, U. Chgo., 1977. Rsch. assoc. U. Wis., Madison, 1977-82; asst. prof. Roswell Park Cancer Inst., Buffalo, 1982-87, assoc. prof., 1987-91, prof., 1992—; sr. v.p. research adminstrn. Leukemia & Lymphoma Soc., White Plains, NY; CEO Nat. Hemophilia Found., NYC, 2005—. Mem. adv. bd. Assn. for Rsch./Childhood Cancer, Buffalo, 1990—; mem. hematology rev. bd. VA, Washington, 1990-93. Recipient Louis Pasteur award U. Ill., 1973. Mem. AAAS, Am. Assn. Microbiology, Am. Assn. Cancer Rsch., N.Y. Acad. Sci. Achievements include discovery of introns in mRNA precursors, B-thalassemia is an RNA processing disorder; discovery that DNA triplexes increase transcription of proto-oncogenes. Office: Roswell Park Cancer Inst Elm And Carlton St Buffalo NY 14263-0001 also: Nat Hemophilia Found 116 W 32nd St 11th Fl New York NY 10001 Office Phone: 212-328-3700. Office Fax: 212-328-3777.

KINNIBURGH, LEAH HUGHES, education educator; b. Selma, Ala., Dec. 24, 1957; d. Miriam Powers and George Webb Hughes; m. James Earl Kinniburgh, Oct. 7, 2000; children: Tyler Webb Robbins, Avery Karen Robbins. PhD, U. Ala., 1998. Cert. tchr., adminstr. State Dept. of Edn. Elem. tchr. Dallas County Sch. Sys., Selma, Ala., 1978—83, Athens (Ala.) City Sch. Sys., 1983—95, elem. sch. prin., 1995—97, asst. prof. edn., 1997—2001, elem. prin., 1995—97; asst. prof. edn. Athens State U., 1997—2001; assoc. prof. edn. Lynn U., Boca Raton, Fla., 2001—. Editor: (college literacy textbooks) Chapter Editing. Office: Lynn Univ 3601 N Military Trail Boca Raton FL 33431 Office Phone: 561-237-7082. Personal E-mail: lkinniburgh@bellsouth.net. E-mail: lkinniburgh@lynn.edu.

KINNIER, EMILY P., artist; d. Nelson Palmore and Elizabeth Bott; m. Eugene Howard Kinnier, Feb. 4, 1939. Grad., Pan Am. Bus. Coll., Richmond, VA, 1935; Studied, Art Students League, N.Y.C., 1953—70. Treas. patterson nj br. Nat. League of Am. Penwomen, Patterson, NJ, 1968—69; treas. Richmond br. Nat. League of Am. Pen Women (Hdgs.), Washington, 1977—78. Studied with Laura Glenn Douglas, Washington, 1950—50; studied with Vytlacil, Kantor, Hovannes, Ben Cunningham, Hale Art Students League, N.Y.C., 1953—72; studied with Burgoyne Diller Studio Atlantic Highlands, Atlantic Highlands, NJ, 1960—64; studied with Laura Pahris Richmond Printmaking Workshop, Richmond, Va., 1980—82. One-woman shows include Middle St. Gallery, Wash., Va., 1996—98, exhibited in group shows, 2000, 2002, exhibitions include Juried Show, Newark Mus., 1964 (Second Prize in Watercolor), State Juried Show, Montclair Mus., 1964 (2nd prize on watercolor), Montclair Mus., N.J., 1964, Jersey City Mus., 1965, Festival of Arts, Monmouth Coll., N.J., 1966, Middle St. Gallery, Wash., Va., 1995, 1708 Gallery, Richmond, Va., 1996—2004, Nations Bank Gallery, 1998. Arts bd. St. Pauls Episc. Ch., Richmond, Va., 1982—84. Mem.: Nat. League of Am. Pen Women Richmond Br., Art Students League N.Y.C. (life). Avocations: travel, gardening. Home: 812 N Tilden Richmond VA 23221-1517

KINNISON, ROBERT WHEELOCK, retired accountant; b. Des Moines, Sept. 17, 1914; s. Virgil R. and Sopha J. (Jackson) K.; m. Randi Hjelle, Oct. 28, 1971; children: Paul F., Hazel Jo Lewis. BS in Acctg., U. Wyo., 1940. CPA, Wyo., Colo. Ptnr. 24 hour auto service, Laramie, Wyo., 1945-59; pvt. practice acctg. Laramie, Wyo., 1963-71, Las Vegas, Nev., 1972-74, Westminster, Colo., 1974-76, Ft. Collins, Colo., 1976-97; ret., 1997. Served with U.S. Army, 1941-45, PTO. Mem. Wyo. Soc. CPAs, Am. Legion (past comdr.), Laramie Soc. CPAs (pres. 1966), VFW, Laramie Optimist Club (pres. 1950), Sertoma Club. Home: 401 N Timberline Rd Lot 288 Fort Collins CO 80524-1431

KINNISON, WILLIAM ANDREW, retired university president; b. Springfield, Ohio, Feb. 10, 1932; s. Errett Lowell and Audrey Muriel (Smith) K.; m. Lenore Belle Morris, June 11, 1960; children— William Errett, Linda Elise, Amy Elisabeth. AB, Wittenberg U., 1954, BS in Edn., 1955; MA, U. Wis., 1963; PhD (1st Flesher fellow), Ohio State U., 1967; postgrad., Harvard U. Inst. Ednl. Mgmt., 1970; LL.D., Calif. Luth. Coll., 1983; Th.D., John Carroll U., 1983; LLD, Lenoir-Rhyne Coll., 1987; LHD, Capital U., 1995. Asst. dean admissions Wittenberg U., Springfield, 1958-65, asst. to pres., 1967-70, v.p. for univ. affairs, 1970-73, v.p. adminstrn., 1973, pres., 1974-95, pres. emeritus, 1995—; pres., CEO Heritage Ctr. of Clark County, 1997—2002. Author: Samuel Shellabarger: Lawyer, Jurist, Legislator, 1969, Building Sullivant's Pyramid: An Administrative History of the Ohio State University, 1970, Concise History of Wittenberg University, 1976, An American Seminary, 1980, Springfield and Clark County: an Illustrated History, 1985, also articles. Asst. to dir. Sch. Edn. Ohio State U., Columbus, 1965-67; past chmn. Assn. Ind. Colls. and Univs. Ohio; trustee Ohio Found. Ind. Colls., 1974-95, chair bd. trustees, 1995; chmn. standing com. Luth. World Ministries, 1976-82; mem. exec. coun. Luth. Ch. in Am., 1978-86; mem., chmn. Commn. for a New Luth. Ch., 1982-86; bd. dirs. Am. Assn. Colls., 1982-84. With U.S. Army, 1956-58. Mem. Clark County Hist. Soc. (trustee 1963—), Orgn. Am. Historians, Blue Key, Phi Beta Kappa, Phi Delta Kappa, Kappa Phi Kappa, Pi Sigma Alpha, Tau Kappa Alpha, Delta Sigma Phi, Omicron Delta Kappa. Clubs: Cosmos, Rotary. Home: 1820 Timberline Dr Springfield OH 45504-1236

KINO, GORDON STANLEY, electrical engineering educator; b. Melbourne, Australia, June 15, 1928; came to U.S., 1951, naturalized, 1967; s. William Hector and Sybil (Cohen) K.; m. Dorothy Beryl Lovelace, Oct. 30, 1955; 1 child, Carol Ann. B.Sc. with 1st class honours in Math, London (Eng.) U., 1948, M.Sc. in Math, 1950; PhD in Elec. Engring, Stanford U., 1955. Jr. scientist Mullard Research Lab., Salford, Surrey, Eng., 1947-51; research asst., then research assoc. Stanford U., 1951-55, research assoc., 1957-61, mem. faculty, 1961—, prof. elec. engring., 1965—, assoc. dean facilities and planning Sch. Engring., 1986-92, assoc. chmn. elec. engring., 1984-88, W.M. Keck Found. chair engring., 1992-97, W.M. Keck Found. chair engring. emeritus, 1997—; dir. Ginzton Lab., 1994-96. Mem. tech. staff Bell Telephone Labs., 1955-57; cons. to industry, 1957— Author: (with Kirstein, Waters) Space Charge Flow, 1968, Acoustic Devices, 1987, (with Corle) Confocal Scanning Optical Microscopy and Related Imaging Systems, 1996; also numerous papers on microwave tubes; electron optics, plasma physics, bulk effects in semiconductors, acoustic surface waves, acoustic imaging, optical microscopy, fiber optics, non-destructive testing, optical storage. Guggenheim fellow, 1967-68; recipient Applied Research Achievement award Am. Soc. Non-destructive Testing, 1986. Fellow IEEE (Centennial medal, Sonics and Ultrasonics Group Achievement award 1984), Am. Phys. Soc., AAAS; mem. Nat. Acad. Engring. Inventor Kino electron gun, 1959; co-inventor real-time scanning optical microscope, 1987, solid immersion lens, 1989, microfabricated miniature microscope, 1995. Home: 867 Cedro Way Stanford CA 94305-1002 Office Phone: 650-723-0205. Business E-Mail: kino@stanford.edu.

KINOSHITA, TOICHIRO, physicist; b. Tokyo, Jan. 23, 1925; came to U.S., 1952; s. Tsutomu and Fumi (Ueda) K.; m. Masako Matsuoka, Oct. 14, 1951; children: Kay, June, Ray. BS, Tokyo U., 1947, PhD, 1952. Mem. Inst. for Advanced Study, Princeton, N.J., 1952-54; postdoctoral fellow Columbia U., N.Y.C., 1954-55; rsch. assoc. Cornell U., Ithaca, N.Y., 1955-58, asst. prof., 1958-60, assoc. prof., 1960-63, prof., 1963-92, Goldwin Smith prof., 1992-95, Goldwin Smith prof. emeritus, 1995—. Mem. tech. adv. panel U.S. Dept. Energy, Washington, 1982-83; com. fundamental constants Nat. Rsch. Coun., Washington, 1984-86. Author: Quantum Electrodynamics, 1990; contbr. over 100 articles to profl. jours. Guggenheim fellow, 1973-74; recipient Sun-Amco medal Internat. Union Phys. & Applied Sci., 1998. Fellow NAS, AAAS, Am. Physical Soc. (Recipient J.J. Sakurai prize 1990). Democrat. Home: 5 Winthrop Pl Ithaca NY 14850-1740 Office: Cornell U Newman Lab Ithaca NY 14853 Business E-Mail: tk@hepth.cornell.edu.

KINS, JURIS, lawyer; b. Jelgava, Latvia, Apr. 24, 1942; came to U.S., 1949; s. Arnolds and Zenta (Dunis) K.; m. Olita Gita Kakis, Oct. 11, 1969; children: Aleksis A., Mikus N. BSChemE, U. Wis., 1964; MSChemE, U. Mich., 1965; JD, U. Wis., 1969. Bar: Wis. 1969, Ill. 1969. Assoc. ptnr. Chadwell & Kayser, Ltd., Chgo., 1969-90; ptnr. Vedder, Price, Kaufman & Kammholz, Chgo., 1990-93; Abramson & Fox, Chgo., 1993—. Pres. Latvian Peoples Support Group, Chgo., 1991—. Mem. ABA, Chgo. Bar Assn., Ill. Bar Assn., Wis. Bar Assn., Latvian Bar Assn. Avocations: tennis, skiing. Office: Abramson & Fox One E Wacker Dr Ste 3800 Chicago IL 60601 E-mail: juriskins@aol.com.

KINSBRUNER BUSH, JENNIFER, lawyer; AB in History & Latin Am. Studies summa cum laude, Princeton U., 1996; Fulbright Scholar, Universidad Católica, Santiago, Chile, 1996—97; JD, Yale Law Sch., 2000. Bar: Calif., US Ct. of Appeals, Federal Circuit. Rsch. assoc. Wiggin & Dana; summer assoc. Kirkland & Ellis, 1998, Cleary Gottlieb, 1999; law clerk to Judge Stanley Marcus US Ct. of Appeals, 11th Circuit, 2000—01; assoc. Irell & Manella, 2001—02; assoc., intellectual property litigation Fish & Richardson, San Diego, 2002—. Office: Fish & Richardson 12390 El Camino Real San Diego CA 92130 Office Phone: 858-678-5070. Office Fax: 858-678-5099. Business E-Mail: bush@fr.com.

KINSELLA, THOMAS, poet; b. Dublin, May 4, 1928; s. John Paul and Agnes (Casserly) K.; m. Eleanor Walsh, 1955, 3 children. With Irish Civil Svc., 1946-65, asst. prin. officer Dept. Fin., 1960-65. Artist in residence So. Ill. U., 1965-67, prof. English, 1967-70; prof. Temple U., Phila., 1970-90; dir. Dolmen Press Ltd., Cuala Press Ltd, Dublin; founder Peppercanister, Dublin, 1972. Author: Poems, 1956, Another September, 1958, Downstream, 1962, Nightwalker and Other Poems, 1968, Notes from the Land of the Dead, 1972, Butcher's Dozen, 1972, Finistere, 1972, New Poems, 1973, Selected Poems 1956-68, 1973, Song of the Night and Other Poems, 1978, The Messenger, 1978, Fifteen Dead, 1979, One and Other Poems, 1979; Songs of the Psyche, 1984; Her Vertical Smile, 1984; St. Catherine's Clock, 1987; Out of Ireland, 1987, Blood and Family, 1988, Poems From Center City, 1990, Personal Places, 1990, Madonna and Other Poems, 1991, Open Court, 1991, From Centre City, 1994, The Dual Tradition: an Essay on Poetry and Politics in Ireland, 1995, Collected Poems, 1996, The Pen Shop, 1997, The Familiar, 1999, Godhead, 1999, Citizen of the World, 2000, Littlebody, 2000, Collected Poems 1956-2001, 2001; editor: Selected Poems of Austin Clarke, 1976; (with Sean O'Tuama) Poems of the Dispossessed 1600-1900 with translations, 1980; The New Oxford Book of Irish Verse (with translations), 1986; transl. (from Old Irish) The Tain, 1970. Recipient Guinness Poetry award, 1958, Triennial Book award, Irish Arts Coun., 1960, Denis Devlin Meml. award, 1966, 1969, 1988, 1994, Field Day/Keough-Notre Dame Centre/Commons Tundish award, 2001; Guggenheim fellow, 1968—69, 1971—72, hon. sr. fellow, Sch. of English, Univ. Coll., Dublin, 2003. Mem.: Irish Acad. Letters, Am. Acad. Arts and Scis. Home: 639 Addison St Philadelphia PA 19147

KINSER, CYNTHIA D., state supreme court justice; b. Pennington Gap, Dec. 20, 1951; d. Morris and Velda (Myers) Fannon; m. H. Allen Kinser, Jr., March 17, 1974; children: Charles Adam, Terah Diane. Student, Univ. of Ga., 1970-71; BA, Univ. of Tenn., 1974; JD, Univ. of Va., 1977. Bar: Va. 1977, U.S. Dist. Ct. (we. dist.) Va. 1977, U.S. Ct. Appeals (4th cir.) 1977, U.S. Supreme Ct. 1988. Law clk. to Judge Glen M. Williams U.S. Dist. Ct., 1977-78; pvt. law practice, 1978-90; commonwealth's atty. Lee County, Va., 1980-83; magistrate judge U.S. Dist. Ct. (we. dist.) Va., Abingdon, 1990-98; justice Va. Supreme Ct., Richmond, 1998—. Trustee Chapter 7 Panel, U.S. Bankruptcy Ct., 1979-90. Mem. Va. Bar Assn., Va. Trial Lawyers Assn., Am. Bar Assn. Methodist. Office: Va Supreme Ct PO Box 1315 Richmond VA 23218-1315

KINSER, KATHERINE ANNE, lawyer; b. Russellville, Ark., Apr. 25, 1954; d. Thomas Kinser and Nancy (Seminatore) Barber; m. Frank W. Sullivan III, Aug. 19, 1988. BA, U. Ark., Little Rock, 1979; JD, So. Meth. U., 1984. Bar: Tex. 1984, U.S. Supreme Ct. 1990; cert. family law specialist, Tex. Assoc. Michael F. Pezzulli, P.C., Dallas, 1984-86; pvt. practice, Dallas, 1986; ptnr. McCurley, Kinser, McCurley & Nelson, L.L.P., Dallas, 1986—. Speaker in field. Contbr. articles to legal publs. Fellow Am. Acad. Matrimonial Lawyers; mem. ABA, State Bar Tex. (family law coun.), Tex. Acad. Family Law Specialists, Tarrant County Family Law Bar Assn., Dallas Bar Assn. (family law sect., sec. 1988-89, v.p. 1990-91, pres. 1991-92, mock trial com. 1987—), Sports Lawyers Assn., Phi Alpha Delta. Avocation: scuba diving.

KINSEY, CHARLES JOHN, industrial auctioneer, consultant, farmer, cattle breeder; b. Regina, Sask., Can., Aug. 4, 1922; came to U.S., 1929; s. Alfred Richardson and Lola Mae (Lagergren) K.; m. Shirley Elaine Grady, June 25, 1950; children: Rebecca Diane, David Allan, Jane Elizabeth, Thomas Charles. BS, U. Ill., 1951. Fieldman Am. Hampshire Swine Registry, Am. Hampshire Herdsman, Peoria, Ill., 1946—48; exec. sec. Park Ridge C. of C., Ill., 1953; indsl. auctioneer S.L. Winternitz & Co., Inc., Chgo., 1954—57; ptnr. Kinsey-Koploy Co., Detroit, 1957—65; pres., prin. Charles Kinsey & Co., Inc., Detroit, 1965—; pres. Mich. Auctioneers Assn., 1960—61; v.p. Mich. Angus Assn., 1963. Cons. A-Line Mfg. Co., Centralia, Ill., 1982—. Author: The Lives and The Times of The Kinsey Brothers, Ernest and Alfred, 1997. Mem. First Presbyn. Ch. Choir, Farmington Hills, Mich., 1959—. Served U.S. Army, 1944-46, Persian Gulf Command, ETO. Recipient Am. Farmer Degree FFA Vocat. Agrl., Urbana, 1940, State PRes. Ill. Assn. Future Farmers Am., 1940-41, Thomas E. Wilson award Ill. 4H Club, Chgo., 1943, State Ill. 4H Livestock Champion, Nat. Hampshire Pig Club contest winner, 1939. Mem. U. Ill. Alumni Assn. (life), Sigma Phi Epsilon (life). Independent. Avocations: baritone soloist, creative writing, voice concerts. Home and Office: Charles Kinsey & Co Inc 40011 Jefferson Novi MI 48375-2026

KINSEY, DONNA LEE, music educator; b. Punxsutawney, Pa., Dec. 18, 1947; d. Donald Joseph White and Sarah Leona Gromley; m. William Robert Kinsey, Mar. 30, 1970; stepchildren: Sheryl Ann Mock, Merrilee Kay Saccol. BS in Music Edn., Ind. U. Pa., 1969; MusM, W.Va. Univ., 1979. Cert. tchr. W.Va. Organist/choir dir. St. John's Luth. Ch., Kittanning, Pa., 1969—71; music tchr. Latrobe Jr. High, Pa., 1971—72; pastoral musician St. Theresa's Roman Cath. Parish, Morgantown, W.Va., 1972—2003, St. Francis de Sales, 2004—; music tchr. Armstrong Sch. Dist., Kittanning, 1969—71, Monongalia County Schs., Morgantown, 1993—. Asst. organist, choir dir. 1st Presbyn. Ch., Greensburg, Pa., 1971—72; music tchr. St. Francis Ctrl. Sch., Morgantown, 1973—92; chair Music Commn. Diocese, Wheeling/Charleston, W.Va., 1973—99; program chair Nat. Pastoral Musicians Music Edn. Bd., 1992—2002; cons. Schulmerick Carillons, Inc. Mem. bd. W.Va. Children's Chorus Bd., 1992—95, 2003—. Mem.: Choristers Guild, Am. Guild Organists, Am. Guild English Handbell Ringers (chair 2002—03, mem. spl. events com.), Music Edn. Assn., Nat. Pastoral Musicians (Nat. Cath. Music Educator of the Yr. 2001—02), Am. Choral Dirs. Assn. Republican. Methodist. Home: 2594 Grafton Rd Morgantown WV 26508 Office: St Francis de Sales 1 Gutherie Ln Morgantown WV 26508

KINSEY, JAMES LLOYD, chemist, educator; b. Paris, Tex., Oct. 15, 1934; s. Lloyd King and Elaine Mills K.; m. Berma McDowell, July 28, 1962; children: Victoria, Samuel, Adam. BA, Rice U., 1956, PhD, 1959; NSF fellow, U. Uppsala, Sweden, 1959-60; postdoctoral fellow, U. Calif., Berkeley, 1960-62. Asst. prof. dept. chemistry M.I.T., 1962-67, assoc. prof., 1967-74, prof., 1974-88, chmn. dept., 1977-82; D.R. Bullard-Welch Found. prof. sci. Rice U., Houston, 1988—; dean natural scis., 1988-98; interim provost Rice U., Houston, 1993-94. Cons. Los Alamos Nat. Labs., external rev. com. chemistry and laser sci. divsn., 1983—89; Miller rsch. fellow, 1960—62; mem. NAS-NRC Bd. Chem. Scis., 1980—83, co-chmn., 1981—83, mem., 2004—; mem. steering com. U.S. Army Basic Sci. Rsch.-NRC, 1981—86; mem. oversight rev. com. chemistry divsn. NSF, 1989; mem. vis. com. for divsn. chemistry and chem. engring. Calif. Inst. Tech., 1999—2004; mem. com. of chemistry facilities and infrastructure U. Calif.-Berkeley, 1992—93; mem. corp. vis. com. for dept. chemistry MIT, 1994—; vis. com. for chemistry Stanford U., 1993—96; mem. external rev. com. for chemistry U. Pa., 2000; mem. adv. com. on rsch. projects State of Tex. Higher Edn. Coordinating Bd., 2000—02; mem. adv. bd. for engring. and scis. Internat. U. Bremen, Germany, 2000—. Assoc. editor Jour. Chem. Physics, 1981-84; mem. editorial adv. bd. Jour. Phys. Chemistry, 1984-88, Ann. Rev. Phys. Chemistry, 1985-89; mem. adv. editorial bd. Chem. Physics Letters, 1992-97; mem. Coun. of Am. Acad. of Arts and Scis., 1997-2001; contbr. articles to profl. jours. Recipient E.O. Lawrence award U.S. Dept. Energy, 1987; Alfred P. Sloan fellow, 1964-68, Guggenheim fellow, 1969-70. Fellow AAAS, Am. Phys. Soc. (exec. com. divsn. chem. physics 1985-88, Earle K. Plyler prize 1995), Am. Acad. Arts and Scis.; mem. NAS, Am. Chem. Soc. (chmn. divsn. phys. chemistry 1985, Nobel Laureate Signature award for grad. edn. 1990), Acad. Medicine, Engring. and Sci. Tex., Sigma Xi. Office: Rice U MS-600 PO Box 1892 Houston TX 77251-1892 Business E-Mail: jlkinsey@rice.edu.

KINSEY, JOHN ALLEN, systems engineer, technical director; b. Salem, N.J., Jan. 24, 1933; s. Charles Allen Kinsey and Margaret Elizabeth Summerlin; m. Becky Lou Schergens, Jan. 1, 1994; children from previous marriage: Steven A., John D., Robert G. BSME, Rutgers U., 1954; postgrad., N.Mex. A&M U., 1955—56, U. Calif., Santa Barbara, 1972—73, U. Houston, Clear Lake, 1989—90, George Mason U., 1991. Test engr. Texaco, Inc., Beacon, NY, 1954—55; sr. design engr. Gen. Dynamics/Convair, Edwards Rocket Base, Calif., 1957—61; mgr. The Aerospace Corp., Vandenberg AFB, Calif., 1961—75, systems engring. dir. El Segundo, Calif., 1975—79, prin. dir. Johnson Space Ctr., Tex., 1979—91, prin. dir., program exec. Arlington, Va., 1991—2004; tech. dir. Futron Corp., Bethesda, Md., 2004—. Rules com. Homeowners Assn., Arlington, Va., 1998—99, landscape com., 2002—03, cmty. rep., 2002—03. 1st lt., test engr. U.S. Army, 1955—57, White Sands Proving Ground. Fellow: AIAA (assoc.); mem.: Women in Aerospace, Am. Rocket Soc. Avocations: bridge, boating, reading. Home: 1541 22d St N Arlington VA 22209 Office: Futron Corp 7315 Wisconsin Ave Ste 900Wl Bethesda MD 20814-3202 Office Phone: 301-280-2650. Business E-Mail: jkinsey@futron.com.

KINSINGER, JACK BURL, chemist, educator; b. Akron, Ohio, June 23, 1925; s. William Franklin and Idelle (Althaus) K.; m. Addie Jean Parker, Sept. 2, 1946 (div. 1987); children: Paul Craig, Amy Jo; m. Gladys Styles Johnston, 1997. BA, Hiram Coll., 1948; MS, Cornell U., 1951; PhD, U. Pa., 1958. Group leader rsch. Rohm & Haas Co., Phila., 1951-56; from asst. prof. to prof. chemistry Mich. State U., East Lansing, 1957-82, assoc. chmn. dept. chemistry, 1965-69, chmn. dept., 1969-75, asst. v.p. rsch. and devel., 1977, assoc. provost, 1977-82; prof. chemistry Ariz. State U., Tempe, 1982-87, v.p.

acad. affairs, 1982-87; pres., CEO, Chgo. Osteo. Health Systems and Midwestern U., 1987—96, pres. emeritus, 1996—. Cons. Union Carbide Co., 1958-80, vice chmn. div. polymer chemistry, 1966-68, chmn., 1969; dir. chemistry div. NSF, 1975-77; trustee Kirksville Osteo. Med. Coll., 1984-87, Ariz. State U. Res. Park; exec. com. Fed. Independent Colls. and Univs., 1993-95. Editor computer symposium Jour. Polymer Sci., 1968. 2nd lt. USAAF, 1943-45. Recipient Disting. Alumnus award Hiram Coll., 1984. Fellow AAAS; mem. Am. Chem. Soc., Coun. Chem. Rsch. (vice chair exec. com. 1980-81). Home: 24548 N 121st Pl Scottsdale AZ 85255 Personal E-mail: jbkgsj623@msn.com.

KINSINGER, ROBERT EARL, property company executive, educational consultant; b. Chgo., Aug. 5, 1923; s. Elmer John and Frances Louise (Ballenger) K.; m. Sylvia Kading, May 20, 1950; children: William, Candace, Lisa. AB, Stanford U., 1948, MA, 1951; Ed.D., Columbia U., 1958; LL.D., Simpson Coll., 1977; L.H.D., Hahnemann U.; Litt.D., Thomas Jefferson U., 1986. Staff mem. U.S. del. 3d Gen. Assembly UN, Paris, France, 1948; regional field rep., mgr. chpt. and regional blood center ARC, Boise, Ida., 1949-56; lectr. Columbia U., 1956, Queens Coll., 1957; ednl. cons. Nat. League Nursing, 1957-60; dir. health careers project SUNY, 1960-66; program dir. W.K. Kellogg Found., Battle Creek, Mich., 1966-70, v.p., 1970-83; chmn. Ednl. Services for the Professions, Inc., 1983-87; pres. Kinland Properties. Cons. in field; vice-chmn., adv. coun. Mich. Comprehensive Health Planning Bd.; chmn. Commn. on Physicians Assts.; dir. Jossey-Bass Inc., Publs., 1982-89; dir., chmn., trustee, exec. com. Fielding Grad. Inst., 1985-92, 95-2002; adv. com. Corp. Cmty. Coll. TV; trustee Aviation Safety Inst. Author: Education for Health Technicians-An Overview, 1965; co-author: Clinical Nursing Instruction by Television, 1965; Editor: Career Opportunities for Health Technicians, 1971. Chmn. bd. overseers U. of State of N.Y. Regents Coll.; mem. exec. com. Commn. for a Nation of Lifelong Learners; dir. Sierra Repetory Theatre; trustee Excelsior Coll.; chmn., trustee Sierra Nonprofit Support Ctr.; counselor Svc. Corps of Ret. Exec. Lt. USNR, World War II. Recipient commn. of honor SUNY, Farmingdale, 1970; Man of Yr. award Nat. Council Community Services, 1971; Honors of Soc. award Am. Soc. Allied Health Professions. Fellow: Am. Soc. Allied Health Profls.; mem.: Village West Yacht Club. Avocation: hot-air balloons (piloted first balloon flight over the magnetic north pole 1994). Home and Office: 21901 Confidence Rd Twain Harte CA 95383-9688 E-mail: rkinsinger@compuserve.com. *While the "Golden Rule" should always guide one's relationships, of equal importance is steadfast delivery of what you promise to yourself and to others, and a constant effort to exceed the original promise.*

KINSLEY, MICHAEL E., newspaper editor, former magazine editor; b. Detroit, Mar. 9, 1951; s. George and Lillian (Margolis) K.; m. Patty Stonesifer, 2002. AB, Harvard U., 1972, JD, 1977; postgrad., Magdalen Coll., Oxford U., Eng., 1972-74. Bar: D.C. Mng. editor The Washington Monthly, 1975, The New Republic, Washington, 1976-79, editor, 1979-81, 85-89, sr. editor, 1989-95; editor Harper's Mag., N.Y.C., 1981-83; Am. Survey editor The Economist, London, 1988-89; contbg. writer Time mag., 1987—; Editor Slate Mag., 1996—2002, contbg. editor, 2002—04; editl. and opinion editor LA Times, 2004—. Co-host CNN Crossfire, 1989-95. Office: Editorial and Opinion Los Angeles Times Times Mirror Square Los Angeles CA 90001*

KINSLEY, WILLIAM BENTON, literature educator; b. Montpelier, Vt., Sept. 11, 1934; emigrated to Can., 1965; s. Benton Rufus and Ann Magadline (Finnegan) K.; m. Therese Huang, Dec. 30, 1964 (dec. Mar. 1996); children: Anne-Marie, Claire, Eliane. Student, Wesleyan U., 1952—55; BA, U. Toronto, 1958; postgrad., U. Lyon, France, 1959; PhD, Yale U., 1965. Instr. St. Michael's Coll., Winooski, Vt., 1958-59, U. Rochester, N.Y., 1963-64; asst. prof. English lit. U. Montreal, Que., Can., 1965-71, assoc. prof., 1971-81, prof., 1981-2001, chmn. dept. etudes anglaises, 1970-71, 75-79, 90-91, 98-99; ret., 2001. Editor: Contexts 2: The Rape of the Lock, 1979. Warden St. Pascal-Baylon Catholic Ch., Montreal, 1981-84, 2003. Can. council fellow, 1972-73 Mem. MLA, Am. Soc. Eighteenth Century Studies (pres. English 1974-75), Can. Soc. Eighteenth Century Studies, Assn. Can. Coll. and Univ. Tchrs. English, Can. Comparative Lit. Assn. Home: 3782 Kent Ave Montreal PQ Canada H3S 1N3 Office: U Montreal Etudes Anglaises Case Postale 6128 Sta A Montreal PQ Canada H3C 3J7 Office Phone: 514-343-5615. E-mail: wkinsley@cam.org.

KINSLOW, MARGIE ANN, volunteer; b. Salt Lake City, Dec. 7, 1931; d. Diamond and Sarah (Chipman) Wendelboe; m. James Ferol Kinslow, Apr. 6, 1954 (dec. July 1982). Student, U. Utah, 1949—53. Jr. vol. chmn. various hosps., Okla., Mont., Colo., 1967—87; pres. Ch. Woman's Orgn., Bartlesville, Okla., 1968; fin. advisor, jr. v.p., vol. chmn. Swedish Med. Ctr., Englewood, 1971—92; pres. Delta Gamma Alumnae, Denver, 1975—76; jr. vol. chair Colo. Assn. Hosp. Aux., Denver, 1977—82, 2d v.p., 1982—84; transp. chair, master class chmn. Rocky Mountain Regional Auditions, Met. Opera, Denver, 1986—. Office vol. Rep. Office, Billings, Mont., 1969-70, Colo. Senator, Denver, 1974-76; vol. various polit. candidates, Denver, 1974-90; various offices Newcomers, Okla., Mont. and Colo., 1967-75; bd. dirs. Anchor Ctr. for Blind Children, 2000—, Denver Lyric Opera, 2002—. Recipient Stellar award, 1979, Cable award, 1991. Mem. PEO, Gen. Fedn. of Women's Clubs (bd. dirs. 1994—, corr. sec. Western region), Colo. Gen. Fedn. of Women's Clubs (pres. 1994-96, various offices 1986-94), Denver Lyric Opera Guild (bd. dirs. 2002—), Cherry Creek Woman's Club (pres. 1985, Hoby corp. bd. 1997—), Littleton Rep. Women's Club. Episcopalian. Avocations: bridge, travel, people, the arts.

KINSLOW, MONICA M., forensic specialist; b. Chgo., Feb. 19, 1956; d. Chris C. and Martha Stratton; m. Keith Kinslow, Mar. 8, 1975; children: Aisha Ebony, Naomi Alice, Miles Keith. BS in Chemistry, Chgo. State U., 1981. Criminalist Chgo. Police Dept., 1988-96; forensic scientist Ill. State Police, Chgo., 1996—. Mem. Midwestern Assn. Forensic Scientists, Am. Chem. Soc. Avocations: church activities, reading. Office: Ill State Police Forensic Sci Ctr 1941 W Roosevelt Rd Chicago IL 60608-1246

KINSMAN, ROBERT PRESTON, biomedical plastics engineer; b. Cambridge, Mass., July 25, 1949; s. Fred Nelson and Myra Roxane (Preston) Kinsman. BS in Plastics Engring., U. Mass. Lowell, 1971; MBA, Pepperdine U., 1982. Cert. biomed. engr., Calif.; lic. real estate sales person, Calif. Product devel. engr., plastics divsn. Gen. Tire Corp., Lawrence, Mass., 1976—77; mfg. engr. Am. Edwards Labs. divsn. Am. Hosp. Supply Corp., Irvine, Calif., 1978—80, sr. engr. Am. Edwards Labs. divsn., 1981—82, mgr. mfg. engring. Edwards Labs., Inc. subs. Añasco, PR, 1983; project mgr. Baxter Edwards Critical Care divsn. Baxter Healthcare Corp., Irvine, 1984—87, mgr. engring. and prodn. Baxter Edwards Critical Care divsn., 1987—93; pres. Kinsman & Assocs., Irvine, 1993—, Billerica, Mass., 2001—; expert/auditor Med. Device Certification GmbH, Memmingen, Germany, 1985—; dir. engring. CardioVasc. Dynamics, Inc., Irvine, 1997—2000, HemoDynamics, Inc., Irvine, 1999—2000; dir. biomaterials engring. Anchor Med. Tech., Inc., Irvine, 2000—01; dir. ops. Triage Med., Irvine, 2001. Mgmt. adv. panel Modern Plastics mag., N.Y.C., 1979-80; elected Nat. Hon. Soc., 1967. Vol. worker VA, Bedford, Mass., 1967-71; instr. first aid ARC, N.D., Mass., Calif., 1971-82; pres., bd. dirs. Lakes Homeowners Assn., Irvine, 1985-91; chmn., bd. dirs., newsletter editor Paradise Park Owners Assn., Las Vegas, Nev., 1988-99; bd. dirs. Orange County (Calif.) divsn. Am. Heart Assn., 1991-2001, chmn. devel. com., 1993-95, v.p. bd. dirs., 1993-94, chmn.-elect bd. dirs., 1994-95, chmn. bd. dirs., 1995-96, adv. coun. rep., 1994-96, immediate past chmn. bd. dirs., 1996-97, nominating com., 1995-98, chmn. nominating com., 2000-01, strategic planning com., 1998-2001, Golden Gavel emeritus mem. bd. dirs., 2001; steering com. Heart and Sole Classic fundraiser, 1988-2001, event chmn., 1991-92, 2001, devel. com. Calif. affiliate, 1993-95; bd. dirs. Billerica Hist. Soc., Mass., 2001-, treas., 2001-02, pres., 2002—; mem. Town of Billerica 350th Anniversary Celebration Com., 2003—, co-treas., 2003—; chmn. Beginnings of Billerica, 350th Anniversary Signature Event. Capt. USAF, 1971-75, USAFR, 1975-81. Recipient Cert. of Appreciation, VA, 1971, Am. Heart Assn., 1991-95, Outstanding Svc. award., 1996, Cert. of Recognition, U.S. Dept. Def., 2002; selected Community Hero Torchbearer 1996 Olympic Games, United Way Am. and Atlanta Com. for Olympic Games. Baxter/Allegiance Found. Community Svc . grantee, Deerfield, Ill., 1992, 93. Mem. Soc. Plastics Engrs. (sr., Mem. of Month So. Calif. sect. 1989), Soc. for Biomaterials, Soc. Mfg. Engrs. (sr.), Am. Mgmt. Assn., Am. Soc. Quality (sr.), Arnold Air Soc. (comptr. 1969, pledge tng. officer 1970), Plastics Acad., Demolay, Profl. Ski Instrs. Am., Mensa (life), Am. Legion, Elks, Phi Gamma Psi. Avocations: skiing, scuba diving, marathon running, golf, music. Office: Kinsman & Assocs PO Box 505 Billerica MA 01821-0505 Office Phone: 978-764-7587. E-mail: kinsmanassociates@comcast.net.

KINSOLVING, AUGUSTUS BLAGDEN, lawyer; b. Boston, Jan. 19, 1940; s. Arthur Lee and Mary Kemp (Blagden) K.; m. Monique Berard, Dec. 21, 1974; children: Isabelle, Arthur. BA, Yale U., 1961; MA, Oxford U., 1963; LLB, Harvard U., 1965. Bar: N.Y. 1965. Assoc. Davis Polk & Wardwell, N.Y.C., 1965-70; v.p. Donaldson Lufkin & Jenrette Inc., N.Y.C., 1970-74; v.p., gen. counsel Asarco Inc., N.Y.C., 1975-99; ptnr. Brock Ptnrs. LLP, N.Y.C., 2002—; mng. dir. Brock Capital Group LLC, 2002—. Dir. Adobe Air, Inc., 2000—, Equipment Support Svcs., Inc., 2000—. Trustee Down Town Assn., 1975-91. Rhodes scholar, 1961. Mem. Am. Assn. Rhodes Scholars (dir. Claremont, Calif. chpt. 1975-90), Assn. Gen. Counsel (emeritus mem.), Coun. of the Ams. (adv. bd. 1991-99), Nat. Ctr. for State Cts. (corp. counsel com. 1997-99), Warren E. Burger Soc., N.Y. Yacht Club, Cruising Club of Am. Avocation: sailing.

KINSOLVING, CHARLES MCILVAINE, JR., marketing executive; b. N.Y.C., Jan. 27, 1927; s. Charles McIlvaine and Florence Natalie (Hogg) K.; m. Coral May Eaton, July 13, 1963 (dec. Jan. 1988); m. Jolie Brockman Hammer, Apr. 26, 1993 (dec. Aug. 1995); m. Jacqueline Wolf Vogelstein, Aug. 22, 1998. Student, U. Paris, 1948; AB, U. Pa., 1949; postgrad., Harvard Med. Sch., 1949-50, Columbia U., 1951-53. Stockholder rels. AT&T, N.Y.C., 1950-51; rsch. assoc. Young & Rubicam, Inc., N.Y.C., 1951-53; asst. mgr. media rsch. McCann-Erickson, Inc., N.Y.C., 1953-58; mgr. plans devel. Nat. Broadcasting Co., N.Y.C., 1958-60; v.p., mktg. new tech. Newspaper Advt. Bur., N.Y.C., 1960-87, sr. v.p. mktg. group, 1987-92; ind. comm. investor N.Y.C., 1992—. Media cons. U.K., Belgium, South Africa; speaker Internat. Fedn. of Editors and Jours. Contbr. articles to profl. jours. Dem. candidate for State Assembly, Manhattan, 1954, 98; 1st vice chmn. N.Y. County Dem. Exec. Com., N.Y.C., 1963-71; mem., chmn. Planning Bd. #6 Manhattan, N.Y.C., 1969-84. Served with U.S. Army, 1945-46. Mem. Am. Mktg. Assn., Am. Assn. pub. Opinion Rsch., Nat. Cable TV Assn., Am. Newspaper Assn. (tech. com. 1983-92, telecom. com. 1982-92), Union Club, Century Assn., Dutch Treat Club (bd. govs. 1994-99), City Club (v.p. 1987-89), Coffee House Club (bd. dirs. 1984—), St. Anthony Club Phila., St. Paul's Sch. Alumni Assn. (exec. com. 1994-99, v.p. 1995-99), Phi Beta Kappa, Delta Psi. Episcopalian. Avocations: travel, photography, stamp collecting/philately. Mailing: 1107 5th Ave New York NY 10128-0145 Home: 27 Horseshoe Dr N East Hampton NY 11937 Personal E-mail: cjkinsolving@nyc.rr.com.

KINSOLVING, SYLVIA CROCKETT, musician, educator; b. Berkeley, Calif., Sept. 30, 1931; d. Harold Waldo and Louise (Effinger) Crockett; m. Charles Lester Kinsolving, Dec. 18, 1953; children: Laura Louise, Thomas Philip, Kathleen Susan. AA in Voice, Piano magna cum laude, No. Va. Community Coll., 1983; BA, U. Calif., Berkeley, 1953. Solo vocalist various chs., Va., 1982—; pvt. tchr. piano Vienna, Va., 1983—. Singer, soloist Unity Ch., Oakton, Va., 1980—, St. Andrew's Anglican Ch., Alexandria, Va., 1985—; active numerous local musical prodns., 1959—. Tour leader Vienna Newcomers, 1980. Mem. PEO, U. Calif. Alumni Club, Fairfax West Music Fellowship (sec. 1990—), Phi Theta Kappa, Pi Beta Phi. Democrat. Episcopalian. Avocations: walking, swimming, music, reading. Home: 1517 Beulah Rd Vienna VA 22182-1417

KINSTLER, EVERETT RAYMOND, artist; b. N.Y.C., Aug. 5, 1926; s. Joseph E. and Essie K.; m. Lea C. Nation, June 23, 1958 (div. 1984); children: Katherine G., Dana C.; m. Peggy Chartier, 1996. Ed., Art Students League, NYC, 1943—45; D (hon.), Rollins Coll., 1983, Lyme Acad. Art, 2002. Started career as illustrator, N.Y.C., 1943; began specializing in portraiture, 1955; instr. Art Students League, N.Y.C., 1969-74. Portraits include over 50 U.S. cabinet officers, ofcl. White House portrait former Pres. Gerald R. Ford, former Pres. Ronald Reagan, former Pres. Richard Nixon, J. Edgar Hoover, Richard K. Mellon, Mrs. Irenee duPont, Jr., Kurt Waldheim, sec.-gen. UN, Casper Weinberger, sec. of def., William Casey, dir. CIA, Cyrus Vance, sec. of state, Astronaut Alan B. Shepard, Jr., William Bowen, pres. Princeton U., James Cagney, John D. Rockefeller III, Byron Nelson, Frank Cary, pres. IBM, Charles Scribner, Jr., John Wayne, John Kemeny, pres. Dartmouth Coll., William Simon, sec. Treasury, Elliot Richardson, ambassador to Gt. Britain, Tennessee Williams, John Connally, gov. of Tex., Charles Brown, CH., ATT, Russel Long, U.S. Senator, Morris Udall, mem. U.S. Congress, Katharine Hepburn, Gregory Peck, former Pres. Richard M. Nixon; Bartlett Gramatti, pres. Yale U., George P. Shultz, former U.S. Sec. of State, Paul Newman, Thomas Kean, former Gov. N.J., former Pres. George Bush, Arthur Ashe, Tony Bennett, Carol Burnett, Elizabeth Dole, Betty Ford, Lady Bird Johnson, William Webster, Ruth Simmons Pres. Smith Coll., former dir. CIA, Harry Blackmun, U.S. Supreme Ct. Justice, former U.S. Sec. of State Warren Christopher, Placido Domingo, President Bill Clinton, Gene Hackman, Ruth Bader Ginsburg, U.S. Supreme Ct. Justice, Donald Rumsfeld U.S. Sec. Def., U.S. Senator Daniel Patrick Moynihan, NY Gov. George Pataki, Peter O'Toole, Sen. Robert Dole, Lawrence Summers, pres. Harvard U., John D. Ong, U.S. amb. to Norway, Dave Brubeck, Donald Trump, Charles Osgood, pres. U. Pa. Judith Rodin, also numerous others; represented in permanent collections, Butler Inst. Am. Art, Nat. Portrait Gallery, Washington, Nat. Acad. Design, Mus. City N.Y., Met. Mus. Art, N.Y.C., The Pentagon, Am. Embassy, Paris, Carnegie Mus., N.Y. Stock Exchange, Bklyn. Mus., White House, Smithsonian Instn., Retrospective Exhibition Boston U., Butler inst. Am. Art, Fairfield, Conn., 1999; numerous colls., univs., bus. firms; author: Painting Portraits, 1971, Painting Faces, Figures, Landscapes, 1981, My Brush with History, 2005; (documentary) An Artists Journey, PBS, 2001, PBS documentary, 2004—. Recipient Artists' Fellowship Medal, 1986, Nat. Arts Club medal, 1993, Allied Artists medal, 1997, Copley medal Nat. Portrait Gallery, 1999, Lifetime Achievement medal Salmagundi Club, 2002, medal honoree Nat. Acad. Design, 2002. Mem. Allied Artists Am. (dir. 1958-60), Artists Fellowships, Inc. (pres. 1967-70), Am. Watercolor Soc., Pastel Soc. Am., Audubon Artists, NAD, Actor's Fund Am. (life), Soc. Illustrators (hon.), Copley Soc. Boston (life), Lambs Club (N.Y.C.) (life),), Century Assn. Club (N.Y.C.), Lotos Club (N.Y.C.) (life), Nat. Arts Club (N.Y.C.)), Dutch Treat Club (N.Y.C.), Players Club (life), Yale Club N.Y. (life). Office: care Nat Arts Club 15 Gramercy Park S New York NY 10003-1705

KINSTLINGER, JACK, engineering executive, consultant; b. Antwerp, Belgium, Mar. 02; came to U.S., 1939; s. Joseph and Rose (Lichtblau) K.; m. Marilyn Wiseman, July 16, 1967; children: Michael, Jeremy. BSCE, Rensselaer Polytechnic Inst., 1952; MSCE, MIT, 1954. Registered profl. engr., N.Y., Pa., Wash., N.H., Colo., Del., Md., Mass., Fla., N.J. Assoc. Tippetts, Abbett, McCarthy, Stratton, N.Y.C., 1957-68; dep. sec. Pa. Dept. Transp., Harrisburg, 1968-75; state hwy. dir. State of Colo., Denver, 1975-82; v.p. Daniel-Mann-Johnson-Mendenhall, Denver, 1982-84; CEO KCI Techs., Inc., Balt., 1984-99, chmn. bd. dirs., chmn. emeritus, 2000—. Bd. dirs. Am. Jewish Com., Balt.; mem. adv. bd. Rensselaer Poly. Inst., Morgan State U. Fellow ASCE, Am. Cons. Engrs. Coun.; mem. Am. Rds. and Transp. Builders Assn. (vice chair, bd. dirs.), High Speed Ground Transp. Assn. (bd. dirs.), Md. Assn. Non-Profit Orgns. (bd. dirs.). Office: KCI Techs Inc 10 N Park Dr Hunt Valley MD 21030-1841 Office Phone: 410-316-7803. Business E-Mail: jkinstlinger@kci.com.

KINTNER, PHILIP L., history professor; b. Canton, Ohio, Jan. 23, 1926; s. William Wagner and Effie (Erwin) K.; m. Anne Genung, Dec. 27, 1951 (dec. June 2003); children: Karen, Judith, Jennifer. BA, Wooster Coll., 1950; MA, Yale U., 1952, PhD, 1958. Instr. Trinity Coll., Hartford, Conn., 1954-56, Reed Coll., Portland, Oreg., 1957-58, Trinity Coll., 1958-59, asst. prof., 1959-64; vis. assoc. prof. U. Iowa, Iowa City, 1964-65; assoc. prof. Grinnell (Iowa) Coll., 1964-69; coll. entrance bd. exam commissioner European History, Princeton, N.J., 1968-70; chief reader advanced placement European history, 1969-72; ACM prof. Florence (Italy) Program, 1989-90; prof. Grinnell Coll., 1970-96, Rosenthal prof. humanities, 1976-96; prof. emeritus, 1996—. With U.S. Army, 1944-46. Recipient numerous travel/study grants for rsch. in Germany. Mem. Sixteenth Century Studies Conf. Avocations: woodworking, cooking, mineral hunting. Home: 716 Broad St Grinnell IA 50112-2226 Office: Grinnell Coll PO Box 805 Grinnell IA 50112-0805 E-mail: kintner@grinnell.edu.

KINTSCH, WALTER, retired psychology professor; b. Temesvar, Romania, May 30, 1932; arrived in US, 1955; s. Christof and Irene (Hollerbach) Kintsch; m. Eileen Hoover, June 27, 1959; children: Anja, Julia. PhD, U. Kans., 1960. Prof. U. Colo., Boulder, 1968—94; ret. Editor: Pyschol Rev, 1989—94; author: books. Office: U Colo Dept Psychology Institute Cognitive Scis Boulder CO 80309-0344 Business E-Mail: wkintsch@psych.colorado.edu.

KINTZEL, ROGER S., publishing executive; b. July 9, 1943; m. Lee; 2 children. BA, Wright State U., 1970. Reporter Xenia (Ohio) Daily Gazette, 1970-72; from police reporter to bus. editor Richmond (Va.) News-Leader, 1973-79; fin. editor Dayton (Ohio) Jour.-Herald Cox Enterprises, 1979-81, bus. mgr. Dayton Newspapers, 1981-83, publ. Springfield (Ohio) News-Sun, 1983-85, pres. Cox Ariz. Publs., publ Mesa Tribune, 1985-86, publ. Austin Am.-Statesman, 1986-95, publ. Atlanta Jour.-Constitution, 1995—2004, sr. pub. Cox Newspapers Inc., 2004—, S.E. rep. Assoc. Press Nominating Com. Bd. dirs. Newspaper Assn. Am. Found., Rsch. Atlanta; bd. councilors Carter Ctr.; mem. exec. com. Ctrl. Atlanta Progress. Mem. Atlanta C. of C. (mem. exec. com.), So. Newspaper Publ. Assn. (bd. dirs.). Office: Cox Newspaper Inc 72 Marietta St NW Atlanta GA 30303-2804

KINTZELE, JOHN ALFRED, lawyer; b. Denver, Aug. 16, 1936; s. Louis Richard and Adele H. Kintzele; children: John A., Marcia A., Elizabeth A.; m. Suzanne Hinsberger; stepchildren: William Karp III, Christopher Karp. BS in Bus., U. Colo., 1958, LLB, 1961. Bar: Colo. bar 1961. Assoc. James B. Radetsky, Denver, 1962-63; pvt. practice law Denver, 1963—. Corp. officer, dir. Kintzele, Inc.; rep. 10th cir. U.S. Ct. of Claims Bar. Chmn. Colo. Lawyer Referral Service, 1978-83, Election commr., Denver, 1975-79, 83-86 Mem. ATLA, ABA, Colo. Bar Assn., Denver Bar Assn., Am. Judicature Soc., Roscoe Pound Found. Democrat. Roman Catholic. Home: 10604 E Powers Dr Englewood CO 80111-3957 Office: 1317 Delaware St Denver CO 80204-2704 Office Phone: 303-892-6494. E-mail: kintzeles@aol.com, jkintlaw@aol.com.

KINZER, KERIN OVERFELT, elementary school educator; b. Great Falls, Mont., July 29, 1952; d. Lee A. and Dona Mae Overfelt; m. Michael Kinzer, Mar. 29, 1991; children: Brytt Irene Kinzer-Neuman, Kylee Rose. BA in Edn., U. Mont., 1974. Cert. ednl. specialist Wyo., 1974. Tchr. spl. edn. Natrona County Sch. Dist. #1, Casper, Wyo., 1974—79; learning specialist Sheridan County Sch. Dist. #2, Sheridan, 1979—. Coach Wyo. Spl. Olympics, Casper, 1974—79. Contbr. intervention team for at risk students. Precinct com. woman Sheridan County Elections, 2002—05. Mem.: Internat. Reading Assn. Democrat. Avocations: swimming, skiing, hiking, reading, travel. Home: 2 Sunset Ln Sheridan WY 82801 Office: Sheridan County Sch Dist #2 1301 Avon Sheridan WY 82801 Office Phone: 307-672-2113. Personal E-mail: kerinkinzer@bresnan.net. E-mail: kinzerk@scsd2.com.

KINZER, WILLIAM LUTHER, lawyer; b. Mifflintown, Pa., Jan. 25, 1929; s. John Raymond and Ethel Naomi (Sellers) K.; m. Ann Marie Rosato, May 3, 1958; children: Karen, Carolyn, Cynthia, Matthew, Mark. BA, Dickinson Coll., Carlisle, Pa., 1950; LLB, Temple U., 1956; LLM, Georgetown U., 1961. Bar: D.C. 1957, Ga. 1962. Atty. IRS, Washington, 1956-62; assoc. Powell, Goldstein, Frazer & Murphy, Atlanta, 1962-65, ptnr., 1965-2000, of counsel, 2000—04, Powell Goldstein LLP, 2004—. Author miscellaneous tax articles, 2 BNA Tax Portfolios. Capt. USAF, 1951-53. Mem. ABA (com. chmn. 1987-89), Fed. Bar Assn., Ga. Bar Assn., Atlanta Bar Assn., Atlanta Tax Forum (pres. 1980, trustee 1978-81), Cherokee Town and Country Club (Atlanta). Roman Catholic. Avocation: golf. Home: 904 Spring Valley Woodstock GA 30189-6102 Office: Powell Goldstein LLP One Atlantic Ctr 14th Fl 1201 W Peachtree St NW Atlanta GA 30309-1740 Office Phone: 404-572-6614. E-mail: wkinzer@pogolaw.com.

KINZEY, BERTRAM YORK, JR., architect, educator; b. Holden, Mass., Sept. 25, 1921; s. Bertram York and Gertrude Sargent (Sampson) K.; m. Ellen Virginia Smith, Nov. 24, 1944; children: Bertram York III, Douglas Webster. BS, Va. Poly. Inst., 1942, MS, 1943. Registered architect, Fla., Va. Asst. naval architect Norfolk Naval Yard, Portsmouth, Va., 1943-45; draftsman, jr. structural engr. Baskervill & Sons, Architects, Richmond, Va., 1945-47; assoc. prof. architecture Va. Poly. Inst., Blacksburg, 1947-59; prof. architecture U. Fla., Gainesville, 1959-85, prof. emeritus, 1985—. Cons. in archtl. acoustics, Gainesville, 1960—. Co-author: Environmental Technologies in Architecture, 1963; contbr. to encys. in field. Fellow Acoustical Soc. Am.; mem. ASHRAE (life), Nat. Coun. Acoustical Cons., AIA (sec. 1969-71, chpt. dir. 1971-74, state dir. 1974-75, Award of Honor Fla. chpt. 1975). Avocations: organ playing and building, woodworking. Home and Office: 212 SW 42nd St Gainesville FL 32607-2769 Office Phone: 352-378-1878. E-mail: bkinzey@ftd.net.

KINZIE, BRENDA ASBURRY, counselor; b. Roanoke, Va., Oct. 25, 1945; d. Omar Lee and Nadine Myrl (Sublett) Asburry; m. Samuel Joseph Kinzie, Mar. 30, 1973. BA, Hollins (Va.) U., 1990; MS, Radford (Va.) U., 1991. Case mgr./counselor Total Action Against Poverty, Roanoke, 1993-95; interagy. case coord. City of Roanoke, 1995-98. Vol. Am. Cancer Soc. Mem.: ACA, Hunting Hills Garden Club. Democrat. Divine Sci. Ch. Avocations: music, reading, walking, flower gardening. Home: 1051 Starmount Ave Roanoke VA 24019-3135

KINZIE, JACK L., lawyer; b. Ponca City, Okla., Sept. 3, 1948; BS, Okla. State Univ., 1971; JD, Univ. Okla., 1975. Bar: Okla. 1976, Tex. 1989, US Dist. Ct. (no., so., ea., we. dist. Tex., no., we. dist. Okla.), US Ct. Appeals 3d, 5th, 10th cir. Ptnr., mem. exe. com., chmn. bankruptcy & insolvency practice & ptnr. in charge Dallas office Baker Botts LLP, Dallas. Editor (assoc.): Okla. Law Rev. Dir. Greater Dallas C. of C., Dallas Ctr. for Contemporary Art; mem. Dallas Citizens Council. Named a Texas Super Lawyer, Texas Monthly mag. & Law & Politics mag., 2003—04. Mem.: Order of the Coif. Office: Baker Botts LLP 2001 Ross Ave Dallas TX 75201-2980 Office Fax: 214-953-6727, 214-661-4727. Business E-Mail: jack.kinzie@bakerbotts.com.

KINZIE, JEANNIE JONES, oncologist; b. Great Falls, Mont., Mar. 14, 1940; d. James Wayne and Lillian Alice (Young) Jones; m. Joseph Lee Kinzie, Mar. 26, 1965 (div. Sept. 1982); 1 child, Daniel Joseph; m. Johnson Wachira, Oct. 7, 1991. Student, Oreg. State U., 1960; BS, Mont. State U., 1961; MD, Washington U., 1965; MBA, U. Phoenix, 1997. Diplomate Am. Bd. Radiology; diplomate Am. Bd. Nuclear Medicine; cert. advanced master gardener Colo. State U., 1997. Intern. in surgery U. N.C., Chapel Hill, 1965-66; resident in therapeutic radiology Washington U., St. Louis, 1968-71, instr. in radiology, 1971-73; asst. prof. in radiology Med. Coll. of Wis., Milw., 1973-75, U. Chgo., 1975-78, assoc. prof. in radiology, 1978-80; assoc. prof. of radiation oncology Wayne State U., Detroit, 1980-85; prof. radiology U. Colo., Denver, 1985-95; dir. radiation oncology U. Hosp., Denver, 1985-91; fellow in nuclear medicine U. Colo., 1996-98, asst. clin. prof. nuclear medicine, 1998—2005; staff radiologist Denver Vets. Hosp., Denver, 2003—. Cons. Denver Vets. Hosp., 1985-98, Denver Gen. Hosp., 1985-95, Rose Med. Ctr., 1986-95, FDA Ctr. for Devices and Radiologic Health, 1986-2003; mem. sci. adv. bd. Cancer League Colo., 1985-88; examiner Am. Bd. Radiology, 1985-88; adv. physician Colo. Med. Found., 1988-98; chmn. faculty promotion com. U. Colo. Health Scis. Ctr., 1988-89. Assoc. editor Internat. Jour. Radiation Oncology Biology and Physics, 1985-95; contbr. articles to profl.

jours.; chpts. to books. Mem. Faith Bible Chapel Ch. NIH grantee, 1973-75. Fellow: Am. Coll. Radiology; mem.: AMA, Am. Cancer Soc. (bd. dirs. Denver unit 1986—87), Am. Soc. Therapeutic Radiologists, Rocky Mountain Oncology Soc. (bd. dirs. 1989—93, pres. 1991—93), Soc. Nuclear Medicine, Colo. Radiol. Soc., Denver Med. Soc., Colo. Med. Soc. (del. or alt. del. to Colo. Med. Soc. Ho. of Dels. 1989—), Am. Coll. Nuclear Physicians. Republican. Avocations: stamp collecting/philately, gardening, rug latching, mountain climbing. Personal E-mail: jeannie.kinzie@att.net.

KINZLER, THOMAS BENJAMIN, lawyer; b. N.Y.C., June 19, 1950; s. David and Rhoda Lenore (Wolgel) K.; m. Carol Ada Loebel, Aug. 24, 1975; children: Katherine Diane, David James. BA, Columbia Coll., 1971; JD, Boston U., 1975. Bar: N.Y. 1976, U.S. Dist. Ct. (no., so., ea. and we. dists.) N.Y. 1976, U.S. Ct. Appeals (2d cir.) 1976. Assoc. Kreindler, Relkin & Goldberg, N.Y.C., 1975-77, Arthur, Dry & Kalish, N.Y.C., 1977-80, Kelley Drye & Warren LLP, N.Y.C., 1980-85; ptnr. Kelley Drye & Warren, N.Y.C., 1985—. Mem. ABA, Assn. of the Bar City of N.Y.C. (products liability com. 1983-86, com. on state legis. 1978-80). Office: Kelley Drye & Warren 101 Park Ave Fl 30 New York NY 10178-0062

KIPERSZTOK, SIMON, reproductive endocrinologist, educator; s. Jacob and Rachel Kipersztok; m. Micki Alice Kantrowitz, Mar. 31, 1985; children: Amy Beth, Lisa Gail, William Aaron, Hannah Rose. BA, Brandeis U., 1979; MD, Tufts U., 1983. Diplomate in ob-gyn. and in reproductive endocrinology and infertility Am. Bd. Ob-Gyn. Prof. ob-gyn U. Fla., Gainesville, 1992—. Pres. Fla. Soc. Reproductive Endocrinology and Infertility, 2001—02. Mem.: Alpha Omega Alpha. Office: U Fla 1600 SW Archer Rd Gainesville FL 32610 Office Phone: 352-392-5680. E-mail: skiper@ufl.edu.

KIPFERL, CHRISTIANA A., special education educator; b. Elmira, N.Y., June 6, 1953; d. Martin Joseph and RosaLea (VanMarter) Burke; m. H. LaVerne Kipferl, Aug. 9, 1986; stepchildren: Kevin, Keith, Kayla, Kerry, Kory, Kelly. AA, Corning C.C., 1973; BS, Mansfield State Coll., 1975, MEd, 1993. Sr. exec. sec., travel coord. Imaging & Sensing Technology Corp., Horseheads, N.Y., 1988-95; resource rm. tchr. Elmira (N.Y.) City Sch. Dist., 1995-96; affective educator Steuben-Allegany BOCES, Bath, N.Y., 1996-97; learning support resource rm. tchr. North Tioga Sch. Dist., Westfield (Pa.) Area Elem. Sch., 1997—2000; primary life skills tchr. Clark Wood Elem. Sch., Elkland, Pa., 2003—. Sunday sch. tchr. Jackson Summit (Pa.) Bapt. Ch.; mem. Corning C.C. Alumni Chorus. Mem. Coun. Exceptional Children. Republican. Baptist. Avocations: fishing, music, camping, working with children, reading. Home: RR 1 Box 32K Millerton PA 16936-9712

KIPHART, RICHARD P., finance company executive; Prin. William Blair & Co. LLC, 1972—. Bd. dir. Concord EFS, Inc., Memphis, chmn. bd., 2003—; bd. dir. Photo Control Corp., Advanced Biotherapy, Inc. Office: Concord EFS Inc 2525 Horizon Lake Dr Ste 120 Memphis TN 38133

KIPKE, MICHELE DIANE, education and social services administrator, former hospital director; b. Glendale, Calif., Mar. 4, 1962; d. Arthur Harold and Anne Stuart (Mills) K. BA, NYU, 1984; PhD, Yeshiva U., 1989. Rsch. asst. Montefiore Med. Ctr., Bronx, N.Y., 1984-86; psychology intern Albert Einstein Coll. Medicine, Bronx, 1986-87; dir. AIDS prevention Montefiore Med. Ctr., Bronx, 1987-89; coord. substance abuse program Childrens Hosp. L.A., Calif., 1990-92, assoc. dir. rsch. and evaluation, 1992-98; dir. bd. rsch. children, youth & families Nat. Res. Council, Washington, 1998—. Cons. HHS, SAMSA, HRSA, Washington, 1990—; coun. rep. elect Homeless Caucus, APHA, 1992-93; peer reviewer NIH, Washington, 1993—; cons. WHO/Mentor Found., Geneva, 1994—; spl. advisor Primary Health Care Initiative, Office of Treatment Improvement, Alcohol, Drug Abuse and Mental Health Adminstrn.; presenter in field. Reviewer AIDS Edn. and Prevention: An Interdisciplinary Jour., Jour. Adolescent Health Care; contbr. articles to profl. jours. Grantee Ctrs. for Disease Control (AIDS Evaluation of Street Outreach Project), 1992-95, Universitywide AIDS Rsch. Program (HIV Prevention Intervention Study with Seropositive Youth, 1993-95, Nat. Inst. on Drug Abuse (Investigation of Drug Use and HIV-Risk Sexual Behaviors Among Homeless Youth, 1993—, Substance Abuse and Mental Health Svc. Adminstrn./Ctr. for Substance Abuse Treatment, 1993—, Health Resources and Svcs. Adminstrn./Bur. Health Cre and Delivery and Assistance, 1993—, others. Mem. APA, Soc. Adolescent Medicine (ad hoc com. on health needs of homeless youth). Office: Childrens Hosp LA Mail Stop #2 PO Box 54700 Los Angeles CA 90054-0700*

KIPLINGER, KNIGHT AUSTIN, journalist, publishing executive; b. Washington, Feb. 24, 1948; s. Austin Huntington and Mary Louise (Cobb) K. BA, Cornell U., 1969; postgrad., Princeton U., 1969-70. Reporter Montgomery County Sentinel, Rockville, Md., 1970; Washington corr. Griffin-Larrabee News Bur., Washington, 1970-73, bur. mgr., 1976-78; Washington bur. chief, chief news svc. Ottaway Newspapers div. Dow Jones & Co., Washington, 1978-83; with Kiplinger Washington Editors, Washington, 1983—, v.p. for publs., 1983-89, exec . v.p., 1989-92, pres., 1992—; assoc. editor The Kiplinger Letter, Washington, 1983-99, editor-in-chief, 1999—; editor in chief Kiplinger's Personal Fin. Mag., Washington, 1985—. Author: World Boom Ahead, 1998; co-author: Washington Now, 1975, The New American Boom, 1986, America in the Global '90s, 1989. Bd. dir. The Washington Chorus, 1975—85, chmn., 1991—99; mem. adv. bd. Levine Sch. Music, Washington, 1975, Mount Vernon Ladies' Assn., 1986—92; bd. trustees White Ho. Hist. Assn., 2003—, Landon Sch., 1995—2000, chmn., 2003—. Mem. Soc. Profl. Journalists, Soc. Am. Bus. Editors and Writers, Nat. Press Club. Office: Kiplinger Washington Editors 1729 H St NW Washington DC 20006-3925

KIPNEES, ROBERT J., lawyer, educator; b. Bklyn., Jan. 23, 1956; s. Jerome J. and Pearl Brown Kipnees; m. Helane A. Asnis, June 11, 1977; children: Joshua, Gabriel, Shira. BA cum laude, Cornell U.; JD cum laude, Harvard U., 1980. Bar: N.J. 1981, N.Y. 1981, U.S. Ct. Appeals (3d cir.) 1985, U.S. Supreme Ct. 1992. Assoc. Marshall Bratter et al., N.Y.C., 1980-82; asst. U.S. atty. Newark, 1982-85; assoc. U.S. atty., 1985-87; ptnr. Greenbaum, Rowe, Smith et al., Woodbridge, N.J., 1988—. Adj. prof. Seton Hall Law Sch., Newark, 1993—. Author: Criminal Trial Preparation, 2000. Trustee Jewish Edn. Assn., Whippany, N.J., 1997—, chair Ctr. for Spl. Edn. com., 1996—. Recipient Spl. Achievement award U.S. Dept. Justice, 1985. Mem. ABA, Phi Beta Kappa. Office: Greenbaum Rowe Smith et al Metro Corp Campus PO Box 5600 Woodbridge NJ 07095 Fax: (732) 549-1881. E-mail: rkipnees@greenbaumlaw.com.

KIPNESS, ROBERT, painter; b. Brooklyn, N.Y., 1931; s. Sam and Stella Kipness; m. Jean Prutton, 1954 (div. 1982); 4 children; m. Laurie Lisle, 1994. BA, Univ. Iowa, 1952, MFA, 1954. Exhibitions include The Contemporaries, NYC, 1959-67, FAR Gallery, NYC, 1968-75, AAA, NYC, 1977, Hirschl & Adler, NYC, 1977-80, Jane Haslem Gallery, Washington, 1976-98, Redfern Gallery, London, 1995-98, Butler Inst. Am. Art, 1999, Weinstein Gallery, San Francisco, 2000-04, Beadleston Gallery, NYC, 2003; represented in collections of Art Inst. Chgo., Bibliotheque National de France, British Mus., Brooklyn Mus. Art, Carnegie Mus. Art Pitts., Fitzwilliam Mus. Cambridge, Libr. Congress, Met. Mus. Art NYC, Mus. Fine Arts Boston, NAD NYC, Nat. Mus. Am. Art Washington, N.Y. Pub. Libr., Phila. Mus. Art, Ashmolean Mus. Oxford, Victoria & Albert Mus. London, Whitney Mus. Am. Art NYC. Q.M.C. U.S. Army, 1956—58. Recipient Speicher-Hassam Purchase award, Am. Acad. & Inst. Arts & Letters, 1988, Daniel Serra-Badue Memorial award, Audubon Artists, 1998, Rembrandt Graphics award, Boston Printmakers, 1999. Mem.: Royal Soc. Painter Printmakers, U.K., NAD (academician, Cannon prize 1999). Mailing: Davidson Galleries 313 Occidental Ave S Seattle WA 98104*

KIPNIS, DAVID MORRIS, physician, educator; b. Balt., May 23, 1927; s. Rubin and Anna (Mizen) Kipnis; m. Paula Jane Levin, Aug. 16, 1953; children: Lynne, Laura, Robert. AB, Johns Hopkins U., 1945, MA, 1949; MD, U. Md., 1951. Intern Johns Hopkins Hosp., 1951—52; resident Duke Hosp., Durham, NC, 1952—54, U. Md. Hosp., 1954—55; asst. prof. medicine Washington U. Sch. Medicine, St. Louis, 1958—63, assoc. prof., 1963—65, prof., 1965—, Busch prof., chmn. dept. medicine, 1972—92; disting. prof. medicine Washington U. Sch. of Medicine, St. Louis, 1992—; asst. physician Barnes Hosp., assoc. physician, 1963—72, physician-in-chief, 1972—93, disting. univ. prof., 1993—. Chmn. endocrine study sect. NIH, 1963—64, diabetes tng. program com., 1970—; chmn. Nat. Diabetes Adv. Bd. Editor: Diabetes, 1973; mem. editl. bd.: Am. Jour. Medicine, 1973, Am. Jour. Med. Scis.; contbr. articles to profl. jours. Served with U.S. Army, 1945—46. Named Banting lectr., Brit. Diabetes Assn., 1972; scholar Markle scholar in med. scis., 1957—62. Mem.: NAS (coun. mem. 1997—2000), Nat. Acad. Scis., Inst. Medicine, Am. Acad. Arts and Scis., Am. Soc. Biol. Chemists, Endocrine Soc. (Oppenheimer award 1965), Am. Diabetes Assn. (Lilly award 1965, Banting medal 1977, Best medal 1981), Am. Fedn. Clin. Rsch., Assn. Am. Physicians (Kober medal 1994), Am. Soc. Clin. Investigation. Home: 7200 Wydown Blvd Saint Louis MO 63105-3023 Office: Barnes Hosp Dept Medicine PO Box 8212 660 S Euclid Ave Saint Louis MO 63110-1010

KIPNISS, ROBERT, artist; b. N.Y.C., Feb. 1, 1931; s. Sam and Stella Anita K.; m. Jean Elizabeth Prutton, July 6, 1954 (div. 1982); children: Max, Ivan, Ruby, Benjamin; m. Laurie Lisle, 1994. Student, Wittenberg Coll., 1948-50; PhD (hon.), Wittenberg U., 1980; BA, U. Iowa, 1952, MFA, 1954; PhD (hon.), Ill. Coll., 1989. One man exhbns. include Museo de Arte Moderno, Cali, Columbia, 1977, Kalamazoo Art Inst., Canton Art Inst., Enatsu Galerie, Tokyo, Gallery New World, Dusseldorf, Germany, Redfern Gallery, London, Venable Neslage, Washington, Hexton Gallery, N.Y.C., Tyler (Tex.) Mus., 1999, Butler Art Inst., Ohio, 1999, Bassenge Gallery, Berlin, 1999, Beadleston Gallery, N.Y.C., 2001, 03, Weinstein Gallery, 1999, 2000, 01, 02, 04; represented in permanent collections Chgo. Art Inst., Whitney Mus. Am. Art, N.Y.C., Nat. Collection Fine Arts, Victoria and Albert Mus., London, Libr. of Congress, L.A. County Mus., Detroit Inst. Art, Cleve. Mus., N.Y. Pub. Libr., Butler Art Inst., De Young Mus., Fogg Mus., Cambridge, Mass., Boston Mus. Fine Arts, Indpls. Mus. Art, Portland Mus. Art, Yale Mus., New Haven, Conn., Brit. Mus., London, The Fitz William Mus., Cambridge, U.K., New Orleans Mus. Art, Met. Mus. Art., Biblioteque Nat. France, Paris, Carnegie Mus., Pitts., Fine Arts Mus. San Francisco, Everson Mus., Syracuse, N.Y., Nelson-Atkins Mus., Kansas City, Mo., Pinakothech der Moderne, Munich. Served with U.S. Army, 1956-58. Recipient Ralph Fabri prize in lithography Nat. Acad. Design, 1976, James R. Marsh Meml. award in lithography Audubon Artists, 1978, Charles M. Lea prize Print Club Phila., 1978, prize for lithography Soc. Am. Graphic Artists, 1979, Medal of Honor in Graphics Audubon Artists, 1983, Childe Hassam purchase award Am. Acad. Arts and Letters, 1988, The Cannon prize Nat. Acad. Design, 1999, Graphics award Boston Printmakers, 1999, Daniel Serra-Badue Meml. award Audobon Artists, 1998, Medal of Honor, Audobon Artists, 1999, 2000, Purchase prize Delta Nat., 2001, Ark. State U., Prints U.S.A., 2001, Springield Mus. of Art, Mo., Leo Meissner award Nat. Acad., 2003. Mem. Nat. Acad. Design, The Century Assn., Soc. Am. Graphics Artists, Royal Soc. Painter Printmakers (London), The Boston Printmakers. Personal E-mail: rkipniss@msn.com.

KIPPER, BARBARA LEVY, wholesale distribution executive; b. Chgo., July 16, 1942; d. Charles and Ruth (Doctoroff) Levy; m. David A. Kipper, Sept. 9, 1974; children: Talia Rose, Tamar Judith. BA, U. Mich., 1964. Reporter Chgo. Sun-Times, 1964-67; photo editor Cosmopolitan Mag., N.Y.C., 1969-71; vice chmn. Chas Levy Co., Chgo., 1984-86, chmn., 1986—. Trustee Spertus Inst. Jewish Studies, Chgo.(Ill.) Hist. Soc., Golden Apple Ind., Joffrey Ballet of Chgo.; bd. dirs. Lincoln Park Zoo. Recipient Deborah award Com. Women's Equality, Am. Jewish Congress, 1992, Shapiro Human Rels. award The Anti-Defamation League of B'nai B'rith, Personal PAC's Leadership award, 1996, Disting. Cmty. Leadership award, ADL, Jewish Culture, 2004; named Nat. Soc. Fund Raising Execs. Disting. Philanthropist, 1995. Mem.: Nat. Found. Jewish Culture (Golden Sceptre award), Chgo. Network, Coun. on Founds., Com. of 200, Chgo. Coun. on Fgn. Rels., Internat. Women's Forum, Econ. Club of Chgo., Execs. Club of Chgo., The Standard Club. Jewish. Office Phone: 708-356-3601. Business E-Mail: bkipper@chaslevy.com.

KIPSHIDZE, NICHOLAS NODAR, cardiologist; b. Tbilisi, Republic of Georgia, Oct. 12, 1952; came to the U.S., 1992; s. Nodar N. and Leli A. (Cheishvili) K.; m. Elena V. Vinogradova, May 2, 1992; 1 child, Nodar Sean. BS, High Sch. N:1, Tbilisi, 1970; MD, Tbilisi State Med. Sch., 1975; PhD in Cardiology, Bakulev Inst., 1982, DSc, 1989. Intern Rsch. Inst. Clin. & Exptl. Therapy, Tbilisi, USSR, 1974-75; resident Bakulev Inst. Cardiovascular Surgery, Moscow, USSR, 1975-78, postdoctoral fellow in cardiology and radiology, 1975-78, rsch. and clin. scientist, 1978-82, sr. rsch. and clin. scientist, 1982-92, assoc. prof. cardiology, 1986-92; project rschr. Med. Coll. Wis., Milw., 1993-94, vis. prof. medicine and surgery, 1994—. Author: Laser Treatment of Coronary Artery Disease, 1992; contbr. articles to profl. jours. Grantee C.R. Bard, 1992-95, Global Theropeutics, 1995-97, AVI Biopharma, 1997—, Cook Inc., 1998—. Fellow Am. Coll. Cardiology, Am. Coll. Angiology, Internat. Coll. Angiology; mem. Latin Am. Soc. Angiology. Christian Orthodox. Achievements include patents for method to treat arterial obstructions, laser catheter method for sealing blood vessel puncture sites, method and apparatus for minimizing restenosis coating intraluminal stents. Office: Med Coll Wis 9200 W Wisconsin Ave Milwaukee WI 53226-3522

KIRAZ, BAHRI, plastics engineer, mechanical engineer, consultant; b. Adana, Karatas, Turkey, Jan. 3, 1950; s. Rabia Kirnik and Kemal Kiraz; m. Gülden Kaya, Nov. 11, 1988; children: Talha, Yasin, Furkan, Kadir, Emine Nisanur. Degree in mech. engring., Cukurova U., Adana, 1975; degree in plastics engring., Fachhochschule Darmstadt, Germany, 1986. Process engring. WOCO, Steinau an der Strasse, Germany, 1986—88, dir. assembling tech. dept., 1988—90; tchr. Tech. Sch. for Plastics Enginring., Weissenburg, Germany; dir. tech. innovation and cons. Alfmeier Corp., Greenville, SC, 2004—. Cons. WOCO, Bad Soden-Salmünster, Hessen, 1990—93, dir. of process engring. dept., 1993—97; devel. engr. Alfmeier Präzision, Treuchtlingen, Germany, 1997—98, cons., 1998—99; dir. tech. innovation and cons. Alfmeier Präzion AG, Treuchtlingen, Mexico, 1999—. Composer: (song) Yok yok deme; prodr.: (devel.) template-ruler for kids; contbr. articles to profl. jours. Lt. Aircraft, 1975—77, Ankara. Mem.: VDI German Engring. Club. Muslim. Achievements include development of Control unite for Sitting comfort; research in Assistance diploma study cross linked polyethylen for joining technology; invention of Development Barb For Joining Technology; Assistance diploma study: Design of Experiment solve (finding the best set up for different processes); TolPro (tolerance program for thermoplastic parts); it is availible on the market; zero-defect Floats production made of NBR foam with my own DOE program; development of Testing method for Floats, hoses, resistor cards for tanks; Design standards for tank valves made of Polyethylen; Geometry for rotation welding (Tube-Fitting); research in Assistance Of Diploma Study For Rotation Welding Process; Assistance of diploma study about Orientation of extruded hoses; design of Design Of Barb For Rotation Welding; development of Finding The Best Process For Rotation Welding; research in Assistance diploma study process technology for rotation welding process; Assistance diploma study Orientation status in tubes for rotation weldig. Avocations: swimming, movie, music, playing guitar. Home: 202 Teaticket Ct Simpsonville SC 29681 Office: Alfmeier Corp 120 Ellcon Dr Greenville SC 29605 Office Phone: 864-299-6300 105. Office Fax: 864-422-5705. E-mail: bahri.kiraz@alfmeier.com.

KIRBERGER, ELIZABETH, lawyer, consultant; b. Tulsa, Okla., 1965; d. Robert Earl Jr. and Phyllis Kirberger. BA in Philosophy and Lit., Wheaton Coll., 1987; JD, Georgetown U., 1990; MPH, Columbia U., 1997. Bar: N.Y., 1991. Law clk. to chief justice Okla. Supreme Ct., Okla. City, 1989; with Herbert Barrett Mgmt. Inc., N.Y.C., 1990—93, Population Coun., N.Y.C., 1993—94, Columbia U. Ctr. for Study of Human Rights, N.Y.C., 1995, Internat. Planned Parenthood Fedn., N.Y.C., 1996—98, AVSC Internat., N.Y.C., 1998—99; pres. Kirberger P.C., N.Y.C., 1998—. Editor Georgetown Internat. Environ. Law Rev., 1988-90; contbr. articles to profl. journals Mem. ABA, N.Y. State Bar Assn., Assn. Bar N.Y.C, Am. Immigration Lawyers Assn. Office Phone: 718-222-3610. Business E-Mail: k@immigration-lawyer.com.

KIRBERGER, MICHAEL PATRICK, application developer, researcher, chemist; b. Meadville, Pa., Nov. 23, 1965; s. Brian Dale and Judith Lee Kirberger; m. Barbara Joie Sliter, June 10, 1994; children: Connor Padraic, Caoilinn Joie, Logan Michael. BA in Journalism, Pa. State U., 1988; postgrad., Dekalb Tech. Coll., 1995—97, Ga. State U., 2004—. Application programmer Suntrust Enterprise Info. Sys., Atlanta, 1998—2004; chemistry grad. rsch. asst., software devel. Ga. State U., Dept. Chemistry, Atlanta, 2004—. Bioinformatics lab. rsch. asst. drug design ctr. Ga. State U., Atlanta, 2002—05, organic chemistry tutorial instr., 2004. Active Am. Indian Relief Coun., Rapid City, SD, 2002—03, Fernbank Mus., Atlanta, 2003—04, Zoo Atlanta, 2003—04. Mem.: Am. Chem. Soc., Am. Mensa, Golden Key Internat. Honor Soc. Avocations: Karate (black belt), reading, writing. Home: 1303 Foxvale Dr Hampton GA 30228 Office: Ga State U 540 General Classroom Bldg 38 Peachtree Center Ave Atlanta GA 30302 Business E-Mail: mkirberger@student.gsu.edu.

KIRBY, ALLAN PRICE, JR., investment company executive; b. Wilkes-Barre, Pa., June 18, 1931; s. Allan Price and Marian (Sutherland) K.; children: Jessie Ann, Allan Price III, Slater Baran, Coray Sutherland, Milan Stanton. BA, Lafayette Coll., 1953. Pres. Liberty Sq., Inc., Mendham, NJ, 1960—; dir., chmn. exec. com. Alleghany Corp., 1987—. Chmn. bd. dirs. A.P. Kirby Jr. Found. Inc., 1989—. Lt. (j.g.) USNR, 1953-55. Mem. Mendham (N.J.) Golf and Tennis Club, Morris County Golf Club (Convent, N.J.), Yale Club (N.Y.C.), Black River Fish and Game Club (Pottersville, N.J.), Delta Kappa Epsilon. Office: 14 E Main St PO Box 90 Mendham NJ 07945-0090

KIRBY, CHARLES WILLIAM, JR., dancer, choreographer; b. Little Rock, Apr. 28, 1926; s. Charles William and Eva Rose (Horton) K. AA, Little Rock Jr. Coll., 1945. Adv. bd. George Brown Coll. Tech., Toronto; exec. com. Canadian Actors Equity Assn.; pres. Southeastern Regional Ballet Festival Assn., 1965; co-founder, co-owner (with Jacques Wensvoort) Abundance Restaurant, Inc., Toronto, 1980— Prin. soloist Ballet Soc. Ark., 1947, assoc. dir. Acad. Ballet Arts, Little Rock, 1948-50, prin. dancer Ark. State Musicals, 1949, Memphis Open Air Theatre, 1950, co-dir. Acad. Dance Arts, Memphis, 1950-65, prin. dancer, costume designer, choreographer Front St. Theatre, Memphis, 1954-64, choreographer Memphis Opera Theatre, 1954-64, performer Dallas Summer Musicals, 1964; co-organizer, choreographer ballets Memphis Civic Ballet, 1953-65; mem. Nat. Ballet Can., 1965-72, soloist, 1972-76, prin. dancer, 1976-85, prin. character artist, 1985-98; appeared: CBS-TV spls. Swan Lake, 1967, Cinderella, 1968 (Emmy award), Sleeping Beauty, 1972 (Emmy award), Giselle, 1975, La Fille Mal Gardee, 1979, Onegin, 1985, The Merry Widow, 1987, The Planets, 1994; choreographer: CBC-TV spls. CBC Opera prodn. La Rondine, 1971, Maurice Ravel Centennial Concert, 1975, summer opera festivals, Nat. Arts Centre, Ottawa, Can., Canadian Opera Co.; co. mgr. Dance Repertory Co., N.Y.C., 1972; author:, dir., choreographer, narrator: spl. ednl. program Spectrum: A Retrospective Look at Dance, 1973. Served with AUS, 1944. Recipient key to City of Little Rock, 1965 Mem.: Assn. Canadian TV and Radio Artists. Episcopalian. Home: 7518 Silver Trumpet Ln # 101 Naples FL 34109

KIRBY, DAVID STEPHEN, music educator; s. Carroll S. and Fay S. Kirby. MusB, Applachian State U., Boone, NC, 1988; MusM, U. Cin., 1991, Mus D, 1995. Artist in residence Nat. Endowment Arts, Dodge City, Kans., 1992—93; dir. bands Brevard Coll., Brevard, NC, 1993—2004, South Stokes H.S., 2004—. Performer: Western Piedmont (NC) Symphony.

KIRBY, DAVID V., prosecutor; b. 1950; BA, Pomona Coll.; JD, Northwestern U. Chief criminal divsn. US Dept. Justice, Burlington, Vt., asst. U.S. atty, 1996—2001, acting U.S. Atty., 2001, 1st asst. U.S. Atty., 2001—04, U.S. atty., 2004—. Office: Office US Atty 11 Elmwood Ave 3rd Fl PO Box 570 Burlington VT 05402-0570 Office Phone: 802-951-6725. Office Fax: 802-951-6540.

KIRBY, DEBORAH MACDONALD, rehabilitation psychologist; b. Washington, May 19, 1948; d. Robert Angus and Margarett Mary (Harrison) MacDonald; m. Stephen Edward Kirby, Sept. 6, 1980; 1 child, Jessica Lynn. BA, George Washington U., 1970; MEd, Am. U., 1972. Lic. profl. counselor. Psychiat. asst. Chestnut Lodge Psychiat. Hosp., Rockville, Md., 1969—70; rsch. psychologist Dept. Army, 1970; clin. intern Counseling Ctr. Am. U., 1972; clin. psychologist Bay County Guidance Clinic, Panama City, Fla., 1974; rehab. psychologist Woodrow Wilson Rehab. Ctr., Fisherville, Va., 1975—84; dir. Shenandoah Counseling Assocs., P.C., 1981—, pres., 1989—. Mem. med. staff Augusta Med. Ctr., Fisherville, Va., 1982—; mem. psychiat. and substance abuse com. Contbr. articles to profl. jours. Bd. dirs. health adv. bd. Augusta County Sch., 1993—. Fellow: Am. Bd. Med. Psychotherapists; mem.: APA, Va. Counselors Assn., Va. Psychol. Assn., Va. Assn. Clin. Counselors, Nat. Beagle Club, Skyline Kennel Club, Charlottesville-Albernarle Kennel Club, Kappa Alpha Theta. Democrat. Office: Shenandoah Counseling Assocs PC PO Box 696 1048 W Beverley St Staunton VA 24402-0696 E-mail: kirbyd@adelphia.net.

KIRBY, DOROTHY MANVILLE, social worker; b. Burke, SD, Oct. 23, 1917; d. Charles Vietz and Gail Lorena (Coonen) Manville; m. Sigmund Kirby, July 11, 1941 (div. 1969); children: Paul Howard, Robert Charles. BA, Wayne State U., 1970, MSW, 1972. Cert. social worker, Mich.; lic. marriage and family therapist, Mich. Pvt. practice social work, Allen Park, Mich., 1973—. Instr. stress, personal effectiveness and comm. Pres. Allen Park Symphony Orch., 1990-92. Mem.: LWV (pres. Allen Park 1965—66), NASW (clin.), AAUW, Mich. Assn. Marriage and Family Therapy (sec. 1982), Nat. Assn. Marriage and Family Therapy. Presbyterian. Avocation: playing violin. Home and Office: 15720 Wick Rd Allen Park MI 48101-1535 Office Phone: 313-382-0623. E-mail: dmkirby@ameritech.net.

KIRBY, EMILY BARUCH, psychologist, writer; b. N.Y.C., Apr. 16, 1929; d. Paul Ludwig and Aimee Augusta (Mayer) Baruch; m. Frank Eugene Kirby, Aug. 17, 1952; children: Russell Steven, Nicholas Quentin, Paula Rachel, Nathaniel Benedict. BA, NYU, 1952, MA, 1953; PhD, Northwestern U., 1974. Instr. psychology Elmhurst Coll., Ill., 1965—68, asst. prof., 1968—74; dir. instnl. rsch. Ctrl. YMCA C.C., Chgo., 1974—77; dir. instnl. rsch. and evaluation Oakton C.C., Morton Grove, Ill., 1977—80; v.p. faculty and acad. affairs Hudson Valley C.C., Troy, NY, 1980—84; mgr. Midwest Odyssey Tours, Inc., 1985—87; pres. Emily Enterprises, 1987—. Adj. faculty Women's Mgmt. Program, Mundelein Coll., Chgo., 1977-79, Northeastern Ill. U., 1994; mem. Off Campus Writers Workshop, Winnetka, Ill.; mem. subcom. on employment and pensions Ill. Commn. on Status of Women, region IV N.Y. planning bd. Bd. Coop. Edn. Svcs., 1981-83; cons. orgn. devel. Prefabets, Czestochowa, Poland, summer 1990, also various not-for-profit orgns., 1990—; bd. dir. The Josselyn Ctr. Mental Health, Northfield, Ill. Author: Yes You Can: The Working Woman's Guide to Her Legal Rights, Fair Employment and Equal Pay, 1984. Contbr. articles to profl. jours., also popular publs. Bd. dirs. North Shore Ecology Ctr., Glencoe, Ill., 1977-80, 83—, So. Sch., Chgo., 1987-92, Antioch Coll. Alumni Bd., 2005—; vol. Earthwatch, 1996-2004, Bosnian survivors of torture, 1998 Mem. AAAS, AAUW, APA (chmn. com. ednl. psychologists in cmty. colls. 1978-80), Am. Ednl. Rsch. Assn. (chairperson newsletter editl. com., spl. interest group com. coll. res. for North Ctrl. region 1978-79), Women in Mgmt. (North Shore chpt. bd.), Women of Achievement (North Shore chpt., Academia award 1989), Orgn. Devel. Network, Chgo., N.Y. Acad. Scis., Antioch Coll. Alumni Assn. (chmn. Chgo. cmty. 1986-88), Northwestern Club Chgo., Phi Delta Kappa Democrat. Unitarian Universalist. Home: 2000 Greenbriar Ln Riverwoods IL 60015-3855 Office Phone: 847-945-7268. *Nothing is wasted; every experience is useful. Life's main challenge is to synthesize, then integrate ideas and events, adding large dollops of humor.*

KIRBY, FRED MORGAN, II, manufacturing executive; b. Wilkes Barre, Pa., Nov. 23, 1919; s. Allan P. and Marian G. (Sutherland) K.; m. A. Walker Dillard, Apr. 30, 1949; children: Alice Kirby Horton, Fred Morgan III, Dillard, Jefferson. Grad., Lawrenceville Sch., 1938; AB, Lafayette Coll., Easton, Pa., 1942; postgrad., Harvard Grad. Sch. Bus., 1947; LLD, Lafayette Coll., 1984; LHD, Drew U., 1997; LLD, St. Joseph's U., 1981, Wake Forest U., 2002. From v.p. to pres., bd. dirs. Allan Corp., 1953-75; pres., chmn. bd. dirs. Filtration Engrs., Inc., 1951-56; dir. Alleghany Corp., 1958-61, 63—, v.p., 1961, exec. v.p., 1963-67, chmn. bd., 1967—, pres., 1968-77, mem. exec. com., 1968—. Pres., bd. dirs. F.M. Kirby Found., Inc.; bd. dirs. Nat. Football Found. and Coll. Hall of Fame, Inc. Served to lt. (s.g.) USNR, 1942-46. Recipient 25th Anniversary citation NCAA, 1966, Silver Anniversary All-Am. award Sports Illustrated, 1966, Gold medal Pa. Soc., 1982, Gold medallion Internat. Swimming Hall of Fame, 1989, Gold medal Nat. Football Found. and Coll. Hall Fame, Inc., 2000, Lawrenceville medal Lawrenceville Sch., 2001. Mem. Westmoreland Club, (Pa.), Spring Valley Hounds (N.J.), Treyburn Country Club (N.C.), Morris County Golf Club (N.J.), Zeta Psi. Office: PO Box 151 17 Dehart St Morristown NJ 07963-0151

KIRBY, HARMON E., retired ambassador; b. Hamilton, Ohio, Jan. 27, 1934; s. Cecil and Julia Emma Catherine (Tucker) Kirby; m. Françoise Rolande Chatelain, Dec. 26, 1963; children: Caroline Patricia, Christopher Harmon. AB, Harvard U., 1952; MA, George Washington U., 1977. With pers. and labor rels. Diamond Nat. Corp., Middletown, Ohio, 1959-60; exec. asst. to exec. v.p. Hudson Pulp and Paper Co., N.Y.C., 1960-61; joined Fgn. Svc., Dept. State, 1961; vice consul U.S. Mission, Geneva, 1961-63, U.S. Consulate Gen., Madras, India, 1964-66; internat. rels. officer Dept. State, 1966-69; polit. officer U.S. Embassy, New Delhi, 1969-72, Micronesia Status Negotiations, 1973; Turkish desk officer Dept. of State, 1974-76, dir. Pakistan/Afghanistan/Bangladesh affairs Washington, 1982-84, dir. UN polit. affairs, 1987-89, dir., performance evaluation, 1989-90; polit. counselor U.S. Mission European Cmtys., Brussels, 1976-79; counselor, dep. chief of mission U.S. Embassy, Khartoum, 1979-81, min.-counselor dep. chief of mission Rabat, Morocco, 1984-87; sr. seminar Nat. and Internat. Affairs, Washington, 1981-82; amb. to Togo, 1990-94; ret., 1995. With State Dept., Washington, 1996—. Bd. dirs. Internat. Eye Found. Fellow: Tangier Am. Legation Mus. Soc.; mem.: Am. Fgn. Svc. Assn., Diplomatic and Consular Officers Ret., Phi Beta Kappa. Avocations: travel, photography, tennis, swimming. Home: 6811 Barrett Ln Bethesda MD 20814-1205

KIRBY, JOHN JOSEPH, JR., lawyer; b. Washington, Oct. 22, 1939; s. John Joseph and Rose Elizabeth (Mangan) Kirby; m. Susan Rita Cullman; children: John Pickens, Timothy James, Perrin Patricia Lucia. BA, Fordham Coll., 1961; BA (Rhodes scholar), Oxford U., 1964, MA, 1967; LLB, U. Va., 1966. Bar: Va 1966, NY 1969. Asst. prof. law U. Va., 1966-67; spl. asst. civil rights divsn. U.S. Dept. Justice, Washington, 1967-68; assoc. Mudge Rose Guthrie Alexander & Ferdon, N.Y.C., 1968-70, ptnr., 1971-95, chmn., 1991-95; ptnr. Latham & Watkins, N.Y.C., 1995—. Dep dir Pres's Comn Campus Unrest, 1970. Bd dirs Georgetown Univ, 1976—92, Fordham Univ, 1994—2000, Merton Col Charitable Corp, 1995—, Fund Modern Cts, 1998—. Mem.: ABA, DC Bar, Va State Bar, Asn Bar City NY. Home: 812 Park Ave New York NY 10021 also: 88 Saddle Rock Rd Stamford CT 06902 Office: Latham & Watkins 885 3d Ave Ste 1000 New York NY 10022-4834 Office Phone: 212-906-1222. E-mail: john.kirby@lw.com.

KIRBY, KENT BRUCE, artist, educator; b. Fargo, N.D., Dec. 31, 1934; s. Harold Ely and Vida Nicola (Vennerstrom) K.; m. Lynn Rennetha Schutte, Sept. 1, 1956 (div. 1981); children: Kalin Louise, Jeffrey Bruce, Kristin Beth; m. Carrie Anne Parks, 1983 BA, Carleton Coll., 1956; MA, U. N.D., 1959; M.F.A., U. Mich., 1970. Tchr. Benjamin Franklin Jr. High Sch., Fargo, 1956-59; instr. in art, acting head dept. art Muskingum Coll., 1959-61; instr. Wilkes Coll., 1961-62; faculty art Alma (Mich.) Coll., 1962-90, prof., 1971—, chmn. dept. art and design, 1962—, chmn. div. fine arts, 1973-75, Charles A. Dana prof. art, 1976. One-man shows Grand Rapids Art Mus., 1981, U. N.Mex., 1980, Ctr. for Creative Studies, Detroit, 1982, Ctrl. Mich. U., Mt. Pleasant, 1990, New Eng. Sch. Photography, Boston, 1992, Alma Coll., 2003; group shows include, 2d Internat. Exhbn. Prints and Drawings, Wesleyan U., 1982, Color Print U.S.A., Tex. Tech U., Lubbock, 1983, 20th Bradley Nat. Print and Drawing Exhbn., 1985, 4th Rockford Internat. Biennale, 1985, Nat. Invitational Print Exhbn., U. Ala., 1988; exhibited Nat. Mus. Am. History, Washington, 1988-89, Stockton Nat. Print and Drawing Exhbn., Haggin Mus. of Art, 1990, "A Decade of Mich. Printmaking", Detroit Inst. Art, 1992, 2001, Nat. Small Print Exhbn., U. Wis., Parkside, 1994, 95, 97, 2002, 2003, Fla. Nat., 1997, Art Link Nat. Exhbn., 2001, 02, 04; represented in permanent collections, Chgo. Art Inst., Detroit Art Inst., Smithsonian Inst., Brit. Mus., London; author: Studio Collotype: Continuous Tone Printing for the Artist, Printmaker and Photographer, 1988. Chmn. museums com., mem. Mich. State Council for Arts, 1966—68. Research fellow Newberry Library, 1974; Mich. Council for Arts grantee, 1975, 78; Nat. Endowment for Arts grantee, 1976 Mem. AAUP, Coll. Art Assn., Mid-Am. Print Coun. Home: 9667 W Van Buren Rd Riverdale MI 48877-9707

KIRBY, MARCIA KAREN, library and information scientist; b. Williamsburg, Va., Oct. 23, 1952; d. Marion O. and Rita S. Smith; m. Garnett E. Kirby, Jr., Aug. 18, 1979; children: Jon-David G., Phillip E. Libr. clk. Williamsburg Regional Libr., Va., 1975—80; libr. tech. Navelex Tech. Libr., Portsmouth, Va., 1982—83; libr. clk. Hampton U. Libr., Va., 1985—87; libr. tech. Internat. Telephone Telegraph, Hampton, Va., 1987—91; libr. clk. Hampton U. Libr., Va., 1992—95; tchr. resource ctr. clk. Newport News Pub. Schs., Va., 1995—96; libr. clk. Gildersleeve Mid. Sch., Newport News, Va., 1995—97; libr. practitioner I Coll. of William & Mary Libr., Williamsburg, Va., 1997—. Mem.: Classified Staff Assn. (corr.; pres. 2000—01, sec. 2003). Avocations: reading, photography, videography, piano.

KIRBY, ODELL, retired small business owner, newswriter, writer; b. Vivan, Okla., 1921; s. Auda and Matilda (Brasfield) Kirby. Student, Inst. of Children's Lit., West Redding, Conn. Printer's devil Indian Jour., Eufaula, Okla., 1936; with various newspapers, 1936—72; owner vacuum cleaner sales and svc. bus., 1972—97.

KIRBY, PAUL H., composer, tax specialist; b. Detroit, Mar. 23, 1946; s. Sigmund and Dorothy Kirby. MusB, U. Mich., 1967; MusM, Mich. State U., 1968, Rice U., 1979; D in Musical Arts, CUNY, 1996. Tchr. Battle Creek (Mich.) Lakeview HS, 1970—77; music dir. Houston Youth Symphony, 1979—87; asst. prof. music Iowa State U., Ames, 1986—89; tax preparer N.Y.C., 1995—. Composer: (albums) Sonata for Trumpet. Composer in residence Our Saviors Atonement Luth. Ch., N.Y.C., 2000—. Mem.: ASCAP, Condrs. Guild, Musicians Club N.Y. Avocation: bridge. Home and Office: 360 Cabrini Blvd # 1D New York NY 10040

KIRBY, RONALD EUGENE, fish and wildlife research administrator; b. Angola, Ind., Nov. 26, 1947; s. Robert Waye and Lorraine Alice (Hoag) Kirby; m. Dona J. Kirby; children: Cyrus Robert, William Emil, Peter Waye, Joshua M. Brosten, Emily A. Brosten, Andrew J. Brosten. BS, Duke U., 1969; MA, So. Ill. U., 1973; PhD, U. Minn., 1976. Staff biologist Coop. Wildlife Rsch. Lab., So. Ill. U., Carbondale, 1969-72; collaborating biologist U.S. Forest Svc., St. Paul and Cass Lake, Minn., 1970-72; rsch. biologist Antarctic Rsch. Program NSF, McMurdo Station, Antarctica, 1974; NIH rsch. trainee dept. ecology and behavioral biology U. Minn., Mpls., 1972-76; wildlife biologist, Patuxent Wildlife Rsch. Ctr. U.S. Fish and Wildlife Svc., Laurel, Md., 1976-80, population mgmt. specialist div. refuge mgmt. Washington, 1980-82, rsch. coord. Nat. Wildlife Refuge System, 1982-83, regional assistance biologist, office info. transfer Ft. Collins, Colo., 1983-88, leader info. transfer sect., 1988-90; asst. dir. No. Prairie Wildlife Rsch. Ctr., Jamestown, ND, 1991-92, dir., 1993; dir. U.S. Nat. Biol. Svc. No. Prairie Sci. Ctr., Jamestown, ND, 1993-96; dir. U.S. Geol. Survey No. Prairie Wildlife Rsch. Ctr., Jamestown, ND, 1997-2001; dir. U.S. Geol. Survey Forest and Rangeland Ecosys. Sci. Ctr., Corvallis, Oreg., 2001—03; sr. adv. biologist We. regional office U.S. Geol. Survey, Seattle, 2003—04, sci. quality coord., 2004—. Mem. waterfowl adv. com. Minn. Dept. Natural Resources, 1970—72; mem. black duck subcom. Atlantic Flyway Coun., 1976—80; mem. tech. sect. Central Flyway, 1991—. Editorial referee to sci. jours. and profl. reports; contbr. to numerous profl. publs. Active Boy Scouts Am., 1984—. Grantee AEC, 1972—76. Mem.: The Wildlife Soc., Lambda Chi Alpha. Avocations: hiking, camping, birdwatching, motorcycling, hunting. Office: Western Regional Office US Geol Survey 909 1st Ave Ste 800 Seattle WA 98104 Office Phone: 206-220-4640. Business E-Mail: ronald_kirby@usgs.gov.

KIRBY, RUSSELL STEPHEN, epidemiologist, researcher, geographer; b. New Haven, June 8, 1954; s. Frank Eugene and Emily (Baruch) K.; m. Elizabeth Margaret Ivens, July 9, 1977; children: Rachel Anne, Amelia Jeanne, Jocelyn Eileen. BA, U. Wis., 1974, MS, 1977, PhD, 1981, MS, 1991. Lectr. U. Wis., Madison, 1980, 82-83; rsch. analyst 3 Wis. Ctr. for Health Stats., Madison, 1981-83, rsch. analyst 5, 1983-85, rsch. analyst 6 maternal and child health statistician, 1985-88; sr. rsch. analyst maternal and child health Ark. Ctr. Health Statistics, Little Rock, 1988-91; instr. dept. pediat. U. Ark. Med. Scis., Little Rock, 1989-93, asst. prof., 1993-96; assoc. prof. dept. ob.-gyn. Milw. Clin. Campus U. Wis. Med. Sch., 1996-01, prof., 2001—02; prof., vice chair dept. maternal and child health, dept. of pediat. Sch. Publ. Health U. Ala. at Birmingham, 2002—. Vis. asst. prof. Beloit Coll., 1987—88; adj. asst. prof. U. Ark., Little Rock, 1988—95; adj. assoc. prof. Coll. Bus. and Mgmt. Cardinal Stritch U., 2000—02; sci. dir. Ark. Reproductive Health Monitoring Sys., 1991—94, dir., 1994—96, cons., 1996—. Book rev. editor Jour. Perinatology, 1992-99; mem. bd. editors Jour. Childs Health, 2003—, Birth, 2003—, Pediatric and Perinatal Epidemiology, Am. Jour. Perinatology, 2005-; contbr. articles to profl. jours. Recipient Callon-Leonard award Wis. Assn. for Perinatal Care, 1994, Byron L. Hawks award Ark. Perinatal Assn., 1995, Fraternalist of Yr. award Ct. Razorback Ind. Order Foresters, 1996; named Vol. of Yr. SE chpt. Wis. March of Dimes Birth Defects Found., 1998, Outstanding Advocate for Maternal and Child Health Wis. Maternal and Child Health Coalition, 1999. Fellow Am. Coll. Epidemiology; mem. APHA, Assn. Am. Geographers (life), Agrl. History Soc. (life), So. Hist. Soc. (life), Wis. Assn. for Perinatal Care (bd. dirs. 1996-2002, pres.-elect 1998-99, pres. 1999-2000, past pres. 2000-01, Pres. award, 2003), Perinatal Found. (bd. dirs. 1996-2002, treas. 2000-2002), Ark. Perinatal Assn. (pres. 1991-92), Soc. for Epidemiologic Rsch., Nat. Perinatal Assn. (bd. dirs. 1990-92, 95-98, ann. conf. chair 1999), Nat Birth Defects Prevention Network (pres. 1999, past pres. 2000, exec. com. 1997—), Soc. for Pediatric and Perinatal Epidemiologic Rsch. (exec. com. 2000-04), Teratology Soc., Ala. chpt. Mar. of Dimes (bd. dirs. 2002—, chpt. chair 2005—), Assn. Tchrs. of Maternal and Child Health (treas. 2005-). Avocations: camping, writing book reviews, computer cartography and graphics, used books. Home: 713 Kendall Dr Vestavia Hills AL 35226 Office: RPHB 320 1530 3rd Ave S Birmingham AL 35294-0022 Office Phone: 205-934-2985. Business E-Mail: rkirby@uab.edu.

KIRBY, SARAH ANN VAN DEVENTER, librarian, aerospace engineer; b. Champaign, Ill., Mar. 10, 1961; d. David Bruce Kirby and Florence May Van Deventer. BS in Aerospace Engring., U. Mich., 1983; MEd, U. Houston, Clear Lake, 1989; MLS, U. Wis., Milw., 2003. Space systems ops. engr. NASA/JSC-MOD, Houston, 1983-99; mgr. E-commerce Moore N.Am., Bannockburn, Ill., 1999—2000; libr. Boelter & Yates, Park Ridge, Ill., 2000—. Contbr. articles to profl. jours. Bd. dirs. Hidden Cove Homeowners Assn., Friendswood, Tex., 1991-96. Avocations: genealogy, theology, tutoring math, softball, golf. Home: 613 Creekside Cir Gurnee IL 60031-2058 Office: Boelter & Yates 1300 Higgins Rd Park Ridge IL 60068

KIRCH, DARRELL GENE, academic administrator, dean; b. Denver, May 3, 1949; m. Deborah M. Kirch; children: Samantha M., Madeline A. BA in Philosophy, U. Colo., 1973, MD magna cum laude, 1977. Diplomate Am. Bd. Psychiatry and Neurology. Resident in psychiatry U. Colo. Health Scis. Ctr., Denver, 1977—82; med. staff fellow adult psychiatry br. NIMH, Washington, 1982—84, sr. staff fellow neuropsychiatry br., 1984—87, med. dir. Neuropsychiat. Rsch. Hosp., 1987—89, dep. scientific dir. Bethesda, Md., 1992—93; prof. Sch. Grad. Studies, prof. dept. psychiatry Med. Coll. Ga., Augusta, 1994—2000, dean Sch. Medicine, 1994—2000, dean Sch. Grad. Studies, 1995—99, sr. v.p. for clin. activities, 1998—2000; prof. dept. psychiatry, sr. v.p. for health affairs Pa. State U., Hershey, 2000—, dean Coll. Medicine, 2000—; CEO Milton S. Hershey Med. Ctr., 2000—. Examiner Am. Bd. Psychiatry and Neurology, Deerfield, Ill., 1985—; chaor sec. on med. schs. AMA, 1998—99; mem. coun. deans adminstrv. bd. Assn. Med. Colls., 2000—. Assoc. editor: Psychopharacology Bull., 1990—98, Schizophrenia Bull., 1989—95. Capt. USPHS, 1986—94. Decorated Commendation medal. Mem.: AMA, Assn. of Am. Med. Coll. (chair 2003), Soc. for Exec. Leadership in Acad. Medicine, Pa. Psychiat. Soc., Pa. Med. Soc., Am. Soc. Clin. Psychopharmacology, Am. Psychiat. Assn. Home: 651 Olde Ventura Farm Rd Hummelstown PA 17036 Office: Pa State U H162 P O Box 850 500 University Dr Hershey PA 17033*

KIRCH, DONALD ALLEN, writer, composer; b. Culver City, Calif., Jan. 24, 1967; s. Donald Raymond and Ruth Mae (White) K. Student, United Broadcast Sch., 1989. FCC permit. Author: Still Waters, 1997, KA-RE, 2000, A Stake in Murder, 2001, A Port By Any Other Name, 2002, A Funny Thing Happened on the Way to Roswell, 2003; songwriter This Is America, 1991, The Working Man, 1991, Oh What A Gift is Christmas Day, 1991, The Miracle of Christmas, 1999. Mem. Titanic Hist. Soc. Roman Catholic. Avocations: history, film, naval ships and history of naval ships, sherlock holmes mysteries, study of strange phenomena. Home: 311 E 91st Ter Kansas City MO 64114-3738 Office Phone: 816-523-3945. E-mail: dkirch@hotmail.com.

KIRCH, PATRICK VINTON, anthropology educator, archaeologist; b. Honolulu, July 7, 1950; s. Harold William and Barbara Ver (MacGarvin) Kirch; m. Debra Connelly, Mar. 3, 1979 (div. 1990); m. Therese Babineau, Feb. 6, 1994. BA, U. Pa., 1971; MPhil, Yale U., 1974, PhD, 1975. Assoc. anthropologist Bishop Mus., Honolulu, 1975-76, anthropologist, 1976-82, head archaeology div., 1982-84, asst. chmn. anthropology, 1983-84; dir., assoc. prof. Burke Mus. U. Wash., Seattle, 1984-87, prof., 1987-89, U. Calif., Berkeley, 1989—, prof. anthropology, endowed chair, 1994—; curator Hearst Mus. Anthropology, 1989—, dir., 1999—2002. Adj. faculty U. Hawaii, Honolulu, 1979—84; mem. lasting legacy com. Wash. State Centennial Commn., 1986—88; pres. Soc. Hawaiian Archaeology, 1980—81; vis. prof. Ecole des Hautes Etudes en Scis. Sociale, Paris, 2002. Assoc. editor Internat. Encyclopedia of the Behavioral and Social Scis., 2002; editor: Island Societies, 1986; co-editor (with Terry L. Hunt): Historical Ecology in the Pacific Islands: Prehistoric Environmental and Landscape Change, 1997; co-editor: (with Eric Conte) Archaeological Investigations in the Mangareva Islands, 2004; co-author (with Peter S. Chapman): Archaeological Excavations at Seven Sites, Southeast Maui, Hawaiian Islands, 1979; co-author: (with Terry L. Hunt) Archaeology of the Lapita Cultural Complex: A Critical Review, 1989; co-author: (with Marshall Sahlins) Anahulu: The Anthropology of History in the Kingdom of Hawaii, Vol. 1: Historical Ethnography, 1992, Anahulu: The Anthropology of History in the Kingdom of Hawaii, Vol. 2, 1992; co-author: (with Roger C. Green) Hawaiki, Ancestral Polynesia: An Essay in Historical Anthropology, 2001; author: Marine Exploitation in Prehistoric Hawaii: Archaeological Investigations at Kalahuipua'a Hawaii Island, 1979, Island Societies: Archaeological Approaches to Evolution and Transformation, 1986, Niuatoputapu: The Prehistory of a Polynesian Chiefdom, 1989, The Evolution of the Polynesian Chiefdoms, 1989, Wet and the Dry: Irrigation and Agricultural Intensification in Polynesia, 1994, Anahulu: The Anthropology of History in the Kingdom of Hawaii, 1994, Feathered Gods and Fishhooks: An Introduction to Hawaiian Archaeology and Prehistory, 1995, Legacy of the Landscape: An Illustrated Guide to Hawaiian Archaeological Sites, 1996, Lapita Peoples: Ancestors of the Oceanic World, 1996, On the Road of the Winds: An Archaeological History of the Pacific Islands Before European Contact, 2000; contbr. articles to profl. pubs. Trustee Berkeley Art Mus. and Pacific Film Archives, 1999—2002, Ctr. for Advanced Study in Behavioral Scis., 2003—. Recipient J.I. Staley prize in anthropology, Sch. Am. Rsch., 1998; fellow, Ctr. for Advanced Study in Behavioral Scis., 1997—98; grantee, NSF, 1974, 1976, 1977, 1982, 1987, 1988, 1989, 1993, 1996, 1998, 2001, NEA, 1985, NEH, 1988, 1999, Hawaii Com. for Humanities, 1981; rsch. grantee, Nat. Geog. Soc., 1986, 1989, 1996, Wenner-Gren Found. for Anthropol. Rsch., 1998. Fellow: NAS (John J. Carty medal for the advancement of sci. 1997), AAAS, Calif. Acad. Scis. (trustee 1999—2003), Am. Philos. Soc., Am. Anthrop. Assn., Am. Acad. Arts and Scis.; mem.: Polynesian Soc., Assn. Field Archaeology, Sigma Xi. Democrat. Avocation: gardening. Office: U Calif Dept Anthropology 232 Kroeber Hall Berkeley CA 94720-3710

KIRCHER, CHRISTOPHER, neurologist, consultant; b. Niagara Falls, N.Y., May 30, 1942; s. Charles Edmund and Nancy Page Kircher; m. Amy Nichols Kircher, May 8, 1982; children: Caroline Anna, Madeline Catherine. BS, Xavier U., Cin., 1963; MD, Ind. U., 1973. Diplomate Am. Bd. Psychiatry and Neurology. Clin. clk. Nat. Hosp. Nervous and Mental Disorders, London, 1973; intern St. Joseph Infirmary, Louisville, 1973—74; resident in neurology U. Minn., Mpls., 1974—75; sr. and chief resident U. Cin., 1975—77; vis. fellow Cleve. Clinic, 1977; neurologist Mayfield Clinic, Cin., 1977—97; neurology and clin. rsch. Riverhills Healthcare, Cin., 1997—2001. Dir. med. adv. bd. Alzheimer's Corp., Albuquerque, 1999—; dir. clin. adv. bd. Panacea Pharm., Gaithersburg, Md., 2001—; cons. ProScan Imaging, Cin., 2002—; co-developer nuclear scanning method Dual Tracer Emission Computer Tomography, 1998; moderator Challenging Views of Alzheimer Disease Conf., 2001—04; lectr. in field; reviewer rsch. grants Alzheimer's Assn., 2004—. Editor: (book) Readings in Neurophysiology, 1968; contbr. articles to profl. jours. Active leadership tng. program Sch. Creative and Performing Arts, Cin., 2001—02. Fellow, NIH, 1965—68; scholar, Cmty. Inst. Cooperation, U. Mich., 1966—67. Mem.: Am. Acad. Neurology. Republican. Avocations: golf, travel, reading. Home: 3444 Arnold St Cincinnati OH 45208-4408 Office: Cincinnati Bio-Med and Fin Cons Ltd 3444 Arnold St Cincinnati OH 45208-4408 E-mail: ckircher@one.net.

KIRCHER, JOHN JOSEPH, law educator; b. Milw., July 26, 1938; s. Joseph John and Martha Marie (Jach) K.; m. Marcia Susan Adamkiewicz, Aug. 26, 1961; children: Joseph John, Mary Kathryn. BA, Marquette U., 1960, JD, 1963. Bar: Wis. 1963, U.S. Dist. Ct. (ea. dist.) Wis. 1963, U.S. Ct. Appeals (7th cir.) 1992. Sole practice, Port Washington, Wis., 1963-66; with Def. Research Inst., Milw., 1966-80, research dir., 1972-80; with Marquette U., 1970—, prof. law, 1980—, assoc. dean acad. affairs, 1992-93. Chmn. Wis. Jud. Council, 1981-83. Author: (with J.D. Ghiardi) Punitive Damages: Law and Practice, 1981, 2d edit (with C.M. Wiseman), 2000; editor Federation of Defense and Corporate Counsel Quarterly; mem. editorial bd. Def. Law Jour.; contbr. articles to profl. jours. Recipient Teaching Excellence award Marquette U., 1986, Disting. Service award Def. Research Inst., 1980, Marquette Law Rev. Editors' award, 1988. Mem. ABA (Robert B. McKay Professor award 1993), Am. Law Inst., Wis. Bar Assn., Wis. Supreme Ct. Bd. of Bar Examiners (vice chair 1989-91, chair 1992), Am. Judicature Soc., Nat. Sports Law Inst. (adv. com. 1989—), Assn. Internationale de Droit des Assurances, Scribes. Roman Catholic. Office: PO Box 1881 Milwaukee WI 53201-1881 Office Phone: 414-288-7095. Business E-Mail: john.kircher@marquette.edu.

KIRCHHEIMER, ARTHUR E(DWARD), lawyer, finance company executive; b. N.Y.C., June 26, 1931; s. Arthur and Lena K.; m. Esther A. Jordan, Sept. 11, 1965. BA, Syracuse U., 1952, LL.B., 1954. Bar: N.Y. 1954, Calif. 1973. Ptnr. Block, Kirchheimer, Lemax & Failmezger, Syracuse, N.Y., 1954-70; corp. counsel Norwich Pharmacal Co., N.Y., 1970-72; sr. v.p., gen. counsel Wickes Cos., Inc., San Diego, 1972-84; prin. Arthur E. Kirchheimer, Inc., P.C., San Diego, 1984-90; writer, cons. in bus. matters La Jolla, Calif., 1990—. Sec., dir. Corp. Fin. Council San Diego, 1975 Pres. Mental Health Assn. Onondaga County, 1970; chmn. Manlius (N.Y.) Planning Commn., 1969-72; mem. Alternatives to Litigation Spl. Panel, 1984—; mem. San Diego County Grand Jury, 1991-92. Mem. ABA, Calif. Bar Assn. Home and Office: 2876 Palomino Cir La Jolla CA 92037-7066

KIRCHHOF, MARY TERESA, special education educator; d. Robert Louis Hughes and Rita Anne Pottner Hughes; m. Calvin Earl Kirchhof, June 19, 1976; children: Joseph Matthew, Timothy John. BS, St. Cloud (Minn.)State U., 1974; MA, St. Thomas U., 1996. Cert. tchr. Minn. Dept. of Edn., 1996, tchr. specific learning disabilities Minn. Dept of Edn., 1996, tchr. early childhood spl. edn. Minn. Dept. of Edn., 1986, tchr. mild, moderate, severe mental handicap Minn. Dept. of Edn., 1974. Tchr. Intermediate Dist., Plymouth, Minn., 1974—91, Edina (Minn.) Pub. Schs., 1991—99, literacy leader, 1999—. Ednl. trainer SOS Seminars, Apple Valley, Minn., 2001—02; adj. instr. Hamline U., St. Paul, 2003—; statewide facilitator Tchrs. as Leaders and Learners Edn. Minn., St. Paul, 2002—; spkr. in field; cons. in field. Active Boy Scouts, Minnetonka, Minn., 1987—2002; sec. Sowers Justice St. Therese, Deephaven, Minn., 1996—2005; action writer Amnesty Internat., Minn., 2000—05. Grantee, Minn. Dept. of Edn., 1997—98, Intermediate Dist. 287, 2002, Fulbright Found., 2003, Edn. Minn. Found. Excellence in Tchg. and Learning, 2004—. Mem.: ASCD, Minn. Reading Assn., Edn. Minn. (goverance bd. 2002—04, presenter, profl. devel. activist), Internat. Reading Assn. Roman Catholic. Avocations: reading, gardening, walking, photography, travel. Office: Edina Public Schools 5701 Normadale Road Edina MN 55424 Office Phone: 952-848-4940.

KIRCHHOFF, MICHAEL KENT, economic development executive; b. Effingham, Ill., Apr. 3, 1963; s. Robert D. and Violet M. (Baumann) K; m. Lynn Reilly, May 27, 1989; children, Amelia Elizabeth, Caroline Rebekah. BA in Econ., BS in Bus., East Ill. U., 1986; postgrad., U. Okla., 1995. Cert. econ. developer; cert. Ill. Assessing Officer. Owner, mgmt. cons. Spectrum Cons., Springfield, 1985-90; intern govs. office Ill. Dept. Revenue, Springfield, 1986-87, property tax analyst, 1987-89; econ. devel. prof. Dept. Commerce and Community Affairs, Springfield, 1989-92; data analyst Ill. Dept. Pub. Aid, Springfield, 1992; mkt. devel. rschr. Ill. Power Co., Decatur, 1992-95; joint purchasing coord. State of Ill., Springfield, 1995-96; owner Phoenix Assocs., Springfield, 1995-96; exec. dir. Tuscola (Ill.) Area Improvement Assn., 1996-97, program mgr. Mainstreet Tuscola, 1996-97; exec. dir. Jacksonville (Ill.) Area Econ. Devel. Coun., 1997-99, Jacksonville (Ill.) Regional Econ. Devel. Corp., 2000—; owner DPI Group, 2004—. Asst. scoutmaster, asst. explorer advisor, scoutmaster, dist. chmn. Okaw dist. Boy Scouts Am., 1997, dist. chmn. Honest Abe dist., 1998—2000, exec. bd. mem. Abraham Lincoln coun., 1998—2004, coun. commr., 2003; mem. Big Bros./Big Sisters, I-Search for Children, Project Safeplace; treas., bd. dirs. Ctrl. Ill. Youth Svc. Bur., Ctrl. Ill. Workforce Prep.; vice chair Douglas County Tourism Com.; advisor Tuscola Tourism Com.; mem. Ill. Enterprise Zone Assn., Nat. Main St. Network; bd. mem. Ill. Rural Ptnrs., 1996—, membership chair, 1997—99; bd. dirs. Jacksonville Main St., 1998—; v.p. Sangamon County Reps., Operation Snowball. Recipient Charles Carter Meml. award InterFraternity Coun., 1984; named one of 40 Under 40 Springfield Bus. Jour., 2000. Mem.: Mid Am. InterFraternity Coun. Assn. (Outstanding State Coord. 1984, Outstanding Area V.P. 1985), Acad. Polit. Sci., Jacksonville Area Indsl. Corp. (sec. 1997—99), Mid-Am. Econ. Devel. Coun., Ill. Devel. Coun. (chmn. govt. affairs com. 1998—2000, bd. dirs. 2001—03, chair edn. com. 2002—), Cmty. Devel. Soc., Internat. Econ. Devel. Coun. (cert. bd. 2002—, bd. dirs. 2004—), Am. Econ. Devel. Coun. (bd. dirs. 2000—01), Am. Soc. Pub. Adminstrn., Order of Omega, Nat. Trust for Hist. Preservation, Rotary, Jacksonville Country Club, Springfield Jaycees, Beta Sigma Psi, Omicron Delta Epsilon. Lutheran. Home: 1225 W College Ave Jacksonville IL 62650-2214 Office: Jacksonville Regional Econ Devel Corp 200 W Douglas Ave Jacksonville IL 62650-2012 E-mail: mike@jredc.org.

KIRCHICK, WILLIAM DEAN, lawyer; b. Oceanside, NY, Nov. 20, 1950; s. Julian Gilbert and Jean (Kostinsky) K.; m. Carol Bonnie Rudnick, May 29, 1977; children: James Rory, Jeffrey Scott. BA in Polit. Sci. magna cum laude, U. Mich., 1973; JD cum laude, Boston Coll., 1976. Bar: Mass. 1978, Ill. 1976, U.S. Dist. Ct. Mass. 1978, U.S. Ct. Appeals (1st cir.) 1978, U.S. Tax Ct. 1976, U.S. Supreme Ct. 1982; accredited estate planner designation. Assoc. Arnstein, Gluck, Lehr & Milligan, Chgo., 1976-77; assoc., ptnr. Peabody &

Brown, Boston, 1977-88; ptnr. Bingham Dana LLP, Boston, 1988—2002, Bingham McCutchen LLP, Boston, 2002—. Mem. Boston Probate and Estate Planning Forum, 1987—, program events coord., 1989-90, moderator, 1990-91; mem. Boston Estate Planning Coun., 1986—, exec. com., 1989-92, sec. 1995-96, treas., 1996-97, v.p. 1997-98, pres.-elect, 1998-99, pres. 1999-2000; mem. Norfolk and Plymouth Bus. and Estate Planning Coun., 1990—; mem. Planned Giving Group of New Eng., Inc., 1997-; curriculum adv. com. for Mass. Continuing Legal Edn., Inc. Contbg. author: Estate and Protective Planning Techniques in Massachusetts, 1990, A Practical Guide to Estate Planning in Massachusetts, 1996, Preparing Estate Tax Returns, 1997, Drafting Wills and Trusts in Massachusetts, 2002; contbr. articles to profl. jours. Chmn. young lawyers team spl. events com. Combined Jewish Philanthropies of Greater Boston, Inc., 1982-84, chmn. young lawyers team, 1984-85, mem. lawyers team cabinet, 1985-89, 91-94; trustee The CJP Disabilities Trust, 1998--, The Acorn Found., 2000-03. Recipient Campaign Leadership award Combined Jewish Philanthropies of Greater Boston, Inc., 1984, Estate Planner of Yr. award Boston Estate Planning Coun., 2004. Fellow Am. Coll. Trust and Estate Counsel; mem. ABA (mem. sect. probate, trusts and real property), Mass. Bar Assn. (mem. tax sect. exec. com. 1989-92, probate sect. exec. com. 1992-93), Boston Bar Assn. (mem. estate planning com. 1981—, chmn. 1984-88, chmn. subcom. to study income, gift and estate tax proposals of Tax Reform Act of 1986 1985-86, chmn. subcom. on proposed temporary regulations concerning Chpt. 13 Internal Revenue Code 1988-89, mem. probate sect. 1978—), U. Mich. Club Greater Boston, Boston Coll. Law Sch. Alumni Assn. Phi Beta Kappa, Phis Eta Sigma. Avocations: jogging, swimming, walking, skiing. Office: Bingham McCutchen LLP 150 Federal St Fl 15 Boston MA 02110-1726 Office Phone: 617-951-8590. Business E-Mail: william.kirchick@bingham.com.

KIRCHMAN, ERIC HANS, lawyer; b. Washington, May 2, 1962; s. Charles Vincent and Erika Ottilie (Knoeppel) K.; m. Hillary Bronkie Hutson, Apr. 19, 1991; children: Erika B., Thomas E., Kristen N. BA, Univ. Md., 1985; JD, Univ. Balt., 1990. Bar: Md. 1990, U.S. Dist. Ct. Md. 1991, U.S. Ct. Appeals (4th cir.) 2000, U.S. Dist. Ct. D.C. 2005. Assoc. Hillel Abrams, Rockville, Md., 1990-92; ptnr. Kirchman & Kirchman, Wheaton, Md., 1992—. Of counsel Md. Coun. for Gifted and Talented Children, Inc., Silver Spring, 1994. With U.S. Army Reserve, 1985-98. Mem.: Montgomery County Bar Assn., Md. State Bar Assn. Office: Kirchman & Kirchman 11141 Georgia Ave Ste 403 Wheaton MD 20902-4659

KIRCHNER, JAMES WILLIAM, retired electrical engineer; b. Cleve., Oct. 17, 1920; s. William Sebastian and Marcella Louise (Stuart) K.; m. Eda Christene Landfear, June 11, 1950 (dec. May 1977); children: Kathleen Ann Kirchner Duda, Susan Lynn Kirchner Buonpane; m. Mary Jane Freebairn, Sept. 17, 2004; children: Lisa Ann Freebairn, Robert V. Freebairn III. BS in Elec. Engring., Ohio U., 1950, MS, 1951. Registered profl. engr., Ohio. Instr. elec. engring. Ohio U., Athens, 1950-52; mgr. liaison engring. Lear Siegler Inc., Maple Heights, Ohio, 1952-64; coordinator engring. services Case Western Res. U., Cleve., 1964-72, gen. mgr. Med. Ctr. Co. (CWRU), 1972-91; ret., 1991; sec. of corp. Thermagon, Inc., Cleve., 1992. Mem. Portage County Republican Exec. Com., 1961-62; treas. PTA, Aurora, Ohio, 1963-65, v.p., 1965-66; mem. The Ch. in Aurora, 1956—. Served with USAAF, 1942-45, PTO Mem. NSPE (life), IEEE (life), VFW (life), Ohio Soc. Profl. Engrs. (life), Cleve. Engring. Soc. (chmn. environ. com. 1976), Am. Soc. Engring. Edn. (life). Home: Reserves of Aurora 535 Treetop Ct Aurora OH 44202-7317 Personal E-mail: jwkfph@aol.com.

KIRCHNER, LISA BETH, actress, vocalist; b. L.A. d. Leon and Gertrude (Schoenberg) K. BA, Sarah Lawrence Coll., N.Y., 1975. Picture rschr. McGraw-Hill, 1985-87, John Wiley & Sons, 1988, Simon & Schuster/Globe Book Co., 1992—2000, Chelsea House Pubs., 1987-94, Oxford Univ. Press, 1997, Facts on File, 2001—02, Greenwood Pub. Co., 1997, Lazard Freres, 1998—, The Oryx Press, 1999—, Abbeville Press, 2001—02. Songwriter, BMI. Broadway appearances include The Threepenny Opera, 1975, The Human Comedy, 1985; off-Broadway appearances include the Radiant City, 1993, Hotel for Criminals, 1974, The American Imagination, others; TV shows include Songs From the Heart, Another World, The Guiding Light, As The World Turns, Out of Our Father's House; appearances at The White House and Gracie Mansion; performed as featured soloist and back-up singer with Judy Collins (numerous TV appearances); prodr., solo vocalist CD releases (Albany Records) entitled One More Rhyme, 1999, When Lights Are Low, 2002. Mem. AFTRA, SAG, BMI, Equity, Actor's Equity Assn. Avocations: painting, crafts, poetry. E-mail: kirchl@aol.com.

KIRCHNER, PETER THOMAS, nuclear medicine physician, educator, consultant; b. July 2, 1939; s. Elek and Julia (Kossy) K.; m. Mary Coleman Kirchner, Dec. 18, 1965; children: David, Annette, Julie. BA Physics, Yale U., 1960; MD, Columbia U., 1964. Diplomate Am. Bd. Internal Medicine, Am. Bd. Nuclear Medicine (sec. 1992-94, chmn. exem. com. 1991-94, vice chmn. 1994, 95). Intern, then resident, chief resident in internal medicine Nat. Naval Med. Ctr., Bethesda, Md., 1964-70; fellow in nuclear medicine Johns Hopkins U., Balt., 1970-72; head nuclear medicine Nat. Naval Med. Ctr., Bethesda, Md., 1972-77; asst. prof. radiology George Washington U., Washington, 1974-77; assoc. dir. nuclear medicine U. Chgo., 1978-81, assoc. prof. radiology, 1977-81, U. Iowa, Iowa City, 1981-84, prof. radiology, 1984—, prof. medicine, 1989—; dir. nuclear medicine U. Iowa Hosps. and Clinics, Iowa City, 1981-98; IPA contractee Dept. of Energy, Germantown, Md., 1998—. Mem. radiology study sect. NIH, 1995-99; bd. dirs. Joint Rev. Com. Nuclear Medicine Tech., exec. com., 1996—; mem. nat. adv. com. Nat. Isotope Ctr., Dept. Energy, 1996-98; mem. Accreditation Coun. for Grad. Med. Edn. Editor Nuclear Medicine Review Syllabus, 1980; co-editor Nuclear Medicine Self Study I, 1988, Self Study II, 1996; author more than 80 sci. articles, 12 book chpts. Ea. Iowa alumni schs.com. chair Yale U., 1989-94. Capt. USNR, 1963-92. Out Svc. Tng. grantee USN, 1970; recipient Von Hevessy award Hungarian Soc. Nuclear Medicine, 1993. Fellow ACP (hon.), Am. Coll. Nuc. Physicians (hon., chmn. quality assurance and practice cert. com. 1993-95, bd. regents 1993—), Am. Coll. Radiology (hon.); mem. Radiol. Soc. N.Am. (sci. program com. 1992-98), Inst. Clin. Positron Emission Tomography (bd. dirs. 1992-97, pres. 1993-94), Soc. Nuc. Medicine (exec. com. 1988-93, bd. dirs. 1993-97, house of dels. 1993—, chair sci. program com. 1988-90, v.p. 1992-93, pres. 1995-96, gen. program chair 1999—, bd. dirs. 1999—). Avocation: tennis.

KIRDANI, ESTHER MAY, retired school counselor; b. Nunda, N.Y., Aug. 27, 1936; d. Herbert Stewart and Sarah Edith (Veley) Stewart Kernahan; m. Rashad Y. Kirdani, Aug. 16, 1958; children: Lavinia Helen, Leila Andrea. BS in Home Econs. Edn., SUNY, Buffalo, 1958; EdM in Secondary Guidance, U. Buffalo, 1972. Permanent cert. home econs. edn. and secondary sch. guidance. Tchr. home econs. Royalton-Hartland (N.Y.) Ctrl. Sch., 1958-60; tchr. math. Grafton (Mass.) Jr. H.S., 1962-65, Clarence (N.Y.) Jr. H.S., 1967-68; sch. counselor West Seneca (N.Y.) Sch. Dist., 1973—2002; ret., 2002. Mem. ACA, Am. Sch. Counselor Assn., Western N.Y. Guidance Dirs. and Chairpersons (coord. 1987-94), Western N.Y. Sch. Counselors Consortium, Western N.Y. Sch. Counselors Assn. (Sch. Counselor of Yr. 2001-02). Avocations: gardening, travel, knitting, doll collecting. Home: 44 Buttonwood Ln East Amherst NY 14051-1642

KIRDAR, NEMIR AMIN, banker; b. Kirkuk, Iraq, Oct. 28, 1936; s. Amin and Nuzhet (Mohamad Ali) K.; m. Nada Adnan Shakir, Feb. 1, 1967; children: Rena, Serra. BA, Coll. of the Pacific, 1960; MBA, Fordham U., 1972; postgrad., Harvard U., 1979. Trainee, asst. treas., asst. v.p. Allied Bank Internat., N.Y.C., 1969-73; v.p. Nat. Bank N.Am., N.Y.C., 1973-74; v.p., head Gulf Div., Chase Manhattan Bank, N.Y.C., 1974-81; pres., chief exec. officer INVESTCORP Bank E.C., Manama, Bahrain, 1982—; also bd. dirs. Chmn. Advisory Council Center for Contemporary Arab Studies, Georgetown U. Contbr. articles to profl. jours. Trustee London Philharmonic Trust, London. Mem. Overseers Committee on University Resources, Harvard U., Bd. Advs. World Economic Forum, Switzerland, Internat. Bd. Councillors Center for Strategic and Internat. Studies, Washington, D.C., Visiting Committee Fordham U., visiting committee JFK Sch. of Govt., Harvard U., bd. Trustees Heart Research Found. N.Y.C.; Friend of Somerville, Somerville Coll. Oxford U. Clubs: Metropolitan. Office: Investcorp 37th Fl W 280 Park Ave Rm 37W New York NY 10017-1216 also: Investcorp PO Box 5340 Manama Bahrain

KIRGIS, FREDERIC LEE, law educator; b. Washington, Dec. 29, 1934; s. Frederic Lee Sr. and Kathryn Alice (Burrows) K.; children: Julianne, Paul Frederic. BA, Yale U., 1957; JD, U. Calif.-Berkeley, 1960. Bar: Colo. 1961, Va. 1983. Atty. Covington & Burling, Washington, 1964-67; from asst. prof. to prof. law U. Colo., Boulder, 1967-73; prof. law UCLA, 1973-78; from prof. law to prof. emeritus Washington & Lee U., Lexington, Va., 1978—2005, prof. emeritus, 2005—, dir. Frances Lewis Law Ctr., 1978-83, dean law sch., 1983-88. Author: International Organizations in their Legal Setting, 1977, 2d edit. 1993, Prior Consultation in International Law, 1983; contbr. articles to profl. jours. Pres. Maury River Soccer Club, Lexington, 1978-85. Served to capt. USAF, 1961-64 Recipient Deak award 1974; research fellow NATO, Brussels, 1978 Mem. Am. Soc. Internat. Law (v.p. 1985-87, sec. 1994—), Am. Law Inst., Internat. Law Assn. (Am. br.), Am. Jour. Internat. Law (bd. editors 1984-96, 98-2003, hon. editor 2003—), State Bar Va., Order of Coif. Democrat. Presbyterian. Home: 15 Grey Dove Rd Lexington VA 24450-2269 Office: Washington and Lee U Sch of Law Lexington VA 24450 Business E-Mail: kirgisr@wlu.edu.

KIRICK, DANIEL JOHN, agronomist; b. Port Jervis, N.Y., Nov. 8, 1953; s. Daniel and Mary Theresa Kirick; m. Jean Marie Guse, Sept. 27, 1986; children: Nicholas, John, Kristina, Kimberly. BA in Biology, History, U. Minn., Duluth, 1976; BS in Agronomy, U. Minn., St. Paul, 1977. Cert. profl. agronomist. Agronomist Delft (Minn.) Farm Chems., 1978, Skelly Fertilizer, Trimont, Minn., 1978-80, Mower County Svc. Co., Sargeant, Minn., 1980-86, Cenex Supply, Ellis, S.D., 1986-88, Rice (Minn.) Farm Supply, 1988-91, Kirick Agronomy Svcs., St. Cloud, Minn., 1992—. Mem. Comty. Edn. Devel. Adv. Coun., Sauk Rapids, Minn., 1990-94, Youth Devel. Bd., Sauk Rapids, 1990, Benton County Ext. Com., 1993-98, Ctrl. Minn. Forage Coun., 1994—. Mem. AAAS, Weed Sci. Soc. Am., Soil Sci. Soc. Am., Crop Sci. Soc. Am., Am. Soc. Agronomy. Roman Catholic. Home: PO Box 206 Rice MN 56367-0206 Office: Kirick Agronomy Svcs 9144 County Road 4 Saint Joseph MN 56374-9748

KIRILOVA, SVETLANA NIKOLOVA, psychologist, consultant; b. Vetrino, Bulgaria, Feb. 14, 1962; d. Nikola Stanev Nedelchev and Bistra Stankova Bodurova; m. Stanimir Naskov Kirilov, Nov. 12, 1990; 1 child, Atanas. MA in Psychology, Sofia U., 1988. Psychologist, cons. House of Creativity, Sofia, 1988-90; h.s. tchr. Vetrino, Bulgaria, 1990-93; psychologist Roli OOD, Sofia, 193-94, United Avio-Med. Rsch. Inst., Sofia, 1995-97; chief psychologist Bulgarian Air Forces, Sofia, 1997—. Psychology advisor Ministry of Def. Hdqrs. of Bulgarian Army, 1996—. Cons., image maker Presdl. Elections, Sofia, 1995; mem. Mensa Internat. 1st lt. Air Force, 1997-2000. Mem. AAAS. Avocations: archaeology, Eastern philosophy, martial arts. Home: 15127 NE 24th St PMB #484 Redmond WA 98052 E-mail: svetlanakirilova@hotmail.com.

KIRK, BALLARD HARRY THURSTON, architect; b. Williamsport, Pa., Apr. 1, 1929; s. Ballard and Ada May (DeLaney) K.; m. Vera Elizabeth Kitchener, Mar. 13, 1951; children: Lisa Lee, Kira Alexandria, Dayna Allison, Courtlandt Blaine. BArch, Ohio State U., 1959. Pres. Kirk Assocs., Architects, Columbus, Ohio, 1963—. Mem. Ohio Bd. Bldg. Standards, Columbus, 1973-78, 92-99; pres. Nat. Coun. Archtl. Registration Bds., Washington, 1983-84, Ohio Bd. Examiners Architects, Columbus, 1973-93; bd. dirs. Nat. Archtl. Accrediting Bd., Washington, 1986-89. Mem. AIA (bd. dirs. Columbus chpt. 1988-92), Coll. of Fellows. Republican. Mem. Brethern Ch. Home: 2557 Charing Rd Columbus OH 43221-3673 Office Phone: 614-486-7241. Personal E-mail: kirkarch@sbcglobal.net.

KIRK, CAROL, lawyer; b. Henry, Ill., Dec. 23, 1937; d. Howard P. and Mildred Root McQuilkin; m. Robert James Kirk, Aug. 20, 1961; children: Kathleen, Nancy, Sally. BS in Music Edn., U. Ill., 1960; JD, Ind. U., Indpls., 1989. Bar: Ind. 1989. Pvt. piano tchr., 1957-85; pub. sch. music tchr., 1960-62; dir. Ind. State Ethics Commn., Indpls., 1989-97; atty. and investigator Disciplinary Commn., Supreme Ct. Ind., Indpls., 1997—. Pres. Coun. on Govtl. Ethics Laws, (Internat.), 1993-94. Exec. editor Articles & Prodn. Ind. Law Rev., 1988-89. Mem. Met. Devel. Commn., Indpls., 1982-87; chairperson Pub. Radio Adv. Bd., Indpls., 1983-84, treas. Cmty. Svc. Coun., Indpls., 1988-91. Invitee to Nat. 4H Congress, Chgo., 1956; named 4H Family of Yr., Washington Twp., 4-H, Indpls., 1980, Vol. of Week, Voluntary Action Ctr., Indpls., 1980. Mem. LWV (pres. Indpls. 1979-83), Ind. Bar Assn., Indpls. Bar Assn., Phi Alpha Delta, Mu Phi Epsilon. Avocation: choir singing. Office: Discip Commn Supreme Ct Ind 1165 South Tower 115 W Washington St Indianapolis IN 46204-3420 E-mail: rkirk1937@aol.com.

KIRK, CASSIUS LAMB, JR., retired lawyer, investor; b. Bozeman, Mont., June 8, 1929; s. Cassius Lamb and Gertrude Violet (McCarthy) K. AB, Stanford U., 1951; JD, U. Calif., Berkeley, 1954. Bar: Calif. 1955. Assoc. Cooley, Godward, Castro, Huddleson & Tatum, San Francisco, 1956-60; staff counsel for bus. affairs Stanford U., 1960-78; chief bus. officer, staff counsel Menlo Sch. and Coll., Atherton, Calif., 1978-81; chmn. Eberli-Kirk Properties, Inc. (dba Just Closets), Menlo Park, 1981-94; ret. Faculty Coll. Bus. Adminstrn. U. Calif., Santa Barbara, summers 1967-73; past adv. bd. Allied Arts Guild, Menlo Park; past nat. vice-chmn. Stanford U. Annual Fund; past pres. Menlo Towers Assn.; endowed 2 professorships Stanford U., 2004 Past v.p. Palo Alto C. of C. With U.S. Army, 1954-56. Mem. VFW, Stanford Faculty Club, Order of Coif, Phi Alpha Delta. Republican. Home: 1330 University Dr Apt 52 Menlo Park CA 94025-4241

KIRK, CHARLOTTE LEIDECKER, director; b. Sheffield, Ala., Feb. 11, 1949; d. Boyd Frank and Mildred Wiley Leidecker; m. Clinton Dale Kirk, Sept. 8, 1967 (div. Mar. 1996); 1 child, Chad E. BS magna cum laude, Murray State U., 1976, MA in Edn., 1980, MA in Sch. Adminstrn., 1986. Kindergarten tchr. Crittenden County Bd. Edn., Marion, Ky., 1977—86; primary tchr. Ft. Thomas (Ky.) Bd. Edn., 1986—88, Harrodsburg (Ky.) Bd. Edn., 1988—89; spl. edn. cons. Ky. Dept. Edn., Frankfort, 1989—94; dir. state and fed. programs Hickman County Bd. Edn., Clinton, Ky., 1994—96; dir. spl. edn. McCracken County Bd. Edn., Paducah, Ky., 1996—2000; asst. supt. Hickman County Bd. Edn., Clinton, 2000—01; dir. spl. edn. Covington (Ky.) Bd. Edn., 2001—. Charter mem. Ky. Assn. Sch. Admin. Inst. for Women in Adminstrn., 1978—2002; pres., sec. Western Ky. Assn. Sch. Adminstr., Paducah, 1995—2000; mem. adv. bd. Ky. Dept. Juvenile Justice, Frankfort, 1998—2001; cons. Trimble County Bd. Edn., Bedford, Ky., 2003; com. mem. Devel. of Ky. Adminstrv. Regulations for Spl. Edn.; presenter Ky. Assn. Gifted Edn. Rec. sec. Marion (Ky.) Woman's Club, 1980—86. Mem.: Kappa Delta Phi, Phi Delta Kappa. Democrat. Baptist. Avocations: sailing, reading, golf. Home: 1204 Aspen Pines Dr Newport KY 41071 Office Phone: 859-392-1137.

KIRK, CONNIE ANN, writer; b. Wellsville, N.Y., Feb. 14, 1957; d. Leonard A. and Mary Arlene Lewis; m. Kenneth Andrew Kirk, May 21, 1983; children: Benjamin Lewis, Johnathan Patrick. BA in English and Creative Writing, Binghamton U., 1986, MA in English and Creative Writing, 1988, PhD in English and Creative Writing, 2004. Adj. prof. English Mansfield (Pa.) U., 1988—2004. Designer, tchr. 1st online English course Mansfield U. Author: (children's nonfiction) First Peoples: The Mohawks of North America, 2001, (young adult biography) J. K. Rowling: A Biography, 2003, Emily Dickinson: A Biography, 2004, Sylvia Plath: A Biography, 2004, (children's picture book) Sky Dancers, 2004. Mem.: MLA, Author's Guild, Soc. of Children's Book Writers and Illustrators, Am. Lit. Assn., Emily Dickinson Internat. Soc. Office: P O Box 337 Painted Post NY 14870

KIRK, DENNIS DEAN, lawyer; b. Pittsburg, Kans., Dec. 13, 1950; s. Homer Standley and Maida Corena (Rouse) K.; 1 child, Dennis Dean II. AA, Hutchinson Cmty. Jr. Coll., 1970; BS with distinction, No. Ariz. U., 1972; JD, Washburn U., 1975. Bar: Kans. 1975, U.S. Dist. Ct. Kans. 1975, D.C. 1977, U.S. Ct. Appeals (D.C. cir.) 1978, U.S. Supreme Ct. 1979, U.S. Ct. Appeals (5th cir.) 1981, U.S. Dist. Ct. Md. 1984, U.S. Tax Ct. 1984, U.S. Claims Ct. 1984, U.S. Ct. Appeals (fed. cir.) 1984, U.S. Ct. Mil. Appeals 1984, Va. 1990, U.S. Ct. Appeals (4th cir.) 1990; lic. pvt. investigator; lic. personal protection specialist. Trial atty. ICC, Washington, 1975-77; assoc. Goff, Sims, Cloud & Stroud, Washington, 1977-82; pvt. practice Washington, 1982-90; ptnr. Slocum, Boddie, Murry & Kirk, Falls Church, Va., 1990-93; pvt. practice Falls Church, Va., 1993—2005; spl. counsel to gen. counsel Pentagon U.S. Army, Washington, 2005—. Pres. Law Facilities, Inc., Washington, 1982-2005 Vol. parole and probation officer Shawnee County, Kans., 1973-74; citizens adv. task force group Md. Nat. Park and Planning Commn., 1978-80; citizens task force on gen. plan amendments study Fairfax County Coun., Va., 1981-82; active Seven Corners Task Force, Fairfax County, 1981-82, chmn. transp. and housing subcoms.; pres. Seven Springs Tenants Assn., College Park, Md., 1976-80, Ravenwood Park Citizens Assn., 1981-82; dir. Greenwood Homes, Inc., Fairfax County Dept. Housing and Cmty. Devel., 1983—2005; mem. gala com. Spotlight the Kennedy Ctr., Pres. Adv. Com. on the Arts, 1986-87, Mason Dist. Rep. Com., 1981-91, Fairfax County Young Reps., Fairfax County Rep. Com., 1982—; founding chmn., charter mem. Mason Dist. Jaycees, 1984-86; sec., gen. counsel, bd. dirs. U.S. Assocs. for the Cultural Triangle in Sri Lanka, 1983-90; commr. Consumer Protection Commn., Fairfax County, 1982—, chmn., 1996-97; vice chmn., 2004, towing adv. bd. Fairfax County, 1993-; Ravenwood precinct chmn. Rep. Orgn., Falls Church, 1982-90, 94—2005; bd. dirs. PTA Baileys Elem. Magnet Sch., 1995-99, v.p., 1996-97; spl. litigation coun. Pa. Bush-Cheny '04. Named to Honorable Order Ky. Cols. Mem. ABA, NRA (life), Am. Fedn. Musicians (life, emeritus), Assn. Former Intelligence Officers, Masons (Grand Sword Bearer 1992), Shriners, Tall Cedars, Scottish Rite, Moose, Royal Arch, Rep. Nat., Rep. Nat. Lawyers Assn. (adv. coun.), Rep. Nat. Com. (life), Phi Kappa Phi, Phi Alpha Delta (nat. capital area alumni chpt. justice 1984-86, 94-96) Methodist. Avocation: music. Home: 6315 Anneliese Dr Falls Church VA 22044-1620 Office: Office Gen Counsel US Army 104 Army Pentagon 3C546 Washington DC 20310-0104 Office Phone: 703-695-1277. Business E-Mail: dennis.kirk@hqda.army.mil.

KIRK, DONALD, journalist; b. New Brunswick, NJ, May 7, 1938; s. Rudolf and Clara (Marburg) K.; m. Susanne Smith, May 31, 1965 (div.); m. Emiko Hayashi, Dec. 12, 1985 (div.); children: James Paul, John Winston, Christian Daryl. AB, Princeton U., 1959; MA, U. Chgo., 1965; postgrad. (Ford Found. fellow), Columbia U., 1964-65. Reporter Chgo. Sun-Times, 1960-61, N.Y. Post, 1961-64; free lance corr., writer, 1965—; Asia corr. Washington Star, 1967-70; Far East corr. Chgo. Tribune, 1971-74, N.Y. and UN corr., 1975-76; world editor, spl. corr. USA Today, 1982-90; Seoul corr. Internat. Herald Tribune, 1998—2003. Vis. fellow Cornell U., Ithaca, N.Y., 1986-88; Fulbright rschr., Philippines, 1995-96. Author: Wider War: The Struggle for Cambodia, Thailand and Laos, 1971, Tell It To The Dead: Memories of a War, 1975, Korean Dynasty: Hyundai and Chung Ju Yung, 1994, Tell It To The Dead: Stories of a War, 1996, Looted: The Philippines After the Bases, Business Guide to the Philippines, 1998, Korean Crisis: Unraveling of the Miracle in the IMF Era, 2000. Recipient Page One award Chgo. Newspaper Guild, 1960; citations Overseas Press Club, 1967, 72, 73, Best Asia article award 1974; George Polk Meml. award for fgn. reporting, 1975, Fulbright scholar, New Delhi, India, 1962-63; Edward R. Murrow fellow Coun. Fgn. Rels., N.Y.C., 1974-75. Mem. Am. Soc. Journalists and Authors, Soc. Profl. Journalists. Clubs: Nat. Press (Washington); Overseas Press (N.Y.C.); Fgn. Corrs. (Hong Kong); Internat. House of Japan. Home: 4343 Davenport St NW Washington DC 20016-4513

KIRK, EDGAR LEE, retired musician, educator; b. Harrisburg, Pa., May 28, 1923; s. Arthur Lee and Bertha May (Berthel) K.; m. Ellen Calhoun Gray, June 18, 1947; children: Arthur Lee, Douglas Gray. MusB, Eastman Sch. Music, U. Rochester, 1947, MusM, 1948, PhD, 1957. Mem. faculty Mich. State U., East Lansing, 1948-89, now emeritus, prof. bassoon, chmn. applied music, 1973-89, chmn. grad. studies, 1978-87, dir. admissions dept. music, 1982, assoc. chmn., 1987-88; prof. bassoon Eastman Sch. Music, U. Rochester, summers, 1954-65; instr. bassoon Interlochen Arts Acad., 1975-79; ret., 1989. Bassoonist, Rochester (N.Y.) Philharmonic Orch., 1946-47, 54-55, staff bassoonist, radio sta. WHAM, Rochester, 1947-48, 1st bassoonist, Lansing (Mich.) Symphony Orch., 1960-73, 87-89, mem., Richards Woodwind Quintet, 1965-88; Rec. artist: Wind Quintets of Peter Muller, Crystal Records, Anton Reicha, Wind Quintets Opus 99, No. 2 and Opus 100, No. 6, Mus. Heritage Soc. With U.S. Army, 1943-46. Mem. Internat. Double Reed Soc. (pres. 1973-74) Home: 1281 Scott Dr East Lansing MI 48823-5213 Business E-Mail: kirk1@msu.edu.

KIRK, JACKIE, artist, educator; b. Oakland, Calif., July 28, 1929; d. Arthur and Naomi Randolph Karbach; m. Neal Kirk (div.); children: Bobbi Keene, Tom; m. Philip Rosenfeld. A, U. Minn., 1949; B, Sonoma State Univ., Santa Rosa, Calif., 1970; M, U. Calif., Davis, 1975. Painting tchr. Coll. of Marin, Kentfield, Calif., 1979—87, U. Calif., Santa Cruz, 1985—98, Sonoma State Univ., 1986—88, U. Calif., Carmel, 1988; pvt. painting tchr. Calif., 1989—2000; painting tchr. San Quentin (Calif.) State Prison, 1998. Lectr. U. Calif., Santa Cruz, Theatre Artaud, San Francisco, 1990, Kaiser Hosp., Oakland, 1991, Calif. Palace of Legion of Honor, San Francisco, 1991, Soc. Arts in Health Care, Greenbrae, Calif., 1994. One-woman shows include San Francisco Palace of Legion of Honor, 1991, Duke U. Mus. Art, 1996, exhibited in group shows at Butler Inst. Art, Youngstown, Ohio, Represented in permanent collections San Francisco Palace of Legion of Honor, Women's Mus. Art, Washington, California Nature Series (Purchase award San Francisco Art Commn., 1988); author: Witness: The Artist's Vision in the Face of AIDS, The Story of Bird. Grantee The Flow Fund, 1995; Individual Artists grantee, Marin Arts Coun., 1991. Home: 53 Taylor Dr # 318 Fairfax CA 94930

KIRK, JANE SEAVER, municipal government administrator; b. Boston, May 12, 1928; d. Howard Wesley and Ruth (Seaver) K. BA, Duke U., 1950; MS, Springfield (Mass.) Coll., 1956. Ctr. dir. ARC, Korea, Japan, France, Morocco, 1951-60; dep. dir. internat. group YMCA of the U.S.A., Chgo., 1961-93; chair selectmen Town of Nelson, NH, 1997—. Bd. dirs. N.E. Delta Dental, Concord, NH, 1998—; incorp Monadnock Family Svcs., 2001—02. Trustee Hist. Soc. Cheshire County, Keene, NH, 1995—2001, Springfield Coll., 1973—2000; pres. Granite Lake Assn., Munsonville, NH, 1995—2000; bd. dirs. Duke Ctr. for Living, Durham, NC, 1995—2001. Recipient Fundraising Achievement award N.Am. YMCA Devel. Officers, 1991. Mem. AAUW, DAR, ARCOA, NAFYR, Daus. of Founders and Patriots, Order Eastern Star, Union League Club Chgo., Coll. Club of Boston, Descendants of Colonial Clergy, Women's Aux., Mass. Ancient and Honorable Artillery Co., Edmund Rice (1638) Assn., Ladies Charitable Soc., Bay State African Violet Soc., Walpole Hist. Soc., Rotary Club of Keene (Paul Harris fellow), Phi Beta Kappa. Republican. Baptist. Avocations: photography, gardening, travel, walking. Home: 543 Granite Lake Rd Nelson NH 03457-5121 Personal E-mail: janekirk@msn.com.

KIRK, JILL, management consultant; BA, U. Oreg. Corp. dir. human resources/orgnl. devel. Tektonix, Inc., group human resources mgr.; dir. cmty. affairs Tektronix, Inc., 1994; exec. dir. Tektronix Found., 1991; founder The Kirk Group LLC, 1999—; ptnr. Lindberg/Kirk/Millar, 2000—; v.p. Oreg. Bus. Coun., 2005—. Mem. bd. dirs., exec. bd., govt. affairs com. Am. Electronics Assn.; bd. dirs. Associated Oreg. Industries; chair deputies com. Oreg. Bus. Coun., vice chair edn. com., mem. higher edn. task force, mem. pub. fin. com. Mem. Oreg. State Bd. Edn., 1996—, chairperson, 2001—, mem. exec. com., mem. joint bds. working group, mem. econ. devel. joint bds. working group; trustee Portland Art Mus., 1998—2001, 2001—; mem. adv. com. Portland Ctr. for the Performing Arts; bd. dirs. Portland Youth Philharm.; mem. strategic planning com. United Way Columbia-Willamette; active Oreg. Profl. Devel. Coun.; bd. chair Lintner Ctr. for Advanced Edn.; active Govs. Task Force on Higher Edn., Govs. Task Force on Quality Edn.;

bd. dirs. Japanese Garden Soc., 2001, STARS, Portland Edn. Network, N.W. Bus. for Culture and the Arts, Nat. Alliance Bus. Western Region. Mem.: Portland C. of C. (bd. dirs.). Office: Oreg Bus Coun 1100 SW 6th Ave Ste 1608 Portland OR 97204-1090

KIRK, JOHN MACGREGOR, lawyer; b. Flint, Mich., Mar. 9, 1938; s. R. Dean and Berenice E. (Mac Gregor) K.; m. Carol Lasko, June 8, 1971; children: John M. Jr., Caroline Dwyer. BA, Washington & Lee U., 1960, LLB, 1962; LLM in Taxation, NYU, 1967. Bar: Mich. 1962, U.S. Ct. Mil. Appeals 1966, U.S. Supreme Ct. 1966, U.S. Tax Ct. 1969, U.S. Dist. Ct. (ea. dist.) Mich. 1982, U.S. Ct. Appeals (6th cir.) 1983. Trial atty. tax divsn. U.S. Dept. Justice, Washington, 1967-72; assoc. Boyer & Briggs, Bloomfield Hills, Mich., 1972-74; ptnr. Butzel, Long, Gust, Klein & Van Zile, Detroit, 1975-78; mem. Meyer, Kirk, Snyder & Lynch P.L.L.C., Bloomfield Hills, 1978—. Mem., past pres. Friends of Baldwin Pub. Libr., Birmingham, Mich., 1972—. Mem. ABA, State Bar Mich., Oakland County Bar Assn., Detroit Bar Assn., Birmingham Rotary, Walloon Yacht Club (treas., past commodore 1960-2004). Republican. Presbyterian. Home: 4350 Yale Ct Bloomfield Hills MI 48302-1669 Office: Meyer Kirk Snyder and Lynch PLLC 100 W Long Lake Rd Ste 100 Bloomfield Hills MI 48304-2773 E-mail: jkirk@meyerkirk.com.

KIRK, JOHN ROBERT, JR., lawyer; b. Stuart, Va., June 21, 1935; s. John Robert and Mary Elise (Mustaine) K.; m. Margarite Conover Kirk; children: Karen Louise, Laura Elise, Rebecca Elizabeth. Student, Rice Inst., 1953-56; BSChemE, U. Tex., 1959; JD, U. Houston, 1966. Bar: Tex. 1966, U.S. Patent and Trademark Office 1967, U.S. Supreme Ct. 1973, U.S. Dist. Ct. (so. dist.) Tex. 1974, U.S. Ct. Claims 1975, U.S. Dist. Ct. (no. dist.) Tex. 1977, U.S. Ct. Appeals (5th cir.) 1980, U.S. Ct. Appeals (11th cir.) 1981, U.S. Ct. Appeals (Fed. cir.) 1983. Patent atty. Jefferson Chem. Co., Houston, 1966-69; mgr. patent divsn., 1969-72; mem. Pravel, Gambrell, Hewitt, Kirk & Kimball, P.C., Houston, 1972-84; ptnr., 1973-84, Baker & Kirk, P.C., 1984-87, Baker, Kirk & Bissex, P.C., 1987-90, Baker, Kirk & Lindsay, P.C., 1990-93, Jenkens & Gilchrist, 1993—. Dir. Nat. Inventors Hall of Fame Found, Inc., 1979-82, 87-97, treas., 1983-84, v.p., 1984-86, pres., 1986-87; adv. bd. Intellectual Property Law Program U. Houston, 1991-2000, John Marshall Law Sch., 1999—, chair; adv. bd. Gulf Coast Regional Small Bus. Devel. Ctr., 1994—2004, Tex. Mfg. Assistance Ctr., Inc., 1995—. Lt. USMCR, 1958-60. Fellow: Coll. State Bar Tex., Houston Bar Found. (life), Tex. Bar Found. (life); mem.: ABA (com. chmn. 1982—90, intellectual property law sect. coun. 1990—94, vice chmn. 1994—95, chmn. 1996—97, com. chmn. sect. on specialization 2002—03, standing com. on specialization 2002—05), Am. Intellectual Property Law Assn., State Bar Tex. (chair intellectual property law sect. 1977—78), Nat. Inventive Thinking Assn. (adv. dir. 1990—2000), Licensing Exec. Soc., Houston Bar Assn., Houston Intellectual Property Law Assn. (bd. govs. 1986—92, pres. 1990—91), Commn. of Patents Edn. Roundtable (commr. 1987—95), Nat. Coun. Intellectual Property Law Assns. (vice chmn. 1986—87, chmn. 1987—88), Garden of the Gods Club, Lakeside Country Club, Union League Club Chgo. Republican. Baptist. Office: 1401 McKinney St Ste 2600 Houston TX 77010-4035 Office Phone: 713-951-3388. E-mail: jkirk@jenkens.com.

KIRK, LYNDA POUNDS, biofeedback therapist, neurotherapist, counselor; b. Corpus Christi, Tex., Dec. 17, 1946; d. James Arthur and Elizabeth Pauline (Sanders) Pounds; children: Leslie Jennifer, Edward Christopher. BA, U. Tex., Austin, 1977; MA, St. Edwards U., 1996. Lic. profl. counselor. Therapist Austin (Tex.) State Hosp., 1977-80; dir. stress mgmt. The Hills Med./Sports Complex, Austin, 1980-82; founder, owner Austin Biofeedback Ctr., 1982—, Health Mastery Concepts, Austin, 1982—, Optimal Performance Inst., 2000—; CEO Healthy Life Options, Inc., Austin, 1998—. Cons. State of Tex., Austin, 1983—, City of Austin, 1985—, Lower Colo. River Authority, Austin, 1984—. Author: (book/cassette series) Regenerative Relaxation, 1981; Urological Applications of Biofeedback, Stress Mastery and Peak Performance, 1986. Bd. dirs. South Austin Civic Club, 1983—, pres., 1987; bd. dirs., treas. Texans for the Preservation of Hist. Structures, 1990—; bd. dirs. Austin Ctr. for Attitudinal Healing, 1992—. Fellow Biofeedback Cert. Inst. Am. (sr.), Internat. Soc. for Neuronal Regulation (pres. 1997-98); mem. Assn. Applied Psychophysiology and Biofeedback (pres. 2003-2004, found. bd. 2005), Internat. Soc. for Study of Subtle Energies and Energy Medicine, Biofeedback Soc. Tex. (pres. 1995-97, exec. bd., citation award 1989), Behavioral Medicine Soc. Am., Am. Holistic Med. Assn., Diplomate Cert. Quantitative Electroencephalography Technologists, Acad. Cert. Neurotherapists, Phi Beta Kappa Episcopalian. Avocations: jogging, snorkeling, mountain biking, designs for world peace. Home: 420 Brady Ln Austin TX 78746-5502 Office: Austin Biofeedback Ctr 3624 N Hills Dr Ste B205 Austin TX 78731-3061

KIRK, MARK STEVEN, congressman; b. Champaign, Ill., Sept. 15, 1959; s. Francis Gabriel and Judith Ann (Brady) Kirk; m. Kimberly Vertolli. BA, Cornell U., 1981; MS, London Sch. of Econs., 1982; JD, Georgetown U., 1992. Bar: Ill. 1992, D.C. 1993. Parliamentary aide Julian Critchley, London, 1982-83; chief of staff U.S. Rep. John Porter, Washington, 1984-90; officer World Bank, Washington, 1990; spl. asst. to asst. sec. of state US Dept. State, Washington, 1991-93; atty. Baker & McKenzie, Washington, 1993-95; counsel Ho. Internat. Rels. Com., Washington, 1995-99; mem. U.S. Congress from 10th Ill. dist., Washington, 2001—; mem. armed svcs. com., transp. and infrastructure com., budget com.; mem. Ho. appropriations com. Bd. dirs. Population Resource Ctr., Princeton, N.J. Contbr. articles to various newspapers. Organizer Bush/Quayle Campaign, No. Ill., 1988, Dole for Pres., 1988, various states; campaigner Porter for Congress, No. Ill., 1984-90. Lt. USNR, 1989—. Kellogg Fellow, Chgo., 1980, Radm James Fellow, Washington, 1984; recipient Coun. of Jewish Fedn. award Washington, 1988. Mem. Navy League, Naval Res. Assn., New Trier Rep. Orgn. Republican. Presbyterian. Avocations: backpacking, skydiving. Office: 1531 Longworth Ho Office Bldg Washington DC 20515 Home: 275 Whistler Rd Highland Park IL 60035-5947

KIRK, NANCY A., state legislator, nursing home administrator; m. Henry Kirk. BS, Ill. State U., 1964; MSW, U. Kans., 1976. Nursing home adminstr.; mem. from dist. 56 Kans. State Ho. of Reps., Topeka. Address: 932 SW Frazier Ave Topeka KS 66606-1948

KIRK, REA HELENE (REA HELENE GLAZER), special education educator; b. N.Y.C., Nov. 17, 1944; d. Benjamin and Lillian (Kellis) Glazer; 3 stepdaughters. BA, UCLA, 1966; MA, Ea. Mont. Coll., 1981; EdD, U. So. Calif., 1995. Cert. spl. edn. tchr., Calif., Mont. Spl. edn. tchr., L.A., 1966-73; clin. sec. speech and lang. clinic Missoula, Mont., 1973-75; spl. edn. tchr. Missoula, Gt. Falls, Mont., 1975-82; br. mgr. YWCA of L.A., Beverly Hills, Calif., 1989-91; sch. adminstrn., ednl. coord. Adv. Schs. of Calif., 1991-94; dir. Woman's Resource Ctr., Gt. Falls, Mont., 1981-82, Battered Woman's Shelter, Rock Springs, Wyo., 1982-84, Battered Woman's Program, Sweetwater County, Wyo., 1984-88, San Gabriel Valley, Calif., 1988; with Spl. Edn., Pasadena, 1994-96, prin., 1995; asst. prof. U. Wis., Platteville, 1996—2003, assoc. prof., 2003—. Mem. Wyo. Commn. Aging, Rock Springs; vis. prof. U. Wuhan, China, 2003—04, Miss. Valley State U., Itta Bena, 2005; adv. bd. New Tchr. Advocate. Pres., bd. dir. battered woman's shelter, Gt. Falls; pres. Women's Resource Ctr., Gt. Falls, Religious Congregation, Rock Springs; founder, advisor Rape Action Line, Gt. Falls; founder Jewish religious svcs., Missoula; 4-H leader; hostess Friendship Force; Friendship Force ambassador, Wyo., Fed. Republic Germany, Italy; v.p. Coun. Devel. Disabilities, Wis.; bd. dir. Coun. Children with Behavior Disorders, Wis., Family Advocates, Platteville, 1996—; organizer Women's Readers Theater, Platteville, Wis.; active YWCA Mont. and Wyo., Cmty. Action Bd. City of LA. Recipient Gladys Byron scholar U. So. Calif., 1993, Dept. Edn. scholar U. So. Calif., 1994, honors Missoula 4-H, Underkoffler Tchg. Excellence award U. Wis., 2000, named advisor of yr., 2000, nominee, 2003, 04, 05; recognized as significant Wyo. woman as social justice reformer and peace activist Sweetwater County, Wyo.; nominated Wyo. Woman of the Yr., 1981, 82; honored by L.A. Mayor Bradley for Anti-Poverty work. Mem. Coun. for Exceptional Children (v.p. Gt. Falls 1981-82, bd. dir., Professionally Recognized Spl. Educator 1998), Wis. Coun. Exceptional Children (bd. dir., pres. S.W. region), Wis. Divsn. Mentally Retarded/Developmentally Disabled), Wis. Assn. Children with Behavior Disorders, Assn. Children with Learning Disabilities (Named Outstanding Mem. 1982), Pioneer Svc. Club (adv.), Phi Delta Kappa, Delta Kappa Gamma (sec. 2002—), Phi Kappa Phi, Kappa Delta Pi (co-counselor 2000—, sec. 2002—), Pi Lamda Theta. Office Phone: 608-342-1279. Business E-Mail: kirkr@uwplatt.edu.

KIRK, RICHARD DILLON, lawyer; b. Washington, Jan. 23, 1953; s. William Edward and Mary Elizabeth (Dillon) K.; m. Bridget Louise Stillwagon, June 27, 1981; children: Catherine Dillon, Suzanne Grace. AB, Georgetown U., 1975; JD, U. Va., 1978. Bar: Del. 1978, U.S. Dist. Ct. Del. 1980, U.S. Ct. Appeals (3rd cir.) 1984, U.S. Supreme Ct. 1984. Law clk. Del. Supreme Ct., Wilmington, 1978-79; assoc. Richards, Layton & Finger, Wilmington, 1979-82; dep. atty. gen. Del. Dept. Justice, Wilmington, 1982-84; assoc. Morris, James, Hitchens & Williams, Wilmington, 1984-86, ptnr., 1987—. Mem. Del. State Bar Assn. (pres. 1993-94, New Lawyers Disting. Svc. award 1988). Democrat. Roman Catholic. Office: Morris James Hitchens & Williams 222 Delaware Ave Wilmington DE 19801-1621 E-mail: rkirk@morrisjames.com.

KIRK, SHERWOOD, retired librarian; b. Kermit, W.Va., July 12, 1924; s. James Douglas and Magdalene (Elkins) Kirk; m. Ora Ward, Jan. 9, 1958; children: Diana, James Sherwood, Philip Lindsey. Student, Mich. State U., 1944; AB, U. Ky., 1949; postgrad., U. Ill., 1949-50. Student asst. U. Ky., 1946-49; circulation asst. U. Ill., 1949-51; head reference and circulation Marshall U., 1951-52; sr. asst., agrl. libr. U. Neb., 1952-54; spl. project asst. Nat. Agr. Libr., Washington, 1954-55; reference asst., liaison loan div. Libr. Congress, 1955-56, catalog asst., 1956-57; coord. pub. libr. svcs. Ky. Dept. Librs., Frankfort, 1957-63, asst. state libr., 1963-69; state libr. Fla., 1969-71; assoc. dir. libr. ops. Ill. State Libr., Springfield, 1971-82; exec. dir. Western Ill. Libr. System, Monmouth, 1982-94; delivery cons. Alliance Libr. Sys., 1994-95, Galesburg, Ill., 1994-95; ret., 1995. Mem. Ky. Gov.'s Planning Com. Librs., 1968; scholarship com. Ill. State Libr.; chmn. com. libr. svc. to state govt. Fla. Sec. of State, 1970; pres. Ill. Book Pac; vol. cataloger Bartow Fla. Pub. Libr.; adv. com. libr. svcs. and constrn. Fla. State Libr.; sec., adv. com. edn. Resource Sharing Alliance W. Ctrl. Ill.; bd. dirs. Friends of Lincoln Libr., Springfield, Ill., 1977—, Aledo-Mercer Carnegie Pub. Libr. Dist., 1997—. Recipient plaques for outstanding libr., Ky. Libr. Trustee Assn., 1968. Mem.: ALA (coun. 1967—69), Assn. State Libr. Agys. (administrv. bd.), Ill. Libr. Assn. (chmn. local arrangement 1974, mem. bicentennial com. 1974—, mem. legis.-libr. devel. com., chair pub. policy com. 1991, Robert R. McClarren Legis. award 1990), Fla. Libr. Assn., Ky. Libr. Assn. (pres. 1965—66), Springfield Lit. Club (pres. 1972), Optimist, Shriners, Masons. Home: 527 Eastlake Dr Haines City FL 33844-6339 E-mail: kirk@ithink.net, sherd@copper.net.

KIRK, SUSANNE SMITH, editor; b. Washington; d. Harold Clair and Theodora Smith; m. Donald Kirk, 1965 (div. 1985); m. Samuel Alexander Tomlinson III, 1989. Student, Kaiserin-Theophanu Sch., Cologne, W.Ger., 1958; AB, Smith Coll., 1963; cert., Goethe Inst., Berlin, 1963; MS, Columbia U., 1965. Reporter South China Morning Post, Hong Kong, 1965-67; corr. German News Agy., Saigon, Vietnam, 1968-69; editor Charles Tuttle Pubs., Tokyo, 1972-74; freelance journalist, 1965-74; asst. editor Charles Scribner's Sons (now Scribner div. Simon & Schuster), N.Y.C., 1975, editor, 1976-80, asst. v.p., 1977-98, fgn. rights dir., 1978-82, sr. editor, 1980-85, exec. editor, 1985—2004, v.p., exec. editor, 1998—2004, editl. cons., 2004—. Spkr. various writers' confs. Contbr. articles to newspapers. Mem. Mystery Writers Am. (Ellery Queen award 2000), Crime Writers Assn. (U.K.), Internat. Assn. Crime Writers, Snarks Ltd. (N.Y.C., v.p. 1983-84, pres. 1985-86), Columbia Club, Pilgrimage Garden Club (Natchez), Smith Coll. Club (N.Y.C.). Home: PO Box 2056 Natchez MS 39121-2056 Personal E-mail: suskirk@aol.com.

KIRK, THOMAS GARRETT, JR., librarian; b. Phila., Aug. 2, 1943; s. Thomas Garrett and Bertha (C.) K.; m. Elizabeth B. Walter, Aug. 29, 1964; children: Jennifer E., Cynthia M., Kristen A. BA, Earlham Coll., Richmond, Ind., 1965; MA, Ind. U., 1969; postgrad., Drexel U., 1987-88. Sci. libr. Earlham Coll., 1965-79; libr. cons. Richmond, Ind., 1972—; acting dir. librs. U. Wis., Parkside, Kenosha, 1979-80; dir. libr. Berea (Ky.) Coll., 1980-94, Earlham (Ind.) Coll., 1994-2000, dir. librs., coord. info. svcs., 2001—. Vis. instr. Ind. U. Libr. Sch., summers 1977, 78; bd. dirs SOLINET, 1981-84, 85-86, treas., 1982-84; bd. dirs. Ky. Libr. Network, 1985-87, 91-93, OCLC Mems. Coun., 1986-92, 1999-2005, exec. com. 2001-02, mem. standing joint com. on membership, 2003-05, mem. fin. com., 2003—05; v.p. Pvt. Acad. Libr. Network Ind., 1995-96, pres., 1996-97, 2005—, OCLC Strategic Directions and Governance Adv. Com., 2000-01; adv. bd. OCLC Coll. and Univ. Librs., 1995-98. Author: Library Research Guide to Biology, 1978, College Libraries in Encyclopedia Library of Information Science, 2003; editor: Course-related Library and Literature Instruction, 1979, Increasing the Teaching Role of Academic Libraries, 1984; editl. bd. Coll. and Rsch. Librs., 1996-2002, Internet Reference Svcs. Quar., 1996-2002, Info. Literacy Adv. Comm., 2000-02. Mem. steering com. Coll. Libr. Dirs. Mentor Program, 2002—; mem. adv. com. Midwest Instr. Tech. Ctr., 2002—; mem. exec. com. Acad. Librs. Ind., 2003—05; sr. advisor Coun. Ind. Colls., 2003—. Mem. ALA (coun. 1986-90), Assn. Coll. Rsch. Librs. (v.p., pres.-elect 1992-93, pres. 1993-94, exec. com. 1984-85, 86-90, 92-95, rep. to Coalition for Networked Info. 1990-95, Miriam Dudley Bibliog. Instrn. Libr. of Yr. award 1984, Acad./Rsch. Libr. of Yr. 2004), Inst. for Info. Literacy (adv. com. 1998-2003, chair 2001-03), Ind. Libr. Fedn., Ind. Coop. Libr. Svcs. Authority (exec. com. 1999-2001), Ky. Libr. Assn. (Acad. Libr. of Yr. award 1984), Phi Kappa Phi. Mem. Soc. Of Friends. Office: Earlham Coll Lilly Libr Richmond IN 47374 Office Phone: 765-983-1360. Business E-Mail: kirkto@earlham.edu.

KIRKBY, MAURICE ANTHONY, oil industry executive; b. Southwell, Notts, U.K., Apr. 12, 1929; emigrated to Can., 1983; s. George Sydney and Rose (Marson) K.; m. Muriel Beatrice Longmire, 1954; children: Peter Michael, Susan Margaret. BA with 1st class honors in Mech. Sci., King's Coll., Cambridge, Eng., 1952, MA, 1955. Chief petroleum engr. Brit. Petroleum Co. p.l.c., London, 1969-74, gen. mgr. exploration and prodn. dept., 1976-80, dirs.' support staff, 1982-83; gen. mgr. BP Petroleum Devel., Aberdeen, Scotland, 1974-76; sr. v.p. oil and gas Standard Oil Co., Cleve., 1980-82; pres., chief exec. officer, dir. BP Can. Inc., Calgary, Alta., Can., 1983-88; chmn., chief exec. officer Hope Brook Gold Inc., Calgary, Alta., Can., 1986-88; dep. chmn. N.Am. Gas Investment Trust, London, 1989-95. Contbr. articles to profl. jours. Mem. Bus. Council on Nat. Issues, Ottawa, Ont., Can., 1983-88. Served with RAF, 1947-49. Fellow Inst. Mining and Metallurgy (dir. 1980), Royal Acad. Engring.; mem. Inst. Mech. Engrs., Soc. Petroleum Engrs. (dir. 1980, 81-83).

KIRK-DUGGAN, MICHAEL ALLAN, retired law, economics and computer sciences educator; b. Stevens Point, Wis., Dec. 15, 1931; s. Frank E. and Dorothy Ada (Darrow) Duggan; m. Shirley M. Spencer, July 1956 (div. Jan. 1981); children: Michelle, Cheryl, Michael, Christopher, Robert, Siobhan, Mary; m. Cheryl Ann Kirk, Jan. 1, 1983. BS in Math., Coll. Holy Cross, 1953; postgrad., U. Minn., 1953—55; JD, LLB, Boston Coll., 1956; M in Patent Law, Georgetown U., 1959. Bar: Mass. 1956, U.S. Supreme Ct. 1961; qualified trial/def. counsel Gen. Cts. Martial, 1965; cert. cmty. based conflict resolution, 1994. Sr. engr. Sylvania Programming Lab., Needham, Mass., 1960—61; trial atty. antitrust divsn. U.S. Dept. Justice, 1961—67; asst. prof. econs. Whittemore Sch. U. N.H., Durham, 1967—69; comdr. U.S. Naval Intelligence Res., 1956—78; adminstrv. judge Atomic Safety and Licensing Bd. Panel, Washington, 1972—89; prof. bus. law and computer scis. U. Tex., Austin, 1969—93, prof. emeritus, 1993—. Apptd. adv. procurator Tribunal, Diocese of Raleigh, 1995-97, 2004—; editor-in-chief Computing Revs., N.Y.C., 1969-74. Author: Antitrust & U.S. Supreme Court, 1829-1984, 1984, Computer Utility, 1972, Law and the Computer, 1973, Paul Robeson Movies and Discography, 1998, Amazon Reviews; editor: Legal Developments, Jour. Mktg., 1967-93, Legal Comments; contbr. articles to profl. jours. Head profs. Johnson, Durham, 1968; vol. IRS Vol. Income Tax Assistance, 1993—97; del. Tex. Dem. Com., Austin, Tex., 1972; eucharistic min., lector and lay pres. St. Columba Cath. Ch., Oakland, Calif., 1997—2004, Holy Cross Cath. Ch., Durham, NC, 1993—97, 2004—. Mem. Mensa, Friend of Bill W. Democrat. Avocations: computer guru/hacker, semi-pro photographer, choral. Home: 5117 Spoolin Ct Raleigh NC 27604-6126 Personal E-mail: mkirkduggan@nc.rr.com.

KIRKEY, JOSEPH BENJAMIN, mechanical engineer, educator; b. Chgo., Nov. 1972; s. Hanford Myles and Lois Suzanne Kirkey; m. Ana Jimena Chavez Boada, June 21, 2002. BS in Engring., U. Ill., Urbana-Champaign, 1995; MEd in Instrnl. Leadership, U. Ill., Chgo., 2004. EIT Ill. Mfg. engr. Panduit, Tinley Park, Ill., 1996—99; mech. engr. Richco, Chgo., 1999—2000; tchr. R.N. Dett Elem. Sch., Chgo., 2002—03; math tchr. Thurgood Marshall Mid. Sch., Chgo., 2003—04, Port Charlotte Mid. Sch., Fla., 2004—. Math counts coach Port Charlotte Mid. Sch., Fla., 2003—; mentor tchr. U. Ill., Chgo., 2004. Recipient Nat. Engring. Design award - Bronze, James F. Lincoln Arc Welding Found., 1996. Avocations: travel, camping, fishing, reading, hiking.

KIRKGAARD, VALERIE ANNE, media group executive, syndicated talk radio host, writer, producer, consultant; b. Merced, Calif., Aug. 18, 1940; d. Basil Stuart and Audrey (Thompson) Coghlan; m. Alonzo Bryson Kirkgaard, Oct. 6, 1962 (div. Aug. 1983); children: Jennifer Alexandra, John Erik. AA, Santa Monica City Coll., 1961; BA, UCLA, 1968; M of Counseling, Goddard Coll., L.A., 1982; M. of Enlightenment, Sci. of Mind Ch., San Diego, 1992; PhD, Harrington U., 1999. Bd. and care organizer Norwalk State Hosp., L.A., 1976-78; liaison to bd. dirs. Gay and Lesbian Cmty. Svcs. Ctr., 1976—79; therapist in pvt. practice Kirkgaard & Assocs, Pasadena, Pacific Palisades, Santa Monica, Calif., 1975—; pvt. practice matrimonial cons., 1976—; CEO Kirkgaard Media Group. Ear coning educator, mfr., 1992—; prodr., host radio and TV Waking Up In America, 1987—; radio prodr. Terry Cole Whittaker; radio prodr./host Open Forum, Waking Up In America, 2 programs for KFNX, Phoenix, Ariz., KTBC, Albuquerque; spkr. in field; also VoiceAmerica.com. Author: Breakfast At Bob's, 1982, Take Two Breaths and Call Me in the Morning, 1988,environ. editor United Fitness Mag., 1992; columnist Hollywood Times, 1976, Century City News, 1990-92, Topanga Messenger, 1996—; author numerous articles; numerous appearances and interviews; inventor in field. Founder Golden Hearts Found. Olympic Torch bearer Olympic Com., Santa Fe Springs, Calif., 1984. Mem. Calif. Assn. Marriage Family and Child Counselors, Women's Mus. of Art, Los Angeles County Mus. Art, World Vision, State of the World Forum, The Hunger Project, Mus. of Tolerance, Greater L.A. Press Club, Scriptwriters Network, Pacific Palisades C. of C., Roar Found., Global Security Inst. Avocations: horseback riding, hiking, reading, gardening. Office: Kirkgaard & Assocs 869 Via De La Paz Ste F Pacific Palisades CA 90272-5202 Office Phone: 340-455-8623. E-mail: valkirkgaard@msc.com.

KIRKHAM, D. COLLIER, lawyer; b. Ames, Iowa, May 29, 1947; AB magna cum laude, Harvard Coll., 1969; MS, Stanford Univ., 1971; JD with highest distinction, Univ. Iowa, 1975. Bar: NY 1976. Assoc. Cravath Swaine & Moore LLP, NYC, 1975—82, ptnr., corp., 1982—. Articles editor Iowa Law Rev. Mem.: ABA, NY State Bar Assn. Office: Cravath Swaine Moore LLP Worldwide Plz 825 Eighth Ave New York NY 10019-7475 Office Phone: 212-474-1204. Office Fax: 212-474-3700. Business E-Mail: ckirkham@cravath.com.

KIRKHAM, JAMES ALVIN, manufacturing executive; b. Sumner County, Tenn., June 18, 1935; s. Shirley Barnes and Ouida Redempta (Bursby) Kirkham; m. Shirley Ann Clouse, Sept. 3, 1954; children: Denise Anne, James Alvin II, Hughe Allan. Welder Ind. Wire Co., 1952-54; driver Arthur Lowe Cigar & Candy Co., 1954-56; time study Insley Mfg. Co., 1957; salesman Am. Chicle Co., 1958-59; mgr. Ace Battery, Inc., Indpls., 1967—; v.p. L. P. Industries, Inc., Indpls., 1977—; pres. Rubber Recycling Corp., 1989—; ptnr. TKT Leasing, Indpls., 1978—, LDJ Leasing, Indpls., 1979—, Vets. Interstate Plan, Inc. Chmn. fundraising equestrian events 10th Pan Am. Games; sec. Johnson County Pk. Bd.; bd. dirs. English Ave. Boys Club, State 4-H Horse and Pony Orgn.; pres. bd. dirs. Ind. Horse Coun. Found., Inc.; pres. PTO Clark Twp. Sch. Dist.; v.p. Johnson County 4-H Fairboard; active Boy Scouts Am.; treas. Ind. Horse Coun. Inc. Named Outstanding Show Mgr., Ind. State Fair, 1971; named to Ind. Horseman Hall of Fame, 1998; recipient Golden Boy award, Indpls. Boys Club Alumni Assn., 1970. Mem.: Indpls. Motor Truck Assn., Ind. Motor Truck Assn., Ind. Saddle Horse Assn., Am. Horse Show Assn., Indpls. C. of C., U.S. C. of C., Ind. Shetland Pony Breeders Club, Ind. Pony Am. Club, Am. Hackney Club, Ind. Pony Exhibitors Club, Moose, Shriners, Masons. Home: 1213 N Matthews Rd Greenwood IN 46143-8343 Office: 2166 Bluff Rd Indianapolis IN 46225-1983 Office Phone: 317-786-2717. E-mail: acebattslaes@sbcglobal.net.

KIRKHAM, JOHN SPENCER, lawyer, director; b. Salt Lake City, Aug. 29, 1944; s. Elbert C. and Emma Kirkham; m. Janet L. Eatough, Sept. 16, 1966; children: Darcy, Jeff, Kristie. BA with honors, U. Utah, 1968, JD, 1971. Bar: Utah 1971, U.S. Dist. Ct. Utah 1971, U.S. Ct. Appeals (10th cir.) 1990, U.S. Supreme Ct. 1991. Assoc. Senior & Senior, Salt Lake City, 1971-73; ptnr. VanCott, Bagley, Cornwall & McCarthy, Salt Lake City, 1973-92, Stoel Rives LLP, Salt Lake City. Mem. exec. bd. Great Salt Lake coun. Boy Scouts Am., 1987— (exec. com. v.p. legal, 2003-); mem. Utah Statewide Resource Adv. Coun., 1995-97; trustee Met. Water Dist. Salt Lake and Sandy, 2003—. Mem. Utah Bar Assn., Utah Mining Assn. (bd. dirs. Salt Lake City chpt. 1987—), Rocky Mountain Mineral Law Found. (trustee 1989-92). Republican. Mem. Lds Ch. Office: Stoel Rives LLP 201 S Main St Ste 1100 Salt Lake City UT 84111-4904 Office Phone: 801-328-3131. E-mail: jskirkham@stoel.com.

KIRKHAM, M. B., plant physiologist, educator; b. Cedar Rapids, Iowa; d. Don and Mary Elizabeth (Erwin) K. BA with honors, Wellesley Coll.; MS, PhD, U. Wis. Cert. profl. agronomist. Plant physiologist U.S. EPA, Cin., 1973-74; asst. prof. U. Mass., Amherst, 1974-76, Okla. State U., Stillwater, 1976-80; from assoc. prof. to prof. Kans. State U., Manhattan, 1980—. Guest lectr. Inst. Water Conservancy and Hydroelectric Power Rsch., Inst. Farm Irrigation Rsch., China, 1985, Inst. Exptl. Agronomy, Italy, 1989, Agrl. U. Wageningen, Inst. for Soil Fertility, Haren, The Netherlands, 1991, Massey U., New Zealand, 1991, Lincoln U., New Zealand, 1998, Environ. and Risk Mgmt. Group Hort. Rsch., 1998, Palmerston North, New Zealand, 1998; U. Hannover, Germany, 2003; William A. Albrecht seminar spkr. U. Mo., 1994; vis. scholar Biol. Labs., Harvard U., 1990; vis. scientist environ. physics sect. dept. sci and indsl. rsch., Palmerston North, New Zealand, 1991, The Horticulture and Food Rsch. Inst. New Zealand, Ltd., Crown Rsch. Inst., Palmerston North, 1998, Landcare Rsch., Lincoln, New Zealand, 1998; mem. peer rev. panel USDA/Nat. Rsch. Initiative, Washington, 1994; mem. rev. panel USDA Office Sci. Quality Rev. Water Quality Nat. Program, 2001, apptd. mem. U.S. Nat. Com. for Soil Sci. of NAS, 2001-04; participant confs. and symposia; spkr., presenter in field. Author: Principles of Soil and Plant Water Relations, 2005; editor: Water Use in Crop Production, 1999; co-editor: (with I.K. Iskandar) Trace Elements in Soil, 2001; cons. editor Plant and Soil Jour., 1979-; mem. editl. bd. BioCycle, 1978-82, Field Crops Rsch. Jour., 1983-91, Soil Sci., 1997-, Jour. Crop Improvement, 1998-, Jour. Environ. Quality, 2002-, Crop Sci., 2004—; mem. editl. adv. bd. Internat. Agrophysics, 2000—, Australia Jour. Soil Rsch., 2004; contbr. more than 220 articles and papers to sci. jours. Recipient Best Reviewer award, Water Resources Engring. divsn. Jour. Irrigation and Drainage Engring., ASCE, 1996, grad. faculty tchg. award, Coll. of Agr., Kanas State Univ., 2001; grantee, NSF, USDA, U.S. Dept. Energy, Dept. Sci. and Indsl. Rsch., New Zealand; NSF postdoctoral fellow, U. Wis., 1971—73, NDEA fellow, E.I. du Pont de Nemours and Co. summer faculty fellow, 1976. Fellow AAAS, Am. Soc. Agronomy (editl. bd. 1985-90), Soil Sci. Soc. Am. (travel grantee to internat. congress Japan 1990), Royal Meteorol. Soc., Crop Sci. Soc. Am. (editl. bd. 1980-84, 2004-); mem. Am. Soc. Plant Physiology (editl. bd. 1982-87), Am. Soc. Hort. Sci., Internat. Soil Tillage Rsch. Orgn., Internat. Union Soil Sci. (1st vice chmn. commn. soil physics 1994-98, sec. commn. on soils, food security and human health 2002—), Bot. Soc. Am., Am. Meteorol. Soc., Société Française de Physiologie Végétale, Japanese Soc. Plant Physiology, Scandinavian Soc. Plant Physiology, N.Y. Acad. Sci., Soc. for Exptl. Biology (London), Growth Regulator Soc. Am., Water Environment Fedn., Am.

Phytopathol. Soc., Internat. Assn. Vegetation Sci., Am. Geophys. Union, Internat. Water Resources Assn., Royal Soc. New Zealand, Internat. Assn. Hydrol. Sci., Am. Phys. Soc., Am. Math. Assn., Am. Chem. Soc., Phi Kappa Phi (scholar award 2000), Gamma Sigma Delta (Disting. Faculty award Kans. State U. chpt., 2001), Sigma Xi (sec. chpt. 1997-99, Outstanding Sr. Scientist award 2002). Home: 1420 McCain Ln Apt 244 Manhattan KS 66502-4680 Office: Kans State U Dept Agronomy Throckmorton Hall Manhattan KS 66505-5501 Office Phone: 785-532-0422. Business E-Mail: mbk@ksu.edu.

KIRKLAND, GEOFFREY ALAN, motion picture production designer; b. Derby, Eng., Oct. 7, 1939; came to U.S., 1980; s. Cyril George and Florence Kathleen Kirkland; m. Elspeth Mary Kennedy, Mar. 23, 1970. AA, Royal Coll. of Art, London, 1961. Designer BBC, London, 1961-66; freelance art dir. London, 1966-75; freelance prodn. designer L.A., 1975—. Prodn. designer: (films) Bugsy Malone, 1975 (British Film Academy award, 1975); Midnight Express, 1978; Fame, 1980; Shoot the Moon, 1982; The Right Stuff, 1983 (Academy award nomination best art direction, 1983); Birdy, 1984; Leonard Part 6, 1987; Journey to the Center of the Earth, 1987; Mississippi Burning, 1988; Wildfire, 1989; Come See the Paradise, 1990; Renaissance Man, 1994; Space Jam, 1996; Desperate Measures, 1998; Angela's Ashes, 1998 (Best Art Direction award, British Acad.); The Life of David Gale, 2001; After the Sunset, 2001; Glory Road, 2004.

KIRKLAND, JOHN C., lawyer; b. Omaha, Nebr., Dec. 28, 1963; s. John and Marilou (Witt) K. AB, Columbia U., 1986; JD, UCLA, 1990. Bar: Calif. 1990. Assoc. Cadwalader Wickersham & Taft, L.A., 1990-97; of counsel Weissmann Wolff Bergman Coleman & Silverman, LLP, Beverly Hills, Calif., 1997-2000; ptnr. Brown Raysman Millstein Felder & Steiner LLP, L.A., 2000-01; shareholder Greenberg Traurig LLP, L.A., 2001—. Bd. dirs. Oaktree Found., Inc. Mem. ABA, L.A. County Bar Assn., Beverly Hills Bar Assn. Home: 754 Swarthmore Ave Pacific Palisades CA 90272-4355 Office: 2450 Colorado Ave Ste 400E Santa Monica CA 90404 E-mail: kirklandj@gtlaw.com.

KIRKLAND, JOHN DAVID, oil and gas company executive, lawyer; b. McAllen, Tex., June 6, 1933; s. O.D. and Daisy (Donohoe) K.; m. Ann Wales, June 15, 1957 (div. Feb. 1985); children: David, Solace, Robert; m. Kate Sayen, May 15, 1993. BA, Yale U., 1955, LLB, 1958. Bar: Tex. 1958. Atty. Baker, Botts, Shepherd & Coates, Houston, 1958-67; v.p. in charge fin. Pennzoil Co., Houston, 1967-73, exec. v.p., dir., 1973-78; dir. exec. edn. Jones Sch. Mgmt. and Adminstrn. Rice U., Houston, 1978-79; vice chmn., dir. Sandefer Oil & Gas, Inc., Houston, 1980; exec. v.p., dir. Roy M Huffington, Inc., Houston, 1980-86; chmn. Heritage Trust Co., Houston, 1986-89; chmn., CEO Antara Resources Inc., Houston, 1996-2000; chmn. Huntington Exploration, Inc., 2002—. Pres. Houston Ballet Found., 1972-74, trustee, 1979-, chmn., 1979-84; treas., chmn. fin. com. United Way of Houston, 1983-84; trustee Chinquapin Sch., 1991-94; bd. dirs. Houston chpt. Juvenile Diabetes Found., 1995-97; mem. adv. coun. Ctr. for Am. History, U. Tex. at Austin, 2002-. Mem. Tex. Bar Assn. Office: 989 S Post Oak Ln Houston TX 77056-2203 Office Phone: 713-888-0120. E-mail: kirkland.johnd@sbcglobal.net.

KIRKLAND, NANCY CHILDS, secondary education educator, consultant; b. Ideal, Ga., July 20, 1937; d. Millard Geddings and Bessie Vioda (Forbes) C.; m. Allard Corley French, Jr., Apr. 22, 1961 (div. Dec. 7, 1978); children: Vianne Elizabeth French Marchese, Nancy Alysia French Joyce; m. Clarence Nathaniel Kirkland, Jr., Dec. 12, 1987. AB in Speech and Religious Edn., LaGrange Coll., 1959; MS, Troy State U., 1977; EdD in Child and Youth Studies, Nova U., 1993. Cert. tchr. English, Religion, instr. Profl. Refinements in Developing Effectiveness, Tchr. Effectiveness and Classroom Handling. Dir. Christian edn. First Meth. Ch., Thomson, Ga., 1959; tchr. English Flanagan (Ill.) Jr.-Sr. H.S., 1962—63; tchr. English and social studies Woodland Jr. H.S., Streater, Ill., 1963—64; tchr. 5th grade Sheridan Elem. Sch., Bloominton, Ill., 1964—65; tchr. English Samson (Ala.) H.S., 1965, Choctawhatchee H.S., Fort Walton Beach, Fla., 1966—68, Marianna (Fla.) H.S., 1972—77; dir. devel. reading lab. Chiefland (Fla.) H.S., 1979—82; tchr. English Buchholz H.S., Gainesville, 1982—. Co-founder, cons. KPS Leadership Specialists, Jonesboro, Ga., 1993—; chairperson Buchholz facilitis com., Gainesville, Fla., 1993—; instr. English Santa Fe C. C., Gainesville, Fla., 1982-87, 96; asst. chairperson Buchholz English Dept., Gainesville, Fla., 1989-92. Contbr. articles to profl. jours. Sec., co-chmn., mem. Buchholz sch. adv. coun., Gainesville, 1994-95; tchr., dir., tchr. trainer Sunday sch., vacation sch., Fla.; actress, dir. Little Theaters, ch. groups, Ill., Ga., Ala.; coord. Gainesville Sister Cities Youth Correspondence Program, 1991-93. Mem. AAUW, ASCD, Alachua Multicultural Coun. (grantee 1992), Nat. Coun. Tchrs. English, Fla. Coun. Tchrs. English, Altrusa Internat. Gainesville (sec. 2004-), Alachua Coun. Tchrs. English (v.p. 1991-92, pres. 1992-93), Gainesville C. of C., Altrusa Internat. Gainesville (sec. 2002). Methodist. Avocations: crafts, sewing, fishing, travel. Home: 1728 NW 94th St Gainesville FL 32606-5570 Office: Buchholz H S 5510 NW 27th Ave Gainesville FL 32606-6405 E-mail: Kirkland@gator.net.

KIRKLAND, REBECCA TRENT, endocrinologist; b. Durham, N.C., Dec. 27, 1942; d. Josiah Charles Trent and Mary Duke (Biddle) Trent-Semans; m. John Lindsey Kirkland III, June 24, 1965. BA, Duke U., 1964, MD, 1968. Intern Baylor Coll. Medicine, 1968-69, resident in pediatrics, 1969-70, fellow in pediatric endocrinology, 1971-73, asst. prof. dept. pediatrics, 1975-81, assoc. prof., 1981-88, prof., 1988—, sr. assoc. dean med. edn. London, 2000; registrar Guy's Hosp., Hosp. for Sick Children, London, 1970; with U. Pa. Sch. Medicine, 1973-74, fellow, 1974-75. Asst. physician divsn. endocrinology Children's Hosp. Phila., 1973-75; mem. staff Tex. Children's Hosp., 1975—, Harris County Hosp. Dist., 1975—; head ambulatory svcs. Tex. Children's Hosp., 1984—, dir. jr. league outpatient dept., 1984—. Contbr. articles and revs. to profl. jours. Active Leadership Tex., Leadership Houston; pres. Greater Houston Women's Found., 1994—96; bd. dirs. AVANCE, Inc., 1992, YWCA, 1992; trustee Mus. Med. Sci., 1984—88; pres. Josiah C. Trent Meml. Found., Inc., 1983—, v.p., 1977—83; bd. dirs. Am. Leadership Forum, 1991, mem. selection com., 1989, 1990, sec. bd. dirs. Houston/Gulf Coast chpg., 1989, 1990, pres.-elect, 1991, pres., 1991—93; bd. dirs. Mus. Health and Med. Scis., 2001—. NIH fellow, 1971-73; recipient Alumnae award Baldwin Sch., 1983, Disting. Alumni award Durham Acad., 1984, Goodheart Humanitarian award B'nai B'rith, 1986, Disting. Svc. award Duke U. Med. Alumni Assn., 1992, Recognition award Ctr. for Interaction: Man, Sci. and Culture, 1993, One Voice for Children award Tex. Network for Medically Fragile and Chronically-Ill Children, 1993; named one of five Outstanding Women of Yr. Channel 13, Houston, 1984, Woman on the move Houston Post, 1989. Fellow Am. Acad. Pediatrics; mem. Endocrine Soc., Am. Fedn. For Clin. Rsch., So. Soc. for Pediatric Rsch., Lawson-Wilkins Pediatric Endocrine Soc., Houston Pediatric Soc., Tex. Pediatric Soc., Tex. Med. Assn., Soc. for Pediatric Rsch., Pediatric Endocrinology Soc. Tex., Ambulatory Pediatric Assn., Am. Pediatric Soc., Am. Acad. Pediatrics (pediatric endocrine sect.) 1990), Tex. Diabetes and Endocrine Assn. Office: Baylor Coll Medicine 1 Baylor Plz Houston TX 77030-3411 Office Phone: 832-822-3441. Business E-Mail: rebeccak@bcm.tmc.edu.

KIRKLAND, RICHARD IDE (RIK), JR., magazine editor; b. Ithaca, N.Y., May 11, 1951; s. Richard Ide and Alice Creel Kirkland; m. Jo ann Fulk, June 4, 1973 (div. 1978); m. Virginia Gonzalez, Jan. 30, 1982; children: Matthew, James, Allegra. BA, Birmingham-So. Coll., 1973; MA, Duke U., 1978. Instr. U. N.C., Greensboro, 1978; reporter Fortune Mag., N.Y.C., 1978-81; writer Fortune, N.Y.C., Washington, 1981-85, European editor London, 1985-89, sr. editor N.Y.C., 1989-95, asst. mng. editor, 1995, dep. mng. editor, 1996-2001; dep. mng. editor Bus. Info. Group Time Inc., 1997—98; mng. editor Fortune, N.Y.C., 2001—05, global editor, 2005—. Named Outstanding Student Ala., Birmingham News, 1969, Distinguished Alumnus, Birmingham-So. Coll., 1999. Mem. Am. Soc. Mag. Execs., Coun. Fgn. Rels. Avocations: rhythm & blues guitar (in band the Prowlers), reading, gardening, hiking.

KIRKLAND, RODNEY F., information technology executive, consultant; s. Robert Jennings and Martha Ann Kirkland; m. Gretchen Lorraine Kirkland, Apr. 25, 1980; children: Jeffrey Bayler, Scott Bayler. AS, BS in Aeronautics Tech. and Commerce, Fla. Inst. Tech., 1974; MA in Social Sci. and Pub. Adminstrn., U. No. Colo., 1978; MBA, Calif. Coast U., 1987, DBA, 1999. Cert. EMT; comml. pilot, project mgmt. profl., in project mgmt. Program mgr. Litton PRC Advanced Tech., Reston, Va., 1980—89, AT&T/Boeing Computer Svcs., Vienna, Va., 1990—94; sr. program mgr. Hewlett Packard, Reston, 1994—. Mem. Rep. Nat. Com., Washington, 1988. Recipient Commendation Heroism award, U. Nat. Bank, 1971. Mem.: US Naval Inst., Project Mgmt. Inst. (licentiate), NRA Inst. for Legis. Action (life). Independent-Republican. Achievements include design and development of the project management system for Federal Telecommunications System (FTS) switched voice projects; design of program management system for Seawolf and Ohio Class submarine design and construction; design and development of the international logisticis system to provision contract procurements within HP; design and development of the program management system for large prime defense and commercial systems contracts within HP. Office: Hewlett Packard 10700 Parkridge Blvd Ste 500 Reston VA 20191 Office Phone: 240-744-8277. E-mail: rod.kirkland@hp.com.

KIRKLAND, STARR MELANIE, librarian, writer; b. Camden, NJ, Oct. 29, 1947; d. David Thomas and Myrtle Celeste Watson; 1 child, Atiya Jamila. AA, C.C. of Phila., 1969—71; BA, Livingston Coll. - Rutgers U., 1971—73; MLS, Rutgers U. Sch. of Communication, Info. and Libr. Studi, 1975—77. Public Library NJ., 1977, School Media Specialist NJ., 1977, Secondary Education - English NJ., 1973. Head children's libr. Camden Free Pub. Libr., NJ, 1977—79; circulation libr. Atlanta Met. Coll., Atlanta, 1979—81; h.s. libr. Katzenbach Sch. for the Deaf, West Trenton, NJ, 1981—85; Riverfront State Prison NJ. Dept. of Corrections, Camden, 1985—90; dir. Glassboro Pub. Libr., NJ, 1991—95; libr. Lawnside Sch., NJ, 1995—98, Tucson, Ariz. Dept. of Corrections, 1998—2000; program assoc. Literacy Volunteers of Tucson, 2000—02; children's libr. Pennsauken Free Pub. Libr., NJ, 2002—. Author: (novels) A Tearful Journey to Joy. Mem. State Commn. of Cmty. Affairs, Camden, NJ, 1982—85. Buddhist. Avocations: choreography, dance, curriculum development, tutor. Office Phone: 856-665-5959 6. Personal E-mail: stardyes@yahoo.com.

KIRKLAND, VIRGIL WAYNE, electrical engineer; b. Carthage, Tex., July 29, 1939; s. J.B. and Evelyn Virginia K.; 1 child, Olga Lynn. BSEE, Lamar State U., 1962. With Hughes Aircraft Co., Fullerton, Calif., 1962-94, mgr. tech. staff, 1979-94, asst. program mgr., 1995; with Butler Svc. Group Consulting, Orange, Calif., 1995; ret. Hughes Aircraft Co., Orange, 1995. Republican. Baptist.

KIRKLAND-CUFFEE, RANA ANTOINETTE, art educator; b. NYC, Oct. 6, 1966; d. Richard Anthony and Sheryl A. Kirkland; 1 child, Elijah Cuffee. BA in Comms., U. So. Calif., L.A., 1989. Founder, owner Rana's Arts Club, L.A., 2000—. Author: Mad About Monologues, 2001; co-prodr., host: (video) I Can Do Yoga.

KIRKPATRICK, ANDREW BOOTH, JR., lawyer; b. Asheville, N.C., Jan. 16, 1929; s. Andrew Booth and Gertrude Elizabeth (Ingle) K.; m. Frances Gordon Cone, Oct. 9, 1954; children: Christine, Melissa, Charles. BS cum laude, Davidson Coll., 1949; LLB magna cum laude, Harvard U., 1954. Bar: Del. 1954, Fla. 1955. Law clk. U.S. Ct. Appeals 3d Cir., 1954-55; assoc. Morris, Nichols, Arsht & Tunnell, Wilmington, Del., 1955-58, ptnr., 1958-95, of counsel, 1995—. Chmn. censor com. Supreme Ct. Del., 1970-78. Trustee U. Del., chmn., 1988-99; trustee Unidel Found., Inc.; pres. Young Republicans of New Castle County, 1957-58; chmn. Kennett Pike Assn., Wilmington, 1967-68; chmn. Gov.'s Commn. on Organized Crime, 1972-73; trustee Tatnall Sch., Inc., 1972-82. 1st lt. inf. U.S. Army, 1951-53. Fellow Am. Coll. Trial Lawyers; mem. Del. Bar Assn. (pres. 1978-79), Wilmington Club, Wilmington Country Club, Vicmead Hunt Club, Phi Beta Kappa. Presbyterian. Home: 9 Barley Mill Dr Wilmington DE 19807-2217 Office: Morris Nichols Arsht & Tunnell PO Box 1347 Wilmington DE 19899-1347

KIRKPATRICK, ANNE SAUNDERS, systems analyst; b. Birmingham, Mich., July 4, 1938; d. Stanley Rathburn and Esther (Casteel) Saunders; children: Elizabeth, Martha, Robert, Sarah. Student, Wellesley Coll., 1956-57, Laval U., Quebec City, Can., 1958, U. Ariz., 1958-59; BA in Philosophy, U. Mich., 1961. Sys. engr. IBM, Chgo., 1962-64; sr. analyst Commonwealth Edison Co., Chgo., 1981-97. Treas. Taproot Reps., DuPage County, Ill., 1977—80; pres. Hinsdale (Ill.) Women's Rep. Club, 1978—81. Mem.: Wellesley Chgo. (bd. dirs. 1972—73). Home: 222 E Chestnut St Unit 8B Chicago IL 60611-2376 Personal E-mail: a.kirkpatrick@sbcglobal.net.

KIRKPATRICK, CHARLES HARVEY, public health service officer, immunologist, researcher; b. Topeka, Nov. 5, 1931; s. Hazen Leon and Clarice Opal (Privott) K.; m. Janice Faye Fosha, July 11, 1959; children: Heather, Michael, Brian. BA, U. Kans., 1954; MD, U. Kans., Kansas City, 1958. Diplomate Am. Bd. Internal Medicine, Am. Bd. Allergy and Immunology. Asst. prof. U. Kans., Kansas City, 1965-68, assoc. prof., 1967; sr. investigator Nat. Inst. Allergy and Infectious Diseases, NIH, Bethesda, Md., 1968-79; dir. allergy and clin. immunology Nat. Jewish Ctr., Denver, 1979-93; prof. U. Colo., Denver, 1979—; dir. rsch. Innovative Therapeutics, Inc., 1993-96; pres. Cytokine Sci., Inc., Denver, 1996-99. Active NIH study sects., Bethesda. Editor: 4 books; contbr. numerous articles to profl. jours. NIH research grantee, 1981-86. Fellow ACP, Am. Acad. Allergy and Immunology, Molecular Med. Soc.; mem. Am. Soc. Clin. Investigation, Am. Assn. Immunologists. Episcopalian. Avocations: enology, antique corkscrews, antique automobiles. Office Phone: 303-315-6596. Business E-Mail: charles.kirkpatrick@uchsc.edu.

KIRKPATRICK, DONALD ROBERT, secondary school educator; b. Ft. Belvoir, Va., Aug. 15, 1956; s. Robert Wilbur and Marsha Beatrice (Watson) K. BS, James Madison U., 1979; postgrad., U. Kans., 1979-81; MEd, U. S.C., 1994. Aid dept. paleobiology Nat. Mus. Natural History, Washington, 1979; rsch. asst. U. Kans., Lawrence, 1979-81; sci. tchr. 8th grade Johnakin Mid. Sch., Marion, SC, 1989—2003; sci. tchr. grades 9-12 Marion HS, 2003—. Rsch. assoc. Horry County Mus., Conway, 1990—; fossil collector/donor Nat. Mus. Natural History, 1979—; presenter in field; instr. part-time Coastal Carolina U., Conway, S.C., 1992—. Francis Marion U., Florence, S.C., 1998—. Lt. USNR, 1981-89. Mem.: ASCD, NEA, Planetary Soc., Nat. Ctr. Sci. Edn., Soc. Vertebrate Paleontology, Paleontol. Rsch. Inst., Astron. Soc. Pacific, S.C. Acad. Sci., S.C. Sci. Coun., Nat. Assn. Biology Tchrs., Nat. Sci. Tchrs. Assn. Episcopalian. Avocations: collecting fossils, walking, reading, swimming. Home: 1321 Snider St Conway SC 29526-3120 Office: Marion High Sch 1205 S Main St Marion SC 29571 Office Phone: 843-423-2571. Personal E-mail: drki@verizon.net. Business E-Mail: dkirkpatrick@marion1.k12.sc.us.

KIRKPATRICK, EDWARD THOMSON, retired academic administrator, mechanical engineer; b. Cranbrook, B.C., Can., Jan. 15, 1925; arrived in U.S., 1954, naturalized, 1981; s. John Thomson and Mary Pauline (Jones) Kirkpatrick; m. Barbara Jane Kelsberg, May 22, 1948; children: Allan, Karen, Ann, Keith. BA in sci., U. B.C., 1947; MS, Carnegie Inst. Tech., 1956, PhD, 1958. Registered profl. engr., N.Y., Ohio. Sales engr., mgr. F.D. Bolton, Ltd., Vancouver, Canada, 1948—54; asst. prof. Carnegie Inst. Tech., Pitts., 1954—58; dept. head U. Toledo, 1958—63; engring. dean Rochester Inst. Tech., NY, 1963—71; pres. Wentworth Inst. Tech., Boston, 1971—90, ret., 1990. Contbr. articles to profl. publs.; author: 1620 Fortran II-D Program, 1963. Recipient Outstanding Civilian Svc. award, U.S. Army, 1971. Fellow: Am. Soc. Engring. Edn. (bd. dirs. 1982—86); mem.: ASME, Nat. Soc. Profl. Engrs. Republican. Episcopalian. Avocations: homebuilt aircraft, flying, travel. Home: 40 Radcliffe Rd Weston MA 02493-1024 Office: Wentworth Inst Tech Office of Pres 550 Huntington Ave Boston MA 02115-5998

KIRKPATRICK, GARLAND PENN, retired pediatrician; b. Chgo., Aug. 23, 1932; m. Dorothy Ann McCluster, Jan. 31, 1958; children: Garland Penn, Dawn Annette. AB, Talladega (Ala.) Coll., 1954; BS, U. Ill., Chgo., 1956, MD, 1958. Diplomate Am. Bd. Pediatrics. Fellow in devel. and behavioral pediatrics U. N.C., Chapel Hill; clin. instr. pediatrics U. Ill. Coll. Medicine, Chgo., 1959-64; pvt. practice pediatrics Kirkpatrick & Germain, Chgo., 1963-89; clin. asst. prof. pediatrics U. Chgo., 1983; clin. assoc. prof. pediatrics Northwestern Med. Sch., Chgo., 1985; clin. asst. prof. pediatrics U. Mich. Sch. Medicine, Ann Arbor, 1995, asst. clin. prof. pediatrics, 1996—2003, ret., 2003. Chmn. dept. pediatrics USAF Hosp., Richards Gebaur AFB, 1961-63; cons. Chgo. Bd. Edn., 1983-84; spkr. in field. Contbr. articles to profl. jours. Capt. USAF Med. Corps. Fellow Am. Acad. Pediatrics (exec. com. Ill. chpt. 1984); mem. AMA, Nat. Med. Assn., Soc. for Behavioral and Devel. Pediatrics. Baptist. Avocations: chess, gardening, reading, music: classical, jazz and gospel.

KIRKPATRICK, JAMES JOSEPH, psychologist; b. Washington, Aug. 3, 1922; s. Luther James and Helen Jordan Kirkpatrick; m. Shirley Ann Mathews, Dec. 31, 1965; children: Martha M., Alan, Lori, James. AB in Psychology, U. Tenn., 1948, MA in Psychology, 1949; PhD in Psychology, Syracuse U., 1953. Diplomate Indsl. Psychology, Am. Bd. Examiners in Profl. Psychology. Project dir. Am. Inst. Rsch., Pitts., 1952—54; v.p. Harless & Kirkpatrick, Assocs., Tampa, Fla., 1954—65; assoc. prof. NYU, N.Y.C., 1965—67; prof. Calif. State U., Long Beach, 1967—87, prof. emeritus, 1987—. Expert witness on equal employment opportunity issues, 1967—2001; cons. U. Chgo. IRC, 1975—81. Contbg. author: Readings Psych Tests and Measures, 1964, sr. author: Testing and Fair Employment, 1968, contbg. author: Comparative Studies of Blacks and Whites, 1973. Pilot USAF, WW II. Named Boss of Yr., Am. Bus. Women's Assn., 1962. Fellow: APA (chair ethics); mem.: Fla. Psychology Assn. (pres. elect 1965), Kiwanis. Democrat. Baptist. Avocations: photography, tennis. Office Phone: 562-596-9926. Personal E-mail: volunteers1@mac.com.

KIRKPATRICK, JEANE DUANE JORDAN, political scientist, federal official; b. Duncan, Okla. d. Welcher F. and Leona (Kile) Jordan; m. Evron M. Kirkpatrick; children: Douglas Jordan, John Evron, Stuart Alan. AA, Stephens Coll.; AB, Barnard Coll.; MA, PhD, Columbia U.; postgrad. (French govt. fellow), Inst. Polit. Sci., U. Paris; LHD (hon.), Georgetown U., U. Pitts., U. Charleston, Hebrew U., Colo. Sch. Mines, St. John's U., Universidad Francisco Marroquin, Guatemala, Coll. of William and Mary, U. Mich., Syracuse U.; hon. degree, Loyola U., Chgo., U. Rochester. Asst. prof. polit. sci. Trinity Coll., 1962-67; assoc. prof. polit. sci. Georgetown U., Washington, 1967-73, prof., 1973—, Leavey prof., 1978—2002, prof. emeritus, 2002—; sr. fellow Am. Enterprise Inst. for Pub. Policy Rsch., 1977—; mem. cabinet U.S. permanent rep. to UN, 1981-85; mem. Def. Policy Rev. Bd. (DPB), 1985-93; chair Commn. on Fail Safe and Risk Reduction (FARR), 1990-92; mem. Pres.'s Fgn. Intelligence and Adv. Bd. (PFIAD), 1985-89; head U.S. Delegation to Human Rights Commn., 2003. Author: Elections USA, 1956, Perspectives, 1962, The Strategy of Deception, 1963, Mass Behavior in Battle and Captivity, 1968, Leader and Vanguard in Mass Society; The Peronist Movement in Argentina, 1971, Political Woman, 1974, The New Presidential Elite, 1976, Dismantling the Parties: Reflections on Party Reform and Party Decomposition, 1978, The Reagan Phenomenon, 1983, Dictatorships and Double Standards, 1982, Legitimacy and Force (2 vols.), 1988, The Withering Away of the Totalitarian State, 1990; syndicated columnist, 1985-97; contbr. articles to profl. jours.; editor, contbr. various pubs. Trustee Helen Dwight Reid Ednl. Found., 1972—, pres., 1990—. Recipient Disting. Alumna award Stephens Coll., 1978, B'nai B'rith Humanitarian award, 1982, Award of the Commonwealth Fund, 1983, Gold medal VFW, 1984, French Prix Politique, 1984, Dept. Def. Disting. Pub. Svc. medal, 1985, Bronze Palm, 1992, Disting. Svc. medal Mayor of N.Y.C., 1985, Presdl. Medal of Freedom, 1985, Jamestown Freedom award, 1990, Centennial medal Nat. Soc. DAR, 1991, Disting. Svc. award USO, 1994, Laureate of the Lincoln Acad. of Ill., Medallion of Lincoln, 1996, Jerusalem 2000 award, 1996, Casey medal of hon., 1998, Tomas Garrigue Masaryk Order, 1998, Chauncey Rose award Rose-Hulman Inst. Tech., 1999, Hungarian Presdl. Gold medal, 1999, Living Legends medal Libr. Congress, 2000, Grand Officier du Wissam Al Alaoui medal King of Morocco, 2000; Kirkpatrick professorship of internat. affairs chair established in her honor Harvard U., 1999; Coun. on Fgn. Rels. established Jeane Kirkpatrick chair in nat. security, 2002. Mem. Internat. Polit. Sci. Assn. (exec. coun.), Am. Polit. Sci. Assn. (Hubert Humphrey award 1988), So. Polit. Sci. Assn. Office: Am Enterprise Inst 1150 17th St NW Washington DC 20036-4603 E-mail: jkirkpatrick@aei.org. *My experience demonstrates to my satisfaction that it is both possible and feasible for women in our times to successfully combine traditional and professional roles, that it is not necessary to ape men's career patterns,— -starting early and keeping one's nose to a particular grindstone, but that, instead, one can do quite different things at different stages of one's life. All that is required is a little luck and a lot of work.*

KIRKPATRICK, JIM C., secondary school educator; s. Jess James Kirkpatrick and Margaret Dane Payne; m. Stephane K. Kirkpatrick, Jan. 10, 1990; 1 child, Kelsey. BA, Okla. U.; MA, So. Meth. U. Golf player PGA; designer LTV Aerospace, Grand Prairie; art dealer Dr. Pepper Co.; tchr. Chapel Hill Ind. Sch. Dist., Mt. Pleasant, Tex. Owner Jim Kirkpatrick Advt. Inc., Dallas, Internat. Buffalo Parts, Muskee, Tex. Mem.: VASE, Dallas Art Club. Republican. Calvanist. Avocations: golf, fishing, swimming, archery, bowling. Home: PO Box 363 Golden TX 75444 Office: Chapel Hill ISD PO Box 1257 Mount Pleasant TX 75456

KIRKPATRICK, JOHN ELSON, retired oil industry executive, retired naval reserve officer; b. Oklahoma City, Feb. 13, 1908; s. Elmer Elsworth and Claudia (Spencer) K.; m. Eleanor Blake, June 20, 1932; 1 child, Joan Elson. Student, U.S. Mil. Acad., 1925-26; BS, U.S. Naval Acad., 1931; postgrad., Harvard U. Grad. Sch. Bus. Adminstrn., 1935-36; LLD, Oklahoma City U., 1963; HHD, Bethany Nazarene Coll., 1967. Founder, v.p., treas. Allied Steel Products Corp., Tulsa, 1936-41; v.p., treas. Kirkpatrick & Bale Oil Co., Oklahoma City, 1945-50; ptnr. Kirkpatrick Oil Co., Oklahoma City, 1950-95. Emeritus dir., Bank One, Okla. Chmn. Kirkpatrick Found.; hon. consul Republic of Korea, 1974-2003; life trustee Okla. Zool. Soc.; mem. life bd. Oklahoma City Mus. Art; mem. Okla. Heritage Assn., Allied Arts Found.; hon. dir. Okla. State Fair; former mem. sr. adv. bd. Frontiers of Sci. Found.; hon. chmn. bd. dirs.; past pres. Presbyn. Homes; founder, bd. dirs. Oklahoma City Cmty. Found.; former mem. Bus. Com. for Arts, Inc.; hon. chmn. Lyric Theatre Okla.; hon. life trustee, dir. emeritus Nat. Cowboy and Western Heritage Mus.; donor Kirkpatrick Auditorium at Oklahoma City U., 1965; dir. Kirkpatrick Sci. and Air Space Mus. at Omniplex; mem. adv. bd. Okla. Health Scis. Ctr.; hon. trustee Tulsa Cmty. Found. Decorated Bronze Star with V; recipient Disting. Svc. award Okla. U., 1959, Sweet Success vol. award, 1998, Nat. Brotherhood citation NCCJ, 1962, AIA award, 1963, Outstanding Okla. Oil Man award Okla. Petroleum Coun., 1974, Merit award Okla. Hosp. Assn., 1974, Esquire/Bus. Com. for the Arts award, 1974, 75, Evergreen Disting. Svc. award for pub. svc., 1982, Okla. Charitable Achiever awards cert. of recognition Pearl M. & Julia J. Harmon Found., 1988, Patrick Henry medal Mil. Order of World Wars Okla. City chpt., 1989, Ptnrs. award World Neighbors, 1991, Henry G. Bennett Distng. Svc. award Okla. State U., 1992, Achievement award Okla. City Fedn. of Colored Womens Clubs, 1992; named to Okla. Hall of Fame, 1962, Okla. Commerce and Industry Hall of Fame, 1985, Wall of Fame Okla. City Pub. Sch. Found., 1990, Humanitarian award Nat. Arthritis Found. Okla. Chpt., 1993; named Outstanding Philanthropist Okla. chapter Nat. Soc. Fund Raising Execs., 1986, Arts Advocate of Yr., SW Theatre Assn. Performing Arts for Children Divsn., 1993, Disting. Philanthropy award Am. Assn. Mus., 1995, Disting. Friends award Okla. City U., 1997; named Hon. USN Master Chief Petty Officer, 2000; donor Kirkpatrick Ctr. bldg. Okla. Ctr. Sci. and Arts, 1978; John E. Kirkpatrick Horticulture Ctr. Okla. State U. Tech. named in his honor, 1990; recognized by Profl. Photographers of Am. Inc. for meritorious contributions to profl. photography Nat. award; recipient John E. Kirkpatrick Humanitarian Oklahoma City Rotary, 1994; honored by Kappa Sigma; named to The Okla. Mil. Hall of Fame, 1999, Tulsa Hall of Fame, 1999, Okla. Higher Edn. Hall of

Fame, 2000. Mem. Ind. Petroleum Assn. (past dir.), Oklahoma City C.of C. (life dir.), Okla. Hist. Soc. (dir. emeritus), Okla. County Hist. Soc. (Cardinal Svc. award 1989), Harvard Area Group, Asia Soc. Okla. (Civic Leader award 1991), 45th Inf. Divsn. Mus. (hon. life, bd. dirs.), Assn. Grads. USAF Acad. (hon.), Rotary, Oklahoma City Petroleum Club (pres. 1959-60). Office: 1001 W Wilshire Blvd # 201 Oklahoma City OK 73116

KIRKPATRICK, JOHN EVERETT, lawyer; b. Meadville, Pa., Aug. 20, 1929; s. Francis Earl and Marjorie Eloise (Roudebush) K.; m. Patricia Ann Benkert, Aug. 9, 1952 (div. June 1963); children: Amy Kirkpatrick Fidler, John Scot, Ann Kirkpatrick Mullen; m. Phyllis Jean Daeuble, Aug. 31, 1963. AB, Amherst Coll., 1951; JD, Harvard U., 1954. Bar: Ohio 1955, Ill. 1962. Assoc. Squire, Sanders & Dempsey, Cleve., 1954-61, Kirkland, Ellis, Hodson, Chaffetz & Masters, Chgo., 1962-64; sr. ptnr. Kirkland & Ellis, Chgo., 1965—95, of counsel, 1995—. Contbr. articles on tax and estate planning to profl. jours. Mem. Cen. DuPage Hosp. Devel. Commn., Winfield, Ill.; elder 1st Presbyn. Ch., Wheaton, Ill., 1983—. Mem. ABA, Ill. State Bar Assn., Chgo. Bar Assn., Chgo. Golf Club, Mid Am. Club, Glen Oak Club, Lago Mar Club. Republican. Avocation: golf. Office: Kirkland & Ellis 200 E Randolph St Fl 54 Chicago IL 60601-6636 Office Phone: 312-861-2060. E-mail: jkirkpatrick@kirkland.com.

KIRKPATRICK, KAREN COFFEY, language educator; AA, Mid. Ga. Coll., Cochran, 1998; BS in Edn., Ga. Southwestern, Americus, 2000, MEd, 2003. English tchr. Dodge County HS, Eastman, Ga., 2000—01; English tchr., yearbook advisor Houston County HS, Warner Robins, Ga., 2001—. Vol. Pulaski County 4-H, Howkinsville, Ga., 1996—. Mem.: Journalism Educators Assn., Profl. Assn. Ga. Educators, Nat. Coun. Tchrs. English. Office: Houston County HS 920 Hwy 96 Warner Robins GA 31088 Office Phone: 478-988-6340. Business E-Mail: kkirkpatrick@hche.net.

KIRKPATRICK, ROBERT HUGH, communications executive; b. Kingston, NY, Mar. 3, 1954; s. Oscar Hugh and Ann (Page) K.; m. Debra Cook, Oct. 25, 1986; 1 child, Page. BA in Polit. Sci. with high honors, SUNY, Oneonta, 1977; M in Pub. and Pvt. Mgmt., Yale U., 1979. Cert. comml. pilot. Policy analyst edn. com. N.Y. State Assembly, 1977; mgr. mktg. Cummins Engine Co., Columbus, Ind., 1980-81, mgr. mktg. ops., 1982-83, dir. electronics mktg., 1984-86, dir. bus. devel. Svc. Products Co. subs., 1987-89; pres. Intelesis Inc., Columbus, 1989-97, CEO, 1996-97; pres. transp. and power divsn. AFFINA Corp., Columbus, 1998-2000; ptnr. Intelesis LLC, Columbus, 2001—03; COO, Servco LLC, Indpls., 2002—. Cons. in field. Contbr. articles to bus. jours. Trustee SUNY, Albany, 1975-76; pres. Student Assn. State Univ., Inc., 1975-76, v.p. 1974-75; vice-chmn. Nat. Student Lobby, 1976-77; pres. Columbus Arts Guild, 1981-82; treas. San Souci, Inc., Columbus, 1983-85; allocations com. United Way, 1990-92; mem. City Transp. Commn., Oneonta, N.Y., 1973-74; bd. dirs. Leadership Bartholomew County Alumni Assn., 1991-92, Young Mothers' Ednl. Devel., Inc., 1994-96; adminstrv. bd. First United Meth. Ch., 1994-96, trustee 1997-99; exec. com. ABC-Stewart Montessori Sch., 1996-99, sec. 1997; vol. pilot Angel Flight Am., 2001—, Ind. Wing Leader, 2003—05. Mem. Yale Club Ind. (treas. 1981-85), Rotary (bd. dirs. 1994-2000, pres. 1996-97, treas. 1997-99), Flying Rotarians Internat. Fellowship (bd. dirs. Americas 2004—). Methodist. Home: 9727 Summerlakes Dr Carmel IN 46032 Office: Servco LLC 720 N High School Rd Indianapolis IN 46214 Office Phone: 317-814-0034.

KIRKPATRICK, R(OBERT) JAMES, geology educator; b. Schenectady, NY, Dec. 31, 1946; s. Robert James and Audrey (Rech) K.; m. Susan A. Wilson, Sept. 4, 1968 (div. 1984); children: Gregory Robert, Geoffrey Stephen; m. Carol A. Hanna, Sept. 3, 1985. AB, Cornell U., 1968; PhD, U. Ill., 1972. Asst. U.S. Geol. Survey, Denver, 1968; rsch. and teaching asst. U. Ill., Urbana, 1968-72, asst. prof. dept. geology, 1978-80, assoc. prof., 1980-83, prof., 1983-88, prof., head dept., 1988-97, R.E. Grim prof., 2005—, exec. assoc. dean Coll. Liberal Arts & Scis., 1997—; sr. rsch. geologist prodn. rsch. div. Exxon, Houston, 1972-73; rsch. fellow in geophysics Harvard U., Cambridge, 1973-75; asst. rsch. geologist Scripps Instn. Oceanography, La Jolla, Calif., 1976-78. Mem. ocean crust panel Joint Oceanographic Instns. for Deep Earth Studies, 1977-78, active margin panel, 1978, downhole measurements panel, 1977-78; cons. various corps. Editor: Initial Reports of the Deep Sea Drilling Project, Vols. 46 and 55, 1979, 80; co-editor: Kinetics of Geochemical Processes, 1981; assoc. editor American Mineralogist, 1987-90; contbr. over 200 articles to profl. jours. Overseas fellow Churchill Coll., Eng., 1985-86; rsch. grantee NSF, 1977—, Dept. Energy, 2000—, various other orgns., 1978—. Fellow Geol. Soc. Am., Mineral. Soc. Am. (councillor 1990-93, Dana medal 2004), Am. Ceramic Soc.; mem. Am. Geophys. Union (VGP award com. 1985-88, chmn. 1986-88), Internat. Mineral. Assn. (alt. U.S. del. 1982, coord. com. 1986 meeting, chmn. program com. 1986, U.S. rep. Commn. on Crystal Growth, v.p. 1986-90, sec. Commn. on Mineral Physics 1986-91). Office: U Ill Dept Geology Urbana IL 61801 E-mail: kirkpat@uiuc.edu.

KIRKPATRICK, SUSAN, Spanish literature educator; b. Newcastle, Wyo., Jan. 16, 1942; d. James Wilson and Rosemary Jane (Russell) K.; 1 child, Taylor Darwin Berg-Kirkpatrick. BA, U. Wyo., 1963, Cambridge (Eng.) U., 1965; PhD, Harvard U., 1972. Instr. Brandeis U., Waltham, Mass., 1970-71; asst. prof. U. Calif. San Diego, La Jolla, 1971-78, assoc. prof., 1978-88, prof., 1988—, dept. chair, 1988-91. Author: Larra: Romantico liberal, 1977, Las Romanticas: Women Writers in Spain, 1989, Antología poética de escritoras dels. XIX, 1992; Spanish editor European Women Writers in Translation series U. Nebr. Press, 1985—. Fulbright fellow U.S. Govt., 1963-65, Guggenheim fellow Guggenheim Found., 1986-87. Mem. MLA (exec. coun. 1993—). Office: U Calif San Diego La Jolla CA 92093

KIRKSEY, AVANELLE, nutrition educator; b. Mulberry, Ark., Mar. 23, 1926; BS, U. Ark., Fayetteville, 1947; MS, U. Tenn., Knoxville, 1950; PhD, Pa. State U., 1961; postdoctoral, U. Calif., Davis, 1976; DSc honoris causa, Purdue U., 1997. Assoc. prof. Ark. Polytechnic U., Russellville, 1950—55; rsch. asst. Pa. State U., University Park, 1956—58, fellow Gen. Foods, 1958—60; assoc. prof. Purdue U., West Lafayette, Ind., 1961—69, prof. nutrition, 1970—85, disting. prof., 1985—96, disting. prof. emeritus, 1997. Prin. investigator nutrition project in rural Egypt; coord. nutrition program Indonesian Univs., 1987-91 Contbr. articles to profl. jours. Recipient Borden award, Am. Home Econs. Assn., 1980. Fellow Am. Inst. Nutrition (Lederle award 1994); mem. N.Y. Acad. Scis., Phi Kappa Phi, Sigma Xi. Office: Purdue U Dept Food Nutrition West Lafayette IN 47907

KIRKSEY, J. MICHAEL, metal products executive; CPA. Acct. Arthur Andersen LLP, 1976-89; various positions Keystone Internat., 1989-96; sr. v.p., CFO Metals USA, Inc., Houston, 1996-99, pres., CEO, 1999—, also bd. dirs. Office: Metals USA Inc 3 Riverway Ste 600 Houston TX 77056

KIRKWOOD, HAROLD PETER, JR., library science educator; b. Cleve., Mar. 25, 1968; s. Harold Peter Kirkwood Sr. and Kathleen Marie White; children: Garrett Douglas, Mackenzie Lynne; m. Monica Christine Turner, 2005 BA, Ind. U., 1990; MLS, U. S.C., 1993. Asst. ref. libr. SUNY, Geneseo, NY, 1994-96, info. tech. libr., 1996-97; assoc. prof. libr. scis. Purdue U., West Lafayette, Ind., 1997—. Webmaster Bus. & Fin. divsn. Spl. Librs. Assn., 1995-2001; chmn. Ctrs. of Excellence Awards, 2003-05; pres. Bschool.com, Inc., 1998—. Contbr. articles to profl. jours. Mem. Spl. Librs. Assn. (chmn.-elect bus. and fin. divsn. 2005—) Independent. Avocations: bicycling, foosball, travel. Office: Purdue U Mgmt & Econ Libr 504 W State St KRAN West Lafayette IN 47907 Office Phone: 765-494-2921. E-mail: kirkwood@purdue.edu.

KIRKWOOD, JOHN, medical association administrator; Mem. program staff Am. Lung Assn. of Metro. Chgo., 1968, assoc. dir. ednl. svcs., dir. dept. environ. health, exec. dir., 1975—2001; CEO Am. Lung Assn., N.Y.C., 2001—; dir. congl. and intergovtl. rels. Region V U.S. EPA, 1972—75.

KIRKWOOD, ROBERT KEITH, applied physicist; b. Santa Monica, Calif., Mar. 10, 1961; s. Robert Lord and Patricia Cathrine (Keith) K.; m. Kimberly DeNeve Saunders, May 2, 1991; children: Rebekah Marie, Rachel Kathryn. BS, UCLA, 1982, MS, 1984; PhD, MIT, 1989. Rsch. asst. dept. elec. engring. UCLA, 1982-84; mem. tech. staff TRW Space and Tech. Group, Redondo Beach, Calif., 1984-85; rsch. asst. MIT, Cambridge, 1985-89, vis. scientist Plasma Fusion Ctr., 1992-94; postdoctoral fellow Calif. Inst. Tech., Pasadena, 1989-91; rsch. assoc. geophysics divsn. Air Force Phillips Lab., Hanscom AFB, Mass., 1991-92, physicist, 1992-94, Lawrence Livermore (Calif.) Lab., 1994—. Contbr. articles to Nuc. Fusion, Physics of Plasmas, Rev. Sci. Instruments, Physics Letters A, Phys. Rev. Letters. Recipient Rsch. Associateship award NRC, 1991; postdoctoral fellow Dept. Energy, 1989; doctoral fellow TRW Space and Tech. Group, 1985. Mem. Am. Phys. Soc. (Simon Ramo award in plasma physics 1991), Am. Geophys. Union. Achievements include development of wave transmission diagnostics for plasmas and demonstration of the interaction between multiple laser beams in plasmas. Office: Lawrence Livermore Lab L-479 PO Box 808 Livermore CA 94551-0808 Office Phone: 925-422-1007. E-mail: kirkwood1@llnl.gov.

KIRPES, ANNE IRENE, elementary school educator; b. Dubuque, Iowa, Oct. 6, 1966; d. Raymond Louis and Norma Jean Margaret (Kern) K. BA, U. No. Iowa, 1989; EdM, Harvard U., 1997. Lic. elem. edn. Tchr. 1st grade Western Ave Sch., Sch. Dist. 161, Flossmoor, Ill., 1989-93, Serena Hills Sch., Sch. Dist. 161, Chicago Heights, Ill., 1993-96; tchr. 3d grade Wheelock Lab. Keene (N.H.) State Coll., 1997-98; reading/lang. arts test devel. specialist Riverside Pub. Co., Itasca, Ill., 1998—2002; reading test devel. dir. Data Recognition Corp., Maple Grove, Minn., 2002—. Exch. team mem. Rotary Group, Paris, 1995. Recipient Silver Congl. award U.S.A., 1988, Gold Congl. award, 1991; Young Alumni award U. No. Iowa Alumni Assn., Cedar Falls, 1994. Mem. ASCD, Nat. Coun. Tchrs. English, Whole Lang. Umbrella, Internat. Reading Assn., Kappa Delta Pi (internat. nominations com. 1988-90), Phi Delta Kappa, Alpha Upsilon Alpha (ad hoc com. mem., 2005—), Omicron Delta Kappa. Avocations: reading, travel, puzzles, butterfly memorabilia, board games. Home: 9461 Jewel Ln North Maple Grove MN 55311 Office Phone: 763-268-2007.

KIRSCH, DONALD, financial consultant; b. NYC, Oct. 9, 1931; s. William and Eva (Wasserman) K.; m. Dorothy Ann Tejw, June 6, 1959; children: Mark Adam, Karen Rebecca Hoffman, Jonathan Bradford. BS, NYU, 1952. Editorial staffer Wall Street Jour., N.Y.C., 1952-53; writer AP, N.Y.C., 1954-55; pres. Wall Street Cons., N.Y.C., 1955—; chmn. Wall St. Group, Calif., Inc., Los Angeles, 1963—; chmn., pres. The Wall Street Group, Inc., N.Y.C., 1959—. Adj. assoc. prof. NYU Grad. Sch. Arts and Sci., 1974-79; founding chmn. Typesetting Products, Inc., Talleres Graficos de Interamericanos, Inc., San Juan, P.R., 1962-80; chmn. Eurofinancing Ltd., 1968; bd. dirs. Co*star Entertainment Inc., MedNet Inc. (chmn. strategic planning com.), Medi-Mail Inc., Dialscan Systems, Audiofidelity Enterprises Inc., Interstate Nat. Dealers Svcs., Inc. Author: FInancial and Economic Journalism: Analysis Interpretation and Reporting, 1978 (Librarians Assn. award 1978), Investor Relations for the Over-the-Counter or Newly Public Company, (with others) The Handbook of Investor Relations; contbr. numerous articles to profl. jours. Trustee Nat. Symphony Orch. of the John F. Kennedy Ctr. for Performing Arts, treas. bd. trustees, 1996-98; trustee Big Bros.; mem. bd. mgrs. Episcopal Social Svcs., N.Y. Mem. N.Y. Soc. Security Analysts, Met. Pres'. Orgn., Young Pres. Orgn. (chmn. met. chpt. 1976-77), Chief Execs. Orgn., Am. Assocs. Royal Acad. Trust (mem. nat. coun.), Econs. Club N.Y., Friar's Club, The Metropolitan (N.Y.C.), Masons. Office: The Wall St Group Inc 32 E 57th St New York NY 10022-2513 Personal E-mail: dkirsch1@aol.com.

KIRSCH, LAURENCE STEPHEN, lawyer; b. Washington, July 20, 1957; s. Ben and Bertha (Gomberg) K.; m. Celia Goldman, Aug. 19, 1979; children: Rachel Miriam, Max David. BAS, MS, U. Pa., 1979; JD, Harvard U., 1982. Bar: D.C. 1982, U.S. Ct. Appeals (3d cir.) 1983, (5th cir.) 1997, (9th cir.) 2001, U.S. Dist. Ct. D.C. 1985, U.S. Ct. Appeals (D.C. cir.) 1985, U.S. Supreme Ct. 1987; registered environ. assessor, Calif. 1988. Law clk. to presiding judge Pa. Dist. Ct., Phila., 1982-83; vis. asst. prof. law U. Bridgeport (Conn.) Law Sch., 1983-84; assoc. Cadwalader, Wickersham & Taft, Washington, 1984-90, ptnr., 1991—2002; with Shea Gardner, Washington, 2002—04, Goodwin Procter LLP, 2004—. Chmn. steering coms. Superfund. *Mr. Kirsch is an environmental litigator, counselor and transactional attorney. His litigation victories include three appellate decisions overturning site listings on the National Priorities List, including the first such decision in the history of the Superfund program, and opinions on the interaction of bankruptcy and environmental law. He negotiates with government agencies and private parties, advises on environmental implications of real estate and corporate transactions, and performs environmental assessments. Mr. Kirsch lectures widely on environmental law subjects and taught a law school course on Law, Science and Technology. He was interviewed as an expert in environmental law by CBS News, the MacNeil-Lehrer Report, and numerous radio shows and newspapers.* Editor-in-chief Indoor Pollution Law Report, 1987-91; mng. editor Harvard Environ. Law Rev., 1981-82; contbr. articles to profl. jours. Mem. ABA, Fed. Bar Assn., AAAS, Air and Waste Mgmt. Assn. (indoor air quality com.), Environ. Law Inst., Nat. Inst. Bldg. Scis. (indoor air quality com.), Am. Soc. Testing and Measurement (indoor air quality com.), Phi Beta Kappa. Home: 7212 Longwood Dr Bethesda MD 20817-2122 Office: Goodwin Procter 901 New York Ave NW Washington DC 20001 Office Phone: 202-346-4440. Office Fax: 202-346-4444. E-mail: lkirsch@goodwinprocter.com.

KIRSCH, LYNN, lawyer; b. New Orleans, Oct. 31, 1964; d. Henry C. and Therese M. ((Guenther) K. BS in Bus. Mgmt., Fla. State U., Panama City, 1992; JD, U. Ariz., 1995. Bar: Nev. 1995, U.S. Dist. Ct. Nev. 1995, U.S. Ct. Fed. Claims 1997, U.S. Ct. Appeals (9th cir.) 1998, U.S. Supreme Ct. 1999. Law clk. U.S. Atty.'s Office, Phoenix, 1993, Slutes, Sakrison, Evan, Grant & Pelander, Tucson, 1993-94, Lionel, Sawyer & Collins, Las Vegas, 1994; judicial extern Fed. Dist. Ct., Tucson, 1994; rsch. asst. U. Ariz., Tucson, 1994-95; law clk. Jacob & Fishbein, Tucson, 1994-95; assoc. Goold, Patterson, DeVore & Rondau, Las Vegas, 1995-97, Curran & Parry, Las Vegas, 1997-99, Bernhard & Bradley, Las Vegas, 1999—2001; gen. counsel Unlt. Holdings, Inc., 2001—04; ptnr. Lynn Kirsch Chtd., 2004—. Mem. Justice of the Peace pro-tempore panel, Las Vegas Twp., County of Clark, 1998-2000; alt. mcpl. ct. judge City of Las Vegas, 1999-2004; vol. mediator clerk county social svs. Neighborhood Justice Ctr.; arbitrator BBB AutoLine; instr. The Nonprofit Corp., Nevada, UNLV Continuing Edn., 2002, 03, 05. Article editor U. Ariz. Law Rev., 1994-95. Mem. Jr. League of Las Vegas, 1998—, league atty., 2000—; mem. State of Nev. Commn. on Postsecondary Edn., 1998-01, Social Register of Las Vegas, House of Blues Found. Adv. Bd. Recipient Cert. Appreciation, U.S. Atty.'s Office, Phoenix, 1993, AmJur award Lawyers Coop. Publ., Tucson, 1993. Mem. ABA (litigation sect., assoc. editor The Affiliate 1999-2000), ATLA, State Bar Nev. (chair young lawyers sect. 1999-2000, so. Nev. disciplinary bd., fee dispute arbitration com.), Clark County Bar Assn. (trial by peers com., cmty. svc. com.), Nev. Trial Lawyers Assn., So. Nev. Assn. Women Attys. Avocations: horseback riding, hiking, skydiving. Office: 1342 S Decatur Blvd Las Vegas NV 89102 Office Phone: 702-459-5455. Personal E-mail: lynn@lynnkirsch.com.

KIRSCH, MARK A., lawyer; b. Washington, Sept. 25, 1958; BA cum laude, Univ. Rochester, 1980; JD, George Washington Univ., 1984. Bar: DC 1985, Md. 1985, Va. 2003, US Dist. Ct. (DC, Md. dist.) 1985. Ptnr., co-chmn. Consumer practice group DLA Piper Rudnick Gray Cary, Reston, Va. Contbr. articles to profl. jours. Mem.: ABA, Md. State Bar Assn. (chmn. com. on franchise & distribution law 1999—2001), DC Bar Assn., Va. Bar Assn. Office: DLA Piper Rudnick Gray Cary Suite 400 1775 Wiehle Ave Reston VA 20190-5159 Office Phone: 703-773-4241. Office Fax: 703-773-5052. Business E-Mail: mark.kirsch@dlapiper.com.

KIRSCH, ROBERT L., lawyer; b. Methuen, Mass., Aug. 23, 1957; s. Richard Alan and Gloria Maria (Russo) K.; m. Anne Elizabeth Renner, Nov. 18, 1989; children: Samuel, Jack. BS in Polit. Sci., Middlebury Coll., 1979; JD, Cornell Law Sch., Ithaca, N.Y., 1983. Bar: Mass. 1983, U.S. Dist. Ct. Mass. 1983, U.S. Ct. Appeals (1st cir.) 1983, N.H. 1985, U.S. Dist. Ct. N.H. 1985. Assoc. Hale and Dorr, Boston, 1983—92, ptnr., 1992—2004; ptnr., chmn. Environ. dept., mem. Litigation dept. & Energy Law group Wilmer Cutler Pickering Hale & Dorr, Boston, 2004—. Pres. exec. com. Mt. Washington Obs., North Conway, N.H., trustee, 1985—. Named a Mass. Super Lawyer, Boston Mag., 2004. Mem. ABA, NH Bar Assn., Boston Bar Assn., Phi Beta Kappa. Office: Wilmer Cutler Pickering Hale & Dorr 60 State St Boston MA 02109-1816 Office Phone: 617-526-6779. Office Fax: 617-526-5000. Business E-Mail: rob.kirsch@wilmerhale.com.

KIRSCH, ROGER ALLEN, principal; b. Evansville, Ind., Feb. 16, 1949; s. Walter Henry Vaentine and Dorothy Alice Kirsch; m. Trudy Mae Rawlings, Nov. 25, 1972; children: Ryan Christopher, Alison Marie. MA, Concordia U., River Forest, Ill., 1976. Tchr. St. Peter Luth. Sch., Schaumburg, Ill., 1972—85, prin. Home: 275 Thrasher St Bloomingdale IL 60108 Office: St Peter Luth Sch 208 E Schaumburg Rd Schaumburg IL 60194 E-mail: rkirsch@stpeterlcms.com.

KIRSCH, ROSLYN RUTH, artist, educator, painter, printmaker; b. NYC, Dec. 30, 1928; d. Harry Morris and Lillian (Zemachson) Friedenberg; m. Louis Kirsch, Dec. 26, 1948; children: Libby Ann, Andrew Lawrence. Student, Queens Coll., 1946-48; BA, Hunter Coll., 1950. Art dir. Ladies' Ready-to-Wear Buying Office, N.Y.C., 1948-50; art educator Armory Art Ctr., West Palm Beach, Fla., 1987—, Boca Raton Mus. Art Sch., Boca Raton, Fla., 1990—. Presenter in field; condr. painting workshops. One-person shows include J&W Gallery, New Hope, Pa., Capitol Gallery, Tallahassee, Fla., Peter Drew Galleries, Fla., Ken Elias, Habitat Gallery, West Palm Beach, Fla., Joel Kessler Gallery, Fla., Indigo Gallery, Fla., Palm Beach Internat. Airport; exhibited in group shows Ann. Hortt Exhbn., Mus. of Art, Ft. Lauderdale, 1994 (award), Nat. Assn. Women Artists, West Palm Beach, 1995 (award), Mus. Art, Ft. Lauderdale, 1998, Boca Raton Mus. Art, Fla., 1999; represented in permanent collections including Mus. Art., Ft. Lauderdale, Boca Raton Mus. Art. Recipient Honorable Mention award Mus. Art, Ft. Lauderdale, 1994, others. Mem. Nat. Assn. Women Artists, Boca Raton Mus. Artists Guild, others. Avocations: golf, fundraising. E-mail: kirschfineart@yahoo.com.

KIRSCH, SCOTT DOUGLAS, family practice physician; b. Bronx, N.Y., Nov. 4, 1946; s. Max Milton Kirsch and Linda Paley Sokoloff; m. Bonnie E. Becker; children: Geoffrey Z., Laura G. BA, Queens Coll., 1967; MD, SUNY, Buffalo, 1971. Diplomate Am. Bd. Family Practice. Asst. dir. family practice residency program South Nassau Cmtys. Hosp., Oceanside, NY, 1980—82, dir., 1982—99, dir. dept. family practice, 1989—99, emeritus mem. dept. family practice, 2001—; assoc. dir. family practice residency program Southside Hosp., Bayshore, 1999—. Recipient award for dedication to Hispanic Cmty., Nat. Hispanic Med. Assn., 2002, legis. resolution for disting. svc., N.Y. State Senate, 1999. Mem.: N.Y. State Acad. Family Physicians (pres. 2001—02, Family Practice Educator of Yr. 2005), Am. Acad. Family Physicians (del. to nat. conv. 1999—, mem. commn. on continuing med. edn. 2002—, chair adv. bd. home study program 2004—). Avocations: history, travel, baseball, boxing, martial arts. Home: 63 Crossbow Ln Commack NY 11725 Office: Southside Hosp 301 E Main St Bay Shore NY 11706 Office Phone: 631-968-3294. Personal E-mail: scottkirsch@optonline.net.

KIRSCH, STEVEN JAY, lawyer; b. St. Louis, Aug. 31, 1951; BS, U. Mo., 1973; JD, Hamline U., 1976. Bar: Minn. 1976, U.S. Dist. Ct. Minn. 1976, U.S. Ct. Appeals (8th cir.) 1977. Ptnr. Murnane, Conlin, White, & Brandt, St. Paul, 1976—. Adj. prof. law Hamline U., St. Paul, 1979-83; mem. adv. bd. Advanced Legal Edn., 1982—. Author: (novel) Oath of Office, 1988, Minnesota Methods of Practice, 3d edit., 1989. Fellow Am. Coll. Trial Lawyers. Avocations: reading, writing, books, sports. Home: 3612 Oak Creek Ter Saint Paul MN 55127-7034 Office: Murnane Law Firm 444 Cedar St 1800 US Bancorp Saint Paul MN 55101 Office Phone: 651-227-9411. E-mail: skirsch@murnane.com.

KIRSCH, THORSTEN, cell biologist, educator; s. Heinz and Ingeborg Kirsch; m. Renee Y. Kirsch, Aug. 17, 2002. PhD, Friedrich-Alexander U., Erlangen, Germany, 1992. Asst. prof. Pa. State Coll. of Medicine, Hershey, 2000—02; assoc. prof. U. Md. Sch. Medicine, Baltimore, 2002—, dir. orthopaedic rsch. Rsch. grant, NIH, 1999, 2003, Arthritis Found., 2003. Mem.: Orthop. Rsch. Soc. (life). Office Phone: 410-706-2417. Business E-Mail: tkirsch@umoa.umm.edu.

KIRSCH, WILLIAM S., insurance company executive, lawyer; b. July 28, 1956; Grad., Northwestern U.; JD, Stanford U. With Kirkland & Ellis, 1981—2003, mng. ptnr., 1986—2003, mem. mgmt. com., co-chair, fin. com., mem. compensation com.; acting gen. counsel Conseco, Inc., Carmel, Ind., 2003, exec. v.p., gen. counsel, sect., 2003, pres., CEO, 2004—, bd. dir., 2004—. Office: Conseco Inc 11825 N Pennsylvannia St Carmel IN 46032*

KIRSCHBAUM, ALAN IRA, air force officer, systems integration specialist; b. Balt., Oct. 3, 1948; s. Marvin and Nadine (Gross) K.; m. Cheryl Louise Demming, Sept. 2, 1984. BME, U. Md., 1971; MBA, N.Mex. Highlands U., 1984; diploma, Def. Systems Mgmt. Coll., Alexandria, Va., 1981, Nat. Def. U., Washington, 1986. Registered profl. engr., Ohio. Commd. 2d lt. U.S. Air Force, 1971, advanced through grades to col., 1993, engine performance analyst aero. systems div. Dayton, Ohio, 1971-76, space def. project mgr., space div. L.A., 1976-79, satellite integration mgr., space div., 1979-81, concept devel. br. chief, weapons lab. Albuquerque, 1981-84, advanced systems integration chief, rsch. office Washington, 1985-89; chief seismic systems acquisition div. USAF Tech. Applications Ctr., Melbourne, Fla., 1989-93; dep. dir. Acquisitions Tech. Applications Ctr., Melbourne, Fla., 1991-93; dep. dir. tech. Ballistic Missile Def. Orgn., Washington, 1993-95; dir. systems engring. Space and Missile Systems Ctr. USAF, L.A., 1995—98; program mgr. space sys. and tech. AT&T Govt. Solutions, Santa Barbara, Calif., 1999—. Adviser Program Mgmt. Assistance Group, Dayton, 1981, Launch Readiness Rev., L.A., 1977. Contbr. articles to profl. jours. Big brother, Big Bros. Am., L.A., 1978; judge Internat. Sci./Engring. Fair, L.A., 1978; assoc. Kennedy Ctr. Performing Arts, Washington, 1985; grant evaluation panel United Way Santa Barbara County Cmty., 2001-05. Decorated Legion of Merit. Fellow AIAA (assoc., orgn. rep. 1977-79); mem. ASME, Air Force Assn., Mil. Ops. Rsch. Soc., Bard House Officers Club, Temple Beth Torah Brotherhood, Tau Beta Pi, Pi Tau Sigma, Omicron Delta Kappa. Home: 2210 Bermuda Dunes Pl Oxnard CA 93036-2778 E-mail: akirschbaum@att.com.

KIRSCHBAUM, LAURENCE J., publishing executive; Grad., U. Mich., 1966. Corr. Newsweek, Detroit, San Francisco; with mktg. dept. Random Ho., 1970; v.p. mktg. Warner Books, 1974—84, pres., 1984—96; chmn. CEO Time Warner Book Group, N.Y.C., 1996—. Office: Time Warner Book Group 1271 AVe of Ams New York NY 10020

KIRSCHBAUM, MYRON, lawyer; b. NYC, Nov. 20, 1949; s. Jonas and Doris (Rose) K.; m. Esther Weiner, June 23, 1971; children: Rachel, Shoshana Stein, Yisrael. BA, Yeshiva U., 1971; JD, Harvard U., 1974. Bar: N.Y. 1975, U.S. Dist. Ct. (so. dist.) N.Y. 1975, U.S. Dist. Ct. (no. dist.) Calif. 1989, U.S. Ct. Appeals (2d cir.) 1975, U.S. Ct. Appeals (9th cir.) 1990, U.S. Ct. Appeals (fed. cir.) 1994, U.S. Ct. Appeals (3d cir.) 2001. Law clk. U.S. Ct. Appeals (2d cir.), N.Y.C., 1974-75; assoc. Kaye, Scholer, Fierman, Hays & Handler, N.Y.C., 1975-82, ptnr., 1983—. Editor Harvard Law Rev., 1972-73, case and comment editor, 1973-74. Mem.: ABA, Dept. Disciplinary Com. Appellate Divsn. 1st dept., Assn. Bar City NY. Office: Kaye Scholer LLP 425 Park Ave New York NY 10022-3506 Office Phone: 212-836-8159. Business E-Mail: mkirschbaum@kayescholer.com.

KIRSCHBAUM, RONALD IRA, lawyer; b. Sebring, Fla., Oct. 13, 1942; s. Jack and Gertrude (Sager) Kirschbaum; m. Jan Ellen Kirschbaum, Nov. 28, 1999; children from previous marriage: Frank S., Cynthia D., Stephen L. AB,

Emory U., 1964; JD, U. N.C., 1967; LLM in Taxation, NYU, 1968. Bar: N.C. 1967, Mo. 1968, Fla. 1969. Assoc. Hoskins, King, Springer, McGannon & Hahn, Kansas City, Mo., 1968—69, Culverhouse, Tomlinson, Taylor & DeCarion, Miami, 1969—71; ptnr. Ragsdale & Kirschbaum P.A., Raleigh, NC, 1971—. Adj. prof. Campbell Sch. Law. Contbr. articles to profl. jours. Chmn. adv. bd. N.C. Anti-Defamation League, 1979—89; mem. Raleigh City Coun., 1973—77. Home: 4621 Grenadine Ct Raleigh NC 27612-4142 Office: Kirschbaum Manning Keenan & Griffin PA 2418 Blue Ridge Rd Raleigh NC 27607

KIRSCHENBAUM, HOWARD, education educator; b. NYC, Oct. 6, 1944; s. Abraham Irving and Theone (Hamburger) K.; m. Barbara Linell Glaser, Mar. 2, 1972 (div. 1985); 1 child, Kimara Linell; m. Mary M. Rapp, July 30, 1988. BA, New Sch. for Social Rsch., 1966; MS, Temple U., 1968, EdD, 1975. Tchr. Abington (Pa.) H.S., 1966-68, New Lincoln Sch., N.Y.C., 1968-69; instr. Temple U., Phila., 1969-71; exec. dir. Nat. Humanistic Edn. Ctr., Upper Jay, N.Y., 1971-77, Sagamore Inst., Raquette Lake, N.Y., 1977-90; pres. Values Assocs., Rochester, N.Y., 1990-97; prof. Warner Grad. Sch. Edn. U. Rochester, 1997—, chair counseling and human devel. dept., 2000—. Adj. faculty SUNY Brockport, 1992-97; dir. White Pine Camp Mus., Paul Smiths, N.Y., 1994-97. *A leader in the values education and character education movement from the 1970s on. One of the world's leading authorities on the life and work of humanistic psychology pioneer Carl Rogers (1902-1987).* Author: 100 Ways to Enhance Values and Morality in Schools and Youth Settings, 1995, On Becoming Carl Rogers, 1979; co-author: Values Clarification, 1972, 3rd edit., 1995, others; contbr. articles to profl. jours. Founder, pres. Adirondack Archtl. Heritage, Keeseville, N.Y., 1990-97; former bd. dirs., v.p. Adirondack Nature Conservancy and Land Trust, Keene Valley, N.Y. Mem. ACA, Author's Guild, Assn. Counselor Edn. and Supervision, Character Edn. Partnership, Nat. Eagle Scout Assn. Avocations: hiking, travel, historic preservation. Office: Warner Grad Sch Edn Univ Rochester Rochester NY 14627 Office Phone: 585-275-5077. Business E-Mail: Howard.Kirschenbaum@rochester.edu.

KIRSCHENMANN, HENRY GEORGE, JR., management consultant, former government official, accountant; b. Bklyn., June 11, 1930; s. Henry Godfrey and Eva Helen (Gellert) Kirschenmann; m. Pam Hirst; children: Victoria Mary, Henry George III, Ronald William. BS, Md. U.; MPA, Am. U. CPA; cert. gov. fin. mgr. Mem. auditor staff Price Waterhouse & Co., Washington; mem. auditor staff U.S. Army Audit Agy.; mem. internal auditor staff Martin-Marietta Co., Orlando, Fla.; various fin. and adminstrv. positions HEW, Washington; dep. asst. sec. HHS, Washington; assoc. cons. Bearing Point, Inc., Tyson's Corner, 1988—. Bd. dirs., assoc. dir. tng. Pub. Svc. Inst., Silver Spring, Md.; exec. dir. Nat. Edn. Inst., Rockville, Md. Pres. Support Groups, Inc.; dir. Soc. Not for Profit Orgns.and Cmtys., Inc. Recipient Superior Svc. award, HHS, Disting. Svc. award, Presdl. Rank award. Mem.: AICPA, Md. Assn. CPA, Inst. Cost Analysis, Assn. Govt. Accts., Nat. Grants Mgmt. Assn. (bus. officer 1997—2001, bd. dirs.), Soc. Rsch. Adminstrs.

KIRSCHNER, BARBARA STARRELS, gastroenterologist; b. Phila., Mar. 23, 1941; m. Robert H. Kirschner (dec.). MD, Women's Med. Coll. Pa., 1967. Diplomate Am. Bd. Pediatrics; cert. in pediatric gastroenterology and nutrition. Intern U. Chgo., 1967-68, resident, 1968-70; mem. staff U. Chgo. Children's Hosp., 1977-83, asst. prof. pediatrics, 1984-88, prof. pediatrics and medicine, 1988—, mem. com. on nutrition and nutritional biology. Contbr. articles to profl. jours. Pediatric Gastroenterology fellow U. Chgo., 1975-77; recipient Davidson award in Pediatric gastroenterology Acad. Pediatrics, 1993, Joseph Brenneman award Chgo. Pediat. Soc., 2001. Mem. Am. Gastroenterologic Assn., N.Am. Soc. Pediatric Gastroenterology, Soc. Pediatric Rsch., Alpha Omega Alpha. Office: U Chgo Med Ctr 5839 S Maryland Ave # MC 4065 Chicago IL 60637-5417 Office Phone: 773-702-6152.

KIRSCHNER, MARC ALAN, neuroscientist; b. Cin., July 3, 1956; s. Jack Robert and Lucretia (Einstein) K. BA, Middlebury Coll., 1978; MD, Case Western Res. U., 1982. Neurology resident McGill U., 1987; postdoctoral fellow Howard Hughes Med. Inst., New Haven, Conn., 1988-89; assoc. rsch. scientist Yale U., New Haven, 1989-91; instr. Oreg. Health Scis. U., Portland, 1991-92, asst. prof., 1992—. Rsch. asst. prof. Vollum Inst. for Advanced Biomed. Rsch. Mem. Am. Acad. Neurology, Soc. for Neurosci. Achievements include research in isolation and characterization of mouse high-affinity excitatory amino acid transporters. Office: Oreg Health Scis Univ Vollum Inst 3181 SW Sam Jackson Park Rd Portland OR 97201-3011

KIRSCHNER, RONALD ALLEN, osteopathic plastic surgeon, ophthalmologist, educator; b. N.Y.C., Jan. 18, 1942; s. Hyman C. and Eleanor (Pinkus) K.; m. Olivia Barbara Schlesinger, June 27, 1964; children: Andrew Scott, Julie Renee. AB, NYU, 1962; DO, Phila. Coll. Osteo. Medicine, 1966, MS in Otolaryngology, 1972. Diplomate Am. Osteo. Bd. Otolaryngology. Intern LeRoy Hosp., N.Y.C., 1966-67; resident Grandview Hosp., Dayton, Ohio, 1967-68, Phila. Coll. Osteo. Medicine, 1970-72, asst. prof., 1972-74, assoc. prof., 1974-76, clin. assoc. prof., 1976-85, clin. prof., 1985-90, prof., chmn. dept. otolaryngology, bronchoesophalogy and facial plastic surgery, 1990-92, dir. emerging tech., 1992—; pvt. practice in plastic, otolaryngology and laser surgery Bala Cynwyd, Pa., 1976—. Dir. neurosensory unit, 1973-76; chmn. laser surgery City Ave. Hosp., Grad. Health System, 1994—; NIH fellow Armed Forces INst. Pathology, Washington, 1971; attending physician Grad. Hosp., 1991—, Suburban Gen. Hosp., chief ear, nose, and throat and plastic surgery, 1976-96, chmn. divsn. surgery, 1983-89, exec. com., 1983-89; attending physician, cons. Del. Valley Med. Ctr., 1985-92, Presbyn.-U. Pa. Med. Ctr., 1987—, Hosp. of Phila. Coll. Osteo. Medicine, chmn. laser and endoscopy com., 1987-89, 91—, mem. exec. com., 1990-92; v.p., chief med. adv. Courtlandt Group, 1979-85, exec. v.p., 1985-86, also dir. rsch. and edn., 1986; otolaryngologist Pa. Hearing Assn., 1986—; preceptor Xanar Laser Divsn., Johnson & Johnson, 1982; design cons. Philling Inc., 1982-87, Inframed Inc., 1985-97, Sigma Dynamics Inc., Rhein Med., Inc., 1988-97; otologic cons. Children's Hearing Aid Bank; pres. Kirschner Design Group, Inc., 1987—; bd. dirs. KDG-Rotem U.S.A., Pa. Acad. Cosmetic Surgery; dir. head and neck YAG laser protocol Cooper Lasersonics, 1983-88; chmn. med. symposium Internat. Conf. on Applied Laser Electro Optics, 1986, 87, 91; session chair Medtech '89, Freie Univ., Berlin, 1989; vis. prof. internat. sch. for quantum electronics Ettore Majorana Nato, Erice, Sicily, 1990; cons. Bur. Vocat. Rehab., Imunodiagnostics Lab., Allergy Mgmt. Systems Inc., dir. 1st World Congress on Cosmetic Laser Surgery, 1992; workshop dir. Internat. Conf. on Occuloplastic Surgery, 1995. Med. editor Med. Portfolio, 1980-85; guest editor Surg. Clinics of N.Am., 1984; monthly columnist Photonics Spectra, 1987-91; contbg. editor Photonics Spectra, 1988-94; med. editl. bd. Pa. Osteo. Med. Jour., Laurin Publs., 1987-94, Laser Applications; contbr. articles to med. jours., chpts. in med. texts; developer various med. instruments. Served with M.C., USN, 1968-70; lt. comdr. Res. Recipient award for disting. tchg. Lindbach Found., 1973, Legion of Honor, Chapel of Four Chaplains, 1982; Survivor of Yr. award, 1984; named Disting. Practitioner Am. Acads. of Practice. Fellow Pan Am. Allergy Assn., Phila. Acad. Facial Plastic Surgery, Phila. Laryngologic Soc., Phila. Coll. Physicians, Am. Soc. Lasers in Medicine and Surgery, Am. Auditory Soc., Am. Acad. Otolaryngology-Head and Neck Surgery, Soc. Ear, Nose, and Throat Advances in Children, Am. Acad. Facial Plastic Surgery (assoc.), Soc. Photo Optical Engrs., Osteo. Coll. Ophthalmology and Otorhinolaryngology, Am. Acad. Cosmetic Surgery; mem. AMA, Am. Osteo. Assn. (editl. cons. Jour. 1977—, editl. referee 1980—), Am. Soc. Esthetic and Reconstructive Surgery, Pa. Med. Soc., Pa. Acad. Otolaryngology, Pa. Acad. Cosmetic Surgery (bd. dirs. 1990—), Internat. Soc. Cosmetic Plastic Surgeons (bd. dirs. 1990-94), Internat. Soc. Cosmetic Plastic Surgery, Philadelphia County Osteo. Med. Assn. (chair laser com.), Centurian Club of Deafness Rsch. Found., Internat. Assn. Logopedics and Phoniatrics, Midwestern Biolaser Inst., Inst. for Applied Laser Surgery (pres.), Pa. Osteo. Med. Assn. (chmn. com. otolaryngology 1984-88, 90-92, chmn. com. promotion of rsch. 1985-88), Am. Acad. Osteopathy Survivors Club of Phila. Coll. Osteo. Medicine (pres. 1981-82), Internat. Soc. for Optical Engring., AAAS, AMA, Acad. Surg. Rsch., N.Y. Acad. Scis., Am. Soc. Liposuction Surgery, Laser Assn. Am. (sec. 1985-88), Laser and Electro Optics Mfs. Assn., Am. Assn. Advancement Med. Instrumentation, Am. Soc. Cosmetic Surgeons, Pa. Hearing Aid Soc. (otologist), Pa. Am. Assn. Otolaryngology and Bronchoesophagology, Pa. Acad. Ophthalmology and Otolaryngology, Pa. Osteo. Med. Soc. (chmn. com. otolaryngology 1984-88, 90—, chmn. med. adv. bd.), Del Valley Tinnitus Assn., Laser Inst. Am. (sr. Outstanding Svc. award 1986, chmn. lasers 1987-89, bd. dirs. 1989—, dir., chmn. com. on biology and medicine 1989-92), Pa. Acad. Cosmetic Surger (bd. dirs.), Am. Acad. Cosmetic Laser Surgery (bd. dirs. 1991-94), Pa. Med. Soc., Montgomery County Med. Soc., Variety Club, NYU Club, Vesper Club, Pickwick Club of Phila., Masons, Shriners, Sigma Xi, Sigma Chi, Lambda Omicron Gamma (pres. 1981-82, Disting. Svc. award Caduceus chpt. 1982). Jewish. Office: 2 Bala Cynwyd Plz Ste 17il Bala Cynwyd PA 19004

KIRSCHNER, STANLEY, chemist; b. N.Y.C., Dec. 17, 1927; s. Abraham and Rebecca K.; m. Esther Green, June 11, 1950; children— Susan Joyce, Daniel Ross. BS magna cum laude, Bklyn. Coll., 1950; AM, Harvard U., 1952; PhD, U. Ill., 1954. Research chemist Monsanto Chem. Co., Everett, Mass., 1951; teaching asst. in chemistry Harvard U., 1950-52, U. Ill., Urbana, 1952-54; mem. faculty dept. chemistry Wayne State U., Detroit, 1954—, prof., 1960—, prof. emeritus, 1992—. Vis. prof. U. London, 1963-64, U. Florence, Italy, 1976, U. Sao Paulo, Brazil, 1969, Tohoku U., Sendai, Japan, 1978, Tech. U. Lisbon, Portugal, 1984, U. Porto, Portugal, 1984 Author: Advances in the Chemistry of Coordination Compounds, 1961, Coordination Chemistry, 1969, Inorganic Syntheses, Vol. 23, 1985; contbr. articles to profl. jours. Served with USN, 1945-46. Recipient Pres.'s award for excellence in teaching Wayne State U., 1979, Gold award Engring. Soc. of Detroit, 1995, Heyrovsky medal Czechoslovak Acad. Scis., 1978, Catalyst award in chem. edn. Chem. Mfrs. Assn., 1984, Faculty Svc. award Wayne State U. Alumni Assn., 1986; fellow Fulbright Found., 1963-64, NSF, 1963-64, Ford Found., 1969-70. Fellow AAAS, Am. Inst. Chemists, N.Y. Acad. Scis.; mem. AAUP, Am. Chem. Soc. (chmn. divsn. edn., bd. dirs. 1985-93, Henry Hill award 1995, Brazilian Acad. Scis., Internat. Conf. Coordination Chemistry (permanent sec. 1966-89, emeritus 1990), Internat. Union Pure and Applied Chemistry (com. nomenclature of inorganic chemistry 1991-93), Chem. Soc. Chile (hon.), Chem. Soc. (London). Office: Dept Chemistry Wayne State Univ Detroit MI 48202

KIRSCHSTEIN, RUTH LILLIAN, physician; b. Bklyn., Oct. 12, 1926; d. Julius and Elizabeth (Berm) Kirschstein; m. Alan S. Rabson, June 11, 1950; 1 child, Arnold. BA magna cum laude, L.I. U., 1947; MD, Tulane U., 1951, LLD, PhD, Tulane U., 1997; DSc (hon.), Mt. Sinai Sch. Medicine, 1984; LLD, Atlanta U., 1985; DSc (hon.), Med. Coll. Ohio, 1986; LHD (hon.), L.I. U., 1991; PhD (hon.), U. Rochester Sch. Medicine, 1998, Brown U., 1999; DSc (hon.), Spelman Coll., 2001, Georgetown U., 2001. Intern Kings County Hosp., Bklyn., 1951-52; resident pathology VA Hosp., Atlanta, Providence Hosp., Detroit, Clin. Ctr., NIH, Bethesda, Md., 1952-57; fellow Nat. Heart Inst. Tulane U., 1953-54; asst. dir. div. biologics standards NIH, 1971-72; dep. dir. Bur. Biologics, FDA, 1972-73, dep. assoc. commr. sci., 1973-74; acting assoc. dir. woman's health NIH, Bethesda, 1974-93, acting dir., 1993, dep. dir., 1993—99, acting dir., 2000—02, sr. advisor to dir., 2003—. Chmn. grants peer rev. study team NIH; mem. Inst. Medicine NAS, 1982—; co-chair, sec. Spl. Emphasis Oversight com. on Sci. and Tech., 1989—; mem. Office Tech. Assessment Adv. Com. on Basic Rsch., 1989—; co-chair PHS Coordinating Com. on Women's Health Issues, 1990—. Recipient Superior Svc. award, 1980, 1993, Presdl. Disting. Exec. Rank award, 1985, 1995, Pub. Svc. award, Fedn. Am. Soc.s Exptl. Biology, 1993, Nat. Pub. Svc. award, Am. Pub. Adminstrn./Nat. Acad. Pub. Adminstrn., 1994, Roger W. Jones award for exec. leadership, Am. U., 1994, Georgeanna Seegar Jones Women's Health Lifetime Achievement award, 1995, Albert Sabin Hero of Sci. award, 2000, Women Achievement award, Anti-Defamation League, 2001, J. Richard Nesson award, Harvard Med. Sch., 2002, Pub. Svc. award, Am. Soc. for Biochemistry and Molecular Biology, 2003. Mem.: NAS-IOM, AMA (Dr. Nathan Davis award 1990), Am. Acad. Arts and Scis., Am. Acad. Microbiology, Am. Assn. Pathologists, Am. Assn. Immunologists. Office: NIH 1 Center Dr Msc 0148 Rm 158 Bethesda MD 20892-0001 Business E-Mail: rk25n@nih.gov.

KIRSHBAUM, HOWARD M., retired judge; b. Oberlin, Ohio, Sept. 19, 1938; s. Joseph and Gertrude (Morris) K.; m. Priscilla Joy Parmakian, Aug. 15, 1964; children: Audra Lee, Andrew William. BA, Yale U., 1960; AB, Cambridge U., 1962, MA, 1966; LLB, Harvard U., 1965. Ptnr. Zarlengo and Kirshbaum, Denver, 1969-75; judge Denver Dist. Ct., 1975-80, Colo. Ct. Appeals, Denver, 1980-83; justice Colo. Supreme Ct., Denver, 1983-97; arbiter Jud. Arbiter Group, Inc., Denver, 1997—, sr. judge, 1997—. Adj. prof. law U. Denver, 1970-; dir. Am. Law Inst. Phila., 1982-2002, Am. Judicature Soc., Chgo., 1979-2002, Colo. Jud. Inst. Denver, 1979-89; pres. Colo. Legal Care Soc., Denver, 1974-75. Bd. dirs. Young Artists Orch., Denver, 1976-85; pres. Cmty. Arts Symphony, Englewood, Colo., 1972-74; dir. Denver Opportunity, Inc., Denver, 1972-74; vice-chmn. Denver Coun. on Arts and Humanities, 1969. Mem.: ABA (standing com. pub. edn. 1996—2001), Assn. for Conflict Resolution, Denver Bar Assn. (trustee 1981—83), Colo. Bar Assn. Avocation: music performance. Office: Jud Arbiter Group Inc 1601 Blake St Ste 400 Denver CO 80202-1328 Office Phone: 303-572-1919.

KIRSHBAUM, JON ALAN, systems analyst, consultant, retired systems administrator; b. L.A., Nov. 5, 1942; s. George Alexander and Mary Elizabeth (Ball) K.; m. Anne Nofrey, Aug. 11, 1961 (div.); 1 child, Warren Ashley (dec.); m. Linda Louise Carl, Dec. 15, 1976; stepchildren: Gary Nicholas, Grant Adam. BS in Comprehensive Mktg., No. Ill. U., 1965, MBA in Fin., 1971, postgrad., 1988-93; MDiv, McCormick Theol. Seminary, Chgo., 1980. Cert. chief sch. bus. ofcl., data warehouse cons. IRD sales/DPD br. office adminstr. IBM Corp., Chgo., 1965-67, systems analyst/sr. assoc. planner Endicott, N.Y., 1967-71; seminary asst. Lincoln Park Presbyn. Ch., Chgo., 1972-73; team/project leader Chgo. Pub. Schs., 1974-89, data base adminstr., 1989-92, supr. desktop pub., 1992-94, core team mem., Time re-engring. project, 1994-95; project leader Info. Technologies, Chgo., 1995-96; prin. cons. Keane, Inc., Lisle, Ill., 1996-99; sr. analyst Mantiss a Dynegy Co., Chgo., 2000-2001. Freelance travel writer and editor, 1998—. Mng. editor: Today's Traveler Mag., Chgo., 1991-92, exec. editor/v.p. mktg., 1992-97. Mem. DuPage County (Ill.) Geneal. Soc. (bd. dirs. 1986-89, pres. 1989-90), DuPage County Hist. Soc., Glen Ellyn (Ill.) Hist. Soc., Salem (Ohio) Hist. Soc., Project Mgmt. Inst. (Chicagoland chpt.), Soc. Profl. Journalists, Chgo. Headline Club, N.Am. Travel Journalists Assn. (regional v.p. 1993-94), East West News Bur. Internat., US Lighthouse Soc., New Dungeness Light Sta. Assn., Dama Internat. (Chgo. chpt.), River Ctr. Found., Near East Archaeol. Soc. Republican. Presbyterian. Avocations: fishing, genealogy, travel, weaving. E-mail: jon_kirshbaum@usa.net.

KIRSHBAUM, LAURENCE J., book publishing executive; Degree, U. Mich., 1966. Reporter Newsweek Mag., Detroit and San Francisco, 1966—69; asst. sales mgr. Random House, 1970—74; dir. mktg. Ballantine Books, 1970—74; from v.p. mktg. to pres. Warner Books, Warner Pub. Svcs., 1974—82; v.p., circulation dir. Conde Nast Pubs., 1982—83; pub., COO Warner Books, 1983—84, pres., 1984—95, chmn., 1996—2005. Co-author: Is the Library Burning?, 1970.

KIRSHBAUM, LAWRENCE G., investment company executive; CFO Prescott, Ball & Turben, Cleve., 1974-87, chmn., CEO, 1987-90; CFO, exec. pres. John Hancock Freedom Securities, N.Y.C., 1991—, dir., Tucker Anthony Inc., Freedom Capital Mgmt. Office: John Hancock Freedom Securities Corp One World Financial Center 200 Liberty St Fl 3 New York NY 10281-1074

KIRSHENBAUM, RICHARD IRVING, retired public health physician; b. Bklyn., Aug. 19, 1933; s. Joseph and Anne (Hantman) K.; m. Jean Shicher, Aug. 17, 1957; children: Miriam, Susan, Rachel. AB, Temple U., 1955; DO, Phila. Coll. Osteo. Medicine, 1959; MPH, Columbia U., 1971. Diplomate Am. Bd. Preventive Medicine. Resident intern Met. Hosp., Phila., 1959-60; pvt. practice medicine Bklyn., 1960-70; resident in pub. health N.Y.C. Dept. Health, 1970-73, pub. health physician, 1973-81, regional health dir. for Queens County, 1977-80, chief epidemiologist for Manhattan Borough, 1980-81; pub. health physician N.Y. State Dept. Health, N.Y.C., 1981-98; retired, 1998. Contbr. articles to profl. jours. Lt. col. Med. Corps N.Y. Army NG, 1981-91, USAR, 1991-93. Recipient Physician's Recognition award AMA 1973, 76, 79, 82, 85, 88, 90, 93, 96, 98. Home: 313 Whitman Dr Brooklyn NY 11234-6935 Personal E-mail: bd67124@optonline.net.

KIRSHNER, ALAN I., insurance company executive; Grad., Vanderbilt Univ. Dir. Markel Corp., Glen Allen, Va., 1978—, pres., 1979—92, chmn., CEO, 1986—. Office: Markel Corporation 4521 Highwoods Pkwy Glen Allen VA 23060*

KIRSNER, JOSEPH BARNETT, physician, educator; b. Boston, Sept. 21, 1909; s. Harris and Ida (Waiser) K.; m. Minnie Schneider, Jan. 6, 1934 (dec. Dec. 4, 1998); 1 son, Robert S. MD, Tufts U., 1933; PhD in Biol. Scis., U. Chgo., 1942; DSc (hon.), Tufts U., 1993. Intern Woodlawn Hosp., Chgo., 1933—34, resident in internal medicine, 1934—35; asst. in medicine U. Chgo., 1935—37, from asst. prof. to assoc. prof., 1937—51, prof., 1951—, Louis Block Disting. Service prof. medicine, 1968—, chief of staff, also dep. dean for med. affairs, 1971—76. Cons. NIH, 1956-69; hon. pres. Gastrointestinal Research Found., 1961-; Mem. drug efficacy adv. com. to NRC; chmn. adv. group Nat. Commn. on Digestive Diseases, 1978; chmn. emeritus sci. adv. com. Nat. Found. Ileitis and Colitis. Editor, author: Kirsner's Inflammatory Bowel Disease, 6th edit., 2004, The Growth of Gastroenterologic Knowledge During the 20th Century, 1994, Early Days of American Gastroenterology, 1996; contbr. more than 800 articles to profl. jours. Served with M.C. AUS, 1943-46, ETO, PTO. Recipient Julius Friedenwald medal disting. work gastroenterology, 1975, Horatio Alger award, 1979, hon. Gold Key for Disting. Service U. Chgo. Med. Alumni Assn., 1979, Alumni medal U. Chgo. Alumni Assn., 1989, Disting. Educator award Am. Gastroenterological Assn., 1999; Joseph B. Kirsner award for excellence in rsch. in clin. gastroenterology established in his honor, Am. Gastroent. Assn., 1990; G. Brohée lectr. World Cong. Gastroenterology, 1994, Laureate award Lincoln Acad. Ill. Mem. Am. Assn. Physicians, ACP (master, John Phillips award), Am. Gastroent. Assn. (past pres., governing bd.), Am. Gastroscopic Soc. (past pres.), Am. Soc. Gastrointestinal Endoscopy (past pres., Rudolf Schindler award), Am. Soc. Clin. Investigation, Ctrl. Soc. Clin. Rsch., Chgo. Soc. Internal Medicine (past pres.), Inst. Medicine Chgo. (George H. Coleman medal, Lifetime Achievement award 2004) Achievements include rsch. in gastrointestinal disorders, inflammatory disease of gastrointestinal tract. Home: 5805 S Dorchester Ave Top C Chicago IL 60637-1730 Office: U Chgo Med Ctr 5841 S Maryland Ave MC 2200 Chicago IL 60637-1470 Office Phone: 773-702-6101. Business E-Mail: jkirsner@medicine.bsd.uchicago.edu. *We need a return to higher standards, personally and professionally. Striving for personal excellence and achievement promotes universal excellence and peace.*

KIRSTEUER, ERNST KARL EBERHART, biologist, curator; b. Vienna, Sept. 28, 1933; came to U.S., 1965; s. Ernst and Barbara (Reichhalter) K.; m. Erika Stepnitz, Jan. 18, 1958. PhD (research fellow 1958-60), U. Vienna, 1961. Instr. U. Vienna, 1961-62; prof. marine biology U. Cumana, Venezuela, 1963-65; asst. curator Am. Mus. Natural History, N.Y.C., 1965-70, assoc. curator, 1970-75, curator, 1975-87, chmn., 1977-84, ret., 1987. Contbr. articles to profl. jours. NSF grantee, 1968-71.

KIRTLAND, MICHAEL ARTHUR, lawyer; b. St. Louis, Oct. 27, 1951; s. John Thornton and Joan Reichert Kirtland; m. Kay Tegman Kirtland, May 17, 1975; children; David Arthur, James Michael. BA, Coe Coll., 1974; MPA, U. Colo., 1981; JD, Faulkner U., 1993; LLM, U. Ala., 1999. Bar: Ala. 1994, U.S. Dist. Ct. (mid. dist.) Ala. 1994, U.S. Supreme Ct. 1997, U.S. Ct. Appeals (11th cir.) 1998. Commd. 2d lt. USAF, 1974, advanced through grades to lt. col., 1990, retired, 1995; atty. pvt. practice, Montgomery, Ala., 1995—. Editor: Air University Review Index, 1990, Air Power Journal Index, 1992. Active Laubruch Literacy Coun., Montgomery, 1996—. Mem. ABA, Nat. Assn. Estate Planners & Counsels, Nat. Acad. Elder Law Attys., Air Force Assn. (life), Retired Officers Assn. Office: 2835 Zelda Rd Montgomery AL 36106-2667

KIRTLEY, JANE ELIZABETH, law educator; b. Indpls., Nov. 7, 1953; d. William Raymond and Faye Marie (Price) Kirtley; m. Stephen Jon Cribari, May 8, 1985. BS in Journalism, Northwestern U., 1975, MS in Journalism, 1976; JD, Vanderbilt U., 1979. Bar: N.Y. 1980, U.S. Dist. Ct. (we. dist.) N.Y. 1980, DC 1982, U.S. Dist. Ct. DC 1982, U.S. Ct. Claims 1982, U.S. Ct. Appeals (4th cir.) 1982, U.S. Ct. Appeals (DC cir.) 1985, U.S. Supreme Ct. 1985, Va. 1995, U.S. Ct. Appeals (10th cir.) 1996, U.S. Ct. Appeals (5th cir.) 1997, U.S. Ct. Appeals (6th and 11th cirs.) 1998. Assoc. Nixon, Hargrave, Devans & Doyle, Rochester, NY, 1979-81, Washington, 1981-84; exec. dir. Reporters Com. for Freedom of Press, Arlington, Va., 1985-99; Silha prof. media ethics & law Sch. Journalism & Mass Comm. U. Minn., Mpls., 1999—, mem. affiliated faculty Law Sch., 2001—; dir. Silha Ctr. Study Media Ethics and Law, Mpls., 2000—. Mem. adj. faculty Am. U. Sch. Comm., 1988—98; mem. affiliated law faculty U. Minn., 2001—; disting. vis. prof. Suffolk U. Law Sch., 2004. Exec. articles editor: Vanderbilt U. Jour. Transnational Law, 1978—79; editor: The News Media and the Law, 1985—, The First Amendment Handbook, 1987, 4th edit., 1995, Agents of Discovery, 1991, 1993, 1995, Pressing Issues, 1998—99; columnist: NEPA Bull., 1988—89, Va.'s Press, 1991—99, Am. Journalism Rev., 1995—, W.Va.'s Press, 1997—99, Tenn. Press, 1997—99, mem. editl. bd.: Comm. Law and Policy. Bd. dirs. Sigma Delta Chi Found., Indpls. Mem.: ABA, Va. State Bar Assn., DC Bar Assn., N.Y. State Bar Assn., Sigma Delta Chi. Home: 3645 46th Ave S Minneapolis MN 55406-2937 Office: 111 Murphy Hall 206 Church St SE Minneapolis MN 55455-0488 Office Phone: 612-625-9038. Business E-Mail: kirtl001@tc.umn.edu.

KIRTON, JENNIFER MYERS, artist; b. Berwick, Pa., Sept. 16, 1949; d. Fred H. and Jean I. Myers; m. Timothy Kirton, Aug. 8, 1970; children: Timothy James, Andrea Jolene, Andrew Joseph. Diploma, Orange Meml. Sch. Nursing, Orlando, Fla., 1970. RN. Galleries in Paris; represented by Mt. Dora (Fla.) Creative Framing Gallery, Met. Art and Antiques Gallery, art-exchang.com, IRRA Registry, Ormond Beach, Leesburg Ctr for Arts, NMWA Gallery Artisan Inn, Deland. Tchr. drawing Mt. Dora Ctr. for Arts; overseas prodn. exhibitor, Paris, 1992—; lectr. in field; chair, judge juried art shows. *Jennifer Kirton, having had only one year of high school art under Robert McGee, who is still an influence, has spent years experimenting, exploring, and perfecting her talent on a daily quest of self-improvement. She was mentored early in her career by artists, Charles Turzak, Joy Pastle and Don Harris, who encouraged and taught her not only technique but passion and dedication to art. Kirton has raised a family, overcome a visual impairment, and recovered from a nearly career-ending injury to her drawing arm. Her art is in prominent collections, but one of her greatest fulfillments is encouraging other artists.* Exhibited in group shows at Nat. Red Cross Scholastic (Nat. award, 1961), Apopka Art & Foliage (1st Place, 1975, 1982, Purchase award, 1978, 3rd Place, 1983, Hon. Mention, 1980, 1986), Winter Park Mall (Best of Show, 1977), Longwood ALOC/CFA (3rd Place, 1980), Colonial Plz. (Hon. Mention, 1982, 1st Place, 1988, 1989), Springs Plz. (Hon. Mention, 1983), Howell Branch Plz. (1st Place, 1984), Under the Trees (2nd Place, 1984, Special Judges award, 1985), Fashion Sq. (Hon. Mention, 1986), Artist League (Hon. Mention, 1986), Centrust (1st Place, 1988), Lake County Art Show (Hon. Mention, 1992), Working Area Artist, Altamonte Libr., Pine Hills, Fiesta in Pk., Art Addiction Sweeden, Mount Dora Ctr. Arts (hon. mention), Internat. Judeo Christian Upstream Gallery, MDCA Permanent Collection, Artists Fla., Vol. IV, 1994—95, one-woman shows include Meritor Bank, Seminole CC, 5th St., Overseas European Corp., Mayor's Show Apopka City Hall, Fruitland Park Libr., Winter Barn Fine Art Gallery, Biennial Deland Mus. Art, Miami Serious Studios, mural, Apopka H.S. Stadium, Represented in permanent collections City of Apopka, Mt. Dora Ctr. for Arts, exhibited in group shows at Galveston Serious Studio. Named Artist of Month, artexchange website, artisrepublik.com, Co-artist of Month, Legacy Fine Art. Mem.: Internat. Registry Artist and Artwork, Art Exch., Leesburg Art Assn., Ctrl. Fla. Artists, Orange County League Artists (past pres.), Nat. League Pen Women, Nat. Mus. Women Arts (mem. Fla. com., historian ecentfl.com, historian). Baptist. Avocation: collecting fine art. Home: 4700 Meadowland Dr Mount Dora FL 32757-9661 Office Phone: 407-353-8332. Personal E-mail: kirtonart@aol.com.

KIRTON, ORLANDO CECILIO, surgeon, educator; b. Gamboa, Panama, Sept. 14, 1958; s. Leafton and Ruth Isabel (Atkinson) K.; m. Jillian Euphemia, July 4, 1987; children: Phillip, Briana, Emily. BA in Biochemistry, Brown U., 1978; MD cum laude, Harvard U., 1983. Diplomate Am. Bd. Surgery. Intern SUNY Health Sci Ctr., Bklyn., 1983-84; resident in surgery SUNY, Bklyn., 1984-85, 87-89, chief resident in surgery, 1989-90; clin. instr., rsch. fellow dept. pathology Children's Hosp., Boston, 1985-87; fellow surg. critical care dept. surgery Jackson Meml. Hosp./U. Miami Sch. Medicine, 1990-91; fellow surgery trauma Jackson Meml. Hosp./U. Miami, 1991-92; med. dir. advanced trauma life support Jackson Meml. Hosp./U. Miami Sch. Medicine, 1996—99; asst. prof. clin. surgery dept. surgery U. Miami Sch. Medicine, 1992-97, coord., undergraduate edu. for trauma svcs., 1993—97, assoc. prof. surgery, 1997-99; assoc. dir. surg. intensive care Jackson Meml. Med. Ctr., 1992—; assoc. dir. dept. surgery, chief gen. surgery Hartford (Conn.) Hosp., 1999—2002, active, asst. staff, dept. surgery, 1999—2001, chief, Red Svc. and Red Svc. Clinic, 1999—2001, assoc. dir., surgical intensive care unit, 1999—, chief, divsn. gen. surgery, 1999—, attending physician, trauma, critical care svcs., 1999—, chairperson, quality assurance subcom., exec. com., dept. surgery, 1999—, active, assoc. staff, dept. emergency medicine, 2001—, acting dir., dept. surgery, 2002—; med. student site dir. Darmouth Med. Sch.; assoc. prof. surgery U. Conn. Sch. Medicine, Farmington, Conn., 1999—2003, vice-chmn., dept. surgery, assoc. prof. surgery, dept. trauma and emergency med. svcs., 1999—, assoc. program dir., integrated gen. surgery residency training program, 1999—, prof. surgery, dept. surgery, 2003—; site dir., integrated gen. surgery residency training program Hartford Hosp., Conn., 1999—; course dir. ATLS-Am. Coll. Surgeons Conn. Com. on Trauma, Hartford Hosp., Conn., 2001—. Attending trauma surgeon Jackson Meml. Ctr., 1992-99, mem. faculty, gen. surg. & trauma critical care, 1992-99, mem. faculty anesthesia critical care, 1992-99, assoc. dir., surgical intensive care unit, 1992-99, assoc. dir. trauma intensive care unit, 1992-97, attending physician, nutritional and metabolic support svcs., 1993-99, attending physician dept. hyperbaric medicine, 1995-99; attending surgeon VA Hosp., Miami, 1995-99; attending physician, U. Miami and Clinics/Sylvester Comprehensive Cancer Ctr., 1993-99; interim chief, divsn. trauma, U. Miami Sch. of Medicine/Jackson Meml. Med. Ctr., dept. surgery, 1996; med. dir. trauma ICU Jackson Meml. Med. Ctr., 1997—; chmn. Trauma Quality Mgmt. Com., Ryder Trauma Ctr., Jackson Meml. Med. Ctr., 1996-97, interim dir., trauma ward unit, 1997, med. dir., trauma intensive care unit, 1997-99; spkr. and moderator in the field; vis. prof. Roanoke Meml. Hosp., dept. surgery, Va., 1995, Orlando Regional Med. Ctr., dept. surgery, Fla., 1997, Grant/Riverside Methodist Hospitals, dept. surgery, Columbus, Ohio, 1997, Integrated Gen. Surgery Residency program, U. Conn. Sch. Medicine, Hartford Hosp., New Britain Gen. Hosp., New Britain Gen. Hosp. and St. Francis Hosp. and Med. Ctr. Hartford and New Britain, Conn., 1999, Baystate Med. Ctr., dept. surgery, Springfield, Mass., 1999, Bridgeport Hosp., dept. surgery, Yale, New Haven Health, Conn., 2000, Surgical Critical Care, dept. surgery and anesthesia, U. Rochester Sch. Medicine, Strong Meml. Hospital, NY, 2001, Sect. Trauma and Critical Care, Yale U. Sch. Medicine, New Haven, Conn., 2003; various com. memberships and adminstrv. responsibilities for U. Miami Sch. Medicine/Jackson Meml. Hosp., U. Conn. Sch. Medicine, Hartford Hosp., Hartford, Conn. Cons. (manuscript reviewer) editor Chest, 1996-, Critical Care medicine, 1997-, Intensive Care Medicine, 2000-, Jour. Trauma, 2001; contbr. articles to profl. jours.; co-author of books, chpts. of books, and monographs. Spkr. 4th Ann. Black History Month program Miami Arena, 1995; mem. Chapman Premedical Soc. and Med. Magnet Program, Miami North Western Sr. High Sch., 1992-95, Dade County Trauma adv. com., 1996-, Anesthesiology and Respiratory Therapy Devices Panel of Med. Devices Adv. Com., Ctr. for Devices and Radiological Health, Food and Drug Adminstrn., 1994-, Assn. Program Dirs. in Surgery Task Force on Short and Long Term Planning Issues, 2001-; chmn. membership com., Coon. Chpt., Am. Col. Surgeons, 2001-; fellowship site reviewer, Soc. Surgical Oncology, Residency Review Com. Commd. as major US Army Reserve Med. Corp., 1992—. Nat. AMEDD Augmentation Detachment, Fort Gillem, Forest Park, Ga. Recipient H. Quillian Jones award Fla. Com. Trauma, 1991, Disting. Svc. award South Fla. Coalition Black Trade Unionists, 1993; grantee Nat. Rsch. Svc., 1985-87, Merck & Co., 1993, Zeneca Pharms., 1995—; rsch. fellow NY Dept. Health, 1979; merit scholar, Henry J. Kaiser Family Found. Assoc. fellow and fellow ACS (candidate group 1984-92); fellow Am. Coll. Critical Care Medicine, Am. Coll. Chest Physicians (Dupont Pharma. Young Investigator award, 1993, Critical Care Rsch. award, 1995, finalist, Alfred Soffer Rsch. award, 1995); mem. AMA, Nat. Med. Assn.(William H. Sinkler Meml. Lectr., 2001, co-chair, critical care symposium, surgery sect., 1999-, Charles Drew Surgical Rsch. Forum, surgical sect.), Am. Trauma Soc., Am. Assn. Surgery Trauma, Assn. Acad. Surgeons, Soc. Critical Care Medicine (abstract reviewer 1994-98, editor surg. sect. newsletter 1995-97, Presdl. Citation award, 1997. 98. 2000, & 2001, annual edu. and scientific symposium program subcom., co-chmn., 1998-2001, coun. 2001-, dir. edu. affairs divsn., 2002-, vice-chair, membership com., 2002-03, chair, 2003-, pub. policy com., 1998-99, chmn. surgical sect., 1998-99), So. Med. Assn., Eastern Assn. Surgery Trauma (bd. dirs. 1998-2001, annual prog. com. 1997-2000, chmn. membership com., 1998-2001, multi-institutional trials subcom., 1997-, publications com., 2000-, nominating com., 2002-), Assn. Surg. Edn., Nat. Assn. Residents and Interns, Fla. Com. on Trauma (assoc. mem.), Surgical Infection Soc., Soc. U. Surgeons, Hartford Cty. Med. Assn., New England Surgical Soc., Alpha Omega Alpha. Office: Hartford Hosp Dept Surgery Bliss 501 PO Box 5037 80 Seymour St Hartford CT 06102-5037 Office Phone: 860-545-4189. Office Fax: 860-545-1568.

KIRVEN, TIMOTHY J., lawyer; b. Buffalo, Wyo., May 26, 1949; s. William J. and Ellen F. (Farrell) K.; m. Elizabeth J. Adams, Oct. 31, 1970; 1 child, Kristen B. BA in English, U. Notre Dame, 1971; JD, U. Wyo., 1974. Bar: Wyo. 1974. Ptnr. Kirven & Kirven, PC, Buffalo, 1974—. Author Rocky Mountain Mineral Law, 1982. Mem. Johnson County Libr. Br., Buffalo. Mem. ABA (ho. of dels. 2002—), Wyo. State Bar (pres. 1998-99), Johnson County Bar Assn., Western States Bar Conf. (pres. 1998-99), Rotary (pres. Buffalo club 1988-89, youth exch. program chmn. 1993-98). Home: PO Box C Buffalo WY 82834-0060 Office: Kirven & Kirven PC 104 Fort St PO Box 640 Buffalo WY 82834-0640*

KIRWAN, BETTY-JANE, lawyer; b. Rockeville Center, N.Y., Feb. 4, 1947; d. Franklin Ira and Pearl Elias; m. Ralph D. Kirwan (div.); children: Katherine, Andrew, Kerrigan; m. John Terence Hanna, Sept. 15, 1985. AB, U. Calif., Berkeley, 1968, JD, 1971. Bar: Calif. 1972, U.S. Dist. Ct. (cen. dist.) Calif. Atty. McCutchen, Black, Verleger, Shea, L.A., 1972-85; founding ptnr. McClintock, Kirwan, Benshoof, Rochefort, Weston, L.A., 1985-89; environ. atty., chair dept. environment L.A. office Latham & Watkins, L.A., 1989—, ptnr., 1989—. Pres. Boalt Hall Alumni Assn., Berkeley, 1983-84; vice chair Hathaway Children's Svcs., L.A., 1984-89. Bd. dirs. Hathaway Children's Svcs., 1985-90, PLI Environ. Law Adv. Com., 1992—. Mem. ABA (vice chair air quality com. Natural Resource sect. 1980-88, chair environ. quality com. Natural Resource sect., chair environ. controls com. Bus. Law sect. 1986-90, coun. Bus. Law sect. 1990-94), Boalt Hall Alumni Assn. (pres. 1984). Home: 1480 Lomita Dr Pasadena CA 91106-4341 Office: Latham & Watkins 633 W Fifth St Ste 4000 Los Angeles CA 90071 Office Phone: 213-485-1234. Business E-Mail: bj.kirwane@lw.com.

KIRWAN, KATHARYN GRACE (MRS. GERALD BOURKE KIRWAN JR.), retired small business owner; b. Monroe, Wash., Dec. 1, 1913; d. Walter Samuel and Bertha Ella (Shrum) Camp; m. Gerald Bourke Kirwan Jr., Jan. 13, 1945. Student, U. Puget Sound, 1933-34; BA, BS, Tex. Woman's U., 1937; postgrad., U. Wash., 1941. Libr. Brady (Tex.) Sr. High Sch., 1937-38, McCamey (Tex.) Sr. High Sch., 1938-43; mgr. Milady's Frock Shop, Monroe, 1946-62, owner, mgr., 1962-93. Mem. Monroe Breast Cancer Screening Project cmty. planning group Fred Hutchinson Cancer Rsch. Ctrs., 1991-93; meml. chmn. Monroe chpt. Am. Cancer Soc., 1961-93; co-chair hon. com. YMCA Pool program, 2005-; mem. Snohomish County Police Svcs. Action Coun., 1971; mem. Monroe Pub. Libr. Bd., 1950-65, pres. bd., 1964-65; mem. Monroe City Coun., 1969-73; mayor City of Monroe, 1974-81; commr. Snohomish County Hosp. dist. 1, 1970-90, chmn. bd. commrs., 1980-90; mem. East Snohomish County Health Planning Com., 1979-81; mem. Snohomish County Law and Justice Planning Com., 1974-78, Snohomish County Econ. Devel. Coun., 1975-81, Snohomish County Pub. Utility Dist. Citizens Adv. Task Force, 1983; sr. warden Ch. of Our Saviour, Monroe, 1976-77, 89, sr. warden, 1976-77, 89-90; co-chair hon. com. pool program YMCA, 2005. With USNR, 1943-46. Recipient Malstrom award for Hist. Homes and Bldgs. of Monroe, 2000, award of project excellence Washington Mus. Assn., 2000. Mem. AAUW, U.S. Naval Inst., Ret. Officers Assn., Naval Res. Assn., Bus. and Profl. Women's Club (2d v.p. 1980-82, pres. 1983-84), Washington Gens., Snohomish County Pharm. Aux., C. of C. (pres. 1972), Valley Gen. Hosp. Guild (pres. 1994, 95, 96), Valley Gen. Hosp. Found. (sec. 1993-97). Episcopalian. Home: 538 S Blakeley St Monroe WA 98272-2402

KIRWAN, R. DEWITT (KYLE KIRWAN), lawyer; b. Albany, Calif., Aug. 30, 1942; s. Patrick William and Lucille Anne (Vartanian) K.; m. Betty-Jane Elias, June 29, 1969 (div. 1982); children: Katherine DeWitt, Andrew Elias; m. Nancy Jane Evers, Oct. 27, 1984; 1 child, Fletcher Evers. BA, U. Calif., Berkeley, 1966; JD, U. San Francisco, 1969. Bar: Calif. 1971, U.S. Dist. Ct. (ctrl. dist.) Calif. 1971, U.S. Ct. Appeals (9th cir.) 1971. Assoc. Schell & Delamer, L.A., 1971-73; ptnr. Lillick & McHose, L.A., 1973-90, Pillsbury Madison & Sutro, L.A., 1990-98, Akin, Gump, Strauss, Hauer & Feld, L.A., 1998—. Chmn., exec. bd. U. Calif., Berkeley, 1988-97, trustee U. Calif. Berkeley Found., 1995-98; bd. dirs., trustee Pacific Crest Outward Bound Sch., 1993-99; bd. dirs. L.A. Philharm. Assn., 1985-89, pres., 1986-88, mem. bus. and profl. com.; bd. dirs. Pasadena (Calif.) Symphony Assn., 1978-82; adv. bd. OpusAlliance.com., 1999-2001. Capt. USAR, 1966-71. Mem.: ABA, Am Bd. Trial Advs., Calif. Club. Democrat. Roman Catholic. Avocations: fly fishing, mountain climbing, hunting, skiing. Office: Akin Gump Strauss Hauer & Feld Ste 2400 2029 Century Park E Los Angeles CA 90067-3012 Office Phone: 310-229-1050. Business E-Mail: rkirwan@akingump.com.

KIRWAN, WILLIAM ENGLISH, II, mathematics professor, academic administrator; b. Louisville, Apr. 14, 1938; s. Albert Dennis Kirwan and Elizabeth (Heil) Kirwan; m. Patricia Ann Harper, Aug. 27, 1960; children: William English III, Ann Elizabeth. BA, U. Ky., 1960; MS (NDEA fellow 1960-63), Rutgers U., 1962, PhD, 1964. Instr. Rutgers U., 1963—64; mem. faculty U. Md., College Park, 1964, prof. math., 1972, chmn. dept., 1977—81, vice chancellor for acad. affairs, 1981—86, provost, 1986—88, acting pres., 1988—89, pres., 1989—98, Ohio State U., Columbus, 1998—2002; chancellor U. Md., 2002—. Vis. lectr. London U., 1966—67; program dir. NSF, 1975—76. Contbr. articles to profl. jours. MS 2000 Com. for NRC; mem. adv. bd. Montgomery County (Md.), 1975—79; bd. dirs. Nat. Assn. State Univs. and Land Grant Colls., 1995—, Greater Washington YMCA, 1994—; World Trade Ctr. Inst., 1990—. Decorated officer Order King Leopold II (Belgium); named Disting. Alumnus, U. Ky., 1989, Rutgers U.; recipient First Citizen of Md. award, Md. State Senate, 1998, Nat. Innovators award, Minority Access, Inc., 2004, Career Achievement award, Rutgers U. Fellow: Am. Acad. of Arts & Sciences; mem.: NCAA (pres. commn. 1995—), Coun. for the Internat. Exch. of Scholars, Math. Assn. Am., Am. Assn. Colls. and Univs. (bd. dirs. 1993—, 1994—), Am. Math. Soc. (coun. 1980—82, editor Proc. 1977—82). Office: University System of Maryland Chancellor's Office 3300 Metzerott Rd, Suite 2C Adelphi MD 20783

KIRWIN, KENNETH FRANCIS, law educator; b. Morris, Minn., May 10, 1941; s. Francis B. and Dorothy A. (McNally) K.; m. Phyllis J. Hills, June 2, 1962; children— David, Mark, Robert. BA, St. John's U., 1963; JD, U. Minn., 1966. Bar: Minn. 1966, U.S. Dist. Ct. Minn. 1968, U.S. Ct. Appeals (8th cir.) 1969. Law clk. to assoc. justice Supreme Ct., Minn., 1966-67; assoc. Lindquist & Vennum, Mpls., 1967-70; prof. law William Mitchell Coll. Law, St. Paul, 1970—. Staff dir. Uniform Rules Criminal Procedure, 1971-74, reporter, 1982-87; reporter Uniform Victims of Crime Act, 1991-92; adj. prof. U. Minn. Law Sch., 1977, 80; active Minn. Lawyers Profl. Responsibility Bd., 1975-81, Minn. Bd. Continuing Legal Edn., 1975-83. Author: (with Maynard E. Pirsig) Cases and Materials on Professional Responsibility, 1984. Mem. Ramsey County Bar Assn., Minn. State Bar Assn. (chair rules of profl. conduct com., 2002-05, co-chair multi jurisdictional practice task force, 2005-), ABA (mem. standing com. on discipline 1983-89), Am. Law Inst. Home: 1418 Brookshire Ct New Brighton MN 55112-6390 Office: William Mitchell Coll Law 875 Summit Ave Saint Paul MN 55105-3030 Office Phone: 651-290-6346. Business E-Mail: kkirwin@wmitchell.edu.

KIRYLO, JAMES DAVID, education educator, consultant; b. Livorno, Italy, Feb. 12, 1958; arrived in U.S., 1976; s. Walter John and Maria Christina Kirylo; m. Anette Aquino Kirylo, Dec. 26, 2003. BS in Elem. Edn., Weber State U., 1981; MEd in Curriculum and Instrn., U. New Orleans, 1990, MEd in Ednl. Adminstrn., 1993, PhD in Curriculum and Instrn., 1997. Tchr. elem. sch. Carbon County Pub. Schs., Price, Utah, 1981—83, St. Joseph Missionary Sch., Holy Trinity, Ala., 1983—84, Cath. Sch., New Orleans, 1984—86, Jefferson Parish Pub. Schs., Harvey, La., 1986—99; asst. prof. U. Ala., Birmingham, Ala., 1999—2001; prof. Evang. U. Paraguay, Asunción, 2001—02; asst. prof. U. South Ala., Mobile, Ala., 2003, Southeastern La. U., Hammond, La., 2003—. Mem. tchr. forum U.S. Dept. Edn., Washington, 1997. Author: Teaching, Learning, and Reflecting: Essays on Education, 2004; contbr. articles to profl. jours. Vol. Habitat for Humanity, Paraguay, 2001. Named State Elem. Tchr. of Yr., La. Dept. Edn., 1997; named one of 40 Under 40, Gambit Weekly, 1997; recipient Excellence in Edn. award, C. of C. and Cox Cable Comms., 1997, La. Jacees Outstanding Edn. award, 1997; grantee, Dept. State, 2004. Mem.: Assn. Childhood Edn. Internat., Am. Ednl. Rsch. Assn. (conf. proposal reviewer 2004, conf. proposal reviewer Mid-South chpt. 2004), Phi Delta Kappa. Roman Cath. Avocations: running, reading, movies. Office: Southeastern Louisiana Univ Dept Tchg and Learning SLU 10749 Hammond LA 70402 Personal E-mail: jkirylo@yahoo.com.

KIRY-RYAN, RITA IRENE, computer scientist, educator; b. St. Louis, July 12, 1960; d. Joseph and Annie Marie (Lorenz) Kiry; m. Thomas Ryan, May 26, 1989; children: Tommy Ryan, Jenny Ryan. BS in Mktg., St. Louis U., 1982, MBA in Internat. Bus., 1988. Maj. account rep. Konica Bus. Machines, St. Louis, 1988—90; store mgr. U.S. Shoe Corp., 1990—93, Charming Shoppes Inc., St. Louis, 1993—94; instr. Sterling Coll., St. Louis, 1996—97, Sanford Brown Coll., St. Louis, 1994—99, ITT Tech. Inst., St. Louis, 1996—2004, faculty advisor, 2001—, chair Sch. Bus., 2004—. Vol. Long Elem. Sch., Crestwood, Mo.; mem. Celiac Sprue Assn., St. Louis, 2003. Mem.: Am. Assn. Profs., St. Louis U. Alumni Assn. Roman Catholic. Avocation: travel. Office: ITT Tech Inst 13505 Lakefront Dr Earth City MO 63045 Office Phone: 314-298-7800 ext. 152. Business E-Mail: rkiry@itt-tech.edu.

KIRZ, JANOS, physicist; b. Budapest, Hungary, Aug. 11, 1937; came to U.S., 1957; s. Andras and Emma (Teller) K.; m. Micheline Barthez, Dec. 19, 1964 (div. Aug. 1985); 1 child, Steven; m. Regina Moreno, Jan. 5, 1988. BA, U Calif., Berkeley, 1959; PhD, U Calif., 1963. Physicist Lawrence Berkeley Lab., Berkeley, Calif., 1964-67; lectr. U. Calif., Berkeley, 1967; assoc. prof. SUNY, Stony Brook, 1968-72, prof., 1973—, Disting. prof., 1995—, chmn. dept. physics and astronomy, 1988—2001; acting divsn. dir., Advanced Light Source Divsn. Lawrence Berkeley Lab., 2004—. Contbr. articles to profl. jours. Fellow Woodrow Wilson Found., 1959, A.P. Sloan Found., 1970, Guggenheim Found., 1985; recipient A.H. Compton Advanced Photon Source award, 2005 Fellow AAAS, Am. Physical Soc.; mem. Optical Soc. Am. Achievements include development of scanning X-ray microscope. Office: MS 80R0114 Lawrence Berkeley Lab Berkeley CA 94720

KISCHER, CLAYTON WARD, human embryologist, educator; b. Des Moines, Mar. 2, 1930; s. Frank August and Bessie Erma (Sawtell) K.; m.Linda Sese Espejo, Nov. 7. 1964; children: Cynthia Ann, Eric Armine, Frank Henry. BS in Biology, U. Omaha, 1953; MS, Iowa State U., 1960, PhD, 1962. Asst. prof. biology Ill. State U., 1962-63; rsch. assoc. Argonne (Ill.) Nat. Lab., 1963; asst. prof. zoology Iowa State U., 1963-64; NIH postdoctoral fellow in biochemistry M.D. Anderson Hosp, Houston, 1964-66; chief sect. electron microscopy S.W. Found. Rsch. and Edn., San Antonio, 1966-67; assoc. prof. anatomy U. Tex. Med. Br., Galveston, 1967-77, U. Ariz. Coll. Medicine, Tucson, 1977—95, prof. emeritus, 1995—. Dir. Scanning electron microscopy lab. Shrine Burns Inst., Galveston, 1969-73, cons. Am. Life League, Stafford, Va., other right to life groups; chmn. Am. Bioethics Adv. Commn. Co-author: The Human Development Hoax: Time to Tell the Truth; author sci. and pub. policy; contbr. articles to profl. jours. Cubmaster pack 107 Island Dist., Galveston, 1974-76; bd. dirs. YMCA. With USN, 1947-49. NIH Rsch. grantee, 1968-89; Morrison Trust grantee, 1975-76. Mem. SAR, Galveston Rsch. Soc. (pres. 1971-72), Am. Soc. Cell Biology, Electron Microscopy Soc. Am., Am. Assn. Anatomists, Tex. Soc. Electron Microscopy (hon.) (editor newsletter 1969-73, pres. 1975-76), Ariz. Soc. Electron Microscopy (pres. 1980-81), Gamma Pi Sigma. Home: 6249 N Camino Miraval Tucson AZ 85718-3024 Office: U Ariz Coll Medicine Dept Cell Biology and Anatomy Tucson AZ 85724-0001 Office Phone: 520-626-6084. Personal E-mail: wkisch@netzero.net.

KISCHUK, RICHARD KARL, insurance company executive; b. Detroit, Mar. 14, 1949; s. Russell and Aubrey Ann (Artt) K.; m. Sandra Jean Dierkes, June 26, 1971; children: Robert Charles, Kirsten Grace, Erin Michelle, Danielle Laraine, Russell Olan, Erika Anne. BS, U. Mich., 1969, M in Actuarial Sci., 1971; MS in Bus. Adminstrn., Ind. U., 1979. Enrolled actuary. Actuarial trainee Lincoln Nat. Life, Ft. Wayne, Ind., 1971-72, actuarial asst., 1972-1973, asst. actuary, 1973-77, asst. v.p., 1977-80, 2d v.p., 1980-82; v.p. Lincoln Nat. Corp., Ft. Wayne, Ind., 1982-86; v.p., dir. Lincoln Nat. Health and Casualty Ins. Co., 1985-87, Lincoln Nat. Life Reins. Co., 1985-87, Lincoln Nat. Adminstrv. Service; chief operating officer, dir. Lincoln Intermediaries, Inc., 1985-87, Spl. Pooled Risk Adminstrs., Inc., 1985-87, Underwriters and Mgmt. Services, Inc., 1985-87; pres. Crown Point Mgmt. Cons., Inc., 1987—, Benefficient Solutions, Inc., 1998—. Mem. editorial adv. bd. CLU Jour., 1983-91; contbr. articles to profl. jours. Fellow Soc Actuaries (chmn. fin. reporting sect. 1982-85, bd. govs. 1986-89), mem. Am. Acad. Actuaries. Avocations: camping, backpacking, canoing, photography. Office: Crown Point Mgmt Cons Inc PO Box 355 Pendleton IN 46064-0355 Office Phone: 765-778-4340. E-mail: rkischuk@umich.edu.

KISE, JAMES NELSON, architect, urban planner; b. Trenton, May 2, 1937; s. Charles Richard and Gladys May (Doll) K.; m. Rachel Bok, Dec. 20, 1958 (div.); children: Jefferson Bok, Charles Curtis; m. Sarah Ludlow Ogden Smith, June 15, 1974; children: Laura Ludlow Susanna, Anthony Lawrence Triplett. BArch, U. Pa., 1959, MArch, 1963, M in City Planning, 1964; postgrad., U. Rome, 1959-60. Registered architect, Pa., N.J., Maine, Del. New town planner Harvard-MIT Joint Ctr. of Urban Studies Ciudad Guayana Project, Caracas, Venezuala, 1961-62; ctr. city planner Phila. City Planning Commn., 1962-66; project dir. Wallace McHarg Roberts & Todd, Phila., 1966-67; dir. urban design ctr. Nat. Urban Coalition (formerly Urban Am., Inc.), Washington, 1967-70; ptnr. Kise Straw & Kolodner, Phila., 1970—. Lectr. U. Pa., 1962-67, 95—; adj. instr. urban design Drexel U., 1974-76; dir. Curtis Pub. Co., 1970-75. Work includes master plans for Schukill River Park, Phila., 1965, Downtown Harrisburg, Pa., 1975, Sadat City, Egypt, 1977, Acad. Ctr. for Performing Arts, 1981, Atlantic City Master Plan, 1986, South Broad St. Design, Phila., 1991, Schuylkill Heritage Corridor Plan, 1995, Lakewood Ranch Town Ctr. Plan, Fla., 1996, Independence Mall Masterplan, 1997, Riverside Master Plan, Jefferson Co., Ky., 2001, Phila. 2024 Plan for Olympic Games, 2004. Pres. Fleisher Art Meml., 1982—94, Historic Rittenhouse Town, 2000—; bd. overseers Grad. Sch. Fine Arts U. Pa., 2002—; Bd. dirs. Settlement Music Sch., 1963—83, Phila. Mus. Art, 1975—, Ebenezer Maxwell Mansion, 1980—93, Ctrl. Phila. Devel. Corp., 1989—, The Found. for Architecture, 1991—2002, Preservation Pa., 1991—, Phila. Soc. Preservation of Landmarks, 1993—99; Fleisher Art Meml., 1970—; bd. dirs. Washington Cmty. Sch. Music, 1967—70, pres. bd., 1968—70. Mem.: AIA, Am. Inst. Planners, Grad. Sch. Fine Arts U. Pa. Alumni Assn. (pres. 2000—02), Phila. Cricket Club, Phila. Club, Tau Sigma Delta, Franklin Inn. Democrat. Episcopalian. Home: 1530 Locust St Apt 12A Philadelphia PA 19102 Office: 123 S Broad St Ste 1270 Philadelphia PA 19109-1024 E-mail: JKise@ksk1.com.

KISELEV, SERGEI BORISOVICH, thermophysics engineering educator; b. Djankoi, Crimea, Russia, Feb. 16, 1953; arrived in US, 1995; s. Boris Danilovich and Ljudmila Antonovna Kiselev; m. Olga Fedorovna Kiselev; 1 child, Irina. PhD in Thermophysics, High Temperature Inst. of the USSR Acad. of Sci., Moscow, 1981; MS in Thermophysics, Moscow Power Engring. Inst., 1984; DSc in Physics and Math., High Temperature Inst. of the USSR Acad. of Sci., 1991. Cert. assoc. prof. of physics, prof. of physics. Rsch. engr. High Temperature Inst. of the USSR Acad. of Sci., Moscow, 1974—75, Nat. Inst. for Phys. and Tech. Measurements, Mendeleevo, Russia, 1975—83; assoc. prof. Moscow State Acad. of Oil and Gas (Gubkin's Inst.), 1983—91, prof. of physics, 1991—92; vis. prof., guest rschr. Inst. for Phys. Sci. and Tech., U. Md., College Park, 1992—93; sr. fellow scientist Oil and Gas Rsch. Inst. of the Russian Acad. of Scis., Moscow, 1993—95; guest rschr. Nat. Inst. of Stds. and Tech., Boulder, 1995—98; rsch. assoc. prof. Colo. Sch. of Mines, Golden, 1998—. Part-time prof. physics Moscow State Acad. of Oil and Gas, 1993—95. Contbr. articles to books and profl. jours. Mem.: AAAS, AIChE. Office Phone: 303-279-2390. Business E-Mail: skiselev@mines.edu.

KISER, BRENDA HATHAWAY, freelance/self-employed writer, editor; b. Corpus Christi, Tex., Mar. 13, 1944; d. Loren Hall and Marjorie Hathaway Kiser; life ptnr. David Lubman. BA, Fla. State U., 1966. Asst. editor Lippincott-Raven Pubs., Brea, Calif., 1993—. Editor: The Guide to Biomedical Standards, 21st edit., (newsletter) Clinical Lab Letter; contbr. articles to mags. and newsletters, columns to newspapers. Coord. Self-Help Interfaith Program, Huntington Beach, 2000—02; sec. Profl. Writers of Orange County, Orange, Calif., 1997—99. Episcopalian. Avocations: music, travel, crafts. Personal E-mail: brendakiser@ix.netcom.com.

KISER, CHÉRIE RENEE, lawyer; b. 1958; BA, Univ. Minn., 1983; JD specialization in Comm., Catholic Univ. Am., 1987. Bar: Pa. 1987, D.C. 1988. Law clk. to Commr. Dennis R. Patrick FCC, Washington; sr. regulatory atty. Sprint Comm. Co.; ptnr. Mintz Levin Cohn Ferris Glovsky & Popeo PC, Washington, mng. ptnr. D.C. office. Chmn. comm. sect. Mintz Levin Cohn Ferris Glovsky & Popeo PC, chmn. diversity com., mem. policy com. Contbr. articles to profl. jour. Mem.: Fed. Comm. Bar Assn. Office: Mintz Levin Cohn Ferris Glovsky & Popeo 701 Pennsylvania Av NW Washington DC 20004 Office Phone: 202-434-7325. Office Fax: 202-434-7400. Business E-Mail: crkiser@mintz.com.

KISER, DANIEL, music educator, musician; s. Howard Wayne and Ruth Ann Kiser; m. Ruth Witter. MusB, So. Ill. U., 1982, MusM, 1983; D of Musical Arts, U. of Ill., 1987. Cert. tchr. music State of N.C., 1993. Asst. prof. of music N.D. State U., Fargo, ND, 1985—92; chair of the sch. of fine arts, dir. bands Lenoir-Rhyne Coll., Hickory, NC, 1992—. Office: Lenoir-Rhyne College Sch of Fine Arts PO Box 7355 Hickory NC 28603

KISER, GLENN AUGUSTUS, retired pediatrician, entrepreneur; b. Bessemer City, N.C., July 13, 1917; s. Augustus B. and May (Carpenter) K.; m. Katherine Parham, June 13, 1941 (dec. 1972); m. Muriel Coykendall, Feb. 4, 1973. BS, MD, Duke U., 1941. Diplomate Nat. Bd. Med. Examiners. Resident physician Duke Hosp., Durham, N.C., 1946-48, Johns Hopkins U., Balt., 1946; pvt. practice Salisbury, N.C., 1947-55; freelance investor, 1955—. Founder stockholder Food Lion, Inc.; med. cons. State of N.C., Raleigh, 1961-64, 75-76, New River Mental Health Ctr., Boone, N.C., 1976-77; chief pediat. dept. Rowan Meml. Hosp., Salisbury, 1947-55, chief of staff, 1951-52, pres. Watauga County (N.C.) Med. Soc., 1978. Author: The Good Doctor--The Life and Times of Dr. Glenn A. Kiser, 1999. Bd. advisors Chowan Coll., Murfreesboro, N.C., 1977-78; trustee Rowan Regional Med. Ctr. Found., Salisbury, Kiser Med. Office Bldg. at Rowan Regional Med. Ctr.,

Kiser Welcome Ctr. at Duke U. Children's Hosp. Surgeon USPHS, 1941-46. Recipient Exemplary Life Svc. award Catawba Coll., 1995, N.C.'s Philanthropist of Yr. award, 1996, Order of the Long Leaf Pine award State of N.C., 1996, Disting. Svc. award Duke U. Med. Ctr., 2000; named Salisbury's Man of Yr., 1998. Mem. AMA, N.C. Med. Soc., Pinnacle Club Duke Med. Ctr. (charter), Duke Med. Ctr. Alumni Assn. (coun. 1988), Duke U. Founders Soc., Lions (dep. dist. gov. N.C. chpt. 1959), James B. Duke Soc. (pres. Milford Hills chpt. 1959, zone chmn. 1959, dep. dist. gov. 1960, internat. amb. 1961), Salisbury Country Club. Presbyterian. Achievements include Achievements include development of the concept of childproof safety caps; one of the first pediatricians to point out the extreme danger of lye poisoning in children. Avocations: photography, boating, music, bicycling. Home: PO Box 68 Spencer NC 28159

KISER, JACKSON L., federal judge; b. Welch, W.Va., June 24, 1929; m. Carole Gorman; children: Jackson, William, John Michael, Elizabeth Carol. BA, Concord Coll., 1951; JD, Washington and Lee U., 1952. Bar: Va. Asst. U.S. atty. Western Dist. Va., 1958-61; assoc., then ptnr. R.R. Young, Young, Kiser, Haskins, Mann, Gregory & Young P.C., Martinsville, Va., 1961-82; judge U.S. Dist. Ct. (we. dist.) Va., 1982-93, chief judge, 1993-97, sr. judge, 1997—. Mem. Martinsville City Sch. Bd., 1971-77. With JAGC U.S. Army, 1952-55, capt. Res., 1955-61. Mem. Am. Coll. Trial Lawyers (state com.), Va. Bar Assn. (exec. com.), Va. State Bar, Va. Trial Lawyers Assn., 4th Cir. Jud. Conf. (permanent), Martinsville-Henry County Bar Assn., Order of Coif. Office: US Dist Ct PO Box 3326 700 Main St Danville VA 24543-3326 Office Phone: 434-799-8700.

KISER, NAGIKO SATO, retired librarian; b. Taipei, Republic of China, Aug. 7, 1923; came to U.S., 1950; d. Takeichi and Kinue (Soma) Sato; m. Virgil Kiser, Dec. 4, 1979 (dec. Mar. 1981). Secondary teaching credential, Tsuda Juku U., Tokyo, 1945; BA in Journalism, Trinity U., 1953; BFA, Ohio State U., 1956, MA in Art History, 1959; MLS, cert. in library media, SUNY, Albany, 1974. Cert. community coll. librarian, Calif., cert. jr. coll. tchr., Calif., cert. secondary edn. tchr., Calif., cert. tchr. library media specialist and art, N.Y. Pub. rels. reporter The Mainichi Newspapers, Osaka, Japan, 1945-50; contract interpreter U.S. Dept. State, Washington, 1956-58, 66-67; resource specialist Richmond (Calif.) Unified Sch. Dist., 1968-69; editing supr. CTB/McGraw-Hill, Monterey, Calif., 1969-71; multi-media specialist Monterey Peninsula Unified Sch. Dist., 1975-77; librarian Nishimachi Internat. Sch., Tokyo, 1979-80, Sacramento City Unified Sch. Dist., 1977-79, 81-85; sr. librarian Camarillo (Calif.) State Hosp. and Devel. Ctr., 1985-93. Editor: Short Form Test of Academic Aptitude, 1970, Prescriptive Mathematics Inventory, 1970, Tests of Basic Experience, 1970. Mem. Calif. State Supt.'s Regional Coun. on Asian Pacific Affairs, Sacramento, 1984-91. Library Media Specialist Tng. Program scholar U.S. Office Edn., 1974. Fellow Internat. Biog. Assn. (life); mem. ALA, Am. Biog. Inst. (life, dep. gov. 1988—), Libr. Congress (nat. mem.), Calif. Libr. Assn., Med. Libr. Assn., Asunaro Shogai Kyoiku Kondankai (Lifetime Edn. Promoting Assn., Japan), The Mus. Soc., Internat. House of Japan, Matsuyama Sacramento Sister City Corp., Japanese Am. Citizens League, Japanese Am. Nat. Mus., Japanese Am. Cultural and Cmty. Ctr., Ikenobo Ikebana Soc. Am., L.A. Hototogisu Haiku Assn., Ventura County Archeol. Soc., Internat. Soc. Poets, AAUW, Ventura County Chpt. Mem. Christian Science Ch. Avocations: flower arranging, ballroom dance, classical music.

KISER-MILLER, KATHY JOY, humanities educator; b. Dayton, Ohio, Feb. 18, 1956; d. Fred Cecil and Joyce Arlene Kiser; m. Daniel Patrick Miller, Aug. 22, 1981; children: Alexander Ross Miller, Davis Noel Miller. BA, Otterbein Coll., 1978; MFA, U. Wis., 1981. Cert. secondary theatre. Sales-kitchen design Matercraft Industries, Boulder, Colo., 1981—83; sales Ford Mktg. Inst., Denver, 1983—84; prof. humanities Colo. Mountain Coll., Steamboat Springs, 1985—. Forensic dir. Colo. Mountain Coll., Steamboat Springs, 1989—95, theatre dir., 1995—, comm. and humanities discipline coord., Glenwood Springs, 1999—; humanities state chair Colo. State Faculty, 1999—2003; adjudicator Theatre Masters, Aspen, Colo., 2003—; judge scholarships Perry Mansfield Performing Arts Camp, Steamboat Springs; mem. adj. faculty Front Range C.C., Westminster, Colo., 1989—95, Regis U., Denver, 1990—94; artist in residence Boulder Valley Schs., 1987—88. Actor: Actors Theatre of Louisville, Midwest Playwright Lab., Germinal Stage, Nat. Pub. Radio-Shakespeare Series, The Changing Scene; mem. editl. adv. bd.: Collegiate Press, 1998—2001. Mem. performing arts guild Steamboat Springs Arts Coun., 1999—2000. Recipient Voice of Democracy Citation, VFW Womens Aux., 1990. Mem.: NEA, C.C. Humanities Assn., Colo. Edn. Assn., Nat. Women in the Arts, U.S. Ski Assn. (sec. 2002—), Theatre Comm. Guild, Kiwanis (pres. 2000—01, sec. 1998—99), Steamboat Springs Winter Sports Club (chair winter carnival sales 1999). Office: Colorado Mountain College 1330 Bob Adams Dr Steamboat Springs CO 80487

KISKA, TIMOTHY OLIN, communications educator, radio producer; b. Detroit, July 26, 1952; s. Edward Frederick and Mary Clare (Barnhart) K.; m. Patricia Irene Anstett, May 23, 1981; children: Caitlin, Amy, Eric. BA, Wayne State U., 1980, MA, 1995, PhD, 2003. Mem. staff Detroit Free Press, 1970-74, reporter, 1974-85, automotive writer, 1985-87; columnist Detroit News, 1987—2002. Asst. prof. comm. U. Mich., Dearborn, 2001-; mem. student newspaper publs. bd. Wayne State U., 1994-97, 99-2001; prodr. Sta. WWJ, 2004-. Author: Detroit's Powers and Personalities, 1989; From Soupy to Nuts! A History of Detroit TV, 2005. Mem.: Assn. Edn. in Journalism and Mass Communication. Home: 20050 Marford Ct Grosse Pointe Woods MI 48236-2324 Office: Univ Mich Dearborn 4901 Evergreen Rd Dearborn MI 48128 Office Phone: 313-583-6381. Business E-Mail: tkiska@umd.umich.edu.

KISKER, CARL THOMAS, pediatrician, educator; BA, Johns Hopkins U., 1958; MD, U. Cin. Coll. Medicine, 1962. Diplomate Am. Bd. Pediatrics, Am. Bd. Pediatric Hematology-Oncology. Lic. physician Ohio, Iowa. Intern U. Oreg. Coll. Medicine, 1962-63; sr. asst. surgeon NIH, 1963-65; jr. resident pediat. Children's Hosp., Cin., 1965-66, sr. resident pediat., 1966-67, fellow pediat. hematology, 1967-69, asst. attending pediatrician, 1968-69, attending pediatrician, 1969-73, dir. hemophilia project, 1971-73, dir. clin. hematology lab., 1972-73; asst. prof. pediat. U. Cin., 1969-72, assoc. prof. pediat., 1972-73, U. Iowa, Iowa City, 1973-79, dir. divsn. pediat. hematology-oncology, 1973-97, prof. pediat., 1979—. Med. lectr. various student and profl. groups; active mem. Pediat. Hematology-Oncology Group, Cin., Children's Cancer Study Group, L.A.; pres. Midwest Blood Club.; mem. adv. coun. Nat. Hemophilia Ctrs., 1979—.$D Mem. editl bd. Pediat. Today; contbr. numerous sci. papers to profl. jours. and chpts. in books. Mem. Iowa Found. Fund Raising Com. Lederle Med. Student Rsch. fellow, 1959; recipient state and fed. grants, Alumni of Yr. award U. Cin. Coll. Medicine, 2002. Mem. Am. Soc. Hematology, Mid-west Soc. for Pediat. RSch., Am. Fedn. for Clin. RSch., Am. Heart Assn., Internat. Soc. Thrombosis and Haemostasis (sub-com. on neonatal hemostasis), Ctrl. Soc. for Pediat. Rsch., Soc. Pediat. Rsch., Johnson County Med. Soc., Prairie Region Affiliated Blood Svcs., Am. Pediat. Soc. Office: Univ Iowa Hosp 2520 Jcp Iowa City IA 52242 E-mail: c-kisker@uiowa.edu.

KISLAK, JEAN HART, art director; b. 1931; d. Frank Ernest and Isabelle Tayor (Ellis) Hart; m. William I. Herendeen, Aug. 23, 1952 (div. Feb. 1956); m. Louis G. Johnson, Jan. 31, 1959 (div. Feb. 1975); 1 child, Jennifer Taylor Johnson; m. Jay Kislak, Apr. 7, 1985. Student, Peace Jr. Coll., Raleigh, N.C., Queens Coll., Charlotte, N.C. With Storer Broadcasting Co., Miami, Fla., S.E. Banks, N.A., Miami, 1974-84, art dir., 1974-84; mem. Gov. Fla. Panel Visual Arts, 1979-81; art cons., 1974—. Internat. rep. Christies, Inc., 1998—2001; mem. art and archtecture com. Libr. of Congress, Washington, 2003. Bd. dirs. Viscaya Mus., Miami, 1963, Beaux Arts, U. Miami, 1968, Theatre Art Patrons, Miami, 1968, Theatre Art Patrons, Miami, 1965, NEH, Fla., 1992; trustee Dade County Zool. Soc., 1988—, Miami Art Mus., Barry Coll. Charter Sch.; mem. Bacardi Imports Art Bd., 1983-89, 98—, Fla. State Bd. Art Coun., 1987, Miami Art Mus. (formerly Dade County Ctr. for the Arts Bd.), 1989-99; bd. dirs. Nat. Wildflower Assn., 1991; mem. exec. bd. Zool. Soc. Fla., 1994; mem. Fla. Humanities Bd., 1994; mem. visual arts com. Libr. Congress, 2002. Recipient Gov. Fla. award art, 1976, 79, Miami Dade Pub. Libr. award, 1978, Bus. Com. for Arts award, 1975-79, WPBT Pub. TV award, 1976, 77, 80, Lowe Gallery, U. Miami cert. recognition, 1980, Dade County Art in Pub. Places cert. recognition, 1981, 82. Mem. 1805 Club (London) (hon. v.p. 1993—), Kislak Found. (bd. dirs. 1997—). Address: 720 NE 69th St Miami FL 33138-5738

KISOR, HENRY DU BOIS, editor, columnist, critic, writer; b. Ridgewood, N.J., Aug. 17, 1940; s. Manown and Judith (Du Bois) K.; m. Deborah L. Abbott, June 24, 1967; children: Colin, Conan. BA, Trinity Coll., 1962, LittD (hon.), 1991; MS in Journalism, Northwestern U., 1964. Copy editor Wilmington News-Jour. (Del.), 1964-65, Chgo. Daily News, 1965-73, book editor, 1973-78, Chgo. Sun-Times, 1978—. Adj. prof. Medill Sch. Journalism Northwestern U., Evanston, Ill., 1979-82 Author: What's That Pig Outdoors?: A Memoir of Deafness, 1990, Zephyr: Tracking a Dream Across America, 1994, Flight of the Gin Fizz; Midlife at 4,500 Feet, 1997, Season's Revenge, 2003, A Venture into Murder, 2005. Bd. dirs. Chgo. Hearing Soc., 1975-76. Recipient Stick-O-Type award Chgo. Newspaper Guild, 1981, 85, Outstanding Achievement award Ill. UPI, 1983, 85, 1st pl. award Ill. UPI columns divsn., 1985, James Friend Meml. Critic award Friends of Lit., 1988, Best Non-fiction award, 1991; finalist Pulitzer Prize nomination in criticism Columbia U., 1981; named to Chgo. Journalism Hall of Fame, 2001; NEH seminar fellow, 1978. Office: Chgo Sun-Times 350 N Orleans St Chicago IL 60654

KISS, RONALD K., naval architect; b. Newark, Feb. 19, 1941; s. Koloman G. and Elsie M. (Kleschitz) K.; m. June Carol Wanner, June 29, 1963; children: Thomas, Timothy, Karen. BS, Webb Inst., 1963; MS, U. Calif., 1966. From naval architect to acting assoc. adminstr. Maritime Adminstrn., Washington, 1963-82; from asst. dep. comdr. to exec. dir. Naval Sea Sys. Command, Arlington, Va., 1982-86; dir. ship programs ASN Shipbuilding & Logistics, Arlington, 1986-90; dep. asst. sec. ship programs ASN Rsch. Devel. Acquisition, Arlington, 1990-96; cons. Rockville, Md., 1996-97; v.p. systems devel. Syntek, Inc., 1997-98; exec. v.p. to pres. Webb Inst., 1998—2005, pres. emeritus, 2005—. Fellow Soc. Naval Architects & Marine Engrs. (past pres., Emory Scott Land medal for accomplishment in marine industry); mem. Am. Soc. Naval Engrs., Royal Inst. Naval Architects, U.S. Naval Inst., Navy League, Surface Navy Assn. Roman Catholic. Avocations: sailing, fishing, golf, stamp collecting/philately.

KISSA, ERIK, retired chemist, consultant; b. Apr. 7, 1923; came to U.S., 1951, naturalized, 1956; s. Mats and Selma (Jakobson) K.; m. Selma Alide Tamm, Sept. 6, 1952; children: Erik Harold, Karl Martin. MS, Tech. U., Karlsruhe, Germany, 1951; PhD, U. Del., 1956. Rsch. chemist E. I. du Pont de Nemours & Co. Inc., Wilmington, Del., 1951-67, sr. rsch. chemist, 1967-74, rsch. assoc. Jackson Lab., 1974-86, sr. rsch. assoc., 1986-90, rsch. fellow, 1990-93; ret., 1994. Cons., 1994—; UN tech. expert, India, 1978, 79, China, 1982, Korea, 1986-88. Author: Fluorinated Surfactants, 1993, Dispersions, 1999, Fluorinated Surfactants and Repellents, 2001; editor: Detergency Theory and Technology, 1987; contbr. articles, chpts. on surface chemistry, textile chemistry, and analytical chemistry to profl. publs.; U.S. and internat. patentee in field. Recipient Soap and Detergent Assn. award, 1991. Mem.: Am. Chem. Soc., Del. Photographic Soc., Du Pont Country Club. Lutheran. Home and Office: 1436 Fresno Rd Wilmington DE 19803-5122 Personal E-mail: ekissa@aol.com.

KISSA, KARL MARTIN, electrical engineer; b. Wilmington, Del., June 5, 1961; s. Erik and Selma (Tamm) Kissa; m. Wendy Sue Earle, Mar. 8, 2003; 1 child, Emily Elisabeth. BS, Duke U., 1982; MEE, U. Del., 1986, PhD, 1989. Tech. staff C.S. Draper Lab., Cambridge, Mass., 1989-94; photonic device engr. United Techs. Photonics, Bloomfield, Conn., 1994-95; sr. optical engr. JDS Uniphase, Bloomfield, 1995—. Vol. Harvard Sq. Meals Program, Cambridge, Mass., 1991-94. Mem. IEEE, Phi Beta Kappa, Tau Beta Pi, Eta Kappa Nu. Congregationalist. Home: 1 Grant Estate Dr West Simsbury CT 06092-2101 Office: JDS Uniphase 45 Griffin Rd S Bloomfield CT 06002-1302

KISSEBERTH, PAUL BARTO, retired publishing executive; b. Tiffin, Ohio, July 5, 1932; s. Roscoe Paul and Mary Margaret (Barto) K.; m. Ann Capps Grinton, June 26, 1954; children: Mary, Katharine, Michael, John. BA, Ohio Wesleyan U., 1954. With McGraw Hill Inc., 1956-89; Western field sales mgr. Fleet Owner Mag., Chgo., 1974-76, advt. sales mgr. N.Y.C., 1976-78, pub., 1978-89, v.p., pub., 1986-89; chmn. McGraw-Hill Pubs., 1981-82; v.p., assoc. pub. Aviation Week & Space Tech., 1987-89; sr. v.p., pub. Fleet Owner Mag., FM Bus. Publs., 1989, pres. transp. and trucking divsn. N.Y.C., 1989-91; pub. Fleet Owner mag. Intertec Pub. Inc., White Plains, N.Y., 1992-96; ret., 1996. Lay leader First United Methodist Ch., Stamford, Conn., 1980-83. Served to 1st lt. USAF, 1954-56. Mem. Associated Bus. Press, Beta Theta Pi. Home: 39 Happy Hill Rd Stamford CT 06903-1203 E-mail: PBK1932@optonline.net.

KISSEL, DONALD EUGENE, retired art educator; b. Indpls., Nov. 21, 1932; s. Walter Peter and Lois Ferguson Kissel; m. Kenneth Wilma Harold Donald. BS, Ball State U., 1957; MEd, Kent State U., 1960. Pvt. practice art tchr., Cleve., 1960—73, Brecksville, Ohio, 1973—85; ret., 1985. Coach tennis Brecksville (Ohio) H.S., 1975—85; driver Meals on Wheels, North Port, Fla., 2001—05; vol. Habitat for Humanity, Fla., 2000—05. With U.S. Army, 1954—56. Mem.: Kiwanis, Masons (master 1983). Presbyn. Home: 4298 Corvette Lane North Port FL 34287-7235

KISSEL, HOWARD WILLIAM, drama critic; b. Milw., Oct. 29, 1942; s. Leo and Ruth (Miletzky) K.; m. Christine Buck, May 5, 1974. BA, Columbia U., 1964; MS in Journalism, Northwestern U., 1966. Arts editor Women's Wear Daily, N.Y.C., 1971-86; drama critic N.Y. Daily News, 1986—97, 2001—, columnist, 1997—2001. Juror Pulitzer Prize for Drama, 1994; bd. dirs. Theater Devel. Fund., 1982-; adj. prof. Marymount Manhattan, 1998-01. Author: David Merrick, The Abominable Showman; Dictionary of Literary Biography, 1982-97; editor: Stella Adler: The Art of Acting. Named to Hall of Achievement Northwestern U., 1997. Mem. N.Y. Drama Critics Circle (pres. 1984-86), N.Y. Film Critics Circle (chmn. 1975, 82), Players Club. Jewish. Home: 275 Central Park W New York NY 10024-3015 Office: NY Daily News Inc 450 W 33rd St Fl 3 New York NY 10001-2681 Office Phone: 212-210-1541.

KISSEL, LYNN ANNE, music educator; b. Ithaca, N.Y., June 15, 1958; d. James David and Edna Ann (Zebrowski) Michael; m. William Stephen Kissel, Aug. 9, 1996; children from previous marriage: Andrea Marie Britt Rigdon, James Michael Britt. BMus with distinction, Eastman Sch. Music U. Rochester, N.Y., 1981; MEd, Roberts Wesleyan Coll., Rochester, N.Y., 1996. Cert. tchr. music k-12 N.Y., 1993, tchr. elem. n-6 N.Y., 1993. Accounts receivable Matthews and Boucher, Inc., Rochester, NY, 1984—86; accounts receivable and purchasing Tapecon, Inc., 1988—92; tchr. instrumental music Barnard Elem. Greece Ctrl. Sch. Dist., 1993—2003, Longridge Elem. Greece Ctrl. Sch. Dist., 2003—. Prin. flutist Greece Symphony Orch., Rochester, NY, 1985—89; master tchr. student tchr. mentor Greece Ctrl. Sch. Dist., 1997—; adjudicator N.Y. State Sch. Music Assn., 1998—. Contbg. editor: Sharing Our Best Cookbook, 2000; performer: Music for Guitar and Flute, 1989. Co-pres. Barnard Elem. PTA, Rochester, NY, 1999—2000; eucharistic minister Our Mother of Sorrows Cath. Ch., 1996—98. Nominee Golden Apple Tchr. of Yr., 2000. Mem.: N.Y. State Sch. Music Assn., Percussive Arts Soc., Nat. Assn. Music Edn., N.Y. State Band Dirs. Assn. Avocations: cooking, performing, walking, gardening, needlecrafts. Home: 309 Gallup Rd Spencerport NY 14559-9598 Office: Longridge Elem Sch 190 Longridge Ave Rochester NY 14616

KISSEL, PETER CHARLES, lawyer; b. Watertown, N.Y., Sept. 29, 1947; s. Laurence Haas and Catherine Cantwell (Weldon) Kissel; m. Sharon Darlene Murphy, June 14, 1970. AB, Syracuse U., 1969; JD, Am. U., 1972. Bar: DC 1973, US Court Claims 1976, US Court Appeals (3d cir) 1976, US Supreme Court 1978, US Dist Ct DC 1979, US Ct Appeals (9th cir) 1979, US Ct Appeals (DC cir) 1983, US Ct Appeals (5th cir) 1988. Atty.-advisor Fed. Power Commn., Washington, 1972-74; atty. pub. utilities, 1974-77; assoc. O'Connor & Hannan, Washington, 1977-79, ptnr., 1979-87, Baller Hammett, Washington, 1987-93; ptnr., CFO, Grammer, Kissel, Robbins, Skancke & Edwards (GKRSE), Washington, 1993—. Co-bus mgr Energy Law Jour, Washington, 1981, asst editor, 1982—89, bus. mgr., 1989—92. Contbr. articles profl jours. Mem Washington adv. bd. Syracuse U., 1995—, mem. chancellor's coun.; mem. adv. bd. Maxwell Sch. Citizenship and Pub. Affairs, 2002—; bd. dirs. Episcopal Caring Response to AIDS Inc., 1988—93, v.p., 1990—91, pres., 1992, mem. exec. com., 1990—93; mem vestry St Patrick's Episcopal Ch, Washington, 1975—78, chmn. ann. fundraising campaign, 1987—89; bd. dirs. PRISM, 1996—97, Waterpower XII Steering Com., 2000—01. Recipient Spl Award, Fed Power Comn, 1973. Mem.: Syracuse Univ. Chancellors Coun., Syracuse Univ. Soc. Fellows, Bar Assn. DC, John Sherman Myers Soc., Nat. Hydropower Assn., Energy Bar Assn. (vice chmn com on publs 1984—85, chmn com on hydroelectric regulation 1991—92), Phi Kappa Psi. Democrat. Episcopalian. Avocations: gardening, American history, Irish history, Irish music. Home: 5604 Utah Ave NW Washington DC 20015-1230 Office: GKRSE 1500 K St NW Ste 330 Washington DC 20005 Office Phone: 202-408-5400. Business E-Mail: pckissel@GKRSE-law.com.

KISSEL, RICHARD JOHN, lawyer; b. Chgo., Nov. 27, 1936; s. John and Anne T. (Unichowski) K.; m. Donna Lou Heidersbach, Feb. 11, 1961; children: Roy Warren, David Todd, Audrey Anne. BA, Northwestern U., 1958; JD, Northwestern U., Chgo., 1961. Assoc. Peterson, Lowrey, Rall, Barber & Ross, Chgo., 1961-65; divsn. counsel Abbott Labs., North Chicago, Ill., 1965-70; mem. Pollution Control Bd., Chgo., 1970-72; adminstrv. asst. Gov.'s Staff, Chgo., 1972; ptnr. Martin, Craig, Chester & Sonnenschein, Chgo., 1973-88, Gardner, Carton & Douglas, Chgo., 1988—2000, chmn. mgmt. com., 1996-98, of counsel, 2000—. Adj. prof. U. Ill. Sch. Pub. Health, Chgo., 1973-76; instr. Kent. Sch. Law, Ill. Inst. Tech., Chgo., 1974-78; mem. vis. com. Northwestern U. Law Sch., 1996-99. Recipient Ill. award IAWA, 1996. Contbr. articles to profl. jours. Mem. Lake Forest (Ill.) Sewer Adv. Com.; bd. dirs. Lake Forest Lake Bluff Sr. Citizens Found. Fellow Internat. Soc. Barristers; mem. Ill. State Bar Assn., Chgo. Bar Assn., Ill. State C. of C. (chmn. environ. affairs 1973-76), Com. on Cts. for 21st Century, Knollwood Club (Lake Forest; gov. 1976-82), Lake Forest/Lake Bluff Sr. Citizens Found (bd. dirs.), 100 Club of Lake County (bd. dirs.), Harbour Ridge Yacht & Country Club. Roman Catholic. Office: Gardner Carton & Douglas 191 N Wacker Dr Chicago IL 60606-1698 Office Phone: 312-569-1442. Personal E-mail: richardj.kissel@gmail.com. Business E-Mail: rkissel@gcd.com.

KISSEL, WILLIAM THORN, JR., sculptor; b. Feb. 6, 1920; s. William Thorn and Frances A. (Dallett) K.; m. Barbara Eldred Case, June 17, 1943 (dec. June 1978); children: William Thorn III (dec.), Michael C. Grad., Choate Sch., 1939; BA, Harvard U., 1944; postgrad., Pa. Acad. Fine Arts, 1951-53; grad., Barnes Found., 1953, Rinehart Grad. Sch. Sculpture, Balt., 1958; BFA (hon.), Md. Inst. Coll. Art, 1996. T. Exhibited sculpture Lever House, N.Y.C., N.A.D., N.Y.C., Balt. Sculptor's Exhibit, York, Pa., Beverly, Mass., Gloucester, Woodmere Gallery, Germantown, Pa.; represented in pvt. collections, U.S.; executed large granite meml., Montclair, N.J.; also many animal sculpture studies and commns. Pilot, lt. (j.g.) USNR, 1943-45. Recipient Mass. Sculptor's award Regional Exhibit, 1958, Speyer award NAD, 1966, 68, Am. Artists Profl. League award, 1966; fellow Pa. Acad. Fine Arts, 1951-53. Fellow Am. Artists Profl. League, Nat. Sculpture Soc. Republican. Episcopalian. Home: 601 Brightwood Club Dr Lutherville MD 21093

KISSINGER, HENRY ALFRED, international consulting company executive, former secretary of state; b. Fuerth, Germany, May 27, 1923; came to U.S., 1938, naturalized, 1943; s. Louis and Paula (Stern) K.; m. Ann Fleischer, Feb. 6, 1949 (div. 1964); children: Elizabeth, David; m. Nancy Maginnes, Mar. 30, 1974. AB summa cum laude, Harvard U., 1950, MA, 1952, PhD, 1954. Exec. dir. Harvard Internat. Seminar, 1951-69; mem. faculty dept. govt., Ctr. for Internat. Affairs Harvard U., 1954-69; dir. def. studies program Harvard Internat. Seminar, 1958-69, assoc. prof. govt., 1959-62, prof., 1962-69; faculty Ctr. Internat. Affairs, Harvard U., 1960-69; asst. to Pres. for nat. security affairs Nat. Security Coun., Washington, 1968—75; sec. US Dept. State, Washington, 1973-77; founder, chmn. Kissinger Assocs., Inc., N.Y.C. Chmn. Nat. Bipartisan Commn. on Ctrl. Am., 1983-84; study dir. nuclear weapons and fgn. policy Coun. Fgn. Rels, 1955-56; dir. spl. studies project Rockefeller Bros. Fund, Inc., 1956-58; cons. Ops. Rsch. Office, 1950-61; cons. to dir. Psychol. Strategy Bd., 1952; cons. Ops. Coordinating Bd., 1955, Weapons Systems Evaluation Group, 1959-60, US Dept. State, 1965-69; hon. chmn. World Cup USA, 1994; advisor to bd. Am. Express Co., Forstmann Little & Co.; internat. coun. J.P. Morgan Chase, Am. Internat. Group; trustee Ctr. Strategic and Internat. Studies; bd. mem. ContiGroup Companies; exec. com. Trilateral Commn.; chair Eisenhower Exch. Fellowship; chancellor Coll. William and Mary; bd dirs. Internat. Rescue com.; U.S. Olympic Com. Author: Nuclear Weapons and Foreign Policy, 1957, A World Restored: Castlereagh, Metternich and the Restoration of Peace, 1812-22, 1957, The Necessity for Choice: Prospects of American Foreign Policy, 1961, The Troubled Partnership: A Reappraisal of the Atlantic Alliance, 1965, White House Years, 1979, For the Record, 1981, Years of Upheaval, 1982, Observations: Selected Speeches and Essays, 1984, Diplomacy, 1994, Years of Renewal, 1999, Does America Need A Foreign Policy?, 2001, Ending the Vietnam War, 2003, Crisis, 2003; Editor: Problems of National Strategy: A Book of Readings, 1965, Confluence, An Internat. Forum, 1951-58; contbr. to profl. jours. Hon. mem. Internat. Olympic Com. Recipient citation Overseas Press Club, 1958, Woodrow Wilson prize for best book fields of govt., politics, internat. affairs, 1958, Disting. Pub. Svc. award Am. Inst. Pub. Svc., 1973, Nobel Peace Prize, 1973, Presdl. Medal of Freedom, 1977, Medal of Liberty, 1986; named Hon. Knight Comdr. of St. Michael and St. George, 1995; Guggenheim fellow, 1965-66. Mem. Am. Polit. Sci. Assn., Council Fgn. Relations, Am. Acad. Arts and Scis., Phi Beta Kappa. Clubs: Metropolitan (Washington); Century, River Club, Brook Club (N.Y.C.), Bohemian (San Francisco). Republican.

KISSINGER, WALTER BERNHARD, retired automotive test and service equipment manufacturing executive; b. Furth, Germany, June 21, 1924; came to U.S., 1938, naturalized, 1939; s. Louis and Paula (Stern) K.; m. Eugenie Van Drooge, July 4, 1958; children: William, Thomas, Dana Marie, John. BA, Princeton U., 1951; MBA, Harvard U., 1953; PhD (hon.), Hofstra U., 2001. Asst. to v.p. fgn. operations Gen. Tire & Rubber Co., Akron, Ohio, 1953-56; pres. Advanced Vacuum Products Co., Stamford, Conn., 1957-62; exec. v.p., dir. Glass-tite Industries, Providence, 1960-62; asst. to pres. Jerrold Corp., 1963-64; exec. v.p., Chmn. exec. com., dir. Jervis Corp., Hicksville, N.Y., 1964-68; chmn., pres., chief exec. officer Allen Group Inc., Melville, N.Y., 1969-88; pres. WBK Assocs., Melville, N.Y., 1988—. Chmn. bd. of the Long Island Res. Inst., Melville, NY, 1992-98; vice chmn. bd. of trustees & chmn. of academic affairs comm., Hofstra U. Dir. Kissinger Family Found., mem. bd. Stony Brook Found.; served to capt. AUS, 1943-46, 50. Decorated Commendation medal. Mem.: The Lakes (Palm Desert, Calif.), Princeton Club of N.Y. Home: Lower Dr Huntington NY 11743 also: Lazy K Ranch Divide CO 80814 Office: WBK Assocs 200 Broadhollow Rd Melville NY 11747-4806 E-mail: ludwigwbk@aol.com.

KISSLING, FRED RALPH, JR., publishing executive, insurance agency executive; b. Nashville, Feb. 10, 1930; s. Fred Ralph and Sarah Elizabeth (FitzGerald) K.; m. Mary Jane Gallaher (dec. 1999); children: Sarah FitzGerald, Jayne Kirkpatrick. BA, Vanderbilt U., 1952, MA, 1958. Spl. agt. Northwestern Mut. Life Ins. Co., Nashville, 1953-58, gen. agt. Lexington, Ky., 1962-80, New Eng. Mut. Life Ins. Co., 1981-87; mgr. life dept. Bennett & Edwards, Kingsport, Tenn., 1958-62; pres. Employee Benefit Cons., Inc., Lexington, 1961—. Owner Lexington House, Inc., 1966—, Kennington Assocs., 1967—; prin. Kissling Orgn., 1980—, pub. Leader's mag., 1967—, editor, 1996—; owner, editor Fin. and Estate Planners Quar., 1993—; owner and pub. Fin. Svcs. Advisor, 1993—, Fraternal Monitor, 1999—; owner, pub., editor Probe Pub. Inc., 1997—; pub. Estate Rsch. Inst. Inc. Author: Sell and Grow Rich, 1966; editor: Questionnaire in Pension Planning, 1970, Questionnaire in Estate Planning, 1971. Adv. bd. Salvation Army, Lexington, 1971—, chmn., 1988-91; gen. chmn. United Way of Blue Grass, 1975, bd. dir., 1975-78, 80-83; trustee, chmn. bd. Lexington Children's Theatre, 1979-81, pres., 1981-83. Mem. Am. Soc. CLU's (chpt. pres. 1969-70, 80-81, 2001-02, regional v.p. 1971-73), Ky. Gen. Agts. and Mgrs. Assn. (pres. 1965-66), Million Dollar Round Table (life mem., v.p., program chmn. 1976), Assn. for Advanced Underwriting (bd. dirs. 1976-84, pres. 1982-83), Am. Soc. Pension Actuaries (bd. dir. 1971-78, pres. 1974-90), U. Akron Sales Insts. (adv. dir. 1996-2004), Am. Philatelic Soc., Sigma Chi, Lexington Club, Iroquois Hunt Club, Spindletop Hall, Masons, Shriners, Thoroughbred Club Am. Avocation: horse breeding. Office: 98 Dennis Dr Lexington KY 40503-2915 Office Phone: 859-277-8059. E-mail: fred@kisslingorganization.com.

KISTENBROKER, DAVID H., lawyer; BA magna cum laude, U. Wis., 1975; MA, Marquette U., 1977, JD, 1980. Bar: Ill. 1980, Wis. 1980, US Ct. Appeals, 2nd, 6th and 7th Cir., US Dist. Ct., No. Dist. Ill., US Dist. Ct., We. Dist. Mich., US Supreme Ct. Ptnr., chmn. Securities Litig. Practice, co-chair Corp. Governance Practice, mem. exec. com. and bd. dirs. Katten Muchin Zavis Rosenman, Chgo. Office: Katten Muchin Zavis Rosenman 525 W Monroe St Chicago IL 60661 Office Phone: 312-909-5452. Office Fax: 312-577-4481. E-mail: david.kistenbroker@kmzr.com.

KISTER, JAMES MILTON, retired mathematician, educator; b. Cleve., June 29, 1930; s. James Leonard and Katherine Alice (Sherrick) K.; m. Susan Spence, 1956; 1 dau., Karen Lynn; m. Jane Bridge; 1978. BA, Coll. of Wooster, 1952; MA, U. Wis., 1956, PhD, 1959. Rsch. asst. Los Alamos (N.Mex.) Sci. Lab., 1953-55; mem. faculty U. Mich., Ann Arbor, 1959-98, prof. math., 1966-98, chmn. dept., 1971-73; ret., 1998. Assoc. Office Naval Rsch., U. Va., 1960-61; mem. Inst. Advanced Study, Princeton, N.J., 1962-64; vis. prof. UCLA, 1967; vis. fellow Clare Hall, Cambridge (Eng.) U., 1970; vis. mem. Institut des Hautes Etudes Scientifique, 1974; vis. prof. U. Calif. at Berkeley, summer 1975; vis. fellow Wolfson Coll., Oxford U., 1977, 85-86. Assoc. editor: Duke Math. Jour, 1972-75; assoc. editor: Mich. Math. Jour, 1976-78, mng. editor, 1978, 82-88. Hon. rsch. fellow Univ. Coll., London, 1993. Mem. Am. Math. Soc., Math. Assn. Am.

KISTIAKOWSKY, VERA, retired physics researcher, retired educator; b. Princeton, NJ, Sept. 9, 1928; d. George Bogdan and Hildegard (Moebius) K.; m. Gerhard Emil Fischer, June 16, 1951 (div. 1970); children: Marc Laurenz Fischer, Karen Marie Fischer. AB, Mt. Holyoke Coll., 1948, ScD (hon.), 1978; PhD, U. Calif., Berkeley, 1952. Staff scientist U.S. Naval Rsch. Def. Lab., San Francisco, 1952-53; fellow U. Calif., Berkeley, 1953-54; rsch. assoc. Columbia U., N.Y.C., 1954-57, instr., 1957-59; asst. prof. Brandeis U., Waltham, Mass., 1959-62, adj. assoc. prof., 1962-63; staff mem. MIT, Cambridge, 1963-69, sr. rsch. scientist, 1969-72, prof. physics, 1972-94, prof. emerita, 1994—; ret., 1994. Author: Atomic Energy, 1959, One Way Is Down, 1967; contbr. articles on nuc. and elem. particle physics and astrophysics to profl. jours. Dir. Coun. for a Liveable World, 1983—, dir. Edn. Fund, 1983—2001, pres., 1997—2000. Recipient Centennial award, Mt. Holyoke Coll., 1972. Fellow AAAS, Am. Phys. Soc. (councilor 1974-77); mem. Assn. for Women in Sci. (pres. 1982-83), Phi Beta Kappa (vis. scholar 1983-84, senator 1988-96), Sigma Xi (lectr. 1990-92). Business E-Mail: verak@mit.edu.

KISTLER, LORETTA M., social worker, consultant; b. Lehighton, Pa., Oct. 1, 1960; d. Wayne R. Behler and Carolyn A. Walck, James E. Ahner and Maryellen L. Behler; m. John Kistler, Nov. 13, 1982 (div. Dec. 16, 1989). BA, Cedar Crest Coll., 1982; MSW, Marywood U., 1984. Lic. social worker Pa., LCSW N.J. Psychiat. social worker Wiley Ho., Bethlehem, Pa., 1984—88; adolescent addictions evaluator Good Samaritan Hosp., Pottsville, Pa., 1988—89; clin. coord. Renewal Centers, Quakertown, Pa., 1989—91, Vitae Ho., Glenmore, Pa., 1991—95; program coord., therapist Cath. Charities-Diocese of Metuchen, Perth Amboy, NJ, 1995—2002; chief social worker Easton (Pa.) Hosp., 2002—. Faculty liasion Marywood U., Scranton, Pa., 1995—2002; program developer Regional Devel. Corp., Pottsville, 1993; addictions group educator Bethesda Treatment Programs, Lehighton, Pa., 1984—89. Sec., past dir. LV K-9 Therapy Assn., Nazareth, Pa., 1997—2003. Mem.: NASW. Lutheran. Avocations: river rafting, camping, therapy dog community education and visiting, cooking. Office: Easton Hosp 250 21st St Easton PA 18042 Personal E-mail: rett60@yahoo.com.

KISTLER, RIVES, state supreme court justice; BA, Williams Coll., 1971; MA, U. N.C., 1978; JD, Georgetown U. Law Sch., 1981. Law clerk Chief Judge Charles Clark U.S. Ct. of Appeals Fifth Circuit; law clerk Justice Lewis F. Powell, Jr. U.S. Supreme Ct.; litigation assoc. Stoel Rives, Portland, Oreg., 1983—87; asst. atty. gen. Oreg. Dept. Justice, 1987—99; judge Oreg. Ct. of Appeals, 1999—2003; justice Oreg. Supreme Ct., 2003—. Adjunct prof. constitutional law Lewis & Clark Law Sch., Portland, Oreg.; former mem., vice-chair Oreg. Bd. of Bar Examiners; former mem. Nat. Assn. of Attorneys Gen. Working Groups. Office: Oreg Supreme Ct 1163 State St Salem OR 97301 Office Phone: 503-986-5713. Business E-Mail: rives.kistler@state.or.us.

KISTNER, DAVID HAROLD, biology professor; b. Cin., July 30, 1931; s. Harold Adolf and Hilda (Gick) K.; m. Alzada A. Carlisle, Aug. 8, 1957; children— Alzada H., Kymry Marie Carlisle. AB, U. Chgo., 1952, BS, 1956, PhD, 1957. Instr. U. Rochester, 1957-59; instr., asst. prof. biology Calif. State U., Chico, 1959-64, assoc. prof., 1964-67, prof., 1967-92, prof. emeritus, 1992—; rsch. assoc. Field Mus. Natural History, 1967—, Atlantica Ecol. Rsch. Sta., Salisbury, Zimbabwe, 1970-95; CEO Kistner family Trust, 1982—. Dir. Shinner Inst. Study Interrelated Insects, 1968-75; cons.-developer DowAgro Scis., Indpls., 1995—. Author: (with others) Social Insects, Vols. 1-3; editor Sociobiology, 1975—; contbr. articles to profl. jours. Patron Am. Mus. Natural History; life mem. Republican Nat. Com., 1980—. Recipient Outstanding Prof. award Calif. State Univs. and Colls., L.A., 1976; John Simon Guggenheim Meml. Found. fellow, 1965-66; grantee NSF, 1960-92, Am. Philos. Soc., 1972, Nat. Geog. Soc., 1988. Fellow Explorers Club, Calif. Acad. Scis.; mem. AAUP, AAAS, Entomol. Soc. Am., Pacific Coast Entomol. Soc., Kans. Entomol. Soc., Am. Soc. Naturalists, Am. Soc. Zoologists, Soc. Study of Systematic Zoology, Internat. Soc. Study of Social Insects, Field Mus. Natural History (life, rsch. assoc.), Chico State Coll. Assocs. (charter). Home: 3 Canterbury Cir Chico CA 95926-2411 Business E-Mail: dkistner@csuchico.edu.

KISVARSANYI, EVA BOGNAR, retired geologist; b. Budapest, Hungary, Dec. 18, 1935; arrived in U.S., 1957; d. Kalman and Ilona (Simon) Bognar; m. Geza Kisvarsanyi, July 3, 1956; 1 child, Erika G. Student, Eotvos Lorand U., Budapest, 1954-56; BS in Geology, U. Mo., Rolla, 1958, MS, 1960. Geologist Mo. Geol. Survey, Rolla, 1959-68; from rsch. geologist to sect. chief Mo. Dept. Natural Resources/Geol. Survey Program, Rolla, 1968-90; asst. dir. MODNR/Geol. Survey Program, Rolla, 1990-93; cons. Sarasota, Fla., 1993—; exec. dir. Hungarian-Am. Cultural Assn., Inc., 1995—; tchr. Sarasota County Pub. Sch. Sys., Sarasota, 1994-98; dir. comm. NEM, Inc., 1998—2001; ret., 2001. Editor: geol. guidebooks, 1976—; contbr. articles to profl. jours. Fellow: Soc. Econ. Geologists (mem. rsch. com. 1989—92), Geol. Soc. Am. (mem. rep. 1985—93); mem.: AAUW, Sigma Xi (pres. Rolla chpt. 1990—91). Avocations: travel, music. E-mail: evakis@prodigy.net.

KISZKA, SONIA ANN, nurse practitioner, educator; b. NYC, Apr. 4, 1938; d. Hermann William and Gertrude (Hohensteiner) Schumann; m. David F. Madden, Feb. 16, 1957 (div. Oct. 1975); children: David F., Michael P., Daniel J., Lisa M.; m. Lawrence F. Kiszka, Nov. 27, 1975; stepchildren: Lawrence V., Patricia, Valerie. AAS in Nursing cum laude, Maria Coll., Albany, NY, 1973; BS, Skidmore Coll., 1991; MEd, St. Michael's Coll., Colchester, Vt., 1995. Nat. cert. nurse practitioner in adult medicine, physician asst. Intensive/critical care nurse, dept. medicine Ellis Hosp., Schenectady, NY, 1979-80, nurse practitioner dept. medicine, 1980-82, dir employee/student health svcs., 1982-85; asst. dir. health svc., health educator Skidmore Coll., Saratoga Springs, NY, 1985-89, dir. Health and Wellness Ctr., 1997—2000; dir. health svcs., health educator St. Michael's Coll., 1989-97, GlaxoSmithkline Pharmaceuticals Vaccine Divsn., Phila., 2000—04; P.N. program coord., asst. prof. nursing Maria Coll., Albany, NY, 2004—. Cons., spkr. in field. Contbr. articles to profl. jours. Bd. dirs. N.Y. State Coalition Nurse Practitioners, 1985-90, 98—, pres. Saratoga/Warren/Washington chpt., 1998—; bd. dirs. New England Coll. Health Assn., 1994-97; active Vt. State HIV/AIDS Task Force. Recipient award for HIV/AIDS edn., Vt. Dept. Health/Dept. Edn., 1995. Mem. Vt. State Nurses Assn. (bd. dirs. 1990-93), Am. Coll. Health Assn. (Vt. rep., chair task force on campus violence, rep./spkr. internat. conf. on sexual assault on campus), New Eng. Coll. Health Assn. (bd. dirs. 1994-97), Vt. Nurse Practitioners Assn. (v.p. 1991-92), Nat. Commn. Certification Physician Assts., NY State Coll. Health Assn. (chair Capital Region 1999-2000), NY State Coalition Nurse Practitioners, NY State Physician Asst. Assn. Roman Catholic. Avocations: needlecrafts, swimming, travel. Fax: 518-580-2339. Office Phone: 518-438-3111 ext 253. Business E-Mail: skiszka@mariacollege.edu.

KIT, SAUL, retired biochemist, educator; b. Passaic, NJ, Nov. 25, 1920; s. Isadore and Minnie (Darvick) K.; m. Dorothy Anken, Sept. 28, 1945; children: Sally, Malon, Gordon. AB, U. Calif.-Berkeley, 1948, PhD, 1951. Post-doctoral fellow U. Chgo., 1951-52; rsch. assoc. biochemistry dept. U. Tex./M.D. Anderson Hosp. and Tumor Inst., Houston, 1953-55, asst. biochemist dept. biochemistry, 1956-57, assoc. biochemist, 1957-60, biochemist and chief sect. nucleoprotein metabolism, 1961-62; asst. clin. prof. biochemistry Baylor U. Coll. Medicine, Houston, 1956-57, assoc. clin. prof., 1957-58, vis. prof. virology and epidemiology dept., spring 1962, prof. biochemistry and head divsn. biochem. virology, 1962-92, prof. emeritus, 1993—; ret., 1993. Vis. prof. Inst. Venez Olano, Caracas, Venezuela, 1971, U. Buenos Aires, 1971, Calouste Gulbenkian Found., Lisbon, 1973; disting. vis. prof. La Trobe U., Victoria, Australia, 1982; mem. del. U.S.-Soviet Health Exch. in Virology, 1967; mem. del. on indsl. biochemistry Program to People's Republic of China, 1990; chmn. pathobiol. chemistry study sect., 1975-79; cons. NIH, 1970-92; sci. adv. bd. Am. Genetics Internat., Inc., 1981-84, Novagene Inc., 1983—. Assoc. editor: Cancer Research, 1960-79; mem. editorial bd. Intervirology, 1972-85, Internat. Jour. Cancer, 1964-90; contbr. 250 articles to profl. jours. With AUS, 1942—46. Recipient Rsch. Career award NIH, 1962-88, Disting. Inventor of 1987 award Intellectual Property Owners, Inc. Mem. Am. Soc. Cell Biology (treas. 1965-68, pres. 1970), Am. Assn. Cancer Rsch. (pres. S.W. sect. 1965-66), Am. Soc. Biol. Chemists, Am. Chem. Soc., Am. Soc. Microbiology, Am. Soc. Virology, Argentine Soc. Virology (corr.), Am. Assn. Vet. Lab. Diagnostics. Achievements include patents in field. Home: 11935 Wink Rd Houston TX 77024-7134 Personal E-mail: saulkit@aol.com.

KITADA, SHINICHI, biochemist; b. Osaka, Japan, Dec. 9, 1948; came to U.S., 1975; s. Koichi and Asako Kitada. MD, Kyoto U., 1973; MS in Biol. Chemistry, UCLA, 1977, PhD, 1979. Intern Kyoto U. Hosp., Japan, 1973-74; resident physician Chest Disease Research Inst., 1974-75; rsch. scholar lab. nuclear medicine and radiation biology UCLA, 1979-87, rsch. scholar Jules Stein Eye Inst., 1988-91; rsch. biochemist La Jolla (Calif.) Cancer Rsch. Found., 1992—. Author papers in field. Japan Soc. Promotion Sci. fellow 1975-76. Mem. Am. Oil Chemists Soc., N.Y. Acad. Scis., Sigma Xi. Office: The Burnham Inst 10901 N Torrey Pines Rd La Jolla CA 92037-1062 E-mail: skitada@ljcrf.edu.

KITAGAWA, AUDREY EMIKO, retired lawyer; b. Mar. 31, 1951; d. Yonoichi and Yoshiko Kitagawa. BA cum laude, U. So. Calif., 1973; JD, Boston Coll., 1976. Bar: Hawaii 1977, U.S. Dist. Ct. Hawaii 1977. Assoc. Rice, Lee & Wong, Honolulu, 1977-80; pvt. practice Honolulu, 1980-96; ret., 1996. Advisor Office of Spl. Rep. of Sec. Gen. Children and Armed Conflict UN, exec. coun. Spiritual Caucus; mem. internat. adv. coun. Internat. Caring Cmtys., Toda Inst. Peace and Global Policy Rsch.; exec. coun. World Commn. Global Consciousness and Spirituality. Nat. coun. Global Action to Stop War; founder, dir. Vision for Humanity; co-facilitator, mem. subcom. spirituality, values and global challenges at the UN United Religions Initiative, UN Cooperation Cir.; spiritual council subcomittee Ohio Spirituality, Values and Global Challenges at the UN; mem. spiritual coun. subcom. on spirituality, values and global challenges UN; bd. dirs. Wall St. Rotary, Apeadu Children's Peace Ctr., Varonne Drau Acad., Vt. Peace Acad. Mem.: ABA, Women Internat. Security, Hawaii Bar Assn., Honolulu Club. Republican. Office Phone: 212-963-0984. E-mail: dmaudrey@aek9.net.

KITAHATA-SPORN, AMY, movement educator; b. Kyoto, Sept. 1, 1957; came to U.S. 1960; d. Luke Masahiko and Carolyn Dawson (Massey) Kitahata; m. Lee Stuart Sporn, Sept. 26, 1981. BA, Oberlin Coll., 1979; tchrs. cert., Am. Ctr. for the Alexander Technique, 1983, Ctr. for Study of Authentic Movement, 1991. Pvt. practice in Alexander Technique, N.Y.C., 1983—; mem. faculty Am. Ctr. for Alexander Technique, N.Y.C., 1984-90, The Juilliard Sch., N.Y.C., 1984—; pvt. instr. creative movement N.Y.C., 1988—. Mem. Am. Ctr. for the Alexander Technique (bd. dirs. 1984-86), N.Am. Soc. Tchrs. of Alexander Technique, Nature Conservancy, Sierra Club. Avocations: yoga, authentic movement, hiking, biking, dance. Office: The Juilliard Sch Lincoln Ctr New York NY 10023

KITASHIRAKAWA, MICHIHISA, head of religious order; b. Tokyo, Feb. 5, 1937; m. Shimazu Kieko, 1967; children: Naoko, Nobuko, Akiko. Degree in politics and econs., Gakusshuin U. Mng. dir. bd. trustees Toshiba Internat. Found.; 5th head Imperial Ho. Kitashirakawa, 1940—; chief priest Grand Ise Shrine (Shinto), 2001—. Office: Peace Summit Secretariat 301 E 57th ST New York NY 10022

KITCH, EDMUND WELLS, law educator; b. Wichita, Kans., Nov. 3, 1939; s. Paul R. and Josephine (Pridmore) K.; m. Joanne Steiner, 1966 (div. 1976); 1 child, Sarah; m. Alison Lauter, Jan. 29, 1978 (div. 2000); children: Andrew, Whitney; m. Gail Lettwich Apr. 26, 2003. BA, Yale U., 1961; JD, U. Chgo., 1964. Bar: Kans. 1964, Ill. 1966, US Supreme Ct. 1973, Va. 1986. Asst. prof. law Ind. U., 1964-65; mem. faculty U. Chgo., 1965-82, prof., 1971-82, dir. law & economics program, 1980—82; mem. Ctr. Advanced Studies U. Va., Charlottesville, 1982-85; prof. U. Va. Sch. Law, 1982—85, Joseph M. Hartfield prof., 1985—2003, Sullivan and Cromwell rsch. prof., 1996-99, Mary and Daniel Loughran prof. law, 2003—, E. James Kelly, Jr. - Class of 1965 rsch. prof., 2003—. Vis. prof. Bklyn. Law Sch., 1995, Northwestern U., 1996, Georgetown U., 2002, U. Nebr., 2002; spl. asst. to solicitor gen. US Dept. Justice, 1973-74; exec. dir. Adv. Com. on Procedural Reform CAB, 1975-76; reporter Com. on Pattern Jury Instruction, Ill. Supreme Ct., 1966-69; mem. com. on pub.-pvt. sector rels. in vaccine innovation Inst. of Medicine, NAS, 1982-85, mem. com. on evaluation polio vaccine, 1987-88. Co-author: (with Harvey Perlman) Intellectual Property and Unfair Competition, 5th edit., 1997, (with Paul Goldstein) Selected Statutes and International Agreements on Unfair Competition, Trademarks, Copyrights and Patents, 2000. Mem. ABA, Va. Bar Assn., Am. Law Inst., Order of Coif, Phi Beta Kappa. Office: U Va Sch Law 580 Massie Rd Charlottesville VA 22903-1789 Office Phone: 434-924-7047. E-mail: ewk@virginia.edu.*

KITCH, PAUL R., lawyer; b. Southfield, Mich., Apr. 1, 1966; BSEE summa cum laude, U. Mich., 1989, MBA with high distinction, JD, U. Mich., 1993. Bar: Ill. 1993, US Ct. Appeals Fed. Cir., US Dist. Ct. No. Dist. Ill., registered: US Patent & Trademark Office. Shareholder Jenkens & Gilchrist, P.C., Chgo., 2001—, firm co-leader intellectual property practice group. Mem.: ABA, Intellectual Property Law Assn. Chgo., Am. Intellectual Property Law Assn., Chgo. Bar Assn. Office: Jenkens & Gilchrist PC Ste 2600 225 W Washington St Chicago IL 60606-3418 Office Phone: 312-425-8517. Office Fax: 312-425-3909. Business E-Mail: pkitch@jenkens.com.

KITCH, RHONDA K., registrar; d. Clenton C. and Ruth E. Horob; m. Travis M. Kitch, May 14, 1994; 1 child, Carson N. BS in Edn., Minot State U., 1995; MS, Minn. State U., Moorhead, 1999; postgrad., ND State U., 2003—. Residence hall dir. Minot (ND) State U., 1994—96; admission counselor Mayville (ND) State U., 1996—97; asst. direct of admission ND State U., Fargo, ND, 1999—2004, asst. registrar, 2004—. Named Apple Polisher, ND State U. Bison Ambassadors, 2004; recipient Tapestry of Diverse Talents award, ND State U., 2001. Mem.: Am. Assn. Collegiate Registrars and Admissions Officers (assoc.), Am. Coll. Pers. Assn. (assoc.), Nat. Assn. of Student Pers. Administrators (assoc.), Phi Kappa Phi (assoc.). Office: ND State U PO Box 5196 Fargo ND 58105 Office Phone: 701-231-7987.

KITCHEN, CHRISTINA MICHELLE RAMIREZ, biostatistics professor, consultant; d. Raul and MaryAnne Ramirez; m. Scott Kitchen, May 0, 2000. BS, U. Tex., Austin, Tex.; MS, PhD, Calif. Inst. of Tech., Pasadena, Calif., 1999. Postdoctoral fellow UCLA Dept. of Biostatistics, L.A., 1999—2001, asst. prof., 2001—. Cons. Wadsworth Ctr.- NY State Dept. of Health, Albany, NY, 1999—. Contbr. articles pub. to profl. jour. Mem. Jr. League, L.A., 2004—05. Recipient Travel Award, Internat. AIDS Soc., 2004, Thomas Everhart Disting. Grad. Student, Caltech, 1999; grantee AIDS Inst. Seed Grant, U. Calif., 2002-2003; Grad. Fellowship, James Irvine Found. Mem.: Am. Statis. Assn. Achievements include patents for Analysis of coreceptor use in the clin. care of HIV-1-infected patients. Avocations: horseback riding, travel. Office: UCLA Dept of Biostatistics 650 Charles E Young Dr Los Angeles CA 90095-1772

KITCHEN, E.C. DEENO, lawyer; b. Tallahassee, May 1, 1942; s. Oscar Edward and Rose (Deeb) K.; m. Patricia Gautier, June 22, 1968; children: Anne-Elizabeth K. Williams, Kimberly Gautier K. Robson, William Gautier, Deeb-Paul II. JD cum laude, U. Fla., 1967. Bar: 1968, U.S. Dist. Ct. (no. and ctrl. dists.) Fla., U.S. Ct. Appeals (3d and 11th cirs.), U.S. Supreme Ct., 1975. Ptnr. Ervin, Varn, Jacobs, Odom & Kitchen, Tallahassee, 1971-88, Kitchen & High, Tallahassee, 1988-93, Kitchen, Judkins, Simpson & High, Tallahassee, 1993—2004; ptnr. Dobson, Kitchen & Smith, Tallahassee, 2004—. Chmn. professionalism com. 2d Jud. Cir. of Fla. Past mem. editl. bd. U. Fla. Law Rev. Chmn. exec. com., Leon County (Fla.) Dem. Party, 1971-73, mem. state exec. com., 1971-75; trustee U. Fla. Law Ctr. Assn. Listed in The Best Lawyers in Am., Woodward/White Inc., N.Y.C.; listed among Florida's "Legal Elite" trial lawyers by Fla. Trend Mag.; listed among Florida's 908 top lawyers by Florida Monthly Mag., Nov. 2004. Master Tallahassee Am. Inn of Ct. (charter); fellow Am. Coll. Trial Lawyers, Internat. Soc. Barristers, Am. Bar Found., Fla. Bar Found.; mem. ABA (bd. regents Nat. Coll. Criminal Def., 1981-84, litigation and criminal justice sects.), Am. Bd. Trial Advocates (charter, Tallahassee chpt., advocate, pres. 1996), Nat. Assn. Criminal Def. Lawyers, Acad. Fla. Trial Lawyers (bd. dirs. 1983-85, past Eagle sponsor), Florida Bar (bd. cert. trial lawyer 1983, exec. coun. trial lawyers sect. 1980-88, chmn. steering com. trial lawyers sect., chmn. trial advocacy program 1982, 88, faculty mem., lectr. 1979—, faculty advanced trial advocacy program, exec. coun. criminal law sect. 1976-85, chmn. legis. com., chmn. grievance com. 2d Jud. Cir. Fla. 1979-80, mem. 1977-80), chmn. Professionalism Com., 2nd Jud. Cir. Fla. (by appt. of Chief Judge), Leading Am. Attys. (adv. bd.), Order of Coif, Phi Kappa Phi, Phi Alpha Delta (past pres.). Avocations: karate (black belt cuong nhu oriental martial arts, black belt isshin-ryu karate). Office: Dobson Kitchen & Smith 610 N Duval St Tallahassee FL 32301 Office Phone: 850-224-2683. Office Fax: 850-224-2283. Business E-Mail: dkitchen@dkslaw.org.

KITCHEN, JAMES R., academic administrator; BS, Ea. Ill. U., 1971; MS in Edn., Ea. Ilinois U., 1972; EdD in Higher Edn. Adminstrn., No. Ariz. U., 1986. Assoc. dean students and dir. student devel. ctr. U. Nev., Las Vegas, 1990—94; assoc. vice chancellor student affairs and dean students U. Kans., Lawrence, 1997—2000, dean dept. student life, 1996—97; v.p. student affairs San Diego State U., 2000—. Co-chair Coun. Calif. State U. V.P.'s, Calif., 2002—. Mem. NAACP, San Diego, 2001, San Diego Hispanic C. of C., 2000, San Diego Black C. of C., 2000; bd. mgrs. Jackie Robinson Family YMCA, San Diego, 2002—04. Named to Moberly Area C.C. Basketball Hall of Fame, Moberly Area C.C., 1992; recipient Basketball Coach Yr. award, Ea. Ill. U., 1971—72, Harvey Goodfriend award, San Diego State U., 2002. Mem.: Nat. Acad. Advising Assn. (commn. on multicultural concerns 1988—2000), Nat. Assn. Student Pers. Adminstrs. Office: San Diego State Univ 5500 Campanile Dr San Diego CA 92182-7430

KITCHEN, JOHN HOWARD, economist; b. New Castle, Pa., 1957; s. Robert Henry and Betty Lee K.; m. Rose Gemma Dukauskas. BA in Econs. and History, Coll. of William and Mary, 1979; MA in Econs., U. Pitts., 1982, PhD in Econs., 1983. Asst. prof. Washington and Jefferson Coll., Washington, Pa., 1983-84; economist Econs. Rsch. Svc. USDA, Washington, 1984-91; sr. economist Pres.'s Coun. Econ. Advisors, 1991-93; economist U.S. Dept. Treasury, Washington, 1993—2002; chief economist budget com. U.S. Ho. Reps., Washington, 2002—. Elder Presbyn. Ch. Mem. Am. Econ. Assn., Nat. Assn. Bus. Economists. Republican. Office: US Treasuy Dept Main Treasury Rm 4453 Washington DC 20220-0001

KITCHEN, JOHN MARTIN, historian, educator; b. Nottingham, Eng., Dec. 21, 1936; s. John Sutherland and Margaret Helen (Pearson) K. BA with honors, U. London, 1963, PhD, 1966. Mem. Cambridge (Eng.) Group Population Studies, 1965-66; mem. faculty Simon Fraser U., Burnaby, Canada, 1966—. Author: The German Officer Corps 1890-1914, 1968, A Military History of Germany, 1975, Fascism, 1976, The Silent Dictatorship, 1976, The Political Economy of Germany 1815-1914, 1979, The Coming of Austrian Fascism, 1980, Germany in the Age of Total War, 1981, British Policy Towards the Soviet Union During the Second World War, 1986, The Origins of the Cold War in Comparative Perspective, 1988, Europe Between the Wars, 1988, A World in Flames, 1990, Empire and After: A Short History of the British Empire and Commonwealth, 1994, Nazi Germany at War, 1994, The Cambridge Illustrated History of Germany, 1996, Empire and Commonwealth, 1996, Kaspar Hauser, 2001, The German Offensives of 1918, 2001, Nazi Germany: A Critical Introduction, 2004. Fellow Royal Hist. Soc., Royal Soc. Can. Home: 24B-6128 Patterson Ave Burnaby BC Canada V5H 4P3 Office: Simon Fraser U Dept History Burnaby BC Canada V5A 1S6 Office Phone: 604-291-3521. Business E-Mail: kitchen@sfu.ca.

KITCHEN, MICHAEL B., bank executive; b. Toronto, Can., 1945; Degree, Ryerson Polytech. U., 1968. Pres. CUNA Mutual Ins. Soc., Madison, Wis., 1995—, CEO, 1995—. Mem.: Am. Ins. Assn. (bd. dirs.), U.S. C. of C. (bd. dirs.). Office: CUNA Mutual Group 5910 Mineral Point Rd Madison WI 53701-0391

KITCHEN, OTIS DORSEY, music educator; b. Williamsport, Md., July 5, 1931; s. Paul Dorsey Kitchen and Estella Oneil Byers; m. Alma Irene Phibbs, June 18, 1955 (div. Mar. 13, 1979); children: Sharon Lynn Cole, Gary Wayne. BS, Bridgewater Coll., Bridgewater, VA, 1953; AG, Navy Sch. of Music, Washington, DC, 1955; MusD (hon.), Nat. Conservatory of Mex., Mexico City, 1982. Pub. sch. tchr. Greensville County Schools, Emporia, Va., 1953—54; dir. army band sch. U.S. Army Ft. Jackson, Columbia, SC, 1954—55; pub. sch. tchr. William Fleming H.S., Roanoke, Va., 1956—65; coll. prof. Elizabethtown Coll., Elizabethtown, Pa., 1965—96; ch. organist St. Paul's United Meth., Lancaster, Pa., 1966—; prof. emeritus Elizabethtown Coll., Elizabethtown, Pa., 1966—, free lance music dir., 1966—. Music dir. All Am. Honors Musicians, Worldwide, 1980—98, Mexican Invitational Festival, Mexico City, Mexico, 1978—88, London and Vienna Festivals, London, 1987—99; dir. of lancaster youth symhony Musical Art Soc., Lancaster, Pa., 1966—85. Dir. of music Elizabethtown Music Found., Elizabethtown, Pa., 1966—71; music cons. For Kids' Sake (Messiah Benefit), Hershey, Pa., 1985—98, Rotary Club, Elizabethtown, Pa., 1996. Specialist U.S. Army, 1954—56, U.S.A. Recipient Citation of Excellence, Nat. Band Assn., 1979, Phi Beta Mu Band Frat., 1985, Music Educators Assn., 1996. Mem.: Am. Band Masters Assn., Nat. Music Educators Assn. (Citation 1996), Elizabethtown PA Rotary Club (Citation 1975), Nat. Band Assn. (bd. of directors 2002—02). R-Consevative. Protestant. Achievements include

Founder of Elizabethtown College Community Symphony Orchestra; Founder of Lancaster County Music Camp; Director of Music for festivals held in Mexico, Europe, China, Rusia and the United States. Avocations: travel, tennis, elderhostel teaching, guest conducting and adjudicating. Office: Elizabethtown College 1 Alpha Drive Elizabethtown PA 17022 E-mail: kitcheod@etown.edu.

KITCHEN, PAUL HOWARD, hockey historian; b. Toronto, Ont., Can., Nov. 14, 1937; s. Percy Floyd and Mary Henrietta (Price) K.; m. Anne Margaret Heaney, Aug. 23, 1963; children: Kevin, Peter. BA, Carleton U., 1963; BLS, U. B.C., 1964. Librarian Nat. Library Can., Ottawa, 1964-66, chief bibliography div., 1966-70, spl. asst to nat. librarian, 1970-72, liaison officer govt. libraries, 1972-75; exec. dir. Can. Library Assn., Ottawa, 1975-85; pres. Paul Kitchen and Assocs., Ottawa, 1986-98. Dir. Book and Periodical Devel. Council, Toronto, 1975-85. Ann. contbr. Am. Library Assn. Yearbook, 1975-85. Recipient Brian McFarlane award for outstanding rsch. and writing (hockey), 2000. Mem. Soc. for Internat. Hockey History Rsch. (pres. 1996-2000). Personal E-mail: pkitchen@magma.ca.

KITCHEN, PETER CHARLES, elementary school educator; b. Battle Creek, Mich., Dec. 1972; s. Paul and Phyllis Kitchen; m. Elizabeth Ann Clark, July 29, 1995; children: Clark Charles, Carson Clare. BS in Edn., Huntington (N.Y.) Coll., 1995; MEd in Curriculum and Instrn., Ind. Wesleyan U., 2000. Lic. tchr. Ind., 2000. Tchr. elem. sch. Huntington (Ind.) Co Cmty. Sch. Corp., 1995—. Coach h.s. tennis Huntington (Ind.) North H.S., 1997—2000. Mem. pk. bd. Huntington (Ind.) Pks. and Recreation Dept., 2001—05. Named Tennis Coach of the Yr., Olympic Athletic Conf., 2003. Home: 1944 Bedford Ct Huntington IN 46750 Office: Flint Springs Elementary School 1360 E Tipton St Huntington IN 46750 Office Phone: 260-356-7612. Personal E-mail: pkitchen@hccsc.k12.in.us.

KITCHENS, DEAN J., lawyer; b. Nov. 4, 1952; BA, Univ. Calif., Berkeley, 1974; JD, UCLA, 1978. Bar: Calif. 1978, Calif. Supreme Ct., Ct. of Appeals (ninth cir.). Assoc. Gibson Dunn & Crutcher LLP, LA, 1978—86, ptnr. litig. dept., 1986—, also gen. counsel to the firm, 2000—. Mem. exec. com. Gibson Dunn & Crutcher, LA, 1996—2000, LA, 2003—, mem. mgmt. com., 1998—. Articles editor UCLA Law Rev. Mem.: LA County Bar Assn. (past mem. Judicial appointments com.), Order of Coif. Office: Gibson Dunn & Crutcher 333 S Grand Ave Los Angeles CA 90071-3197 Office Phone: 213-229-7416. Office Fax: 213-229-6416. Business E-Mail: dkitchens@gibsondunn.com.

KITCHENS, FREDERICK LYNTON, JR., retired insurance company executive; b. Detroit, Sept. 30, 1940; s. Frederick Lynton and Madeline Dorothy (Jacobs) Kitchens; m. Carol Ann Crane, Dec. 22, 1961; children: Frederick Lynton, Anne LeBaron, Susan Elizabeth. BA, Mich. State U., 1962. CPCU. Mgr. underwriting Royal Ins. Co., N.Y.C., 1968—70; asst. to pres. Grow, Keller, Englebert & Freese, Detroit, 1970—71; v.p. Dobson McOmber, Inc., Ann Arbor, Mich., 1971—73; exec. v.p. Hylant MacLean, Inc., Toledo, 1973—83; chmn., CEO Cherokee Ins. Co., Nashville, 1983—84; chmn. Coastal Plains Ins., Jacksonville, Fla., 1984—92; exec. v.p., dir. Brown & Brown, Inc., Jacksonville, 1992—99; ret., 2000. Instr. Coll. Ins., N.Y.C., 1969—70. Trustee Jacksonville Country Day Sch., 1985—90, Hope Haven Children's Clinic, 1988—91; dir. Jacksonville Commodores League; mem. Fla. Aviation Adv. Coun., 1990—94, Leadership Jacksonville, 1991. Capt. U.S. Army, 1962—67, Vietnam. Decorated Bronze Star; recipient Commendation medal, NATO, 1965. Master: Mason (scottish rites 32d degree, york rites); mem.: Lloyd's of London (underwriting mem.), Jacksonville C. of C. (cmty. devel. bd. 1986), Safari Club Internat. (dir., pres. N. Fla. chpt. 1990—92), Fla. Yacht Club, LA Yacht Club (commodore 1989—90). Republican. Presbyterian. Avocations: flying, safari hunting. Address: 66 Cavanaugh Lake Rd Chelsea MI 48118-9732 also: PO Box 278 Ranburne AL 36273

KITCHENS, FREDERICK LYNTON, III, education educator, researcher; s. Frederick Lynton Kitchens, Jr. and Carol Ann (Crane) Kitchens. BBA, Ga. So. U., 1984—88. MBA, 1991—92; PhD, U. of Miss., 1994—2000. PIA; Comml. Ins. Profl. Ins. Agents, 1988, Ins. Inst. of Am., 1988. Am. scholar Lloyd's of London, 1987—87; comml. underwriter Fireman's Fund Ins. Co., Atlanta, 1988—90; temp. instr. Ga. So. U., Statesboro, 1993—94; grad. instr. The U. of Miss., Oxford, 1996—2000; asst. prof. Ball State U., Muncie, Ind., 2000—05, assoc. prof., 2005—. Asst. underwriter Cherokee Ins. Co., Nashville, 1984—84; mgmt. trainee Hamilton-Lines Mfg., Bognor, England, 1985—85; asst. agt. Coastal Plains Ins. Assoc, Jacksonville, Fla., 1986; v.p. to pres. Doctoral Student Orgn., Oxford, Miss., 1998—99; dir. Cluster Computing Rsch. Project, Muncie, Ind., 2001—; advisor Assn. of Info. Tech. Professionals, Muncie, 2001—; adv. software development FSA BAsed Lang. Translator, 2002. Author: (book chpt.) Neural Networks in Bus.: Techniques and Applications, Encyclopedia of Information Science and Technology, 2005; contbr. articles to profl. jours. including Rev. of Bus. Rsch., Jour. Info. Tech. Edn., Asian Jour. Info. Sys., Jour. Enterprise Info. Mgmt., Electronic Jour. E-Learning, Jour. Computer Info. Sys., others. Recipient Eagle Scout, Boy Scouts of Am., 1982, First Pl. award, Ind. Cyberstar Awards, 2002, Innovation in Leadership of Bus. Edn. award, The Assn. Advance Collegiate Schs. Bus., 2003, Disting. Paper award, Decision Scis. Inst., 2004, Internat. Acad. Bus. and Pub. Adminstrn., 2005; grantee George A. and Frances Ball Rsch. Grant, Ball State U., 2001, Miller Coll. Bus., 2005. Mem.: Omicron Delta Kappa (assoc.), Mu Kappa Tau (assoc.), Beta Gamma Sigma (assoc.). Avocation: travel. Office: Ball State U WB 203 Muncie IN 47306

KITCHENS, WILLIAM CHARLIE, accountant; b. Jacksonville, Fla., Oct. 21, 1945; s. William Othar and Mazie Alice (Dugger) K. BBA, postgrad., Ga. Coll., Milledgeville, 1981. Cert. enrolled agt., accredited tax advisor. Income tax practitioner H&R Block, Macon, Ga., 1976-86; cost acct., dept. head West Point Pepperell, Milledgeville, 1981-82; asst. fin. examiner Ga. Dept. of Banking and Fin., Dublin, 1980; tax acct. Ga. Farm Bur. Fedn., Macon, 1982-97; pvt. practice income tax svc. Macon, 1997—. Served as staff sgt. USAF, 1965-68. Mem. Nat. Assn. Enrolled Agts., Ga. Assn. Enrolled Agts., Nat. Soc. Pub. Accts., Nat. Assn. Income Tax Practitioners. Republican. Baptist. Home and Office: Bill Kitchens Income Tax Svcs 544 Orange St Macon GA 31201-8622 Address: PO Box 7885 Macon GA 31209-7885 E-mail: billkitc@bellsouth.net.

KITCHENS, WILLIAM H., lawyer; b. Newnan, Ga., Aug. 3, 1948; BA with high honors, Emory U., 1970; JD, U. Ga., 1973. Bar: Ga. 1973. Mng. ptnr. Arnall Golden Gregory, LLP, Atlanta. Adj. prof. food and drug law Emory U. Sch. Law, 1979—; bd. dirs. Ga. Biomed. Partnership; mem. Metro Atlanta Biosci. Coun.; mem. S.E. task force Med. Tech. Leadership Forum. Notes editor Ga. Law Review, 1972-73; mem. editl. adv bd. Food and Drug Law Jour., 1981-87, 96-2001; author: Georgia Environmental Law Jour., 1995, 96, The Georgia Environmental Law Handbook, 1996, FDA Regulation of Tissue Engineering in Synthetic Biodegradable Polymer Scaffolds, 1997; contbr. articles to profl. jours. Mem. Leadership Atlanta. Mem. ABA, Am Judicature Soc., State Bar Ga., Lawyers Club Atlanta, Atlanta Bar Assn, Food and Drug Law Inst., Met. Atlanta C. of C. (bd. advisors), Omicron Delta Kappa Office: Arnall Golden & Gregory LLP 171 17th St NW Ste 2100 Atlanta GA 30363-1031 Office Phone: 404-873-8500.

KITE, MARILYN S., state supreme court justice, lawyer; b. Laramie, Wyo., Oct. 2, 1947; BA with honors, U. Wyo., 1970, JD with honors, 1974. Bar: Wyo. 1974. Sr. asst. atty. gen. State of Wyo., 1974—78; mem. Holland & Hart, Jackson, Wyo., 1979—2000; justice Wyo. Supreme Ct., 2000—. Contbr. articles to profl. jours. Mem. ABA (nat. resources sect., litigation sect.), Wyo. State Bar. Address: Wyo Supreme Ct 2301 Capitol Ave Cheyenne WY 82002

KITE, STEVEN B., lawyer; b. Chgo., May 30, 1949; s. Ben and Dolores (Braver) K.; m. Catherine Lapinski, Jan. 13, 1980; children: David, Julia. BA, U. Ill., 1971; JD, Harvard U., 1974. Bar: Ga. 1974, U.S. Dist. Ct. Ga. 1974, U.S. Ct. Appeals (5th and 11th cirs.) 1981, Ill. 1985, Fla. 1986. Ptnr. Kutak Rock, Atlanta, 1974—84, Gardner Carton & Douglas LLP, Chgo., 1984—2005, Sonnenschein Nath & Rosenthal LLP, Chgo., 2005—. Author, editor: Law For Elderly, 1978; author: Tax-Exempt Financing for Health Care Organizations, 1996; co-author: Bond Financing, 1994. Bd. dirs. Atlanta Legal Aid Soc., 1979-84; trustee Sr. Citizens Met. Atlanta, 1980-83. Mem. ABA, Ill. Bar Assn., State Bar Ga., Chgo. Bar Assn., Fla. Bar Assn., Nat. Assn. Bond Lawyers. Avocations: travel, sports, reading. Office: Sonnenschein Nath & Rosenthal LLP 233 S Wacker Dr Ste 8000 Chicago IL 60606 Office Phone: 312-876-8195. E-mail: skite@sonnenschein.com.

KITELEY, BRIAN ALAN, English literature educator, writer; b. Mpls., Minn., Sept. 26, 1956; s. Murray James and Jean (Vettel) K.; m. Cynthia Coburn, Aug. 27, 1991. BA, Carleton Coll., 1978; MA, CCNY, 1985. Lectr. Am. U. Cairo, 1987-89; asst. prof. Ohio U., Athens, 1992-94, U. Denver, 1994-98, assoc. prof., 1998—. Author: Still Life with Insects, 1989, I Know Many Songs, But I Cannot Sing, 1996, The 3 A.M. Epiphany, 2005. Recipient Nat. Endowment Arts, 1991, Guggenheim Fellowship, 1992, Whiting Found. Writers award, 1996. Office: U Denver English Dept Pioneer Hall Denver CO 80208 E-mail: bkiteley@du.edu.

KITNER, DAVID N., lawyer; b. Brownwood, Tex., Aug. 25, 1948; BA, Rice U., 1970; JD with honors, U. Tex., 1973. Bar: Tex. 1973; bd. cert. labor and employment law, Tex. Bd. Specialization. Mem. Strasburger & Price L.L.P., Dallas. Instr. trial advocacy So. Meth. U., 1982-86. Named Tex. Super Lawyer, Tex. Monthly Mag. Fellow Am. Coll. Trial Lawyers, Tex. Bar Found. (life); mem. Tex. Assn. Def. Counsel, Dallas Bar Assn., Order Coif, Defense Rsch. Inst.; fellow Tex. Bar Found. Office: Strasburger & Price LLP 901 Main St Ste 4300 Dallas TX 75202-3724 E-mail: david.kitner@strasburger.com.

KITNER, HAROLD, artist, educator; b. Cleve., May 18, 1921; s. Isaac and Frieda Kitner; m. Joyce Lapaz, Nov. 30, 1946; children: Jon, Ann, Kathi. MA, Case Western Res. U., 1947; postgrad., Cleve. Inst. Art, Ohio U., Cleve. Coll., Washington and Lee U.; D Equivalency, Kent State U., 1949. Chmn. fine arts Kent (Ohio) State U., 1950-74, dean Honors Coll., 1970-72, prof. emeritus, 1980. One-man shows include Cleve. Mus., Kent State U. Mus., Libr. Congress; represented in permanent collections at Akron Art Mus., Canton Art Inst., Cleve. Mus., Dayton Art Inst., Akron U., Kent State U. Negotiator, pres. faculty union AAUP, Kent., 1977-80; founder Blossom Festival Sch., Cleve., 1967. Jewish. Home: 2274 Ashley River Rd Apt 1007 Charleston SC 29414

KITSON, DON E., music educator; b. Providence, Oct. 15, 1950; s. William J. and Constance H. Kitson; m. Donna Jean Vasil, Apr. 26, 1973; children: Tamara Jean, Tanya Maria, Tasha Anne. MusB, Boston Conservatory Music, 1973; MA, U. Conn., 1978. Band dir. Mohawk Tr. Regional Sch. Dist., Shelburna Falls, Maine, 1973—78, music dir., 1978—80; band dir. N. Franklin Sch. Dist., Connell, Wash., 1980—85, music dir., 1985—93; band dir. Charlotte County Pub. Sch., Punta Gorda, Fla., 1993—. Adminstrv. asst. N.E. Music Camp, Ware, Mass., 1980—89. Recipient Tchr. of Yr., Mohawk Tr. Regional Sch. Dist., 1980. Mem.: NEA, Fla. Bandmasters Assn., Fla. Music Educators Assn., Masons. Avocation: model railroads. Office: Punta Gorda Mid Sch 825 Carmelita St Punta Gorda FL 33950

KITSOPOULOS, NICHOLAS, composer; b. Summit, NJ, Oct. 8, 1962; s. Sotirios Constantine and Antonia Kitsopoulos. Composer self employed freelancer, N.Y.C., NY, 1980—. Judge Daytime Emmy Awards, N.Y.C., NY, 2000—05. Orchestrater: Broadway plays Pucciais La Boheme, 2003 (Tony award nominee, 2003); composer: (TV Spl.) Victoria's Secret Fashion Show, 2003, (TV) A & E Biography Tony Blair, 2002 (Biograpy of Yr. nominee, 2002). Recipient Communicator award, The Communicator Awards, 2002. Mem.: Local 802 N.Y. Musicians Union, Am. Soc. Composers, Authors and Publishers, SAG. E-mail: nkmusic@earthlink.net.

KITT, OLGA, artist; b. N.Y.C., July 29, 1929; d. Elias and Mary (Opiela) K.; m. Nicholas Rawluk, Aug. 6, 1955 (div. 1960); 1 child, Wade. BA, Queens Coll., 1951; MA, State U. Iowa, 1952; studied with Meyer Schapiro, N.Y.C., 1954; studied with Hans Hofmann, N.Y.C., Provincetown, 1954-55; postgrad., Inst. Fine Arts, NYU, 1955, NYU, 1960-62; studied with Robert Beverly Hale, N.Y.C., 1979. Gallery asst. Chappellier Gallery, N.Y.C., 1952—53; asst. to Walter Pach NY, 1953—56; tchg. asst. CCNY, 1953—58; tchr. art NY, 1962—80. One-woman shows include CCNY, 1957, Manhattan Coll., Riverdale, N.Y., 1980, Blackout Gallery, N.Y.C., 1997, Coll. Mt. St. Vincent, 2001, 2002, 2003, The Corridor Gallery of Riverdale Temple, 2001, 2002, The Corridor Gallery of Interchurch Ctr., 2002, exhibited in group shows at Whitney Mus., 1954, Bronx County Hist. Soc., 1978, Mus. Modern Art, N.Y.C., 1978, Art Students League, 1979, Bronx Mus. Arts, 1979, Coll. Mt. St. Vincent, 2000, Broome St. Gallery, N.Y.C., 2002, one-woman shows include Borough Pres. Carrion Gallery, 2005, exhibited in group shows at Broome St. Gallery, 2003, 2004, Represented in permanent collections Bronx Council of the Arts, Bronx Arts Ensemble, Riverdale Press, Riverdale YM-YWHA, U. Iowa, Iowa City, Fordham U., Fordham Prep. Sch., Hostos Coll., N.Y.C., Harris Sch. of Art, Tenn., numerous pvt. collections, exhibitions include Starving Artists Gallery, N.Y.C., 2005. Home: Apt 4D 5610 Netherland Ave Bronx NY 10471-1703 Studio: 495 S Broadway Yonkers NY 10705-3221 E-mail: olgakitt2@cs.com.

KITT, SANDRA ELAINE, writer, library specialist; b. N.Y.C., June 11, 1947; d. Archie Benjamin Nathaniel and Annabelle Clementine (Wright) Kitt. AA, Bronx (NY) C.C., 1968; BFA, CCNY, 1970, MFA, 1975. Sec., asst. Philip Gips Design Studio, N.Y.C., 1970—73; info. operator NY Telephone Co., N.Y.C., 1965—67; part-time asst. Am. Mus., N.Y.C., 1969—71; freelance graphic designer N.Y.C., 1971—90; libr. specialist Am. Mus. Natural History, N.Y.C., 1973—2003. Author: Rites Of Spring, 1984, Adam and Eva, 1984, All Good Things, 1984, Perfect Combination, 1985, Only With The Heart, 1985, With Open Arms, 1987, An Innocent Man, 1989, The Way Home, 1990, Someone's Baby, 1991, Lover Everlasting, 1993, Love Is Thanks Enough, 1993, Serenade, 1994, Sincerely, 1995 (Waldenbooks award, 1995), The Color of Love, 1995, Someone's Baby, 1996, Sweet Dreams, 1996, Suddenly, 1996, Significant Others, 1996, Celebration, 1996, Homecoming, 1996, Adam and Eva, 1997, Family Affairs, 1999, Heart of the Matter, 1999, Close Encounters, 2000, She's the One, 2001, Just Passing Through, 2002, Southern Comfort, 2004, The Next Best Thing, 2005. Recipient Keys to the city of East Orange, Women of Excellence, Mayor of N.Y.C., Lifetime Achievement award, Romantic Times. Mem.: Novelist Inc., Romance Writers Am. (Spl. Svc. award, Lifetime Achievement (N.Y. chpt.)), Spl. Librs. Assn. (pres. NY chpt. 1999—2000). Avocations: travel, cooking. Office: PO Box 403 New York NY 10024 Office Phone: 917-669-6395. Personal E-mail: sandikitt@hotmail.com.

KITT, WALTER, psychiatrist; b. NYC, Dec. 18, 1925; s. Elias and Mary (Opiela) K.; m. Terry Escorcia, May 15, 1955 (dec. 1974); 1 child, Gregory; m. Sally Anderson Chappell, June 22, 1977. Student, CCNY, 1942-44; AB magna cum laude, Syracuse U., 1948; MD, Chgo. Med. Sch., 1952. Diplomate Am. Bd. Psychiatry and Neurology. Resident Neuropsychiat. Inst., Chgo., 1953-56; practice medicine specializing in psychiatry Chgo., 1956—62, Park Ridge, Ill., 1992—97; psychiatrist Lakeside VA Med. Ctr., Chgo., 1981-92, acting chief psychiat. svcs., 1986-87; ret., 1998. Asst. prof. clin. psychiatry U. Ill. Med. Ctr., Chgo., 1958-64, Northwestern U., Chgo., 1974-96, asst. prof. emeritus 1996-2005; chmn. divsn. psychiatry Our Lady of Mercy Hosp., Dyer, Ind., 1970-72; practice medicine specializing in Psychiatry, Munster, Ind., 1962-80. Mem. Am. Psychiat. Assn.

KITTEL, PETER, research scientist; b. Fairfax, Va., Mar. 23, 1945; s. Charles and Muriel K.; m. Mary Ellen, Aug. 12, 1972; 1 child, Katherine. BS, U. Calif., Berkeley, 1967; MS, U. Calif., La Jolla, 1969; PhD, Oxford U., 1974. Rsch. asst. U. Calif., La Jolla, 1967-69, Oxford (Eng.) U., 1969-74; rsch. assoc., adj. assoc. prof. U. Oreg., Eugene, 1974-78; rsch. assoc. Stanford (Calif.) U., 1978; rsch. assoc. Nat. Rsch. Coun. Ames Rsch. Ctr. NASA, Moffett Field, Calif., 1978-80, rsch. scientist, 1980—2004, Ames assoc., 2005—. Dir. Internat. Cryogenic Engring. Conf., 1998—, Cryogenic Engring. Conf., 1983-89, 92—, internat. CryoCooler conf., 1996—; co-chmn. Internat. CryoCooler conf., 1996-98. Adv. editor: Cryogenics, 1987—; editor: Advances in Cryogenic Engineering, 1992-98; contbr. articles to profl. jours. Fellow Oxford U., 1972-74, Nat. Rsch. Coun., 1978-80; recipient medal for Exceptional Engring. Achievement NASA, 1990, Space Act award NASA, 1989, 91. Fellow: Cryogenic Soc. Am.; mem.: AAAS, Am. Phys. Soc. Home: 3132 Morris Dr Palo Alto CA 94303-4037 Office: NASA 244-10 Ames Research Ctr Moffett Field CA 94035-1000 Office Phone: 650-604-4297. Business E-Mail: pkittel@mail.arc.nasa.gov.

KITTEL, ROBERT NORVELLE, lawyer; b. Balt., June 27, 1945; s. Robert John and Ida Virginia (Oursler) K.; m. Barbara Lee Mason, Sept. 5, 1975; children: Jennifer LaPlante, Robert W. Kittel, Megan C. Kittel. BS in Pol. Sci., Loyola Coll., Balt., 1967; JD, Villanova Law Sch., 1970; LLM, George Washington U. Law, 1980. Bar: Pa., 1970, U.S. Supreme Ct., U.S. Ct. of Claims. Asst. staff judge advocate USARD-NACU Support C., Rep. of Vietnam, 1971-72; post judge advocate Seneca Army Depot, Romulus, N.Y., 1972-73; trial atty. Army Regulatory Law Office, Washington, 1974-75; asst. staff judge advocate U.S. Army Support Command Hawaii, Honolulu, 1975-78; counsel Armed Forces Inst., Washington, 1978-79; asst. counsel Naval Facility Engring. Command, Alexandria, Va., 1979-83, assoc. counsel, 1983-86, dep. counsel, 1986-93; sr. exec. svc. office JAG U.S. Army, Arlington, Va., 1993—, spl. asst. to JAG regulatory law and intellectual property. Office: Office of JAG 2200 Army Pentagon Washington DC 20310

KITTELBERGER, LARRY E., engineering executive; B of Computer Sci., Pa. State U.; MBA in Fin. and Quantitative Analysis, Old Dominion U. Various leadership positions Tenneco, Inc.; sr. v.p., chief info. officer AlliedSignal, Inc., 1994—99, Lucent Techs., Inc., 1999—2001; sr. v.p. adminstrn., chief info. officer Honeywell Internat., Inc., Morristown, NJ, 2001—. Office: Honeywell Internat 101 Columbia Rd Morristown NJ 07962

KITTELSEN, RODNEY OLIN, lawyer; b. Albany, Wis., Mar. 11, 1917; s. Olen B. and Nellie Winifred (Atkinson) K.; m. Pearle M. Haldiman, Oct. 12, 1940; children: Gregory S., James E., Bradley J. PhB, U. Wis., 1939, LLB, 1940. Spl. agt. FBI, Washington, 1940-46; ptnr. Kittelsen, Barry, Ross, Wellington & Thompson, Monroe, Wis., 1946—. Dist. atty. Green County, Monroe, 1947-53; pres. State Bar Wis., Madison, 1976-77, 83-85; dir. Wis. Law Found., Madison, 1992—. Pres. Monroe Police and Fire Commn., 1947—; legal counsel X-FBI Inc., Quantico, Va., 1986—; mem. Am. Coll. Trust and Estate Coun., Chgo., 1983—. Recipient Outstanding Citizen award Monroe Jaycees, 1977, Outstanding Svc. award Albany FFA, 1991, Disting. Svc. award U. Wis. Law Sch., 1995, Disting. Svc. award U. Wis. Law Alumni Assn., 1995, Hon. Am. Famer award, 2003, award Wilaw Found., 2005. Fellow: Am. Bar Found.; mem.: Wis. Bar Found., Wis. Law Found. (life), Wis. Bar Assn. Home: 708 26th Ave Monroe WI 53566-1620 Office: 916 17th Ave Monroe WI 53566-2003 Office Phone: 608-325-2191.

KITTERMAN, RALPH DONALD, retired member of clergy; b. Kingsley, Iowa, July 1, 1919; s. Elmer Silas Kitterman and Kathryn Featherston; m. Gertrude Helen Thompson, Aug. 12, 1942 (dec. Aug. 1985); children: Ronald Ray, James Richard. BA, Morningside Coll., 1940; MST, Boston U., 1943; DD (hon.), Morningside Coll., 1960. Ordained to ministry Meth. Ch., 1943. Minister various churches throughout Iowa, 1943-84; retired, 1984. Prison chaplain. Mem. Masons. Avocations: music, art, gems and minerals, book collector, history. Address: Friendship Haven 420 Kenyon Rd Fort Dodge IA 50501-5749

KITTLE, CHARLES FREDERICK, surgeon; b. Athens, Ohio, Oct. 24, 1921; s. Frederick F. and Ida (Falls) K.; m. Jeane Mignon Groenier, 1945 (div. 1973); children: Candace Mignon, Bradley Dean, Leslie Jeane, Brian David; m. Ann Catherine Bates, 1981. AB with honors, Ohio U., Athens, 1942, LLD, 1967; MD with honors, U. Chgo., 1945; MS in Surgery, U. Kans., 1950. Diplomate Am. Bd. Surgery, Am. Bd. Thoracic Surgery (mem. bd. 1967-75, chmn. 1973-75). Intern U. Chgo. Clinics, 1945-46; resident gen. and thoracic surgery U. Kans. Med. Center, 1948-52; spl. tng. radio-isotopes for med. use Oak Ridge Inst. Nuclear Studies, 1950, cons. med. div., 1950-55; mem. faculty U. Kans. Sch. Medicine, 1950-66; assoc. prof. surgery, lectr. history medicine, 1959-66; cons. thoracic surgery VA Hosp., Wadsworth, Kans., 1954-57, cons. gen. surgery, 1957-60; attending gen. surgery VA Hosp. Kansas City, Mo., 1954-66, Wichita, Kans., 1955-62; prof. surgery, head sect. thoracic and cardiovascular surgery U. Chgo. Clinics, 1966-72; prof. surgery, dir. thoracic surgery sect. Rush Med. Coll. and Presbyn.-St. Luke's Hosp., 1973-92, prof. emeritus, 1992—; dir. Rush Cancer Ctr., 1978-86; mem. staff McNeal Hosp., Berwyn, Ill., 1986-92. Cons. Mcpl. TB Sanatorium, Chgo., 1968-74, Hines VA Hosp., Maywood, Ill., 1973-92; spl. rsch. cardiovascular surgery, control of blood flow. Life trustee Newberry Libr., Chgo. Served as lt. (j.g.) USNR, 1946-48. Recipient Konneker award Ohio U., 2004; clin. fellow Am. Cancer Soc., 1950-52; Markle scholar med. scis., 1952-58. Mem. AAAS, ACS (bd. dirs. Kans. 1965-68), Am. Assn. History Medicine, Am. Assn. Thoracic Surgery, Am. Coll. Cardiology (bd. dirs. Kans. 1963-66), Chgo. Surg. Soc. (pres. 1972-73), Am. Heart Assn. (chmn. program com. cardiovasc. surgery 1965-88, exec. com. cardiovasc. surgery coun. 1962-74, chmn. coun. 1972-74), Am. Physiol. Assn., Cen. Surg. Soc., Chgo. Med. Soc., Am. Surg. Assn., Internat. Cardiovasc. Soc. (sec. 1965-71), Internat. Soc. Surgery, Soc. Med. Hist. (pres. Chgo. 1983-85), N.J. Thoracic Surgery Soc., Ill. Thoracic Surgery Soc. (pres. 1983-84), Soc. Clin. Surgery, Soc. Surg. Oncology, Soc. Vascular Surgery, Soc. Univ. Surgeons (pres. 1966-67), Soc. Thoracic Surgery, Univ. Village Assn. (bd. dirs. 1986-89, pres. 1989), Arthur Conan Doyle Soc., Caxton Club (pres. 1999-2001), Chgo. Literary Club, Hounds of Baskerville, Baker Street Irregulars, Grolier Club, Phi Beta Kappa, Sigma Xi, Alpha Omega Alpha. Home: 856 S Laflin St Chicago IL 60607-4026 Office Phone: 312-243-4310. E-mail: kittle856@mindspring.com.

KITTLES, KERRY, professional basketball player; b. Dayton, Ohio, June 12, 1974; s. Acosta and Mary Kittles. Degree in mgmt., Villanova U., 1996. Basketball player N.J. Nets, East Rutherford, 1996—2004, L.A. Clippers, 2004—. Eucharistic Min. Roman Catholic Ch. Named La's. Mr. Basketball, 1992, Second Team All-Am. by the AP, 1995, First Team All-Am., 1996, NBA co-Rookie of the Month for Dec. 1996; NBA All-Rookie Second Team, 1996-97. Set NBA rookie record 1996-97 for most 3 point shots made, had his number 30 retired by Villanova U., 1998. Office: c/o Los Angeles Clippers 1111 S Figueroa st ste1100 Los Angeles CA 90015

KITTLESON, HENRY MARSHALL, lawyer; b. Tampa, Fla., May 13, 1929; s. Edgar O. and Ardath (Ayers) K.; m. Barbara Clark, Mar. 20, 1954; 1 dau., Laura Helen. BS with high honors, U. Fla., 1951, JD with high honors, 1953. Bar: Fla. 1953. Ptnr. Holland & Knight, Lakeland and Bartow, Fla., 1955—. Mem. adv. bd. Fla. Fed. Savs. & Loan Assn., 1974-86; mem. Fla. Law Revision Commn., 1967-76, vice chmn., 1969-71; mem. Gov.'s Property Rights Study Commn., 1974-75, Nat. Conf. Commrs. Uniform State Laws, 1982—. Mem. coun. U. Fla. Law Ctr., 1974-77. Served to maj. USAF, 1953-55. Fellow Am. Bar Found.; mem. ABA (chmn. standing com. on ethic and profl. responsibility 1980-81), Am. Law Inst., Am. Coll. Real Estate Lawyers, Fla. Bar (chmn. standing com. profl. ethics 1965-66, tort litig. rev. commn. 1983-84), Blue Key, Sigma Phi Epsilon, Phi Delta Phi, Phi Kappa Phi, Beta Gamma Sigma, Lakeland Yacht and Country Club. Presbyterian. Home: 1111 S Lakemont Ave Apt 511 Winter Park FL 32792 Office: Holland & Knight PO Box 32092 92 Lake Wire Dr Lakeland FL 33815-1510 Business E-Mail: henry.kittleson@hklaw.com.

KITTLESON, MARK DOUGLAS, veterinary cardiologist, veterinary medicine educator; b. Sherburn, Minn., Sept. 21, 1950; s. Norman Leonard and Lavonne Elaine Kittleson; m. Judith Ann Knobloch, June 11, 1972; children: Ashlie Ann, Natalie Jean. BS, U. Minn., 1972, DVM, 1974; PhD, Ohio State U., 1982. Diplomate Am. Coll. Vet. Internal Medicine. Staff veterinarian Westfield (N.J.) Vet. Group, 1974-76; resident in vet. internal medicine Kans. State U., Manhattan, 1976-78; rsch. assoc. Ohio State U.,

Columbus, 1978-80; asst. prof. Mich. State U., East Lansing, 1980-84; from asst. prof. to assoc. prof. U. Calif., Davis, 1984-92, prof., 1992—. Cons. Vet. Info. Network, Davis, Calif.; Buchanan lectr. Coll. Vet. Medicine, Mich. State U., 1996; assoc. dir. Vet. Med. Tchg. Hosp., 1996-2000. Author: (book) Small Animal Cardiovascular Medicine, 1998; assoc. editor: Jour. Vet. Internal Medicine, 1986-90; contbr. over 90 articles to sci. jours., chpts. in books. Recipient Small Animal Rsch. award Ralston Purina, 1989. Mem. Am. Coll. Vet. Internal Medicine (bd. cert. in cardiology, pres. 1984-87, v.p. 1998-99, pres.-elect 1999-2000, pres. 2000-01, chmn. bd. 2001-2002). Avocations: basketball, computers. Business E-Mail: mdkittleson@ucdavis.edu.

KITTLITZ, RUDOLF GOTTLIEB, JR., chemical engineer, researcher; b. Waco, Tex., Apr. 19, 1935; s. Rudolf Gottlieb and Lena Hulda (Landgraf) K.; children: Lenell, Theresa, Liesel, Rolf. BSChemE, U. Miss., 1957; MS in engring., U. Ala., 2003. Registered profl. engr., Calif. Engr., polychems. research E.I. du Pont de Nemours & Co., Wilmington, Del., 1957-60, engr., textile fibers dept. Seaford, Del., 1960-62, sr. engr., textile fibers dept., 1962-67, Chattanooga, 1967-68, sr. research engr., 1968-83, sr. research engr. textile fibers Seaford, 1983-87, research assoc. textile fibers, 1987-92, sr. rsch. assoc. fibers, 1992-94, Chattanooga, 1995—2000; statis. cons. Rudy Kittlitz & Assocs., Alpine, Tex., 2001—. Lectr. in field; adj. prof. U. Tenn.-Chattanooga, 1980—82, Sul Ross State U., 2001—; Citizen Am. Program del. to Russia, 1991. Co-author: Quality Assurance for the Chemical and Process Industries--A Manual of Good Practices, 1987, 2d edit., 1999, ANSI/ASQC Q90/ISO 9000: Guidelines for Use by the Chemical and Process Industries, 1992, Specifications for the Chemical and Process Industries--A Manual for Development and Use, 1996, Glossary and Tables for Statistical Quality Control, 4th edit., 2004. Vice chmn. Cmty. Action Com., Seaford, 1966; mem. Alpine Pks. and Recreation Bd., 2001—, chmn., 2005—; chmn. U.S. tech. adv. group to tech. com. Internat. Orgn. Standardization, 2001—. Fellow: Am. Soc. for Quality (cert. quality and reliability engr., chmn. Chattanooga sect. 1975—76, councilor region 11 chem. divsn. 1975—80, chmn. Del. sect. 1984—85, exec. regional dir. 1987—91, dir.-at-large 1991—93, parliamentarian 1993—99, 2000—, W.G. Hunter award 1989); mem.: Internat. Orgn. for Standardization, Am. Statis. Assn., Nat. Assn. Parliamentarians. Democrat. Baptist. Home: 2006 Ceredo Dr Alpine TX 79830 Office: 117 N 2d St # 2207 Alpine TX 79830-4701 Office Phone: 432-837-9937.

KITTO, JOHN BUCK, JR., mechanical engineer; b. Evanston, Ill., Dec. 22, 1952; s. John Buck and Marie (Comstock) K.; children: Christopher Daniel, Andrew Comstock. BSME, Lehigh U., 1975; MBA, U. Akron, 1980. Registered profl. engr., Ohio, Pa. Sr. engr. McDermott Tech. Inc. subs. Babcock & Wilcox Co., Alliance, Ohio, 1975-80, research engr., 1980-81, program mgr., 1981-94, bus. devel. specialist, 1995-99; bus. devel. mgr. The Babcock and Wilcox Co., Barberton, Ohio, 1999—. Editor: Heat Exchangers for Two Phase Flow, 1983, Two-Phase Heat Exchanger, 1985, Maldistribution of Flow, 1987, Steam: Its Generation and Use, 2005; author and patentee in field. Fellow ASME (chmn. chpt. 1983-84, chmn. exec. com. of heat transfer divsn. 1992-93, v.p. region V 1992-95, officer bd. comms. 1991-95, sr. v.p. 1995-98, mem. bd. govs. 1998-2002, Prime Movers award 1992, Dedicated Svc. award 1992, George Westinghouse Silver medal 1991); mem. Air Waste Mgmt. Assn., Tau Beta Pi, Pi Tau Sigma, Beta Gamma Sigma, Sigma Iota Epsilon. Republican. Avocations: reading, hiking, board games, coaching soccer. Home: 1225 Arrowhead Dr SW Dellroy OH 44620 Office: Babcock & Wilcox Co PO Box 351 20 S Van Buren Ave Barberton OH 44203-0351 Office Fax: 330-860-1409.

KITTREDGE, NANCY, artist; b. Ellsworth, Maine, Nov. 12, 1938; m. Robert Kaye Jellison, Apr. 7, 1979. BA in Theatre Arts, U. Maine, 1961; MA, U. Miami, Fla., 1963; student U. N.H., 1957-59. Solo exhbns. Triad Gallery, San Diego, 1976, Designbank, San Diego, 1978, Challis Gallery, Laguna Beach, 1980, San Diego Mus. Art, 1981, John Douglas Cline Gallery, Phoenix, 1982, Suzanne Brown Gallery, Scottsdale, Ariz., 1983, Joy Horwich Gallery, Chgo., 1984, 88, San Francisco Art Exch., 1986, J.J. Brookings, San Jose, Calif., 1987, Mira Costa Coll., San Marcos, Calif., 1990, David Zapf Gallery, San Diego, 1993, 96, 99, 2001, 05; group shows include U. Maine, Orono, 1961, U. Miami, Fla., 1963, La Jolla Mus. Art, 1975, Laguna Beach Mus. Art, 1976, San Diego Artists Guild, 1976, San Diego-Yokohama Invitational, Japan, 1979, Gallery, One, San Francisco, 1981, Riggs Gallery, San Diego, 1981, John Douglas Cline Gallery, Phoenix, 1981, Ankrum Gallery, L.A., 1982, Maple Creek Gallery, San Diego, 1982, Deicas Art Gallery, La Jolla, 1983, Alexandria (La.) Mus. Art Internat. Exhbn., 1986, Riverside (Calif.) Mus. Art., 1987, J.J. Brookings and Co. Gallery, San Jose, 1987, Newport Harbor Mus., Newport Beach, Calif., 1988, Schwartz Cierlak Gallery, Santa Monica, Calif., 1988—, Orlando Gallery, L.A., 1988—, Joy Horwich Gallery, Chgo., 1988, 91, Calif. Ctr. for the Arts, Escondido, 1992, BCA Gallery, Boston, 1995, L.A. Mcpl. Gallery, 1998, Oceanside Mus. Art, 2000, San Diego Mus. Art, 2002; represented in permanent collections at Household Corp., Chgo., Morton Foods, Dalas., Capital Intermediaries, Des Moines, Laguna Mus. Art, Laguna Beach, Calif., San Deigo Mus. Art, others; cover Contemporary Women Artists Calendar, 1986. Mem. San Diego Artists Guild (bd. dirs. 1975-76, 80-81), Artists Equity Assn., Phi Kappa Phi. Episcopalian. E-mail: nkart@san.rr.com.

KITTREDGE, WILLIAM ALFRED, humanities educator; b. Portland, Oreg., Aug. 14, 1932; s. Franklin Oscar and Josephine (Miessner) K.; m. Janet O'Connor, Dec. 8, 1952 (div. 1968); children: Karen, Bradley. BS, Oreg. State U., 1953; MFA in Creative Writing, U. Iowa, 1969. Rancher Warner Valley Livestock, Adel, Oreg., 1957-67; prof. U. Mont., Missoula, 1969—, now Regents Prof. emeritus. Author: The Van Gogh Field, 1979, We Are Not In This Together, 1984, Owning It All, 1987, Hole in the Sky, 1992, Who Owns the West, 1996, The Portable Western Reader, 1997, Taking Care, 1999, Balancing Water, 2000, The Nature of Generosity, 2000, Southwestern Homelands, 2002, The Best Stores of William Kittredge, 2003. With USAF, 1954-57. Recipient award for lit. Gov. of Mont., 1988, Charles Frankel prize in Humanities, NEH, 1994; named Mont. Humanist of Yr., 1989. Home: 143 S 5th St E Missoula MT 59801-2719 Office Phone: 406-549-6605. Personal E-mail: kittredgeb@aol.com.

KITTRELL, STEVEN DAN, lawyer; b. Winfield, Kans., Aug. 4, 1953; s. William Dan and Jeanette E. (Miller) Kittrell; m. Susan K. Hattan, May 30, 1987. BA cum laude, Baylor U., 1974; JD cum laude, George Washington U., 1978; LLM in Taxation, Georgetown U., 1981. Bar: DC 1978, Md. 1991, US Ct. Fed. Claims 1979, US Tax Ct. 1979, US Supreme Ct. 1984. Legis. asst. to senator Bob Dole of Kans. US Senate, Washington, 1976-78; assoc. O'Connell & Associates, Washington, 1978-84; ptnr. O'Connell & Kittrell, Washington, 1984-88, Golden, Freda & Schraub, Washington, 1989-91, McGuire, Woods, Battle & Boothe LLP (now McGuireWoods LLP), Washington, 1991—, mng. ptnr. DC office. Mem. ABA (mem. sections of gen. practice & tax, 1978-, chmn. sect. taxation com. on domestic rels. tax problems 1984-86), DC Bar Assn. (mem. sect. taxation), Delta Theta Phi. Republican. Baptist. Avocation: Tae Kwon Do. Office: McGuireWoods LLP Washington Sq 1050 Conn Ave NW, Ste 1200 Washington DC 20036-5317 Office Phone: 202-857-1701. Office Fax: 202-828-2975. Business E-Mail: skittrell@mcguirewoods.com.

KITTRIE, NICHOLAS, international lawyer, writer; b. en route Bilgoraj, Silesia, Mar. 26, 1930; (parents Brit. citizens); s. S.K. Kronenbergh and Perla F. (Ver Standijk) K.; m. Sara Yudovic de Burak, June 1, 1962; children: Orde Felicien, Norda Nicole, Zachary McNair. Student, U. Cairo, 1946, U. London, 1947; LLB, U. Kans., 1950, MA, 1951; postgrad., U. Chgo., 1954-55; LLM, Georgetown U., 1963, SJD, 1968. Bar: Kans. 1953, D.C. 1958, U.S. Supreme Ct. Instr. Western civilization dept. U. Kans., 1948-50; legal analyst Kans. Govt. Rsch. Ctr., 1951-54; asst. to dir. legis. svc. ABA, 1955-56, project dir., 1956-58; rsch. assoc. Yale Law Sch., 1958; legal counsel to U.S. Senator Wiley, 1959; counsel to U.S. Senator Estes Kefauver, antitrust and monopoly subcom. U.S. Senate, 1959-62; ptnr. DeGrazia & Kittrie, Washington, 1962-67; prof. criminal and comparative law Washington Coll. Law, Am. U., 1963—, dir. Inst. for Advanced Studies in Justice, 1970-78, dean, 1977-79, Mooers scholar and prof. law, 1983—; univ. prof. Am. U., Washington, 1994—. Lectr. U. Ottawa, summer 1966; vis. lectr. Salzburg Law Sch., summers 1999—; rsch. scholar Univs. Warsaw and Berlin, summers 1967, 68; rsch. assoc. Ctr. Studies Criminal Justice U. Chgo., 1967-68; dir. Law and Policy Inst., Jerusalem, summers 1970-76, Inst. Law and Mass Media, 1978—; chmn. Eleanor Roosevelt Inst. for Justice and Peace, 1989—; vis. fellow Inst. Advanced Legal Rsch. U. London, 1973-74, Nat. Inst. Justice U.S. Dept. Justice, 1979-80; vis. prof. London Sch. Econs., 1974; prof. internat. criminal law, Salzburg Law Sch., 2000-; cons. Pres.'s Commn. Marijuana and Drug Abuse, 1972, v.p.'s commn. to combat terrorism, 1985; permanent rep. of AIDP to UN Social and Econs. Coun., 1975—; mem. task force on role of psychology in criminal justice Am. Psychol. Assn.; dir. Dulles Internat. Bank, 1998-, Bank of Chios, Athens, Greece; dir., gen. counsel Liberty House Investments; chmn. KVK Communications Ltd.; chmn. finance com. U. Bridgeport, 1998—. Author: International Legal Responsibility for Colonial People, 1951, The Mentally Disabled and the Law, 1959, The Right to be Different: Deviance and Enforced Law, 1971, The Comparative Law of Israel and the Middle East, 1971, The Real Estate Settlement Process and Its Cost, 1972, Crescent and Star: Arab-Israeli Perspectives on the Middle East Conflict, 1972, Medicine, Law and Public Policy, 1975, The Tree of Liberty: Rebellion and Political Crime in America, 1986, 2d edit., 1998, The Uncertain Future: Gorbachev's Eastern Bloc, 1988, The War Against Authority: From the Crisis of Legitimacy to a New Social Contract, 1995, Rebels With a Cause: The Minds and Morality of Political Offenders, 2000, Sentencing, Sanctions and Corrections: Federal and State Law, Policy and Practice, 2002, The Future of Peace in the 21st Century, 2003, International Criminal Law and Procedure, 2003, International Crimes and Punishments: Laws of Peace and Laws of War, 2004; chmn. editl. bd. Jour. Criminology, 1973-75; mem. editl. bd. Law and Human Behavior, 1976-80; mem. editl. adv. bd. The Washington Times; mem. exec. bd. Paragon House Pubs.; sr. cons. U.S. News and World Report Books; contbr. articles to profl. jours. Chmn. UN Alliance of NGOs on Crime Prevention and Criminal Justice, 1998—, sci. com. U. Messina, Italy. Served with Brit. Middle East Command. Raymond fellow U. Chgo., 1954-55; rsch. fellow Yale Law Sch., 1955; sr. fellow NEH, 1973-74. Mem. ABA, AAAS (mem. coun. 1972—), Am. Soc. Criminology (pres. 1975), Internat. Assn. Penal Law (v.p. Am. sect., sec.-gen. 1975-80), Internat. Assn. Comparative Pub. Law (bd. dirs. 1976—), Am. Soc. Pub. Adminstrn., Am. Soc. Internat. Law (chair interest group on status of minorities), Internat. Inst. Space Law, Inter-Am. Bar Assn., Kans. Bar Assn., D.C. Bar Assn., Manorial Soc. Gt. Britian, Knight, Order of St. John, Rose Haven Yacht Club (bd. dirs.), Cosmos Club, Phi Delta Phi (Sam Green award). Home: 6908 Ayr Ln Bethesda MD 20817-4902 also: Ramsbridge Farm Cochran Mill Rd Leesburg VA 20175-4617 Office: Am U Sch Law 4801 Massachusetts Ave NW Ste 354 Washington DC 20016 Fax: 202-387-3629. Office Phone: 202-387-4346. E-mail: genih@aol.com.

KITTROSS, JOHN MICHAEL, retired communications educator; b. NYC, Apr. 25, 1929; s. John H. and Lucile S. (Vossen) K.; m. Sally Sprague, Dec. 27, 1951; children: David M., Julia Ann. AB, Antioch Coll., 1951; MS, Boston U., 1952; PhD, U. Ill., 1960. Various positions broadcasting, summer stock, motion picture prodn., 1946-52; rsch. asst. U. Ill. Inst. Comm. Rsch., Urbana, 1955-59; from instr. to assoc. prof. dept. telecomm. U. So. Calif., 1959—68; prof. comm. Temple U., 1968-85, asst. dean Sch. Comm. and Theater, 1971-73, assoc. dean, 1973-80; dean Emerson Coll., Boston, 1985, provost, v.p. acad. affairs, 1985-87, prof. dept. mass comm., 1987-93. Vis. prof., dir. Temple U. Sch. Comm. and Theater London Programme, 1994; mng. dir. K
≥ Assocs., 1995—. Author: Television Frequency Allocation Policy in the United States, 1979; co-author: Stay Tuned: A Concise History of American Broadcasting, 1978, 3d edit., 2002, Controversies in Media Ethics, 1996, 2nd edit., 1999; editor: Free and Fair: Courtroom Access and the Fairness Doctrine, 1970, Jour. Broadcasting, 1960-72, Documents in American Telecommunications Policy, 1977, Administration of American Telecommunications Policy, 1981; editor: Media Ethics, 1989—; compiler: Bibliography of Theses and Dissertations in Broadcasting, 1920-73, 1978; contbg. editor: Comm. Booknotes Quar., 1997—; contbr. articles to profl. jours. Trustee Upper Moreland Free Pub. Library, 1976-82. Served with AUS, 1952-54. Mem. AAUP, Broadcast Edn. Assn. (Disting. Broadcast Edn. award 1990), Assn. Edn. in Journalism and Mass Comm., Radio-TV News Dirs. Assn., Soc. Profl. Journalists, ACLU. Unitarian (trustee ch. 1966-68). Home: 164 High St Acton MA 01720-4218

KITTS, JAMES A., education educator; b. Rochester, NY, Aug. 31, 1971; s. Frank Anthony and Beverly Ann (Shoenberger) Cuomo. BA in Environ. Studies, Oberlin Coll., 1992; MS in Natural Resources, U. Mich., 1995; MA in Sociology, Cornell U., 1998, PhD, 2001. Tchg. fellow U. Mich., Ann Arbor, 1993—95, Cornell U., Ithaca, NY, 1995—2000; prof. U. Wash., Seattle, 2000—05. Chmn. faculty coun. on ednl. tech. U. Wash., Seattle, 2002—05. Mem. editl. bd.: Computational Math. Orgn., 2003—; contbr. chapters to books. Grantee, NSF, 1998, 2004; Buttrick-Cripper fellow, Cornell U., 1997—98. Mem.: Acad. Mgmt., Am. Sociol. Assn. (Best Paper award 1999). Office: Univ Washington Box 353340 202 Savery Hall Seattle WA 98195-3340

KITZ, RICHARD JOHN, anesthesiologist, educator; b. Oshkosh, Wis., Mar. 25, 1929; s. Edward G. and Lona M (Schneider) Kitz; m. Jeanne Hogan, Feb. 27, 1954; 1 child, Anne Marie. BS, Marquette U., 1951, MD, 1954; MA (hon.), Harvard U. Med. Sch., 1969; DSc (hon.), Marquette U., 2000. Diplomate Am. Bd. Anesthesiology (dir.). From intern in surgery to assoc. prof. Columbia U., 1954—66, assoc. prof., 1966—69; prof. rsch. and tchg. in anesthesia Harvard U.-MIT, co-dir. divsn. health scis. tech., 1985—91; anaesthetist-in-chief Mass. Gen. Hosp., Boston, 1969—94; from prof. to prof. emeritus Med. Sch. Harvard U., 1969—2004, prof. emeritus Med. Sch., 2004—. Cons. FDA; prin. investigator Harvard Anaesthesia Rsch. and Rsch. Tng. Ctr., 1969—93. Editor: This is No Humbug! Reminiscences of the Department of Anesthesia at the Massachusetts General Hospital, 2002; editor: (with E.M. Papper) Uptake and Distribution of Anesthetic Agents, 1963; editor: (with M.B. Laver) Sci. Basis of Anesthesia; editor-in-chief Jour. Clin. Anesthesia, 1987—95; contbr. articles to profl. jours. Served with M.C. USN, 1955—57. Fellow: Coll. Anesthesiologists; mem.: Harvard Club (Boston), Royal Coll. Surgeons Ireland (hon. mem. faculty anesthetists), Mass. Soc. Anesthesiologists, Am. Soc. Anesthesiologists, Royal Coll. Anesthetists Eng. (hon.), Japan Soc. Anesthesiologists (hon.), German Soc. Anesthesiologists and Intensive Care (hon.), Australian Soc. Anesthetists (hon.), Assn. Univ. Anesthetists, AMA, Inst. Medicine, NAS, Blue Water Sailing Club, Beverly Yacht Club. Roman Catholic. Home: 6 Pond St Dover MA 02030-2432 Office: Mass Gen Hosp Dept Anesthesia Boston MA 02114 Business E-Mail: richard_kitz@hms.harvard.edu, rkitz@partners.org.

KITZES, WILLIAM FREDRIC, lawyer, advocate, researcher; b. Bklyn., Nov. 24, 1950; s. David Louis and Rhoda Rachel (Feldman) K; m. Sandra Shimasaki, Apr. 7, 1979: children: Justin, Dana. BA, U. Wis., 1972; JD, Am. U., 1975. Bar: D.C. 1977. Legal advisor on product recalls U.S. Consumer Products Safety Commn., Washington, 1975-77, program mgr., 1977-80, regulatory counsel, 1980-81; v.p., gen. mgr. Inst. for Safety Analysis, Rockville, Md., 1981-83; prin. Consumer Safety Assocs., Potomac, Md., Boca Raton, Fla., 1983—. Cons. Toro Co., Bloomington, Minn., 1987, Vendo Co., Fresno, Calif., 1987, Nat. Assn. Attys. Gens., Washington, 1987, Arctic Cat, Inc., Thief River Falls, Minn., 1995—, Global Furniture, Toronto, Ont., 1997, Product Safety Online, Boca Raton, 1997—, Cisco Sys., Inc., San Jose, Calif., 2001-. Contbg. columnist CCH Product Safety Guide and Products Liability Reporter, 2000-01. Counsel Friends of Charlie Gilchrist, Montgomery County, Md., 1983; chmn. Fla. Consumers Coun., 1995—. Recipient silver medal for meritorious svc. U.S. Consumer Products Safety Commn., 1976. Mem. Am. Soc. Safety Engrs., Human Factors Soc., System Safety Soc., Nat. Safety Coun., Internat. Consumer Product Health and Safety Orgn. Home and Office: Consumer Safety Assocs 4501 NW 25th Way Boca Raton FL 33434-2506 Office Phone: 561-241-1900. Business E-Mail: kitzes@productsafety.com.

KITZHABER, JOHN ALBERT, former governor, emergency physician, former state senator; b. Colfax, Wash., Mar. 5, 1947; s. Albert Raymond and Annabel Reed (Wetzel) K.; m. Sharon Lacroix; 1 child, Logan. BA, Dartmouth Coll., 1969; MD, U. Oreg., 1973. Intern Gen. Rose Meml. Hosp., Denver, 1976-77; Emergency physician Mercy Hosp., Roseburg, Oreg., 1974-75; mem. Oreg. Ho. of Reps., 1979-81, Oreg. Senate, 1981—93, pres., 1985—93; former gov. State of Oregon, 1995—2003; pres. Estes Park Inst., Englewood, Colo., 2003—; endowed chair Found. for Med. Excellence, Portland, Oreg., 2003—. Assoc. prof. Oreg. Health Sci. U., 1989-1995; MD chmn. health policy Found. Med. Excellence, 2003-. Pres. Estes Park Inst., Colo., 2003—. Mem. Am. Coll. Emergency Physicians, Douglas County Med. Soc., Physicians for Social Responsibility, Am. Council Young Polit. Leaders, Oreg. Trout. Democrat. Office: Found Med Excellence Ste 800 1 SW Columbia St Portland OR 97258

KITZKE, EUGENE DAVID, research and development company executive; b. Milw., Sept. 2, 1923; s. Leo R. and Regina R. (Tomczyk) Kitzke; m. Lorraine Grace Shummon, Sept. 2, 1946; children: Mary Victoria, Paul Simon, Patrice Lynn, Jerome Peter. BS, Marquette U., 1945, MS, 1947; diploma in basic clin. sci., Med. Coll. Wis., 2002. Instr. microbiology St. Mary's Sch. Nursing, Grand Rapids, Mich., 1946-47; assoc. prof. Aquinas Coll., 1947-51; lab researcher S.C. Johnson & Son, Inc., Racine, Wis., 1951-57, research mgr., 1957-76, v.p. corp. R&D, 1976-81; pres. Oak Crete Block Corp., South Milwaukee, Wis., 1980—; developer Wind Crest Subdiv., Wind Lake, Wis., 1993. Adj. prof. dept. environ. medicine Med. Coll. Wis., Milw., 1973—81; owner Danel Enterprise, South Milwaukee; judge Marquette U. Sci. Fair; bd. dirs. Songcards, inc. Author: (book) For the Next Generation, 1986; contbr. articles to tech. jours., fiction and poetry to mags.;, author pubs. in field. Mem. pres.' coun. Alverno Coll., 1979—87. Recipient H. F. Johnson Cmty. Svc. award, 1996; Disting. scholar, Marquette U., 1995. Mem.: AAAS, Hist. Sci. Soc., Palm Soc. (exec. bd., past pres.), Sigma Xi, Sigma Tau Delta, Phi Sigma. Roman Catholic. Achievements include patents in field. Home: 616 Aspen St South Milwaukee WI 53172-1702 Office: PO Box 413 South Milwaukee WI 53172-0413 also: 7101 S Pennsylvania Ave Oak Creek WI 53154-2439 *Honor thyself. Be in control. Be paid.*

KIVEL, PAUL, writer; 3 children. Trainer, activist, writer, co-founder Oakland Men's Project, Volcano, Calif., 1979—90. Author: You Call This Democracy, Boys Will Be Men, Uprooting Racism, I Can Make My World A Safer Place, Men's Work; co-author (with Allen Creighton): Making the Peace, Helping Teens Stop Violence, Young Men's Work; co-author: (with Allen Creighton & Ralph Cantor) Days of Respect; co-author: (with M. Nell Myhand) Young Women's Lives. Office: Paul Kivel & Assoc 658 Vernon St Oakland CA 94610

KIVELL, WAYNE M., music educator, choral conductor; b. LeRoy, Minn., July 5, 1939; s. Elmer R. and Elsbeth E. Kivell; m. Alyce M. Thompson, June 17, 1967; children: Brent E., Julie M. BA, Luther Coll., 1961; MS in music edn., U. Wis., 1965; MA in Musicology, U. Minn., 1983. Vocal music dir. Lakefield HS, Lakefield, Minn., 1961—65, Emmetsburg HS and C.C., Emmetsburg, Iowa, 1965—69, Northfield HS, Northfield, Minn., 1969—94; asst. dir. Dale Warland Singers, St. Paul, 1972—83; music libr. asst. St. Olaf Coll., Northfield, Minn., 1989—2001; founder, music dir. I Cantanti Chamber Choir, Northfield, Minn., 1988—; exec. sec. Am. Choral Dir. Assn. of Minn., 1997—. Editor (arranger) choral music. Mission trips to Nicaragua Interfaith Svc. to Latin Am., 2003—05; active with Habitat for Humanity, Rice City, Minn., 2002—. Recipient F. Melius Christiansen award, ACDA of Minn., 2000. Mem.: NEA, Minn. Music Educators Assn., Am. Choral Dir. Assn. Avocations: tennis, woodworking, MG automobiles. E-mail: kivellw@rconnect.com.

KIVELSON, MARGARET GALLAND, physicist; b. NYC, Oct. 21, 1928; d. Walter Isaac and Madeleine (Wiener) Galland; m. Daniel Kivelson, Aug. 15, 1949; children: Steven Allan, Valerie Ann. AB, Radcliffe Coll., 1950, AM, 1951, PhD, 1957. Cons. Rand Corp., Santa Monica, Calif., 1956-69; asst. to geophysicist UCLA, 1967-83, prof., 1983—, also chmn. dept. earth and space scis., 1984-87, acting dir. Inst. Geophys. Planet Physics, 1999—2000; prin. investigator of magnetometer, Galileo Mission Jet Propulsion Lab., Pasadena, Calif., 1977—2004. Overseer Harvard Coll., 1977-83; adv. coun. NASA, 1987-93; chair atmospheric adv. com. NSF, 1986-89, Com. Solar and Space Physics, 1977-86, com. planetary exploration, 1986-87, com. solar terrestial physics, 1989-92; adv. com. geoscis. NSF, 1993-97; space studies bd. NRC, 2002-05. Editor: The Solar System: Observations and Interpretations, 1986; co-editor: Introduction to Space Physics, 1995; contbr. articles to profl. jours. Named Woman of Yr., LA Mus. Sci. and Industry, 1979, Woman of Sci., UCLA, 1984; recipient Grad. Soc. medal Radcliffe Coll., 1983, 350th Anniversary Alumni medal Harvard U., 1986, Alfvén medal European Geophys. Union, 2005. Fellow AAAS, NAS, Internat. Inst. Astronautics, Am. Geophys. Union (Fleming medal 2005), Am. Acad. Arts and Scis., Am. Phys. Soc., Am. Philisophical Soc., Royal Astron. Soc.; mem. Am. Astron. Soc. Office: UCLA Dept Earth & Space Scis 6847 Slichter Los Angeles CA 90095-0001 Office Phone: 310-825-3435. Business E-Mail: mkivelson@igpp.ucla.edu.

KIZER, CAROLYN ASHLEY, poet, educator; b. Spokane, Wash., Dec. 10, 1925; d. Benjamin Hamilton and M. (Ashley) K.; m. Stimson Bullitt, Jan., 1948 (div.); children: Ashley Ann, Scott, Jill Hamilton; m. John Marshall Woodbridge, Apr. 11, 1975. BA, Sarah Lawrence Coll., 1945; postgrad. (Chinese govt. fellow in comparative lit.), Columbia U., 1946-47; studied poetry with Theodore Roethke, U. Wash., 1953-54; LittD (hon.), Whitman Coll., 1986, St. Andrew's Coll., 1989, Mills Coll., 1990, Wash. State U., 1991. Specialist in lit. U.S. Dept. State, Pakistan, 1964-65; first dir. lit. programs Nat. Endowment for Arts, 1966-70; poet-in-residence U. N.C. at Chapel Hill, 1970-74; Hurst Prof. Lit. Washington U., St. Louis, 1971; lectr. Spring Lecture Series Barnard Coll., 1972; acting dir. grad. writing program Columbia U., 1972; poet-in-residence Ohio U., 1974; vis. poet Iowa Writer's Workshop, 1975; prof. U. Md., 1976-77; poet-in-residence, disting. vis. lectr. Centre Coll., Ky., 1979; disting. vis. poet East Wash. U., 1980; Elliston prof. poetry U. Cin., 1981; Bingham disting. prof. U. Louisville, Ky., 1982; disting. vis. poet Bucknell U., Pa., 1982; vis. poet SUNY, Albany, 1982; prof. Columbia U. Sch. Arts, 1982; prof. poetry Stanford U., 1986; sr. fellow in humanities Princeton U., 1986; vis. prof. writing U. Ariz., 1989, 90, U. Calif., Davis, 1991; Coal Royalty chair U. Ala., 1995. Participant Internat. Poetry Festivals, London, 1960, 70, Yugoslavia, 1969, 70, Pakistan, 1969, Rotterdam, Netherlands, 1970, Knokke-le-Zut, Belgium, 1970, Bordeaux, 1992, Dublin, 1993, Glasgow, 1994; sr. fellow humanities council Princeton U., 1986. Author: Poems, 1959, The Ungrateful Garden, 1961, Knock Upon Silence, 1965, Midnight Was My Cry, 1971, Mermaids in the Basement: Poems for Women, 1984 (San Francisco Arts Commn. award 1986), Yin: New Poems, 1984 (Pulitzer prize in poetry 1985), The Nearness of You, 1987 (Theodore Roethke prize, 1988); Proses: On Poems & Poets, 1994, Picking & Choosing: Prose on Prose, 1995, Harping On: Poems 1985-1995, 1996, The Complete Pro Femina, 2000, Cool, Calm and Collected Poems, 1960-2000; editor: Woman Poet: The West, 1980, Leaving Taos, 1981, The Essential Clare, 1993, 100 Great Poems by Women, 1995; translator Carrying Over, 1988; founder, editor: Poetry N.W., 1959-65; contbr. poems, articles to Am. and Brit. jours. Recipient award Am. Acad. and Inst. Arts and Letters, 1985, Pres.'s medal Ea. Wash. U., 1988, 5 Gov.'s awards State of Wash., 1965, 85, 95, 98, 2001, Silver medal Commonwealth Club, 1997, 2002, Aiken Taylor prize Sewanee Rev., 1998, Patterson prize, 2002, Western State Lifetime Achievement award, 2002, 1st prize Ind. Pub. Book award, 2002, L.A. Times Top Ten Books award, 2002, Acad. prize, 2003, Poets' prize, 2003. Mem. PEN, Amnesty Internat., Poetry Soc. Am. (Masefield prize 1983, Frost medal 1988). Episcopalian. Address: 19772 8th St E Sonoma CA 95476-3849

KIZER, JOHN OSCAR, lawyer; b. Wheeling, W.Va., Mar. 6, 1913; s. Edwin O. and Laura E. (Dennis) K.; m. Lillian Taylor Cart, Sept. 15, 1934; children: Nora Kizer Bell, Stephen. AB, W.Va. U., 1934, LLB, 1936. Bar: W.Va. 1936. Dir. safety responsibility dept. W.Va. Rd. Commn., 1936-39; assoc. Clark, Woodroe & Butts, Charleston, W.Va., 1939; ptnr. Campbell,

Love, Woodroe & Kizer and predecessor firms, Charleston, 1939-75, Love, Wise, Robinson & Woodroe, Charleston, 1976-83, Love, Wise & Woodroe, Charleston, 1983-89, Kay, Casto, Chaney, Love & Wise, Charleston, 1989—. Gen. receiver Cir. Ct. Kanawha County, 1953-98; dir. emeritus Charleston Nat. Bank. Bd. dirs., past pres., co-incorporator Children's Mus., Charleston; co-incorporator Sunrise Found.; bd. dirs. Daywood Found. Recipient Spl. Achievement award for Pub. Svc. W.Va. U. Coll. of Law, 1991, W.Va. Bar Assn. Lifetime Achievement award, 1998. Mem. ABA, W.Va. Bar Assn., W.Va. State Bar (chmn. com. legis. 1960-71, mem. com. legal ethics, 1964-84, chmn. 1968-84), Berry Hills Country Club, Delta Tau Delta. Presbyterian. Office: Kay Casto & Chaney 1600 Bank One Ctr Charleston WV 25301-2723 Address: Kizer % Bell PO Box 9593 Roanoke VA 24020-1593

KIZER, JORGE R., cardiologist, epidemiologist; arrived in U.S., 1979; s. Saul Kizer and Fanny Dejman; m. Carol A. Lillienstein, May 28, 2000; 1 child, Jacqueline Elizabeth. BS, SUNY, Stony Brook, 1990; MD, U. of Pa., 1994; MSc, Harvard U., 1999. Diplomate internal medicine Am. Bd. of Internal Medicine, cardiovasc. disease Am. Bd. of Internal Medicine. Medicine intern and resident Brigham and Women's Hosp./Harvard Med. Sch., Boston, 1994—97; fellow in cardiovasc. medicine U. of Pa. Med. Ctr., Phila., 1997—2001; asst. prof. medicine and pub. health Weill Med. Coll. of Cornell U., N.Y.C., 2001—, Bruce B. Lerman clin. scholar, 2004—. Recipient Mentored Patient-Oriented Rsch. Career Devel. award, NIH, 2002—07. Mem.: Phi Beta Kappa, Alpha Omega Alpha. Achievements include peer-reviewed publs. association between pulmonary fibrosis and coronary artery disease; role of cardiac troponin T in the long-term risk stratification of patients undergoing percutaneous coronary intervention; limitations of current risk-adjustment models in the era of coronary stenting. Avocations: jogging, swimming, reading, languages, travel. Home: 430 E 63rd St Apt 6N New York NY 10021-7927

KIZER, KENNETH WAYNE, emergency physician, medical educator, academic administrator; b. Decatur, Ind., May 28, 1951; s. Homer Martin Kizer and Ellen Hope Howland; m. Suzanne A. Stoddard, Aug. 26, 1972; children: Kelli Christina, Kimberly Casey. BS with honors, Stanford U., 1972; MD with honors, MPH in Epidemiology, UCLA, 1976. Rotating internship Naval Regional Med. Ctr., Portsmouth, Va., 1977; undersea medicine fellowship Naval Undersea Med. Inst., Groton, Conn., 1977; resident in diagnostic radiology U. Calif, San Francisco, 1980-81, resident in occupl. medicine, 1982-83; firefighter; emergency physician; dir. Emergency Med. Svcs. Authority State of Calif., 1983-84; chief dep. dir. and chief of pub. health Calif. Dept. Health Svcs., Sacramento, 1984-85, dir., 1985-91; prof., chmn. dept. cmty. and internat. health U. Calif., Davis, 1991-94; undersec. for health Dept. Vets. Affairs, Washington, 1994-99; dir. Health Sys. Internat., Inc., 1994-97; pres., CEO Nat. Quality Forum, Washington, 1999—. Contbr. numerous articles to profl. jours., chpts. to books. Chair Radiation Emergency Screening Team, 1988-91, Hazardous Waste Appeal Bd., 1990; co-chair Calif. AIDS Leadership Com.; mem. Diving Control Bd. U. Calif., 1980-91, Gov.'s Emergency Ops. Exec. Coun., 1984-91, Governing Bd. Calif YMCA Model Legislature Program, 1986-90, Chem. Emergency Planning and Response Commn., 1988-90; chair S.W. Low Level Radioactive Waste Compact Commn., 1990-91, tobacco edn. oversight com. State Calif., 1990-91, bd. dirs. Calif. Wellness Found., 1992-2003, Matthews Found., 1991-94, Ctr. for AIDS Rsch., Edn. and Svcs., 1992-94, Infection Control Coun., 1991-94; mem. adv. bd. Preventive Sports Medicine Inst., 1991-94. Lt. USN, 1976-80. Recipient Humanitarian Svc. medal Dept. of Def., 1979, Spl. Recognition award No. Calif. Emergency Med. Care Coun., 1984, Golden State Med. Assn., 1986, Calif. Div. Am. Lung Assn., 1988, Calif. Health Fedn., 1988, cert. of Recognition Calif. Asian Pacific Health Coalition, 1989, Spl. Achievement award Calif. Emergency Physician Med. Group, 1989, Jean Spencer Felton award for Excellence in Sci. Writing, 1989, spl. awards from March of Dimes, Am. Cancer Soc., Calif. State Senate, Calif. Conf. Local Health Officers, others, 1991—, Healthcare Heroes award Calif. State Assembly, 1996, Cert. of Recognition award, 1996, Dr. Nathan Davis award AMA, 1998, Literacy Achievement award Am. Coll. Physician Execs., 1998, Founders award Wilderness Med. Soc., 1998, Lifetime Achievement award Assn. Health Systems Pharmacists, 2002, Founders award Am. Coll. Med. Quality, 2004, Gustov O. Lienhand award, Inst. Medicine/Nat. Acad. Scis., 2004; named Toll fellow Coun. State Govts., 1987. Fellow Am. Coll. Preventive Medicine, Am. Coll. Emergency Physicians, Am. Coll. Occupl. Environ. Medicine, Am. Acad. Clin. Toxicology, Royal Soc. Health, Royal Soc. Medicine, Am. Coll. Med. Toxicology, Am. Coll. Physician Execs., Am. Acad. Med. Adminstrs., Explorers Club; mem. APHA, Internat. Soc. Toxicology, Inst. Medicine NAS, Wilderness Med. Soc., Undersea and Hyperbaric Med. Soc., Nat. Soc. YMCA Youth Govs., Nat. Assn. Underwater Instrs. (Outstanding Contribution to Diving award 1984), Inst. Medicine, Delta Tau Delta (Beta Rho chpt. Hall of Fame 1987), Alpha Omega Alpha, Delta Omega. Independent. Avocations: scuba diving, hiking and backpacking, photography, racquet sports, book collecting. Office: Nat Quality Forum Ste 500 North 601 13th St NW Washington DC 20005 Office Phone: 202-783-1300. Personal E-mail: kwkizer@cs.com. Business E-mail: kwkizer@qualityforum.org.

KIZER, NANCY ANNE, music educator, musician; b. Richmond, Calif., July 30, 1940; d. Benjamin Harrison Pilgrim and Doris Mabel (Parnell) Pilgrim-Myers; children: Kevin John Keuning, Stephen Douglas Keuning. MusB, U. of the Pacific, Stockton, Calif., 1958—62. Cert. secondary music tchr. Musician/violist Stockton Symphony Orch., Stockton, Calif., 1959—; music tchr./grades 7-9 Stockton Unified Sch. Dist., Stockton, Calif., 1962—64; music tchr./grades kindergarten-12 Lincoln Unified Sch. Dist., Stockton, Calif., 1983—95; coord./summer arts program Stockton Arts Commn., Stockton, Calif., 1987—2002; instr./string ensemble San Joaquin Delta Coll., Stockton, Calif., 1995—97; music libr. Stockton Symphony Assn., Stockton, 1996—2002, pers. mgr., 1999—; instr./string ensemble San Joaquin Delta Coll., Stockton, Calif., 2002—04; music tchr./HS Stockton Unified Sch. Dist., Stockton, Calif., 2002—. Recipient Music Honor Student, Santa Cruz HS, 1958. Mem.: Mortar Bd./Sr. Women's Honor Soc. (mem. 1962), Am. Fedn. Musicians, Nat. Educators Assn. (licentiate), Music Educators Nat. Conf. (licentiate), Mu Phi Epsilon/Nat. Music Fraternity (mem. 1959—). Home: 2424 North Center St Stockton CA 95204 Office: Stockton Symphony 46 West Freemont St Stockton CA 95202 Personal E-mail: vlanancy@inreach.com. Business E-Mail: personnel@stocktonsymphony.org.

KIZILISIK, AYDIN TARIK, surgeon, researcher; b. Istanbul, Turkey, July 20, 1959; s. Karani Ozer Akra and Gulen Kizilisik, Suat Kizilisik (Stepfather); m. Semiha Reha Duldur, Nov. 19, 1984; 1 child, Basak. MD, Ankara U. Med. Sch., 1984; M in Exptl. Surgery, U. Alta., Edmonton, Alta, Can., 1994. Intern Ankara U. Hosps., 1983—84; resident in surgery Gulhane Mil. Med. Acad. and Hosps., Ankara, 1986—91; sr. med. examiner, med. advisor to the gov. Tosya, Kastamonu, Turkey, 1984—86; fellow in liver transplantation U. Alta. Hosps., 1991—93; cons. liver transplant and hepatobiliary surgeon King Fahad N.G. Hosp., Riyadh, Saudi Arabia, 1994—98; fellow in multiorgan transplantation U. Tenn. Hosps., Memphis, 1999—2001, transplant surgeon, 2001—02; asst. prof. surgery Vanderbilt U. Med. Ctr., Nashville, 2002—; attending transplant surgeon VA Med. Ctr., Nashville, 2002—, St. Thomas Hosp., Nashville, 2002—. Instr. ACLS program King Fahad N.G. Hosp., Riyadh, 1994—98, instr. advanced trauma life support program, 1994—98; presenter in field. Contbr. more than 50 articles to profl. jours. Helen Boone scholar, Nora's Life Gift Found., 1999. Fellow: ACS, Internat. Coll. Surgeons, Am. Soc. Transplant Surgeons, Internat. Soc. Surgery, Am. Soc. Transplantation (Trainee Travel award 2000), Transplantation Soc.; mem.: European Soc. Organ Transplantation, Internat. Liver Transplantation Soc., Mid. Ea. Soc. Organ Transplantation, Turkish Nat. Soc. Surgery, NY Acad. Scis., Turkish Med. Assn. Achievements include research in graft versus host disease after small bowel transplantation; analysis of donor criteria and its implications on the outcome of liver transplants; development of microsurgery training for transplantation research purposes; research in impact of long term chronic immunosuppressive therapy on health and quality of life after orthotopic liver transplantation; development of pancreas transplantation with portal-enteric drainage. Office: Vanderbilt U Med Ctr 912 Oxford House Nashville TN 37232-4750 Office Phone: 615-936-0404. Office Fax: 615-936-0409. E-mail: tarik.kizilisik@vanderbilt.edu.

KJELDSBERG, KARL R., lab administrator, physician, educator; MD, U. Edinburgh, Scotland. Cert. in Anatomic and Clin. Pathology, in Hematology. Prof., pathology, chmn., dept. pathology U. Utah Sch. Medicine, adj. prof., internal medicine; pres., CEO ARUP Labs., Salt Lake City, 2003—. Rev. pathologist Southwest Oncology Group Lymphoma Com.; rev. pathologist, Non-Hodkin's Lymphomas Children's Cancer Study Group, mem., non-Hodgkin's Lymphoma strategy com. Fellow: Coll. Am. Pathologists, Am. Soc. Clin. Pathologists (chmn., hematology coun.); mem.: Am. Assn. Blood Banks, Internat. Acad. Pathologists, Am. Soc. Hematology, Soc. Hematopathology. Office: ARUP Labs 500 Chipeta Way Salt Lake City UT 84108

KJELL, BRADLEY PRYOR, computer scientist, educator; b. Rockford, Ill., Apr. 14, 1948; s. Clifford George and Dorothy Pryor Kjell. BA in physics, U. Ill., 1970; MS in physics, Ill. State U., 1971; MA in libr. sci., No. Ill. U., 1973, MS in computer sci., 1979; PhD, U. Wis., 1985. Software engr. Mark Controls Corp., Northbrook, Ill., 1976—78; asst. prof. George Mason U., Fairfax, Va., 1985—92; prof. Ctrl. Conn. State U., New Britain, 1992—. Mem.: IEEE (sec. of the soc. for social implications of tech. 2002). Office: Ctrl Conn State Univ 1615 Stanley St New Britain CT 06050-4010 Office Phone: 860-832-2717. Personal E-mail: kjell@ieee.org.

KJELLMARK, ERIC W., JR., management consultant, performing company executive; b. New Rochelle, N.Y., May 14, 1928; s. Eric William and Anna Sophia (Fogelstrom) K. BCE, Cornell U., 1950. Mgr. mktg. planning E. I. DuPont de Nemours, Wilmington, Del., 1980-87, dir. Far East task force, 1987-89; gen. dir. Opera Del., Inc., Wilmington, 1985-95; cons. Condux, Inc., Wilmington, 1985-94. Cons. Monkman-Rumsey, Inc., Wilmington, 1986-92. Treas., v.p. Grand Opera House, Inc., Wilmington, 1971-91, bd. trustees 1992—2004; panelist Del. State Arts Coun., Wilmington, 1987-89, 96, 97; sec.-treas. Opera Del., 1994-96, bd. dirs., 1956-2004, Wilmington Waterways, Inc., 1985-89; chmn. oversight com. Delaware Art Stabilization, 1993-96, chmn. level IV cos. Opera Am., 1989-91, bd. dirs., 1991-94; panelist Mid-Atlantic States Arts Consortium, 1990, NEA, 1991-94; pres. Opera for Youth, 1997-2000; bd. dirs. Nat. Opera Assn., 1998, 99. Recipient W.W. Laird award DE, 1992, Partners in Excellence award Opera Guild Internat., 1994. Mem. Am. Chem. Soc., Am. Inst. Chem. Engrs., Alpha Chi Sigma. Republican. Episcopalian. Office: 3300 NE 36th St #821 Fort Lauderdale FL 33308

KJELSTRUP, CHERYL ANN, retired librarian; b. Madison, Wis., Sept. 23, 1947; d. Robert A. and Katherine E. (Benish) Heiman; m. Glen W. Wildenberg, Apr. 6, 1968 (div. June 1984); 1 child, William G. Wildenberg; m. Rod R. Kjelstrup, Jan. 3, 1987; children: Christopher M., Andrew J. BA in Social Scis., Kans. State U., 1970; student, U. Wis., Oshkosh, 1983; M of Libr. and Info. Sci., U. Wis., Milw., 1997. Cert. K-12 libr. and computer instr., Wis. Libr. aide Two Rivers (Wis.) Pub. Schs., 1976-88; libr. Wrightstown (Wis.) Cmty. Schs., 1988-90; libr., computer coord. Brillion (Wis.) Schs., 1990—2005, ret., 2005. Bd. dirs. Cmty. Concerts Assn., Manitowoc, Wis., 1980-88, Manitowoc-Calumet County Libr., 2001—; long-rang planning com. Brillion Pub. Libr., 1993-94. Delta Kappa Gamma Sigma scholar, 1994-95. Mem. Wis. Ednl. Media Assn. (mem. info. literacy com. 1992-93), Brillion Fedn. Tchrs. (pres. local 1994-96, 98-2000), Delta Kappa Gamma (pres. 1992-94). Avocations: hunting, pistol shooting, needlework, sewing. Home: 14415 Jambo Creek Rd Mishicot WI 54228-9734

KJOK, SOL, artist, art educator; b. Lillehammer, Norway, Mar. 16, 1968; d. Erik and Ingunn (Haugsrud) K. BA in French Lit., U. Vienna, Austria, 1991; M in French Lit., U. Paris, 1992; MA in Romance Lang. and Lit., U. Cin., 1993, MA in Art History, 1996; MFA in Painting, Parsons Sch. Design, N.Y.C., 1998. Cert. govt. authorized translator and interpreter. Graphic designer Agence Karen, Paris, 1988; tchg. asst. art history U. Cin., 1995-96, dir. ind. studies of Norwegian lang./culture, 1993-96; resident Larroque Artists' Colony, Urt, France, 1997-98; tchg. asst. painting Parsons Sch. Design, N.Y.C., 1997-98. Lectr. in field. Contbr. articles to profl. jours.; translator: French/Norwegian, Paris, 1988; Spanish/Norwegian translator/interpretor Medellin, Bogota, Colombia, 1993; translator English, German novels, articles, short stories into Norwegian, various pub. houses, 1985—; one-woman shows include Brodie Gallery, Cin., 1996, Kreditkassen, Bagn, Norway, 1987, Tegnerforbundet Gallery, Oslo, 2001, Samuel S.T. Chen Fine Arts Ctr., Conn., 2005, Galleri 27, Oslo, Norway, 2005; exhibited in group shows at Gjensidigegården, Fagernes, Norway, 1985, Valdrestunet, Bagn, 1987, Art et Dessin, Paris, 1988, Mus. of U. Medellin, 1993, KZF Gallery, Cin., 1994, 840 Gallery, Cin., 1995-96, Machina dell'Arte, Cin., 1996, Schoharie County Arts Coun., 1996, Gallery Alexy, Phila., 1996, Glenn Eure's Ghost Fleet Gallery, Nags Head, NC, 1996, 98, Amos Joseph Fine Art, Santa Fe, 1996, NJ Ctr. Visual Arts, 1997, Pleiades Gallery, NYC, 1997, Viridian Artists, Inc., 1997, Akademie der bildenden Künste Munich, 1997, AIR Gallery, NYC, 1997, 2000, Artists' Space, NYC, 1997, Brenda Taylor Gallery, NYC, 1998, Cmty. Cultural Ctr., Phila., 1998, Manefisken Galleri, Oslo, 1998, Valdres Kunstforening's Gallery, Norway, 1998, PS 122 Gallery, NYC, 1998, Cameron/Weiland Gallery, NYC, 1998, Galeri Steen, Oslo, Norway, 1999, Pleiades Gallery, NYC, 1999, Galleri Steen, Oslo, 2001, Goldstrom Gallery, NYC, 2001, Seaside Art Gallery, Nags Head, NC, 2002, Painted Bride Art Ctr., Phila., 2002, Arnot Art Mus., 2003, House of America, Madrid, 2004, Romo Gallery, Atlanta, 2005, others; works in pvt. collections including: USA, Austria, Belgium, Colombia, Eng., Francy, Germany, Norway & Sweden; works in pub. collections including: Cin. Art Mus., Tekningsmuseet, Sweden Mem. Cin. Artists Group Effort, 1994—. Recipient Alpha Kappa Alpha Grad. Merit award; grantee Ga. Rotary Student Program, 1989, Lise & Arnfinn Heje's Legacy, Oslo, 1990, Thom Wilhelmsen's award, Oslo, 1991, Knut Hamsun's Legacy, Oslo, 1992, Olav and Lizzie Juvkam's legacy, 1990-94, Einar Storsveen's Legacy, 1992-94; Cin. Women's Club scholar, 1995, U. Cin. scholar, 1993-96, Parsons scholar, 1997-98; AAUW fellow, 1997-98; Joahn Jorgen Brochs Legat. grant, 1998, Rsch. grant Astrup-Fearnley, Oslo, 1996, Thesis Rsch. grant Astrup-Fearnley Found., Oslo, 1996, Artist grant Norwegian Ministry Culture, 1998, Exhbn. grant, Arts Council, Norway, 1999, Public Project grant, Am.-Scandinavian Found., NYC, 2005; recipient Edwin Gould Found. award Nat. Arts Club, NYC, 1998, Excellence in Drawing award Internat. Icarus Exhbn., 1998, Spl. Gallery prize Contemporary Realism III Exhibit, Phila., 1998, Honorable Mention award in Exhbn. Am. Art, RIC Inst., Chgo., 2004, others. Mem. Internat. Assn. Univ. Women, Coll. Art Assn., Norwegian Soc. Young Artists, Norwegian Visual Artists, Drawing Assn. Norway. Avocation: long distance running. Home: 44 Eagle St Brooklyn NY 11222-1013 Office Phone: 718-389-8228. Personal E-mail: sol.kjok@rcn.com.

KLAAS, NICHOLAS PAUL, management consultant; b. Kieler, Wis., June 25, 1925; s. Paul Francis and Ida Klaas; m. Ruth Elizabeth Barry, Nov. 5, 1949; children: Paul, Patricia, Kathleen, James. BA, Loras Coll., 1945; PhD, U. Notre Dame, 1948. Registered to practice before U.S. Patent Office, 1970. Product mgr. Rohm & Haas Co., Phila., 1948-52; mgr. research and devel. 3M Co., St. Paul, 1952-65; exec. v.p., dir. Wyomissing Corp., West Reading, Pa., 1965-71, v.p. comml. develop., 1972—74; group v.p. chems. GAF Corp., N.Y.C., 1974—77; gen. mgr. splty. chems. Ga. Pacific Corp., Portland, Oreg., 1977; pres. J.T. Baker Chem. Co., Phillipsburg, N.J., 1977-84; chmn. bd. J.T. Baker B.V., Deventer, Netherlands, 1978-84; pres. Klaas Assocs., 1984—. Adj. prof. chemistry San Diego State U., 1985-98; mem. bd. visitors chair, undergrad. rsch. com. U. N.C., Asheville, 1986-91, Council for Chem. Research, 1987-98. Patentee in field; contbr. articles to profl. jours. Trustee St. Joseph Hosp., Reading, Pa., 1968-71; bd. regents Loras Coll., Dubuque, Iowa, 1974-76. Mem. AAAS, Synthetic Organic Chem. Mfg. Assn. (dir. 1974-77), Asphalt Roofing Mfrs. Assn. (dir. 1974-77), Am. Chem. Soc. Clubs: Smoke Rise. Address: 51 Hoot Owl Ter Kinnelon NJ 07405-2409 E-mail: npaulklaas@aol.com.

KLAAS, PAUL BARRY, lawyer; b. St. Paul, Aug. 9, 1952; s. N. Paul and Ruth Elizabeth (Barry) K.; m. Barbara Ann Bockhaus, July 30, 1977; children: James, Ann, Brian. AB magna cum laude, Dartmouth Coll., 1974; JD cum laude, Harvard U., 1977. Bar: Minn. 1977, U.S. Dist. Ct. Minn. 1977, U.S. Ct. Appeals (8th cir.) 1979, U.S. Ct. Appeals (10th cir.) 1980, U.S. Supreme Ct. 1982, U.S. Ct. Appeals (9th cir.) 1989, U.S. Ct. Appeals (fed. cir.) 1994. Assoc. Dorsey & Whitney, Mpls., 1977-82, ptnr., trial group, 1983—. Chair trial dept., co-chair Internat. Arbitration and Litigation Practice Group; adj. prof. William Mitchell Coll Law, St. Paul, 1980-85. Fellow: Am. Coll. Trial Lawyers; mem.: Phi Beta Kappa. Office: Dorsey & Whitney 50 S 6th St Ste 1500 Minneapolis MN 55402-1498 Office Phone: 612-340-2817. Office Fax: 612-340-2868. E-mail: klaas.paul@dorsey.com.

KLAASSEN, PAUL, personal care industry executive; m. Terry Klaassen. Founder, chmn., CEO Sunrise Sr. Living, 1981—. Founding chmn., dir Assisted Living Fed. Am.; bd. trustees Hudson Inst., Inst. Am. Values, Ethics Public Policy Ctr., Trinity Forum; adv. com. Dept. Healthcare Policy Harvard Univ. Med. Sch. Office: Sunrise Sr Living 7902 Westpark Dr Mc Lean VA 22102 Office Phone: 703-273-7500. Office Fax: 703-744-1601.

KLAEHNE, EBERHARD O.W., pharmaceutical executive, chemist; b. Hamburg, Germany, Jan. 31, 1951; arrived in U.S., 1993; s. Walter and Hedwig (Jaster) Klaehne; m. Soumontha Phommachack, Dec. 21, 1987; m. Gabriele Jacobsen (div.); children: Maurice Nicolas, Somsay Phommachack. Diploma in chemistry, U. Hamburg, 1977, Dr. rerum naturalium, 1982. Dir. quality control Ichthyol Gesellschaft Cordes, Hermanni and Co., Hamburg, 1982—85; dir. quality control/quality assurance LTS Lohmann Therapie Systeme AG, Neuwied, Germany, 1985—93; dir. quality assurance LTS Lohmann Therapy Systems Corp., West-Caldwell, NJ, 1993—96; dir. quality control, clin. supply LTS Lohmann Therapie Systeme AG, Andernach, Germany, 1996—2001, dir. quality assurance, 2001—02; exec. dir. quality Mylan Technologies Inc., St. Albans, Vt., 2002—. Rsch. assoc. DFG German Rsch. Soc., U. of Hamburg, Hamburg, Germany, 1977—77; sci. asst. lectr. U. of Hamburg, Hamburg, Germany, 1977—78; predoctoral rsch. assoc. Centre d'Etudes Nucléaires de Saclay, Saclay, 1979; rsch. assoc. DFG, German Rsch. Soc., Hamburg, Hamburg, Germany, 1980; sci. asst. U. of Hamburg, Hamburg, Germany, 1979—81; presenter in field. Contbr. articles to profl. jours. Leader table tennis sporting group Glashuetter Sporting Club, 1968—74. Scholar, DAAD German Academic Exch. Svc., 1978, DAAD German Academic Exch. Svc., Centre d' Etudes Nucléaires de Saclay, Paris, France, 1979. Achievements include research in synthesization and characterization of novel class of neutral, anionic and cationic trigonal-bipyramidal coordinated Uranium(IV) organyls; photo reduction of Uranium(IV) to U(III) organyls with Trispentahaptocyclopentadienyl U(IV)alkyls; homolytic cleavage of U(IV)-C bonds with excess of Li-organyls. Personal E-mail: eklaehne@web.de.

KLAERNER, CURTIS MAURICE, gas industry executive; b. Fredericksburg, Tex., Sept. 7, 1920; s. Elgin and Irene (Wagner) K.; m. Aileen E. Eitt, Sept. 4, 1942 (dec. Oct. 1998); children: Sherilyn Kay, Curtis Elgin; m. Jean L. Patton, Aug. 26, 2000. BS in Chem. Engring, U. Tex., 1942; grad. program sr. execs., Mass. Inst. Tech., 1956. Process engr., then chief process engr. Magnolia Petroleum Co., 1942-53; refinery mgr., then mgr. Eastern region mfg. Socony Mobil Oil Co., 1953-59; regional exec., then regional v.p. Mobil Internat. Oil Co., 1959-61; pres. Mobil Inner Europe, Geneva, Switzerland, 1962-65; corp. v.p. charge marine transp. and internat. sales Socony Mobil Oil Co., 1965-69; exec. v.p. internat. div. Mobil Oil Corp., 1969-72, pres., 1972-79, also exec. v.p., dir., mem. exec. com. corp.; vice chmn., dir. Commonwealth Oil Refining Co., San Antonio, 1979, pres., chief operating officer, 1979-83; ret., 1983; pres. Klaerner Enterprises, 1984—; vice chmn. Weed Instrument Co.; dir. Belgian Refining Corp., Antwerp, 1984—, W.I. Oil Corp., Antigua, 1984—, Nat. Petroleum Ltd., Bermuda, 1986—. Mem. adv. coun. Engring. Found., U. Tex., Austin. Recipient Disting. Grad. award Coll. Engring., U. Tex., 1983 Mem. Phi Eta Sigma, Omega Chi Epsilon, Phi Kappa Sigma. Clubs: Circumnavigators (N.Y.C.); Oak Hills Country, Optimists, Exchange, Petroleum (San Antonio), Country Club San Antonio. Republican. Episcopalian. Home: 11 Chelsea Way San Antonio TX 78209-7400

KLAFTER, CARY IRA, lawyer; b. Chgo., Sept. 15, 1948; s. Herman Nicholas and Bernice Rose (Maremont) K.; m. Kathleen Ann Kerr, July 21, 1974; children: Anastasia, Benjamin, Eileen. BA, Mich. State U., 1968, MS, 1971; JD, U. Chgo., 1972. Bar: Calif. 1972. Assoc. Morrison & Foerster, San Francisco, 1972-79, ptnr., 1979-96; v.p. legal and govt. affairs, dir. corp. affairs, corp. sec. Intel Corp., Santa Clara, Calif., 1996—. Lectr. law Stanford Law Sch., 1990-99. Capt. USAR, 1971-78. Mem.: Soc. Corp. Secs. and Governance Profls.

KLAHR, GARY PETER, retired lawyer; b. N.Y.C., July 9, 1942; s. Fred and Frieda (Garson) K. Student, Ariz. State U., 1958—61; LLB with high honors, U. Ariz., 1964. Bar: Ariz. 1967, U.S. Dist. Ct. Ariz. 1967. Assoc. Brazlin & Greene, Phoenix, 1967—68; sr. ptnr. Gary Peter Klahr, P.C., Phoenix, 1968—2002; owner Klahr Paralegal Svc., 2002—. *Has made substantial appellate law in the area of juvenile delinquency and dependency, elections law, and student rights cases. Filed suit to re-apportion the Arizona Legislature which ended up at the Supreme Court under Klahn vs. Ely. Defended youth in the areas of curfew laws and student dress, especially opposing mandatory uniforms. Several cases were on national media including a suit to dissolve Town of Apache Junction (1981 — David Brinkley's Journal — NBC).* Asst. editor Ariz. Law Rev., 1963-64; contbr. articles to profl. jours. Bd. dirs. CODAMA, 1975-89, pres., 1980-81; bd. dirs. Tumbleweed Runaway Ctr., 1972-76; mem. bd. dirs. Internat. Found. Anti-Cancer Drug Discovery, 1998-2002, chair exec. com., 1999-2002; chmn. Citizens Criminal Justice Commn., 1977-78; elected Phoenix City Coun., 1974; co-chmn. delinquency subcom. Phoenix Forward Task force; vol. referee Maricopa County Juvenile Ct., 1969; mem. City Coun., Phoenix, 1974-1976; vol. adult probation officer; vol. counselor youth programs Dept. Econ. Security and Dept. of Corrections, Phoenix; ex-officio mem., spl. cons. Phoenix Youth Commn.; mem. citizen adv. coun. Phoenix Union H.S. Dist., 1985-90, 95-99, co-chmn. 1998-99, elected Governing Bd., 1991-95, 2001-05, v.p., 1992-95, co-chmn. citizens adv. com., 1970-72; mem. rev. bd. Phoenix Police Dept., 1985-94; bd. dirs. Metro Youth Ctr., 1986-87, mem. bd. dirs.Svc./Employment/Redevel. (SER) Jobs for Progress, Phoenix, 1985-90, pres., 1986-87; bd. dirs. East McDowell Youth Assn., 1992-94; v.p. local chpt. City of Hope, 1985-86; Justice of the Peace pro tem Maricopa County Cts., 1985-89; mem. City License Appeals Bd., 1987-97, vice chmn. 1988-93, chmn. 1993-97; juvenile hearing officer Maricopa County Juvenile Ct., 1985-89; v.p., co-founder Cmty. Leadership for Youth Devel. (CLYDE); del. Phoenix Together Town Hall on Youth Crime, 1982. Named 1 of 3 Outstanding Young Men of Phoenix, Phoenix Jaycees, 1969; recipient Disting. Citizen award Ariz. chpt. ACLU, 1976. Mem. ACLU (v.p. ctrl. chpt. Ariz. 1990-95, pres. 1995-2001, mem. state bd. 1990-2001), Ariz. State Bar (past sec., bd. dirs. young lawyers sect., co-chmn. unauthorized practice com. 1988-89, mem. other coms.), Maricopa County Bar Assn. (past sec., bd. dirs. young lawyers sec., vice-chmn. juvenile practice com. 1998-99), Am. Judicature Soc., Jewish Children's and Family Svc., Joint Jewish Task Force on Pub. Edn., Common Cause, NAACP, Ariz. ConsumersCoun., Phoenix Jaycees, Temple Beth Israel, Order of the Coif, Phi Alpha Delta. Democrat. Jewish. Office: 317 E Berridge Ln Phoenix AZ 85012 Office Phone: 602-265-3150. Personal E-mail: garyk57647@aol.com.

KLAIN, RONALD ALAN, lawyer; b. Indpls., Aug. 8, 1961; s. Stanley Hugh and Sarann (Horwitz) K.; m. Monica Medina, June 22, 1986; children: Hannah, Michael, Daniel. BA summa cum laude, Georgetown U., 1983; JD magna cum laude, Harvard U., 1987. Bar: Pa., 1992, D.C. 1999. Law clk. Hon. Byron R. White, Washington, 1987-89; spl. asst. Senate Judiciary Com., Washington, 1986-87, chief counsel, 1989-92; assoc. general counsel for Washington issues Clinton/Gore Campaign, 1992; assoc. counsel to the Pres. The White House, Washington, 1993-94; chief of staff and counselor for Atty. Gen., Janet Reno Dept. Justice, Washington, 1994-95; staff dir. Senate Dem. Leadership Com., Washington, 1995; chief of staff Vice President Gore, The

White House, Washington, 1995-99; gen. counsel Gore-Lieberman Recount Com., Tallahassee, 2000; ptnr. O'Melveny & Myers LLP, Washington, 1999-2000, 01—, chair strategic counseling practice group. Legis. dir. and legis. asst. for telecommunications policy to Rep. Ed Markey. Editor: Harvard Law Review, 1985—86. Commr. Pres.'s Commn. on Fed. Appointments Process, Washington, 1990; dir. debate preparation Kerry-Edwards for Pres., Washington, D.C., 2004. Named Lawyers of the Yr., Nat. Law Jour., 2000, Top Lawyer in Washington Under the Age of 40, Washingtonian; named one of 50 Most Promising Leaders in Am. Under the Age of 40, Time Mag., Top 20 Young Lawyers Nationwide. Mem.: ABA. Democrat. Jewish. Home: 3912 Rosemary St Chevy Chase MD 20815 Office: O'Melveny & Myers LLP 1625 Eye St NW Washington DC 20006 Office Phone: 202-383-5317. Office Fax: 202-383-5414. Business E-Mail: rklain@omm.com.*

KLAINER, PETER SCOTT, plastic surgeon; b. Boston, Mass. MD, Columbia Coll.of Physicians and Surgeons, 1984—88. MD Bd. of Med. Examiners, 1988. Plastic and reconstructive surgeon Chrysalis Plastic Surgery, Sterling, Va., 2000—. Tchg. cons. Cynosure Lasers, Inc., Chelmsford, Mass., 2000—. Fellow: Am. Coll. Surgeons, Am. Soc. for Laser Medicine and Surgery; mem.: Va. Med. Soc., Am. Soc. Plastic Surgeons. Office: Chrysalis Plastic Surgery 46396 Benedict Dr #330 Sterling VA 20164 Office Phone: 703-421-6000. Office Fax: 703-421-6100. E-mail: chrysalisplastic@prodigy.net.

KLAMANN, JOHN MICHAEL, lawyer; b. Fresno, Calif., Aug. 23, 1952; s. Michael J. and Jacqueline C. K.; m. Brigid A. Cleary, Apr. 17, 1982; children: Conor, Seth, Zachary, Hannah, Kaitlin, Abbye. BS in Psychology, Kans. State U., 1974; JD, U. Kans., 1978. Bar: Mo. 1978, Kans. 1979. Atty. Popham Law Firm, Kansas City, Mo., 1978-88, Payne and Jones, Overland Park, Kans., 1989-96, Klamann and Hubbard, P.A., Overland Park, 1996—. Adj. prof. U. Mo., Kansas City Sch. of Law, 1998-2001. Author: (with others) Am Jur Trials, 1988, 90, 92. Mem. ABA, ATLA, Mo. Assn. Trial Attys., Kans. Trial Lawyers Assn., Mo. Bar Assn., Kans. Bar Assn. Home: 70 Dunfold Cir Kansas City KS 64112 Office: Klamann and Hubbard PA 7101 College Blvd Ste 120 Overland Park KS 66210 Fax: 913-327-7800. E-mail: jklamann@kh-law.com.

KLAMMER, JOSEPH FRANCIS, retired management consultant; b. Omaha, Mar. 25, 1925; s. Aloys Arcadius and Sophie (Nadolny) K. BS, Creighton U., 1948; MBA, Stanford U., 1950; cert. in polit. econs. Grad. Inst. Internat. Studies, U. Geneva, 1951. Cert. mgmt. cons. Adminstrv. analyst Chevron Corp., San Francisco, 1952-53; staff asst. No. Natural Gas Co., Omaha, 1953-57; mgmt. cons. Cresap, McCormick and Paget, Inc., N.Y.C., 1957-75, v.p., mgr. San Francisco region, 1968-75, bd. dirs.; mgmt. cons., prin. J.F. Klammer Assocs., San Francisco, 1975-2000; semi-ret. practice mgmt. cons., San Francisco, 2000—03; ret., 2003. Bd. dirs. Conard House. Mem. adv. coun. Creighton U. Coll. Arts and Scis., 2000—03; CEO.pres. Broadway Towers Homeowners Assn., San Francisco, 1993—94, mem. maintenance com., 2000—, bd.dirs., 2002—, sec., 2005—, mem. rules com., 1995—96; apptd. and attended U.S. Mil. Acad., West Point, NY, bd. dirs., mem. fin. com., 1994—95. 1st lt. USAAF, 1943—46, lt. col. USAF, ret. Recipient Sovereign Mil. Hospitaller Order of St. John of Jerusalem of Rhodes and of Malta, Alumni Merit award Creighton U. Coll. Arts and Scis., 1998. Mem. Knights of Malta, Alpha Sigma Nu. Republican. Roman Catholic. Home: 1998 Broadway St #805 San Francisco CA 94109-2281

KLAMON, LAWRENCE PAINE, lawyer; b. St. Louis, Mar. 17, 1937; s. Joseph Martin and Rose (Schimel) K.; m. Jo Ann Karen Beatty, Nov. 1957 (div. Feb. 1974); children: Stephen Robert, Karen Jean, Lawrence Paine; m. Frances Ann Estes, Mar. 1980. AB, Washington U., St. Louis, 1958; JD, Yale U., 1961. Bar: N.Y. 1964, Ga. 1992. Confidential asst. Office Sec. Def., Washington, 1961-62, spl. asst. to gen. counsel, 1962-63; asso. Cravath, Swaine & Moore, N.Y.C., 1963-67; v.p., gen. counsel Fuqua Industries, Inc., Atlanta, 1967-73, sr. v.p. fin. and adminstrn., 1971-81, pres., 1981-89, chief exec. officer, 1989-91; chmn., 1991; sr. counsel Alston & Bird, Atlanta, 1991-95; pres., CEO Fuqua Enterprises, Inc., Atlanta, 1995-97. Chmn. Gov.'s Internat. Adv. Coun., 1992-95. Mem. bd. editors Yale Law Jour., 1959-61. Mem. State Bar Ga., Order of Coif, Phi Beta Kappa, Omicron Delta Kappa.

KLAMPE, CRAIG ALLEN, composer; b. San Diego, Apr. 14, 1957; s. Dean Gordon and Shirley Lorraine Klampe; m. Katherine Anne Kampmann, July 22, 1978; children: Gordon Dean, Ian Joseph. BA, U. Calif., San Diego, 1978; MA, Claremont Grad. U., 1983. Choirmaster All Saints Luth. Ch., San Diego, 1988—2005; co-dir. St. Anthony Antiochian Orthodox Ch., La Jolla, Calif., 1995—2000. Composer: (choral) O Lord, teach me to seek, 1995, Intimam, 2001, O splendor of the Father's light, 2002, I will sing, 2002, Ely Canticles, 1996, How Great is Your Goodness, 2005. Mem.: Am. Choral Dirs. Assn. (life). Personal E-mail: craigklampe@msn.com.

KLAPER, MARTIN JAY, lawyer; b. Chgo., Jan. 12, 1947; s. Carl and Kate F. (Friedman) K.; m. Julia Warner, Nov. 14, 1973. BS in Bus. summa cum laude, Ind. U., 1969, JD summa cum laude, 1971. Bar: Ind. 1971, U.S. Dist. Ct. (no. and so. dists.) Ind. 1971, U.S. Ct. Appeals (7th cir.) 1972, U.S. Supreme Ct. 1979. Law clk. to justice U.S. Ct. Appeals (7th cir.), 1971-72; ptnr. Ice Miller, Indpls., 1972—. Mem. ABA, Ind. Bar Assn. Office: Ice Miller PO Box 82001 Indianapolis IN 46282-2001 Office Phone: 317-236-2322. Personal E-mail: Klaper@comcast.net. Business E-Mail: Klaper@Icemiller.com.

KLAPPA, GALE E., corporate financial executive; BA in mass communications, U. Wis.-Milw., 1972. Pres., CEO, SWEB; pres. N.Am. Group, Mirant; with So. Co., Atlanta, 1974—2003, chief mktg. officer, chief strategic officer, exec. v.p., CFO, treas.; pres., CEO, Wis. Electric Power and Wis. Gas Co. (We Energies), 2003—, chmn., 2004—. Dir. Edison Electric Inst.; vice chmn. Nuclear Electric Ins. Ltd. Adv. coun. U Wis.-Milw. Sch. Bus.; bd. dir. United Way Greater Milw., Met. Milw. Assn. Commerce. Office: Wis Energy Corp 231 W Michigan St Milwaukee WI 53203*

KLAPPER, BYRON D., finance company executive; b. NYC, May 2, 1938; s. Irving and Lottie K.; m. Karin I. Klapper, June 28, 1964; children: Kimberly, Lonn-Eric. BS in Journalism, U. Kans., 1964; cert. Wharton Sch., U. Pa., 1974. Reporter Topeka Daily Capitol, Kans., 1963, U.P.I., Kans. City, Mo.; editor Am. Cyanamid Co., Wayne, NJ, 1964-67; media rels. staff Bethlehem Steel Corp., NYC, 1968; speech writer Burlington Ind., Inc., NYC, 1969; reporter Wall St Jour., NYC, 1970-80; sr. v.p. Std. and Poors Corp., NYC, 1980-90; mng. dir. Fitch Investors Svc., NYC, 1990-98, Am. Capital Access, Inc., 1998—2001. Columnist skiing Morristown Daily Record, 1988-2001, Editor-in-chief, SnoSports., Internet Ski Mag.; bd. dir. Powell Techs., Inc., Visions West, Inc. Contbg. editor Barron's NYC, 1967-69; pub. S&P's Creditweek, 1981-90; publ. Creditweek Internat., 1983, Mcpl. Bond Book, 1984, S&P's Creditwire, 1986; original author of the anticipated novel: "Fuel or Fool Your Mind". Recipient Nat. Journalism award, William Randolph Hearst Found., 1960, 62, New Products award, McGraw Hill, 1986. Mem. Ea. Ski Writers Assn. (dir. 1985-91), Govt. Fin. Officers Assn., Pub. Securities Assoc., Bond Market Assn., Downtown Athletic Club, Fgn. Corres. Club Japan (hon.), N.Am. Snowsports Journalists Assn. (dir. 1998-2001). Avocations: writing, photography, skiing, computers, triathlon. Home: 37 Tara Ln Montville NJ 07045-9699

KLAPPER, MOLLY, lawyer, educator; b. Berlin; came to U.S., 1950; d. Elias and Ciporah (Weber) Teicher; m. Jacob Klapper; children: Rachelle Hannah, Robert David. BA, CUNY, MA, 1964; PhD, NYU, 1974; JD, Rutgers U., 1987. Bar: N.J. 1987, U.S. Dist. Ct. N.J. 1987, N.Y. 1989, U.S. Dist. Ct. (so. and ea. dists.) N.Y. 1989, D.C. 1989, U.S. Supreme Ct. 1991, U.S. Ct. Appeals (2d cir.) 1992; cert. arbitrata, Better Bus. Bur., 2000, cert. arbitrator (NASD) Nat. Assn. of Security Dealers, 2003, N.Y. Stock Exchange, 2005. Arbitrator, mediator NYSE; prof. English Bronx C.C., CUNY, 1974-84; law intern U.S. Dist. Ct. N.J., Newark, 1987; law sec. to presiding judge appellate div. N.J. Supreme Ct., Springfield, 1987-88; assoc. Wilson, Elser, Moskowitz, Edelman and Dicker, N.Y.C., 1988-96; adminstrv. law judge Dept. Finance, N.Y.C., 1997—; adj. prof. law Touro Law Ctr., Huntington, NY, 2001—04; lectr. Potsdeur U.; law judge Taxi and Limousine Commn., 2004. Small claims ct. arbitrator, 1994—; mediator comml. divsn. N.Y. State Supreme Ct., 2000—, ct. evaluator, 2003; mediator civil, equity and probate cases N.J. Superior Ct.; jud. nominee State Supreme Ct., 2d dist., 1999; mediator Nat. Assn. Sec. Dirs., 2002—; spkr. ABA Midwinter Conf., 2004; arbitrator, mediator NYSE, 2004—; coach, mediator, skills trainer, 2005; presenter in field; mediator U.S. Dist. Ct. NY Bankruptcy Ct., 2005. Author: The German Literary Influence on Byron, 1974, 2d edit., 1975, The German Literary Influence on Shelley, 1975; contbr. to profl. publs. NEH fellow, 1978; grantee Am. Philos. Soc., 1976. Mem. Assn. Bar of City of N.Y., Assn. Profl. Ins. Women (Pres. Cir. award, 2003), ABA. Avocations: bicycling, skiing, swimming, walking, hiking. Office: 720 Ft Washington Ave New York NY 10040-3708

KLAPPER, RICHARD H., lawyer; b. White Plains, NY, 1954; AB, Hamilton Coll., 1975; MA, JD, Yale U., 1979. Bar: NY 1981. Assoc. Sullivan & Cromwell, NYC, 1980—87, ptnr., 1987—, mng. ptnr. litig. practice group, 1999—2004. Mem.: Fed. Bar Coun., Am. Law Inst. Office: Sullivan & Cromwell 125 Broad St Fl 28 New York NY 10004-2489 Office Phone: 212-558-3555. Office Fax: 212-558-3588. Business E-Mail: klapper@sullcrom.com.

KLAPPERICH, FRANK LAWRENCE, JR., investment banker; b. Oak Park, Ill., Oct. 11, 1934; s. Frank Lawrence and Marjorie (Doan) K.; m. Margaret Monroe Touborg, Mar. 9, 1957; children: Margaret Friis, Susan Doane, Frank Lawrence III, Elizabeth Monroe. AB, Princeton U., 1956; MBA, Harvard U., 1961, postgrad., 1979. With Kidder, Peabody & Co., Inc., Chgo., 1961—, v.p., 1964—, dir., 1972-86, mng. dir., 1986-88, sr. v.p., 1988-90, ret., 1990; pres. Charter Capital Corp., 1991—. Governing mem. Orchestral Assn. Chgo. Symphony Orch., 1995—; vice chmn. governing mems., 1996-98; bd. dirs. Cmty. Found. Collier County, 2005— With USN, 1956—59, ret. LCDR USNR. Mem. Investment Analysts Soc. Chgo., Securities Industry Assn. (chmn. Ctrl. States dist. 1986-87), Inst. Chartered Fin. Analysts, Harvard Bus. Sch. Assn. Chgo., English Speaking Union (bd. dirs. Naples (Fla.) chpt. 2005—), Classic Chamber Concerts Inc. (bd. dirs. 2005—), Harvard Bus. Sch. Alumni Assn. (bd. dirs. 2005—), Princeton Club (Chgo., pres. 1970-71), Charter Club (governing bd. 1987-97), Chgo. Club, Mid-Day Club (trustee 1987-90), Bond Club (pres. 1983-84), Econ. Club, Forum Club S.W. Fla. (bd. dirs. 2002-05), Harvard Club of Naples (Fla., pres. 2001-03), Princeton Club of S.W. Fla. (bd. dirs. 2003—, v.p. 2005—), Indian Hill Club (Winnetka, Ill.), Hole-in-the-Wall Golf Club (Naples). Home: 345 Woodley Rd Winnetka IL 60093-3740 Office Phone: 312-984-0984.

KLARE, GEORGE ROGER, retired psychology professor; b. Mpls., Apr. 17, 1922; s. George C. and Lee (Launer) K.; m. Julia Marie Price Matson, Dec. 24, 1946; children: Deborah, Roger, Barbara. Student, U. Nebr., 1940-41, U. Minn., 1941-43, U. Mo., 1943; BA, U. Minn., 1946, MA, 1947, PhD, 1950. Instr. U. Minn., 1948-50; staff psychologist Psychol. Corp., N.Y.C., 1950-51; research assoc. U. Ill., 1952-54; asst. prof. dept. psychology Ohio U., Athens, 1954-57, assoc. prof., 1957-62, prof., 1962-79, Disting. prof., 1979-89, Disting. prof. emeritus, 1989—, chmn. dept., 1959-63, acting dean Coll. Arts and Sci., 1965, 85-86, dean, 1966-71, media coordinator, 1972-75, acting assoc. provost for grad. and research programs, 1986-87; research assoc. Harvard U., 1968-69; vis. prof. State U. N.Y. at Stony Brook, 1971-72, U. Iowa, 1979-80. Staff mem. N.Y.C. Writers Conf., 1956-57; cons., lectr. Nat. Project Agr. Communication, 1957-59, Com. on World Literacy and Christian Lit., 1958-62; exec. asst., sr. rsch. engr. Autonetics, 1960-61; cons. Resources Devel. Corp., 1962-65, Boston Pub. Sch., 1968, D.C. Heath Co., 1971, Western Electric, 1973, Westinghouse, 1975, Human Resources Rsch. Orgn., 1978-79, U.S. Navy, 1975, Armed Svcs. Readability Rsch., 1975, Center for Ednl. Exptl., Devel. and Evaluation, 1978-79, 81, U.S. Army, 1979, Bell System Center for Tech. Edn., 1975-80, Time, Inc., 1977-79, AT&T, 1979-81, 83,84, Coll. Osteo Medicine, Ohio U., 1987-89; lectr. Open Univ., Eng., 1975, NATO Conf. Visual Presentation of Info., The Netherlands, 1978, Beijing Normal U., 1990. Author: (with Byron Buck) Know Your Reader, 1954, The Measurement of Readability, 1963, (with Paul A. Games) Elementary Statistics: Data Analysis for the Behavioral Sciences, 1967, A Manual for Readable Writing, 1975, 4th edit., 1980, How to Write Readable English, 1985, Assessing Readability-Citation Classic, 1988; mem. editorial bd. Info. Design Jour., 1979—, Instrl. Sci., 1975-93, Reading Tchr., 1981-82, Reading Rsch. and Instrn., 1985-87, The Literacy Dictionary, 1993 (invited essay 1995). Served to 1st lt. USAAF, 1943-45. Decorated Air medal, Purple Heart; Fulbright travel grantee U.S.-U.K. Ednl. Commn. to Open U., 1977-81 Fellow Am. Psychol. Assn.; mem. Nat. Reading Conf. (invited address 1975, Oscar Causey award for outstanding contbns. to reading research 1981), Internat. Reading Assn. (elected to Hall of Fame 1997), Am. Ednl. Research Assn., Phi Beta Kappa, Delta Phi Lambda, Psi Chi, Phi Delta Kappa. Home and Office: 8800 Johnson Rd Ste 108 The Plains OH 45780-1277 Business E-Mail: klare@ohio.edu.

KLARE, MICHAEL THOMAS, social sciences educator, director; b. N.Y.C., Oct. 14, 1942; s. Charles and Mildred (Smith) K. BA, Columbia U., 1963, MA, 1968; postgrad., Yale U., 1963-65; PhD, Union Inst., 1976. Instr. Parsons Sch. Design, N.Y.C., 1967-70; research dir. N.Am. Congress on Latin Am., Berkeley, Calif., 1970-76; vis. lectr. Tufts U., 1973; vis. fellow Center of Internat. Studies, Princeton U., 1976-77; program dir. Inst. Policy Studies, Washington, 1977-84; prof. peace & world security studies Hampshire Coll., Amherst, Mass., 1985—, dir. 5 colls. program in peace and world security studies, 1985—. Vis. assoc. prof. of peace studies Wellesley Coll., 1992-93; def. corr. The Nation, 1983—. Author: War Without End, 1973, Supplying Repression, 1978, Beyond the Vietnam Syndrome, 1981, American Arms Supermarket, 1985, Rogue States and Nuclear Outlaws, 1995, Resource Wars, 2001, Blood and Oil, 2004; co-author: A Scourge of Guns, 1996; editor: Peace and World Security Studies: A Curriculum Guide, 6th edit., 1994; co-editor: Low Intensity Warfare, 1988, Peace and World Security Studies: A Curriculum Guide, 5th edit., 1989, World Security: Challenges for a New Century, 1991, 3d edit., 1998, Lethal Commerce: The Global Trade in Small Arms and Light Weapons, 1995, Light Weapons and Civil Conflict, 1999; contbg. editor Current History. Bd. dirs. Arms Control Assn., 1994—. Home: 17 Columbus Ave Northampton MA 01060-4252 Office: Hampshire Coll Sch Social Sci Amherst MA 01002 Office Phone: 413-559-5563. E-mail: mklare@hampshire.edu.

KLARFELD, JONATHAN MICHAEL, journalism educator; b. Springfield, Mass., Dec. 11, 1937; m. Patricia Holland, Sept. 7, 1974; children: Victoria, Alexander. AB, Colgate U., 1960. Reporter, editor Holyoke (Mass.) Transcript-Telegram, 1962-65, UPI, Springfield, Boston, 1965-66, Boston Globe, 1966-68; press sec. Boston Parks/Redevel. Auth., 1968-70; reporter, writer Boston Record-Am., 1970-72; mgr. pub. info. Mass. Blue Cross, 1972-74; assoc. professor journalism Boston U., 1975—, dir. print journalism, 1979-96, dir. print and online journalism program, 1996—. Editl. cons. Lawyers Weekly Pubs., Boston, Lansing, Mich., Richmond, Va., Providence, 1983-92; press analyst Oxbow Corp., West Palm Beach, Fla., 1984-96; news media critic/columnist Boston Herald, 1994, 95; cons. in libel and invasion of privacy cases. Contbr. articles to numerous newspapers, periodicals. Mem. New Eng. Gilbert and Sullivan Soc., Sorcerers Rugby Club (pres. 1974-80), Newton Squash and Tennis Club (bd. govs. 1999-2003), Delta Kappa Epsilon. Avocations: squash, tennis, Gilbert and Sullivan. Office: Boston U Sch Journalism Boston MA 02215 Office Phone: 617-353-4978. E-mail: jklar@bu.edu.

KLARFELD, PETER JAMES, lawyer; b. Holyoke, Mass., Aug. 19, 1947; s. David Nathan and Gloria (Belsky) K.; m. Mary Myrtle, July 7, 1985; children: Peter Marcus (dec.), Mary Elizabeth, Louis Edward. BA, U. Va., 1969, JD, 1973; MA, U. Chgo., 1970. Bar: Va. 1973, D.C. 1975, U.S. Dist. Ct. D.C. 1977, U.S. Dist. Ct. (ea. dist.) Va. 1977, U.S. Dist. Ct. (ea. dist.) Wis. 1987, U.S. Dist. Ct. (no. dist.) Calif. 1990, U.S. Ct. Appeals (4th cir.) 1978, U.S. Ct. Appeals (3rd & 9th cirs.) 1986, U.S. Ct. Appeals (2d cir.) 1998, U.S. Ct. Appeals (7th cir.) 2003, U.S. Supreme Ct. 1977. Law clk. to Hon. Robert R. Merhige, Jr. U.S. Dist. Ct. (ea. dist.) Va., Richmond, 1973-74; atty., office of legal counsel U.S. Dept. Justice, Washington, 1974-76; ptnr. Brownstein Zeidman & Lore, Washington, 1977-96, Wiley, Rein &Fielding LLP, Washington, 1996—. Editor: Covenants Against Competition in Franchise Agreements, 2002; contbr. articles to profl. jours. Trustee Dalkon Shield Other Claimants Trust, Richmond, 1990-96, chmn., 1991-96. Mem. ABA. Home: 434 E Columbia St Falls Church VA 22046-3501 Office: Wiley Rein & Fielding 1776 K St NW Washington DC 20006-2304 E-mail: pklarfeld@wrf.com.

KLARICH, DAVID JOHN, lobbyist, lawyer; b. Hamilton, Ohio, July 17, 1963; s. Victor Martin and Janet Dawn (Carlson) K.; m. Cheryl Ruth O'Donnell, June 18, 1988. BA in Biology and Chemistry, U. Mo., 1985; MA in Pub. Policy, JD, Regent U., 1990. Bar: Mo. 1990. Mem. Mo. Ho. of Reps. from 92nd & 94th dists., Jefferson City, 1990-94, Mo. Senate from 26th dist., Jefferson City, 1994—2002, Riezman and Berger, P.C., Clayton, Mo., 1995—2002; apptd. commr. Mo. Indsl. Rels., 2002—; mng. mem. Citizens for Policy Reform, LLC. Chmn. judiciary com. Mo. State Senate, 2001—02. Chmn. judiciary com. Mo. State Senate, 2001—02; chmn. West County Rep. Orgn. Recipient Adminstrn. of Justice award Jud. Conf. Mo., 1991, 99, Mo. Bar award, 1993, 97, 2000, 01, Mo. Hosp. Assn. award, 1995, Jud. Conf. award, 2000, 02, Legal Svcs. award, 2000, award Mo. Assn. Probate and Assoc. Cir. Judges, 2001; named Mo. Bar Outstanding Legis. of Yr., 1996, Voice of Bus. award Assoc. Industries, 1998. Mo. Lawyers weekly v.p. and coming Lawyer Mem. Bar Assn. Met. St. Louis, Young Lawyers Assn., Vol. Lawyers Assn., St. Louis Lawyers Assn., Mo. Assn. Trial Attys., ABA, St. Louis Eagle Scout Assn., Nat. Eagle Scout Assn., Jaycees, Lions, Mo. C. of C. (Spirit of Enterprise award 1997), Theta Xi. Mem. Assembly of God Ch. Office Phone: 636-394-9809. E-mail: dklarich@sbcglobal.net.

KLARIK, BELA WILLIAM JAMES CLARK, retired school system administrator; b. Masontown, Pa., Aug. 7, 1931; s. Louis Klarik and Margaret Irma (Soltesz) Clark; children: Frank, Roxana, Steven, Louis M. AB in Edn. cum laude, Fairmont State Coll., 1957; postgrad., Antioch Coll., 1960, U. Md., 1965—75, W.Va. U., 1958—59, postgrad., 1963; MEd, U. Ga., 1961. Cert. ednl. supr. and adminstr., math. sci. and phys. edn. tchr. Ohio, Md. Profl. baseball player minor leagues Bklyn. Dodgers, 1953-55; tchr. math., coach Madison (Ohio) Meml. HS, 1957-60; tchr. math. and sci. Euclid (Ohio) City Schs., 1961-62; head dept. math. Richard Montgomery High Sch., Montgomery County Pub. Schs., Rockville, Md., 1962-65; Nat. Assn. Secondary Sch. Prins. adminstrv. intern John F. Kennedy HS, Silver Spring, Md., 1965-66; vice-prin. Col. E. Brooke Lee Jr. HS, Silver Spring, 1966-67; supr. math. Montgomery County Pub. Schs., Rockville, 1967-75, dir. dept. acad. skills, 1975-91; ret., 1991. Leader Md. delegation People to People Internat. Am.-Soviet Youth Exch., 1987; mem. edn. policy fellowship Inst. for Ednl. Leadership, 1988—89; mem. Md. Stds. for Schs. Com., 1989—91. Staff sgt. USAF, 1949—52. NSF Summer Inst. fellow, Antioch Coll., 1960, NSF Acad. Yr. Inst. fellow, U. Ga., 1960—61, NSF fellow, W.Va. U., 1963, U. Ga. fellow, 1961. Mem.: Inst. for Ednl. Leadership, Burnt Store Isles (Fla.) Assn., Montgomery County Ret. Sch. Employees Assn., Md. Ret. Pub. Sch. Employees Assn., Burnt Store Isles Boat Club, Am. Legion. Democrat. Roman Catholic. Avocations: travel, boating, sports, gourmet cuisines and wines. Home: 5006 Ovideo St Punta Gorda FL 33950-8000 E-mail: ldsleigh@comcast.net.

KLARMAN, MICHAEL JOSEPH, law educator; b. NYC, June 27, 1959; s. Herbert Elias and Muriel (Friedman) K.; m. Lisa Leigh Landsverk, May 15, 1985; children: Muluwork Tibebu, Rachel Emily. BA, MA, U. Pa., 1980; JD, Stanford U., 1983; DPhil, Oxford (Eng.) U., 1987. Law clk. to Judge Ruth Bader Ginsburg, U.S. Ct. Appeals, Washington, 1983-84; asst. prof. law U. Va., Charlottesville, 1987-92, prof., 1992—98, 1996 rsch. prof. law, 1993—96, F. Palmer Weber rsch. prof. of civil liberties & human rights, 1997—2000, Elizabeth D. & Richard A. Merrill rsch. prof., 2003—. James Monroe Disting. prof. law, 2003—, prof. history, 2003—. Editl. bd. Law & History Rev. U. Va. Contbr. articles to law jours.; author: From Jim Crow to Civil Rights: The Supreme Court and the Struggle for Racial Equality, 2004 (Bancroft Prize, 2005). Named scholar, Brit. Marshall Fund, 1984—87; recipient Roger & Madeleine Traynor Faculty Award for Excellence Legal Scholarship, U. Va., 1996, All-Univ. Achievement Award, 1997, State Coun. Higher Edn. Faculty Award, 1997. Mem. Am. Soc. Legal Historians, Order of Coif, Phi Beta Kappa. Democrat. Avocations: reading, travel. Office: U Va Sch Law 580 Massie Rd Charlottesville VA 22901-1789 Office Phone: 434-924-3771. E-mail: mjk6s@virginia.edu.*

KLAS, ROBERT RAYMOND, architect; b. Colome, S.D., May 28, 1936; s. Raymond Charles and Alice Elizabeth (Holden) K.; m. Rosemarie Stach, July 6, 1947; children: John Robert, Paul Anthony, Julie Anne. BArch, U. Oreg., 1966. Lic. architect, Oreg., Wash., Calif., Nev, Idaho. Staff asst. Lane County Planning Dept., Eugene, Oreg., 1963-64; work/study program U. Oreg., Eugene, 1965-66; job capt. Louis C. Gilham, Portland, 1966-68; assoc. Williams & Ehmann & Assocs., Portland, 1999—2005; assoc. prin., pres., CEO EKA Architects, 1980—. Cons. STOA-EKA Architects, 1980—. Campaign worker United Fund, Portland, 1968-69; leader Boy Scouts Am., Beaverton, Oreg., 1976-78, com. mem., 1978-81, com. chmn., 1981-83. With U.S. Army, 1959-61. Recipient Cert. of Achievement, U.S. Army So. European Task Force, 1962, Cert. merit Constrn. Specifications Inst., 1979, Cert. Appreciation, 1982, Tech. Excellence award, 1986. Mem. AIA, Constrn. Specifications Inst. (chpt. pres. 1978-79, dir. 1976-79, tech. chmn. N.W. region 1985-87), Chancellor Club. Republican. Roman Catholic. Home: 13283 SW Scotts Bridge Dr Tigard OR 97223-7811 Office: EKA Architects 6775 SW 111th Ave Beaverton OR 97008-5382 E-mail: eka.architects@verizon.net.

KLASKO, HERBERT RONALD, lawyer, educator, writer; b. Phila., Nov. 26, 1949; s. Leon Louis and Estelle Lorraine (Baratz) K.; m. Marjorie Ann Becker, Aug. 27, 1977; children: Brett Andrew, Kelli Lynn. BA, Lehigh U., 1971; JD, U. Pa., 1974. Bar: Pa. 1974, U.S. Dist. Ct. (ea. dist.) Pa. 1974, U.S. Ct. Appeals (3d cir.) 1981. Assoc. Fox, Rothschild, O'Brien & Frankel, Phila., 1974-75; ptnr., chmn. immigration dept. Abrahams & Loewenstein, Phila., 1975-88, Dechert, Price & Rhoads, Phila., 1988—2003; mng. ptnr. Klasko, Rulon, Stock & Seltzer, LLP, Phila., 2004—. Instr., mem. adv. bd. Inst. for Paralegal Tng., Phila., 1974-81; instr. Temple Law Sch. Grad. Legal Studies, Phila., 1984; adj. prof. Villanova U. Law Sch., Pa., 1985-90. Co-author: (with Matthew Bender and Hope Frye) Employer's Immigration Compliance Guide, 1985; bd. editors: Immigration Law and Procedure Reporter. Exec. committeeman, bd. dirs. Jewish Cmty. Rels. Coun., Phila., 1977—; chmn. exec. com., com. on unprosecuted Nazi war criminals Nat. Jewish Cmty. Rels. Adv. Coun., NYC, 1983-90; v.p. Hebrew Immigrant Aid Soc., Phila., 1977—; pres. Coun. of Tenants Assn., Southeastern Pa., 1980-81. Recipient Legion of Honor award Chapel of Four Chaplains, 1977. Mem. ABA (coordinating com. on immigration), Phila. Bar Assn., Am. Immigration Lawyers Assn. (chmn. Phila. chpt. 1980-82, bd. govs. 1980—, nat. sec. 1984-85, 2d v.p. 1985-86, 1st v.p. 1986-87, pres.-elect 1987-88, pres. 1988-89, exec. com. 1984-90, 96-99, gen. counsel 1996-99, Founders award 1999), Am. Immigration Law Found. (bd. dirs. 1987-90). Avocations: politics, sports, travel, organizations. Office: Klasko Rulon Stock & Seltzer LLP 1800 JFK Blvd Ste 1700 Philadelphia PA 19103 Office Phone: 215-825-8608. Business E-Mail: rklasko@klaskolaw.com.

KLASNA, GORDON SCOTT, assistant principal; b. Billings, Mont., June 4, 1972; s. Jonathan Joseph and Jacqueline Ann Klasna; m. Sheri McKinley, June 16, 1995; children: Caleb Scott, Areya Kae. BS, U. Mary, 1995; MEd, U. Mont., 2004. Lic. educator Mont., 1996. Music tchr. Yellowstone Edn. Ctr., Billings, Mont., 1994—95; choral dir. Hermiston H.S., Oreg., 1995—96, Lewistown Sch. Dist. No. 1, 1996—2004; asst. prin. Billings West H.S., 2004—. Mem.: Nat. Assn. Secondary Sch. Prins. (assoc.). Office: Billings West HS 2201 St John's Ave Billings MT 59102 Office Phone: 406-655-1317. Office Fax: 406-655-3100. Personal E-mail: gklasna@bresnan.net. Business E-Mail: klasnag@billings.k12.mt.us.

KLASS, SHEILA SOLOMON, English language educator, writer; b. NYC, Nov. 6, 1927; d. Abraham Louis and Regina (Glatter) Solomon; m. Morton Klass, May 2, 1953; children: Perri, David, Judy. BA, Bklyn. Coll., 1949; MA, State U. Iowa, 1951, MFA, 1953. English tchr. Julia Ward Howe Jr. H.S., N.Y.C., 1951-57; prof. English, Borough of Manhattan C.C./CUNY, N.Y.C., 1965-2000; prof. writer N.Y.C., 1950—. Author: (young adult novels) Nobody Knows Me in Miami, 1981, To See My Mother Dance, 1981, Alive and Starting Over, 1983, The Bennington Stitch, 1985, Page Four, 1986, Credit-Card Carole, 1987, Kool Ada, 1991, Rhino, 1993, Next Stop: Nowhere, 1995, A Shooting Star, 1996, Little Women Next Door, 2000; (adult novels) Come Back on Monday, 1960, Bahadur Means Hero, 1969, A Perpetual Surprise, 1981, In a Cold Open Field, 1997; (juvenile) The Uncivil War, 1997; (memoir) Everyone in This House Makes Babies, 1964. Mem. Learning Leaders Vol. Program, N.Y.C., 1990—. Mem. PEN. Jewish. Avocation: travel. Home: 900 W 190th St Apt 2O New York NY 10040-3653

KLATELL, ROBERT EDWARD, lawyer, educator; b. Tampa, Fla., Dec. 11, 1945; s. Jack S. and Arla M. (Bragin) K.; m. Penelope E. Manegan, June 14, 1970; children: Christopher J., James M., Jeremy N. BA, Williams Coll., 1968; JD, NYU, 1971. Bar: N.Y. 1972. Asso. Kramer, Lowenstein, Nessen, Kamin & Soll, N.Y.C., 1970-76; gen. counsel Arrow Electronics, Inc., N.Y.C., 1976—2002, v.p., 1979-88, sr. v.p., 1988-93, treas., 1990-96, CFO, 1992-96, exec. v.p., 1993—2003, ret., 2004, cons., 2003—. Bd. dirs. Datascape Corp., TTM Techs., Inc., Mechagrif Interactive Techs. Inc. Mem. ABA, Assn. Bar City N.Y., Fin. Execs. Inst.

KLATSKY, ARTHUR LOUIS, cardiologist, epidemiologist; b. N.Y.C., Oct. 24, 1929; s. Martin Max and Rose M. (Hurwitz) Klatsky; m. Eileen Selma Rohrberg, June 21, 1953; children: Jennifer Ann, Benjamin Paul. BA, Yale U., 1950; MD, Harvard U., 1954. Diplomate Am. Bd. Internal Medicine, Am. Bd. Cardiovascular Disease. Intern in medicine Boston City Hosp., 1954-56; resident in internal medicine and cardiology Boston VA Hosp., 1958-60; trainee in cardiology U. Calif., San Francisco, 1960-61; clin. instr. in medicine U. Calif. Med. Ctr., San Francisco, 1961-68, asst. clin. prof. medicine, 1968-80; staff physician internal medicine and cardiology Kaiser Found. Hosp., Oakland, Calif., 1961-80, sub-chief dept. medicine, 1973, chief divsn. cardiology, 1978-94; assoc. divsn. rsch. Kaiser Permanente Med. Care Program, Oakland, 1975—; sr. cons. in Cardiology, 1995—. Mem. med. adv. coun. Wine Inst., San Francisco, 1978—. Contbr. articles to profl. jours., chpts. to books. Mem. profl. edn. com. Alameda County Heart Assn., 1969—. With Med. Corps, 1956-58. Recipient rsch. award, Med. Friends of Wine, 1984, 1st Thomas Turner award for Excellence in Alcohol Rsch., Alcoholic Beverage Med. Rsch. Found., 1992, Morris Collen Lifetime Rsch. Achievement award, 2004; fellow Am. Heart Assn. Coun. on Epidemiology, 1975—. Fellow ACP, Am. Coll. Cardiology; mem. Am. Wine Alliance for Rsch. and Edn. (bd. dirs. 1989—), Disting. Practioner in Medicine, Nat. Acad. of Practice (Disting. Practitioner award 1995). Avocations: long distance running, music, gardening, travel. Office: Kaiser Found Hosp 280 W Macarthur Blvd Oakland CA 94611-5642 Office Phone: 510-752-6538.

KLATT, WAYNE ROY, editor, writer; b. Chgo., Sept. 11, 1940; s. Waldemar George Klatt and Agnes Sophie Scannell; m. Marilyn Louise Koeppel, Aug. 7, 1965; children: Theresa Ann, Catherine Louise, Jennifer Marie. BS in Comm., U. Ill., 1962. Reporter City News Bureau of Chgo., 1963—64, editor, 1965—. Co-author: Freed to Kill, 1990, I Am Cain, 1994, Homicide: 100 Years of Murder in America, 1998; contbr. articles to mags. Recipient Short Story Contest awards, U. Ill., 1958, 1st prize, Nit & Wit Mag., 1983. Mem.: Chgo. Press Vets. Assn. Avocations: reading, history, literature, films, psychology. Home: 4722 N Avers Ave Chicago IL 60625-6201 Office: City News Service Tribune Tower 435 N Michigan Ave Chicago IL 60611 Office Phone: 312-222-5555.

KLATTEN, SUSANNE QUANDT, pharmaceutical executive; b. Bath Homburg, Germany, Apr. 28, 1962; d. Herbert Quandt and Johanna; married; 3 children. MBA, IMD Bus. Sch. Lausanne. Mem. adv. bd., majority shareholder Altana Group, Bod Homburg, Germany; mem. supervisory bd. BMW. Chmn. bd. counsellors Herbert-Quandt-Stiftung Found. Named one of World's Richest People, Forbes Mag., 2003—04, most powerful people, Forbes mag., 2005. Office: Herbert-Quandt-Stiftung Herbert-Quandt-Haus Am Pilgerrain 15 Bad Homburg D-61352 Germany Office Phone: 49-06172-1712500. Office Fax: 49-06172-1712545. Business E-Mail: h-quandt-stiftung@altana.de.*

KLATZKY, ROBERTA LOU, psychologist, educator; b. Duluth, Minn., Jan. 6, 1947; d. Arnold and Rena (Brusin) Klatzky. BS, U. Mich., 1968; PhD, Stanford U., 1972. Asst. prof. U. Calif., Santa Barbara, 1972-77, assoc. prof., 1977-82, prof. psychology, 1982-93; prof. Carnegie Mellon U., Pitts., 1993—, head dept., 1993—2003. Author: Human Memory, 1980, Memory and Awareness, 1983. Ctr. Advanced Study fellow, Stanford, Calif., 1982. Fellow: AAAS (chair psychol0gy sect. 2000—01), APA (bd. sci. affairs 2005), Am. Psychol. Soc. (treas. 1999—); mem.: Vision Scis. Soc., Soc. Exptl. Psychologists, Internat. Soc. Attention and Performance (mem. exec. com. 2001—), Psychonomic Soc. (chmn. governing bd. 1998), Phi Beta Kappa. Avocation: piano. Office: Carnegie Mellon Univ Dept Psychology Pittsburgh PA 15213 Office Phone: 412-268-8026. Business E-Mail: klatzky@cmu.edu.

KLAUBERG, WILLIAM JOSEPH, information technology executive; b. N.Y.C., June 30, 1926; s. Leo V. and Marian (Casey) K.; m. Kathleen Kelly, Feb. 18, 1950; children: Christine Anne, Kathleen Noel, Angela Ellen, William Jr. BS in Nautical Sci., Mcht. Marine Acad., 1947; BS in Fgn. Svc., Georgetown U., 1949. Mgr. US Lines, Inc., Japan, 1949-65, v.p. Tokyo, 1965-68, v.p. European Div. London, 1968-71, v.p. West Coast Div. San Francisco, 1971-73, v.p. East Coast Div. N.Y.C., 1973-81; project mgr. Vinnell Corp., Balt., 1981-82, v.p. Fairfax, Va., 1982-83, exec. v.p., 1983-88, pres., CEO, 1988-93, chmn., chief exec. officer, 1993-94; chmn., 1994-97. Lt. (j.g.) USNR, 1947-52.

KLAUCK, JUDITH LYNN, middle school educator; b. East St. Louis, July 26, 1945; d. James L. and Lydia L. (Arnold) K. BS in Home Econs. Edn., So. Ill. U., 1969, MS in Home Econs. Edn., 1978; cert. in guidance, So. Ill. U., Edwardsville, 1989. Cert. tchr., Ill. Home econ. tchr. Althoff Cath. H.S., Belleville, Ill., 1969—89, guidance counselor, 1989—98; family and consumer sci. tchr. North Jr. H.S., Collinsville, 1998—2004, Collinsville Mid. Sch., 2004—. Mem. Am. Assn. Family and Consumer Scis. (past pres., treas. Dist. 5 chpt. 1969—), Delta Kappa Gamma Soc. Internat. (chpt. pres. 2000-04).

KLAUS, BENJAMIN ERNST, music educator; b. Milwaukee, Wis., Oct. 21, 1980; s. Ernst and Cathleen Klaus. BBS, Amb. Bapt. Coll., 1999—2003. Music dir. Parkdale Bapt. Ch., Gastonia, NC, 2001—02, Shining Light Bapt. Ch., Monroe, NC, 2002—03. Pvt. music instr. Waukesha County Conservatory of Music, Hartland, Wis., 2004—. Vocalist Florentine Opera Co., Milwaukee, Wis., 2004—05. Conservative-R. Bapt. Home: W31403 Winkler Ct Mukwonago WI 53149 Office: Waukesha County Conservatory of Music 1125 James Dr Hartland WI 53029 Office Phone: 262-367-5333. Personal E-mail: bklaus1@juno.com.

KLAUS, CHARLES, retired lawyer; b. Freiburg, Baden, Germany, Feb. 11, 1935; came to U.S., 1939; children: Charles, Kathryn, Richard; m. Elaine S. Jones, Jan. 6, 2002. BA, Cornell U., 1956, MBA, JD with distinction, 1961; postdoctoral, Case Western Res. U., 1964, Lakeland Cmty. Coll., 1976, 2004. Bar: Ohio 1961, U.S. Dist. Ct. (no. dist.) Ohio 1962. Assoc. Baker & Hostetler, Cleve., 1961-71, ptnr., 1972-94, formerly mng. ptnr. Cleve. office, retired, 1995. Past hon. trustee and pres. Cleve. Music Sch. Settlement; past trustee Cleve. Audubon Soc.; past trustee, sec. Cleve. Area Arts Coun., Lake Erie Opera Theatre, N.E. Ohio chpt. Arthritis Found.; former mem. Group Svc. Coun. Welfare Fedn. Cleve.; corp. mem. Holden Arboretum, 1993—, mem. coun., 2003—. Recipient Award of Merit, Cleve. Audubon Soc., 1979. Mem. Millard Fillmore Soc., Rowfant Club (past sec.), Kirtland Country Club (past dir., past sec., Willoughby, Ohio).

KLAUS, WILLIAM ROBERT, lawyer; b. Phila., Jan. 19, 1926; s. William Anthony and Amanda (Pusey) K.; m. Janet Lois Scoggins, Aug. 18, 1951; 1 child, Kenneth Springfield. LLB, Temple U., 1951. Bar: Pa. 1952. Assoc. Pepper, Hamilton & Scheetz, Phila., 1952-59, ptnr., 1959—95, retired, chmn. emeritus, 1995—. Bd. dirs. Pa. Warehousing, Co., Phila. Co-author: Practical Guide to U.C.C., 1969. Chmn. Phila. Comm. Legal Svcs., Inc., 1966-83, Phila. Legal Assistance Corp., 1995-2000. Staff sgt. U.S. Army, 1943-46, ETO. Faculty fellow U. Pa. Law Sch., 1973. Mem. ABA (chmn. com. legal aid 1978-79), Nat. Legal Aid Defenders Assn. (pres. 1978), Pa. Bar Assn., Phila. Bar Assn. (chancellor 1974), Phila. Club (chmn. house com. 1979-2002), Little Egg Harbor Yacht Club (commodore 1991), Merion Cricket Club. Avocations: skiing, sailing, archeology, music, antiques.

KLAUSEN, RAYMOND, theatre set designer, television production designer, sculptor; b. Jamaica, N.Y., May 29, 1949; s. Jens and Ane Kathrine (Jensen) K. BA, Hofstra U., 1961; MA in Art, NYU, 1963; MFA in Theatre Design, Yale U., 1967. Prodn. designer TV and theater. Hoffman eminent scholar prof. theatre, Fla. State U., 1993—. Theatrical set designer, 1967—, freelance TV art dir., 1970—; designer sets for Dreams, Soul Possessed, Brother's of the Knight, Pepito's Story, Kennedy Ctr., Waiting in the Wings, Comedy Tonight, Broadway, A Few Good Men...Dancin', New Victory Theatre, My Favorite Broadway, Ira Gershwin at 100, Carnegie Hall, Jubilee!, Bally's Grand, Las Vegas, Hello Hollywood, Hello!, MGM Grand, Reno, Jazz Legs, Berlin, Pete 'N' Keely, off Broadway, The Subject Was Roses, How to Succeed in Business Without Really Trying, You Can't Take it With You, Mary, Mary, Gypsy, John Drew Theatre, Scenes Formthe Life of Ggalileo, Johnny Johnson, Yale U., Summer and Smoke, Palmer Theatre, New Haven, Conn.; numerous TV series, individual spls. for Sammy Davis Jr., Elvis Presley, Neil Diamond, Bing Crosby, Perry Como, Jackie Gleason, Cher, Smothers Brothers, Pearl Bailey, The Muppets, Natalie Cole, Roberta Flack, Lynda Carter, plus the Kennedy Ctr. Honors, Omnibus, AFI Tributes to Bette Davis, John Huston, Fred Astaire, Jimmy Stewart, Henry Fonda, Alfred Hitchcock and Elizabeth Taylor, also Nat. Tours for Lionel Richie, Kenny Rogers, Julio Iglesias, Travis Tritt, Bally's Casino Prodns., The Kennedy Ctr. Homors, Gala for the Pres. at Ford's Theatre, Night of 100 Stars, The Tony Awards (2 times), The Am. Music Awards Show (28 times), The Academy Awards Show (9 times), Miss America (5 times), The 50th Anniversary of TV, Texaco Salutes Broadway, Happy Birthday Hollywood, (series) Vibe; solo exhbns. include LBJ Gallery, Newport Beach, Calif., 1990, Wade Gallery, L.A., 1991, Gallery Sanyo, Tokyo, 1991, 92, Ruth Bachofner Gallery, L.A., 1992, 95, Fla. State U. Mus., Tallahassee, 1993,; group exhbns. include Zantman Galleries, Carmel, Calif., 1991, Long Beach (Calif.) Mus. Art, 1992, Ward-Nasse Gallery, N.Y.C., 1992, Ettinger Gallery, Laguna Beach, Calif., Boise (Idaho) State U. Art Gallery, 1993, LACE, L.A., 1993, Alder Gallery, Eugene, Or., 1993, Clara Kott Von Storch Gallery, Mich.,1993, Michael Stone Collection, Va., 1993, San Diego Art Inst., Calif., 1993, Roy G. Biv Gallery, Palm Springs, Calif., 1994, Palm Springs Desert Mus., Calif., 1994, La Quinta Sculpture Park, La Quinta, Calif., 1994, Quietude Garden Gallery, East Brunswick, N.J., 1995, Hunter Mus. Am. Art, Chatanooga, Tenn., 1995, SUNY Plattsburg Art Mus., 1995, San Bernadino Coungy Mus., Calif., 1995, Paris Gibson Mus., Great Falls, Mont., 1995, Eva Cohen Gallery, Chgo., Ill., 1995, D.O.C.S. Gallery, New Orleans, 1997. With U.S. Army, 1962-63. Bates Travel fellow Europe, 1967; TDK Corp. grantee, 1991, 92; recipient 3 Nat. Acad. TV Arts and Sci. Emmy awards for Cher series, 1976, Acad. awards, 1982, 83, nominations for 1980, 91 Acad. Awards and Lynda Carter's Celebration, 1981, Kennedy Ctr. Honors, 1984, 86, Am. Music Awards, 1985, 90, Happy Birthday Hollywood, 1987, Acad. awards, 1991, 96. Home and Office: # 9B 514 West End Ave New York NY 10024-4344 also: 325 S Swall Dr Apt 503 Los Angeles CA 90048-3078

KLAUSMEYER, DAVID MICHAEL, scientific instruments manufacturing company executive; b. Indpls., Aug. 29, 1934; s. David M. and V. Jane (Donnellan) K.; m. Julie Ann Johnson, Oct. 29, 1955; children: Kathleen M., Kevin M., Gregory J. BSS, Georgetown U., 1955. Asst. to pres. White Cons. Ind., Cleve., 1957; auditor Ernst & Ernst, Cleve., 1957-59; pres. Photopipe, Inc., Cleve., 1960-63; v.p. McGregor & Werner Internat., Inc., Washington, 1964-70; internat. cons. Stratford of Tex., Houston, 1971-72; pres. FLR Corp., Houston, 1972-74, Southwest Cons., Houston, 1981-86, Imaging Products, Houston, 1987-90; sec. Nanodyanmics, Inc., N.Y.C., 1988—, also bd. dirs.; pres. Corp. Devel., Houston, 1974-81; ptnr. Klausmeyer & Assoc., Houston, 1970—2001; ret., 2001. Dir. U.S. investment banking Secured Electronic Global Order Execution Sys. Securities, Grand Cayman Island, 1995—2001; bd. dirs. S.ure Reification, Houston. Bd. dirs. Cath. Endowment Found. Galveston-Houston, 1999-2002; mem. nat. fin. and ops. com. St. Vincent de Paul Soc., St. Louis, 2004—. With USCG, 1955-57. Republican. Roman Catholic. Home: 288 Litchfield Ln Houston TX 77024-6035 Office: Nanodynamics Inc 34 East 29th St New York NY 10016 Office Phone: 713-827-8947. E-mail: dklausmeyer@houston.rr.com.

KLAUSNER, JACK DANIEL, lawyer; b. N.Y.C., July 31, 1945; s. Burt and Marjory (Brown) K.; m. Dale Arlene Kreis, July 1, 1968; children: Andrew Russell, Mark Raymond. BS in Bus., Miami U., Oxford, Ohio, 1967; JD, U. Fla., 1969. Bar: N.Y. 1971, Ariz. 1975, U.S. Dist. Ct. Ariz. 1975, U.S. Ct. Appeals (9th cir.) 1975, U.S. Supreme Ct. 1975. Assoc. counsel John P. McGuire & Co., Inc., N.Y.C., 1970-71; assoc. atty. Hahn & Hessen, N.Y.C., 1971-72; gen. counsel Equilease Corp., N.Y.C., 1972-74; assoc. Burch & Cracchiolo, Phoenix, 1974-78, ptnr., 1978-98; judge pro tem Maricopa County Superior Ct., 1990—, Ariz. Ct. Appeals, 1992—; ptnr. Warner Angle, Phoenix, 1998—. Bd. dirs. Hunter Contracting Co. Bd. dirs. Santos Soccer Club, Phoenix, 1989-90; bd. dirs., pres. south Bank Soccer Club, Tempe, 1987-88. Office: Warner Angle Hallam Jackson & Formanek 3550 N Central Ave Ste 1500 Phoenix AZ 85012-2112 Home: 1702 E Becky Cir Payson AZ 85541-3363

KLAUSNER, MICHAEL DAVID, law educator; b. Phila., Dec. 12, 1954; s. Gilbert and Edith (Quitman) Klausner; m. Barbara Ann-Pei Sih, Sept. 2, 1984; children: Jill, Gregory. BA in Polit. Sci./Urban Studies, summa cum laude, U. Pa., 1976; MA in Economics, JD, Yale U., 1981. Bar: DC 1983. Law clk. to Judge David Bazelon US Ct. Appeals DC Cir., 1981-82; law clk. to Justice William Brennan US Supreme Ct., 1983-84; vis. scholar & lectr. dept. law Peking U., China, 1984-85; assoc. Paul, Weiss, Rifkind, Wharton & Garrison, Washington, 1982—83, Gibson, Dunn & Crutcher, Washington, Hong Kong, 1986-89; White House fellow, dep. assoc. dir. Office Policy Devel. White House, Washington, 1989-90; asst. prof. to prof. NYU Sch. Law, 1991—97; prof. law Stanford Law Sch., 1997—, Bernard D. Bergreen faculty scholar, 1997—2003, Nancy and Charles Munger prof. bus., 2003—, assoc. dean rsch. and academics, 2004—. Vis. prof. Stanford Law Sch., 1995—96. Avocation: scuba diving. Office: Stanford Law Sch Crown Quadrangle 559 Nathan Abbott Way Stanford CA 94305-8610 Office Phone: 650-723-6433. E-mail: klausner@stanford.edu.*

KLAUSNER, RICHARD D., cell biologist, researcher; b. New York, N.Y., Dec. 22, 1951; BS, Yale U., 1973; MD, Duke U. Med. Sch., 1976. Rsch. assoc. Harvard Med. Sch., 1977-79; rscher., med. officer, mathematical biology program Nat. Insts. Health, Bethesda, Md., 1979-84; branch chief, cell biology, metabolism branch Nat. Inst. of Child Health and Human Develop., Bethesda, Md., 1984-95; dir. Nat. Cancer Inst., Bethesda, Md., 1995—2001; exec. dir. Global Health (Bill and Melinda Gates Found.), Seattle, 2002—. Chmn., Scientific Advisory Bd., Ariad Pharmaceuticals, 1991. Medicine, 1976; numerous articles in prof. journals. Recipient Meritorious Svc. Award, 1986, PHS, Damashek Prize, 1992, Am. Soc. for Hematology Mem. NAS, Am. Soc. for Clinical Investigation, Inst. Medicine. Office: The Bill & Melinda Gates Found PO Box 23350 Seattle WA 98102

KLAUSNER, SAMUEL ZUNDEL, sociologist, educator; b. Bklyn., Dec. 19, 1923; s. Edward Solomon and Bertha (Adler) K.; m. Bracha Turgeman, Oct. 26, 1948 (div. 1960); children: Rina Ellen Klausner Spence, Jonathan David; m. Madeleine Suringar, Feb. 20, 1964 (div. 1982); children: Daphne Klausner Genyk, Tamar; m. Roberta Sands, Nov. 26, 1992. BS, NYU, 1947; MA, Columbia U., 1951, EdD, 1952, PhD, 1963. Cert. psychologist, N.Y., D.C. Lectr. edn. CCNY, 1951-52, 55-57; lectr. sociology Columbia U., 1957-63; instr. psychology Hebrew U., Jerusalem, 1952-53; lectr. religion and psychiatry Union Theol. Sem., 1961-63; assoc. prof. sociology U. Pa., Phila., 1967-70, prof., 1970-96; dir. Ctr. for Rsch. on the Acts of Man, 1971-88, chmn. grad. group in sociology, 1984-86; prof. emeritus U. Pa., Phila., 1996—. Clin. psychologist Govt. Mental Hosp., Jerusalem, 1954-55; program dir. Bur. Applied Social Rsch., Columbia U., 1956-61; sr. rsch. assoc. Bur. Social Sci. Rsch., Washington, 1964-67; exec. sec. Soc. for Study of Religion, 1964-70; cons. U.S. Dept. Commerce, 1968-69, U.S. Naval Chaplains Sch., 1973-81, Nat. Libr. Medicine, 1969, NRC, 1967-81, others; vis. prof. Al Mansoura U., Egypt, 1983, Muhammad V. Univ., Morocco, 1986. Author: Psychiatry and Religion, 1964, The Quest for Self-Control, 1965, The Study of Total Societies, 1967, Why Man Takes Chances, 1968, Society and Its Physical Environment, 1970, On Man in His Environment, 1971, Eskimo Capitalists, 1981; author, editor: The Nationalization of the Social Sciences, 1986; also articles. With USAAC, 1943-45; with Israel Air Force, 1947-48. Ford Found. area rsch. fellow, 1952-53; Fulbright scholar, 1983. Mem. APA, AAAS, Am. Sociol. Assn., Assn. Sociol. Study of Jewry (pres. 1980), Soc. Sci. Study of Religion (v.p. 1974), Am. Vets. Israel (pres. 1951, 98-2000, newsletter editor 1998—). Jewish. Home: 7055 Greenhill Rd Philadelphia PA 19151-2322 E-mail: sklausner@ucwphilly.rr.com. *My ideals of social conduct have not been designed to assist in attaining professional success. Judaism is a central guiding reference and though I may deviate from its principles in my daily behavior for reasons of good sense and self interest, they remain normative. My professional station arises from an obsession with the requirements of scholarship. A willingness to be critical of current social institutions has brought social attention but not professional advancement.*

KLAUSS, KENNETH KARL, composer, music educator; b. Parkston, S.D., Apr. 8, 1923; s. Christian and Paulina (Engel) Klauss. MusB in Composition, U. So. Calif., 1946. Tchr. composition and piano, L.A., 1946-50; composer Lester Horton Theater, L.A., 1949-50; tchr. music San Francisco, 1950-61; composer, educator L.A., 1961—; lectr. in music for dance Idyllwild (Calif.) Sch. Music and Arts, 1967-74; lectr. in music history So. Calif. Inst. Architecture, Santa Monica, 1970-76. Composer in residence Perry/Mansfield Camp, Steamboat Springs, Colo., 1966; guest performer, composer, lectr. Libr. Congress, Am. U., Washington, 1996; guest lectr. U. S.D., Vermillion, 2002. Composer: (opera) Fall of the House of Usher, 1952, harpsichord/violin composition commd. by U. S.D., 2001; author, composer: (poetry/music orchestration) Story of the World Vols. I to VIII, 1952-86; performances by Rawlins Trio of U. S.D., Mpls., Omaha and Vermillion, 2005. Founder, patron Klauss/James Archive and Art Mus., Parkston, 1995—. Recipient hon. mention opera competition Ohio U., Athens, 1954. Democrat. Avocations: history, poetry. Home: 440 Wren Dr Los Angeles CA 90065-5040 Office Phone: 605-928-3366. Personal E-mail: kkennkarl@aol.com. Business E-Mail: musicart@santel.net.

KLAVITER, HELEN LOTHROP, magazine editor; b. Lima, Ohio, Mar. 5, 1944; d. Eugene H. and Jean (Walters) Lothrop; m. Douglas B. Klaviter, June 7, 1969 (div. 1982); 1 child, Elizabeth. BA, Cornell Coll., Mt. Vernon, Iowa, 1966. Communication specialist Coop. Extension Service, Urbana, Ill., 1969-71; mng. editor Poetry Mag., Chgo., 1973—. Editorial cons. Harper & Row, N.Y.C., 1983-87. Bd. dirs. Ill. Theatre Ctr., 1989-95, St. Clement's Open Pantry, 1990—, Episc. Diocese of Chgo. Hunger Commn., 1992—, Comms. Commn., 1993—. Episcopalian. Office: Poetry Mag The Poetry Found 1030 N Clark St Ste 420 Chicago IL 60610 Office Phone: 312-799-8004. Business E-Mail: hklaviter@poetrymagazine.org.

KLAW, BARBARA ANNE, language educator; b. Chgo., Mar. 22, 1957; BA cum laude in French, No. Ill. U., 1979; postgrad., Northwestern U., 1982-83; MA in French lit., U. Pa., 1985, PhD in French, 1990. Teaching asst. Northwestern U., Evanston, Ill., 1982-83; teaching asst. U. Pa., Phila., 1983-84, 84-85, 1986-87; lectr. Université de Dijon, Dijon, France, 1985-86, U. Pa., Phila, 1987-88; teaching asst. Penn-in-Tours program Faculté des Lettres, Tours, France, summer 1988; asst. prof. French No. Ky. U., Highland Heights, 1990-96; assoc. prof. No. Ky. Univ., 1996—. Faculty advisor Internat. Student Union, No. Ky. U., 1991-98; participant com. for modification of tng. program for new tchg. assts. Northwestern U., spring 1983. Author: Le Paris de Beauvoir; mem. editl. bd. Women in French Studies, 1999—; mem. adv. bd. Simone de Beauvoir Studies, 2002—; numerous presentations in French and on French subjects; contbr. articles to profl. jours. No. Ky. U. summer fellow, 1991, 94, 97, Am. Philos. Soc. grantee, 1997; NEH grantee, 2001-04. Mem. MLA, Simone de Beauvoir Soc., Alliance Française de Cin. (bd. dirs.), Am. Assn. Tchrs. French, Women in French (treas. 1992—98), French-Am. C. of C. in Cin., Ky. World Lang. Assn. E-mail: klaw@nku.edu.

KLAWE, MARIA MARGARET, engineering and computer science educator; b. Toronto, Ontario, Can., July 5, 1951; d. Janusz Josef and Kathleen Wreath (McCaughan) K.; m. Nicholas John Pippenger, May 12, 1980; children: Janek, Sasha. BSc in math., U. Alberta, 1973; PhD, U. Alberta, Edmonton, Can., 1977; PhD (hon.), Ryerson U., 2001, U. Waterloo, 2003, Queens U., 2004. Asst. prof. dept. math. sci. Oakland U., Rochester, Mich., 1977-78; asst. prof. dept. computer sci. U. Toronto, Canada, 1979-80; rsch. staff mem. IBM Rsch., San Jose, Calif., 1980-89, mgr. discrete math., 1984-88, mgr. dept. math., related computer sci., 1985-87; prof., head dept. computer sci. U. BC, Vancouver, 1988-95, v.p. student and acad. svcs., 1995—98, dean sci., 1998—2002; dean Sch. Engring & Applied Sci. Princeton U., 2003—, prof. dept. computer sci., 2003—. Mem. adv. bd. univ. rels. IBM Toronto Lab., 1989; mem. sci. adv. bd. Dimacs NSF Sci. Tech. Ctr., New Brunswick, NJ, 1989-95; mem. adv. bd. Geometry Ctr., 1991-95; mem. BC Premier's Adv. Coun. on Sci. and Tech., 1993—2001, Provincial Adv. Com. on Edn. Tech., 1993; founder, dir. E-GEMS project U. BC, 1992-2002; Chair for Women in Sci. and Engring. Nat. Sciences and Engring. Rsch. Coun. of Can.(NSERC)-IBM, 1997-2002; co-founder, chmn. bd. Silicon Chalk, Vancouver.; bd. trustees Math. Sciences Rsch. Inst., chair bd. trustees Anita Borg Inst. Women and Tech. Palo Alto Calif.; trustee Inst. Pure and Applied Math. LA. Editor: (jours.) Combinatorica, 1985—, SIAM Jour. on Computing, 1986-93, SIAM Jour. on Discrete Math., 1987-93; contbr. articles to profl. jours. Named Can. New Media Educator of Yr., 2001, BC Sci. Coun. Champion of Yr., 2001; recipient Women of Distinction Award in Sci. and Tech., Vancouver YWCA, 1997, Can. Wired Woman Pioneer Award, 2001, Disting. Alum. Award, U. Alberta, 2003, Nico Habermann award, 2004; INCO scholar, 1968—71, NRC Can. fellow, 1973—77. Fellow Assn. Computing Machinery (mem. coun. 1998-2000, v.p. 2000-02, pres. 2002-04); mem. Am. Math. Soc. (bd. trustees 1992-97, chmn. 1995-96), Can. Math. Soc., Can. Heads Computer Sci. (pres. 1990-91), Assn. Women Math., Computing Rsch. Assn. (mem. bd. 1990-96), Soc. Indsl. and Applied Math. Avocations: running, painting, kayaking, windsurfing. Office: Princeton U Sch Engring & Applied Sci C-230 EQuad Princeton NJ 08544-5263 Office Phone: 609-258-2660. Office Fax: 609-258-7305. Business E-Mail: klawe@princeton.edu.*

KLAWITER, DONALD CASIMIR, lawyer; b. Phila., Feb. 26, 1950; s. Joseph C. and Frances J. (Koniecki) K.; m. Marie M. Gabuzda, Jan. 2, 1982; children: Joseph, Jeffrey. BA, MA, U. Pa., 1972, JD, 1975. Bar: Pa. 1975, U.S. Supreme Ct. 1979, D.C. 1987, U.S. Dist. Ct. D.C. 1987, U.S. Ct. Appeals (4th and 8th crcts.) 1988, U.S. Ct. Appeals (9th crct.) 1993. Trial atty. antitrust div. U.S. Dept. Justice, Phila., 1975-78, spl. asst. operations antitrust div. Washington, 1978-80, chief antitrust Dallas, 1980-82, sr. trial atty. Washington, 1982-86; of counsel Morgan, Lewis & Bockius LLP, Washington, 1986-88; ptnr. Morgan, Lewis & Bockius, Washington, 1988—. Chair bd. dirs. Pinecrest Sch., Annandale, Va., 1998-2004; chair bd. trustees Commonwealth Acad., Alexandria, Va., 2001—; mem. bd. trustees Browne Acad.,

Alexandria, 2005-. Mem. ABA (litigation, antitrust law and bus. law sects., chair criminal practice and procedure com. sect. antitrust law 1995-97, mem. governing coun. sect. antitrust law 1997—, sec. sect. antitrust law 2000-01, program officer sect. antitrust law 2001-03, vice chmn. 2003-04, chair-elect 2004-05, chair 2005—), Internat. Bar Assn. (legal practice divsn., antitrust coms). Roman Catholic. Home: 5930 Munson Ct Falls Church VA 22041-2443 Office: Morgan Lewis & Bockius 1111 Pennsylvania Ave NW Washington DC 20004 Office Phone: 202-739-5222. Business E-Mail: dklawiter@morganlewis.com.

KLAYMAN, BARRY MARTIN, lawyer; b. Montclair, NJ, Sept. 26, 1952; s. Max M. and Sylvia (Cohen) K.; m. Anna Kornbrot, June 8, 1975; children: Alison Melissa, Matthew Daniel. BA magna cum laude, Columbia U., 1974; JD cum laude, Harvard U., 1977. Bar: Pa. 1977, Del. 1998, U.S. Dist. Ct. (ea. dist.) Pa. 1977, U.S. Dist. Ct. Del. 1998, U.S. Ct. Appeals (3d cir.) 1978. From assoc. to ptnr. Wolf, Block, Schorr & Solis-Cohen LLP, Phila., 1977—. Bd. dirs. BBYO, Inc. Contbr. articles to profl. jours. Bd. dirs. Akiba Hebrew Acad., 1991—, sec., 1994-95, v.p., 1995-96, 98-2000, treas. 1996-98, pres. 2000-03; dir. B'nai B'rith Youth Orgn. Inc., 2002—; mem. cmty. planning and allocations com. Jewish Fedn. Greater Phila., 1997-2003, trustee, 2000-05, mem. com. on nat. svcs., 1991-2003, chair, 1998-2003, mem. com. on formal Jewish edn., 2000-03, mem. com. on policy, strategy and funding, 2003—; exec. com. United Jewish Cmtys. Nat. Funding Coun., 2002-. Mem. ABA (litig. sect., torts and ins. practice sect.), Del. Bar Assn., Phila. Bar Assn., Pa. Bar Assn., Assn. Trial Lawyers Am., B'nai B'rith Youth Orgn. (bd. dirs. Phila. region 1984—, chmn. 1991-95, mem. Internat. Youth Commn. 1991-2001, exec. com., 1996-2001), B'nai B'rith (coun. v.p. 1996-97, mem. Justice Lodge 1992-2003), Phi Beta Kappa. Office: Wolf Block Schorr & Solis-Cohen LLP 1100 N Market St Ste 1001 Wilmington DE 19801 Office Phone: 302-777-0313. Business E-Mail: bklayman@wolfblock.com.

KLAYMAN, LARRY ELLIOTT, lawyer, legal association administrator; b. Phila., July 20, 1951; s. Herman Klayman. AB with honors, Duke U., 1973; JD, Emory U., 1977. Bar: Fla. 1977, D.C. 1980, U.S. Ct. Internat. Trade 1982, U.S. Ct. Appeals (fed. cir.) 1983. Assoc. atty. Blackwell, Walker, Gray et al, Miami, Fla., 1977-78; trial atty. U.S. Dept. Justice Antitrust Div., Washington, 1979-81; assoc. atty. Busby, Rehm & Leonard, P.C., Washington, 1981-83; pvt. practice Washington, 1984-85; pres., chief exec. officer Klayman & Gurley, P.C., Washington, 1985-89, Klayman & Assocs., P.C., Washington, 1989—2002; founder The Klayman Law Firm, 2002—; founder, gen. counsel, chmn. Judicial Watch, 1994—2003. Pres., chief exec. officer Free Trade Enterprises, Ltd., Washington, Internat. Design Enterprises, Ltd., Internat. Food Enterprises, Ltd. Contbr. article to profl. jour. Mem. Nat. Press Club, Capitol Hill Club. Achievements include Republican candidate for U.S. Senate, FL., 2004.

KLEBANOFF, SEYMOUR JOSEPH, medical educator; b. Toronto, Ont., Can., Feb. 3, 1927; s. Eli Samuel and Ann Klebanoff; m. Evelyn Norma Silver, June 3, 1951; children: Carolyn, Mark. MD, U. Toronto, 1951; PhD in Biochemistry, U. London, 1954. Intern Toronto Gen. Hosp., 1951—52; postdoctoral fellow dept. path. chemistry U. Toronto, 1954—57; postdoctoral fellow Rockefeller U., N.Y.C., 1957—59, asst. prof., 1959—62; assoc. prof. medicine U. Washington, Seattle, 1962—68, prof., 1968—2000, prof. emeritus, 2000—. Mem. adv. coun. Nat. Inst. Allergy and Infectious Diseases, NIH, 1987—90. Author: The Neutrophil, 1978; contbr. over 200 articles to profl. jours. Recipient Merit award, NIH, 1988, Mayo Soley award, Western Soc. for Clin. Investigation, 1991, Bristol-Myers Squibb award for Disting. Achievement in Infectious Disease Rsch., 1995. Fellow: AAAS; mem.: NAS, Am. Acad. Arts and Scis., Inst. of Medicine, Soc. for Leukocyte Biology (Marie T. Bonazinga rsch. award 1985), Endocrine Soc., Infectious Diseases Soc. Am. (Bristol award 1993), Assn. Am. Physicians, Am. Soc. Biol. Chemists, Am. Soc. Clin. Investigation. Home: 509 Mcgilvra Blvd E Seattle WA 98112-5047 Office: U Wash Dept Medicine Div Al & Infectious Disease PO Box 357185 Seattle WA 98195-7185 Office Phone: 206-685-1876. Business E-Mail: seym@u.washington.edu.

KLEBBA, RAYMOND ALLEN, property manager; b. Chgo., Apr. 16, 1934; s. Raymond Aloysius and Marie Cecelia (Tobin) K.; m. Barbara Ann Gurbal, Oct. 7, 1961; children: Anne, Daniel, Mary, Theresa. Student, Loyola U., Chgo., 1954-56; cert. property mgr., Inst. Real Estate Mgmt., 1970. Corr., rep. Western R.R. Assn., Chgo., 1956-61; pres. Midland Warehouses, Chgo., 1961-68; v.p., gen. mgr. Strobeck, Reiss Sch. Mgmt. Co., Chgo., 1968-70, real estate mgr., broker, 1970—83; v.p., dir. Mid-Am. Nat. Bank, Chgo., 1983-90; br. mgr. Bank of Highwood/Deerfield, Ill., 1990-94; v.p. sales First Colonial Mortgage Corp., Chgo., 1994-95; bus. mgr. St. Matthias Parish, Chgo., 1995-98; real estate broker Tempo Real Estate, Inc., Chgo., 1998—. Mem. Chgo. Bd. Realtors (vice chmn. comml. and indsl. leasing and property mgmt. coun.), Inst. Real Estate Mgmt. (life; chmn. chpt. of yr. com. 1975-76), Rotary, Moose, KC. Avocations: bowling, golf, gardening, fishing (Chicago land individual casting champion 1999. Home: 4933 N Leavitt St Chicago IL 60625-1308 Office Phone: 773-271-3200.

KLEBER, HERBERT DAVID, psychiatrist, educator; b. Pitts., June 19, 1934; s. Max J. and Dorothea (Schulman) K.; m. Joan Louise Fox, Sept. 9, 1956 (div. Jan. 1988); children: Elizabeth, Marc, Pamela. BA in Psychology cum laude, Dartmouth Coll., 1956; MD, Jefferson Med. Coll., 1960; MA (hon.), Yale U., 1975; PhD (hon.), N.Y. Med. Coll., 1990. Lederle rsch. fellow Jefferson Med. Coll., 1959-60; rotating intern Health Ctr. Hosps. of U. Pitts., 1960-61; resident in psychiatry Yale U., New Haven, 1961-64; surgeon, chief receiving svc. USPHS Hosp., Lexington, Ky., 1964-66; asst. chief Hill-West Haven divsn. Conn. Mental Health Ctr., 1966-67, outpatient and admissions coord., 1967-68, dir., founder drug dependence unit, 1968-75, dir. substance abuse treatment unit, 1975-89; exec. dir. psychiatry emergency rm. svc. Yale-New Haven Hosp., 1967-68; from asst. prof. to assoc. prof. Yale U. Sch. Medicine, New Haven, 1966-75; prof. Yale U., 1975-91; exec. v.p., med. dir. Ctr. on Addiction and Substance Abuse Columbia U., 1992—; prof., dir. divsn. substance abuse N.Y. State Psychiat. Inst., 1991—; prof. psychiatry Columbia U. Coll. Phys. and Surg., N.Y.C., 1991—; attending psychiatrist Columbia-Presbyn. Med. Ctr., 1992—. U.S. presdl. appointee Office Nat. Drug Control Policy, dep. dir., 1989-91; founder APT Foudn., Inc., 1970, CEO, 1982-89; dir. NIDA Clin. Rsch. Ctr. for Treatment of Opioid and Cocaine Abuse, Yale U., 1986-89, dir. rsch. tng. fellowship in substance abuse, 1988-89; mem. drug abuse adv. com. FDA, 1987-90; mem. bd. of sci. counselors Addiction Rsch. Ctr, Nat. Inst. on Drug Abuse, 1982-85; mem. exec. instns. rev. groups NIMH and Nat Inst. on Drug Abuse; Nolan D.C. Lewis vis. prof. Carrier Found., 1985; dir. Nat. Inst. Drug Abuse Medication Devel. Ctr., 1994—, Columbia U., Rsch. Training Fellowship program, Columbia U., 1993—; lectr. and presenter in field. Contbr. chpts.: Opiate Addiction: Origins and Treatment, 1973, Treatment Aspect of Drug Dependence, 1978, Clinical Psychiatric Medicine, 1981, Cocaine: Scientific and Social Dimensions, 1992, Drugs, Alcohol and Tobacco: Making the Science and Policy Connections, several others; editor: APA Treatment Manual for Substance Abuse Disorders, APA Textbook of Substance Abuse Treatment, Clinician's Guide to Cocaine Abuse Treatment; (with others) APA Textbook-Treatment of Psychiatric Disorders: Treatment of Substance Abuse; assoc. editor Am. Jour. Drug and Alcohol Abuse and Addictive Behaviors, mem. edit. bd.; rsch. editor Jour. Substance Abuse Treatment, mem. edit. bd. Am. Jour. Addictions, Advances in Alcohol Actions/Misuse, Harvard Rev. of Psychiatry; edit. cons. Archives Gen. Psychiatry, Conn. Medicine, Med. Letter, Jour. Maintenance in the Addictions, Sci.; contbr. over 200 articles to profl. jours. Exec. com. Com. on Problems of Drug Dependence, Inc.; co-chmn. Mayor's Task Force on Drugs, City of New Haven; mem. adv. bd. Rand Drug Policy Rsch. Ctr.; mem. Gov.'s Drug Adv. Coun., State of Conn., 1970-76; mem. nat. adv. coun. Nat. Inst. of Drug Abuse, Alcohol, Drug Abuse and Mental Health Adminstrn., 1975-79, NIMH, 1977-79. Recipient Meritorious Svc. award Lapides Found., 1979, Families in Action Drug Prevention award, 1990, Gov.'s award for outstanding svc. in field of substance abuse State of Conn., 1987, Nyswander and Dole award, 1986, Alcohol, Drug Abuse, Mental Health Agy. award for pub. svc., 1986. Fellow ACP, Am. Psychiat. Assn. (mem. coun. on addiction, cons. joint commn. on pub. affairs, task force on benzodiazepine dependency, Gold award 1975, Found.'s Fund prize 1981), Am. Coll. Neuropsychopharmacology (Eddy award of Coll. on Problems of Drug Dependence 1995), N.Y. Acad. Medicine, Am. Acad. Psychiatrists in Alcoholism and Addictions (founding, Founders award 1987); mem. Inst. of Medicine (substance abuse coverage com., medication devel. for substance abuse com.). Republican. Jewish. Avocations: swimming, cross country skiing. Office: Columbia U Coll Phys/Surgns 1051 Riverside Dr New York NY 10032-1013

KLECK, ROBERT ELDON, psychology professor; b. Archbold, Ohio, Aug. 3, 1937; AB in Philosophy, Denison U., 1959; PhD in Social Psychology, Stanford (Calif.) U., 1963. Postdoctoral fellow Stanford U., 1963-64; asst. prof. Williams Coll., Williamstown, Mass., 1964-66; asst. to assoc. prof. Dartmouth Coll., Hanover, N.H., 1966-75, prof. psychology, 1975—, John Sloan Dickey Third Century Prof. of Social Scis., 1985-90, chmn. dept. psychology, 1993-99. Vis. rsch. prof. Boy's Town Ctr. Study of Youth Devel., Stanford U., 1974-75; cons. VA Stroke Project, 1983-86, Disadvantaged Children in N.H., 1974, Bur. Devel. Disabilities, Concord, N.H., 1975-80, Crotchet Mountain Rehab. Ctr., 1973, Abilities, Inc., Albertson, N.Y., 1979-81, Can. Rsch. Coun., NSF, USPHS; faculty sponsore USPHS Post-doctoral fellowship, 1977-78. Cons. editor Jour. Personality and Social Psychology, 1974-78, assoc. editor 1971-72; mem. editorial bd. Jour. Nonverbal Behavior, 1990-93; mem. editorial adv. bd. Action for Children's TV, 1975-79; editorial cons.various jours.; contbr. articles to profl. jours. Danforth fellow, 1959-63; Gen. Motors scholar, 1955-59. Mem. Am. Psychol. Soc., Internat. Soc. Rsch. on Emotion, Soc. Experimental Social Psychology, New Eng. Psychol. Assn., Soc. Kent and Danforth Fellows, Sigma Xi, Phi Beta kappa. Home: 6207 Moore Hall Hanover NH 03755-3578 Office: Dartmouth Coll Dept Of Psychology Hanover NH 03755 Office Phone: 603-646-2056. Business E-Mail: r.kleck@dartmouth.edu.

KLECKER, BEVERLY MCCAULEY, academic administrator; d. Franklin James and Dorothy (Camden) McCauley. PhD, Ohio State U., 1996. Lic. Profl. Clin. Counselor Ky., 2005. Grad. rsch. assoc. Ohio State U., Columbus, Ohio, 1992—95; asst. prof. Ea. Ky. U., Richmond, Ky., 1996—99. Rschr., evaluator, grants Morehead State U., Morehead, Ky., 2001—. Ky. rep. Mid-South Ednl. Rsch. Assn., Gatlinburg, Tenn., 2003—05; bd. mem. Cath. Social Svcs., Columbus, Ohio, 1987—90. Recipient Outstanding Dissertation, Phi Delta Kappa, 1996. Office: Morehead State U 503 Ginger Hall Morehead KY 40313 Office Phone: 606-783-2536.

KLECKNER, ROBERT GEORGE, JR., retired lawyer; b. Reading, Pa., Mar. 14, 1932; s. Robert George and Elizabeth (Endlich) K.; m. Carol Espie, June 15, 1955; children: Anthony Savage, Susan Duffield. BA, Yale U., 1954; LLB, U. Pa., 1959. Bar: Pa. 1960, NY 1964. Pvt. practice, Reading, 1960-63; assoc. Sullivan & Cromwell, NYC, 1963-70; house counsel Goldman, Sachs & Co., NYC, 1970-78; cons. NYC, 1978-80; house counsel Johnson & Higgins, NYC, 1980-97; sr. atty. legal dept. Marsh & McLennan Cos., Inc., NYC, 1997; ret., 1997. 1st lt. USAR, 1955-57, Korea. Mem. ABA, Assn. Bar City of NY, Berks County Bar Assn., Union Club, Univ. Club, Mill Reef Club, Phi Beta Kappa. Republican. Lutheran. Home: 80 East End Ave New York NY 10028-8004

KLECZKA, GERALD DANIEL, former congressman; b. Milwaukee, Wis., Nov. 26, 1943; s Harry J. and Agnes P. (Dusza) Kleczka; m. Bonnie L. Scott, 1978. Ed., U. Wis., Milw. Mem. Wis. Assembly, 1968-74; mem. Wis. Senate, 1974-84, U.S. Congress from 4th Wis. dist., Washington, 1984—2005. Mem. ways and means com., ways and means health subcom., house budget com. Mem. Wis. Dem. Com., Milwaukee County Dem. Com. With Air N.G., 1963-69. Mem. LaFarge Lifelong Learning Inst., Thomas More Found., Polish Nat. Alliance-Milw. Soc., Polish Am. Congress. Democrat.

KLEE, CAROL ANNE, foreign language educator; b. Royal Oak, Mich., Sept. 6, 1953; d. Lewis Emil and Anne Perna (Marino) K.; m. Luis Alberto Ramos-García, Dec. 30, 1987; 1 child, Camille Anne Ramos-Klee. BA, Coll. Wooster, 1975; MA, U. Tex., 1980, PhD, 1984. Rsch. asst. S.W. Ednl. Devel. Lab., Austin, Tex., 1980-83; asst. prof. U. Ill., Urbana-Champaign, 1983-85, U. Minn., Mpls., 1985-90, assoc. prof., 1990—. Co-author: Lingüística aplicada: la adquisición del español como segunda lengua, 2003; editor: Sociolinguistics of the Spanish Speaking World, 1991, Faces in a Crowd: The Individual Learner in Mulisection Courses, 1994; editor Hispanic Linguistics, 1988-95; contbr. articles to profl. jours. Mem. MLA, Am. Coun. on the Tchg. Fgn. Langs., Am. Assn. U. Suprs., Coords. and Dirs. Lang. Programs (pres. 1996-97), Am. Assn. Tchrs. Spanish and Portuguese (exec. coun. 1994-96), Minn. Coun. on the Tchg. Fgn. Langs. (adv. bd. 1986-88, Emma Birkmaier award 1997), Phi Beta Kappa. Office: U Minn Dept Spanish & Portuguese 34 Folwell Hall Minneapolis MN 55455 Office Phone: 612-625-9521. Business E-Mail: klee@umn.edu.

KLEE, CLAUDE BLENC, medical researcher; MD, U. Marsailles, France, 1959. Chief lab. chemistry, chief protein biochemistry sect. Nat. Cancer Inst., 1974—. Recipient Women's Excellence in Scis. award, Fedn. Am. Soc. for Exptl. Biology, 1997. Fellow: AAAS; mem.: Inst. Medicine, Nat. Acad. Sci. Office: Nat Cancer Inst-Biochem Lab 9000 Rockville Pike Bethesda MD 20892-0001*

KLEE, VICTOR LA RUE, mathematician, educator; b. San Francisco, Sept. 18, 1925; s. Victor La Rue and Mildred (Muller) K.; BA, Pomona Coll., 1945, DSc (hon.), 1965; PhD, U. Va., 1949; Dr. honoris causa, U. Liège, Belgium, 1984, U. Trier, Germany, 1995. Asst. prof. U. Va., 1949-53; NRC fellow Inst. for Advanced Study, 1951-52; asst. prof. U. Wash., Seattle, 1953-54, assoc. prof., 1954-57, prof. math., 1957-97, adj. prof. computer sci., 1974—98, prof. applied math., 1976-84; prof. emeritus, 1998—. Vis. asso. prof. UCLA, 1955-56; vis. prof. U. Colo., 1971, U. Victoria, 1975, U. Western Australia, 1979; cons. IBM Watson Research Center, 1972; cons. to industry; mem. Math. Scis. Research Inst., 1985-86; sr. fellow Inst. for Math. and its Applications, 1987. Co-author: Combinatorial Geometry in the Plane, 1963, Old and New Unsolved Problems in Plane Geometry and Number Theory, 1991, Convex Polytopes, 2003; contbr. more than 200 articles to profl. jours. Recipient Rsch. prize U. Va., 1952, Vollum award for disting. accomplishment in sci. and tech. Reed Coll., 1982, David Prescott Burrows Outstanding Disting. Achievement award Pomona Coll., 1988, Max Planck rsch. prize, 1992; NSF sr. postdoctoral fellow, Sloan Found. fellow U. Copenhagen, 1958-60, fellow Ctr. Advanced Study in Behavioral Scis., 1975-76, Guggenheim fellow, Humboldt award U. Erlangen-Nürnberg, 1980-81, Fulbright fellow U. Trier, 1992. Fellow AAAS (chmn. sect. A 1975), Am. Acad. Arts and Scis.; mem. Am. Math. Soc. (assoc. sec. 1955-58, mem. exec. com. 1969-70), Math. Assn. Am. (pres. 1971-73, L.R. Ford award 1972, Disting. Svc. award 1977, C.B. Allendoerfer award 1980, 99), Soc. Indsl. and Applied Math. (mem. coun. 1966-68), Internat. Linear Algebra Soc., Phi Beta Kappa, Sigma Xi (nat. lectr. 1969). Home: 13706 39th Ave NE Seattle WA 98125-3810 Office: U Wash Dept Math PO Box 354350 Seattle WA 98195-4350 Office Phone: 206-363-1850. E-mail: jmklee@worldnet.att.net.

KLEEBLATT, NORMAN L., museum curator; AB in Art History, Rutgers U., 1971; diploma in conservation, MA, NYU, 1975. Conservator The Jewish Mus., N.Y.C., 1975-80, curator collections/conservator, 1981-87, curator collections, 1987-94, Susan and Elihu Rose curator fine arts, 1995—. Mem. sci. coun. Mus. Art and History of Judaism; cons. Montclair (N.J.) Art Mus., 1975. Author: An Expressionist in Paris: the Paintings of Chaim Soutine, 1988; co-author: Treasures of the Jewish Museum, 1986; contbg. author: Gonn Mosny: Atmen und Malen, 1989, Pre-Raphaelite Art in its European Context, 1995, L'Affaire Dreyfus de A & Z: histoire et dictionnaire, 1994, L'Affaire Dreyfus et l'opinion publique en France et à l'étranger, 1995, Diaspora and Modern Visual Culture: Representing African and Jewish Diaspora, 1998; editor: The Dreyfus Affair, 1987; (catalogue) Mirroring Evil: Nazi Imagery/Recent Art, 2001; co-editor: Painting a Place in America, 1991; exhibits include The Paintings of Moritz Daniel Oppenheim: Jewish Life in 19th Century Germany, 1981, Too Jewish? Challenging Traditional Identities, 1996, Mirroring Evil: Nazi Imagery/Recent Art, 2002; reviewer in field. Recipient Hon. Mention, Henry Allen Moe Prize, 1985, 88, Nat. Jewish Book award, 1992, Second prize Henry Allen Moe Prize, 1992, Présidence d'honneur Com. Sci. Soc. Internat. d'Histoire de l'Affaire Dreyfus, 1994—; post-grad. fellow Nat. Mus. Fellowship Act, 1975-76; fellow mus. profls. Nat. Endowment Arts, 1996. Mem. Internat. Assn. Art Critics (Am. sect.), Am. Assn. Mus., Coll. Art Assn. Office: The Jewish Mus 1109 5th Ave New York NY 10128-0118

KLEEMAN, CHARLES RICHARD, medical educator, nephrologist, researcher; b. L.A., Aug. 19, 1923; m. 1945; 3 children. BS, U. Calif., 1944, MD, 1947. Rotating intern San Francisco City Hosp., 1947-48; asst. resident pathology Mallory Inst.-Boston City Hosp., 1948-49; resident in medicine Newington VA Hosp., 1949-51; from instr. to asst. prof. metabolism Yale U. Sch. Medicine, 1953-56; assoc. prof. UCLA Sch. Medicine, 1956—60, prof. medicine Cedars-Sinai Med Ctr., 1961—72, prof., dir. dept. internal medicine, 1972—94, prof. emeritus, 1994—. Nephrologist VA Med. Ctr., West L.A., 1993—; prof. medicine, dept. chief Hadassah Med. Sch.-Hebrew U., Israel, 1972-75; vis. prof. Beilinson Hosp.-Tel Aviv U., 1968, St. Francis Hosp., Honolulu, 1968, U. Queensland, 1966; chief metabolic sect. VA Hosp., L.A. 1956-60, cons., 1962—; chief metabolic sect. Wadsworth VA Med. Ctr., L.A., 1956-60. Upjohn-Endocrine Soc. scholar U. London, 1960-61. Mem. AMA, Am. Physiol. Soc., Inst. Medicine-NAS, Am. Soc. Clin. Investigation, Endocrine Soc., Am. Assn. Physicians. Office: VAMC West LA Med Divsn Nephr W111L, 11301 Wilshire Blvd Los Angeles CA 90073 Business E-Mail: ckleeman@ucla.edu.

KLEES, JULIA ELENA, physician; b. Phila., Jan. 7, 1961; d. Athanasius C. and Katherine E. Klees. BA, Lehigh U., Bethlehem, Pa., 1982; MD, Hahnemann U., Phila., 1984; MPH, U. Calif., Berkeley, 1989. Diplomate Am. Bd. Internal Medicine, Am. Bd. Occupl. Medicine. Resident Mayo Grad. Sch. Medicine, Rochester, Minn., 1984-87; fellow U. Calif., San Francisco, 1987-89; med. dir. occupl. health svc. Albert Einstein Med. Ctr., Phila., 1989-91; asst. prof. medicine Jefferson Med. Coll., Phila., 1991-95; assoc. corp. med. dir. BASF Corp., Rockaway, NJ, 1995—. Contbr. articles to profl. jours. Fellow Am. Coll. Occupl. and Environ. Medicine (del. 1993-95); mem. AMA, APHA, Am. Coll. Physicians, Am. Med. Women's Assn. Office: BASF Corp 333 Mount Hope Ave Rockaway NJ 07866

KLEESPIES, GAVIN W., historian; b. Cambridge, Mass., Jan. 28, 1975; s. Philip M. and Penelope M. Kleespies. BA, Bard Coll., 1996; MA, U. Chgo., 1999. Editl. asst. Hudson Valley Regional Rev., Annandale, NY, 1994—96; archival asst. Cambridge (Mass.) Hist. Commn., 1996—98, curatorial asst., 1997—98; exec. dir. Mt. Prospect (Ill.) Hist. Soc., 1999—. Author: Images of America, Mount Prospect, 2003. Avocation: furniture design and construction. Office Phone: 847-392-9006. E-mail: kleespiesmedist@wowown.com.

KLEFFNER, GREGORY WILLIAM, retail executive, accountant; b. St. Louis, Nov. 21, 1954; s. Francis R. and Charlotte P. (Petersen) Kleffner; m. Renee A. Drake, June 10, 1993; children: Patricia Elaine, Laura Elizabeth, Michael Gregory. BSBA, Washington U., 1977. Staff Arthur Andersen & Co., St. Louis, 1977-79, sr. acct., 1979-81, mgr. to ptnr. and head audit dept., 1981—2002; v.p., controller Kellwood Co., St. Louis, 2002—, corp. officer and v.p. finance, 2005—. Bd. mem. Grand Center, Inc., St. Louis County Industrial Develop. Authority, St. Louis County Business Finance Co. Mem. Am. Inst. CPA's, Mo. Soc. CPA's, St. Louis County Econ. Devel. Assn. (loan rev. com. 1986-87), Am. Y-Flyer Yacht Racing Assn. (sec.-treas 1984—). Avocations: sailing, golf. Office: Kellwood Co 600 Kellwood Parkway Chesterfield MO 63017 Business E-Mail: gregkleffner@kellwood.com.

KLEIDON, AXEL, geographer, educator; b. Hamburg, Germany, Apr. 16, 1969; m. Ma-Li G. Kleidon; children: Maximilian, Sophie. BSc in Physics, U. Hamburg, Germany, 1992, PhD, 1998; MSc in Physics, Purdue U., 1994. Post doctoral scientist Stanford (Calif.) U., 1998—2000; asst. prof. U. Md., College Park, 2001—. Editor: Non-Equilibrium Thermodynamics and The Production of Entropy: Life, Earth, and Beyond, 2005. Office: Univ Md Dept Geography 2181 Lefrak Hall College Park MD 20742 Office Phone: 301-405-3203. Office Fax: 301-314-9299. E-mail: akleidon@umd.edu.

KLEIM, E. DENISE, city official; BA in Econs. cum laude, San Jose State U., 1975; MBA, Willamette U., 1982. Mgmt. asst. Urban Renewal Agy. City of Salem, Oreg., 1976-78, grant adminstr. dept. cmty. devel., 1978-80, asst. to dir. dept. cmty. devel., 1981-84, lobbyist, 1980-83; sr. mgmt. analyst Bur. Bldgs., City of Portland, Oreg., 1984-86, adminstrv. mgr., 1986-99, mgr. adminstrv. svcs. bur. devel. svcs., 1999—. V.p. Montclair After Sch. Care Assn., Portland, 1995-96; mem. Atkinson Soc., Salem, 1995-97. Office: City of Portland Bur Devel Svc 1120 SW 5th Ave Portland OR 97204-1912

KLEIMAN, ALAN BOYD, artist; b. Bklyn., Feb. 20, 1938; s. Louis and Alfreda (Belowsky) K.; m. Audrey Barbara Code, Feb. 9, 1963; 1 dau., Andrea Kristin. B.F.A., Va. Commonwealth U., 1951; M.F.A., Cranbrook Acad. Art, 1953. Asst. publicity dir. Artist Tenents Assn., 1960-67; v.p. Grand St. Artist Group, 1970-75; chmn. Soho Artifacts, 1971-75. Author: Painting Provincetown Water, 1961, Investigations into the Light of Red Color, 1968, Light, Dazzle and Glow, 1970; one-man show includes Elizabeth Harris Gallery, N.Y.C., 1995, Ohara Gallery, N.Y.C., 1996, Robert Steel Gallery, N.Y.C., 1997, 2003, 04, Kouros Gallery, N.Y.C., 2000; group shows include Nexus Gallery, Boston, 1959, Betty Parsons Gallery, N.Y.C., 1961, 79, Sun Gallery, 1962, New Gallery, Provincetown, Mass., 1961-62, Marino, N.Y.C., 1966, Warren Benedek, N.Y.C., 1972, Landmark Gallery, N.Y.C., 1975-76, Renaissance Soc., Chgo., 1979, Art U.S.A. '80, U.S., Can., Sweden, Siegel Gallery, N.Y.C., 1983, Michael Walls Gallery, N.Y.C., 1989, Robert Steel Gallery, N.Y.C., 1997; represented in permanent collections Mus. Modern Art, Whitney Mus., Am. Arts, Met. Mus. Art, N.Y.C., Carnegie Mus., Pitts., Boston Mus. Fine Arts, William Patterson Coll., Wayne, N.J.; 169 self portraits at Clocktower, N.Y.C., 1985—; retrospective 1960-86 at P.S.I., N.Y.C., 1986. Served with U.S. Army, 1953-55. Recipient 1st prize Boston Arts Festival, 1954; N.Y. State Council Arts grantee, 1977-78; Curtral Council Found. awardee, 1978; grantee Esther and Adolph Gottleib Found., 1985, Pollack-Krasner Found., 1987, NEH, 1989-90. Mem. Theatre of Artists League (v.p. 1972), Orgn. Ind. Artists, Am. Abstract Artists, Nat. Endowment for Arts. *My creative drive has at times thrived on procrastination, anger, jealousy, rage, talent and plain hard work. Balancing emotion and intelligence make the tension expressed in my painting. I want to make more and better art.*

KLEIMAN, BERNARD, lawyer; b. Chgo., Jan. 26, 1928; s. Isidore and Pearl (Wikoff) Kleiman; m. Gloria Baime, Nov. 15, 1986; children: Leslie, David. BS, Purdue U., 1951; JD, Northwestern U., 1954. Bar: Ill. 1954. Practice law in assn. with Abraham W. Brussell, 1957-60; dist. counsel United Steel Workers Am., 1960-65, spl. counsel, 1997—, gen. counsel, 1965-97; ptnr. Kleiman, Cornfield & Feldman, Chgo., 1960-75; prin. B. Kleiman (P.C.), 1976-77, Kleiman, Whitney, Wolfe & Elfenbaum, P.C., 1978-99. Mem. collective bargaining coms. for nat. labor negotiations in basic steel, tire mfg., and shipbuilding industries. Contbr. articles to legal jours. Served with U.S. Army, 1946—48. Mem.: ABA, Allegheny County Bar Assn. Office Phone: 412-562-2305.

KLEIMAN, GARY HOWARD, broadcast, advertising and cellular communications consultant; b. Phila., Jan. 24, 1952; s. Leon and Martha (Rubin) K.; m. Annette Suzanne Vranich, Sept. 23, 1978; children: Aaron Jay, Jared Adam. Diploma, Am. Acad. Broadcasting, Phila., 1969, Pa. State Fire Sch., Media, 1969; BS, Temple U., 1972. Cert. radio mktg. cons., Radio Advt. Bur., NYC. Gen. mgr. Sta. WFEC, Harrisburg, Pa., 1974-75; local sales mgr. Sta. WYSP-FM, Phila., 1976-79; pres. A.S.K. Advt., King Prussia, Pa., 1976-80; v.p., gen. mgr. Sta. WGLU-FM, Johnstown, 1980-82, Sta. WAJE, Edensburg, Pa., 1982-84, Sta. WSBY-WQHQ-AM-FM, Salisbury, Md., 1984-86; mgr. Sta. WJDY, Salisbury, 1986-87; pres. IDEAS Unltd. Mktg. and Advt. Co., Salisbury, 1986—; gen. mgr. Sta. WACS-FM, Schenectady, 1988-89; v.p., gen. mgr. Sta. WDLE-FM, Federalsburg, Md., 1989-91; area mgr. Bell Atlantic Mobile Sys., 1992—93; pres. CellComm Mobile/Cellular One, 1993—; gen. mgr. Shore-Trade Exchange, LLC, 2005—. Media cons. Sta. WMDT-TV, Salisbury, 1988; dir., tchr. Am. Acad. Broadcasting, Phila., 1976-79 Contbr. articles to profl. publs. Com. chmn. Salisbury Revitalization, 1984—; mem. Bennett Mid. Sch. Parents, Tchrs., Students Assn., pres., 1994-95; bd. dirs. Salisbury Regional Urban Design Action Team, 1984-89, Deers Head Hosp. Found., Am. Heart Assn.; co-sponsor projects Lower Shore Easter Seals, Salisbury, 1985, Am. Cancer Soc., 1984-85, Kidney Found., 1985, Epilepsy Assn., 1985, Johnstown Area Regional Industries, 1981-84; promotion coord. Salisbury Festival com., 1985, 87-91, vice chmn., 1985-90; exec. com. Lower Shore chpt. March Dimes, 1984-89; scout leader Boy Scouts Am., 1988-90; adult leader 4-H, 1988-2001; mgr. area Little League; active campaigner Cambria County Dem. Com., 1982-84, Wicomico County Dem. Com., 1991-2004. Squadron comms. officer, pub. affairs officer, air crew ground team search rescue MDWG USAF aux./CAP, 1997-2003; adv. bd. Wicomico Mentoring Project, 1994-2004, co-chair, 1996-2001, chmn. 2000-01; vice chmn. bd. dirs. Jr. Achievement, 2000-01; mem. Cmty. Emergency Response Team, 2004— Recipient numerous awards from local civic orgns., 1981—. Mem. Downtown Salisbury Assn. (bd. dirs., v.p. 1997-98, pres. 1999-00), Fruitland C. of C. (bd. dirs. 1996-2000, v.p. 1999-2000), Salisbury Area C. of C. (bd. dirs. 1989-92, 98-2001), Caroline County C. of C. (bd. dirs. 1989), Salisbury Jaycees (Springboard award 1985), Johnstown Jaycees, Salisbury State U. Athletic Club (pres. 1985), Tall Timber Park Assn. (pres. 1992-94). Democrat. Jewish. Avocations: photography, camping, skiing, softball, volleyball. Home: 115 Tall Timber Ln Fruitland MD 21826-1318 Office: CellComm Mobile Ste 103 City Ctr on Plaza Salisbury MD 21801 also: IDEAS Unltd Broadcast Cons City Center Ste 103 Salisbury MD 21801 Office Phone: 410-546-0500. Personal E-mail: gkleimancap@yahoo.com. E-mail: phoneman@cellcomm-mobile.com. *To me success is not measured in money, it's measured in how others perceive you in your community. To me, a business day starts at 7:30 and ends when all of my clients and customers are happy and all problems have been solved.*

KLEIN, ANA MARIA V., mathematics professor; arrived in US, 2000, arrived in U.S., 2000; d. Nicholas Klein and Klara Unger; m. Tito Graffe, Dec. 1, 1971; 3 children. BA in Modern Langs., Met. U.; MA in Ednl. Psychology; D, McGill U., Montreal, Can., 2000. Asst. prof. SUNY, Fredonia, 2001—. Author: Children's Math Problem Solving, 2004, Cultural Awareness in Higher Education, 2005. Mem.: Nat. Assn. Math. Edn., Tchg. English Rsch. Other Langs., Am. Edn. Rsch. Assn. Avocations: swimming, reading, writing. Office: SUNY Fredonia E 242 Thompson Fredonia NY 14063 Home: 70 Greco Ln. #52 D Dunkirk NY 14048 Mailing: 645 Prince Arthur W 7 Montreal H2X 1T9 Canada

KLEIN, ANDREW MANNING, lawyer; b. New Rochelle, N.Y., Dec. 28, 1941; s. Arthur Manning and Ethelyn (Lappe) K.; m. Christine DeBow, Mar. 14, 1970 (div. Aug. 1990); children: Emily DeBow, Adrienne Manning; m. Mary Manning, Apr. 4, 1992. AB, U. Chgo., 1963, JD, 1966. Bar: N.Y. 1967, D.C. 1980. Assoc. Lovejoy, Wasson, Lundgren & Ashton, N.Y.C., 1966-73; spl. counsel Office of Market Structure, 1973-74, asst. dir. Office of Market Structure and Trading Practices, 1974-75, assoc. dir. Office of Market Structure and Trading Practices, 1975-77, dir. Div. Market Regulation, SEC, Washington, 1977-79; ptnr. Schiff Hardin & Waite, Chgo., 1979-81, Washington, 1981—. Mem. adv. bd. Securities Regulation and Law Report, Bur. Nat. Affairs; contbr. articles to legal jours. With USNG, 1966-67. Mem. ABA (subcom. market regulation, co-chmn. task force on manipulation), Fed. Bar Assn. (exec. coun. securities com.), George Town Club (Washington), University Club (Washington). Office: Schiff Hardin & Waite 1101 Connecticut Ave NW Ste 600 Washington DC 20036-4390

KLEIN, ARNOLD SPENCER, lawyer; b. N.Y.C., Mar. 10, 1951; s. Paul and Ethel (Cooper) K.; m. Arlene Sandra Feinberg, Aug. 14, 1977; children: Jeffrey Daniel, Rachel Pauli. BA, SUNY, Stony Brook, 1974; JD cum laude, N.Y. Law Sch., 1977. Bar: N.Y. 1978, Fla. 1984, U.S. Dist. Ct. (so. and ea. dists.) N.Y., U.S. Dist. Ct. (so. dist.) Fla., U.S. Ct. Appeals (2d cir.), U.S. Supreme Ct. Mem. Kelley, Drye & Warren, N.Y.C., 1977-85, ptnr., 1986-94, Meltzer, Lippe & Goldstein, LLP, Mineola, NY, 1994—2004; atty. The Law Offices of Kenneth Koopersmith, LLC, Garden City, NY, 2004—. Mem. ABA, N.Y. State Bar Assn., Nassau County Bar Assn. Office: Law Offices of Kenneth Koopersmith LLC 200 Garden City Plz Garden City NY 11530 Office Phone: 516-354-0800. Business E-Mail: akleinesq@hotmail.com.

KLEIN, ARNOLD WILLIAM, dermatologist; b. Mt. Clemens, Mich., Feb. 27, 1945; s. David Klein; m. Malvina Kraemer. BA, U. Pa., 1967, MD, 1971. Intern Cedars-Sinai Med. Ctr., L.A., 1971—72; resident in dermatology Hosp. U. Pa., Phila., 1972—73, UCLA, 1973—75; pvt. practice Beverly Hills, Calif., 1975—. Prof. dermatology/medicine U. Calif. Ctr. Health Scis.; mem. med. staff Cedars-Sinai Med. Ctr.; asst. clin. prof. dermatology Stanford U., 1982—89; from asst. clin. to prof. dermatology/medicine UCLA, trustee David Geffen Sch. Medicine, 2003—; mem. adv. bd. Botox, Allergan Inc.; retained cons., investigator Elan Pharms.; cons., investigator Inamed Aesthetics, Q-Med, Medicis, Skin-Medica, Ortho-Neutrogena; presenter seminars in field. Assoc. editor: Jour. Dermatologic Surgery and Oncology, reviewer: Jour. Sexually Transmitted Diseases, Jour. Am. Acad. Dermatology; mem. editl. bd. Men's Fitness mag., Shape mag., Archives Dermatology; contbr. articles to profl. jours. Mem. CAlif. State Adv. Com. Malpractice, 1983—89; med. adv. bd. Skin Cancer Found., Lupus Found. Am.; founder R. Tarlow/Dr. Arnold Klein Fund Breast Cancer Treatment. Mem.: AFTRA, AMA, Am. found. AIDS Rsch. (founder, bd. dirs.), Soc. Cosmetic Chemists, Am. Venereal Disease Assn., Jennifer Jones Simon Found. (trustee), Hereditary Disease Found. (bd. dirs.), Discovery Fund Eye Rsch. (bd. dirs.), Lupus Found., Internat. Psoriasis Rsch. Inst., Scleroderma Found., Dermatology Found., Am. Acad. Dermatology, Met. Dermatology Soc., Am. Coll. Chemosurgery, LA Med. Assn., Assn. Sci. Advisors, Am. Assn. Cosmetic Surgeons, Internat. Soc. Dermatologic Surgery, Am. Soc. Dermatologic Surgery, Calif. Med. Assn., Children's Mus. LA (founder), Dance Gallery LA (founder), LA Mus. Contemporary Art (founder), Friars Club, Delphos, Phi Beta Kappa, Sigma Tau Sigma. Office: 435 N Roxbury Dr Ste 204 Beverly Hills CA 90210-5004 Office Phone: 310-275-5136. Personal E-mail: awkleinmd1@aol.com. *The sincerest form of respect is trust. Being a Physician is all about serving this trust. Also, it is about dedication, observation, obsession and creative intelligence. Who and what I am...where I begin and where I end...is all about being a physician.*

KLEIN, BARBARA A., information technology executive; BS, Marquette U.; MBA, Loyola U., Chgo., 1977. CPA. Former exec. Pillsbury, Sears, Roebuck and Co.; former v.p., corp. contr. Ameritech Corp.; former v.p. fin., CFO Dean Foods Co.; sr. v.p., CFO CDW Computer Ctrs., Vernon Hills, Ill., 2002—. Mem.: AICPA. Office: CDW 200 N Milwaukee Ave Vernon Hills IL 60061

KLEIN, BENJAMIN, economics professor, consultant; b. N.Y.C., Jan. 29, 1943; s. Hyman and Beartha (Kristel) K.; m. Lynne Schneider; children: Franz, Emily, Amanda. ABA in Philosophy, Bklyn. Coll., 1964; MA in Econs., U. Chgo., 1967, PhD in Econs., 1970. Asst. prof. UCLA, 1968-72, assoc. prof., 1973-78, prof. econs., 1978—; faculty rsch. fellow Nat. Bur. Econs., N.Y.C., 1971-72, rsch. assoc., 1976-77; pres. Econ. Analysis Corp., L.A., 1980—2004; dir Law and Econs. Consulting Group, 2004—. Vis. prof. U. Wash., Seattle, 1978; cons. FTC, Washington, 1976-86, bd. govs. FRS, Washington, 1973-75. Contbr. articles to profl. jours. Ford Found. fellow, 1967-68, Scaiffe Found. fellow, 1975-76, Law and Econs. fellow U. Chgo. Law Sch., 1979; grantee Sloan Found., 1981-87; recipient ann. prize for disting. scholarship in law and econs. U. Miami Law and Econ. Ctr., 1978-79, ann. award for best articles Western Econ. Assn., 1979. Mem. Am. Econs. Assn. Office: UCLA Dept Econs 405 Hilgard Ave Los Angeles CA 90095-9000 Office Phone: 310-556-0709. Business E-Mail: bklein@lecg.com.

KLEIN, BENJAMIN GARRETT, mathematics professor, consultant; b. Durham, N.C., Jan. 24, 1942; s. James Raymond and Lenetta Mae (Garrett) K.; m. Rosemary Therese McAndrew, June 19, 1971; children: David Garrett, Peter Raymond. BA, U. Rochester, 1963; MA, Yale U., 1965, PhD, 1968. Lectr., asst. prof. NYU, N.Y.C., 1967-71; asst. prof. to prof. math. Davidson Coll., N.C., 1971—, vice chmn. faculty, 1985-88, appt. Dana prof. math., 1990-93, appt. Dolan prof. math., 1993—, chair dept. math., 1994-98, mem. advanced placement calculus devel. com., 1999—2003. Cons. N.C. Dept. Pub. Instrn., Raleigh, 1981-85, 90—. Mem. editl. bd. The Coll. Math. Jour. Elder Davidson Coll. Presbyterian Ch., 1981-83, 87-89, 94-96. Named N.C. Prof. of Yr., Coun. Advancement and Support of Edn., 1991; recipient Thomas Jefferson award, 1990;, 1990, Hunter-Hamilton Love of Tchg. award, 2004. Mem.: N.C. Assn. Advanced Placement Math. Tchrs., N.C. Coun. Tchrs. Math., Nat. Coun. Tchrs. Math., Math. Assn. Am. (chair S.E. sect. 1993—95, gov. S.E. sect. 2003—), Am. Math. Soc. Democrat. Office: Davidson Coll PO Box 6937 Davidson NC 28035-6937 Office Phone: 704-894-2318. Business E-Mail: beklein@davidson.edu.

KLEIN, BERNARD, publishing company executive; b. N.Y.C., Sept. 20, 1921; s. Joseph J. and Anna (Wolfe) K.; m. Betty Stecher, Feb. 17, 1946; children: Cheryl Rona, Barry Todd, Cindy Ann. BA, CCNY, 1942. Founder, pres. U.S. List Co., Boca Raton, Fla., 1946—; founder, pres., chief editor B. Klein Publs., Delray Beach, Fla., 1953—. Cons. direct mail advt. and reference book pub. to pubs., industry, 1950— Author: all biennials Ency. of American Indian, 1954—; Guide to American Directories. Served with AUS, 1942-45, ETO. Mem. Direct Mail Advt. Assn. Lodges: Masons. Home: 12727 Coral Lakes Dr Boynton Beach FL 33437-4143 Office Phone: 561-496-3316.

KLEIN, CALVIN RICHARD, fashion designer; b. N.Y.C., Nov. 19, 1942; s. Leo and Flore (Stern) K.; m. Jayne Centre, Apr. 26, 1964 (div. 1974); 1 dau., Marci; m. Kelly Rector, Sept. 1986 (div. 1996). AA, Fashion Inst. Tech., 1962. Founder, pres., designer Calvin Klein Ltd., N.Y.C., 1968—2003; sold company to Phillips-Vanteusen, 2003. Critic Parsons Sch. Design; critic, cons. Fashion Inst. Tech.; launched fragrance lines for men and women, Obsession, Eternity, Escape, Contradiction, Truth Calvin Klein. Recipient Coty award, 1973, 74, 75, Woolmark award for Career Achievement, 1987, FIT Pres. award, 2002; named Outstanding Am. talent in women's fashion design Coun. Fashion Designers of Am., 1982, 83, 86, America's 25 Most Influential People, Time, Womenswear/Menswear Designer of the Year, Coun. Fashion Designers of Am., 1993. Mem. Council Fashion Designers, Mus. Modern Art, Met. Mus. Art, Whitney Mus., Guggenheim Mus. Office: Calvin Klein Inc 205 W 39th St 4 New York NY 10018-3102 Address: Calvin Klein Europe Via Montenapoleone 29 20121 Milano Italy

KLEIN, CHARLOTTE CONRAD, public relations executive; b. Detroit, June 20, 1923; d. Joseph and Bessie (Brown) K. BA, UCLA, 1945. Corr. UPI, Los Angeles, 1945-46; staff writer CBS, Los Angeles, 1946-47; publicist David O. Selznick Studios, Culver City, Calif., 1947-49, Foladare and Assocs., Los Angeles, 1949-51; publicist to v.p. Edward Gottlieb & Assocs., N.Y.C., 1951-62; v.p. to sr. v.p. Harshe Rotman & Druck, N.Y.C., 1962-78; dir. press/govt. affairs Sta. WNET-TV, N.Y.C., 1978-79; pres. Charlotte C. Klein Assocs., N.Y.C., 1979-84; sr. v.p., group supr. Porter Novelli, N.Y.C., 1984-89; prin. Charlotte Klein Assocs., N.Y.C., 1989—. Adj. prof. pub. rels. NYU; bd. dirs. U.S. Trademark Assn., 1959-62, Am. Arbitration Assn., 1970-80 (exec. com. 1980-82); mem. adv. bd. Coll. and Cmty. Fellowship Grad. Ctr., CUNY, 2002—; cons. Ctr. for Advancement of Women, 2003-04. Contbr. articles to profl. jours. Bd. dirs. Manhattan chpt. Am. Cancer Soc., 1988-92. Recipient Cine Golden Eagle, 1977, Matrix award Women in Comms., 1975, Honor award Coll. and Cmty. Fellowship, 2004, Keeper of the Flame award Nat. Women's Hall of Fame, 2005. Mem. Pub. Rels. Soc. Am. (accredited; pres. N.Y. chpt. 1985-86, Silver Anvil award 1978, John Hill award 1988), Women's Forum (bd. dirs. N.Y. chpt. 1986-87, 96-98), Internat. Women's Forum (leadership com. chair dialogue for democracy 1993-98, co-chair task force on violence against women globally, 1998-2001), Women Execs. in Pub. Rels. (pres. 1965). Avocations: painting, stamp collecting/philately. E-mail: kleintravis@earthlink.net.

KLEIN, CHARLOTTE FEUERSTEIN, art consultant; b. Stoneham, Mass., June 3, 1931; d. Harold and Esther B. (Franks) Feuerstein; m. Philipp Hillel Klein, June 21, 1953; children— Joshua David, Daniel William, Jonathan Henry. BS, Boston U., 1953. Tchr. pub. schs., Scotia, Schenectady, Niscayuna, NY, 1953-56, Newton, Mass., 1974-75; ptnr., art cons. Washington Graphics, Washington, 1979-82; dir., art adviser CFK Assocs., Washington, 1982— . Mem. AAUW, AFI Silver Theatre and Cultural Ctr., Washington Opera Soc., The Phillips Collection, Friends of Kennedy Ctr., Washington, Nat. Symphony Orch. Assn., Holocaust Mus., Textile Mus., Washington, Corcoran Gallery Art, Smithsonian Assn. Mem. Nat. Bldg. Mus.

KLEIN, CHUCK, retired private investigator, writer; b. Cin., 1942; s. Charles H. and Ruth Emily Klein; m. Annette Margolis Levine, Aug. 18, 1996; children: Trey, Jay, Todd, Amy, Brad. LLB, Blackstone Law Sch., 1972. Cert. police officer, Ohio; cert. fire fighter, Ind.; cert. firearms instr. NRA; lic. pvt. investigator; cert. instinct shooting instr. Tactical Def. Inst., Ohio. Firearms editor P.I. Mag., Toledo, Ohio, 1988—. Author: (fiction) Circa 1957, 1990, (non-fiction) Instinct Combat Shooting, 1986, Klein's Firearm Manual, 1997, Klein's C.C.W. Handbook, 1998, (fiction) The Power of God, 1999, (non-fiction) Lines of Defense, 2000, (fiction) The Way it Was, 2003. Mem. Am. Soc. Law Enforcement Trainers, Internat. Assn. Law Enforcement Firearms Instrs., Fairfield Sportsman Assn., Kiwanis Club of Cin. (pres. 2002-03). Avocations: golf, skeet.

KLEIN, CYNTHIA, art appraiser; BA in Art Hist., BS in Bus. Adminstrn., Mktg. with honors, Univ. Mass., Amherst; grad studies in Art Hist., Rutgers Univ. Specialist, paintings dept. to dir., prints dept. C.G. Sloan & Co. Auctioneers, N. Bethesda, Md., 1991—2000; v.p., dir., prints dept. Doyle New York, 2000—. Prints appraiser Antiques Roadshow, WGBH-PBS. Mem.: Am. Hist. Prints Collectors Soc., Soc. for Japanese Arts, Phi Beta Kappa. Office: Doyle New York 175 E 87th St New York NY 10128 Office Phone: 212-427-4141 ext. 246. Office Fax: 212-369-0892. Business E-Mail: prints@doylenewyork.com.*

KLEIN, DALE EDWARD, federal agency administrator; b. Cooper County, Mo., July 6, 1947; BS, U. Mo., 1970, MS, 1971, PhD in Nuclear Engring., 1977. Design engr. Procter & Gamble Co., 1970-72; teaching and rsch. asst. nuclear engring. U. Mo., Columbia, 1973-77; asst. prof. U. Tex., Austin, 1977-82, assoc. prof., 1982-90, prof., 1990—, dir. nuclear engring. teaching program, 1988-94, assoc. dean rsch. coll. engring.; asst. secy. for nuclear, chem. and bio. defense programs U.S. Dept. Defense, Washington, 2001—. Named Young Engr. of Yr., Travis chpt. Tex. Soc. Profl. Engring., 1982, Engr. of Yr., 1990, Tex. Engr. of Yr., 1992. Mem. ASME (Edwin F. Church award 1988, Gustus L. Larson Meml. award 1990). Achievements include research in thermal analysis of nuclear shipping containers, heat transfer augmentation for flow over rough surfaces, liquid metal flows through a packed bed under the influence of a transverse magnetic field, and nuclear waste disposal. Office: US Dept Defense Nuclear Chem and Bio Defense Programs 3150 Defense Pentagon Washington DC 20301-3150

KLEIN, DEBORAH RAE, nurse; b. Detroit, Mar. 29, 1951; d. Chester Anthony and E. Jacquelyn (Hollenbeck) Simpson; m. Robert Joseph Klein, Apr. 15, 1977; 1 child, Jeffrey. BS in Nursing, Mich. State U., 1974; MS in Health Adminstrn., U. Houston, 1984. Grad. nurse St. Mary's Hosp., Livonia, Mich., 1974; RN U.S. Army, Ft. Polk, La., 1974-78; DON Byrd Meml. Hosp., Leesville, La., 1978-79, Alvin (Tex.) Cmty. Hosp., 1979-83; adminstrn. resident Katy (Tex.) Med. Ctr., 1983-84, DON, 1984-85, COO, DON, 1985-90; v.p. Doctors' Hosp., Tulsa, 1990-97; dir. ops. improvement Okla. divsn. Columbia HCA, 1997-98; v.p., COO SouthCrest Hosp., Tulsa, Okla., 1998—2001; chief nursing officer Vaughn Regional Med. Ctr., Selma, Ala., 2002—03; dir. Tulsa Regional Med. Ctr., Tulsa, Okla., 2000—01; v.p. clin. integration Hillcrest HealthCare Sys., Tulsa, 2000—01; nurse mgr. VAMC, Salem, Va., 2003—. Cons. in field; diplomat Am. Coll. Healthcare Execs.; adj. faculty Bartlesville Wesleyan Coll., 1999-2001. Sec., treas. Sam Houston coun. Boy Scouts Am., 1984-88. Capt. U.S. Army, 1972-78. With U.S. Army Nurse Corps, 1974—78. Recipient Commendation medal, U.S. Army. Mem.: Emergency Nurses Assn. Republican. Roman Catholic. Avocations: reading, crafts. Home: 532 Santee Rd Roanoke VA 24019-4928

KLEIN, EDWARD JOEL, literature educator, writer; b. Yonkers, N.Y., Oct. 19, 1936; s. Meyer I. and Gertrude (Axelrod) K.; m. Emiko Oshikiri, June 25, 1963 (div. 1975); children: Karen, Alec; m. Tessa Namuth, Mar. 20, 1978 (div. 1981); m. Dolores Jones Barrett, Oct. 24, 1987. BS, Columbia U., 1960, MS, 1961. Copy boy, feature writer N.Y. Daily News, N.Y.C., 1957-60; reporter World Telegram & Sun, N.Y.C., 1960-61; reporter, editor Japan Times, Toyko, 1961-63; fgn. corr. UPI, Tokyo, 1963-64; editor The Shipping and Trade News, Toyko, 1964-65; assoc. editor Newsweek Mag., N.Y.C., 1965-69, fgn. editor, 1969-76, asst. mng. editor, 1976-77; editor N.Y. Times Mag., N.Y.C., 1977-87; contbg. editor Vanity Fair, N.Y.C., 1988—, Parade, N.Y.C., 1991—; columnist Walter Scott's Personality Parade, 1991—. Author: (with Robert Littell and Richard Chesnoff) If Israel Lost the War, 1969, The Parachutists, 1981, All Too Human: The Love Story of Jack and Jackie Kennedy, 1996, Just Jackie: Her Private Years, 1998, The Kennedy Curse: Why Tragedy Has Haunted America's First Family for 150 Years, 2003, Farewell, Jackie: A Portrait of Her Final Days, 2004, The Truth About Hillary: What She Knew, When She Knew It, and How Far She Will Go to Become President, 2005; editor: (with Don Erickson) About Men. Mem. Coun. on Fgn. Rels., PEN Am. Ctr., Am. Motorcyclist Assn., The Oversease Press Club N.Y. E-mail: meiji@aol.com.

KLEIN, EMILEE, professional golfer; b. Santa Monica, Calif., June 11, 1974; Student, Ariz. State U. With LPGA, 1994—; mem. U.S. Solheim Cup Team, 2002. Named two-time All-American, 1993, 94, Collegiate Player of the Year, 1994. Achievements include Winner PING/Welch's Championship, 1995, Weetabix Women's British Open, 1995; recorded four top-20 finishes in 1995; third place Rolex Rookie of the Year standings, 1995. Office: LPGA 100 International Golf Dr Daytona Beach FL 32124-1092 also: Callaway Golf 2285 Rutherford Rd Carlsbad CA 92008-8815

KLEIN, ERIC A., lawyer; b. NYC, July 3, 1959; AB, Princeton, 1981; JD, Boston U., 1985. Bar: Calif. 1986. Ptnr. corp. group, leader west coast mergers and acquisitions and securities practices Katten Muchin Zavis Rosenman, LA. Mem.: ABA (mem. Intellectual Property Law Sect., Intellectual Tech. Transfer). Office: Katten Muchin Zavis Rosenman Ste 2600 2029 Century Park E Los Angeles CA 90067 Office Phone: 310-788-4640. Office Fax: 310-712-8482. E-mail: eric.klein@kmzr.com.

KLEIN, GABRIELLA SONJA, retired communications executive; b. Chgo., Apr. 11, 1938; d. Frank E. Vosicky and Sonja (Kosner) Becvar; m. Donald J. Klein. BA in Comm. and Bus. Mgmt., Alverno Coll., 1983. Editor, owner Fox Lake (Wis.) Rep., 1962-65, McFarland (Wis.) Cmty. Life and Monona Cmty. Herald, 1966-69; bur. reporter Waukesha (Wis.) Daily Freeman, 1969-71; cmty. rels. staff Waukesha County Tech. Coll., Pewaukee, Wis., 1971-73; pub. rels. specialist JI Case Co., Racine, Wis., 1973-75, corp. publs. editor, 1975-80; v.p., bd. dirs. publs. Image Mgmt. Valley View Ctr., Milw., 1980-82; pres. Comm. Concepts Unltd., Racine, 1983-98; ret., 1998. Past pres. Big Bros./Big Sisters Racine County; past v.p. devel. Girl Scouts Racine County, bd. dirs.; steering com. Racine Cmty. Coalition for Youth; bd. dirs. Root-Pike Watershed Initiative Network; steering com. Racine County Youth As Resources. Recipient award Wis. Press Assn., Nat. Fedn. Press Women, Silver medal Ad Club Racine, 1998, Outstanding Alumna award Alverno Coll., 1999, Edn. Cmty. Leader of Yr., Racine Area Mfrs. and Commerce, 2000, Thanks Badge award Girl Scouts of Racine County, 2000, Cmty. Trustee award Leadership Racine, 2004, Thanks Badge II award Girl Scouts Racine County, 2005; named Wis. Woman Entrepreneur of Yr., 1985, Vol. of Yr. Racine Area United Way, 1994, Woman of Distinction Bus., Racine YWCA, 1995 Home: 3045 Chatham St Racine WI 53402-4001

KLEIN, GAIL BETH MARANTZ, freelance/self-employed writer, animal breeder; b. Bklyn., Dec. 1, 1946; d. Herbert and Florence (Dresner) Marantz; m. Harvey Leon Klein, Mar. 17, 1979. AB cum laude, U. Miami, Coral Gables, Fla., 1968, MEd, 1969, MBA, 1977. Cert. residential contractor, Fla.; notary pub. Asst. dir. student activities Miami-Dade Community Coll., 1969-79, instr. photography for mentally retarded adults, 1974, acting dir. student activities, 1976, acting advisor student publs., 1979; dog breeder Vizcaya Shepherds, Palm Beach Gardens, Fla., East Hampton, Conn., 1979—; trainer Dog Obedience and Conformation Show Handling, West Palm Beach, 1980—; owner, CEO Word Master Profl. Comm. Freelance writer WordMaster Profl. Comms.; mgr. proposal devel., specialist Profl. Food-Svc. Mgmt., Inc., 1994—97; spl. projects-ops. Chartwells, 1997—98; proposal and resource libr. mgmt., proposal writer Wackenhut Corp., Inc., 1998—2000; cons. Universal Staffing Svcs., 2001; sr. tech. cons. Belcan Corp., 2001—02; tech. publs. analyst-mil. engines Pratt & Whitney, 2002—04, tng. coord. Turbine Module Ctr., 2004—; spke in field; appeared on various radio talk shows. Editor (booklet) 1978 Consumers Guide to Banking, 1978, (newsletter) Newsletter of German Shepherd Dog Club Ft. Lauderdale, Inc., 1980-83, Sunshine State Shepherd, 1988-89; contbr. articles to newspapers and mags. Chair spl. events com. Third Century U.S.A., Dade County, Fla., 1976; mem. adv. com., mktg. cons. YWCA of Greater Miami, 1976-79; mem. comty. rels. com. Greater Miami Jewish Fedn., 1976-79; mem. Met. Miami Art Ctr., 1977-79; vice chair, chair appeals bd. Palm Beach County Animal Care and Control, 1989-97, mem. pet overpopulation com., 1991-93; co-developer, co-adminstr. OFA Verifications for German Shepherd Dogs, 1985—; pub. info. coord. Am. Kennel Club, Palm Beach County, 1991-94. Recipient Job Training Partnership Act Employee of Yr. award State of Fla., 1994. Mem.: Am. Sewing Guild, Palm Beach Users Group, Conformation Judges Assn. Fla., Inc., Nat. Assn. Dog Obedience Instrs., Assn. Proposal Mgmt. Profls., Fla. Freelance Writers Assn., Hadassah (life), Wolf Song of Alaska (grant/proposal writer), Treasure Coast German Shepherd Dog Club (charter), Jupiter-Tequesta Dog Club, Inc. (pres. 1984—85, bd. dirs., various other offices, Gaines Sportsmanship award 1993), German Shepherd Dog Club of Can., Inc., German Shepherd Dog Club of Greater Miami (life; rec. sec. 1977—78, corr. sec. 1978—80, bd. dirs. 1981—82, 1989—94), German Shepherd Dog Club Am., Inc. (hip dysplasia/orthopedic com. 1987—89), German Shepherd Dog Club Eastern Conn., Obedience Tng. Club Palm Beach County, Inc. (AKC Cmty. Achievement Merit award 1994), Mortar Board, Phi Kappa Phi, Epsilon Tau Lambda, Alpha Lambda Delta. Republican. Jewish. Avocations: reading, computers, crafts, photography, sewing. Home: 12 Comstock Trl East Hampton CT 06424-2304 Personal E-mail: gailklein@aol.com.

KLEIN, GARNER FRANKLIN, cardiologist, internist; b. San Pedro, Calif., June 21, 1933; s. John William and Anna Louise K.; m. Nancy Shank, Aug. 19, 1985; children: Kevin Wayne, Samuel Kyle, Lisa K., Garner F. BA in Biology, North Tex. State U., 1953; MA in Anatomy, U. Tex. Med. Br., Galveston, 1956, MD, 1958. Diplomate Am. Bd. Internal Medicine. Intern U.S. Naval Hosp., Camp Pendleton, Calif., 1958—59; resident in internal medicine VA Hosp./Southwestern Med. Sch., Dallas, 1962—66; cardiologist Valley Diagnostic Clinic, Harlingen, Tex., 1966—2002, Valley Bapt. Med. Ctr., Harlingen, 1966—, chief dept. medicine, 1982—84, 1992—94, 2002—04, chief med. staff, 1994—96; pres. Valley Diagnostic Med. and Surg. Clinic, 1992—96; med. dir. Valley Health Plans, 2002—. Cons. in cardiology Dolly Vinsant Meml. Hosp., San Benito, Tex., 1966-2000, South Tex. Hosp., Harlingen, 1966-2000; med. dir. South Tex. Emergency Care Found., 1991—, Valley Diagnostic Clinic, 1996-99, Los Fresnos Rural Health Clinic, 1996-2000; clin. prof. medicine U. Tex. Health Sci. Ctr., San Antonio, 1999—, Regional Acad. Health Ctr., Harlingen, Tex. Mem. Wesley United Meth. Ch., Harlingen. Lt. comdr. M.C., U.S. Navy, 1958-66. Named Profl. Vol. of Yr., Tex. affiliate Am. Heart Assn., 1983. Fellow ACP, Am. Coll. Cardiology, Acad. for Healthcare Mgmt.; mem. AMA, Tex. Med. Assn., Nat. Assn. EMS Physicians, Air Med. Physician Assn., Nat. Assn. Managed Care Physicians, Am. Coll. Managed Care Medicine, Tex. Soc. Internal Medicine

(Amb. Leadership award 1998), Am. Heart Assn. (pres. Tex. affil. 1980-81), Am. Stroke Assn., Am. Coll. Physician Execs., Cameron-Willacy County Med. Soc. (pres. 1978), Sigma Xi, Alpha Omega Alpha. Avocations: hunting, fishing, gardening. Office: Valley Health Plans 2005 Ed Carey Dr Harlingen TX 78550 Business E-Mail: garner.klein@valleybaptist.net.

KLEIN, GARY, dentist; Grad., U. Western Ontario. Founder Smilesolvers, Toronto, Canada. Clin. instr./demonstrator U. Toronto. Mem.: Ontario Dental Assn., Periodontal Assocs. Study Club, Toronto Crown & Bridge Study Club, Alpha Omega Dental Fraternity. Avocations: running, cycling, skiing, tennis, water-skiing, swimming. Office: 1268 St Clair Ave West Toronto ON Canada M6E 1B9 also: 8601 Warden Ave Markham ON Canada L3R 2L6 Office Phone: 416-658-8885, 905-940-9988. Office Fax: 416-658-4402, 905-415-5982.*

KLEIN, GEORGE, manufacturing company executive, systems analyst, consultant; b. Budapest, Hungary, Aug. 4, 1944; arrived in US, 1950; s. Louis and Sue (Fleiner) Klein; m. Marcella E. Baum, Aug. 23, 1964; children: Diane L., Elliot C., Louis H., David A. BEE, CUNY, 1964; MBA, Hofstra U., 1971. Registered profl. engr., NY. Gen. mgr. Alphanumerics, Inc., Lake Success, NY, 1967—70; founder, officer, dir. Catoptrics, Inc., New Hyde Park, NY, 1970—72; consulting engr. G. Klein & Assocs., New Hyde Park, 1972—77, 1978—81; v.p. engring. Codata Corp., Larchmont, NY, 1977—78; founder, sr. v.p., CEO DCS Controls Corp., Great Neck, NY, 1981—86; founder, pres., dir. Landmark Systems, Inc., NYC, 1986—. Pres. Klein and Labiak, Inc., 1992, Dura BioMed., Inc.; founder, pres., dir. GPK Technologies Corp., New Hyde Park, NY, 1986—; prin. Stack, Klein and Labiak Fin. and Mgmt. Cons.; co-founder, dir. SatQuest.com. Contbr. articles to profl. jours. Served with U.S. Army, 1957—59. Mem.: ASHRAE, IEEE, Am. Energy Engrs. Achievements include patents for signal measurement system in 1972, communications network in 1979 and universal input/output device in 1983. Avocations: weightlifting, racquetball, squash, reading. Home: 159 Robby Ln New Hyde Park NY 11040-1105

KLEIN, GERHART LEOPOLD, public relations executive; b. Phila., July 24, 1948; s. Joseph G. and Liselotte M. (Peschke) K.; m. Anne Sceia, July 19, 1976. BS cum laude, Temple U., 1970, JD, 1980. Bar: Pa. 1980, N.J. 1980, U.S. Dist. Ct. (ea. dist.) Pa. 1980, U.S. Dist. Ct. N.J. 1980, U.S. Ct. Appeals (3d cir.) 1982, U.S. Supreme Ct. 1985, U.S. Tax Ct. 1985. News anchor WAMS, Wilmington, Del., 1967-68; news anchor, disc jockey WRCP AM & FM, Phila., 1968-70, news dir., 1970; editor, writer, reporter, news anchor WCAU (CBS) Radio, Phila., 1970-72; dir. pub. info., press sec. Pa. Dept. Pub. Welfare, Harrisburg, 1972-73; freelance journalist Phila., 1973-75; asst. editor Focus Mag., Phila., 1974-75; editor, writer, reporter, news anchor KYW Newsradio, Phila., 1975-77; atty. Montgomery, McCracken, Walker & Rhoads, Phila., 1980-85; v.p., gen. mgr. to exec. v.p. Anne Klein & Assocs., Inc., Marlton, NJ, 1985—. Mem. Environ. Commn., Mt. Laurel Twp., N.J., 1988-92; mem. water quality com. Old Taunton Colony Club, 1995—. Recipient Phila. Trial Lawyers Assn. Barrister award, 1980. Mem. Pub. Rels. Soc. Am. (chmn. task force on ethics bd. confidentiality 1991-92, mem. body of knowledge bd. 1994-98, author PR Law Sect. of Accreditation Handbook 1990, Phila. chpt. Pepperpot awards, Presdl. citation 1991, 92), Pub. Rels. Soc. Am. Counselors Acad. (chmn. tech. com.), Pub. Rels. Profls. So. N.J. (treas. 1990-92), Soc. Profl. Journalists, Broadcast Pioneers, Pinnacle Worldwide (treas. 1994-96, pres.-elect 1996-98, pres. 1998-2000, chmn. 2000-02, chmn. emeritus 2002-). Office: Anne Klein & Assocs Inc 10 Lake Ctr Ste 108 Marlton NJ 08053-3424 Office Phone: 856-988-6560. E-mail: gklein@akleinpr.com.

KLEIN, HARVEY, medical educator; b. N.Y.C., Aug. 29, 1937; s. Emanuel and Rose (Sanderman) K.; m. Phyllis Levine, Sept. 22, 1963; children: Laura, Daniel. SB, U. Chgo., 1959; MD, Harvard U., 1963. Diplomate Am. Bd. Internal Medicine. Intern N.Y.-Cornell, N.Y.C., 1963-64, asst. resident, 1964-65, sr. resident, 1967-68, chief resident, 1968-69, fellow in medicine, 1969-70; asst. prof. medicine Cornell U. Med. Coll., N.Y.C., 1970-75, assoc. prof., 1975-88, William S. Paley prof. clin. medicine, 1992—. Capt. USAF, 1965-67. Office: Cornell U Med Coll 525 E 68th St New York NY 10021-4870 Office Phone: 212-746-4101.

KLEIN, HENRY, lawyer; b. N.Y.C., Oct. 6, 1949; s. Leo Herman and Florence (Silver) K.; m. Ann Laura Hallasey, July 30, 1972; children: Lauren Jennifer, Benjamin Jason. BA, SUNY, Albany, 1971; JD, U. San Diego, 1975. Bar: Calif. 1975, U.S. Ct. Customs and Patent Appeals 1976, U.S. Ct. Appeals (Fed. cir.) 1985, U.S. Dist. Ct. (cen. dist.) Calif. 1986. Trademark atty. U.S. Patent Office, Washington, 1975-77; ptnr. Ladas & Parry, Los Angeles, 1978—2002; private practice 2002-. Mem. San Diego Law Rev., 1974-75; editor-in-chief Trademark Soc. Newsletter, 1977. Mem. U. San Diego Civil Legal Clinic, 1974, Civil Rights Research Council, San Diego, 1974, Calif. Pub. Interest Research Group, San Diego, 1975. N.Y. State scholar, 1967-71; Tex. State legal scholar State of Tex., 1972; recipient Am. Jurisprudence award Bancroft-Whitney Co. and Lawyer Co-Op. Pub. Co., Lubbock, Tex., 1972; Patent Trademark Spl. Achievement awards U.S. Dept. Commerce, Washington, 1976, 77. Mem. U.S. Trademark Assn. (v.p. 1976, pres., chmn. 1977), Los Angeles Patent Law Assn., Phi Delta Phi. Republican. Jewish. Home: 10427 Vivienda St Alta Loma CA 91737-1755 Office: Law Offices of Henry Klein 10427 Vivienda St Alta Loma CA 91737-1755

KLEIN, HENRY, architect; b. Cham, Germany, Sept. 6, 1920; came to U.S., 1939; s. Fred and Hedwig (Weiskopf) K.; m. Phyllis Harvey, Dec. 27, 1952; children: Vincent, Paul, David. Student, Inst. Rauch, Lausanne, Switzerland, 1936-38; BArch, Cornell U., 1943. Registered architect, Oreg., Wash. Designer Office of Pietro Belluschi, Architect, Portland, Oreg., 1948-51; architect Henry Klein & Assoc., Architects, Mt. Vernon, Wash., 1952—78; pvt. practice architect Henry Klein Partnership, 1978—. Bd. dirs. Wash. Pks. Found., Seattle, 1977-92, Mus. N.W. Art, 1988-95. With U.S. Army, 1943-46. Recipient Louis Sullivan award Internat. Union Bricklayers and Allied Craftsmen, 1981; Presdl. Design award Nat. Endowment Arts, 1988; George A. and Eliza Howard Found. fellow. Fellow AIA (Seattle chpt. medal 1995). Jewish. Home: 21625 Little Mountain Rd Mount Vernon WA 98274-8003 Office: Henry Klein Partnership 314 Pine St Mount Vernon WA 98273-3852

KLEIN, HERBERT GEORGE, newspaper editor; b. LA, Apr. 1, 1918; s. George and Amy (Cordes) K.; m. Marjorie Galbraith, Nov. 1, 1941; children: Joanne L. (Mrs. Robert Mayne), Patricia A. (Mrs. John Root). AB, U. So. Calif., 1940; Hon. Doctorate, U. San Diego, 1989. Reporter Alhambra (Calif.) Post-Advocate, 1940-42, news editor, 1946-50; spl. corr. Copley Newspapers, 1946-50, Washington corr., 1950; with San Diego Union, 1950-68, editl. writer, 1950-52, editl. page editor, 1952-56, assoc. editor, 1956-57, exec. editor, 1957-58, editor, 1959-68; mgr. comm. Nixon for Pres. Campaign, 1968-69; dir. comm. Exec. Br., U.S. Govt., 1969-73; v.p. corp. rels. Metromedia, Inc., 1973-77; media cons., 1977-80; editor-in-chief, v.p. Copley Newspapers, Inc., San Diego, 1980—2003; nat. fellow Am. Enterprise Inst., 2004—; cons. Copley Newspapers, Inc., San Diego, 2004—. Publicity dir. Eisenhower-Nixon campaign in Calif., 1952; asst. press sec. V.P. Nixon campaign, 1956; press sec. Nixon campaign, 1958; spl. asst., press sec. to Nixon, 1959-61; press sec. Nixon Gov. campaign, 1962; dir. comm. Nixon presdl. campaign, 1968; mem. Advt. Coun., N.Y. Author: Making It Perfectly Clear, 1980. Trustee U. So. Calif.; past chmn. Holiday Bowl; bd. dirs. Greater San Diego Internat. Sports Coun.; mem. com. Super Bowls XXII, XXIII, and XXXVII; active Olympic Tng. Site Com.; trustee U. So. Calif.; trustee U. Calif. San Diego Found; bd. dirs. San Diego Econ. Devel. Com. With USNR, 1942-46; comdr. Res. Recipient Fourth Estate award U. So. Calif., 1947, Alumnus of Yr. award U. So. Calif., 1971, Gen. Alumni Merit award, 1977, Spl. Svc. to Journalism award, 1969, Headliner of Yr. award L.A. Press Club, 1971, San Diego State U. First Fourth Estate award, 1986, Golden Man award Boys and Girls Club, 1994, Newspaper Exec. of Yr. award Calif. Press Assn., 1994; named Cmty. Champion, Hall of Champions, 1993, Mr. San Diego, 2001. Fellow Am. Enterprise Inst.; mem. Am. Soc. Newspaper Editors (past dir.), Calif. Press Assn., Pub. Rels. Seminar, Gen. Alumni U. So. Calif. (past pres.), Alhambra Jr. C. of C. (past pres.), Greater San Diego C. of C. (mem. exec. com.), Bohemian Club, Fairbanks Country Club, Kiwanis, Rotary (hon.), Sigma Delta Chi (chmn. nat. com., chmn. gen. activities nat. conv. 1958), Scripps Inst. (dir.'s cabinet Oceanography), Delta Chi. Presbyterian. Home: 5110 Saddlery Sq PO Box 8935 Rancho Santa Fe CA 92067-8935 Office: 750 B St Ste 2380 San Diego CA 92101-8114 Office Phone: 619-702-1141. Business E-Mail: hklein@hgk.sdcoxmail.com. *As I look back on a lifetime in journalism and politics, the thesis which has most effected my career has been a desire to be a thoughtful "man in the arena". To leave a legacy, you cannot be bland. I believe one must develop a philosophy endowed with principle which allows him to take a stand, popular or not, on issues in which he or she believes.*

KLEIN, HOWARD BRUCE, lawyer, law educator; b. Pitts., Feb. 28, 1950; s. Elmer and Natalie (Rosenzweig) K.; m. Lonnie Jean Wilets, Dec. 12, 1977; children: Zachary B., Eli H. Student, Northwestern U., 1968-69; BA, U. Wis., 1972; JD, Georgetown U., 1976. Bar: Wis. 1976, Pa. 1981, U.S. Ct. Appeals D.C., 1978, U.S. Dist. Ct. Pa. 1981, U.S. Ct. Appeals (3rd cir.) 1982, U.S. Supreme Ct. 1983. Law clk. to justice Robert Hansen Wis. Supreme Ct., Madison, 1976-77; asst. atty. gen. dept. justice State of Wis., 1977-80; chief criminal divsn. U.S. Atty.'s Office, Phila., 1980-87; ptnr. Blank, Rome & McCauley, Phila., 1987-96, chmn. litigation dept., 1991-94; prin. Law Offices of Howard Bruce Klein, Phila., 1996—; dir. in house tng. Am. Law Inst.-ABA, 1996—. Regional, nat. instr. Nat. Inst. Trial Advocacy, Phila. and Boulder, Colo., 1987-98; adj. prof. evidence and trial advocacy Temple U. Law Sch., 1984—; instr. Atty. Gen. Advocacy Inst., Washington, 1983-87; lectr. pub. corruption and trial advocacy; cons. Pa. Valley Neighborhood Assn., 1984—. Contbr. to profl. jours. Advisor Phila. Police Dept. Reform Commn., 1986—; campaign issues dir. Pa. Atty. Gen. campaign, Phila., 1988, 92; bd. dirs. Citizens Crime Commn. Delaware Valley, Phila. Mem. Fed. Bar Assn. (chmn. criminal law com.), Phila. Bar Assn., Wis. Bar Assn., D.C. Bar Assn., U.S. Attys. Alumni Assn. (co-founder, exec. bd.), Vesper Club (Phila.). Democrat. Jewish. Avocations: golf, basketball, hiking. Office: 1700 Market St Ste 2632 Philadelphia PA 19103-3903 Office Phone: 215-972-1411. Personal E-mail: howbrklein@aol.com.

KLEIN, IDA, elementary school educator; arrived in US, 1960; d. Sandor Klein and Sarah Weiss. BA, Sir George Williams Coll., 1959. Tchr. H.B. Milnes Elem. Sch., Fair Lawn, NJ, 1960—2005; ret., 2005. Mem.: NEA, N.J. Edn. Assn. Achievements include introduction of chess into first grade classes in 1986 to help integrate emigre students from Russia and Israel. Avocation: music.

KLEIN, IRMA MOLLIGAN, career planning administrator, consultant; b. New Orleans, Jan. 5, 1929; d. Harry Joseph and Gesina Francis (Bauer) Molligan; m. John Vincent Chelena (dec. 1978); 1 child, Joseph William Chelena; m. Chris George Klein, Aug. 14, 1965; 1 stepchild, Arnold Conrad. BS in Bus., Augustine Coll.; postgrad., Mktg. Inst., Chgo., Loyola U., Realtors Inst., Baton Rouge. Mgr. Stan Weber & Assocs., Metairie, La., 1971-75, tng. dir., 1975-81; cons. Coldwell Banker Comml. Co., New Orleans, 1981; dir. career devel. Coldwell Banker Residential Co., New Orleans, 1982-85; pres. Irma Klein Career Devel., Inc., 1994-95, Klein Enterprises, Inc., 1994—. Instr. U. New Orleans, Realtors Inst., La. Real Estate Commn. Author: Training Manual, 1978, Career Development, 1982, Obtaining Listings, 1986, Participative Marketing, 1986, Marketing & Servicing Listings, 1987, Designing Training Curriculum, 1987, Participative Management. Mem. La. Hist. Assn. Meml. Hall Found. Mem.: CRS (pres. La. chpt. 1988—90), CRB (pres. La. chpt. 1982—83, chmn. edn.), Confederate Lit. (pres. New Orleans 2001—), Antique Study Group (pres. 2001—03), Les Quarante Ecolieres (pres. 1994—96), La. Dental Assts. Assn. (pres. 1964), Am. Dental Assts. Assn., Nat. Assn. Realtors (nat. conv. spkr. 1986), Realtors Nat. Mktg. Inst. (residential specialist 1977, amb. Tex. and La. 1985—, cert. broker 1980, Outstanding Achievement award 1985), Edn. and Resources (pres. La. chpt., cert.), Jefferson Bd. Realtors (v.p. 1984), La. Realtors Assn. (bd. dirs. 1973—74, grad. Realtors Inst. 1976), Metairie Woman's Club (sec. 1997—99, pres.-elect 1999, pres. 2000—01), Rsch. Club New Orleans (pres. 1984—85), Odyssey Ho. La. Republican. Roman Catholic. Avocation: antiques. Personal E-mail: cgkimk@cox.net.

KLEIN, JASON EVAN, publishing executive; b. N.Y.C., May 11, 1960; s. William Louis and Bernice Carol (Tick) K.; m. Robin Fern Nash, July 23, 1989; children: Michael Louis, Jill Lauren. AB, Dartmouth Coll., 1982; MBA, Harvard U., 1986. Assoc. cons. Bain & Co., Palo Alto, Calif., 1982-84; sr. engagement mgr. McKinsey & Co., N.Y.C., 1986-93; dir. strategy Times Mirror, N.Y.C., 1993-95; pres., group pub. Field & Stream/Outdoor Life and Today's Homeowner, N.Y.C., 1995—99; pres., CEO, Times Mirror Mags., N.Y.C., 1999—2001, Healthy Living Media, N.Y.C., 2001—03, Newspaper Nat. Network, N.Y.C., 2003—. Dir. Am. Advt. Found. Trustee N.Y.C. Police Found.; bd. dirs. Am. Advt. Found.; bd. dirs. emeritus Recreation Roundtable. Mem. Phi Beta Kappa. Office: Newspaper Nat Network 20 W 33d St 7th Fl New York NY 10001 E-mail: jklein@mba1986.hbs.edu.

KLEIN, JEFFREY PETER, investor; b. NYC, June 29, 1943; s. Seymour M. and Ruth (Liberman) Klein. BA, Colgate U., 1965; MBA, Columbia U., 1967. Exec. Mr. Ephram, Inc., N.Y.C., 1967—69; account exec. Thomson-Leeds Co., 1969—79; officer M.K.B. Group, Inc., N.Y.C., 1979—2000. Trustee, com. chmn. Collegiate Sch., N.Y.C., 1976—85, 1991—98, pres. bd. trustees, 1994—98; bd. dirs., com. chmn. 92d St. YMHA, 1980—; chmn. bd. dirs. NY Chamber Symphony, 1993—2002; pres. Bertha & Isaac Liberman Found., 1983—. Mem.: Mus. Modern Art, Conservation Com., Contemporary Arts Coun., Arch. and Design Com., Colgate Club (N.Y.C.), Harmonie Club (bd. dirs. 2002—), Sunningdale Country Club (Scarsdale, N.Y.) (bd. dirs. 1980—85). Avocations: golf, photography, travel, reading. Home: 480 Park Ave New York NY 10022-1613 Office: 200 Park Ave S Ste 13H New York NY 10003-1503 Personal E-mail: jpk480@aol.com.

KLEIN, JEFFREY RICHARD GEORGE, school psychologist; s. John Robert Mathew and Patricia Lucile Klein; m. Angela Holt Klein, Sept. 23, 1995; children: Grant Elijah, Lauryn Elizabeth, Carter Joseph. BS in Ednl. Psychology, Brigham Young U., Provo, Utah, 1993—97; MEd in Sch. Psychology, U. Calif., Santa Barbara, 1997—99, PhD in Edn., 1997—2002. Cert. Sch. Psychologist Calif., 2000, Mo., 2002; in Spl. Edn. Utah, 1997. Sch. psychology intern L.A. Unified Sch. Dist., 1999—2000; sch. psychologist Panama-Buena Vista Union Sch. Dist., Bakersfield, Calif., 2000—02; dir., rsch., evaluation, and assessment Pk. Hill Sch. Dist., Kansas City, Mo., 2002—. Contbr. articles to profl. jours. Exec. sec. Ch. of Jesus Christ of Latter-Day Saints, Platte City, Mo., 2004—05. Mem.: NASP, ASCD, Dirs. Rsch. and Evaluation, Nat. Assn. Test Dirs., Am. Ednl. Rsch. Assn. Independent. Mem. Lds Ch. Avocations: golf, yoga, swimming. Office: Park Hill Sch Dist 7703 NW Barry Rd Kansas City MO 64153 Office Phone: 816-741-1521. E-mail: kleinj@parkhill.k12.mo.us.

KLEIN, JERRY EMANUEL, insurance and financial planning executive; b. Cin., Apr. 4, 1933; s. Milton H. and Ida S. (Dunsker) K.; m. Arlene Ruth Rosen, July 3, 1957 (dec. Nov. 1974); children: Marjorie, Bradley, Amy; m. Nancy Cohen Hahn, Aug. 7, 1982. BMech. Engring., Cornell U., 1956; MBA, Ohio State U., 1959. CLU, ChFC. Fin. engring. Avco Electronics, Cin., 1959-61; fin. rep. Northwestern Mut. of Milw., Cin., 1961—. Vice chmn. Am. Jewish Com., 1978; pres. Social Health Assn., 1964—66; bd. dirs. Jewish Vocat. Svc., 1964—92, pres., 1978—80, Cancer Family Care, 1981—83; chmn. fin. com. Jewish Fedn., 1981—83, treas., mem. exec. com., 1981—84; bd. dirs. Children Psychiat. Ctr., 1973—86, Jewish Family Svc., 1984—94, Cin. Jewish Fedn., 1972—92, Halom Ho., 1992, treas., 1998—; chmn. HILB Scholarship Com., 1985—; bd. dirs. Radio Reading Svc., 1997, Cin. Assn. Blind, 1999—, TriCounty Parkinson Wellness Assn., 2004—. 1st lt. USAF, 1956—58. Recipient Kate S. Mack award Jewish Fedn., 1975, Human Rels. award NCCJ, 1992 Mem. Million Dollar Round Table (life), Nat. Assn. Life Underwriters, Estate Planning Coun. Cin., Assn. CLUs. Jewish. Office: Northwestern Mut Fin Network Rookwood Tower 2d Fl 3805 Edwards Rd Cincinnati OH 45209 Office Phone: 513-366-3667.

KLEIN, JOEL IRWIN, school system administrator; b. N.Y.C., Oct. 25, 1946; s. Charles Samuel and Claire (Hofstein) K.; m. Linda Kay Davis, June 26, 1971 (div. May 1977); m. Harriet Howard Davis, Mar. 8, 1980; 1 child, Julia. BA magna cum laude, Columbia Coll., 1967; JD magna cum laude, Harvard U., 1971. Rsch. asst. Ctr. for Advance Study of Behavior Scis. Stanford U., 1971-72; Fredrick Sheldon traveling fellow Harvard U., 1972-73; law clk. U.S. Ct. Appeals, D.C. cir., 1973-74, U.S. Supreme Ct., 1974-75; with Mental Health Law Project, Washington, 1975-76; mem. Rogovin, Stern & Huge, Washington, 1976-81; ptnr. Klein, Farr, Smith & Taranto, Washington, 1981-93; dep. counsel to pres. Exec. Office of the Pres., Washington, 1993-95; prin. dep. asst. atty. gen. antitrust div., U.S. Dept. Justice, Washington, 1995—96, acting asst. atty. gen., 1996—97, asst. atty. gen., antitrust div., 1997—2001; chmn., CEO Bertelsmann, Inc., 2001—02; chancellor NYC Dept. Edn., 2002—. Vis. and adj. prof. law Georgetown U. Law Ctr., 1987—; lectr. Stanford U. Law Sch., 1972; treas. World Fedn. Mental Health, 1985-87. Contbr. articles and book revs. to profl. jours. Mem. U.S. Dept. of State, Office of Human Rights, Delegation to Rev. Psychiat. Abuse in the Former Soviet Union, 1989; active D.C. Big Bros. program, 1990—; mem., ex-officio mem., chairperson. The Green Door, 1976—. Recipient Vol. Recognition award Nat. Assn. Attys. Gen., 1993, Isaac Ray award Am. Psychiat. Assn., 1994. Mem. ABA, Am. Law Inst., Am. Psychiat. Assn. Avocations: tennis, reading. Office: NYC Dept Edn 52 Chambers St New York NY 10007

KLEIN, JOHN JACOB, retired economist; b. Chgo., Aug. 30, 1929; s. John and Mathilda (Keller) K.; m. Sylvia Elvine Knauss, Nov. 25, 1953; children: Leslie Klein Funk. BA cum laude, Northwestern U., 1950; MA, U. Chgo., 1952, PhD, 1955. Asst. prof. econs. Okla. State U., Stillwater, 1957-60; assoc. prof. econs. Fordham U., N.Y.C., 1960-67; prof. econs. Ga. State U., Atlanta, 1967—94, prof. econs. emeritus, 1994—. Author: (with M. Friedman) Studies in the Quantity Theory of Money, 1956, (with Leftwich, Trenton, Poole) The Oklahoma Economy, 1963; author: Money and the Economy, 6th edit. 1986; contbr. articles to profl. jours. With U.S. Army, 1955-57. Mem. Am. Econ. Assn., So. Econ. Assn., Phi Beta Kappa, Pi Mu Epsilon. Republican. Avocation: music. Home: 855 Oakhaven Dr Roswell GA 30075-1248

KLEIN, JONATHAN, broadcast executive; BA magna cum laude, Brown U., 1990. News writer, editor CBS Nightwatch; exec. v.p. CBS News, 1996—98; founder, CEO FeedRoom Inc., 1999—2004; pres. CNN/U.S., 2004—. Prodr.: CBS Morning News, CBS Weekend News, 48 Hours, Coast to Coast, Public Eye with Bryant Gumbel; writer: (TV films) The Buffalo Soldiers, 1997; writer, dir., prodr. Before Your Eyes: One Last Chance, 1998. Recipient 2 Peabody awards, 3 Emmy awards. Office: CNN One CNN Ctr Atlanta GA 30303 Office Phone: 404-827-1500.

KLEIN, JONATHAN D., finance company executive; Various Hambros Bank Ltd., 1983-93; co-founder Getty Investment Holdings L.L.C., 1993-95; joint chmn., co-founder Getty Commns. plc, 1995-96, CEO, dir., 1996-98; co-founder, CEO, dir. Getty Images, 1998—. Dir. Hambros Bank Ltd., 1989-98; bd. dir. Getty Investments L.L.C., A Contemporary Theatre, Realnetworks. Office: Getty Images 601 N 34th St Seattle WA 98103*

KLEIN, JOSEPH, retired mining executive; b. NYC, Nov. 9, 1921; s. Erwin Wolffe and Ada (Black) K.; m. Betty Evelyn Northington, Dec. 24, 1948; children: Kathryn Ann Zornes (dec.), Elizabeth Ellen Scahill, Joseph Mark, Jr., Timothy Northington. Certificate in fgn. trade, Am. Grad Sch. Internat. Mgmt., 1947; D Internat Laws (hon.), Am. Grad. Sch. Internat. Mgmt., 1993. Vice pres. internat. ops. Clary Corp., San Gabriel, Calif., 1948-60, dir., 1967-70; dir. internat. ops. Remington Rand Corp., N.Y.C., 1961-62; pres. NBC Internat. Ltd.; v.p. NBC News, N.Y.C., 1962-66; exec. v.p., dir. Cyprus Mines Corp., Los Angeles, 1966-79; chmn. bd. Hawaiian Cement Corp., 1969-79; ret. pres., dir. Pluess-Staufer Industries, Inc., Los Angeles, 1979-91, sr. fin. cons., bd. dirs., 1991-99. Dir. Mission Ins. Group, Inc.; mem. Pres.'s Export Expansion Council, 1971-74; vice-chmn. bd. trustees Am. Grad. Sch. Internat. Mgmt., 1975-83, chmn. bd. trustees, 1983-88. Served pvt. to capt. U.S. Army, 1940-46. Decorated Silver Star, Bronze Star with oak leaf cluster, Purple Heart, Combat Inf. Badge, Croix de Guerre; recipient Jonas B. Mayer Outstanding Alumni award, Am. Grad. Sch. Internat. Mgmt., 1974, So. Calif. Alumni Assn. award, 1974. Mem. AIME, The Ret. Officers Assn. (pres. dir. west L.A. area chpt.), Town Hall, Mil. Order Purple Heart (comdr. Ariz. 1949-50, Hollywood chpt. 1987-88), Am. Legion (post comdr. 1990-91, trustee 1991—2004), Elks. Republican. Presbyterian. Home: 1071 Villa View Dr Pacific Palisades CA 90272-3949 Personal E-mail: jmk6500@aol.com.

KLEIN, JULIA MEREDITH, freelance journalist; b. Phila., Dec. 11, 1955; d. Abraham and Murielle (Pollack) Klein. BA magna cum laude, Harvard U., 1977. Copy editor J.B. Lippincott, Phila., 1977; features reporter The Oakland Press, Pontiac, Mich., 1978; freelance writer, researcher, editorial cons., 1978—; reporter, critic and editor The Phila. Inquirer, 1983-2000. Nat. Arts Journalism Program fellow, 1996-97, John J. McCloy fellow in journalism, 1998, Alicia Patterson Found. fellow, 2000, Western Knight Ctr. fellow for Specialized Journalism, 2001; Fulbright German Studies Seminar, 2004. Mem. Soc. Profl. Journalists (2d pl. award for criticism 1998, 2003, 3d Pl. award for criticism 1999), Am. Soc. Journalists and Authors, N.Am. Travel Journalists Assn., Journalism and Women Symposium, Nat. Book Critics Cir., Phi Beta Kappa Home and Office: 307 Monroe St Philadelphia PA 19147-3211 Office Phone: 215-733-0761. Personal E-mail: julklein@juno.com.

KLEIN, LAURA COLIN, publishing executive; With Levine, Huntley, Schmidt & Beaver Advt., N.Y.C., 1985—86; nat. sales mgr. Andrew's Mag., 1986—89; acct. mgr. ELLE Mag., 1989—92; Ea. sales mgr. Woman's Day, N.Y.C., 1992—96, v.p., ad dir., 1996—2000, v.p., pub., 2002—; pub. Family Life, 2000. Office: Womans Day Mag Hachette Filipacchi Mags Inc 1633 Broadway 42d Fl New York NY 10019 Office Phone: 212-767-6000. Office Fax: 212-767-5610.*

KLEIN, LAWRENCE ALLEN, accounting educator; b. Harrisburg, Pa., Jan. 14, 1946; s. Samuel Edward and Ella Violet (Loeb) K. AB, Franklin and Marshall Coll., 1969; MBA, Pa. State U., 1974, PHD, 1978. Adminstrv. asst. dept. acctg. and mgmt. info. sys. Pa. State U., State College, 1975-76; asst. prof. acctg. U. Houston, 1978-79, U. Wyo., Laramie, 1982-84; asst. prof. bus. adminstrn. Franklin and Marshall Coll., Lancaster, Pa., 1979-82; assoc. prof. accountancy Bentley Coll., Waltham, Mass., 1984—. Vis. prof. econ. and mgmt. Vesalius Coll., Brussels, 1996; presenter in field. Author study guides for books in field; co-editor conf. procs., 1976. Program/conf. coord. N.E. Am. Acctg. Assn., State College, 1976; small bus. coun. Laramie Area C. of C., 1973-74. With USAF, 1969-70. Grantee Am. Acctg. Assn., Hasking & Sells Found. Mem. AAUP, NRA (life), AARP, Nat. Retired Tchrs. Assn., Inst. Mgmt. Accts. (I. Wayne Keller award, Ray E. Longnecker award 1980, Cert. Merit Manuscript award), Am. Acctg. Assn. (Sectional Best Paper award 1987), Decision Scis. Internat. (chmn. acctg. track N.E. sect. 1992), Mass. Soc. CPAs (acad. assoc.), Fin. Execs. Internat., Am. Legion (life), Am. Inst. Physics, U.S. Golf Assn., U.S. Tennis Assn. (life), Elks (permanent benefactor), Marine Meml. Club (perpetual benefactor), Jewish War Vets. (life), Beta Gamma Sigma, Beta Alpha Psi, Omicron Delta Kappa. Republican. Jewish. Avocations: tennis, golf, reading, swimming. Home: 521 Katahdin Dr Lexington MA 02421-6452 Office Phone: 781-891-2776. E-mail: lklein@bentley.edu.

KLEIN, LAWRENCE ROBERT, economist, educator; b. Omaha, Sept. 14, 1920; s. Leo Byron and Blanche (Monheit) Klein; m. Sonia Adelson, Feb. 15, 1947; children: Hannah, Rebecca, Rachel, Jonathan. BA, U. Calif.-Berkeley, 1942; PhD, MIT, 1944; MA, Lincoln Coll., Oxford U., 1957; LLD (hon.), U. Mich., 1977, Dickinson Coll., 1981; ScD (hon.), Widener Coll., 1977, Elizabethtown Coll., 1981, Ball State U., 1982, Technion, 1981, U. Nebr., 1983; D (hon.), U. Vienna, 1977; EdD, Villanova U., 1978; D (hon.), Bonn U., 1974, Free U. Brussels, 1979, U. Paris, 1979, U. Madrid, 1980; DSc, Nat. Central Univ. Taiwan, 1985; DHC, So. Helsinki Sch. Econs., 1986; Dr. Humane Letters, Bard Coll., 1986, Bilkent U., 1989, St. Norbert Coll., 1989;

DHC, Univ. Lodz, 1990; D. Litt, Univ. Glasgow, 1991; DSc, Rutgers Univ., 1992; PhD (hon.), Bar Ilan U., 1994; D. honors (hon.), Carleton Univ., 1997; DHC, U. Piraeus, 1999, Acad. Economic Studies, Romania, 1999, U Toronto, 2002, Konan U., Japan, 2002, Keio U., 2002. Faculty U. Chgo., 1944—47; research assoc. Nat. Bur. Econ. Research, 1948—50; faculty U. Mich., 1949—54; research assoc. Survey Research Center, 1949—54, Oxford Inst. Stats., 1954—58; faculty U. Pa., Phila., 1958—, prof., 1958—, Univ. prof., 1964—, Benjamin Franklin prof., 1968—, prof. emeritus; vis. prof. Osaka U., Japan, 1960, U. Colo., 1962, CUNY, 1962-63, 82, Hebrew U., 1964, Princeton U., 1966, Stanford U., 1968, U. Copenhagen, 1974; Ford vis. prof. U. Calif. at Berkeley, 1968, Inst. for Advanced Studies, Vienna, 1970, 74; hon. prof. Shanghai Jiao Tong Univ., 1984; honorary prof. Nankai Univ., 1993, Shanghai Acad. Soc. Sci., 1994; dir. and chmn. econ. policy com. W.P. Carey & Co., 1984—; adv. State Information Ctr., Beijing, 1992—; hon. chmn. Pa. Inst. for Econ. Rsch. Adv. Bd., 2002—. Cons. Can. Govt., 1947, UNCTAD, 1966, 75, 77, 80, McMillan Co., 1965—74, E.I. du Pont de Nemours, 1966—68, State of N.Y., 1969, AT&T, 1969, Fed. Res. Bd., 1973, UNIDO, 1973—75, Congl. Budget Office, 1977—, Coun. Econ. Advisers, 1977—80; chmn. bd. trustees Wharton Econometric Forecasting Assocs., Inc., 1969—80, chmn. profl. bd., 1980—; trustee Maurice Falk Inst. for Econ. Rsch., Israel, 1969—75; adv. coun. Inst. Advanced Studies, Vienna, 1977—; chmn. econ. adv. com. Gov. of Pa., 1976—78; mem. com. on prices Fed. Res. Bd., 1968—70; prin. investigator econometric model project Brookings Instn., 1963—72, Project LINK, 1968—; sr. adviser Brookings Panel on Econ. Activity, 1970—; mem. adv. com. Inst. Internat. Econs., 1983; hon. mem. Chinese Bd. Soc. Scis., 1997, Romanian Acad., 1999—; coord. Jimmy Carter's Econ. Task Force, 1976; mem. adv. bd. Strategic Studies Ctr., Stanford Rsch. Inst., 1974—76; corr. fellow Brit. Acad., 1991—. Author: The Keynesian Revolution, 1947, Textbook of Econometrics, 1953, An Econometric Model of the United States, 1929-1952, 1955, Wharton Econometric Forecasting Model, 1967, Essay on the Theory of Economic Prediction, 1968, An Introduction to Econometric Forecasting and Forecasting Models, 1980; author, editor: Brookings Quar. Econometric Model of U.S., Ecometric Model Performance, 1976, Lectures in Econmetrics, 1983; editor: Internat. Econ. Rev., 1959—65; assoc. editor:, mem. editl. bd.: Empirical Econs., 1976—. Recipient William F. Butler award, N.Y. Assn. Bus. Economists, 1975, Golden Slipper Club award, 1977, Pres.'s medal, U. Pa., 1980, Alfred Nobel Meml. prize in econs., 1980. Fellow: Nat. Assn. Bus. Economists, Am. Acad. Arts and Scis., Econometric Soc. (past pres.), Brit. Acad. (corr.); mem.: NAS, Russian Acad. Sci. (fgn.), Ea. Econ. Assn. (pres. 1974—76), Am. Econ. Assn. (exec. com. 1966—68, pres. 1977, John Bates Clark medalist 1959), Social Sci. Rsch. Coun. (fellow 1945—46, 1947—48, com. econ. stability, dir. 1971—76), Am. Philos. Soc. Achievements include creation of econometric models and the application to the analysis of economic fluctuations and economic policies. Office: U Pa Mc Neil Bldg Rm 335 3718 Locust Walk Philadelphia PA 19104-6209 Address: WP Carey 50 Rockefeller Plaza New York NY 10020*

KLEIN, LINDA ANN, lawyer; b. N.Y.C., Nov. 7, 1959; d. Gerald Ira Klein and Sandra Florence Fishman; m. Michael S. Neuren, Sept. 23, 1985. BA cum laude, Union Coll., 1980; JD, Washington & Lee U., 1983. Bar: Ga. 1983, D.C. 1984, U.S. Dist. Ct. (no. and mid. dist.) Ga. 1985, U.S. Ct. Appeals (11th cir.) 1986. Assoc. Nall & Miller, Atlanta, 1983-86, Martin, Cavan & Andersen, Atlanta, 1986-90, ptnr., 1990-93; mng. ptnr. Gambrell & Stolz, 1993—. Instr. Nat. Ctr. Paralegal Tng., Atlanta, 1986. Mem.: ABA (editor Trial Techniques newsletter 1989, vice chmn. trial techniques com. 1989—90, chair 1991—92, vice chair fidelity and surety com. 1994—97, chair ann. meeting 1996—97, mem. coun. tort and ins. practice sect. 1998—, ho. of dels. 1998—, chair tort and ins. practice sect. 2003—04, Margaret Brent Women Lawyers of Achievement award 2004), Am. Law Inst. (mem. 2003—), Coun. of Superior Cts. Judges (ex-officio uniform rules com.), Atlanta Bar Assn. (chair commn. on uniform rules of ct. 1986, bd. dirs. Atlanta Coun. on Young Lawyers 1986—89), Inst. for CLE (chair Ga. br. 1998—2000), Nat. Conf. Bar Pres. (exec. coun. 1998—2001), State Bar of Ga. (chair study com. on rules of practice 1987—94, bd. govs. 1989—, mem. exec. com. 1992—99, sec. 1994—96, pres. 1997—98, vice chair profl. liability com.), Pi Sigma Alpha, Phi Alpha Delta. Office Phone: 404-577-6000. Business E-Mail: lklein@gambrell.com.

KLEIN, LIVIU, cardiologist; b. Brasov, Brasov, Romania, Aug. 27, 1974; s. Tiberiu and Cameluta Silvia Ioana Klein; m. Oana Lacramioara Nica-Mihailescu, June 14, 1997. BS in Math. and Computer Programming, Info. Tech. Lyceum, Romania, 1998; MD, Carol Davila Sch. Medicine, Romania, 1998; MS in Clin. Investigation, Northwestern U., 2005. Diplomate Am. Bd. Internal Medicine. Intern U. Hosp., Bucharest, Romania, 1999—2000; resident Adv. Ill. Masonic Med. Ctr., U. Ill., Chgo., 2000—03; NRSA fellow in cardiovasc. disease epidemiology and prevention Northwestern U. Feinberg Sch. Medicine, Chgo., 2003—05, fellow in cardiovasc. disease, 2005—. Recipient Peer Recognition award, Adv. Ill. Masonic Med. Ctr., U. Ill., Chgo., 2002—03, Outstanding Sr. Resident award, 2003; grantee, Heart Failure Soc. Am., Mpls.-St. Paul, 2003, Am. Heart Assn., Dallas, 2004; Merit scholar, Carol Davila Sch. Medicine, Bucharest, 1994—97. Mem.: ACP (assoc. 3d prize Clin. Poster Competition 2002, 1st prize Clin. Poster Competition 2003), Am. Heart Assn. (coun. epidemiology and prevention), Heart Failure Soc. Am., Ill. Med. Soc., Chgo. Med. Soc. Jewish. Office: Northwestern U 201 E Huron St Galter 10-240 Chicago IL 60611 Office Phone: 312-503-0197. Office Fax: 312-908-9588, 312-604-7380. E-mail: lklein@northwestern.edu.

KLEIN, LLOYD WILLIAM, cardiologist, researcher; b. N.Y.C., Sept. 29, 1952; s. Julian and Zali (Heimlich) K.; m. Barbara Joyce Visocan, Sept. 4, 1982; children: Laura, Jenny. AB cum laude with honors in Chemistry, Kenyon Coll., 1973; MD, U. Cin., 1977. Diplomate Am. Bd. Internal Medicine with subspecialty in cardiovascular disease, Nat. Bd. Med. Examiners. Intern/resident Albert Einstein Coll. Medicine/Bronx Mcpl. Hosp. Ctr., 1977-80; clin. fellow in cardiology Mt. Sinai Med. Ctr./CCNY, N.Y.C., 1980-82; attending physician emergency rm. Bronx Mcpl. Hosp. Ctr., 1980-83; assoc. dir. cardiac catheterization labs. Phila. Heart Inst./Presbyn.-U. Pa. Med. Ctr., 1983-88; dir. interventional cardiology, dir. rsch./edn. Cardiac Catheterization Labs., Northwestern Meml. Hosp., Chgo., 1988-90; dir. divsn. cardiology VA Lakeside Med. Ctr., Chgo., 1989-90; med. dir. Rush Heart Inst./Oak Park Hosp./Rush Sys. for Health, Oak Park, Ill., 1998—2001; dir. interventional cardiology Rush-Presbyn.-St. Luke's Med. Ctr., Chgo., 1990—, co-dir. Cardiac Catheterization Labs., 1990—2004, assoc. dir. cardiology sect., dir. clin. svcs., 2001—04; dir. rsch. Gottlieb Meml. Hosp., Melrose Pk., Ill., 2004—, dir. prof. devel., 2004—. Instr. medicine, clin. assoc. cardiology Mt. Sinai Sch. Medicine/CCNY, 1982-83; asst. prof. clin. medicine U. Pa., Phila., 1983-88; assoc. prof. medicine Northwestern U., Chgo., 1988-90, Rush U. Med. Sch., Chgo., 1990-97, prof., 1997—. Editor: Quick Reference to Internal Medicine, 1994, Coronary Stenosis Morphology: Analysis and Clinical Implication, 1997, Resource Utilization in cardiac Disease, 1998; contbr. numerous articles and abstracts to profl. jours., chpts. to books; editl. review cons. Annals of Internal Medicine, Circulation, Am. Heart Jour., Archives of Internal Medicine, Jour. of Heart and Lun Transplantation, Critical Care Medicine, Chest; editl. bd. Jour. Am. Coll. Cardiology, 1990-94, 95—, Am. Jour. Cardiology, 1989—, Catheterization and Cardiovascular Diagnosis, 1994—, Cardiac Chronicle, 1990-94, Cardiovascular Therapeutics, 1997; contbg. editor: Year Book of Critical Care Medicine, 1990-94; assoc. editor Jour. Juosie Cardiology, 2001— Mem. Tobacco Free Ill. Named One of Best Cardiologists in Chgo., Chgo. Mag., 1995, 2004; recipient award Am. Chem. Soc., AMA Physician's Recognition award; George Gund scholar; grantee N.Y. Heart Found., 1982-83, Am. Heart Assn. Southeastern Pa., 1984-85, ADAC Labs., Inc., 1985-87, Glaxo Inc. G.B., 1986-87, Philips, Inc., 1990-92, Boston Sci., Inc., 1990-92, Baxter, Inc., 1994-96, Rush U. Com. on Rsch., 1996-98, Smith-Klein, 1997—, Robert Wood Johnson Found., 1994-98. Fellow ACP, Am. Coll. Cardiology (mem. database com., database devel. and outcomes assessment subcom. 1996—, Ill. chpt. bd. councilors 1997—, mem. program com. 1995—, rsch. presentation evaluation com. 1995—), Coun. on Clin. Cardiology of Am. Heart Assn., Soc. for Cardiac Angiography and Interventions (registry, program and interventional cardiology com. 1995—, chair 2000—), Coun. on Circulation of Am. Heart Assn.; mem. Am. Fedn. Clin. Rsch., Am. Heart Assn. of Met. Chgo. (chmn. tobacco issues com. 1993-96, pub. policy and gove. rels. com. 1991-2004, vice chair 1995-97), Am. Heart Assn. (West Suburban divsn. founding pres. 1998), Philander Chase Soc., Alpha Omega Alpha, Sigma Chi. Avocations: reading, skiing, chess, classical music. Office: Clinical Cardiology Assocs Gottlieb Meml Hosp Profl Bldg Room 314 701 North Ave Melrose Park IL 60160 Office Phone: 708-681-7878. Business E-Mail: iklein@rpslmc.edu. E-mail: lloydklein@comcast.net.

KLEIN, LUELLA VOOGD, obstetrics-gynecology educator; b. Walker, Iowa, Oct. 24, 1924; d. Elmer De Witt and Leah (Stunkard) Bare; m. Alfred O. Colquitt. BA, U. Iowa, 1947, MD, 1949. Diplomate Am. Bd. Ob-Gyn. Intern Western Res. U., Cleve., 1949—50; resident in medicine, surgery and ob-gyn Cleve. City Hosp., 1950—55; U.S. Sr. Fulbright Rsch. scholar U. London Postgrad. Med. Sch., 1955—57; obstetric cons. Ga. Dept. Pub. Health, Atlanta, 1958—60; pvt. practice Atlanta, 1960—65; asst. dir. clin. rsch. Bristol Labs., Syracuse, NY, 1965—67; prof., dir. maternal and infant care project Emory U. Grady Meml. Hosp., Atlanta, 1967—; co-dir. Regional Perinatal Ctr., Charles Howard Candler prof., chmn. dept. ob-gyn Emory U. Sch. Medicine, Atlanta, 1986—93. Gen. bd. dirs., bd. dirs. divsn. maternal-fetal medicine Am. Bd. Ob-Gyn.; bd. dirs. Alan Guttmacher Inst., N.Y.C., chmn., vice chmn.; Maternal and Child Health Care governing coun. Am. Hosp. Assn., Chgo.; chmn. FDA Ob-Gyn Device Com., Washington, 1986—88. Recipient Elizabeth Blackwell award, Am. Women's Med. Assn., 1986, Atlanta Woman History Maker award, Am. Women's Assn., 1987, Emory medal, 1988, Daggett Harvey award, Chgo. Maternity Ctr., Northwestern U., 1991, 40th Anniversary award, Fedn. Internat. Gynecology and Obstetrics, 1994. Fellow: ACOG (pres., v.p., asst. sec. 1982—85, Disting. Svc. award 1994); mem.: AMA, Inst. Medicine, Med. Assn. Ga. (chair maternal and child health care com.), Atlanta Obstet. and Gynecol. Soc. (pres.), Ga. Obstet. and Gynecol. Soc. (pres.), Marietta (Ga.) Country Club. Office: Grady Meml Hosp DeptGyn/Ob 69 Jesse Hall Dr SE Atlanta GA 30303-3033

KLEIN, LYNN ELLEN, artist; b. San Francisco, Apr. 14, 1950; BA in Studio Arts, U. Minn., 1974, MFA in Design, 1976. Instr. art edn. U. Minn., Mpls., 1976-78, lectr. in design, 1974-84; vis. artist U. Iowa, Ames, 1984—, Textile Ctr. of Minn., 2003. Resident Cité Internat. des Arts, Paris, 1984-86, summer 1998, vis. artist Textile Arts Ctr. of Minn., 2003. One-woman shows include Rochester (Minn.) Fine Arts Ctr., 1976, Northrup Gallery, U. Minn., Mpls., 1976, Allrich Gallery, San Francisco, 1982, 1988, Coffman Gallery, U. Minn., 1982, The Print Club, Phila., 1985, Foster-White Gallery, Seattle, 1989, Carolyn Ruff Gallery, Mpls., 1994, Robert Green Fine Arts, 2000, exhibited in group shows at Mpls. Inst. Arts, 1976, 1988, Franklin Inst. Sci. Mus., Phila., 1984, Minn. Mus. Art, St. Paul, 1990, Textile Arts Internat., 1990, 1992, San Francisco Bay Area Women Artists Mentors, 1994, USART San Francisco Internat. Art Expo, I. Wolk Gallery, St. Helena, Calif., 1996, Robert Green Fine Arts, Mill Valley, Calif., 1996, 2002, Craftsman's Guild and Calif. Heritage Gallery, 1998, Ren Brown Collection, Bodega Bay, Calif., 1998, Gensler Architecture-Material Matters, San Francisco, 1998, San Jose Mus. Art, Visible Rhythm, 2001, 2003, Kala Art Inst., 2002, Pyramid Atlantic Book Arts Fair, Wash., 2002, Brave New World Print Portfolio, NY Print Fair, 2004, Neomodern Calif. Abstraction Crocker Art Mus. to Monterey Mus., Sacramento, 2005, Represented in permanent collections Mpls. Inst. Arts, Oakland (Calif.) Mus., Bibliotéque Nat., Dept. des Estampes et de lá Photographie, Paris, Phila. Mus. Art, Walker Art Ctr., Mpls., Achenbach Found., Fine Arts Mus. San Francisco, San Jose Mus. Art., Calif., NY Pub. Libr., Rutgers Univ. Ctr. for Innovative Prints, Crocker Art Mus., Sacramento, San Diego Mus. Art, print publs., Double/Absent, edit. 15, 1983 (Calif. Phelan award for printmaking), Untitled, edit. 10, 1992, Wild Women Portfolio, edit. 20, 2002, Brave New World, edit. 20, 2004, commns., Miami Internat. Airport, 2000, Caesar's Palace, Las Vegas, 2001, Fairmount Mayakoloa, Cancun, Mex., 2004, Ritz Carelton, Palm Beach, Fla., 2005, numerous others. Recipient J.D. Phelan award World Print Coun., 1983; Minn. State Arts Bd. Grantee, 1978; Photography fellow, St. Paul, 1984; Rockefeller Found. fellow, Am. Ctr., 1984-86, Jerome Found. Printmaking fellow, Kala Inst., Berkeley, 1989; Amity Art Found. grant, Woodbridge, Conn., 2003. Mem.: Achenbach Graphic Arts Coun.

KLEIN, MARC S., editor, publishing executive; b. Feb. 16, 1949; married; 2 children. BA in Journalism, Pa. State U., 1970. Bur. chief Courier-Post, Camden, N.J., 1970-75; asst. mng. editor Phila. Bull., 1975-81; editor Jewish Exponent, Phila., 1981-83; editor, pub. Jewish Bull. of No. Calif., San Francisco, 1984—. Pub. j. the Jewish news weekly of No. Calif.; mem. exec. com. Jewish Telegraphic Agy. Past pres. Temple Israel, Alameda; former bd. dirs. Oakland-Piedmont Jewish Community Ctr. Recipient 1st place awards Phila. Press Assn., 1973, 1st place award N.J. Press Assn., 1973; Wall St. Jour. Newspaper Fund intern, fellow, 1969. Mem. Am. Jewish Press Assn. (pres.), Soc. Profl. Journalists (past bd. dirs.). Office: 225 Bush St Ste 1480 San Francisco CA 94104-4216 E-mail: marc@jweekly.com.

KLEIN, MARTIN I., lawyer; b. N.Y.C., Nov. 12, 1947; m. Diane Levbarg. BA, Lehigh U., 1969; JD, Am. U., 1972. Bar: N.Y. 1973, Fla. 1978, Calif. 1981, D.C. 1981; solicitor Supreme Ct. Eng., 1996—. Mem. profl. staff U.S. Senate Com. on Labor and Pub. Welfare, 1969-72; legis. aide U.S. Senator Jacob K. Javits, 1969-72; ptnr., head creditors' rights dept. Dreyer & Traub, N.Y.C., 1980-93; ptnr., head dept. bankruptcy Shea & Gould, N.Y.C., 1993—95; pvt. practice Martin I. Klein, P.C., 1995—. Lectr. Am. Law Inst.-ABA Com. on Continuing Profl. Edn., 1975—, The Practising Law Inst., 1975—, Mathematica, 1981—; adj. assoc. prof. law Benjamin Cardozo Sch. Law, Yeshiva U., 1980—; lectr. Columbia U. Sch. Law, 1980—; mem. med. malpractice mediation panel appellate div. Supreme Ct. State N.Y. 1980—; trustee, treas., pres. Cen. Synagogue, N.Y.C., 1986-98; arbitrator, N.Y.C. Small Claims Ct. Contbr. articles on fin. real estate and comml. law to profl. jours. Del. White House Conf. on Youth, 1971; chmn. Town of Palm Beach Zoning Commn., 1994-2001. Mem. ABA, N.Y. State Bar Assn., Fla. Bar Assn., Calif. Bar Assn., D.C. Bar Assn., N.Y. County Lawyers Assn. (mem. com. on bankruptcy), Am. Arbitration Assn. (mem. comml. panel). Address: 21st Fl 780 Third Ave New York NY 10017

KLEIN, MARTIN JESSE, physicist, educator, science historian; b. N.Y.C., June 25, 1924; s. Adolph and Mary (Neuman) K.; m. Miriam June Levin, Oct. 28, 1945 (div. 1973); children: Rona F., Sarah M. Klein Zaino, Nancy R. Klein; m. Linda L. Booz, Oct. 8, 1980; 1 child, Abigail M. AB, Columbia U., 1942, MA, 1944; PhD, MIT, 1948. With OSRD for USN, 1944-45; research assoc. in physics MIT, Cambridge, 1946-49; instr. physics Case Inst. Tech., Cleve., 1949-51, asst. prof., 1951-55, assoc. prof., 1955-60, prof., 1960-67, acting dept. head, 1966-67; prof. history physics Yale U., New Haven, 1967-74, Eugene Higgins prof. history physics and prof. physics, 1974-91, 95-99, Bass prof. history sci., prof. physics, 1991-95, chmn. dept. history sci., 1971-74, William Clyde De Vane prof., 1978-81, prof. emeritus, 1999—. Van der Waals guest prof. U. Amsterdam, 1974, Pieter Zeeman guest prof., 1993; vis. prof. Harvard U., 1989-90, Rockefeller U., 1975, adj. prof. 1976-79. Author: Paul Ehrenfest, Vol. I: The Making of a Theoretical Physicist, 1970; editor: Collected Scientific Papers of Paul Ehrenfest, 1959; sr. editor The Collected Papers of Albert Einstein, 1988-97; editorial adviser Ency. Brit, 1956-76; translator: Letters on Wave Mechanics, 1967; contbr. articles to profl. jours. NRC fellow Dublin (Ireland) Inst. Advanced Studies, 1952-53; Guggenheim fellow Leyden, Netherlands, 1958-59; Guggenheim fellow Yale, 1967-68 Fellow Am. Acad. Arts and Scis., Am. Phys. Soc.; mem. NAS, AAUP, History of Sci. Soc., Am. Assn. Physics Tchrs., Internat. Acad. History of Sci., Phi Beta Kappa, Sigma Xi. Home: 1 Caroline Meadows Apt 104 Chapel Hill NC 27517-8508 Office: Yale U Dept Physics PO Box 208120 New Haven CT 06520-8120 E-mail: blawett_klein@bellsouth.net.

KLEIN, MARTIN SAMUEL, management consulting executive; b. N.Y.C., Dec. 8, 1932; s. David and Dorothy (Manheim) K.; m. Elizabeth Jann Perks, Dec. 19, 1964 (dec. Aug. 1994); children: Sarah Madeline, Dorothy Ann. AB, Harvard U., 1954, MBA, 1962. V.p. United Rsch., Cambridge, Mass., 1962-69, Boston Cons. Group, 1969-73; pres. Instnl. Strategy Assocs., Belmont, Mass., 1973—. Cons. Brookings Instn., Washington, 1963-64. Author: (with others) Impact of Transportation on Development, 1964, Combining Public Health Nursing Agencies, 1964; contbr. articles to profl. jours. Bd. dirs. Vis. Nurse Assn., Boston, 1972-82, Harvard Cmty. Health Plan, Boston, 1978-93; vice chmn. Harvard Cmty. Health Plan Found., 1986-93, Cambridge Ctr. for Adult Edn., 1983-85; sec.-treas. Ctr. for Effective Philanthropy, Cambridge, 1982-98; trustee Mt. Auburn Hosp., Cambridge, 1995-, Big Sister Assn. Greater Boston, 1996-99; counselor to bd. trustees Aga Khan U., Karachi, 1993-2002. Sr. fellow Cheswick Ctr., 1980—, trustee; Harvard Coll. scholar, 1954, Fulbright scholar, Australia, 1954-55, George F. Baker scholar Harvard Bus. Sch., 1962. Mem. Am. Hosp. Assn. (com. on governance 1998-2001), Mass. Hosp. Assn. (trustee adv. coun. 2002--), Harvard Club (N.Y.C. and Boston), Belmont Hill Club (treas. 1979-80), Harvard Travellers Club (Boston), Kirribilli Club (Sydney, Australia). Jewish. Office: Instl Strategy Assocs Inc 43 Village Hill Rd Belmont MA 02478-2117

KLEIN, MARY ANN, special education educator; b. Ridgewood, N.J., Jan. 31, 1956; d. Julius R. and Nancy M. Pascuzzo; m. Thomas F. Klein, July 16, 1983. B in Elem. Edn. & Spl. Edn., Adelphi U., Garden City, N.Y., 1978; M in Spl. Edn. & Reading, Adelphi Univ., Garden City, N.Y., 1980. Cert. in spl. edn. Learning disabilities specialist Merrick UFSD, Merrick, NY, 1978—. Swimming instr. disabled children and adults Village of Garden City, 1974—79; pvt. piano instr., NY, 1978—82; clinician & diagnostician Adelphi U. Reading Clinic, Garden City, 1980—84; ednl. cons. BOCES of Nassau County, Merrick, NY, 1993—94, SETRC of Nassau County, Westbury, NY, 1995—96; founder peer tutoring program Birch Sch., Merrick, NY; spl. edn. rep. Birch Child Study Team, Merrick, NY. Co-author: (curriculum guide) Foundations for Learning, 1991; author: (resource guide) Strategies to Assist Learning Disabled Children in the Classroom Setting, 1995. Mem. Merrick PTA, 1978—, tchr. liaison, 1994—97; mem. Merrick SEPTA, 1983—, Com. on Spl. Edn., 1983—, Nassau Reading Coun., 1996—; co-founder Students Against Destructive Decision-Making, Birch Sch., Merrick, NY; apptd. Crisis Mgmt. Team, Birch Sch. Mem.: State Congress of Parents & Tchrs. (hon.), Coun. for Exceptional Children, Kappa Delta Pi. Avocations: piano, travel.

KLEIN, MICHAEL, art center administrator; b. N.Y.C., Jan. 23; MA, Williams Coll., 1977. Curator Microsoft Corp., Redmond, Wash., 1999—2004; exec. dir. Internat. Sculpture Ctr., Hamilton, NJ, 2005—. Office: Internat Sculpture Ctr 14 Fairgrounds Rd Ste B Hamilton NJ 08619 Office Fax: 609-689-1061. Personal E-mail: kleinm52@hotmail.com. Business E-Mail: mklein@sculpture.org.

KLEIN, MICHAEL D., lawyer; b. Wilkes-Barre, Pa., June 9, 1951; BA magna cum laude, King's Coll., 1973; JD, Dickinson Sch. Law, 1976. Bar: Pa. 1976, U.S. Ct. Appeals (3rd cir.) 1984, U.S. Dist. Ct. (mid. dist.) Pa. 1984, U.S. Dist Ct. (ea. dist.) Pa. 1994. Asst. atty. gen. Commonwealth of Pa., Harrisburg, 1976-82; mgr. corp. affairs, corp. sec. Pa. Am. Water Co., Hershey, 1982-89; ptnr. LeBoeuf, Lamb, Greene & MacRae LLP, Harrisburg, Pa., 1991—, mng. ptnr. Harrisburg office, 1991—. Mem. Pa. Bar Assn., Am. Water Works Assn. Office: LeBoeuf Lamb Greene & MacRae LLP 200 N Third St Ste 300 Harrisburg PA 17101 Office Phone: 717-232-8199. Office Fax: 717-232-8720. Business E-Mail: mklein@llgm.com.

KLEIN, MICHAEL ELIHU, physician; b. NYC, Apr. 6, 1946; s. Leo and Edith (Rigrod) K.; m. Elizabeth Angela McGehee, Oct. 8, 1988; children: Michael, Debra, Daniel. BA, Wesleyan U., Middletown, Conn., 1967; MD, MPH, Yale U., 1972. Diplomate Am. Bd. Internal Medicine. Asst. dir. hematology U. Md., Balt., 1979-83; sr. investigator U. Md. Cancer Ctr., Balt., 1979-83; pvt. practice specializing in hematology/oncology Cowley Assocs., Camp Hill, Pa., 1983-97, Ctrl. Pa. Hematology & Oncology, Lemoyne, 1997—; chief hematology Pinnacle Health Systems, Harrisburg, Pa., 2002—; assoc. clin. prof. Univ. Pa., Hersey, 2004—; asst. clin. prof. Pa. Coll. Osteopathic Medicine, 2004—. Cons. in hematology and oncology Holy Spirit Hosp., Camp Hill, Pa., 1983—, chmn. blood usage com., 1998—2000, Camp Hill, 2003—; cons. in hematology and oncology Pinnacle Health System, Harrisburg, 1983—, chief hematology, 2002—, chmn. blood utilization com., 1988—. Author: Political Dynamics National Health Insurance in New York, 1972; contbr. articles to profl. jours., chpts. to books. Founder, bd. dirs. Number Nine, New Haven, 1971. Comdr. lt. USPHS, 1974-77. Fellow Internat. Acad. Clin. and Applied Thrombosis/Hemostasis; mem. AMA, Am. Soc. Clin. Research, Am. Soc. Clin. Oncology, Am. Soc. Hematology, Am. Legion, Balt. Blood Club (pres. 1979-83). Avocations: stamp collecting/philately, baseball, reading. Office: Ctrl Pa Hematology & Oncology 50 N 12th St Ste 100 Lemoyne PA 17043-1440 Office Phone: 717-737-5767. E-mail: orioledh@aol.com.

KLEIN, MICHAEL LAWRENCE, research chemist, educator; b. London, Mar. 13, 1940; s. Julius and Bessie (Bloomberg) K.; m. Brenda May Woodman, June 3, 1962; children— Paula Denise, Rachel Anne B.Sc., Bristol U., Eng., 1961; PhD, Bristol U., 1964. Research fellow CIBA-GEIGEY, Genoa, Italy, 1964-65; research fellow Imperial Chem. Industries (UK), Bristol, Eng., 1965-67; research assoc. Rutgers U., New Brunswick, N.J., 1967-68; research officer NRC of Can., Ottawa, Ont., 1968-87; prof. chemistry U. Pa., Phila., 1987—91, William Smith prof. chemistry, 1991—93, Hepburn prof. phys. scis., 1993—, dir. Lab. for Rsch. on the Structure of Matter. Part-time prof. chemistry Mc Master U., Hamilton, Ont., 1977-89; mem. internat. relations com. Natural Scis. and Engring. Research Council, Ottawa, 1982-84, mem. NSERC chem. panel, 1985-86, NSF panels, 1993—, NIH panels, 1996—; mem. FDA Panel, 1999; vis. prof., Paris, Lyon, France, Kyoto, Japan, Amsterdam, Canberra, Australia, Florence, Italy; fellow commoner Trinity Coll., Cambridge, Eng., 1985-86; dir. NSF Materials Rsch. Lab., 1993-96, NSF MRSEC, 1996—; Miller prof. U. Calif., Berkeley, 1997, Linnett prof. U. Cambridge, 1998; fellow Sydney-Sussex Coll., Cambridge, U.K., 1998. Editor: Rare Gas Solids, Vol. I, 1976, Vol. II, 1977, Inert Gases, 1984; mem. editl. bd. Chem. Physics, 1986—, Physics Reports, 1986—, Jour. Phys. Chemistry, 1990-95, Molecular Physics, 1992-99, Computational Materials Sci., 1992—, Jour. Chem. Soc. Farady Trans., 1993-98, Jour. Phys. Condensed Matter, 1994-97, Phys. Chemistry Chem. Physics, 1999—, Accounts of Chem. Rsch., 2004—, Chem. Physics Letters, 2003—, Jour. Chem. Physics, 2003—; contbr. numerous articles to profl. jours. Recipient Alder prize CECAM, 2004; IBM World Trade fellow, 1970, Guggenheim fellow, 1989, Humboldt fellow, 1995; grantee Natural Scis. and Engring. Rsch. Coun., 1979-89, NSF, 1988—, NIH, 1988—. Fellow Royal Soc. Can., Royal Soc. London, Inst. Physics, Chem. Inst. Can., Am. Phys. Soc. (Rahman prize 1999), Am. Acad. Arts and Scis.; mem. Am. Chem. Soc. (Phila. Sect. award 1998), Royal Soc. Chemistry (U.K.). Office: Univ Pa 141 CHEM/6323 Philadelphia PA 19104

KLEIN, MICHAEL ROGER, foundation administrator, lawyer, investor; b. N.Y.C., Apr. 10, 1942; s. Jesse and Stephanie (Siegel) K.; m. Joan Ilona Fabry, Feb. 19, 1977; children: Nicholas Jesse, Alexander Fabry. BBA, U. Miami, Coral Gables, Fla., 1963, JD, 1966; LLM, Harvard U., 1967. Bar: Fla. 1966, D.C., 1969, U.S. Dist. Ct. (D.C. cir.) 1970, U.S. Supreme Ct., 1970. Asst. prof. law La. State U., Baton Rouge, 1967-69; assoc. Wilmer, Cutler & Pickering, Washington, 1969-74, ptnr., 1974—. Chmn. Zenith Gallery, Inc., Washington, 1978—, LePavillon of D.C., Washington, 1983-89; co-founder, chmn. bd. CoStar Group Inc., 1988—, vice-chmn. bd. dirs. Perini Corp. 1991—, lead dir.; bd. dirs. SRA Internat. Inc.; co-founder, chmn. bd. Precept Corp., 1999—; co-founder, chmn., CEO Le Paradou, LLC, 2003-; co-owner, dir. Astar Air Cargo, Inc., 2003—. Author: Eminent Domain, 1969; contbr. articles to profl. jours. Trustee Ctr. for Law in the Pub. Interest, L.A., 1975-91, Am. Himalayan Found., 1996—; pres. PEN Faulkner Found., 2005—; chmn. bd. trustees Advocates for Pub. Interest, Washington, 1986-89; dir. Support Ctr. of D.C., Inc., 1991-95. Mem. Am. Law Inst. Jewish. Office: Pen Faulkner Found 901 Fifteenth St NW Washington DC 20005

KLEIN, MILES VINCENT, physics professor; b. Cleve., Mar. 9, 1933; s. Max Ralph and Isabelle (Benjamin) K.; m. Barbara Judith Pincus, Sept. 2, 1956; children: Cynthia Klein-Banai, Gail. BS, Northwestern U., 1954; PhD, Cornell U., 1961. NSF postdoctoral fellow Max Planck Inst., Stuttgart, Germany, 1961; prof. U. Ill., Urbana, 1962—. Co-author: Optics, 1986; contbr. articles to profl. jours. A.P. Sloan Found. fellow, 1963. Fellow AAAS, Am. Phys. Soc. (Frank Isakson prize 1990), Am. Acad. Arts and Scis.; mem. IEEE (Sr.), Nat. Acad. Scis. Office: Materials Rsch Lab 104 S Goodwin Ave Urbana IL 61801-2902 Office Phone: 217-333-1744. E-mail: mvklein@uiuc.edu.

KLEIN, NANCY KIRKLAND, choral music educator; b. Alexandria, Va., Dec. 3, 1954; d. Robert Carey and Roma Susan (Sanders) Kirkland; m. Robert Chandler Klein, Feb. 25, 1984; children: Carey Elizabeth, William Chandler. BA, U. Richmond, 1976; M in Vocal Performance, Ea. Ky. U., 1982; PhD in Music, NYU, 1986. Cert. music tchr., Va., Ky, N.Y., N.C., Tenn., Calif., 15 other states. Music educator Boyle County Schs., Danville, Ky., 1976—83; asst. dir. NYU Choral Arts Soc., 1983—85, acting dir., 1985—86; assoc. prof. music Old Dominion U., Norfolk, Va., 1986—, grad. program dir., 1988—. Pvt. practice, N.Y.C., 1983-86; cons. choral clinican and adjudicator, 1987—; adv. bd. for musical publs., N.Y.C., 1985-87. Contbr. articles to profl. jours.; conducted numerous choral concerts in U.S., England, Ireland, Wales, Japan, Scotland and Turkey. Active Kempsville Presbyn. Ch., Va. Beach, Va., dir. of choirs and orcht. Mem. Music Educators Nat. Conf., Va. Music Educators Conf. (editor choral rev. 1988—, past pres. coll. sect.), Am. Choral Dirs. Assn., Golden Key, Omicron Delta Kappa, Phi Delta Kappa, Pi Kappa Lambda. Avocations: swimming, painting, family activities. Office: Old Dominion U Music Dept Norfolk VA 23508 Office Phone: 757-683-4061. Personal E-mail: drnancyk@aol.com. Business E-Mail: nklein@odu.edu.

KLEIN, NEIL CHARLES, physician; b. N.Y.C., Jan. 6, 1935; s. Martin and Jeannette F. (Pazow) K.; divorced; children: Lisa, Susie, David; m. Phyllis Klein, Nov. 26, 1989. AB, Columbia U., 1956; MD, Cornell U., 1960. Diplomate Am. Bd. Internal Medicine, Am. Bd. Gastroenterology, Nat. Bd. Med. Examiners. Intern N.Y. Hosp., 1960-61, resident, 1964-67; fellow in medicine Cornell Med. Coll., 1965-67, clin. instr. in medicine, 1967-70, asst. clin. prof. medicine, 1970-77; assoc. clin. prof. medicine N.Y. Med. Coll., 1977-84, clin. prof. medicine N.Y.C., 1984—98, Columbia U., N.Y.C., 1998—; asst. clin. attending physician N.Y. Hosp., 1970-77, St. Joseph's Hosp., Stamford, Conn., 1967-72; from asst. to assoc. attending physician Stamford (Conn.) Hosp., 1967—, assoc. chief medicine, 1972-75, chief divsn. gastroenterology, 1978-84. Bd. dirs. Conn. Med. Ins. Co., 1988-2002, fin. com., 1988-2002, sec., 1990-2002; bd. dirs. Stamford Health Network, 1987-93, chmn. fin. com., 1994-2001; mem. sci. adv. coun. Fairfield-Westchester Ileitis-Colitis Found., 1982—; mem. Commn. of Aging, Stamford, 1971-82. Fellow ACP, Am. Coll. Gastroenterology, Royal Soc. Tropical Medicine and Hygiene; mem. Fairfield County Med. Assn. (trustee 1980-87, chmn. bd. trustees 1984-85, pres. 1985-86), Conn. State Med. Assn., Am. Soc. Gastrointestinal Endoscopy, Am. Gastrointestinal Assn., Cornell Med. Coll. Alumni Assn. (pres. 1976-78, sr. advisor 1978—), Stamford Med. Soc. (pres. 1990-91). Office: Shoreline Med Group 1450 Washington Blvd Stamford CT 06902-2451 Office Phone: 203-327-9321. Business E-Mail: neilklein@shorelinemedicalllp.com.

KLEIN, OTTO GEORGE, III, lawyer; b. Berkeley, Calif., Dec. 7, 1950; BA, U. Wash., 1973; JD, Yale U., 1976. Bar: Wash. 1976. Atty. Perkins Coie, 1976-81; ptnr. Syrdal, Danelo, Klein, Myre & Woods, 1981—88, Heller Ehrman, 1988-97; mem. Summit Law Group, Seattle, 1997—. Office: Summit Law Group Ste 1000 315 5th Ave S Seattle WA 98104-2679 Office Phone: 206-676-7000. Business E-Mail: ottok@summitlaw.com.

KLEIN, PAUL E., lawyer; b. N.Y.C., Apr. 26, 1934; AB, Cornell U., 1956; JD, Harvard U., 1960. Bar: Mich. 1960, Ill. 1965, N.Y. 1967, U.S. Supreme Ct. 1977, U.S. Ct. Appeals (2d cir.) 1980. Atty. Dow Chem. Co., Midland, Mich., 1960-65; assoc. Gunther & Choka, Chgo., 1965-66; atty. Esso Rsch. & Engring. Co., Linden, N.J., 1966-67; sr. mng. editor Matthew Bender & Co., N.Y.C., 1967-72; assoc. gen. counsel N.Y. Life Ins. Co., 1972-80, v.p., assoc. gen. counsel, 1980-84; v.p., counsel Huggins Fin. Svcs., Inc., 1984-86; exec. corp. tax. div. Ernst & Young, 1986-95; pvt. practice White Plains, 1995—2004; ret., 2004. Adj. asst. prof. L.I. U., 1972-79, adj. assoc. prof., 1979-80; adj. assoc. prof. acctg. and taxation, Fordham U. at Lincoln Ctr. grad. sch. of bus. adminstrn., 1995-2003. Former columnist Jour. Real Estate Taxation; writer; editor. Mem. ABA (past chmn. subcom. on life ins. products/ins. cos. com., sect. taxation), Assn. Bar City N.Y. (past chair subcom. on life and health ins. of the com. on ins. law), Assn. Life Ins. Counsel (sec.-treas. 1979-83, bd. govs. 1983-87), N.Y. State Bar Assn. E-mail: pek34@optonline.net.

KLEIN, PETER MARTIN, lawyer, retired transportation executive; b. N.Y.C., June 2, 1934; s. Saul and Esther (Goldstein) K.; m. Ellen Judith Matlick, June 18, 1961; children: Amy Lynn, Steven Ezra. AB, Columbia U., 1956, JD, 1962. Bar: N.Y. 1962, D.C. 1964, U.S. Supreme Ct. 1966. Asst. proctor Columbia U., 1959-62; asst. counsel Mil. Sea Transp. Svc., Office Gen. Counsel, Dept. Navy, Washington, 1962-65; trial atty. civil div. U.S. Dept. Justice, N.Y.C., 1966-69; gen. atty. Sea-Land Svc., Inc., Menlo Park, N.J., 1969-76, v.p., gen. counsel, sec., 1976-79, Sea-Land Industries, Inc., Menlo Park, 1979-84; assoc. gen. counsel R.J. Reynolds Industries, Inc., Winston-Salem, N.C., 1978-84; sr. v.p., gen. counsel, sec. Sea-Land Svc., Inc. (formerly Sea-Land Corp.), Charlotte, N.C., 1984-94, sr. v.p.-law, sec., 1994-95, ret., 1996—. Mem. adv. com. on pvt. internat. law Dept. State, 1974-95; mem. U.S. delegation UN Conf. of Trade and Devel., UN Commn. on Internat. Trade Law, 1975-76, trade regulation adv. bd. Bur. Nat. Affairs, 1986-88; alt. mem. N.Am. coun. London Ct. of Internat. Arbitration, 1988-95. Trustee Jewish Edn. Assn. Met. N.J., 1973-76; trustee Temple B'nai Abraham of Essex County, N.J., 1973—, v.p., 1976-81, pres. 1981-83; mem. Essex County Dems. Com., 1986-88; mem. Livingston Twp. Planning Bd., 1996—, vice chmn. 1997-99, chmn., 2000—. With USN, 1956-59, Antarctica. Mem. ABA, FBA, Am. Maritime Assn. (bd. dirs., chmn. coms. on law and legis. 1974-78), Am. Polar Soc. (life), Navy League U.S. (life), U.S. Naval Inst. (life), N.Y. State Bar Assn., D.C. Bar Assn., Internat. Bar Assn., Maritime Law Assn. Home: 22 Sandalwood Dr Livingston NJ 07039-1409

KLEIN, PHILIP ALEXANDER, economist; b. Austin, Tex., Oct. 8, 1927; s. David Ballin and Rose (Schaffer) K.; m. Margaret A. McCormack, May 20, 1961; children— Kathleen Monico, Alan Schaffer BA, U. Tex., 1948, MA, 1949; PhD, U. Calif., Berkeley, 1958. Instr. Carleton Coll., Northfield, Minn., spring 1955; mem. faculty Pa. State U., State College, 1955—, prof. econs., 1965—2000, emeritus prof. econs., 2000—; rsch. assoc. Nat. Bur. Econ. Rsch., 1955-70, 73-79, Ctr. Internat. Bus. Cycle Rsch., Columbia U., 1979-96, Econ. Cycle Rsch. Inst., 1996—. Vis. prof. San Francisco State U., summer 1963, U. Hawaii, summer 1967, Inst. Europeen D'Adminstrn. des Affairs, Fontainbleau, France, 1963-64, 65, 66, 67, U. Osijek, Yugoslavia, 1970, Mills Coll., spring 1982; acad. visitor London Sch. Econs., 1973-74, 81; disting. Fulbright fellow U. Siena, Italy, 1989; adj. scholar Am. Enterprises Inst., Washington, 1976—; cons. UN, Ctr. Devel. Planning Projections Policies, 1973, OECD, Paris, 1978-81, EEC, Brussels, 1979-82, World Bank, Washington, 1986, 87, 88 Mem. editorial bd. Internat. Jour. Forecasting, 1986—, Jour. Econ. Issues, 1976-81, 85-87; author books in field; contbr. articles to profl. jours., chpts. to books. With M.C., AUS, 1946-47. Recipient Distinction in Social Scis. award Pa. State U., 1981, Veblen-Commons award Assn. Evolutionary Econs., 1990; Fulbright fellow France, 1963, Yugoslavia, 1970, Italy, 1989. Mem. Econs. Assn., Assn. Evolutionary Econs. (pres. 1977, Veblen-Commons award 1990), Assn. Comparative Econs., Phi Beta Kappa (pres. chpt. 1981). Home: 719 S Sparks St State College PA 16801-4114 Office: Pa State U Dept Econs 516 Kern Grad Bldg University Park PA 16802 Office Phone: 814-865-5781. Business E-Mail: pak11@psu.edu.

KLEIN, R. KENT, lawyer; b. Richmond, Mo., Feb. 11, 1944; BA with distinction, U. Ariz., 1965, JD, 1968. Bar: Ariz. 1968. Atty. State Compensation Fund Ariz., 1968-74, Lewis & Roca, Phoenix, 1974—2002, Klein, Lundmark, Barberich & La Mint, P.C., Phoenix, 2002—. Mem. State Bar Ariz. Office: Klein Lundmark Barberich & La Mont PC Ste B-112 5333 N 7th St Phoenix AZ 85014 Office Phone: 602-279-9777. Business E-Mail: rkklein@klbllaw.com.

KLEIN, RICHARD DANIEL, law educator; b. N.Y.C., June 21, 1943; s. Abraham Ehrenfeld and Anna (Rubin) K.; m. Janet Lee Benshoof, Mar. 27, 1971; children: David and Eli (twins). BS, U. Wis., 1964; M in Internat. Affairs, Columbia U., 1969, EdD in Comparative Edn. and Internat. Affairs, 1970; JD, Harvard U., 1972. Bar: N.Y. 1973, U.S. Dist. Ct. (ea. and so. dists.) N.Y. 1976, U.S. Ct. Appeals (2d cir.) 1976, U.S. Supreme Ct. 1979. Vol. U.S. Peace Corps, Somalia, Africa, 1964-66; sr. atty. Legal Aid Soc., N.Y.C., 1972-82; prof. Hofstra Law Sch., Hempstead, N.Y., 1982-83, Touro Law Sch., Huntington, N.Y., 1983—. Contbr. articles to profl. jours. Dem. County Committeeman, N.Y.C., 1983—. Internat. Devel. fellow Ford Found., 1966-70. Mem. ABA, Nassau County Bar Assn., Nat. Assn. Criminal Def. Lawyers (spl. adv. com.), Assn. Trial Lawyers Am. Jewish. Avocations: skiing, music. Office: Touro Law Sch 300 Nassau Rd Huntington NY 11743-4346 Home: Apt 33J 60 E 8th St New York NY 10003 Office Phone: 631-421-2244. E-mail: klein@lawyer.com.

KLEIN, RICHARD S., lawyer; b. NYC, Nov. 27, 1947; BA, CUNY, 1968; JD, Bklyn. Law Sch., 1973. Bar: NY 1974, US Dist. Ct. Ea. Dist. NY, US Dist. Ct. So. Dist. NY. Ptnr. Wilson, Elser, Moskowitz, Edelman & Dicker LLP, NYC. Mem.: ABA, NY State Bar Assn. Office: Wilson Elser Moskowitz Edelman & Dicker LLP 23rd Fl 150 E 42nd St New York NY 10017-5639 Office Phone: 212-490-3000 ext. 2280. Office Fax: 212-490-3038. Business E-Mail: kleinr@wemed.com.

KLEIN, RICHARD TEMPLE, JR., hand tool manufacturing executive; b. Evanston, Ill., May 17, 1956; s. Richard Temple and Donna Grace (Hoyt) K.; m. Risa L., June 18, 1978; children: Richard Temple III, Jason Lewit, Jonathan Hoyt. BBA, U. Miami, Fla., 1978. Dir. Mr. Tool Mfg., Roselle, Ill., Klein Tools Inc., Midwest Grinding, Inc., Skokie, Ill. Contbr. articles to profl. jours. Active Civil Air Patrol. Mem. Soc. Mfg. Engrs. Office: Klein Tools Inc 7200 N Mccormick Blvd Chicago IL 60659

KLEIN, ROBERT, comedian, actor; b. N.Y.C., Feb. 8, 1942; s. Benjamin and Frieda (Moskowitz) K.; m. Brenda Boozer, Apr. 29, 1973 (div.); 1 child, Alexander Stewart. BA, Alfred (N.Y.) U., 1962; student, Yale U. Sch. Drama, 1962-63; DHL (hon.), Alfred U., 1980. Mem. Second City Theatrical Co., Chgo., 1965-66. Stage appearances include 20,000 Frozen Grenadiers with Second City Theatrical Co., Chgo., 1965 (debut); Broadway appearances include The Apple Tree, 1966, New Faces of 1968, 1968, Morning, Noon and Night, 1969, They're Playing Our Song, 1979 (Tony award nomination best actor in a musical 1979), The Robert Klein Show! 1985-86, The Sisters Rosensweig, 1993; film appearances include The Landlord, 1970, The Owl and the Pussycat, 1970, Rivals, 1972, Hooper, 1978, The Bell Jar, 1979, Nobodys Perfekt, 1981, The Last Unicorn (voice), 1982, Tales from the Darkside-The Movie, 1990, Radioland Murders, 1993, Mixed Nuts, 1994, Jeffrey, 1995, Next Stop Wonderland, 1996, One Fine Day, 1997, Primary Colors, 1997, Suits, 1998, Goosed, 1998, Labor Pains, 1998; records include Child of the Fifties, 1973 (Grammy award nominee), Mind Over Matter, 1974 (Grammy award nominee), New Teeth, 1975, Let's Not Make Love; frequent TV and concert appearances including (video) Tax Attack 87, (HBO spl.) Robert Klein on Broadway, 1987; TV series include Comedy Tonight, 1970 (host), TV's Bloopers and Practical Jokes, 1984 (host), Robert Klein Time, Dead Comics Society, Stand-Up/Sit Down Comedy, A&E Rev., Sisters, 1993-96; TV movies include Your Place of Mine?, 1983, Poison Ivy, 1985, This Wife for Hire, 1985: radio work includes The Robert Klein Radio Show; videos include Robert Klein: Child of the 50s, Man of the 80s, 1984, Robert Klein on Broadway, 1986, Tax Attack, 1987; author: (memoir) The Amorous Busboy of Decatur Avenue, 2005. Mem. Actors Equity Assn., Screen Actors Guild, AFTRA, Am. Guild Variety Artists, Writers Guild. Office: c/o Mel Berger William Morris Agy 1325 6th Ave New York NY 10019-6026*

KLEIN, ROBERT NICHOLAS, II, real estate developer; 3 children. BA in History with honors, JD, Stanford U. Pres. Klein Fin. Corp., Palo Alto Calif., Klein Fin. Resources. Bd. dirs. Global Security Inst.; participated in drafting of legis. to create the Calif. Housing Fin. Agy., past bd. dirs.; co-author Proposition 71, Calif., 2004; chmn. Yes on Proposition 71 campaign for the Calif. Stem Cell Rsch. & Cures initiative, 2004; interim pres. Calif. Inst. for Regenerative Medicine, 2004—05, chmn. ind. citizens oversight com., 2004—. Named one of 100 Most Influential People of 2005, Time mag. Office: Klein Fin Corp Ste 330 550 Calif Ave Palo Alto CA 94306*

KLEIN, SAMI WEINER, librarian; b. Worcester, Mass., July 6, 1939; d. Phillip and Barbara Rose (Ginsburg) Weiner; m. Eugene Robert Klein, Oct. 22, 1961; children: Pamela, Jeffrey, Elizabeth. BS, Simmons Coll., 1961; MLS, U. Md., 1973; postgrad., Johns Hopkins U., 1976-78. Chemist Hercules, Wilmington, Del., 1961-62, FDA, Washington, 1965-66; libr. NSWC, White Oak, Md., 1973-78; chief Hdqs. Libr. EPA, Washington, 1978-82; chief rsch. info. svcs. Nat. Inst. Svcs. and Tech., Gaithersburg, Md., 1982-95; chief rsch. libr. and info. program, rsch. libr. Nat. Inst. Stds. and Tech., Gaithersburg, Md., 1995-99; retired Nat. Inst. Svcs. and Tech., Gaithersburg, Md., 1999. Cons. in field; mem. librs. exec. coun. Met. Washington Coun. of Govts., 1981-82; elected mem. com. Fed. Libr. Info. Ctr., 1993-95, chair, budget and fin. working group, 1994-98. Editor OIS Sci.-Tech Info, 1982-95; mem. editorial bd. Assn. Ofcly. Analyt. Chemists, 1985-92, Sci. and Tech. Librs., 1996—. Fed. govt. rep. Inst. for Sci. Info. Internat. Users Group, 1985—86; mem. info. tech. com. Candlelight Concert Soc.; chmn. Howard County Holocaust Remembrance Program, 2003; 2d v.p. Bet Aviv Congregation, pres., 2004—; mem. edn. com. Fed. Libr. and Info. Ctr. Com., 1987—91. Recipient Gold medal Am. Soc. Chemists, 1961, Engring. award Govt. Iindustry Data Exch. Program, 1997. Mem. ALA (sec.-treas. Fed. Librs. Round Table 1983-84, rep. to NTIS 1984-90, bd. dirs. 1986-89, v.p. 1991, pres. 1991-92, nominations chair 1992-93, scholar 1994-96, chair privatization com. 1995-97, chair co-awards com. 1996—, 1st FLRT Disting. Svc. award 1995), Spl. Librs. Assn. (treas. info.-tech. group 1986-87, student loan com. 1984-85), D.C. Law Librs. Soc. (NIST v.p. standards com. for women 1988, pres. 1989, bd. dirs. Comstar Credit Union 1994-2000), Fed. Libr. and Info. Network (exec. adv. com. 1989-91, sec. 1989, vice chair 1990-91), Jewish Mus. Md. (bd. dirs. 1999—), Beta Phi Mu. Democrat. Jewish. Home: 11041 Wood Elves Way Columbia MD 21044-1002 E-mail: swklein@comcast.net.

KLEIN, SHIRLEY SNYDERMAN, retail executive; b. Balt., Oct. 23, 1929; d. Julius Herman and Fannie (Dannenberg) Snyderman; m. Ralph Lincoln Klein, Jan. 4, 1953; children: Andrew P., Michael J., Howard S. BA, Towson State Tchr.'s Coll., 1951. Office staff accts. receivable, jr. controller Klein's Tower Plz., Inc., Forest Hill, Md., 1952-60, jr. buyer, 1960-70, v.p., buyer children's, ladies, linens, 1970—; chmn. Upper Chesapeake Health Found., 1993—2001; bd. mem. Upper Chesapeake Health Sys. (2 Hosp.), 1994. Treas. Mortgage Svc. Co., Inc., 1956—64; v.p. Klein's Supermarkets, 1979—, Colgate Investments, 1970—. Pres. Hadassah Harford County, 1966-68; v.p.;, adv. bd. John Carroll Sch., Md. Diocese, 1967, bd. mem., 1970; chmn. Retinitis Pigmentosa Found., Harford County, Md., 1971; bd. dirs. Harford Opera Theatre Guild, 1976-79; treas. Harford County Commn. for Women, 1977-82; v.p. Jewish Nat. Fund., Balt., 1990-95, bd. dirs., 1993-2000; vice chair Israel Bonds Balt., 1980-97. Recipient Goldie Myeir award, 1996. Mem.: LWV. Home: 109 W Jarrettsville Rd Forest Hill MD 21050-1319 Office: 2101 Rockspring Road Forest Hill MD 21050 Fax: 410-838-5592.

KLEIN, SNIRA L(UBOVSKY), Hebrew language and literature educator; came to U.S., 1959, naturalized, 1974; d. Avraham and Devora (Unger) Lubovsky; m. Earl H. Klein, Dec. 25, 1975. Tchr. cert., Tchrs. Seminar, Netanya, Israel, 1956; B. Rel. Edn., U. Judaism, 1961, M in Hebrew Lit., 1963; BA, Calif. State U., Northridge, 1966; MA, UCLA, 1971, PhD, 1983. Tchg. asst. UCLA, 1969-71; instr., continuing edn. U. Judaism, L.A., 1971-76, 94—, instr., 1975-84. Vis. lectr. UCLA, 1985-91; adj. asst. prof. U. Judaism, 1984-94; adj. prof. Bibl. Acad. Jewish Religion, 2001-. Mem. Assn. for Jewish Studies, Nat. Assn. of Profs. of Hebrew, World Union of Jewish Studies. Jewish. Avocations: gardening, music. Office: U Judaism 15600 Mulholland Dr Los Angeles CA 90077-1519

KLEIN, SOPHIA H., entrepreneur; b. Dayton, Ohio, Aug. 17, 1915; d. Felix Frank Borkowski, Helen Marie Sichujainska; children: Helen Marie, Betty Jean. Owner Oak Hill Optical, Dayton, Town & Country Water Softener, Dayton, Klein Enterprises, Dayton, Country Squire Supper Club, Dayton, Bagel Connection, Dayton, Exquisitely Yours Jewelers, Dayton. Mem.: Dayton Cath. Bus. Women's Club (pres., Dayton Woman of Yr. 1988), Holy Seplecher (Lady of the Cross 1987—, U.S. Rep. Millennium visit to Vatican 2000). Democrat. Roman Catholic. Avocation: golf. Home: 20 Oak Knoll Dr Dayton OH 45419

KLEIN, STACY A., theater director; b. Balt., Nov. 16, 1956; d. Belman Aaron and Carole Lee (Sollins) Klein; m. Carlos Uriona, Oct. 4, 2002; children: Tadea, Cariel stepchildren: Manuel Uriona, Eugenio Uriona. BFA, Boston U., 1979; MA, Goddard Coll., 1980; PhD, Tufts U., 1987; cert. in Hebrew Lang., Hebrew U., Warsaw U. Asst. dir. Little Flags Theater, Boston, 1979—82; founder, artistic dir. Double Edge Theatre, Boston, 1982—. Dir.: (plays) The Song Trilogy, 1988—98 (Best of Boston award), The Garden Cycle, 1998—. Recipient Artistic Excellence award, State of Mass., 1997, Doris Duke Newgen Mentorship award, TCG; grantee, NEA, 1998—2004. Mem.: Theater Comm. Group. Jewish. Avocations: languages, reading, travel. Office: Double Edge Theatre 948 Conway Rd Ashfield MA 01330 Office Phone: 413-628-0277. E-mail: sklein@doubleedgetheatre.org.

KLEIN, STACY LYNN, educational consultant; b. Framingham, Mass., Aug. 17, 1970; d. Stuart Matthew and Sheryl G. AA, Palm Beach C.C., 1990; BS in Adminstrn. Studies, Nova U., 1992; MIBA, Nova Southeastern U., 1994. Office mgr. Unitech Mgmt., Hollywood, Fla., 1993-95; prodr. Image Com, Inc., Ft. Lauderdale, Fla., 1994-96; admissions counselor Keiser Coll., Ft. Lauderdale, Fla., 1996-97; univ. rep. Nova Southeastern U., Ft. Lauderdale, Fla., 1997-99, student advisor, 1999—. Adj. faculty Fla. Nat. Coll., Miami, 1999—, Broward C.C., Ft. Lauderdale, 1999— Avocations: sailing, biking, tennis. Home: 452 Palo Alto Dr Palm Springs FL 33461-1518 Office: Nova Southeastern U 3301 College Ave Fort Lauderdale FL 33314-7796

KLEIN, STEPHEN THOMAS, performing arts executive; b. Cleve., Mar. 9, 1947; s. Howard B. and Lilly (Gatchell) K.; m. Mary Ussery, Nov. 19, 1972; children— William Howard, Sarah Katherine. B.F.A., Boston U., 1970. Orch. Mgr. Cleve. Orch., 1978-82; exec. dir. Denver Symphony Orch., Colo., 1982-85, Nat. Symphony Orch., Washington, 1985-94; mng. dir. Pitts. Pub. Theater, 1994—.

KLEIN, SUSAN ELAINE, librarian; b. Cedar Falls, Iowa, Aug. 5, 1952; d. Elmo Calvin and Mabel Audrey (Taylor) Boone; m. Richard Joseph Klein II, Oct. 16, 1982; children: Michael Joseph, Christopher James. BA, U. No. Iowa, 1974. Reporter The No. Iowan, Cedar Falls, summer 1972; res. desk clk. U. No. Iowa Libr., Cedar Falls, summer 1974; paralegal for migrant action program VISTA, Muscatine, Iowa, 1975-76; office asst. Cedar Falls Pub. Libr., 1976-77, libr. asst., 1977-78, cataloger, 1978-86, libr. asst., 1986-87, young adult libr., 1988—. Mem. Iowa Libr. Assn. (cert.). Democrat. Avocations: cooking, bicycling, gardening, canoeing, reading.

KLEIN, T(HEODORE) E(IBON) D(ONALD), writer; b. N.Y.C., July 15, 1947; s. Richard and Norma (Kashins) K. AB, Brown U., 1969; M.F.A., Columbia U., 1972. Asst. story editor Paramount Pictures, N.Y.C., 1972-75; editor-in-chief Twilight Zone Mag., N.Y.C., 1981-86; editor CrimeBeat mag., N.Y.C., 1991-93; editor mag. Sci-Fi Entertainment, Herndon, Va., 1995. Author: (novel) The Ceremonies, 1984, (story collection) Dark Gods, 1985; screenwriter: (feature film) Trauma, 1994; contbr. fiction to anthologies; author articles in mags., newspapers. Recipient novel award Brit. Fantasy Soc., 1985, novella award World Fantasy Soc., 1986. Mem. Phi Beta Kappa Home: 210 W 89th St New York NY 10024-1805 Personal E-mail: metronetwork@att.net.

KLEIN, WARD, consumer products company executive; With Ralston Purina Co., 1979, Energizer Holding, 1986—, vice-pres. mktg., 1992—94, vice-pres., gen. mgr. global lighting prods., 1994—96, pres., CEO, 2000—, also chmn., 2004—. Chmn. various foreign divisions Energizer Holdings. Office: Energizer HQ 533 Marryville University Saint Louis MO 63141 Office Phone: 800-383-7323.*

KLEIN, WILLIAM M. (BILL KLEIN), information technology executive; B in acctg., Calif. State U.; completed, Stanford Exec. Program, 1999. CPA. Sr. mgr. Price Waterhouse, San Jose, Calif.; sr. mgmt. positions Hewlett-Packard, 1986—2000; exec. v.p., CFO BEA Systems, Inc., San Jose, 2000—. Office: BEA Systems Inc 2315 N First St San Jose CA 95131 Office Phone: 800-817-4BEA, 408-570-8000. Office Fax: 408-570-8901.

KLEINBARD, EDWARD D., lawyer; b. N.Y.C., Nov. 6, 1951; s. Martin L. and Joan K.; m. Norma F. Cirincione, Oct. 17, 1947. BA, MA, Brown U., 1973; JD, Yale U., 1976. Bar: N.Y. 1977. Assoc. Cleary, Gottlieb, Steen & Hamilton, N.Y.C., 1977—84, ptnr., 1984—. Book rev., article editor Yale Law Jour., 1975-76; contbr. articles to profl. jours. Fellow Am. Coll. Tax Counsel; mem. ABA, N.Y. State Bar Assn. (co-chmn. fin. instruments com. 1989-91), Assn. Bar City of N.Y., Internat. Assn. Fin. Engrs., Internat. Fiscal Assn. Office: Cleary Gottlieb Steen & Hamilton LLP 1 Liberty Plz Fl 38 New York NY 10006-1470 E-mail: ekleinbard@cgsh.com.*

KLEINBERG, BRENDA LOUISE, writer, philanthropist; b. Seymour, Ind., Oct. 24, 1954; d. Henry Lawrence and Dorothy Mae Pottschmidt; m. Charles L. Bochantin Sr., Oct. 27, 1981 (div. Nov. 1994); 1 child, Charles Lawrence Jr.; m. Douglas Raymond Kleinberg, May 12, 1995 (div. Jan. 2000); 1 child, Donovan Scott. Author: Love Will Come Tomorrow, 1983, The Charlie Books - a Collection of Children's Stories, 1988 (VIP award 1992), Poems for Tuesdays, Fridays and Saturdays, 1983 (Golden Poet award 1988, 89, 91), A Simple Expression - a Collection of Short Stories, 1991, Pieces of My Heart--Thoughts and Reflections of a Christian Mother, 1999; essayist: The Christian Connection Newspaper, 1999; writer poems and songs, 1986—. Recipient Literary award Grand Prize for poem "Sidewalk Royalty" Iliad Press, 1999. Avocation: the outdoors. Address: PO Box 121 Knob Lick MO 63651-0121

KLEINBERG, HOWARD J., newspaper columnist; b. N.Y.C., Oct. 23, 1932; s. Benjamin and Ruth (Wile) K.; m. Natalie Bernstein, Feb. 22, 1953; children: Linda Kleinberg Landy, Eliot, Eileen Kleinberg Newmark, David. Student pub. schs. Mem. staff Miami (Fla.) News, 1950-65, 66-88, mng. editor, 1968-76, editor, 1976-88; nat. columnist Cox Newspapers, Miami, 1988—; history columnist Miami Herald, 1989—. Author: Miami, The Way We Were, 1985, The Great Florida Hurricane and Disaster, 1993, Miami Beach, A History, 1994. Mem. Orange Bowl Com. Served with AUS, 1953-55, Korea. Recipient 1st pl. award Fla. Edn. Assn., 1985, Miami Urban League Black Awareness award, 1975, 1st pl. awards for column writing, Cox Newspapers, 1987, 88.

KLEINBERG, LAWRENCE H., investor, consultant; b. N.Y.C., Dec. 20, 1943; s. Paul and Gertrude (Voron) Kleinberg; m. Lois Helene Kass, June 10, 1967; children: Brian Andrew, Rachel Adele. BA in Econs., Adelphi U., 1965, MBA, 1969. Analyst, Pfizer, Inc., N.Y.C., 1965-69; various fin. mgmt. positions Beech-Nut, Inc., N.Y.C., 1969-73; v.p., controller Life Savers, Inc., N.Y.C., 1973-79, sr. v.p. fin., 1979-83, exec. v.p., 1983, pres., 1984, divsn. pres. Nabisco Brands, Inc., 1984-87; v.p., corp. controller Nabisco Brands, Inc., Parsippany, NJ, 1987-88; sr. v.p. fin. Nabisco Foods Group, Parsippany, 1988-94; sr. v.p. planning Nabisco, Inc., Parsippany, 1995-96; pvt. investor, cons., 1996—. Bd. dirs. Stravina Oper. Co. Home: 13285 Verdun Dr Palm Beach Gardens FL 33410 E-mail: lhk43@aol.com.

KLEINBERG, NORMAN CHARLES, lawyer; b. Phila., July 18, 1946; s. Frank and Mildred Brosnan (Hill) K.; m. Marcia Sue Topperman, Jan. 31, 1971; children: Lauren Blythe, Joanna Leigh. AB, Tufts U., 1968; JD, Columbia U., 1972. Bar: N.Y. 1973, U.S. Supreme Ct., U.S. Ct. Appeals (1st, 2d, 3d, 5th, and fed. cirs.), U.S. Dist. Ct. (so. and ea. dists.) N.Y., U.S. Tax Ct., U.S. Dist. Ct. (ea. dist.) Wis., U.S. Dist. Ct. (no. dist.) Calif., U.S. Dist. Ct. (ea. dist.) Mich. Law clk. to judge U.S. Dist. Ct. (so. dist.) N.Y., N.Y.C., 1972-74; assoc. Hughes Hubbard & Reed, N.Y.C., 1974-80, ptnr., 1980—. Articles editor Columbia Jour. Law and Social Problems, 1971-72. Served to staff sgt. USAR, 1968-74. Fellow Am. Coll. Trial Lawyers; mem. ABA, Fed. Bar Coun., Assn. Bar of City of N.Y. (com. on state cts. of superior jurisdiction, com. profl. responsibility, com. profl. and jud. ethics., com. on jud., coun. on jud. adminstrn.), Internat. Bar Assn., N.Y. State Bar Assn., Def. Rsch. Inst. Home: 460 E 79th St New York NY 10021-1443 Office: Hughes Hubbard & Reed 1 Battery Park Plz Fl 12 New York NY 10004-1482 Business E-Mail: kleinber@hugheshubbard.com.

KLEINE, HERMAN, economist; b. N.Y.C., Mar. 6, 1920; s. Max and Fannie (Schechter) K.; m. Paula Stein, June 16, 1962; children— Joseph, Michael. BS, State U. N.Y. at Albany, 1941; MA, Clark U., 1942, PhD, 1951. Researcher for Nat. Indsl. Conf. Bd., 1946; instr. to asst. prof. Worcester Polytech. Inst., 1946-49; economist ECA, Mut. Security Agy., The Hague, Netherlands, 1949-53; internat. relations and econs. FOA, ICA, Washington, 1953-57; dir. U.S. Ops. Mission to Ethiopia, ICA, 1957-59, asst. dep. dir. for ops., 1959-61; Nat. War Coll., 1961-62; AID adviser U.S. Mission to UN, N.Y.C., 1962-64; dep. asst. adminstr. for Africa AID, Washington, 1964-67; dep. dir. U.S. AID mission to Brazil, 1967-69; asso. U.S. coordinator Alliance for Progress, 1969-70; dep. U.S. coordinator, asst. adminstr. Latin Am. Bur. AID, Washington, 1971-76; advisor to controller Interam. Devel. Bank, 1976-84; dir. internship programs Ctr. Immigration Policy and Refugee Assistance, Georgetown U., 1984-86; cons., mediator, 1986—. Mem. U.S. delegation UN Gen. Assembly, 1962, 63 Served from pvt. to capt. USAAF, 1942-46. Recipient AID Distinguished honor award, 1973, Adminstrs. Distinguished Career Service award, 1976, Superior Honor award Dept. State, 1976, Distinguished Alumnus award State U. N.Y. at Albany, 1977; duPont fellow, 1948; named to Hempstead, N.Y. Sch. Dist. Hall Fame, 1986. Mem. Kappa Phi Kappa. Jewish. Home and Office: 100 Hilary Cir Fairfield CT 06825

KLEINER, DIANA ELIZABETH EDELMAN, art historian, educator, academic administrator; b. N.Y.C., Sept. 18, 1947; d. Morton Henry and Hilda Rachel (Wyner) Edelman; m. Fred S. Kleiner, Dec. 22, 1972; 1 child, Alexander Mark. BA magna cum laude, Smith Coll., 1969; MA, MPhil, Columbia U., 1970, 74, PhD, 1976; MA (hon.), Yale U., 1989. Lectr., asst. prof. U. Va., Charlottesville, 1975-76, 76-78; vis. asst. prof. U. Mass., Boston, 1979; Mellon faculty fellow Harvard U., Cambridge, Mass., 1979-80; asst. prof. Yale U., New Haven, 1980-82, assoc. prof., 1982-89; fellow Whitney Humanities Ctr., Yale U., New Haven, 1984-87; master Pierson Coll., Yale U., New Haven, 1986-87; dir. grad. studies dept. history of art Yale U., New Haven, 1988-90; prof. history of art and classics Yale U., New Haven, 1989-95, dir. grad. studies dept. classics, 1991-94, chair dept. classics, 1994-95, Dunham prof. classics and history of art, 1995—, dep. provost for the arts, 1995—2003; liaison for faculty programs AllLearn, 2000—. Mem. adv. bd. Archaeol. News, Tallahassee, 1980-2000, Am. Jour. Archaeology, Boston, 1985-98; mem., chair program for ann. meetings com. Archaeol. Inst. Am., Boston, 1988-93. Author: Roman Group Portraiture, 1977, The Monument of Philopappos in Athens, 1983, Roman Imperial Funerary Altars with Portraits, 1987, Roman Sculpture, 1992, paperback edit., 1994, Cleopatra and Rome, 2005; editor: I, Clavdia: Women in Ancient Rome, 1996, I Clavdia II: Women in Roman Art and Society, 2000, (electronic courses for AllLearn: eClavdia: Women in Ancient Rome, 2001—, Brainy and Battered Third-Century Women, 2003-, Pompeii!, 2004-. Bd. dirs. Westville Cmty. Nursery Sch., New Haven, 1989-90, The Foote Sch., New Haven, 1994-2000; regional rep. Deerfield (Mass.) Acad., 2001—, mem. parent's com., 2002-04, trustee, 2004-. Grantee: Am. Coun. Learned Socs., 1979, NEH, 1980, 95, Am. Philos. Soc. 1982, The John Paul Getty Trust, 1992. Mem. Archaeol. Inst. Am., Coll. Art Assn. Home: 102 Rimmon Rd Woodbridge CT 06525-1941 Office Phone: 203-432-2673. Business E-Mail: diana.kleiner@yale.edu.

KLEINER, FRED SCOTT, art historian, archaeologist, educator, editor; b. N.Y.C., Apr. 29, 1948; m. Diana Elizabeth Edelman, Dec. 22, 1972; 1 child, Alexander Mark. BA with honors, U. Pa., 1968; MA, Columbia U., 1969, PhD, 1973. Agora fellow Am. Sch. Classical Studies, Athens, Greece, 1973-75; asst. prof. art history and archaeology U. Va., Charlottesville, 1975-78; asst. prof. Boston U., 1978-81, assoc. prof., 1981-86, prof., 1986—, dir. grad. studies dept. art history, 1979-81, 99, chmn. dept. art history, 1981-85, sr. fellow Soc. Fellows Humanities, 1985-86. Excavator, Cosa, Italy, 1969-70; vis. prof. Yale U., New Haven, 1997. Author: Greek and Roman Coins in the Athenian Agora, 1976, The Early Cistophoric Coinage, 1977, Medieval and Modern Coins in the Athenian Agora, 1978, The Arch of Nero in Rome, 1985, Art Through the Ages, 1996, Art Through the Ages--The Western Perspective, 2002, Art Through the Ages, 12th edit., 2005 (Texty Prize, 2001, McGuffey Prize, 2001), Art Through the Ages--Non-Western Perspectives, 2005, Art Through the Ages--A Concise History, 2005; editor-in-chief: Am. Jour. Archaeology, 1985—98; contbr. articles to profl. jours., to other books, encyclopedias and exhbn. catalogues. Bd. dirs. Yale Youth Hockey Assn., 1994-97, v.p., 1996-97; co-founder, mgr. Conn. Ice Dogs, 1997-2001. Grantee Am. Philos. Soc., 1971, 80, Am. Coun. Learned Socs., 1978, 82; Guggenheim fellow, 1988-89; fellow Asian Cultural Coun., 2004. Mem.: Tex. and Acad. Authors Assn. (awards com. 2002—), Soc. Acad. Authors (awards com. 2002—), Coll. Art Assn. (Morey Book award com. 1999—2000, chair 2001—03), Archaeol. Inst. Am. (chmn. fellowship com. 1985, publs. com. 1985—98, numismatics com. 2000—03). Home: 102 Rimmon Rd Woodbridge CT 06525-1941 Office: Boston U Dept Art History Boston MA 02215 Office Phone: 617-353-1455. Business E-Mail: fsk@bu.edu.

KLEINER, JANELLYN PICKERING, librarian; b. Harrisburg, Ill. d. Herschel Laurence and Hester Perle (Rutherford) Pickering; m. Arthur A. Kleiner (div.); children: Richard, Arthur, Mark L. BA, MLS, MA, La. State U. News reporter Morning Adv.-State Times, Baton Rouge; with pub. rels. and advt. dept. Hundemer Advt. Agy., Baton Rouge; head circulation dept. La. State Libraries, Baton Rouge, head interlibrary loan dept., prin. searcher, head reference svcs., 1985—, assoc. dean librs., 1999—. Library cons. Oak Ridge (Tenn.) Associated Univs., 1987-88. Mem. exec. bd. faculty senate La. State U. Mem. ALA (reference and adult svcs. div., MARS editor, exec. com. 1986-89, chair codes com. 1988—, chair 1988-89, numerous other com. and offices). Avocations: bicycling, reading.

KLEINER, MADELEINE A., lawyer; b. 1951; Graduate, Cornell U.; JD, Yale Law Sch. Clk. to Hon. William P. Gray U.S. Dist. Ct. for Ctrl. Dist. of Calif.; assoc. Gibson, Dunn and Crutcher, L.A., 1977—83, ptnr., 1983—95; sr. exec. v.p., chief adminstrv. officer, gen. counsel H.F. Ahmanson & Co., 1995—2001; exec. v.p., gen. counsel, corp. sec. Hilton Hotels Corp., Beverly Hills, Calif., 2001—. Bd. advisors UCLA Med. Ctr. Asst. sec. Performing Arts Coun., L.A. Music Ctr. Office: Hilton Hotels Corp 9336 Civic Ctr Dr Beverly Hills CA 90210

KLEINFELD, ANDREW J., federal judge; b. 1945; BA magna cum laude, Wesleyan U., 1966; JD cum laude, Harvard U., 1969. Law clk. Alaska Supreme Ct., 1969—71; U.S. magistrate U.S. Dist. Ct. Alaska, Fairbanks, 1971—74; pvt. practice law Fairbanks, 1971—86; judge U.S. Dist. Ct. Alaska, Anchorage, 1986—91, U.S. Ct. Appeals (9th cir.), San Francisco, 1991—. Contbr. articles to profl. jours. Mem.: Tanana Valley Bar Assn. (pres. 1974—75), Alaska Bar Assn. (pres. 1982—83, bd. govs. 1981—84), Phi Beta Kappa. Republican. Office: US Ct Appeals 9th Cir Courthouse Sq 250 Cushman St Ste 3-a Fairbanks AK 99701-4665

KLEINFELD, ELIZABETH ANNE, writing and literature educator; b. Hempstead, NY, June 18, 1969; d. Robert J. and Therese (O'Regan) K.; m. Travitt Lee Hamilton, Mar. 16, 1992. BS in History, Bradley U., 1992; MS in English, Ill. State U., 1994. Editor-in-chief Broadside Literary Jour., Peoria, Ill., 1988—91; instr. of English Ill. State U., Normal, 1993-94, Red Rocks C.C., Lakewood, Colo., 1995—; resident instr. English C.C. of Aurora, Colo., 1996—2000. Editor-in-chief Inscape Lit. Mag., 1997—2000. Mem.: MLA, Nat. Coun. Tchrs. English. Office: Red Rocks CC 13300 W 6th Ave Lakewood CO 80228 Home: 411 Pearl St Denver CO 80203-3807

KLEINFELD, ERWIN, mathematician, educator; b. Vienna, Apr. 19, 1927; came to U.S., 1940; s. Lazar and Gina (Schönbach) K.; m. Margaret Morgan, July 2, 1968; children— Barbara, David. BS, CCNY, 1948; MA, U. Pa., 1949; PhD, U. Wis., 1951. Instr. U. Chgo., 1951-53; asst. prof. Ohio State U., 1953-56, asso. prof., 1957-60, prof., 1960-62; prof. math. Syracuse U., 1962-67, U. Hawaii, 1967-68, U. Iowa, 1968—2002, prof. emeritus, 2002—. Vis. lectr. Yale, 1956-57; cons. Nat. Bur. Standards, summer 1953; research specialist U. Conn., summer 1955; research mathematician Bowdoin Coll., summer 1957; research asso. Cornell U., summer 1958, U. Calif. at Los Angeles, summer 1959, Stanford, summer 1960, Inst. Def. Analysis, summer 1961, 62, AID-India, summer 1964, 65; vis. prof. Emory U., 1976-77; Cons. Edn. IX Project, World Bank, U. Indonesia, 1985-86, Mucia/Ind. U.-(ITM) Shah Alam, Malaysia Project, 1988-89. Editorial bd. Jour. Algebra-Academic Press; cons. editor, Merrill Pub. Co.-Div. Bell & Howell. Contbr. articles research jours. Served with AUS, 1945-46. Wis. Alumni Rsch. Found. fellow, 1949-51, vis. rsch. fellow U. New Eng., Australia, 1992; grantee U.S. Army Rsch. Office, 1955-70, NSF, 1970-75. Mem. Am. Math. Soc., Sigma Xi. Home: 1555 N Sierra 120 Reno NV 89503 Office Phone: 775-337-0196. Business E-Mail: kleinfld@math.uiowa.edu.

KLEINFELD, KLAUS, electronics executive; b. Bremen, Germany, Nov. 6, 1957; s. Klaus Joachim and Elisabeth Berta (Freier) K.; m. Birgit Henriette Müeller, July 27, 1982; children: Hannah, Lena. Diploma-Kaufmann, U. Goettingen (Germany), 1982; Dr. rer. pol., U. Wuerzburg (Germany), 1992. Researcher U. Muenster, Germany, 1980-82; cons. Inst. Prof. Bergler, Nuernberg, Germany, 1982-85; product strategy Ciba-Geigy, Basle, Switzerland, 1985-86; cons. Siemens, Munich, 1987, corp. strategies mgr., personnel dept. corp. planning and devel., 1988—94, head corp. projects, corp. planning and devel., 1994, head corp. cons., 1995, head fluoroscopy & imaging, angiogrpahy div., med. engr. group, 1998—2000, mem. group exec. mgmt., med. solutions group, 2000; COO Siemens Corp., 2001, CEO, 2002—; mng. bd. Siemens AG, Germany, 2002—. Spkr. in field. Author: Argwohn, 1980, Strategic Management and Corporate Identity, 1992; contbr. articles to profl. jours. Office: Siemens Corp 153 E 53rd St New York NY 10022

KLEINGARTNER, ARCHIE, founding dean, educator; b. Gackle, N.D., Aug. 10, 1936; s. Emanuel and Ottile (Kuhn) K.; m. Dorothy Jean Hanselmann, Sept. 21, 1957; children: Elizabeth, Thomas. BA, U. Minn., 1959; MS, U. Oreg., 1961; PhD, U. Wis., 1965. Asst. and assoc. prof. UCLA, 1964-69, assoc. dean, chmn., 1969-71, prof., 1971-75, 83—, dir. entertainment mgmt. program, 1988—, founding dean Sch. Pub. Policy and Social Rsch. Berkeley, 1994—; v.p. U. Calif. Sys., Berkeley, 1975-83. Cons. in field, 1967—; arbitrator in field, 1971—; chmn. Global Window Ptnrs., Inc., 1998—. Mem. labor mgmt. disputes panel City of L.A., 1978—. With U.S. Army, 1954-56. Mem. London Sch. Econs., Alpha Kappa Psi. Republican. Methodist. Avocations: tennis, biking, gardening. Home: 12258 Montana Ave #103 Los Angeles CA 90049 Office: UCLA Sch Pub Policy Social Rsch PO Box 951656 Los Angeles CA 90095-1656 Office Phone: 310-825-2527. Business E-Mail: akleinga@ucla.edu.

KLEINHENZ, CHRISTOPHER, foreign language educator, researcher; b. Indpls., Dec. 29, 1941; m. Margaret Ellen Zechiel, Aug. 1, 1964; children: Steven Russell, Michael Thomas. BA, Ind. U., 1964, MA, 1966, PhD, 1969. Asst. prof., dir. Bologna program Ind. U., 1970-71; instr. U. Wis., Madison, 1968-69, asst. prof., 1969-70, asst. prof., dept. French and Italian, 1971-75, assoc. prof., 1975-80, chmn. medieval studies program, 1975-80, 81-84, 89-95, 96—, prof., 1980—, chmn. dept., 1985-88, Carol Mason Kirk prof. Italian, 2000—. Dir. devel. grant NEH, Madison, 1976-79, co-dir. rsch. tools grant, 1980-84. Author: The Early Italian Sonnet, 1986; editor: Medieval Manuscripts and Textual Criticism, 1976, Medieval Studies in North America, 1982, Routledge Studies in Medieval Literature, 1986-2002, Dante Studies, 1988-2003, Medieval Italy: An Encyclopedia, 2004; co-editor: Saint Augustine the Bishop: A Book of Essays, 1994, Routledge Medieval Casebooks, 1991—, Fearful Hope: Approaching the New Millennium, 1999; assoc. editor: Dante Ency., 2000; chmn. editl. bd. Medieval Acad. Reprints for Teaching, 1981-93; bibliographer MLA, N.Y.C., 1981-88, BIGLLI, Rome, 1994—, Dante Studies, 1984-2002, ICLS, 2002—; book rev. editor Italica, 1984-93; co-translator: Dante Alighieri, Il Fiore and the Detto d'Amore, 2000. Chmn. com. on ctrs. and regional assns. Medieval Acad., 1993-99. Recipient Chancellor's Disting. Tchg. award, 2004, Leonard Covello Lifetime Achievement award, 2005; Newberry Libr./NEH grantee, 1988-89. Mem. Medieval Assn. of Midwest (pres. 1984-85, 2003-04), Dante Soc. Am. (mem. coun. 1985-91), Am. Boccaccio Assn. (v.p. 1987-93, pres. 1993-97), Am. Assn. Tchrs. of Italian (v.p. 1993-98, pres. 1999-2003). Avocations: sports, stamp collecting/philately, photography, travel. Home: 2247 Fox Ave Madison WI 53711-1922 Office: U Wis Dept French and Italian 1220 Linden Dr Madison WI 53706-1525 Office Phone: 608-262-3941. Business E-Mail: ckleinhe@wisc.edu.

KLEINKNECHT, KENNETH SAMUEL, retired air transportation executive; b. Washington, July 24, 1919; s. Christian Frederick and Nell May (Barr) K.; m. Patricia Jean Todd, May 24, 1947; children: Linda May, Patricia Ann, Frederick William. BSM.E., Purdue U., 1942. Project engr. NACA Lewis Research Center, Cleve., 1942-51; aero. research scientist NASA Flight Research Ctr., Edwards AFB, Calif., 1951-59; successively mgr. Mercury Project, dep. mgr. Gemini Program, mgr. command and service modules NASA Johnson Space Ctr., 1959-70, mgr. Skylab Program, 1970-74, dir. flight ops. Houston, 1974-76, asst. mgr. Orbiter Project, 1976-77; head constrn. space shuttle orbiter NASA Johnson Space Center, 1979-81; dep. assoc. adminstr. for space transp. systems European ops. to European Space Agy., Paris NASA Hdqrs., Washington, 1977-79; mgr. program engring., sr. space transp. system tech. adviser Denver div. Martin Marietta Aerospace, 1981-83, mgr. mfg. procurement and testing, 1983-84, dir. design to cost/productivity Space Sta. Project, 1984-88; mgr. laser project Zenith Star Program, 1988-90, ret., 1990. Exec. bd. Sam Houston Area council Boy Scouts Am., Houston, 1972-77. Recipient (with others) Group Achievement award for Mercury Project NASA, 1962, NASA medal for outstanding leadership Pres. of U.S., 1963, 81, John J. Montgomery award San Diego chpt. Nat. Soc. Aerospace Profls., 1963, (with others) Group Achievement award for X-15 Rsch. Airplane Flight Test Orgn., 1964, for Gemini Program, 1966, Exceptional Svc. medal NASA, 1969, Disting. Svc. medal NASA, 1969, 73 Fellow Am. Astron. Soc. (W. Randolph Lovelace II award 1975), AIAA (assoc.); mem. Internat. Acad. Astronautics, Kiwanis, Masons (33rd degree) Home: 825 Front Range Rd Littleton CO 80120-4005 Office Fax: 303-734-3633. E-mail: ksklein@worldnet.att.net. *As a member of the team that made lunar and space shuttle missions successes, I believe that my "formula for success" is one part high goal and one hundred parts persistence. I have always believed in establishing principles, high ideals of conduct as structures to direct our lives. It is voluntary total dedication to valid ideals, attention to detail, discipline and accepting accountability that will bring success on every level. To reach beyond one's present grasp is to assure ever higher attainments in the future.*

KLEINLEIN, KATHY LYNN, training and development executive; b. S.I., NY, May 2, 1950; d. Thomas and Helen Mary (O'Reilly) Perricone; m. Kenneth Robert Kleinlein, Oct. 30, 1983. BA, Wagner Coll., 1971, MA, 1974; MBA, Rutgers U., 1984; MA in Theology, Barry U., 1998; EdD, Grad. Theol. Found., 2004. Cert. secondary tchr., N.Y., N.J., Fla. Tchr. English N.Y.C. Bd. Edn., S.I., 1971-74, Matawan (N.J.) Bd. Edn., 1974-79; instr. English Middlesex County Coll., Edison, N.J., 1978-81; med. sales rep. Pfizer/Roerig, Bklyn., 1979-81, mgr. tng. ops. N.Y.C., 1981-86; dir. sales tng. Winthrop Pharms. divsn. Sterling Drug, N.Y.C., 1986-87; dir. tng. Reuters Info. Sys., NYC, 1987—90; pres., dir. tng. Women in Transition, 1990—98; pastoral min., dir. religious edn. St. Raphael's Ch., 1998—2001; diocesan dir. catechetical ministry Diocese of Venice, Fla., 2001—. Pres. Kleinlein Cons.; pers. mgmt. officer USAR, NJ, 1981-86; cons. Concepts & Prodrs., NYC, 1981-85; bd. regents Blessed Edmund Rice Sch. for Pastoral Ministry; bd. dirs. Campaign for Human Devel. Trainer United Way, 1982-83, polit. action com., 1982—85; mem. Rep. Presdl. Task Force, Washington, 1983—; chair Sarasota Library Adv. Bd.; sec. Intracoastal Civic Assn.; reinventing govt. coun. Sarasota County Planning Commn., exec. bd. Edn. Found., St. Joseph Bon Secours Hosp.; grievance com. Fla. Bar; bd. regents Blessed Edmund Rice Sch. for Pastoral Ministry. Mem. Sarasota County Sch. Bd., 2002—. Capt. U.S. Army, 1974—78. First woman in N.Y. N.G., 1974; first woman instr. Empire State Mil. Acad., Peekskill, N.Y., 1976. Mem.: Sarasota Women's Alliance, Rep. Women's Club, Alpha Omicron Pi. Republican. Roman Catholic. Office: Diocese Venice Cath Ctr 1000 Pinebrook Rd Venice FL 34292 Office Phone: 941-484-9543. Business E-Mail: kleinlein@dioceseofvenice.org.

KLEINMAN, ARTHUR MICHAEL, medical anthropology and psychiatry educator; b. N.Y.C., Mar. 11, 1941; s. Marcia F. (Kaplan) K.; m. Joan Andrea Ryman, Mar. 20, 1965; children: Peter John, Anne Simone. AB, Stanford U., 1962, MD, 1967; MA, Harvard U., 1974. Diplomate Nat. Bd. Med. Examiners, Am. Bd. Neurology and Psychiatry. Med. intern Yale-New Haven Hosp., 1967-68; surgeon USPHS, Bethesda, Md., 1968-70; resident in psychiatry Mass. Gen. Hosp., Boston, 1972-75; assoc. prof. U. Wash., Seattle, 1976-79, prof. psychiatry and anthropology, 1979-82; prof. med. anthropology and psychiatry Harvard Med. Sch., Boston, 1982—; chmn. dept. social medicine, prof. anthropology Harvard U., Cambridge, Mass., 1991-2000, Maude and Lillian Presley prof. med. anthropology and psychiatry, 1993—2002, Esther and Sidney Rabb prof. anthropology, 2002—, chair dept. anthropology, 2004—. Co-chair com. on culture, health and devel. Social Sci. Rsch. Coun., 1990. Author: Patients and Healers in the Context of Culture, 1980 (Wellcome medal Royal Anthrop. Inst.), Social Origins of Distress and Disease, 1986, The Illness Narratives, 1988, Rethinking Psychiatry, 1988, Writing at the Margin, 1995; co-editor: Relevance of Social Science for Medicine, 1981, Culture and Depression, 1985, Pain as Human Experience, 1992, Science and Ethics of the Placebo, 2002, Reducing Suicide, 2002; editor-in-chief: Culture, Medicine and Psychiatry: A Jour. of Internat. Cross-Cultural Rsch., 1976-86. Recipient Rsch. award NIMH, 1977-79, Rockefeller Found., 1983-86, 89-91, NSF, 1983-86, R.W. Johnson Found., 1989, 94; grantee NIMH, 1984—, Carnegie Corp., 1990-92, MacArthur Found., 1992-94, Rockefeller Found., 1992-94; NIH fellow, 1968-70, Guggenheim fellow, 1992. Fellow AAAS, Am. Psychiat. Assn. (vice chmn. coun. on global psychiatry 2002-05), Am. Anthrop. Assn., Inst. Medicine of NAS (chmn. com. on chronic pain, illness behavior and disability, co-chmn. com. preventing suicide), Royal Anthrop. Inst., Am. Acad. Arts and Scis. (Franz Boas award), Am. Anthrop. Assn. Office: Harvard U 330 William James Hall 33 Kirkland St Cambridge MA 02138-2019 Business E-Mail: Kleinman@wjh.harvard.edu.

KLEINMAN, STUART BRUCE, physician; b. N.Y.C., June 21, 1959; s. Gerald and Sally (Lebenson) K. BA, Lehigh U., 1981; MD, Med. Coll. of Phila., 1983. Diplomate Am. Bd. Psychiatry and Neurology. Intern in psychiatry and medicine Pa. Hosp., Phila., 1983-84; residency in psychiatry Inst. of Pa. Hos., Phila., 1984-87; fellow in forensic psychiatry Ctr. for Social Legal Studies U. Pa., Phila., 1986-87; fellow in psychiatry and law NYU Med. Ctr., Bellevue Hosp., N.Y.C., 1987-88; med. dir. Crime Victims Ctr./Victim Svcs. Agy., Bklyn., 1988-96; attending psychiatrist Forensic Psychiatry Clinic Criminal/Supreme Cts. Manhattan, N.Y.C., 1988-94; instr. in clin. psychiatry Columbia U. Coll. Physicians and Surgeons, N.Y.C., 1988-90, asst. prof. clin. psychiatry, 1990—; adj. instr. in psychiatry NYU Sch. Medicine, 1989—. Clin. asst. attending psychiatrist Bellevue Hosp. Forensic Psychiatry Clinic, 1994-99. Recipient Therman award Pa. Hosp., 1987, Kenneth Appel award Phila. County Med. Soc., 1987, Menninger award Cen. Neuropsychiat. Assn., 1987; named Outstanding Alumnus U. Pa. Ctr. for Social and Legal Studies, 1990. Mem. Am. Acad. Psychiatry and Law (chmn. com. on trauma and stress, pres. Tri-state chpt. 1996-98), Internat. Soc. for Traumatic Stress Studies (pres. N.Y. chpt. 1993-95), Am. Psychiat. Assn., Phi Beta Kappa, Alpha Omega Alpha, Sigma Tau Delta. Jewish. Avocations: literature, cinema, travel. Office: 315 Central Park West New York NY 10045

KLEIN-SEETHARAMAN, JUDITH, biochemist; b. Cologne, Nord-Rhein Westfalen, Germany, May 30, 1971; d. Clementine Klein; m. Sridhar Seetharaman, Mar. 5, 1971; 1 child, Roshan. PhD, MIT, 1996—2000. Humboldt fellow Goethe Universitaet Frankfurt, Frankfurt/Main, Germany, 2001—; rsch. scientist Carnegie Mellon U., Pittsburgh, 2001—; asst. prof. U. Pitts., Pa., 2002—. Co-director Ctr. Biol. Lang. Modeling, Pittsburgh, 2002—; vis. rschr. Forschungsinstitut Juelich, Nordrhein-Westfalen, Germany, 2002—. Author: (computer game) Biomedical Problem Solving Environment. Recipient Sofja Kovalevskaja Prize, Humboldt-Found. and Bundesregierung Deutschland, 2001; fellow Predoctoral Fellowship, Howard Hughes Med. Inst., 1996-2000; grantee Computational Learning and Discovery in Biol. Sequence, Structure and Function Mapping, NSF, 2002-2007. Mem.: Biophysical Soc., Protein Soc. Achievements include research in analysis of conformational changes in g protein coupled receptors and other signaling proteins using biochemical, biophysical and computational approaches; use of analogy between language and biology for the mapping of sequence to structure, function and dynamics of proteins.

KLEINSMITH, BRUCE JOHN See NUTZLE, FUTZIE

KLEINSORGE, WILLIAM PETER, metallurgical engineer; b. San Francisco, Feb. 10, 1941; s. William P. Kleinsorge; m. Kathryn Deane Vincent, Nov. 14, 1966; children: Elizabeth Louise, Victoria Anne. BS in Metall. Engring., U. Nev.-Reno, 1964. Registered profl. engr., S.C., Calif. Welding engr. Mare Island Naval Shipyard, Vallejo, Calif., 1965—69, Charleston Naval Shipyard, 1969—70; supervisory welding engr. U.S. Naval Ship Repair Facility, Subic Bay, Philippines, 1970—72; head welding engr. Charleston Naval Shipyard, 1972—79; metall. engr. U.S. Nuc. Regulatory Commn., Atlanta, 1979—99; ret., 1999. With Nat. Guard U.S. Army, 1965—72. Mem.: Am. Soc. Mil. Engrs., Am. Welding Soc., Am. Soc. Metals, Masons.

KLEISNER, TED J., hotel executive; b. Chgo., Sept. 5, 1944; Student, U. Denver. Chmn. Human Devel. Bur. Greater Washington Bd. of Trade, 1980—84; chmn. Pvt. Industry Coun., Washington, 1981—83; pres., mng. dir. The Greenbrier, White Sulphur Springs, W.Va.; pres. Greenbrier Resort Mgmt. Co., White Sulphur Springs; pres., COO Americas Hotel Group/Starwood Hotels Worldwide, Inc., White Plains, NY. Bd. dirs. Hersney Entertainment and Resorts Co. Bd. dirs. Appalachian Tourism Ctr., Discover the Real W.Va. Found. Named Ind. Hotelier of World, Hotels mag., 1993, Resort Exec. of Yr., 1994. Mem.: W.Va. Found. for Ind. Colls. Assn. (bd. dirs.), W.Va. C. of C. (bd. dirs.), W.Va. Roundtable (bd. dirs.). Office: 300 W Main St White Sulphur Springs WV 24986

KLEJNOT, GETHA JEAN, school nurse practitioner, music educator; b. Stroudsburg, Pa., July 28, 1950; d. Robert Roger and Betty Wilson Snyder; m. Gerald Francis Klejnot, Sr., Feb. 14, 1986 (div. Apr. 2, 1998); 1 child, Andrew Robert. AA in nursing, C.C. Balt., 1976; MusB, Peabody Conservatory, 1980. RN Md., 1976, CPR, Am. Heart Assn., 1976. Oncology and bone marrow transplant nurse Johns Hopkins Hosp., Balt., 1976—80; head nurse Balt. City Hospitals, 1980—84; home health nurse Bay Area Home Health, Annapolis, 1984—85; icu-ccu nurse SRT Med Staff, Balt.; pvt. piano tchr. for large studio Annapolis, 1987—; sch. health nurse Anne Arundel County Health Dept, 1995—. Tchg. asst. pre-sch. music theory Eastman Sch. Music, U. Rochester, NY, 1968—70. Mem.: Nat. Guild Piano Tchrs. Achievements include Piano study with Maria Luisa Faini, Julio Esteban, Alexander Paskanov; Harpsichord study with Shirley Matthews; Piano pedagogy with Tinka Knopf; Master classes with Eugene List and Ignor Kipnis. Avocation: kayaking. Home: 1217 Plateau Pl Annapolis MD 21401 Office Phone: 410-222-7134. Personal E-mail: gesny@comcast.net.

KLEM, CHRISTOPHER A., lawyer; b. Morristown, N.J., Nov. 1, 1952; s. Walter and Mary Elizabeth (Jacoby) K.; m. Susan Mary Morser, Aug. 21, 1976; children: Eric Christopher, Catherine Mary. AB magna cum laude, Harvard U., 1974, JD magna cum laude, 1977. Bar: Mass. 1977. Assoc. Ropes & Gray, Boston, 1977-85, ptnr. corp. dept., 1985—, head ednl. inst practice group & co-head securities & pub. co. practice group. Contbr. articles to profl. jours. Commr. Conservation Com., Lincoln, Mass., 1989-95; trustee, v.p. Fenn Sch., 1996-98; chmn. Lincoln Cmty. Preservation Action Com., 2000-2002; trustee St. Mark's Sch., 2002-; council mem. Mass. Audubon Soc., 2003-. Mem. ABA (chmn. com. ins. regulation sect. adminstrv. law 1989-91, vice chmn. 1985-89), Boston Bar Assn., Belmont Hill Club, Boston Econs. Club, Phi Beta Kappa. Office: Ropes & Gray One International Pl Boston MA 02110 Office Phone: 617-951-7410. Office Fax: 617-951-7050. Business E-Mail: christopher.klem@ropesgray.com, cklem@ropesgray.com.

KLEMA, DONALD DAVID, architect; b. Oak Ridge, Tenn., June 28, 1956; s. Ernest Donald and Virginia Clyde (Carlock) Klema; m. Martha Louise Wetherill, May 22, 1994; 1 child, Madeleine Wetherill. BA with honors, Princeton U., 1978; postgrad., Rice U., 1978-79; MArch, MIT, 1982. Registered arch., Mass. Intern Morris-Aubry Architects, Houston, 1979-80; arch. Ann Beha Assocs., Boston, 1982-86; assoc. William Rawn Assocs., Boston, 1986-89, DiMella Shaffer, Boston, 2004—; sr. assoc. Kallmann, McKinnell & Wood Architects, Boston, 1989—2004. Design studio instr. Boston Archtl. Ctr., 1989—90, thesis advisor, 1990, vis. archtl. critic, MIT, Mass. Coll. Art, Roger Williams Coll., Wentworth Inst. Tech., 1982—. Prin. works include Charlestown Navy Yard Rowhouses (AIA Honor award, 1994), Marx Hall, Princeton (N.J.) U. (Boston Soc. Archs. award, 1996), Miller Performing Arts Ctr., Alfred U. (AIA/Brick Inst. Am. award, 2001, Boston Soc. Archs. award, 1999), Ewing Marion Kauffman Found. Hdqs., Kansas City, Mo., World Trade Ctr. W., Boston (award Assoc. Gen. Contr. Am., 2003, Boston Soc. Archs. award, 2004). Travel grantee, Aga Khan Found., 1982. Mem.: AIA (found. scholar 1981—82), Boston Soc. Archs., Phi Beta Kappa. Democrat. Home: 26 Butman St Beverly MA 01915-4649 Office: DiMella Shaffer 286 Congress St Boston MA 02210 Business E-Mail: dklema@dimellashaffer.com.

KLEMA, ERNEST DONALD, nuclear physicist, educator; b. Wilson, Kan., Oct. 4, 1920; s. William W. and Mary Bess (Vopat) K.; m. Virginia Clyde Carlock, May 23, 1953; children: Donald David, Catherine Marion. AB in Chemistry, U. Kans., 1941, MA in Physics, 1942; postgrad., Princeton U., 1942, U. Ill., 1946-49; PhD in Physics, Rice U., 1951. Staff scientist Los Alamos Sci. Lab., 1943-46; sr. physicist Oak Ridge Nat. Lab., 1950-56, prin. physicist, 1958; assoc. prof. nuclear engring. U. Mich., 1956-58; prof. nuclear engring. Northwestern U., 1959-68, chmn. dept. engring. scis., 1960-66; prof. engring. sci. Tufts U., 1968-86, dean Coll. Engring., 1968-73, adj. prof. internat. politics Fletcher Sch. Law and Diplomacy, 1973-83, dean emeritus, prof. emeritus Coll. of Engring., 1987—. Vis. scholar physics Harvard U., 1985-86; chmn. subcom. on neutron standards and measurements NRC, 1958-62; del. Internat. Atomic Energy Agy. symposium neutron detection, dosimetry and standardiazation, Harwell, Eng., 1962; cons. Oak Ridge Nat. Lab., Argonne Nat. Lab. Author articles fission cross-sects., gamma-gamma angular correlations, empirical nuclear models, thermal neutron measurements, semi-conductor radiation detectors.;patentee purification hydrogen-argon mixtures. Fellow Am. Phys. Soc., Am Nuclear Soc.; mem. IEEE (sr.), Phi Beta Kappa, Sigma Xi, Pi Mu Epsilon, Alpha Chi Sigma. Clubs: Harbor (Seal Harbor, Me.).

KLEMANN, GILBERT LACY, II, lawyer; b. New Rochelle, N.Y., July 26, 1950; s. N. Robert and Rosemary Virginia (Gerard) K.; m. Patricia Louise Hild, June 16, 1973; children: Tricia Rosemary, Gilbert Hild. AB, Coll. Holy Cross, 1972; JD, Fordham U., 1975. Bar: N.Y. 1976, U.S. Dist. Ct. (so. and ea. dists.) N.Y. 1976, Conn. 1988, U.S. Supreme Ct. 1991. Assoc. Chadbourne & Parke, N.Y.C., 1975-83, ptnr., 1983-90, of counsel, 2000; sr. v.p., gen. counsel Fortune Brands, Inc. (formerly Am. Brands Inc.), Old Greenwich, Conn., 1991-97, exec. v.p. strategic and legal affairs, 1998, exec. v.p. corp., mem. bd. dirs., 1999; sr. v.p., gen. counsel, sec. Avon Products, Inc., N.Y.C., 2001—. Bd. dirs. N.Am. Galvanizing and Coatings, Inc., Standard Comml. Corp. Editor Fordham Law Rev., 1974-75. Mem. Conn. Bar Assn., Greenwich (Conn.) Country Club, Nassau Club (Princeton, N.J.), Longboat Key Club (Fla.). Republican. Roman Catholic. Avocation: golf. Home: 25 Hope Farm Rd Greenwich CT 06830-3331 also: 415 L'Ambiance Dr Longboat Key FL 34288 Office: Avon Products Inc 1345 Ave of the Americas New York NY 10105-0196 Personal E-mail: gilbert.klemann@avon.com.

KLEMENS, PAUL GUSTAV, physicist, researcher; b. Vienna, May 24, 1925; came to U.S., 1959, naturalized, 1968; s. Walter and Ida (Klug) K.; m. Ruth Hannah Wiener, July 30, 1950; children: Michael Walter, Susan Margaret. BSc, U. Sydney, 1946, MSc, 1948; PhD, Oxford U., 1950. With Nat. Standards Lab., Sydney, Australia, 1950-59, research officer, 1950-52, sr. research officer, 1952-57, prin. research officer, 1957-59; physicist Westinghouse Research Lab., Pitts., 1959-64, mgr. transport properties of solids dept., 1964-67; prof. physics U. Conn., 1967-91, prof. emeritus, 1991—, head dept. physics, 1967-74. Vis. prof. Leiden (The Netherlands) U., 1963-64, City U., London, 1989, U. Nottingham, Eng., 1992; mem. adv. bd. on heat Nat. Bur. Standards, 1967-70, mem. adv. bd. on cryogenics, 1974-79; mem. governing bd. Internat. Thermal Conductivity Confs., 1973—; mem. adv. bd. associateship program NRC, 1983-87; mem. standing com. on accreditation Conn. Bd. Higher Edn., 1980-86; cons. Los Alamos Nat. Lab., 1972-97. Contbr. articles to sci. jours. Recipient Y.S. Touloukian award Heat Transfer div. ASME, 1988. Fellow Am. Phys. Soc.; mem. Conn. Acad. Sci. and Engring. (fin. com. 1998-2002) Clubs: Cosmos Washington. Achievements include The Internat. Conference on Phonon Scattering in Condensed Matter decided in 2001 to name its trienniel award the Klemens Award, to recognise his early work in the field. Home: 21 Timber Dr Storrs Mansfield CT 06268-1210 Office: U Conn Dept Physics Storrs Mansfield CT 06269-3046 Personal E-mail: klemens@rcn.com.

KLEMENS, THOMAS A., insurance company executive; b. 1951; Degree, Calif. Polytechnic U. CPA. From v.p. to CFO First American Corp., Santa Ana, Calif., 1985—93, CFO, 1993—, sr. exec. v.p., 2003—. Bd. dir. First American Title Ins. Co. Mem.: AICPA, Nat. Assn. Accts., Calif. Soc. CPAs. Office: First American Corp One First American Way Santa Ana CA 92707

KLEMENS, THOMAS LLOYD, editor; b. Pitts., Mar. 28, 1952; s. Robert F. and Ann E. (Lacy) K.; m. Norreen McLellan, Aug. 4, 1973; children: Jonathan, Zachary. BFA, Carnegie-Mellon U., 1974; BSCE, U. Pitts., 1983; postgrad., Roosevelt U., Chgo., 1990-91. Registered profl. engr., Ill. Choir dir., tchr. Wellsville (Ohio) H.S., 1975-76; asst. band dir., tchr. North Hills H.S., Ross Twp., Pa., 1976-79; field engr. S.J. Groves & Sons, Pitts., 1983; structural engr. Sargent & Lundy, Chgo., 1983-87; field engr. Structural Preservation Systems, Inc., Margate, N.J., 1987; project mgr. Northwest Group, Inc., West Chicago, Ill., 1987; engr., purchasing agt. L.J. Keefe Co., Mt. Prospect, Ill., 1987-89; from assoc. editor to editor Hwy. & Heavy Constrn. Cahners Pub., Des Plaines, Ill., 1989-91, editor Hwy. & Heavy Constrn. Products, 1991-93, sr. editor Consulting/Specifying Engr., 1993-94; co-owner Wordwright, Palatine, Ill., 1993—. Instr. Motorola U., 1996-98; com. on constrn. equipment Transp. Rsch. Bd., Washington, 1991-93 adj. faculty William Rainey Harper Coll., Palatine, 1997—. Author Hwy. and Heavy Constrn., 1989-91, editor, 1991-92; author, editor Infrastructure, 1992-93; sr. editor Cons./Specifying Engr., 1993-94; editor PM Engr., Bus. News Pub., 1994-96, Plumbing Engr., TMB Pub., 1996-2003; sr. editor engring. HanleyWood LLC, 2003—. Mem. ASCE, Am. Concrete Inst., Am. Soc. Testing and Materials. Office: 426 S Westgate Addison IL 60101-4546 Office Phone: 630-705-2611. E-mail: tklemens@hanleywood.com.

KLEMENT, VERA, artist; b. Gdansk, Dec. 14, 1929; d. Klement and Rose (Rakovchik) Shapiro; divorced; 1 son, Max Klement Shapey. Cert. in fine arts, Cooper Union Sch. Art and Architecture, 1950. Prof. art U. Chgo., 1969—95. Residency and stipend Camargo Found., Cassis, France. One woman shows include RoKo Gallery, N.Y.C., 1958, 60, Bridge Gallery, N.Y.C., 1965, Artemisia Gallery, Chgo., 1974, Chicago Gallery, 1976, Marianne Deson Gallery, 1979, 81, Goethe Inst., 1981, CDS Gallery, N.Y.C., 1981, 84, Roy Boyd Gallery, Chgo., 1983, 85, 87, 89, 90, 91, 92, 93, Spertus Mus., Chgo., 1987, retrospective exhbn., 1953-86, Renaissance Soc., Chgo., 1987, Brody's Gallery, Washington, 1992, Fassbender Gallery, Chgo., 1994, 95, 96, 97, Chgo. Cultural Ctr., 1999, retrospective exhbn., 1965-99, Fassbender, 1999, 2001, Ft. Wayne (Ind.) Mus. Art, 2001, Block Mus., Northwestern U., Evanston, Ill., 2001, U. Ariz. Mus. Art, Tucson, 2001, Tarble Arts Ctr., Ea. Ill. U., Charleston, 2002, Brauer Art Mus., Valparaiso (Ind.) U., 2002, Eric Yake Kenagy Gallery, Goshen (Ind.) Coll., 2003, Miami U. Mus. Art, Oxford, Ohio, 2004, Maya Polsky Gallery, Chgo., 2004, Frederick Baker, Chgo. 2004, Printworks, Chgo., 2004, Daum Mus. Contemporary Art, Sedalia, Mo., 2004, DCS Gallery, N.Y.C., 2005; group shows include Mus. Modern Art, N.Y.C., 1954, 55, Bklyn. Mus., 1950-60, Dallas Mus. Fine Arts, 1954, Tate Gallery, London, 1956, Museo de Arte Moderno, Barcelona, Spain, 1955, Musee d'Art Moderne, Paris, 1955, U. Ky., 1959, Art Inst. Chgo., 1967, Walker Art Ctr., Mpls., 1977, U. Mo., 1978, Detroit Inst. Arts, 1978, Ukrainian Inst. Art, Chgo., 1978, Jewish Mus., N.Y.C., 1982, Kunstverein, Munich, Germany, 1987, Amerika Haus, Berlin, 1987, Terra Mus. Am. Art, Chgo., 1988, Corcoran Gallery, Washington, 1994, Cultural Ctr., Chgo., 1994, former IBM Gallery, N.Y.C., 1995, Virginia Beach Ctr. Arts, 1995, Fischer Art Gallery U. So. Calif., 1995, Portland (Oreg.) Mus. Art, Evanston Art Ctr., Mus. Contemporary Art, Chgo., 1996, Block Gallery Northwestern U., Evanston, 1996, Riva Yares Gallery, Santa Fe, 2002, Klein Artworks, Chgo., 2002, Maya Polsky Gallery, Chgo., 2002; represented in permanent collections Mus. Modern Art, N.Y.C., Phila. Mus. Art, Print Club, Phila., Ill. State Mus., Springfield, U. Tex., Nat. Mus. Am. Art, Washington, Jewish Mus., N.Y.C., Art Inst. Chgo., Philip Morris, N.Y.C., Smart Mus. U. Chgo., Sch. Social Svc. Adminstrn. U. Chgo., Mus. Contemporary Art, Chgo., Mary and Leigh Block Gallery, Evanston, Mus. Art U. Ariz., Tucson, Union Club League Chgo., Daum Mus. Contemporary Art, Sedalia, Mo., Kresge Mus. Art, East Lansing, Mich., U. Miami Mus. Art, Oxford, Ohio; also pvt. collections. Recipient Pollock/Krasner Found. award, 1998; Louis Comfort Tiffany Found. fellow, 1954, Guggenheim fellow, 1981-82, Nat. Endowment for the Arts fellow, 1987; Ill. Arts Coun. grantee, 1988. Personal E-mail: veraklement@aol.com.

KLEMIN, LAWRENCE R., lawyer; b. New Rockford, N.D., Mar. 31, 1945; s. Lawrence R. Klemin and Carol M. (Cook) Roaldson; m. Rita R. DiPalma, Sept. 2, 1970; children: Laura K., Peter L. BA in English, U. N.D., 1967, JD with distinction, 1978. Bar: N.D. 1978, U.S. Dist. Ct. N.D. 1978, U.S. Ct. Appeals (8th cir.) 1987, U.S. Supreme Ct. 1988. Hearing officer N.D. Employment Security Bur., Bismarck, 1971-75; assoc. Atkinson & Dwyer, Bismarck, 1978-81; ptnr. Atkinson, Dwyer & Klemin, Bismarck, 1981-82, Dwyer & Klemin, Bismarck, 1982-86; pres. Lawrence R. Klemin, P.C., Bismarck, 1986-92, Bucklin & Klemin, P.C., Bismarck, 1992-96, Bucklin, Klemin & McBride, P.C., Bismarck, 1996—. Pres. Title and Escrow Co., Bismarck, 1988-98, Litigation Svcs., Inc., Bismarck, 1995—; state rep. N.D. legis assembly, 1998—; commr. Nat. Conf. of Commrs. on Uniform State Laws, 1999—; mem. state adv. coun. N.D. Office Adminstrv. Hearings, Bismarck, 1993-98. Author: Small-Case Litigation Forms, 2004; author, editor Civil Practice of North Dakota, 1993— Bd. dirs. N.D. March of Dimes, Bismarck, 1994-2002, Burleigh-Morton chpt. Am. Red Cross, 2002—; mem. Corpus Christi Parish Coun., Bismarck, 1996-2002. With U.S. Army, 1967-70, Vietnam. Mem. State Bar Assn. N.D. (chair adminstrv. law com. 1996-98), N.D. Land Title Assn. (legis. com. 1990-99), Bismarck Mandan C. of C. (bd. dirs. 1996-98), Optimist Internat. (bd. dirs. 1985-86), Elks, Eagles. Roman Catholic. Avocations: antique auto restoration, astronomy, camping. Home: 1709 Montego Dr Bismarck ND 58503-0856 Office: Bucklin Klemin & McBride PC 400 E Broadway #500 PO Box 955 Bismarck ND 58502-0955 Office Phone: 701-258-8988. Business E-Mail: lklemin@bkmpc.com.

KLEMP, BARBARA ANNE, music educator; b. Morristown, N.J., Oct. 10, 1960; d. Carl William and Edith Nathalie Klemp. BA in Music Edn., Rutgers U., 1982, MusM, 2004. Cert. K-12 vocal/instrumental music comprehensive tchr. N.J. Tchr. music Shore Regional H.S., West Long Branch, NJ, 1982—84; tchr. elem. music Bartle Sch., Highland Park, NJ, 1986—88; tchr. music, dir. H.S. Choral Activities Sch. Dist. of Chathams, Chatham, NJ, 1988—. Choreographer, Chatham, 1990—; composer/arranger, Chatham, 1995—; clin. music edn., Chatham, 1991—; guest ncondr. Messiah sing-in Lincoln Ctr., N.Y.C., 2004. Composer ednl. choral publs.; condr. Mesiah Sing In, Lincoln Ctr., 2004. Vol. America Sings! Inc., Alexandria, Va., 1990—. Named conductor, Morris-Union Jointure Commn., 1992-1998; recipient Svc. and Leadership Recognition award, 1995. Mem.: Internat. Assn. Jazz Educators (condr. N.J. All-State Jazz Choir 2001), Am. Choral Dirs. Assn., Music Educators Nat. Conf., N.J. Music Educators Assn. (condr. All-N.J. Region I Choirs 1994, 2000), N.J. Edn. Assn. (condr. Messiah Sing-In, Lincoln Ct., N.Y.C. 2004). Republican. Avocations: bicycling, walking, rollerblading, reading. E-mail: bkjerzshore@aol.com.

KLEMP, PETER S., music educator, composer; s. Paul A. and Katherine A. Klemp; m. Gail M. Newman, Oct. 6, 1990; children: Zachary, Alexandra, Noah. BA in Music Edn., Concordia Coll., St. Paul, 1992. Cert. tchr. Minn., Wis. Band dir. Trinity Lone Oak Luth. Sch., Eagan, Minn., 1988—91; music dir., composer Youth Performance Co., Mpls., 1989—92; choir dir. Bethel Luth. Ch., St. Paul, 1990—91, Trinity Luth. Ch., Rochester, 1998—2001; music dir. Rochester (Minn.) Ctrl. Luth. Sch., 1992—2002, Racine (Wis.) Luth. H.S., 2002—. Composer: Liturgy for the Family of God, 2003; rec.: 3 albums with Klemp Family Singers. Pit orch. dir. Rochester Civic Theatre, 1998; instrumentalist Rochester Civic Band, 1994—2002, Racine Concert Band, 2004—05; elder St. John's Luth. Ch., Racine, 2003—05. Mem.: Wis. Music Educators Assn., Nat. Band Assn., Music Educators Nat. Conf. Lutheran. Office Phone: 262-637-6538.

KLEMPERER, WILLIAN, chemistry professor; b. N.Y.C., Oct. 6, 1927; s. Paul and Margit (Freund) K.; m. Elizabeth Cole, Jan. 12, 1949; children: Joyce Hillary, Paul, Wendy Judith. AB, Harvard U., 1950; PhD, U. Calif., Berkeley, 1954; DSc, U. Chgo., 1996. Instr. chemistry Harvard U., Cambridge, Mass., 1954-57, asst. prof., 1957-61, assoc. prof., 1961-65, prof., 1965—. Asst. dir. NSF, Washington, 1979-81; vis. scientist Bell Tel. Lab., 1963-83; Evans lectr. Ohio State U., 1981, Pratt lectr. U. Va., 1984, Rollefson lectr. U. Calif., 1985, Oesper lectr. U. Cin., 1987, Kolthoff lectr. U. Minn., 1987, Mary E. Kapp lectr. Va. Commonwealth U., 1987, Linus Pauling Disting. lectr. Oreg. State U., 1988, Harry Emmett Gunning lectr. U. Alta., Can., 1988, Fritz London Meml. lectr. Duke U., 1989, Hinshelwood lectr. Oxford U., Eng., 1989, Neckers lectr. So. Ill. U., 1990; George C. Pimentel meml. lectr. U. Calif., Berkeley, 1992, vis. Miller prof., 1998; Joe L. Franklin meml. lectr. Rice U., 1994, E.K.C. Lee Fellowship lectr. U. Calif., Irvine, 1994; Richard C. Lord lectr. MIT, Cambridge, Mass., 1997; Bernstein lectr. UCLA, 1997. Served with A.C., USN, 1944-46. Recipient Wetherill medal Franklin Inst., 1978, Disting. Svc. medal NSF, 1981, Bomem Michelson award Coblentz Soc., 1990, Faraday Medal and Lectureship Royal Soc. Chemistry, 1995, Ioannes Marcus Marci medal Prague, 2004; named hon. citizen City of Toulouse, France, 2000. Fellow Am. Phys. Soc. (Earle Plyler prize 1983); mem. NAS, Am. Acad. Arts and Scis., Am. Chem. Soc. (Irving Langmuir award 1980, Peter Debye award in phys. chemistry 1994, E. Bright Wilson award in spectroscophy 2001, Remsen award Md. sect. 1992). Achievements include research in molecular structure, energy transfer and intermolecular forces using experimental spectroscopic methods; modelling molecule formation and detection in the interstellar medium. Home: 53 Shattuck Rd Watertown MA 02472-1310 Office: Harvard U Dept Chemistry and Chem Biology 12 Oxford St Cambridge MA 02138-2902 Office Phone: 617-495-4094. Business E-Mail: klemperer@chemistry.harvard.edu.

KLENK, JAMES ANDREW, lawyer; b. Evergreen Park, Ill., July 18, 1949; s. Paul Theodore and Joan (Launspach) K.; m. Carol Evans, Aug. 26, 1972; children: Paul Andrew, Matthew Evans. BA, Beloit Coll., 1971; JD, U. Wis., 1974. Bar: Ill. 1974, Wis. 1974, U.S. Supreme Ct. 1978. Law clk. to Judge Thomas E. Fairchild U.S. Ct. Appeals (7th cir.), Chgo., 1974-75; assoc. Kirkland & Ellis, Chgo., 1975-78; ptnr. Reuben & Proctor, Chgo., 1978-86, Isham, Lincoln & Beale, Chgo., 1986-88, Sonnenschein, Nath & Rosenthal, Chgo., 1988—. Articles editor Wis. Law Rev. Mem. ABA (litigation sect., torts and ins. practice sect., bus. law sect.), Ill. Bar Assn. (anti-trust law sect., litigation sect., torts and ins. practice sect., intellectual prop.), Libel Def. Resource Ctr. (def. counsel sect.), Order of Coif, Phi Beta Kappa. Office: Sonnenschein Nath & Rosenthal 8000 Sears Tower Chicago IL 60606 Office Phone: 312-876-8062. Business E-Mail: jklenk@sonnenschein.com.

KLENK, TIMOTHY CARVER, lawyer; b. Glen Cove, N.Y., Apr. 29, 1939; s. Horace I. and Laura (Dugan) K.; m. Ann Ruth Schuessler, 1961 (dec. 1966); 1 child, Carolyn; m. Margaret Jo Garrett, Aug. 30, 1969. AB, Wheaton Coll., 1961; JD, Northwestern U., 1967. Bar: Ill. 1967, U.S. Dist. Ct. (no. dist.) Ill. 1968, U.S. Dist. Ct. (cen. dist.) Wis. 1976, U.S. Dist. Ct. (cen. dist.) Ill. 1981, U.S. Ct. Appeals (7th cir.) 1979, U.S. Supreme Ct. 1980. Systems engr. IBM, N.Y.C., 1961-62; assoc. Kirkland & Ellis, Chgo., 1967-70, Pope, Ballard, Shepard & Fowle Ltd., Chgo., 1970-74, ptnr., 1974-77, dir., 1977-94, mng. dir., 1993-94; ptnr. Ross & Hardies, Chgo., 1994—2003, McGuireWoods LLP, 2003—. Bd. dirs. Living Bibles Internat. U.S., Naperville, Ill., 1983-91, also v.p. 1st lt. U.S. Army, 1962-64. Mem. ABA, Ill. Bar Assn., 7th Cir. Bar Assn., Am. Judicature Soc., Christian Legal Soc. (bd. dirs. 1986—, pres. 1988-90), Am. Arbitration Assn. (arbitrator), Order of Coif. Republican. Avocations: flying, water sports, skiing. Office: Ross & Hardies 150 N Michigan Ave Ste 2500 Chicago IL 60601-7567 E-mail: tklenk@mcguirewoods.com.

KLENKE, DEBORAH ANN, band director, choral director, department chairman; b. Oak Park, Ill., May 20, 1958; d. Myron and Rita Frances Joshel; children: S. Joel, Jeremy. BS, Elmhurst Coll., 1986. Dir. music, dept. chmn. Faith Christian Elem.- Jr. HS, Geneva, Ill., 1987—2003; dir. bands St. Peter Sch., Geneva, Ill., 1991—99. Prin. flutist West Suburban Symphony, Hinsdale, 1991—2003; freelance flutist. Mem.: Ill. Grade Sch. Music Assn., Ill. Music Educators Assn., Chgo. Flute Club. Office: Faith Christian Elem - Jr HS 1745 Kaneville Rd Geneva IL 60134 Personal E-mail: debklenke@yahoo.com.

KLENKE, ROBERT HUGH, computer engineer, educator, electronics engineer, consultant; b. Huntington, N.Y., Apr. 27, 1960; s. Robert Herman Klenke and Patricia Ann Hassel; m. Janet Kelso Kelso, June 20, 1993; children: Barbara Kelso, Robert Louis. PhD, U. Va., 1993. Prin. scientist U. Va., Charlottesville, Va., 1993—98; assoc. prof. Va. Commonwealth U., Richmond, Va., 1998—. Cons. Sci. Applications Internat. Corp., Hampton, Va., 2001—04. Contbr. articles to profl. jours. Lt. USN, 1982—87. Decorated Navy Achievement medal U.S. Navy. Mem.: IEEE (sr.). Office: Virginia Commonwealth University 601 West Main St Richmond VA 23284-3072 Office Phone: 804-827-7007.

KLEPINGER, JOHN WILLIAM, trailer manufacturing company executive; b. Lafayette, Ind., Feb. 7, 1945; s. John Franklin and R. Wanda (North) K.; m. Mary Patricia Duffy, May 1, 1976; 1 child, Nicholas Patrick. BS, Ball State U., 1967, MA, 1968. Sales engr. CTS Corp., Elkhart, Ind., 1969-70; exec. v.p. Woodlawn Products Corp., Elkhart, 1970-78; v.p. Period Ind., Henderson, Ky., 1976-78, Sotebeer Constrn. Co., Inc., Elkhart, 1978-81; gen. mgr. Wells Industries Inc., Ogden, Utah, 1981—2000; regional mgr. Wells Cargo, Inc., Phoenix, 1995—, Carbondale, Pa., 1999—2003. Regional dir. Zion's First Nat. Bank, Ogden, 1986-99. Bd. dirs. St. Benedict's Hosp., Ogden, 1986-94, chmn., 1987-94; bd. dirs. Weber County Indsl. Devel. Corp., Nat. Job Tng. Partnership Inc., 1986-89; mem. Weber-Morgan Pvt. Industry Coun., 1983-96, Utah Job Tng. Coordinating Coun., 1988-96, chmn. 1993-94; co-chmn. Surgebaake Coalition, 1999—, Trailer Safety Industry Coalition, 2004—. Named Ogden Bus. Man of Yr., Weber County Sch. Dist., 1984. Mem. Nat. Assn. Trailer Mfrs. (bd. dirs., vice chmn. 1994-95, chmn. 1995-97, sec., treas. 1998-99, tech. and maintenance coun. task force 1999--), Weber County Prodn. Mgrs. Assn. (pres. 1984-85, 92-93), Nat. Assn. Pvt. Industry Couns. (bd. dirs. 1986-96, pres. 1988-92), Nat. Alliance Bus. (bd. dirs. 1987-90), Soc. of Automotive Engrs. (trailer com. 1999—), Trailer Safety Ind. Coalition (co-chmn. 2004-05), Surge Brake Coalition (co-chmn. 1999—), Ogden Area C. of C. (bd. dirs. 1986-96, treas. 1986-89), Phoenix C. of C., Exch. Club (bd. dirs. Ogden 1984-86). Roman Catholic. Avocations: finance, community service, leadership, sports, travel. Office: Wells Cargo Inc 6902 W Hadley St Phoenix AZ 85043-4300

KLEPNER, JERRY D., federal agency administrator; b. St. Louis, Dec. 4, 1944; s. Philip and Theresa (Smith) K.; m. Bonnie Klepner, July 1, 1966 (div. 1980); children: Robert, Melissa; m. Karetta Hubbard, June 6, 1981. BA, Washington U., 1967, postgrad., 1966—67. Nat. exec. v.p., dir. legislation Nat. Treasury Employees Union, Washington, 1971-84; ptnr. Anderson, Benjamin, Read & Haney, Washington, 1986-87; staff dir. U.S. Ho. of Reps. Subcom. on Compensation and Employee Benefits, Washington, 1984-86; dir. legislation Am. Fedn. State, County and Mcpl. Employees, Washington, 1987-93; asst. sec. legislation Dept. Health and Human Svcs., Washington, 1993-96; sr. v.p. Ketchum Pub. Rels., Washington, 1996-98; mng. dir. Black, Kelly, Scruggs & Healey, Washington, 1998—. Commr. Va. Statewide Health Coordinating Coun., Richmond, 1986-87; dir. No. Va. Health Systems Agy., Fairfax, 1984-87. Democrat. Jewish. Achievements include boating, fishing, swimming, photography, hist. non-fiction and fiction. Office: Black Kelly Scruggs & Healey 1801 K St NW Ste 901-1 Washington DC 20006-1301

KLEPPA, OLE J., chemistry professor; b. Oslo, Feb. 4, 1920; married; 2 children. MS, Norwegian Inst. Tech., 1946, DS, 1956. Union Carbon and Carbide postdoctoral fellow, instr. U. Chgo. Inst. Study of Metals, 1948-50; rsch. supr. divsn. chemistry and metallurgy Norwegian Def. Rsch. Establishment, 1950-51; asst. prof. U. Chgo., 1952-57, assoc. prof., 1958-62, prof. dept. chemistry, 1962-90, prof. dept. geophys. scis., 1968-90, prof. emeritus, 1990—, assoc. dir. James Franck Inst., 1968-71, dir., 1971-77, dir. materials rsch. lab., 1984-87. Cons. Argonne Nat. Lab., 1959-71; dir. The Calorimetry Conf., 1963-69, chmn., 1966-67; vis. prof. Japan Soc. Promotion of Sci., 1975, U. Paris, Orsay, 1977; presenter confs. in field. Bd. editors Jour. Chem. Physics, 1965-67, Jour. Chem. Thermodynamics, 1981-87, Jour. Phase Equilibria, 1995—; contbr. articles to profl. jours. Recipient Huffman Meml. award, 1982, U.S. Sr. Sci. Humboldt award, 1983-84. Fellow AAAS, Am. Soc. Metals; mem. Am. Chem. Soc., Am. Ceramic Soc., Soc. Norwegian Engrs., Royal Norwegian Soc. Sci. and Letters, Norwegian Acad. Tech. Scis., Minerals, Metals, and Materials Soc. (Hume-Rothery award 1994). Achievements include pioneering development of new technique of high-temperature oxide melt solution calorimetery; being the first person to extensively apply the Calvét-type twin microcalorimeter in high temperature thermochemistry; originator of a novel high-temperature reaction calorimeter suitable for continuous use at temperatures up to about 1500K; applying new calorimeter in extensive studies of binary alloys of transition metals and rare earth metals with Group VIII transition metals and with noble metals. Office: U Chgo James Franck Inst 5640 S Ellis Ave Chicago IL 60637-1433 Business E-Mail: Kleppa@control.uchicago.edu.

KLEPPE, JOAN MARIE, entertainment executive; b. Lomira, Wis., Aug. 22, 1925; d. George Jacob and Susan Elizabeth (Welsch) Steiner; m. Albert Wilhey Wellander, June 10, 1950 (div. Mar. 1960); children: Thomas A., Alan G., Barbara Sue; m. Willard Earl Kleppe, Sept. 18, 1978 (dec. Mar. 1988). Degree magna cum laude, Fond du Lac (Wis.) Comml Coll., 1943; BS in Music Edn., U. Wis., 1947; postgrad., Second City, Chgo., 1976-78. Cert. exec. sec., Ill. Adminstrv. asst. to pres. Canvas Products Corp., Fond du Lac, Wis., 1947-50; jr. exec. corp. offices Sears, Roebuck and Co., Chgo., 1950-54; exec. dir. Lake View Citizens' Coun., Chgo., 1963-67; exec. sec. Chgo. Police Dept., 1967-72, founder, dir. boys' a capella choir, 1970-72; polygraph interviewer, reporter Inst. Lie Detection, Chgo., 1972-75; exec. sec., adminstrv. asst. Electro Brand, Inc. importers, Chgo., 1975-80, Gen. Instrument Corp., Chgo., 1980-85; founder, exec. dir., musician Spring Valley Concert Band, Schaumburg, Ill., 1994—. Entertainer St. Andrew Players, Chgo., 1965-74; trombonist Ukrainian Cathedral Concert Band, Chgo., 1968-70; performer, dir., costumer St. Marcelline Prodns., Inc., Schaumburg, 1989-95; performer, bd. dirs. Silver Foxes Theatrical Troupe, Streamwood, Ill., 1992-96. Author, dir. children's theatrical prodns. Let Freedom Ring, 1966, A Fractured Fairy Tale, 1967; author: Kids 'n' Kops, 1997; writer, dir. musical comedy Talent, of Chorus, 1989, Puttin' on the Bits, 1990; composer music anthem Chgo.: I Will, 1970; columnist Chgo. police dept. publ. The Star, 1968-72. Coord. neighborhood groups Lake View Citizens Coun., Chgo., 1963-67; sec., youth liaison youth com. Chgo. Police Dept., 1967-72; founding mem. Schaumburg Arts Collective, 1996—; mem., liaison Schaumburg Sister Cities, 1995—; coord. benefit performances; bd. dirs. St. Marcelline Prodns.; mem. Prairie Center Arts Found., 1997—, Assn. Concert Bands, Inc., 1998—. U. Wis. scholar, 1943, Pi Rho Zeta scholar, 1942; named Vol. of Yr. Kiwanis, 1970, Most Valuable Civilian Employee Chgo. Police Dept., 1970. Republican. Roman Catholic. Avocations: acting in community theater, freelance writing, costume design, singing, fishing. Home: 607 N Walnut Ln Schaumburg IL 60194-2636 Office: Spring Valley Concert Band Inc PO Box 68901 Schaumburg IL 60168-0901 Office Phone: 847-289-4227. Personal E-mail: jkleppe1@sbcglobal.net.

KLEPPE, JOHN ARTHUR, electrical engineer, educator, engineering executive; b. Oakland, Calif., Feb. 21, 1939; s. Arthur William and Musa (Anderson) K.; m. Julianna Marie Galli, Aug. 12, 1961; children: John Frederick, Johanna Beth, Judith Anne. BSEE, U. Nev., 1961, MSEE, 1967; PhD, U. Calif., Davis, 1970. Registered profl. engr., Nev., Calif. Prof. elec. engring. U. Nev., Reno, 1970—, dir. Engring. Research and Devel., 1976-88; pres., research cons. Sci. Engring. Instruments, Inc., Reno, 1968-97; pres. Klepco, Inc., 1976—. Cons.; chief engr. NSF weather expdn. to Antarctica, 1977; del. White House Conf. Small Bus., 1980 Author: (textbook) Engineering Applications of Acoustics, 1989; contbr. articles, papers to publs. and confs. around the world. Served to lt. C.E. USN, 1961-65. Recipient Outstanding Engring. Achievement award for Nev., 1981, 84; Inventor of Yr. award, 1985 Mem. IEEE, Nev. Innovation and Tech. Coun. (pres. 1981-93, pres. 1996-97), Sigma Xi, Tau Beta Pi. Home: 2776 Spinnaker Dr Reno NV 89509 Office: U Nev Dept Elec Engring MS 260 Reno NV 89557-0153 Business E-Mail: kleppe@ee.unr.edu.

KLEPPER, ELIZABETH LEE, physiologist; b. Memphis, Mar. 8, 1936; d. George Madden and Margaret Elizabeth (Lee) K. BA, Vanderbilt U., 1958; MA, Duke U., 1963, PhD, 1966. Rsch. scientist Commonwealth Sci. and Indsl. Rsch. Orgn., Griffith, Australia, 1966-68, Battelle Northwest Lab., Richland, Wash., 1972-76; asst. prof. Auburn (Ala.) U., 1968-72; plant physiologist USDA Agrl. Rsch. Svc., Pendleton, Oreg., 1976-85, rsch. leader, 1985-96. Assoc. editor Crop Sci., 1977-80, 88-90, tech. editor, 1990-92, editor, 1992-95; mem. editl. bd. Plant Physiology, 1977-92, Irrigation Sci., 1987-92; mem. editl. adv. bd. Field Crops Rsch., 1983-91; contbr. articles to profl. jours., chpts. to books. Mem. Unatilla Basin Watershed Coun., 2005—. Marshall scholar Brit. Govt., 1958-59; NSF fellow, 1964-66; Recipient First Citizen award, Pendleton, 2005, White Rose award, March of Dimes, Portland, 2005. Fellow: AAAS, Am. Soc. Agronomy (monograph com. 1983—90, bd. dirs. 1995—98), Soil Sci. Soc. Am. (fellows com. 1986—88), Crop Sci. Soc. Am. (fellows com. 1989—91, pres.-elect 1995—96, pres. 1996—97, Monsanto Disting. Career award 2004); mem.: Agronomic Sci. Found. (bd. dirs. 1993—99), Sigma Xi. Home: 1454 SW 45th Pendleton OR 97801 Office: USDA Agrl Rsch Svc PO Box 370 Pendleton OR 97801-0370 E-mail: klepperb@uci.net.

KLEPPNER, DANIEL, physicist, researcher; b. N.Y.C., Dec. 16, 1932; s. Otto and Beatrice (Taub) K.; m. Beatrice Spencer; children: Paul, Sofie, Andrew. BS, Williams Coll., 1953; BA, Cambridge (Eng.) U., 1955; PhD, Harvard U., 1959. Asst. prof. physics Harvard U., Cambridge, Mass., 1962-66; assoc. prof. MIT, Cambridge, 1966-73, prof., 1974—, Lester Wolfe prof. physics, 1986—, assoc. dir. Rsch. Lab. of Electronics, 1987—. Author: Introduction to Mechanics, 1973, Quick Calculus, 1986. Recipient Oersted medal, AAPT, 1996. Fellow Am. Phys. Soc. (Davisson-Germer prize 1986, Julius Edgar Lilienfeld prize 1991), AAAS, Optical Soc. Am. (William F. Meggars award 1991), Am. Acad. Arts and Scis.; mem. NAS, Am. Assn. Physics Tchrs. (Oersted medal). Office: MIT Dept Physics 77 Mass Ave Rm 26237 Cambridge MA 02139-4307

KLESIUS, PHILLIP HARRY, microbiologist, researcher; b. Phila., Mar. 1, 1938; s. Phillip M. and Mary Hoagen (Plummer) K.; m. Patricia Ann Wood, Oct. 31, 1969; children— Stephen, Patrick BS, Fla. So. U., Lakeland, 1961; MS, Northwestern State U., Natchitoches, La., 1963; PhD, U. Tex., Austin, 1966; postgrad., U. Calif.-San Francisco, 1967. Hon. diplomate Am. Coll. Vet. Microbiologists. Asst. prof. microbiology U. Tex., Austin, 1967-68; asst. prof microbiology U. Ariz., Tucson, 1968-72; asst. chief strep sect. USPHS, Fort Collins, Colo., 1972-73; research microbiologist U.S. Dept. Agr., Auburn, Ala., 1973-82, dir., 1982—. Adj. prof. Auburn U., 1974—; adj. assoc. prof. Med. Coll. S.C., Charleston, 1975—; visting prof. Tuskegee Inst., Ala., 1974— Contbr. articles to profl. jours. Recipient Technology Transfer award USDA, 1999; named USDA Scientist of Yr., 1994, 99. Fellow Am. Acad. Microbiology, Am. Assn. Vet. Immunologists (dir. 1985—), Am. Assn. Vet. Pathologists, Am. Assn. Vet. Parasitologists, Am. Soc. Microbiologists. Office: Aquatic Animal Disease Rsch Lab PO Box 952 Auburn AL 36831-0952 Home: 2009 Hillbrook Cir Auburn AL 36830-7657 Business E-Mail: klesiph@vetmed.auburn.edu. E-mail: klesiph@charter.net.

KLESKO, RYAN, professional baseball player; b. Westminster, Calif., June 12, 1971; Right field Atlanta Braves, 1992—99, San Diego Padres, 2000—. Spokesperson Make-A-Wish Found. Avocations: hunting, fishing. Office: 100 Park BLVD San Diego CA 92101-7405

KLESSE, WILLIAM R., energy executive; BS in Chemical Engineering, Univ. of Dayton, 1968; M.B.A., West Texas State Univ., 1973. With Diamond Shamrock (now Valero Energy Corp.), 1969—; sr. v.p./Group Executive Diamond Shamrock Corp., 1989—95, exec. v.p., 1995—96; exec. v.p., Refining, Product Supply and Logistics Ultramar Diamond Shamrock Corp., San Antonio, 1996—98, exec. v.p., operations, 1999—2001; chmn. Shamrock Logistics GP, LLC, 1999—2001; exec. v.p., coo Valero Energy Corp, 2001—. Office: Valero Engeryg Corp PO Box 500 San Antonio TX 78292

KLESZYNSKI, KENNETH, music educator, conductor; b. Chgo., Jan. 27, 1950; s. Leonard Aloysius and Mildred Kleszynski; m. Barbara Jean Alex, Nov. 12, 1994; children: Keith Leonard, Jan Aileen. BA, MusB Edn., Benedictine Coll., 1972; MA, Ariz. State U., 1976; PhD, Mich. State U., 1984. Gen. music tchr. TG Barr Sch., Phoenix, 1972—73; orch./asst. band dir. McClintock H.S., Tempe, Ariz., 1973—78; asst. prof. music Olivet (Mich.) Coll., 1978—84, Otterbein Coll., Westerville, Ohio, 1984—87; prof. of music U. Portland, Oreg., 1987—, dir. music edn. and music grad programs, 1987—, dir. univ. core program, 2002—04. Condr. cmty. and chamber orchs. U. Portland; condr. Westerville Civic Symphony. Prodr. and sponsor U. Portland / Portland Polish Festival Polish Music Concert, 1998—2003. Recipient Bronze award, Coun. for Advancement and Support of Edn. Dist. VIII, 2000, Culligan award for Distg. Svc., U. Portland, 2001; grantee, Burlington No. Found., 1989, Jackson Found., 1989, Arthur Butine Devel. Fund, U. Portland, 1999, 1990, 1992—94, 1996. Avocations: fly fishing, collecting CDs, reading, food and wine, golf. Home: 5606 SW Riverside Ln Unit 4 Portland OR 97239 Office: U Portland 5000 N Willamette Blvd Portland OR 97203 Office Phone: 503-943-7294. Business E-Mail: kkleszyn@up.edu.

KLETT, EDWIN L., lawyer; b. Clearfield, Pa., Dec. 8, 1935; s. John L. and Gertrude Elizabeth (Larson) K.; m. Janis Lynn Gibson; children: David, Lauren, Krista, Kirklin, Keenan. BS in Commerce and Finance, Bucknell U., 1957; JD, Dickinson Sch. Law, Carlisle, Pa., 1962. Bar: Pa. 1963, U.S. Dist. Ct. (we. dist.) Pa. 1963, U.S. Dist. Ct. (mid. dist.) Pa. 1995, U.S. Dist. Ct. (ea. dist.) Pa. 2000, U.S. Ct. Appeals (3d cir.) 1967, U.S. Ct. Appeals (6th cir.) 1985, U.S. Ct. Appeals (11th cir.) 2001, U.S. Supreme Ct. 1983. Assoc. Eckert, Seamans, Cherin & Mellott, Pitts., 1962, ptnr., 1969; sr. ptnr., chmn. Klett Rooney Lieber & Schorling P.C., Pitts., 1989—. Trustee Dickinson Sch. Law, 1982-2005, Bucknell U., 2004, Bucknell U., 2004-2008; mem. civil procedural rules com. Pa. Supreme Ct., 1986-99, vice chair, 1989-92, chair, 1993-99. Mem. Pa. State Transp. Adv. Bd., Harrisburg, Pa., 1985—88, Rep. State Fin. Com., Harrisburg, Pa., 1986—91, Allegheny County Rep. Fin. Com., Pitts., 1987—92. Fellow Internat. Acad. Trial Lawyers, Am. Coll. Trial Lawyers (Pa. state com. 1994-99, state chair 1996-98), Am. Bd. Trial Advs., Am. Bar Found., Am. Bar Inst., Pa. Bar Found., Alletheny County Bar Found.; mem. ABA (ho. dels. 1999-2000), Am. Bd. Trial Advs., Acad. Trial Lawyers Allegheny County (bd. govs. 1986-89, pres. 1988-89), Am. Judicature Soc., Allegheny County Bar (bd. govs. 1989-92, 99-02, pres. 1999-01). Home: 151 Ordale Blvd Pittsburgh PA 15228-1525 Office: Klett Rooney Lieber & Schorling 1 Oxford Ct Fl 40 Pittsburgh PA 15219-1407 Office Phone: 412-392-2178. Business E-Mail: elklett@klettrooney.com.

KLETT, GORDON A., retired savings and loan association executive; b. Galva, Iowa, Apr. 29, 1925; s. Ernest and Frieda (Gutknecht) K.; m. Edna Mae Klett, June 11, 1950; children: Joel G., Kristin F., Andrea E. BA, Valparaiso U., 1949; MA, UCLA, 1951. With U.S. Weather Bur., St. Paul, 1941-42; vis. lectr. U. Ceylon, Colombo, 1951-52; fgn. service officer U.S. Dept. State, Mex., 1956-58; with Glendale (Calif.) Fed. Savs. and Loan Assn., 1953-56, 59-84, pres., chief operating officer, 1980-84. Served with USAAF, 1943-46.

KLETZIEN, SHARON BENGE, language educator, department chairman; d. Robert Kenney Benge and Mary Sue Reynolds; m. S. Damon Kletzien, June 25, 1967; children: Jonathan Burk, Christopher Damon. BA, West Tex. State U., 1961; MA, Am. U., 1971; PhD, Temple U., 1988. Supervisory Certificates for Reading, Curriculum and Instruction Pa. Dept. of Edn., 1992, Teaching Reading, English, French Pa. Dept. of Edn., 1977. Instr. U. Tunis - Peace Corps, 1964—66; tchr., reading specialist Springfield Sch. Dist., Pa., 1977—91; prof., dept. chair West Chester U., 1991—. Editl. rev. bd. Jour. Literacy Rsch., Jour. Adolescent & Adult Literacy, The Thinking Classroom, Yearbook Nat. Reading Conf.; presenter edn. workshop Reading Writing Critical Thinking. Co-author: Informational Text in K-3 Classrooms; contbr. articles to profl. jours., chpts. to books. Pres. LWV, Springfield, Pa., 1990—91. Recipient Outstanding Student Rsch., Am. Ednl. Rsch. Assn., Divsn. C, 1988, Program of Excellence, Pa. Coun. Social Studies, 1995, Nat. Coun. Social Studies, 1996. Mem.: Nat. Reading Conf., Internat. Reading Assn. Office: West Chester U Dpt Literacy - Recitation Hall West Chester PA 19383 Office Phone: 610-436-2877. Personal E-mail: skletzien@wcupa.edu.

KLEVORICK, ALVIN K., law and economics educator; b. 1943. BA, Amherst Coll., 1963; MA, 1965; PhD, Princeton U., 1967. Lectr. econs. Princeton U., 1966-67; asst. prof. econs. Yale U., 1967-70, assoc. prof. econs., 1970-73, vis. lectr. law, 1972-73, assoc. prof. law and econs., 1973-75, prof. law and econs., 1975-86; John Thomas Smith prof. law and econs., 1986—; dep. dean, 1994-99; dir. Cowles Found. for Rsch. in Econs., 1984-96; dir. Div. Social Scis., 1998-. Fellow Ctr. for Advanced Study in Behavioral Scis., 1975-76. Mem. Am. Econ. Assn., Econometric Soc. Office: Yale Law Sch PO Box 208215 New Haven CT 06520 E-mail: alvin.klevorick@yale.edu.*

KLEWANS, SAMUEL N., lawyer; b. Lock Haven, Pa., Mar. 2, 1941; s. Morris and Ruth N. Klewans; children: Richard Bennett, Ruth Elise, Paul Henry, Margo Ilene. AB, U. Pa., 1963; JD, Am. U., 1966. Bar: Va. 1966, U.S. Dist. Ct. (ea. dist.) Va. 1966, U.S. Dist. Ct. D.C. 1967, U.S. Ct. Appeals D.C. 1967, U.S. Ct. Appeals (4th cir.) 1967, U.S. Supreme Ct. 1971. Law clk. U.S. Dist. Ct. (ea. dist.) Va., 1966-67; ptnr. Fried, Fried & Klewans, Springfield, Va., 1970-86; prin. Klewans & Assocs., 1986-91; shareholder, ptnr. Grad, Logan & Klewans, P.C., Alexandria, Va., 1991—. Lectr. No. Va. Inst. Continuing Med. Edn., No. Va. Ctr. Quality and Health Edn. Contbr. articles to profl. jours. 1st lt. JAGC-USAR, 1966-72. Office: 1421 Prince St Ste 320 Alexandria VA 22314-2805 Office Phone: 703-535-5399. E-mail: sklewans@glklawyers.com.

KLEWENO, GILBERT H., lawyer; b. Endicott, Wash., Mar. 21, 1933; s. Melvin Lawrence and Anna (Lust) K.; m. Virginia Symms, Dec. 28, 1958; children: Stanley, Douglas, Phillip. BA, U. Wash., 1955; LLR, U. Idaho, 1959. Bar: Wash. 1960. Assoc. Read & Church, Vancouver, Wash., 1960-68, Boettcher, LaLonde & Kleweno, Vancouver, Wash., 1968-99; sole practitioner Vancouver, 1999—. Part-time U.S. Magistrate Judge, 1979. Chmn. Bd. Adjustors, Vancouver, Civil Svc. Commn., Vancouver. Mem. Wash. State Bar Assn., Elks, Gyro Club. Office: 211 E McLoughlin Blvd #130 Vancouver WA 98663

KLEY, JOHN ARTHUR, banker; b. Jericho, NY, Oct. 24, 1921; s. John and Annie (Upton) K.; m. Florence Elizabeth Cannon, Sept. 1, 1945 (dec. Apr. 1983); 1 dau., Martha Anne; m. Edna C. Dornhoefer, June 1984 (div. June 1987); m. Lorelei W. Lasecki. Apr. 1989. Grad., Stonier Grad. Sch. Banking, Rutgers U., 1952; B.P.S., Pace U., 1974. With Washington Irving Trust Co. (and successor County Trust Co.), White Plains, N.Y., 1937-76, asst. treas., asst. v.p., v.p., 1947-57, exec. v.p., 1957-60, pres., 1960-72, chmn. bd., 1972-76; v.p. Bank N.Y. Co., 1968-74, vice chmn., 1974-77; dir. Bank of N.Y., 1973-77. Past chmn. bd. trustees, trustee emeritus Westchester C.C.; past pres., chmn. Westchester C.C. Found.; past pres. Legal Aid Soc. West County; past chmn. bd. regents Stonier Grad. Sch. Banking, Rutgers U. Served from pvt. to maj. USAAF, 1942-46; lt. col. Res., 1946-51. Recipient Leffinqwell medal, 1960 Mem. ABA (com. on mechanization of check handling, chmn. tech. com. 1954-64, NY State Bankers Assn. (pres. 1969-70), Imperial Golf Club (Naples), Whippoorwill Club (Armonk, N.Y.). Episcopalian. Home: 7515 Pelican Bay Blvd Apt 303 Naples FL 34108-6518

KLIEBENSTEIN, DON, lawyer; b. Marshalltown, Iowa, May 3, 1936; s. Donald B. and Gertrude E. (Skeie) K.; m. Mary L. Delfs, June 11, 1960; 1 child, Julie Ann. Student, Grinnell Coll., 1953-55; BA, U. Iowa, 1957, JD, 1961. Bar: Iowa 1961, U.S. Dist. Ct. (no., so. dists.) Iowa 1961, U.S. Supreme Ct. 1971. Pvt. practice, Grundy Center, Iowa, 1961-67; ptnr. Kliebenstein & Heronimus, Grundy Center, 1967-77, Kliebenstein, Heronimus & Schmidt, Grundy Center, 1977-98, Kliebenstein Heronimus Schmidt and Harris, Grundy Center, 1999—2003; of counsel Kliebenstein, Heronimus, Schmidt and Harris, 2004—. Bd. dirs. Grundy Nat. Bank, Grundy Ctr.; county atty. Grundy County, 1965-98. Mem. ABA, Iowa State Bar Assn., Grundy County Bar Assn. (pres. 1979-80), 1st Jud. Dist. Bar Assn. (pres. 1975-76). Republican. Methodist. Home: 701 9th St Grundy Center IA 50638-1238 Office: Kliebenstein Heronimus Schmidt & Harris 630 G Ave PO Box 365 Grundy Center IA 50638-0365 Office Phone: 319-824-6951.

KLIEBHAN, SISTER M(ARY) CAMILLE, academic administrator; b. Milw., Apr. 4, 1923; d. Alfred Sebastian and Mae Eileen (McNamara) K. Student, Cardinal Stritch Coll., Milw., 1945-48; BA, Cath. Sisters Coll., Washington, 1949; MA, Cath. U. Am., 1951, PhD, 1955. Joined Sisters of St. Francis of Assisi, Roman Catholic Ch., 1945; legal sec. Spence and Hanley (attys.), Milw., 1941-45; instr. edn. Cardinal Stritch Coll., 1955-62, assoc. prof., 1962-68, prof., 1968—, head dept. edn., 1962-67, dean students, 1962-64, chmn. grad. div., 1964-69, v.p. for acad. and student affairs, 1969-74, pres., also bd. dirs., 1974-91, chancellor, 1991—. Mem. TEMPO, 1982—2001, bd. dirs., 1986—89; bd. govs. Wis. Policy Rsch. Inst., 1987—97; bd. dirs. Goals for Milw. 2000, 1980—83; treas. Wis. Found. Ind. Colls., 1974—79, 1987—90, v.p., 1979—81, pres., 1981—83; bd. dirs. DePaul Hosp., 1982—91, Sacred Heart Sch. Theology, 1983—2004, dir. emerita, 2004; bd. dirs. Viterbo Coll., 1990—98, Milw. Cath. Home, 1991—2001, St. Ann Ctr. for Intergenerational Care, 1991—99, Wis. Psychoanalytic Found., 1989—96, St. Coletta's of Mass., 1995—98, Internat. Inst. Wis., 1984—94, Milw. Achiever Program, Inc., 1983—2003, dir. emerita, 2004; bd. dirs. Franciscan Pilgrimage Programs, Inc., 1997—, Friends of Internat. Inst. Wis., 1994—, Mental Hea.th Assn. Milwaukee County, 1983—87, Pub. Policy Forum, 1987—90, Better Bus. Bur. of Wis., Inc., 1989—2001, YWCA Greater Milw., 1996—2001, St. Camillus Campus, 1996—2001, mem. adv. bd., 1989—96. Mem. Am. Psychol. Assn., Rotary Club of Milw. (v.p., pres. elect 1992-93, pres. 1993-94), St. Mary's Acad. Alumnae Assn., Phi Delta Kappa, Delta Epsilon Sigma, Psi Chi, Delta Kappa Gamma, Kappa Delta Pi. Business E-Mail: ckliebhan@stritch.edu. *It is because of my faith that I can meet every condition with courage.*

KLIEFOTH, A(RTHUR) BERNHARD, III, neurosurgeon; b. San Antonio, Nov. 26, 1942; S. Arthur Bernhard, Jr. and Pauline (Gray) K.; m. Ingrid R. Kunde, Apr. 22, 1968; children: Karena, Tanya. AB in Chemistry, Princeton U., 1965; MD, U. Tex. Med. Br., Galveston, 1970. Diplomate Am. Bd. Neurol. Surgery. Intern Naval Hosp., Oakland, Calif., 1970-71, resident gen. surgery San Diego, 1972-73; neurosurg. tchr. Washington U., St. Louis, 1973-78, rsch. fellow dept. radiation scis., 1977-78; commd. ensign USN, 1969, advanced through grades to comdr., 1977; staff neurosurgeon Naval Regional Med. Ctr., Oakland, 1978-81; capt. USNR, 1985; practice medicine specializing in neurosurgery Knoxville, Tenn., 1981—; mem. staff U. Tenn. Hosp., St. Mary's Hosp.; chmn. dept. surgery, 1989-90; clin. assoc. prof. surgery U. Tenn. Bd. dirs. Tenn. Donor Svcs., Cole Neurosci. Found., Knoxville Donor Svcs., Epilepsy Found. Ea. Tenn., vis. prof. Bethesda Naval Hosp. (Nat. Naval Med. Ctr.). Pres. Princeton Alumni Assn. Knoxville and Ea. Tenn., Exec. Com. West Hills Assn. Recipient Disting. Southern Neurosurgeon award, So. Neurosurgery Soc., 2003—. Fellow ACS, Stroke Coun. Am. Heart Assn.; mem. AMA, Am. Assn. Neurol. Surgeons, Am. Soc. Stereotactic and Functional Neurosurgery, Tenn. Neurosurg. Soc., World Soc. Stereotactic and Functional Neurosurgery, Congress Neurol. Surgeons, So. Neurosurg. Soc., So. Med. Assn., Tenn. Med. Assn., Knoxville Acad. Medicine, San Francisco Neurol. Soc., Soc. Med. Cons. to Armed Forces, Assn. Mil. Surgeons U.S., Soc. Neurosci. Office: 6901 Office Park Cir Knoxville TN 37909-1162 Address: PO Box 51648 Knoxville TN 37950-1648 Office Phone: 865-524-9400.

KLIEMAN, RIKKI JO, lawyer, legal analyst; b. Chgo., May 13, 1948; d. Ben and Jeannette (Wiener) K.; m. Philip A. Brady, Sept. 20, 1987 (div.); m. William J. Bratton, April 30, 1999 BS, Northwestern U., Evanston, Ill., 1970; JD, Boston U., 1975. Bar: Mass. 1975, Colo. 1977, U.S. Dist. Ct. Mass. 1975, U.S. Ct. Appeals (1st cir.) 1976, U.S. Ct. Appeals (11th cir.) 1984. Law clk. to Hon. Walter J. Skinner U.S. Dist. Ct., Boston, 1975-76; asst. dist. atty. Middlesex County, Cambridge, Mass., 1977-79, Norfolk County, Dedham, Mass., 1979-81; assoc. Choate, Hall & Stewart, Boston, 1981-84; ptnr. Friedman & Atherton, Boston, 1984-89, Klieman & Lyons, Boston, 1989—94; of counsel Klieman, Lyons, Schindler & Gross (formerly Klieman & Lyons), Boston, 1994—; anchor Court-TV, 1994—2003, legal analyst, 2003—, The Today Show, 2003—. Instr. Bosto U. Sch. Law, 1977-79, 86-, tchr. Continuing Legal Edn., 1979—, adj. prof. Columbia Law Sch., 1996-2003 Author:(autobiography) Fairy Takes Can Come True-How A Driven Woman Changed Her Fate, 2003; Author/editor: Woman Trial Lawyers, 1987—; editor Mass. Lawyers Weekly, 1981-85; contbr. articles to profl. jours.; Film appearances include The Cable Guy, 1996, A Civil Action, 1998, 15 Minutes, 2001; TV appearances include The D.A., 2004, Dr. Vegas, 2004, Las Vegas, 2005, NYPD Blue, 2005; TV miniseries An American Tragedy, 2000 Exec. com. for civil rights Anti Defamation League, Boston, 1991—; dir., clk. Shepherd Ho., Boston, 1986—. Named One of Top Five Female Trial Attys. in U.S.A., Time Mag., 1983. Mem. ABA, Nat. Assn. of Criminal Def. Lawyers (bd. dirs. 1983-88), Boston Bar Assn., Mass. Bar Assn. (criminal justice coun. 1982-84), Women's Bar Assn., Mass. Assn. of Women Lawyers, Mass. Acad. of Trial Attys. Avocations: jogging, aerobics, theater, film. Office: Klieman Lyons Schindler & Gross 21 Custom House St Boston MA 02110

KLIGER, MILTON RICHARD, diversified financial services company executive; b. N.Y.C., Sept. 26, 1922; s. David and Sadie (Zelikow) K.; m. Ruth Salkind, Jan. 30, 1944 (dec. July 1991); children: Alan S., Sandra F.; m. Gladys Duarte, Sept. 26, 1992. BBA, Bernard Baruch Coll., 1947. Acct. Shipowners Agy. Inc., N.Y.C., 1946-48; chief acct. Am.-Israeli Shipping Co. Inc., N.Y.C., 1948-53; exec. v.p. Maritime Overseas Corp., N.Y.C., 1953-87, also bd. dirs.; CFO, sr. v.p., treas. Overseas Shipholding Group Inc., N.Y.C., 1970-87, also bd. dirs.; pres. OSG Internat. Inc., 1980-87; sr. v.p. Argent Group, Ltd., N.Y.C., 1988-89; pres. Milton Kliger Mgmt. Svcs., Inc., N.Y.C., 1989-93. Marine Equity Corp., N.Y.C., 1990—. Home: 7000 Island Blvd Apt 909 Aventura FL 33160

KLIGERMAN, MORTON M., radiologist; b. Phila., Dec. 26, 1917; s. Samuel and Dorothy (Medvene) K.; m. Barbara B. Coleman, Mar. 14, 1956; children: Hilary, Thomas A., Valli á Court. BS, Temple U., 1938, MD, 1941, MSc, 1949; MA (hon.), Yale U., 1958; D.F.A. (hon.), New Sch. Music, 1985; MA (hon.), U. Pa., 1986. Instr. radiology Temple U., Phila., 1947-48, Columbia U., N.Y.C., 1948-50, asst. prof. radiology, 1950-53, assoc. prof., 1953-58; Robert E. Hunter prof. radiology, chmn. dept. radiology Yale U., New Haven; also radiologist-in-chief Yale-New Haven Hosp., 1958-72; dir. Cancer Research and Treatment Center U. N.Mex., Albuquerque, 1972-80, prof. radiology, 1972-80; asst. dir. for radiation therapy Los Alamos Sci. Lab., 1972-80; chief div. radiation oncology Bernalillo County Med. Center, Albuquerque, 1972-80; prof. radiation oncology U. Pa., Phila., 1980—, Henry K. Pancoast prof. research oncology, 1984-88; prof. emeritus, 1988—. Cons. on staff Presbyn. Hosp., Lovelace-Bataan Med. Center, St. Joseph Hosp., VA Hosp., all Albuquerque, Los Alamos Med. Center. Contbr. articles to profl. jours. Bd. dirs. Santa Fe Opera, 1975-80, mem. nat. adv. bd., 1980-89; bd. dirs. Santa Fe Opera Found., 1976-80, also pres.; bd. dirs. N.Mex. divsn. Am. Cancer Soc., 1972-76, Phila. divsn., 1985-89, Pa. Ballet, 1985-89; bd. advisors Annenberg Ctr., U. Pa., 1987-2001, bd. overseers, 2001-03, Phila. Scholar Fund, 1992—. With M.C., U.S. Army, 1944-47. Recipient Disting. Alumni award Temple U., 1964; Silver Medallion Columbia U., 1967; Grubbe Gold Medal award Chgo. Med. Soc.-Chgo. Radiol. Soc., 1976; Disting. Alumnus award Temple U. Med. Sch., 1986; named Med. Alumnus of Yr. Temple U. Med. Sch., 1989; Morton M. Kligerman endowed chair radiation oncology U. Pa. Med. Sch., 2003. Fellow Am. Coll. Radiology, Coll. Physicians Phila.; mem. Pa. Med. Soc., Philadelphia County Med. Soc., Am. Assn. Cancer Rsch., Am. Radium Soc. (v.p. 1976-77, pres. 1982-83, Janeway medal 1981), Am. Soc. Therapeutic Radiologists (pres. 1968-69, Gold medal 1982), Am. Legion, Alpha Omega Alpha. Home: 220 W Rittenhouse Sq Philadelphia PA 19103-5737 Office: Hosp of Univ Pa Dept Radiation Oncology 3400 Spruce St Philadelphia PA 19104-4283 Office Phone: 215-662-6463. Business E-Mail: kligerman@xrt.upenn.edu.

KLIMAN, SYLVIA MAY STERN, communications executive; b. Boston, July 16, 1934; d. Edward I. and Bernice Stern; m. Allan Kliman, June 24, 1956; children: Gilbert Harrow, Douglas Hartley. AB, Vassar Coll., 1956. Editl. asst. Harvard Law Sch. profs., Cambridge, Mass., 1956-58; editor Vassar Micellany News, Poughkeepsie, N.Y., 1953-56; editor, founder Park Parent, Brookline, Mass., 1968-73; pres. Sylvia S. Kliman Real Estate Brokerage, Brookline, 1971—. Pres. Dunewind Films, 1979—, creative cons. for feature films & TV, 1977—. Vol. Mass. ARC blood program, 1970-73; polit. speechwriter, 1960—; mem. Barn Gallery, Ogunquit Mus. of Art, Friends of Vassar Art Gallery; trustee Park Sch., Brookline, 1970-73; bd. friends Peter Bent Brigham Hosp., 1970-75; bd. dirs. Spl. Com. to Restore Ogunquit Dunes, 1975—. Mem. Park Sch. Parents Assn. (pres. 1968-70), Norfolk Dist. Med. Soc. Womens Aux., Boston Mus. Fine Arts, Vassar Club (bd. dirs.), Coll. Club. Unitarian. Home: 40 Newton St Brookline MA 02445-7407 also: Dunewind Ogunquit ME 03907

KLIMAS, ELIZABETH JOLANTA, accountant, lawyer, economist; d. Anna Z. (Klimas) Sarwaryn. BSc in Bus, Law, Calif. State U. Northridge, 2002; attended, UCLA. Cert. Acctg. Assn., 1992; Summa Pub./NY 1999, Summa Pub./NY 2000. Sr. acctg. staff Motion Picture Industry, Los Angeles, Calif., 1992—. Founder, owner Elizabeth Klimas & Assocs. USA Corp. Author: (poetry) The Best Poems & Poets Of 2001 (Internat. Poet Of Merit Award, 2002), Tender Moments (Bronze Commemorative Award Medallion, 2001), (law and taxation) IRS Revealed: Money For Sex, (articles) on taxation and tax law/Los Angeles Daily News, (book) The New World Book of Klimases, A Celebration of Klimases, The Klimases Since 1912. Silver leader DAV, Calif., 1996—2005; vol. Getty Mus., Los Angeles, Calif., 1999—2005; 1996 campaign advisor Rep. Senatorial Inner Cir., Washington DC, Md., 1996—96. Nominee For Appointment as Citizen of the Yr. 1994 for Outstanding Services and Contbn. to Internat. Affairs, H.R.H. Kevin, Prince Regent, Hutt River Province Principality, 1995; recipient Order of the Legion of Merit, The Rep. Senatorial Inner Cir., 1998, Rep. Senatorial Medal of Freedom, Rep. Senatorial Inner Cir., 1999, Wall of Tolerance honoree, Civil Rights Meml. Ctr., Montgomery, Ala., 2005. Mem.: Humane Soc. of US (HSUS ORG.), The Smithsonian Instn. (assoc.; nat. assoc. mem. 1996—), So. Poverty Law Ctr. (assoc.; mem. 2001—03, Cert. for Outstanding Support of the work of the So. Poverty Law Ctr. & Tchg. Tolerance 2002), The Libr. of Congress (assoc.; mem. 1996—2003), ABA (assoc.; j.d. mem. 1996—2002), Rep. Presdl. Task Force (life; platinum mem. 1992—2005, Cert. of Membership 2003). Independent Thinkers. Catholic. Avocations: cmty. TV for So. Calif. KCET, Am. for fair taxation, natural history preservation, nat. wildlife federation/defenders of wildlife, guiding eyes for the blind/ASPCA. Home: PO Box 56944 Sherman Oaks CA 91413 Personal E-mail: elzaklimas@yahoo.com.

KLIMEK, DEBORAH LYNN, ophthalmologist; b. Minn. BA, St. Olaf Coll., 1992; MD, U. Minn., 1997. Diplomate Am. Bd. OPhthalmology. Pediat. intern, resident U. Minn., Mpls., 1997—98; resident in ophthalmology St. Louis U., 1998—2001; fellow in pediat. ophthalmology U. Iowa, Iowa City, 2001—02; pediat. ophthalmologist Acuity Eye Care, Danbury, Conn., 2002—03; pvt. practice ophthalmology South Charleston, W.Va., 2003—. Investigator Pediat. Eye Disease Investigators Group. Mem.: Am. Acad. Ophthalmology, Am. Assn. Pediat. Ophthalmology and Strabismus, Alpha Omega Alpha. Office: Children's Eye Care and Adult Strabismus Surgery 24 MacCorkle Ave SW #203 South Charleston WV 25303 Office Phone: 304-720-7001.

KLIMEK, JOSEPH JOHN, physician, educator; b. Wilkes-Barre, Pa., Sept. 14, 1946; s. Joseph John and Frances Carol (Pavloski) K.; m. Jane Marie Stout, June 26, 1971 (div.); 1 child, Adam. AB cum laude, Princeton U., 1968; MD, Pa. State U., 1972. Diplomate Am. Bd. Internal Medicine, Am. Bd. Infectious Diseases. Intern, resident in internal medicine Hartford U., Conn., then fellow in infectious disease, 1972—76, chief epidemiology, 1976—87, dir. subsplty. medicine, 1985—87, assoc. dir. medicine, 1987—90, assoc. dir. dept. medicine and chmn. AIDS program, 1987—90, dir. dept. medicine, 1990—, chmn. AIDS task force, 1985—90, assoc. chmn. dept. medicine, 1995—; asst. prof. medicine U. Conn., Farmington, 1977—84, assoc. prof., 1984—90, prof., 1990—; assoc. chmn. dept. medicine U. Conn. Sch. Medicine, 1995—. Conn. mem. numerous faculties pharm. industry. Sr. assoc. editor Am. Jour. Infection Control, 1980-95; med. editor Asepsis, The Infection Control Forum; also mem. numerous editl. bds. in field; contbr. articles to med. jours. Recipient Disting. Alumnus award, 1978, ARC award, 1986. Fellow ACP, Infectious Disease Soc. Am.; mem. APHA, AAAS, Am. Profls. in Infection Control, Am. Soc. Microbiology, Am. Fedn. Clin. Rsch., Soc. Hosp. Epidemiologists Am., Am. Venereal Disease Assn., Am. Med. Writers Assn. Achievements include integrated internal medicine residency of Hartford Hospital with University of Connecticut School of Medicine; developed hospital community linkage network for AIDS care in Greater Hartford; introduced primary care medicine practice model to all ambulatory services; expanded care to indigent with two bilingual satellite practices; developed hospital cardiac services product line; developed hospital-wide Program in Integrative Medicine; initiated formal hospitalist program for care of inpatients; facilitation of hospital-wide program in palliative medicine. Home: 31 Main St Farmington CT 06032-2229 Office: Hartford Hosp 80 Seymour St Hartford CT 06115-2701 Office Phone: 860-545-2085. Business E-Mail: jklimek@harthosp.org.

KLIMENT, ROBERT MICHAEL, architect; b. Prague, Czechoslovakia, June 9, 1933; came to U.S., 1950; s. Felix and Sophie (Baltinester) K.; m. Janet McClure, Sept. 12, 1959 (div. 1968); 1 child, Nicholas McClure; m. Frances Halsband, May 1, 1971; 1 child, Alexander Halsband. BA, Yale U., 1954, MArch, 1959. Registered architect Penn., N.Y., N.J., Mass., Conn., Ohio, Va., D.C., N.C., N.H., Md., Ill., Miss.; cert. Nat. Coun. Archtl. Registration Bds. Architect Mitchell/Giurgola Architects, Phila., 1961-66, architect, assoc. N.Y.C., 1967-71; ptnr. R.M. Kliment Architect, N.Y.C., 1972-78, R.M. Kliment & Frances Halsband Architects, N.Y.C., 1978—. Instr. U. Pa., Phila., 1963-66, vis. prof., 1972-73; asst. prof. Columbia U., N.Y.C., 1966-70, vis. prof., 1977, 84; vis. prof. MIT, Cambridge, Mass., 1970, Yale U., New Haven, 1972-74, N.C. State U., Raleigh, 1978, Rice U., Houston, 1979, U. Va., Charlottesville, 1979-80, Harvard U., Cambridge, 1980-81. Works include Computer Sci. Bldg. Princeton U. (Nat. Honor award AIA 1994), U. Va. Life Scis. Bldg., Columbia U. Computer Scis. Bldg. (Nat. Honor award AIA 1987, award NYSAA 1985, Tucker award Bldg. Stone Inst. 1985, other awards), Mercantile Exch. Bldg., N.Y. (Bard award for excellence in architecture City Club N.Y. 1989), Burke Chemistry Bldg., Dartmouth Coll., Adelbert Adminstrn. Bldg., Case Western Res. U. (AIA Nat. honor award 1994), Sudikoff Computer Sci. Bldg., Dartmouth Coll., MTA/L.I. R.R. Entrance Bldg., Penn Sta., N.Y. (Bard award for excellence in architecture City Club N.Y. 1995, AIA nat. honor award 1996, NYSAA & NYC AIA awards 1995), Ebert Art Ctr., Coll. of Wooster, U.S. Courthouse and post office, Bklyn., U.S. Courthouse Gulfport, Miss., Yale Divinity Sch., Franklin and Marshall Coll. Roschel Performing Arts Ctr., N.Y.C. Primary Sch. 54, N.Y.C. Priamry Sch. 178, N.Y.C. Monroe H.S.; exhibited in group shows at Bklyn. Mus., 1977, The Drawing Ctr., 1977, Cooper Hewitt Mus., 1977-78, Mus. Finnish Architecture, Helsinki, Finland, 1980, Harvard Grad. Sch. Design, 1981, NAD, 1981, 87, Smith Coll. Mus. Art, 1981, Rice U. Farrish Hall Gallery, 1983, Columbia U. Low Libr., 1986, Parrish Art Mus., 1987, German Architecture Mus., Frankfurt, 1989, Rotunda Gallery, Bklyn., 1995. With U.S. Army, 1955-57. Fulbright scholar, Italy, 1959-60; AIA Archtl. Firm award, 1997, Medal of Honor NYC AIA, 1998. Fellow AIA, Century Assn. Office: R M Kliment & Frances Halsband Architects 255 W 26th St New York NY 10001-8001

KLIMENT, STEPHEN ALEXANDER, architect, editor, journalist; b. May 24, 1930; s. Felix and Sophia (Baltinester) K.; m. Felicia Drury, Dec. 24, 1957; children: Pamela Drury, Jennifer Anne. Student, Ecole Speciale d'Architecture, Paris, 1948-49; BArch, MIT, 1953; MFA in Arch., Princeton U., 1957. Draftsman Jean Labatut, Princeton, N.J., 1957; designer Skidmore, Owings & Merrill, N.Y.C., 1957-59, Reeb-Draz Assos., Cleve., 1959-60; editor Archtl. and Engring. News, 1961-69; v.p. Caudill Rowlett Scott, N.Y.C., 1969-72; architect, cons., 1972-78; editor in chief Advt. & Pub. News, 1978-80; exec. editor Whitney Libr. of Design, 1981-85; v.p., editl. dir. Practice Mgmt. Assocs., Ltd., 1985-87; editor sci. and tech. div. John Wiley & Sons, 1987-90; editor-in-chief Archtl. Record, 1990-96; arch., journalist, 1996—. Adj. prof. Sch. Architecture and Environ. Studies, City Coll. of CUNY, 1997—; lectr. U. Oreg., Carnegie-Mellon U., U. Ariz., Yale U., Harvard U., Washington U., St. Louis, U. Tex., U. Nebr., Ariz. State U., N.C. State U., Tex. A&M U., Miss. State U. Author: Writing for Design Professionals, 1998, Creative Communications for a Successful Design Practice, Into the Mainstream: Syllabus for a Barrier-Free Environment, Architectural Sketching and Rendering: Techniques for Designers and Artists; (with R.H. McNulty) Neighborhood Conservation; editor: Design Principal's Report, 1998—; founding editor Building Type Basics Series, John Wiley & Sons, Inc.; contbr. articles to profl. jours. Chmn. adv. coun. Princeton U. Sch. Architecture and Urban Planning, 1973-84. With AUS, 1953-55. Fellow AIA (chmn. OCULUS adv. bd. NY chpt. 2002-05); mem. Univ. Club (NYC). Episcopalian. Home and Office: 1255 5th Ave New York NY 10029-3850

KLIMI, GJERGJ, mathematics professor; b. Tirana, Albania, Apr. 10, 1947; s. Vlash and Violeta Klimi; m. Dorina Paco, June 5, 1952; children: Iven, Hiperion. BS in Physics, U. Tirana, Albania, 1969, PhD in Physics, 1999. Cert. English lang. tchr. U. Tirana, 1978. Tchr. physics H.S. Lac, Albania, 1970—72; math. and physics faculty Mil. Acad. Tirana, Albania, 1972—88; physics instr. Mil. Acad. of Gen. Staff, Tirana, Albania, 1988—92; chair dept. physics Mil. Acad. of Tirana, Tirana, Albania, 1988—93; math. faculty Pace U., N.Y.C., 2000—, math. lab. specialist, 2001—04. Sr. officer Com. of Sci. and Tech., Tirana, Albania, 1993—95; dir. Tempus Office, Ministry of Higher Edn., Tirana, Albania, 1995—97. Author: (book) Elements of Applied Probability. Active in the processes of destruction of the communist dictatorship in Albania, and in the Dem. reformation of the mil. Dem. Movement, Tirana, Albania, 1990—92; acting dir. Albanian Relief Found., Tirana (N.Y.C. NGO), Albania, 1993—95; vice chmn. Helping Handicapped People, Tirana, Albania, 1992—95. Recipient Gold Medal of Eagle, Pres. Of Republic of Albania, 1996, Outstanding Contbn. award, Pace U., 2003. Achievements include research in the field of the military. Office Phone: 212-346-1280.

KLIMIS, MANNY JOHN, social sciences educator; b. Gary, Ind., Aug. 16, 1949; s. John E. and Mary J. Klimis; m. Litsa S. Johnson Gout, Dec. 30, 1995; children: Staci M., Joni A. BS in Social sci., Ind. U., Bloomington, 1972; MEd in Social sci., U. S. Fla., Tampa, 1976. Social sci. tchr. Clearwater Mid. Sch., Fla., 1973—78; adj. instr. Pasco-Hernando CC, West Pasco, Fla., 1976—78; GED instr. Pinellas Co., Clearwater, Fla., 1976—79; social sci. tchr. Tarpon Springs Mid. Sch., Fla., 1979—. Author: My Life As a Public School Teacher: Leave No Teacher Behind, 2005. Congl. lobbyist NEA, Washington, 1980—85. Mem.: Pinellas Classroom Tchrs. Assn. (faculty rep. 1973—). Democrat. Greek Orthodox. Home: PO Box 392 Tarpon Springs FL 34688 Office: Tarpon Springs Mid Sch 501 N Florida Ave Tarpon Springs FL 34688

KLIMKO, AMANDA RABB, music educator; b. Birmingham, Ala., Dec. 5, 1956; d. William Earl Kelly and Grace Ann (Moon) Rabb; m. Benhamin Richard Klimko, Dec. 11. MusB, Samford U., 1978. Educator elem. music Jefferson County Schs., Birmingham, Ala., 1978—85; dir. children's choir St. Mary's Episcopal Ch., 1982—85; educator mid and jr. high music Hewett Mid. Sch., Trussville, 1985—86; educator jr. high music Simmins Jr. High Sch., Hoover, 1986—89; choral dir. Hewitt-Trussville High Sch., 1989—; choir dir. Grace Presbyn. Ch., 1996—. Vol. Ea. Area Christian Mins., Birmingham, 1999—; bd. dirs. Carnington Homeowners Assn., Trussville, 2002—03. Mem.: Am. Choral Dirs. Assn., Music Educators Nat. Assn., Ala. Vocal Assn. (dist. chair 1994—98). Presbyterian. Avocations: music, piano, singing, needlecrafts, gardening. Office: Hewitt-Trussville High Sch 5275 Trussville-Clay Rd Trussville AL 35173

KLIMLEY, (ABBOTT) PETER, marine biologist, educator; s. Stanley P. and Dorothy A. Klimley; m. Patricia M. Klimley, Apr. 7, 1971. BS in Zoology, SUNY, Stony Brook, 1970; MS in Biol. Oceanography, U. Miami, 1976; PhD in Marine Biology, U. Calif., La Jolla, 1982. Tchr. chemistry Hackley Prep. Sch., N.Y.C., 1971—72; tchr. marine biology and oceanography Oceanics Sch., N.Y.C., 1972—73; rsch. asst. Rosenstiel Sch. Atmospheric Sci. U. Miami, 1973—76; grad. rsch. asst. Scripps Instn. Oceanography, U. Calif., San Diego, 1977—82, postgrad. rschr., 1982—84, asst. rsch. scientist, 1984—87; asst. rsch. behaviorist Bodega Marine Lab., U. Calif., Davis, 1987—95, assoc. rsch. behaviorist, 1996—2001; adj. assoc. prof. depet. wildlife, fish and conservation biology U. Calif., Davis, 1999—; sr. fisheries ecologist H.T. Harvey & Assocs., San Jose, Calif., 2001—02. Rsch. assoc. Pt. Reyes Bird Obs., Bolinas, Calif., 1991—; adj. faculty mem. Centro de Investigaciones de Biologicas, La Paz, Mexico, 1993—; rsch. assoc. Inst. Marine Sci. U. Calif., Santa Cruz, 1999—; spkr. in field. Cons. editor Animal Behavior & Marine Biology, 1995—, off-bd. editor Oceologia, 1997—, reviewer numerous jours.; contbr. over 50 articles to profl. jours.; editor: Great White Sharks: The Biology of Carcharodon Carcharias, 1996; author: The Secret Life of Sharks: A Leading Biologist Reveals the Mysteries of Shark Behavior, 2003. Recipient Sci. Achievement award, So. Calif. Acad. Sci., 1981, SNAP EXCEL Silver award, Am. Scientist mag., 1995, cert. of excellence, Bookbuilders West Book Show, 1998; grantee, NSF, 1993—95, 1997—98, 1997—99, Nat. Marine Fisheries Svc., 1994—96, Sea World, San Diego, 1995—98, U. Calif., Santa Cruz, 1997—99, Dept. of Def., 1997—99, Nat. Undersea Rsch. Program, 1997—98, 1998—2000, Nat. Geog. Soc., 1999—2000, 2001—03, U. Calif., Davis, 2000—01, CVPIA Program, Calif., 2001—02, UC Mexus, 2003—04, CALFED ERP program, Calif., 2003—05, U. Calif. Stream Pulsed Flow Program, 2004—, David and Lucile Packard Found., 2004—05, numerous others. Mem.: AAAS, Assn. for Study of Animal Behavior, Am. Soc. Ichthyologists and Herpetologists, Am. Elasmobranch Soc., Sigma Xi. Achievements include research in animal behavior and behavioral ecology of marine vertebrates; conservation; marine fisheries biology, ecology and oceanography. Avocations: skiing, scuba diving. Office: U Calif Dept Fish Wildlife & Conservation Biology Biotelemetry Lab 1334 Academic Surge Davis CA 95616

KLINCK, CYNTHIA ANNE, library director; b. Salamanaca, N.Y., Nov. 1, 1948; d. William James and Marjorie Irene (Woodruff) K.; m. Andrew Clavert Humphries, Nov. 26, 1983. BS, Ball State U., 1970; MLS, U. Ky., 1976. Reference/ young adult libr. Bartholomew County Libr., Columbus, Ind., 1970-74; dir. Paul Sawyier Pub. Libr., Frankfort, Ky., 1974-78, Washington-Centerville Pub. Libr., Dayton, Ohio, 1978—. Libr. bldg. cons.; libr. cons., trainer OPLIN Task Force. Contbr. articles to profl. jours. Bd. dirs. Bluegrass Cmty. Action Agy., Frankfort, Ky., 1971-73; founder, bd. dirs. FACTS, Inc. (info. & referral), Frankfort, 1972-74; co-founder, bd. dirs. Seniors, Inc., Dayton, Ohio, 1980-81, 91—; trustee, officer South Cmty., Inc. Mental Health Ctr., Dayton, 1980-89; pres. Miami Valley Librs.; mem. govt. affairs com., ann. conf. planning com., fin. resources task force conf. presenter Ohio Libr. Coun.; program presenter Ohio Libr. Coun. Confs.; del. to Am. Libr. Assn. Congress on Profl. Edn. Recipient Vol. of Yr., So. Metro Regional C. of C. Mem. ALA, Am. Soc. for Info. Sci., Am. Soc. for Pers. Adminstrn., Ohio Libr. Assn. (chmn. legis. com.), South Metro Regional C. of C. (exec. com., bd. dirs., chmn. edn. com., chair), Rotary (bd. dirs.), Pub. Libr. Assn. Mng. for Results (trainer). Office: Washington-Centerville Pub Libr 111 W Spring Valley Rd Dayton OH 45458-3761 Office Phone: 937-435-7375.

KLINE, CELESTE MARIE, librarian; b. Daggett, Mich., July 25, 1945; d. Lamiel Bernard and Martha Elizabeth Kline; divorced; 1 child, Tanya Gypsy. Profl. lifetime libr. cert., Wash.; cert. profl. libr., Mich. Coord. children's svcs. Peter White Pub. Libr., Marquette, Mich., 1972-75, Josephine County Libr. Sys., Grants Pass, Oreg., 1975-80, head Ill. Valley br. Cave Junction, Oreg., 1980-85, head reference/adult brs. Grants Pass, 1985-91, libr. dir., 1991-92, Ellensburg (Wash.) Pub. Libr., 1992—. Chair children's sect. Oreg. Libr. Assn., 1980-82; sec. So. Oreg. Libr. Fedn., 1981-83, pres., 1983-85. Mem. Friends of the Libr., 1992—; mem. Interagy Coun., Ellensburg, 1992—; Bd. dirs. Kittitas County Bd. Health Adv. Com., Ellensburg, 1998—2000; bd. dirs. Cmty. Health and Safety Network, Ellensburg, 1997—99. Mem. LWV, Wash. Libr. Assn., Rotary Club Ellensburg. Roman Catholic. Avocations: travel, reading, church activities, family, internet. Office: Ellensburg Pub Libr 209 N Ruby St Ellensburg WA 98926-3338 E-mail: klinec@ellensburg.library.org.

KLINE, DAVID ADAM, lawyer, educator, writer; b. Keota, Okla., Sept. 27, 1923; s. David Adam and Lucy Leila (Wood) K.; m. Ruthela Deal, Aug. 25, 1947; children: Steven, Timothy, Ruthanna. JD, Okla. U., 1950. Bar: Okla. 1949. Law clk., spl. master U.S. Dist. Ct. Okla., 1952-61; 1st asst. U.S. atty. We. Dist. Okla., 1961-69; judge We. Dist. Okla. U.S. Bankruptcy Ct., Oklahoma City, 1969-82; sr. shareholder Kline Kline Elliott & Bryant, PC, Oklahoma City, 1983—. Pres. Nat. Conf. Bankruptcy Judges 1977-78; mem. arbitration panel program U.S. Dist. Ct. (we. dist.) Okla., 1985— mem. faculty Fed. Jud. Ctr., Washington, Nat. Seminar Bankruptcy Judges, 1971-86; adj. prof. law Oklahoma City U., 1980-84; cons. Norton Bankruptcy Law and Practice, 1986, Callaghan & Co.; bd. dirs. Consumer Credit Counseling Svc. Ctr., Okla., 1973-2001, chmn., 1992. Author: (non-bankruptcy): A Little Book (A New Thing in the Earth), 1993, A Little Book II (The Blood of the Lion), 1995, A Little Book III (The Revelation), 1997, A Little Book IV (A Still Small Voice), 1998, A Little Book V (Law and Liberty), 2003, electronic edit.; co-author: Briefcase, 1988—2000; mem. editl. bd. Am. Bankruptcy Law Jour., 1974—77, contbg. author Cowan's Bankruptcy Law and Practice, 1983, 2d edit., 1986. Fellow: Am. Coll. Bankruptcy Class II. Office: Kline Kline Elliott & Bryant PC Kline Law Bldg 720 NE 63rd St Oklahoma City OK 73105-6405 Office Phone: 405-848-4448. Business E-Mail: dkline@klinefirm.org.

KLINE, DONALD, food company executive; b. Chgo., July 6, 1948; s. Ralph Waldo and Theresa (Donato) K.; m. Christine Janet Kennedy, Aug. 23, 1972; children: Bethany Amber, Torah-Ann Shiloh, Nathaniel Darwin Kennedy, Abraham Newton Kennedy, Seth-Andrew Brigham Kennedy. AA, South Suburban Coll., 1969; AS, Kishwaukee Coll., 1971; BS, Roosevelt U., 1974, No. Ill. U., 1974; cert. thermal process control of low-acid canned foods, U. Wis., 1974. Quality control chemist Syntex Labs., Elgin, Ill., 1972-75; quality control mgr. Gt. China Food Products Co., Chgo., 1975; quality assurance mgr. TV Time Foods, Inc. subs. McCormick & Co., Inc., Bremen, Ind., 1975-80; pres. Abinadi Enterprises Internat. Corp., Nappanee, Ind., 1980-82; quality assurance/rsch. and devel. mgr. Snyder's of Hanover, Inc., Hanover, Pa., 1982-92; sr. rsch. assoc. Nabisco Biscuit Co., East Hanover, N.J., 1992-94; dir. quality assurance and tech. svcs. Hanover (Pa.) Foods Corp., 1994-95; dir. quality assurance UTZ Quality Foods, Inc., Hanover, 1995—2002, dir. tech. svcs., 2002—. Elder Ch. Jesus Christ of Latter-day Saints, 1976—, pres. Sunday sch., 1979-80, project coord., purchasing agt. ch. fund raising projects, 1980-82, exec. sec., 1981-82, pub. rels. dir., 1982-83, 91-92, mission leader for Gettysburg-Hanover, Pa., 1983-85, Gettysburg ward mission leader, 2000-03, Gettysburg ward fin.clk., 2003-04; chmn., pack and troop treas. Boy Scouts of Am., 1985-92, Webeloes leader, 1987-89, merit badge counselor, 1988-92; citizen adv. coun. Spring Grove Area Sch. Dist., 1988-92, ch. employment dir., 1991-92, ch. phys. facilities fin. clk. for York, Pa., 1992-93; dir. Hanover/Gettysburg, Pa. Church Family History Ctr., 1996-2000; sustaining mem. Rep. Nat. Com. Mem. Inst. Food Technologists (profl.), Snack Food Assn. (sci. rev. 1996—), Am. Assn. Nutritional Cons. (cert. nutritional cons.), Nat. Assn. Cert. Natural Health Profls. (cdet. nat. health profl.). Republican. Achievements include development of one hundred different snack foods marketed in U.S. and fgn. countries; development of first product line of flavored sour-dough pretzels. Office: Utz Quality Foods Inc 900 High St Hanover PA 17331-1639 Home: 10 Kevin Dr New Oxford PA 17350-9186 Office Phone: 800-367-7629 367. E-mail: donkcncfoodtec@yahoo.com, dkline@utzsnacks.com.

KLINE, EILEEN MARY, secondary school educator; b. Astoria, NY, Sept. 5, 1949; d. William Terence and Dorothy Mary Gillis; m. Edward Charles Kline, July 24, 1971; children: Kevin, Patrick, Kathleen, Megan. BA, Queens Coll., 1971; MA, Adelphi U., 1977. Math. tchr. Weber Jr. H.S., Port Washington, NY, 1971—78; math. instr. State U. Old Westbury, NY, 1983, Adelphi U., Garden City, NY, 1994—. Mem.: Math. Assn. Am., Nat. Coun. Math. Tchrs. Roman Cath. Avocation: golf. Office: Adelphi U South Ave Garden City NY 11530

KLINE, EUGENE MONROE, lawyer; b. N.Y.C., May 22, 1914; s. Lewis R. and Hattie (Wachter) K.; m. Harriet Meyer, July 2, 1939; children: Robert A., Thomas R. AB, Columbia U., 1933, LLB, 1935. Bar: N.Y. 1935, U.S. Dist. Ct. (so. dist.) N.Y. 1945, U.S. Dist. Ct. (ea. dist.) N.Y. 1955, U.S. Supreme Ct. 1973. Atty. Charter Rev. Commn., N.Y.C., 1935; assoc. Greenbaum, Wolf & Ernst, N.Y.C., 1935-37, Wagner, Quillinin and Rifkind, N.Y.C., 1937-40; atty. SEC, N.Y.C. and Washington, 1941-43; from assoc. to ptnr. Phillips Nizer LLP, N.Y.C., 1943—. With U.S. Army, 1943. Office: Phillips Nizer LLP 666 5th Ave New York NY 10103-0084 E-mail: ekline@phillipsnizer.com.

KLINE, FRANK MENEFEE, psychiatrist; b. Cumberland, Md., May 14, 1928; s. Frank Huber and Margaret (Menefee) K.; m. Shirley Steinmetz, June 27, 1953; children: Frank F., Margaret L. BS, U. Md., 1950, MD, 1952; PhD, So. Calif. Psychoanalytic Inst., 1977. Diplomate Am. Bd. Psychiatry and Neurology (examiner 1970—). Intern Cin. Gen. Hosp., 1952-53; resident Brentwood VA Med. Ctr., West L.A., 1955-58; regional chief West Ctrl. Mental Svc., L.A. County Dept. Mental Health, L.A., 1967-68; assoc. dir. adult psychiatry out-patient dept. L.A. County, U. So. Calif. Med. Ctr., 1968-77, acting dir. adult psychiat. dept., 1977; chief psychiatry VA Med. Ctr., Long Beach, Calif., 1977-91. Clin. prof., vice-chair U. Calif., Irvine, 1978—91, prof. emeritus, 1995—, U. So. Calif.; clin. prof. Drew King, 1992—2004; reviewer Hosp. Cmty. Psychiatry, 1978—, Am. Jour. Psychiatry, 1978—, Readings, 1995—2002; cons. Los Angeles County Dept. Mental Health, 1992—. Editor: A Handbook of Group Psychotherapy, 1983. 1st lt. M.C., U.S. Army, 1953-55. Office: San Pedro Cmty Mental Health Ctr 150 W 7th St San Pedro CA 90731 Office Phone: 310-519-6100. Personal E-mail: frank.kline1@cox.net.

KLINE, GEORGE LOUIS, writer, translator, retired philosophy and literature educator; b. Galesburg, Ill., Mar. 3, 1921; s. Allen Sides and Wahneta (Burner) K.; m. Virginia Harrington Hardy, Apr. 17, 1943; children: Brenda Marie, Jeffrey Allen, Christina Hardy (Mrs. Francis C. Hanak). Student, Boston U., 1938-41; AB with honors, Columbia Coll., 1947; MA, Columbia U., 1948, PhD, 1950. Instr. philosophy Columbia U., 1950-52, 53-54, asst. prof., 1954-60; vis. asst. prof. U. Chgo., 1952-53; assoc. prof. philosophy and Russian Bryn Mawr Coll., 1960-66, prof. philosophy, 1966-81, Milton C. Nahm prof. philosophy, 1981-91, chmn. dept., 1977-82, chmn. dept. Russian, 1990-91, Milton C. Nahm prof. emeritus of philosophy, 1991—, Katharine E. McBride prof. of philosophy, 1992-93; adj. rsch. prof. history Clemson U., 2005—. Lectr. Free U., West Berlin, Heidelberg U., Marburg U., Germany, London Sch. Econs. and Polit. Sci., Mid East Tech. U., Ankara, Turkey, Oxford (Eng.) U., Queens U., Belfast, Trinity Coll., Dublin, U. Belgrade, U. Zagreb, Yugoslavia, U. P.R., Uppsala U., Sweden; participant internat. confs. Austria, Can., Denmark, France, Germany, The Netherlands, Italy, Mex., Eng., Scotland, Russia. Author: Spinoza in Soviet Philosophy, 1952, 1981, Religious and Anti-Religious Thought in Russia, 1968; author (with others) Continuity and Change in Russian and Soviet Thought, 1955, Marx and the Western World, 1967, Hegel and the Philosophy of Religion, 1970, Sartre: A Collection of Critical Essays, 1971, Hegel and the History of Philosophy, 1974, Dissent in the USSR: Politics, Ideology, and People, 1975, Speculum Spinozanum, 1977, Western Philosophical Systems in Russian Literature, 1979, Vico and Marx: Affinities and Contrasts, 1983, Nineteenth Century Religious Thought in the West, 1985, Spinoza nel 350 anniversario della nascita, 1985, Hegel and Whitehead: Contemporary Perspectives on Systematic Philosophy, 1986, George Lukács and His World: A Reassessment, 1987, Dictionary of Literary Biography Yearbook, 1987, 1988, Europa und die Folgen: Castelgandolfo-Gespräche, 1987, 1988, Hegel and His Critics, 1989, Brodsky's Poetics and Aesthetics, 1990, Spinoza: Issues and Directions, 1990, Histoire de la littérature russe, 1990, The Trotsky Reappraisal, 1992, Metaphysics as Foundation: Essays in Honor of Ivor Leclerc, 1993, Philosophical Imagination and Cultural Memory, 1993, Hryhorij Savyč Skovoroda: An Anthology of Critical Articles, 1994, Phenomenology and Skepticism: Essays in Honor of James M. Edie, 1996, Russian Religious Thought, 1996, Iosif Brodskii: Trudy i dni, 1998, J. M. Bochenski: The Man and His Work, 2001, A William Ernest Hocking Reader, 2004; translator: History of Russian Philosophy (V.V. Zenkovsky), 1953, 2003, Boris Pasternak: Seven Poems, 1969, 1972, Joseph Brodsky: Selected Poems, 1973; co-translator: A Part of Speech (Joseph Brodsky), 1980, To Urania (Joseph Brodsky), 1988; editor: Soviet Education, 1957, Alfred North Whitehead: Essays on his Philosophy, 1963, 1989; editor, contbr.: European Philosophy Today, 1965; co-editor: Iosif Brodskii: Ostanovka v pustyne, 1970, 2000; co-editor, contbr.: Russian Philosophy, 1965, 1969, 1976, 1984, Explorations in Whitehead's Philosophy, 1983, Philosophical Sovietology, 1988; co-editor: Jour. Philosophy, 1959—64; cons. editor:, 1964—78, Ency. Philosophy, 1962—67, Studies in Soviet Thought (now Studies in East European Thought), 1962—, Jour. Value Inquiry, 1967—, Process Studies, 1970—, Soviet Union, 1975—80, Philosophy Research Archives (now Jour. Philos. Rsch.), 1975—, Jour. History of Ideas, 1976—86, 1988—98, Slavic Review, 1977—79, Soviet Studies in Philosophy (now Russian Studies in Philosophy), 1987—, History of Philosophy Quar., 1990—93, Skepsis, 1990—, Symposion: A Journal of Russian Thought, 1996—, cons. editor philosophy: Current Digest of Soviet Press, 1961—64; contbr. articles to nat. and internat. jours. and reference works;

writings translated into numerous fgn. langs. Served with USAAF, 1942-45. Decorated D.F.C, 1944; Cutting traveling fellow Paris, 1949-50; Fulbright fellow Paris, 1950, 79; Ford fellow Paris, 1954-55; Rockefeller fellow USSR and East Europe, 1960; Nat. Endowment for Humanities sr. fellow, 1970-71; Guggenheim fellow, 1978-79. Mem. Am. Philos. Assn. (exec. com. Ea. div. 1990-93), Metaphys. Soc. Am. (councillor 1969-71, 78-82, v.p. 1984-85, pres. 1985-86, del. to Am. Coun. Learned Socs., 1994-97), Philosophy Edn. Soc. (pub. Rev. Metaphys., dir. 1966-90), Soc. Phenomenology and Existential Philosophy, Am. Assn. Advancement Slavic Studies (dir. 1972-75, award for Disting. Contbns. to Slavic Studies 1999), Hegel Soc. Am. (councillor 1968-70, 74-78, v.p. 1971-73, pres. 1984-86), Soc. Advancement Am. Philosophy, Phi Beta Kappa. Home: 2812 Echo Trl Anderson SC 29621-1911

KLINE, GINGER B., academic administrator; b. Wilkes Barre, Pa., May 4, 1970; d. Kenneth and Bonita Dean; m. Forrest Kline, Sept. 16, 2000. AAS, Luzerne County C.C., Nanticoke, Pa., 1995; BAS, King's Coll., Wilkes Barre, Pa., 2000. Fin. aid clk. Luzerne County C.C., Nanticoke, 1989—99; dir. fin. assistance and planning Keystone Coll., La Plume, Pa., 1999—. Mem.: AAUW, Nat. Assn. Fin. Aid Adminstrs., Pa. Assn. Fin. Aid Adminstrs. (support staff tng. com. chair 2004—, mem. Pa. tng. com. 2005—, fin. aid basics com. 2004—), Ea. Assn. Fin. Aid Adminstrs. (assoc.; leadership devel. com. 2004—). Office: Keystone Coll One College Green La Plume PA 18440 Office Phone: 570-945-8130. Office Fax: 570-945-8967. E-mail: ginger.kline@keystone.edu.

KLINE, J. PETER, hotel executive; BS in Hotel Adminstrn., MS in Acctg., Cornell U. CPA, Tex. With Laventhol & Horwath, ptnr., mgr. cons. divsn. Tex., 1976-80; founding ptnr. Harvey Hotel Co., Dallas, 1981—; pres., CEO Bristol Hotels & Resorts, Dallas, chmn., CEO Addison, Tex., 1998. Mem. N.Y. Hospitality Coun.; bd. dirs. North Tex. Commn.; adv. bd. U. North Tex., U. Tex.-Dallas Sch. Mgmt.; co-chmn. 2d Ann. Cornell U. Conf. on Hospitality Ind. Strategy, 1998. Mem. Internat. Assn. Holiday Inss, U.S. C. of C. (mem. regulatory affairs and econ. policy coms.).

KLINE, JAMES EDGAR, actor; b. Beach Grove, Ind., Feb. 22, 1932; s. Charles Raymond and Edna Marie (Pollack) K.; m. Phyliss Dawn Schneider, Nov. 8, 1952; children: Timson, James Jr., Peggy, Daniel, Andrew, Mary, Jon. Lectr. in field; judge Nat. Prospectors and Treasure Convention, 1989-90. Appeared in films Coming Home, 1978, Comes A Horseman, 1979, Electric Horseman, 1980, China Syndrome, 1981, Tom Horn, 1982, Weekend in the Country, 1997, It's My Party, 1997, City of Angels, 1998, various other films, TV programs, comml.s.; screenwriter, exec. prodr., actor motion picture Father Dad; author (as James Klein): Where to Find Gold in Southern California, 1975, Where to Find Gold in the Desert, 1977, Where to Find Gold in Nevada, 1985, How to Find Gold, 1997, Gold Rush (childrens), 1998, Follow the Padres (childrens), 1999; other mag. articles and short stories. With U.S. Army, 1952-53. Recipient Cert. of Achievement, Am. Cancer Soc., 1977, Disneyland, 1983, City of Anaheim, 1984, also various schs. Office Phone: 818-769-9111. Personal E-mail: jklein49er@juno.com.

KLINE, JAMES EDWARD, lawyer; b. Fremont, Ohio, Aug. 3, 1941; s. Walter J. and Sophia Kline; m. Mary Ann Bruening, Aug. 29, 1964; children: Laura Anne Kline, Matthew Thomas, Jennifer Sue. BS in Social Sci., John Carroll U., 1963; JD, Ohio State U., 1966; postgrad., Stanford U., 1991. Bar: Ohio 1966, NC 1989, US Tax. Ct. 1983. Assoc. Eastman, Stichter, Smith & Bergman, Toledo, 1966-70; ptnr. Eastman, Stichter, Smith & Bergman (name now Eastman & Smith), Toledo, 1970-84, Shumaker, Loop & Kendrick, Toledo, 1984-88; v.p., gen. counsel Aeroquip-Vickers, Inc. (formerly Trinova Corp.), Toledo, 1989-99; exec. v.p. Cavista Corp., 2000—01; dir. devel. Toledo Mus. Art, 2002—03; v.p., gen. counsel, sec. Cooper Tire and Rubber Co., Findlay, Ohio, 2003—. Corp. sec. Sheller-Globe Corp., 1977—84; adj. prof. U. Toledo Coll. Law, 1988—94; bd. dirs. Plastic Techs., Inc.; trustee Promedica Health Edn. and Rsch. Corp., 2002—. Author: (with Robert Seaver) Ohio Corporation Law, 1988. Trustee Kidney Found. of Northwestern Ohio, Inc., 1972-81, pres., 1979-80; bd. dirs. Toledo Botanical Garden (formerly Crosby Gardens), 1974-80, pres., 1977-79; bd. dirs. Toledo Zool. Soc., 1983-96, 99—2004, pres., 1991-93; bd. dirs. Toledo Area Regional Transit Authority, 1984-90, pres., 1987-88; bd. dirs. Home Away From Home, Inc. (Ronald McDonald House NW Ohio), 1983-88; trustee Toledo Symphony Orch., 1981—, St. John's H.S., 1988-91; trustee Lourdes Coll., 1988-96, chmn., 1994-96; trustee Ohio Found. Ind. Colls., 1991-2000, ProMedica Health, Edn. and Rsch. Corp., 2002—, Toledo Opera, 2003-05. Fellow Ohio Bar Found.; mem. ABA, Nat. Assn. Corp. Dirs., Ohio Bar Assn. (corp. law com. 1977—, chmn. 1983-86), NC Bar Assn., Mfrs. Alliance (chair Law Coun. II 1997-99), Toledo Area C. of C. (trustee 1994—, chmn. 2000-01), Confrerie des Chevaliers du Tastevin, Inverness Club, Toledo Club (trustee 1990-97), Stone Oak Country Club, Ottawa Skeet Club, Fiddlers Creek Club, Answer Club Roman Catholic. Home: 216 Treetop Pl Holland OH 43528-8451 Office: Cooper Tire & Rubber Co 701 Lima Ave Findlay OH 45840 Office Phone: 419-427-4757. Personal E-mail: jektreetop@sbcglobal.net. Business E-Mail: jekline@coopertire.com.

KLINE, JERRY ROBERT, retired administrative judge, ecologist; b. Mpls., May 20, 1932; s. Frederick Andrew and Margaret (Wicklund) K.; m. Alice Nell Reed, Sept. 4, 1954; children: Steven, Jennifer, Robert, Neil, Daniel. BS, U. Minn., 1957, MS, 1960, PhD, 1964. Postdoctoral rsch. assn. Argonne Nat. Lab., Ill., 1964-65, group leader rsch., 1968-74; scientist, dir. Rainforest Project P.R. Nuclear Ctr., 1965-68; sr. scientist Nuclear Regulatory Commn., Washington, 1974-80, adminstrv. judge, 1980-98. Contbr. articles to profl. jours., chpts. to books. Bd. dirs., chmn. Cedar Lane Unitarian Ch. Served with U.S. Army, 1950-53. Recipient NRC Spl. Achievement award, 1979. Mem. Nature Conservancy, Sigma Xi. Avocations: travel, gardening. Home: 13624 Middlevale Ln Silver Spring MD 20906-2123 Personal E-mail: KJerry@verizon.net.

KLINE, JOHN, congressman; b. Allentown, Pa., Sept. 6, 1947; m. Vicky Kline; children: Kathy, Dan. BA in Biology, Rice U., 1969; MPA, Shippensburg U. Pa., 1988. Mem. US Ho. Reps. from Minn. 2nd dist., 2003—. Military aide to Pres. Carter; military aide to Pres. Reagan. Active USMC, 1969—94, retired as Colonel USMC. Recipient Hero of the Taxpayer award, Small Bus. Adv. award, Spirit of Enterprise award, True Blue award, Family Rsch. Coun. Republican. Responsibilities while military aide to pres. included carrying "nuclear football" — package containing launch codes for nuclear attack. Office: 1429 Longworth House Office Bldg Washington DC 20515*

KLINE, JOHN WILLIAM, retired military officer, management consultant; b. Zanesville, Ohio, June 26, 1919; s. Gerry William and Lillian Elizabeth (Scheiderer) K.; m. Katherine Edmond Winton, Oct. 24, 1942; children: Susan Isabel (Mrs. John Farris Morehead), Flora Edmond (Mrs. Richard Crandall Creighton), Elizabeth Gerry (Mrs. Paul Sweeney). Student, Ohio U., 1937-40; grad., Primary, Basic and Advanced Flying Schs., 1941, Air Command and Staff Sch., 1949, Air War Coll., 1959; BA, La. Tech. U., 1971. Commd. 2d lt. USAAF, 1941; advanced through grades to maj. gen. USAF, 1968; comdr. (2d Bomb Wing), Hunter AFB, Ga., 1961-63, (397th Bomb Wing), Dow AFB, Maine, 1963-64; dir. operations, chief staff Hdqrs. 8th Air Force, Westover AFB, Mass., 1964-66; vice comdr. 3d Air Div., Andersen AFB, Guam, 1966-68; asst. dep. chief staff ops. Hdqrs. SAC, Offutt AFB, Nebr., 1968-69; vice-comdr. 2d Air Force, Barksdale AFB, La., 1969-72; ret., 1972; v.p., mgmt. cons. Paul R. Ray, Inc., Ft. Worth, 1972—; pres. Mapotec, Inc., Daytona Beach, Fla., 1974, Precision Aerial Surveys, Inc., 1975-85; v.p. ops. Aero Service, Houston, 1976-80, v.p. new ventures and planning, 1980-82. Decorated D.S.M., Legion of Merit with 3 oak leaf clusters, Air medal with oak leaf cluster, Air Force Commendation medal; Air Force Distinguished Service Order Republic Vietnam). Mem. Oak Hills Golf Club, Guadalajara Golf Club, Beta Theta Pi. Presbyterian. Home: One Towers Park Ln # 912 San Antonio TX 78209-

KLINE, KATY, museum director; Curator, coord. spl. projects List Visual Arts Ctr., MIT, Cambridge, dir., 1986—98, Bowdoin Coll. Mus. Art, Brunswick, Maine, 1998—. Review panelist Nat. Endowment for Arts, Inst. Mus. Svcs., Adolph and Esther Gottlieb Found.; juror Del. Art Mus. Biennial, Mid Atlantic Arts Found., RI Sch. Design Mus. Art, McKnight Found.; vis. com. Williams Coll. Mus. Art. Mem. City of Lowell's Pub. Art Adv. Bd. Recipient Gyorgy Kepes Fellowship Prize, 1995. Office: Bowdoin Coll Mus Art 9400 College Station Brunswick ME 04011*

KLINE, KENNETH ALAN, mechanical engineering educator; b. Chgo., July 11, 1939; s. George Lester and Beverly Gretchen (Hanson) K.; m. Nancy Ann Bixler, June 25, 1960; children: Lisa Suzanne, John Kenneth, Jeffery Eastbury, Gretchen Mary. BS, U. Minn., 1961, PhD, 1965. Rsch. asst. U. Minn., Mpls., 1961-62, rsch. fellow, 1962-65; sr. rsch. engr. Esso Prodn. Rsch. Co., Houston, 1965-66; assoc. prof. Wayne State U., Detroit, 1966-73, prof. mech. engring., 1973—, interim chair dept. mech. engring., 1986-87, chair, 1987-95, interim dean of engring., 1996—, chair mech. engring., 1997—. Cons. Ford Motor Co., Detroit, 1976—, vis. scientist, 1984-85; vis. prof. U. Munich, 1972-73. Editor Proc. 6th Internat. Conf. Vehicle Structures, 1986; contbr. articles to profl. jours. Patentee ops. in submarine wells, layng pipes in water. Rep. precinct del., Grosse Pointe Park, Mich., 1982-84; vol. Grosee Pointe Neighborhood Club, 1973-82. A.P. Sloan Found. nat. scholar, 1959-61; NSF fellow 1961-64, NASA fellow 1964-65; recipient Sr. U.S. Sci. award Alexander von Humboldt-Stiftung, Fed. Republic Germany, 1972; prin. investigator NSF Rsch. Experiences for Undergrad. Sites, 1995—. Fellow ASME (chair 1974-75, 89-91, program chair winter ann. meeting 1993, gen. chair internat. mech. engring. congress & expo. 1994, nat. nominating com. 1997—, chair nat. dept. heads com., 1998—, Dedicated Svc. award 1996), AIAA, Soc. Automotive Engrs. (chair 1984-86, Forest R. McFarland award 1993), Soc. Rheology, Engring. Soc. (vice chair Detroit 1988—). Avocations: bird watching, tree farming, reading, swimming. Office: Wayne State U Engring Rm 2105 Detroit MI 48202 Business E-Mail: kline@eng.wayne.edu.

KLINE, KEVIN DELANEY, actor; b. St. Louis, Oct. 24, 1947; s. Robert Joseph and Peggy (Kirk) K.; m. Phoebe Cates, Mar. 5, 1989; 2 children: Owen, Greta. BA in Speech and Theatre, Ind. U.; adv. program diploma, Juilliard Sch. Drama Divsn., N.Y.C., 1972. Founding mem. The Acting Co., N.Y.C., 1972-76. Apptd. artistic assoc. N.Y. Shakespeare Festival, 1993. Actor Broadway prodns.: On the Twentieth Century, 1978 (Tony award), Loose Ends, 1979, Pirates of Penzance, 1980 (Tony award, Obie award), Arms and the Man, 1985, The Play What I Wrote, 2003; off-Broadway: Richard III, 1983, Henry V, 1984, Hamlet, 1986 (Obie award), Much Ado About Nothing, 1988; actor, dir. off-Broadway: Hamlet, 1990; actor, dir. TV special: Hamlet, 1990; actor (Broadway) Ivanov, 1997, Henry IV, Parts I & II, 2003 (Tony nom. best actor in a play, 2004, Drama Desk award best actor, 2004), (off-Broadway) Measure for Measure, 1993, The Seagull, 2001; motion picture appearances include: Sophie's Choice, 1982, Pirates of Penzance, 1983, The Big Chill, 1983, Silverado, 1985, Violets are Blue, 1985, Cry Freedom, 1987, A Fish Called Wanda, 1988 (Academy award Best Supporting Actor 1989), The January Man, 1989, I Love You To Death, 1989, Soapdish, 1991, Grand Canyon, 1991, Consenting Adults, 1991, Chaplin, 1992, Dave, 1993, George Balanchine's The Nutcracker (voice only), 1993, Princess Caraboo, 1994, French Kiss, 1995, The Hunchback of Notre Dame (voice only), 1996, Fierce Creatures, 1997, In & Out, 1997, The Ice Storm, 1997, A Midsummer Night's Dream, 1999, Wild Wild West, 1999, The Road to El Dorado (voice), 2000, The Anniversary Party, 2001, Life as a House, 2001, The Emperor's Club, 2002, De-lovely, 2004, As You Like It, 2005; dir. (TV movie) Hamlet, 1990. Office: William Morris Agy 1325 Avenue Of The Americas New York NY 10019-6026

KLINE, KIP L., philosophy educator; b. South Bend, Ind., Sept. 17, 1971; s. Richard Dale and Kay Ellen Kline; life ptnr. Nicole Teresa Lee. BS, Taylor U., 1994; MA, Ball State U., 2002; postgrad., Ind. U., 2002—. English tchr. Shelbyville (Ind.) H.S., Greenfield (Ind.) Ctrl. H.S., Greenville, Ind., Center Grove H.S., Greenwood, Ind., 1998—2002; assoc. instr. Ind. U., Bloomington, 2002—. Mem.: Philosophy of Edn. Soc. Home: 329 W 24th Pl Chicago IL 60616 Office: Ind U Bloomington IN 47403 Personal E-mail: clkline@indiana.edu.

KLINE, LEE B., retired architect; b. Renton, Wash., Feb. 2, 1914; s. Abraham McCubbin and Pearl Kline; m. Martha Myers, Aug. 29, 1936 (div. Oct. 1995); children— Patricia, Joanne Louise Kline Kresse; m. Marilyn Gibson, May 7, 1997. B.Arch., U. So. Calif., 1937. Draftsman, designer, 1937-43; pvt. archtl. practice Los Angeles, 1943-2001; ret., 2001. Instr. engring. extension U. Calif., 1947-53; mem. panel arbitrators Am. Arbitration Assn., 1964— Pres. LaCanada Irrigation Dist., 1966-96, dir., 1963-96; bd. dirs. Foothill Mcpl. Water Dist., 1980-96, LaCanada br. ARC, 1959-81. Recipient Disting. Service citation Calif. council AIA, 1960, honor awards AIA, 1957, 59, Sch. of Month awards Nation's Schools, 1964, 71 Fellow AIA (pres. Pasadena chpt. 1957, pres. Calif. council 1959) Home: 526 W Huntington Dr Unit F Arcadia CA 91007-3443 Office: Kline Enterprises Inc 969 Colorado Blvd Los Angeles CA 90041-1773

KLINE, LOWRY F., beverage company executive, lawyer; Sr. v.p., gen. counsel Coca-Cola Enterprises, Atlanta, 1996-97, exec. v.p., gen. counsel, 1997-99, exec. v.p., chief adminstrv. officer, 1999-2001, elected to bd., vice chmn., 2000—02, vice chmn., CEO, 2001—02, chmn., CEO, 2002—. Bd. dirs. Dixie Group, Jackson Furniture Industries. Office: Coca-Cola Enterprises 2500 Windy Ridge Pkwy SE Atlanta GA 30339-5677

KLINE, MABLE CORNELIA PAGE, retired secondary school educator; b. Memphis, Aug. 20, 1928; d. George M. and Lillie (Davidson) Brown; 1 child, Gail Angela Page. Student, LeMoyne Coll.; BSEd, Wayne State U., 1948, postgrad. Tchr., Flint, Mich., 1950—51, Pontiac, Mich., 1953—62; tchr. 12th grade English Cass Tech. H.S., Detroit, 1962—95, coord. Study Skills program, mem. English book selection com., 1986—; ret., 1995. Mem.: ASCD, NEA (life), YWCA (life), NAACP (life), Nat. Coun. Tchrs. English, Am. Fedn. Tchrs., Sayne State U. Alumni Assn., Delta Sigma Theta. Episcopalian. Home: 555 Brush St Apt 1512 Detroit MI 48226-4354 Office: Cass Tech High Sch English Dept 2421 2nd Ave Detroit MI 48201-2697

KLINE, MARK WENDEL, pediatric medicine educator; b. Corpus Christi, Tex., Jan. 31, 1957; s. William Marshall and Elsie Marie (Ford) K. BA, Trinity U., 1978; MD, Baylor Coll. Medicine, 1981. Diplomate Am. Bd. Pediat., Pediatric Infectious Diseases. Intern and resident in pediat. Baylor Coll. Medicine, Houston, 1981-85, postdoctoral fellow infectious diseases, 1985-87; asst. prof. pediat. St. Louis (Mo.) U. Sch. Medicine, 1987-89, Baylor Coll. Medicine, Houston, 1990-92, assoc. prof. pediat., 1993-97, prof. pediat., 1997—. Assoc. dir. Gen. Clin. Rsch. Ctr., Baylor Coll. Medicine, Tex. Children's Hosp., Houston, 1992—; dir. AIDS Internat. Tng. and Rsch. Program, 1999—. Contbr. chpts. to books and articles to profl. jours. Named One of Five Outstanding Young Texans, Tex. Jr. C. of C., 1993. Fellow Am. Acad. Pediat., Infectious Disease Soc. Am., Am. Pediatric Soc., Soc. for Pediatric Rsch.; mem. Am. Soc. for Microbiology. Office: Baylor Coll Med Dept Peds MC1-4000 6621 Fannin St Houston TX 77030-2303

KLINE, MARY KENEALY, school system administrator; b. Herkimer, N.Y., May 20, 1954; d. Robert J. and Gertrude C. Kenealy; m. Lawrence Scott Kline, Aug. 21, 1982; 1 child, Andrew Robert. BA, Nazareth Coll., Rochester, N.Y., 1976; MS, SUNY, Cortland, 1981, Cert. Advanced Study, 1992. Cert. nursery-grade 6 elem. edn. N.Y., 1976, reading tchr. N.Y., 1981, sch. dist. adminstr. N.Y., 1992. Migrant tutor Herkimer (N.Y.) County BOCES, 1979—80, curriculum specialist, 1980—83, coord., 1983—2000, dir., 2000—. Bd. mem. N.Y. State Reading Assn., Albany, 1990—, conf. coord., 1993—96, pres., 2001—02, N.Y. State Migrant Consortium, Albany, 1993—95. Bd. dirs. Mohawk Valley Reading Coun., Utica, NY, 1982—; trainer Literacy Vols. Am., Utica, 1985—90; rep. Clinton (N.Y.) Elem. Sch., 1994—96; treas. Mid York Child Care Coordinating Coun., Rome, NY, 1995—2000; bd. dirs. Cornell Coop. Ext., Herkimer, 1995—96, Mohawk Vally Cmty. Action Agy., Rome, 2002—. Recipient Outstanding NY State Migrant Educator award, Nat. Assn. State Migrant Edn. Dirs., 1990, Coun. Svc. award, N.Y. State Reading Assn., 1993, 2002. Mem.: ASCD, Mohawk Valley Sch. Adminstrs. Orgn., N.Y. State Assn. Continuing and Cmty. Educators, Nat. Even Start Assn., Internat. Reading Assn., Sch. Adminstrs. Assn. N.Y. State. Home: 223 Homewood Dr Clinton NY 13323 Office: Herkimer County BOCES 352 Gros Blvd Herkimer NY 13350

KLINE, NANCY MATTOON, librarian; b. Providence, Oct. 9, 1937; d. Donald Potter and Lillian Hortense (Groux) Mattoon; m. Kenneth Ernest Kline, June 20, 1959. BS, U. Conn., 1959, MS, 1961; MLS, U. R.I., 1973; PhD, U. Conn., 1994. Map libr. U. Conn. Libr., Storrs, 1970-79, dept. head, 1979-88, asst. to dir. libr., 1989-90, reference librarian, 1991-93, reference collection coord., 1993—, acting reference dept. head, 1995-96. Contbr. articles to profl. jours., 1973—. Bd. dirs. Mansfield (Conn.) Libr., 1978-83; libr. Mansfield Hist. Soc., 1969-79; com. mem. Planning for Year 2002, Mansfield, 1989-92 Mem. ALA, Spl. Librs. Assn. (assoc. editor bulletin 1973-77, editor 1976-79), Conn. Libr. Assn. (pres. 1980-81), Assn. Coll. and Rsch. Librs. (New Eng. chpt., chair collection devel. interest group 1995—), New Eng. Libr. Assn., Beta Phi Mu, Phi Kappa Phi, Phi Delta Kappa. Office: U Conn Libr 369 Fairfield Storrs Mansfield CT 06269-6016 Home: PO Box 577 Storrs Manfld CT 06268-0577

KLINE, NANCY MEADORS, non-profit company executive, consulting executive, writer; b. Clovis, N.Mex., May 1, 1946; d. Max Irby and Edelweiss (Corbin) Meadors; m. Peter Lee Kline, June 27, 1972 (div. 1986); m. Christopher Alexander Spence, June 9, 1990. BA in Literature, Scripps Coll., Claremont, Calif., 1968. Tchr. Sandy Spring (Md.) Friends Sch., 1968-70, Madeira Sch., Greenway, Va., 1970-72; founding dir. Thornton Friends Sch., Silver Spring, Md., 1973-84, The Leadership Inst., Sandy Spring, 1984-92; pres. Time to Think, Inc., Oxfordshire, Eng., 1992—; dir. Leadership 2020, London, 1995—. Author: Physical Movement for the Theater, 1969, Enjoying the Arts: Dance, 1973, Women and Power: How Far Can We Go?, 1993; author BBC-TV program Breaking Glass: Women and Men in Leadership, 1995, Time to Think: Listening to Ignite the Human Mind, 1999. Mem. P.E.O. Women, Inst. Personal & Devel. In Practice (London), NOW. Democrat. Mem. Soc. Of Friends. Avocations: writing, gardening. Home: 63 Preston Crowmarsh Wallingford Oxfordshire OX10 6SL England Office: Time to Think Inc 6004 Rhode Island Ave Riverdale MD 20737-1936

KLINE, NORMAN DOUGLAS, retired judge; b. Lynn, Mass., Dec. 28, 1930; s. Samuel and Ida (Luff) K.; m. Betty Toba Feldman, Feb. 27, 1966; children: Sarah, Samuel. AB, Harvard Coll., 1952, postgrad., 1952-53; JD, Boston U., 1959. Bar: Mass. 1959. Pvt. practice, Boston, 1959-60; atty. U.S. Dept. Army, Cleve., 1960; trial atty. FMC, Washington, 1960-72, adminstrv. law judge, 1972-92, chief adminstrv. law judge, 1992—2005. With U.S. Army, 1953-55. Mem. Fed. Adminstrv. Law Judges Conf. Avocations: classical music, collecting cds.

KLINE, PAUL CONLEY, lawyer; s. Joseph Nathaniel and Florence (Conley) Kline; m. Martha Elena Morales, Nov. 22, 1975; children: Samara Kathryn, Paul Conley Jr., Joseph Nathaniel IV. BA in Latin Am. studies, Monterey Inst. Internat. Studies, Calif., 1974; MPA, Harvard U., Cambridge, 1990; JD, U. San Diego, 1994. Bar: Calif. 1999. Fgn. svc. officer U.S. Dept. State, 1976—99; founder, atty. Calif. Bus. Immigration, Bonita, 1999—. Bd. dirs. San Diego-Shannon Partnership, 2002—. Editor: (book) Perspectives on Change in Contemporary Mexico, 1974. Recipient Meritorious Hon. Award, U.S. Dept. State, 1986, 1998, Commendation, Drug Enforcement Adminstrn., Mex., 1989, Certificate of Appreciation, U.S. Southern Command, Panama, 1998. Mem.: Am. Immigration Lawyers Assn., Diplomatic Consular Officers, San Diego County Bar Assn., Am. Fgn. Svc. Assn., Harvard Club of San Diego. Republican. Roman Catholic. Avocations: genealogy, hiking. Office: Calif Bus Immigration 5035 Central Ave #F Bonita CA 91902 E-mail: paulckline@aol.com.

KLINE, PHILLIP D., state attorney general; b. Kansas City, Kans., Dec. 31, 1959; s. James R. and Janet S. (Shirley) K.; m. Deborah Suzanne Shattuck, July 22, 1989; 1 child, Jacqueline Hillary. BS in Pub. Rels. and Polit. Sci., Cen. Mo. State U., 1982; JD, U. Kans., 1987. Bar: Kans. 1987, U.S. Ct. Appeals (10th cir.), U.S. Dist. Ct. Kans. News reporter WHB Radio, Kansas City, Mo., 1981-82; pub. rels. rep. Mid-America, Inc., Kansas City, Mo., 1982-84; assoc. Blackwell, Sanders, Matheny, Weary & Lombardi, Overland Park, Kans., 1987—95; legislator State of Kans., 1992—2000, atty. gen., 2003—. Nominee Kans. 2d Congl. Dist., 1986; former chmn. taxation com.; fin. chmn. Johnson County Reps., 1990-91; chmn. Shawnee Reps., 1991-92; chmn., co-chmn. Corp. Woods Charity Jazz Festival, Overland Park, 1991-95; bd. dirs. Shawnee Mission Edn. Found., 1994-95, Rep. Ho. Campaign Com. Mem. Johnson County Bar Assn., Kans. Bar Assn., Rotary (bd. dirs., v.p. 1991-93, pres. 1994-95, Disting. Svc. award 1991). Republican. Methodist. Avocations: history, reading, athletics. Office: Atty Gen 120 SW 10th Ave, 2nd Fl Topeka KS 66612-1597

KLINE, RAYMOND ADAM, professional organization executive; b. New Ringgold, Pa., Sept. 14, 1926; s. Raymond Adam and Helen Marie (Herb) K.; m. Jeanelle Batley, Apr. 26, 1958; children— Robin Jeanelle, Raymond Ashley. AB, Lebanon Valley Coll., 1950, LLD (hon.), 1990; LLB, George Washington U., 1957, JD (hon.), 1982. Bar: D.C. 1958. Mgmt. analyst Army Missile Command, Huntsville, Ala., 1958-61; chief mgmt. devel. office Marshall Space Flight Ctr., Huntsville, 1961-66; asst. assoc. adminstr. for systems mgmt. NASA Hdqrs., Washington, 1967-75, asst. adminstr. instl. mgmt., 1975-77, assoc. adminstr. mgmt. ops, 1977-79; dep. adminstr. GSA, 1979-84, acting adminstr., 1981, 1984-85; pres. Nat. Acad. Pub. Adminstrn., 1985-92. Instr. in polit. sci. U. Ala., 1958-63 Served with U.S. Army, 1944-46, 50-51. Mem. D.C. Bar, Phi Delta Phi, Pi Gamma Mu. Home: 15432 Carrolton Rd Rockville MD 20853-1703

KLINE, RICHARD L., retired music educator; b. West Reading, Pa., Feb. 11, 1930; s. Leroy C. and Elda R. Kline; m. Barbara Sue Metzger, June 13, 1953; children: Susan K. Liberati, David R. BS in Music Edn., Lebanon Valley Coll., 1951; MA in Music Edn., Columbia U., 1952. Music educator Pequea Valley H.S., Intercourse, Pa., 1956—57, Hempfield Sch. Dist., Landisville, Pa., 1957—87; musical dir. Actors County Pa., Lancaster, 1989—97; ret. Organist Grace Luth. Ch., Lancaster, 1959—78; substitute organist local chs. With USAF, 1952—56. Recipient Red Rose award, The Lancaster New Era, 2000. Mem.: Pa. State Educators Assn., Pa. Music Educators Assn. (Disting. Svc. award Dist. 7 2000). Democrat. Lutheran. Avocations: travel, ballroom dancing, exercise, theater, reading. Home: 18 St Peter Cir Lititz PA 17543

KLINE, RICHARD STEPHEN, public relations executive; b. Brookline, Mass., June 20, 1948; s. Paul and Helen (Chartoff) K.; m. Carroll Potter, (dec. Apr. 1984); m. Sharon Tate, June 16, 1985; stepchildren: Allison, Kevin. BA, U. Mass., 1970. Reporter, photographer Worcester (Mass.) Telegram & Gazette, 1970-71; account exec. Wenger-Michael Advt., L.A., 1971; pub. rels. dir. Oakland (Calif.) Symphony Orch., 1972; asst. v.p., dir. promotions Gt. Western Savs. and Loan, Beverly Hills, Calif., 1972-75; v.p., dir. mktg. Union Fed. Savs. and Loan, L.A., 1975-78; chmn. bd. dirs. Berkhemer & Kline, L.A., 1978-88, Berkhemer Kline Golin/Harris, L.A., 1988-93; COO Golin/Harris Comm., Chgo., 1992-95; pres. Shandwick U.S.A., N.Y.C., N.Y., 1995-96, Kline Consulting Group, L.A., 1997; regional pres., sr. ptnr. Fleishman-Hillard, Inc., L.A., 1997—. Former instr. Am. Savs. and Loan Inst.; bd. dirs. Golin/Harris Communications; exec. com. Santa Barbara Old Spanish Days Fiesta Rodeo, 1992. Past pres., mem. exec. com. Big Bros. L.A.; bd. dirs. Am. Cancer Soc., L.A., Solvang (Calif.) TheatreFest; mem. Town Hall Forum, L.A.; commr. Parks and Recreation, City of Oakland, 1973-74; bd. dirs. United Way, 1988-93, TheaterFest, 1990-94, LA's Best, LA C. of C.; exec. com. Ctrl. City Assocs. Recipient Pres.'s Club award Big Bros. Greater L.A., 1987, 88, Best in West Pub. Svc. award Am. Advt. Fedn.,

San Francisco, 1975, Commitment to Youth award Big Bros. Greater L.A., 2001. Mem. Nat. Investor Rels. Inst., Pub. Rels. Soc. Am. (Disting. Cmty. Svc. award 1987), Internat. Assn. Bus. Communicators, Motor Press Guild, Newcomen Soc., Nat. Cattlemen's Assn., Arthur W. Page Soc., Calif. Cattlemen's Assn., Am. Quarter Horse Assn., Rancheros Visitadores, Vaqueros de Los Ranchos, Publicity Club L.A., Jonathan Club. Avocations: horseback riding, fishing. Office: Fleishman-Hillard Inc 515 S Flower St Ste 700 Los Angeles CA 90071-2209

KLINE, SIDNEY DELONG, JR., lawyer; b. West Reading, Pa., Mar. 25, 1932; s. Sidney D. and Leona Clarice (Barkalow) Kline; m. Barbara Phyllis James, Dec. 31, 1955; children: Allison S. McCanney, Leslie S. Davidson, Lisa P. Gallen. BA, Dickinson Coll., 1954, LLD (hon.), 1998; LLB, The Dickinson Law Sch., 1956, LLD (hon.), 1994. Bar: Pa. 1956, U.S. Dist. Ct. (ea. dist.) Pa. 1961, U.S. Supreme Ct. 1967. Assoc. Stevens & Lee, Reading, Pa., 1958-62, ptnr., shareholder, 1963-97, pres., 1977-93, chmn., 1993-97, counsel, 1998—. Bd. dirs. Reading Eagle Co. Pres. United Way Berks County, Reading, 1972—74, campaign chmn., 1986; bd. dirs. Reading Ctr. City Devel. Fund, 1976—98, pres., 1992—97; bd. dirs. Greater Berks Devel. Fund, 1998—; gov. Dickinson Sch. Law, 1978—, sec., 1988—2003; trustee Dickinson Coll., 1979—, chmn., 1990—98. With U.S. Army, 1956—58. Recipient Doran award, United Way Berks County, 1978, Richard J. Caron Cmty. Svc. award, Caron Found., 1993, Thun Cmty. Svc. award, 1995, William Strong Cmty. Svc. award, 2002. Fellow: Berks County Bar Assn., Pa. Bar Assn., Nat. Soc. Fund Raising Execs. (Outstanding Vol. Fund Raiser Greater Northeastern Pa. chpt. 1992), Am. Coll. Trust and Estate Coun., Club at Pelican Bay (Naples, Fla.), Moselem Springs Golf Club (Fleetwood, Pa.), Berkshire Country Club (Reading). Republican. Lutheran. Office: PO Box 679 111 N 6th St Reading PA 19603-0679 Office Phone: 610-478-2200. Business E-Mail: sdk@stevenslee.com.

KLINE, SUSAN ANDERSON, medical educator, internist; b. Dallas, June 4, 1937; d. Kenneth Kirby and Frances Annette (Demorest) Anderson; m. Edward Mahon Kline, Dec. 26, 1964 (dec. July 1990). BA, Ohio U., 1959; MD, Northwestern U., 1963. Diplomate Am. Bd. Internal Medicine, Nat. Bd. Med. Examiners (bd. dirs. 1977-81). Asst. physician NY Hosp., 1967—68, physician-to-outpatients, 1968—69, electrocardiographer, 1968—70, asst. attending physician, 1969—76, physician-in-charge cardiopulmonary lab., 1970—71, dir. adult cardiac catheterizaion lab., 1970—71, dir. adult cardiac catheterization lab., 1971—79, assoc. attending physician, 1976—85, emeritus attending physician, 1985—, emeritus dir. adult cardiac catheterization lab., 1985—; assoc. dean student affairs Cornell U. Med. Coll., N.Y.C., 1974—78; assoc. dean admissions and student affairs Cornell Med. Sch., Ithaca, NY, 1978—80; mgr. occupl. med. programs GE Co., 1980—84; sr. assoc. dean student affairs N.Y. Med. Coll., Valhalla, 1984—94, interim dean, v.p. med. affairs, 1994—96, exec. vice dean acad. affairs, vice provost univ. student affairs, 1996—. Chmn. unmatched student com. Nat. Residency Matching Program, 1998—2000, chmn., second match com., mem. exec. com., 2003—, pres.-elect, 2004—05, pres., 2005; mem. test com. Ednl. Commn. on Fgn. Med. Grads., Phila., 1985—92; US Med. Licensing Exam test accommodations com. Nat. Bd. Med. Examiners, Phila., 1992—97; bd. dirs. Nat. Resident Matching Program, exec. com., 2003—, chair 2nd match com., 2004; mem. Liaison Com. on Med. Edn., 1998—2004, chair ad hoc subcom. rev. accreditation stds., 2000—01, exec. com., 2002—04; policy com. Liaiaon Com. on Med. Edn., 2003—04; chmn. adv. com. Electronic Residency Application Svc., 1996—2001. Bd. visitors Coll. Arts, Ohio U., Athens, 1981—91; bd. dirs. Burke Rehab. Hosp., White Plains, 1997—. Recipient Leaders of the Future award, Nat. Coun. Women, N.Y.C., 1978, Cert. of Appreciation, Ohio U., 1978. Fellow: ACP, Am. Soc. Internal Medicine, Am. Coll. Cardiology; mem.: Phi Kappa Phi, Am. Assn. Med. Colls. (chmn. 1989—93, chmn. N.E. group on student affairs, mem. sr. mgmt. adv. com. 2001—), N.Y. Cardiologists Soc., Am. Heart Assn. (fellow coun. on clin. cardiology), Cruising Club Am., Alpha Omega Alpha, Phi Beta Kappa. Avocation: sailing. Home: 561 Pequot Ave Southport CT 06490-1366 Office: NY Med Coll Sunshine Cottage Valhalla NY 10595 Office Phone: 914-594-4500. Business E-Mail: kline@nymc.edu.

KLINE, SYRIL LEVIN, writer, educational consultant; b. Washington, Oct. 19, 1953; d. Irvin and Blanche Levin; children: Seth Adam Lessans, Jonathan Rafael Lessans; m. Peter Lee Kline, Dec. 28, 1989 BS, U. Md., 1975. Cert. integrative learning master facilitator, 1990. Tchr. Hebrew Washington Hebrew Congregation, 1974-80; sec., realtor Colquitt-Carruthers Inc., Montgomery County, Md., 1974-80; adminstrv. asst. Bd. Jewish Edn., Silver Spring, Md., 1980-81; tchr. presch. and kindergarten Children's Learning Ctr., Rockville, Md., 1982-89; curriculum designer, dir. integrative learning Nat. Acad. Integrative Learning, Rochester, N.Y., 1990-92; ednl. cons. Integra Learning Systems, South Bend, Ind., 1992—; free-lance radio and print writer South Bend, 1992—. Ednl. cons. Integrative Learning Systems, Damascus, Md., 1988-89; ind. cons., course designer Prince George's County (Md.) Libr., 1989, North Syracuse (NY) Schs., 1989-92, Oswego (NY) Cmty. Schs., 1989-92, Xerox, Rochester, NY, 1990-92, Eastman Kodak, Rochester, 1990-92, Penn Yann (NY) Schs., 1991, Utica (NY) Schs., 1991, City of Rochester Schs., 1991, Bellcore, Elizabeth, NJ, 1991, Alliant Tech Sys., St. Paul, 1991, Paramus (NJ) Cmty. Schs., 1992, Govt. Can., 1992, Project Read, San Francisco, 1992, Sandia Labs, Santa Fe, 1992, City of Elkhart, Ind., 1992-94, Trinity Corp., Joliet, Ill., 1995, Scottsdale Mall, South Bend, 1995, Pathfinders, Plymouth, Ind., 1996; assessment designer Integra Learning Systems, 1995; asst. childrens program coord. Brookside Gardens, Wheaton, Md.; presenter in field Co-author: (novel) The Butterfly Dreams, 1998; featured commentator Sta. WVPE, 1995-98; columnist Action Line; soprano Ind. Opera North; author: The Changeling, 2003, 2d edit., 2005, The Fortunate Unhappy, 2003 Spkr., presenter Little Bear Child Abuse Prevention Program, Madison Ctr. Hosp., South Bend, 1993-95; vol. fundraiser Jewish Fedn. St. Joseph Valley, South Bend, 1995-96; mem. com., writer, presenter Holocaust Commemoration; actress, dir. Osceola Players, South Bend Civic Theatre; cantorial soloist Temple Beth El, South Bend, 1997 Mem. Hadassah (life, corres. sec. 1994-95), Omicron Nu. Democrat. Avocations: radio commercial voices, singing, theater, pets, travel. Office: 1404 Billman Ln Silver Spring MD 20902

KLINE, THOMAS R., lawyer; b. NYC, 1947; AB, Columbia Coll., 1968; JD, Columbia U., 1975. Bar: DC 1976, NY 1976, Md. 1996. Trial atty. US Dept. Justice, Civil Divsn., Fed. Program Branch, 1979—81; ptnr., Litig. Andrews Kurth LLP, Washington. Adj. lectr. Am. U., 1977—81, George Mason U., 1986; adj. asst. prof. George Washington U., 2000—. Mem., editl. bd. Columbia Law Rev., 1974—75. Vol. mediator Alternate Dispute Resolution Program, USDC, Washington, 1996—; bd. dir. Washington Coun. Lawyers, 1984—. James Kent Scholar, 1974—75, Harlan Fiske Stone Scholar, 1972—73, 1973—74. Mem.: CPR Inst. Dispute Resolution (regional panal of disting. neutrals for Washington DC 1999—), ABA (co-chmn. energy resources law com. 1989—98, Tort & Ins. Practice Sect.), NY State Bar, Md. State Bar, DC Bar. Fluent in French. Office: Andrews Kurth LLP 1701 Pennsylvania Ave NW Ste 300 Washington DC 20006 Office Phone: 202-662-2716. Office Fax: 202-974-9512. Business E-Mail: tkline@andrewskurth.com.

KLINE, THOMAS RICHARD, lawyer; b. Hazleton, Pa., Dec. 18, 1947; s. Isadore J. and Jeanne (Levin) K.; m. Paula Wolf, Dec. 25, 1972; children: Hilary, Zachary. AB, Albright Coll., 1969; MA, Lehigh U., 1971; JD, Duquesne U., 1978. Bar: Pa., NY, U.S. Supreme Ct., U.S. Dist. Ct. (ea. dist.) Pa., U.S. Dist. Ct. (we. dist.) Pa., U.S. Ct. Appeals (3rd cir.). Tchr. Hazleton Area Sch. Dist., 1969-74; lectr. Lehigh U., Bethlehem, Pa., 1974; law clk. to Hon. Thomas W. Pomeroy Pa. Supreme Ct., Pitts., 1978; atty. Beasley Casey Colleran Erbstein Thistle & Kline, Phila., 1980-94; ptnr. Kline & Specter, 1995—. Adj. prof. sch. law Temple U.; chmn. fed. jud. nominations com. Ea. Dist., U.S. Dist. Ct. of Pa. Named Top Lawyer in Pa., survey by Law & Politics, 2004, 2005; named one of 10 Top Litigators in Am., Nat. Law Jour., 2000. Fellow: Internat. Acad. Trial Lawyers, Am. Coll. Trial Lawyers; mem.: ATLA, U. Pa. Inn of Cts., Inner Circle of Advocates, Phila. Trial Lawyers Assn., Pa. Trial Lawyers Assn., Phila. Bar Assn., Pa. Bar Assn., ABA. Office: 1525 Locust St Philadelphia PA 19102-3732 Office Phone: 215-772-1000. Business E-Mail: tom.kline@klinespecter.com.

KLINEDINST, JOHN DAVID, lawyer; b. Washington, Jan. 20, 1950; s. David Moulson and Mary Stewart (Coxe) K.; m. Cynthia Lynn DuBain, Aug. 15, 1981. BA cum laude in History, Washington and Lee U., 1971, JD, 1978; MBA in Fin. and Investments, George Washington U., 1975. Bar: Calif. 1979, U.S. Dist. Ct. (so. dist.) Calif. 1979, U.S. Ct. Appeals (9th cir.) 1987. With comml. lending dept. 1st Nat. Bank Md., Montgomery County, 1971-74; assoc. Ludecke, McGrath & Denton, San Diego, 1979-80; ptnr. Whitney & Klinedinst, San Diego, 1980-83, Klinedinst & Meiser, San Diego, 1983-86; CEO Klinedinst PC, San Diego, 1986—. Mem. bd. trustees Phi Kappa Psi Endowment Fund, 2004—. Mem. law coun. Washington and Lee U., 1993-97, vice chmn. law campaign, 1991-94, bd. trustees, 2001—; vice chmn. bd. dirs. ARC of San Diego/Imperial, 1991-97; pres. House Corp. Calif. Lambda, Phi Kappa Psi, 1999—. Recipient Disting. Alumnus award Washington and Lee U., 1993. Mem. ABA (standing com. on legal profl. liability), Order of the Coif (hon.), Calif. Bar Assn., San Diego Bar Assn., San Diego Def. Lawyers, San Diego/Tijuana Sister Cities Soc., Washington Soc. (bd. dirs. 1997—), Washington and Lee U. Alumni Assn. (bd. dirs. 1986-90, pres. 1989-90), Washington and Lee U. Club (pres. San Diego chpt. 1980-87, San Diego Dialogue of U. Calif. San Diego), La Jolla Beach and Tennis Club, Fairbanks Ranch Country Club, Bohemian Club, Phi Kappa Psi (bd. trustees endowment fund 2003—) Republican. Episcopalian. Home: 6226 Via Dos Valles Rancho Santa Fe CA 92067-9999 Office: Klinedinst PC 501 W Broadway Ste 600 San Diego CA 92101-3584 Office Phone: 619-239-8131. Business E-Mail: jklinedinst@klinedinstlaw.com.

KLINEDINST, THOMAS JOHN, JR., insurance agency executive; b. Cin., Aug. 2, 1942; s. Thomas John and Betty Ann (Broeman) K.; m. Diana Lowry McCarroll; children: Thomas John III, Margaret Lucie, George Calvin. BA, Georgetown U., 1965. Spl. agt. Fidelity & Deposit Co. Md., Cleve., 1965-67; account exec. Thomas E. Wood, Inc., Cin., 1967-71, asst. v.p., 1971-73, v.p., 1973-79, exec. v.p., 1979-87, pres., 1987-95, pres., chmn., CEO, 1995—, also bd. dirs. Cons. Airport Operators Coun. Internat., Washington, 1979-95; pres. Ohio CAP Ins. Co., Ltd., 1988—; dir. Star Banc Corp., 1993—, Star Bank Cinti, 1993—, Employers Resource Assn., 1994—, Franciscan Health Sys. of Ohio Valley, 1994—, chmn., 1997; exec. com. USI Ins. Svc. Corp., 1995—. Pres. Travelers Aid-Internat. Inst., Cin., 1980-84; pres.-elect Fedn. Cath. Cmty. Charities, Cin., 1980-81; pres. Terrace Park Swim Club, Cin., 1980-82; trustee Cin. Better Bus. Bur., 1991—, dir. Project Encor, 1991—; bd. dirs. Hamilton County Hosp. Commn., 1996, chmn., 1997 Named Young Agt. of Yr., Cin. Ins. Bd., 1977. Mem. Coun. Ins. Agts. and Brokers (mem. bd. dirs. 1984-94), Ind. Ins. Agts. Assn. Ohio, Cin. Ins. Bd. (trustee 1980-85, pres. 1984-85), Queen City Club, Cin. Country Club, Friars Club (pres. 1974-78, Friars award 1977), Rotary. Republican. Roman Catholic. Office: Thomas E Wood Inc 312 Elm St Fl 24 Cincinnati OH 45202-2739

KLINEFELTER, GARY V., lawyer; b. 1948; Bar: Ariz. 1975. With Amerco, Reno, 1978, sec., gen. counsel, 1988—; sec. U-Haul, Ariz., 1990—, gen. counsel, 1988—. Office: Amerco 1325 Airmotive Way Reno NV 89502*

KLINEFELTER, JAMES LOUIS, lawyer; b. L.A., Oct. 8, 1925; s. Theron Albert and Anna Marie (Coffey) K.; m. Joanne Wright, Dec. 26, 1957 (div.); children: Patricia Anne, Jeanne Marie, Christopher Wright; m. Mary Lynn S. Klinefelter, Aug. 19, 1971; 1 child, Mary Katherine. BA, U. Ala., 1949, LLB, 1951. Bar: Ala. 1951, U.S. Dist. Ct. (no. dist.) Ala. 1959, U.S. Ct. Appeals (11th cir.) 1983. Regional claims rep. State Farm Mut. Auto Ins. Co., Anniston, Ala., 1951-54; ptnr. Burnham & Klinefelter, Anniston, 1954—2003; mem. Sides, Oglesby, Held and Dick, 2003—. Mem. adv. com. Supreme Ct. Ala. Mem. Ala. Dem. Exec. Com., 1964—, chmn. legis. rev. com., 1964—; past chmn. Calhoun County Dem. Exec. Com., 1964—; mem. Anniston City Sch. Bd. Lt. (j.g.) USNR, 1943-46. Mem. ABA, Assn. Def. Trial Attys., Ala. Bar Assn. (mem. task force on jud. selection, mem. long-range planning task force), Calhoun County Bar Assn., Ala. Def. Lawyers Assn. (past pres.), Ala. Law Inst. (bd. dirs.), Ala. Sch. Bd. Attys. (past pres.), Internat. Assn. Def. Counsel, Kiwanis (past pres.), Anniston Country Club, Phi Kappa Sigma, Phi Alpha Theta. Avocations: tennis, swimming, reading. Home: 1412 Christine Ave Anniston AL 36207-3924 Office: Sides Oglesby Held and Dick 1310 Leighton Ave PO Box 1849 Anniston AL 36202-1849 Office Phone: 256-237-6611. E-mail: sohd@cableone.net. *When obligations or obnoxious tasks are accepted gratefully as opportunities, one's life can be turned about, and bitterness and resentment changed into joyful satisfaction. Hard tasks are the food of growth.*

KLINEFELTER, SARAH STEPHENS, retired dean, broadcast executive; b. Des Moines, Jan. 30, 1938; d. Edward John and Mary Ethel (Adams) Stephens; m. Neil Klinefelter. BA, Drake U., 1958; MA, U. Iowa, 1968; postgrad., Harvard U., 1984, U. Wis., 1987, Vanderbilt U., 1991-92. Chmn. humanities dept. High Sch. Dist. 230, Orland Pk., Ill., 1958-68; chmn. communications and humanities div. Kirkwood Community Coll., Cedar Rapids, Iowa, 1968-78; prof. English Sch. of the Ozarks, Point Lookout, Mo., 1978-86; gen. mgr. Sta. KSOZ-FM, Point Lookout, 1986-90; dean div. of performing and profl. arts Coll. of the Ozarks, Point Lookout, 1989-2001. Commr. Skaggs Cmty. Hosp., Branson, Mo., 1986—; chmn. Branson Planning and Zoning Commn., 1983; project dir. Mo. Humanities Bd.; commr., examiner North Cen. Assn. Higher Edn., 1978-85; commr. Iowa Humanities Bd., 1971-78; mem. Taney County Planning and Zoning Commn., 1989-98, 2005—; pres. Branson Arts Coun., 1997—2002; co-chair Taney County Bd. Adjustment; FDA noro-virus grant coord. Branson City Health Dept., 2003-04. Democrat. Presbyterian. Home: 182 Hensley Rd Forsyth MO 65653-5137 Personal E-mail: sarahk@tri-lakes.net.

KLINE-KOENIG, BARBARA A., medical/surgical nurse; b. Pitts., July 11, 1958; d. Robert T. and Janet (Falkenstein) K. BSN, Cedar Crest Coll., Allentown, Pa., 1982; MSA in Health Adminstrn., West Chester U., 1988; postgrad., U. Pa., 1995—, postgrad. Cert. med.-surg. nurse, ACLS. Staff nurse Crozer-Chester Med. Ctr., Upland, Pa.; primary nurse Paoli (Pa.) Meml. Hosp.; mktg. dept. liaison U. Pa. Med. Ctr.; clin. resource mgr. adminstrn. Hosp. of U. Pa., Phila., 1994—, mgr. denials and appeals. Named Nurse of Hope, Am. Cancer Soc., 1984.

KLING, CARL ANDREW, music educator; b. Ft. Worth, June 18, 1968; s. Alvin Andrew and Karen Elaine Kling; m. Jennifer Rae Milles, June 14, 2003. B in Music Edn., Tex. We. U., 1991; MA in Music, Stephen F. Austin State U., 1993; postgrad., Ind. U., 2001—. Asst. dir. bands Georgetown (Tex.) Jr. High Sch., 1993—94; assoc. dir. bands Cleburne (Tex.) H.S., 1994—2000; dir. bands H.F. Stevens Mid. Sch., Crawley, Tex., 2000—01; asst. instr. Ind. U., Bloomington, 2001—04; dir. bands N.W. Mo. State U., Maryville, 2004—, dir. summer music camp, 2004—. Contbr. chapters to books. Grantee, N.W. Mo. State U., 2004. Mem.: Music Educators Nat. Conf., Coll. Band Dir. Assn., Nat. Band Assn., Kappa Kappa Psi, Pi Kappa Lambda. Avocations: camping, hiking, model railroading. Home: 609 S Buchanan St Maryville MO 64468 Office: NW Mo State Univ 800 University Dr Maryville MO 64468 Office Phone: 660-562-1794.

KLING, LEWIS, multi-industry executive; BSEE, Rensselaer Polytechnic Inst.; MBA, Stetson U. From computer engr. to several managerial positions Apollo div. (later Simulation and Control Systems) GE, 1966—90; v.p., gen. mgr. electronic systems div. Harris Corp., Melbourne, Fla., 1990—95; sr. v.p., gen. mgr. Commercial Avionics Systems AlliedSignal Aerospace, Ft. Lauderdale, Fla., 1995—97, chmn. bd. American Russian Integrated Avionics JV; pres. Dielectric Communications General Signal (merged with SPX corp. 1998), Raymond, Maine, 1997; corp. v.p., officer SPX Corp., 1999—2004; COO Flowserve Corp., Irving, Tex., 2004—05, CEO, pres., mem. bd. dirs., 2005—. Office: Flowserve Corp 5215 N O Connor Blvd Ste 2300 Irving TX 75039 Office Phone: 972-443-6505. Business E-Mail: lkling@flowserve.com.

KLING, MERLE, political scientist, university official; b. Russia, June 15, 1919; came to U.S., 1921, naturalized, 1927; s. Saul and Dina (Hoffman) K.; m. Ann Ruth Yasgur, Jan. 1, 1948 (dec. June 1976); 1 child, Arnold Saul; m. Sandra Perlman, Aug. 26, 1978 (dec. Aug. 1990). AB, Washington U., St. Louis, 1940, MA, 1941, PhD, 1949; DHC (hon.), Washington U., 1983; LLD (hon.), Mercy Coll., 1985. Mem. faculty Washington U., 1946—, asst. prof. polit. sci., 1950-54, asso. prof., 1954-61, prof., 1961-83, prof. emeritus, 1983—; dean Washington U. (Faculty Arts and Scis.), 1966-69, 73-76, provost, 1976-79, exec. vice chancellor, provost, 1979-83, acting chmn. dept. polit. sci., 1970-71; pres. Mercy Coll., Dobbs Ferry, N.Y., 1984-85. Vis. prof. U. Ill., 1961; research asso. Center Internat. Studies, Princeton U., 1964-65 Author: The Soviet Theory of Internationalism, 1952, A Mexican Interest Group in Action, 1961; contbr. articles to profl. jours. Served with AUS, 1942-45. Merle Kling professorship of Modern Letters established in honor, Washington U., 1983. Mem. Am. Polit. Sci. Assn. (council 1967-69), Midwest Polit. Sci. Assn. (editor jour. 1965-66, pres. 1969-70), Phi Beta Kappa, Alpha Kappa Delta, Omicron Delta Kappa. Home: 20 N Kingshighway Blvd Saint Louis MO 63108-1366

KLING, PHRADIE (PHRADIE KLING GOLD), small business owner, educator; b. N.Y.C., July 2, 1933; d. Samuel A. and Mary Leah (Cohen) Kling; m. Lee M. Gold, Sept. 5, 1955 (div. 1976); children: Judith Eileen, Laura Susan, Stephen Samuel, James David. BA, Cornell U., 1955; MA in Human Genetics, Sarah Lawrence Coll., 1971. Genetic counselor assoc. Coll. Medicine and Dentistry N.J., Newark, 1970—73; assoc. genetic counselor Sarah Lawrence Coll., Bronxville, NY, 1970—73; genetic counselor N.Y. Fertility Rsch. Found., N.Y.C., 1971—73; staff assoc., genetic counselor depts. pediatrics, ob-gyn and neurology Columbia U. Coll. Physicians and Surgeons, N.Y.C., 1973—78; asst. in genetics St. Luke's Hosp. Ctr., N.Y.C., 1977—79; health program assoc. Conn. Dept. Health Svcs., Hartford, 1978—84; edn. cons. Conn. Traumatic Brain Injury Assn., Rocky Hill, 1984—85; office mgr. Anderson Turf Irrigation Inc., Plainville, Conn., 1986—92; owner, mgr. KlingWorks, contract adminstrn., Avon, Conn., 1992—. Spkr., instr. health and health ethics issues, Conn., NY, NJ, 1971—85; dir. confs. genetics and traumatic brain injury, 1980—85; project dir. ednl. field testing Biol. Scis. Curriculum Study, 1981—83; scientist AAAS Sci.-by-Mail, 1991—2000. Active Farmington River Watershed Assn., Simsbury, Conn., 1988—; docent Sci. Mus. Conn., West Hartford, 1989—90. Recipient citation for dedicated svc., Conn. Safety Belt Coalition, 1985. Mem.: Conn. Assn. Jungian Psychology (bd. dirs.), Bus. and Profl. Microcomputer Users Group (bd. dirs.), Am. Human Genetics Soc., Am. Mensa (chpt. coord. gifted children 1985—), Cornell Club Greater Hartford. Home and Office: 33 Hunter Rd Avon CT 06001-3618

KLING, SUSAN SCHAEFER, librarian; b. Lincoln, Nebr., May 25, 1948; d. Victor Frederick and Rosa Florence (Klein) Schaefer; m. William Albert Kling, May 29, 1970; children: Kenneth William, Thomas Schaefer. BS in Elem. Edn., U. Nebr., 1970; MLS, Emporia State U., 1977. Interlibrary loans libr. Nebr. Libr. Commn., Lincoln, 1970-72, abstractor, indexer Nebr. state publ. checklist, 1973-74, supr. N.E. publs. clearinghouse, 1974-78, divsn. chief reference/interloan divsn., 1978-84, dir. libr. operation, 1984-86; dir. Marion (Iowa) Pub. Libr., 1987—. Pres. Nebr. Libr. Assn., 1985-86. Recipient Exemplary Mem. award Cornhusker chpg. Nat. Micrographics Assn., 1981. Mem. ALA (mem. GODORT election com. 1975-76), Iowa Libr. Assn. (exec. bd. 1992-94, conf. exhibits coord. 1989-96), Mountain Plains Libr. Assn. (state libr. sect. 1974-85, chair 1974-75, chair JMRT 1976-77), Iowa Libr. Assn. (pres. 1998), Beta Phi Mu. Office: Marion Pub Libr 1095 6th Ave Marion IA 52302-3428 Home: 2790 Brandon Ct Marion IA 52302-6267 Office Phone: 319-377-6200 24. Business E-Mail: klings@mail.crlibrary.org.

KLING, VINCENT GEORGE, architect; b. East Orange, N.J., May 9, 1916; s. George Nelson and Pauline (Geiger) K.; m. Caperton Booth, June 20, 1942; children— Vincent George, Robert Booth. B.Arch., Columbia U., 1940; M.Arch., MIT, 1942. Registered architect, Pa. Founder, sr. ptnr. Kling Partnership, Phila., 1946—64; prin. Vincent G. King & Assoc., 1964—73, Kling-Lindquist Inc., 1973—86, Kling-Lindquist Partnership Inc., 1986—87. Cons. architect Community Coll., Phila., 1979—, MARTA, Atlanta, 1975—, Seattle Transit, 1983— Chmn. Charlestown, Twp. Planning Commn., Chester Springs, Pa., 1985; mem. Chester County Area Airport Authority, Pa., 1978—, Mayor's Commn. on 21 Century, Phil., 1985. Served to lt. USN, 1941-46 Recipient AIA Lifetime Achievement award, 2003, Frank P. Brown award Franklin Inst., 1982, Alumni medal Columbia U., 1984, Gold medal Tau Sigma Delta, 1976, award of excellence Artists Guild of Delaware Valley, 1976, Gold medal and diploma of honor City Council of Quito, Ecuador, 1961 Fellow AIA; mem. AIA (Phila. chpt.)(pres. 1965-66), NAD (assoc.1987-91, academician, 1991-; Samuel F.B. Morse award 1968, 72), Fountainebleau Fine Arts and Music Schs. Assn., Soc. Am. Registered Architects Clubs: MIT of Phila., Columbia of Phila. Lodges: Lions. Republican. Avocations: aviation, farming, music, cars, swimming.*

KLING, WILLIAM HUGH, broadcast executive; b. St. Paul, Apr. 29, 1942; s. William Conrad and Helen A. (Leonard) Kling; m. Sarah Margaret Baldwin, Sept. 25, 1976. BA in Economics, St. John's U., 1964; MA in Comm., Boston U., 1966. Pres. Minn. Pub. Radio, Inc., St. Paul, 1966—, Greenspring Co., 1986—, Am. Pub. Media Group, 1999—; founding dir. Nat. Pub. Radio, 1968-70, dir., 1977-80; founding pres. Pub. Radio Internat., 1982-86, vice chmn., 1986-93; co-founder, chmn. Gather.com. Bd. dirs. St. Paul Travelers Co., Wenger Corp., Irwin Fin.; mem. various fund bds. Capital Gropu Am. Funds, chmn. New Econ. Fund, chmn. Small Cap World Fund. Bd. dirs. Minn. Orch., 1987—93; trustee J. L. Found., 1988—; bd. dirs., chmn. Fitzgerald Theater Corp., 1983—; mem. James Madison coun. Libr. of Congress, 1992—94; trustee St. John's U., 2005—. Named Disting. Minnesotan, 1995; named one of 100 Disting. Minnesotans of the Century, Mpls. Star Tribune, 2000; named to Minn. Broadcasters Hall of Fame, 2004; recipient Edward R. Murrow award, 1981, award for Excellence, Channels Mag., 1987. Mem.: Mpls. Club. Office: Am Pub Media Group 45 7th St E Saint Paul MN 55101-2274

KLINGBIEL, PAUL HERMAN, retired information scientist; b. Watertown, Wis., Nov. 3, 1919; s. Herman Carl and Elsa Helen (Zilisch) K.; m. Mildred Louise Wells, Nov. 30, 1968; stepchildren: Alice J. Blessley, Jo Ann Grayson. PhB, U. Chgo., 1948, BS, 1950; MA, Am. U., 1966. Abstractor Armed Svcs. Tech. Info. Agy., Dept. Def., Washington, 1953-58; editor Tech. Abstract Bull., 1958-60; dir. Office of Lexicography, 1960-66; phys. sci. adminstr., linguistics rsch. Def. Documentation Ctr., 1966-79; sr. cons. Aspen Systems Corp., 1979-81; systems analyst PRC Data Svcs. Co., Linthicum Heights, Md., 1981-82; lectr. Am. U., Washington, 1966-69; cons. divsn. med. scis. NAS, 1969-70; ret., 1981. Contbr. articles to profl. jours. With AUS, 1943-46. Recipient Meritorious Civilian Svc. award, 1974, Disting. Career award, 1979. Fellow AAAS; mem. Assn. Computational Linguistics, N.Y. Acad. Scis. Lutheran. Achievements include research in the field of computational linguistics. Home: 700 Mease Plz Apt 417 Dunedin FL 34698-6629 Personal E-mail: phk19@ij.net.

KLINGENSMITH, MICHAEL, publishing executive; BA, Univ. Chgo., 1975, MBA, 1976. Pres., pub. Entertainment Weekly Mag. Time Inc., N.Y.C., 1990—96, pres. Entertainment Weekly, 1996—98, pres. Sports Illustrated, 1998—2001, exec. v.p., 2001—. Trustee Univ. Chgo., amfAR; dir. YMCA of Greater NY. Office: Time Inc 1271 Avenue of the Americas New York NY 10020-1300*

KLINGER, ALAN MARK, lawyer; b. Bklyn., July 19, 1956; s. David and Gloria (Feldman) K.; m. Susan Debra Wagner, Aug. 29, 1982; children: Zachary Wagner, Jesse Wagner. AB, Princeton U., 1978; JD, NYU, 1981. Bar: N.Y. 1982, N.J. 1982, U.S. Dist. Ct. N.J., U.S. Dist. Ct. (so., ea. and we. dists.) N.Y. 1982, U.S. Ct. Appeals (2d cir.) 1985, U.S. Supreme Ct. 1989. Law clk. to judge NJ Supreme Ct., Trenton, 1981-82; assoc. Stroock & Stroock & Lavan, NYC, 1982-90, ptnr., employment law, benefits, litig., 1990—, mem. operating exec. com. Rep. United Jewish Appeal, N.Y.C., 1985—. Mem. ABA, N.Y. State Bar Assn., Fed. Bar Council, Assn. of Bar of City of N.Y.,

ACLU. Avocations: chess, table-tennis, basketball. Office: Stroock & Stroock & Lavan 180 Miaden Ln New York NY 10038-4982 Office Phone: 212-806-5818. Office Fax: 212-806-6006. Business E-Mail: aklinger@stroock.com.

KLINGER, MARILYN SYDNEY, lawyer; b. N.Y.C., Aug. 14, 1953; d. Victor and Lillyan Judith Klinger. BS, U. Santa Clara, 1975; JD, U. Calif., Hastings, 1978. Bar: Calif. 1978. Assoc. Chickering & Gregory, San Francisco, 1978-81, Steefel, Levitt & Weiss, San Francisco, 1981-82, Sedgwick, Detert, Moran & Arnold, San Francisco and L.A., 1982-87, ptnr. San Francisco, 1988-98, L.A., 1998—. Guest lectr. Stanford U. Sch. Engring. Vol. atty. Lawyers Commn. on Urban Affairs, San Francisco, 1978-80. Mem. ABA (tort and ins. practice sect., chair surety and fidelity com. 2003-04, constrn. forum, pub. contracts sect.), Internat. Assn. Def. Counsel (chmn. fidelity and surety com. 1996-98), Nat. Bond Claims Assn. (spkr.), Surety Claims Inst. (spkr.), No. Calif. Surety Underwriters Assn., No. Calif. Surety Claims Assn. (lectr., pres. 1989-90), Surety Assn. L.A. (spkr.). Avocations: reading, hiking, golf. Home: 939 15th St # 10 Santa Monica CA 90403-3146 Office: Sedgwick Detert Moran & Arnold 801 S Figueroa St Fl 18 Los Angeles CA 90017-2573 Office Phone: 213-615-8038. Business E-Mail: marilyn.klinger@sdma.com.

KLINGER, RONALD FRED, neurologist; b. Bklyn., June 14, 1958; s. Erwin and Roberta May (Haagman) K.; m. Ruth Ann Gargan, Jan. 18, 1986; children: Sarah, Jessica, Joshua. BS in Chemistry, Pace U., 1978; MD, Bowman Gray-Wake Forest U., 1982. Diplomate Am. Bd. Neurology. Intern Brookdale Hosp., Bklyn., 1982-83; resident in neurology North Shore Hosp., Manhasset, N.Y., 1983-86; pvt. practice in neurology L.I., 1986—. Clin. instr., N.Y. Hosp. Mem. Am. Acad. Neurology. Republican. Jewish. Avocations: antiques, collectibles. Office Phone: 516-541-0300.

KLINGHOFFER, DAVID, journalist; b. Santa Monica, Calif., Oct. 31, 1965; s. Paul and Carol (Bernstein) Kaye. AB magna cum laude, Brown U., 1987. Film and TV critic Washington Times, 1990-92; editl. asst. Nat. Rev., N.Y.C., 1987, asst. book editor, 1987-89, lit. editor, 1992-98, sr. editor, 1998-99, contbg. editor, 2000-01; editl. dir. Toward Tradition, 2001—02. Author: The Lord Will Gather Me In: My Journey to Jewish Orthodox, 1998, The Discovery of God: Abraham and the Birth of Monotheism, 2003, Why the Jews Rejected Jesus: The Turning Point in Jewish History, 2005. Jewish.*

KLINGHOFFER, JUDITH APTER, historian, cross cultural consultant; b. Sept. 4, 1946; d. Abraham Apter and Rachel (Preisler) Basch; m. Arthur Jay Klinghoffer, May 18, 1969; 1 child, Joella. BA, Hebrew U., 1967; MA in Pub. History, Rutgers U., 1986, PhD in History, 1994. Pub. historian, Cherry Hill, 1986-90; asst. prof. Rowan U., Glassboro, N.J., 1991-92; staff mem. Ctr. Hist. Analysis, Rutgers U., New Brunswick, N.J., 1994-95; pres. Global Perspectives, Cherry Hill, 1997—. Vis. lectr. Beijing, China, 1992-93; Fulbright prof., Aarhus, Denmark, 1996. Co-author: Israel and the Soviet Union, 1985, International Citizens' Tribunals: Mobilizing Public Opinion to Advance Human Rights, 2002; author: The Citizen Planner, 1989, Vietnam, The Jews and The Middle East: Unintended Consequences, 1999; contbr. articles to profl. jours., to online jours. E-mail: klinghof@crab.rutgers.edu.

KLINGLE, PHILIP ANTHONY, law librarian; b. Bklyn., July 24, 1950; s. Lorin Russell and Therese Margaret (Meehan) K.; m. Rachelle Phyllis Miller, Nov. 20, 1977; children: David Adam, Michael Matthew, Anne Elizabeth. BA, Fordham U., 1971; MA, NYU, 1973; MS, Columbia U., 1976. Asst. reference libr. N.Y. Hist. Soc., N.Y.C., 1973-77; libr. Bklyn. Pub. Libr., 1977-78; reference libr., asst. prof. John Jay Coll. Criminal Justice CUNY, 1978-81; libr. Inst. Jud. Adminstrn. Sch. of Law NYU, 1981-82; sr. law libr. ct. libr. N.Y. State Supreme Ct., S.I., 1982—. Editor: jour. The Literature of Criminal Justice, 1980-81, IJA Report, 1981-82. Mem. ALA, Am. Assn. Law Librs., Law Libr. Assn. Greater N.Y., Libr. Assn. CUNY (mem. exec. coun. 1978-81). Office: NY State Supreme Ct Libr Richmond County Courthouse Staten Island NY 10301 Office Phone: 718-390-5291.

KLINGLER, GWENDOLYN WALBOLT, state representative; b. Toledo, May 28, 1944; d. L. Byron and Elizabeth (Brown) Walbolt; m. Walter Gerald Klingler, June 11, 1966; children: Kelly Michelle, Lance, Jeffrey. BA, Ohio Wesleyan U., 1966; MA, U. Mich., 1969; JD, George Washington U., 1981. Bar: Ill. Rsch. assoc. U. Mich., Ann Arbor, 1966-71; abstractor Year Book Med. Pub., Chgo., 1972-75; law clk. FDA, Rockville, Md., 1980; atty. Atty. Gen.'s Office State of Ill., Springfield, 1981-84, appellate prosecutor, 1984-92; ptnr. Boyle, Klingler & McClain, Springfield, 1992-95. Mem. Springfield Bd. of Edn., 1987-91, pres., 1988; alderman Springfield City Coun., 1991-95; Rep. Ill. Ho. of Reps., 100th Dist., 1995-2003. Recipient Woman of Achievement award in Govt., Women-in-Mgmt., 1994, Disting. Alumni award Leadership Springfield, 1996. Mem. AAUW, Cen. Ill. Women's Bar Assn. (chair membership com.), Sangamon County Bar Assn., Greater Springfield C. of C., Women-in-Mgmt. Republican. Presbyterian (elder). Home: 1600 Ruth Pl Springfield IL 62704-3362 E-mail: klingler@housegopmail.state.il.us.

KLINGLER, STACY LYNN, museum director; b. Tulsa, Feb. 29, 1976; d. Carole and Robert Klingler; m. Richard Anthony Lynch, Aug. 4, 2002. BA, Gonzaga U., 1998; MA, U. Ill., 2002. Asst. dir. Gen. Lew Wallace Study and Mus., Crawfordsville, Ind., 2003—, Mont. County Hist. Soc., Crawfordsville, Ind., 2003—04; dir. Putnam County Mus., Greencastle, Ind., 2004—. Profl. exhibit co-coord. Crawfordsville Art League, 2004. Dir.: (museum exhbn.) Barns Make the Farm. Psycholinguistics Tng. grant, NSF, 2001. Mem.: Am. Assn. State and Local History, Assn. Ind. Mus. Avocation: dance. Office Phone: 765-653-8419. E-mail: pcmuseum@ccrtc.com.

KLINGMAN, JOHN PHILIP, architect, educator; b. Phila., July 31, 1947; s. John Philip and Ethel Iva (Serfas) K. BSCE, Tufts U., 1969; postgrad., Stanford U., 1969-70; MArch, U. Oreg., 1983. Registered architect, La. Constrn. coord., project mgr. Payette Assocs., Inc., Boston, 1972-81; mem. design team Fairchild Biochemistry Bldg. Harvard U., 1977—78; project architect LaBouisse & Waggonner Inc. Architects, New Orleans, 1986-89; cons. architect Waggonner & Ball, Inc. Architects, New Orleans, 1990-96; design, planning and preservation U.S. Customhouse, New Orleans, 1996—. Asst. prof. Sch. Architecture Tulane U., New Orleans, 1983-90, assoc. prof., 1990-96, prof., 1996—, Faunt prof., 2002—, assoc. dean, 1991-93; chmn. archtl. rev. com. Historic Dists. Landmarks Commn., 1995—. Author: New New Orleans Architecture, New Orleans Mag., annually, 1997-; co-editor: Talk About Architecture: A Century of Architectural Education at Tulane, 1993. Recipient GSA Honor award for customhouse projects, 1996. Avocation: wood sculpture. Home: 1309 Harmony St New Orleans LA 70115-3424 Office: Tulane U Sch Architecture New Orleans LA 70118 Office Phone: 504-314-2339. Business E-Mail: jklingm@tulane.edu.

KLINGSBERG, DAVID, lawyer; b. N.Y.C., Feb. 4, 1934; m. Fran Sue Morganstern, Aug. 16, 1959; 3 children. LL.B., Yale U., 1957; BS, NYU, 1954. Bar: N.Y. 1958. Law clk. to U.S. Dist. Judge, N.Y., 1957-58; atty. U.S. Dept. Justice, Office Dep. Atty. Gen., Washington, 1958-59; asst. U.S. atty. criminal div. So. Dist. N.Y., 1959-61; chief appellate atty. U.S. Atty. Office, NY, 1961-62; assoc. Kaye Scholer LLP, NYC, 1962—65, ptnr., 1966—2004, chmn. exec. com., 1997—2004, spl. counsel, 2005—. Vis. lectr. Rutgers Sch. Law, 2005—. Contbr. articles to legal jours.; mem. editorial bd. Yale Law Jour, 1956-57. Bd. dirs. Legal Aid Soc. NY, 2001—. Recipient Pub. Interest Leadership award, Legal Aid Soc., 2001. Fellow Am. Coll. Trial Lawyers; mem. ABA, Assn. Bar City N.Y. (chmn. anti-trust and trade regulation com. 1986-89, Thurgood Marshall award for representation in death sentence cases 1998), N.Y. State Bar Assn., Fed. Bar Coun. Office: Kaye Scholer LLP 425 Park Ave New York NY 10022-3506 Office Phone: 212-836-8281.

KLINK, FREDRIC J., lawyer; b. N.Y.C., Oct. 4, 1933; s. Frederick Carl and Sophia Adelaide (Wolf) K.; children: Christopher, Charles; stepchildren: Kirsten Morehouse, Trina Morehouse. AB, Columbia U., 1955, LL.B., 1960. Bar: N.Y. 1960. Practiced in, N.Y.C.; ptnr. firm Dechert, Price & Rhoads, 1989—2001, of counsel, 2001—. Editor: Columbia U. Law Rev, 1959-60. Served as lt. (j.g.) USNR, 1955-57. Mem. Am. Law Inst., Am., Internat., N.Y. C. bar assns. Office: Dechert LLP 4675 McArchur Ct Newport Beach CA 92660 Home: 23655 Tampico Bay Dana Point CA 92629 Office Phone: 949-442-6012. Business E-Mail: fredric.klink@dechert.com.

KLINK, ROBERT MICHAEL, consulting engineer, management consultant, financial consultant, property developer; b. Hamilton, Ind., Sept. 5, 1939; s. Robert Eli and Marie Ann Klink; m. Jesse Joyce Plummer, Sept. 10, 1960 (dec. Feb. 1966); children: Kevin Mark, Kent Michael, Kelly Martin, Kris Montgomery, Jeffrey Arthur; m. Mary Louise Mauldin, Oct. 30, 1999. Student, Tri State Coll., Angola, Ind., 1957; degree in Hwy. Engring., Purdue U., 1959; cert. in grad. sch. mgmt., Harvard U., 1976. Cert. behavorial cons. Hwy. engr. Ind. State Hwy. Commn., Ft. Wayne, 1959-65; staff engr. Cities Svc. Oil Co., Inc., South Bend, Ind., 1965-66; client svcs. mgr., asst. to v.p. Clyde E. Williams & Assocs., South Bend, 1966-72; pres. Alpha Devel. Corp., South Bend, 1970-72; sr. v.p., CFO Snell Environ. Group, Inc., Lansing, Mich., 1972-77; pres. Klink Devel. Co., Dayton, Ohio, 1972-91; pres., chmn. Solar GeoThermo Energy Systems, Inc., Dayton, 1982—; pres., mng. ptnr. Klink Enterprises Co., Dayton, 1977—; pres., chmn. bd. Design Enterprise, Ltd., Dayton, 1977-91; chmn., pres. Cons. Info. Agy., Chattanooga, 1991—. Cons. engr. in mech., elec., civil, hwy., environ., sanitary, transp., archtl., planning and surveying engring.; bd. dirs. Pono Kai Resort, Kapaa, Kauai, Hawaii, Imperial Hawaii, Honolulu; cons. World Bank/USAID, Dacca, Bangladesh, Country of Brazil, Rio de Janeiro; cons. engr., mgmt. cons., project developer, cons. to govtl. agys. and Fortune 500 cos.; lectr., spkr. in field. Patentee Solar and Geo Thermo Energy System; co-author: Water Handling Handbook, 1977. Trustee Centerville (Ohio) Cmty. Ch., 1982-88, Okemos (Mich.) Cmty. Ch., 1972-77; mem. The Presdl. Roundtable, Washington, 1989—, Rep. Senatorial Inner Circle, Washington, 1985—, Nat. Rep. Congrl. Com., 1986—, The Presidents Assn.; tchr. Woodland Park Bapt. Ch., Chattanooga; mem. Woodland Park Bapt. Ch. Chattanooga, 1998—; mem. Downtown Kiwanas Club Chattanooga. Recipient Outstanding Citizen award Am. Legion, Butler, Ind., 1953, Resolution of Appreciation Centerville City Coun., 1978, Resolution of Appreciation Greene County, 1989; named Hon. Citizen of Tenn., Nashville, 1989. Mem. Am. Water Works Assn. (life), Nat. Water Pollution Control Fedn., Profl. Svcs. Mgmt. Assn. (com. chair), Soc. for Mktg. Profl. Svcs. (com. chair), Ind. Hoosier Assocs., Ohio Early Birds. Christian and Missionary Alliance. Avocations: gardening, landscaping, woodworking, classic automobiles, golf.

KLINKE, LOUISE HOYT, volunteer; b. Rochester, N.Y., Nov. 16, 1933; d. Martin Breck Hoyt and Evelyn Louise Moone; children: Geoffrey P., David H., Debra L. Tice. AA, Rochester Bus. Inst., 1952. Dir. fin. and pers. Landmark Soc. Western N.Y., Rochester, 1965—85; ret., 1985. Vol. Landmark Soc. Preservation Issues Com., Nathaniel Rochester Soc., Rochester Inst. Tech., Arts and Cultural Coun. Devel. Com., Hillside's Campaign Com.; vol. chmn. Hillside's Bldg. Com.; mem. Meml. Art Gallery, Eastman House, Strong Mus., Nat. Trust for Hist. Preservation, Preservation League N.Y. State, Smithsonian Inst., Met. Mus., Rochester Area Cmty. Found.; treas. Rochester Contemporary; mem. adv. bd. MECA, 2005—; bd. dirs. Art Walk, Race and Reconciliation, Keuka Coll., 1982—, Hillside Children's Ctr., 1982—, treas.; former v.p. Hillside Children's Found.; bd. dirs. Women's Found. Genesee Valley, Rochester Hist. Soc., 1984—, former treas.; bd. dirs. Alzheimer's Assn., former treas.; bd. dirs. Pyramid Arts Ctr., former treas.; bd. dirs. Opera Theatre Rochester, treas.; former bd. dirs. Friends Eastman Opera; bd. dirs. Garth Fagan Dance, 2001—. Mem.: BOA, Geva Theatre Rochester City Ballet, Assn. Fund Raising Profls., Chatterbox Club. Democrat. Episcopalian. Home: 1400 East Ave #203 Rochester NY 14610

KLINKOSUM, MAITRI (MIKE KLINKOSUM), lawyer; b. Winston-Salem, N.C., Mar. 18, 1970; s. Nithi and Elizabeth Hopkins Klinkosum. BA, U. N.C., Chapel Hill, 1992; JD, U. Miami, 1995. Bar: Ill. 1995, U.S. Dist. Ct. (no. dist.) Ill. 1997, N.C. 1998, U.S. Dist. Ct. (we. dist.) N.C. 1998. Asst. pub. defender Kane County Pub. Defender's Office, St. Charles, Ill., 1996, Cook County Pub. Defender's Office, Chgo., 1996—98; assoc. Willardson, Lipscomb & Beal, Wilkesboro, NC, 1998—99, Vannoy, Colvard, Tripelett & Vannoy, North Wilkesboro, NC, 1999—2001; solo practitioner Wilkesboro, 2001—03; asst. capital defender Office of the Capital Defender, Durham, NC, 2002—. Author articles to profl. jours. Mem.: ACLU, ATLA, Fla. Assn. Criminal Def. Lawyers (Student Award for Outstanding Advocacy), N.C. Acad. Trial Lawyers (chairperson criminal def. sect. 2004—05), Nat. Assn. Criminal Def. Lawyers. Democrat. Avocations: racquetball, martial arts. Office: Ste 4001 123 W Main St Durham NC 27701 Office Phone: 919-560-5837. E-mail: mklinkosum@yahoo.com.

KLINMAN, JUDITH POLLOCK, biochemist, educator; b. Phila., Apr. 17, 1941; d. Edward and Sylvia Pollock; m. Norman R. Klinman, July 3, 1963 (div. 1978); children: Andrew, Douglas. BA, U. Pa., 1962, PhD, 1966; PhD (hon.), U. Uppsala, Sweden, 2000. Postdoctoral fellow Weizmann Inst. Sci., Rehovoth, Israel, 1966—67; postdoctoral assoc. Inst. Cancer Rsch., Phila., 1968—70, rsch. assoc., 1970—72, asst. mem., 1972—77, assoc. mem., 1977—78; asst. prof. biophysics U. Pa., Phila., 1974—78; assoc. prof. chemistry U. Calif., Berkeley, 1978—82, prof., 1982—, prof. molecular and cell biology, 1993—, chair chem. dept., 2000—03, Joel Hildebrand chair, 2002—03, Miller prof., 2003—04. Mem. ad hoc biochemistry and phys. biochemistry study sects. NIH, 1977—84, phys. biochemistry study sect., 1984—88. Mem. editl. bd.: Jour. Biol. Chemistry, 1979—84, Biofactors, 1991—98, European Jour. Biochemistry, 1991—95, Biochemistry, 1993—, Ann. Rev. Biochemistry, 1996—2000, Accts. Chem. Res., 1995—98, Current Opinion in Chemical Biology, 1997—, Chemical Record, 2000—, Advances in Physical Organic Chemistry, 2003—; contbr. articles to profl. jours. Fellow, NSF, 1964, NIH, 1964—66, Guggenheim, 1988—89. Mem.: NAS, Am. Philos. Soc., Am. Soc. Biochemistry and Molecular Biology (membership com. 1984—86, pub. affairs com. 1987—94, program com. 1995, pres.-elect 1997, pres. 1998, past pres. 1999), Am. Acad. Arts and Scis., Am. Chmn. Soc. (exec. coun. biol. divsn. 1982—85, chmn. nominating com. 1987—88, program chair 1991—92, Repligen award 1994), Sigma Xi. Office: U Calif Dept Chemistry Berkeley CA 94720-0001 Office Phone: 510-642-2668.

KLIPPEL, CHARLES H, lawyer, insurance company executive; With Aetna Inc. Law Dept., 1981—, with internat. law group, 1988; chief counsel global investment mgmt. network Aetna Inc., gen. counsel internat. divsn., 1996—2000, v.p., dep. gen. counsel, 2000—. Adj. prof. of health law U. Conn. Sch. of Law; mem. leadership coun. Harvard Sch. of Pub. Health; pres. Harvard-Radcliff Club of No. Conn. Office: Aetna Inc 151 Farmington Ave Hartford CT 06156

KLIPPEL, JOHN H., physician, healthcare association executive; Bachelor degree, Bowling Green State U.; MD, U. Cin. Coll. Medicine. Bd. cert. in rheumatology. Resident in internal medicine Yale-New Haven Hosp.; fellow in rheumatology Nat. Inst. Health, U. Calif., San Diego; clinical dir. Nat. Inst. Arthritis and Musculoskeletal and Skin Diseases (component of Nat. Inst. Health, NIH); med. dir. Arthritis Found., 1999—2003, pres., CEO, 2003—. Author numerous sci. and clinical publ. Recipient Burroughs-Wellcome Vis. Prof. award, Royal Soc. Medicine, London. Fellow: ACP, Am. Coll. Rheumatology; mem.: Am. Bd. Internal Medicine (diplomat). Office: Arthritis Found PO Box 7669 Atlanta GA 30357-0669 Office Phone: 404-965-7671. E-mail: jklippel@arthritis.org.

KLIPPER, MITCHELL S., book publishing executive; b. 1957; BS, U. Buffalo, 1979. Audit mgr. KMG Main Hurdman, N.Y.C., 1979-86; v.p., contr. Barnes & Noble Bookstores, Inc., N.Y.C., 1986-88, exec. v.p., CFO, 1988—. Office: Barnes & Noble Inc 122 5th Ave Fl 2 New York NY 10011-5693

KLIPPERT, RICHARD HOBDELL, JR., engineering executive; b. Oakland, Calif., Jan. 25, 1940; s. Richard Hobdell and Carol Ione K.; m. Penelope Ann Barker, Sept. 5, 1979; children: David, Deborah, Candice, Kristina. BS in Bus., Oreg. State U., 1962; postgrad. in Polit. Sci., U. Calif., Berkeley, 1968—69; postgrad. in Mgmt., George Washington U., 1972—73; grad., Naval War Coll., 1973. Cert. Program Mgr. IBM, 1993, Program Mgr. III SAIC, 2002, Answer Group Mgr. SAIC, 2003. Commd. ensign USN, 1962, advanced through grades to comdr., ret., 1982, expert Antisubmarine Warfare; mem. Combat Search and Rescue Southeast Asia, 1964—67; exec. officer H.S. Squadron, 1974; mem. Flag Staff, 1974—79; chief engr. Light Airborne Multipurpose Sys. MK-III IBM, Washington, 1979—82, mgr. HH-60 sys. engring., 1984—85, mgr. V-22 engring., 1985—88, program mgr. Document Mgmt. Sys. Integration, 1988—, dir. publ. solutions, 1990—; program mgr. USDA SCOAP/ASCS Programs, 1992, SAIC, Sacramento, 1997—, divsn. mgr., dir. instrnl. tech., mgr. divsn. Capture mgr. WARSIM Program, 1994; loaned exec. Boulder County United Way, 1993; dir. USDA FSA programs Unisys Fed. Sys., 1995-97; acct. exec. FDA. Author: The Moon Book, 1971; contbr. articles to profl. jours. Loaned exec. Boulder County United Way, 1993. Decorated Silver Star USN. Mem. Soc. Naval Engrs., Assn. Image and Info. Mgmt., Soc. Automotive Engrs., Project Mgmt. Inst., Naval Inst., Sigma Chi. Republican. Congregationalist. Avocations: golf, tennis, photography, bridge. E-mail: rklippert@earthlink.net.

KLIR, GEORGE JIRI, systems science educator; b. Prague, Czechoslovakia, Apr. 22, 1932; arrived in U.S., 1966, naturalized, 1972; s. Jan and Emilie (Přitasilová) K.; m. Milena Řeholová, Jan. 26, 1962; children: Jane, John. MSEE, Czech Tech. U., Prague, 1957; PhD, Czechoslovak Acad. Scis., Prague, 1964; D (hon.), Prague U. Econs., 1994, Tech. U. in Brno, 1997, Czech Tech. U., 1998, U. Ostrava, 2003, U. Western Bohemia, 2004. Rsch. fellow Inst. Computer Research, Prague, 1960-64; lectr. U. Baghdad, Iraq, 1964-66, UCLA, 1966-68; assoc. prof. Fairleigh Dickinson U., 1968-69, Sch. Advanced Tech., SUNY, Binghamton, 1969-72, prof. systems sci., 1972—, disting. prof. T.J. Watson Sch., 1984—, chmn. dept. systems sci., 1977-94. Dir. Internat. Conf. Applied Gen. Systems Rsch., 1977, Ctr. for Intelligent Systems, T.J. Watson Sch., 1995-2000. Author: Cybernetic Modelling, 1967, An Approach to General Systems Theory, 1969, Methodology of Switching Circuits, 1972, Architecture of Systems Problem Solving, 1985, 2d edit., 2003, Fuzzy Sets, Uncertainty, and Information, 1988, Facets of Systems Science, 1991, 2d edit., 2001, Fuzzy Measure Theory, 1992, Fuzzy Sets and Fuzzy Logic, 1995, Uncertainty-Based Information, 1998, 2d edit, 1999, Fuzzy Sets, 2000, Uncertainty and Information, 2005; author, co-author or editor other books; editor-in-chief: Book Series on Basic and Applied General Systems Research, 1978-82, Book Series on Frontiers in System Science: Implications for the Social Sciences, 1978-84, International Jour. Gen. Systems, 1974—, IFSR Book Series on Systems Science and Engineering, 1984—; mem. editl. bds. other profl. jours.; contbr. numerous articles to profl. jours Recipient award for outstanding contbns., Austrian Soc. Cybernetics, 1976, award, Netherland Soc. Sys. Rsch., 1976, Bernard Bolzano gold medal in math. scis., Czech Acad. Scis., 1994, Lotfi A. Zadeh Best Paper award, 1994, award for highest achievement in scholarship, Simon Bolivar U. in Caracas, 1997, Arnold Kaufmann's Gold Medal prize for excellence in uncertainty rsch., 2000, CASYS award for outstanding work on anticipatory and intelligent sys., 2001, Chancellor's award excellence in scholarship, creative activities., SUNY, 2005; fellow rsch., IBM, 1969, Netherlands Inst. Advanced Studies, 1975—76, 1982—83, Japan Soc. for Promotion of Sci., 1980. Fellow: IEEE (life), Internat. Fuzzy Systems Assn. (pres. 1993—95, Outstanding Achievement award 2005); mem.: N.Am. Fuzzy Info. Processing Soc. (pres. 1988—91), Internat. Fedn. Sys. Rsch. (pres. 1980—84), Internat. Soc. Sys. Scis. (mng. dir., v.p. 1978—80, pres. 1980—81, Disting. Leadership award 1994, 1994), AAAS. Home: 401 Manchester Rd Vestal NY 13850-3606 Office: SUNY/Dept Sys Sci/Indsl Eng Thomas J Watson Sch Engring and Applied Sci Binghamton NY 13902-6000 Business E-Mail: gklir@binghamton.edu. *The main force behind my intellectual development has been my passion for discovery and integration in science and technology. The most precious values in professional life are for me scientific honesty and tolerance.*

KLISZUS, EDWARD A., JR., school system administrator; b. Elizabeth, NJ, Aug. 8, 1953; s. Edward Anthony and Irene Kliszus; m. Lisa L Ippolito, Feb. 14, 2004; children: Erika Anne, Jeffrey Edward. MusB, Nyack Coll., 1971—75; MusM, Manhattan Sch. of Music, 1975—76; PhD, NY U., 1993—2000. Teacher of Music NJ., 1976, NY, 1976, Principal/Supervisor NJ, 1992. Tchr. of music Twp. of Union Pub. Schools, Union, NJ, 1977—86, dir. of music, 1986—2000, dir. of k-8 gifted & talented and computer edn., 1990—94, elem. sch. prin., 1994—2003; supt. of schools Belleville Twp. Bd. of Edn., Belleville, 2004—. Adj. prof. of music Kean U., Union, NJ, 2000—03; dir. and ceo Union Music Sch., NJ, 1986—2000; condr. & music dir. Union Symphony Orch., NJ, 1986—2000; adj. prof. of music Bergen C.C., Paramus, NJ, 1999—2000; coord. union h.s. alternative h.s. Twp. of Union Pub. Schools, Union, NJ, 1992; supt. of schools Denville Twp. Bd. of Edn., Denville, NJ, 2003—04. Author: (educational horizons) Politics and Educational Policy: A School Survival Kit; composer: Fanfare for Chamber Ensemble, 1993, Eclipse, 1994, Light & Shadows, 1996, Ballade for Alto Saxophone & Piano, 1996, Scherzo & prestissimo, 1997, Synapse for C Flute and Piano, 1997, Three Short Pieces for Doublebass & Piano, 1998, Flying. Pres. NJ. Music Administrators Assn., 1994—96. Mem.: Am. Assn. Composers, Authors and Pubs., Pi Lambda Theta (assoc.), Phi Delta Kappa (assoc.). Office Phone: 973-450-3500.

KLITENIC, JASON, lawyer; BA, Johns Hopkins U., 1989; JD, Balt. Sch. Law, 1993. Ptnr. Alston & Bird LLP, Atlanta; dep. assoc. atty gen. US Dept. Justice, Washington, 2002—03; dep. gen. counsel US Dept. Homeland Security, Washington, 2003—. Mem. strategic mgmt. task force Dept. Justice, 2002—03, mem. trade policy rev. group, 2002—03. Mem.: ABA. Office: US Dept Homeland Security 3801 Nebraska Ave NW Washington DC 20528*

KLITZKE, THEODORE ELMER, arts consultant, retired college dean; b. Chgo., Nov. 4, 1915; s. John Frederick and Edith (Bachmann) K.; m. Margaret Bridget Gaughan, Feb. 23, 1946; children: Annetta, Margaret. B.F.A., Chgo. Art Inst., 1940; BA, U. Chgo., 1941, PhD, 1953; D.F.A. (hon.), Kansas City Art Inst., 1980, Md. Inst., Coll. Art, 1982. Instr. art history U. Chgo., 1946-47; edn. adviser U.S. Armed Forces in Germany, Nurnberg, 1948-51; asst. prof. art history N.Y. State Coll. Ceramics, SUNY, Alfred, 1953-59; prof. art history, chmn. dept. U. Ala., 1959-68; v.p. acad. affairs, dean Md. Inst., Coll. Art, 1968-82, pres., 1977-78, Balt. News Network, 1989-97; mem. accessions com. Balt. Mus. Art, 1979-82. Juried art exhbn. Art Inst. of Chgo. & Univ. Chgo., 1938—41. Author: Melville Price Retrospective, 1970; contbg. author: Festschrift Ulrich Middeldorf, 1968, Lothar Strauch: 1907-91, Plastik und Graphik, 1993; contbr. articles to profl. jours. and ency. Bd. dirs. Ala. chpt. ACLU, 1965-68; bd. dirs. S.W. Ala. Self-Help Housing, 1966-68. Served with AUS, 1942-46. Recipient First Annual Peace and Freedom award Democratic Student Orgn., U. Ala., 1968, first prize design competition for altar symbols, Rockefeller Meml. Chapel, Univ. Chgo., 1941; citation Civil Liberties Union Ala. Mem. AAUP, Southeastern Coll. Art Conf. (pres. 1961-62), Coll. Art Assn., Nat. Assn. Schs. Art (dir. 1971-74, mem. commn. on accreditation 1975-78, treas. 1980-82, fellow 1981), Print and Drawing Soc. of Balt. Mus. Art (pres. 1974-76), Union Ind. Colls. Art (chmn. planning com. 1977-80), Am. Studies Assn., Coll. Art Assn. Am., Johns Hopkins Club (Balt.). Home: 7918 Sherwood Ave Baltimore MD 21204-3600 Office Phone: 410-828-0735. E-mail: tklitzke@bcpl.net.

KLITZMAN, BRUCE, physiologist, plastic surgery educator, researcher; b. Dayton, Ohio, Nov. 4, 1951; m. Hardee Burt Brown; children: Rachel Hardee, Page Hardee. BS in Biomed. Engring. cum laude, Duke U., 1974; PhD, U. Va., 1979. Rsch. assoc. physiology U. Ariz. Coll. Medicine, Tucson, 1979-81; asst. prof. physiology, biophysics La. State U. Sch. Medicine, Shreveport, 1981-85; assoc. prof., 1985; sr. dir. Kenan plastic surgery rsch. labs., asst. rsch. prof. surgery and biomed. engring., assoc. prof. cell biology and biochem. engring. Duke U. Med. Ctr., Durham, NC, 1985—. Adj. prof. biomed. engring. La. Tech. U., Ruston, 1982-86; session chmn. Third, Fourth and Fifth World Congresses for Microcirculation, 1984, 87, 91; speaker, lectr. various symposia and seminars. Contbr. articles to profl. jours., chpts. to books; assoc. editor Jour. Reconstructive Microsurgery; editl. bd. Cell Transplantation, Am. Jour. Physiology, Jour. Reconstructive Microsurgery,

Microvascular Rsch., Microcirculation. Recipient Instl. Nat. Rsch. Svc. award NIH, 1974-81, Machiko-Kuno Med. Student Rsch. award, U. N.C. at Chapel Hill, 1992, first prize investigator category, Plastic Surgery Ednl. Found., 1988; fellow U. Va., 1979, NATO, 1980; grantee Am. Heart Assn., 1982-85, NIH, 1985—. Mem. Am. Physiol. Soc., Am. Heart Assn. (circulation coun. 1984, grantee 1982-85, rsch. com. La. chpt. 1985), Am. Soc. Reconstructive Microsurgery (chmn. sci. session), Microcirculatory Soc. (sec. 1993-97, program com. 1983-84, mem. com. 1984-87, pres. 1998-99), Soc. Biomaterials, Plastic Surgery Rsch. Coun. (sci. adv. bd. 1998), European Soc. Microcirculation (travel award 1980), Internat. Soc. Oxygen Transport to Tissue, Controlled Release Soc. Home: 3015 Wade Rd Durham NC 27705-5630 Office: Duke U Med Ctr Plastic Surgery Rsch Lab PO Box 3906 Durham NC 27710-0001 E-mail: Klitz@duke.edu.*

KLOB, HANS RUDOLPH, economist, consultant; b. Windischgarsten, Austria, Nov. 11, 1945; s. Olav M. and Maria A. Klob; m. Adelheid Klob, June 2, 1971; children: Verena-Maria, Bernhard O.R. BS in Applied Econs., U. San Francisco, 1986; PhD, U. Vienna, Austria, 1970. Rsch. asst. Dept. Minerology Vienna Nat. Hist. Mus., 1970—71; expert minerologist German Tech. Asst. to Turkey, Ankara, 1971—72; govt. advisor, project dir. Austrian Tech. Asst. to Rwanda, Kigali, 1973—77; sr. exploration geologist OMV-AG, Vienna, 1978—81; sr. geologist, mgr. devel. Sohio Petroleum Corp., San Francisco, 1981—84; prin. cons., geologist HRK Internat. Geological Cons. Svcs., San Francisco, 1984—; gen. mgr., pres. Argosy Mining Ltd., Vienna, 1995—; gen. mgr., ptnr. M2TL Multimedia Telecomm. Cons., San Francisco, 2003—; sr. v.p., exploration Empire Gold Corp., Vancouver, Canada, 1997—2002. Author: (novels) Lost in the Yellow Room, 2000. Fellow, U. Edinburgh, 1970—71. Avocations: music, painting, writing, skiing. Office Phone: 415-681-7753. Personal E-mail: hrkinter@aol.com.

KLOBASA, JOHN ANTHONY, lawyer; b. St. Louis, Feb. 15, 1951; s. Alan R. and Virginia (Yager) Klobasa. BA in Econs., Emory U., 1972; JD, Wash. U., 1975. Bar: Mo. 1975, U.S. Dist. Ct. (ea. dist.) Mo. 1975, U.S. Ct. Appeals (8th cir.) 1976, U.S. Supreme Ct. 1979, U.S. Tax Ct. 1981, U.S. Ct. Appeals (9th cir.) 1990, U.S. Ct. Appeals (10th cir.) 1993. Assoc. Kohn, Shands, Elbert, Gianoulakis & Giljum LLP, St. Louis, 1975—80, ptnr., 1981—. Spl. counsel City of Town and Country, Mo., 1987; spl. counsel City of Des Peres, Mo., 1987, alderman, 1989-91. Mem.: ABA, Met. St. Louis Bar Assn., Mo. Bar Assn., Order of Coif, Phi Beta Kappa. Republican. Office: Kohn Shands Elbert Gianoulakis & Giljum LLP One US Bank Plz Ste 2410 Saint Louis MO 63101-1643 Office Phone: 314-241-3963. Business E-Mail: jklobasa@ksegg.com.

KLOBE, TOM, art gallery director; b. Mpls., Nov. 26, 1940; s. Charles S. and Lorna (Effertz) K.; m. Delmarie Pauline Motta, June 21, 1975. BFA, U. Hawaii, 1964, MFA, 1968; postgrad., UCLA, 1972-73. Vol. peace corps, Alang, Iran, 1964-66; tchr. Calif. State U., Fullerton, 1969-72, Santa Ana (Calif.) Coll., 1972-77, Orange Coast Coll., Costa Mesa, Calif., 1974-77, Golden West Coll., Huntington Beach, Calif., 1976-77; art gallery dir. U. Hawaii, Honolulu, 1977—. Acting dir. Downey (Calif.) Mus. Art, 1976; exhibit design cons. Honolulu Acad. Arts, 1998—, Mission Houses Mus., 2003-04, Hawaii State Art Mus., 2002; exhibit designer John Young Mus., U. Hawaii, 1998; cons. Judiciary History Mus., Honolulu, 1982-96, Maui (Hawaii) Arts and Cultural Ctr., 1984-94, curator Keia Wai Ola: This Living Water, 1994; exhbn. coord. Schaefer Portrait Challenge, 2003; exhibit designer Inst. for Astronomy, Honolulu, 1983-86; exhibit design cons. Japanese Cultural Ctr. Hawaii, 1993—; juror Print Casebooks; project coord. Crossings '97: France/Hawaii, Crossings 2003: Korea/Hawaii. Recipient Best in Exhbn. Design award Print Casebooks, 1984, 86, 88, Vol. Svc. award City of Downey, 1977, Chevalier l'Ordre des Arts et des Letters, France, 2000, Robert W. Clopton award for Disting. Cmty. Svc., 2003; named Living Treasure of Hawaii, Honpa Hongwanji: Mission of Hawaii, 2005; grantee NEA, 1979-93, State Found. Culture and the Arts, 1977—. Mem. Hawaii Mus. Assn. Roman Catholic. Office: U Hawaii Art Gallery 2535 The Mall Honolulu HI 96822-2233 Office Phone: 808-956-6888. Business E-Mail: gallery@hawaii.edu. *Personal philosophy: Nothing is impossible. Believe in yourself and in each other. Each of us has the ability to shape our destiny.*

KLOCK, JOHN HENRY, lawyer; b. Gouverneur, NY, Mar. 29, 1944; s. John F. and Patricia M. (Chateau) K.; m. Connie E. McLaughlin, May 31, 1969; children: Thomas, Jacqueline. BA, St. Bonaventure U., 1966; postgrad., U. Va., 1967; MA, NYU, 1970; JD, Rutgers U., 1976. Bar: N.J. 1976, U.S. Dist. Ct. N.J. 1976, N.Y. 1977, U.S. Ct. Appeals (3d cir.) 1979, U.S. Dist. Ct. (ea. dist.) N.Y. 1981, U.S. Supreme Ct. 1981, U.S. Dist. Ct. (so. dist.) N.Y. 1982, U.S. Dist. Ct. (no. dist.) N.Y. 1988, U.S. Dist. Ct. (we. dist.) N.Y. 2002; cert. civil trial atty. N.J. Law clk. to judge U.S. Dist. Ct. N.J., Newark, 1976-77; assoc. Gibbons, Del Deo, Dolan, Griffinger & Vecchione, Newark, 1977-83, ptnr., 1983—. Author: New Jersey Practice Court Rules (5th edit.), vol. 1, 1A, 2, 2A, 2000, New Jersey Practice Evidence Rules, 4th edit., 2002, New Jersey Practice Trial Lawyers Manual, vol. 2E, 2005; contbr. articles to profl. jours. Active Scotch Plains Hist. Commn. Named Super Lawyer constrn. law, NJ Mag., 2005. Mem. ABA, N.J. Bar Assn., N.Y. Bar Assn., U.S. Supreme Ct. Hist. Soc., N.J. Hist. Soc., Plainfield Country Club. Roman Catholic. Achievements include patents for quick release automatic chauk gun. Avocations: golf, gardening. Home: 1800 Lake Ave Scotch Plains NJ 07076-2920 Office Phone: 973-596-4757. E-mail: jklock@gibbonslaw.com.

KLOCK, JOSEPH PETER, JR., lawyer; b. Phila., Mar. 14, 1949; s. Joseph Peter and Mary Dorothy (Fornace) K.; m. Susan Marie Girsch, Mar. 17, 1979; children: Susan Elizabeth, Kathleen Marie, Robert Charles, Peter Joseph II. BA in Philosophy with honors, LaSalle Coll., 1970; JD cum laude, U. Miami, Fla., 1973; DHL (hon.), LaSalle U., 1999. Bar: Fla. 1973, Pa. 1973, D.C. 1978. Ptnr. Steel, Hector & Davis LLP, Miami, Fla., 1977-79, adminstrv. ptnr., 1978-82, chmn., mng. ptnr., 1982—2004, chmn., 2004—05; gen. counsel, chief legal officer Flo-Sun, Inc., 1991—. Adj. prof. U. Miami Law Sch., 1974-84; bd. dirs. Nat. Beverage Corp., Premier Hotel Corp., Fla. Partnership for the Americas, FTAA Adminstrv. Secretariat, Inc., St. Thomas Human Rights Inst.; chmn. bd. dirs. Baypoint Sch., Inc.; mem. Fed. Jud. Nominating Com. of Fla., 1993-97. Trustee Belen Jesuit Prep. Sch., St. Joseph's Preparatory Sch., 1998-2004, Barry U., Collins Ctr., Miami Art Mus., Fundacion Mir, New Hope Charities, Inc.; chmn. bd., trustee Carrollton Sch., 1982-98. Fellow Am. Bar Found.; mem. ABA (chmn. Caribbean law com. internat. law sect. 1991-92), Fla. Bar (chmn. civil procedure rules com. 1979-82), D.C. Bar, Dade County Bar Assn., Assn. Bar City of N.Y., Am. Law Inst., Am. Assn. Sovereign Mil. Order Malta, Iron Arrow Honor Soc., Westview Country Club, Sailfish Club Palm Beach, Govs. Club West Palm Beach, Miami City Club (pres. 1994-97), Phi Alpha Delta, Phi Kappa Phi, Omicron Delta Kappa. Democrat. Roman Catholic. Home: 5095 SW 82nd St Miami FL 33143-8503 Office: 200 S Biscayne Blvd Fl 41 Miami FL 33131-2398 also: Ste 200 One North Clematis St West Palm Beach FL 33401 Office Phone: 305-577-2877. Business E-Mail: jpk@steelhector.com.

KLOCK, MARK STEVEN, finance educator; b. Plattsburg, N.Y., Sept. 2, 1958; s. Benny LeeRoy and Margaret Ann (Sherman) K.; m. Pamela Anne Megna, July 10, 1982; children: Nathan Vincent, Ethan Brian, Justin James, Leanne Linda. BA, Pa. State U., 1978; JD, U. Md., 1988; PhD, Boston Coll., 1983. Bar: Md. 1988, D.C. 1989. Rsch. assoc. Nat. Bur. Econ. Rsch., Cambridge, Mass., 1980-81, John Hancock, Boston, 1982-83, MCR, Inc., Falls Church, Va., 1983-84; asst. prof. Univ. of Balt., 1984-87; prof. George Washington U., Washington, 1987—. Mng. editor Md. Jour. of Internat. Law and Trade, Balt., 1987-88; editorial rev. bd. Midwest Jour. of Econs. and Bus., Mankato, Minn., 1991; cons. in field. Contbr. articles to profl. jours. Recipient Am. Jurisprudence prize U. Md. Law Sch., Balt., 1986, 87, Bernstein prize, 1988. Mem. Am. Econ. Assn., Am. Fin. Assn., Fin. Mgmt. Assn., Md. State Bar Assn. (free legal advisor, Silver Spring, Md., 1989), D.C. Bar Assn., Ea. Fin. Assn. Avocations: scuba diving, tropical fish, spelunking. Office: George Washington U 2023 G St NW # 101 Washington DC 20006-4205 Office Phone: 202-994-8342.

KLODOWSKI, HARRY FRANCIS, JR., lawyer; b. Pitts., June 18, 1954; s. Harry F. and Nancy (Coll) K.; m. Amy Martha Auslander, Nov. 12, 1983; children: Deborah, Daniel. BA, SUNY, Buffalo, 1976, JD, 1979. Bar: Pa. 1979, U.S. Dist. Ct. (we. dist.) Pa. 1979, U.S. Tax Ct. 1979, U.S. Ct. Appeals (3d cir.) 1979. Assoc., then ptnr. Berkman, Ruslander, Pohl, Lieber & Engel, Pitts., 1979-88; prin. Doepken, Keevican & Weiss, P.C., Pitts., 1988-93, Picadio McCall Kane & Norton, Pitts., 1993-94; pvt. practice, Pitts., 1994—. Assoc. editor Pitts. Legal Jour., 1979—; contbr. articles to profl. jours. Mem. ABA, Pa. Bar Assn., Allegheny County Bar Assn. (chmn. environ. law sect. 1997), Environ. Law Inst. (assoc.), Air and Waste Mgmt. Assn. (chmn. pub. info. com. 1996—), Rivers Club. Avocations: skiing, racquetball. Home: 615 Sandy Hill Rd Valencia PA 16059-2731 Office: 6400 Brooktree Ct Ste 250 Wexford PA 15090 E-mail: harry@klodowskilaw.com.

KLOEPFER, MARGUERITE FONNESBECK, writer; b. Logan, Utah, Nov. 13, 1916; d. Leon and Jean (Brown) Fonnesbeck; m. Lynn William Kloepfer, Aug. 6, 1937; children: William Leon, Kenneth Lynn, Kathryn Kloepfer Ellis, Robert Alan. BS, Utah State U., 1937. Legal sec. Lynn W. Kloepfer, Atty., Ontario, Calif., 1958-74; freelance writer, novelist Ontario, Calif., 1974—. Author: (novels) Bentley, 1979, Singles Survival, 1979, But Where is Love, 1980, The Heart and the Scarab, 1981, Schatten in der Wuste, 1983, In A Pickle, 2003, Hope's Beat, 2003; contbr. short stories, articles. Pres. Foothill chpt. Nat. Charity League Inc., Ontario, 1965-67, nat. pres., 1968-70; pres. Interfraternity Mother's Clubs council U. So. Calif., Los Angeles, 1971-72. Clubs: Friday Afternoon (West San Bernardino County) (pres. 1986-87). Home: 306 E Hawthorne St Ontario CA 91764-1749

KLOEPPER, DAVID ALAN, retired management consultant; b. Colby, Kans., Dec. 8, 1945; s. Robert Mayer and Justine (Peterson) Kloepper; m. Evelyn Maria Gritzbach, June 27, 1969. BS in Metallurgy, MIT. Process devel. engr. Grumman Aerospace, Bethpage, N.Y., 1968-72; mgr. svc. engring. Hilti, Inc., Stamford, Conn., 1972-79; nat. sales mgr. F & S Cen. Mfg., Bklyn., 1979-82; v.p. ops. and adminstrn. Imperial Bolt & Mfg. Co., South Plainfield, N.J., 1982-85; nat. sales mgr. Indsl. Bolt & Nut, Irvington, N.J., 1985-86, T.A. & D.A. Troy, Fairfield, N.J., 1986-87; project mgr. Don Aux Assocs., Hasbrouck Heights, NJ, 1987—2001, practice leader, 1992—2001; ret., 2001. Pres. Van Vorst Pk. Neighborhood Assn., Jersey City, 1981—82; v.p., bd. dirs. Los Alamos (N.Mex) Concert Assn., 2002—; bd. dirs. Citizen Support Civic Ctr., Inc., 2003—05; commr. Los Alamos Planning and Zoning Commn., 2002—03; mem. adv. com. Los Alamos Comprehensive Plan, 2002—03. Republican. Avocations: movies, classical music. Home: 570 Rim Rd Los Alamos NM 87544 E-mail: d.kloepper@losalamos.com.

KLOER, PHILIP BALDWIN, popular culture critic; b. Honolulu, Sept. 13, 1955; s. Baldwin Ernest and Betty Louise (Burger) K.; m. Heather Ann Windsor, May 14, 1976; 1 child, Amanda Cynthia. BA, Ind. U., 1976. Writer Stillwater (Okla.) News-Press, 1976-78; film critic, columnist Fla. Times-Union, Jacksonville, 1978-85; arts editor Atlanta Constitution, 1985-87, TV critic, 1987—. Contbr. TV Guide, 1990. Recipient Olive Br. award Ctr. for War, Peace & Media, NYU, 1991, finalist Green Eyeshade award Sigma Delta Chi, 1986; named TV Critic of Yr., Nat. TV Movie Festival, 1990, Critic of Yr., Fla. Soc. Newspaper Editors, 1985. Office: Atlanta Constitution 72 Marietta St NW Atlanta GA 30303-2804

KLOESS, LAWRENCE HERMAN, JR., retired lawyer; b. Mamaroneck, NY, Jan. 30, 1927; s. Lawrence H. and Harriette Adelia (Holly) K.; m. Eugenia Ann Underwood, Nov. 10, 1931; children: Lawrence H. III, Price Mentzel, Branch Donelson, David Holly. AB, U. Ala., 1954, JD, 1956; grad., Air Command & Staff Coll., 1974, Air War Coll., 1976; grad. Indsl. Coll. of the Armed Forces, Nat. Def. U., 1977. Bar: Ala. 1956, U.S. dist. Ct. (no. dist.) Ala. 1956, U.S. Ct. Appeals (5th cir.) 1957, U.S. Ct. Mil. Appeals 1971, U.S. Supreme Ct. 1971, U.S. Ct. Appeals (11th cir.) 1981. Sole practice, Birmingham, Ala., 1956-60, 62-66; corp. counsel Bankers Fire and Marine Ins. Co., 1961-62; dist. counsel for Ala. Office Dist. Counsel U.S. Dept. Vets. Affairs, Montgomery, 1966-95. Contbr. articles to profl. jours. Vice chmn. Salvation Army adv. bd., 1981, bd. dirs., 1978-81; nat. conf. bar pres.'s ABA, 1981—; adminstrn. bd. Frazer Meml. United Meth. Ch., 1987-90, 92—; mem. adv. coun. Ret. and Sr. Vol. Program, Montgomery, 1997—; active Montgomery Symphony League, 2000—; bd. dirs., sec. Air Force Judge Adv. Gen. Sch. Found., 1996—. Col. Judge Adv. Gen. USAFR, 1954-86, ret. Decorated Legion of Merit, Meritorious Svc. medal with oak leaf cluster, USAF Commendation medal; named Outstanding Judge Advocate USAFR, 1977, 79. Mem.: ABA (pres. nat. conf. bar 1981—), VFW (life), Wynlakes Residential Homeowners Assn. (bd. dirs), English Speaking Union (bd. dirs. 1997), Ala. Spl. Camp for Children and Adults (bd. dirs. 1999), Svc. Corps of Ret. Execs. Assn. (bd. dirs. 1996—), Farrah Law Soc., Citizens Conf. on Criminal and Juvenile Justice (staff mem. 1974), Citizens Conf. on Ala. Ct. (exec. com., sponsor new jud. article to state constitution 1973), Fed. Bar Assn. (pres. Montgomery chpt. 1973), Montgomery County Bar Assn. (chmn. law day com. 1972, chmn.state bar liason com. 1975, chmn. bd. dirs. 1977, bd. dirs. 1979, chmn. and editor Montgomery County Bar Jour. (ABA Merit award) 1979—80, v.p. 1980, pres. 1981), Ala. Law Found. (trustee), Ala. State Bar Assn. (editl. bd. 1970—82, chmn. law day com. 1973, chmn.citizen edn. com. 1974, chmn. editl. adv. bd. Ala. Lawyer 1975—79, mem. adv. com. CLE 1983, character and fitness com.), Am. Legion, Air Force Assn., Mystic Soc. (krewe of phantom host), Blue-Gray Cols. Assn., Montgomery Country Club, Maxwell-Gunter Officers, Montgomery, Res. Officers Assn. of U.S. (chpt. pres. 1978, state pres. 1982), Ret. Officers Assn. (life), Air War Coll. Alumni Assn. (life), Air Force Ret. Judge Advocate Assn., Capital City Club, The Club, Inc Birmingham, Montgomery Rotary Club (v.p. 1996, pres. 1998), Montgomery Capital Rotary Club (pres. 1979, Paul Harris fellow), Hon. Order Ky. Cols., Theta Chi (Outstanding Alumni award 1976), Sigma Delta Kappa (pres. U. Ala. chpt.). Republican. Home: 7157 Pinecrest Dr Montgomery AL 36117-7413 Personal E-mail: kloess2@aol.com.

KLOHN, EARLE JARDINE, retired engineering company executive, consultant; b. Winnipeg, Man., Can., Aug. 14, 1927; s. August Frank and Florence (McLeod) K.; m. Beryl MacRae, Aug. 8, 1950 (dec. Nov. 19, 1963); children: James Kimberley, Douglas Alan, Barbara Marjorie; m. Lorna Charles, Oct. 2, 1964; 1 child, Michael. BSCE with distinction, U. Alta., Edmonton, Can., 1950, MSCE, 1952. Registered profl. civil engr., Can. Found. engr. O.J. Porter & Co. Ltd., Sacramento, Calif., 1950, R.M. Hardy and Assocs. Ltd., Edmonton, 1951, Klohn Leonoff Ltd., Vancouver, 1952-55, sr. engr., 1955-60, ptnr. Richmond, B.C., Can., 1960, pres., 1970-87, chmn., CEO, 1987-93; pres., CEO Klohn-Crippen Cons. Ltd., Vancouver, B.C., 1988-97, chmn. emeritus, 1997-2000; ret., 2000. Past chmn. Can. Nat. Com. on Large Dams; past mem. com. on tailing dams Internat. Commn. on Large Dams; mem. numerous cons. rev. bds. for earthfill dams; geotech. cons. Revelstoke Dam, Site C Dam, Stikine-Iskut devel. for BC Hydro, numerous others; internat. cons. design and constrn. tailing dams; past chmn. Vancouver Geotech. Group; presenter papers at various seminars, profl. meetings and confs. Contbr. numerous articles to profl. publs. Recipient Alfred A. Raymond award Raymond Internat., 1960, award Vancouver Geotech. Soc., 1998, Legget award Can. Geotech. Soc., 1990, McPartland Meml. medal, 1992, Pub. Paper award Can. Dam Safety Assn., 1995, Meritorious Achievement award Cons. Engrs. of B.C., 2002. Fellow ASCE, Engring. Inst. Can. (past chmn. Vancouver br., Leonard medal 1972), Can. Acad. Engring.; mem. Assn. Cons. Engrs. Can., Can. Inst. Mining and Metallurgy, Assn. Profl. Engrs. B.C. (Meritorious Achievement award 1982), Alaska Soc. Profl. Engrs., Internat. Soc. Soil Mechanics and Found. Engring. Mem. United Ch. Can.

KLOIN, JAY ELLIOT, physician; b. Bklyn., Feb. 27, 1947; s. Leo H. and Beatrice (Baram) K.; div. May 1995; children: Jennifer, Jacquelyn. MD, U. Paris, 1975. Physician Med. Assoc. of Lehigh Valley, Emmaus, Pa., 1978—; internist Dept. Vets. Affairs, Allentown, Pa., 1979—; chief med. officer outpatient clinic, 1999—; staff physician Lehigh Valley Hosp., Allentown, Pa., 1978—, St. Luke's Hosp., 1979—. Asst. clin. prof. medicine Drexel U. Sch. Medicine, Phila., 1980—; clin. asst. prof. medicine Pa. State U., Hershey, 1995—; mem. geriatrics adv. com., dept. medicine divsn. internal medicine and geriatrics, Greater Lehigh Valley Independent Practice Assn.; adj. asst. clin. prof. medicine Temple Univ. Med. Sch., 2005—. Physician Parkland High Sch. Sys. Fellow Am. Coll. Physicians; mem. Am. Soc. Internal Medicine. Office: 431 Chestnut St Emmaus PA 18049-2401

KLONER, ROBERT A., cardiologist, researcher, educator; b. Buffalo, Oct. 8, 1949; s. Philip and Shirley (Miller) K.; m. Judith A. Kloner, July 24, 1977; children: Alissa, Susan. BS, Northwestern U., 1971, PhD, 1974, MD, 1975. Med. house officer Peter Bent Brigham Hosp., Boston, 1975-76, from asst. resident to sr. resident, 1976-78, rsch. clin. fellow in cardiology, 1979; clin. fellow in medicine Harvard Med. Sch., Boston, 1975-78, rsch. fellow in medicine, 1978-79, asst. prof. medicine, 1979-84, assoc. prof. medicine, 1984; prof. medicine Wayne State U., Detroit, 1985-88, U. So. Calif., L.A., 1988—. Dir. rsch. Heart Inst. Hosp. of Good Samaritan, L.A., 1988—. Author: The Beta Virus, 1996, Mind Cure, 1998, Viagra, 1998, The Deity Genes, 2001; editor: The Guide to Cardiology, 1984, 3d edit., 1995, Cardiovascular Trials Review, 1996-2004, Heart Disease and Erectile Dysfunction, 2004; co-editor: Stunned Mycardium, 1993, Ischemic Preconditioning, 1994; assoc. editor Jour. Cardiovascular Pharmacology and Therapeutics, 1995, Internat. Jour. Impotence Rsch., 2004; mem. editl. bd. Circulation, Circulation Rsch., Jour. Am. Coll. Cardiology, Am. Jour. Cardiology, Am. Heart Jour., Heart Disease, Heart, Jour. Molecular and Cellular Cardilogy, Am. Jour. Geriat. Cardiology; contbr. over 660 articles and chpts. to profl. jours., books, monographs. Recipient Sheard-Sanford award ASCP, 1976, Merck award, 1975; named highlycited.com Inst. Sci. Info., 2002, Inaugural fellow Coun. on Basic Cardiovascular Sci. of Am. Heart Assn., 2001. Fellow Am. Coll. Cardiology; mem. Am. Heart Assn. (established investigator award 1981-86), N.Y. Acad. Scis., Am. Fedn. Clin. Rsch., Am. Soc. Clin. Investigators, Alpha Omega Alpha. Office: Good Samaritan Hosp Heart Inst 1225 Wilshire Blvd Los Angeles CA 90017 Business E-Mail: rkloner@goodsam.org.

KLONOFF-COHEN, HILLARY SANDRA, epidemiologist; d. Harry and Mary Klonoff; m. Randy Earl Cohen, Aug. 31, 1981; 1 child, Auroraleigh Camillia. BA in Psychology, U. B.C., Vancouver, 1976; MS in Biology, U. Bridgeport, 1985; PhD in Epidemiology, U. of NC, Chapel Hill, 1987. Cert.Human Nutrition U. of Bridgeport, Conn., 1984. Staff epidemiologist Eisenhower Med. Ctr., Rancho Mirage, Calif., 1988—89; prof. U. of Calif., San Diego, La Jolla, Calif., 1990—. Cons. San Bernardino County Med. Ctr., Calif., 1989—91, Infant Mortality Rev. Program Adv. Com., San Diego, 1994—96; com. mem. Office of Environ. Health Hazard Assessment, Devel. and Reproductive Toxicants Identification (DART) Com., Sacramento, 1999—, Sys. Wide Cancer Rsch. Coord. Com., U. of Calif., Office Pres., Calif., 1994—. Contbr. articles to med. and sci. jours. Recipient Career Devel. award, Calif. Tobacco-Related Disease Program, 1992—94; grantee Calif. Breast Cancer Rsch. Program, 2005—, U. of Calif. Acad. Senate award, 1996, Calif. Tobacco-Related Disease Rsch. Program. Supplemental Minority Tng. grant, 1993-1994, Calif. Tobacco-Related Disease Rsch. Program. New Investigator award, 1990-1992, EPA -Biomarkers for the Assessment of Exposure and Toxicity in Children — STAR award, 2003—, Calif. Tobacco-Related Disease Rsch. Program, 2003-2006, Save Our Children's Sights (SOCS), Mobile Pre-school Eye Care, First Five Commn. of San Diego, 2003—05, Tobacco-Related Disease Rsch. Program, 2004—, Calif. Tobacco-Related Disease Rsch. Project, 1999-2002, Calif. Breast Cancer Rsch. Program. Translational Rsch. Collaboration award, 1999-2003, Calif. Tobacco-Related Disease Rsch. Program, 1998—2003, 1993-1999. Mem.: APHA, Soc. for Reproductive Endocrinology & Infertility, Am. Soc. for Reproductive Medicine, Pub. Health Alumni Assn., U. of NC, Chapel Hill, Assn. for Women in Sci., Cancer Ctr., U. of Calif., San Diego, Soc. of Epidemiologic Rsch., So. Calif. Pub. Health Assn. Office: Univ Calif San Diego Dept Family & Preventive Medicine 9500 Gilman Drive La Jolla CA 92093-0607 Office Phone: 858-534-8654. E-mail: hklonoffcohen@ucsd.edu.

KLOOSTER, JUDSON, retired dean; b. La Combe, Alta., Can., Dec. 24, 1925; s. Henry J. and Evelyn Mae (Eglin) K.; m. Arlene Jean Madsen, Nov. 28, 1948; children: Cherylin Klooster Peach, Lynette Carol Tibbetts, Terrill Ann Klooster McClanahan Hannum. Student, Andrews U., 1942-43, Pacific Union Coll., 1943—44; DDS, U. of the Pacific, 1947; MMS, Tulane U., 1968; D of Pub. Svc. (hon.), U. of the Pacific, 1992. Pvt. practice dentistry, San Francisco, 1947-49, Escondido, Calif., 1949-67; part-time mem. faculty Loma Linda (Calif.) U. Sch. Dentistry, 1956-67, full-time prof. restorative dentistry, 1967—97, dir. continuing edn., 1968-72, dean, 1971-94, dean emeritus, 1994—, emeritus prof. dentistry, 1997—. Mem. faculty U. Pacific Sch. Dentistry, 1947—49; cons. USPHS, VA. Treas. Am. Fund for Dental Health, 1987-89, v.p. 1990-91, pres., 1992-93. Lt. Dental Corps USNR, 1953-55. Fellow Am. Coll. Dentists, Internat. Coll. Dentists (councillor 1993-97, Lifetime Achievement award 2004); mem. ADA, Calif. Dental Assn. (chmn. coun. dental edn. 1972-75), Tri-County Dental Soc. (ex officio dir. 1971-94, pres.-elect 1978-79, pres. 1979-80), Rotary (pres. San Bernardino South club 1977-78), Xi Psi Phi. Republican. Mem. Seventh Day Adventist Ch. (elder 1969—). Home: 25131 Crestview Dr Loma Linda CA 92354-3508

KLOOSTERHUIS, ROBERT JOHN, publishing association company executive; b. Kalamazoo, Aug. 22, 1932; BA, Emmanuel Missionary Coll., Berrien Springs, Mich., 1954; MA, Andrews U., Berrien Springs, 1965; PhD (hon.), Andrews U., 2000. Ordained minister Seventh-day Adventist Ch., 1966; lic. pilot. Pres. Franco-Haitian Sem., Port-au-Prince, Haiti, 1960-61; sec.-treas. Franco-Haitian Union, Port-au-Prince, 1961-64; pastor Ill. Conf., Brookfield, 1965-70, youth ministries stewardship dir., 1970-76; pres. Franco-Haitian Union, Port-au-Prince, 1976-80, African Indian Ocean Divsn., Abidjan, Ivory Coast, 1980-85; gen. v.p. Gen. Conf. Seventh-day Adventists, Silver Spring, Md., 1985-2000; chmn. bd. Pacific Press Pub. Assn., Nampa, Idaho, 1985-2000, Andrews U., Barrien Springs, Mich., 2000—. Office: Gen Conf Seventh Day Adventists 12501 Old Columbia Pl Silver Spring MD 20904

KLOPF, JOHN FRANCIS, JR., management consultant; b. Huntingdon Valley, Pa., Apr. 2, 1963; s. John Francis Sr. and Elizabeth Dorothea (Campion) K.; m. Maria Ignacia Bravo Pariente, Nov. 25, 1989. AB Am. Studies cum laude, Georgetown U., 1984; MA Internat. Studies, MBA Multinat. Mgmt., U. Pa., 1993. Sr. creative cons. The Cutting Corp., Washington, 1984-85; metrodesk copyaide The Washington Post, Washington, 1985-86; program mgr. Georgetown Grads. in Latin Am., Peru, 1986-87; coord. media campaign Refugee Voices, Washington, 1988-91; strategic planning analyst Seagram Latin Am., Coral Gables, Fla., summer 1992; mgmt. cons. Halcyon Inc., Washington, 1993-97; sr. assoc. cons. AT&T Solutions, Washington, 1997-98; cons. IBM Consulting Group, 1998—. Alt. del. Va. Dem. Party, Richmond, 1997. Scholar CSX Corp., Georgetown U., 1982-84, Anheuser-Busch Corp., Georgetown U., 1992-93. Mem. Wharton Club Washington, Arlington Dems. Roman Catholic. Avocations: tennis, basketball, golf, politics. Office: IBM Consulting Group 1301 K St NW Washington DC 20005-3317

KLOPFENSTEIN, MARK WILLIAM, secondary school educator; b. Bellefonte, Pa., Oct. 3, 1962; s. William Elmer and Carol Forbes Klopfenstein; m. Susan Kathleen Shade, June 3, 1989; children: Kathleen Ann, Caleb James. BA in Polit. Sci., Crime & Delinquency Studies, U. Kans., 1983; BS in Edn., Kans. State U., Manhattan, 1988; MA in History, U. Mo., Kansas City, 1997. Tchr.US history Blue Valley HS, Stilwell, Kans., 1989—, tech. integration specialist, 2003—. Vision champion Hillcrest Covenant Ch., Prairie Village, Kans., 2003—05. Recipient Discourse Challenge award, Hewlett-Packard, Ednl. Testing Svc., 2004; grantee, Blue Valley Edn. Found., 2003, Learn.com, 2005. Mem.: Found. for Tchg. Economics (assoc.), Kans. Coun. for the Social Studies (assoc.), Assn. of Am. Educators (assoc.), Smithsonian Instn. (assoc.). Evangelical. Avocations: woodworking, running. Office: Blue Valley High Sch 6001 W 159th St Stilwell KS 66085 Office Phone: 913-239-4964.

KLOPFENSTEIN, REGINALD LEE, music educator; b. Fort Wayne, Ind., Nov. 2, 1957; s. Calvin G. and Marilyn G. Klopfenstein; m. Kay Teresa Grabill, June 23, 1984; children: Matthew Lee, Joshua Ian. MusB, Wheaton Coll. Conservatory, 1980; cert. in Performance, Ind. U., 1981, MusM, 1982, MusD, 1995. Assoc. instr. Ind. U., Bloomington, Ind., 1991—94; assoc. prof. music Bethel Coll., Mishawaka, Ind., 1996—. Assoc. faculty Ind. U., South Bend, Ind., 2003—04; freelance musician, 1982—. Musician: Honolulu (Hawaii) Symphony Orch., 1982—91, Columbus (Ind.) Philharmonic, 1994—96, South Bend (Ind.) Symphony, 1997—; contbr. articles to profl. jours. Mem.: Am. Fedn. Musicians, Percussive Arts Soc. Avocations: basketball, tennis, reading, camping. Office: Bethel College 1001 West McKinley Ave Mishawaka IN 46545

KLOPFENSTEIN, REX CARTER, electrical engineer; b. Pittsfield, Mass., Mar. 3, 1938; s. Glenn A. and Jasmine V. (Carter) Klopfenstein; m. Linda Gilgore, Oct. 6, 1962; children: Mark W., Eric G. BSEE, U. Conn., 1959; MEE, Syracuse (NY) U., 1963. Engr. GE, Syracuse, 1959-63; lab. mgr. Melpar Divsn. E Sys., Falls Church, Va., 1963-70; mgr. hardware engring. Logicon Inc., Fairfax, Va., 1977-78; software and test mgr. Acuity Sys. Inc., Reston, Va., 1978-81; engring. mgr. AMF Electronic Rsch. Lab., Sterling, Va., 1981-82; tech. staff The MITRE Corp., McLean, Va., 1970-77, lead engr., 1982-96, Mitretek Sys., Inc., McLean, 1996—. Sec. tech. com. X3K5 Am. Nat. Stds. Inst., Washington, 1992-94. Co-author: Microcomputer Design and Application, 1977; contbr. articles to profl. jours. Mem. Rep. Nat. Com., chmn. honor roll, 1997. Named Engr. of Yr., DC Coun. Engring. and Archtl. Socs., 2000. Fellow: Washington Acad. Scis. (bd. mgrs. 1996—98, pres.-elect 1998, pres. 1999—2000, v.p. adminstrn. 2004—); mem.: IEEE (sr., life) (No. Va. sect. sec. 1991—92, vice-chmn., treas. 1992—93, chmn. 1993—94, nat. area coun. vice-chmn. 1994—95, chmn. 1995—96, web site mgr. 1997—, editor 1998—99, bd. dirs. 2002—, assoc. editor, Third Millennium medal 2000), Assn. Computing Machinery, Chi Phi, Tau Beta Pi. Avocation: photography. Home: 4224 Worcester Dr Fairfax VA 22032-1140 Office: Mitretek Systems Inc 3150 Fairview Pk Dr S Mc Lean VA 22042-4519 Office Phone: 703-610-1534. Personal E-mail: r.klopfenstein@ieee.org.

KLOPFENSTEIN-FLETCHER, KRISTINE SUE, music educator, librarian, bassoonist; b. Iowa City, Oct. 5, 1951; d. Frederick Joseph Klopfenstein and M. June Collins; m. Richard Wesley Fletcher, May 28, 1972; 1 child, Evan Paul Fletcher. MusB in Music Edn., U. Iowa, 1973, MA in Bassoon Performance, 1975, D of Musical Arts, 1986; M of Libr. and Info. Sci., U. Wisc., 1998. Instr. music U. the Ozarks, Clarksville, Ark., 1976—79; grad. tchg. asst. U. Iowa, Iowa City, 1981—82; sr. lectr. in music U. Wis., Eau Claire, Wis., 1982—; libr. svcs. specialist Luther-Midelfort Med. Libr., Eau Claire, 1999—99. Sr. lectr. Wis. in Scotland, Dalkeith, Midlothian, 1994; music instr. Internat. Music Camp, Manitoba, Canada, 1992—96, Indianhead Arts Camp, Shell Lake, Wis., 1992—94. Contbr. articles to profl. jours.; author: The Paris Conservatoire and The Contest Solos for Bassoon, 1988; musician: (compact disc) Zodiac, Eau Claire Chamber Orchestra Live!, Music by Allan J. Segall, Clearly Three: Music for Clarinet, Bassoon and Piano, Clearly Three: Trios from the Twentieth Century, 2005, Eau Claire Chamber Orch.; musician: (bassoonist) Wis. Woodwind Quintet. Vis. fellow, Tokyo Nat. Fine Arts and Music, 1988. Mem.: Music Libr. Assn., Internat. Double Reed Soc., Beta Phil Mu, Pi Kappa Lambda. Office: Univ Wis Dept Music and Theatre Arts Eau Claire WI 54702 Office Phone: 715-836-4954.

KLOPFLEISCH, STEPHANIE SQUANCE, social services agency administrator; m. Randall Klopfleisch; children: Elizabeth, Jennifer, Matthew. BA, Pomona Coll., 1962; MSW, UCLA, 1966. Social worker Los Angeles County, 1963-67, program dir. day care, vol. svcs., 1968-71; divsn. chief children's svcs. Dept. Pub. Social Svcs., Los Angeles County, 1971-73, dir. bur. social svcs., 1973-79; chief dep. dir. dept. cmty. svcs. Los Angeles County, 1980-96, dir., 1996-2001. With Area 10 Devel. Disabilities, 1981-82; bd. dirs. L.A. Fed. Emergency Mgmt. Act, 1985-91, pres., 1987; bd. dirs. L.A. Shelter Partnership, Pomona Coll. Assocs., 1988—. Mem. Calif. Commn. on Family Planning, 1976-79; chmn. L.A. Commn. on Children's Instns., 1977-78; bd. dirs. United Way Info., 1978-79; chmn. L.A. County Internat. Yr. of Child Commn., 1978-79; bd. govs Sch. Social Welfare, UCLA, 1981-84; bd. dirs. Calif. Soc. Welfare Archives, 1999—, pres.2002—; mem. Brentwood Symphony, 1999—, bd. dirs., 2004; mem. L.A. Valley Symphony, 2004. Mem. NASW, L.A. Philharm. Affiliates, Soroptimist Internat. (bd. dirs. 1989—, pres. L.A. chpt. 1993).

KLOPMAN, GILLES, chemistry professor; b. Brussels, Feb. 24, 1933; came to U.S., 1965; s. Alge and Brana Klopman; m. Malvina Pantiel, Sept. 5, 1957. BA, Athenee d'Ixelles, Belgium, 1952; lic. chemistry, U. Brussels, 1956, D in Chemistry, 1960. Rsch. scientist Cyanamid European Rsch. Inst., Geneva, 1960-67; postdoctoral fellow U. Tex., 1964-65; assoc. prof. Case Western Res. U., Cleve., 1967-69; prof. chemistry Case We. Res. U., Cleve., 1969—, chmn. dept., 1981—86, interim dean sci. and math., 1986—88, C.F. Mabery prof. of rsch., chmn. dept., 1988—2003, C.F. Mabery prof. rsch. emeritus, 2003—. V.p. Biofor, Ltd., PA, 1986-95; pres. Discovery Software Inc., 1991-93, Multicase, Inc., 1995—. Author: All Valence Electrons SCF Calculations, 1970, Chemical Reactivity and Reaction Paths, 1974; contbr. articles to profl. jours. Recipient Kahlbaum prize, Swiss Chem. Soc., 1971; grantee NSF, NIH, EPA, PRF, ONR. Mem. AAUP, Am. Chem. Soc. (Morley medal 1993, Patterson-Crane award, 2005), Brit. Chem. Soc., Belgium Chem. Soc., Sigma Xi. Office: Case Western Res U 10900 Euclid Ave Cleveland OH 44106-1712 E-mail: klopman@po.cwru.edu, klopman@multicase.com.

KLOPOTT, R. BETH, historical consultant, jewelry maker; b. Bklyn., Nov. 18, 1949; d. Kermit and Jacqueline (Lasher) Obstgarten; m Zvi S. Klopott, Aug. 8, 1971; children: Shayna, Freeman. BA, SUNY, Binghamton, 1971; MA, SUNY, Albany, 1975, PhD, 1981. Rsch. assoc. Hanford (N.Y.) Mus., 1990-91, Jewish Mus., N.Y.C., 1988-92; rsch. assoc. and quest curator Albany Inst. of History and Art, 1987—93. Contbr. articles to Hudson Valley Regional Rev. Pres. Congregation Ohev Shalom, Albany, 1994-96. Mem. Orgn. Am. Historians, Am. Assn. State and Local History. Home: 144 Dumbarton Dr Delmar NY 12054-4426

KLOPOTT, ZVI SIMCHA, psychiatrist; b. Petah-Tikva, Israel, Nov. 6, 1948; d. Ludwig Eliezer and Sarah Klopott. BA, SUNY, Binghamton, 1970; MD, Albany Med. Coll., 1974. Diplomate Am. Bd. Psychiatry and Neurology, Am. Bd. Child Psychiatry. Consulting psychiatrist Samaritan Hosp., Troy, N.Y., 1978; attending psychiatrist Capital Dist. Psychiatric Ctr., Albany, N.Y., 1977-78; fellow in child psychiatry Albany Med. Coll., 1978-81; co-med. dir. Unified Svcs. for Children and Adolescents of Rensselaer Co., Troy, 1981-86, med. dir., 1986—; cons. child psychiatrist Project Strive, Albany, 1981-97, Jewish Family Svcs., Albany, 1986-91; pvt. practice Albany, N.Y., 1981—; cons. child psychiatrist QUESTAR III, Schodac, N.Y., 1997—. Assoc. clin. prof. Albany Med. Coll., 1977; cons. child psychiatrist Wildwood Sch., Niskayuna, N.Y., 1986—, Cmty. Maternity Svcs., 1991—; cons. Psych.-Residential Opportunities, Inc., 1992—; lectr. local and nat. confs. on childhood psychopathology, dual diagnosis and emotional disturbance. Named Disting. Tchr. Psychiatry Dept. Albany Med. Coll., 1977. Fellow Am. Psychiatric Assn., Am. Acad. of Child and Adolescent Psychiatry; mem. Capital Dist. Council for Child and Adolescent Psychiatry (pres. 1987-89). Avocations: reading, sailing, cross country skiing. Office: Bldg 5 Pine West Plz Ste 508 Albany NY 12205-5516 Office Phone: 518-452-4232.

KLOS, JEROME JOHN, lawyer, director; b. La Crosse, Wis., Jan. 17, 1927; s. Charles and Edna S. (Wagner) K.; m. Mary M. Hamilton, July 26, 1958; children— Bryant H., Geoffrey W. BS, U. Wis., 1948, JD, 1950. Bar: Wis. 1950. Pres. Klos, Flynn and Papenfuss, La Crosse, 1950—. Bd. dirs. Union State Bank, West Salem, Wis. Mem. LaCrosse County Bd., 1957-74, vice chmn., 1972-74; pub. adminstr. La Crosse County, 1962-73; bd. dirs. West Salem Area Growth, Inc., La Crosse Area Growth, Inc.; trustee Sander and McKinly Scholarship Funds of West Salem Sch. Dist. Fellow Am. Coll. Real Estate Lawyers, Am. Coll. Probate Counsel, Wis. Law Found.; mem. Wis. Bar Assn., Elks, KC. Office: 800 Lynn Tower Bldg La Crosse WI 54601 E-mail: kfpatts@aol.com.

KLOSE, KEVIN, broadcast executive; b. Toronto, Ont., Can., Sept. 1, 1940; came to U.S., 1942; s. Willard and Virginia Taylor K.; m. Eliza Kellogg, Sept. 1964; children: Nina, Brennan, Chandler. BA in English Lit., Harvard U., 1962; DHL (hon.), Union Coll., 2000. Staff reporter Washington Post, 1967-77, Moscow bur. chief, 1977-81, midwest corr. Chgo., 1983-87, deputy nat. editor, 1987-91; dir. Radio Free Europe/Radio Liberty, Munich, 1992-94, pres. Prague, Czech Republic, 1994-97; dir. U.S. Internat. Broadcasting Bur., Washington, 1997-98; assoc. dir. U.S. Info. Agy., Washington, 1997-98; pres., CEO Nat. Pub. Radio, Washington, 1998—. Bd. dirs. E, Independent Sector, Washington; trustee Arthur F. Burns Fellowship Program, 1999-2002; mem. Internat. Rsch. & Exchs. Bd., Washington, 1999—. Author: Russia and The Russians, 1984; co-author: I Will Survive, 1962, The Typhoon Shipments, 1974, Surprise! Surprise!, 1977, Freedom's Child, 1987. With USN, 1962—64. Woodrow Wilson Nat. fellow, 1983-87. Avocations: skiing, sailing. Office: Nat Pub Radio 635 Massachusetts Ave NW Washington DC 20001-3753 Office Phone: 202-513-2000. Business E-Mail: kklose@npr.org.

KLOSKA, RONALD FRANK, manufacturing executive; b. Grand Rapids, Mich., Oct. 24, 1933; s. Frank B. and Catherine (Hilaski) K.; m. Mary F. Minick, Sept. 7, 1957; children: Kathleen Ann, Elizabeth Marie, Ronald Francis, Mary Josephine, Carolyn Louise. Student, St. Joseph Sem., Grand Rapids, Mich., 1947-53; PhB, U. Montreal, Que., Can., 1955; MBA, U. Mich., 1957. Staff acct. Coopers & Lybrand, Niles, Mich., 1957, staff to sr. acct., 1960—63; treas. Skyline Corp., Elkhart, Ind., 1963, v.p., treas., 1964—67, exec. v.p. fin., 1967—74, pres., 1974—85, pres., chief ops. officer, 1985—91, vice chmn., chief adminstrn. officer, 1991—94, vice chmn., chief adminstrn. officer, sec., 1994—95, vice chmn., dep. CEO, chief adminstrn. officer, 1995—98, vice chmn., CEO, chief adminstrn. officer, 1998—2001, dir., cons., 2001—. With U.S. Army, 1957—60. Mem. Mich. Soc. CPAs, Ind. Soc. CPAs, South Bend Country Club. Roman Catholic. Home: 1329 E Woodside St South Bend IN 46614-1455 Office: Skyline Corp 2520 Bypass Rd Elkhart IN 46514-1584

KLOSS, LINDA L., medical association administrator; Former sr. mgr. MediQual Systems, Inc., Mass., InterQual, Inc., Chgo.; exec. v.p., CEO Am. Health Info. Mgmt. Assn., Chgo., 1995—. Bd. dirs. Am. Health Info. Mgmt. Assn., 1980—86, pres. bd. dirs., 1985. Office: Am Health Info Mgmt Assn 233 N Michigan Ave Ste 2150 Chicago IL 60601-5519 Business E-Mail: lkloss@ahima.org.

KLOSSON, MICHAEL, foreign service officer; b. Washington, Aug. 22, 1949; s. Boris Hansen and Harriet Fraser (Cheston) K.; m. Bonita L. Bender; children: Emily C., Karen Lee Bender. BA, Hamilton Coll., 1971; M.P.A., Woodrow Wilson Sch., Princeton U., 1974; MA, Princeton U., 1975. Asst. lectr. Hong Kong Baptist Coll., 1971-72; commd. fgn. service officer Dept. State, 1975, staff asst. to asst. sec. of state for East Asian affairs Washington, 1975-77; Chinese Lang. trainee Fgn. Service Inst., Taichung, Taiwan, 1977-78; polit. officer Am. embassy, Taipei, Taiwan, 1978-80; polit. officer office Japanese affairs Dept. State, Washington, 1980-81, spl. asst. to sec. of state, 1981-83; Pearson fellow U.S. Senate, 1983-84; dep. dir. for polit. affairs Office European Security and Polit. Affairs Dept. State, Washington, 1984-87, dir., secretariat staff, 1987-90; dep. chief of mission Am. Embassy, Stockholm, 1990-92, chargé d'affaires, 1992-93, charge d'affaires The Hague, 1993-94, dep. chief of mission, 1994-96; dep. asst. sec. of state for legis. affairs Dept. of State, Washington, 1996-99; cons. genl. U.S. Consulate, Hong Kong, 1999—2002; amb. Republic of Cyprus, 2002—05; faculty adv., state dept. chair Nat. Defense U., 2005—. Herbert H. Lehman fellow, 1971, Winston Churchill fellow, 1972-74. Mem. Am. Fgn. Svc. Assn., Phi Beta Kappa. Home: 15437 Narcissus Way Rockville MD 20853 Office Phone: 202-685-4771. Personal E-mail: mklosson@hotmail.com.

KLOSTER, CAROL GOOD, wholesale distribution executive; b. Richmond, Va., Aug. 18, 1948; d. David William and Lucy (McDowell) Good; m. John Kenneth Kloster III, Feb. 15, 1975; children: John Kenneth IV, Amanda Aileen. AB, Coll. William and Mary, 1970. Personnel supr. Charles Levy Circulating Co., Chgo., 1974-75, warehouse supr., 1976-77, warehouse mgr., 1978-80, dir. sales, 1980-83, asst. v.p., dir. mktg., 1984; v.p., gen. mgr. Video Trend of Chgo., 1985-86; v.p. gen. mgr. Levy Home Entertainment, 1986-92; pres., CEO Chas Levy Co., 1992—. Mem. bd., Family Focus Inc. Recipient Algernon Sidney Sullivan award Coll. William and Mary, 1970. Presbyterian. Home: 619 W North St Hinsdale IL 60521-3152 Office: Charles Levy Co 1200 N North Branch St Chicago IL 60622-2493

KLOTMAN, ROBERT HOWARD, music educator; b. Cleve., Nov. 22, 1918; s. Louis Klotman and Pearl (Warshawsky) Kaplan; m. Phyllis Helen Rauch, Apr. 4, 1943; children: Janet Lynn, Paul Evan. BS in Music Edn., Ohio No. U., 1940; MA in Music, Case-Western Res. U., 1950; EdD, Columbia U., 1956; MusD (hon.), Ohio No. U., 1984. Supr. music pub. schs., Dola, Ohio, 1940-42; tchr. instrumental, vocal music pub. schs. Euclid, Ohio, 1942, 46; tchr. instrumental music pub. schs. Cleveland Heights, Ohio, 1946-59; dir. music edn. pub. schs. Akron, Ohio, 1959-63; divisional dir. music edn. pub. schs. Detroit, 1963-69; prof., chmn. dept. music edn. Ind. U., Bloomington, 1969-83, prof. emeritus, 1987—. Vis. prof. Shanghai Conservatory of Music, 1985, U. Alta., Edmonton, Can., summer 1991; guest lectr. U. Bar-Ilan, Israel, 1984; ednl. dir. firm Scherl & Roth (string importers), Cleve., 1956-70; mem. adv. bd. Contemporary Music Project, Ford Found., 1964-65; ednl. cons. Summy-Birchard Co. (music pubs.); mem. bicentennial com. J. C. Penney Co., 1974-76. Condr.: Akron Youth Symphony Orch., 1959—63, Oak Park (Mich.) Symphony, 1967—69, Bloomington Youth Symphony Orch., 1969—75, Terre Haute Youth Symphony, 1992, Great Lake Music Camp Orch., 1982—96; author: Learning to Teach Through Playing: String Techniques and Pedagogy, 1971, The School Music Administrator and Supervisor: Catalysts for Change in Music Education, 1973, Teaching Strings, 1996; author: (with others) Humanities Through the Black Experience, Foundations of Music Education, 1983, 1988; co-author: Administrating and Supervising Music, 1991; contbg. author: Ency. of Edn., 1971; editor: Orch. News, 1959—70; mem. editl. bd.: Music Educators Jour., 1962—64, Instrumentalist, 1974—91; editor (with others): Scheduling Music Classes, 1968; editor, contg. author: Music Performance Trust Funds Guide; composer: Action with Strings, 1962, Renaissance Suite, 1964, String Literature for Expanding Technique, 1973. Bd. dirs., sec. Ind. U. Credit Union, 1974-87; chmn. ednl. com. Chamber Music Am., 1993-95. With inf. AUS, 1942-46, ETO, PTO. Recipient citation Nat. Assn. Negro Musicians Inc., 1966, citation Black Music Caucas, 1978, Outstanding Hoosier Musician award, 1986, Disting. Service award Am. String Tchrs. Assn., 1987, Sagamore of the Wabash Govs. award, 1991, medal of honor Midwest Orch./Band Conf., 2003; named to MENC Hall of Fame, 2004; Lowell Mason fellow, 2005. Mem. Chamber Music Am. (chair edn. com. 1993-95), Am. String Tchrs. Assn. (pres. 1962-64, dir. pubs. 1985-94, chmn. past pres. coun. 1998-2000), Music Educators Nat. Conf. (chmn. commn. on tchr. edn. 1968-72, pres. 1976-78, Disting. Svc. award 1989, chmn. Hall of Fame com. 1996-2002, Hall of Fame 2004), Rotary, Phi Mu Alpha Sinfonia, Phi Delta Kappa. Democrat. Jewish. Avocations: tennis, swimming, reading mystery novels. E-mail: Klotman@indiana.edu.

KLOTT, DAVID LEE, lawyer; b. Vicksburg, Miss., Dec. 10, 1941; s. Isadore and Dorothy (Lipson) Klott; m. Maren J. Randrup, May 25, 1975. BBA summa cum laude, Northwestern U., 1963; JD cum laude, Harvard U., 1966. Bar: Calif. 1966, U.S. Ct. Claims 1968, U.S. Supreme Ct. 1971, U.S. Tax Ct. 1973, U.S. Ct. Appeals (fed. cir.) 1982. Ptnr. Pillsbury Winthrop, San Francisco, 1966—. Mem. tax adv. group to sub-chpt. C J and K, Am. Law Inst.; instr. Calif. Continuing Edn. Bar, Practising Law Inst., Hastings Law Sch.; exec. v.p., sec. Global Ctr. Inc., 2000—01; vice-chmn. HL Ventures, LLC, 2000—05. Commentator Calif. Nonprofit Corp. Law. Mem.: ABA, Calif. State Bar Assn., Internat. Wine and Food Soc. (bd. dir., exec. com., sr. vice chmn., bd. gov. Ams.), Am.-Korean Taekwondo Friendship Assn. (1st dan-black belt), Harbor Point Racquet and Beach Club, Olympic Club, Northwestern Club, Harvard Club, Beta Alpha Psi, Beta Gamma Sigma (pres. local chpt.). Office: Pillsbury Winthrop LLP 17 Wolfback Ridge Rd Sausalito CA 94965

KLOTTER, JAMES C., historian, educator; b. Lexington, Ky., Jan. 17, 1947; s. John Charles K. and Marjorie Virginia (Gibson) Gabbard; m. Freda Jean Campbell, Dec. 28, 1966; children: Karen, Christopher, Katherine. BA, U. Ky., 1968, MA, 1969, PhD, 1975; LittD, Ea. Ky. U., 1997, Union Coll., 1998. Rsch. analyst Ky. Hist. Soc., Frankfort, 1973-75, asst. editor, 1975-78, mng. editor, 1978-80, state historian, 1980-88, asst. dir., 1988-90, dir., state historian, 1990-98; state historian, prof. history Georgetown Coll., 1998—. Chmn. bd. dirs. Farmers State Bank, Booneville, Ky.; bd. dirs. Hyden (Ky.) Middlefork Fin., Collaborative Tchg. and Learning. Author: William Goebel: Politics of Wrath, 1977, co-author: A New History of Kentucky, 1997; editor: Our Kentucky: Study of Blue Grass State, 2000. Sec. Ky. Civil War Roundtable, Lexington, 1984-94, pres. 1994—. Mem. So. Hist. Assn., Ky. Assn. Tchrs. History (pres. 1986-87), Ky. Coun. on Archives (chmn. 1980-81), Ky. Oral History Commn. Bd., Ky. Hist. Soc. Found., U. Ky. Libr. Assn. (pres. 1984-85). Office: 400 E College St # 244 Georgetown KY 40324-1628 Business E-Mail: james_klotter@georgetowncollege.edu.

KLOTTER, JOHN CHARLES, retired law educator; b. Louisville, Nov. 6, 1918; s. John J. and Lillie R. (Fischer) K.; m. Jane Riddle, Nov. 2, 1954 (dec.); children: James C., Douglas A., Ronald L. AB, Western Ky. U., 1941; JD, U. Ky., 1948. Bar: Ky. 1948, U.S. Supreme Ct. 1967. Tchr. pub. schs., Louisville, 1941-42; spl. agt. FBI, 1948-50; legal officer Ky. State Police, 1951-52; dir. divsn. probation and parole State of Ky., Frankfort, 1952-56; assoc. dir. So. Police Inst., U. Louisville, 1957-71, dir. So. Police Inst., prof., dean Sch. Justice Adminstrn., So. Police Inst., 1971-81. Editorial dir. criminal justice text series W.H. Anderson Co., 1970-76; chmn. Louisville-Jefferson County Criminal Justice Commn., 1974-76; mem. Ky. Crime Commn., 1971-75, Ky. Law Enforcement Coun., 1971-81, Atty. Gen.'s Prosecutors Adv. Coun., 1970-82. Author: Techniques for Police Instructors, 1963; (with Kanovitz) Constitutional Law, 1968, 9th edit., 2001, Criminal Evidence, 1971, 8th edit., 2004, Legal Guide for Police, 1978, 6th edit., 2002, Criminal Justice Instructional Techniques, 1979, Legal Aspects of Private Security, 1981, Criminal Law, 1983, 8th edit., 2003. Capt. U.S. Army, 1942-46; col. Res. ret. Ford Found. grantee, 1968 Mem. Ky., Louisville bar assns., Res. Officers Assn., Soc. Former Spl. Agts. FBI. Home: 2103 Starmont Rd Louisville KY 40207-1140 E-mail: jk40207@aol.com.

KLOTZ, ANN MARIE, director; b. Detroit, Mich., Feb. 18, 1979; d. Charles Giacolone and Katherine (Klotz) Giacalone. BA Polit. Sci., Women Studies, Grand Valley State U., Allendale, Mich., 2002; MA Student Affairs Adminstrn., Mich. State U., 2004. Dir. residence hall Ball State U., Muncie, Ind., 2004—. Named Advisor of the Yr., 2005; recipient Max Raines Most Outstanding First Yr. Grad. Student in Student Affaris adminstrn., Mich. State U., 2003. Mem.: Am. Coll. Personnel Assn., Phi Kappa Phi. Democrat. Avocations: politics, reading, musicals, exercise, entertaining. Home: 1089 Beaconsfield Grosse Pointe MI 48230 Office: Ball State Univ 400 Schmidt Hall Muncie IN 47306 Office Phone: 765-285-5042. E-mail: aklotz@bsu.edu.

KLOTZ, CHARLES RODGER, water transportation executive, investment company executive; b. Englewood, N.J., Apr. 14, 1942; s. George Edward and Beryl Edith (Cullingford) K.; m. Deborah Goodwin, June 25, 1966; children: Christine, Suzanne. BS, Trinity Coll., Hartford, Conn., 1964; MBA, Dartmouth Coll., 1966. Officer Bank of Boston Corp., 1969—85; pres., chief exec. officer Gulf Resources & Chem. Corp., Boston, 1985—89, also bd. dirs.; chmn. bd., CEO Spartan Madison Corp., 1991—2002. Chmn. bd. G.L. Holdings Corp., 1988—; chief exec. officer, chmn. bd. Gotaas Larsen Shipping Corp., 1988-97, also bd. dirs.; pres., bd. dirs. Tec Capital Ltd., 2000—; bd. dirs., dep. chmn. Trigen Holding AG. Lt. USCG, 1966-69. Mem. Flyfisher's Club (London), Wellesley Country Club, Coral Beach and Tennis Club (Bermuda), Pocasset Golf Club. Episcopalian. Office: Bingham McCutchen 150 Federal St Fl 15 Boston MA 02110-1726

KLOTZ, EDNA MAY, retired librarian; b. Corry, Pa., July 20, 1922; d. Milton Edward and Ethyl May Robbins; m. Donald L. Klotz, Sept. 9, 1950. BA, Hiram Coll., 1944; BSLS, Western Reserve U., Cleve., 1945. Student asst. Hiram (Ohio) Coll., 1941-44; head cataloguer Baldwin Wallace Coll. Library, Berea, Ohio, 1945-48; circulation librarian Ohio State U., Columbus, 1948-52, special collection librarian, 1952-57; asst. librarian Worthington Pub. Library, Worthington, 1957-68; circulation librarian Capital U. Library, 1968-80, acquisitions librarian Bexley, 1980-89; ret., 1989—. Methodist. Home: 1937 Harwitch Rd Columbus OH 43221-2812

KLOTZ, FLORENCE, costume designer; b. N.Y.C., Oct. 28, 1928; d. Philip K. and Hannah Kraus. Student, Parsons Sch. Design, 1941. Designer: Broadway shows Take Her She's Mine, 1960, Never Too Late, 1962, Nobody Loves An Albatross, 1963, On An Open Roof, 1963, Owl and the Pussycat, 1964, One by One, 1964, Mating Dance, 1965, The Best Laid Plans, 1966, Superman, 1966, Paris Is Out, 1970, Norman Is That You, 1970, Legends, Follies, 1971 (Drama Desk award, Tony award), A Little Night Music, 1973 (Drama Desk award, Tony award), Side By Side Sondheim, 1975, Pacific Overtures, 1976 (Drama Desk award, Tony award, Los Angeles Critic Circle award), On the 20th Century, 1978 (Drama Desk award), Broadway Broadway, Dancin' In The Streets, 1982, Grind, 1984 (Tony award), Jerry's Girls, 1985; (ballet-jazz opus) Antique Epagraph, N.Y.C.; Broadway musicals Rags, 1986, Roza, 1987; Ctr. prodns. Carousel, 1956, Oklahoma, 1956, Annie Get Your Gun, 1956, 4 Baggatelle; movies Something for Everyone, 1969, A Little Night Music, 1976 (Oscar nomination, Los Angeles Critic Circle award); ice shows John Curry's Ice Dancing, 1979; Broadway musical A Doll's Life; ballet 8 Lines, 1986, I'm Old Fashioned (Jerome Robbins), Ives Songs (Jerome Robbins), City of Angels, 1989 (Tony award nominee, Outer Critics Circle award), Kiss of the Spider Woman, 1989 (Tony award 1989, Drama Desk award 1989), Show Boat, Toronto, Can., 1993, Broadway, 1994-95 (N.Y. Outer Critics Cirlce award 1995, Drama Desk award 1995, Tony award 1995, Theatre L.A. Ovation award 1997, Jessie award 1996), Whistle Down the Wind, 1996. Recipient Life Achievement award Theatre Crafts Internat., 1994, L.A. Ovation award, 1997, award NAACP, 1997, Dramalogue, 1997, L.A. Drama Desk, 1997; inducted into Theatre Hall of Fame, 1997, Patricia Zipprodt award, Fashion Inst. of Techn., 2002, Irene Sharaff award, 2005. Democrat. Home: 1050 Park Ave New York NY 10028-1031

KLOTZ, KEVIN MICHAEL, music educator; b. Houston, Tex., July 11, 1976; BM Piano, Houston Bapt. U., 1995—99; MM Conducting, U. Houston, 2002. Music dir. St. Lawrence Cath. Ch., Sugarland, Tex., 1999—. Composer (arranger) Liturgical Music. Named to Dean;s List in Musicology Theory, Performane, Houston Bapt. U., 1995—99, Dean's list, U. Houston, 2001—02. Mem.: Am. Choral Dirs. Assn., Nat. Pastoral Musicians. Achievements include artistic dir. and conductor of St. Lawrence Chamber Singers, profl. vocal ensemble. Avocations: music, movies, outdoors. Home: 1102 Meadowlark Ln Sugar Land TX 77478 Office: St Lawrence Cath Ch 3100 Sweetwater Blvd Sugar Land TX 77479 E-mail: PianomanKMK@aol.com.

KLOTZ, MARTIN B., lawyer; b. 1950; BA, Yale U., 1971, PhD, 1976, JD, 1981. Bar: NY 1982. With Paul, Weiss, Rifkind, Wharton & Garrison; asst. US atty. So. Dist. NY, 1988—91; ptnr., litig. dept. Willkie Farr & Gallagher LLP, NYC. Office: Willkie Farr & Gallagher LLP 787 Seventh Ave New York NY 10019 Office Phone: 212-728-8688. Office Fax: 212-728-9688. E-mail: mklotz@willkie.com.

KLOVES, STEVEN, film director, scriptwriter; b. Austin, Texas, Mar. 18, 1960; m. Kathy Kloves; 1 child, Callie. Screenwriter: (films) Racing With the Moon, 1984; adapted screenwriter Wonder Boys, 2000; Harry Potter and the Sorceror's Stone, 2001; Harry Potter and the Chamber of Secrets, 2002; Harry Potter and the Prisoner of Azkaban, 2004; screenwriter, dir. The Fabulous Baker Boys, 1989; Flesh and Bone, 1993.

KLOWDEN, MICHAEL LOUIS, think-tank executive; b. Chgo., Apr. 7, 1945; s. Roy and Esther (Siegel) K.; m. Patricia A. Doede, June 15, 1968; children: Kevin B., Deborah C. AB, U. Chgo., 1967; JD, Harvard U., 1970.

Bar: Calif. 1971. From assoc. to ptnr. Mitchell, Silberberg & Knupp, L.A., 1970-78; mng. ptnr. Morgan, Lewis & Bockius, L.A., 1978-95; vice chmn. Jefferies & Co., Inc., L.A., 1995-96; pres., COO Jefferies Group, Inc. and Jefferies Co., Inc., L.A., 1996-2000, vice chmn., 2000—01; pres., CEO Milken Inst., 2001—. Trustee U. Chgo., 1986—. Office: Milken Institute 1250 Fourth St Santa Monica CA 90401 E-mail: mklowden@milkeninstitute.org.

KLUCKING, GAIL MARIE, education educator; b. Trenton, NJ, Feb. 17, 1958; d. Laurence Patrick and Christina Thelma Minnick; m. Tony Vaughn Klucking, June 5, 1987; 1 child, Sara. BA, Mo. Bapt. Coll., 1984; MPA, Troy State U., 1991; MPhil, U. Oxford, England, 1993; PhD, Auburn U., 1999. Instr. English Kubaski H.S., Okinawa, Japan, 1987-89; founding dir., com. mem. Taylor Rd. Kindergarten, Montgomery, Ala., 1988-98; tchr. Eastwood Christian Sch., 2000—05. Adj. instr. Auburn U., Montgomery, 1993—; field rep. European Region Troy State U., Upper Heyford, England, 1990-91; adv. 21st century adminstr. evaluatin program task force State of Ala., Dept. Edn., Taylor Rd. Edn. Adhoc Com., Montgomery. Sunday sch. tchr. O'Fallon (Ill.) Bapt. Ch., 1980-85, Taylor Rd. Bapt. Ch., 1994-2002; coach Spl. Olympics, Seattle, 1987; pres. Student Govt. Assn., Mo. Bapt. Coll., 1984. With USAF, 1985-87. Mem.: Am. Soc. Pub. Adminstrn., Phi Kappa Phi, Phi Sigma Alpha. Republican. Avocations: fitness training, reading.

KLUG, AARON, molecular biologist; b. Aug. 11, 1926; s. Lazar and Bella (Silin) Klug; m. Liebe Bobrow, 1948; 2 children. B.Sc., U. Witwatersrand; M.Sc., U. Cape Town; PhD, DSc, Cambridge U.; DSc (hon.), U. Chgo., 1978, Columbia U., 1978; D (hon.), U. Strasbourg, 1978; DSc (hon.), Stockholm U., 1980, U. Witwatersrand, 1984, Hebrew U., Jerusalem, 1984, Hull U., 1985, U. St. Andrews, 1987, U. Western Ont., 1991, Warwick U., 1994, Capetwon U., 1997; D Litt, Cambridge U., 1998, Stirling U., 1998; DSc (hon.), London, 2000, Oxford, 2001. Jr. lectr., 1947-48; rsch. student Cavendish Lab. Cambridge (Eng.) U., 1949-52; Rouse-Ball rsch. student Trinity Coll., 1949-52; Colloid Sci. dept., 1953; Nuffield rsch. fellow Birkbeck Coll., London, 1954-57, dir. virus structure rsch. group, 1958-61; mem. staff Med. Rsch. Coun. Lab. Molecular Biology, Cambridge U., 1962—, joint head div. structural studies, 1978-86, dir., 1986-96. Leeuwenhoek lectr. Royal Soc., 1973; Dunham lectr. Harvard U. Med. Sch., 1975; Harvey lectr., N.Y.C., 1979, Lane lectr. Stanford U., 1983; Silliman lectr. Yale U., 1985; Cetus lectr. Berkeley U., 1986; Pauli lectr., Zürich, 1986; Nishina Meml. lectr., Tokyo, 1986; J. T. Baker lectr. Cornell U., 1987; Jean Weigle lectr., Geneva, 1989, Steenbock lectr. U. Wis., Madison, 1989; Innovators in Biochem. lectr. U. Va., Richmond, 1990; Calbiochem. lectr. U. Calif., San Diego, 1991; Neurath lectr. U. Wash., Seattle; Blackett lectr. Delhi, 1997. Contbr. articles to sci. jours. Recipient Heineken prize Royal Netherlands Acad. Sci., 1979, Louisa Gross Horwitz prize Columbia U., 1981, Nobel prize in chemistry, 1982, Gold medal of Merit, U. Cape Town, 1983, Copley medal Royal Soc., 1985, Harden medal Biochem. Soc., 1985; Knight, 1988, Order of Merit, 1995. Fellow Royal Soc. (pres. 1995-2000), Peterhouse (Cambridge hon.), Royal Coll. Physn, (hon., Baly medal 1987), Royal Coll. Pathologists (hon.), Trinity Coll. (Cambridge, hon.), Birkbeck Coll. (London, hon.); mem. Am. Acad. Arts and Scis. (fgn. hon.), French Acad. Scis. (fgn. assoc.), Max-Planck-Gesellschaft (fgn. assoc.), NAS (fgn. assoc.), Am. Philos. Soc. (fgn. mem.), Japan Acad. (hon.). Office: Med Rsch Coun Lab Molecular Biology, Hills Rd Cambridge CB2 2QH England

KLUG, SCOTT LEO, former congressman; b. Milwaukee, Wis., Jan. 16, 1953; s. Ralph William Klug and Josephine (Farrell) Weber; m. Tess Summers, Mar. 4, 1978; children: Keefe, Brett, Collin Phillip. BA, Lawrence U., 1975; MS in Journalism, Northwestern U., 1976; MBA, U. Wis., 1990. Reporter TV sta., Wausau, Wis., 1976-78; reporter Sta. KING-TV, Seattle, 1978-81; investigative reporter Sta. WJLA-TV, Washington, 1981-88; anchor, reporter Sta. WKOW-TV, Madison, Wis., 1988-90; v.p. pub. fin. dept. Blunt, Ellis & Loewi, Madison, 1990; mem. 102nd-105th U.S. Congress from 2d Wis. dist., Washington, D.C., 1991-98, mem. commerce com.; publ., CEO Trails Media Group Inc., Madison, 1999—; pub. affairs counsel Foley and Lardner, Washington, 1999—. Reporter, producer documentaries (Emmy awards 1989, 90). Named Nat. Humanitarian of Yr., Humane Soc., 1986; John McCloy fellow Columbia U. Sch. Journalism, 1987. Republican. Avocations: tennis, basketball, cooking. Office: Trails Media Group PO Box 317 Black Earth WI 53515 also: Foley and Lardner Verex Plaza 150 E Gilman St Madison WI 53703*

KLUGE, JOHN WERNER, broadcasting and advertising executive; b. Chemnitz, Germany, Sept. 21, 1914; s. Fritz and Gertrude (Donj) K.; children: Samantha, Joseph B. Student, Wayne U.; BA (4 year honor scholar), Columbia, 1937. Vice pres., sales mgr. Otten Bros., Inc., Detroit, 1937-41; pres., dir. radio sta. WGAY, Silver Spring, Md., 1946-59, St. Louis Broadcasting Corp., Brentwood, Mo., 1953-58, Pitts. Broadcasting Co., 1954-59; pres., treas., dir. Capitol Broadcasting Co., Nashville, 1954-59, Assoc. Broadcasters, Inc., Ft. Worth-Dallas, 1957-59; partner Western N.Y. Broadcasting Co., Buffalo, 1957-60; pres., dir. Washington Planagraph Co., 1956-60, Mid.-Fla. Radio Corp., Orlando, 1952-59; treas., dir. Mid-Fla. Television Corp., 1957-60; owner Kluge Investment Co., Washington, 1956-60; partner Nashton Properties, Nashville, 1954-60, Texworth Investment Co., Ft. Worth, 1957-60; chmn. bd. Seaboard Service System, Inc., 1957-58; chm. bd., pres., CEO Metromedia Inc., Secaucus, N.J., 1959-86; former gen. ptnr., chm. bd., pres., CEO Metromedia Co., now chmn. and pres. East Rutherford, NJ; now pres., chmn. bd. Benale Holdings Corp., Dallas; also chmn., dir. LDDS Comm., Jackson, Miss.; investor, operator N.Y./N.J. Metro Stars, Secaucus, N.J., 1995. Pres. New Eng. Fritos, Boston, 1947-55, N.Y. Inst. Dietetics, N.Y.C., 1953-60; chmn. bd., pres., dir. Metromedia, Inc., N.Y.C., Metromedia, Inc. (including met. broadcasting div., world wide broadcasting div. and Foster & Kleiser div., outdoor advt.); chmn. bd., treas., dir. Kluge, Finkelstein & Co. (food brokers), Balt.; chmn. bd., treas. Tri-Suburban Broadcasting Corp., Washington, Kluge & Co.; chmn. bd., pres., treas. Washington, Silver City Sales Co., Washington; dir. Marriott-Hot Shoppes, Inc., Chock Full O' Nuts Corp., Nat. Bank Md., Waldorf Astoria Corp., Just One Break, Inc., Belding Heminway Co., Inc.; mem. adv. council Mfrs. Hanover Trust Co.; Mem. Washington Bd. Trade. Bd. dirs. Brand Names Found., Inc., Shubert Found.; v.p., bd. dirs. United Cerebral Palsy Research and Ednl. Found., 1972—; trustee Strang Clinic Miliken U.; bd. govs. N.Y. Coll. Osteo. Medicine. Served to capt. U.S. Army, 1941-45. Mem. Nat. Food Brokers Assn., Washington Food Brokers Assn. (pres. 1958), Grocery Wheels Washington, Grocery Mfrs. Reps. Washington, Advt. Club Washington, Nat. Assn. Radio and Television Broadcasters, Advt. Council N.Y.C., Nat. Sugar Brokers Assn. Clubs: Army and Navy (Washington), University (Washington), Figure Skating (Washington), National Capital Skeet and Trap (Washington), Broadcasters (Washington); Metropolitan (N.Y.C.), Columbia Associates (N.Y.C.), University (N.Y.C.); Olympic (San Francisco); Marco Polo (N.H. gov.).*

KLUGER, ALAN M., academic administrator; b. Bklyn., Feb. 9, 1949; s. Morris and Sarah Kluger; m. Nancy Gail Schrager; 1 child, Samantha. BA, SUNY, Binghamton, 1970; MBA, CUNY, N.Y.C., 1975. CPA Ariz., 1986. Acct. Alan Kluger, CPA, Scottsdale, Ariz., 1986—92; CFO We. Internat. U., Phoenix, 1993—95; CEO Huron (S.D.) U., 1995—96; CFO S.W. Naturopathic Med. Coll., Tempe, Ariz., 1997—99, COO, 1999—2001; exec. dir. Ariz. Automotive Inst., Glendale, 2001—. Nominee U.S. Congress, NY, 1976. Avocations: reading, exercise, tennis. Home: PO Box 4702 Scottsdale AZ 85261 Office: Ariz Automotive Inst 6829 N 46th Ave Glendale AZ 85301

KLUGER, JEFFREY, reporter, author; Licensed atty.; adj. instr., sci. journalism NYU; writer, editor NY Times Bus. World Mag.; staff writer Discover Mag.; contbr. Time Mag., 1996—98, sr. writer, 1998—. Co-author (with Jim Lovell): Lost Moon: The Perilous Voyage of Apollo 13 (basis for movie, Apollo 13), 1994; co-author: (with Ron Howard) The Apollo Adventure: The Making of Apollo Space Program and the Movie Apollo 13, 1995; author: Journey Beyond Selene, 1999, Splendid Solution: Jonas Salk and the Conquest of Polio, 2005. Co-recipient First Place, Whitman Bassow award, Overseas Press Club, 2002. Office: Sr Writer Time Mag 1271 Ave of Americas New York NY 10020-1393 Office Phone: 212-522-1212.*

KLUGER, RICHARD, writer, editor; b. Paterson, N.J., Sept. 18, 1934; s. David and Ida (Abramson) K.; m. Phyllis Schlain, Mar. 23, 1957; children—Matthew Harold, Leonard Theodore. AB cum laude, Princeton, 1956. Copy editor Wall St. Jour., 1956-57; editor, pub. County Citizen, New City, N.Y., 1958-60; staff writer N.Y. Post, 1960-61; asso. editor Forbes mag., 1962; gen. books editor N.Y. Herald Tribune, 1962-63, book editor, 1963-66; editor Book Week, 1963-66; sr. editor Simon and Schuster, 1966-68, mng. editor, 1968, exec. editor, 1968-70; editor-in-chief Atheneum Pubs., 1970-71; pres., pub. Charterhouse Books, 1971-73. Author: When the Bough Breaks, 1964, National Anthem, 1969, Simple Justice, 1976, Members of the Tribe, 1977, Star Witness, 1979, Un-American Activities, 1982, The Paper: The Life and Death of the New York Herald Tribune, 1986, The Sheriff of Nottingham, 1992, Ashes to Ashes: America's Hundred-Year Cigarette War, 1996; co-author: (with Phyllis Kluger) Good Goods, 1982, Royal Poinciana, 1988. Recipient George Polk award, 1987, Pulitzer prize Gen. Non-Fiction, 1997; Nat. Am. Book Non-Fiction award nominee, 1976, 86; nominee Nat. Book Critics Cir. award, 1997. Home: 1307 Acton St Berkeley CA 94706

KLUGHART, TONI ANNE, music educator, musician; b. Detroit, Mich., Dec. 5, 1964; d. Eugene Stanley McGuire Jr. and Rose Marie (Williams) McGuire; m. Charles Edward Klughart, Dec. 5, 1998; children: Nathaniel, Edward, Nathaniel Edward. AA Fine Arts, No.Va. C.C., 1983. Piano and voice instr., owner Ten Fingers Piano Studio, Fairfax, Va., 1986—96; asst. mgr. Music & Arts, Springfield, Va., 1986—88; piano instr., accompanist Comm. Music Sch., Richmond, Va., 1996—97; owner, faculty Klughart Music Sch., Atlanta, 1998—2003; office asst. Mobility Products Unlimited, LLC, Sparta, Tenn., 2003—; piano, guitar, voice, clarinet instr. Klughart Music Sch., Sparta, Tenn., 2003—. Singer (composer): (CD) Christmas and Lullabys. Scholar Organ Study scholarship, Am. Guild of Organists, 1995. Avocations: exercise, reading, crocheting, composing. Office: Mobility Products Unltd Klughart Music 337 Burley St Sparta TN 38583 Office Fax: 931-837-2388. Business E-Mail: klughartmusic@hotmail.com.

KLUGMAN, STEPHAN CRAIG, newspaper editor; b. Fargo, N.D., May 11, 1945; s. Ted and Charlotte (Olson) K.; m. Julie Sue Terpening, Sept. 18, 1971; children: Josh, Carrie. BA in Journalism, Ind. U., 1967. Copy editor Chgo. Sun-Times, 1967-68, asst. telegraph editor, 1968-72, telegraph editor, 1972-74, city editor, 1974-76, asst. mng. editor features, 1976-78; asst. prof. Medill Sch. Journalism, Northwestern U., Evanston, Ill., 1978-79, dir. undergrad. studies, 1979-82; editor Jour.-Gazette, Ft. Wayne, Ind., 1982--. Mem. Am. Soc. Newspaper Editors. Office: Jour-Gazette 600 W Main St Fort Wayne IN 46802-1408 Office Phone: 260-461-8853. Business E-Mail: cklugman@jg.net.

KLUM, HEIDI, model, actress; b. Bergisch-Gladbach, Germany, June 1, 1973; d. Gunther and Erna Klum; m. Ric Pipino, Sept. 6, 1997 (div. 2003); 1 child, Leni; m. Seal, May 10, 2005; 1 child. Model Victoria's Secret Fashion Show, 2001, 2002, 2003; appeared on covers of major mags. including Elle, Sports Illustrated (Swimsuit Edit.), Mademoiselle, Glamour, Bride's, Cosmopolitan; appeared in campaigns including Bonne Bell, Finesse, Gerry Webber, Givenchy, Amerige, INC, Am. Express, Kathleen Madden, Katjes, Nike, Otto, Peek&Cloppenburg, Swatch, Victoria's Secret; launched line of perfume, 2002; co-creator jewelry collection The Heidi Klum Collection for Mouawad; designer of a line of Birkenstocks. Actor: (films) 54, 1998, Blow Dry, 2001, Ella Enchanted, 2004, The Life and Death of Peter Sellers, 2004; (TV films) Spin City, 1998—99; exec. prodr., host (TV series) Project Runaway, 2004, TV appearances include Sex and the City, 2001, Malcolm in the Middle, 2002, Yes, Dear, 2002, CSI: Miami, 2003; host: (TV series) Project Runway, 2005—; author (with Alexandra Postman): Heidi Klum's Body of Knowledge: 8 Rules of Model Behavior (to Help You Take off on the Runway of Life), 2004. Charity involvements include ARC, Elizabeth Glazer Pediatric AIDS Found. Office: William Morris Agy One William Morris Pl Beverly Hills CA 90212*

KLUN, JEROME ANTHONY, entomologist, researcher; b. Ely, Minn., May 4, 1939; s. Anton Dominic and Julia (Pishler) K.; m. Phyllis Ruth VanRiper, Mar. 18, 1989 (div.); children: Curt Anthony, Eric Leslie, Toinette Marie; m. Harriet Lee Rosenfeld, May 30, 1993. BA, U. Minn., 1961; PhD, Iowa State U., 1965. Rsch. assoc. entomology dept. Iowa State U., Ames, 1961-65, assoc. prof. entomology, 1968-77; rsch. entomologist agrl. rsch. USDA, Ankeny, Iowa, 1965-77, Beltsville, Md., 1977—. Panel chmn. Agy. for Internat. Devel., Washington, 1990-92, rsch. panel leader, 1996-98. Contbr. 105 articles to profl. jours. Mem. AAAS, Am. Chem. Soc., Entomol. Soc. Am. Achievements include patents for defined chemistry of many important insect, insect and plant, insect interaction. Home: 11621 Springridge Rd Potomac MD 20854-1110 Office: USDA Beltsville Agrl Rsch Ctr 10300 Baltimore Ave Beltsville MD 20705-2350

KLUNZINGER, THOMAS EDWARD, writer, actor, film director; b. Ann Arbor, Mich., Sept. 11, 1944; s. Willard Reuben Klunzinger and Katherine Eileen (McCurdy) Klunzinger Scholtz. BA in Advt. cum laude, Mich. State U., 1966. Copywriter Campbell-Ewald Advt. Co., Detroit, 1966-70; travel cons. Moorman's Travel Svc., Detroit, 1973-74; media dir. Taylor for Congress Campaign, East Lansing, Mich., 1974; comms. specialist House Republican Staff, Lansing, Mich., 1975-80; trustee Meridian Twp., Ingham County, Mich., 1980-84; vice chmn. Econ. Devel. Corp., 1982-84; compliance officer The Eyde Co., Lansing, 1985-88; legis. aide Mich. Ho. of Reps., Lansing, 1988-90; comm. officer Ingham Regional Med. Ctr., 1994—96, 2000—03, Schultz Investment Advisors, 2003, Eaton Rapids med. Ctr., 2004—. Author: Chester!, 1981, Heavy Lady, 1983, Double Standards, 1985, A Villa in Unadilla, 1985, Losing It, 1987, The Wizards of Kyshtym/Deine Kleine Beine, 1988, Lounge Lizards/Managing Gran, 1989, Like A Brother, 1989, Loose Dogs Will Bite, 1990, Beloved Friend, 1990, To Be Announced, 1991, Okemos Passing, 1992, Song of the Whale, 1993, Mimsy Borogroves and the Tooth Fairy, 1993, What About the Hungarian?, 1995, The Passion of Richard II, 1996, The Hunchback of Notre Dame, 1997, Out at Home, 1998, The Real Boy's Pirate Show, 1998, As I Was Saying..., 1999, Breakfast in Berlin, 1999, Folles, 2000, Blond Ambition, 2000, Rock the Cradle, 2000, In Pain, 2001, Butterknife, 2002, Better Than Never, 2003, American Burkha, 2003, Rush Limbaugh in Hell, 2003, Not My Baby, 2004, Abe Lincoln on Speed, 2005, Something Wonderful, 2005. Mem. Ingham County Bd. Canvassers, 1993—96; treas. Meridian Twp., 1996—2000; pres. Riverwalk Theatre, 1990—92, sec., 1993—95; mem. Ingham County Rep. Com., 1976—2004, sec., 1986—88, 1991—92, 1996, treas., 2001—02, Mich. Rep. State Com., 1981—85, 6th Dist. Rep. Com. sec., 1989—93; bd. dirs. Capital Area Transp. Authority, 1999—2001. Mem.: Mich. Numis Soc. (sec. 1991—96, editor 1993—2004, 1st v.p. 2003—04, 50th ann. coord. 2004—), Am. Numis. Assn. (region 4 coord. 1997—), Dramatists Guild. Address: PO Box 585 Okemos MI 48805-0585 E-mail: teklunzinger@yahoo.com.

KLURFELD, JAMES MICHAEL, journalist; b. N.Y.C., May 15, 1945; s. Herman and Jeanette (Garfield) K.; m. Judith E. Freiband, July 23, 1967; children: Jennifer, Jason. BA, Syracuse U., 1967. Tchr. N.Y. Bd. Edn., 1967-68; reporter Newsday, Melville, N.Y., 1968-73, Albany bur. chief, 1973-76, Washington bur. chief, 1981-86, assoc. editor, 1986-87, editor editorial pages, 1987—, v.p., 1998—. Recipient Pulitzer prize, 1969, Award for Nat. Corr. Sigma Delta Chi, 1983, Disting. Writing award Am. Soc. Newspapers Editors, 1987. Office: Newsday Inc 235 Pinelawn Rd Melville NY 11747-4250

KLUTTZ, WANDA BARRINGER, elementary school educator; b. Rowan County, N.C., June 11, 1954; d. Banks Ray and Edna Marie (Kasten) Barringer; m. Ronald Steve Kluttz, July 30, 1976; children: Jennifer Marie, Bryan Michael. BA, U. N.C., 1976; postgrad., Catawba Coll., 1989. Cert. elem. tchr., sci. 4-9, N.C, cert. AIG tchr. AIG instr. K-5 Faith Elem. Sch.; AIG coord. Rowan-Salisbury Schs., NC. Active County-Wide Think-a-Thon 1988-89, Summer SPEC camp for gifted 1989; Knowledge Master Instr. 1989. Named Tch. of the Yr. 1987, Rowan County Schs., Time Warner Start Tchr., 2003. Mem. NEA, N.C. Assn. Educators, Parents for the Advancement Gifted Edn. (pres. 1991). Address: 1000 School St Faith NC 28041

KLYATIS, LEV MATUSOVICH, test and reliability scientist; b. Kiev, Ukraine, Mar. 4, 1933; arrived in US, 1993, naturalized, 2000; s. Matus I. Klyatis and Dina Sifry; m. Nellya V. Klyatis, Aug. 31, 1956; children: Irina, New York, Evgeny, Karmiel. MS in Engring. Tech., Agrl. Inst., 1953—58; PhD in Engring. Tech., Belorussia State U., 1962—63; D of Tech. Scis., Leningrad Agrl. U., 1981—82; Dr.Ing., Latvia State U., 1992—93. Over 20 cert., Am. Soc. Quality, SAE Internat., IEEE. Test engr. Govtl. Test Ctr., Kiev, 1958-62, prin. engr. Kalinin, Russia, 1962-65; prin. specialist Ministry of Agr., Moscow, 1965-68, head of dept., 1968-73; lead scientist, head of dept. All-USSR Agrichem. Inst., Moscow, 1973-86; head of dept. All-USSR Industry Inst., Moscow, 1986-90; prof. U. Agrl. Engring., Moscow, 1988—90; chmn. State Enterprise Testmash, Moscow, 1990-93; head of dept. ECCOL Inc., NYC, 1997—. Bd. dirs. Internat. Assn. Arts and Scis. Inc., NYC, 1997—; academician Acad. for Quality Russian Fedn., 1998—; expert U.S. tech. adv. group to Internat. Electrotech. Commn., 2000—; mem. World Quality Coun., 2001—; expert ISO/IEC Joint Study Group Safety Aspects of Risk Assessment, 2004—; bd. of reviewers Quality Press Pub., 2003—. Author: Methods of Accelerated Testing, 1969, Accelerated Evaluation of Farm Machinery, 1985, Trends in the Development of Testing Technique, 1991, Step-by-Step Accelerated Testing, 1999, Successful Accelerated Testing Part 1, 2002, Foundation of Farm Machinery Accelerated Testing, 1980, others; over 30 patents in field; contbr. over 200 articles to profl. books, papers and jours. Recipient Aerospace Outstanding Contbn. award, Tech. Stds. Bd., 2003. Mem.: Soc. Reliability Engrs., Soc. Automotive Engrs. Internat. (governing bd. 2003—), Am. Soc. Quality (sr.; exec. bd. 2002—, rsch. grant 1998, special svc. award 2002, Allen Chop award in reliability 2003). Achievements include development of 15 advanced technological systems of simulation of field input influences; 12 new types of testing equipment; new methodology of accelerated reliability; invention of cost-effective technology of accelerated quality improvement, including high correlation between accelerated testing results and field results; new approach in accurate physical simulation of field input influences in the laboratory; industrial technology of product accelerated reliability testing. Avocation: running. Home: 72 Montgomery St Apt 1311 Jersey City NJ 07302-3827 Personal E-mail: lklyaxis@agoron.com.

KLYOSOV, ANATOLE ALEX, biochemist, researcher; b. Chernyakhovsk, Russia, Nov. 20, 1946; arrived in US, 1990, naturalized; s. Alexey Ivan and Tamara Michael (Kuz) K.; m. Gail Michael Muratov, Dec. 28, 1967; children: Svetlana, Yuri. MS, Moscow State U., 1969, PhD, 1972, DSc, 1978. Scientist Moscow State U., 1969—72, asst. prof., 1972—75, sr. scientist, 1975—79, prof., 1979—81; prof., head Carbohydrate Rsch. Lab. Acad. Sci. USSR, Moscow, 1981—92; prof. biochemistry Harvard Med. Sch., Boston, 1990—; mgr. biochem. rsch., v.p. Kadant Composites, 1996—; chief scientist Pro-Pharmaceuticals, Inc., Boston, 2000—. Vis. lectr. biochemistry Harvard U., 1974-75; adv. bd. Coun. Biotech. Acad. Sci. USSR, 1981-90, chmn. commn. cellulose bioconversion, 1982-90; expert panel Biofocus Found., Stockholm, Washington, 1991—. Author: The Practical Course of Chemical and Enzyme Kinetics, 1976, Enzyme Catalysis, 1980, Enzymatic Degradation of Polymers, 1984, Enzyme Engineering at the Industrial Level, 1989. Recipient Lenin Komsomol Nat. prize USSR in Sci. USSR Govt., Moscow, 1978, Nat. prize in Sci., 1984, Sci. and Tech. Gold medal, 1988. Mem.: World Acad. Arts and Scis., Internat. Orgn. Biiotech. Bioengring., Am. Chem. Soc. Avocations: science, tennis, running. Home: 36 Walsh Rd Newton MA 02459-3529 Office: Kadant Composites 8 Alfred Cir Bedford MA 01730-2340 also: Pro-Pharmaceuticals 189 Wells Ave Newton MA 02459 Office Phone: 781-275-3600. Personal E-mail: aklyosov@comcast.net. Business E-Mail: aklyosov@kadantcomposites.com. E-mail: klyosov@pro-pharmaceuticals.com.

KMENTA, JAN, economics professor; b. Prague, Czechoslovakia, Jan. 3, 1928; came to U.S., 1963; m. Joan Helen Gaffney, Aug. 9, 1959; children: David, Steven. B in Econs. with 1st class honors, Sydney U., 1955; MA, Stanford U., 1959, PhD, 1964; hon. doctorate, U. Saarland, Germany, 1989. Lectr. U. N.S.W., Sydney, 1957-61; sr. lectr. Sydney U., 1961-63; asst. prof. U. Wis., Madison, 1963-65; prof. Mich. State U., East Lansing, 1965-73, U. Mich., Ann Arbor, 1973—. Vis. prof. U. Bonn, Germany, 1971-72, 1979-80, U. Saarland, Saarbrucken, Germany, 1984, 85, 86. Author: Elements of Econometrics, 2d edit., 1986; editor: (with others) Evaluation of Econometric Models, 1980, Large-Scale Macro-Econometric Models, 1981; contbr. articles to profl. jours. Recipient U.S. Sr. Scientist Prize, Humboldt Found., Bonn, 1979; Fulbright scholar, 1957-59. Fellow Am. Statis. Assn., Econometric Soc.; mem. Am. Econ. Assn., Czechoslovak Soc. Arts and Scis. in Am. Home: 2511 Londonderry Rd Ann Arbor MI 48104-4017 Office: U Mich Dept Econs Ann Arbor MI 48109

KMETZ, DONALD R., retired academic administrator; Dean Sch. Medicine U. Louisville, 1981-98; ret.; v.p. health affairs U. Louisville, 1992-98; ret. Office: U Louisville Sch Medicine Health Scis Ctr 323 E Chestnut St Louisville KY 40202-1823

KMIEC, EDWARD URBAN, bishop; b. Trenton, N.J., June 4, 1936; s. John and Thecla (Czupta) K. Ed., St. Charles Coll., Catonsville, Md., 1956, St. Mary's Sem., Balt., 1958; STL, Gregorian U., Rome, 1962. Ordained priest Roman Cath. Ch., 1961. Ordained titular bishop Simidicca and aux. bishop Trenton, 1982-92; bishop of Nashville, 1992—; bishop of Buffalo, 2004—. Roman Catholic. Address: The Catholic Center 795 Main St Buffalo NY 14203 Office Phone: 716-847-5500.

KNABE, GEORGE WILLIAM, JR., pathologist, educator; b. Grand Rapids, Mich., June 29, 1924; s. George William and Dorothy Emma (Fischofer) K., m. Lorine Jeanette Moffit, Jan. 16, 1954; children: Katharine J., Elizabeth J., Ann C., Dorothy M. Student, Mich. State U., 1942-43, The Citadel, Charleston, SC, 1943-44, Johns Hopkins U., 1944-45; MD, U. Md., 1949. Diplomate Am. Bd. Pathology. Intern Balt. City Hosp., 1949-50; resident pathology Cleve. Clin. Found., 1950-51, Henry Ford Hosp., Detroit, 1953-54; chief lab. svc. VA Ctr., Dayton, Ohio, 1955-57; vis. prof. pathology U. El Salvador Sch. Medicine, 1957-59; asst. prof. pathology U. P.R. Sch. Medicine, 1959-60; prof., chmn. dept. pathology Sch. Medicine, U. S.D., 1960-68, dean., 1967-72; dir. med. edn. St. Luke's Hosp., Duluth, 1972-78; prof. pathology U. Minn.-Duluth Sch. Medicine, 1972—, assoc. dean clin. affairs., 1972-76; chief. dept. pathology Virginia (Minn.) Regional Med. Ctr., 1978-98; pres. Range Pathology, 1998—. Bd. dirs Health Sys. Agy. of Western Lake Superior, Duluth 1975-82, No. Lakes Health Care Consortium, 1984—, U. Minn. Health and Med. Sch. Adv. Groups 1972—. 1st lt. to capt. M.C., USAF, 1951-53; surgeon to capt., USPHS Res., 1957—. Mem. AMA, U.S. and Can. Acad. Pathology, Am. Soc. Clin. Pathologists, Coll. Am. Pathologists. Avocations: art, horticulture, photography. Home: 1008 S 7th Ave Virginia MN 55792-3151 Office: Range Pathology 1008 7th Ave S Virginia MN 55792-3151 Office Phone: 218-749-3341. E-mail: knabegw@yahoo.com.

KNABLE, MICHAEL, medical researcher; BS, DO, Ohio U. Med. dir. Stanley Med. Rsch. Ctr., 1998—2003, exec. dir., 2003—; clin. instr. dept. psychiatry George Wash. U. Med. Ctr.; dep. med. dir. Nat. Inst. Mental Health, 1992—98. Bd. dir. Ahead with Autism Found., Psychiatric Genomics, Inc., DarPharma, Inc. Co-author (with E. Fuller Torrey): Surviving Manic Depression, 2001. Office: Stanley Med Rsch Inst 5430 Grosvenor Ln Ste 200 Bethesda MD 20814

KNACHEL, PHILIP ATHERTON, librarian; b. Indpls., June 23, 1926; s. Firman F. and Mary Esther (Atherton) K.; m. Pierrette Annie Roy, July 1, 1955; children— Sylvette, Eric BS, Northwestern U., 1948; cert., Institut de

Tours, France, 1951; MA, Johns Hopkins U., 1952, PhD, 1954; MSLS, Syracuse U., 1959; LittD (hon.), Amherst Coll., 1984. Instr. history Hunter Coll., NYC, 1954-57; historian Rome (NY) Air Devel. Ctr., 1957-59; chief tech. svcs. Folger Shakespeare Libr., Washington, 1959-61, asst. dir., to 1969, assoc. dir., 1969-93; freelance French translator, 1993—. Adj. prof. history U. Md., College Park, 1967-69; French translator cons. Author: England and the Fronde, 1967; editor: Eikon Basilike, 1966, The Case of the Commonwealth of England Stated, 1967 Served with USN, 1944-46 Avocations: piano, travel. Home: 5807 Phoenix Dr Bethesda MD 20817-3401

KNACKSTEDT, MARY V., interior designer; b. Harrisburg, Pa., Oct. 26, 1940; d. Harry and Veronica Knackstedt. Student, Pratt Inst., 1957-59, Cooper Union, Phila. Coll. Art. Pres. Knackstedt Inc., Harrisburg, N.Y.C., 1958—. Adv. bd. PNC Bank, N.A., Camp Hill, Pa., 1981—; lectr. bus. practices Harvard U., 1988—; cons., speaker in field. Author: Interior Design for Profit, 1980, Profitable Career Options for Designers, 1985, The Interior Design Business Handbook, 1988, 4th edit., 2005, Marketing and Design Services: The Designer Client Rlationship, 1993, Interior Design and Beyond, 1995; prin. works include Hershey Med. Ctr., Milton Hershey Sch., founder's Hall, Hershey, Pa., Hershey Pub. Libr. Bus. devel. program founder Riverfront Peoples Park, Harrisburg, 1980-90; bd. dirs. Harrisburg Symphony Assn., 1983-89; founder, pres. Profl. Cath. Women's Forum; devel. coun. Bishop McDevitt Sch., Harrisburg. Fellow Internat. Interior Design Assn., Am. Soc. Interior Designers (past officer); mem. Internat. Furnishings and Design Assn., Illuminating Engring. Soc. N.Am., Interior Design Soc., Pres.'s Assn., Am. Mgmt. Assn. Home and Office: 2901 N Front St Harrisburg PA 17110-1223 Address: 161 E 61st St New York NY 10021-8125 Office Phone: 717-233-6575. Personal E-mail: maryknackstedt@aol.com.

KNAFF, JOHN ALBERT, meteorologist, aerospace scientist; b. Denver, Colo., May 5, 1967; s. Lawrence Charles and Elizabeth Ann Knaff; m. Laura Anne Majeski, July 23, 1994; children: Rachel Anne, Rebecca Marie. BS in meterology, Tex. A&M U., 1985—89; MSc, Colo. State Univ., 1989—92; PhD. in atmospheric sci., Colo. State U., 1992—97. Post doctoral fellow Coop. Inst. for Rsch. in the Atmopsphere, Fort Collins, Colo., 1997—99, rsch. scientist, 1999—. Cons. Sci. and Tech. Corp. - MetSat, Fort Collins, Colo., 2000—. Recipient David Johnson award, Nat. Oceanic and Atmospheric Adminstrn., 2004; Global Change fellowship, NASA, 1993. Mem.: Am. Geophys. Union (assoc.), Am. Meteorol. Soc. (assoc.). Achievements include development of a statistical typhoon intensity prediction scheme for the western North Pacific. Home: 2455 Cheviot Dr Fort Collins CO 80526 Office: CIRA Colorado State Univ Foothills Campus Fort Collins CO 80523-1375 Office Phone: 970-491-8881. Office Fax: 970-491-8241. E-mail: knaff@cira.colostate.edu.

KNAG, PAUL EVERETT, lawyer; b. Flushing, N.Y., Feb. 26, 1948; s. Howard Alf and Charlotte (Rausch) Knag; m. Maryann McCaffrey, June 27, 1970; children: Paul Everett, Peter, Kathleen, John. BA magna cum laude, Queens Coll., 1967; JD cum laude, Harvard U., 1970. Bar: N.Y. 1970, Conn. 1971, DC 1983. Law clk. U.S. Ct. Appeals (2nd cir.), N.Y.C., 1970-71; ptnr. Cummings & Lockwood, Stamford, 1979—2002, Murtha Cullina LLP, New Haven, 2002—. Author: HIPAA: A Guide to Healthcare Privacy and Security Law, 2002. Mem.: Conn. Health Lawyers Assn., Am. Health Lawyers Assn., Regional Bar Assn., Conn. Bar Assn., Boston Bar Assn., Mass. Bar Assn., Quinnipiack Club, Harvard Club Fairfield County, Middlesex Club Darien, Dunes Club (Naragansett, R.I.), Officer's Club Hartford. Republican. Office: 99 High St Boston MA 02110-2320 also: 177 Broad St Stamford CT 06905 Office Phone: 203-772-7711. Business E-Mail: pknag@murthalaw.com.

KNAKE, MICHAEL WILLIS, music educator; b. Springfield, Nebr., Feb. 25, 1964; s. Willis Dean Walter and Sharon Kay (Dodson) Knake; children: Hillary Kay, Heidi Ann. BFA, Peru State Coll., 1989. Nebraska Teaching Cert. Music tchr. Dawson-Verdon Cons. Schools, Dawson, Nebr., 1990; band dir. Tecumseh Public Schools, 1991; music tchr. Chester-Hubbell Buron Public Schools, 1992—93; band dir. Lexington Pub. Schools, 1994; customer svc. rep. Coleman Powermate Corp., Kearney, Nebr., 1995—97; music tchr. Loup City Pub. Schools, 1998—2000; band dir. Bayard Pub. Schools, 2001—. Mem. Bayard Public Schools Tech. Com., 2001—; founder Western Nebr. Jr. High Band, 2001—. Mem.: Nebr. Music Educators Assn., Nebr. State Bandmasters Assn., Music Educators Nat. Conf., Fraternal Order of Eagles, Internat. Assn Lions Clubs. Democrat. Meth. Home: 819 Ave C Bayard NE 69334

KNAPE, HERBERT FRITZ, engineering executive; b. Grand Rapids, Mich., Dec. 24, 1922; s. John C. and Mayme J. Knape; m. Glenna S. Knape, Feb. 12, 1950; children: John, Judy, Mary Lou, Jim, Bill, Betsy, Robert. BS in Engring., MIT, 1944. Process engr. Jarecki Machine & Tool, Grand Rapids, Mich., 1945-55; v.p. engring. Knape and Vogt Mfg., Grand Rapids, 1955-65; pres. Knape Industires, Inc., Rockford, Mich., 1965—2001, chmn. bd., 2001—. Mem. Soc. of Vacuum Coaters (bd. dirs.), Am. Welding Soc. (bd. dirs.), Employers Assn. (bd. dirs.), Spring Lake Yacht Club (bd. dirs.), Grand Rapids Yacht Club, Spring Lake Country Club. Roman Catholic. Avocations: sailing, yachting. Home: 435 Edgemere Dr SE Grand Rapids MI 49506-2904 Office: Knape Industries Inc 10701 Northland Dr NE Rockford MI 49341-8008 Office Phone: 616-866-1651. Personal E-mail: knapeind@wmis.net. Business E-Mail: herbandglenna@yahoo.com.

KNAPP, ALBERT BRUCE, gastroenterologist; b. NYC, Aug. 9, 1955; s. Russell Sage and Bettina (Liebowitz) K.; m. Alice Anne Cohen, Sept. 7, 1986. BA, Columbia U., 1975, MD, 1979. Intern, resident Albert Einstein Med. Ctr., N.Y.C., 1979-82; fellow in gastroenterology Brigham & Women's Hosp. and Harvard Med. Sch., Boston, 1982-85; attending Lenox Hill Hosp., NYC, 1985—, St. Vincent's Hosp., N.Y.C., 1985—; asst. prof. NYU Med. Sch., N.Y.C., 1990—2004; asst. attending NYU Med. Ctr., NYC, 2002—, assoc. prof. medicine, 2005—. Author textbook in field, 1982; contbr. numerous articles to profl. jours. Trustee N.Y. Police Found., N.Y.C., 1991—. NIH rsch. grantee, 1982. Fellow ACP (jour. reviewer Annals of Internal Medicine 1985—); mem. Am. Gastroenterol. Assn. (jour. reviewer Gastroenterology 1985—), Am. Assn. Gastrointestinal Endoscopy, Am. Assn. for Study of Liver Disease (Rsch. award 1984). Office: 21 E 79th St New York NY 10021-0125 E-mail: albert@knappmd1.com.

KNAPP, AMY K., insurance company executive; With health maintenance orgn., Fla.; pres., CEO United Healthcare N.E., N.Y.C. Office: United Healthcare NE 2 Penn Plz Fl 7 New York NY 10121

KNAPP, CHARLES BOYNTON, economist, educator, former university president; b. Ames, Iowa, Aug. 13, 1946; s. Albert B. and Anne Marie (Taff) K.; m. Lynne Vickers, Aug. 25, 1967; 1 dau., Amanda. BS, Iowa State U., 1968; MA, PhD, U. Wis., 1972. Asst. prof. econs., research assoc. Ctr. for Study of Human Resources, U. Tex., Austin, 1972-76; spl. asst. to Sec. of Labor Dept. Labor, Washington, 1977-79, dep. asst. sec. labor, 1979-81; assoc. prof. pub. policy George Washington U., 1981-82; assoc. prof. econs. Tulane U., New Orleans, 1982-87, sr. v.p., 1982-85, exec. v.p., 1985-87; pres., prof. econs. U. Ga., Athens, 1987-97, prof. emeritus, 2005—; pres. Aspen Inst., 1997-99; ptnr. Heidrick & Struggles Internat., Inc., Atlanta, 2000—04; dir. ednl. devel. CF Found., Inc., Atlanta, 2004—. Bd. dirs. AFLAC Inc. Contbr. articles to profl. jours. Office: CF Found Inc 3445 Peachtree Rd NE Ste 175 Atlanta GA 30326 Business E-Mail: cknapp@cffdn.org.

KNAPP, CHARLES LINCOLN, law educator; b. Zanesville, Ohio, Oct. 22, 1935; s. James Lincoln and Laura Alma (Richardson) K.; m. Beverley Earle Trott, Aug. 23, 1958 (dec. 1995); children: Jennifer Lynn, Liza Beth. BA, Denison U., 1956; JD, NYU, 1960. Bar: N.Y. 1961. Assoc. Paul, Weiss, Rifkind, Wharton & Garrison, N.Y.C., 1960-64; asst. prof. law NYU Law Sch., N.Y.C., 1964-67, assoc. prof., 1967-70, prof. law, 1970-88, Max E. Greenberg prof. contract law, 1988-98, Max E. Greenberg prof. emeritus contract law, 1998—, assoc. dean, 1977-82. Vis. prof. law U. Ariz. Law Sch., Tucson, 1973, Harvard U. Law Sch., Cambridge, Mass., 1974—75, Bklyn. Law Sch., 2003, U. Copenhagen, 2004, Hastings Coll. Law, San Francisco, 1996—97, disting. prof. law, 1998—2000, Joseph W. Cotchett Disting. prof. law, 2000—. Author: Problems in Contract Law, 1976, (with N. Crystal and H. Prince) 5th edit., 2003; editor-in-chief: Commercial Damages, 1986. Mem. Am. Law Inst., Order Coif, Phi Beta Kappa. Office: Hastings Coll Law 200 McAllister St San Francisco CA 94102-4707 E-mail: knappch@uchastings.edu.

KNAPP, CHRISTIAN JAKOB, lawyer; b. Speyer, Rheinland Pfalz, Germany, Sept. 12, 1967; s. Hans Juergen and Edda Knapp. BA, Calif. State U.; JD, U. Pacific, McGeorge Sch. Law, 1994; grad. with honors, Judge Adv. Gen.'s Sch., 1997; LLM in Taxation, Wash. Sch. Law, 1998. Bar: Calif. 1994, U.S. Supreme Ct., U.S. Dist. Ct. (cen. dist.) Calif. Real estate agt. Sun View Realty, Helendale, Calif., 1987—91; law clk. Calif. EPA, Sacramento, 1993; assoc. atty. Thompson and Thompson Law Office, Victorville, 1994—95; legal specialist US Army, Ft. Hood, Tex., 1996—97, staff judge adv. and legal assistance atty. Ft. Monmouth, NJ, 1997—98, claims judge adv. and mil. magistrate, 1998—99; assoc. atty. Pursley and Glaeser Law Offices, 1999—2000; staff atty. Social Security Adminstrn., Office Hearings and Appeals, Stockton, 2000—01, supervisory atty., 2001—. Capt. U.S. Army, 1995—99. Recipient Judge Paul W. Brosman award highest class standing criminal law, US Ct. Appeals armed forces, 1997. Office: Social Security Adminstrn 401 N San Joaquin St Stockton CA 95202

KNAPP, CLEON TALBOYS, publishing executive; b. Los Angeles, Apr. 28, 1937; s. Cleon T. and Sally (Brasfield) K.; m. Elizabeth Ann Wood, Mar. 17, 1979; children: Jeffrey James, Brian Patrick, Aaron Bradley, Laura Ann. Student, UCLA, 1955-58. With John C. Brasfield Pub. Corp. (purchased co. in 1965, changed name to Knapp Comm Corp. 1977, sold to Condé Nast Publs. in 1993); pres. Talwood Corp., Knapp Found., L.A. Bd. visitors John E. Anderson Grad. Sch. of Mgmt., UCLA; chmn. bd. trustees Art Ctr. Coll. Design. Mem. Bel Air Country Club, Regency Club, Country Club of the Rockies, Eagle Springs Golf Club. Office: Talwood Corp 10100 Santa Monica Blvd Los Angeles CA 90067-4003

KNAPP, CRAIG BRIAN, music educator, musician; b. Rockville Centre, N.Y., Feb. 4, 1975; s. Howard Lee and Miriam Gertrude Knapp. AA, Suffolk CC, 1997; BM, Suny, 1998, MA, 2002; cert., Tech. Inst. Music Educators; cert. in level 1 and 2, Orff-Schulwerk. Music tchr. Rocky Point Pub., Rocky Point, NY, 1998—. Pres. Ants Marching Entertainment, LLC. Mem.: Suffolk County Music Educator's Assn. (asst. to v.p. festivals), N.Y. State Sch. Music Assn., Music Educators Nat. Conf. Home: 124 Lakeside Trail Ridge NY 11961 Office: Rocky Point Schools Joseph Edgar Bldg 525 Route 25 A Rocky Point NY 11778 Office Phone: 631-744-1600 ext. 3168. E-mail: mrknappl@aol.com.

KNAPP, DAVID ALLAN, pharmaceutical educator, researcher; b. Cleve., Feb. 25, 1938; s. Frederick Allan and Ethel R. (Ogden) K.; m. Deanne Evander, June 2, 1962; 1 child, Wendy Kay Knapp Steagall. BS, Purdue U., 1960, MS, 1962, PhD, 1965. Lic. pharmacist. Asst. prof. Coll. Pharmacy Ohio State U., Columbus, 1964-67, assoc. prof., 1967-71; assoc. prof., now prof. Sch. Pharmacy U. Md., Balt., 1971—, assoc. dean grad. edn. and rsch., 1981-83, chmn. dept. pharm. practice and adminstrn. sci., 1987-91, dir. Ctr. on Drugs and Pub. Policy, 1987-96, acting dean Sch. Pharmacy, 1989-91, dean, 1991—. Vis. scholar U. Mich. Sch. Pub. Health, 1970-71, Agy. Healthcare Rsch. and Quality, HHS, 2001-02; intramural researcher Nat. Ctr. for Health Svc. Rsch., Dept. HHS, Hyattsville, Md., 1978; scholar in residence Am. Assn. Colls. Pharmacy, Alexandria, Va., 1986-87. Author: Pharmacy Drugs and Medical Care, 5 edits., 1972-92; contbr. articles to profl. jours. Recipient numerous grants and contracts; named Disting. Alumnus, Purdue U., 1986. Fellow AAAS, APHA, Am. Assn. Pharm. Scientists, Am. Found. Pharm. Edn. (bd. dirs. 1994-96, exec. com. 1995-96); mem. Am. Assn. Colls. Pharmacy (bd. dirs. 1986-89, 93-96, Volwiler Rsch. Gold medal 1986, pres. 1994-95, commn. to stimulate change in pharm. edn. 1989-95, commn. future grad. edn. pharm. scis. 1996-98, chair arugur commn. 1993-99), Am. Pharm. Assn. (rsch. achievement award 1984), Am. Soc. Hosp. Pharmacists (commn. on goals 1996, com. credentialing 1996-99), Sigma Xi, Rho Chi. Unitarian Universalist. Office: Sch Pharmacy U Md 20 N Pine St Baltimore MD 21201-1142 Business E-Mail: dknapp@rx.umaryland.edu.

KNAPP, DAVID HEBARD, retired banker; b. N.Y.C., May 22, 1938; s. Alfred John and Doris (Hebard) K.; m. Letitia Lykes, Aug. 18, 1959; children— Genevieve, Christopher, Breckenridge. BA, Williams Coll. With Rotan, Mosle, Houston, 1960-62; asst. cashier, mgr. credit dept. Fannin Bank, Houston, 1962-64, asst. v.p. comml. loans, 1964-66, v.p. comml. loans, 1968-70, vice chmn. bd., 1970-82; co-chmn. exec. com. Interfirst Bank Fannin, 1982-83; ret. Devel. loan officer AID, Rio de Janeiro, Brazil, 1966-68; pres. Penta Internat., Inc., Houston, 1979-82; dir. Lykes Bros. Inc., Tampa, Fla., First Fla. Banks, Tampa, Interocean Steamship Co., Tampa, Lykes Bros. Steamship Co., New Orleans Trustee St. Lukes Episcopal Hosp., Houston, St. John's Sch., Urban Affairs Corp.; trustee Armand Bayou Nature Center, Pasadena, Tex., pres., 1977-79. Mem.: Houston Country (Houston). Office: 2807 Bammel Ln Houston TX 77098-1105 Home: 3227 Huntingdon Pl Houston TX 77019-3925

KNAPP, DAVID WILLIAM, lawyer, writer; b. San Jose, Calif., Jan. 5, 1922; s. John Fletcher and Emma Elizabeth (Tonkin) Knapp; m. Lucille Elizabeth Schulz, July 17, 1943; children: David William Jr., Gregory John, Jonathan Roy. Student, San Jose State U.; LLB, LaSalle U., Chgo., 1952. Bar: Supreme Ct. of U.S. Clk. superior ct. Calif. Superior Ct., County Santa Clara; trial lawyer Rankin, Oneal, Etal, San Jose; atty. at law Knapp & Knapp, San Jose; trial atty. Calif. Trial Lawyers Assn., San Jose. Judge pro temp Superior Ct. Author: (books) Herr Doe - The Silent Facade, 2002, Moses Del Rio-An American, 2003, When Darkness Comes, 2003. Chmn., civil svc. Santa Clara County, San Jose, 1957—63; scoutmaster Boy Scouts Am.; chmn. Dem. for Reagan, San Jose, Dem. for Nixon. 1st lt. USAF, WWII. Mem.: San Jose Elks (exalted ruler 1962—63), Masonic Lodge Golden Rule #479 (master scottish rite bodies 1974—75, 33 degree). Independent. Avocations: farming, cattle rancher. Home: 1784 Santa Barbara Dr San Jose CA 95125 Office: Law Offices Knapp & Knapp 1093 Lincoln Ave San Jose CA 95125 Office Phone: 408-298-3838. E-mail: dedeknapp@aol.com.

KNAPP, ELLEN M., financial company executive; 2 children. BS, U. SC, 1974. With Computer Scis. Corp. NASA Goddard Space Fligth Ctr.; with Booz-Allen & Hamilton; vice chmn., tech. Coopers & Lybrand, N.Y.C., 1992—98; chief knowledge officer, global CIO PriceWaterhouse Coopers, N.Y.C., 1998—. Mem. bd. assessment Nat. Rsch. Coun.; session chmn. Internat. Conf. on Future of Industry in Advanced Socs. MIT; guest lectr. Columbia U., Dartmouth U., Oxford U.; juror Lemelson-MIT award for Invention and Innovation, 1996, 97; keynote spkr. 10 Anniversary Symposium computer sci. and telecomms. bd. NAS, 1996; keynote spkr. numerous confs. Co-author: Every Manager's Guide to Business Processes, 1995; contbr. articles, chapters to books. Office: PriceWaterHouseCoopers 1301 Ave of Ams New York NY 10019-6022

KNAPP, GEORGE GRIFF PRATHER, retired insurance executive; b. New Rochelle, N.Y., June 26, 1923; s. Griff Prather and Lucy Chadbourne (Norvell) K.; m. Eva Witte, May 30, 1953; children: Edward, Wesley, Helen, Elizabeth. BA, Harvard U., 1945; postgrad., Law Sch., 1946. With Chubb & Son, N.Y.C., 1947-88, mgr. personal lines dept., 1966-73, asst. to pres., 1973, Can. zone officer, 1974-78, N.Y. zone officer, 1978-83, sr. v.p., 1968-88, nat. producer liaison, 1984-88; sr. v.p. Fed. Ins. Co., 1968-88, dir., 1970-88; exec. dir. Excess Line Assn. N.Y., 1988-90; cons. ins. advisor Westchster County vol. hosp. Arbitrator for major property/casualty ins. co. Gov. Lawrence Hosp., 1968-75. Served with U.S. Army, 1943-46. Mem.: Bronxville Field Club, Harvard Club (N.Y.C.), Phi Beta Kappa. Republican. Roman Catholic. Home: 23500 Cristo Rey Dr Unit 312D Cupertino CA 95014-6527 Personal E-mail: george.knapp@ispwest.com.

KNAPP, GEORGE M., lawyer; b. Inglewood, Calif., June 19, 1954; BA magna cum laude, UCLA, 1975; JD, George Washington U., 1978. Bar: Calif. 1978, D.C. 1979. Law clk. to Hon. Jon G. Lotis Fed. Energy Regulatory Commn., 1978-79, dep. asst. gen. counsel, 1980; sr. atty. FPL Energy, LLP, Juno Beach, Fla. Mem. ABA (vice chmn. alt. energy sources com. sect. of environ., energy, and resources, 1980-85, chmn. 1985-89, mem. coun. 1989-92, chmn. membership com. 1992-94, chmn. strategic planning com. 1994-96, vice chmn. sect. 1996-97, chmn.-elect sect. 1997-98, chmn. sect. 1998-99), State Bar Calif., D.C. Bar, Energy Bar Assn. (chmn. program com. 1991-92, chmn. internat. energy transactions com. 1995-97), Phi Beta Kappa. Office: FPL Energy LLC 700 Universe Blvd Juno Beach FL 33408 Office Phone: 561-304-5146. Business E-Mail: george_knapp@fpl.com.

KNAPP, HOWARD RAYMOND, internist, clinical pharmacologist; b. Red Bank, N.J., Oct. 5, 1949; s. Howard Raymond and Jane Marie (Ray) K.; m. Brenda Louise Carr, 1984; 1 child, Matthew. AB in Biology, Washington U., St. Louis, 1971; MD, Vanderbilt U., 1977, PhD in Pharmacology, 1984. Diplomate Am. Bd. Internal Medicine. Asst. prof. medicine and pharmacology Vanderbilt U., Nashville, 1984-89, assoc. prof., 1990; assoc. prof. internal medicine and pharmacology U. Iowa, Iowa city, 1990-97, prof. internal medicine and pharmacology, 1997-2000, assoc. dir. NIH Clin. Rsch. Ctr., 1997-2000; exec. dir. Deaconess Billings (Mont.) Clin. Res. Divsn., 2000—. Mem. NIH Nutrition Study Sect., Bethesda, Md., 1994—96; cons. pharm. firms, grant orgns. and govtl. entities; mem. applied pharmacol. task force Nat. Bd. Med. Examiners, 1997—2000; mem. expert panel on cardiovasc. and renal drugs U.S. Pharmacopeia, 2000—. Editor-in-chief Lipids, 1995—; contbr. numerous articles to profl. jours., chpts. to books. Grantee NIH, Am. Heart Assn., others. Fellow ACP, Am. Heart Assn. (vascular biol. rsch. rev. com. 1993-95, arteriosclerosis coun.); mem. Ctrl. Soc. for Clin. Rsch. (chair clin. pharmacol. sect. 1992-95), Am. Soc. for Clin. Pharmacology and Therapeutics. Achievements include first demonstration that calcium ionophores stimulate eicosanoid synthesis; first evidence that N-3 fatty acids reduce platelet activation and blood pressure in patients; first demonstration of the effects of 5-lipoxygenase inhibition in humans. E-mail: hknapp@billingsclinic.org.

KNAPP, J. BARCLAY, entrepreneur; married; 2 children. BA in Math., John Hopkins U.; MBA, Harvard U. Formerly with Planning Rsch. Corp., Va.; founding mem. Cellular Comm., Inc., 1983—96; co-founder NTL, N.Y.C., 1993—2003, pres., CEO, 1997—2003. Pres., CEO Cellular Comm., P.R., CoreComm Ltd. Trustee Johns Hopkins U.; founding mem., past nat. chair Krieger Schs. Second Decade Soc.

KNAPP, JAMES IAN KEITH, judge; b. Bklyn., Apr. 6, 1943; s. Charles Townsend and Christine (Grange) K.; m. Joan Elizabeth Cunningham, June 10, 1967 (div. Mar. 1971); 1 child, Jennifer Elizabeth; m. Carol Jean Brown, July 14, 1981; children: Michelle Christine, David Michael Keith AB cum laude, Harvard U., 1964; JD, U. Colo., 1967; M in Law in Taxation, Georgetown U., 1989. Bar: Colo. 1967, Calif. 1968, U.S. Supreme Ct. 1983, D.C. 1986, Ohio 1995. Dep. dist. atty. County of L.A., 1968-79; head dep. dist. atty. Pomona br. office, 1979-82; dep. asst. atty. gen. criminal divsn. U.S. Dept. Justice, Washington, 1982-86, dep. assoc. atty. gen., 1986-87, dep. asst. atty. gen. tax divsn., 1988-89, acting asst. atty. gen. tax divsn., 1989, acting dep. chief organized crime sect. criminal divsn., 1989-91, dep. dir., asset forfeiture office criminal divsn., 1991-94; adminstrv. law judge Social Security Adminstrn., 1994—. Editor: California Uniform Crime Charging Standards and Manual, 1975 Vice chmn. Young Reps. Nat. Fedn., 1973-75; pres. Calif. Young Reps., 1975-77; mem. exec. com. Rep. State Ctrl. Com., Calif., 1975-77; pres. Miami Valley Episc. Russian Network, 2004—. Mem.: DC Bar Assn., Calif. Bar Assn. Episcopalian. Avocations: travel, reading. Office: Office of Hearings & Appeals 110 N Main St Ste 800 Dayton OH 45402-1786

KNAPP, MARK LANE, communications educator, consultant; b. Kansas City, Mo., July 12, 1938; s. Herbert H. and Mary Ellen (Coleman) K.; m. Cynthia Lackie Dennis, Jan. 27, 1963 (div. Aug. 1974); children: Hilary A. Cellard, Eric C.; m. Lillian J. Davis, Aug. 8, 1975 (div. July 2002; 1 child, Avery K. Davis. BS, U. Kans., 1962, MA, 1963; PhD, Pa. State U., 1966. From instr. to asst. prof. U. Wis., Milw., 1965-70; from assoc. prof. to prof. Purdue U., West Lafayette, Ind., 1970-80; prof. SUNY, New Paltz, N.Y., 1980-83; disting. vis. prof. U. Vt., Burlington, 1983; vis. prof. U. Tex., Austin, 1983-85, sr. lectr., 1985-87, prof., 1987-89, Jesse H. Jones Centennial prof. in comm., 1989—, U. Tex. Disting. Tchg. prof., 1999—. Cons., lectr. in field. Author: Nonverbal Communication in Human Interaction, 1972, 6th edit. (with J. Hall), 2005, Japanese edit., 1979, Spanish edit., 1980, Chinese edit., 1999, Portuguese edit., 1999, Polish edit., 2000, Russian edit., 2004, Social Intercourse: From Greeting to Goodbye, 1978, Essentials of Nonverbal Communication, 1980, Interpersonal Communication and Human Relationships, 1984, 4th edit. (with A. Vangelisti), 2005, (with J.C. McCroskey and C.E. Larson), An Introduction to Interpersonal Communication, 1971; editor: (with G.R. Miller) Handbook of Interpersonal Communication, 1985, 2d edit., 1994, 3d edit. (with J.A. Daly), 2002; contbr. articles to profl. jours., chpts. to books. With U.S. Army, 1957-59. Recipient Outstanding Young Tchr. award Ctrl. States Speech Assn., 1969; Ea. Comm. Assn. scholar, 1982-83. Fellow Internat. Comm. Assn. (pres. 1975-76); mem. Nat. Comm. Assn. (pres. 1989-90, Golden Anniversary award 1974, Disting. Scholar award 1993, Robert J. Kibler Meml. award 1993, Ecroyd award 2004), Assn. Comm. Adminstrs. (pres. 1997), Coun. Comm. Assns. (vice chair 1997). Achievements include research in interpersonal communication, nonverbal communication, communication in developing and deteriorating relationships, lying and deception, communication and the process of aging, communication behavior in organizational settings. Home: 5804 Rising Hills Dr Austin TX 78759-5513 Office: U Tex Dept Comm Studies Austin TX 78712 Office Phone: 512-471-3787. Business E-Mail: mlknapp@mail.utexas.edu.

KNAPP, MILDRED FLORENCE, retired social worker; b. Detroit, Apr. 15, 1932; d. Edwin Frederick and Florence Josephine (Antaya) K. BBA, U. Mich., 1954, MA in Cmty. and Adult Edn., 1964, MSW, 1967. Dist. dir. Girl Scouts Met. Detroit, 1954-63; planning asst. Coun. Social Agys. Flint and Genessee Counties, 1965; sch. social worker Detroit (Mich.) Pub. Schs., 1967-98, ret., 1998. Field instr. Mem. alumnae bd. govs. U. Mich., 1972-75, scholarship chmn., 1969-70 76-80, chair spl. com. women's athletics, 1972-75, class agt. fund raising Sch. Bus. Adminstrn., 1978-79; mem. Founders Soc. Detroit Inst. Art, 1969—, Friends Children's Mus. Detroit, 1978— Women's Assn., Detroit Symphony Orch., 1982-89, Mich. Humane Soc., 1991—; vol. Coun. Detroit Symphony Orch., 1990—; trustee, fin. chmn. Children's Mus. Recipient Appreciation cert.; fellow, Mott Found., 1964; grantee, HEW, 1966. Mem. NASW, Acad. Cert. Social Workers, Nat. Cmty. Edn. Assn. (charter), Sch. Social Work Assn. Am. (charter), Outdoor Edn. and Camping Coun. (charter), Mich. Sch. Social Workers Assn. (pres. 1980-81), Detroit Sch. Social Workers Assn. (past pres.), Detroit Assn. U. Mich. Women (pres. 1980-82), Detroit Fedn. Tchrs., Madame Alexander Doll Club. Methodist. Home: 702 Lakepointe St Grosse Pointe Park MI 48230-1706

KNAPP, PAUL RAYMOND, think-tank executive; b. Long beach, Calif., Sept. 8, 1945; s. Franklin L. and Ella Jo (Andrews) K.; m. Shirley K. Wheeler, July 16, 1967 (div. 1987); children: Michele Ann, Erica Elizabeth, Matthew Gary; m. Nancy Jane Gift, May 1, 1988. BS, Calif. State U., Chico, 1970; MBA magna cum laude, U. Chgo., 1977. With Kemper Corp., various locations, 1969-77; sr. v.p., cFO Kemper Fin. Svcs., Inc., Chgo., 1977-87; pres., CEO Kessler Asher Group, Chgo., 1988-90; dir., chmn., pres., CEO, Catalyst Inst., Chgo., 1991—. Bd. dirs. Berger Mut. Funds, Denver, Futures Industry Inst., Washington, 1992—, Internat. Fedn. for Bus. Edn., Kansas City, Mo., 1993—. U.S. nat. com. for Pacific Econ. Cooperation, Washington, 1995—; bd. dirs. Allendale Assn., Lake Villa, Ill., 1988—. Home: 1410 N State Pkwy Chicago IL 60610-1512

KNAPP, PEGGY DURDA, international company administrator; b. Mpls., Jan. 2, 1944; d. Joseph and Dolores Catherine Durda; m. Bobby Lee Knapp, Apr. 16, 1966 (div. Feb. 1973); 1 child, Noelle Catherine. Attended, U. Minn., Mpls., 1961-64, Christian Life Sch. Theology, 1996—. Stewardess Northwest Airlines, Mpls., 1964-66; sales mgr. LDS, Dallas; aeration ind. internat. dir. Chaska, Minn. Divsn. Mem. bd. dirs. Joseph Durda Found., Mpls. Contbr. articles to profl. jours. Vol. Minn. AIDS Project, Mpls., 1993-95, Parkland Hosp., Dallas, 1986-88; Christian Ch. counselor, 1998—; vol. pre-sch. spl. needs children, 1997—; lic. min., treas. bd. dirs. Heart's Cry Internat. Ministry, 1999. Mem. Nat. Assn. Golf Supts., Nat. Golf Found., Assn. Women Execs. Republican. Avocations: reading, painting, crafts, floral design. Office: Aeration Industries Inc 4100 Peavey Rd Chaska MN 55318-2386

KNAPP, RICHARD MAITLAND, association executive; b. Hartford, Conn., July 23, 1941; s. Maitl K.; m. Elizabeth Burgoyne, Apr. 1969; children: Heather, Peter. BA, Marietta (Ohio) Coll., 1963; MA, U. Iowa, 1965, PhD in Hosp. and Health Adminstrn., 1968. Trainee USPHS, 1964-65; project dir. Tchg. Hosp. Info. Ctr., Coun. of Tchg. Hosps., Assn. Am. Med. Colls., Washington, 1968-69; dir. divsn. tchg. hosps. Assn. Am. Med. Colls., Washington, 1969-73, dir. dept. tchg. hosps., 1973-87, sr. v.p., 1987-93, exec. v.p., 1994—; mem. adv. com. ambulatory dental svcs. program Robert Wood Johnson Hosp., 1978-83. Bd. dirs. Nat. Assn. Biomed. Rsch., chmn. exec. com. 1993-95; chmn. exec. com. Ad Hoc Group for Med. Rsch., 1992—. Contbr. articles to profl. jours.; mem. editl. bd. Inquiry, 1983-88. Bd. dirs. Hosp. Fund, Inc., 1984-2000; adv. com. The Commonwealth Fund Exec. Nurse Devel. Program, 1984-93; trustee Inova Health Sys. Bd., 1986—, chmn., 1999-2003; trustee Inova Health Care Svcs. Bd., 1982-98, chmn. 1993-98; mem. oper. bd. Fairfax Hosp., 1987-92, sec. bd., 1987-89, chmn. bd., 1990-92; mem. vestry St. Anne's Episc. Ch., Reston, Va., 1979-83. Mem.: Va. Hosp. and Health Care Assn. (bd. dirs. 2001—03), Inst. Medicine of NAS, Am. Hosp. Assn., W.Va. Thoroughbred Breeders Assn., Md. Horse Breeders Assn., Throughbred Owners and Breeders Assn., Hidden Creek Country Club, Cosmos Club, Delta Upsilon. Office: Assn Am Med Colls 2450 N St NW Washington DC 20037-1167 Office Phone: 202-828-0410. Business E-Mail: rmknapp@aamc.org.

KNAPP, ROBERT CHARLES, retired obstetrics and gynecology educator; b. NYC, Jan. 19, 1927; s. Jack and Hilda (Knapp); m. Miriam Hermanos, Nov., 1955; children: Louise, Jennifer, Michael. AB, Columbia U., 1949; MD, SUNY Downstate Med. Center, Bklyn., 1953; MA, Harvard U., 1982; DSc (hon.), SUNY, Bklyn., 2003. Diplomate Am. Bd. Ob-Gyn. Intern Kings County Hosp., Bklyn., 1953-54, resident, 1954-58; instr. ob-gyn SUNY, Bklyn., 1958-62, Am. Cancer Soc. fellow, 1962-63, asst. prof. ob-gyn, 1962-63; asst. prof. Cornell U., 1963-69, assoc. prof., 1969-70; chmn. dept. ob-gyn. Nassau County Med. Center, East Meadow, N.Y., 1967-70; assoc. prof. ob-gyn. Harvard Med. Sch., Boston, 1970-75, William H. Baker prof. gynecology, 1975-93, William H. Baker prof. emeritus, 1993—; asso. chief of staff Boston Hosp. for Women, 1975-80; dir. gynecology surgery and oncology Brigham and Women's Hosp., Boston, 1980-89. Dir. gynecology Sidney Farber Cancer Inst., 1975-89. Served with U.S. Army, 1944-46. Fellow ACOG, ACS; mem. AAAS, Am. Soc. Clin. Oncology, Am. Fedn. Clin. Rsch., Obstet. Soc. Boston, Am. Radium Soc., Boston Surg. Soc. Soc. Gynecologic Oncology, Am. Assn. for Cancer Rsch., Soc. Surg. Oncologists, Internat. Soc. Gynecologic Oncologists. Home: 20 Sutton Pl S New York NY 10022-4165 Business E-Mail: robert_knapp_ma82@post.howard.edu.

KNAPP, ROBERT STANLEY, English language educator; b. Alamosa, Colo., Mar. 29, 1940; s. Stanley Osgood and Pearl (Betts) K.; m. Christine Knodt, June 17, 1965. BA, U. Colo., 1962; MA, U. Denver, 1963; PhD, Cornell U., 1968. Instr. Princeton U., 1966-68, asst. prof., 1968-74; asst. prof. English Reed Coll., Portland, 1974-77, assoc. prof. English, 1977-83, prof. English, 1983—. Author: Shakespeare - the Theater and the Book, 1989; contbr. articles to profl. jours. NEH fellow, 1979-80. Mem. MLA, Shakespeare Assn. Am. Home: 3735 SE Woodstock Blvd Portland OR 97202-7537 Office: Reed Coll 3203 SE Woodstock Blvd Portland OR 97202-8138 Office Phone: 503-771-1112.

KNAPP, ROSALIND ANN, lawyer; b. Washington, Aug. 15, 1945; d. Joseph Burke and Hilary (Eaves) K. BA, Stanford U., 1967, JD, 1973. Bar: Calif. 1973, D.C. 1980. With U.S. Dept. Transp., Washington, 1973—, asst. gen. counsel legislation, 1979-81, dep. gen. counsel, 1981—. Mem. D.C. Bar Assn., Calif. Bar Assn. Office: Dept Transp Office of the General Counsel 400 7th St SW Washington DC 20590-0003 Office Phone: 202-366-4713. Business E-Mail: lindy.knapp@dot.gov.

KNAPP, THOMAS JOSEPH, lawyer; b. Chgo., Aug. 27, 1952; s. William Bernard and Jeannette Cecilia (Zarnowiecki) K.; m. Lee Ann Schiller, Sept. 27, 180; children: Brian Thomas, Terrence Joseph, Christopher Ryan, Katharine Cannon. BA, U. Ill., 1974; JD, Loyola U., Chgo., 1977. Bar: Ill. 1977, Fla. 1979, D.C. 1979, Tex. 1987, U.S. Dist. Ct. (no. and cen. dists.) Ill., U.S. Ct. Appeals (5th, 7th, 8th and 9th cirs.), U.S. Supreme Ct. 1986. Law clk. to presiding justice Cir. Ct. Cook County, Chgo., 1977-78; asst. atty. gen. consumer protection div. Atty. Gen. Ill., Chgo., 1978-80; atty. Burlington No. R.R. Co., Chgo., 1980-83, asst. gen. solicitor, 1983-85, asst. gen. counsel Ft. Worth, 1985-86, assoc. gen. counsel, 1986-88, labor counsel, 1988-95; of counsel Paul, Hastings, Janofsky & Walker, L.L.P., Washington, 1996-98, 2000—02; asst. gen. counsel The Boeing Co., Seattle, 1998—2002; v.p., gen. counsel Northwestern Energy Corp., Sioux Falls, SD, 2002—. Commr. Village of Wilmette, Ill., 1985; mem. cable TV adv. bd. City of Bedford, 1992-94. Mem. ABA, Assn. Trial Lawyers Am., Nat. Assn. R.R. Trial Counsel, Ill. Trial Lawyers Assn., Chgo. Council of Lawyers, Commn. of Airline R.R. Labor Lawyers. Clubs: Tavern (Chgo.), Union League of Chgo. Roman Catholic. Avocations: sailing, golf, photography. Home: 7116 Darby Rd Bethesda MD 20817-2914 Office: Northwestern Corp 125 S Dakota Ave Sioux Falls SD 57104-6403 Office Phone: 605-978-2930.

KNAPPE, CARLETON FOSS, lawyer; b. Snohomish, Wash., May 7, 1948; s. Ford Carleton and Dorothy (Heaton) K.; m. Caryl Conley, June 11, 1977; children: Alyson, Rachel. BS, Willamette U., 1970, JD, 1974. Surveyor U.S. Soils Conservation Svc., Snohomish, 1965-67; worker Standard Oil, Point Wells, Wash., 1968-70; clk. Washington County, Hillsborough, oreg., 1971-74; ptnr. Knappe & Knappe Inc. P.S., Snohomish, 1974—. City atty. City of Monroe, Wash., 1974-86; legal counsel Snohomish Pub. Hosp. Dist. # 1, Monroe, 1975—. Bd. dirs. Deaconess Children's Svcs., Everett, Wash., 1988-94. Sgt. USNG, 1974-80. Recipient Golden Hand award Deaconess Children's Svcs., 1994. Mem. Exch. Club. Presbyterian. Avocations: golf, stamp collecting/philately, reading, chess. Office: Knappe & Knappe Inc PS 90 Avenue A Snohomish WA 98290-2999

KNAPPENBERGER, PAUL HENRY, JR., science museum director; b. Reading, Pa., Sept. 5, 1942; s. Paul Henry and Kathryn (Medrick) K.; m. Naomi Knappenberger; children— Paul Charles, Timothy Alan, Shannon Rose Lalor, Heidi Kathrin. AB in Math, Franklin and Marshall Coll., 1964; MA in Astronomy (NASA fellow), U. Va., 1966, PhD in Astronomy, 1968. Astronomer Fernbank Sci. Center, Atlanta, 1968-72; instr. Emory U. and Ga. State U., Atlanta, 1970-72; dir. Sci. Mus. of Va., Richmond, 1973-91; pres. The Adler Planetarium, Chgo., 1991—. Asst. prof. Va. Commonwealth U., U. Richmond, 1973-81; bd. dirs. Assn. Sci. and Tech. Centers, pres., 1985-87; instr. astronomy Yellowstone Inst.; former v.p. Midlothian Athletic Assn.; mem. council Nat. Mus. Act, 1984-86. Former mem. bd. dirs. Mus. Film Network, Exhibit Research Collaborative; co-founder Planetarium Show Network; dir. Informal Sci. Instructional Services, Ltd. NSF Sci. Edn. grantee, 1971-72; grantee NEH, Inst. Mus. Services. Mem. Am. Astron. Soc., AAAS, Internat. Planetarium Soc., Va. Acad. Sci., Va. Assn. Museums (council 1979-91), Am. Assn. Museums, Great Lakes Planetarium Assn. Home: 6n488 Splitrail Ct Saint Charles IL 60175-6928 Office: Adler Planetarium 1300 S Lake Shore Dr Chicago IL 60605-2489

KNATTERUD, MARY E., editor, educator, writer; b. Pipestone, Minn., Mar. 21, 1954; BA, Concordia Coll., 1974; MA, U. Minn., 1979, PhD, 1997. Editor/writer U. Minn. Pub. Ctr., Mpls., 1981—86; user documentation tng. specialist Higher Edn. Assistance Found., St. Paul, 1986—87; assoc. prof./sr. rsch. assoc. U. Minn., Dept. Surgery, Mpls., 1987—. Author: First Do No Harm: Empathy and the Writing of Medical Journal Articles, 2002. Fellow: Am. Med. Writers Assn. (pres. north ctrl. chpt. 1992—93, Pres.'s award 2002); mem.: 4Cs, Nat. Coun. Tchrs. English. Democrat. Lutheran. Office: U Minn Dept Surgery MMC 195 420 Delaware St SE Minneapolis MN 55455

KNAUER, GEORG NICOLAUS, philologist; b. Hamburg, Germany, Feb. 26, 1926; came to US, 1975. s. Georg A. and Ilse M. (Groothoff) K.; m. Elfriede Regina Overhoff, Aug. 3, 1951; 1 child, Georg Lorenz. DrPhil, U. Hamburg, 1952. Rsch. asst. Thesaurus Linguae Latinae, Munich, 1952-54; asst. Freie U., Berlin, 1954—61, privatdozent, 1961-64, assoc. prof., 1964-66, prof., 1966-74; prof. classical studies U. Pa., Phila., 1975-88, prof. emeritus, 1988—, chmn. dept. classical studies, 1978-79, 80-82, 85-88; resident Rockefeller Found., Bellagio Study and Conf. Ctr., Como, Italy, 1989. Brit. Coun. scholar U. London, 1957-58; vis. prof. Yale U., 1965-66; Nellie Wallace lectr. Oxford (Eng.) U., 1969; mem. Inst. Advanced Study, Princeton, NJ, 1973-74; vis. prof. Columbia U., fall 1976; mem. Notgemeinschaft für eine freie Universität, Berlin, 1969-90; mem. Bund Freiheit der Wissenschaft, Bonn, 1970—; mem. Internat. Coun. on Future of Univ., NYC. Author: Psalmenzitate in Augustins Konfessionen, 1955, 2d edit. under title Three Studies, 1987, Die Aeneis und Homer, 1964, 2d edit. 1979. Served with German Army, 1944-45. Guggenheim fellow, 1979-80, NEH fellow, 1984-85, Herzog August Bibliothek fellow, Germany, 1991, 97, 2002; vis. scholar Am. Acad., Rome, 1979-80, 90, 97, 2003, resident in classics, 1985 Mem. Am. Philol. Assn., Berliner Wissenschaftliche Gesellschaft, Am. Renaissance Soc. Home: The Quadrangle Apt 3314 3300 Darby Rd Haverford PA 19041-1070 Office: U Pa Dept of Classical Studies Logan Hall Philadelphia PA 19104-6304 Business E-Mail: gknauer@sas.upenn.edu.

KNAUER, JAMES PHILIP, physicist; b. Sandusky, OH, May 12, 1950; s. William David Sr. and Alice Roselyn (Mowry) Knauer; m. Susan Diana Holmes, Apr. 8, 1974. BS, MIT, 1972; MS, U. Hawaii, 1974, PhD, 1977. Rsch. asst. MIT, Cambridge, Mass., 1971-72; grad. tchg. asst. U. Hawaii, Honolulu, 1972-74, 74-77, jr. researcher, 1978-79; rsch. investigator U. Pa., Phila., 1977-78; assoc. rsch. scientist Lockheed Missiles & Space Co., Palo Alto, Calif., 1979-86, rsch. scientist, 1979-86; scientist Lab. Laser Energetics U. Rochester, NY, 1986-99, sr. scientist, 1999—. Mgr. Nat. Laser Users Facility, Rochester, 1986—96. Leader 4-H Club, Monroe County, NY, 1987—. Mem.: Carriage Assn. Am., Am. Driving Soc., Am. Phys. Soc. (Excellence in Plasma Physics Rsch. award 1995), N.Y. State Horse Coun., Sigma Xi. Republican. Avocation: riding and driving horses. Office: Lab for Laser Energetics Univ of Rochester 250 E River Rd Rochester NY 14623-1212 Office Phone: 585-275-2074. Business E-Mail: jkna@lle.rochester.edu.

KNAUER, LEON THOMAS, lawyer; b. N.Y.C., July 16, 1932; s. Lawrence R. and Loretta M. (Trainor) K.; m. Traude Kunz, Sept. 11, 1976; children: Robert A., Katrine M. BS in Math., Fordham U., 1954; JD, Georgetown U., 1961. Bar: Conn. 1961, D.C. 1961, U.S. Supreme Ct. 1965. Law clk. U.S. Dist. Ct. (D.C.), 1960-61; assoc. Wilkinson, Barker & Knauer LLP, Washington, 1961-68, ptnr., 1968-82, Wilkinson Barker Knauer, LLP, Washington, 1982—. Instr. Georgetown U. Law Center, 1964-65. Editor: Telecommunications Act Handbook: A Complete Reference for Business, 1996, Telecommunications Act of 1996-A Domestic and International Prospective for Business, 1998. Pres. Catholic Apostolic Mass Media, 1974-76, Knights of Malta, 1979—, Thomas More Soc. of U.S., 1984-85. Lt. USMC, 1954-57. Recipient award for outstanding legal svc. in media area NAACP, 1973, Officer's Cross for legal svcs. to Austria, 1992. Mem. Fed. Comms. Bar Assn. (editor Comms. Bar Jour. 1960-69, treas. 1980-82, mem. exec. com. 1982-84), Washington Golf and County Club, Cosmos Club Washington, Fordham U. Alumni of Washington (pres. 1982-85). Republican. Roman Catholic. Office: 2300 N St NW Ste 700 Washington DC 20037-1122

KNAUER, VIRGINIA HARRINGTON (MRS. WILHELM F. KNAUER), advocate, retired federal agency administrator; b. Phila., Mar. 28, 1915; d. Herman Winfield and Helen (Harrington) Wright; m. Wilhelm F. Knauer, Jan. 27, 1940; children: Wilhelm F., Valerie H. (Mrs. I. Townsend Burden III). BFA, U. Pa., 1937; grad., Pa. Acad. Fine Arts, 1937; postgrad., Royal Acad. Fine Arts, Florence, Italy, 1938-39; LL.D. (hon.), Phila. Coll. Textiles and Sci., St. Francis de Sales, Widener Coll., Chester, Pa., Tufts U.; Litt.D. (hon.), Drexel U.; L.H.D. (hon.), Russell Sage Coll., Pa. Coll. Podiatric Medicine; L.H.D., Jacksonville U.; LLD (hon.), U. Pa., 1971. Dir. Pa. Bur. Consumer Protection, 1968-69; spl. asst. to Pres. for consumer affairs The White House, 1969-77; dir. U.S. Office Consumer Affairs, Washington, 1971-77, 81-88; spl. adv. to Pres. for consumer affairs The White House, 1981-88; chair ABRH Inc., Washington, 1988-91; consumer cons. Haney and Knauer, Inc., Washington, 1991-93. Pres. Virginia Knauer & Assocs., Inc., Washington, 1977-81; chmn. Coun. for Advancement of Consumer Policy, 1979-81; U.S. rep., vice chmn. consumer policy com. OECD, 1970-77, 81-88; mem. Coun. Wage and Price Stability, 1974-77; vice-chmn. Philadelphia County Rep. Com., 1958-77; pres. Phila. Congress Rep. Women's Councils, 1958-77; dir. Pa. Coun. Rep. Women, 1963-80; founder N.E. Phila. Coun. Rep. Women, pres., 1956-68 Bd. dirs. Hannah Penn House, 1956—, v.p., 1971; chmn. Knauer Found. Hist. Preservation, 1963—; nat. chmn. to promote no fault automobile ins. Project New Start, 1988-91; bd. dirs. Nat. Coalition for Cancer Survivorship; mem. city coun., Phila., Pa., 1960-68. Recipient Gimbel-Phila. award, 1977, Ind. Achievement in Govt. award Soc. Consumer Affairs Profls., 1983; named Disting. Dau. Pa., 1969; named to Disting. Women's Com., Northwood U., 1997. Mem. Nat. Trust Hist. Preservation, Am. Assn. Ret. Persons, Internat. Neighbors Club, Exec. Women in Govt., Penn Women (trustees coun.), Consumers for World Trade (bd. dirs.), Zeta Tau Alpha, Kappa Delta Epsilon (hon.). Episcopalian.

KNAUS, TIM, political organization administrator; Chmn. Jefferson County Dem. Com., Colo. State Dem. Party, 1999—. Office: Ste 200 770 Grant St Denver CO 80203-3517 also: Colorado Democratic Party 777 Santa Fe Drive Denver CO 80204

KNAUSS, JOHN ATKINSON, retired federal agency administrator, oceanographer, educator, retired dean; b. Detroit, Sept. 1, 1925; s. Karl Ernst and Loise (Atkinson) K.; m. Marilyn Mattson, Sept. 6, 1954; children: Karl, William. BS, MIT, 1946; MS, U. Mich., 1949; PhD, U. Calif., 1959; DSc (hon.), U R.I., 1992. Oceanographer Navy Electronics Lab, San Diego, 1947, Office Naval Rsch., 1949-51, Scripps Instn. Oceanography, 1951-52, 55-62; prof. Grad. Sch. Oceanography, U. R.I., Narragansett, 1962-90, dean, 1962-87, provost for marine affairs, 1969-82, v.p. marine programs, 1982-87, prof., dean emeritus, 1990—; undersecretary for oceans and atmosphere Dept. Commerce, Washington, 1989-93; adminstr. Nat. Oceanic and Atmospheric Adminstrn., Washington, 1989-93; U.S. commr. Internat. Whaling Commn., 1991-93; rsch. assoc. Scripps Inst. Oceanography U. Calif., San Diego, 1993—2004. Leader 10 oceanographic expdns. to study oceanic circulation, 1955-65; chair U.S. phys.-chem. panel Internat. Indian Ocean Expdn., 1959-62; mem. Pres's. Commn. on Marine Scis., Engring. and Resources, 1967-68; mem. State Dept. Pub. Adv. Com. on Law of Sea, 1970-82; chair sr. adv. com. on environ. scis. Ctr. for Energy and Environ. Rsch., U. P.R., 1977-80; mem. Nat. Adv. Com. on Oceans and Atmosphere, 1978-85, vice chair, 1979-81, chair 1981-85; chair bd. govs. Joint Oceanographic Instns., Inc., 1978-80; co-founder Law of Sea Inst., mem. exec. bd. 1965-76, 82-87; bd. dirs. Coun. for Ocean Law, 1983-89, 94-01; chair marine divsn. Nat. Assn. State U. and Land Grant Colls., 1984-85; chair Joint Oceanographic Instns. for Deep Earth Sampling, 1984-86; bd. dirs. Harbor Br. Oceanographic Instn., 1987-89; 1st vice chmn. Intergovernmental Oceanographic Commn., 1991-93; mem. bd. trustees Bermuda Biological Sta. Rsch., 1995-05, life trustee, 2005-; mem. ocean rsch. adv. panel Nat. Oceanographic Rsch. Leadership Coun., 1998-02, chair, 1998-02, Sea Grant adv. com., 2003-05. U.S. Congress renamed its Sea Grant fellowship the Dean John A. Knauss Fellowship program in 1987. With USNR, 1943-46, 53-54. Named to R.I. Heritage Hall of Fame, 1983; recipient Albatross award Am. Miscellaneous Soc., 1959, Nat. Sea Grant award, 1974. Fellow AAAS (v.p. 1972-73), Am. Geophys. Union (pres. oceanography sect. 1965-67, pres-elect 1996-98, pres. 1998-2000, Ocean Sci. award 1988); mem. Am. Meteorol. Soc. (hon., coun. 1980-82). Home: 126 Willett Rd Saunderstown RI 02874-3810

KNAUSS, ROBERT LYNN, independent corporate director; b. Detroit, Mar. 24, 1931; s. Karl Ernst and Loise (Atkinson) K.; m. Angela Tirola Lawson, Feb. 21, 1973; children by previous marriage: Robert B., Charles H., Katherine E.; 1 stepson, Ian T. Lawson. AB, Harvard U., 1952; JD, U. Mich., 1957. Bar: Calif., Tenn., Tex. Assoc. Pillsbury, Madison & Sutro, San Francisco, 1958-60; prof. law U. Mich., 1960-72, v.p. student svcs., 1970-72; dean, prof. law Vanderbilt U., Nashville, 1972-79; dean U. Houston Law Ctr., 1981-93, disting. univ. prof., 1981-95. Vis. prof. Vt. Law Sch., South Royalton, Amos Tuck Sch. Bus. Adminstrn., Dartmouth Coll., Hanover, NH, 1979—81; chmn., CEO Baltic Internat. USA/Inc., 1994—2003; chmn., prin. exec. officer Phillips Svcs. Corp., 2002—03; bd. dirs. Mex. Fund, Equus II, Inc., XO Comm. Inc. Editor: Small Business Financing, 4 vols., 1966, Securities Regulation Sourcebook, 1970-71, (with others) Cases and Materials on Enterprise Organizations, 1987; contbr. articles to profl. jours. Regent Nat. Coll. Dist. Attys., 1981-95. Lt. (j.g.) USN, 1952-55. Fellow Tex. Bar Found., Am. Bar Found; mem. Calif. Bar Assn., Tenn. Bar Assn., Tex. Bar Assn. (chmn. corp. coun. sect. 1991), Am. Law Inst. (life), Order of Coif. Home: PO Box 40 ThreeCreek Ranch Burton TX 77835-0040 Office Phone: 979-289-4000. E-mail: BOBKNAUSS@CS.COM.

KNEALE, DENNIS RANDALL, publishing executive; b. July 24, 1957; s. Doreen (Treshan) and Donald R. Kneale. Grad., U. Fla. With The Wall Street Journal, 1982—98, sr. ed., Tech., Sci. & Hlth. section, 1993—98; exec. ed. Forbes, 1998—2000, mng. ed., 2000—. Office: Forbes 60 Fifth Ave New York NY 10011

KNEALE, JAMES C., gas company executive; V.p., CFO, treas. Oneok Inc., Tulsa, Okla., 1999—. Office: Oneok Inc 100 W Fifth St Tulsa OK 74103

KNEAVEL, ANN CALLANAN, humanities educator, communications consultant; b. Balt., Oct. 29, 1946; d. James Michael and Ann (Ijams) Callanan; m. Thomas Charles Kneavel, Jr., Dec. 18, 1970; children: Meredith Elizabeth, Thomas Charles III, Rebecca Ann. BA, Coll. Notre Dame Md., 1968; MA in Am. Lit., U. Md., 1970; PhD in Modern Brit. Lit., U. Ottawa, 1979. Instr. U. Md., College Park, 1968—71, U. Ottawa, 0971—1972, Wilmington Coll., Del., 1976—79, Del. Tech. and C.C., Dover, 1975—79; asst. prof. Widener U., Chester, Pa., 1981—82; prof. Goldey-Beacom Coll., Wilmington, 1981—; dir. satellite campuses Total Quality Master's Program, Falmouth, Mass., 1995—. Contbr. articles to profl. jours. Trustee Hockessin (Del.) Pub. Libr., 1981-93, Alpha Tau Omega Fraternity, Wilmington, 1994—; mem. Friends of Hockessin Libr., 1981—. Mem. MLA, Nat. Coun. Tchrs. English, Conf. on Christianity and Lit., Am. Culture Assn., C.C. Humanities Assn., Alpha Chi (faculty sponsor, Svc. award 1994, v.p. region VI 2000-02, pres. region VI, 2002-04, nat. coun. 2003—), Nat. Coun. 2003-. Roman Catholic. Home: 7 Arthur Dr Hockessin DE 19707-1012 Office: Goldey-Beacom Coll 4701 Limestone Rd Wilmington DE 19808-1927 Business E-Mail: kneavela@gbc.edu.

KNEAVEL, THOMAS CHARLES, JR., psychologist, educator; b. Balt., Oct. 30, 1941; s. Thomas Charles and Caroline Frances (Noha) K.; m. Ann Callanan, Dec. 18, 1970; children: Meredith, Thomas, Rebecca. BS, Loyola Coll., Balt., 1963, MEd, 1968; PhD, U. Ottawa, 1979. Diplomate Am. Bd. Forensic Examiners; lic. psychologist, Del. Tchr. Ridge Sch., Towsen, Md., 1961-65; psychologist Balt. City Schs., 1965-69; clin. psychologist D.C. Children's Ctr., Laurel, Md., 1969-70; psychology intern Child Study Ctr. U. Ottawa, 1970-71; psychology intern Child Diagnostic and Devel. Clinic Children's Hosp. of Ea. Ont., Ottawa, 1971-72; sch. psychologist Cape Henlopen Sch. Dist., Nassau, Del., 1972-79; psychologist Comty. Mental Health Clinic, Beebe Hosp., Lewes, Del., 1973-79; program dir. child crisis unit Terry Children's Psychiat. Ctr., New Castle, Del., 1979-86, chief psychologist, 1982-86; pvt. practice, 1983—; psychologist Christina Sch. Dist., 1986—98; clin. dir. adolescent programs Meadow Wood Hosp., New Castle, Del., 1993—94; dir. psychol. svcs. Med. Ctr. Del. Dept. Adolescent Medicine 1st State Sch., 1995—99; psychologist Thomas A. Edison Charter Sch., Wilmington, 2000—03; cons. psychologist United Spine Ctr., 2005—. Cons. on compulsive gambling to dir. Del. Divsn. Mental Health; cons. Joseph Ho., Balt., 1969—70; mem. citizens adv. bd. Cmty. Mental Health Clinic Beebe Hosp., 1974—79; adj. faculty dept. psychiatry and human behavior Thomas Jefferson U. Med. Sch., 1980—86; frequent nat. presenter on treating oppositional disorders in children and adolescents, 1980—82; apptd. by Gov. DuPont and Gov. Castle Del. Devel. Disabilities Planning Coun., 1982—84, vice chmn., 1983—85, chmn., 1985—87; state rep. Nat. Assn. Devel. Disabilities, Washington, 1984—87, mem. child devel. com.; mem. state genetics adv. coun. A.I. DuPont Inst. and State of Del., 1986—94; clin. cons. Turnabout Counseling Ctr., Seaford, Del., 1987—91; apptd. by Gov. Castle State Bd. Psychol. Examiners, 1989, v.p., 1991—92, pres., 1992—94; adj. prof. Widner U., 1995—99. Mem. APA, Del. Psychol. Assn., Falmouth Inst. Quality Sys. Mgmt. (bd. dir. 1997—), Nat. Assn. Sch. Psychologists (charter), Del. Sch. Psychologists Assn. (pres. 1976-77), Del. Psychol. Inc. (bd. dir. 1987-89), Nat. Grad. Sch. for Quality Mgmt. (bd. dir. 1997-, bd. chair 2003-, bd. mem. 1990-, chmn. bd. trustees 2003-), Nat. Eagle Scout Assn. Roman Catholic. Home: 7 Arthur Dr Hockessin DE 19707-1012 Office: 17-C Trolley Sq Wilmington DE 19806 Office Phone: 302-654-7155. E-mail: dockneavel@yahoo.com.

KNEBEL, DONALD EARL, lawyer; b. Logansport, Ind., May 26, 1946; s. Everett Earl and Ethel Josephina (Hultgren) K.; m. Joan Elizabeth Vest, June 5, 1976 (div. 1980); 1 child, Mary Elizabeth; m. Jennifer Colt Johnson, Sept. 25, 1999. BEE with highest distinction, Purdue U., 1968; JD magna cum laude, Harvard U., 1974. Bar: Ind. 1974, U.S. Ct. Appeals (7th cir.) 1980, U.S. Ct. Appeals (3rd cir.) 1986, U.S. Ct. Appeals (6th cir.) 1987, U.S. Ct. Appeals (fed. cir.) 1988, U.S. Ct. Appeals (4th cir.) 2005. Assoc. Barnes, Hickam, Pantzer & Boyd, Indpls., 1974-81; ptnr. Barnes & Thornburg LLP, Indpls., 1981—. Contbr. articles on intellectual property, antitrust and distbn. law to profl. publs. Trustee Indpls. Civic Theatre, 1986—95, chmn., 1988—91, hon. trustee, 1995—2002, Trustee, 2002—, chmn., 2002—05. Mem.: ABA, TechPoint (dir. 2003—), TechLaw Group (v.p. 2002—03, pres. 2004—), 7th Cir. Bar Assn., Indpls. Bar Assn., Ind. Bar Assn., Columbia Club, Kiwanis (pres. 1991—92). Presbyterian. Office: Barnes & Thornburg LLP 11 S Meridian St Indianapolis IN 46204-3535 Office Phone: 317-231-7214. Business E-Mail: dknebel@btlaw.com.

KNEBEL, JACK GILLEN, lawyer; b. Washington, Jan. 28, 1939; s. Fletcher and Amalia Eleanor (Rauppius) K.; m. Linda Karin Ropertz, Feb. 22, 1963; children: Hollis Anne (dec.), Lauren Beth. BA, Yale Coll., 1960; LLB, Harvard U., 1966. Bar: Calif. 1966, U.S. Dist. Ct. (no. dist.) Calif. 1966, U.S. Ct. Appeals (9th cir.) 1966. Assoc. McCutchen, Doyle, Brown & Enersen, San Francisco, 1966-74, ptnr., 1974-94, of counsel, 1994-99; owner Artema, 1999—; dir. litigation tng. Brigham, McCutchen, San Francisco, 2002—. Exec. com. San Francisco Lawyers Com. for Urban Affairs, 1991-93; adv. coun. Hastings Coll. Trial Advocacy, San Francisco, 1981-91, chair, 1990-91; mediator, arbitrator Am. Arbitration Assn., 1989—; lectr. Law Sch. Stanford U., 1998-2001, Harvard U., 2002—. Bd. dirs., pres. Orinda (Calif.) Assn., 1972-74, Sea Ranch (Calif.) Assn., 1978-79; co-chmn. Citizens to Preserve Orinda, 1983-85. Ensign lt. (jg) USN, 1960—63, ensign lt. (jg) USNR, 1963—66. Fellow Am. Coll. Trial Lawyers (mem. com. on fed. rules civ. pro 1990-93); mem. ABA, Maritime Law Assn. of U.S. Democrat. Home: PO Box 220 Islesboro ME 04848 Office: Bingham McCutchen Three Embarcadero Ctr Ste 1800 San Francisco CA 94111 Office Phone: 415-393-2000. Business E-Mail: jack.knebel@bingham.com.

KNEBEL, JOHN ALBERT, lawyer, retired government agency administrator; b. Tulsa, Oct. 4, 1936; s. John Albert and Florence Julia (Friend) K.; m. Zenia Irene Marks, June 6, 1959; children— Carrie, John Albert III, Clemens. BS, U.S. Mil. Acad., 1959; MA in Econs, Creighton U., 1962; JD, Am. U., 1965. Bar: D.C. bar 1966, U.S. Ct. Appeals bar 1966. Asst. to Rep. J.E. Wharton of N.Y., Washington, 1963-64; asso. mem. law firm Howrey, Simon, Baker & Murchison, Washington, 1965-68; asst. counsel Com. on Agr., U.S. Ho. Reps., Washington, 1968-71; gen. counsel SBA, Washington, 1971-74, U.S. Dept. Agr., Washington, 1973-75; under sec. Dept. Agr., 1975-76, sec. of agr., 1976-77; ptnr. firm Baker & McKenzie, Washington, 1977-86; pres. Am. Mining Congress, Washington, 1986-95; exec. v.p. Nat. Assn. Broadcasters, Washington, 1995—. Served to 1st lt. USAF, 1959-62. Mem. Fed. Bar Assn. (past pres.), Am., D.C. bar assns., Delta Theta Phi, Omicron Delta Gamma. Home: 1418 Laburnum St Mc Lean VA 22101-2523 Office: Nat Assn Broadcasters 1771 N St NW Washington DC 20036-2891

KNECHT, BEN HARROLD, surgeon; b. Rapid City, S.D., May 3, 1938; m. Jane Bowles, Aug. 27, 1961; children: John, Janelle. BA, U. S.D., 1960; MD, U. Iowa, 1964; cert. total quality mgmt., U. Wash., 1998. Diplomate Am. Bd. Surgery. Intern L.A. County Gen. Hosp., 1964—65; resident in surgery U. Iowa Sch. Medicine, Iowa City, 1968—72; surgeon Wenatchee Valley Clinic, Wash., 1972—; med. dir. Wenatchee Valley Hosp., 1997—; chmn. med. informatics Wenatchee Valley Clinic, 1995—2000, chmn. gen.-vasc. surg. dept., 1996—2001; mem. risk mgmt. commn. Wenatchee Valley Med. Clinic., 1999—, med. dir. group, 2004—; clin. prof., dept. surgery U. Wash. Dir. emergency rm. Ctrl. Wash. Hosp., Wenatchee, 1972-79, chmn. libr., 1976-86, chief surgery, 1983-86; chmn. claims rev. panel Wash. State Med. Assn., Seattle, 1979-82, prof. liability com. risk mgmt., 1985-90; clin. prof. surgery U. Wash.; mem. adv. risk mgmt. com. Wash. State Physicians Ins. Subscribers, 1990-98, regional adv. com. Nat. Libr. Medicine, 1991-93. Fundraiser Ctrl. Wash. Hosp. Found., 1987; del. Gov.'s Conf. on Libr., 1991; bd. dir. United Way, 1974-77; chmn. North Ctrl. Healthcare Skills Panel, 2003—; mem. founding bd. Cascade Unitarian Fellowship, 1986-88; mem. ad hoc com. on tchg./learning Wenatchee H.S., 1999-2002, mem. prin.'s adv. com., 2002—; post leader Med. Explorers, 1973-76; mem. Wash. State Healthcare Personnel Shortage Task Force, 2005-. Lt. comdr. USN, 1965-68, Vietnam. Recipient AMA Physicians Recognition Award, 1992—2006, WSMA Disting. Svc. award, 1997, Chelan-Douglas County Med. Soc. Appreciation award, 1997. Mem. AMA (alt. del. 1985-87, del. 1988-98, surg. caucus exec. com. 1991-94, group adv. com. 2004—), ACS (bd. dir. Wash. chpt. 1981-84), Am. Coll. Physician Exec., Am. Soc. Quality, Am. Med. Group Assn. (chief med. officer panel 2004—), North Pacific Surg. Assn., Wash. State Med. Assn. (trustee 1979-98), Chelan-Douglas County Med. Soc., Am. Soc. Gen. Surgery (founding bd. 1994-2001, bd. dirs. 1992-2001), Henry A. Harkins Surg. Soc., Rotary (chmn. youth com. 1976-78), Wenatchee C. of C. (Greater Wenatchee and Cmty. Devel. 2000-02), Alpha Tau Omega. Avocations: snow and water skiing, reading, hiking, computing. Office: Wenatchee Valley Clinic 820 N Chelan Ave Wenatchee WA 98801-2028

KNECHT, JAMES HERBERT, retired lawyer; b. L.A., Aug. 5, 1925; s. James Herbert and Gertrude Martha (Morris) K.; m. Margaret Paton Vreeland, Jan. 3, 1953 (dec. 1994); children— Susan, Thomas Paton, Carol. BS, UCLA, 1947; LLB, U. So. Calif., 1957. Bar: Calif. bar 1957, U.S. Supreme Ct. bar 1969. Mem. firm Forster, Gemmill & Farmer, Los Angeles, 1957-84; sole practice, 1985—2004; ret., 2004. Chmn. bd. Templeton (Calif.) Nat. Bank, 1992-95. Fellow Am. Bar Found. (life); mem. ABA, San Luis Obispo County Bar Assn., Legion Lex, Caltech Assocs., L.A. Area C. of C. (dir. 1979-83), Beta Theta Pi. E-mail: jknecht@ccaccess.net.

KNECHT, JOHN H., artist, filmmaker, educator; b. Iron Ridge, Wis., Mar. 5, 1947; s. Henry C. and Laverne A. (Qualmann) K.; m. Lynn Schwarzer, Mar. 18, 1984; children: Anna, Benjamin. BSA, U. Wis.-Oshkosh, 1972; MFA, Idaho State U., 1974. Asst. prof. film U. Okla., Norman, 1974-79; vis. lectr. Brown U., Providence, 1981; asst. prof. fine arts/film Colgate U., Hamilton, N.Y., 1981-86, assoc. prof., 1986-92, prof., 1992—, chair dept. of art and art history, 1991—99, prof. art and art history, endowed chair, 2005—. Screenings/exhbns. include: San Francisco Cinematheque, 1979—, Athens Film Festival (Golden Athens award), 1978, 2004, Mus. Modern Art, N.Y.C., 1985—, Edinburgh Internat. Film Festival, Scotland, 1981, 84, Dallas Video Festival, 2004, 05, Carnegie Art Ctr., 2005; dir., writer: Aspects of a Certain History, 1984, Worldwide Video Festival, 1996, European Media Arts Festival, 1996, Brooklyn Mus., 1997. With U.S. Army, 1966-68, Vietnam. N.Y. Found. for the Arts fellowship, 1989, 97; Jerome Found. grantee, 1979; Lightworks grantee, 1982. Home: PO Box 83 Hamilton NY 13346-0083 Office Phone: 315-228-7636. Business E-Mail: jknecht@mail.colgate.edu.

KNECHT, MELISSA, music educator, musician; b. Wooster, Ohio, Feb. 23, 1954; d. Richard Boid and Joy (Brand) Gerber; m. John David Robinson, Aug. 20, 1985 (div. Dec. 12, 1988); m. Sam James Knecht, Nov. 28, 1998; children: Lydia Joy, Katherine Ruth. MM, Ind. U., 1979; BME, U. Mich., 1976, PhD, 1992. Tchg. asst. U. Mich., Ann Arbor, 1986—90; adj. prof. U. Toledo, 1995—96, Siena Heights Coll., Adrian, Mich., 1996—97, Hillsdale Coll., Mich., 1993—97, vis. prof., 1997—98, asst. prof., 1998—2002, assoc. prof., 2002—. Music dir. Tampa Theatre, Fla., 1980—81; orch. conductor Livonia Youth Philharm. Orch., Mich., 1991—96; dir. edn. and outreach Toledo Symphony, 1999—; presenter in field; violinist/violist Spoleto Festival, Italy, 1978, Philharmonica de Caracas, Venezuela, 1981, Jacksonville Symphony, 1978—89, Fla. Philharmonic, 1979—82, Am. Chamber Orch., Chgo., 1983—84, Toledo Symphony, 1991—2001. Grantee, CETA, 1978—79. Mem.: Coll. Music Soc., Am. String Tchrs. Assn. Avocation: running. Office: Hillsdale Coll 81 E College Hillsdale MI 49242

KNECHT, RICHARD ARDEN, family practitioner; b. Grand Rapids, Mar. 7, 1929; s. Fredrick William and Eva Rae (Blakley) K.; m. Joan Matson, Dec. 26, 1951 (div. 1975); children: Richard Arden, Karrie Jo, Jeffrey Paul; m. Patricia Irene Gilmore, Aug. 14, 1976; 1 child, Kimberly Kahler. BS, U. Mich., 1951, MD, 1955. Diplomate Am. Bd. Family Practice, Am. Bd. Geriatric Medicine; cert. med. dir. Intern St. Mary Hosp., Grand Rapids, Mich., 1955-56; pvt. practice, Fife Lake, Mich., 1956—. Fellow Am. Acad. Family Physicians, Am. Geriatric Soc., Royal Soc. Medicine; mem. Mich. Med. Soc. (com. on aging 1988—), Mich. Acad. Family Practice (chmn. com. on aging 1986-88, pub.'s award 1988), Mich. Med. Dirs. Assn. (pres. 1996-97). Avocations: archaeology, geology, hunting, fishing. Home and Office: PO Box 130 125 Morgan St Fife Lake MI 49633 Personal E-mail: r.knecht@charter.net.

KNECHT, ROBERT LEE, archivist; b. Kansas City, Mo., Feb. 14, 1949; s. Claude Robert and Walterene Knecht; m. Margaret Gale Briggs, May 23, 1981; children: Anna, John. BA, Baker U., 1971; MA, Emporia State U., 1987. Archives aid Fed. Recs. Ctr., Kansas City, 1973—75; archives tech. Fed. Archives and Recs. Ctr., 1975—77, archivist, 1977—79; archivist II, libr. II Kans. State Hist. Soc., Topeka, 1979—, head archival arrangement and description sect., 1999—. Instr. U. Mo. Extension Svc., Sedalia, 1976—80, Lincoln U., 1976—80; rschr. Hearne Bros., Warren, Mich., 1984—86; guest lectr. Emporia State U., Kans., 1990—91; mem., chair Johnson County Archives and Recs. Mgmt. Adv. Bd., Olathe, Kans., 1990—2000; mem. Haskell Indian Nations U. Archives Adv. Bd., 1997—99; presenter in field. Contbr. articles to profl. jours. Vestry mem. St. Augustine's, Topeka, 1990—. With USAR, 1971—77. Scholar, Baker U., 1967—71. Fellow: Kansas City Area Archivists (chair, mem. edn. membership and steering coms. 1976—, co-chair 1988—90); mem.: State Hist. Soc. Mo., Midwest Archives Conf., Kans. State Hist. Soc., Kans. History Tchrs. Assn. (mem. exec. com. 1984—87, 2005—), Am. Assn. State and Local History, Alpha Sigma Delta, Phi Alpha Theta. Anglican. Avocations: piano, organ, travel. Office: Kans State Hist Soc 6425 Southwest 6th Ave Topeka KS 66615

KNECHT, TIMOTHY HARRY, lawyer; b. Flint, Mich., Nov. 6, 1953; s. Wayne Warren and Nancy Jane (Post) K.; m. Linda Marie D'Appolonia, Aug. 14, 1976; children: Nicole Constance, Colleen Lin, Patric Timothy. BA in Econs., Duke U., 1975; JD, Detroit Coll. of Law, 1979. Shareholder Cline, Cline & Griffin, Flint, 1979—. Bd. dirs. Flint Inst. Arts, 1985-91, trustee, 1985-91; bd. dirs. Friends of Modern Art, Flint, 1980-86, Flint Environ. Action Team, 1985-93, treas., 1985-88, pres. 1988-93; legal com. rep., Flint Area Health Fedn., 1986-92; century mem. Boy Scouts Am.; trustee Grand Blanc Cmty. Fund, 1993—, pres., 1998-99; trustee Family Svc. Agy., 1993—, pres., 1998-99. Mem. ABA, Def. Rsch. Inst., Mich. Def. Trial Counsel, Genesee County Bar Assn.(treas. 1986-87, dir. 1988-91, state bar negligence law sect. 1995—, officer 1999—), Mich. Bar Assn., Flint Golf Club. Avocations: skiing, water sports, sailing, swimming, aviation. Home: 13084 Log Cabin Ptd Fenton MI 48430 Office: Cline Cline & Griffin 1000 Mott Foundation Bldg Flint MI 48502-1861 E-mail: TKnecht@ccglawyers.com.

KNEE, RUTH IRELAN (MRS. JUNIOR K. KNEE), social worker, health care consultant; b. Sapulpa, Okla., Mar. 21, 1920; d. Oren M. and Daisy (Daubin) Irelan; m. Junior K. Knee, May 29, 1943 (dec. Oct. 1981). BA, U. Okla., 1941, cert. social work, 1942; MA in Social Svcs. Adminstrn., U. Chgo., 1945. Psychiat. social worker, asst. supr. Ill. Psychiat. Inst., U. Ill., Chgo., 1943-44; psychiat. social worker USPHS Employee Health Unite, Washington, 1944—49; social work assoc. Army Med. Ctr., Walter Reed Army Hosp., Washington, 1949-54; psychiat. social work cons. HEW, Region III, Washington, 1955-56; with NIMH, Chevy Chase, Md., 1956-72; chief mental health care adminstrn. br. Health Svcs. and Mental Health Adminstrn., USPHS assoc. dep. adminstr., 1972-73; dep. dir. Office of Nursing Home Affairs, 1973-74; long-term mental health care cons.; mem. com. on mental health and illness of elderly HEW, 1976-77; mem. panel on legal and ethical issues Pres.'s Commn. on Mental Health, 1977-78; liaison mem. Nat. Adv. Mental Health Coun., 1977-81. Mem. editl. bd. Health and Social Work, 1979-81. Bd. dirs. Hillhaven Found., 1975-86, governing bd. Cathedral Coll. of the Laity, Washington Nat. Cathedral, 1988-94, Cathedral Fund Com., 1997—,bd. of visitors sch. of social work, Univ. of Okla., 2000— Recipient Edith Abbott award, U. Chgo. Sch. Social Svc. Adminstrn., 2001, Disting. Alumna award, U. Okla. Coll. Arts and Scis., 1999. Fellow APHA (sec. mental health sect. 1968-70, chmn. 1971-72), Am. Orthopsychiat. Assn. (life), Gerontol. Soc. Am., Am. Assn. Psychiat. Social Workers (pres. 1951-53); mem. Nat. Conf. Social Welfare (nat. bd. 1968-71, 2d v.p. 1973-74), Inst. Medicine/NAS (com. study future of pub. health 1986-87), Coun. on Social Work Edn., Nat. Assn. Social Workers (sec. 1955-56, nat. dir. 1956-57, 84-86, chmn. competence study com., practice and knowledge com. 1963-71, presdl. award for exemplary svc. 1999), Acad. Cert. Social Workers (NASW Found. co-chair social work pioneers 1993—), Am. Pub. Welfare Assn., DAR, U. Okla. Assocs., Woman's Nat. Dem. Club (mem. gov. bd. 1992-95, ednl. found. bd. 1992-2000), Cosmos Club (Washington, chair program com. 1998-2001), Phi Beta Kappa (fellow), Psi Chi. Address: 8809 Arlington Blvd Fairfax VA 22031-2705

KNEE, STUART EUGENE, historian, educator; b. N.Y.C., Nov. 16, 1945; s. Harold Edward and Mae (Sharff) Knee; m. Sonya Siegel, Jan. 24, 1971; children: Karen Lisa, Mark Adam, Eric Andrew. BA, Queens Coll./CUNY, Flushing, 1967, MA, 1969; PhD, NYU, 1974. Adj. asst. prof. Queens Coll. CUNY, Flushing, 1971—75; vis. asst. prof. U. Toledo, 1978—79, Ctrl. Mich. U., Mt. Pleasant, 1980, LeMoyne Coll., Syracuse, NY, 1980—83; adj. asst. prof. Syracuse U., NY, 1980—83; assoc. prof. Coll. Charleston, SC, 1986—93, prof. history, 1993—, dir. Jewish studies program, 1986—92. Author: The Concept of Zionist Dissent in the American Mind 1917-1941, 1979, Hervey Allen (1889-1949): A Literary Historian in America, 1988, Christian Science in the Age of Mary Baker Eddy, 1994; contbr. articles to profl. jours. Mem., donor Boys' and Girls' Town, Omaha, 1979—, DAV, Cin., 1980—, So. Poverty Law Ctr., Montgomery, Ala., 1983—; mem. Am. Jewish Congress, World Jewish Congress. Recipient Founder's Day award, NYU, 1974; grantee, NEH, 1994. Mem.: Assn. Jewish Studies, Am. Hist. Assn., So. Jewish Hist. Soc. (exec. bd. 1986—92). Avocations: poetry, tennis, walking, decorative shell bottles, photography. Home: 5 Brisbane Dr Charleston SC 29407 Office: Coll Charleston Dept History 66 George St Charleston SC 29424 Office Phone: 843-953-5938. Office Fax: 843-953-6349. Business E-Mail: knees@cofc.edu.

KNEEDLER, ALVIN RICHARD (RICHARD KNEEDLER), former academic administrator; b. Ruffsdale, Pa., Apr. 8, 1943; s. Alvin Raymond and Louise (Mac Innes) Kneedler; m. Suzette Gallagher, June 17, 1967; children: Eric, Rebecca. AB, Franklin and Marshall Coll., 1965; MA in French Lang. and Lit., U. Pa., 1967, PhD in French Lang. and Lit., 1970; cert. in Ednl. Mgmt., Harvard U., 1975; DHL (hon.), Tohoku Gakuin U., 1993; LHD (hon.), Franklin and Marshall Coll., 2002. Instr. French Franklin and Marshall Coll., Lancaster, Pa., 1968—70, asst. prof. French, 1970—72, asst. to. dean, 1971—74, asst. to pres., 1974—77, sec. coll., 1977—79, v.p. adminstrn., 1979—84, v.p. devel., 1984—88, sec. bd. trustees, 1974—88, pres., 1988—2002, pres. emeritus, 2002—; cons. Coun. of Ind. Colls., 2002—. Mem. exec. com. Assn. Ind. Colls. and Univs. Pa., 1989—98, 2000—02, chmn., 1996—97; exec. com. Nat. Assn. Ind. Colls. and Univs., 1999, chair policy and pub. rels. com., 99, mem. coun. ind. coll. dir., 2000—02; chair Pa. Gov.'s Training, Am.'s Tchrs. Commn., 2005—. Mem. Lancaster City Planning Commn., 1980—85, chmn., 1983—85; v.p., bd. dirs. Hist. Preservation Trust, Lancaster, 1984—87; sec., bd. dirs. Pa. Sch. Arts, Lancaster, 1985—89; bd. dirs. St. Joseph Hosp., 1991—95, Lancaster Area Arts Coun., 1987—91, Louise Von Hess Found. for Med. Edn., 1990—, Urban League Lancaster County, 1991—93, United Way, 1993—98, Urban Alliance, 1998—2002; chmn. Cmty. Cultural Planning Com., 1989—90; mem. Downtown Task Force, 1989—90; trustee Kiski Sch., 1988—95; chmn. exec. bd. Commonwealth Partnership, 1997—98; mem. adv. bd. PRIME, Inc., 1991—98; bd. dirs. Lancaster-York Hist. Reegion, 2001—. Mem.: Lancaster Pa. Soc., Mid. States Assn. Schs. and Coll. (vol. evaluator 1986—), Sons of Revolution (mem. exec. com. 2005), Lancaster C. of C. and Industry (bd. dirs. 1990—92, mem. exec. com.), Phi Alpha Theta, Phi Beta Kappa. Democrat. Presbyterian. Home: 1416 Newton Rd Lancaster PA 17603-2461 Office Phone: 717-393-6899. Business E-Mail: richard.kneedler@fandm.edu.

KNEEDLER, EDWIN S., federal agency administrator; b. 1946; BS, Lehigh U.; JD, U. Va. Bar: Oreg. 1975. Asst. to the solicitor gen. US Dept. Justice, Washington, 1979—93, dep. solicitor gen., 1993—. Professor law George Washington U. Office: US Dept Justice 950 Pennsylvania Ave NW Ste 5143 Washington DC 20530

KNEELAND, DOUGLAS EUGENE, retired newspaper editor; b. Lincoln, Maine, July 27, 1929; s. Vernis Bruce and Sadie Jane (Curtis) K.; m. Anne Packard Libby, Sept. 8, 1951 (dec. Nov. 1989); children: Debra Jo Kneeland Wentz, Libby Kneeland Williams, Bruce, Wayne; m. Barbara Jordan Lees, May 24, 1997. BA in Journalism, U. Maine, 1953, LittD (hon.), 2005. Reporter Bangor Daily News, Maine, 1951-53, Worcester Telegram, Mass., 1953-56; city editor, news editor Lorain Jour., Ohio, 1956-59; copy editor, nat. corr., dep. nat. editor N.Y. Times, N.Y.C., Kansas City, San Francisco and Chgo., 1959-81; nat.-fgn. editor Chgo. Tribune, 1981-82, assoc. mng. editor, 1982-87, assoc. editor, 1987-90, pub. editor, 1990-93; vis. lectr. journalism U. Maine, Orono, 1993—2003. Columnist Lincoln News, Maine, 1995—2001. Served with AUS, 1947-49, Korea, Japan. Home: 31 Albert Dr Lincoln ME 04457-9601 E-mail: dougk@midmaine.com.

KNEEN, JOHN W., venture capitalist; b. Detroit, Sept. 3, 1952; s. Russell Packard and Joyce (Knapper) Kneen; m. Mary Ellen Raphael, June 18, 1983 (div. Sept. 1998). BA, Coll. Wooster, 1974; MBA, Northwestern U., Evanston, Ill., 1976. CPA Ill., 1978. CPA Coopers & Lybrand, Chgo., 1976—88; v.p. Prime Group, Inc., Chgo., 1988—89; sr. v.p. devel. Evergreen Healthcare, Inc., Carmel, Ind., 1990—96; CFO Alterra Healthcare, Inc., Brookfield, Wis., 1996—97; mng. dir. Beecken Petty & Co., Chgo., 1997—. Bd. trustees Wooster Coll., 2003—. Mem.: Western Golf Assn. (bd. dirs. 1995—), Coll. Wooster Alumni Assn. (pres. 1999—2000), Union League Club Chgo., Medinah Country Club (bd. dirs. 1994—96). Republican. Methodist. Avocations: golf, skiing. Home: 2337 N Cambridge Chicago IL 60614 Office: Beecken Petty & Co 200 W Madison Chicago IL 60606 Business E-Mail: jkneen@bpcompany.com.

KNEESE, CAROLYN CALVIN, retired education educator; b. Austin, Sept. 16, 1941; d. Elmer Ben and Agnes Standlee Calvin; children: Kyle Calvin, Reagan Scott. BA, U. Tex., Austin, 1962; MA, Houston Baptist U., 1990; EdD, U. Houston, 1994. Cert. real estate broker Tex., 1988. Tchr. Austin Sch. Dist., Tex., 1963—64, Highland Park Sch. Dist., Dallas, 1964—67; translator, rschr. Methodist Hosp., Houston, 1969—70; rsch. asst. U. Houston, 1993—94; rsch. assoc. Tex. A&M U., College Station, 1994, asst. prof. Commerce, 1998—2002, assoc. prof. ednl. adminstrn., 2003—04, ret., 2004. Author: numerous jour. articles and publs. Fundrasier Partnership Baylor Coll. Medicine, Houston, 2004; past bd. mem. Houston Symphony. Mem.: AAUW, Tex. Real Estate Commn., Phi Delta Kappa. Home: 1100 Uptown Park Blvd Houston TX 77056 Personal E-mail: cckneese@aol.com.

KNEESHAW, STEPHEN JOHN, history professor, editor; b. Tacoma, Wash., Oct. 14, 1946; s. John Francis and Lois Jean Kneeshaw; m. Bobara Ann Bliss, Aug. 16, 1969; children: Daniel Ryan, Christine Bliss Kneeshaw-Yokley, Brianne Marie. BA, U. Puget Sound, 1968; MA, U. Colo., 1969, PhD, 1971. Instr. history U. Colo., Boulder, 1971—72; prof. history Coll. of Ozarks, Point Lookout, Mo., 1972—. Nat. adv. bd. Nat. Coun. for History Edn., 1990—; adj. curator for exhibits Ralph Foster Mus., Point Lookout, Mo., 1995—. Author: (scholarly monograph (book) In Pursuit of Peace: The American Reaction to the Kellogg-Briand Pact, 1928-1929 (Nominee for Mo. Book award, 1992), (review essay) Voices from Vietnam: The New Literature from America's Longest War in Teaching History, (collection of essays) Resources for Teachers of History: K-12 and College in The History Highway 2000, Briinging the Internet and World Wide Web into the History Classroom, in History.Edu: Essays on Teaching with Technology, Resources for Teachers of History: K-12 and College, in The History Highway 3.0, (op-ed essay) Some Thoughts on American Education and on American Teachers in Teaching History, (essay) The Internet, E-Mail, and the Environment in OAH Magazine of History, (annotated film guide) A Selected Listing of Films, with Annotations in Instructor's Manual for America's History, Volumes One and Two, (encyclopedia entry) Missouri The Show Me State in World Book Encyclopedia, (review essay) Recasting World War II: Using Oral Histories to Understand the Greater War in Teaching History; editor: Teaching History: A Journal of Methods, 1976—. Instr. ARC, Branson, Mo., 1981—95; chair constn. bicentennial com. City of Branson, Mo., 1986—91; cmty. adv. bd. Tri-Lakes Newspapers, Branson, Mo., 1992—94; extraordinary min. and ch. coun. Our Lady of the Lake Ch., Branson, Mo., 1980—2005; Llittle League coach Branson Pks. and Recreation, Mo., 1979—98; classroom vol. Branson R-IV Schs., Mo., 1988—2005. Named one of Outstanding Young Men of Am., 1979 and 1982; fellow West Point ROTC fellow in Mil. History, U.S. Mil. Acad., 1996; NDEA Title IV fellow, U. Colo., 1968-1971, Rsch. Grant, 1970-1971, NEH fellow, Newberry Libr., Chgo., 1979, Wye Faculty fellow, Aspen Inst., 1989. Mem.: C.C. Humanities Assn., Wash. State Coun. for Social Studies, SW.W. Mo. Dist. Social Studies Assn., Nat. Coun. for History Edn. (nat. adv. bd. 1990—2005), Am. Hist. Assn., Soc. for Historians of Am. Fgn. Rels. (membership com. 1978—84), Orgn. Am. Historians (nat. chmn. membership com. 2004—), Phi Alpha Theta (chpt. advisor 1973—2005), Sigma Nu (divsn. comdr. 1976—88, Man of Yr. 1968). Roman Catholic. Avocations: travel, reading, sports card collecting, photography. Home: 153 Raspberry Ln Branson MO 65616 Office: College of Ozarks Dept History Point Lookout MO 65726 Office Phone: 417-334-6411 x4264. Office Fax: 417-335-2618. Business E-Mail: kneeshaw@cofo.edu.

KNEEZEL, RONALD D., lawyer; b. 1956; BA, U. Ill., 1978, MBA, 1982, JD. Bar: 1982. Atty. Foley & Lardner Attys. at Law, Milw., 1982—88; v.p., gen. counsel Banta Corp., Menasha, Wis., 1988—, sec., 1991—. Named one of 300 top-paid corporate gen. counsels, Corp. Counsel Mag., 2000. Mem.: ABA. Office: Banta Corp 225 Main St PO Box 8003 Menasha WI 54952-8003 Office Phone: 920-751-7708. Office Fax: 920-751-7790.

KNEIPPER, RICHARD KEITH, lawyer; b. Kenosha, Wis., June 18, 1943; s. Richard F. and Esther E. (Beaster) K.; m. Sherry Hayes, Dec. 16, 1977; children: Ryan Hayes, Lindsey Merrill. BS, Washington and Lee U., 1965; JD, Cornell U., 1968. Bar: Tex. 1982, U.S. Dist. Ct. (so. dist.) N.Y. 1968, U.S. Ct. Appeals (2d cir.) 1971. Atty. Chadbourne & Parke, N.Y.C., 1968-81, Jones Day, Dallas, 1981-99; chief adminstrv. officer PHNS, Dallas, 1999—. Mem. Bd. Mgrs. Parkland Health and Hosp. Sys. Contbr. numerous articles to profl. jours. Mem. profl. adv. group Save Outdoor Sculpture!; chmn., co-founder Dallas Adopt-a-Monument; bd. dirs., mem. adv. coun. Appalachian Coll. Assn., Inc., Sch. Visual Arts, U. North Tex.; former mem. adv. com. Nat. Arts Edn. Initiative, Nat. Mus. Am. Art, Smithsonian Instn. Mem. ABA, N.Y. Bar Assn., Tex. Bar Assn., Tex. Sculpture Assn., Assn. of Bar of City of N.Y. Episcopal. Office: PHNS Inc 5400 LBJ Freeway Ste 200 Dallas TX 75240

KNEISEL, EDMUND M., lawyer; b. Atlanta, Feb. 21, 1946; s. John F. and Mary E. (Moore) K.; m. Leslie A. Jones, June 19, 1976; 1 child, Mary Kathleen. AB, Duke U., 1968; JD, U. Ga., 1974. Bar: Ga. 1974, U.S. Dist. Ct. (no. and mid. dists.) Ga., U.S. Ct. Appeals (1st, 2d, 4th, 5th, 6th and 11th cirs.), U.S. Supreme Ct. 1984. Law clk. to Hon. R.C. Freeman U.S. Dist. Ct. (no. dist.) Ga., Atlanta, 1974-76; assoc. Kilpatrick & Cody, Atlanta, 1976-82; ptnr. Kilpatrick Stockton LLP, 1982—. Mng. editor Ga. Law Rev., Athens, 1973-74; contbr. articles to profl. jours. Lt. USNR, 1968-71. Mem. ABA, Lawyers Club Atlanta, Druid Hills Golf Club. Office: Kilpatrick Stockton LLP 1100 Peachtree St NE Ste 2800 Atlanta GA 30309-4530 E-mail: ekneisel@kilpatrickstockton.com.

KNEISER, RICHARD JOHN, accountant; b. Milw., Nov. 20, 1938; s. Frank Edward and Esther (Sobek) K.; m. Caroline Irene Stahl, Aug. 22, 1959; children: Richard J. Jr., Ronald V., Robert C. BS in Acctg., Marquette U., 1960. CPA. Staff mem. Arthur Andersen & Co., Milw., 1960-65, audit mgr., 1965-73, ptnr., 1973-94. Mem. exec. bd. Wis. Pub. Utility Inst., Madison, 1982-94; advisor acctg. practices com. U.S. Cath. Conf., 1989-2001; mem. adv. bd. Biltmore Investors Bank, 1995-97, N.Am. Clutch Corp., dir.and sec., 2003—; pres. The Carowoods Corp., 1990—. Dir. Skylight Opera Theatre, Milw., 1987-95; active Marquette U. Pres. Exec. Senate, Milw. 1987-94; trustee Village of Oconomowoc Lake, Wis., 1991-95, 97—, mem. planning commn., 1989-93, 97—, chmn. fin. com., 1991-93, mem., 1993—; bd. dirs. Oconomowoc Meml. Hosp. Found., Inc., 1996-99, treas., 1997-98, v.p., 1998-99. Mem. AICPA, Wis. Inst. CPA, Oconomowoc Lake Club (bd. dirs. 1988-97, officer, 1989-95, commodore 1994-95), Beta Gamma Sigma, Beta Alpha Psi. Avocations: antiques, fishing, tennis, golf, gardening. Home: 35920 Pabst Rd Oconomowoc WI 53066-4519 Office Phone: 262-567-6461. Business E-Mail: rkneiser@execpc.com.

KNELLER, JOHN WILLIAM, academic administrator, retired language educator; b. Oldham, Eng., Oct. 15, 1916; s. John William and Margaret Ann (Truslove) K.; m. Alice Bowerman Hart, Apr. 30, 1943; 1 dau., Linda Hart. AB, Clark U., 1938, LittD, 1970; AM, Yale U., 1948, PhD, 1950; French Govt. and Fulbright fellow, U. Paris, France, 1949-50. Asst. in instrn. Yale U., 1947-49; instr. French Oberlin Coll., 1950-52, asst. prof., 1952-55, assoc. prof., 1955-59, prof. French, 1959-65, chmn. dept. Romance langs., 1958-65, dean Coll. Arts and Scis., 1967-68, provost, 1965-69; pres. Bklyn. Coll., CUNY, 1969-79, pres. emeritus, 1979—. Univ. prof. humanities and arts Hunter Coll. and Grad. Ctr., CUNY, 1979-95, prof. emeritus, 1995—; mng. editor French Rev., 1962-65, editor-in-chief, 1965-68; co-chair bd. dirs. Henri Peyre Inst. for the Humanities, 1980-2001; cons. NEH; chmn. subcom. on enrollment goals and projections N.Y. State Edn.; Commr.'s Adv. Coun. on Higher Edn., Adv. Coun. on Higher Edn. Co-author: Initiation au francais, 1963, Introduction a la poesie francaise, 1962; assoc. editor Yale French Studies, 1948-50, gen. editor, Henri Peyre: His Life in Letters, 2005; contbr. articles to jours. in field. Bd. dirs. Independence Savs. Bank. Sgt. AUS, 1942-46. Decorated comdr. Ordre des Palmes Académiques (France). Mem. Am. Assn. Tchrs. French (exec. council 1962-68), Modern Lang. Assn. (exec. council 1965-69), Yale Grad. Sch. Assn. (exec. com. 1967, 71), Bklyn. C. of C. (dir.), Kappa Delta Pi (hon.), Alpha Sigma Lambda (hon.) Clubs: Century (N.Y.C.), Yale (N.Y.C.), Southport Racquet. Personal E-mail: jkneller@optonline.net.

KNELLER, MICHAEL, transportation services executive; m. Andrea Kneller. Grad., Yale U.; JD, Stanford U., 2000. Assoc. Debevoise & Plimpton LLP, NYC; v.p., gen. counsel, sec. Landstar System, Inc., Jacksonville, 2005—. Mem.: ABA, NY State Bar Assn. Office: Landstar System Inc 13410 Sutton Pk Dr S Jacksonville FL 32224 Office Phone: 904-398-9400. Office Fax: 904-390-1437.

KNEPP, CHRISTOPHER A., lawyer; b. Balt., Sept. 22, 1954; BA, U. N.C., 1976; JD cum laude, Harvard U., 1979. Bar: Tex. 1979, U.S. Supreme Ct. 1984. Mem. Hughes & Luce LLP, Austin, Tex.; ptnr. Vinson & Elkins LLP, Austin, Tex. Mem. ABA, State Bar Tex., Phi Beta Kappa. Office: Vinson & Elkins LLP Ste 100 2801 Via Fortuna Austin TX 78746 Office Phone: 512-542-8437. E-mail: cknepp@velaw.com.

KNEPPER, GEORGE W., historian, educator; b. Akron, Ohio, Jan. 15, 1926; s. George W. and Grace (Darling) K.; m. Phyllis Watkins, Aug. 21, 1949; children: Susan Lynne, John Arthur. BA, U. Akron, 1948; MA, U. Mich., 1950, PhD, 1954. Mem. faculty U. Akron, 1948-49, 54-92, assoc. prof. history, head dept., 1959-62; dean U. Akron (Coll. Liberal Arts), 1962-67, prof. history, 1964-88, disting. prof. history, 1988-92. Author: New Lamps for Old, One Hundred Years of Urban Higher Education at the University of Akron, 1970, An Ohio Portrait, 1976, Akron: City at the Summit, 1981, Ohio and Its People, 1989, Summit's Glory: Sketches of Buchtel Coll. and the University of Akron, 1990, Ohio Lands Book, 2002; editor: Travels in the Southland; The Journal of Lucius Verus Biérce 1822-23, 1966. Served to ensign USNR, 1943-46. Fulbright fellow U. London, Eng., 1953-54 Mem. Am., So. hist. assns., Orgn. Am. Historians, Ohio Acad. History, Omicron Delta Kappa, Alpha Tau Omega, Phi Alpha Theta, Alpha Sigma Lambda. Home: 88 Ridge Side Ct Munroe Falls OH 44262-1076 Office: Univ Akron Coll Liberal Arts Dept History Akron OH 44325-0001

KNERLY, STEPHEN JOHN, JR., lawyer; b. Lakewood, Ohio, Dec. 15, 1949; s. Stephen John Sr. and Mary Louise (Johnson) K.; m. Catherine Arion de Bravura; 1 child, Alexandra M. C. AB summa cum laude, Bowdoin Coll., 1972; AM, Fletcher Sch. Law & Diplomacy, 1973; JD, Case Western Res. U., 1976. Bar: Ohio 1976. Law clk. Stephen J. Knerly and Assocs., Cleve., 1973-74, Hahn, Loeser, Freedheim, Dean et al, Cleve., 1975-76, assoc., 1976-83; ptnr. Hahn, Loeser & Parks, Cleve., 1984—; CEO, mng. ptnr. Hahn, Loeser & Parks, LLP, Cleve., 1993—. James Bowdoin scholar Bowdoin Coll., 1972; named Consul Honoraire de France, Cleve. Mem. French-Am. C. of C., Phi Beta Kappa. Home: 10390 Mitchells Mill Rd Chardon OH 44024-8613 Office: Hahn Loeser & Parks LLP 3300 BP Tower 200 Public Sq Ste 3300 Cleveland OH 44114-2301

KNERR, ANTHONY DAVID, financial consultant; b. Bellefonte, Pa., Dec. 7, 1938; s. Henry William Knerr and Catherine Margaret Conner; m. Katrina Ely Carter, June 22, 1963 (div. July 1974); children: Christopher Hamilton, Theodore Gabriel; m. Susanne E. Kastler, Apr. 20, 2002. BA magna cum laude, Yale U., 1960, MA cum laude, 1964; PhD, NYU, 1978. Tchr. Milton (Mass.) Acad., 1961-63; program officer Internat. Exchange Program, N.Y.C., 1965-67; assoc., cons. Booz Allen & Hamilton, N.Y.C., 1967-70; vice chancellor for budget and planning CUNY, N.Y.C., 1970-77; spl. asst. to acting pres. Yale U., New Haven, 1977-78; exec. v.p. fin., treas. Columbia U., N.Y.C., 1978-88; pres. Publ. Group Inc., N.Y.C., 1988-90; mng. dir. Anthony Knerr & Assocs., N.Y.C., 1990—. Lectr. Columbia U., N.Y.C., 1986-88; pres. emeritus Caribbean Conservation Corp., 1993-2001; vice chmn. Humanity in Action, 2000—; bd. dirs. Del. Mut. Funds. Author: Shelley's Adonais: A Critical Edition, 1984. Bd. dirs. N.Y. Soc. Libr., 1983—,; pres. emeritus United Neighborhood Houses, 1994—; vice chmn. Humanit in Action, 1997—. Mem. The Century Assn., Keats-Shelley Assn. (bd. dirs. 1983—), Grolier Club, Phi Beta Kappa. Home: 115 E 70th St New York NY 10021-5020 Office: Anthony Knerr & Assocs 485 5th Ave 3rd Flr New York NY 10017

KNESEL, ERNEST ARTHUR, JR., health facility administrator, chemicals executive; b. New Orleans, Dec. 11, 1945; s. Ernest Arthur and Catherine Charlotte (Maier) K.; m. Lavina Lynn Menge, June 2, 1968; children: Eric Ernest, Tami Lynn, Bradley William. Student, Armstrong Coll., 1963-64; BS, Fairleigh Dickinson U., 1968, MS, 1970. Cert. clin. chemist. Technologist Am. Biol. Control Lab., Tenefly, N.J., 1966-68; sr. technologist Englewood (N.J.) Hosp., 1968-69; founder, v.p. Biomed. Reference Labs., Inc., Burlington, N.C., 1969-82; sr. v.p. Roche Biomed. Labs., Inc., Burlington, 1982-95; pres., founder Roche Image Analysis Sys., Inc., Elon College, N.C., 1989-96; exec. v.p., founder Autocyte, Inc., Elon College, 1996-99; v.p., founder TriPath Imaging, 1999-2000; cons. True North Group, 2000—01; founder, pres. Select Diagnostics Inc., 2001—; co-founder, pres. Synermed Select Ptnrs., Inc., 2003—. Inventor serum filter/dispenser vial, automated aliquoting system, cyto-rich automated cytology preparation system and simultaneous machine and human interactive cytology evaluation system. Mem. Am. Assn. Clin. Chemistry, Am. Soc. Clin. Pathologists (assoc.). Roman Catholic. Avocation: magic. Office: Select Diagnostics Inc 1100 Revolution Mill Dr Greensboro NC 27405 Personal E-mail: eknesel1@aol.com.

KNETTER, MICHAEL MARK, dean, economics professor; b. Rhinelander, Wis., Apr. 8, 1960; s. Edmund David and Margaret Helen Knetter; m. Karen Joy Goedewaagen, July 31, 1988; children: Maxine, Lillian. BA in Math. and Econs., U. Wis., Eau Claire, 1983; PhD, Stanford U., 1988. Asst. prof. econs. Dartmouth Coll., Hanover, NH, 1988—94, assoc. prof. econs., vice chair dept. econs., 1994—97, assoc. dean MBA program, prof. internat. econs., Amos Tuck Sch. Bus., 1997—2002; dean, prof. fin., investment, and banking U. Wis. Sch. Bus., Madison, 2002—. Rsch assoc. Nat. Bur. Econ. Rsch., 1992-; trustee Lehman Bros./First Trust Income Opportunity Fund, Lehman Bros. Liquid Assets trust; former sr. staff economist Pres.' Coun. Econ. Advisors for George H.W. Bush and Bill Clinton. Contbr. articles to profl. jours. Rsch. fellow German Marshall Fund, 1991; Pub. Policy grantee Lynde and Harry Bradley Found., 1991. Mem. Am. Econ. Assn. Office: Sch Bus U Wis 5110 Grainger 975 Univ Ave Madison WI 53706

KNETZER, KATHLEEN S., mathematics educator; d. James L and Ruby E Hopper; m. James W Knetzer, June 28, 1969; children: Kristofer J, Kara L. BA, Blackburn Coll., Carlinville, Ill., 1972; MS, So. Ill. U., Edwardsville, 1977. Cert. adminstr. Ill., 1977, tchr. Ill. Math. tchr. Carlinville H.S., 1972—. Scholastic bowl coach Carlinville H.S., 1990—, student coun. sponsor, 2004—. Sunday sch. tchr. Emmanuel Bapt. Ch., Carlinville, Ill., 1983—2004. Named Outstanding Math. Tchr., So. Ill. U., 1998. Baptist. Avocations: reading, sewing. Office: Carlinville High School 829 W Main St Carlinville IL 62626 Office Phone: 217-854-3104.

KNEZ, BRIAN J., publishing executive; Various positions including v.p. Harcourt Coll. Pub., pres. Harcourt, Inc. Sci., Tech. & Med. Group Harcourt Brace & Co., Chestnut Hill, Mass., 1987-95, CEO, bd. dirs., 1995-97, pres., co-COO, 1997-99, co-CEO, 1999—. Office: 275 Washington St Newton MA 02458-1646

KNICELY, CARROLL FRANKLIN, publishing executive; b. Staunton, Va., Dec. 8, 1928; s. Bernard Clyde and Violet Iona Phillips-K.; m. Evelyn Virginia Furr, Feb. 4, 1948; children: Kaye Gaines, Brenda Kramer, Beverley White, Carroll Jr., Daryl. BS, Barry U., 1982. Bus. mgr. News-Virginian, Waynesboro, Va., 1952-57; pres., pub. Glasgow (Ky.) Daily Times, 1957-76, Associated Pubs., Glasgow, 1960—. Regent Western Ky. U., Bowling Green, 1976-80; cons. Aquila Mut. Funds, N.Y.C., 1988-98, trustee, 1998—; chmn. Vision 2020, Inc., Bowling Green, Ky., 1998—. Dir. Citizens TransFin./Star Bank, Glasgow & Bowling Green, 1976-98; commr. commerce Commonwealth of Ky., Frankfort, 1979-80, sec. of commerce, 1983-88; postmaster U.S. Postal Svc., Glasgow, 1965-67; mem. Barren River Area Devel. Dist., 1994; trustee Campbellsville (Ky.) U. 1997—. Mem. Ky. Press Assn. (pres. 1978-79), Glasgow C. of C. (pres. 1978-79), Rotarian, Mason. Baptist. Avocations: bicycling, travel, writing. Home: 505 Augusta Cir Glasgow KY 42141-8272 Office: Associated Pubs Inc 211 S Green St PO Box 335 Glasgow KY 42142-0335 E-mail: srknicely@glasgow-ky.com.

KNICKEL, CARIN S., oil industry executive; b. Powell, Wyo. BA in Mktg. and Stats., U. Colo.; M.Mgmt., MIT. Mktg. account mgr. ConocoPhillips, 1979—87, area dir. light oil sales product supply and trading, 1987, gen. mgr. bus. develop. for refining and mktg. in Europe London, gen. mgr. refining, mktg., and transp., pres. specialty bus. divsn., 2001—03, v.p. human resources Houston, 2003—. Chmn. rodeo run com. ConocoPhillips; bd. dirs. Colo. Spl. Olympics. Office: ConocoPhillips 600 N Dairy Ashford Rd Houston TX 77079

KNICKERBOCKER, ROBERT PLATT, JR., lawyer; b. Hartford, Conn., Sept. 23, 1944; s. Robert P. and Audrey Jane (Stempel) K.; m. Kathleen A. Sakal (div. May 1985); children: Sarah, Abigail, Jonathan; m. Barbara Denise Whinnem, Oct. 3, 1987. BA, Cornell U., 1966; JD, U. Conn., 1969. Bar: Conn. 1969, U.S. Dist. Ct. Conn. 1969, U.S. Ct. Appeals (2d cir.) 1970. Law clk. to presiding justice Conn. Supreme Ct., Hartford, 1968-69; ptnr. Day, Berry & Howard, Hartford, 1969—. Mem. State Implementation Plan Regulation Adv. Commn., 1979-90. Chmn. Town Plan and Zoning Commn., Glastonbury, Conn., 1975-79, Glastonbury Bd. Edn., 1982-86. Mem. Conn. Bar Assn., Greater Hartford C. of C. (state legis. com.). Republican. Episcopalian. Office: Day Berry & Howard Cityplace Hartford CT 06103-3499 Office Phone: 860-275-0122. Business E-Mail: knicker@dbh.com.

KNICKREHM, GLENN ALLEN, management executive; b. LA, Mar. 27, 1948; s. Allen F. and Evelyn Knickrehm. BA magna cum laude, Occidental Coll., 1971; BS, Columbia U., 1971, MBA, 1973. Analyst Exxon Co., N.Y.C. and L.A., 1971-72; cons. Boston Cons. Group, Boston and Munich, 1973-77, mgr. Boston, 1977-83; pres., chmn. Our Market Supermarket, Inc., 1980-81; pres. Bay Resource Corp., 1983—2002. Chmn. Apex Internat. Alloys, Inc., 1986-89; pres. Mashamoquet Holdings, Inc., 1995—; adv. Beach Brook Prodns., 1995—; pres. Constellation Prodns., Inc., 1996—; dir. Scuola il Bisonte, Florence, Italy, 1998—; bd. dirs. Am. Repertory Theatre, Mus. Fine Arts; trustee Westfield Ctr. for Early Keyboard Studies, 1999—. Dir. New Eng. Theater Guild, Inc., 1985-89, Samuel Bronfman fellow, 1972; pres. Constellation Charitable Found., 2001--. Mem. Boston Anthenaeum, Columbia U. Faculty Club, Phi Beta Kappa, Tau Beta Pi, Beta Gamma Sigma, Sigma Pi Sigma, Pi Mu Epsilon, Kappa Mu Epsilon. Office: Constellation Productions Inc 161 First St Cambridge MA 02142 Office Phone: 617-939-1900.

KNIES, ROBERT CARL, JR., critical care nurse; b. Wilkes-Barre, Pa., Sept. 7, 1960; s. Robert Carl and Alice Ann (Swartman) K.; m. Lisa Ann Stumhofer, May 17, 1986; 1 child, Kayleigh Ann Elisabeth. Diploma, St. Joseph Hosp. Sch. Nursing, Reading, Pa., 1983; BSN, Pa. State U., 1990; MSN, Villanova U., 1996. Cert. emergency nurse, CPR instr., emergency med. technician, instr., ACLS. Staff nurse St. Joseph Hosp., Reading, 1983-84; clin. nurse Community Gen. Hosp., Reading, 1984-89; nurse Med. Pers. Pool, Allentown, Pa., 1989-91, Pottstown (Pa.) Meml. Med. Ctr., 1990-96; clin. nurse specialist emergency svcs. Health Sys. Minn., 1996-2000; clin. mgr. emergency svcs. Stevens Hosp., Edmonds, Wash., 2000—04, dir. emergency svcs., 2001—04; clin. prof. LaSalle U., Phila., 2004; dir. trauma svcs. St. Mary Med. Ctr., Langhorne, Pa., 2004—. Adj. faculty Reading Area C.C., 1991-95, Seattle Pacific U., 2001. Mem. Nat. Assn. Clin. Nurse Specialists (bd. dirs. 1999-01), Emergency Nurses Assn. (pres. Twin-Cities chpt. 2000, pres.-elect Minn. coun. 2000), Sigma Theta Tau, Alpha Sigma Lambda. Personal E-mail: rck_cns@hotmail.com.

KNIESNER, JOHN THOMAS, librarian; b. Berea, Ohio, Dec. 19, 1949; s. Albert Henry and Elizabeth (Leonard) K.; m. Patti-Jo Samo, Sept. 8, 1979; children: Janet Deborah, Joseph David. BA, Kent State U., 1971; MLS, U. Mich., 1972. Profl. libr. I Columbus (Ohio) Met. Libr., 1972-76, profl. libr. II, 1977-78, profl. libr. III, 1979-85; dir. Bellaire (Ohio) Pub. Libr., 1986—. Computer cons. Toledo-Lucas County Pub. Libr., Ohio, 1979, Richardson-Smith Indsl. Design, Columbus, 1984; libr. Ctrl. Ohio Transit Authority, Columbus, 1981-84. Film reviewer The News, 1985-86; contbr. articles to librs. Mem. steering com. Always a River, 1991; mem. adv. com. Ohio Humanities Coun., Columbus, 1993-94; water safety instr. ARC, Columbus and Bellaire, 1984—. Recipient Civitan award PTA, Bellaire, 1992, 97, plaque for saving lives, Am. Red Cross, Wheeling, W.Va., 1987, commendation Columbus Area Shared Use Automated Resources, 1976. Mem. Ohio Libr. Coun. (facilitator 1981-82, 92), S.E. Ohio Libr. Orgn. (pres. 1988-89, 2000-2001, chair compact disc com. 1990-98, chair policy com. 2000-2003), No. Ohio Valley Astronomy Educators (pub. rels. officer 1994-97), Ednl. Film Libr. Assn. (film judge 1980-83), Pi Sigma Alpha. Republican. Roman Catholic. Avocations: ice skating, swimming, reading, chess, tennis. Office: Bellaire Pub Libr 330 32nd St Bellaire OH 43906-1571 Office Phone: 740-676-9421. Personal E-mail: jkniesner@hotmail.com.

KNIFFEN, DONALD AVERY, astrophysicist, educator, researcher; b. Kalamazoo, Apr. 27, 1933; s. Frederick Bowerman and Eva Virginia (Arp) Kniffen; m. Janis Kay Nesom, June 14, 1952; children: Karyol Kniffen Poole, Donald Avery Jr., Kimberly Kniffen Giesbrecht. BS magna cum laude, La. State U., 1959; AM, Washington U., St. Louis, 1960; PhD, Cath. U. Am., 1967. Astrophysicist Goddard Space Flight Ctr., Greenbelt, Md., 1960-91; lectr. physics U. Md., College Park, 1978-87; project scientist Compton Gamma Ray Obs., 1979-91; William W. Elliott prof., chmn. dept. physics and astronomy Hampden-Sydney Coll., Va., 1991-2001; rsch. prof. George Mason U., 2002—05; sr. rsch. scientist NASA Hdqrs., 2005—. Vis. scientist NASA/USRA, Greenbelt, 1997—98; astrophysics cons. NASA/HSTX, NASA/USRA, 1991—98; program scientist NASA Hdqrs., 1999—2005; sr. rsch. scientist NASA/USRA, 2005—. Contbr. articles to profl. jours. Served with USN, 1952-56. Recipient Medal for Outstanding Leadership NASA, 1992, Laurel award Space/Missiles, Aviation Week & Space Tech., 1991. Fellow Royal Astron. Soc.; mem. AAUP, Am. Phys. Soc., Am. astron. Soc., Internat. Astron. Union, Sigma Xi. Democrat. Avocations: travel, reading, gardening. Home: 2814 Andy Ct Crofton MD 21114-3157 Office: Code 661 NASA Goddard Space Flight Ctr Greenbelt MD 20771-0001 Personal E-mail: dkniffen1@verizon.net. Business E-Mail: dak@milkyway.gsfe.nasa.gov.

KNIFFIN, PAULA SICHEL, insurance sales executive; b. NYC, Oct. 2, 1941; d. Harold M. and Edith (Sachnoff) Sichel; m. Richrd G. Kniffin, Aug. 3, 1963; children: Douglas, Kelly. BA, Bucknell U., 1963. CLU, cert. fin. planner. Tchr. New Cumberland (Pa.) Jr. High Sch., 1963-64, Meadowbrook Jr. High Sch., East Meadow, N.Y., 1964-67; real estate salesperson Claire Sobel Real Estate, Syosset, N.Y., 1979-80; sales force recruiter Mut. of N.Y. Life Ins. Co., Jericho, 1981-82; head of life and health ins. dept., employee benefit cons. The Viking Agy., Inc., Syosset, N.Y., 1983—. Mem. Soc. Fin. Svc. Profls., Fin. Planning Assn., Women Life Underwriters Conf. (pres. 1988-89), Nat. Assn. Ins. and Fin. Advisors (bd. dirs. 1988-89), Nat. Assn. Ins. and Fin. Advisors, Ladies Golf Com. (chair 1990-93), Nassau Country Club, Mayacoo Lakes Country Club. Republican. Avocations: golf, tennis, bridge, reading. Office: The Viking Agy 117 Oak Dr Syosset NY 11791-4625 Office Phone: 516-496-7711. E-mail: paula@vikingagency.com.

KNIGHT, ATHELIA WILHELMENIA, journalist; b. Portsmouth, Va., Oct. 15, 1950; d. Daniel Dennis and Adell Virginia (Savage) K. BA with honors in English, Norfolk State Coll., 1973; MA with honors in Journalism, Ohio State U., 1974. Cert. tchr. Va. Aide D.C. Coop. Extension Service, 1969-72; sub. tchr. Portsmouth Pub. Schs., 1973; reporter Virginian Pilot, Norfolk, 1973, Chgo. Tribune, 1974; met. desk reporter Washington Post, 1975-81, investigative reporter, 1981-94, sports writer, 1994-2000; asst. dir. Washington Post Young Journalists, 2000—03, dir., 2003; adj. prof. Georgetown U., 2002—. Vis. prof. journalism Hampton U., 2001. Mem. Herb Block Found. Recipient Mark Twain award, 1982, 87, Front Page award Washington-Balt. Newspaper Guild, 1982, Nat. award for edn. Edn. Writers Assn., 1987, Pub. Svc. award Md.-Del.-D.C. Press Assn., 1990, 93, 1st Pl. award for spot news, 1997; Ohio State U. fellow, 1974, Nieman fellow Harvard U., 1985-86. Maynard Mgmt. at the Kellogg Sch. of Mgmt. N.W. U., 2003. Mem.: Assn. Women in Sports Media, Investigative Reporters and Editors, Nat. Assn. Black Journalists, Women in Comm. Methodist. Office: Washington Post 1150 15th St NW Washington DC 20071-0002

KNIGHT, BETTY, journalist, educator, advocate; b. Little Rock, Sept. 5, 1925; d. Charles Roscoe Knight and Ethel Emmaline Horn. AA, L.A. City Coll., 1951; BA, L.A. State Coll., 1953; MA, UCLA, 1957. Cons. to prof. L.A. City Coll., 1965—2000. Contbr. articles and short stories to profl. jours.; author: numerous poems. Sec. Com. for Rights of Disabled, L.A., 1967—68; pres. Inner City L.A. NOW, 1985—93. Named winner writing contest, L.A. State Coll., 1952; Will Rogers fellow, UCLA, 1956—57. Mem.: ACLU, L.A. Sci. Fantasy Soc., Ams. for Dem. Action, Gray Panthers. Democrat. Avocations: science fiction fantasy, music, art. Home: 3565 Berry Dr Studio City CA 91604-3882

KNIGHT, BOBBY (ROBERT MONTGOMERY KNIGHT), college basketball coach; b. Massillon, Ohio, Oct. 25, 1940; s. Carroll and Hazel (Henthorne) K.; m. Nancy Lou Knight, Apr. 17, 1963 (div.); m. Karen Edgar, 1988. BS, Ohio State U., 1962. Asst. coach Cuyahoga Falls (Ohio) High Sch., 1962-63; freshman coach U.S. Mil. Acad., West Point, N.Y., 1963-65, head basketball coach, 1965-71, Ind. U., Bloomington, 1971-2000, Tex. Tech. U., Lubbock, 2001—. Speaker clinics in field; condr. tng. clinics for coaches and players. Trustee Naismith Meml. Basketball Hall of Fame. Served U.S. Army. Recipient Big Ten Coach-of-Year award, 1973, 75, 76, 81, 89; named unanimously Nat. Coach of Year, 1975, 89, Nat. Coach of Yr. AP and Basketball Weekly, 1976; recipient appreciation plaque from team, 1979; elected to Basketball Hall of Fame, 1991. Mem. Nat. Assn. Basketball Coaches (bd. dirs.) Methodist. Achievements include coaching U.S. team to gold medal 1984 Olympics; coached Ind. U. to NCAA Championship, 1976, 81, 87; college basketball's winningest active coach (one of only 12 NCAA coaches to have won 700 or more games). Office: Tex Tech U Mens Basketball United Spirit Ctr Indiana Ave Lubbock TX 79409

KNIGHT, CHRISTINA RAE LAMBERT, nurse, educator, personal care industry executive; b. Daytona Beach, Fla., July 12, 1969; d. Richard Ray and Patricia Sue Lambert; m. Michael David Knight, Mar. 30, 1995; children: Alexis Nicole, McKenzie Danielle. AS in Nursing, Daytona Beach CC, 1991. Certified Emergency Nurse, Emergency Nurses Assn., 1996. Rn, 1990—; pres. Mid-Atlantic Consulting, Inc, Monroe, NC, 2001—. Lectr., NC, 2003—. Pres. Greater Charlotte Chpt. of Am. Assn. of Legal Nurse Cons., Charlotte, NC, 2006, sec. treas., 2004—. Mem.: Emergency Nurses Assn. (assoc.). Office: Mid-Atlantic Consulting Inc 2118 Genesis Dr Monroe NC 28110 Office Phone: 704-289-4284. Office Fax: 704-289-4284. E-mail: chris@midatlconsulting.com.

KNIGHT, CHRISTOPHER NICHOLS, lawyer; b. New Haven, Sept. 7, 1946; s. Douglas Maitland and Grace Wallace (Nichols) K.; m. Emily Byrn Turner, Oct. 20, 1979; children: Ethan Douglas, Benjamin Walker Lester, Christopher N. Jr. BA, Yale U., 1968; JD, Duke U., 1971. Bar: Wis. 1971, U.S. Dist. Ct. (ea. dist.) Wis. 1973, U.S. Ct. Appeals (7th cir.) 1977, N.C. 1979, U.S. Dist. Ct. (mid. dist.) N.C. 1979, Minn., 1980, U.S. Supreme Ct. 1980, U.S. Ct. Appeals (4th, 8th cirs.) 1980, U.S. Dist. Ct. Minn. 1980, Ill. 1982, N.Y., 1996. Assoc. Quarles & Brady, Milw., 1971-78, ptnr., 1978-79, Smith & Moore LLP, Greensboro, NC, 1979—80, Kutak Rock, Mpls., 1980-82, Isham Lincoln & Beale, Chgo., 1982-88, Hopkins & Sutter, Chgo., 1988-2001, Foley & Lardner LLP, Chgo., 2001—, mng. ptnr., 2003—04. Bd. dirs. Lyric Opera Chgo., 2003—, bd. trustees; bd. dirs. Chgo. Humanities Festival, 2005—; bd. trustees Writers' Theatre, 2004—. Mem. ABA, Ill. State Bar Assn., Minn. State Bar Assn., NY State Bar Assn., NC State Bar Assn., State Bar Wis., Am. Bar Found., Nat. Assn. Bond Lawyers, Chicagoland C. of C. (bd. dirs. 2004—), Econ. Club of Chgo. Congregationalist. Office: Foley & Lardner LLP Ste 2800 321 N Clark St Chicago IL 60610-4764 Office Phone: 312-832-4515. E-mail: cknight@foley.com.

KNIGHT, CRANSTON S., history professor; b. Chgo., Sept. 10, 1950; m. J. Dolores Anderson, Aug. 5, 1978; children: Jason J., Illya A., Ashiyrah H. Ramirez-Knight de Torres. BA, So. Ill. U.; MA, Northeastern Ill. U., Chgo., 1990; PhD, Loyola U., Chgo., 2005. Adj. prof. history Loyola U., Chgo., 1992—95; prof. history Columbia Coll., Chgo., 2000—02, Chgo. City Colls., 2001—. Cons. Chgo. Pub. Schs., 1992—93; mem. coun. ethics and internat. affairs Carnegie. Author: (poetry) La Brigada; Spain 1936-1939, On the Borders of Hiroshima: I heard a Rumor of War, In the Garden of the Beast: Vietnam Cries A Love Song, Freedom Song; editor: (anthology) Tour of Duty: Vietnam in the Words of Those Who Were There. Oganizer Orgn. of N.E., Chgo., 1998—2003. Recipient Creative Arts award, Benjamin Henry Matchett Found. for Creative Arts, 1989, Humanities and Letters award, U. Ill., 1997, Edn. Excellence award, Henry Horner Alumni and Assocs.: Youth Acad., 1999; Writers Completion grant, Ill. Arts Coun., 1996, 1998. Mem.: Acad. Political Sci., Assn. Asion Studies, Chgo. Coun. Fgn. Rels., Phi Beta Delta Honor Soc. Internat. Scholars. Roman Catholic. Avocations: writing, travel, movies, photography. Home: 1300 W Hood Chicago IL 60660 Office: Chgo City Colls 1900 W Van Buren Chicago IL 60612 Office Phone: 312-850-7113. Personal E-mail: savingnet2@yahoo.com. Business E-Mail: cknight@ccc.edu.

KNIGHT, EDWARD R., judge, psychologist, law educator; b. Milw., Oct. 5, 1917; s. Harry and Lillian (Bachman) K.; m. Judith A. Weidberg, July 6, 1941; 1 child, Barbara Jane. AB, U. Wis., 1940, JD, 1941; AM, NYU, 1942, PhD, 1943. Bar: Wis. 1941, N.J. 1976; diplomate Am. Bd. Profl. Psychology. Master Oxford Acad., Pleasantville, NJ, 1941, psychologist, 1942, head psychologist, 1943, asst. headmaster, 1945-47, headmaster, 1947-73, emeritus, 1973—. U.S. magistrate judge, 1976—; judge Mcpl. Ct., Margate City, N.J., 1976-81; ptnr. Fox, Rothschild, Atlantic City, N.J., 1976—; dir. First Fidelity Bank, 1950-90. Pres., bd. govs. Atlantic City Med. Ctr., 1973-87, chmn. emeritus, 1987—; chmn. Master Planning Bd., Egg Harbor Twp., N.J., 1961-73; chmn. Atlantic County (N.J.) Charter Study Commn., 1973-74, treas. bd. Atlanticare, 1993—. Author: Self-Discipline and Academic Failure; mem. editl. bd. Parental Delinquency; contbr. articles on edn. and psychology to profl. jours. Capt., USAAF, 1943-45; personnel com., personnel div. ATSC, Wright Field. Named Trustee of Century, Atlantic City Med. Ctr., 1998. Fellow APA (sch. psychologists div.); mem. Ea. N.J. psychol. assns., Nat. Assn. Ind. Schs., N.J. Assn. Sch. Psychologists, Interam. Soc. Psychology, Boarding Sch. Headmasters Assn. Mid. States (pres. 1966-67), Wis. Alumni Assn., U. Wis. Mem. Union (life), Atlanticare Health Sys. (vice-chmn. bd.), Phi Delta Kappa, Kappa Delta Pi. Home: 7 N Thurlow Ave Margate City NJ 08402-1213 Office: US Dist Ct 1301 Atlantic Ave Fl 3 Atlantic City NJ 08401-7207

KNIGHT, EDWARD S., lawyer, federal official; b. Amarillo, Tex., Jan. 20, 1951; m. Amy Knight; 1 child, Travis. BA in Latin Am. Studies with honors, U. Tex., Austin, 1973; JD, U. Tex., 1976. Bar: Tex., D.C., Supreme Ct. With Akin, Gump, Strauss, Hauer and Feld, Washington, 1978-82, ptnr., 1982-93; exec. sec., sr. adv. to sec. Treasury U.S. Dept. Treasury, Washington, 1993-94, gen. counsel, 1994-99; exec. v.p., chief legal officer NASD, Washington, 1999—; exec. v.p., gen. counsel NASDAQ, 2000—. Alumni bd. dirs. U. Tex.; bd. dirs. Software and Info. Industry Assn. Mem. ABA, Supreme Ct. Bar Assn., D.C. Bar Assn., Tex. Bar Assn. Office: NASDAQ 9513 Key West Ave Rockville MD 20850

KNIGHT, FRANK BARDSLEY, mathematics professor; b. Chgo., Oct. 11, 1933; s. Frank Hyneman and Ethel Eunice (Verry) K.; m. Ingeborg G. Belz, Aug. 30, 1971; children: Marion A., Marc A., Ellen D. BA, Cornell U., 1955; PhD, Princeton U., 1959. Instr. math. U. Minn., Mpls., 1960-61, asst. prof., 1962-63; asst. prof. math. U. Ill., Urbana, 1964-66, assoc. prof., 1967-71; prof. U. Ill, Urbana, 1971-91, prof. emeritus, 1991—. Author: Essentials of Brownian Motion and Diffusion, 1981, Essays on the Prediction Process,

1981, Foundations of the Prediction Process, 1992. Sloan fellow, 1968-71; NSF grantee, 1981-89. Mem. Am. Math. Soc., Inst. Math. Stats., Am. Alpine Club. Office: U Ill 1409 W Green St Urbana IL 61801-2943 Business E-Mail: f-knight@math.uiuc.edu.

KNIGHT, FRANKLIN W., historian, educator; b. Mile Gully, Manchester, Jamaica, Jan. 10, 1942; came to U.S., 1964; s. Willis Jefferson and Irick May (Sanderson) K.; m. Ingeborg Bauer, June 11, 1965; children: Michael, Brian, Nadine. BA with honors, U. West Indies, Jamaica, 1964; MA, U. Wis., 1965, PhD, 1969. From asst. to assoc. prof. SUNY, Stony Brook, 1968-73; assoc. prof. Johns Hopkins U., Balt., 1973-77, prof., 1977-91, Stulman prof. History, 1991—, dir. Latin Am. Studies Program, 1992-95; v.p. Latin Am. Studies Assn., 1997-98; pres., 1998-00. Author: Slave Society in Cuba, 1970 (Black Acad. award 1971), The Caribbean, 1990; co-editor: The Modern Caribbean, 1989, Atlantic Port Cities, 1991; editor: Caribbean Slave Societies, 1997. Active Md. Quincentenary Com., 1992. Named Disting. Grad. U. West Indies, Jamaica, 1992. Mem. The Hist. Soc. (pres. 2004—), Latin Am. Studies Assn., Assn. Caribbean Historians. Office: Johns Hopkins U 3400 N Charles St Baltimore MD 21218-2680 Office Phone: 410-516-7591. Business E-Mail: fknight@jhu.edu.

KNIGHT, GARY, lawyer, educator, writer; b. St. Joseph, Mo., Dec. 8, 1939; s. Herbert S. and Iris (Crawford) K.; m. Rebecca Emelie Forrester, Nov. 24, 1962; children: Kevin Crawford, David Forrester, Jonathan Gary. Student, Westminster Coll., 1957-59; AB in Polit. Sci., Stanford U., 1961; JD, So. Meth. U., 1964. Bar: Calif. 1965. Assoc. Nossaman, Thompson, Waters and Moss, L.A., 1964-68; mem. faculty La. State U. Law Center, Baton Rouge, 1968-85, assoc. prof., 1971-75, prof. law, 1975-85, Campanile prof. marine resources law, 1971-85; owner Jonathan Pub. Co., 1981—. Mem. adv. com. on law of sea Nat. Security Council Inter-Agy. Law of Sea Group, 1972-81; cons. CIA, 1977-85; mem. Gulf of Mex. Fishery Mgmt. Coun., 1981-84. Author: The Future of International Fisheries Management, 1975, Managing the Sea's Living Resources, 1977, The International Law of the Sea: Cases, Documents and Readings, 1991, Marine Fisheries Management Reporter, 1981-94; assoc. editor: Ocean Development and International Law: A Jour. of Marine Affairs, 1972-85. Trustee Wimberley Village Libr., 2005—. Mem. ABA (com. on law of sea 1971-80, com. marine resources 1967-71), Am. Soc. Internat. Law (bd. rev. and devel. 1975-80, panel on law of sea 1972-80), Internat. Law Assn. (com. on law of sea 1974-81), Law of Sea Inst. (exec. bd. 1975-81), Order of Coif, Phi Alpha Delta, Omicron Delta Kappa, Beta Theta Pi.

KNIGHT, GLADYS (GLADYS MARIA KNIGHT), singer; b. Atlanta, May 28, 1944; d. Merald and Elizabeth (Woods) Knight, Sr.; m. Barry Hankerson, Oct. 1974 (div. 1979); 1 child, Shanga Hankerson; m. William McDowell, Apr. 2001. Grad. coll.; degree (hon.), Shaw U. Author: lyrics Way Back Home, others; first pub. recital, Mt. Mariah Bapt. Ch., Atlanta, 1948; toured with Morris Brown Choir, 1950-53, recitals local chs. and schs., 1950-53; winner grand prize Ted Mack's Amateur Hour 1952; jazz vocalist, Lloyd Terry Jazz Ltd., 1959-61, mem. Gladys Knight and the Pips (formerly Pips Quartet), 1953—, concert appearances in Eng., 1967, 72, 73, 76, Australia, Japan, Hong Kong, Manila, 1976; rec. artist, Brunswick, 1957-61, Fury, 1961-62, Everlast, 1963, Maxx and Bell, 1964-66, Motown, 1966-73, Buddah, Capitol, Columbia, MCA, 1988; albums with the Pips include Best of Gladys Knight and the Pips, All the Great Hits, If I Were Your Woman, 1989, Soul Survivors: The Best of Gladys Knight and the Pips 1973-1988, 1990, Blue Lights in the Basement, 1996, Imagination, 1996, The Lost Live Albums, 1996; solo albums include Good Woman, 1991, One Voice, 2005; TV appearance Charlie & Co., 1985; produced, appeared in HBO film Sisters in the Name of Love, 1986. Winner 6 gold Buddah records, 1 gold, 1 platinum Buddah album; 4 Grammy awards; named Top Female Vocalist, Blues and Soul mag. 1972; spl. award Washington City Coun. for inspiration to youth in city, 1972; other awards include Clio, AGVA, NAACP Image, Ebony Music, Cashbox, Billboard, Record World, Rolling Stone, Ladies Home Jour., Am. Music award (with Pips), 1984, 1988, Core award B'nai B'rith award; inducted into Rock and Roll Hall of Fame, 1996. Address: Care Shakeji Inc 3221 LaMirada Ave Las Vegas NV 89120

KNIGHT, H. STUART, law enforcement official, consultant; b. Sault St. Marie, Ont., Can., Jan. 6, 1921; s. Alexander G. and Muriel C. (Breathwaite) K.; m. Betty Cooley, June 29, 1946; children: Suzanne Cawley, Bill, Bob, John, Barbara Powell. BS, Mich. State U., 1948; postgrad., Princeton U., 1965-66. With U.S. Secret Svc., 1950-82, dir., 1973-82. Vice chmn. Guardsmark Inc., Memphis, 1984—; v.p. Interpol, Paris, 1974-81; disting. faculty fellow Fed. Execs. Inst., Charlottesville, Va., 1981; mem. adv. bd. Am. Products Devel. Co.; mem. steering com. Ctr. for Strategic and Internat. Studies. Bd. dirs. Falls Church (Va.) Homeowners Assn., 1982-84; bd. dirs., pres. INKODE Govt. Sys.; mem. lottery bd. State of Va. Staff sgt. U.S. Army, 1942-46, PTO. Decorated Silver Star, Bronze Star, Purple Heart; named original mem. Gallery of Fame, Mich. State U., to Wall of Fame, 2001, Fed. Exec. of Yr., 1982; recipient Mr. Sam award, Touchdown Club, Washington, 1979. Mem. Internat. Assn. Chiefs of Police (life, mem. bd. officers 1974-81), Nat. Sheriffs Assn. (life), Civitan. Avocations: bicycling, golf, puzzles. Office: Guardsmark Inc 22 S 2nd St Memphis TN 38103-2695

KNIGHT, HENRY L., minister; b. Monroville, Ala., Nov. 10, 1933; s. Cullin Knight, Queen (Bolar) Knight; m. Carrie Mural Agee, Apr. 9, 1955 (div. May 2002); 1 child, Darlene Marie Knight Wooten; children: Karen L. Knight Mayo, Darryl D. Mayo. BA, L.I.F.E. of L.A., 1975; MA, Azusa Pacific U., 1984; HDL (hon.), St. Stephens Ednl. Coll., 1994. Cert. Pastoral cert., Ordination bd. cert. U.S. Chaplain Assn. Tchr. Lockhaven Christian Sch., Inglewood, Calif., 1975—76; tchr., counselor West Angeles Ch., L.A., 1977—89; pastor, counselor Greater True Light Tabernacle, L.A., 1989—. Hosp. med. coord. L.A. County Health Dept., 1958—93; tchr., chaplain Union Rescue Mission, L.A., 1993—95; care giver Feed the Children, L.A., 1998—. Author: What is Preaching, 1999, Unique Bible Study, 1987, The Solution, 1986. E-5 U.S. Army, 1956—58. Recipient Good Conduct medal, U.S. Army, 1958. Democrat. Mem. Ch. Of God In Christ. Avocations: singing, walking, skating. Office: Greater True Light Tabernacle 5426 S Vermont Ave Los Angeles CA 90037-3532 Home: PO Box 7749 Los Angeles CA 90007-0749

KNIGHT, JAMES ATWOOD, manufacturing executive; b. Providence, Apr. 26, 1954; s. Richard Brayton and Louise (Atwood) K.; m. Cynthia Forbes Olney, June 11, 1983; children: Hilary Atwood, James Atwood Jr., Remington Forbes, William Olney, Elsie Lawson. BS, Boston U., 1975; MBA, Dartmouth Coll., 1984. Sr. assoc. Strategic Decisions Group, Menlo Park, Calif., 1984-88; mgr. Apple Computer, Cupertino, Calif., 1988-90; with Holt, Chgo., 1990, Boston Cons. Group, Chgo., 1991-95; v.p. SCA Consulting L.L.C., Chgo., 1995-97, mng. ptnr., 1997—2001; ptnr. Mercer Cons., 2001—02; chmn., CEO Knight Industries, Northfield, Ill., 2002—; chmn. Knight-Celotex, 2002—; chmn., CEO Knight-Rikett, LLC, 2002—; chmn. Internat. Constrn. Supplies, LLC, 2003—, Freightsource LLC, 2003—, Rikett Global BV, Rikett Tech. AS; CEO Rikett Asia LTD. Dir. Stay Focused, LLC. Author: Value Based Management, 1997; contbr. chpt. to book. Avocations: skiing, squash. Office: Knight Industries LLC One Northfield Plz Ste 400 Northfield IL 60093 Home: 11 Downing Rd Hanover NH 03755 E-mail: jknight@aknightcompany.com.

KNIGHT, JOHN ALLAN, clergyman, theology studies educator; b. Mineral Wells, Tex., Nov. 8, 1931; s. John Lee and Beulah Mae (Bounds) K.; m. Justine Anne Rushing, Aug. 22, 1958; children— John Allan, James Alden, Judith Anne. BA, Bethany Nazarene Coll., 1952; MA, Okla. U., 1954; B.D., Vanderbilt U., 1957, PhD, 1966. Ordained to ministry Ch. of Nazarene, 1954; pastor Tenn. Dist. Ch. of Nazarene, 1953-61, 71-72; prof., chmn. dept. philosophy and religion Trevecca Nazarene Coll., Nashville, 1957-69; chmn. dept. philosophy and religion Mt. Vernon (Ohio) Nazarene Coll., 1969-71, pres., 1972-75; pastor Grace Nazarene Ch., Nashville, 1971-72; pres. Bethany (Okla.) Nazarene Coll., 1976-85; gen. supt. Internat. Ch. of the Nazarene, 1985—2001, vice chair Bd. Gen. Supts., 1990-92, chair Bd. Gen. Supts., 1992-94; ret., 2001. Coordinator U.S. Govt. Project Studying Possible Coop. Ventures for Tenn. Colls. and Univs., 1969; mem. gen. bd. Internat. Ch. of Nazarene, 1980-85 Author: Commentary on Philippians, 1968, The Holiness Pilgrimage, 1971, In His Likeness, 1976, Beacon Bible Expositions, Vol. 9, 1985, What the Bible Says About Tongues - Speaking, 1988; co-author: Sanctify Them -- That the World May Know, 1987; co-author: Go -- Preach, The Preaching Event in the 90s; author: All Loves Excelling, 1995, Bridge to Our Tomorrows, 2000; editor-in-chief: Herald of Holiness, Kansas City, Mo., 1975-76. Pres. bd. govs. Okla. Ind. Coll. Found., 1979-81; trustee So. Nazarene U., Okla. Recipient Lily Found. Theology award Vanderbilt U., 1958-59; Carré fellow Vanderbilt U., 1960-62 Mem. Soc. Sci. Study Religion, Am. Acad. Religion, Wesley Theol. Soc. (pres. 1979), Evang. Theol. Assn. Clubs: Kiwanis Internat. Mem. Ch. Of Nazarene. Office: Internat Ch of the Nazarene 6401 Paseo Blvd Kansas City MO 64131-1213 E-mail: jkharlo@aol.com.

KNIGHT, KAREN ANNE MCGEE, artist, educator, educational research administrator; b. Florence, Ala., July 5, 1956; d. Glenn Houston and Juanita May (Fowler) McGee; m. Charles Ronald Knight, June 3, 1980; 1 child, Lara-Elizabeth. AA, Fla. Coll., 1976; BS, U. N. Ala., 1978, MA in Edn., 1994. Cert. tchr., Tenn., Ala. Title I reading aide Florence City Schs., 1978—79, 1st grade tchr., 1980—83; pre-kindergarten tchr. Belmont Weekday Sch., Nashville, 1984—85; kindergarten tchr. Metro-Davidson County Schs., Nashville, 1985—87; freelance watercolorist Shoals Artist's Guild, Florence, 1992—, Westat/quality control monitor, 1997—98, Westat/assessment adminstr., 1998—2001, Westat/field supr., 2001—. Chair Shoals Artists Guild, 1993—, v.p., 1996, pres., 1998. Sunday sch. tchr. Placed in watercolor competition N. Ala. State Fair, 1993. Mem. Nat. Mus. Women in Arts, Watercolor Soc. Ala. (N.W. Ala. area rep. 1996-2000), Tenn. Valley Art Assn., So. Watercolor Soc., Tenn. Valley Art Assn. Guild Avocations: herb and perennial gardening, genealogy. Home: 111 Snell Dr Florence AL 35630-6257

KNIGHT, KENNETH VINCENT, entrepreneur, venture capitalist; b. Jersey City, Mar. 30, 1944; s. Julian (Konopacki) and Ellen (Gordon) Knight; m. Karen Keenan, June 1, 1968 (div. June 1978); 1 child, Karisa M.; m. Maria H. Herrera, June 17, 1983; children: Alexander, (adopted) Maria B. Barroso, Christina M. Barroso. Student, Northwestern Coll., Iowa, 1962-65; BS in Mgmt., N.Y. Inst. Tech., N.Y.C., 1973; MBA, Nova Southeastern U., Ft. Lauderdale, Fla., 1977; grad., Officer Candidate Sch., FARNG, 1968. Mgr., customer/corp. rels. Cavanaugh Corp., Miami, Fla., 1967; asst. dir. corp. svcs. Burger King Corp., Miami, 1968-70; asst. to sr. v.p. investor rels. Deltona Corp., Miami, 1970-74; dir. corp./investor rels. Gen. Devel. Corp., GDV Corp., Miami and N.Y.C., 1974-78; v.p. resort affiliations, stockholder Interval Internat., Miami, 1978-79, sr. v.p. mktg., 1979-82, exec. v.p., chief ops., 1983-84; pres., chief ops. Interval Internat. & Worldex, Miami, 1984-87, pres., major shareholder, 1987—89, vice chmn., 1989-92; founder, gen. ptnr. Leisure Fund, Ltd., Miami, 1992—95; founder, pres., CEO Leisure Founders, Inc., 1992—96; founder, sr. ptnr. Leisure Fund Assoc., L.P., 1995—; founder, chmn., CEO Leisure Corp. Internat., 1996—; pres. KFH Mgmt., Inc., 1995—. Founder, chmn, CEO, co-founder Worldex Corp., Miami, 1982-92, Worldex Travel Ctrs., 1983-92, Leaguestar Plc, London, 1988-92; co-founder Worldex Corp., Denver and L.A., Worldex Europe Ltd., London, Intercambico Internat. de Vacienes, SA, Mexico City, 1985-92, Interval Austrailasia Pty. Ltd., Sydney, 1980-91, Leisurecorp Internat., 1992—; bd. advisors Property Planning, Inc., 1972-75, Interval Internat., 1975-78; founder, forum participant Time Share Inst., 1978-92; sr. founder, forum participant, Moderator Am. Resort Developers Assn., Washington, 1978-91; Ecotourism Natureshare Assn., Stowe, Vt., 1990, Interval/CUC Internat. Merger Acquisition, Stamford and London, 1992; II Merger, 1994, Vacation Accommodation Directory, Tampa, 1992, Condo Network, Inc., Kansas City, 1992, Brentwood Equities/ALA Healthcare, LA, 1993-95, Vryex Corp. Bridge, La Jolla, Calif., 1996, Nextec Corp./Erose Capital, LA, 1997—, Voice Track Corp., Dallas, 1997, Hawaiian Water Bridge, Honolulu, 1998, InterLink Acquisition Restructure, Denver, 1999, I-Mind Edn. Sys. Syndication, San Francisco, 2000; bd. govs. Nova U. Grad. Sch. Bus. Century Found., 1987-91, Nova Southeastern Wayne Hurizenga Grad. Sch. Bus. and Entrepreneurship, 1992—, adv. bd.; spkrs. forum Dave Thomas's Ambs. Enterprise Program, Nova Southeastern U., 1995, bd. dirs. South Fla. Alumni; mem. Farquhar Undergrad. Pres. Search Com., 1998, bd. trustees audit com., 1998—; trustee Nova Southeastern U., 1994, vice-chair strategic planning, 1996; Fla. venture forum Fla. Internat. U., 1995—, Small Bus. Devel. Ctr., U. Ctrl. Fla., 1996—, Assoc. Gov. Bds. Univs. and Colls., 1995—; spkr., lectr. in field. Founder: (mags.) The Leisure Society, Dreamweavers; exec. pub.: (newspaper) Timesharing Times, 1980; (mag.) Timeshare Traveler, 1984-90, Directory Resorts, 1980-90; mem. editl. bd. Vacation Industry Rev., 1985— (most traveled exec. 1984); author: Best Use for Resort Condominiums, 1972, Time Sharing—What It Is and How It Works, 1974, MBA Mag., Timesharing for Land Devel. Industry, 1974, Timesharing—Alternatives for Low Cost Vacations and Second Homes, Graduate Business Jour., 1977, Timesharing Times, Quality First for Interval and Knight, 1980, Travelmost Mag., 1982, Fla. Trend, The Achievers Sharing the Honors in a Time-Share Success, 1982, Timesharing Institute, The State of the Industry, 1983, Timeshare Encyclopedia, Volume II, Marketing & Sales, 1979, Volume IV, Finance & Servicing, Receivables, 1980, U.S. Congressional Record, 1987, Leisure Sharing for the 21st Century, NYU Hospitality Conference, 1992. 2d lt. U.S. Army, 1966-67; 1st lt. Fla. Army N.G., 1970-72, ret. 1993. Recipient Achievers award Fla. Trend mag., 1983, 88, Inc. 500 award Inc. mag., 1984, The Capital award Nat. Leadership Coun., 1991, Nova U. Alumni award, 1992; named Fla.'s Best Internat. Co., Prestige Internat. mag., 1985, Alumni of Yr., Nova Southeastern U., 1993. Roman Catholic. Avocations: adventure travel, cruising, skiing. Office: LeisureCorp Internat 6278 N Federal Hwy #294 Fort Lauderdale FL 33308 Home: 3674 Loquat Ave Miami FL 33133-6228 E-mail: knightnsu@aol.com, leisurefund@aol.com.

KNIGHT, MARY ANN, school system administrator; b. Dubuque, Iowa, Nov. 5, 1944; d. Harold V. and Grace C. (Riley) McMahon; m. George Everett Knight, June 10, 1967; children: Michelle, Suzanne, Thomas. BA in English, Clarke Coll., Dubuque; MA, SUNY, New Paltz. Cert. in English edn., N.Y., N.J. Journalist Advertiser-Photo News, Warwick, N.Y., 1974-80; tchr. English St. Stephen's Sch., Warwick, 1980-82; tutor in composition Warwick, 1982-84; tchr. writing SUNY, New Paltz, 1984-86; tchr. English Goshen (N.Y.) High Sch., 1987—2001; sch. adminstr. Goshen Ctrl. Sch. Dist., 2001—. Trustee Albert Wisner Pub. Library, Warwick, 1974-81. Mem. AAUW (past officer), Sigma Tau Delta. Roman Catholic. Home: 10 Lakeview Dr Warwick NY 10990-3026 Office: Goshen Intermediate Sch 13 McNally St Goshen NY 10924

KNIGHT, MORRIS HOMER, composer, educator; b. Charleston, S.C., Dec. 25, 1933; s. Moaris H. and Dorothy Eudora Knight; m. Kay E. Knight, June 10, 1955; children: Priscilla, Cassandra, Audrey. BFA, U. Ga., 1955; MFA, Ball State U., 1966. Dir. program WRFC Radio, Athens, Ga., 1956—63, KSFR Radio, San Francisco, 1963—64; tchr. Ball State U., Muncie, Ind., 1964—88; composer in residence Sebago Lake Region Chamber Festival, Harrison, Maine, 1970—. Author: Aural Comprehension, 1966; composer: over 100 works. Mem.: Am. Soc. Composers, Authors, Pubs. Home: 595 Norway Rd Harrison ME 04040

KNIGHT, NORMAN, volunteer, retired broadcast executive; b. July 24, 1924; LLD (hon.), Northeastern U.; DBA (hon.), Nathaniel Hawthorne Coll.; DCS (hon.), Merrimack Coll.; DHL (hon.), Suffolk U.; DCC (hon.), Anna Maria Coll. News reporter, scriptwriter Sta. WEW, WIL, WTMV, 1938-41; Announcer, host-producer Sta. WTMV, 1942; announcer, promotion mgr., news reporting continuity dir. Sta. KTHS, 1943; announcer Sta. WMC, 1943; announcer, news writer, reporter, salesman Sta. WMMN, 1944; gen. mgr. Sta. WAJR, 1944-46; Eastern dir. sta. relations MBS, 1946-49; v.p. sales, advt. and promotion Sponsor Publs., Inc., 1950-53; gen. mgr. Sta. WABD (now WNYW-TV), 1953-54; exec. v.p., gen. mgr. Yankee Network div. RKO Teleradio Pictures, Inc. (operating Yankee Network WNAC, WRKO, WNAC-TV); also dir. Yankee Network; v.p. RKO Teleradio Pictures, 1954-60; pres. Yankee div. RKO Teleradio Pictures, Inc., 1957-60, Yankee div. RKO Gen., Inc., 1958-60; treas., chmn. Knight Sales, Inc.; chmn., treas. Knight Radio, Inc. (WEZF, WGIR and WGIR-FM), Knight Broadcasting N.H, Inc. (WHEB-FM, WXHT, WTMN); pres., treas. Knight Communications Corp. (WTAG and WSRS). Chmn. Caribbean Communications Corp.; tv and radio advisor John F. Kennedy. Established first complete TV sta.: pub. affairs film unit which produced Brotherhood Series: River of Life, Wershmeitz (only film 1956 Hungarian revolt), Suffer the Little Children, Breast Cancer, over 100 programs Dangers of Apathy; TV documentaries, 1953-60; Author: (sales techniques radio/TV) The Cause of All Mankind, (film and TV) A Storm is Always a Challenge, Awake America, others. Radio-TV chmn. United Fund Greater Boston, Mass. Cancer Soc., ARC chpt. Met. Boston, Met. Boston chpt. ARC; bus. chmn. Easter Seal Soc.; radio chmn. Salvation Army; dir. Strawberry Banke; bd. dirs. New Eng. Nephrosis Found.; pres., founder New Eng. Kidney Disease Found.; founder, chmn. Nat. Kidney Disease Found.; pres. Norman Knight Charitable Found.; trustee Mass. Bd. Regional Community Colls., Agassiz Village Camps, Crippled Children's Non-Sectarian Fund, Boys and Girls Camps, Inc.; mem. nat. council, exec. com. New Eng. council Boy Scouts Am.; exec. com., dir. Rescue, Inc.; exec. com. The Jimmy Fund; exec. com., trustee Children's Cancer Research Found., Dana Farber Cancer Inst.; mem. fin. com. Com. Econ. Devel.; mem. devel. council Boston U.; mem. pres.'s council Boston Coll.; bd. dirs. Freedoms Found.; also nat. co-chmn. Am. Freedom Ctr.; chair, pres. Mass. Fallen Firefighters Meml. Fund, 2001. Recipient Americanism award Am. Heritage Com., 1959, awards from VFW, Am. Legion, Amvets, Am. Legion Aux., 1959-60, award for contbn. to radio and TV industry Alpha Epsilon Rho; Golden Mike award Broadcasters Found., 1996; named one of ten Outstanding Yougn Men, Boston Jr. C. of C., 1956, Man of Yr., Italian-Am. Police Assn., Humanitarian award ARC, 1998; Norman Knight Camping Fund for less priviledged established in his honor, 1958, Norman Knight Hyperbaric Medicine Ctr., Mass. Eye and Ear Infirmary established in his name, 1999, Norman Knight Endowment Fund for batter women and children established in his honor, 1999, chair and pres. Mass. Fallen Firefighters Meml., Inc., 2001—; established Knight Nursing Ctr. at Mass. Gen. Hosp., 2004-05. Mem. Radio-TV Execs. Sec., Young Pres.'s Orgn., Broadcast Pioneers, AIM, Alpha Epsilon Rho. Clubs: Variety (Boston); Broadcasting Execs. New Eng, 100 of Mass. (co-founder, pres., dir.), 100 of N.H. (life), 100 of Vt. (life). Office: 63 Bay State Rd Boston MA 02215-1802

KNIGHT, NORMAN GLADSTONE, minister; b. Bklyn., May 22, 1953; s. Herman Gladstone Knight and Blanca Velez; m. Heather Joy Knight; children: Raaqim, Siraaj, Jamaal, Lauren, Johanna stepchildren: Matthew Mayne, Holly Mayne, Micah Mayne. BA in Bus. Adminstrn., Park U., 1976; MDiv, Andrews U., 1989; DMin, Trinity Bible Coll. and Seminary, 2004. Ordained to ministry Seventh-day Adventist Ch., Berkeley, Calif., 1992. Sales rep. Proctor & Gamble, Inc., Cin., 1976—78; dir. partnership program U. Calif., San Diego, 1978—86; outreach officer Andrews U., Berrion Springs, Mich., 1986—88; pastor 7th Day Adventist Ch., Pleasant Hill, Calif., 1988—; cons., ptnr. Knight Cons., Stockton, Calif. Regional coord. Calif. Gear Up U. Calif. Office of Pres., Oakland, 2002—; chaplain Vallejo (Calif.) Police Dept., 1993—, U. Pacific, Stockton, 2004, Kaiser Hosp./Sutton Hosp., Vallejo, 1995—; prison chaplain Calif. Med. Facility, Vacaville, 1990—. Advisor Black Student Union, U. Calif., San Diego; mem. sch. bd. Napa Adventist Jr. Acad., Rio Lindo Acad., Golden Gate Acad., mem. mgmt. team; mem. exec. com. NCC Seventh-day Adventist, Operation Reachback. Recipient Role Model of Yr. award, Nat. Assn. Negro Bus. and Profl. Women's Club, Inc., Assoc. Pastor award, Market St. Seventh Day Adventist Ch., Outstanding Pastoral Svc. award, Berea Seventh Day Adventist Ch., Bible Tchr. Svc. award, Golden Gate Acad. Mem.: Greater Bay Ministerial Assn., Vallejo Ministerial Assn., Sacramento Urban League, No. Calif. Conf. Black Ministerial Fellowship, Black Faculty and Staff Assn. (pres.), Omicron Psi, Alpha Phi Alpha. Democrat. Home: 10431 Big Oak Cir Stockton CA 95209 Office Phone: 209-477-1570. Office Fax: 209-477-2188. E-mail: nknight263@aol.com.

KNIGHT, PATRICIA MARIE, optics scientist, consultant; b. Schnectady, N.Y., Jan. 25, 1952; BS in Engring. Sci., Ariz. State U., 1974, MSChemE, 1976; PhD in Biomed. Engring., U. Utah, 1983. Teaching and rsch. asst. Ariz. State U., Tempe, 1974-76; product devel. engr. Am. Med. Optics, Irvine, Calif., 1976-79, mgr. materials rsch., 1983-87; rsch. asst. U. Utah, Salt Lake City, 1979-83; dir. materials rsch. Allergan Surg. Products, Irvine, 1987-88, dir. rsch., 1988-91, v.p. rsch., devel. and engring., 1991—2002; v.p. rsch., devel. Advanced Med. Optics, Santa Ana, Calif., 2002—03; cons. biomed. product rsch. and devel. Laguna Niguel, Calif., 2003—. Contbr. articles to profl. jours. Mem. Soc. Biomaterials, Am. Chem. Soc., Soc. Women Engrs., Assn. Rsch. in Vision and Opthalmology, Biomed. Engring. Soc. E-mail: pkbiomed@cox.net.

KNIGHT, PHILIP HAMPSON, apparel executive; b. Portland, Oreg., Feb. 24, 1938; s. William W. and Lota (Hatfield) Knight; m. Penelope Parks, Sept. 13, 1968; children: Matthew, Travis. BBA, U. Oreg., 1959; MBA, Stanford U., 1962. CPA Oreg. Co-founder Nike, Inc. (formerly Blue Ribbon Sports, Inc.), 1962; chmn. Nike, Inc., Beaverton, Oreg., 1967—, CEO, 1967—2004, pres., 1968—90, 2000—04. Bd. dirs. U.S.-Asian Bus. Coun., Washington. 1st lt. AUS, 1959—60. Named Oreg. Businessman of Yr., 1982; named one of 1988's Best Mgrs., Bus. Week Magazine. Mem.: AICPA. Republican. Episcopalian. Avocations: tennis, running, golf. Office: Nike Inc One Bowerman Dr Beaverton OR 97005*

KNIGHT, RAYMOND SCOTT, music educator; b. St. Marys, Pa., Apr. 9, 1957; s. Donald and Rose Knight; m. Lisa Ann Knight, July 5, 1998; children: Lucas Ryan, Lexi Rose. Grad., Clarion U., 1979, grad., 1984. Instr. music Elk County Cath. High Sch. Dir. chorus ECCAS, St. Marys, Pa., 1993—; dir. band ECES, 1984—, St. Leos, 1984—. Mem.: Nat. Educators Nat. Conf., Pa. Music Educators Assn. Roman Catholic. Avocations: hunting, fishing, music, woodworking. Home: 185 Little Bear Run Rd Saint Marys PA 15857 Office: Elk County Cath High Sch 600 Maurus St Saint Marys PA 15857

KNIGHT, RITA CECILIA, school librarian; b. Jerseyville, Ill., Aug. 19, 1958; d. Cecil Jesse and Rita Lenora Knight; m. Gary Dean Mertens, June 19, 1982; children: Rita Elena Mertens, Jane Eliza Mertens, Ellis William Mertens. MLS, Dominican U., River Forest, Ill., 1982. Catalog libr. Okla. State U., Stillwater, 1982—84; prin. catalog libr. U. Ariz., Tucson, 1984—93; catalog libr. Grinnell Coll., Iowa, 1993—. Author: (chpt.) Cataloging Special Materials: Critiques and Innovations, 1986, Library User Education: Powerful Learning, Powerful Partnerships, 1987, Library Services for Hispanic Children: a Guide for Public and School Libraries, 1987; contbr. articles to profl. jours. Troop leader and svc. unit mem. Girl Scouts Am., Grinnell, Iowa, 1996—2005. Mem.: Iowa Libr. Assn. Assn. of Coll. and Rsch. Libraries. (newsletter com. 1993—96), ALA Assn. for Libr. Collections and Tech. Svcs. (continuing edn., tng. and recruitment for cataloging 1996—2002), ALA Assn. of Coll. and Rsch. Librs. (bibliographic instrn. sect. continuing edn. com. 1987—89, budget and fin. com. 1993—95, newsletter com. 1993—96, chair coll. librs. discussion group 1998—2002, exec. coun. 1998—2002, budget and fin. com. 1999—2003, task force on funding and orgnl. models 2001—02). Avocations: camping, bicycling, travel, cooking, hiking. Home: 1433 West St Grinnell IA 50112 Office: Grinnell Coll Burling Libr 1111 Sixth Ave Grinnell IA 50112 Office Phone: 641-269-3368. Business E-Mail: knight@grinnell.edu.

KNIGHT, ROBERT EDWARD, bank executive, educator; b. Alliance, Nebr., Nov. 27, 1941; s. Edward McKean and Ruth (McDuffee) K.; m. Eva Sophia Youngstom, Aug. 12, 1966. BA, Yale U., 1963; MA, Harvard U., 1965, PhD, 1968. Asst. prof. U.S. Naval Acad., Annapolis, Md., 1966-68; lectr. U. Md., 1967-68; fin. economist Fed. Res. Bank of Kansas City, Mo., 1968-70, rsch. officer, economist, 1971-76, asst. v.p., sec., 1977, v.p., sec., 1978-79; pres. Alliance Nat. Bank, 1979-94, also chmn., 1983-94; pres. Robert E. Knight & Assocs., banking and econ. cons., Cheyenne, Wyo., 1979—. Chmn. Eldred Found., 1985—; vis. prof., chmn. banking and fin. East Tenn. State U., Johnson City, 1988; faculty Stonier Grad. Sch. Banking, 1972-2002, Colo. Grad. Sch. Banking, 1975-82, Am. Inst. Banking, U. Mo.,

Kansas City, 1971-79, Prochnow Grad. Sch. Banking, U. Wis., 1980-84; extended learning faculty Park Coll., 1996—; mem. Coun. for Excellence for Bur. Bus. Rsch. U. Nebr., Lincoln, 1991-94, mem. Grad. Sch. Arts and Scis. Coun., Harvard, 1994—; chmn. Taxable Mcpl. Bondholders Protective Com., 1991-94. Contbr. articles to profl. jours. Bd. dirs. Stonier Grad. Sch. Banking, 1979-82, Nebr. Com. for Humanities, 1986-90, People of Faith (Royal Oaks) Found., 2000-04; trustee Knox Presbyn. Ch., Overland Park, Kans., 1965-69; bd. regents Nat. Comml. Lending Sch., 1980-83; mem. Downtown Improvement Com., Alliance, 1981-94; trustee U. Nebr. Found., 1982-94; fin. com. United Meth. Ch. Alliance, 1982-85, trustee, 1990-93; mem. Box Butte County Indsl. Devel. Bd., 1987-94; bd. mem. Homeowners Assn. Found., Sun City, Ariz., 2005-; chmn., CEO Eldred Found. Woodrow Wilson fellow, 1963—64. Mem. Am. Econ. Assn., Am. Fin. Assn., So. Econ. Assn., Nebr. Bankers Assn. (com. state legis. 1980-81, com. comml. loans and investments 1986-87), Am. Inst. Banking (state com. for Nebr. 1980-83), Am. Bankers Assn. (econ. adv. com. 1980-83, cmty. bank leadership coun.), Western Econ. Assn., Econometric Soc., Rotary, Masons. Home and Office: 429 W 5th Ave Cheyenne WY 82001-1249

KNIGHT, ROBERT G., mayor, investment banker; b. Wichita, Kans., July 31, 1941; s. Edwar G. and Melba (Barbour) K.; m. Jane Carol Benedick, Aug. 12, 1967; children— Jennifer, Amy, Kristin BA, Wichita State U. Rep. First Securities Co., Wichita, Kans., 1970-76, v.p., 1984—, Mid-Continent Mcpls., Wichita, Kans., 1977-82, Ranson & Co., Wichita, Kans., 1982-84; mayor City of Wichita, 1980-81, 84—. Trustee Salvation Army, Wichita, 1980—, Urban Ministeries, Wichita, 1980—, Southwestern Coll., Winfield, Kans., 1980—; bd. dirs. Kans. Water Authority, Topeka, 1983—; commr. City of Wichita, 1979—. Served with USMCR, 1962-66 Recipient award of honor Concerned Citizens for Community Standards, 1982 Mem. Nat. League Cities, Kans. League Municipalities Republican. Methodist. Avocation: sports. Office: Mayors Office City Hall 1st Fl 455 N Main St Wichita KS 67202-1600

KNIGHT, ROBERT HUNTINGTON, lawyer, bank executive; b. New Haven, Feb. 27, 1919; s. Earl Wall and Frances Pierpont (Whitney) K.; m. Rosemary C. Gibson, Apr. 19, 1975; children: Robert Huntington, Jessie Valle, Patricia Whitney, Alice Isabel, Eli Whitney. Grad., Phillips Acad., Andover, Mass., 1936; BA, Yale, 1940; LL.B., U. Va., 1947, LLM, 1949. Bar: N.Y. bar 1950. With John Orr Young, Inc. (advt. agy.), 1940-41; asst. prof. U. Va. Law Sch., 1947-49; assoc. firm Shearman & Sterling & Wright, N.Y.C., 1949-55, ptnr., 1955-58; dep. asst. sec. def. for internat. security affairs Dept. Def., 1958-61; gen. counsel Treasury Dept., 1961-62; ptnr. firm Shearman & Sterling, N.Y.C., 1962-80, sr. ptnr., 1980-85, of counsel, 1986—; dep. chmn. Fed. Res. Bank N.Y., 1976-77, chmn., 1977-83. Counsel to bd. United Technologies Corp., 1974-85; dir. internat. bd. Owens-Corning Fiberglas Corp., 1989—; dir. I-Corps, Nat. Leadership Bank, Mercator, Inc., Citizen Exchange Coun.; mem. Intelsat Arbitration Panel, 1971-91. Bd. dirs. Internat. Vol. Services; chmn. bd. dirs. U. Va. Law Sch. Found., 1970-90; bd. dirs. Asia Found. Served to lt. col. USAAF, 1941-45. Mem. ABA, Fed. Bar Assn., Internat. Bar Assn., Inter-Am. Bar Assn., Assn. of Bar of City of N.Y., N.Y County Lawyers Assn., Internat. Law Assn., Washington Inst. Fgn. Affairs, Council Fgn. Relations, Pilgrims Club, Links Club, World Trade Ctr Club, River Club (N.Y.C.), Army and Navy Club, Met. Club (Washington), Round Hill Club (Greenwich, Conn.), Ocean Club (Ocean Ridge, Fla.), Farmington Club (Va.). also: 570 Park Ave New York NY 10021-7370 also: 6767 N Ocean Blvd Ocean Ridge FL 33435-3314 Office: 599 Lexington Ave New York NY 10022-6030

KNIGHT, ROBERT MILTON, journalist, educator; b. Tacoma, Dec. 2, 1940; s. Lawrence Leslie Knight and Marian Delphine (Humphrey) Gordy, (stepmother) Margaret Irene (Michael) K.; m. Susan Jan Guthrie, July 3, 1965; children: Kelly Leslie, Leigh April. BS in Journalism, U. Colo., 1967; MA in Integrated Profl. Studies, De Paul U., 1996. Statehouse reporter The New Mexican, Santa Fe, 1968-70; gen. newsman Sta. KOB-TV and Radio, Albuquerque, 1970-71; statehouse corr. Sta. KOAT-TV, Albuquerque, 1971-73; freelance journalism Chgo., 1973-74; product mgr. Deltak, Inc., Schiller Park, Ill., 1974-76; mgr. corp. comm. Advanced Sys., Inc., Elk Grove Village, Ill., 1976-79; account exec. Hill & Knowlton, Inc., Chgo., 1979-81; freelance writer Knight, Writer, Chgo., 1981-94; sr. editor City News Bur. of Chgo., 1994-98. Mem. adv. bd. PC/Expo Chgo., 1989-90; lectr. Northwestern U., 1984-98; lectr. journalism and English, Gettysburg Coll., 1998—. Author: A Journalistic Approach to Good Writing: The Craft of Clarity, 1998; contbr. articles to newspapers and mags. With USN, 1959-61. Mem. Soc. Profl. Journalists (bd. dirs. Chgo. Headline Club chpt. 1992—, regional conf. chairperson 1993, chpt. pres. 1994-95), Ind. Writers Chgo. (bd. dirs. 1983-85, program chairperson 1991-93). Home: 1225 Beecherstown Rd Biglerville PA 17307-9511 E-mail: RKnight@gettysburg.edu. *Personal philosophy: Question. Question everything, but don't be afraid to believe an answer. Don't be afraid to believe--in a religion, in a philosophy, in an institution, in a person, in yourself. Be prepared, however, to give up your most cherished belief if you must. If answers to your questions prove the belief to be false, then get rid of it.*

KNIGHT, SHIRLEY, actress; b. Goessel, Kans., July 5, 1936; d. Noel Johnson and Virginia (Webster) K.; m. Eugene Persson, 1959 (div., 1969) m. John R. Hopkins (dec., 1998); children: Kaitlin, Sophie. D.F.A., Lake Forest Coll., 1978. Actress theatre and films. Theater debut in Look Back in Anger, Pasadena (Calif.) Playhouse, 1958, N.Y.C. debut in Journey to the Day, 1963; other N.Y.C. theater appearances include The Three Sisters, 1964, Rooms, 1966, We Have Always Lived in the Castle, 1966, The Watering Place, 1969, Kennedy's Children, 1975 (Tony award), Happy End, 1977; with Bristol (Eng.) Old Vic Theatre in And People All Around, 1967; other appearances in Eng. include A Touch of the Poet, 1970, Antigone, 1971, Economic Necessity, 1973; other U.S. theater appearances include A Streetcar Named Desire, Princeton, N.J., 1976, Happy End, N.Y.C., 1977, Landscape of the Body, Chgo., then N.Y.C., 1977, A Lovely Sunday for Creve Coeur, Charleston, S.C., then N.Y.C., 1979, Losing Time, N.Y.C., 1979, I Won't Dance, Buffalo, 1980, Come Back Little Sheba, N.Y.C., 1984, Women Heroes, N.Y.C., 1986, The Depot, N.Y.C., 1987; film appearances include: Five Gates to Hell, 1959, Ice Palace, 1960, The Dark at the Top of the Stairs, 1960, The Couch, 1962, Sweet Bird of Youth, 1962, House of Women, 1962, Flight from Ashiya, 1964, The Group, 1966, Petulia, 1966, Dutchman, 1967, The Rain People, 1969, Secrets, 1971, The Counterfeit Killer, 1970, Juggernaut, 1974, Beyond the Poseidon Adventure, 1979, Prisoners, 1981, Endless Love, 1981, The Sender, 1982, The Secret Life of Houses, 1994, Benders, 1994, Color of Night, 1994, Stuart Saves His Family, 1995, Death In Venice, CA, 1994, Diabolique, 1996, As Good as it Gets, 1997, The Man Who Counted, 1998, 75 Degrees in July, 2000, Angel Eyes, 2001, The Salton Sea, 2002, P.S. Your Cat is Dead, 2002, Divine Secrets of the Ya-Ya Sisterhood, 2002, Fly Cherry, 2003, A House on a Hull, 2003, Sexual Life, 2005, To Lie in Green Pastures, 2005; TV films include: The Outsider, 1967, Shadow Over Elveron, 1968, The Counterfeit Killer, 1968, Majesty, 1968, The Lie, 1971, The Country Girl, 1973, Friendly Persuasion, 1975, Medical Story, 1975, Return to Earth, 1976, 21 Hours at Munich, 1976, The Defection of Simas Kudirka, 1978, Champions: A Love Story, 1979, Playing for Time, 1980, With Intent to Kill, 1984, Sweet Scent of Death, 1984, Billionaire Boys Club, 1987, Bump in the Night, 1991, Shadow of a Doubt, 1991, To Save a Child, 1991, A Mother's Revenge, 1993, Hoggs' Heaven, 1994, Baby Brokers, 1994, The Yarn Princess, 1994, A Part of the Family, 1994, Fudge-A-Mania, 1995, Dad, the Angel & Me, 1995, Children of the Dust, 1995, Indictment: The McMartin Trial, 1995 (Emmy award), Stolen Memories: Secrets From the Rose Garden, 1996, A Promise to Carolyn, 1996, Somebody Is Waiting, 1996, Little Boy Blue, 1997, The Wedding, 1998, If These Walls Could Talk, 1996, The Univited, 1996, Mary & Time, 1996, Dying to be Perfect: The Ellen Hart Pena Story, 1996, Convictions, 1997, A Father for Brittany, 1998, A Marriage of Convenience, 1998, My Louisiana Sky, 2001, Shadow Realm, 2002, Mrs. Ashboro's Cat, 2003; (TV series) Buckskin, 1958, Angel Falls, 1993, Maggie Winters, 1998; (TV mini series) When Love Kills: The Seduction of John Hearn, 1993; guest appearances includeRawhide, 1959, The Fugitive, 1964, 1965, 2001, Marcus Welby, M.D., 1974, Barnaby Jones, 1975, Spenser: For Hire, 1985, 1987, thirtysomething, 1987, Murder She Wrote, 1990, Matlock, 1990, Law & Order, 1991, 2001, Law & Order: Special Victims Unit, 2003, L.A. Law, 1993, NYPD, 1995, Ally McBeal, 2002, ER, 2002, Crossing Jordan, 2004, Cold Case, 2004, House, M.D., 2005, Desperate Housewives, 2005 and several others. Active Com. for Handgun Control, nat. civil rights orgns., worker for peace. Recipient Tony award (Antoinette Perry for Supporting or Featured Actress), 1976, Emmy award for Outstanding Guest Performer in Comedy Drama or Series, 1988, Emmy award for Outstanding Guest Performer in a Drama Series (NYPD Blue), 1995.*

KNIGHT, TIMOTHY P., publishing executive; b. Flint, Mich., Aug. 24, 1965; BA in Acctg., Marquette U., 1987; JD, DePaul U., 1990. Sr. corp. assoc. Skadden, Arps, Slate, Meagher & Flom, Chgo. and London, 1992—96; mergers and acquisitions counsel Tribune Co., Chgo., 1996—97; v.p. affiliates and bus. devel. Classified Ventures, Chgo., 1997—98; v.p. strategy and devel. Tribune Pub. Co., Chgo., 1998—2001; head interactive ops. Chgo. Tribune, 2001—03, v.p. strategic mktg., devel. and fin., 2001—03; exec. v.p., gen. mgr. Newsday, Melville, NY, 2003—04, COO, 2004, pres., 2004—, pub., CEO, 2004—. Chmn.'s coun. Heckscher Mus. Art, Huntington, NY. Office: Newsday 235 Pinelawn Rd Melville NY 11747*

KNIGHT, WALKER LEIGH, publishing executive, minister; b. Henderson, Ky., Feb. 6, 1924; s. Cooksey Bennett and Rowena (Henderson) K.; m. Iva Nell Moseley, Nov. 10, 1943; children: Walker Leigh, Kenneth Wayne, Nelda Denise, Emily Jill. BA, Baylor U., 1949. Ordained min. Bapt. Ch., 1948. Reporter Henderson Gleanor and Jour., 1942; pastor in Dale, Tex., 1948-49; editor Falls County Record, Marlin, Tex., 1948-49; assoc. editor Bapt. Std., Dallas, 1950-59; editl. dir. So. Bapt. Home Mission Bd., Atlanta, also editor Missions U.S.A. mag. and Atlanta bur. chief Bapt. Press News Service, 1959-83; editor, pub. Bapts. Today (formerly SBC Today), 1983-89, pub., 1989-93, pub. emeritus, 1994—. Author: Panama, The Land Between, 1965, Struggle for Integrity, 1969, See How Love Works, 1971, Seven Beginnings, 1976, Chaplaincy, Love on the Line, 1978, Tell the People, 1986; contbr.: Southern Baptists Observed, 1992, Struggle for the Soul of the SBC, 1993; editor: The Whitsitt Jour., 1995-98. With USAAF, 1943-45. Home and Office: 1008 Forrest Blvd Decatur GA 30030-4732

KNIGHT, W.H., JR., (JOE KNIGHT), dean, law educator; m. Susan Mask; children: Michael, Lauren. BA in Econs., Speech and Polit. Sci., U. N.C., 1976; JD, Columbia U. Prof. U. Iowa Coll. Law, 1983—2001, vice provost, 1997—2000; dean U. Wash. Law Sch., 2001—. Vis. prof. Washington U., St. Louis, Duke U. Schs. Law; assoc. counsel, asst. sec. Colonial Bancorp. Mem.: ABA, Nat. Bar Assn., Nat. Conf. on Black Lawyers, Soc. Am. Law Tchrs., Am. Law Inst., N.Y. Bar, State Farm Mutual Automobile Ins. Co. Office: U Washington Sch Law William H Gates Hall Box 353820 Seattle WA 98195-3020 Office Phone: 206-543-2586. Office Fax: 206-616-5305. Business E-Mail: whknight@u.washington.edu.

KNIGHT, WILLIAM R., research scientist, educator; b. Burbank, Calif., Feb. 8, 1949; s. Jack D. and Rose T. Knight; m. Lucy Jo Bennett, July 20, 1980; 1 child, Michael. BA in Physics, U. Calif., San Diego, 1976, MS in Physics, 1978. Sr. mem. tech. staff Hewlett Packard, Corvallis, Oreg., 1979—2002; rsch. asst. Oreg. State U., Corvallis, 2002—03; phys. scientist Nat. Weather Svc., Palmer, Alaska, 2003—. Educator 509J Pub. Sch. Dist., Corvallis, 1991—2000, mem. sch. site coun., 1992—95. Contbr. articles to profl. jours. With USAF, 1969—72. Fellow, Fanny/John Hertz Found., 1978. Mem.: AAAS. Achievements include creation of a numerical modeling program for a major high-tech company; creation of a unique science/math education program for K-6 public education; patents for focussing in micro-electron devices. Home: PO Box 1942 Palmer AK 99645-1942 Office: NWS-WWCATWC 910 S Felton St Palmer AK 99645 Personal E-mail: wknights@gci.net.

KNIGHTLEY, KEIRA, actress; b. Teddington, Middlesex, Eng., Mar. 26, 1985; d. Will Knightley and Sharman Mcdonald. Actor: (films) A Village Affair, 1994, Innocent Lies, 1995, Star Wars: Episode I - The Phantom Menace, 1999, The Hold, 2001, Deflation, 2001, New Year's Eve, 2002, Bend it Like Beckham, 2002, Thunderpants, 2002, Pure, 2002, The Seasons Alter, 2002, Pirates of the Caribbean: The Curse of the Black Pearl, 2003, Love Actually, 2003, King Arthur, 2004, Stories of Lost Souls, 2005, The Jacket, 2005, Pride and Prejudice, 2005; (TV films) Royal Celebration, 1993, Treasure Seekers, 1996, Coming Home, 1998, Princess of Thieves, 2001; (TV miniseries) Oliver Twist, 1999, Doctor Zhivago, 2002. Office: PMK Pub Rels 33rd Fl 650 Fifth Ave New York NY 10019*

KNIGHTON, BARBARA MCLEOD, occupational health specialist, risk specialist; b. Regina, Sask., Can. d. Alan Donald and Jeanne-Marie (Smith) McLeod; m. James Edward Knighton, Feb. 9, 1979; children: Skye Alan, Aren James, Taylor William. BS, U. B.C., Vancouver, Can., 1976; MS, Calif. State U., Northridge, 1992. Tchg. asst. U. Wash., Friday Harbor, 1976; rsch. asst. Controlled Environ. Pollution Expt., Vancouver, 1976, Can. Fisheries and Marine Svc., Vancouver, 1977-78, U. Tex. Med. Br., Galveston, 1979-80; mem. tech. staff Los Angeles County Dept. Pub. Works, Alhambra, Calif., 1992-95, safety officer, 1995-97, risk mgr., 1997—. Asst. scoutmaster Boy Scouts Am., La Crescenta, Calif., 1996—. Mem. Am. Soc. Safety Engrs., Am. Indsl. Hygiene Assn., Am. Conf. Govtl. Indsl. Hygienists. Avocations: camping, hiking. Office: Los Angeles County Dept Pub Works 900 S Fremont Ave Alhambra CA 91803-1331

KNIGHTS, EDWIN MUNROE, pathologist; b. Providence, Dec. 25, 1924; s. Edwin Munroe and Viola Ruth (Koreb) K.; m. Ruth Lindsay Currie, Sept. 23, 1961; children: Edwin B., Jessie B., Ross D., David J. (dec. 1979). AB, Brown U., 1948; MD, Cornell U., 1948. Intern Bellevue Hosp., N.Y.C., 1948-49; resident in pathology R.I. Hosp., Providence, 1949-50, Henry Ford Hosp, Detroit, 1952-54; assoc. pathologist Harper Hosp., Detroit, 1954; dir. labs. Hurley Hosp., Flint, Mich., 1957-62, Providence Hosp., Southfield, Mich., 1963-75; dir. Northland Oakland Med. Labs., Southfield, Mich., 1964-75, Bio Sci. Labs., Detroit, 1975-85, Smith Kline Bio-Sci. Labs, Detroit, 1985-89; dir. labs. Kern Hosp., Warren, Mich., 1977-81; pres. Coll. Terr. Inc., Flint, Mich., 1968—2003; dir. Performance Assurance Profls., Bloomfield Hills, Mich., 1988-94; pres. Life Sci. Inc., Flint, 1971-72, Vet. Med. Labs., 1973-75; clin. prof. pathology Mich. State U., 1974-75; rep. Comprehensive Health Planning Coun. S.E. Mich., 1973-85, trustee, 1986-87; mem. lab. peer rev. com. Mich. Dept. Social Svcs., 1979-84; med. dir. Smith Kline Beecham Labs., Detroit, 1990-92, Nat. Health Labs., Flint, 1992-94. Pres. Life Sci. Inc., Grantham, 1996-98; pathologist Project Hope, Indonesia and Vietnam, 1961, Peru, 1962, Ecuador, 1964; bd. dirs. GeneSaver DNA Preservation Svcs., 1996—. Author: Ultramicro Methods for Clinical Laboratories, 1957, 2d edit., 1962; editor: Minicomputers in the Clinical Laboratory, 1970, Lifelines, 1971-75,For Want of an "A" Confusion Reigns. The Day Nature Goofed, 2004; contbg. editor Jour. Foot Surgery, 1983-89; contbr. articles to profl. jours. and mags.; patentee in field. Emeritus mem. adv. coun. New Eng. Hist. Geneal. Soc., trustee, 2001—; mem. long range planning com. Eastman Cmty. Assn., 1997-2003. Lt. MC USNR, 1944-46, 50-52, ETO, Korea. USPHS grantee, 1957-66. Fellow ACP, Coll. Am. Pathologists, Am. Soc. Clin. Pathology (Mich. councillor 1966-68); mem. AMA, Am. Coll. Med. Genetics (affil. doctoral mem.), Oakland County Med. Soc. (pres. 1974), Mich. Soc. Pathologists (pres. 1970, del. Mich. State Med. Soc. 1986-93), Internat. Acad. Pathology, Mich. State Med. Soc., Assn. Clin. Scientists, Gen. Soc. Mayflower Descs., Roger Williams Family Assn., Wardroom Club (Boston). Home and Office: 125 Hawthorne Village Rd Nashua NH 03062

KNIGHTS, MAYVELLA R., Spanish language educator; b. Caribou, Maine; m. Joseph C. Knights, May 15, 1971; children: Holly, Kristina. BA, Ricker Coll., 1971. Spanish tchr. Massabesic H.S., Waterboro, Maine, 1983—. Advisor fgn. lang. club Massabesic H.S., chmn. dept. fgn. langs. Mem.: Maine Edn. Assn., NEA. Avocations: travel, reading, crossword puzzles, puzzles.

KNILANS, MICHAEL JEROME, food products executive; b. Columbus, Ohio, Mar. 3, 1927; s. Alfred Sidney and Bernice (Meyers) K.; m. Anne Eberhardt, June 15, 1947; children: Michael, Kyleen, Christine, Timothy, Suzanne. BS, Ohio State U., 1949. With Big Bear Stores Co., Columbus, 1942-89, mdse. mgr., 1952-61, v.p., 1961-70, exec. v.p., 1970-76, pres., 1976-89, dir. Bd. dirs. Price Chopper Supermarkets, Schenectady, N.Y. Chmn. bd. Ohio Workers Compensation Bd., 1989-95; bd. dirs. Children's Hosp., Columbus, Mt. Carmel Coll. Nursing, Columbus; v.p. East Ctr. region Boy Scouts Am. With USNR, 1944-46, PTO. Mem. Ohio Coun. Retail Mchts. (treas.), Better Bus. Bur. (pres. 1978), C. of C., Masons, Shriners, Jesters, Rotary (pres. 1981—, dist. gov. 1993-94). Republican. Home: 1119 Kingsdale Ter Columbus OH 43220-4946 Office Phone: 614-451-1293. Personal E-mail: mknilans@aol.com.

KNISELY, RALPH FRANKLIN, retired microbiologist; b. Altoona, Pa., Mar. 30, 1927; s. Calvin Ross and Frieda Pauline (Neher) K.; m. Joan Marie Fitzgerald, Jan. 29, 1949 (div. 1955); 1 child, Patricia Ann; m. Ann Martin, May 21, 1960. BS, postgrad., Pa. State U., 1953. Bacteriologist Altoona Hosp., 1953-56, adminstrv. asst. to pathologist, 1957-59; microbiologist Chem. Corps Dept. Army, Ft. Detrick, Md., 1959-72; rsch. microbiologist Edgewood Arsenal, Aberdeen Proving Ground, Md., 1972-86. Contbg. author: Rapid Identification of Biological Agents, 1966; contbr. articles to Jour. Bacteriology, European Jour. Microbiology. Pres. Eastview Civic Assn., Frederick, Md., 1968-69; mem. Srs. and Lawmen Together Coun., Frederick City Police and Frederick County Sheriffs Office. With USN, 1945-46, 50-51; capt. Res. ret., 1945-87. Mem.: AARP (bd. dirs. chpt. 636 1990—92, chpt. pres. 1995—96, bd. dirs. chpt. 636 1997—98), Rsch. Soc. Am. (emeritus), Am. Soc. for Microbiology (emeritus), N.Y. Acad. Sci. (life), Assn. Mil. Surgeons U.S. (life), Philalethes Soc., Knisely Reunion Assn. (historian 1993—, pres. 1994—95), Internat. Platform Assn., Ret. Officers Assn. (chpt. v.p. 1969—70, pres. 2002—03), Nat. Assn. Ret. Fed. Employees (life; pres. chpt. 409 1995—97, bd. dirs. 1997—98), Am. Legion (life), Am. Philatelic Soc. (life), Sampson WWII Vets. (life; Md. dir.), Fleet Res. Assn., Nat. Sojourners (pres. chpt. 354 1965, 1981, sec. 1986—), Masonic Rsch. Soc., Legion of Honor (comdr. 2002—03), Korean Vets., Quatour Coronati Corr. Cir. (London), Keystone Kopps (pres. 2002), George Washington Masonic Stamp Club (pres. 1978—80, sec. 1988—98), KT, Scottish Rite, Order of Quetzalcoatl, Tall Cedars of Lebanon, Shriners, Masons, Elks (life). Republican. Lutheran. Avocations: family genealogy, amateur radio. Home: 7400 Skyline Dr Frederick MD 21702-3652

KNISPEL, HOWARD EDWARD, lawyer; b. Bklyn., Apr. 22, 1959; s. Joseph and Irene K.; m. Marisa Gonzalez, July 5, 1987; children: Jennifer, Stephen. BA, Rochester Inst. Tech., 1981; JD, NYU, 1988. Bar: N.Y. 1989, U.S. Dist. Ct. (so. and ea. dist.) 1990, U.S. Supreme Ct. 2002. Assoc. Lipsig, Sullivan & Liapakis, N.Y.C., 1988-89, Fein & Steinberg, Bklyn., 1990-91; pvt. practice N.Y.C., 1991-96, Sunrise, Fla., 1996-98; assoc. Assocs. and Bruce Sheiner, Ft. Myers, Fla., 1998, Feldman, Kramer & Monaco P.C., Hauppauge, NY, 1998—2000; pvt. practice Commacle, NY, 2000—. Instr. N.Y. Paralegal Sch., N.Y.C., 1994-96; adminstrv. law judge N.Y.C. Taxi Limousine Comm., 1995-96. Bd. dirs. Eisenhower Coll. Alumni Assn., Seneca Falls, N.Y., 1998. Democrat. Jewish. Office Phone: 631-864-7589. E-mail: hekesg@heleesq.com.

KNIZE, DAVID MAURICE, plastic surgeon; b. Ennis, Tex., Apr. 2, 1938; s. Joseph Fred and Mary Elizabeth (Vavra) K.; m. Barbara Ruth Reed BA, Tex. U., 1959; MD, Southwestern Med. Coll., 1963. Resident in Orthopedic surgery Duke U., Durham, N.C., 1964-66; resident gen. surgery U. Colo., Denver, 1966-68; resident plastic surgery N.Y.U., 1970-74; assoc., prof. surgery U. Colo., Denver, 1974--. Contbr. articles to profl. jours. Lt. comdr. USN, 1969—71. Mem.: AMA, Colo. State Soc., Am. Soc. Plastic and Reconstructive Surgeons. Republican. Avocations: bicycling, windsurfing, scuba diving, glider flying. Office: 3555 S Clarkson St Englewood CO 80110-3909 Home: 4545 S Monaco St Unit 446 Denver CO 80237-3463

KNIZESKI, JUSTINE ESTELLE, insurance company executive; b. Glen Cove, NY, June 4, 1954; d. John Martin and Elsie Beatrice (Gozelski) Knizeski. BA, Conn. Coll., 1976; M in Mgmt., Northwestern U., 1981. Customer svc. supr. Brunswick Savs., Freeport, Maine, 1977-79; investment analyst Bankers Life and Casualty Co., Chgo., 1980-83, dir. corp. planning and analysis, 1983-87; dir. budgets, cost acctg. Blue Cross/Blue Shield of Ill., 1987-97, dir. planning, budgets and analysis, 1997—, exec. dir. budgets and analysis, 2002—, divsn. v.p. corp. budgets and procurement, 2003—04, v.p., chief procurement officer, 2004—. Sec. Alternatives, Inc., Chgo., 1991—92, vice chmn., 1987—91, 2002—04, chair fin. com., 2002—05, ad hoc fin. com., 1998—2001; active Chgo. Coun. Fgn. Rels., 2002—; ad hoc fin. com. Alternatives, Inc., 2005—, chmn. bd. dir., 1984—87, bd. dir., 1983—84, 2001—02, Non-Profit Fin. Ctr., 2000—03, treas., 2002—03. Mem.: Planning Forum. Avocations: travel, sailing, bicycling, travel, painting. E-mail: knizeskij@bcbsil.com.

KNOBBE, LOUIS JOSEPH, lawyer, educator; b. Carroll, Iowa, Apr. 6, 1932; s. Louis C. and Elsie M. (Praeger) Knobbe; m. Jeanette M. Sganga, Apr. 3, 1954; children: Louis, Michael, Nancy, John, Catherine. BSEE, Iowa State U., 1953; JD, Loyola U., L.A., 1959. Bar: Calif. 1960, U.S. Supreme Ct. 1963, U.S. Patent and Trademark Office. Tech. staff Bell Tel. Labs., 1953-54; patent engr. GE, Washington, 1955—56, N.Am. Aviation, Downey, Calif., 1956-59; patent lawyer Beckman Instruments, Fullerton, Calif., 1959-62; co-founder, ptnr. Knobbe, Martens, Olson & Bear, Newport Beach, Calif., 1962—2002, of counsel, 2003—. Lectr. Computer Law Assn., Inc., L.A., L.A. Intellectual Property Law Assn., San Diego Bar Assn.; adj. prof. Sch. Law San Diego U., 1987—2003; mem. engring. adv. bd. U. Calif., Irvine. Co-author: (book) Attorney's Guide to Trade Secrets, 1972, 2d edit., 1996, update, 2002, How to Handle Basic Patent, 1992; contbg. author (book) Using Intellectual Property Rights to Protect Domestic Markets, 1986; contbr. articles to profl. jours. Bd. dirs. Orange County (Calif.) Performing Arts Ctr., 1975—83; past pres. Philharm. Soc. Orange County; past bd. mem., past v.p. Opera Pacific, Orange County; bd. visitors Loyola Law Sch., 2000—. Recipient Jurisprudence award, Anti-Defamation League, 1988, Lifetime Contbn. award, Forum for Corp. Dirs., 2005. Fellow: Inst. Advancement Engring.; mem.: IEEE (past chmn. Orange County sect., Centennial medal 1984), ABA, Licensing Execs. Soc., Orange County Patent Law Assn. (lectr.), Orange County Bar Assn., State Bar Calif., Am. Arbitration Soc. (panel neutrals), Am. Intellectual Property Law Assn. (lectr.), Pacific Club, First Friday Friars, Santa Ana North Rotary, Eta Kappa Nu, Tau Beta Pi, Phi Kappa Phi. Avocations: boating, still and video photography, travel and exploration in lake powell, death valley, deserts of Arizona and Baja California. Office: 2040 Main St Fl 14 Irvine CA 92614 Office Phone: 949-760-0404. Business E-Mail: LKnobbe@kmob.com.

KNOBEL, DALE THOMAS, historian, educator, university president; b. East Cleveland, Ohio, Sept. 14, 1949; s. Harry Spencer and Gwynne Ann K.; m. Tina Jamieson, June 19, 1971; children: Allison. BA, Yale U., 1971; PhD, Northwestern U., 1976. Asst. prof. history Northwestern U., Evanston, Ill., 1976-77, Tex. A&M U., College Station, 1977-84, assoc. prof. history, 1984-96, dir. univ. hons. prog., 1987-92, exec. dir. honors programs and acad. scholarships, 1992-95, assoc. provost for undergrad. programs, 1995-96; provost, dean of faculty, prof. history Southwestern U., Georgetown, Tex., 1996-98; pres., prof. history Denison U., Granville, Ohio, 1998—. Author: America for the Americans: The Nativist Movement in the United States, 1996, Paddy and the Republic: Ethnicity and Nationality in Antebellum America, 1985; co-author: Prejudice, 1982; contbr. Immigrant America, 1994, Fleeing the Famine, 2003; book rev. editor Jour. of Early Republic, 1987-89; contbr. articles to profl. jours. Chmn. Bryan Hist. Landmark Commn., 1987-93; trustee Bryan Tx.Pub. Libr., 1989-92, Brazos Valley Mus. of Natural History, 1994-96, Inst. for Internat. Edn. Students, Chgo., 1999—, Newark Midland Theater Assn.,1999; pres. Denison Univ. Rsch. Found., 1998—, North Coast Athletic Conf., 2004—, Five Colls. Ohio, Inc., 2004—; vice chmn. Ohio Found of Ind. Coll., 2002—. Am. Assn. State and Local History grantee, 1984; NEH grantee, 1978; NSF grantee, 1972-74; W.K. Kellogg

Found. grantee, 1985-87. Mem. Nat. Collegiate Honors Coun., Orgn. Am. Historians, Immigration History Soc., Soc. for Hist. of the Early Am. Republic, Great Lakes Colls. Assn. (treas. 2004—), Union Club Cleve., Univ. Club Chgo., Rocky Fork Hunt and Country Club, Phi Beta Kappa, Phi Alpha Theta, Omicron Delta Kappa, Phi Kappa Phi, Phi Beta Delta. Methodist. Home: 204 Broadway W Granville OH 43023-1120

KNOBLAUCH, MARK GEORGE, librarian, consultant; b. Ft. Wayne, Ind., Oct. 8, 1947; s. Marcus George and Helen Edna (Helmke) K. BA, Valparaiso U., 1969; A.M.L.S., U. Mich., 1970. Cataloger Chgo. Pub. Library, 1970-73, head serials dept., 1973-78, head acquisitions div., 1978-84, dir. tech. svcs., 1985-91, dir. collection mgmt., 1992-96; dep. exec. dir. Pub. Libr. Assoc., 1997-99. Columnist Arts Sect., Chgo. Tribune newspaper, 1981-91, Booklist Mag., 2000—; cons. BJ Chakiris Corp., 1997—. Contbr. articles to profl. jours. Judge U.S. Indsl. Film Festival, Chgo., 1976-90; chmn. 1st St. Paul's Luth. Ch., Chgo., 1979-83; bd. dirs. Printer's Row Book Fair, 1986—. Mem.: Beta Phi Mu. Home: 435 W Surf St Chicago IL 60657-6132 E-mail: mark@knoblauch.us.

KNOBLAUCH, MARY REILLY (MARY LOUISE REILLY), retired music educator, writer; b. Montrose, Mo., Feb. 21, 1922; d. John Henry Welling and Sylvesta Lesmeister; m. Charles A. Knoblauch, Apr. 7, 1996; m. Barney E. Reilly, Dec. 28, 1946 (dec. July 30, 1991); 1 child, Marguerite Ann. BS in Music Edn., St. Mary Coll., Leavenworth, Kans., 1944; MA in Edn., Immaculate Heart Coll., L.A., Calif., 1956; LHD (hon.), St. Mary Coll., Leavenworth, Kans., 2002. Tchr. music French Inst. Notre Dame De Sion, Kansas City, Mo., 1944—46, L.A. City Schs., 1946—54, supr. music ctrl. dist., 1954—55; asst. prof. music L.A. State Coll., 1955—57; assoc. prof. music San Fernando State Coll., Northridge, Calif., 1957—74; prof. music Calif. State U., Northridge, 1975—92, prof. emeritus, 1992. Music cons. L.A. Parochial Schs., 1963—73; adv. bd. Cultural Ctr., Woodland Hills, Calif., 1960; v.p. edn. Opera Guild, L.A., 1970. Author: (tchr.'s materials) It's Time for Music, 1985, (textbooks) World of Music K-6, 1988, Music Connection Series K-6, 1995—98. Grant dir. L.A. Mcpl. Arts, 1978; mem. Liturgical Music Comm., L.A., 1972—79; dir. Docent Ministry, St. Francis of Assisi, 1999—; mem. Comprehensive Arts Ctr. State Dept. of Edn., Sacramento, 1976. Recipient Disting. Prof. award, Calif. State U., 1979, St. Cecilia's award Docent Ministry, 2002, Lifetime Achievement award, Calif. Music Educators Hall of Fame, 2002. Mem.: La Quinta Arts Found., Sigma Alpha Iota (award of Honor 1961), Delta Kappa Gamma (grad. scholarship 1955). Achievements include development of music framework for Calif. schs., State Dept. Edn., 1970. Avocations: reading, piano, dance, gardening. Home: 48 605 Vista Tierra La Quinta CA 92253

KNOBLOCH, CHARLES SARON, lawyer, geophysicist; b. Wayne, Mich., May 11, 1959; s. Faustyn Edwin and Ameaila Caroline (Marquardt) K. BS in Applied Geophysics with honors, Mich. Tech. U., 1980; JD, U. Houston, 1991, Coll. of William and Mary, Madrid, 1990; diploma in internat. law, U. San Diego, Russia, 1991. Bar: Tex. 1992; cert. patent atty. U.S. Patent & Trademark Office, 1994, Coll. of State Bar of Tex., 1994-96. Pvt. practice, Houston, 1992—. With DuPont/Conoco, Houston/Jakarta, 1980-2002; CEO Leading Edge Measurements, Inc., 2003; exec. dir. Insights and Innovations, LLC, 2004—; adv. bd. Tex. Accts. and Lawyers for the Arts, 1997; pres. Omnilaw.com, 1993—; indsl. adv. bd. Mich. Tech. U., 2005; bd. dirs. Autonomous Devices, Inc., 2005. Chmn. M.D. Anderson Cancer Ctr. Network, Houston, 1997; nominated attendee John Ben Shepperd Pub. Leadership Forum, Austin, Tex., 1995; mem. Lakewood Ch., 2001—; mem. indsl. adv. bd. Mich. Tech. U., 2005—. Recipient Engrg. Excellence award DuPont, Imaging Tech. award, 1996; inducted Acad. Geol. and Engring. and Scis., Mich. Tech. U., 2004. Mem. Houston Intellectual Property Law Assn., Indonesian Petroleum Assn. (data mgmt. com., ad hoc legal com. 1999), ABA (corp. law com.), Am. Assn. Petroleum Geologists (co-chair data mgmt. Bali 2000), Inodnesian Am. Bus. Assn. (bd. dirs. 2003-05), Drilling Engrs. Assn., Soc. Exploration Geophysicists Office Phone: 713-202-9898. E-mail: knoblcs@omnilaw.com.

KNOBLOCH, FERDINAND J., psychiatrist, educator; b. Prague, Czech Republic, Aug. 15, 1916; emigrated to Can., 1970; s. Ferdin and Marie (Verunac) K.; m. Susana Hartman (dec. 1944 victim of Holocaust); m. Jirina Skorkovska, Sept. 5, 1947; children: Katerina, Yohana. Maturity degree, Realgymnasium, Prague, 1935; student, Charles U. Med. Sch., Prague, 1935—46; psychoanalytic tng., Charles U. Med. Sch., 1945-53, 1945—53. Successively lectr., asst. prof., assoc. prof. psychiatry Charles U., Prague, 1946-70; mem. faculty U. B.C., Vancouver, Canada, 1970—, prof. psychiatry, 1971-83, prof. emeritus, 1983—; clin. dir. Day House Univ. Hosp., 1972-90. Vis. prof. U. Havana, 1963, U. Ill., Chgo., 1968-69, Columbia U., 1969-70, Albert Einstein Med. Coll., 1970; pres. European seminar mental health and family WHO, 1961, 3d Internat. Congress Psychodrama, 1968; co-chmn. Internat. Symposium Non-Verbal Aspects and Techniques of Psychotherapy, 1974; hon. dir. psychodrama Moreno Inst., NYC, 1974. Author: (with Jirina Knobloch) Forensic Psychiatry, 1967 (award Czechoslovak Med. Soc. 1968), Psychotherapy, 1968, Neurosis and You, 1962, 63, 68, Integrated Psychotherapy, 1979 (transl. into German 1983, Japanese 1984, Czech 1993, Chinese, 1995), Integrated Psychotherapy in Action, 1999; contbr. articles on psychotherapy integration, psychology of music and evolutionary psychology to profl. jours. Polit. prisoner of Gestapo, 1943-45. Fellow Am. Pscyhiat. Assn. (disting. life); mem. Czechoslovak Soc. Advancement Psychoanalysis and Integration of Psychotherapy (pres. 1968-72), Am. Acad. Psychoanalysis, Polish Psychiat. Assn. (corr.), Can. Psychiat. Assn., Am. Group Psychotherapy Assn., Can. Soc. for Integrated Psychotherapy and Psychoanalysis (pres. 1972—), World Psychiat. Assn. (co-chmn. sect. psychotherapy 1983-93, chmn. 1993-96).

KNOBLOCH, MARCIA M. (MARTA KNOBLOCH), writer; b. Montgomery, Ala., July 7, 1939; d. Kenneth Floyd Musick and Mary Cherry Phelps; m. William W. Knobloch; children: Charles Wayne, Mark David. Student, Coll. Notre Dame of Md., Balt. Vis. poet Fondazione Il Fiore, Florence, Italy, 2003, Festival of Poetry and Poets, St. Mary's Coll. of Md., 1992, Gunston Day Sch. Book and Authors Day, 1999; lectr. and condr. workshops in field; judge poetry contests; curator Emmina Verzella's personal exhbn., NYU and Instituto Italiano di Cultura, 1993; writing instr. Writer's Ctr., Bethesda, Md., 1998—99. Author: (fables) Tales of Five Continents, 1999, (play) La Virago, 2001, (artist book) Quetzal, 2001; contbr. poetry, short stories, critical essays and revs. numerous lit. mags. and anthologies including Balt. Rev., Md. Poetry Rev., numerous others.; guest editor Lite, 2002; contbr.: Md. Poetry Rev., 1988—98; one of founding editors Chesapeake mag., 1993, Passager: A Jour. of Remembrance and Discovery, 1990; editl. asst.: The Spirit of Italy in American Art 1716-1945, 1990, The Shaping Hand of Italy in American Art; A Dictionary of American Artists of Italian Heritage 1776-1945, 1993; co-editor: Margaret, Remembering A Life That Was Poetry, 1998; assoc. editor East of the Bay, A Chester River Anthology, 1999. Asst. to exec. dir. fundraising campaign Lyric Found.; bd. dirs. ARTSCAPE Lit. Arts Com. of Mayor's Adv. Com. on Arts and Culture of Balt., 1989—91, Balt. City Arts Grants Com., 1990, The Sun A.D. Emmart Award Co., Balt.; exec. bd. Balt. Heritage, Balt. Planning Com., Theatre of Nations Festival, Christine di Pizan Soc. for Humanities Steering Com., Coll. Notre Dame of Md., The Women's Assn. of Balt. Symphony, Women's Com. of Balt. Mus. Art, Young Assocs. of Balt. Symphony. Recipient Premio Donna, Lions Castello Ferrara, 1995, Columbia Book award, 1993, Il Premio Nazionale di Arti e Ambiente di Italia, 1991, Lit. Arts award, Balt. ARTSCAPE, 1988. Mem.: Acad. Am. Poets, Poetry Soc. Am., Nat. League of Am. PEN Women, Writers Ctr. Bethesda, Balt. Bibliophiles, Hamilton St. Club, Johns Hopkins Club, Arts Seminar Group.

KNOBLOCH, NEIL A., education educator; s. Ezra J and Marie E Knobloch; m. June R Mogler; children: Grant A, Nelson A, Kedron R. BS, Iowa State U., 1988—92, MS, 1992—97; PhD, Ohio State U., 1999—2002. Tchr. Mid-Prairie Cmty. Sch., Wellman, Iowa, 1992—99; lectr. Ohio State U., 1999—2002; asst. prof. U. of Ill., 2002—. Pres. Actimax Learning, Inc., Champaign, Ill., 2004—. Author: (facilitator's guide) Reap: A Business Management Simulation, (book) Supervising and Mentoring the Beginning Teacher; contbr. articles to profl. jours. Tchr. Apostolic Christian Ch., Champaign, Ill., 2003—05. Nat. Project of Learner-Centered Tchg. Approaches, USDA, 2003—, grant, U. of Ill., 2003—04, Ill. State Bd. of Edn., 2002—. Mem.: Am. Assn. for Agrl. Edn. (rsch. com. chair 2004—05, Outstanding Rsch. Presentations 1998, 2001, 2003), Am. Edn. Rsch. Assn., Nat. Assn. of Agrl. Educators (life Oustanding New Tchr. 1998), Omicron Tau Theta, Gamma Sigma Delta. Achievements include patents pending for. Office: University of Illinois 139 Bevier Hall 905 S Goodwin Ave Urbana IL 61822 Office Phone: 217-244-8093. E-mail: nknobloc@uiuc.edu.

KNOEBEL, SUZANNE BUCKNER, cardiologist, educator; b. Ft. Wayne, Ind., Dec. 13, 1926; d. Doster and Marie (Lewis) Buckner. AB, Goucher Coll., 1948; MD, Ind. U.-Indpls., 1960. Diplomate: Am. Bd. Internal Medicine. Asst. prof. medicine Ind. U., Indpls., 1966-69, assoc. prof., 1969-72, prof., 1972-77, Krannert prof., 1977—. Asst. dean rsch. Ind. U., Indpls., 1975-85; assoc. dir. Krannert Inst. Cardiology, Indpls., 1974-90; asst. chief cardiology sect. Richard L. Roudebush VA Med. Ctr., Indpls., 1982-90; editor-in-chief ACC Current Jour. Rev., 1992-2000. Fellow Am. Coll. Cardiology (v.p. 1980-81, pres. 1982-83); mem. Am. Fedn. Clin. Research, Assn. Univ. Cardiologists Office: Krannert Inst 1701 N Senate Ave Indianapolis IN 46202 Office Phone: 317-962-0061. Business E-Mail: sknoebel@iupui.edu.

KNOEDLER, ELMER L., retired chemical engineer; b. Gloucester, N.J., Feb. 12, 1912; s. Elmer L. and Carolyn (Belle) K.; m. Mabel Dyer Todd, Jan. 15, 1966 (dec. July 2003); children: Dianne, Homer. ME, Cornell U., 1934, MS, 1936; PhD, Columbia, 1952. Registered profl. engr., 3 states. With Atlantic Mfg. Co., 1934-35; asst. supt. charge Davis Emergency Equipment Co., 1937-38; charge rsch. and devel. metal powder process Metals Disintegrating Co., 1939-41, cons. chem. engr., sr. field engr., 1941-82; ptnr. Sheppard T. Powell & Assocs., Balt. Past mem. Md. Bd. for Registration Engrs. and Land Surveyors. Contbr. numerous articles to tech. and profl. jours. Fellow Am. Inst. Chemists, ASME (past chmn. com. water conditioning and indsl. waste); mem. Am. Inst. Chem. Engrs. (chmn. Balt. sect. 1953), Am. Chem. Soc., Am. Inst. Cons. Engrs., Sigma Xi, Phi Lambda Upsilon. Home: 400 Avinger Ln Apt 321 Davidson NC 28036-9759 Office: 1915 Aliceanna St Baltimore MD 21231-3014

KNOELKER, MICHAEL T.F., science observatory director; b. Feb. 9, 1953; Diploma in Physics, U. Göttingen, Germany, 1978; PhD in Physics, U. (Germany) Freiburg, 1983. Asst. prof. U. Göttingen, 1983—90; astronomer Kiepenheuer-Instut Sonnenphysik, Freiburg, 1990—; vis. scientist High Altitude Obs. Nat. Ctr. Atmospheric Rsch., Boulder, Colo., 1987—94, affiliate scientist High Altitude Obs., 1994—95, sr. scientist, dir. High Altitude Obs., 1995—. Mem., steering com. Solar Magnetism Initiative, 1995—; mem. Assn. of Univs. for Rsch. in Astronomy (AURA) Observatory Vis. Com., 1996—. Office: NCAR PO Box 3000 Foothills Lab High Altitude Obs 3450 Mitchell Ln Boulder CO 80307

KNOEPFLMACHER, ULRICH CAMILLUS, literature educator; b. Munich, June 26, 1931; U.S. citizen; s. George A. and Hilde (Weiss) K.; married; 4 children. AB, U. Calif., Berkeley, 1955, MA, 1957; PhD, Princeton U., 1961. From instr. to assoc. prof. U. Calif., Berkeley, 1961-69, Humanities Rsch. prof., 1966-67, 77; asst. dean U. Calif. Coll. Letters and Sciences, Berkeley, 1967-71; prof. U. Calif., Berkeley, 1969-79; prof. English Princeton U., 1979—, now William and Annie S. Paton Found. prof. ancient and modern lit. Vis. prof. Harvard U., 1971; Grad. prof. Tulsa U., 1979, Bread Loaf Sch. English, 1981, 83, 85, 87, NYU, 1982, Johns Hopkins U., 1983; adv. bd. Publs. MLA, 1977-81, SEL, 1979— VIJ, 1982—, Children's Lit., 1987—; dir. NEH summer seminars, 1975, 84, 86, 89, 90, 91, 95, 99. Author: Religious Humanism and the Victorian Novel, 1965, George Eliot's Early Novels: The Limits of Realism, 1968, Laughter and Despair: Readings in Ten Novels of the Victorian Era, 1971, Emily Bronte's Wuthering Heights, 1988, Wuthering Heights: A Study, 1994, Ventures into Childland: Victorians, Fairy Tales, and Femininity, 1998; editor: Francis Newman: Phases of Faith, 1970, George MacDonald's Fairy Tales, 1999, Frances Hodgson Burnett's A Little Princess, 2002; co-editor: Nature and the Victorian Imagination, 1977, The Endurance of Frankenstein: Essays on Mary Shelley's Novel, 1978, Forbidden Journeys: Fairy Tales and Fantasies by Victorian Women Writers, 1992, Cross-Writing the Child and the Adult, 1997; cons. editor Teaching Children's Literature: Issues, Pedagogy, Resources, 1992; edit. bd. publs. MLA, 1981-83. Recipient Disting. Tchg. award Acad. Senate U. Calif., 1977; Am. Coun. Learned Soc. fellow, 1965, Guggenheim fellow, 1969-70, 87-88, sr. fellow NEH, 1972-73, 91-92, sr. fellow Humanities Coun., Princeton U., 1975, Rockefeller Found. sr. fellow, 1983-84, Nat. Humanities Ctr. fellow, 1996. Mem. MLA, Nat. Coun. Tchrs. English, N.E. Victorian Assn., N.Am. Victorian Studies Assn., Children's Lit. Assn. Office: Princeton U Dept English McCosh Hall Princeton NJ 08544-1016 E-mail: uknopf@princeton.edu.

KNOKE, DAVID HARMON, sociology educator; b. Phila., Mar. 4, 1947; s. Donald Glenn and Frances Harriet (Dunn) Knoke; m. Joann Margaret Robar, Aug. 29, 1970; 1 child, Margaret Frances. BA, U. Mich., 1969, MSW, 1971, PhD, 1972; MA, U. Chgo., 1970. Asst. prof. sociology Ind. U., Bloomington, 1972-75, assoc. prof., 1975-81, prof., 1981-85, dir. Inst. Social Rsch. and Ctr. for Survey Rsch., 1982-84; prof. sociology U. Minn., Mpls., 1985—, chmn., 1989-92, undergrad. dir., 1995-98, grad. dir., 1998—2002. Mem. sociology program rev. panel NSF, 1981-83; mem. sociology rev. panel Fulbright Scholars, 1993-95; mem. sociology com. Grad. Records Exams., 1998-2000. Author: Change and Continuity in American Politics, 1976, (with Peter J. Burke) Log-Linear Models, 1980, (with James R. Wood) Organized for Action, 1981, (with George W. Bohrnstedt and Alisa Potter Mee) Statistics for Social Data Analysis, 1982, 4th edit., 2002, (with James H. Kuklinski) Network Analysis, 1982, (with Edward O. Laumann) The Organizational State, 1987, Organizing for Collective Action, 1990, Political Networks, 1990, (with George W. Bohrnstedt) Basic Social Statistics, 1991, (with Franz Pappi, Jeffrey Broadbent and Yutaka Tsujinaka) Comparing Policy Networks, 1996, (with Arne Kalleberg, Peter Marsden and Joe Spaeth) Organizations in America, 1996, (with Peter Capelli, Laurie Bassi, Harry Katz, Paul Osterman and Michael Useem) Change at Work, 1997, Changing Organizations, 2001. Recipient NIMH Rsch. Scientist Devel. award, 1977-82; 12 rsch. grants NSF; Nat. Merit scholar, 1965-69, Fulbright Sr. Rsch. scholar, Germany, 1989, scholar of the Coll. U. Minn., 1996-99; Ctr. for Advanced Study in the Behavioral Scis. fellow, 1992-93. Mem. Am. Sociol. Assn. (chair orgns. and occupation sect. 1992-93), Sociol. Rsch. Assn., Acad. of Mgmt., Internat. Network for Social Network Analysis, European Group for Orgnl. Studies. Unitarian Universalist. Home: 7305 Wooddale Ave S Minneapolis MN 55435-4157 Office: U Minn Dept Sociology Minneapolis MN 55455 Office Phone: 612-624-4300. Business E-Mail: knoke@atlas.socsci.umn.edu.

KNOLES, GEORGE HARMON, history educator; b. Los Angeles, Feb. 20, 1907; s. Tully Cleon and Emily (Walline) K.; m. Amandalee (Barker), June 12, 1930; children: Ann Barker (Nitzan), Alice Laurane (Simmons). AB (hon.), Coll. of Pacific, 1928, AM, 1930; PhD, Stanford U., 1939. Instr. history Union High Sch., Lodi, Calif., 1930-35; history asst. Stanford, 1935-36; history instr., 1937-41; asst. prof., 1942-46; assoc. prof., 1946-51; prof. history, 1951-72; Margaret Byrne, prof. Am. history, 1968-72; emeritus, 1972—; chmn. history dept., 1968-72. Dir. Inst. Am. History, 1956-72; prof. history; chmn. div. social sci. State Coll. Edn., Greeley, Colo., 1941-42; summer tchr. Central Wash. Coll. Edn., Ellensburg, 1939, State Coll., Flagstaff, Ariz, 1940, 1941, U. Calif. at Los Angeles, 1947; Stanford U., Tokyo U.; Am. Studies Seminars, Tokyo, 1950-52, 56, U. Wyo., 1955; cons. acad. history Hdq. USAF, 1950-52; dir. summer Inst. Tchrs. Am., Alpach, Austria, 1965; Blazer lectr. U. Ky., 1961; Throchmorton lectr. Lewis an Clark Coll., 1965; Fulbright distinguished lectr., Japan, 1971 Author: The Presidential Campaign and Election of 1892, 1942; Readings in Western Civilization, (with Rixford K. Snyder), 1951; The Jazz Age Revisited, 1955, The New United States, 1959; Editor: The Crisis of The Union, 1860-61, 1965; Sources in American History, 10 vols, 1965-66, The Responsibilities of Power, 1900-1929, 1967; Essays and Assays: California History Reappraised, 1973; Contbg. articles to profl. jour. Lt., USNR, 1944-46. Mem. Am. So. Hist. Assn.; Orgn. Am. Historians (exec. com. 1950-54, bd. editors rev. 1955-58); Am. Studies Assn. (council 1952-54); Soc. of Am. Historians. Clubs: Commonwealth. Methodist. Home: 850 Webster St Apt 220 Palo Alto CA 94301-2878

KNOLL, ANDREW HERBERT, biology professor; b. West Reading, Pa., Apr. 23, 1951; s. Robert Samuel and Anna Augusta (Meyer) K.; m. Marsha Craig, June 22, 1974; children: Kirsten C., Robert A. BA with highest honors, Lehigh U., 1973; MA, Harvard U., 1974, PhD, 1977; PhD (hon.), Uppsala U., Sweden, 1996; DSc (hon.), Lehigh U., 1998. Asst. prof. geology Oberlin Coll., Ohio, 1977-82; assoc. prof. Harvard U., Cambridge, Mass., 1982-85, prof. biology, 1985-2000, curator bot. mus., 1985—, prof. earth and planetary sci., 1985—, chmn. dept. organismic and evolutionary biology, 1992-98, 2004—05, Fisher prof. natural history, 2000—, assoc. dean faculty Arts and Scis., 2000—03. Mem. com. on planetary biology U.S. Space Sci. Bd., 1982-88, NRC Bd. on Earth Scis., 1987-88, 92-95, space studies bd., 1989-90, 97-2000; Crosby vis. lectr. MIT, 1999; mem. sci. team NASA MER 2003 Mars Mission. Assoc. editor Paleobiology, 1980-92, Precambrian Rsch., 1985—, Trends in Ecology and Evolution, 1987-92, Rev. of Palaeobotany and Palynology, 1987—, Am. Jour. Sci., 1990—, Geology, 1992-98, Palaios, 1996-2002, Palaeography Palacoclimatology Palaeocology, 1997—, Internat. Jour. Plant Scis., 1998—; contbr. articles to profl. publs. Bd. dirs. U.S. Nat. Mus. Nat. Hist., 1993-97. Named one of Time/CNN America's Best Scientists, 2002; recipient Walcott medal, Nat. Acad. Scis., 1987, Chang prize in paleontology, Am. Mus. Natural History, 2001, Moore Medal, Soc. Sedimentary Geology, 2005, medal, Paleontological Soc., 2005, Bownocker medal, Ohio State U., 2005; fellow, Geol. Soc. Am., Linnean Soc., London, Am. Acad. Arts and Scis., 1987, Guggenheim, 1987, AAAS; Vis. fellow, Gonville and Caius Coll., Cambridge, Eng., 1991—92. Fellow AAAS, European Union Geoscis. (hon.); mem. NAS, Bot. Soc. Am., Am. Philos. Soc., Paleontol. Soc. (Schuchert award 1987), Soc. Study Evolution, Phi Beta Kappa (book award in sci. 2003), Sigma Xi. Avocations: travel, reading, cooking, choral music. Office: Harvard Univ Botanical Museum 26 Oxford St Cambridge MA 02138-2902

KNOLL, CHARLES D., priest, educator, musician; b. Chicora, Pa., Feb. 14, 1927; s. Francis A. Knoll and Mary A. Black. BA in Philosophy, St. Fidelis, 1951; MA in Theology, Capuchin Coll., 1955; MusM, Cath. U., 1968; diploma in Music, Cologne Hochschule, 1963. Prof. St. Fidelis Coll., Pa., 1956—66, Capuchin Coll., DC, 1967—72, music confessor, 2001—05; music cons. Parish Diocese, Pa., 1972—79; music editor Paluch World Libr. Publ., Ill., 1979—84; parish ministry St. Peter Paul, Cumberland, Md., 1984—92; confessor Nat. Shrine Franciscan Conception, DC, 2001—. Music therapist Duquesne U., Pa., 1992—93; organist in field. Poet: chpt. book Purple Twilight, 1995. Chaplain Peace Pilgrims, Fatima, Portugal, 2003. Named Artist of Yr., Cumberland Arts, 1986; Fulbright music scholar, Cologne Nochschule, 1962—63. Roman Catholic. Avocations: swimming, golf, photography, stamp collecting/philately. Home: Capuchin Coll 4121 Harawood Rd US Washington DC 20017 Personal E-mail: cknoll75@yahoo.com.

KNOLL, DAELYNN ADELE, music educator; b. Clarkston, Wash., Dec. 28, 1969; d. LaVerne Ray and Diane Carol Walker; married, Aug. 17, 1996; children: Adelyn Adele, Kyler Nathan. BA in vocal music edn., U. Idaho, 1995. Classroom and playground aide Moscow (Idaho) Sch. Dist., 1996—99; music specialist grades K-8 Asotin (Wash.) Sch. Dist., 1999—. Sec. local chpt. Asotin Edn. Assn., Asotin, 2000. Drum grant, Asotin Edn. Found., 2003. Avocations: singing, camping, skiing. Office: Asotin-Anatone Edn Found 314 1st St Asotin WA 99402 Office Phone: 509-243-4151. Business E-Mail: dknoll@aasd.wednet.edu.

KNOLL, JAMES LEWIS, lawyer; b. Chgo., Oct. 5, 1942; AB, Brown U., 1964; JD, U. Chgo., 1967. Bar: Ill. 1967, Oreg. 1971, Wash. 1984, Alaska 1993. Mediator, arbitrator, Portland, Oreg. Adj. prof. law Northwestern Sc. Law, Lewis and Clark Coll., 1982-91. Mem. ABA (mem. TIPS coun. 1989-92, chair property ins. com. 1984-85, mem. fidelity surety com., chair comml. tort com. 1985-86), Oreg. State Bar (editor 2 vol. text on ins. 1983, 96), Wash. State Bar, Oreg. Assn. Def. Coun. (pres. 1984). Office: 1500 SW Taylor St Portland OR 97205-1819 E-mail: jim@hamiltonmediation.com.

KNOLL, JEANNETTE THERIOT, state supreme court justice; b. Baton Rouge, La. m. Jerold Edward Knoll; children: Triston Kane, Eddie Jr., Edmond Humphries, Blake Theriot, Jonathan Paul. BA in Polit. Sci., Loyola U., 1966; JD, Loyola U. Sch. of Law, 1969; LLM in Jud. Process, U. Va. Sch. of Law, 1996; studied with Maestro Adler, Mannes Coll. of Music, 1962-63. Criminal defense atty., first asst. dist. atty. Twelfth Jud. Dist. Ct. Avoyelles Parish, 1972-82; gratuitous atty., advisor U.S. Selective Svc., Marksville, La.; judge (3d cir.) U.S. Ct. of Appeal, 1982-93; assoc. justice La. Supreme Ct., 1997—. Instr. La. Jud. Coll.; chair CLE La. Ct. of Appeal Judges; former mem. state bd. of La. Commn. on Law Enforcement & Criminal Justice; former mem. Past pres. Bus. and Profl. Women's Club; Marksville C. of C.; active Am. Legion Aux.; dir. Arts & Humanities Council of Avoyelles, Inc.; former chmn. La. March of Dimes. Named La. Crimefighters' Outstanding Jurist of Yr., 2000; named to La. Political Hall of Fame, 2000; recipient Met. Opera Assn., New Orleans Opera Guild Scholarship, Outstanding Jud. award, Victims & Citizens Against Crime, Inc., 1995, 2002. Mem.: La. State Bar Assn. Office: La Supreme Ct 400 Royal St New Orleans LA 70130*

KNOLL, MICHAEL STEVEN, law educator; b. Bronx, N.Y., Apr. 23, 1957; s. Alvin D. and Donna A. (Miller) K. AB, U. Chgo., 1977, AM, 1980, PhD in Econs., 1983, JD, 1984. Bar: Ill., N.Y., D.C. Law clk. to hon. Alex Kozinski US Ct. Appeals (9th cir.), Pasadena, Calif., 1986; legal advisor to vice chmn. US Internat. Trade Commn., Washington, 1984-87; assoc. Debevoise & Plimpton, NYC, 1987-89; of counsel, assoc. Irell & Manella, L.A., LA, 1989-95; asst. prof. U. So. Calif. Law Ctr., LA, 1990-92, assoc. prof., 1992-95, prof., 1995-2000; prof. real estate Wharton Sch., U. Pa., Phila., 2000—; Earle Hepburn prof. law U. Pa. Law Sch., Phila., 2000—, assoc. dean, 2004—. Contbr. articles to profl. jours. Mem. Am. Fin. Assn., Am. Econ. Assn. Fin. Mgmt. Assn., Order of Coif. Office: U Pa Law Sch 3400 Chestnut St Philadelphia PA 19104 Office Fax: 215-573-2025.*

KNOLLENBERG, JOSEPH (JOE KNOLLENBERG), congressman; b. Mattoon, Ill., Nov. 28, 1934; m. Sandie Knollenberg; children: Martin, Stephen. Student, Eastern Ill. U. CLU. Agent, owner ins. co., 1960-93; mem. 103rd-106th Congresses from 9th Mich. Dist. (formerly 11th), 1993—, mem. budget com. appropriations, mem. stds. of offcl. conduct coms. Past chmn., Birmingham Cable TV Community Adv. Bd., 18th Dist. Rep. Com., Rep. Com. Oakland County, 1978-86; past pres. St. Bede's Parish Coun., Evergreen Sch. PTA (Birmingham Sch. Dist.), Bloomfield Glens Homeowner's Assn., Cranbrook Homeowner's Assn.; past coord. Southfield Ad Hoc Park and Recreation Devel. Com.; past mem. Southfield Mayor's Wage and Salary Com.; chmn. Candidate Assistance Com./State Com., Oakland County Campaign, 1978; former regional/vice chair 17th Dist. Com., 1975-77; mem. Rep. State Com; exec. com. mem. and fin. com. Rep. Com. Oakland County; founder, mem. Rep. Leadership Com. Oakland County, 1984—; mem. Allstate Ins. Co's P.A.C.; del. Rep. Nat. Conv., 1980; del. to every state convention since 1974. Named chmn. of one of the top twenty-five counties in the country by Rep. Nat. Com. Mem. Am. Soc. Chartered Life Underwriters, Detroit Assn. Life Underwriters, Oakland County Lincoln Rep. Club, Troy C. of C. (current vice chmn.). Republican. Office: US Ho Reps 2349 Rayburn HOB Washington DC 20515-2211 also: 30833 Northwestern Hwy Ste 100 Farmington Hills MI 48334*

KNOLLER, GUY DAVID, lawyer; b. N.Y.C., July 23, 1946; s. Charles and Odette Knoller; children: Jennifer Judy, Geoffrey David. BA cum laude, Bloomfield (N.J.) Coll., 1968; JD cum laude, Ariz. State U., 1971. Bar: Ariz. 1971, U.S. Dist. Ct. Ariz. 1971, U.S. Supreme Ct. 1976. Trial atty. atty. gen.'s hons. program Dept. Justice, 1971-72; atty., adv. NLRB, 1972-73, field atty. region 28 Phoenix, 1972-74; assoc. Powers, Ehrenreich, Boutell & Kurn, Phoenix, 1974-79; ptnr. Froimson & Knoller, Phoenix, 1979-81; sole practice Phoenix, 1985—; of counsel Burns & Burns. Mem. bd. visitors Ariz. State U. Coll. Law, 1975-76; pres. Ariz. Theatre Guild, 1990, 91. Fellow Ariz. Bar Found.; mem. ABA, State Bar Ariz. (chmn. labor rels. sect. 1977-78), Ariz. State U. Coll. Law Alumni Assn. (pres. 1977). Office: 2828 N Central Ave Ste 1110 Phoenix AZ 85004-1028 Office Phone: 602-230-1099. Business E-Mail: gdkpc@pcslink.com.

KNOOP, VERN THOMAS, civil engineer, consultant; b. Paola, Kans., Nov. 19, 1932; s. Vernon Thomas and Nancy Alice (Christian) K. Student, Kans. U., 1953-54; BSCE, Kans. State U., 1959. Registered profl. engr., Calif. Surveyor James L. Bell, Surveyors and Engrs., Overland Park, Kans., 1954; engr. asst. to county engr. Miami County Hwy. Dept., Paola, 1955; engr. State of Calif. Dept. Water Resources, L.A., 1959-85, sr. engr., 1986-88, chief, water supply evaluations sect. L.A., Glendale, 1989—. Hydrology tchr. State of Calif. Dept. Water Resources, L.A., 1984; mem. Interagency Drought Task Force, Sacramento, 1988-91. Mem. Jefferson Ednl. Found., Washington, 1988-91, Heritage Found., Washington, 1988—, Nat. Rep. Senatorial Com., Washington, 1990—, Rep. Presdl. Task Force, Washington, 1990-91. With U.S. Army, 1956-57. Decorated Good Conduct medal U.S. Army, Germany, 1957. Mem. ASCE (life, dir. L.A. sect. hydraulics/water resources mgmt. tech. group 1985-86, chmn. 1984-85), Profl. Engrs. Calif. Govt. (dist. suprs. rep. 1986—), Am. Assn. Individual Investors (life), L.A. World Affairs Coun., Singles Internat. Baptist. Home: 2851 Hermosa Ave Glendale CA 91214-3906 Office: State Calif Dept Water Resources 770 Fairmont Ave Glendale CA 91203-1035 E-mail: vernk@charter.net, vernk@msn.com.

KNOPF, ALFRED, JR., retired publisher; b. White Plains, N.Y., June 17, 1918; s. Alfred A. and Blanche (Wolf) K.; m. Alice Laine, July 27, 1952; children— Alison, Susan, David. Grad., Phillips Exeter Acad., 1937; AB, Union Coll., Schenectady, 1942. With Atheneum Pubs., N.Y.C., 1959-88, chmn. bd., 1964-88. Vis. chmn. Scribner Book Cos.; sr. v.p. MacMillan Pub. Co. (ret.). Capt. USAAF, 1941-45. Mem. Delta Upsilon. Clubs: Dutch Treat (N.Y.C.); Tavern (Chgo.). Home: 530 E 72nd St Apt 18F New York NY 10021-4864

KNOPF, CLAIRE, editor, writer; b. Passaic, N.J., Apr. 22, 1939; d. Isadore and Helen Knopf. *Ancestor, Rabbi Uri of Strelisk, was a philosopher, writer and Kabbalist. A rabbi's prediction that he would be born with a unique soul that would light up the world came to pass. He became known as Ha-Saraf (the fierce angel). His enthusiastic prayers, which lasted for many hours, were joined by tens of thousands of Jews. His spiritual discourses appear in Hasidic Anthology, by L.I. Newman and Tales of Hasidim, by Martin Buber. A biography of Rabbi Uri is written in Encyclopedia Judaica.* Student, Mich. State U., 1957—59, U. Calif., Berkeley, 1960—61, Columbia U., N.Y.C., 1962—63, Parsons Sch. Design, 1995—96. Freelance copy editor Massada Pub. Co., The Magnes Press, The Hebrew U., Israel, 1970—79; writer Edrei-Sharon Publs., Israel, 1970—79; copy editor Time Mag., Time Warner, Inc., N.Y.C., 1980—96; freelance copy editor New Woman Mag., 1997—2000; copy editor, writer, reporter Salt Lake Olympic Winter Games and Paralympic Winter Games, Salt Lake City, 2000—02; writer, reporter, rschr. Internat. Figure Skating Mag., 2002—; freelance copy editor US Weekly, BabyTalk, Woman's World, In Touch Weekly, Quest, Food & Wine, Ladies' Home Jour., Psychology Today Mag., NYC2012, U.S. Candidate City for Olympic Games, others. Mem.: Soc. Children's Book Writers and Illustrators, Time-Life Alumni Soc., N.Y. Press Club, Inc. Avocations: art, writing children's books, ice skating, cross country skiing. Home and Office: 6040 Boulevard East Apt 14M West New York NJ 07093 Personal E-mail: claireknopf@earthlink.net.

KNOPF, KENYON ALFRED, economist, educator; b. Cleve., Nov. 24, 1921; s. Harold C. and Emma A. (Underwood) K.; m. Madelyn Lee Siddy Trebilcock, Mar. 28, 1953 (dec. June 1999); children— Kristin Lee, Mary George. AB magna cum laude with high honors in Econs., Kenyon Coll., 1942; MA in Econs.; PhD, Harvard U., 1949; LLD (hon.), Kenyon Coll., 1993. Mem. faculty Grinnell Coll., 1949-67, prof. econs., 1960-67, Jentzen prof., 1961-67, chmn. dept., 1958-60, chmn. div. social studies, 1962-64, chmn. faculty, 1964-67; dean coll. Whitman Coll., Walla Walla, Wash., 1967-70, prof. econs., 1967-89, Hollon Parker prof. econs., 1985-89, prof. emeritus, 1989—, provost, 1970-81, dean faculty, 1970-78, acting pres., 1974-75; pub. interest dir. Fed. Home Loan Bank, Seattle, 1976-83. Mem. council undergrad. assessment program Ednl. Testing Service, 1977-80 Author: (with Robert H. Haveman) The Market System, 4th edit, 1981; A Lexicon of Economics, 1991; editor: Introduction to Economics Series (9 vols.), 1966, 2d edit., 1970-71; co-editor: (with James H. Strauss) The Teaching of Elementary Economics, 1960. Mem. youth coun. City of Grinnell, 1957—59; mem. Walla Walla County Mental Health Bd., 1968—75, Walla Walla Civil Svc. Commn., 1978—84, chmn., 1981—84; mem. Grinnell City Coun., 1964—67; pres. Walla Walla County Human Svcs. Adminstrv. Bd., 1975—77; mem. Ia. adv. coun. SBA; tax aide AARP/IRS Tax Counseling for Elderly, 1987—98, local coord., 1990—91, assoc. dist. coord. S.E. Wash., 1991—94, assoc. dist. coord. tng., 1994—98; bd. dirs. Skagit County Boys & Girls Club, 2001—, Walla Walla United Fund, 1968—76, pres., 1973; bd. dirs. Shelter Bay Cmty., Inc., 1995—2003, v.p., 1995—97, pres., 1997—2003; bd. dirs. La Conner Cmty. Scholarship Found., 1997—, La Conner Boys and Girls Club, 1999—, pres., 2001—03. With USAF, 1942—46, PTO. Social Sci. Rsch. Coun. grantee, 1951-52. Mem.: Am. Conf. Acad. Deans (exec. com. 1970—77, chmn. 1975), Am. Assn. Ret. Persons, Kiwanis (pres. LaConner club 2003—04), Phi Beta Kappa. Office: 223 Skagit Way La Conner WA 98257-9602

KNOPF, MATTHEW J., lawyer; b. 1956; BA summa cum laude, SUNY, Stony Brook, 1981; JD, Univ. Chgo., 1986. Bar: Ill. 1986, Minn. 2000. Sr. v.p., gen. counsel County Seat Stores, Inc; atty. Skadden, Arps Law, NYC; ptnr., mergers, acquisitions corp. group Dorsey & Whitney LLP, Mpls., and co-chair, bus. restructuring practice group. Bd. dir. Minnetonka Ctr.Arts. Office: Dorsey & Whitney LLP Ste 1500 50 S Sixth St Minneapolis MN 55402-1498 Office Phone: 612-340-5603. Office Fax: 612-340-2868. Business E-Mail: knopf.matthew@dorsey.com.

KNOPF, PAUL MARK, immunoparasitologist, neuro-immunologist; b. Trenton, N.J., Apr. 4, 1936; s. David and Beatrice Knopf; m. Carol Lois Harrison, June 29, 1958; children: Jeffrey William, Steven Harrison, Rachel Analiese. BSc, MIT, 1958, PhD, 1962. Postdoctoral fellow MRC Lab. Molecular Biology, Cambridge, Eng., 1962-64; spl. research assoc. Salk Inst., La Jolla, Calif., 1964-72; prof. med. sci. Brown U., Providence, 1972—2003, Charles A. and Helen B. Stuart prof. med. sci., 1992—2003, chmn. sect. molecular, cellular and devel. biology, 1990-94, chmn. dept. molecular microbiology and immunology, 1994-97, prof. emeritus med. sci., 2003—. Mem. study sect. on parasitic disease NIH, 1985—87. Recipient Career Devel. award NIH, 1966-72; named Tchr. of Yr. in Life Scis., Brown U., 1998; grantee NIH, 1966-76, 84-88, 91-99, Rockefeller Found., 1972-80, Edna McConnell Clark Found., 1976-85, WHO, 1979-94, MS Soc., 1989-90; Fulbright-Hays sr. fellow, 1978-79, Fogarty sr. internat. fellow, 1986-87. Mem. AAAS, Am. Assn. Immunologists, Am. Soc. Tropical Medicine and Hygiene, Soc. Neurosci., Am. Soc. Microbiology, New Eng. Assn. Parasitology. Office: Brown U Divsn Biology and Medicine PO Box G-B4 Providence RI 02912-9107 Office Phone: 401-863-1607. Business E-Mail: Paul_Knopf@Brown.edu.

KNOPF, ROBERT MICHAEL, theater educator, theater director; b. NYC, July 16, 1961; s. Richard Leon and Florence Klein Knopf; m. Elizabeth Pascal, July 31, 1994; children: Amelia, Lara. BA, Oberlin Coll., 1983; JD, Duke U., 1987; MFA, U. Wis., 1991; PhD, U. Mich., 1996. Atty. Baker & Hosteter, Washington, 1987—88; vis. asst. prof. theater Purdue U., West Lafayette, Ind., 1996—98; asst. prof. theater U. Mich., Ann Arbor, Mich., 1998—2000; assoc. prof. theater Conn. Coll., New London, Conn., 2000—04; prof. and theatre and dance dept. chair SUNY, Buffalo, 2004—. Dir. grad. studies theater U. Mich., 1998—2000, assoc. chair, 1999—2000; artistic assoc. Circle Repertory Co., N.Y., 1991—92, Brave New World Theater Marathon, NY, 2002; dir., creator Neo/Retro/Woyzeck, NY Fringe Festival, 2003. Author: The Theater and Cinema of Buster Keaton, 1999, Theater of the Avant-Garde, 1890-1950, 2001, Theater and Film, 2004, The Director as Collaborator, 2005. Avocations: skiing, golf, bowling. Office: Univ Buffalo, SUNY Dept Theatre Dance 285 Alumni Arena Buffalo NY 14260 Office Phone: 716-645-6898 x 1334. Business E-Mail: rknopf@buffalo.edu.

KNOPIK, ROBERT, retail executive, consultant; b. Chgo., Nov. 29, 1945; s. Walter Robert and Josephine Kay Knopik; m. Penelope Gretchen Kraft, Nov. 13, 1993; children: Tracy, Cory, Kimberly. BS, Drake U., 1967. Tchr. Greenbrook North H.S., Northbrook, Ill., 1967—72; various mgmt. positions Inland Steel, Chgo., 1972—91; v.p. Inland Steel Industries, Chgo., 1991—98; exec. search cons. Boyden, Chgo., 1998; pres. Creative Apparel & Design, Rockford, Ill., 1999—2001, The Leadership Search Group, North Barrington, Ill., 2000—01, mng. dir., 2001—. Pres. Wynstone Homeowners Assn., Barrington, 1999—. Mem.: Wynstone Golf Club (bd. dirs. 2002—). Republican. Roman Catholic. Avocations: golf, skiing, gardening. Home: 19 Lakeside Ln North Barrington IL 60010 Office: The Leadership Search Group 300 Village Green Dr Lincolnshire IL 60069 E-mail: rwk72949@aol.com.

KNOPMAN, DAVID S., neurologist; b. Phila., Oct. 6, 1950; AB, Dartmouth Coll., 1972; MD, U. Minn., 1975. Diplomate Am. Bd. Psychiatry and Neurology. Intern Hennepin County Med. Ctr., 1975-76; resident U. Minn., 1976-79, asst. prof. neurology Mpls., 1980-86, assoc. prof. neurology, 1986-98, prof., 1998—2000; cons. dept. neurology Mayo Clinic, Rochester, Minn., 2000—; prof. Mayo Clinic Coll. Medicine, Rochester, 2000—. Office: Mayo Clinic Dept Neurology Rochester MN 55905 Office Phone: 507-284-2511.

KNOPMAN, DEBRA SARA, environmental scientist, director, hydrologist, policy analyst; b. Phila., Aug. 13, 1953; d. Harold L. and Minnette (Smulyan) Knopman; m. Donald Weightman, Sept. 29, 1985; children: Leah Alana, David Atwood. BA, Wellesley Coll., 1975; MSCE, MIT, 1978; PhD, Johns Hopkins U., 1986. Sci. writer and editor, Washington, 1975-78; legis. asst. Daniel P. Moynihan, Washington, 1979-80; prof. staff mem. U.S. Senate Com. on Environ. and Pub. Works, Washington, 1980-83; student asst., office of groundwater U.S. Geol. Survey, Reston, Va., 1984-85, rsch. hydrologist, nat. rsch. program, 1985-86, hydrologist, br. of systems analysis, 1987-91, chief, br. or systems analysis, 1991-93; dep. asst. sec. water and sci. Dept. Interior, 1993-95; dir. Progressive Policy Inst. Ctr. for Innovation and Environ., 1995—. Mem. Nuclear Waste Tech. Rev. Bd., 1997—. Editor: Scientific Research in Israel, 1976; editor Geophysics News, 1990-92; contbr. articles to profl. jours. Mem. commn. on geoscis., environment and resources NRC, 1995-98. Henry R. Luce Found. scholar, Taiwan, 1978-79. Mem. Am. Geophys. Union (chair pub. info. com. 1990-92). Democrat. Jewish. Address: Progressive Policy Inst 600 Pennsylvania Ave SE Ste 400 Washington DC 20003-4350

KNOPP, ALEX, lawyer, mayor; b. Manchester, Conn., Sept. 23, 1947; m. Betty L. Bono, 1984. BA, Wesleyan U., 1969; JD, George Washington U., 1981. Councilman-at-large Common Coun., Norwalk, Conn., 1983-85, pres., 1985-86; mem. Conn. Ho. of Reps., 1987—2001; pvt. practice Norwalk, 1981—; mayor of Norwalk, 2001—. Mem. Order of Coif, Phi Beta Kappa. Address: 35 5th St Norwalk CT 06855-2402

KNOPP, MARVIN ISADORE, mathematics professor; b. Chgo., Jan. 4, 1933; s. Mitshel and Minnie (Israel) K.; m. Josephine Zadovsky, June 9, 1957 (div. 1998); children: Seth David, Yudah Benjamin, Abby Alissa, Elana Melissa. BS, U. Ill., 1954, A.M., 1955, PhD, 1958. Rsch. mathematician Space Tech. Labs., L.A., 1958-59; NSF postdoctoral fellow Inst. Advanced Study, Princeton, N.J., 1959-60; asst. prof. U. Wis., 1960-62, assoc. prof., 1962-67, prof., 1967-72; mathematician Nat. Bur. Standards, Washington, 1963-64; vis. prof. U. Basel, Switzerland, 1968-69; prof. U. Ill., Chgo., 1970-76, Temple U., Phila., 1976—, Bryn Mawr (Pa.) Coll., 1988-89. Mem. Inst. Advanced Study, Princeton, N.J., 1975, 78, 88; vis. prof. Ohio State U., spring 1979 Author: Theory of Area, 1969, Modular Functions in Analytic Number Theory, 1970, 2d edit., 1993; editor Ill. Jour. Math., 1971-78, The Ramanujan Jour., 1995—, Procs. of Conf. in Analytic Number Theory, 1981, others; contbr. articles to profl. jours. NSF grantee, 1960-90, Fulbright-Hays grantee NRC, 1975-76, Nat. Security Agy. grantee, 1990-93. Mem. Am. Math. Soc., London Math. Soc. Democrat. Jewish. Home: 410 Lancaster Ave Apt 221 Haverford PA 19041-1326 Office: Temple U Dept Math Philadelphia PA 19122 Office Phone: 215-204-7589.

KNORTZ, WALTER ROBERT, accountant, retired insurance company executive; b. Bklyn., July 15, 1919; s. John Walter and Elizabeth Anna (Grotyohann) K.; m. Muriel Clancy, Oct. 14, 1950 (dec.); children: Deborah Ann, Kenneth Robert, Pamela Jane; m. Dorothy E. Lauterborn, Nov. 17, 1962. BBA, St. Johns U., 1942; MBA, N.Y. U., 1949. Acct. Consol. Edison Co., N.Y.C., 1936-45; mng. acct. S.D. Leidersdorf & Co., N.Y.C., 1945-53; with Equitable Life Assurance Soc. of U.S., N.Y.C., 1953-82, 2d v.p., 1969-73, v.p., assoc. controller, 1973-75, v.p., fin. officer investment ops., 1975-82; asst. treas., treas. Equitable Life Holding Corp., 1971-75; comptroller Equitable Life Mortgage & Realty Investors, 1970-75; v.p., treas. Equitable Life Community Enterprises Corp., 1970-75, Student Life Funding, Inc., 1970-75; v.p., dir. Equico Lessors, Inc., Mpls., 1974-78; v.p. Equico Securities, Inc., 1970-80, Planters Devel. Corp., St. Louis, 1972-81. Mem. Phila. Stock Exchange, Inc., 1971-78. Pres. Leisure Towne Civic League, 1983-84, treas., 1985-86; mem. bldg. fund com. Holy Eucharist Ch., chmn. fin. com., 1984-89. Served with AUS, 1942-45. Mem. AICPA, Tax Execs. Inst., Fin. Execs. Inst., Beta Rho Kappa, Delta Mu Delta. Roman Catholic. Home: 41 Finchley Ct Southampton NJ 08088-1006

KNOS, ANYA DOZIER, academic administrator, director; d. Edward P. and Marianne Dozier; m. Terry Enos, Apr. 29, 1983; children: Lisa Enos, Pasquala Enos. Assoc. Fine Arts, Inst. Am. Indian Arts, 1984; BA, Coll. Sante Fe, 1984; MA, St. John's Coll., 1987; PhD, U. Ill., 1998. Cert. tchr. N.Mex. Sr. rschr. Circles of Wisdom Santa Fe (N.Mex.) Indian Sch., 1998—2002, dir. Cultivating Our Own to Lead program, 2001—05, co-principal investigator and project dir. N.Mex. Tribal Coalition, 2001—. Adj. faculty Coll. Santa Fe, 1996—; founding bd. mem. Tewa Women United, San Ildefonso Pueblo, N.Mex. Mem. Betterment Edn., Santa Clara Pueblo, N.Mex., 1999—2000; bd. dir. Santa Clara Pueblo (N.Mex.) Libr., 1996—2000; co-chmn. Santa Fe (N.Mex.) County Maternal Child Health Coun., 1996—98. Fellow, U.S. Dept. Edn., 1993—96; grantee, 2001—05, NSF, 2001—05. Mem.: ASCD, Am. Ednl. Rsch. Assn., Nat. Indian Edn. Assn. Office: Santa Fe Indian School 1501 Cerrillos Rd PO Box 5340 Santa Fe NM 87505 Office Phone: 505-989-6340.

KNOSPE, WILLIAM HERBERT, medical educator; b. Oak Park, Ill., May 26, 1929; s. Herbert Henry and Dora Isabel (Spruce) K.; m. Adris M. Nelson, June 19, 1954. BA, U. Ill., Chgo. and Urbana, 1951; BS, U. Ill., 1952; MD, U. Ill., Chgo., 1954; MS in Radiation Biology, U. Rochester, 1962. Diplomate Am. Bd. Internal Medicine and Subspecialty Bd. on Hematology. Rotating intern Upstate Med. Ctr. Hosps-SUNY-Syracuse, 1954-55; resident in medicine Ill. Central Hosp., Chgo., 1955-56, VA Research Hosp-Northwestern U. Med. Sch., Chgo., 1956-58; investigator radiation biology Walter Reed Army Inst. Research, Washington, 1962-64, investigator hematology, asst. chief dept. hematology, 1964-66; attending physician med. service Walter Reed Gen. Hosp., Washington, 1963-64, fellow in hematology, 1964-65; asst. chief hematology service, chief hematology clinic Walter Reed Army Inst. of Rsch., Washington, 1964-66; asst. attending staff physician Presbyn. St. Luke's Hosp., Chgo., 1967-68, asst. dir. hematology radiohematology lab., 1967-74, assoc. attending staff physician, 1968-74, sr. attending staff physician, 1974—; asst. prof. medicine U. Ill.-Chgo., 1967-69, assoc. prof., 1969-72; assoc. prof. medicine Rush Med. Coll., Chgo., 1971-74, prof. medicine, 1974—; dir. sect. hematology Rush-Presbyn.-St. Luke's Med. Ctr., Chgo., 1974-93; Elodia Kehm prof. hematology Rush-Med. Coll., Chgo., 1986-94, prof. emeritus, 1994—; prof. medicine U. N.Mex., Albuquerque, 1994—2002, emeritus, 2002—. Speaker at profl. confs. U.S. and abroad; vis. prof. medicine dept. hematology U. Basel, Switzerland, 1980-81, Cancer Ctr., U. N.Mex., 1992-93. Contbr. numerous articles to profl. publs. Trustee Ill. chpt. Leukemia Soc. Am., 1977-88, v.p., 1979-80; trustee Bishop Anderson House (Rush-Presbyn.-St. Luke's Med. Ctr.), 1980-94. Served to capt. M.C., USAR, 1958-61, to lt. col., U.S. Army, 1961-66. Fellow ACP; mem. Am. Fedn. Clin. Research, AMA, Am. Soc. Hematology, Am. Soc. Clin. Oncology, Central Soc. Clin. Research, Chgo. Med. Soc., Inst. Medicine Chgo., Internat. Soc. Exptl. Hematology, Radiation Research Soc., Southeastern Cancer Study Group, Polycythemia Vera Study Group, Eastern Coop. Oncology Group, Ill. State Med. Soc., Assn. Hematology-Oncology Program Dirs., Sigma Xi, Chgo. Literary Club. Office: 310 Big Horn Ridge Dr NE Albuquerque NM 87122-1455

KNOTT, ANNE MARIE, finance educator; d. Robert T. and Mary Patricia Knott; 1 child, Nicholas Pulos. PhD, UCLA, 1996. Project mgr. Hughes Aircraft Co., Canoga Park, Calif., 1978—93; asst. prof. The Wharton Sch., U. Pa., Phila., 1995—. Author: (textbook) Venture Design, 2001. Mem.: Coll. of Orgn. Sci. (chair). Achievements include patents pending for the method for reversing induced discrimination. Office: The Wharton Sch Univ Pa 2023 Steinberg Hall-Dietrich Hall Philadelphia PA 19104-6370

KNOTT, BILL, poet, literature educator; MFA, Norwich U. Instr. Columbia Coll., 1972—75, Thomas Jefferson Coll., 1975, Emerson Coll., 1975—77, 1981—83, poet, assoc. prof. writing Boston, 1984—; instr. Wright State U., 1978, New Eng. Coll., 1979, Centrum Arts Ctr., 1980, YHMA/WA Poetry Ctr., 1981; instr. Writers Workshop U. Iowa, 1983—84; instr. U. Ala., 2001. Author: The Naomi Poems, 1968, Auto-necrophilia, 1971, Rome in Rome, 1976, Selected and Collected Poems, 1977 (Elliston prize, 1979), Becos, 1983, Poems 1963-1988, 1989, Outremer, 1989, The Quicken Tree, 1995, Laugh at the End of the World: Collected Comic Poems, 2000, The Unsubscriber, 2004. Fellow, John Simon Guggenheim Meml. Found., 2003; grantee, Nat. Endowment for the Arts, 1980, 1985. Office: Emerson Coll 120 Boylston St Boston MA 02116-4624

KNOTT, DOUGLAS RONALD, dean, agricultural sciences educator, researcher; b. Fraser Mills, B.C., Can., Nov. 10, 1927; s. Ronald David and Florence Emily (Keeping) K.; m. Joan Madeline Hollinshead, Sept. 2, 1950 (dec.); children: Holly Ann, Heather Lynn, Ronald Kenneth, Douglas James (dec.); m. Pat Decker, June 1, 2002 (dec.) BSA, U. B.C., 1948; MS, U. Wis., 1949, PhD, 1952. Asst. prof. U. Sask., Saskatoon, 1952-56, assoc. prof., 1956-65, prof., 1965-93, head dept. crop sci., 1965-75, assoc. dean rsch. Coll. Agr., 1988-93; prof. emeritus, 1993—. Author: The Wheat Rusts—Breeding for Resistance, 1989; also numerous papers. Named to Saskatchewan Agr. Hall of Fame. Fellow Am. Soc. Agronomy, Agrl. Inst. Can.; mem. Can. Soc. Agronomy, Genetics Soc. Can., Order of Can. Mem. United Ch. of Can. Avocation: tennis. Office: U Sask Dept Plant Scis 51 Campus Dr Saskatoon SK Canada S7N 5A8 Office Phone: 306-966-5004. E-mail: dougknott@shaw.ca.

KNOTT, JOHN RAY, JR., language educator; b. Memphis, July 9, 1937; s. John Ray and Wilma (Henshaw) K.; m. Anne Percy, Dec. 5, 1959; children: Catherine, Ellen, Walker, Anne. AB, Yale U., 1959, Carnegie fellow, 1960; PhD, Harvard U., 1965. Instr. Harvard U., 1965-67; mem. faculty U. Mich., Ann Arbor, 1967—, prof. English, 1976—, chmn. dept., 1982-87, assoc. dean Coll. Arts and Scis., 1977-80, acting dean Coll. Arts and Scis., 1980-81, interim dir. Inst. for Humanities, 1987-88, interim dir. Program in the Environment, 2001—02. Dir. region IV Mellon Fellowship Selection Com., 1989-94. Author: Milton's Pastoral Vision, 1971, The Sword of the Spirit, 1980, Discourses of Martyrdom in English Literature, 1563-1694, 1993, Imagining Wild America, 2002; editor: The Triumph of Style, 1967, Mirrors: An Introduction to Literature, rev. edit., 1987, The Huron River: Voices From the Watershed, 2000, Reimagining Place, 2001; contbr. articles on Abbey, Berry, Browne, Bunyan, Fox, Foxe, Milton, and Spenser to scholarly jours. Woodrow Wilson fellow, 1960-61; NEH fellow, 1974 Mem. MLA, Milton Soc., Sierra Club. Office: Univ Mich Dept English Ann Arbor MI 48109

KNOTT, KENNETH, industrial engineering educator, consultant; b. Dudley, Worcestershire, Eng., Mar. 6, 1929; arrived in U.S., 1977; s. John Peter Grainger and Sarah (Turner) K.; m. Margaret Knott, Apr. 22, 1957; children: DiLwyn John, Tracy James. Diploma in Grad. Studies, Engring. Prodn., U. Birmingham at Edgbaston, Eng., 1956; MS in Indsl. Engring., Pa. State U., 1966; PhD in Engring. Prodn., Tech. U. Loughborough, Eng., 1983. Apprentice British Thompson Houston Co. Ltd., Birmingham, 1944-48, Coventry, Eng., 1948-50; design draftsman New Conveyor Co. Ltd., Smethwick, Eng., 1952-53; tech. asst. to gen. mgr. N. Hingley and Sons, Netherton, Eng., 1953-55; prodn. engr. Chubb and Sons, Ltd., Wolverhampton, Eng., 1955-56; plant mgr. John Morris Electrical Engring., Bilston, Eng., 1956; lectr. in prodn. engring. Dudley and Staffordshire Tech. Coll., Dudley, Eng., 1956-63; instr. in indsl. engring. Pa. State U., State College, 1963-66; mng. dir. Maynard Tng. Ctr., Birmingham, 1966-70, Kenneth Knott Ltd., Birmingham, 1966-77, Work Study Contract Svcs., Birmingham, 1970-77; asst. prof. indsl. and mgmt. systems engring. Pa. State U., 1977-84, assoc. prof. indsl. and mgmt. engring., 1984-87, prof. indsl. and mgmt. engring., 1987-95, emeritus prof. indsl. engring., 1996—. Mem. editorial bd. Internat. Jour. Prodn. Rsch., Loughborough, 1984—; mem. robotics sub-com. Welding Rsch. Coun., N.Y.C., 1977-79, welding processes sub-com., 1977-83; mem. com. maintenance in mfg. Nat. Mfg. Engring. Ctr., Ann Arbor, Mich., 1989-90. Author: Job Analysis Procedure Manual, 1970, (with others) A Comparison of Alternative Time Slotting Systems for Indirect Time Standards Work Measurement, 1986, An Analytical Approach to Designing and Testing Time Slotting Systems, 1986; co-author: Laboratory Manual Manufacturing Processes, 1965, Principles and Practice of MTM-2, 1970, Principles and Practice of MTM-3, 1971, Manufacturing Processes Associate Degree Program, 1980; editor Metods Time Measurement Jour., 1982-90; contbr. tech. papers to profl. jours. Recipient AT&T Found. Outstanding Teaching award Am. Soc. Engring. Edn., 1991, Lenhard Teaching fellowship Lenhardt Ctr. Innovative Teaching Pa. State U., 1992. Fellow Inst. Indsl. Engrs. (panel rsch. in work measurement work measurement and methods engring. divsn. 1981-83, assoc. editor IIE Transactions 1982-92, program chmn. 1983-87, rsch. chmn. 1984-89, reorganization com. 1988, divsn. dir. 1982-83, honors chmn. 1991—, pres. Ctrl. Pa. chpt. 1982-83, Phil Carroll award 1986, Tech. Innovation in Indsl. Engring. award 1993), World Acad. Productivity Sci., Soc. Am. Magicians, Pa. Soc. Profl. Engrs., Fedn. Productivity Scis. (hon., London), Methods Time Measurement Assn. (editor Methods Time Measurement Jour., chmn. midland region United Kingdom divsn. 1967-72, internat. com. investigation into Application Handbook Requirements 1970, tech. panel United Kingdom divsn. 1969-77, tng. and qualifications com.), Soc. Mfg. Engrs. (continuing edn. chmn. Ctrl. Pa. chpt. 1987, sec. 1993—), Internat. Brotherhood Magicians, Inner Magic Cir. (decorated Silver Star), Kano Soc., Sigma Xi, Alpha Pi Mu. Avocations: magic, Judo. Home: PO Box 234 Pine Grove Mills PA 16868-0234 Office: Pa State U 207 Hammond Bldg University Park PA 16802-1401 Office Phone: 814-234-2713. Personal E-mail: k.knott@fimexpert.com. Business E-Mail: kok@psu.edu.

KNOTT, WILEY EUGENE, retired electronics engineer; b. Muncie, Ind., Mar. 18, 1938; s. Joseph Wiley and Mildred Viola (Haxton) K.; 1 child, Brian Evan. BSEE, Tri-State U., 1963; postgrad., Union Coll., 1970-73, Ga. Coll., 1987. Assoc. aircraft engr. Lockheed-Ga. Co., Marietta, 1963-65; tech. publs. engr. GE, Pittsfield, Mass., 1965-77, sr. publs. engr., 1977-79, group leader, 1967-79; specialist engr. Boeing Mil. Airplane Co., Wichita, Kans., 1979-81, sr. specialist engr., 1981-84, 89-90, logistics mgr., 1984-85, customer support mgr., 1985-89, base mgr. Castle AFB, 1990-91; facilities plant ops. and maintenance engr. Boeing Comml. Airplane Co., Everett, Wash., 1991-92, lead engr., 1992-93, prin. engr., 1993-95, ret., 1995; part-time bus. cons., 1972—2003. Active Jr. Achievement, 1978-79, Am. Security Coun., 1975-90, Nat. Rep. Snatori al Com., 1979-86, Nat. Rep. Congl. Com., 1979-87, Rep. Nat. Com., 1979-87, Rep. Presdl. Task Force, 1981-86, Joint Presdl./Congl.

Steering Com., 1982-86, Rep. Polit. Action Com., 1979-86, Mus. of Aviation, 1987-95; state advisor U.S. Congl. Adv. Bd., 1981-86; adviser Jr. Achievement, 1978-79. Mem. Sr. Coalition, Traditional Values Coalition. With AUS, 1956—59. Mem.: Assn. U.S. Army, Amvets, Nat. Def. Indsl. Assn. (life), Air Force Assn. (life), Christian Srs. Assn., Overseas Brats, Heidelberg Am. H.S. Alumni Assn., Mil. Brats, Ill. Rlwy. Mus., PGA Tour Ptnrs. (life), U.S. Golf Assn., Perry Country Club. E-mail: wileyknott@cox.net.

KNOTT, WILLIAM ALAN, library director; b. Muscatine, Iowa, Oct. 4, 1942; s. Edward Marlan and Dorothy Mae K.; m. Mary Farrell, Aug. 23, 1969; children: Andrew Jerome, Sarah Louise. BA in English, U. Iowa, 1967, MA in L.S., 1968. Asst. dir. Ottumwa (Iowa) Pub. Libr., 1968-69; libr. cons. Iowa State Libr., Des Moines, 1968-69; dir. Hutchinson (Kans.) Pub. Libr., S. Cen. Kans. Libr. Sys., 1969-71, Jefferson County Pub. Libr., Lakewood, Colo., 1971—. With USAR, 1965—67. Mem.: ALA, Urban Librs Coun., Colo. Libr. Assn. Office: Jefferson County Pub Libr 10200 W 20th Ave Lakewood CO 80215-1402 Office Phone: 303-275-2200. Business E-Mail: wknott@jefferson.lib.co.us.

KNOTTS, DUSTY MARIE, literature and language educator; BA, U. Tex., Tyler, 2000. Tchr. English Martin's Mill Ind. Sch. Dist., Benwheeler, Tex., 2001—03, Ennis Ind. Sch. Dist., 2003—. Mailing: Ennis Jr HS 501 N Gaines St Ennis TX 75119-3841

KNOTTS, ROBERT SPENCER (BOB KNOTTS), writer, playwright; b. Detroit, Mich., Dec. 9, 1952; s. John William and Elizabeth Jeanette Knotts. Writer various Vt. newspapers, Burlington, Vt., 1980—83; reporter, anchor WJOY Radio, Burlington, 1983—86; reporter WCAX-TV, Burlington, 1986—89; writer, reporter South Fla. Sun-Sentinel, Fort Lauderdale, Fla., 1989—94; writer Fort Lauderdale, Fla., 1994—. Author: (book) Super Eight: Today's Hottest Sports Stars, 1999, The Summer Olympics, 2000, Pocket Guide to the 2000 Olympics, 2000, Martial Arts, 2000, Equestrian Events, 2000, Weightlifting, 2000, Track and Field, 2000, Hard News, 2001, Florida History, 2002, Florida Plants and Animals, 2002, Florida Native Peoples, 2002, All Around Florida, 2002, Uniquely Florida, 2002, People of Florida, 2002;: (plays) Never Nothin' Again No More, 2001, In Mordant Whispers, 2003, Empath 52 Equals You, 2004; State of Fla. Divsn. Cultural Affairs, 2005; contbg. editor: Arthur Frommer's Budget Travel; contbr. articles to mags. including Sports Illustrated, Travel & Leisure, USA Weekend, N.Y. Times, Family Circle, Reader's Digest;, author 10 juvenile novels under pen name M.D. Spenser. Recipient Various Writing & Journalism awards, Fla. Mag. Assn., 2001, Associated Press, 1984, 1985, 1986, Vt. Broadcasters Assn., 1984, 1985, 1986. Mem.: PEN Fla. (sec., treas.), Poets, Playwrights, Editors, Essayists, Novelists, Dramatists Guild of Am., Authors Guild. Avocations: music, auto racing, weightlifting. Office Phone: 954-205-2722. Business E-Mail: bob@bobknotts.com.

KNOTT-TWINE, LAURA MAE, director; b. Hartford, Conn., Nov. 11, 1946; m. Richard Graham Twine, Jan. 26, 1973; children: Edward Dean, Susan Helene. BA, Norwich U., 1996—98, MA, 1998—99. Pres. and owner Orchard Ho. Weavers, Windham Ctr., 1980—85; founder, exec. dir. & ceo Windham Textile and History Mus., Inc., 1980—95; dirctor of SBA Women's Bus. Ctr. U. of Hartford, Conn., 2000—; faculty- undergraduate Union U./Vt. Coll., Monpelier, Vt., 2002—. Pres., v.p. & sec. Handweavers Guild of Conn., Glastonbury, Conn., 1979—84; v.p. NE CT Tourism Dist., Windham, Conn., 1984—86; advisor Nat. Heritage Corrior Pk. Bd., Hartford, Conn., 1988—95; paliamentarian Assn. of Girl Scouts Exec. Staff, North Haven, Conn., 1997—98; mem. Windham, Conn. Econ. Devel. Com., Windham, Conn., 1988—95; founder Windham Textile and History Museum, Inc.; instr. bus. Vermont Coll. Handweaver, Colonial Handweaving. Mem. Nat. Heritage Corridor Bd., Hartford, Conn., 1988—95; advisor Nat. Inst. of Puppetry at U. of Conn., Storrs, Conn., 1990—96; mem. Assn. of Women's Bus. Centers, Boston, 2000—03; program officer Museums of NE Conn. Assn., 1989—95; mem. SBA Women Bus. Advocate, Conn., 2002; life mem. Girl Scouts of Am., NYC, 1998—2003. Independent. Catholic. Avocations: handweaving, handspinning, reading, travel. Home: 32 Gray Pine Common Avon CT 06001 Office: The Entrepreneurial Center U Hartford 50 Elizabeth St Hartford CT 06105 Office Phone: 860-768-5663. Personal E-mail: rltwine@comcast.com. E-mail: knotttwin@hartford.edu.

KNOUS, PAMELA K., wholesale distribution executive; Student, Carleton Coll.; Degree in Math., Bus. Adminstrn., Acctg., U. Ariz. Ptnr. KPMG Peat Marwick, L.A.; group v.p. finance The Vons Companies, Inc., 1991—94; sr. v.p., CFO The Vons. Companies, Inc., 1994; exec. v.p., CFO The Vons Companies, Inc., 1995—97, Supervalu Inc., Mpls., 1997—.

KNOWLES, ALISON, artist; b. NYC, Apr. 29, 1933; m. Dick Higgins, 1960; children: Hannah, Jessie. Student, Middlebury Coll., 1952-54; BFA with honors, Pratt Inst., 1956; student, Manhattan Sch. Printing, 1962. Executed: large canvas Mother of the Great Train Robbery; active in starting Fluxus Movement in Europe, 1962; one-woman shows include Nonagon Gallery, NYC, 1958, Judson Gallery, NYC, 1962, Phase 11 Gallery, Toronto, Ont., Can., 1967, Guggenheim Mus., 1969, Gallerie Inge Baecker, Germany, 1973, 85, Galerie Rene Block, Germany, 1974, De Appel Galerie, Amsterdam, 1974, 76, Gallerie 38, Copenhagen, 1976, Vehicule Gallerie, Montreal, 1976, Aalborg Kunstmuseum, 1987, Galerie Schüppenhauer, 1992, Emily Harvey Gallery, 1999, Gallerie Beim Steinernen Kreuz, Bremen, Germany, 2003; exhibited at Studio Spichernstrasse 28, Cologne, Germany, 1962, Rolf Nelson Gallery, LA, 1963, Fluxhall, NYC, 1964, Phila. Mus. Art, 1966, Something Else Gallery, NYC, 1966, Stedelijk van Abbemuseum, Eindhoven, Netherlands, 1967, Chgo. Mus. Contemporary Art, 1967, Duchamp Festival, U. Calif., Irvine, 1972, Mercer Art Ctr., Goddard Coll., NYC, 1972, Galerie Rene Block, NYC, 1974, 76, 80, Women's House Exhbn., Calif., 1975, Bklyn. Mus., 1976, The New Sch., 1976, Whitney Mus., NYC, 1977, 99, Grommet Theatre, NYC, 1977, Franklin Furnace, NYC, 1978, LA Inst. Art, 1978, the Kitchen, NYC, 1979, U. Calif. Sacramento, 1979, Dartmouth Coll., Hanover, NH, 1979, Art Inst. Detroit, 1980, Exptl. Intermedia Found., NYC, 1980, 84, NY Avant Garde Festival, 1968-80, SUNY, Purchase, 1982-83, Emily Harvey Gallery, NYC, 1987, Mus. Modern Art, NYC 1987, Acustica Festival, Whitney Equitable Mus., 1990, LA Mus. Contemporary Art, 1998, Drawing Ctr., N.Y., 2001 others; represented in permanent collections Aalborg Nordyllands Mus., Aarhus Mus., Archive De Appel, Bibliothèque Nat. de Paris, Calif. Inst. Arts; author: The Canned Bean Rolls, 1963, The T Dictionary in The Four Suits, 1965, By Allison (one 1) Knowles, 1965, The House of Dust, 1969, Journal of the Identical Lunch, 1970, Proposition VI, 1970, Proposition IV, 1973, The Identical Lunch, 1973, Women's Work, 1975, More By Alison Knowles (again, one 1), 1976, Gem Duck, 1977, The Bean Concordance, 1983; A Finger Book, 1988, The Book of Bean, 1990, Spoken Text and Event Scores, 1993, Footnotes, 2000, Left Hand Books, 1995; exhibited at Donguy Galerie, Paris, Hundertmark Gallery, Cologne, Neuberger Mus., NY, Guggenheim Mus., NY, Fluxus Festival, Wiesbaden, Germany, Sweden, Copenhagen, North Water Song, Appolohuis, Holland, SUNY Brockport, Samaya Found., radio Köln, Kunsthalle Kiel and Gadok, Lubeck, Sommerakademie Salzburg, 1990, Fluxus Pavilion, Venice Biennale The Book of Bean, 1990, Salzburg Acad. der Kunst, Austria, U. Conn., Storrs, 1992; teaching residency, 1990; resident Banff Centre, Alta., Can., 1991. Recipient Karl Sczuka Radio award Sta. WDR, Fed. Republic Germany, 1982; Guggenheim fellow, 1968, 70; grantee Nat. Endowment for Arts, 1981, 85, Deutscher Akademischer Austauschdienst, 1984. Address: 122 Spring St New York NY 10012-3815

KNOWLES, BEYONCÉ GISELLE See BEYONCÉ

KNOWLES, CHARLES TIMOTHY, lawyer, state legislator, military officer, educator; b. Providence, Aug. 21, 1949; s. Charles Timothy and Olga (Dower) K.; m. Sandra J. Bellem; children: Justin, Jennifer. BA, U. R.I., 1971; JD cum laude, New Eng. Sch. Law, 1977; MSS, U.S. Army War Coll., 2000. Bar: R.I., U.S. Dist. Ct. (R.I.), U.S. Supreme Ct. Assoc. Robinson & Resnick, Warwick, RI, 1977-79, Haronian & Paquin, Warwick, 1979-84; ptnr. Knowles & Bissonnette, Warwick, 1984—; mem. R.I. Ho. of Reps., Providence, 1989-97, chmn. jud. com., 1993-97; ret.; legal counsel corp. com. R.I. Ho. of Reps., 2000—; adj. prof. Johnson and Wales U., 2001—. Sec. Narragansett (R.I.) Dem. Ctrl. Com., 1982-93; vice-chmn. Narragansett Zoning Bd., 1982-88; coach Narragansett Little League, 1982-88. 1st lt. U.S. Army, 1971-73; col. R.I. ARNG, 1974-99, brig. comdr., 1997-99; comdr. 1021st civil affairs group, 1999-2001. Decorated Legion of Merit, Meritorious Svc. medal (3), Master Parachutist Wings, Spl. Forces; named to St. Andrew's Hall of Fame, 2002. Mem. R.I. Bar Assn., Am. Legion, Save the Bay, Lions, St. Andrew's Alumni Assn. (sec.). Episcopalian. Home: 56 Fowler St North Kingstown RI 02852-5010 Office: Knowles and Bissonnette 3214 Post Rd Warwick RI 02886-7129 Office Phone: 401-738-5200. E-mail: ctkcolinf@aol.com.

KNOWLES, EDWARD F(RANK), architect; b. Bklyn., Aug. 12, 1929; s. Frank W. and Isabel (Leudesdorff) K.; m. Barbara Lee DuPree, Mar. 14, 1953; children: Christopher, Sarah, Mary, Emily. BArch, Pratt Inst., 1951. Registered architect, N.Y. Pvt. practice in architecture, N.Y.C., 1960—; ptnr. Macfayden & Knowles, N.Y.C., 1965-68; instr. architecture Pratt Inst., 1959-60, Cooper Union Coll., N.Y.C., 1960-64, Columbia U., N.Y.C., 1965-66. Cons. N.Y. State Council Arts, Bklyn. Inst., Man and Sci., San Francisco, Arts Resources Devel. Com., Richmond Found., N.Y.C. Dept. Parks. Prin. works include Holy Trinity Episc. Ch., Hicksville, N.Y., Manhattan Sch. of Music, Bklyn. Acad. Music, The Leperc Space Lobby Restoration, City Ctr. of Music and Drama, new Boston City Hall, The Drawing Ctr., N.Y.C., Pine Manor Jr. Coll., 21 McGill Club, Toronto, IBM World Trade Corp., Myron Minskoff, MCA Broadcasting, First Rock Fin. Corp., Equilease Corp., Litton Industries, McDonough, Marcus, Cohn and Tretter, Fleischman Shopping Ctr., Naples, Fla., Exotic Gardens, East Norwich, L.I., N.Y., Duff's Restaurant, N.Y.C., Abel's Restaurant, Newark, N.J., Casey's Restaurant, N.Y.C., Ferdinand Coudert residence, Lowell Nesbitt residence, Catherine Cahill and William Bernhard residence, Mr. and Mrs. Henry Stifel residence, Mr. and Mrs. Harvey Lichtenstein residence, Luigo de la Huerta residence, Harvey Smith residence, Wallace Forbes residence, Guido diBenedetto residence, Dorothea Tanning residence, Alvin Friedman-Klein residence, Hamilton Fish Kean residence, Baron Lambert chalet, Gstaad, Switzerland, Altman residence, N.Y.C., Gillespie residence, Prout's Neck, Maine, Robert residence, Nantucket, Phyllis Vineyard residence, Ont., Mr. and Mrs. Robert Greenhill residences, Moosehead Lake, Maine, Fla., Nantucket, Alison Flemer residence, Vieques. Mem. Rembrandt Club (Bklyn.). Office: 127 W 56th St New York NY 10019-3809 *Significant architecture must express the emotional factors of the problem in addition to the obvious requirements of program, site, budget, and structure, or it ceases to be an art form. The rejection of any of the phenomena that are experienced at any point in history is short-sighted.*

KNOWLES, ELIZABETH PRINGLE, museum director; b. Decatur, Ill., Jan. 9, 1943; d. William Bull and Elizabeth E. (Pillsbury) Pringle; m. Joseph E. Knowles; 1 child, Elizabeth Bakewell. BA in Humanities with honors, Stanford U., 1964; MA in Art History, U. Calif., Santa Barbara, 1968; grad., Mus. Mgmt. Inst., 1984; MBA, Rensselaer Poly. Inst., 1999. Cert. jr. coll. tchr. Calif. Instr. art history Murray State U., Murray, Ky., 1967-68; instr. Santa Barbara Art Inst., 1969, Santa Barbara City Coll., 1969-70, 76-78, instr. cont. edn., 1973-86; from staff coord. docents to curator edn. Santa Barbara Mus. Art, 1974-86; assoc. dir. Meml. Art Gallery, Rochester, N.Y., 1986-88; instr. mus. studies Calif. State U., Long Beach, 1989; exec. dir. Lyman Allyn Art Mus., New London, Conn., 1989-95; pres. Only In Conn. Spl. Interest Tours, Chester, 1995-97; supr. mus. edn. programs Mystic (Conn.) Seaport Mus., 1996-2001; exec. dir. Wildling Art Mus., Los Olivos, Calif., 2001—. Instr. continuing edn. Santa Barbara City Coll., 1973—86. Contbr. essays to art catalogues. Bd. dirs., chmn. Met. Transit Dist., Santa Barbara, 1978—80; commr. Santa Barbara City Planning Commn., 1975—77; founding pres. Santa Barbara Contemporary Arts Forum, 1976—78. Fellow Kellogg Found., Smithsonian Inst., 1985. Mem.: New Eng. Mus. Assn. (v.p. 1993—95), Coll. Art Assn., Am. Assn. Mus. (treas. edn. com. 1986—88). Office Phone: 805-688-1082. E-mail: Penny@wildlingmuseum.org.

KNOWLES, JAMES KENYON, mechanical engineer, educator; b. Cleve., Apr. 14, 1931; s. Newton Talbot and Allyan (Gray) K.; m. Jacqueline De Bolt, Nov. 26, 1952; children: John Kenyon, Jeffrey Gray, James Talbot. SB in Math., MIT, 1952, PhD, 1957; DSc (hon.), Nat. U. Ireland, 1985. Instr. math. MIT, Cambridge, 1957-58; asst. prof. applied mechanics Calif. Inst. Tech., Pasadena, 1958-61, assoc. prof., 1961-65, prof. applied mechanics, 1965—, William R. Kenan Jr. prof., 1991—, William R. Kenan Jr. prof. emeritus, 1996—. Vis. prof. MIT, 1993-94; cons. in field. Contbr. articles to profl. jours. Recipient Eringen medal, Soc. Engring. Sci., 1991, Goodwin medal, MIT, 1955. Fellow: AAAS, ASME (Koiter medal 2002), Am. Acad. Mechanics. Office: Calif Inst Tech Divsn Engring & Applied Sci 104-44 1201 E California Pasadena CA 91125-0001 Office Phone: 626-395-4135. Business E-Mail: knowles@caltech.edu.

KNOWLES, JEFFREY D., lawyer; b. Washington, Apr. 22, 1949; BA, Columbia Univ., 1971; JD, NY Law Sch., 1975. Bar: NY 1976, DC 1977. Co-founder, gen. counsel Electronic Retailing Assn., 1990—2003; ptnr., govt. divsn. Venable LLP, Washington, and head, advt., mktg. practice group. Mem.: ABA, Promotion Mktg. Assn., Direct Mktg. Assn., Electronic Retailing Assn. (bd. dir.). Office: Venable LLP 575 Seventh St NW Washington DC 20004 Office Phone: 202-344-4860. Office Fax: 202-344-8300. Business E-Mail: jdknowles@venable.com.

KNOWLES, JEREMY RANDALL, chemist, educator; b. Rugby, England, Apr. 28, 1935; came to U.S., 1974; s. Kenneth Guy Jack Charles and Dorothy Helen (Swingler) K.; m. Jane Sheldon Davis, July 30, 1960; children: Sebastian David Guy, Julius John Sheldon, Timothy Fenton Charles. BA, Balliol Coll., Oxford (Eng.) U., 1958; MA, D.Phil., Christ Ch., 1961; Doctor honoris causa, U. Edinburgh, 1992, ETH, Switzerland, 2001. Research fellow Calif. Inst. Tech., 1961-62; fellow Wadham Coll., Oxford U., 1962-74, univ. lectr., 1966-74; vis. prof. Yale U., 1969, 71; Sloan vis. prof. Harvard U., 1973, prof. chemistry, 1974—, Amory Houghton prof. chemistry and biochemistry, 1979—, dean faculty of arts and scis., 1991—2002, disting. svc. prof., 2003—. Newton-Abraham vis. prof. Oxford U., 1983-84; hon. fellow Balliol Coll., Oxford U., Wadham Coll., Oxford U. Author papers, revs. bioorganic chemistry. Served as pilot officer RAF, 1953-55. Recipient Prelog medal ETH, Switzerland, CBE award (Queen's Birthday Honours), Eng., 1993, Welch award Robert A. Welch Found., 1995, Harvard medal, 2002. Fellow: Royal Soc. (Davy medal 1991), Am. Acad. Arts and Scis., Royal Chem. Soc. London (hon. Charmian medal); mem.: NAS (fgn. assoc.), Am. Philos. Soc., Am. Soc. Biol. Chemists, Am. Chem. Soc. (Nakanishi award 1999, Bader award 1989, Cope Scholar award 1989, Repligen award 1992), Biochem. Soc. London. Home: 67 Francis Ave Cambridge MA 02138-1911 Office: Harvard U Wadsworth House Cambridge MA 02138-5722 Office Phone: 617-496-9137.

KNOWLES, JULIE NALL, secondary school educator; b. Webb, Ala., Nov. 5, 1941; d. Ealie Edward and Creola (Carter) Nall; m. William Durwood Knowles, Jan. 17, 1970. BS in Edn. magna cum laude, Troy State U., 1965; MA in English, Samford U., 1969; PhD in English, Auburn U., 1980; AA in Music, Chattahoochee Valley C.C., Phenix City, Ala., 1999. Cert. tchr. Ala., Ga., Fla. Tchr. Ahrens H.S. Jefferson County Schs., Louisville, 1975—76; instr. Auburn U., Ala., 1981—82; assoc. prof. Stillman Coll., Tuscaloosa, Ala., 1983—85; asst. prof. Mercer U., Macon, Ga., 1986—87; prof. Troy State U., Phenix City, Ala., 1987—99; tchr. Camden County H.S. Camden County Schs., Kingsland, Ga., 1999—2000; tchr. Paxon Sch. Advanced Studies Duval County Sch. Sys., Jacksonville, Fla., 2000—04; prof. Bapt. Coll. of Fla., Graceville, 2005—. Editor, creator: The Chariot, 1988-91; contbr. articles to mags. Ch. pianist Turners Station (Ky.) Bapt Ch., 1973—76, Union Grove Bapt. Ch., Opelika, Ala., 1976—82, Hatchechubbee (Ala.) Bapt. Ch., 1988—95; mem. choir Folkston (Ga.) Bapt. Ch., 2000—. Rsch. grantee Troy State U., 1992; recipient Woodrow Hale Meml. Prize # 1 Green River Writers, 1996. Mem. Profl. Assn. Ga. Educators, Phi Theta Kappa, Phi Kappa Phi, Kappa Delta Pi (counselor Rho Phi chpt. 1989-92, Point of Excellence award 1993). Democrat. Southern Baptist. Avocations: motorcycling, piano, fishing. Home: 10076 E State Hwy 52 Webb AL 36376 Office Phone: 850-263-3261 x467.

KNOWLES, LYNDA HETTICH, lawyer; b. Louisville, Nov. 12, 1959; d. Gilbert Lee Hettich and Marilyn Ann Lattis; children: Jessie Jane, Anna Leigh. Student, U. Dallas, 1977-79; BA in Polit. Sci., U.N.C., 1980; JD, U. Denver, 1985. Bar: Colo. 1985, U.S. Dist. Ct. Colo. 1986, U.S. Ct. Appeals (10th cir.) 1986. Practice law, Littleton, 1985-95; mem. staff Time Warner Telecom, Littleton, 1999—2003, atty., 2003—. Mem. Colo. Bar Assn. Roman Catholic. Avocations: piano, running. Office: Time Warner Telecom 10475 Park Meadows Dr Littleton CO 80124-5433

KNOWLES, MARIE L., transportation executive; Sr. fin. analyst Arco Transp. Co., Long Beach, Calif., 1972-1986; asst. treas. for banking, 1986-1988; v.p. of fin., planning and control ARCO Internat. Oil and Gas Co., 1988-90; v.p. and controller ARCO, 1990-93; sr. v.p. and pres. ARCO Transp. Co., 1993-96, exec. v.p., CFO L.A., 1996—. Office: Atlantic Richfield 4 Centerpointe Dr La Palma CA 90623-2502

KNOWLES, MARJORIE FINE, law educator, dean; b. Bklyn., July 4, 1939; d. Jesse J. and Roslyn (Leff) Fine; m. Ralph I. Knowles, Jr., June 3, 1972. BA, Smith Coll., 1960; LLB, Harvard U., 1965. Bar: Ala., N.Y., D.C. Teaching fellow Harvard U., 1963-64; law clk. to judge U.S. Dist. Ct. (so. dist.), N.Y., 1965-66; asst. U.S. atty. U.S. Atty.'s Office, N.Y.C., 1966-67; asst. dist. atty. N.Y. County Dist. Atty., N.Y.C., 1967-70; exec. dir. Joint Found. Support, Inc., N.Y.C., 1970-72; asst. gen. counsel HEW, Washington, 1978-79; insp. gen. U.S. Dept. Labor, Washington, 1979-80; assoc. prof. U. Ala. Sch. Law, Tuscaloosa, 1972-75, prof., 1975-86, assoc. dean, 1982-84; law prof., dean Ga. State U. Coll. Law, Atlanta, 1986-91, law prof., 1986—. Cons. Ford Found., N.Y.C., 1973-98, 2000-03, trustee Coll. Retirement Equities Fund, N.Y.C., 1983-2002; mem. exec. com. Conf. on Women and the Constn., 1986-88; mem. com. on continuing profl. edn. Am. Law Inst.-ABA, 1987-93. Contbr. articles to profl. jours. Am. Council Edn. fellow, 1976—77, Aspen Inst. fellow, Rockefeller Found., 1976. Mem. ABA (chmn. new deans workshop 1988), Ala. State Bar Assn., N.Y. State Bar Assn., D.C. Bar Assn., Am. Law Inst., Tchrs. Ins. Annunity Assn. (trustee 2003-). Office: Ga State U Coll Law University Plz Atlanta GA 30303 Office Phone: 404-651-2081.

KNOWLES, RICHARD ALAN JOHN, language educator; b. Southbridge, Mass., May 17, 1935; s. Clarence Fay and Mildred Elizabeth (Branniff) K.; m. Jane Marie Boyle, Sept. 1, 1958; children: Jonathan Edwards, Katherine Mary. BA magna cum laude, Tufts U., 1956; MA, U. Pa., 1958, PhD, 1963. Physics asst. Tufts U., Medford, Mass., 1954-56; asst. instr. English U. Pa., Phila., 1956-60; from asst. prof. to prof. U. Wis., Madison, 1962-90, Dickson-Bascom prof. humanities, 1990—. Vis. lectr. U. Pa., 1967, George Washington U., Am. U., 1969, Cath. U., Washington, 1985; manuscript reader various univs., 1965—; cons. Am. Players Theater, Spring Green, Wis., 1980-83; poetry judge Brittingham Poetry Prize, Madison, 1986—, NEH referee, panelist, Washington, 1988—. Author: (with others) Shakespeare Variorum Handbook, 1971; author: Shakespeare Variorum Handbook, rev., 2003; editor: (with others) English Renaissance Drama, 1978; editor: New Variorum As You Like It, 1977; co-editor New Variorum Shakespeare, 1978—; mem. editl. bd. Shakespeare Notes, 1996—. Officer, prodr. Madison Savoyards, Wis., 1978—; pres. Friends U. Wis. Librs., Madison, 1982—84. Folger Libr. fellow, Washington, 1968, Guggenheim fellow, N.Y., 1976-77; NEH fellow 1983-87; Rsch. fellow Humanities Rsch. Inst., Madison, 1990. Mem. MLA, Shakespeare Assn. Am., Internat. Assn. Univ. Profs. English, Assn. Lit. Scholars and Critics, Nakoma Country Club. Democrat. Avocations: theater, chamber music, opera, gardening, carpentry. Home: 2226 Commonwealth Ave Madison WI 53726-5302 Office: U Wis Dept English 600 N Park St Madison WI 53706-1403 E-mail: rknowles@facstaff.wisc.edu.

KNOWLES, RICHARD NORRIS, chemist; b. Wilmington, Del., Aug. 8, 1935; s. Francis and Dorothy Edith Knowles; m. Alice Keith Pfohl, Aug. 30, 1957 (div. May 1987); children: Elizabeth Nelson, Dorothy Lawrence, Cynthia Norris; m. Claire Elaine Frerichs, Dec. 31, 1988; 1 stepchild, Christine J. Stoelting. BS, Oberlin Coll., 1957; PhD, U. Rochester, 1961. With DuPont Co., Wilmington, Del., 1960-96; asst. works mgr. Chambers Worls, NJ, 1980-83; mgr. Niagara Falls (N.Y.) Plant, 1983—87, Belle (W.Va.) Plant, 1987-95; dir. cmty. awareness emergency response & industry outreach Wilmington, 1995-96; work with Chem. Mfrs. Assn. in Responsible Care; assoc. Dalmau Network; prin. Richard N. Knowles & Assocs.; advisor to mayor Niagara Falls, 1999—2004; founder, dir. Ctr. Self-Orgnl. Leadership, 2001—; ptnr. Soliance Group, U.S.A. Author: The Leadership Dance, Pathways to Extraordinary Organizational Effectiveness, 2002; (feaures include) The New Pioneers, 1998, The Soul at Work, 2000; contbr. articles to profl. jours. Elder Presbyn. Ch.; bd. dirs. Nat. Inst. Chem. Studies, Du Versity, Inst. for the Study of Coherence and Emergence. Recipient Chem. Emergency Planning and Preparedness Ptnr. award, EPA, 1995, 1996. Mem.: Almost Heaven Hammered Dulcimer Soc., Nature Conservancy (DuPont Agrl. Products Crystal award 1991), Am. Chem. Soc. Achievements include 40 patents in field. Office: 6989 Rebecca Dr Niagara Falls NY 14304-3050 Office Phone: 716-731-2917. Personal E-mail: rnknowles@aol.com. E-mail: rnknowles@aol.com.

KNOWLES, TONY, former governor; b. Tulsa, Jan. 1, 1943; m. Susan Morris; children: Devon, Lucas, Sara. BA in Econs., Yale U., 1968. Co-owner Downtown Deli, Anchorage, 1976—; mayor Municipality of Anchorage, 1981-87; gov. State of Alaska, 1994—2002. Dem. candidate for Alaska U.S. Senate seat, 2004. Mem. citizen's com. to develop comprehensive plan for growth and devel., Anchorage, 1972; mem. Borough Assembly, Anchorage, 1975—79. With 82d Airborne U.S. Army, 1961—65, Vietnam. Named Child Advocate of the Yr., Child Welfare League Am., 1999; recipient Silver Medal of Merit, VFW, 2001. Democrat. Home: 1146 S Street Anchorage AK 99501*

KNOWLES, WILLIAM LEROY (BILL KNOWLES), television news producer, journalism educator; b. L.A., June 23, 1935; s. Leroy Edwin and Thelma Mabel (Armstrong) K.; children from previous marriage: Frank, Irene, Daniel, Joseph, Ted; m. Sharon Weaver, Dec. 28, 1990. BA in Journalism, San Jose State Coll., 1959; postgrad., U. So. Calif., 1962—63. Reporter, photographer, prodr. KSL-TV, Salt Lake City, 1963-65; prodr., editor, writer WLS-TV, Chgo., 1965-70; news writer ABC News, Washington, 1970-71, assoc. prodr., 1971-75, ops. prodr., 1975-77, So. bur. chief Atlanta, 1977-81, Washington bur. chief, 1981-82, West Coast bur. chief, 1982-85; prof. U. Mont., Missoula, 1986—; jazz writer and historian; chair Radio-TV dept. U. Mont., 2000—03. Advisor U. Mont. Student Documentary Unit; chair faculty senate, 2003-04. Served with U.S. Army, 1959-62. Decorated Commendation medal; Gannett fellow Ind. U., 1987; Media Mgmt. fellow Poynter Inst. Media Studies, 1988. Mem. Assn. for Edn. in Journalism (head radio-TV divsn. 1995-96). Office: U Mont Radio-TV Dept Missoula MT 59812-6480 Office Phone: 406-243-4747. Business E-Mail: bill.knowles@umontana.edu.

KNOWLES, WILLIAM STANDISH, retired chemist; b. Taunton, Mass., June 1, 1917; married; 4 children. BS in Chemistry, Harvard U., 1939; PhD in Steroid Chemistry, Columbia U., 1942. Postdoct. fellow Harvard U., Cambridge, Mass., 1951; chemist Monsanto, St. Louis, 1942—86, ret., 1986. Recipient St. Louis award, St. Louis sect. ACS, 1978, IR 100 awards for Asymmetric Hyrogenation, 1974, Monsanto Thomas and Hochwalt award, 1981, ACS Award for Creative Invention, 1982, Paul N. Rylander award, Organic Reactions Catalysis Soc., 1996, Nobel Prize in Chemistry, Royal Swedish Acad., 2001. Avocations: fly fishing, hiking, bicycling. Home: PO Box 71 Kelly WY 83011-0071*

KNOWLTON, GRACE FARRAR, sculptor, photographer, painter; b. Buffalo, Mar. 15, 1932; d. Frank Neff and Esther Sargeant (Norton) Farrar; m. Winthrop Knowlton, July 8, 1960 (div. 1980); children: Eliza, Samantha. BA,

Smith Coll., 1954; MA, Columbia U., 1981. Asst. to curator of graphic arts Nat. Gallery of Art, Washington, 1955-57; tchr. art Arlington (Va.) Pub. Schs., 1957-60; sculptor, photographer, painter, 1960—; tchr. art Art Students League, N.Y.C., 1999—. One-woman shows include Katonah (N.Y.) Mus., 1993, Smith Coll. Mus., Northampton, Mass., 1993, Hirschl & Adler Modern, N.Y.C., 1997, Bates Coll. Mus., Lewiston, Maine, 2002, Neuberger Mus., Purchase, N.Y., 2002, Represented in permanent collections Corcoran Gallery Art, Washington, D.C., Met. Mus., N.Y.C., Storm King Art Ctr., Mountainville, N.Y., Victoria & Albert Mus., London, Eng., Yale U. Mus. Art, New Haven, Conn., Houston (Tex.) Mus. Fine Arts. Home: 67 Ludlow Ln Palisades NY 10964-1606 Personal E-mail: graceknowlton@earthlink.net.

KNOWLTON, LESLIE BROOKS, journalist; b. Orange, N.J., July 18, 1952; d. Bruce Douglas and Elizabeth (Snow) Knowlton; m. Charles Gottlieb Herzog, Dec. 27, 1979 (div. 1992); 1 child, Siri Whitney Herzog. BA, U. Conn., 1977; MA, Calif. State U. Long Beach, 1983; postgrad., City Coll., 1998. Dir. rsch. Grubb & Ellis Co., Newport Beach, Calif., 1985-87; reporter Orange County Businessweek, Irvine, Calif., 1987-89; reporter/desk asst. LA Times, Costa Mesa, Calif., 1989-90, free lance journalist, 1990—, Psychiat. Times, 1990—, N.Y. Daily News, 1990—, Cosmopolitan Mag., 1990—, Fitness Mag., 1990—, NY Acad. Sci. Faculty scholar, U. Conn., 1976, Univ. scholar, 1976. Mem.: Nat. Writers Union, Author's Guild, Am. Soc. Journalists and Authors, Deer Isle Yacht Club, N.Y. Newswomen's Club, Psi Chi, Phi Kappa Phi. Avocations: reading, boating, hiking. E-mail: lk@leslieknowlton.com.

KNOWLTON, SYLVIA KELLEY, physician; b. Huntington, Ind., June 8, 1949; d. Darwin Newton and Mary Lucille (Wilson) Kelley; m. R. A. Levinson, Dec., 1971 (div. 1988); 1 child, Diana Nicole Levinson; m. Donald William Knowlton, Apr. 20, 1989; children: Fred, Bill. BS, Ind. U., 1977, MD, 1975. Diplomate Am. Bd. Internal Medicine, Am. Bd. Allergy and Immunology. Intern in internal medicine Mt. Sinai Med. Ctr., Miami Beach, Fla., 1976; resident in internal medicine U. Mich., Ann Arbor, 1976, U. Calif., Davis, 1976-77; fellow Nat. Jewish Hosp., Denver, 1977-79; pvt. practice Boca Raton, Fla., 1980—. Republican. Avocations: singing, sailing, poetry. Office: Delmar Office Park 7301 W Palmetto Park Rd Ste 10 Boca Raton FL 33433-3458

KNOWLTON, THOMAS A., dean, retired food products executive; b. Toronto, Ont., Can., June 16, 1946; s. William George and Grace K.; m. Janice Elizabeth Knowlton, June 8, 1968; children: Kimberly, Tricia, Jeffrey, Andrea. BA, U. Windsor, Ont., 1968, MBA, 1970. Brand mgr. Colgate Palmolive, Toronto, 1970-73; product mgr. Gen. Foods, Toronto, 1973-75; v.p., dir. client services Leo Burnett, Toronto, 1975-79; sr. v.p. mktg. and sales Kellogg Salada Can. Inc., Rexdale, Ont., 1979-82, pres., chief exec. officer, 1983-88; v.p. Kellogg Co., 1984—; mng. dir. Kellogg Co. of Gt. Britain Ltd., 1989-90, chmn., 1990-94, exec. v.p., area dir. Europe, 1992-94; corp. exec. v.p., pres. Kellogg N.Am., 1994-99; ret., 1998; dean faculty bus. Ryerson U., Toronto, 2000—. Bd. dirs. Wm. Wrigley Jr. Co., AIM Trimark Funds Mgmt., Toronto, Sun Rype Products, Hudson's Bay Co. Mem. Young Pres.'s Orgn., York Downs Golf and Country Club (Unionville, Ont.), Sanctuary Golf Club (Sanibel, Fla.).Hudsons Bay Co. Home: 123 Cheltanham Ave Toronto ON Canada M4N 1R1

KNOWLTON, WILLIAM ALLEN, federal agency administrator, educator; b. Weston, Mass., June 19, 1920; s. Frank Warren and Isabelle (Riese) K.; m. Marjorie Adams Downey, Nov. 27, 1943; children: William Allen, Davis Downey, Timothy Riese, Hollister Knowlton Petraeus. BS, U.S. Mil. Acad., 1943; MA, Columbia U., 1957; grad., Nat. War Coll., 1960; LLD (hon.), Akron U., 1972. Commd. 2d lt. U.S. Army, 1943, advanced through grades to gen., 1976; with 7th Armored Div., World War II, Army Gen. Staff, 1947-49, SHAPE, France, 1951-54; assoc. prof. social scis. U.S. Mil. Acad., 1955-58, supt., 1970-74; bn. comdr. 3d Armored Cav. Regt., 1958-59, mil. attache, 1961-63; brig. comdr. Ft. Knox, Ky., 1963-64; with Office Chief Staff U.S. Army, 1964-65; mil. asst. to spl. asst. to sec. and dept. sec. def. Office Sec. Def., 1965-66; sec. Joint Staff, dir. pacification support, dep. asst. chief staff for civil ops. revolutionary devel. support U.S. Mil. Assistance Command, Vietnam, 1966-67; asst. div. comdr. 9th Inf. Div., Vietnam, 1968; sec. gen. staff Office Chief Staff U.S. Army, 1968-70; chief staff hdqrs. U.S. European Command, Stuttgart, W.Ger., 1974-76; comdr. Allied Land Forces Southeast Europe, Izmir, Turkey, 1976-77; U.S. rep. NATO Mil. Com., Brussels, 1977-80; ret., 1980; cons. on internat. affairs and strategic intelligence R & D Assocs., Marina del Rey, Calif.; sr. assoc. Burdeshaw Assocs. Ltd., 1981-91; dir. Aeronca Inc., 1982-86, Chubb Corp., Fed. Ins. Co., Vigilant Ins. Co., Chubb Life Am., 1983-93; sr. fellow CAPSTONE course Nat. Def. U., 1984-95, sr. fellow emeritus CAPSTONE course, 1995—. Sr. rsch. fellow Inst. Advanced Technology U. Tex., Austin, 1998—; lectr. Am. U., 1995—1998 Contbr.: Ency. Americana and nat. mags. Trustee Davis and Elkins Coll., 1982-90. Decorated Def. D.S.M., Army D.S.M., Silver Star with 2 oak leaf clusters, Legion of Merit with oak leaf cluster, D.F.C., Bronze Star with V device, Air medal with 9 oak leaf clusters, Army Commendation medal with oak leaf cluster, knight comdr. cross Order Merit W. Ger., officer Legion of Honor France, Vietnamese Nat. Order and Gallantry Cross with palm; recipient George Washington honor medal Freedoms Found., Valley Forge, 1957, 58, Lemnitzer award, 1994, Disting. Grad. award, U.S. Mil. Acad., 2004; named Hon. Col. Regiment, 40th armor Berlin. Mem. Am. Mil. Inst., 7th Armored Divsn. Assn. (hon. pres.), Coun. Fgn. Rels., Soc. Mayflower Descs., Washington Inst. Fgn. Affairs (v.p. 1998), S.R., Soc. Colonial Wars, Univ. Club (N.Y.C.), Army and Navy Club (Washington), Phi Kappa Phi. Home: Goodwin House #452 4800 Fillmore Ave Alexandria VA 22311 Personal E-mail: genbill@aol.com.

KNOX, CHARLES GRAHAM, lawyer; b. Erie, Pa., June 10, 1948; s. William Wallace and Agnes Ruth (Graham) K.; m. Jill Ann Poole, Mar. 22, 1975; children: Stephanie Marie, William Wallace II. BA, Williams Coll., 1970; JD, U. Mich., 1973. Bar: Pa. 1973, U.S. Dist. Ct. (we. dist.) Pa. 1973. Assoc. Buchanan Ingersoll P.C., Pitts., 1972-81, shareholder, 1981-97; ptnr. Marcus & Shapira, LLP, Pitts., 1997—. Pres., bd. trustees Parkwood United Presbyn. Ch., Allison Pk., Pa., 1991, treas., bd. dirs. Wildwood Golf Club, Allison Pk., Pa., 2001— Mem.: ABA, Allegheny County Bar Assn., Pa. Bar Assn. Home: 4230 Wembleton Dr Allison Park PA 15101-1564 Office: Marcus & Shapira LLP 301 Grant St Ste 35 Pittsburgh PA 15219-1407 Office Phone: 412-338-5217. E-mail: knox@marcus-shapira.com.

KNOX, GERTIE R., compliance executive, accountant; b. Rossville, Tenn., Feb. 2, 1960; d. Columbus and Mabel (Strickland) K.; m. Micheal F. Coley, Sept. 1, 1990. BBA, U. Memphis, 1982; MBA, Colo. State U., 1998. CPA, Calif. Contracts and fin. adminstr. Textron Aerostructures, Nashville, 1983-86; ptnr. PricewaterhouseCoopers LLP, Irvine, Calif., 1986-2001; COO, Global Social Compliance LLC, L.A., 2001—. Mem.: AICPA. Avocations: reading, travel. Home: Irvine CA 92606 Fax: 213-362-6012. E-mail: gknox@gsocialc.com.

KNOX, HELENE MARGRETHE, poet; b. Sacramento, Calif., May 1, 1943; d. James Dale and Helen Margrete K. BA with honors, U. Calif., 1965, MA, 1968, PhD, 1979; MDiv, Starr King Sch. for Ministry, Berkeley, Calif., 1994. Assoc., instr., sect. leader dept. English U. Calif., Berkeley, 1972-74, 77-78; Fulbright lectr. in Am. studies U. Perpignan, France, 1972-73, U. Augsburg, Fed. Republic Germany, 1980-81; lectr. English U. San Francisco, 1979; vis. asst. prof. English Drexel U., Phila., 1981-82; asst. prof. English and creative writing Muhlenberg Coll., Allentown, Pa., 1982-86; ind. poet, essayist, tchr., scholar, editor, interviewer Oakland, Calif., 1987—; instr. Starr King Sch. for Ministry, 1991. Presenter pub. readings of original poetry, U.S., Europe and Tunisia, 1970—; lectr. on lit., U.S. and Europe, 1972-89; presenter papers at profl. meetings. Contbr. poetry to lit. mags. and anthologies; contbg. editor Standing Before Us: Unitarian Universalist Women and Social Reform, 1776-1936, 2000, The Role of the Dissenter in Western Christianity: From Jesus Through the 16th Century, 2004; contbr. stories, scholarly articles to various publs. Recipient Feminist Theology award Unitarian Universalist Women's Fedn., Boston, 1991. Mem.: PEN, Nat. Writers Union. Mem. Green Party. Unitarian Universalist. Avocations: music, organic gardening. Office: 2625 Alcatraz #181 Berkeley CA 94705-2702 Office Phone: 510-654-1667. E-mail: hknox@juno.com.

KNOX, JAMES EDWIN, lawyer; b. Evanston, Ill., July 2, 1937; s. James Edwin and Marjorie Eleanor (Williams) Knox; m. Rita Lucille Torres, June 30, 1973; children: James Edwin III, Kirsten M., Katherine E., Miranda G. BA in Polit. Sci., State U. Iowa, 1959; JD, Drake U., 1961. Bar: Iowa 1961, Ill. 1962, Tex. 1982. Law clk. to Hon. Tom C. Clark, U.S. Supreme Ct., Washington, 1961-62; assoc., then ptnr. Isham, Lincoln & Beale, Chgo., 1962-70; v.p. law N.W. Industries, Inc., Chgo., 1970-80; exec. v.p., gen. counsel Lone Star Steel Co., Dallas, 1980-86; sr. v.p. law Anixter Internat. Inc., Chgo., 1986—2002. Instr. contracts and labor law Chgo. Kent Coll. Law, 1964—69; arbitrator Nat. Rlwy. Adjustment Bd., 1967—68; ptnr. Mayer, Brown & Platt, Chgo., 1992—96; gen. counsel Arris Group, Inc., 1996—2002. Mem.: ABA, Ill. Bar Assn., Phi Beta Kappa, Order of Coif. Republican. Office: Anixter Internat Inc 2301 Patriot Blvd Glenview IL 60025-8020 Office Phone: 224-521-8796.

KNOX, JAMES MARSHALL, lawyer; b. Chgo., Jan. 12, 1944; s. Edwin John and Shirley Lucille (Collett) K.; m. Janine Foster, July 18, 1964; children: Erik M., Christian S. BA, U. Ill., 1968; MA in Libr. Sci., Rosary Coll., 1973; JD, DePaul Coll. Law, 1979. Bar: Ill. 1979, U.S. Dist. Ct. (no. dist.) Ill. 1979, U.S. Ct. Appeals (7th cir.) 1980. Head reference Northbrook (Ill.) Pub. Libr., 1973-76; asst. dir. hdqrs. Jackson (Miss.) Met. Libr. Sys., 1976-77; assoc. Fishman & Fishman, Ltd., Chgo., 1979-91; prin. Law Office James M. Knox, 1991—. Gen. counsel Deerfield (Ill.) Pub. Libr., 1994—. Commr. Evanston Preservation Commn., 1991-98; sustaining mem. Miss. Hist. Soc. Mem. ABA, Ill. State Bar Assn., Ill. Trial Lawyer's Assn., Chgo. Bar Assn., U. Ill. Alumni Assn. (dir. 1986-91). Home: 121 W Chestnut #3104 Chicago IL 60610 Office: Chestnut Tower 121 W Chestnut Chicago IL 60610 Office Phone: 312-587-1356. Personal E-mail: KawOxford@aol.com.

KNOX, LANCE LETHBRIDGE, venture capitalist; b. Hartford, Conn., Sept. 25, 1944; s. Robert Chester and Leonice Katherine (Merrels) K.; children: Michele Merrels, Elizabeth McVarish; m. Mary E. Lambert, 1981. BA, Williams Coll., 1966; MBA, NYU, 1970. Asst. cashier Citibank, N.C., N.Y.C., 1968-70, asst. v.p., 1970-72, v.p., 1972-74, sr. credit officer, 1973-74; v.p. fin. GATX Corp., Chgo., 1974-77; pvt. investor venture capital, 1978—. Pres. Bistrot Zinc, Chgo.

KNOX, MICHAEL DENNIS, medical educator, research center administrator; b. Wyandotte, Mich., May 9, 1946; s. Harold L. and Mary (Latta) K.; m. Lucinda Carol Page, May 6, 1972; children: John M.P., James R. S. BA, Ea. Mich. U., 1968; MSW, U. Mich., 1971, MA in Psychology, 1973, PhD in Psychology, 1974. Lic. clin. psychologist, Fla., Va. Dir. Applied Sci., Inc., Ann Arbor, Mich., 1974-76; clin. dir. Community Mental Health Ctr., Inc., Huntington, W.Va., 1976-78; clin. instr. Marshall U. Sch. Medicine, Huntington, 1977-78; dir. Western Tidewater Mental Health Ctr., Suffolk, Va., 1978-86; asst. prof. Eastern Va. Med. Sch., Norfolk, 1979-86; assoc. prof., chmn. dept. cmty. mental health U. South Fla., Tampa, 1986-91, prof., chmn. dept. cmty. mental health, 1991-95, prof. dept. cmty. mental health, 1991—2001, dir. Ctr. for HIV Edn. and Rsch., 1988—, prof. medicine dept. internal medicine Coll. Medicine, 1994—, disting. univ. prof. cmty. and family health Coll. Pub. Health, 1997—2004, disting. prof. dept. mental health law and policy Louis de la Parte Fla. Health Inst., 2001—, disting. prof. global health, coll. public health, 2004—, courtesy disting. prof. gerontology, 2005—. Chmn., bd. dirs. Applied Sci. Corp., Tampa, 1985-99; adj. disting. prof. psychology Marshall U., 1977-78, U. South Fla., 1988—; mem. faculty senate, exec. com. mem., 1992-99, pres. faculty senate, 1995-97, courtesy disting. prof. gerongoloty, 2002—; chmn. adv. coun. faculty senate Fla. State U. Sys., 1996-98; cons. USPHS, Bethesda, Md., 1990—, NIMH, Rockville, Md., 1990-98; lectr. in field, 1980—; tech. advisor state and local govts.; dir. Fla./Caribbean AIDS Edn. and Tng. Ctr., 1999-; vis. scholar dept. psychiatry Oxford (Eng.) U., summer 1999; prin. investigator more than 50 rsch. grants, 1988—. Author books including: Last Wishes: A Handbook to Guide Your Survivors, 1995, HIV and Community Mental Healthcare, 1998; contbr. more than 60 articles on AIDS and psychology; invited reviewer 5 acad. jours., internat. spkr. 1982—. Advisor Joint Commn. on Accreditation of Hosps., Chgo., 1982-84; bd. dirs. U.S. Power Squadron, Raleigh, N.C., 1983-84; co-chair Am. Found. for AIDS Rsch. 16th Nat. HIV/AIDS Update Conf., 2004; mem. steering com. S.E. Region STD/HIV Prevention Tng. Ctr., 2004—; mem. U.S. Power Squadron. Recipient Disting. Svc. award Nat. Coun. Cmty. Mental Health Ctrs., 1984, resolution of appreciation, 1993; grantee Emory U., 1988-91, NIMH, 1991-93, U. Miami, 1991-99, HHS, 1999—. Fellow APA, Am. Psychol. Soc.; mem. Internat. AIDS Soc., U. Mich. Alumni Assn., U.S. Power Squadron, Sigma Xi. Achievements include significant research findings in the area of HIV/AIDS risk factors for the seriously mentally ill, HIV/AIDS risk reduction, AIDS prevention, knowledge and attitudes regarding AIDS among treatment providers. Office: U South Fla Fla Mental Health Inst MHC 1700 13301 Bruce B Downs Blvd Tampa FL 33612-3807 Business E-Mail: knox@fmhi.usf.edu.

KNOX, MICHAEL JOHN, academic administrator; b. Coleman, Tex., Sept. 4, 1971; s. Eldon Beck and Mary Margaret Korenek Knox; m. Erica Leigh Stocker, July 5, 2003. B in Edn., Tex. A&M U., 1994; MEd, U. Pa., 1999. Tchr. Huntington Indep. Sch. Dist., Tex., 1996—98; asst. dir. student activities U. Ky., Lexington, 1999—2002; asst. dean students, dir. student activities Bellarmine U., Louisville, 2002—. Mem.: Nat. Orienation Dirs. Assn., Nat. Assn. Student Pers. Adminstrs. Roman Catholic. Avocations: golf, travel. Office: Bellarmine Univ 2001 Newburg Rd Louisville KY 40205 E-mail: mknox@bellarmine.edu.

KNOX, PAUL L., architecture educator, dean; B, PhD in Geography, U. Sheffield, Eng. Prof. dept. urban affairs and planning Va. Tech, assoc. dean acad. affairs, 1993—98, dir. PhD program in environ. design and planning, univ. disting. prof., interim dean Coll. Architecture and Urban Studies, 1998—99. Lectr. in field. Author 12 books; contbr. articles to profl. jours. Mem.: Va. Soc. AIA (hon.). Office: Coll Architecture and Urban Studies Va Tech 202 Cowgill Hall 0205 Blacksburg VA 24061

KNOX, ROBERT SEIPLE, physicist, researcher; b. Franklin, N.J., July 13, 1931; s. Harvey Stoll and Laura (Seiple) K.; m. Myrta I. Borges, Sept. 1, 1954; children: Bruce Robert, Wayne Harvey, Lee Benjamin. BS in Engring. Physics, Lehigh U., 1953; PhD in Physics and Optics, U. Rochester, 1958. Rsch. assoc. U. Ill., 1958-59, rsch. asst. prof., 1959-60; mem. faculty U. Rochester, N.Y., 1960—, assoc. prof. dept. physics, 1963-68, prof., 1968-97; sr. scientist Lab. for Laser Energetics, 1985—; chmn. dept. physics and astronomy U. Rochester, 1969-74, assoc. dean spl. programs Coll. Arts and Scis., 1982-87, faculty sr. assoc., 1997-2001, prof. emeritus, 1997—. Cons. solid state sci. divsn. Argonne Nat. Lab., 1959—69, Naval Rsch. Lab., 1960—70; NSF sr. fellow U. Leiden, 1967—68. Author: Theory of Excitons, 1963, (with A. Gold) Symmetry in the Solid State, 1964, (with D.L. Dexter) Excitons, 1965; also articles. Japan Soc. Promotion of Sci. fellow Kyoto U., 1979, Royal Soc. Guest Rsch. fellow, Fulbright fellow Imperial Coll. (London), 1993. Fellow Am. Phys. Soc. (Biol. Physics prize 1994), Am. Soc. Photobiology, Am. Assn. Physics Tchrs., Biophys. Soc., Internat. Soc. Photosynthesis Rsch. Achievements include research in atomic spectra and structure, absorption and luminescence spectra ionic and molecular crystals, photosynthesis theory, picosecond spectroscopy. Office: U Rochester Dept Physics & Astronomy Rochester NY 14627-0171 Business E-Mail: rsk@pas.rochester.edu.

KNOX, SIMMIE LEE, artist; b. 1936; BFA, MFA, Temple U. Tyler Sch. of Art, Phila. Staff mem. Museum of African Art, Washington; portrait artist, 1981—. Portrait commissions include, Martin Luther King, Jr., Bowie State Coll., 1974, Frederick Douglass, Museum of African Art, Wash., DC, 1975, Judge H. Carl Moultrie, The H. Carl Moultrie Courthouse, 1985, Supreme Court Justice Thurgood Marshall, 1989, Dorothy Height, Nat. Council of Negro Women, 1989, David & Joyce Dinkins, The Schomburg Collection, 1993, Col. Rosemary McCarthy, U.S. Army Nurse Corp, 1994, John V. Atanasoff, Cosmos Club, 1995, Muhammad Ali, Michigan, 1995, Hank & Billye Aaron, Georgia, 1996, Melvin Sabshin, Am. Psychiatric Assn., 1997, Official White House portrait, Pres. William Clinton & First Lady Hillary Clinton, 2004.

KNOX, THOMAS PATRICK, lawyer; b. St. Louis, Mo., July 1, 1943; s. Russell Anthony and Marguerite Therese Knox; m. Michele Drury Knox. BA, Cardinal Glennon, 1965; JD, Woodrow Wilson Coll. of Law, 1975. Gen. counsel United Family Life Ins. Co., Atlanta; asst. gen. counsel Creditor Resources, Atlanta; pres. Thomas P. Knox PC, Cumming, Ga.; rep. Ga. Gen. Assembly, Cumming; pres. Jackson and Knox PC, Cumming; sr. ptnr. Knox and Sudman LLC, Cumming. Pres. Forsyth County Assn. of Criminal Defense Lawyers, Cumming, Ga., 1999. Chmn. Forsyth County Rep. Party, Cumming. Recipient Ronald Reagan award, Forsyth County Rep. Party, 2004. Mem.: Criminal Defense Bar (pres. 1999), County and State Bar Assn., Upper Chattahoochee Riverkeepers, River Bend Gun Club. Republican. Avocations: boating, sailing, skiing, reading, politics. Office: Knox and Sudman 302 Tribble Gap Rd Cumming GA 30040 Office Phone: 770-887-0400. Office Fax: 770-889-8122. E-mail: knoxsudman@bellsouth.net.

KNOX, WILLIAM ARTHUR, judge; b. Fargo, N.D., Jan. 8, 1945; BS, N.D. State U., 1966; JD, U. Minn., 1968. Law specialist USCG, Boston, 1968—69, Juneau, Alaska, 1970—72; prof. Law Sch., U. Mo., Columbia, 1972—85; magistrate judge U.S. Cts., Jefferson City, Mo., 1985—. Author: West's Federal Criminal Forms, 2002, West's Missouri Criminal Practice, 2005. Office: 131 W High St Jefferson City MO 65101-1557 Office Phone: 573-634-3418. Business E-Mail: william.knox@mow.uscourts.gov.

KNOX, WILLIAM DAVID, publishing company executive; b. Sault Ste. Marie, Mich., June 9, 1920; s. Victor A. and Bertha V. (Byers) K.; m. Jane Edith Shaw, June 15, 1941; children: Georgia Knox Mode, William David II, Randall S., Brian V. BS, Mich. State U., 1941; postgrad., Harvard U., 1943-44; LLD (hon.), U. Wis., 1973. Youth editor Hoard's Dairyman mag., W.D. Hoard & Sons Co., Fort Atkinson, Wis., 1941-42, asso. editor, 1946-49, editor, 1949—, pres., treas., gen. mgr., 1972—. Pres. Nat. Brucellosis Com., 1955-66, chmn. Wis. com., 1951-60; mem. nat. agrl. adv. com., 1961-62, nat. adv. com. on trade negotiations, 1976-82; bd. dirs. First Am. Bank and Trust, D.C.I. Mktg., Inc. Pres. Fort Atkinson Bd. Edn., 1948-59; bd. visitors U. Wis., 1979-84; trustee Univ. Rsch. Park, Inc., 1984-93; bd. dirs. Wis. Taxpayers Alliance, 1976-98. Lt. USNR, 1942-46. Recipient Disting. Svc. award Nat. Brucellosis Com., 1957, Pure Milk Assn., 1966, Am. Dairy Sci. Assn., 1970, Wis. Farm Bur. Fedn., 1974, Nat. Assn. Animal Breeders, 1981, Nat. Assn. Livestock Records, 1983, Wis. Agri-Bus. Coun., 1992, Nat. Agri-Mktg. Assn., 1992, Outstandin ANR Patriarch award Alumni assn. Coll. of Agr. and Natural Resources, Mich. State U., 1992; service citations Fla. Dairy Farmers Fedn., 1962, Wis. Farm Bur. Fedn., 1956, Nat. Plant Food Coun., 1963, Dairy Coun. Ctrl. Ga., 1967, Mid-Am. Dairymen Salute award, 1977, Nat. 4-H Alumni award, 1965, Mich. State U. Disting. Alumnus award, 1966; named Tri-State Man of Yr., 1966, Milw. Milk Prodrs. Assn. Man of Yr., 1976. Fellow Am. Dairy Sci. Assn.; mem. Agrl. Publs. Assn. (pres. 1979-81), Am. Newspaper Pubs. Assn., Am. Vet. Med. Assn. (hon.), Am. Jersey Cattle Club (hon.), Am. Agrl. Econs. Assn., Wis. Vet. Med. Assn. (hon.), Rotary (Internat. Svc. citation 1956), Alpha Gamma Rho, Alpha Zeta (Centennial Honor Roll award 1997). Republican. Episcopalian. Home: 703 Robert St Fort Atkinson WI 53538-1150 Office: Hoard's Dairyman W D Hoard & Sons Co PO Box 801 Fort Atkinson WI 53538-0801

KNOX, WYCKLIFFE AUSTIN, JR., lawyer; b. Augusta, Ga., Nov. 1, 1940; s. Wyckliffe Austin Knox Sr. and Byrnece (Purcell) Swanson; m. Shell Hardman, Apr. 15, 1967; children: Wyckliffe Austin III, Dorothy Shell, John Hardman, Davis Purcell. BBA, U. Ga., 1962, JD, 1964. Bar: Ga. 1964, U.S. Dist. Ct. (so. dist.) Ga. 1964, U.S. Ct. Appeals (5th cir.) 1966, U.S. Ct. Claims 1973, U.S. Supreme Ct. 1973, U.S. Ct. Appeals (11th cir.) 1981, U.S. Ct. Appeals (4th cir.) 1983. Assoc. Hull, Towill & Norman, Augusta, 1964-67; ptnr. Hull, Towill, Norman, Barrett & Johnson, Augusta, 1967-76, Knox & Zacks, Augusta, 1976-77, pres., 1977—94; ptnr. Kilpatrick & Cody, 1994—97; ptnr., litig. practice Kilpatrick Stockton LLP, Augusta & Atlanta, 1997—, past chmn. exec. com. Chmn. bd. dirs. 1st Union Nat. Bank of Ga., Augusta, Knox-Rivers Constrn. Co., Thomson, Ga. Mem. bd. visitors sch. law U. Ga., Athens, 1973-76, bd. dirs. athletic assn., 1975-85, emeritus dir. 1985-; mem. jud. com. Bus. Council Ga., Atlanta, 1986—; pres. Ga. council Boy Scouts Am., Augusta, 1974-75; pres.Richmond/Columbia County unit Am. Cancer Soc., Augusta, 1985, chmn. bd. dirs. 1986—; trustee Richard B. Russell Found., Atlanta, 1971—; pres. Georgians for Better Transp.; founding dir. & past chmn. Ga. Lottery Corp.; mem Met. Atlanta Olympic Games Auth.; mem. Commn. for a New Ga.; dir. Ga. C. of C. Fellow Am. Bar Found., Ga. Bar Found; mem. Augusta Bar Assn. (pres. 1984), Ga. Bar Assn., Ga. Acad. Hosp. Attys. (bd. dirs. 1979-80), Am. Acad. Healthcare Attys., Ga. Def. Lawyers Assn. (bd. dirs. 1973-76), YPO. Clubs: Piedimont Driving (Atlanta), Augusta Country (pres. 1988), Pinnacle (Augusta). Lodges: Rotary (pres. local club 1979-80). Methodist. Avocations: fishing, skiing, golf. Office: Kilpatrick Stockton LLP Ste 1400 Wachovia Bank Bldg 699 Broad St Augusta GA 30901-1453 also: Kilpatrick Stockton LLP Ste 2800 1100 Peachtree St Atlanta GA 30309-4530 Office Phone: 706-823-4200, 404-815-6387. Office Fax: 706-828-4461. Business E-Mail: wknox@kilpatrickstockton.com.

KNOXVILLE, JOHNNY (PHILIP JOHN CLAPP), actor; b. Knoxville, Tenn., Mar. 11, 1971; s. Phil and Lemoyne; m. Melanie Knoxville, May 1995; 1 child, Madison. Student, Am. Acad. Dramatic Arts. Actor: (films) Desert Blues, 1995, Coyote Ugly, 2000, The Tree, 2001, The Ringer, 2001, Life Without Dick, 2001, Don't Try This at Home, 2001, Big Trouble, 2002, Deuces Wild, 2002, Men in Black 2, 2002, Grand Theft Parsons, 2003, Walking Tall, 2004, A Dirty Shame, 2004, Lords of Dogtown, 2005, The Dukes of Hazzard, 2005; writer, prodr., actor: Jackass: The Movie, 2002; creator, writer, prodr.: (TV series) Jackass, 2000—02. Office: Creative Artists Agy 9830 Wilshire Blvd Beverly Hills CA 90212*

KNUDSEN, CHILTON ABBIE RICHARDSON, bishop; b. Sept. 29, 1946; m. Michael J. Knudsen, May 29, 1971; 1 child, Daniel. BA, Chatham Coll., Pitts., 1968; MDiv, Seabury-Western Theol. Sem., Evanston, Ill., 1980. Ordained deacon, 1980, priest, 1981; pastoral care officer Episcopal Diocese of Chgo.; consecrated bishop, 1998; bishop Episcopal Diocese of Maine, Portland, 1998—. Episcopalian. Office: Episcopal Diocese of Maine 143 State St Portland ME 04101 Office Phone: 207-772-1953. Office Fax: 207-773-0095.*

KNUDSEN, GENE ARTHUR, school system administrator; b. Sioux City, Iowa, Oct. 19, 1948; arrived in Germany, 1976, arrived in Germany, 1976; s. Donald Arthur and Leola (May) Knudsen; m. Debra Jane Anderson, May 27, 1972; children: Kyle Anderson, Sean Arthur. BS, Morningside Coll., 1971; MEd, U. So. Calif., 1981, EdD, 1985. Secondary tchr. Akron (Iowa) Pub. Sch. Sys., 1971-76, Darmstadt (W. Germany) Jr. H.S., 1976-82, Ramstein (W. Germany) H.S., 1982-85; ednl. program mgr. Landstuhl (W. Germany) Mid. Sch., 1985-87; asst. prin. Kaiserslautern (W. Germany) H.S., 1987-91; prin. Augsburg (W. Germany) H.S., 1989-91; asst. supt. Munich Sch. Dist., 1991-92, Hessen (Germany) Sch. Dist., 1992—2001, Heidelberg Sch. Dist., Germany, 2001—. Tchr., cons. Germany Writing Project, 1979—98, co-dir., 1999—; photographer, writer Dept. Def. Dependent Schs., Germany, 1985—91. Author: (book) Holistic Writing, 1985, Writing Is..., 1987; editor: (newsletter) Dept. Def. Dependent Schs. Jour., 1988—89. Mem. Sch. Adv. Coun., Landstuhl, 1985—87, PTA, Kaiserslautern, 1987—88. Recipient Major Gen. Keith L. Ware Journalism award, 2004. Mem.: Assn. Supervision and Curriculum Devel. (grantee 1984), Nat. Coun. Tchrs. English (Richard Mead award 1989), Phi Delta Kappa (grantee 1985). Methodist. Avocations: photography, writing, travel. Home: CMR-419 Box 781 APO AE 09102 Office: Heidelberg DSO Unit 29237 APO AE APO AE 09102 E-mail: gene_knudsen@eu.odeddoe.edu.

KNUDSEN, LAURA GEORGIA, linguist; b. Kenosha, Wis., Sept. 21, 1969; d. Richard Dennis and Georgia Elizabeth (Perrin) Wright; m. Martin Christian Knudsen, Aug. 20, 1994. BA in Linguistics, Ind. U., 1991, MA in Linguistics, 2001. Linguist Ind. U., Bloomington, 1987—, tchr. ESL, Ctr. for English Lang. Tng., 1995—; tchr. ESL Aichi U., Toyohashi, Japan, 1998, Ind. U./ Purdue U. Indpls., 2002; tchr. Aikido Ind. U., 2001—. Presenter in field Contbr. articles to profl. jours. Fulbright scholar IIE, Budapest, 1996-97; FLAS fellow U.S. Dept. Edn., Ind. U., 1993-94, GANN fellow, 1991-92. Mem. Linguistic Soc. Am., Ind. U. Linguistic Club (sec. 1996, pres. 1998), INTESOL (student rep. 1999, rec. sec. 2002-03). Avocation: Aikido. Office: Ind U Ctr English Lang Tng Meml Hall 317 Bloomington IN 47405

KNUDSEN, WILLIAM CLAIRE, geophysicist, researcher; b. Provo, Utah, Dec. 12, 1925; s. Nels William and Julia A. (Brown) K.; m. Ruth Crandall, Aug. 31, 1948; children: Linda, Ruthanne, Guy, Grant. BS, Brigham Young U., 1950; MS, U. Wis., 1952, PhD, 1954. Sr. rsch. physicist Calif. Rsch. Corp., La Habra, 1954-62; staff scientist Lockheed Palo Alto Rsch. Lab., Palo Alto, Calif., 1962-84, Knudsen Geophys. Rsch. Inc., Monte Sereno, Calif., 1984-95; ret., 1995. Adj. prof. Brigham Young U., 1997, Utah State U., 1997. Patentee in field. With Signal Corps U.S. Army, 1944-46. Mem. Am. Geophys. Union, Sigma Xi. Mem. Lds Ch. E-mail: wcknudsen@msn.com.

KNUDSON, ALFRED GEORGE, JR., medical geneticist; b. LA, Aug. 9, 1922; s. Alfred George and Mary Gladys (Galvin) Knudson; m. Anna T. Meadows, June 20, 1977; children from previous marriage: Linda, Nancy, Dorene. BS, Calif. Inst. Tech., 1944, PhD, 1956; MD, Columbia U., 1947; PhD (hon.), Thomas Jefferson U., 1992, U. Oslo, 2000. Chmn. dept. pediat. City of Hope Med. Ctr., Duarte, Calif., 1956—62, chmn. dept. biology, 1962—66; assoc. dean Health Sci. Ctr., SUNY, Stony Brook, 1966—69; dean Grad. Sch. Biomed. Scis., U. Tex. Health Sci. Ctr., Houston, 1970—76; dir. Inst. Cancer Rsch., Fox Chase Cancer Ctr., Phila., 1976—83, sr. mem., 1976—, disting. sci., 1992—, pres., 1980—92. Mem. Assembly Life Scis. NRC, 1975—81. Author: Genetics and Disease, 1965; contbr. articles to profl. jours. Recipient Charles S. Mott prize, GM Cancer Rsch. Found., 1988, medal of honor, Am. Cancer Soc., 1989, Charles Rodolphe Brupbacher Found. prize, 1995, Gairdner Found. Internat. award, 1997, Albert Lasker Clin. Med. Rsch. award, Lasker Found., 1998, John Scott award, City of Phila., 1999, Lila Gruber Meml. Cancer Rsch. award, Am. Acad. Dermatology, 2000, Kyoto prize, 2004. Fellow: AAAS; mem.: NAS, Am. Soc. Pediatric Hematology/Oncology (Disting. Career award 1999), Am. Assn. Cancer Rsch., Am. Pediat. Soc., Assn. Am. Physicians, Am. Soc. Human Genetics (pres. 1978, Allan award 1991), Internat. Soc. Pediatric Oncology, Am. Acad. Arts and Scis., Am. Philos. Soc. Achievements include research in genetics of human cancer. Office: Inst Cancer Rsch 7701 Burholme Ave Philadelphia PA 19111-2412 Office Phone: 215-728-3642. Business E-Mail: ag_knudson@fccc.edu.

KNUDSON, MARK BRADLEY, health products executive, venture capitalist; b. Libby, Mont., Sept. 24, 1948; s. Melvin R. and Helga Jean (Joice) K.; m. Susan Jean Voorhees, Sept. 12, 1970; children: Kirstin Sue, Amy Lynn. BS, Pacific Luth. U., 1970; PhD, Wash. State U., 1974. Lectr. Wash. State U., Pullman, 1973-75; rsch. assoc. U. Wash., Seattle, 1976-78, asst. prof., 1976-79; physiologist Cardiac Pacemakers Inc., St. Paul, 1979-80, mgr. rsch., 1980-82, dir. applied rsch., 1982-83; pres., chmn. bd. SenTech Med. Corp., St. Paul, 1983-86; pres. Arden Med. Systems Inc. subs. Johnson & Johnson, 1986-89; pres., dir. Johnson & Johnson Profl. Diagnostics Inc., Raritan, N.J., 1988-89; ptnr. Med. Innovation Ptnrs., 1989-99; gen. ptnr. Med. Innovation Fund, 1999—; chmn., CEO Venturi Group LLC, 1999—; pres., CEO Pi Med., Inc., 1999—2002; exec. chmn. Restore Med., Inc., 2002—. Bd. dirs. Diametrics Inc.; lectr. in field. Contbr. articles to profl. jours.; patentee in field. Chmn., bd. dirs. Luth. Sem. Fellow, NIH, Wash. State U., 1974—75, U. Wash., 1975—76. Fellow Am. Heart Assn.; mem. AAAS, Sigma Xi. Republican. Lutheran. Office: Venturi Group LLC 2800 Patton Rd Saint Paul MN 55113-1100

KNUDSON, ROZANNE RUTH, writer; b. Washington, June 1, 1932; d. James K. and Ruth (Ellsworth) K. BA in English, Brigham Young U., 1954; MA, U. Ga., 1956; PhD in English Edn., Stanford U., 1963. Tchr. Key West High Sch., Miami Edison Jr. High Sch.; instr. Stanford U., Adelphi U., Purdue U.; supr. Hicksville (L.I.) Schs.; asst. prof. CUNY-York Coll. Vis. scholar Stanford U.; writer in residence Kean Coll., N.J.; speaker Women in Sports Conf. Evergreen State Coll., Washington; executor Literary Estate of May Swenson, 1990-. Author: of poems, May Swenson: A Poet's Life in Photos, 1996, The Wonderful Pen of May Swenson, 1993, Coaching Evelyn, 1991, American Sports Poems, 1988, Julie Brown: Racing Against the World, 1988, Rinehart Shouts, 1987, Frankenstein's 10 K, 1986, A Waterpower Workout, 1986, Martina Navratilova: Tennis Power, 1986, Zan Hagen's Marathon, 1984, Babe Didrikson: Athlete of the Century, 1985, Speed, 1983, Punch, 1983, Muscles, 1983, Just Another Love Story, 1982, Rinehart Lifts, 1980; (from the estate of May Swenson) Nature, The LOve Poems of May Swenson, Poems of May Swenson. Fellow MacDowell Colony Va. Ctr. for Creative Arts, Ragdale, Dorland Mountain Colony, Cummington Cmty. of Arts, Hambidge Ctr., Villa Montalvo. Home: 73 The Blvd Sea Cliff NY 11579-1027 E-mail: cberglie@netscape.net.

KNUDSON, RUTHANN, environmental consultant, anthropologist, archaeologist; b. Milw., Oct. 24, 1941; d. Sidney Olaus and Clara Ruth (Tappe) K. BA Liberal Arts, Hamline U., St. Paul, 1959—61; BA in anthropology magna cum laude, U. Minn., 1961—63, MA in anthropology, 1963—66; PhD in anthropology, Wash. State U., 1968—73; postgrad. hydrogeology, U. Idaho, Moscow, 1988—88. Cert. profl. archaeologist. Seasonal ranger Bandelier Nat. Monument Nat. Park Svc., N.Mex., 1963; instr. U. No. Colo., Greeley, 1966—68; asst. rsch. prof. U. Idaho, Moscow, 1974—79, assoc. rsch. prof., 1979—81; dir. cultural resource svcs. Woodward Clyde Cons., San Francisco, 1981—86, v.p., shareholder, 1985—88; arch. Nat. Park Svc., Washington, 1990—96; supr. Agate Fossil Beds Nat. Monument, 1996—2005; prin. Knudson Assoc. (formerly Paleo-Designs), 1974—; res. assoc. Calif. Acad. Sci., 1986—. Vis. asst. prof. Wright State U., Dayton, Ohio, 1974; cons. Am. Folklife Ctr., Washington, 1981-83, NRC, Washington, 1982-83; resource cons. Calif. Heritage Task Force, 1983-94, Office Tech. Assessment, Washington, 1986; Woodward lectr., 1985; chmn. bd. dirs. No. Great Plains Inventory and Monitoring Program, 2004-05. Author: Cambria Village Ceramics, 1967, Organizational Variability in Late Paleo-Indian Assemblages, 1983, Contemporary Cultural Resource Management, 1986; co-editor: The Public Trust and the First Americans, 1995, The 10,000 year old Lubbock Artifact Assemblage, 1998, Using Cultural Resources to Enhance Ecosystem Management, 1999, Using the Past to Shape National Park Service Policy for Wildlife, 1999, Cultural Resource Management in Context, 2000, Medicine Creek is a Paleoindian Cultural Ecotone: The Red Smoke Assemblage, 2002, Ecologically Based Archaeology in a Public Context, 2003, Marie Wormington, 2005. Bd. dirs. Preservation Action, Washington, 1980-85, 89-90, Californians for Preservation Action, 1981-82; sec.-treas. Idaho NOW, 1977-78; co-chmn. Nebr. Panhandle Tourism Coalition, 1996-2005, co-chmn., 1998-2000; Bridges to Buttes Scenic Byway Mgmt. Team, 1999-2005, Friends of the Intertribal Gathering, 2003-, Indians & Pioneers Tourism Marketing Com., 2003-, Friends of Mo. Breaks, 2005-. Recipient Preservation award Nat. Conf. State Historic Preservation Officers, 1981, Conservation award Am. Soc. Conservation Archaeology, 1981; Frison Inst. vis. sr. fellow, 2004. Mem. Plains Anthropol. Soc. (bd. dirs. 2003—), Soc. Applied Anthropology, Am. Anthropol. Assn. (Margaret Mead award 1983), Soc. Am. Archaeology (exec. bd. 1979-81, exec. com. 1983-85, legis. coord. 1979-82, chmn. com. pub. archaeology 1980-82, 84-85), Women's Coun. Energy and Environ. (bd. dirs. 1994-96), Geol. Soc. Am., Phi Beta Kappa. Democrat. Methodist. Home and Office: 3021 Fourth Ave S Great Falls MT 59405-3329 Personal E-mail: paleoknute@3rivers.net.

KNUTH, DEAN LESLIE, research and development company executive, golf consultant, writer; b. Eau Claire, Wis., Apr. 29, 1947; s. Herbert LaVerne and Betty Lou Knuth; m. Suzanne Yavorsky, May 15, 1998; children: Alison Stewart Brown, Gregory Scott, Stephen Matthew. BS, U.S. Naval Acad., 1970; MS in Engring., U.S. Naval Postgrad. Sch., 1978. Commd. ensign USN, 1970, advanced through grades to capt., 1990; sr. dir. US Golf Assn., Far Hills, NJ, 1981—97; bus. develop. exec. Northrop Grumman Corp., San Diego, 1997—; ret. USN, 1998. Cons. Callaway Golf, 1999—2002. Author: USGA Handicap and Course Rating manuals; contbg. editor: Golf Digest Mag., 1999—. Decorated Legion of Merit Pres. of the U.S.; named one of Greatest Inventions in 25 Years, Golf Digest Mag., 2002. Mem.: Golf Writers Assn. Am., Royal and Ancient Golf Club of St. Andrews, Century Club San Diego. Achievements include first to golf handicap course rating and slope rating system used worldwide; invention of golf handicap system; patents for golf club heads. Avocation: golf. Home: 4392 Colling Rd E Bonita CA 91902 Office: Northrop Grumman Corp 9326 Spectrum Ctr Blvd San Diego CA 92123 Office Phone: 858-514-9816. Personal E-mail: dknuth@cox.net. E-mail: dean.knuth@ngc.com.

KNUTH, DONALD ERVIN, computer sciences educator; b. Milw., Jan. 10, 1938; s. Ervin Henry and Louise Marie (Bohning) Knuth; m. Jill Carter, June 24, 1961; children: John Martin, Jennifer Sierra. BS, MS, Case Inst. Tech., 1960; PhD, Calif. Inst. Tech., 1963; DSc (hon.), Case Western Res. U., 1980, Luther Coll., Decorah, Iowa, 1985, Lawrence U., 1985, Muhlenberg Coll., 1986, U. Pa., 1986, U. Rochester, 1986; DSc, U. Paris-Sud, Orsay, 1986; DSc (hon.), SUNY, Stony Brook, 1987, Oxford (Eng.) U., 1988, Brown U., 1988, Valparaiso U., 1988, Grinnell Coll., 1989, Dartmouth Coll., 1990, Concordia U., Montréal, 1991, Adelphi U., 1993, Masaryk U., Brno, 1996, Duke U., 1998, St. Andrews U., 1998, Williams Coll., 2000, U. Tubingen, 2001, Athens U. Econ., 2001, U. Oslo, 2002, Harvard U., 2003, U. Thessaloniki, 2003, U. Antwerp, 2003, U. Montréal, 2004; DSc, Armenian Acad. Sci., 2005; D Tech., Royal Inst. Tech., Stockholm, 1991; Pochetnogo Doktora, St. Petersburg U., Russia, 1992; DLitt (hon.), U. Waterloo, 2000. Asst. prof. Calif. Inst. Tech., Pasadena, Calif., 1963—66, assoc. prof., 1966—68; prof. Stanford U., Calif., 1968—92, prof. emeritus, 1993—. Cons. Burroughs Corp., Pasadena, Calif., 1960—68. Author: The Art of Computer Programming, 1968 (Steele prize, 1987), Computers and Typesetting, 1986. Recipient Nat. medal of Sci., Pres. James Carter, 1979, Disting. Alumni award, Calif. Inst. Tech., 1978, Priestley award, Dickinson Coll., 1981, Franklin medal, 1988, J.D. Warnier prize, 1989, Adelsköld medal, Swedish Acad. Sci., 1994, Harvey prize, Israel Inst. Tech., 1995, Kyoto prize, Inamori Found., 1996; fellow, Guggenheim Found., 1972—73. Fellow: Brit. Computer Soc., Assn. for Computing Machinery (Grace Murray Hopper award 1971, Alan M. Turing award 1974, Computer Sci. Edn. award 1986, Software Sys. award 1986), Am. Acad. Arts and Scis., The Computer Mus.; mem.: NAS, IEEE (hon. McDowell award 1980, Computer Pioneer award 1982, von Neumann medal 1995), Acad. Sci. (fgn. assoc. Paris, Oslo, Munich, London), Nat. Acad. Engring. Lutheran. Avocation: playing pipe organ. Office: Stanford Univ Computer Scis Dept Stanford CA 94305-9045

KNUTH, ELDON LUVERNE, engineering educator; b. Luana, Iowa, May 10, 1925; s. Alvin W. and Amanda M. (Becker) K.; m. Marie O. Parrat, Sept. 10, 1954 (div. 1973); children: Stephen B., Dale L., Margot O., Lynette M.; m. Margaret I. Nicholson, Dec. 30, 1973. BS, Purdue U., 1949, MS, 1950; PhD (Guggenheim fellow), Calif. Inst. Tech., 1953. Aerothermodynamics group leader Aerophysics Devel. Corp., 1953-56; asso. research engr. dept. engring. UCLA, 1956-59, asso. prof. engring., 1960-65, prof. engring. and applied sci., 1965-91, prof. emeritus, 1991—, head chem., nuclear thermal div. dept. engring., 1963-65, chmn. energy kinetics dept., 1969-75, head molecular-beam lab., 1961-88. Gen. chmn. Heat Transfer and Fluid Mechanics Inst., 1959; vis. scientist, von Humboldt fellow Max-Planck Inst. für Strömungsforschung, Göttingen, Fed. Republic Germany, 1975-76; mem. Internat. Adv. Com. Internat. Symposium Rarefied Gas Dynamics., 2000—. Author: Introduction to Statistical Thermodynamics, 1966, Who Wrote Those Letters?, 2005, Auf den Spuren von Jürnjakob Swehn, 2005; also numerous articles; patentee radial-flow molecular pump Served with AUS, 1943-45. Recipient Fritz Reuter medal, Landsmannschaft, Mecklenburg, 2002. Mem. AIAA, Am. Soc. Engring. Edn., Am. Inst. Chem. Engrs., Combustion Inst., Soc. Engring. Sci., AAAS, Am. Phys. Soc., Am. Vacuum Soc., Sigma Xi, Tau Beta Pi, Gamma Alpha Rho, Pi Tau Sigma, Sigma Delta Chi, Pi Kappa Phi. Clubs: Gimlet (Lafayette, Ind.). Home: 18085 Boris Dr Encino CA 91316-4350

KNUTH, JOSHUA WAYNE, special education educator; b. Clinton, Iowa, Nov. 16, 1977; d. William Robert Knuth and Susan Fay Ashby Richardson. BS, U. Dubuque, 2001. Spl. edn. tchr. Savanna (Ill.) H.S., 2001—, head varsity basketball coach, 2001—05. Asst. football coach West Caroll Thunder, Savanna, 2003—05; baseball coach Mount Carroll (Ill.) H.S., 2004—05; mem. adv. bd. Waterfowl USA, Carroll County, Ill.; coach all-star basketball game Shoot the Bull Hame of Fame, Thomson, Ill., 2004. Mem.: Football Coach Assn., Coun. Exceptional Children, Moose. Democrat. Methodist. Avocation: sports. Office: Savanna High Sch 500 Cragmoor 61074

KNUTH FISCHER, CYNTHIA STROUT, environmental consultant; b. Walpole, Mass. d. Harold A. and Doris A. (Kendall) Strout; m. Adam Knuth (dec.); m. Charles S. Fischer. BA, Middlebury Coll., 1948; MA in Internat. Law and Govt., NYU, 1965. Adminstrv. asst. FAO Mission to Iraq, Baghdad, 1950—53; internat. conf. precis-writer Copenhagen, 1954—56; exec. sec. to UN legal counsel, 1956—62; exec. sec. to pres. Gen. Assembly UN, N.Y.C., 1962—63; exec. sec. UN Devel. Program, N.Y.C., 1964—69; adminstrv. asst. Ctr. for Internat. Affairs, Harvard U., Cambridge, Mass., 1976—82; founder, pres. Friends of Native Ams., 1986—. Founder Menotomy Indian Day, Arlington, Mass., 1991, Aberjona Indian Day, Winchester, Mass., 1992; founder, pres. Ctr. for Environ. Edn., East Coast, 1990—; sec. to bd. dirs. UN Assn. Greater Phila., 1998—2002; publicity chair, bd. dirs. Valley Forge Audubon Soc., 1996—2000; environ chair Lions Club of West Chester, Pa., 1996. Vol. Chadds Ford Hist. Soc., Second Reading Bookstore to benefit Sr. Ctr. of West Chester, 1998—; founder Friends of Indigenous Peoples, 2000—; vol. Phila. Hospitality, 2002—; mem. Coalition for A Strong UN, 1980—; vol. Meals on Wheels CC Hosp., 2003—. Mem. Common Cause (exec. bd. Mass. 1986), Mass. UN Assn. (exec. bd. 1970), Boston Jazz Soc. (exec. bd. 1975), Mystic River Watershed Assn. (exec. bd. 1991), Phi Delta Kappa (2d v.p. Harvard U. chpt. 1990-92), Sierra Club/Thoreau Group (chair 1993), Walden Forever Wild (exec. bd. 1993-95). Home: 956 Conner Rd West Chester PA 19380-1810 E-mail: cknuth@aol.com.

KNUTSEN, ALAN PAUL, pediatrician, immunologist, allergist; b. Mpls., July 21, 1948; s. Donald Richard and Shirley Marie (Erickson) K.; m. Kim A.; children: Laura Joelle, Brian A., Benjamin C., Elizabeth G., Katherine M., Amy S., Summer A. BA in Biology, U. Calif., 1971; MD, St. Louis U., 1975. Resident pediatrics St. Louis U. Med. Ctr., 1975-78; fellow allergy Duke U. Med. Ctr., Durham, N.C., 1978-80;, 1980-93; dir. dept. allergy and immunology St. Louis U. Med. Ctr., 1985—; prof. St. Louis U., 1993—, 1993—. Mem. credentials com. St. Louis U. Med. Ctr., 1980—, infectious disease com., 1980—; dir. pediatric immunology lab, 1983—; dir. pediatric allergy/immunology trng. program. Contbr. articles to profl. jours. Mem. Am. Acad. Allergy/Immunology, Clin. Immunology Soc., Phi Beta Kappa, Alpha Omega Alpha. Democrat. Lutheran. Home: 10 Orchard Way Saint Louis MO 63122-6920 Office: St Louis U Pediatric Rsch Inst 1465 S Grand Blvd Saint Louis MO 63104-1003 Business E-Mail: knutsenm@slu.edu.

KNUTSON, GEORGIANNA (GEEGEE) (GEEGEE KNUTSON), retired small business owner; b. Mitchell, S.D., Sept. 9, 1937; m. Thomas R. Knutson, 1958 (div. 1981); children: Tami Ann Carter, Nancy J.Gresham, Carey Lynn Clark. BFA in Music Edn., U. S.D., 1959; grad., Eastern Mich. U.; grad. in music, U. Mich. Tchr. music Rapid City (S.D.) Sch. Sys., 1959-60, Bedford (Ind.) Jr. High Sch., 1960-61, Redford Union Schs., Detroit, 1973-77; substitute tchr. Mich., 1977—79; temp. office worker Olsten Temp., Atlanta, 1981—84; adminstr. customer support Harris Adacom, Atlanta, 1984-92; owner Word P Pro, Decatur, Ga., 1989-94; ret., 1994. Pub. I Can Color, 1993. Past adult leader, trainer, day camp dir., neighborhood chair Girl Scouts U.S., 1971-81; active Parents Without Ptnrs., 1982-91, state v.p. family activities, 1987-88; mem. Internat. K-Kids Com., 2003— (chmn. 2005-), K-Kids Kiwanis adv., 2000-. Mem. Kiwanis Internat. (sec. Northlake 1993-97, 99—, pres. 1997-98, divsn. 14 sec. 1995-2003, adminstrv. asst. Builders Club/K-kids 1999-2004, internat. K-Kids com., 2003-05, chmn. 2005—, dist. adminstr. Ga. dist. K-Kids, 2005—, K-Kids advisor, 2000-05, Dist. Leadership award, 1998, 2003, Hixson award, 1999). Mem. Eckankar Ch. E-mail: geegeek@bellsouth.net.

KNUTZEN, MARTHA LORRAINE, lawyer; b. Bellingham, Wash., Aug. 28, 1956; BA in Polit. Sci., Scripps Coll., 1978; MA in Polit. Sci, Practical Politics, JD, U. San Francisco, 1981. Bar: Calif. 1981. Lawyer, mgr. legal computer support svcs., San Francisco, 1981—. Mem. San Francisco Citizens' Adv. Com. on Elections, 1994-96; 3d vice chair Dem. Party, San Francisco, 1996-2000, mem. Resolution Com., Calif. Dem. Party, 2001—; chair San Francisco Human Rights Commn., 1996—; cmty. organizer. Recipient Civil Rights Leadership award Calif. Assn. Human Rights Commn., 1996. Office: Office Atty Gen 455 Golden Gate San Francisco CA 94102-2230 Home: Apt 44 601 Van Ness Ave San Francisco CA 94102-3263

KO, CHIA-WEN, biostatistician, researcher; b. Changhua, Taiwan, Dec. 15, 1965; d. Wu-Hsiang Ko and Yen Lin; m. Christopher John Endres, May 22, 1993; children: Claire Yvonne Endres, Eleanor Marie Endres, Angela Anna Endres. BS, Nat. Ctrl. U., 1988, MS, 1990; PHD, U. Wis., 1996. Statistician Walter Reed Army Med. Ctr., Washington, 1998—99; rsch. biostatistician Organon Pharmaceuticals, Inc, West Orange, NJ, 2002—. Cons. Organon Pharmaceuticals, Inc, 2002—; reviewer Walter Reed Army Med. Ctr., 1998—99; mentor NIH, Bethesda, Md., 1999—2001. Recipient Excellent Tchg. asst., U. Wis., Madison, 1993—94, Intramural Rsch. Tng. award, Found. For Advanced Edn. In Sci., 1997—99; fellow, NIH, 1997—98, 1999—2002; scholar, Bd. Edn., 1985—89. Mem.: Internat. Chineses Statis. Assn., Soc. Clin. Trials, Internat. Biometrics Soc., Am. Statis. Assn. Achievements include research in Published Or Submitted 20 Scientific Articles In The Past Two Years; development of Quality Of Life Instruments To Be Used For Male Hypogonadism; discovery of The Genetic And Environmental Risk Factors For Birth Defects And Newborn Hearing Screening Failures. Avocations: reading, movies, travel. Office: Organon Pharmaceuticals Inc 375 Mt Pleasant Ave West Orange NJ 07052 E-mail: c.ko@organonusa.com.

KO, GWANGPYO, public health service officer, educator; b. Seoul, Republic of Korea, Jan. 29, 1970; arrived in U.S., 1994; s. Yeonjoo Ko and Mongsoon Son; m. Soeun Joo, Feb. 13, 1974; children: Alex, Michelle. BS, Seoul Nat. U., 1992, MS, 1994, Harvard U., 1996, PhD, 2000. Asst. prof. U. Tex., Houston, 2003—. Contbr. articles to profl. jours., chapters to books. Pres. Harvard Korean Soc., Cambridge, Mass., 1998—99. Fellow, Harvard U., Boston, 2000—01, U. N.C., Chapel Hill, 2001—03; grantee, AWARE/EPA, 2005—. Mem.: Am. Soc. Microbiology. Office: U Tex 1200 Herman PRessler W-634 Houston TX 77225 Office Phone: 713-500-9282. E-mail: gko@uthouston.edu.

KO, WEN-HSIUNG, electrical engineering educator; b. Shang-Hong, Fukien, China, Apr. 12, 1923; came to U.S., 1954, naturalized, 1963; s. Sing-Ming and Sou-Yu (Kao) K.; m. Christina Chen, Oct. 12, 1957; children: Kathleen, Janet, Linda, Alexander. BSEE, Nat. Amoy U., Fukien, China, 1946; MS, Case Inst. Tech., 1956, PhD, 1959. Engr., then sr. engr. Taiwan Telecommunication Adminstrn., 1946-54; mem. faculty Case Inst. Tech., Cleve., 1956-93; prof. elec. and biomed. engring. Case Western Res. U., Cleve., 1967-93, prof. emeritus, 1994—, dir. engring. design center, 1970-82; pres., prin. Wen H. Ko & Assocs., Cleve., 1996—. Cons. NSF, N.Am. Mfg. Co., NIH, 1966-82; pres. Transducer Rsch. Found., 1986—; rschr. in med. implant electronics, telemetry and stimulation, microsensors and microactators, micro-electro-mech.-sys. Recipient career achievement award Transducer Internat. Conf., Chgo., 1997. Fellow IEEE, AIMBE; mem. Instrument Soc. Am., Bio-Med. Engring. Soc., Sigma Xi, Eta Kappa Nu. Home: 1356 Forest Hills Blvd Cleveland OH 44118-1359 Office: Case Western Res U EECS Dept Cleveland OH 44106 Business E-Mail: whk@cwru.edu.

KOBAK, ALFRED JULIAN, JR., obstetrician, gynecologist; b. Chgo., Feb. 10, 1935; s. Alfred J and Rose B (Baron) Kobak; m. Sue B Stein, May 3, 1959; children: William, Steven, Jane, Deborah. BS, U. Ill., 1957, MD, 1959. Diplomate Am Bd Ob-Gyn. Intern Michael Reese Hosp., Chgo., 1959-60; resident Cook County Hosp., 1960-62, 64-65; practice medicine specializing in ob-gyn. Valparaiso, Ind., 1965—. Mem. med. staff Porter Meml. Hosp., Valparaiso, 1965—, chmn. dept. OB/GYN, pres. med. staff, 1981—82; clin. assoc. prof. ob-gyn. Ind. U. Sch. Medicine; pres. Ob-Gyn. Assocs., 1970—2005. Contbr. articles to profl jours. Bd. dirs. N.W. Ind. Jewish Fedn., 1970—84, Porter County Bd. Health, 1991—, pres., 1997; bd. dirs., past pres. Porter County Health Dept. Capt USAF, 1962—64. Fellow: ACS, Am. Coll. Ob-Gyn., Internat. Coll. Surgeons; mem.: AMA, Chgo. Gynecol. Soc. (v.p. 1998—99), Porter County Med Soc (pres. 1979, 1986), Ctrl. Assn. Obstetricians and Gynecologists, Ind. Med. Assn., Am. Soc. Reproductive Medicine, Sand Creek Club. Office: 1101 Glendale Blvd Valparaiso IN 46383-3724 Office Phone: 219-462-6144.

KOBAK, JAMES BENEDICT, management consultant; b. St. Louis, Mar. 4, 1921; s. Edgar and Evelyn (Hubert) K.; m. Hope McEldowney, June 13, 1942; children: James Benedict, John D. (dec.), Thomas M. BS, Harvard U., 1942; postgrad., Pace Coll., 1946—49. CPA, N.Y., La., Union S.Africa. Assoc. J.K. Lasser & Co., N.Y.C., 1946-71, partner, 1954-64, adminstrv. partner, 1964-71; internat. adminstrv. partner Lasser, Harmood Banner, Dunwoody, N.Y.C., 1964-71; pres. James B. Kobak & Co., Darien, Conn., 1971—. Ptnr. James B. Kobak Bus. Models Co., 1972-82; founder Kobak Open. Author: How to Start a Magazine and Publish It Profitably, 2002. Chmn. mag. com., mem. bus. com. Nat. council Boy Scouts Am.; co-founder, sec.-treas. John D. Kobak Appalachian Edn. Found., Darien; trustee Hill Sch., Pottstown, Pa. Served to capt., F.A. AUS, 1942-46. Mem. AICPA, N.Y. State Soc. CPAs, Transvall Soc. Accts., Harvard Club (N.Y.C.), Wee Burn Country Club (Darien), Hapenny Bay Beach Club (St. Croix), Carambola Golf Club, St. Croix Country Club. Home and Office: 6 Hale Ln Darien CT 06820 Home: Sweet Lime Village # 29 Kingshill VI 00850 Personal E-mail: jimkobak@aol.com.

KOBAK, JAMES BENEDICT, JR., lawyer, educator; b. Alexandria, La., May 2, 1944; s. James Benedict and Hope (McEldowney) K.; m. Carol Johnson, June 11, 1966; children: James Benedict III, Katherine Jean, Marcie Ann. BA magna cum laude, Harvard U., 1966; LLB, U. Va., 1969. Bar: U.S. Dist. Ct. (so. and ea. dists.) N.Y. 1972, U.S. Supreme Ct. 1977, U.S. Ct. Appeals (2nd cir.) 1973, (5th cir.) 1982, U.S. Dist. Ct. (no. dist.) Calif. 1983, N.J. 1996. Asst. prof. U. Ala., 1969-70; assoc. Hughes Hubbard & Reed LLP, N.Y.C., 1970-77, ptnr., 1977—. Lectr. in law U. Va., 1986-2000; adj. assoc. prof. Fordham U., 1986—; arbitrator Am. Arbitration Assn. Editor: Misuse: Licensing and Litigation, 2000; mem. bd. editors Va. Law Rev., 1967-69, assoc. editor, 1968-69; contbr. articles to profl. jours., mags., treatises and newspapers. Trustee Morristown-Beard Sch., 1995—2001, Jersey City Mus., 2002—. Mem. ABA (antitrust sect., former chair intellectual property com.), Assn. Bar City N.Y., N.Y. County Lawyers Assn. (bd. dirs. 1988-93, 95-97, 2001—, chmn. trade regulation com. 1987-88, chmn. com. on changing trends in the profession 1990-93, chmn. com. on law reform 1994-98, exec. com. 1996-98, chair libr. com. 1998—), Order of Coif, Am. Law Inst., Adirondack 46ers Club, Keene Valley Country Club (trustee 1995-98), Harvard Club (N.Y.). Home: 206-95 W Shearwater Ct Jersey City NJ 07305 Office: Hughes Hubbard & Reed 1 Battery Park Plz Fl 12 New York NY 10004-1482 Business E-Mail: kobak@hugheshubbard.com.

KOBASHIGAWA, JON AKIRA, internist, cardiologist, researcher, educator; b. Honolulu, Sept. 25, 1954; s. Eikichi and Alice K. BS, Stanford U., 1976; MD, Mt. Sinai Sch. Medicine, 1980. Diplomate Am. Bd. Internal Medicine, Am. Bd. Cardiology. Intern, resident, cardiology fellow UCLA Med. Ctr., 1980-86; from clin. instr. medicine to clin. prof. UCLA, 1986-99, clin. prof. medicine, 1999—, med. dir. heart transplant program, 1994—, chief divsn. clin. faculty medicine, 1998—. Contbr. articles to profl. jours. Upjohn clin. scholar, 1980; grantee in field. Mem. AAAS, Am. Coll.

Cardiology (chmn. heart failure and transplant com.), Internat. Soc. Heart Lung Transplantation (bd. dirs., program chair 1999—, pres. 2004), Am. Soc. Transplantation, Am. Heart Assn. (chair 1998—), Alpha Omega Alpha. Office: Univ Cardiovasc Med Group 100 Ucla Med Plz Ste 630 Los Angeles CA 90095-0001 Office Fax: 310-794-1211. Business E-Mail: jonk@mednet.ucla.edu.

KOBAYASHI, ALBERT SATOSHI, mechanical engineering educator; b. Chgo., Dec. 9, 1924; s. Toshiyuki and Taka (Torii) K.; m. Elizabeth Midori Oba, Sept. 24, 1953; children: Dori Kobayashi Ogami, Tina, Laura. BS in Engring., U. Tokyo, 1947; MSME, U. Wash., 1952; PhD, Ill. Inst. Tech., 1958. Position II engr. Konishiroku Photo Industry, Tokyo, 1947-50; design engr. Ill. Tools Works, Chgo., 1953-55; rsch. engr. Armour Rsch. Found., Ill. Inst. Tech., Chgo., 1955-58; from asst. prof. to assoc. prof. dept. mech. engring. U. Wash., Seattle, 1958-64, prof., 1964-97, Boeing Pennell prof. structural mechanics, 1988-95, prof. emeritus, 1997—. Coll. faculty assoc.The Boeing Co. Seattle, 1958—76; cons. Math. Sci. Northwest, Bellevue, Wash., 1962—82, UN Devel. Program, NY, 1984; vis. scholar U. Tokyo, 1969, 77; program dir. mech., structural and materials engring. divsn. NSF, 1987—88. Contbr. over 480 papers to Fracture Mechanics, Exptl. Mechanics Biomechanics and numerical analysis. Recipient F. G. Tatnall award Soc. Exptl. Stress Analysis, 1973, B.J. Lazan award, 1981, R. E. Peterson award, 1983, William Murray Lecture medal, 1983, Burlington Resources Found. Faculty Achievement award, 1992, M. M. Frocht award, 1995, G. E. Sr. Rsch. award Am. Soc. Engring. Edn., 1995, Disting. Alumni award Univ. Student Club (UW), 1997; decorated Order of Rising Sun, gold rays with neck ribbons Emperor of Japan, 1997. Fellow ASME, Soc. Exptl. Mechanics (hon. life mem., pres. 1989-90); hon. fellow Internat. Congress on Fracture, 2005. Home: 15420 62nd Pl NE Kenmore WA 98028-4312 Office: U Wash Dept Mech Engring Box 352600 Seattle WA 98195-2600 Office Phone: 206-543-5488. Business E-Mail: ask@u.washington.edu.

KOBAYASHI, HERBERT SHIN, electrical engineer; b. Webster, Tex., Feb. 6, 1929; s. Mitsutaro and Moto Kobayashi; m. Haruko Orita; children: June, Naomi, Ken. BSEE, U. Houston, 1951; MSEE, U. Mich., 1958, MS in Indsl. Engring., 1969. Design engr. SIE, Houston, 1960-61, Boeing Aerospace, Huntsville, Ala., 1961-62, New Orleans, 1962, Lockheed Electronics, Houston, 1963; aerospace technologist NASA, Houston, 1963—2002; pres. Kobayashi Inc., Webster, Tex., 1960—. Patentee in field. Mem. planning and zoning commn., Webster, 1993-94. With U.S. Army, 1954-56. Mem. IEEE, AIAA. Achievements include development of technique to make stronger concrete slabs, to separate dirt from rock by smaller, lighter machinery, pulse width modulation for servo loop (closed or open) more efficiency. Home: 1428 NASA Pkwy Webster TX 77598-4702

KOBAYASHI, HISASHI, computer scientist, dean; b. Tokyo, June 13, 1938; arrived in U.S., 1965; m. Masaye Okubo. BS, U. Tokyo, 1961, MS, 1963; MA, Princeton U., 1966, PhD, 1967. Radar system designer Toshiba, Kawasaki, Japan, 1963-65; mem. rsch. staff IBM, Yorktown Heights, NY, 1967-86; dir. Japan Sci. Inst. IBM Japan Ltd., 1982-86; Sherman Fairchild U. prof. elec. engring., computer sci. Princeton (N.J.) U., 1986—, dean Sch. Engring. and Applied Sci., 1986-91. Vis. asst. prof. UCLA, 1969—70; vis. prof. U. Hawaii, 1975, Tech. U. Darmstadt, Germany, 1979—80, U. Victoria, Canada, 1998, U. Tokyo, 1991—92; cons. prof. Stanford U., 1976; internat. prof. U. Libre de Bruxelles, Belgium, 1980; mem. computer sci. panel NRC, 1981—82; mem. adv. bd. Inst. Sys. Sci., Nat. U. Singapore, 1986—, Advanced Sys. Found., Vancouver, Canada, 1986—98; mem. adv. bd. dep. elec. engring. U. Pa., 1986—91; mem. sci. adv. com. Stanford Rsch. Inst. Internat., Menlo Park, Calif., 1986—91; sci. adv. bd. NASA, Washington, 1990—92; external examiners rev. bd. Ctr. Sys. Sci. Simon Fraser U., 1990—92; mem. Premier's Coun., Ont., Canada, 1990—91; bd. advisors Bower award and prize Franklin Inst., Phila., 1990—; bd. dirs. gov. Internat. Coun. Computer Comms., Washington, 1992—2005. Author: (book) Modeling and Analysis, 1978; assoc. editor: IEEE Trans Info. Theory, 1980—83, editor-in-chief: Performance Evaluation, 1981—86; contbr. articles to profl. jours. Recipient David Sarnoff RCA award, 1960, Invention award, IBM, 1971, 1973, Outstanding Contbn. award, 1975, 1984, Humboldt award, 1979, Silver Core award, IFIP, 1980, Edward Rhein Tech. award, 2005. Fellow: IEEE (life; chmn. Richard Hamming award 1990—91), Inst. Electronic, Info. and Comms. Engrs. Japan, Engring. Acad. Japan (Edward Rhein Tech. award 2005); mem.: Internat. Coun. Computer Comm. (gov. 1993—2005), Internat. Fedn. Info. Processing (chmn. working group 1982—86), Internat. Union Radio Sci. (vice chmn. commn. C 1978—81). Achievements include patents in field. Home: PO Box 384 New Brunswick NJ 08903-0384 Office: Princeton U B323 Engring Quadrangle Princeton NJ 08544-5263 Office Phone: 609-258-1984. Business E-Mail: hisashi@princeton.edu.

KOBAYASHI, NORITAKE, business educator; b. Tokyo, Feb. 23, 1932; s. Daijyo and Makiko (Tadokoro) K.; m. Mieko Mary Margaret Nishino, May 21, 1960; children: Norikazu, Sumiko, Kumiko. AB cum laude, Harvard U., 1953, postgrad., 1953-54; LLB, Keio U., Japan, 1954, PhD, 1973. Lectr. Keio U., 1956-62, assoc. prof. Yokohama, 1962-73, prof. Grad. Sch. Bus. Adminstrn., 1973-96, dir. sch. bus., 1980-83, dean Grad. Sch. Bus. Adminstrn., 1987-91, Mitsubishi chair, prof. Tokyo, 1991-96, prof. emeritus, 1996—; dean Shukutoku U. Coll. of Cross-Cultural Comm. and Bus., Saitama, 1996—2000, Shukutoku U. Grad. Sch. Internat. Bus. and Culture, 2000—02; prof. Shukutoku U., 2002—03. Vis. prof. Ind. U., Bloomington, 1968, Asian Inst. Mgmt., Philippines, 1970, Internat. Mgmt. Inst., Geneva, 1974, UCLA, Anderson Sch. Mgmt., L.A., 2004; bd. dirs. Mazda Motor Corp., 1980-96, Bosch Japan K.K. 1992—, Fuji Xerox Co., Ltd., 1999-2002, corp. auditor, Fuji Xerox Co., Ltd., 2002-03, adviser, 2003-04. Author: Joint Venture in Japan, 1967, The World of Japanese Business, 1969, International Business, 1972, Japanese Multinational Enterprises, 1980, Management, A Global Perspective, 1997. Trustee emeritus Brown U.; bd. dirs. Inst. for Internat. Studies and Training, 2005—. Recipient Mgmt. Sci. Pub. Prize Nihon Keiei Kyokai, 1981. Fellow Acad. Internat. Bus.; Workshop to Study Multinat. Enterprises (hon. pres.); mem. Comparative Law Assn. Japan, Mgmt. Assn. Japan, Am. Acad. Polit. and Social Sci., Japan-Am. Soc., Keio U. Alumni Assn., Tokyo-Am. Club, Harvard Club, Tokyo Club. Home: 2070 Stradella Rd Los Angeles CA 90001 also: 304 5-17-1 Higashi gotauda Shinagawa Tokyo 141-0022 Japan E-mail: n.kobayashi@alea.ne.jp.

KOBAYASHI, RIKI, retired chemical engineer, educator; b. Webster, Tex., May 13, 1924; s. Mitsutaro and Moto (Shigeta) K.; m. Barbara Joan Stevens, June 1, 1957; children: James Brock, Alec Stevens; m. Lee Mary Parker Lovejoy; children: Susan, Anne. BSChemE, Rice U., 1944; MS, U. Mich., 1947, PhD in Chem. Engring., 1951. Faculty dept. chem. engring. Rice U., Houston, 1951-94, Louis Calder prof., 1967-94, prof. emeritus, 1994—; ret. D.L. Katz disting. lectr. U. Mich., 1975; hon. chmn., honoree Symposia on Thermodynamics, Chromatography & Transport Phenomena, Am. Inst. Chem. Engrs. Spring Meeting, 1987; plenary lectr. Chemicon '89 Trivandrum, India; Lindsay disting. lectr. Tex. A&M U., 1985; cons. in field. Author: (with others) Handbook of Natural Gas Engineering, 1959; Contbr. over articles to profl. jours. Served with AUS, 1945-46. Recipient Meritorious award Cyrogenic Engring. Conf. Com., 1966, 1st Donald L. Katz award Gas Processors Assn., 1985, Outstanding Engring. Alumni award Rice U., 1985; Japan Soc. Promotion of Sci. fellow, 1985. Fellow AICE, Am. Inst. Chemists; mem. AIME, NAE, Am. Inst. Physics, Am. Chem. Soc., Japan Inst. Chem. Engring. (hon.), Nat. Acad. Engring., Sigma Xi, Alpha Chi Sigma, Tau Beta Pi, Phi Lambda Upsilon, Phi Kappa Phi. Unitarian Universalist. Achievements include co-invention of diffl. kinetics. Home: 348 Piney Point Rd Houston TX 77024-6506

KOBAYASHI, ROGER HIDEO, allergy and immunology educator, microbiologist, educator; b. Honolulu, May 21, 1947; s. Roy T. and Setsuko (Ebesugawa) K.; m. Ai Lan Doan, May 21, 1974; children: Lisa, Timothy. MS in Physiology, U. Hawaii, 1975; MD, U. Nebr., 1975. Diplomate Am. Bd. Allergy and Immunology, Am. Bd. Pediatrics, Nat. Bd. Med. Examiners. Asst. prof. pediatrics U. Nebr. Med. Ctr., Omaha, 1980-84, asst. prof. medical microbiology, 1980-85, dir. pediatric allergy and immunology, 1980-88, assoc. prof. pediatrics, 1984-88, assoc. prof. pathology and microbiology, 1985-88; assoc. prof. pediatrics UCLA, 1988-90, assoc. clin. prof. pediatrics, 1990-95, clin. prof. pediatrics, 1995—. Bd. dirs. Am. Lung Assn. Nebr., Asthma and Allergy Found. Am., Am. Lung Assn. Nebr.; cons. physician Children's Hosp., 1980—, Rare Antibody and Antigen Corp., Shanghai, ZLB Biologic Divsn., 1996—, Immune Deficiency Found., 1997—, Bayer Biologics, 2000—;mem. U. Nebr. Chancellor's Com. on Rural Health, 1982-88. Grantee Enzon Inc., 1986-88, Sandoz, Inc. 1986-87, 88-92, Schering Co. 1987-88, 90-93, NIH 1982, Mead-Johnson 1983-84, Fisons, Inc. 1990-92, Pfizer 1990-91, Rorer Pharm. 1993-97, Glaxo Inc., 1993-98, Genentech, 1994-96, Smith Kline Beecham, 1994-97, Miles Labs., 1995, Hoechst, 1995-96, McNiel, 1995, Muro, 1996—, Zeneca, 1996—, Bayer Pharm., 1996—. Fellow Am. Acad. Pediatrics (sec.-treas. Nebr. chpt. 1985-88), Am. Acad. Allergy and Immunology; mem. Nebr. Allergy Soc. (pres. 1981-84), Am. Fedn. Clin. Rsch., Am. Soc. Microbiology, Clin. Immunol. Soc. Avocations: fly fishing, wine collecting, tennis, golf. Home: 9942 Lafayette Ave Omaha NE 68114-2132

KOBAYASHI, SEIEI, English literature educator; b. Maebashi, Gunma, Japan, Nov. 22, 1941; s. Mokuhei and Shizuko (Yamada) K.; m. Chieko Ohto, Apr. 4, 1970; children: Shigehisa, Naoki. BA, U. Tokyo, 1965, MA, 1969. Lectr. Kyoritsu Women's Jr. Coll., Tokyo, 1970—74, asst. prof., 1974—80, Hosei U., Tokyo, 1980—81, prof., 1981—93; prof. English lit. Chuo U., Tokyo, 1994—; Vis. scholar U. Cambridge (Eng.), 2003. Author: An Essay on Shakespeare's History Plays, 1981; contbg. author: The Discourse of Vision-The Meeting Point of Popular Culture and Art (ed. Y. Midzunoe), 1994, Essays on World Modern Drama (ed. M. Osada), 1996, Celtic Illusion (ed. Y. Midzunoe), 1998, A Dictionary of English and American Drama, 1999, The Kenkyusha Dictionary of Shakespeare, 2000, New Phases of Modern Drama (ed. M. Osada), 2001, The Still Centre: Reading English Literature (ed. A. Kudo), 2001, The Discourse of English Literature-from Midieval Drama to Modern Poetry, 2004; co-editor: Kadokawa—Scott Foresman English-Japanese Dictionary, 1992; co-translator: Joseph Zsuffa, Béla Balázs The Man and Artist, 2000. Mem. English Lit. Soc. Japan, Shakespeare Soc. Japan, Renaissance Inst. Avocations: music, photography. Office: Chuo U Faculty Sci & Tech 1-13-27 Kasuga Bunkyo 112-0003 Japan

KOBAYASHI, SUSUMU, retired computer company executive; b. Kumamoto, Japan, Apr. 3, 1939; s. Senkichiro and Michiko Kobayashi. BS, Tokyo Inst. Tech., 1963. Programmer Osaka (Japan) Gas Co., Ltd., 1963-65, C. Itoh Computing Svcs. Co., Ltd., Tokyo, 1965-67; applications analyst, systems engr. Control Data Far East, Inc., Tokyo, 1967-75; asst. gen. mgr. systems dept. JMA Sys., Inc., Tokyo, 1975-79; dir. Nuc. Data Corp., Tokyo, 1979-89, Yokogawa Supertek Corp., Tokyo, 1989-90; tech. advisor sales divsn. Yokogawa Cray ELS Ltd., Tokyo, 1990-92; tech. advisor Cray Rsch. Japan Ltd., Tokyo, 1990-96; advisor Tsukuba Press Ltd., Tsukuba-shi, Japan, 1996-97; pres. Tera Computer Japan (now called Cray Japan, Inc.), Tokyo, 1997—2000, 2000—02, chief scientist Tsukuba-shi, 2002—04, rep., 2004—05; ret. Translator, editor: book Fortran 4 (D. D. McCracken), 1968, Lisp 1.5 Primer (C. Weissman), 1970, A Few Good Men from Univac (D. E. Lundstrom), 1992, The Official Computer Widow's (and Widower's) Handbook (by Experts on Computer Widow/Widowerhood), 1992, Future Computer Opportunities (Jack Dunning), 1993, Enabling Technologies for Petaflops Computing (T. Sterling, P. Messina, P. H. Smith), 1997, The Supermen (Charles J. Murray), 1998; contbr. articles to electronic mags. Mem.: IEEE, AIAA, Astron. Soc. Pacific, Am. Assn. Artificial Intelligence, Japan Info. Processing Soc., Japan Math. Soc., Assn. Computing Machinery. Avocations: motoring, audio/visual. Home: 85-2-206 Migawa 2-chome Mito Ibaraki 310-0912 Japan

KOBBEROE, BIRTHE, corporate financial executive, accountant; b. Copenhagen, June 17, 1937; arrived in U.S., 1983, permanent resident, 1996; d. Gustav Carl Andersen and Britta Madsen; m. John Kobberoe, Mar. 4, 1961; children: Michael, Lise. Student, Nelholt & Son, 1954—58; diploma, Copenhagen Trade Sch., Denmark, 1955; diploma in English, Berlitz Sch. Lang., 1956, U. Nev., Las Vegas, 1984. Acct. Hoffman & Sons, Copenhagen, 1958, Jens Pedersen Forwarder, Copenhagen, 1958—59, Nordic Antenna Man, Copenhagen, 1959—63; acct., CFO Ratel Radio, Copenhagen, 1963—83, Ratel Radio, Cons., Las Vegas, 1983—. Editor bi-monthly Danish Am. newspaper; pub. (CD with Poems), 2002; author: (book of poetry) A Lifetime of Poetry, 2003, The Silence Within, 2004, Diamond Pearls, 2004, Eternal Portraits, 2004, The Colors of Life, 2004, Invoking the Muse, 2005. Culture leader Scandinavian Club of Las Vegas, 1986—90. Recipient Nat. Libr. Poetry Editor's Choice award, 1997, 2001—03, Internat. Poet of Merit award, 2002, Congl. Order of Merit, 2003. Mem.: The Great Book Found., Nev. State Garden Club (environment chmn. 1988—90, auditor), Sunset Garden Club. Republican. Lutheran. Avocations: swimming, painting, writing books, poetry, piano. Home: 1995 Hallwood Dr Las Vegas NV 89119 E-mail: susdane@kobberoe.com.

KOBDISH, GEORGE CHARLES, lawyer; b. Casper, Wyo., June 30, 1950; s. Richard Matthew and Jo Earl (Uttz) K.; m. Mary Ellen Griffith, Jan. 24, 1969; children: George Charles, Jr., Kelly Rebecca, Kimberle Nelle. BBA with honors, U. Tex., 1971, JD, 1974. Bar: Tex. 1974, U.S. Dist. Ct. (no. dist.) Tex. 1975. Asst. atty. gen. State of Tex., Austin, 1974—76; assoc. McCall, Parkhurst & Horton LLP, Dallas, 1976—80, ptnr., 1981—. Bd. dirs. North Dallas Shared Ministries, 1993—2000, pres., 1996—98; lay gen. chairperson Cath. Cmty. Appeal, 2000—01; bd. dirs. Notre Dame of Dallas Schs, Inc., 2000—, pres., 2004—. Mem. Am. Coll. Bond Counsel, Nat. Assn. Bond Lawyers, Tex. Bar Assn., Dallas Bar Assn., Royal Oaks Country Club, Tower Club, Dallas Friday Group, Serra Internat. (Dallas bd. dirs., pres. 1998-99, U.S.A. coun., gov. Dist. 46, 2002-03), Phi Delta Theta. Roman Catholic. Home: 7147 Araglin Ct Dallas TX 75230-2097 Office: McCall Parkhurst & Horton LLP 717 N Harwood St Ste 900 Dallas TX 75201-6586 Office Phone: 214-754-9236. Business E-Mail: ckobdish@mphlegal.com.

KOBE, DONALD HOLM, physics professor; b. Seattle, Jan. 13, 1934; s. Kenneth Albert and Jeneva Katherine (Holm) K. BS, U. Tex., Austin, 1956; MS, U. Minn., 1959; PhD, 1961. Vis. asst. prof. Ohio State U., Columbus, 1961-63; rsch. assoc. Quantum Chemistry Group, Uppsala, Sweden, 1964-66; vis. asst. prof. H.C. Oersted Inst., Copenhagen, 1966-67; Northeastern U., Boston, 1967-68; prof. No. Tex. State U., Denton, 1968-88, U. North Tex., Denton, 1988—. Fulbright lectr., Taipei, Taiwan, 1963-64, Nat. Acad. Sci. lectr., Yugoslavia, 1973; Fulbright lectr./researcher São Paulo, Brazil, 1988-89. Contbr. articles to profl. jours. Fellow Am. Sci. Affiliation; mem. Am. Phys. Soc., Am. Assn. Physics Tchrs., Sigma Xi. Home: 1704 Highland Park Rd Denton TX 76205-6972 Office: Univ of North Tex Dept of Physics Denton TX 76203-1427 Office Phone: 940-565-3272. Business E-Mail: kobe@unt.edu.

KOBE, LAN, medical physicist; b. Semarang, Indonesia; naturalized; d. O.G. and L.N. (The) Kobe. BS in Physics, IKIP U., Bandung, Indonesia, 1964, MS in Physics, 1967; MS in Med. Physics and Biophysics, U. Calif., Berkeley, 1975. Physics instr. Sch. Engring. Tarumanegara U., Jakarta, Indonesia, 1968-72; rsch. fellow dept. radiation oncology U. Calif., San Francisco, 1975-77; clin. physicist in residence dept. radiation oncology UCLA, 1977-78, asst. hosp. radiation physicist, 1978-80, hosp. radiation physicist, 1980—. Instr. radiation oncology physics to resident physicians and med. physics grad. students. Contbr. articles to profl. jours. Newhouse grantee U. Calif., Berkeley, 1974-75, grantee dean grad. divsn. U. Calif., Berkeley, 1975; recipient Pres. Work Study award U. Calif., Berkeley, 1974-75, Outstanding Svc. award, 1986, Devel. Achievement award, 1988. Mem. Am. Soc. for Therapeutic Radiology and Oncology, Am. Assn. Physicists in Medicine (nat. and So. Calif. chpts.), Am. Bd. Radiology (cert.), Am. Assn. Individual Investors (life). Office: UCLA Dept Radiation Oncology Los Angeles CA 90095-6951

KOBER, ARLETTA REFSHAUGE (MRS. KAY L. KOBER), supervisor; b. Cedar Falls, Iowa, Oct. 31, 1919; d. Edward and Mary (Jensen) Refshauge; m. Kay Leonard Kober, Feb. 14, 1944; children: Kay Mary, Karilyn Eve. BA, State Coll. Iowa, 1940; MA, U. No. Iowa. Tchr. HS, Soldier, Iowa, 1943—50, 1965—67; coord. Office Edn. Waterloo (Iowa) Cmty. Schs., 1967—84; head dept. coop. career edn. West HS, Waterloo, 1974—84. Mem. Waterloo Sch. Health Coun.; mem. nominating com. YWCA, Waterloo; Black Hawk County chmn. Tb Christmas Seals; ward chmn. ARC, Waterloo; co-chmn. Citizen's Com. Sch. Bond Issue; pres. Waterloo PTA Coun., Waterloo Vis. Nursing Assn., 1956—62, 1982—, Kingsley Sch. PTA, 1959—60; v.p. Waterloo Women's Club, 1962—63, pres., 1963—64, trustee bd. clubhouse dirs., 1957—58; mem. Gen. Fedn. Women's Clubs, Nat. Congress Parents and Tchrs.; bd. dirs. United Svcs. Black Hawk County, Broadway Theatre League, St. Francis Hosp. Found., Black Hawk County Rep. Women, 1952—53; del. Iowa Rep. Convs., 1996, 1998; Presbyterial world svc. chmn. Presbyn. Women's Assn.; deacon Westminister Presbyn. Ch., 1995—98. Mem.: LWV (dir. Waterloo 1951—52), NEA, AAUW (v.p. Cedar Falls 1946—47), Black Hawk County Hist. Soc. (charter), Internat. Platform Assn., Town Club (dir.), P.E.O., Elklets, Dleta Kappa Gamma, Delta Pi Epsilon (v.p. 1966—67). Home: 3436 Augusta Cir Waterloo IA 50701-4608 Office: 503 W 4th St Waterloo IA 50701-1554

KOBETZ, RICHARD WILLIAM, criminologist, consultant; b. Chgo., Oct. 23, 1933; s. Nestor Joseph and Mary (Zurek) K.; m. Eleanore Marian Sever, Oct. 8, 1960 (div. Dec. 1995); children: Kevin, Kimberly and Candice (twins). AA, Chgo. City Jr. Coll., 1959; student, Ill. Tchrs. Coll., 1964-66; MS in Pub. Adminstrn., Ill. Inst. Tech., 1968; D of Pub. Adminstrn., Nova U., 1978. Diplomate Am. Bd. Forensic Examiners; cert. personal protection specialist. Police officer Winnetka (Ill.) Police Dept., 1954-55; from police officer to sgt. to lt. Chgo. Police Dept., 1955-68; asst. dir. Internat. Assn. Chiefs of Police, Washington, 1968-79; capt. Gretna (La.) Police Dept. Exec. dir., trainer, cons. Exec. Protection Inst., Berryville, Va., 1979—; dir., trainer, cons. North Mountain Pines Tng. Ctr., Winchester, Va., 1979—; security cons. numerous U.S. corps., 1979—; active various security and enforcement agys., 1979—; del. Interpol; spkr. UN, Vienna; cons. security Olympic Games Author: The Police Role and Juvenile Delinquency, 1971, Juvenile Justice Administration, 1973, Target Terrorism: Providing Protective Services, 1979, Providing Executive Protection, 1990, Vol. II, 1994; contbr. articles to profl. jours., chpts. to books. Acad. Security Educators and Trainers disting. fellow, 1987. Mem. Acad. Security Educators and Trainers (pres., v.p. 1982—), Internat. Assn. Chiefs of Police (Achievement award 1979), Am. Soc. Indsl. Security, Am. Soc. Criminology, Am. Soc. for Pub. Adminstrn. Clubs: Nine Lives Assocs. (Berryville) (exec. sec. 1978—). Republican. Roman Catholic. Avocations: shooting, camping, travel. Home and Office: Highlander Lodge 276 Journeys End Ln Bluemont VA 20135-1862 Office Phone: 540-554-2540. E-mail: rwk@crosslink.net.

KOBLER, JOHN F., priest, researcher; b. Chgo., June 16, 1925; s. Leo Peter Kobler and Ella O'Donnell. MA, St. Louis U., 1957. Ordained Passionists, Louisville, 1954; cert. tchr. h.s. Mo., 1957. Sem. lector in Latin and Greek Mother of Good Coun. Sem., Warrenton, Mo., 1956—65; tchr. Latin Bellarmine Coll., Louisville, 1965—67; superior Immaculate Conception monastery, Chgo., 1968—71, Immaculate Conception Monastery, Chgo., 1975—79; fund raiser CP missions, Birmingham, Ala., 1972—75, pres. Province Senate, 1973—76; rschr. Vatican II Chgo., 1979—. Tchr. med. ethics St. Mary's Infirmary, St. Louis, 1956—57, St. Mary's and Elizabeth Hosp., Louisville, 1966; cons. Nat. Method Inst., Charlottenburg, Denmark, 1963—67; chaplain Fort Leonard Wood, Whiteman AFB, Fort Knox; superior, founder province devel. office CP Monastery, Chgo., 1975—79; assoc. editor Soc. Justice Rev., St. Louis, 2001—; assoc. dir. Holy Cross Retreat House, Cin., 1971; mem. extraordinary chpt. acad. formation and fin. com. Senate of Holy Cross Province, 1969; trustee Cath. Theol. Union, Chgo., 1970—71. Author: Vatican II and Phenomenology, 1985, Vatican II, Theophany and Phenomenon of Man, 1991; contbr. more than 80 articles to profl. jours. here and abroad. Recipient Golden Heart award, Immaculate Conception Monastery, 1975. Mem.: Am. Cath. Philos. Assn., Soc. Cath. Social Scientists, Fellowship of Cath. Scholars, C.G. Jung Inst. of Chgo., Lumen Christi Inst. Cath. Faith, Thought and Culture, The Acton Inst. Study of Religion and Liberty, Cath. Hist. Soc., The Metaphysical Soc. Am. Achievements include research in use of a phenomenological style in Vatican II's reflection. Avocation: philosophy. Home and Office: Immaculate Conception Monastery 5700 N Harlem Ave Chicago IL 60631 E-mail: irenebh@juno.com.

KOBLIK, STEVEN S., academic administrator; Pres. Reed Coll., Portland, Oreg., 1992—2001, The Huntington Library, Art Collections, and Botanical Gardens, San Marino, Calif., 2002—. Office: Reed Coll Office Pres 3203 SE Woodstock Blvd Portland OR 97202-8199

KOBLUK, MICHAEL DANIEL, retired municipal official; b. Trail, B.C., Can., Dec. 10, 1937; came to U.S., 1956; BA, Gonzaga U., 1969. Owner Am. Theater Prodns., N.Y.C., 1965-69; dir. opera house and convention ctr. City of Spokane (Wash.), 1974-79; dir. entertainment facilities, 1979-2000; retired, 2000—. Dir. performing and visual arts Expo 74, Spokane, Wash., 1971-74. Entertainer The Chad Mitchell Trio, 1958-69; recs. include: An Evening with the Chad Mitchell Trio—Live at the Birchmere, The Chad Mitchell Trio, The Best of the Chad Mitchell Trio—The Mercury Years, Blowin' in the Wind, The Chad Mitchell Trio at the Bitter End, Mighty Day on Campus, The Very Best of the Chad Mitchell Trio, The Chad Mitchell Trio Collection—The Original Kapp Recordings; (with John Denver) Mighty Day—The Chad Mitchell Trio Reunion, The Chad Mitchell Trio Reunion...Part 2. Alumni dir. Gonzaga U., 1970-71. Recipient Disting. Svc. award State of Wash., 1974, Disting. Alumni award Gonzaga U., 1999; inductee Hall of Fame, Trail, 1999; named Profl. of Yr., Spokane Conv. and Visitors Bur., 1999, one of 80 Most Important and Influential People of Century for Spokane, spl. millenium edit. Inlander, 1999. Mem. Internat. Assn. Assembly Mgrs. (pres. 1990-91).

KOBRIN, LAWRENCE ALAN, lawyer; b. N.Y.C., Sept. 14, 1933; s. Irving and Hortense (Freezer) K.; m. Ruth E. Freedman, Mar. 5, 1967; children: Jeffrey, Rebecca, Debra. AB in History summa cum laude, Columbia U., 1954, JD, 1957. Bar: N.Y. 1957, U.S. Dist. Ct. (so. dist.) N.Y. 1958, U.S. Dist. Ct. (ea. dist.) 1958, U.S. Ct. Appeals (2d cir.) 1959, U.S. Supreme Ct. 1966. Assoc. Cahill, Gordon, Reindel & Ohl, N.Y.C., 1958-59, Arthur D. Emil, N.Y.C., 1959-63; ptnr. Emil & Kobrin, N.Y.C., 1963-79, Milgrim, Thomajan, Jacobs and Lee, N.Y.C., 1979-83, Cahill Gordon & Reindel LLP, N.Y.C., 1984—. Bd. dirs. Wurzweiler Sch. of Social Work, vice-chmn., 1994-98; dir. UMB Bank and Trust Co., 1978-91; treas. The Jewish Week, N.Y.C., 1992-96, chmn., 1996—. Notes editor Columbia U. Law Rev.; mng. editor Tradition, 1961-64, editl. com. 1964—; contbr. articles to profl. jours. V.p., assoc. treas., chmn. dist. com. Fedn. Jewish Philanthropies, N.Y.C., 1981-84, com. long range planning, 1985-86, com. inner city, 71-76; chmn. Ramaz Sch., N.Y.C., 1978-83; sec. to bd. Bar Ilan U., N.Y.C., 1972-80; pres. The Jewish Ctr., N.Y.C., 1987-90, N.Y.C. UJA-Fedn., chmn. communal planning com., 1988-91, chmn. com. on cmty. couns., 1996-98; v.p. Union Orthodox Jewish Congregations, 1968-74; chmn. campus com., 1962-66, chmn. Israel com., 1967-72, chmn. pub. com., 1972-78; pres. Massad Camps, 1971-77; bd. dirs. Am. Friends Pardes, 1991-96, Histadrut Ivrit., 1991-2003; pres. Ariel Am. Friends of Midrasha and United Instns., 1991-95, chmn., 1995-2001, Beth Din of Am., 1994-96, chmn. exec. com., 1997-02, exec. com. Orthodox Caucus, 1995—, bd., exec. com., Edah, 1994—; mem. exec. com. Columbia Barnard Hillel, 1995—. Kent scholar, 1954-55, Stone scholar, 1954-55. Mem. Nat. Assn. Coll. and Univ. Attorneys (1973-80), Am. Coll. Real Estate Lawyers. Home: 15 W 81st St New York NY 10024-6022 also: 8 Popple Swamp Rd Cornwall Bridge CT 06754-1135 Office Phone: 212-701-3337. Business E-Mail: lak56@columbia.edu, lkobrin@nysbar.org. E-mail: kobrinL@mindspring.com, Lkobrin@cahill.com.

KOBS, JAMES FRED, direct marketing consultant; b. Chgo., June 27, 1938; s. Fred Charles and Ann (Ganser) K.; m. Nadine Schumacher, May 18, 1963; children: Karen, Kathleen, Kenneth. BS in Journalism, U. Ill., 1960. Copywriter Rylander Co., Chgo., 1960-62; mng. dir. Success Mag., Chgo., 1963-65; mail order mgr. Am. Peoples Press, Westmont, Ill., 1966-67; exec. v.p. Stone & Adler Advt., Chgo., 1967-78; chmn. Kobs & Brady Advt., Inc.

(now Draft Direct Worldwide), Chgo., 1978-88; vice chmn. Kobs & Brady Advt., Inc. (now Draft Worldwide), Chgo., 1988; chmn. Kobs Gregory & Passavant, Chgo., 1989—2001; pres. Kobs Strategic Cons., Chgo., 2002—. Guest lectr. U. Wis., U. Ill., NYU; adj. prof. direct mktg. Northwestern U. Medill Sch. Journalism Grad. Program; instr. U. Chgo. Strategic Direct Mktg. Cert. Program; internat. lectr. in field. Author: Profitable Direct Marketing, 2d edit., 1991, 24 Ways to Improve Your Direct Mail Results, 99 Proven Direct Response Offers; contbr. articles to periodicals. Past chmn. Direct Mktg. Ednl. Found. Recipient numerous local and nat. advt. awards; named to Direct Mktg. Hall of Fame. Mem. Direct Mktg. Assn. (dir., sec., mem. exec. com., recipient Silver and Gold Mailbox, Gold Medallion, Gold Echo, Ed Mayer award), Chgo. Assn. Direct Mktg. (past pres., Direct Marketer of Yr.), Boys and Girls Clubs of Chgo. (corp. bd.), Alpha Delta Sigma. Office: Kobs Strategic Consulting 155 N Michigan Ave Chicago IL 60601

KOBUS, RICHARD LAWRENCE, architect, industrial designer; b. Chgo., Nov. 19, 1952; BS in Architecture, U. Ill., 1974; MArch, Harvard U., 1978. Registered architect, Mass., N.H., Maine, Ill., Pa., R.I., Ohio, N.J., Conn., Wash., Mo., N.Y., Vt. Designer Metz, Train, Olsen & Youngren, Chgo., 1974-75, Shepley, Bulfinch, Richardson & Abbott, Boston, 1978-79; assoc. Skidmore, Owings and Merrill, Boston, 1979-83; pres., prin., founder Tsoi/Kobus & Assocs., Inc., Cambridge, Mass., 1983—. Archtl. prin. healthcare acad., corp., and rsch. facilities U.S., Europe, Asia. Mem. permanent bldg. com. Town of Belmont, 1999—2003; bd. trustees Buckingham, Browne and Nichols, 1999—2005, Mass. Eye and Ear Infirmary, 1999—; pres. Major's Cove Assn., Edgartown, Mass., 1997—2001. Julia Amory Appleton fellow Harvard U., 1978-79; recipient Gov. Design award, 1986, Modern Healthcare Nat. Design award, 1988, 94, 98, AIA.Boston Soc. Architects Healthcare Assembly Design award, 1997, 98, 99, 2001, PCI Design award, 1995, 98, AIA Honor Design award, 1994, 97, 98, 99, Am. Sch. and Univ. Archtl. Portfolio award, 1989, 90, Small Bus. of Yr. award Greater Boston C. of C., 2000. Mem.: AIA (mem. Acad. on Arch. for Health 1997—, Healthcare Assembly Design award 1997, 1998, 1999, 2001), Soc. Campus and Univ. Planning, Urban Land Inst., Boston Soc. Archs. (sec. bd. dirs. 2000—01), Am. Coll. Healthcare Archs. (founding mem. and fellow), Nat. Assn. Indsl. and Office Parks. Avocations: sailing, rowing, photography, auto racing. Office: Tsoi/Kobus & Assocs Inc PO Box 9114 One Brattle Sq Cambridge MA 02238-9114 E-mail: rkobus@tka-architects.com.

KOBUSKIE, JOHN ARNOLD, retired elementary school educator, retired athletic director; b. Gloversville, N.Y., July 6, 1973; s. Joseph Kobuskie and Henrietta Walther; m. Irene McIntyre, Aug. 19, 1944 (dec. 1996). BS, SUNY, Cortland, 1948; M, SUNY, 1956. Phys. edn. tchr., coach Dodeville Ctrl., 1948; tchr. 7th grade spl. edn. Gloversville Pub. Schs., 1949—52, tchr. 6th grade, tchr. 7th grade math., 1952—55, tchr. phys. edn. grades 1-6, 1956—74, athletic dir., 1974—80. Founding mem. Big Bros., Gloversville, 1966—70. Named to Hall of Fame, Cortland Coll., 1974, Gloversville H.S., 2005. Mem.: Pinebrook Golf Club (course record holder 1970). Republican. Lutheran. Home: 142 Strawberry Hill Rd Gloversville NY 12078 Home (Winter): 11216 28th St Cir E Parrish FL 34219

KOBYLARSKI, REBECCA LEE, music educator; b. New Brunswick, NJ, July 5, 1960; d. Ruth and William Arthur Newman; m. William James Kobylarski, Sept. 17, 1989; children: Dana Ann, Jaclyn Page. AA, Brookdale C.C., 1979—80; BA, Stonybrook, 1980—83. Early Childhood Education Musikgarten/ NC, 2002. Adminstrv. asst. Skeets/ Briarcreek, New York, NY, 1983—84; salesperson Am. Office Equipment, Freehold, NJ, 1985; trade recorder NY Merc. Exch., NYC, 1986; trader asst. MBF Trading, Inc., NYC, 1986—90, commodities trader, 1989—90; music tchr. Adventure Bay Preschool, Boca Raton and Coconut Creek, Fla., 1995—97; pvt. classical piano instr. Jupiter, Fla., 1997—; pres., instr. of music and movement classes for young children and parents Baby Grand of Boca, Inc., Jupiter, Fla., 2002—; children's fitness instr. My Gym, Jupiter, Fla., 2004—. Mem. Nat. Guild of Piano Teachers, Austin, Tex., 2002—. D-Liberal. Jewish. Avocations: swimming, running, biking. Home: 114 Via Santa Cruz Jupiter FL 33458 Personal E-mail: kobylarski@bellsouth.net.

KOBZA, DENNIS JEROME, architect; b. Ullysses, Nebr., Sept. 30, 1933; s. Jerry Frank and Agnes Elizabeth (Lavicky) K.; m. Doris Mae Riemann, Dec. 26, 1953; children: Dennis Jerome, Diana Jill, David John. BS, Healds Archtl. Engring., 1959. Draftsman, designer B.L. Schroder, Palo Alto, Calif., 1959-60; sr. draftsman, designer Ned Abrams, Architect, Sunnyvale, Calif., 1960-61, Kenneth Elvin, Architect, Los Altos, Calif., 1961-62; ptnr. B.L. Schroder, Architect, Palo Alto, Calif., 1962-66; pvt. practice architecture Mountain View, Calif., 1966—. Served with USAF, 1952-56. Recipient Solar PAL award, Palo Alto, 1983, Mountain View Mayoral award, 1979. Mem. C. of C. (dir. 1977-79, Archtl. Excellence award Hayward chpt. 1985, Outstanding Indsl. Devel. award Sacramento chpt., 1980), AIA (chpt. dir. 1973), Constrn. Specifications Inst. (dir. 1967-68), Am. Inst. Plant Engrs., Nat. Fedn. Ind. Bus. Orgn., Rotary (dir. 1978-79, pres. 1986-87). Home: 3840 May Ct Palo Alto CA 94303-4545 Office: 2083 Old Middlefield Way Mountain View CA 94043-2465 Office Phone: 650-961-6103. Business E-Mail: dkarch@kobza.com. E-mail: dkobza@kobza.com.

KOC, LORRAINE K., lawyer; b. Gulfport, Miss., Jan. 29, 1958; BA magna cum laude, MA, Univ. Pa., 1979, JD, 1983. Bar: Pa. 1983. Gen. counsel Deb Shops, Inc., Phila., 1985—. Adj. faculty Pa. State Univ., Abington, 1989—. Mem.: Pa. Bar Assn., Nat. Assn. Women Lawyers (pres. 2005—), ABA, Soc. Human Resource Mgmt., Phila. Bar Assn. (Disting. Svc. award 1988). Office: Deb Shops Inc 9401 Bluegrass Rd Philadelphia PA 19114 Office Phone: 215-676-6000. Business E-Mail: lkoc@debshops.com.

KOCAOGLU, DUNDAR F., engineering management educator, industrial engineer, civil engineer; b. June 1, 1939; came to U.S., 1960; s. Irfan and Meliha (Uzay) K.; m. ALev Baysak, Oct. 17, 1968; 1 child, Timur. BSCE, Robert Coll., Istanbul, Turkey, 1960; MSCE, Lehigh U., 1962; MS in Indsl. Engring., U. Pitts., 1972; PhD in Ops. Rsch., 1976. Registered prof. engr., Pa., Oreg. Design engr. Modjeski & Masters, Harrisburg, Pa., 1962-64; ptnr. TEKSER Engring. Co., Istanbul, Turkey, 1966-69; project engr. United Engrs., Phila., 1964-71; rsch. asst. U. Pitts., 1972-74; vis. asst. prof., 1974-76; assoc. prof. indsl. engring., dir. engring. mgmt., 1976-87; prof., chmn. engring. and tech. mgmt. dept. Portland State U., 1987—. Pres., CEO TMA-Tech. Mgmt. Assocs., Portland, Oreg., 1973—; pres, CEO Portland Internat. Conf. Mgmt. Engring. and Tech., 1990—. Editor: Management of R&D and Engineering, 1992; co-editor: Technology Management-The New International Language, 1991, Innovation in Technology Management-The Key to Global Leadership, 1997, chnology and Innovation management, 1999, Technology Management in the Knowledge Era, 2001, Technology Management for Reshaping the World, 2003; series editor: Wiley Series in Engring. and Tech. Mgmt., 1984-98; contbr. articles on tech. mgmt. to more than 100 profl. jours. Lt. C.E., Turkish Army, 1966-68. Fellow IEEE (Centennial medal 1984, Millennium medal, 2000); editor-in-chief trans. on engring. mgmt. 1986—2002, Millennium medal, 2000); mem. Informs (chmn. Coll. Engring. Mgmt. 1979-81), Am. Soc. Engring. Edn. (chmn. engring. mgmt. div. 1982-83), IEEE Engring. Mgmt. Soc. (fellow, publs. dir. 1982-85), ASCE (mem. engring. mgmt. bd. govs. 1988-93), Muhendis, Ilim Adamlari ve Mimarlar Dernegi Soc. Turkish Engrs. and Scientists (hon.), Am. Soc. Engring. Mgmt. (dir. 1981-86), Omega Rho (pres. 1984-86). Office: Portland State U Engring & Tech Mgmt Program PO Box 751 Portland OR 97207-0751 Office Phone: 503-725-4660. Business E-Mail: kocaoglu@etm.pdx.edu.

KOCAREV, LJUPCO, engineering educator, researcher; b. Skopje, Macedonia, Feb. 25, 1955; s. Milco and Nadezda Kocarev; m. Radica Kocareva; children: Saso, Neda Kocareva. PhD, U. Kiril i Metodij, Macedonia, 1989. Prof. Grad. Sch., Faculty Elec. Engring., Skopje, Macedonia, 1990—2004; rsch. scientist UCSD, La Jolla, Calif., 2000—. Achievements include research in nonlinear systems and circuits, chaos theory, coding theory, cryptogrpahy, networking. Office: UCSD 9500 Gilman Dr La Jolla CA 92093-0402 Office Phone: 858-822-2011. E-mail: lkocarev@ucsd.edu.

KOCH, CHARLES DE GANAHL, industrial company executive; b. Wichita, Kans., Nov. 1, 1935; s. Fred Chase and Mary Clementine (Robinson) K. BS in Gen. Engring, MIT, 1957, MS in Mech. Engring., 1958, MS in Chem. Engring., 1959; DSc (hon.), George Mason U.; JD (hon.), Babson Coll.; PhD in Commerce (hon.), Washburn U. Engr. Arthur D. Little, Inc., Cambridge, Mass., 1959-61; v.p. Koch Engring. Co., Inc., Wichita, 1961-63, pres., 63-71, chmn., 1967-78; pres. Koch Industries, Inc., Wichita, 1966-74, chmn., CEO, 1967—. Bd. dirs. Intrust Bank, N.A., Mercatus Ctr. Chmn. Inst. Humane Studies, Claude R. Lambe Charitable Found., Charles G. Koch Charitable Found. Recipient Entrepreneurial Leadership award, Nat. Found. for Teaching Entrepreneurship, Adam Smith award, Am. Legislative Exchange Council, Brotherhood/Sisterhood award, Nat. Conference of Christians and Jews, Distinguished Citizen award, Boy Scouts of Am., Free Enterprise award, Council for Nat. Policy, Spirit of Justice award, Heritage Found., Director's award for global vision in energy, NY Mercantile Exchange, 1999, Nat. Distinguished Service award, Tax Found., 2000. Mem.: Flint Hills Nat., Mt. Pelerin Soc., The Vintage Club. Named one of World's Richest People by Forbes in 1999, 2000, 01, 02, 03, 04. Office: Koch Industries PO Box 2256 4111 E 37th St N Wichita KS 67220

KOCH, CHARLES JOHN, credit agency executive; Pres., COO, CEO Charter One Bank FSB, 1976—; pres. Charter One Fin. Inc., Cleve., First Fed. Savings Ball. Office: Charter One Fin Inc 1215 Superior Ave E Cleveland OH 44114-3249

KOCH, CRAIG R., automobile rental and leasing company executive; b. 1946; married BS, Lehigh U., 1968, MBA, 1971. Mktg. assoc. RCA Corp., 1971-72; mgr. fleet planning Hertz Corp., 1972-73, mgr. fleet ops. adminstrn., 1973-77, div. v.p. fleet ops. adminstrn., 1977-78; div. v.p. Hertz Europe Ltd., 1978-80; v.p. Rent-A-Car div. Hertz Corp., 1980-83, exec. v.p. Rent-A-Car div., 1983-87, pres., Rent-A-Car div., 1988—93, pres., COO, 1993—2000, CEO, 2000—. Office: Hertz Corp 225 Brae Blvd Park Ridge NJ 07656-1888

KOCH, DAVID HAMILTON, chemical company executive; b. Wichita, Kans., May 3, 1940; m. Julia Koch; children: David Jr., Mary Julia. BS in Chem. Engring., MIT, 1962, MS in Chem. Engring., 1963. Rsch. engr. and process design engr. Amicon Corp., Cambridge, 1963-64, Arthur D. Little, Inc., Cambridge, Mass., 1964-67, Halcon Internat., Inc., NYC, 1967-70, Scientific Design Comp. (affiliate of Halcon Internat., Inc.), NYC; with Koch Industries, Inc., Wichita, Kans., 1970—, exec. v.p., 1981—, also bd. dir.; chmn. bd. dir., CEO Chemical Technology Group, LLC, subsidiary Koch Industries, Inc. Bd. trustees NYU Med. Ctr., NYC, Meml. Sloan Kettering, NYC, House Ear Inst., LA, John Hopkins U., Prostate Cancer Found., LA; gov. NY Presbyterian Hosp., NYC, Deerfield Acad., Mass.; bd. dirs. Am. Mus. Natural History, NYC, Aspen Inst., Colo., Inst. Human Origins, Phoenix, Ariz, Rockefeller U., NYC, MIT (life mem. of corp.), Reason Found., Santa Monica, Calif., CATO Inst., Washington, DC; bd. overseers, WGBH, Channel 2, Boston; bd. visitor, M.D. Anderson Cancer Advisory Bd., Houston, Tex.; bd. assoc., Whitehead Inst., Cambridge, Mass.; bd. advisors John Hopkins Med. Ctr.; mem. chairman's coun. Metropolitan Mus. Art, NYC; mem. Libertarian Party Candidate for VP of US, 1980; vice-chmn., bd. dir Am. Ballet Theatremem; mem. Nat. Cancer Advisory Bd.; nat. dinner chmn. Rep. Governor's Assn., 1999; mem. James Madison Coun., Libr. Congress, Washington, DC. Named a honoree, NY Acad. Medicine's 10th Ann. Gala, 2004; named in honor David H. Koch Bldg., MIT; recipient Businessman of Yr., Manhattan Rep. Party, 2002, Corp. Citizenship award, Woodrow Wilson Internat. Ctr. for Scholars, 2004, Entrepreneurial Leadership award, Nat. Found. for Teaching Entrepreneurship. Mem. River Club (NY), Racquet & Tennis Club (NY), Explorers Club (NY), numerous others. Named one of World's Richest People by Forbes in 2001, 02, 03, 04. Address: Koch Industries, Inc 667 Madison Ave Fl 22D New York NY 10021-8029 Office: Koch Industries, Inc 4111 E 37th St N Wichita KS 67220 Office Phone: 212-319-1100, 316-828-5500.

KOCH, EDWARD IRVING, lawyer, former mayor; b. N.Y.C., Dec. 12, 1924; s. Louis and Joyce Koch Student, Coll. City N.Y.; LLB, NYU, 1948. Bar: N.Y. State 1949. Pvt. practice, N.Y.C., 1949-64; democratic dist. leader Greenwich Village, 1963-65; sr. partner firm Koch Lankenau Schwartz & Kovner, N.Y.C., 1965-69; mem. N.Y.C. Council, 1967-68, 91st-92nd Congresses from 17th Dist. N.Y., 1969-72, 93d-95th congresses from 18th Dist. N.Y., 1973-77, mem. appropriations com., sec. N.Y. Congl. del.; mayor N.Y.C., 1978-89; ptnr. Bryan Cave LLP, N.Y.C., 1990—. Author: Mayor, 1984, Politics, 1985, His Eminence and Hizzoner, 1989, All the Best, Letters from a Feisty Mayor, 1990, Citizen Koch, 1992, Ed Koch on Everything, 1994, Murder at City Hall, 1995, Murder on Broadway, 1996, Murder on 34th Street, 1997, The Senator Must Die, 1998, Giuliani Nasty Man, 1999, I'm Not Done Yet!, 1999, (with Pat Koch Thaler) Eddie, Harold's Little Brother, 2004. Served with AUS, World War II. Recipient: NY Fed. Bar Coun. Emory Buckner medal for Outstanding Pub. Svc., 2004 Office: Bryan Cave LLP 1290 Ave Americas Fl 33 New York NY 10104-3300 Business E-Mail: eikoch@bryancave.com.

KOCH, EDWIN ERNEST, artist, interior designer; b. Bronx, N.Y., Feb. 21, 1915; s. Henry Koch and Elsie Ziegenbalg. One-man shows include Mus. of Hudson Highlands, 1986; exhibited in group shows at Met. Mus. Art, 1952, Bklyn. Mus., 1953, Pa. Acad., 1953, NAD, 1958, Am. Watercolor Soc.; represented in permanent collections Butler Art Inst., Youngstown, Ohio. With AUS, 1942-46. Recipient Top Best in Show awrd Middle Town Art Soc., 1980's, Nat. Arts Club, 1989. Mem. Audubon Artists Am., Nat. Soc. Painters in Casein and Acrylic (bd. dirs. 1975-76), Painters and Sculptors Soc. N.J. (v.p. 1978), Knickerbocker Artists, Artists Equity. Home: 109 Old Hoagerburgh Rd Wallkill NY 12589-3430 E-mail: eek@frontier.net.

KOCH, GEORGE WILLIAM, lawyer; b. Cin., Apr. 8, 1926; s. George Earl and Lucille (Arnold) K.; m. Helen Lawton, July 29, 1950; children: Jorie, Danny, P.C., Bobby, Monte, Lucy. B.B.S, U. Cin., 1948, LL.B., JD, 1950. Bar: Ohio 1950. Asst. city atty., Cin., 1950-54; assoc. dir. Ohio Council Retail Merchants, Columbus, 1954-59; dir. fed. affairs Sears, Roebuck & Co., Washington, 1959-65; pres., chief exec. officer Grocery Mfrs. Am., Inc., Washington, 1966-90; ptnr. Kirkpatrick Lockhart, 1990—. Chmn. Congl. Charity Tennis Tournament, Congl. Charity Golf Tournament. Served with USNR, World War II. Mem. Nat. Press Club, Union League, City Tavern Club, Congl. Country Club, Greenbrier Golf and Tennis Club. Home: 10837 Stanmore Dr Potomac MD 20854-1521 Office: Kirkpatrick & Lockhart 1800 Massachusetts Ave NW Fl 2 Washington DC 20036-1806 Office Phone: 202-778-9110.

KOCH, JAMES VERCH, academic administrator, economist; b. Springfield, Ill., Oct. 7, 1942; s. Elmer O. and Wilma L. K.; m. Donna L. Stickling, Aug. 20, 1967; children: Elizabeth, Mark. BA, Ill. State U., 1964; PhD, Northwestern U., 1968. From asst. prof. to prof. econs. Ill. State U., 1967-78, chmn. dept., 1972-78; dean Faculty Arts and Scis., R.I. Coll., Providence, 1978-80; prof. econs., provost, v.p. acad. affairs Ball State U., Muncie, Ind., 1980-86; pres. U. Mont., Missoula, 1986-90, Old Dominion U., Norfolk, Va., 1990-2001, prof. econs., 2001—. Author: Industrial Organization and Prices, 2d edit, 1980, Microeconomic Theory and Applications, 1976, The Economics of Affirmative Action, 1976, Presidential Leadership, 1996, The Entrepreneurial President, 2003. Mem. Am. Econ. Assn. Lutheran. Office: Old Dominion U Dept Econs Norfolk VA 23529 Office Phone: 757-683-3458. Business E-Mail: jkoch@odu.edu. *Survival in the 21st century, whether in higher education or in automobile production, demands and requires quality. Excellence must be our goal in all that we undertake. This is an attitude that must be instilled in the home, in our schools, and throughout society so that it permeates our lives.*

KOCH, JANE ELLEN, secondary school educator; b. Evansville, Ind., Sept. 11, 1947; d. Mason Irwin and Mary Louise (Westfall) Price; m. Donald Lawrence Koch, Dec. 26, 1970; children: Christopher Evan, Darren Nicholas. BA in Edn., U. Evansville, 1970, MA in Edn., 1973. English tchr. Princeton (Ind.) Cmty. H.S., 1970-72, North Posey H.S., Poseyville, Ind., 1972-76; English tchr., libr. New Harmony (Ind.) Sch., 1989—. Roman Catholic. Avocations: reading, organ, piano. Home: 176 N Cale Poseyville IN 47633-0532 Office: New Harmony Sch 1000 E St New Harmony IN 47631 Office Phone: 812-682-4401. E-mail: kochj2@ccsi.tds.net, kochj@nharmony.k12.in.us.

KOCH, JESSICA BETH, music educator, director; b. Oak Lawn, Ill., June 11, 1981; d. Byron Leo and Linda Marie Yehling; m. Brendan Justin Koch, July 24, 2004. BA cum laude in Music, St. Xavier U., 2003. Asst. choir dir. Bethel Ref. Ch., Chgo., 2000—02; dir. of music St. Cajetan Parish, Chgo., 2002—04; dir. music ministries Our Lady of Brook Parish, Northbrook, Ill., 2005—. Freelance vocal coach, Ill., 1999—; freelance piano tchr., Chgo., 1999—. Tchr. religious edn. St. George Sch., Tinley Park, Ill., 2000—03. Named Honors Recital Performer, St. Xavier U., 2000; recipient Sr. Music award, Carl Sandburg H.S., 1999; grantee, VanderCook Coll. Music, 2005—; scholar, St. Xavier U., 1999—2003; Presdl. scholarship, 1999—2003, O'Donahue Piano scholarship, 1999—2003. Mem.: Nat. Pastoral Musicians, Music Educators Nat. Conf. (pres. chpt. 2002—03). Republican. Roman Catholic. Avocations: quilting, needlecrafts, pilates, cooking, baking. Office: Our Lady of the Brook Parish 3700 Dundee Road Northbrook IL 60062 Office Phone: 847-272-5686. Office Fax: 847-498-0899. E-mail: jkoch@olbparish.org.

KOCH, KATHERINE ROSE, communications executive; b. Pitts., Apr. 21, 1949; d. Irving Samuel Stapsy and Betty Ruth (Sachs) Blake; m. Stanley Christopher Brown, July 26, 1986; 1 child, Matthew. BFA, Rochester Inst. Tech., 1973. Instr. Ivy Sch. Profl. Art, Pitts., 1973-74; advt. dir. Buhl Optical Co., Pitts., 1974-77; pres., creative dir. Ambit Mktg. Comm., Ft. Lauderdale, Fla., 1977—. Instr. Point Park Coll., Pitts., 1977-78. Bd. dirs. United Way, Broward County, 1995—, Broward C.C. Found., 2002, Broward Coordinating Coun., 1994—, Broward Alliance, Ft. Lauderdale Mus. Art. Mem.: Tower Forum (bd. dirs. 1995—), Womens Exec. Club (pres. 1995—96). Office: Ambit Mktg Comm 2455 E Sunrise Blvd Ste 711 Fort Lauderdale FL 33304-3110

KOCH, KATHLEEN DAY, lawyer; b. St. Louis, Nov. 27, 1948; d. Edward J. and Margaret (Beckmeier) D.; children: Stefan, Martha, Rebecca. Student, Concordia Coll., River Forest, Ill., 1966-69; BS in Edn., U. Mo., 1971; JD, U. Chgo., 1977. Bar: Ill. 1977, D.C. 1978. Atty. HUD, Washington, 1977-79, U.S. Merit Sys. Protection Bd., Washington, 1979-84; sr. atty., personal law divsn. U.S. Dept. Commerce, Washington, 1984-87; assoc. counsel to pres. White House, Washington, 1987-88; gen. counsel Fed. Labor Rels. Authority, Washington, 1988-91; spl. counsel Office Spl. Counsel, Washington, 1991-97; chief OEEOA FBI, Washington, 1997—; dep. gen. coun., equal opportunity & adminstr. law U.S. Dept. Housing and Urban Development, Washington. Recipient Disting. Alumni award U. Mo., St. Louis, 1990. Office: US Dept Housing and Urban Develop Rm 10110 451 7th St SW Washington DC 20410-0001 Office Phone: 202-708-3250. Office Fax: 202-708-3389. Business E-Mail: kathleen_d._koch@hud.gov.

KOCH, KEVIN M., pharmacist, researcher; s. Mark William and Aileen (Leo) Koch; m. Kathleen R. Maloney, Aug. 31, 1986; 1 child, Mark M. PhD, U. Wash., 1985. Registered Pharmacist Wis., 1978. Clin. pharmacokineticist MerckSharpe&Dohme Rsch. Labs., West Point, Pa., 1985—88; asst. dir., clin. pharmacokinetics Glaxo Inc, Research Triangle Park, NC, 1988—95; sr. clin. pharmacokineticist GlaxoWellcome, Research Triangle Park, 1995—2000; dir., clin. pharmacokinetics GlaxoSmithKline, Research Triangle Park, 2000—. Mem.: Am. Assn. Pharm. Scientists.

KOCH, LYNN ARTHUR, music educator; b. Springville, NY, Apr. 30, 1954; s. Carl Henry and Letha Mary Koch; m. Deborah June Bergan Kenyon, July 22, 2000; children: Gavin Earl Kenyon, Amalia May Kenyon, Jessica Rue Kenyon, Gillian Mary, Devon Rathlyn. MusB, SUNY, Potsdam, 1976; MusM, Westminster Choir Coll., 1981. Vocal music tchr. Trenton City Schs., Trenton, NJ, 1982—87, Cincinnatus Ctrl. Sch., Cincinnatus, NY, 1987—. Performer of folk music KinderFolk Music Productions, Marathon, NY, 1983—; organist, choir dir. McGrawville Bapt. Ch., McGraw, NY, 1991—. Composer: (organ works) From Heaven Above, (organ work) Azmon, (choral work) Sometimes a Light Surprises, God of the Earth, the Sky, the Sea, The Summer Days are Come Again, O Lamb of God: Partite for Organ and Choir, (organ works) Handworks, (choral work) Morning Song; musician: (recording) Labor of Love, The Fox, Old Blue and Dinosaurs Too; author: (article) Old Time Herald; author: (compiler) (folk song collection) Folk Songs of Upstate New York; composer: (choral work) The Irish Blessing, (organ work) Passacaglia and Fugue in C Minor. Recipient ASCAPlus award, Am. Soc. of Composers, Authors and Publishers, 2004. Mem.: Am. Soc. of Composers, Authors and Publishers (ASCAPlus Award 2004), Music Educators Nat. Conf. Home: 1875 E Freetown Rd Marathon NY 13803 Office: KinderFolk Music Productions 1875 E Freetown Rd Marathon NY 13803 Office Phone: 607-849-3435. Personal E-mail: lynndeborahk2@aol.com.

KOCH, MARGARET RAU, writer, artist, historian; b. Sacramento; d. George James Rau and Callista Marie Martin; children: Edward James, Kathleen, Thomas C. Student, U. Calif., Berkeley, 1936-38. Mem. editl. staff Santa Cruz (Calif.) Sentinel, 1958-76. Author: Santa Cruz County, Parade of the Past, 1973, 74, 77, 81, 91, 99, They Called It Home, 1974, Walk Around Santa Cruz, 1978, Going To School in Santa Cruz County, 1978, The Pasatiempo Story, 1990, Santa Cat-Behind the Lace Curtains, 2001; exhibited in group shows at Sedona Arts Ctr., Yavapai County Arts Fair, Ft. Verde Art Show, 1997, 98, 99, 2000. Organizer, first pres. Santa Cruz Hist. Soc. Recipient 3 Mixed Media Watercolor awards Yavapai County Art Fair, Ariz., 2 Watercolor awards Fort Verde Art Show, Ariz. Mem. No. Ariz. Watercolo Soc., Pen Women, Santa Cruz Art League, Sedona Art Ctr. Home: 2307 Town Center Dr Klamath Falls OR 97601-7142

KOCH, PAUL CHARLES, academic administrator, psychology professor; b. Springfield, Mass., Sept. 3, 1958; s. Richard Charles and Lois Jean K.; m. sherree Beth Boysen, Mar. 10, 1979; children: Melinda, Andrew, Kristin. BS, Morningside Coll., 1983; MS, Iowa State U., 1985, PhD, 1987. Prof. psychology St. Ambrose U., Davenport, Iowa, 1988—, dean arts and scis., 1998—. ILI grantee NSF, 1990-92. Mem. Am. Psychol. Assn., Midwestern Psychol. Assn., Rotary Club, Phi Eta Sigma, Psi Chi, Phi Kappa Phi. Office: St Ambrose U 518 W Locust St Davenport IA 52803

KOCH, PHILIP FREDERICK, artist; b. Rochester, N.Y., Mar. 30, 1948; s. George Julian Koch and Elizabeth (Capstaff) Koch Bellins; m. Alice Jonas, May 8, 1982; 1 child, Susan; 1 stepchild, Louisa Jonas. BA cum laude, Oberlin Coll., 1970; MFA, Ind. U., 1972. Instr. painting Cen. Wash. State Coll., Ellensburg, 1972-73, Md. Inst. Coll. of Art, Balt., 1973—. One-man shows include Univ. Md., 2004, Cape Mus. Fine Art, Mass., 2003, Earlham Coll., Ind., 2002, Rahr West Art Mus., Manitowoc, Wis., 1999, Lyon Weir Gallery, Chgo., 1999, Blanden Meml. Art Mus., 1998, Saginaw Art Mus., Mich., 1997, Washington County Mus. of Fine Arts, Md., 1995, Midwest Mus. of Am. Art, Ind., 1995, Butler Inst. of Am. Art, Salem, Ohio, 1995, Swope Art Mus., Ind., 1995, 2001, Cedar Rapids (Iowa) Mus. of Art, 1994, Payne Gallery Moravian Coll. Bethlehem, Pa., 1990, Sazama Gallery, Chgo., 1991, Meredith Long & Co., Houston, 1984, 86, 88, 92, C. Grimaldis Gallery, Balt., 1981, 83, Jane Haslem Gallery, Washington, 1989, 91, Alpers Fine Art, Andover, Mass., 2004, Berkshire Mus., Pittsfield, mass., 2005. Recipient Mellon grantee, 1984, Ford grantee, 1979. Office Phone: 410-486-2161. E-mail: info@philipkoch.com.

KOCH, ROBERT CHARLES, lawyer, community activist; b. Berwyn, Ill., Apr. 7, 1947; s. Eugene William and Ellen Marie (Hudec) K.; m. Sharon Smith, June 27, 1970; children: Jason, Ryan, Lindsay. BS, Ill. Inst. Tech., 1969; JD, Coll. William and Mary, 1972. Bar: Ill. 1972, Okla. 1978, N.Y. 2003, Fla. 2003. Assoc. Bell, Boyd & Lloyd, Chgo., 1972-78; staff atty. Phillips Petroleum Co., Bartlesville, Okla., 1978-81, sr. atty., 1986-90, sr.

counsel, 1990—2002; counsel Phillips Petroleum Co. Europe & Africa, London, 1981-86; mng.ptnr. Koch Law Office, 2002—. Author of Sunday sch. curriculums. Chmn. Washington County Dem. Party, Bartlesville, 1993-97; pres., dir. Westside Cmty. Assn., Bartlesville, 1997—2002. Mem.: ATLA, ABA, Okla. Bar Assn., N.Y. State Bar Assn., Fla. Bar, Am. Legion. Democrat. Presbyterian. Avocations: church youth ministry, travel. Home: 839 Berkeley St Boca Raton FL 33487 Office: 7401 N Federal Hwy Boca Raton FL 33487 Mailing: PO Box 81041 Boca Raton FL 33481-0841 E-mail: BobKoch@KochLawOffice.com.

KOCH, ROBERT LOUIS, II, manufacturing company executive, mechanical engineer; b. Evansville, Ind., Jan. 6, 1939; s. Robert Louis and Mary L. (Bray) K.; m. Cynthia Ross, Oct. 17, 1964; children: David, Kevin, Kristen, Jennifer. BSME, U. Notre Dame, 1960; MBA, U. Pitts., 1962; D of Tech. (hon.), Vincennes U., 1992. Registered profl. engr., Ind. V.p. Ashdee Corp., Evansville, 1962-68, pres., 1968-82; ptnr. Fesk Partnership, Evansville, 1964—; chmn., CEO Gibbs Die Casting Corp., Henderson, Ky., 1976—; pres., CEO Koch Enterprises, Inc., Evansville, 1982—; chmn., dir. UNISEAL, Inc., Evansville, 1984—; v.p., dir. Brake Supply Co., Evansville, 1986—; chmn. bd. Marco Sales, Inc., St. Louis, 1997—. Exec. in residence U. So. Ind., Evansville, 1967; bd. dirs. Fifth-Third Bacnorp, Cincinnati, Ohio, Bindley Western Industries, Indpls., So. Ind. Properties, Inc., Evansville, So. Ind. Minerals, Inc., N.Am. Green, Inc., Audubon Metals LLC, Vectren Corp.; chmn. bd. dirs. Uniseal Rubber Products, Inc., Arnold, Mo., 1988-95. Inventor, patentee water purifier, drying oven, powder coating booth, electro painting system. Contr., dep. mayor City of Evansville, 1976-80; active Gov.'s Fiscal Policy Adv. Com., Indpls., 1978-89, Pres. Adv. Coun. Indiana Univ., 1992—, Purdue U., 1992—, parents exec. com., West Lafayette, 1985-88, sch. bd. nominating com., 1987-89; vice-chmn. bd. trustees U. Evansville, 1985-92, chmn. bd. trustees, 1993-96; pres. Signature Learning Ctr. Inc., Evansville, 1994—; vice-chmn. bd. trustees Evansville Mus. Arts and Scis., 1982-92; bd. dirs. SW Ind. Pub. Broadcasting, 1985-89, Pub. Edn. Found., Evansville, 1986-88, Hoosiers for Higher Edn., 1991-98, Commit, Inc., Cmty. Alliance Found., 1991—, Ind. Colls. Ind., 1992—, Found. for Ind. Higher Edn., 1996—, Project E, 2000; treas. Vanderburgh County Rep. Com., Evansville, 1984-88; pres. Cath. Edn. Found., Evansville, 1978-82; chmn. Ind. Econ. Devel. Coun., 1991-92, Ind. Humanities Coun. Bus. Forum, 1999, United Way of Southwestern Ind. Campaign, 1998; co-chmn. Ind. Bus. Higher Edn. Forum, 1991-96; pres. Cath. Found. Southwestern Ind., 1992—; v.p. Ind. Acad., Indpls., 1999--; pres. Evansville Regional Bus. Com., 2002--. 1st lt. USAR, 1961-67. Recipient Challenger award Nat. Assn. Woodworking Machinery Mfrs., Louisville, 1980, Boy Scout's Disting. Citizen's award, 1991, Rotary Club Citizenship award, 1991, Sagamore of the Wabash, 1999; named Exec. of Yr. Profl. Secs. Assn., 1984, Knight of the Order of the Holy Sepulchre, 1996, Entrepreneur of Yr., Ind. Mfg., 1998, Ind. Bus. Leader of Yr. Ind. C. of C., 2002. Mem. Metro Evansville C. of C. (bd. dirs. Met. 1983-96, named Bus. Person of Yr. 1998), Ind. C. of C. (bd. dirs., chmn. 1991—), Young Pres. Orgn., World Pres. Orgn., Evansville Country Club, Victoria Nat. Golf Club. Avocations: golf, tennis, skiing. Office: Koch Enterprises Inc 10 S 11th Ave Evansville IN 47744-0001

KOCH, ROBERT MICHAEL, research scientist, consultant, educator; b. Mineola, N.Y., Apr. 19, 1964; s. Roy Arthur and Ellen Anne (Trimble) K.; m. Laureen Theresa Chase, July 6, 1991. BSME, Poly. U., Bklyn., 1986, PhD in Applied Mechanics, 1991. Profl. engr., R.I. Mech. engr. Vernitech Corp., Deer Park, N.Y., 1983-85; instr. Poly. U., Bklyn., 1986-91; chief rsch. scientist Naval Undersea Warfare Ctr., Newport, RI, 1991—. Cons. Beltran, Inc., Bklyn., 1988-91; adj. prof. Roger Williams U., Bristol, R.I., 1993—. Teaching fellow Poly. U., 1986-90, rsch. fellow, 1987, 90, Fed. Engr. of Yr. NSPE, 2005. Mem. AIAA, ASME, Acoustical Soc. Am., N.Y. Acad. Scis., Sigma Xi. Republican. Roman Catholic. Achievements include research in undersea propulsion, underwater shock analysis, underwater structural acoustics, adaptive procedures in h-and p-version finite element analysis, rapid prototyping with stereolithography, probabilistic structural mechanics, ultrasonic wave propagation in elastic solids. Home: 304 White Horn Dr South Kingstown RI 02881-1829 Office: Naval Undersea Warfare Ctr Code 8232 Bldg 1302 Newport RI 02841-0001

KOCH, SEBASTIAN, neurologist; b. Kinshasa, Democratic Republic of Congo, Oct. 31, 1966; s. Benno and Ebba Koch; m. Peangchai Magner, Jan. 25, 2000; children: Maia, Lukas. MD, Wake Forrest Sch. of Medicine, 1993. Lic. Am. Bd. Medicine and Psychiatry, 1997. Asst. prof. neurology U. Miami, Sch. of Medicine, Fla., 1999—. Rsch. grant, Dana Found., 2002-2004. Office: U Miami Sch Medicine 1150 NW 14th St Miami FL 33136 Office Phone: 305-243-6733. Office Fax: 305-243-7615. E-mail: skoch@med.miami.edu.

KOCH, STEPHEN BAYARD, writer, language educator; b. St. Paul, May 8, 1941; s. Robert Fulton and Edith (Bayard) K.; m. Frances Bernard Cohen, Apr. 25, 1987. BA, CCNY, 1962; MA, Columbia U., 1963, postgrad., 1963-66. Instr. English dept. SUNY, Stony Brook, 1965-70; adj. prof. Columbia U., N.Y.C., 1978-89, acting chmn., then chmn. writing div. Sch. Arts, 1989—98. Lectr. creative writing program Princeton (N.J.) U., 1979-86. Author: Night Watch, 1970, Stargazer: Andy Warhol's World and His Films, 1973, 3d edit., 1991, The Bachelors' Bride, 1986, Double Lives, 1994, The Modern Library Writer's Workshop: A Guide to the Craft of Fiction, 2003, The Breaking Point: Hemingway, Dos Passos, and the Murder of Jose Robles, 2005; contbr. articles to numerous publs. Democrat. Episcopalian. Address: 1100 Madison Ave New York NY 10028 Office Phone: 212-249-7199. Personal E-mail: stephenkock41@msn.com.

KOCH, STEVEN, lawyer, investment banker, finance company executive; b. Evanston, Ill., Feb. 9, 1956; s. David and Sylvia (Kurtzon) K.; m. Ellen Liebman, May 17, 1986. BA, Hampshire Coll., Amherst, Mass., 1977; MBA, JD, U. Chgo., 1982. Bar: Ill. 1982. Law clk. to judge U.S. Ct. Appeals (7th cir.), 1982—83; assoc. Lehman Bros. Kuhn Loeb, N.Y.C., 1983—85; joined First Boston (now Credit Suisse First Boston), 1985, mng. dir., 1989—93, co-head mergers and acquisitions group, 1993—2000, co-chmn. mergers and acquisitions group, 2000—; vice chmn. Credit Suisse First Boston, 2000—. Bd. mem. Mount Sinai Hosp. Med. Ctr., Chgo., Greater Chgo. Food Depository, NYC2012. Office: Credit Suisse First Boston 227 W Monroe St Chicago IL 60606-5016 Office Phone: 312-750-3000. E-mail: Steven.Koch@csfb.com.

KOCH, TAD HARBISON, chemistry professor, researcher; b. Mount Vernon, Ohio, Jan. 1, 1943; s. Justin Louis and Mary Fosdick (Grove) K.; m. Carol Ann Kuban, May 28, 1976 BS, Ohio State U., 1964; PhD, Iowa State U., 1968. Asst. prof. chemistry U. Colo., Boulder, 1968-74, assoc. prof., 1974-82, prof., 1982—, chmn. dept. chemistry and biochemistry, 1983-86; fellow U. Colo. Cancer Ctr., 1997—; mem. grad. sch. faculty Sch. Pharmacy, U. Colo. Health Scis. Ctr., 1999—. Contbr. numerous articles to profl. jours.; patentee in field Grantee U.S. Army Med. Comd., 1998, 2001, NSF, 1985, 89, 92, NIH, 1985, 87, 93, 98, 2001, Coun. Tobacco Rsch., 1992, 96, Petroleum Rsch. Fund, 1997, Am. Cancer Soc., 1997. Mem. AAAS, Am. Chem. Soc., Am. Assn. Cancer Rsch., Am. Soc. Photobiology. Office: U Colo 215 UCB Boulder CO 80309-0215 E-mail: tad.koch@colorado.edu.

KOCH, THOMAS FREDERICK, lawyer; b. Hackensack, NJ, Nov. 24, 1942; s. Elmer J. and Evelyn (Zombeck) K.; m. Sally J. Tucker, June 6, 1970; children: Christine E., Donald T. AB, Middlebury Coll., 1964; JD, U. Chgo., 1967. Bar: Vt. 1967, U.S. Dist. Ct. Vt. 1971. Assoc. firm Free and Bernasconi, Barre, Vt., 1970-74; ptnr. Bernasconi & Koch, Barre, 1974—. Mem. jud. nominating bd. State of Vt., 1979-81; mem. Vt. Ho. of Reps., 1977-80, 97—, mem. mcpl. corps and elections, judiciary, house rules and joint rules coms. health and welfare, chmn., 2001-04, human svcs. com., joint com. on health access oversight, chair, 2004; moderator Town of Barre, 1984-; chmn. Vt. Rep. Platform com. 1984. Del. nat. convs. of Assn. of Evang. Luth. Chs., 1978, 84, 86; del. to constrn. conv. of Evang. Luth. Ch. in Am., 1987-94; mem. churchwide assemblies, 1991, 97, 99; mem. New Eng. synod coun. Evang. Luth. Ch. Am., 1987-94; mem. churchwide assemblies, 1991, 97; scoutmaster Boy Scouts Am., Barre, 1989-93, dist. chmn. 1993-96, 98-2000; mem. exec. bd. Green Mountain Coun., 1997—, v.p. for dist. ops., 2002-03, v.p. for adminstrn., 2004—. Mem. Vt. Bar Assn., Washington County Bar Assn., Barre Lions Club (pres. 1977-78). Republican. Home: 326 Lowery Rd Barre VT 05641-9090 Office: 101 N Main St PO Box 892 Barre VT 05641-0892 E-mail: tfklaw@sover.net.

KOCH, WILLIAM ALBERT, JR., theme park manager; b. Huntingburg, Ind., Oct. 22, 1961; s. William Albert and Patricia Ann (Yellig) K.; m. Lori Ann Morris, May 18, 1985; children: Lauren Rosalee, Leah Clarice, William A. Koch III. BSEE, U. Notre Dame, 1984; MS in Computer Sci., U. So. Calif., L.A., 1986. Mem. tech. staff TRW Electronics & Def., Redondo Beach, Calif., 1984-86; pres., gen. mgr. Holiday World Theme Park, Santa Claus, Ind., 1987—. Mem. Ind. State Bldg. Commn., 1997—; chmn. tourism task force Lincolnland Econ. Devel. Corp. Mem. Tau Beta Pi, Optimist. Republican. Avocations: photography, computers, golf. Home: 27 Balthazar PO Box 356 Santa Claus IN 47579-0356 Office: Holiday World Highway 162 # 36 Santa Claus IN 47579

KOCHAN, THOMAS A., business educator; b. Manitowoc, Wis., Sept. 28, 1947; s. Leo H. and Loretta M. K.; m. Kathryn A. Otis, Aug. 23, 1969; chldren: Andrew, Sarah, Samuel, Jacob, Benjamin. PhD, U. Wisc., 1973; hon. degree, U. San Martin de Porres, 1999. Asst./asoc. prof. Cornell U., Ithaca, N.Y., 1973-80; prof. MIT Sloan Sch. Mgmt., Cambridge, Mass., 1980—. Arbitrator Am. Arbitration Assn., Boston. Author: The Transformation of American Industrial Relations, 1986 (award Best Book on Mgmt. 1988), The Changing Nature of Work, 2000 (award Nat. Acad. Scis. Com. Report), Restoring the American Dream, 2005; editor: Perspectives on Work mag., 1997. Advisor AFL-CIO, Washington, 1983-88, Fed. Mediation and Conciliation Svc., Washington, 1993—; commn. mem. Nat. commn. on the Future of Worker Mgmt. Rels., Washington, 1993-95; cons. U.S. Sec. Labor, Washington, 1979-80. Recipient Cushing Gavin award Labor Guild of the Archdiocese of Boston, 1998. Mem. Indsl. Rels. Rsch. Assn. (pres. 1999-2000), Soc. Profls. Dispute Resolution (task force chair on workplace 1999, Bill Abner award 1974), Internat. Indsl. Rels. Assn. (pres. 1992-95), Nat. Acad. Human Resources. Democrat. Roman Catholic. Avocations: travel, reading. Office: MIT Sloan Sch Mgmt 50 Memorial Dr Cambridge MA 02142 Office Fax: 617 253 7696. E-mail: tkochan@mit.edu.

KOCHANEK, PATRICK MICHAEL, pediatrician, educator; b. Detroit, July 1, 1954; s. Julius E. and Stella A. (Mrowiec) K.; m. Denise Marie Kochanek; children: Ashley, Stanton, Jillian. BS, U. Mich., 1976; MD, U. Chgo., 1980. Intern, then resident U. Calif., San Diego, 1980-83; fellow pediatric critical care medicine Children's Hosp. Nat. Med. Ctr., Washington, 1983-86; guest scientist Naval Med. Rsch. Inst., Bethesda, Md., 1983-86; from asst. prof. to prof. U. Pitts., 1986—2002, prof., 2002—, dir. Safar Ctr. for Resuscitation Rsch., 1994—; dir. pediatric critical care medicine rsch. Children's Hosp. Pitts., 1992—. Editor in chief Pediatric Critical Care Medicine, 2000—. Recipient Investigator award Soc. Critical Care Medicine, 1994—. Office: Safar Ctr Resuscitation Rsch 3434 5th Ave Pittsburgh PA 15260 Office Phone: 412-383-1900. Business E-Mail: kochanekpm@ccm.upmc.edu.

KOCHANSKI, LOIS WHIDDEN, foundation administrator; b. San Angelo, Tex., Aug. 21, 1923; d. James Edgar and Bessie Mae (Mullican) Whidden; m. Joseph Thaddeus Kochanski, Jan. 21, 1949; children: Mary Ann Daly, James T., Constance Wetterer. BA, U. Tex., 1945. Intelligence analyst U.S. Office of Naval Intelligence, Arlington, Va., 1960-64; asst. to v.p. for acad. affairs George Washington U., Washington, 1964-67; exec. dir. Found. for Advanced Edn. in Scis., Bethesda, Md., 1970—. Author: The Mullican Family of Warren County, Tennessee, 1991 Mem. AAUW, NIH Camera Club, Soc. of Mayflower Descendants. Avocations: photography, piano, genealogy, bridge, swimming. Home: 5301 Westpath Way Bethesda MD 20816-2212

KOCHAR, MAHENDR SINGH, physician, educator, health facility administrator, writer, research scientist, consultant; b. Jabalpur, India, Nov. 30, 1943; arrived in U.S., 1967, naturalized, 1978; s. Harnam Singh and Chanan Kaur Kochar; m. Arvind Kaur, 1968; children: Baltej (Baj), Ajay (Jay). MB, BS, All India Inst. Med. Scis., New Delhi, 1965; MSc, Med. Coll. Wis., 1972; MBA, U. Wis., Milw., 1987. Diplomate Am. Bd. Internal Medicine, Nephrology and Geriat., Am. Bd. Family Practice, Am. Bd. Mgmt., Am. Bd. Clin. Pharmacology. Intern All India Inst. Med. Scis. Hosp., New Delhi, 1966—67, Passaic Gen. Hosp., NJ, 1967—68; resident medicine Allegheny Gen. Hosp., Pitts., 1968—70; fellow clin. pharmacology Milw. VA Med. Ctr., 1970—71, attending physician, 1973; fellow nephrology and hypertension Milw. County Gen. Hosp., 1971—73, attending physician, 1973—95, St. Michael Hosp., Milw., 1974—, dir. hemodialysis unit, 1975—80; clin. asst. prof. medicine and pharmacology and toxicology Med. Coll. Wis., Milw., 1973—75, asst. prof., 1975—78, assoc. prof., 1978—84, prof., 1984—, assoc. dean continuing med. edn., 1985—86, assoc. dean grad. med. edn., 1987—99, sr. assoc. dean acad. affairs, 1994—95, sr. assoc. dean grad. med. edn., 1999—. Attending physician St. Joseph's Hosp., Milw., 1975—; chmn. medicine Northpoint Med. Group, Milw., 1974-75; dir. Milw. Blood Pressure Program, 1975-78; dir. Hypertension Clinic, Milwaukee County Downtown Med. and Health Services, 1975-79; chief hypertension. VA Med. Ctr., Milw., 1978-2000, assoc. chief staff for edn., 1979-2000; exec. dir. Med. Coll. Wis. Affiliated Hosps. Inc., Milw., 1987—. Author: Hypertension Control, 1978, 2nd rev. edit., 1985; editor: Textbook of General Medicine, 1983, Concise Textbook of Medicine, 2d edit., 1990, 3d edit. 1998, 4th edit., 2003. Recipient Grad. of Last Decade award U. Wis., Milw., 1998, Disting. Alumnus award, 2004. Fellow ACP (pres., gov. Wis. chpt. 1994-98, bd. regents 1997-2003, chmn. bd. govs. 1998-99, Laureate award 2000, Key Contact award 2001, master 2004), Am. Coll. Cardiology (gov. dept. vets. affair, 1999-2000), Am. Acad. Family Physicians, Royal Coll. Physicians Can., Am. Coll. Clin. Pharmacology, Am. Heart Assn. (high blood pressure coun.), Royal Coll. Physicians (London), Am. Coll. Physician Execs.; mem. AMA (del. Wis., mem. coun. on med. edn. 2005—), Am. Assn. Physicians from India (pres. Wis. chpt. 1995-97, Most Disting. Physician award 2004), Am. Fedn. Med. Rsch., Milw. Acad. Medicine (pres. 1996-97, trustee 1997-2003, pres.'s award 1998), Milwaukee County Med. Soc. (bd. dirs. 2000-2002, pres. elect 2002-03, pres. 2003, Disting. Svc. award 2005), Wis. Med. Soc. (dels. AMA, bd. dirs., Disting. Svc. award 2001), Soc. Tchg. Scholars. Office: Med Coll Wis 8701 Watertown Plank Rd Milwaukee WI 53226

KOCHER, CYNTHIA, investment specialist; b. Lompoc, Calif., May 6, 1954; d. John Wayland and Marjorie (Bartle) K. BA in Asian Studies, U. Oreg., 1976; MBA in Internat. Mgmt., Am. Grad. Sch. Internat. Mgmt., 1978; MBA in Fin. Planning, City U., 2002. CFP. Comml. asst., mgr. Far East imports Barber S.S. Lines, N.Y.C., 1978-80; asst. sec. internat. cash mgmt. Mfrs. Hanover Trust Co., N.Y.C., 1980-84; sales staff Century 21-Gordon Agy., 1984-86; broker, salesperson Forest Hill Realty, Newark, 1986-90; owner, operator Oregon Cafe, Jersey City, 1988-90; comms. analyst and onboard svc. mgr. Northwest Airlines, N.Y., Minn., Japan, 1990-93; personal fin. advisor, project mgr., internat. promotions Am. Express Fin., Advisor, Inc., Mpls., 1993-98; pres. The Mil. Retirees' Bed and Breakfast Club, Inc., 1998-99; ind. distbr. Rexall Showcase Internat., 1998-99; sr. investment specialist Charles Schwab and Co., Inc., 2000—03; v.p. investment and ins. office First Horizon Investment Svcs. (divsn. First Tenn. Brokerage, Inc.), Bellevue, Wash., 2003—. Recipient 5th pl. award Internat. Speech Contest in Japanese, Asahi Shimbun, 1975. Mem. NAFE, DAR (geneal. records chmn. 1985-86, schs. chmn. 1985-86, yearbook co-chmn. 1983-87, rec. sec. 1986-87), Rotary (Maple Grove club chmn. com. internat. svc. 1998-99), Kiwanis (Bellevue Sunrise). Office: 111 108th Ave NE Ste 150 Bellevue WA 98004 Personal E-mail: cyndykocher@yahoo.com.

KOCHER, JUANITA FAY, retired auditor; b. Falmouth, Ky., Aug. 9, 1933; d. William Birgest and Lula (Gillespie) Vickroy; m. Donald Edward Kocher, Nov. 18, 1953. Grad. high sch., Bright, Ind. Cert. internal auditor and compliance officer. Bookkeeper Mchts. Bank and Trust Co., West Harrison, Ind., 1952-56, teller, asst. cashier, 1962-87, br. mgr., 1979-87, internal auditor, 1987-96, ret., 1996; bookkeeper Progressive Bank, New Orleans, 1956-58; with proof dept. 1st Nat. Bank, Cin., Ohio, 1958-59, teller Harrison, Ohio, 1959-62. Bookkeeper Donald E. Kocher Constrn., Harrison, 1981—. Mem. Am. Bankers Assn., Ind. Bankers Assn. Home: 11277 Biddinger Rd Harrison OH 45030

KOCHER, MININDER SINGH, pediatric orthopaedic surgeon, epidemiologist; b. Rochester, N.Y., Dec. 23, 1966; s. Haribhajan Singh and Ranjit Kaur Kocher; m. Michele Mary Dupre, June 4, 1994; children: Ava Dupre children: Sophia Dupre, Isabelle Dupre, Calvin Dupre. AB, Dartmouth Coll., 1989; MD, Duke U., 1993; MPH, Harvard U., 2000. Bd. cert. Am. Bd. Orthopaedic Surgeons, 2002. Intern Beth Israel Hosp./Harvard Med. Sch., 1993—94; resident Harvard Combined Orthop. Surgery Residency program, 1994—98; fellow pediat. orthop. surgery Boston Children's Hosp., 1998—99; fellow sports medicine Steadman Hawkin's Clinic, 1999—2000; pediatric orthop. surgeon Children's Hosp. Boston, 2000—; asst. prof. orthop. surgery Harvard Med. Sch., Boston, 2000—; cons. Steadman Hawkins Sports Medicine Found., Vail, Colo., 2000—. Dir. Children's Hosp. Orthop. Inst. for Clin. Effectiveness, Boston, 2000—; asst. dir. divsn. sports medicine Children's Hosp., Boston, 2005—. Sci. adv. com. Steadman Hawkins Sports Medicine Found., Vail, Colo., 2000; med. adv. com. LeadingMD.com, L.A., 2001. Recipient Wilburt Davidson award, Duke U. Sch. Medicine, 1993, Harris Yett award, Harvard Combined Orthop. Program, 1994, Von Meyer award, Children's Hosp. Boston, 1998, Zimmer award, Am. Orthop. Assn., 1999, Richard Kilfoyle award, New Eng. Orthop. Soc., 1999, Clin. Rsch. prize, Arthroscopy Assn. N.Am., 2000, 2001, Vernon Thompson award, Western Orthop. Assn., 2000, Kappa Delta award, Otherpedic Rsch. and Edn. Found., 2005; Nat. Honor Soc. scholar, LG Balfour, 1985—89, Nat. Merit Scholarship, 1985—89, Rufus Choate scholar, Dartmouth Coll., 1988—99. Fellow: Am. Acad. Orthop. Surgeons (Kappa Delta Clin. Rsch. award 2005); mem.: Am. Orthop. Soc. for Sports Medicine, Anterior Cruciate Ligament Study Group, Pediat. Orthop. Soc. N.Am. (clin. effectiveness com. 2002—, bd. dirs. 2005, Angela Kuo award 2004), Phi Beta Kappa. Office: Childrens Hosp Boston 300 Longwood Ave Boston MA 02135 Office Phone: 617-355-7497. Business E-Mail: mininder.kocher@childrens.harvard.edu.

KOCHEVAR, NANCY L., elementary school educator; d. Albert Frank and Adeline Kochevar. BA in English, Colo. State U., Pueblo, 1970; MA, No. Ariz. U., 1986. Reading tchr. Rangely (Colo.) Schs., 1970—73; title i tchr. Pueblo (Colo.) Sch. Dist. #70, 1973—76; tchr. Dolores (Colo.) Schs., 1979—82; tchr., curriculum chair Bloomfield (N.Mex.) Schs., 1982—. Recipient PAC Mem. of Yr. award, Bloomfield Bilingual Com., 1989. Master: Nat. Assn. Tchrs. Math. (assoc.); mem.: Assn. Supervision and Curriculum Devel. (assoc.), Internat. Reading Assn. (assoc.), Nat. Edn. Am. (assoc.; pres. 1980—81), Phi Delta Kappa (assoc.). Avocations: travel, swimming, reading.

KOCHI, JAY KAZUO, chemist, educator; b. Los Angeles, May 17, 1927; s. Tsuruzo and Shizuko (Moriya) K.; m. Marion Kiyono, Mar. 1, 1959; children: Sims, Julia. Student, Cornell U., 1945; BS, UCLA, 1949; PhD, Iowa State U., 1952. Faculty Harvard U., 1952-55; NIH fellow Cambridge U., Eng., 1956; mem. faculty Iowa State U., 1956; with Shell Devel. Co., 1957-61; mem. faculty dept. chemistry Case Western Res. U., Cleve., 1962-69, prof., 1966-69; prof. chemistry Ind. U., Bloomington, 1969-74, Earl Blough prof. chemistry, 1974-84; Robert A. Welch Disting. prof. chemistry U. Houston, 1984—. Cons. chemist, 1964— Mem. Am. Chem. Soc., Chem. Soc. (London), Nat. Acad. Scis., Sigma Xi. Achievements include research on mechanism of catalysis of organic reactions, organometallics, electrochemistry and photochemistry, time-resolved spectroscopy, and x-ray crystallography of reactive intermediates. Home: 4372 Faculty Ln Houston TX 77004-6601 Office: U Houston Dept Chemistry 4800 Calhoun Rd Houston TX 77204-5003 Office Phone: 713-743-3293. Business E-Mail: jkochi@uh.edu.

KOCIAN, CHARLOTTE THERESA, owner operator, consultant; b. Phila., Aug. 11, 1947; d. Charlotte Theresa Keich. BSChemE, U. South Fla., 1972, postgrad., 1992—, Temple U., 1979, Rutgers U., 1981. Lic. ins. agt.; real estate agt. Engr. Procter & Gamble, Cin., 1972-77, Johnson & Johnson, Princeton, N.J., 1977, FMC Corp., Princeton, 1977-79, Getty Oil & Refining, Wilmington, Del., 1979-80; engr., cons. Marlton, N.J., 1980-87; pres. C.T. Kocian Inc., Tampa, Fla., 1987—; co. pres., registered securities prin. Investment Counselors, Tampa, Fla., 1989. Engring. expert witness, Cherry Hill, 1980—; pres. C.T. Kocian Inc., Tampa, Fla., 1987—. Mem. LWV, Am. Inst. Chem. Engrs. (reg. securities prin. investment counselor), Nat. Assn. Securities. Democrat. Avocations: chess, biking, gardening, dog breeding, swimming, reading.

KOCIS, JANET KAY, elementary school educator; b. Litchfield, Ill., May 6, 1951; d. Thomas Dewey Allan and Loeta Joyce Jones; m. Peter Anthony Kocis, Apr. 12, 1975; children: Nichol Antonacci, Amanda. MusB, So. Ill. U., 1973; M in Tchr. Leadership, U. Ill., Springfield, 2004. Tchr. music Sch. Dist. #7, Gillespie, Ill., 1973—76; tchr. 5th and 6th grades Sts. Simon and Jude, 1979—84; tchr. music St. ALoysius Sch., Springfield, 1986—93; tchr. 6th grade sci. Enos Sch., 1997—2002; tchr. 6th grade math., lang. arts Grant Mid. Sch., 2002—03, tchr. 7th and 8th grade math., 2003—05, coach math., 2005—. Mem.: Nat. Coun. Tchrs. Math. Office: US Grand Mid Sch 1800 W Monroe St Springfield IL 62704 Office Phone: 217-525-3170.

KOCIUBES, JOSEPH LEIB, lawyer; b. Frankfurt, Fed. Republic, Germany, June 16, 1947; s. Max and Rachel (Ackermn) Kociubes; m. Peggy Ann Roth, May 18, 1969; children: Lisa Roth, Adam Roth. BA, U. Pitts, Pitts., Pa., 1969; JD, Harvard U., 1974. Bar: Mass./ US Dist. Ct. 1974, Mass./ US Ct. Appeals (1st cir.) 1974, US Supreme Ct. 1981, Mass./ US Ct. Appeals (6th cir.) 1987, Mass./ US Ct. Appeals (4th cir.) 1988. Assoc. Bingham, Dana & Gould, Boston, 1974—81, ptnr., 1981, mem. mgmt. com., 1984—96; faculty various programs Mass. continuing Legal Edn., 1989—; trial practice adv. Harvard Law Sch., 1985—; adj. prof. Northeastern Law Sch., 2001—. Gen. counsel ACLU of Mass.; dir., mem. exec. com. Greater Boston Legal Svc., 1989; dir. Vol. Lawyers Project, 1985—95. Fellow: Internat. Acad. Trial Lawyers; mem.: Boston Bar Assn. (v.p. 2000—01, mem. 2000—03, pres.-elect 2001—02, pres. 2002—03, dir. lawyers com. for civil rights under law), Mass Bar Found., Am. Bar Found., Mass. State Com., Am. Coll. Trial Lawyer, Boston Bar Found. (trustee 1997—2000, 2001), Mass. State Com., Am. Coll. Trial Lawyer (fellow). Office: Bingham McCutchen 150 Federal St Boston MA 02110-1726 Office Phone: 617-951-8688. E-mail: joe.kociubes@bingham.com.

KOCOL, ROBERT S., information technology executive; BS, Miss. State U; MBA, Fla. Tech. U. CPA. Fin. analyst Gen. Motors, Miss.; program mgmt., controller, printer opers. Storage Tek, Louisville, Colo., 1980—91, dir., fin. opers. to dir., worldwide field opers. fin. and adminstrn., 1991—96, v.p., fin. planning and opers., 1996—98, corp.v.p., CFO, 1998—. Office: Storage Technology One Storage Tek Dr Louisville CO 80028

KOCSIS, JAMES PAUL, artist; b. Buffalo, Apr. 27, 1936; Grad., U. of the Arts, 1958. Illustrator children's books, 1961-68; illustrator, designer Random House Publ., 20th Century Fox, 1967; pub. Kocsis catalogues, books, color prints and posters. Instr. drawing and pictorial composition, lectr. U. of Arts, Phila., 1965-67; lectr. Kutztown State Tchrs. Coll., civic and social grps. Works included in pub. collections: Lessing J. Rosenwald, Nat. Gallery Art, Washington, Library of Congress, Washington, Albright-Knox Art Gallery, Buffalo, Victoria and Albert Mus., London, Kendal (Eng.) Mus., Bodleian Library Oxford U., Eng.; pvt. collections Her Royal Highness Elizabeth Queen of Eng., His Royal Highness Charles, Prince of Wales, Right Hon. Lord Kenneth Clark, Nancy and Ronald Reagan Presdl. Collection, White House, Lehigh Valley (Pa.) Hosp., 1989, Lehigh Valley Internat. Airport, Allentown, Pa., others; one-man shows Igneous Man Exhbn.1, Columbia (S.C.) Mus. Art, 1974, Crucifixion Exhbn.-Memory of Phila. Scourge Period 1972, U. of Arts, 1976, Igneous Man Exhbns. 2-31, Harvard U., 1976, Sydney (Australia) Opera House, 1979, Dhahran (Saudi Arabia) Cen. Library, 1982, Jilin U., Changchun, China, 1982, 13th Ann. Festival Arts, United World Coll SE Asia, 1984, Italsider Steel Co., Genoa and Alessandria, Italy, 1985, United

World Coll. Adriatic, Trieste, Italy, 1985, United World Coll. So. Africa, Mbabane, 1985, Internat. Music & Art Festival, Glamorgan, Wales, 1985, U.S. Internat. U.-Europe, London, 1985, U. Glasgow, Scotland, 1985, James Joyce Mus., Dublin, Ireland, 1985, Kendal (Eng.) Mus., 1986, Internat. Pub. Rels. Conv., Harare, Zimbabwe, 1987, Trinity Coll. Oxford U., 1988, Imo State Libr., Owerri, Nigeria, 1989, Progress Bank of Nigeria Ltd., Lagos, 1989, Nat. Arts Theatre, Lagos, 1989, Freedom Hall, Martin Luther King, Jr. Ctr. Nonviolent Social Change and Atlanta-Fulton Pub. Libr., Atlanta, 1990, U.S. Mission to the UN, N.Y.C., 1991, UN, N.Y.C. (first Am. honored with one-man exhbn., 1991), Sopot, Poland, 1991, Gdansk, Poland, 1991, German-Am. Inst., Saarbrucken, Germany, 1992, Amerika Haus, Frankfurt, Germany, 1992, Zentral-Bibliothek, Cologne, Germany, 1993, Freie Universitat Berlin, Universitatbibliothek, Berlin, 1994, Igneous Man Exhbn./India, Gandhi Peace Found., New Delhi, 1995, Internat. India Ctr., New Delhi, 1995, Nat. Mus. and Libr. Casa de la Cultura Ecuatoriana Benjamin Carrion, Quito, Ecuador, South Am., 1998, Benjamin Franklin Libr., Mexico City, 1998, Inst. de Investigaciones Esteticas, U. Nacional de Mex., Mexico City, 1998, La Casa de Cultura, Jesus Reyes Heroles, Coyoacan, Mex., 1999, Libr. of Nat. Acad. Athens, 2003, Elefterios Venizelos Internat. Airport, 2003, Vikelaia Libr., Crete, 2003, Acad. Athens (Greece) U., 2003, The Hermitage Mus., St. Petersburg, Russia, 2005, Dostoevsky Mus., St. Petersburg, Russia, 2005, Russian Acad. Arts, St. Petersburg, Russia, 2005 Recipient Biannual award Am. Inst. Graphic Arts, 1968, Letters of Recognition Lord Kenneth Clark, 1981, Her Royal Highness Elizabeth, The Queen of Eng., His Royal Highness, Charles, Prince of Wales, 1983. Achievements include inventing new art form: psychic impressionism. Home and Office: PO Box 905 Allentown PA 18105-0905 E-mail: kocsis@jamespaulkocsis.org.

KOCUREK, MICHAEL J., former foundation administrator; b. N.Y.C., Jan. 6, 1943; s. Michael Stephen and Celeste (Ruthkoski) K.; m. Margaret Carroll Hatton, Aug. 6, 1967; children: Monica, Anne, Michael-Justin. BS in Paper Sci. and Engring. cum laude, Syracuse U., 1964, MS in Paper Sci. and Engring., 1968, PhD in Paper Sci. and Engring., 1970. Asst. prof. chemistry U. Wis., Stevens Point, 1970-75, assoc. prof. paper sci., 1975-80, prof., 1980-86, chmn. paper sci., 1973-86; exec. dir. Charles H. Herty R&D Found., Savannah, Ga., 1986—. Mem. univ. planning com. U. Wis., 1977-86, chmn., 1979-81, mem. U. Wis.-system task force, 1980-81, chmn. discipline coord. group, 1981-84, mem. various univ. coms.; adj. prof. Ga. Inst. Tech., 1988—, Ga. So. U., 1988—, Inst. Paper Sci. & Tech., 1996—; cons., seminar leader in field; mem. Gov.'s Coun. on Sci. & Tech.; chair Ga. Pulp & Paper Consortium. Series editor: Pulp & Paper Manufacture, 3d edit., 1979-92; rev. editor: Pulp & Paper Technologists Handbook, 1st edit., 1982; prodr., author (videotape course) Introduction to Pulp & Paper, 1982, 86, (videotape series) Paper Quest, 1986—; prodr., host (videotape series) Personalities In Paper, 1984-86; co-prodr., author (videotape series) Pulp Mill Quality, 1989—. Fellow Tech. Assn. Pulp and Paper Industry (mem. acad. adv. coun. 1970-87, chmn. ednl. activities Lake State chpt. 1973-77, mem. profl. devel. ops. coun. 1976-81, chmn. continuing edn. divsn. 1976-78, chmn. LSOC task force young profls. 1978-81, chmn. tech. ops. coun. 1985-87, mem. human resources divsn. 1988—, bd. dirs. 1992—, mem. various coms., rev. editor Introduction to Pulp & Paper Interactive Videodisc 1986, Disting. Svc. award 1992). Office: Herty Pulp & Paper Devel Ctr PO Box 7798 Garden City GA 31418-7798

KODAMA, YUJI, mathematics professor; b. Beppu, Oita, Japan, Mar. 10, 1951; d. Migaku and Ayako (Motokawa) K. BEE, Yamanashi U., Kofu, Japan, 1973; MEE, Osaka U., Toyonaka, Japan, 1975; DS in Physics, Nagoya U., Aichi, 1978; PhD in Math., Clarkson U., Potsdam, N.Y., 1980. Asst. prof. math. Clarkson U., 1979-80, Ohio State U., Columbus, 1982-83, 85-87, assoc. prof., 1987-92; prof. Osaka U., Suita, 1996—98, Ohio State U., Columbus, 1992—. Postdoctoral fellow Bell Labs., Murray Hill, N.J., 1980-82, cons., 1982-90; rsch. assoc. physics Nagoya U., Aichi, Japan, 1983-88. Referee jour. The Phys. Rev., 1981—; Am. Phys. Soc., 1981—, contbr. articles to math. and physics jours. NSF grantee, 1984—. Mem. Soc. Indsl. and Applied Math., Am. Math. Soc. Office: Ohio State U Dept Math Columbus OH 43210

KODIS, MARY CAROLINE, marketing consultant; b. Chgo., Dec. 17, 1927; d. Anthony John and Callis Ferebee (Old) K.; student San Diego State Coll., 1945-47, Latin Am. Inst., 1948. Controller, div. adminstrv. mgr. Fed. Mart Stores, 1957-65; controller, adminstrv. mgr. Gulf Mart Stores, 1965-67; budget dir., adminstrv. mgr. Diana Stores, 1967-68; founder, treas., controller Handy Dan Stores, 1968-72; founder, v.p., treas. Handy City Stores, 1972-76; sr. v.p., treas. Handy City div. W.R. Grace & Co., Atlanta, 1976-79; founder, pres. Hal's Hardware and Lumber Stores, 1982-84; retail and restaurant cons., 1979— . Treas., bd. dirs. YWCA Watsonville,1981-84, 85-87; mem. Santa Cruz County Grand Jury, 1984-85. Recipient 1st Tribute to Women in Internat. Industry, 1978; named Woman of the Yr., 1986. Mem. Ducks Unltd. (treas. Watsonville chpt. 1981-89). Republican. Home and Office: 5500 NE 82nd Ave #103 Vancouver WA 98662-9410

KOEDEL, JOHN GILBERT, JR., retired metal products executive; b. Pitts., June 25, 1937; s. John Gilbert and Elizabeth Marie (Kramer) K.; m. Fay Birren, Dec. 21, 1963; 1 son, John III. BS in Commerce, Washington and Lee U., 1959. V.p. Pitts. Nat. Bank, 1960-68; various positions up to pres. Nat. Forge. Co., 1968-95. Bd. dirs. The RCR Group, Inc. Served to sgt., U.S. Army, 1960-65. Mem. Fishing Bay Yacht Club, Conenango Club, Masons. Republican. Presbyterian. Avocations: sailing, wood working. Home: PO Box 877 Deltaville VA 23043-0877

KOEDEL, ROBERT CRAIG, minister, historian, educator; b. Tarentum, Pa., July 1, 1927; s. Theodore and Evelyn (Dagan) K.; m. Barbara Ellen Wood, Jan. 6, 1962. BA, Wheaton Coll., Ill., 1949; M.Div., Pitts. Theol Sem., 1953; MA, U. Pitts., 1964; postgrad., Temple U., 1964-70. Ordained to ministry Presbyn. Ch. U.S.A., 1953. Pastor Monaghan Presbyn. Ch., Dillsburg, Pa., 1956-59; asst. pastor Mt. Calvary Presbyn. Ch., Corapolis, Pa., 1959-60; assoc. pastor Dormont Presbyn. Ch., Pitts., 1960-64; mem. faculty Atlantic Community Coll., Mays Landing, N.J., 1966-92, prof. social sci., history, religion, 1978-92, chmn. dept. history, 1969-70, 78-79, asst. dean instrn., 1970-72; lectr. in history Stockton State Coll., 1985-86; clergyman Pitts. Presbytery. Author: South Jersey Heritage: A Social, Economic and Cultural History, 1977, God's Vine in This Wilderness: Religion in South Jersey to 1800, 1980, Following the Water: The Shellfish Industry in South Jersey, 1983, Becoming a Presbyterian, 1993, Letters from Wheaton by a Forty-Niner, 1997, The Sky Pilot Said It: Memoires of an Air Force Chaplain, 2001; contbr. articles to profl. jours., articles to newspapers. Mem. Atlantic County Cultural and Heritage Adv. Bd., 1991. Served as chaplain USAF, 1953-56. N.J. Hist. Commn. research grantee, 1974, 84. Mem. United Teaching Professions, N.J. Hist. Soc. (trustee 1985-88), Atlantic County Hist. Soc. (editor jour. 1983-91), Gloucester County Hist. Soc., Pitts. Presbytery, Hist. Soc. Western Pa. (rsch. historian). Home: 1 Unger Ln Pittsburgh PA 15217-1018

KOEGEL, WILLIAM FISHER, lawyer; b. Washington, Aug. 18, 1923; s. Otto Erwin and Rae (Fisher) K.; m. Barbara Bixler, Feb. 2, 1946 (dec. 1968); children: John Bixler, Robert Bartlett; m. Ruth Swan Boynton, June 21, 1969 (dec. 1983); m. Irene Lawrence, Aug. 4, 1984. BA, Williams Coll., 1944; LL.B., U. Va., 1949. Bar: N.Y. 1950. From assoc. to ptnr. Clifford Chance US LLP (formerly Rogers & Wells), N.Y.C., 1949—88, head litigation dept., 1977-88, sr. counsel, 1989—. Chmn. Scarsdale (N.Y.) Republican Town Com., 1965-71; pres. trustees Hitchcock Presbyn. Ch., Scarsdale, 1970-73, 78-79, 82-83. Served with AUS, 1943-45, ETO. Fellow ACTL; mem. ABA, N.Y. State Bar Assn., Bar Assn. City N.Y., Order of Coif. Clubs: Town (Scarsdale) (pres. 1976-77); Williams (N.Y.C.); Shenorock Shore, Fox Meadow Tennis, The Moorings. Home: 7 Chesterfield Rd Scarsdale NY 10583-1619 Office: Clifford Chance US LLP 31 West 52nd St New York NY 10014

KOEGEN, ROY JEROME, lawyer; b. Spokane, Wash., Mar. 1, 1949; s. Frank J. and Jeanne (Bardsley) K.; m. Ann Martinelli, Aug. 28, 1970; children: Jennifer, Christopher. BA, Gonzaga U., 1971; JD, U. Calif., San Francisco, 1974. Bar: Calif. 1974, Wash. 1979, U.S. Supreme Ct. 1982. Assoc. Wilson, Jones, Morton & Lynch, San Mateo, Calif., 1974-78, Blair & Koegen, Spokane, 1978-80; ptnr. Preston, Thorgrimson, Ellis & Holman, Spokane, 1980-90, Perkins Coie LLP, Seattle, Spokane, 1990—2002, Lukins & Annis, PS, Spokane, 2002—05, Koegen Edwards LLP, 2005—. Author: Washington Municipal Financing Deskbook, 1992. Chmn. exec. com. Cmty. Alcohol Ctr., Spokane, 1982—84, Century II Park Dist., Spokane, 1982—84; bd. dirs. Nature Conservancy, Wash. Nat. Pk. Found. Mem. ABA, Wash. Bar Assn., Calif. Bar Assn., Nat. Assn. Bond Lawyers, The Nature Conservancy (bd. dirs.). Roman Catholic. Office: Koegen Edwards LLP 1001 Fourth Ave Ste 2580 Seattle WA 98154 Office Phone: 509-455-9555, 206-381-1818. Business E-Mail: rkoegen@lukins.com, roy@koegenedwards.com.

KOEHLER, JANE ELLEN, librarian; b. Belleville, Ill., Oct. 18, 1944; d. Edward William and Elizabeth Ellen (Sanford) Hindman; m. Robert Philip Koehler, Feb. 18, 1936; children: Clare Anne, Beth Ellen. BS, Eastern Ill. U., 1967; MS, U. Ill., 1970. Cert. edn. educator. Library asst. Belleville (Ill.) Pub. Library, 1964-65; tchr. librarian Sch. Dist. 72, Woodstock, Ill., 1966-73; dir. library services Sch. Dist. 200, Woodstock, 1969-73; dir. youth services Woodstock Pub. Library, 1980-89, asst. dir., 1989—. Author: (short story) Northwest Herald, 1980; columnist Woodstock Ind., 2001—. Bd. dir. Auxillary Mem. Hosp.; vol. Turning Point (Crisis Intervention), 1978-88; mem. Ill. Literary Heritage Com., 1984-85; chmn. Mem. Hosp. for Mem. Library Adminstr. Coun. of Northern Ill. (sec. 1990), Woodstock Fine Arts Assn. Republican. Roman Catholic. Avocations: writing, swimming, skiing, guilting, travel, theater. Home: 13171 Hickory Ln Woodstock IL 60098-3617 Office: Woodstock Pub Library 414 W Judd St Woodstock IL 60098-3131

KOEHLER, REGINALD STAFFORD, III, lawyer; b. Bellevue, Pa., Dec. 29, 1932; s. Reginald S. and Esther (Hawken) K.; m. Ann Ellsworth Rowland, June 15, 1956; children: Victoria Elizabeth, Cynthia Rowland, Robert Steven. BA, Yale U., 1956; JD, Harvard U., 1959. Bar: N.Y. 1960, Calif., Fla., D.C. 1979, Wash. 1984, Oreg. 1985, Alaska 1985, U.S. Supreme Ct. 1973. Assoc. Davis Polk & Wardwell, N.Y.C., 1959-68; ptnr. Donovan Leisure Newton & Irvine, N.Y.C., 1968-84, Perkins Coie, Seattle, 1984—. Author: The Planning and Administration of a Large Estate. Fellow Am. Coll. Trust and Estate Counsel; mem. N.Y. State Bar Assn., Calif. Bar Assn., D.C. Bar Assn., Wash. Bar Assn., Oreg. Bar Assn., Alaska Bar Assn., Chi Psi. Episcopalian. Office: Perkins Coie 1201 3rd Ave Fl 48 Seattle WA 98101-3029 Office Phone: 206-359-8632.

KOEHLER, ROBERT BRIEN, priest; b. Hastings, Nebr., Aug. 26, 1950; s. Robert Joseph and Melba Deloris (Morey) K.; m. Terry Ellen Collins; children: Gregory, Michael, Louisa. BA cum laude, U. Dallas, 1972; postgrad., U. Wis., 1973; MDiv, Nashotah Ho., 1976. Chaplain DeKoven Found., Racine, Wis., 1976-81; Curate Emmanuel Ch., Rockford, Ill., 1978-81; Rector St. Raphael's Ch., Ft. Myers Beach, Fla., 1981-84; Vicar Ch. Holy Cross, Burleson, Tex., 1984-87; Canon to the Ordinary, Diocese of Ft. Worth, 1987-93; Rector St. Luke's Ch., Ft. Myers, Fla., 1993—2001, Baton Rouge, 2001—. Exec. dir. Episc. Synod Am., Ft. Worth, 1991-93. Dist. chmn. Boy Scouts Am., Ft. Myers, 1993-96; trustee Nashotah (Wis.) House, 1994—; bd. dirs. Interfaith Vol. Care Givers, 1996-99, Goodwill Industries, S.W. Fla., 1999-2001; instl. review com. Lee Meml. Health Sys., 1999-2001. Mem. SAR, Soc. Holy Cross, Soc. Colonial Wars. Office: St Luke's Episc Ch 8833 Goodwood Blvd Baton Rouge LA 70806 E-mail: frkoehler@stlukesbr.org.

KOEHLER, ROBERT H., lawyer; b. Kansas City, Kans., Sept. 22, 1941; AB, Marquette Univ., 1963; JD, Univ. Kans., 1966. Bar: Kans. 1966, DC 1973, Va. 1999, DC Ct. Appeals, Va. Supreme Ct., US Ct. Mil. Appeals, US Ct. Appeals (1st, 4th, 5th, 6th, 10th, DC, Fed. cir.), US Supreme Ct. 1973. Ptnr., Govt. Contracts, Def. & Nat. Security Affairs practices, mem. mgmt. com., office mng. ptnr. Patton Boggs LLP, McLean, Va. Dir., mem. exec. com., former chmn. USO of Metro. Washington. Served U.S. Army, 1967—73. Decorated Bronze Star, Meritorious Svc. award, Army Commendation medal, Vietnam Svc. medal. Office: Patton Boggs LLP 9th Fl 8484 Westpark Dr Mc Lean VA 22102-5117 Office Phone: 703-744-8005. Office Fax: 703-744-8001. Business E-Mail: rkoehler@pattonboggs.com.

KOEHLER, WALLACE, library and information scientist, educator, researcher; b. Chgo., Apr. 2, 1945; s. Wallace and Mirjam Koehler; m. Vera Blair; children from previous marriage: Ingrid, William. PhD, Cornell U., 1973—77; MS, U. Tenn., 1993—97. Asst. prof. SLIS U. Okla., Norman, 1997—2001; assoc. prof., dir. MLIS program Valdosta State U., Ga., 2001—. Author: Fundamentals of Informational Studies: Understanding Information and Its Environment, 2003, (article) Library Management, 2000 (Highly Commended Paper award, 2000); contbr. articles to profl. jours. With U.S. Army, 1966—68. Office: Valdosta State U 1500 N Patterson St Valdosta GA 31698 Business E-Mail: wkoehler@valdosta.edu.

KOEHN, DONNA SCOTT, assistant principal, counseling administrator; b. Cleve., Apr. 7, 1951; d. Donald Bennett and Beulah Mae Scott; m. Calvin Elliott Koehn, Aug. 4, 1973; children: Coreen Elizabeth, Stephen Matthew. EdB, Kent State U., 1973; MS in Ednl. Adminstrn., U. Akron, 1991, postgrad. Cert. secondary edn., vocat. edn., elem. prin. Tchr. East Cleveland (Ohio) City Schs., 1979—83, Parma Heights (Ohio) Christian Acad., 1987—91, prin., adminstr., 1992—96; asst. prin. Maple Heights (Ohio) City Schs., 1997—98; asst. prin., guidance counselor Greater Cleveland Christian Sch., Middleburg Heights, Ohio, 2002—. Mem. sch. bd. Parma Heights Christian Acad., 1990—92; founding bd. dirs. Greater Cleveland Christian Schs., Middleburg Heights, 1993—96. Mem.: ASCD, E-Docs. Home: 4635 Fulton Rd Cleveland OH 44144 Personal E-mail: dsk4635@yahoo.com.

KOEHN, ENNO, engineering educator, researcher; b. Flushing, N.Y., Apr. 29, 1936; s. Theodore J. and Anna M. (Sievers) K.; m. Carol Ann Butcher, Nov. 25, 1967; children: William Enno, James Frederick. BCE, CUNY, 1958; MS, Columbia U., 1960; PhD, Wayne State U., 1975. Registered profl. engr., Tex., Ind., Ohio. Engring. inspector Bd. Water Supply, N.Y.C., 1957; rsch. engr. N.Am. Rockwell, Columbus, Ohio, 1958-59; asst. prof. L.I. U., Greenvale, N.Y., 1960-66; specialist IBM, Burlington, Vt., 1966-67; prof. civil engring. Ohio Northern U., Ada, 1967-79; assoc. prof. civil engring. Purdue U., West Lafayette, Ind., 1979-84; prof., chair dept. civil engring. Lamar U., Beaumont, Tex., 1984—2003, prof., 2003—. Rsch. cons. Atomic Internat., Canoga Park, Calif., 1962, GM Corp., Warren, Mich., 1973, Bechtel Corp., Ann Arbor, Mich., 1978-81, U.S. Army Rsch. Lab., Champaign, Ill., 1983-88; program evaluator Accreditation Bd. for Engring. and Tech. Contbr. articles to profl. jours. Active Alumni Rep. Com. Columbia U., N.Y.C., 1990—; sustaining mem. Boy Scouts Am. Troop Com., 1980—; pres., campaign chairperson United Way, Ada, 1975-77, Lamar Engring., Beaumont, 1984-86. Fellow ASCE (Best Paper nomination); mem. NSPE, Am. Soc. Engring. Edn. (Best Paper nomination), Assn. Advancement Cost Engring. Internat., Rotary Internat. (dir. 1970-73), Tau Beta Pi (chpt. adviser), Sigma Xi (Membership award), Chi Epsilon (Honor Membership award). Episcopalian. Avocations: reading, gardening, walking, travel. Office: Lamar U Civil Engring Dept PO Box 10024 Beaumont TX 77710-0024

KOEHN, WILLIAM JAMES, lawyer; b. Winterset, Iowa, Mar. 24, 1936; s. Cyril Otto and Ilene L. (Doop) K.; m. Francia C. Leeper, Sept. 6, 1958; children: Cynthia Rae, William Fredric, James Anthony. BA, JD cum laude, U. Iowa, 1963. Bar: Iowa 1963, U. S. Ct. Appeals (8th cir.) 1971, U.S. Ct. Appeals (10th cir.) 1972, U.S. Ct. Appeals (2d cir.) 1972, U.S. Ct. Appeals (5th cir.) 1977, U.S. Supreme Ct. 1971. Of counsel Davis, Brown, Koehn, Shors & Roberts, P.C., Des Moines, 1963—. Prof., lectr. in U.S., Can., Europe. Bd. editors Iowa Law Rev., 1961-63; contbr. articles to profl. jours. Co-founder Big Bros.-Sisters of Greater Des Moines, 1969, pres., 1976-77; chmn. Des Moines Friendship Commmn., 1970-71; bd. dirs. Greater Des Moines YMCA, 1983-90; co-chmn. Des Moines Bicentennial Commn., 1975-76; chmn. Environ. and Pub. Works Commn.; mem. adv. com. civil justice reform act, 1990; chmn. worldwide dispute resolution com., Lex Mundi, 1989-94, bd. dirs., 1992-96; arbitrator AAA Comml. Sect., 2004. Lt. USNR, 1958-61. Mem. ABA (environ. litigation sub-com., construction com., internat. lit. environ. commn.), Iowa Bar Assn. (environ. coun. 1989-92, 1999-2001, litigation com. 1992-95, proflism. com. 1994-2002, chmn. internat. law sect. 2005—), Polk County Bar Assn., Iowa Trial Lawyers Assn., Order of Coif. Republican. Office: Fin Ctr 666 Walnut St Des Moines IA 50309-3904 Home: 29980 Nantucket Dr PO 669 Pacific City OR 97135 Office Phone: 515-288-2500. Business E-Mail: wk@lawiowa.com.

KOEHN, WILLIAM W., pharmacist, consultant; b. Sioux Falls, SD, Apr. 28, 1948; s. Alfred and T. Madelyn Koehn; m. Laura J. Krafcsik, Oct. 5, 1980; children: Adrienne, Peter. BS, SD State U., Brookings, 1971; MS in pharmacy, U. Mo., Kansas City, 1982; postgrad., Rockhurst U., Kansas City, Mo., 2003—. Cert. Am. Soc. Clin. Pathologists, bd. cert. oncology pharmacy, registered pharmacist Mo., 1982, Kans., 1983, SD, 1983. Med. tech. Kans. U. Hosp., Kansas City, 1973—83, pharmacist, 1983—93, pharmacy dir., 1993—. Chief pharmacy svcs. USAR, Independence, Mo., 1988—; cons. in field. Maj. USAR, 1988—. Mem.: Am. Soc. Clin. Oncology, Assn. Mil. Surgeons U.S., Am. Soc. Hosp. Pharmacists. Republican.

KOELBL, JAMES J., dean; Faculty mem. U. Ill., Loyola U., U. Louisville; group assoc. dir. profl. svc. ADA; dean Sch. Dentistry W.Va. U., 1999—. Mem.: W.Va. State Dental Assn. (v.p. 2004—). Office: W Va Univ Sch Dentistry Robert C Byrd Health Sci Ctr Med Ctr Dr Morgantown WV 26506-9400

KOELLER, KELLY KARL, radiologist; s. Roy Gustav and Barbara Jeanne Koeller. MD, U. Tenn., Memphis, 1978—82; BSEE, U. Memphis, 1978. Diplomate Am. Bd. Radiology, 1990, cert. in neuroradiology Am. Bd. Radiology, 2004. Fellow, neuroradiology sect. U. Calif., San Francisco, 1990—92; neuroradiologist Naval Med. Ctr., Oakland, Calif., 1992—93, neuroradiologist, dept. radiology San Diego, 1993—96, chief of neuroradiology, dept. radiology, 1994—96; chief of neuroradiology, dept. radiologic pathology Armed Forces Inst. Pathology, Washington, 1996—, assoc. chmn., dept. radiologic pathology, 1999—2001, chmn., dept. radiologic pathology, 2001—. Mem. editl. bd. Radiographics, Bethesda, Md., 2001—. Capt. USN, 1982—2005, Washington, D.C. Decorated Fleet Marine Force Ribbon Dept. Def., Navy and Marine Corps. Commendation Medal, Joint Meritorious Unit Award, Joint Svc. Commendation Award. Fellow: Am. Coll. Radiology; mem.: Radiol. Soc. N.Am., Assn. Program Dirs. Radiology (exec. com. 2001—05), Am. Soc. Spine Radiology, Am. Soc. Head and Neck Radiology, Am. Soc. Neuroradiology (acr councilor 2001—05), Omicron Delta Kappa, Alpha Epislon Delta (pres. 1977—78), Tau Beta Pi, Mortar Bd. Office: Armed Forces Inst Pathology 14th St at Alaska Ave NW Washington DC 20306-6000 Office Phone: 202-782-2166.

KOELLER, ROBERT MARION, lawyer, director; b. Quincy, Ill., Apr. 8, 1940; s. Marion Alfred and Ruth (Main) K.; m. Marlene Meyer, June 1962; children: Kristin, Katherine, Robert. AB, MacMurray Coll., 1962; LLB, Vanderbilt U., 1965. Bar: Ind. 1968. Asst. gen. counsel Nat. Homes Acceptance Corp., Lafayette, Ind., 1967-70; gen. counsel, sec. Herff Jones Co., Indpls., 1970-74; ptnr. Warren, Snider, Koeller & Warren, Indpls., 1974-76; pvt. practice Indpls., 1976—; mem. Coons, Maddox & Koeller, Indpls., 1993-96, Maddox, Koeller Hargett & Caruso, 1996—2002, Ittenbach Johnson Trettin & Koeller, Indpls., 2002—. Dir. various cos. Mem. ABA, Ind. Bar Assn., Indpls. Bar Assn., Hillcrest Country Club. Republican. Methodist. Office: Ste 4 6350 N Shadeland Ave Indianapolis IN 46220 Office Phone: 317-842-5235. Business E-Mail: rkoeller@ijtklaw.com.

KOELLNER, LAURETTE, human resources specialist, aerospace transportation executive; b. Bklyn., Oct. 21, 1954; B in Bus. Mgmt., U. Ctrl. Fla.; MBA, Stetson U. Cert. contracts mgr. Nat. Contracts Mgmt. Assn. Analyst contracts, advanced to various positions McDonnell Douglas, 1978—86, mgr. contracts and pricing missle sys. co. Titusville, Fla., 1986—88, bus. mgr. Tomahawk Cruise Missle prog., 1988—89, dir. strategic and bus. planning, 1989—90, head internal support and svcs. ops. missle prodn. facility, 1990—92; budget mgr. McDonnell Douglas Aerospace, St. Louis, 1992—94, dir. human resources divisn., 1994—96, v.p., gen. auditor, 1996—97, Boeing Co. (formerly McDonnell Douglas), St. Louis, 1997—99, v.p., corp. controller, 1999—2004, exec. v.p., 2004—; pres. Connexion by Boeing, 2004—. Bd. dirs. Sara Lee Corp., Exostar, Chgo. Coun. Fgn. Rels., Chicagoland C. of C.; mem. bd. regents U. Portland; mem. dean's exec. coun. coll. bus. adminstrn. U. Ctrl. Fla. Named to Hall of Fame, U. Ctrl. Fla., 2003. Mem.: Economic Club Chgo. Office: Boeing World Hdqs 100 N Riverside Chicago IL 60606 Office Phone: 312-544-2000.

KOELMEL, LORNA LEE, data processing executive; b. Denver, May 15, 1936; d. George Bannister and Gladys Lee Steuart; m. Herbert Howard Nelson, Sept. 9, 1956 (div. Mar. 1967); children: Karen Dianne, Phillip Dean, Lois Lynn; m. Robert Darrel Koelmel, May 12, 1981; stepchildren: Kim, Cheryl, Dawn, Debbie. BA in English, U. Colo., 1967. Cert. secondary English tchr. Substitute English tchr. Jefferson County Schs., Lakewood, Colo., 1967—68; sec. specialist IBM Corp., Denver, 1968—75, pers. administr., 1975—82, asst. ctr. coord., 1982—85, office systems specialist, 1985—87, backup computer operator, 1987—; computer instr. Barnes Bus. Coll., Denver, 1987—92; owner, mgr. Lorna's Precision Word Processing and Desktop Pub., Denver, 1987—89; computer cons. Denver, 1990—. Editor newsletter Colo. Nat. Campers and Hikers Assn., 1992-94. Organist Christian Sci. Soc., Buena Vista, Colo., 1963-66, 1st Ch. Christ Scientists Thornton-Westminster, Thornton, Colo., 1994—; chmn. bd. dirs., 1979-80. Mem. NAFE, Nat. Secs. Assn. (retirement ctr. chair 1977-78, newsletter chair 1979-80, v.p. 1980-81), Am. Theatre Organ Soc. (Rocky Mountain chpt.), Am. Guild Organists, U. Colo. Alumni Assn., Avon Ind. Sales Rep and Pres. Club, Alpha Chi Omega (publicity com. 1986-88). Clubs: Nat. Writers. Lodges: Job's Daus. (recorder 1953-54). Republican. Avocations: quilting, piano, bridge, logic problems, golf.

KOELTL, JOHN GEORGE, federal judge; b. NYC, Oct. 25, 1945; s. John J. and Elsie (Bender) K. AB summa cum laude, Georgetown U., 1967; JD magna cum laude, Harvard U., 1971. Bar: N.Y. 1972, U.S. Dist. Ct. (so. and ea. dists.) N.Y. 1975, U.S. Ct. Appeals (2d cir.) 1975, U.S. Supreme Ct. 1978, U.S. Ct. Appeals (5th and 11th cirs.) 1981, U.S. Ct. Appeals (4th cir.) 1992, U.S. Dist. Ct. (no. dist.) N.Y. 1982. Law clk. to Judge U.S. Dist. Ct. (so. dist.), N.Y.C., 1971-72; law clk. to Justice Potter Stewart U.S. Supreme Ct., Washington, 1972-73; asst. spl. prosecutor Watergate Spl. Prosecution Force, Dept. Justice, Washington, 1973-74; assoc. Debevoise & Plimpton, N.Y.C., 1975-78, ptnr., 1979-94; judge U.S. Dist. Ct. (so. dist.), N.Y.C., 1994—. Adj. prof. law NYU Law Sch., 1999—. Mem. bd. editors Manual for Complex Litigation 4th edit.; contbr. articles to profl. jours. Mem.: ABA (bd. editors jour. 1991—97, vice chmn. securities com. adminstrv. law sect. 1979—81, co-dir. divsn. publs. litigation sect. 1982—84, coun. mem. litigation sect. 1984—87, assoc. editor Litigation jour. 1975—78, exec. editor 1978—80, editor-in-chief 1980—82, chmn. 1st amendment com. 1987—89, chmn. spl. pubs. com. 1989—92, dir. divsn. publs. litigation sect. 1992—93), Am. Law Inst., Harvard Law Sch. Assn. N.Y. (v.p. 1993—94), N.Y. County Lawyers Assn. (mem. fed. cts. com. 1984—87), N.Y. State Bar Assn., Assn. Bar N.Y.C. (mem. com. on fed. legislation 1976—78, sec. 1978—81, mem. com. profl. and jud. ethics 1981—84, fed. cts. com. 1984—86, chmn. 1986—89, mem. com. on profl. responsibility 1991—94, mem. com. on internat. dispute resolution 2000—). Office: US Courthouse 500 Pearl St Rm 1030 New York NY 10007-1316

KOELZER, GEORGE JOSEPH, lawyer; b. Orange, N.J., Mar. 21, 1938; s. George Joseph and Albertina Florence (Graul) Koelzer; m. Patricia Ann Kilian, Apr. 8, 1967; 1 child, James Patrick. AB, Rutgers U., 1962, LLB, 1964. Bar: N.J. 1964, DC 1978, N.Y. 1980, Calif. 1993, registered: Eng. (fin. lawyer) 2001. Assoc. Louis R. Lombardino, Livingston, NJ, 1964-66, Lum Biunno & Tompkins, Newark, 1971-73, Giordano, Halleran & McOmber, Middletown, NJ, 1973-74; asst. U.S. atty. for N.J. U.S. Dept. Justice, 1966-71; ptnr. Evans, Koelzer, Osborne & Kreizman, N.Y.C. and Red Bank,

N.J., 1974-86, Ober, Kaler, Grimes & Shriver, N.Y.C., 1986-92, Lane Powell Spears Lubersky, L.A., 1993-97, Hancock, Rothert & Bunshoft, L.A., 1997-2000, Coudert Bros., L.A., London, 2000—. Adj. prof. Seton Hall U. Sch. Law, 1989—92; mem. lawyers adv. com. U.S. Ct. Appeals (3d cir.), 1985—87, vice chmn., 1986, chmn., 87; mem. lawyers adv. com. U.S. Dist. Ct. N.J., 1984—92; permanent mem. Jud. Conf. U.S. Ct. Appeals (3d cir.); del. jud. conf. U.S. Ct. Appeals (2d cir.), 1987—89. Recipient Atty. Gen.'s award, 1970. Fellow: Am. Bar Found.; mem.: ABA (co-chmn. com. admiralty and maritime litig. 1979—82, mem. nominating com. 1982, dir. divsn. IV procedural coms. 1982—85, chmn. 9th ann. meeting sect. litig. 1984, mem. nominating com. 1984, mem. coun. sect. litig. 1985—88, advisor standing com. lawyer competence 1986—2001, mem. nominating com. 1987, dir. divsn. I adminstrn. 1988—89, co-chmn. com. admiralty and maritime litig. 1989—90, sect. litig.), Assn. Bus. Trial Lawyers, Assn. Average Adjusters U.S., Assn. Average Adjusters Gt. Britain, Comml. Bar Assn. (London), Fed. Bar Coun., DC Bar Assn., Assn. Bar City of N.Y. (mem. admiralty com. 1987—90), N.Y. State Bar Assn. (chmn. admiralty com., comml. and fed. litig. sect. 1989—92), State Bar Calif., Maritime Law Assn. U.S. (vice chmn. com. maritime fraud and crime 1989—94, chmn. 1994—98, bd. dirs. 1998—2001, mem. ABA rels. com., mem. fed. procedure com.), Civil Justice Inst., L.A. World Affairs Coun., Jonathan Club (L.A.), Mid-Ocean Club (Bermuda). Republican. Roman Catholic. Home: 521 S Orange Grove Blvd 100 Pasadena CA 91105-3528 Office Phone: 213-229-2921. Business E-Mail: gkoelzer@coudert.com.

KOEN, BENJAMIN DAVID, musician, educator, writer; s. Leon and Thelma Jean Koen; m. Elham Saba Yazdanpour, Apr. 4, 1998; children: Naseem Serene, Solya Taj. BMus in Jazz Studies/Performance, Ohio State U., Columbus, 1987—90, MA in Cognitive Ethnomusicology, 1998—2000, PhD in Cognitive/Med. Ethnomusicology, 2000—03. Fgn. expert in music Lioaning Youth Mgmt. Engring. Coll., Shenyang, China, 1996—97; musician, composer, rec. artist Green Mountain Records, Tallahassee, 1987—; instr., grad. tchg. assoc., music Ohio State U., Columbus, 1998—2003, rsch. assoc., cognitive ethnomusicology lab., 2000—01; med. ethnomusicologist Humanities Project for Ctrl. Asia-Aga Khan Found., Dushanbe & Khoroq, Tajikistan, 2001; music presenter Smithsonian Instn., Washington, 2002; asst. prof., ethnomusicology Fla. State U. Sch. Music, Tallahassee, 2003—. Musician: (albums) William Parker's Sunrise in the Tone World, Songs From Green Mountain, Reliance, 110 Bridge St.; contbr. articles to profl. jours. Musician, lectr., workshop presenter One Human Family Workshops Inc., Columbus, Ohio, 2000—02; music and healing spkr. Leon County Libr. Sys., Tallahassee, 2004; music performance for the elderly Blossom Nursing Home/Altercare of Alliance, Ohio, 1980—87; music performer for the elderly St. George on the Commons, Columbus, Ohio, 1999—2003; music presenter Soul Miners Project, Columbus, Ohio, 2000—01; sec. Dorothy Baker Tng. Inst., Columbus, Ohio, 1996—2002. Grantee, Assn. for the Study of Persian Speaking Socs., 2002. Mem.: Soc. for the Study of Persian Socs. (assoc.), Coll. Music Soc. (assoc.), Soc. for Med. Anthropology (assoc.), Soc. for Ethnomusicology (assoc.), Kappa Lambda (assoc.), Phi Kappa Phi (assoc.). Avocations: taiji, swimming, dance, oragami. Office: Fla State Univ Sch Music Tallahassee FL 32306-1180 Office Phone: 850-644-4642. Office Fax: 850-644-2033. Business E-Mail: bkoen@fsu.edu.

KOEN, BILLY VAUGHN, mechanical engineering educator; b. Graham, Tex., May 2, 1938; s. Ottis Vaughn and Margaret (Branch) Koen; m. Deanne Rollins, June 3, 1967; children: Kent, Douglas. BA in Chemistry, BS in Chem. Engring., U. Tex., 1961; S.M. in Nuclear Engring., MIT, 1962, Sc.D. in Nuclear Engring., 1968; Diplome d'ingeneiur en Genie Atomique, L'institut National des Scis. et Techniques Nucleaires, France, 1963. Registered profl. engr., Tex. Asst. prof. mech. engring. U. Tex., Austin, 1968-71, assoc. prof., 1971-80, Minnie S. Piper prof., 1980, prof., 1981—; dir. Bur. Engring. Teaching U. Tex.-Austin, 1973-76. Prof. Ecole Centrale, Paris, 1983; undergrad advisor mech. engring., 1988-92; vis. prof. Tokyo Inst. Tech., 1994 (summer), 1998-99, 2001 (summer); cons., lectr. in field. Author: Definition of the Engineering Method, 1985, Discussion of the Method, 2003; contbr. articles to profl. jours. Bd. dirs. Oak Ridge Associated Univs., 1975-76. Recipient Standard Oil Ind. award, 1970, W. Leighton Collins Distinguished and Unusual Service awd., Am. Soc. for Engineering Education, 1992. Fellow Am. Soc. Engring. Edn. (v.p. 1987-93, Chester Carlson award 1980, Ben Dasher best paper award 1985, 86, Helen Plants award 1986, William Elgin Wickenden best paper award 1986, Olmsted award, dir. 1982-84, W. Leighton Collins award 1992, Centennial medallion 1993), Am. Nuc. Soc.; mem. N.Y. Acad. Sci., Association des Ingenieurs en Genie Atomique, Rotary Club (Austin; Internat. fellow 1962), Phi Beta Kappa, Sigma Xi (disting. lectr. 1981-83), Tau Beta Pi. Mem. Soc. Of Friends. Achievements include development of computer algorithm for calculation of nuclear system reliability. Office: U Tex Dept Mech Engring Etc 5160 Austin TX 78712 Business E-Mail: koen@uts.cc.utexas.edu.

KOEN, ROBERT G., lawyer; b. 1946; BA with honors, U. Wis., 1968; JD, Georgetown U., 1972. Bar: NY 1973, US Tax Ct. 1974, NJ 1974. Ptnr. LeBoeuf, Lamb, Leiby & MacRae, NYC, Akin Gump Strauss Hauer & Feld LLP, NYC; now ptnr., comml. real estate DLA Piper Rudnick Gray Cary, NYC, 2004—. Editor Internat. Law Jour. Georgetown, 1971-72, Real Estate Fin. Jour. Law fellow Georgetown Law Sch., 1971-72. Mem.: ABA, Comml. Real Estate Secondary Mkt. and Securitization Assn., NY State Bar Assn., Assn. of Bar of NYC. Office: Piper Rudnick 1251 Ave of the Americas New York NY 10020-1104 Office Phone: 212-835-6187. Office Fax: 212-884-8487. Business E-Mail: robert.koen@piperrudnick.com.

KOENEMAN, DONALD W., marketing executive; b. Chester, Pa., Sept. 3, 1951; s. Harry S. and Edith J. Koeneman; m. Cynthia E. Barratt, Dec. 22, 1973; 1 child, Todd D. None, US Navy, 1975. Regional sales mgr. AMETEK Drexelbrook, Horsham, Pa., 1978—96, sr. product mgr., 1996—. Contbr. articles to tech. jours. Petty officer USN, 1969—75. Mem.: Instrument Soc. of Am. Achievements include development of Continuouos RF sensing element for non metallic vessels. Office: AMETEK Drexelbrook 205 Keith Valley Rd Horsham PA 19044 Office Phone: 215-674-1234. Office Fax: 215-674-2731. E-mail: don.koeneman@ametek.com.

KOENIG, ALLEN EDWARD, higher education consultant; b. Feb. 11, 1939; s. Edward and Eva (Barnes) Koenig; m. Judy Lynn Gill, June 8, 1969; children: Wendy, Jody, Mark. BA, U. So. Calif., 1961; MA, Stanford U., 1962; PhD, Northwestern U., 1964. Asst. prof. speech Ea. Mich. State U., Ypsilanti, 1964—65, U. Wis.-Milw., 1965—67, Ohio State U., Columbus, 1967—69; dir. comm. AAUP, Washington, 1969—70; v.p. devel. Capital U., Columbus, 1970—74; exec. v.p. Marycrest Coll., Davenport, Iowa, 1974—75; assoc. dir. U. So. Calif.-Idyllwild Camps, 1975—76, exec. dir., 1976—79; pres. Emerson Coll., Boston, 1979—89, Chapman U., Orange, Calif., 1989—91; sr. assoc. Thomas H. Langevin & Assoc., 1992—2002; sr. cons. R.H. Perry & Assocs., 1993—. Prof. cons. radio TV stas. Appalachia Ednl. Lab., Charleston, W.Va., 1967—69; mem. commn. on leadership devel. Am. Coun. on Edn., Washington, 1984—86; co-founder Registry Coll. and U. Pres., 1992, vice chmn., 2003—; vis. prof. mass comm. Boston U., 1991—92. Sr. editor: The Farther Vision: Educational Television Today, 1967; editor: Broadcasting and Bargaining: Labor Relations in Radio and Television, 1970, Jour. Ednl. Broadcasting Rev., 1967—69; contbr. articles to profl. jours. Bd. mem., v.p., treas., pres. Profl. Arts Consortium, Boston, 1981—89; exec. bd. dirs. pres.'s steering com. Boston Pub. Schs., 1982—86; trustee Marycrest Coll., Davenport, 1982—86. Recipient Broadcast Preceptor award, San Francisco State Coll., 1969, 1971. Mem.: NATAS (bd. govs. New Eng. chpt. 1980—84, pres. 1988—89), Mass. Corp. for Ednl. Telecomm. (chmn. 1989), Assn. Ind. Colls. and Univs. in Mass. (exec. com. 1983—89), Alpha Kappa Delta, Alpha Epsilon Rho. Office Phone: 614-798-0538. E-mail: akoenig@columbus.rr.com.

KOENIG, ELDO C., computer engineer, research scientist; BSEE, Washington U., St. Louis, 1943; MSEE, Ill. Inst. Tech., Chgo., 1949; MSE, U. Wis., Madison, 1951, PhD, 1956. Scientist Manhattan project U.S. War Dept., N.Y.C.; faculty U. Wis., Madison, 1962—. Author (with Charles H. Davidson): Computers; Introduction to Computers and Applied Computing Concepts, 1967, Japanese edit., 1970; contbr. scientific papers, articles to profl. jours. Recipient Allis Chalmers Fellowship award, 1952, Alfred Noble prize, ASCE, 1951. Fellow: AAAS; mem.: IEEE (sr.), Assn. Computing Machinery, Eta Kappa Nu, Sigma Xi, Tau Beta Pi. Home: 35005 Fairview Rd Oconomowoc WI 53066-3312 E-mail: koenigec@execpc.com.

KOENIG, HAROLD MARTIN, former United States Navy surgeon general; b. Salinas, Calif., Feb. 28, 1940; m. Deena Prescott; children: Steven Fillmore, Scott Osborne, Grant Matthew. BS, Brigham Young U., 1962; MD, Baylor U., 1966. Diplomate Am. Acad. Pediatrics, Pediatric Hematology and Oncology. Commd. lt. USN, 1958, advanced through grades to vice adm.; gen. med. officer Fleet Activities, Sasebo, Japan, 1967-69; resident, fellow Naval Hosp., San Diego, 1969-73, head pediatric, hematology-oncology div., 1973-80; chief pediatrics Naval Regional Med. Ctr., Oakland, Calif., 1980-83; dir. med. svcs. Naval Hosp., Oakland, 1983-84, exec. officer Portsmouth, Va., 1984-85, comdg. officer San Diego, 1985-87, Naval Health Scis. Edn. and Tng. Command, Bethesda, Md., 1987-88; dir. health care ops. div. Office of Surgeon Gen./Naval Medicine, Washington, 1988-90; dep. asst. sec. def. Health Svcs. Ops., Office of Sec. Def., Washington, 1990-94; surgeon gen. USN, Washington, 1994-98, ret., 1998. Contbr. articles to profl. jours. Decorated Def. Superior Svc. medal, Legion of Merit (2); recipient 4 other personal awards, Navy disting. svc. medal. Fellow Am. Acad. Pediatrics (chmn. mil. sect. 1982-84), Am. Soc. Hematology; mem. AMA, other med. socs. Home: 4933 Marlborough Dr San Diego CA 92116-2346 Personal E-mail: eaglesct@cox.net.

KOENIG, HAROLD PAUL, management consultant, ecologist, evangelist, writer; b. Mason City, Iowa, Apr. 22, 1926; s. Reuben Harold and Dorothea (Paule) K.; m. Barbara Anne Rucker, June 29, 1974; children: Kimberley Anne, Joseph Paul, Liberty U. Student, Ohio Wesleyan U., 1944-45; BS, Iowa State U., 1947; MS, Ill. Inst. Tech., 1956. Registered profl. engr., Iowa, Minn., Ill., Ind., Fla.; ordained to ministry Bapt. Ch., 1994. Chief engr. Grain Processing Corp., Muscatine, Iowa, 1948-50; engr. mgr. Standard Oil Co. Ind., Whiting, Ind., 1953-56; with Booz, Allen & Hamilton, Chgo. and Genoa, Italy, 1956-64; v.p. Dresser Industries, Inc., Dallas, 1964-67; founder, chmn., pres., CEO Ecol. Sci. Corp., Miami and Lugano, Switzerland, 1967-73, Tele-Optics, Inc., West Palm Beach, Fla., 1986-90; chmn., pres., CEO Unionam., Inc. subs. Windham Power Lifts, Elba, Ala., 1974-76; dir. gen., CEO Matisa, S.A., Lausanne, Switzerland, 1977-78; dir. gen. Canron Pipe & Hydraulics, Montreal, Que., Can., 1978-80; COO Tel-Tech Devices, Inc., Ft. Lauderdale, Fla., 1984-86; chmn. H.P. Koenig Mgmt. Cons., Miami, 1980-84, Jupiter, Satellite Beach, Fla., 1990—. Cert. trainer Evang. Explosion Internat., Ft. Lauderdale, 1981—, cert. Evang. Explosion lectr., West Palm Beach, 1991—; advisor Citizens Democracy Corps, Russia, 1996-97, Ukraine, 1998; lectr. in field. Author: Winning Against Satan-Applying Military Principles to Spiritual Warfare, 1991; contbr. articles to profl. jours. Witness on environ. and ecol. matters U.S. Congress, Washington, 1969-71; adv. for founding Earth Day, 1970; mem. Citizens Democracy Corps, Khabarovsk, Sakhalin Island, Russia, 1996, Velikie Luki, Russia, 1997, Odessa and Nikolaev, Ukraine, 1998; adv. for Drug Treatment Fla., 1998-; mem. Pres. Nixon's Com. on Environ. Quality, 1969-72; deacon Bapt. Ch., missionary to Kenya; founder, pres., CEO H.E.A.R.T. (Help Early Addicts Receive Treatment), 1999-; scoutmaster, Iowa, 1949-50. Lt. comdr. USNR, 1943-46; PTO Seabees, 1951-53. Recipient Eagle Scout award with bronze, silver, gold palms, Boy Scouts Am., 1942, Meritorious Svc. award, Govt. of Italy, 1962, Ziegenhein award, PREVENT, 2005. Mem. Phi Gamma Delta (Golden Owl award), Gideon. Republican. Avocations: tennis, bridge, golf. Home and Office: 705 Palmer Way Melbourne FL 32940 Office Phone: 321-752-4485.

KOENIG, JOHN M., ambassador; b. Tacoma, 1958; m. Natalie Koenig; children: Ted, Alex. Staff asst. Bur. East Asian and Pacific Affairs US Dept. State, Washington, watch officer, Am. vice consul to Manila Philippines, Am. political officer to East Berlin, Am. political officer to Jakarta, Am. sr. political officer to Nicosia, Am. political-military officer, dep. political counselor Athens, Greece, dep. chief of US Mission to NATO, acting permanent representative, US Mission to NATO. Office: Bureau European and Eurasian Affairs US Dept State 2201 C St NW Rm 4515 Washington DC 20520*

KOENIG, LOUIS WILLIAM, political science professor, writer; b. Poughkeepsie, N.Y., May 28, 1916; s. Casper and Pauline (Graf) K.; m. Eleanor Margaret White, July 30, 1945; 1 child, Juliana. BA, Columbia U., 1938, MA, 1940, PhD, 1944; LHD (hon.), Bard Coll., 1960. Adminstrv. addt. Nat Resources Planning Bd., Washington, 1941; legis. analyst U.S. Bur. Budget, Washington, 1941-42; procedures analyst Office Price Adminstrn., Washington, 1943-44, assoc. adminstrv. history project, 1944-46; instr., asst. prof. Bard Coll., Annandale-on-Hudson, N.Y., 1944-50; assoc. prof., prof. polit. sci. NYU, N.Y.C., 1950-86, adj. prof., 1986—. Mem. fgn. affairs task force Hoover Commn., Washington, 1948-49; intelligence analyst Dept. State, Washington, 1950; staff assoc., cons. Fund for Advancement Edn., Ford Found., N.Y.C., 1954-55; lectr. exec. seminars CSC, King's Point, N.Y., Oak Ridge, Tenn., U. Va., Charlottesville, 1964—; lectr. Nat. War U., Washington, 1966—, Air War Coll., 1965—; vis. prof. Columbia U., N.Y.C., 1965, 78, CUNY, 1968, C.W. Post Ct., L.I. U., Brookville, N.Y., 1986—; instr. non-fiction writing Bread Loaf Writers' Conf., Middlebury Coll., 1960; cons. program in polit. theory and constl. law Rockefeller Found., N.Y.C., 1962-63; cons. N.Y.C. Charter Revisin Commn., 1987-88; dir. seminar for coll. tchrs. NEH, Washington and N.Y.C., 1976, 77, 79, 81; dir. seminar on polit. parties, Robert A. Taft Inst., N.Y.C., 1982; commentator on presdl. inauguration, author and performer NBC-TV, 1969. Author: The Presidency and the Crisis: From the Invasion of Poland to Pearl Harbor, 1944, The Truman Administration, 1956, repub. 1979, The Presidency Today, 1956, The Invisible Presidency, 1960, The Chief Executive, 1964, 6th edit., 1996, Congress and the President, 1965, Bryan, A Political Biography of William Jennings Bryan, 1971, paperback edit. 1975, Toward a Democracy, 1973, An Introduction to Public Policy, 1986; co-author: Congress, the Presidency, and the Taiwan Relations Act, 1985; chmn. bd. editors Presdl. Studies Quar., 1972-94. Chmn. concerned Christian for social responsibility Cmty. Ch., Garden City, N.Y., 1968-74, chmn. bd. missions, 1976-80. Gilder fellow Columbia U., 1940. Mem. ASPA, Am. Polit. Sci. Assn., Phi Beta Kappa. Avocations: gardening, stamp collecting/philately, travel. Home: 135 Chestnut St Garden City NY 11530-6424

KOENIG, ROBERT AUGUST, minister, educator; b. Red Wing, Minn., July 14, 1933; s. William C. and Florence E. (Tebbe) Koenig; m. Pauline Louise Olson, June 21, 1962. BS cum laude, U. Wis., Superior, 1955; MA in Ednl. Adminstrn., U. Minn., 1965, PhD, 1973; MDiv magna cum laude, San Francisco Theol. Sem., 1969; postgrad. (John Hay fellow), Bennington Coll., summer, 1965. Ordained to ministry Presbyn. Ch., 1970. Supr. music Florence (Wis.) H.S., 1955—56; dir. instrumental music Chetek (Wis.) Pub. Schs., 1958—62; tchr. instrumental music and humanities Palo Alto (Calif.) Sr. H.S., 1962—65; asst. to min. St. John's Presbyn. Ch., San Francisco, 1964—65; min. Sawyer County (Wis.) larger parish, 1969—74; tchr. gen. music Jordan Jr. H.S., Palo Alto, 1966—69; instr. Coll. Edn. U. Minn., 1969—71; adminstv. asst. to pres. Lakewood State C.C., White Bear Lake, Minn., 1971—72; asst. to exec. dir. Minn. Higher Edn. Coord. Bd., St. Paul, 1972, coord. commn. and pers. svcs., 1972—74; instr. Inver Hills C.C., Inver Grove Heights, Minn., 1974; pastor First Presbyn. Ch. of Chippewa Falls (Wis.), 1974—85; sr. pastor Grove Presbyn. Ch., Danville, Pa., 1985—88, First Presbyn. Ch., South St. Paul, Minn., 1988—98; stated supply pastor Couderay and Radisson Presbyn. Chs., Wis., 1999—. Mem. study com. Presbytery of Chippewa, 1973—74, mem. min. rels. com., 1974—77; adj. asst. prof. ednl. adminstrn. U. Minn., Mpls., 1976—77; mem. faculty U. Wis. Ext., Eau Claire, 1977; chmn. 3d Ann. Bibl. Sem., 1977; mem. faculty Communiversity, 1977—85; mem. ministerial rels. com. Presbytery of No. Waters, 1977—82, chmn., 1981—82, moderator, 1983; mem. internat. coord. com. ch. mission Synod Lakes and Prairies, 1978—79; chmn. Synod Designation Pastor Plan Cabinet, 1982—84, Presbytery Coun., 1982—84, mem., 1987—88; chairperson Christian edn. com. Presbytery of Northumberland, 1987—88; mem. Christian edn. com. Synod of the Trinity, 1987—88; mem. com. ministry Presbytery of Twin Cities Area, 1999—2001, Danville-Riverside Area Ministerial Assn., 1985—88, pres., 1987—88; mem. South St. Paul Ministerial Assn., 1988—98, pres., 1989—90. Contbr. articles to profl. jours. Bd. dirs. N. Ctrl. Career Devel. Ctr., Mpls., 1978—84, chmn. fin. com., 1979—84, bd. dirs. devel. found., 1983—85; pres. Chippewa Valley Ecumenical Housing Assn., 1984—85; bd. dirs. Coll. Edn. and Human Devel. Alumni Soc. U. Minn., 1999—2005, mem. exec. com., 2001—05, v.p., 2001—02, pres., 2002—04. With U.S. Army, 1956—58, Korea. Mem.: Elks (Danville chpt.), Masons (grand chaplain Wis. chpt. 1977—80, 1983—85), Phi Delta Kappa (U. Minn. Twin Cities chpt.). Home: 6045 Bowman Ave E Inver Grove Heights MN 55076-1502

KOENIG, RODNEY CURTIS, lawyer, rancher; b. Black Jack, Tex., Nov. 21, 1940; s. John Henry and Elva Marguerite (Oeding) K.; m. Mary Mishler, May 1, 1993; children: Erik Jason, Jon Todd. BA, U. Tex., 1962, JD with honors, 1969; postgrad., Auburn U., 1965-67. Bar: Tex. 1969, U.S. Dist. Ct. (so. dist.) Tex. 1970, U.S. Ct. Appeals (5th cir.) 1970, U.S. Tax Ct. 1980, U.S. Ct. Mil. Appeals 1986. Ptnr. Fulbright & Jaworski, LLP, Houston, 1969—. Asst. prof. Auburn U., 1965-67; lectr. in field Contbr. articles to profl. jours. Pres. Houston Navy League, 1979-81; commr. Battleship Texas Commn.; Houston Saengerbund; bd. dirs. Houston divsn. Am. Heart Assn., Fayette Heritage Mus.; dir. Advanced Estate Planning and Probate Course, 1988; trustee Luck and Loessin Collection Trust, Luth. Found. of the S.W., treas., exec. com.; active Tex. Luth. U. Corp.; mem. Planned Giving Adv. Coun., U. Tex., 2005-. With USN, 1962-67; capt. JAGC, USNR, 1967-89. Recipient Fed. Republic of Germany Order of Merit, 1994. Fellow Am. Coll. Trust and Estate Counsel, Coll. State Bar Tex. (charter); mem. ABA, Internat. Acad. Estate and Trust Law (academician), Tex. Judge Adv. Res. Officers Assn., German Texan Heritage Soc. (pres. 1997-2000), Tex. German Soc. (founding dir.), Res. Officers Assn., Sons of Republic of Tex., Wednesday Tax Forum (past chmn.), German Gulf Coast Assn. (pres. 1989-93), Bach Soc. (bd. dirs.), English Speaking Union (bd. dirs.), Houston Early Music (pres. 2000-04), Houston Karneval Verein (prince 1994-95), USS San Jacinto Com. (treas.), Houstonian Club, Frisch Auf Valley Country Club, Order of Coif, U.S. Naval Order, U.T. NROTC Alumni Assn. (pres. 2000-02), Fayette Meml. Found. (bd. dirs.), Phi Delta Phi, Omicron Delta Kappa. Lutheran. Home: 2720 University Blvd Houston TX 77005-3440 Office: Fulbright & Jaworski LLP 1301 Mckinney St Fl 51 Houston TX 77010-3031 Office Phone: 713-651-5333. E-mail: rkoenig@fulbright.com.

KOENIGSKNECHT, ROY A., dean; b. Fowler, Mich., Dec. 27, 1942; s. Joseph I. and Katherine (Zimmermann) K.; m. Marilie A. Dani, Aug. 20, 1966; children: John, Adam, Amanda. AB in Psychology, Central Mich. U., 1964; MA in Speech and Lang. Pathology, Northwestern U., 1965, PhD in Communicative Disorders, 1968. Head speech and lang. pathology Northwestern U., Evanston, Ill., 1973-78, prof. speech and lang. pathology, 1975-85, chair communicative disorders, 1978-81, assoc. dean Grad. Sch., 1981-85; prof. speech and hearing sci. Ohio State U, Columbus, 1985—; dean Grad. Sch. Ohio State U., Columbus, 1985-95; v.p. Ohio State U. Rsch. Found., Columbus, 1985-95. Mem. Grad. Record Exams. Bd., 1991-95, NIH adv. bd. on deafness and other communicative disorders, 1990-95; cons. evaluator Commn. on Instns. Higher Edn., 1996—. Author: Developmental Sentence Analysis, 1974; Interactive Language Development, 1975. Contbr. articles to profl. jours. Mem. adv. coun. on grad. study Ohio Bd. Regents, Columbus, 1985-95; bd. dirs. Friends of Evanston Pub. Libr., 1984, Evanston Pub. Libr., 1985. Recipient Disting. Alumni award Central Mich. U., 1977; Fulbright fellow, 1982. Fellow Am. Speech-Lang. Hearing Assn. (exec. bd. 1986-91, pres. 1990), AAU Assn. Grad. Schs.), Com. on Instnl. Cooperation Grad. Deans (chair 1985-86), Nat. Assn. State U. and Land Grant Colls.-Coun. Rsch. Pol. and Grad. Edn. (exec. com. 1995-96). Avocations: golf, skiing. Home: 720 Gatehouse Ln Columbus OH 43235-1732 Office: Ohio State U 105 Pressey Hall Columbus OH 43210-1335 Business E-Mail: koenigsknecht.1@oso.edu.

KOENKER, DIANE P., history professor; b. Chgo., July 29, 1947; m. Roger Koenker; 1 child. AB in History, Grinnell Coll., 1969; AM in Comparative Studies in History, U. Mich., 1971, PhD in History, 1976. From asst. prof. to assoc. prof. in history Temple U., Phila., 1976-83; asst. prof. history U. Ill., Urbana-Champaign, 1983-86, assoc. prof., 1986-88, prof. history, 1988—, dir. Russian and East European Ctr., 1990-96, editor Slavic Rev., 1996—. Vis. lectr. history U. Ill., Urbana-Champaign, 1975; vis. fellow Australian Nat. U., 1989; Fulbright-Hays Faculty Rsch. Abroad, 1993; lectr. in field. Author: Moscow Workers and the 1917 Revolution, 1981, paperback edit., 1986, (with William G. Rosenberg) Strikes and Revolution in Russia 1917, 1989, Republic of Labor: Russian Printers and Soviet Socialism, 1918-1930, 2005; editor: Tret'ya Vserossiiskaya Konferentsiya Professional'nykh Soyuzov 1917, 1982, (with William G. Rosenberg and Ronald Grigor Suny) Party, State and Society in the Russian Civil War: Explorations in Social History, 1989, (with Ronald D. Bachman) Revelations from the Russian Archives, 1997; editor, translator: (with S.A. Smith) Notes of a Red Guard, 1993; mem. editl. bd. Cambridge Soviet Paperbacks; mem. adv. bd. Soviet Studies in History, 1986-89; book reviewer to numerous jours.; contbr. articles to profl. jours. Rsch. fellow Temple U., 1977, 82, Sr. fellow Russian Inst.-Columbia U., 1977-78, Individual fellow NEH, 1983-84, Rsch. fellow NEH, 1984-85, 94-95, MUCIA Exch. fellow Moscow State U., 1991; grantee Am. Coun. Learned Socs.-Social Sci. Rsch. Coun., 1977-78, Temple U., 1979-81, 82-83, William and Flora Hewlett Internat. Rsch. grantee, 1986, 91, Nat. Coun. for Soviet and East European Rsch. grantee, 1989, IREX Travel grantee, 1993; recipient Fulbright-Hays Faculty Rsch. award for USSR, 1989, Arnold O. Beckman Rsch. Bd. award, 1990-91, 2002-. Mem. Am. Hist. Assn. (mem. membership com. 1996-98, European History sect. chair 2001, Chester Higby prize European sect. 2003), Am. Assn. Advancement Slavic Studies (bd. dirs. 1996—), Midwest Workshop of Russian and Soviet Historians, Assn. Women in Slavic Studies. Office: U Ill Slav Rev 57 E Armory Ave Champaign IL 61820-6601 also: U Ill Dept History 309 Gregory Hall 810 S Wright St Urbana IL 61801-3644

KOEPFF, PAUL R., lawyer; b. Morristown, NJ, 1947; BA cum laude, Lehigh U., 1969, MBA in Econs., 1970; JD, Duke u., 1973. Bar: NY 1974, US Dist. Ct. (So. and Ea. Districts NY) 1974, US Ct. Appeals (1st, 2nd, 3rd, 4th, 5th, 6th, & 9th Circuits) 1974, US Supreme Ct. 1978, NJ 1992, US Dist. Ct. (Western Dist. Michigan) 1994. Ptnr. litig. O'Melveny & Myers LLP, NYC, chair insurance and mass torts practice. Rsch. and mng. editor Duke Law Jour., 1972—73, contbg. author (to chapters of a treatise) NY Insurance Law. Mem.: Defense Research Inst., Federation of Insurance and Corp. Counsel, Assn. of the Bar of the City of NY (past mem.), NY State Bar Assn. (past mem.), ABA (litig. sect. and Tort and Insurance Practice Sect.). Office: O'Melveny & Myers LLP Times Square Tower 7 Times Square New York NY 10036 Office Phone: 212-326-2189. Office Fax: 212-326-2061. Business E-Mail: pkoepff@omm.com.

KOEPFINGER, JOSEPH LEO, retired utilities executive; b. Sewickley, Pa., May 6, 1925; s. Joseph P. and Mary M. (O'Hanlon) K.; m. Genevieve C. Strobel, Oct. 1, 1955; children: Nancy, Joseph, Margaret, Patricia, James, Paul. BSEE, U. Pitts., 1949, MSEE, 1953. Jr. devel. engr. Duquesne Light Co., Pitts., 1949-52, devel. engr., 1952-54, sr. devel. engr., 1954-57, project engr., 1957-61, sr. project engr., 1961-64, product and comml. engr., 1964-80, dir. project and comml. dept., 1980-85, dir. sys. studies and rsch., 1985-2000, ret., 2000, ind. cons., 2000—. Chmn. accredited std. com. C62, Am. Nat. Std. Inst.; bd. dirs. Mehta Tech. Inc.; U.S. tech. adv. Internat. Electrotech. Commn., 1979—, sec. for IEC 37, 1996—; advisor to Lane dept. computer sci. and elec. engring. acad. W.Va. U., IEEE Power Engring. Soc. disting. lectr. Prin. writer standard Guide for Surge Withstand Capability Test, 1974 Pres. Moon Area Sch. Dist., Moon Twp., Pa., 1978-79. With U.S. Army, 1943-45, ETO. Fellow IEEE (mem. emeritus stds. bd., Charles P. Steimetz award 1989), IEEE Power Engring. Soc. (Excellence in Power Distbn. Engring. award 1998). Democrat. Roman Catholic. Home: 119 Windy Willow Dr Coraopolis PA 15108-2945

KOEPKE, ALLEN HENRY, music educator, composer; b. Chgo., Apr. 20, 1939; s. Henry Emil and Dorothy Laura Frieda (Theel) Koepke; m. Sherril Lynn Head, June 8, 1986; children: Scott, Amy Koepke Hanisch, Ann, Stephen stepchildren: Amy Reedy Davis, Chad Reedy, Ryan Reedy. BA, Luther Coll., Decorah, Iowa, 1960; MA, U. Northern Iowa, Cedar Falls, 1967. Cert. permanent tchg. Iowa Dept. Edn., 1967. Dir. choral activities Clear Lake Cmty. Schs., Clear Lake, Iowa, 1960—67, Jefferson H.S., Cedar Rapids, 1967—80, Kirkwood C.C., 1980—96; choir dir. Springfield Luth. Ch., Decorah, 1957—58, Calmar Luth. Ch., 1958—60, First Congregational Ch., Clear Lake, 1960—67, St. Stephens Luth. Ch., Cedar Rapids, 1967—72, Trinity Meth. Ch., 1972—83, All Saints Cath. Ch., 1983—85, St. John's Christ Episcopal Ch., 1985—97, St. Mark's Luth. Ch., Iowa, 1998—. Musical and tour dir. The Young Americans, L.A., Calif., 1969; mem. artistic com. Cedar Rapids Symphony Orch., 1998—; bd. dir. Heuer Publs., Iowa. Composer: Missa Brevis, 1995, In Praise of Music, 1996, A Vision, A Dream, 1996, over 60 published works. Initiator Show Choir, Iowa, 1968, Collegiate Jazz Choir, Iowa, 1983; musical dir. Cedar Rapids Follies, 1979—83, NAACP prodn. Kismet, Cedar Rapids, 1982. Recipient Iowa Prof. of Yr., Carnegie Found. Advancement of Tchg., 1996, Innovator of Yr., League for Innovation, 1996. Mem.: Am. Choral Dirs. Assn., Iowa Choral Dirs. Assn. (Robert M. McCowen Meml. award 1997). Lutheran. Avocations: reading, golf, crossword puzzles. Personal E-mail: ahkoepke@aol.com. E-mail: allen@koepkemusic.com.

KOEPKE, JOHN ARTHUR, hematologist, clinical pathologist; b. Milw., Mar. 25, 1929; s. Elmer Paul and Meta Clara (Jennrich) K.; m. Evelyn Mae Lovekamp, June 18, 1955; children: Mary Evelyn, John Frederick, Mark David, James Robert. BA, Valparaiso U., 1951; MD, U. Wis., 1956; MS, Marquette U., 1964. Intern, resident in clin. pathology and internal medicine Milw. Hosp., 1956-60; mem. faculty U. Ky. Coll. Medicine, 1961-71, assoc. prof., 1965-71; dir. clin. pathology, prof. pathology U. Iowa, Iowa City, 1972-79, vice chmn. dept., 1972-79; prof. pathology, assoc. prof. internal medicine Coll. Medicine, Duke U., Durham, N.C., 1979-94; dir.clin. transfusion svc. hematology lab. Duke U. Med. Ctr., 1979-88, prof. emeritus, 1994—. Vis. scientist Karolinska Inst., Stockholm, 1967-68, Royal Postgrad. Med. Sch., London, 1978. Author 7 books in field; editor 6 books; bd. editors Am. Jour. Clin. Pathology, 1976—, Clin. and Lab. Hematology, 1978-94, Blood Cells, 1985-98; assoc. editor Cytometry, 1993-1998, Comms. in Clin. Cytometry, 1994-99, Lab. Hematology, 1994—; contbr. over 250 articles to profl. jours., 25 chpts. to books. Recipient Pres.'s award Valparaiso U., 1951, also Disting. Alumnus award, 1980. Fellow Am. Soc. Clin. Pathology, Coll. Am. Pathologists; mem. AMA, Internat. Coun. for Standards in Hematology (secretariat 1978—, v.p. 1990-92, pres. 1992-94). Lutheran. Home: 3924 Saint Mark's Rd Durham NC 27707-5015 E-mail: nckoepke@mindspring.com.

KOEPP, DAVID, screenwriter; Grad., UCLA. Screenwriter: (with Martin Donovan) Apartment Zero, 1989 (also prodr.), Bad Influence, 1990, (with Daniel Petrie Jr.) Toy Soldiers, 1991, (with Donovan) Death Becomes Her, 1992, (with Michael Crichton) Jurassic Park, 1993, Carlito's Way, 1993, (with Stephen Koepp) The Paper, 1994 (also co-prodr.), The Shadow, 1994, Mission: Impossible, 1996, The Trigger Effect, 1996 (also dir.), The Lost World: Jurassic Park, 1997, Snake Eyes, 1998, Stir of Echoes, 1999 (also dir.), Panic Room, 2002 (also prodr.), Spider-Man, 2002, Secret Window, 2004, War of the Worlds, 2005, (TV films) Hack, 2002 (also exec. prodr.), (TV series) Hack, 2002-04 (also exec. prodr.). exec. prodr., dir. (TV films) Suspense, 2003.*

KOEPP, DONNA PAULINE PETERSEN, librarian; b. Clinton, Iowa, Oct. 8, 1941; d. Leo August and Pauline Sena (Outzen) Petersen; m. David Ward Koepp, June 5, 1960 (div. June 1984). BS in Edn., U. Colo., 1967; MA in Libr., U. Denver, 1974; postgrad., U. Colo., 1984-85. Subject specialist govt. publs., map dept. Denver Pub. Libr., 1967-85; head govt. documents, map libr. U. Kans., Lawrence, 1985-2000, map and geomedia svcs. libr., 2000—02. Head govt. document, microforms, reference instrn. Soc. Sci. Program Harvard U., 2002-; apptd. Fed. Depository Libr. Coun. to Pub. Printer, 1998-2001. Prodn. mgr. Meridian Jour., 1988-93, 96-99; editor: Index and Carto-Bibliography of Maps, 1789-1969, 1995. Recipient Documents to the People award Congl. Info. Svc./Govt. Documents Round Table/ALA, 1999. Mem. Map & Geography Round Table of Am. Libr. Assn. (chmn. 1986-87, Outstanding Contbn. to Map Librarianship 1991), Govt. Documents Round Table of Am. Libr. Assn., Western Assn. Map Librs. (sec. 1983-84). Office: Govt Documents Microforms Libr Lamont Libr Lower Level U Harvard College Libr Cambridge MA 02138- Office Phone: 617-495-2105. Business E-Mail: koepp@fas.harvard.edu.

KOEPPE, PATSY PODUSKA, internist, medical educator; b. Memphis, Nov. 18, 1932; d. Ben F. and Lily Mae (Reid) Poduska; m. Douglas F. Koeppe Sr., Sept. 8, 1967; 1 child, Douglas F. Jr. BA, Tex. Woman's U., 1954; MD, U. Tenn., 1957. Intern Roanoke (Va.) Meml. Hosp., 1960-61; resident in internal medicine VA Teaching Group Hosp., Memphis, 1961-62, Lahey Clinic, Boston, 1962-63; fellow in endocrinology and metabolism U. Tex. Med. Br., Galveston, 1963-65; pvt. practice Kingsville, Tex., 1972-73; dir. Women's Health Care Ctr., College Park, Md., 1974-77; instr. internal medicine and endocrinology U. Tex., Galveston, 1965-69; asst. prof. endocrinology Med. Br., U. Tex., Galveston, 1969-72, asst. prof. internal medicine, 1969-72, 78-87; assoc. prof. U. Tex., Galveston, 1987-93, prof., 1994-98; mem. grad. faculty biomed. sci. Med. Br., U. Tex., Galveston, 1983-98, acting dir. div. geriatrics, 1991-92. Hon. mem. med. staff Med. Br. U. Tex., 1998—. Mem. Am. Geriatric Soc., Tex. Med. Assn., Tex. Med. Found., Galveston County Med. Soc. Presbyterian. Home: 1101 Skyline Ridge Lookout Wimberley TX 78676-6041 E-mail: pkoeppe@pol.net.

KOEPPEL, GARY MERLE, publishing executive, art gallery owner, writer; b. Albany, Oreg., Jan. 20, 1938; s. Carl Melvin and Barbara Emma (Adams) K.; m. Emma Katerina Koeppel, May 20, 1984. BA, Portland State U., 1961; MFA, State U. Iowa, 1963. Writing instr. State U. Iowa, Iowa City, 1963-64; guest prof. English U. P.R., San Juan, 1964-65; assoc. prof. creative writing Portland (Oreg.) State U., 1965-68; owner, operator Coast Gallery, Big Sur, 1971—, Pebble Beach, Calif., 1986—, Maui, Hawaii, 1985—, Hana, Hawaii, 1991—, Carmel, Calif., 2003—; owner Coast Pub. Co., Coast Seri Graphics, Coast Advt., Coast Lic., 1991—. Editor, pub. Big Sur Gazette, 1978-81; producer, sponsor Maui Marine Art Expo., 1984-95, Calif. Marine Art Expo., Paris Marine Art Expo., Hawaiian Cultural Arts Expo., 1993; founder, pres. Global Art Expos1994, Planet Big Sur, 1996, Coast Constrn., 1998; founder ideasbank.com, 1999, investmentart.com, 2001; co-founder Automotive Expo, 2004. Author: Sculptured Sandcast Candles, 1974, Henry Miller, The Paintings, 1991. Founder Big Sur Vol. Fire Brigade, 1975; chmn. coordinating com. Big Sur Area Planning, 1972-75; chmn. Big Sur Citizens Adv. Com., 1975-78. Mem. Am. Soc. Appraisers, Big Sur C. of C. (pres. 74-75, 82-84), Big Sur Grange, Phi Gamma Delta, Alpha Delta Sigma. Address: Coast Gallery PO Box 223519 Carmel CA 93922-3519 Business E-Mail: gary@coastgalleries.com.

KOEPPEL, JOHN A., lawyer; b. Jersey City, Aug. 9, 1947; s. A.J. and Florence (McDonald) K.; m. Susan Lynn Rothstein, Nov. 12, 1972; children: Adam, Leah. BA in Govt. cum laude, U. Notre Dame, 1969; MA in Internat. Law, Tufts U., 1970; JD, U. Calif., San Francisco, 1976. Bar: Calif. 1976, D.C. 1980, U.S. Dist. Ct. (no. dist.) Calif. 1976, U.S. Supreme Ct. 1980. Assoc. Barfield, Barfield, Dryden & Ruane, San Francisco, 1976-80; from assoc. to shareholder Ropers, Majeski, Kohn & Bentley, San Francisco, 1980—, resident dir., 1992-95, 97-99; mediator San Francisco Superior Ct., 1993—. Arbitrator San Francisco Superior Ct., 1979—; legal counsel San Francisco Jaycees, 1980-81, Friends of the Americas, San Francisco, 1982-84; bd. dirs. ST. Francis Homes Assn., 1985-88; instr. Hastings Coll. Advocacy, San Francisco, 1988-91; lectr. U. Calif., San Francisco, 1990-95; sec. San Francisco Casualty Claims Assn., 1993-95; bd. dirs. and legal counsel Or Shalom, 2002—05; bd. dirs. Ropers Majeski Kohn & Bentley, 1992-99, 2003—. Bd. dirs. Active Youth Sports Coaching 1990-2000, San Francisco Sch., 1998-2000, San Francisco Food Bank, 2005-. Mem. Nat. Bd. Trial Advocacy, Calif. State Bar (certificate of recognition for pro bono legal work, 1989), D.C. Bar, San Francisco Bar Assn. (Outstanding Vol. of Yr. 2004). Avocations: running, skiing, hiking, rowing, travel. Office: Ropers Majeski Kohn & Bentley 333 Market St Ste 3150 San Francisco CA 94105-2132 Office Phone: 415-543-4800. Personal E-mail: johnkoeppel@sbcglobal.net. Business E-Mail: jkoeppel@ropers.com.

KOEPPEL, NOEL IMMANUEL, financial planner, securities and real estate broker; b. NYC, Apr. 30, 1930; s. Eziel and Anna (Bodian) K.; divorced; children: Thomas Joseph, Elizabeth Mansfield, Roberta Sharon. BA, U. Wis., 1952; MBA, Wharton U. of Pa., 1957. CFP. V.p. E. Koeppel, Inc., Jamaica, N.Y., 1956-77; account exec. First Investors Corp., N.Y.C., 1977-79, Ross Stebbins Co., N.Y.C., 1980-82; account exec., CFP Advest Inc., Forest Hills, N.Y., 1982-83, Donald & Co. Securities Inc., Jersey City, N.J., 1983-90, Stuart Coleman Co. Inc., N.Y.C., 1990-97; account exec. Brill Sec. Inc., N.Y.C., 1998—. Lt. (j.g.) USN, 1952-56. Mem.: Fin. Planners Assn. N.Y., Inst. CFPs, Penn Club N.Y. Avocations: skiing, sailing, hiking, classical music and art. Home: 130 E End Ave New York NY 10028-7553 Office: Brill Sec Inc 152 W 57th St Fl 16 New York NY 10019-3310

KOEPSEL, KEITH ROBERT, music educator; b. Sheboygan, Wis., May 30, 1960; s. Robert John Koepsel and Virginia Ellen Kading. B in Music Edn., U. Wis., 1982; M in Music Edn., U. No. Colo., 1991. Band tchr. Dededo (Guam) Mid. Sch., 1984—89; music tchr. Rangely (Colo.) Sch. Dist., 1989—92, REIJ Sch. Dist., Gunnison, Colo., 1992—. Music tchr. on leave Moravian Mission Sch., Leh, Ladakh, India, 2002—03; adj. instr. Western State Coll., Gunnison, 1999—. Author: Tradition Folk Music of Ladakh, 2004. Clarinet player WSC Band, Gunnison, 1992—; children worker Trinity Bapt. Ch., Gunnison, 1992—. Mem.: Colo. Music Educators Assn. (dist. 7 rep. 1993—2005). Republican. Avocations: stamp collecting/philately, travel, backpacking.

KOEPSEL, WELLINGTON WESLEY, electrical engineering educator; b. McQueeney, Tex., Dec. 5, 1921; s. Wesley Wellington and Hulda (Nagel) K.; m. Dorothy Helen Adams, June 25, 1950; children: Kirsten Marta, Gretchen Lisa, Wellington Lief. BSEE, U. Tex., 1944, MS, 1951; PhD, Okla. State U., 1960. Engr. City Pub. Svc. Bd., San Antonio, 1946—47; rsch. sci. Mil. Physics Rsch. Lab. U. Tex., 1948—51; rsch. engr. North Am. Aviation, Downey, Calif., 1951; asst. prof. So. Methodist U., 1951—59; assoc. prof. U. N.Mex., Albuquerque, 1960—63, Duke U., 1963—64; prof., head dept. elec. engring. Kans. State U., Manhattan, 1964—76, prof. elec. engring., 1976—84, prof. emeritus, 1984—; pres., owner Mutronic Sys., Austin, Tex. Contbr. articles profl. jours. Served from ensign to lt. (j.g.) USNR, 1944-46. Mem. IEEE (sr.), Sigma Xi, Eta Kappa Nu. Achievements include research on microcomputer simulation and modeling of electromagnetic (microwave) sensor systems; digital signal processing; development of R.F. wireless data transmission and computer software for systems simulation. Address: PO Box 26806 Austin TX 78755-0806 Personal E-mail: wkoepsel@ieee.org.

KOERNER, EDWARD C., automotive executive; BS in Mech. Engring., Mich. State U., 1973; post grad., Pa. State U., 1990. Lab. tech. GM Oldsmobile Div., Lansing, Mich., 1969; asst. chief engr. base engine GM Powertrain, Detroit, 1987—94, chief engr. product line exec., 1994—98; dir. chassis GM Truck Group, 1998—2001; exec. dir. chassis GM North Am., 2001; exec. dir. vehicle systems. GM North Am Vehicle Orgn., 2001—02; exec. dir. engring. GM Powertrain, Detroit, 2002—03; v.p. engring. ops. GM Powertrain., 2003—.

KOERNER, WENDELL EDWARD, JR., lawyer, mediator; b. Mexico, Mo., July 22, 1938; s. Wendell Edward and Dorothy Irene Koerner; m. Mary Jo Maday, Sept. 29, 1973 (dec. Jan. 1998); children: Jennifer L. Wolfe, R. John Maday, Greg S. Maday, Ryan E. Koerner. BS in Indsl. Mgmt., U. Kans., 1960; JD, U. Mo., Columbia, 1968. Bar: Mo. 1968, U.S. Dist. Ct. (we. dist.) Mo. 1968, U.S. Ct. Appeals (8th cir.) 1973, U.S. Dist. Ct. Kans. 1998. Assoc. Brown, Douglas & Brown, St. Joseph, Mo., 1968-71, ptnr., 1972-98, Franke & Schultz, P.C., Kansas City, Mo., 1999—. Vol. legal counsel YWCA, St. Joseph, 1983-92; temple atty. Moila Shrine Temple, St. Joseph, 1993-97; spkr. in field. Bd. dirs. Ecumenical Corp. for Housing Opportunity, St. Joseph, 1997—; vol. in probation and parole The Mo. Bar, 1971-73. Recipient Lon O. Hocker Meml. Trial Lawyer award Mo. Bar Found., 1973. Fellow Am. Coll. Trial Lawyers; mem. Mo. Bar, St. Joseph Bar Assn. (pres. 1985), Mo. Orgn. Def. Lawyers (pres. 1995-96), Internat. Assn. Def. Counsel, Am. Bd. Trial Advocates, Masons, Shriners. Mem. Chjistian Ch. (Disciples of Christ). Avocations: golf, fishing. Home: 4005 Miller Rd Saint Joseph MO 64505-1541 Office: 21st Fl Comerce Tower 911 Main St Kansas City MO 64105 E-mail: wkoerner@micro.com.

KOERSELMAN, CORNELIUS GERRIT, voice educator; b. Sioux Center, Iowa, Jan. 3, 1960; s. Cornie Gerrit and Elizabeth Johanna Koerselman; m. Sherri Ann Van Der Vliet, July 8, 1977; children: Stephanie Dawn Ingram, Beau James, Kaitlin Elizabeth. BA in Music and Psychology, Northwestern Coll., Orange City, Iowa, 1982; MEd in Guidance and Counseling, N.W. Mo. State U., Maryville, Mo., 1986. Lic. secondary tchr. and guidance counselor 7-12 Dept. Of Ed. State of Iowa, 1987. Vocal music tchr. Sibley-Ocheyedan H.S., Sibley, Iowa, 2001—, guidance counselor, 1987—2001. Pvt. counselor, cons., Sibley, Iowa, 1987—. V.p. First Ref. Ch., Sibley, Iowa, 1991—93; program developer Kiwanis Club, Sibley, Iowa, 1987—2005. R-Consevative. Reformed Church In America. Avocations: singing, golf, theater. Home: 413 13th Ave Sibley IA 51249 Office: Sibley-Ocheyedan High School 120 11th Ave NE Sibley IA 51249 Office Phone: 712-754-3601. Home Fax: 712-754-2534; Office Fax: 712-754-2534. Personal E-mail: corky@sibley-ocheyedan.k12.ia.us.

KOESER, LORI ANN, music educator; b. Sac City, Iowa, Jan. 30, 1965; d. Eldon Elnor and Darlene Eleanore Hecht; m. Leland James Koeser, July 5, 1996; 1 child, Nicholas James. B in music edn., Morningside Coll., 1987. Lic. profl. tchg. K-12 music Colo. Vocal music tchr. Battle Creek Schs., Battle Creek, Iowa, 1987—90, Kuemper Cath. HS, Carroll, Iowa, 1990—94, Spencer HS, Spencer, Iowa, 1994—96, Eastwood Local Schs., Pemberville, Ohio, 1996—2002, Dist. II Schs., Colo. Springs, Colo., 2003—. Independent. Luth. Home: 5966 Dolores St Colorado Springs CO 80922 Office: Sabin Middle Sch 3605 N Carefree Cir Colorado Springs CO 80917 Office Phone: 719-328-7081. E-mail: lakoeser@adelphia.net.

KOESSEL, DONALD RAY, retired bank executive; b. Grand Rapids, Mich., May 15, 1929; s. Fred Christian and Erna Wilhelmina (Grein) K.; m. Jeannine C. Koessel; children: Martin, Kathryn. BA, Yale U., 1951; MBA, Harvard U., 1955. Copywriter Grand Rapids Press, 1951-52; public relations rep. Smith Kline & French Labs., 1952-53; money market analyst Nat. Shawmut Bank of Boston, 1955-58; asst. sec. 1st Bank System, Mpls., 1958-62, asst. v.p., 1962-65; with 1st Nat. Bank Mpls., 1965-85, exec. v.p., 1975-85, chmn. trust com., 1979-85. Home: 18064 N Somerset Dr Surprise AZ 85374-6446

KOESTER, FREDERICK. H., aviation systems engineer; b. Mt. Vernon, N.Y., Aug. 28, 1932; s. Frederick H. and Frances A. (Moore) K.; m. Eileen R. Bobb, Dec. 30, 1961; children: Robert J., John M., Thomas E. BS in Naval Sci., US Naval Acad., 1955; BSEE, Naval Postgrad. Sch., Monterey, Calif., 1962; MS in Adminstrn., Systems Mgmt., George Washington U., 1967. Commd. ensign USN, 1955, advanced through grades to lt. comdr., ret., 1975; sr. engr. Booz-Allen & Hamilton, Bethesda, Md., 1975-79, ManTech Internat., Washington, 1979-82, Raytheon Svc. Co., Washington, 1982-84, 86-90; task mgr., sr. engr. Quest Rsch. Corp., McLean, Va., 1984-86; sr. systems engr. MiTech Inc., Rockville, Md., 1990-93; knowledge strategist, systems engr. Titan Systems Corp., Washington, 1993—. Editor: Digital Symposium Proceedings, 1966; contbr. articles to profl. jours. Mem. Soc. Competitive Intelligence Profls. Republican. Roman Catholic. Avocations: golf, investing, history. Home: 7601 Gaylord Dr Annandale VA 22003 Office: Fed Aviation Adminstrn Fed Office Bldg 10-A 800 Independence Ave Washington DC 20005

KOESTER, HELMUT HEINRICH, history professor; b. Hamburg, Germany, Dec. 18, 1926; came to U.S., 1958; s. Karl and Marie-Luise (Eitz) K.; m. Gisela G. Harrassowitz, July 8, 1953; children: Reinhild, Almut, Ulrich, Heiko. Dr. theol., U. Marburg, Germany, 1954; Privatdozent, U. Heidelberg, Germany, 1956; Dr. theol. (hon.), U. Geneva. Ordained to ministry Luth. Ch., 1956; asst. pastor Hannover, Germany, 1951-54; teaching asst., then asst. prof. U. Heidelberg, 1954-56, 56-58, 59; mem. faculty Harvard U. Div. Sch., 1958-98, John H. Morison prof. N.T. studies, 1964-98, Winn prof. ecclesiastical history, 1968-98, rsch. prof., 2000—. Vis. prof. U. Heidelberg, 1963, Drew U., 1966, U. Minn., 1990, Free U. Amsterdam, 1992, Boston U., 2000, Williams Coll., 2001. Author: Synoptische Ueberlieferung bei den Apostolischen Vaetern, in Texte und Untersuchungen, 1957, (with James M. Robinson) Trajectories through Early Christianity, 1971, Einfuehrung in das Neue Testament, 1979, Introduction to the New Testament, 1982, Ancient Christian Gospels, 1990, (with Francois Bovon) Genèse de l'écriture chrètienne, 1991, History, Religion and Culture of the Hellenistic Age, 1995, History and Literature of Early Christianity, 2000, (CD-Rom) The Cities of Paul, 2004; editor Harvard Theol. Rev., 1975-99, Hermeneia, Archaeol. Resources for New Testament Studies. Asso. trustee Am. Schs. Oriental Research, 1974-75; trustee William F. Albright Inst. Archaeol. Research, 1974-80. Served with German Navy, 1944-45. Guggenheim fellow, 1964-65; Am. Coun. Learned Socs. fellow, 1971-72, 78-79. Fellow Am. Acad. Arts and Scis.; mem. Soc. Bibl. Lit. (pres. 1990-91), Soc. Novi Testamenti Studiorum. Home: 12 Flintlock Rd Lexington MA 02420-1704 Office: 45 Francis Ave Cambridge MA 02138-1911 Business E-Mail: helmut_koester@harvard.edu.

KOESTER, JOLENE, academic administrator; BA magna cum laude, U. Minn., 1970; MA in Communication Arts, U. Wis., Madison, 1971; PhD in Speech Communications, U. Minn., 1980. Asst. prof. speech and drama U. Mo., Columbia, 1980—83; asst. prof. communication studies Calif. State U., Sacramento, 1983—85, assoc. prof. communication studies, 1985—89, dept. chair communication studies, 1986—89, prof. communication studies, 1989—2000, asst. v.p. academic affairs, 1989—91, assoc. v.p. academic affairs, 1991—93, v.p. academic affairs, 1993—2000, provost, 1996—2000; pres. Calif. State U. Northridge, 2000—. Office: Calif State U UN 200 18111 Nordhoff St Northridge CA 91330-8230

KOESTER, TRYSCH, jewelry designer, educator; b. Miami, Sept. 4, 1959; d. Romayne Pennywell; life ptnr. Brenda Manies. M in Christian Edn., D In Christian Edn., Andersonville Theol. Sem., Camilla, Ga., 2004. Instr. musical theatre Dillard Sch. of the Arts, Ft. Lauderdale, 1995—99; music educator Highlands Christian Acad., Pompano Beach, Fla., 1999—2005; jewelry designer and instr. Jewelaerie, A Well-Wrapped Design Co., Ft. Lauderdale, 2003—. Editor: Fort Dix Military Police Training Manual; author: Manual for Special Operations in Security; composer: (music) Joseph's March, Angels on Pointe. Specialist US Army, 1977—79, Camp Zama, Japan. Mem.: NRA (cert. instr. 1990), Fla. Bandmasters Assn., Fla. Orch. Assn., Fla. State Music Tchrs. Assn. (chmn. manual Student Day Performance Eval. Rules, Strings and Woodwind), Am. Soc. for Composers, Arrangers and Publishers. Avocations: reading, computer programming. Personal E-mail: trysch@jewelaerie.com.

KOESTNER, CAROL ANN, information technology manager, consultant; d. Edward Richard and Ileita P. Koestner; adopted children: Tamera A. Hough, Sheryl D. Fox, Charles R. Shumate. BA in Math., U. of South Fla., 1969, Roanoke Coll., 1967. Programmer May Plant DuPont Data Sys., Camden, SC, 1969—71; analyst May Plant Nylon Info. Sys., Camden, 1971—74; from sr. analyst to sr. specialist DuPont Nylon Info. Sys., Camden, 1974—84, sr. specialist, 1984—89; sys. cons. DuPont Textiles & Interiors Nylon Info. Sys., Camden, 1990—. Bus. cons. applied economics class Jr. Achievement Camden (S.C.) HS, 1987—99. Musician at various venues songs. Pres. band booster club Camden (S.C.) HS, 1979—80; campaign leader breast cancer Am. Cancer Soc., Columbia and Camden, SC, 2001—02; mem. coun. on ministries Lyttleton St. United Meth. Ch., Camden, 1980—83; vol. grant writer. Vet.'s Formation, Columbia, SC, 2002—03. Recipient Jake Watson award, United Way of Kershaw County, 1987, 1993, Svc. award, Jr. Achievement. Republican. Methodist. Avocations: travel, volunteer work, crafts. Home: 2204 Elkridge Drive Camden SC 29020-2016 Office: DuPont Textiles & Interiors PO Drawer 7000 Camden SC 29020-7000 Personal E-mail: ckoestner@aol.com.

KOETTER, CORNELIA M., lawyer; b. Durham, NC, Apr. 25, 1958; BA, Loyola Coll., 1980; JD, U. Md., 1985. Bar: Md. 1986, DC 1990. Assoc. Nolan, Plumhoff & Williams, Chartered. Mem.: Md. Bar Assn. Office: Nolan, Plumhoff & Williams, Chartered Ste 700, Nottingham Ctr 502 Washington Ave Towson MD 21204-4528 E-mail: ckoetter@nolanplumhoff.com.

KOFF, FRED WILLIAM, retired research chemist; b. Haapsalu, Estonia, July 21, 1922; s. Fritz and Matilde (Lindström) K.; m. Annemarie Fehmel, June 13, 1947 (div. Apr. 1989). Degree in marine navigation, Merchant Marine Acad., Tallinn, Estonia, 1944. Rsch. chemist Chem. Rsch. Ctr. Allied Chem. Corp., Morristown, N.J., 1959-84. Contbr. articles to profl. jours. including Hydrometallurgy, Jour. Am. Chem. Soc.; patentee in field. Freedom fighter against Russian encroachment into the affairs of the Baltic States, Ctrl. and East European Coalition in U.S., N.Y.C., 1994—. Lutheran. Avocations: sailing, classical music. Home: 19804 Rhea See Dr Lutz FL 33548-4281

KOFF, HOWARD MICHAEL, lawyer; b. Bklyn., July 25, 1941; s. Arthur and Blanche Koff; m. Linda Sue Bright, Sept. 10, 1966; 1 son, Michael Arthur Bright. BS, NYU, 1962; JD, Bklyn. Law Sch., 1965; LLM in Taxation, Georgetown U., 1968. Bar: N.Y. 1965, D.C. 1966, U.S. Supreme Ct. 1969, U.S. Ct. Appeals (2d, 3d, 4th, 5th, 7th, 9th and D.C. cirs.), U.S. Dist. Ct. (no. dist.) N.Y. 1981. Appellate atty. tax divsn. U.S. Dept. Justice, Washington, 1965-69; tax supr. Chrysler Corp., Detroit, 1969-70; chief tax counsel Conn. Gen. Life Ins. Co., Hartford, Conn., 1970-77, Rohm & Haas Co., Phila., 1977-78; ptnr. Dibble, Koff, Lane, Stern and Stern, Rochester, 1978—81; pres. Howard M. Koff, P.C., Albany, NY, 1981—. Lectr. tax matters. Editor-in-chief Bklyn. Law Rev., 1964—65, chartrer mem. editl. adv. bd. Jour. Real Estate Taxation; contbr. articles to legal jours. Chmn. pub. adv. coun. N.Y. State Ethics Commn. Recipient Founders Day award, NYU, 1962, Lawyers Coop. award for gen. excellence, Lawyers Coop. Pub. Co., 1965. Mem. ABA (past chmn. subcom. on partnerships tax sect.), FBA (past pres. Hartford County chpt.), Albany County Bar Assn., Estate Planning Coun. Ea. N.Y., Albany Area C. of C., Rotary, Colonie Guilderland N.Y. Club. Republican. Home: 205 W Bentwood Ct Albany NY 12203-4905 Office: 600 Broadway Albany NY 12207-2205 Office Phone: 518-463-5530.

KOFF, ROBERT HESS, academic administrator, adult education educator; b. Chgo., June 5, 1938; s. Arthur Karl and Dorothy (Hess) K. BA, U. Mich., 1961; MA, U. Chgo., 1962, PhD, 1966. Lic. psychologist, Calif. Instr., counselor S. Shankman Orthogenic Sch. U. Chgo., 1961—64; tchr. U. Chgo. Lab. Sch., 1963—64; instr. U. Ill., Champaign, 1964, U. Chgo., 1964—66; vis. scientist, Lab. for Hypnosis Rsch., asst. prof. Stanford U., Calif., 1966—72; prof., dean Roosevelt U., Chgo., 1972—79; univ. dean SUNY, Albany, 1979—92; program dir., sr. v.p. Danforth Found., St. Louis, 1992—2003; prof., asst. vice chancellor Ctr. Advanced Learning Washington U., St. Louis, 2003—. Vis. scholar Oxford U., Eng., 1965; chmn. N.Y. State Ednl. Conf. Bd., Albany, 1981-92. Mem. Nat. Adv. Coun. on Edn. of Disadvantaged Children, Washington, 1979-82, Gov.'s Adv. Commn. on Children and Youth, Albany, 1981-92. Mem. APA (com. chmn.), Am. Ednl. Rsch. Assn., Nat. Register Health Svc. Providers in Psychology. Office: Ctr for Advanced Learning/Washington U Campus Box 1135 Saint Louis MO 63130 Office Phone: 314-935-5946.

KOFF, SHIRLEY IRENE, writer; b. Oakland, Calif., Aug. 31, 1948; d. Lawrence Ray and Stella Pauline (Durham) Butler; m. Robert Allen Koff, June 12, 1971; children: Jennifer, Katherine. BA, Calif. State U., 1971, MA, 1972. Adj. prof. Pellissippi State U., Knoxville, 1989-93; asst. mgr. Adolfo II, Pigeon Forge, Tenn., 1994-98. Poet, writer; tchr. adult religious edn. classes and seminars; expert info. provider internet resource AskAnything.com. Tchr., lay min., bd. dirs. First Assembly of God Ch., Sevierville, 1996-99; core group leader, founding mem. Wellspring Congregation, United Meth. Ch., 1999-2001. Mem.: AAUW, Knoxville (Tenn.) Writers Guild, Tenn. Writers Alliance, Appalachian Writers Assn., Mensa. Democrat. Avocations: writing, speaking, teaching. Home: 1214 Amber Ln Sevierville TN 37862-6101 E-mail: sikoff@chartertn.net.

KOFFEL, MARTIN M., engineering company executive; b. 1939; MS, MBA, Stanford U., 1971. With Homestake Mining Co., 1974-81, Cooper Labs., Inc., 1981-84, Gilette Corp., 1984-86, Cooper Vision Inc., 1986-88; chmn. bd., pres., CEO URS Corp., San Francisco, 1989—. Bd. dir. McKesson Corp., San Francisco, 2000—02, James Hardie Industries N.V., Mission Viego, Calif., 2001—02. Adv. coun. McLaren Sch. Bus., U. San Francisco; trustee Am. Enterprise Inst. Pub. Policy, Washington. Office: URS Corp 600 Montgomery St 25th Fl San Francisco CA 94111-2727 Office Phone: 415-774-2700. Office Fax: 415-398-1905.

KOFMAN, MIKHAIL, economist, engineering executive; b. Nikolaev, Ukraine, Oct. 14, 1961; s. Efim and Tatiana K.; m. Anna Barybina, Ju. 4, 1982; children: Julia, Yuri. Degree in Econs./Electronics, Nikolaev (Ukraine) C.C., 1981; BS in Econs., BSc Electronics/Digital Satellite Sys., Ukrainian State Maritime Tech., Nikolaev, 1990. Mgr., gen. mgr. Chernomorsky Shipbuilding Yard, Nikolaev, 1983-88; pres. Astra Inc., Nikolaev, 1988-94; prin., owner New EVE, Corp., Springfield, Mass., 1994-96; pres. Elithan United, Inc., Springfield, Mass., 1996-97; CEO 9 Net Ave, Inc., Fort Lee, N.J., 1997-99; dir. engring. Concentric Network Corp., San Jose, Calif., 1999-2000; owner, founder, CEO, 3WCorp, Inc., Fort Lee, N.J., 2000—, Data Peer Inc., Fort Lee, 2000—. With USSR Army, Ukraine. Office: DataPeer Inc 2115 Linwood Ave 5th Fl Fort Lee NJ 07024 E-mail: mkofman@mkofman.com.

KOFNOVEC, DONNA ANN See HANOVER, DONNA

KOFORD, STUART KEITH, electronics executive; b. North Hollywood, Calif., Oct. 25, 1953; s. Kenneth Harold and Theresa (Sutton) K.; m. Gail Anne Joerger, Dec. 28, 1985; 1 child, Michelle Anne. BSME, Mich. Tech. U., 1976. Engr. Motorola, Schaumburg, Ill., 1976-77, sr. engr., 1977-79; engring. project mgr. Amphenol, Cicero, Ill., 1979-80, mgr. R & D, 1980-82, mgr. engring. Broadview, Ill., 1982—91; pres. Koford Engring., Lisle, Ill., 1982-2001; product gen. mgr. MK-Koford, Des Plaines, Ill., 2001—04; ptnr., sec.-treas. Micro-Lungo, 1998—; pres. Koford Engring., Winchester, Ohio, 2004—. Contbr. articles to profl. jours.; patentee in field. Mem. IEEE (program com. Electronic Components Conf. 1979-91), Soc. Plastic Engrs., ASME, Electronic Connector Study Group (program chmn. 1982-84). Republican. Avocation: slot car racing (world champion 1989). Home: 1239 Cheshire Ave Naperville IL 60540-5724 Office: Koford Engring LLC 1441 Dorcey Rd Winchester OH 45697

KOFRANEK, ANTON MILES, floriculturist, educator; b. Chgo., Feb. 5, 1921; s. Antonin J. and Emma (Rehorek) K.; children— Nancy, John A. BS, U. Minn., 1947; MS, Cornell U., 1949, PhD, 1950. Asst. prof. to prof. U. Calif., Los Angeles, 1950-68, prof. hort. dept. Davis, 1968-87, ret. prof. emeritus, 1987. Vis. prof. U. Wageningen, Netherlands, 1958, Cornell U., 1966, Hebrew U., Rehovot, Israel, 1972-73, Lady Davis fellow, 1980; vis. prof. Glasshouse Crops Research Inst., Littlehampton, U.K., 1980, AID, Egypt, 1978-82, FAO-UN, India, 1985 Co-author: (with Hartmann, Rubatzky and Flocker) Plant Science— Growth, Development and Utilization of Cultivated Plants, 2d edit., 1981; co-editor: (with R. A. Larson) U. Calif. Azalea Manual, 1975; contbr. articles to profl. jours. Served with AUS, 1942-45, ETO; Served with AUS, PTO. Recipient rsch. awards of merit Calif. State Florist Assn., 1966, Garland award 1974; named Young Man of Yr. Westwood Jr. C. of C., 1956; recipient rsch. and tchng. award Soc. Am. Florists, 1993. Fellow Am. Soc. Hort. Sci (dir., sectional chmn. 1973-74); mem. Sigma Xi, Pi Alpha Xi. Office: U Calif Dept Environ Hort Davis CA 95616 *Always give dollar value for the work you promise to perform.*

KOGA, ROKUTARO (ROCKY KOGA), physicist; b. Nagoya, Japan, Aug. 18, 1942; came to U.S., 1961, naturalized, 1966; s. Toyoki and Emiko (Shinra) K.; m. Cordula Rosow, May 5, 1981; children: Evan A., Nicole A. BA, U. Calif., Berkeley, 1966; PhD, U. Calif., Riverside, 1974. Rsch. fellow U. Calif., Riverside, 1974-75; rsch. physicist Case Western Res. U., Cleve., 1975-79, asst. prof., 1979-81; physicist Aerospace Corp., L.A., 1981-96, sr. scientist, 1996-2000, dsting. scientist, 2000—. Contbr. articles to profl. confs. Mem. IEEE, Am. Phys. Soc., Am. Geophys. Union, N.Y. Acad. Scis., Sigma Xi. Achievements include research on gamma-ray astronomy, solar neutron observation, space sciences, charged particles in space and the effect of cosmic rays on microcircuits in space. Office: Aerospace Corp Space Scis Lab Los Angeles CA 90009 Business E-Mail: rocky.koga@aero.org.

KOGAN, PAVEL, conductor; b. Moscow, June 6, 1952; s. Leonid and Elizaveta (Gilels) K.; m. Ljubov Kazinskaja, Dec. 21, 1977 (div. Sept. 1984); 1 child, Dmitri. Masters degree, Moscow Conservatory, 1976. Music dir., chief conductor Zagreb (Yugoslavia) Philharm. Orch., 1988-90, Moscow State Symphony Orch., 1989—. Named People's Artist of Russian Fedn., 1994. Achievements include opened Bolshoi Operas, 1988-1989. Office: Moscow State Symphony Orch 1/2 Spartakovskaja Sq 103009 Moscow Russia*

KOGAN, RICHARD J., former pharmaceutical company executive; b. N.Y.C., June 6, 1941; s. Benjamin and Ida K.; m. Susan Linda Scher, Aug. 29, 1965. BA, CCNY, 1963; MBA, NYU, 1968. V.p. planning and adminstrn. pharm. divsn. Ciba-Geigy Ltd., Summit, NJ, 1975-76, pres. Can. pharm. ops., 1976—79, pres. U.S. pharm. divsn., 1979—82; exec. v.p. pharm. ops. Schering-Plough Corp., Kenilworth, NJ, 1982—86, pres., COO, 1986—96, pres., CEO, 1996—2003, chmn. bd. dirs., 1998—2002. Bd. dirs. Colgate-Palmolive Co., The Bank of NY Co., Inc., NYU; trustee St. Barnabas Corp. and Med. Ctr. Trustee NYU, bd. overseers Stern Sch. Bus. Mem.: Coun. Fgn. Rels.

KOGER, MICHAEL PIGOTT, physician, writer; b. Balt., Jan. 20, 1953; s. Linwood Jr. and Margaret (Pigott) K.; children: Michael Pigott Koger Jr. Student, Morgan State U., 1970, Fisk U., 1971-73, MIT, 1973-74; MD, Meharry Med. Coll., 1979; BA Journalism, Ga. State U., 2001, BA in Spanish, 2002; MA in Health Sci., U. Ala., 2003, postgrad., 2002—. Internal med. resident Franklin Sq. Hosp., Balt., 1979—82; attending physician Provident Hosp., Balt., 1982-85, VA Hosp., Marion, Ill., 1986-88, Central State Hosp., Milledgeville, Ga., 1988—92, Northwest Ga. Regional Hosp., Rome, 1992—96, Complete Wellness Med. Ctr., Atlanta, 1997; news dir. Sta. WRAS, Ga. State U., Atlanta, 2000—02; with Applied Rsch. Ctr., Ga. State U., 1999—2002; announcer WVUA FM Tuscaloosa New Rock 90.7 FM, 2002—03. Chmn. dept. quality assurance and utilization review Hancock Meml. Hosp., Sparta, Ga., 1985-86; mem. sci. adv. bd. Nutrition Superstore-.com, 1999-2001. Columnist Sparta Ishmaelite, 1985-86, Signal (Ga. State U.), 2000. Vol. com. Olympic Games, Atlanta, 1996, Hands on Atlanta, 1996-97, Atlanta Cmty. Food Bank, 1996-97, organizing com. Atlanta Paralympic, 1996, Am. Heart Assn., Marietta, Ga., 1996. Mem. AMA, Soc. Profl. Journalists, Journalism History Soc. Home: PO Box 21260 Tuscaloosa AL 35402 Office: Univ Ala Dept Health Scis Tuscaloosa AL 35402 E-mail: mkoger@alum.mit.edu.

KOGGE, PETER MICHAEL, computer scientist, educator; b. Washington, Dec. 3, 1946; s. Roy and Louise (McGrath) K.; m. Mary Ellen Clarke, June 12, 1971; children: Peter Michael, Mary Elizabeth, Timothy McGrath. BSEE, U. Notre Dame, 1968; MS in Systems Info. Scis., Syracuse U., 1970; PhDEE, Stanford U., 1973. Jr. engr. IBM, Owego, N.Y., 1968-72, staff engr., 1972-74, adv. engr., 1974-76, sr. engr., 1976-81, mem. sr. tech. staff, 1981-93; IBM fellow, 1993; McCourtney prof. computer sci. U. Notre Dame, Ind., 1994—, interim dept. chair computer sci. dept., 2000—01, prof. elec. engring., assoc. dean rsch. Coll. Engring, 2001—. Adj. prof. computer scis. SUNY, Binghamton, 1977—94; past mem. rev. com. NSF Computing Divsn.; program chair 6th Symposium on Frontiers of Massively Parallel Computation, 1996; disting. vis. scientist NASA Jet Propulsion Lab., 1997; program com. Supercomputing, 1998, 99, 2000, 02, Internat. Symposium on Computer Arch., 1999; program vice chair 7th Symposium on Frontiers of Massively Parallel Computation, 1999; program co-chmn. Great Lakes Conf. on VLSI, 2002. Author: Architecture of Pipelined Computers, 1980, Architecture of Symbolic Computers, 1991; editor conf. proc. Internat. Conf. on Parallel Processing, 1988. Recipient IBM Outstanding Innovation awards for Space Shuttle, IOP, 3838 Array Processor, AI Parallel Processor, Pres.'s award for patents, Daniel L. Slotnick award for most original paper Internat. Conf. Parallel Processing, 1994, Outstanding Computer Sci. and Engring. Dept. Instrn., 1999. Fellow IEEE; mem. Assn. for Computing Machinery, Am. Assn. Artificial Intelligence, IBM Acad. Tech. Roman Catholic. Office: U Notre Dame Dept Computer Sci and Engring 384 Fitzpatrick Hl Engrng Notre Dame IN 46556-5637 E-mail: kogge@cse.nd.edu.

KOGLIN, TERRY LEE, mechanical engineer, consultant; b. Janesbille, Wis., May 6, 1948; s. Charles Leroy and Patricia Ann (Dean) Koglin; m. Jane Ann Oakey (div.). BS, U. Wis. Madison, 1975. EIT NJ, Pa., Fla., NY, Wash., Ohio. Mchanical engr. Finnish Nat. Railways, Helsinki, Finland, 1975, Airpax Electronics, Cambridge, Md., 1976—78, Earle Gear and Machine, Phila., 1978—82; cons. Steinman Boynton Granquist and Birdsall, N.Y.C., 1982—99, Parsons Brinckerhoff Quade and Douglas, N.Y.C., 1999—. Author: Financing High Speed Rail System: High Speed Rail Association Symposium, 1992, Preserving Williamsburg's Cabels Civil Engineering, 1996, High Speed Rail Project for New York City: Symposium on Urban Transportation, 2000, Movable Bridge Engineering, 2003. Com. mem. Am. Railway Engring., Wash., DC, 1999—; lectr. Princeton U., Princeton, NJ, 1997—99. Mem.: Heavy Movable Structures Ins., Am. Railway Engring. and Maintenance Way Assn., Internat. Assn. for Bridges and Structural Enging. Republican. Achievements include invention of railroad-highway crossing; movable bridge ctr. lock. Avocations: travel, writing, reading, politics, history. Home: 2833 Calgary Ln Janesville WI 53545 Office Phone: 212-465-5184. E-mail: koglin@yahoo.com.

KOGOD, ROBERT P., philanthropist, former real estate company executive; b. 1931; m. Arlene R. Kogod, 1956; 3 children. BS, Am. U., 1962, LLD (hon.), 2000. Joined Charles E. Smith Companies, 1959; co-chmn. & co-CEO Charles E. Smith Residential Realty Inc., 1967—2001; merged with Archstone Communities Trust to become Archstone-Smith Trust, 2001, bd. trustees, 2001—; co-chmn. & co-CEO Charles E. Smith Comml. Realty LP, 1997—2001; merged with Vornado Realty Trust, 2002, bd. trustees, 2002—. Bd. regents Smithsonian Instn., 2005—; advisor to pres. Am. U., 2003—; has contbd. to Smithsonian Instn., Signature Theatre, Wooly Mammoth Theatre, Am. U., U. Md. Clarice Smith Performing Arts Ctr., many others. Named one of Top 200 Collectors, ARTnews mag., 2004. Avocation: Collector modern and contemporary art, especially Am. Office: Vornado Realty Trust 888 7th Ave New York NY 10019*

KOGOVSEK, DANIEL CHARLES, lawyer; b. Pueblo, Colo., Aug. 4, 1951; s. Frank Louis and Mary Edith (Blatnick) K.; m. Patricia Elizabeth Connell, June 30, 1979; 1 child, Ryan Robert. BA, U. Notre Dame, 1973; JD, Columbia U., 1976. Bar: Colo. 1976, U.S. Dist. Ct. Colo. 1976, U.S. Ct. Appeals (10th cir.) 1978, U.S. Supreme Ct. 1983. Ast. atty. gen. Colo. Dept. Law, Denver, 1976-79; campaign mgr. Congressman Kogovsek, Pueblo, 1980, 82; dir. Office Consumer Svcs., Denver, 1981; mem. firm Fish & Kogovsek, Denver, 1983-84; sr. assoc. Petersen & Fonda, P.C., Pueblo, 1985-89; mem. firm Kogovsek & Higinbotham, P.C., Pueblo, 1989—2002; mem. firm. Kogovsek Law Firm, P.C., Pueblo, 2002—; county atty. Pueblo County, 2001—. Mem. ABA, Colo. Bar Assn., Pueblo Bar Assn. Home: 584 W Spaulding Ave S Pueblo West CO 81007-1874 Office: Ste 202 830 N Main St Pueblo CO 81003-0202 E-mail: kog-law@aculink.net.

KOGUT, JOHN ANTHONY, wholesale distribution executive; b. Lackawanna, N.Y., Dec. 8, 1942; s. John J. and Rose J. (Gaj) K.; m. Deborah A. Hillman; children: David J., Robert J., Katherine A., Lindsey A., Kimberly M. BS in Pharmacy, U. Buffalo, 1965; MBA, Syracuse U., 1978. Pharmacist, mgr. Fay's Drug Co., Liverpool, N.Y., 1969-75, v.p., 1975-82, sr. v.p., 1982-89, pres., 1989-95; pres. Health Mart divsn., v.p. Franchise Svcs. FoxMeyer Corp., 1995-96; pres. Health Mart Divsn., v.p. mktg. McKesson Corp., 1996-99; pres. pharmac ops. Cmty. Health Svcs., Inc., Chgo., 1999—. Mem. N.Y. State Bd. Pharmacy, 1987-95. Served to capt. U.S. Army, 1966-69 Mem. Am. Pharm. Assn., Pharm. Soc. of State N.Y., Am. Mgmt. Assn., Nat. Assn. Chain Drug Stores (pharmacy affairs com. chmn. 1982-83), N.Y. State Bd. Pharmacy. Republican. Roman Catholic. Office Phone: 315-595-6170. Business E-Mail: jkogut@pharmacyaide.com.

KOGUT, KENNETH JOSEPH, consulting engineer; b. Chgo., Dec. 3, 1947; s. Joseph Henry and Estelle Theresa (Swiercz) K.; m. Darlene Agnes Jedlicka, June 15, 1974. Student, Lewis Coll., 1966—68; BME, U. Detroit, 1971, ME, postgrad., U. Detroit, 1972—. Registered profl. engr., Ill.; cert. energy mgr. Mech. engr. Fluor Pioneer Inc., Chgo., 1972-73, cons. engr., 1973-75; project mgr. Engring. Corp. Am., Chgo., 1976-77; sr. cons. pub. utilities DeLoitte, Haskins & Sells, Chgo., 1977-79; individual practice as energy and mgmt. cons., 1979—. Author: Energy Management for the Community Bank. Alfred P. Sloan fellow, 1971-73; reciepient award Pres.'s Program for Energy Efficiency, Corp. Energy Mgmt. award, 1981, Regional Energy Profl. Devel. award, 1984, Regional Energy Engr. of Yr. award, 1987, Ill. Energy award, 1988, Illiana Energy Mgmt. Exec. of Yr. award Assn. Energy Engrs., 1992, 96, Disting. Svc. award Assn. Energy Engrs., 1999, Excellence in Engring. award Am. Soc. Heating Refrigeration and Air-Conditioning Engrs. Ill. chpt., 1994, Energy Mgrs. Hall of Fame, 2002. Mem. Am. Nuclear Soc., Nat., Ill. socs. profl. engrs., Assn. Energy Engrs. (pres. Chgo. chpt. 1985, pres Ill. chpt. 1990-93, regional v.p. 1993-95, dir. chpt. devel., 1996, internat. pres-elect 1997, internat. pres. 1998, energy policy com.), Environ. Engrs. and Mgrs. Inst., Demand-Side Mgmt. Soc., Exec. Hosp. Engrs. Soc. Ill., Energy Svcs. Mktg. Soc., Blue Key, Tau Beta Pi, Pi Tau Sigma, Polish Nat. Alliance. Address: 5232 170th Pl Oak Forest IL 60452-4450

KOGUT, LIOR, mechanical engineer, researcher; b. Haifa, Israel, Nov. 3, 1973; s. Judith and Shlomo Kogut; m. Merav Avital, Apr. 22, 1973; children: Dean, Daniella. BS, Technion - Israel Inst. of Tech., 1991—95, MS, 1997—98, PhD, 1999—2002. R&d engr. Israeli Def. Force, Tel-Aviv, Israel, 1995—99; post-doctoral fellow U. of Calif. at Berkeley, 2002—. Sec., contact mechanics com. of theASME tribology divsn. ASME, 2002. Mem.: ASME. Office: Univ of California at Berkeley Dept of Mechanical Engineering Berkeley CA 94720-1740 Business E-Mail: kogut@newton.berkeley.edu.

KOH, CHYE HOCK, lawyer; b. Taiping, Malaysia, Sept. 23, 1961; BA, U. Utah, 1983, MA, 1986; LLB, U. Wales, 1989; LLM, Georgetown U., 1991. Bar: Va. 1993, U.S. Ct. Appeals (4th cir.) 1993, Malaysian Cert. Legal Practice 1996. Profl. legal specialist Cleary, Gottlieb, Steen & Hamilton, Washington, 1992—94; legal mgr. Occidental Oil and Gas Corp., Malaysia and Bangladesh, 1994—99; legal dir., internat. counsel Unocal Offshore Svcs., Ltd., Sugarland, Tex., 1999—. Avocations: reading, writing, music, cooking. Office: Unocal Offshore Svcs Ltd 14141 Southwest Fwy Sugar Land TX 77478 E-mail: ckoh@unocal.com.

KOH, HAROLD HONGJU, dean, law educator; b. Cambridge, Mass., Dec. 8, 1954; s. Kwang Lim and Hesung (Chun) Koh; m. Mary-Christy Fisher, Feb. 19, 1984; children: Emily J.Y., William H.W. BA cum laude, Harvard U., 1975, JD, 1980; BA, Magdalen Coll., Oxford U., 1977; MA (hon.), Yale U., 1990; LLH (hon.), CUNY-Queens Law Sch., 1998, Suffolk Law Sch., 1999, U. Conn., 2000, Conn. Coll., 2001, Skidmore Coll., 2002; LHD (hon.), Albertus Magnus Coll., 1999, Dickinson Coll., 2000. Bar: N.Y. 1981, D.C. 1981, U.S. Dist. Ct. D.C. 1981, U.S. Ct. Appeals (D.C. cir.) 1981, U.S. Ct. Claims 1982, Conn. 1985, U.S. Supreme Ct. 1985, U.S. Dist. Ct. Conn. 1987. Law clk. to judge U.S. Ct. Appeals (D.C. cir.), Washington, 1980-81; law clk. to Justice Harry A. Blackmun U.S. Supreme Ct., Washington, 1981-82; assoc. Covington & Burling, Washington, 1982-83; atty.-advisor Office of Legal Counsel, Dept. Justice, Washington, 1983-85; assoc. prof. law Yale Law Sch., New Haven, 1985-90, prof., 1990-93, dir. Orville H. Schell Jr., Ctr. Internat. Human Rights, 1993—98, Gerald C. and Bernice Latrobe Smith Prof. internat. law, 1993—, dean, 2004—. Adj. asst. professorial lectr. law George Washington U. Nat. Law Ctr., 1982—85; vis. prof. internat. law U. Toronto, 1990, 2002; vis. prof. Hague Acad. Internat. Law, 1993; vis. fellow All Souls Coll., Oxford U., 1996—97; Waynflete Lectr. Magdalen Coll., Oxford U., 1996—97; asst. sec. state for Democracy, Human Rights and Labor U.S. Dept. State; commr. Commn. for Security and Cooperation in Europe; U.S. delegate UN Gen. Assembly (Third Com.), UN Human Rights Commn., Orgn. Am. States, Coun. Europe, Orgn. for Security and Cooperation in Europe, UN Com. Against Torture, 1998—2001, Inaugural Cmty. of Democracies Meeting, Warsaw, 2000, UN Conf. on New and Restored Democracies, Cotonou, Benin, 2000. Author: The National Security Constitution, 1990, Transnational Legal Problems, 1994, International Business Transactions in United States Courts, 1998, (with Ronald C. Slye) Deliberative Democracy and Human Rights, 1999, The Human Rights of Persons with Intellectual Disabilities: Different But Equal, 2003, Transnational Business Problems, 2003; bd. editors Am. Jour. Internat. Law, Human Rights Quarterly, Foundation Press; contbr. articles to profl. jours. Bd. dirs. Human Rights Watch, Arms Control Assn. Co-recipient Human Rights Award, Am. Immigration Lawyers' Assn., 1992, Trial Lawyer of Yr. Award, Trial Lawyers for Pub. Justice, 1995; named Public Sector 45, American Lawyer mag., 1997; recipient Richard E. Neustadt Award, Am. Polit. Sci. Assn., 1991, Justice in Action Award, Asian-Am. Legal Defense & Edn. Fund, 1993, Korean Am. Coalition Pub. Service Award, 2001, John Quincy Adams Freedom Award, Amisad Am., 2002, Arthur J. Goldberg Award, Jacob Fuchsberg Law Ctr., Touro Law Sch., 2000, Wolfgang Friedmann Award, Columbia Jour. Transnational Law, 2003, Villanova Medal, Villanova Law Sch., 2000; grantee Marshall scholar, Oxford U., 1977. Fellow: Am. Acad. Arts and Scis; mem.: Am. Soc. Internat. Law., Am. Law Inst., Twentieth Century Fund. Office: Yale Law Sch PO Box 208215 New Haven CT 06520-8215 E-mail: harold.koh@yale.edu.

KOH, JASON, orthopedic surgeon; BA magna cum laude, Harvard U., 1990; MD, Johns Hopkins U., 1994. Lic. Nat. Bd. Med. Examiners. Clin. fellow Mass. Gen. Hosp., Harvard Med. Sch., Boston, 1994—95; clin. fellow, chief resident Hosp. for Spl. Surgery, Cornell Med. Sch., N.Y.C., 1995—99; clin. fellow Cleve. Clinic, 1999—2000; asst. prof. Northwestern U. Med. Sch., Chgo., 2000—; orthopaedic cons. Chgo. Cubs, 2000—03; med. dir. Joffrey Ballet, Chgo., 2000—. Coauthor Charles Neer award, Am. Shoulder and Elbow Soc. Pres. med. faculty senate Northwestern U., Chgo., 2003—04. Recipient John Harvard scholarship, Harvard U., 1986—90, Harvard Coll. scholarship, 1990, Patellofemoral Found. Traveling fellowship, 2005, Richard O'Connor award, Arthroscopy Assn. N.Am., John J. Fahey N.Am. traveling fellowship, Am. Orthopaedic Assn. Fellow: Am. Acad. of Orthopaedic Surgery; mem.: Am. Bd. of Orthopaedic Surgery (task force mem. 2004—05), Arthroscopy Assn., ACL Study Group, Am. Orthopaedic Soc. for Sports Medicine, Internat. Cartilage Repair Soc. Achievements include research in; John J. Fahey, MD, North American Traveling Fellowship, American Orthopaedic Association. Avocation: travel. Office: Northwestern Meml Faculty Found 17-100 675 N St Clair Chicago IL 60611 Office Phone: 312-695-6800.

KOH, STEVE Y., lawyer; b. Seattle, Aug. 20, 1967; BBA magna cum laude, U. Wash., 1989; JD, Yale U., 1992. Bar: Wash., US Supreme Ct., US Ct. Appeals (5th Cir.), US Ct. Appeals (9th Cir.), US Dist. Ct. (We. Dist.) Wash. Intern to Hon. Jose A Cabranes US Dist. Ct., (Dist. Conn.), 1990; summer assoc. Cravath Swaine & More, NY, 1991; law clk. to Hon. Patricia Wald US Ct. Appeals (DC Cir.), 1992—93; atty. US Dept. Justice, Fraud Sect., 1993—95; ptnr., mem exec. com. Perkins Coie LLP, Seattle, chmn. hiring com. Articles editor Yale Law Jour. Bd. trustees Childhaven. Named a Super Lawyer, Wash. Law& Politics; named to best lawyers under 40, Nat. Asian-Pacific ABA. Mem.: Fed. Bar Assn. (trustee), Wash. State Bar Assn., Asian Bar Assn. Office: Perkins Coie LLP 1201 Third Ave Ste 4800 Seattle WA 98101-9000 Office Phone: 206-359-8530. Office Fax: 206-359-9000. Business E-Mail: skoh@perkinscoie.com.

KOHAN, BETSY BURNS, lawyer; b. La Mesa, Calif., Jan. 24, 1949; d. William Richard and Winifred Marion Burns; m. Dennis Lynn Kohan, Mar. 8, 1986; children: Toni Kick, Bart, Elyse, David Karowsky. BA, Stanford U., 1971; JD, U. Colo., 1974. Bar: Colo. 1974, Calif. 1985. Ptnr. Karowsky, Witwer & Oldenburg, Greeley, Colo., 1974-82; pvt. practice, Greeley, 1983-84; v.p., assoc. gen. counsel Sun Savs., San Diego, 1985-86; v.p., asst. gen. counsel Imperial Savs. & Loan Assn., San Diego, 1986-88, Am. Real Estate Group, Irvine, Calif., 1988-90, Columbia Savs. & Loan Assn., Irvine, 1990-91; staff atty. FDIC, Irvine, 1991-94; prof. Anhui Inst. Fin. and Trade, Bengbu, China, 1994, Guangzhou (China) Inst. Fgn. Trade, 1995; sr. counsel Nissan N.Am., Inc., Torrance, Calif., 1996—. Mem. Commn. on Legal and Jud. Edn., Colo. Supreme Ct., Denver, 1983-84. Contbr. articles to legal publs. Chmn. Colo. Commn. on Women, Denver, 1978-80; vice chmn. bd. trustees U. No. Colo., 1980-84. Named Outstanding Coloradoan, Colo. Jaycees, 1980, Outstanding Young Lawyer, Colo. Bar Assn., 1979. Mem. L.A. Bar Assn. (comml. law com. 1997—). Home: 525 E Seaside Way Unit 204 Long Beach CA 90802-8001 Office: Nissan NAm Inc 990 W 190th St Fl 8 Torrance CA 90502-1046 Office Phone: 310-719-8282. Business E-Mail: betsy.kohan@nissan-usa.com.

KOHAN, DENNIS LYNN, finance educator; b. Kankakee, Ill., Nov. 22, 1945; s. Leon Stanley and Nellie K.; m. Julianne Johnson, Feb. 14, 1976 (dec. Sept. 1985); children: Toni, Bart, Elyse; m. Betsy Burns, Mar. 8, 1986; 1 child, David. BA, Ill. Wesleyan U., 1967; postgrad., John Marshall Law Sch., 1971—74; MPA, Gov.'s State U., 1975. Police officer Kankakee County, 1967-75; loan counselor, security officer Kankakee Fed. Savs. & Loan, Kankakee, 1975-76; mgr. Bank Western, Denver, 1976-85; mgr. real estate lending dept. Ctrl. Savs., San Diego, 1985-87; maj. loan work-out officer Imperial Savs., San Diego, 1987-88; cons. Equity Assurance Holding Corp., Newport Beach, Calif., 1987-88; compliance officer Am. Real Estate Group and New West Fed. Savs. and Loan, Irvine, Calif., 1988-90; co-founder Consortium-Real Estate Asset Cons., Costa Mesa, Calif., 1990-91; investigator, criminal coord. Resolution Trust Corp., Newport Beach, 1991-94; instr. for Internat. Trade Anhui Inst. Fin. and Trade, Bengbu, China, 1994-95; instr. Guangzhou Inst. Fgn. Trade, China, 1995—; owner Kohan Internat. Bus. Forensics, 1995—; investigator Office Insp. Gen. LA Unified Sch. Dist., 2000—. Instr. U. No. Colo. Coll. Bus., Greeley, 1981-85; chmn. bd. North Colo. Med. Ctr., Greeley, 1983-85; pres. bd. Normedco, Greeley, 1984-85; part-time prof. bus. pub. adminstrn. So. Calif. Internat. Coll., 1998—. Vol. cons., chmn. ARC, Colo., 1979-85; campaign mgr. Donley Senatorial campaign, Colo., 1982, Kinkade City Coun. campaign, Colo., 1983; chmn. Weld County Housing Authority, 1981. Staff sgt. U.S. Army, 1969-71, Vietnam. Mem. Nat. Assn. Realtors, Shriners, Kiwanis. Office Phone: 213-241-7741. Personal E-mail: dkohan@earthlink.net.

KOHEL, EDWARD ARLEN, music educator; b. Lincoln, Nebr., Jan. 3, 1946; s. Edward and Lulu Louise Kohel; m. Rhonda Marthena Grooms, June 20, 1970; children: Scott Edward, Kimberly Ann, Laura Marie. BS in Music Edn., Midland Luth. Coll., 1970; MS in Edn., Chadron (Nebr.) State Coll., 1981, specialist degree in ednl. adminstrn., 1986. Supt. schs. Wolbach (Nebr.) Pub. Schs., 1990—91; tchr. K-12 music Ansley (Nebr.) Pub. Schs., 1991—92; tchr. K-12 music, K-12 guidance counselor Arcadia (Nebr.) Pub. Schs., 1992—96; ins. salesman Mason City, Nebr., 1996—97; tchr. K-12 music, h.s. prin. Elba (Nebr.) Pub. Schs., 1997—2000; instrumental music dir. Elm Creek (Nebr.) Pub. Schs., 2000—. Pvt. counselor, Mason City, 1991—2000; mem. adv. com. Ednl. Svc. Unit 10 Vocat. Consortium, Kearney, Nebr., 1998—2001; mem. dist. music contest com. Nebr. Sch. Activities Assn., Lincoln, Nebr., 2001—. Mem.: Nebr. Bandmasters Assn., Nebr. Music

Educators, Eagles, Lions. Methodist. Avocations: singing, camping, outdoor work. Office: Elm Creek Pub Schs 230 Calkins Elm Creek NE 68836 Office Phone: 308-856-4300. Office Fax: 308-856-4907. E-mail: edkohel@csu10.org.

KOHEL, RUSSELL JAMES, geneticist; b. Omaha, Nov. 30, 1934; married; 3 children. BS, Iowa State U., 1956; MS, Purdue U., 1958, PhD, 1959. Supervisory rsch. geneticist Argrl. Rsch. Svc. USDA, College Station, Tex., 1959—. Fellow Am. Soc. Agronomy; mem. Am. Soc. Plant Physiologists, Am. Genetic Assn., Genetics Soc. Am. Office: USDA So Plains Agrl Rsch Ctr Crop Germplasm Rsch Unit 2765 F&B Rd College Station TX 77845-9593

KOHEN, ELLI, science educator; b. Istanbul, Turkey, Oct. 2, 1930; arrived in US, 1969; s. Yasef and Vida Kohen; m. Cahide Bahar Kohen, June 21, 1957; 1 child, Dahlia Kohen-Gordon. MD, U. Istanbul, 1954; D in Exptl. Pathology, Karolinska Inst., Stockholm, 1973. Resident in pathology Springfield (Mass.) Hosp., 1956—57, Westfield (Mass.) State Sanat., 1958—60; house physician in pathology Sarafand Hosp., Israel, 1957—58; fellow in pharmacol. Baylor Sch. Med., Houston, 1960—61; from fellow in biophysics to rsch. assoc. U. Pa. Johnson Found. Sch. Med., Phila., 1961—66; vis. scientist Karolinska Inst., Stockholm, 1966—69; sr. scientist, disting. scientist Cancer Rsch. Inst., Miami, Fla., 1969—84; prof. biology U. Miami, Coral Gables, Fla., 1981—2001, prof. emeritus, 2002—. Workshop dir. in field. Author: Cell Structure and Function By Microspectrofluorometry, 1989, Analytical Use of Fluorescent Probes in Oncology, 1996, Histological Correlates of Cellular Detoxification, 1997, Applications of Optical Engineering To The Study of Cellular Pathology, Vol. I, 1997, Ladino/English-English/Ladino Dictionary, 2000, La Concierge, 2001, Fluorescence Probes in Oncology, 2002, World History and Myths of Cats, 2003; contbr. chapters to books, articles to profl. jours. 1st lt. MC Turkish Army, 1954—55. Grantee, NIH, Am. Cancer Soc., Cystic Fibrosis Found., Nat. Sci. Found. on Metabolism. Mem.: European Acad. Sci., Arts and Letters (corr.). Jewish. Achievements include research in microspectrofluorometry and microinjection of single living cells; first to in subdisciplines of cell biology: cell biochemistry, cellular pathology and cellular pathopharmacology. Avocations: history, travel, coin collecting/numismatics, cruising, linguistics. Office: Univ Miami Dept Chemistry Physics Bldg Coral Gables FL 33146 Office Phone: 305-284-1881. Business E-Mail: ekohen@umiami.ir.miami.edu.

KOHEN, MARTHA, architecture educator; Grad., U. de la Republica, Montevideo, Uruguay; postgrad. diploma, Cambridge (Eng.) U. Arch., tchr., Paysandu, Uruguay, 1971—76; arch., cons. Matto Grosso, Brazil, 1976—84, Sao Paulo, Brazil, 1976—84; asst. prof. Sommer and Sprechmann Studio, Sch. Arch., 1985—94; assoc. prof. Otero Studio, Sch. Arch., Montevideo, 1994—98; dir. acad. cooperation unit faculty arch. Univ. de la Republica, Uruguay, 1998—2003; dir. and prof. Sch. Arch., Coll. Design, Constrn. and Planning U. Fla., 2003—; founding mem. Kohen-Otero Archtl. Studio, Montevideo, 1989—. Dep. bd. mem. Internat. Coun. Urban Planners, 1994, nat. mem., 1995—2000; vis. prof. Internat. Seminars Arch. e Citta U. degli Studi di Napoli Federico II, Italy, 1991—93; vis. lectr. Sch. Arch., Rosario, Argentina, 1992, Rosario, 1996—98, NYU Internat. Ctr. for Advanced Studies, 2000; mem. jury Fourth Internat. Seminary, Napoli, Italy, 1992; vis. prof. 7th Internat. Seminary, Napoli, Italy, 1998; vis. prof. dept. arch. U. Hong Kong, 2002. Recipient First prize, Barao de Rio Branco Square, Rio de Janeiro, 1995, Meml. of the Disappeared Detained Citizens, City of Montevideo, 1996, Hdqrs. of URAGUA, 2000, Spl. Mention, The Cerrillos Masterplan, Portal del Bicentenario, Santiago de Chile, 2001, First prize landscape arch., Quito Internat. Biennale, 2002, First prize, Sao Paulo Biennal of Arch., 2003. Mem.: Uruguayan Archtl. Assn. (mem. Coll. Cons., mem. Coll. Juries 1995—), Soc. for Internat. Devel. (Uruguayan chpt.). Office: Univ Fla Sch Arch PO Box 115702 Gainesville FL 32611-5702

KOHL, BENEDICT M., lawyer; b. 1931; AB, Brown U., 1952; LL.B. cum laude, Harvard U., 1955. Bar: D.C. 1955, U.S. Supreme Ct. 1962, N.J. 1963. Partner Lowenstein, Sandler, Kohl, Fisher & Boylan, Roseland, N.J.; atty. interpretative div. Office Chief Counsel, IRS, 1957-60, Office of Tax Legis. Counsel, U.S. Treasury Dept., 1960-62. Nat. v.p. Am. Jewish Com., former N.J. pres.; former trustee Overlook Hosp. Mem. ABA, N.J. State, Essex County bar assns. Office: Lowenstein Sandler Kohl et al 65 Livingston Ave Ste 9 Roseland NJ 07068-1725

KOHL, BENJAMIN GIBBS, historian, educator; b. Middletown, Del, Oct. 26, 1938; s. Victor Philip and Catherine B. (Carpenter) K.; m. Judith Ann Cleek, Jan. 2, 1961; children: Benjamin Gibbs, Laura Ann Kohl Ball. AB with honors, Bowdoin Coll., 1960; MA, U. Del., 1962; PhD, Johns Hopkins U., 1968. Adj. instr. Franklin and Marshall Coll., Lancaster, Pa., 1961-62; instr. history Johns Hopkins U., Balt., 1965-66, Vassar Coll., Poughkeepsie, NY, 1966-68, asst. prof., 1968-74, assoc. prof., 1974-81, prof., 1981-2001, chmn. dept. history, 1979-82, 88, 1993-96, Andrew W. Mellon prof. of humanities, 1994-2001, prof. emeritus, 2001—. Pres. Am. Friends of Warburg Inst., NYC, 1994-96; adv. bd. Renaissance Studies, 1988—; pres., Hedgelawn Found., Worton, Md., 2003—. Author: Renaissance Humanism, Bibliography of Materials in English, 1985, Padua Under the Carrara, 1998, The Records of the Venetian Senate on disk 1335-1400, 2000, Culture and Politics in Early Renaissance Padua, 2001; co-author: (with A.A. Smith), Major Problems in the History of the Italian Renaissance, 1995, (with A. Mozzatto and M. O'Connoll) Rulers of Venice, 1332-1524, 2005; co-editor: (with R.G. Witt) The Earthly Republic, 1978; co-editor Centennial Directory of the American Academy in Rome, 1995, Weyer on Witchcraft, 1998; contbr. more than 20 scholarly essays and more than 50 books revs. on medieval and Renaissance history to profl. jour Historian, City of Poughkeepsie, 1971-77. Fulbright fellow, Padua, Italy, 1964-65; Am. Acad. fellow, Rome, 1970-71; Delmas fellow, Venice, 1978. Fellow Royal Hist. Soc.; mem. AAUP (pres. chpt. 1987-89, 95-98, Medieval Acad. Am. (life), Renaissance Soc. Am. (life), Am. Hist. Assn. (life). Democrat. Episcopalian. Avocations: reading, bicycling, gardening. Home: PO Box 166 One Bayview Rd #8 Betterton MD 21610-0166 Office Phone: 410-348-5858. Personal E-mail: kohlinmd@dmv.com.

KOHL, HERBERT, senator, professional sports team executive; b. Milw., Feb. 7, 1935; BA, U. Wis., 1956; MBA, Harvard U., 1956. Owner Milw. Bucks (NBA) Milw. Brewers; U.S. senator from Wis., 1989—; pres. Herbert Kohl Investments. State chmn. Dem. Party, Wis., 1975-77; mem. com. on aging, appropriations com., senate Dem. steering & coordination com., com. on judiciary, 1989; ranking minority mem. jud. subcom. on terrorism, tech. & govt. info. With USAR, 1958-64. Democrat. Office: US Senate 330 Hart Senate Office Bldg Washington DC 20510-0001 also: Milw Bucks Bradley Ctr 1001 N 4th St Milwaukee WI 53203-1314*

KOHL, JOHN PRESTON, finance educator, consultant; b. Allentown, Pa., Dec. 26, 1942; s. Claude Evan and Edna Lenoir (Woodland) Kohl; m. Nancy Ann Christensen, Mar. 11, 1967; children: John P. Jr., Mark C. BA, Moravian Coll., 1964; MDiv, Yale U., 1967; MS in Mgmt., Am. Tech. U., 1974, MS in Counseling, 1976; PhD in Bus. Adminstrn., Pa. State U., 1982. Ordained to ministry United Ch. of Christ, 1967. Min. Christ Congl. Ch., New Smyrna Beach, Fla., 1968-71, First Congl. Ch., Hutchinson, Minn., 1971-73; instr. Pa. State U., University Park, 1978-82; asst. prof. mgmt. U. Tex., El Paso, 1982-85; assoc. prof. San Jose State U., 1985-87; prof., chmn. dept. mgmt. U. Nev., Las Vegas, 1988-99; dean Grad. Sch. Internat. Trade & Bus. Adminstrn. Tex. A&M Internat. U., Laredo, 1999—2003, interim provost, v.p. acad. affairs, 2002; dean Coll. Bus. and Econs., Calif. State U.-East Bay, Hayward, 2005—. Cons. in field. Co-author: Personnel Managment, 1986; contbr. articles to profl. jours. Capt. U.S. Army, 1973—78, col. USAR, 1993—99. Decorated Nat. Def. Svc. medal, Meritorious Svc. medal, Army Commendation medal. Mem.: Am. Acad. Mgmt. Home: 3030 Deer Meadow Dr Danville CA 94506 Office: State Univ East Bay Dean Coll Bus and Econ Hayward CA 94542-3066 Office Phone: 510-885-3291. Business E-Mail: john.kohl@csueastbay.edu.

KOHL, ROBERT L., lawyer; b. NYC, Mar. 19, 1944; s. Sol and Mimi K.; m. Enid H. Kohl, Aug. 26, 1967; children: David, Lauren. BA, Queens Coll., 1965; JD, Harvard U., 1968. Bar: NY 1968, US Dist. Ct. (ea. dist.) NY 1971. Assoc. Beekman & Bogue, NYC, 1968-75, ptnr., 1975-81, Gaston & Snow, NYC, 1981-91, Rosenman & Colin, NYC, 1991—2002, Katten Muchin Rosenman LLP, NYC, 2002—. Mem. ABA (com. on fed. regulation of securities, subcom. on 33 Act gen.). Avocations: skiing, tennis, running, biking. Office: Katten Muchin Rosenman LLP 575 Madison Ave New York NY 10022 Office Fax: 212-940-8776. Business E-Mail: robert.kohl@kattenlaw.com.

KOHLBERG, JAMES A., venture capitalist; BA, Golden Gate U.; MBA, NYU. With Merrill Lynch, Kohlberg Kravis Roberts & Co., NYC, 1984—87; co-founder, mng. prin. Kohlberg & Co., Mt. Kisco, NY, 1987—. Bd. dirs. Allied Aerospace Engring., Inc., Applied Graphics Tech., Inc., CUSA Busways, LLC, Holley Performance Products, Inc., Innotek, Inc., Katy Industries, Inc., Nancy's Specialty Foods, Inc., Nevamar Co., LLC, Orion Food Sys. LLC, Simplicity Mfg. Inc., Tinnerman Palnut Engineered Products LLC, KTTI Holding Co., Inc. Office: Kohlberg & Co 111 Radio Cir Mount Kisco NY 10549 Office Phone: 914-241-7430. Office Fax: 914-241-7476.

KOHLBERG, JEROME, JR., (JERRY KOHLBERG), venture capitalist, lawyer; b. N.Y.C., 1925; married; 4 children. Grad., Swarthmore Coll., 1946; MBA, Harvard Bus. Sch.; JD, Columbia U., 1950. Bar: N.Y. Formerly with Bear Stearns & Co., Inc.; sr. founding ptnr. Kohlberg, Kravis, Roberts & Co., N.Y.C., 1976-87; chmn. Houdaille Industries, Inc., Fort Lauderdale, Fla., exec. com.; chmn., co-founder Kohlberg and Co., Mt. Kisco, NY, 1987—94; spl. limited principal Kohlberg & Co., 1994—. Bd. dirs. Sterndent Corp. Founder Kohlberg Found., Campaign for America, Campaign Reform Project; bd. managers Swarthmore Coll. Named to Private Equity Hall of Fame, 1994. Achievements include forming the Campaign Reform project which was pivotal in passing The McCain-Feingold campaign finance reform bill. Office: Kohlberg & Co 111 Radio Circle Mount Kisco NY 10549*

KOHLENBERG, STANLEY, corporate financial executive; b. Bklyn., Aug. 19, 1932; s. Max and Minnie (Roth) K.; m. Ruth Barbara Itkin, Dec. 11, 1955; children: Robin sue, Mark Stuart, Howard Scott. BS, Columbia U., 1953; postgrad., NYU, 1956-58. Acct. supr. L.W. Frohlich, N.Y.C., 1959-62; advt. mgr. Pfizer Pab., N.Y.C., 1962-63; mktg. dir. Tussy Cosmetics, N.Y.C., 1964; sr. v.p., dir. client svc. Sudler & Hennessey, N.Y.C., 1964-66; pub. Cosmetics Fair mag., N.Y.C., 1966-68; exec. v.p. Spectrum Cosmetics, N.Y.C., 1968-70; pres. Coty, Inc., N.Y.C., 1970-72; exec. v.p. Revlon, Inc., N.Y.C., 1972-76; pres. Calvin Klein Cosmetics, Inc., N.Y.C., 1977-79, CFT Mktg., Inc., N.Y.C., 1980-84, Sanofi Beauty Products, Inc., N.Y.C., 1984-88; pres., CEO Alfin, Inc., N.Y.C., 1988-92; exec. v.p. Tottenham & Co., N.Y.C., 1992-96; chmn. bd., CEO Trans World Gaming Corp., N.Y.C., 1996-99; pres., CFO DP Parfume Corp., 1999—. With M.D., AUS, 1953-55. Office Phone: 212-685-0773. Personal E-mail: stanley.kohlenberg@verizon.net.

KOHLER, FRED CHRISTOPHER, tax specialist; b. Cleve., Oct. 21, 1946; s. Fred Russell and Ruth Mary (Harris) Kohler; m. Kuo-Jung Chang. BS (Austin scholar), Northwestern U., 1968; MBA (Faville fellow), Stanford U., 1970. Sr. analyst adminstrv. svcs. dissn. Arthur Andersen & Co., San Francisco, 1970-75; fin. systems analyst, sr. cost acct. Hewlett Packard Co., Palo Alto, Calif., 1975-77, internat. mktg. systems adminstr., 1977-80, sr. planning and reporting analyst corp. hdqrs., 1980-86, fin. planning and reporting mgr., 1986-90, tax mgr., 1990-92, sr. tax mgr., 1992—. Mem. World Affairs Coun. No. Calif., Commonwealth Club, Churchill Club, Northwestern U. Alumni Club No. Calif., Stanford U. Alumni Assn., Beta Gamma Sigma. Home: 315 Homer Ave Unit 201 Palo Alto CA 94301-2761 Office: 3000 Hanover St Palo Alto CA 94304-1112

KÖHLER, HORST, President of Federal Republic of Germany; b. Skierbieszów, Poland, Feb. 22, 1943; m. Eva Luise Köhler; two children. PhD in Econs. and Polit. Scis., U. Tübingen, Germany, 1977. Rsch. asst. Inst. for Applied Econ. Rsch., 1969—76; various positions German Ministries Econs. and Fin., 1976—93; German dep. min. fin., 1990-93; pres. German Savings Bank Assn., 1993-98, European Bank for Reconstruction and Devel., 1998-2000; mng. dir., chmn. exec. bd. Internat. Monetary Fund, 2000—04; pres. Fed. Republic Germany, 2004—. Rep. fed. chancellor preparation Group Seven Econ. Summits, Houston, 1990, London, 1991, Munich, 1992, Tokyo, 1993; hon. prof. U. Tübingen, 2003. Office: Bundespraesidialamt 11010 Berlin Germany

KOHLER, LAURA E., human resources executive; married; 3 children. Grad., Duke U., 1984; MFA, Cath. U., 1987. Past tchr. Chgo. Pub. Schs.; past corp. team facilitator; past mgr. Nat. Players, Washington; past residence mgr. Olney (Md.) Theatre; founder Chgo.; past exec. dir. Kohler Found., Inc.; v.p. human resources Kohler Co., 1990—, past v.p. comm., 1994—99, sr. v.p. human resources, also bd. dirs. Office: Kohler Co 444 Highland Dr Kohler WI 53044-1500

KOHLER, PETER OGDEN, internist, educator, academic administrator; b. Bklyn., July 18, 1938; s. Dayton McCue and Jean Stewart (Ogden) K.; m. Judy Lynn Baker, Dec. 26, 1959; children: Brooke Culp, Stephen Edwin, Todd Randolph, Adam Stewart. BA, U. Va., 1959; MD, Duke U., 1963; PhD in Pub. Svc. (hon.), U. Portland, 2003. Diplomate Am. Bd. Internal Medicine and Endocrinology. Intern Duke U. Hosp., Durham, N.C., 1963-64, fellow, 1964-65; clin. assoc. Nat Cancer Inst., Nat Inst. Child Health and Human Devel., NIH, Bethesda, Md., 1965-67, sr. investigator, 1968-73, head endocrinology service, 1972-73; resident in medicine Georgetown U. Hosp., Washington, 1969-70; prof. medicine and cell biology, chief endocrinology divsn. Baylor Coll. Medicine, Houston, 1973-77; prof., chmn. dept. medicine U. Ark., 1977-86, interim dean, 1985-86; chmn. Hosp. Med. Bd., 1980-82, chmn. council dept. chmn., 1979-80; prof., dean Sch. Medicine, U. Tex., San Antonio, 1986-88; pres. Oreg. Health & Sci. U., Portland, 1988—. Cons. endocrinology merit rev. bd. VA, 1985—86; mem. bd. sci. counselors NICHD, 1987—92, chair, 1990—92; chair task force on health care delivery AAHC, 1991—92; Inst. Medicine bd. dirs. Stds. Ins. Co.; bd. dirs. Portland br. Fed. Res. Bank of San Francisco; chair Task Force on Improving Quality of Long-Term Care, 1994; mem. adv. bd. Loaves and Fishes, 1989—99; mem. Gov.'s adv. com. Commn. on Tech. Edn., 1989—92; chair Oreg. Health Coun., 1993—95; various positions Am. Bd. Internal Medicine, 1987—93, NIH; mem. numerous bd. dirs. and adv. bds. Editor: Current Opinion in Endocrinology and Diabetes, 1994-97, Diagnosis and Treatment of Pituitary Tumors, (with G. T. Ross), 1973, Clinical Endocrinology, 1986; assoc. editor: Internal Medicine, 1983, 87, 90, 94, 98; contbr. articles to profl. jours. Mem. campaign cabinet United Way, 1999—2004. With USPHS, 1965-68. NIH grantee, 1973—; Howard Hughes Med. Investigator, 1976-77; recipient NIH Quality awrds, 1969, 71, Disting. Alumnus award Duke Med. Sch., 1992, MRF Mentor award, Med. Rsch. Found., 1994, Humanitarian award Am. Lung Assn., 1996, Jewish Nat. Fund Tree of Life award, 1998, Internat. Citizens award Oreg. Consular Corps., 1999, Human Rels. award Am. Jewish Com., 2002, Leadership award Coun. for Advancement and Support of Edn., 2004; named Honored Citizen, Archl. Found. Oreg., 2002; named one of Twenty Leaders of Change, The Bus. Jour., 2004. Fellow ACP; mem. AMA (William Beaumont award 1988), Inst. Medicine, Am. Soc. Clin. Investigation, Am. Fedn. Clin. Rsch. (nat. coun. 1977-78, pres. so. sect. 1976), So. Soc. Clin. Investigation (coun. 1979-82, pres. 1983, Founder's medal 1987), Am. Soc. Cell Biology, Assn. Acad. Health Ctrs. (chmn. 1998-99, bd. dirs.), Assn. Am. Physicians, Am. Diabetes Assn., Endocrine Soc. (coun. 1990-93), Raven Soc., Phi Beta Kappa, Sigma Xi, Alpha Omega Alpha, Omicron Delta Kappa, Phi Eta Sigma. Methodist. Office: Oreg Health & Sci U Office of Pres L101 3181 SW Sam Jackson Park Rd Portland OR 97239-3098

KOHLI, GURMANDER S., plastic surgeon; b. Quetta, India, Oct. 27, 1945; s. Asa Singh Kohli and Jaswant Kaur Sethi; m. Maninder Kaur Dutta, Apr. 13, 1975; children: Sanjivan, Moneet, Manpreet, Harjivan, Sukhjivan. MBChB, U. Glasgow, 1973. Diplomate Am. Bd. Plastic Surgery, 1984, lic. Mass., Calif., England, Lithuania. Resident Boston Med. Ctr., 1975—79, 1979—81; plastic surgeon pvt. practice, Boston, 1981—2004; chief plastic surgery Boston Regional Med. Ctr., Stoneman, 1989—99, Whidden Meml. Hosp., Everett, 1992—2001; asst. clin. prof. surgery Tufts U. Sch. Medicine, Boston, 2002—; asst. clin. prof. plastic surgery U. Calif., San Diego, 2004—; plastic surgeon pvt. practice, Irvine, Calif., 2004—. Fellow, Plastic Surgery Ednl. Found., 2002—, Nat. Endowment Plastic Surgery, 2002—. Fellow: Am. Coll. Surgeons; mem.: Mass. Soc. Plastic Surgeons, New Eng. Soc. Plastic Surgeons, Am. Soc. Plastic Surgeons, Mass. Med. Soc. Sikh. Home: 3 Hollinwood Irvine CA 92618-4070 E-mail: gsk@kohli.com.

KOHLI, HARINDER S., economist, corporate executive; b. Apr. 11, 1945; s. Ujagar Singh and Jogingar (Anand) Kohli; m. Paulina Ledergerber; children: Harpaul Alberto, Monica Sarita. BSc, Punjab (India) U., 1966; MBA, Harvard U., 1972. Mktg. exec. Union Carbide India, New Delhi, 1967-70; dir. The World Bank, Washington, 1986-93, sr. adv., 1994-98; pres., CEO Centennial Group, Inc., Washington, 1998—. Spkr., author (books, articles) fin., infrastructure. energy, litig. and econ. devel. Baker scholar, Harvard U., 1972. Mem.: Emerging Markets Forum, India Software Group, First Ea. Investment Group (Hong Kong), Optimos and Internat. Devel. Bus. Cons. Home: 6516 Deidre Ter Mc Lean VA 22101-1605 Office Phone: 202-393-6663. E-mail: harinder@centennial-group.com.

KOHLI, SANDEEP, materials scientist, researcher; b. Delhi, India, 1970; arrived in U.S., 1999; BS in Physics, U. Delhi, 1990; MS in Physics, U. Delhi, 1992, PhD, 1997. Rsch. assoc. Nat. Phys. Lab., New Delhi, 1996—99; rsch. scientist Colo. State U., Fort Collins, 1999—. Chmn. session on nanomaterials Internat. Conf. on Composites/Nano Engring., 2003. Contbr. articles to profl. jours. Fellow, IKY, Greece; Nat. Rsch. Assoc. fellow, Coun. Of Sci. And Indsl. Rsch., India, 1997—99. Mem.: IEEE (sr.), Internat. Ctr. for Diffractions Data. Office: Colo State U Dept Chemistry Fort Collins CO 80523 Office Phone: 970-491-4076. Business E-Mail: sandeep.kohli@colostate.edu.

KOHLMANN, SUSAN J., lawyer; b. Jan. 15, 1958; BA, Yale Univ., 1979; JD, Columbia Univ., 1982. Bar: NY 1983. Ptnr., chmn. Intellectual Property dept., office mng. ptnr. Pillsbury Winthrop Shaw Pittman, NYC. Editor (Casenote & Comment): Columbia Jour. Transnational Law. Mem. bd. legal adv. NOW Legal Def. & Edn. Fund. Mem.: Internat. Trademark Assn., Assn. Bar City of NY (co-chmn. Com. on Women & the Law 1999—2001, mem. exec. com.). Office: Pillsbury Winthrop Shaw Pittman 1540 Broadway New York NY 10036 Office Phone: 212-858-1707. Office Fax: 212-858-1500. Business E-Mail: susan.kohlmann@pillsburylaw.com.

KOHLMEIER, JADA, social studies educator; b. Washington, Aug. 28, 1970; d. Marvin and Karen Kohlmeier. BA in history, Kans. State U., 1988—92; MA in tchg., Wash. U., 1992—93; PhD, U. of Kans., 1997—2003. Secondary social studies tchr. Concordia Sch. Dist., Kans., 1993—97, De Soto Sch. Dist., Kans., 1997—2003; asst. prof. secondary social sci. edn. Auburn Univ., Ala., 2003—. Sunday sch. tchr. Trinity Luth. Ch., Auburn, Ala., 2003—05, Bethany Luth. Ch., Overland Pk., Kans., 2000—03. Recipient Milken Family Found. Nat. Educator award, Milken Family Found., 2001; James Madison Meml. fellowship, James Madison Found., 1992. Office: Auburn Univ 5040 Haley Ctr Auburn AL 36849 Office Phone: 334-844-4434.

KOHLMEIER, LOUIS MARTIN, JR., newspaper reporter; b. St. Louis, Feb. 17, 1926; s. Louis Martin and Anita (Werling) K.; m. Barbara Anne Wilson, Nov. 15, 1958; children— Daniel Kimbrell, Ann Werling. B.Journalism, U. Mo., 1950. Staff writer Wall St. Jour., St. Louis and Chgo., 1952-57, Washington, 1960—; staff writer St. Louis Globe-Democrat, 1958-59. Author: The Regulators Watchdog Agencies and the Public Interest, 1969. Served with AUS, 1950-52. Recipient Nat. Headliners Club award nat. reporting, 1959, Sigma Delta Chi award Washington corr., 1964, Pulitzer prize nat. reporting, 1964 Home: # 105 11400 Strand Dr Apt 105 Rockville MD 20852-2942

KOHLOSS, FREDERICK HENRY, retired engineer; b. Ft. Sam Houston, Tex., Dec. 4, 1922; s. Fabius Henry and Rowena May (Smith) K.; m. Margaret Mary Grunwell, Sept. 9, 1944; children: Margaret Ralston, Charlotte Todesco, Eleanor. BS in Mech. Engring., U. Md., 1943; M in Mech. Engring., U. Del., 1951; JD, George Washington U., 1949. Engring. faculty George Washington U., Washington, 1946-50; devel. and stds. engr. Dept. Def., 1950-51; chief engr. for mech. contractors Washington, 1951-54, Cleve., 1954-55, Honolulu, 1955-56; cons. engr., 1956-61; pres. Frederick H. Kohloss & Assocs., Inc., Cons. Engrs., Honolulu, 1961-91; chmn. Lincolne, Scott & Kohloss Inc, Cons. Engrs., Honolulu, 1991-97, sr. cons., 1997-2001, cons. engr., 2001—03, ret., 2003. Contbr. articles to profl. jours. Served with AUS, 1943-46. Fellow ASME, ASHRAE, Chartered Inst. Bldg. Svcs. Engrs., Instn. Engrs. Australia, Australian Inst. Refrigeration, Air Conditioning, Heating; mem. IEEE (sr.), NSPE, Soc. Fire Protection Engrs., Oahu Country Club (Honolulu). Home: 2500 N Rosemont Blvd #433 Tucson AZ 85712 Office Phone: 520-325-4753. E-mail: fredpeg@cox.net.

KOHLSTEDT, JAMES AUGUST, lawyer; b. Evanston, Ill., June 1, 1949; s. August Lewis and Deloris (Weichelt) K.; m. Patricia Ann Lang, Oct. 8, 1977; children: Katherine, Matthew, Lindsey, Kevin. BA, Northwestern U., 1971; JD, MBA, Ind. U., 1976. Bar: U.S. Dist. Ct. (no. dist.) Ill. 1976, U.S. Tax Ct. 1978. Tax specialist Peat Marwick, Mitchell & Co., Chgo., 1976-77; assoc. Bishop & Crawford Ltd., Oak Brook, Ill., 1977-83, 1984-85; ptnr. Arnstein, Gluck, Lehr & Milligan, Oak Brook, 1985-87, Keck, Mahin and Cate, Oak Brook, 1987-96, McBride Baker & Coles, 1996-2001, mem. mgmt. com., 1997; chair McBride Baker & Coles Trade and Profl. Assn. Practice Group; sr. ptnr. The Kohlstedt Law Firm LLC, 2001—. Bd. dirs. Nat. Entrepreneurship Found., Bloomington, Ind., 1981-92, Camp New Hope Devel. Bd., Oak Brook, 1983; mem. sch. bd. Lyons Twp. H.S. Dist. 204, La Grange, Ill., 1985—, Hinsdale (Ill.) Cmty. House Coun., 1991-94; mem. area leadership com. Superconducting Super Collider, 1987-88; mem. citizens adv. com. on edn. to U.S. Congressman Harris Fawell, 1986-93; bd. dirs. Ill. Corridor Partnership for Excellence in Edn., 1988-94, DuPage Conv. and Visitors Bur., 1997-2001; mem. exec. bd. Visit Ill., 1997-2003; mem. planned giving com. Elmhurst Coll., 1986—; mem. citizens adv. panel U.S. Army ROTC Cadet Command, 1991-94; bd. dirs. Ill. Math and Sci. Acad. Alliance, 1989—; del. White House Conf. Travel and Tourism, 1995; mem. allied adv. bd. midwest chpt. Am. Soc. Travel Agents, 1995; Collegiate Edn. adv. com. Dept. Def., 1995. Recipient Outstanding Young Citizen of Chgo. award 1987. Mem. ABA, Ill. Travel and Tourism Assn., Ill. Bar Assn., DuPage Estate Planning Coun., Oak Brook Jaycees (pres. 1984—, chmn. bd. 1985, trustee 1985-86), Beta Gamma Sigma. Republican. Lutheran. Office Phone: 630-571-0793. E-mail: jim@ktlawpro.com.

KOHLSTEDT, SALLY GREGORY, historian, educator; b. Ypsilanti, Mich., Jan. 30, 1943; BA, Valparaiso U., 1965; MA, Mich. State U., 1966; PhD, U. Ill., 1972. Asst. prof. Simmons Coll., Boston, 1971-75; assoc. prof. to prof. Syracuse (N.Y.) U., 1975-89; prof. history of sci. U. Minn., Mpls., 1989—; dir. Ctr. for Advanced Feminist Studies, 1997-98. Vis. prof. history of sci. Cornell U., 1989, Amerika Inst. U. Munich, 1997; vis. assoc. Calif. Inst. Tech., 2004, lectr. in field Author: The Formation American Scientific Community: AAAS, 1848-1860, 1976; editor: (with Margaret Rossiter) Historical Writing on American Science, Osiris, 2d Series, 1, 1985, (with R.W. Home) International Science and National Scientific Identity: Australia between Britain and America, 1991, The Origins of Natural Science in the United States: The Essays of George Brown Goode, 1991, (with Barbara Haslett et al.) Gender and Scientific Authority, 1996, (with Helen Lonino) The Women, Gender, and Science Question, 1997, The History of Women in Science: An Isis Reader, 1999, (with Bruce Leavenstein and Michael Sokal) The Establishment of Science in America: The American Association for the Advancement of Science, 1999; contbr. articles to profl. jours.; mem. editl. bd. Signs, 1980-88, 90-93, Sci., 1980-81, News and Views: History of Am. Sci. Newsletter, 1980-86, Sci., Tech. and Human Values, 1983-90, Syracuse Scholar, 1985-88, chair, 1988, Minerva, 2000—, Isis, 2002-; assoc. editor

Am. Nat. Biography, 2d edit., 1988-98, consulting edit., 1993-99; Gruphon Press Reprints in the History of Science, 1993-98; reviewer books, articles, proposals for NSDF, NEH, U. Chgo. Press, others; editor sci. biography series Cambridge U., 1997-2003. NSF grantee, 1969, 78-79, 84, 93-95, 2002, Smithsonian Instn. predoctoral fellow, 1970-71, Danforth Assoc., 1975-82, Syracuse U. grantee, 1976, 82, Am. Philos. Soc. rsch. grantee, 1977, Haven fellow Am. Antiquarian Soc., 1982, Fulbright Sr. fellow U. Melbourne, Australia, 1983, Woodrow Wilson Ctr. fellow, 1986, Smithsonian Instn. Sr. fellow, 1987. Fellow AAAS (nominating com. 1980-83, 96-98, sect. chair 1986, bd. dirs. 1998-2002, chair divsn. on sci., ethics and religion 2003—, coun. 2004—), Am. Hist. Assn. (profl. com. 1974-76, rep. U.S. Nat. Archives Adv. Coun. 1974-76), Berkshire Conf. Women Historians (program com. 1974), Forum on the History Sci. in Am. (coord. com. 1980-86, chair 1985, 86), History of Sci. Soc. (sec. 1978-81, coun. 1982-84, 89-91, 94-96, com. on publs. 1982-87, chair nominating com. 1985, 99, women's com. 1972-74, vis. lectr. 1988-89, chair edn. com. 1989, pres. 1992, 93), Internat. Congress for History of Sci. (U.S. del. 1977, 81, vice chair 1985) Orgn. Am. Historians (chair com. on status of women 1983-85, endowment fund drive, auction subcom. 1990-91). Lutheran. Home: 4140 Edmund Blvd Minneapolis MN 55406-3646 Business E-Mail: sgk@umn.edu.

KOHN, A. EUGENE, architect; b. Phila., Dec. 12, 1930; s. William Bernard and Hannah (Steinberg) K.; m. Barbara S. Kohn; children: Brian, Steve, Laurie. BArch, U. Pa., 1953, MArch, 1957. Registered architect Ala., Calif., Colo., Conn., Del., D.C., Fla., Ga., Idaho, Ill., Kans., Ky., Md., Mass., Mich., N.J., N.Y., N.C., Ohio, Okla., Pa., Tenn., Tex., Va., Wis., Minn., U.K., Japan; lic. profl. planner, N.J. With Nolan Swinburne, 1957-60; project designer, project mgr. Nolan & Swinburne, Architects, Phila., 1958-60; project designer, studio designer head Vincent G. Kling Architects, Phila., 1960-64; designer Kahn & Jacobs Architects, N.Y.C., 1964-65; dir. design Welton, Becket & Assocs., N.Y.C., 1965-67; pres., prin. John Carl Warnecke & Assocs., N.Y.C., Los Angeles, San Francisco, 1967-76; founder, pres. Kohn Pedersen Fox Assocs. PC, Architects and Planners, N.Y.C., 1976—. Mem. archtl. rev. panel N.Y. Port Authority; guest lectr. Bucknell U., U. Ky., UCLA, U. Pa., Miami U., Oxford, Ohio, Kent State U., U. Tenn., N.Y. Inst. Tech., Clemson U., Pa. State U., U. Fla., Washington U., St. Louis, U. Chgo., Ill. Inst. Tech., U. Wis., Pratt U., Harvard U., Kuala Lumpur, Australia, New Zealand, Japan, Russia, Hong Kong; spkr. in field; archtl. critic various univs.; exec. fellow Harvard Design Sch. Former bd. dirs. Sheltering Arms Children Svc., Archtl. League, Chgo. City Ballet; chmn. bd. overseers Grad. Sch. Fine Arts, trustee U. Pa., adv. bd. MS in Real Estate Devel.; trustee Columbia U. Grad. Sch. Arch. and Planning, Silvermine Art Guild; mem. bd. advisors com. on the Art Gallery and Brit. Arts Ctr. Yale U.; bd. trustees Mus. African Art, N.Y.C., Nat. Bldg. Mus. Lt. comdr. USN, 1953—56. Recipient Receiving the Flame of Truth award, Fund for Higher Edn., 1987, GSA award, Ellis Island Medal of Honor, 1998; Theopolis Parsons Chandler fellow. Fellow: AIA (pres. N.Y. chpt. 1987—88, internat. steering com., honor design awards 1962, 1984, 1987); mem.: Mcpl. Art Soc. N.Y., Nat. Coun. Archtl. Registration Bds., N.Y. State Assn. Archs., N.Y. Bldg. Congress, Urban Land Inst. (trustee), Royal Inst. Brit. Architects, Octagon Soc. of the AIA, University (N.Y.C.), City Club N.Y., TAu Sigma Delta. Avocations: painting, music, tennis, golf, skiing. Home: 570 Park Ave New York NY 10021 Office: Kohn Pedersen Fox Assocs PC 111 W 57th St New York NY 10019-2211 Office Phone: 212-237-3330. E-mail: gkohn@kpf.com.

KOHN, ADAM M., lawyer; b. 1973; BS in Economics, U. Pa., 1995; JD, Yeshiva U., 1998. Bar: DC, NY, US Supreme Ct. Assoc. Shaw Pittman LLP, Washington; assoc., health care practice group Sonnenschein Nath & Rosenthal LLP, Washington, 2003—. Mem.: ABA (mem. health law sect.), Assn. Clin. Rsch. Professionals, Am. Health Lawyers Assn. Office: Sonnenschein Nath & Rosenthal LLP Ste 600, E Tower 1301 K St NW Washington DC 20005 Office Phone: 202-408-9163. Office Fax: 202-408-6399. Business E-Mail: akohn@sonnenschein.com.

KOHN, ALFIE, writer, educator; b. Miami Beach, Fla., Oct. 15, 1957; s. Stewart L. and Estelle E. (Kauffman) K.; m. Alisa Harrigan, June 25, 1994. BA, Brown U., 1979; MA, U. Chgo., 1980. Vis. lectr. Phillips Acad., Andover, Mass., summers 1978-85, Tufts U., Medford, Mass., 1983, 84; lectr. in field. Author: No Contest: The Case Against Competition, 1986 (Nat. Pub. award 1987), The Brighter Side of Human Nature, 1990, You Know What They Say, 1990, Punished by Rewards, 1993, Unconditional Parenting: Moving from Rewards and Punishment to Love and Reason, 2005; contbg. editor Psychology Today, 1987-89; mem. editorial com. Coop. Learning mag., 1989—; contbr. articles to profl. jours. Mem. nat. adv. bd. Peace Edn. Found. Mem. Internat. Assn. for Study Cooperation in Edn. Avocations: composing, performing satiric songs.*

KOHN, DAVID SAMUEL, finance educator, banker; b. Paterson, N.J., Jan. 4, 1944; s. Nathan Stolzer Kohn and Edith Koggin; m. Marilyn Andrea Primoff, Sept. 2, 1979; 1 child, Douglas Samuel. BA, C. W. Post Coll., 1967; MBA, L.I. U., 1969; diploma, Pace U., 1972; PhD, NYU, 1995. CPA, N.Y.; cert. N.Y. state real estate broker, N.Y. state mortgage banker; cert. N.J. mortgage banker. Asst. prof. Pace U., N.Y.C., 1978-87; CPA Primoff & Co., N.Y.C., 1980-89; treas., ptnr. Vehicle Parts Warehouse, Astoria, N.Y., 1985-95; ptnr. 107 W. 109th St. Assocs., N.Y.C., 1980—, 1505 Lexington Ave. Assocs., N.Y.C., 1980—; chmn., CEO Continental Mortgage Bankers, Westbury, N.Y., 1988-98; chmn. Charles Booth Profl. Hair Products, Inc., N.Y.C., 1998—; chmn., prof. acctg. dept. U. Bridgeport (Conn.), 2002—. Cons., N.Y.C., 1980—; adj. prof. Yeshiva U., N.Y.C., 1997-98; chmn., CEO CPA Internetwork Ltd., N.Y.C., 1999—. Cash chmn. United Jewish Appeal, Westchester County, Rockland County, Putnam County, N.Y., 1973-75; bd. dirs. Quaker Bridge Camp, Ossining, N.Y., 1974-85, Congregation Anshe Dorche Emes, Ossining, 1976-84, B'nai Brith, 1989-92, Westchester Rockland, Pulman Ctr. Meadowbrook Bank scholar, 1969. Mem. AICPA, Mortgage Bankers Assn. Am., N.Y. State Soc. CPA (lectr., mem. real estate com.), Delta Pi Epsilon. Avocations: golf, fishing, tennis. Fax: 914-235-4366. E-mail: DSKohn9021@aol.com.

KOHN, DONALD L., economist, federal agency administrator; b. Phila., Pa., Nov. 7, 1942; m. Gail Kohn; children: Laura, Jeffrey. BA in econ., Coll. Wooster, 1964; PhD in econ., U. Mich., 1971. Fin. economist Fed. Reserve Bank of Kans. City, 1970—75; economist Divsn. Rsch. and Stats., FRS, 1975—78, chief of capital markets, 1978—81, assoc. dir., 1981—83; dep. staff dir. for monetary and fin. policy FRS, 1983—87, dir., divsn. of monetary affairs, 1987—2001, sec. of fed. open market com., 1987—2002, advisor to bd. monetary policy, 2001—02, mem. bd. govs. Washington, 2002—. Contbr. articles to profl. jours. Recipient Disting. Alumni award, Coll. Wooster, 1998, Disting. Achievement award, Money Marketeers of NYU, 2002. Office: FRS Marriner S Eccles Fed Reserve Bd Bldg 20th and C Sts NW Washington DC 20551

KOHN, IMMANUEL, lawyer; b. Jerusalem, Dec. 6, 1926; arrived in US, 1934; s. Hans and Yetty (Wahl) Kohn; m. Vera Sharpe, July 22, 1950; children: Gail, Peter, Sheila, Robert. Grad., Deerfield Acad., 1944; BA summa cum laude, Harvard U., 1949; LL.B cum laude, Yale U., 1953. Bar: NY 1955, US Dist. Ct. (Ea. Dist.) NY 1955, US Dist. Ct. (So. Dist.) NY 1957, US Ct. Appeals (2nd Cir.) 1966, US Supreme Ct. 1972. Assoc. Cahill Gordon & Reindel LLP, NYC, 1953-62, ptnr., Corp. Practice Area, 1962, mem. exec. com., 1972—, chmn. exec. com., 1991—. Trustee Inst. Advanced Study, Princeton, NJ, 1997—. Editor: Yale U. Law Jour., 1951—53. Ensign US Maritime Svc., 1946. Sheldon travelling fellow, 1949—50. Mem.: Order of Coif, Downtown Assn., Beden Brook Club (NJ), Sky Club, Met. Opera Club, Phi Beta Kappa. Office: Cahill Gordon & Reindel LLP 80 Pine St Fl 17 New York NY 10005-1790 Office Phone: 212-701-3803. Office Fax: 212-378-2232. Business E-Mail: ikohn@cahill.com.

KOHN, JEAN GATEWOOD, retired health facility administrator, pediatrician; b. Chgo., July 8, 1926; d. Gatewood and Esther Lydia (Harper) Gatewood; m. Martin M. Kohn, Feb. 10, 1951; children: Helen, Joel, Michael, David. BS, U. Chgo., 1948, MD, 1950; MPH, U. Calif., Berkeley, 1973. Diplomate Am. Bd. Pediatrics. Physician Permanente Med. Group, San Leandro, Calif., 1953-60; pediatric cons. Calif. Children Svcs., 1961-72; lectr. maternal and child health U. Calif., 1973-91; med. advisor rehab. engring. ctr. Packard Children's Hosp. at Stanford, Calif., 1976-97, med. dir. child prosthetic clinic, 1977-97, ret., 1997, pediatrician Mary L. Johnson Infant Devel. Unit, 2000—. Asst. neurologic diagnostic ctr. U. Calif., San Francisco, 1960-72; pediatric cons. Project HOPE, Nicaragua, 1966, Peru, 1962; pediatric cons. sch. pub. health U. Hawaii, Okinawa, 1975. Contbr. chpts. to books and articles to profl. jours. Mem. adv. panel State of Calif. Dept. Spl. Edn., Calif. Children Svcs.; bd. dirs. Mental Health Assn., United Cerebral Palsy Assn., Head Start, San Mateo County, 1993—. Recipient Lyda M. Smiley award Calif. Sch. Nurses Orgn., 1987. Fellow Am. Acad. Pediats., Am. Acad. Cerebral Palsy and Devel. Medicine; mem. Project HOPE Alumni Assn. (pres. 1988-92). Office Phone: 650-725-8995.

KOHN, JEFFREY IRA, lawyer; b. N.Y.C., Mar. 10, 1959; s. Howard Sanford and Arlene Vivian (Kostrinsky) K.; m. Martha C. Obler, Aug. 12, 1984; children: Brian Edward, Alexandra Hannah. BS in Indsl. and Labor Rels., Cornell U., 1981; JD, George Washington U., 1984. Bar: N.Y. 1985, U.S. Dist. Ct. (so. and ea. dists.) N.Y. 1985, N.J. 1988, U.S. Ct. Appeals (2d cir.) 1991, U.S. Supreme Ct., 1992, U.S. Ct. Appeals (3d cir.) 1993. Assoc. O'Melveny & Myers, N.Y.C., 1984-92, ptnr., 1992—. Adj. prof. N.Y. Law Sch., 1989—91, adj. instr. law, 1986—89. Author: (book chpt.) NLRA Law and Policy, 1992; supplemental author: Modern Law of Employment Relations, 1990—. Mem.: ABA (employment and labor law com. 1991—, co-chair employment law com. 2000—03). Avocations: tennis, baseball, photography. Home: 4 Stony Hollow Rd Chappaqua NY 10514-2014 Office: O'Melveny & Myers LLP 153 E 53rd St Fl 53 New York NY 10022-4688 E-mail: jkohn@omm.com.

KOHN, MARTIN F., theater critic, journalist; b. Bklyn., May 29, 1945; s. Philip and Bertha G. Kohn; m. Laura Sacks, May 31, 1980; children: Maggie P., Anna R. BA, Bklyn Coll., 1966; MA, Syracuse U., 1968. Reporter, editor Detroit Free Press, 1977—98, theater critic, 1998—. Singer, guitarist The Roughstone Ramblers, Providence, 1973—76; contbg. editor Parents Mag., N.Y.C., 1991—99; columnist Back Stage, N.Y.C. Author: (book) Family Fare, 1988, Family Fare 2, 1993; editor: VideoHound's Family Video Guide, 1996; musician (singer, prodr.): (CD) Drawerful of Fives, 2003. Recipient Deems Taylor award, ASCAP, 1995; Critic fellow, Eugene O'Neill Theatre Ctr., Waterford, Conn., 2001. Mem.: Am. Theatre Critics Assn., TWIA (life), Mensa. Office: Detroit Free Press 600 W Fort St Detroit MI 48226

KOHN, RICHARD H., historian, educator; b. Chgo., Dec. 29, 1940; s. Henry L. and Kate K.; m. Lynne Holtan, Aug. 15, 1964; children: Abigail, Samuel. AB, Harvard U., 1962; MS in History, U. Wis., 1964, PhD in history, 1968. Asst. prof. history CCNY, 1968-71; from asst. prof. to prof. Rutgers U., New Brunswick, N.J., 1971-84; Harold Keith Johnson vis. prof. mil. history U.S. Army Mil. History Inst., Army War Coll., Carlisle Barracks, Pa., 1980-81; chief of Air Force history USAF, Washington, 1981-91; adj. prof. Nat. War Coll., Washington, 1985-90; from assoc. prof. to prof. history U. N.C., Chapel Hill, 1991—, chair, curriculum in peace, war and defense, 1992—. Expert witness U.S. Indian Claims Commn., Washington, 1974; cons. to various def. and hist. agys. and orgns., 1972—; vis. scholar strategic studies Johns Hopkins U. Sch. Advanced Internat. Studies, 1991; dir. Triangle Inst. for Security Studies, 1992-2000; bd. visitors Air Univ. USAF, 1996-2001. Author: Eagle and Sword: The Federalists and the Creation of the Military Establishment in America, 1783-1802, 1975; co-author: The Exclusion of Black Soldiers from the Medal of Honor in World War II, 1997; editor (reprint series) The American Military Experience, 1979; editor: The U.S. Military under the Constitution of the United States, 1789-1989, 1991; co-editor: (books) Air Superiority in World War II and Korea, 1983, Air Interdiction in World War II, Korea, and Vietnam, 1986, Strategic Air Warfare, 1988, Soldiers and Civilians, 2001; contbr. articles to profl. jours., chpts. to books. Recipient cert. for patriotic civilian service Dept. of Army, 1981, 96, Orgnl. Excellence award Dept. Air Force, 1990, Exceptional Civilian Svc. award Dept. Air Force, 1991, Edward F. Miller History prize Naval War Coll., 2005. Mem. Air Force Hist. Found. (Pres.' award 1987), Am. Antiquarian Soc., Am. Hist. Assn. (coun. 1986-89), Orgn. Am. Historians (Binkley-Stephenson award 1973, pub. history com. 1989-92, chair 1991-92), Soc. for Mil. History (trustee 1981-89, 95-99, parliamentarian 1982-89, pres. 1989-93, chair nom. com. 2000-2003), World War II Studies Assn. (bd. dirs. 1985-88, 91-97, 2000—). Office: U NC Curriculum Peace War Defense Cb # 3200 Chapel Hill NC 27599-3200

KOHN, ROGER ALAN, surgeon; b. Chgo., May 1, 1946; s. Arthur Jerome and Sylvia Lee (Karlen) K.; m. Barbara Helene, Mar. 30, 1974; children: Bradley, Allison. BA, U. Ill., 1967; MD, Northwestern U., 1971. Diplomate Am. Bd. Ophthalmology. Internship UCLA, 1971-72; residency Northwestern U., Chgo., 1972-75; fellowship U. Ala., Birmingham, 1975, Harvard Med. Sch., Boston, 1975-76; chmn. dept. ophthalmology Kern Med. Ctr., Bakersfield, Calif., 1978-87; asst. prof. UCLA Med. Sch., 1978-82, assoc. prof., 1982-86, prof., 1986—. Vice chmn. dept. ophthalmology Santa Barbara Cottage Hosp., 2004—05. Author: Textbook of Ophthalmic Plastic and Reconstructive Surgery, 1988; contbr. numerous articles to profl. jours.; author chpts. in 16 additional textbooks; patentee in field. Bd. dirs. Santa Barbara (Calif.) Symphony, 1990—. Capt. USAR, 1971-77. Name applied to med. syndrome Kohn-Romano Syndrome. Mem. Am. Soc. Ophthalmic Plastic and Reconstuctive Surgery (cert.), Am. Acad. Ophthalmology (Honor award 1995), Santa Barbara Ophthalmologic Soc. (pres. 1998), Pacific Coast Ophthal. Soc. (bd. dirs. 1986—, 1st v.p. 1990). Jewish. Avocations: guitar, tennis. Office: 525 E Micheltorena St Ste 201 Santa Barbara CA 93103-4212

KOHN, SHALOM L., lawyer; b. Nov. 18, 1949; s. Pincus and Helen (Roth) K.; m. Barbara Segal, June 30, 1974; children: David, Jeremy, Daniel. BS in Acctg. summa cum laude, CUNY, 1970; JD magna cum laude, MBA, Harvard U., 1974. Bar: Ill. 1975, U.S. Dist. Ct. (no. dist.) Ill. 1975, U.S. Ct. Appeals (7th cir.) 1976, U.S. Supreme Ct. 1980, N.Y. 1988, U.S. Dist. Ct. (so. dist.) N.Y. 1988, others. Law clk. to chief judge U.S. Ct. Appeals (2d cir.), N.Y.C., 1974-75; assoc. Sidley & Austin, Chgo., 1975-80, ptnr., 1980—. Exec. com. Adv. Coun. Religious Rights in Eastern Europe and Soviet Union, Washington, 1984-86; bd. dirs. Brisk Rabbinical Coll., Chgo. Contbr. articles to profl. jours. Mem. ABA, Chgo. Bar Assn. Office: Sidley Austin Brown & Wood Bank One Plz 10 South Dearborn Chicago IL 60603 also: 787 Seventh Ave New York NY 10019 Office Phone: 312-853-7756, 212-839-5440. Business E-Mail: skohn@sidley.com.

KOHN, STEVEN M., lawyer; b. Chgo., June 19, 1942; m. Dorine Kohn; 3 children. BA, UCLA, 1965, MBA in fin., 1967; JD, U. San Francisco, 1974. Bar: Calif. 1974. With Crosby Heafey Roach & May (combined with Reed Smith in 2003), 1977—2003, chair products liability practice group; ptnr. Reed Smith LLP, Oakland, Calif., 2003—, practice group leader products liability group, 2003—. Mem.: ABA, Def. Rsch. Inst. (mem. drug and med. device litig. steering com., chair warnings subcom.), Internat. Assn. Def. Counsel, Alameda Bar Assn., San Francisco Bar Assn. Avocations: reading, photography, endurance sports. Office: Reed Smith LLP 1999 Harrison St Ste 2400 Oakland CA 94612-3572 Office Phone: 510-466-6727. Office Fax: 510-273-8832. Business E-Mail: skohn@reedsmith.com.

KOHN, WALTER, physicist, retired educator; b. Vienna, Mar. 9, 1923; m. Mara Schiff; children: J. Marilyn, Ingrid E.Kohn Katz, E. Rosalind. BA, U. Toronto, Ont., Can., 1945, MA, 1946, LLD (hon.), 1967; DSc (hon.), U. Paris, 1980; PhD (hon.), Hebrew U. Jerusalem, 1981; DSc (hon.), Queens U., Kingston, Can., 1986, Fed. Inst. of Tech., Zurich, 1994, U. Wuerzburg, 1995, Tech. U. Vienna, 1996, Carnegie Mellon U., 1999, Rutgers U., 2001, Oxford U., 2001, U. Sherbrooke, Canada, 2002, Free U., Berlin, 2003; DSc, Tech. U., Dresden, 2003; PhD in Physics, Harvard U., 1948; PhD (hon.), Brandeis U., 1981, Weizmann Inst., Israel, 1997, Tel Aviv U., 1999. Indsl. physicist Sutton Horsley Co., Canada, 1941—43; geophysicist Koulomzine, Canada, 1944—46; instr. physics Harvard U., Cambridge, Mass., 1948—50; asst. prof. physics Carnegie Mellon U., Pitts., 1950—60, assoc. prof. physics, 1953—57; prof. physics U. Calif., San Diego, 1960—79, chmn. dept. physics, 1961—63; dir. Inst. for Theoretical Physics, U. Calif., Santa Barbara, 1979—84; prof. dept. physics U. Calif., Santa Barbara, 1984—91, prof. of physics emeritus, rsch. prof. of physics, 1991—; rsch. physicist Ctr. for Quantized Electronic Structures, U. Calif., Santa Barbara, 1991—. Vis. scholar U. Pa., U. Mich., U. Wash., U. Paris, U. Copenhagen, U. Jerusalem, Imperial Coll., London, ETH, Zurich, Switzerland; cons. Gen. Atomic, 1960—72, Westinghouse Rsch. Lab., 1953—57, Bell Telephone Labs., 1953—66, IBM, 1978; mem. or chmn. rev. coms. Brookhaven Nat. Labs., Argonne Nat. Labs., Oak Ridge Nat. Labs., Ames Lab., Tel Aviv U. (physics dept.), Brown U., Harvard U., U. Mich., Simon Frazer U., Tulane U., Reactor Divsn. NIST, Gaithersburg, Md.; chmn. S.D. divsn. Acad. Senate, 1968—69; dir. NSF Inst. Theoretical Physics U. Calif. Santa Barbara, 1979—84; mem. senate rev. com. U. Calif. Mgmt. Nat. Labs., 1986—89; adv. bd. Statewide Inst. Global Conflict and Cooperation, 1982—92; mem. bd. govs. Weizmann Inst. Sci., 1996—. Contbr. over 200 sci. articles and revs. to profl. jours. With Can. Army Inf., 1944—45. Recipient Buckley prize, 1960, Davisson-Germer prize, 1977, Nat. medal of Sci., 1988, Feenberg medal, 1991, Niels Bohr/UNESCO Gold medal, 1998, Nobel prize in Chemistry, 1998; fellow Lehman, Harvard U., 1946, NRC, 1950—51, sr., NSF, 1958, Guggenheim, 1963, sr. postdoctoral, NSF, 1967; grantee Oersted Fellow, Copenhagen, 1951—52. Fellow: AAAS, Am. Acad. Arts and Scis., 1963, Am. Phys. Soc. (counselor-at-large 1968—72); mem.: NAS, 1969, Bavarian Acad. Scis. (corr. mem. 2003—), Royal Soc. of London, 1998, Am. Philos. Soc., Internat. Acad. Quantum Molecular Scis., 1991. Achievements include research in electron theory of solids and solid surfaces. Office: U Calif Dept Physics Santa Barbara CA 93106*

KOHN, WILLIAM IRWIN, lawyer; b. Bronx, N.Y., June 27, 1951; s. Arthur Oscar and Frances (Hoffman) K.; m. Karen Mindlin, Aug. 29, 1974; children: Shira, Kinneret, Asher. Student, U. Del., 1969—71; BA with honors, U. Cin., 1973; JD, Ohio State U., 1976. Bar: Ohio 1976, US Dist. Ct. (no. dist.) Ohio 1976, Ind. 1982, US Dist. Ct. (no. and so. dists.) Ind. 1982, D.C. 1992, US Supreme Ct., 1992, Ill. 1994, US Dist. Ct. (no., ctrl., and so. dists.) Ill.; cert. Bus. Bankruptcy Law Am. Bankruptcy Bd. Cert. Ptnr. Krugliak, Wilkins, Griffith & Dougherty, Canton, Ohio, 1976-82, Barnes & Thornburg, Chgo., 1982—2001, Sachnoff & Weaver Ltd., Chgo., 2002, Schiff Harden LLP, Chgo., 2002—. Adj. prof. law U. Notre Dame, Ind., 1984—90. Author: West's Indiana Business Forms, West's Indiana Uniform Commercial Code Forms; contbr. articles to profl. jours. Bd. dirs. Family Svcs., South Bend, 1985—94, Jewish Fedn., Highland Park United Way, Jewish Family and Cmty. Svcs. Mem. ABA (bus. bankruptcy subcom.), Am. Bankruptcy Inst. (insolvency sect.), Ill. Bar Assn., Chgo. Bar Assn., Comml. Law League, Am. Bd. Certification (dir., std. com.). Office: Schiff Hardin LLP 6600 Sears Tower Chicago IL 60606 Office Phone: 312-258-5796. E-mail: wkohn@schiffhardin.com.

KOHNE, HEIDI ANN, church musician; b. Salem, Oreg., Sept. 15, 1974; d. Wilmar Allison and Karen Lee Kohne. MusB in organ performance, DePauw U., 1997; MusM in organ and ch. music, Ind. U., 1999. Organist St. Paul's Cath. Ch., Greencastle, Ind., 1994—97; concert office employee Interlochen Ctr. for the Arts, Interlochen, Mich., 1996—97, stage crew employee, 1998; organist Covenant Presbyn. Ch., Gresham, Oreg., 1999—2001; Kresge auditorium stage mgr. Interlochen Ctr. for the Arts, 1999—2003; organist Mt. Tabor Presbyn. Ch., Portland, Oreg., 2001—02, dir. music ministries, organist, 2003—. Program com. mem. Am. Guild of Organists, Portland, Oreg., 2001—02, sub dean, 2002—04, dean, 2004—. Computer graphics: Interlochen Stage Charts, 2003. Stage hand Portland Baroque Orch., Portland, Oreg., 2003—; accompanist Mt. Tabor Mid. Sch. Choir, Portland, Oreg., 2003—. Mem.: PEO, Am. Guild English Handbell Ringers, Presbyn. Assn. Musicians, Am. Guild Organists (cert. svc. playing). Presbyterian. Home: 1917 NE 77th Ave Portland OR 97213 Office: Mt Tabor Presbyn Ch 5441 SE Belmont Portland OR 97215 Office Phone: 503-234-6493. E-mail: hkohne@theinter.com.

KOHNEN, CAROL ANN, librarian; b. St. Louis, Apr. 8, 1948; d. Joseph William and Josephine (Strenfel) Licavoli; m. Richard Joseph Kohnen, May 9, 1970; children: Jill Patricia, Douglas Richard. BA, St. Louis U., 1970; MA in Libr. Sci., U. Mo., 1994. Cert. tchr., secondary English Mo., libr. K-12 Mo. Programmer, cons., Creve Coeur, Mo., 1981-90; audio-visual technician Parkway Schs., Chesterfield, 1989-92; libr. St. Joseph's Acad., Frontenac, 1992-98, Parkway No. HS, 1998—2004; coord. libr., media and instrl. tech. Parkway Sch. Dist., 2004—. Co-chair telecomms, users group Coop. Sch. Dists., St. Louis County, 1995—99; dept. leader Parkway No. HS, 1999—2004; mem. tech. coun. Parkway Sch. Dist., 2002—, chmn. tech. integration and facilitation com., 2004—. Am. memory fellow, Libr. Congress, 1998—99. Mem.: ISTE, Mo. Assn. Sch. Librs., St. Louis Suburban Sch. Librs. Assn. (sec. 1993—95, membership chmn. 2001—03), Mo. Assn. Sch. Librs. (Webmaster, bd. dirs. 2003—), Am. Assn. Sch. Librs., ASCD, ALA, Beta Phi Mu, Phi Beta Kappa. Avocations: reading, genealogy, web browsing. Office: Parkway School Dist Libr Media Svcs 455 North Woods Mill Rd Chesterfield MO 63017 Business E-Mail: ckohnen@pkwy.k12.mo.us.

KOHNSTAMM, ABBY E., marketing executive; b. Los Angeles, Calif. married; 2 children. BA, Tufts U.; MA in Edn., MBA, NYU. Various mktg. positions including sr. v.p. cardmember mktg. Am. Express, 1979—93; v.p. corp. mktg. Internat. Bus. Machines Corp., Armonk, NY, 1993—98, sr. v.p. corp. mktg., 1998—. Bd. of overseers Arts & Sci. Tufts U., NYU Stern Sch. of Bus.; bd. dirs. IBM Credit Corp., Tiffany & Co. Mem. Assn. Nat. Advertisers. Avocations: family acitivies, music, theater. Office: Internat Bus Machines Corp New Orchard Rd Armonk NY 10504-1722 Office Phone: 914-765-1900. E-mail: abby@us.ibm.com.

KOHORN, ERNEST I., obstetrician, gynecologist; b. Trutnov, Czechoslovakia, Oct. 9, 1928; s. Leo and Hilda (Ullmann) K.; m. Margot L. Kohorn, May 28, 1993; children: Ruth, Bruce. MB, Cambridge (Eng.) U., 1952, MChir, 1962, MA, 1963. Intern London U. Hosp., 1952-54; resident in surgery London Sick Children's Hosp., 1957-58, Univ. Coll. Hosp., London, 1958-61; resident in ob-gyn. Charlottes/Chelsea Hosps., London, 1961-62; fellow in gynecol. oncology Middlesex Hosp., London, 1962-64; mem. staff Yale-New Haven Hosp.; prof. ob-gyn. Yale U. Sch. Medicine. Fellow Royal Coll. Surgeons (Eng.), Royal Coll. Ob-Gyn.; mem. Soc. Pelvic Surgeons, Soc. Gynecol. Surgeons (pres. 1996), Soc. Gynecologic Investigation, Am. Urogynecologic Soc. (pres. 1992). Jewish. Office: Yale U Sch Med Dept Ob-Gyn PO Box 208063 333 Cedar St New Haven CT 06510-3206

KOHRING, VICTOR H., state legislator; b. Waukegan, Ill., Aug. 2, 1958; s. Heinz H. and Dolores E. Kohring. AAS in Bus. Adminstrn., Matanuska-Susitna C.C., Palmer, Alaska, 1985; BA in Mgmt. Sci., Alaska Pacific U., 1987, MBA, 1989. State legislator Ho. of Reps., Dist. 26 Wasilla and Peters Creek/Chugiak, AK, 1994, re-elected 1996, 98—; mem. ho. fin. com. Ho. of Reps., 1994, 96, 98—. Chmn. house budge subcoms. for dept. edn., 1995-96, adminstrn., 1995-96, environ. conservation, 1997-98, cmty. and regional affairs, 1997-98, commerce and econ. devel., 1997-98, law, 1999—, natural resources, 1999—; constn. exec., 1978—; real estate developer, 1978-82. Bd. dirs. Alaska Housing Fin. Corp., Anchorage, 1991-94; vice chmn., mem. Iditarod Trail Com.; mem. Matanuska-Susitna Borough Econ. Devel. Commn., 1993-94; mem. Wasilla Planning and Utilities Commn., 1991-94; chmn., mem. Alaska del. Rep. Nat. Conv., Dallas, 1984, dist. del. rep., 1984, 86, 90, 92; treas. Rep. Party Alaska, Mat-Su, 1990, fin. chmn., 1990-91. Mem. NRA, Christian Businessman's Assn., Greater Wasilla C. of C., Chugiak-Eagle River C. of C., Anthony J. Dimond H.S. Alumni Assn., Pioneers of Alaska. Republican. Home: PO Box 870515 Wasilla AK 99687-0515 Office: Alaska Ho of Reps State Capitol Bldg Juneau AK 99801

KOHRMAN, ARTHUR FISHER, pediatrics educator; b. Cleve., Dec. 19, 1934; s. Benjamin Myron and Leah (Fisher) K.; m. Claire Hoffenberg, Nov. 10, 1955; children: Deborah, Benjamin, Ellen, Rachel. BA, BS, U. Chgo., 1955; MD, Western Res. U., 1959. Diplomate Am. Bd. Pediatrics. Lic. Ill.,

Ind. Intern Cleve. Met. Gen. Hosp., 1959-60; resident in pediatrics Case Western Res. U., Cleve., 1960—62; post doctoral fellow Stanford U., Palo Alto, Calif., 1965-68; from asst. prof. to prof. Mich. State U., East Lansing, 1968—81, assoc. chmn. dept. human devel., 1968—78, assoc. dean Coll. Human Medicine, 1977—81; prof., assoc. chmn. dept. pediatrics U. Chgo., 1981-96; pres. La Rabida Children's Hosp. and Research Ctr., Chgo., 1981-96; prof. pediatrics, assoc. chmn. Northwestern U. Sch. Medicine and Children's Meml. Hosp., Chgo., 1997—2002; prof. preventive medicine Sch. Medicine, Northwestern U., Chgo., 2000—02, prof. emeritus pediatrics and preventive medicine, 2003—. Congl. fellow Office Tech. Assessment, U.S. Congress, 1980-81; pres. Children's Hospice Internat., 1983-86; chmn. instl. rev. bd. U. Chgo., 1986-96. Contbr. numerous scholarly articles to profl. jours. Served to capt. USAF, 1962-65. Recipient Outstanding Service award Am. Diabetes Assn. Mich. chpt., 1977. Fellow Am. Acad. Pediatrics (chmn. com. on bioethics 1990-94); mem. Am. Pediatric Soc., Ambulatory Pediatric Assn., Soc. Pediatric Rsch., Lawson Wilkins Pediatric Endocrine Soc., Alpha Omega Alpha.

KOHRT, CARL FREDRICK, research and development company executive; b. Normal, Ill., Dec. 18, 1943; s. Carl Fred and Catherine Elizabeth (Traughber) K.; m. Margaret Lynne McCartney; children: Kristopher Alan, Brian Douglas, Jason Ivor. BS, Furman U., 1965; PhD, U. Chgo., 1971; MS, MIT, 1991. Postdoctoral fellow James Franck Inst., U. Chgo., 1970—71; sr. scientist rsch. labs. Eastman Kodak, Rochester, NY, 1971-76, rsch. lab. head, 1977-79, asst. div. dir. rsch. labs., 1979-84, asst. to vice chmn. Kodak office, 1984-85, div. dir. electronic rsch. labs., 1985-87, dir. rsch. photographic rsch. labs., 1987-90; Kodak's mem. of Sloan fellow program MIT, Cambridge, 1990—91, gen. mgr. health scis. divsn., 1991-95; exec. v.p., asst. COO, 1995-98; exec. v.p., asst. COO, chief tech. officer, 1998-2000; pres., CEO Battelle Meml. Inst., Columbus, Ohio, 2001—. Vice chmn., bd. dirs., Brookhaven Sci. Assocs., chair bd. trustees COSI Columbus; bd. trustees Furman U.; bd. dirs. Pharos LLC; chair bd. govs. UT-Battelle LLC. Contbr. articles to profl. jours.; patentee in field. Chmn. sustaining membership Boy Scouts Am., Rochester, 1988, scoutmaster, Pittsford, NY, 1976-88, mem. exec. bd. Otetiana coun., 1997; chair Cmty. Needs Study, Greece, NY, 1973; bd. dirs. Greater Columbus C. of C; trustee Ohio Bus. Roundtable. Woodrow Wilson fellow (hon.), 1965, NSF Grad. fellow, 1965—70. Mem.: Indsl. Rsch. Inst. (alt. rep.). Presbyterian. Avocations: backpacking, whitewater canoeing, music. Office: Battelle Mem Inst 505 King Ave Columbus OH 43201

KOHUT, ROBERT IRWIN, otolaryngologist, educator; b. Chgo., Nov. 29, 1932; s. Emil and Ruth Irene Kohut; m. Joanne Kay Hughes, Dec. 26, 1953 (dec. Oct. 1982); children: James, Paul, Robert, John; m. Frances Irene Speas, June 6, 1983 (div. 1999). BA, Wittenburg Coll., 1956; MD, U. Chgo., 1960. Diplomate Am. Bd. Otolaryngology (bd. dirs. 1979). Intern U. Chgo., 1961-62, resident in otolaryngology, 1962-65, NIH fellow, 1965-66, instr. in otolaryngology, 1965-66; assoc. prof. U. Fla., Gainesville, 1966-68, 1968-71, assoc. prof., acting chmn., 1971-72; prof., chief otolaryngology U. Calif., Irvine, 1972-79; prof., chmn. otolaryngology Wake Forest U. Sch. Medicine, Winston-Salem, 1979-99, prof. emeritus, chair, 1999—. Mem. study sect. Nat. Insts. Neurol. and Communicative Disorders and Stroke/NIH, Bethesda, Md., 1981—86; cons. NASA, 1982—84; mem. adv. bd. Nat. Inst. Deafness and Other Comm. Disorders, 1991—94; exec. v.p. med. affairs, med. dir. Deafness Rsch. Found., 1999—2001. Contbr. numerous chpts. to books and articles to profl. jours.; editor otology divsn. Head and Neck Surgery-Otolaryngology; mem. editorial bd. Am. Jour. Otology, 1992-2000, Am. Jour. Otolaryngology, 1982-2000, Archives of Otolaryngology, 1980-2000, Laryngoscope, 1976-2000. With USAF, 1950-53. Recipient Norvel Pierce award Chgo. Laryngological Soc., 1965, Basic Rsch. award Acad. Ophthalmology and Otolaryngology, 1968. Mem. ACS, Soc. Univ. Otolaryngologists (pres. 1978-79), Barany Soc., Am. Laryngological, Rhinological and Otological Soc. (exec. coun. 1987-90, Edmund Fowler award 1974, Guest of Honor, So. sect. 1996), Am. Broncho-Esophagological Ass., Am. Neurotology Assn., Otosclerosis Study Group, Am. Otological Soc. (sec.-treas. 1987-92, pres.-elect 1992-93, pres. 1993-94), Assn. Acad. Depts. Otolaryngology, Pacific Coast Oto-Ophthalmol. Soc., Forsyth County Med. Soc., N.C. Med. Soc., N.C. Soc. Otolaryngology Head and Neck Surgery (v.p. 1985, pres. 1986-87), Assn. for Rsch. in Otolaryngology, Am. Acad. Otolaryngology-Head and Neck Surgery, Am. Soc. Head and Neck Surgery, Internat. Fedn. Oto-Rhino-Laryngological Soc. (chmn. emeritus standing com. edn. 2004), others. Avocations: fishing, hunting, sailing. Office: Wake Forest U Sch Medicine Dept Otolaryngology Medical Center Blvd Winston Salem NC 27157-0001 E-mail: rikohut@direcway.com.

KOIDE, FRANK TAKAYUKI, electrical engineering educator; b. Honolulu, Dec. 25, 1935; s. Sukeichi and Hideko (Dai) K.; children: Julie Anne M., Cheryl Lynne K. BSEE, U. Ill., 1958; MEE, Clarkson U., Potsdam, N.Y., 1961; PhD, U. Iowa, 1966. Publs. engr. to electronics engr. Collins Radio Co., Cedar Rapids, Iowa, 1958-61; tchr. Cedar Rapids Adult Edn. Sch., 1960-61; lab. instr. U. Iowa Coll. Medicine, 1963-64; asst. prof. Iowa State U., 1966-69; prin. biomed. engr. Tech., Inc., San Antonio, 1968-69; mem. faculty U. Hawaii, 1969—2002, prof. elec. engring. and physiology, 1974—95, prof. emeritus, 2002—. Cons. in field. Author papers, reports in field. NIH predoctoral fellow, 1966; NASA-Am. Soc. Engring. Edn. Space systems Design Inst. fellow, 1967; NSF Digital and Analogue Electronics Inst. fellow U. Ill., 1972. Mem. IEEE. Office: U Hawaii Dept Electrical Engring 2540 Dole St Honolulu HI 96822-2303 Office Phone: 808-956-7406. Business E-Mail: koide@spectra.eng.hawaii.edu.

KOIWA, HISASHI, science educator; s. Masahiro and Yukiko Koiwa; m. Nami Kimura, May 20, 2003. PhD, Kyoto U., Japan, 1993—96. Rsch. assoc. Purdue U., West Lafayette, Ind., 1996—2002; asst. prof. Tex. A&M U., College Station, 2002—04. Grantee, NSF, 2004. Mem.: Japanese Soc. Plant Physiologist, Am. Soc. Plant Biologist, Sigma Xi. Achievements include research in Plant C-terminal domain phosphatases. Office: Dept Horticultural Scis 2133 Tamu College Station TX 77843-2133 Office Phone: 979-845-5282. Office Fax: 979-845-0627.

KOJIMA, TAKESHI, law educator, arbitrator, writer; b. Yokohama, Japan, Sept. 1, 1936; s. Buzaemon and Maki Kojima; m. Shigeko Niwa, May 3, 1966; children: Natsuko, Haruka. BA, Chuo U., Tokyo, 1959, LLM, 1961, LLD, 1978; qualified lawyer, Inst. Legal Tng. and Rsch., Tokyo, 1963. Rschr. U. Mich., Ann Arbor, 1966-68; asst. prof. law Chuo U., 1960-64, assoc. prof., 1964-71, prof., 1971—, councilor, 1995—, chmn. grad. sch., 1997—. Vis. prof. U. Florence, Italy, 1974, Columbia U., N.Y.C., 1988; guest prof. Aix-Marseille (France) U., 1983, Frankfurt (Germany) Goethe U., 1991-92; examiner nat. jud. exam. Ministry Justice, Tokyo, 1984-90, acting chmn. Study Commn. on Issue Fgn. Lawyers (with Ministry Justice, Japan Fedn. Bar Assns.), 1992-94, chmn. Study Commn. on Representation in Internat. Arbitration (with Ministry Justice, Japan Fedn. Bar Assns.), 1994-95; chmn. Study Commn. on Fgn. Lawyers (with Ministry Justice, Japan Bar Assns.), 1996—, acad. councillor Ctr. Internat. Civil & Comml. Law, 1996—; trustee Ctr. Automobile Product Liability, 1995—; chmn. study commn. on issue fgn. lawyers Ministry of Justice, Japan Fedn. Bar Assns., 1996—; legis. coun. Ministry of Justice, 1997—; expert mem. coun. for screening newly founded univs. and other schs., Ministry Edn., 1990-95; dir. Japan Inst. Comparative Law, Tokyo, 1987-90. Co-author: Access to Justice, Vol. I, 1978, Small Claims Courts, 1991; editor: Perspectives on Civil Justice and ADR, 1990, The Grand Design of America's Justice System, 1995; contbr. articles to profl. jours. Spl. arbitrator Ctrl. Tribunal, Ministry Constrn., Tokyo, 1990—; spl. mem. coun. on indsl. structure Ministry Internat. Trade and Industry, Tokyo, 1991-94; mem. Nat. Tribunal Constrn. Procurement, Office of Prime Min., Tokyo, 1991-96; insp. Govtl. Sch. Insp., Ministry Edn., Tokyo, 1993—, chmn. collaborators conf. for rsch. legal edn. reform; coun. legis. on civil procedure, Ministry Justice, 1997—. Mem. Japanese Assn. Civil Procedure Law (pres. 1995-98), Japanese Assn. Pvt. Law (bd. dirs. 1983-87), Japan Legal Aid Assn. (mng. trustee 1993—), Japan Negotiation Assn. (v.p. 1993—), Japan Assn. Lawyers (trustee 1975—), Japanese-Am. Assn. for Legal Studies (councilor 1991—), Am. Law Inst. Buddhist. Avocations: golf, travel. Home: 1013 Shinyoshida-machi Yokohama Kohoku 223 Japan Office: Chuo U 742-1 Higashinakano Hachioji Tokyo 192-03 Japan

KOK, FRANS JOHAN, investment banker; b. Zaandam, Netherlands, May 14, 1943; came to U.S., 1963; s. Cornelis and Aaf K.; m. Mary M. Shirley, Dec. 23, 1971. BA in Econ., Occidental Coll., L.A., 1967; MA in Econs., Calif. State U., L.A., 1969; MBA, Insead, Fontainebleau, France, 1971, Harvard U., 1972. Assoc. Booz, Allen & Hamilton, Washington, 1974-78; chief economist EPA, Washington, 1978-80; CFO, co-founder Long Lake Energy Corp., N.Y.C., 1980-83; mng. dir. Ferris, Baker-Watts, Inc., Balt., 1983-89, 1st Nat. Bank Md., Balt., 1989-94; chmn., CEO, Johan Hekelaar, Inc., Chevy Chase, Md., 1994—; chmn. MarinaLife LLC, Balt. Bd. dirs. MaxPitch Media, Inc., Richmond, Va. Home: PO Box 423 Philomont VA 20131 Office Phone: 301-656-7870.

KOK, HANS GEBHARD, consulting engineer; b. Potshausen, Germany, Apr. 5, 1923; came to U.S., 1951, naturalized, 1959; s. George J. and Anitina K. (Janssen) K.; m. Roselle V. Venier, June 22, 1960; Children: George H., Karen R. Student, Suderburg Engring. Coll., Germany, 1940-42, Hamburg Engring Coll., 1945-46; Dipl.Ing, Technische Hochschule, Aachen, Germany, 1950. Registered profl. engr., N.Y., Pa., Ind., Mich., Calif., Fla., N.J., Ariz., Md. Design engr. Lummus Co., N.Y.C., 1951-53; structural engr. M.H. Treadwell Co., N.Y.C., 1953-56, head structural engring. sect., 1956-62, chief structural engr., 1962-63; mgr. plant design divsn. Treadwell Corp., N.Y.C., 1963-69, asst. v.p. engring., 1969-73, v.p. engring., 1973-83; pres. Treadwell Corp. Mich., Inc., 1974-83; dir. BassetMiller Treadwell Pty. Ltd., 1973-83; cons. engr., 1983—. Chmn. exec. com. Coun. Engring. Laws, 1976. Contbr. articles to profl. jours. Recipient 1st award James F. Lincoln Arc Welding Found., 1966. Fellow ASCE; mem. Nat. Soc. Profl. Engrs., N.Y. State Soc. Profl. Engrs., Am. Inst. Mining, Metall. and Petroleum Engrs. (chmn. materialshandling com.), Am. Mining congress, Am. Mgmt. Assn. Home: 4438 Meager Cir Port Charlotte FL 33948-9495

KOKALJ, JAMES EDWARD, retired aerospace administrator; b. Chgo., Oct. 29, 1933; s. John and Antoinette (Zabukovec) K. AA in Engring., El Camino Coll., Torrance, Calif., 1953. Dynomometer lab. technician U.S. Electric Motors, L.A., 1953-54; devel. lab. technician AiResearch divsn. Garrett, L.A., 1956-59; tech. rep. McCulloch, L.A., 1959-65; dist. mgr. Yamaha Internat., Montebello, Calif., 1965-67; salesman Vasek Polak BMW, Manhattan Beach, Calif., 1967-68; sr. svc. rep. Stratos-We. div. Fairchild, Manhattan Beach, 1968-70; asst. regional mgr. we. states J.B.E. Olson div. Grumman, L.A., 1970-71; gen. mgr. Internat. Kart Fedn., Glendora, Calif., 1971-73; logistics support data specialist Mil. Aircraft divsn. Northrop Grumman, Hawthorne, Calif., 1974-95; ret., 1995. Author: Technical Inspection Handbook, 1972; contbr. articles to profl. jours. With USN, 1954-56. Mem. U.S. Naval Inst., Internat. Naval Rsch. Orgn., Nat. Maritime Hist. Soc., So. Calif. Hist. Aircraft Found., Found. L.A. Maritime Mus. Republican. Roman Catholic. Avocations: woodworking, ship modeling, maritime history, auto and aircraft restoration. Home: 805 Bayview Dr Hermosa Beach CA 90254-4147

KOKE, RICHARD JOSEPH, writer, curator; b. NYC, Sept. 19, 1916; s. Joseph and Emily Josephine (Chevrolet) K.; m. Mary A. Kimbley, Jan. 1, 1955. Student, Art Students League, 1935, Cooper Union Art Inst., 1935-37; AB, NYU, 1941; MA, Columbia U., 1947. Historian, Bear Mountain (N.Y.) Trailside Hist. Mus., 1935-37; curator Stony Point (N.Y.) Battlefield Mus., summers 1937-41; research cons. Hudson Valley Survey, 1946-47; historian Saratoga Nat. Hist. Park, 1947; curator mus. N.Y. Hist. Soc., 1947-83, curator emeritus, 1983—. Conducted archaeol. investigations on Revolutionary War mil. sites in Highlands of the Hudson, N.Y., 1935-41 Author: Accomplice in Treason; Joshua Hett Smith and the Arnold Conspiracy, 1973, Corridor Through the Mountains, 1998; editor: Scenic and Historic America, 1938; contbr. mags. and revs.; compiler American Landscape and Genre Painting in the New York Historical Society, 3 vols., 1982. Served with AUS, 1942-45; art dir, in charge cartographic dept. M.C. 1942-44; battlefield history research analyst. hist. sect. Hdgrs. 1944-45; engaged in collection and editing of mil. data pertaining to tactical operations Am. forces, preparation ofcl. army histories of Services of Supply, 1st, 3d, 7th, 9th, 15th armies World War 11, Western European Front. Recipient 1st prize hist. essay contest sponsored by Colonial Dames of N.Y., 1940 Home: PO Box 700 Peru NY 12972-0700 Office: 170 Central Park W New York NY 10024-5152

KOKEN, M. DIANE, state commissioner; b. Lancaster, Pa., Dec. 29, 1952; d. James E. Koken and Helen Sotiro; m. John K. Herr III; children: Kathryn, Rebecca. BS magna cum laude, Millersville U., 1972; JD, Villanova U., 1975. Counsel, v.p., corp. sec. Provident Mutual Ins. Co., Phila., 1975-97; commr. Pa. Ins. Dept., Harrisburg, 1997—. Mem. ABA, Phila. Bar Assn., Internat. Claims Assn. Office: Pa Insurance Dept 1326 Strawberry Sq Harrisburg PA 17120-0046 Office Phone: 717-783-0442.

KOKOTOVIC, PETAR V., electrical and computer engineer, educator; b. Mar. 18, 1934; Dipl.Eng., U. Belgrade, Yugoslavia, 1958, Magistar (Elec. Engring.), 1963; Candidate of Tech. Scis., Russian Acad. Scis., Moscow, 1965. Prof. elec. engring. U. Ill., Urbana, 1966-91, Grainger prof. emeritus, 1991—; prof. elec. and computer engring. U. Calif., 1991—; dir. Ctr. for Control Engring. and Computation. Recipient Quazza medal Internat. Fedn. Automatic Control, 1990, IEEE Control Sys. Field award, 1995. Fellow: IEEE (Engring. Outstanding AC Transactions Paper award 1982—83, Axelby Outstanding Paper award 1991—92, H. Bode Prize lecture 1991, James H. Mulligan, Jr. Edn. medal 2002, Richard E. Bellman Control Heritage award 2002); mem.: NAE. Office: U Calif Electrical & Comp Eng Dept Santa Barbara CA 93106

KOLA, ARTHUR ANTHONY, lawyer; b. New Brunswick, N.J., Feb. 16, 1939; s. Arthur Aloysius and Blanche (Raym) K.; m. Jacquelin Lou Draper, Sept. 3, 1960; children— Jill, Jean, Jennifer; m. Anna Molnar, Apr. 15, 1977 AB, Dartmouth Coll., 1961; LLB, Duke U., 1964. Bar: Ohio 1964, U.S. Dist. Ct. (no. dist.) Ohio 1969, U.S. Ct. Appeals (6th cir.) 1971, U.S. Supreme Ct. 1972. Assoc. Squire, Sanders & Dempsey, Cleve., 1964-65, assoc., 1968-74, ptnr., 1974-94; pvt. practice Kola Law Office, Cleve., 1994—. Asst. prof. law Ind. U., Bloomington, 1967-68; instr. labor law Case Western Res. U., Cleve., 1976 Bd. visitors Duke U. Sch. Law, 1985—. Served to capt. U.S. Army, 1965-67 Mem. Ohio Bar Assn., Cleve. Bar Assn. (chmn. labor and employment law sect. 1993-94), Am. Arbitration Assn. (bd. dirs. 1991-97). Office: Kola Law Office 6100 Oak Tree Blvd Ste 200 Independence OH 44131-6914 Office Phone: 216-328-2009.

KOLAKOWSKI, DIANA JEAN, county commissioner; b. Detroit, Aug. 28, 1943; d. Leo and Genevieve (Bosh) Zyskowski; m. William Francis Kolakowski, Jr., Oct. 22, 1966; children: Wiliam Francis III, John. BS, U. Detroit, 1965. Lab. asst. chemistry dept. U. Detroit, 1961-65; rsch. chemist Detroit Inst. Cancer Rsch., Mich. Cancer Found., 1965-70; substitute tchr. Warren (Mich.) Consol. Schs., 1979-81; mem. Macomb County Bd. Commrs., Mt. Clemens, Mich., 1983—, vice chmn., 1993-95, chmn., 1995-97. Dir. S.E. Mich. Transp. Authority, Detroit, 1983—85; trustee Macomb County Ret. System, Mt. Clemens, 1988—91, 1992—95, 2003—; del. S.E. Mich. Coun. Govts., Detroit, 1987—, vice chmn., 1995—99, chmn., 1999—2000, Regional Transit Coord. Coun., 1995—97; bd. dirs. Creating a Healthier Macomb, 1996—2001, Macomb Bar Found., 1996—. Contbr. articles to sci. jours. Trustee Myasthenia Gravis Found., Southfield, Mich., 1964-71; dir. Otsikita coun. Girl Scouts Am., 1995-96; mem., sec. Sterling Heights (Mich.) Bd. Zoning Appeals, 1978-83; mem. Macomb County Dem. Exec. Com., Mt. Clemens, 1982—, 10th and 12th Dem. Congl. Dist. Exec. Com., Warren, 1982—, del. 1996 Dem. Nat. Conv.; mem. behavioral medicine adv. coun. St. Joseph Hosp. Named Woman of Distinction, Macomb County Girl Scouts U.S.A., 1996, Woman of Yr., Am. Fedn. State, County and Mcpl. Employees 411, 2004; recipient Leadership award, Cath. Social Svcs. Macomb, 1997, Polish Pride award, Polish Am. Citizens for Equity, 1997, Excellence in County Govt. award, 1997, Regional Ambassador award, S.E. Mich. Coun. Govt., 2005; GM scholar, U. Detroit, 1961—65. Mem. Nat. Assn. Counties, Mich. Assn. Counties, Mich. Assn. Planning Ofcls., Am. Polish Cultural Ctr., Polish Am. Congress, Alpha Sigma Nu. Roman Catholic. Avocations: singing, piano, crossword and jigsaw puzzles. Home: 33488 Breckenridge Dr Sterling Heights MI 48310-6082 Office: Office Bd Commrs Macomb Co Adminstrn Bldg 1 S Main St Fl 9 Mount Clemens MI 48043-2306 Office Phone: 586-469-5125.

KOLAKOWSKI, JANE STEFFEN, elementary school educator; b. Reedsburg, Wis., June 9, 1951; d. John Andrew and Jean (Schoonover) Steffen; m. Peter Ritson Kolakowski, June 16, 1973; children: Christopher Lee, Kathryn Steffen. AB, Ripon Coll., 1973; MEd, George Mason U., 1991. Cert. tchr., Va. Sec. Ctrl. Rappahannock Libr., Fredericksburg, Va., 1973, children's storyteller, 1974; elem. tchr. Stafford County Pub. Schs., Va., 1974—76, 1983—. Cons. for tchr. tng., various Va. sch. dists., 1990—; mem. clin. faculty Mary Washington Coll., Fredericksburg, 1990-2004. Author: Linking Math with Literature, 1992, vol. 2, 1994, Selected Literature for Language Skills, 1992. Recipient various awards. Mem. NEA, Va. Educators Assn., Nat. Coun. Tchrs. English, Va. State Reading Assn., Rappahannock Reading Coun., Phi Delta Kappa (Cert. Recognition 1992). Presbyterian. Avocations: reading, art history, visiting museums, French history, travel. Home: 2 Bainbridge Ln Fredericksburg VA 22407-1301 Office: Falmouth Elem Sch 1000 Forbes St Falmouth VA 22405-1494 E-mail: jskola@msn.com.

KOLANSKY, HAROLD, physician, psychiatrist, psychotherapist; b. Carbondale, Pa., Aug. 15, 1924; s. Abe and Miriam (Raker) K.; m. Elsa Harwitz, June 8, 1948; children: Jeffrey, Betta, Daniel. Student, U. Scranton, 1942-44; MD cum laude, Georgetown U., 1948. Rotating intern Walter Reed Army Hosp., Washington, 1948-49; resident Coatesville (Pa.) VA Hosp. and Deans' Com. Program, Phila., 1949-52; practice medicine specializing in psychiatry and psychoanalysis Phila., 1952—, Elkins Park, Pa., 1959—; clin. assoc. prof. psychiatry U. Pa. Sch. Medicine, 1972-77, clin. prof., 1977, 91—, mem. steering com. Psychoanalytic Cluster, 1991—, chair steerimg com. Psychoanalytic Cluster, 1997-99; prof. psychiatry and human behavior Jefferson Med. Coll., Thomas Jefferson U., Phila., 1977-91, dir. sect. child and adolescent psychoanalysis, 1980-90, dir. sect. psychoanalysis, 1982-90; mem. faculty child and adolescent psychiatry Children's Hosp. of Phila., 1991—. Mem. psychiatry staff Albert Einstein Med. Ctr., 1952-69, 82—, sr. attending, 1983—, dir. divsn. child psychiatry, 1955-69, acting chmn. dept. psychiatry, 1968-69, dir. child psychiatry fellowship, 1960-69, dir. ctr. for psychoanalysis, 1991—, mem. exec. com., ednl. com. and curriculum com., 1991—; mem. faculty Inst. Phila. Assn. Psychoanalysis, 1960—, chmn. administrv. bd., 1966-69, dir. divsn. childrn and adolescent psychoanalysis, 1975-84, tng. and supervisory analyst, 1976—, chmn. tng. analyst com., 1982-83, 93-94, 95-96, chmn. curriculum com., 1982-88, dir. consultation and evaluation divsn., 1988-89, mem. ednl. com., 1989-94, mem. ednl. com., vice chmn., 1997, mem. ednl. com., 1997-2000, chmn. edn. com., 2000-2001, vice-chmn., 1997-2001, chmn. faculty com., 1997—, chmn., liaison com. med. edn., 1994—, chair ednl. com., 2000-01; mem. staff psychiatry Phila. Psychiat. Ctr., 1952-81; pres. Regional Coun. Child Psychiatry, Pa., S.E. N.J., Del., 1967-68, 72-73, chmn. exec. com., 1970-73; chmn. med. bd. Ea. State Sch. and Hosp., Trevose, Pa., 1966-69; asst. prof. psychiatry Hahnemann Med. Coll. and Hosp., Phila., 1952-60; mem. Pa. Task Force on Mental Health Children, 1971-74; vis. prof. psychiatry U. P.R. Sch. Medicine, 1982—; mem. steering com. psychoanalytic cluster U. Pa. Sch. Med., 1991—, chmn., 1997-99. Contbg. author to numerous texts on psychoanalysis and psychiatry including: A Handbook of Child Psychoanalysis, 1968, Behavior Pathology of Childhood and Adolescence, 1973, Controversy in Psychiatry, 1978, Prognosis, 1981; contbr. numerous articles on child and adult psychiatry and psychoanalysis to profl. jours. Capt. M.C., U.S. Army, 1950-51, Korea. Recipient 1st prize biochemistry Georgetown U., 1945, Robert Waelder award for Teaching Excellence in Psychiatry Thomas Jefferson Med. Coll., 1987, Dedication to Edn. award, 1990, award for tchg. excellence dept. psychiatry Albert Einstein Med. Ctr., 1993, award for tchg. excellence, 1996, 2000, 02, 04, Outstanding Tchr. award Children's Hosp. of Phila. 2003; 1st pl. U.S. in Surgery Nat. Bd. Med. Examiners, 1948. Fellow: Phila. Coll. Physicians, Am. Acad. Child Psychiatry (chmn. com. continuing med. edn. 1974—82, councillor, citation for developing continuing med. edn. program 1976), Am. Psychiat. Assn.; mem.: AMA, Phila. County Med. Soc., Pa. Med. Soc., Am. Psychoanalytic Assn. (exec. counselor 1969—73, 1977—82, fellow bd. profl. standards 1983—89, 1992—98, mem. com. on child and adolescent analysis 1984—90, 1999—, acting fellow bd. on profl. standards 1989, mem. univ. and med. edn. com. 1995—2000, budget and fin. com. 1996—98, all exec. counselor 1999—2001, Edith Sabshin Teaching award 2000), Internat. Psychoanalytic Assn., Phila. Psychiatric Soc. (Psychiat. Educator award 2002), Assn. Child Psychoanalysis, Phila. Assn. Psychoanalysis (bd. dirs. 1984—86, pres. 1984—86, Gersld Pearson prize award 1960).

KOLAR, MARY JANE, trade and professional association executive; b. Benton, Ill., Aug. 9, 1941; d. Thomas Haskell and Mary Jane (Sanders) Burnett; m. Otto Michael Kolar, Aug. 13, 1966; children: Robin Lynn, Deon Michael. BA with high honors, So. Ill. U., 1963, MA with highest honors, 1964. Tchr. pub. schs., Benton and Zeigler, Ill., 1960-63; grad. asst. and grad. fellow So. Ill. U., Carbondale, 1963-64; instr. Ridgewood High Sch., Norridge, Ill., 1964-67, Maine Twp. High Sch., Des Plaines, Ill., 1967-70; freelance writer plumbing, heating & cooling industry couns. Chgo., 1970-71; ednl. coord. Am. Dietetic Assn., Chgo., 1971-72; dir. profl. devel. Am. Dental Hygienists Assn., Chgo., 1972-78; dir. Learning Ctr. div. Am. Coll. Cardiology, Bethesda, Md., 1978-80; dir. edn. Nat. Moving and Storage Assn., Alexandria, Va., 1980-82; exec. dir. Women in Communications, Inc., Austin, Tex., 1982-84, Altrusa Internat., Chgo., 1984-87, Assn. Govt. Accts., Alexandria, Va., 1987-90, Bus./Profl. Advt. Assn., Alexandria, 1991-92, Am. Assn. Family and Consumer Scis., Alexandria, 1992-96, dir. Project Taking Charge Adolescent Pregnancy Prevention Program, 1993-95; pres., CEO The Alexandria Group, Inc. (charter accredited co., Am. Soc. Assn. Execs.), 1996—. Mem., chair Accreditation Commn. for Assn. Mgmt. Cos., 2005—; cons. spkr. various profl., philanthropic and trade assns., ednl. instns. and fed agys. Contbr. articles to profl. jours. and assn. mags., chapters to books. Mem. adv. council Accrediting Commn., Assn. of Ind. Colls. and Schs., 1980-88; treas. Pub. Employees Roundtable, 1988-90, Hollin Hills Civic Assn., 1989-90. Fellow Am. Soc. Allied Health Professions (dir. 1978-79), Am. Soc. Assn. Execs. (charter accredited; cert. commr. accreditation commn. for assn. mgmt. cos. 2002—, Key Profl. Assn. coun. 1994-96, peer rev. com., 1997-2000, rsch. com. 1996-2000, strategic leadership forum com. 1996-97, awards com. 1992-93, univ. affairs commn. 1986-92, chair 1990-91, found. bd. 1987-91, chmn. edn. sect. 1982-83, bd. dirs. 1983-86, chair higher edn. task force 1990-91, chair fellows 1987, Educator of Yr. award 1978, Key award 1990, pres., CEO); mem. Greater Washington Soc. Assn. Execs. (edn. com. 1979-82, CEO com. 1990-92, 94-96, vice chair 1995-96, strategic planning com. 1994-95, exec. search com. 1994-96), Future Home Makers Am. (bd. dirs. 1992-96), Alexandria C. of C. (assn. coun. 1990-96, steering com. 1993-96), Women in Comm. (newsletter editor, legis. and career re-entry chair, chair ERA task force, dir. Washington profl. chpt. 1981-83, program com. Chgo. chpt. 1984-86), So. Ill. U. Alumni Assn. (bd. dirs. 1984-89, v.p. 1986-89, presdl. search com. 1986-87). Office: 526 King St Ste 405 Alexandria VA 22314-3143 Business E-Mail: mjkolar@alexandriagroup.com. *Being a professional means many things. It means adhering to an ethical code, having high standards of quality, striving toward excellence through basic and ongoing preparation for the profession I have chosen to practice. It means having goals and being willing to contribute to solving the social, economic and political problems of the society of which I am a part. Professionalism is more than acceptance of responsibility, more than doing one's duty, more than being good at what one does. Professionalism requires a commitment to what you do and to the future. It carries with it obligation and risk. It necessitates service to the profession— a willingness to be a leader— and a desire to meet the needs of others.*

KOLASKY, WILLIAM JOSEPH, JR., lawyer; b. Springfield, Vt., Mar. 26, 1946; s. William J. Sr. and Valentina (Stankiewicz) K.; m. Mary L. Coyne, Jan. 16, 2001; children: Robert, Caroline, Ethan. AB magna cum laude, Dartmouth Coll., 1968; JD magna cum laude, Harvard U., 1971. Bar: Mass. 1971, D.C. 1975, U.S. Dist. Ct. D.C. 1975, U.S. Ct. Appeals (D.C. cir.) 1976, U.S. Supreme Ct. 1976. Law clk. Chief Judge Bailey Aldrich, US Ct. Appeals (1st cir.), Boston, 1971—72; asst. to gen. counsel U.S. Dept of Army, Washington, 1972—75; assoc. Wilmer, Cutler & Pickering, Washington, 1975-78, ptnr., 1979—2001, 2002—04; dep. asst. atty. gen., internat. enforcement Antitrust Div., U.S. Dept. Justice, Washington, 2001—02; ptnr., co-chmn. Antitrust & Competition dept. Wilmer Cutler Pickering Hale & Dorr LLP, Washington, 2004—. Instr. Am. Univ. Washington Coll. Law. Note editor Harvard Law Rev., 1969-70; contbr. legal articles to profl. jours. Capt. U.S. Army, 1972—75. Mem. ABA (antitrust sect.), D.C. Bar Assn., Phi Beta Kappa, Omicron Delta Epsilon. Office: Wilmer Cutler Pickering Hale & Dorr LLP 2445 M St NW Washington DC 20037-1487 Office Phone: 202-663-6357. Office Fax: 202-663-6363. Business E-Mail: william.kolasky@wilmerhale.com.

KOLATCH, ALFRED JACOB, publisher; b. Seattle, Jan. 2, 1916; s. Sander and Yetta (Jacobs) K.; m. Thelma Rubin, June 16, 1940; children: Jonathan, David. BA, Yeshiva U., 1937; Rabbi, Jewish Theol. Sem., 1941. Ordained rabbi, 1941; rabbi Columbia, S.C., 1941-43, Kew Gardens, N.Y., 1946-48; founder, pres. Jonathan David Pubs., Middle Village, N.Y., 1949—. Author: These Are the Names, 1948, Who's Who in the Talmud, 1964, The Name Dictionary, 1967, Jewish Information Quiz Book, 1967, The Family Seder, 1968, Names for Pets, 1971, JD Dictionary of First Names, 1980, Jewish Book of Why, 1981, Complete Dictionary of English and Hebrew First Names, 1984, The Second Jewish Book of Why, 1985, Today's Best Baby Names, 1986, This Is the Torah, 1987, The New Name Dictionary, 1989, The Jewish Home Advisor, 1990, The Jewish Child's First Book of Why, 1992, The Jewish Mourner's Book of Why, 1992, Classic Bible Stories for Jewish Children, 1994, The Jewish Heritage Quiz Book, 1995, Great Jewish Quotations, 1996, Let's Celebrate Our Jewish Holidays, 1997, A Child's First Book of Jewish Holidays, 1997, Best Baby Names for Jewish Children, 1998, What Jews Say About God, 1999, The Presidents of the United States and the Jews, 2000, The Masters of the Talmud, 2003, (paperback edit.) The Jewish Book of Why: The Torah, 2004, The Jewish Books of Why Library, 2004, The Comprehensive Dictionary of English and Hebrew First Names, 2004, A Handbook for the Jewish Home, 2005, Inside Judaism: An Encyclopedia of Customs, Concepts, and Ceremonies, 2005. Served as chaplain U.S. Army, 1943-46. Mem. Rabbinical Assembly, Assn. Jewish Chaplains (past pres.), Mil. Chaplains Assn. (past v.p.) Home: 72-08 Juno St Forest Hills NY 11375-5930 Office: 68-22 Eliot Ave Middle Village NY 11379 Personal E-mail: rabbiajk@aol.com.

KOLATCH, MYRON, magazine editor; b. Bklyn., Sept. 26, 1929; s. Philip S. and Rebecca (Langberg) K.; m. Francine Ruth Miller, Jan. 28, 1951; children: Barry Steven, Jonathan Lee, Sari Elana. B.A, N.Y. U., 1950, postgrad in English, 1950-51. Mem. staff New Leader, 1953—, mng. editor, 1960-61, exec. editor, 1961—. Bd. dirs. Tamiment Inst. Served with AUS, 1951-53. Home: 18622 Radnor Rd Jamaica NY 11432-5829 Office: 275 7th Ave New York NY 10001-6708 Office Phone: 212-807-8240. Business E-Mail: mkolatch@thenewleader.com.

KOLATTUKUDY, PAPPACHAN ETTOOP, medical center executive, biochemist, educator; b. Cochin, Kerala, India, Aug. 27, 1937; came to the U.S., 1960; m. Marie M. Paul. BS, U. Madras, 1957; B in Edn., U. Kerala, 1959; PhD, Oreg. State U., 1964. Prin. jr. HS, India, 1957-58; HS chemistry tchr., 1959-60; asst. biochemist Conn. Agrl. Experiment Sta., New Haven, 1964-69; assoc. prof. Wash. State U., Pullman, 1969-73, prof. biochemistry, 1973-80, dir. inst. biol. chemistry, 1980-86; dir. Ohio State Biotech. Ctr., Columbus, 1986-95, dir. Neurobiotech. Ctr., dir. med. biotech., 1995—2003; dir. Biomolecular Sci. Ctr., chair dept. molecular biology and microbiology U. Ctrl. Fla., Orlando, 2003—04, Dean, Burnett Coll. Biomed. Scis., 2004—. Cons. Analabs, New Haven, Allied Chem. Corp., Solvay, N.Y., Genencor Corp., South San Francisco, Calif., Monsanto Co., St. Louis; mem. Overseas Adv. Com., India; mem. Edison Bio-Tech. Ctr., Cleve., trustee; mem. adv. com. to MUCIA on Sci. and Tech., Nat. Agrl. Biotech. Consortium; Ohio rep. to Midwest Plant Biotech. Consortium. Contbr. over 300 articles to profl. jours.; patentee in field. Recipient Golden Apple award Wash. State Apple Commn., President's Faculty Excellence award Wash. State U.; grantee NIH, NSF, Am. Heart Assn., Am. Cancer Soc., DOE. Mem. Fedn. Am. Socs. for Exptl. Biology, Am. Soc. Plant Physiologists, Am. Soc. Microbiology. Home: 1112 Cherry Valley Way Orlando FL 32828 Office: U Ctrl Fla Coll Biomed Scis Biomolecular Sci Bldg Rm 136 4000 Central Florida Blvd Orlando FL 32816

KOLAYA, MARGARET HELEN BOUTWELL, librarian; b. Concord, N.H., Apr. 15, 1947; d. Harvey B. and Margaret A. Boutwell; m. John L. Kolaya, June 20, 1970; children: Lauren B., Timothy A. BA in History, Bucknell U., 1969; MLS, Rutgers U., 1979. Manuscripts asst. Yale U. Libr., New Haven, 1969-70; head libr. The Wardlaw-Hartridge Sch., Edison and Plainfield, N.J., 1983-96; supervising libr. Rockwood Meml. Libr., 1996-97; dir. Clark Pub. Libr., 1997—2002, Scotch Plains (NJ) Publ Libr., 2002—. Bd. dirs. Hist. Soc. Plainfield, 1973-97, pres., 1987-88; bd. dirs. Catherine Webster Home, Inc., Plainfield, 1993-2002. Mem. ALA, N.J. Libr. Assn., Third N.J. Regiment (Brigade of the Am. Revolution). Home: 1081 Oakland Ave Plainfield NJ 07060-3411 Office: Scotch Plains Pub Libr 1927 Bartle Ave Scotch Plains NJ 07076-

KOLB, CHARLES CHESTER, foundation administrator; b. Erie, Pa., Sept. 4, 1940; s. John Christian and Edna Lucille (Church) K.; m. Joy Bilharz, June 3, 1972 (div. Mar. 1991); 1 child, Nancy Gwenyth; m. P. Jean Drew, July 20, 1991; 1 child, Catherine Claire Fraley. BA in History, Pa. State U., 1962, PhD in Archaeology and Anthropology, 1979. Instr. anthropology Pa. State U., University Park, 1966-69, Bryn Mawr (Pa.) Coll., 1969-73; from instr. to asst. prof. anthropology Pa. State U., Erie, 1973-84; dir. rsch. and grants Mercyhurst Coll., 1984-89, asst. dir. Hammermill Libr., 1989; humanities adminstr. program officer divsn. state programs NEH, Washington, 1989-91, program officer divsn. preservation and access, 1991-96, sr. program officer, 1997—, Recovering Iraq's Past Initiative, 2003—, Rediscovering Afghanistan Initiative, 2004—. Manuscript reviewer Holt, Rinehart and Winston, Inc., 1977-89, Prentice-Hall, Inc., 1979-85, William C. Brown, Pubs., 1982-85, U. Tex. Press, 1988—, U. Utah Press, 1991—, U. Press of Fla., 1994—, AltaMira Press/Sage, 1995—, U. Pa. Mus. Applied Sci. Ctr. Archaeology, 1996—, Dover Pub., 1996—, U. Press Colo., 2003—, Centro de Estudios Arqueológicos el Colegio de Michoacán, Mex., 2004, U. Ariz. Press, 2005; grant proposal reviewer NEH, 1981-89, NSF, 1982—, Social Sci. Humanities Rsch. Coun. Can, 2003-, Can. Found. Innovation, 2004—, Wenner-Gren Found. for Anthropol. Rsch., 1987-89, Nat. Geog. Soc. Rsch., Conservation and Exploration Grants, 2005-; co-founder, ann. symposium co-organizer Ceramic Studies Interest Group, 1986—. Author: Marine Shell Trade and Classic Teotihuacan, 1987; editor: A Pot for All Reasons, 1988, Ceramic Ecology, 1988, 89, 97; contbr. articles to profl. jours., chpts. to books; book and film reviewer Sci. Books and Films, 1977—; manuscript reviewer Am. Antiquity, 1978—, Current Anthropology, 1979—, Ancient Mesoamerica, 1990—, Ethnohistory, 1995—, Jour. Material Culture, 1995—, Hist. Archaeology, 1995—, L.Am. Antiquity, 1995—, H-Net Revs., 1996-, Jour. Archaeol. Sci., 1998—, Jour. Am. Inst. for Conservation, 2001—; abstractor Ceramic Abstracts, 1990-96, Art and Archaeology Technical Abstracts, 1996—; regional editor La Tinaja: Newsletter of Archaeol. Ceramics, 1991—; N.Am. corr. Old Potter's Almanack, 1992—; reviewer CHOICE, 1992—, ScienceNETLinks, 1999—, Transoxiana: E-journal de Estudios Orientales, 2003—, Central Asian Rsch. Rev., 2003—; contbr. Ency. of Modern Asia, 2002, Ency. World's Minorities, 2003, Dictionary of American History, 2002, Ency. Modern Middle East and North Africa 2d edit., 2004, Ency. of Developing World, 2005, Ency. of World Geography, 2005. Mem. Commonwealth Pa., Gov.'s Conf. on Librs. and Info. Systems, 1989. Nat. Geographic Soc. rsch., conservation and exploration grantee, 2005—. Fellow AAAS (panelist sci. journalism awards 2003—), Royal Anthrop. Inst. Gt. Britain and Ireland, Am. Anthrop. Assn.; mem. ALA, Am. Ceramic Soc., Am. Chem. Soc., Am. Ethnological Soc., Am. Soc. Ethnohistory, Archaeol. Inst. Am., Assn. Field Archaeology, Coun. Mus. Anthropology, Materials Rsch. Soc., Prehist. Ceramic Rsch. Group, Soc. Am. Archaeology, Soc. Archaeol. Scis. (life, bd. dir. 1998--, assoc. editor for archaeol. ceramics Bull. 1997—), Soc. Hist. Archaeology, Soc. Am. Archivists, Register Profl. Archaeologists, U.S. Naval Inst. (life), Soc. for Pa. Archaeology, N.Y. State Archaeol. Assn., Paleopathology Assn., Assn. Moving Image Archivists, Pearl Harbor History Assocs. (life), Naval Hist. Found., Ctrl. Eurasian Studies Soc., Am. Inst. Afghanistan Studies, Sigma Xi, Alpha Kappa Delta, Phi Kappa Phi, Pi Gamma Mu. Achievements include rsch. in tech. and cultural interpretations of archaeol. ceramics by using physiochem. analyses and petrographic microscopy, ceramics from Afghanistan, Ctrl. Asia, Mexico, Guatemala, East Africa, Great Lakes Basin. Home: 1005 Pruitt Ct SW Vienna VA 22180-6429 Office: NEH Divsn Preservation & Access 1100 Pennsylvania Ave NW Washington DC 20506-0001 Business E-Mail: ckolb@neh.gov.

KOLB, CHARLES EDWARD MEALEY, federal government official, lawyer; b. Salisbury, Md., Nov. 6, 1950; s. Stanley Denmead and Kathryn Beatrice (East) K.; m. June Joelynn Fletcher, July 25, 1976 (div. 1983); m. Ingrid Ann Christner, Aug. 27, 1988. AB, Princeton U., 1973; BA with honors, Balliol Coll. Oxford U., Eng., 1975, MA, 1980; JD, U. Va., 1978. Assoc. Cahill, Gordon & Reindel, N.Y.C., 1978; law clk. to Hon. Joseph H. Young U.S. Dist. Ct. Md., Balt., 1978-79; assoc. Covington & Burling, Washington, 1979-82, Foreman & Dyess, Washington, 1982-83; asst. gen. counsel U.S. Office Mgmt. and Budget, Washington, 1983-86; dep. gen. counsel for regulations and legis. U.S. Dept. Edn., Washington, 1986-88, dep. under sec. for planning, budget and evaluation, 1988-90; dep. asst. for domestic policy to the Pres. of U.S. The White House, 1990—. Bar: D.C. 1978, Md. 1978. Contbr. articles to profl. jours. Sec. bd. dirs. Internat. Human Rights Law Group, Washington, 1983-91. Mem. Soc. of the Cincinnati, Princeton Club N.Y. Republican. Episcopalian. Office: The White House Office Policy Devel 2nd Fl W Wing Washington DC 20500

KOLB, DAVID ALLEN, psychologist, educator; b. Moline, Ill., Dec. 12, 1939; s. John August and Ethel May (Petherbridge) K.; m. Alice Yoko; 1 son, Jonathan Demian. AB cum laude, Knox Coll., 1961; PhD, Harvard U., 1967; ScD (h.c.), U. N.H., 1984; PhD (h.c.), Internat. Mgmt. Ctr., Buckingham, 1988; LittD (h.c.), Franklin U., 1994; DHL (h.c.), SUNY, 1996. Asst. prof. organizational psychology MIT, Cambridge, 1965-70, assoc. prof., 1970-75; prof. organizational behavior and mgmt. Case Western Res. U., Cleve., 1976—, deWindt Prof. Leadership and Enterprise Devel. Weatherhead Sch. Mgmt., 1992-97, chmn. dept., 1984-90. Vis. prof. mgmt. London Grad. Sch. Bus., 1971; dir. Devel. Research Assos., 1966-80; mgmt. cons., U.S., Australia, N.Z., Indonesia, Singapore, Malaysia, Thailand, Japan. Author: Experiential Learning: Experience as the source of learning and development, 1984, Kolb Learning Style Inventory 3.1, 2005; co-author: Organizational Behavior: An Experiential Approach, 7th edit, 2001, Organizational Behavior: A Book of Readings, 7th edit, 2001, Changing Human Behavior: Principles of Planned Intervention, 1974, Innovation in Professional Education: Steps on Journey from Teaching to Learning, 1995, Conversational Learning: An Experiential Approach to Knowledge Creation, 2002. Woodrow Wilson fellow, 1962. Mem. Internat. Assn. Applied Social Scientists (charter), Soc. Intercultural Edn., Tng. and Rsch. (charter), Coun.l Advancement of Experiential Learning (Research Excellence award 1984, Morris T. Keaton Adult and Experiential Learning award 1991, Case Weatherhead Rsch. Recognition award 2002-03). Office: Case Western Res U Dept of Orgn Behavior Cleveland OH 44106 E-mail: dak5@msn.com.

KOLB, DOROTHY GONG, elementary school educator; b. San Jose, Calif. d. Jack and Lucille Gong; m. William Harris Kolb, Mar. 22, 1970. BA with highest honors, San Jose State U., 1964; postgrad., U. Hawaii, Calif. State U., L.A.; MA in Ednl. Tech., Pepperdine U., 1992. Cert. in elem. edn., edn. for mentally retarded, edn. for learning handicapped pre-sch., adult classes, resource specialist, English lang. devel., specially designed acad. instrn. in English, 2000, 2003. Tchr. Cambrian Sch. Dist., San Jose, 1964-66, Ctrl. Oahu Sch. Dist., Wahiawa, Hawaii, 1966-68, Montebello (Calif.) Unified Sch. Dist., 1968—. Recipient Very Spl. Person award, Calif. PTA, 1998, Hon. Svc. award, 2003; Walter Bachrodt Meml. scholar. Mem.: Tau Beta Pi, Pi Tau Sigma, Kappa Delta Pi, Pi Lambda Theta.

KOLB, FELIX OSCAR, physician; b. Vienna, Nov. 12, 1921; arrived in U.S., 1938; s. Leon and Hilde (Grunwald) K.; m. Susan L. Goldberger, July 1, 1966; children: Lisa F., Marc E. AB, U. Calif., Berkeley, 1941; MD, U. Calif., San Francisco, 1943. Diplomate Am. Bd. Internal Medicine, Am. Bd. Endocrinology and Metabolism. Intern San Francisco Gen. Hosp., 1943-44; clin. asst. U. Calif. Med. Ctr., San Francisco, 1946-47; med. resident VA Hosp., U. Calif., San Francisco, 1947-49, New Eng. Ctr. Hosp., Boston, 1949-50; grad. asst. endocrine svc. of Dr. Fuller Albright Mass. Gen. Hosp., Boston, 1950-51; attending physician U. Calif. Hosp., San Francisco, 1952—; asst. chief, assoc. chief, sr. dept. of medicine Mt. Zion Hosp., San Francisco, 1952-98, emeritus, 1998—; asst. assoc. dir. metabolic rsch. unit U. Calif., San Francisco, 1952-85, clin. prof. medicine, 1969-99, clin. prof. medicine emeritus, 1999—, asst. assoc. dir. metabolic rsch. unit, 1952-85; pvt. practice in endocrinology and metabolism San Francisco, 1952-99; retired. Cons. physician Shriners Hosp., San Francisco, VA Hosp., San Francisco, Children's Hosp., San Francisco, Letterman Hosp., San Francisco, Marshal Hale Hosp., San Francisco, Calif. Pacific Med. Ctr., San Francisco. Co-author, author 3 text book chpts.; contbr. numerous articles to profl. jours.; editl. bd. Metabolism, Reviewer for Ann. and Arch. Internal Medicine, Calcified Tissue Internat. Capt. U.S. Army, 1944-46. Fellow ACP; mem. AMA, Calif. Med. Assn., San Francisco Med. Assn., Am. Diabetes Assn., Endocrine Soc., Am. Fedn. for Clin. Rsch., We. Soc. for Clin. Rsch., Am. Soc. Internal Medicine, Calif. Soc. Internal Medicine, San Francisco Soc. Internal Medicine, Am. Soc. for Bone and Mineral Rsch., Alpha Omega Alpha (sec.-treas. 1955-56), Phi Delta Epsilon. Democrat. Jewish. Avocations: piano, golf. Home: 9 Starboard Ct Mill Valley CA 94941-3210 Fax: 415-383-1013. E-mail: FOKolbmd@yahoo.com.

KOLB, GLORIA RO, medical products executive; BS in mech. engring., MIT, 1994; MS in mech. engring., Stanford U., 1995; MBA in entrepreneurship, Babson Coll., 2001. Founder, pres. Fossa Med., Inc., 2001—. Named one of Top 100 Young Innovators, MIT Tech. Review, 2004. Office: Fossa Med 13 Highland Cir Needham MA 02494

KOLB, GWIN JACKSON, language professional, educator; b. Aberdeen, Miss., Nov. 2, 1919; s. Roy Rolly and Nola Undine (Jackson) K.; m. Ruth Alma Godbold, Oct. 11, 1943; children: Gwin Jackson II, Alma Dean. BA, Millsaps Coll., 1941; MA, U. Chgo., 1946, PhD, 1949; LHD, Millsaps Coll., 1991. Editorial asst. Modern Philology, 1946-56; mem. faculty U. Chgo., 1949-89, prof. English, 1961-77, Chester D. Tripp prof. humanities, 1977-89, emeritus, 1990—, chmn. dept., 1963-72, chmn. coll. English staff, 1958-60, head humanities sect. in coll., 1960-62. Vis. assoc. prof. Northwestern U., winter 1958, Stanford U., spring 1960; vis. prof. U. Wash., summers 1967, 73, Ohio State U., spring 1987, Peking U., fall 1994, U. Evansville, winter, spring 1996, Huntingdon Coll., winter, spring 1997, U. Ga., winter 1998, Berry Coll., winter, spring 2000. Co-author: Dr. Johnson's Dictionary, 1955, Reading Literature: A Workbook, 1955; editor: (Samuel Johnson) Rasselas and Other Tales, 1990; co-editor: A Bibliography of Modern Studies Complied for Philological Quarterly, 1951-65, 3 vols., 1962, 72, Modern Philology, 1973-89, Approaches to Teaching the Works of Samuel Johnson, 1993. Served with USNR, 1942-45. Frederick A. and Marion S. Pottle fellow Beinecke Libr. Yale U., 1993; recipient Quantrell award U. Chgo., 1955, Medal of Honor U. Evansville, 1992, Alumni award Millsaps Coll., 1967; Guggenheim fellow, 1956-57; grantee Am. Coun. Learned Socs., 1961-62. Mem. MLA, Midwest MLA (pres. 1964-65), Johnson Soc. Ctrl. Region (pres. 1965-66), Nat. Coun. Tchrs. English (bd. dirs. coll. sect. 1966-68), Am. Soc. 18th Century Studies (exec. bd. 1973-76, pres. 1976-77), The Johnsonians, Assn. Depts. English (pres. 1968), Caxton Club, Quadrangle. Home: 609 Ridge Rd Kenilworth IL 60043-1042

KOLB, HAROLD HUTCHINSON, JR., language educator; b. Boston, Jan. 16, 1933; BA in English with honors, Amherst Coll., 1955; MA in Am. Studies, U. Mich., 1960; PhD in British and Am. Lit., Ind. U., 1968. Instr. English Valparaiso U., 1960-62; teaching assoc. Ind. U., 1962-65; from asst. prof. to prof. English U. Va., Charlottesville, 1967-99, prof. emeritus, 2000—, dir. Ctr. for Liberal Arts, 1984-99. Project dir. NEH, 1972-76, 85-99; dir. Canadian Judicial Writing Program, 1981-84; guest prof. Am. studies U. Bonn, 1982; chmn. MLA Delegate Assembly Steering Com., 1984-85. Author: The Illusion of Life-American Realism as a Literary Form, 1969, A Field Guide to the Study of American Literature, 1976, A Writer's Guide: The Essential Points, 1980; co-author: A Handbook for Research in American Literature and American Studies, 1994; contbr. articles to scholarly and other publs. Naval aviator USN, 1955—59. Recipient Armstrong prize in English, Amherst Coll., 1952, James A. Work prize, Ind. U., 1965, Guggenheim fellowship, 1970-71, Faculty Leadership award Am. Assn. Higher Edn., Carnegie Found. for Advancement of Teaching and Change mag., 1986, Citation for Leadership in Rejuvenation of Secondary and Elem. Edn., Va. Bd. Edn., 1987, Phillip E. Frandson award for Innovation and Creative Programming, Nat. U. Continuing Edn. Assn., 1988, Outstanding Faculty award, Va. Coun. Higher Edn., 1988. Office Phone: 434-293-7398. Business E-Mail: hhk6s@virginia.edu.

KOLB, JAMES A., science foundation director, writer; b. Berkeley, Calif., May 31, 1947; s. James DeBruler and Evelyn (Thomas) K.; m. Mary Catherine Eames; children: Thomas, Catherine Mary. BA in Zoology, BA in Biol. Sci., Ecology, U. Calif., Berkeley, 1970, MS in Wildland Resource Sci., 1972. Rsch. asst. Sagehen Creek Rsch. Sta. U. Calif., Berkeley, 1970, tchg. asst. dept. wildlife & fisheries, 1970-71, rsch. assoc. air pollution resource ctr. Berkeley, Riverside, 1971; tchr. secondary sci. Hayward (Calif.) Unified Sch. Dist., 1972-77; dir. Marine Sci. Ctr., Poulsbo, Wash., 1981-92; exec. dir. Marine Sci. Soc. Pacific Northwest, Poulsbo, 1992-95, For Sea Inst. Marine Sci., Indianola, Wash., 1995—98; dir. academic studies West Sound Academy, Poulsbo, 1998—. Project dir. Marine Sci. Project FOR SEA, Poulsbo, 1978-81; mem. Wash. State Environ. Edn. Task Force, Olympia, 1986—, Puget Sound Water Quality Authority Edn. & Pub. Involvement, Olympia, 1987-91, Marine Plastics Debris Task Force, Olympia, 1987; dir. acad. studies, West Soun Acad., Poulsbo, 1998-; cons., tchr., trainer Hood Canal Wetlands Project, Hoodsport, Wash., 1990. Author: Marine Science Activities, 1979 (NSTA award 1986), Marine Biology and Oceanography, 1979, 80, 81 (NSTA award 1985, 86), Marine Science Career Awareness, 1984 (NSTA award 1985), The Changing Sound, 1990, Puget Soundbook, 1991, Life in the Tidal Zone, 1995, The Sea Around Us, 1995, Life in the Estuary, Begining in the Watershed, 1995, Life With Pagoo, 1995, Investigating the Ocean Planet, 1995, Ocean Studies, Ocean Issues, 1995, Marine Biology and Oceanography, 1995, Marine Explorations CD-ROM, 1997, The Tuna/Dolphin Controversy CD-ROM, 1998, Marine Science Clip Art Portfolio CD-ROM, 1998, Marine Biology and Oceanography CD-ROM, 2000, Ocean Studies, Ocean Issues CD-ROM, 2001; co-author: A Salmon in the Sound, 1991, Discovering Puget Sound, 1991, The Puget Sound Book CD-Rom, 2003, The Electronic Whale Gray Whale Migration Simulation CD-ROM, 2004. Mem. NSTA, ASCD, Internat. Reading Assn., Nat. Marine Educators Assn. (Marine Edn. award 1997), Northwest Assn. Marine Educators (past pres.), Wildlife Soc., People for Puget Sound (v.p.).

KOLB, JANICE GRAY, writer; b. Phila., Dec. 23, 1933; d. Ellis George and Violet Matilda Gray; m. Robert Alexander Kolb Jr., Jan. 7, 1955; children: June, Laurel, Barbara, George, Jessica, Janna. Diploma in dental hygiene, Temple U., 1953. Cert. dental hygienist. Author: Whispered Notes, 1990, Compassion for All Creatures, 1997, Journal of Love, 2000, The Enchantment of Writing, 2001, Higher Ground, 2001, Beneath the Stars and Trees, 2002, Silent Violence, 2002, Beside the Still Waters, 2003, In Corridors of Eternal Time, 2003, Solace of Solitude, 2005; contbr. articles to profl. jours. Mem.: N.H. Writers Group. Avocation: animal rights. Personal E-mail: jan@janicegraykolb.com.

KOLB, JOHN E., lawyer; b. Argenta, Tex., Aug. 19, 1928; s. Luther T. and Gladys (Bomer) K.; m. Joy Voltz, Aug. 16, 1947; children: Susan Kolb Dunwoody, Jay T., Paul M., Ellen Kolb Klepacki, Ann Kolb Cuclis. BBA, U. Tex., 1949; LLB, U. Houston, 1955. From assoc. to ptnr. Vinson & Elkins, Houston, 1955—. Bd. dirs. Adobe Resources Corp., N.Y.C. Regent U. Houston System, 1981-87; bd. dirs. W.M. Keck Found., Los Angeles, 1986—. Recipient Disting. Alumnus award U. Houston Alumni Assn., 1984. Mem. ABA, Tex. Bar Assn., Houston Bar Assn. Mem. Disciples of Christ Ch. Clubs: Ramada (Houston), River Oaks Country. Address: 10 S Briar Hollow Apt 59 Houston TX 77027

KOLB, KEITH ROBERT, architect, educator; b. Billings, Mont., Feb. 9, 1922; s. Percy Fletcher and Josephine (Randolph) K.; m. Jacqueline Cecile Jump, June 18, 1947; children: Brooks Robin, Bliss Richards. Grad. basic engring., US Army Specialized Training Rutgers U., 1944; BArch cum laude, U. Wash., 1947; MArch, Harvard U., 1950. Registered arch., Wash., Mont., Idaho, Calif., Oreg., Nat. Coun. Archtl. Registration Bds. Draftsman, designer various archtl. firms, Seattle, 1946-54; draftsman, designer Walter Gropius and Archs. Collaborative, Cambridge, Mass., 1950-52; prin. Keith R. Kolb, Arch., Seattle, 1954-64, Keith R. Kolb Arch. & Assocs., Seattle, 1964-66; ptnr. Decker, Kolb & Stansfield, Seattle, 1966-71, Kolb & Stansfield AIA Archs., Seattle, 1971-89; pvt. practice Keith R. Kolb FAIA Archs., Seattle, 1989—. Instr. Mont. State Coll., Bozeman, 1947-49; asst. prof. arch. U. Wash., Seattle, 1952-60, assoc. prof., 1960-82, prof., 1982-90, prof. emeritus, 1990—. Design arch. Dist. II Hdqrs. and Comm. Ctr., Wash. State Patrol, Bellevue, 1970 (Exhbn. award Seattle chpt. AIA), Hampson residence, 1970 (nat. AIA 1st honor 1973, citation Seattle chpt. AIA 1980), Acute Gen. Stevens Meml. Hosp., 1973, Redmond Pub. Libr., 1975 (jury selection Wash. coun. AIA 1980), Tolstedt residence, Helena, Mont., 1976, Herbert L. Eastlick Biol. Scis. Lab. bldg. Wash. State U., 1977, Redmond Svc. Ctr., Puget Sound Power and Light Co., 1979, Computer and Mgmt. Svcs. Ctr., Paccar Inc., 1981 (curatorial team selection Mus. History and Industry exhbn. 100th anniversary of AIA 1994), Seattle Town House, 1960 (curatorial team selection Mus. History and Industry exhbn. 100th anniversary of AIA 1994), Comm. Tower, Pacific N.W. Bell, 1981 (nat. J.F. Lincoln bronze), Forks br. Seattle 1st Nat. Bank, 1981 (commendation award Seattle chpt. AIA 1981, nat. jury selection Am. Architecture, The State of the Art in the '80's 1985, regional citation Am. Wood Coun. 1981), Reg. ops. Control Ctr. Sacramento Dist. Corps Engrs. McChord AFB, Wash., 1982, Puget Sound Blood Ctr., 1983-88, expansion vis./dining/recreation facilities Wash. State Reformatory, Monroe, 1983, Univ. Sta. P.O., U.S. Postal Svc., Seattle, 1983, Guard Towers, McNeil Island Corrections Ctr. Wash., 1983, Magnolia Queen Anne Carrier Annex, U.S. Postal Svc., Seattle, 1986, Tolstedt residence, Seattle, 1987, Maxim residence, Camano Island, Wash., 1991, Carmean residence alterations/additions, Seattle, 1995, 96, 97, 2001, 2002, Susanna Burney and Bliss Kolb residence, Seattle, 2001-04. Pres. Laurelhurst Cmty. Club, Seattle, 1966. Served with U.S. Army, 1943-45, ETO. Decorated Bronze Star medal ETO; recipient Alpha Rho Chi medal; selected Am. Archs., Facts on File, Inc., 1989. Fellow AIA (dir. Seattle chpt. 1970-71, sec. Seattle chpt. 1972, Wash. state coun. 1973, pres. sr. coun. Seattle chpt. 1994-96, trustee Seattle Archtl. Found. 1994-96, Citation award Seattle chpt. for a Seattle 1960 Town House, 1990, honored Living Legends Series 2002); mem. U. Wash. Archtl. Alumni Assn. (pres. 1958-59), Phi Beta Kappa, Tau Sigma Delta. Home and Office: 3379 47th Ave NE Seattle WA 98105-5326 Office Phone: 206-527-7544.

KOLB, KEN LLOYD, writer; b. Portland, Oreg., July 14, 1926; s. Frederick Von and Ella May (Bay) K.; m. Emma LaVada Sanford, June 7, 1952; children: Kevin, Lauren, Kimrie. BA in English with honors, U. Calif., Berkeley, 1950; MA with honors, San Francisco State U., 1953. Cert. jr. coll. English tchr. Freelance fiction writer various nat. mags., N.Y.C., 1951-56;

freelance screenwriter various film and TV studios, LA, 1956-81; freelance novelist Chilton, Random House, Playboy Press, N.Y.C., 1967—. Instr. creative writing Feather River Coll., Quincy Calif., 1969; min. Universal Life Ch. Author: (teleplay) She Walks in Beauty, 1956 (Writers Guild award 1956), (feature films) Seventh Voyage of Sinbad, 1957, Snow Job, 1972, (novels) Getting Straight, 1967 (made into feature film), The Couch Trip, 1970 (made into feature film), Night Crossing, 1974; contbr. fiction and humor to nat. mags. and anthologies. Foreman Plumas County Grand Jury, Quincy, 1970; chmn. Region C Criminal Justice Planning Commn., Oroville, Calif., 1975-77; film commr. Plumas County, 1986-87. Served with USNR, 1944-46. Established Ken Kolb Collection, Boston U. Libr., 1969. Mem. Writers Guild Am. West, Authors Guild, Plumas Ski Club (pres. 1977-78), Mensa, Phi Beta Kappa, Theta Chi. Democrat. Avocations: skiing, tennis, travel. Home and Office: PO Box 30022 Cromberg CA 96103-3022 Office Phone: 530-836-2332. *The true measure of success is not the attainment of great wealth or a position of power over others, but the quality of one's own life. I'm grateful for the money and honors I've had from writing, but more important to me is my ongoing love affair with my wife and the loving friendship of my grown children. I believe in God and a sense of humor as guiding principles, but I can't explain either one.*

KOLB, NATHANIEL KEY, JR., architect; b. Sherman, Tex., Aug. 17, 1933; s. Nathaniel Key and Nelcine (Dial) K.; m. Catherine Conner, Nov. 24, 1958; children: Nathaniel Key, Mary Catherine, Amy Monica, Peter Paul, John Conner, Elizabeth Dial. BArch, Tex. A&M U., 1957; MArch, U. Pa., 1960. Registered architect, Tex. With CRSS, Houston, 1955-58, Vincent G. Kling, Phila., 1958-61, William B. Tabler, N.Y.C., 1961-63; chmn. bd., pres. Omniplan, Inc., Dallas, 1963-99. Instr. Tex. A&M Univ., Coll. Station, 1957-58; adj. asst. prof. Columbia U., N.Y.C., 1961-62; bd. dirs. Fidelity Bank, Dallas, 1985-98; mem., chmn. Urban Design Task Force, Dallas, 1974-83; dir., mem. exec. com. Greater Dallas Planning Coun., 1982-85; mem. adv. coun. Ryan Real Estate Coun., U. Tex., Arlington, 1985-88; bd. dirs. Peacock Alley, 1998—. Chmn. Hist. Landmarks Com., Dallas, 1977-79; pres., dir. Dallas Ballet, 1982-87. Recipient Outstanding Alumni award, Coll. Architecture, A&M U./ Tex., 2003, Disting. Alumni award, Sherman HS, 2002. Fellow AIA; mem. Tex. Soc. Architects, Dallas chpt. AIA (dir. 1976-80, pres. 1979), Dallas Club (pres., dir. 1980-86) Office: Omniplan 1845 Woodall Rogers Fwy Dallas TX 75201

KOLB, SHARON MARIE, education educator, director, consultant; b. Kenosha, Wis., Sept. 6, 1966; d. Darrell Anthony and Colleen Faith Kolb; life ptnr. Britta Jan Johnson; 1 child, Kelly Kolb-Johnson; 1 child, Shelby Kolb-Johnson. BS, U. Wis. Eau Claire, Eau Claire, 1988; MS, U Wis. Whitewater, 1993; PhD, U Wis., 2000. Tchr. Beaver Dam Unified Sch., Wis., 1988—2000; lectr. U. Wis., Whitewater, 2000—01, asst. prof., coord. cognitive disabilities program, 2001—05, assoc. prof. spl. edn., licensure and field experience coord., 2005—. Cons. Statewide Transition Consortium"Wis. Healthy and Ready to Work Project", Madison, 2002—; spkr. in field. Contbr. chapters to books A Practitioner's Guide to Facilitating the Role of Families in the Transition Process, 2003, articles profl. jours., rsch. papers to numerous confs. Mem. Am. Legion Auxiliary, Wis., 1973—, Rainbow Families of Wis., Madison, Wis., 1997—. Recipient Transition:18-21 Age Group, Dept. of Pub. Instr., 2002—03. Mem.: Coun. Exceptional Children, Phi Kappa Phi. Democrat. Lutheran. Avocations: parent volunteer, volleyball, softball, guitar. Home: 335 Huntsville Ridge Sun Prairie WI 53590 Office: Dept of Special Education 800 West Main Street Whitewater WI 53190 Office Phone: 262-472-4831. Business E-Mail: kolbs@uww.edu.

KOLB, VERA M., chemist, educator; b. Belgrade, Yugoslavia, Feb. 5, 1948; arrived in U.S., 1973; d. Martin A. and Dobrila (Lopicic) Kolb; m. Cal Y. Meyers, 1976 (div. 1986); m. Michael S. Gregory, 1997 (div. 1999). BS, Belgrade U., 1971, MS, 1973; PhD, So. Ill. U., 1976. Fellow So. Ill. U., Carbondale, 1977-78, vis. faculty lctr., 1978-85; assoc. prof. chemistry U. Wis., Parkside, 1985-90, prof. chemistry, 1990—, dept. chair, 1995-97. Vis. scientist Salk Inst. Biol. Studies U. Calif., San Diego, 1992—94; instr. San Francisco State U., 1997; vis. scholar Northwestern U., 2002—03. Editor: (book) Teratogens, Chemicals which Cause Birth Defects, 2nd edit., 1993, 1988; contbr. articles to profl. jours.; musician (violinist): Racine Symphony Orch., Parkside Cmty Orch., 2002—05. Assoc. dir. higher edn. Wis. Space Grant Consortium, 1995—97, assoc. dir. for special initiatives, 2002—05; violinist Racine (Wis.) Symphony Orch., Parkside Cmty. Orch. Recipient Higher Edn. awards, Wis. Space Grant Consortium, 1999—2003, Hall of Fame, Southeastern Wis. Educators, 2002; fellow NASA, 1992—94; grantee Fulbright, 1973—76, NIH, 1984—87, Am. Soc. Biochemistry and Molecular Biology, 1988. Mem.: Am. Chem. Soc. (task force occupl. safety and health 1980—94). Achievements include patents in field. Office: Univ Wis Parkside Dept Chemistry PO Box 2000 Kenosha WI 53141-2000

KOLBAS, ROBERT MICHAEL, electrical engineering educator; b. Syracuse, N.Y., Nov. 13, 1953; s. John Michael and Frances C. (Woityra) K.; children: Michael Thomas, Daniel Robert, Sarah Anne, Mary Chen; m. Dahua Zhang. BS in Engring., Cornell U., 1975; MS in Physics, U. Ill., 1977, PhD, 1979. Rsch., teaching asst. U. Ill., Urbana, 1975-79; prin. rsch. scientist Honeywell, Inc., Bloomington, Minn., 1979-83, sr. prin. rsch. scientist, 1983-85; assoc. prof. N.C. State U., Raleigh, 1985-90, prof. elec. and computer engring., 1990—, head elec. and computer engring. dept., 1995-2000. Contbr. articles to profl. publs.; patentee in field. Mentor to high sch. students, N.C. Sch. Sci. and Math., Durham, 1988-91. Kodak doctoral fellow U. Ill./Kodak, 1978. Fellow IEEE; mem. Tau Beta Pi, Sigma Xi. Office: N C State U PO Box 7911 Raleigh NC 27695-0001 E-mail: kolbas@eos.ncsu.edu.

KOLBE, JAMES THOMAS, congressman; b. Evanston, Ill., June 28, 1942; s. Walter William and Helen (Reed) K. BA in Polit. Sci., Northwestern U., 1965; MBA in Econs., Stanford U., 1967. Asst. to coordinating architect Ill. Bldg. Authority, Chgo., 1970-72; spl. asst. to Gov. Richard Ogilvie Chgo., 1972-73; v.p. Wood Canyon Corp., Tucson, 1973-80; mem. Ariz. State Senate, 1977-83, majority whip, 1979-80; mem. U.S. Congress from 8th dist. Ariz., 1985—; mem. appropriations com.; chmn. appropriations subcom. treasury, postal svc., gen. gov. Trustee Embry-Riddle Aero. U., Daytona Beach, Fla.; bd. dirs. Community Food Bank, Tucson; Republican precinct committeeman, Tucson, 1974—. Served as lt. USNR, 1968-69, Vietnam. Republican. Methodist. Office: 237 Cannon HOB Washington DC 20515-2542

KOLBE, KARL WILLIAM, JR., lawyer; b. Passaic, NJ, Sept. 29, 1926; s. Karl William Sr. and Edna Ernestine (Rumsey) K.; m. Barbara Louise Bogart, Jan. 28, 1950 (dec. Aug. 1992); children: Kim E., William B., Katherine B.; m. Patricia L. Coward, Apr. 30, 1994. BA, Princeton U., 1949; JD, U. Va., 1952. Bars: N.Y. 1952, D.C. 1976, U.S. Supreme Ct. 1966. Ptnr. Thelen, Reid & Priest, N.Y.C., 1966-92, of counsel, 1993—. Dir. Bessemer Trust Co. (N.A.), N.Y.C.,1977-97, Carolinas Cement Co., 1994-98, World Trade Corp., 1987-2002; vice-chmn. The Friends of Thirteen Inc. Bd. dirs. N.J. Ballet Co., West Orange, 1970-98, Ocean Liner Mus., 1992-2003. With USN, 1944-46. Mem. ABA (chmn. pub. utility law sect. 1984-85). Clubs: Univ. (N.Y.C.); Metro. (Washington). Home: PO Box 278 111 Old Chester Rd Essex Fells NJ 07021-1625 Office: Thelen Reid & Priest 875 Third Ave New York NY 10022 Office Phone: 212-603-2306. Business E-Mail: wkolbe@thelenreid.com.

KOLBE, RONALD LYNN, research engineer; b. Washington, June 3, 1950; s. Casper Maul and Ruthlee (Cade) K.; m. Margaret Garret, Mar. 16, 1984; 1 child, Katharine Lynn. BSME, U. Md., 1973; MS in Nuclear Engring., Purdue U., 1976; PhD in ME, U. Tenn., 1986. Mech. engr. Burns & Roe, Oradell, NJ, 1981—84; asst. prof. engring. U.S. Mcht. Marine Acad., Kings Point, NY, 1984—87; asst. prof., dir. engr. Shepherd Coll., Sheperdstown, W.Va., 1987—88; staff scientist Berkeley Rsch. Assocs., Springfield, Va., 1989—91; mech. engr. Naval Rsch. Lab., Washington, 1991—97; sr. software engr. ManTech, Lexington Park, Md., 1997—2000; sr. scientist Sci. Applications Internat. Corp., McLean, Va., 2000—05; engr. Northrop Grummen, Alexandria, Va., 2005—. Mem.: ASME, AIAA, Sigma Xi. Republican. Methodist. Office Phone: 703-971-3103 239. E-mail: ronald.kolbe@ngc.com.

KOLBERT, KATHRYN, lawyer, educator; b. Detroit, Apr. 8, 1952; d. Melvin and Rosalie Betty (Frank) K.; children: Samuel Kolbert-Hyle, Kate Kolbert-Hyle. BA, Cornell U., 1974; JD, Temple U., 1977. Bar: Pa. 1977, U.S. Dist. Ct. (ea. dist.) Pa. 1977, U.S. Ct. Appeals (3d cir.) 1977, U.S. Supreme Ct. 1985, U.S. Dist. Ct. N.D. 1991, U.S. Ct. Appeals (5th cir.) 1991, U.S. Ct. Appeals (10th cir.) 1994, U.S. Ct. Appeals (8th cir.) 1994. Atty. Community Legal Svcs., Phila., 1977-79, Women's Law Project, Phila., 1979-88; co-founder, dir. policy Women's Agenda, Phila., 1984-88; atty. pvt. practice, Wyndmoor, Pa., 1997. Cons. Planned Parenthood Fedn., N.Y.C., 1988-89, Nat. Abortion Rights Action League, Washington, 1987; cons. reproductive freedom project ACLU, N.Y.C., 1988-89, state coordinating counsel, 1989-92; v.p. Ctr Reproductive Law & Policy, N.Y., 1992-97; lectr. dept. women's studies U. Pa., 1978-86, 90-91, lectr. Sch. Law, 1989-91, sr. rsch. adminstr. Annenberg Pub. Policy Ctr., 1998—; Open Soc. Inst. fellow, 1998-2000. Exec. prodr. (radio series on constnl. law) Justice Talking; contbr. chpts. to books. Founder, Commn. to Elect Women Judges, Women Judges Pac, Phila, 1984; bd. dirs. Com. to Elect the Casey 5, Phila. Recipient Dedicated Advocacy award Nat. Abortion Rights Action League Pa., 1986, Pa. Coalition Against Domestic Violence, 1986, Luth. Settlement House Women's Program, 1987, Am. Dem. Action award, 1989, honoree Women's Way, 1991; named One of 100 Most Influential Lawyers in Am., Nat. Law Jour. Democrat. Jewish. Business E-Mail: KKOLBERT@asc.upenn.edu.

KOLBESON, MARILYN HOPF, holistic practitioner, educator, artist, advertising executive, poet; b. Cin., June 9, 1930; d. Henry Dilg Hopt and Carolyn Josephine (Brown) Hopf; children: Michael Llen, Kenneth Ray, Patrick James, Pamela Sue Kolbeson Lang, James Allan. Student, U. Cin., 1947—48, student, 1950. Cert. holistic memory release practitioner. Interior decorator Metro Carpet, 1971-77; sales and mktg. mgr. Cox Patrick United Van Lines, 1977-80; sales mktg. mgr. Creative Incentives, Houston, 1980-81; pres. Ad Sense, Inc., Houston, 1981-87, M.H. Kolbeson & Assocs., Houston, 1987, Seattle, 1987—, The Phoenix Books, Seattle, 1987-90, METASELF Healing, Seattle, 1999—. Bd. dirs. Umbrella Prodns.; cons. N.L.P. Practitioner and Cons.; Aircraft bus. mgmt. cons., Seattle, 1988—90; holographic memory release practitioner, 1996—; cooking demonstrator, nutritional advisor Puget Consumers Coop., Seattle, 1991—2002; lectr., cons. in field. Pub.: You Make the Difference in Nat. Lit. Poetry Anthology, Morning Song, 1996,: Moving On in Nat. Libr. Poetry, 1998; contbr. poetry to A Place at the Table, 1999; Heart Button Technique, 1995, Om Art angel meditation balls, 2002; mgr., assoc. prodr.: (mus. comedy) Times Three, 1999; prodn. mgr. Of a Certain Age, 2002, 2004; Green Scythe, 2004; instrument keeper (group shows) Gentle Wind Project, 1999—, creator, artist Art in the Round. Vol. Seattle Pub. Schs., 1992—2005; mem. citizens adv. bd. Arcola (Ill.) Sch. Dist., 1964—66; mem. ARC, Seattle; charter mem. Rep. Task Force; mem. adv. bd. Alief Ind. Sch. Dist., 1981—87, pres., 1983—84; bd. dirs. Santa Maria Hostel, 1983—86, v.p., 1983—84; mem. citizen's adv. bd. Am. Inst. Achievement, 1986—87; bd. dirs. Breighton Found. Sr. Housing Devel., Seattle, 2000—05, S.E. Seattle Sr. Found., 2000—; founder, pres. Mind Force, Houston, 1978—87, Seattle, 1987—95; founder META Group, Seattle, 1991—, Meta-Self Healing Ministries, Seattle, 1997—. Mem.: Nat. Sch. Pub. Rels. Assn., Internat. Soc. Poets, Inst. Noetic Scis., Houston Advt. Splty. Assn. (bd. dirs. 1984—87, treas. 1985, v.p. 1986—87), Internat. Platform Assn., World Future Soc., Nat. Assn. Mentally Ill. (Wash.), Toastmasters (area gov. 1978), Galleria Area C. of C. (bd. dirs. 1986—87), Fair and Tender Ladies Book Group Seattle, Lakewood Seward Park Cmty. Club (bd. dirs.), Grand Club (v.p. 1986). Republican. Universalist. Office: 5253 S Brandon St Seattle WA 98118-2522 Office Phone: 206-723-3588. Personal E-mail: mhk99@comcast.net.

KOLCZYNSKI, PHILLIP JOHN, lawyer; b. Cleve., Dec. 9, 1947; s. Peter Raymond and Emily Agnes (Magielski) K.; m. Kathleen Anne Dacey, June 6, 1987. BA, Marquette U., 1969; JD, Case-Western Res. U., 1977. Bar: Ohio 1977, D.C. 1978, Calif. 1984. Litigation atty. FAA, Washington, 1977-79; assoc. Arent, Fox, Kitner, Plotkin & Kahn, Washington, 1979-80; trial atty. aviation unit, civil div. U.S. Dept. Justice, Washington, 1980-83; ptnr. Engstrom, Lipscomb & Lack, L.A., 1983-88, Speers, Dana, Teal, Balfour & MacDonald, Costa Mesa, Calif., 1988-94; sole practitioner Irvine, Calif., 1994—. Instr., lectr. U.S. Justice Dept., Washington, 1981-83, chmn. Nat. Symposium on Aviation and Admiralty Law, 1982; instr. aviation law U. So. Calif.; lectr., Calif. Continuing Edn. of the Bar (CEB), settlement negotiations, advanced product liability. Author: Preparing a Case for Trial in Federal Court, 1995; contbr. articles to law rev. and profl. jours. Maj. USMC, 1969-74. AV rated, Martindale Hubbell Bar Register of Pre-eminent Attys. Mem. ABA (vice chmn. aviation sect. 1989-92), Orange County Bar Assn. (chmn. aviation sect. 1990-91, 2001—), Los Angeles County Bar Assn. (arbitrator 1987-91). Avocations: fishing, boating, squash, woodworking. Office: Philip Kolczynski Law Corp 3 Hutton Ctr Ste 900 Santa Ana CA 92707

KOLDA, THOMAS JOSEPH, non-profit organization executive; b. Chgo., Dec. 1, 1939; s. Amos Joseph and Cecilia Marie (Baxa) K.; m. Gail Judith Kettler, June 30, 1962; children: Brian Joseph, Jeffrey Thomas. BA, Coe Coll., 1961, MA, 1984; PhD in Adminstrn. and Fin. Mgmt., Columbia Pacific U., 1986. Cert. fund raising exec. Dir. devel./pub. rels. Mt. Mercy Coll., Cedar Rapids, Iowa, 1965-69; v.p. delve. St. Mary's Coll., Orchard Lake, Mich., 1969-71; dir. devel. Roman Catholic Diocese, Tucson, 1971-74; dir. devel./pub. rels. The Pontifical Coll. Josephinum, Columbus, Ohio, 1975-77; dir. trusts and estates Ohio State U. Devel. Fund, Columbus, 1977-85; v.p. devel. Coe Coll., Cedar Rapids, Iowa, 1985-87; dir. trusts and estates Marquette U., Milw., 1987-92; pvt. practice cons. fin. and charitable gift planning, 1992-98; dir. Coll. Edn. Advancement and Univ. Planned Giving U. Wis., Whitewater, 1999—2004; dir. gift planning Case Western Res. U., Cleve., 2005—. V.p. Whitewater City Coun., Wis. Mem. Nat. Soc. Fund Raising Execs. (past pres. Ctrl. Ohio chpt.), Internat. Assn. Fin. Planning (bd. dirs. 1991-95), Coun. Advancement and Support Edn., Nat. Com. on Planned Giving. Office: Adelbert Hall 409 10900 Euclid Ave Cleveland OH 44106 E-mail: koldat@case.edu, koldat@adelphia.net.

KOLDE, RICHARD ARTHUR, insurance company executive, consultant; b. Pomona, Calif., Jan. 25, 1944; s. Arthur and Rosemary (Decker) K.; children: Nicole Rochelle, Eric Christian, Katarina R. AA, Mt. San Antonio Coll., 1963; BS, U. So. Calif., 1965; AS, Mira Costa Coll., 1979. Lic. CPCU. Asst. mgr., mgr. Lord Rebel Ind., Montclair, Costa Mesa and Carlsbad, Calif., 1971-74; agt. Conn. Mut. Life Ins. Co., San Diego and Carlsbad, 1974-77; pres., owner Investment Assocs., Carlsbad, 1977-82, 93—; mng. gen. agt. E.F. Hutton Life Ins. Co., San Diego, 1982—. Cons. Hansch Fin. Group, Laguna Hills, Calif., 1984; cons., recruiter Ky. Gen. Life Ins. Co., 1990-92; mng. gen agt. N.W. Life of Can. Ins. Co, 1991—; v.p. Zoomer's Inc.-West Coast, 2005 Bd. dirs. Boys Club Am., Carlsbad, 1980-84, adv. bd., 1984—; bd. dirs. YMCA, Pomona, 1960-64. With USAF, 1966-71. Decorated Outstanding Unit award Small Arms Expert award Security 1 & 2 Protection of Pres. U.S. award. Mem. Nat. Assn. Life Underwriters (legis. officer 1974—), Calif. Assn. Life Underwriters, Internat. Assn. Fin. Planners (Mem. of Yr. award 1977), U.S. Gymnastics Fedn. (coaching credentials, ofcl. judge collegiate level), VFW, Rotary, Phi Sigma Beta. Republican. Avocation: NRA firearms instr. and range safety officer. Personal E-mail: rkolde@surfbest.net.

KOLE, JANET STEPHANIE, lawyer, writer; b. Washington, Dec. 20, 1946; d. Martin J. and Ruth G. (Goldberg) K. AB, Bryn Mawr Coll., 1968; MA, NYU, 1970; JD, Temple U., 1980. Bar: Pa. 1980, N.J. 1994, N.Y. 2000. Assoc. editor trade books Simon & Schuster, N.Y.C., 1968-70; publicity dir. Am. Arbitration Assn., N.Y.C., 1970-73, freelance photojournalist, 1973-76; law clk. Morgan Lewis & Bockius, Phila., 1977-80; assoc. Schnader, Harrison, Segal & Lewis, Phila., 1980-85; ptnr. Cohen, Shapiro, Polisher, Shiekman & Cohen, Phila., 1985-95; ptnr., chmn. environ. practice group Klehr, Harrison, Harvey, Branzburg & Ellers, Phila., 1995-97; pvt. practice, 1997-2001; chmn. environ. dept. Cooper, Levenson, April, Niedelman & Wagenheim, Atlantic City/Cherry Hill, NJ, 2001—03; chmn. environ. dept., shareholder Flaster Greenberg, PC, Cherry Hill, NJ, 2003—. Chmn. environ. practice group Flaster Greenberg, PC. Author: Post Mortem, 1974; editor Environmental Litigation, 1991, 99; contbr. numerous articles to profl. jour.; past mem. editl. bd. New Am. Rev. Mem. Mayor's Task Force on Rape, N.Y.C., 1972-77; adv. Support Ctr. Child Advs., Phila., 1980—; mem. Phila. Vol. Lawyers for Arts. Fellow Acad. Advocacy, Am. Bar Found.; mem. ABA (former co-chair individual and small firm, former co-chair environ. litigation com., former dir., publs., former coun. mem. sect. litigation, dir. publs., former co-divsn. dir. substantive areas litigation, former editor litigation news, former chmn. com. monographs and unpublished papers, com. spl. pubs., co-chair electronic publ. com., vice-chair, special com. on smart growth and urban policy), ATLA. Office: 3d Fl 1810 Chapel Ave West Cherry Hill NJ 08002 Office Phone: 856-382-2230. Business E-Mail: janet.kole@Flastergreenberg.com.

KOLE, JULIUS S., lawyer; b. Chgo., July 27, 1953; s. Jack H. and Ruth (Rakowsky) K.; m. Dorie Elrod, June 27, 1976; children: Ryan, Frederick, Abby. BS in Fin., U. Ill., Chgo., 1975; JD, John Marshall Law Sch., 1978. Bar: Ill. 1978. Asst. pub. defender Cook County Pub. Defender, Chgo., 1978-80; prin. Law Offices of Julius S. Kole, Buffalo Grove, Ill., 1980—. Fellow Ill. State Bar Assn., Lake County Bar Assn. Jewish. Avocations: sports, reading, motorcycling. Office: 750 W Lake Cook Rd Ste 135 Buffalo Grove IL 60089-2075 Office Phone: 847-541-2204.

KOLEK, ROBERT EDWARD, lawyer; b. Chgo., June 1, 1943; s. Joseph and Mary Kolek; m. Linda L. Bernicchi, Aug. 27, 1966; children: Kimberley M. Szalkus, Robert E. Jr. BBA, Loyola U., Chgo., 1965, JD, 1968. Bar: Ill. 1968. Law clk. to Hon. Thomas Kluczynski, Ill. Supreme Ct., Chgo., 1968-70. Mem. ABA, Chgo. Bar Assn. Roman Catholic. Avocation: photography. Office: Schiff Hardin LLP 6600 Sears Tower Chicago IL 60606 Office Phone: 312-258-5500. E-mail: rKolek@schiffhardin.com.

KOLENDA, JOANNE L., elementary school educator, secondary school educator, volunteer; b. Des Moines; d. Ralph J. and Marian L. Schindler; m. David J. Kolenda; children: Christopher, Daniel, Mark, Laura Reilly. BA, Creighton U., 1964; MA, Nebr. U., 1984. Cert. tchg. English, History, French, Iowa, Nebr. Tchr. English Omaha Pub. Schs., Nebr.; tchr. U. Nebr., Omaha No. H.S., Omaha Tech H.S., Omaha Ctrl. H.S. Author: The Theory of Transcendence, 1984, Testing, Testing: One, Two, Three, 1985. Recipient Rsch. award, Sorbonne U., 1995. Mem.: Act II Playhouse Guild (life), Joslyn Art Mus. Women's Assn. (life), Am. Lawyers Aux. (life), Opera Vols. Internat. (life), Alpha Sigma Alpha (life), Alpha Sigma Nu (life).

KOLER, ROBERT DONALD, medical educator; b. Casper, Wyo., Feb. 14, 1924; s. Joseph Leonard and Nellie (Hayes) K.; m. June Rogers, June 23, 1945; children— Thomas E., Mary L. BA, U. Oreg., 1945, MD, 1947. Intern U. Oreg. Med. Sch., Portland, 1947-48, resident, 1948-49, 51-53, asst. prof. medicine, 1956-59, assoc. prof., 1959-64, prof. medicine, head hematology and exptl. medicine, 1964-69, prof. medicine, head med. genetics, 1967-87, 1976-77, interim v.p. acad. affairs, 1987-89, prof. emeritus, 1989—, assoc. v.p. acad. affairs, 1989—. Mem. cancer research center com. Nat. Cancer Inst., 1968-72 Contbr. articles to profl. jours. Mem. Oreg. Bd. Social Protection, 1967-70. Served to capt. M.C. AUS, 1949-51. Fellow A.C.P., Western Soc. Clin. Research (councilor 1964-66), Western Assn. Physicians (councilor 1975-78); mem. Am. Fedn. Clin. Research, Am. Soc. Hematology, Am. Soc. Human Genetics, Phi Beta Kappa, Alpha Omega Alpha. Home: 9680 NE Blackcap Ln Newberg OR 97132-7115

KOLESAR, PETER JOHN, finance educator, engineering educator, entrepreneur; b. N.Y.C., Nov. 25, 1936; s. John Michael and Agnes (Vajda) K.; m. Nicole Bordat, May 30, 1969 (div. 1981); children: Lara, Alexandre; m. Miriam Larsson, June 18, 1988; 1 child, Angelica. BA, Queens Coll., 1959; BS in Indsl. Engring., Columbia U., 1959, MS, 1962, PhD, 1964. Systems analyst Procter & Gamble, Cin., 1959-61; lectr. Imperial Coll., London, 1964-65; asst. prof. Sch. Engring. Columbia U., N.Y.C., 1965-70, prof. Grad. Sch. Bus., 1975—, rsch. dir. Deming Ctr. Quality Mgmt., 1990; sr. analyst Rand Corp., N.Y.C., 1971-74. Examiner Malcolm Baldrige Nat. Quality Award, 1990-91; chmn. mgmt. com. Mont. Fly Co., LLC, 1999-2003; pres., Montgomery Lake Assn., 2001—; bd. dirs. The Juran Inst.; cons. in field. Assoc. editor Mgmt. Sci.; editor-at-large Interfaces, 1991—; contbr. articles to profl. jours. Recipient Systems Sci. prize NATO, 1976 Fellow AAAS; mem. Ops. Research Soc. Am. (council 1980-83, Lanchester prize 1976), Inst. Mgmt. Scis., Am. Statis. Assn., Am. Soc. Quality Control. Home: 410 Riverside Dr New York NY 10025-7974 Office: Columbia U 408 Uris Hall New York NY 10027 Office Phone: 212-854-4105.

KOLET, MICHELLE L., mathematics educator; d. Fran and Jerry Kolet. BS in Math., Bradley U., Ill., 1992; MS in Math., No. Ill. U., 1997; MA in Ednl. Leadership, Roosevelt U., Ill., 2003. Math. educator Ottawa Twp. H.S., Ill., 1992—94, Schaumburg H.S., Ill., 1994—. Office: Schaumburg High Sch 1100 West Schaumburg Rd Schaumburg IL 60194 Office Phone: 847-755-4600. Office Fax: 847-755-4623.

KOLFF, WILLEM JOHAN, retired internist, medical educator; b. Leiden, Holland, Feb. 14, 1911; arrived in U.S., 1950, naturalized, 1956; s. Jacob and Adriana (de Jonge) Kolff; m. Janke C. Huidekoper, Sept. 4, 1937; children: Jacob, Adriana P., Albert C., Cornelis A., Gualtherus C.M. Student, U. Leiden Med. Sch., 1930—38; MD summa cum laude, U. Groningen, 1946; MD (hon.), U. Turin, Italy, 1969; MD (hon.), Rostock (Germany) U., 1975, U. Bologna, Italy, 1983; DSc (hon.), Allegheny Coll., Meadville, Pa., 1960; DSc (hon.), Tulane U., 1975; DSc (hon.), CUNY, 1982, Temple U., 1983; DSc (hon.), U. Utah, 1983; D. of Tech. Scis. (hon.), Tech. U. Twente, Enschede, The Netherlands, 1986; DSc (hon.), U. Athens, 1988, Aix-Marseille II, 1993. Internist, head med. dept. Mcpl. Hosp., Kampen, Holland; dir. divsn. artificial organs Cleve. Clinic Found., 1950—67; privaat docent, dept. medicine U. Leiden, 1950—67; prof. surgery U. Utah Coll. Medicine, Salt Lake City, 1967—, Disting. prof. medicine and surgery, 1979—, prof. internal medicine, 1981—, dir. Kolff's Lab., 1986—, dir. Inst. Biomed. Engring., dir. divsn. artificial organs, 1967—86, ret. Decorated commandeur Order Van Oranje Netherlands, Orden de Mayo al Merito en el Grade de Gran Official Argentina; named one of Utah's Most Disting. Achievers, 1996; named to, Nat. Inventors Hall of Fame, 1985, 1995, On the Shoulders of Giants Hall of Fame, Cleve., 1989; recipient Landsteiner medal for establishing blood banks during German occupation in Holland, Netherlands Red Cross, 1942, Cameron prize, U. Edinburgh, Scotland, 1964, Gairdner prize, Gairdner Found., 1966, Valentine award, N.Y. Acad. Medicine, 1969, 1st Gold medal, Netherlands Surg. Soc., 1970, Leo Harvey prize, Technion, Israel, 1972, Sr. U.S. Scientist award, Alexander Von Humboldt Found., 1978, Austrian Gewerbeverein's Wilhelm-Exner award, 1980, John Scott medal, City of Phila., 1984, Japan prize, Japan Found. Sci. and Tech., 1986, Rsch. prize, Netherlands Royal Inst. Engrs., 1986, 1st Jean Hamburger award, Internat. Soc. Nephrology, 1987, 1st Edwin Cohn-De Laval award, World Apheresis Assn., 1990, Fed. prize, Fedn. Sci. Med. Assn., 1990, Father of Artificial Organs award and medal, Internat. Soc. Artificial Organs, 1992, Christopher Columbus Discovery award in biomed. rsch., NIH, 1992, Legacy of Life award, LDS Deseret Found., 1995, Lifetime Achievement award, Ahmedabad, India, 1996, Russ prize, Ohio U. and Nat. Acad.of Engring., 2003, The Lasker Award, 2002. Mem.: ACP, NAE (City of Medicine award 1989), AAUP, AAAS, AMA (Sci. Achievement award 1982), European Dialysis and Transplant Assn., Nat. Kidney Found., Am. Soc. Artificial Internal Organs, N.Y. Acad. Scis., Soc. Exptl. Biology and Medicine, Am. Physiol. Soc., Academia Nacional de Medicine (hon.; Colombia), Austrian Soc. Nephrology (hon.), Rotary. Achievements include patents for ventricular assist device and method of manufacturing; collapsible artificial ventricle and pumping shell; ventricular assist device with volumne displacement chamber; electrohydraulic heart with septum mounted pump; muscle and air powered left ventricular assist device; development of artificial kidney for clinical use, 1943; heart-lung machine, 1949; first membrane oxygenator, 1955; disposable twin-coil kidney, 1956; balloon pump, 1962; wearable artificial kidney (WAK), 1981; artificial heart, 1958; human implantation, Dr. Barney Clark, 1982.*

KOLIANI, LEONARDI, physician; b. Athens, Greece, Sept. 13, 1956; cmae to U.S., 1958; s. Ismet and Nezaqet (Kaso) K.; m. Syzana Koliani, July 19, 1980; children: Andrew, Jenna, Tara, Brett. BS, U. Conn., 1978; MD, U. del Noreste, Tampico, Mex., 1983. Diplomate Am. Bd. Internal Medicine. Intern, resident in medicine St. Mary's Hosp., Waterbury, Conn., 1984-87; pvt. practice, Waterbury, Conn., 1987—. Office: Phoenix Internal Med Assocs 500 Chase Pkwy Waterbury CT 06708-3019 Office Phone: 203-754-5504.

KOLIN, RANDY RANDALL ROSS, psychologist; b. Columbus, Ohio, Jan. 20, 1967; s. Barry Ronald and Ceilia Tema Kolin; m. Mellisa Paige Rubin, June 29, 1997; children: Madelyn Haley, Samantha Lee. BA in Psychology, Ohio State U., 1989; MEd, DePaul U., Ill., 1992; D of Psychology, Ill. Sch. of Profl. Psychology, 2000. Lic. Psychologist Calif. Bd. of Psychology, 2002. Clinnical mgr. Ctr. for Drug Free Living, Orlando, Fla., 2000—00; psychologist - dept of psychiatry chem. dependency svcs. Kaiser Permanent, Union City, Calif., 2001—02; psychologist San Quentin State Prison, Calif., 2002—04; adj. faculty prof. New Coll. Of Calif., San Francisco, 2002—04; psychologist Randy Kolin Psy.D, Lafayette, CA, Calif., 2004—. Avocations: gardening, exercise. Office: Randy Kolin PsyD 3182 Old Tunnel Rd Lafayette CA 94549 Office Phone: 925-437-3314. Office Fax: 925-376-5199. Personal E-mail: randy_kolin@yahoo.com.

KOLINSKY, MICHAEL ALLEN, emergency physician; b. Phila., Dec. 23, 1947; s. Maurice and Lenore (Rose) K.; m. Barbara Victorine, June 20, 1981; children: Nicole, Daniel, Samuel. BA, U. Wis., 1970; MD, Rush U., 1979. Diplomate Am. Bd. Emergency Medicine. Staff physician emergency dept. River Parishes Hosp., LaPlace, La., 1982-85; co-med. dir. emergency dept. Meadowcrest Hosp., Gretna, La., 1985-92; co-med. dir. City of New Orleans Emergency Med. Svcs., 1987—2004; med. dir. emergency dept. Tulane U. Med. Ctr., New Orleans, 1992—. Fellow Am. Acad. Emergency Medicine. Office: Tulane Med Ctr Emergency Dept 1415 Tulane Ave New Orleans LA 70112-2600 E-mail: kolinsky@tulane.edu.

KOLKER, ADAM ROSS, plastic surgeon; s. Paul and Susan Kolker; m. Lauren Pia Silverman, Jan. 27, 2001. BS in Bio Arts, Union Coll., NY, 1988; MD cum laude, Albany Med. Coll., 1990. Diplomate Am. Bd. Plastic Surgery, Am. Bd. Surgery, Nat. Bd. Med. Examiners. Clin. asst. prof. surgery Mt. Sinai Sch. Medicine. Attending plastic surgeon St. Vincent's Hosp. and Med. Ctr., N.Y.C., NYU Downtown Hosp., Manhattan Eye, Ear and Throat Hosp., The Mt. Sinai Hosp. Fellow, Harvard Med. Sch., U. Melbourne, Australia. Fellow: ACS; mem.: Am. Soc. Aesthetic Plastic Surgeons, Am. Soc. Plastic Surgeons.

KOLKER, ALLAN ERWIN, ophthalmologist; b. St. Louis, Nov. 2, 1933; s. Paul P. and Jean Kolker; m. Jacquelyn Krupin, Dec. 8, 1957; children: Robin, Marci, David, Scott. AB, Washington U., St. Louis, 1953, MD, 1957. Diplomate Am. Bd. Ophthalmology (dir. 1994-98). Intern St. Louis Children's Hosp., 1957-58; resident in ophthalmology Washington U./Barnes Hosp., St. Louis, 1960-65; glaucoma fellow Washington U., St. Louis, 1963—64, staff, faculty, 1964—, prof. ophthalmology, 1974-96, clin. prof. ophthalmology, 1996—. Med. dir. The Glaucoma Inst., pvt. practice; mem. glaucoma com. Prevent Blindness Am. Author: (with J. Hetherington) Becker and Shaffer's Diagnosis and Therapy of the Glaucomas, 3d, 4th, 5th edit., 1983, (with T. Krupin) Complications in Ophthalmic Surgery, 1999; contbr. numerous articles to profl. jours., chpts. to books. Served with USPHS, 1958-60. NIH spl. fellow, 1963-65; grantee, 1969-80; 1st Disting. Eye Alumni award Washington U., 1990, Alumni/Faculty award Washington U. Sch. Medicine, 2002. Mem. AMA, Assn. Rsch. in Vision and Ophthalmology, Am. Acad. Ophthalmology (mem. coun. 1986-92, trustee 1994-98, Life Achievement award 2002), Am. Bd. Ophthalmology (dir. 1994-98), Am. Ophthal. Soc., Am. Glaucoma Soc. (founding mem., pres. 1992-94, Spl. Honor award 2002), Mo. Ophthal. Soc. (pres. 1986-87), St. Louis Med. Soc. Home: 176 Plantation Dr Saint Louis MO 63141-8352 Office: Glaucoma Cons Midwest 12601 Olive Blvd Saint Louis MO 63141-6313 Office Phone: 314-878-7962.

KOLKER, CHARLES JOHN, lawyer; b. Lawton, Okla., Nov. 8, 1940; s. Charles Hohn and Rosemary (Brown) K.; m. Catherine Sue Martin, June 2, 1990; children: Charles John III, Cynthia Lynn, Christopher Thomas. BS, St. Louis U., 1962, JD, 1968. Bar: Ill. 1968, Mo. 1969, U.S. Dist. Ct. (so dist.) Ill. 1969, U.S. Ct. Appeals (7th cir.) 1972, U.S. Supreme Ct. 1976. Ptnr. Carr, Raffaelle, Cook & Kolker, East St. Louis, Ill., 1968-71; pvt. practice East St. Louis, Bellville, Ill., 1971—. Chmn. Upjohn Home Health Care Adv. Com., St. Clair, Ill., 1985-87, corp. counsel, dir. legal dept. City of East St. Louis, 1971-75; atty. 23 local chpts. Am. Fedn. Tchrs., Union Privilege Legal Svcs. Bd. dirs. East St. Louis chpt. NAACP, 1984-97; organizer, dir. over 12 ind. Dem. orgns., St. Clair and Madison County, Ill., 1965—; candidate for justice Ill. Supreme Ct., 1988; mem. adv. com. Gibson Home Health Care, St. Clair County, Ill., 1990—; bd. dirs. Racial Harmony, 1993—. Mem. ATLA, Ill. Bar Assn., Mo. Bar Assn., Wildwood Lake Estates Assn. (pres. 1995-97). Roman Catholic. Avocation: flying. Office: 9423 W Main St Belleville IL 62223-1712

KOLKER, LAWRENCE PAUL, lawyer; b. Huntington, N.Y., Aug. 1, 1956; s. Justin William and Sondra Geraldine (Budow) K.; m. Emily Diane Porter, June 14, 1981; children: Danielle, Jeremy, Madeline. BA, SUNY, Binghamton, 1978; JD, Bklyn. U., 1983. Bar: N.Y. 1984, U.S. Dist. Ct. (so. and ea. dists.) N.Y. 1984, U.S. Dist. Ct. (we. dist.) Mich. 1992, U.S. Ct. Appeals (2d cir.) 1989, U.S. Ct. Appeals (11th cir.) 1992. Clk. Hon. Henry F. Werker, N.Y.C., 1981-82; asst. corp. counsel N.Y.C. Law Dept., 1983-87; assoc. Hill, Betts & Nash, N.Y.C., 1987-89; ptnr. Wolf, Haldenstein, Adler, Freeman & Herz, LLP, N.Y.C., 1989—. Mem. N.Y. State Bar Assn., Assn. of Bar of City of N.Y. Avocations: carpentry, cooking, guitar, cross country skiing, tennis. Office: Wolf Haldenstein Adler Freeman & Herz LLP 270 Madison Ave New York NY 10016-0601 E-mail: kolker@whafh.com.

KOLKEY, DANIEL MILES, former judge, lawyer; b. Chgo., Apr. 21, 1952; s. Eugene Louis and Gilda Penelope (Cowan) K.; m. Donna Lynn Christie, May 15, 1982; children: Eugene, William, Christopher, Jonathan. BA, Stanford U., 1974; JD, Harvard U., 1977. Bar: Calif. 1977, U.S. Dist. Ct. (ea. dist.) Calif. 1978, U.S. Dist. Ct. (cen. dist.) Calif. 1979, U.S. Ct. Appeals (9th cir.) 1979, U.S. Dist. Ct. (no. dist.) Calif. 1980, U.S. Supreme Ct. 1983, U.S. Dist. Ct. Ariz. 1992, U.S. Dist. Ct. (so. dist.) Calif. 1994. Law clk. U.S. Dist. Ct. judge, N.Y.C., 1977-78; assoc. Gibson Dunn & Crutcher, L.A., 1978-84, ptnr., 1985-94; counsel to Gov., legal affairs sec. to Calif. Gov. Pete Wilson, 1995-98; assoc. justice Calif. Ct. Appeal, 3rd Appellate Dist., Sacramento, 1998—2003; ptnr. Gibson, Dunn & Crutcher, San Francisco, 2003—. Arbitrator bi-nat. panel for U.S.-Can. Free Trade Agreement, 1990—94; commr. Calif. Law Revision Commn., 1992—94, vice chair, 1993—94, chair, 1994; mem. Blue Ribbon Commn. on Jury Sys. Improvement, 1996; adj. prof. McGeorge Sch. Law, 2001—04; mem. Calif. State-Fed. Jud. Coun., 2001—03. Co-editor: Practitioner's Handbook on International Arbitration and Mediation, 2002; contbr. articles to profl. jours. Co-chmn. internat. rels. sect. Town Hall Calif., L.A., 1985—90; chmn. internat. trade legis. subcom., internat. commerce steering com. L.A. Area C. of C., 1983—91, law and justice com., 1993—94; adv. coun., exec. com. Asia Pacific Ctr. for Resolution of Internat. Bus. Disputes, 1991—94; mem. L.A. Com. on Fgn. Rels., 1983—95, Pacific Coun. Internat. Policy, 1999—; gen. counsel Citizens Rsch. Found., 1990—94; assoc. mem. ctrl. com. Calif. Rep. Party, 1983—94, mem. ctrl. com., 1995—98; dep. gen. coun. credentials com. Rep. Nat. Conv., 1992, alt. Calif. Delegation, 1992, Calif. del., 1996; bd. dirs. L.A. Ctr. for Internat. Comml. Arbitration, 1986—94, treas., 1986—88, v.p., 1988—90, pres., 1990—94. Master Anthony Kennedy Inns. of Ct., 1996-99. Mem. Am. Arbitration Assn. (panel of arbitrators, arbitrator large complex case dispute resolution program 1993-94), Am. Law Inst., Chartered Inst. Arbitrators, London (assoc. 1986-94), Friends of Wilton Park So. Calif. (chmn. exec. com. 1986-94, exec. com. 1986—). Office: Gibson Dunn & Crutcher LLP One Montgomery St 31st Fl San Francisco CA 94104-4505

KOLKIN, MITCHELL, lawyer; b. Mar. 12, 1950; BA, U. Pa., 1971; JD, Duke U., 1976. Bar: Calif. 1976, Md. 1981. Ptnr., transactional bus. Venable LLP (formerly Venable, Baetjer & Howard), Balt. Note, comment editor Duke Law Jour., 1975-76. Mem. ABA, Md. State Bar Assn., Bar Assn. Balt. City, State Bar Calif., Phi Beta Kappa. Address: Venable LLP 1800 Mercantile Bank & Trust Blg 2 Hopkins Plz Baltimore MD 21201-2930 Office Phone: 410-244-7656. Office Fax: 410-244-7742. Business E-Mail: mkolkin@venable.com.

KOLKO, GABRIEL, historian, educator; b. Paterson, N.J., Aug. 17, 1932; s. Philip and Lillian Kolko; m. Joyce Manning, June 11, 1955. BA, Kent State U., 1954; MS, U. Wis., 1955; PhD, Harvard U., 1962. Assoc. prof. U. Pa., 1964-68; prof. history SUNY-Buffalo, 1968-70, York U., Toronto, Ont., Can., 1970-92, Disting. research prof., 1986-92, prof. emeritus, 1992—. Author: Wealth and Power in America, 1962; The Triumph of Conservatism, 1963; author: Railroads and Regulations, The Politics of War, 1968, The Roots of American Foreign Policy, 1969, The Limits of Power, 1972, Main Currents in Modern American History, 1976, Anatomy of a War, 1985, Confronting the Third World, 1988, Century of War, 1994, Vietnam, Anatomy of a Peace, 1997, Another Century of War?, 2002; contbr. articles to profl. jours. Fellow Social Sci. Research Council, 1963-64; Guggenheim fellow, 1966-67; fellow Am. Council Learned Socs., 1971-72; Killam fellow, 1974-75, 82-84 Fellow Royal Soc. Can. Home: Wittenburgergracht 53 1018 MX Amsterdam Netherlands E-mail: kolko@chello.nl.

KOLLAER, JIM C., real estate executive, architect; b. Amarillo, Tex., Jan. 5, 1943; s. Walter W. and Margaret M. Kollaer; 1 child, Andrew N. Student, Amarillo Coll., 1960-62, La. State U., 1962-65; BArch, Tex. Tech. U., 1969. Lic. architect, Tex.; lic. broker, Tex. V.p., dir. urban design RKA Inc. Assoc., Dallas, 1969-75; sr. planner CRS Inc., Houston, 1975-76, assoc., 1976-77, v.p., dir. mktg., 1977-80; pres. Houston divsn. Henry Miller Co., Houston, 1980-85; pres. Henry S. Miller/Grubb & Ellis, 1985-89, Kollaer Internat., 1989-90; pres., CEO Greater Houston Partnership, 1990—. Past chmn. Tex. Bus. Hall of Fame; bd.dir. Ctr. Houston's (Tex.) Future; cons. and lectr. in field. Sr. fellow Am. Leadership Forum. Fellow AIA; mem. Am. C. of C. Execs. (bd. dirs.), Tex. Soc. Archs., Urban Land Inst., Tex. Assn. Realtors, Nat. Assn. Realtors, Houston Wilderness (bd. dirs.), U.S. C. of C. (bd. dirs.), Chamber Found. (bd. dirs.), Coronado Club. Republican. Presbyterian. Office: Greater Houston Partnership 1200 Smith St Ste 700 Houston TX 77002-4400 E-mail: jkollaer@houston.org.

KOLLAR, LINDA RANDLETT, lawyer; b. Malden, Mass., Nov. 24, 1944; d. Arthur Myrle and Nathalie Marie Randlett. BA with honors, Scripps Coll., 1966; JD cum laude, Pepperdine U., 1985. Bar: Calif. 1986, U.S. Dist. Ct. (ctrl. dist.) Calif. 1988, U.S. Ct. Appeals (9th cir.) 1990. Staff family crisis intervention Dept. Social Svcs., L.A., 1967—76; juvenile ct. dependency case worker L.A. County, 1976—79; investigator Juvenile Ct., L.A., Calif., 1979—82; extern, pub. defender Ventura County, 1983; clk. Nordman, Cormany, Hair & Compton, Oxnard, Calif., 1984; assoc. Price Postel & Parma, Santa Barbara, Calif., 1985—87, Silver & Arsht, Westlake Village, Calif., 1987—93; ptnr. Weinhart & Riley, L.A., 1993—97, Hooper, Lundy & Bookman, L.A., 1997—. Mem. Alliance Children and Family Svcs., Sacramento, 1999—; pres., bd. dirs., co-founder Western Child Welfare Law Ctr., Pasadena, Calif., 1999—; bd. profl. stds. Pepperdine U. Sch. Law; presenter in field. Contbr. chapters to books, articles to profl. jours. Recipient award for contbn. to providers of foster care and role model for young women, David and Margaret Home, LaVerne, Calif., 2000. Mem.: ABA, L.A. County Bar Assn., Calif. Acad. Health Care Attys., State Bar Calif., Phi Delta Phi. Office: Hooper Lundy & Bookman 1875 Century Park East #1600 Los Angeles CA 90067

KOLLAR, RENE M, religious studies educator, historian; b. Hastings, Pa., June 21, 1947; s. Matthew J Kollar and Bernice C Kosic. BA, St. Vincent Coll., 1970; MDiv, St. Vincent Seminary, 1973; MA, U. Md., 1975, PhD, 1981. Asst. prof. hist. St. Vincent Coll., Latrobe, Pa., 1982—85, assoc. prof. hist., 1985—91, chmn., dept. hist., 1991—2004, prof. hist., 1991—; prof. church hist. St. Vincent Seminary, 1997—; dean, sch. humanities and fine arts St. Vincent Coll., 2004—. Mem. St. Vincent Coll. Corp. Bd. Incorporators, 1990—96, 1997—; vis. scholar Heythrop Coll., U. London, 1996—97. Mem. editl. bd. Am. Benedictine Rev., 1990—94, 2001—; author: (book) Westminster Cathedral from Dream to Reality, 1987, The Return of the Benedictines to London, 1990, Searching for Raymond: Anglicanism Spiritualism and Bereavment Between the World Wars, 2002; contbr. over 150 articles and book reviews. Co-recipient Freedom Project Tchg. grant, John Templeton Found., 2001; hon. rsch. fellow, King's Coll., U. London, 1987—88, Faculty Develop. grant, St. Vincent Coll., 1984—89, 1993, 1994, 1996, 2001, 2002. Mem.: Am. Cath. Hist. Assn., Royal Hist. Soc., Am.Hist. Assn. Roman Cath. Avocations: reading, jogging, travel. Home: St Vincent Archabbey Latrobe PA 15650 Office: St Vincent Coll 300 Fraser Purchase Rd Latrobe PA 15650 Office Phone: 724-805-2343. Business E-Mail: rkollar@stvincent.edu.

KOLLAR-KOTELLY, COLLEEN, federal judge; b. Apr. 17, 1943; m. John T. Kotelly. BA, Cath. U., 1965, JD, 1968. Law clerk to Hon. Catherine Kelly, Dist. Columbia Ct. Appeals, 1968—69; atty. criminal divsn. US Dept. Justice, 1969-72; chief legal counsel St. Elizabeth's Hosp., 1972-84; judge DC Superior Ct., 1984-97, dep. presiding judge, criminal divsn., 1995—97; dist. judge US Dist. Ct. DC, 1997—. Apptd. mem. Judicial Conf. Com. Fin. Disclosure by Chief Justice Rehnquist, 2000—02; apptd. to presiding judge US Foreign Intelligence Surveillance Ct. by Chief Justice Rehnquist, 2002—09; adj. prof. joint tchg. program on mental health and the law Georgetown U. Sch. Medicine, chair bd. art trust for superior ct. Fellow: ABA; mem.: Thurgood Marshall Inn of Ct. (founding mem.). Office: 333 Constitution Ave NW Washington DC 20001-2802

KOLLER, DAPHNE, computer scientist; BS in Math. and Computer sci., Hebrew U., Jerusalem, Israel, 1985, MSc in Computer sci., 1986; PhD, Stanford U., Calif., 1993; postdoctoral fellow, UC Berkeley, 1993—95. Asst. prof., computer sci. Stanford U., Calif., 1995—2001, assoc. prof., computer sci., 2001—. Author: published in jour. such as Games and Economic Behavior, Artificial Intelligence, Science, and Nature Genetics. Named a MacArthur Fellow, 2004; recipient Young Investigator award, Office of Naval Rsch., 1999. Office: Computer Sci Dept Stanford U 353 Serra Mall Stanford CA 94305-9025

KOLLER, LOREN D., veterinary medicine educator; b. Pomeroy, Wash., June 16, 1940; s. Edwin C. and Doris K. (Shelton) K.; m. Kathleen Noel Ringness, Sept. 7, 1963; children: Susan E., Michael D., Christopher L. DVM, Wash. State U., 1965; MS, U. Wis., 1969, PhD, 1971. Head diagnostic and comparative pathology Nat. Inst. Environ. Health Scis., Research Triangle Park, NC, 1971-72; rsch. assoc. dept. vet. medicine Oreg. State U., Corvallis, 1972-76, assoc. prof., 1976-78, prof., 1995—2001, dean Coll. Vet. Medicine, 1985-95; assoc. prof. dept. vet. medicine, asst. dean U. Idaho, Moscow, 1978-81, assoc. prof., assoc. dean, 1981-82, prof., assoc. dean, 1982-85; owner Loren Koller & Assocs., LLC, 2001—. Rsch. asst. dept. vet. sci. U. Wis., Madison, 1968-71; assoc. veterinarian Blue Cross Vet. Clinic, Corvallis, 1965-66; mem. Nat. Adv. Com. to Establish Acute Exposure Guidelines for Hazardous Substances Commn. Contbr. articles to profl. jours., chpts. to books. Served to capt. M.C., U.S. Army, 1966-68. Grantee NIH, USDA, Dow Chem. Co., EPA, WHO, FDA, Merck Sharp & Dohme, Warner-Lambert, Pew Found. Fellow Acad. Toxicol. Sci.; mem. AVMA, NAS (mem. com. toxicology and Inst. of Medicine). Personal E-mail: kollerl@pacifier.com.

KOLLER, MATTHEW C., music educator; b. Camden, NJ, July 20, 1973; s. Charles H and Sharon M Koller; m. Christina R Spear, July 27, 1996; 1 child, Christian Alexander. MusB, Westminster Choir Coll. of Rider U., 1991—95. Dir. of choral activities and band dir. Ctrl. Mid. Sch., Stirling, NJ, 1998—; musical dir. Watchung Hills Regional H.S., Warren, NJ, 1998—. Musical director Jekyll and Hyde (Paper Mill Playhouse Rising Star award for Outstanding Musical Direction, 2002), Godspell (Paper Mill Playhouse Rising Star award Nomination for Outstanding Musical Direction). Recipient Champion of Children, Long Hill Twp. Bd. of Edn., 2005. Mem.: Am. Choral Directors Assn. R-Consevative. Roman Catholic. Office Phone: 908-647-2311.

KOLLER, SHIRLEY LEAVITT, sculptor; b. Youngstown, Ohio, Apr. 6, 1921; d. Benjamin Harrison and Rose (Cohen) Leavitt; m. Herbert Richard Koller Mar. 7, 1943 (dec. June 1988); children: Donald Lee, Susan Koller Van Horne, Laura Frances. Diploma, Cleve. Inst. Art, 1942; BS, Western Res. U., Cleve., 1942; MFA, Am. U., 1972. Lectr. No. Va. C.C., Alexandria, 1977-92; curator art program AAAS, 1997—. Lectr. sr. citizens Jewish Cmty. Ctr. of Greater Washington, Rockville, Md., 1990, 95, Washington Hebrew Congregation, Washington, 1995, Georgetown, 2001; appearance on Peter Jennings/ABC World News Tonight, 1991, Arlington Cable, 1990, Voice of Am. Radio, 1992; adj. faculty Md. Coll. of Art & Design, 1991-93; vis. artist Fairfax County Pub. Schs., 1982-85; visual art specialist, Fillmore Arts Ctr., Washington, 1977-81; spkr. in field. Artist: (3-D wall installation) The Joy of Transportation, 1989-93 (comm. 1989); writer: (newsletter) Eye Wash, 1990-92; curator Tri-State Ednl. Assn. exhibits, Washington; one-woman shows include Watkins Gallery, Am. U., 1972, Gate House Gallery, Washington, 1994, Mansion Art Gallery, Rockville, 1993, Friedholm Fine Arts Gallery, Asheville, NC, 1991, O Street Studios, Washington, 1990, AAAS/Atrium Gallery, Washington, 1989-90, Artisans of Va. Invitational, 2004—, others; exhibited in group shows at Gallery 10, Washington, 1998, Tri-State Sculptors Ednl. Assn., Washington, 1997, Associated Artists of Winston-Salem, NC, 1996, 99, Tri-State Sculptors Conf., U. SC, Spartenburg, 1996, ARTS 901 E Street, Washington, 1996, AAAS, Washington, 1995-96, Newhouse Ctr. for Contemporary Art, S.I., NY, 1995-96, Mill River Gallery, Ellicott City, Md., 1999, Tysons Galleria II, Vienna, Va., 1999, Washington Sculptors Group, 1998-2000, Coastal Carolina U., Myrtle Beach, 1999, Grounds for Sculpture, Hamilton, NJ, 2000, 02, Mus. Art, Beijing, 2001, Brookside Gardens, 2002-03, Meridith Coll., Raleigh, NC, 2003, Artists In Our Midst, Washington, 2003, Capetown (South Africa) U., 2003, Washington Sculptors Group Ann. Exhbn., Washington, 2004, Tri-State Sculptors Conf., Winston-Salem, NC, 2004, Am. Ctr. for Physics, College Park, Md., 2004-05, others; work collected at Ballston Metro Sta., Arlington, Va., First Am. Bank, Va. Commonwealth U., U. Md., AAAS/Washington, Akin Group, Law Offices, Washington, IBM Rsch. Hdqrs., Durham, NC, Internat. Sculpture Ctr., Hamilton NJ, Tri State Sculptors Edn. Assn., U. NC, Brevard, Am. Ctr. for Physics, 2004-05, others. Finalist Best Pub. Art Sculpture award, Rockville, 2004; named to Hall of Fame, Shaker Heights (Ohio) H.S., 2001; recipient Editor's Choice award, Internat. Libr. Photography, 1998. Mem. Tri-State Sculptors Ednl. Assn. (life), Washington Sculptors Group. Democrat. Jewish. Avocations: travel, lecturing, gourmet cooking. Home: 2700 Virginia Ave NW Washington DC 20037-1908 E-mail: shirleyartkoller@metronets.com.

KOLLI, SAI, publishing executive; b. Hyderabad, India, July 28, 1966; arrived in U.S., 1989; s. Koteswara R. and Lakshmi B. Kolli; m. Rajeswari R. Rao, May 24, 1968; children: Vivek, Divya. M in Mgmt. Studies, Birla Inst. Tech. and Sci., Pilani, India, 1987, M in Engring., 1988; MS, U. Louisville, 1992, PhD, 1994. Grad. asst. U. Louisville, 1990-94; lectr. U. Tex., Dallas, 1995-2001; sr. analyst Am. Airlines, Ft. Worth, 1995-98, mgr. fin. analysis, 1998-2000, contr., 2000-01, dir., 2001—03; dir. ops. Dallas Morning News, 2003—. Author: (book) Management Consulting, 2000, Production and Operations Management, 2000; editor: Manufacturing Decision Support Systems, 1997. All. Am. scholar, U.S. Achievement Acad. Univs., 1993. Mem.: INFORMS (cluster chmn. meeting 1999, sec. Dallas-Ft. Worth chpt. 1995—97, pres. Dallas-Ft. Worth chpt. 1998), Alpha Pi Mu (sec. student chpt. 1991—92, newsletter editor enging. economy divsn. 1993—94). Home: 437 Waterview Dr Coppell TX 75019 Office: Dallas Morning News PO Box 655237 Dallas TX 75265 Business E-Mail: skolli@dallasnews.com. E-mail: ukolli@comcast.net.

KOLLIAS, JIM HARRY, music educator; b. Laguna Beach, Calif., Jan. 4, 1966; s. Harry D. and Linda Kollias; m. Doris C. Kateyiannis, Aug. 20, 1989; 1 child, Christina Eleftheria; 1 child, Harrison James. BA in Music, UCLA, 1987; MS in Music Edn., U. Ill., Champaign-Urbana, 1996. Cert. profl. clear single subject instrn. credential, music Calif. Instrumental music dir. Vina Danks Mid. Sch., Ontario, Calif., 1988—94, Columbus Tustin Mid. Sch., Tustin, 1994—2004, C. E. Utt Mid. Sch., Tustin, 1994—96; orch. dir. Tustin H.S., Calif., 2000—; dir. bands and orch. Beckman H.S., 2004—. Guest condr. San Bernardino County H.S. Honor Orch., Calif., 1998, San Bernardino County Concert Orch., Calif., 2000; mentor tchr. Ontario Montclair Sch. Dist., Ontario, 1993—94, Tustin Unified Sch. Dist., 1996—97; chairperson Tustin Unified Sch. Dist. Facilities Com., 1995—96; presenter in field. Composer: (music) Everyone Can Play in Twelve Keys, 1990; contbr. articles to profl. jours. Named Toast of the Town, Town & Country Com., Orange County Philharm. Soc., 2001; recipient Pied Piper award, So. Calif. Sch. Band & Orch. Assn., 1996, PTSA Hon. Svc. award, Vina Danks Mid. Sch. PTSA, 1992; grantee, Orange County Philharm. Soc., Tustin Pub. Schs. Found. Mem.: Calif. Music Educators Assn., San Bernardino County Music Educators Assn. (secondary orch. rep. 1993—94), So. Calif. Sch. Band & Orch. Assn. (v.p. elem. & mid. sch. edn. 1999—2001). Personal E-mail: jhkollias@yahoo.com. Business E-Mail: jkollias@tustin.k12.ca.us.

KOLMAN, KATHLEEN, music educator; b. Butte, Mont., Dec. 16, 1956; d. William Charles and Leocadia Ramirez Kolman; 1 child, Rose Elizabeth Kimbell. BS, Coll. Life Long Learning, 2003; MA, Lesley U., 2005. Profl. seamstress, Plymouth, NH, 1990—2002; singer, rec. artist, 1990—2005; tchr. music Vintage Fret Shop, Ashland, 2003—05, John Stark Regional High Sch., Weare, 2003—05. Bd. dirs. CLL Alumni Bd., Bow, NH; v.p. Vocal Jazz Coalition, N.Y.C., 2003—05. Singer: (albums) The Dreamer, 1999; singer: (dancer) USO. Mem.: Internat. Assn. Jazz Educators, Music Educators Nat. Com., Alpha Sigma Lambda. Avocations: tai chi, jazz, dance. Home: PO Box 843 Plymouth NH 03264 Office: John Stark Regional High Sch 618 N Stark Hwy Weare NH 03281

KOLMAN, MARK HERBERT, lawyer; b. Balt., Aug. 24, 1946; s. Lester Norman and Jeannette (Carmel) K.; m. Susan Dellheim, July 26, 1998; 1 child, Margaret Carmel. BA in History, Bucknell U., 1968; JD, U. Md., 1971. Bar: Md. 1972, D.C. 1991, U.S. Dist. Ct. Md. 1980, U.S. Ct. Appeals (4th cir.) 1980, U.S. Supreme Ct. 1980, U.S. Dist. Ct. D.C. 1991. Asst. state's atty. City of Balt., 1971-75, County of Balt., Towson, Md., 1975-80; asst. fed. defender Pub. Defender's Office, Balt., 1980; asst. U.S. atty. Balt., 1980-84; assoc. Gordon, Feinblatt, Rothman, Hoffberger & Hollander, Balt., 1984-86, ptnr., 1986-91, chmn. litigation dept., 1991; ptnr. Anderson Kill Olick & Oshinsky, P.C., Washington, 1991-96, Dickstein Shapiro Morin & Oshinsky, Washington, 1996—. Trustee Md. chpt. Leukemia Soc. Am., 1987-91; mem. adv. bd. Greenebaum Cancer Ctr.; bd. dirs. Nat. Coalition for Cancer Survivorship, 1993-95. Mem. ABA, Fed. Bar Assn. (chmn. bd. govs. 1990-91, pres. Md. chpt. 1994-95, 4th cir. officer 1995-96), Md. Bar Assn., Balt. County Bar Assn., Md. State's Attys. Assn. (bd. dirs. 1976-91), Md. Trial Lawyers Assn., Md. Criminal Def. Attys. Assn. Avocations: golf, swimming, scuba. Home: 9775 Polished Stone Columbia MD 21046-2800 Office: Dickstein Shapiro Morin Oshinsky 2101 L St NW Washington DC 20037-1526

KOLMES, STEVEN ALBERT, biologist, educator; b. Poughkeepsie, NY, Sept. 17, 1954; s. Isaac and Beatrice (Stoller) K.; m. Linda Ann Fergusson, June 20, 1987; children: Sara Kjellaug, Elijah John. BS in Zoology, Ohio U., 1976; MS, U. Wis., 1978, PhD, 1984. Lectr. U. Wis., Madison, 1983-84; asst. prof. biology Hobart & William Smith Colls., Geneva, NY, 1984-89, chmn. biology dept., 1988-90, assoc. prof., 1989-94, prof., environ. studies coord., 1994-95; Molter chair sci., environ. studies dir., prof. biology U. Portland, Oreg., 1995—. Vis. scientist Univ. Coll., Cardiff, Wales, 1987, Simon Fraser U., Burnaby, BC, 1985, BC, 86; biology coord. Simcalc Project, Dartmouth, Mass., 1994—95, mem. adv. bd., 1993—95; mentor Oreg. Collaborative Excellence in Preparation of Tchrs., 1995—99; mem. Willamette River and Lower Columbia River Salmonid Tech. Recovery Team, 2000—; mem.

toxicology tech. adv. com. Dept. Environ. Quality, 2001—03; mem. exec. com. Edn. Sustainable Western Network, 2005—. Issue editor Coun. on Undergrad. Rsch. Quar., 1996-98; contbr. articles to profl. jours. Mem. vestry St. Peter's Ch., Geneva, 1992-95. Fulbright rsch. scholar, 1991; grantee USDA, 1993-95, NSF, 1996-98, NOAA, 2001-03. Mem. AAAS, Animal Behavior Soc. (mem. membership com. 1993-96), Entomol. Soc. Am., Fulbright Assn. (life). Democrat. Episcopalian. Achievements include research in inactive constituents of pesticide formulations, honeybee colonies containing behaviorally distinct patrilines. Office: Univ Portland Dept Biology 5000 N Willamette Blvd Portland OR 97203-5743 Business E-Mail: kolmes@up.edu.

KOLODEY, FRED JAMES, lawyer; b. LaCoste, Tex., Mar. 5, 1936; s. Raymond and Mamie V. (Newman) K.; children: Trecia Anne Estep, Michele Leigh Winn; m. Helen Gable McIntosh, June 10, 1989. BA, Tex. Christian U., 1962; LL.B., So. Methodist U., 1964. Bar: Tex. 1964. Since practiced in, Dallas; ptnr. Kolodey & Thomas, 1975-83, of counsel, 1983-94, Thomas, Sheehan & Culp, 1994—2001, Kolodey, Thomas & Blackwood, 2001—. Pres. Dallas Jr. Bar Assn., 1969 Comments editor: Southwestern Law Jour, 1963-64. Mem. dist. hearing office panel Dallas Community Coll., 1974, Democratic precinct chmn., 1968-73. Mem. Tex., Dallas bar assns., Delta Theta Phi (pres. 1963, Nat. award 1964), Alpha Chi, Pi Sigma Alpha. Home: 540 Mariah Bay Dr Heath TX 75032-7626 Office Phone: 214-782-1610.

KOLODNER, RICHARD DAVID, biochemist, educator; b. Morristown, N.J., Apr. 3, 1951; s. Ignace Izack and Ethel (Zelnick) Kolodner; m. Karin Ann Gregory, Aug. 6, 1983 (div. May 1991). BS, U. Calif., Irvine, 1971, PhD, 1975; MS (hon.), Harvard U., 1988. Rsch. fellow Harvard U. Med. Sch., Boston, 1975-78; asst. prof. Dana Farber Cancer Inst. and Harvard U. Med. Sch., Boston, 1978-83, assoc. prof., 1983-88, prof. biochemistry, 1988-97; chmn. divsn. cellular molecular biology Dana-Farber Cancer Inst., Boston, 1991-94, head x-ray crystallography lab., 1991-97, chmn. divsn. of human cancer genetics, 1995-97; prof. medicine, mem. Cancer Ctr. U. Calif. Med. Sch., San Diego, 1997—; mem. Ludwig Inst. Cancer Rsch., San Diego, 1997—, assoc. dir. N.Y., 2004—. Editor: PLASMID Jour., 1986—95; assoc. editor: Cancer Rsch. Jour., 1995—2000, Cell jour., 1996—; mem. editl. bd. Molecular Cellular Biology Jour., 1999—, Jour. Biol. Chemistry, 2000—05, DNA Repair Jour., 2003—; contbr. articles to sci. jours. Recipient Jr. Faculty Rsch. award, Am. Cancer Soc., 1981, Faculty Rsch. award, 1984, Merit award, NIH, 1993, Charles S. Mott prize, GM Cancer Rsch. Found., 1996; grantee, NIH, 1978—; rsch. grantee, Am. Cancer Soc., 1980—82. Fellow: Am. Acad. Microbiology; mem.: NAS, Am. Assn. Cancer Rsch., Genetic Soc. Am., Am. Soc. Microbiology, Am. Soc. Biochemistry and Molecular Biology. Home: 13468 Kibbings Rd San Diego CA 92130-1231 Office: Ludwig Inst for Cancer Rsch 9500 Gilman Dr CMME 3058 La Jolla CA 92093-0669 Business E-Mail: rkolodner@ucsd.edu.

KOLODNY, EDWIN HILLEL, neurologist, geneticist, director; b. Boston, Mar. 15, 1936; s. Myer Zeman and Naomi Lillian (Zalkind) K.; m. Roselyn Leinwand, May 31, 1958; children: Nancy, Leonard Benjamin, Robin, Noah Jacob. AB in Econs. cum laude, Harvard Coll., 1957; MD with honors, NYU, 1962. Diplomate Am. Bd. Psychiatry and Neurology, Am. Bd. Med. Genetics. Intern, resident in internal medicine Bellevue Hosp., N.Y.C., 1962-64; resident in neurology Mass. Gen. Hosp., Boston, 1964-67; spl. fellow lab. neurochemistry Nat. Inst. Neurol. Diseases, Bethesda, Md., 1967-70; asst. prof. neurology Harvard Med. Sch., Boston, 1970-76, assoc. prof., 1976-85, prof., 1985-91; Bernard and Charlotte Marden prof., chmn. dept. neurology NYU Med. Ctr., N.Y.C., 1991—. Vice-chmn. exec. com. Med. Bd. Tisch Hosp., N.Y., 1993-97, chmn., 1997-99; vis. prof. Weizmann Inst. Sci., Rehovot, Israel, 1988, 90; assoc. dir. Eunice Kennedy Shriver Ctr., Mental Retardation, Inc., Waltham, Mass., 1976-83, acting dir., 1983-84, dir., 1984-90; assoc. neurologist Mass. Gen. Hosp., Boston, 1976-87, neurologist, 1988-91; chmn. com. Rsch. Ctrs. Forward Planning Mental Retardation, Nat. Inst. Child Health and Human Devel., 1983-84; cons. pres.'s com. Mental Retardation, 1982; adv. genetic svcs. Dept. Pub. Health Mass., 1977-80; mem. Mass. Nat. Inst. Health Centennial Com., 1987-88, profl. adv. bd. Internat. Rett Syndrome Assn., 1986-94, sci. adv. bd. United Leukodystrophy Found., 1986-94, sci. med. adv. com. Canavan Found., 1994—; mem. expert com. Gaucher Initiative Project Hope, 2000—; mem. steering com. Global Orgn. for Lysosomal Diseases, 2002—. Mem. editl. bd. Annals of Neurology, 1984-89; contbr. articles to profl. jours. Mem. sci. adv. bd. Nat. Tay Sachs and Allied Diseases Assn., 1970—; mem. med. adv. bd. Dysautonomia Found., 2001—; v.p., trustee Temple Emanuel, Newton, Mass., 1983—89; trustee Hebrew Coll., Brookline, Mass. Recipient Solomon A. Berson Med. Alumni Achievement award clin. sci. NYU Sch. Medicine, 1993, Above and Beyond award Nat. Tay Sachs and Allied Diseases Assn., 2003, Disting. Svc. award ROFEH Internat., 2004. Fellow Am. Coll. Med. Genetics, Am. Acad. Neurology (S. Wier Mitchell award 1970); mem. Am. Assn. Neuropathology (Moore award 1975), Am. Neurol. Assn., Am. Soc. Human Genetics, Am. Soc. Neurochemistry, Child Neurology Soc., Harvard Varsity Club (Cambridge), Assn. for Rsch. in Nervous and Mental Diseases (bd. dirs. 1993—), Alpha Omega Alpha. Avocations: judaica, photography. Home: 110 Bleecker St Apt 24D New York NY 10012-2106 Office: NYU Med Ctr 550 1st Ave New York NY 10016-6402 Office Phone: 212-263-6347. Business E-Mail: edwin.kolodny@med.nyu.edu.

KOLODNY, RICHARD, finance educator; b. Jersey City, May 13, 1943; s. Harry and Mildred Kolodny; m. Alene Judith Kolodny, Feb. 2, 1969. BSBA, Northwestern U., 1965; MBA, NYU, 1967, PhD, 1972. Asst. prof. fin. SUNY, Binghamton, 1972-76, assoc. prof. fin., 1976-78, U. Md., College Park, 1978-82, prof. fin., 1982—, chair dept. fin., 1989-98. Cons. in field. Assoc. editor Fin. Mgmt., Jour. Acctg. Pub. Policy; contbr. articles to profl. jours. Grantee NSF, 1978-82, U. Md., 1980, 85; PhD fellow NYU; recipient research awards SUNY-Binghamton, 1975, 76, 77. Mem. Am. Fin. Assn., Fin. Mgmt. Assn., Ea. Fin. Assn. (bd. dirs. 1984-88), So. Fin. Assn. Office: Univ of Maryland Coll Of Business & Mgmt College Park MD 20742-0001

KOLODNY, STANLEY CHARLES, oral surgeon, retired military officer; b. N.Y.C., Feb. 22, 1923; s. Aaron and Lea (Stern) K.; m. Mary Kathryn Leigh, Feb. 22, 1947; children: Kathleen Susan, Carter Leigh, Stanley Charles. BA, U. Tex., 1944; D.D.S., Baylor U., 1947; MS, U. Ill., 1961. Diplomate: Am. Bd. Oral and Maxillofacial Surgery. Commd. 1st lt. USAF, 1951, advanced through grades to maj. gen., 1981; cons. in oral surgery Surgeon Gen. U.S. Air Force, 1966; chmn. dept. oral surgery Wilford Hall USAF Med. Center, San Antonio, 1969-75, dir. dental services, 1975-77; asst. surgeon gen. for dental services Bolling AFB, Washington, 1979-82. Clin. prof. dept. surgery U. Tex. Dental Br., Houston, 1969-77; clin. asso. prof. dept. surgery U. Tex. Med. Sch., San Antonio, 1969-77 Contbr. chpt. to book, articles to profl. jours. Bd. dirs. Am. Cancer Soc., 1970-77. Decorated D.S.M., Legion of Merit with oak leaf cluster, Air Force Commendation medal; recipient cert. of achievement for outstanding oral surgery USAF. Fellow Am. Coll. Dentists, Am. Assn. Oral and Maxillofacial Surgeons; mem. ADA, Soc. Air Force Clin. Surgeons. Home: 6401 Red Bud Dr Flower Mound TX 75022-5859

KOLODNY, STEPHEN ARTHUR, lawyer; b. Monticello, N.Y., 1940; BA in Bus. Adminstrn., Boston U., 1963, JD, 1965. Bar: Calif., 1966; U.S. Dist. Ct. (cen. dist.) Calif. 1966, U.S. Supreme Ct. 2004; cert. family law specialist. Sole practice, L.A., 1966—95; partner Kolodny and Anteau, L.A., 1995—. Lectr. family law subjects; adj. prof. U. Houston; ABA Trial Advocacy Inst., 1989—, co-chair, 1997—. Author: Evidence ABA Adv., 1996, (ann. publ.) Family Law Contempts; co-author: The Divorce Trial Manual, 2003 Named Number One Family Law Trial Lawyer, Calif. Lawyer Mag., Aug. 1999; named one of Top 10 Lawyers in U.S.A., Town and Country Mag., 1998, Worth Mag., 2002; recipient Silver Shingle award for disting. svc. to profession Boston U. Sch. Law, 2003. Mem. Am. Acad. Matrimonial Lawyers (past pres. So. Calif. chpt.), Am. Coll. Family Trial lawyers (founding dir. and diplomate), Internat. Acad. Matrimonial Lawyers (bd. gov., past pres. U.S.A. chpt.), Calif. State Bar Assn. (cert. family law specialist 1980—; lectr. State Bar panel, CEB programs, family law sect., article author), L.A. County Bar Assn. (lectr., past chmn. family law sect.), Beverly Hills Bar Assn. (lectr., family law sect.). Office Fax: 310-271-3918. Business E-Mail: kolodny@kolodny-anteau.com.

KOLODZEI, NATALIA A., art association administrator, art historian, curator; b. Moscow, Jan. 8, 1974; d. Tatiana A. and Alexander D. Kolodzei. BA in Art History with honors, State U. N.J., 1998. Exec. dir. Kolodzei Art Found., Inc., Highland Park, N.J., 1991—; curator Bergen Mus. Art and Sci., Chelsea Art Mus., NYC, 2005. Mem. adv. bd. Russian Am. Forum, N.Y., 1995—. Contbr. articles to exhbn. catalogs, art mags. Art Chronika, Iskusstvo; editor: (catalogs and books) Oley Vassiliev: Memory Speaks. Themes and Variations, 2004, Art Constitution. Named Hon. Citizen of State of Okla., Gov. of Okla., 1993. Mem. Am. Assn. for Advancement of Slavic Studies, Internat. Salon Soc. (ambassador 1996—), Internat. Art Fund, Print Club N.Y. (bd. dirs.), N.Y. Russian Club (bd. dirs.), Golden Key Nat. Honor Soc., Phi Beta Kappa. Avocation: collecting russian and eastern european art. Home: 123 S Adelaide Ave Apt 1N Highland Park NJ 08904-1615 Fax: 732-545-8428. Office Phone: 732-545-8425. E-mail: kolodzei@kolodzeiart.org.

KOLODZIEJ, EDWARD ALBERT, political scientist, educator; b. Chgo., Jan. 4, 1935; s. Albert Stanley and Anna Caroline (Chudzik) K.; m. Antje Heberle, Aug. 15, 1959; children: Peter, Andrew, Matthew, Daniel. BS summa cum laude, Loyola U., Chgo., 1956; MA, U. Chgo., 1957, PhD, 1961. Analyst nat. security fgn. affairs div. Congl. Research Service, Library of Congress, Washington, 1960-62; asst. prof. polit. sci. U. Va., Charlottesville, 1962-67, assoc. prof., 1967-73, chmn. dept. govt. and fgn. affairs, 1967-69, prof. polit. sci., 1973-83; head dept. U. Ill., Urbana, 1973-77, dir. Office Arms Control, Disarmament and Internat. Security, 1983-86, research prof. polit. sci., 1983—2001, elected univ. scholar, 1988; dir. Ctr. Global Studies, 2001—. Vis. prof. LaTrobe, Melbourne, 1999, Senshu U., Tokyo, 2001; cons. in field Author: The Uncommon Defense and Congress, 1966, French International Policy under de Gaulle and Pompidou: The Politics of Grandeur, 1974, Making and Marketing Arms: The French Experience and Its Implications for the International System, 1987; editor: American Security Policy, 1979, Security Policies of Developing States, 1981, Limits of Soviet Power in the Developing World, 1987, Security and Arms Control: Guide to National and International Policy-Making, 2 vols., 1989, Cold War as Cooperation, 1991, Coping with Conflict After the Cold War, 1996, Power, Politics and Promise of Human Rights, 2003, International Relations and Security, 2005; mem. editl. bd. Internat. Studies Quar., Defence and Peace Econs., Contemporary Security Policy, European Security; contbr. articles on fgn. and security policy and decision-making to profl. jours., U.S., Europe; also contbg. author books. Mershon Postdoctoral fellow nat. security Ohio State U., 1964-65, Rockefeller Postdoctoral fellow in internat. rels., Paris, 1965-66, Ford Found. fellow in social sci., 1969-71, Fulbright Rsch. fellow, 1986; NSF grantee, 1971, Deutscher Akademischer Austauschdienst grantee, 1975, Ford Found. Internat. Arms Control Competition grantee, 1976, Ctr. for Advanced Study, U. Ill., 1979, 95—, Rockefeller Found. grantee, 1980, grantee NEH, 1981, Woodrow Wilson Ctr., 1987, U.S. Inst. Peace grantee, 1987, 91, grantee Ford Found., 1993; recipient Burlington award for outstanding tchg. and scholarship, 1985. Mem. Internat. Inst. Strategic Studies London, Council Fgn. Relations N.Y., Am., Midwest internat. polit. sci. assns., Internat. Studies Assn. Home: 711 W University Ave Champaign IL 61820-3919 Office: U Ill Dept Polit Sci Urbana IL 61801 Business E-Mail: edkoloj@uiuc.edu.

KOLOJEJCHICK, ANDREW J., music educator; b. Sawyersville, Pa., July 30, 1969; s. John Andrew and Alberta Louise Kolojejchick; m. Diane Catherine Ameri-Kolojejchick, July 12, 1997. B of Music Edn., Wilkes U., 1991. Dir. band Wyoming Valley West High Sch., Plymouth, Pa., 1994—2005. Mem.: Pa. Music Educators Assn. (dist. 9 v.p. 2004).

KOLOMBATOVIC, VADJA VADIM, retired management consulting company executive; b. Belgrade, Serbia, Yugoslavia, Jan. 20, 1924; came to U.S., 1944; s. George Steven and Antigona (Kefala) K.; m. Virginia Doris Carter, 1946; children: Vadja Vadim Jr., Mimi Carter. BS, U. Ill., 1948; cert. in personnel mgmt., U. Richmond, Va., 1949. Office mgr. State Farm Ins. Co., Richmond, 1948-49; spl. agt. FBI, N.Y.C. and San Francisco, 1949-66, asst. legal attache Paris, 1966-69, legal attache Madrid, Spain, Paris, 1969-75, chief liaison sect. Washington, 1975-76; v.p. for internat. affairs Intertel, Washington, 1976-83, sr. v.p., 1983-85, exec. v.p. Rockville, Md., 1985-89, pres., 1989-92, pres., CEO, 1993-2000, also bd. dirs. V.p. Chalk's Internat., Miami, Fla., 1976-91; sr. internat. cons. Served to lt. U.S. Army, 1946-47. Mem. Am. Legion, Soc. Former Spl. Agts., Assn. Former Intelligence Officers, Assn. Former Legats, REs. Officers Assn., Masons (32 deg.), Shriners (Fairfax, Va.), McLean C. of C. Republican. Avocations: stamp collecting/philately, gardening. Home: 1171 Dolley Madison Blvd Mc Lean VA 22101-3019

KOLOMIYSKY, ARKADIY NAUMOVICH, physicist, researcher, educator; b. Potsdam, Germany, July 26, 1947; arrived in Russia, 1950; arrived in US, 2001. s. Naum Veniaminovich Kolomiysky and Shuamis Zimelevna Lin. MS/Engr. in Physics, Moscow Inst. Physics & Tech., 1971; PhD in Physics and Math., I.V. Kurchatov Atomic Energy Inst., Moscow, 1981. Rsch. engr. I.V. Kurchatov Atomic Energy Inst., Moscow, 1971-73; rsch. scientist Br. I.V. Kurchatov Atomic Energy Inst., Troitsk, Moscow, Russia, 1973-83, group leader Troitsk/Moscow, 1983-87, sr. scientist Troitsk, 1987-90; lead scientist Troitsk Inst. Innovation and Fusion Rsch., Troitsk, 1990—2001; sr. scientist Altair Ctr., Shrewsbury, Mass., 2001—03; security officer Allegiance Security Corp., 2004—. Assoc. prof. Moscow Inst. Physics and Tech., 1978—. Contbr. articles to profl. jours. Avocations: literature, theater, travels. Address: 92 Hamilton St Apt 3 Worcester MA 01604 Personal E-mail: arkolom@yahoo.com.

KOLOSKI, JOHN WILLIAM, language educator, writer; s. John William and Elsie Elmina (Sutton) Koloski; m. Diane Carol Di Phillips, Aug. 26, 1989; children: Julia, David, Madison. BA in English Lit., Binhamton U., 1986; cert. in tchg. English, Marywood U., 1998. Features writer, editor Chitra Publs., Montrose, Pa., 1988—90; network mgr. Angelo Ventresca Assocs., Montrose, 1990—98; tchr. English Montrose Area Sch. Dist., 1998—. Recipient St. Pious X CCO Tchg. award, Diocese of Scranton, 1999. Mem.: Nat. Conf. Tchrs. English, Am. Mensa. Republican. Roman Catholic. Avocations: writing, reading. Home: RR5 Box 53D Montrose PA 18801 Office: Montrose Area Sch Dist 50 High School Rd Montrose PA 18801

KOLOVICH, MARCIA A., middle school educator; b. Shamokin, Pa., Aug. 2, 1939; d. William and Veronica Madlyn (Nawrocki) K.; m. Joseph M. Allison, Oct. 23, 2004 BS in Edn. with honors, Youngstown (Ohio) U., 1962, AB in Sociology with honors, 1963. Cert. tchr., Ohio. Educator St. Rose Sch., Girard, Ohio, 1958-61, Holy Family Sch., Poland, Ohio, 1961-62, Palmetto Sch., Fontana, Calif., 1963-66, Roosevelt/Reed Mid. Sch., Hubbard, Ohio, 1966—2004; ret. Editor YAC Newsletter, 1992—. Active YWCA Aux. (named Woman of Yr. 1996). Recipient Positive Media Image award, 1997, also various awards and scholarships, HCIA Tchr. of Yr., 1998; named Women of Yr. Am. Biog. Inst., 1996, 97, 98, 2000, Internat. Woman of Yr. Biog. Ctr., Cambridge, Eng., 1997, 98, 2000 Outstanding Women of 20th Century. Mem. Altrusa Internat. (v.p. 1993-95, Altrusan of Yr. 1994, pres. 1995-97, chmn. dist. 5 new club bldg-ext., bd. dirs. 1992—, chmn.), Northeastern Ohio Edn. Assn., Polish Am. Hist. Assn., Trumbull County Ednl. Svc. Ctr. (mem. mentorship program, sch. dist. mentor com.), Nat. Ohio Hubbard Edn. Assn., Angels of the World (SGA dir.), Noetic Scis., Assn. Rsch. and Enlightenment, Am. Chronic Pain assn., Angel Collectors Club Am., Delta Kappa Gamma, Phi Delta Kappa. Avocations: community service, writing, wellness, angelology, travel.

KOLSBY, HERBERT F., lawyer, educator; b. Phila., July 10, 1926; s. Leonard H. and Josephine R. (Refsen) K.; m. Hermine W. Kolsby, Sept. 5, 1948; children: Dana Kolsby Edenbaum, Robert, Paul. JD, Temple U., 1951. Bar: Pa. 1951. Ptnr. Kolsby Gordon Robin & Shore, Phila., 1954—. Prof. law, dir. LLM in trial advocacy Temple U. Sch. Law, Phila., 1991-97. Gen. chmn. Fedn. Jewish Agys., Phila., 1989-90; pres. Temple Adath Israel, Phila., 1993-94. Recipient Justice Michael A. Musmanno award as outstanding trial lawyer Phila. Trial Lawyers Assn., 1993; Herbert F. Kolsby disting. lectureship in trial advocacy at Temple U. Sch. Law established in his honor, 2001. Fellow Am. Coll. Trial Lawyers, Internat. Acad. Trial Lawyers; mem. Inner Circle Advocats, White Manor Country Club (pres. 1968-69). Democrat. Avocation: golf. Office: Kolsby Gordon Robin Et Al 1650 Market St Fl 22D Philadelphia PA 19103-7301 Home: 3101 Boardwalk 2403-2 Atlantic City NJ 08401-5100

KOLSTAD, MICHAEL LAMAR, music educator; b. Casper, Wyo., May 17, 1966; s. Terry LaMar and Peggy June Kolstad; m. Paula Kay Hopper, Dec. 19, 1987; children: Madison Marie, Chase Miguel. MusB in Edn., Evangel U., 1988; MusM, U. N.C., 1990, MusD, 1996. Assoc. prof. music Evangel U., Springfield, Mo., 1991—; adj. prof. music Drury U., Springfield, Mo., 1995—2002. Dir. instrumental music Ctrl. Assembly of God, Springfield, Mo., 2000—. Musician (condr.): various performances. Condr. fine arts festival orch. Assembly of God Youth Dept., Springfield, Mo., 2003—05. Recipient Young Alumnus award, Evangel U., 2000. Independent. Home: 1180 Vineyard Drive Nixa MO 65714 Office: Evangel University 1111 N Glenstone Springfield MO 65802 Office Phone: 417-865-2815. Office Fax: 417-865-9599. E-mail: kolstadm@evangel.edu.

KOLTNOW, PETER GREGORY, engineer, consultant; b. N.Y.C., Apr. 14, 1929; s. Harry George and Fay (Richman) Koltnow; m. Dorothy D. Witter, Oct. 27, 1950; children: Nan Koltnow Chase, Nina. BS, Antioch Coll., 1951; MS, U. Calif. at Berkeley, 1956. Engr. City of Dayton, Ohio, 1953-55; traffic engr. County of Fresno, Calif., 1956-62, Auto Club of So. Calif., 1962-67; dir. urban div. Automotive Safety Found., Washington, 1967-69, Hwy. Users Fedn., 1970-71, v.p., 1971-74, pres., 1974-84; counselor to pres. Am. Trucking Assns., 1985-90. Guest lectr. various univs., 1965—; chmn. Transp. Rsch. Bd., 1979. Contbr. articles to profl. jours. Pres. Candlelighters, 1970—71. With Ordnance Corps U.S. Army, 1951—53. Recipient Disting. Svc. award, Transp. Rsch. Bd., 1982. Mem.: ASCE (James Laurie prize 1984), Nat. Acads. (nat. assoc.). Unitarian Universalist. Home and Office: 3100 N Leisure World Blvd Apt 401 Silver Spring MD 20906

KOLVE, V. A., English literature educator; b. Taylor, Wis., Jan. 18, 1934; s. Amos and Gunda (Lien) K. BA, U. Wis., 1955; BA with honors, Oxford U., 1957, MA, DPhil, Oxford U., 1962. From asst. prof. to assoc. prof. English Stanford (Calif.) U., 1962-69; prof. English U. Va., Charlottesville, Va., 1969-78, Commonwealth prof. English, 1979-86, chmn. dept. English, 1979-81; found. prof. English UCLA, 1986—2001, prof. emeritus, 2001—. Guggenheim Found. ednl. adv. bd., 1988—; The Alexander Lectures, U. Toronto, 1993, The Clark Lectures, Cambridge U., 1994. Author: The Play Called Corpus Christi, 1966, Chaucer and The Imagery of Narrative, 1984; author, editor: (with Glending Olson) Norton Critical Edition: Chaucer: The Canterbury Tales, 1989, 2d expanded edit., 2005. 1st lt. U.S. Army, 1959. Recipient Brit. Coun. Humanities prize, 1985, Harbison Teaching award Danforth Found., 1972, UCLA Disting. Teaching award, 1995, Disting. Faculty award, 1999; Jenkins Rsch. fellow Oxford U., 1958-62, Guggenheim fellow, 1968, Sr. fellow Ctr. Advanced Studies in Visual Arts, Nat. Gallery, 1984, fellow Ctr. Advanced Study in Behavioral Scis., Stanford U., 1985; Rhodes scholar, 1955-58. Fellow Medieval Acad. Am. (pres. 1992), Am. Acad. Arts and Scis.; mem. MLA (chair exec. com. Chaucer divsn. 1973-77, 86-90, James Russell Lowell prize 1985), New Chaucer Soc. (trustee 1988-92, pres. 1994-96), Early English Text Soc., AAUP, Phi Beta Kappa. Democrat. Home: 2034 Outpost Dr Los Angeles CA 90068-3726 E-mail: kolve@ucla.edu.

KOLVENBACH, PETER HANS, priest, religious order superior; b. Druten, The Netherlands, 1928. Student U. Nijmegen (Netherlands), theology St. Joseph U., Beirut, linguistics, Paris, 1963-67. Joined Jesuit Order Netherlands; ordained priest Roman Cath. Ch., 1961; prof. linguistics St. Joseph U., Beirut, 1968-81; provincial superior Beirut, 1974-81; rector Pontifical Oriental Inst., Rome, 1981-83; superior-gen. Soc. of Jesus, 1983—; consultor Congregation for Oriental Chs., mem. Congregation for Evangelization of Peoples, mem. Orthodox-Cath. dialogue, 1983—. Author: In Cammino Verso La Pasqua, 1988, Men of God: Men for Others, 1990, El Padre Kolvenbach en Colombia, 1990, Kolvenbach en México, 1990, Cinco mensajes universitarios, 1991, Seleccion de escritos 1983-90, also various articles and revs. in field of linguistics and spiritual theology; mem. of commns. Cath. Orthodox dialogue books. Address: Borgo Santo Spirito 4 00193 Rome Italy Business E-Mail: infosj@sjcuria.org.

KOLYER, JOHN MCNAUGHTON, materials scientist, retired chemist; b. East Williston, N.Y., June 30, 1933; s. John and Mildred (McNaughton) K.; children: Scott McNaughton, Paul Franklin, Craig David, Jeffrey John. BA, Hofstra U., 1955; PhD, U. Pa., 1960. Technician Olin-Mathieson Chem. Corp., Port Washington, N.Y., 1955-56; rsch. chemist FMC Corp., Princeton, N.J., 1960-62; tech. supr. Allied Chem. Corp., Morriston, N.J., 1964-71; mem. tech. staff Rockwell Internat., Anaheim, Calif., 1973-96; scientist, engr. Boeing Co., Anaheim, 1997—2002; ret. Author: many technical articles and works of fiction and verse; patentee in field; author: Engaged to be Dead, 2004. Mem.: N.Y. Acad. Scis., Soc. for Advancement Materials Processing and Engrng., Am. Chem. Soc., Phi Lambda Upsilon, Kappa Mu Epsilon, Sigma Kappa Alpha. Office: 1455 Superior Ave Apt 124 Newport Beach CA 92663-6107

KOMAR, VITALY, artist; b. Moscow, Sept. 11, 1943; Student, Stroganov Inst. Art and Design, Moscow, 1967. Ptnr. Komar & Melamid Studio, N.Y.C., 1973—2003. Instr. visual art Moscow Regional Art Sch., 1968-76. Exhibitions include Wadsworth Atheneum, Hartford, Conn., 1978, Mus. Modern Art, Oxford Eng., Mus. Decorative Art, Paris, 1985, Neuen Gesellschaft für Gildende Kunst, Berlin, 1988, Bklyn. Mus., 1990, Alternative Mus., N.Y.C., 1994, Storefront for art and architecture, N.Y.C., 1995, Ukraine State Mus., Kiev, 1995, Mus. Modern Art, Cologne, Germany, 1997, Kunsthalle, Vienna, Austria, 1998; exhibited in group shows at Met. Mus. Art, N.Y.C., 1982, 84, Chrysler Mus., Norfolk, Va., 1983, Sydney, Australia, 1986, Kassel, Documenta 8, Germany, 1987, Solomon R. Guggenheim Found., 1987, FIAC, Paris, 1989, Bklyn. Mus., 1990, Venice Bienalle, 1997, 99, Yeshiva U. Mus., N.Y.C., 2002-03; represented in permanent collections Whitney Mus. Am. Art, N.Y.C., Stedeliyk Mus., Amsterdam, The Netherlands, Guggenheim Mus., Mus. Modern Art, Met. Mus. Art; commns. include mural Unity, 1st Interstate Bank Bldg., L.A., 1993, murals Liberty as Justice, N.Y., Bronx Housing Ct., 1994-98. Grantee Nat. Endowment Arts, 1982. Office Phone: 212-777-6653. Fax: 212-777-6653. E-mail: komar@maxf.net.

KOMAROFF, LINDA, curator; Joined faculty dept. art Hamilton Coll., NY, 1986; with Met. Mus. Art, NYC; joined LA County Mus. Art, 1995, curator Islamic art, head dept. ancient and Islamic art. Author: The Golden Disk of Heaven: Metalwork of Timurid Iran, 1992; Co-curator (with Stefano Carboni) (exhibitions) The Legacy of Genghis Kahn: Courtly Art and Culture in Western Asia, 1256-1353 (Alfred H. Barr Jr. Award for exhbn. catalogue, Coll. Art Assn., 2004). Recipient Media Award, Muslim Pub. Affairs Coun., 2003; Fulbright Scholar Grant, 1980—81, 1988—89. Office: LA County Mus Art 5905 Wilshire Blvd Los Angeles CA 90036*

KOMAROFF, STANLEY, lawyer; b. Bklyn., Apr. 1, 1935; s. William Ralph and Fanny (Wein) K.; m. Rosalyn Steinglass, Dec. 25, 1960; children: William Charles, Andrew Steven. BA, Cornell U., 1956, JD, 1958. Bar: N.Y. 1959. Assoc. Proskauer Rose LLP, N.Y.C., 1958-68, ptnr., 1968—, chmn., 1991-99; sr. advisor Henry Schein, Inc., Melville, NY, 2004—. Mem. hosp. rev. and planning coun. N.Y. State, 1982-92; trustee Beth Israel Med. Ctr., 1984—, vice chair, 1999—; trustee St. Lukes-Roosevelt Hosp. Ctr., Continuum of Health Ptnrs. Inc.; mem. bd. regents L.I. Coll. Hosp., 2001—; bd. dirs. Edmond de Rothschild Found., Club Med, Inc., 1984-95, Overseas Shipholding Group, Inc., Westhampton Beach Performing Arts Ctr.; chmn.

ann. fund Cornell U. Law Sch., 1991-93, mem. adv. coun. 1st lt. USAR, 1958. Fellow Am. Bar Found.; mem. N.Y. State Bar Assn., Assn. Bar City of N.Y., N.Y. County Lawyers Assn., Order of Coif, Sunningdale Country Club, Phi Kappa Phi. Home: 910 Park Ave Apt 5-s New York NY 10021-0255 Office: Henry Schein Inc 135 Duryea Rd Melville NY 11747 Office Phone: 631-843-5907. Business E-Mail: Stanley.Komaroff@Henryschein.com.

KOMAROV, ANDREI M., science educator; b. Frunze, Russia, Sept. 22, 1961; arrived in US, 1992; s. Mikhail I. Komarov and Emma G. Komarova; m. Natalia V. Kouznetsova; 1 child, Valeria. MD, Russian State Med. U., Russia, 1984; PhD, Inst. of Chem. Physics, Acad. of Scis., Russia, 1988. Vis. scientist Med. Coll. of Wis., Milw., 1992—94; sr. rsch. scientist George Wash. U., Wash., DC, 1994—97, asst. rsch. prof., 1998—. Ad hoc referee Free Radical Biology and Medicine, Newton, Mass., 1996—, Ctr. for Scientific Review, NIH, Bethesda, Md., 2000—, NSF, Arlington, Va., 2000—. Contbr. articles various profl. jours., chapters to books various profl. text books. Recipient Diploma of Sr. Scientist in Biophysics award, State Attestation Commn., Russia, 1992, Faculty Rsch. award, George Wash. U., 1998. Mem.: Oxygen Club of Greater Wash., DC. Achievements include development of nitric oxide trapping agents for nitric oxide detection and scavenging; studies on the role of nitric oxide in inflammation. Office: George Wash U Dept of Biochemistry 2300 Eye St NW Ross Hall 441 Washington DC 20037 E-mail: phyamk@gwumc.edu.

KOMEN, LEONARD, lawyer; b. St. Louis, May 31, 1943; s. Meyer and Yetta (Ellman) K.; m. Sandra Gail Cytron, June 8, 1969; children: Douglas Steven, Matthew Todd. BA, U. Mo., 1965, JD, 1970. Bar: Mo. 1970, U.S. Dist. Ct. (ea. dist.) Mo. 1971, U.S. Supreme Ct. 1973, U.S. Ct. Appeals (8th cir.) 1985, U.S. Claims Ct. 1992. Assoc. Susman, Willer & Rimmel, St. Louis, 1970-74, Susman Schermer Rimmel & Parker, St. Louis, 1974-77, ptnr., 1977-80; prin., v.p. Selner, Glaser, Komen, Berger & Galganski, P.C., St. Louis, 1980-96; prin. mgr. Komen, Berger & Cohen, L.C., 1996-99; prin. Law Offices of Leonard Komen, P.C., 1999—. Ct.-apptd. trustee, examiner, receiver U.S. Bankruptcy Ct., 1988—. bd. dirs. Zeta Beta Tau Frat. Inc., 1984—, nat. sec., 1989-90, nat. v.p., 1990-92, nat. pres., 1992-94; mem. supervisory bd. Nat. Interfraternity Coun. Legal Advocacy Fund, 1993-98. Pres. Creve Coeur Hockey Club Inc., St. Louis, 1987-88, bd. dirs., 1989-93; coord. Parkway North Hockey Club, 1989-91; pres., bd. dirs. Roswell Messing Ednl. Found., 1989—; bd. dirs. Zeta Beta Tau Centennial Found. 1990-98. Recipient Merit citation Zeta Beta Tau Frat., Inc., 1977, 91, 92, 2002. Mem.: Mo. Bankers Assn., Comml. Law League Am. Jewish. Home: 14385 Stablestone Ct Chesterfield MO 63017-2502 Office: Law Offices of Leonard Komen PC 7733 Forsyth Blvd Ste 300 Clayton MO 63105 Office Phone: 314-863-9191. Business E-Mail: lenkomen@komenlaw.com.

KOMENAKA, IAN K., medical and surgical educator; s. Ian H and Diane K Komenaka; m. Sonal G Gandhi. BA in Chemistry, Cornell U., 1993; MD, John A. Burns Sch. of Medicine, 1997. Fellow, attending surgeon Columbia U.- Presbyn. Med. Ctr., N.Y.C., 2002—03; asst. prof. surgery Ind. U./Purdue U., Indpls., 2004—. Dir. Wishard Hosp. Breast Surgery Clinic, Indpls., 2004—. Contbr. articles to med. jours. Recipient Best Chief Resident Surgeon award, NY Meth. Hosp., 2002; Breast Surgery fellow, Columbia U. - Presbyn. Med. Ctr., 2002—03. Mem.: ACS, AMA, Am. Soc. Breast Surgeons. Home: 225 E North St Indianapolis IN 46204 Office: Ind U Cancer Pavilion 535 Barnhill Dr Rm 431 Indianapolis IN 46202 Office Phone: 317-630-8409. Office Fax: 317-630-8721. E-mail: komenaka@hotmail.com.

KOMIE, STEPHEN MARK, lawyer; b. Chgo., Jan. 22, 1949; s. Leonard D. and Miriam (Wineberg) K. BA, U. Ariz., 1970, MA in Russian History, 1973; JD, DePaul U., 1976. Bar: Ill. 1976, U.S. Dist. Ct. (no. dist.) Ill. 1976, U.S. Ct. Appeals (7th cir.) 1976, U.S. Ct. Appeals (8th cir.) 1982, U.S. Dist. Ct. (ctrl. dist.) Ill. 1984, U.S. Dist. Ct. (no. dist.) Ind. 1985, U.S. Ct. Appeals (6th cir.) 1989, U.S. Dist. Ct. (ea. dist.) Mich. 1995, U.S. Supreme Ct. 1993. With Komie & Assocs., Chgo., 1976—; prin. Buffalo Grove (Ill.) Law Offices Ltd., 1977-86. Prin. Drunken Drivers Def. Lawyers of Ill. Ltd., Chgo., 1982—. Recipient Nat. Pub. Svc. award ATLA, 1994. Mem. ABA (solo practice and small firm practice task force 1990-92, elected mem. criminal justice sect. coun., 1995—), Ill. Bar Assn. (mem. assembly 1985-91, vice chmn. 1988-89, chmn. 1989-90, vice chmn. com. professionalism 1990-91, chair 1991—, bd. govs. 1992-98, 99—, sec. 1997-98), Chgo. Bar Assn. (chmn. criminal law com. 1983-84, def. of prisoners com. 1986-87), Nat. Assn. Criminal Def. Lawyers (parliamentarian 1988-89, 90-91, bd. dirs. 1983-86), Ill. Bar Found. (bd. dirs. 1988-90, 92—), Ill. Attys. for Criminal Justice (treas. 1991-92), Lincoln Inn of Ct., Internat. Bar Assn. (vice-chair family law com.). Office: 1 N La Salle St Ste 4200 Chicago IL 60602-4097

KOMISAR, ARNOLD, otolaryngologist, educator; b. N.Y.C., Nov. 27, 1947; s. Samuel and Sonia (Schwartz) K.; children: Alexandra Danielle, Jonathan Reed. BS, Bradley U., 1968; DDS, NYU, 1972, MS in Health Care Policy Mgmt., 2004; MD, Hahnemann Med. Coll., 1975. Diplomate Am. Bd. Otolaryngology. Resident in surgery Beth Israel Med. Ctr., N.Y.C., 1975-76; resident in otolaryngology Mt. Sinai Med. Sch., N.Y.C., 1976-79; asst. prof. otolaryngology Albert Einstein Coll. Medicine, N.Y.C., 1979-85, assoc. prof., 1985-86, assoc. clin. prof., 1986-90; assoc. dir. head and neck surgery Albert Einstein Affiliated Hosps., N.Y.C., 1982-86; attending otolaryngologist Montefiore Hosp. and Med. Ctr., N.Y.C., 1979-90, Bronx Mcpl. Hosp. Ctr., N.Y.C., 1979-90, North Ctrl. Bronx Hosp., N.Y.C., 1979-90, N.Y. Hosp.-Cornell U. Med. Ctr., N.Y.C., 1997—; clin. assoc. prof. otolaryngology Cornell U. Med. Coll., N.Y.C., 1994—98, clin. prof., 1998—2000; attending otolaryngologist N.Y. Hosp.-Cornell U. Med. Ctr., N.Y.C., 1997—2000; clin. prof. otolaryngology NYU, 2000—. Otolaryngologist Lenox Hill Hosp., N.Y.C., 1986—, asst to dir. resident edn. dept. otolaryngology, 1986—, adj. otolaryngologist, 1987—, attending otolaryngologist, 1989—, assoc. dir. otolaryngology, 1990—; cons. otolaryngology N.Y. Eye and Ear Infirmary, N.Y.C., 1986-89; courtesy staff surgery-otolaryngology Drs. Hosp., N.Y.C., 1986-90; attending staff Manhattan Eye Ear and Throat Hosp., 1995—; attending otolaryngologist N.Y. Hosp. Cornell U. Med. Ctr., 1997-2000; presenter in field. Author: Glossary, 2004, On the Same Shore, 2005; contbr. articles to profl. jours. Recipient Centurion award Bradley U., 1997. Fellow Am. Coll. Surgeons, Am. Soc. Head and Neck Surgery, Am. Acad. Facial Plastic and Reconstructive Surgery, Am. Acad. Otolaryngology/Head and Neck Surgery (Honor award), Triological Soc. (Mosher award), Am. Bronchoesophagological Soc., NY Acad. Medicine, Am. Laryngol. Assn.; mem. AMA, Am. Acad. Anti-Aging Medicine, Pan-Am. Soc. Brochoesophagology, Soc. Univ. Otolaryngologists, NY Head and Neck Soc., Med. Soc. NY, NY Laryngol. Soc., NY County Med. Soc. Avocations: reading, travel. Office: 1317 3d Ave New York NY 10021-2995 Office Phone: 212-861-8888. Personal E-mail: axk2@aol.com.

KOMISAR, DAVID DANIEL, retired university provost; b. N.Y.C., July 20, 1917; s. Jacob and Yetta (Jacobson) K.; m. Beatrice Liebman, Aug. 15, 1940 (dec. Sept. 1981); children— Jack Lloyd, June Diana; m. Molly Komisar, Nov. 1984 BSS., Coll. City N.Y., 1937, MS, 1940; postgrad., U. Glasgow, 1945, Sorbonne, 1946; PhD, Columbia U., 1953. With Civil Service, N.Y.C., 1939-42; indsl. personnel work, 1943-44; counselor vocational rehab. U.S. Army, 1943-46; dir. guidance Mohawk Coll., 1946-48; dir. guidance, chmn. dept. psychology Champlain Coll., State U. N.Y., Plattsburg, 1948-53; chmn. dept. psychology U. Hartford, 1953—, pres. univ. faculty senate, 1964-65; dean U. Hartford (Sch. Arts and Scis.), 1966-67, dean of faculties, 1967-70, v.p. acad. affairs, 1970-71, provost, 1972-80, Univ. prof., 1980-84, prof. and provost emeritus, 1984—; mem. Conn. Civil Service Commn., 1980-84; pres. Emeriti Assn., 1989-91; cons. Palm Beach County Mental Health Assn., 1991—. Project dir. research in mental retardation Office Vocat. Rehab., Dept. Health, Edn. and Welfare, 1964-65, psycho-social com. social rehab. services, 1968-74; head New Eng. Conf. Mental Retardation, 1960, Conn. Task Force on Mental Retardation, 1960-61; Conn. rep. Nat. Def. Edn. Act, 1960-61; research fellow U.S. Office Vocational Rehab., 1962-63; Conn. Citizens Com. on State Welfare, 1967-69; mem. standing com. accreditation Conn. Commn. High Edn., 1969-75. Contbr. articles on testing, therapy, vocational selection to profl. jours. Co-chmn. Citizens Charter Com. Hartford, 1959; mem. bd. Hartford Jewish Cmty. Ctr., 1955-63, v.p., 1963-78, life officer 1978—; mem. bd. Mental Health Assn., 1959-62; bd. dirs. Inst. of New Dimensions, Palm Beach Cmty. Coll., 1994—. Recipient rsch. grant for study residential care retarded children HEW, 1965-69, Disting. Svc. medal U. Hartford, 1990, Univ. medal U. Hartford, 1991; elected to Townsend Harris Hall of Fame, 1998. Mem. Conn. Valley Assn. Psychologists (past pres.), Am. Psychol. Assn., Conn. Psychol. Assn. (council; pres.), Nat. Vocational Guidance Assn., Am. Personnel and Guidance Assn., Sigma Xi. Clubs: Connecticut Valley Torch (past pres.), Probus (past pres.) (Hartford).

KOMISARJEVSKY, CHRISTOPHER P.A., retired public relations executive; b. Feb. 16, 1945; BS in Polit. Sci., MBA; postgrad. German Lit./Internat. Affairs, U.S./Europe. Hill and Knowlton, Inc., 1972-92, pres., CEO Europe, Mid. East and Africa ops., CEO Carl Byoir & Assocs.; pres., CEO Gavin Anderson & Co. Omnicom, 1992-95; pres., CEO Burson-Marsteller U.S., N.Y.C., 1995-99, Burson-Marsteller Worldwide, N.Y.C., 1998—2004. Chmn. Burson-Marsteller Global Corp. Practice, 1995-99. Co-author: Peanut Butter and Jelly Management, 2000; contbr. articles to profl. jours.; lectr. at Spain's Instituto de Empresa, Switzerland's Internat. Inst. for Mgmt. Devel., N.Y.U. Grad. Sch. Bd. dirs. several non-profit orgs.; trustee EQ Advisors Trust. Capt. U.S. Army, 1967-72 (Vietnam). Recipient Ellis Island Medal of Honor, 1996. Personal E-mail: chris.komisarjevsky@gmail.com.

KOMLOS, PETER, violinist; b. Budapest, Hungary, Oct. 25, 1935; s. Laszlo and Franciska (Graf) K.; m. Edit Feher, 1960; 2 sons; m. Zsuzsanna Arki, 1984; 1 son. Educated, Budapest Music Acad. Founded Komlos String Quartet, 1957; 1st violinist Budapest Opera Orchestra, 1960; leader Bartok String Quartet, 1963; extensive concert tours to USSR, Scandinavia, Italy, Austria, W.Ger., Czechoslovakia, 1958-64, to U.S., Can., N.Z., Australia, 1970, Japan, Spain, Portugal, 1971; Far East, U.S., Europe, 1973; recordings include Beethoven's string quartets for Hungaroton, Budapest; Bartok's string quartets for Erato, Paris, all Bartok's Quartets, 1991-92, Different Haydn Quartets, Canyon Classic-Japan, Mendelssohn-Schonberg Pieces, Hunghroton, 1992. Recipient 1st prize Internat. String Quartet Competition, Liè ge, 1964, Liszt prize, 1965, Gramopone Record prize of Germany, 1969, Kossuth prize, 1970, second Kossuth prize, 1997, UNESCO Music Coun. placque, 1981; named Eminent Artist, 1980. Office Phone: 36 26 360 697. E-mail: stradivari@avelert.nu.

KOMM, KERMIT MATTHEW, software engineer; b. LaGrange, Ill., Apr. 9, 1964; s. Charles Paul and Dorothy Anna Jean (Groves) K. BS in Elec. Engring., UCLA, 1986. Dir. ops. Leviathan Devel., L.A., 1986-90; software engr. FortuNet, Las Vegas, Nev., 1991; v.p. software engring. Future Techs., Las Vegas, 1991-95; v.p. engring. Innovation Mgmt. Group, Las Vegas, 1995—. Author: (software) My-T-Mouse, 1993, Joystick-to-Mouse, 1995, My-T-Soft AT, 1998, The Magnifier, 1998. Avocations: travel, driving, hiking. Office: Innovation Mgmt Group Inc 4425 E Sahara Ave Ste 9 Las Vegas NV 89104-6357

KOMMALAPATI, RAGHAVA RAO, civil engineer, environmental engineer, educator; s. Kommalapati. BSCE, Nagarjuna U., Andhra Pradesh, India, 1988; M.Tech in Engring. Structures, Kakatiya U., Andhra Pradesh, 1990; MS, La. State U., Baton Rouge, 1994, PhD, 1995. Asst. prof. Prairie View (Tex.) A&M U., 1998—2004, assoc. prof., 2004—. STI coord. Prairie View A&M U., 2000—. Contbr. more than 50 articles to profl. jours. Mem.: ASCE (faculty advisor 2002—05), Am. Assn. of Environ. Engring. and Sci. Profs., Am. Water Works Assn., Water Environment Fedn., Phi Kappa Phi. Office: Prairie View A&M University Dept of Civil Engineering P O Box 4249 Prairie View TX 77446-4249 Office Phone: 936-857-2418. Office Fax: 936-857-4125. E-mail: r_kommalapati@pvamu.edu.

KOMMEDAHL, THOR, plant pathology educator; b. Mpls., Apr. 1, 1920; s. Thorbjørn and Martha (Blegen) K.; m. Faye Lillian Jensen, June 2, 1924; children: Kris Alan, Siri Lynn, Lori Anne. BS, U. Minn., 1945, MS, 1947, PhD, 1951. Instr. U. Minn., St. Paul, 1946-51, asst. prof. plant pathology, 1953-57, assoc. prof., 1957-63, prof., 1963-90, prof. emeritus, 1990—; asst. prof. plant pathology Ohio Agrl. Research and Devel. Ctr., Wooster, 1951-53, Ohio State U., Columbus, 1951-53; prof. Univ. Coll., U. Minn., St. Paul, 1990—. Cons. botanist and taxonomist Minn. Dept. Agr., 1954-60, Sci. Mus. Minn., 1990—; 7th A.W. Dimock lectr. Cornell U., 1979; external assessor U. Pertanian Malaysia, 1994-97. Author: Pesky Plants, 1989; co-author: Scientific Style and Format, 1994; editor Minn. Fulbright newsletter, 1995-2002, Procs. IX Internat. Congress Plant Protection, 2 vols., 1981, Corn Disease newsletter, 1970-76; assoc. editor The Boghopper, 1996—; cons. editor McGraw Hill Ency. Sci. and Tech., 1972-78; editor-in-chief Phytopathology, 1964-67; sr. editor: Challenging Problems in Plant Health, 1982, Plant Disease Reporter, 1979; contbr. articles to profl. jours. Bd. mem. Park Bugle, 1998—. Recipient Elvin Charles Stakman award, 1990, Award of Merit, Gamma Sigma Delta, 1994; Guggenheim fellow, 1961, Fulbright scholar, 1968. Fellow AAAS, Am. Phytopathol. Soc. (councilor 1958-60, pres. 1971, publs. coord. 1978-84, Disting. Svc. award 1984, 93, sci. adv. 1984—, adv. bd. office internat. programs 1987-93, editor Focus 1981—); mem. Am. Inst. Biol. Scis., Bot. Soc. Am., Coun. Sci. Editors, Internat. Soc. Plant Pathology (councilor 1971-78, sec.-gen. and treas. 1983-88, treas. 1988-93, editor newsletter 1983-93), Mycol. Soc. Am., Minn. Acad. Sci., N.Y. Acad. Scis., Weed Sci. Soc. Am. (award of excellence 1968), Fulbright Assn. (editor newsletter Minn. chpt. 1995-2002). Baptist. Home: 1666 Coffman St Apt 322 Saint Paul MN 55108-1340 Office: U Minn Dept Plant Pathology 495 Borlaug Hall 1991 Upper Buford Cir Saint Paul MN 55108-6030 Office Phone: 612-625-3164. Office Fax: 612-625-9728. Business E-Mail: thork@umn.edu.

KOMODORE, BILL G., painter; b. Athens, Greece, Oct. 23, 1932; came to U.S, 1947; s. Konstantine B. and Dina K. (Mentis) Koumoundouros; m. Marianne Aulow (div.); children: Charles, Alexander. Student art, Hans Hofmann Sch.; studied with George Rickey, Mark Rothko, David Smith. Painter, full prof. So. Meth. U., 1990. One-man shows include Haydon Calhoun Gallery, Dallas, 1961, Howard Wise Gallery, N.Y.C., 1964, 67, Automation House, N.Y.C., 1972, Mary Washington Coll., 1975, Stephen Austin U., Nacogdoches, Tex., 1980, D.W. Gallery, Dallas, 1981, 83, 84, Sheraton Gallery, Dallas, 1986, Eugene Binder Gallery, Dallas, 1987, Longview (Tex.) Mus., 1988-89; group shows include Mus. Modern Art, N.Y.C., 1964, Cin. Art Mus., 1965, Albright-Knox Gallery, Buffalo, 1956, Whitney Mus., N.Y.C., 1965, 67, Bertrand Russell Centenary Exhbn., London, 1972, U. Tex, 1979, Dallas Mus. Fine Arts, 1980, San Francisco Mus. Modern Art, 1988, First Tex. Triennial Contemporary Art Mus., Houston, 1988 (travel through 1989); represented in permanent collections Nat. Gallery Art, Washington, Walker Art Ctr., Mpls., Whitney Mus. Am. Art, Des Moines Art Ctr., Milw. Mus. Art, Minn., Hamilton (Ont., Can.) Gallery Art, Dallas Mus. Art acquires large work GAIA, 1990; illustrator: Fishes of Lake Pontchartrain, 1954, A Ballad of a Sweet Dream of Peace (Robert Penn Warren), 1981; contbr. to books in field; tchr. Newcomb Art Sch., 1955-57, Northwood Inst., Dallas, 1969; vis. artist Mary Washington Coll., 1973-77, Richland Coll., Dallas, 1977-79, Cedar Valley Coll., So. Meth. U., 1980, Brookhaven Coll., 1981-90 Emmy awards judge, 1971 With Greek underground, World War II. Recipient Bausch & Lomb Sci. award, 1950, Houston Mus. award, 1960 Home: 5946 Oram St Dallas TX 75206-7232 *To shape tomorrow's world for the better, the artist must forget "modern" art, which is already old, and look around intensely at the world, its people and what is left of nature.*

KOMORNY, KENNETH MICHAEL, pharmacist; b. Toledo, May 16, 1970; s. Robert Edgar and Veronica Komorny; m. Lynn Marie Pyles, Mar. 19, 1994; children: Hannah Noel, Grace Nicole. BS in Pharmacy, U. Toledo, 1993; PharmD, U. Cin., 1995. Registered pharmacist Ohio State Bd. of Pharmacy, 1993, cert. pharmacotherapy specialist Bd. of Pharm. Specialties, 1999. Cert. specialist of poison info. Cin. Drug and Poison Info. Ctr., 1993—97; clin. pharmacist St. Luke Hosp. - East, Ft. Thomas, Ky., 1995—97; clin. lead pharmacist Summa Health Sys., Akron, Ohio, 1997—99, ednl., investigational, and clin. coord., 1999—. Author: (presentation) The Akron Area Society of Pharmacy Technicians - Spring Conference, Lupus Foundation of America Akron Area Chapter, American Heart Association 4th Ann. Stroke Symposium, Cuyahoga Falls, Ohio, Ohio College of Clinical Pharmacy Spring Meeting 2002, Plain City, Ohio, 36th Ann. ASHP Midyear Clinical Meeting - Management Case Studies, New Orleans, Louisiana, West Side Family Practice - Education Spring Retreat, (poster presentation) 38th Ann. ASHP Midyear Clinical Meeting, New Orleans, Louisiana, 34th Ann. ASHP Midyear meeting, Orlando, Fla.; contbr. articles to profl. jours. Mem. coun. Jerusalem Evangel. Luth. Ch. Mem.: Pharmacy and Therapeutics Soc. (assoc.), Ohio Coll. Clin. Pharmacy (assoc.), Am. Coll. Clin. Pharmacy (assoc.). Achievements include nvestigator at Summa Health System, National Nosocomial Resistance Surveillance Group (NNRSG): A Multicenter, Prospective, Cross-Sectional Study of the Clinical and Economic Impact of Methicillin Res. Home: 8760 Guilford Rd Seville OH 44273 Office: Summa Health Sys 525 E Market St Akron OH 44309-2090 Office Phone: 330-375-4397. Personal E-mail: komorny@earthlink.net. E-mail: komornyk@summahealth.org.

KOMOSKI, PAUL KENNETH, educational association administrator, researcher, volunteer; b. Jersey City, Nov. 20, 1928; s. Louis Stanislaw and Stelle Marie (Norwich) K.; m. Isabel Jane Parrish, Mar. 24, 1952 (dec. Mar. 1970); children: Christina, William; m. Joanna Monica Anthony, June 15, 1972; 1 child, Mara Mia. BA, Acadia U., 1950, MA, 1952. Tchr. Morristown (N.J.) Sch., 1950-52; tchr., head mid. sch. Collegiate Sch., N.Y.C., 1952-60; pres. Ctr. for Programmed Instrn., N.Y.C., 1960-64; assoc. dir. Inst. for Ednl. Tech. Columbia U., N.Y.C., 1963-66; pres., exec. dir. Ednl. Products Info. Exch. Inst., Hampton Bays, N.Y., 1967—. Pres., founder Learning and Info. Networking Cmty. Tech. (LINCT) Coalition, Hampton Bays, 1994—, U.S. Environ. Protection Agy., Washington, 1986-88, NSF, Washington, 1992-93. Founder, exec. editor www.eLearningspace.org, 2000—. Bd. mem. Children Uniting Nations; overseer Friends World Program, Southampton Coll., LIU, 1992-. Mem. ASCD, Am. Edn. Rsch. Assn., Assn. Ednl. Comm. and Tech. (Lifetime Achievement 1981), Internat. Soc. for Performance and Instrn. (Lifetime Achievement award 1979). Quaker. Avocations: tennis, jazz vocalist, song writer. Home: 355 Sebonac Rd Southampton NY 11968-2720 Office: EPIE Inst PO Box 590 Hampton Bays NY 11946 Office Phone: 631-728-9100. E-mail: kkomoski@epie.org.

KOMP, BARBARA ANN, writer; b. La Porte, Ind., Nov. 3, 1954; d. Gerald Lee and Betty Mae (Schelin) K. BA in Elem. Edn., Ball State U., 1977; cert. in lang. arts/reading competencies, 1977. Quality control insp. Foreman Mfg. Co., Rolling Prairie, Ind., 1978-80; quality control inspector Weil-McLain, Michigan City, Ind., 1980-81, jr. quality control engr., 1981-84, tech. writer, 1984-88, mgr. tech. pubs., 1988-97, mktg. comms. specialist, 1997-2000; tech. writer C.E. Niehoff & Co., Evanston, Ill., 2000—. Advisor Jr. Achievement, Michigan City, 1982-84; mem. bd. dirs. Mich. City YMCA, 1992-93; mem. bd. dirs. Christmas-in-April, Michigan City, chair in-kind donations com., 1993-95, bd. sec. 1994-95. Mem.: Soc. Tech. Comm. (sr.; competition judge 1994, 2005, Tech. Manual Achievement award 1986, Tech. Manual Merit award 1990, 1992—93, 1996, Tech. Manual Excellence award 1996, Tech. Manual Disting. award 2005, Tech. Manual Achievement award 1996), Mensa. Avocations: jazz aerobics, photography, volleyball. Office: C E Niehoff & Co 2021 Lee St Evanston IL 60202 Office Phone: 847-866-1507. E-mail: bkomp@ceniehoff.com, centwriter11@comcast.net.

KOMPASS, EDWARD JOHN, consulting editor; b. Jersey City, Dec. 22, 1926; s. Edward F. and Margaret A. (Doran) K.; m. Amelia M. Heubel, Sept. 22, 1951; children: Christine (Mrs. Kevin Scully), Daniel E., Andrew J., Timothy M., Matthew P., Julie A. (Mrs. Matthew Wilhm). Degree in mech. engring., Stevens Inst. Tech., 1951. Jr. engr. Intelectron Inc., N.Y.C., 1951-52; engr. De Florez Co., N.Y.C., 1952-54; asst. editor control engring., McGraw-Hill Pub. Co., N.Y.C., 1954-60, assoc. editor, 1960-65; mng. editor control engring., Dun-Donnelley Pub. Corp., N.Y.C., 1965-72; editor control engring., Tech. Pub., Barrington, Ill., 1972-86; editorial dir. control engring. Cahners Publ., 1986-87, cons. editor, 1987—, forum discussions moderator, control engring online, 1997. Co-organizer ann. advanced control confs. Purdue U., Lafayette, Ind., 1974-77, 79-93; conf. dir. Internat. Control. Engring. Expn. and Conf., Chgo., 1992-94; mem. adv. coun. Indsl. Automation Conf., 1994, 95, 96. Editor, contbr. profl. articles and editorials to jours.; editorial advisor Detroit Engr. With USNR, 1944-46. Recipient 19th Ann. Crain award Assn. Bus. Pubs., 1987. Mem. IEEE, Am. Soc. Bus. Paper Editors, Instrument Soc. Am., Engring. Soc. Detroit, Am. Legion, VFW, Rotary Internat., Beta Theta Pi. Roman Catholic. Home and Office: 678 Cobb Hill Rd Lincoln VT 05443-9699 E-mail: ekompass@gmavt.net.

KON, ALEXANDER A., pediatrician, educator; BA, U. Calif., Berkeley, 1989; MD, CM, McGill U., Montreal, Can., 1994. Diplomate Nat. Bd. Med. Examiners, 1995, gen. pediat. Am. Bd. Pediat., 2000, pediatric critical care medicine Am. Bd. Pediat., 2002. Resident in pediat. Stanford U., Palo Alto, Calif., 1994—97; clin. fellow, pediatric critical care medicine U. Calif., San Francisco, 1997—2000, fellow, program in bioethics, 1997—2000; asst. prof. clin. pediat. U. of Calif., Davis, 2000—, aux. faculty mem., 2001—. Rsch. asst. U. Calif., San Francisco, 1987—88; vis. scholar Harvard U.-MIT, 1992; Sir William Osler spkr. McGill U. Faculty Medicine, 1992; lectr. in field. Contbr. articles to profl. jours., including Neurology, others. Mem. profl. edn. workgroup Calif. Coalition for Compassionate Care, 2002—; mem. hosp. ethics com. U. Calif. Med. Ctr., San Francisco, 1998—2000, U. Calif. Davis Med. Ctr., 2000—, mem. pediatric ICU adv. com., 2000—, mem. pediatric ICU clin. practice com., 2000—, mem. pediatric ICU morbidity and mortality com., 2000—, mem. pediatric critical care faculty search com., 2000—, chair pediatric ICU visitation com., 2002, mem. pediatric ICU pain mgmt. com., 2002, chair ethics com., subcom. on edn., 2003—, mem. adv. com. Gen. Clin. Rsch. Ctr., 2004—. Recipient Tchg. award, Am. Acad. Family Physicians, 2001; grantee Minor's Understanding of Clin. Rsch., Children's Miracle Network, 2003—. Fellow: Am. Acad. Pediat.; mem.: Calif. Thoracic Soc. (steering com. 2002—), Am. Soc. for Bioethics and Humanities (accreditation coun. for grad. med. edn. 2002—), Soc. of Critical Care Medicine (patient and family support com. 2002—, Rsch. award 2001). Office: U Calif Davis 2516 Stockton Blvd Sacramento CA 95817

KONA, MARTHA MISTINA, librarian, freelance information consultant; b. Banovce, Slovakia; came to U.S., 1950; d. Albert and Anna (Kubrican) Mistina; m. William Kona, Aug. 6, 1955 (dec. Dec. 1989); children: Olivia, Lindy Anne. Student, U. Salzburg, 1950; BA, Rosary Coll., 1953, MA, 1958; postgrad., Roosevelt U., 1980. Libr. instr., prof. Univ. Ill., Chgo., 1958-63; rsch. libr. Cen. Soya Chemurgy, Chgo., 1965-73; asst. dir. Rush Univ. Libr., Chgo., 1973-78; pvt. practice cons., info. specialist Wilmette, Ill., 1980; pvt. practice author and lectr., 1985—. Cons., liaison Matica Slovenska, Slovak Nat. Libr. and Archives, Martin, Slovak Republic, Slovac World Congress, 1991-98. Author: Soybean Proteins, 1969, Multi Media Catalog, 1975, Health Science Librarians of Illinois, 1977, Slovak Americans and Canadians, 1985; co-author, editor: Archbishop Dr. Karol Kmetko, 1989, PhD Dissertations in Slovakiana in the Western World: Bibliography, 1996; contbr. articles to profl. jours. Bd. dirs. Slovak Am. Found. Edn. and Sci., Inc., 1994; Slovak rep. European-Am. adv. bd. Archdiocese Chgo. Mem. AAUW, AAUP (chair bylaws com. 1975-77), Health Sci. Librs. Ill. (co-founder, archivist 1970-77), Slovak World Congress (chair heritage and culture commn. 1990—), First Slovak League of Am., Slovak Cath. Falcon, Ill. Audio Visual Assn. (pres. 1975-77), Soveriegn Mil. Order of Temple of Jerusalem (Grand Cross, 1975, Order of Merit in Grade and Rankd of Grand Comdr., 1999—, Grand Magistral Liaison, 1989-96), Slovak Inst. (Rome), Imperial Order of Constantine the Great and St. Helen (bd. dirs. 1977—), Dames of the Order in the U.S.A. (Lady Comdr.), Order St. John Jerusalem, Woman's Club Wilmette Philanthropy (chair 1991-93), Pi Gamma Mu. Avocations: reading, travel, classical music, physical fitness, beachcombing. Home: 600 3rd St Wilmette IL 60091-1921

KONAN, DENISE, academic administrator, economics professor; BA, Goshen Coll.; MA, PhD, Univ. Colo., Boulder. Prof. econ. Univ. Hawaii, Manoa, 1993—, asst. vice chancellor, 2002—05, interim chancellor, 2005—. Contbr. articles in profl. jours., chapters to books. Office: Univ of Hawaii Manoa Chancellor's Office 2500 Campus Rd Honolulu HI 96822*

KONATE, DIALLA, mathematician, educator; b. Bafoulabe, Mali, Sept. 10, 1953; s. Zegue Konate and Morimoussou Dansira; m. Habsatou Ba, Sept. 24, 1977; children: Ramata, Mariam, Aicha, Ibrahim. DEA, U. Lyon, France, 1978; Doctorate, U. Lyon, 1979. Lectr. U. Grenoble, France, 1976-78; sr. lectr. U. Lyon, 1978-80; asst. prof. ENIG, Gabes, Tunisia, 1980-83, chair dept. math., 1980-84; dir., sci. rschr. LICIA, Paris, 1984-96, ICTA, Washington, 1998—; prof. UAG, France; prof. math. dept. Va. Polytechnic Inst. State U., Blacksburg, Va.; dir. inst. high performance computing applications Winston-Salem State U., SC. Chair sci. program INTI, Africa, 1998—; mem. anti-corruption forum World Bank Mali Govt., 1998-2000; UNDP vis. prof. U. Mali, 1998—; devel. project supr. World Bank, Africa, 1999—. Editor Techinche-Technologie-Development, 1987. Achievements include research in singular perturbation; developing a new technique in singular perturbation that is now considered as an appreciable advance in field. Business E-Mail: dkonate@vt.edu, konated@wssu.edu.

KONCHITSKY, ALON, electronics engineer, communications executive; PhD, Bournemouth (Eng.) U.; MA in Mgmt., Bournemouth (Eng.)U.; BSc in Computer Sci., Tel Aviv (Israel) U.; degree in Elec. Engring., Tel Aviv (Israel) Inst. of Tech. Rschr. DSP Comm., Tel Aviv; tech. leader Nokia, San Diego; chief wireless arch. Advanced Radio Solutions, Cupertino, Calif., 2002—05, chief tech. officer. Cons. Goldman Sachs, Fidelity, VCs, San Diego; dir. Digital Comm. Sys., v.p. engring. tech. rsch. Recipient Tech. award, USAF, 1995. Mem.: IEEE, U. Calif. San Diego Connect. Constitution. Achievements include development of digital radio. Personal E-mail: dr.alon.konchitsky@ieee.org.

KONDOS, GREGORY, painter, art educator; b. Lynn, Mass., 1923; m. Moni Van Camp. BA, MA, Calif. State Univ., Sacramento. Faculty Sacramento City Coll., 1956—62, chmn. Art dept., 1962—82. Artist in residence Yosemite Nat. Park; guest instr. Univ. Calif., Berkeley, Univ. Fla., Monterey Mus. Art. Exhibition at Am. Acad. Arts & Letters, NYC, 1993 With USN, 1942—46. Recipient Dillon Collection prize, Winter Invitational, Calif. Palace, Legion of Honor. Mem.: NAD (academician 1995—). Office: Gregory Kondos Art Gallery 3835 Freeport Blvd Sacramento CA 95822*

KONDRACKE, MORTON MATT, journalist; b. Chgo., Apr. 28, 1939; s. Matthew and Genevieve Marta (Abrams) K.; m. Millicent Martinez, Oct. 7, 1967; children: Alexandra, Andréa. AB, Dartmouth Coll., 1960. Corr. Chgo. Sun Times, Chgo. and Washington, 1963-77; exec. editor The New Republic, Washington, 1977-85; columnist Wall Street Jour., Washington, 1980-85, United Features Syndicate, Washington, 1983-85; Washington bur. chief Newsweek Mag., Washington, 1985-86; sr. editor The New Republic, Washington, 1986—91; exec editor & columnist Roll Call, 1991—; co-host, The Beltway Boys Fox News Channel, 1996—. Radio commentator Nat. Pub. Radio and Sta. WRC-AM, Washington, 1978-83; TV commentator McLaughlin Group, Washington, 1981—96, PBS; author Saving Milly, 2001. Panelist presdl. debate, Kansas City, Mo., 1984; bd. dirs. Freedom House, 1984— . Served with U.S. Army, 1960-63 Mem.: Michael J. Fox Found for Parkinson's Rsch, Parkinson's Action Network. Office: Roll Call Suite 700 50 F St NW Washington DC 20001*

KONDRACKI, EDWARD ANTHONY, lawyer; b. Camden, N.J., Oct. 10, 1946; s. Edward S. and Helen J. (Roman) K.; m. Mary A. Russo, Aug. 3, 1974; children: Elysia A., Michelle A. BA, Rutgers U., 1968, JD, 1971. Bar: N.J. 1971, U.S. Dist. Ct. N.J. 1971, U.S. Supreme Ct. 1977, U.S. Ct. Appeals (3d cir.) 1980. Law clk. U.S. Dist. Ct., Camden, N.J., 1971-72; assoc. Davis & Reberkenny, Cherry Hill, N.J., 1972-75, mem., dir., 1975-99; mem. Law Offices of Edward A. Kondracki, L.L.C., Medford, N.J., 2000—. Counsel Evesham Mcpl. Utilities Authority, Bordentown Sewerage Authority, Mt. Holly Mcpl. Utilities Authority, Bordentown City Water Utility, Moorestown Twp. Water & Sewer Utility; mem. Am. Cancer Soc.; chair parents adv. com. Keuka Coll. Mem. ABA, Assn Environ. Authorities (chmn. legal com. 1981-97, trustee 2000—), Trial Attys. N.J. (trustee 1985-90), N.J. State Bar Assn., Burlington County Bar Assn. Roman Catholic. Home: 68 Fawn Ct Medford NJ 08055-8344

KONECK, JOHN MICHAEL, lawyer; b. Mpls., Aug. 16, 1953; s. Robert W. and Bernice V.; m. Debra K. Plotz, Aug. 16, 1980; 1 child, Robert John. BS, N.D. State U., 1975; JD, Yale Law Sch., Mpls., 1978. Bar: N.D. 1978, Minn. 1979. Jud. law clk. N.D. Supreme Ct., Bismarck, 1978-79; ptnr. Fredrikson & Byron, Mpls., 1979—. Real property law specialist, mem. Minn. Bd. Legal Cert., Supreme Ct. Minn., 1994-99, chmn., 1996-99; mem. Vol. Lawyers Network; assoc. prof. William Mitchell Coll. Law, 1997—. Mem. ABA (chair litig. and dispute resolution, com. of sect. real property, probate and trust law 1995-98, chief editor newsletter of litig. and dispute resolution com. 1991-93, vice chair 1991-95), Am. Coll. Real Estate Lawyers, Minn. State Bar Assn. (co-chair real property cert. coun. 1990—, mem. rules of profl. conduct com.), State Bar Assn. N.D., Hennepin County Bar Assn. (co-chair rules of profl. conduct com. 1994-96). Office: Fredrikson & Byron 200 S 6th St Ste 4000 Minneapolis MN 55402-1425 Office Phone: 612-492-7038. E-mail: jkoneck@fredlaw.com.

KONECNI, VLADIMIR J. J. CH. S. (GRAF KONECNI), psychologist, educator, writer; b. Belgrade, Yugoslavia, Oct. 27, 1944; s. Josip J. and Dora D. (Vasic) Konecni; m. Daiva K. Stasiulis, Jan. 3, 1973 (div. Apr. 7, 1977); m. Marie Gabrielle Frey, May 11, 1987 (dec. Oct. 1, 1989); m. Mirjam Christina Dolman, Nov. 27, 1993; 1 child, Dusan A. V. C. B. BSc magna cum laude, Belgrade U., Yugoslavia, 1968; MA, U. Toronto, Can., 1971, PhD, 1973. Asst. prof. U. Calif. San Diego, La Jolla, 1973—78, assoc. prof., 1978—82, prof. psychology, 1982—; prof. methodology in psychology Belgrade U., Serbia and Montenegro, 1994—. Vis. prof. Sydney U., Australia, 1979, U. Western Australia, Perth, 1979, Pontifica U. Catolica, Rio de Janeiro, 1980, London Sch. Econs., 1980—81, Free U. Berlin, 1986, Hebrew U., Jerusalem, 1986, U. Cape Town, South Africa, 1987, U. Amsterdam, Netherlands, 1991, Tartu U., Estonia, 2002—; fellow John Simon Guggenheim Meml. Found., N.Y.C., 1979—80; vis. scientist Russian Acad. Scis., St. Petersburg, 1993. Author, producer, director: (performance pieces) Paat (The Boat), 2001; author, director, producer (performance pieces) Beckett v. Duchamp, 2002, author, producer, director Dvojnost (Duality), 2003; one-man shows include Of Nuns, Spices, and Boiling Mud, 1982, West Hollywood Art Galleries, 1986, Blue and brown, Tallinn City Mus., Estonia, 1999; poet (prin. works) Port-au-Prince, 1996, Door, 1997. Fellow, John Simon Guggenheim Meml. Found., 1979—80. Mem.: Internat. Informatization Acad., European Psychology-Law Assn., Internat. Assn. Aesthetics. Libertarian. Serbian Orthodox. Avocations: mountain climbing, horseback riding, swimming, chess, fencing.

KONENKAMP, JOHN K., state supreme court justice; b. Oct. 20, 1944; m. Geri Konenkamp; children: Kathryn, Matthew. JD, U. S.D., 1974. Dep. state's atty., Rapid City; pvt. practice, 1977-84; judge SD Cir Ct. (7th cir.), 1984—88, presiding judge, 1988-94; assoc. justice SD Supreme Ct., Pierre, 1994—. Bd. dirs. Alt. Dispute Resolution Com., Adv. Bd. for Casey Family Program. Served in USN. Mem. Am. Judicature Soc., State Bar S.D., Pennington County Bar Assn., Nat. CASA Assn., Am. Legion. Office: SD Supreme Ct 500 E Capitol Ave Pierre SD 57501-5070

KONETY, BADRINATH R., surgeon, researcher; s. R. S. and Prabha R. Konety; m. Suma H. Murthy, Oct. 1992; children: Isha R., Arjun S. BA, St. Joseph's Coll., Bangalore, India, 1984; MD, Bangalore U., 1990; MBA, U. Pitts., 2000. Diplomate Am. Bd. of Urology, 2003. Asst. prof. U. of Iowa, 2001—; chief, sect. of urology Vets. Adminstrn. Med. Ctr., 2002—. Recipient Resident Essay Contest, Am. Urologic Assn. NE Sect., 1998, Pfizer Scholars in Urology award, Pfizer Inc., 1998, Frederick N. Schwentker Endowment award, U. Pitts., 1998; fellow Jahnigen Rsch. scholar, Am. Geriat. Soc., 2004—; grantee New Investigator award, Dept. of Def., 2004—. Fellow: ACS (assoc.); mem.: Soc. for Basic Urologic Rsch., Soc. of Urologic Oncology, Am. Urologic Assn. Achievements include development of Urinary tumor marker BLCA-4 for bladder cancer; EAU-AUA Exchange Fellow year 2004; research in American Foundation for Urologic Disease Research Scholar Award; Ferdinand Valentine Fellowship. Office: Univ Iowa Dept of Urology 3236 RCP 200 Hawkins Dr Iowa City IA 52242 Office Phone: 319-356-1974.

KONETZNI, ALBERT H., JR., career officer; b. N.Y.C., Nov. 16, 1944; s. Albert H. Sr. and Adeline E. (Gergel) K.; m. Shirley A. Lane, Nov. 21, 1995; children: Albert H. III, Kristen, Kiera, Kyle. BS, U.S. Naval Acad., Annapolis, Md., 1966; MS in Pers. Adminstrn., George Washington U., 1972. Commd. ensign U.S. Navy, 1966, advanced through grades to vice adm., 2001; submarine office, comdr. U.S.S. Grayling, Charleston, S.C., 1981-84; comdr. Submarine Squadron 16, Kingsbay, Ga., 1987-89; asst. chief pers. for policy, plans, career progression U.S. Navy, Washington, 1994-95; comdr. Submarine Group Seven, Yokosuka, Japan, 1995-98; comdr. submarine force U.S. Pacific Fleet, Harbor, Hawaii, 1998-2001; dep. commdr. in chief, chief of staff U.S. Atlantic Fleet, 2001—. Co-author: Command At Sea, 1980. Office: USN 1562 Mitscher Ave Ste 250 Norfolk VA 23551-2489

KONG, ADA, chemist; b. Canton, China, Aug. 9, 1964; arrived in U.S., 1979; d. Suk Ming Kong and Wai Chun Mui; m. Wing L. Cheung, Aug. 22, 1983; children: Greg K. Cheung, Brian W. Cheung. BS cum laude, SUNY, Fredonia, 1986. Chemist Chemtech Consulting Group, Inc., N.Y.C., 1986—87; asst. lab. dir. Interstate Sanitation Commn., N.Y.C., 1987—89; chemist U.S. Dept. Energy/Environ. Measurements Lab., N.Y.C., 1989—2003, U.S. Dept. Homeland Security/Environ. Measurements Lab., N.Y.C., 2003—. Contbr. articles to profl. jours. Vol. tchr. Ming Yuen Chinese Sch., N.Y.C., 2000—. Mem.: Chinese Am. Soc. Mass Spectrometrists (pres. 2001—03, adv. com. mem. 2004—), Am. Soc. for Mass Spectrometry. Office: US DHS/EML 201 Varick Street 5th Fl New York NY 10014-4811 Office Phone: 212-602-6247. Office Fax: 212-620-3600. Business E-Mail: ada.kong@dhs.gov.

KONG, LAURA S. L., geophysicist; b. Honolulu, July 23, 1961; d. Albert T.S. and Cordelia (Seu) K.; m. Kevin T.M. Johnson, Mar. 3, 1990. ScB, Brown U., 1983; PhD, MIT/Woods Hole Oceanog. Inst., 1990. Grad. rschr. Woods Hole (Mass.) Oceanog. Instn., 1984-90; postdoctoral fellow U. Tokyo, 1990-91; geophysicist Pacific Tsunami Warning Ctr., Ewa Beach, Hawaii, 1991-93; seismologist U.S. Geol. Survey Hawaiian Volcano Obs., 1993-95; rschr. U. Hawaii, Honolulu, 1996-99; environ. specialist Dept. Transp., Honolulu, 2000—05; dir. Internat. Tsunami Info. Ctr., Honolulu, 2005—. Chair Hawaii Earthquake Adv. Bd., 1994—; tsunami advisor State of Hawaii, 1999—; mem. equal opportunity adv. bd. Nat. Earth Svc. Pacific Region, Honolulu, 1992-93, Asain-Am.-Pacific Islander spl. emphasis program mgr., 1992-93; mem. steering com. U.S. Nat. Tsunami Hazard Mitigation Program; mem. Hawaii State Hazard Mitigation Forum, Hawaii Multi-Hazard Sci. Adv. Com.; legis. rschr. Hawaii Senate, 1996-98. Contbr. articles to profl. jours.; spkr., editl. reviewer in field. Rsch. fellow Japan Govt.-Japan Soc. for Promotion of Sci., 1990; recipient Young Investigator grant Japan Soc. for Promotion of Sci., 1990. Mem. Am. Geophys. Union, Seismol. Soc. Am., Hawaii Ctr. for Volcanology, Assn. Women in Sci., Sigma Xi. Avocation: sports. Office: Nat Weather Svc Internat Tsunami Info Ctr 737 Bishop St Ste 220 Honolulu HI 96813 E-mail: laura.kong@fhwa.dot.gov.*

KONG, NORMAN, chemist; b. Qufu, Shandong, China, Mar. 26, 1964; arrived in US, 1995; s. Fanyi Kong; m. Jingyi Li, Feb. 13, 1989; children: Eddie, Brandon. BSc, Shandong U., Jinan, China, 1984, MSc, 1989; PhD, U. Alta., Edmonton, Can., 1995. Postdoctoral fellow SUNY, Buffalo, 1995—96, sr. postdoctoral fellow, 1996—97; prin. scientist Hoffmann-La Roche, Nutley, NJ, 1997—2001, sr. prin. scientist, 2001—. Contbr. articles to profl. jours. Mem.: N.Y. Acad. Sci., Am. Chem. Soc. Achievements include patents in field. Avocations: music, fishing, hiking, golf. Office: Hoffmann-La Roche 340 Kingsland Nutley NJ 07110 E-mail: nkong2000@yahoo.com.

KÖNIG, PETER, pediatrician, educator; b. Cluj, Romania, Feb. 14, 1938; came to U.S., 1976; s. Rudolf and Irina (Grünwald) K.; m. Lea Schiffer, Sept. 30, 1965; 1 child, Orly. Graduate, Timisoara Med. Sch., Romania, 1959; MD, Hebrew U., Jerusalem, 1966; PhD, U. London, 1974. Resident Hadassah Hosp., Jerusalem, 1969—70, Bikur Cholim Hosp., Jerusalem, 1970-71, staff, 1974-76; fellow in pulmonary diseases Brompton Hosp., London, 1971-74; asst. prof. child health U. Mo., Columbia, 1976-80, assoc. prof. child health, 1980-84, prof. in child health, 1984—. Fellow Am. Acad. Allergy; mem. Am. Thoracic Soc., Acad. Allergy, Soc. Pediatric Research, Chilean Asthma Found., Sigma Xi. Home: 1310 Vintage Dr Columbia MO 65203-4878 Office: U Mo Child Health 1 Hospital Dr Columbia MO 65212-5276 Office Phone: 573-882-6978. Business E-Mail: KonigP@health.missouri.edu.

KONIGSBERG, ALLEN STEWART See ALLEN, WOODY

KONIGSBURG, ELAINE LOBL, writer; b. N.Y.C., Feb. 10, 1930; d. Adolph and Beulah (Klein) Lobl; m. David Konigsburg, July 6, 1952; children— Paul, Laurie, Ross. BS, Carnegie Mellon U., 1952; postgrad., U. Pitts., 1952-54; DHL (hon.), U. North Fla., 2001. Author: juveniles Jennifer, Hecate, Macbeth, William McKinley and Me, Elizabeth, 1967 (Newbery Honor Book), From The Mixed-Up Files of Mrs. Basil E. Frankweiler, 1967 (Newbery medal 1968), About the B'nai Bagels, 1969, (George), 1970, Altogether, One at a Time, 1971, A Proud Taste for Scarlet and Miniver, 1973 (Nat. Book award nominee), The Dragon in the Ghetto Caper, 1974, The Second Mrs. Giaconda, 1975, Father's Arcane Daughter, 1976, Throwing Shadows, 1979 (Am. Book award nominee), Journey to an 800 Number, 1981, Up From Jericho Tel, 1986, Samuel Todd's Book of Great Colors, 1990, Samuel Todd's Book of Great Inventions, 1991, Amy Elizabeth Explores Bloomingdale's, 1992, T-backs, T-shirts, COAT and Suit, 1993, TalkTalk, 1995, The View From Saturday, 1996 (Newbery medal 1997), Silent to the Bone, 2000, The Outcasts of 19 Schuyler Place, 2004. Recipient Regina medal, Cath. Libr. Assn., 2001; named to State of Fla. Hall of Fame, 2000.

KONING, HENDRIK, architect; arrived in U.S., 1979; BArch, U. Melbourne, Australia, 1978; MArch II, UCLA, 1981. Lic. architect Calif., 1982, contractor, 1984; registered architect, Australia; cert. Nat. Coun. Archtl. Registration Bds. Prin. in charge of tech., code, and prodn. issues Koning Eizenberg Architecture, 1981—, v.p. Santa Monica, Calif., 1990—. Mem. U.S. Green Bldg. Coun., instr. UCLA, U. B.C., Harvard U., MIT; lectr. in field. Exhibited works at Bannatyne Gallery, 1991, Gagosian Gallery, 1992, The Contemporary Arts Ctr., 1993, Wexnet Ctr., 1994, MOCA Taipei and Mus. of Art Macau, 2003, Nat. Bldg. Mus., 2004, others; prin. works include The Standard Downtown L.A., Farmers Market Expansion, L.A. (ULI award fr excellence), Avalon Hotel, Beverly Hills (AIA/L.A. Design award, WUF prize), Digital Domain renovation and screening rm., Santa Monica, Lightstorm Entertainment offices and THX theater, Santa Monica, Gilmore Bank, (with RTA) Materials Rsch. Lab. U. Calif., Santa Barbara, Ken. Edwards Ctr. Cmty. Svcs., Santa Monica, Peck Park Cmty. Ctr. Gymnasium, San Pedro, Calif., Sepulveda Recreation Ctr. Gymnasium, L.A., (Nat. Concrete/Masonry award 1996, AIA Calif. Coun. Honor award 1996, AIA L.A. Chpt. Merit Award, 1997, L.A. Bus. Coun. Beautification awrd 1996, AIA/SFV Design award 1995), PS# 1 Elem. Sch., Santa Monica, Famers Market additions and master plan, L.A. (Westside Urban Forum prize 1991), Simone Hotel, L.A. (Nat. Honor award AIA 1994), Boyd Hotel, L.A. Cmty. Corp. Santa Monica Housing Projects, 5th St. Family Housing, Santa Monica, St. John's Hosp. Replacement Housing Program, Santa Monica, Liffman House, Santa Monica, (with Glenn Erikson) Electric Artblock, Venice (Beautification award L.A. Bus. Coun. 1993), 6th St. Condominiums, Santa Monica, Hollywood Duplex, Hollywood Hills (Record Houses Archtl. Record 1988), Tarzana House (Merit award L.A. chpt. AIA 1991, Merit Award AIA Calif. Coun., 1998, Sunset Western Home awards 1993-94), 909 Ho., Santa Monica (Merit award L.A. chpt. AIA 1991), 31st St. House, Santa Monica (Honor award AIACC 1994, Record House 1995, Nat. AIA Honor award 1996), others. Recipient 1st award Progressive Architecture, 1987; named one of Domino's Top 30 Architects, 1989. Fellow AIA (juror San Diego design awards 1992, panelist honor awards 1994, Calif. coun. spl. awards 1997, nat. interior design awards 1997), Royal Australian Inst. Archs.; mem. Nat. Trust for Hist. Preservation, So. Calif. Assn. Non-Profit Housing, L.A. Conservancy. Office: Koning Eizenberg Architecture 1454 25th St Santa Monica CA 90404-3008 E-mail: info@kearch.com.

KONISHI, MASAKAZU, neuroscientist, educator; b. Kyoto, Feb. 17, 1933; BS, Hokkaido U., Japan, 1956, MS, 1958, LLD (hon.), 1991; honoris causa, Hokkaido U., 1991; PhD in Zoology, U. Calif., Berkeley, 1963. Postdoctoral fellow Alexander von Humboldt Found., 1963-64; fellow Internat. Brain Rsch. Orgn. and UNESCO, 1964-65; asst. prof. zoology U. Wis., 1965-66; asst. to assoc. prof. biology Princeton U., NJ, 1970-75; prof. biology Calif. Inst. Tech., Pasadena, 1975-79, Bing prof. behavioral biology, 1979—. Mem. Salk Inst., 1991—. Assoc. editor Jour. Neurosci., 1980-89, sect. editor, 1990-93; mem. editl. adv. bd. Jour. Comparative Physiology. Recipient Elliot Coues award, Am. Ornithologists Union, 1983, F.O. Schmitt prize, 1987, Internat. prize for biology Japan Soc. for Promotion Sci., 1990, David Sparks award in Integrative Neurophysiology U. Ala., 1992, Charles A. Dana award for Pioneering Achievements in Health and Edn., 1992, Sci. Writing prize Acoustical Soc. Am., 1994, Found. Ipsen prize, 1999, Kresge/Mirmelstein award for Excellence in Auditory Rsch., 2001, Lewis S. Rosenstiel award for Disting. Work in Basic Med. Sci., Brandeis U., 2004, Edward M. Scolnick prize in Neuroscience, McGovern Inst., MIT, 2004, Gerard prize, Soc. Neuroscience, 2004, Karl Spencer Lashley award, Am. Philos. Soc., 2004. Mem.: Internat. Soc. Neuroethology (pres. 1986—89), Am. Acad. Arts and Scis., Nat. Acad. Scis. Office: Calif Inst Tech Divsn Biology 1200 E California Blvd Pasadena CA 91125-0001

KONKASHBAEV, ISAK KAZHKENOVICH, physicist; b. Almaty, Kazakhstan, Mar. 28, 1943; s. Kazhken Konkashbaev and Zhaiza Zhumanova; m. Rauza Sagievna Nurkeeva, Nov. 5, 1971; children: Askar Isakovich Konkachbaev, Anuar Isakovich Konkachbaev. Bachelors Degree, Novosibirsk State U., Russia, 1963, MS, 1965; PhD, Moscow State U., 1672; DSc, Kurchatov Inst. of Atomic Energy, 1989. Scientist Budker Inst. of Nuc. Physics, Novosibirsk, Russia, 1968—71, Kurchatov Inst. of Atomic Energy, Moscow, 1971—75, heat of theoretical group Troitsk, Moscow Region, Russia, 1975—89; head of theoretical lab. Troitsk Inst. for Innovation and Fusion Rsch., 1990—2002; vis. scientist Karlsruhe Forshungzentrum, Karlsruhe, Germany, 1992—98; physicist Argonne Nat. Lab., Ill., 1998—. Mem.: Am. Nuc. Soc. (assoc.). Achievements include patents for Fusion Systems. Home: 143D Enclave Cir Bolingbrook IL 60440 Office: Argonne Nat Lab 9700 South Cass Ave Argonne IL 60439 Office Phone: 630-252-9171. Home Fax: 630-252-3250; Office Fax: 530-252-3250. Personal E-mail: isak@anl.gov.

KONKEL, MARY SUSAN, library administrator; b. Portland, Oreg., Jan. 7, 1957; d. William Eugene Konkel and Carole Barbara Lehman; m. Steven Andrew Balcken, Dec. 19, 1981; 1 child, Dianna Lynn Balcken. BA in Spanish and Portuguese, U. Wis., Milw., 1979, MLS, 1981; MA in Comm. Studies, Governors State U., University Park, 1992; cert. in Computer Info. Systems, Coll. of DuPage, Ill., 2003. Libr. tech. asst. U. Wis., Milw., 1976-81, original cataloger, acad. specialist, 1982-85; fieldworker Am. Geog. Soc. Collection, Milw., 1980-81; head monographic cataloging unit, asst. libr. U. Cin., 1985-87; head cataloging, libr., univ. prof. Governors State U., 1987-92; head cataloging, asst. prof. bibliography U. Akron, Ohio, 1992-98, assoc. prof. bibliography, 1999-2001; head tech. svcs., assoc. prof. Coll. of DuPage, Ill., 2001—. Pres. Online Audiovisual Catalogers, Inc., 1994-95, cataloging policy com., 1989-93; presenter in field. Contbr. articles to profl. jours. Vol. Inventure Pl. Nat. Inventors Hall of Fame Mus., Akron, 1995-2000; bd. dirs. Suburban Libr. Sys., Burr Ridge, Ill., 1989-92; trustee Richton Park (Ill.) Pub. Libr., 1989-92; founding mem. YMCA Trailblazers Oreg. Trail Bunkhouse, 1993-96. Mem. ALA (treas., video round table), Assn. Coll. and Rsch. Librs. (chair media resources com.), Assn. Libr. Collections and Tech. Svcs., Acad. Libr. Assn. Ohio (pres. 1998-99, bd. dirs. 1995-97, chair pub. rels. com. 1996-97, archivist 1999-2001). Avocations: camping, mall shopping, movies, music, reading. Office: Library Coll of DuPage 425 Fawell Blvd Glen Ellyn IL 60137-6599 Business E-Mail: konkel@cdnet.cod.edu.

KONNAK, JOHN WILLIAM, surgery educator; b. Racine, Wis., June 28, 1937; s. William Frank and Ruth Viola Konnak; m. Betty LaFleur, June 9, 1962; 1 child, William. BS, U. Wis., 1959, MD, 1962. Diplomate Am. Bd. Urology. Intern Phila. Gen. Hosp., 1962-63; asst. resident Harbor Gen. Hosp., Torrance, Calif., 1965-66; resident U. Mich. Hosp., Ann Arbor, 1966-69, attending staff mem., 1969—99; prof. surgery U. Mich. Med. Sch., Ann Arbor, 1982—2001, emeritus prof. urology, 2001—. Served with USPHS, 1963-65. Fellow ACS; mem. Cen. Surg. Assn., Am. Urol. Assn., Mich. Urol. Assn. (pres. 1991-92), Transplantation Soc. Mich. (pres. 1981-83), Alpha Omega Alpha. Republican. Avocation: scuba diving. Home: 2906 Parkridge Dr Ann Arbor MI 48103-1737

KONNER, JOAN WEINER, academic administrator, educator, television producer, writer, television executive; b. Paterson, N.J., Feb. 24, 1931; d. Martin and Tillie (Frankel) Weiner; children: Rosemary, Catherine (dec.); m. Alvin H. Perlmutter. Student, Vassar Coll., 1948—49; BA, Sarah Lawrence Coll., 1951; MS, Columbia U., 1961. Editl. writer, columnist, reporter Hackensack (N.J.) Record, 1961-63; prodr., reporter WNDT Ednl. Broadcasting Corp., N.Y.C., 1963-65; prodr., writer, reporter NBC News, N.Y.C., 1965-77; exec. prodr. nat. pub. affairs programs WNET Ednl. Broadcasting Corp., N.Y.C., 1977-78, exec. prodr. Bill Moyers Jour., 1978-81, v.p. met. programming, 1981-84; exec. prodr., pres., co-founder Pub. Affairs TV with Bill Moyers PBS; prof. broadcast and journalism, dean emerita Grad. Sch. Journalism Columbia U., N.Y.C., 1988-97, pub. Columbia Journalism Rev., 1988-99. Prof. Grad. Sch. Journalism, Columbia U., N.Y.C., 1988—. Bd. dirs. Hudson River Found., Contemplative Mind in Society, Florence and John Schumann Found.; past trustee Providence Jour., Columbia U., Rockland Ctr. for Arts, Sarah Lawrence Coll., Religion Writers Found., Radio and TV News Dirs. Found., Pulitzer Prize Bd. Recipient 16 Emmy awards NATAS, Columbia-du Pont award, Peabody award, Gavel award ABA, Edward R. Murrow award, others. Mem. Dirs. Guild, Writers Guild, Soc. Profl. Journalists, Newspaper Women's Club of N.Y.C., Century Assn., Cosmopolitan Club. Office: Columbia U Grad Sch Journalism Journalism Bldg New York NY 10027

KONNEY, PAUL EDWARD, consumer products company executive, lawyer; b. Hartford, Conn., June 24, 1944; s. William Frederick and Dorothy (Dittmer) K.; m. Elizabeth Buhl Wright Temple, July 27, 1968 (div. 1979); m. Barbara Jean Greaves, June 2, 1979; children: Gretchen Blair, Tyler Wingard. AB cum laude, Harvard U., 1966; JD, U. Pa., 1969. Bar: N.Y. 1973. Law clk. to Hon. Chief Judge William Hastie U.S. Ct. Appeals, Phila., 1969-70; assoc. Debevoise & Plimpton, N.Y.C., 1971-81; v.p., gen. counsel Tambrands Inc., Lake Success, N.Y., 1982-83, v.p., gen. counsel, sec. White Plains, N.Y., 1983-89, sr. v.p., gen. counsel, sec., 1989-93; v.p., gen. counsel Quaker State Corp., Oil City, Pa., 1994, v.p., gen. counsel, sec. Irving, Texas, 1995, sr. v.p., gen. counsel, sec., 1996-98, Estee Lauder Cos. Inc., N.Y.C., 1999—. Bd. dirs. Taylor & Dodge Inc., N.Y.C.; mem. U.S. Del. US/USSR Legal Exchange, Russia, 1988; internat. policy com. U.S. C of C, Washington, 1989—. Article and book rev. editor U. Pa. Law Rev., 1968-69. Bd. dir. Visiting Nurse Assn., Dallas, 1996-99. Mem. U.S. delegation to 1st U.S.-USSR legal seminar. Mem. ABA, Am. Soc. Corp. Secs., U.S. C. of C. (internat. policy com.). Episcopalian. Office: The Estee Lauder Cos Inc 767 5th Ave New York NY 10153-0003 E-mail: pekonney@aol.com.

KONNYU, ERNEST LESLIE, former congressman; b. Tamasi, Hungary, May 17, 1937; arrived in US, 1949; s. Leslie and Elizabeth Konnyu; m. Lillian Muenks, Nov. 25, 1959; children: Carol, Renata, Lisa, Victoria. Student, U. Md., 1960-62; BS in Acctg., Ohio State U., 1965. Mem. Calif.

Assembly, Sacramento, 1980-86, 100th Congress from 12th Calif. dist., 1987-89; CEO Konnyu Financials and Taxes, Inc. Chmn. Assembly Rep. Policy Com. of State Assembly, Sacramento, 1985-86; vice chmn. Assembly Human Svcs., Sacramento, 1980-86; vice chmn. Policy Rsch. Com., Sacramento, 1985-86. Mem. Rep. State Cen. Com., Calif., 1977-88, Rep. Cen. Com., Santa Clara County, Calif., 1980-88; mem. adv. bd. El Camino Hosp., Mountain View, Calif., 1987-89. Served to maj. USAF, 1959-69. Recipient Nat. Def. Medal, 1968, Disting. Service award U.S. Jaycees, 1969, Nat. Security award Am. Security Council Found., 1987; named lifetime senator U.S. Jaycees, 1977. Mem. Am.- Hungarian C. of C. (v.p. 1995-97). Republican. Roman Catholic. Avocations: politics, golf. Office Phone: 408-244-3299. Personal E-mail: konnyu@sbcglobal.net.

KONOLA, CLAUDETTE JUNE, finance company executive, consultant; b. Deadwood, SD, Sept. 2, 1948; d. Donald John Konola and Rose Marie Larive-Konola. BSc, Univ. Colo., 1981. Mgmt. trainee Am. Nat. Bank, Denver, 1974-80; training coord. loan analysis United Bank Denver, 1980-81; asst. v.p. Canadian Commercial Bank, Denver, 1981-83, First Interstate Bank Denver, 1983-88; v.p. Ctrl. Bank Denver, 1988-93; revolving loan fund adminstr. Mesa county Western Colo. Bus. Devel. Corp., Grand Junction, Colo., 1994-96; southwest regional dir. Cmty. Reinvestment Fund, Inc., Mpls., 1996—2002, nat. dir. tng. and assistance, 2002—. Pres. Downtown Denver Bus. and Profl. Women, 1985—87; treas. Women's Bean Project, Denver, 1991—93; sec., treas. Riverside Task Force, Grand Junction, 1995—98; co-founder Colo. Women's Hall of Fame, 1986. Democrat. Office: Cmty Reinvestment Fund PO Box 552 Clifton CO 81520-0552 Office Phone: 970-434-5318. Personal E-mail: claudette@crfusa.com.

KONOPINSKI, VIRGIL JAMES, industrial hygienist, consultant; b. Toledo, July 11, 1935; BSChemE, U. Toledo, 1956; MSChemE, Pratt Inst., 1960; MBA, Bowling Green State U., 1971. Registered profl. engr., Ohio, Ind., Calif., cert. indsl. hygienist, safety profl. Assoc. engr. Owens Ill., Toledo, 1956, 60; real estate developer Grand Rapids, Ohio, 1961; chem. engr. USPHS, Cin., 1961-64; sr. environ. engr. Vistron Corp., Lima, Ohio, 1964-67; environ. specialist, asst. to dir. environ. control Owens Corning Fiberglas, Toledo, 1967-72; gen. mgr. Midwest Environ. Mgmt., Maumee, Ohio, 1972-73; staff specialist, indl. hygienist Williams Bros. Waste Control, Tulsa, 1973-75; dir. divsn. indsl. hygiene and radiol. health Ind. State Bd. Health, Indpls., 1975-87; exec. v.p. ACT Ind., Indpls., 1987-89; sr. cons. Occusafe, Chgo., 1990-91; regional safety engr., human resources analyst/safety U.S. Postal Svc., Bloomingdale, Ill., 1991—2003; cons. in field, 2003—. Bd. dirs. IOSHA Indsl. Hygiene, 1975—83; cons. indoor air, radon, occupl. health, Zionsville, 1987—91, Cary, 1991—2003, Maumee, Ohio, 2003—. Contbr. articles to profl. jours. With USNR, 1956—59. Mem.: Am. Soc. Safety Engrs., Mil. Officers Assn., Naval Res. Assn. Republican. Roman Catholic. Home and Office: 7206 Longwater Dr Maumee OH 43537 Office Phone: 419-878-3158.

KONOW, JAMES DOUGLAS, economist, educator; b. Phoenix, Mar. 7, 1955; s. Albert Henry Sr. and Nancy (Brown) K.; m. Petra Liedke, Apr. 8, 1982; 1 child, Alexander Ian. BA in Econs., Ariz. State U., 1977; MA in Econs., U. Calif., San Diego, 1983; PhD in Econs., UCLA, 1989. Fin. analyst Ford Motor Co., Cologne, Germany, 1979-82; asst. prof. Loyola Marymount U., L.A., 1989-96, assoc. prof., 1996-2001, prof., 2001—, chair dept. econs., 2004—. Vis. fgn. scholar Osaka U., Japan, 2004. Assoc. editor Social Justice Rsch.; contbr. articles to Am. Econ. Rev., Econ. Inquiry, Jour. Econ. Behavior and Orgn., Jour. Econ. Lit. Bd. dirs. UCLA Ctr. Governance, 2000—. Fulbright-Hayes scholar, 1978; Russell Sage Found. grantee, 1999; fellow Loyola Marymount U., 1999, grantee, 2000. Mem. Am. Econ. Assn., Econ. Sci. Assn., Pub. Choice Soc., Phi Beta Kappa, Omicron Delta Epsilon, Phi Kappa Phi Avocations: squash, reading, cooking, wine, hiking. Office: Loyola Marymount U Dept Econs One LMU Dr Ste 4200 Los Angeles CA 90045 E-mail: jkonow@lmu.edu.

KONOWIECKI, JOSEPH SAMUEL, lawyer, health facility administrator; b. Albany, NY, May 17, 1953; BA in polit. sci. magna cum laude, UCLA, 1975; JD, U. Calif. Hastings Coll. Law, San Francisco, 1978. Bar: Calif. 1978, DC. Ptnr. K & R Law Group (formerly Konowiecki & Rank LLP), LA, 1980—2001; gen. counsel PacifiCare Health Systems, Inc., Calif., 1989—, sec., 1993—, exec. v.p., 1999—, full-time exec. v.p., gen. counsel, sec., 2002—. Adv. bd. ForestWeb Inc., 2000—. Founding editor Hastings Comm. and Entertainment Law Jour.; contbr. articles to Practicing Law Inst., law journals. Office: PacifiCare Health Sys Inc 5995 Plaza Dr Cypress CA 90630

KONRADI, DONNA BETH, nurse, educator; b. Chgo., Mar. 18, 1954; d. Loren Lee and Viola (Sopocy) Brandt; m. Eugene Dennis Konradi, July 21, 1984; children: Anna, Andrew. BSN, No. Ill. U., 1976; MSN, U. Ill., Chgo., 1983; D of Nursing Sci., Ind. U., 1994. RN, Ill. From instr. to asst. prof. St. Francis Med. Ctr. Coll. Nursing, Peoria, Ill., 1985-89; clin. part-time faculty Ind. U. Sch. Nursing, Indpls., 1989-91; staff devel. cons. St. Vincent Hosp. and Health Care Ctr., Indpls., 1990-94; asst. prof. Bradley U., Peoria, 1994-99; grad. dir., asst. prof. Mennonite Coll. Nursing, Ill. State U., Normal, 1999-2001. Vis. lectr. Ind. U. Sch. Nursing, 1992-94; cons. test constrn. Regents Coll., Albany, N.Y., 1993-2000. Contbr. articles to profl. jours. Mem. rsch. com. St. Francis Med. Ctr., 1997-2001; mem. com. Ctrl. Ill. Stroke Coun., Peoria, 1997-99. Recipient rsch. grants Ind. U. Sch. Nursing, 1993-94, Ill. State U., 2000, Ill. State U. Assessment Office, 2001. Mem. ANA, Ill. Nurses Assn. (Dist. 6 treas./bd. dirs. 1997-99), Midwest Nursing Rsch. Soc. (rsch. sect. chair/co-chair 1998-2001), Sigma Theta Tau (Alpha chpt. counselor/bd. dirs. 1992-93). Home: 1800 Continental Dr Zionsville IN 46077-8707 Fax: 309-438-2620. E-mail: dbkonra@ilstu.edu.

KONSELMAN, DOUGLAS DEREK, lawyer; b. Tampa, Fla., Oct. 3, 1958; s. Derek Konselman and Linda (Horton) Fisher. BA in Biology, U. South Fla., 1981; JD, Loyola U., New Orleans, 1984; LLM, Georgetown U., 1996. Bar: Fla., 1984, N.J. 1985, N.Y. 1985, D.C. 1985, U.S. Supreme Ct. 1986. Ptnr. Konselman & Co., Washington, 1991-96; mng. ptnr. Konselman & Ptnrs., N.Y.C., 1996—. Mem. Practicing Law Inst., N.Y.C., 1985—. Contbr. articles to law jours. Bd. dirs. Boca Raton (Fla.) Mus. Art, 1987, Market Square West, 1995-98, 99—. Mem. Am. Corp. Counsel Assn., Am. Soc. Internat. Law, Internat. Assn. Fin. Engrs., Fgn. Law Soc., Soc. for Internat. Devel., Asia Soc., Mensa. Republican. Presbyterian. Avocations: foreign languages, russian, french, german. Office: 801 Pennsylvania Ave NW Washington DC 20004-2615

KONSKI, JAMES LOUIS, civil engineer; b. N.Y.C., Nov. 4, 1917; s. Herbert D. and Ruby (Louis) K.; children: Alexander (dec.), Christina, Marguerite. BS in Civil Engring., U. Mo., 1950, MS in Civil Engring., 1951; PhD, European Inst. Cycle Engring., Essex, England, 1985. Registered profl. engr., N.Y., Ky., R.I., Kans. registered profl. surveyor. Engr., Bur. Yards and Docks, Washington, 1951; structural engr. Sanderson & Porter, N.Y.C., 1951-52; field engr. Ebasco Services, Inc., Owensboro, Ky., 1952-53; chief structural engr. Berger Assos., Syracuse, N.Y., 1953-54, Endman, Anthony & Hosley (formerly Berger Assos.), Syracuse, 1954-57; pres. Konski Engrs. Profl. Corp., Syracuse, 1957—; prin. Konski Engrs. Internat., 1965—. Cons. engr. U.S. Trade Mission to Africa, 1965, to Far East, 1970; speaker Met. Assn. Urban Designers and Environ. Planning Conf., Eng., 1974, Netherlands, 1975 Contbr. articles to profl. jours. Served with USMC, 1939-46; maj. Res. ret. Recipient Honor Award for Disting. Service in Engring., U. Mo., 1986. Fellow ASCE (v.p. 1972-73, nat. dir. 1966-70), Am. Cons. Engrs. Council (past chpt. pres.); mem. Internat. Assn. Bridge and Structural Engrs., NSPE (past chpt. pres., Engr. of Yr. award Cen. N.Y. chpt., 1991), Am. Concrete Inst., Prestressed Concrete Inst., Am. Congress Surveying and Mapping, Am. Mil. Engrs., Am. Water Works Assn., Am. Road Builders Assn., Am. Soc. Photogrammetry, League Am. Wheelman (area rep. 1967-77), U.S. Cycling Fedn., Am. Coll. Sports Medicine, Internat. Randonneurs (dir. USA/Can.), Sigma Xi, Tau Beta Pi, Chi Epsilon, Pi Mu Epsilon. Achievements include participating in Paris-Breast-Paris Bicycle Race, 1975, 79, 83, 87; directing Internat. Randonneurs (U.S.), 401 Man Cycle Team, France, 1991, 95). Office: Old Engine House #2 727 N Salina St Syracuse NY 13208-2510

KONSLER, KRISTEN NICOLE, human resources specialist; b. Lake Forest, Ill., Dec. 30, 1975; d. Rodney, Sr. and Constance Konsler. BA in Psychology, No. Ill. U., 1998; MA in Indsl./Orgnl. Psychology, U. N.C., 2005. Orgnl. effectiveness specialist St. Agnes Med. Ctr., Fresno, Calif., 2002—04; orgnl. effectiveness mgr. Blue Shield Calif., Woodland Hills, 2004—. Recipient Academic Excellence award, No. Ill. U., 1994, 1995; scholar, 1998. Mem.: Orgnl. Devel. Network (assoc.), Soc. Indsl. Orgnl. Psychology (assoc.), Campus Activities Bd. (assoc.; coord. of spl. events and travel 1996—98), Golden Key Nat. Honors Soc. (assoc.), Psychology Nat. Honors Soc. (assoc.; pres. and treas. 1996—98). Office Phone: 818-228-2422.

KONSTAN, DAVID, classics and comparative literature professor, researcher; b. N.Y.C., Nov. 1, 1940; s. Harry and Edythe (Wahrman) K.; m. Pura Nieto; children: Eve Anna, Geoffrey Theodore. Instr. Bklyn. Coll., 1965-67; prof. Wesleyan U., Middletown, Conn., 1967-87; prof. classics and comparative lit. Brown U., Providence, 1987—. Author: Epicurean Psychology, 1973, Roman Comedy, 1983, Simplicius Physics 6, 1989, Sexual Symmetry, 1994, Greek Comedy and Ideology, 1995, Friendship in The Classical World, 1997, Philodemus on Frank Criticism, 1998, Pity Transformed, 2001. Mem. Am. Philol. Assn. (pres. 1999). Avocation: cooking. Home: 70 Westford Rd Providence RI 02906-2515 Office: Brown U 48 College St Providence RI 02912-1856 Office Phone: 401-863-3140. Business E-Mail: dkonstan@brown.edu.

KONTIO, PETER, lawyer; b. Fitchburg, Mass., Jan. 7, 1948; AB in Econ. cum laude with high honors, Clark Univ., 1970; JD, Univ. Chgo., 1973. Bar: Ga. 1973. Ptnr., trial and litig., internat. litig., telecom. groups Alston & Bird LLP, Atlanta. Mem. Chgo. Law Rev. Mem.: ABA, Atlanta Bar Assn., Federal Defender Program, Inc. (pres.), Univ. Chgo. Law Sch. Atlanta Area Alumni Assn. (pres.), Lawyers Club Atlanta, Phi Beta Kappa, Omicron Delta Epsilon, Psi Chi. Office: Alston & Bird LLP One Atlantic Ctr 1201 W Peachtree St NW Atlanta GA 30309-3424 Office Phone: 404-881-7172. Office Fax: 404-881-7777. Business E-Mail: pkontio@alston.com.

KONTNY, VINCENT L., rancher, retired engineering executive; b. Chappell, Nebr., July 19, 1937; s. Edward James and Ruth Regina (Schumann) K.; m. Joan Dashwood FitzGibbon, Feb. 20, 1970; children: Natascha Marie, Michael Christian, Amber Brooke. BSCE, U. Colo., 1958, DSc honoris causa, 1991. Operator heavy equipment, grade foreman Peter Kiewit Son's Co., Denver, 1958-59; project mgr. Utah Constrn. and Mining Co., Western Australia, 1965-69, Fluor Australia, Queensland, Australia, 1969-72; sr. project mgr. Fluor Utah, San Mateo, Calif., 1972-73; sr. v.p. Holmes & Narver, Inc., Orange, Calif., 1973-79; mng. dir. Fluor Australia, Melbourne, 1979-82; group v.p. Fluor Engrs., Inc., Irvine, Calif., 1982-85, pres., chief exec. officer, 1985-87; group pres. Fluor Daniel, Irvine, Calif., 1987-88, pres., 1988-94, Fluor Corp., Irvine, 1990-94, vice chmn., 1994; ret., 1994; bd. dirs. Chgo. Bridge & Iron Co., Plainfield, Ill., 1997—; COO Washington Group Internat., Inc., Boise, Idaho, 2000—03. Purchased Last Dollar Ranch, Ridgway Co. 1989, Centennial Ranch, Colona Co., 1992, owner Double Shoe Cattle Co. Contbr. articles to profl. jours. Mem. engring. devel. coun., U. Colo.; mem. engring. adv. coun., Stanford U. Lt. USN, 1959-65. Mem.: Nat. Acad. Constrn., Center Club (Costa Mesa, Calif.). Republican. Roman Catholic. Avocation: skiing. Home: 35000 S Highway 550 Montrose CO 81401-8477 Personal E-mail: vincekontny@starband.net.

KONTOS, GEORGE JOHN, JR., surgeon; b. Chgo., May 26, 1958; s. George John and Sherry Knox Kontos; m. Sherry Knox Reed, Aug. 24, 1991; children: Alexis Reed, Nicholas John. BA, Northwestern U., 1977—79; MD, Loyola U., Maywood, Ill., 1979—82. Diplomate Am. Bd. Thoracic Surgery, 1992, Am. Bd. Surgery, 1988. Resident, gen. surgery Mayo Clinic, Rochester, Minn., 1982—88; resident, cardiac surgery U. Ala., Birmingham, 1988—91; cardiovasc. and thoracic surgeon Midwest Cardiovasc. Ctr., Sioux Falls, SD, 1992—94, Ctrl. Ala. Thoracic and Cardiovasc. Surgery, Montgomery, 1994—2002; surgeon U. Tenn., Memphis, 2002—03; thoracic, cardiovasc. surgeon Helena Surgery Assoc., Ariz., 2004—. Guest reviewer Jour. Applied Physiology, Houston, 1991—92, Transplantation, Boston, 1991—97, Am. Jour. Cardiology, Dallas, 2001, 2002, 2004. Mem. Am. Hellenic Philanthropic Orgn., Montgomery, Ala., 1994—2002. Grantee, Am. Heart Assn., 1992. Fellow: Am. Coll. Chest Physicians, Am. Coll. Cardiology, Southeastern Surg. Congress, Am. Coll. Surgeons; mem.: Johns Hopkins Med. and Surg. Assn., Priestly Soc., Mayo Clinic, N.Y. Acad. Scis., Soc. Thoracic Surgeons. Greek Orthodox. Avocations: fountain pen collector, water sports, sailing. Home: 429 Greenfield Rd Memphis TN 38117 Office: Helena Surgery Assoc 1805 Martin Luther King Dr-PO Box 224 Helena AR 72342 Office Phone: 870-338-7000. Office Fax: 870-338-7005. Personal E-mail: geokontos@cox-internet.com.

KONWINSKI, JACQUELINE MARIE KORALEWSKI, secondary school educator; b. Toledo, Ohio, Apr. 11, 1943; d. Michael Joseph and Anne Rose (Drabik) Koralewski; m. James Robert Konwinski, June 25, 1966; 1 child, John Robert. BA, Mary Manse Coll., 1965; MA, U. Toledo, 1986. Cert. tchr., Ohio. Tchr. Summerfield High Sch., Petersburg, Mich., 1965-66, Ctrl. Cath. High Sch., Toledo, 1966-67, McAuley High Sch., Toledo, 1979-83, Notre Dame Acad., Toledo, 1987—2005. Recipient Platinum award, Doors to Diplomacy, 2005. Mem. Nat. Coun. Social Studies, Ohio Coun. Social Studies, Polish Geneal. Soc. Mich., Friends Lathrop House. Democrat. Roman Catholic. Office: Notre Dame Acad 3535 W Sylvania Ave Toledo OH 43623-4479 Office Phone: 419-475-9359. Business E-Mail: jkonwinski@nda.org.

KONZ, GERALD KEITH, retired manufacturing company executive; b. Racine, Wis., Apr. 3, 1932; m. Marianne Bubolz; children: Richard C., Brenda S. BS in Econs., U. Wis., 1957, LLB, 1960. V.p. in charge corp. tax dept. S.C. Johnson & Son, Inc., Racine, 1982-98, chmn. bd. trustees pension trust, employee profit sharing and savs. plan, 1982-98. Bd. dirs. Johnson Family Funds, Inc., Racine, Wis. Pub. Expenditure Survey, Madison, 1982-92; mem. adv. bd. Venture Investors, Inc., Madison, Wis., 1997—98. Treas. St. Catherines H.S. Found., Racine, 1994—97, pres., 1997—2001; bd. dirs. YMCA, Racine, 1988—98. Mem. ABA, Tax Execs. Inst. (pres. Wis. chpt. 1972), Wis. Bar Assn., Racine-Kenosha Estate Planning Coun. (pres. 1980). Office: 3515 Taylor Ave Racine WI 53405-4727 Office Phone: 262-554-7796. E-mail: gkonz@wi.rr.com.

KOO, ANTHONY YING CHANG, economist, educator; b. Shanghai, Nov. 22, 1918; came to U.S., 1940; s. Vee-Sing and Tseng (Soo) K.; m. Delia Zung-Fung Wei, June 6, 1943; children: Victoria M., Margery E., Emily D. BA, St. John's U., Shanghai, 1940; MS, U. Ill., 1941; MA, Harvard U., 1943, PhD, 1946. Prof. econs. U. Mich., Ann Arbor, 1964-67; from asst. prof. to prof. Mich. State U., East Lansing, 1950-64, prof. econs., 1967—. Cons. The East-West Ctr., Honolulu, 1963, Internat. Labor Orgn., Geneva, 1965-66, U.S. Dept. Energy, Washington, 1980-82; vis. prof. Nat. Taiwan U., 1969-70, Indonesia 2d U. Project, 1989, Wuhan U. and Zhongshan U., China, 1990; adj. prof. econs. Fla. State U., 1990—. Author: Land Market Distortion and Tenure Reform, 1982; editor: Selected Essays of Gottfried Haberler, 1986; editor/author: The Liberal Economic Order, 1993; contbr. articles to profl. jours. Grantee, Soc. Sci. Coun., 1953, 1957, 1964, 1968, Ford Found., 1956—57, 1961—62, NSF, 1965—67. Mem. Am. Econ. Assn., Econometric Soc., Acad. Sinica. Office: Mich State U Dept Of Econs East Lansing MI 48824 also: Fla State U Dept Econs Tallahassee FL 32306 Business E-Mail: koo@msu.edu.

KOO, GEORGE PING SHAN, business consultant; b. Changting, China, June 4, 1938; came to the U.S., 1949, naturalized, 1955; s. Ted Swei Yen and Pei-Fen (Yang) K.; m. May Jen, May 5, 1962; children: Denise, Douglas, Alyssa. BS, MIT, 1960, MS, 1962; DSc, Stevens Inst. Tech., 1969; MBA, U. Santa Clara, 1975. Mgr. Allied Chem. Corp., 1963-71; assoc. dir. SRI Internat., 1972-78; v.p. Chase Manhattan Bank, 1978-79; mng. dir. Bear-Stearns China Trade, 1979-82; v.p. Bear-Stearns & Co., 1982-83; pres. Microelectronic Bus. Internat., Inc., Mountain View, Calif., 1983-85; v.p. Tiara Computer Sys., Inc., 1985-86; mng. dir. internat. svcs. H&Q Tech. Ptnrs., Inc., 1987; mng. dir., CEO Internat. Strategic Alliances, Inc., 1988-99; dir. Chinese svcs. group Deloitte & Touche LLP, San Jose, Calif., 1999—. Cons., chair on Asian Fin. and Alliances, Santa Clara, Calif., 1990-93. Human rels. commr. City of Mountain View, 1994-98. Mem. Asian Am. Mfrs. Assn. (chmn. 1996-97), mem. com. of 100 (dir. 1998—, vice chair, 2003-). Home: 1819 Van Buren Cir Mountain View CA 94040-4054 Office Phone: 650-255-6902. Personal E-mail: geopkoo@yahoo.com.

KOO, HARRY PONTAHK, physician, surgeon, educator; s. Jay J. and Jungwoo Koo; m. Yoon-Mie Rhee, Nov. 5, 1988; children: Irene Younghee, Daniel Jinmoe. BA, Williams Coll., Williamstown, Mass., 1982; MD, Univ. of Rochester Sch Medicine, Rochester, N.Y., 1987. Diplomate Am. Bd. of Urology / MD, 1997. Asst. prof. of surgery U. Mich. Med. Sch., Ann Arbor, Mich., 1995—2000; assoc. prof. surgery Va. Commonwealth U. Med. Coll. of Va., Richmond, Va., 2000—04, prof. surgery, 2004—. Barbara and william thalhimer chmn. of urology Va. Commonwealth U. Med. Coll. of Va., Richmond, Va., 2004—. Editor: (on-line textbook) emedicine textbook of Pediatrics; contbr. articles pub. to profl. jour. Grantee Pediat. Nephrology Mentor Grant, NIH, 2002-2004, Rsch. Grant in Pediat. Urology, Nat. Kidney Found., 1993-1994, VCU Faculty Rsch. Grant, Va. Commonwealth U. Med. Coll. of Va., 2002-2003. Fellow: ACS, Am. Acad. of Pediat.; mem.: Am. Urol. Assn. Mid Atlantic Sect. (by laws com. 2004), Am. Urol. Assn. Office: Divsn of Urology 1200 East Broad St Richmond VA 23298 Office Phone: 804-828-5318. Office Fax: 804-828-2157. Business E-Mail: hpkoo@vcu.edu.

KOO, JOHN YING MING, psychiatrist, dermatologist; b. Tokyo, Jan. 9, 1955; arrived in U.S., 1967; s. Kwang Ming Koo and Amy Tsai Ma; m. Nancy Chiang, July 7, 1978; children: Kathie, Jennifer, Jocelyn, Jonathan, Karina. *Father, Kwang Ming Koo, is advisor to Taiwan president; He is widely regarded as the "Father of Taiwan Independence Movement," Uncle, Chen-Fu Koo is the Chairman of The Chinese National Association of Industry and Commerce. Cousin, Jeffrey Koo is CEO of China Trust Bank. Brother, Richard Koo is a well known economist in Japan. Wife, Nancy Koo is Senior Director of GAP Computer dept & 1999 recipient of Asian-American Achievement Award. Daughter, Kathie Koo, is a recipient of "Women who can be president" award from League of Women Voters and a Harvard University graduate.* BA in Biochemistry, U. Calif., Berkeley, 1977; MD, Harvard U., 1981. Cert. psychiatry and dermatology. Intern UCLA Ctr. Health Scis., 1981—82; resident in psychiatry UCLA Neuropsychiatric Inst., 1982—85; resident in dermatology U. Calif.-San Francisco Med. Ctr., 1985—88; dir. Psoriasis and Skin Treatment Ctr., U. Calif., San Francisco, 1988—; prof. and vice chmn. dept. dermatology, prof. U. Calif., San Francisco, 1989—. Cons. in field to numerous pharm. cos.; med. adv. bd. Nat. Psioriasis Found., Portland, Oreg., 1995. *With extensive background in Science including medicine and psychiatry and avid interest in moral/religious/philosophical issues, John Koo M.D. is hoping to formulate a Moral Science concept that integrates Science and religion on a rational basis--"rational religion".* Mem. editl. bd.: Jour. Am. Acad. Dermatology, 1994; editor: Dermatology and Psychosomatics, 1999. Scholar Harvard Nat. scholar, Harvard Med. Sch., Boston, 1981. Mem.: Am. Psychiat. Assn., Am. Acad. Dermatology, Assn. for Psychocutaneous Medicine N.Am. (founder). Avocations: studying philosophy and religion, military history. Office: U Calif San Francisco Psoriasis and Skin Treatment Ctr 515 Spruce St San Francisco CA 94118 Office Phone: 415-476-4701. Office Fax: 415-502-4126.

KOOB, CHARLES EDWARD, lawyer; b. Kansas City, Mo., Aug. 31, 1944; s. Charles H. and Adeline (Meinert) K.; m. Pamela Ann (Nabseth), June 26, 1971; children: Jason Wyeth, Peter Nabseth. BA, Rockhurst Coll., 1966; JD, Stanford U., 1969. Bar: Calif. 1970, N.Y., 1972 U.S. Dist. Ct. (so. and ea. dist.) N.Y. 1973, U.S. Ct. Appeals (2d cir.) 1975, U.S. Ct. Appeals (5th cir.) 1979, U.S. Supreme Ct. 1988, U.S. Ct. Claims 1988, U.S. Ct. Appeals (3d cir.) 1985. Assoc. Simpson, Thacher, and Bartlett, N.Y.C., 1970—76, ptnr., 1976—, co-head litig. group. Mem. ABA, N.Y. State Bar Assn., Calif. State Bar Assn. Office: Simpson Thacher and Bartlett 425 Lexington Ave Fl 15 New York NY 10017-3954 Office Phone: 212-455-2970. Office Fax: 212-455-2502. Business E-Mail: ckoob@stblaw.com.

KOOB, ROBERT DUANE, chemistry professor, academic administrator; b. Graetinger, Iowa, Oct. 14, 1941; s. Emil John and Rose Mary (Slinger) Koob; m. E. Yvonne Ervin, June 9, 1960; children: Monique, Gregory, Michael, Eric, David; children: Angela, Julie. BA in Edn., U. No. Iowa, 1962; PhD in Chemistry, U. Kans., 1967. From asst. prof. to prof. chemistry ND State U., Fargo, 1967—90, chmn. dept. chemistry, 1974—78, 1979—81, dir. Water Inst., 1975—85, dean Coll. Sci. and Math., 1981—84, v.p., 1985—90, interim pres., 1987—88; v.p. for acad. affairs, sr. v.p. Calif. Poly. State U., San Luis Obispo, 1990—95; pres. U. No. Iowa, Cedar Falls, 1995—, prof., 1995—. Cons. TransAlta, Edmondton, Alta., Canada, Alta. Rsch. Coun., Mitre Corp., Washington; bd. dirs. State Bank Fargo, Fargo Cass County Econ. Devel. Corp.; chair bd. dirs. Cal Poly Found.; chair Iowa Coordinating Coun. for Post-H.S. Edn., 1996—97. Contbr. articles to profl. jours. V.p. Crookston Diocesan Sch. Bd., Minn., 1982; pres. elem. sch. bd., St. Joseph's Ch., Moorhead, Minn., 1982, parish coun., Moorhead, Minn., 1983; pres. bd. Shanley H.S., Fargo, 1985; serves on Cedar Valley Promise, Cedar Valley Alliance, Cedar Valley United Way, Opportunity Works, Am. Coun. Edn., Am. Assn. of States Colls. and Univs. Named to Cedar Valley Bus. Hall of Fame; grantee in field. Mem.: Iowa Assn. Coll. Pres. (pres. 1996). Roman Catholic. Avocations: reading, flying, sailing, racquet sports, bicycling. Office: Univ of Northern Iowa 1227 W 27th St Cedar Falls IA 50614-0002 Office Phone: 319-273-2566. E-mail: bob.koob@uni.edu.

KOOGLE, TIMOTHY K., communications executive; MS in Engr., Stanford U. Pres. Intermec Corp.; corp. v.p. Western Atlas Inc.; with Motorola Inc.; chmn., CEO Yahoo! Corp., Santa Clara, Calif., 1999—. Chmn. bd. dirs. AIM. Office: Yahoo Inc 701 First Ave Sunnyvale CA 94089-1019

KOOIJMANS, PIETER HENDRIK, judge International Court of Justice; b. Heemstede, The Netherlands, July 6, 1933; m. A. Kooijmans-Verhage; 4 children. Degree, Free U., Amsterdam, The Netherlands, 1964. Mem. Faculty of Law Free U. of Amsterdam, 1960-65, prof. European law and pub. internat. law, 1965-73; state sec. for fgn. affairs Govt. of The Netherlands, 1973-77; prof. pub. internat. law U. Leiden, The Netherlands, 1978-92, 95-97; minister of fgn. affairs Govt. of The Netherlands, 1993-94; judge Internat. Ct. of Justice, The Hague, The Netherlands, 1997—. Author textbooks in field; contbr. articles to profl. jours. Head Netherlands del. to UN Commn. on Human Rights, 1982-85, 92, chair commn., 1984-85, spl. reporter on questions relevant to torture, 1985-92; mem. various UN and Orgn. on Security and Coop. in Europe missions to former Yugoslavia, 1991-92. Office: care Internat Ct of Justice Peace Palace 2517 KJ The Hague Netherlands

KOOIMA, LINDA KAY, neonatal and pediatrics nurse; b. Rock Valley, Iowa, Aug. 26, 1948; d. Thomas and Frances Mae (Harmelink) K.; m. Orlando Sabas Arroyo, Apr. 12, 1976; children: Annie Josephine, Solomon Jordan. Dipl. nursing, Northwestern U., 1969; BA in Spanish, S.D. State U., 1989. RN, Ill., S.D., Ariz., Calif., Fla., N.Y. Critical care nurse Children's Meml. Hosp., Chgo., 1969-70; nurse neonatal ICU, Moffitt Hosp. U. Calif., San Francisco, 1970-76; clinic nurse S.D. State U., Brookings, 1985-88; mother and baby nurse Santa Barbara (Calif.) Cottage Hosp., 1988-89; neonatal nurse Santa Ana (Calif.) Hosp. and Med. Ctr., 1990, Hoag Presbyn. Meml. Hosp., Newport Beach, Calif., 1991; pediatric camp nurse Camp Gulliver, Coral Gables, Fla., 1993-95; utilization rev. nurse Initial Health Care, Miami, 1995-98; travel nurse mother/baby Star-Med Co., 1998-99, U.S.

Nursing Corp., 2000—; travel nurse Vassar Brothers Hosp., Poughkeepsie, NY, 2001—. Travel nurse mother-baby unit Cedars-Sinai Med. Ctr., L.A., 2002—03. Republican. Avocation: scuba diving. Home: 801 Brickell Key Blvd #2302 Miami FL 33131

KOOISTRA, ANDREW J., painter, sculptor; b. Whitinsville, Mass., July 8, 1924; s. Henry A. Kooistra and Tillie A. Frieswyck; m. Ingeberg H. Kooistra, May 30, 1968; children: Andrea, Katharine. BFA, Tufts U., Medford, Mass., 1951; postgrad., Harvard U., 1952; MFA, U. So. Calif., L.A., 1953. Tchr. art Ellenville Ctrl. Sch., NY, 1953. One-man shows include Woodstock (N.Y.) Artists Assn., 1953, 2003, Ellenville Pub. Libr. and Mus., 1987, Petrucci Gallery, Saugerties, N.Y., 1989, Schenectady Mus. and Planetarium, N.Y., 1989, Whitinsville Social Libr., Mass., 1989, Sullivan County Art Mus., Hurleyville, N.Y., 1990, Fletcher Gallery, Woodstock, N.Y., 1996, exhibited in group shows at Hawthorn Gallery, Woodstock, 1988, Provincetown Art Assn. and Mus. Bd. dirs. Woodstock Artists' Assn., 1985. With USAAF, 1943—46. Episcopalian. Avocation: book and print collecting. Home: PO Box 203 Napanoch NY 12458

KOOKEN, JOHN FREDERICK, retired bank holding company executive; b. Denver, Nov. 1, 1931; s. Duff A. and Frances C. K.; m. Emily Howe, Sept. 18, 1954; children: Diane, Carolyn. MS, Stanford U., 1954, PhD, 1961. With Security Pacific Nat. Bank-Security Pacific Corp., L.A., 1960-92; exec. v.p. Security Pacific Corp., L.A., 1981-87, CFO, 1984-92, vice chmn. Los Angeles, 1987-92; ret., 1992. Bd. dirs. Golden State Bancorp., 1992-2002, ACE Ltd., 1985-91 Centris Group, 1986-99, Pacific Gulf Properties, 1994-2001, East West Bancorp, 2002-; lectr. Grad. Sch. Bus. U. So. Calif., 1962-67; chmn. Bank Adminstrn. Inst., 1989-90. Pres. bd. dirs. Children's Bur., L.A., 1981-84; bd. dirs. United Way, L.A., 1982-89, Huntington Meml. Hosp., Pasadena, 1985—, chmn., 1999—2002; bd. dirs. So. Calif. Healthcare Systems, 1993—2005, chmn. 2001—2005. Lt. (j.g.) USNR, 1954-57. Mem.: Fin. Execs. Inst. (pres. LA chpt. 1979—80, dir. 1981—84).

KOOL, ERIC T., chemist, educator; b. 1960; BS, Miami U., Ohio, 1982; PhD, Columbia U., 1988. Prof. dept. chemistry Stanford (Calif.) U. Contbr. articles to profl. jours. Recipient faculty award Am. Cyanamid, 1994, Pfizer award Am. Chem. Soc., 2000; named Young Investigator, Office Naval Rsch., 1992, Young Investigator, Beckman Found., 1992, Young Investigator, Army Rsch. Office, 1993; Dreyfus Found. Tchr.-scholar, 1993, Arthur C. Cope scholar Am. Chem. Soc., 2000; Alfred P. Sloan Found. fellow, 1994. Achievements include research on design, synthesis and study of molecules that mimic complex biological functions such as replication. Office: Stanford U Dept Chemistry Stauffer I Rm 103 Stanford CA 94305-5080 E-mail: kool@leland.stanford.edu.

KOOLURIS DOBBS, LINDA KIA, artist; b. Orange, N.J., Jan. 28, 1949; m. Kildare Dobbs, May 7, 1981. AA, Pine Manor Coll., 1968; Cert., Sorbonne, 1968-69; BFA with honors, Sch. Visual Arts, 1972. Tchg. staff various colls., 1975—; tchg. staff fashion dept/ Ryerson U., 1980—2003; tchg. staff Avenue Rd. Art Sch., 1999—. Exhibitions include Mus. of Textiles, Toronto, ArtCanadiana.com, Bronxville Art and Frame Gallery, Atrium Gallery, Chubb Group of Ins. Cos., Warren, N.J., Vancouver Art Gallery, Newbury Fine Arts, Boston and Edgartown, Mass., Art Gallery of Hamilton, Toronto Watercolour Soc., Vancouver Maritime Mus., Ceperley House of Visual Arts Burnaby, B.C., Sutton Gallery, The Granary, Port Hope, Ont., The Hummingbird Centre, Carrier Gallery, Columbus Ctr., First Canadian Pl. Gallery, Toronto, Harry Ransom Humanities Rsch. Ctr., U. Tex., Austin, Represented in permanent collections AT&T, Artform, Norway, Glaxo Wellcome Inc., Inland Pacific Enterprises, Temple Scott & Assocs., Uniglobe, Advance Travel, AGF Mgmt. Ltd., Toronto Stock Exch., Ont. Govt. Art Collection, Parliament Bldg., Queen's Park, Pine Manor Coll., U.S., Mt. Sinai Hosp., Merrill Lynch, Aon Reed Stenhouse, U. Toronto, Scotia McLeod, Probyn & Co., numerous others, prin. works include portrait commns. the Hon. Henry N. R. Jackman, the Hon. Edwin A. Goodman, the Hon. Barbara McDougall, others, the Hon. David Peterson, Prof. Vern Krishna; contbr. to and features in art periodicals and publications; featured in water color books, Splash 3, 4, 5 & 8, featured in, Can. Bus. Mag.; photographer The Nat. Post, The Fin. Post., Verve Mag., Can. Bus. Mag. Recipient Ann. Art Purchase prize Pine Manor Coll., 1968, 2d prize Fin. Post Ann. Reports awards, 1981. Mem. Toronto Watercolour Soc. (Hon. Mention, Ann. Fall Show 1991, Best in Architecture 1994). Address: 484 Avenue Rd Ste 609 Toronto ON Canada M4V 2J4 Office Phone: 416-960-8984.

KOOMEN, CORNELIS JAN, telecommunications and electronics executive; b. Zaandam, The Netherlands, Sept. 25, 1947; s. C.J. and G. (Dykman) K.; m. Jantiena Catharina de Jong; children: Casper Jan, Jeroen. MS, Tech. U., Delft, The Netherlands, 1972, PhD, 1982. Rschr. RVO/TNO, The Hague, The Netherlands, 1973-74, Philips Rsch. Labs., Eindhoven, 1974-83, mgr., 1987-89; sys. engr. Philips Telecom. and Data Systems, Hilversum, The Netherlands, 1983-84, semiconductor exec., tech. mgr., dir., 1989-90; software coord. Philips Electronics, Eindhoven, 1984-86; dir. Philips Comm. Systems, Hilversum, 1990-91; dir., v.p. Philips Semiconductors, Eindhoven, 1991-94, exec. v.p., 1995-98, chmn. N.Am., 1996-98; pres. and CEO digital video group Philips Consumer Electronics, Palo Alto, Calif., 1998-2000; chmn. Securealink, Los Gatos, Calif., 2000—02, SafeNet Europe, 2002—03, sr. v.p., 2002—03; chmn. XCeive, Santa Clara, Calif., 2004—; pres., CEO ComDyke, Los Gatos, Calif., 2004—. Prof. Tech. U., Eindhoven, The Netherlands, 1984-2001; module dir. Found. Toptech Studies, Delft, 1987-92. Author: The Design of Communicating Systems; editor Internat. Fedn. of Info. Processing Computer Hardware Description Langs. conf. proc., 1985-87; patentee in field; contbr. articles to profl. jours. Chmn. Gen. Edn. Com., Waalre, The Netherlands, 1977-81. Named Prof. Bahlerprice, Royal Inst. Engrs., 1986. Mem. IFIP WG 10.2, Soc. for Gen. Edn. (chmn. 1985-88). Avocations: aquarel painting, photography. Office: Xceive 2730 San Tomes Exp Way #210 Santa Clara CA 95051 Home: 15415 Via Caballero Monte Sereno CA 95030-2101

KOONCE, CALVIN SCOTT, brokerage firm executive, physicist; b. Columbus, Ga., Dec. 9, 1937; s. Loftin Burns and Virginia (Scott) K.; m. Janet Elizabeth Bell, July 22, 1967: children: Elizabeth Ann, Kathleen Sharon, Franklin Scott. BS, MIT, 1960; PhD, U. Calif., Berkeley, 1967. Physicist Nat. Bur. Standards, Gaithsburg, Md., 1967-75; pres. Koonce Securities, Inc., Bethesda, Md., 1979-99, chmn., 1999—; pres. Montgomery Investment Mgmt., Bethesda, 1989—. Contbr. articles to profl. jours. Recipient Disting. Young Scientist award Md. Acad. Scis., 1969; fellow NSF, 1963. Mem. Am. Phys. Soc., Security Traders Assn. of Washington (pres. 1987), Beta Theta Pi. Republican. Presbyterian. Home: 9101 Kendale Rd Potomac MD 20854-4512 Office: Koonce Securities Inc 6550 Rock Spring Dr Ste 600 Bethesda MD 20817-1185 Business E-Mail: calvin@koonce.net.

KOONCE, NEIL WRIGHT, lawyer; b. Kinston, N.C., July 8, 1947; s. Harold Wright and Edna Earle (Regan) K.; m. Virginia Gayle Evans, Feb. 27, 1993; children: Channing, Carl Younger, Ginny Younger. AB, U. N.C., 1969; JD, Wake Forest U., 1974; postgrad. exec. program, U. Va., 1983. Bar: N.C. 1973, U.S. Dist. Ct. (mid. dist.) N.C. 1975, U.S. Ct. Appeals (4th cir.) 1978, U.S. Supreme Ct. 1981. Atty. Cone Mills Corp., Greensboro, N.C., 1974-81, sr. atty., 1981-85, asst. gen. counsel, 1985-87, gen. counsel, 1987—, v.p., 1989—, v.p., gen. counsel, corp. sec., 1999—2004; v.p. Internat. Textile Group, Inc., Greensboro, 2004—, gen. counsel, 2004—. Bd. dirs. Family and Children's Svcs., Greensboro, 1981-89, S.C. Energy Users Com., Columbia, S.C., 1984-89, Carolina Utility Customer's Assn., Raleigh, 1983-90, 94—, N.C. Found. for Rsch. and Econ. Edn., 1986-87, 93—, Electricity Consumers Resource Coun., Washington, 1987, 92—, vice chmn., 1990, chmn., 1991; bd. dirs. N.C. Citizens for Bus. and Industry, Raleigh, 1991-96, Met. YMCA, Greensboro, 1991-95, Salvation Army Boys and Girls Clubs, Greensboro, 1996—, S.C. Mfrs. Alliance, 1998—. With AUS, 1970-71. Mem. ABA, N.C. Bar Assn., N.C. Textile Mfrs. Assn. (bd. dirs. 1998—, vice chmn. 2004), Greensboro Bar Assn., Rotary (sec. 1983-86, bd. dirs. 1985-90, pres. 1988). Democrat. Presbyterian. Home: 200 Irving Pl Greensboro NC 27408-6510 Office: International Textile Group Inc 804 Green Valley Rd 300 Greensboro NC 27408-7020

KOONS, IRVIN LOUIS, graphics designer, consultant, marketing professional; b. Harrisburg, Pa., Mar. 14, 1922; s. Frank and Rose (Silver) K.; m. Leah Fay, Dec. 25, 1949; children: Adam, Jonathan, Joshua. Grad., Pratt Inst., 1942, New Sch., N.Y., 1946; student and instr., Ecole Des Beaux Arts, Fontainebleau, France, 1948-50; student, others schs. in France, Switzerland and Italy, 1947-49. Designer, chief exec. officer Irv Koons Assocs. (subs. Saatchi and Saatchi Worldwide, since 1983), N.Y.C., 1950-89; sr. advisor to adminstr. UN Devel. Program, N.Y.C., 1989—. Sr. advisor Div. for Pvt. Sector in Devel. and UNISTAR, UNDP; founder, co-dir. Internat. Design Assistance Commn., 1984—; sr. advisor to adminstr. UN Devel. Programme, 1989—; past cultural attache, spl. cons. U.S. Dept. State, India; dir. 1st internat. packaging exhbn. USIA; tchr. various art schs.; advisor Inferential Focus Forum; lectr. mktg. NYU, U. Pa., Columbia U., U. Tel Aviv, Northwestern U. and others in Eng., Holland, France, Switzerland, Brazil, China, India; expert legal witness corp. and product image/identity. Exhibited paintings and drawings in group shows in U.S. and France, represented in permanent collections including Mus. Modern Art, Cooper Hewitt Nat. Design Mus., the Jewish Mus., Yeshiva U. Mus.; complete collection of works on 7,000 slides plus several thousand sketches and finished itmes at Hagley Mus. and Libr., Wilmington, Del.; slides also available on CD-Rom; prin. works include Life of Moses series, 1975-78, stained glass wall for Fedn. Jewish Philanthropies, 1975, series coord. Torah ornaments for Temple Emmanuel, N.J., 1986; designed stage sets for traveling shows of original broadway casts: Harriette, Three Sisters, Blythe Spirit, Springtime for Henry, others; illus. many books and mags. including Ladies Home Jour., Good Housekeeping, Fortune, Seventeen, Sports Illustrated; designer 1st Daily offset newspaper in world, Middletown Daily Record, 1956 (Ayer Cup best design 1957, 58), redesign Washington Star, 1969; cons. editor Graphis Packaging, Switzerland, 1970; art critic The Statesman newspaper, India, 1946; contbr. articles on mktg. to profl. jours.; subject one-man articles in mags. including Graphis, Idea, 1976, others; 40-min. multi-image show of life and work produced by PDC, 1982. Founder, co-dir. Internat. Design Assistance Commn.; bd. dirs., exec. com. Found. for Future Generations; past bd. dirs. Am.-Israel Cultural Found.; bd. dirs., trustee Temple Emanuel, Englewood N.J., 1987; trustee Art Ctr. No. N.J., Englewood, 1960-68; artist in residence Melton Orgn., 2003; contbr. logo and trade mark designs and graphic comms. to non-profit civic orgns. including Am. Cancer Soc., Fedn. Jewish Philanthropies, World Hunger, Sloan-Kettering Meml. Hosp., United Cerebral Palsy, Jewish Theol. Sem., many others. With inf. U.S. Army, 1942-46, CBI. Recipient Best Ann. Report Design, 1957, 59, 61, Silver award Variety Store Merchandisers, 1967, Gold award Variety Store Merchandisers, 1970, Gold award Internat. Folding Carton Competition, 1964, Gold award Paperboard Packaging Council, 1974, awards N.Y. Art Dir.'s Club, 1958, 59, 63, 76, 77, 79 (2), awards Am. Inst. Graphic Arts, 1955, 58, 59, 60 (3), 61, 65 (2), 72, awards Soc. Illustrators, 1959, 68, Communication Arts awards, 1960, 64, 66, 67, 71, awards N.J. Art Dir.'s Club, 1962, 65 (3), 68, awards Package Design Mag., 1963-68, 70 (3),Indsl. Design awards, 1968, 75, Package of Yr. award, 1968, awards NYU, 1973, 74, Best Bottle of Yr. award, 1975, Clio award, 1976, 77, 81, Gold awards Package Design Council, 1977, 79, 80 (2), 87 (2), Gold Clio award, 79, 84, 88, Nat. Printing award, 1981, Desi award 1981, Best of Best 1985, Pratt. Inst. Alumni Achievement award, 1998; named one of 2000 Outstanding Designers and Artists of 20th Century, Cambridge Internat. Biographical Ctr., 2005, (2)others. Mem. Package Designers Coun. (Person of Yr. 1982, bd. dirs. 1962—), Indsl. Design Soc. Am., Packaging Inst., Am. Inst. Graphic Arts. Avocations: collecting historical packages, rewriting and illustrating legends, fables and fairy tales from India. Home: 213 Engle St Tenafly NJ 07670-2139 Office: Irv Koons Assocs 213 Engle St Tenafly NJ 07670-2139 Office Phone: 201-568-7387. Personal E-mail: ikadesign@aol.com.

KOONS, JEFF, artist; b. York, Pa., 1955; One person shows include New Mus. Contemporary Art, N.Y., 1980, Internat. With Monument, N.Y., 1985, Feature Gallery, N.Y., 1985, Daniel Weinberg Gallery, L.A., 1986, MCA, Chgo., 1988, Sonnabend Gallery, N.Y., 1988, 91, Max Hetzler Gallery, Cologne, Germany, 1988, 91, Donald Young Gallery, Chgo., 1988, Venster Gallery, Rotterdam, The Netherlands, 1989, Lehmann Gallery, Lausanne, Switzerland, 1992, Christophe Van de Weghe, Brussels, 1992, San Francisco Mus. Modern Art, 1992, 93, Walker Art Ctr., Mpls., 1992, Stedelijk Mus., Amsterdam, 1992, Mus. Contemporary Art, Sydney, 1996, Per Skarstedt Fine Art Gallery, N.Y.C., 1996, Guggenheim Mus., Bilbao, Spain, 1997, Sonnabend Gallery, N.Y.C., 1999, Rockefeller Ctr., 2000, others; exhibited in group shows at P.S. 1, Long Island City, N.Y., 1981, Annina Nosei Gallery, N.Y., 1981, Barbara Gladstone Gallery, N.Y., 1981, Renaissance Soc., Chgo., 1982, 85, Espace Lyonnais d'Art Contemporain, Lyon, France, 1982, Artists Space, N.Y., 1983, LACE, L.A., 1983, White Columns, N.Y., 1984, Hallwalls, Buffalo, 1984, Features Gallery, Chgo., 1985, Whitney Mus., N.Y., 1985, 87, 89, 90, Michael Kline Gallery, N.Y., 1985, Galerie Crousel-Hussenot, Paris, 1985, New Mus., N.Y., 1985, Fundacion Caixa de Pensiones, Madrid/Barcelona, 1985, ICA, Boston, 1985, 88, Prospect Gallery, Frankfurt, Germany, 1985, Centro Reina Sofia, Madrid, 1987, Saatchi Collection, London, 1987, 88, LACMA, L.A., 1987, Centre Pompidou, Paris, 1987, John & Marble Ringling Mus. Art, Sarasota, Fla., 1987, Carnegie Internat., Pitts., 1988, Ctr. Nat. des Art Plastiques, Paris, 1988, MCA, Chgo., 1988, Kunsthalle, Dusseldorf, Germany, 1988, Roseum, Malmo, 1988, MOCA, L.A., 1989, Kunstverein, Hamburg, 1989, Kunsthalle, Basel, Switzerland, 1989, Mus. Modern Art, N.Y.C., 1989, 90, Biennale, Venice, Italy, 1990, Mus. Haus Lange and Mus. Haus Esters, Krefeld, 1990, Pharmakon, Tokyo, 1990, Biennial, Sydney, 1990, Thaddaeus Ropac Gallery, Salzburg, Austria, 1990, Stedelijk Mus., Amsterdam, 1990, Israel Mus., Tel Aviv, 1990, Deste Found., Athens, Greece, 1990, Mus. Art, Indpls., 1991, Martin-Gropius-Bau, Berlin, 1991, Mus. voor Hedendaagse Kunst, Hertogenbosch, The Netherlands, 1992, Anthony d'Offay Gallery, London, 1992, Musee d'Art Contemporain Pully/Lausanne, 1992, Ctr. Curatorial Studies Mus., Bard Coll., Annondale-on-Hudson, N.Y., 1996-97, Mus. Modern Art, 1997-98, Whitney Mus. Am. Art, N.Y.C., 1990-2000, James Cohan Gallery, 2000, Mus. Contemporary Art, Chgo., 2000, Royal Acad. Arts, London, 2000, others; author: (book) The Jeff Koons Handbook, 1993; co-author: (with Thomas Kellein) Jeff Koons: Pictures 1980-2002, 2003 (with Robert Rosenblum and David Sylvester) Jeff Koons: Easy Fun Ethereal, 2003. Studio: Jeff Koons Prodns Inc 600 Broadway Fl 2 New York NY 10012-3206

KOONS, STEPHEN ROBERT, lawyer; b. Elmira, N.Y., Apr. 28, 1948; s. Robert Oscar and Katheryn Elizabeth (Norris) K.; m. Kathleen Marie Brooks Burman, Aug. 24, 1968 (div. July 1991); 1 child, David Robert; m. Laurene Ann Valdez, June 25, 1994; 1 child, Daniel Justin. BS, Fla. State U., 1970, JD, 1973. Bar: Fla. 1973, U.S. Dist. Ct. (so. dist.) Fla. 1974, U.S. Dist. Ct. (mid. dist.) Fla. 1974, U.S. Supreme Ct. 1978; bd. cert. civil lawyer. Asst. atty. gen. State of Fla., West Palm Beach, 1973, asst. state atty., 1975-77; assoc. Weathers & Narkier, West Palm Beach, 1977-78; ptnr. Davis, Rose & Koons, West Palm Beach, 1978-81, Mgee, Jordan, Shuey & Koons, Lake Worth, Fla., 1981-88, Stephen R. Koons, P.A., West Palm Beach, 1988-90, 93-97, Powers & Koons, West Palm Beach, 1990-93, Koons & Volpi, West Palm Beach, 1997—. Gen. counsel First Fed. Savs. & Loan, Lake Worth, 1982-87; mem. Criminal Justice Commn., Palm Beach County, 1987-92; bd. dirs., sec. Treasure Pride Probation Svc., Palm Beach County, 1983-95; adj. instr. Fla. Atlantic U., Boca Raton, Fla., 1995-97. Author seminar material. Fedn. chief Indian Guides, YMCA, West Palm Beach, 1977-82; mem. pres.'s cir. Republican Party of Palm Beach County; chmn. Lake Worth Civil Svc. Bd., 1982-82, 88. Recipient Svc. award Lake Worth Bar Assn., 1985, Pride Probation Svcs., 1991, Lake Worth Civil Svc. Bd., 1992. Mem. Fed. Bar Assn. (pres. Gold Coast chpt. 1988), Acad. Fla. Trial Lawyers (chair pro bono com. 1986—, lectr. continuing legal edn. 1984-95, Svc. award Spkrs. Bur. 1988). Avocations: golf, tennis, skiing, travel. Office: Ste G 25 W New Haven Ave Melbourne FL 32901-4463

KOONTZ, ALFRED JOSEPH, JR., financial analyst, consultant; b. Balt., Mar. 6, 1942; s. Alfred J. and Mary Agnes (Valis) K.; m. Kay Francis Frank, Aug. 4, 1962; children— Debbie Kay, Denise Marie, Stacey Lynn, Alfred Joseph, III. BSBA, Pa. State U., 1964. CPA, Md. Mgr. Price Waterhouse & Co., Balt., 1964-73, sr. mgr. N.Y.C., 1973-74, Morristown, N.J., 1974-75; v.p. fin Piper Aircraft Corp., Lock Haven, Pa., 1975-80, sr. v.p. fin., 1980-85, sr. v.p. fin., treas., 1985-86, exec. v.p., chief operating officer Vero Beach, Fla., 1987-88; pres., dir. Piper Acceptance Corp., Lakeland, Fla., 1985-88; sr. v.p. fin. and adminstrn., treas., bd. dirs. Todd Shipyards Corp., Seattle, 1988-91; exec. v.p., CFO Pay'N Pak Stores Inc., Bellevue, Wash., 1992-93; pres. Alfred J. Koontz & Assoc., Vero Beach, 1993—; co-owner, CFO Pub. Telecomm. Providers, Inc., Vero Beach, 1993-97; co-owner, operator A&K Enterprises of Vero, Inc., 1994—. Client rels. exec. Diamond Cluster Internat., Chgo., 1998-2003; CFO Wannabe's, LLC, 1999, acting CFO TEF, Inc, 2005. Mem.: AICPA. Home: 1790 Sand Dollar Way Vero Beach FL 32963-2723 E-mail: akeovi@aol.com.

KOONTZ, CARL LENNIS, II, investment counselor; b. Oct. 28, 1942; s. Carl Lennis and Jessie Marie (Rhodes) K.; m. Rose Marie Catalano, May 6, 1978. BS, U. Tenn., 1964, MS magna cum laude, 1968. Quality control analyst Ford Motor Co., Cin., 1965-66; mgmt. trainee Abbott, Procter & Paine, Richmond, Va., 1968-70; v.p. pension cons. Paine, Webber, N.Y.C., 1970-76; asst. v.p. Scudder, Stevens & Clark, N.Y.C., 1976-78, v.p. investments, 1978-85, mng. dir., 1985-87; v.p. Scudder, Stevens & Clark of Can., Toronto, Ont., 1984-87, Smith Barney Capital Mgmt., 1987-92; v.p. investment policy com. Capital Mgmt. Assocs., N.Y.C., 1992, sr. v.p., 1993; pres. Capital Mgmt. Mid-Cap Fund, 1994, co-head equity investments, 1996, co-chief investment officer, mng. dir., 1998; pres. Capital Mgmt. Small-Cap Fund, 1998; mng. dir. Weiss, Peck & Greer, 2000—03, head Large Cap Growth Group, 2001—03, mgr. Large-Cap Growth Fund, 2001—03; mng. dir. asset mgmt. Bank of N.Y., 2004—, chief investment officer Large-Cap Growth, 2004—, mgr. Hamilton Large Cap. Growth Fund, 2005—. Mem. dean's adv. coun. Col. of Bus., U. Tenn. With U.S. Army ANG, 1965-70. Fellow Fin. Analysis Fedn. (chartered fin. analyst); mem. Investment Counsel Assn. Am. (chartered investment counselor), N.Y. Soc. Security Analysts, Madison Ave. Sports Car Driving and Chowder Soc., Holland Lodge, Univ. Club, Antique Automobile Club Am., Pontiac Oakland Club Internat., Bond Club N.Y. Avocations: antique cars, model railroading, photography, swimming, tennis. Home: 373 Middlesex Rd Darien CT 06820-2518 Office Phone: 212-237-0900. Business E-Mail: ckoontz@bankofny.com.

KOONTZ, DEAN RAY, writer; b. Everett, Pa., July 9, 1945; s. Raymond and Florence (Logue) K.; m. Gerda Ann Cerra, Oct. 15, 1966. BS, Shippensburg U., 1966, LittD (hon.), 1989. Tchr. Appalachian Poverty Program, Saxton, Pa., 1966-67, Mechanicsburg (Pa.) Sch. Dist., 1967-69; freelance writer Orange, Calif., 1969—. Author of over 59 novels including Star Quest, 1968, The Fall of the Dream Machine, 1969, Fear That Man, 1969, Anti-Man, 1970, Beastchild, 1970 (Hugo award nomination 1971), Dark of the Woods, 1970, The Dark Symphony, 1970, Hell's Gate, 1970, The Crimson Witch, 1971, A Darkness in My Soul, 1972, The Flesh in the Furnace, 1972, Starblood, 1972, Time Thieves, 1972, Warlock, 1972, A Werewolf Among Us, 1973, Hanging On, 1973, The Haunted Earth, 1973, Demon Seed, 1973, rev. edit., 1997, After the Last Race, 1974, Nightmare Journey, 1975, Night Chills, 1976, The Vision, 1977, Whispers, 1980, Phantoms, 1983, Darkfall, 1984, Twilight Eyes, 1985, Strangers, 1986, Watchers, 1987, Lightning, 1988, Servants of Twilight, 1989, The Bad Place, 1990, Cold Fire, 1991, Hideaway, 1992, Dragon Tears, 1993, Mr. Murder, 1993, Winter Moon, 1994, Dark Rivers of the Heart, 1994, Strange Highways, 1995, Intensity, 1996, Santa's Twin, 1996, Fear Nothing, 1997, Tick Tock, 1997, Sole Survivor, 1997, From the Corner of His Eye, 2000, Icebound, 2000, False Memory, 2000, One Door Away from Heaven, 2001, By the Light of the Moon, 2002, The Face, 2003, The Taking, 2004, Life Expectancy, 2004, Velocity, 2005 (Publishers Weekly bestseller list); (with Kevin Anderson) Dean Koontz's Frankenstein: Book One: Prodigal Son, 2005; (children's books) Robot Santa: The Further Adventures of Santa's Twin, 2004; others under pseudonyms David Axton, Brian Coffey, Deanna Dwyer, K.R. Dwyer, John Hill, Leigh Nichols, Anthony North, Richard Paige, and Owen West.*

KOONTZ, LAWRENCE L., JR., state supreme court justice; b. Roanoke, Va., Jan. 25, 1940; BS, Va. Polytech. U., 1962. Asst. commonwealth's atty., Roanoke, 1967—68; judge Va. Juvenile & Domestic Rels. Dist. Ct., 1968—76, Va. Cir. Ct. (23rd cir.), 1976—85, Ct. Appeals of Va., 1985—95; justice Va. Supreme Ct., 1995—. Mem.: ABA. Office: Va Supreme Ct PO Box 1315 Richmond VA 23218-1315 Office Phone: 540-387-6082.

KOOP, C. EVERETT (CHARLES EVERETT KOOP), surgeon, educator, former Surgeon General of the US; b. Bklyn., Oct. 14, 1916; s. John Everett and Helen (Apel) K.; m. Elizabeth Flanagan, Sept. 19, 1938; children: Allen van Benschoten, Norman Apel, David Charles Everett, Elizabeth. AB, Dartmouth Coll., 1937, DSc (hon.) (hon.), 1989; MD, Cornell U., 1941; DSc in Medicine, U. Pa., 1947, DSc (hon.) (hon.), 1990; LLD (hon.) (hon.), Ea. Bapt. Coll., 1960, Phila. Coll. Osteo. Medicine, 1979, LaSalle Coll., 1983, Colby-Sawyer Coll., 1988, Princeton U., 1989, Hahnemann U., 1989, U. Miami, 1991, U. Cin., 1991; MD (hon.) (hon.), U. Liverpool, Eng., 1968; LHD (hon.) (hon.), Wheaton Coll., 1973, Phila. Theol. Sem., 1980, Chgo. Med. Sch., 1988, Brown U., 1990; DSc (hon.) (hon.), Gwynedd Mercy Coll., 1978, Washington and Jefferson Coll., 1979, Marquette U., 1983, Ea. Mich. U., 1985, N.Y. Med. Coll., 1985, Ball State U., 1987, Kirksville Coll. Osteo. Med., 1988, Albany Med. Coll., 1988, Colby Coll., 1988, Yeshiva U., 1988, Phila. Coll. Pharmacy and Sci., 1988, Baylor Coll. Medicine, 1988, U. Mass., Boston, 1989, Brandeis U., 1990, Northwestern U., 1990, U. New England, 1991; D. Pub. Svc. (hon.) (hon.), George Washington U., 1991; DPH, Cedar Crest Coll., 1995; D in Humanities, So. Utah U., 1997; LLD, Med. Coll. Pa., 1997. Diplomate Am. Bd. Surgery, Nat. Bd. Med. Examiners. Intern Pa. Hosp., Phila., 1941-42; fellow in surgery U. Pa. Hosp., Phila., 1942-47; fellow in pediat. surgery Children's Hosp., Boston, 1946; surgeon-in-chief Children's Hosp. of Phila., 1948-81; with U. Pa. Sch. Medicine, 1942-85, prof., 1959-85; former dep. asst. sec. for health HHS; surg. gen. of U.S. US Dept. Health & Human Services, 1981-89; former dir. internat. health USPHS, from 1982; chair Safe Kids Nat. Campaign, Washington; dir. Elizabeth De Camp McInery prof. surgery C. Everett Koop Inst. Dartmouth-Hitchkock Med. Ctr., Hanover, N.H., 1993—. Cons. USN, 1964—81; sr. scholar C. Everett Koop Inst. at Dartmouth; dir. Ready to Learn Program Carnegie Found., 1993—95; McEnerny prof. surgery Dartmouth Med. Sch. Author: Visible and Palpable Lesions in Children, The Right to Live, The Right to Die, 1976, The Right to Live, The Right to Die, rev. edit., 1980, Smoking: The New Book of Knowledge, 1989; author: (with E. Koop)) Sometimes Mountains Move, 1979; author: (with F. A. Schaeffer)) Whatever Happened to the Human Race?, 1979; author: Koop: The Memoirs of America's Family Doctor, 1991; author: (with T. Johnson)) Let's Talk, 1992; editor: surgery sect. Jour. Clin. Pediatrics, 1961—64; mem. edit. bd.: Zeitschrift fur Kinderchirurgie and Grenzqebiete, 1964—81, editor-in-chief: Jour. Pediatric Surgery, 1965—77, editl. cons.: Japanese Jour. Pediatric Surgery and Medicine, 1970—81, chmn. editorial bd.: PHS Reports, 1982—89, mem. editorial adv. bd.: Tobacco Control: An Internat. Jour.; contbr. publs. in surg. physiology, biomed. ethics, physiology of surg. neonate, tech. advances in pediatric surgery. Bd. dirs., pres. Nat. Health Mus. Inc.; bd. dirs., chmn. sci. adv. com. Biopure; chmn. Patient Med. Edn., 1993—96, Patient Med. Record, Inc., 1997—; Bd. dirs. Med. Assistance Programs, Inc., Brunswick, Ga., Friends Nat. Libr. of Medicine. Decorated chevalier Legion of Honor France, Order Duarte, Sanchez and Mella Dominican Republic, Chevalier French Legion of Honor; named Hon. Citizen, City of Balt., 1985; recipient medal, City of Marseille, Presbyn. Man of Yr. award, Presbyn. Social Union Phila., 1975, Super Achiever of Yr. award, Phila. chpt. Juvenile Diabetes Found., 1975, Man of Yr. award, Jewish Community Chaplaincy Svc. Phila., 1975, Copernicus medal, Polish Surg. Soc., 1977, Gold medal, Children's Hosp. Phila., 1981, Sec. of Health of Commonwealth of Pa. award, 1981, Thomas Linacre award, Nat. Fedn. Cath. Physicians Guild, 1981, Key to City of St. Louis, 1985, Award of Distinction, Alumni Assn. Cornell U. Med. Coll., 1988, Humanitarian Svc. award, City of

Boston, 1989, Harry S. Truman award, City of Independence, Mo., 1990, Daniel Webster award, Dartmouth Coll., 1990, John Wiley Jones Disting. Lectr. award, Rochester Inst. Tech., 1990, NAS Public Welfare medal, 1990, Tyler prize, U. So. Calif., 1991, Albert Schweitzer prize, Johns Hopkins U., 1991, Person of Yr. award, Nat. Hosp. Orgn., 1991, C. Everett Koop Hon. Lectr. medal named in his honor, Anchor & Caduceus Soc., 1991, C. Everett Koop Health Adv. award named in his honor, Am. Soc. for Health Care Mktg. and Pub. Rels., Gustav O. Lienhard award, Inst. Medicine, 1992, Presdl. medal of Freedom, 1995, Heinz Found. award, 1995, Medal of Honor, Am. Cancer Soc., 2000, Presdl. Medal of Freedom; scholar Disting. scholar to Carnegie Found. for advancement of teaching. Fellow: ACS, Am. Acad. Pediatrics (William E. Ladd Gold medal), Royal Coll. Physicians and Surgeons of Glasgow (hon.), Royal Coll. Surgeons Eng. (hon.); mem.: AMA, Societé Suisse De Chirurgie Infantile, Deutschen Gesselschaft für Kinderchirugi, Societé Française de Chirurgie Infantile, Assn. Mil. Surgeons U.S. (pres. 1982, 1987, Founders medal), Internat. Soc. Surgery, Brit. Assn. Pediatric Surgeons (Dennis Browne Gold medal), Soc. U. Surgeons, Royal Soc. Medicine, Am. Surg. Assn., Sigma Xi. Office: Dartmouth Coll Dartmouth-Hitchcock Ctr C Everett Koop Inst Hanover NH 03755

KOOPERSMITH, KIM, lawyer; b. Lake Success, NY, Aug. 11, 1959; d. Kenneth and Marcia Ilene (Shapiro) K.; m. William J. Borner, June 19, 1983; children: Meredith Lee, Charlotte Jane. BA cum laude, U. Pa., 1981; JD, Fordham U., 1984. Bar: NY 1985, US Dist. Ct. (so. and ea. dists.) NY 1985, US Ct. of Appeals (2nd cir.). Ptnr. Anderson Kill Olick & Oshinsky, P.C., NYC, 1984; now ptnr. litig. and mem. mgmt. com. Akin Gump Strauss Hauer & Feld LLP, NYC. Contbr. articles to profl. publs. Mem. NY State Bar Assn., Assn. of Bar NYC Office: Akin Gump Strauss Hauer & Feld LLP 590 Madison Ave New York NY 10022-2524 Office Phone: 212-872-1060. Business E-Mail: kkoopersmith@akingump.com.

KOOPMAN, BARBARA GOLDENBERG, psychiatrist; b. Boston; d. Morris and Fannie (Goretsky) Goldenberg; m. Philip Koopman, Dec. 19, 1967 (div. Oct. 1981); m. Morris Klein, Dec. 30, 1985 (dec.). BS, Simmons Coll., 1944; MA, Smith Coll., 1945; PhD in Lit., Columbia U., 1951; MD, Tufts U., 1957. Diplomate Am. Bd. Psychiatry and Neurology. Lecturer Columbia U., N.Y.C., 1948-50; sr. psychiatrist Manhattan State Hosp., N.Y.C., 1961-62; clinical asst. psychiatry Mt. Sinaii Hosp., N.Y.C., 1961-66; attending staff psychiatry Brookdale Hosp., Bklyn., 1962-71; faculty Inst. Short-Term Dynamic Psychotherapy St. Clare's Hosp., Denville, NJ, 1991—95. Translator: The Impulsive Character, 1974; editor Jour. Orgonomy, 1967-92; editor, co-translator: The Final Appeal to Mankind, 1997; contbr. articles to profl. jours. Fellow Mt. Sinai Hosp., 1959-61, trustee fellow Columbia U., 1948-51. Mem. Am. Psychiatric Assn. (life), Am. Coll. Orgonomy (pres. 1986-87). Avocations: fine arts, alternative healing. Home: 222 Riverside Dr New York NY 10025-6809 Office: 222 Riverside Dr New York NY 10025-6809 Office Phone: 212-222-3265. Personal E-mail: mozq7@aol.com.

KOOPMAN, RICHARD NELSON, engineer, consultant; b. Buffalo, N.Y., Nov. 26, 1945; s. Richard John Walter and Nellie Elkins (Wisbrock) K.; m. Mary Margaret Blume, July 17, 1970; Anthony Blake (dec.), Laura Nicole. BSME, Washington U., 1968; MSME, U. Minn., 1969, PhD, 1975. Registered profl. engr., Ill., Minn. Engr. Honeywell, Inc., Mpls., 1973-75, Argonne (Ill.) Nat. Lab, 1975-80; mem. tech. staff, supr. Bell Labs, Naperville, Ill., 1980-85; sr. cons. Engring. Sys. Inc., Aurora, 1996—2002, dir. mech. and elec. engring., 2002—; dir. McDonald's Corp., Oakbrook, Ill., 1985-96; v.p. Fla. Plastics Internat., Inc., Evergreen Park, Ill., 1999—2001. Contbr. articles to profl. jours.; patentee in field. Mem. Hinsdale (Ill.) Planning Commn., 1992-95, Zoning Bd. Appeals, 1995-96; bd. dirs. Bradley U. Parents Orgn., 1995-99, career com. chair, 1996-98, GraueMill Mus., 1984-91. Named Supr. of Yr., INROADS-Chgo., 1991. Mem. ASME (section chmn. 1980-81), Nat. Soc. Profl. Engrs., Hinsdale Jaycees (treas. 1980-83), Woodlands Home Owners Assn. (treas. 1998—), Tau Beta Pi, Omicron Delta Kappa, Pi Tau Sigma. Mem. United Ch. of Christ. Office: Engring Sys Inc 3851 Exchange Ave Aurora IL 60504 Office Phone: 630-851-4566. E-mail: rnkoopman@prodigy.net.

KOOPMAN, WILLIAM JAMES, medical educator, internist, immunologist; b. Lafayette, Ind., Aug. 19, 1945; s. William James and Barbara Mary (Morehouse) K.; m. Lilliane Kathryn Desimone, June 15, 1968; children: Benjamin, Anna, Rebecca, Steven. BA, Washington and Jefferson U., 1967; MD, Harvard U., 1972. Diplomate Am. Bd. Internal Medicine. Intern/resident in medicine Mass. Gen. Hosp., Boston, 1972-74; rsch. fellow NIH, Bethesda, Md., 1974-77; from asst. prof., assoc. prof. to prof. medicine specializing in rheumatology and clin. immunology U. Ala., Birmingham, 1977—, Howard L. Holley prof. medicine, 1988-95, dir. Multipurpose Arthritis Ctr., 1983-96; chmn. Dept. Medicine, 1995—. Mem. nat. adv. coun. Nat. Inst. Arthritis, Musculo-skeletal and Skin Diseases, 1987-90; chmn. bd. sci. counselors, NIH, NIAMS, 1991-95. Editor: Arthritis and Rheumatism jour., 1985—90, Arthritis and Allied Conditions, 14th edit.; contbr. more than 250 articles to profl. jours. Recipient Carol Nachman Rsch. prize Fed. Republic Germany, 1982. Fellow ACP (master), Am. Coll. Rheumatology (pres. Southeastern region 1986-87, treas. 1992-94, 2nd v.p. 1994-95, pres.-elect 1995-96, pres. 1996-97); mem. ACP (master), Am. Soc. Clin. Investigation (pres. 1990-91), Assn. Am. Physicians, Am. Assn. Immunologists, Inst. of Medicine, Birmingham Area C. of C. Presbyterian. Avocations: fishing, gardening. Office: U Ala Sch Medicine DERB 1808 7th Ave S # Bdb420 Birmingham AL 35233-1912

KÖÖRNA, ARNO, economist, educator; b. Tallinn, Estonia, Feb. 2, 1926; s. Artur and Anna-Helena (Schultz) K.; m. Eha Lind, Dec. 28, 1946; children: Silvia, Vello. PhD, Tartu U., Estonia, 1955; academician, Estonian Acad. Scis., Tallinn, 1973, PhD in Econs., 1970. Prof. Tartu U., 1972-75; sec. gen. Estonian Acad. Scis., 1973-82, v.p., 1982-91, pres., 1991-94, ex-pres., 1995. Author: Economic Motivation of Quality, 1978, Science in Estonia, 1993, Estonian Science in Transition, 1994; contbr. articles to profl. jours. Mem. Mem. Estonian Parliament, Tallinn, 1985—90; chmn. Estonian Sci. Coun., Estonia, 1992—94. Mem. Internat. Assn. IUS Primi Viri (mem. standing com.), World Futures Studies Fedn., Russian Acad. Humanities, Ctrl. European Acad. Sci. and Art (hon.). Home: Kapi 9-22 10136 Tallinn Estonia Office: Estonian Acad Scis Kohtu 6 10130 Tallinn Estonia Office Phone: 6115801. E-mail: arno.koorna@mail.ee.

KOOSER, TED (THEODORE J. KOOSER), poet; b. Ames, Iowa, Apr. 25, 1939; s. Theodore B. and Vera (Moser) Kooser; m. Kathleen Rutledge. BS, Iowa State U., 1962; MA, U. Nebr., 1968. Former v.p. Lincoln Benefit Life; 13th Poet Laureate Cons. in Poetry to the Libr. of Congress, 2004—05; founder Am. Life in Poetry project, 2005—. Vis. prof. English U. Nebr., Lincoln. Author: (poetry collections) Official Entry Blank, 1969, A Local Habitation and a Name, 1974, Not Coming to Be Barked At, 1976, Sure Signs, 1980 (Soc. of Midland Authors Poetry Prize, 1980), One World at a Time, 1985, The Blizzard Voices, 1986, Weather Central, 1994, Winter Morning Walks: One Hundred Postcards to Jim Harrison, 2000 (Nebr. Book Award for poetry, 2001), Delights & Shadows, 2004 (Pulitzer Prize for poetry, 2005); co-author (with Jim Harrison): Braided Creek: A Conversation in Poetry, 2003 (Soc. Midland Authors Poetry Prize, 2004); author: (chapbooks/spl. editions) Grass County, 1971, Twenty Poems, 1973, Shooting a Farmhouse/So This is Nebraska, 1975, Old Marriage and New, 1978, Etudes, Bits Press, 1992, A Book of Things, 1995, A Decade of Ted Kooser Valentines, 1996, Flying at Night: Poems, 1965-1985, 2005; co-author (with Harley Elliott): Voyages to the Inland Sea, 1976; co-author: (with William Kloefkorn) Cottonwood County, 1979; author: (essay collection) Local Wonders: Seasons in the Bohemian Alps, 2002 (Nebr. Book Award for nonfiction, 2003, Gold Award for Autobiography, ForeWord mag. Book of Yr. Awards), (non-fiction) The Poetry Home Repair Manual: Practical Advice for Beginning Poets, 2005. Recipient Prairie Schooner Prize in Poetry, 1976, 1978, Stanley Kunitz Poetry Prize, Columbia Mag., 1984, Pushcart Prize, 1984, Nebr. Governor's Art Award, 1988, Mayor's Art Award, Lincoln, Nebr., 1989, Richard Hugo Prize, Poetry N.W., 1994, James Boatwright Award, Shenandoah, 2000, Merit Award in Poetry, Nebr. Arts Coun., 2000, Mari Sandoz Award, Nebr. Libr. Assn., 2000; writing fellowship, Nat. Endowment Arts, 1976, 1984.*

KOPE, JOSEPH B., retired humanities educator; b. Youngstown, Ohio, Aug. 5, 1926; s. Joseph Bartholomew and Veronica Pauline Kope. AB Hist., Univ. PA, Philadelphia, PA, 1951; BS Educ., Youngstown Univ., Youngstown, OH, 1961; MA English educ., Ohio State Univ., Columbus, OH, 1971. Educator English, social studies Youngstown Ohio Bd. of Ed., 1962—89; tchr. Savs. and Loan Inst. Pres. Youngstown Teachers of English, Youngstown, Ohio, 1967—69; chmn. dept. english Woodrow Wilson H.S., Youngstown, Ohio, 1969—79; chmn. history dept. Volney Rogers H.S., Youngstown, Ohio, 1984—89; adv. Jr. Achievement. Cpl. U.S. Army, 1945—46, W. Pacific & Philippine Islands. Martha Holden Jennings scholar. Mem.: Nat. Coun. Tchrs. English, Mahoning County Ret. Teachers, Polish-Am. Hist. Assn., Am. Coun. of Polish Culture, Butler Mus. of Am. Art, Kosciuszko Found. of NYC, Cleve. Mus. of Art, Mahoning Valley Hist. Soc., Saybrook Beach Club, Sr. Citizens Club, Polish Arts Club (bd. of dirs. 1992—96), Saxon Club, Alpha Phi Omega, Kappa Delta Pi. Roman Catholic. Avocations: gardening, reading, art & stamp collecting, piano, accordion. Home: 284 Wilcox Road Austintown OH 44515

KOPE, SHANE BRIEN, lawyer; b. Ft. Lauderdale, Fla., Aug. 2, 1974; s. Davis Brien and Georgia Kay (Corcoran) Kope. JD, Dickinson Sch. Law, 2002. Lic.: Pa. (atty.) 2004. Law clk. Cumberland County Cts., Carlisle, Pa., 2001—04; atty., owner Law Office of Davis Brien Kope & Georgia Kay Kope-Corcoran, Camp Hill, Pa., 2004—. CLE Web devel. asst. Pa. Bar Inst., Mechanicsburg, 2003—. Vol. Harrisburg Soup Kitchen, Pa., 2002—. Fellow Cherie T. Millage fellowship, for law clerking for the Cherokee Nation, Okla., 1999. Mem.: Cumberland County Bar Assn., ABA, Pa. Bar Assn., Dauphin County Bar Assn. Liberal. Office: Law Office of Shane B Kope 4660 Trinble Rd Ste 201 Harrisburg PA 17011 Office Phone: 717-761-7573. Office Fax: 717-761-7572. E-mail: sbkope@comcast.net.

KOPEC, JOHN WILLIAM, research scientist; b. Chgo., Nov. 5, 1936; s. John Frank and Marie Eva (Wreshnig) K.; m. Jean Elois Prather, Dec. 28, 1958 (div. June 1977); children: Brian More, Vaune Estra. AA, Chgo. City Coll., 1974; student, Ill. Inst. Tech., Chgo., 1974-80. Systems analyst Motorola, Chgo., 1959-61; asst. exptl. engr. Ill. Inst. Tech. Rsch. Inst., Chgo., 1961-68, extpl. engr., 1968-74, liaison engr. Chgo. and Geneva, Ill., 1974-81; supr. Riverbank Acoustical Labs., Ill. Inst. Tech. Rsch. inst., Chgo. and Geneva, Ill., 1986-94, lab. mgr., 1994—, ret., 1998. Author: The Sabines at Riverbank, 1997; contbr. articles to Jour. Acoustical Soc. Am.; paper reviewer, contbr. articles Internat. Noise Control Engrs. With USAF, 1955-59. Fellow: Acoustical Soc. Am. (chmn. archives and history 1992—94, sec. tech. com. 1991—94, mus. curator 1985—98, co-chmn. tech. program 2001, Silver cert. 2002); mem.: ASTM (chmn. awards com., sec. E 33.01 1980—98, appreciation award 1994), Can. Acoustical Soc., Soc. Automotive Engrs. (task group, paper reviewer), N.Y. Acad. Scis. Achievements include one of first smokeless fires for firefighters of U.S. Navy and U.S. Air Force; one of first to discover ionization of turbulent flow in a hypersonic wind tunnel; discovered Wallace Clement Sabine files previously thought destroyed; developed one of first rapid transit speech noise floor's, also an industrial colored noise floor map. Home: 5206 S Lotus Ave Chicago IL 60638-1632

KOPEC, JOSEPH A., public relations executive; b. Cardale, Pa., June 22, 1946; s. Joseph Andrew and Mary Louise (Kovall) K.; m. Karen K. Sauke, Oct. 25, 1969; children: Stephen William, David Alexander. BA in Journalism, Ohio State U., 1971. Dir. com. Atty. Gen. of Ohio, Columbus, 1972-76; v.p. Harshe-Rotman & Druck Inc., Chgo., 1976-80; sr. cons. Hay Group/Saatchi & Saatchi, Chgo., 1980-82; sr. v.p., mng. dir. Hill and Knowlton, Chgo., 1982-91; exec. v.p. Edelman PR Worldwide, Chgo., 1991-93; prin. The Dilenschneider Group, Chgo., 1993—97; pres. Kopec Assocs., Inc., Chgo., 1998—. Mem. Pub. Rels. Soc. Am. (accredited), Nat. Investor Rels. Inst. (bd. dirs.), Econ. Club Chgo. Episcopalian. Office: Kopec Assocs Inc Ste 1802 330 S Michigan Ave Chicago IL 60604

KOPEC-GARNETT, LINDA, nursing administrator, researcher; d. Frank J. and Anna Paul Kopec; m. Thomas R. Garnett, Oct. 6, 1990. BSN cum laude, Fitchburg State Coll., Mass., 1983; MS Health svc. adminstrn., Ctrl. Mich. U., 1996. RN in Va. Nurse intern Med. Coll. Va. Hosp., Richmond, Va., 1983, nurse clinician in neurosci. ICU, 1984-86; terr. mgr., patient care specialist Kinetic Concepts Therapeutic Svc., Richmond, Va., 1986-89; rsch. coord. neurology dept. Med. Coll. Va. and Va. Commonwealth U., Richmond, 1989—; assoc. adminstr. neurology dept. Va. Commonwealth U., Richmond, 2001—. Mem.: Am. Epilepsy Soc., Sigma Theta Tau.

KOPEL, DAVID BENJAMIN, lawyer; b. Denver; s. Gerald Henry and Dolores B. Kopel; m. Deirdre Frances Dolan, Apr. 5, 1987. BA in History, Brown U., 1982; JD, U. Mich., 1985. Bar: Colo. 1986, N.Y. 1986, U.S. Dist. Ct. (ea. and so. dists.) N.Y. 1986, U.S. Ct. Appeals (2d cir.) 1988, U.S. Dist. Ct. Colo. 1988, U.S. Ct. Appeals (10th cir.) 1988, U.S. Ct. Appeals (D.C. cir.) 1997, U.S. Ct. Appeals (5th cir.) 1999, U.S. Ct. Appeals (4th cir.) 2003. Assoc. Sullivan & Cromwell, N.Y.C., 1985-86; asst. dist. atty. Manhattan Dist. Atty., N.Y.C., 1986-88; asst. atty. gen. Colo. State Atty. Gen., Denver, 1988-92; rsch. dir. Independence Inst., Golden, Colo., 1992—. Adj. prof. NYU Sch. of Law, 1998-99. Democrat. Avocations: skiing, golf, amateur radio. Office: Independence Inst 13952 Denver West Pkwy Ste 400 Golden CO 80401

KOPELL, NANCY, mathematician, education educator; b. N.Y.C., Nov. 8, 1942; BS in Math., Cornell U.; PhD, U. Calif.-Berkeley, 1967. C.L.E. Moore Instructorship MIT, Cambridge, 1967—69; faculty mem. Northeastern U., 1969—78, prof. math., 1978—86, Boston U., 1986—. Co-dir. Ctr. for BioDynamics Boston U.; vis. prof. Centre National de la Recherche Scientifique France, 1970, MIT, 1975, 1976—77, Calif. Inst. Tech., 1976; Wolmer Fries Meml. lectr. Rensselaer Polytechnic Inst.; Mark Kac Meml. lectr. Los Alamos Nat. Labs.; Univ. lectr. Boston U., 1993. Named William Goodwin Aurelio Prof. of Math. and Sci., Boston U., 2000; fellow, Gugenheim Found., Sloan Found., MacArthur Found., 1990—95. Mem.: NAS. Office: CAS Math and Stats Boston Univ 111 Cummington St Boston MA 02215

KOPELMAN, IAN STUART, lawyer; b. Chgo., Oct. 11, 1949; s. Ted and Norma (Hyman) K.; m. Nancy Henriette Stamp, Mar. 18, 1984; children: Meredith Samantha, Jason Lee. BA cum laude, Knox Coll., 1971; JD with distinction, U. Iowa, 1974. Bar: Ill. 1974, U.S. Dist. Ct. (no. dist.) Ill. 1974, U.S. Tax Ct. 1974. Ptnr. Arnstein & Lehr, Chgo., 1979-88; prin. Shefsky & Froelich Ltd., Chgo., 1988-96; ptnr., co-chair employee benefits/exec. compensation group Altheimer & Gray, Chgo., 1996-99; ptnr., chair employee benefits/exec. compensation group Rudnick & Wolfe, Chgo., 1999-2000; ptnr., co-chair employee benefits/exec. compensation dept. Piper, Marbury, Rudnick & Wolfe (now DLA Piper Rudnick Gray Cary), Chgo., 2000—. Adj. prof. law John Marshall Law Sch., 2004—; lectr. in field. Contbr. articles to profl. publs. Pres. Chgo.-Knox Coll. Alumni Assn., Chgo., 1978-79. Recipient commendation Internat. Acad. Trial Lawyers, 1974, award Iowa Acad. Trial Lawyers. Mem. ABA, Ill. Bar Assn., Chgo. Bar Assn. (chmn. employee benefits com. 1981-82, commendation 1986), Profit Sharing Coun. Am. (legal and legis. com. 1990—, bd. dirs. 1997-2005, legal counsel 2005—), Midwest Benefits Coun. (chmn. legal and legis. com. 1991-93), Chgo. Assn. Commerce and Industry, Phi Sigma Alpha, Omicron Delta Kappa, Phi Delta Phi. Jewish. Avocations: theater, history, reading, sports. Office: DLA Piper Rudnick Gray Cary Suite 1900 203 N La Salle St Chicago IL 60601-1293 Office Phone: 312-368-2161. Office Fax: 312-236-7516. Business E-Mail: Ian.Kopelman@dlapiper.com.

KOPELMAN, LEONARD, lawyer; b. Cambridge, Mass., Aug. 2, 1940; s. Irving and Frances Estelle (Robbins) K.; m. Carol Hunsberger. BA cum laude, Harvard U., 1962, JD, 1965. Bar: Mass. 1966. Assoc. Warner & Stackpole, Boston, 1965-73; sr. ptnr. Kopelman and Paige, Boston, 1974—. Lectr. Harvard U., 1965—; permanent master Mass. Superior Ct., 1971—; gen. counsel Emerson Coll.; hon. consul gen. of, Finland, Mass., 1975—; U.S. del. Soc. for Internat. Devel.; Chmn. Mass. Jud. Selection Com. for the Fed. Judiciary, 1971—; chief counsel AAUP; dean consular corps of Boston, 2001—. Trustee Cathedral of the Pines, 1972; pres. Hillel Found. of Cambridge, Inc., 1973—; trustee Faulkner Hosp., 1974—, Parker Hill Med. Ctr., 1976—; dir. gen. Consular Corps Coll. NEH grantee, 1975; named one of the 12 most powerful lawyers in Mass. Nat. Law Jour. Mem. ABA (exec. coun. 1969—), Mass. Bar Assn. (chmn. mcpl. law sect.), Am. Judges Assn., Mass. C. of C. (pres. 1974-77), Harvard Faculty Club, Algonquin Club (pres.), Harvard Club, Union Club, Hasty Pudding Club, St. Botolph Club. Home: 33 Yarmouth Rd Chestnut Hill MA 02467-2815 Office: Kopelman and Paige 31 St James Ave Boston MA 02116-4101

KOPELMAN, RICHARD ERIC, management educator; b. NYC, May 31, 1943; s. Seymour H. and Leona L. (Quint) K.; m. Carol Fialkov, June 7, 1970; children: Joshua Marc, Michael Adam. BS, U. Pa., 1965, MBA, 1967; DBA, Harvard U., 1974. Instr. bus. C.C. Phila., 1967-69; instr. mgmt. Baruch Coll./CUNY, N.Y.C., 1973-74, asst. prof., 1974-77, assoc. prof., 1978-80, prof., 1981—. Cons. in field; corp. dir. Aleph Null Corp., 1979-88, Applied Photonics, Inc., 1986-91, Infodex Sys., Inc., 1986-88, EMS Devel. Corp., 1992-96; pres. Cube One, Inc., 1998—; acad. co-dir. MS in Indsl. Rels. program Baruch/Cornell U., 1985-97, acad. co-dir. Baruch exec. MS in Indsl. Rels. program, 1994-2000; acad. dir. Baruch exec. MS in Indsl. and Labor Rels. program, 2000—. Author: The Management of Productivity: A Practical People-Oriented Perspective, 1986; mem. editl. rev. bd. Jour. Social Behavior and Personality, 1985-89, Nat. Productivity Rev., Jour. Orgnl. Behavior Mgmt., Perceptions, 1991-94, Jour. Psychology, 1999—, Jour. Orgnl. Excellence, 2000—; contbr. numerous articles to profl. and acad. jours. Bd. dirs. Day Care Coun., Nassau County, 1979-82; Nassau Symphony Orch., 1984-85. Recipient Pres. award for excellence in tchg. Baruch Coll., 1987, Pres. award for excellence in scholarship, 2005, Tchg. Excellence award, 1989, 91, 92, 93, CUNY Excellence Award for Rsch., Sch. Bus. and Pub. Adminstrn. Tchg. and Svc., 1999; William B. Harding fellow Harvard U. Mem. APA, Acad. Mgmt., Decision Scis. Inst., Soc. for Human Resource Mgmt. (accredited pers. diplomate, sr. profl. in human resources), Am. Compensation Assn., Met. N.Y. Assn. for Applied Psychology (sec. 1986-87, treas. 1987-88, v.p. 1988-89, pres. 1989-90), Sigma Iota Epsilon (faculty advisor Baruch Coll. chpt. 2003-). Home: 65 Colgate Rd Great Neck NY 11023-1501 Office: Baruch Coll Zicklin Sch Bus/Dept Mgmt 1 Bernard Branch Way New York NY 10010-5518 Office Phone: 646-312-3629. Business E-Mail: richard_kopelman@baruch.cuny.edu. E-mail: rekopelman@managingperformance.com.

KOPELSON, ARNOLD, film producer; b. New York, NY, Feb. 14, 1935; BS, N.Y.U.; JD, N.Y. Law Sch., 1959. Prodr. (film) Foolin' Around, 1980, Dirty Tricks, 1981, Gimme an F, 1984, Platoon, 1986 (Acad. awd Best Picture), Triumph of the Spirit, 1989, Out for Justice, 1991, Falling Down, 1993, The Fugitive, 1993 (Acad. award nom Best Picture), Outbreak, 1995, Seven, 1995, Eraser, 1996, Murder at 1600, 1997, Mad City, 1997, The Devil's Advocate, 1997, U.S. Marshals, 1998, A Perfect Murder, 1998, Don't Say A Word, 2001, Joe Somebody, 2001, Twisted, 2004; exec. prodr. (film) Lost and Found, 1979, The Legacy, 1979, Night of the Juggler, 1980, Final Assignment, 1980, Dirty Tricks, 1980, Model Behavior, 1984, Warlock, 1989, Fire Birds, 1990; exec. prodr. (TV) Past Tense, 1994, The Fugitive, 2000, Thieves, 2001.*

KOPENHAVER, PATRICIA ELLSWORTH, podiatrist; Student, Columbia U., 1950-53; BA, George Washington U., 1954; MA, Columbia U., 1956; Dr. Podiatric Medicine, N.Y. Coll. Podiatric Medicine, 1963, postgrad., 1980; LLD (hon.), Barry U., 1998; MD (hon.) (hon.), Internat. U. Health Scis. Sch. Medicine, 2001; MD (hon.), Internat. Univ. of the Hlth. Sci., 2001. Diplomate Nat. Bd. Podiatry Examiners. Pvt. practice podiatry, Greenwich, Conn., 1964—; staff podiatrist Havenhealth Care Ctr., Greenwich, 2003—. Mem. staff Laurelton Convalescent Hosp., Greenwich; trustee N.Y. Coll. Podiatric Medicine, 1998. Bd. dirs. Monmouth Opera Guild, 1965; trustee Monmouth Opera Festival, 1966, v.p., 1964; mem. Greenwich Arts Coun.; program chmn. Greenwich Women's Rep. Club, 1983-84, 4th dist. rep., 1984-85, 87—; trustee N.Y. Coll. Podiatric Medicine, 1998—. Recipient Hosp. Fund award for med. research translations ARC, Alumni award of distinction N.Y. Coll. Podiatric Medicine, 1997; scholarship named in her honor N.Y. Coll. Podiatric Medicine, 1997. Mem. AAUW (v.p. 1991, pres. Greenwich br. 1992-94, bd. dirs. 1996), NOW, Conn. Podiatric Med. Assn., Hist. Soc., Asian Soc., Fairfield Podiatry Assn., Am. Assn. Women Podiatrists (founding charter pres. 1969-78), Acad. Podiatry, Am. Podiatry Coun., UN Assn. U.S.A., Acad. Podiatric Medicine (chmn. nominating com. 1981, 1st v.p. 1983-84, chmn. fundraising 1984-85, chmn. women's issues 1985, chmn. cmty. edn. 1989), Am. Acad. Sports Medicine, Am. Acad. Podiatric Sports Medicine (assoc. 1989), George Washington U. Alumni Assn., Columbia Alumni Assn., Fairfield County Alumni Assn. Columbia U., Coast Soc. of Founders Barry U. (treas. 1998), Nat. Fedn. Rep. Women, Bruce Mus., Nature Conservancy, Federated Garden Clubs Conn., St. Mary Ladies Guild, Greenwich Gardeners, Womans' Club (ways and means com. 1989, pres.), English Speaking Union, Soroptimists Internat. Am. (pres. Greenwich br. 1990—, bd. dirs. 1997-98), Inc. (vice chmn. program com. 1985—, regional med. scholarship chmn. 1987, med. scholarship chmn. N.E. region 1988, program dir. 1988—, pres. Greenwich br. 1990-92), Toastmasters, Travel Club (program com. 1984—), Soroptimist (bd. dirs. 1997, 2000—), Greenwich Woman's Club (chair gardeners judges 2001—), Pi Epsilon Chi. Home: 2 Sutton Pl S New York NY 10022-3070 also: 8 Dearfield Dr Greenwich CT 06831-5348 Office Phone: 203-661-9311. Office Fax: 203-869-5096.

KOPF, GEORGE MICHAEL, retired ophthalmologist; b. Chilton, Wis., Oct. 20, 1935; s. George and Mary (Schmid) K.; m. Sandra Mary Nolte, Dec. 29, 1962; children: Karen, Jennifer, Nancy. BS, U. Wis., 1958, MD, 1961. Diplomate Am. Bd. Ophthalmology. Intern Luther Hosp., Eau Claire, Wis., 1961-62; resident Milw. County Hosp., 1962-63, Detroit Gen. Hosp., 1965-68; ophthalmologist pvt. practice, Zanesville, Ohio, 1968—; ret., 1999. Mem. med. staff Bethesda Hosp., Zanesville; mem. med. Staff Good Samaritan Med. Ctr., Zanesville, pres., 1978, sec. bd. dirs., 1986-96. Capt. USAF, 1963-65. Fellow ACS, Am. Acad. Ophthalmology; mem. Ohio Ophthalmology Soc. (pres. 1976-77), Muskigum County Acad. Medicine (pres. 1983), Ohio State Med. Assn., Rotary. Republican. Roman Catholic. Avocations: tennis, swimming, hiking, reading, travel. Home: 2950 Ash Meadows Blvd Zanesville OH 43701-9081

KOPF, RANDI, family and oncology nurse practitioner, lawyer; b. Jersey City, Mar. 30, 1953; d. Soloman and Sydell Kopf. BS, MS, SUNY, Stony Brook, 1978; JD, U. Md., Balt., 1989. Bar: Md., 1989, D.C., 1991; cert. family nurse practitioner. Pvt. practitioner allergy and dermatology, 1982-83; pvt. cons. practice as oncology nurse practitioner; legal intern Office of Gen. Counsel, NIH, 1988; legal assoc., health svcs. group Nixon, Hargrave, Devans & Doyle, Washington, 1990-93; prin. atty., founder Kopf HealthLaw Group, Bethesda, Md., 1995; pvt. law practice, 1995—. Lectr., cons. Am. Cancer Soc.; mem. faculty Georgetown U., U. Md., Adelphi U.; nat. lectr. on med. legal topics. Author: Handbook of Nursing Physical Assesment, 1987, Before You Sign...Managed Care Contract Review for Health Care Providers, 1996; editor, contbg. author Jour. Nursing Law, 1993—; contbr. articles to nat. profl. jours. Recipient Alumni award for Outstanding Volunteerism, Cornell U., 1998. Mem. D.C. Bar Assn., Md. Bar Assn., Am. Hosp. Atty. Assn., Chesapeake Nurse Atty. Assn. (pres., bd. dirs.), Am. Health Lawyers Assn. Home: 511 Golden Oak TER Rockville MD 20850-7801

KOPF, RICHARD G., federal judge; b. 1946; BA, U. Nebr., Kearney, 1969; JD, U. Nebr., Lincoln, 1972. Law clk. to Hon. Donald R. Ross US Ct. Appeals (8th cir.), 1972-74; ptnr. Cook, Kopf & Doyle, Lexington, Neb., 1974-87; U.S. magistrate judge, 1987-92; fed. judge US Dist. Ct. (Nebr. dist.), 1992—, chief judge, 1999—2004. Mem. ABA, ABA Found., Nebr. State Bar, Nebr. State Bar Found. Office: US Dist Ct 586 US Courthouse 100 Centennial Mall N Lincoln NE 68508-3859 Office Phone: 402-437-5252. Business E-Mail: richard_kopf@ned.uscourts.gov.

KOPLAN, STEVEN, federal government commissioner; Children: Michael, Bruce, David, Adam. BA, Brandeis U.; JD, Boston U. Sch. Law; M of Laws in Taxation, N.Y.U. Prosecutor tax divsn. U.S. Dept. Justice; legislative rep. AFL-CIO; staff atty. U.S. Senator Lee Metcalf; v.p. governmental affairs Joseph E. Seagram & Sons, Inc.; principal Bayh & Connaughton, McNair Law Firm, Washington; dir. governmental affairs Safari Club Internat.; chmn. U.S. Internat. Trade Commn., 2000—02, 2000—. Democrat.

KOPLEWICZ, HAROLD SAMUEL, child and adolescent psychiatrist; b. Bklyn., Jan. 12, 1953; s. Joseph and Romana (Magid) K.; m. Linda Jane Sirow, June 22, 1980; children: Joshua, Adam, Sam. BS, U. Md., 1973; MD, Albert Einstein Coll. of Medicine, 1978. bd. cert. Psychiatry, Neurology in Psychiatry; Diplomate Am. Bd. Psychiatry and Neurology, 1983, Am. Bd. Child Psychiatry, 1984. Med. dir. preschool hyperactivity program NY State Psychiat. Inst., NYC, 1982-85, med. dir. children's anxiety clinic, 1983-86; dir. gen. residency tng. child psychiatry Columbia Coll. Physicians and Surgeons, NYC, 1985-86; chief divsn. child and adolescent psychiatry Schneider Children's Hosp. and Hillside Hosp. of L.I. Jewish Med. Ctr., NYC, 1986-96; editor Youth Mental Health Update, 1989-96; assoc. prof. psychiatry Albert Einstein Coll. Medicine, NYC, 1991-96; dir. child and adolescent psychology divsn. NYU Med. Ctr./Bellevue Hosp. Ctr., NYC, 1996—; prof. clin. psychiatry and pediatrics, vice chmn. psychiatry NYU Sch. Medicine, 1996—, founder, dir. NYU Child Study Ctr. NYC, 1997—, Arnold & Debbie Simon prof. child & adolscent psychiatry, prof. pediatrics, 2000—. Cons. Riverdale Cmty. Ctr., 1981-86, The Dalton Sch., 1991-96, The N.Y. Infirmary, 1991, The Family Acad., 1991-96, Jewish Child Care Assn., 1992-96, Health Edn. Task Force, Roslyn Sch. Dist., 1993-96; dir. Nat. Child Mental Health Inst., 1999—; Richard B. Richter vis. prof. in child psychiatry Ind. U., 2005. Author: It's Nobody's Fault: New Hope and Help for Difficult Children and Their Parents, 1996, Childhood Revealed: Art Expressing Pain, Hope and Discovery, 1999, Trubulent Times Prophetic Dreams, 2000, More Than Moody: Recognizing and Treating Adolescent Depression, 2002; editor NYU Child Study Ctr. Letter, 1996—; editor-in-chief: Jour. Child and Adolescent Psychopharmacology, 1997—; mem. adv. bd. Parents Mag., 1996—, Parents In Action, 1996—; mem. profl. adv. bd. Big Apple Parent Paper, 1995—, NYC chpt. Nat. Alliance for Mentally Ill, 2001—. Bd. dirs. Raoul Wallenberg New Leadership Soc., 1983-87, Cmty. Mainstreaming Assocs., 1990; chmn. Simon Wiesenthal Ctr., 1984-86; commr. NY State Commn. for Study of Youth Crime and Violence and Reform of the Juvenile Justice Sys., 1993-96; prin. investigator Developing Innovative Mental Health Care Delivery for Adolescents, Hewlett-Woodmere Sch. Dist., 1992; adv. bd. Our Children's Found., 1996-97. Recipient Hulse award NY Coun. Child and Adolescent Psychiatry, 1995, Exemplary Psychiatrist award Nat. Alliance Mentally Ill, 1997, Contbns. to Humanity award Marymount Manhattan Coll., 1999, Am. Grand Hope award 2000. Fellow Am. Acad. Child and Adolescent Psychiatry (Reiger award 1997), Am. Psychiat. Assn.; mem. Soc. Profs. Child and Adolescent Psychiatry, Am. Bd. Psychiatry and Neurology (examiner 1988-98), Nat. Bd. Med. Examiners (mem. psychiatry com. 1993-96), Nat. Found. Depressive Illness (nat. bd. dirs. 1992—), Mental Health Assn. of N.Y. (profl. adv. bd. 1997—). Office: NYU Child Study Ctr 577 1st Ave New York NY 10016 Fax: 212-263-0484. E-mail: harold.koplewicz@nyumc.org.

KOPLIK, MICHAEL R., durable goods company executive; s. Perry H Koplik. Sales manager Castle & Overton Inc., NYC, 1957—60; dir., v.p. Perry H. Koplik & Sons Inc., NYC, 1960—78, pres., CEO, 1978—2001, 2003—. Office: Perry H Koplik & Sons Inc 450 Park Ave New York NY 10022-2605

KOPLIN, DONALD LEROY, health products executive, consumer advocate; b. Greenleaf, Kans., Dec. 31, 1932; s. Henry G. Koplin and Edith Mary Stevens; m. Patricia Joynes, June 2, 1962 (div. Aug. 1974); children: Marie Claire, Marie Joelle (adopted); m. Joan Freudenthal, June 28, 1997. Student, U. San Diego, 1956-59, 67-68. Electronics test insp. Gen. Dynamics, San Diego, 1956-59; cryptographer Dept. of State, Washington, 1959-67, communications program officer France, Angola, Madagascar, Qatar, India, Oman, Benin and the Bahamas, 1977-86; tech. writer Ryan Aero. Corp., San Diego, 1967-68; comml. dir., tech. advisor, pub. rels. officer Societe AGM, San Francisco, Athens, Greece, Antananarivo and Morondava, Dem. Republic of Madagascar, 1968-72; founder, dir. Soc. Bells, Cyclone & Akai, Antananarivo, 1972-74; founder, ptnr., assoc. editor Angola Report, Luanda, 1974-75; polit. reporter Angola Report, Reuters, AP, UPI Corr., BBC, Luanda; supr. Tex. Instruments, Lubbock, 1976-77; exec. Dial A Contact Lens, Inc., La Jolla, Calif., 1986-90, Assn. for Retarded Citizens, San Diego, 1991-92, Club Med, Copper Mountain, Colo., 1992-94; CEO Vient Inc., 1994-97, Koplin Kollection Fine Arts Gallery, La Jolla, Calif., 1996-98. Active San Diego Zool. Soc. With USN, 1951-55, Korea. Mem.: Am. Fgn. Svc. Assn. Avocation: writing. Home: 6718 Evergreen Ave Oakland CA 94611-1518 Personal E-mail: dojokop@webtv.net.

KOPLOS, JANET, editor, art critic; BA in Journalistm, Univ. Minn., Mpls.; MA in Art Hist., Ill. State Univ., 1984. Editor Minichi Daily News, Tokyo, Art Material Trade News, Atlanta; contbg. editor Fiberarts, Art Papers, New Art Examiner; sr. editor Art in America, NYC, 1990—. Writer, lectr., critic in field, 1976—; author: Contemporary Japanese Sculpture, 1991; co-author: Unexpected: Artists' Ceramics of the 20th Century, 1999, Laura De Santillana Works, 2002. Recipient Nat. Endowment Arts award, Arts Critic's Fellowship. Office: Art in America Brant Art Publications 575 Broadway New York NY 10012 Office Phone: 212-941-2800. Office Fax: 212-941-8885.

KOPLOVITZ, KAY, television network executive; b. Milw, Apr. 11, 1945; d. William E. and Jane T. Smith; m. William C. Koplovitz Jr., Apr. 17, 1971. BS, U. Wis., 1967; MA in Comms., Mich. State U., 1968. Radio and TV producer, dir. Sta. WTMJ-TV, Milw., 1967; editor Comm. Satellite Corp., Washington, 1968-72; dir. cmty. svc. UA Columbia Cablevision, Oakland, NJ, 1973-75; v.p., exec. dir. UA Columbia Satellite Services Inc., Oakland, NJ, 1977-80; founder, chmn., CEO USA Networks and Sci-Fi Channel, NYC, 1977—98; CEO Koplovitz & Co., NYC, 1998—; chmn. bd Reality Central, 2003—. Founder Springboard 2000; bd. dirs. Springboard Enterprises, Liz Claiborne, Instinet. Mem. bd. overseers NYU Grad. Sch. Bus., 1984-90; bd. dir. Nat. Jr. Achievement, 1986-1996. Named to Entrepreneur oHall of Fame, Babson Coll., 2001, Cable Hall of Fame, 2001, Broadcasting Mag. Hall of Fame, 1992; recipient Outstanding Alumnus award, Mich. State U. Grad. Sch. Bus., 1985, Oustanding Corp. Social Responsibility, CUNY, 1986, Women Who Run the World award, Sara Lee Corp., 1987, Muse award, N.Y. Women in Film and TV, 1992, Ellis Island medal of honor, 1993, Crystal award, Women in Film, 1993. Mem.: Com. of 200, Nat. Acad. Cable Programming (bd. dirs. 1984—87), Cable Advt. Bur. (bd. dirs., exec. com., treas. 1981—87, Chmn.'s award for leadership 1987), Women in Cable (founding bd. dirs., membership chmn. 1979—80, v.p. 1981—82, pres. 1982—83), Nat. Acad. TV Arts and Scis. (chmn. 1994—97, bd. dirs. 1984—93), Internat. Coun., Advt. Coun. Inc. (chmn. 1992—93, bd. dirs. 1985—94), Nat. Cable TV Assn. (bd. dirs. 1984—98), N.Y.C. Partnership (bd. dirs. 1987—), Womens Forum. Avocations: tennis, skiing, travel. E-mail: kay@koplovitz.com.

KOPLOWITZ, STEPHAN, choreographer; b. 1956; Choreographer and dance dir. Packer Collegiate Inst., 1983—. Founding mem. Webbed Feats. Choreographer (multimedia works) seen at Grand Ctr. Terminal, Lincoln Ctr., Bryant Pk., N.Y.C., Nat. History Mus., London, Brit. Libr., Germany. Recipient N.Y. Dance and Performance award for Sustained Achievement in Choreography, 2000, Alpert award, 2004; fellowship, John Simon Guggenheim Meml. Found., 2003.

KOPP, CHARLES GILBERT, lawyer; b. Hartford, Conn., Jan. 10, 1933; s. Henry and Grace (Goldberg) K.; m. Ann Weiss, June 10, 1962 (div. 1963) BA, Amherst Coll., 1955; JD, U. Pa., 1960. Bar: Pa. 1961. Sr. counsel Wolf, Block, Schorr and Solis-Cohen LLP, Phila., 1960—. Vis. lectr. Villanova (Pa.) Univ., 1981. Contbr. articles to profl. jours. Commr. Delaware River Port Authority, 1986-87; co-chmn. select com. of U.S. Embassy, Bern, Switzerland, 1985; mem. Pa. Gov.'s Spl. Tax Commn., 1980; mem. fin. com. Rep. State Com., 1984-98, mem. leadership com.; bd. dirs. Pennsylvanians for Effective Govt., Harrisburg, 1987-99; mem. Pa. Electoral Coll., 1988; mem. adv. bd. region I, Resolution Trust Corp., 1990-93; mem. coun. The Pa. Soc., 1991-98; trustee Thomas Jefferson U. Hosp., 1988—, Pop Warner Little Scholars; mem. adv. bd. PNC, Phila., 1992-2000. 1st lt. USAF, 1955-57. Recipient Pop Warner Gold Football award, 1988. Mem.: ABA, Phila. Bar Assn., Pa. Bar Assn., Greater Phila. C. of C. (exec. com. 1988—96), Vesper Club, Pyramid Club. Republican. Jewish. Home: 210 W Rittenhouse Sq Apt 3306 Philadelphia PA 19103-5780 Office: Wolf Block Schorr and Solis Cohen LLP 1650 Arch St Fl 22 Philadelphia PA 19103-2003

KOPP, EUGENE HOWARD, electrical engineer; b. N.Y.C., Oct. 1, 1929; s. Jacob and Fanny (Lipschitz) K.; m. Claire Bernstein, Aug. 31, 1950; children: Carolyn, Michael, Paul. B.E.E., CCNY, 1950, M.E.E., 1953; PhD in Engring, UCLA, 1965. Registered profl. engr., Calif. Project engr. Polarad Electronics Corp., Long Island City, N.Y., 1950-53, Kaye Halbert Corp., Culver City, Calif., 1953-55; chief engr. Precision Radiation Instruments, Inc., Los Angeles, 1955-58; mem. faculty sch. engring. Calif. State U., Los Angeles, 1958-74, assoc. prof., 1962-66, prof., 1966-74, dean engring. Sch., 1967-73; v.p. acad. affairs West Coast U., Los Angeles, 1973-79; sr. scientist Hughes Aircraft Co., 1980-85, mgr. research and devel., 1985-93, dir. advanced programs, 1994-95; v.p. mobile satellites Boeing Satellite Systems, 1996-97, chief scientist comml. satellites, 1998—2002; chief scientist homeland security The Boeing Co., 2003—. Lectr. evening divsn. CCNY, N.Y.C., 1950-53; lectr. UCLA, 1979-91. Vis. research fellow U. Leeds, Eng., 1966-67 Mem. IEEE, AIAA, Tau Beta Pi, Eta Kappa Nu, Pi Tau Sigma. Avocation: flying. Office: The Boeing Co PO Box 1351 South Pasadena CA 91031-1351

KOPP, EUGENE PAUL, lawyer; b. Charleston, W.Va., Nov. 20, 1934; s. Eugene Alexander and Virginia Elizabeth (King) K.; m. Katherine Patricia Rogers, July 1, 1967; 1 son, Eugene Paul. BA, U. Notre Dame, 1957, MA, 1958; JD, W.Va. U., 1961. Ba: W.Va. 1961, D.C. 1977, Tex. 1980. Law clk. U.S. Dist. Ct. W.Va., 1961-62; trial atty. Dept. Justice, Washington, 1962-69; dep. dir. USIA, 1973-77, acting dir., 1976-77; assoc. gen. counsel Champlin Petroleum Co., Ft. Worth, 1977-81; v.p. Washington affairs Union Pacific Corp., Washington, 1981-87; dep. dir. U.S. Info. Agy., 1989-93; exec. dir. MFJ Task Force, 1993-94; of counsel Clarendon Assocs., Inc., 1995-97, Ruddy and Muir, 1998—2004; vice chmn. Nexphase Comms., Inc., 2000—01; ptnr. Kopp, Kramer, Quinn LLC, Wash., DC, 2004—; of counsel Sale and Quinn, 2004—. Cons. nat. Security Council, Washington, 1981, mem. transition team, 1980. Mem.: Washington Inst. Fgn. Affairs, DC Bar Assn., Tex. Bar Assn., W.Va. Bar Assn., Capitol Hill Club, Dacor Club (Washington), Met. Club (Washington), Belle Haven Country Club. Roman Catholic. Home: 508 Cathedral Dr Alexandria VA 22314-4706 Office Phone: 202-833-4170. Personal E-mail: kopponbeat@aol.com.

KOPP, ILYA ZINOVIJ, environmental engineer; b. Tashkent, Uzbekistan, Aug. 1, 1929; s. Zinovij Il'ich and Anna Hanna-Bath Abramovna K.; 1 child, Victor. MS in Engring., Navy Architecture U., St. Petersburg, Russia, 1951; DSc, State Tech. U., Russia, 1961; PhD, Moscow (Russia) Aviation Inst., Tech. U., 1988. Head rsch. dept. North-West Politechnical Inst., St. Petersburg, 1957-86; prof. State Tech. U., St. Petersburg, 1986-97. Dep. dir., head theoretical dept. Sci. and Rsch. Inst. of Atmospheric Air Protection, St. Petersburg, 1988-97. Author: Progress of the Theory of Heat for New Technology, 2003, Effective Surfaces for Heat Transfer, 2002, Decline of the Nuclear Century or?, 2002, Power Installations for Energy Supply and Environment, 1992, Heat Power Installation for Energy Supply and Environment Protection, 1988, Foundation of the Theory of the Environmental Protection, 1993 (2nd prize 1994), Energy and Environment, 1982, Foundations of Thermodynamics and Energy Equipment for Nuclear Power Installations, 1989, others; contbr. over 170 articles to profl. jours.; patentee in field. Mem. AAAS, N.Y. Acad. Sci., Internat. Info. Acad. Home: 36-19 Bowne St #5F Flushing NY 11354 E-mail: ilkopp@hotmail.com.

KOPP, NANCY KORNBLITH, state official; b. Coral Gables, Fla., Dec. 7, 1943; d. Lester and Barbara M. (Levy) Kornblith; m. Robert E. Kopp, May 3, 1969; children: Emily, Robert E. III. BA with honors, Wellesley Coll., 1965; MA, U. Chgo., 1968; LittD (hon.), Hood Coll., 1988; LHD (hon.), Towson U., 2001; JD (hon.), U. Md., Balt., 2001. Instr. polit. sci. U. Ill., 1968-69; staff spl. subcom. on edn. U.S. Ho. of Reps., Washington, 1970-71; legis. staff Md. Gen. Assembly, Annapolis, 1971-74; mem. Md. Ho. of Dels., 1974—2002, spkr. pro tem, 1991-93, chmn. appropriations subcom on edn. and devel., chmn. spending affordability joint com.; state treas. State of Md., Annapolis, 2002—. Chmn. Md. Coll. Savings Plans. Mem. State Retirement and Pension Bd.; vice chmn. Capital Debt Affordability Com., chmn.; mem. Nat. Assessment Governing Bd., Md. Supplemental Retirement Bd., Md. Higher Edn. Investment Bd. Mem.: N.E. State Treas. Assn. (chmn. capital debt affordability com., vice chmn. state ret. and pension bd.). Democrat. Jewish. Office: Treasury Building 80 Calvert St Annapolis MD 21401 Office Phone: 410-260-7160. E-mail: nkopp@treasurer.state.md.us.

KOPP, RICHARD EDGAR, electrical engineer; b. Bklyn., July 12, 1931; s. Edgar A. and Anna M. (Barto) K.; m. Elaine Hecker, June 14, 1953; children: Debra, Richard (dec.), Lisa, Barbara. BEE, Poly. Inst. Bklyn., 1953, MS, 1957, DEE, 1960. Rsch. engr. Grumman Aerospace Corp., Bethpage, N.Y., 1953-58, head computing rsch. group, 1958-65, head systems rsch. lab., 1965-70, dir. systems scis. rsch., 1970-89, dir. sci. adv. bd., 1989-90, pvt. cons., 1990—. Mem. adv. com. Poly. Inst. Imaging Scis.; adj. prof. Poly. Inst. Bklyn., 1961-70. Contbr. articles to profl. jours. Fellow AIAA (assoc.); mem. IEEE (sr.). Home: 119 Constantine Way Mount Sinai NY 11766 E-mail: rekopp@aol.com.

KOPP, ROBERT WALTER, lawyer; b. Boston, Feb. 21, 1935; s. Robert A. and Marie (Powers) K.; m. Carol A. Rosenberger, Aug. 22, 1959; children: Robert A., Christopher F., J. Brian, David W., Karen A. BS in Physics, Holy Cross Coll., 1957; LLB, Georgetown U., 1963. Bar: N.Y. 1963. Sr. ptnr. Bond, Schoeneck & King, Syracuse, N.Y., 1963—; gen. counsel Pay Bd. Econ. Stabilization Program Phase II, Washington, 1972-73. Lt. (j.g.) USN, 1957-62. Fellow Am. Bar Found., Coll. Labor and Employment Law (founding); mem. ABA (coun. sect. labor and employment law 1980-88, sect. governance liaison 1989-90, 94-2000, sect. del. to ho. of dels. 1990-93), N.Y. State Bar Assn. Roman Catholic. Home: 1 Lincoln Ctr Syracuse NY 13202-1324 Office: Bond Schoeneck & King 1 Lincoln Ctr Fl 18 Syracuse NY 13202-1324

KOPP, WENDY, teaching program administrator; b. Austin, Tex., June 29, 1967; BA, Princeton U., 1998; degree (hon.), Conn. Coll., Drew U. Pres. and founder Teach For America, 1989—. Bd. dirs. New Tchr. Project, The Learning Project, Kipp Acad. Recipient Nat. Acad. fellow, 1990, Jefferson Award for Pub. Svcs., Woodrow Wilson award, 1993, Aetna's Voice of Conscience award, 1994, Citizen Activist award, 1994, Kilby Young Innovator award; named to Time Mag. Roster of Am. Most Promising Leaders Under 40, 1994, Woman of Yr. Glamour mag., 1990. Office: Teach For America 315 W 36th St Fl 6 New York NY 10018-6404

KOPPEL, LOWELL B., chemical engineer; b. Chgo., Sept. 13, 1935; s. Maurice G. and Mynn S. (Schultz) K.; m. Barbara Jane Parker, June 12, 1957; children: Steven P., Sharon M. Grottkau, Michael D., Lowell B. Jr. BS in Chem. Engring., Northwestern U., 1957, PhD, 1960; MS in Chem. Engring., U. Mich., 1958. Instr., fellow Calif. Inst. Tech., Pasadena, 1960-61; from asst. to prof. chem. engring. Purdue U., 1961-85, head Sch. Chem. Engring., 1973-81; sr. cons. Setpoint, Inc., Houston, 1985-90, dir., 1990-95; v.p. Aspen Tech., Inc., Cambridge, Mass., 1996-00; prin., owner Value Techniques, LLC, Winchester, Mass., 2000—. Author: Process Control, 1965, Control Theory, 1968; contbr. numerous articles to profl. jours. Recipient Lecturship award Am. Soc. Energy Edn., 1982, Outstanding Personal Achievement award McGraw-Hill Chem. Engring., 1994. Mem. AIChE. Home: 16 Hastings Rd Winchester MA 01890-3859 Office: Value Techniques LLC 16 Hastings Rd Winchester MA 01890-3859 E-mail: koppel@valuetechniques.com.

KOPPEL, TED, newscaster; b. Lancashire, Eng., Feb. 8, 1940; arrived in U.S., 1953; m. Grace Anne Dorney, 1963; 4 children, Andrea, Deirdre, Andrew, Tara. BA in speech, Syracuse U., 1960; MA in mass comm. rsch. & polit. sci., Stanford U., 1962. News corr., writer Sta.-WMCA, NYC, 1963; with ABC News, 1963—, former gen. assignment corr., former Vietnam war correspondent, Miami bur. chief, 1968—69, Hong Kong bur. chief, 1969—71, chief diplomatic corr., 1971—80, anchor The ABC Saturday Night News, 1975—77, anchor Nightline, 1980—; also mng. editor. Corr. for TV spls. including The People of People's China, 1973, Kissinger: Action Biography, 1974, Second to None, 1979, The Koppel Reports, 1988—90. Co-editor: The Wit and Wisdom of Adlai Stevenson, 1965; co-author (with Marvin Kalb): In The National Interest, 1977; author: Nightline: History in the Making and the Making of Television, 1996. Named Chevalier de l'Ordre des Arts et des Lettres, Republic of France, 1994; named to Broadcasting Hall of Fame; recipient George Polk Awards for TV reporting, 1981, George Polk Awards for network TV reporting, 1985, Sol Taishoff Award for Excellence in Broadcast Journalism, Nat. Press Found., 1984, 37 Emmy awards, Acad. TV Arts and Scis., 6 George Foster Peabody Awards, 10 duPont-Columbia Awards, 9 Overseas Press Club Awards, 2 Sigma Delta Chi Awards, Soc. Profl. Journalists, numerous others. Office: Nightline 1717 De Sales St NW Washington DC 20036-4401*

KOPPELMAN, ANDREW MARTIN MAYER, law educator; b. Nyack, NY, Aug. 29, 1957; s. George Irving and Ruby Etta (Lee) K.; m. Valerie Jane Quinn, June 24, 1989; 1 child, John Miles Isidore. AB, U. Chgo., 1979; MA in Polit. Sci., Yale U., 1986, JD, 1989, PhD, 1991. Bar: Conn. 1990, NY 1991. Law clk. to Chief Justice Ellen A. Peters conn. Supreme Ct., 1991—92; asst. prof. politics Princeton U., NJ, 1992—97; asst. prof. law and polit. sci. Northwestern U., Chgo., 1997—2000, assoc. prof., 2000—03, George C. Dix prof. constitutional law, 2000—00, prof. law, 2003—. Vis. prof. law U. Tex. at Austin, 1997. Author: Antidiscrimination Law and Social Equality, 1996 (Myers Center Award, 1997), The Gay Rights Question in Contemporary American Law, 2002; contbr. articles to profl. jours. Summer rsch. fellow Ctr. for Studies in Law, Econs. and Pub. Policy Yale U., 1988, 90, 91, NEH summer rsch. stipend fellow, 1993, Harvard U. Program in Ethics and Professions fellow, 1994-95. Office: Northwestern U Sch Law 357 E Chicago Ave Chicago IL 60611 Office Phone: 312-503-8431. E-mail: akoppelman@northwestern.edu.*

KOPPELMAN, CHAIM, artist, educator; b. Bklyn., Nov. 17, 1920; s. Samuel and Sadie (Mondlin) K.; m. Dorothy Myers, Feb. 13, 1943; 1 child, Ann. Student, Bklyn. Coll., 1938, Am. Artists Sch., 1939; student Aesthetic Realism, with Eli Siegel, 1940-78; student, Art Coll. Western Eng., Bristol, 1944, Ecole des Beaux-Arts, Rheims, 1945, Art Students League, 1946, Amedée Ozenfant Sch., 1946-49; student Aesthetic Realism, with Ellen Reiss, 1978—. Art instr. N.Y. U., 1947-55, N.Y. State U., New Paltz, 1952-58; instr. Sch. Visual Arts, N.Y.C., 1959—. Cons. Aesthetic Realism Found., N.Y.C., 1971— Author: This is the Way I See Aesthetic Realism, 1969; illustrator: Definition, 1972; contbr. articles to profl. jours.; Bibliographies of his work The Indignant Eye (Ralph Shikes), 1969, The New Humanism (Barry Schwartz), 1974, The Art of the Print (Fritz Eichenberg), 1976, American Prints and Printmakers (Una Johnson), 1980, Hilla Rebay: In Search of the Spirit in Art (Joan Lukach), 1983; one man shows include Asso. Am. Artists Gallery, 1973, Terrain Gallery, N.Y.C., 1974, 83, Warwick (Eng.) Gallery, 1975, Merida Rapp Graphics, Louisville, 1985, Print Club, Phila., Beatrice Conde Gallery, 2000, others; group shows include Purdue U., 1972, Utah State U., 1972, Arte Fiera, Bologna, 1978, NAD, N.Y.C., 1983, Print Club, Phila., 1988, Alternative Mus., N.Y.C., 1988, Art Mus., Bogota, 1996; represented in permanent collections Victoria and Albert Mus., London, Mus. Fine Arts, Caracas, Venezuela, Mus. Modern Art, N.Y.C., Met. Mus. Art, N.Y.C., Library of Congress, Washington, Los Angeles County Mus. Art, Phila. Mus. Art, Guggenheim Mus., others; sculptor Eli Siegel Meml., Druid Hill Park, Balt., 2002. Served with USAF, 1942-45. Decorated Bronze Star; recipient N.Y. State Creative Artists Pub. Svc. award, 1976, prize Soc. Am. Graphic Artists, Fabri prize Nat. Acad. Ann., 1989, Cook prize, 1998, Lifetime Achievement award Soc. Am. Graphic Artists, 2004; Louis Comfort Tiffany grantee, 1956, 59, Documenta II, Kassel, 1961. Mem. Nat. Acad. Design. Home and Office: 498 Broome St New York NY 10013-2213 E-mail: pierodella@aol.com. *I learned from Eli Siegel, the great American poet and critic, the most important thing an artist can know-this Aesthetic Realism statement: "All beauty is a making one of opposities and the making one of opposites is what we are going after in ourselves." Every artist is trying to put together opposites such as sameness and difference, warm and cool, freedom and order, and every person and artist is trying to put these same opposites together in his life.*

KOPPELMAN, CHARLES A., record company executive; Chmn. O.Y., N.Y.C.; chmn., CEO EMI Records Group, N.Y.C., 1994—97, EMI Music Publishing, 1990—94, CAK Entertainment Co.; former dir., chmn. Steve Madden Ltd., 2000—04; cons. Martha Stewart Living Omnimedia, Inc., 2003—, vice chmn., 2003—05, chmn., 2005—. Bd. trustees Hofstra U. Dean's Coun. Hofstra Law Sch. Recipient Abe Olman Publishers award, Songwriters Hall of Fame, Humanitarian of the Year, T.J. Martell Found. Leukemia, Cancer and AIDS Rsch. Achievements include formerly singer with trio Ivy; song previewer, then with Don Kirshner as dir. of music pub. co. Office: Martha Stewart Living Omnimedia Inc 11 W 42nd St New York NY 10036 Office Phone: 212-827-8000. Office Fax: 212-827-8204.*

KOPPELMAN, DOROTHY MYERS, artist, consultant; b. NYC, June 13, 1920; d. Harry Walter and May (Chalmers) Myers; m. Chaim Koppelman, Feb. 13, 1943; 1 child, Ann. Student, Bklyn. Coll., 1938-42, Am. Artists Sch., 1940-42, Art Students League, 1942; student of Aesthetic Realism, with Eli Siegel, 1942-78, with Ellen Reiss, 1978—. Instr. art Bklyn. Coll., 1952-75; dir. Terrain Gallery, N.Y.C., 1955-83, Visual Arts Gallery., Sch. Visual Arts, 1961-62; pres. Aesthetic Realism Found., 1973-85, cons., 1973—. Instr. Nat. Acad. Sch. of Design, 1988—89, 1996, 98. One-woman shows include Terrain Gallery, 1961, Rina Gallery, Jersey City, 1961, Atlantic Gallery, 1999; exhibited in group shows at Mus. Modern Art, N.Y.C., 1962, Balt. Mus., 1962, Bklyn. Mus., 1962, N.J. State Mus., Jersey City, 1959, San Francisco Art Inst., 1961-62, 65, Butler Art Inst., Youngstown, Ohio, 1966, Nat. Acad. of Design Juried Ann., 1986, 90, 99, 2000, Swiss Inst., N.Y.C., Susan Teller Gallery, N.Y.C., 1993, 95, Drawing Ctr., N.Y.C., Audubon Soc. ann., N.Y.C., 1995-96, 98, Chuck Levitan Gallery, N.Y.C., 1996, Washington Square East Gallery, N.Y.C., 1992, 96, Am. Soc. Contemporary Artists Anns., 1994-96, 97, 98, 99, 2000, 01, 02, 03, 04, Atlantic Gallery, 1998—, Beatrice Conde Gallery, 2000, Terrain Gallery, 2001, 02, 03,04, 05, Sarah Lawrence Gallery, 2001, Denise Bibro Gallery, 2001; represented in permanent collections Hampton U., Nat. Mus. Women in the Arts, Mus. Jewish Family, Durham, N.C., Savannah Coll. Art and Design, Washington County Mus. Art, Md., Libr. Congress, Washington, N.Y. Hist. Soc.; author Poems and Prints, 2000; co-author: Aesthetic Realism: We Have Been There - Six Artists, 1969; illustrator Children's Guide to Parents (by Eli Siegel), 1971, 2d edit., 2003. Recipient Theresa Lindner award for painting ASCA, 1996, Clara Shainness award for painting, 1999; Tiffany grantee for painting, 1965. Home: 498 Broome St New York NY 10013-2213 Office: Aesthetic Realism Found Inc 141 Greene St New York NY 10012-3201 Personal E-mail: pierodella@aol.com.

KOPPELMAN, LEE EDWARD, regional planner, educator; b. NYC, May 19, 1927; s. Max and Madelyn Judith (Eisenberg) K.; m. Constance E. Lowinger, June 18, 1948; children: Leslie, Claudia, Laurel, Keith. BEE, CCNY, 1950; MS, Pratt Inst., 1964; D in Pub. Adminstrn., NYU, 1970; LLD,

L.I. U., 1978; DHL, Dowling U., 1991. Cert. landscape architect, NY; cert. profl. planner, NJ. Cons. on site planning and landscape architecture, 1950-60; dir. planning Suffolk County Planning Dept., 1960-88; exec. dir. LI Regional Planning Bd., 1965—; leading prof. polit. sci., dir. ctr. regional policy studies SUNY, Stony Brook, 1967—. Adj. prof. environ. sci. Syracuse U., 1976-83; cons. US Dept. Housing and Urban Devel., 1972-78, UN on Land Use and Coastal Zone Planning; mem. Coastal Zone Mgmt. Adv. Com., 1973-75, Nassau/Suffolk Comprehensive Health Planning Council, Melville, NY, 1973-76, Nat. Shoreline Erosion Adv. Panel, 1974-81; exec. dir. tax relief on LI Bi-County State Commn., 1991-92; adv. coun. Sch. of Art, Architecture and Planning Cornell Univ., 1995—. Co-author: Planning Design Criteria, 1968 (3rd edit. 1981), Housing: Planning and Design, 1974, A Methodology to Achieve the Integration of Coastal Zone Science and Regional Planning, 1974, The Urban Sea: Long Island Sound, 1976, Site Planning Criteria, 1978, Long Island Comprehensive Waste Treatment Management Plan, Vol. 1 and 2, 1979, Time Saver Standards for Site Planning, 1982, Long Island Segment of the Nationwide Urban Runoff Program, 1982, Financing Government on Long Island, 1992, The Long Island Comprehensive Special Groundwater Protection Area Plan, 1992, Airport Joint Use Feasibility Study: Calverton Airport, 1993, Financing Government on Long Island, working paper, vols. 1, 2, and 3, 1993, Groundwater and Land Use Planning Experience from North Am., 1996, Town of East Hampton comprehensive Plan, 2002, Fire Island National Seashore-1964-2004: An Adminstrative History, 2005. Recipient cert. of tribute Temp. State Commn. on Water Resources Planning, 1964, career achievement medal Engring. and Archtl. Alumni CCNY, 1977, Disting Alumnus award NYU, 1985, medal of honor LI Assn., 1987, Lone Eagle award Pub. Rels. Soc. Am., 1987, Disting. Leadership award nat. honors program Am. Planning Assn., 1989, Disting. Svc. award NY met. chpt. Am. Planning Assn., 2000, Disting. Svc. medal Found. for LI State Parks, 2001, Career Achievement medal, Pratt Inst. Sch. of Arch.; Paul Harris fellow, 2002; named Citizen of Yr. LI chpt. NSPE, 1983. Mem. Am. Inst. Architects (hon.), Am. Inst. Planners, NY State County Planners Assn. (pres. 1967-68), Internat. Fedn. Planning and Housing, Assn. Architecture and Engr., Sigma Xi. Home: 2 Dune Ct East Setauket NY 11733-1527 Office: SUNY Ctr Regional Policy Studies Stony Brook NY 11794-0001

KOPPEN, HANS T., information technology executive; B of Econs., U. Rotterdam; B in Elecs., Inst. Tech. Rotterdam; M in Mgmt. Sci., Boston U. Various mgmt. positions Control Data Corp., 1971—98; pres. GE Capital Info. Tech. Solutions, 1971—98; sr. v.p., pres. L.Am. Ingram Micro, Inc., exev. v.p., pres. Asia-Pacific Santa Ana, Calif., 2002—. Office: Ingram Micro Inc 1600 E St Andrew Pl PO Box 25125 Santa Ana CA 92799

KOPPERMAN, PAUL EDWARD, history professor; b. Barranquilla, Colombia, Aug. 29, 1945; s. Abraham and Elsa Lehman Kopperman; m. Diane Harris, June 15, 1983; children: Melissa, Aaron. BA, Queens Coll., 1966, MA, 1967; PhD, U. Ill., 1972. Asst. prof. history U. Ill., Urbana, 1978—78; prof. history Oreg. State U., Corvallis, 1978—. Author: (monograph) Braddock at the Monongahela, (biography) Sir Robert Heath, 1575-1649: Window on an Age, (booklet) Ashes and Smoke: The Holocaust in Its History; contbr. articles to profl. jours. Advisor Hillel at Oreg. State U., Corvallis, 1980—2001; chair Holocaust Meml. Program, Corvallis, Oreg., 1987—2005. Recipient C. Warren Hovland Svc. award, Coll. of Liberal Arts, Oreg. State U., 1997, Master Tchr. award, 2005; fellow, David Libr. of the Am. Revolution, 2002; fellowship, Burroughs-Wellcome Found., 1998, Francis Clark Wood Inst. Libr. Residence Rsch. fellowship, Coll. of Physicians of Phila., 2001. Republican. Jewish. Avocations: reading, bicycling. Home: 1925 NW Fourteenth St Corvallis OR 97330 Office: Oreg State Univ Dept History Corvallis OR 97331-5104 Office Phone: 541-737-1265. Office Fax: 541-737-1257. Business E-Mail: pkopperman@oregonstate.edu.

KOPPES, CLAYTON R., academic administrator; s. Clinton and Effie Koppes. Grad., Bethel Coll., 1967; MA, Emory Coll., 1968; PhD, U. Kans., 1974. Sr. rsch. fellow Calif. Inst. Tech.; mem. faculty Oberlin (Ohio) Coll., 1978—, Irvin E. Houck prof. humanities, 1986—91, dean Coll. Arts and Scis., 1996—2004, v.p. acad. affairs, provost, 2004—. Author: JPL and the American Space Program, 1982 (Dexter prize Soc. for the History of Tech.); co-author: Hollywood Goes to War: How Politics, Profits & Propaganda Shaped World War II Movies, 1987. Office: Oberlin Coll 173 W Lorain St Oberlin OH 44074

KOPPES, RICHARD H., lawyer; b. Norfolk, Va. BA, Loyola Marymount U., 1968; JD, U. Calif., 1971. Bar: Calif. 1971. Dep. dir., gen. counsel Dept. Health Svcs., Calif., 1977—85, chief adminstrv. law judge, 1985—86; dep. exec. officer, gen. counsel CalPERS, 1986—96; of counsel Jones Day, San Francisco. Co-dir. exec. edn. programs Stanford U., coord. instl. investor's forum and fiduciary coll., cons. prof.; bd. dirs. Valeant Pharmaceuticals Internat. (formerly ICN Pharmaceuticals, Inc.), Orange County, Calif., Apria Healthcare Group, Orange County, Calif., Am. Soc. Corp. Secretaries, Investor Responsiblity Rsch. Ctr., Washington, Internat. Corp. Governace Network, London; mem. bd. govs. legal advisory com. NYSE, 1994—97; mem. advisory bd. Nat. Assn. Corp. Dirs.; dir. Found. Fiduciary Studies; mem. standing advisory group Pub. Co. Acctg. Oversight Bd.; spkr. in field. Contbr. articles to profl. jours. Named one of 100 Most Influential Lawyers, Nat. Law Jour., 1994. Mem.: ABA (immediate past vice chmn. corp. counsel com.), Nat. Assn. Pub. Pension Attys. (founder, past pres., adminstrv. officer). Office: Jones Day 555 California St 26th Fl San Francisco CA 94104 Office Phone: 415-875-5865. Office Fax: 415-875-5700. E-mail: rkoppas@jonesday.com.

KOPROSKI, ALEXANDER ROBERT, real estate company executive; b. Stamford, Conn., Apr. 6, 1934; s. Alexander J. and Gladys J. (Kryger) Koproski; m. Patricia A. Velliquette; children: Lisa, Susan, Gregory, Beth. Student, U. Conn., 1952-54; BS in Mktg. and Fin., Tri-State U., Angola, Ind., 1959. Lic. real estate broker Conn., N.Y. Comml. and indsl. broker S.H. Silberman, Inc., Stamford, 1960-73; owner, CEO, comml. and indsl. broker Al Koproski Realty, Stamford, 1973—. Mem. Coastal Mgmt. Adv. Com. Nat. v.p. Polish Nat. Youth Baseball Found., 1997; co-chmn. nat. coun. Kosciuszko Found.; past pres. Holy Name Home and Sch. Assn.; past chmn. Kosciuszko Pk. Meml. Com., Stamford Pulaski Meml. Com., Hartford; past mem. Stamford Bicentennial Com., Resource Recovery Task Force, Polish Am. Affairs Coun., Mayor's South End. Adv. Com., Stamford C.E.T.A. Manpower Program; mem. South End Revitalization Com., Stamford, 1996—; past bd. dirs. Polish Am. Congress Conn., Polish Am. Ctrl. Com. Stamford; bd. dirs. Polish Slavic Info. Ctr., Stamford, 1975—, Am. Ctr. Polish Culture, Washington, 1990—, treas., fund raiser; chmn. Little League, Dzialdowo, Poland; grand marshal N.Y.C. Pulaski Parade, 2000; mem. com. dedication of Pope John Paul II statue, Stanford; past chmn. Poles for Ford Com.; mem. Poles for Bush, 2000; past chmn. lay adv. bd., past chmn. 75th ann. yr. book Holy Name of Jesus Cath. Ch., Stamford, lay adv. bd., mem. 100th anniversary com., 2002—03; mem. com. statue dedication Pope John Paul II statue, Stamford, Conn., 2004; mem. Polish studies adv. com. Ctrl. Conn. State U., 1994. With U.S. Army, 1955—57. Named Citizen of Yr., Polish Am. World, N.Y.C., 1978, Layman of Yr., Stamford Kiwanis Club, 1979; recipient Krzyzem Kawwalerskim Orderu Zaslugi Rzeczypospolitej Polskeij medal, Govt. of Poland, 1994, Ellis Island Medal of Honor, 1998, Excellence award Inst. for Religious Edn. and Pastoral Studies, Sacred Heart U., 2001, Polish Govt. medal, 2001, Urzad Kultury Fizcznej i Sportu award, Govt. of Poland, 2001, REAPS award for excellence, Sacred Heart U. Bapt. Ct., 2001, Baseball field in Dizialdowo, Poland named "Al Koproski Stadium", 2003. Mem.: Stamford Bd. Realtors, Stamford Hist. Soc., Stamford Old Timers Athletic Assn. (v.p. 2005—), Polish Am. Cultural Soc. (historian, pres. 2002—, Citizen of the Yr. 1975), St. Davids Bluff Homeowners Assn. (pres.), Oceanview Beach and Tennis Club (past pres.), Polish Am. Bus. and Profl. Club (past pres.), Holy Name Athletic Club (pres., CEO, past pres., Citizen of the Yr. 1982), Exch. Club, Am. Coun. Polish Cultural Club (nat. fundraising chmn. Washington project), Am. Assn. Mil. Order of Malta. Republican. Roman Catholic. Achievements include honor by dedication of Al Koproski Little League Baseball Stadium, Dzialdowo Poland. Avocations: swimming, fundraising, travel. Home: 222 Ocean Dr E Stamford CT 06902-8134 Office: Polish Slavic Info Ctr PO Box 631 Stamford CT 06904-0631 Office Phone: 203-323-9944.

KOPROWSKI, HILARY, microbiologist, educator; b. Warsaw; s. Pawel and Sonia (Berland) K.; m. Irena Grasberg; children: Claude Eugene, Christopher Dorian. BA, Nikolaj Rej Gymnasium of Luth. Congregation, Warsaw; MD, U. Warsaw; grad., Warsaw Conservatory Music and Santa Cecilia Acad., Rome; DSc (hon.), Ludwig-Maximilian U., Munich, Widener Coll.; D of Medicine and Surgery, U. Helsinki, Finland; MD (hon.), U. Uppsala, Sweden; LittD (hon.), Thomas Jefferson U.; DMS (hon.), U. Lublin, Poland, Univ. Coll. Dublin, U. Poznan, Poland, U. Warsaw Acad. Medicine, La Salle U. Rsch. asst. dept. exptl. and gen. pathology U. Warsaw, 1936—39; staff Yellow Fever Rsch. Svc., Rio de Janeiro, 1940—44; staff rsch. divsn. Am. Cyanamid Co., 1944—46; asst. dir. viral and rickettsial rsch. Lederle Lab., Pearl River, NY, 1946—57; dir. Wistar Inst., Phila., 1957—91, prof., 1957—93, prof. laureate, 1993—; Wistar Inst. prof. of rsch. medicine U. Pa., 1957—; prof. microbiology and immunology Thomas Jefferson U., Phila., 1992—; dir. Ctr. Neurovirology, Biotech. Found. Labs., 1992—. Cons. WHO, 1950—; mem. microbiology study sect. NIH, 1956-60; mem. PAHO; mem. adv. com. Nat. Multiple Sclerosis Soc., 1970-78; mem. immunobiology adv. com. NIH, USPHS, 1975-76; mem. bd. sci. counselors div. cancer etiology Nat. Cancer Inst., 1982-86, chmn., 1987-90; mem. biol. response modifiers program decision network com. NIH, 1985-87; mem. immunobiol. adv. com. NIH, USPHS, 1975-76. Co-editor: Methods in Virology, Viruses and Immunity, Current Topics in Microbiology and Immunology, 1965—. Hon. trustee Kosciuszko Found., 1993—. Decorated commandeur Order du Mérite pour la Rsch. et l'Invention, chevalier Order Royal De Lion Belgium, officer Order of the Polish Republic, comdr. Order of The Lion of Finland, chevalier Legion d'honneur (France), Greater Order of Merit Poland; named hon. trustee, Kosciuszko Found., 1993; recipient Alvarenga prize, Coll. Physicians Phila., 1959, Alfred Jurzykowski Found. Polish Millenium prize, 1966, Felix Wankel Tierschutz prize, 1979, Phila. Cancer Rsch. award, Phila. Cancer Club, 1989, San Marino award, 1989, Nicolaus Copernicus medal, Polish Acad. Scis., 1989, The Phila. award, 1990, John Scott award, 1990, Andrzeja Drawicza award, 2005, Lifetime Achievement award, Monte Jade Sci. and Tech. Assn. Mid-Atlantic, Alexander von Humboldt Sr. U.S. Scientist award; scholar Fulbright scholar, Max Planck Inst. für Verhaltensphysiologie, Seewiesen, Fed. Republic Germany, 1971. Fellow AAAS, N.Y. Acad. Medicine, Phila. Coll. Physicians; mem. NAS, Nat. Acad. Arts and Scis., Yugoslavian Acad. Scis., Polish Acad. Scis., Russian Acad. Med. Scis., Finnish Acad. Arts and Scis., N.Y. Acad. Scis. (pres. 1959, trustee 1960-72), Order of the Smile. Achievements include development of first oral polio vaccine which ultimately led to elimination, in 1992 of polio from the Americas; development of new rabies vaccine for humans, reducing the number of injections and of oral vaccine in bait for immunization of wildlife; research on mechanism of damage of cells in brain in neurotropic virus infection; development of first monoclonal antibody for treatment and cure of colorectal cancer. Office: Thomas Jefferson U Dept Microbiology and Immun JAH-M85 1020 Locust St Philadelphia PA 19107 Office Phone: 215-503-4761. Business E-Mail: hilary.koprowski@jefferson.edu.

KOPSKY, PATRICIA MILLS, art educator; b. Granite City, Ill., July 20, 1959; d. Henry Sam and Lorayne Gabriel Mills; m. Damon Wood Kopsky, June 27, 1981. BS, So. Ill. U., 1981. Cert. tchr. Ill., Mo. Instr. basic skills edn. program Temple U., Bamberg, Germany, 1982; art tchr. Big Bend C.C., Bamberg, 1983; instr. ESL Belleville (Ill.) Area Coll., 1985—86; art tchr. Granite City H.S., 1986—. Mem.: Am. Fedn. Tchrs. Avocations: drawing, painting, aerobics, gardening, travel. Home: 53 Janday Ln Granite City IL 62040 Office: Granite City HS 3101 Madison Ave Granite City IL 62040

KORAL, ALAN MAX, lawyer; b. N.Y.C., July 10, 1941; s. Max and Sylvia (Stoffman) K. AB with highest honors, U. Rochester, 1962; postgrad., Princeton U., 1962-65; JD, U. Chgo., 1975. Bar: Ill. 1975, N.Y. 1977, U.S. Dist. Ct. (no. dist.) Ill. 1975, U.S. Dist. Ct. (so. dist.) N.Y. 1978, U.S. Dist. Ct. (no. dist.) N.Y. 1981, U.S. Dist. Ct. (ea. dist.) N.Y. 1986, U.S. Ct. Appeals (11th cir.) 1987, U.S. Ct. Appeals (2nd cir.) 1990, U.S. Ct. Appeals (3d and 4th cirs.) 1995. Assoc. Vedder, Price, Kaufman & Kammholz, Chgo., 1975-76, Vedder, Price, Kaufman, Kammmholz & Day, N.Y.C., 1976-81, ptnr., 1982-2000, Vedder, Price, Kaufman & Kammholz, N.Y.C., 2000—03, voting shareholder, 2003—. Author: Conducting the Lawful Employment Interview, 1st edit., 1984, 4th edit., 1992, Employee Privacy Rights, 1988. Mem. N.Y. State Human Rights Adv. Coun., N.Y.C., 1985. Recipient Cmty. Svc. award Bar Assn. Human Rights Greater N.Y., 1988. Mem. ABA, N.Y. State Bar Assn. (chair CLE com., mem. exec. com. labor and employment sect.), Assn. Bar City N.Y. Office: Vedder Price Kaufman & Kammholz 805 3rd Ave New York NY 10022-7513 Office Phone: 212-407-7750. E-mail: akoral@vedderprice.com.

KORALL, ELIZABETH A., elementary school educator; b. Rochester, NY., Apr. 29, 1957; d. Donald Peter Reinhardt and Elizabeth Louise Landry; m. Richard D. Kovall, Dec. 30, 1978; children: Nicholas, Jessica, Stephen. BS in Spl. Edn., Buffalo State Coll., 1981; M in Reading, Elmira Coll., 1985. Tchr. elem. edn. Tioga Ctr. Sch. Dist., NY, 1983—2005. Roman Catholic. Home: 1759 W River Rd Nichols NY 13812

KORANYI, ADAM, mathematics professor; b. Szeged, Hungary, July 13, 1932; came to U.S., 1957, naturalized, 1963; s. Jeno and Vilma (Szigethy) K.; m. Anna Eiben, Mar. 16, 1968; children— Peter, Daniel. Diploma, U. Szeged, 1954; PhD, U. Chgo., 1959. Instr. Harvard, 1959-60; asst. prof. U. Calif. at Berkeley, 1960-64; vis. asst. prof. Princeton, 1964-65; faculty Belfer Grad. Sch. Sci., Yeshiva U., N.Y.C., 1965-79, prof. math., 1968-79, Washington U., St. Louis, 1979-85; Disting. prof. Lehman Coll. CUNY, 1985—. Contbr. articles to profl. jours. Mem. Am. Math. Soc., Acad. Scis. Hungary. Home: 26 Royden Rd Tenafly NJ 07670-1010 Office: CUNY Lehman Coll Bronx NY 10468

KORB, DONALD L., federal agency administrator, lawyer; b. Cleve., Apr. 29, 1948; s. Max E. and Frances A. (Wright) K.; m. Patricia A. Krawulski, June 24, 1972; children: Patrick, Laurel. BA, John Carroll U., 1970; JD, Case Western Res. U., 1973; LLM in Taxation, Georgetown U., 1977. Bar: Ohio 1973, DC 1978. Atty.-advisor Office Chief Counsel, IRS, Washington, 1974-77, asst. to IRS commr., 1984-86; assoc. Thompson, Hine and Flory, Cleve., 1978-81, ptnr., 1981—84, Thompson, Hine and Flory LLP, Cleve., 1986—97, Thompson Hine LLP, 1998—2004; tax ptnr. Cooper & Lybrand, Cleve., 1997—98; chief counsel, IRS, asst. gen. counsel US Dept. Treasury, Washington, 2004—. Spkr. in field. Contbr. articles to profl. jours. Mem. exec. com. Cuyahoga County Republican Orgn., 1998—2004, mem. fin. com., 1994, 2003—04; chair, Long-Range Strategic Planning Com. of the Bd. Trustee Cleve. Opera, 2001, trustee, 1999—2004. 1st lt. U.S. Army, 1973. Fellow Am. Coll. Tax Counsel (regent 2001-04); mem. ABA (mem. 1978-, tax sect., chmn. adminstrv. practice com. 1992-94, vice chair com. ops. 2000-02, coun. dir. 1996-99, LMSB Divsn. Coord. 2003-04), Cleve. Bar Assn., Cleve. Tax Club, Union Club Cleve., Soc. for Am. Baseball Rsch. Republican. Roman Catholic. Avocations: collecting recordings and librettos of Broadway musicals; US Commemorative and airmail postage stamps and US postal stationary; lionel trains; books about subjects such as baseball, presdl. elections, Cleve. history, H.L. Mencken, passenger trains and 20th century US History; political board/computer games. Office: IRS Rm 3026 1111 Constitution Ave NW Rm 3026 Washington DC 20224-0002 Office Phone: 202-622-3300. Office Fax: 202-622-4277. Business E-Mail: donald.l.korb@irscounsel.texas.gov.

KORB, HAROLD, physicist, consultant; b. Cando, N.D., Oct. 1, 1942; s. Leo and Eleanor Korb; m. Anne Douglas, Sept. 7, 1968; children: Laura Ferris, Kathleen Sullivan, Jennifer McPheeters. BS, N.D. State U., 1964; MA, Dartmouth Coll., 1966; PhD, U. Ill., 1971. Mem. tech. staff Bell Tel. Labs., Allentown, Pa., 1966-74; rsch. specialist, rsch. mgr. Monsanto Co., St. Louis, 1974-89; rsch. dir. MEMC Electronic Materials, Inc., St. Peters, Mo., 1989-98; owner Korb Consulting, LLC, Town and Country, Mo., 1998—. Mem. IEEE, Electrochem. Soc. Achievements include patents for integrated circuits and silicon materials. Office: Korb Consulting LLC 13717 Benwirth Ct Chesterfield MO 63017-8434 Fax: 314-469-3104. E-mail: Harold.Korb@usa.net.

KORB, WILLIAM BROWN, JR., retired manufacturing executive; b. Warren, Pa., Apr. 27, 1940; s. William Brown and Helen (Haslett) K.; m. Dorothy Wendell Trout, June 11, 1962; children: Karen Michel, David Wendell, Christine Leigh. BS in Indsl. Engring, Pa. State U., 1962; grad., Advanced Mgmt. Program, Harvard U., 1979. With Reliance Electric Co. div. Exxon, 1962-86, gen. mgr. mech. group, Mishawaka, Ind., 1977-79, operating v.p., Cleve. Cleve., 1979-86; pres., CEO, bd. dirs. Gilbarco, Inc., Greensboro, N.C., 1987-99, Marconi Commerce Systems, Inc., 1999—2001; ret., 2001. Bd. dirs. Cambrex Corp., Premier Farnell plc. Bd. visitors Greensboro Coll. Mem.: Greensboro Country Club. Home: 2704 Lake Forest Dr Greensboro NC 27408-3805

KORBER, BETTE TINA MARIE, chemist; b. Long Beach, Calif., 1958; d. George Korber. BS in chemistry, Calif. State U., 1981; PhD in chemistry in the field of immunology, Calif. Inst. Tech., 1988. Postdoctoral fellow Los Alamos Nat. Lab., 1990, tech. staff scientist theoretical biology and biophysics (T10) group, 1993—. Elizabeth Glaser scientist Pediatric AIDS Found., 1997—2003; external faculty Santa Fe Inst., N.Mex. Nominee Rave award in Medicine, WIRED, 2005; recipient Los Alamos Nat. Achievement award, 1996, 2002, Elizabeth Glaser Scientist for the Pediatric AIDS Found., 1997—2003, Outstanding Alumnus award for Sch. Natural Scis., Calif. State U., Long Beach, 2001, Ernest Orlando Lawrence award, US Dept. Energy, 2004; fellow, Leukemia Soc., Harvard U., 1988—90, Dir. Funded Postdoctoral Fellow, Los Alamos Nat. Lab, 1990—92; grantee Los Alamos Nat. Lab. Fellow, 2002. Achievements include publishing over 100 sci. papers that have been cited over 3,700 times; conducting pioneering studies delineating the genetic characteristics of the virus population; developing the Los Alamos HIV database, a foundation for HIV research for scientific community; internationally recognized AIDS researcher. Office: Los Alamos Nat Lab MS K710 T 10 Theoretical Divsn Los Alamos NM 87545 Office Phone: 505-665-4453. Office Fax: 505-665-3493. Business E-Mail: btk@lanl.gov.*

KORBER, LOUISE ANN, artist; b. Wilmington, Del., Oct. 23, 1934; d. Stanley Kasmir and Margaret Helen (Kelly) Czajkowski; m. Ernest Andrew Korber, Oct. 28, 1961; children: Edward Andrew, Jonathan Paul, Ann Louise. BA, U. Del., 1956, MA, 1962; postgrad., U. Pa., 1959, 60, Pa. Acad. Fine Arts, 1960-61, 62-63. Elem. art instr. Oak Grove Sch., Elsmere, Del., 1956-57; elem. and middle sch. art instr. Wilmington Friends Sch., 1957-60. Recipient Winsor Newton '89 Award. Exhibited in juried shows Pa. Watercolor Soc., Harrisburg, 1982, Galerie Triangle, 1982, 96, and Martin Luther-King Meml. Libr., Washington, 1983, Ctr. for the Creative Arts, Hockessin, Del., 1985, Sketch Club, Phila., 1993, 95, Chester County Art Assn., West Chester, Pa., 1987, 88, 89, 90, 91, 94, 95, 96, 97, 98, West Chester U., 1987, Balt. Watercolor Soc., 1987, 88, 89, 96, Mayflower Hotel, Washington, 1988, J. Low Art Gallery, 1989; represented in permanent collections Univ. Del., Del. Trust Co., Prudential Savs. Bank, Hotel duPont, Wilmington Trust Co., Hempt Bros., Inc., Chem. Bank, Skadden, Arps, Slate, Meagher & Flom, Texaco, AmeriHealth Inc., others. Mem. Studio Group (pres. 1996-98), Balt. Watercolor Soc., Phila. Watercolor Club, Pa. Watercolor Soc. (signature). Roman Catholic. Home: 212 Unami Trl Newark DE 19711-7509

KORBITZ, BERNARD CARL, retired oncologist, hematologist, educator, consultant; b. Lewistown, Mont., Feb. 18, 1935; s. Fredrick William and Rose Eleanore (Ackmann) K.; m. Constance Kay Bolz, June 22, 1957; children: Paul Bernard, Guy Karl. B.S. in Med. Sci., U. Wis.-Madison, 1957, M.D., 1960, M.S. in Oncology, 1962; LL.B., LaSalle U., 1972. Asst. prof. medicine and clin. oncology, U. Wis. Med. Sch., Madison, 1967-71; dir. medicine Presbyn. Med. Ctr., Denver, 1971-73; practice medicine specializing in oncology, hematology, Madison, 1973-76; med. oncologist, hematologist Radiologic Ctr. Meth. Hosp., Omaha, 1976-82; practice medicine specializing in oncology, hematology, Omaha, 1982-95, ret., 1995; sci. advisor Citizen's Environ. Com., Denver, 1972-73; mem. Meth. Hosp., Omaha, 1977—; dir. Bernard C. Korbitz, P.C., Omaha, 1983-96; bd. dirs., pres. B.C. Korbitz P.C., ret., 1996. Contbr. articles to profl. jours. Webelos leader Denver area Council, Mid. Am. Council of Nebr. Boy Scouts Am.; bd. elders King of Kings Luth. Ch., Omaha, 1979-80; bd. elders St. Mark Luth. Ch., Omaha, 1993-98; mem. People to People Del. Cancer Update to People's Republic China, 1986, Eastern Europe and USSR, 1987; mem. U.S. Senatorial Club, 1984, Republican Presdl. Task Force, 1984. Served to capt. USAF, 1962-64. Named Medford (Wis.) H.S. Athletic Hall of Fame, 1997. Fellow ACP, Royal Soc. Health; mem. Am. Soc. Clin. Oncology, Am. Soc. Internal Medicine, AMA, Nebr. Med. Assn., Omaha Med. Society, Omaha Clin. Soc., Phi Eta Sigma, Phi Beta Kappa, Phi Kappa Phi, Alpha Omega Alpha. Avocations: photography, fishing, travel. Home: 9024 Leavenworth St Omaha NE 68114-5150

KORC, MURRAY, endocrinologist; b. Gunsburg, Fed. Republic of Germany, Apr. 3, 1947; came to U.S., 1960; m. Antoinette Korc. BA, Bklyn. Coll., 1968; MD, Albany (N.Y.) Med. Coll., 1974. Intern, then resident Albany Med. Ctr. Hosp., 1974-77; endocrinology fellow U. Calif., San Francisco, 1977-79, from prof. to chief divsn. endocrinology, diabetes and metab Irvine, 1989—.

KORCHIN, JUDITH MIRIAM, lawyer; b. Kew Gardens, N.Y., Apr. 28, 1949; d. Arthur Walter and Mena (Levisohn) Goldstein; m. Paul Maury Korchin, June 10, 1972; 1 son, Brian Edward. BA with high honors, U. Fla., 1971, JD with honors, 1974. Bar: Fla. 1974, U.S. Ct. Appeal (2d, 5th and 11th cirs.), U.S. Dist. Ct. (so., mid. and no. dists) Fla. Law clk. to judge U.S. Dist. Ct., 1974-76; assoc. Steel, Hector & Davis, Miami, Fla., 1976-81, ptnr., 1981-87, Holland and Knight, Miami, 1987—. Author, exec. editor U. Fla. Law Rev., 1973—74; contbr. chapters to books, articles to profl. jours. Mem. U. Fla. Law Ctr. Coun., 1980-83; pres. alumni bd. U. Fla. Law Rev., 1983; bd. dirs. Fla. Film & Rec. Inst., 1982-84. Named Best of the Bar, So. Fla. Bus. Jour., 2004; named one of Fla. Trend's Legal Elite, 2004; recipient Trail Blazer Award, The Women's Com. of 100, 1988. Fellow: Fla. Bar Found. (subcom. legal assistance for poor 1988—90), Am. Bar Found.; mem.: ABA (sect. alternative dispute resolution, vice chmn. 1994—95, co-chmn. fed. ct. mediation com. 1995, sect. labor and employment law, sect. litig.), Fla. Bar Assn. (vice chmn. jud. nominating procedures com. 1982, civil procedure rules com. 1984—89, 1993—95), Nat. Assn. Bank Women (TV panelist greater Miami chpt. 1987), Nat. Assn. Women Bus. Owners (adv. coun. 1987—88), Dade County Bar Assn. (bd. dirs. 1981—82, treas. 1982, sec. 1983, 3d v.p. 1984, 2d v.p. 1985, 1st v.p. 1986, pres. 1987), CPR Inst. for Dispute Resolution (nat. panelist 1994—, exec. com. 2003—), Am. Arbitration Assn. (employment law panel, s.e. 1993—, comml. law panel 1993—), Greater Miami C. of C. (com. profl. devel. 1988—90), Rabbinical Assn. Greater Miami (TV panelist Still Small Voice 1987), City Club (bd. dirs. 1988—93), Phi Kappa Phi, Phi Beta Kappa, Order of Coif. Office: Holland & Knight PO Box 015441 701 Brickell Ave Ste 3000 Miami FL 33131-2898 Office Phone: 305-789-7764. Business E-Mail: judith.korchin@hklaw.com.

KORCHYNSKY, MICHAEL, metallurgical engineer; b. Kiev, Ukraine, Apr. 11, 1918; arrived in U.S., 1950, naturalized, 1956; s. Michael and Jadwiga (Zdanowicz) K.; m. Taisija Lapin, Nov. 22, 1951; children: Michael, Marina, Roksana Dipl. Ing. in Metals Tech., Tech. U. Lviv, 1942. Lectr. Tech. U. Lviv, 1942-44; chief engr. C.E., U.S. Army, Fed. Republic Germany, 1945-50; rsch. metallurgist Union Carbide Co., Niagara Falls, NY, 1951-61; rsch. supr. Jones & Laughlin Steel Corp., Pitts., 1962-68, dir. product rsch., 1969-72; dir. alloy devel. metals divsn. Union Carbide Co., N.Y.C., 1973-77, Pitts., 1978-86; cons., prin. Korchynsky and Assocs., Pitts., 1986—. Metall. cons. Strategic Minerals Corp.-STRATCOR, 1986—; lectr. Niagara U., 1957—58. Recipient Achievement award, Vamidinm Internat. Tech. Com., 2003, China Fgn. Specialist award, 2004; Sr. fellow, Union Carbide, 1979. Fellow Am. Soc. Metals Internat. (Andrew Carnegie lectr. 1973, W.H.

Eisenman medal 1984, F.C. Bain award 1986); mem. AIME (Howe meml. lectr. 1983, Robert Earll McConnell engring. achievement award 1991) Iron and Steel Soc., SAE Internat., Am. Iron and Steel Inst. (medalist), Acad. Engring. Scis. of Ukraine, Ukrainian Technol. Soc., Polish Soc. Metallurgical Assn. (hon.). Achievements include patents for alloy design and processing tech. of a family of micro-alloyed high-strength low alloy steel. Home: 2770 Milford Dr Bethel Park PA 15102-1763 Business E-Mail: michael.korchynsky@stratcor.com.

KORDANA, KEVIN A., law educator; b. 1969; BA, Yale U., 1991, JD, 1995. Law clk. to Hon. Richard A. Posner US Ct. Appeals 7th Cir., Chgo., 1995—96; asst. prof. U. Va. Sch. Law, 1996—97, assoc. prof., 1997—2001, prof., 2001—. Vis. prof. U. So. Calif. Law Sch., George Wash. U., 2003—04. Mem.: Am. Econ. Assn., Am. Law & Econ. Assn., Phi Beta Kappa. Office: U Va Sch Law 580 Massie Rd Charlottesville VA 22903 Office Phone: 434-924-3680. E-mail: kk3t@virginia.edu.

KORDASH, DOROTHY MAE, artist; b. St. Joseph, Mo., Sept. 7, 1927; d. Perle Elisha and Carrie Allene (Womach) Reece; m. James A. Kordash, Apr. 20, 1956. Art studies, various workshops, U.S., Can., Eng. Acctg. clk. Interstate Bakeries, Kansas City, Mo., 1946-50; adminstrv. clk. Ford Motor Co., Lenexa, Kans., 1951-82; freelance artist Leawood, Kans., 1972—. Treas. Art Images Gallery, Kansas City, 1982-86. One-woman shows include Grand Opening Macy's Dept. Store, Overland Park, Kans., 1975, Arte Ctr., Plano, Tex., 1997, exhibited in group shows at Knickerbocker Artists, Salmagundi Club, N.Y.C., 1983, Art-A-Fair, Laguna Beach (Best Abstract award, 1997, 1998, 1999, Best Mixed Media award, 1999, 2000, 2001, 2003, 2004), Town Art Show, Leawood, Kans., 2002 (Best of Show in Two-Dimensional Art award, 2002), Ariz. Fine Art Expo, Scottsdale, 2005; contbr. paintings to Pub. TV Art Auction, Kansas City, 1985—90; artist commemorative bicentennial book, Johnson County, Kans., 1975, invitation cover Truman Med. Ctr., Kansas City, 1988, Celebration of Fine Art, Scottsdale, Ariz., 1991—2002; Represented in permanent collections Ford Motor Co., Claycomo, Mo., Volume Shoe Co., Topeka. Mem. Internat. Soc. Exptl. Artists, Ariz. Art Guild, Kans. Watercolor Soc. (signature, Purchase awards 1973, 75, 77, 83), Greater Kansas City Art Assn. (Best of Show award 1983), Sonoran Arts Guild Avocation: photography. Home: 8624 Reinhardt Ln Leawood KS 66206-1455

KORDESTANI, OMID, information technology executive; BSEE, San Jose (Calif.) State U.; MBA, Stanford U. Former positions in mktg., product mgmt., and bus. devel. 3DO Co., Go Corp., and Hewlett-Packard; dir. OEM sales Netscape, 1996—97, v.p. bus. devel. sales, 1998—99; sr. v.p. worldwide sales and field ops. Google Inc., Mountain View, Calif., 1999—. Office: Google Inc 1600 Amphitheatre Pky Mountain View CA 94043

KORDONS, ULDIS, lawyer; b. Riga, Latvia, July 9, 1941; arrived in U.S., 1949; s. Evalds and Zenta Alide (Apenits) Kordons; m. Virginia Lee Knowles, July 16, 1966. AB, Princeton U., 1963; JD, Georgetown U., 1970. Bar: N.Y. 1970, Ohio 1978, Ind. 1989. Assoc. Whitman, Breed, Abbott, N.Y.C., 1970-77, Anderson, Mori & Rabinowitz, Tokyo, 1973-75; counsel Armco Inc., Parsippany, NJ, 1977-84; v.p., gen. counsel, sec. Sybron Corp., Saddle Brook, NJ, 1984-88, Hillenbrand Industries Inc., Batesville, Ind., 1989-92; pres. Plover Enterprises, Cin., 1992—96, Kordons & Co., LPA, Cin., 1996—. Adj. prof. Xavier U., Cin., 2004—, Duke U. Law Sch., 2005—. Lt. USN, 1963—67. Mem.: ABA, Ind. Bar Assn., Ohio Bar Assn., N.Y. Bar Assn. Office: 8238 Wooster Pike Cincinnati OH 45227-4010 Office Phone: 513-272-1636. Business E-Mail: kordonslaw@cinci.rr.com. E-mail: ukordlaw@aol.com.

KOREMAN, DOROTHY GOLDSTEIN, physician, dermatologist; b. Bklyn., Nov. 1, 1940; d. Benjamin and Ida (Krenick) Goldstein; m. Neil M. Koreman, Aug. 16, 1964; children: Elizabeth Koreman Landau, Robert Stephen. BA, Bklyn. Coll., 1961; MD, SUNY, Bklyn., 1965. Diplomate Am. Bd. Dermatology. Intern pediatrics Kings County Hosp. Ctr., Bklyn., 1965-66; resident dept. dermatology Wayne State U. Sch. Medicine, Detroit, 1966-69; clin. instr. dermatology Sch. Medicine Wayne State U., Detroit, 1969-71; asst. clin. prof. dermatology U. Miami, 1971-75, assoc. clin. prof. dermatology, 1975-82, clin. prof. dermatology and cutaneous surgery, 1982—. Mem. Miami Dermatol. Soc. (pres. 1978-79). Avocations: travel, cooking, reading, skiing, needlepoint. E-mail: skinkor40@aol.com.

KOREN, EDWARD BENJAMIN, cartoonist, educator; b. NYC, Dec. 13, 1935; s. Harry L. and Elizabeth (Sorkin) K.; m. Catherine Curtis Ingham; children: Nathaniel, Alexandra, Benjamin. BA, Columbia U., 1957; student, Atelier 17, Paris, 1957-59; M.F.A., Pratt Inst., 1964; D.H.L. (hon.), Union Coll., 1984. Cartoonist, staff artist New Yorker mag., N.Y.C., 1962; mem. faculty Brown U., 1964—, asso. prof. art, 1969-77, adj. assoc. prof., 1977—. Disting. visitor Am. Acad. in Berlin, 2003. One-man travelling exhbn. Art Gallery, SUNY, Albany, 1982; exhibited in group shows including Expn. Dessins d'Humeur, Soc. Protectrice d'Humeur, Avignon, France, 1973, Biennale Illustration, Bratislav, Czechoslovakia, 1973, Art from the New York Times, Soc. Illustr., N.Y.C., 1973, Art from the New Yorker, Grolier Club, 1975, Terry Dintinfass Gallery, N.Y.C., 1975-77, 79, 91, Virginia Lynch Gallery, 1992, 94, 2000, 2002, Wash. Art Assn., Conn., 2004,; work appears in Fogg Mus., Princeton U. Mus., RISD Mus., Fitzwilliam Mus., Swann Collection Cartoon and Caricature, Libr. of Congress; contbr.: drawings to various publs. including The Nation, Time mag., Newsweek mag., Fortune mag., N.Y. Times, Sports Illustrated mag., Vogue mag., Vanity Fair mag.; illustrator: Don't Talk to Strange Bears, 1969, The People Maybe, 1974, Cooking for Crowds, 1975, Noodles Galore, 1977, How to Eat Like a Child, 1978, Dragons Hate to be Discrete, 1978, Teenage Romance, 1981, Do I Have to Say Hello?. 1989, A Dog's Life, 1995, Dear Bruno, 1996, Pet Peeves, 2000, The New Legal Seafoods Cookbook, 2003, Travelling While Married, 2003; author, illustrator: Behind The Wheel, 1972; author: Do You Want to Talk About It?, 1977, Are You Happy?, 1978, Well, There's Your Problem, 1980, Caution, Small Ensembles, 1983, What About Me?, 1989, Quality Time, 1995, The Hard Work of Simple Living, 1998, Very Hairy Harry, 2003. John Simon Guggenheim fellow, 1970-71 Mem. Author's League, Soc. Am. Graphic Artists. Personal E-mail: eddo@sover.net.

KOREN, EDWARD FRANZ, JR., lawyer; b. Eustis, Fla., Aug. 6, 1946; s. Edward Franz Sr. and Frances (Boyd) K.; m. Louise Poole, June 19, 1970; children: Daniel Edward, Susan Louise. BSBA in Acctg., U. Fla., 1971, JD with high honors, 1974. Bar: Fla. 1975, U.S. Dist. Ct. (Mid. Dist.) Fla. 1977, U.S. Supreme Ct. 1980, U.S. Ct. Appeals (11th cir.) 1981, U.S. Tax Ct. 1985, U.S. Ct. Claims 1986. Instr. tax U. Fla., Gainesville, 1974-75; assoc. Holland & Knight, Lakeland, Fla., 1975-79, ptnr., 1980—, chmn. trusts and estates dept., 1983—; chair, private wealth svcs. Adj. prof. graduate tax program U. Fla., Gainesville, 1996; adj. prof. grad. estate planning program U. Miami Law Sch., 2000-. Exec. editor U. Fla. Law Review, 1973—74, lead author, editor Estate and Personal Financial Planning (West), 1988—2003; author: 13th edit., 2001; contbr. articles to profl. jours. Capt. U.S. Army, 1971—72. Fellow: Am. Bar Found., Am. Coll. Tax Counsel (bd. cert. estate planning & probate lawyer, Fla. bar bd. legal specialization and edn.); mem.: ABA (chmn. marital deduction com. 1991—95, supervisory coun. 1995—2001, mem. exec. coun. 1995—, rep. to the Nat. Conf. of Attys. and Corp. Fidcuiaries 1998—, vice chmn. probate and trust divsn. 2001—03, real property, probate and trust law sect. 2001—, chair, real property, probate and trust law sect. 2004—), Am. Judicature Soc., Hillsborough County Bar Assn., Lakeland 10th Jud. Cir., Fla. Inst. CPAs, Am. Assn. Attys. and CPAs, Fla. Bar Assn. (chmn. 1982—84, vice-chmn., bd. certification, designation and advertising 1984—88, chmn. real property, probate and trust law sect. 1988—89, chmn. tax sect. 1990—91, active various sects. and coms., mem. continuing legal edn. com.), Am. Coll. Trust and Estates Counsel (mem. bus. planning com. 1994—, regent 1997—2003, immediate past chmn. estate and gift tax com. 2001—04), Fla. Blue Key, Centre Club, Tampa Club, Lakeland Yacht and Country Club, Phi Delta Phi, Phi Kappa Phi, Order of Coif. Republican. Presbyterian. Home: 114 Hickory Creek Dr Brandon FL 33511-8012 Office: Holland & Knight LLP 92 Lake Wire Dr PO Box 32092 Lakeland FL 33815 Address: Holland & Knight LLP 100 N Tampa St Ste 4100 Tampa FL 33602 Office Phone: 863-682-1161, 863-499-5314, 813-227-6655. E-mail: ekoren@hklaw.com.*

KOREN, YORAM, mechanical engineering educator; b. Tel Aviv, Aug. 1, 1938; came to U.S., 1985; s. Shlomo and Bathia (Rabinowitz) Shterwzis; m. Aliza Halina Palyard, Apr. 3, 1963; children: Shlomik, Esther. Prof. U. Mich., Ann Arbor. Cons. Ford, Coldy Internat., Cybernet System, Metcut, SKF, Frat, 1980—. Author: Computer Control of Manufacturing Systems, 1983, Robotics for Engineers, 1985, Numerical Control of Machine Tools, 1978; contbr. articles to profl. jours.; patentee in field. Sgt. maj. USAF, 1957-61. Fellow SME, ASME; mem. IEEE (sr.), CIRP. Home: 4101 Thornoaks Dr Ann Arbor MI 48104-4255 Office: U Mich 2250 GG Brown Bldg Ann Arbor MI 48109-2125

KORENEV, SERGEY ALEXANDROVICH, physicist; b. Sretensk, Russia, May 27, 1951; s. Anna K.; m. Valentina Perelevskay, Apr. 24, 1951; children: Anton, Ivan. MS, Tech. U. Moscow, 1976; PhD, Joint Inst. Nuclear Rsch., Dubna, Russia, 1987, DSc, 1995. From scientist to prin. scientist Joint Inst. Nuclear Rsch., 1976-98; prof. physics N.J. Inst. Technology, Newark, 1996-98; mgr. radiation physics STERIS Corp., Libertyville, Ill., 1998-2000, dir. R&D Ctr. for Radiation Physics, 2000—03, dir. rsch. ctr., 2003—04, dir. rsch. & devel., 2004—. Author: Discovery of New Physical Phenomena: Explosive Ion Emission, 1985, Discovery of New Physical Phenomena: Vacuum Condensation in the Ion Diode with Explosive Pulsed Emission, 1988, Creation of Physical Principles of Forming High Current Pulsed Ion Beams, 1995, Creation of Physical Principles of Surface Modification of Materials by Pulsed Electron/Ion/Cluster Beams in Adiabatic Conditions, 1998; contbr. articles to profl. jours. Recipient Silver medal USSR Ctrl. Exhbn., 1985. Mem. IEEE (sr.), Nuc. and Plasma Soc., Am. Phys. Soc., Am. Vacuum Soc, Materials Rsch. Soc. Achievements include patentee in field (45). Office: 2500 Commerce Dr Libertyville IL 60048-2494 Office Phone: 847-573-3223. E-mail: sergey@korenev.com.

KORENGOLD, GEORGE MATTHEW, physician; b. N.Y.C., Dec. 16, 1946; s. Marvin Curtis and Edna (Gerler) K.; m. Barbara Lynn Korengold, Aug. 23, 1970; children: Adam Stuart, Erin Carol. BA, U. Pa., Phila., 1968; MD, George Washington U., 1992. Diplomate Am. Acad. Pediatrics. Pediatric resident Children's Nat. Med. Ctr., Washington, 1972-75; pediatrician Korengold, Mayol, Deutsh, Walters & Gatto, MDs, Bethesda, Md., 1975—. Mem. Montgomery County Med. Soc., Montgomery-Prince George's Pediatric Soc. (pres. 1990). Office: Ste 238 11325 Seven Locks Rd Potomac MD 20854-3205 Office Phone: 301-299-8930. E-mail: gmbpk@aol.com.

KORENIC, LYNETTE MARIE, librarian; b. Berwyn, Ill., Mar. 29, 1950; d. Emil Walter and Donna Marie (Harbutt) K. m. Jerome Dennis Reif, Dec. 31, 1988. BS in Art, U. Wis., 1977, MFA, 1979, MA in LS, 1981, MA in Art History, 1984. Asst. art libr. Ind. U., Bloomington, 1982-84; art libr. U. Calif., Santa Barbara, 1984-88, head Arts Libr., 1988-99; art libr. U. Wis., Madison, 1999—. Author articles. Mem. Art Librs. Soc. N.Am. (sec. 1983-84, v.p. 1989, pres. 1990), Beta Phi Mu. Office Phone: 608-263-2256. E-mail: lkorenic@library.wisc.edu.

KORETSKY, SIDNEY, internist, educator, paper historian; b. Chelsea, Mass., Dec. 30, 1921; s. Harry and Rachel (Greenfield) K.; m. Elaine Ruth Stern, Feb. 22, 1953; children: Peter Austin, David Stuart, Donna Monel. AB, Harvard U., 1943; MD, Jefferson Med. Coll., 1946. Intern Springfield (Mass.) Hosp., 1946-47; resident Boston City Hosp., 1949-52, New England Med. Ctr., Boston, 1952-53; clin. instr. in medicine Tufts U. Sch. Medicine, Boston, 1953—; pvt. practice internist Boston, 1953—; sr. physician Beth Israel Deaconess Med. Ctr., Boston, 1992—. Rschr. in heart disease, Beth Israel Deaconess Med. Ctr., 1953-68. Contbr. numerous articles to profl. med. jours.; editor, graphic designer, photographer: The Goldbeater of Mandalay, 1991, and other books dealing with the history of hand papermaking. Former pres. Greater Boston Med. Soc. Capt., U.S. Army Med. Corps, 1947-49, Korea, Japan. Mem. AMA, Internat. Assn. Paper Historians, Dard Hunter Paper History Soc., Mass. Med. Soc., Mass. Horticultural Soc., Harvard Club of Boston. Avocations: horticulture, high adventure travel, photography. Home and Office: 756 Washington St Brookline MA 02446-2109

KORF, CLIFFORD DEAN, physician assistant; b. Garden City, Kans., Jan. 10, 1951; s. Lloyd James and Virginia Lee (Thomas) K.; m. Lavetta Mae Ruth Whitesell, Mar. 19, 1977; children: Jonathan David, Benjamin Joseph, Rachel Elizabeth. A in nursing, Garden City Cmty. Jr. Coll., 1975; B in health sci., Wichita State U., 1980. Reg. nurse St. Catherine Hosp., Garden City, 1975-77; RN Wesley Med. Ctr., Wichita, 1977-80; physician asst., dir. Wichita County Med. Ctr., Leoti, Kans., 1980-81; physician asst., supr. Cardiovascular Med. Group, Wichita, Kans., 1981-93; physician asst. Cardiovascular Cons. of Kans., Wichita, 1993—. Clin. instr. Wichita State U., 1985-95; affiliate to med. staff St. Francis Reg. Med. Ctr., 1981—; instr. Adv. Cardiac Life Support, Wichita, 1983—; allied health profl. rev. com. Via Christi Reg. Med. Ctr. St. Francis campus, Wichita, 1986—. Den leader Boy Scouts Am., Wichita, 1994-97, adult scouter-leader, 1995-97, asst. leader Pathfinders, 1997—. Fellow Am. Acad. Physician Assistants; mem. Kansas Acad. Physician Assistants. Republican. Seventh-Day Adventist. Avocations: scouting, gardening, camping, family activities, flowers. Office: Cardiovascular Cons Kans 1035 N Emporia St Ste 210 Wichita KS 67214-2992

KORF, GENE ROBERT, lawyer; b. Greenville, S.C., June 2, 1952; s. Norman and Paula (Heller) K.; m. Madeline Jane Hammer, June 20, 1976; children: Scott, Neil. BA summa cum laude, Hunter Coll., 1974; JD, Bklyn. Law Sch., 1977; LLM in Taxation, NYU, 1983. Dir. Korf & Rosenblatt, Morristown, N.J. Prodr. (mus. rev.) And the World Goes Round (Drama Desk award 1990, 91, Outer Critics Cir. award 1990, 91), The Kentucky Cycle, 1993 (Tony award nominee 1994), The Crucible, 2002 (Tony award nominee 2002). Long Day's Journey Into Night, revival, 2003 (Tony award 2003). Trustee Roundabout Theatre Co., 1993—, Harold Wetterberg Found., 1991—, Blanche and Irving Laurie Found., 1991—, Schulman Family Found., 1993. Recipient City Ctr./Leonard Harris award 2001. Jewish. Office: Korf & Rosenblatt 89 Hdqrs Plz North Tower 14th Fl Morristown NJ 07960-1734 Office Phone: 973-993-1743.

KORF, JEAN PRINZ, retired theater educator; b. New Albany, Ind., Oct. 28, 1925; d. Winfield Henry and Waneta Sadler Prinz; m. Leonard Lee Korf, Aug. 15, 1949; children: Kerry Lee, William Milton, Geoffrey Leonard. BA, UCLA, 1947, MA, 1953; MS in Edn., U. So. Calif., 1963. Theater prodn. mgr. Whittier (Calif.) H.S., 1949-52; drama tchr. Calif. H.S., Whittier, 1953-66; theater arts prof. Rio Hondo Coll., Whittier, 1966-90. Founder TheaterCreations Unltd., 1990—; guest dir. La. State U., Baton Rouge, 1990, 91, St. Barts Playhouse, N.Y.C., 1992, U.S. State Dept. Arts Am., Bialystok, Poland, 1993. Commr. Whittier Cultural Arts Commn., 1993-2005; bd. dirs. Whittier Cultural Arts Found., 1990—. Fellow Coll. Fellows Am. Theater (dean 1994-96), Rio Hondo Coll.; mem. Los Angeles County Mus. Art, Nat. Mus. Women in the Arts, UCLA Theater Film & TV Alumni Assn. (bd. dirs. 1991-2000), Nat. Theatre Conf., Nature Conservancy, World Wildlife Fund, Save the Children. Democrat. Unitarian Universalist. Avocations: theatre going, attending cultural events, conservation, travel, genealogy. Home: 9811 Pounds Ave Whittier CA 90603-1616 Personal E-mail: jeankorf@aol.com.

KORF, RICHARD PAUL, mycology educator; b. Bronxville, N.Y., May 28, 1925; s. Frederick and Evelyn F. (Krug) K.; m. Kumiko Tachibana, June 27, 1959; children: Noni, Mia, Ian, Mario. BSc, Cornell U., 1946, PhD, 1950. Lectr. botany U. Glasgow, Scotland, 1950-51; asst. prof. Cornell U., Ithaca, N.Y., 1951-55, assoc. prof., 1955-61, prof. mycology, 1961-92, chmn. theatre arts, 1985-86, prof. emeritus, 1992—. Fulbright rsch. prof. Yokohama (Japan) Nat. U., 1957-58; cons. prof. U. Ryukyus, Ryukyu Islands, 1969; adjunktvikar U. Copenhagen, 1973; Fulbright rsch. scholar U. Louvain, Belgium, 1972-73; dir. Exe Island Biol. Sta., Portland, Ont., 1973—; mem. sci. coun. Academia Sinica, Beijing, China, 1985-90. Editor Mycotaxon, 1974-91; book rev. editor Mycologia, 1972-80; corr. editor Mycological Rsch., 1996-98; mem. editl. bd. Persoonia, 1987—, Mycosystema, 1988-94. State vice chair Liberal party, NY, 1968. Sr. postdoctoral fellow NSF, Yokohama, 1957; recipient SUNY Chancellor's award for excellence in teaching, 1992. Fellow Br. Mycol. Soc. (Centennial); mem. Internat. Mycol. Assn. (nomenclature chmn. 1971-84), Internat. Assn. Plant Taxonomy (mem. gen. com. 1975-91); Mycol. Soc. Am. (pres. 1971, Disting. Mycologist Award 1991). Avocations: acting, contract bridge, naturism. Home: 316 Richard Pl Ithaca NY 14850-3129 Office: Cornell U Plant Pathology Plant Sci Bldg Ithaca NY 14853 Business E-Mail: rpk1@cornell.edu.

KORFMACHER, WALTER AVERILL, chemist, researcher; b. St. Louis, Nov. 6, 1951; s. William Charles and Louise Trowbridge (Averill) K.; m. Madeleine Marie Deutsch, June 1, 1974; children: Mary Averill, Joseph Deutsch. BS in Chemistry, St. Louis U., 1973; MS in Chemistry, U. Ill., 1975, PhD in Chemistry, 1978. Lab. instr. St. Louis U., 1970—72; tchg. asst. U. Ill., Urbana, 1973—75; grad. rsch. asst. Colo. State U., Ft. Collins, 1976—78; rsch. chemist Nat. Ctr. for Toxicol. Rsch., Jefferson, Ark., 1976—91; dir. Dept. Drug Metabolism Schering-Plough Rsch. Inst., Kenilworth, NJ, 1991—. Adj. assoc. prof. U. Tenn. Coll. Pharmacy, Memphis, 1988-91; adj. asst. prof. dept. chemistry U. Ark., Little Rock, 1983-91; adj. assoc. prof. dept. toxicology U. Ark. Med. Scis., Little Rock, 1991. Contbr. more than 100 articles to profl. jours. Recipient Plaque award USPHS, 1989, Commendable Svc. award FDA, 1990, Regional Achievement award N.J., 2002. Mem. AAAS, Am. Chem. Soc., Am. Soc. Mass Spectrometry, Assn. Ofcl. Analytical Chemists, N.Y. Acad. Scis., Phi Beta Kappa, Sigma Xi. Roman Catholic. Achievements include research in area of analytical methods development, particularly trace organic analysis, utility of GC-MS and LC-MS as well as tandem mass spectrometry. Office: Schering Plough Rsch Inst Dept Drug Metabolism 2015 Galloping Hill Rd Dept Drug Kenilworth NJ 07033-1300 Business E-Mail: walter.korfmacher@spcorp.com.

KORG, JACOB, English literature educator; b. N.Y.C., Nov. 21, 1922; s. Reuben and Mary (Lehrman) K.; m. Cynthia Stewart, Jan. 21, 1952; 1 dau., Nora Francis. BA, CCNY, 1943; MA, Columbia U., 1947, PhD, 1952. Instr. English Bard Coll., 1947-49, CCNY, 1950-55; from asst. prof. to prof. U. Wash., Seattle, 1955-68, prof. English, 1970-91, prof. emeritus, 1991—; prof. English U. Md., 1968-70. Vis. prof. Nat. Taiwan U., 1960. Author: George Gissing, A Critical Biography, 1963, Dylan Thomas, 1965, Language in Modern Literature, 1979, rev. edit., 1992, Browning and Italy, 1983, Ritual and Experiment in Modern Poetry, 1995, Winter Love: Ezra Pound and H.D., 2003, also articles, revs.; editor: London in Dickens' Day, 1960, George Gissing's Commonplace Book, 1962, The Force of Few Words, 1966, Twentieth Century Views of Bleak House, 1968, Poetry of Robert Browning, 1971; co-editor: George Gissing on Fiction, 1978; mem. editl. bd. Victorian Poetry, 1979-2002, Nineteenth-Century Lit., 1983-95, Rivista di Studi Vittoriani. Served with AUS, 1943-46. Mem.: MLA, Assn. Literary Scholars and Critics. Office: Univ Wash Dept English Seattle WA 98195-0001 Home: 900 University St Apt 14-0 Seattle WA 98101 E-mail: korg@u.washington.edu.

KORIA, PATRICIA MARIA, librarian; b. Lebanon, Pa., May 21, 1947; d. Wilmer Edwin and Cecilia (Shanahan) Kohl. BS, Shippensburg State U., 1969; MA in Edn., Del. State Coll. Libr. Christina Sch. Dist., Newark, Del. Mem. NEA, ASCD, ALA, Am. Assn. Sch. Librs., Children's Lit. Assn., Del. State Edn. Assn., Christina Edn. Assn., Internat. Reading Assn. Home: 55 South Dr Earleville MD 21919-2242

KORJUS, CHRISTOPHER NELSON, lawyer; b. Atlanta, Dec. 21, 1958; s. James H. and Margaret (Marr) K. BA in Polit. Sci., Old Dominion U., 1983; JD, Coll. William and Mary, 1986. Bar: D.C. 1987, Va. 1986, Md. 1994, U.S. Supreme Ct. 1996; CFP. Law clk. Dept. Justice, Washington, 1986; assoc. Ernst & Whinney, Washington, 1986-88; ptnr. Cowles, Rinaldi, Judkins & Korjus, Ltd., Fairfax, Va., 1988—, lectr. constrn. law, 1991—. Adj. prof. No. Va. C.C., Alexandria, 1997—; arbitrator Am. Arbitration Assn., 1997—; lectr. SBA, Arlington, Va., 1995; mem. membership com. Met. Sub-Contractors Assn., Annandale, Va., 1996—. Author: Virginia Mechanics Lien Can Trap the Unwary, 1992, 150 Day Rule - Virginia Mechanics Liens, 1993, others; co-author: Construction Law in Virginia, Maryland and District of Columbia, 1992-97. With USN, 1977-80. Mem. ABA, Va. Bar Assn., Md. Bar Assn., D.C. Bar. Office: Cowles Rinaldi Judkins & Korjus Ltd 10521 Judicial Dr Ste 204 Fairfax VA 22030-5160

KORKMAZ, TURGAY, education educator; s. Ziyaettin and Guner Korkmaz; m. Fatma Turkay Arslan; 1 child, Zeynep. PhD, U. Of Ariz., 1998—2002. Rsch. asst. U. Of Ariz., 1998—2002; asst. prof U. Of Tex., San Antonio, 2002—. Contbr. scientific papers. Achievements include research in QoS routing algorithms. Office: Univ of Tex at San Antonio 6900 North Loop 1604 West San Antonio TX 78249 Office Phone: 210-458-7346. Office Fax: 210-458-4437. Personal E-mail: korkmaz@cs.utsa.edu.

KORKMAZIAN, GAYANE K., music educator; b. Fresno, Calif., Sept. 3, 1947; d. Michael and Florence Artenian; m. Frank A. Korkmazian, Jr., May 19, 1984. BA in music, Calif. State U., 1969, life credential in elem. edn., 1970. Music tchr. Fresno Unified Sch. Dist., 1971—82; cultural arts coord. City of Fresno, 1986—94; pvt. music tchr. Self-Employed, 1970—. Exec. officer Calif. Orch. Dir., 1975—2000; festival coord. Calif. Music Educators Assn., 1986—; Sunday sch. music tchr. St. Gregory Armenian Ch., Fowler, Calif., 1988—. Mem. Sunnyside Citizens Patrol, Fresno, Calif., 1997—; vol. PBS TV Sta., Fresno; treas. St. Gregory Ch. Ladies Soc., Fowler, Calif., 2000—04; bd. mem. Calif. Armenian Home for the Aged Home Guild, Fresno, 2000—05, treas., 2002—03, pres., 2004—05; Armenian Ch. N. Am. Western Diocese Ladies Soc. Ctrl. Coun., 2004—. Recipient Vol. of the Yr., PBS TV Sta., 1998, Pres. award, Calif. Assn. Music Educators, 2005. Mem.: Fresno-Madera Counties Music Educators Assn. (sec. 2004—), Am. String Tchrs. Assn., Music Edn. Nat. Conf., Mu Phi Epsilon Internat. Profl. Music Fraternity. Democrat. Orthodox Armenian. Avocations: reading, needlecrafts, travel. Home and Office: 289 S Armstrong Fresno CA 93727

KORMAN, BARBARA, sculptor; b. N.Y.C., Apr. 8, 1938; d. David and Rose (Katz) K. BFA cum laude, N.Y. State Coll. Ceramics, 1959, MFA, 1960. Sculptor Barbara Korman Design Studio, N.Y.C., 1960—. Educator sculpture and design N.Y.C. Bd. Edn., 1961-91; photographer, prodr. audio-visual ednl. packages, N.Y.C., 1973-89; designer, producer wearable sculpture, 1992—. One-woman shows include Overseas Press Club, N.Y.C., 1988, Tiffany & Co. Windows, 1992, U.S. Mil. Acad., West Point, N.Y., 1996, Westchester C.C., Valhalla, N.Y., 2003, Krause Gallery, Providence, 2003, Piero Gallery, South Orange, N.J., 2004, exhibited in group shows at Met. Mus. Art, N.Y.C., 1976, Nat. Arts Club, 1976, Hudson River Mus., Yonkers, N.Y., 1978, Queens Mus., Flushing, N.Y., 1981, Heckscher Mus., Huntington, N.Y., 1996, Grounds for Sculpture, Hamilton, N.J., 2001, Yosemite Gallery, Yosemite Nat. Park, Calif., 2002, Hammond Mus., North Salem, N.Y., 2004, Arts Exch., Westchester Arts Coun., White Plains, N.Y., 2004. Recipient Excaliber Foundry award for bronze casting, 1998, BRIO award for sculpture, 1997-98, Jeffrey Childs Willis Meml. prize for Sculpture, 1984, Outstanding Art Educator award Sch. Art League, 1977, Internat. Woman's Yr. award for Outstanding Cultural Contbns., 1975, 76, House of Heydenryk prize for Sculpture, 1974, Yosemite Renaissance XVII award, 2002, Coun. Am. Artist Socs. award, 2002; materials grantee Formica Corp., 1985. Mem. Nat. Assn. Women Artists, Internat. Sculpture Ctr., Katonah Mus. Artist Assn. (bd. dirs.), Bronx Coun. of Arts. Studio: 357 E 201st St Bronx NY 10458-2205 E-mail: kormanstudio@aol.com.

KORMAN, EDWARD R., federal judge; b. NYC, Oct. 25, 1942; s. Julius and Miriam Korman; m. Diane R. Eisner, Feb. 3, 1979; children: Miriam M., Benjamin E. BA, Bklyn. Coll., 1963; LL.B., Bklyn. Law Sch., 1966; LL.M., NYU, 1971. Bar: NY 1966, admitted to practice: US Supreme Ct. 1972. Law clk. to judge N.Y. Ct. Appeals, 1966-68; assoc. Paul, Weiss, Rifkind, Wharton and Garrison, 1968-70; asst. U.S. atty. Eastern Dist. N.Y., 1970-72; asst. to solicitor gen. of U.S., 1972-74; chief asst. U.S. atty. Eastern Dist. N.Y., 1974-78, U.S. atty., 1978-82; ptnr. Stroock & Stroock & Lavan, NYC, 1982-84; prof. Bklyn. Law Sch., 1984-85; U.S. dist. judge Eastern Dist. N.Y., 1985—, chief judge, 2000—. Chmn. Mayor's Com. on NYC Marshals, 1983—85; mem. Temporary Commn. of Investigation of State of NY, 1983—85. Jewish. Office: US Dist Ct US Courthouse 225 Cadman Plz E Brooklyn NY 11201-1818 Office Phone: 718-260-2470. Business E-Mail: edward_korman@nyed.uscourts.gov.

KORMAN, JAMES WILLIAM, lawyer; b. Washington, Apr. 29, 1943; s. Milton D. and Bernice (Rosensweig) K.; m. Barbara Dale Lewis, June 11, 1967; 1 child, Katherine Korman Frey. AB, Coll. William & Mary, 1965; JD, George Washington U., 1968. Bar: Va. 1968, D.C. 1970, U.S. Supreme Ct. 1972, U.S. Ct. Appeals (4th cir.) 1974, U.S. Dist. Ct. (ea. dist.) Va. 1975. Assoc. Kinney, Smith and Barham, Arlington, Va., 1968-73, ptnr., 1973-78; pres. Bean, Kinney & Korman, Arlington, 1979—; neutral case evaluator Fairfax Cir. Ct., 1995—. Mem. Va. Bar Coun., 1983-89, 98-2004, 10th dist. grievance com., 1978-81; mem. adv. bd. Bank of Arlington, Va., 1977-78; lectr. various civil litigation topics continuing legal edn.; contbg. atty. Mathew Bender's Fed. Practice Forms, 1978; panelist Va. Conf. Nat. Assn. Bank Women, 1984; adj. prof. George Mason U. Law Sch., 1996—; mem. faculty Va. State Bar Profl. Course, 1998-2001. Contbr. articles to profl. jours. Bd. dirs. No. Va. Jewish Cmty. Ctr., 1985-91; mem. adv. bd. Sch. Contemporary Edn., Springfield, Va., 1985-91; mem. Va. Commn. on Women and Minorities in the Law, 1988-92. Capt. JAG, USAR, 1972-74. Recipient Meritorious Svc. award Legal Aid Bur., 1968, Adult Leadership award Boy Scouts Am., 1972; named One of 50 Top Divorce Lawyers Washingtonian Mag., 2000, 04, Washington's Best Lawyers, 2004; One of Best Lawyers in Am., 1995, 97, 99, 2001, 03, 05. Fellow: Am. Bar Found., Va. Law Found., Am. Acad. Matrimonial Lawyers (Va. chpt. v.p. 1996—99, pres. 2001—03, cert. arbitrator); mem.: ATLA, ABA, Plaintiffs Bar Ltd., Va. Trial Lawyers Assn. (jud. task force 1998—, 2002), Arlington Bar Found. (bd. dirs. 1990—, pres. 2000—01), Arlington Bar Assn. (bd. dirs. 1977—81, pres. 1981—82, Robert J. Arthur Disting. Svc. award 2002), Va. State Bar (pro bono steering com. 1992—93, bd. govs. family law sect. 2005—). Democrat. Avocation: collecting political buttons. Home: 2450 N Wakefield Ct Arlington VA 22207-3554 Office: Bean Kinney & Korman 2000 N 14th St Ste 100 Arlington VA 22201-2552 Office Phone: 703-525-4000. Business E-Mail: jkorman@beankinney.com.

KORMAN, MARTIN, lawyer; b. Phila., Oct. 10, 1963; AB, Stanford U., 1985; JD, Yale U., 1989. Bar: NY 1990, Calif. 1994. Ptnr. Wilson Sonsini Goodrich & Rosati. Named one of 45 Under Forty-Five, Am. Lawyer, 2003. Office: Wilson Sonsini Goodrich & Rosati 650 Page Mill Rd Palo Alto CA 94304-1050 Office Phone: 650-493-9300.

KORMAN, NATHANIEL IRVING, research and development company executive; b. Providence, Feb. 23, 1916; s. William and Tillie (Jacobs) K.; m. Ruth C. Kaplan, Apr. 6, 1941; children: Michael, Robert. BS summa cum laude, Worcester Poly. Inst., 1937; MS (Coffin fellow), MIT, 1938; PhD, U. Pa., 1958. Dir. advance mil. systems RCA Corp., 1958-67. Chmn. radar panel U.S. R&D Bd., 1948-56; lectr. U. Pa. Evening Grad. Sch., 1967-68; cons. in field Color Sci., 1968-83; pres. Ventures R&D Group; cons. to Satellite Wholesale of N.Mex., 1991—. Author: The Evolution of Human Society, 1998; patentee in field. Mem. Citizens Com. for Better Schs., Moorestown, N.J., 1958. Recipient Merit award RCA, 1951. Fellow IEEE; mem. Sigma Xi. Home: 5700 Teakwood Trl NE Albuquerque NM 87111-6225

KORMONDY, EDWARD JOHN, retired academic administrator, retired science educator; b. Beacon, NY, June 10, 1926; s. Anthony and Frances (Glover) Kormondy; m. Peggy Virginia Hedrick, June 5, 1950 (div. 1989); children: Lynn Ellen, Eric Paul, Mark Hedrick. BA in Biology summa cum laude, Tusculum Coll., 1950, DSc (hon.), 1997; MS in Zoology, U. Mich., 1951, PhD in Zoology, 1955. Tchg. fellow U. Mich., 1952-55; instr. zoology, curator insects Mus. Zoology, 1955-57; from asst. prof. to assoc. prof. Oberlin (Ohio) Coll., 1957—67, prof., 1967-69, acting assoc. dean, 1966-67; dir. Commn. Undergrad. Edn. Biol. Scis., Washington, 1968-72; dir. Office Biol. Edn. Am. Inst. Biol. Scis., Washington, 1968-71; mem. faculty Evergreen State Coll., Olympia, Wash., 1971-79, interim acting dean, 1972-73, v.p., provost, 1973-78; sr. profl. assoc., directorate sci. edn. NSF, 1979; provost, prof. biology U. So. Maine, Portland, 1979-82; v.p. acad. affairs, prof. biology Calif. State U., L.A., 1982-86; sr. v.p., chancellor, prof. biology U. Hawaii-West Oahu and U. Hawaii, Hilo, 1986-93, chancellor emeritus, 2000—; pres. U. West L.A., 1995-97; spl. asst. to pres. Pacific Oaks Coll., 2000—. Author: Introduction to Genetics: A Program for Self Instruction, 1964, Readings in Ecology, 1965, General Biology, A Book of Readings, 1966, Concepts of Ecology, 1969, 4th edit., 1996, General Biology: The Integrity and Natural History of Organisms, 1977, Handbook of Contemporary World Developments in Ecology, 1981, International Handbook of Pollution Control, 1989, Biology, 1984, 1988, Fundamentals of Human Ecology, 1998, University of Hawaii-Hilo: A College in the Making, 2001; contbr. articles to profl. jours. With USN, 1944—46. Postdoctoral fellow, U. Ga., 1963—64, Vis. Rsch. fellow, Georgetown U., 1978—79, Rsch. grantee, NAS, Am. Philos. Soc., NSF. Fellow: AAAS; mem.: So. Calif. Acad. Scis. (bd. dirs. 1985—86, 1993—97, v.p. 1995—96), Nat. Assn. Biology Tchrs. (pres. 1981), Ecol. Soc. Am. (sec. 1976—78), Sigma Xi (Rsch. grantee). E-mail: ekor@aol.com.

KORN, DAVID, pathologist, educator; b. Providence, Mar. 5, 1933; s. Solomon and Claire (Liebman) Korn; m. Phoebe Richter, June 9, 1955 (div. Dec. 1993); 1 adopted child, Joanna M. Fiduccia children: Stephen James, Daniel Clair, Michael Philip; m. Carol Scheman, Dec. 24, 1997. BA, Harvard U., 1954, MD, 1959. Intern Mass. Gen. Hosp., Boston, 1959—60, resident in Pathology, 1960—61; rsch. assoc. NIH, 1961—63, asst. pathologist, 1963—68; mem. staff Lab. Biochem. Pharmacology; prof. pathology Sch. Medicine, Stanford (Calif.) U., 1968—97, chmn. dept. pathology Sch. Medicine, 1968—84; physician-in-chief pathology Stanford Hosp., 1968—84, dean Sch. Medicine, 1984—85, v.p., dean, 1986—95; cons. pathology Palo Alto VA Hosp., 1968—84; sr. v.p. biomed. and health scis. rsch. Assn. Am. Med. Colls., 1997—. Sr. surgeon USPHS, 1961—66; cell biology study sect. NIH, 1973—77, chmn., 1976—77; bd. sci. counselors divsn. cancer biology and diagnosis Nat. Cancer Inst., 1977—82, chmn. divsn. cancer biology and diagnosis, 1980—82; chmn. Nat. Cancer Adv. Bd., 1984—91; disting. scholar-in-residence Assn. Am. Med. Colls., 1995—97; sr. fellow sci. and health policy Assn. Acad. Health Ctrs., 1995—97. Mem. editl. bd. Human Pathology, 1969—74, assoc. editor, 1974—88, mem. editl. bd. Jour. Biol. Chemistry, 1973—79. Founding mem., chmn. bd. Calif. Transplant Donor Network, 1987—95. Recipient Disting. Young Scientist award, Md. Acad. Sci., 1967. Fellow: AAAS, Am. Soc. Clinical Pathology (hon.); mem.: Assn. Pathology (chmn. 1999), Inst. Medicine (Disting. Svc. award 1999), Fedn. Am. Soc. Exptl. Biology (bd. dirs., exec. com.), Am. Soc. Investigative Pathology (Gold-headed Cane award 2003), Am. Soc. Biochemistry and Molecular Biology. Home: 3827 Cathedral Ave NW Washington DC 20016 Office: AAMC 2450 N St NW Washington DC 20037-1167 Office Phone: 202-828-0509. Business E-Mail: dkom@aamc.org.

KORN, EDWARD DAVID, biochemist; b. Phila., Aug. 3, 1928; s. Joel and Carrie (Goldman) K.; m. Muriel Evelyn Fisher, June 23, 1950; children: Elizabeth Gail, Sarah Harris Korn Gilchrist. BA, U. Pa., 1949, PhD, 1954. Scientist Nat. Heart, Lung, Blood Inst., Bethesda, Md., 1954-69; vis. scientist Cambridge (Eng.) U., 1958-59, 69-70; prof. FAES Grad. Program, Bethesda, 1966-76; head sect. on cell biology Nat. Heart Lung and Blood Inst., Bethesda, 1969—, chief lab. of cell biology, 1974—, sci. dir., 1989-99. Editor: (book series) Methods in Membrane Biology, 1974-79; assoc. editor Jour. Biol. Chemistry, 1977-93; contbr. numerous sci. articles to jours. in field, 1953—. Recipient Superior Svc. award USPHS, 1980, Presdl. Meritorious Exec. Rank award, 1987; Mider lectr. NIH, 1985. Mem. NAS, Am. Soc. for Biochemistry and Molecular Biology, Biophys. Soc., Am. Soc. Cell Biology, Found. Advanced Edn. in Scis. (bd. dirs. 1977-92). Office: NIH 9000 Rockville Pike Bldg 50 Bethesda MD 20892-0001 E-mail: edk@nih.gov.

KORN, JESSICA SUSAN, research scientist, educator; b. L.A., Aug. 16, 1968; d. Lester B. and Carolbeth (Goldman) K. BA in Sociology, UCLA, 1990, MA in Edn., 1992, PhD in Philosophy, 1996. Actor Curb-Esquire Films, Burbank, Calif., 1984; exec. asst. Korn Capital Group, Inc., L.A., 1991; tchg. asst. Grad. Sch. Edn. and Info. Studies UCLA, 1995, rsch. analyst Grad. Sch. Edn. and Info. Studies, 1992—96, postdoctoral fellow Higher Edn. Rsch. Inst., 1996—97, tchg. assoc., 1997; rsch. scientist, affiliate asst. prof. U. Wash., 1997—99; v.p. instnl. rsch. Eckerd Coll., St. Petersburg, Fla., 1999—2005; rsch. scientist, assoc. dir. instnl. rsch. Loyola U. Chgo., 2005—. Internat. election observer Orgn. for Security and Cooperation in Europe, 1997, 98, 2000, 02. Contbr. articles to profl. jours. Jr. assoc. Big Sisters Am., L.A., 1994-98. Mem. AAUW, Am. Ednl. Rsch. Assn., Assn. Study of Higher Edn., Assn. for Instnl. Rsch., Nat. Coun. Rsch. on Women, Screen Actors Guild Am. Avocations: working with rape and other trauma survivors, humanitarian aid work, travel, yoga.

KORN, LAURENCE, health products executive; PhD, Stanford U. Hellen Hay Whitney postdoctoral fellow Carnegie Instn. of Washington; staff scientist MRC Lab. of Molecular biology, Cambridge, England; asst. prof. Stanford U., Calif., head rsch. lab., 1981—86; dir., chmn. bd. Protein Design Labs, Inc., Fremont, Calif., 1986—, CEO, 1987—. Office: Protein design Labs Inc 34801 Campus Dr Fremont CA 94555*

KORN, LESTER BERNARD, diversified financial services company executive; b. N.Y.C., Jan. 11, 1936; BS with honors, UCLA, 1959, MBA, 1960; postgrad., Harvard Bus. Sch., 1961. Mgmt. cons. Peat, Marwick, Mitchell & Co., L.A., 1961-66, ptnr., 1966-69; founder, CEO Korn/Ferry Internat., L.A., 1969-91, chmn. emeritus, 1991—; U.S. amb. and U.S. rep. Econ. and Social Coun. UN, 1987-88; chmn., founder Korn Tuttle Capital Group, Inc., 1991; alt. rep. 42d and 43d UN Gen. Assembly. Chmn., CEO Korn Tuttle Capital Group, Inc., 1991; bd. dirs. Continental Am. Properties, Coun. Am. Ambs., Music Ctr. Operating Co. L.A., Performing Arts Ctr., L.A., Tenet Healthcare Corp., RAND-Ctr. for Russian and Eurasian Studies; mem. U.S. Presdl. Del. to Observe Elections in Bosnia, 1996. Author: The Success Profile, 1989. Trustee UCLA Found.; bd. overseers and bd. visitors Anderson Grad. Sch. Mgmt., UCLA; trustee, founding mem. Dean's Coun. UCLA, Performing Arts Cen. L.A., 1999—; mem. adv. coun. Am. Heart Assn.; spl. advisor, del. UNESCO Inter-gov. Conf. on Edn. for Internat. Understanding, Coop., Peace, 1983; adv. bd. Women in Film Found., 1983-84; chmn. Commn. on Citizen Participation in Govt., State of Calif., 1979-82; bd. dirs. John Douglas French Found. for Alzheimer's Disease; mem. Republican Nat. Exec. Fin. Com., 1985, Pres.'s Commn. White House Fellowships, Republican Eagles; hon. chairperson 50th Am. Presdl. Inaugural, 1985; co-chmn. So. Calif. region NCCJ; mem. U.S. Presdl. Del. to observe elections in Bosnia, 1996. Recipient Alumni Profl. Achievement award UCLA, 1984, Superior Honor award U.S. Dept. State, 1988, Neil H. Jacoby Internat. award, 1990, Internat. Citizen of Yr. award Internat. Visitors Coun., 1991; Korn Convocation Hall at UCLA dedicated in his honor, 1995. Mem. AICPAs, Calif. Soc. CPAs, Am. Bus. Conf. (founding mem.), Coun. Am. Ambs., Prodrs. Guild of Am., Hillcrest Country Club, Rockefeller Ctr. Club.

KORN, PETER A., arbitrator, mediator, educator; b. N.Y.C., Sept. 16, 1939; s. Samuel S. and Sylvia Korn; m. Marian Bell, Dec. 24, 1967; 1 child, Sheryl Robin. BBA, CCNY, 1961; M.G.A., U. Pa., 1962. Exec. asst. City of Rochester, N.Y., 1962-64, budget dir., 1964-69, city mgr., 1980-85; mgr. City of Long Beach, N.Y., 1970-71; adminstr. Jersey City, 1972-75, Broward County, Fla., 1975-76; prof., asst. to pres. Nova U., Ft. Lauderdale, Fla., 1976-80; v.p. electronic tng. div. Kodak Corp., Rochester, 1986-87, cons. state and local services, electronic tng. div., 1987-89; prof. pub. adminstrn. SUNY, Brockport, 1987-90; city mgr. City of Peoria, Peoria, Ill., 1990-96, City of New Rochelle, 1996—2002; labor arbitrator, 2002—. Adj. prof. polit. sci. Iona Coll., 2003—. Author: Financing City and Schools in Yonkers NY, 1976 Mem.: Indsl. Rels. Rsch. Assn., Am. Arbitration Assn. Avocation: boating.

KORNBERG, ALAN WILLIAM, lawyer; b. NYC, Dec. 11, 1952; s. Peter and Selma (Borden) K. AB, Brandeis U., 1974; JD, NYU, 1977. Bar: N.Y. 1978, D.C. 1993. Assoc. Milbank, Tweed, Hadley & McCloy, N.Y.C., 1977-86, ptnr., 1986-90, Paul, Weiss, Rifkind, Wharton & Garrison, LLP, N.Y.C., 1990—. Fellow Am. Coll. Bankruptcy, 1995; adj. instr. law Yeshiva U., N.Y.C., 1984-85. Bd. dirs. Lubovitch Dance Found., Inc., 1988-98, Photographers & Friends United Against AIDS, 1989-92, Classical Action, 1993-98; trustee Bennington Coll., Vt., 2004—. Mem. ABA, N.Y. Bar Assn., Assn. of Bar of City of N.Y., Akin Hall Assn. Home: 975 Park Ave New York NY 10028 Office: Paul Weiss Rifkind Wharton & Garrison LLP 1285 Avenue Of The Americas New York NY 10019-6064 Office Phone: 212-373-3209. Business E-Mail: akornberg@paulweiss.com.

KORNBERG, ARTHUR, biochemist, educator; b. Bklyn., Mar. 3, 1918; s. Joseph and Lena (Katz) Kornberg; m. Sylvy R. Levy, Nov. 21, 1943 (dec. 1986); children: Roger, Thomas Bill, Kenneth Andrew; m. Charlene Walsh Levering, 1988 (dec. 1995); m. Carolyn Frey Dixon, 1998. BS, CCNY, 1937, LLD (hon.), 1960; MD, U. Rochester, 1941, DSc (hon.), 1962, U. Pa., U. Notre Dame, 1965, Washington U., 1968, Princeton U., 1970, Colby Coll., 1970; LHD (hon.), Yeshiva U., 1963; MD honoris causa, U. Barcelona, Spain, 1970. Intern in medicine Strong Meml. Hosp., Rochester, NY, 1941—42; commd. officer USPHS, 1942, advanced through grades to med. dir., 1951; mem. staff NIH, Bethesda, Md., 1942—52, nutrition sect., div. physiology, 1942—45; chief sect. enzymes and metabolism Nat. Inst. Arthritis and Metabolic Diseases, 1947—52; guest research worker depts. chemistry and pharmacology coll. medicine NYU, 0466; dept. biol. chemistry med. sch. Washington U., 1947; dept. plant biochemistry U. Calif., 1951; prof., head dept. microbiology, med. sch. Washington U., St. Louis, 1953—59; prof. biochemistry Stanford U. Sch. Medicine, 1959—88, chmn. dept., 1959—69, prof. emeritus dept. biochemistry, 1988—. Mem. sci. adv. bd. Mass. Gen. Hosp., 1964—67; bd. govs. Weizmann Inst., Israel. Author: For the Love of Enzymes, 1989; contbr. sci. articles to profl. jours. Lt. (j.g.), med. officer USCGR, 1942. Co-recipient Nobel prize in physiology or medicine, 1959; named Arthur Kornberg Med. Rsch. Bldg. at U. Rochester in his honor, 1999; recipient Paul-Lewis award in enzyme chemistry, 1951, Max Berg award prolonging human life, 1968, Sci. Achievement award, AMA, 1968, Lucy Wortham James award, James Ewing Soc., 1968, Borden award, Am. Assn. Med. Colls., 1968, Nat. medal of sci., 1979, Gairdner Found. Internat. Awards, 1995. Mem.: NAS, Am. Philos. Soc., Am. Acad. Arts and Scis., Royal Soc., Harvey Soc., Am. Chem. Soc., Am. Soc. Biol. Chemists (pres. 1965), The Japan Soc. (hon.), Alpha Omega Alpha, Sigma Xi, Phi Beta Kappa. Office: Stanford U Sch Med Dept Biochemistry Beckman Ctr Rm B400 Stanford CA 94305-5307 E-mail: akornberg@stanford.edu.*

KORNBERG, FRED, electronics executive; b. Lemberg, Poland, Jan. 28, 1936; s. Karl Kalman and Edith (Keller) K.; m. Rowena Birnbach, June 15, 1958; children: Michelle Caren, Matthew Eric, Tara Kim. BSEE, NYU, 1958, MSEE, 1959. Staff rsch. scientist Coll. Engring. NYU, Bronx, N.Y., 1958-59; sr. staff engr. Radio Engring. Labs., L.I., N.Y., 1956-62, dir. rsch., 1962-69; gen. mgr., v.p. Nardcom Group, Melville, N.Y., 1969-71; exec. v.p. Comtech Telecommunications Corp., Melville, N.Y., 1971-76, pres., 1976—; also bd. dirs. Mem. IEEE (sr. mem.), Armed Forces Communication and Electronics Assn. (sr. mem.). Republican. Jewish. Avocations: jogging, reading, swimming. Home: 17 Palatine Ct Syosset NY 11791-1105 Office: Comtech Telecommunications Corp 105 Baylis Rd Melville NY 11747 Business E-Mail: fkornberg@comtechtel.com.

KORNBERG, SIR HANS LEO, biochemist, educator; b. Herford, Germany, Jan. 14, 1928; s. Max and Margarete (Silberbach) K.; m. Monica Mary King, Oct. 6, 1956 (dec. June 1989); children: Julia Margaret, Rachel Elizabeth, Jonathan Paul, Simon Alexander; m. Donna Haber, July 28, 1991. BSc, U. Sheffield, 1949, PhD, 1953, DSc (hon.), 1979; MA, Oxford U., 1959, DSc, 1961; ScD, Cambridge U., 1975; DSc (hon.), Warwick U., 1975, Leicester U., 1979, Bath U., 1980, Strathclyde U., 1985, South Bank U., 1994, Leeds U., 1995, La Trobe U., 1997; D.U. (hon.), Essex U., 1979; MD (hon.), Leipzig U., 1984; LLD (hon.), Dundee U., 1999. John Stokes rsch. fellow U. Sheffield, 1951—53; Commonwealth Fund fellow Yale U., U. Calif., Berkeley, Pub. Health Rsch. Inst., 1953—55; mem. sci. staff M.R.C. cell metabolism rsch. unit Oxford, 1955—60; prof. biochemistry U. Leicester, 1960—75; Sir William Dunn prof. biochemistry Cambridge U., England, 1975—95, fellow Christ's Coll. England, 1975—, Master, 1982—95. Lectr. Worcester Coll. Oxford, 1958-60; Leeuwenhoek lectr. Royal Soc., 1972; Weizmann Meml. lectr., Rehovot, 1975; mem. Sci. Rsch. Coun., 1967-72, chmn. sci. bd., 1969-72; mem. U.G.C. Biol. Sci. Com., 1967-76; U.K. rep. NATO-ASI Panel, 1970-76, chmn., 1974-75; chmn. Royal Commn. on Environ. Pollution, 1976-81; mem. Agrl. Rsch. Coun., 1981-84; mem. Priorities Bd. for Rsch. and Devel. in Agr., 1984-90; chmn. adv. com. on Genetic Modification, 1986-95. Author: (with Hans Krebs) Energy Transformations in Living Matter, 1957; contbr. articles to profl. jours. Mng. trustee Nuffield Found., 1972-93; gov. Hebrew U. Jerusalem, 1976-97, hon. gov., 1997—; sci. gov. Weizmann Inst. Sci., Rehovot, Israel, 1981-90, emeritus gov., 1990—; trustee Marine Biol. Lab., Woods Hole, Mass., 1982-87, 88-93, Wellcome Trust, 1990-92; gov. Wellcome Trust Ltd., 1992-95; bd. dir. U.K. Nirex Ltd., 1986-95; pres. Biochem. Soc. U.K., 1990-95, Assn. Sci. Edn., 1991-92, Internat. Union of Biochemistry and Molecular Biology, 1991-94. Recipient Colworth medal Biochem. Soc., 1963, Otto Warburg medal German Biochem. Soc., 1973; created knight bachelor, 1978; hon. fellow Worcester Coll., Oxford, 1981, Brasenose Coll., Oxford, 1982, Wolfson Coll., Cambridge, 1990. Fellow Royal Soc. (coun. 1975-77), Inst. Biology (hon., v.p. 1970-72), Royal Soc. Arts, Royal Coll. Physicians (London) (hon.), Am. Acad. Microbiology; hon. mem. Am. Soc. Biochemistry and Molecular Biology, Am. Acad. Arts and Scis. (fgn. assoc.), German Soc. Biol. Chemists, Japanese Biochem. Soc., Biochem. Soc. U.K., Brit. Assn. Advancement Sci. (hon., pres. 1984-85); mem. NAS (fgn. assoc.), Am. Philos. Soc., German Acad. Scis. (Leopoldina), Italian Nat. Acad. Sci. (Lincei), Phi Beta Kappa. Office: The University Professors Boston U 745 Commonwealth Ave Boston MA 02215-1401 Office Phone: 617-353-4020. Business E-Mail: hlk@bu.edu.

KORNBERG, ROGER DAVID, biochemist, structural biologist; b. St. Louis, Apr. 24, 1947; s. Arthur and Sylvy Ruth (Levy) K.; m. Yahli Deborah Lorch, Sept. 18, 1984; children: Guy Joseph, Maya Lorch, Gil Lorch.adr BS, Harvard U., 1967; PhD, Stanford U., 1972. Mem. sci. staff MRC Lab. Molecular Biology, Cambridge, Eng., 1974-75; asst. prof. biol. chemistry Harvard Med. Sch., Cambridge, Mass., 1976-77; prof. cell/structural biology Stanford (Calif.) U., 1978—, chmn. dept., 1984-92. Contbr. articles to profl. jours. Recipient Eli Lilly award, 1981, Passano award, 1982, Ciba-Drew award, 1990, Harvey prize Technion, 1997, Gairdner Internat. award, 2000, Welch award in chemistry, 2001. Mem. NAS. Office: Stanford U Dept Structural Biology Fairchild Bldg D-123 Stanford CA 94305-5400 E-mail: kornberg@stanford.edu.

KORNBERG, WARREN STANLEY, journalist; b. N.Y.C., June 21, 1927; s. Murray and Helen (Blumberg) K.; m. Felice Sher, June 15, 1952; children: Lisa Kornberg, Jena Talarico, Eva Polston. BA, Adelphi Coll., 1950; MA, Columbia, 1952; postgrad., U. Mo., 1954-55. Reporter Fall River (Mass.) Herald News, 1955-58, Boston Herald, 1958-59, Washington Post, 1960-61; Washington corr.-sci. editor McGraw Hill Publs., Washington, 1962-66; editor Sci. News, Washington, 1966-70; writer syndicated column Warren Kornberg on Science, 1969-70; sci. editor pub. affairs NSF, Washington, 1970-75; editor NSF mag. Mosaic, Washington, 1975—93; book rev. editor Physics Today, 1993—2003. Home: 11017 Kenilworth Ave Garrett Park MD 20896-0153

KORNBLATT, DAVID, corporate financial executive; BS, Drexel U. CPA. Sr. tax mgr. KPMG, 1987—93; dir. taxes The Gillette Co., London, 1998—2002; from dir. taxes to CFO York (Pa.) Internat., 1993—2003, v.p., CFO, 2002—. Office: York International 631 South Richland Ave York PA 17403 Office Phone: 717-771-7008. E-mail: davidkornblatt@york.com.

KORNBLAU, DAVID LEON, lawyer; b. Phila., Apr. 18, 1961; s. Marvin and Lois (Bookman) K. AB cum laude, Princeton U., 1983; JD cum alude, Harvard U., 1986. Bar: N.Y. 1987, U.S. Ct. Appeals (9th cir.) 1987, U.S. Dist. Ct. (so. and ea. dists.) N.Y. 1988. Law clk. to presiding judge U.S. Ct. Appeals (9th cir.), San Francisco, 1986-87; assoc. Paul Weiss Rifkind Wharton & Garrison, N.Y.C., 1987—95; trial atty SEC, 1995—2000, chief litigation counsel, Divsn. Enforcement, 2000—05; 1st v.p., head of regulatory affairs Merrill Lynch & Co., Inc., N.Y.C., 2005—. Chief counsel The Jury Project, 1993—94. Mem. bd. editors Harvard Law Rev., 1984-86; contbr. articles to profl. jours. Mem. ABA. Office: Merrill Lynch & Co Inc 4 World Financial Ctr 250 Vesey St New York NY 10080*

KORNBLEET, LYNDA MAE, insulation, fireproofing and acoustical contractor; b. Kansas City, Kans., June 15, 1951; d. Seymour Gerald Kornbleet and Jacqueline F. (Hurst) Kornbleet Malka. BA, U. St. Thomas, Houston, 1979. Lic. real estate salesperson; Disadvantaged Bus. Cert., State of Tex. Temporary counselor Lyman's Pers., Houston, 1974-75; real estate salesperson Coldwell Banker, Houston, 1975-77; sales, office mgr. Acme Insulation, Dallas, also Houston, 1977-79; owner, pres. Payless Insulation Inc., Houston, 1979—; contractor City of Houston, 1985—; owner, founder Superior Air Ducts, Houston, 2002—, Eco Air. Cotton duct mfr.; HVAC contractor. Active Houston Ind. Sch. Dist., 1989—. Recipient award Internat. Cellulose 12,000,000 sq. ft., 2003; named Contractor of Yr., Sears Home Improvement, 1988. Mem. Houston Air Conditioning Coun. (bd. dirs. 1982-83), Cellulose Insulation Contractors (chmn. Houston 1981-82), Houston Bus. Coun., Insulation Contractors Assn. Greater Houston (pres. 1991-94, award for Top 50 Woman-Owned Cos. 1995), Women in Constrn. (bd. dirs. 1998-2000, sec.). Democrat. Avocations: bridge, golf. Office: Payless Insulation 1331 Seamist Dr Houston TX 77008-5017 Office Phone: 713-868-1021. Business E-Mail: LMK@paylessinsulation.com.

KORNBLET, DONALD ROSS, communications company executive; b. St. Louis, Nov. 7, 1943; s. Louis Yale and Mildred Fayette (Levey) K.; m. Ann Louise Vogel, Dec. 30, 1973; children: Ben Michael, David, Sarah. BA, Yale U., 1966. Dir. pub. info. Urban League St. Louis, 1968—71; midwestern dir. Coro Found., 1971—76; v.p., ptnr. Fleishman-Hillard, Inc., 1976—84; pres., co-owner USA-800, Inc., Kansas City, Mo., 1984—86; pres., owner BRI, St. Louis, 1986—2002; sr. v.p. Americall Group, Inc., 2002—. Mem. chancellor's coun. U. Mo., St. Louis, 1982-85; bd. dirs. Zelda Epstein Day Care Ctr., St. Louis, 1989; pres. Wellington Way Condominium, 1989; bd. dirs. Better Bus. Bur. Ea. Mo., 1990-2000, chmn., 1994-95, Coun. Better Bus. Burs., 1997-2005, The Nat. Conf., 1990, Coro Found., Midwestern Ctr., 1992, bd. trustees Coro Found., 1998; trustee Laumeier Sculpture Park, St. Louis County. Recipient merit award Opportunities Industrialization Ctr., St. Louis, 1984; named One of Top 25 Small Bus. Owners, St. Louis U., 1988. Mem. Direct Mktg. Assn. (Direct Marketer of Yr. 1995), Bus. Mktg. Assn., St. Louis Club, Yale Univ. Club Washington Jewish. Office: Americall Grop Inc 1100 Corporate Square Dr Saint Louis MO 63132-2908 Office Phone: 314-213-7871. E-mail: kfornblet@americallgroup.com.

KORNBLUTH, FRANCES HELEN SCHACHTER, artist; b. NYC, July 26, 1920; d. Jacob and Sarah (Goodstone) Schachter; m. Marvin Hubert Kornbluth, Nov. 21, 1942; children: Bruce Ian, Jane Allyse Cathy. BA, Bklyn. Coll., 1940; MA in Edn., Pratt Inst., 1962. Cert. early childhood tchr., N.Y., Conn. Painter and sculptor, 1958—; tchr. Mineola (N.Y.) Pub. Schs., 1959-67; supr. student tchrs. Mills Coll., N.Y.C., 1966-68; instr. Art Edn. Hofstra U., Hempstead, N.Y., 1967-68, Adelphi U., Garden City, N.Y., spring 1968; instr. Art Dowling Coll., Oakdale, N.Y., 1967, U. Conn., Storrs, spring 1970; tchr. dir. gifted Thompson (Conn.) Elem. Sch., 1972-75; instr. Annhurst Coll., Woodstock, Conn., spring 1980. Lectr. in field. One-woman shows include Works on Canvas Cambridge (Mass.) Art Assn., 1976, Landscape is Alive and Well in Northeastern Connecticut, Women's Ctr. U. Conn., 1978, Path Artworks Gallery, Hartford, 1981, Works on Paper Galeria Prin., Dominican Republic, 1985, Collages, 1986, Selections Artworks Gallery, Hartford, 1991, Visions of Our Land Legis. Office Bldg., Hartford, Conn., 1992, U. Mass. Med. Sch., Worcester, 1997, Showcase for Collage, Providence, Points of

Departure, Slater Meml. Mus., Norwich, Conn., 2001, Edge of the Sea Arts, Worcester, Mass., 2002, Atrium Gallery, Danielson, Conn., 2003, exhibited in group shows at Small Works on Paper Concordia Gallery, Bronxville, NY, 1992, Art for AIDS Sake, Worcester, Mass. Mem. Thompson Hist. Soc., 1989—. With OSS, Army, 1943-45. Recipient Charles H. Woodbury Meml. Prize for a Landscape, 1975, Helen Henningson Meml. Prize for Oil, 1977, Elizabeth Morse Genius Found. Prize-Works on Paper, 1982, 1st prize, Collage N.E. Conn. Art Guild, 1992, Miriam E. Halpern Meml. award, 1992, Lifetime Achievement award, Bklyn. Coll., 2000, 1st prize painting, Slater Meml. Mus., Norwich, 2000, Graphics award, Conn. Acad. Fine Arts, 2004. Mem. Conn. Acad. Fine Arts, Nat. Assn. Women Artists (2 Gold medals of Honor), Women Artists of Monhegan Island, Arts Worcester, ART XII. Democrat. Avocations: music, movies. Home: 134 Buckley Hill Rd North Grosvenordale CT 06255-1803 Studio: Monhegan Island Monhegan ME 04852

KORNEGAY, HORACE ROBINSON, trade association administrator, congressman, lawyer; b. Asheville, NC, Mar. 12, 1924; s. Marvin Earl and Blanche Person (Robinson) K.; m. Annie Ben Beale, Mar. 25, 1950; children: Horace Robinson, Kathryn Elder Kornegay Cozort, Martha Beale Kornegay Howard. BS, Wake Forest U., 1947, JD, 1949. Bar: NC 1949, U.S. Supreme Ct. 1959, DC 1979. Practice in, Greensboro, NC; asst. solicitor Superior Ct. Guilford County, 1951-53; dist. solicitor 12th Solicitorial Dist., 1955-60; mem. 87th-90th Congresses from 6th Dist. NC, NC; v.p., counsel The Tobacco Inst., Washington, 1969-70, pres., exec. dir., 1970-81, chmn., 1981-86; counsel Adams Kleemeier Hagan Hannah & Fouts, Greensboro, NC, 1987-2000; ret., 2000. Bd. dirs. Greensboro Mcht. Assn. Pres. Guilford Young Dem. Club, 1952, N.C. Young Dem. Clubs, 1953-54; chmn. bd. visitors Sch. Law, Wake Forest U., 1979-93; past chmn. adminstrv. bd. Concord-St. Andrew's United Meth. Ch., Bethesda, Md.; mem. adminstrv. bd. West Market St. United Meth. Ch., Greensboro. With AUS, 1943-46. Decorated Purple Heart, Bronze Star, Combat Inf. badge, Expert Infantryman's badge; recipient Americanism award Anti-Defamation League, B'nai B'rith, Washington, 1985. Mem. ABA, Fed. Bar Assn., NC Bar Assn. (chmn. dispute resolution com. 1989-92), Greensboro Bar Assn. (pres. 1992-93), DC Bar Assn., Am. Judicature Soc., Wake Forest Univ. Lawyers Alumni Assn. (past pres.), SAR (trustee), Alpha Sigma Phi Edn. Found. (trustee), Am. Legion, VFW, Royal Brit. Legion (hon.), Congl. Country Club, Greensboro Country Club, Masons, Shriners, Rotary, Phi Delta Phi, Alpha Sigma Phi. Home: 12 St Augustine Sq Greensboro NC 27408-3834 Personal E-mail: hokorn@bellsouth.com.

KORNELL, RONALD FRANK, economist; b. Chgo., June 4, 1935; s. Benedyct John and Esther Klimek-Wiorski; m. Patty Wilson, Oct. 17, 1963 (dec.); 1 child, E. Michael; m. Alyne Vidal, Jan. 5, 1977; 1 child, Nathalie. BA Econs./Internat. Affairs, U. Ill., 1957, MA Econs., 1958; Ops. Rsch., U. Mich., 1966; postgrad., Am. U., 1969-71. Internat. banking officer Bank of Am., San Francisco, 1962; project fin. officer Export-Import Bank, Washington, 1962-65; economist/planner Litton Industries, L.A., Athens, 1965-69; dir. internat. fin. Northrop-Page Comms., Vienna, Va., 1971-77; economist/aid coord. O.E.C.D., Paris, 1977-79; dir. E. Africa Louis Berger S.A., Paris, 1979-80; v.p. East and Southern Africa Louis Berger Internat., Inc., Nairobi, Kenya, 1980-85, group v.p. Asia-Pacific ops. Bangkok, Thailand, 1985—. Mem. Am. Soc. Civil Engring., Am. Econ. Assn., Road Engring. Assn. Asia and Australasia, Am. C. of C. in Thailand, Transp. Rsch. Bd., The Asia Soc. Home: Jaspal Apt 7A 34 Soi 23 Sukumvit Rd Bangkok 10110 Thailand Office: Louis Berger Group Inc 38 Convent Rd Bangkok 10500 Thailand E-mail: rkornell@louisberger.com.

KORNFELD, NEIL S., lawyer; b. June 12, 1963; BS, Northwestern U., 1985; JD, Boston U., 1988. Bar: NY 1989, US Dist. Ct. Ea. Dist. NY, US Dist. Ct. So. Dist. NY. Asst. dist. atty. NY County Dist. Atty.'s Office, NYC, 1988—93; ptnr. Wilson, Elser, Moskowitz, Edelman & Dicker LLP, NYC. Mem. faculty NY Coll. Podiatric Medicine. Mem.: NY County Law Assn., NY State Bar Assn. Office: Wilson Elser Moskowitz Edelman & Dicker LLP 23rd Fl 150 E 42nd St New York NY 10017-5639 Office Phone: 212-490-3000 ext. 2505. Office Fax: 212-490-3038. Business E-Mail: kornfeldn@wemed.com.

KORNFELD, ROBERT JONATHAN, playwright, photographer; b. Newtonville, Mass., Mar. 3, 1919; s. Lewis Felix and Lillian (Seiferth) K.; m. Celia Seiferth Kornfeld, Aug. 23, 1945; 1 child: Robert J. Jr. AB, Harvard Coll., 1941. Script writer Sta. XEQ, Mexico City, 1938-39; editor Fed. Writers Project, New Orleans, 1941-42; reporter The Examiner, San Francisco, 1942-43; copy writer Conner Co., San Francisco, 1944, Albert Frank Agy., N.Y.C., 1945-47, Agrl. Adv. & Rsch., N.Y.C., 1947-50, Knox Kornfeld & Smith, N.Y.C., 1950-60; writer Robert Kornfeld Assoc., N.Y.C., 1961-78, playwright, 1979—. Vis. artist Am. Acad. in Rome, 1996; adviser Classic Stages of La.; play reader, 2004—05. Author: Landmarks of the Bronx, 1990, (plays) The Art of Love, 1988 (1st prize San Francisco Playwrights Ctr., 1988), Three Byk, 1993, Nadezhda, 1994, 616 Royal Street, 1994, Matisse, 1995, The Hanged Man, 1996, Acting Out, 1996, Queen of Carnival, 1997, Father New Orleans, 1997, Hot Wind from the South, 1998, The Celestials, 1998, Retrospective, 1999, Passage in Purgatory, 2000, The Celestials, 2005, The Gates of Hell, 2000; photographer (group shows) The Mask, 2000, Photographs, 2001, The Gates of Hell, 2002, Starry Night, 2003; dir.: (plays) Theater for the New City; author (libretto): (Operas) A Dream Within a Dream, 1985. Chmn. Riverdale Hist. Dist., 1975—, Toscanini Collection, 1984—87, Landmarks Task Force, 1975—99; bd. dirs. Hist. Dist. Coun., 1978—; mem. Time Sq. Playwrights, 2005—; bd. dirs. Riverdale Nature; active Bronx County Dem. Com.; mem. Benjamin Franklin Dem Club, Dem. County Com., 2004—; bd. dirs. Riverdale Neighborhood Ho., 1968—90, Theater for the New City, NYC, 1992—2005, Met. Historic Structures Assn. Pvt. U.S. Army, 1939—40. Recipient proclamation of thanks N.Y. City Coun. for Toscanini Collection, 1984, Preservation award Met. Hist. Structures Assn., 1989, award for establishing Riverdale Hist. Dist. N.Y. City Coun., State Assembly, Riverdale Neighborhood House, 1990, Bronx Landmarks Guardian award Bronx Borough pres., 1995. Mem. Dramatists Guild, N.Y. Theatre League, PEN (freedom to write com.), Harvard Club (N.Y.C.), Riverdale Yacht Club, Nat. Arts Club (co-chair lit. com.), Harvard Ind. Film Group, Sierra Club, Times Square Playwrights. Home: Withers Cottage 5286 Sycamore Ave Bronx NY 10471-2838 E-mail: rojokosr@aol.com.

KORNFELD, STUART A., hematology educator; b. St. Louis, Mo., Oct. 4, 1936; AB, Dartmouth Coll., 1958; MD, Washington U., 1962. Rsch. asst. biochemistry dept. sch. medicine Washington U., St. Louis, 1958-62, from instr. to asst. prof. medicine, 1966-70, from asst. to assoc. prof. biochemistry, 1968-72, prof. medicine dept. internal medicine, 1972—, prof. biochemistry, co-dir. divsn. hematology and oncology, 1976—, dir. divsn. oncology, 1973-76; intern med. ward Barnes Hosp., 1962-63, asst. resident, 1965-66; rsch. assoc. nat. inst. arthritis and metabolic disease NIH, 1963-65. Faculty rsch. assoc. Am. Cancer Soc., 1966-71; mem. cell biology study sect. NIH, 1974-77; mem. bd. sci. counselors Nat. Inst. Arthritis, Diabetes & Digestive & Kidney Disease, 1983-87; mem. sci. rev. bd. Howard Hughes Med. Inst., 1986—; mem. bd. sci. advisers Jane Coffin Childs Meml. Fund. Res., 1987—; Jubilee lectr. Biochemistry Soc., 1989. Assoc. editor Jour. Clin. Investigation, 1977-81, editor, 1981-82; assoc. editor Jour. Biol. Chemistry, 1982-87; author 145 publs. Recipient Borden award, 1962, Rsch. Career Devel. award NIH, 1971-76; named Harden Medallist, Biochemistry Soc., 1989, Passano Found. laureate, 1991. Mem. NAS (mem. inst. medicine), Am. Soc. Clin. Investigation (counselor 1972-75), Am. Soc. Hematology, Am. Soc. Biol. Chemists, Assn. Am. Physicians (sec. 1986—), Am. Acad. Arts and Sci., Am. Chem. Soc., Sigma Xi. Achievements include research in the structure, biosynthesis and function of glycoproteins, especially those which are found on the surface of normal and malignant cells, targeting of newly synthesized acid hydroloses to lysosomes. Office: 8826 Clin Scis Res Bldg PO Box 8125 Saint Louis MO 63156-8125*

KORNGOLD, GERALD, dean, law educator; BA, U. Pa., 1974, JD, 1977. Bar: Pa. 1977, D.C. 1979, Ohio, 1995. Atty. Wolf, Block, Schorr & Solis-Cohen, Phila., 1977-79; asst. prof. to prof. N.Y. Law Sch., N.Y.C., 1979-87, assoc. dean for acad. affairs, 1984-86; prof. Case Western Res. U. Sch. Law, Cleve., 1987—, Everett D. and Eugenia S. McCurdy prof., 1994—, dean, 1997—. Author: Private Land Use Arrangements: Easements, Covenants, and Equitable Servitudes, 1990, (with Paul Goldstein) Real Estate Transactions, 1993. Mem. Am. Law Inst., Phi Beta Kappa Office: Case Western Res U Sch Law 11075 East Blvd Cleveland OH 44106-5409 Office Phone: 216-368-3283. E-mail: slb11@case.edu.

KORNGUTH, STEVEN EDWARD, biologist; b. NYC, Dec. 1, 1935; s. Eugene Irving and Helen (Pardes) K.; m. Margaret Livens, Aug. 29, 1958; children: Ingrid Laura Taylor, David Gregory. BA, Columbia Coll., 1957; PhD, U. Wis., 1961. Rschr. Psychiat. Inst. Columbia U., N.Y.C., 1961-62; from asst. prof. to prof. neurology and physiol. chmn. U. Wis., Madison, 1963-98; dir. neurol. scis. NSF, Washington, 1981-83; dir. Biol. Scis. Inst. Advanced Tech., prof. pharmacy U. Tex., Austin, 1985—. Cons. Army Sci. Bd. Editor: Prof. Scholar, 1991; contbr. over 110 articles to profl. jours.; patentee in field. Mem. Rotary. Avocations: piano, bicycling, reading. Business E-Mail: steve_kornguth@iat.utexas.edu.

KORNHAUSER, LEWIS, law educator; b. 1950; BA, MA, Brown U.; JD, U. Calif., Berkeley, 1976, PhD, 1980. Bar: Calif. 1976. Asst. prof. NYU Sch. Law, NYC, 1977-81, assoc. prof., 1981-82, prof. law, 1982—, now Albert B. Engelberg prof. law. Fellow Ctr. Advanced Study Behavioral Sciences, Palo Alto, Calif., 1981-82. Office: NYU Sch Law Vanderbilt Hall Rm 314E 40 Washington Sq S New York NY 10012-1099 Office Phone: 212-998-6175. E-mail: lewis.kornhauser@nyu.edu.*

KORNICK, MICHAEL, chef; Grad., Culinary Inst. Am., 1982. Chef Quilted Giraffe, NY, Windsor Ct. Hotel, New Orleans; mng. ptnr. KDK Restaurant Group; exec. chef Gordon, 1985, Lettuce Entertain You Enterprises, Four Seasons Hotel Aujord'hui, Boston, 1991, Marche, Red Light; owner, chef MK the Restaurant, Chgo., 1998—. Named Best New Chef de Cuisine, Boston mag., 1992; recipient award, James Beard Found., 2001. Office: 868 N Franklin Chicago IL 60610

KORNICKER, LOUIS SAMPSON, museum curator; b. N.Y.C., May 23, 1919; s. Howard and Lena (Cohen) K.; m. Beatrice Nyman; children: Lance, Steven, William. BS, U. Ala., 1941; BSChemE, 1942; MA, Columbia U., 1954; PhD, 1957. Tech. group supr. Hercules Powder Co., Chattanooga, Tenn., 1942-45; sr. process engr., pilot plant supt. Cities Svc. Refining Co., Lake Charles, La., 1945-48; sec., treas. Uncle Sam Chem. Co., N.Y.C., 1948-57; asst. dir. Inst. Marine Sci. U. Tex., Port Aransas, 1957-60; geologist Office Naval Rsch., Chgo., 1960-61; prof. oceanography Tex. A&M U., College Station, 1961-64; curator dept. invertebrate zoology Smithsonian Inst., Washington. Adj. prof. biology George Washington U., 1968—. Author: Antarctic Ostracoda (Myodocopina), 1975, Research: Revision, Distribution, Ecology and Ontogeny of the Ostracode Subfamily Cyclasteropinae, 1981, Antrctic and Subantarctic Myodocipina (Ostracoda), 1993; assoc. editor: Biology and Paleobiology of Ostracoda, 1975; mem. editl. bd. Palaeogeography, Palaeoclimatology and Palaeocology, 1960-87; mem. bd. assoc. editors Antarctic Research Series Am. Geophys. Union, 1978-90. Mem. Soc. Systematic Zoology, Crustacean Soc., Sigma Xi. Office: Smithsonian Instn Nat Mus Natural History Washington DC 20560-0001 E-mail: kornicker.louis@nmnh.si.edu.

KORNILOWICZ, MARIAN ANDREW, lawyer; b. Niskayuna, NY, May 17, 1954; s. Mieczyslaw and Zdzislawa Biedul-Kornilowicz; m. Teresa L. Paris, Apr. 15, 1989; children: Olivia Grazyna Paris-Kornilowicz, Andrzej Mateo Paris-Kornilowicz. Student, Jagiellonian U., Krakow, Poland, 1974—75; BS in Engring. Sci, B.S. in Polit. Sci. and History, Rensselaer Poly. Inst., 1977; LLM, U. Pa., 1982; JD, Suffolk U., Boston, 1980. Bar: Mass. 1980, Pa. 1982, NY 1985, NJ 1990. Ptnr. Lightman Manochi & Kornilowicz, Phila., 1991—2001; ptnr., dept. chmn. Cohen Seglias Pallas Greenhall & Furman, Phila., 2001—. Dir. Preservation Alliance, Phila., 2003—, chmn. bd., 2005—; dir. Jagiellonian Law Soc., Phila. Home: 1929 Bainbridge St Philadelphia PA 19146 Office: Cohen Seglias Pallas Greenhall & Furman 30 S 17th St 19 Fl Philadelphia PA 19103 Office Phone: 215-564-1700. Personal E-mail: mak@cohenseglias.com.

KORNMAN, ELSIE FRY, retired elementary education educator; b. Kirkland Lake, Ont., Can., Jan. 17, 1933; arrived in U.S., 1969; d. Bert and Ethel May (Wilson) Fry; divorced; children: Scott Elbert, Stacy Marie Kornman Webb. AA, Graceland Coll., Lamoni, Iowa, 1953; cert. in teaching, North Bay (Ont.) Tchrs. Coll., 1955; BS in Edn., Memphis State U., 1973-77; MS in Edn., S.W. Mo. State U., 1982. cert. Ontario, Can., Mo., Utah, New Mexico. Tchr. Brethour (Ont.) Twp. Sch. Dist., 1951; tchr. 2d grade Burford (Ont.) Sch. Dist., 1955-57; tchr. Hamilton (Ont.) Sch. Dist., 1957-60; grad. asst. S.W. Mo. State U., Springfield, 1979-80; reading specialist Willard (Mo.) R-2 Schs., 1980-82; tchr. Granite Sch. Dist., Salt Lake City, 1985-88; tchr. grade 1 Aztec (N.Mex.) Sch. Dist., 1988—98, ret., 1998. Author ch. sch. material. Dir. craft and religious classes Cmty. of Christ, 1989-92; peer counselor New Horizons, Durango, Colo., 1989-92; tchr. craft Getaway Ft. Lewis Coll., Durango, summers 1990, 91, 93; dir. Camp Quality Internat., Western Colo., 1990-94. Avocations: knitting, quilling. Home: 720 W Fairmont St Longview TX 75604

KORNREICH, EDWARD SCOTT, lawyer; b. Bklyn., Apr. 18, 1953; s. Lawrence and Selma K.; m. Shirley (Werner), Feb. 28, 1982; children: Mollie, Davida, Lawrence. BA magna cum laude (hon.), Columbia U., 1974; JD, Harvard U., 1977. Bar: NY 1978, US Dist. Ct., NY, Southern & Eastern Dist., US Ct. Appeals, Second Circuit. Appellate atty. Legal Aid Soc., NYC, 1977-79; assoc. atty. Rosenman and Colin, NYC, 1979-84; v.p., legal affairs, gen. counsel St. Luke's-Roosevelt Hosp. Ctr., NYC, 1984-87; mem. Garfunkel, Wild, and Travis, P.C., Gt. Neck, NY, 1987-90; ptnr., co-chair health care law dept. Proskauer Rose, LLP, NYC, 1990—. Joint com. on health care decisions near end of life ABA and Hastings Ctr., 1992-95; sr. adv. com. Robert Wood Johnson N.Y. Acad. Medicine Project. Trustee, post grad. Ctr. Mental Health, N.Y.C., 1992-99. Mem. Am. Health Lawyers Assn.; N.Y. State Bar Assn. (chair provider's com. health law sect. 2002—); Assn. of Bar City of N.Y. (com. on medicine and law 1985-88, chmn. health law com. 1991-94, AIDS com. 1986-97); Phi Beta Kappa. Avocation: running. Office: Proskauer Rose LLP 1585 Broadway Fl 27 New York NY 10036-8299 Office Phone: 212-969-3395. Business E-Mail: ekornreich@proskauer.com.

KORNS, LEOTA ELSIE, writer, mountain land developer, insurance broker; b. Canton, Okla., Jan. 19, 1916; d. James Abraham and Ida Agnes (Engel) Klopfenstine; m. Richard Francis Korns, July 1, 1943 (wid. Dec. 17, 1988); 1 child, Michael Francis. BS, Pitts. State U. of Kans., 1966. Sec. various firms, Kans. City, Mo., 1937-45; cons. Electrolux Corp., St. Paul, 1946-49; sec. health, safety and waste IAEA, Vienna, Austria, 1959-60; tchr. Montezuma-Cortez H.S., Cortez, Colo., 1966-67; ins. agent Korns Ins. Agy., Durango, Colo., 1968—; owner, pres. Korns Investments, Inc., Durango, Colo., 1970—. Bd. dirs. LaPlata County Landowners Assn., Durango, 1981-87; writer, instr. women's history course U. N.Mex., Albuquerque, Ft. Lewis Coll., Durango, Colo., and Mesa (Ariz.) C.C., 1970-75; also spkr. in field. Author: (novels) Yesterday Should Have Been Over, 1965, Somewhere Out in the West, 2002; (play) Angry Young Men, 1957; writer numerous short stories including The Combine, 1947. Convenor, mem. NOW, Durango, 1970—; precinct capt. La Plata County Rep. Party, 1981—. Mem. Unity Sch. Christianity, Trimble Hot Springs. Avocations: mountain walking, swimming, piano, cross country skiing. Home: 556 2d Ave Durango CO 81301-5604 Office Phone: 970-247-0532. E-mail: leotakorns@frontier.net.

KOROBKIN, BARRY JAY, architect; b. N.Y.C., Dec. 9, 1949; s. Raymond Lawrence and Leanore Anne (Kaplan) K.; m. Laura Hanft, Aug. 27, 1977; children: Rachel Tess, Robert Benjamin. BA magna cum laude, Williams Coll., 1971; MArch, Harvard U., 1976. Registered architect, Mass., N.Y., Fla. Planner M. Paul Friedberg and Assocs., N.Y.C., 1972; architect Herman Hertzberger, Amsterdam, The Netherlands, 1976-77; lectr. Harvard Grad. Sch. Design, Cambridge, Mass., 1977-79; ptnr. KJA Architects, Somerville, Mass., 1979-89, Linden Properties Inc., Somerville, 1983—; prin. Korobkin Assocs., Somerville, 1990—. Author: Images for Design, 1974; prin. works include Eldridge House, 1981 (AIA award 1982, Mass. Gov.'s award 1987), Maxim House, 1984 (New England AIA award 1987). Recipient AIA medal Harvard U. Grad. Sch. Design, 1976; Sheldon fellow Harvard U., 1977. Mem. AIA (chmn. housing com. 1987-90, rsch. fellow 1973), Boston Soc. Architects (bd. dirs. 1990-92), Phi Beta Kappa. Democrat.

KOROLOGOS, ANN MCLAUGHLIN, communications executive; b. Newark, Nov. 16, 1941; d. Edward Joseph and Marie (Koellhoffer) Lauenstein; m. John McLaughlin, 1975 (div. 1991); m. Tom C. Korologos, 2000. Student, U. London, 1961-62; BA, Marymount Coll., 1963; postgrad., Wharton Sch., 1987. Supr. network comml. schedule ABC, N.Y.C., 1963-66; dir. alumnae relations Marymount Coll., Tarrytown, N.Y., 1966-69; account exec. Myers-Infoplan Internat. Inc., N.Y.C., 1969-71; dir. comm. Presdl. Election Com., Washington, 1971-72; asst. to chmn. and press sec. Presdl. Inaugural Com., Washington, 1972-73; dir. Office of Pub. Affairs, EPA, Washington, 1973-74; govt. rels. and comm. exec. Union Carbide Corp., N.Y.C. and Washington, 1974-77; pub. affairs, issues mgmt. counseling McLaughlin & Co., 1977-81; asst. sec. for pub. affairs Dept. of Treasury, Washington, 1981-84; under sec. Dept. of Interior, Washington, 1984-87; cons. Ctr. Strategic and Internat. Studies, Washington, 1987; sec. labor Dept. of Labor, Washington, 1987-89; vis. fellow Urban Inst., 1989-92; pres., CEO New Am. Schs. Devel. Corp., 1992-93; ret., 1993. Mem. def. adv. com. Women in the Svcs., 1973—74; mem. Am. Coun. Capital Formation, 1976—78; mem. environ. edn. task force HEW, 1976—77; chair Pres.'s Commn. Aviation Security and Terrorism, 1989—90; bd. dirs. Fannie Mae, Kellogg Co., Host Marriott Corp., Am. Airlines, AMR Corp., Harman Internat. Industries, Inc., Microsoft; pres. Fed. City Coun., 1990—95; chair Aspen Inst., 1996—2000, vice-chair, 1996; chmn. RAND. Bd. dirs. Charles A. Dana Found. Mem.: Sulgrave Club, Met. Club, Cosmos Club. Republican. Roman Catholic.

KOROLOGOS, TOM CHRIS, ambassador; b. Salt Lake City, Apr. 6, 1933; s. Chris T. and Irene (Kolendrianos) K.; m. Carolyn Joy Goff, June 16, 1960 (dec. Jan. 1997); children— Ann, Philip Chris, Paula; m. Ann McLaughlin, Dec. 9, 2000. BA, U. Utah, 1955; MS (Grantland Rice Meml. fellow 1957; Pulitzer traveling fellow 1958), Columbia, 1958. Reporter Salt Lake Tribune, 1950-56, 59-60; reporter N.Y. Herald Tribune, 1958; account exec. David W. Evans & Assos., Salt Lake City, 1960-62; asst. to Senator Wallace Bennett of Utah, Washington, 1962-71; dep. asst. Pres. Nixon, 1971-74; asst. to Pres. Ford, 1974-75; cons. Timmons and Co., Washington, 1975—2003; sr. advisor to Bob Dole, 1996; sr. counselor to Amb. Paul Bremer Office of Coalition Provisional Authority, Baghdad, Iraq, 2003; US amb. to Belgium US Dept. State, Brussels, 2004—. Dir. congl. rels. Pres.-Elect Reagan; former chmn. U.S. Adv. Commn. Pub. Diplomacy. Former chmn. bd. trustees Am. Coll. of Greece; former mem. bd. dirs. Internat. Media Fund; mem. Internat. Broadcasting Bd. Govs., 1995-2002. With USAF, 1956-57. Recipient Disting. Alumnus award U. Utah, 1989, Hon.Doctorate in Human Letters, 2003. Mem. Ahepa. Greek Orthodox. Office: Am Embassy Brussels Belgium PSC 82 Box 002 APO AE 09710

KOROMA, ABDUL G., judge International Court of Justice; b. Freetown, Sierra Leone, Sept. 29, 1943; Student, Kings Coll., U. London, Kiev State U. Bar: Lincoln's Inn, High Ct. Sierra Leone. Joined Govt. of Sierra Leone, 1964, various positions, 1964-69; with Ministry Foreign Affairs, 1969; del. UN Gen. Assembly; dep. permanent rep. to UN Govt. of Sierra Leone, 1978-81, permanent rep. to UN, 1981-85, former amb. to EEC, permanent rep. to UNESCO, 1985—88, amb. to Ethiopia and Orgn. African Unity, 1988—92; high commr. to Zambia and Tanzania, 1988; judge Internat. Ct. of Justice, The Hague, 1994—. Mem. Internat. Law Com., chair 43d session; mem. dels. to 3d UN Conf. on Law and the Sea, UN Conf. on Succession of States in Respect to Treaties, UN Commn. on Internat. Trade Law, Spl. Com. on the Rev. of UN Charter and on Strengthening Role of Orgn. Com. on Peaceful Uses of Outer Space; vice chair UN Charter Legal Com., 1978; chmn. UN Spl. Com. of 24, UN 6th Com.; lectr. numerous univs.; mem. internat. planning coun. Internat. Ocean Inst. Contbr. articles to profl. jours. Pres. Henry Dunant Ctr., Geneva. Decorated insignia Comdr. of Rokel. Mem. Am. Soc. Internat. Law, Inst. Internat. Law, Lincoln's Inn (hon. bencher). Office: Internat Ct of Justice Peace Palace Carnegieplein 2517 KJ The Hague Netherlands

KORONES, SHELDON BERNARR, pediatrician, educator; b. N.Y.C., Apr. 26, 1924; s. Samuel Aaron and Estelle (Goldstein) K.; m. Judith Ann Kest, June 15, 1952; children: David N., Susan Gifford. BS, U. Tenn., 1944; MD, U. Tenn., Memphis, 1947. Diplomate Am. Bd. Pediatrics, Am. Bd. Neonatal/Perinatal Medicine. Intern Boston City Hosp., 1948-49; asst. resident pediat. Babies Hosp., N.Y.C., 1950-51, 53-54; asst. in pathology Children's Med. Ctr., Boston, 1949-50; asst. clin. prof. pediat. U. Tenn., 1961-68, assoc. prof. newborn svcs. dept. pediats., 1968-72, prof. pediats., dir. newborn svcs., 1972-89, prof. ob-gyn., 1982-89, alumni disting. svc. prof. pediat. ob-gyn., 1989—. Project dir., prin. investigator collaborative perinatal project NIH, Bethesda, 1960-75; dir. newborn ctr. Regional Med. Ctr. Memphis, 1968-2004; perinatal adv. com. State Tenn., 1974—, chmn. subcom. standards regionalization perinatal care, 1975—, subcom. liaison, legis. funding and cmty. edn., 1979—, subcom. perinatal transp., 1979-86, gov.'s task force prevention mental retardation, 1980-83, gov.'s task force healthy children, 1983-86, subcom. follow-up, 1983-86, subcom. evaluation, 1983-86, subcom. med. home., 1983-86, task force child devel. standards dept. human svcs., 1984-86; med. svc. adv. com. March of Dimes, 1974-78, edn. adv. com., 1979-1987, exec. com. west Tenn. chpt., 1986-92; bd. examiner oral exams maternal and fetal medicine Am. Bd. Ob-Gyn., Chgo., 1975; study panel bur. med. devices diagnostic products FDA, 1976-93; prin. investigator Nat. Heart, Lung, Blood Inst., Bethesda, Md., 1976-83, Coop. Multictr. Network Neonatal Intensive Care Rsch., Bethesda, 1986-2001; profl. edn. rsch. com. Am. Lung Assn. Tenn., 1977-81; pres.-elect med. staff Regional Med. Ctr. Memphis, 1982-83, pres. 1983-84; adv. bd. Office Drug Policy, Memphis, 1991; subcom. ob-gyn. newborn svcs. TLC Family Care Healthplan, Memphis, 1994—; mem. perinatal com. devel. clin. practice guidelines TennCare, First Mental Health, Inc., 1996; spkr., cons. in field. Author: High Risk Newborn Infants: The Basis for Intensive Nursing Care, 1972, 4th edit., 1986, Spanish translation, 1979, Russian translation, 1981; co-author: Neonatal Decision Making, 1993; author, co-author: (chpts.) Synopsis of Pediatrics, 1963, 6th edit., 1984, Resuscitation of the Newborn, 3d edit., 1973, Iatrogenic Problems in Neonatal Intensive Care, 1976, Current Diagnosis, 1977, Standards and Recommendations for Hospital Care of Newborn Infants, 6th edit., 1977, Current Therapy in Obstetrics and Gynecology, 1980, 83, Assisted Ventilation of the Newborn, 1981, The Use of Computers in Perinatal Medicine, 1982, Parent-Baby Attachment in Premature Infants, 1983, Infant Stress under Intensive Care, 1985, Gynecology and Obstetrics, Vol. 2, 1985, Teratogen Update: Environmentally Induced Birth Defect Risks, 1986, Assisted Ventilation of the Neonate, 1988, 4th edit., 2003, Comprehensive Pediatrics, 1990; author: (introduction) Planning and Design for Perinatal and Pediatric Facilities, 1977; editor Ross Labs., Columbus, Ohio, 1975-82, Perinatal Press, U. Tenn., Memphis, 1976-78, Brentwood Pub. Corp., L.A., 1977-88, Am. Baby Hosp. Network Adv. Bd., 1984—, Jour. Perinatology-Neonatology, 1988—, Am. Baby Mag., 1992—; reviewer C.V. Mosby Co., 1976-77, 81, 83, J.B. Lippincott Co., 1979, Williams and Wilkins Co., 1981, Polymorph films, 1985, Pediats., 1974—, New Eng. Jour. Medicine, 1975—, Am. Jour. Ob-gyn., 1979, 92, 97, Jour. Pediats., 1997, Pediat. Nephrology, 1997-2004, Pediat. Infectious Disease Jour. 1997-2000, 2003-04, Arch. Pediat. and Adolescent Medicine, 1999, Jour. Perinatology, 2001-04, Acta Paediatrica, 2003; contbr. over 300 articles to profl. publs. Bd. dirs. Memphis Orch. Soc., 1961-70. With USPHS, 1951-53. Named Citizen of Yr. Newspaper Guild Memphis, 1974, Who's Who in Medicine, Memphis Mag., 1984-88, Top Doctors, 1996; recipient Myrtle Wreath award Hadassah,

1976, Contribn. to Perinatal Medicine commendation Commr. Pub. Health Tenn., 1978, Cmty. Svc. award Nat. Conf. Christians and Jews, 1982, City Coun. Memphis, 1982, L.M. Graves Meml. Health award Mid-South Med. Ctr. Coun., Inc., 1984, Cert. Appreciation, Gov. Lamar Alexander, 1986, Key to City Memphis, Mayor Richard Hackett, 1988, Alumni Svc. award U. Tenn. Nat. Alumni Assn., 1989, Themis award March of Dimes, 1991, Meritorious Svc. commendation State Tenn. Ho. of Reps., 1992, Person of Vision award Alliance for Blind Visually Impaired, 1994, Meritorious Svc. award Tenn. Hosp. Assn., 1995; Sheldon B. Korones Chair Neonatology U. Tenn. Coll. Medicine named in his honor, 1989, Sheldon B. Korones Newborn Ctr. named in his honor, 2004; grantee NIH, 1960-75, 1971-75, 1985-2001, Merck, Sharpe and Dohme, 1970-73, Tenn. Dept. Health, 1970—, Memphis Regional Med. Program, 1972-75, Tenn. Dept. Human Svcs., 1972—96, March of Dimes, 1973-80, Nat. Heart, Lung, Blood Inst., 1976-83, Nat. Inst. Child Health Human Devel., 1986-91, 91-96, 96—, Tenn. Dept. Children's Svcs., 1996-2001. Fellow Am. Coll. Ob-Gyn. (assoc.); mem. So. Soc. Pediat. Rsch., Am. Acad. Pediats. (com. fetus and newborn 1969-75, liaison com. perinatal health Am. Coll. Ob-Gyn. 1965-74, rep. to joint com. newborn hearing Am. Speech Hearing Assn., Am. Acad. Ophthalmology Otolaryngology 1969-75, task force on circumcision 1973-74), Tenn. chpt. Pediatrician of Yr. 1994), Tenn. Pediat. Soc., Memphis Pediat. Soc., Am. Pediat. Soc., Tenn. Perinatal Assn. (bd. dirs. 1983—), Russian Perinatologists Assn. (hon. pres. 1996), Nat. Assn. Perinatal Social Workers (hon. 1980), Sigma Xi, Alpha Omega Alpha. Office: U Tenn 853 Jefferson Ave Rm 201 Memphis TN 38103-2807 Office Phone: 901-448-5950. Business E-Mail: skorones@utmem.edu.

KOROS, WILLIAM JOHN, chemical engineering educator; b. Omaha, Aug. 31, 1947; s. William Alexander and Mary Ellen (Roth) K.; m. Ann Marie Teahan, Dec. 19, 1970. BSChemE, U. Tex., 1969, MSChemE, 1975, PhDChemE, 1977. Registered profl. engr., Tex. Chem. engr. E.I. DuPont, Wilmington, Del., 1969-71, cons., 1982—, engr. Camden, S.C., 1971-73; research asst. U. Tex., Austin, 1973-77; asst. prof. chem. engring. N.C. State U., Raleigh, 1977-80, prof., 1980-83; prof. chem. engring. U. Tex., Austin, 1983—2001, B.F. Goodrich prof. material engring., 1986—2001, chmn. chem. engring., 1993-97, Roberto C. Goizueta chair in chem. engring., 2001—. Editor in chief Jour. Membrane Sci. Recipient Sigma Xi Research award, 1980, Young Investigators award NSF, 1983, Alcoa Found Research award N.C. State U., 1983. Fellow AIChE (Inst. award for excellence in indsl. gas separations 1995, Gerhold award 1999), AAAS; mem. Am. Chem. Soc., Nat. Acad. Engring. Office Phone: 404-385-2684. Business E-Mail: unk@che.gatech.edu.

KOROSEC, KENNETH DAVID, lawyer, director; b. Cleve., Oct. 15, 1943; s. Frank A. and Marion (Dunn) K.; m. Constance E. Johnson, June 25, 1966; children: Jason A., Jill A. BA cum laude, Case Western Res. U., 1963; JD cum laude, Cleve. State U., 1967. Bar: Ohio 1967, U.S. Dist. Ct. (no. dist.) Ohio 1976, U.S. Supreme Ct. 1986. Legal counsel Cleve.-Seven County Transp. Land Use Study, 1967-69, N.E. Ohio Area Wide Coord. Agy., 1969-71; county adminstr. Geauga County, Ohio, dir. County Planning Commn., 1971-75; gen. practice Chesterland, Ohio, 1967—. Bd. dirs. Chardon Tool & Supply Co., Inc.; counsel Geauga County Community Improvement Corp., 1971— . Contbr. articles to profl. jours. Mem. ABA, Ohio Bar Assn., Geauga Bar Assn., N.E. Running Club (chmn. bd. dirs.), Chesterland C. of C. Home: 11919 Caves Rd Chesterland OH 44026-1711 Office: Diplomat Bldg 12573 Chillicothe Rd Chesterland OH 44026-2536 Office Phone: 440-729-1414. Personal E-mail: kdklaw@sbcglobal.net.

KOROT, BERYL, artist; b. N.Y.C., Sept. 17, 1945; d. George and Frieda (Braunstein) K.; m. Steve Reich, May 30, 1976; 1 child, Ezra. Student, U. Wis., 1963-65; BA, Queens Coll., 1967. Chief, co-founder Radical Software, 1970-73; co-editor Video Art, 1976. Exhibitions include 4 channel video work Dachau 1974, exhibitions include 5 channel video work, weavings, drawings Text and Commentary, Kitchen, N.Y.C., 1975, exhibitions include Everson Mus. Art, Syracuse, N.Y., 1975, 1977, Documenta 6, Kassel, Germany, 1977, Videopoints, Mus Modern Art, N.Y.C., 1978, Mickery Theatre, Holland, 1978, Whitney Mus., N.Y.C., 1980, San Francisco Art Inst., 1981, Leo Castelli Gallery, N.Y.C., 1977, Mus. Fine Arts, Montreal, 1979, John Weber Gallery, 1986, Jack Tilton Gallery, 1987, Carnegie Mus. Art, 1990, Long Beach Mus. Art, 1988, Jewish Mus., N.Y.C., 1988, Video Skuptur, Kunstverein, Koln, 1989, The Cave, 1993, Reina Sofia Mus., Madrid, 1993—94, Dusseldorf Kunsthalle, Whitney Mus. Am. Art, N.Y.C., Carnegie Mus. Art, ICC Gallery, Tokyo, 1997, Hindenburg, 1998, Bklyn. Acad. Music, 1998, Spoleto Festival, 1998, Mass. Coll. Art, 1999, Historischen Mus., Frankfurt, 2000—01, Whitney Mus., N.Y.C., 2000, 2001, Jewish Mus. Paris, 2002—03, short commd. work, Art 21, PBS, 2002, web project, Holocaust, 2005; video artist (video installation) Dachau, 1974. Fellow, N.Y. State Coun. on Arts, 1978, Creative Artist Pub. Svc., 1975, 1979; grantee, Rockefeller Found., 1989, 1998, Andy Warhol Found., 1991, NEA, 1991—92; artist fellow, 1975, 1977, 1979, Guggenheim fellow, 1994, Montgomery fellow, Dartmouth Coll., 2000. Home: 258 Broadway New York NY 10007-2315 Personal E-mail: bkorot@aol.com.

KOROTENKO, KONSTANTIN ALEX, research scientist; b. Novorosysk, Russia, Dec. 26, 1949; arrived in U.S., 1999; s. Alex and Nadezhda Ivan Korotenko; m. Lioudmila Alex Zinchak, Mar. 13, 1982; 1 child, Irina. MS in Physics, Moscow State U., 1978; PhD in Phys. Engring., Shirshov Inst. Tech., 1983, DS in Phys. Engring., 1998. Leading scientist Shirshev Inst. Tech., Moscow, 1980—99; rsch. assoc. Dartmouth U., Thayer Sch. Engring., Hanover, NH, 2002—; sr. rsch. assoc. NOAA/AOML/PHOD, Miami, 2004—05. Vis. prof. U. Miami, 1999—2000; vis. rschr. RIKZ Reijknalerstaat, Hague, Netherlands, 1993—99, U. du Littoral, Lille, France, 1999—, U. R.I., Narragansett, 2000—01. Author: Investigation of Infusion Processes in Coastal Zone of the Black Sea, 1989; contbr. scientific papers. Recipient award, Nat. Rsch. Coun., 2004—05; fellow, Fulbright Found., 1999—2000. Mem.: Am. Geophys. Union, Moscow Phys. Soc. (mem. exec. bd. 1996—). Avocations: tennis, computers. Office: Dartmouth Coll Thayer Sch Engring 8000 Cummings Hall Hanover NH 03755

KOROTEV, RANDALL L., science educator, editor; b. Green Bay, Wis., May 15, 1949; s. Jordan R. and Nadine F. Korotev; m. Elizabeth L. Lobos, July 13, 1974. Ph.D., U. Wis., Madison, 1976. Rsch. assoc. prof. Washington U., St. Louis, 1979—. Assoc. editor Meteoritics & Planetary Sci. Jour., Tucson, 2002—. Treas. Webster Groves (Mo.)Nature Study Soc., 1996—2005; Mo. editor, Christmas bird counts Nat. Audubon Soc., NYC, 2002—05. Achievements include research in lunar geochemistry. Office: Washington Univ 1 Brookings Dr Saint Louis MO 63130 Office Phone: 314-935-5637. E-mail: korotev@wustl.edu.

KOROTKIN, FRED, writer, philatelist; b. Duluth, Minn., Oct. 25, 1917; s. Morris and Ethel (Billert) K. BA, U. Minn., 1949. Writer-instr. Palmer Writers Sch., Mpls., 1961-66; editor Finance & Commerce, and Daily Market Record, Mpls., 1966-67; stamp editor Mpls. Star, 1970-74, White Bear Press, 1976, Minn. Suburban Newspapers, Inc., 1983-85, The Enterpri$e, 1988-89, Post Publs. Weekend, 1989-91. Mem. philatelic adv. panel Am. Revolution Bicentennial Commn., 1971-74, Am. Revolution Bicentennial Adminstrn., 1974, philatelic advisor, 1974-76; regional rep. Interphil '76, 1974-76, USO, AARP, So. Poverty Law Ctr./Klanwatch Project. Contbr. revs., articles to popular mags., newspapers. Pres. North High Alumni Assn., Mpls., 1946-47; mem. nat. adv. bd. The Generation After; assoc. Simon Wiesenthal Ctr. for Holocaust Studies; mem. St. Louis Park Centennial Commn., 1985-86; charter mem. U.S. Holocaust Meml. Mus., U.S. World War II Meml., Air Force Meml. Found., Nat. D-Day Mus.; founding mem. F.D.R. Meml., Nat. Campaign for Tolerance, William J. Clinton Presdl. Found.; mem. Ret. Sr. Citizens League. Recipient Disting. Topical Philatelist Hall of Fame award, medal, 2004, and invited to sign Disting. Topical Philatelist scroll of honor, 1962, Silver medal for Keeping Posted column in Mpls. Star Am. Philatelic Soc.-Chgo. Philatelic Soc. Conv., 1974, Silver award for Keeping Posted column in Post Publs. Weekend, sponsored by Coun. Philatelic Orgns., 1989, True Grit award Grit Mag., 1997, 98. Mem.: DAV (life; comdr. Mpls. chpt. No. 1 1986), Internat. Assn. Philatelic Journalists, Internat. Philatelic Press Club (gov.), Am. Philatelic Soc. (life; spkrs.' bur. 1977—, writers unit), Ret. Sr. Citizens' League, Father Solanus Guild, People for the Am. Way, Internat. Platform Assn., Jerusalem Instn. for the Blind, Keren Or, Inc., Camera, Holocaust Survivors Assn. USA (nat. adv. bd.), Alliance Ret. Ams., Am. United for Separation of Ch. and State, Nat. Com. to Preserve Social Security, Statue of Liberty-Ellis Island Found. Inc. (charter), Mid. East Media Rsch. Inst., Am. Topical Assn. (founding pres. chpt. 1957—61, nat. pres. 1968—70, 1970—72, dir., nat. adv. com.), Paralyzed Vets. Am. (hon.), Manuscript Soc., Collectors Club N.Y., Royal Philatelic Soc. New Zealand, Christchurch Philatelic Soc., Inc., New Zealand Stamp Collector's Club (hon.; anonymously donated ann. Fred Korotkin Cup for best thematic entry 1966—). Home: Apt 512 4925 Minnetonka Blvd Minneapolis MN 55416-2271 also: PO Box 11053 Minneapolis MN 55411-0053 *Ever since I was a youngster I've tried to determine what character traits help make a person successful. I've come to believe that the most important combination is still confidence in self, stick-to-itiveness, and that other winning ingredient which can be called aim, direction or goal.*

KOROTKIN, MICHAEL PAUL, lawyer; b. N.Y.C., Oct. 5, 1937; m. Marcia Ellen, Aug. 28, 1960; children: Darryl, Alan, Alyssa. AB, Duke U., 1959; LLB, NYU, 1962. Bar: N.Y. 1963. Ptnr. Kramer, Levin, Naftalis & Frankel LLP, N.Y.C., 1973—. Office: Kramer Levin Naftalis & Frankel LLP 1177 Ave of the Americas New York NY 10036 Office Phone: 212-715-9155. E-mail: mkorotkin@kramerlevin.com.

KOROW, ELINORE MARIA, artist, educator; b. Akron, Ohio, July 31, 1934; d. Alexander and Elizabeth Helen (Doszpoly) Vigh; m. John Henry Korow, Sept. 28, 1957 (div. Oct. 1980); children: Christopher, David, Daniel; m. Harry Edward Bieber, Aug. 1, 1982 (dec. May 1994). Student, Siena Heights Women's Coll., 1952-53; diploma, Cleve. Inst. Art, 1957, Sawyer Coll. Bus., 1976. Staff artist Am. Greetings Corp., Cleve., 1957-58, designer, 1970-73; owner Elinore Korow: Portraits, Shaker Heights, Ohio, 1973-94, Akron, 1994—. Instr. painting Cuyahoga CC, Cleve., 1979—, chmn. sr. excellence art exhbn.; instr. U. Akron, 1995—; dir. spl. exhbns. Massillon Art Mus., Canton Mus. Art, 2000—; lectr. in field. Exhibited in group shows at 17th Ann. Russell Art Exhibit, Novelty, Ohio, 1992, Ohio Regional Painting Exhbn., 1993, Beck Ctr. Cultural Arts, Lakewood, Ohio, 1993, Canton Art Inst., Butler Inst. Am. Art, Youngstown, Nat. Acad. Design, N.Y.C., Lynn Kottler Galleries, World Trade Ctr., others, one-woman shows include Cuyahoga Valley Art Ctr., Cuyahoga Falls, Ohio, 1995, Akron Woman's City Club, 1996, others, Represented in permanent collections Blue Cross/Blue Shield N.E. Ohio, Am. Greetings Corp., U. Akron Alumni Ctr., Cleve. Playhouse, Temple Emanuel, Cleveland Heights, Ohio, Kent State U., 1st Congl. Ch., Akron. Women's com. Cleve. Orch., 2002; rep. Women's Art League Akron Area Arts Alliance, 2001; charter mem. Alliance Visual Arts, 1999—2000; bd. dirs. Akron Soc. Artists and Women's Art League, 2001—, Cuyahoga Valley Art Ctr., 2005. Recipient 2d pl., 17th Ann. Russell Show, Novelty, 1992, 1st pl. award, 1993, 3d pl., Valley Art Ctr., Cuyahoga Falls, 1994, 1st prize cash award, AIDS Benefit, Ohio, 2000, 1st prize, All Mem. Show, 2001, 1st pl., Lawrence Churski Gallery, 2002. Mem.: Boardroom Group, Akron Soc. Artists (signature), Ohio Watercolor Soc. (charter), Women's Art Club Cleve. (past pres. 1970—71), Women's Art League (past pres. 1999—2000), Am. Soc. Portrait Artists (assoc.), Women's Network. Avocations: music, travel. Home: 923 Mayfair Rd Akron OH 44303-1317 Office Phone: 330-867-8796.

KORPAL, EUGENE STANLEY, banker, military officer; b. St. Louis, Sept. 1, 1931; s. Stanley Anthony and Mary Ann (Bronakowski) K.; m. Lily M. Alder, July 17, 1954; children: Teresa Kaye, Karla Jeannine. BS, U. Mo., 1953. Commd. officer U.S. Army, 1954, advanced through grades to maj. gen.; served with inf. div., 1964-67; comdr. 1st Bn., 29th Arty. Ft. Carson, Colo., 1969-70; comdr. 3d Bn., 319th Arty. Vietnam, 1970-71; comdr. 3d Inf. Div. Arty., 1973-75; chief Joint U.S. Adv. Group, 1978-80; asst. div. comdr. 25th Inf. Div. Schofield Barracks, Hawaii.; comdg. gen. Ft. Sill, Okla., 1985-87; adv. dir., v.p. Ft. Sill Nat. Bank, 1987—2002, dir., 2002—. Decorated DSM, Legion of Merit with oak leaf cluster, Bronze Star, Air medal, others. Mem. Assn. U.S. Army, Field Arty. Assn.

KORPAN, RICHARD, retired energy executive; Exec. v.p., CFO Fla. Progress Corp., 1989-91, pres., COO, 1991-97, chmn., CEO, 1997—2000; ret., 2000. Bd. dirs. Progress Energy Corp., 2000—01, Black Hills Corp., Rapid City, SD, 2003—. Address: PO Box 33028 Saint Petersburg FL 33733-8028 Office: Black Hills Corp PO Box 1400 Rapid City SD 57709 Office Phone: 605-721-1700.*

KORPI, MEG, research and development company executive; d. Urho John and Laura Korpi; m. Rusty Wright. BA with honors, U. Calif., 1977; EdS, Stanford U., 1982, PhD, 1988. Asst. rsch. scientist Dallas Ind. Sch. Dist., Dallas, 1977—79; evaluation cons. Menlo Park, Calif., 1981—92; faculty mem. Stanford U. Sch. of Edn., Stanford, Calif., 1988—89; sr. rsch. assoc. ETR Assoc., Scotts Valley, Calif., 1992—2003; prin. Character Rsch. Inst., Scotts Valley, Calif., 2003—; exec. dir. Ctr. for Youth Devel. Rsch., Scotts Valley, Calif., 2005—. Evaluation adv. com. Joseph P. Kennedy Jr. Found., Cmty. of Caring, Washington, 2000—01; assessment adv. com. Character Edn. Partnership, Washington, 2001—01; mem. nat. experts panel Ctr. for the 4th and 5th Rs, Cortland, NY, 2002—05; reviewer Jour. of Rsch. in Character Edn., Waco, Tex., 2003—. Author: (rsch. instruments) Social Emotional Academic Learning Survey (SEALS); co-author: Character Education Evaluation Toolkit; author: CRI Social Climate Surveys for Secondary and Elem. Sch. Internat. host Nat. Prayer Breakfast, Washington, 2003—05; founding bd. mem. Kesed Seminars, Pleasanton, Calif., 1997; english tchr. Ednl. Svcs. Exch. with China, Ganzhou, China, 1990—90. Rsch. grant, Annie E. Casey Found., 1997-2002, Sweetland Found., 2003-2005, Rsch. Fellowship, Kings Coll., U. of Aberdeen, Scotland, 1986-87. Mem.: Am. Evaluation Assn., Character Edn. Partnership, Am. Ednl. Rsch. Assn., Soc. for Prevention Rsch. Independent. Avocations: hiking, international travel, scuba diving. Office: Character Rsch Inst 146 Bean Creek Rd Ste D3 Scotts Valley CA 95066 Office Phone: 831-359-8359. E-mail: mkorpi@characterresearch.org.

KORS, MICHAEL (KARL ANDERSON JR.), fashion designer; b. Long Island, NY, Aug. 9, 1959; s. Joan Kors. Student, Fashion Inst. Tech., 1977. Designer, buyer, display dir. Lothar's Boutique, NYC, 1978-81; founder Kors by Michael Kors, 1981—. The first women's ready-to-wear designer House of Celine, Divsn. Moët Hennessy Louis Vuitton, 1997, creative dir., 99; released signature fragrance for women, Michael Kors, 2000; released signature fragrance for men, Michael Kors, 01. Named Womenswear Designer of Yr., Coun. Fashion Designers Am., 1999, Menswear Designer of Yr., 2003; recipient First Am. Original award, DuPont, 1983, Elle/Cadillac Fashion award for Excellence, 1995, Lifetime Achievement award, Lighthouse Internat., 1999, NY award, NY Mag., Golden Hanger award for best designer, E! TV Networks, Women's Fragrance Star of Yr. for MICHAEL, Fragrance Found., 2000, Men's Fragrance Star of Yr. for MICHAEL for Men, Best New Women's Fragrance for MICHAEL, Cosmetic Exec. Women, Best New Men's Fragrance for MICHAEL for Men. Mem.: Coun. Fashion Designers Am. (exec. v.p., bd. dir.). Office: 550 7th Ave Fl 7 New York NY 10018-3203

KORS, R. PAUL, search company executive; b. Pontiac, Mich., June 12, 1935; s. Ralph Dewey and Lydia Elizabeth (Shavlik) K.; m. Carol Jayne Kullick, July 17, 1966; children: Kristen Patricia, Shannon Elizabeth. BBA, U. Mich., 1958; MBA, U. So. Calif., 1965. Salesman Nalco Chem. Co., LA, 1958-66; investment mgr. Dean Witter & Co., LA, 1966-73; sr. assoc. Korn Ferry Internat., LA, 1973-74, v.p. Houston, 1974-77, v.p., mgr., 1977-78; founder, pres., CEO Kors Montgomery Internat., Houston, 1978—. Chmn. ITP Worldwide, 2003—. Served to 1st lt. U.S. Army, 1958. Mem.: Palmas del Mar Country Club. Avocations: skiing, golf, tennis, films, reading. Home: 14306 Heatherfield Dr Houston TX 77079-7407 Office: Kors Montgomery Internat 14811 Saint Marys Ln # 280 Houston TX 77079-2908 Office Phone: 713-840-7101. Business E-Mail: pkors@korsmontgomery.com.

KORSCHOT, BENJAMIN CALVIN, retired investment company executive; b. LaFayette, Ind., Mar. 22, 1921; s. Benjamin G. and Myrtle P. (Goodman) K.; m. Marian Marie Schelle, Oct. 31, 1941; children: Barbara E. Korschot Haehlen, Lynne D. Korschot Gooding, John Calvin. BS, Purdue U., 1942; MBA, U. Chgo., 1947. V.p. No. Trust Co., Chgo., 1947-64; sr. v.p. St. Louis Union Trust Co., 1964-73; exec. v.p. Waddell and Reed Co., Kansas City, Mo., 1973-74, pres., 1974-79, vice-chmn. bd., 1979-85; pres. Waddell & Reed Investment Mgmt. Co., 1985-86; chmn. bd. Waddell & Reed Asset Mgmt. Co., 1973-86, retired, 1986. Pres. United Group of Mut. Funds, Inc., Kansas City, Mo., 1974-85, chmn., 1985-86; vice-chmn. Roosevelt Fin. Group, St. Louis, 1968-91, chmn. adv. bd., 1991-92; treas. Helping Hand of Goodwill Industries, 1993-95, chmn. investment com., 1995-2004; bd. dirs. Mo. United Meth. Found., 1995-2004, chmn. investment com., 2001-2004; chmn. bd. govs. Investment Co. Inst., 1980-82; chmn. bd. Fin. Analyst Fedn., 1978-79. Contbr. articles on investment fin. to profl. publs.; author autobiography, 1997. Mem. Civic Coun. Greater Kansas City, Mo., 1974-85; chmn. fin. com. ARC Retirement Sys., 1986-87. With USN, 1942-45, 50-52. Mem. Inst. CFAs, Fin. Execs. Inst., Kansas City Soc. Fin. Analysts, Lakewood Oaks Golf Club. Republican. Home: 101 NW Hackberry St Lees Summit MO 64064-1477 Personal E-mail: bckorschot@yahoo.com. *A happy Christian home environment, the adversity of the depression of the 30's, the challenges of competitive sports, the desire to achieve knowledge, recognition and responsibilities, a devoted wife and three children who made our marriage most meaningful have been the dominant influences of my life.*

KORST, CHRISTOPHER A., lawyer, rental company executive; V.p., asst. gen. counsel Thorn Americas, 1992—96, v.p. bus. devel., 1996, v.p. Thorn Auto, 1996—97; COO AdvantEdge Quality Cars, 1997—99, prin., owner, 2000—01; sr. v.p. Rent A Ctr., Plano, Tex., 2001—, gen. counsel, 2001—. Office: Rent A Center 5700 Tennyson Pkwy Plano TX 75024*

KORST, HELMUT HANS, mechanical engineer, educator; b. Vienna, Jan. 4, 1916; came to U.S., 1948; married, 1942; 4 children. Diploma in Engring., Vienna Tech. U., 1941, Dr. Tech. Sci., 1947, Golden Dr. diploma, 1997. Rsch. engr. Maschinenfabrik Augsburg-Nurnberg AG, Germany, 1941-45; asst. prof. mech. engring. Vienna Tech. U., 1945-48, vis. lectr. gas dynamics, 1948-49; from assoc. prof. to prof. mech. engring. U. Ill., Urbana, 1949-84, head dept. mech. and indsl. engring., 1962-74, prof. emeritus, 1984—; chair naval air power engring. USN Postgrad. Sch., Monterey, Calif., 1979; Ebaugh Chair Mech. Engring. U. Fla., Gainesville, 1984; pvt. practice cons. Urbana, 1956—. Vis. prof. Kans. State U., Manhattan, 1950, Va. Poly. Inst. and State U., Blacksburg, 1954; design specialist Gen. Dynamics Convair, Ft. Worth, 1955; propulsion specialist Rocketdyne div. N.Am. Aviation, 1960, 65-68; cons. GE, 1959, Adv. Group Aeronautical R & D NATO, 1964, U.S. Missile Command, 1971—. Sr. postdoctoral fellow NSF, 1957; recipient ASEE Centennial medal 1993, Daniel Guggenheim medal in aviation, 1994. Fellow: AIAA, ASME; mem.: ASME Internat. (hon.), Am. Soc. Engring. Edn., Sigma Xi. Achievements include research on internal and external aerodynamics, jet and rocket propulsion, and heat transfer. Address: 3 Eton Ct Champaign IL 61820-7602 Business E-Mail: H-korst@uiuc.edu.

KORSYN, KEVIN ERNEST, music educator; s. Felix Korsyn and Irene Marshall. BA, U. Pa., 1973; MPhil, Yale U., 1978, PhD, 1983. Faculty U. North Tex., Denton, Tex., 1984—, U. Mich., Ann Arbor, 1992—. Author: Decentering Music, 2003; mem. editl. bd.: Theoria, 1985—, Music Theory Spectrum, 2000—03; contbr. articles to profl. jours. Recipient Disting. Faculty award, Mich. Assn. Governing Bds., 1997. Fellow: Mich. Soc. Fellows (sr.); mem.: Am. Musicol. Soc., Soc. for Music Theory (awards com. 1992—95, Emerging Scholar award 1991). Avocations: philosophy, poetry. Home: Apt 25 D 555 E William Ann Arbor MI 48104 Office: Sch Music Univ Mich Ann Arbor MI 48109 Business E-Mail: kkorsyn@umich.edu.

KORT, WESLEY ALBERT, religious studies educator, writer; b. Hoboken, N.J. s. Arthur Henry Kort and Jantina Schrik; m. Phyllis May Hoekstra, Dec. 17, 1960; children: Anne Catherine Rankowitz, Eva Deane, Alexander Wesley. BA, Calvin Coll., 1956; BD, Calvin Theol. Sem., 1959; MA, U. Chgo., 1961, PhD, 1965. Instr. Princeton U., NJ, 1963—65; asst. to assoc. prof. Duke U., Durham, NC, 1965—77, prof., 1977—. Author: Shriven Selves: Religious Problems in Recent American Fiction, 1972, Narrative Elements and Religious Meaning, 1975, Moral Fiber: Character and Belief in Recent American Fiction, 1982, Modern Fiction and Human Time: A Study in Narrative and Belief, 1985, Story, Text, and Scripture: Literary Interests in Bibical Narrative, 1988, Bound to Differ: The Dynamics of Theological Discourses, 1992, Take, Read: Scripture, Textuality and Cultural Practice, 1996, C.S. Lewis Then and Now, 2001, Place and Space in Modern Fiction, 2004; contbr. essays and reviews to profl. jours. Fellow: Soc. of Arts, Religion and Contempory Culture, Erasmus Inst.; mem.: Ctr. Theol. Inquiry. Home: 308 Old Buggy Tr Hillsborough NC 27278 Office: Duke Univ Dept Religion Box 90964 Durham NC 27708 Office Phone: 919-660-3514. Office Fax: 919-660-3530. Business E-Mail: wkort@duke.edu.

KORTE, JEFFREY EDWERTH, epidemiologist, educator; BA in Psychology, Rice U., 1992; MS in Pub. Health, U. NC, Chapel Hill, 1997, PhD in Epidemiology, 1999. Postdoctoral fellow Internat. Agy. for Rsch. on Cancer, Lyon, France, 1999—2001; asst. prof. U. Tex. Health Sci. Ctr., San Antonio, 2001—. Office: U Tex Health Sci Ctr 7703 Floyd Curl Dr San Antonio TX 78229 Office Phone: 210-567-4960. Business E-Mail: kortej@uthscsa.edu.

KORTEPETER, KARL NURI, dietician; b. London, Eng., Dec. 21, 1957; arrived in U.S., 1967; s. Carl Max and Cynthia Ann Kortepeter; m. Tamara Jean Jenkins (div.); 1 child, Derek. BS in math., MIT, 1979, BS in econs., 1980; MBA, U. So. Calif., 1995; BS in food and nutrition cum laude, SUNY, 2002; MS in nutrition, Case Western Reserve U., Cleve., 2004. Cert. computer sys. Computer Learning Ctr., Calif., 1986; registered dietitian Dietetics Reg. Am. Dietetics Assn., 2004. Sci. analyst Western Space and Missile Ctr., Vandenberg AFB, Calif., 1979—83; law clk. Law Offices Henry Himmelfarb, LA, 1984—86; legal analyst Fed. Litigator's Group, Beverly Hills, 1986—87; transaction processing facility programmer II Sys. One Corp., El Segundo, Calif., 1987—91; programmer, analyst May Dept. Stores Co., North Hollywood, Calif., 1991; referral sys. coord. Ea. Adirondack Healthcare Network, Plattsburgh, NY, 1998—2000; dietetic intern VA, Cleve., 2002—03, dietitian, 2004—; adminstrv. asst. Case Western Res. Sch. Medicine, Cleve., 2003—05. Exec. v.p. Optimum Nutrition, Plattsburgh, NY, 1997—. Author: Keynes Generalized Excess Demand Inflation Theory, 1982, Porsche Carrera Consumer Behavior, 1997, EAHCN Referral System, 2000. Br. chief, sr. instr. Army Nat. Guard, 3d Info. Operations Battalion, Northfield Falls, Vt., 1998—2002; target analyst, divsn. artillery 42d Infantry Divsn., Troy, NY, 2002—03; sys. svc. officer Joint Forces Headquarters, Columbus, Ohio, 2003—05. Capt. USAF, 1979—83. Alumni Scholarship, Case Western Reserve U. Dept. Nutrition, 2003, AFROTC scholarship, 1977—79. Mem.: Nat. Guard Assn., Mil. Officer's Assn. of Am. (N.Y. state dir. 2002—04), Am. Dietetics Assn. Republican. Presbyterian. Avocations: swimming, military history, hiking, cooking, oriental carpet collecting. Office Fax: 216-368-3970. E-mail: karldekorte@aol.com.

KORTH, CHARLOTTE WILLIAMS, furniture and interior design firm executive; b. Milw.; d. Lewis C. and Marguerite Peil Brooks; m. Robert Lee Williams, Jr., Oct. 25, 1944 (dec.); children: Patricia Williams, Melissa Williams O'Rourke, Brooks Williams; m. Fred Korth, Aug. 23, 1980. Student, U. Wis., 1941. Owner Charlotte's Inc., El Paso, Tex., 1951—, chmn., CEO, 1979—; pres. Paso del Norte Design, Inc., El Paso, 1978-81; mem. adv. com. for interior design program El Paso C.C., 1981—; mem. adv. bd. S.W. Design Inst., 1982—; ptnr. Wilko Partnership, 1981-98; mem. adv. bd. Mountain Bell Telephone Co., 1976-79; mem. Sch. Architecture Found. Adv. Coun. U. Tex. Austin, 1985-91. Charter mem. Com. of 200, 1982—, Nat. Mus. Women in the Arts, 1985—; mem. Renaissance 400, El Paso, El Paso Women's Symphony Guild, El Paso Mus. Art. Recipient of Silver plaque Gifts and Decorative Accessories Mag., 1978; named Woman of Yr. by El Paso Am. Bus. Women's Assn., 1978, Outstanding Woman of Yr. by Women's Polit. Caucus, 1979. Mem. Am. Soc. Interior Designers (bd. dirs. Tex. chpt.

1977-82), El Paso Women's C. of C. (hon.), El Paso C. of C. (dir. 1976-82), Coronado Country Club, Internat. Club, El Paso Country Club, Santa Teresa Country Club (N.Mex.). Avocations: travel, antiques, collectibles. Home: 6041 Torrey Pines Dr El Paso TX 79912-2029 Office: Charlotte's Inc 5411 N Mesa St Ste 7 El Paso TX 79912-5495

KORTH, FRITZ-ALAN, lawyer; b. Ft. Worth, Aug. 29, 1938; s. Fred and Vera (Connell) K.; m. Penne Percy, Dec. 15, 1965 (div. 1997); children: Fritz-Alan Jr., Maria Eleanor, James Frederick. AB, Princeton U., 1961; LLB cum laude, U. Tex., 1964; HHD (hon.), U. Americas, 1982. Bar: Tex. 1964, D.C. 1964. Asst. sec. OKC Corp., Dallas, 1964-65; ptnr. Korth & Korth, Washington, 1965—; pres. Wilmar Corp., Port Chester, N.Y., 1980—. Founder, sec., bd. dirs. Women's Nat. Bank, Washington, 1978-85, chmn. bd. First WNB Corp., 1982-85; bd. dirs. Trans Leisure Corp., N.Y.C., 1970-75, chmn. bd., 1973-75; bd. dirs. Del Norte Tech., Inc., Dallas., 1969—, chmn., 1982-98, vice chmn. bd. dirs., 1998—; bd. dirs. Del Norte Tech. Ltd., Swindon, Eng.; trustee Meridian Internat. Ctr., 2003—. Registrar St. John's Episcopal Ch., Washington, 1968-70, vestryman, 1970-74, treas., 1973-77; chmn. fin. com., mem. diocesan coun. Episcopal Diocese Washington, 1973-77; trustee, treas. Cathedral chpt. Washington Nat. Cathedral, 1977-84; pres. U. Americas Found., 1969-84; bd. assocs. U. Americas, Puebla, Mex., 1969—; bd. dirs. Travelers Aid Soc. Washington, 1969-86, pres., 1973-75; dir. Southwestern Exposition and Livestock Show, 1987—; charter commr. U.S.-Mex. Commn. for Ednl. and Cultural Exch., 1991-97; pres. AMMA Found., Inc., 1994—, dir. 1989. Mem. ABA, Inter-Am. Bar Assn., D.C. Bar, Tex. Bar Assn., Am. Law Inst., Am. Soc. of Most Venerable Order of Hosp. of St. John of Jerusalem, Phi Delta Phi. Clubs: Met. (Washington), Chevy Chase (Washington); Argyle (San Antonio); Steeplechase (Ft. Worth); Princeton (N.Y.C.); Gymkhana Club (Mauritius). Mailing: PO Box 65482 Washington DC 20035-5482 also: 888 17th St NW Ste 608 Washington DC 20006-3313

KORTHALS, CANDACE DURBIN, lawyer; b. Tampa, Fla., Oct. 3, 1948; d. Robert F. and Geraldine B. Durbin; children: John Kristofor, Kathryn Elizabeth. BA in Internat. Studies, Ohio State U., 1969, BS in Edn., 1970; JD cum laude, Nova U., 1982. Bar: Fla. 1982. Tchr. Palatka (Fla.) Mid. Sch., 1970-72, Dillard H.S., Ft. Lauderdale, Fla., 1974-79; atty. Broward County Pub. Defenders, 1982-84, Grimmett & Korthals, 1984-90, Gunther & Whittaker, 1990-94, Law Office of John Camillo, 1994-99, Neale & De Almeida, 1999-2000, Heinrich, Gordon, Hargrove, Weihe & James, 2000—02, Barnett & Barnard, Hollywood, 2002—. Staff mem. Nova Law Rev., 1981, 82. Office: Barnett & Barnard 4601 Sheridan St #505 Hollywood FL 33021 Office Phone: 954-463-3449. Business E-Mail: ckorthals@bbslawfirm.com.

KORTLANDER, WILLIAM CLARK, painter; b. East Grand Rapids, Mich., Feb. 9, 1925; s. Claude Emperor and Daisy Maude Kortlander; m. Elizabeth Abercrombie Fisher, Apr. 26, 1952; children: Susan Elizabeth, John William. BA, Mich. State U., 1949; MA, U. Iowa, 1954, PhD, 1958. Rsch. asst. U. Iowa, 1950—51, tchg. asst., 1951—54; art hist. instr. Lawrence U., Appleton, Wis., 1954—56; asst. prof. art history U. Tex., 1956—61; prof. art Ohio U., 1961—94; vis. asst. prof. Mich. State U., 1960; prof. emeritus Ohio U., 1994—. Contr. Ohio Hist. Soc., 2003—. Author: (book) Painting with Acrylics, 1973; one-man shows include Otterbein Coll., Westerville, Ohio, 1965, Denison U., Granville, Ohio, 1965, Bryson Gallery, Columbus, Ohio, 1965, Art Inst. Zanesville, Ohio, 1965, Batelle Meml. Inst., Columbus, Ohio, 1966, Art. Inst. Zanesville, Ohio, 1966, W. Va. State Coll. Inst., 1966, Western Electric Co., Columbus, 1966, Bennett Gallery, Toledo, Ohio, 1966, A.M. Sachs Gallery, N.Y., 1967, 1968, Merida Gallery, Louisville, Ky., 1967, Montana State U., 1969, Gallery 200, Columbus, Ohio, 1974, Springfield Art Ctr., 1974, Northern Ohio U., 1974, Ohio U., 1975, Haber Theodore Gallery, NY, 1980, 1982, 1984, Cultural Ctr. of Southeastern Ohio, Athens, 1984, Foster Harmon Gallery, Sarasota, Fla., 1986, Worthington Arts Coun., Ohio, 1998, Fitton Ctr. for Creative Arts, Hamilton, Ohio, 2004, two-person shows, Gallery V., Columbus, Ohio, 1993, 1994, 1995, 1998, three-person shows, 2000, exhibited in group shows at Des Moines Art Ctr., U. Tex., Southern Meth. U., Southwestern La. Inst., Dallas Mus. Contemporary Art, Laguna Gloria Mus., Waco Mus., Witte Mus., Dallas Mus. Fine Arts, Huntington Mus., Dayton Art Inst., La Jolla Mus., U. Maine, et. al. Pfc infantry, 1943—46, Europe. Decorated Combat Infantry badge, Bronze star; recipient Baker award, Ohio U., 1967, Painting of the Yr., Mead Corp., 1965. Avocations: tennis, reading. Home: 7414 Angel Ridge Rd Athens OH 45701 Office Phone: 740-593-7660.

KORVIN, CATHERINE MADELEINE, editor; arrived in U.S., 1982; d. Charles Guit and Madeleine Finkel; m. Andrew Peter Korvin, Dec. 18, 1981; children: David, Steven. BA in German Studies, U. Sorbonne, 1976, BA in Russian Studies, 1978, MA in Russian Studies, 1980; diploma, Inst. Nat. Techniques Documentation, 1980; MLS, St. John's U., 1986. Tchr. French Rutgers U., Newark, 1983—86, Alliance Francaise, N.Y.C., 1983—86; asst. editor Pub. Affairs Info. Svcs., Inc., N.Y.C., 1986—90, assoc. editor Pub. Affairs, 1990—97, editor, dep. exec. dir. Pub. Affairs, 1997—. Head info. svc. GFC-BTP, Paris, 1980—82. Trustee Demarest Pub. Libr., NJ, 1998—2000. Avocations: travel, reading. Office: OCLC Pub Affairs Info Svc 521 W 43d St New York NY 10036 Office Phone: 212-736-4161. Personal E-mail: catherine_korvin@hotmail.com.

KORY, MARIANNE GREENE, lawyer; b. N.Y.C., 1931; d. Hyman Louis and Belle (Rome) Greene; children: Erich Marcel, Lisa. BA, CCNY; JD, N.Y. Law Sch., 1976; LLM, U. Wash., 1986. Bar: Ohio 1977, D.C. 1979, N.Y. 1983, Vt. 1994, U.S. Dist. Ct. (so. and ea. dists.) N.Y. 1983, U.S. Dist. Ct. Vt. 1994. Hearing examiner Ohio Bd. Employee Compensation, Columbus, 1977; atty. advisor Office Hearings and Appeals Social Security Adminstrn., Cin. and N.Y.C., 1977-78; gen. atty. labor Office of Solicitor U.S. Dept. of Labor, N.Y.C., 1978-82; pvt. practice N.Y.C., 1983—; adminstrv. Seattle, 1989-91, Burlington, Vt., 1994—. Founder Cin. chpt. Amnesty Internat., 1977. Alvin Johnson fellow in Philosophy; grad. faculty New Sch. for Social Rsch. Mem. NOW, Nat. Abortion Rights Action League, Feminist Majority Found., Vt. Bar Assn., Planned Parenthood, Wilderness Soc., Defenders of Wildlife, Ctr. for Marine Conservation, Nat. Wildlife Fedn., Humane Soc., Emily's List, Phi Beta Kappa. Office: 1361 S Ocean Blvd #202 Pompano Beach FL 33062-8022 Office Phone: 954-781-2820. E-mail: mariannekory@aol.com.

KORZAN, BARBARA K., music educator; b. Columbus, Ga., June 24, 1937; d. Olaf and Ruth (Henderson) Krogland; m. Frederick Richard Korzan, Nov. 27, 1959; children: Frederick Richard Jr., Thomas Olaf, Anna Ruth. B in Music Edn., Fla. State U., 1959; MEd in Music, Columbus (Ga.) State U., 1980. Pub. sch. music tchr. Bay County Sch. Bd., Panama City, Fla., 1959-61; instr. piano McGee Music Conservatory, Columbus, 1961-62, Columbus, 1962—; instr. Kindermusik, 1989-997—. Mem. Music Tchrs. Nat. Assn. (cert. piano tchr.), Orpheus Federated Music Club (dir. Orpheus Singers 1994-96, past sec., program chair, v.p.), Ga. Music Tchrs. Assn. (cert., state certification chair 1987-90), Columbus Music Tchrs. Assn. (past pres., sec., treas., certification chair), Sigma Alpha Iota. Episcopalian. Avocations: travel, gardening. Home: 2700 Barbara Ave Columbus GA 31907-2508

KOSACZ, BARBARA A., lawyer; b. Pawtucket, RI, Feb. 16, 1958; BA, Stanford U., 1980; JD, U. Calif., Berkeley, 1988. Bar: Calif. 1988. Ptnr. Cooley Goodward LLP (formerly Cooley Godward Castro Huddleson & Tatum), Palo Alto, Calif., 1995—, mgmt. com. mem., 1997—98. V.p. bus. devel., gen. counsel iScribe, Inc., 2001; guest lectr. Boalt Hall Law Sch., Santa Clara Law Sch., Stanford Law Sch. Sr. article editor High Tech. Law Jour., 1987—88. Office: Cooley Godward LLP Five Palo Alto Sq 3000 El Camino Real Palo Alto CA 94306-2155 Office Phone: 650-843-5000. E-mail: bkosacz@cooley.com.

KOSAR, KEVIN RICHARD, writer, consultant; b. Akron, Ohio, Mar. 15, 1970; s. Michael Henry and Shirley Rae Kosar; m. Laura Hoguet, June 19, 2004. BA, Ohio State U., 1993; MA, NYU, 1995, PhD, 2003. Lectr., adviser to pres. Met. Coll. of N.Y., N.Y.C., 2002—03; analyst in am. nat. govt. Congl. Rsch. Svc., Washington, 2003—. Lectr. in pub. policy NYU, N.Y.C., 2002—03. Editor: (nonfiction book) Bridging the Gap: Higher Education and Career-Centered Welfare Reform, 2003; author: Failing Grades: Education Standards and Federal Politics, 2003. Fellow, Lynde and Henry Bradley Found., 1993—94, 1997—98; Presdl. Mgmt. Fellow, U.S. Govt., 2003—05. Mem.: Am. Polit. Sci. Assn., Assn. of Pub. Policy Analysis and Mgmt. Achievements include research in the governance of governmental entities. Home: 617 F St NE Washington DC 20002 Office: Congl Rsch Svc 101 Independence Ave SE Washington DC 20540 Office Phone: 202-707-3968.

KOSASKY, HAROLD JACK, fertility researcher; b. Winnipeg, Man., Can., Oct. 19, 1927; s. Jack and Lillian (Resnick) K.; m. Shirley Anne Johnston, Sept. 3, 1955; children: Julia, Leah, Robert. BA, U. Manitoba, Can., 1948; MD, U. Manitoba, 1953. Diplomate Am. Bd. Ob-gyn.; lic. Coll Physicians and Surgeons Can., Med. Coun. Can., Ky. State Bd. Health, Idaho State Bd. Health, Mass. Bd. Registration in Medicine. Intern Deer Lodge VA and Grace Hosps., Winnipeg, Man., Can., 1952-53; resident in gen. surgery Col. Belcher Hosp., Calgary, Alta., Can., 1953-54; resident in psychiatry Warren (Pa.) State Hosp., 1955-56; jr. asst. resident, asst. resident, sr. resident in ob-gyn. Chgo. Lying-In Hosp., 1956-59; exch. fellow in ob-gyn. Newcastle Gen. Hosp., U. Durham, Eng., 1959-60; asst. and assoc. prof. U. Louisville Sch. Med., 1961-65; asst. and assoc. in ob-gyn. various hosps., Boston, 1966-81; gynecologist, obstetrician Boston Hosp. for Women, 1965-81; gynecologist Brigham & Women's Hosp., Boston, 1981—; instr. ob-gyn. Harvard U., 1965—; pres., CEO Boston Rheology, 2000—. Cons. Ovutime, Boston, 1972-82; pres. Saltime Co., 1994, chmn. 1999-2000; asst. vis. surgeon Boston City Hosp., 1967-69; mem. Ky. Govs. Task Force on Mental Retardation, 1964-65, Com. on Malignancy, chmn., 1963-65; CEO, pres. Boston Rheology, 2000—. Contbr. articles to profl. jours.; co-inventor Ovutime; inventor Saltime Ovulation group of instruments. Fellow ACS, Royal Coll. Surgeons of Can. (cert.), Royal Soc. Health, Boston Obstetric Soc. (emeritus); mem. AAAS, Gen. Med. Coun. Gt. Britain (lic.), Royal Coll. Obstetricans and Gynecologists, Assn. Prof. Ob-gyn., Louisville Obstet. and Gynecol. Soc. (sec., treas. 1962-65), Louisville Med. Forum (v.p.). Clubs: Harvard. Episcopalian. Office: Ste 207 830 Boylston St Chestnut Hill MA 02467 Office Phone: 617-556-6680.

KOSCHEYEV, VICTOR S., emergency physician, researcher; s. Semon M. Koscheyev and Polina I. Pavlova; m. Margarita A. Volostnikova, Mar. 24, 1962; 1 child, Inna Linder. MD, PhD, Inst. of Biophysics, Moscow, DSc, 1979. Mem. Med. Acad. of Sci. (Russia), 1986. Head dept. human protection Inst. of Biophysics, Moscow, 1975—89; dir. Ctr. for Disaster Medicine, Moscow, 1989—92; dept. head Ministry Health, Moscow, 1991—92; prof. and fellow Radiobiology Rsch. Inst., Bethesda, 1993—94; lab. head health and human performance in extreme environments U. of Minn., Mpls., 1995—. Cons. 3M, Mpls., 1987—92. Contbr. articles to profl. pubs. Chmn. Nat. Commn. Sci. Degree Certification, Moscow, 1988—92. Recipient Nat. prize, U.S.S.R., 1979, Nat. medal, 1987, 1988; grantee, NASA, 1995—98, 3M Corp., 1998, NASA, 1999—2002, 2003—05, U. Minn., 2002-2004. Mem.: Aerospace Med. Assn., World Assn. for Disaster and Emergency Medicine (assoc.). Office: U Minn 1901 University Ave SE Minneapolis MN 55455 E-mail: kosch002@umn.edu.

KOSCHMANN, J. VICTOR, history professor, academic program director; Student, Lewis and Clark Coll., 1960-62; BA in Social Scis., Internat. Christian U., Tokyo, 1965; MA in Internat. Studies, Sophia U., Tokyo, 1971; PhD in History, U. Chgo., 1980. Translator, assoc. editor Japan Interpreter, Tokyo, 1971-77; Asian studies instr. Sophia U., Tokyo, 1975-76; social sci. lectr. U. Chgo., 1978-80; asst. prof. Japanese history Cornell U., Ithaca, N.Y., 1980-86, assoc. prof. Japanese history, 1986-94, prof. Japanese history, 1994—, dir. East Asia program. Fulbright fellow, vis. rsch. assoc. faculty law and politics Rikkyo U., Tokyo, 1983-84; vis. lectr. Internat. U. Japan, Niigata, 1983-84; vis. prof. Kyoto Ctr. for Japanese Studies, 1990-91; guest prof. faculty lit., U. Kyoto, 1990-91; vis. rschr. Tokyo U. Fgn. Studies, 1995-96; vis. prof. Japanese studies Nat. U. Singapore, 1999; cons. CBS News, N.Y. Times, Tokyo Broadcasting Sys.; manuscript and proposal reader for numerous instns., including Cambridge U. Press, Princeton U. Press, Cornell U. Press, Calif. U. Press, N.C. U. Press, Cornell East Asia Papers series, Sociol. Forum, East Asia Cultures Critique, Jour. Asian Studies, Pacific Affairs, Jour. Japanese Studies, Columbia East Asian Inst., Social Scis. and Humanities Rsch. Coun. Can., NEH, others; lectr., panel mem., participant NEH Seminar on Japanese Intellectual History, Hawaii, 1976, SSRC/ACLS, Monterey, 1978, Assn. for Asian Studies conv., Toronto, 1981, Cornell U., 1981-83, 85, 87-89, U. Chgo., 1982, 85, McGill U., Montreal, 1982, Harvard U., 1983, U. Calif., Berkeley, 1983, Hokkaido Nat. U., Sapporo, Japan, 1984, Japan Fgn. Svc. Tng. Inst., Tokyo, 1984, U. Seiji Kenkyukai, Atami, Japan, 1984, Rikkyo U. Internat. Symposium, Tokyo, 1985, Am. Hist. Assn., N.Y.C., 1985, San Francisco, 1989, Assn. Asian Studies, Boston, 1987, Chgo., 1990, Duke U., 1988, Smithsonian Instn., Airlie, Va., 1988, Sweet Briar Coll., 1989, Harvard U., 1989, U. Calif., San Diego, 1989, Columbia U., 1989, SUNY, Binghamton, 1990, Hokkaido U., 1991, U. Mich., 1993, Princeton U., 1994, U. Wash., 1995, Heidelberg, 1995, Rikkyo U., Tokyo, 1996, UCLA, 1997, Nat. U. Singapore, 1999, Australia Nat. U., 2001, others. Author: The Mito Ideology: Discourse, Reform and Insurrection in Late Tokugawa Japan, 1790-1864, 1987, Revolution and Subjectivity in Postwar Japan, 1997; editor: Authority and the Individual in Japan: Citizen Protest in Historical Perspective, 1978, Conflict in Modern Japanese History: The Neglected Tradition, 1982, International Perspectives in Yanagita Kunio and Japanese Folklore Studies, 1985, Total War and Modernization, 1998; contbr. articles to profl. jours. Fellow U. Chgo., 1976-79, Ctr. for Far Eastern Studies, 1978, 1979-80, Japan Found., 1979, 95-96, Cornell U., 1985-86; grantee Social Sci. Rsch. Coun., 1983-84, NEH, 1987-88, 92, 1983, Japan-U.S. Edn. Commn., 1983-84, Cornell U., 1984-85, 91, Japan Found., 1989, 94, Assn. for Asian Studies, 1985. Office: Cornell Univ Hist Dept 320 Mcgraw Hall Ithaca NY 14853-4601

KOSCIELAK, JERZY, research scientist; b. Lodz, Poland, Sept. 6, 1930; s. Jozef and Regina (Pokrzywa) K.; m. Anna Kitaszewska, 1969 (div. 1974); 1 child, Katarzyna. MB, Med. Acad., Warsaw, Poland, 1953, MD, 1960, DrSci, 1966. Asst. dept. physiol. chemistry Med. Acad., Warsaw, 1950-51; asst. and sr. asst. dept. biochemistry Inst. of Hematology, Warsaw, 1951-67; rsch. fellow Harvard Coll., Cambridge, 1964-65; head immunochem. lab. Inst. of Hematology, Warsaw, 1968-69, head dept. biochemistry, 1969—2002. Sci. sec. Inst. of Hematology, Warsaw, 1969-97, dir., rsch. 1997—, prof., 1973—. Editor-in-chief Acta Haematologica Polonica jour., 1976-85; contbr. articles to profl. jours. Mem. Polish Biochem. Soc. (chmn. Warsaw divsn. 1967-69), Forum of Carbohydrates Coming of Age (FCCA), Polish Acad. Sci., Internat. Glycoconjugate Orgn. (Polish rep. 1988—, pres. 1993-95), Found. for Glycobiology Glyco XII (founder, pres. 1993—). Avocation: history. Office: Inst of Hematology Chocimska 5 00957 Warsaw Poland Office Phone: 004822 8489515. Business E-Mail: kosci@atos.warman.com.pl.

KOSE, SAMET, psychiatrist; b. Gaziantep, Turkey, Oct. 10, 1966; s. Muhammed Selim and Ayse Kose; m. Nurgun Uckan, Sept. 3, 1994; 1 child, Omay Ege. MD, Hacettepe U., Ankara, Turkey, 1989. Lic. specialist in psychiatry Republic of Turkey Ministry of Health. Gen. practitioner emergency svc. Birecik State Hosp., S. Urfa, Turkey, 1990—91; resident in psychiatry dept. psychiatry Dokuz Eylul U., Faculty of Medicine, Izmir, Turkey, 1991—96; staff psychiatrist Baskent U. Zubeyde Hanim Edn. and Rsch. Ctr., Izmir, 1996—99; postdoctoral fellow in psychiat. neuroimaging Med. U. of S.C., Charleston, 2000—. Onsite rsch. coord. Med. U. of S.C., Charleston, 2001—05. Author: (poetry book) E. E. Cummings: A Profile of a Poet. Recipient Best Rsch. Study award, Bull. Clin Psychopharmacology, 2005, Grant-in-Kind, Ctr. for Advanced Imaging at Med. U. of S.C., 2001—05, Young Investigator award, NARSAD, 2003, Scholars award, Health Emotions Rsch. Inst., Jr. Investigators Rsch. Colloquium award, APA, 2005; grantee, NIH, 2001—05, Nat. Alliance for Rsch. on Schizophrenia and Depression, 2003—05, NIH/NICHD, 2004—05. Mem.: Am. Psychiatry Assn., Turkish Psychiatry Assn., Turkish Med. Assn., E.E. Cummings Soc. Office: Med U of SC Rm 502 N 67 President St Charleston SC 29425 Office Phone: 843-792-9222. Office Fax: 843-792-5702.

KOSEK, WAYNE RICHARD, retired secondary school educator; b. Chgo., Aug. 11, 1946; s. Louis Frank and Alice Lorraine (Jerabek) Kosek; m. Susan Jean Schikora, June 1971 (div. June 1980); 1 child, Kersten; m. Konnie Gale Lorenz Benedict, Mar. 19, 1982; children: Derek, Jenna. BS in Edn., Ill. State U., 1964; MS in Edn., No. Ill. U., 1986. Cert. secondary edn. tchr. Ill. Tchr. Cmty. HS, West Chicago, Ill., 1968—2005; ret., 2005. Contbr. articles to profl. jours. Parent rep. Strikers-Fox Valley F.C., Batavia, Ill., 1992—94, bd. dirs., 1994; computer cmty. chair Louise White PTO, Batavia, 1993—94. Mem.: NEA, Ill. Assn. Tchrs. English, Nat. Coun. Tchrs. English/Interdisciplinary (Tchr. of Excellence award 2004), West Chicago Sch. Tchrs. Assn. (v.p. 1989—93, pres. 1993—97), Ill. Edn. Assn. Avocations: tennis, golf, cross country skiing, reading. Home: 1311 Davey Dr Batavia IL 60510-8626 E-mail: wkosek@comcast.net.

KOSEL, RENÉE, state representative; b. Chgo., Apr. 3, 1943; m. Alfred Kosel; 3 children. BS in Edn., Western Ill. U. Bd. dirs. Lincoln-Way H.S. Dist. Recipient numerous awards. Mem.: local cmty. orgns. Republican. Lutheran. Office: 221-N Stratton Office Bldg Springfield IL 62706 Address: 19201 S LaGrange Rd Ste 204B Mokena IL 60448 Office Phone: 708-479-4200. E-mail: rkosel@aol.com.

KOSHALEK, RICHARD, academic administrator, former museum director, consultant; b. Wausau, Wis., Sept. 20, 1941; s. H. Martin and Ethel A. (Hochtritt) K.; m. Elizabeth J. Briar, July 1, 1967; 1 child, Anne Elizabeth. Student, U. Wis., 1960-61, MA, 1965-67; BA, U. Minn., 1965. Curator Walker Art Ctr., Mpls., 1967-72; asst. dir. NEA, Washington, 1972-74; dir. Ft. Worth Art Mus., 1974-76, Hudson River Mus., Westchester, N.Y., 1976-80, Mus. Contemporary Art, L.A., 1980-99, Pasadena Design Ctr.; pres. art ctr. Coll. of Design, Pasadena, Calif., 1999—. Mem. Pres.' Coun. on Arts, Yale U., New Haven, Conn., 1989-94; mem. internat. bd. Biennale di Venezia, Italy, 1992-93; mem. internat. adv. bd. Wexner Ctr., Ohio State U., Columbus, 1990—; mem. com. of assesors The Tate Gallery of Art, London; mem. internat. jury Philip Morris Art award, 1996; commr. Kwangju Biennale, 1997; mem. screening com. Osaka Triennale, 1997; selection com. Museo de Art Contemporaneo de Monterrey prize, 1997-98; panel chair Phila. Exhbns. Initiative, 1998, fed. adv. com. for internat. exhbns. Nat. Endowment for the Arts, 1997; bd. mem. Am. Fedn. of Arts, 2001—, Internat. Design Conf., Aspen, 2001; juror Chrysler Design awards, 2002, La Biennale De Venezia, 2002; del., panelist, World Econ. Forum, 2002—; cons. in field. Co-curator (exhibitions and books) Panza Collection, 1986, Ad Reinhardt, 1991, Arata Isozaki, 1991, Louis I. Kahn, 1992, Robert Irwin, 1993, At the End of the Century: One Hundred Years of Architecture, 1998, Richard Serra, 1998. Mem. Chase Manhattan Bank Art Com., N.Y.C., 1986—; chmn. architect selection Walt Disney Concert Hall, L.A., 1988-90; mem. adv. Neighborhood Revitalization Bd. for Pres. Clinton, Little Rock, Ark., 1993; bd. dirs. Am. Ctr. in Paris, 1993—. Recipient Parkinson Spirit of Urbanism award U. So. Calif. Archtl. Guild, 1996; NEA fellow, 1972, Durfee Found. fellow, 1992, Design fellow IBM, 1984; Chevalier Des Arts et Lettres, French Govt., 1999. Mem. Am. Assn. Mus. Dirs. Office: Office of the President Art Center Coll of Design 1700 Lida St Pasadena CA 91103*

KOSHIMITSU, KEIKO, artist; b. Tokyo, Sept. 21, 1958; arrived in U.S., 1984; d. Minoru and Sumiko Koshimitsu; m. Aldo E. Garay, June 1, 1995; children: Kazuki Aldo Garay Jr., Rina Angelica Garay. BFA, Tama Art U., Tokyo, 1981; MA in Edn., Yokohama (Japan) Nat. U., 1983. Supr. The Bank of Yokohama, N.Y.C., 1997—2002, asst. v.p., 2003. One-woman shows include JTB Equitable Ctr., N.Y., 1992, exhibitions include Tokyo Prefecture Mus., 1979, 1980, 1982, Bronx Mus., N.Y., 1994, exhibited in group shows at Sanaa Gallery, Tokyo, 1981, Sumitomo Bldg. Gallery, 1981, Kanagawa Prefecture Gallery, Yokohama, 1982, Yokohama Gallery, 1982, 1983, 1984, 1985, 1986, Mitsubishi Gallery, Tokyo, 1983, Cast Iron Gallery, N.Y., 1992, 1996, El Bohio C.C., 1992, Tenri Gallery, 1992, Klein Landaw Fine Arts, 1992, Japan Consulate, 1993, 2004, Walter Wickiser Gallery, N.Y., 1993, 1995, 1999, 2000, 2001, Gallery One Twenty Eight, 1994, Liver House, 1994, Krasdale Gallery, 1995, Ise Gallery, 1996, 1997, Kaoru Gallery, Tokyo, 1997, Broome St. Gallery, N.Y., 1999, New Century Artist Gallery, 2000, Caelum Gallery, 2001, Tenri Gallery, 2001, 2002, 2003, 2004. Mem.: Japanese Artists Assn. (treas. 1991—99, pres. 2000—), Tama Art U. Alumni Assn. (v.p., treas. 2003). Home: 175 Maplewood Ave Bogota NJ 07603 Office: Japanese Artist Assn NY Inc 175 Maplewood Ave Bogota NJ 07603 E-mail: keikokoshimitsu@optonline.net.

KOSHIOL, JILL, epidemiologist; d. Thomas and Brenda Covert; m. Paul Koshiol. BS, BA, William Jewell Coll., 1999; MSPH, U. N.C., 2002. Lab. technician Flexcell Internat. Corp., Hillsborough, NC, 2000—00; tchg. asst. dept. biology U. N.C., Chapel Hill, 2000—00; rsch. asst. dept. epidemiology U. N.C. Sch. Pub. Health, 2001—02, study mgr. dept. epidemiology, 2002—03, tchg. asst. dept. epidemiology, 2003—03, rsch. asst. dept. epidemiology, 2003—04; rsch. asst. GlaxoSmithKline, WorldWide Epidemiology, Rsch. Triangle Pk., 2001—. Composer (musician). Grantee, Nat. Cancer Inst., 2001—05. Mem.: Epidemiology Student Orgn. (treas. 2002—03), Alpha Epsilon Lambda. E-mail: koshiol@email.unc.edu.

KOSHLAND, DANIEL EDWARD, JR., biochemist, educator; b. N.Y.C., Mar. 30, 1920; s. Daniel Edward and Eleanor (Haas) Koshland; m. Marian Elliott, May 25, 1945 (dec. 1997); children: Ellen, Phyllis, James, Gail, Douglas; m. Yvonne Cyr, Aug. 27, 2000. BS, U. Calif., Berkeley, 1941; PhD, U. Chgo., 1949; PhD (hon.), Weizmann Inst. Sci., 1984, U. Mass., 1992, Ohio State U., 1995, Brandeis U., 2000, Scripps Inst., 2003; ScD (hon.), Carnegie Mellon U., 1985; LLD (hon.), Simon Fraser U., 1986; LHD (hon.), Mt. Sinai U.; LLD (hon.), U. Chgo., 1992. Chemist Shell Chem. Co., Martinez, 1941—42; rsch. assoc. Manhattan Dist. U. Chgo., 1942—44; group leader Oak Ridge Nat. Labs., 1944—46; postdoctoral fellow Harvard, 1949—51; 51staff Brookhaven Nat. Lab., Upton, NY, 1951—65; affiliate Rockefeller Inst., N.Y.C., 1958—65; prof. biochemistry U. Calif., Berkeley, 1965—97, prof. molecular biology, 1997—, chmn. dept., 1973—78. Fellow All Souls Oxford U., 1972; Phi Beta Kappa lectr., 76; John Edsall lectr. Harvard U., 1980, Robert Woodward vis. prof., 86; William H. Stein lectr. Rockefeller U., 1985; G. N. Lewis lectr.U U. Calif., Berkeley. Author: Bacterial Chemotaxis as a Model Behavioral System, 1980; mem. editl. bd. jours.: Accounts Chem. Rsch., Jour. Chemistry, Jour. Biochemistry; editor: jour. Procs. NAS, 1980—85, Sci. mag., 1985—95. Recipient T. Duckett Jones award, Helen Hay Whitney Found., 1977, Nat. Medal of Sci., NSF, 1990, Merck award, Am. Soc. Biochemistry and Molecular Biology, 1991, Westheimer award, Harvard U., 2002, Clark Kerr award, U. Calif., 1994, Lasker Found. award, 1998; fellow Guggenheim Found., 1972. Mem.: Acad. Forum (chmn.), Am. Acad. Arts and Scis. (coun.), Am. Philos. Soc., Am. Chem. Soc. (Edgar Fahs Smith award 1979, Pauling award 1979, Rosentiel award 1984, Waterford prize 1984, Seaborg medal 2000), Royal Swedish Acad. Scis. (hon.), Japanese Biochem. Soc. (hon.), NAS, Am. Soc. Biol. Chemists (pres.), Alpha Omega Alpha (hon.). Home: 3991 Happy Valley Rd Lafayette CA 94549-2423 Office: U Calif Dept Molecular Cell Biology 406 Barker Hall #3202 Berkeley CA 94720-3202 Office Phone: 510-642-0416. E-mail: dek@berkeley.edu.

KOSHMANOVA, TETYANA S., education educator, researcher; d. Sergey Nikolayevich Koshmanov and Austra Arnoldovna Averkiyeva; 1 child, Olena Y. PhD, Inst. for Rsch. on Prof. Edn., Acad. Pedagogical Scis., Kyiv, Ukraine, 2001, PhD, 2002; habilitated D of Pedagogical Sciences, Inst. for Rsch. on Prof. Edn., Acad. Pedagogical Scis., 2003. Cert. profl. edn. of tchrs. Highest Attestation Commn. of Ukraine, 2003. Prof. Ivan Franko Nat. U., L'viv, Ukraine, 1991—; asst. prof. Western Mich. U., Kalamazoo, 2001—. Prof., dissertation sci. adviser dept. pedagogy Ivan Franko Nat. U. L'viv, 2001—; presenter in field. Author: The Development of Teacher Education in the U.S.A (1960 1998), 1999, On the Way to Innovative Teacher Education:

Michigan State University, 2000, Models of Teaching. Book of Methods for Teacher Education Students - Prospective Teachers, 2002; co-editor (with C. Clark): Culture and Community in Learning to Teach: Ukraine and the U.S.A., 2000; contbr. articles to profl. jours. Fellow Contemporary Issues, IREX, Dept. of State, 2000; grantee Fulbright, 1996—97; Publ. grantee, Fulbright, Dept. of State, 1999, Travel grantee, 2003, Publ. grantee, IREX Dept. of State, 2003, FRACAS rsch. grantee, Western Mich. U., 2004. Mem.: AAUP, Peace Edn., Am. Ednl. Rsch. Assn., Centarl Eurasian Studies Soc. Office: Western Michigan Univ 2431 Sangren Hall College of Education Kalamazoo MI 49008 Office Phone: 269-387-3508. Office Fax: 269-387-2882. Business E-Mail: tkoshman@wmich.edu.

KOSHY, ACHAMMA G., chemistry educator; b. Venmoney, Kerala, India, May 25, 1948; arrived in US, 1981; d. Cherian Jacob and Mary John; m. George Koshy, Nov. 15, 1971; children: Rachel Koshy Dong, Renny K. Bagchi, Ruben G. BSc, Ravishankar U., 1967, MSc, 1969. Cert. Secondary Tchr. Northeastern U. Ill., 1986. Chemistry lectr. Cochin Coll., U. Kerala, India, 1971—81; chemistry tchr. St. Scholastica HS, Chgo., 1981—82, St. Ignatius Coll. Prep. Sch., Chgo., Resurrection HS, Chgo., 1984—, discipline bd. mem. Avocations: reading, gardening, cooking, exercise. Home: 4635 W Birchwood Skokie IL 60076 Office: Resurrection HS 7500 W Talcott Ave Chicago IL 60631-3742

KOSIK, EDWIN MICHAEL, federal judge; b. 1925; BA, Wilkes Coll., Wilkes-Barre, Pa., 1949; LLB, Dickinson Sch. Law, Carlisle, Pa. Asst. U.S. atty. Pa. State Workmen's Compensation Bd., 1953-58, chmn., 1964-69; pvt. practice Needle, Needle & Needle, 1958-64; pres. judge 45th Jud. Dist. Ct. Common Pleas, 1979-86; judge U.S. Dist. Ct. (mid. dist.) Pa., Scranton, 1986—, now sr. judge. Office: US Dist Ct US Courthouse PO Box 856 Scranton PA 18501-0856 Office Phone: 570-207-5730. E-mail: chambers_of_edwin_m._kosik@pamd.uscourts.gov.

KOSKI, WALTER S., chemistry educator, scientist; b. Phila., Dec. 1, 1913; s. Bruno and Helen (Laskowska) Stankiewicz; m. Helen Ireton Tag, May 11, 1940; children— Carol Lee, Ann Louise, Nancy Cheryl, Phyllis Ireton. PhD, Johns Hopkins, 1942. Research chemist Hercules Powder Co., 1942-43; group leader Los Alamos Sci. Lab., 1944-47; physicist Brookhaven Nat. Lab., 1947-48; asso. prof. Johns Hopkins, 1947-55; prof. chemistry Johns Hopkins (Grad. Sch.), 1955—, B.N. Baker prof. chemistry, 1975—, chmn. dept., 1958-69. Fellow Am. Phys. Soc.; mem. Am. Chem. Soc. (merit award Md. sect), Phi Beta Kappa. Office: Johns Hopkins U 3400 N Charles St Baltimore MD 21218-2680

KOSKINEN, JOHN ANDREW, foundation executive; b. Cleve., June 30, 1939; s. Yrjo Alfred and Irja (Danska) K.; m. Patricia Salz, June 15, 1963; children: Jeffrey, Cheryl. BA magna cum laude, Duke U., 1961; JD cum laude, Yale U., 1964; postgrad., Cambridge U., Eng., 1964-65. Bar: Calif. 1965, Conn. 1972. Clk. to presiding judge U.S. Ct. Appeals, Washington, 1965-66; lawyer Gibson, Dunn & Crutcher, L.A., 1966-67; spl. asst. to dep. exec. dir. Nat. Adv. Commn. Civil Disorders (also called Kerner Commn.), Washington, 1967-68; legis. asst. to Mayor John Lindsay N.Y.C., 1968-69; adminstrv. asst. to Senator Abraham Ribinoff Conn., 1969-73; v.p. Palmieri Co., Washington, 1973-77, pres., chief operating officer, 1977-79, pres., chief exec. officer, 1979-94; dep. dir. for mgmt. Office of Mgmt. and Budget, Washington, 1994-97; asst. to Pres., chmn. President's Coun. on Year 2000 Conversion, Washington, 1998-2000; dep. mayor, city adminstr. DC, 2000—03; pres. U.S. Soccer Found., Washington, 2004—. Bd. dirs. AES Corp., 2004—. Mem. Pres.'s Mgmt. Improvement Coun., 1979-80; bd. dirs. Nat. Captioning Inst., 1979-91, chmn., 1986-87, vice-chmn., 1979-86; trustee Coop. Assistance Fund, 1982-93; trustee Duke U., 1985-97, vice chmn. 1993-94, chmn. 1994-97; chmn. Washington 1994 World Cup Commn., 1989-94, Washington Olympic Football Organizing Com., 1993-96; vice chmn. Am. Soccer League, 1987-91; dir. U.S. Soccer Found., 1993-94, 2001—; pres. Washington Met. Area Coun. Govt., 2003. Fellow Nat. Acad. Pub. Adminstrn., Phi Beta Kappa; mem. Duke U. Gen. Alumni Assn. (pres. 1980-81), Soccer Hall of Fame, Va. Avocations: soccer, tennis, music. Office: US Soccer Foundation Ste 210 1050 17th St NW Washington DC 20036 Office Phone: 202-872-6657. Personal E-mail: johnkosk@aol.com.

KOSLOW, JONATHAN L., lawyer; b. N.Y.C., 1953; BA magna cum laude, NYU, 1974; JD, Boston U., 1977; LLM in Estate Planning, U. Miami, 1978. Bar: NY 1978. Ptnr.-in-charge trusts and estates Skadden, Arps, Slate, Meagher & Flom LLP, NYC. Contbr. articles to profl. publs. Mem.: NY State Bar Assn. (mem., trusts and estates law sect.), ABA (mem., real property, probate and trust law sect.). Office: Skadden Arps Slate Meagher & Flom LLP 4 Times Sq New York NY 10036 Office Phone: 212-735-2810. Office Fax: 917-777-2810. Business E-Mail: jkoslow@skadden.com.

KOSLOW, SALLY, editor-in-chief; BA, U. Wis. Editor-in-chief McCall's mag., N.Y.C., 1994—2001; editor-in-chief Lifetime mag. The Hearst Corp., N.Y.C., 2002—, editor Mary Emmerling's Country, 2002—. Office: Lifetime mag The Hearst Corp 1790 Broadway New York NY 10019

KOSLOW, STEPHEN HUGH, health science administrator, pharmacologist; s. Julius and Lillian Koslow; m. Diane Heisler, Aug. 18, 1962; children: Karin, James. BS, Columbia U., 1962; PhD, U. Chgo., 1967. Internat. postdoctoral fellow Swedish Med. Rsch. Coun., Karolinski Inst., 1968-69; pharmacologist, chief neurobiology unit St. Elizabeth's Hosp., Washington, 1970-77; chief biol. rsch. sect. Clin. Rsch. br. NIMH, Rockville, Md., 1975-81, chief Neurosci. Rsch. br., 1981—85, chief Basic Scis. Neurosci. Rsch., 1985—88, dep. dir. divsn. Basic Brain and Behavioral Scis., 1989—90; dir. divsn. Basic and Clin. Neurosci. Rsch. NIMH-NIH, Rockville, 1990—99; assoc. dir., dir. office neuroinformatics NIMH, Rockville, 1999—2004; dir. external rels. Allen Inst. Brain Sci., Washington, 2005—. Project dir. NIHM-CRB Collaborative Program on Psychobiology of Depression-Biol. Study, 1975-85; mem. adv. bd. Tourette Syndrome Assn., Bayside, N.Y., 1984; chair fed. coordinating com. on the Human Brain Project, 1991—; chair neuroinformatics subgroup of Office Econ. Coop. & Devel., Megasci. Forum, Biol. Working Group, 1996-99; co-chair US/EC com. on neuroinformatics, 1998—, chair global sci. forum neuroinformatics working group, 2000-02. Mem. editl. bd. Neuropsychopharmacology, 1987-92, Critical Revs. in Neurobiol., 1991-2004, Human Brain Mapping, 1993-2004, Psychopharm. Bull., 1989-99, Neuroimage; series editor Progress in Neuroinformatics Rsch., 1996-2001, Neuroimage, 1995-2001, CNS Drug Revs., 1995-99, Biomednet, 1999-2003; editor: Databasing the Brain From Data to Knowledge, 2005; assoc. editor Jour. Integrative Neurosci. Recipient NIMH Quality Increase award, 1977-78, Health Adminstr.'s award for Meritorious Achievement, 1986, Pub. Health Svc. Spl. Recognition award, 1992, Alumni Achievement award U. Chgo. Club of Washington, 1995, two Dir.'s awards NIH, 1996, Pres. award Internat. Neural Network Soc., 2001; Swedish Med. Rsch. Coun. internat. postdoctoral fellow, 1968-69, Spl. NATO fellow, 1969. Fellow AAAS, Am. Coll. Neuropsychopharmacology, Am. Coll. Med. Informatics; mem. Am. Soc. for Neurochemistry, Am. Soc. Pharmacology and Exptl. Therapeutics, Collegium Internat. Neuro Psychopharmacologium, Soc. for Neurosci., Soc. Biol. Psychiatry. Office: Allen Inst Brain Sci 551 N 34th St Seattle WA 98103 Office Phone: 206-548-7038. Office Fax: 206-548-7071. Business E-Mail: steveko@aooeninstitute.org.

KOSLYN, PAMELA, lawyer; b. Cleve., Dec. 20, 1960; d. Robert Koslovsky and Edith Berkowitz Weiss. BA in Psychology, Columbia U., 1982; JD, U. So. Calif., 1985. Bar: Calif. 1985, U.S. Ct. Appeals (9th cir.) 1985. Assoc. Herzig & Yanny, L.A., 1986-87, Freshman, Marantz et al, Beverly Hills, Calif., 1987-88, Menes Law Corp., L.A., 1988-90; of counsel Simon & Simon Ltd., Manhattan Beach, Calif., 1990-95, Cohen and Cohen, L.A., 1995—; pvt. practice, L.A., 1990—. Grader Com. Bar Examiners, San Francisco, 1987; media cons. USA Today, People, E! Entertainment, Entertainment Tonight, L.A., 1995—. Exec. prodr., project coord. prodn. screening series featuring films directed by women, Cinewomen Screening Series, 1994-97. Vol. Vols. in Parole, Ventura, Calif., 1987-89, Childhelp USA, L.A., 1998-99. Office: 740 N La Brea Ave Fl 2D Los Angeles CA 90038-3339 Fax: 323-936-6354. E-mail: pkoslyn@pacbell.net.

KOSMOPOULOU, GEORGIA, economics professor; m. Dimitrios Vassilios Papavassiliou. BA, U. Piraeus, Greece, 1989; MS, U. Ill., 1992; PhD, U. Ill., Urbana Champaign, 1996. Vis. asst. prof. Va. Poly. Inst. and State U., Blacksburg, Va., 1996—97; asst. prof. U. Okla., Norman, Okla., 1997—2003, U. Piraeus, Piraeus, Greece, 2003—04; assoc. prof. U. Okla., Norman, Okla., 2003—. Contbr. scientific papers pub. to profl. jour. Office: Univ Okla 729 Elm Ave Norman OK 73019 E-mail: georgiakosm@yahoo.com.

KOSNER, EDWARD A(LAN), editor; b. N.Y.C., July 26, 1937; s. Sidney and Annalee (Fisher) Kosner; m. Alice Nadel, Feb. 1, 1959; children: John Robbins, Anthony William; m. Julie Baumgold, Nov. 19, 1978; 1 child, Lily. BA, CCNY, 1958. CCNY corr. N.Y. Times, 1957—58; rewriteman, asst. city editor N.Y. Post, 1958—63; assoc. editor Newsweek Mag., N.Y.C., 1963—67, gen. editor, 1967—69, nat. affairs editor, 1969—72, asst. mng. editor, 1972, mng. editor, 1973—75, editor, 1975—79, N.Y. Mag., 1980—93, pub., 1986—91, pres., 1991—93; editor-in-chief Esquire Mag., N.Y.C., 1993—97; editor N.Y. Sunday Daily News, N.Y.C., 1998—99; editor-in-chief N.Y. Daily News, N.Y.C., 2000—03. Recipient various journalism awards. Mem.: Am. Soc. Mag. Editors (pres. 1984—86, exec. com.), Century Club. Personal E-mail: edsquire@aol.com.

KOSOBAYASHI, KEVAN TAKASHI, music educator; b. St. Louis Park, Minn., May 1, 1971; s. Tomoyoshi and Sumiko Kosobayashi; m. Megumi Kabayama, June 21, 2003. B of Music, Northwestern U., 1994; MA, Columbia U., 2000. Cert. Ill. State Bd. Edn. Dir. orch. Batavia Pub. Schs., Ill., 1994—95; asst. lang. tchr. Hiroshima Bd. Edn., Japan, 1995—97; dir. orch. Schaumburg High Sch., Ill., 1998—2004, Buffalo Grove High Sch., 2004—; dir., conductor Schaumburg Youth Orch., Chamber Strings, Ill., 2002—. Recipient Elsie Eckstein award, Northwestern U., Evanston, Ill., 1989—93, George Patterson award, 1994. Mem.: Music Educators Nat. Conf., Am. String Tchrs. Assn., Pi Kappa Lambda. Avocation: travel. Office: Buffalo Grove High Sch 1100 W Dundee Rd Buffalo Grove IL 60089 Office Phone: 847-718-4047. E-mail: kevan.kosobayas@d214.org.

KOSOVICH, DUSHAN RADOVAN, psychiatrist; b. Trepca, Niksic, Yugoslavia, Dec. 23, 1926; came to U.S., 1967, naturalized, 1972; s. Radovan Dj and Djurdja K. (Bacovic) K.; children— Jasmine, Nicholas. MD, Belgrade U., 1954, postgrad., 1954-57; certificate, Am. Inst. for Psychoanalysis and Postgrad. Center, 1972. Resident in neuropsychiatry, Belgrade, Yugoslavia, 1954-57; resident in psychiatry Bellevue Med. Center, N.Y.C., 1957-59, McGill U., Montreal, Que., Can., 1965-67; founder, chief neuropsychiatric service for inpatient and outpatients Gen. Hosp., Titograd, Montenegro, Yugoslavia, 1960-65; staff psychiatrist Bellevue Med. Center, N.Y.C., 1967-73; dir. inpatient psychiat. service Lincoln Hosp., Bronx, N.Y., 1973-75; chief inpatient services Methodist Hosp., Bklyn., 1975-76, acting dir. psychiat dept., 1976-78, dir., 1978-84; pvt. practice N.Y.C., 1984—. Clin. asso. prof. dept. psychiatry Downstate Med. Center, State U. N.Y., 1975—; Psychoanalyst Karen Horney Psychoanalytic Inst., N.Y.C. Author: Stress, 1989, Optimistic Psychoanalysis, 1989, It Drives Me Crazy, 1997, The Stress in the Vortex of Global Anomie, 2000, The Paradoxes of Dushan Kosovich, 2003; contbr. articles to profl. jours. Served with Yugoslavian Army, 1944-46 Recipient City of Titograd award for best sci. achievement, 1964 Fellow Assn. for Advancement Psychoanalysis, Karen Horney Psychoanalytic Inst. and Ctr., Am. Acad. Psychoanalysis; mem. Am. Acad. Clin. Psychiatrists, N.Am. Acad. for Auricular Medicine, Am. Acad. Psychiatry and Law, World Psychiat. Assn., Am. Yugoslav Med. Soc. Home: Trump World Tower Apt 21D 845 United Nations Plz New York NY 10017 Office: 333 E 46th St Apt 1E New York NY 10017 E-mail: dkosovich@msn.com.

KOSOWSKY, NINA, secondary school educator; b. Derby, Conn., Feb. 15, 1946; d. Frank and Helen (Statkevich) K. BS, Cen. Conn. State Coll., 1967; MS, U. Bridgeport, Conn., 1968; cert. in reading, So. Conn. State U., 1972. Cert. tchr., Conn. Substitute tchr. Shelton (Conn.) Bd. Edn., 1967-68, Seymour (Conn.) Bd. Edn., 1967-68; with Oxford (Conn.) Bd. Edn., 1968—, remedial reading tchr., 1972—, gifted and talented tchr., 1985-90. Reading curriculum coord. Oxford Bd. Edn., 1981-89; reading cons. 1972—. Rec. sec. com. Three Saints Ch., 1975-89, pres., 1995—; rec. sec. Fellowship of Orthodox Chs. in Conn., 1999-2002, pres., 2002—. Mem. Oxford Edn. Assn., Conn. Edn. Assn., NEA, Internat. Reading Assn. Russian Orthodox. Avocations: travel, arts and crafts, reading.

KOSS, LEOPOLD G., pathologist, educator; b. Gdansk, Poland, Oct. 2, 1920; arrived in U.S., 1947, naturalized, 1952; s. Abram and Rose (Merenholc) Kon; m. Lydia Palla; children: Michael S., Andrew C., Richard P. MD, U. Berne, Switzerland, 1946; Doctorate (hon.), Pomeranian Med. Acad., Poland, 2002. Intern, Lincoln Hosp., NYC, 1947-48; tng. pathology St. Gallen, Switzerland, 1946-47, Kings County Hosp., Bklyn., 1949-52; instr. pathology LI U. Coll. Medicine, NY, 1949-52; mem. staff Meml. Hosp. Cancer and Allied Diseases, NYC, 1952-70, attending pathologist, 1961-70, chief cytology svc., 1961-70; pathologist-in-chief Sinai Hosp. Balt., 1970-73; prof., chmn. dept. pathology Montefiore Hosp., Med. Ctr. Albert Einstein Coll. Medicine, Bronx, NY, 1973-92, prof., chair emeritus, 1993—. Hon. prof. pathology Severance Med. Coll., Seoul, Korea, 1956; assoc. mem. Sloan-Kettering Inst. Cancer Research, NYC, 1957-70; assoc. prof. pathology Sloan-Kettering div. Postgrad. Sch. Med. Sci., Cornell U., 1957-70; prof. pathology Jefferson Med. Coll., Phila., 1970-73; clin. prof. pathology U. Md. Med. Sch., 1971-73; vis. pathologist James Ewing Hosp., NYC, 1952-60; former cons. pathologist NY State Dept. Health, Hosp. Spl. Surgery, NYC; cons. pathologist Walter Reed Army Med. Ctr., Nassau County Med. Ctr.; Frost lectr., Balt., 1999. Author: Diagnostic Cytology and Its Histopathologic Bases, 4th rev. edit. 1992, Tumors of the Urinary Bladder, 1975, Supplement, 1984, Aspiration Biopsy: Cytologic Interpretation and Histologic Bases, 2nd rev. edit. 1992, Introduction to Gynecologic Cytology, 1999; editor: Advances in Clinical Cytology, Vol. I, 1981, Vol. II, 1984, Papillomaviruses and Human Diseases, 1987, Errors and Pitfalls in Diagnostic Cytology, 1997; contbr. over 365 articles to profl. jour. and 40 chpts. to books also monographs. Served to maj. M.C., AUS, 1955-57. Recipient Wien award Papanicolaou Cancer Inst., 1963, Alfred P. Sloan award cancer rsch., 1964, Fred Stewart award, 1984, Vandenbergne-Hill award, 1984, Meritorious medal U. Brussels, 1987, Jurzykowski award, 1991, Disting. Pathologist award US and Can. Acad. Pathology, 2001, Disting. Pathologist award Assn. Pathology Chairs, 2002, Doctor Honoris Causa, Pomeranian Med. Acad., Poland, 2002. Fellow: AAAS, Internat. Acad. Cytology (Goldblatt award 1962, Kazumasa Masubuchi Life-Time Achievement award in clin. cytology 1995), Coll. Am. Pathologists, Am. Soc. Clin. Pathology, Royal Coll. Pathologists (hon. Found. lectr. 1997), Royal Coll. Pathologists (hon.); mem.: AMA, Am. Soc. for Colposcopy and Cervical Pathology (Disting. Svc. award 1996), Internat. Soc. of Urol. Pathology (F.K. Mostofi Disting. Svc. award 1995), German Acad. Sci. (Leopoldina), Peruvian Soc. Ob-Gyn., Polish Soc. Pathology, Japanese Soc. Pathology, Argentinian Soc. Cytology, Mex. Soc. Cytology, Brit. Soc. Clin. Cytology (hon.), Royal Acad. Medicine Spain (corr.), Korean Med. Assn., NY State Soc. Pathology (Lansky-Ratner award 1989), NY Pathology Soc. (pres. 1985—87, Middleton-Goldsmith lectr. 1992), Internat. Acad. Pathology (Maude Abbott lectr. 1989), Am. Soc. Cytology (pres. 1962, Papanicolaou award 1966), James Ewing Soc., Am. Soc. Exptl. Pathology (Gold Cane award 1993). Office: Montefiore Med Ctr 111 E 210th St Bronx NY 10467-2401 Office Phone: 718-920-5185. Business E-Mail: lkoss@montefiore.org.

KOSS, ROSABEL STEINHAUER, retired health and physical education educator; b. Phila., Sept. 3, 1913; d. Arthur H. and Agnes (Temple) Steinhauer; m. Franklyn C. Koss, July 6, 1947 (dec. 1987); children: C. Lynn Knauff, Susan Kreiner, Carolyn Ruef, Rosalind Diehl. BS, Coll. of N.J., 1935; MA, Columbia U., N.Y.C., 1942; DEd, Columbia U., 1964; diploma, Hasmors Gym Leaders Inst., Lilsved, Sweden, 1970, Pensioner's Program, Lilsved, 1972. Cert. health edn. specialist, 1989. Supr. health and phys. edn. Flemington (N.J.) Pub. Schs., 1935-37; tchr. health and phys. edn. Ridgewood (N.J.) High Sch., 1937-40, Passaic Valley Regional High Sch., Little Falls, N.J., 1940-48; asst. prof. Montclair State Coll., Upper Montclair, N.J., 1958-61, Upsala Coll., East Orange, NJ, 1964—71; assoc. to full prof. Ramapo Coll of N.J., Mahwah, N.J., 1971-84, dir. tchr. edn., 1974-79, prof. emeritus, 1985; adj. prof. Richard Stockton Coll. of N.J., Pomona, 1985-95. Asst. sport attachee Royal Swedish Embassy, N.Y.C., 1964-74. Author: (with others) Dance for Older Adults, 1988, Mature Stuff. Physical Activity for Older Adults, 1989, Exercise for the Older Adult, 1998; contbr. articles profl. jours. Mem. Little Falls (N.J.) Bd. Edn., 1954-63; trustee, treas. Bergen County (N.J.) Ret. Sr. Vol. Program, 1979-84; mem. recreation adv. com. Stone Harbor Bd. Health, v.p., 1995; mem. Cape May County Freeholders Adv. Commn. on Women, 1986—, Cape May County Human Svcs. Adv. Coun., 1989—; vestrywoman St. Mary's Episcopal Ch., Stone Harbor; mem. N.J. Commn. on Aging, 1992-98, chmn., 1996-98; mem. Health Promotion and Planning Lab, State of N.J., 1998; del. White House Conf. on Aging, 1995; mem. adv. com. Cape May Human Svcs. Named Gerontologist of Yr., Soc. on Aging N.J., 1993; named to Athletic Hall of Fame, Coll. N.J., 1980, Trenton State Coll. Alumni Athletic Hall of Fame, 1987, Nat. Women's Wall of Fame, 1994, Athletic Hall of Fame Ramapo Coll. N.J., 2003; recipient Athletic Alumni Women's award, Coll. N.J., 1976, citation, State of N.J. Senate and Gen. Assembly, 1994, Cape Women's Resource Honor award, 1994, Alice Stokes Paul award, Cape May County Adv. Commn. on Status Women, 2003; grantee, The Royal Swedish Consulate, N.Y.C., 1968, 1970, 1972. Fellow: Assn. for Gerontology in Higher Edn.; mem.: AAUW, AAHPERD (life; coun. on aging and adult devel., profl. achievement award, N.J. 1973, honor award fellow 1979, merit award Ea. Dist. 1980, disting. leadership award 1996, Rosabel Koss award named in her honor), Vols. in Medicine, Internat. Soc. Comparative Phys. Edn. and Sport, Nat. Coun. on Aging, N.J. AHPERD (Disting. Leadership award), Gerontol. Soc. N.J. (parliamentarian 1988—89), Wetlands Inst. (docent), Cape May County LWV, Stone Harbor Women's Civic Club, Garden Club. Avocations: travel, gardening, salt marsh ecology, swimming. Home: 150 91st St Stone Harbor NJ 08247-2016 Home (Winter): 30 Andrews Ave The Grove Apt 0 Delray Beach FL 33483 Personal E-mail: rosabelk@fcc.net.

KOSSAR, RONALD STEVEN, lawyer; b. Ellenville, N.Y., May 30, 1948; s. Emanuel and Helen (Panken) K.; m. Sandra Perlman, Aug. 25, 1973. BA cum laude, Boston U., 1970; JD, Am. U., 1973. Bar: N.Y. 1974, D.C. 1974, U.S. Dist. Ct. (no. dist.) N.Y. 1974, U.S. Tax Ct. 1974, U.S. Ct. Appeals D.C. 1974. Tax law specialist Office Asst. Commr. (Tech.), IRS, Washington, 1973-75; sole practice Middletown, NY, 1976—. Dir. Newburgh (N.Y.) Realty Corp. Mem. ABA, N.Y. State Bar Assn., Orange County Bar Assn., Middletown Bar Assn., D.C. Bar. Jewish. Office: 402 E Main St Middletown NY 10940-2516 Office Phone: 845-343-5111. Office Fax: 845-343-5222. Business E-Mail: rsklaw@warwick.net.

KOSSLER, WILLIAM JOHN, physics professor; b. Charleston, S.C., Mar. 26, 1937; s. William John and Lois Covil (Gordon) K.; m. Margaret O'Neil; children: Neil, William, Paul. BS, MIT, 1959; PhD, Princeton U., 1964. Grad. asst. Princeton (N.J.) U., 1962-64; asst. prof. MIT, Cambridge, Mass., 1966-69, Coll. William & Mary, Williamsburg, Va., 1969-70, assoc. prof., 1970-78, prof. physics, 1978—. Author: Low Magnetic Fields in Anisotropic Super Conductors, 1995; contbr. articles to profl. jours. Fellow Am. Phys. Soc. Avocation: sailing. Home: 496 Burnham Rd Williamsburg VA 23185-4749 Office: PO Box 8795 Williamsburg VA 23187

KOSSLYN, STEPHEN M., psychologist, educator; b. Santa Monica, Calif., Nov. 30, 1948; s. S. Duke and Rhoda Kosslyn; m. Robin S. Rosenberg, Mar. 28, 1982; children: Justin Lewis, David Alan, Nathaniel Solté. BA in Psychology, UCLA, 1970; PhD in Psychology, Stanford U., 1974. Asst. prof. psychology The Johns Hopkins U., 1974-77; assoc. prof. psychology Harvard U., 1977-81; rsch. affiliate of the Ctr. for Cognitive Sci. MIT, 1980-94; assoc. prof. psychology Brandeis U., 1981-82; prof. psychology Harvard U., 1983—, chmn. Dept. Psychology, 2005—; co-dir. James S. McDonnell Found. Summer Inst. in Cognitive Neuroscience, 1987; assoc. psychologist in neurology Mass. Gen. Hosp., 1990—. Vis. asst. prof. psychology U. Calif., Berkeley, 1976; vis. prof. psychology The Johns Hopkins U., 1982-83, Maitre de Conference, Coll. de France, 1997-98; cons. Consulting Statisticians, Inc., 1977-83; mem. governing bd. Cognitive Sci. Soc., 1989-95. Author: Image and Mind, 1980, Ghosts in the Mind's Machine, 1983, Wet Mind: The New Cognitive Neuroscience, 1992, Image and Brain, 1994, Elements of Graph Design, 1994, (with R. Rosenberg) Psychology: The Brain, The Person, The World, 2001, 2d edit., 2003; editor: (with others) Tutorials in Learning and Memory: Essays in Honor of Gordon H. Bower, 1983, Quantitative Analyses of Behavior, Vol. 9: Computational and Clinical Approaches to Pattern Recognition and Concept Formation, 1989, An Invitation to Cognitive Science: Visual Cognition and Action, 1990, Essays in Honor of William K. Estes, 1992, Frontiers in Cognitive Neuroscience, 1992, The Neuropsychology of Mental Imagery, 1996; contbr. articles to profl. jours. Recipient Boyd R. McCandless Young Scientist award divsn. 7 APA, 1978, Initiatives in Rsch. award NAS, 1983, Cattell award for sabbatical leave, 1991, J-L Signoret prize Fondation Ipsen/Am. Acad. Arts and Scis., 1995; Guggenheim fellow. Mem. AAAS, APA, Am. Psychol. Soc., Mass. Neuropsychol. Soc., Cognitive Sci. Soc., Psychonomic Soc., Soc. for Neurosci., Am. Acad. Arts and Scis., Soc. Exptl. Psychologists. Avocations: classical music, French, bass guitar. Office Phone: 617-495-3932. Business E-Mail: smk@wjh.harvard.edu.

KOSSMAN, NINA, writer, translator; b. Dec. 17, 1959; BA, Bennington Coll., 1980; MA, U. Pitts., 1990. Author: Pereboi, 1990, Behind the Border, 1994, Po Pravuyu Ruku Sna, 1996; translator: In the Inmost Hour of the Soul, 1989, Poem of the End (Marina Tsvetaeva), 1998; anthologist: Gods and Mortals (Modern Poems on Classical Myths), 2000.

KOSTEL, GRACE M., botanist; b. Wagner, SD, May 7, 1957; d. Ernest E. and Lucille M. Kostel. BS magna cum laude, U. Ark., 2003. Botanist U.S. Forest Svc., Hot Springs, SD, 2001—. Scholar, Morris K. Udall Found., 2000. Mem.: Ecol. Soc. Am., Am. Inst. Biol. Sics., Am. Soc. Plant Taxonomists, Phi Beta Kappa. Home: 655 N Cedar St Laramie WY 82072 Office: U Wyo Aven Nelson Blvd Laramie WY 82072

KOSTELANETZ, BORIS, lawyer; b. St. Petersburg, Russia, June 16, 1911; came to U.S., 1920, naturalized, 1925; s. Nachman and Rosalia (Dimschetz) K.; m. Ethel Cory, Dec. 18, 1938; children: Richard Cory, Lucy Cory. B.C.S., N.Y. U., 1933, BS, 1936; JD magna cum laude, St. John's U., 1936, LL.D. (hon.), 1981. CPA N.Y.; bar: N.Y. 1936. With Price, Waterhouse & Co., C.P.A.'s, N.Y.C., 1934-37; asst. U.S. atty. So. Dist. N.Y.; also confidential asst. to U.S. atty, 1937-43; spl. asst. to atty. gen. U.S., 1943-46; chief war frauds sect. Dept. Justice, 1945-46; spl. counsel com. investigate crime in interstate commerce U.S. Senate, 1950-51; ptnr. Kostelanetz Ritholz Tigue & Fink, N.Y.C., 1946-89, of counsel, 1990-94, Kostelanetz & Fink, N.Y.C., 1994—. Instr. acctg. N.Y. U., 1937-47, adj. prof. taxation, 1947-69; Mem. com. on character and fitness Appellate div. Supreme Ct. N.Y., 1st dept., 1974—, chmn., 1985-98. Author: (with L. Bender) Criminal Aspects of Tax Fraud Cases, 1957, 2d edit., 1968, 3d edit., 1980; Contbr. articles to legal, accounting and tax jours. Chmn. Kefauver for Pres. Com. N.Y. State, 1952. Recipient Meritorious Svc. award NYU, 1954, John T. Madden Meml. award, 1969, Pietas medal St. John's U., 1961, medal of honor, 1983, James Madison award, 1988, Torch of Learning award Am. Friends of Hebrew U. Law Sch., 1979, N.Y.U. Presdl. citation, 1990, N.Y. State Bar Assn. Fifty-Yr. Lawyer award, 1990, ABA Sect. Taxation Distinguished Svc. award, 1999. Fellow Am. Coll. Trial Lawyers, Am. Coll. Tax Counsel, Am. Bar Found.; mem. ABA (coun. sect. taxation 1978-81, ho. of dels. 1984-89), Fed. Bar Assn., Internat. Bar Assn., Soc. King's Inn, Ireland (hon. bencher 1995), N.Y. State Bar Assn., N.Y. State CPAs, N.Y. County Lawyers Assn. (v.p. 1966-69, pres. 1969-71, bd. dirs. 1958-64, 66-69, 71-74, chmn. judiciary com. 1965-69), Assn. of Bar of City of N.Y., NYU Sch. Commerce Alumni Assn. (pres. 1951-52), NYU Alumni Fedn. (pres. 1989-92), St. John's U. Law Sch.

Alumni Assn. (pres. 1955-57). Home: 37 Washington Sq W New York NY 10011-9181 Office: Kostelanetz & Fink 530 5th Ave Fl 22 New York NY 10036-5101 Office Phone: 212-808-8100.

KOSTELANETZ, RICHARD, writer, artist; b. N.Y., May 14, 1940; s. Boris and Ethel (Cory) K. AB with honors, Brown U., 1962; postgrad. (Fulbright scholar), King's Coll., U. London, 1964-65; MA, Columbia U., 1966. Program assoc. thematic studies John Jay Coll. CUNY, 1972-73; sr. staff Ind. U. Writers' Conf., 1976; vis. prof. English and Am. studies U. Tex. at Austin, 1977; vis. prof. of theater Hunter Coll., CUNY, 2002; guest Mishkenot Sha'ananim, Jerusalem, 1979, 86, DAAD Berliner Kunstlerprogramm, 1981-83; master artist Atlantic Ctr. for the Arts, 2001. Co-propr. Assembling Press, 1970-82; lit. dir. The Future Press, 1976—; propr. Wordsand Music (ASCAP), 1982—; Archae Editions, 1978— guest artist WXXI-FM, Rochester, 1975, 76, Synapse, Syracuse U., 1975, Cabin Creek Ctr. for Work and Environ. Studies, 1978, Electronic Music Studio of Stockholm, 1981, 83, 84, 86, 88, Bklyn. Coll. Ctr. for Computer Music, 1984, Dennis Gabor Lab. Mus. of Holography, 1985, 89, Exptl. TV Lab., Owego, N.Y., 1985, 86, 87, 89, 90, 91, Real Art Ways, 1988, Film/Video Arts, 1989, Inst. Electronic Arts, Alfred U., 2004. Author: Music of Today, 1967, The Theatre of Mixed Means, 1968, 81, Master Minds: Portraits of Contemporary American Artists & Intellectuals, 1969, Visual Language, 1970, In the Beginning, 1971, The End of Intelligent Writing, 1974; 2d edit. as Literary Politics in Am, 1977; I Articulations/Short Fictions, 1974, Recyclings, vol. 1, 1974, complete text, 1984, Openings & Closings, 1975, Extrapolate, 1975, Come Here, 1975, Modulations, 1975, Portraits from Memory, 1975, Constructs, 1976, Rain Rains Rain, 1976, Numbers: Poems and Stories, 1976, Numbers Two, 1977, Illuminations, 1977, One Night Stood, 1977, Grants & the Future of Literature, 1978, Constructs Two, 1978, Tabula Rasa, 1978, Inexistences, 1978, Wordsand, 1978, Twenties in the Sixties, 1979, "The End" Appendix, 1979, "The End" Essentials, 1979, And So Forth, 1979, Exhaustive Parallel Intervals, 1979, More Short Fictions, 1980, Metamorphosis in Arts, 1980, The Old Poetries and the New, 1981, Autobiographies, 1981, Reincarnations, 1982, Turfs/Arenas/Fields/Pitches, 1983, American Imaginations, 1983, Epiphanies, 1983, Autobiographien New York Berlin, 1986, Prose Pieces/After Texts, 1987, The Old Fictions and the New, 1987, The Grants-Fix, 1987, Conversing with Cage, 1988, rev. edit., 2002, On Innovative Music(ian)s, 1989, Unfinished Business, 1990, The New Poetries and Some Olds, 1991, Politics in the African-American Novel, 1991, Constructs Three, 1991, Constructs Four, 1991, Constructs Five, 1991, Constructs Six, 1991, Fifty Untitled Constructivist Fictions, 1991, Intermix, 1991, Flipping, 1991, Published Encomia, 1991, Solos, Duets, Trios & Choruses, 1991, On Innovative Art(ist)s, 1992, A Dictionary of the Avant-Gardes, 1993, 2d edit., 1999, Wordworks: Poems New & Selected, 1993, On Innovative Performance(s), 1994, One Million Words of Booknotes 1958-1993, 1996, Minimal Fictions, 1994, Crimes of Culture, 1995, Fillmore East: Recollections of Rock Theater Twenty-Five Years After, 1995, Radio Writings, 1996, Openings, 1997, Thirty Years of Critical Engagements with John Cage, 1997. An ABC of Contemporary Reading, 1995, John Cage (Ex)plain(ed), 1996, 3-Element Stories, 1998, Vocal Shorts: Collected Performance Texts, 1998, Which Witch?, 1999, Political Essays, 1999, 3 Canadian Geniuses, 2001, More Wordworks, 2004, 35 Years of Visible Writing, 2004, SoHo: The Rise and Fall of an Artists Colony, 2003, Autobiographies at 60, 2004, Contagion: A Novel, 2004, Reimagining Rockaway Postcards, 2004, Erotic Minimal Fictions, 2005, The East Village, 1969-70, 2004, Autobiographies at 50, 2005, Kaddish and Other Audio Writings, 2005, numerous others, works included in various anthologies; editor, contbr.: On Contemporary Literature, 1964, 69, The New American Arts, 1965, Twelve from the Sixties, 1967, The Young American Writers, 1967, Beyond Left & Right: Radical Thought for Our Times, 1968, Imaged Words & Worded Images, 1970, Moholy-Nagy, 1970, 91, John Cage, 1970, 91, Possibilities of Poetry, 1970, Social Speculations, 1971, Human Alternatives: Visions for Us Now, 1971, Future's Fictions, 1971, Seeing Through Shuck, 1972, Breakthrough Fictioneers, 1973, The Edge of Adaptation, 1973, Essaying Essays, 1975, Language & Structure, 1975, Younger Critics in North America, 1976, Esthetics Contemporary, 1977, 88, Assembling Assembling, 1978, Visual Literature Criticism, 1979, Text-Sound Texts, 1980, Scenarios, 1980, The Yale Gertrude Stein, 1980, A Critical Assembling, 1980, Aural Literature Criticism, 1981, American Writing Today, 1981, The Avant-Garde Tradition in Literature, 1982, Gertrude Stein Advanced, 1990, Merce Cunningham, 1992, 98, John Cage: Writer, 1993, Writings AboutJohn Cage, 1993, 2000, Nicolas Slonimsky: The First 100 Years, 1994, A Portable Baker's Biographical Dictionary of Musicians, 1995, AnOther E.E. Cummings, 1998, Writing on Glass, 1997, Classic Essays on 20th Century Music, 1996, A B.B. King Companion, 1997; A Frank Zappa Companion, 1997, Virgin Thomson: A Reader, 2002, The Gertrude Stein Reader, 2002, An Aaron Copland Reader, 2003, others; composer: Praying to the Lord, 1977, 81, Invocations, 1981, 84, The Gospels/Die Evangelien, 1982, The Eight Nights of Hanukah, 1983, New York City, internat. version, 1984, Am. version, 1987, A Special Time, 1985, Baseball: Americas' Game, 1988, 2nd edit., 1998, Onomatopoeia, 1988, Kaddish, 1990, Acoustic Fiction I: Ululation, 1992, No, I'm Not Richard Kostelanetz, 1993; producer numerous audiotapes, films, videotapes, extended radio features for stas. in Australia, Fed. Republic Germany, Sweden, U.S.; filmmaker: (with others) Openings & Closings, 1978, Constructivist Fictions, 1978, Epiphanies, 1981-94, Ein Verlorenes Berlin/A Berlin Lost/Berlin Perdu/Ett Forlorat Berlin/El Berlin Perdido/Berlin Sche-Einena Jother, 1984-88 (prizewinner Ann Arbor, Mich., Film Festival); video art: Three Prose Pieces, 1975, Kinetic Writings, 1989, Video Strings, 1989, Stringsieben, 1989, Turfs/Grounds/Lawns, 1989, Invocations, 1988, Seductions, 1988, The Gospels Abridged, 1988, Relationships, 1988, Two Erotic Videotapes, 1988, Two Sacred Texts, 1988, Partitions, 1986, Onomatopoeia, 1989, Kaddish, 1991, Openings & Closings, 1975, Video Writing, 1987, Declaration of Independence, 1979, Epiphanies, 1980, Home Movies Reconsidered, 1992, Americas' Game. 2001, Video Poems, 2004, Video Stories, 2004, More or Less, 2004; contbg. editor: Pushcart Prize; writer, narrator: Camera Three, WCBS-TV, 1974; co-founder, compiler Assembling, 1970-82; co-pub., editor: Precisely, A Critical Jour., 1977—; contbr. articles, poems, revs., photographs and essays to mags.; numerous group exhbns. visual poetry, visual fiction, audiotapes, videotapes, films, holograms and numerical art; comprehensive exhbn.: Wordsand, at Simon Fraser U., U. Alta., Cornell Coll., Vassar Coll., U. N.D., Calif. State U., Bakersfield, Dade County C.C., Miami, Fla., 1978-81; retrospectives of video art Anthology Film Archives, 1994, Bumbershoot, Seattle, 1991, Festival de la Baite, Geneva, 1989, U. of S.C., 1978. Woodrow Wilson fellow, 1962-63, Pulitzer fellow in critical writing, 1965-66, fellow Guggenheim Meml. Found., 1967-68, Fund for Investigative Journalism, 1980, Vogelstein Found., 1980, Internat. fellow Columbia U., 1963-64, Editors fellow CCLM, 1983, Ivri-Nasawi fellow, 2000—; Visual Arts grantee Nat. Endowment of Arts, 1976, 78, 79, 85, 86, 90, Media Arts grantee Nat. Endowment of Arts, 1981, 82, 84, 91; N.Y. State Regents scholar, 1963-64, Am. Pub. Radio Program Fund, 1984; Pollock-Krasner fellow, 2001; recipient Standard award ASCAP, 1983-92, 94— (annually). Mem. Nat. Coalition Ind. Scholars, Internat. Assn. Art Critics, Soc. for Origination of Horspiel in Am., Phi Beta Kappa. Address: PO Box 444 Prince St New York NY 10012-0008 *To do what has not been done in several domains and in the course of that adventure to discover new possibilities in art, in writing, and in myself.*

KOSTELNIK, MICHAEL CHARLES, retired military officer; b. Harlingen, Tex., May 15, 1946; s. Michael and Nita Louise K.; m. Barbara Lynn Brychta, Dec. 23, 1966; 1 child, Khristine Lynn Kostelnik Carlson. BS in Mech. Engring., Tex. A&M U., 1969; MS in Indsl. and Mgmt. Engring., U. Iowa, 1970; grad., USAF Test Pilot Sch., 1977; post grad., U. Fla., 1980; grad., Nat. Def. U., 1981, USAF Instrument Pilot Instrs. Sch., Indsl. Coll. of Armed Forces, 1986, Def. Sys. Mgmt. Coll., 1989; grad. sr. exec. devel. program, U. NH, 1993; grad., Syracuse U., 1996. Commd. 2nd lt. USAF, 1969, advanced through grades to maj. gen., 1994; pilot trainee Vance AFB, Okla., 1970-71; with 18th Tactical Reconnaissance Squadron, Shaw AFB, SC, 1971-72; aircraft comdr., instr. pilot, wing flight examiner 10th Tactical Reconnaissance Wing, Alconbury, England, 1972-75; ctr. test project pilot 4485th Test Squadron, Tactical Air Warfare Ctr., Eglin AFB, Fla., 1975-76; squadron ops. officer 3246th Test Wing, Eglin AFB, 1977-81; tactical fighter requirements officer Office Dep. Chief of Staff for Rsch., Devel. and Acquisition, Washington, 1981-85; dir. combined test forces Edwards AFB, Calif., 1986-87; comdt. USAF Test Pilot Sch., Edwards AFB, 1987-89; dep. program dir. F-16 Sys. Program Office, Wright-Patterson AFB, Ohio, 1989-91; program dir. Short Range Attack Missile II, SRAM-Tactical Sys. Program Office Aero. Sys. Divsn., Air Force Sys. Command, Wright-Patterson AFB, 1991-92; First Sys. Program dir., Aircraft Sys. Program Office Aero. Sys. Ctr., Air Force Material Command, Wright-Patterson AFB, 1992-93; vice comdr. Warner Robins Air Logistics Ctr., Robins AFB, Ga., 1993-94; dir. spl. programs Office Under Sec. of Def., The Pentagon, Washington, 1994-95; dir. plans Hdqs. Air Force Materiel Command, Wright-Patterson AFB, Ohio, 1995—97; vice comdr. Air Force Materiel Command, Wright Paterson AFB, 1997—98, comdr. Air Force Devel. Test Ctr. Eglin AFB, Fla., 1998—99, comdr. Air Armanent Ctr., 1999—2002; dep. assoc. adminstr. for space shuttle and internat. space sta. Hdqrs. NASA, Washington, 2002—. Assoc. editor Whispering Wind, 1992—; contbr. articles to profl. mags. Decorated Def. Disting. Svc. medal, Air Force Disting. Svc. medal with oak leaf cluster, Legion of Merit, Meritorious Svc. medal with two oak leaf clusters, Air Force Commendation medal with oak leaf cluster; recipient Marie Radice award Am. Indianist Soc., 1985, Les Bircher award, 1987, Nat. Def. Indsl. Assoc. gold medal, 2001, Air Force Assoc. Jerry Waterman award, 2001, NAACP Cleophs McIntosh Armed Svcs. award, 2000, NDIA Moseley Munitions Mgmt. award, 2000, NASA Outstanding Leadership award, 2002, Computer Week Fed. 100 award, 2004; named 1st Disting. Grad. of Mary Carroll H.S., Corpus Christi, 2004; named to Acad. Dist. Grads., Mech. Engring., Tex. A&M U., 2004. Mem. Soc. Exptl. Test Pilots (sect. chmn.), Order of Daedalions. Roman Catholic. Avocations: golf, alpine skiing, Native American crafts and culture, fishing. Office: NASA 300 E Str SW Washington DC 20546 Office Phone: 202-358-4424.

KOSTEN, THOMAS R., psychiatrist, educator; b. Bklyn., Feb. 16, 1951; s. Richard Kosten; m. Therese Kosten, Aug. 12, 1978; children: Molly, Neal. MD, Cornell, N.Y., 1977. Lic. Psychiatry Am. Bd. Psychiatry And Neurology, 1984, Addiction Psychiatry Am. Bd. Of Psychiatry And Neurology, 1993. Chief of psychiatry VA Conn., West Haven, Conn., 1996—2000; prof. Yale U., New Haven, 1983—. Congl. fellow, u.s. ho. of rep. Ho. Subcommittee on Human Resources (Christopher Shays, Chair), Washington, 1998—99. Recipient America's Top Drs., Second Edit.; Top Doctors: N.Y., Sixth Edit., Castle Connolly Med. Ltd., 2002. Fellow: Am. Acad. of Addiction Psychiatry (pres. 1998—2000). Achievements include research in 1993 Joel Elkes Internat. award for outstanding contrb. to Psychopharmacology, American Coll. of Neuropsychopharmacology 2000-on Sr. Scientist Award, Nat. Inst. on Drug Abuse. Avocations: tennis, ice skating. Office: VA Conn- Psychiatry 151D 950 Campbell Ave - Bldg 35 New Haven CT 06511

KOSTER, BARBARA, insurance company executive; Acct. Chase Manhattan Bank, 1976—87, v.p. fin. sys., 1980—85, v.p. info. svcs., 1985—88, pres., Chase Access Svcs., 1988—95; v.p., policy adminstrn. and mgmt. info. systems Prudential Financial, 1995—97, v.p., Individual Fin. Svcs., 1997—2000, chief info. officer, individual life ins. systems Newark, 2000—03, sr. v.p., chief info. officer, 2004—. Recipient award Women in Sci. & Tech., 1999. Office: Prudential Ins Co Am 751 Broad St Newark NJ 07102-3714*

KOSTER, ELAINE, publishing executive; b. NYC; BA, Barnard Coll. Pres., pub. Dutton Signet, N.Y.C.; head Elaine Koster Literary Agy. LLC, N.Y.C. Office: Elaine Koster Literary Agy LLC 55 Central Park W Ste 6 New York NY 10023-6003

KOSTER, EMLYN HOWARD, geologist, educator; b. Suez Canal Zone, Egypt, Mar. 18, 1950; arrived in Eng., 1953, Canada, 1971, came to U.S., 1996; s. Douglas Albert and Dorothy Muriel (Roberts) Koster; m. Maryse Rémillard Koster, May 22, 1974; children: Véronique Justina, Simon Emlyn. BSc with spl. honours in Geology, U. Sheffield, Eng., 1971; PhD in Geology, U. Ottawa, 1977. Rsch. scientist terrain scis. divsn. Geological Survey of Can., Ottawa, 1973-74; cons. Geo-Analysis Ltd., Ottawa, 1975-76; asst. prof. dept. geology Concordia U., Montreal, Canada, 1976-77; asst. prof. dept. geol. scis. U. Sask., Saskatoon, Canada, 1977-80; rsch. officer, project mgr. Alta. Geol. Survey, Alta. Rsch. Coun., Edmonton, Canada, 1980-86; dir. Royal Tyrrell Mus. of Palaeontology, Drumheller and Field Sta., Dinosaur Provincial Park, UNESCO World Heritage Site, Alta., 1986-91; dir. gen. Ont. Sci. Centre, Agy. Govt. Ontario, Toronto, Canada, 1991-96; pres., CEO Liberty Sci. Ctr., NJ, 1996—. Mem. Challenger Ctr. for Space Sci. Edn., Va., 1993—2002, Can.-China Dinosaur Expdn. to Gobi Desert, China, 1987; vis. prof. U. Buenos Aires, 1988; pres. Geol. Assn. Can., 1996—97; mem. adv. com. Mus. Mgmt. Inst., Getty Leadership Inst., Calif., 1997—99; bd. dirs. Assn. Sci.-Tech. Ctrs., Washington, 1993—2001; v.p. Giant Screen Theatre Assn., Minn., 2003—; mem. Interdisciplinary Planning Com. for Liberty State Park, NJ, 1999—; Prin.-for-a-Day NY Pub. Schs., 2001; mem. sr. adv. bd. Flandrau Sci. Ctr., Ariz., 2002—; vis. prof. Inst. Marine and Coastal Studies, Rutgers U., NJ, 2002—; bd. dirs. Prosperity N.J.; mem. adv. coun. Met. Waterfront Alliance for N.Y. Harbor; advisor Coll. Sci. and Math., Montclair State U., 2004—; keynote spkr. Internat. Forum on Culture of Sci., Tech. and Innovation in Soc., Bogota, Colombia, 2004. Contbr. papers in sci. jours.; author numerous field guidebooks, book reviews; many interviews in field; internat. spkr. at more than 125 sci. confs., assn. events, convs., workshops. Mem. leadership council UNA of the USA; advisor NJ Gov.'s Commn. on Victims Meml. to the World Trade Ctr. disaster, 2001; bd. dirs. Hudson County C. of C., 1997—, Save Ellis Island! Found., NJ, 2000—; mem. bd. regents St. Peter's Coll., NJ, 1998—2003. Decorated chevalier Ordre des Palmes Academiques (France); recipient Tracks award Can. Soc. Petroleum Engrs., 1984, John Cotton Dana award N.J. Assn. Mus., 2003. Fellow: Explorers Club; mem.: AAAS (com. on pub. awareness of sci. 2003—), N.Y. Soc. Assn. Execs. (bd. dirs. 2004—). Avocations: ecology, culture, tourism. Office: Liberty Sci Ctr Liberty State Pk 251 Phillip St Jersey City NJ 07305-4600 Business E-Mail: ekoster@lsc.org.

KOSTERE, KIM MARTIN, psychologist, consultant; b. Detroit, Jan. 22, 1954; d. Walter Thomas and Shirley Marian (Goebel) K. BA, Mercy Coll., 1977; MA, Ctr. Humanistic Studies, Detroit, 1983; PsyS, Ctr. Humanistic Studies, 1986; PhD, Union Inst., Cin., 1989. Therapist Metro T.A.G., Livonia, Mich., 1978-81, Highland Waterford Ctr., Waterford, Mich., 1981-83; psychologist, v.p. substance abuse svcs. Square Lake Counseling Ctr., Bloomfield Hills, Mich., 1983-90; psychologist, co-dir. Counseling Ctr., P. C., Bloomfield Hills, Mich., 1991-99; cons., 1999—. Co-founder, dir. Ont. (Can.) NLP Inst., 1979-80; adj. faculty in psychology Edison C.C., Naples, Fla., 1999—, Capella U., Mpls. Author: A Brief Account of the Center for Humanistic Studies, 1987; co-author: Get the Results You Want, 1987, Maps, Models and the Structure of Reality, 1989, Utilizing the Metaphor: An Ericksonian/NLP Approach, 1992. Democrat. Roman Catholic. Personal E-mail: kimk@cyberisle.com.

KOSTIĆ, NENAD MIODRAG, chemist, educator; b. Belgrade, Yugoslavia, Nov. 18, 1952; arrived in U.S., 1978; s. Miodrag N. and Vera (Klujic) K.; m. Dragana J. Dimitrijevic, Jul. 18, 1976; children: Dimitrije N., Bogdan N. BS, U. Belgrade, 1976; PhD, U. Wis., 1982. Rsch. fellow Calif. Inst. Tech., Pasadena, 1982—84; prof. chemistry Iowa State U., Ames, 1984—. Vis. prof. Leiden U., Leiden, The Netherlands, 1994. Contbr. articles to profl. jours. Recipient Presdl. Young Investigator award NSF, 1988, Sci. and Rsch. award Karić Found., Belgrade, 2001; rsch. fellow A.P. Sloan Found., 1991 Fellow AAAS; mem. Am. Chem. Soc., Serbian Chem. Soc, Serbian Acad (external) Achievements include many research publications in inorganic, organometallic biological, physical, organic, and bioinorganic chemistry and invited lectures in the U.S. and abroad. Home: 4104 Quebec St Ames IA 50014-3869

KOSTIS, JOHN BASIL, cardiologist; b. Yannina, Greece, June 14, 1936; came to U.S., 1964; s. Basil John and Vasiliki Ilia (Masouras) K.; m. Barbara Charleston, June, 1969; children: William Jason, Steven Lawrence. MD, U. Salonica, Greece, 1960; student, USAF Sch. Aerospace Medicine, 1963, U. Pa., 1967-68. Diplomate Am. Bd. Internal Medicine, subspecialty cardiovascular disease. Resident internal medicine Evangelismos Hosp., 404 Gen. Hosp., Athens and Larissa, Greece, 1963-64; intern Bklyn.-Cumberland Med. Ctr., 1964-65, med. resident, 1965-67; fellow cardiology Phila. Gen. Hosp., 1967-69; instr. physiology and aviation medicine Sch. Aviation Medicine, Athens, 1969-70; assoc. clin. medicine, asst. prof. medicine U. Pa., Phila., 1971-72; assoc. prof. Coll. Medicine and Dentistry N.J.-Rutgers Med. Sch., New Brunswick, 1972-76; chief cardiology Robert Wood Johnson U. Hosp., New Brunswick, 1980—. Adj. prof. biomed. engring. Rutgers U. Coll. Engring., Piscataway, N.J., 1975—, Grad. Sch. Biomed. Engring., 1976—; prof. medicine U. Medicine and Dentistry N.J.-Robert Wood Johnson Med. Sch., New Brunswick, 1976—, chief div. cardiovascular disease, 1982-84, chief div. cardiovascular disease and hypertension, 1984-97, prof. pharmacology, 1986—, John G. Detwiler prof. cardiology, 1987—, chmn. dept. medicine, 1990—; cons. pharm. industry. Co-editor: Essentials of Cardiovascular Diagnosis, 1984, Beta Blockers in the Treatment of Cardiovascular Disease, 1984, The Pharmacological Treatment of Cardiovasuclar Diseases, 1986, Angiotensin Converting Enzyme Inhibitors, 1987, The Prevention of Sudden Cardiac Death, 1990, Disease Mgmt. and Clin. Outcomes, 1997—; mem. editorial bds. Am. Jour. Cardiology, Clin. Therapeutics, Cardiovascular Drug Reviews, others; co-inventor device noninvasive diagnostic system for coronary artery disease. Grantee pharm. industry, NHLBI, NIH, NIA. Fellow ACP, Am. Coll. Cardiology; mem. Am. Heart Assn. (disting. leadership in rsch. award 1986), Assn. U. Cardiologists, Am. Coll. Angiology, Am. Coll. Chest Physicians, Am. Soc. Hypertension, Internat. Soc. Hypertension, Assn. Profs. of Medicine. Office: U Med and Dentistry NJ Robt Wood Johnson Med Sch PO Box 19 New Brunswick NJ 08903-0019 Office Phone: 732-235-7685. Business E-Mail: kostis@umdnj.edu.

KOSTKA, RONALD WAYNE, marketing consultant; b. Chgo., Sept. 13, 1931; s. James V. and Marie (Zvolanek) K.; m. Madonna Lou Miller, June 8, 1957 (div. Dec. 1980); children: Paul, Daniel, Jane; m. Irene Mary Harnett, Sept. 14, 1991. BS in journalism, U. Ill., Urbana, 1957. Reporter Champaign News Gazette, Champaign, Ill., 1956-57; copy editor Mpls. Tribune, Mpls., 1957-58; pub. rels. mgr. 3M Co., St. Paul, Minn., 1958-92; cons. mktg. Pub. Rel., Minnetonka, Minn., 1992—. Contbr. articles to profl. jours. Firearms safety instr. State of Minn., Minnetonka, 1967-77. Staff Sgt. USAF, 1951-55, Korea. Decorated Air medal (4 OLC), Purple Heart, Hwarang (Republic of Korea). Mem. DAV, Nat. Muzzle Loading Rifle Assn., NRA, Soc. of Profl. Jours. (cert 1957), Rice Lake Rod and Gun Club, Brill Area Sportsman's Club. Avocations: canoeing, hunting, competitive skeet shooting. Home: 1909 22-1/2 St Rice Lake WI 54868-9092

KOSTLAVY, WILLIAM CHARLES, school librarian, archivist; b. Marshfield, Wisc., May 19, 1952; s. Henry Kostlevy and Dorothy Ellen Stave; m. Gari-Anne Patzwald, Aug. 6, 1978. AB, Asbury Coll., 1977; MA, Marquette U., 1979; MA in Theology, Batlery Theol. Sem., 1982; PhD, U. Notre Dame, 1996. Pastor Florence Ch. Brethren, Constantine, Mich., 1982—88; archivists Aubery Theol. Sem., Wilmore, Ky., 1988—2004; libr. Fuller Theol. Sem., Pasadena, Calif., 2004—. Author: Holiness Manuscripts, 1994, Historical Dictionary of the Holiless Movement, 2001, Hisotry of Breslow Theological Seminary, 2005. Chmn. Bretlreb Hist. Coms., 1997—. Mem.: Am. Soc. Ch. History, Conf. Fath and History, Am. Hist. Assn., Ky. Coun. Archivists (chmn. 1997, 2001), Wesleyan Theol. Soc. (sec. 1991—, treas. 1991—). Avocations: reading, baseball. Office: Fuller Theol Seminary 135 N Oakland Ave Pasadena CA 91182

KOSTOULAS, IOANNIS GEORGIOU, physicist; b. Petra, Pierias, Greece, Sept. 12, 1936; arrived in U.S., 1965, naturalized, 1984; s. Gerogios Ioannou and Panagiota (Zarogiannis) Kostoulas; m. Katina Sioras Kay, June 23, 1979; 1 child, Alexandra. Diploma in physics, U. Thessoloniki, Greece, 1963; MA, U. Rochester, 1969, PhD, 1972; MS, U. Ala., 1977. Instr. U. Thessaloniki, 1963—65; tchg. asst. U. Ala., 1966—67, U. Rochester, 1967—68; guest jr. rsch. assoc. Brookhaven Nat. Lab., Upton, NY, 1968—72; rsch. physicist, lectr. UCLA, U. Calif.-San Diego, 1972—76; sr. rsch. assoc. Mich. State U., East Lansing, 1876—1978, Fermi Nat. Accelerator Lab., Batavia, Ill., 1976—78; rsch. staff mem. MIT, Cambridge, 1978—80; sr. sys. engr., physicist Hughes Aircraft Co., El Segundo, Calif., 1980—86; sr. physisict electro-optics and space sensors Rockwell Internat. Corp., Downey, Calif., 1986—96, Boeing Corp., Downey, 1996—98; scientist Raytheon Sys. Co., El Segundo, Calif., 1998—2000; engring. specialist Northrop-Grumman Corp., Azusa, Calif., 2000—04; sr. project engr. Aerospace Corp., El Segundo, 2005—. Contbr. articles to profl. jours. With Greek Army, 1961—63. Rsch. grantee, U. Rochester, 1968—72. Mem.: Internat. Soc. Optical Engring., N.Y. Acad. Scis., Am. Phys. Soc., Pan Macedonian Assn., Hellenic U. Club, Ahepa Lodge, Sigma Pi Sigma. Home: 2404 Marshallfield Ln # B Redondo Beach CA 90278-4406 Office: Aerospace Corp 2350 E El Segundo Blvd Bldg A8 M8-227 El Segundo CA 90245 Office Phone: 310-416-1611. E-mail: yannismacedon@aol.com.

KOSTYO, JACK LAWRENCE, physiology educator; b. Elyria, Ohio, Oct. 1, 1931; s. Louis and Matilda (Thomasko) K.; m. Shirlianne Guth, June 10, 1953; children: Cecile A., Louis C. AB, Oberlin Coll., 1953; PhD, Cornell U., 1957; MD (hon.), U. Göteborg, 1978. NRC fellow Harvard Med. Sch., Boston, 1957-59; asst. prof., then prof. physiology Duke U., 1959-68; prof., chmn. dept. physiology Emory U., Atlanta, 1968-79; prof. physiology U. Mich. Med. Sch., Ann Arbor, 1979-94, chmn. dept. physiology, 1979-85, active prof. emeritus in internal medicine, 1995—; assoc. dir. Mich. Diabetes Rsch. and Tng. Ctr., Ann Arbor, 1986-97, dir. grants program, 1997—. Mem. endocrinology study sect. NIH/USPHS, 1967-71, internat. and coop. projects study sect., 1992-96; mem. physiology test com. Nat. Bd. Med. Examiners, 1974-77, mem. comprehensive part II com., 1986-91, U.S. Med. Licensure Examination Step 2 Com., 1990-91. Editor in chief Endocrinology, 1978-82; sect. editor Ann. Rev. Physiology, 1982-86; mem. editorial bd. Growth Regulation, 1990-97; contbr. articles to profl. jours. Mem. adv. bd. Searle Scholars, 1982-85. Recipient Lederle Med. Faculty award, 1961, Ernst Oppenheimer Meml. award Endocrine Soc., 1969 Mem. Endocrine Soc. (editl. bd., coun., chmn. awards com.), Am. Physiol. Soc. (editl. bd., coun., chmn. standing com. on edn., mem. coun. of endocrinology and metabolism sect., chmn. endocrinology and metabolism sect. 1990-91, rep. to Coun. Acad. Socs. of Assn. Am. Med. Colls., mem. AAAS sect. on med. scis., editor Handbook of Physiology sect. 7, Endocrinology, vol. 5), Soc. for Exptl. Biology and Medicine (editl. bd.), Internat. Union Physiol. Scis. (commn. on med. edn.), Assn. Chmn. Depts. Physiology (pres. 1979, coun.), Am. Diabetes Assn., Coun. Acad. Socs. (adminstrv. bd. 1983-86), Sigma Xi. Office: Mich Diabetes Rsch-Tng Ctr U Mich Med Sch 1331 E Ann St 0580 Ann Arbor MI 48109 Office Phone: 734-763-5730. E-mail: jkostyo@umich.edu.

KOSZARSKI, RICHARD, art historian, curator; b. N.Y.C., Dec. 18, 1947; s. Casimir and Janina (Orzechowski) K.; m. Diane Kaiser, 1975; 1 child, Eva. BA, Hofstra U., 1969; MA, NYU, 1974, PhD, 1977. Lectr. Sch. Visual Arts, N.Y.C., 1974-84, NYU, 1976, 97, Columbia U., N.Y.C., 1980-86; historian Astoria Motion Picture & TV Found., N.Y.C., 1977-81; curator of film Am. Mus. Moving Image, N.Y.C., 1981-92, exhbn. curator Masterpieces of Moving Image Tech., 1988, head collections and exhbns., 1992-96, sr. historian, 1996-97; assoc. prof. English Rutgers U., 1998—. Author: (books) Hollywood Directors 1914-40, 1976, The Rivals of D.W. Griffith, 1976, Hollywood Directors 1941-76, 1977, Universal Pictures: 65 Years, 1977, The Man You Loved to Hate, 1983, The Astoria Studio and Its Fabulous Films, 1983, An Evening's Entertainment: The Age of the Silent Feature Picture, 1915-1928, 1990, Von: The Life and Films of Erich von Stroheim, 2001, Fort Lee: The Film Town, 2004; (documentary films) Roger Corman, Hollywood's Wild Angel, 1978, The Man You Loved to Hate, 1979; editor-in-chief Film History, An Internat. Jour., N.Y.C., 1986—. Mem. Ft. Lee Film Commn. Rsch. associateship Am. Film Inst., 1971, 72; rsch. grantee Am. Coun. Learned Socs., 1978; recipient Nat. Film Book award Nat. Film Soc., 1984, award Prix Jean Mitry, 1991; NEH fellow, 2003. Mem. Polish Inst. Arts and Scis., Antique Wireless Assn., Kosciuszko Found., Assn. Moving Image Archivists.

KOSZEWSKI, BOHDAN JULIUS, retired internist, medical educator; b. Warsaw, Dec. 17, 1918; Came to U.S., 1952; s. Mikolaj and Helen (Lubienski) K.; children Mikolaj, Joseph, Wanda Marie, Andrzej Bohdan. MD, U. Zurich, Switzerland, 1946; MS, Creighton U., 1956. Resident in pathology U. Zurich, 1944-46, resident in internal medicine, 1946-50, assoc. in medicine, 1950-52; intern St. Mary's Hosp., Hoboken, N.J., 1953; practice medicine specializing in internal medicine Omaha, 1956-90. Mem. staff St. Joseph's Hosp., Mercy and Meth. Hosps.; instr. internal medicine Creighton U., 1956-57, asst. prof., 1957-65, assoc. prof. internal medicine, 1965-90; cons. hematology Omaha VA Hosp., 1957-90. Author: Prognosis in Diabetic Coma, 1952; contbr. numerous articles to profl. jours. Served with Polish Army, 1940-45. Fellow ACP, Am. Coll. Angiology; mem. AAAS, Am. Fedn. Clin. Research, Internat. Soc. Hematology, Polish-Am. Congress Nebr. (pres. 1960-68, 82-92). Home: 1400 Broadmoor Ave Lincoln NE 68506

KOTA, SREENIVAS, civil engineer, consultant; s. Gangiah Kota and Kota Sumitra; m. Savita Bharathy, July 1, 1975. BECE, Osmania U., Hyderabad, India, 1991; MSCE, U. N.Mex., 1993; PhDCE, NC State U., 1998. Registered profl. engr., Del., 2002. Project engr. Malcolm Pirnie, Inc., Fair Lawn, NJ, 2001—03; project mgr. URS Corp., Wayne, NJ, 2003—. Recipient Best Student Paper award, Am. Geophys. Union, 1997, Outstanding Student Achievement award, State of Andhra Pradesh, India, 1985. Mem.: ASCE, Interstate Tech. Regulatory Coun., Nat. Groundwater Assn. (pub. awareness com. 2002). Office Phone: 973-812-6852.

KOTAS, ROBERT VINCENT, pediatrician, educator; b. Buffalo, Nov. 26, 1938; s. Vincent John and Regina K.; m. Ilona Rae Fielding, Mar. 2, 1968; children: Nicole, Timothy, Robert, Rebecca. BS, Canisius Coll., 1959; MD, U. Buffalo, 1963. Diplomate: Am. Acad. Pediatrics. Research assoc. McGill U., 1969-70; intern Buffalo Children's Hosp., 1963-64; resident in pediatrics Johns Hopkins Hosp., Balt., 1964-66; asst. prof. pediatrics U. Okla. Med. Sch., 1970-72, dir. newborn services, 1970-72; dir., div. devel. physiology; career investigator W.K. Warren Med. Research Center, Tulsa, 1972-76, sci. dir., 1976-80; dir. William and Natalie Warren Med. Inst., Tulsa, 1980-83; chief pediatrician Ella Austin Health Ctr., San Antonio, 1989-95, med. dir., 1993-95; lab. dir., 1993-95; pediatrician UTHSC-SA Primary Care Cmty. Pediat., San Antonio, 1995-98, Minor Emergency Ctr., San Antonio, 1998-99; assoc. Fernando A. Guerra, MD, San Antonio, 1998-99, Lonestar Pediats., Kaufman, Tex., 1999—2002; lead staff physician Cmty. Outreach Clinic/Bluitt-Flowers, Dallas, 2002—. Clin. prof. pediats. U. Okla. Med. Sch., Tulsa, 1977-99; clin. instr. pediats. U. Tex. Southwestern Med. Ctr., Dallas, 2002—; assoc. prof. pediats. U. Tex. Health Sci. Ctr., San Antonio, 1983-98, dir. rsch. devel., 1993-94, also med. dir.; guest scientist Nat. Inst. Child Health and Human Devel., Bethesda, Md., 1975-77, also cons.; cons. Am. Lung Assn., others; cons. pediatrician San Antonio Ind. Sch. Dist. Contbr. articles to profl. jours. and books. Served as capt. USAF, 1966-68. Recipient continuing edn. awards AMA; Best M.D. Written Book award Am. Med. Writers Assn., 1980; Mosby scholar, 1963; grantee NIH, 1969-70, 75-79, 84-88; grantee USPHS, 1968-69, 91-95; others. Fellow Am. Coll. Obstetricians and Gynecologists (assoc.); mem. Johns Hopkins Med. and Surg. Assn., So. Soc. Pediatric Rsch., Soc. Pediatric Rsch., Am. Physiol. Soc., Soc. Gynecol. Investigation. Home: 604 Courageous Dr Rockwall TX 75032-5768 *Grateful for the excitement of impending discovery which characterizes my work with its promise of surprise in the midst of daily routine, I am indebted for the guidance and inspiration that my present and past associates have given me to deal effectively with the diversity and perversity of experience.*

KOTCHER, SHIRLEY J.W., lawyer; b. June 6, 1924; m. Harry A. Kotcher; children: Leslie Susan, Dana Anne. BA, NYU; JD, Columbia U. Bar: N.Y. In-house counsel Booth Meml. Med. Ctr., Flushing, N.Y., 1975-83, gen. counsel, 1983-91; v.p., gen. counsel the N.Y. Hosp. Med. Ctr. Queens, 1991-97; advisor health care Borough Pres. Queens, 1978. Author: Hidden gold and Pitfalls in New Tax Law, 1970. Mem. North Hempstead Sr. Citizen Commn., Manhasset, NY, 1999—; mem. affordable sr. housing endowment adv. com. Town of North Hempstead, 1999—; bd. dirs. Denton Green Housing Co. Inc., Garden City Park, NY, 1999—. Mem. ABA (health law forum com.), Nat. Health Lawyers Assn., Am. Acad. Hosp. Attys., Am. Soc. Law and Medicine, Am. Soc. Health Care Risk Mgmt., Assn. for Hosp. Risk Mgmt. N.Y., Greater N.Y. Hosp. Assn. (legal adv. com. 1976-97).

KOTEFF, ELLEN, periodical editor; b. Harvey, Ill. d. Walter Peter and Florence (Walz) K. BS in Journalism, U. Fla. Editor Palm Beach (Fla.) Daily News; met. editor Daily Record, Parsippany; exec. editor Nation's Restaurant News, NYC, editor, 2004—. Former v.p. Internat. Foodservice Editl. Coun.; mem. jury IFMA Silver Plate. Bd. dirs. Women's Foodservice Forum, 2003. Recipient Jesse H. Neal award, 2002, 2004, McAllister Editl. fellowship award, 2002. Office: Nations Restaurant News 425 Park Ave New York NY 10022-3506 Office Phone: 212-756-5186. Business E-Mail: ekoteff@nrn.com.

KOTELLY, GEORGE VINCENT, editor, writer, electrical engineer; b. Boston, Aug. 27, 1931; s. James Visar and Pauline (Plaha) K.; m. Shirley Elizabeth Mullo, June 14, 1959; children— Kenneth James, William John, Douglas George, Joanne Elizabeth BSE.E., Tufts U., 1953. Publs. engr. Raytheon, Burlington, Mass., 1970-73; tech. writer USM Corp., Beverly, Mass., 1973-75; engring. writer Analogic, Wakefield, Mass., 1975-77; tech. editor Computer Design Mag., Littleton, Mass., 1977-79; sr. editor Edn. Mag., Boston, 1979-83; editor-in-chief Mini-Micro Systems Mag., Cahners Pub. Co., Boston, 1983-88; mng. editor Lightwave Jour. PennWell Pub. Co., Westford, Mass., 1988-89; sr. editor Lincoln Lab. MIT, Lexington, 1989-91; editor COMDEX Preview and Show Daily The Interface Group, Needham, Mass., 1991-93; exec. editor Lightwave Jour. PennWell Pub. Co., Nashua, N.H., 1993-97; editor-in-chief Vision Systems Design Mag., 1997—2003; tech. editor Advanced Imaging Mag., Cygnus Pub., Melville, NJ, 2004—05; pres. Koty Assocs., 2005—. Contbr. numerous articles to tech. jours. Sgt. U.S. Army, 1954-56. Mem. IEEE. Republican. Mem. Albanian Orthodox Ch. Avocations: golf, bowling, chess, jogging, baseball. Home: 12 Scotch Pine Ln Merrimack NH 03054-3900 Office Phone: 603-429-2838. Personal E-mail: geoshirl1@msn.com.

KOTEN, JOHN, editor-in-chief; With Wall St. Jour., 1977—92, reporter, sr. writer, Chgo. bureau chief, sr. editor; editor Worth mag., 1992—2002; editor-in-chief Inc Mag., 2002—, Fast Company Mag., 2005—; CEO Mansueto Ventures, 2005—. Regular guest CNBC. Contbg. editor: Smart Money mag. Named one of 100 Most Influential Journalists, Journalist and Fin. Reporting Group. Office: Inc Magazine 375 Lexington Ave New York NY 10017*

KOTHARI, CARTIK RAY, electrical engineer, researcher; arrived in U.S., 1997; s. Saravana and Gomathy Saravana Muthu. BS in Engring., Osmania U., 1995; MS, U. Memphis, 1999, MS, 2000. Sales svc. engr. Usha Drager Ltd, Hyderabad, India, 1995—97; web developer CDI Innovantage Inc., Salt Lake City, 2001; rsch. asst. Dept. Elec. Engring. U. Memphis, 2002—. Contbr. articles to profl. jours. Office: Department of Electrical Engineering The University of Memphis Memphis TN 38152

KOTHARI, MILIND JAGDISH, neurologist, consultant; b. India, Sept. 26, 1962; came to U.S., 1970; s. Jagdish V. and Jyotsna J. (Mehta) K.; m. Smeeta M. Shah, Sept. 3, 1989; children: Sonia, Saira. BA cum laude, CUNY, 1983; DO, N.Y. Inst. Tech., 1988. Diplomate Am. Acad. Neurology, Am. Bd. Electrodiagnostic Medicine. Intern Coney Island Hosp., Bklyn., 1988-89; resident Booth Meml. Hosp., Flushing, N.Y., 1989-90, NYU Med. Ctr., N.Y.C., 1990-92, chief resident, 1992-93; tchg. asst. in neurology NYU Sch. Medicine, 1992-93; fellow in neurophysiology and neuromuscular disease Brigham & Women's Hosp., Boston, 1993-95; clin. fellow in neurology Harvard Med. Sch., Boston, 1993-95; prof. neurology Pa. State U. Coll. Medicine, Hershey, 1995—. Contbr. articles to profl. jours.; lectr. in field. Mem. Am. Acad. Neurology, Am. Assn. Electrodiagnostic Medicine (Jr. Mem. Recognition award 1995), Ctrl. Pa. Neurol. Soc. Avocations: tennis, bike riding. Office: Penn State U Coll Medicine Dept Neurology 500 University Dr Hershey PA 17033-2360

KOTHARY, PIYUSH C., research scientist; b. Yangon, Myanmar, Sept. 4, 1940; s. Chamanlal D. and Labhuben C. Kothary; m. Sarla P. Parekh, Feb. 21, 1943; children: Shilpa, Priya. PhD magna cum laude, La Salle U., 1994. Demonstrator St. Xavier's Coll., Bombay, 1963—71; sr. rsch. assoc. U. Mich., Ann Arbor, 1971—. Dir. rsch. Skillman Lab. Kellogg Eye Ctr., Ann Arbor, 1994—. Grantee, NIH, 1990—95, 1993. Mem.: Assn. for Rsch in Vision and Ophthalmology (presenter 1994—2005). Office: 521 Kellogg Eye Ctr 1000 Wall St Ann Arbor MI 48105 Personal E-mail: Piyush0940@aol.com. Business E-Mail: kotha@umich.edu.

KOTHE, CHARLES ALOYSIUS, lawyer; b. Jersey City, Oct. 12, 1912; s. Charles A. and Lillian (Hansen) K.; m. Janet Fleming, Feb. 19, 1937; children: Diane, Charles F., James R., David J. Student, Bucknell U., 1930-33; AB, U. Tulsa, 1934; scholarship, U. Heidelberg, Germany; JD with honors, U. Okla., 1938. Bar: Okla. 1938. Staff counsel Mid-Continent Petroleum Co., Tulsa, 1939-41; gen. counsel Macnick Co., Tulsa, 1941-43; v.p. indsl. rels. NAM, N.Y.C., 1959-65; atty., v.p., dir. Coburn Optical Industries, 1966-76; dir. T.D. Williamson Co.; of counsel Pray, Walker, Jackman Law Firm, Tulsa, 1990—. Mem. faculty labor law dept. Tulsa Law Sch., 1939-60; dean indsl. rels. dept. Okla. Sch. Acctg., 1960-65; founding dean O.W. Coburn Law Sch.; mem. Faculty Univ. Ctr. at Tulsa, 1989—; mem. panel Am. Arbitration Assn., Fed. Mediation and Conciliation Svc.; spl. cons., 1966-90; fedd. mediator EEOC, 1999—; chmn. Pub. Employees Rels. Bd., 1989—; mem. Fed. Svc. Impasses Panel, 1991-95. Author: Industrial Relations in thc Non-Union Plant, 1960, NLRB and the Rights of Management, 1966; Editor: Tale of 22 Cities, 1964. Co-founder, 2d pres. Effective Citizens Orgn., 1957; mem. Tulsa Civil Svc. Commn., 1980-85. Named Citizen of Year Tulsa, 1946 Mem. ABA (10th Circuit councilman 1940), Okla. Bar Assn. (chmn. labor law section), U.S. Jr. C. of C. (v.p. 1956), Okla. Jr. C. of C. (pres. 1955), Tulsa Jaycees (pres. 1954), Jr. Bar Conf. Okla. (pres. 1946), U. Tulsa Alumni Assn. (pres. 1957, distinguished alumnus 1974), Order of Coif, Tulsa Club, So. Hills Country Club, Nat. Lawyers Club, Masons, Shriners, Sigma Alpha Epsilon, Phi Delta Phi, Beta Gamma Sigma. Office: 900 Oneok Bldg 100 W 5th St Tulsa OK 74103-4240

KOTIN, PAUL, pathologist; b. Chgo., Aug. 13, 1916; s. Elias and Rose (Spunt) K.; m. Pauline H. Stephan, Dec. 12, 1970; children: Joel Tepper, David Bernard. BS, U. Ill., 1937, MD, 1940. Intern Deaconess Hosp., Chgo., 1939-40, resident pathology, 1940-41; pvt. practice pathology and internal medicine San Luis Obispo, Calif., 1946-48; researcher pathology U. So. Calif., 1949-50; med. microbiologist Los Angeles County Hosp., 1950-51, attending staff pathologist, 1951-62; mem. faculty U. So. Calif., 1951-62, prof. pathology, 1959-60, Paul Pierce prof. pathology, 1960-62; chief carcinogenesis studies br. Nat. Cancer Inst., 1962-63, asso. dir. for field studies, 1963-64, sci. dir. for etiology, 1964-66; dir. div. environ. health scis. NIH, 1966-69; dir. Nat. Inst. Environ. Health Scis., 1969-71; v.p. for health scis., dean Sch. Medicine, Temple U., Phila., 1971-74; sr. v.p. health, safety and environment Johns-Manville Corp., 1974-81. Edgar Allen Meml. lectr. Yale Sch. Medicine, 1957; vis. prof. oncology U. Wis., 1959-60; vis. prof. pathology U. N.C., also Duke U., 1967-71; Harry Shay Meml. lectr. Temple U., 1964; Sappington Meml. lectr. Am. Occupational Medicine Assn., Anaheim, Calif., 1979, Gehrmann lectr., Nashville, 1981; chmn. Gordon Research Conf. Cancer, 1965, Beryllium Industry Sci. Adv. Com., 1995—; adj. prof. pathology U. Colo., 1974—; Cons. air pollution med. program, div. spl. health service USPHS, 1958-62; mem. sci. adv. bd. Council Tobacco Research-U.S.A., 1952-65; adv. com. r.r. diesel gases and dust Calif. Pub. Utilities Commn., 1956-62; adv. com. research pathogenesis cancer Am. Cancer Soc., 1962-65; pathology study sect. NIH, 1962-66, lung cancer task force, 1967-68; corr. mem. permanent European com. Research Chronic Hazards, 1960—; cancer prevention com. UICC, 1962-66, com. on exptl. design and methodology in carcinogenesis, 1967-70; sci. com. Inst. Occupational and Environ. Health, Quebec. Asbestos Mining Assn., 1966-75; mem. Fed. Com. Pest Control, 1964-71; program com. Tenth Internat. Congress, 1967-70; mem. Expert Panel on Carcinogenicity, 1962-70, Nat. Environ. Health Scis. Center, 1965, Nat. Adv. Com. Occupational Safety and Health, 1975-78, Armed Forces Epidemiol. Bd., 1976-80; chmn. Beryllium Industry Sci. Adv. Com., 1990—. Editorial adv. bd.: Cancer Research, 1957-61, Internat. Rev. Exptl. Pathology, 1968—; editorial bd.: AMA Archives Pathology, 1965-71, Environ. Research, 1966—, Am. Jour. Pathology, 1971-82; Contbr. articles to med. jours. Served with AUS, 1941-46. Recipient Superior Service award HEW, 1966, Disting. Service award, 1969; Sr. postdoctoral fellow NSF, 1959-60; named Alumnus of Yr. U. Ill. Coll. of Medicine, 1990. Fellow Coll. Am. Pathologists, N.Y. Acad. Scis., Am. Acad. Occupational Medicine; mem. AMA (com. research on tobacco and health 1966-78), Am. Assn. Cancer Research (dir.), Am. Assn. Pathologists and Bacteriologists, AAAS, Am. Indsl. Hygiene Assn. (hon.), Am. Occupational Medicine Assn. (Knudsen award 1981), Sigma Xi, Alpha Omega Alpha. Home: 540 Camino Los Altos Santa Fe NM 87501 Office Phone: 505-984-8064.

KOTKIN, DAVID **See COPPERFIELD, DAVID**

KOTKOV, BENJAMIN, retired clinical psychologist; b. Boston, Apr. 8, 1910; s. Moses and Annie (Hopner) K.; m. Sally B., Jan. 28, 1941; children: Ralph, Frank. AB, Cornell U., 1929; MA, Harvard U., 1934; PhD, Ottawa U., Ont., Can., 1954. Diplomate Am. Bd. Clin. Psychology, Am. Bd. Profl. Psychology, Am. Bd. Med. Psychotherapists, Am. Bd. Disability Cons., Am. Bd. Prescribing Psychologists, Am. Coll. Forensic Examiners, Serious Mental Illness, Am. Coll. Advanced Practice Psychologists, Am. Bd. Psychologist-Physicians, Am. Bd. Psychotherapy, Am. Bd. Hypnotherapy. Staff to chief Nerve Clinic, New Eng. Med. Ctr., Boston, 1934-42, VA Mental Hygiene Unit, Boston, 1946-52; chief psychologist Mental Hygiene Clinics, State of Del., 1952-53; clin. exec. Child Guidance Ctr., Brattleboro, Vt., 1954-64; staff to prof. and faculty head Windham Coll., Putney, Vt., 1964-76; pvt. practice Brattleboro, 1976—2005; ret., 2005. Internat. adv. bd. Acad. of Psychoanalysis, Germany, 1969—86. Contbr. numerous articles to profl. jours. Lt. U.S. Army, 1942—46. Recipient Editor's award Internat. Jour. Profl. Hypnosis, 1977, medallion Acad. Psychosmatic Medicine, 1979, Membership Leader award Vt. Lions, 1993-94, Outstanding Premier Leadership award in psychopharmacology for professional psychologists, 1998; NEA grantee, 1956-57. Fellow Am. Psychol. Soc., Internat. Soc. Profl. Hypnosis, Acad. Sci. Hypnotherapy, Am. Assn. Applied and Prevention Psychology, Acad. Clin. Psychology; mem. AAUP (emeritus), APA (life), Am. Philos. Assn., Soc. Personality Assessment (life), Vt. Psychol. Assn. (pres. 1968-69, chmn. cert. bd. 1974-76), New Eng. Soc. Clin. Hypnosis (pres. 1988), DAV (life), Lions (pres. 1973-74, 84-85, 94-97), Elks, Am. Legion. Home and Office: 70 Orchard St Brattleboro VT 05301-2678 E-mail: bkotkov2@juno.com.

KOTLARCHUK, IHOR O. E., lawyer; b. Ukraine, July 31, 1943; came to U.S., 1946, naturalized, 1957; s. Emil and Lidia N. (Maceluch) K. BS in Fin., Fordham U., 1965, JD, 1968; LLM, Georgetown U., 1974, MA in Govt., 1982; MEd, Mary Washington Coll., 2003. Bar: N.Y. 1969, D.C. 1972, Va. 2001, U.S. Ct. Mil. Appeals, U.S. Tax Ct., U.S. Supreme Ct. Sr. trial atty. criminal sect. tax divsn. U.S. Dept. Justice, Washington, 1973-78, civil sect. tax divsn., 1978-80, fraud sect. criminal divsn., 1980-84, internal security sect. criminal divsn., 1984-97; ret., 1999; sr. internat. law enforcement adv. on tax policy/enforcement U.S. Treasury Dept., 2000—; pvt. practice law Alexandria, Va., 2001—. Tchr. social studies, Stafford, Va., 2003—. Pres. The Washington Group, 2000—. With U.S. Army, 1969-73, Vietnam; judge advocate gen.; ret. col. USAR. Decorated Bronze star, Legion of Merit. Mem. ABA, N.Y. State Bar Assn., Va. State Bar Assn., Va. Trial Lawyers Assn., D.C. Bar Assn., Res. Officers Assn., Ukrainian Assn. Washington D.C. (pres. 2000-01), Phi Alpha Delta. Ukrainian Catholic. Address: 205 S Lee St Alexandria VA 22314-3307 Office: 109 S Fairfax St Alexandria VA 22314-3307 Fax: 703-548-1861.

KOTLER, LAWRENCE JOEL, lawyer; b. Johannesburg, Jan. 8, 1965; arrived in US, 1967; s. Morris Nathan and Marcie Susan K.; m. Rita M. Eichman, Apr. 17, 1993; children: Julia Renee, Theodore George. BA, U. Pa., 1986; JD, Boston U., 1989. Bar: Pa. 1989, NY 2001, Del. 2002, US Dist. Ct. Ea. Dist. Pa. 1990, US Dist. Ct. Mid. Dist. Pa. 1996, US Dist. Ct. So. Dist. NY, US Ct. Appeals 3rd Cir. 1996. Assoc. Sprecher, Felix, Visco, Hutchison & Young, Phila., 1989-91, Adelman Lavine Gold & Levin, P.C., Phila., 1991-93, Buchanan Ingersoll, P.C., Phila., 1993—99, counsel, 2000, shareholder, 2001; ptnr. Duane Morris LLP, Phila., 2001—. Bd. dirs. Consumer Bankruptcy Assistance Project. Mem.: ABA, Ea. Dist. Pa. Bankruptcy Conf. (chmn. pro bono com.), Phila. Bar Assn., NY Bar Assn., Pa. Bar Assn., Del. Bar Assn. Office: Duane Morris LLP One Liberty Pl Philadelphia PA 19103-7396 Office Phone: 215-979-1514. Office Fax: 215-979-1020. Business E-Mail: ljkotler@duanemorris.com.

KOTLER, MILTON, marketing company executive; b. Chgo., Mar. 15, 1935; s. Maurice and Betty (Bubar) K.; m. Greta Smith, July 11, 1976; children: Anthony, Joshua, Jonathan, Rebecca. BA, U. Chgo., 1954, MA in Polit. Sci, 1957, postgrad. (Jane Morton fellow), 1957-59. Asst. prof. Chgo. City Coll., 1961-63; resident fellow Inst. for Policy Studies, Washington, 1963-77; exec. dir. Inst. Neighborhood Studies, Washington, 1972-75, Nat. Assn. Neighborhoods, Washington, 1975-81; v.p. Ctr. for Responsive Governance, Washington, 1981—, treas., 1980—; pres. Kotler Mktg. Group, Washington, 1984—. Beijing, Shenzhen. Vis. prof. U. Calif., Berkeley, 1968, George Washington U., 1985; adj. prof. Am. U., Washington, 1976—, U. Md., 1980— Author: Neighborhood Government, 1969, 2d edit., 2005, Building Neighborhood Organization, 1983; co-editor: Clear Sighted View of Chinese Marketing, 2005; co-editor Jour. Community Action, 1981—; contbr. chpts. to books. V.p. Alliance for Voluntarism, 1979-80; chmn. bd. Washington Symphony Orchestra, 1992—. Office: 925 15th St NW 4th Flr Washington DC 20005 Office Phone: 202-331-0555. Business E-Mail: mkotler@kotlermarketing.com. *I have sought in all my work to empower the neighborhood community as a sphere of our personal responsibility. I have done this so that we may become more human through that responsibility to our neighbors.*

KOTLER, PHILIP, marketing educator, writer; b. Chgo., May 27, 1931; s. Maurice and Betty (Bubar) K.; m. Nancy Ruth Kellum, Jan. 30, 1955; children: Amy Elizabeth, Melissa Eve, Jessica Kellum. Student, DePaul U., 1948-50; MA, U. Chgo., 1953; PhD, MIT, 1956; postgrad., U. Chgo., 1957, Harvard, 1960; PhD (hon.), DePaul U., 1988, U. Zurich, Switzerland, 1989, Athens U. Econs. and Bus., 1995, Stockholm U., 1998, Crackow U. Econs., 1998; PhD (hon.), Budapest Sch. Econ. Sci. and Pub. Policy, B.I. Norwegian Sch. Mgmt. Sch. analyst Westinghouse Corp., Pitts., 1953; asst., then assoc. prof. Roosevelt U., Chgo., 1957-61; from asst. prof. to prof. marketing Northwestern U., Evanston, Ill., 1962-69, A. Montgomery Ward prof. marketing, 1969-73, Harold T. Martin prof. marketing, 1973-88, S.C. Johnson & Son disting. prof. internat. mktg., 1989—. Adv. mktg. editor Holt, Rinehart and Winston, 1965-78; chmn. Coll. on Mktg., Inst. Mgmt. Scis., 1968; mem. adv. bd. Yankelovich Ptnrs. Author: Simulation in Social and Administrative Science, 1971, Creating Social Change, 1971, The New Competition, 1985, Marketing for Health Care Organizations, 1986, Marketing Models, 1992, Marketing for Congregations: Serving People More Effectively, 1992, Strategic Marketing for Education Institutions, 1995, High Visibility, 1997, Standing Room Only: Strategies for Marketing the Peforming Arts, 1997, The Marketing of Nations, 1997, Museum Strategy and Marketing, 1998, Kotler on Marketing, 1999, Marketing Places Europe, 1999, Marketing Asian Places, 2001, Marketing Moves, 2002, Repositioning Asia, 2002, Marketing Professional Services, 2002, Social Marketing: Improving the Quality of Life, 2002, A Framework for Marketing Management, 2003, Marketing Places: Attracting Investment, Industry and Tourism to Cities, States, and Nations, Marketing for Hospitality and Tourism, 2003, Marketing Global Biobrands, 2003, Rethinking Marketing, 2003, Marketing Insights A to Z, 2003, Lateral Marketing, 2003, Strategic Marketing for Nonprofit Organizations, 2003, Ten Deadly Marketing Sins, 2004, Attracting Investors, 2004, Corporate Social Responsibility: Doing the Most Good for Your Company and Your Cause, 2005, Principles of Marketing, 2005, Marketing Management: Analysis, Planning and Control, 2005, According to Kotler, 2005. Bd. govs. Sch. of Art Inst. Chgo., 1985-2004. Mem. Am. Mktg. Assn. (bd. dirs. 1970-72, First Disting. Mktg. Educator 1985), Inst. Mgmt. Scis., Marketing Sci. Inst. (trustee 1974-84), Phi Beta Kappa. Office: Northwestern U Kellogg Sch Mgmt Evanston IL 60208-0001 Home: 1241 Gulf of Mex Dr Longboat Key FL 34228

KOTLER, RICHARD LEE, lawyer; b. L.A., Apr. 13, 1952; s. Allen S. Kotler and Marcella (Fromberg) Swartz; m. Cindy Jasik, Dec. 9, 1990; children: Kelsey Elizabeth, Charles Max. BA, Sonoma State Coll., 1976; JD, Southwestern U., 1979. Bar: Calif. 1980, U.S. Dist. Ct. (cen. dist.) Cal. 1980; cert. family law specialist. Sole practice, Newhall, Calif., 1980-83, 88—; sr. ptnr. Kotler & Hann, Newhall, 1983-88; pvt. practice Law Offices of Richard L. Kotler, Newhall, 1984-86. Judge pro temp Municipal Ct., 1981-84, Superior Ct., 1985—. Chmn. Santa Clarita Valley Battered Women's Assn., Newhall, 1983-87; bd. dirs. Santa Clarita Valley Hotline, Newhall, 1981-83. Recipient Commendation award L.A. County, 1983; named SCV Paintball champion. Mem. Santa Clarita Valley Bar Assn. (v.p. 1985—), L.A. Assn. Cert. Family Law Specialists, Los Angeles Astronomy Soc., Newhall Astronomy Club. Avocations: astronomy, classic cars, collecting stamps, precious metals, trout fishing. Office: Ste 204 24881 San Fernando Rd Santa Clarita CA 91321-4172

KOTLER, STEVEN, investment banker; b. N.Y.C., Jan. 9, 1947; s. Louis and Etta (Smeltzer) K.; m. Carolyn Miller, Sept. 26, 1973; children: William, Thomas. BBA, CCNY, 1967. V.p. N.Y. Hanseatic Corp., N.Y.C., 1967-74; with Schroder Wertheim & Co. Inc., N.Y.C., 1974—, gen. ptnr., 1979—, mng. dir., 1981—, pres., 1987—, CEO, 1996-99; vice chmn. Gilbert Global Equity Capital, LLC, N.Y.C. Bd. dirs. Birch Telecom, CPM Holdings; bd. dirs., co-chmn. True Temper Sports; bd. govs. Am. Stock Exch., 1992-97; coun. pres. The Woodrow Wilson Internat. Ctr. for Scholars, 1999-02; mem. infrastructure and housing task force NYC Partnership, NYC C. of C.; bd. overseers Calif. Inst. Arts. Served with USAR, 1967-72. Mem.: Coun. on Fgn. Rels.

KOTLIAR, B. GABRIEL, physics professor; b. Feb. 26, 1957; BSc in Physics and Math., Hebrew U., 1979, MSc in Physics, 1980; PhD in Physics, Princeton U., 1983. Postdoctoral fellow Inst. for Theoretical Physics U. Calif., Santa Barbara, 1983—85; asst. prof. MIT, 1985—88; assoc. prof. Rutgers U., Piscataway, NJ, 1988—92, prof. I, 1992—96, prof. II, 1996—. Assoc. editor Phys. Rev. Letters, 1996—97; cons. ATT Bell Labs., 1988—97, Los Alamos Nat. Labs., 1991—98. Editor (with D. D. Sarna and Y. Tokura): (book) Monographs in Condensed Matter Science, 1997. Recipient Guggenheim fellowship, 2003, Alfred P. Sloan rsch. fellowship, 1986—88, Presdl. Young Investigator award, 1987—92, Lady Davies fellowship, 1994—95. Fellow: Am. Phys. Soc. Office: Rutgers U Serin Physics Lab Piscataway NJ 08855-0849

KOTLOWITZ, ALEX, writer, journalist; Student, Wesleyan U. Former prodr. segments TV series MacNeil/ Lehrer NewsHour; former reporter The Wall Street Jour.; former contbr. NPR. Writer-i-residence Northwestern U.; Welch chmn. in Am. studies U. Notre Dame, South Bend, Ind. Author: There Are No Children Here: The Story of Two Boys Growing Up In the Other America, 1991 (Helen Bernstein award Excellence Journalism N.Y. Pub. Libr. 1992), The Other Side of the River: A Story of Two Towns, a Death and America's Dilemma, 1998 (Heartland prize for nonfiction Chgo. Tribune 1998), Never a City So Real, 2004; contbr. various mags., including The New Yorker, The N.Y. Times Mag., This Am. Life. Recipient George Polk award TV reporting Long Island U. Journalism dept. work on MacNeil/Lehrer NewsHour, 1984, Robert F. Kennedy award Coverage of Disadvantaged, George Foster Peabody award 2003. Office Phone: 708-445-8805. E-mail: akotlowitz@aol.com.

KOTLOWITZ, ROBERT, writer, editor; b. Paterson, N.J., Nov. 21, 1924; s. Max and Debra (Kaplan) K.; m. Carol Naomi Leibowitz, Oct. 15, 1950; children— Alexander William, Daniel Justin. BA, Johns Hopkins, 1947; preparatory diploma, Peabody Conservatory Music, 1941. Asso. editor Pocket Books, Inc., 1950-55, Discovery, 1952-55; mgr. press and information RCA Victor Records, 1955-60; sr. editor Show mag., 1960-64, Harper's mag., 1965-67, mng. editor, 1967-71; sr. v.p., dir. programming Sta. WNET/ Channel 13, N.Y.C., 1971-91, editorial advisor, 1991—. Guest lectr. Queen's Coll., 1954-55; author monthly column Performing Arts, 1966— Author: novel Somewhere Else, 1972, The Boardwalk, 1977, Sea Changes, 1986, His Master's Voice, 1992, (memoire) Before Their Time, 1997; Contbg. editor: Atlantic Monthly, 1971-74; Contbr. nat. publs. Served with inf. AUS, 1943-46. Recipient Edward Lewis Wallant award for novel, 1972, Nat. Jewish Book award, 1972, Nat. Emmy award, 1973; sr. fellow Freedom Forum, Columbia U., 1993; fellow Am. Acad., Berlin, 1998. Mem. Century Assn. Home: 54 Riverside Dr New York NY 10024-6509 Office Phone: 212-787-0239.

KOTOSKE, ROGER ALLEN, artist, educator; b. South Bend, Ind., Jan. 4, 1933; s. Michael and Louise (Gallo) K.; 1 child, Tamara. Student, U. Notre Dame, 1950-52; BFA, U. Denver, 1955, MA, 1956. Instr. Fitzsimons Army Hosp., Denver, 1956-58, U. Denver, 1958-68; mem. faculty U. Ill., 1968—; now assoc. prof. Vice pres., artist Denver Nat. Sculpture Symposium, 1968 One man shows James Yu Gallery, N.Y.C., 1974, Hiestand Gallery, Miami U., Oxford, Ohio, 1978, Hilton Center for Performing Arts, St. Louis, 1979, group shows include, Galex Nat. 23, Galesburg, Ill., 1989, Greater Midwest Internat. III, Warrensburg, Mo., 1988, SUNY, Potsdam, 1975, Grey Gallery, N.Y.C., 1976, Illinois Painters III, 1980; exhibited in group show U. Del., Newark, 1986, U. of Ill. Faculty Internat. Exchange Exhbn., Chinese Fine Arts Mus., Beijing, China, 1987, Art Yard, Denver, 1996, Vanguard Art in Colo. 1940-1970, Boulder Mus. Contemporary Art, 1999; represented in permanent collections Rock Hill Nelson Gallery, Kansas City, Mo., SUNY, Oswego, Denver Art Mus., others. Ford Found. grantee, 1975-78 Home: 1611 W White St Champaign IL 61821-3017

KOTOVSKY, KENNETH, psychology educator; b. Pitts., July 5, 1939; s. Jacob and Dorothy (Friedland) K.; m. Avis Brenda Lovit, June 10, 1962; children: Laura Lovit, Jack. BS in Econs./Polit. Sci., MIT, 1961; MS in Psychology, Carnegie Mellon U., 1970, PhD In Psychology, 1983. Systems analyst Stanford Rsch. Inst.-Control Systems Lab., Menlo Park, Calif., 1962-64 summers; USPHS trainee Biophys. Lab. Eye & Ear Hosp. of Pitts., Pitts., 1963-64; instr. biology C.C. Allegheny County, Pitts., 1966-70, asst. prof. biology and psychology, 1970-75, assoc. prof., chmn. psychology, 1976-81, prof. psychology, 1981-89; assoc. prof., dir. undergrad. studies Carnegie Mellon U., Pitts., 1989—2000, prof. psychology, 2000—. Rsch. assoc. psychology Carnegie Mellon U., Pitts., 1983-88, adj. prof. psychology, 1988-89. Editor: (with David Klahr) Complex Information Processing: The Impact of Herbert A. Simon, 1989, (with B. Fischhoff, H. Tuma and J. Bielak) A Two State Solution in the Middle East: Prospects and Possibilities, 1993; contbr. articles to profl. jours. Bd. dirs. Mid. East Forum, Pitts., 1987—; chmn. Troop com. Boy Scouts Am., Pitts., 1984-86; mem. Reizenstein Consortium Community Orgns., Pitts., 1979-82; com. on planning and allocation Pvt. Industry Coun. Allegheny County, 1988-91. Recipient Advising award Carnegie Mellon U., 1986, Best Paper award Xerox, 1993; fellow NSF, 1964-66, grantee, 1981, 85-87 Mem. APA, Am. Psychol. Soc., Cognitive Sci. Soc. Democrat. Jewish. Avocations: skiing, bicycling, canoeing, sailing. Home: 1310 Murray Ave Pittsburgh PA 15217-1223 Office: Carnegie Mellon U Psychology Dept Pittsburgh PA 15213 Office Phone: 412-268-8110. Business E-Mail: kotovsky@cmu.edu.

KOTSAY, MARK STEVEN, professional baseball player; b. Woodler, Calif., Dec. 2, 1975; Student, Calif. State U., Fullerton. Ctr. field, right field Fla. Marlins, 1996—2000, San Diego Padres, 2000—03, Oakland Atheletics, 2004—. Named Most Outstanding Player Coll. World Series, 1995; recipient Golden Spikes award, USA Baseball, 1995. Achievements include being a mem. of U.S. Olympic Baseball Team, 1996; being tied for Ea. League for double plays by outfielder with four, 1997. Mailing: care Oakland Atheletics Network Assoc Coliseum 7000 Coliseum Way Oakland CA 94621*

KOTSOVOS, JERRY FRANK, retired secondary school educator, writer; b. Portland, Oreg., May 20, 1946; s. John Gerald and Bernice Marie Kotsovos; m. Sharon Irene Brumfield, Aug. 10, 1967; children: Darren Wade, Laura Eve. BS, U. Oreg., 1968; MS, So. Oreg. U., 1971. Cert. tchr. Oreg. Social studies tchr. Marshfield H.S., Coos Bay, Oreg., 1968—2003; ret., 2003. Cons. advanced placement program Coll. Bd., Princeton, NJ, 1984—2001. Author: Comfortable Lies and Uncomfortable Truths, 2005. Mem. walkathons March of Dimes, Coos Bay; mem. Tchr. Participation in Presdl. Classroom, Washington, 1974; campaign worker Dem. Party, Coos Bay, 1972. Recipient Tchr. Recognition award, U.S. Dept. Edn., 1999. Mem.: NEA, Coos Bay Edn. Assn. (rep. 1970). Achievements include topic of Time mag. article, 1977. Avocations: travel, distance running. Home: 5508 NW Jackson St Camas WA 98607 Personal E-mail: jskots@aol.com.

KOTT, ALAN, state agency administrator; b. Bronx, N.Y., Mar. 8, 1948; s. Murray and Lee (Raffelson) K.; m. Carol Mary Portanova, Nov. 4, 2000; children: Joni, Amy, Greg, Tyler, Corbin. BA in Psychology, Queens Coll., Flushing, N.Y., 1970; MA in Psychology, New Sch. for Social Rsch., N.Y.C., 1972; PhD, NYU, 1990. Psychometrician L.I. Jewish-Hillside Med. Ctr., Glen Oaks, N.Y., 1971-74; from rsch. scientist to unit chief Office of Alcoholism and Substance Abuse Svcs. State of N.Y., N.Y.C., 1974-86, asst. dir., 1987—2003; dir. Office of Alcoholism and Substance Abuse Svcs. State of N.Y., N.Y.C., 2004—. Prin. investigator Narcotic and Drug Rsch., Inc., N.Y.C., 1985-87; chmn. Evaluation Subcom. Task Force on Integrated Projects, N.Y.C., 1987-94; mem. Task Force Youth Substance Abuse State of N.Y., Albany, 1986-87, Combined Psychiat. and Addictive Disorders, N.Y.C., 1986-88; mem. rsch. Task Force Mentally Impaired Chem. Abusers, 1989-93; chmn. Evaluation Systems Program Adv. Com., 1995—; project dir. N.Y. State Treatment Outcomes and Performance Pilot Studies II, 1998-2002; chmn. N.Y. State Office of Alcoholism and Substance Abuse Svcs. IMPALA Adv. Com., 1999-2002. Mem.: AIAA, AAAS, Nat. Space Soc., Banner House. Office Phone: 518-485-7189. E-mail: alankott@oasas.state.ny.us.

KOTT, DAVID RUSSELL, lawyer; b. Trenton, N.J., Jan. 22, 1952; s. Maurice G. and Ruth (Shulman) K.; m. Lauren Handler, Aug. 24, 1980; children: Emily R., Adam J. BA, Am. U., 1973; JD, Rutgers U., 1977. Bar: N.J. 1977, U.S. Dist. Ct. N.J. 1977, U.S. Ct. Appeals (3d cir.) 1980, N.Y. 1984, U.S. Dist. Ct. (so. and ea. dists.) N.Y. 1985; cert. civil trial atty. Law clk. to justice N.J. Supreme Ct., Morristown, 1977-78; from assoc. to ptnr. McCarter & English LLP, Newark, 1978—. Sustaining mem. Product Liability Adv. Coun. Fellow Am. Coll. Trial Lawyers; mem. ABA, Am. Bd. Trial Advocates, N.J. Bar Assn., Essex County Bar Assn., Assn. Def. Trial Lawyers Attys., Trial Lawyers N.J., Fedn. Ins. and Corp. Attys., Def. Rsch. Inst., The Newark Club, Club at World Trade Ctr. Republican. Jewish. Office: McCarter & English LLP 4 Gateway Ctr 100 Mulberry St Newark NJ 07102-4004 Office Phone: 973-622-4444. Business E-Mail: dkott@mccarter.com.

KOTTAMASU, MOHAN RAO (K.V.R. MOHAN RAO), physician, health facility administrator; b. Gudivada, India, Jan. 13, 1947; arrived in U.S., 1973; s. Janardana Rao and Kantharatnamma (Maddi) Kottamasu; m. Sarada Devi Vusirikala, Dec. 20, 1992; children: Pallavi, Aamani. MBBS, Gulbarga Med. Coll., 1972. Diplomate Am. Bd. Internal Medicine, 1977, in pulmonary disease Am. Bd. Internal Medicine, 1980. House surgeon Govt. Gen. Hosp., Gulbarga, India, 1971-72; intern St. Vincent's Med. Ctr. Richmond, S.I., NY, 1973-74, resident, 1974-76, chief resident, 1976-77; pulmonary diseases fellow Lahey Clinic and Deaconess Hosp., Boston, 1977-79; clin. fellow Harvard Med. Sch., Boston, 1978-79; assoc. Valley Pulmonary and Med. Assocs., Springfield, Mass., 1979-81, ptnr., v.p., 1981—. Adj. asst. prof. clin. pharmacy Mass. Coll. Pharmacy and Allied Health Scis., 1984—; pres. med. staff Mercy Hosp., Springfield, 1989—91. Pres. house staff St. Vincent's Med. Ctr., 1976; founding pres. Indian Assn. Greater Springfield, 1985—86. Fellow: ACP, Am. Coll. Chest Physicians; mem.: AMA, Hampden Dist. Med. Soc. (pres.-elect 1999, pres. 2000—01, Cmty. Clinician of the Yr. 2001), Mass. Med. Soc., Am. Thoracic Soc. Hindu. Avocations: chess, gardening. Home: 112 Twin Hills Dr Longmeadow MA 01106-2952 Office: Valley Pulmonary Med Assocs 222 Carew St Springfield MA 01104-4103 Office Phone: 413-739-5661.

KOTTAS, JOHN FREDERICK, business administration educator; b. Hampton, Va., Apr. 18, 1940; s. Harry and Johnny (Edwards) K.; m. Betty Ann Hokenson, Aug. 7, 1965; children: John Bohlin, Ellen Elizabeth, Katherine Caroline, Paul Frederick. BS, Purdue U., 1962; MS, Northwestern U., 1964, PhD, 1968. Lectr. Wharton Sch., U. Pa., Phila., 1966-68; asst. prof. Sch. Bus. Adminstrn., U. N.C., Chapel Hill., 1968-73; adj. assoc. prof. Boston U. Overseas Grad. Program, Heidelberg, W. Ger., 1973-74; asso. prof. coordinator mgmt. sci. and info. systems Sch. Bus. Adminstrn., U. Mo., St. Louis, 1974-79; Zollinger prof. bus. adminstrn. Coll. William and Mary, Williamsburg, Va., 1979—. Presented three-day mgmt. seminar on Inventory Mgmt. and Control at numerous univs., U.S. and Can., 1976-78; cons. in field. Co-author: Production/Operations Management: Contemporary Policy of Managing Operating Systems, 1972, Cases and Applications in Lotus 1-2-3 (for DOS), 1995, Cases and Applications in Lotus 1-2-3 (for Windows), 1996, Cases and Applications in Microsoft EXCEL 5.0, 1996; contbr. articles to various publs. NDEA fellow, 1962-65; Walter P. Murphy fellow, 1962 Home: 109 Maxwell Pl Williamsburg VA 23185-5523 Office: Coll of William and Mary Sch Bus Adminstrn Williamsburg VA 23187 Office Phone: 757-221-2868. Personal E-mail: jfkott@cox.net. Business E-Mail: john.kottas@business.wm.edu.

KOTTER, JOHN PAUL, organizational behavior educator, management consultant; b. San Diego, Feb. 25, 1947; s. Paul Henry and Louise (Churchill) K.; m. Nancy Dearman; children: Jonathan, Caroline. BS, MIT, 1968, MS, 1970; D.BA, Harvard U., 1972. Rsch. fellow Harvard Bus. Sch., Boston, 1972-73, asst. prof., 1973-77, assoc. prof., 1977—80, prof., 1980—90, named Konosuke Matsushita Prof. of Leadership, 1990; ret. Cons. in field. Author: The General Managers, 1982, Power and Influence, 1985, The Leadership Factor, 1988, A Force for Change, 1990, Corporate Culture and Performance, 1992, The New Rules, 1995, Leading Change, 1996, Matsushita Leadership, 1997 (Fin. Times/Booz-Allen and Hamilton Global Bus. Book Award for biography/autobiography, 1998), John P. Kotter on What Leaders Really Do, 1999, The Heart of Change, 2002, others. Named #1 "leadership guru" in Am., Bus. Week mag., 2001; recipient Exxon Award for Innovation in Grad. Bus. Sch. Curriculum Design, Johnson, Smith and Knisely Award for New Perspectives in Bus. Leadership. Office: Harvard Bus Sch Soldiers Fld Boston MA 02163 E-mail: jkotter@hbs.edu.*

KOTTER, RITA JOAN, theatre educator, design consultant; b. Superior, Wis., Aug. 6, 1934; d. Edward Kotter and Mernnie Geraldine Bellino; children: Rebekah West, Laura Majors, Richmond Majors. BA, U. of Wis., 1952—56; MA, U. of Colo., 1959—69. Teacher Certification Colo., 1959. Tchr., theatre, speech, English Beloit Pub. Schools, Wis., 1956—57, Roseville Pub. Schs., Mich., 1957—58, Canon City Pub. Schs., Colo., 1959—60, Brighton Pub. Schs., Colo., 1960—64, Boulder Valley Schs., Colo., 1964—91; fine arts dept. chair Fairview H.S., Boulder, Colo.; parliamentarian U. of Colo. Bd. of Regents, 1999—. Pub. speaking trainer Boulder Bus. & Profl. Women, Boulder, Colo., 1993—; theatre cons. Carousel Dinner Theatre, Ft. Collins, Colo., 1992—94; master artist-in-residence Deer Creek Elem. Sch., Bailey, Colo., 1993—93; student tchr. supr. U. of No. Colo., 1993—94. Pres. Secondary Sch. Theatre Assn., Washington, 1983—85; bd. of nominations chair Am. Theatre Assn., Washington, D.C., 1973—85; pres. Arts & Humanities Assembly of Boulder County, 1965—2005; chair Leadership Boulder-C. of C., 1993—97; parliamentarian Alliance for Colo. Theatre, Denver, 1984—97; treas. Rocky Mountain Theatre Assn., Denver, 1989—93; adjudicator Am. Coll. Theatre Festival, 1972—92, Festival of Am. Cmty. Theatres, Denver, 1980—90. Recipient Women Who Light up the Cmty., Boulder C. of C., 1999, Inaugural Hall of Fame, Colo. Thespian Soc., 2000, AMOCO Gold Medallion of Excellence, Rocky Mountain/Am. Coll. Theatre Festival, 1984, Alpha Psi Omega Outstanding Theatre Student, U. of Wis. at Superior, 1956, Disting. Svc. award, Alliance for Colo. Theatre, 1993. Mem.: Boulder Bus. & Profl. Women (parliamentarian 1994—2000), Am. Alliance for Theatre & Edn. (dir. of stds. 1987—91), Colo. Alliance for Arts Edn (v.p. 2003—04). Avocations: reading, theatre, skating, tennis, dance. Home: 1407 Bradley Dr Boulder CO 80305

KOTTICK, EDWARD LEON, musician, educator; b. Jersey City, June 16, 1930; s. Hyman W. and Frieda M. (Stoller) K.; m. Gloria Astor, May 10, 1953; children: Judith, Janet AB, NYU, 1953; MA, Tulane U., 1959; PhD, U. N.C., Chapel Hill, 1962. Trombonist New Orleans Philharm., 1955-57; asst. prof. music Alma Coll., Mich., 1962-65; vis. prof. music U. Kans., Lawrence, 1965-66; assoc. prof. music U. Mo.-St. Louis, 1966-68; prof. music U. Iowa, Iowa City, 1968-92, prof. emeritus, 1992. Author: The Unica in the Chansonnier Cordiforme, No. 42 of Corpus Mensurabilis Musicae, 1967, Tone and Intonation on the Recorder, 1974, The Collegium: A Handbook, 1977, The Harpsichord Owner's Guide, 1987; author: (with G. Lucktenberg) Early Keyboard Instruments in European Museums, 1997; contbr. articles to profl. jours.; author: A History of the Harpsichord, 2003. With U.S. Army, 1953-55. U. Iowa grantee, 1975, 80, 85, 90, summer fellow, 1976; Galpin Soc. grantee, 1978. Mem. Am. Mus. Instrument Soc. (bd. govs. 1986-90, Am. Musicol. Soc. (chpt. sec. 1961-62, chpt. program com. 1964-66, chair com. 1972-73, 96-97, mem. nat. com. Collegium Musicum 1973-75), Fellowship Makers and Restorers of Hist. Instruments, Galpin Soc., Guild Am. Luthiers, Midwestern Hist. Keyboard Soc. (bd. dirs. 1980-90, 94-97). Home: 502 Larch Ln Iowa City IA 52245-3434 Personal E-mail: ed@kottick.com.

KOTTING, JOEY, artist; Exhibitions include White Columns, White Room Gallery, 1998, Atrocity Exhibition, Yvon Lambert, 2004, Print Publishers Spotlight: Universal Limited Art Editions, Barbara Krakow Gallery, 2004. Fellow Guggenheim Meml. Found., 2004. Mailing: c/o Barbara Krakow Gallery 10 Newbury St Boston MA 02116*

KOTTMEYER, MARTIN S., writer, farmer; b. Breese, Ill., Aug. 11, 1953; s. Martin and Alvera (Woker) K. AS, Kaskaskia Coll., Centralia, Ill., 1973. Engaged in farming, Carlyle, Ill., 1970s—. Contbr. articles to Magonia, The Reall News, Ency. of the Paranormal, Ency. of Extraterrestrial Encounters, others. Recipient Dr. Alexander Imich award Soc. for Enlightenment and Transformation of UN, 1995, Internat. Zurich prize, FundaciOn Anomalla, 1999. Mem. Rational Exam. Assn. of Lincoln Land. Avocations: ufo culture, science fiction, bad movies. Home: 10501 Knolhoff Rd Carlyle IL 62231-3523

KOTTRABA, CARIN, psychologist; b. Balt., June 11, 1976; d. Robert Paul and Mary Brookes Kottraba; m. Scott P. Hill. MA in Clin. Psychology, MS in Indsl./Orgnl. Psychology, Calif. Sch. Profl. Psychology, 2001, PhD in Clin. Psychology, PhD in Indsl./Orgnl. Psychology, 2003. Therapist Villa View Cmty. Hosp., San Diego, 2000—01, Pomerado Hosp., San Diego, 2001—, Palomar Hosp., San Diego, 2002—; clin. psychologist Calif. State Prison, L.A. County, 2003—. Tchg. asst. and rschr. Calif. Sch. Profl. Psychology, San Diego, 2001—02; cons. Calif. State U., San Marcos, Calif., 1998—99, S. Ctrl. L.A. (Calif.) Regional Ctr., 2000—01, Bader Group Cons., San Diego, 2001—02; compensation cons. Bauer & Wilson, Ltd., Balt., 2002—03. Contbr. articles to profl. jours. Fellow, Orgnl. Cons. Ctr., 1998—2000; grantee, Calif. Sch. Profl. Psychology, 2001—03. Mem.: APA, Am. Psychol. Soc., Soc. for Indsl./Orgnl. Psychology (presenter profl. conf. 2004), Ea. Psychol. Assn. Republican. Roman Cath. Avocations: cooking, skiing, snorkeling, scuba diving, skydiving. Office: 44750 60th St W Lancaster CA 93536-7620 E-mail: ckottraba@excite.com.

KOTUK, ANDREA MIKOTAJUK, public relations executive, writer; b. New Brunswick, N.J., Oct. 19, 1948; d. Michael and Julia Dorothy (Muka) Mikotajuk. BA, Douglass Coll., Rutgers U., 1970. Pub. relations asst. Wall St. Jour. Newspaper Fund, Princeton, N.J., 1970; editorial asst. Redbook mag., N.Y.C., 1970-71; asst. pub. relations dir. Children's Aid Soc., N.Y.C., 1971-75; assoc. pub. relations dir. Planned Parenthood, N.Y.C., 1975-80; pres. Andrea & Assocs., N.Y.C., 1980—. Writer publicist for non-profit agys.; contbg. editor Arts Mag., 1970-75. Office: Andrea & Assocs 5th Floor 112 E 23rd St New York NY 10010-4518 Office Phone: 212-353-9585.

KOTULA, MICHAEL ANTHONY, lawyer; b. Rockville Centre, N.Y., Aug. 17, 1965; s. Michael Stanley and Rosemary Therese Kotula. BA, Emory U., 1987; JD with honors, George Washington U., 1990. Bar: N.J. 1990, D.C. 1991, N.Y. 1995, U.S. Dist. Ct. N.J. 1990, U.S. Dist. Ct. D.C. 1992, U.S. Dist. Ct. (ea. and so. dists.) N.Y. 1998, U.S. Ct. Appeals (3rd cir.) 1992. Law clk. Hon. Curtis E. von Kann U.S. Superior Ct. (D.C.), Washington, 1990-91; assoc. Carr, Goodson, Lee & Warner, Washington, 1991-94, Rivkin, Radler, LLP, Uniondale, NY, 1994-98, ptnr., 1998—. Contbg. author: The Law of Liability Insurance, 1999; contbr. articles to profl. jours.; conf. lectr. Recipient Outstanding Advocate award Met. Washington Trial Lawyers Assn., 1990. Mem. N.Y. State Bar Assn. (exec. com. young lawyers sect. 1997-2001, liaison to the environ. law sect. 1997-2001). Avocations: running, weightlifting, travel, sports, kayaking. Office: Rivkin Radler Eab Plz Uniondale NY 11556-0001 E-mail: michael.kotula@rivkin.com.

KOTWAL, RUSS STEVEN, military officer, physician; b. Birmingham, Ala., Sept. 16, 1964; m. Bari Marie Petree, Feb. 16, 1985; children: Ashley Russell, Aaron Steven, Kirstyn Marie. BS, Tex. A&M U., Coll. Sta., Tex., 1985; MD, Uniformed Svcs. U. of the Health Scis., Bethesda, Md., 1996; M in Pub. Health, U. of Tex. Med. Br., Galveston, Tex., 2004. Fellow Am. Acad. of Family Physicians, 2003, Diplomate Am. Bd. of Family Physicians, 1999. Residency in family practice Martin Army Cmty. Hosp., Ft. Benning, Ga., 1996—99; ranger bn. surgeon 3d Bn., 75th Ranger Rgt., Fort Benning, Ga., 1999—2003; residency in aerospace medicine Inst. Naval Operational Medicine, Pensacola, Fla., 2004—05. Adj. asst. prof. Dept. of Mil. and Emergency Medicine, The Uniformed Svcs. Univ. of the Health Sci., 2004—05. Contbr. articles pub. to profl. jour. Maj. U.S. Army, 1985—2005, Tex., Hawaii, Md., Ga., Fla. Decorated 2 Bronze Stars, 1 Meritorious Svc. Medal, 3 Army Commendation Medals, 4 Army Achievement Medals U.S. Army; recipient Chmn. of the Joint Chiefs of Staff Award for Excellence in Mil. Medicine, Dept. of Def., 2000. Mem.: AMA (us army surgeon gen. rep. 1992—96), Uniformed Svcs. Acad. of Family Physicians, Spl. Ops. Med. Assn., Assn. of the US Army, Aerospace Med. Assn., Assn. of Mil. Surgeons of the US, Am. Acad. of Family Physicians, Soc. of US Army Flight Surgeons (life). Achievements include research in Malaria, combat parachute injuries, pain control in combat; Three combat tours, two in Afghanistan and one in Iraq; Sr. mil. parachutist with two combat jumps, one into Afghanistan in October 2001 and one into Iraq in March 2003. Avocations: travel, parachuting, rugby. Office: Naval Operational Medicine Institute 340 Hulse Road Pensacola FL 32508 Office Phone: 850-982-6264.

KOTZ, NATHAN KALLISON (NICK KOTZ), news correspondent; b. San Antonio, Sept. 16, 1932; s. Jacob and Tybe (Kallison) K.; m. Mary Lynn Booth, Aug. 7, 1960; 1 child, Jack Mitchell. AB magna cum laude in Internat. Relations, Dartmouth Coll., 1955; student, London Sch. Econs., 1955-56. Reporter, Des Moines Register, 1958-64, Washington corr., 1964-70; also for other Cowles Publs. (newspapers); nat. corr. Washington Post, 1970-73; adj. prof. Sch. Communication, Am. U., Washington, 1978-86; sr. journalist in residence Duke U., 1983; corr. PBS Frontline, 1992. Farmer, Broad Run, Va., 1980— Free-lance writer, 1973; author: Let Them Eat Promises: The Politics of Hunger in America, 1969, Wild Blue Yonder: Money, Politics, and the B-1 Bomber, 1988, Judgment Days: Lyndon Baines Johnson, Martin Luther King, Jr., and the Laws That Changed America, 2005; co-author: The Unions, 1971, A Passion for Equality: George Wiley and the Movement, 1977. Bd. dirs. Iowa Bds. Internat. Edn., 1962-64, Suburban Md. Fair Housing, 1966-72, Black Student Fund, 1976-86—, Penn-Faulkner, 1986—; bd. dirs. Fund for Investigative Journalism, 1977-86, chmn., 1978-82. Served to 1st lt. USMCR, 1956-58. Recipient Pulitzer prize for nat. reporting, 1968; Raymond Clapper Meml. award, 1966, 68; 2d pl., 1973; Disting. Service award Sigma Delta Chi, 1966; Robert F. Kennedy Journalism award, 1968; Spl. Merit award Am. U., 1981, award for pub. service Nat. Mag., 1985; Adj. Faculty award Am. U., 1985; Olive Branch award NYU Ctr. for War, Peace and News Media, 1989. Mem. Nat. Press Club, Cosmos Club, Phi Beta Kappa. Mailing: Author Mail Houghton Mifflin 222 Berkeley St Boston MA 02116

KOTZ, SAMUEL, statistician, educator, translator, editor; b. Harbin, China, Aug. 28, 1930; s. Boris and Guta (Kahana) K.; m. Roselyn Greenwald, Aug. 6, 1963; children: Tamar Ann, Harold David, Pauline Esther. MSc with honors, Hebrew U., Jerusalem, 1956; PhD, Cornell U., 1960; Dr. honoris causa, U. Athens, 1995, Harbin Inst. Tech., 1984, Bowling Green State U., 1997. Rschr. Israel Meteorol. Svc., 1954-58; lectr. Bar-Ilan U., Israel, 1960-62; postdoctoral Ford fellow U. NC, 1962-63; assoc. prof. U. Toronto, 1963-67; prof. math. Temple U., 1967-79; prof. stats. U. Md., College Park, 1979-97, disting. scholar-tchr., 1984-85. Disting. vis. prof. Bucknell U., 1977, Guelph (Can.) U., 1987; hon. prof. Harbin Inst. Tech., 1987; Eugene Lukacs disting. rsch. prof. Bowling Green (Ohio) State U., 1992; vis. prof. U. Luleå, Sweden, 1993, 95, Hong Kong U., 1994, U. Copenhagen, summer 1996, U. South Brittany, Vannes, France, 1998; vis. prof. econs. and fin. St. Petersburg (Russia) U., summer 1995; vis. rschr. Internat. Statis. Inst., The Hague, summer 1996, U. Paul Sabatier, Toulouse, France, summer 1998, U. York, Eng., 1999, U. Salford, Eng., 1999, 2000, Athens U. Econs., 1999, U. Lund, Sweden, 2000; vis. sr. rsch. scholar George Washington U., 1997—, U. Trento, Italy, summers, 2001, 02, U. Padua, 2002, U. Bologna, 2002. Author, editor 30 books, 4 Russian-English profl. dictionaries, over 130 rsch. papers; translator 18 books; co-editor-in-chief: Encyclopedia of Statistical Sci., 9 vols. and supplement, 1982-89, editor-in-chief up-date vols. 1-3, 1994-98; co-editor: Breakthroughs in Statistics, 3 vol., 1995-98; editor: Leading Statistical Personalities, 1997; co-author: Process Capability Indices, 1993, 98, Applied Bayesian Statistics (in Chinese), 2000, 2d edit., 2001, Extreme Value Distributions, 2000, Correlation and Dependence, 2001, Laplace Distributions and Applications, 2001, Strength-Stress Models, 2003, Statistical Size Distributions in Economics, 2003, Multivariate T-distributions and Applications, 2004, Beyond Beta, 2005; mem. editl. bd. Jour. Quality Rsch. and Tech.; coord. editor Jour. Statis. Planning and Inference, AIEE Transactions; editor-in-chief: Quality Management. Served with Israeli Army, 1950-52. Fellow Am. Statis. Assn., Inst. Math. Stat., Royal Statis. Soc., Washington Acad. Sci. (hon.); mem. Internat. Statis. Inst. (elected mem.). Office: George Washington U Dept Engring Mgmt and Sys Analysis Washington DC 20052-0001 Office Phone: 202-994-7187. Business E-Mail: kotz@gwu.edu.

KOTZWINKLE, WILLIAM, writer; b. Scranton, Pa., Nov. 22, 1938; s. William John and Madolyn (Murphy) K.; m. Elizabeth Gundy. Student, Rider Coll., Pa. State U. Author: The Fireman, 1969, The Ship That Came Down the Gutter, 1970, Elephant Boy: The Story of the Stone Age, 1970, The Day the Gang Got Rich, 1970, The Oldest Man, and Other Timeless Tales, 1971, Elephant Bangs Train, 1971, The Return of Crazy Horse, 1971, Hermes 3000, 1972, The Supreme, Superb, Exalted and Delightful, One and Only Magic Building, 1973, Up the Alley with Jack and Joe, 1974, The Fat Man, 1974, Night-Book, 1974, Swimmer in the Secret Sea, 1975, The Leopard's Tooth, 1976, Doctor Rat, 1976 (World Fantasy award best novel 1977), Fata Morgana, 1977, Herr Nightingale and the Satin Women, 1978, The Ants Who Took Away Time, 1978, Dream of Dark Harbor, 1979, The Nap Master, 1979, Jack in the Box, 1980 (pub. as Book of Love, 1982), Christmas at Fontaine's, 1982, (novelization of screenplay) E.T., The Extra-Terrestrial, 1982 (N.D. Children's Choice award 1983, Buckeye award 1984), (novelization of screenplay) Superman III, 1983, Great World Circus, 1983, Queen of Swords, 1983, Trouble in Bugland: A Collection of Inspector Mantis Mysteries, 1983, E.T., The Book of the Green Planet, 1985, Seduction in Berlin, 1985, Jewel of the Moon, 1985, Heart of Wood, and Other Timeless Tales, 1986, The World Is Big and I'm So Small, 1986, The Exile, 1987, The Midnight

Examiner, 1989, Hot Jazz Trio, 1989, The Empty Notebook, 1990, The Game of Thirty, 1994, The Million Dollar Bear, 1995, Tales from the Empty Notebook, 1996, The Bear Went Over the Mountain, 1996, The Amphora Project, 2005; screenwriter: (films) A Nightmare on Elm Street 4: The Dream Master, 1988, Book of Love, 1991; co-author (with Glenn Murray and Audrey Colman) Walter the Farting Dog, 2001, Walter the Farting Dog: Trouble at the Yard Sale, 2004. Recipient Nat. Mag. award for fiction, 1972, 75; O'Henry prize, 1975. Office: Doubleday 1540 Broadway New York NY 10036-4039

KOUBEK, EKATERINA N., education educator; b. Moscow, Jan. 30, 1971; d. Nadezhda Matveyevna and Nikolay Ivanovich Zagoudaev; m. James David Koubek, Apr. 29, 1997; 1 child, Anna Maria. PhD, U. Nebraska, Lincoln, 2002. Tchr. English Caledonian Sch., Prague, Czech Republic, 1994—97; tchg. asst. U. Nebr., Lincoln, 1998—2002, rsch. assoc., 2002—03, lectr. of Czech, 1998—99, 2003—04; asst. prof. edn./ESL Buena Vista U., Storm Lake, Iowa, 2004—. Contbr. articles to profl. jours. Mem.: MLA. Avocations: travel, languages. Home: 207 Lake Ave Storm Lake IA 50588 Office: 610 W 4th St Storm Lake IA 50588 Office Phone: 712-749-2215. Personal E-mail: koubel@bvu.edu.

KOUCHOUKOS, NICHOLAS THOMAS, surgeon; b. Grand Rapids, Mich., Dec. 26, 1936; s. Thomas Paul and Antoinette (Karver) K.; m. Judith Buell, Aug. 24, 1966; children— Nicholas Thomas, Robert Buell, Thomas Paul. Student (James B. Angell scholar), U. Mich., 1954-57; MD cum laude, Washington U., 1961. Diplomate Am. Bd. Thoracic Surgery (bd. dirs. 1989-96). Intern Barnes Hosp., Washington U. Med. Ctr., St. Louis, 1961-62, asst. resident in surgery, 1962-65, chief adminstrv. resident, 1965-66; sr. clin. trainee in surgery USPHS, 1966-67; asst. in surgery Sch. Medicine Washington U., St. Louis, 1961-65, instr. surgery, 1965-67, John M. Shoenberg prof. cardiovascular surgery, 1984-96, vice chmn. dept. surgery, 1993-96; research fellow surgery Sch. Medicine, U. Ala., Birmingham, 1967-68, instr. surgery, 1967-69, advanced trainee thoracic and cardiovascular surgery, 1968-70, asst. prof. surgery, 1969-71, assoc. prof., 1971-74, prof., vice-dir. div. thoracic and cardiovascular surgery, 1974-81, John W. Kirklin prof. cardiovascular surgery, 1981, clin. prof., 1981-84; cardiovascular surgeon-in-chief Jewish Hosp. of St. Louis, 1984-96, surgeon in chief, 1988-96; mem. cardiovascular research study com. Am. Heart Assn., 1977-79; surgery study sect. USPHS, Bethesda, Md., 1977-80; vice chmn. dept. surgery Washington U. Sch. Medicine, St. Louis, 1991-96. Ad hoc cons. Specialized Centers in Research Arteriosclerosis, Nat. Heart and Lung Inst., Bethesda, 1971-72, mem. ad hoc rev. com. for collaborative studies on coronary artery surgery, 1973-75, surgery A study sect., 1976-77; mem. merit rev. bd. in cardiovascular studies VA, Washington, 1976-78 Editorial bd. Jour. Cardiac Rehab., 1979-84, Current Topics in Cardiology, 1977-92, Circulation, 1978-81, 86-88, Cardiology Update, 1979-92, Annals Thoracic Surgery, 1980-89, Cardiosat, 1984-92; assoc. editor Jour. Thoracic and Cardiovascular Surgery, 1994-98. Fellow: ACS, Am. Coll. Cardiology (asst. treas. 1997—99, sec. 1999—2000, finalist Young Investigators award 1962); mem.: AAUP, AMA, Internat. Cardiovascular Soc., Soc. Vascular Surgery, Soc. Univ. Surgeons, So. Surg. Assn., So. Thoracic Surg. Assn., St. Louis Thoracic Surg. Soc. (pres. 1993—95), Soc. Thoracic Surgeons (treas. 1992—97, v.p. 1998, pres. 1999—2000), John Kirklin Soc., St. Louis Met. Med. Soc., Internat. Surg. Soc., Assn. Acad. Surgery, Assn. Clin. Cardiac Surgeons, Am. Surg. Assn., Am. Assn. Thoracic Surgery, Alpha Omega Alpha, Phi Beta Kappa. Home: 25 Picardy Ln Saint Louis MO 63124-1606 Office: Mo Bapt Hosp 3009 N Ballas Rd Ste 266C Saint Louis MO 63131-2308 Office Phone: 314-996-5287. Personal E-mail: ntkouch@aol.com.

KOUCKY, JOHN RICHARD, metallurgical engineer, manufacturing executive; b. Chgo., Sept. 21, 1934; s. Frank Louis and Ella (Harshman) K.; m. Beverly Irene O'Dell, Aug. 16, 1958 (dec. May 1990); children: Deborah, Diane; m. Beverly Kay Cummins, Apr. 27, 1991 (dec. Jan. 1996); m. Mary Ann Hubbard, Jan. 4, 1997. BS in MetE., U. Ill., 1957; MBA, Northwestern U., 1959. Metallurgist, asst. plant mgr. Fansteel Metall. Corp., North Chicago, Ill., 1957-64; supr. production engring. cen. foundry div. Gen. Motors Corp., Saginaw, Mich., 1964-67; asst. gen. mgr. Marion (Ind.) Malleable Iron, 1967-68; mgr. production engring. tech., plant mgr., v.p. engr. Wagner Castings Co., Decatur, Ill., 1968-79, 83-91; v.p., gen. mgr. Pa. mall iron div. Gulf & Western, Lancaster, 1979-82; v.p. tech. Wagner Laser Techs., 1989-94; v.p. Decatur Mfg. Co., 1993-95, 300 Below, Inc., Decatur, 1993—. 1st lt. U.S. Army, 1957—58. Mem. Am. Soc. Metals (local chmn. 1976—), Am. Foundrymans Soc. (local vice chmn. 1968—), Ductile Iron Soc. (nat. bd. dirs. 1983—), Iron Castings Soc., Soc. Automotive Engrs., U. Ill. Dept. Materials Sci. Alumni Assn. (bd. dirs. 1983-98, Loyalty award 1986), Gray Iron Founders Assn., Soc. for Advancement Material and Process Engring., Country Club Decatur, Decatur Tennis Club (pres. 1976-78), Decatur Racquet Club. Republican. Avocations: tennis, golf, bridge, gardening. Home: 510 Greenway Ln Decatur IL 62521-2533 Office: 300 Below Inc 2999 Parkway Dr Decatur IL 62526 Office Phone: 217-423-3070. E-mail: jkoucky@300below.com.

KOUFIS, JOHN THEODORE, accountant; b. East Lansing, Mich., June 28, 1965; s. Theodore John and Helen Constantinos (Athanasopoulos) K. BS in Acctg., DePaul U., 1987. CPA, Ill. Audit assoc. Coopers & Lybrand, Chgo., 1987-89, audit sr. assoc., 1989-93; asst. contr. NCH Promotional Svcs. divsn. Dun & Bradstreet, Lincolnshire, Ill., 1993-95, contr., 1995-98; CFO Croda Adhesives, Inc., Itasca, Ill., 1998—2001, Knights Apparel LLC, Oakbrook, Ill., 2001—. Mem. AICPAs, Ill. CPA Soc. Avocations: ice hockey, music. Home: 1121 N Thackeray Dr Palatine IL 60067-2751 Office: Knights Apparel LLC 2221 Camden Ct # 390 Oak Brook IL 60523

KOUKLIN, NIKOLAI A., science educator, researcher; m. Irina A. Ionova, Nov. 20, 2000. MS with distinction, Moscow Inst. Physics and Tech., 1998; PhD, U. Nebr., 2001. Prof. U. Wis., Milw., 2005—. Scientist (nanotechnology) 3D Ultra-high dense InGaAsN QDs by nonlithographic technique; contbr. chapters to books. Referee UK Pub. Svc., London, 2002—05. Fellow, Brown U., Providence, 2002—05. Achievements include discovery of Self-assembled nanotube network; development of Second Order Self-Assembly Techniques for Future Electronic Devices; patents for Controlled Assembly of Carbon Nanotube Probes; development of Ultra-dense ZnO Nanowire Array Technology; 3D highly ordered quantum dots. Avocations: swimming, hiking, travel. Office Phone: 414-229-4679.

KOUL, HARI KRISHEN, research scientist, advocate; b. Anantnag, Kashmir, India, Sept. 14, 1963; s. Soom Nath and Shyama (Dulari) K.; m. Sweaty Koul, Apr. 29, 1994; children: Neil, Kashyap. BS in Biology and Chemistry, Kashmir U., 1984, MS in Biochemistry, 1986; PhD in Biochemistry, Postgrad. Inst. Med. Edn. and Rsch., Chandigarh, India, 1990. Jr. rsch. fellow Postgrad. Inst. Med. Edn. and Rsch., 1986-88, sr. rsch. fellow, 1988-90, tutor in biochemistry, 1990-91; postdoctoral fellow in surgery and physiology U. Mass. Med. Sch., Worcester, 1991-94, sr. rsch. assoc. in surgery and physiology, 1994-96, instr. urologic and transplantation surgery, 1996-97; sr. staff scientist, prin. investigator Henry Ford Health Scis. Ctr., Detroit, 1997—2003; prof., dir. rsch. divsn. urology U. Colo. Health Scis. Ctr., Denver, 2003—, program dir. urosciences, 2004—. Program dir. Urolithiasis Rsch. Project, NIH, 1997-2003; mem. NIH-Site visit com. U. Chgo. Program Project, Bethesda, Md., 1999, NIH-Gen. Medicine B-Study sect. and Urology Spl. Emphasis Panel (SEP), 2000, Vet's Health Adminstrn. Rev. Bd., 2004—, various emphasis and rev. panels, NIH, mem. rsch. adv. coun., U. Colo. Sch. Medicine, 2003—, mem. clin. translational rsch. adv. coun., 2004—; vis. prof. Morgan State U., Balt., 2004;mem. U. Colo. Cancer Ctr.; spkr. and lectr. in field. Author: (chpt.) Kidney Stones Medical and Surgical Management, 1996; editl. bd. (journal) Urol. Rsch., 2001; contbr. articles to profl. jours. Pres. Assn. Basic Med. Scientists, Chandigarth, India, 1990-91; mem. Kashmir Overseas Assn., 1991—, ACLU, 1997; founding exec. dir. Save Kashmir Movement, 1999; mem. Am. Friends of India, 2000, India Think Tank, 2000; coord. Panun Kashmir, 2000; mem. Oxalosis and Hyperoxaluria Found., 2001—. Recipient Jr. Rsch. fellowship Coun. Sci. and Indsl. Rsch., New Delhi, 1987, Internat. Scientist of Yr., 2002; Sr. Rsch. fellow Coun. Sci. and Indsl. Rsch., 1988, Postdoctoral fellow U. Mass. Med. Sch., 1991; Rsch. grantee NIH, 1997—. Fellow: Am. Soc. Nephrology, Am. Coll. Nutrition; mem.: AAAS, Soc. of Baric Urologic Rsch., Am. Urological Assn., Soc. Am. Asian Scientists in Cancer Rsch. (bd. dirs. 2004—), Am. Soc. Nephrology, Am. Soc. Biochemistry Molecular Biology, Molecular Medicine Soc., ROCK Soc. (pres. 2005—), Urolithiasis Soc. India, N.Y. Acad. Sci., Am. Chem. Soc., Kashmir Overseas Assn. (bd. dirs. Mich. chpt. 2003, pres.). Avocations: cricket, soccer, international public policy analysis, reading, thinking. Office: Dir Rsch, Divsn Urology and Dept Surgery Univ Colo Sch Medicine 4200 E Ninth Ave, Box C319 Denver CO 80262 Home: 5645 S Havana Ct Englewood CO 80111 Office Phone: 303-315-2385. Business E-Mail: hari.koul@UCHSC.edu. E-mail: harikoul@yahoo.com.

KOURI, DONALD JACK, chemist, educator; b. Hobart, Okla., July 25, 1938; s. Eddie and Theresa LaJuan (Williams) K.; m. Shirley Ann Stewart, Apr. 9, 1965; children: Lisa Renee, David Matthew. BA, Okla. Bapt. U., 1960; MS, U. Wis., 1962, PhD, 1965. Postdoctoral fellow Joint Inst. Lab Astrophysics, U. Colo., 1965-66; asst. prof. chemistry Midwestern U., Wichita Falls, 1966-67, U. Houston, 1967-71, assoc. prof., 1971-73, prof., 1973—, Disting. Univ. prof., 1987-96, Cullen Disting. prof. chemistry and physics, dir. Inst. for Digital Informatics and Analysis. Vis. lectr. U. Ill., 1972; vis. scientist Inst. for Strömungsforschung, Göttingen, Fed. Republic Germany, 1973-74; bd. dirs. Inst. for Digital Informatics and Analysis. Recipient U.S. Sr. Scientist award Alexander von Humboldt Found., 1973-74, Southwestern Tex. sect. award Am. Chem. Soc., 1981, Sigma Xi Rsch. award, 1995; fellow A.P. Sloan Found., 1972-74, Weizmann Inst., 1973, Inst. for Advanced Studies, Hebrew U. Jerusalem, 1978-79, Guggenheim Found., 1978-79. Fellow Am. Phys. Soc. (exec. com. mem., sec.-treas. Few Body Topical group); mem. IEEE, ASCAP, Am. Chem. Soc., Am. Assn. Physics Tchrs. Democrat. Baptist. Office: U Houston Dept Chemistry 4800 Calhoun Rd Houston TX 77204-5003 E-mail: kouri@uh.edu.

KOURIDES, IONE ANNE, endocrinologist, researcher, educator; b. N.Y.C., Sept. 1, 1942; d. Peter T. and Anne E. (Spetseris) K.; m. Charles G. Zaroulis, Nov. 30, 1974; children: Anna Larisa, Andrew, Christina, Peter. BA, Wellesley Coll., 1963; MD, Harvard U., 1967. Diplomate Am. Bd. Internal Medicine, Am. Bd. Endocrinology and Metabolism. Intern Jewish Hosp., Washington U., St. Louis, 1967-68; resident Montefiore, Albert Einstein Med. Sch., Bronx, NY, 1968-69; fellow Beth Israel, Harvard U., Boston, 1970-72; assoc. prof. medicine Cornell U. Med. Coll., N.Y.C., 1981—; sr. med. dir., worldwide team leader endocrine care Pfizer Inc., N.Y.C., 1990—. Mem. editl. bd. Endocrinology, Jour. Clin. Endocrinol Metabolism, also others; contbr. over 100 articles to sci. jours., chpts. to books. Mem. nat. campaign Harvard Med. Sch., Boston, 1986-92; nat. bd. dirs. Philoptochos Soc. Greek Orthodox Archdiocese. Grantee NIH, 1979-84. Fellow ACP; mem. Am. Soc. Clin. Investigation, Am. Assn. Physicians, Am. Thyroid Assn. (coms.), Endocrine Soc. (coms.). Achievements include discovery of alpha-secreting pituitary tumors; demonstrated that measurement of amniotic fluid thyroid stimulating hormone can be used to diagnose hypthyroidism in utero; development of insulin secretagogue Glucotrol XL. Home: 1070 Park Ave New York NY 10128-1000 Office: Pfizer Inc 235 E 42nd St New York NY 10017-5755 Office Phone: 212-573-2178. Business E-Mail: kourii@pfizer.com.

KOURIDES, PETER THEOLOGOS, lawyer; b. Istanbul, Turkey, July 24, 1910; arrived in US, 1912, naturalized, 1931; s. Theologos and Zafiro (Gurlides) Kourides; m. Anna E. Spetseris, Aug. 4, 1938; children: Ione A., P. Nicholas. BA, Columbia, 1931, JD, 1933; HHD (hon.), Hellenic Coll., 1985. Bar: NY 1933. Mem. firm Seward, Raphael & Kourides, NYC, 1935—; gen. counsel Greek Archdiocese N.Am. and S.Am., 1938-96; trustee Hellenic Cathedral City NY, 1938-98; trustee, counsel St. Basil's Acad., Garrison, NY, 1946-97, United Greek Orthodox Charities, 1965-70; counsel World Conf. Religion Peace, 1970-82, Consultate Gen. Greece, NYC, 1963-90. Rep. at enthronement of Athenagoras I Greek Archdiocese of N.Am. and S.Am., Istanbul, 1949. Author: The Evolution of the Greek Orthodox Church in America and Its Current Problems, 1959, The Centennial History of the Archdiocesan Cathedral of the Holy Trinity, 1992. Nat. v.p. Order of Ahepa, 1960; counsel Columbia U. Cancer Clinic, Greece, 1965—70; mem. gen. bd. Nat. Coun. Chs., 1960—82, v.p., 1969—72; del. 3d Assembly World Coun. Chs., New Delhi, 1961, del. 4th Assembly Uppsala, Sweden, 1968, del. 5th Assembly Nairobi, Kenya, 1975, mem. internat. affairs com., 1968—74; del. World Conf. Religion on Peace, Kyoto, 1971; trustee Hellenic Coll., Brookline, Mass., 1968—97. Decorated grand comdr. Knights of Holy Sepulchre Jerusalem, Golden Cross Order of Phoenix King Constantine II of Greece, Titular Archon Megas Nomophylax Ecumenical Patriarchate of Ea. Orthodox Ch. Mem.: ABA, Am. Judicature Soc., Consular Law Soc., NY Bar Assn., Columbia Alumni Assn., Hellenic Am. C. of C. (dir., counsel 1955—). Home: 46 Groton St Forest Hills NY 11375-5921 Office: 110 E 59th St New York NY 10022-1304 Office Phone: 212-355-2880.

KOURILSKY, FRANÇOIS MICHEL, research scientist; b. Paris, Dec. 28, 1934; s. Raoul and Simone (Develay) K.; m. Colette Lucienne Bellegarde, Nov. 7, 1956 (div. Dec. 1985); children: Laurent, Michel; m. Françoise Marie-Noël Gauthier, Aug. 20, 1988. Cert. in Psychophysiology, Faculty Scis., Paris, 1961; Cert. in Immunology, Pasteur Inst., Paris, 1962; MD, Faculty Medicine, Paris, 1966; D (hon.), U. Buenos Aires, 1992. Sr. resident Paris Hosp., 1960-66; rsch. fellow Sch. Medicine, NYU, 1962-63; chef de clinique-attache Faculty Medicine, Paris, 1966-68; rschr. Nat. Inst. Health and Med. Rsch., France, 1967—88, emeritus rsch. dir., 2000—; dir. gen. Nat. Ctr. Sci. Rsch., France, 1988-94; hon. dir. rsch. Inst. Gustave Roussy, Villejuif, France, 1995—2002, emeritus dir. rsch., 2001—. Dir. unit of tumor immunology Nat. Inst. Health and Med. Rsch., U. Paris 7, 1974-76; dir. Inst. Immunology Marseille, France, 1976-85; chmn. sci. coun. coord. Inst. Curie, Paris, 1983-87; dir. Federative Rsch. Inst., Inst. Gustave Roussy, 1996-2000; chmn. sci. coun. firms Immunotech SA, 1982, Epigene SA, 2000-01, IPSOGEN S.A., 2001—. Contbr. over 100 articles to profl. jours. V.p. superior coun. rsch. tech. French Ministry Rsch., 1983-87; chmn. commn. Plan Recherche, 1985; chmn. Rsch. Obs. Midi, Pyrenees, France, 2000-2003; pres. Mediterranean Techs., Provence, Alpes, Cote D'Azur, 2000-2003. Named officer Nat. Order of Merit, France, 1990, officer Legion D'Honneur, France, 1994, comdr. Order of Merit Fed. Republic of Germany, 1995 Home: 21 Blvd Du Montparnasse 75006 Paris France Home Fax: 33-1-428432-26.

KOURLIS, REBECCA LOVE, state supreme court justice; b. Colorado Springs, Colo., Nov. 11, 1952; d. John Arthur and Ann (Daniels) Love; m. Thomas Aristithis Kourlis, July 15, 1978; children: Stacy Ann, Katherine Love, Aristithis Thomas. BA with distinction in English, Stanford U., 1973, JD, 1976; LLD (hon.), U. Denver, 1997. Bar: Colo. 1976, D.C. 1979, U.S. Dist. Ct. Colo. 1976, U.S. Ct. Appeals (10th cir.) 1976, Colo. Supreme Ct., U.S. Ct. Appeals (D.C. cir.), U.S. Claims Ct., U.S. Supreme Ct. Assoc. Davis, Graham & Stubbs, Denver, 1976-78; sole practice Craig, Colo., 1978-87; judge 14th Jud. Dist. Ct., Craig, Colo., 1987-94; arbiter Jud. Arbiter Group, Inc., 1994-95; justice Colo. Supreme Ct., 1995—. Water judge divsn. 6, 1987-94; lectr. to profl. groups. Contbr. articles to profl. jours. Chmn. Moffat County Arts and Humanities, Craig, 1979; mem. Colo. Commn. on Higher Edn., Denver, 1980-81; mem. adv. bd. Colo. Divsn. Youth Svcs., 1988-91; mem. com. civil jury instructions, 1990-95, standing com. gender and justice, 1994-97, chair jud. adv. coun., 1997-2002, chair com. on jury reform, 1996—, chair com. family issues, 2002—; co-chair com. on atty. grievance reform, 1997-2002; mem. long range planning com. Moffat County Sch., 1990; bd. visitors Stanford U., 1989-94, Law Sch. U. Denver, 1997-2002; trustee Kent Denver Sch., 1996-2002, Graland Sch., 2004—. Named N.W. Colo. Daily Press Woman of Yr., 1993; recipient Trailblazer award AAUW, 1998, Mary Lathrop award Colo. Women's Bar Assn., 2001, Jud. Excellence award Acad. Matrimonial Lawyers, 2002, Champion for Children award Rocky Mountain Children's Law Ctr., 2003, Friend of Children award Adv. for Children, 2003. Fellow: Colo. Bar Found., Am. Bar Found.; mem.: N.W. Colo. Bar Assn. (Cmty. Svc. award 1993—94), Dist. Ct. Judges' Assn. (pres. 1993—94), Colo. Bar Assn. (bd. govs. 1983—85, mineral law sect. bd. dirs. 1985, sr. v.p. 1987—88), Rocky Mountain Mineral Found. Office: State Jud Bldg 2 E 14th Ave Denver CO 80203-2115

KOURNIKOVA, ANNA, retired professional tennis player; b. Moscow, June 7, 1981; d. Sergei and Alla Kournikova; m. Sergei Fedorov (div.). Prof. tennis player WTA, 1995—2004. Player Russian Fed Cup team, 1996—97, 2000, Russian Olympic Team, 1996; founder Physical Culture Russian Acad., 1997. Actor: (films) Me, Myself & Irene, 2000. ITF Jr. World champion, 1995, ITF Women's Cir. Satellite Event, Midland, Mich., 1996, title ITF Women's Cir. Satellite, Rockford, Ill.; winner Orange Bowl, 1995, Italian Open Jrs., 1995, European Champaionships, 1995; semi-finalist Wimbledon Jrs., 1995, quarter finalist French Open Jrs.; recipient (with Martina Hingis) WTA Tour Doubles Team of the Year award, 1999; named 1 or top 10 Most Marketable Female Athletes, Sports Business Daily, 2003. Achievements include won 16 career WTA doubles titles including Australian Open, 1999, 2000. Office: c/o Bollettieri Tennis Acad 5500 34th St W Bradenton FL 34210-3506

KOUSSA, HAROLD ALAN, insurance account executive; b. Central Falls, R.I., June 20, 1947; s. Harold Albert and June Joann (John) K. BSEngring. Sci., U. R.I., 1969; MBA Fin., U. Hartford, 1975; MS in Engring. Sci. Nuclear Engring., Rensselaer Poly. Inst., 1977. Lic. property and casualty ins. prodr., Conn. Reactor engring. asst. Conn. Yankee Atomic Power Co., Haddam Neck, 1969-75, reactor engr., 1975-77; staff nuclear engr. Am. Nuclear Insurers, Farmington, Conn., 1977-79, sr. staff nuclear engr., 1979-81, prin. engr., 1981-82, mgr. ops., 1982-89, account exec., 1989-93, cons., 1993-94; account exec. Indsl. Risk Insurers, Hartford, Conn., 1994-97; account mgr., sen. account exec. Arkwright, Waltham, Mass., 1997-99, FM Global (formerly Arkwright), Norwood, Mass., 1999—. Mem East Hampton Rep. Town Com., 1982-88; del. Conn. Rep. Conv., 1982, 84, 86; mem. East Hampton Water Pollution Control Authority, 1982-88, vice chmn., 1984-85, chmn., 1985-88. Capt. USNR, 1982—. Decorated Meritorious Svc. medal, Navy Commendation medal, Navy Achievement medal (4), Nat. Def. Svc. medal, Mil. Outstanding Vol. Svc. medal, Armed Forces Res. medal. Mem. ASME, Am. Nuc. Soc., Am. Soc. Naval Engrs., U.S. Naval Inst., Navy League U.S., Naval Res. Assn., Res. Officers Assn., Masons, U. R.I. Fast Break Club. Home: 105 Sheldonville Rd North Attleboro MA 02760 Office Phone: 781-440-8385. E-mail: harold.koussa@fmglobal.com.

KOUSSER, J(OSEPH) MORGAN, historian, educator; b. Lewisburg, Tenn., Oct. 7, 1943; s. Joseph Maximillian and Alice Holt (Morgan) K.; m. Sally Ann Ward, June 1, 1968; children: Rachel Meredith, Thaddeus Benjamin. AB, Princeton U., 1965; M.Phil., Yale U., 1968, PhD, 1971; MA, Oxford U., Eng., 1984. Instr. Calif. Inst. Tech., Pasadena, 1969-71, assoc. prof. Padadena, 1975-79, prof., 1979—. Vis. prof. U. Mich., Ann Arbor, 1980, Harvard U., Cambridge, Mass., 1981-82, Oxford U., 1984-85, Claremont Grad. Sch., 1993; expert witness Minority Voting Rights Cases; researcher. Author: Shaping of Southern Politics, 1974, Colorblind Injustice: Minority Voting Rights and the Undoing of the Second Reconstruction, 1999. Recipient Lillian Smith award So. Regional Coun., 1999, Ralph J. Bunche award Am. Polit. Sci. Assn., 2000; Guggenheim Found. fellow, 1984-85, Woodrow Wilson Ctr. fellow, 1984-85; grantee NEH, 1974, 82. Mem. Orgn. Am. Historians, Am. Hist. Assn., Social Scis. History Assn., So. Hist. Assn. Democrat. Avocation: running. Office: Calif Inst Tech 228-77 Caltech Pasadena CA 91125-7700 Office Phone: 626-395-4080. E-mail: kousser@hss.caltech.edu.

KOUTS, HERBERT JOHN CECIL, retired physicist; b. Bisbee, Ariz., Dec. 18, 1919; s. Oliver Allen and Lillian (Niemeyer) K.; m. Hertha Pretorius, Feb. 2, 1942; children: Anne Elizabeth, Catherine Jennifer; m. Barbara Stokes, Mar. 27, 1974; stepchildren: Francis Spitzer, Michael Spitzer, Daniel Spitzer. BS, La. State U., 1941, MS, 1946; PhD, Princeton U., 1952. With Brookhaven Nat. Lab., Upton, L.I., N.Y., 1950-73, 77-89, sr. scientist, asso. div. head, 1958-73, chmn. dept. nuclear energy, 1977-88; mem. Def. Nuclear Facilities Safety Bd., U.S. Govt., Washington, 1989-2000; ret. Dir. div. reactor safety rsch. AEC, Washington, 1973-75; dir. Office Nuclear Regulatory Rsch., U.S. Nuclear Regulatory Commn., Washington, 1975-76; mem. adv. com. reactor physics AEC, 1956-63, mem. adv. com. reactor safeguards, 1962-66; mem. European Am. Adv. Com. for Reactor Physics to European Nuclear Energy Agy., 1962-68; mem. internat. nuclear safety adv. group to IAEA, 1985-92. Served with USAAF, 1942-45. Recipient E. O. Lawrence award AEC, 1963, Disting. Service award, 1975; Disting. Service award NRC, 1976, Sec. Energy's Gold medal for achievement, 1999. Mem. Am. Nuclear Soc. (Theos Thompson award in nuclear reactor safety 1983), N.Y. Acad. Scis., Center Moriches Audubon Soc., Nat. Acad. Engring. Home: 249 S Country Rd Brookhaven NY 11719-9704 E-mail: hjckouts@erols.com.

KOUTSKY, DEAN ROGER, advertising executive; b. Omaha, Nov. 17, 1935; s. John Lewis and Ann Helen (Swan) K.; m. Kathryn Junette Strand; children: Linda, Lisa. BFA, Mpls. Coll. Art and Design, 1957. Art dir. Knox Reeves Advt., Inc., Mpls., 1958-65; v.p., exec. art dir. BBDO, Inc., Mpls., 1965-70; v.p., assoc. creative dir. Campbell-Mithun, Inc., Mpls., 1970-80, sr. v.p., creative dir., 1980-83, exec. v.p., exec. creative dir., 1983-85, vice chmn., 1985-89; exec. cons. Campbell-Mithun Esty, Inc., Mpls., 1989-90; ptnr., mgr. Harmon Ct., 1991-97. Bd. trustees Mpls. Coll. Art and Design, 1982-90, chmn., bd. trustees, 1985-89, adj. prof. advt./design divsn., 1995—. Office: 2005 James Ave S Minneapolis MN 55405-2404

KOUTSOBINA, VASSILIKI, musicologist, chemist; d. Thomas Koutsobinas and Helen Koutsobina; m. Argirios Dinopoulos, Oct. 30, 1994; children: Stergios Dinopoulos, Thomas Romanos Dinopoulos. BSc, U. Athens, Greece, 1982—89; MMus, U. Hartford, Hartt Sch. Music, Conn., 1992—94; studied, U. Cin., Conservatory of Music, 2001—05. Music history and theory instr. Synchrono Conservatory, Athens, Greece, 1994—97; musicologist, head of reference svcs. Music Libr. Greece, Athens, 1995—2000; tchg. asst. U. Cin., Coll.-Conservatory of Music, 2001—03. Radio prodr. Third Program/Hellenic Radio, Athens, Greece, 1997—98; recruiting com. Music Libr. Greece, Athens, 1998—2000. Dir., office of ho. rep. Greek Parliament, Athens, Greece, 1986—89. Mem.: Am. Musicological Soc. Avocations: swimming, photography. Home: 70 Terpsitheas St Athens 15341 Greece Personal E-mail: koutsov@email.uc.edu.

KOUVEL, JAMES SPYROS, physicist, educator; b. Jersey City, May 23, 1926; s. Spyros and Ifegenia (Cassianos) K.; m. Audrey Lumsden, June 26, 1953; children: Diana, Alexander. B.Engring., Yale U., 1946, PhD, 1951. Research fellow U. Leeds, Eng., 1951-53, Harvard, 1953-55; physicist Gen. Electric Co. Research and Devel. Center, 1955-69; prof. physics U. Ill.-Chgo., 1969—. Vis. scientist Atomic Energy Rsch. Establishment, Harwell, Eng., 1967-68; vis. prof. U. Paris, Orsay, France, 1981; cons. Argonne (Ill.) Nat. Lab., 1969-89, mem. rev. com., 1970-72, vis. scientist, 1973-74; mem. materials rsch. adv. com. NSF, 1980-82, mem. materials rsch. groups spl. emphasis panel, 1993; mem. evaluation panel NRC, 1981-85. Author papers in field.; Editor: Magnetism Conf. proc, 1965-67; editorial bd.: Jour. Magnetism and Magnetic Materials, 1975— . Served with USNR, 1944-46. Guggenheim fellow, 1967-68; NSF rsch. grantee, 1973-96. Fellow Am. Phys. Soc., AAAS Home: 223 N Euclid Ave Oak Park IL 60302-2107 Office: U Ill Physics Dept Chicago IL 60607-7059 Office Phone: 312-996-5348. Business E-Mail: kouvel@uic.edu.

KOUWENHOVEN, GERRIT WOLPHERTSEN, retired museum director; b. Mt. Kisco, N.Y., May 8, 1939; s. John Atlee and Eleanor Warren (Hayden) K.; m. Ellen Mather Davis, June 17, 1961; children: Derek Gerritsen, Kirsten Elizabeth. BA in English, U. Colo., 1962, postgrad., 1962-64, Seattle Pacific U., 1975-76, Antioch, 1981-82. Human rights intern Eleanor Roosevelt Meml. Found., 1964-65; field rep., investigator equal opportunities divsn. State of Wis. Indsl. Commn., 1964-66; from employment specialist to asst. dir. Seattle Urban League, 1966-73; pvt. practice campaign cons., 1973-75; tchr. English, chair dept. English LaConner (Wash.) High Sch., 1976-78; tchr. English Arlington (Vt.) Meml. High Sch., 1978-79; pvt. practice rschr., 1979-80; dean Ethan Allen C.C., Manchester Center, Vt., 1981-82; with Friends of Hildene, Inc., Manchester, Vt., 1983—2001, exec. dir., 1986—2001, exec. dir. emeritus, bd. advisers, 2002—. Mem. allocations com. United Way Bennington County, 1992—95; mem. bd. advisors Merck Forest and Farmland Ctr., 2002—; mem. adv. coun. Merck Forest & Farmland Ctr.,

2002—05, bd. trustees, 2005—, v.p., 2005—; mem. chancel choir First Congl. Ch., Manchester, 1979—, chair stewardship, 1980—82, 1991—93, bd. trustees, 1981—84, 1991—94, 2004—, co-chair bicentennial steering com., 1983—84, bd. deacons, 1985—88, 1996—99, chair, 1986, chair search com., 1986—88, 1996—98; mem. exec. com. Vt. Conf. United Ch. of Christ, 1999—, chmn., bd. of dirs., 2002—; trustee Dorset (Vt.) Players, Inc., 1983—91, treas., 1986—91; bd. trustees Long Trail Sch., Dorset, 1988—98, vice chair, 1989—90, 1996—97, chair, 1990—96; bd. trustees Am. Theatre Works, Inc., Dorset, 1990—94, chair fin. com., 1992—94; bd. dirs. Preservation Trust Vt., Burlington, 1991—, v.p., 1993, 2005, pres., 1994—2004; bd. trustees United Counseling Svc. Bennington County, Inc., 1992—, sec., 1994—, v.p., 1995, pres., 1996—; bd. trustees Coll. St. Joseph, Vt., 1999—2002; bd. dirs. Vt. Conf. United Ch. of Christ, 1998—, Vt. Alliance of Conservation Voters, 2001—02. Recipient Cmty. Svc. award Manchester C. of C., 1994; recipient Cleveland E. and Phyllis B. Dodge award for Outstanding Cmty. Svc., United Counseling Svc. Bennington County, 2000. Mem. Dorset Nursing Assn. (bd. dirs. 1997—, sec. 1997-2000, pres. 2000-03, v.p. 2003—), Lions (Manchester chpt., bd. dirs. 1984-94, sec. 1984-88, pres. 1991-93). Office: 95A Elm St PO Box 1233 Manchester VT 05254

KOUYATÉ, LANSANA, economist, federal official, diplomat; b. Koba, Guinea, July 15, 1950; married; 3 children. Degree with honors, U. Conakry, 1975. Asst. to dep. dir. Nat. Op. for the Devel. of Rice Culture, 1982—83; counsellor Guinean Embassy, Cote d'Ivoire, 1983—85; with Guinea Fgn. Ministry, 1985—87; permanent rep. to UN Govt. of Guinea, New York, 1992—93, ambassador Cairo, 1987—92; spl. rep. of Sec.-Gen. to Somalia and Rwanda UN, 1993—94, under sec. for political affairs for Africa, Western Asia, and the Middle East, 1994—97; former exec. sec., now sec.-gen. Econ. Cmty. of West African States, Abuja, Nigeria, 1997—2002; spl. rep. of the sec.-gen. Internat. Francophonie Orgn. to Ivory Coast, Paris, 2003—. Author: (Books) International Funding of State-Owned Companies in Guinea: Problems and Prospects, The End of the Cold War and its Impact on Third World Countries. Office: Org Internationale de la Francophonie Cabinet du Secretaire general 28 rue de Bourgogne 75007 Paris France

KOUYMJIAN, DICKRAN, art historian, Orientalist, educator; b. Tulcea, Romania, June 6, 1934; (parents Am. citizens); s. Toros S. and Zabelle I. (Calusdian) K.; m. Angèle Kapoïan, Sept. 16, 1967. BS in European Cultural History, U. Wis., 1957; MA in Arab Studies, Am. U., Beirut, 1961; PhD in Near East Lang. and Culture, Columbia U., 1969. Instr. English and gen. edn. depts. Am. U. Beirut, 1959—61; instr. English Columbia U., N.Y.C., 1961-64; dir. Am. Authors, Inc., N.Y.C., 1965-67; asst. prof. and asst. dir. Ctr. for Arabic Studies Am. U., Cairo, 1967-71; prof., chmn. Armenian Studies dept. Haigazian U., Beirut, 1971-72; assoc. prof. history Am. U. Beirut, 1971-75; prof. art history Am. U., Paris, 1976-77; prof. history and art, dir. Armenian Studies program Calif. State U., Fresno, 1977—. Dir. Ctr. for Armenian Studies, Calif. State U., Fresno, 1990—; Fulbright disting. lectr., prof. Armenian and Am. Lit. Yerevan (Armenia, USSR), 1987; cons. archaeology UNESCO, Paris, 1976; prof., chairholder Armenian Sect., Inst. Nat. des Langs. et Civilisations Orientales, U. Paris, 1988—91; 1st incumbent Haig & Isabel Berberian endowed chair Armenian studies Calif. State U., Fresno, 1989—; 2nd incumbent William Saroyan endowed chair of Armenian studies U. Calif., Berkeley, 1996—97; vis. prof. Oriental Inst. U. Louvain-la-Neuve, Belgium, 2001. Author: Index of Armenian Art, part I, 1977, part II, 1979, The Armenian History of Ghazar P'arpetzi, 1986, Arts of Armenia, 1992; co-author: (with A. Kapoïan) The Splendor of Egypt, 1975, (with M. Stone, H. Lehmann) Album of Armenian Paleography, 2002, (with Giusto Traina, Carlo Franco, Cecilia Veronese Arslan) History of Alexander of Macedonia: An Illustrated Armenian Manuscript of the 14th Century, 2003; author and editor: William Saroyan: An Armenian Trilogy, 1986, William Saroyan: Warsaw Visitor and Tales of the Vienna Streets, 1990; editor: (books) Near Eastern Numistatics, Iconography, Epigraphy and History, 1974, Essays in Armenian Numismatics in Honor of C. Sibilian, 1981, Armenian Studies: In Memoriam Haïg Berbèrian, 1986, Movses of Khoren and Armenian HIstiorigraphy from its Beginnings, 2000; editl. bd. Armenian Rev., 1974—, Ararat Lit. mag., 1975—, Revue des Etudes Armèniennes, 1978—, NAASR Jour. Armenian Studies, Jour. of the Soc. for Armenian Studies, 1995—; contbr. articles to profl. jours. Served with U.S. Army, 1957. Recipient St. Sahag and St. Mesrob medal His Holiness Karekin I, Catholics of All Armenians, 1996, Outstanding Prof. award Am. U., Cairo, 1968-69, 69-70, Hagop Kevorkian Disting. Lectureship in Near Eastern Art and Civilization, NYU, 1979, Arthur H. Dadian Armenian Heritage award Armenian Students Assn. Am., 2003; voted Outstanding Prof. of Yr., Faculty Senate, Calif. State U., Fresno, 1986-87; Fulbright fellow, USSR, 1986-87, Michael Dukakis fellow Am. Coll. Thessaloniki, 2003; grantee NEH, Paris, 1980-81, 95, Bertha & John Garabedian Charitable Found., 1994—; chosen Scholar of U. Phi Beta Phi Calif. State U., 1999; named Man of Yr. Armenian Nat. Com. Calif., 2000. Mem. Am. Oriental Soc., Am. Numismatic Soc., Mid. East Studies Assn. (charter), Coll. Arts Assn., Soc. Armenian Studies (charter, pres. 1985-86, 92-94), Société asiatique (Paris), Internat. Assn. of Armenian Studies, Mid. East Medievalist, Assn. Paléographique Internat., Phi Kappa Phi (nat. scholar Fresno chpt. 1998, Univ. Scholar award chpt. 962 1999). Achievements include selected to serve on jury for annual Francqui Prize, Brussels, 2001. Avocations: music, films, bibliophile. Home: 54 rue Boussingault 75013 Paris France Office: Calif State U Armenian Studies Program 5245 N Backer Ave # PB4 Fresno CA 93740-8001 Office Phone: 559-278-2669. Business E-Mail: dickrank@csufresno.edu.

KOVAC, CAROLINE (CAROL KOVAC), computer company executive; BA, Oberlin Coll.; PhD in Chem., U. So. Calif. Joined IBM, 1983; dir. computational biology IBM Rsch., v.p. tech. strategy, div. operations; gen. mgr. IBM Life Sci., 2000—. Mem.-emeritus IBM Acad. Tech. Named to Hall of Fame, Women in Tech. Internat., 2002. Office: IBM 1133 Westchester Ave White Plains NY 10604

KOVAC, SHIRLEY ANN, retired elementary school educator; b. Sharon, Pa., Feb. 7, 1950; d. Peter and Stella Antos; m. Donald Edward Kovac; children: Shelly, Karen, Donald Jr. BS in Edn., Slippery Rock U., 1972. Libr. aide Sharon City Schs., Pa., 1972—75, substitute tchr., 1975—76; tchr. 1st grade Hadley Elem. Sch., 1976—82, Musser Elem. Sch., 1982—83; tchr. 1st and 2d grade West Hill Elem. Sch., 1983—90; tchr. 5th grade Case Ave. Elem. Sch., 1990—93, tchr. 2d grade, 1993—2005; ret., 2005. Recipient Tchg. and Spl. Student Activities award, Adminstrn. and Bd. Edn., Sharon, 1999. Mem.: NEA, Pa. State Tchrs. Assn., Sharon Tchrs. Assn. Office: Ednl Svc Ctr 215 Forker Blvd Sharon PA 16146

KOVACEVIC, RADOVAN, mechanical engineering educator; b. Niksic, Yugoslavia, July 17, 1947; came to U.S., 1987; s. Bozo and Zagorka (Vujicic) K.; m. Ljiljana Sokic, Dec. 10, 1972; children: Ivana, Jelena. BS, U. Belgrade, Yugoslavia, 1969, MS, 1972; PhD, U. Titograd, Yugoslavia, 1978. From asst. prof. to prof. U. Titograd, Titograd, 1975-86; assoc. prof. Syracuse (N.Y.) U., 1987-90, U. Ky., Lexington, 1991-95, prof., 1995-97; Herman Brown chair prof. So. Meth. U., Dallas, 1997—. Cons. prof. Harbin (China) Inst. Tech., 1994. Co-author: Principles of Abrasive Waterjet Technology, 1998; contbr. over 100 articles to profl. jours. Recipient Taylor Rsch. medal, Soc. Mfg. Engrs., 2000, Adams Meml. Membership award, Am. Welding Soc., 1997. Fellow: ASME. Achievements include patents for high-pressure waterjet-assisted cooling/lubrication system in machining, method of monitoring and control for the 3D shape of wld pool based on vision system, new control of gas metal arc welding. Office: So Meth Univ PO Box 750335 Dallas TX 75275-0335 E-mail: kovacevi@smu.edu.

KOVACEVICH, RICHARD M., bank executive; BA in Industrial Engring., Stanford U., 1965; M in Industrial Engring.; MBA, Stanford U., 1967. Exec. v.p. Kenner div. Gen. Mills, Inc., Mpls., 1967-72; prin. Venture Capital, 1972-75; v.p. consumer services Norwest Corp., Mpls., from 1975, then sr. v.p. N.Y.C. banking group, then exec. v.p., mgr. N.Y.C. bank div., then exec. v.p. mem. policy com., vice-chmn., chief operating officer banking group, 1986—89, pres., COO, vice chmn., 1989—93, CEO, 1993—96, chmn., 1995—96; chmn., CEO Wells Fargo & Co. (merged with Norwest Corp.), 1996—98, pres., CEO San Francisco, 1998—2001, chmn., pres., CEO, 2001—. Mem. bd. dirs. Cargill, Inc., Cisco Systems, Inc., Target Corp.; mem. Federal Reserve's Federal Advisory Council, Calif. Bus. Roundtable, Calif. Commn. for Jobs and Economic Growth; chmn. San Francisco Com. on Jobs. V.p., bd. of govs. San Francisco Symphony; vice chmn., bd. trustees San Francisco Museum of Modern Art. Recipient Banker of the Year, Am. Banker, 2003. Office: Wells Fargo & Co 420 Montgomery St San Francisco CA 94163-1205*

KOVACEVICH, ROBERT EUGENE, lawyer; b. Nov. 9, 1933; s. John Edward and Katrina Margaret K.; m. Yvonne R. Stokke; children: Tawni, Mark, Phillip, Bernhard. Grad., St. Martin's Coll., Lacy, Wash., 1955; JD with honors, Gonzaga U., Spokane, Wash., 1959; LLM in Taxation, NYU, 1960. Bar: Wash., 1960; U.S. Ct. Appeals (9th cir.) 1963, U.S. Ct. Appeals (fed. cir.) 1982, U.S. Ct. Appeals (11th cir.) 1988, U.S. Ct. Appeals (10th cir.) 1993, U.S. Dist. Ct. (ea. dist.) Wash. 1960, U.S. Dist. Ct. (we. dist.) Wash., 1976, U.S. Ct. Claims, 1973, U.S. Tax Ct., 1982, Wash. Supreme Ct., 1959, U.S. Supreme Ct., 1975, Coeur d'Alene, Kalispel and Swinomish Tribal Bars, 2001-03. Lawyer U.S. Supreme Ct., Spokane, 1963-72; ptnr. Kovacevich & Algeo, Spokane, 1972-80; pvt. practice Spokane, 1980—. Instr. Gonzaga U. Sch. Bus., 1967-84; mgr. leasing co.; expert witness U.S. Senate Com. Appropriations, 1976. Mem. ABA, Assn. Trial Lawyers, Fed. Bar Assn. Ea. Wash., Spokane Co. Bar. Assn., Spokane Club. Office: 818 W Riverside Ave Ste 715 Spokane WA 99201-0910 Office Phone: 509-747-2104.

KOVACH, ANDREW LOUIS, human resources specialist, consultant; b. Greensboro, Pa., Feb. 4, 1948; s. Andrew and Pauline (Nassar) K.; m. Cindy Juliani, Nov. 28, 1970; 1 child: Courtney. BS in Indsl. Engineering, W.Va. U., 1969. Engr. DuPont, Martinville, Va., 1970-73; supt. engr. Allied Corp., Syracuse, NY, 1973—75, mgr. employee rels. Morristown, NJ, 1976—80, mgr. orgnl. devel., 1980, dir. human resources N.Y.C., 1981—82, dir. comml. devel., 1983—87; sr. v.p. human resources, info. systems Morristown Meml. Hosp., Morristown, NJ, 1988—96; v.p. human resources and chief adminstrv. officer Atlantic Health Sys., Florham Park, 1996—. Bd. dirs. Allied Office Supplies; mem. ethics com. Morristown Surg. Ctr.; ptnr. Thomas Andrew Assoc., Morristown, NJ, 1987—; co-compliance officer Atlantic Health Sys. Mem.: Park Ave. Club, Morristown Club (bd. dir.). Presbyterian. Office Phone: 973-660-3125.

KOVACH, BILL, educational foundation administrator; b. Greeneville, Tenn., Sept. 16, 1932; s. John and Olga (Sicos) K.; m. Lynne Marie Stamm, Jan. 11, 1956; children: Teresa, David, Charles, John. BS, East Tenn. State U., 1959; LLD (hon.), Colby Coll., 2000. Gen. assignment Press-Chronicle, Johnson City, Tenn., 1959-61; reporter Nashville Tennessean, 1961-68, N.Y. Times, N.Y.C., 1968-79, Washington bur. chief Washington, 1979-86; editor Atlanta Jour.-Constitution, 1986-88; curator Nieman Found., Harvard U., 1989-2000; chmn. Com. of Concerned Journalists, Washington, 1997—; John Seigenthaler chair of excellence in First Amendment studies Middle Tenn. State U., 2004—. Lectr. Ball State U., Muncie, Ind., 1981; chair adv. bd. Internat. Consortium Investigative Journalists; bd. dirs. Ctr. for Pub. Integrity, Harvard Mag. Co-author: The Elements of Journalism, 2001, Warp Speed: America in the Age of Mixed Media, 1999; contbg. author: Assignment America, 1984, The Art of Writing Non-Fiction, 1986, Profiles in Courage for Our Time, 2002. With USN, 1951—55. Stanford Profl. Journalism fellow, 1967-68. Mem. AAAS. Office Phone: 202-293-7394. Business E-Mail: bkovach@journalism.org.

KOVACH, JOSEPH WILLIAM, management consultant, psychologist, educator; b. Hammond, Ind., Oct. 4, 1946; s. William Charles and Florence (Miotke) K. BA in Speech, St. Joseph Coll., Whiting, Ind., 1969; MA in Psychology, Roosevelt U., 1974; PhD, Ill. Inst. Tech., 1981; PhD in Clin. Psychology, Chgo. Sch. Profl. Psychology, 1986. Diplomate Am. Bd. Psychol. Specialties of Am. Coll. Forensic Examiners; lic. sch. psychologist, Ill., Ind., Mo.; cert. marriage and family therapist, Ind. Asst. corp. merchandising mgr. Kroch's & Brentano's, Chgo., 1965—70; regional ops. mgr. Interstate Dept. Stores, Inc., Highland, Ind., 1971—73; prof., chmn. psychology Calumet Coll. St. Joseph, Whiting, 1984—; dir. Ednl. Rsch. Exch., Calumet City, Ill., 1988—; pres. Joseph W. Kovach and Assocs., Ltd., Calumet City, 1969—; dir. Buzan Centre Ltd. Chgo., 1992—. Sr. cons. Calumet City Youth Svc. Bur., 1973-75; supr. Loyola U. Med. Ctr., Maywood, Ill., 1980-83, Northwestern Meml. Hosp., 1973-83, rsch. assoc., 1979-81; pre-doctoral intern Chgo. Read Mental Health Ctr., 1983-84, asst. program dir., 1988-89; sch. psychologist intern Sch. Dist. 163, Park Forest, Ill., 1986; grad. asst. Roosevelt U., Chgo., 1970-71; rsch. assoc. Northwestern U. Med. Sch., 1974-76, Loyola U. Med. Ctr., Maywood, 1976-78; adj. faculty Thornton C.C. (now South Suburban Coll.), South Holland, Ill., 1976, 97-98, Purdue U. Calumet, Hammond, 1976-89; presenter Internat. Conf. of The Role of Social Sci. in the Devel. of Edn., Bus. and Govt. Entering the 21st Century, Kaunas, Lithuania, 1998, 24th Internat. Congress on Arts and Comm., Oxford, Eng.; co-organizer USA Memory Championships; organizer Midwest Memory Championships; chief psychologist establishing nonmil. support svcs. for mil. and families, U.S. 8th Army, Korea, 2001; Oxford Round Table: Women's Rights, Lincoln Coll., Oxford U., Eng., 2004. Columnist: Bus. in Rev./The Times, Munster, Ind., Executive Excellence and Personal Excellence, Provo, Utah, Northwest Ind. Bus. Jour., Talking to the Boss, Skokie, Ill. Mem. APA, Midwest Psychol. Assn., Ill. Sch. Psychologists Assn., Internat. Conf. Police Chaplains Office: PO Box 113 Calumet City IL 60409-0113 Office Phone: 708-862-7777.

KOVACH, ROBERT LOUIS, geophysics educator; b. L.A., Feb. 15, 1934; s. Nicholas Arthur and Stefania Teresa (Rüssler) K.; m. Linda Elly Heyn, Dec. 23, 1960; children: Denise Lynn, Dianne Yvonne, John Robert, Robert John. Geophysical Engring Degree, Colo. Sch. Mines, 1955; MA, Columbia U., 1959; PhD, Calif. Inst. Tech., 1962. Registered geophysicist, Calif. Sr. scientist Jet Propulsion Lab., Pasadena, Calif., 1961-63; asst. prof. Calif. Inst. Tech., Pasadena, 1963-65, Stanford (Calif.) U., 1965-66, assoc. prof., 1966-70, prof. geophysics, 1970—. Prin. investigator Apollo Moon Seismic Expts., 1996-76; cons. DOE, 1996-97. Author: Earth's Fury, 1995, Conflict with the Earth, 1997. Lt. U.S. Army, 1956-58. Fellow John Simon Guggenheim Found., 1971; recipient Exceptional Sci. Achievement award NASA, 1973. Fellow Geol. Soc. Am.; mem. Am. Geophysical Union (pres. seismology sect. 1976-78), Can. Well Logging Soc., Seismol. Soc. Am., Soc. Exploration Geophysicists. Office: Dept Geophysics Stanford University Stanford CA 94305 Office Phone: 415-723-4827. Business E-Mail: kov@pangea.stanford.edu.

KOVACH, RONALD, footwear manufacturing executive; b. N.Y.C., Dec. 22, 1946; s. Edward Joseph and Louise Christine (Ragno) K.; m. Linda Cathrine Clark, May 5, 1969; children: Meredith Alexa, Matthew Alexander. BA with honors, U. Calif., Riverside, 1968, MA, 1970; postgrad., UCLA, 1970-74. Asst. v.p. Big 5 Sporting Goods, El Segundo, Calif., 1972-91; dir., founder Eagle Claw Saltwater Fishing Schs., Huntington Beach, Calif., 1989—; ind. cons. to sporting goods industry Huntington Beach, 1992—. Bd. dirs. Penn Fishing U.; lectr., condr. seminars, Huntington Beach, 1985—; frellance photojournalis, Huntington Beach, 1985—; co-owner FX (fishing expeditions outdoor apparel); bd. dirs. Advt. Maj. Footwear Co.; cons. in field; host Fishing Expdns. on Outdoor Channel. Author: Bass Fishing in California: Secrets of the Western Pros, 1985, Trout Fishing in California: Secrets of the Top Western Anglers, 1987, Saltwater Fishing in California: Secrets of the Pacific Experts, 1989, Serious Bass Fishing: Winning Secrets of Advanced Bass Anglers, 1994, The Serious Pacific Angler: Advanced Secrets of The Eagle Claw Fishing School, 1994; host: Fishing Expeditions Sta. XTRA-sports Radio, L.A.; host: Fishing Expdns. TV; co-host: World of Big Game Fishing Show ESPN-TV; contbr. numerous articles to various publs. Organizer Proposition 132, Calif. anti-gill net initiative, 1990. Calif. State scholar U. Calif., 1970; rsch. NIMH fellow UCLA, 1972. Mem. Internat. Game Fish Assn., Nat. Resource Def. Coun., Calif. Trout, Bass Anglers Sportsman Soc., Outdoor Writers Assn. Am., Outdoor Writers Calif., United Anglers, Pacific Offshore Rsch. Found., Scripps Inst. Oceanography. Avocations: fishing, travel, racquetball. Home: 17911 Portside Cir Huntington Beach CA 92649-4931 Office: 7351 Heil Ave Ste D Huntington Beach CA 92647-4534

KOVACHEVICH, ELIZABETH ANNE, judge; b. Canton, Ill., Dec. 14, 1936; d. Dan and Emilie (Kuchan) Kovachevich. AA, St. Petersburg Jr. Coll., 1956; BBA in Fin. magna cum laude, U. Miami, 1958; JD, Stetson U., 1961, LLD (hon.), 1993. Bar: Fla. 1961, U.S. Dist. Ct. (mid. and so. dists.) Fla. 1961, U.S. Ct. Appeals (5th cir.) 1961, U.S. Supreme Ct. 1968. Rsch. and adminstrv. aide Pinellas County Legis. Del., Fla., 1961; assoc. DiVito & Speer, St. Petersburg, Fla., 1961—62; house counsel Rieck & Fleece Builders Supplies, Inc., St. Petersburg, 1962; pvt. practice St. Petersburg, 1962—73; judge 6th Jud. Cir., Pinellas and Pasco Counties, Fla., 1973—82, U.S. Dist. Ct. (mid. dist.) Fla., Tampa, 1982—96, chief judge, 1996—. Chmn. St. Petersburg Profl. Legal Project-Days in Ct., 1967, Supreme Ct. Bicentennial Com. 6th Jud. Cir., 1975—76. Prodr., coord. (TV prodn.) A Race to Judgement. Bd. regents State of Fla., 1970—72; legal advisor, bd. dirs. Young Women's Residence, Inc., 1968; mem. Fla. Gov.'s Commn. on Status of Women, 1968—71; mem. Pres.'s Commn. on White House Fellowships, 1973—77; mem. def. adv. com. on Women in Svc. Dept. Def., 1973—76; Fla. publicity chmn. 18th Nat. Rep. Women's Conf., Atlanta, 1971; lifetime mem. Children's Hosp. Guild, YWCA of St. Petersburg; charter mem. Golden Notes, St. Petersburg Symphony; hon. mem. bd. of overeers Stetson U. Coll. of Law, 1986. Recipient St. Petersburg Panhellenic Appreciation award, 1964, Pinellas United Fund award in recognition of concern and meritorious effort, 1968, Disting. Alumni award, Stetson U., 1970, Woman of Yr. award, Beta Sigma Phi, 1970, 1970, Am. Legion Aux. Unit 14 Pres. award cmty. svc., 1970, Dedication to Christian Ideals award and Man of Yr. award, KC Dists. 20-21, 1972, USN Recruiting Command Appreciation award, 1975, Woman of Yr. award, Fla. Fedn. Bus. and Profl. Women, 1981, ann. Ben C. Willard Meml. award, Stetson Lawyers Assn., 1983, Alumni of Yr. award, St. Petersburg Jr. Coll., 1994, Cath. Law Person of Yr., Greater Tampa Cath. Lawyer's Guild, 1998, Disting. Svc. award, Fla. Coun. on Crime and Delinquency, 1999, J-Ben Watkins award, Stetson U. Coll. of Law, 1999, Woman of Achievement award, Delta Delta Delta, 2000, Outstanding Jurist award, Hillsborough County, 2000—01, Pub. Svc. award, William Reece Smith, Jr., 2001, Mrs. Charles Ulrick Bay award, St. Petersburg Rotary award, St. Petersburg Quarterback Club award, President's Award, Fed. Bar. Assn., 2001, Presidential Special Recognition Award, 2002. Mem.: ABA, St. Petersburg Bar Assn. (chmn. bench and bar com., sec. 1969), Am. Judicature Soc., Pinellas County Trial Lawyers, Fla. Bar Assn., ATLA. Office: US Dist Ct Fl 17 801 N Florida Ave Tampa FL 33702-3849

KOVACHY, EDWARD MIKLOS, JR., psychiatrist, consultant; b. Cleve., Dec. 3, 1946; s. Edward Miklos and Evelyn Amelia (Palenscar) K.; m. Susan Eileen Light, June 21, 1981; children: Timothy Light, Benjamin Light. BA, Harvard U., 1968, JD, MBA, Harvard U., 1972; MD, Case Western Reserve U., 1977. Diplomate Nat. Bd. Med. Examiners. Resident in psychiatry Stanford U. Med. Ctr., Stanford, Calif., 1977-81; pvt. practice psychiatry, mediation, exec. coaching Menlo Park, Calif., 1981—. Presenter ann. meeting Am. Psychol. Assn., 1998, Calif. Assn. Marriage and Family Therapists, 1999. Co-prodr. Jolson and Company, Century Ctr. for the Performing Arts, N.Y.C., 2002; columnist The Peninsula Times Tribune, 1983-85. Trustee Mid-Peninsula H.S., Palo Alto, Calif., 1990-2001, mem. bd. advisors, 2001—; mem. gift com. Harvard Coll. Class of 1968, 25th reunion chmn. participation, San Francisco, 1993, 30th reunion chmn. participation, West Coast, 1998, nat. co-chmn. participation and assocs. giving, 1999—, nat. co-chmn. participation, 35th reunion, 2003. Recipient Albert H. Gordon award Harvard U., 2000, Joseph R. Hamlen award Harvard U., 2003; named to Hall of Fame, Shaker Heights Alumni Assn., 2003. Mem. Am. Psychiat. Assn. (presenter annual meetings 1984, 98), Physicians for Social Responsibility, Assn. Family and Conciliation Cts., No. Calif. Psychiat. Soc. Presbyterian. Avocations: personal activism, musical comedy, athletics. Office: 1187 University Dr Menlo Park CA 94025-4423 Office Phone: 650-329-0600. Personal E-mail: edkovachy@aol.com.

KOVACIC, WILLIAM EVAN, law educator, lawyer, consultant; b. Poughkeepsie, N.Y., Oct. 1, 1952; s. Evan Carl and Frances Katherine (Crow) K.; m. Kathryn Marie Fenton, May 18, 1985. AB with honors, Princeton U., 1974; JD, Columbia U., 1978. Bar: NY 1979. Law clk. to Hon. Roszel C. Thomsen U.S. Dist. Ct. Md., Balt., 1978—79; atty. planning office bur. competition FTC, Washington, 1979—82, atty. advisor to commr., 1983; assoc. Bryan, Cave, McPheeters & McRoberts LLP, Washington, 1983—86; prof. George Mason U. Sch. Law, Arlington, Va., 1986—99, George Washington U. Law Sch., Washington, 1999—. Mem. U.S. Senate Judiciary Subcom. on Antitrust and Monopoly, Washington, 1975—76; gen. counsel U.S. FTC, 2001—04; cons. in field. Contbr. legal articles to profl. jours. Harlan Fiske Stone fellow, Columbia U., 1976—78. Mem. ABA (antitrust law and pub. contract law sects.), Fed. Bar Assn. Roman Catholic. Office: George Washington U Law Sch 720 20th St NW Washington DC 20052-0001 Office Phone: 202-994-8123. Office Fax: 202-994-5446. Business E-Mail: wkovacic@law.gwu.edu.

KOVACIC-FLEISCHER, CANDACE SAARI, law educator; b. Washington, Mar. 19, 1947; d. Donald George and Martha Eleanora (Saari) K.; m. Walter H. Fleischer; 1 child, Ilona Saari Fleischer. AB, Wellesley Coll., 1969; JD, Northeastern U., 1974. Law clk. to Hon. James L. Oakes U.S. Ct. Appeals (2d Cir.), Brattleboro, Vt., 1974—75; law clk. to Hon. Warren Burger U.S. Supreme Ct., Washington, 1975—76; assoc. Wilmer, Cutler & Pickering, Washington, 1976—80, Cole & Groner, Washington, 1980—81; prof. Am. U. Coll. Law, Washington, 1981—. Vis. prof. UCLA, 1988; moot ct. panelist Nat. Assn. Attys. Gen., Washington, 1986-90; mediator U.S. Ct. Appeals (D.C. cir.). Author (with Leavell, Love and Nelson): Equitable Remedies, Restitution and Damages, 1994, 2000, 2005; contbr. articles to profl. publs. Officer Eisenhower Found. for Prevention of Violence, 1977-81; mem. D.C. Cir. Com. on Bicentennial of Constn., 1986-92. Recipient U. Faculty award for outstanding tchg., Am. U., 1987, student award for outstanding tchg., 1994; Pauline Ruyle Moore scholar, Coll. Law Am. U., Washington, 1984, 1998, 2000, Wellesley scholar, Wellesley Coll., 1968, 1969. Mem.: AAUW, ABA, Am. Law Inst., Women's Bar Assn., Am. Assn. Law Schs. (chair remedies sect. 1990), Cosmos Club. Office: Am U Coll Law 4801 Massachusetts Ave NW Washington DC 20016-8196 Business E-Mail: kovacic@wcl.american.edu.

KOVACIK, NEAL STEPHEN, hotel and restaurant executive; b. Toledo, Mar. 2, 1952; s. Albert Joseph and Phyllis (Lesinski) K.; m. Denise Reichert, Apr. 20, 1974 (div. June 1976). Student, Bowling Green State U., 1971-72, U. Toledo, 1973-74, Owens Tech. Coll., 1975. Dir. food and beverages Motor Inn of Perrysburg, Ohio, 1976-78; v.p. food and beverage ops. Bennett Enterprises, Perrysburg, 1978-82, v.p. hotel and restaurant ops., 1982—. Bd. dirs. Greater Toledo Office of Tourism and Convs., 1994—. Recipient Food and Beverage Dir. of Yr. award Holiday Inns. Inc. and Internat. Assn. Holiday Inns, 1976. Mem. Northwestern Ohio Restaurant Assn. (bd. dirs. 1980-84), Toledo Hotel and Motel Assn. Democrat. Roman Catholic. Avocations: art, wildlife photography. Home: 9640 Monclova Rd Monclova OH 43542-9709 Office: Bennett Enterprises Corp 27476 Holiday Ln Perrysburg OH 43551-3345 E-mail: neal_kovacik@bennett-enterprises.com.

KOVACS, AIMEE, conference speaker, minister; b. Laredo, Tex. d. Arturo and Hilaria; m. James Kovacs; six stepchildren and 1 son. BS, U. Tex.; M in Bibl. Counseling, D in Ministry in D in Ministry in Dance, PhD, Friends Internat. Christian U. Cert. tchr. Tex. and N.J.; cert. min. Eagles House, N.Y. Mktg. staff Abbington Assocs., N.J.; tchr. N.J. Sch. Sys.; min. The Eagle House, N.Y.C.; pres. Kingdom Glory, Inc., West Long Branch, N.J. Pres. World Wide Dominion Dancers, N.J.; mem. mktg. staff Abbington Assocs., N.J.; host TV program on Nigeria, NTV. Author: Dancing Into The Anointing, 1996; choreographer (dance concert) World of Dance, 1967, (play) Monmouth Players; writer, dir. (play) Comedy of Teachers, 1975; prodr. (video) World of Dance, 1998; host, sponsor (TV program) Victory is a Choice,

Nigeria. Team mother West Long Branch (N.J.) Sports, 1984-87; art appreciation vol. West Long Branch Elem., 1987; class mother Rumson Country Day Sch., 1988; choreographer UN, N.Y., 1993; mothers club Christian Bros. Acad., Lincroft, 1995-96; vol. Children of the World Found., 1998. Named Sweetheart, Pan Am. Student Forum, Tex., 1962, Ms. Sail Boat Race, Atlantic Highlands Yacht Club, 1976, Mrs. West Long Branch, Mrs. N.J. Internat. Pageant, 1996, Mrs. Colts Neck, Mrs. N.J. Internat. Pageant, 1997, Mrs. Monmouth County, Mrs. N.J. Internat. Pageant, 1998; Martin High Choir scholar, Laredo, Tex., 1962. Mem. Battle Ground Country Club, Elisha House, B. Hinn Ptnrs. Republican. Avocations: golf, sailing, skiing, dance, gardening. Home and Office: Kingdom Glory Internat Inc PO Box 40 West Long Branch NJ 07764-0040

KOVACS, ALAN L., lawyer; b. N.Y.C., May 21, 1947; s. Edward J. and Hilda Kovacs; m. Caryn R. Bronstein, Aug. 5, 1972; children: Erica, Michele. BA, Amherst Coll., 1969; JD, Columbia U., 1972; LLM, Boston U., 1980. Bar: N.Y. 1973, Mass. 1975. Asst. dist. atty. N.Y.C. Dist. Attys. Office, 1972-75; assoc. Gadsby & Hannah, Boston, 1976-78; asst. atty. gen., chief antitrust divsn. Atty. Gens. Office, Boston, 1978-85; counsel Ferriter, Scobbo, Caruso, Boston, 1985-97; founder Law Office of Alan L. Kovacs, Boston, 1997—. Chmn. Antitrust Task Force Nat. Assn. of Attys. Gen., 1983-85; commr. payment adv. commn. Mass. Hosp., Boston, 1995-97. Dir. Newton (Mass.) Girls Soccer League, 1985—; mem. Newton Dem. Com., 1986—; class agent Amherst (Mass.) Coll. Alumni Fund, 1994—. Mem. ABA, MBA, Boston Bar Assn. Home: 257 Dedham St Newton MA 02461-2044 Office: 2001 Beacon St Ste 106 Boston MA 02135

KOVACS, MALCOLM, social studies educator, religious studies educator; BA in Polit. sci., Roosevelt U., 1965; cert., U. Geneva, 1966; MSc, London Sch. Econs., 1968; postgrad., Rabbinical Coll. Am., Morristown, N.J., 1972—75; PhD in Sociology, Union Grad. Sch., Cin., 1977. Spl. asst., overseas rep. U.S. Nat. Student Assn., Washington, 1966—68; assoc. dir. Washington Urban Coalition, 1967; prof. sociology Montgomery Coll., Rockville, Md., 1970—. Dir. Jewish Roots Ctr. Montgomery Coll., 1975—2003; dir. Torah Edn. and Rsch. Ctr., Balt., 2003—. E-mail: takovacs@comcast.net.

KOVALCHIK, JOHN ROBERT, music educator; b. Pitts., Aug. 8, 1949; s. John James and Marleen Jeannette Kovalchik; m. Joan Elaine Musser, Sept. 4, 1971; children: John, Robert. BS, Pa. State U., 1971, MEd, 1974. Cert. tchr. Pa. Dept. Edn., 1974. Instrumental music tchr. State Coll. (Pa.) Area Sch. Dist., 1971—, asst. marching band dir., 1973—, jazz band dir., 1980—; project chmn., music performance trust funds Local 660, Am. Fedn. of Musicians, State Coll., Pa., 1979—97, pres., 1984—99; cons., performing arts com. of the ctrl. Pa., festival of the arts Ctrl. Pa, Festival of the Arts, State Coll., Pa., 1984—91. Bd. mem. Pa. State Alumni Blue Band Exec. Bd., Univ. Pk., 1985—2001; guest condr. Leonardtown (Md.) Mid. Sch., 1994—94; jazz night coord. Pa. Music Educators Assn., 1997—2002; leader The Tarnished Six Traditional Dixieland Jazz Band, State Coll., Pa., 1997—. Musician: (recording) Prime Cuts, 1980, Movin' Willie's Grave, 1981, Livin' High, 1985, Live at the Nittany Lion Inn, 1986, In the Morning I Sing, 1994, Polished Up, 1994, The Tarnished Six Does Thirty Years, 1997. Pres. Pa. State Blue Band, 1970—71; cons. State Coll. (Pa.) Area Sch. Dist. Citizen's Adv. Bd., 1991—92. Recipient Dist. 4 Citation of Excellence award, Pa. Music Educators Assn., 1997. Mem.: Am. Fedn. Musicians of the U.S. and Can. (conf. del. 1985—97), Internat. Assn. Jazz Educators, Pa. Music Educators' Assn., Pa. State Edn. Assn., NEA, Music Educators' Nat. Conf., Nat. Band Assn., State Coll. Area Edn. Assn. (chmn., extra pay for extra duty com. 1984—85). Avocations: golf, travel, reading, jogging. Home: 345 Koebner Cir State College PA 16801-2518 Office: Mt Nittany Mid Sch 656 Brandywine Dr State College PA 16801 Personal E-mail: jkt6tuba@aol.com. E-mail: jrk11@scasd.k12.pa.us.

KOVALCHUK, BRIAN, beverage company executive; CFO Benetton; acting pres. Pabst Brewing Co., 2001, CEO, pres., 2001—. Office: Pabst Brewing Co Ste 300 121 Interpark Blvd San Antonio TX 78216 Office Phone: 210-226-0231. Office Fax: 210-299-6807.*

KOVALCHUK, ILYA, professional hockey player; b., Tver, Russia, Apr. 15, 1983; Right wing Atlanta Thrashers, 2001—. Recipient Maurice Richard Trophy, 2004. Achievements include the first Russian player to be selected first in an NHL Entry Draft. Office: Atlanta Hockey Club Inc 1 CNN Ctr 13 S Atlanta GA 30303

KOVALCIK, PAUL JEROME, surgeon; b. Buffalo, Apr. 16, 1943; s. Jerome G. and Dorothy I. (Kalinowski) K.; m. Janet I. Howe, Jan. 13, 1968; children: Julia, Peter, John, Matthew, Andrew. BA, CUNY, Flushing, 1965; MD, Georgetown U., 1969. Diplomate Nat. Bd. Med. Examiners, Am. Bd. Surgery, Am. Bd. Colon and Rectal Surgery; ATLS instr. Commd. ensign USN, 1969, advanced through grades to capt., 1984, ret. Med. Corps, 1989; intern medicine and surgery Naval Hosp., Boston, 1969-70, resident gen. surgery, 1970-73, Naval Regional Med. Ctr., Portsmouth, Va., 1973-74; fellow colon and rectal surgery Lahey Clinic, Boston, 1974-75; assoc. prof. surgery Ea. Va. Med. Sch., 1980—, Uniformed Svcs. U. Health Scis., 1986—; head dept. gen. surgery Naval Hosp. Portsmouth, 1985-87. Cons. Naval Hosp. Portsmouth; chmn. ethics com. Maryview Hosp., Portsmouth, 1992-2001, pres. med. staff, 2001-03; assoc. examiner Am. Bd. Colon and Rectal Surgery; vis. prof. Greenville (S.C.) Hosp. System, 1984, U. S.C., Columbia, 1984, W.Va. U. Med. Ctr., Charleston, 1986, East Carolina U., Greenville, 1991, 93; lectr. Georgetown U., Washington, 1985, U.S. Naval Hosp., Guantanamo Bay, Cuba, 1986, U.S. Naval Hosp., Roosevelt Roads, P.R., 1987, U.O.A. Mid-Atlantic Regional Conf., 1987, Acute Combat Symposium Tidewater chpt. AMSUS, Norfolk, 1987, Trauma Symposium Naval Hosp., Roosevelt Roads, 1988, Thomas Jefferson U. Med. Sch., 1988, 90, Acute Combat Trauma Symposium, Norfolk, 1988, Piedmont Soc. Colon and Rectal Surgeons, Williamsburg, Va., 1990, Sardestin, Fla., 1992, Kiawah Island, S.C., 1993, Joseph F. Mulach Med. Lectr. Series St. Clair Hosp., Pitts., 1991, Student Cancer Conf. Ea. Va. Med. Sch., Norfolk, 1994; Thordur Thordarson Meml. lectr., Reykjavik, Iceland, 1987; pres. Portsmouth Acad. Medicine, 1998-99; med. advisor Va. Tumor Registry; chmn. credentials appeals com. United Health Care Va., 2000-2002; lectr. U. Sienna, Italy, 1998, U. Copenhagen, 2002; pres. med. staff Mayview Med. Ctr., 2000-02; chmn. eithics com. Cheszvake Gen. Hosp., 2003—. Contbr. numerous articles to med. jours. Fellow: ACS (surveyor commn. on cancer 2000—), Am. Soc. Colon and Rectal Surgery; mem.: AMA, Va. Surg. Soc., Soc. Am. Gastrointestinal Endoscopic Surgeons (founder), Am. Soc. Colon and Rectal Surgeons (chmn. self-assessment com. 1988—92, mem.-at-large to exec. coun. 1992—, recert. com.), Lahey Clin. Alumni Assn. Republican. Roman Catholic. Avocations: fishing, tennis, gardening, travel, collecting pipes. Home: 4762 River Shore Rd Portsmouth VA 23703-1518 Office: 3105 American Legion Rd Ste A Chesapeake VA 23321-5653 also: 667 Kinsborough Sq Ste 300 Chesapeake VA 23320 Office Phone: 757-686-2687. Personal E-mail: pkovalcik@cox.net.

KOVALESKI, DIANE MARIE, secondary school educator; b. Scranton, Pa., Aug. 17, 1973; d. Joseph Andrew and Mary Patricia Kovaleski. BA in English, Cedar Crest Coll., 1995; MS, Wilkes U., 2004. Cashier KMart, Pittston, Pa., 1989—95; prodn. asst. OCC Sports, L.A., 1995; project mgr. Creative Graphics, Inc., Allentown, Pa., 1995—97; call specialist Notify MD/Ring Med., Moosic, 1997—99; substitute tchr. Pittston Area Sch. Dist., 1999; tchr. bus. Saucon Valley Sch. Dist., Hellertown, 1999—2000, Pen Argyl Area High Sch., 2000—. Mem.: NEA, Nat. Bus. Edn. Assn., Internat. Soc. Tech. Edn. Democrat. Roman Catholic. Avocations: reading, writing, music, scrapbooks. Home: 116 E Center St Nazareth PA 18064 Office: Pen Argyl Area Sch Dist 501 W Laurel Ave Pen Argyl PA 18072

KOVALEV, ALEXEI, professional hockey player; b. Togliatti, Russia, Feb. 24, 1973; Profl. hockey player N.Y. Rangers, 1992—98, Pitts. Penguins, 1998—2003, N.Y. Rangers, 2003—04, Montreal Canadiens, 2004—. Player NHL All-Star game, 2001, 03, Russian Olympic Team, 1992, 2002. Recipient Olympic Gold medal, 1992, Stanley Cup Champion, 1994. Office: c/o Montreal Canadiens 1275 St Antoine St W h3c 5l2 Montreal PQ Canada

KOVARY, LORAINE THERESA, language educator; b. Bethlehem, Pa., Sept. 5, 1948; d. Genero Brita, Incoranata Brita; m. Frank Joseph Kovary, June 10, 1972. BS in Edn., Kutztown U., 1970, MA in Spanish, 1973; student, U. Valencia, Spain, 1969. Tchr. Spanish Wilson H.S., West Lawn, Pa., 1970—. Dir. Wilson Study Tour to Spain Program, West Lawn, 1973—. Recipient Disting. Tchr. award, Hood Coll., 1999. Mem.: Wilson Fedn. Tchrs., Am. Assn. Tchrs. Spanish and Portuguese. Roman Catholic. Avocations: travel, bicycling, skiing. Office: Wilson High Sch 2601 Grandview Blvd West Lawn PA 19609

KOVATCH, CAROL WILHELM, small business owner; b. Albany, N.Y., Jan. 15, 1931; d. John Frederick and Elizabeth Marie (Speck) Wilhelm; m. Jak Gene Kovatch, Dec. 24, 1967. BS, Russell Sage Coll., 1952. Copy editor Textile World mag. McGraw Hill Inc., N.Y.C., 1957-62, assoc. editor Modern Packaging Ency., 1962-64, asst. editor Modern Packaging mag., 1964-68; prodn. editor communications dept. Haskins & Sells, N.Y.C., 1968-73; mgr. graphic design Sikorsky Aircraft div. United Technologies Corp., Stratford, Conn., 1973-87; pres. Carol Kovatch Communications, Westport, Conn., 1987—2001; dir., co-owner The Kovatch Studio, 2001—. Mem. Women in Communications (v.p. com. Fairfield chpt. 1988-89), Conn. Assn. Bus. Communicators (bd. govs. 1977-81, awards chmn. 1978-80, v.p. progs. 1980-81, internat. coun. 1987-88), Entrepreneurial Women's Network, Internat. Assn. Bus. Communications. Home and Office: 34 Sasco Creek Rd Westport CT 06880-6341

KOVATCH, JAK GENE, artist; b. LA, Jan. 17, 1929; s. Jack and La Vinia Blanche (Abernathy) K.; m. Carol Jean Wilhelm, Dec. 24, 1967; 1 son by previous marriage, Jason. Student, UCLA, 1946, Chouinard Art Inst., 1947-49, Calif. Sch. Art, L.A., 1949-50, U. So. Calif., 1951, L.A. City Coll., 1955-56, Art Students League, N.Y.C., 1972, 75. Student asst. Lynton Kistler Studio, L.A., 1952-53; staff animation dept. Walt Disney Prodns., Inc., Burbank, Calif., 1953. Instr. drawing and anatomy Famous Artists Schs., Westport, Conn., 1957-59; tchr. Roger Ludlowe H.S., Fairfield, Conn., 1959-60; extension instr. NYC Coll., 1959-60; instr. sculpture Fairfield U., 1967; faculty U. Bridgeport, Conn., 1962-94, Ethyl prof. design, 1988-94, assoc. prof. dept. design, 1978-88, prof. design, 1988-94; faculty Silvermine Sch. Art, New Canaan, Conn., 1994—; vis. faculty Aldrich Mus. Contemporary Art, Ridgfield, Conn., 1999; fellow Mellon Found.; vis. faculty Yale U., 1979-83; lectr. in field. Stage designer for, Benjamin Zemach, L.A., 1953-54, freelance illustrator, NYC, 1957-58; one-man show Monroe C. Gutman Libr., Harvard U., 2000; exhibited in group shows including Taipei Fine Arts Mus., Taiwan, R.O.C., 1987, 91, Tokyo Met. Mus., Japan, 1985-87, Barbican Arts Ctr., London, 1989, Legislative and State Office Bldgs., Hartford, 1991, Salford Mus., Eng., 1989, Inst. Tech. Aeroespacial, Sao Jose dos Campos, Brasil, 1987, U. Hawaii, 1985, Mus. Modern Art, Wakayama, Japan, 1987, Northeastern U., Boston, 1999, Butler Inst. Am. Art, Youngstown, Ohio, 2002, Boston Printmakers, 2002; represented in permanent collections Fogg Mus. Art, Cambridge, Mass., Libr. Congress, Joseph Hirshhorn Collection, Greenwich, Conn., Fairfield Art Collection, John Slade Ely House Collections, New Haven, Bicentennial Art Collection, Westport (Conn.) Town Hall, U. Miss., Albert Dorne Collection, NYC, others; artist project grant from Conn. Commn. on Arts, Hartford, 1984-85. Selection com. State of Conn. Commn. on Arts, Percent for Art Program, Hartford, 1987-88. Recipient award Boston Mus. Fine Arts, 1954, Wadsworth Atheneum, Hartford, Conn., 1958, 79, Mus. Art, Sci. and Industry, Bridgeport, 1962-63, 65-66, 75, 77, 79, 81-84, 22 awards Fairfield (Conn.) U., 1973-95, award New Haven Paint and Clay Club, 1976, 78, 81, 89-90, 97-98, 2002, spl. recognition award Print Club Albany, Schenectady Mus., 1992, John Taylor Arms Meml. award Audubon Artists, Inc., Nat. Arts Club, N.Y.C., 1993, etching award Stamford (Conn.) Mus., 1994, Painting award New Britain Mus. Am. Art, 1997, awards Brush and Palette Club, New Haven, 2000, 02, more than 180 others. Mem. Soc. Am. Graphic Artists, Boston Printmakers, Audubon Artists (bd. dirs. for graphics 1995), Conn. Acad. Fine Arts, Greenwich Art Soc., LA Printmaking Soc., Phila. Print Club, Silvermine Guild Artists (trustee 1979-83), Westport-Weston Arts Coun. Home: 34 Sasco Creek Rd Westport CT 06880-6341 Office: Silvermine Sch of Art Inc 1037 Silvermine Rd New Canaan CT 06840-4398 Office Phone: 203-259-9461. Personal E-mail: jakkovatch@sbcglobal.net. *I consider my concept of Image Continuum to be a significant consequence of 50 years of painting and printmaking. Six basic components form the foundation of this concept: 1. Use of former images to create new ones; 2. Repetition of a theme (subject matter and symbols repeated); 3. Use of modules; 4. Use of storyboards and grids; 5. Structuring forms transparently; 6. Use of abstraction, animation, distortion. An integral part of Image Continuum is persistent use of multiple images. This means of expression may be directly related to my personal impatience with dwelling too long on one image or idea. I have been able to temper this drive for immediacy and rapid image development by using images in a series or storyboard format.*

KOVEL, RALPH MALLORY, writer, antique expert; b. Milw. s. Lester and Dorothy K.; m. Terry Horvitz; children: Lee R., Karen. Attended, Ohio State U. Pres., chmn. U.S. Brands, Inc.; pres. Lucayan Aquaculture, Freeport, Bahamas. V.p., treas. Antiques, Inc.; trustee WVIZ-TV, Western Res. Hist. Soc., Cleve., Cleve. Pops Orch., Inc., Sara Lee Foods; Hiram fellow, former tchr. course in antiques Western Res. U., John Carroll U. Writer: (with Terry Kovel) syndicated column Kovels Antiques and Collecting, 1955—, Ask the Experts, House Beautiful, 1979-2000, Medio, CD-Rom Mag., 1995, The Kovels on Collecting, Forbes Mag., 2000-02; editor: monthly newsletters Kovels on Antiques and Collectibles, 1974—, Kovels Sports Collectibles, 1992-97; Know Your Antiques, Pub. TV, 1969-70; syndicated TV series Kovels on Collecting, 1981, 87, Collector's Journal TV, 1989-93, Flea Market Finds with the Kovels HGTV, 2000-; numerous appearances on radio and TV talk shows; author: (with Terry Kovel) Kovels' Dictionary of Marks-Pottery and Porcelain, 1953, rev. edit., 1995, Directory of American Silver, Pewter and Silver Plate, 1958, American Country Furniture, 1780-1875, 1963, Kovels' Know Your Antiques, rev. edit., 1993, Kovels Antiques and Collectibles Price List, 37th edit., 2005, Kovels' American Art Pottery, 1993, Kovels' Bid, Buy & Sell Online, 2001, The Kovels' Bottle Price List, 12th edit., 2002, Kovels' Price Guide for Collector Plates, Figurines, Paperweight and Other Ltd. Editions, 1978, Kovels' Collector's Guide to American Art Pottery, 1974, Kovels' Collector's Guide to Limited Editions, 1974, Kovels' Know Your Collectibles, 1981, 1992, Kovels' Book Antique Labels, 1982, Kovels' Depression Glass and Dinnerware Price List, 8th edit. 2004, Kovels' Illustrated Price Guide to Royal Doulton, 2d edit., 1984, Kovels' Organizer for Collectors, rev. edit., 1983, Kovels' Collectors' Source Book, 1983, Kovels' New Dictionary of Marks Pottery and Porcelain, 1850 to the Present, 1986, Kovels' Advertising Collectibles Price List, 1986, 05, Kovels' Guide to Selling Your Antiques and Collectibles, rev. edit., 1990, Kovels' American Silver Marks 1650 to Present, 1989, Kovels' Antiques and Collectibles Fix-It Source Book, 1990, Kovels' Quick Tips: 799 Helpful Hints on How to Care For Your Collectibles, 1995, Kovels' Guide to Selling, Buying and Fixing Your Antiques and Collectibles, 1995, The Label Made Me Buy It, 1998, Kovel's Yellow Pages 2d edit., 2003, Kovel's American Antiques 1750-1900, 2004; (video tape series) Collecting With the Kovels, Art Pottery I, Art Pottery II, 1995, Kovels' Page-A-Day Collectibles Calendar 1990, 1991, Kovels' Antiques and Collectibles 2003 Day-At-A-Time Calendar; contbr. numerous articles on antiques to publs, chapt. to books. Former mem. rev. and allocations com. United Torch Fund, Cleve.; past pres. E. End Neighborhood Settlement House; past chmn. adv. com. Woodhill Homes; past bd. dirs. Soc. Collectors, Silver Mus. Religious Art. Recipient Lane Bryant award, 1966; Peirce Award for Outstanding Cmty. Svc. Sta. WVIZ-TV, 1980, Cleve. Emmy award best entertainment, 1971, Cleve. Emmy award cultural affairs programming, 1987. Mem. Union League Club (Chgo.), Oakwood Club (Cleve.). Office: PO Box 22200 Cleveland OH 44122-0200

KOVEL, TERRY HORVITZ, writer, antiques authority; b. Cleve. d. Isadore and Rix Horvitz; m. Ralph Kovel; children: Lee R., Karen. BA, Wellesley Coll., 1950. Tchr. math. Hawken Sch. for Boys, Shaker Heights, Ohio, 1961-71; now pres. Antiques Inc.; past tchr. course in antiques Western Res. U., John Carroll U. Writer: (with Ralph Kovel) syndicated column Kovels Antiques and Collecting, 1955—, Ask the Experts, House Beautiful, 1979-2000, Medio, CD-Rom mag., 1995, The Kovels on Collecting, Forbes Mag., 2000-02; editor: monthly newsletters Kovels on Antiques and Collectibles, 1974-, Kovels Sports Collectibles, 1992-97; TV series Know Your Antiques, Pub. TV, 1969-70; syndicated TV Series Kovels on Collecting, 1981, 87, Collector's Journal TV, 1989-93, Flea Market Finds with the Kovels HGTV, 2000-; numerous appearances on radio and TV talk shows; author: (with Ralph Kovel) Kovels' Dictionary of Marks-Pottery and Porcelain, 1953, rev. edit., 1995, Directory of American Silver, Pewter and Silver Plate, 1958, American Country Furniture, 1780-1875, 1963, Kovels' Know Your Antiques, rev. edit, 1993, Kovels' American Art Pottery, 1993, Kovels' American Antiques 1750-1900, 2004, Kovels' Antiques and Collectibles Price List, 37th edit., 2005, Kovels' Know Your Collectibles, 1981, 1992, Kovels' Bottle Price List, 12th edit., 2002, Kovels' Organizer for Collectors, 1978, revised, 1983, Kovels' Price Guide for Collector Plates, Figurines, Paperweights and Other Limited Editions, 1978, Kovels' Collector's Guide to American Art Pottery, 1974, Kovels' Collector's Guide to Limited Editions, 1974, Kovels' Depression Glass and Dinnerware Price List, 8th edit., 2004, Kovels' Illustrated Price Guide to Royal Doulton, 2d edit., 1984, Kovels' Collectors' Source Book, 1983, Kovels' New Dictionary of Marks Pottery and Porcelain, 1850 to the Present, 1986, Kovels' Advertising Collectibles Price List, 1986, 2005, Kovels' Guide to Selling Your Antiques and Collectibles, 1987, 2d edit., 1990, Kovels' Book of Antique Labels, 1982, Kovels' American Silver Marks 1650 to the Present, 1989, Kovels' Antiques and Collectibles Fix-It Source Book, 1990, Kovels' Guide to Selling, Buying and Fixing Your Antiques and Collectibles, 1995, Kovels' Quick Tips: 799 Helpful Hints on How To Care for Your Collectibles, 1995, The Label Made Me Buy It, 1998, Kovels' Yellow Pages, 2d. edit., 2003, Kovels' Bid, Buy and Sell Online, 2001; (Video tape series) Collecting With the Kovels, 1995, Art Pottery I, Art Pottery II, Kovels' Page-A-Day Collectibles Calendar 1990, 1991, Kovels' Antiques and Collectibles 2003 Day-At-A Time-Calendar; contbr. numerous articles on antiques to publs, chapt. to books. Trustee Hiram Coll., 1989-99, hon. trustee, 2000; bd. mem. Shaker Hist. Soc. Hiram fellow; recipient Peirce award for outstanding cmty. svc. Sta. WVIZ-TV, 1980, Cleve. Emmy award for best entertainment, 1971, Cleve. Emmy award for cultural affairs programming, 1987; Laurel Sch. Alumanae of Yr. Office: PO Box 22200 Cleveland OH 44122-0200

KOVER, ARTHUR JAY, marketing educator, consultant; b. N.Y.C., June 16, 1932; s. Theodore and Anita Pearl (Robinson) K.; m. Eugenia Marie Wetzel, Jan. 16, 1971 (div.); children: Amy R., Ezra W.; m. Margaret Sater Lord, Mar. 23, 1991. BA, Cornell U., 1953; MA in Sociology, Yale U., 1954, PhD in Sociology, 1970. Sr. project dir. dept. of rsch. Kenyon & Eckhardt, Inc., N.Y.C., 1960-64, v.p., dir. rsch., 1979-81; v.p., mgr. dept. of rsch. Foote, Cone & Belding, N.Y.C., 1964-69; asst prof. orgnl. behavior Cornell U., Ithaca, N.Y., 1970-78; v.p., dir. rsch. devel. J. Walter Thompson Co., N.Y.C., 1978-79; dir. rsch. and strategy planning Cunningham & Walsh, Inc., N.Y.C., 1981-87; sr. v.p.- rsch. N.W. Ayer, Inc., N.Y.C., 1987-91; prof. mktg. grad. sch. bus. adminstrn. Fordham U., N.Y.C., 1991—2001, chair mktg. area, 1993—98; mgmt. fellow Yale Sch. Mgmt., New Haven, 2001—. V.p., assoc. rsch. dir. Benton & Bowles, Inc., N.Y.C., 1972-74; mem. corp. rsch. & devel. com., new bus. com. J. Walter Thompson Co., N.Y.C., 1978-79, strategy planning bd., N.Y. operating com. Kenyon & Eckhardt, Inc., 1979-81; v.p. Cunningham & Walsh, Inc., N.Y.C., 1981, sr. v.p., 1982, trustee profit sharing plan, 1985, mng. dir. bd. dirs. strategy & planning com., quality com., 1986; adj. prof. mktg. grad. sch. bus. adminstrn. NYU, 1985-90; ind. mktg. and orgnl. cons. in field. Author: (with others) America as a Mass Society, 1963; book rev. editor Adminstrv. Sci. Quar., 1971-73; mem. edit. rev. bd. Jour. Advt. Rsch., 1982-92, assoc. editor, 1991—98, editor in chief Jour. Advt. Rsch., 1998—; contbr. articles to profl. jours.; pub. papers; reviewer in field. 1st lt. U.S. Army, 1954—56. N.Y. State Regents scholar, Cornell State scholar, 1949-54, Univ. scholar Yale U., 1954-57; Wilson U. fellow Yale U., 1959, Spl. Rsch. fellow NIMH, Yale U., 1968-70. Fellow Acad. Mktg. Sci., Soc. Applied Anthropology; mem. Am. Mktg. Assn. (exec.), Am. Sociol. Assn., Comm. Rsch. Coun., Market Rsch. Coun. (councilman at large, 1986-87, pres. 1989-90), Assn. Consumer Rsch., Lotos Club, Elizabethan Club, Franklin Inn Club. Office: Fordham U Grad Sch Bus Adminstrn 113 W 60th St New York NY 10023-7484

KOVNER, BRUCE, investment company executive; b. NYC, 1945; BA, Harvard Coll., 1966; student, John F. Kennedy Sch. Govt., 1970. Cons. US Congress, Nat. Sci. Found., Coun. Environ. Advisors for State of NY, Fels Ctr. Govt., U. Pa., 1970—76; v.p. to sr. v.p. Commodities Corp., Princeton, NJ, 1977—83; founder, chmn. Caxton Corp., 1983—. Founder Sch. Choice Scholarships Found., chmn.; mem. bd. Juillard Sch., Am. Enterprise Inst., Manhattan Inst., Philharmonic-Soc., NY, Thomas B. Fordham Found. Achievements include ranked by Forbes as one of the Worlds Richest People, 2002, 03, 04. Office: Caxton Assocs LLC 500 Park Ave New York NY 10022 Office Phone: 212-303-6100.

KOVNER, KATHLEEN JANE, civic worker, portrait artist; b. Cambridge, Mass., Nov. 25, 1919; d. David Leo and Kathleen Elizabeth (Lalley) Lane; m. Benjamin Kovner (dec.), June 20, 1938; children: Kathleen Barbara (dec.), Michael Anthony, Peter Christopher. Student, Art Students League, N.Y.C., 1937-40. Owner, CEO Helen Bennett Ltd., Stamford, Conn., 1948-59; cons. Bride's Mag., N.Y.C., 1967-70; co-chair membership com. Women's Nat. Rep. Club, N.Y.C., 1980-81, chmn. membership com., 1981-87, v.p., 1986-87, also bd. dirs. Ltd. ptnr. 519 8th Ave Corp., N.Y.C., 18-19th St. Corp., N.Y.C., Kaufman Arcade Bldg., N.Y.C., 19th St. Assn., N.Y.C., dir. Nelson Tower Assoc., N.Y.C., 1998, ptnr. 450 Seventh Ave Assoc., N.Y.C. Portrait artist in oils, with various portraits in pvt. collections. Fundraiser St. Ignatius Loyola, N.Y.C., 1960-61, Jeanine Pirro-Campaign for Dist. Atty., Westchester County, N.Y., 1993, 97. Republican. Roman Catholic. Home: 62 Brookridge Dr Greenwich CT 06830-4830 also: 923 5th Ave New York NY 10021-2649

KOWALCHICK, EDWARD M., headmaster; b. Phila., Pa. m. Patricia Perri Kowalchick; 2 children. AB, St. Joseph's U., 1971; MA, Villanova U., 1975. Teacher and sch. administrator Hill Sch. & Rosemont Sch., Pa., 1971—; v.p. for enrollment Lynn University in, Boca Raton, Fla.; head of sch. Brother Rice High Sch., Bloomfield Hills, Mich., 2002—04; headmaster Georgetown Prep, Bethesda, Md., 2004—. Co-founder Internat. Boys' Schools Coalition, 1991—. Office: Georgetown Prep 10900 Rockville Pike Rockville MD 20852*

KOWALKOWSKI, JEFFREY FRANCIS, musician, educator, composer; b. Chgo., July 4, 1967; s. Thomas Francis Kowalkowski and Irene Klepacki; m. Mary Elizabeth Decker, May 1, 1998; children: Caleb Francis, Henry David. MusB, DePaul U., 1989, MusM, 1991; MusD, Northwestern U., 1996. Freelance pianist, Chgo., 1985—; pvt. music tchr., 1986—. Lectr. Depaul U., Chgo., 1996—, Northeastern Ill. U., Chgo., 2000—; composer-in-residence Lucky Pierre Performance Group, Chgo., 2001—. Composer: (sound installation) Gone Overboard, 1996, (songs) Circular Ruins: Three Days, 1996, (albums) Missa Canibus, 1998. Artistic dir. Milkwood Found., Chgo., 1998—. Recipient Cmty. Arts Project award, Starbucks Coffee, 1999, Driehaus Found., 2004; Artist in Edn. grantee, Ill. Arts Coun., 1996—2003. Mem.: Chgo. Fedn. Musicians. Avocation: bicycling.

KOWALSKI, ANTHONY ALBERT, music educator; b. Sandusky, OH, July 19, 1943; s. Albert Stanley and Virginia Rosemary (Passinissi) Kowalski; m. Linda Kay Montgomery, Aug. 31, 1968; children: Brian, Tiffany, Holly, Kristi, Lisa, Leslie. MusB ed., Bowling Green U, Bowling Green, OH, 1968, EdM, 1982. Music instr. Sandusky City Sch., Sandusky, Ohio, 1970—2002. Choir dir. Jackson Jr. High, Sandusky, Ohio, 1995. Author vocal and piano songs. Renovate bldg. and apart., Sandusky, Ohio, 1970. E-5 US Coast Guard, 1967—73, Toledo, OH. Mem.: Music Ed. Nat. Conf. Achievements include

3rd degree black belt in Shotokan Karate and instr. for more than 15 yr. Avocations: Karate, tennis, fishing, piano, performing and composition. Home: 3603 Ann Dr Sandusky OH 44870-2430 Office: Jackson Jr HS 314 W Madison St Sandusky OH 44870-2430

KOWALSKI, DENNIS ALLAN, artist, educator; b. Chgo., May 14, 1938; s. Florian Lawrence and Emily Helen (Sinoga) K.; m. Kathryn Susan Lehar, Mar. 19, 1966; 1 dau., Denise Kathryn. Student, U. Ill., 1955-57; B.F.A., Art Inst. Chgo., 1962, M.F.A. with honors, 1966. Preparator Chgo. Acad. Scis., 1960-62, 64-68; instr. DePaul U., Chgo., 1967-70; asso. prof. U. Ill., 1970—. One-man shows, Marianne Deson Gallery, Chgo., 1978, 81, 83, 86, Artpark, Lewiston, N.Y., 1978, N.A.M.E. Gallery, Chgo., 1980, Foster Gallery, U. Wis., Eau Claire, 1982, group shows include, Mus. Contemporary Art, Chgo., 1976, 79, 84, 85, Indpls. Art Mus., 1978, 86, Manhattan Psychiat. Ctr. for Sculpture Garden, N.Y.C., 1979, 82, Northwestern U., 1980, Stefanotti Gallery, N.Y.C., 1980, Carnegie-Mellon U., Pitts., 1982, Navy Pier, Chgo., 1982, Randolph St. Gallery, Chgo., 1982, U. Md., 1983, Semaphore Gallery, N.Y.C., 1983, Internat. Exptl. Art Exhbn., Young Artists Club, Budapest, Hungary, 1985 Served with U.S. Army, 1962-64. George D. Brown Traveling fellow, 1966; Nat. Endowment for Arts fellow, 1975; Ill. Arts Council fellow, 1980, 84; Ill. Arts Council grantee, 1980 Home: 1102 N Wolcott Ave Chicago IL 60622-3708 Studio: 4401 N Ravenswood Ave Chicago IL 60640-5871

KOWALSKI, KENNETH LAWRENCE, physicist, researcher; b. Chgo., July 24, 1932; s. Florian Lawrence and Emily Helen (Sinoga) K.; m. Audrey Bellin; children: Eric Clifford, Claudia Gail. BS, Ill. Inst. Tech., 1954; PhD, Brown U., 1963. Aero. rsch. scientist Lewis Rsch. Ctr., NACA, 1954-57; rsch. assoc. in physics Brown U., summer 1962, Case Inst. Tech., Cleve., 1962-63, asst. prof. physics, 1963-67, assoc. prof., 1967-73, Case Western Res. U., 1967-73, prof., 1973—, exec. officer dept. physics, 1970-71, chmn. dept. physics, 1971-76. Vis. prof. Inst. Theoretical Physics U. Louvain, Belgium, 1968-69; scientist-in-residence Argonne Nat. Lab., 1986-87, User Fermilab, 1993—. Author: (with S.K. Adhikari) Dynamical Collision Theory and It's Applications, 1991; editor: (with W.J. Fickinger) Modern Physics in America, 1988; contbr. articles to profl. jours. NSF grantee, 1972-96. Mem. Am. Phys. Soc. Achievements include research on theoretical physics. Home: 2172 Bellfield Rd Cleveland Heights OH 44106 Office: Case Western Res U Dept Physics 10900 Euclid Ave Dept Physics Cleveland OH 44106-1712 Office Phone: 216-368-4011. Business E-Mail: klk3@po.cwru.edu.

KOWALSKI, MICHAEL J., retail products executive; Various positions including group v.p. mktg. Tiffany & Co., N.Y.C., 1983-92, exec. v.p. merchandising & mktg., 1992—96, pres., 1996—99, COO, 1997—99, CEO, 1999—, chmn. bd. dirs., 2002—. Bd. dirs. Fairmont Hotels and Resorts, Bank of New York, Tiffany & Co., 1995—. Office: Tiffany & Co 727 5th Ave New York NY 10022*

KOWARSKI, ALLEN AVINOAM, endocrinologist, educator; b. Tel Aviv, Dec. 30, 1927; s. Hanoch and Sima (Tkazh) K.; m. Hanna Rose Zas, Mar. 24, 1950; children: David, Ruth. Student, Hebrew U., Jerusalem, 1946—47, MD, 1955; student, U. Lausanne (Switzerland) Med. Sch., 1949—52. Acad. physician Hebrew U., 1955-62; instr., fellow Johns Hopkins U., Balt., 1962-68, asst. prof., 1968-72, assoc. prof., 1972-81; prof. U. Md., Balt., 1981—; pres. Kay Labs., Inc., 1974—. Patentee in field; contbr. over 170 articles to profl. jours. Grantee NIH, 1979-97, McNeil Pharm., 1984-86, DuPont Critical Care, 1985-90, Genentech Found. for Growth & Devel., 1994-95, Lilly Rsch. Lab. 1996-98. Mem. Am. Pediat. Soc., Soc. Pediat. Rsch., Lawson-Wilkins Pediat. Endocrine Soc., The Endocrine Soc., Am. Fedn. Clin. Rsch., Am. Diabetes Assn. (Diabetes Rsch. award 1983, Charles H. Best medal for disting. svc. 1994). Achievements include invention of nonthromogenic blood withdrawal sys., nonthrombogenic glucose monitor; discovery of DAWN phenomenon in diabetes and bioinactive growth hormone syndrome (Kowarski syndrome); integrated concentration of growth hormone method for diagnosis of growth hormone deficiency. Office: Kay Labs Inc 5801 Nicholson Ln Unit 1135 Rockville MD 20852-5734

KOWEL, STEPHEN THOMAS, electrical engineer, educator; b. Phila., Nov. 20, 1942; s. Abraham and Anna (Forman) K.; m. Janis Zoltan, June 7, 1970; children: Ann, Eugene, Rose. BSEE, U. Pa., 1964; PhD in Elec. Engring., 1968; MSEE, Poly. Univ., 1966. Rsch. assoc. U. Pa., Phila., 1968-69; asst. prof. elec. and computer engring. Syracuse (N.Y.) U., 1969-74, assoc. prof., 1974-79, prof., 1979-84; prof. elec. engring. and computer sci. U. Calif., Davis, 1984-90, vice-chair dept., 1986-90, dir. organized rsch. program on polymeric ultrathin film systems, 1988-90; chmn. elec. and computer engring. U. Ala., Huntsville, 1990-97, dir. PhD program in optical sci. and engring., 1992-97, interim dean engring., 1997—98, dir., lab. for integrated computing and optoelectric systems, 1998-99, prof. elec. and computer engring., 1998-99; dean engring. U. Cin., 1999—2004, prof. elec. engring., 2004—. Vis. prof. Cornell U., Ithaca, N.Y., 1982-83; cons. in field. Contbr. articles to profl. jours.; patentee in field. Grantee NASA, USAF, U.S. Army, NSF, Advanced Rsch. Projects Agy. Fellow OSA, IEEE (Centennial medal 1984); mem. AAUP, Am. Soc. Engring. Edn., Sigma Xi. Home: 3787 Brighton Manor Ln Cincinnati OH 45208-1965 Business E-Mail: Stephen.Kowel@uc.edu.

KOWITZ, ALETHA AMANDA, retired dental librarian; b. Chgo., Sept. 26, 1925; d. William Carl and Amanda Hedwig (Ross) K. AA, Wright Jr. Coll., Chgo., 1945; BS, U. Chgo., 1951; MA, Rosary Coll., 1959. Rsch. chemist Synthetical Labs, Chgo., 1945-50, Glidden Co., Chgo., 1950-54, chem. libr., 1954-59; asst. circulation-reference libr. U. Ill. Med. Ctr., Chgo., 1959-67; periodicals libr. Northwestern U. Med. Libr., Chgo., 1967-70; reference libr. ADA, Chgo., 1970-76, asst. libr. dir., 1976-77, libr. dir., 1977-92; ret., 1992. Sec. St. Pauls House Corp., Chgo., 1979-95, bd. dirs. Author: Dentistry Journals and Serials, 1985; co-author: Dentistry on Stamps, 1990; contbr. articles to profl. jours. Fellow Am. Coll. Dentists (hon.); mem. Am. Chem. Soc., Am. Inst. Chemists, Am. Acad. History Dentistry, Med. Libr. Assn., Odontographic Soc. (hon., merit award 1985), Iota Sigma Pi. Mem. United Ch. of Christ. Personal E-mail: lethalada@aol.com.

KOZACHEK, JANET LYNNE, artist, educator; b. Princeton, N.J., July 27, 1957; d. Walter and Agnes Robb (Davies) Kozachek; m. Nathaniel Owen Wallace, May 26, 1979. BA, Douglass Coll., New Brunswick, N.J., 1980; Cert. Grad. Study, Beijing (China) Ctrl. Art Acad, 1983-85; MFA, Parsons Sch. Design, N.Y.C., 1990. Tchr. English Hebei U., Baoding, China, 1981-82, Jilin U., Changchun, China, 1982-83; lectr. art European divsn. U. Md., 1986-87; arts-in-edn. artist S.C. State Arts Commn., 1993—. Adj. prof. art Mercer County C.C., Trenton, N.J., 1990-91; guest lectr. Penland Sch. Art, N.C., 1985, Bluefield (W.Va.) State Coll., 1991, Kutztown (Pa.) U., 1991. Organizer six-artist show Gibbes Mus. Art, 1995; artist retrospective I.P. Stanback Mus., 1993; solo exhbns. include Gallerie de Vierde Dimensie, Plasmolen, Netherlands, 1989, Johnson and Johnson World Hdqrs., 1993, I.P. Stanback Mus., 1993, Goin Gallery, Charleston, S.C., 1994, Nina Liu Gallery, Charleston, Portfolio Gallery, Columbia, Rabold Gallery, Aiken, S.C., 2005; exhibited in group shows at Alexandria (La.) Mus. Art, 1992, Greenville (N.C.) Mus. Art, 1992, Picolo Spoleto Exhbn., Charleston, 1993, 2003, 2004, 2005, Armory Art Ctr., West Palm Beach, Fla., 1993, Summer Olympic Games, Stone Mountain, Ga., 1996, Eleven Eleven Sculpture Gallery, Washington, D.C., 2002, North Charleston Arts Ctr., 2004, Museo Italo-Americano, San Francisco, Calif., 2004, Thresholds, Southeastern Traveling Exhbn., 2004-06, North Charleston Cultural Arts Ctr., 2004, Ellipse Gallery, Washington, 2005, numerous others; work in numerous pvt. collections and I.P. Stanback Mus. Permanent Collection, Columbia Mus. Arts, Morris Mus. Art, Augusta, Ga., Calhoun County Mus., Painted Bride Art Ctr., Phila., Pa., First Bapt. Ch., Orangeburg, S.C.; featured in publs. Helena Rubinstein scholar, 1989-90; grantee Orangeburg Arts Ctr., 1993, 95, Puffin, 2004; recipient Curator's Choice award Stage Gallery, 2000, Best of Show award S.C. State Fair, 2002, First prize painting, 2004, Puffin Found. award, 2004. Mem.: Soc. Am. Mosaic Artists (pres. 1999—2002, cofounder). Democrat. Avocations: travel, gardening, reading. Home: 639 Wilson St NE Orangeburg SC 29115-4872 Office Phone: 803-534-8007. Personal E-mail: kozachek@bellsouth.net.

KOZAK, ALEXANDER L., engineer; b. Kiev, Ukraine, June 16, 1951; arrived in U.S., 1996; s. Leonid Kozak and Evgenia Gerasimova; m. Evgenia I. Chakshova, Feb. 10, 1973; children: Natalia, Dmitry. MS in Structural Mechanics, Kiev Civil Engring. Inst., 1973, PhD in Structural Mechanics, 1981, DSc in Structural Mechanics, 1995. Sun cert. programmer Java platform. Engr., rschr., sr. rschr., prin. rschr. Struct. Mech. Inst. Kiev State Tech. U. Constrn. and Arch., 1973-95; sr. engr., prin. engr. SC Solutions, Inc., Sunnyvale, Calif., 1996—. Contbr. articles to profl. jours. Avocation: stamp collecting/philately.

KOZAK, HARLEY JANE, actress, writer; b. Wilkes-Barre, Pa., Jan. 28, 1957; d. Joseph Aloysius and Dorothy (Taraldsen) K.; m. Gregory Aldisert, 1997; children: Audrey, Lorenzo and Gianna. Cert., NYU, 1980. Appeared in films Parenthood, 1989, Arachnophobia, 1990, The Taking of Beverly Hills, 1990, The Favor, 1990, Necessary Roughness, 1991, All I Want for Christmas, 1991, Magic in The Water, 1995, TV series Harts of the West, 1993-94, Bringing Up Jack, 1995, You Wish, 1997; author: (novels) Dating Dead Men, 2004, Dating is Murder 2005. Office: Renee Zuckerbrot Lit Agy 115 W 29th St 10th Fl New York NY 10001

KOZAK, JOHN W., lawyer; b. Chgo., July 25, 1943; s. Walter and Stella (Palka) Kozak; m. Elizabeth Mathias, Feb. 3, 1968; children: Jennifer, Mary Margaret, Suzanne. BSEE, U. Notre Dame, 1965; JD, Georgetown U., 1968. Bar: Ill. 1968, DC 1968. Patent advisor Office Naval Rsch., Corona, Calif., 1968-69; assoc. Leydig, Voit & Mayer, Ltd. and predecessor firms, Chgo., 1969-74, ptnr., 1974—, chmn. mgmt. com., 1982-91, pres., 2001—. Mem. United Charities Legal Aid Soc., 1989—2002. Fellow: Am. Coll. Trial Lawyers; mem.: ABA, Chgo. Intellectual Property Law Assn., Licensing Execs. Soc., Am. Intellectual Property Law Assn., Orchid Island (Fla.) Golf and Beach Club, Knollwood Club (Lake Forest), Winter Club (Lake Forest, Ill.), Lawyers Club Chgo., Univ. Club (Chgo.). Office: Leydig Voit & Mayer Ste 4900 2 Prudential Pla Chicago IL 60601 Office Phone: 312-616-5600. Business E-Mail: jkozak@leydig.com.

KOZBERG, DONNA WALTERS, rehabilitation services professional; b. Milford, Del., Jan. 1, 1952; d. Robert Glyndwr and Gailey Ruth (Bedorf) Walters; m. Ronald Paul Kozberg, June 8, 1974; 1 child, Mariel Gailey. BA, U. Fla., 1973, M in Rehab. Counseling, 1974; MFA, CUNY, 1979; MBA, Rutgers U., 1986. Cert. rehab. counselor. Rehab. counselor Office Vocat. Rehab., N.Y.C., 1975-81; area dir. Lift, Inc., Staten Island, N.Y., 1981-83, ea. region dir. pub. relations, advt. Mountainside, N.J., 1983-85, v.p., 1985—, v.p., chief fin. officer, 1988, exec. v.p., 1991-93, pres., 1993; co-founder, mng. dir. Expert Strategies, Inc., Mountainside, N.J., 1992—; self-employed writer, editor, 1975—. Adv. bd. Rutgers Exec. Master Bus. Adminstrn. Contbr. articles to profl. jours.; assoc. editor Parachute mag., 1978; editor-in-chief (newsletter) Counselor Adv, 1980. Pres. Com. on Employment of People with Disabilities; trustee Ctr. for Creative Living; bd. dirs. N.J. Adv. Coun. for Independent Living, adv. panel NYU. Mem. Nat. Rehab. Assn. (Spl. citation 1974, grantee 1973), Nat. Rehab. Adminstrs. Assn., Nat. Rehab. Counselors Assn., N.J. Rehab. Counselors Assn. (pres. 1996), Poets and Writers. Avocations: Tennis, English lit., Tae Kwon Do. Home: 45 Dug Way Watchung NJ 07069-6011 Office: Lift Inc PO Box 4264 Warren NJ 07059-0264 E-mail: dwkozberg@aol.com.

KOZBERG, RONALD PAUL, health and human services administrator; b. N.Y.C., Apr. 8, 1951; s. Raymond and Muriel (Tolmas) K.; m. Donna Lynn Walters, June 8, 1974; 1 child, Mariel Gailey. BA, Queens Coll., 1973; M of Rehab. Counseling, U. Fla., 1974; M of Pub. Health, Columbia U., 1986. Cert. rehab. counselor. Program dir. South Beach Psychiat. Ctr., S.I., N.Y., 1974-76; dir. rehab. svcs. Bklyn. Developmental Ctr., 1976-85; dir. stds. and compliance Bronx Developmental Svcs., 1985-91; pres. Expert Strategies, Inc., Warren, N.J., 1991—. Technology com. chairperson Union County Edn. Coun., Westfield, N.J., 1993—. Author: The Do's and Dont's of Interviewing, 1992. Recipient Dean's Coun. award Dean of Health Related Professions, 1974. Mem. Nat. Rehab. Adminstrs. Assn. (N.E. regional bd. mem. 1982), Nat. Rehab. Counselors Assn. (N.Y. state sec., treas. 1981-82), Nat. Rehab. Assn. (pres., Spl. Citation 1974), Am. Pub. Health Assn. Avocations: golf, tennis, photography. Home: 45 Dug Way Watchung NJ 07069-6011 Office: Expert Strategies Inc PO Box 4264 Warren NJ 07059-0264 E-mail: rpkozberg@aol.com.

KOZIK, JEANNE ANN, elementary school educator; b. Milw., June 21, 1949; d. Lawrence James Anderson and Arleen Myrtle Knutson; m. Jerry Kozik, Aug. 21, 1971; children: Darren, Brad. BS, U. Wis., Milw., 1971. Tchr. Glendale-River Hills Sch., Wis., 1971—76, Big Bend Elem. Sch., Mukwonago, Wis., 1988—. Mem.: Alpha Rho Soc. Avocations: gardening, reading, travel. Home: W 784 Potters Cir East Troy WI 53120

KOZIK, SUSAN S., information technology executive; Grad., Bates Coll. With Cigna Corp.; sr. v.p., chief tech. officer Penn Mut. Life Ins. Co.; v.p. info. tech. ops. and svcs. Lucent Techs.; exec. v.p., chief tech. officer TIAA-CREF, N.Y.C., 2003—. Active, former trustee Bates Coll. Recipient 1st Disting. Young Alumni award, Bates Coll. Office: TIAA-CREF 730 3d Ave New York NY 10017

KOZINSKI, ALEX, federal judge; b. Bucharest, Romania, July 23, 1950; came to U.S., 1962; s. Moses and Sabine (Zapler) K.; m. Marcy J. Tiffany, July 9, 1977; children: Yale Tiffany, Wyatt Tiffany, Clayton Tiffany. AB in Econs. cum laude, UCLA, 1972, JD, 1975. Bar: Calif. 1975, D.C., 1978. Law clk. to Hon. Anthony M. Kennedy U.S. Ct. Appeals (9th cir.), 1975-76; law clk. to Chief Justice Warren E. Burger U.S. Supreme Ct., 1976-77; assoc. Covington & Burling, Washington, 1979-81; asst. counsel Office of Counsel to Pres., White House, Washington, 1981; spl. counsel Merit Systems Protection Bd., Washington, 1981-82; chief judge U.S. Claims Ct., Washington, 1982-85; judge U.S. Ct. Appeals (9th cir.), 1985—. Lectr. law U. So. Calif., 1992. Office: US Ct Appeals Ste 200 125 S Grand Ave Pasadena CA 91105*

KOZITKA, RICHARD EUGENE, retired consumer products company executive; b. Staples, Minn., Apr. 30, 1934; s. Michael V. and Luella H. (Drews) K.; m. Mary Elizabeth Juneau, Sept. 27, 1969; children: Michael Arthur, Laura Juneau Hensley. BA in Journalism, U. Minn., 1956. Program dir. Jr. Achievement of Chgo., 1961-63; mgr. publ./employee communications The Quaker Oats Co., Chgo., 1963-72, dir. employee and audio visual communications, 1972-78, v.p. corp. adminstrv. svcs., 1978-95. Trustee Luth. Social Svcs. Ill. Served with U.S. Army, 1957-61. Mem. Westmoreland Country Club (Wilmette, Ill.), Chgo. Curling Club (Northbrook, Ill.), Univ. Club Chgo., Pelican Strand Country Club (Naples, Fla.), La Playa Beach Club (Naples). Lutheran. Home: 9790 Gulf Shore Dr Unit 205 Naples FL 34108

KOZLOFF, JESSICA S., academic administrator; b. San Antonio, Mar. 29, 1941; d. Robert John and Ann (Acklen) Sledge; m. Stephen R. Kozloff, June 12, 1965; children: Kyle Schaller, Rebecca Esther. BS, U. Nev., 1963, MA, 1964; PhD, Colo. State U., 1983. Prof. polit. sci. U. Northern Colo., Greeley, 1976-89, exec. asst. to pres., 1985-89; v.p. acad. affairs State Colls. in Colo., Denver, 1989-94; pres. Bloomsburg U., 1994—. Mem. Middle States Commn. on Higher Edn., 2000—; bd. dirs. Geisinger Health Plan Bd. dirs. United Way, Bloomsburg, 1994—2000, Boy Scouts Am., Bloomsburg, 1994—2000. Acad. Adminstrn. fellow Am. Coun. on Edn., 1985. Mem.: Geisinger Health Plan (bd. dirs. 2004—), Bloomsburg C. of C., Nat. Collegiate Athletics Assn. (mem. pres. commn. 1996—2001), Am. Assn. State Colls. and Univs. (bd. dirs. Pa. campus 2004—, bd. dirs. 1998—2001), Bloomsburg Rotary Club. Avocations: golf, tennis, skiing, biking, travel. Office: Bloomsburg U 400 E 2nd St Bloomsburg PA 17815-1399 Office Phone: 570-389-4526. Business E-Mail: jkozloff@bloomu.edu.

KOZLOFF, JOYCE, artist; b. Somerville, N.J., Dec. 14, 1942; m. Max Kozloff. BFA, Carnegie Inst. Tech., 1964; MFA, Columbia Univ., 1967. Taught at Chgo. Art Inst., Sch. Visual Arts, NYC, Cooper Union, NYC. Exhibitions include Payson Galleries, NYC, 1995, DC Moore Gallery, NYC, 1996-2001, Boston Univ. Art Gallery, 2000, Whitney Mus. Contemporary Art, NYC, 1999-2000, Nat. Mus. Women in the Arts, Washington, 2001; represented in permanent collections of Met. Mus. Art, NYC, Mus. Modern Art, NYC, Nat. Gallery of Art, Washington; author of Patterns of Desire, 2000; co-author, w. Robert Kushner, of Boy's Art, 2003. Grantee Yaddo Fellowship, Sarasota Springs N.Y., Diane Wood Middlebrook Fellowship, Rockefeller Found., Bellagio, Italy, Jules Guerin Fellowship, Am. Acad., Rome, Italy, Nat. Endowment for the Arts. Mem.: NAD (academician). Home: 152 Wooster St New York NY 10012*

KOZLOFF, LLOYD M., dean, microbiologist, educator; b. Chgo., Oct. 15, 1923; s. Joseph and Rose (Hollobow) K.; m. Judith Bonnie Friedman, June 16, 1947; children: James, Daniel, Joseph, Sarah BS, U. Chgo., 1943, PhD, 1948. Asst., then assoc. prof. biochemistry U. Chgo., 1949-61, prof., 1961-64; prof. microbiology U. Colo., Denver, 1964-80, chmn. dept. microbiology, 1966-76, assoc. dean, prof., 1976-80; dean, prof. U. Calif., San Francisco, 1981-91, prof., dean emeritus, 1991—. Career investigator USPHS, U. Chgo., 1962 Founding editor Jour. Virology, 1966-76; contbr. articles to profl. jours., chpts. to books. Chmn. bd. dirs. Proctor Fund., 1981-91; v.p. San Francisco Alliance for Mental Illness, 1993-96; pres. emeritus U. Calif. San Francisco Faculty Assn., 1996-2000. With USN, 1944-46. Commonwealth Fund fellow, 1953, Lederle Found. fellow, 1954; recipient Disting. Svc. award U. Chgo., 2004. Fellow AAAS, Am. Acad. Microbiol. (hon.); mem. Am. Soc. Biol. Chemistry, Am. Soc. Microbiology (head virology sect. 1974-76), Am. Chem. Soc., N.Y. Acad. Sci. Home: 43000 Lyndon Ln Fort Bragg CA 95437 Office: U Calif Grad Divsn San Francisco CA 94114-2732

KOZLOFF, THEODORE J., lawyer; b. Reading, Pa., 1941; BA, MA in Econ., U. Pa., 1964, LLB cum laude, 1967. Bar: Calif. 1967, N.Y. 1968. Mem. Comm. on Securities Regulation, Assoc. of the Bar of the City of New York, 1981—84, Skadden, Arps, Slate, Meagher & Flom, San Francisco; Board of Overseers University of Pennsylvania Law School, 1986—90; bd. trustees The Hill School, Pottstown, Pa., 1987—. Editor U. Pa. Law Rev., 1966-67. Office: Skadden Arps Slate Meagher & Flom 4 Embarcadero Ctr San Francisco CA 94111-4106

KOZLOV, VIKTOR, professional hockey player; b. Togliatti, Togliatti, Russia, Feb. 14, 1975; Hockey player San Jose Sharks, 1994-98, Fla. Panthers, Sunrise, 1997—2004, New Jersey Devils, 2004—. Player NHL All-Star game, 2000. Office: c/o New Jersey Devils 50 Rt 120 North East Rutherford NJ 07073

KOZLOWSKI, CHERYL M., fixed income analyst; b. Boston, July 19, 1974; d. Leo Dennis and Angeles Zenaida. BA, Middlebury Coll., 1996; postgrad., Harvard Bus. Sch., 2000—02. Lic. pilot. Fin. analyst Merrill Lynch, N.Y.C., 1996-1998; prin. Clayton, Dubilier & Rice, Inc., N.Y.C., 1998-2000; equity analyst Am. Express, 2002—04; fixed income analyst Airlie Opportunity Fund, 2004—. Treas. The Friends of Tolstoy Found., 1998—2002; chmn. Young New Yorkers of N.Y. Philharmonic, 1999—2002; bd. dirs. Shackleton Schs., 2000—. Avocation: skiing. Home: 610 Park Ave Apt 14A New York NY 10021-7080 E-mail: ckozlowski@mba2002.hbs.edu.

KOZLOWSKI, ELLEN RHODA, lawyer; b. N.Y.C., Nov. 1, 1953; d. Kurt Edwin and Ruth Ethel (Mayer) Levy; m. Jeffrey P. Kozlowski, June 27, 1976; children: Sarah Michelle, Daniel Lewis, Noah Matthew. BA in Chemistry, SUNY, Binghamton, 1974; MA in Chemistry, Columbia U., 1975; JD, NYU, 1981. Bar: N.Y. 1982, N.J. 1982. Book review editor R.R. Bowker Co., N.Y.C., 1976-78; assoc. Stroock & Stroock & Lavan, N.Y.C., 1981-93, spl. counsel, 1993-94. E-mail: jkozlow@aol.com.

KOZLOWSKI, MELANIE A., secondary school educator; d. James A. and Eileen H. Richardson; m. Brian C. Kozlowski, Oct. 18, 1997; children: Zachary B., Collin J. BA, U. Wis., Stevens Point, 1996; MA in Edn., Viterbo U., 2005. Tchr. English Wausau (Wis.) West H.S., 1997—98; tchr. lang. arts Lincoln H.S., Wisconsin Rapids, Wis., 1998—. Forensics coach Wausau West H.S., 1997—98; mem. Release Day com. Lincoln H.S., Wisconsin Rapids, 2004—. Recipient Schs. Plus grant, South Wood County Comty. Found., 2000, 2003, endowment fund grant, Wisconsin Rapids Pub. Schs., 2003, 2004; grantee Cen. Wis. Writing Project, U. Wis.-Stevens Point, 1999. Mem.: AAUW, ASCD, Nat. Coun. Tchrs. English. Office: Lincoln H S 1801 16th St S Wisconsin Rapids WI 54494

KOZLOWSKI, RONALD STEPHAN, retired librarian; b. Chgo., Oct. 18, 1937; s. Stephan James and Helen Marie Beck (Tancula) K.; m. Barbara Hartlein, Aug. 8, 1964; children: Ann, Keith, Ellen, Brent. BS in Edn, Ill. State U., 1961; MA in LS, Rosary Coll., 1968. Audiovisual libr. Triton Jr. Coll., River Grove, Ill., 1968-69; br. libr. Evansville (Ind.) Pub. Librs., 1969-70, asst. dir., 1971-74; head reference and acquisitions dept. Ind. State U., Evansville, 1970-71; dir. West Fla. Regional Libr., Pensacola, 1974-77, Louisville Free Pub. Libr., 1977-83, Pub. Libr. Charlotte and Mecklenburg County, NC, 1983-86; exec. dir. Cuyahoga County Pub. Libr., Cleve., 1986-89; dir. Miami-Dade Pub. Libr. Sys., Miami, Fla., 1989-1993; adminstr. Anne Arundel County Pub. Libr., Annapolis, Md., 1993—2002; ret., 2002. Del. White House Conf. on Librs. Mem. ALA, Md. Libr. Assn. Home: 1731 Timberly Waye Richmond VA 23233 Personal E-mail: rskozlowski@comcast.net.

KOZMA, ADAM, electrical engineer; b. Cleve., Feb. 2, 1928; s. Desire and Vera (Nagy) K.; m. Eileen Marie Somogyi, Oct. 24, 1956 (dec. Jan. 1978); children: Paul A. (dec.), Peter A.; m. Rebecca Chelius, Feb. 6, 1993. BSME, U. Mich., 1952, MS in Engring.-Instrumentation Engring., 1964; MS in Engring. Mechanics, Wayne State U., 1961; PhD in Elec. Engring., U. London, 1968; diploma of membership, Imperial Coll., 1969. Design engr. US Broach Co., Detroit, 1951-57; rsch. engr. Inst. Sci. & Tech., Willow Run Labs. U. Mich., Ann Arbor, 1958-69; gen. mgr. Electro Optics Ctr. Harris, Inc., Ann Arbor, 1969-73; sr. rsch. engr. radar div. Environ. Rsch. Inst. Mich., Ann Arbor, 1973-75, mgr. elec. and electromagnetics dept., 1975-76, mgr. tech. staff, 1976-77, v.p., dir. radar div., 1977-85, v.p., corp. devel., 1985-86; v.p., dir. def. electronics engring. div. Syracuse (N.Y.) Rsch. Corp., 1986-88; head intelligence systems dept. MITRE Corp., Bedford, Mass., 1988-89, head advanced systems dept., 1990-93; adj. prof. Coll. Engring. U. Mich., Ann Arbor, 1993—2002, vis. scholar, 2003—. Cons. Conductron Corp., Ann Arbor, 1966, IBM, Endicott, N.Y., 1967-68, U.S. Army Missile Command, Huntsville, Ala., 1974-76, MITRE Corp., 1993-2001, Veridian-ERIM-Internat., Inc., 1998-2001; lectr. various univs.; engring. cons., 1993—. Co-author: Hologram Visual Displays (Motion Picture TV Engrs. honorable mention 1977); patentee in field. With U.S. Army, 1946—47, with USAR, 1947—51, with reserve USAF, 1953—61. Fellow IEEE (life), Optical Soc. Am.; mem. Aero. and Electronics Systems Soc. of IEEE (radar systems panel 1984—, bd. govs. 91-93), Geoscience and Remote Sensing Soc. of IEEE, Am. Def. Preparedness Assn. (chmn. various coms. avionics sect. 1975-88, Ordnance medal 1984), Soc. Photo-Optical Instrumentation Engrs., Sigma Xi. Lutheran. Avocations: tennis, skiing, bicycling. Home and Office: 2996 Appleway Ann Arbor MI 48104-1808 Personal E-mail: akozma@comcast.net. Business E-Mail: akozma@umich.edu.

KOZODOY, NEAL, magazine editor; b. Boston, Apr. 4, 1942; s. Peter H. and Marion (Seder) K.; m. Ruth Lurie, June 7, 1964; children— Sarah Naomi, Peter, Elizabeth. BA, Harvard U., 1963; B.H.L., Hebrew Coll., Boston, 1963; MA, Columbia U., 1966. Mem. editorial staff Commentary mag., NYC, 1966—, exec. editor, 1968-90, editor, 1990-95, chief editor, 1995—; editor

Library Jewish Studies, 1970-95. Vis. lectr. Jewish Theol. Sem., 1974-75, Yale U., 1976; cons. President's Commn. Campus Unrest, 1970, NEH, 1976-82, U.S. Dept. Edn., 1985-88, Office of Nat. Drug Control Policy, 1989-90. Sec. Com. for the Free World, 1981-90. Woodrow Wilson fellow, 1964-65; Danforth fellow, 1965-67 Office: Commentary Am Jewish Com 165 E 56th St New York NY 10022-2709

KOZOL, JONATHAN, writer; b. Boston, Sept. 5, 1936; s. Harry Leo and Ruth (Massell) K. BA, Harvard U., 1958; Rhodes scholar, Magdalen Coll., Oxford U., 1958-59. Tchr. Boston pub. schs., 1964-65, Newton pub. schs., 1966-68; dir., trustee Store-front Learning Center, 1968-74; vis. lectr. Yale U., 1969, numerous univs., 1971-2001; prof. edn. Trinity Coll., 1980. Cons. U.S. Office Edn., 1965-66; inst. Ctr. for Intercultural Documentation, Cuernavaca, Mex., 1969, 70, 74. Author: Death At An Early Age, 1967 (Nat. Book award, 1968), Free Schools, 1972, The Night Is Dark and I Am Far From Home, 1975, Children of the Revolution, 1978, Prisoners of Silence, 1980, On Being A Teacher, 1981, Illiterate America, 1985, Rachel and Her Children, 1988 (Robert F. Kennedy Book award, 1989), Savage Inequalities, 1991 (New Eng. Book award, 1992, Amazing Grace, 1995 (Anisfield-Wolf Book award, 1996), Ordinary Resurrections, 2000 (Christopher award, Harry Chapin award, 2001, Wilbur award, 2001), The Shame of the Nation, 2005; corr.: Los Angeles Times, USA Today, 1982-83; contbr. to N.Y. Times Book Rev., 1968-85; reporter-at-large The New Yorker mag., 1988. Trustee New Sch. for Children, Roxbury, Mass.; bd. dirs. Nat. Literacy Coalition, 1980-83. Recipient Olympia Thousand Dollar award, 1962, Lannan Literary award, 1994; Saxton fellow in creative writing Harper & Row, 1964; Guggenheim fellow, 1970, 84; Field Found. fellow, 1972; Ford Found. fellow, 1974; Rockefeller Found. fellow, 1978, fellow in humanities, 1983. Mem. Nat. Coalition for the Homeless, Fellowship of Reconciliation. Address: PO Box 145 Byfield MA 01922-0145 Office Fax: 978-462-8557. *My concerns are the education, health and housing of low income children.*

KOZOLCHYK, BORIS, law educator, consultant; b. Havana, Cuba, Dec. 6, 1934; came to U.S., 1956; s. Abram and Chana (Brewda) D.; m. Elaine Billie Herman, Mar. 5, 1967; children: Abbie Simcha, Raphael Adam, Shaun Marcie. DCL, U. Havana, 1956; Diplome, Faculte Internat. de Droit, Luxembourg, 1958; LLB, U. Miami, 1959; LLM, U. Mich., 1960, SJD, 1966. Teaching asst. Sch. of Law U. Miami, Fla., 1957-59; asst. prof. law Sch. of Law So. Meth. U., Dallas, 1960-64; resident cons. The Rand Corp., Santa Monica, Calif., 1964-67; dir. Law Reform Project USAID, San Jose, Costa Rica, 1967-69; prof. law Coll. of Law U. Ariz., 1969—. Tchg. asst. Faculte Internat. de Droit Campare, 1958; vis. prof. law Nat. U. of Mex., 1961; vis. exch. prof. law Nat. U. of Chile, Santiago, 1962; guest lectr. Latin Am. Law seminar Stanford (Calif.) U., 1964; guest lectr. extension grad. seminar on Latin Am. law UCLA, 1965; Bailey vis. prof., Tucker lectr. La. State U., 1979; vis. prof. U. Aix en Provence, France, 1985; cons. on legal sys. U.S. Agy. Internat. Devel., 1974-77; legal cons. Overseas Pvt. Investment Corp., 1974; cons. uniformity of comml. laws Orgn. Am. States and U.S. State Dept., 1974-77; expert witness on banking and comml. law and custom issues; advisor Libr. Congress Law divsn.; Joseph Bernfeld Meml. lectr. L.A. Bankruptcy Forum, 1989; magisterial lectr. Nat. U. Mex. Sch. Law, 1989; advisor Project Lao, 1991; lectr. in field. Author of books; bd. mem. Am. Jour. of Comparative Law; mem. editl. bd. Internat. Banking Law Jour.; founder, faculty advisor Ariz. Jour. of Internat. and Comparative Law, 1982-86; reporter Ency. Comparative Law, 1989; contbr. articles to profl. jours. and publs. Selected Nat. U. Mex. rep. First Mexican congress Comml. Law, 1974; pres. Ariz. Friends of Music, 1975-76; hon. chmn. community rels. com. Jewish Fedn. So. Ariz.; mem. adv. com. Ariz.-Mex. Commn. Govs.; legal advisor Ariz.-Mex. Banking com.; del U.S. Coun. on Internat. Banking to ICC; adv. mem. U.S. del. to UNCITRAL Internat. Contract Law, 1989-95; dir., pres., bd. dirs. Nat. Law Ctr. for InterAm. Free Trade, 1992—. Recipient Extraordinary Tchg. and Rsch. Merit award Coll. Law, U. Costa Rica, 1969, Cmty. Svc. award Tucson Jewish Cmty. Coun., 1979, Man of Yr. award, 1982, Commendation award U.S. Dept. Justice, 1979, Disting. Svc. award Law Coll. Alumni Assn., 1990, Commendation award U.S. Dept. State, 1990, Ptnrs. in Democracy award Am.-Israel Friendship League, 2003, cert. of Honor Outstanding Contbn. Civil Rights and Social Justice, Tucson Human Rels. Commn., 2003; named to Hall of Fame Profs. of Comml. Law, Nat. U., Mex., 1987; named One of Most Influential Hispanics, Hispanic Bus. Mag., 1991, Man of Yr., Hispanic Profl. Action Com., 1995; NSF grantee, 1973-75. Mem. ABA (task force for the revision of UCC article 5, Leonard J. Theberge award 2004), State of Ariz. Bar (Honoree at 100 Women and Minority Lawyers Dinner), Inter-ABA (co-chmn. comml. law and procedure sec. 1973-78, Best Book award 1973), Am. Soc. of Internat. Law, Internat. Acad. Comml. and Consumer Law (pres. 1988-90), Am. Acad. Fgn. Law (founding), Am. Law Inst. (consultative com. to UCC articles 3, 4, 4a and 5), Nat. Mexican Notarial Bar Assn. (hon. life 1982), Internat. Acad. Comml. and Consumer Law (elected pres. 1988), Sonora Bar Assn. (1st Disting. Svc. award 1989). Home: 7401 N Skyline Dr Tucson AZ 85718-1166 Office: U Ariz Coll Of Law Tucson AZ 85721-0001 Personal E-mail: b.kozolchyk@worldnet.att.net.

KOZUCH, JAMES JEFFREY, lawyer, engineer; b. Ford City, Pa., Mar. 24, 1950; BSME, Cornell U., 1972; MBA, Lehigh U., 1976; JD, Temple U., 1985. Bar: Pa. 1985, U.S. Dist. Ct. (ea. dist.) Pa. 1985. U.S. Ct. Appeals (3d cir.) 1992, Pa.; registered profl. engr., Pa. Engr. Pa. Power & Light Co., Allentown, 1972-74; asst. sr. engr. Mobil Oil, Princeton, N.J., 1974-77, planner Denver, 1977-79; corp. planner Gulf Oil, Pitts., 1979-80; planning coord. Air Products & Chems., Allentown, 1980-82; assoc. Butz, Hudders, Tallman et al, Allentown, 1985-87, Rawle & Henderson, Phila., 1987—. Appointed Spl. Master U.S. Dist. Ct. (ea. dist.) Pa., 1992. Mem. ABA, Pa. Bar Assn., Lehigh County Bar Assn., ASME (com. on legal affairs), Pa. Def. Inst. Office: Rawle & Henderson 1 S Penn Sq Philadelphia PA 19107-3519

KOZUCH, JULIANNA BERNADETTE, librarian, educator; b. Wallis, Tex., Feb. 16, 1921; d. Felix Joseph and Agnes Mary (Vrana) K. BA in English, Our Lady of the Lake U., San Antonio, 1951; MEd, Our Lady of the Lake U., 1961, MLS, 1972. Joined Sisters of Divine Providence order, Roman Cath. Ch., 1936; cert. tchr., Tex., Okla., La. Tchr. Sts. Cyril & Methodius, Granger, Tex., 1940-41, St. John's Sch., Fayetteville, Tex., 1941-42, 55-56, St. Ferdinand's Sch., San Fernando, Calif., 1942-43, Immaculate Conception, Houston, 1943-52, St. Joseph Meml., Enid, Okla., 1952-55, St. Mary's Sch., Natchitoches, La., 1956-57, St. Francis Sch., Iota, La., 1957-58, St. Joseph's Sch., Abilene, Tex., 1958-59, St. Genevieve, Lafayette, La., 1959-61, St. Peter and Paul Sch., New Braunfels, Tex., 1961-63, St. Pius, Pasadena, Tex., 1963-65, St. Anne's, Houston, 1965-70, Meml. High, Lafayette, La., 1972-73; tchr., libr. St. Mary's, San Antonio, Tex., 1970-72, St. Augustine, Laredo, Tex., 1973-77; with bookstore Our Lady of Lake U., San Antonio, 1977-78, ref. libr., 1978-85; head libr. Worden Sch., San Antonio, 1985—. Mem. ethnic affairs Tex. Cath. Conf., 1978—, treas., 1982—; speaker Tex. Inst. Texan Cultures, 1983; translator for Czechoslovakia refugees, 1981—, Dr. Denton Belk; interviewed on Channel 36 TV, 1982, Channel 12, 1979, 82. Mem. math. textbook com. Galveston (Tex.) Houston Diocese, 1968-70; rep. religious women Bishop's Coun., Corpus Christi (Tex.) Diocese, 1976-77; docent Luth. Youth Conf., Inst. Texan Cultures, 1983. Recipient Disting. Svc. award Bayanihan Dance Troupe, 1977, Margil award Tex. Cath. Conf. on Cmty. Ethnic Affairs, 1985, Papal medal, 1987. Mem. AAUP (sec. 1979-82), Nat. Coun. Math. Tchrs., Nat. Cath. Libr. Assn. (treas. Houston chpt. 1968-70, treas. San Antonio chpt. 1970-72, Community Leader of Am. award 1969), Tex. Libr. Assn., Bexar County Libr. Assn. (membership com. 1970-72), Teenage Libr. Assn. (bd. dirs Houston chpt. 1968-70), Southwestern Libr. Assn., Our Lady of the Lake U. Assn. (sec. San Antonio chpt. 1980-82, historian 1982—), Our Lady of the Lake Sisters Orgn. (social com. 1978-79), Czech-Am. Cultural and Edn. Found. (bd. dirs. 1982—, Svc. award 1987). Democrat. Roman Catholic. Home: 603 SW 24th St San Antonio TX 78207-4621 Office: Our Lady of the Lake U 411 SW 24th St San Antonio TX 78207-4666

KOZYREV, ANDREI NIKOLAEVICH, research scientist; s. Nikolay Konstantinovich Kozyrev and Klavdia Nikolaevna Kozyreva; m. Lyubov P. Lisenkova, Jan. 19, 1979; 1 child, Pavel A. PhD, Acad. Fine Chem. Tech., 1978—83. Sr. scientist Miravant Pharmaceuticals, Inc., Santa Barbara, 2000—; scientist Tef Labs, Austin, 1999—2000. Assoc. prof. Acad. Fine Chem. tech., Moscow, 1984—94. Rsch. grant, Internat. Sci./G.Soros Found., 1993, scholarship, Ministry of High Edn. of USSR/Russia, 1985—86, Rsch. grant, Europien Union Sci. Com., 1992—95. Mem.: Am. Chem. Soc. Achievements include patents for preparation of pyrrolic compounds. Office: Miravant Pharmaceuticals Inc 336 Bollay Dr Santa Barbara CA 93117 Business E-Mail: akozyrev@miravant.com.

KRA, PAULINE SKORNICKI, French language educator; b. Lodz, Poland, July 30, 1934; arrived in US, 1950, naturalized, 1955; d. Edward and Nathalie Skornicki; m. Leo Dietrich Kra, Mar. 10, 1955; children: David Theodore, Andrew Jason. Student, Radcliffe Coll., 1951-53; BA, Barnard Coll., 1955; MA, Columbia U., 1963, PhD, 1968; MA, Queens Coll., 1990. Lectr. Queens Coll., CUNY, 1964-65; asst. prof. French Yeshiva U., N.Y.C., 1968-74, assoc. prof., 1974-82, prof., 1982-99, prof. emerita, 1999—; sr. programmer analyst Dept. Biomed. Informatics Columbia U., N.Y.C., 1998—. *Demonstrated the unity of Montesquieu's Letters Persanes and worked on the annotation of the letters. Studied the bimolecular sub language and wrote a semantic grammar for the extraction of information on molecular interactions from journal articles. The grammar led to the development of the GeneWays database and software.* Author: Religion in Montesquieu's Lettres persanes, 1970; contbr. articles to profl. jours. Mem. MLA, Am. Assn. Tchrs. French, Am. Soc. 18th Century Studies, Société Française d'étude du XVIII Siècle, Soc. Montesquieu, Assn. for Computers and Humanities, Assn. for Lit. and Linguistic Computing, Phi Beta Kappa. Home: 10914 Ascan Ave Forest Hills NY 11375-5370 E-mail: kra@yu.edu.

KRAAKMAN, REINIER HERMAN, law educator; b. Santa Monica, Calif., June 15, 1949; BA in History and Sci., Harvard U., 1971; JD, Yale U., 1979. Law clk. to Hon. Henry J. Friendly US Ct. Appeals, NYC, 1979-80; asst. prof. Yale U., 1980-84, assoc. prof., 1984-85, prof., 1985-87; prof. law Harvard Law Sch., Cambridge, Mass., 1987—, Ezra Ripley Thayer prof. law, 1998—. Vis. prof. Harvard U., 1986-87, Georgetown U., 1993-94, NYU, 1996-98; vis. lectr. Yale U., 1987-88. Co-author: A Guide to the Russian Law on Joint Stock Companies, 1998, Commentaries and Cases on the Law of Business Organization, 2003; co-editor: The Anatomy of Corporate Law: A Comparative and Functional Approach, 2004. Fulbright Fellowship in Sociology, U. Frankfurt, 1971. Office: Harvard Law Sch 1563 Massachusetts Ave Cambridge MA 02138 Office Phone: 617-495-3586. Office Fax: 617-496-6118. Business E-Mail: kraakman@law.harvard.edu.*

KRABBE, JEROEN AART, actor; b. Amsterdam, Dec. 5, 1944; s. Maarten and Margreet (Reiss) K.; m. Herma van Geemert, Dec. 31, 1965; children: Martyn, Jasper, Jakob. Student, Acad. of Fine Arts, Amsterdam, 1980, Acad. of Dramatic Arts, 1965. Actor Rosenberg (Marion) Office, L.A. Actor: (films) Soldier of Orange, 1978, The Fourth Man, 1982 (Best Actor award), No Mercy, 1987, The Living Day Lights, 1987, A World Apart, 1988, Crossing Delancey, 1988, Melancholia, 1989, Till There Was You, 1990, Kafka, 1991, The Prince of Tides, 1991, Robin Hood, 1991, Kakda, King of the Hill, 1992, The Fugitive, 1993, Farinelli, 1994, Immortal Beloved, 1994, Blood of a Poet, 1995, Dangerous Beauty, 1998, The Disappearance of Garcia Lorca, 1997, Ever After, 1998, An Ideal Husband, 1999, The Sky is Falling, 2000, The Discovery of Heaven, 2001, Fogbound, 2002 (also assoc. prodr., dir.), Ocean's Twelve, 2004, Off Screen, 2005, Deuce Bigalo: European Gigolo, 2005, (TV films) Family of Spies, 1990, Robin Hood, 1991, Dynasty: The Reunion, 1991, Stalin, 1992, The Odyssey, 1997, Business for Pleasure, 1997, Only Love, 1998, Jesus, 1999; dir.: (films) The Discovery of Heaven, 2001; dir., prodr. (films) Left Luggage, 1998. Recipient Imagfic '84 award, Madrid, 1984, Vittorio de Sica prize, Sorrento, 1983, Anne Frank prize, Amsterdam, 1985, Rotterdams Golden Heart award, 1986-87, Golden Calf award for life achievement Dutch Film Festival, 1996, The Rembrandt award for life achievement Veronica Broadcasting Corp., 1998, Berlin, Blue Angel award, 1998, Emden, Best Film of Festival; comdr. Order of the Dutch Lion. Office: Marion Rosenberg 8428 Melrose Pl Ste C West Hollywood CA 90069-5308*

KRABBE, THOMAS JOSEPH, music educator; b. Appleton, Wis., Apr. 8, 1967; s. Ralph Joseph and Germaine Judith (Jandrin) Krabbe. MusB, St. Norbert Coll., DePere, Wis., 1989; MusM, Ariz. State U., Tempe, 1991. Cert. tchr. Wis. Music tchr. Kyrene Sch. Dist., Tempe, 1991—94, Neenah Sch. Dist., Wis., 1994—98, Verona Area Sch. Dist., Wis., 1998—99, Madison Met. Sch. Dist., Wis., 1999—. Mem.: Pi Kappa Lambda, Delta Epsilon Sigma, Aristos Scholars. Roman Catholic. E-mail: tjkrabbe@juno.com.

KRABBENHOFT, KENNETH LESTER, radiologist, educator; b. Sabula, Iowa, Jan. 7, 1923; s. Lester Henry and Bessie Grant (Thompson) K.; m. Gloria Darlene Eriksen, June 17, 1944; children: Kenneth Lester, Douglas Harold, Karen Ann Krabbenhoft Caumartin. BA, State U. Iowa, 1943, MD, 1946. Diplomate: Am. Bd. Radiology. Intern Harper Hosp., Detroit, 1946-47, resident in radiology, 1949-52, assoc. radiologist, 1952-57, radiologist, 1957—; practice medicine specializing in radiology Birmingham, Mich., 1957—; prof., chmn. dept. radiology Wayne State U., Detroit, 1969-84; chief radiology Detroit Receiving Hosp.-Univ. Health Center, 1980-84. Cons. radiologist VA Hosp., Allen Park, Mich., Children's Hosp. Mich., Crittenton Gen. Hosp., Herman Kiefer Hosp., Nat. Cancer Inst.; mem. Nat. Cancer Adv. bd., 1970-73; pres. Affiliated Radiologists, Inc., Detroit, 1973-85, Detroit Gen. Hosp. Rsch. Corp., 1974-82; mem. Environ. Radiation Exposure Adv. Com., 1975-78; trustee Am. Bd. Radiology, 1971-93, sec., exec. dir., 1981-93, assoc. exec. dir., 1993-95; treas. Am. Bd. Med. Specialists, 1981-85; alt. del. Internat. Congress Radiology. Cons. editor: Am. Jour. Roentgenology, 1975-81. Served to lt. (j.g.), M.C. USNR, 1947-49. Recipient Disting. Alumnus award M.D. Anderson Cancer Ctr., 1988; Nat. Cancer Inst. grantee, 1971-75; Nat. Cancer Inst. Specialized Cancer Center grantee, 1973-75. Fellow Am. Coll. Radiology (Gold medal 1989); mem. Detroit Acad. Medicine, Detroit Med. Club, AMA (vice chmn. sect. council 1969-71), Mich., Wayne county med. socs., Mich. Radiol. Soc. (pres. 1969-70), Am. Radium Soc., Am. Roentgen Ray Soc. (Silver medal 1962, Gold medal 1983), AAAS, Radiol. Soc. N.Am., Chicago Radiol. Soc. (hon., Gold medal 1992), Inter-Am. Coll. Radiology, Friends of Detroit Public Library, Founders Soc. Detroit Inst. Art, State Hist. Soc. Iowa, Mich. Hist. Soc., Lost Lakes Woods Assn., Sigma Xi, Alpha Omega Alpha. Clubs: Masons. Achievements include exhibited portable radioactive istopes for radiography at Smithsonian Inst., 1964-67. Home and Studio: 4856 Northfield Pkwy C-6 Troy MI 48098-4433 Business E-Mail: ae8724@wayne.edu.

KRABILL, ROBERT ELMER, osteopathic physician; b. Wayland, Iowa, June 4, 1934; s. Robert H. and Amanda (Wyse) K.; m. Ellen Savage, Sept. 1, 1963; children: Keith Andrew, Angela Kay, Valerie Ann, Kelly Dawn. BS, Iowa Wesleyan Coll., 1961; DO, Kirkville Coll. Osteo. Medicine, 1966. Diplomate Am. Bd. Family Practice. Intern Cuyahoga Falls Gen. Hosp., Ohio, 1966—67, mem. staff, 1967—; gen. practice osteo. medicine Uniontown, Ohio, 1967—. Sec., treas. gen. practice dept. Cuyahoga Falls Gen. Hosp., 1985-86. Named one of Outstanding Young Men of Am., U.S. Jaycees, 1969. Mem. Am. Osteo. Assn., Ohio Osteo. Assn., Am. Coll. Gen. Practitioners Osteo. Medicine and Surgery. Mennonite. Home: 3733 N Vista St NW Uniontown OH 44685-8496 Office: PO Box 399 Uniontown OH 44685-0399

KRACH, DALE JAMES, science educator, athletic trainer; b. Phila., Jan. 12, 1947; s. James and Laura Abel Krach; m. Donna Rae Davis, Aug. 1, 1970; children: Joshua Dale, Nathan Jarrett, Amy Meredith. AB in Psychology, W.Va. U., 1970; MS in Environ. Sci., Drexel U., 1977; postgrad. in sports medicine, Pa. State U., 1984; cert. sci. tchr., U. West Ga., 1999, cert. in ednl. leadership, 2002. Cert. athletic trainer Nat. Athletic Trainers Assn., athletic adminstr. Nat. Interscholastic Administrators Assn., EMT Pa. Field supervising environ. protection specialist Bucks County Dept. of Health, Doylestown, Pa., 1971—77; health edn. instr., emergency care program asst. Pa. State U., State College, 1977—84; athletic trauma and rehab. specialist PAPP Clinic, Newnan, Ga., 1984—92; sci. tchr., head athletic trainer Northgate H.S., Newnan, 1996—. Sports medicine cons. U.S. Women's Olympic Weightlifting, Marietta, Ga., 1990—95; sports medicine staff 11th Pan Am. Games, Indpls., 1987; asst. chief athletic trainer, EMT Centennial Olympic Games, Atlanta, 1996. Mem. med. staff Boy Scouts of Am. Nat. Jamboree, Fort A.P. Hill, Va., 1989—2001; athletic trainer, mem. med. staff Ga. State Games, Atlanta and Augusta, 1990—2000; 2d v.p. Lambda Omicron chpt. Alpha Phi Omega, Morgantown, W.Va., 1969—70. Named Eagle Scout, Boy Scouts Am., 1963; recipient Silver Beaver award, 1995. Mem.: AAHPERD (corr.), Ga. Athletic Trainers Assn. (corr.), Nat. Interscholastic Athletic Adminstrs. Assn. (corr.), Nat. Athletic Trainers Assn. (corr.), Nat. Assn. Secondary Sch. Prins. (assoc.), Kappa Delta Pi, Eta Sigma Gamma. Avocations: camping, outdoor sports, military memorabilia, reading, travel. Home: 145 Marsha Way Sharpsburg GA 30277-3377 Office: Northgate HS 3220 Fischer Rd Newnan GA 30265 Office Phone: 770-463-5585. Office Fax: 770-463-4982. Personal E-mail: dkrach@charter.net. E-mail: dale.krach@cowetaschools.org.

KRACH, MITCHELL PETER, b. Westfield, Mass., Nov. 2, 1924; s. John Joseph and Sophie Mary (Swiatlowski) Krach; m. Theresa Florence Sanczuk, May 29, 1957; children: Susan, Gregory, Mitchell, Jonathan, Matthew. Cert., Mass. U. Ext., 1944; grad. Sch. Bus. Adminstrn., Harvard U., 1966. Cert. purchasing mgr., registered and bonded real estate broker Mass. Auditor H.F. Lynch Lumber Co., West Springfield, Mass., 1946—51, dir., 1951—79; treas., chmn. bd. dirs. Nat. Res. Corp., Longmeadow, Mass., 1957—93; ret., 1993. Mgr. purchasing H.F. Lynch Lumber Co., 1951—61, sec. bd. dirs., 1951—79, ctrl. mgr. purchasing, 1961—71, v.p. purchasing, 1971—76, v.p. purchasing and fin., 1976—79, treas. bd. dirs., 1976—79; legal arbitrator bldg. materials Nat. Res. Corp. Contbr. articles to profl. jours. Exec. mem., vice-chmn. bd. govs. Shriners Hosp., Springfield, 1980; mem. Melha Temple. Mem.: Mfrs. Agts. Nat. Assn., Purchasing Mgmt. Assn. Worcester, Purchasing Mgmt. Assn. West New Eng. (pres. 1963—64), Am. Soc. Notaries, Nat. Assn. Purchasing Mgmt. (dir. nat. affairs 1965, nat. lumber chmn. 1970—80), Nat. Fedn. Ind. Bus. (nat. adv. coun. 1978), Am. Turners, 100 Club Mass., Falley Press Club, K.T., Shriners, Masons, Elks (chmn. bd. trustees). Democrat. Roman Catholic. Home: 15 Woodhill Rd Monson MA 01057-9743

KRACKE, ROBERT RUSSELL, lawyer; b. Decatur, Ga., Feb. 27, 1938; s. Roy Rachford and Virginia Carolyn (Minter) K.; m. Barbara Anne Pilgrim, Dec. 18, 1965; children: Shannon Ruth, Robert Russell, Rebecca Anne, Susan Lynn. Student, Birmingham So. Coll.; BA, Samford U., 1962; JD, Cumberland Sch. Law, 1965. Bar: Ala. 1965, U.S. Tax Ct. 1971, U.S. Supreme Ct. 1971. Individual practice law, Birmingham, Ala., 1965—; founding ptnr. Kracke and Thompson, Birmingham, 1980—. Editor, Birmingham Bar Bull, 1974—; bd. editors Ala. Lawyer, 1980-86, 2003—; contbr. articles to profl. jours. Coordinating com. Nat. Conv. of ARC of U.S., 1999—; pres., treas. Nov. Organ Recital Series, 1999—; pres. Housing Agy. Retarded Citizens; pres. Ala. chpt. Nat. Voluntary Health Agys., 1988—89; exec. com. legal counsel Birmingham Opera Theatre, 1983—95; active Dem. Exec. Com., 1970—98; deacon Ind. Presbyn. Ch., Birmingham, 1973—76, elder, 1999—2003, trustee I.P.C. Found., 2004—, pres. adult choir, 1968—99, chief adminstrv. officer, 1970—99, bd. dirs., Ala. Assn. Retarded Citizens, Jefferson County Assn. Retarded Citizens, 1983—91, pres.-elect, 1994—96, pres., 1996—98; bd. dirs., founding pres. Ala. chpt. Juvenile Diabetes Rsch. Found. Internat.; bd. dirs. ARC of Ala., 1996—98, Found.of ARC; v.p., bd. dirs. Mental Retardation/Devel. Disabilities Health Care Authority of Jefferson County, 2003—. With USNR, 1955—61. Mem. Birmingham (exec. com., law libr. chmn., law day 1976, bull., history and archives com.), Ala. Bar Assn., ABA (award merit law day 1976), Am. Judicature Soc., U.S. Supreme Ct. Hist. Soc., Ala. Hist. Assn., So. Hist. Assn., The Club, Phi Alpha Delta (pres. chpt. 1964-65), Rotary (pres. Shades Valley club 1988-89, dir. 2005—, Paul Harris fellow, sec. dist. 6860, 1990-91, dist. coord. comm., bd. dir., sec. ednl. found.), Sigma Alpha Epsilon. Home: 4410 Briar Glen Dr Birmingham AL 35243-1743 Office: Kracke and Thompson Lakeview Sch Bldg 808 29th St S Birmingham AL 35205-1004 Business E-Mail: rkracke@ktlegal.com.

KRACOV, DANIEL A., lawyer; b. NYC, June 30, 1963; BA magna cum laude, Univ. Md., 1985; JD, Univ. Va., 1988. Bar: Va. 1988, DC 1989. Ptnr., Food & Drug Law, Health Care practices, dep. dir. Public Policy & Regulatory dept. Patton Boggs LLP, Washington. Mem. editl. bd. Va. Jour. Internat. Law; contbr. articles to profl. jours. Home: Patton Boggs LLP 2550 M St NW Washington DC 20037-1350 Office Phone: 202-457-5623. Office Fax: 202-457-6315. Business E-Mail: dkracov@pattonboggs.com.

KRAEHE, ENNO EDWARD, history professor; b. St. Louis, Dec. 9, 1921; s. Enno and Amelia Roth (Henckler) K.; m. Mary Alice Eggleston, May 25, 1946; children: Laurence Adams, Claudia. BA, U. Mo., 1943, MA, 1944; PhD, U. Minn., 1948. Instr. history U. Del., 1946-48; asst. prof. history U. Ky., 1948-50, asso. prof., 1950-63, prof., 1963-64, U. N.C., 1964-68, U. Va., 1968-71, Commonwealth prof., 1971-77, William W. Corcoran prof., 1977-91, William W. Corcoran prof. emeritus, 1991—. Vis. prof. U. Mo., 1946, U. Va., 1955, U. Tex., 1955, U. Minn., 1963; U.S. Dept. State Specialist in, Germany, 1953; mem. regional selection com. Woodrow Wilson fellowship Found., 1959-60; mem. Sr. Fulbright-Hayes History Screening Com., 1970-73 Author: Metternich's German Policy Volume I: The Contest with Napoleon 1799-1814, 1963; author: Volume II: The Congress of Vienna, 1814-1815, 1983; editor: The Metternich Controversy, 1971; mem. editl. bd. Ctrl. European History, 1967-72, Austrian History Yearbook, 1969-74; contbr. entries and articles to encys. and hist. jours., U.S. and Europe. Active Charlottesville Com. on Fgn. Rels.; mem. Nat. Coordinating Com. for Promotion of History, mem. policy bd., 1985-88; mem. Met. Opera Guild, Friends of Ky. Ctr. Recipient Best Book award Phi Alpha Theta; Fulbright scholar Austria, 1952-53; Guggenheim fellow, 1960-61, Am. Coun. Learned Socs. fellow, 1969, 73, resident fellow Rockefeller Ctr. in Bellagio, 1983; grantee NEH, 1973, 80, 83, NEH Libr. Preservation Screening Com., 1988 Mem. Am. Hist. Assn., Conf. Group for Ctrl. European History (mem. exec. bd. 1966-68), German Studies Assn. (mem. exec. coun. 1985—), So. Hist. Assn. (chmn. European sect. 1974, 75, Disting. Svc. award European sect.), Colonnade Club, Blue Ridge Swimming Club, Phi Beta Kappa. Episcopalian. Home: 130 Bennington Rd Charlottesville VA 22901-2653

KRAEMER, DAVID C., theology educator; b. Newark, Oct. 23, 1955; s. Paul William and Phyllis (Ferster) K.; m. Susan L. Boxerman, July 21, 1955; children: Talia, Liviya. BA, Brandeis U., 1977; MA, Jewish Theol. Sem., N.Y.C., 1978, PhD, 1984. Asst. prof. theology Jewish Theol. Sem., 1984-90, assoc. prof. theology, 1990-94, prof. theology, 1994—, sem. libr. N.Y.C., 2004—. Cons. The Jewish Mus., N.Y.C., 1990-92, Heritage/WNET, N.Y.C., 1997. Author: Reading the Rabbis, 1996, Responses to Suffering, 1995, The Mind of the Talmud, 1990, The Meanings of Death in Rabbinic Judaism, 2000; editor: The Jewish Family, 1989, Exploring Judaism, 1999. Assn. Jewish Studies, Soc. Bibl. Lit. Democrat. Jewish. Avocations: cooking, family care, pet care, running. Office: Jewish Theological Seminary 3080 Broadway New York NY 10027-4650 Office Phone: 212-678-8075. E-mail: dakraemer@jtsa.edu.

KRAEMER, HARRY M. JANSEN, JR., investment company executive, former medical products executive; BA in Math. and Econs. summa cum laude, Lawrence U., Wis., 1977; M in fin. and acctg., Northwestern U. J.L. Kellogg Grad. Sch. of Mgmt., 1979. CPA Ill. With N.W. Industries, Bank of Am.; dir. corp. devel. Baxter Internat. Inc., Deerfield, Ill., 1982, various positions in domestic and internat. ops., sr. v.p., CFO, 1993-97, mem. Office Chief Exec., 1995—, pres., 1997, CEO, 1999—2004, bd. dirs., 2000, chmn., 2000; exec. ptnr. Madison Dearborn Partners, Chgo., 2005—. Bd. dirs. Comdisco, Inc., MedPtnrs., Inc., Sci. Applications Internat. Corp., Evanston Northwestern Healthcare Science Applications Internat. Corp.; mem. coun. fin. execs. conf. bd.; mem. Bus. Roundtable, Healthcare Leadership Coun. Bd. dirs. Highland Park Hosp., Ill.; bd. trustees, deans' adv. bd. Northwestern U. J.L. Kellogg Grad. Sch. Mgmt.; bd. trustees Lawrence U. Recipient

Schaffner award, Northwestern U. J.L. Kellogg Grad. Sch. Mgmt., 1996. Mem.: Fin. Execs. Inst., Execs. Club Chgo., Mid-Am. Club, Comml. Club Chgo., Chgo. Club. Office: Madison Dearborn Partners Ste 3800 3 First National Plz Chicago IL 60602

KRAEMER, HELENA ANTOINETTE CHMURA, psychiatry educator; Degree, Stanford U., 1963. Prof. biostats. in psychiatry, Dept. Psychiatry and Behavioral Scis. Stanford U. Recipient Harvard award in psychiat. epidemiology and biostats., 2001. Mem.: Inst. Medicine, 2004. Office: Stanford U Dept Psychiatry and Behavioral Scis 300 Pasteur Dr Stanford CA 94305 Business E-Mail: hck@stanford.edu.

KRAEMER, IRA B., symphony conductor; b. Newark, Mar. 25, 1942; s. Alex Kraemer and Rae Warshawski; m. Janet Lynda Ericson, July 7, 1974; children: Erik, Kris, Daryll, Lyndyn. BS in Conducting, Mannes Coll. Music, NYC, 1966; PhD in Music, Buxton U., London, 1994. Music dir., conductor Little Symphony of Newark, 1965—69, Suburban Symphony, Cranford, NJ, 1979—80, Summit Symphony, NJ, 1980—83, Performing Arts Ensemble, Red Bank, NJ, 1991—2002, Young Players Philharmonic, Somerset, NJ, 2001—. Composer: (saxophone quartet) Petite Suite, 1987 (world broadcast, 1988), (viola sonata) Sonata for Viola & Piano, 1988. Supporter Young Players Philharmonic, Somerset, 2001—. Recording grant, Union County Cult. Commn., 1984. Avocation: antiques. Office: 467 Grant Ave Scotch Plains NJ 07076 Office Phone: 908-322-4469. E-mail: ira@mail.eclipse.net, info@ypphilharmonic.org.

KRAEMER, KENNETH LEO, architect, educator, urban planner; b. Plain, Wis., Oct. 29, 1936; s. Leo Adam and Lucy Rose (Bauer) K.; m. Norine Florence, June 13, 1959; children: Kurt Randall, Kim Rene. BArch, U. Notre Dame, 1959; MS in City and Regional Planning, U. So. Calif., 1964, M of Pub. Adminstrn., 1965, PhD, 1967. From instr. to asst. prof. U. So. Calif., L.A., 1965-67; from asst. prof. to prof. U. Calif., Irvine, 1967—, dir. Pub. Policy Research Orgn., 1974-92, dir. Ctr. for Rsch. on Info. Tech. and Orgns., 1992—. Cons. Office of Tech. Assessment, Washington, 1980, 84-85; pres. Irvine Research Corp., 1978—. Author: Management of Information Systems, 1980, Computers and Politics, 1982, Dynamics of Computing, 1983, People and Computers, 1985, Modeling as Negotiating, 1986, Data Wars, 1987, Wired Cities, 1987, Managing Information Systems, 1989, Asia's Computer Challenge, 1998. Mem. Blue Ribbon Data Processing Com., Orange County, Calif., 1973, 79-80, Telecomm. Adv. Bd., Sacramento, 1987-92. Fellow Assn. for Info. Sys.; mem. Am. Soc. for Pub. Adminstrn. (Disting. Research award 1985), Internat. Conf. on Info. Systems, Am. Planning Assn., Assn. for Computing Machinery, Notre Dame Club. Democrat. Roman Catholic. Office: U Calif Ctr Rsch Info Tech & Orgns Berkley Pl N Ste 3200 Irvine CA 92697-0001 E-mail: kkraemer@uci.edu.

KRAEMER, LILLIAN ELIZABETH, lawyer; b. NYC, Apr. 18, 1940; d. Frederick Joseph and Edmee Elizabeth (de Watteville) K.; m. John W. Vincent, June 22, 1962 (div. 1964). BA, Swarthmore Coll., 1961; JD, U. Chgo., 1964. Bar: N.Y. 1965, U.S. Dist. Ct. (so. dist.) N.Y. 1967, U.S. Dist. Ct. (ea. dist.) N.Y. 1971. Assoc. Cleary, Gottlieb, Steen & Hamilton, N.Y.C., 1964-71, Simpson Thacher & Bartlett, N.Y.C., 1971-74, ptnr., 1974-99, of counsel, 2000—. Mem. vis. com. U. Chgo. Law Sch., 1988-90, 91-94, 97-99 Bd. mgrs. Swarthmore Coll., 1993—; warden St. Francis Episcopal Ch., Stamford, Conn., 2001-05; bd. dirs. Turtle Bay Music Sch., 2005— Fellow Am. Coll. Bankruptcy; mem. Lawyers Alliance for N.Y. (bd. dirs. 1996-2001, co-chair capital campaign 2003-05), Assn. Bar City N.Y. (mem. various coms.), Coun. on Fgn. Rels., N.Y. State Bar Assn., Order of Coif, Phi Beta Kappa. Democrat. Avocations: travel, reading, word games. Home: 2 Beekman Pl New York NY 10022-8058 Address: 46 Saddle Rock Rd Stamford CT 06902 E-mail: lkraemer@stblaw.com.

KRAEMER, MICHAEL FREDERICK, lawyer; b. NYC, Jan. 21, 1947; s. Jerome W. and Honey (Dunner) K.; m. Ross Shepard, June 21, 1970; 1 child, Jordan Harriet. BA cum laude, Amherst Coll., 1969; JD, U. Pa., 1972. Bar: Pa. 1972, N.J. 1973, Mass. 2003, RI 2003, U.S. Dist. Ct. (ea. dist.) Pa. 1972, U.S. Dist. Ct. N.J. 1973, U.S. Ct. Appeals (3d cir.) 1974, U.S. Ct. Appeals (2d cir.) 1980, U.S. Ct. Appeals (4th and 7th cirs.) 1981, U.S. Ct. Appeals (6th cir.) 1990, U.S. Ct. Appeals (1st cir.) 2001, U.S. Dist. Ct. Mass. 2003, U.S. Dist. Ct. RI 2003. Assoc. Astor & Weiss, Phila., 1972-75, Pechner, Sacks, Dorfman, Rosen & Richardson, Phila., 1975-76; ptnr. Kleinbard, Bell & Brecker, Phila., 1976-85, White and Williams LLP, Phila., 1985—2002, Hinckley, Allen & Snyder LLP, Providence, 2002—. Bd. dirs. Ctr. City Residents Assn., Phila., 1976-78; Served to 2d lt. USAR, 1972-73. Recipient Disting. Svc. award Amherst Coll. Alumni Coun., 1994. Mem. Amherst Alumni Assn. Phila. (pres. 1977-79), Indsl. Rels. Rsch. Assn., Germantown Cricket Club (Phila.), Univ. Club (Providence). Office: Hinckley Allen & Snyder LLP 1500 Fleet Ctr Providence RI 02903

KRAEMER, WALDRON, lawyer; b. Newark, Apr. 13, 1937; s. Manfred Kraemer and Evelyn C. Waldron; m. Jean A. Rosenberg, June 17, 1962; children: Adam, Elise. BA, Colgate U., 1958; LLB, Harvard U., 1961. Bar: N.J. 1961. Law clk. N.J. Supreme Ct., 1962—63; from assoc. to ptnr. Kraemer, Burns, Mytelka, Lovell & Kulka, P.A. and predecessor firms, Newark/Springfield, NJ, 1963—. Mem., chmn. N.J. Bd. Bar Examiners, 1969—78; pres. Essex County Bar Assn., Newark, 1982—83; mem. N.J. Supreme Ct. Disciplinary Rev. Bd., 1984—87. With USAR. Office: Kraemer Burns Mytelka Lovell & Kulka PA 675 Morris Ave Springfield NJ 07081 Office Phone: 973-912-8700.

KRAETZER, MARY C., sociologist, educator, consultant; b. N.Y.C., Sept. 12, 1943; d. Kenneth G. and Adele L. Kraetzer; m. Kestas E. Silunas. AB, Coll. New Rochelle, 1965; MA, Fordham U., 1967, PhD, 1975. Instr. Mercy Coll., Dobbs Ferry, N.Y., 1969-70, asst. prof., 1970-75, assoc. prof., 1975-79, prof., 1979—, program dir. behavioral sci., 1997—, program dir. grad. programs in health svc. mgmt., 2001—. Rsch. asst. Fordham U., Bronx, N.Y., 1965-67, tchg. asst., 1967-68, tchg. fellow, 1968-69, adj. instr., 1971-75, adj. asst. prof., 1975-76; adj. assoc. prof. L.I. U. Grad. br. Campus Mercy Coll., 1976-79, adj. prof., 1979-81, coord. MS in Cmty. Health Program, 1976-81, adj. prof. Westchester campus, 1988-94; rsch. cons. elem. schoolbooks Nat. Coun. Chs./Ch. Women United Task Force on Global Consciousness, N.Y.C., 1971; mem. adv. com. edn. and society div. Nat. Coun. Chs., 1975-78; mem. evaluation team Middle States Assn. Colls. and Secondary Schs. Commn. on Higher Edn., Monmouth, N.J., 1976; presenter in field. Contbr. chapters to books, articles to profl. jours. Recipient Tchg. Excellence award Mercy Coll., 1999; Bd. Regents scholar, 1961-65, 65-69; Fordham U. scholar, 1965-68; Fordham U. fellow, 1968-69; Mercy Coll. grantee, 1984, 85, 86, 88, 92; Mercy Coll. Faculty Devel. grantee, 1999; NSF summer intern, 1967. Mem. APHA (conf. presenter), Am. Sociol. Assn. (presenter). Office: Mercy Coll 555 Broadway Dobbs Ferry NY 10522-1134 Office Phone: 914-674-7341. Business E-Mail: mkraetzer@mercy.edu.

KRAEUTLER, ERIC, lawyer; b. Newark, Oct. 9, 1954; s. John Howard and Marie (Bevere) K.; m. Jacqueline Maykranz, May 18, 1985; children: Matthew John, Caroline Ann. BA, Princeton U., 1976; JD, U. Va., 1980. Bar: Pa., U.S. Dist. Ct. (ea. dist.) Pa., U.S. Ct. Appeals (3rd cir.), U.S. Ct. Appeals (9th cir.), U.S. Dist. Ct. (no. dist.), Ind., U.S. Supreme Ct. Assoc. Morgan, Lewis & Bockius, LLP, Phila., 1980-84, 1987-90; ptnr. Morgan, Lewis & Bockius, Phila., 1990—, co-leader, intellectual property litigation practice, 1999—, chair firmwide profl. recruiting com., 2000—; asst. U.S. atty. U.S. Atty.'s Office, Phila., 1984-87; spl. dep. atty. gen. Commonwealth of Pa., 1992-94. Trustee Princeton Tower Club, 1980—; trustee Nat. Multiple Sclerosis Soc., 1993—, sec., 1994-96, vice chmn., 1996-98, chmn., 1998-2000; mem. Princeton Alumni Coun. 1984-87, Com. of Seventy, 2001—, exec. com., 2002-. Mem. ABA, Fed. Bar Assn., Phila. Bar Assn., Intellectual Property Owner Assn. Presbyterian. Avocation: running. Home: 35 Wellesley Rd Swarthmore PA 19081-1232 Office: Morgan Lewis & Bockius LLP 1701 Market St Philadelphia PA 19103-2903 Office Phone: 215-963-4840. Business E-Mail: ekraeutler@morganlewis.com.

KRAFKA, MARY BAIRD, lawyer; b. Ottumwa, Iowa, Jan. 4, 1942; d. Glenn Leroy and Alice Erna (Krebill) B.; m. Jerry Lee Krafka, Oct. 14, 1962; children: Lisa Krafka Piper, Gregory D., Jeffrey A., Amy Krafka Pittman. BA in English and Human Rels., William Penn Coll., Oskaloosa, Iowa, 1990; JD, U. Iowa, 1993. Bar: Iowa 1993. Vol. lawyer Legal Svcs. Corp., Ottumwa, 1993-94; pvt. practice, Ottumwa, 1994—. Mem. AAUW, ABA, Iowa Bar Assn., Wapello County Bar Assn., PEO Sisterhood (Iowa chpt. HC 1973). Lutheran. Avocations: sewing, reading, walking, running, people. Home: 931 W Mary St Ottumwa IA 52501-4904 Office: 101 S Market St Ste 203 Ottumwa IA 52501-2933 Business E-Mail: mbkrafka@lisco.com.

KRAFT, ARTHUR, university dean; b. Eden, NY, May 7, 1944; s. Arthur Brauer and Mary Jane (Forti) K.; m. Joan Marie Brown, Sept. 3, 1966; children: Arthur G., Stephen Michael, Leigh Judith. BS, St. Bonaventure U., 1966; MA, SUNY, Buffalo, 1969, PhD, 1970. Asst. prof. Ohio U., Athens, 1969-72, assoc. prof., 1972-75; prof. U. Nebr., Lincoln, 1975-77, assoc. dean Coll. Bus., 1977-83; dean Coll. Bus. and Econs. W.Va. U., Morgantown, 1983-87; dean sch. bus. Rutgers U., New Brunswick, N.J., 1987-93; dean Sch. Mgmt. Ga. Inst. Tech., Atlanta, 1993-97; dean Coll. Commerce, Charles H. Kellstadt Grad. Sch. Bus., DePaul U., Chgo., 1997—. Pension adv. com. Monongalia County Hosp., Morgantown, 1985-87. Recipient NASA fellowship Stanford U., 1973, fellowship Sears-Roebuck Fellowship Found, Washington, 1974-75; named Outstanding Young Individual Jaycees, Lincoln, 1978. Mem. Am. Econ. Assn., Am. Assembly of Collegiate Schs. of Bus. (visitation com. 1977—, continuing accreditation com. 1987, bus. accreditation com. 1995—), North Ctrl. Assn. (evaluator 1986-87), Beta Gamma Sigma. Avocations: trivia, sports. Office Fax: 312-362-5198. Business E-Mail: akraft@depaul.edu.

KRAFT, DONALD EUGENE, architecture and engineering company executive; b. Rochester, N.Y., Aug. 10, 1929; s. Nicholas Raymond and Rosella Theresa (Miller) K.; m. Rosemarie Ursula Kraus, April 24, 1965; children: Eva Maria, Christian Martin, Donald Alexander Nicholas. Student, U. Rochester, 1948-51; BS in Engring., Bus. Adminstrn., Econs., Empire State Coll., 1977. Registered profl. engr., N.Y. Engr. stds. dept. Kodak Park, 1950-52; sales rep. C.A. Brewer, Inc., 1952-56; civil and san. engr. design Lozier Engrs. and Morrison & Morrison, 1956-61; v.p. gen. mgr. Profl. Chem. Corp. Dental Equipment, 1962-65; project engr. new product devel. Caldwell Mfg. Co., Inc., 1965-71; applications engr. Schlegel Corp., 1971-72; pres. Don Kraft Co., Penfield, N.Y., 1973—; sales, design, R&D and project mgr. turnkey automated prodn. equipment Alliance Tool Corp., 1978-81; gen. ptnr. Arens Assoc. Architecture and Engring. Svcs., Penfield, N.Y., 1986—. Cons. in field. Patentee in hydraulics, pneumatics, dental equipment, window hardware, weather seals, automotive & bus. equipment. With USN, 1947-48, USNR, 1947, 48-49, 54-58. Mem. Rochester C. of C., Civic Music Assn., Meml. Art Gallery, Rochester Yacht Club. Republican. Roman Catholic. Achievements include beyond state-of-the-art products, automated production equipment & systems, trisected an angle using only a straight edge and a compass, solving a 2400 year old problem, and working on gravity machine research and development and up-to-date formulas. Home and Office: 1930 Harris Rd Penfield NY 14526-1822 Office Phone: 585-377-9190. E-mail: arens@bluefrognet.net.

KRAFT, GEORGE HOWARD, physician, educator; b. Columbus, Ohio, Sept. 27, 1936; s. Glen Homer and Helen Winner (Howard) K.; children: Jonathan Ashbrook, Susannah Mary. AB, Harvard U., 1958; MD, Ohio State U., 1963, MS, 1967. Diplomate Am. Bd. Phys. Medicine and Rehab. (subspecialty in spinal cord injury medicine), Am. Bd. Electrodiagnostic Medicine. Intern U. Calif. Hosp., San Francisco, 1963—64, resident in phys. medicine and rehab., 1964—65, Ohio State U., Columbus, 1965—67; assoc. U. Pa. Med. Sch., Phila., 1968—69; asst. prof. U. Wash., Seattle, 1969—72, assoc. prof., 1972—76, prof., 1976—, Alvord prof. MS rsch., 2005—; chief of staff U. Wash. Med. Ctr., Seattle, 1993—95. Dir. electrodiagnostic medicine U. Wash. Hosp., 1987—, dir. Multiple Sclerosis Ctr., 1982—; co-dir. Muscular Dystrophy Clinic, 1974—; assoc. dir. rehab. medicine Overlake Hosp., Bellevue, Wash., 1989-2003; bd. dirs. Am. Bd. Electrodiagnostic Medicine, 1993-2000, chmn., 1996-2000. Co-author: Chronic Disease and Disability, 1994, Living with Multiple Sclerosis: A Wellness Approach, 2000; cons. editor: Phys. Medicine and Rehab. Clinics, 1990—, EEG and Clin. Neurophysiology, 1992-96; assoc. editor Jour. Neurol. Rehab. and Neurol. Repair, 1988-2000, Muscle and Nerve, 1998-2000; contbr. articles to profl. jours. Sci. peer rev. com. C Nat. Multiple Sclerosis Soc., N.Y.C., 1990-96, chmn., 1993-96, med. adv. bd., 1991—; bd. sponsors Wash. Physicians for Social Responsibility, Seattle, 1986—. Rsch. grantee Rehab. Svcs. Adminstrn., 1976-81, Nat. Inst. Handicapped Rsch., 1984-88, Nat. Multiple Sclerosis Soc., 1990-92, 94-95, Nat. Inst. Disability and REhab. Rsch., 1998—. Fellow Am. Acad. Phys. Medicine and Rehab. (pres. 1984-85, Zeiter award 1991, Krusen award 2002); mem. Am. Assn. Electrodiagnostic Medicine (pres. 1982-83. Lifetime Achievement award 2004), Assn. Acad. Physiatrists (pres. 1980-81), Am. Acad. Clin. Neurophysiology (pres. 1995-97), Am. Acad. Neurology, Internat. Rehab. Medicine Assn., Alpha Omega Alpha. Episcopalian. Office: Dept Rehab Med U Wash PO Box 956490 Seattle WA 98195 Office Phone: 206-543-7272.

KRAFT, GERALD, economist; b. Detroit, July 1, 1935; s. Jule and Shirley (Schwartz) K.; m. Sandra Doris Johnson, Aug. 7, 1955; children: Michael Stanton, Lynn Barbara. Student, U. Chgo., 1951-52; BA, Wayne U., 1955; MA, Harvard U., 1957. Mng. dir. Harvard U. Statis. Lab., Cambridge, Mass., 1957-58; prin. United Rsch. Inc., Cambridge, 1958-61; sr. rsch. assoc. Sys. Analysis and Rsch. Corp., Boston, 1961-64, Regional and Urban Planning Implementation, Inc., Cambridge, 1964-65; pres., CEO, chmn. Charles River Assocs. Inc., Boston, 1965-92; CEO The GSK Group, Ltd., 1994—; chmn. Modern Broadcast Prodns. Lectr. MIT, Harvard U., U. Pa., Northeastern U.; mem. planning com., dir. Maritime Transp. Rsch. Bd., NRC, 1976-79; mem. Group I Coun., mem. coms. Transp. Rsch. Bd., 1977-80, NRC v.p. program; pres. Transp. Rsch. Forum, 1977; chmn. 2nd Internat. Tungsten Symposium, 1982. Author: (with others) The Role of Transportation in Regional Economic Development, 1971; co-author: Report of Task Force on Transp. to Sci. Adv. panel to Com. on Pub. Works, U.S. Ho. of Reps, 1974; contbr. articles to profl. jours. Trustee, dir., fin. com., exec. com., former chmn. budget subcom., asst. treas. Beth Israel Hosp.; past dir. Beth Israel Corp.; trustee, fin. com., patient care and quality com., audit and compliance com. Beth Israel Deaconess Med. Ctr.; past dir. Med. Care Boston, Inc.; fin. com. Commonwell, Inc.; mem. Harvard U. Grad. Sch. Arts & Scis., adv. com. grad. student life Harvard U.; adv. bd. Medifile, Inc.; mem. allocation subcom. United Way. Mem. AAAS, Am. Econ. Assn., Econometric Soc., Am. Statis. Assn., Inst. Mgmt. Scis., Ops. Rsch. Soc. Am. (Boston Branch), Internat. Wine and Food Soc. (past treas., past pres., past chmn.), Confrerie des Chevaliers du Tastevin, Grand Senechal (past chef du protocole), Sous-Commanderie de Mass.(officier commandeur), Harvard Club Boston, Univ. Club, Rotary (past bd. dirs., trustee student aid fund, Paul Harris fellow), Fine Wine Coun. Mass. (bd. dirs.), Beefeater Club, Chaine des Rotisseurs (vice echanson), L'ordre Mondial, Confraternita Enogastronomica Toscana, Phi Beta Kappa. Home: 60 Scotch Pine Rd Weston MA 02493-1405 Business E-Mail: gkraft@gskgroup.com.

KRAFT, HENRY ROBERT, lawyer; b. L.A., Apr. 27, 1946; s. Sylvester and Freda (Shochat) K.; m. Terry Kraft, July 21, 1968; children: Diana, Kevin. BA in History, San Fernando Valley State Coll., 1968; JD, U. So. Calif., 1971. Bar: Calif. 1972, U.S. Dist. Ct. (ctrl. dist.) Calif. 1985, U.S. Ct. Appeals (9th cir., fed. cir.) 1998, U.S. Dist. Ct. (so., ctrl. and no. dists.) Calif 1998. Dep. pub. defender San Bernardino (Calif.) County, 1972-78; pvt. practice, Victorville, Calif., 1979-96; city atty. Victorville, 1987—2002; of counsel Best Best & Krieger LLP, Victorville, 1996-98; assoc. Parker, Covert & Chidester, Tustin, Calif., 1999-2000; ptnr. Parker & Covert LLP, Tustin, 2000—. Atty. City of Barstow, Calif., 1980-97; instr. Victor Valley Coll., Victorville, 1986—. Atty. Barstow Community Hosp., 1980-88. Mem. FBA, San Bernardino Bar Assn. (fee dispute com., jud. evaluation com.), High Desert Bar Assn. (pres., v.p., sec. 1979-81), Calif. Soc. Health Care Attys., League Calif. Cities, Am. Arbitration Assn. (panel neutral arbitrators). Democrat. Jewish. Avocations: bicycling, travel, wine enthusiast. Office: Parker & Covert LLP East Bldg Ste 204 17862 E Seventeenth St Tustin CA 92780-2164 Office Phone: 714-573-0900. E-mail: hkraft@parkercovert.com.

KRAFT, IRVIN ALAN, psychiatrist; b. Huntington, W.Va., Nov. 20, 1921; m. Shirley Goldin, July 4, 1951; children: Karen Kraft Pennebaker, Joanna Kraft Katz, Elizabeth Kraft Schmachtenberger, Mark. BS, NYU, 1943, MD, 1949. Diplomate Am. Bd. Psychiatry and Neurology, Am. Bd. Child Psychiatry. Chief psychiatry Tex. Children's Hosp., Houston, 1958-65; prof. mental health U. Tex. Sch. Pub. Health, Houston, 1975-91; emeritus prof. mental health U. Tex., Houston, 1991—; assoc. clin. prof. pediatrics Baylor Coll. Medicine, Houston, 1977—, clin. prof. psychiatry, 1977—, U. Tex. Sch. Medicine, Houston, Galveston. Med. dir. Tex. Inst. Family Psychiatry, Houston, 1964-79; dir. Houston Heart Assn., 1969-70; med. dir. Adult Adolescent Rehab. Ctr., Houston, 1982-85; chmn. subcom. Mental Health Needs Coun., Houston, 1988-89. Author: (with others) Adolescent Group Psychotherapy, 1989, Bibliography of Child and Adolescent Psychiatry, 1990; co-editor: Child Group Psychotherapy: Future Tense, 1986; mem. editorial bd. Jour. Child and Adolescent Group Therapy, 1989—. Mem. drug prevention com. High Sch. for Health Professions, Houston, 1989-90; mem. Tex. House Rep. Com. on Edn., 1974. N.Y. Acad. Scis. fellow, 1971—; recipient Gold award Am. Acad. Pediatrics, 1969, cert. of award Am. Group Psychotheraphy Assn., 1970. Fellow Am. Acad. Child and Adolescent Psychiatry (life), Am. Group Psychotherapy Assn. (life), Am. Acad. Psychoanalysis (life), Am. Psychiat. Assn. (life), Houston Group Psychotherapy Soc. (life), Southwestern Group Psychotherapy Soc. (life), Houston Psychiat. Soc. (life), Tex. Soc. Psychiat. Physicians (life), Tex. Soc. of Child and Adolescent Psychiatry (life), Am. Orthopsychiatry Assn. (life). Home: 2423 Gramercy Blvd Houston TX 77030-3105 Office: 4545 Post Oak Pl # 375 Houston TX 77027 Office Fax: 713-668-2555. Personal E-mail: irvkraft@houston.rr.com.

KRAFT, JAMES ALLEN, lawyer; b. Seattle, Mar. 8, 1955; s. Warren Earl and Barbara Anne (Allen) K.; m. Dominique Patricia Posy, Aug. 4, 1984. AB in East Asian Studies cum laude, Harvard U., 1978, JD, 1982. Bars: N.Y. 1982, Wash. 1984. Assoc. Milbank, Tweed, Hadley & Mc Cloy, N.Y.C., 1982-84; assoc. corp. counsel Burlington Northern, Inc., Seattle, 1984-88; sr. corp. counsel Burlington Resources, Inc., Seattle, 1988, asst. v.p. law, 1989; v.p. law and corp. affairs Plum Creek Timber Co., Seattle, 1989—2002, sr. v.p., gen. counsel and sec., 2002—. Contbr. articles to profl. jours. Mem. bd. trustees Pacific Northwest Ballet Co., Seattle, 1986—. Mem. ABA, Wash. State Bar Assn., N.Y. State Bar Assn., Japan Am. Soc. State Wash., (trustee 1987—). Clubs: Lincoln's Inn Soc. (Cambridge, Mass.) (co-chmn. 1981-82). Republican. Avocations: squash, gardening. Office: Plum Creek Timber Co 999 3rd Ave Ste 4300 Seattle WA 98104-4096

KRAFT, KAREN ANN, secondary school educator; b. Bklyn., June 27, 1964; d. Michael John and Barbara Ann (DeMaio) Miele; m. John L. Kraft, June 17, 1989; children: Taylor Michael, Mason Genaro. BS, North Tex. State U., 1986; MA in Edn., U. North Tex., 1990. Lic. provisional tchr. English and Spanish, gifted and talented, Tex. Tchr. Westwood H.S., Palestine, Tex., 1987-88, Allen (Tex.) H.S., 1988-93, Coppell (Tex.) H.S., 1993—. Tchr. Nat. Honor Soc. Faculty Coun., Allen, 1989-93; Nat. Honor Soc. sr. sponsor Coppell H.S., 1994—; facilitator Student Mentorship Course. Mem. ASCD, Nat. Coun. Tchrs. English, Tex. Assn. for Gifted and Talented. Roman Catholic. E-mail: kkraft@coppellISD.com.

KRAFT, KENNETH HOUSTON, JR., insurance agency executive; b. Chgo., Apr. 2, 1934; s. Kenneth Houston and Elizabeth (Preston) K.; m. Ruth Neely, Aug. 11, 1956 (div. Sept. 1979); children: Katherine Elizabeth, Carolyn Ruth, Kenneth Houston III; m. Kathleen Hartung, Mar. 16, 1985. BS in Fin., Purdue U., 1956. Pres., chmn. bd. Kraft Ins. Agy., Inc., Winter Park, Fla., 1960—, KHK Fin. Corp., Winter Park, 1974—; chmn. bd. Echo Pub. Co., Sulfur Springs, Tex., 1970—2000; owner Kraft Cattle Co., 1981—86. Sr. mem., exec., fin., comml. loan, audit and exam. coms. Barnett Bank Cen. Fla., Orlando, 1965-98; founding dirs. Goodings Groceries of Fla., Altamonte Springs, Fla., Schwartz Electro-Optics, Orlando, Internat. Laser Sys., Orlando, KHK Fin. Corp., Carson City, Nev., Princeton Fin. Corp., Orlando, Falcon Aviation, Orlando, TV-9 Inc., ABC affiliate, Orlando, First Ctrl. Corp., Orlando, Inglewood Daily News, Inglewood Citizen Co., LA. Bd. dirs. Winter Park C. of C., 1965-70, Orange County chpt. ARC, Orlando, 1963-65, Orange County chpt. United Way, Winter Park, 1970-72, Winter Park YMCA, 1972-75, citrus grower Kraft Groves, 1966-2000; mem. Fla. Citrus Mut., Lakeland, 1966-2000, Com. of 100 of Orange County, Inc., Orlando, 1983—; bd. trustees Winter Park Meml. Hosp., 1969-88, also exec. com., compensation com., chmn. long range planning com.; chmn. Winter Park Cmty. Trust Fund, 1981-92; mem. grievance com. 9th Jud. Cir., 1987-90; active Boy Scouts Am., Rollins Coll. Fiat Lux Soc., Corp. Coun., Crummer Grad. Sch. Bus., Winter Park, Fla.; mem. selection com. COMPUSA Fla. Citrus Bowl, 1999. Lt. (j.g.) USNR, 1956-58. Named Outstanding Young Man of Winter Park, Winter Park Jaycees, 1970, Citizen of the Yr., Winter Park, Fla., 2002. Mem.: US Navy League, US Naval Inst., So. Grand Bank Owners Assn., Nat. Assn. Ins. Agts., Fla. Assn. Ins. Agts., Ctrl. Fla. Assn. Ins. Agts. (pres. 1963—64), Purdue U. Alumni Assn. (pres. coun., dirs. cir. Krannert Grad. Sch. Mgmt., Deans Club Sch. Sci.), Rotary (bd. dirs. Winter Park Club 1968—74), All-Am. John Purdue Club, Gold Club Purdue Mus. Orgn., Country Club of Orlando (pres. 1994—95), Useppa Island Club, Captiva Island Yacht Club, U. Club, Masons, Delta Delta (chpt. pres. 1956, ctrl. Fla. alumni chpt.pres. 1960), Sigma Chi (Significant SIG award for achievement in profl. career and civic endeavors, presented to few Sigma Chi frat. alumni 2004). Republican. Presbyterian. Home: 231 Chelton Cir Winter Park FL 32789-6004 also: 1765 Venus Dr Sanibel FL 33957-3427 Office: Kraft Ins Agy Inc PO Box 1443 Winter Park FL 32790-1443: 328 Deep Water Drive White Stone VA 22578

KRAFT, MICHAEL EUGENE, political science professor; b. L.A., Nov. 18, 1943; s. Louis and Pearl (Wiener) Kraft. BA, U. Calif., Riverside, 1966; MA, Yale U., 1967, PhD, 1973. Asst. prof. Vassar Coll., Poughkeepsie, N.Y., 1973-76, U. Wis., Green Bay, 1977-79, assoc. prof., 1979-82, prof., 1982—. Vis. disting. prof. Oberlin (Ohio) Coll., 1984-85, U. Wis., Madison, 1987-88. Author: Environmental Policy & Politics, 2001, 3rd edit., 2003; co-author (editor): Technology and Politics, 1988, Public Reactions to Nuclear Waste, 1993, Environmental Policy, 6th edit., 2005, Toward Sustainable Communities, 1999, Public Policy, 2004. Bd. dir. Lake Michigan Fedn., Chgo., 1986—2003. Yale U. fellow, 1966-69, Mem. AAAS, Am. Polit. Sci. Assn., Western Polit. Sci. Assn., Phi Beta Kappa, Phi Kappa Phi. Avocations: photography, music, gardening. Office: U Wis Pub & Environ Affairs/MAC B310 2420 Nicolet Dr Green Bay WI 54311-7001 Office Phone: 920-465-2531. Business E-Mail: kraftm@uwgb.edu.

KRAFT, RICHARD LEE, lawyer; b. Lassa, Nigeria, Oct. 14, 1958; m. Tanya Kraft, July 14, 1984; children: Devin, Kelsey. BA in Fgn. Svc., Baylor U., 1980, JD, 1982. Bar: N.Mex. 1982, U.S. Dist. Ct. N.Mex., U.S. Ct. Appeals, U.S. Supreme Ct. Assoc. Sanders, Bruin & Baldock, Roswell, N.Mex., 1982-87, ptnr., 1987-98, Kraft & Stone, LLP, Roswell, 1998-2000; owner The Kraft Law Firm, 2000—. Vol. lawyer Ea. N.Mex. U., Roswell, 1984-98; bd. dirs. Roswell YMCA, 1983-87, Crimestoppers, 1991-94; pres. Roswell Mens Ch. Basketball League; participant Roswell Mens Ch. Softball League; asst. chair legal div. United Way Drive, 1990; pres. sch. bd. Valley Christian Acad., 2003—. Recipient Outstanding Contbn. award N.Mex. State Bar, 1987, 2000. Mem. N.Mex. Bar Assn. (bd. dirs. young lawyers div. 1983-91, pres. 1986-87, chmn. membership com., bar commr. 1986-87, 91-2003, pres. 1998-99, Outstanding Young Lawyer award 1990), Chaves County Bar Assn. (chair law day activities, chair ann. summer picnic com., rep. bench and bar com.), Roswell Legal Secs. Assn. (hon.), Roswell C. of C. (participant and pres. Leadership Roswell, exec. dir., bd. dirs. 1991-), Sertoma (bd. dirs. Roswell club 1989-91) Valley Christian Acad. (pres., bd. dirs., 2003-). Baptist. Office: The Kraft Law Firm 111 W Third St Roswell NM 88201-4783 Office Phone: 505-625-2000. Business E-Mail: rkraft@thekraftlawfirm.com. E-mail: thekraftlawfirm@aol.com.

KRAFT, ROBERT ARNOLD, retired medical educator, physician; b. Seattle, Mar. 27, 1924; s. Vincent Irving and Blanche (Palmer) K.; m. Robby Lee Roberson, June 12, 1949 (dec. Aug. 2002); children: Angela Kraft Cross, Peter, Darius. BA, U. Wash., 1948, MD, 1954. Diplomate Am. Bd. Pathology, Am. Bd. Nuclear Medicine. Intern USPHS Hosp., Staten Island, N.Y., 1954-55; resident in Pathology Tacoma (Wash.) Gen. Hosp, 1958-60, U. Calif., San Francisco, 1960-62; staff pathologist Peninsula Hosp., Burlingame, Calif., 1962-90, dir. nuclear medicine, 1965-90; asst. clin. prof. nuclear medicine and pathology U. Calif., San Francisco, 1962-90. Bd. dirs. Am. Bd. Nuclear Medicine, L.A., 1990-95. Capt. USAF, 1943-45, ETO. Decorated DFC. Fellow Am. Coll. Nuclear Physicians (regent 1985-91), Coll. Am. Pathologists; mem. Am. Coll. Nuclear Physicians (pres. Calif. chpt. 1972-73), Soc. Nuclear Medicine (trustee 1982-85), South Bay Pathology Soc. (pres. 1966-67). Avocations: golf, astronomy, mining history, orchids. Home: 971 Baileyana Rd Hillsborough CA 94010-6173

KRAFT, ROBERT K., professional sports team executive; b. Brookline, Mass., July 5, 1941; m. Myra Kraft; 4 children. Grad., Columbia U.; MBA, Harvard U. Owner Foxboro (Mass.) Stadium; chmn. Chestnut Hill Mgmt.; pres. New England TV Corp., 1986-91; with Rand-Whitney Group, Inc., Worcester, Mass.; founder Internat. Forest Products, 1972; pres. Internat. Forest Products Group Cos.; chmn. Carmel Container Systems, Ltd., Israel; owner New England Patriots, 1994—. Mem. exec. com. Dana Farber Cancer Inst.; trustee Columbia U.; bd. dirs. Harvard Sch. Bus. Mem. bd. overseers Boston Symphony Orch., Boston Mus. Sci. Avocations: golf, tennis. Office: New England Patriots Gillete Stadium One Patriots Pl Foxboro MA 02035-1388*

KRAFT, ROBERT PAUL, astronomer, educator; b. Seattle, June 16, 1927; s. Victor Paul and Viola Eunice (Ellis) K.; m. Rosalie Ann Reichmuth, Aug. 28, 1949; children: Kenneth, Kevin. BS, U. Wash., 1947, MS, 1949; PhD, U. Calif.-Berkeley, 1955; DSc (hon.), Ind. U., 1995. Postdoctoral fellow Mt. Wilson Obs., Carnegie Inst., Pasadena, Calif., 1955-56; asst. prof. astronomy Ind. U., Bloomington, 1956-58, Yerkes Obs., U. Chgo., Williams Bay, Wis., 1958-59; staff Hale Obs., Pasadena, 1960-67; prof., astronomer Lick Obs., U. Calif., Santa Cruz, 1967-92; astronomer, prof. emeritus, 1992—. Acting dir. Lick Obs., 1968-70, 71-73, dir., 1981-91; dir. U. Calif. Observatories, 1988-91; chmn. Fachbeirat, Max-Planck-Inst., Munich, Fed. Republic Germany, 1978-88; bd. dirs. Cara corp. (Keck Obs.), Pasadena, 1985-91; bd. dirs. AURA, 1989-92. Contbr. articles to profl. jours. Jila vis. fellow U. Colo., Nat. Bur. Stds., Boulder, 1970; Fairchild scholar Calif. Inst. Tech., Pasadena, 1980, Tinsley prof. U. Tex., 1991-92; Henry Norris Russell lectr. Am. Astron. Soc., 1995; recipient Disting. Alumnus award Coll. Arts and Scis., U. Wash., 1995, Catherine Wolfe Bruce Gold medal Astron. Soc. Pacific, 2005. Mem. Nat. Acad. Sci., Am. Acad. of Arts and Scis., Am. Astron. Soc. (pres. 1974-76, Warner prize 1962, Russell prize lectr. 1995), Internat. Astron. Union (v.p. 1982-88, pres.-elect 1994-97, pres. 1997-2000), Astron. Soc. Pacific (bd. dirs. 1981-87), Royal Astron. Soc. (fgn. assoc.). Democrat. Unitarian Universalist. Avocations: contract bridge, art appreciation, classical music, opera, eonology. Office: U Calif Lick Observatory Santa Cruz CA 95064 E-mail: kraft@ucolick.org.

KRAFT, SCOTT COREY, correspondent; b. Kansas City, Mo., Mar. 31, 1955; s. Marvin Emanuel and Patricia (Kirk) K.; m. Elizabeth Brown, May 1, 1982; children: Kate, Kevin. BS, Kans. State U., 1977. Staff writer AP, Jefferson City, Mo., 1976-77, Kansas City, 1977-79, corr. Wichita, Kans., 1979-80, nat. writer N.Y.C., 1980-84; nat. corr. L.A. Times, Chgo., 1984-86, bur. chief Nairobi, Kenya, 1986-88, Johannesburg, South Africa, 1988-93, Paris, 1993-96, dep. fgn. editor, 1996-97, nat. editor, 1997—. Recipient Disting. Reporting in a Specialized Field award Soc. of the Silurians, 1982, Peter Lisagor award Headline Club Chgo., 1985, Feature Writing finalist Pulitzer Prize Bd., 1985, Sigma Delta Chi award, 1993. Office: LA Times Nat Editor 202 W 1st St Los Angeles CA 90012

KRAFT, YVETTE, art educator; b. Washington, Jan. 17, 1945; d. Alvin Abraham and Rena Zlotnick Kraft. Studies with Master Painter Leon Berkowitz, 1982—87; student, Corcoran Coll. of Art and Design, 1992—. Art dir. after-sch. program Georgetown Montessori Sch., 1988; art instr. Washington Home, Sr. Citizen Care Facility, 1989—90; art instr. students with spl. needs Horace Mann Elem. Sch., 1990; art instr. Southeast Asian Refugee Children, 4-H, Arlington, Va., 1989—90; pvt. art instr. ages 2-17, 1990—92; art instr. Janney Elem. Sch., 1991, 1998, 1999, Ben Murch Elem. Sch., 1991; artist-in-residence Anne Beers Elem. Sch., 1992—93; art instr. children and adolescents with emotional disorders Clara Aisenstein, MD, Child Psychiatrist, 1993—96; art instr. Randle Highlands Elem. Sch., 1994, Naylor Rd. Elem. Sch., 1997, Bethany Woman's Shelter, 1998—2000; conduct art classes N St. Village, Washington, 2003—. Fine arts com. Washington Hebrew Congregation, 1979—82; adv. bd. New Art Examiner Mag., Washington, 1985—86; asst. mgr. Americana West Gallery; founder, dir. Project City People, 1992, 93; edn. dir. Fondo del Sol Visual Arts Ctr., 1992—93. One-woman shows include Maret Sch., Washington, DC, 1987, Georgetown Montessori Sch., 1988, Horace Mann Sch., 1989, Fillmore Sch. of Arts, 1991, NIH, Clin. Ctr. Gallery, Bethesda, Md., 1995, Fondo de Sol Visual Arts Ctr., Washington, DC, 1996, DC Arts Ctr., 1999, Nat. Coalition for Homeless, 2001, exhibited in group shows at Am. Art League, 1982—85, Highlights of the Yr. Exhbn., Martin Luther King Libr., 1986—87, Washington Hebrew Congregation, 1986—87, 2002—03, Capricorn Gallery, Bethesda, Md., 1987, Ctr. for Collaborative Art and Visual Edn., Washington, DC, 1999, Capital Children's Mus., 1999, Eight Is An Octive, Nat. Theatre, 2000, Am. Oh Yes Folk Art Gallery, 2000—03, Joy of Motion, 2001, Rockville Arts Pl., Md., 2003. Grantee grant, Cafritz Found., 1990, 1991, Hattie M. Strong Found., 1991, George Preston Marshall, 1991. Independent. Jewish. Avocations: jazz, walking, art museums, sketching, clothing design and coordination. Office Phone: 202-332-0535.

KRAGH, JOHN FREDERICK, JR., orthopedist, educator; b. Newburgh, N.Y., May 1, 1963; s. John Frederick and Maureen Ellen Kragh; m. Gretchen Dawn Garceau, Sept. 24, 1999. MD, Uniformed Services U. Health Scis., 1989. Diplomate Am. Bd. Orthop. Surgery. Commissioned 2d lt. US Army, 1985—, advanced through grades to lt. col., 1999; orthop. surgeon Orthop. Dept., Fort Bragg, NC, 1997—2001; rsch. dir. Orthop. Residency, Fort Sam Houston, Tex., 2001—. Bn. surgeon 3d Ranger Bn., Fort Benning, Ga., 1990—93. Decorated Meritorious Svc. Medal U.S. Army; recipient Surgeon General's Physician Recognition Sabbatical fellowship, 1992, Eisenhower Army Med. Ctr. Rsch. award, 1993, Founders award, Soc. Mil. Orthopedic Surgeons. Fellow: Am. Acad. Orthop. Surgeons. Office: BAMC Orthopedics Rm 129-5 MCHE-SDR 3851 Roger Brooke Dr Fort Sam Houston TX 78234-6200

KRAGNES, EARL NEWTON, retired minister; b. Pitts., Sept. 13, 1921; s. Alfred Martin Kragnes and Margaret Lohr; m. Anna C. Kragnes, Nov. 4, 1943; children: Kathy, Janice, Cheryl, Philip. BA, Johnson Bible Coll., 1944; MA, Phillips Theol. Sem., 1946, B Divinity, 1948. Ordained to ministry Christian Ch. (Disciples of Christ), 1942. Pastor N.E. Christian Ch., Oklahoma City, 1948-49; assoc. min. Crown Heights Christian Ch., Oklahoma City, 1949-53; field rep. Nat. Coun. Chs. N.Y.C., Oklahoma City, 1953-56; dir. religious edn. Mo. Coun. Chs., Jefferson City, 1957-59; exec. dir. Okla. Coun. Chs., Oklahoma City, 1959-74; dir., mgr. interreligious liaison office AARP, Washington, 1974-93; ret. Bd. dirs. Nat. Interfaith Coalition on Aging, Washington, 1974-93. Contbr. chpt. to book. Cons. adv. bd. inst. Lifelong Learning, Montgomery Coll., Rockville, Md., 1997-00. Recipient Spiritual Well-being of Elderly award Nat. Coun. on Aging, Inc., 1993. Avocations: volunteer work, recording for the blind and dyslexic. Home: 407 Russell Ave Apt 601 Gaithersburg MD 20877-2856

KRAHENBUHL, GARY STUART, university administrator; b. DeKalb, Ill., Sept. 11, 1943; s. Orville and Lillian (Wickness) K.; m. Richey Jane Krahenbuhl, Apr. 2, 1966; children: Lisa, Julie, Kevin, Michael. BS in Edn., No. Ill. U., 1965, MS in Edn., 1966; EdD, U. No. Colo., 1969. Asst. prof. U. Hawaii, Honolulu, 1969-73, Ariz. State U., Tempe, 1973-75, assoc. prof., 1975-79, prof. and chair, 1979-84, assoc. dean, 1984-90, dean liberal arts, 1990-2000, sr. v.p., 2001—. Contbr. articles to profl. jours. Convener, CEO, Coun. for the Arts and Scis. in Urban Univs., Wichita, Kans., 1993-98; mem. Higher Edn. Rsch. Adv. Bd., Phoenix, 1992-96; bd. dirs. Ariz. Sr. Olympics, Phoenix, 1985-87; chmn. adminstrv. bd. United Meth. Ch., Tempe, 1997-98. Recipient Award for Outstanding Contbn. to Edn., No. Ill. U., 1996, Difference Maker award Ariz. State U., 2001. Fellow Am. Acad. Kinesiology and Phys. Edn. (pres. 2000-2001), Am. Coll. Sports Medicine (bd. trustees 1988-91); mem. Coun. of Colls. of Arts and Scis. (pres. 1993-94), Am. Acad. Kinesiology and Phys. Edn. (pres. 2000-2001), Soc. for Coll. and Univ. Planning (editl. bd. 1997—). Republican. Avocations: photography, golf, travel, reading history and biographies. Home: 8822 S Oak St Tempe AZ 85284 Office: Ariz State Univ PO Box 872203 Tempe AZ 85287-2203 E-mail: gary.krahenbuhl@asu.edu.

KRAHL, ENZO, retired surgeon; b. Fiume, Italy, Apr. 22, 1924; came to U.S., 1951, naturalized, 1955; s. Massimiliano and Camilla (Aub) K.; m. Anne Katharine Ferbstein, June 14, 1958; children— Edward Alexander, Katharine Frances MD, U. Florence, Italy, 1948. Diplomate Am. Bd. Surgery. Asst. dept. surgery U. Rome, 1948-51; fellow in vascular surgery Columbia Presbyn. Med. Ctr., N.Y.C., 1951-52, fellow in surgery, 1954-55; resident in surgery St. Vincent's Hosp., N.Y.C., 1952-54; chief resident in surgery Akron City Hosp., Ohio, 1957-58; dir. grad. edn. Akron Gen. Hosp., 1959-60; practice medicine specializing in surgery Akron, 1958-60, Superior, Wis., 1960-84; ret., 1984. Mem. staff Superior Meml. Hosp., also bd. dirs.; founder Superior Clinic, 1964; past dir. Blue Cross-Blue Shield United of Wis. Contbr. articles to med. jours. Past v.p. Duluth-Superior Symphony; past mem. exec. com. bd. dirs. Health Systems Agy. Western Lake Superior. Served as capt. M.C., U.S. Army, 1955-57 Recipient United Fund award, 1965, cert. of merit N.Y.C. CD, 1953 Mem. Wis. State Med. Soc., Italian Heritage Soc., Am. Bridge League, Marshwood Country Club, AAD Temple Club, Masons, Shriners. Jewish. Home: 15 Cotton Xing Savannah GA 31411-2504 Personal E-mail: anneande@bellsouth.net.

KRAHMER, JOHANNES ROBERT, lawyer; b. Mannheim, Germany, Feb. 29, 1932; came to U.S., 1938; s. Wolf and Herta C. K.; m. Betty Pease, Aug. 22, 1958; children: Elizabeth M. Krahmer Keating, Andrea Krahmer Cross. AB magna cum laude, Dartmouth Coll., 1953; JD cum laude, Harvard U., 1959. Bar: D.C. 1960, Del. 1965, U.S. Supreme Ct. Assoc. Ivins, Phillips and Barker, Washington, 1959-62; staff atty., tax legis. counsel U.S. Dept. Treasury, Washington, 1962-64; assoc. Morris, Nichols, Arsht and Tunnell, Wilmington, Del., 1964-65; ptnr. Morris, Nichols, Arsht & Tunnell, Wilmington, Del., 1966—. Author tax mgmt. portfolios; contbr. articles to profl. pubs. Trustee Princeton (NJ) Theol. Sem., 1972—, chmn. bd. trustees, 1991-96. Lt. (j.g.) USN, 1953-56. Fellow Am. Coll. Trust and Estate Counsel, Am. Coll. Tax Counsel; mem. ABA (sec. sect. taxation 1986-88). Republican. Presbyterian. Home: 2201 Kentmere Pky Wilmington DE 19806-2017 Office: Morris Nichols Arsht & Tunnell 1201 N Market St Wilmington DE 19801-1347 Office Phone: 302-575-7225. E-mail: jkrahmer@mnat.com.

KRAICHNAN, ROBERT HARRY, physicist, consultant; b. Phila., Jan. 15, 1928; s. Robert Maxwell and Anna (Maximon) Kraichnan; m. Carol Gebhardt, May 22, 1954 (div. 1988); 1 child, John; m. Judy Ellen Moore, June 30, 1989. BS in Physics, MIT, 1947, PhD in Theoretical Physics, 1949. Mem., asst. to Albert Einstein Inst. Advanced Study, Princeton, NJ, 1949-50; mem. tech. staff Bell Tel. Labs., 1950-52; rsch. assoc. Columbia U., N.Y.C., 1952-56; rsch. assoc. Courant Inst. NYU, 1956-58, sr. rsch. scientist Courant Inst., 1958-62; pvt. practice physicist, 1962-80; pres., prin. Robert H. Kraichnan, Inc., Santa Fe, 1980—. Adj. assoc. prof. dept. grad. physics NYU, 1956—57; cons. Naval Rsch. Lab., 1957—59, Inst. Def. Analyses, 1967—70, Los Alamos Nat. Lab., 1979—, Princeton U., 1987—; cons. Inst. Space Studies NASA, 1961—69, contractor, 1967—69; assoc. in physics Woods Hole (Mass.) Oceanographic Inst., 1960—70; contractor Office Naval Rsch., 1962—80; rsch. affiliate meteorology MIT, 1963—. Contbr. articles to sci. jours. Recipient ADION medal, Observatoire de Nice, Dirac prize, Internat. Ctr. Theoretical Physics, 2003; grantee, NSF, 1970—. Fellow: AAAS, Am. Phys. Soc. (Otto Laporte award 1993, Lars Onsager Meml. prize 1997); mem.: NAS. Avocations: mountain hiking, violin, carpentry.

KRAINES, MERRILL M., lawyer; b. NYC, Aug. 3, 1955; BA magna cum laude, Dartmouth Coll., 1976; JD, Columbia U., 1979. Bar: NY 1980. Ptnr. and co-head tech. and emerging companies dept. Fulbright & Jaworski, LLP, NYC. Mem. ABA (sect. corp. banking and bus. law, small bus. com., subcom. emerging growth ventures), NY State Bar Assn. Office: Fulbright & Jaworski LLP 666 5th Ave Fl 31 New York NY 10103-3198 Office Phone: 212-318-3000. Office Fax: 212-318-3400. Business E-Mail: mkraines@fulbright.com.

KRAININ, JULIAN ARTHUR, film director, film producer, cinematographer, writer; b. NYC, Jan. 24, 1941; s. David A. and Anne N. (Wineblatt) K.; m. Martha Wineblatt, June 17, 1967; 1 child, Todd Philip. BS, Allegheny Coll., 1962, HHD (hon.), 1993; MFA, Columbia U., 1965. Prodr. spl. projects Westinghouse Broadcasting Co., N.Y.C., 1967-69, also prodr., dir., writer, 1967—; v.p., exec. prodr. Krainin/Sage Prodns., Inc., N.Y.C., 1969-80, also dir., writer, 1969-80; pres. Krainin Prodns., Inc., N.Y.C., 1976—. Nat. lectr. motion pictures at various univs. and colls., 1967—; cons. on films U. Mass., 1973; juror Mid-West Film Makers and Graphic Arts Festival, 1971-72, Nat. Emmy Awards, 1975-82, 85-90, Dirs. Guild of Am. Awards, 1987-90; mem. journalism adv. bd. Queens Coll., 1987-90; bd. dirs. Bklyn. Ctr. for Families in Crises, 1986-90; journalism adv. bd. Queens Coll. Films include: The Reluctant Revolution, 1968, Exit to Nowhere, 1967, Promises to Keep, 1967, The March, 1965, Nowhere Fast, 1968, Hide and Seek, 1966, (with Jacques Cousteau) Oceans: The Silent Crisis, 1972, Art is (Acad. award nominee, hon. screenings White House, Mus. Modern Art), 1972, The Other Americans (Emmy award), 1969, Princeton: A Search for Answers (Acad. award), 1973, The American Experiment, 1974, Going Metric, 1975, To America, 1976, The Broken Silence, 1976, The World of James Michener: Hawaii Revisited, 1977, The World of James Michener: The South Pacific, End of Eden? (hon. screening Mus. Modern Art), 1978, (with Ed Asner) The Writer, 1980, The Making of an Opera, 1980, Luciano Pavorotti At Home, 1980, La Gioconda miniseries, 1980, Heritage: Civilization and the Jews (Peabody, Christopher awards), 1981-82, PBS series, CBS Reports: Don't Touch that Dial!: The Making of a Television Series (Emmy nominee, TV Guide citation, 1982, The Smithsonian Quadrangle: A View from the Castle, 1984, America Undercover: The Wrong Man, 1985-86, (with Tom Peters) The Power of Excellence, 1987; (with Abba Eban) Heritage: Civilization and the Jews, Disaster at Silo 7, 1988, Memory and Imagination, New Pathways to the Library of Congress, 1990; documentary film: The Television Quiz Show Scandal, 1991, Queen's College, 1993, (feature film) Quiz Show, 1994 (4 Acad. award nominations including Best Picture), The Unabomber: Deadly Mail!, 1996, The Thousand Acre Universe, 1996, George Wallace (Golden Globe, Humanitas, Cable Ace, Peabody awards), The John Glenn Story: Return to Space and Return of the Hero, 1998-99, Something the Lord Made, 2004 (Emmy award, Peabody, Am. Film. Inst., Dir. Guild Am., Christopher, TV Critics Assn., NAACP Image, Freddie, Writers Guild Am., Golden Globe noms.) Recipient numerous awards and citations including Acad. Award, 1973, Emmy Award, 1969, Chgo. Internat. Film Festival award, 1969, 77, 78, Florence Internat. Film Festival award, 1969, Cine Golden Eagle awards, 1969, 72, 73, 74, 76, 78, Photog. Soc. Am. award, 1968, Venice Film Festival award, 1970, Moscow Internat. Film Festival award, 1970, Cindy award Prodrs. Assn. Am., 1971, 76, San Francisco Internat. Film Festival award, 1972, Am. Film Festival award, 1974, 76, 78, Tel Aviv Internat. Film Festival award, 1970, Atlanta Internat. Film Festival award, 1969, 72, Festival of Ams. award, 1976, N.Y. Internat. Film and TV Festival award, 1969, 72, Gabriel award, 1968-70, Oberhausen Internat. Film Festival award, 1969, Columbus Film Festival award, 1973, Mannheim Internat. Film Festival award, 1969, U.S. Indsl. Film Festival award, 1973, Ohio State award, 1967, N.Y. Film Festival at Lincoln Center award, 1970. Mem. Writers Guild Am., Acad. Motion Picture Arts and scis., Photog. Soc. Am., Dirs. Guild Am. (award 1973). Office: 25211 Summerhill Ln Stevenson Ranch CA 91381-2262 Office Phone: 661-259-9700. Business E-Mail: krainin@comcast.net.

KRAJESKI, THOMAS CHARLES, ambassador; b. Groveland, Mass. Joined Fgn. Svc., 1979; with U.S. Embassy, Kathmandu, Nepal, 1980—82, chief counsular sect. Madras, India, 1982—84, dep. chief consular sect. Warsaw, 1985—88; fgn. svc. officer U.S. Dept. State, Washington, 1988—92, U.S. Embassy, Tunis, Tunisia, 1992—93, dep. chief, polit. sect. Cairo, 1993—97; consul gen. Dubai, United Arab Emirates, 1997—2001; dir. No. Gulf affairs bur. Near Ea. affairs U.S. Dept. State, Washington, 2002—04, U.S. amb. to Yemen, 2004—. Office: Am Embassy Sana a Yemen US Dept State Washington DC 20521-6330*

KRAJEWSKI, MICHAEL, conductor; b. Detroit, Mich. m. Darcy Krajewski. Grad, Wayne State U., U. of Cinn. Coll. Conservatory of Music. Music dir. Modesto Symphony Orch.; prin. pops condr. New Mex., Long Beach and Jacksonville Symphonies; asst. condr. Detroit Symphony Orch.; music dir. Detroit Symphony Civic Orch.; resident condr. Fla. Symphony Orch.; prin. pops condr. Houston Symphony Orch., 2000—. Fellowship condr. Detroit Symphony; artist intern Mich. Opera Theatre. Performed with Boston Pops Orch., San Francisco, St. Louis, Detroit, Balt., Atlanta, Minn., Oreg. et al. Recipient awards, Am. Soc. of Composers, Authors and Publishers. Office: Houston Symphony 615 Louisiana St Ste 102 Houston TX 77002*

KRAJICK, KEVIN RUDOLPH, freelance/self-employed journalist; b. Camp Kilmer, N.J., Aug. 10, 1952; s. Rudolph Adam and Katherine Sarah (Distin) Krajick; m. Ruby Jean Kipniss, Sept. 8, 1996; children: Stella, Lydia. BA in Comparative Lit. cum laude, Columbia U., 1976, MS in Journalism, 1977. Assoc. editor Police and Corrections mags., N.Y.C., 1978-84; nat. editor Nat. Law Jour., N.Y.C., 1984-85; assoc. editor Newsweek, N.Y.C., 1988-96; freelance author N.Y.C., 1981—. Author: (book) Barren Lands: An Epic Search for Diamonds in the North American Arctic, 2001; contbr. articles to publs. Recipient Walter Sullivan award for excellence in sci. journalism, Am. Geophys. Union, 1998, 2004, Brock award for agrl. writing, Calif. Poly. U., 1998; Sci. Writing fellow, Marine Biol. Lab., 1996. Mem.: Nat. Assn. Sci. Writers. Home: 245 W 104th St Apt 14B New York NY 10025-4280 Office Phone: 212-666-4824. E-mail: krk4@columbia.edu.

KRAKAUER, HENRY, physics educator; b. Regensberg, Germany, Feb. 14, 1947; came to U.S., 1953; s. Mark and Sara K.; m. Sarah Gordon, Oct. 16, 1971; children: Ilana, Mark, Benajamin. BA, Rutgers U., 1969; PhD, Brandeis U., 1975. Instr. W.Va. U., Morgantown, 1975-77; postdoctoral fellow Northwestern U., Evanston, Ill., 1977-80; asst. prof. Coll. of William and Mary, Williamsburg, Va., 1980-84, assoc. prof., 1984-90, prof., 1990—. Contbr. numerous articles to profl. publs. Fellow Am. Phys. Soc.; mem. Materials Rsch. Soc. Office: Coll of William and Mary Dept Physics Williamsburg VA 23187

KRAKER, DEBORAH SCHOVANEC, special education educator; b. Enid, Okla., May 28, 1960; d. Charles Raymond and Marcella Ruth (Mack) Schovanec; m. Kevin Mark Kraker, July 10, 1987. BS, U. Ctrl. Okla., 1982; postgrad., Okla. State U., Stillwater, 1995—. Cert. tchr. spl. edn., learning disability/mentally handicapped. Customer svc. mgr. Skaggs, Oklahoma City, 1982-92; tchr. spl. edn. Edmond (Okla.) Pub. Schs., 1993—. Tchr. Francis Tuttle Vocat. Tech. Ctr., Oklahoma City, 1993, 94, 95, mem. adv. bd., 1993-96. Mem. adv. bd. Francis Tuttle Vocat. Tech. Ctr., 1993—. Mem. NEA, Okla. Edn. Assn. (del. nat. assembly 1996), Edmond Assn. Classroom Tchrs. (v.p. 1997-98), Coun. for Exceptional Children, Assn. Classroom Mems. (exec. bd.), Okla. Commn. Tchr. Preparation (mem. portfolio rev. team, mem. accreditation rev. team, mem. program accreditation), Learning Disabilities Assn., Kappa Delta Pi. Republican. Roman Catholic. Avocations: reading, sewing, cooking, collecting antiques. Home: 2721 Berkshire Way Oklahoma City OK 73120-2704

KRAKOFF, CHARLES, marketing professional; BA in Anthropology, Reed Coll.; MBA in Fin. and Internat. Bus., Columbia U. Sr. fin. analyst capital appropriations Trans World Airlines, NYC, 1982—83; spl. projects coord. Sherburne Corp., Killington, Vt., 1983—84; cons. William Kent & co., Greenwich, Conn., 1984—87; sr. project officer Botswana Devel. Corp., Gaborone, 1987—89; dir. Botswana Investment Promotion, Hong Kong, 1990—91; sr. assoc. Abt Assoc., Inc., Cambridge, Mass., 1991—97; head Africa cons. svcs. Std. Corp. and Merchant Bank, Johannesburg, 1997—98; mng. dir. C2SI Cons., Johannesburg, 1998—2004; co-founder, dir., CFP Africa Bus. Direct, Johannesburg, 2000—02; chief office for Africa Internat. Trade Ctr., Geneva, 2004; founder, mng. ptnr. Koios Assoc. LLC, 2005—. Avocations: skiing, hiking, reading, jazz, cooking. Home: 8 MacLeod Ln Acton MA 01720

KRAKOFF, ROBERT LEONARD, publishing executive; b. Pitts., May 4, 1935; s. Frank and Della (Zionts) Krakoff; m. Sandra Gusky, June 22, 1958; children: Roger, Hope, Reed. BS with honors, Pa. State U., 1957; MBA, Harvard U., 1959. Staff v.p. mktg. planning TWA, N.Y.C., 1963—70; v.p., contr. consumer product div. Singer, N.Y.C., 1970—71; staff v.p. strategic planning RCA, N.Y.C., 1971—72; pres. Am. Internat. Travel Svc., Boston, 1972—73, Cahners Travel Group, N.Y.C., 1973—74, Cahners Expn. Group, N.Y.C., 1974—86; exec. v.p., COO Reed Pub. U.S.A., Newton, Mass., 1986—89, pres., COO, 1989—91, chmn., CEO, 1991—96, Advanstar, Inc. (formerly Advanstar Holdings, Inc.), Boston, 1996—2003, 2004, Blantyre Ptnrs., Boston, 2004—. Bd. dirs. Freedom Comms., Inc., 1996—. Trustee Beth Israel Deaconess Med. Ctr., 2004—. With USAR, 1957—63. Office: Blantyre Ptnrs 20 Park Plz Ste 481 Boston MA 02116 Office Phone: 617-948-2583. Business E-Mail: rkrakoff@aol.com.

KRAKOWER, BERNARD HYMAN, management consultant; b. N.Y.C., May 11, 1935; s. David and Bertha (Glassman) K.; m. Sondra Joan Fishbein, Apr. 14, 1968; children: Lorna, Victoria, Ariela Shauna. BA in Advt., UCLA, 1959; cert. in real estate, 1966, cert. in indsl. rels., 1972; MBA, Pepperdine U., 1979. Loan officer Lytton Fin. Corp., L.A., 1961-65; mgmt. cons. James R. Colvin & Assocs., L.A., 1965-67; sr. indsl. rels. rep. Sci. Data Systems (Xerox), 1967-68; dir. ops. Tratec, Inc., L.A., 1968-70; chmn. Krakower/Brucker Internat., Inc., L.A., 1970-88; sr. ptnr. Krakower Finnegan Assocs., L.A., 1988-90; pres. Krakower Group, Inc., 1990—. Bd. dirs. Columbia Nat. Bank, Santa Monica, Calif., Elings Park, Santa Barbara, Calif.; mem. adv. bd. Private Financing Group, 2000. Mem. citizens liaison com. L.A. Dept. Recreation and Parks, 1973; apptd. commr., v.p. L.A. Countywide Citizens Planning Coun. by L.A. County Bd. Suprs., 1988-97, v.p., 1991-93, pres. 1993-97; pres., bd. dirs. L.A. Bus. Coun.; mem. bd. visitors Pepperdine U. Graziadio Sch. Bus. and Mgmt., 1997—; leadership mem. Santa Barbara Region Econ. Cmty. Project, 1997; v.p. bd. dirs. Santa Barbara Newcomers, 1999; mem. adv. bd. Calif. Coast Venture Forum, 1999, co-chmn. Santa Barbara Region Tech. Coun., 1999; bd. dirs. Santa Barbara C. of C., 2001. Mem.: Santa Barbara Regional C. of C., So. Calif. Tech. coast Angels, Santa Barbara Regional C. of C. (bd. dirs. 2001—, mem. fin. com. 2001—, mem. exec. com. 2003—, bd. dir. Elings Pk. chpt. 2003—). Personal E-mail: kgi@krakower.net.

KRALLINGER, JOSEPH CHARLES, entrepreneur, consultant, writer; b. Lancaster, Pa., May 29, 1931; s. Ferdinand and Mathilde (Meyer) K.; m. Hilde Eisenhauer, Oct. 1, 1955; children— Joanne, Diane, Robert BS in Econs. cum laude, Franklin and Marshall Coll., 1953. C.P.A. Auditor GAO, Denver, 1953; auditor Army Audit Agy., 1953-55; ptnr. Arthur Andersen & Co., Phila., 1955-76; v.p. strategic planning and acquisitions, chief fin. officer Berwind Corp., Phila., 1976-88; cons. Palm Desert, Calif., 1988—. Dir., bus. advisor and investor various indsl., health care, mining, oil and gas cos., 1976—; cons. in field. Author: An Auditor's Approach to Statistical Sampling, 5 vols., 1967-72, Strategic Planning Workbook, 1989, 2d edit., 1993, How to Acquire the Perfect Business for Your Company, 1991; Planeacion Estrategica Practica, 1991; Mergers and Acquisitions: Managing the Transactions, 1997, Chinese and Spanish edits., 2000; contbr. articles to profl. jours. Bd. dirs. alumni coun. Franklin and Marshall Coll., Lancaster, 1969-75; pres., tchr. religious edn. St. Genevieve Cath. Ch., Flourtown, Pa., 1971-76; bd. dirs. Whitemarsh Twp. Citizens Coun., Plymouth Meeting, Pa., 1972-75;

hon. life mem., past chmn. bd. dirs. Phila. chpt. Am. Cancer Soc. Recipient Nat. Vol. award Am. Cancer Soc., 1985, Crusade award Am. Cancer Soc., 1985, Teaching award St. Genevieve Ch., 1985, Cert. Merit Inst. Mgmt. Accts., 1998. Mem. AICPA (statis. sampling com.), Pa. Inst. CPAs, Nat. Assn. Accts. (past pres. Phila. chpt.), Planning Forum (past pres. Phila. chpt.), Soc. Children's Book Writers and Illustrators, Ironwood Country Club (bd. dirs. 1991-93). Avocations: golf, racquet sports, writing, reading. Home and Office: 48-120 Alder Ln Palm Desert CA 92260-6652

KRAM, SHIRLEY WOHL, federal judge; b. N.Y.C., 1922; Student, Hunter Coll., 1940-41, CUNY, 1940-47; LLB, Bklyn. Law Sch., 1950. Atty. Legal Aid Soc. N.Y., 1951-53, 1962-71; assoc. Simons & Hardy, 1954-55; pvt. practice law, 1955-60; judge Family Ct., N.Y.C., 1971-83, U.S. Dist. Ct. (So. Dist.), NYC, 1983—93, sr. judge, 1993—. Author: (with Neil A. Frank) The Law of Child Custody, Development of the Substantive Law Office: 2101 US Courthouse 40 Centre St New York NY 10007-1581*

KRAMARAE, CHERIS, education educator; b. Brookings, S.D., Mar. 10, 1938; d. William H. Gamble and Deda Rae Smits; m. Dale V. Kramer, Dec. 21, 1960; children: Brinlee, Jana. BS, So. Dakota State, 1960; MS, Ohio Univ., 1963; PhD, U. Ill., Urbana-Champaign, 1975. Prof. communication Univ. Ill., Urbana, Ill., 1985-96, dir. women's studies, 1993-96, jubilee prof., 1993-96; researcher Ctr. for the Study of Women in Soc./U. Oregon, Eugene, 1996—, Internat. dean Internat. Women's Univ., Hamburg, Germany, 1998-00. Author: Women and Men Speaking, 1981; editor: Technology and Women's Voices, 1988; co-editor: The Knowledge Explosion, 1992 (Choice Outstanding Academic Books award, 1994), Routledge International Encyclopedia of Women, 2001. Rsch. scholar AAUW, 1999-2000. Mem.: AAUW. E-mail: cheris@uoregon.edu.

KRAMARSKY, WERNER H., art collector; b. Amsterdam; s. Siegfried and Lola Kramarsky; m. Sarah-Ann Kramarsky; children: Stephen Mortimer, Daniel Jacob, Ann. NY State Commr. Human Rights, 1975—82. Bd. trustees Mus. Modern Art, NYC, 1998—, life trustee, 2003—, mem. drawing com., 1994—, vice chmn., 1998—, mem. com. on archives, library and rsch., 1997—; chmn. bd. Andy Warhol Found.; bd. dirs. UCLA Hammer Mus. Named one of Top 200 Collectors, ARTnews mag., 2004. Avocation: Collector modern and contemporary drawings, especially Am. Office: Andy Warhol Found 66 Bleeker St Fl 7 New York NY 10012*

KRAMER, ADAM MILES, lawyer; b. Montgomery, Ala., Sept. 18, 1972; s. Stephen James and Lauren Paula Kramer; m. Jennifer Lyn Rosenthal, Nov. 2, 2002. JD, U. Tex., 1998. Bar: Tex. 1998. Assoc. Vinson Elkins, Houston, 1998—2004. Editor: Tex. Law Review. Home: 119 Carnarvon Houston TX 77024 Office Phone: 713-758-2222. Office Fax: 713-615-5641. Business E-Mail: akramer@velaw.com.

KRAMER, ALAN SHARFSIN, lawyer; b. N.Y.C., Apr. 28, 1934; s. Michael and Alene (Sharfsin) K. BA, Dickinson Coll., 1956; LL.B., Columbia, 1962, JD, 1969. Bar: N.Y. 1962. Practice in, N.Y.C., 1962-69, 73—; sr. v.p. Am. Medicorp, Inc., N.Y.C., 1969-72; individual practice, 1974-78; pres. Alan S. Kramer (p.c.), 1978—; sr. mng. dir. Bear, Stearns & Co., Inc., 1990-96. Editor: Columbia Law Rev, 1960-62. Mem. nat. coun. Salk Inst.; mem. bd. visitors Columbia Law Sch. Served with M.I. AUS, 1956-58. Mem. Assn. of Bar of City of N.Y. Home: 315 E 86th St New York NY 10028-4714 Office: 500 Marmaroneck Ave 4th Fl Harrison NY 10528

KRAMER, ANDREA S., lawyer; b. Chgo., Mar. 15, 1955; BA summa cum laude with high distinction, U. Ill., 1975; JD cum laude, Northwestern U., 1978. Bar: Ill. 1978, U.S. Tax Ct. 1980, U.S. Ct. Fed. Claims 1982, Ill. Ct. Appeals (no. dist., 7th cir.). With Coffield, Ungaretti & Harris, Chgo.; ptnr. McDermott Will & Emery LLP, Chgo. Adj. law prof. Northwestern U. Sch. Law. Author: Financial Products: Taxation, Regulation and Design, 2000; mem. editorial bd. Jour. Criminal Law and Criminology, 1976-78; contbr. articles to profl. jours., chpts. to books. Founding mem. The Women's Treatment Ctr., Chgo., chmn. bd. dirs.; bd. dirs. Dance Art. Recipient Bronze Tablet, U. Ill., 1975, Unsung Heroine Award, Cook County Bd. Commrs., 2004. Mem. Anti-Defamation League, Internat. Bar Assn., Chgo. Bar Assn. (sect. taxation), Chgo. Fin. Exchange, Alpha Lambda Delta, Phi Alpha Theta, Phi Beta Kappa, Phi Kappa Phi. Office: McDermott Will & Emery LLP 227 W Monroe St Chicago IL 60606-5096 Office Phone: 312-984-6480. Office Fax: 312-984-7700. Business E-Mail: akramer@mwe.com.

KRAMER, ANDREW MICHAEL, lawyer; b. N.Y.C., Nov. 2, 1944; s. Irving and Ida (Kaplan) K.; m. Cheryle Lynn Safran, June 21, 1966; children: Howard, Jennifer; m. Nita Lynne Albert, Mar. 13, 1983; children: Samantha, Stephanie. BA cum laude, Mich. State U., 1966; JD cum laude, Northwestern U., 1969. Bar: Ill. 1969, D.C. 1977, U.S. Ct. Appeals (4th cir.) 1977, U.S. Ct. Appeals (5th cir.) 1972, U.S. Ct. Appeals (6th cir.) 1972, U.S. Ct. Appeals (7th cir.) 1970, U.S. Ct. Appeals (11th cir.) 1982, Ohio 1990. Assoc. firm Seyfarth, Shaw, Fairweather & Geraldson, Chgo., 1969-73, ptnr. Washington, 1974-83; ptnr. client affairs Jones Day, Washington and Cleve., 1983. Exec. dir. Ill. Office Collective Bargaining, Springfield, 1973-74. Contbr. articles to profl. jours. Mem.: ABA, D.C. Bar Assn., Chgo. Bar Assn., Pepper Pike Club (Cleve.), Firestone Country Club, Congl. Country Club (Md.). Office: Jones Day 51 Louisiana Ave NW Washington DC 20001-2113 Office Phone: 202-879-4660. Business E-Mail: akramer@jonesday.com.

KRAMER, BARNETT SHELDON, oncologist; b. Balt., July 29, 1948; s. Mervin and Muriel Hannah (Woolf) K.; m. Ruth Solomon, June 25, 1972; 1 child, Jeremy. Student, Johns Hopkins U., 1966-69, MPH, 1991; MD, U. Md., 1973. Intern Washington U., St. Louis, 1973-74, med. resident, 1974-75; fellow Nat. Cancer Inst., Bethesda, Md., 1975-78, sr. investigator, 1986-90, assoc. dir., 1990-96, dep. dir. Divsn. Cancer Prevention and Control, 1996-97, dep. dir., Divsn. Cancer Prevention, 1997-2000; asst. prof. U. Fla., Gainesville, 1978-83, assoc. prof., 1983-86; editor-in-chief Jour. Nat. Cancer Inst., Bethesda; dir. Office Med. Applications of Rsch. NIH, 2000—, assoc. dir. for disease prevention, 2001—. Prof. medicine Uniformed Svcs. U. Health Scis., Bethesda, Md., 1989-90, clin. prof. medicine, 1990—. Co-editor: (with P. Greenwald and D. Weed) Cancer Prevention and Control, 1995; (with J. Gohagan and P. Prorok) Cancer Screening Theory and Practices, 1999, (with C. Allegra) Understanding Clinical Trials, 2000; assoc. editor Jour. Nat. Cancer Inst., 1988-94, editor-in-chief, 1994—; mem. editl. bd. Physicians Data Query, 1988—, chmn. bd. cancer prevention and screening, 1992—; contbr. articles to profl. publs., chpts. to books. With USPHS, 1975-78. Fellow ACP; mem. Am. Soc. Clin. Oncologists (mem. cancer prevention com.), Am. Assn. Cancer Rsch., Alpha Omega Alpha, Delta Omega. Avocation: fountain pen collecting. Office: NIH Office Disease Prevention Rm 2B-03 6100 Executive Blvd MSC 7523 Bethesda MD 20892-2082 Business E-Mail: kramerb@od.nih.gov, bk76p@nih.gov.

KRAMER, BARRY ALAN, psychiatrist, educator; b. Phila., Sept. 9, 1948; s. Morris and Harriet (Greenberg) K.; m. Paulie Hoffman, June 9, 1974; children: Daniel Mark, Steven Philip. BA in Chemistry, NYU, 1970; MD, Hahnemann Med. Coll., 1974. Resident in psychiatry Montefiore Hosp and Med. Ctr., Bronx, N.Y., 1974-77; practice medicine specializing in psychiatry, N.Y.C., 1977-82; staff psychiatrist L.I. Jewish-Hillside Med. Ctr., Glen Oaks, N.Y., 1977-82; asst. prof. SUNY, Stony Brook, 1978-82; practice medicine specializing in psychiatry, L.A., 1982—; asst. prof. psychiatry U. So. Calif., 1982-89, assoc. prof. clin. psychiatry, 1989-94, prof. clin. psychiatry, 1994-98; ward chief Los Angeles County/U. So. Calif. Med. Ctr., 1982-98. Med. dir. ECT, Cedars Sinai Med. Ctr., 1998—; cons. Little Neck Nursing Home (N.Y.), 1979-82, L.I. Nursing Home, 1980-82; dir. ECT U. So. Calif. Sch. Medicine, 1990. Reviewer Am. Jour. Psychiatry, Hosp. and Cmty. Psychiatry; mem. editl. bd. Convulsive Therapy; contbr. articles to profl. juors., papers to sci. meetings. Grantee NIMH, 1979-80, UCLA/U. So. Calif. Long-Term Gerontology Ctr., 1985-86, NARSAD, 2001-. Fellow Am. Psychiat. Assn., Assn. Convulsive Therapy (editl. bd.); mem. AMA, Soc. Biol. Psychiatry, Calif. Med. Assn., L.A. Med. Assn., Am. Assn. Geriatric Psychiatry, Gerontol. Soc. Am., So. Calif. Psychiat. Soc. (chair ETC com.). Jewish. Office: Cedars Sinai Med Ctr Thalians 306-C 8730 Alden Dr Los Angeles CA 90048 also: PO Box 5792 Beverly Hills CA 90209-5792 Office Phone: 310-423-4014. Personal E-mail: barryakramer@yahoo.com. Business E-Mail: krameb@cshs.org.

KRAMER, BURTON, graphic designer, educator; b. N.Y.C., June 25, 1932; s. Sam and Ida (Moore) K.; m. Irene Margarite Therese Mayer, Feb. 22, 1961; children: Gabrielle Kimberly, Jeremy Jacques. BS in Graphic Design, Ill. Inst. Tech., Chgo., 1954; postgrad. (Fulbright scholar), Royal Coll. Art, London, 1955-56; M.F.A., Yale U., 1957; D (hon.), Ontario Coll. Art and Design, 2003. Registered graphic designer Ont. Designer Will Burtin, NYC, 1957-58; asst. art dir. Arch. Record, NYC, 1959; pres., creative dir. Kramer Design Assoc., Ltd., Toronto, Canada, 1967—2001; designer Geigy Chem. Corp., NYC, 1959-61; dir. corp. graphics Clairtone Sound Corp., Toronto, Canada, 1967; chief designer Halpern Advt., Zurich, Switzerland, 1961-65; instr. Ont. Coll. Art & Design, Ont., Canada, 1978—. Guest lectr. Rochester Inst. Tech., 1976, 81, designer-in-residence, 1981; vis. lectr. U. Cin., 1980; guest lectr., Arnhem, The Netherlands, 1994, Mexico City U. Autonoma, 1995; spkr. 1st Internat. Biennial of Symbols/Logotypes, Ostend, Belgium, 1994; mem. faculty Seneca Coll. Book designer The Art of Norval Morrisseau, 1979, Passionate Spirits, 1980; author Can. sect. Trademarks and Symbols of the World, 1973; co-author: Report on Canadian Road Sign Graphics, 1968; work pub. in numerous nat. and internat. jours., annuals and books; contbr. articles to profl. jours.; major works include signing-info. sys. CBC Broadcast Ctr., Toronto, IBM Tng. Ctr., Centenary Hosp., Scarborough, St. Lawrence Ctr. for Arts, Eaton Ctr., Erin Mills New Town, Mississauga, Metro Ctrl. YMCA, Copps Coliseum, Union Sta.; designer visual identity programs for CBC, N.Am. Life Assurance, Can. Imperial Bank Commerce, Reed Paper, ONEX Packaging Inc., Gemini, Vincor Internat., Can. Sys. Group, Nat. Rsch. Coun. Can., Centrestage, Royal Ont. Mus., Teknion Furniture Sys., Inc., Decoustics, Chartwell I.R.M., Scarborough Bd. Edn., Ont. Edn. Comm. Authority, Can. Crafts Coun., Ont. Guild Crafts, Zoomit Corp.; exhbn. paintings Galerie Wolfgang Exner, Vienna, 1994-95, Pekao Gallery, Toronto, 1999, Peak Gallery, 2002, Kabat Wrobel Gallery, Toronto, 2003, Found. for Constructive Art, Calgary, 2002, Gallery Carrion Vivar, Bogota, 2005, Arta Gallery, Toronto, 2005; work on website Canadian Ctr. for Contemporary Art, www.ccca.ca, 2002, investmentart.com, 2003. Bd. dirs. Arts Toronto. Decorated Order of Ont.; recipient gold medal Internat. Typographic Composition Assn., 1971, gold medal Art Dir. Club Toronto, 1973, medal Leipzig BookFair, Toronto Arts Lifetime Achievement award 1999. Fellow Soc. Graphic Designers Can. (past pres.); mem. Alliance Graphique Internat., Royal Can. Acad. Arts, Assn. Registered Graphic Designers Ont., Nat. Yacht Club. Home: 101 Roxborough St W Toronto ON Canada M5R 1T9 Office: 103 Dupont St Toronto ON Canada M5R 1V4 Office Phone: 416-921-1078 ext. 23. E-mail: burton@kramer-design.com.

KRAMER, CECILE E., retired medical librarian; b. NYC, Jan. 6, 1927; d. Marcus and Henrietta (Marks) K. BS, CCNY, 1956; MS in L.S., Columbia U., 1960. Reference asst. Columbia U. Health Scis. Library, N.Y.C., 1957-61, asst. librarian, 1961-75; dir. Health Scis. Libr. Northwestern U., Chgo., 1975-91, asst. prof. edn., 1975-91, prof. emeritus, 1991—. Instr. library and info. sci. Rosary Coll., 1981-85; cons. Francis A. Countway Library Medicine, Harvard U., 1974. Pres. Friends of Libr., Fla. Atlantic U., Boca Raton. Fellow Med. Libr. Assn. (chmn. med. sch. librs. group 1975-76, editor newsletter 1975-77, instr. continuing edn. 1966-75, mem. panel cons. editors Bull. 1987-90, disting. mem. Acad. Health Info. Profls. 1993—); mem. Biomed. Comm. Network (chmn. 1979-80). Home: 9184 Flynn Cir Apt 4 Boca Raton FL 33496-6675 E-mail: kramer@fau.edu.

KRAMER, DALE VERNON, retired language educator; b. Mitchell, SD, July 13, 1936; s. Dwight Lyman and Frances Elizabeth (Corbin) K.; m. Cheris Gamble Kramarae, Dec. 21, 1960; children: Brinlee, Jana. BS, S.D. State U., 1958; MA, Case Western Res. U., 1960, PhD, 1963. Instr. English Ohio U., Athens, 1962-63, asst. prof., 1963-65, U. Ill., Urbana, 1965-67, assoc. prof., 1967-71, prof. English, 1971-96; prof. emeritus, 1997—; acting head English dept. U. Ill., Urbana, 1982, 86-87, assoc. dean Coll. of Arts & Scis., 1992-95. Chmn. bd. editors Jour. English and Germanic Philology, 1972-95; mem. bd. editors Cambridge Edit. of the Works of Joseph Conrad, 1995—; assoc. vice provost, prof. English, U. Oreg., 1990. Author: Charles Robert Maturin, 1973, Thomas Hardy: The Forms of Tragedy, 1975, Thomas Hardy: Tess of the d'Urbervilles, 1991; editor: Critical Approaches to the Fiction of Thomas Hardy, 1979, Thomas Hardy, The Woodlanders, 1981, 85, Thomas Hardy, The Mayor of Casterbridge, 1987, Critical Essays on Thomas Hardy: The Novels, 1990, The Cambridge Companion to Thomas Hardy, 1999. Served to capt. U.S. Army, 1958-66. Mem. Ctr. for Advanced Study, 1971; Am. Philos. Soc. grantee, 1969, 86, NEH grantee, 1986. Congregationalist.

KRAMER, EDWARD E., screenwriter, editor; b. Bklyn., Mar. 2, 1961; s. Leon A. and Helen M. Kramer. BS in Psychology, Emory U., Atlanta, 1983; MPH in Health Adminstrn. Planning, Emory U., 1994. Cert. addiction counselor - Level II 1987, nat. cert. addiction counselor Level II 1992. Program coord. Met. Atlanta Coun. on Alcohol and Drugs, Atlanta, 1985—87; tech. dir. Met. Regional Ednl. Svc. Agy., 1991—2001; pres. Ed Kramer & Assocs., Inc., Atlanta, 1998—, Psychiatric Healthcare Cons., Atlanta, 1987—98; dir. rsch. Talbott Recovery System, Atlanta, 1988—90; pub. Ora Press, Atlanta, 2003—. Pres. Dragon Con, Inc., Atlanta, 1986—2000; pub. Ora Press, Atlanta, 2003—. Editor: (anthology) Free Space, 1987 (Special Promethius award, 1998), The Sandman: Book of Dreams, 1996, Dark Love, 1996 (Deathrealm award, 1997), The Crow: Shattered Lives and Broken Dreams, 1998, Strange Attraction: Turns of the Midnight Carnival Wheel, 2000. Bd. dirs. Mayor's Taskforce on Domestic Violence, Atlanta, 1983—85; disaster action team mem. ARC, Decatur, Ga., 1982—88, CPR / multi-mediafFirst aid instr. Atlanta, 1980—87; foster care rev. panel co-chmn. Coun. of Juvenile Ct. Judges, Decatur, 1991—98. Fellow Melvin Jones fellow for humanitarian svc., Lions Club Internat. Found., 2000. Mem.: Sci. iction and Fantasy Writers Assn., Horror Writers Assn. (v.p. bd. trustees 1998—2001). Jewish. Avocation: Photography, Travel, Caving. Home: 2480 Honeycomb Way Duluth GA 30096 Personal E-mail: edkramer@edkramer.com.

KRAMER, EDWARD JOHN, materials engineering educator; b. Wilmington, Del., Aug. 5, 1939; s. Edward Noble and Irma (Nemetz) K.; m. Gail Allen Woodford, Aug. 24, 1963; children: Eric Woodford, Jeanne Noble. BChemE, Cornell U., 1962; PhD, Carnegie-Mellon U., 1967. Asst. prof. dept. materials sci. and engring. Cornell U., Ithaca, N.Y., 1967-72, assoc. prof., 1972-79, prof., 1979-88, Samuel B. Eckert prof. materials sci. and engring., 1988-97; prof. dept. materials & chem. engring. U. Calif., Santa Barbara, 1997—. Vis. scientist Argonne (Ill.) Nat. Lab., 1974-75; vis. prof. Akademie der Wissenschaften Inst. Metallphysik, Göttingen, Germany, 1979, Ecole Poly. Federale de Lausanne, Switzerland, 1982, Johannes Gutenberg U., Mainz, Germany, 1987-88. Contbr. over 300 articles to sci. jours. Recipient U.S. Sr. Scientist award Alexander von Humboldt Stiftung, 1987-88, Swinburne award Inst. Materials, U.K., 1996; NATO fellow, 1966-67, John Simon Guggenheim Found. fellow, N.Y.C., 1988. Fellow AAAS, Am. Phys. Soc. (High Polymer Physics prize 1985); mem. NAE, Materials Rsch. Soc., Am. Chem. Soc., Böhmische Phys. Soc. Avocation: masters swimming. Office: Univ Calif Materials Dept Engring II Santa Barbara CA 93106 Office Phone: 805-894-4999. Business E-Mail: edkramer@mrl.ucsb.edu.

KRAMER, ELEANOR, retired real estate broker, tax specialist, financial consultant; b. NYC, Feb. 18, 1939; d. Herman I. Kramer and Fay (Berger) Kramer-Levy; m. Richard H. Fitz-Gerald III, Dec. 24, 1959 (div.); m. Gregory F. Navarro, Oct. 1, 1975 (div. Mar. 1996); children: Brad, Cindy. BA in Speech and Theater, Bklyn Coll., 1975; MS in Urban Affairs, CUNY, Hunter Coll., 1976. Tchr. cultural arts Bronx (N.Y.) Bd. Edn., 1966-70; real estate broker, pres. Tritown Realty Corp., Mamaroneck, N.Y., 1978-83; pvt. practice tax cons. Mamaroneck, 1983—. Adj. prof. sociology Rockland Community Coll., Suffern, N.Y., 1979-85, Westchester Community Coll., Valhalla, N.Y., 1979-85; founder dance therapy St. Vincent's Hosp., N.Y.C.; lectr., demonstrator N.Y.C. Pub. Schs., author, producer, performer, co-creator child edn. programs, 1967-77. Mem. pub. relations com. Bicentennial commn. Village of Mamaroneck, 1976; bd. dirs. Community Action Program, Mamaroneck, 1977-79. Mem.: LWV (bd. dirs. 1977—80), NOW (ad hoc chmn. 1970, co-chair, co-author women's ednl. seminar Libr. of Congress), Nat. Soc. Tax Preparers, Lions (Larchmont, NY). Avocations: puzzles, tennis, antiques, jazz, theater. Office: PO Box 172 Bronx NY 10464-0172

KRAMER, EUGENE LEO, lawyer; b. Barberton, Ohio, Nov. 7, 1939; s. Frank L. and Portia I. (Acker) Kramer; m. JoAnn Stockhausen, Sept. 19, 1970; children: Martin, Caroline, Michael. AB, John Carroll U., 1961; JD, U. Notre Dame, 1964. Bar: Ohio 1964. Law clk. U.S. Ct. Appeals (7th cir.), Chgo., 1964-65; ptnr. Squire, Sanders & Dempsey, Cleve., 1965-91, Roetzel & Andress, A Legal Profl. Assn., Cleve. and Akron, Ohio, 1992-97; spl. counsel Ohio Atty. Gen., 2003. Cons. Ohio Constl. Revision Commn., Columbus, 1970—74. Trustee Regina Health Ctr., 1997—, pres., 2001—04; past pres. HELP Found., Inc., HELP, Inc., Cleve., 1981—92, Playhouse Sq. Assn., Cleve., 1980—84; pres. N.E. Ohio Transit Coalition, 1992—; mem. policy com. Build-Up Greater Cleve. Program, 1982—98; mem. Greater Cleve. Growth Assn.; trustee Consultation Ctr. Diocese Cleve., 1990—96, Citizens League Greater Cleve., 1984—90, 1993—, Citizens League Rsch. Inst., 1995—97, St. Ann Found., 1990—92, Lyric Opera Cleve., 1995—. Recipient Disting. Leadership award, HELP, Inc., 1986, Pioneer Achievement award, HELP-Six Chimneys, Inc., 1986, Disting. Svc. award, Assn. Retarded Citizens, 1990, Vol. Svc. award, City of Lakewood, 2001. Mem.: ABA, Cleve. Bar Assn., Ohio State Bar Assn. (chmn. local govt. law com. 1986—90), Club Key Tower. Democrat. Roman Catholic. Avocations: music, theater, sports, travel. Home and Office: 1422 Euclid Ave Ste 1162 Cleveland OH 44115-2001 Office Phone: 216-621-7974. Personal E-mail: elkramer5@aol.com.

KRAMER, GEORGE P., lawyer; b. Holyoke, Mass., Feb. 22, 1927; m. Elizabeth M. Truax, Oct. 13, 1973; children: Alice S. Truax, R. Hawley Truax, Charles W. Truax. AB, Harvard U., 1950, LL.B., 1953; Cert., Sorbonne, 1948. Bar: N.Y. 1954. Assoc. Watson Leavenworth Kelton & Taggart, N.Y.C., 1953-59, partner, 1960-65, Conboy, Hewitt, O'Brien & Boardman, N.Y.C., 1965-86, Hunton & Williams (merger Conboy, Hewitt, O'Brien & Boardman), N.Y.C., 1986—. Lectr. Practising Law Inst.; bd. dirs. Burleson Corp.; mem. vis. com. Peabody Mus. of Harvard U., 1974-80; mem. N.Y. Cotton Exch., N.Y. Bd. Trade. Author: Misleading Trademarks and Consumer Protection. Trustee Hancock Shaker Village, 1982—; trustee Harvard U. Law Sch. Assn. of N.Y., 1985-87, v.p. 1987-89. Served to lt. USNR, 1945-46. Recipient Congl. Antarctic medal, 1977 Mem. ABA, Internat. Bar Assn., Assn. Bar City N.Y. (sec. 1963-65, exec. com. 1970-74, chmn. various coms.), Am. Law Inst., Internat. Trademark Assn. (dir. 1975-78), Assn. Internationale pour la Protection de la Propriete Industrielle, Harvard U. Alumni Assn. (bd. dirs. 1983-89), Mass. Speleological Soc. (pres.), Antarctican Soc., Am. Polar Soc., Century Assn., Harvard Club (sec. 1972-83, 88-90, bd. mgrs. 1983-86), Harvard Faculty Club. Home: 151 E 79th St New York NY 10021-0417 Office: Hunton & Williams 200 Park Ave Fl 43 New York NY 10166-0005 Office Phone: 212-309-1010. Business E-Mail: gkramer@Hunton.com.

KRAMER, GORDON, mechanical engineer; b. Bklyn., Aug. 1937; s. Joseph and Etta (Grossberg) K.; m. Ruth Ellen Harter, Mar. 5, 1967 (div. June 1986); children: Samuel Maurice, Leah Marie; m. Eve Burstein, Dec. 17, 1988. BS, Cooper Union, 1959; MS, Calif. Inst. Tech., 1960. With Hughes Aircraft Co., Malibu, Calif., 1959-63; sr. scientist Avco Corp., Norman, Okla., 1963-64; asst. divsn. head Batelle Meml. Inst., Columbus, Ohio, 1964-67; sr. scientist Aerojet Electrosystems, Azusa, Calif., 1967-75; chief engr. Beckman Instrument Co., Fullerton, Calif., 1975-82; prin. scientist McDonnell Douglas Microelectronics Co., 1982-83, Kramer and Assocs., 1983-85; program mgr. Hughes Aircraft Co., 1985-96, ret., 1996; personal fin. advisor Ameriprise Fin., 1999—. Cons. Korea Inst. Tech. NSF fellow, 1959-60. Mem. IEEE. Democrat. Jewish. Home: 153 Lake Shore Dr Rancho Mirage CA 92270-4055 Office Phone: 760-340-3903. Personal E-mail: gordeve@aol.com. Business E-Mail: gordon.x.kramer@ampf.com.

KRAMER, HARRY, artist; b. Phila., Mar. 20, 1939; s. Samuel and Clayre (Sumerson) K.; m. Gertrude Murry Cader, Apr. 26, 1969. BFA in Painting, Phila. Coll. Art, 1962; MFA in Painting, Yale U., 1965. Prof. Queens Coll., Flushing, N.Y., 1970-2000; instr. N.Y. Studio Sch., 1968-73, NYU, 1968-69. One-man shows: Brata Gallery, N.Y.C., 1972, 55 Mercer Gallery, N.Y.C., 1973, 74, 76, 81, Forum Gallery, Md., 1977, Ted Greenwald Gallery, N.Y.C., 1983, Gruenebaum Gallery, N.Y.C., 1985, 87, Charles Cowles Gallery, N.Y.C., 1991, 94, 98, 2003, Bill Bace Gallery, 1993, Ameringer and Yohe, 2003; group exhbns. Hudson River Mus., Yonkers, N.Y., 1983, NY Studio Sch., 1985, NAD, 1994, 95, 96, 2001, US Embassy, Vienna, 2002, Ameringer and Yohe Fine Art, NYC, 2002, 03; private collections, Bklyn. Mus. Art, Corcoran Gallery, Met. Mus. Art, NAD, Ketcham and McDougal Found., NJ, Detroit Inst. of Art, Chase Manhattan Bank. Fellow N.Y. State Coun. on Arts, 1973, 77, NEA, 1982. Mem.: NAD (academician 1994—). Avocations: fishing, boating. Mailing: Ameringer and Yohe 20 West 57th St New York NY 10019

KRAMER, ILSE ELISABETH, rare book dealer; b. Duesseldorf, Germany, Feb. 16, 1936; d. Georg Friedrich Karl Kramer and Hilde Adele Emmi Schlieper. MLS, U. Cologne, 1959. Libr. dept. German U. Bonn, Germany, 1959—62; rare book bibliographer John Carter Brown Libr., Brown U., Providence, 1962—91. Translator John Carter Brown Libr., 1962—91; cons. M&S Rare Books and Press, Inc., Providence, 1995—. Author: Die Wunderbare Neue Welt, 1988, Pimpinella, 1996. Archivist Cen. Congrl. Ch., Providence, 1989—. Mem. German-Am. Friends Niederrhein, R.I. Libr. Assn., Writers Clan. Avocations: writing, poetry. Home: 248 Waterman St Providence RI 02906-5203 Office: Cen Congrl Ch 296 Angell St Providence RI 02906 Personal E-mail: ilsekramer@aol.com.

KRAMER, JOHN PAUL, entomologist, educator; b. Elgin, Ill., Mar. 13, 1928; s. Rutherford Hayes and Anna Maria (Burita) K.; m. Jean Kent Simpson, June, 1957 (div. 1973); children: Philip Simpson, Katherine Jean. BS, Beloit (Wis.) Coll., 1950; MS, U. Mo., 1952; PhD, U. Ill., 1958. Asst. prof. entomology N.C. State U., 1958-59; asso. entomologist Ill. Natural History Survey, Urbana, 1959-65; with Cornell U., 1965-90, prof. insect pathology dept. entomology, 1975-90, prof. emeritus, 1990—. WHO traveling cons., 1962, NSF vis. scientist, Japan, 1967; mem. study sect. for tropical medicine and parasitology NIH, 1966-68; vis. scientist Inst. Arctic Biology in Alaska, 1972; vis. prof. entomology Ohio State U., Columbus, 1984; collaborator in parasitology Oswaldo Cruz Inst., Brazil, 1999-2001. Contbr. articles to profl. jours. Served to 1st lt. U.S. Army, 1952-54, Korea. Decorated Bronze Star; recipient Korean Svc. medal with 2 battle stars; NSF fellow, 1967; NIH rsc. grantee, 1959-72; Office of Naval Rsch. grantee, 1971-74; WHO rsch. grantee, 1979-82; USDA rsch. grantee, 1980-90. Mem. Soc. Invertebrate Pathology, N.Y. Entomol. Soc., Am. English Spot Rabbit Club, Am. Cavy Breeders Assn., Am. Rabbit Breeders Assn., N.Y. State Rabbit Breeders Assn. (pres. 1989-90), Taughannock Area Rabbit Breeders Assn. (pres. 1983-84, 91-96), Am. Netherland Dwarf Rabbit Breeders Assn., N.Y. State Cavy Fanciers Club (v.p. 1973-75). Unitarian-Universalist. Home: 115 Hanshaw Rd Ithaca NY 14850-2207 Office: Cornell Univ Dept Entomology 3142 Comstock Hall Ithaca NY 14853-2601

KRAMER, KENNETH BENTLEY, retired federal judge, former congressman; b. Chgo., Feb. 19, 1942; s. Albert Aaron and Ruth (Pokrass) K.; m. Louise Kotoshirodo; children: Kenneth Bentley, Kelly J. BA magna cum laude in Polit. Sci., U. Ill., 1963; JD, Harvard U., 1966. Bar: Ill. 1966, Colo. 1969. Dep. dist. atty. El Paso County, Colo., Colorado Springs, 1970-72; pvt. practice law Colorado Springs, 1972-78; mem. Colo. Ho. of Reps., 1973-78, 96th-99th Congresses from 5th Colo. Dist., 1978-86; asst. sec. Dept. Army, Washington, 1988-89; judge U.S. Ct. of Appeals for Vets. Claims, Washington, 1989-2000, chief judge, 2000—04. Chmn. com. on vets. benefits ABA, 1990-94. Bd. visitors U.S. Air Force Acad., 1979-86; bd. dirs. Pikes Peak

Mental Health Ctr., 1976-78, Mountain Valley chpt. March of Dimes, 1983-85, U.S. Space Found., 1983—; founder U.S. Space Found.; commr. Nat. Coun. on Uniform State Laws, 1977-78. Capt. U.S. Army, 1967-70. Recipient Disting. Civilian Svc. medal. Mem. Phi Beta Kappa.

KRAMER, LARRY, playwright, writer; b. Bridgeport, Conn., June 25, 1935; s. George L. and Rea (Wishengrad) K. BA, Yale U., 1957. Asst. story editor Columbia Pictures Corp., N.Y.C., 1960-61, prodn. exec. London, 1961-65; asst. to pres. United Artists, N.Y.C., 1965-66. Author: Faggots, 1978, Reports from the Holocaust: The Making of an AIDS Activist, 1989, The Tragedy of Today's Gays, 2005; playwright: The Normal Heart, 1985 (Marton award Dramatists Guild 1986, City Lights award 1986, Sarah Siddons award 1986, Olivier award nomination best play 1986), Just Say No, 1988, The Furniture of Home, 1989, The Destiny of Me, 1993; assoc. prodr.: (films) Here We Go Round the Mulberry Bush, 1967; screenwriter, prodr.: (films) Women in Love, 1970 (Academy award nomination best adapted screenplay 1970). Co-founder Gay Men's Health Crisis, Inc., N.Y.C., 1981; founder ACT UP (AIDS Coalition to Unleash Power), N.Y.C., 1988. Recipient Arts and Communication award Human Rights Campaign Fund, 1987; named Man of Yr. Aid for AIDS, Los Angeles, 1986.*

KRAMER, LARRY, dean, law educator, lawyer; b. Chgo., June 23, 1958; m. Sarah Delson, 1996; 1 child, Veronika. BA magna cum laude, Brown U., 1980; JD cum laude, U. Chgo., 1984. Clerk to Judge Henry J. Friendly U.S. Ct. Appeals for the Second Cir., 1984—85; to Justice William J. Brennan, Jr. U.S. Supreme Ct., 1985—86; asst. prof. U. Chgo., 1986—90, prof., 1990—91; vis. prof. U. Mich., 1990—91, prof., 1991—94; vis. prof., Golieb Fellow NYU, 1993—94, Russell D. Niles Prof. Law, 2001—04, assoc. dean Rsch. and Academics, 2002—04; dean, Richard E. Lang Prof. Law Stanford Law Sch., 2004—. Reporter Fed. Cts. Study Com., 1989—90; cons. Mayer, Brown, Rowe & Maw, New York, NY, 1991—2004; assoc. dir., instr. Inst. Judicial Adminstrn., NYU, 1994—98; dir. English-Lang. Studies The Hague Acad. Internat. Law, 1994. Co-author: Conflict of Laws: Cases-Comments-Questions, 1993, 2001; editor: Reforming the Civil Justice System, 1996; author: The People Themselves: Popular Constitutionalism and Judicial Review, 2004. Mem.: ABA, Chgo. Coun. Lawyers (bd. govs. 1989—91), Brennan Ctr. for Jusice (bd. mem. 1995—2004), Am. Assn. Law Schs. (chair Conflict Laws Sec. 1992—93, chair Fed. Cts. Sec. 1996—97), Judicature Soc., NY Bar Assn., Am. Law Inst. Office: Stanford U Sch Law Crown Quadrangle 559 Nathan Abbott Way Stanford CA 94305-4985 Office Phone: 650-723-4985. E-mail: deans.office@law.stanford.edu.*

KRAMER, LAWRENCE STEPHEN, journalist; b. Hackensack, NJ, Apr. 24, 1950; s. Abraham and Ann Eve (Glasser) K.; m. Myla F. Lerner, Sept. 3, 1978; children: Matthew Lerner, Erika. BS in Journalism, Syracuse U., 1972; MBA, Harvard U., 1974. Reporter San Francisco Examiner, 1974-77, exec. editor, 1986-91; reporter Wash. Post, 1977-80, asst. to exec. editor, 1982, asst. mng. editor, 1982-86; exec. editor Trenton Times, NJ, 1980-82; founder, pres., exec. editor DataSport Inc. (acquired by Data Broadcasting Corp.), San Mateo, Calif., 1991-94; v.p. news, sports, mktg. Data Broadcasting Corp., San Mateo, 1994-97; founder, pres., CEO CBS.Marketwatch.com., San Francisco, 1997—2005, pres. digital media, 2005—. Guest lectr. Harvard Bus. Sch.; mem. Pulitzer Prize Jury, 1987—88; founding bd. mem. Online Pub. Assn., 2001. Recipient W.R. Hearst Found. award 1971-72, Gerald Loeb award 1977, Nat. Press Club award; named one of 100 Most Influential Bus. Journalists 20th Century, 2000 Mem. Soc. Profl. Journalists Achievements include created SporTrax; created DBC News, predecessor co. to Market-Watch.com. Home: 8 Auburn Ct Belvedere Tiburon CA 94920-1349

KRAMER, LINDA KONHEIM, curator, art historian; b. N.Y.C., Nov. 8, 1939; d. Clarence John and May (Sternberg) Konheim; m. Samuel R. Kramer, Apr. 24, 1977; 1 child, Nicholas Clarence. BA in Fine Arts and Art History, Smith Coll., 1961; BFA in Painting and Graphic Design, Yale U., 1963; MA in 19th and 20th Century European and Am. Art, NYU, 1968, PhD, 2000. Program adminstr. Solomon R. Guggenheim Mus., 1966—76; cataloger modern drawings Sotheby Park-Bernet, N.Y.C., 1980-82; expert in modern drawings Sotheby's N.Y., 1982-85; curator prints and drawings, dept. head Bklyn. Mus., 1985-94. Tchr. Sch. Visual Arts, N.Y.C., 1977-80, Manhattanville Coll., summer 1995, 96; exec. dir. Nancy Graves Found., N.Y.C., 1996—; mem. adv. bd. Coll. Fine Arts, West Wash. U., Bellingham, 1987-95. Author: books, pamphlets and catalogs; contbr. articles to profl. jours. Grantee Nat. Mus. Act, 1976, 78; Jane and Morgan Whitney fellow Met. Mus. Art, 1995-96. Mem. Am. Assn. Mus., Print Coun. Am., Art Table, Coll. Art Assn. Home: 372 Central Park W New York NY 10025-8240 Office: Nancy Graves Found 450 W 31st St 2d Fl New York NY 10001-4608 Office Phone: 212-560-0602. Business E-Mail: mail@nancygravesfoundation.org.

KRAMER, MARC Z., publishing executive; Grad., SUNY, Albany, N.Y. Law Sch. Lawyer labor dept. N.Y.C. Bd. Edn.; dep. gen. counsel, gen. counsel Mayor's Office Labor Rels., 1985—90; labor assoc. Proskauer Rose Goetz & Mendelsohn, NY, 1990—93; v.p., gen. counsel N.Y. Daily News, 1993—98; v.p. labor rels. N.Y. Times, N.Y.C., 1998—99, prodn. supr., 1999—2001, sr. v.p., 2001—04, sr. v.p. circulation, 2004—. Office: NY Times 229 W 43rd St New York NY 10036-3959

KRAMER, MARY ELIZABETH, state legislator, health services executive; b. Burlington, Iowa, June 14, 1935; d. Ross L. and Geneva M. (McElhinney) Barnett; m. Kay Frederick Kramer, June 13, 1958; children: Kent, Krista. BA, U. Iowa, 1957, MA, 1971. Cert. tchr., Iowa. Tchr. Newton (Iowa) Pub. Schs., 1957-61, Iowa City Pub. Schs., 1961-67, tchr., asst. supt., 1971-75; dir. pers. Younkers, Inc., Des Moines, 1975-81; v.p. Wellmark, Inc., Des Moines, 1981-99; mem. Iowa Senate from 37th dist., Des Moines, 1990—2004; pres. of the senate, 1997—2004; U.S. amb. to Island of Ea. Caribbean, 2004—. Mem. Olympic adv. com. Blue Cross and Blue Shield Assn., Chgo., 1988—92; presdl. appointee White House Commn. on Presdl. Scholars, 2001, now chmn.; Bd. dirs. Polk County Child Care Rsch. Ctr., Des Moines, 1986—96, YWCA, Des Moines, 1989—94. Named Mgr. of Yr. Iowa Mgmt. Assocs., 1985, Woman of Achievement YWCA, 1986, Woman of Vision Young Women's Resource Ctr., 1989. Mem. Soc. Human Resource Mgmt. (Profl. of Yr. 1996), Iowa Mgmt. Assn. (pres. 1988), Greater Des Moines C. of C. (bd. dirs. 1986-96), Nexus, Rotary Internat. Republican. Presbyterian. Avocations: music, public speaking. Office: Iowa State Senate State Capitol Des Moines IA 50319-0001 also: Am Embassy Bridgetown CMR 1014-Exec Fpo AA 34055 Office Phone: 246-436-4950. E-mail: mkramer@legis.state.ia.us, kaynmary@aol.com.

KRAMER, MICHAEL STUART, pediatric epidemiologist; b. N.Y.C., July 8, 1948; arrived in Can., 1978; s. George and Beatrice (Jacobs) K.; m. Claire Yael Sasportas, June 14, 1981; children: Eric, Elise, Philippe. BA, U. Chgo., 1969; MD, Yale U., 1973. Diplomate Am. Bd. Pediatrics, Am. Coll. Epidemiology. Intern in pediat. Yale New Haven (Conn.) Hosp., 1973-74, resident in pediat., 1974-76; fellow clin. epidemiology Yale U., 1976-78; asst. prof. faculty medicine McGill U., Montreal, Que., Can., 1978-82, assoc. prof., 1982-87, prof., 1987—. Com. mem. U.S. Inst. Medicine/NAS, Washington, 1986—; vis. scientist Nat. Perinatal Epidemiology Unit, Oxford, England, 1991—92; cons. WHO, Geneva, 1984—, Nat. Health Rsch. Scientist, Nat. Health R&D Program Can., 1992—97; disting. scientist Can. Inst. Health Rsch., 1997—2002, sr. investigator, 2002—, sci. dir. Inst. Human Devel. and Child and Youth Health, 2003—. Author: Clinical Epidemiology and Biostatistics, 1988, Nutrition During Pregnancy, 1990, Adverse Events Associated With Childhood Vaccines, 1994, Improving Birth Outcomes, 2003, Reducing Birth Defects, 2003. Violinist:New Haven Symphony, 1969-73, I Medici di McGill, Montreal, 1990-94. Nat. Health Rsch. scholar, 1982-88; recipient Prix d'excellence Insvc. Clubs Coun. Que., Montreal, 1987, Chercheur Boursier Sr. FRSQ, Que., 1988-91, Rsch. award Ambulatory Pediatric Assn., 1993. Mem. Soc. Pediatric Rsch. (coun. mem. 1986-89), Soc. Epidemiol. Rsch., Soc. Pediatric and Perinatal Epidemiol. Rsch. (pres. 1997-98). Avocations: chamber music (violin), skiing, hiking, tennis, squash. Office: McGill U 2300 Tupper St Montreal PQ Canada H3H 1P3 Business E-Mail: Michael.Kramer@mcgill.ca.

KRAMER, MICHAEL W., communications educator; s. Howard W. and Valerie E. Kramer; m. Carla J. Aufdemberge, Nov. 27, 1954; children: Jason M., Sarah M. AA, Concordia Jr. Coll., Ann Arbor, Mich., 1974; BA, Concordia Coll., Seward, Nebr., 1976; MA, Northeastern Ill. U., Chgo., 1982; PhD, U. of Tex., 1991. Tchr. Martin Luther H.S., Maspeth, NY, Luther H.S. South, Chgo., 1978—84; prof. Concordia Coll., Austin, Tex., 1984—91, U. of Mo., Columbia, 1991—. Author (rschr.): (scholarly book) Managing Uncertainty in Organizational Communication; contbr. articles to profl. jours. Pres. Alive in Christ Luth. Ch., Columbia, Mo., 1999—2000, Nazareth Luth. Ch., Chgo., 1983—84. Recipient Charles Redding Dissertation award, Internat. Comm. Assn., 1993, Top Rsch. Papers award, Nat. Comm. Assn., 1992, 1994, 1996—97, 2001, 2003. Mem.: Acad. of Mgmt. (assoc.), Internat. Comm. Assn. (assoc.), Nat. Comm. Assn. (assoc.; awards chair 1998—2000). Office: University of Missouri 115 Switzler Hall Columbia MO 65211 Office Phone: 573-882-6980. Business E-Mail: kramerm@missouri.edu.

KRAMER, NOËL ANKETELL, judge; b. Bay City, Mich., Nov. 22, 1945; d. Thomas Jackson and Ruth Genevieve (LeRoux) Anketell; m. Franklin D. Kramer, May 30, 1970; children: Katherine, Christopher. BA with honors, Vassar Coll., 1967; JD with honors, U. Mich., 1971. Bar: D.C. 1972, U.S. Supreme Ct. 1975. Assoc. Wilmer, Cutler & Pickering, Washington, 1971-76; asst. U.S. atty. D.C. US Dept. State, Washington, 1976-84; judge D.C. Superior Ct., Washington, 1984—2005; assoc. judge D.C. Ct. Appeals, Washington, 2005—. Mem. ABA., Nat. Assn. Women Judges, Women's Bar Assn. D.C., D.C. Bar (chair person cts., lawyers and adminstrn. justice div. 1982-84), U. Mich. Law Club Washington (pres. 1976-78). Office: DC Ct Appeals 500 Indiana Ave NW Rm 6000 Washington DC 20001-2131*

KRAMER, ORIN STUART, investment services company executive; b. Maplewood, N.J., June 27, 1945; s. Julian Saul and Ruth (Tantleff) K.; m. Hilary Meg Ballon, Jan. 7, 1989; children: Sophia, Charles. BA, Yale U., 1967; JD, Columbia U., 1970. Atty. Simpton, Thacher & Bartlett, N.Y.C., 1970-71; exec. dir. N.Y. State Commn. on Economy, N.Y.C., 1973-74; assoc. dir. White House Domestic Policy Staff, Washington, 1977-81; cons. McKinsey & Co., N.Y.C., 1981-83, Kramer Assoc., N.Y.C., 1984—; gen. ptnr. Boston Provident Partners, 1992; gen ptnr. Kramer Spellman LP, Fort Lee, NJ, 1995—. Vice chair, exec. dir. N.Y. State Commn. on Liability Ins. and Tort Reform, N.Y.C., 1986, Calif. Workers Compensation Ratemaking Commn., Sacramento, 1986. Author: Rating the Risks, 1990, Rate Suppression and its Consequences, 1991. Home: 261 Glenwood Rd Englewood NJ 07631-1910

KRAMER, PAUL R., lawyer; b. Balt., June 6, 1936; s. Philip and Lee (Labovitz) K.; m. Janet Amitin, Sept. 1, 1957; children: Jayne, Susan, Nancy. BA, Am. U., 1959, JD, 1961. Bar: Md. 1961, D.C. 1962, U.S. Supreme Ct. 1965, U.S. Ct. Appeals (6th cir.) 1962, U.S. Dist. Ct. 1963, U.S. Ct. Appeals (4th cir.) 1964, U.S. Ct. Appeals (9th cir.) 1996. Staff atty., dep. dir. Legal Aid Agy. Fed. Pub. Defender's Office, Washington, 1962-63; asst. U.S. atty. Dist. Md., 1963-69; dep. U.S. atty. Md. Balt., 1969-83; exec. bd. Balt. area coun. Boy Scouts Am., 1970-83, coun. adv. bd. Balt. area, 1983—, N.E. regional adv. bd., 1999—. Mem.-at-large Boy Scouts of Am. Nat., 1992—; instr. U. Md. Sch. Law, 1975-80; assoc. prof. law Villa Julie Coll., 1976-80; assoc. professorial lectr. George Washington U., 1979; instr. Nat. Coll. Dist. Attys., 1979; permanent mem. 4th cir. fed. jud. conf. Mem. ABA, Fed. Bar Assn. (pres. Md. chpt. 1973-74, nat. dep. sec. 1981-82, nat. sec. 1982-83, nat. cir. v.p. 1973-81, 86-87, cir. officer 4th cir. 1992-93, v.p. 4th cir. 1996-02, chmn. nat. cir. v.p. 1978-80, nat. coun. 1973—, jud. selection com. 1971-79, 88-90, faculty Fed Practice Inst. 1981-86, strategic long range planning com. 1995-96, found. charter life fellow 2002—), Md. Bar Assn. (subcom. litig. dist. ct. 1990—, found. fellow 1996—, bd. govs. 2005—), Balt. Bar Assn. (criminal law com., dist. ct. com. 1990—, jud. selection com. 1992—, chair judiciary sub-com. on policy 1993-94, atty. grievance commn. of Md., inquiry com. Balt. City, 1993—, chair criminal law com., drug ct. com. 1994-95), Balt. County Bar Assn., Nat. Assn. Criminal Trial Attys., Md. Trial Lawyers Assn., Md. Criminal Def. Attys. Assn., U.S. Atty. Alumni Assn. (bd. dirs. 2003—), Barrister's Law Club (pres. 2003) Masons (past master). Office Phone: 410-727-5531, 800-794-8095.

KRAMER, PETER DAVID, psychiatrist, psychology professor; b. N.Y.C., Oct. 22, 1948; s. Eric M. and Lore E. Kramer; m. Rachel M. Schwartz, June 29, 1980; children: Sarah Elizabeth, Jacob Aaron, Matthew Charles. AB, Harvard Coll., 1970; postgrad., Univ. Coll., London, 1970-72; MD, Harvard Med. Sch., 1976. Diplomate Am. Bd. Psychiatry & Neurology, Am. Bd. Adolescent Psychiatry. Resident in internal medicine U. Wis. Hospitals, Madison, 1976-77; resident in psychiatry Yale U., New Haven, 1977-80; acting dir. divsn. sci. Alcohol, Drug Abuse, Mental Health Adminstrn., Rockville, Md., 1980-82; outpatient dir. R.I. Hosp., Providence, 1982-84; asst. prof. dept. psychiatry Brown U., Providence, 1982-91, assoc. prof., 1991-95, prof., 1995—; asst. prof. psychiatry George Washington U., 1981-82. Author: Moments of Engagement, 1989, Listening to Prozac, 1993, Should You Leave?, 1997, Spectacular Happiness, 2001, Against Depression, 2005; mem. editl. bd. Psychiat. Times, 1985—, The Psychodynamic Letter, 1990-92, Am. Jour. Psychotherapy, 1996—; contbr. articles to profl. jours. Mem. Am. Psychiat. Assn. (pvt. practice com. 1988-94, chmn. 1992-94), R.I. Med. Soc., R.I. Psychiat. Soc. (pres. 1990-91). Office: 196 Waterman St Providence RI 02906-2212

KRAMER, PETER ROBIN, computer company executive; b. N.Y.C., Sept. 29, 1951; s. Morris and Ruth (Soloway) K.; m. Gerry Festo, Aug. 25, 1985. BA in Fine Arts, SUNY, Stony Brook, 1973; MFA, L.I. U., 1975. Dir., gen. ptnr. Doll & Richards Gallery, Boston, 1979-81; exec. v.p. and dir. Zoom Telephonics, Inc., Boston, 1977—. Bd. dirs. Intermute, Inc. Bd. dirs. Cambridge Art Assn., 1983-86, pres. 1986-88; mem. nat. adv. bd. Coll. Arts and Scis. SUNY, Stony Brook, 1999-; dir. Intermute, Inc., 2000-. Avocations: old houses, fine arts, antiques, tennis, golf.

KRAMER, RICHARD JAY, gastroenterologist, educator; b. Morristown, N.J., Mar. 31, 1947; s. Bernard and Estelle (Mishkin) K.; m. Leslie Fay Davis, June 28, 1970; children: Bryan Jeffrey, Erik Seth Davis. Student, UCLA, 1965-68; MD, U. Calif., Irvine, 1972. Diplomate Am. Bd. Internat. Med., Am. Bd. Gastroenterology. Intern Los Angeles County Harbor Gen. Hosp., Torrance, Calif., 1972-73; resident Santa Clara Valley Med. Ctr., San Jose, Calif., 1973-76; fellow gastroent. Stanford (Calif.) U. Hosp., 1976-78; pvt. practice San Jose, 1978—2003; tchr. gastroenterology Santa Clara Valley Med. Ctr., San Jose, 2003—. Clin. assoc. prof. of medicine Stanford (Calif.) U., 1984—; chmn. med. dept. Good Samaritan Hosp., San Jose, 1988-90. Pres. Jewish Family Service Bd., San Jose, 1974. Recipient Regents scholarship U. Calif., 1965, 68, Mosby Book award, Mosby Books, Inc., Irvine, Calif., 1972. Mem. Am. Coll. Physicians, Calif. Med. Soc., Santa Clara County Med. Soc., No. Calif. Soc. Clin. Gastroenterologists, Internat. Brotherhood Magicians, Mystic 13 (pres. 1986-87, San Jose), Masons, Alpha Omega Alpha. Jewish. Avocations: magic, travel.

KRAMER, ROBERT ALLEN, elementary school educator; b. Waukesah, Wis., June 6, 1958; s. Reuben Albert and Eunice Mae Kramer; m. Crystal Dawn Roemhildt, July 13, 1980; children: Joshua Reuben, Samuel Timothy, Joanna Beth. BS in Edn., Dr. Martin Luther Coll., New Ulm, Minn., 1980; MS in Music, So. Oreg. U., 2004. Music tchr. Minn. Valley Luth. H.S., New Ulm, 1979—80; elem. tchr. Good Shepherd Luth. Sch., Omaha, 1980—86, Immanuel Luth. Sch., Greenville, Wis., 1986—. Condr. Kimberly (Wis.) Cmty. Band, 2001—, Neenah (Wis.) Cmty. Band, 2004—. Mem.: Music Educators Nat. Conf. Republican. Lutheran. Avocation: woodworking. Home: W6461 Summer Wind Ln Greenville WI 54942 Office: Immanuel Luth Sch W7265 School Rd Greenville WI 54942 Office Phone: 920-757-6606. Office Fax: 920-757-1151. Personal E-mail: rkramer6@netscape.net. E-mail: ilsgreen@netscape.net.

KRAMER, SIDNEY B., publishing executive, literary agent, lawyer; b. N.Y.C., 1915; s. Louis and Mildred (Hindin) K.; m. Esther Schlansky, Nov. 23, 1939; children: Wendy Beth Kramer Posner, Mark William. BS, NYU, 1936; JD, Bklyn. Law Sch., St. Lawrence U., 1939. Bar: N.Y. 1940, Conn. 1962, U.S. Supreme Ct. 1975. Practice in, N.Y.C., 1940-45, Westport, Conn., 1963—; founder (1945), sr. v.p. Bantam Books, Inc., N.Y.C., 1945-67; founder (1950), mng. dir. Corgi Books, London, 1960-62; pres., dir. Remarkable Bookshop, 1960-95; pres. New Am. Library, N.Y.C., 1967-72, MEWS Books Ltd., Westport, Conn., 1975—. Mng. dir., cons. Cassell & Collier Macmillan Pubs. Ltd., London, 1973-74; chmn. Nat. Assn. Paperback Pubs., 1945-67 Chmn. Democratic Town Com., also justice peace, Westport, 1960—; chmn. Save Westport Now, 1981— . Recipient Westport Arts Heritage award for Lit., 2001. Mem. Conn. Bar Assn. Office: 20 Bluewater Hill Westport CT 06880-6504 Office Phone: 203-227-1836. Personal E-mail: mewsbooks@aol.com.

KRAMER, SIMON PAUL, writer; b. Cin., Aug. 17, 1914; s. Simon Pendleton and Minnie (Halle) K.; m. Marie Louise Belden, Jan. 5, 1955 (div. 1968); 1 child, Theresa. BA, Princeton U., 1935; MLitt, Trinity Coll., Cambridge, Eng., 1938. Spl. asst. coord. Inter-Am. Affairs, Washington, 1940-43; staff CIA, Washington, 1947-51; ptnr. Auerbach, Pollak and Richardson, N.Y.C., 1954-57; pres. Conporacion Industrial, Panama, 1954-57, Panama Coop. Fisheries, 1957-60; staff cons. IGY-Nat. Acad. Scis., Washington, 1956-57, 60-62. Author: The Last Manchu, 1967, 2d edit. 1987, Latin American Panorama, 1968, The City in American Life, 1970, Nelson Rockefeller and British Security Coordination in Sage Readers in 20th Century History, 1982. Lt. USNR, 1943-46. Republican. Avocations: politics, gardening, bridge. Home and Office: 3023 Dent Pl NW Washington DC 20007-2916 E-mail: sptk@erols.com.

KRAMER, THOMAS GREGORY, lawyer; b. St. Paul, Nov. 29, 1950; s. Wallace Matthew and Gene Conleth (Farrell) K.; m. Mary Ann Kramer, Sept. 19, 1971; children: Jeremy Thomas, Laura Louise, Colin Farrell; 1 foster child, Rebecca Ann DeVries. BA, U. Minn., 1972; JD, William Mitchell Coll. Law, St. Paul, 1976. Bar: Minn. 1976; U.S. Dist. Ct. Minn. 1976. Asst. county atty. Yellow Medicine, Granite Falls, Minn., 1976-79, county atty., 1979—; assoc. Allen Swen Anderson Law Office, Granite Falls, Minn., 1976-77; pvt. practice Granite Falls, Minn., 1977—. Arbitrator Am. Arbitration Assn., Mpls., 1990—. Mem. Kiwanis (past pres.), Granite Falls, Minn., 1976—. Mem. ABA, Minn. State Bar Assn., Minn. Trial Lawyers Assn. Home: PO Box 128 Granite Falls MN 56241-0128 Office: Box 128 132 8th Ave Granite Falls MN 56241-1508 Fax: 320-564-2503. E-mail: tom.kramer@co.yellow.medicine.mn.us.

KRAMER, WILLIAM DAVID, lawyer; b. Anniston, Ala., Feb. 2, 1944; s. John Robert and Janice Marian (Dye) K.; m. Johanna Scalzi, Dec. 1, 1973; children: Elizabeth Annemarie, David MacLaren. Student, Case Western Res. U., 1959-60; AB in Govt. with honors magna cum laude, Oberlin Coll., 1965; JD, M in Pub. Adminstrn., Harvard U., 1969. Bar: Mass. 1969, D.C. 1973, U.S. Ct. Appeals (D.C. cir.) 1974, U.S. Dist. Ct. D.C. 1976, U.S. Ct. Appeals (10th cir.) 1978, U.S. Ct. Internat. Trade 1983, U.S. Ct. Appeals (fed. cir.) 1983. Assoc. dir. Gov.'s Com. on Law Enforcement and Adminstrn. Criminal Justice, Boston, 1969-71, dep. dir., 1971-73; assoc. Squire, Sanders & Dempsey, Washington, 1973-79, ptnr., 1979-92, Baker Botts LLP, Washington, 1992-2000; mem. Verner, Liipfert, Bernhard, McPherson and Hand, Chartered, Washington, 2000—02; ptnr., fed. regulatory matters, internat. trade Piper Rudnick LLP (now DLA Piper Rudnick Gray Cary LLP), 2002—. Mem. internat. law sect. D.C. Bar. Founding pres., chmn. bd. dirs. Children's Chorus of Washington, 1995-97, mem. adv. bd., 1997—. Mem. Phi Beta Kappa. Office: DLA Piper Rudnick Gray Cary LLP Ste 700 1200 19th St NW Washington DC 20036-2412 Office Phone: 202-861-6203. Office Fax: 202-689-8557. Business E-Mail: bill.kramer@dlapiper.com.

KRAMISH, ARNOLD, physicist, historian, writer; b. Denver, June 6, 1923; m. Vivian Ruth Raker, Aug. 19, 1952; children: Pamela, Robert. BS, U. Denver, 1945; A.M., Harvard U., 1947. With Manhattan Project, 1944-46, AEC, 1946-51; sr. staff mem. Rand Corp., Santa Monica, Calif., 1951-68; v.p. Inst. for the Future, Washington, 1968-70; sci. attache U.S. Mission to UNESCO, Paris, 1970-73; counselor for sci. and tech. affairs U.S. Mission to OECD, Paris, 1974-76; sci. research R & D Assocs., Arlington, Va., 1976-81; ind. tech. cons., 1981—; tech. dir. White House Study preliminary to Strategic Def. Initiative, 1981—84; advisor Undersecretary of Def. for Policy, 1984—91; assoc. Global Bus. Access Ltd., 1991—. Prof. UCLA, 1965-66, London Sch. Econs., 1967-68; adj. prof. internat. studies U. Miami, Fla., 1969; fellow Woodrow Wilson Internat. Ctr. for Scholars, 1982-83; Rockefeller scholar, Bellagio, Italy, 1984; pres. Tech. Analysis Internat., 1983—. Author: Atomic Energy for Your Business, 1956, Atomic Energy in the Soviet Union, 1959, The Peaceful Atom in Foreign Policy, 1963, The Future of Non-Nuclear Nations, 1970, The Griffin, 1986; also numerous articles, book chpts.; patentee nuclear radiometer. Sci. advisor European Cmty., 1960-62. With AUS, 1943-46. Carnegie fellow Coun. on Fgn. Rels., 1958-59; John Simon Guggenheim fellow, 1966-67; Rsch. fellow Inst. for Strategic Studies, London, 1966-67; Sr. fellow Global Access Inst., 1994—. Mem. PEN, Authors Guild. Office: PO Box 2621 Reston VA 20195-0621 Business E-Mail: Kramish@post.harvard.edu.

KRAMLICH, C(HARLES) RICHARD (DICK), venture capitalist; b. Green Bay, Wis., Apr. 27, 1935; m. Debra Durban, Apr. 26, 1961 (div.); m. Lynne Kramlich (dec. 1980); m. Pamela Kramlich; children: Mary, Richard Squire, Peter Nard, Christina. BS in History, Northwestern U., 1957; MBA, Harvard U., 1960. With Kroger Co., Cin., 1960—64; joined Gardner & Preston Moss, Boston, 1964, exec. v.p., 1968—69; gen. ptnr. Arthur Rock & Associates, 1969—78; co-founder & gen. ptnr. New Enterprise Associates, Menlo Park, Calif., 1978—. Bd. dirs. Celetronix, Decru, Fabric7Systems, Financial Engines, Force10 Networks, Foveon, Graphic Enterprises, Informative, Zhone Technologies, Visual Edge Tech., Silicon Valley Bancshares, 2005—, adv. mem. bd., 2003—05. Vice chmn. bd. dirs. San Francisco Exploratorium; bd. dirs. UCSF Found., Bay Area Video Coalition; founder New Art Trust, 1997—. Named one of Top 200 Collectors, ARTnews mag., 2004; recipient Lifetime Achievement Award in Entrepreneurship & Innovation, Lester Ctr. for Entrepreneurship & Innovation, Haas Sch. Bus., U. Calif. Berkeley, 2005. Mem.: Nat. Venture Capital Assn. (pres. 1992—93, chmn. 1993—94, Lifetime Achievement Award 2001). Avocation: Collector video and new media art. Office: New Enterprise Associates 2490 Sand Hill Rd Menlo Park CA 94025 Office Phone: 650-854-9499. Office Fax: 650-854-9397.*

KRANE, STEPHEN MARTIN, rheumatologist, educator; b. NYC, July 15, 1927; s. Daniel Golden and Bessie (Berman) K.; m. Cynthia Ramin, June 28, 1952; children: David Alan, Peter Jay, Ian Matthew, Adam. AB, Columbia U., 1946, MD, 1951; A.M. (hon.), Harvard U., 1968; MD (hon.), U. Geneva, 1989, U. Paris, 2003. Intern to chief resident in medicine Mass. Gen. Hosp., Boston, 1951-57, chief arthritis unit, 1961, physician, 1969—2001; research fellow Washington U., St. Louis, 1956; asst. in medicine Harvard U. Med. Sch., Boston, 1958, prof., 1972-87, Persis, Cyrus and Marlow B. Harrison Disting. prof. clin. medicine, 1987—. Contbr. articles to profl. jours. Served with USNR, 1945-46. Recipient Kappa Delta award Orthopedic Rsch. Soc., 1977, Herberden medal Herberden Soc., London, 1980; named Guggenheim fellow Oxford U., 1973-74. Fellow ACP, AAAS, Am. Acad. Arts and Scis., Am. Coll. Rheumatology (master, Disting. Investigator award 1995); mem. Am. Soc. Clin. Investigation, Assn. Am. Physicians, Am. Soc. Biol. Chemistry, Molecular Biology, Soc. Bone Mineral Rsch., Endocrine Soc. Home: 101 Windsor Rd Newton MA 02468-1121 Office: Mass Genl Hosp Boston MA 02114 Business E-Mail: krane.stephen@mgh.harvard.edu.

KRANE, SUSAN, museum director, curator; b. Gary, Ind., June 8, 1954; BA, Carleton Coll., 1976; MA, Columbia U., 1978; MBA, U. Colo., 2000. Rockefeller Found. intern Walker Art Ctr., Mpls., 1978-79; curator Albright-Knox Art Gallery, Buffalo, 1979—87, High Mus. Art, Atlanta, 1987-95; adj. faculty Emory U., 1988-95; dir. U. Colo. Art Mus., 1996—2001; adj. prof. U.

Colo., Scottsdale Mus. Contemporary Art, Ariz., 2001—. Author catalogues: Judy Pfaff, 1982, Surfacing Images: The Paintings of Joe Zucker, 1982, Mario Merz, 1984, Jan Kotik: The Painterly Object, 1984, Hollis Frampton: Recollections Recreations, 1984, The Wayward Muse, 1987, Albright-Knox Art Gallery: The Paintings and Sculpture Collection, 19877, Creighton Michael, 1987, Sherrie Levine, 1988, Houston Conwill, 1989, Ida Applebroog, 1989, Lynda Benglis: Dual Natures, 1991, Joel Otterson, 1991, Max Weber: The Cubist Decade 1910-1920, 1991, Barbara Ess, 1992, Ray Smith, 1993, Alison Saar, 1993, Equal Rights and Justice, 1994, Tampering Artists and Abstraction Today, 1995; contbr. Striking Out: Another American Road Show, 1991, Graven Images, 1991, Conversations at the Castle: Changing Audiences and Contemporary Art, Out of Order: Mapping Social Space, 2000, Lesley Dill: A 10-Year Survey, 2002, Let's Walk West: Brad Kahlhamer, 2004 Office: Scottsdale Mus Contemporary Art 7380 E Second St Scottsdale AZ 85251 Office Phone: 480-874-4632. E-mail: susank@sccarts.org.

KRANITZ, GEORGINA ANN, academic administrator; b. Wallsend, Eng., Oct. 25, 1948; came to U.S., 1957; d. James F. and Mary E. Bage; m. Michael E. Kranitz, Aug. 24, 1968. BA, Grand Valley St. U., 1969; MEd, Ariz. State U., 1982; EdD, Nova/Southeastern U., 1992. Acquisitions control supr. Maricopa C.C. Dist., Tempe, Ariz., 1976-78, sys. implementation supr., 1978-80; dir. admission svcs. S. Mountain C.C., Phoenix, 1980-86, dir. bus. svcs., 1986-91, dean instrn., 1991-92; dean admission/student svcs. Paradise Valley C.C., Phoenix, 1992-99, pres., 1999. Coord. Ariz. Women's Polit. Caucus, Phoenix, 1970-80; precinct committeewoman Dems., Phoenix, 1970-80; bd. dirs. S. Mountain YMCA, 1980-85. Named Top Ten Women Edn. Ariz. Women's Mag., 1997, 98, 99. Mem. Nat. Assn. Coll. and Univ. Bus. Officers (1999—), Western Assn. Coll. and Univ. Bus. Officers (pres. 1994-95), Greater N.E. Phoenix C.C. (dir. 1999), S. Mountain Small Bus. Assn. (bd. dirs. 1980-84). Avocation: reading. Office: Paradise Valley CC 18401 N 32d St Phoenix AZ 85032

KRANITZ, THEODORE MITCHELL, lawyer; b. St. Joseph, Mo., May 27, 1922; s. Louis and Miriam (Saferstein) K.; m. Elaine Shirley Kaufman, June 11, 1944; children: Hugh David, Karen Gail and Kathy Jane (twins). Student, St. Joseph Jr. Coll., 1940-41; BS in Fgn. Svc., Georgetown U., 1948, JD, 1950. Bar: Mo. 1950, U.S. Supreme Ct. 1955. Pres., sr. ptnr. Kranitz & Kranitz, PC, St. Joseph, 1979—. Author: articles in field. Pres. St. Joseph Comty. Theatre, Inc., 1958-60; bd. dirs. United Jewish Fund St. Joseph, 1957—, pres., 1958-63; sec. Boys' Baseball St. Joseph, 1964-68; trustee Temple Adath Joseph, 1970-74, 77-80; bd. dirs. Temple B'nai Sholem, 1976—, Lyric Opera Guild Kansas City, 1980-91; founder, pres. St. Joseph Light Opera Co., Inc., 1989-90; mem. St. Joseph Postal Customers Adv. Coun., 1993-2005, chmn., 1993-95; mem., sec. St. Joseph Downtown Assn., 1995-97 Mem. Mo. Bar, St. Joseph Bar Assn. (pres. 1977-78), Am. Legion, Air Force Assn., B'nai B'rith (dist. bd. govs. 1958-61). Home: 2609 Gene Field Rd Saint Joseph MO 64506-1615 Office: Kranitz & Kranitz PC Boder Bldg 107 S 4th St PO Box 968 Saint Joseph MO 64502-0968 Office Phone: 816-232-4409. Office Fax: 816-232-8558. Business E-Mail: tkranitz@kranitzandkranitzpc.com.

KRANKING, MARGARET GRAHAM, artist, educator; b. Dec. 21, 1930; d. Stephen Wayne and Madge Williams (Dawes) Graham; m. James David Kranking, Aug. 23, 1952; children: James Andrew, Ann Marie Kranking Eggleton, David Wayne. BA summa cum laude (Clendenin fellow), Am. U., 1952. Asst. to head publs. Nat. Gallery Art, Washington, 1952-53. Tchr. art Woman's Club, Chevy Chase, Md., 1976-88, 98—; guest instr. Amherst Coll., 1985, The Homestead, Hot Springs, Va., 1997; judge The Miniature Painters, Sculptors and Gravers Soc. Washington, 69th Ann. Internat. Exhbn., 2002, Bethesda, Md. One-woman shows include Spectrum Gallery, Washington, 1974, 76, 78-79, 83, 85, 87, 90, 92, 95, 97, 2000, Philip Morris, U.S.A., Richmond, Va., 1982-83, 86, Forence (S.C.) Mus., 1991, Lombardi Cancer treatment Ctr., Washington, 1992, Capital Gallery, Frankfort, Ky., 1993, Acad. Arts, Easton, Md., 1999, Warm Springs (Va.) Gallery, 1997-98; exhibited in group shows at Balt. Mus., 1974, 76, Corcoran Gallery Art, Washington, 1952, 72, USIA Traveling Exhbt., C.Am., 1978-79, AARP Traveling Exhbn., 1986; represented in permanent collections U. Va., Philip Morris U.S.A., USCG, AT&T, Freddie Mac, Florence Mus., S.C., Navy Fed. Credit Union Hdqs., Vienna, Va., Marsh and McClennan Co., Washington, The Washington Hilton, D.C., USCG Hall Heroes; traveling exhbn. Nat. Watercolor Soc., Watercolor U.S.A., Am. Watercolor Soc., Am. Artist mag., North Light mag., Adirondacks Nat. Exhbn. of Am. Watercolor, Artitude Internat. Art Competition, N.Y., Shada Gallery, Riyadh, Saudi Arabia, Belle Grove Plantation Invitational, Middletown, Va., Strathmore Hall Arts Ctr., North Bethesda, Md., Wash. Woman mag., Am. Speech-Lang. Hearing Assn., mag., Govt. House, Annapolis, Md. Invitational, 1997-99, Strathmore Hall Arts Ctr., North Bethesda, Md., Montgomery Coll. Invitational, Md., Glen View Mansion Invitational, Rockville, Md., 2000; ofcl. artist USCG; commd. to do painting of military funeral of Lt. Jack Rittichier for USCG Hall of Heroes, 2004; contbr. reproductions and text to numerous books. Recipient George Gray award USCG Art Program, N.Y., 1991, 98. Mem.: Western Fedn. Watercolor Socs., Watercolor Art Soc. Houston, Transparent Watercolor Soc. Am., Am. Watercolor Soc., Washington Soc. Landscape Painters, Potomac Valley Watercolorists (pres. 1981—83), Washington Watercolor Assn., So. Watercolor Soc., Ga. Watercolor Soc., Southwestern Watercolor Soc., Nat. Watercolor Soc. Roman Catholic. Home: 3504 Taylor St Chevy Chase MD 20815-4022

KRANOWITZ, CAROL STOCK, pre-school educator; b. New Haven, Conn., Dec. 3, 1945; d. Herman Edward and Doris Baker Stock; m. Alan Michael Kranowitz, June 25, 1967; children: Jeremy Lewis, David Stock. BA, Barnard Coll., N.Y., 1967; MA in Edn. and Human Devel., George Wash. U., Washington, D.C., 1995. Preschool tchr. St. Columba's Nursery Sch., Washington, 1976—2001; internat. lectr. Sensory Processing Disorder, 1998—. Author: The Out-of-Sync Child: Recognizing and Coping with Sensory Processing Disorder, 1998, The Out-of-Sync Child Has Fun, 2003 (Therapeutic Contbn. award Devel. Delay Resources, 2003), 101 Activities for Kids in Tight Spaces, 1995, The Goodenoughs Get in Sync! A Story for Kids About Sensory Processing Disorder, 2004 (I-Parenting Media award, 2005, Juvenile Non-fiction award, 2004); co-author: Answers to Questions Teachers Ask About Sensory Integration, 2001, Balzer-Martin Preschool Screening, 1992, Hear, See, Play! Music Discovery Activities for Young Children, 1989; editor-in-chief: S.I. Focus Mag., 2004—. Adv. bd. Devel. Delay Resources, Bethesda, Md., 1998—, Nat. Autism Assn., 2004—, S.I. Challenge, Dallas-Ft. Worth, 2000—. Mem.: Nat. Autism Assn. Jewish. Avocation: cello.

KRANTZ, CLAIRE WOLF, artist, freelance critic, curator; b. Chgo., June 22, 1938; d. George and Etta (Shtriker) Kaplan; m. San Robert Wolf, Mar. 8, 1959 (dec. 1973); children: Richard Wolf, Deborah Wolf Blanks, Rachel Wolf; m. David L. Krantz, Dec. 19, 1976. BS in Occpl. Therapy, U. Ill., 1961; post grad., Stanford U., 1977-78; BFA, Sch. Inst. of Chgo., 1979, postgrad., 1980-83. Occpl. therapist, 1961-76. Lectr. at various universities in the U.S., Europe, and Indonesia. Solo and two-person exhbns. include Gallerie S&H De Buck, Belgium, 1989, Galerie Paula Kouwenhoven, Delft, The Netherlands, 1990, Galerie Blankenese, Germany, 1991, Sazama Gallery, Chgo., 1992, Chgo. Cultural Ctr., 1993, Perimeter Gallery, Chgo., 1997, 2002, Bade Mus., Berkeley, Calif., 1997, Wash. State U., Pullman, 1997, Kedia Kabun Gallery, Yogyakarta, Indonesia, 1998, Contemporary Art Ctr. of Peria, Ill., 2000, I. Space Gallery, 2002, Toomey-Tourell Gallery, San Francisco, 2002, Flatfile Photographic Gallery, Chgo., 2004, various others; group exhbns. include Walker Gallery Art, 1981, Art Inst. Chgo., 1981, A.I.R. Gallery, N.Y.C., 1991-2003, Spertus Mus., Chgo., 1994, NY Arts Gallery, N.Y.C., 2003, Clarke House Mus., Chgo., 20094, various others; organized exhibits for institutions including: The Spertus Mus., The State of Ill. Mus., U-Turn E-Magazine, Wood Street Gallery, Ukrainian Inst. Modern Art; freelance art critic for nat. art publs., including Art in America. Mem. Chgo. Art Critics Assn., Phi Kappa Phi. Home and Studio: 711 S Dearborn #401 Chicago IL 60605-2308 Office Phone: 312-753-5071 (also fax). E-mail: cwkrantz@rcn.com.

KRANTZ, DAVID S., psychology educator, researcher; b. N.Y.C., Feb. 9, 1949; s. Robert B. and Beatrice K.; m. Marsha L. Douma, June 27, 1982; children: Michael Douma, Della Krantz. BS, CCNY, 1971; PhD, U. Tex., 1975. Asst. prof. psychology U. So. Calif., L.A., 1975-78; asst. then assoc. prof. Uniformed Svcs. U. Health Scis., Bethesda, Md., 1978-87, prof. med. psychology, 1987—, prof., chmn. dept. med. and clin. psychology, 1999—; prof. psychiatry and medicine Georgetown U. Sch. Medicine, 1999—. Co-author: Behavior, Health and Environmental Stress, 1982, Introduction to Health Psychology, 1989, 97; assoc. editor: Health Psychology, 1988-93, editor-in-chief, 1994—2000; mem. editorial bd.: Psychosomatic Medicine, 1990—; contbr. more than 170 articles and chpts. to profl. publs. Named one of Outstanding Young Scientists in Am., Sci. Digest, 1984. Fellow APA (pres. health psychology divsn. 2005-, Outstanding Contbn. to Health Psychology award 1981, 2000, Disting. Sci. Early Career award 1982), Acad. Behavioral Medicine Rsch. (pres. 1995). Achievements include research on the etiology of myocardial ischemia and arrhythmia, and research in behavioral cardiology. Office: Uniformed Svcs U Health Sci Med Psychology 4301 Jones Bridge Rd Bethesda MD 20814-4712 Office Phone: 301-295-3273. E-mail: dskrantz@usuhs.mil.

KRANTZ, EJNAR SANFRIO, composer, musician, educator; s. Sam Krantz and Hannah Victoria Carlson. MusB, Sherwood Music Sch., Chgo., 1939; MusM, Chgo. Musical Coll., 1943; DFA, Chgo. Musical Coll. Roosevelt U., 1954. Choral dir. Grace Luth. Ch., San Antonio, 1944—47; concert pianist, 1947—54; organist and dir. St. Matthew Luth. Ch., Washington, 1954—55; minister of music First Presbyn. Ch., Battle Creek, Mich., 1955—57; adj. faculty Ind. U. at South Bend, 1962—95; interim asst. prof. music Manchester Coll., 1960—62, Goshen Coll., 1963; minister of music First Presbyn. Ch., South Bend, 1957—60. Contbr. articles to profl. jours.; composer: (vocal solos) Israel's Lament, Restoration/Snow, The Highlands Sing, The Mesa Trail, Vocal Solos by Ejnar Krantz, (choral works) Come Unto Me, Hear My Cry, O God (Psalm 61), In Him Will I Trust (Psalm 91), Lo, I Am With You Alway, Psalm 100: Make a Joyful Noise Unto the Lord, Psalm 121: I Will Lift Up Mine Eyes, Radiance: The Thing Most Beautiful, (piano) All Kinds of Pieces for Little Fingers, An Approach to Fingering in Piano Playing, Two Tone Pictures-Melancholy and Capriccio, Four Little Mood Pictures, Sonorous Sketches from the Four Winds., Three Greetings, (organ) Four Offeratories, Preludes on Four Familiar Hymn Tunes, Toccata Chromatica in A Minir. Recipient Chgo. Artists Assn. award, 1938; Rudolph Ganz ccholar, Chgo. Musical Coll., 1942—43. Avocations: languages, sailing, swimming, reading. Home: 1002 S Ironwood Dr South Bend IN 46615-1616

KRANTZ, JUDITH TARCHER, novelist; b. N.Y.C., Jan. 9, 1928; d. Jack David and Mary (Brager) Tarcher; m. Stephen Falk Krantz, Feb. 19, 1954; children: Nicholas, Anthony. BA, Wellesley Coll., 1948. Fashion publicist, Paris, 1948-49; fashion editor Good Housekeeping mag., N.Y.C., 1949-56; contbg. writer McCalls, 1956-59, Ladies Home Jour., 1959-71; contbg. west coast editor Cosmopolitan mag., 1971-79. Author: Scruples, 1978, Princess Daisy, 1980, Mistral's Daughter, 1982, I'll Take Manhattan, 1986, Till We Meet Again, 1988, Dazzle, 1990, Scruples Two, 1992, Lovers, 1994, Spring Collection, 1996, The Jewels of Tessa Kent, 1998, Sex & Shopping: Confessions of a Nice Jewish Girl, 2000. Office: St Martin Press 175 5th Ave New York NY 10010*

KRANTZ, KERMIT EDWARD, obstetrician, department chairman; b. Oak Park, Ill., June 4, 1923; s. Andrew Stanley and Beatrice H. (Cibrowski) K.; m. Doris Cole Krantz, Sep. 7, 1946; children: Pamela (Mrs. Richard Huffstutter), Sarah Elizabeth, Kermit Tripler. BS, Northwestern U., 1945, BM, MS in Anatomy, Northwestern U., 1947, MD, 1948; LittD (hon.), William Woods Coll., 1971. Diplomate Am. Bd. Ob-Gyn. Intern ob-gyn. N.Y. Lying-In Hosp., 1947-48; asst. resident, asst. ob-gyn. Cornell U. Med. Coll., N.Y. Lying-In Hosp., N.Y. Hosp., 1948-50; fellow, resident in ob-gyn Mary Fletcher Hosp., Burlington, Vt., 1950-51; dir. Durfee Clinic, 1952-55; instr., then asst. prof. U. Vt. Coll. Medicine, 1951-55; asst. prof. U. Ark. Med. Sch., 1955-59; prof., chmn. dept. ob-gyn. U. Kans. Med. Ctr., 1959-90, obstetrician and gynecologist in chief, 1959-90, lectr. history medicine, 1959—, prof. anatomy, 1963—, dean clin. affairs, 1972-74, chief staff, 1972-74, assoc. to exec. vice chancellor for facilities devel., 1974-83, Univ. Disting. prof., 1990—92; univ. disting. prof. emeritus ob/gyn. and anatomy U. Kans., 1994—. Cons. in field. Author numerous articles in field. Mem. Nat. Adv. Child Health and Human Devel. Council, NIH, 1974-76. Named Outstanding Prof. in Coll. of Medicine Nu Sigma Nu, 1955, Charles A. Durham Meml. lectr., Ann. Session Tex. Med. Assn., 1978; recipient Found. award, South Atlantic Assn. Obstetricians and Gynecologists, 1950, Am. Assn. Obstetricians and Gynecologists, 1950, Wyeth-Ayerst Pub. Recognition award, 1st Am. Assn. Prof. of Gynecology and Obstetrics, 1988, Robert A. Ross lectureship award, Armed Forces Dist. meeting Am. Coll. Obstetricians and Gynecologists, 1972, Outstanding Civilian Svc. medal, U.S. Army-Dept. Def., 1985; Bowen-Brooks fellow, N.Y. Acad. Medicine, 1948—50, Markle scholar med. sci., 1957—62, Kermit E. Krantz Soc. established at U. Kans. Med. Ctr., 1982, Arey-Krantz Mus. Anatomy established at Northwestern U. Sch. Medicine, 2004. Founding fellow Am. Coll. Obstetricians and Gynecologists (Kermit E. Krantz Lectureship award established 1973, Outstanding Dist. Services award 1978, 82); fellow ACS, Am. Coll. Ob-Gyn (life); mem. Am. Assn. Anatomists, Am. Fedn. Clin. Research, AMA, Am. Med. Writers Assn., Am. Fertility Soc., AAUP, Soc. Exptl. Biology and Medicine, Aerospace Med. Assn., Endocrine Soc., Soc. Gynecologic Investigation, Central Assn. Obstetricians and Gynecologists, N.Y. Acad. Medicine, N.Y. Acad. Sci., Kans. Med. Soc., Assn. Mil. Surgeons U.S. (sustaining), Kans. Obstet. Soc., Arey-Krantz Mus. Anatomy Northwestern U. Sch. Medicine, Sigma Xi, Alpha Omega Alpha. Home: 441 W 66th St Prairie Village KS 66208 Office: U Kans Med Ctr Kansas City KS 66160-0001 Office Phone: 913-588-6201.

KRANTZ, LINDA LAW, librarian; b. Princeton, N.J., June 19, 1943; d. Harold Bell and Ruth Workman Law; m. David Walter Krantz, July 29, 1967. Student, Mt. Union Coll., 1961-63; BA in French Lit., U. Rochester, 1965; MLS, Rutgers State U., 1967. Libr. asst. Fine Hall Libr. Math. and Physics Princeton U., 1962—66; reference libr. Princeton Pub. Libr., 1966-67; cataloger NASA Lewis Rsch. Ctr., Cleve., 1967; reference libr. sci.-tech. Cleve. Pub. Libr., 1968-69; reference libr. Wright State U. Libr., Dayton, Ohio, 1969-73; libr. dir. Rockbridge Regional Libr., Lexington, Va., 1974—. Bd. dirs. Kendal, sec., 2003—. Musician (violinist): Rockbridge Orch., 1975—96, 1999—, Allegheny-Highlands Symphony Orch., 1997—. Mem.: ALA, Va. Pub. Libr. Dirs. Assn. (pres. 2002—03), Va. Libr. Assn. (legis. co-chair 1997—99, George Mason award 1995), Lexington Rotary Club (bd. dirs. 1997, 2005—, Paul Harris fellow 1996), Omicron Delta Kappa. Avocations: music, nature, reading, cats. Home: 151 Elliots Hill Ln Lexington VA 24450-7203 Office: Rockbridge Regional Libr 138 S Main St Lexington VA 24450-2316 Office Phone: 540-463-4324 100. E-mail: lkrantz@rlib.net.

KRANTZ, STEVEN GEORGE, mathematics professor, writer; b. San Francisco, Feb. 3, 1951; s. Henry Alfred and Norma Oliva (Crisafulli) K.; m. Randi Diane Ruden, Sept. 7, 1974. BA, U. Calif., Santa Cruz, 1971; PhD, Princeton U, 1974. Asst. prof. UCLA, 1974-81; assoc. prof. Pa. State U., University Park, 1981-84, prof., 1984-86; prof. dept. math. Washington U., St. Louis, 1986—, chmn. dept. math., 1999—, divsn. head for sci. depts., 2002—. Adv. bd. Am. Inst. Math., Am. Math. Soc. book series; mng. editor Jour. Math. Analysis and Applications. Founder, mng. editor Jour. Geometric Analysis; editor-in-chief Jour. of Math. Analysis and Apps.; Author: Function Theory of Several Complex Variables (monograph), 1982, 2d edition, 1992, Complex Analysis: The Geometric Viewpoint, 1990, Real Analysis and Foundations, 1991, Partial Differential Equations and Complex Analysis, 1992, A Primer of Real Analytic Functions, 1992, Geometric Analysis and Function Spaces, 1993, How to Teach Mathematics, 1993, 2nd edit., 1999, A Tex Primer for Scientists, 1995, The Elements of Advanced Mathematics, 1995, 2d edit., 2002, Techniques of Problem Solving, 1996, Function Theory of One Complex Variable, 1997, A Primer of Mathematical Writing, 1996; (with H. R. Parks) The Geometry of Domains in Space, 1999, Contemporary Issues in Mathmatics Education, 1999, A Handbook of Complex Variables, 1999, A Panorama of Harmonic Analysis, 1999, Handbook of Typography for the Mathematical Sciences, 2000, The Implicit Function Theorem, 2002, Mathematical Apocrypha, 2002, Graduate School and Careers in Mathematics: A Survival Guide, 2003; cons. editor Birkhäuser Pub., 2002-, McGraw-Hill, 2002-; contbr. numerous rsch. articles to profl. publs. Recipient Disting. Tchg. award, UCLA Alumni Found., 1979:NSF rsch. grantee, 1975—, Kemper grantee, 1994. Richardson fellow Australian Nat. U., 1995; mem. Am. Math. Soc. (prin. organizer summer rsch. inst. 1989), Math. Assn. Am. (Chauvenet prize, Beckenbach prize 1994), Textbook Authors Assn. Business E-Mail: sk@math.wustl.edu.

KRANWINKLE, CONRAD DOUGLAS, lawyer, broadcast executive; b. Elgin, Ill., Oct. 27, 1940; s. Conrad David and Helen Elvira (Walgren) K.; m. Susan Hall Warren, Aug. 24, 1962; children: Mark Conrad, Jane Shafer. BA, Northwestern U., 1962; JD, U. Mich., 1965. Bar: Calif. 1966, U.S. Dist. Ct. (ctrl. dist.) Calif. 1966, U.S. Ct. Appeals (9th cir.) 1966, N.Y. 1995. Law clk. to chief justice U.S. Supreme Ct., Washington, 1966-67; ptnr. Munger, Tolles & Olson, LA, 1967-88, O'Melveny & Myers, 1989—2000, mng. ptnr., 1996—2000; exec. v.p., gen. counsel Univision Comms., Inc., 2000—. Vis. prof. law U. Mich., winter 1993. Pres. Poly. Sch. Bd. Trustees, Pasadena, Calif., 1986-88; mgr. Rep. Gubernatorial campaign, Calif., 1973-74; chmn. U.S. Senate campaign, Calif., 1978. Mem. Am. Law Inst., Coun. on Fgn. Rels., Calif. C. of C. (bd. dirs. 1990-94), Calif. Club, Valley Hunt Club, River Club. Office: Univision Comms Inc Ste 3050 1999 Avenue of the Stars Los Angeles CA 90067 E-mail: dkranwinkle@univision.com.

KRANZDORF, NORMAN M(ELVIN), lawyer, real estate executive; b. Hanover, Pa., Sept. 28, 1930; s. Julius L. and Dora (Kaplan) K.; m. Hermina Goodman, Aug. 28, 1955; children: Betty, Michael. AB, Dickinson Coll., 1952; LLB, U. Pa., 1955. Bar: Pa. 1955. Pres. Amterre Devel. Inc.; v.p., gen. mgr. Food Fair Properties, Inc., counsel; ptnr. The Kranzco Group and Affiliates, Conshohocken, Pa.; CEO, pres. Kranzco Realty Trust, Conshohocken, Pa., 1980-2000; trustee Kramont Realty Trust, Plymouth Meeting, Pa., 2000—. Chmn. Amterre Property Group LLC, 2003-; lectr. continuing edn. programs Mich. State U., U. Ariz.; lectr. Am. Mgmt. Assn., Practicing Law Inst., Aspen Law Inst., N.W. Ctr. for Profl. End., others. Author: Retailer Tenant Bankruptcy, 1997; contbr. articles to profl. jours. Former trustee Internat. Coun. Shopping Ctrs.; bd. govs. Nat. Assn. Real Estate Investment Trusts. Office: Urdang Capital Mgmt Ste 300 630 W Germantown Pike Plymouth Meeting PA 19462-1069 Home: 630 Germantown Pike Plymouth Meeting PA 19462 Office Phone: 610-818-4680.

KRANZOW, RONALD ROY, lawyer; b. Chgo., Aug. 4, 1931; s. Roy Ludwig and Elsie Emma (Hennig) K.; m. Joan Carole Stromberg, June 7, 1952; children: Susan, Kenneth, Jill. Student, De Paul U., 1949-52, Syracuse U., 1952-53, Trinity U., 1953-54, Roosevelt U., 1956, John Marshall Law Sch., 1956-59; JD, Golden Gate U., 1961. Bar: Calif. 1961, Tex. 1977, U.S. Ct. Appeals (9th cir.) 1961, U.S. Ct. Appeals (2d cir.) 1969, U.S. Ct. Appeals (8th cir.) 1976, U.S. Ct. Appeals (fed. cir.) 1982. Sales corr. Internat. Cellucotton Products Co., Chgo., 1949-52; sales asst. Kaiser Aluminum & Chem. Corp., Oakland, Calif., 1956-61, trademark counsel, 1961-68, PepsiCo Inc., Purchase, N.Y., 1968-74, asst. gen. counsel, 1976-86, assoc. gen. counsel, 1986-96; v.p., legal counsel Frito-Lay Inc., Dallas, 1974-89, sr. v.p., legal counsel, 1989-95; assoc. gen. counsel Frito-Lay, Inc., Dallas, 1995-96. Contbr. articles to profl. jours. Trustee Grace Presbyn. Village, Dallas, 1995-96. Mem. ABA, Dallas Bar Assn. (chmn. antitrust and trade regulation sect. 1990-91), Am. Intellectual Property Law Assn., U.S. Trademark Assn. (chmn., com. mem. 1965—, pres., chmn. bd. dirs. 1977-78), Internat. Trademark Assn. Republican. Presbyterian. Avocations: church teaching, sports, reading.

KRAPF, ELIZABETH MARIA, paralegal, musician; b. Bogota, Colombia, Apr. 11, 1980; d. Norbert Alfred and Katherine Ann Krapf. BS in Arts Adminstrn., BA in German, Butler U., 2002. Cert.: Ind. (paralegal) 2004. Paralegal Marion County Prosecutor's Office, Indpls., 2002—03; litig. paralegal Landman & Beatty Lawyers, LLP, Indpls., 2004—. Scholar, Butler U., 1998—2002. Mem.: Phi Theta Kappa (life). Liberal. Roman Catholic. Office: Landman & Beatty Lawyers LLP 151 N Delaware Street Suite 1150 Indianapolis IN 46204 Office Phone: 317-236-1040.

KRARAS, GUST C., hotel executive; b. Terpsithea, Greece, Mar. 4, 1921; came to U.S., 1938; s. Christ I. and Ypapanti (Contos) K.; m. Stella Dialectos, Apr. 28, 1946; children: Christ, Angel, Ypapanti. Owner-operator Lorraine Hotel & Restaurant, Wildwood, N.J., 1955-73, White Star Motel, Wildwood, 1972—; owner-operator Nantucket Motel, Wildwood, 1973—, White Star Tours, Reading, Pa., 1975—; owner Two Mile Landing, Wildwood, 1982—; owner-operator Beach Terrace Motor Inn, Wildwood, 1985—, Rusty Rudder Restaurant, Wildwood, 1985—, Mansion Heights Assocs., Birdsboro, Pa., 1986—. Owner-operator G.C.M., Reading, 1980—, Hopewell Heights, Birdsboro, 1988—. Editor hist. jours., 1954, 70, 75, 89. Pres. St. Constantine Ch., St. Helen Ch., Reading, 1958-59, 77, chpt. 61 Am. Hellenic Ednl. Progressive Assn., Reading, 1957; dist. gov. 5th dist. AHEPA, N.J., Del., 1981-82. With OSS, 1943-45, ETO. Mem. Nat. Tour Assn., Archon Depoutatos of Ecumenical Patriarchate of Constantinople, Masons, Shriners. Democrat. Greek Orthodox. Office: White Star Tours Inc 26 E Lancaster Ave Reading PA 19607-2632 E-mail: gkraras@whitestartours.com.

KRASEAN, THOMAS KARL, historian; b. South Bend, Ind., Feb. 21, 1940; s. William Henry and Rose Ercelia (Mariottini) K.; m. Arleen Ruth Llewellyn, June 19, 1965 (div. Oct. 1970); children: Thomas Karl, David William, Elizabeth Rose; m. Liliane Siahou, Nov. 4, 1972. AA, Kellogg Community Coll., 1960; student, U. Ala., 1960-61; BA, East Mich. U., 1963; MA, Western Mich. U., 1965. Cert. in fund raising mgmt., 1996. Field rep. Ind. State Libr., Indpls., 1965-69, state archivist, 1969-70; dir. Byron Lewis Libr., Vincennes (Ind.) U., 1970-77; field rep. Ind. Hist. Soc., Indpls., 1977-82, dir. field svcs. divsn., 1982-92, dir. cmty. rels. divsn., 1992-97, dir. devel. and membership svcs., 1997—2001, spl. asst. to the pres., 2001—02, dir. planned giving, 2002—. Rep. Ind. Am. Revolution Bicentennial Commn., 1971-77; mem. Adv. Com. Historic Preservation, 1972-73, Adv. Com. Ind. Hist. Bur., 1980-2000; chmn. George Rogers Clark Trail Found., 1972-74; founder, pres. Old N.W. Corp., 1973-77; bd. dirs. Ind. Adv. Com. Nat. Hist. Publs. and Records Commn., 1979-97. Mem. White River Park Task Force, Indpls., 1981-83; bd. dirs. Friends of the State Archives, 2000-. Named Sagamore of the Wabash. Mem. Am. Assn. State and Local History (state chmn. awards com. 1981-92, regional chmn. awards com. 1988-92, nominating com. 1992-95), Soc. Am. Archivists, Midwest Archives Conf. (charter), Ind. Hist. Soc. (adv. coun. Ind. Jr. Hist. Soc. 1971-2001), Ind. Oral History Roundtable (charter), Soc. Ind. Archivists (founder, sec., treas. 1972-92), Civil War Roundtable (pres. 1970-71, 79-80, 93-94), Battle Creek (Mich.) Indpls. Civil War Roundtable (life), Indpls. Lit. Club (pres. 1989, treas. 1991—), Contemporary Club Indpls. (bd. dirs. 1998-2000, pres. 2001-02), Devonshire Neighborhood Assn. (pres. 1998-2000). Republican. Roman Catholic. Avocations: travel, book collecting. Home: 6038 Castlebar Cir Indianapolis IN 46220-4107 Office: Ind Hist Soc 450 W Ohio St Indianapolis IN 46202-3269 E-mail: tkrasean@indianahistory.org.

KRASHESKY, ALAN, newscaster; married; 3 children. BS in Comm. Mgmt., Ithaca Coll., N.Y., 1981. Weekend sports anchor, weathercaster and reporter WBNG-TV, Binghamton, NY, 1981; weathercaster and reporter KTBC-TV, Austin, Tex., 1982; reporter WLS-TV, Chgo., 1982—89, co-anchor morning news, 1989—94, co-anchor 5pm news, 1994—98, co-anchor 6pm news, 1998—, host NewsViews. TV Journalist Francis Cardinal George: Journey of Hope, 1999 (Silver Angels award, 1999), Pilgrimage of Peace: The Pope in the Holy Land, 2000 (Chgo. Emmy award, 2000). Named Alumnus of Yr., Milton Hershey Sch., 2005; recipient Outstanding Young Alumni award, Ithaca Coll., 1992, Father of Yr., Chgo. Father's Day Coun., 1996,

Communicators award, Archdiocese of Chgo., 1997, Heritage Media award, Polish Am. Congress, 1997, Outstanding Achievement in Broadcast Journalism award, Milton Hershey Sch., 1997. Mem.: NATAS (Chgo. chpt.), Chgo. Headfire Club. Office: WLS-TV 190 N State St Chicago IL 60601

KRASIN, MATTHEW J., oncologist; b. El Cajon, Calif., Aug. 21, 1969; m. Audrey L. Rogers. MD, U. Tex. Med. Br., Galveston, 1991—95. Cert. in radiation oncology Am. Bd. Radiology, 2000. Faculty, divsn. radiation oncology St. Jude Children's Rsch. Hosp., Memphis, 2000—. Office: St Jude Children's Rsch Hosp 332 N Lauderdale Memphis TN 38105 Office Phone: 901-495-3596. E-mail: matthew.krasin@stjude.org.

KRASLOW, DAVID, retired publishing executive, writer, consultant, reporter; b. NYC, Apr. 16, 1926; s. Frank and Goldie (Sirota) K.; m. Bernice Schonfeld, Sept. 18, 1949; children: Ellen Anne, Karen Leah, Susan Beth. BA in Journalism, U. Miami, Fla., 1948. Washington corr. L.A. Times, 1963-66, news editor Washington bur., 1966-70, chief Washington bur., 1970-72; asst. mng. editor Washington Star-News, 1972-74; chief Washington bur. Cox Newspapers, 1974-77; pub. Miami News, 1977-88, sports writer, 1947-48; successively sports writer, reporter, Washington corr. Miami Herald, 1948-63; panelist news program Sta. WPBT-TV, Miami, 1979-91; v.p. Cox Newspapers, Miami, 1989-91. Co-author: A Certain Evil, 1965, The Secret Search for Peace in Vietnam, 1968. Life trustee, acad. affairs com., Sch. Medicine com., athletic adv. com. U. Miami; mem. Orange Bowl Com.; bd. dirs. Greater Miami Tennis Found., Inc., Internat. Oceanographic Found., U. Miami, Pub. Health Trust of Miami-Dade County; founding pres. Ctr. for Fine Arts (now Miami Art Mus.), Miami, 1979-84. With USAAF, 1944-46. Recipient George Polk award, 1969; Raymond Clapper award, 1969; Dumont award, 1969; Nieman fellow Harvard U., 1961-62 Mem.: Gridiron Club (Washington). Jewish. Personal E-mail: dkgables@aol.com.

KRASNA, ALVIN ISAAC, biochemist, educator; b. N.Y.C., June 23, 1929; s. Selig and Esther (Finer) K.; m. Elaine C. Cohen, Feb. 27, 1955; children—Susan Roni, Gary Marc, Allen Selig. BA, Yeshiva Coll., 1950; PhD, Columbia U., 1955. Mem. faculty Columbia U., 1956—, prof. biochemistry, 1970—, acting chmn., 1977-78, 88-90, vice chmn., 1978-88, 90—. Contbr. to profl. jours. Predoctoral fellow NSF, 1953; Guggenheim fellow, 1962; research grantee NSF; research grantee NIH; research grantee Am. Cancer Soc.; research grantee AEC, Dept. Energy Mem. Am. Chem. Soc., Am. Assn. Biol. Chemists, AAAS, Harvey Soc., Am. Soc. Microbiology, Sigma Xi. Home: 6 Arbor Dr New Rochelle NY 10804-1101 Office: 630 W 168th St New York NY 10032-3702

KRASNER, DANIEL WALTER, lawyer; b. NYC, Mar. 18, 1941; s. Nathan and Rose Krasner; m. Ruth Pollack, Dec. 20, 1964; children: Jonathan, Lisa, Noah, Rebecca. BA, Yeshiva Coll., 1962; LLB, Yale U., 1965. Bar: N.Y. 1966, U.S. Dist. Ct. (so. dist.) N.Y. 1967, U.S. Dist. Ct. (ea. dist.) N.Y. 1968, U.S. Supreme Ct. 1978, U.S. Ct. Appeals (1st, 2d, 3d, 5th, 6th, 8th-11th dists.). Assoc. Pomerantz Levy Houdek & Block, N.Y.C., 1965-76; sr. ptnr. Wolf Haldenstein Adler Freeman & Herz, N.Y.C., 1977—. Vice chmn. Westchester Day Sch., Mamaroneck, N.Y., 1979-86; v.p., trustee Bd. Jewish Edn., N.Y.C., 1981—. Democrat. Avocations: tennis, golf, sailing. Office: Wolf Haldenstein Adler Freeman & Herz 270 Madison Ave New York NY 10016-0601 Office Phone: 212-545-4600. Business E-Mail: krasner@whafh.com.

KRASNER, JONATHAN B., history educator; b. N.Y.C., Aug. 29, 1964; s. Daniel W. and Ruth S. Krasner; m. Frank P. Tipton, July 16, 2000; 1 child, Ariel Hope. BA, Brandeis U., Waltham, Mass., 1988; EdM, Harvard U., Cambridge, Mass., 1995; PhD, Brandeis U., Waltham, Mass., 2002. Tchr. Charles E. Smith Sch., Rockville, Md., 1988—90, Ramaz Upper Sch., N.Y.C., 1990—94; chmn., history dept. Gann Acad., Waltham, Mass., 1998—2002; asst. prof., Am. Jewish history Hebrew Union Coll., Cin., 2002—. Mem.: Network for Rsch. in Jewish Edn., Am. History Assn., Assn. for Jewish Studies. Office: Hebrew Union Coll 3101 Clifton Ave Cincinnati OH 45220

KRASNO, RICHARD MICHAEL, foundation executive, educator; b. Chgo., Jan. 20, 1942; s. Louis R. K. and Adeline G. (Glassman) Kaplan; children: Jeffrey Patrick, Eric Peter; m. Carin Blucher. BS, U. Ill., 1965; PhD, Stanford U., 1970; LittD (hon.), Coll. St. Rose, 1983; LLD (hon.), Sacred Heart U., 1984. Asst. prof. ednl. psychology U. Chgo., 1970-74; program advisor Brazil Ford Found., Rio de Janeiro, 1974-77, program advisor Latin Am. N.Y.C., 1977, program advisor Mid.-East & Africa, 1978-80; deputy asst. sec. of edn. U.S. Dept. Edn., Washington, 1980-81; exec. v.p. Inst. Internat. Edn., N.Y.C., 1981-83, pres., CEO, 1983-98; pres. Monterey (Calif.) Inst. Internat Stud, 1998-99, Kenan Charitable Trust, Chapel Hill, N.C., 1999—. Commr. U.S.-Brazil Fulbright Commn., 1975-77, U.S. Nat. Commn. UNESCO, 1983; chmn. Internat. Transition Team Dept. Edn., 1979, 80; mem. U.S.-Mex. Bilateral Commn., 1980, 84; sr. Fulbright lectr., 1973-74. Contbr. articles to profl. jours. Trustee Laspau, Cambridge, Mass., 1980—82, Eisenhower Exch. Program, 2002—; chmn. Rhodes Scholars Selection Com., 2001—04; dir. U. NC Healthcare, 2004—. Nat. Defense Edn. fellow U.S. Govt., 1967-68. Mem. Coun. Fgn. Rels., Century Assn., Cosmos Club. Office: The Kenan Ctr PO Box 3858 Chapel Hill NC 27515-3858 Business E-Mail: richard_krasno@unc.edu.

KRASNOFF, ERIC, health products executive; s. Abraham Krasnoff; m. Robin Krasnoff; 2 children. BA in Anthropology, Columbia Univ. Various exec. positions, including v.p., sr. v.p., group v.p., exec. v.p., pres., COO Pall Corp., East Hills, NY, 1975—94, chmn, CEO, 1994—. Chmn. bd. Nat. Blood Found., 2001—; Presdl. adv. bd. Nat. Ctr. for Disability Svcs.; vice chmn. Am. Bus. Conf.; bd. dir. Nassau Healthcare Corp., 2004—. Bd. trustees Long Island Univ., 1992—. Office: Pall Corp 2200 Northern Blvd Greenvale NY 11548-1289 Office Phone: 516-484-5400.*

KRASNOW, ERWIN GILBERT, lawyer; b. Bklyn., Jan. 8, 1936; s. Charles and Etta (Simowitz) K.; m. E. Judith Levine, Sept. 6, 1960 (dec. July 1994); children: Michael Andew, Catherine Beth; m. Jane Gasperini, Nov. 25, 1995. AB summa cum laude, Boston U., 1958; JD, Harvard U., 1961; LLM, Georgetown U., 1965. Bar: Mass. 1961, U.S. Dist. Ct. Mass. 1961, D.C. 1963, U.S. Ct. Appeals (D.C. cir.) 1963, U.S. Supreme Ct. 1965, U.S. Ct. Appeals (4th cir.) 1978, U.S. Ct. Appeals (5th and 11th cirs.) 1982. Rsch. asst. Harvard U. Law Sch., Cambridge, Mass., 1961; adminstr. asst. to Congressman Torbert H. Macdonald, U.S. Ho. of Reps., Washington, 1962—64; ptnr. Kirkland and Ellis, Washington, 1964—76; sr. v.p., gen. counsel Nat. Assn. Broadcasters, Washington, 1976—84; ptnr. Verner, Liipfert, Bernhard, McPherson & Hand, Washington, 1984—2001, Shook, Hardy & Bacon, Washington, 2002—03; owner Garvey Schubert Barer, Washington, 2004—. Vis. prof. Ohio State U., 1974; disting. vis. lectr. Temple U., 1976; adj. prof. Am. U., 1975, Law Ctr., Georgetown U., 1984; professorial lectr. Grad. Sch. Arts and Scis., George Washington U., 1982, 83, adj. prof., 1998; professorial lectr. Sch. Law, Cath. U. Am., 1982; bd. dirs. Broadcast Capital Fund, Inc. (formerly Minority Broadcast Investment Fund), 1978—, treas., 1979-92, vice chmn., 1993—; mem. govt. industry adv. coun. Ctr. for Telecom. Studies, George Washington U., 1980-84; mem. adv. bd. Inst. for Comm. Law, Sch. Law, Cath. U. Am., 1982—; mem. bd. advisors Comm. Media Ctr., N.Y. Law Sch., 1982—; mem. adv. com. comm. law program UCLA, 1983-85. Co-author: A Candidate's Guide to the Law of Political Broadcasting, 1977, 3d edit., 1984, Buying and Building a Broadcast Station, 3d edit., 1987, 100 Ways To Cut Legal Fees and Manage your Lawyer, 1988, Radio Financing: A Guide for Lenders and Investors, 1990, Insider's Guide to Radio Acquisition Contracts, 1992; co-author: FCC Lobbying A Handbook of Insider Tips and Practical Advice, 2001; editor: National Assosication of Broadcasters Legal Guide to FCC Broadcast Rules, Regulations and Policies, 1977; bd. editors Fed. Comm. Bar Jour., 1973-75; mem. editl. adv. bd. Jour. Broadcasting, 1972-85, Telematics and Informatics, 1982—; mem. adv. com. COMM/ENT Law Jour., 1983—; contbr. articles to legal pubs. Mem. ABA (vice chmn. agy. adjudication com. 1974-77, chmn. comm. law com. adminstrv. law sect. 1980-81), FBA (pres. Capitol Hill chpt. 1963-64, dep. co-chmn. comm. law com. 1967-69, co-chmn. 1970-71), Fed. Comm. Bar Assn. (exec. com. 1976-79, 84-85, treas. 1984-85), Capitol Hill Bar Assn. (past pres.), Boston U. Alumni Club Washington (pres. 1967-70), Boston U. Nat. Alumni Assn. (bd. dirs. 1966-68, regional v.p. 1971, 73), Phi Beta Kappa. Home: 3307 Q St NW Washington DC 20007-2717 Office: Garvey Schubert Barer Flour Mill Bldg 5th fl 1000 Potomac St NW Washington DC 20007-3501 Office Phone: 202-298-2161. Business E-Mail: ekrasnow@gsblaw.com.

KRASNOW, RICHARD P., lawyer; b. Bklyn., Feb. 12, 1947; s. Nathan A. and Doris (Pearson) K.; m. Nancy Meyrich, Oct. 3, 1982. AB, U. Chgo., 1968; JD, NYU, 1972. Assoc. Shereff, Friedman, Huffman & Goodman, N.Y.C., 1972-73; ptnr. Weil, Gotshal & Manges, N.Y.C., 1972—. Mem. ABA, N.Y. State Bar Assn., Assn. Bar City of N.Y. Office: Weil Gotshal & Manges 767 5th Ave Fl Concl New York NY 10153-0119

KRASNY, MICHAEL P., investment company executive; BS in Fin., U. Ill., 1975. Founder, chmn., CEO, sec. CDW Computer Ctrs., Vernon Hills, Ill., 1984—2001, pres., 1984—90, bd. mem. emeritus, 2001—; pres. Sawdust Investment Mgmt. Corp. Bd. mem. Kellogg Sch. of Mgmt., Northwestern U. Bd. dirs. Ctr. for Enriched Living, The Anti-Defamation League, B'nai Brith Beber Camp. Recipient Entrepeneur of Yr., Ernest and Young, 1993, CEO of Yr., Fin. World, 1996, Torch award for marketplace ethics, Nat. BBB, 2000. Mem.: Young Pres. Orgn., Econ. Club of Chgo. Office: CDW 200 N Milwaukee Ave Vernon Hills IL 60061-1577 also: Sawdust Investment Mgmt 812 Skokie Blvd Northbrook IL 60062*

KRASNY, MYRON S. (MIKE KRASNY), lawyer; b. Phila., Nov. 15, 1931; s. Maurice and Sara (Krakover) K.; m. C. Althea Jones, Dec. 21, 1958; children: G. Mitchell, Robin Gayle, Scott Douglas, Glenn Steven, Keith Stuart. Cert. Chinese Lang. Sch., Yale U., 1952; BBA, U. Miami (Fla.), 1958, JD, 1960. Bar: Fla. 1960, U.S. Dist. Ct. (mid. dist.) Fla. 1963, U.S. Ct. Appeals (11th cir.) 1975, U.S. Supreme Ct. 1979, Colo. 1997. Law clk. to Judge Harrold Carswell U.S. Fed. Dist. Ct., Tallahassee, 1960-62; ptnr. Kelley Stroud & Krasny, Eau Gallie, Fla., 1962-64, Storms Pappas & Krasny, Melbourne, Fla., 1964-78; ptnr., shareholder Storms Krasny Normile & Dettmer P.C., Melbourne, 1978-88, Krasny & Dettmer, Melbourne, 1988—. City atty. City of Satellite Beach (Fla.), 1964-74; city prosecutor Cities of Melbourne and Eau Gallie, 1964-73; mcpl. judge City of Melbourne Beach, 1965-73. Bd. dirs. Am. Cancer Soc., 1985-96; chmn. bd. dirs. Easter Seal Soc., 1988. With USAF, 1951-55; capt. CAP 1995—. Mem. Inns of Ct. (counsellor, master 1992—), Melbourne Area Pilot's Assn., Satellite Beach Flying Club. Avocations: instrument-rated pilot, scuba diving, bicycling, skiing, weightlifting. Office: Krasny & Dettmer 304 S Harbor City Blvd Ste 201 Melbourne FL 32901-1324 Office Phone: 321-543-2145. E-mail: mkrasny@cfl.rr.com.

KRASNY, PAULA J., lawyer; b. Phila., Pa., Sept. 29, 1963; Student, Harvard U., 1984; AB, Vassar Coll., 1985; JD, Northwestern U., 1988. Bar: Ill. 1988. Atty. McDermott, Will & Emery, Chgo., ptnr., 1995—99, Baker & McKenzie, Chgo., 1999—. Mem. adv. bd. Northwestern Jour. Tech. and Intellectual Property; bd. dir. Frances Lehman Loeb Art Ctr. Vassar Coll. Mem.: ABA, Internat. Trademark Assn., Am.-Israel C. of C. Office: Baker & McKenzie One Prudential Plz 130 East Randolph Dr Chicago IL 60601

KRATHWOHL, DAVID READING, retired education educator; b. Chgo., May 14, 1921; s. Marie (Reimold) Krathwohl; m. Helen Jean Abney, Dec. 20, 1943; children: James D.(dec.), David A., Ruth Anne Krathwohl Cleghorn, Kristin Jeanne. BS, U. Chgo., 1943, MS, 1947, PhD, 1953. Asst. dir. unit on evaluation Bur. Ednl. Research, Coll. Edn., U. Ill., 1949-55, instr., 1949-53; asst. prof., 1953-55; asso. prof. Mich. State U., 1955-58, prof., 1958-65, research coordinator, 1955-63; chmn. Psychol. Found. Edn., 1960-63; dir. Bur. Ednl. Research, 1963-65; dean NYU Sch. Edn., Syracuse, 1965-76, prof., 1965-91, Hannah Hammond prof. edn., 1982-91, Hannah Hammond prof. emeritus, 1991—; ret., 1991. Chmn. bd. trustees Ea. Regional Inst. Edn., 1966—71. Author (with others): Taxonomy of Educational Objectives: Cognitive Domain, 1956; author: Affective Domain, 1964, Social and Behavioral Science Research.: A New Framework for Conceptualizing, Implementing and Evaluating Research Studies, 1985, How to Prepare a Research Proposal, 3d edit., 1988, Methods of Educational and Social Science Research: An Integrated Approach, 2d edit., 1998; author: (with N.L. Smith) How to Prepare a Dissertation Proposal, 2005; editor (with L. W. Anderson): A Taxonomy for Learning, Teaching and Assessing: A Revision of Bloom's Taxonomy of Educational Objectives, 2001. With USAAF, 1943—46. Fellow, Ctr. Advanced Study Behavioral Scis., 1980—81. Fellow: APA (v.p. ednl. psychology divsn.), AAAS; mem.: Am. Psychol. Soc., Am. Ednl. Rsch. Assn. (pres.). Home: 9 Thornwood Ln Fayetteville NY 13066-2529 Office: Syracuse U Sch Of Education Syracuse NY 13244-2340

KRATKA, ILENE, artist, sculptor; b. Bridgeton, NJ, May 31, 1941; d. William Herbert Kratka and Zelda Verna Osdin; life partner Scott Hayes. BA, American U., 1965; postgrad., Corcoran Sch. Art, 1968-71. Presch. tchr. Headstart Program, Washington, 1963-65; pottery tchr. Centering, Cambridge, Mass., 1971-77, Hui Noeau, Maui, Hawaii, 1977-78. Exhibited in group shows including Hawaii Craftsman, 1979, Art Maui, 1989, 2000, Lahaina Arts Soc., 1985, Hui Noeau, 1987, Viewpoints Gallery, 1990, 93, 94, 95; in collections of H.M.S. Assocs., San Francisco, The Willkinsburg Drop-In Ctr., Pitts., County of Maui. Mem. Centering Pottery Coop., Cambridge, Mass., 1970-77. Mem. Centering Pottery (co-founder), Maui Crafts Guild (bd. dirs., display chairperson), Viewpoints Artists Collective (bd. dirs. and installations, pres. 1997). Avocation: writing haiku poetry.

KRATKA-SCHNEIDER, DOROTHY MARYJOHANNA, psychotherapist; b. New Britain, Conn., Apr. 29, 1934; d. Josef Matthew and Mari Catherine (Stifil) Kratka; m. Warren Andrew Schneider, Apr. 26, 1975. BS in Nursing, Columbia U., 1960; MSW, Fordham U., 1969; EdD in Counseling Psychology, U. San Francisco, 1983. RN, Conn.; bd. cert. diplomate in clin. social work. Instr. pub. health nursing U. Conn., Storrs, 1963-64; participant Voter Registration Drive, Greenwood, Miss., 1965; pub. health nurse Jesuit Med. Mission Bd., Tanzania, East Africa, 1965-67; chief psychiat. social worker Knickerbocker Hosp., N.Y.C., 1969-74; coordinator social services Rockefeller U. Hosp., N.Y.C., 1974-77; asst. prof. Calif. State U., Sacramento, 1985-88, assoc. prof., 1985-88; counseling psychologist VA, San Francisco, 1987-89; psychologist, social worker Dept. Transp., 1989-93; pvt. practice Corte Madera, Calif., 1993—. Bd. dirs. Nat. Assn. Soc. Work Referral Service, San Francisco, 1984-86. Bd. dirs. Health Systems Adv. Com., San Francisco, 1978, Cmty. Mental Health, Marin County, Calif., 1998—; mem. Cath. Charities Bd. for Aging, San Francisco, 1985, bd. dirs., 1983-85; apptd. to Marin County Cmty. Mental Health Bd., 1998—; apptd. to Marin County Grand Jury, Superior Ct., 1999—. Grantee, NIMH, 1967—69. Mem. APA, Internat. Assn. Profl. Counselors and Psychotherapists (diplomate psychotherapy), NASW (diplomate in clin. social work), Register for Clin. Social Workers of NASW, Amnesty Internat., Kappa Delta Pi. Democrat. Roman Catholic. Avocations: hiking, watercolors, flying, swimming. Office: 200 Professional Ctr D Ste 200 Novato CA 94947 Office Phone: 415-898-9015 ext. 724. E-mail: dorothyschneider@earthlink.net.

KRATOCHVIL, BYRON GEORGE, chemistry educator, researcher; b. Osmond, Nebr., Sept. 15, 1932; came to Can., 1967; s. Frank James and Mabel Louise (Schneider) K.; m. Marianne Spain; children: Susan, Daniel, Jean, John. BS, Iowa State U., 1957, MS, 1959, PhD, 1961. Asst. prof. chemistry U. Wis.-Madison, 1961-67; assoc. prof. chemistry U. Alta., Edmonton, Canada, 1967-71, prof. chemistry, 1971-98, prof. emeritus, 1998—, dept. chmn., 1989-95, assoc. v.p. rsch., 1996-98, sr. advisor, v.p. rsch., 1998-2001; dir. planning and ops. Alta. Synchrotron Inst., 2002—04. Co-author: (with W.E. Harris) Chemical Analysis, 1969, Chemical Separations and Measurements, 1974, Introduction to Chemical Analysis, 1981-84; analytical editor Can. Jour. Chemistry, Ottawa, Ont., 1985-88, sr. editor, 1988-93; contbr. articles to profl. jours. Recipient Merit award Iowa State U. Alumni, 1990. Fellow AAAS, Chem. Inst. Can. (bd. dirs. 1977-80, Fisher Lectr. award 1990); mem. Am. Chem. Soc. Office: U Alta Dept Chemistry Chemistry Centre Edmonton AB Canada T6G 2G2 Office Phone: 780-492-4665. E-mail: ron.kratochvil@ualberta.ca.

KRATOCHVIL, L(OUIS) GLEN, lawyer; b. Highland, Wis., Oct. 11, 1922; s. John A. and Emma (Pusch) K.; m. Evelyn Gregory, Sept. 12, 1946; 1 son, Louis Glen Jr. LLB, U. Wis., 1951; JD. Bar: Wis. 1951, Tex. 1952, U.S. Dist. Ct. (so. dist.) Tex. 1956, U.S. Ct. Appeals (5th cir.) 1956, U.S. Supreme Ct. 1956, U.S. Dist. Ct. (ea. dist.) Tex. 1961. Landman Shell Oil Co., Houston, 1951-52; assoc. firm Murphy & Crystal, Houston, 1953-55; asst. U.S. atty. So. Dist. Tex., 1955-57; pvt. practice Houston, 1957—99. Pres. McGregor Terr. Civic Club, Houston, 1954, Young Rep. Club U. Wis., 1950. Lt. USNR, 1941-46, PTO. Mem.: FBA, ABA, U. Wis. Alumni Assn. (pres. Houston chpt. 1972—73), Maritime Law Assn., Houston Bar Assn., Wis. Bar Assn., Tex. Bar Assn., Brazos River Club (treas. 1970—99), Lions (pres. 1955), Phi Alpha Delta (chief justice 1950). Home: 302 Kickerillo Dr Houston TX 77079-7412 Office: Kratochvil and Powell 3303 Main St Ste 207 Houston TX 77002-9321

KRATOVIL, JANE LINDLEY, think tank associate, not-for-profit developer; b. Boston, Nov. 25, 1952; 1 child, Lindley. BA, Lynchburg Coll., 1974. Various positions U.S. Ho. of Reps., Washington, 1974-77, The Pittston Co., Greenwich, Conn., 1977-79; assoc. dir. City Sports Mgmt. Inc., Washington, 1979-82; adminstrv. asst. to spl. asst. to pres. for adminstrn. The White House, Washington, 1982-85; exec. asst. to gen. and dep. gen. counsel U.S. Dept. Treasury, Washington, 1985-88; exec. dir., sec. Eisenhower World Affairs Inst., Washington, 1988-2000; pres. Lindley & Assoc., Alexandria, Va., 2000—. Office: 2230 Candlewood Dr Alexandria VA 22308-1505 E-mail: jkratovil@earthlink.net.

KRATT, MARY NORTON, writer; b. Beckley, W.Va., June 7, 1936; d. William Randolph and Martha Hunter (Hood) Norton; m. Emil F. Kratt, Aug. 29, 1959; children: E. William, Laura Catherine, Mary Hunter. BA, Agnes Scott Coll., Decatur, Ga., 1958; MA, U. N.C., 1992. Ednl. cons. Charlotte (N.C.) Landmarks Commn., 1988, 90, Charlotte Pub. Libr., 1986; adj. instr. U. N.C., Charlotte, 1993—96. Author: Marney, 1980, Spirit Going Barefoot (poetry), 1982, Southern Is..., 1985, 14th edit. 1992), Legacy: The Myers Park Story, 1986, The Imaginative Spirit: Literary History of Charlotte and Mecklenburg County, 1988, My Dear Miss Eva, 1990, A Little Charlotte Scrapbook, 1990, A Bird in the House, 1991, Charlotte: Spirit of the New South, 1992, The Only Thing I Fear is A Cow and A Drunken Man, 1991, On The Steep Side, 1993, Small Potatoes, 1999, Valley, 2000, Remembering Charlotte: Postcards from a New South City, 1905-1950, 2000, New South Women: Twentieth Century Women of Charlotte, North Carolina, 2001; poetry, articles pub. numerous lit. mags.; editorial bd. N.C. Lit. Rev. Bd. dirs. Mus. of New South, Charlotte, 1990—92. Recipient Oscar Arnold Young award for best original book of poems North Carolinian, 1983, ACE award for excellence in comm. Women in Comm., 1984, Spl. Merit award, 1990, Peace prize, History Book award N.C. Soc. Historians, 1987, Hist. Preservation award for vol. svc. Charlotte Landmarks Commn., 1990, Fortner award St. Andrews Coll., 1994, MacDowell Colony Artist Residency award N.C. Arts Coun., 1996, Brockman Campbell Poetry Book award, 1999. Mem. N.C. Writers Network (past bd. dirs.), N.C. Writers Conf. (chmn. 1991), Charlotte Writers' Club (pres. 2002-2003), Phi Kappa Phi. Home and Office: 3328 Providence Plantation Ln Charlotte NC 28270-3719 Office Phone: 704-708-8589.

KRATT, PETER GEORGE, lawyer; b. Lorain, Ohio, Mar. 7, 1940; s. Arthur Leroy and Edith Ida (Dietz) K.; m. Sharon Amy Maruska, June 15, 1968; children: Kevin George, Jennifer Ivy. BA, Miami U., Oxford, Ohio, 1962; JD, Case Western Res. U., 1966. Bar: Ohio 1966. Atty. Cleve. Trust Co., 1966-74; assoc. counsel AmeriTrust Co., 1974-84, sec., assoc. counsel, 1985-87, sed., sr. assoc. counsel, 1987-92; ret. v.p., mgr. personal trust adminstrn. Huntington Trust Co., 1993-99. Mem. Am. Soc. Corp. Secs., Ohio Bar Assn., Rotary, Lions. Methodist. Avocations: hiking, gardening. E-mail: pkratt@centurytel.net.

KRAUS, DAVID (DIRK) BRUCE, musician, educator; b. Marysville, Ohio, Dec. 28, 1968; s. Kenneth Martin and Alice Elizabeth Kraus; m. Jennifer Ann Simpson. BA, BS, Ohio No. U., 1992. Piano tchr. Conservatory Piano, Worthington, Ohio, 1996—2001; piano tchr., owner Piano Inst., Ft. Collins, Colo., 2001—. Mem.: Ft. Collins Music Tchrs. Assn. Office: Piano Inst 2839 S College # 3 Fort Collins CO 80525

KRAUS, DAVID ROBERT, lawyer; b. Pitts., July 1, 1960; BA, Dickinson Coll., 1982; JD, Boston U., 1985. Bar: Pa. 1985, U.S. Dist. ct. (mid. dist.) Pa. 1987. Counsel Pa. Bd. Fin. and Revenue, Harrisburg, 1985-87; mng. ptnr. Dechert LLP (formerly Dechert Price & Rhoads), Harrisburg, 1987—. Office: Dechert LLP 30 N 3rd St Harrisburg PA 17101-1703 E-mail: david.kraus@dechert.com.*

KRAUS, DOUGLAS M., lawyer; b. NYC, Jan. 28, 1949; s. Irving R. and Bebe B. (Baron) K.; m. Alice R. Weigle, Mar. 8, 1970; children— Amy Elizabeth, Jonathan Eric. BA magna cum laude, U. Pa., 1970; JD, U. Chgo., 1973. Bar: NY 1974, US Dist. Ct. (so. and ea. dists.) NY 1974, US Ct. Appeals (2d cir.) 1974, US Ct. Appeals (8th cir.) 1981, US Ct. Appeals (DC cir.) 1982, US Ct. Appeals (1st cir.) 1983, US Supreme Ct. 1984. Assoc. firm Skadden, Arps, Slate, Meagher & Flom., NYC, 1973-81, ptnr., 1981—, chmn., pro bono com. Lectr. on bank acquisitions and takeovers Practicing Law Inst., NYC, 1982-84. Assoc. editor, contbr. U. Chgo. Law Rev., 1972-73. mem.,zoning bd. Town of New Castle, Chappaqua, NY, 1974-75, councilman, 1976-80, town justice, 1994-; bd. dir., Legal Aid Society, 1993-, NY Lawyers for the Public Interest, 1994-; mem., bd. advisors, NYU Law Sch. Ctr. for Research in Crime and Justice, 1985-. Mem. ABA (chmn. nat. inst. 1983), Assn. Bar City NY (mem., Com. on Federal Courts, 1984-88). Office: Skadden Arps Slate Meagher & Flom LLP 4 Times Sq New York NY 10036 Office Phone: 212-735-2510. Office Fax: 917-777-2510. Business E-Mail: dkraus@skadden.com.

KRAUS, EDWARD, lawyer; b. Pitts., Pa., May 22, 1967; BA, UC Berkeley, Calif., 1985—89; JD, Santa Clara U. Sch. Law, Calif., 1989—92. Bar: Calif. 1992, US Dist. Ct.: (no. dist.) 1992, (ea. dist.) 1998, US Ct. Appeals: (9th cir.) 1998. Dep. pub. defender Santa Clara County Pub. Defender's Office, San Jose, Calif., 1995—98; assoc. Reed, Elliott, Creech & Roth, San Jose, Calif., 1998—2002; mem. Creech, Liebow & Kraus, San Jose, Calif., 2003—. Bd. mem. Anti-Defamation League, San Francisco, 1995—2001, Jewish Cmty. Rels. Coun., San Jose, Calif., 1995—2001. Mem.: Nat. Assn. of Criminal Lawyers, Santa Clara County Bar Assn., State Bar of Calif., Am. Trial Lawyers Assn. (assoc.). Office: Creech Liebow & Kraus 333 W San Carlos St Ste 1600 San Jose CA 95110 Office Fax: 408-993-1335. Business E-Mail: ekraus@sjlegal.com.

KRAUS, HANS MICHAEL, lawyer; b. Ludwigshafen, Germany, Aug. 20, 1954; came to the U.S., 1983; Referendar, U. Freiburg, Germany, 1978; assessor, State of Rheinland Pfalz, Germany, 1981; M in Comparative Jurisprudence, U. Tex., 1982. Bar: Germany 1982, Ga. 1985. Assoc. Stoffel & Ptnrs., Cologne, Germany, 1982-83; ptnr. Smith Gambrell & Russell, Atlanta, 1983—. Bd. dirs. Brita Ltd., Toronto, Can., USHA Ltd., New Delhi, Loher Drive Sys., Atlanta. Contbr. articles to profl. jours. Mem. Internat. Bar Assn., German Am. C. of C. Office: Smith Gambrell & Russell 1230 Peachtree St NE Ste 3100 Atlanta GA 30309-3592

KRAUS, HERBERT MYRON, public relations executive; b. Cleve., Sept. 21, 1921; s. Joseph Emil and Eva (Meyers) K.; m. Barbara Cohen, Sept. 9, 1945 (div. Jan. 1, 1955); 1 child, Gale Ann Kraus Reinitz; m. Catherine Eugenia Capraro, Mar. 5, 1955; 1 child, Claudia Willa Kraus Piper. BA, U. Ill., 1941. Pub. rels. assoc. Nat. Jewish Hosp., Chgo., 1948-51; dir. pub. rels. State of Israel Bond Dr., Chgo., 1951-54; pvt. practice Chgo., 1954-73; pres.

Manning, Selvage & Lee of Chgo., 1973-82; pvt. practice Chgo., 1982-85; pres. Kraus Dunham Nikolich P.R., Chgo., 1986-88; sr. counselor Weiser Walek Group, Chgo., 1989-92, Fin. Rels. Bd., Chgo., 1992—2001; Herbert M. Krauss & Co., 2002—. Instr. pub. rels. Columbia Coll., Chgo.; adj. prof. pub. rels. Stuart Grad. Sch. Bus., Ill. Inst. Tech., Chgo. Co-chmn. John Fischetti Cartoon Awards Com., Chgo., Comms. Chgo. XV, 1989; pres. Friends of WFMT, Inc., 1989-90; bd. dirs. Victory Gardens Theatre, Chgo., 1978-95, Am. Jewish Com., Chgo., 1989—; del. Rep. Nat. Conv., Detroit, 1980; columnist: Chgo. Journalist; bd. dirs. Emanuel Congregation, 2000-04. Recipient Alschuler award for comty. svc. Am. Jewish Com., 1995. Fellow: Pub. Rels. Soc. Am.; mem.: Chgo. Headline Club, Chgo. TV Acad., Publicity Club Chgo. (pres. 1989—90), Chgo. Press Vets. (bd. dirs. 2000—), Am. Friends of Czech Republic. Avocations: theater, travel, humor writing, poker. Home: 415 W Aldine Ave Apt 7A Chicago IL 60657-3601 Office Phone: 312-578-9114. E-mail: hkraus921@rcn.com.

KRAUS, JILL GANSMAN, former jewelry industry marketing executive; b. Phila., Oct. 25, 1952; d. Lester David and Lois (Singer) Gansman; m. Peter Steven Kraus, July 20, 1980; 2 children, Jason Andrew, Benjamin Michael. BFA, Carnegie Mellon U., 1974; MFA, RISD, 1977. Designer Accesocraft, NYC, 1977-78, Cadoro, NYC, 1978-79; asst. to dir. of design Monet Jewelry, NYC, 1979-81; sr. designer Swank Inc., NYC, 1981-85; named product mktg. mgr. Marvella, NYC, 1985; cons. Liz Claiborne; named v.p. design & training Swarovski Jewelry US Ltd., NYC, 1992. V.p. associates divsn. Jewish Guild for the Blind, NYC, 1983—87; bd. trustees Carnegie Mellon U.; bd. dirs. World Studio Found., NYC; co-chair Friends of the Carnegie Internat.; commd. Kraus Campo garden for Carnegie Mellon U. campus, 2004. Named one of Top 200 Collectors, ARTnews mag., 2004. Democrat. Avocation: Collector Contemporary Art.

KRAUS, JODY S., law educator; b. Indpls., 1960; BA, Ohio State U., 1982; MA, U. Ariz., 1984, PhD, 1987; JD, Yale U., 1990. Bar: Va. 1990, DC 1992. Asst. prof. U. Va. Sch. Law, 1990—95, prof. law and prof. philosophy, 1996—, E. James Kelly, Jr. rsch. prof., 1997—2000, named Caddell & Chapman rsch. prof., 2002. Mem. adv. bd. Legal Theory. Mem.: Am. Philos. Assn., Assn. Am. Law Schools, Am. Law Inst. Office: U Va Sch Law 580 Massie Rd Charlottesville VA 22903-1789 Office Phone: 434-924-3568. E-mail: jsk5g@virginia.edu.

KRAUS, JOHN WALTER, former aerospace engineering company executive; b. N.Y.C., Feb. 5, 1918; s. Walter Max Kraus and Marian Florance (Nathan) Sandor; m. Janice Edna Utter, June 21, 1947 (dec. Feb. 1981); children: Melinda Jean Kraus Peters, Kim Kohl Kraus; m. Jean Curtis, Aug. 27, 1983. BS, MIT, 1941; MBA, U. So. Calif., 1972. From indsl. engr. to indsl. enging. mgr. TRW, Inc., Cleve., 1941-61; spl. asst. Atomics Internat., Chatsworth, Calif., 1961-65; br. chief McDonnell Douglas Astronautics Co., Huntington Beach, Calif., 1966-74; sr. mgr. McDonnell Douglas Space Systems Co., Huntington Beach, Calif., 1983-93; pres. Kraus and DuVall, Inc., Santa Ana, Calif., 1975-83; retired, 1993. Cons. Tech. Assocs. So. Calif., Santa Ana, 1974-75. Author: (handbook) Handbook of Reliability Engineering and Management, 1988. Mem. Nat. Def. Industries Assn. (formally Am. Def. Preparedness Assn., life, chmn. tech. div. 1954-57), Nat. Soc. Profl. Engrs. (life), Oasis Sailing Club (commodore 1996-2002, dir. 1996—), Friends of Oasis (dir. 1999—, treas. 2000-2002, 2004—), MIT Club of So. Calif. Republican. Avocations: sailing, reading, gardening. Home: 2001 Commodore Rd Newport Beach CA 92660-4307 Personal E-mail: skprjohn6@netscape.net.

KRAUS, JOSEPH C., music educator; b. Rochester, NY, Apr. 7, 1955; s. George C and Lucille R Kraus. MusB, U. of Rochester Eastman Sch., 1977; M in Music Theory, Ind. U., 1981; PhD, in Music Theory, U. of Rochester-Eastman Sch., 1987. Prof. of music theory U. Nebr., Lincoln, Nebr., 1984—. Pres. Music Theory Midwest, 2003—05. Contbr. chapters to books, articles to prof. jours. Pres. Lincoln Friends of Chamber Music, Lincoln, Nebr., 1994—2004. Recipient Outstanding Svc. to Students Chancellor award, U. Nebr. Mem.: Soc. for Music Theory (chair, com. mem. 2000—03). Democrat. Achievements include research in Tchaikovsky State House-Mus. Avocations: travel, chamber music (performance). Home: 5211 W Chadderton Circle Lincoln NE 68521-4323 Office: University of Nebraska 230 Westbrook Music Building Lincoln NE 68588-0100 Office Phone: 402-472-5121. Office Fax: 402-472-8962. Business E-Mail: jkraus1@unl.edu.

KRAUS, KRANDALL ANTHONY, writer; b. Santa Rosa, Calif., July 2, 1944; s. Cletus Kraus and Annabel Adams; life ptnr. Paul Alex Borja, Aug. 19, 1991. MA, Ohio U., Athens, OH, 1968. Asst. head of publications/media Libr. of Congress, Washington, 1980—85. Cons. to office of the v.p. The White Ho., Wash., 1975—77; mem. emeritus Ryan White Statewide Working Group, Sacramento, 1991—. Author: (novel) The President's Son, (nonfiction/reference) How To Get A Federal Job, (novel) Bardo, Love's Last Chance (Lambda Lit. Award Finalist, 2000); co-author (nonfiction) It's Never About What It's About (Lambda Lit. Award, 2000); author: (poetry) The Christmas Poems (Lambda Lit. Award Finalist, 2002). Grantee Grant, Pen Am. Ctr., 2003. Home: 664 Church Street San Francisco CA 94114 Personal E-mail: krandallkraus@earthlink.net.

KRAUS, LISA MARIE WASKO, music educator, composer, musician; b. Phila., Oct. 10, 1969; d. Raymond and Muriel Joan Wasko; m. Timothy J. Kraus, Nov. 23, 2002; 1 child, Emily Victoria. AA in Music, Phila. CC, 1987; MusB Magna Cum Laude, Temple U., 1993; MusM Suma Cum Laude, Duquesne U., 2001. Cert. Music K-12 PA, 1993. Tchr. music, art, lit. tchr., program dir. Blair Christian Acad., 1993—95; tchr. orch., choir, music theory Archdiocese of Phila. St. Maria Goretti H.S., 1995—96; tchr. music, musical/vocal dir., asst. dir. musicals Bristol Twp. Sch. Dist., Levittown, 1996—. Studio musician Various Studios, 1987—; composer, arranger She Writes Music, 2001—, Martial Arts Channel, Breakthrough Comm., 2003—. Performer: Pipes and Drums of the Delaware Valley, 1987—2003, Artists Conf., 2001—02. Recipient Musical Achievement Citation, Sen. Tommy Tomlinson, 2001, Performing Arts award, Mayor Bristol Twp., 2000, 2001; scholar Ednl. scholarship, St. Albain Swain Masonic Lodge #529, 2000. Master: TRI M Music Honor Soc. (corr.; soc. sponsor 2001—, Cert. Recognition 2002); mem.: So. Poverty Law Ctr. (award 2004), Found. Ednl. Excellence (Recognition award 1997), Am. Choral Dirs. Assn., Music Educators Nat. Conf. (assoc.; collegiate chpt. treas. 1991—92), Nat. Acad. Recording Arts and Scis. (assoc.). Avocations: antiques, dog show training, painting, scrapbooks, cross stitch.

KRAUS, LORRAINE MARQUARDT, biochemist, researcher; m. Alfred P. Kraus, Sr., May 7, 1944; children: G. Thomas, Alfred P. Jr. BS, Mt. Mary Coll., Milw., Wis., 1943; PhD, U. Tenn., Memphis, Tenn., 1956; BFA, Memphis Coll. Art, Memphis, Tenn., 1982; MFA, Memphis Coll. Art, Memphis, Tenn., 1991. Asst. prof. biochemistry U. Tenn. Health Sci. Ctr., Memphis, 1960—67, assoc. prof. biochemistry, 1967—72, prof. biochemistry, 1972—90, prof. emeritus, 1990—. Adv. com. blood diseases and resources nhlbi NIH, Washington, 1979—83; cons. job corps sickle cell disease program; cons. Indian Health Svc. USPHS, Washington, 1969—90; rsch. grant and contract rev. USPHS NHLBI, 1980—92; cons./ lectr., Japan, China, Jamaica, West Germany, Austria, 1955—2005; chmn., dept biochemistry U. Tenn. Health Sci. Ctr., Memphis, 1982—84. Contbr. scientific papers pub. to profl. jour. Chair camping com. Girl Scout Coun., Memphis, Tenn. Scholar, Mt. Mary Coll., 1939 - 1943; Pre Doctoral Fellow, USPHS Nat. Heart Inst., 1954 -1955, Rockefeller Scholarship, U. Tenn. Health Sci. Ctr., 1950-1952. Mem.: Internat Soc Hematology Am Chemical Soc., Am Soc Hematology, Am. Soc. Biological Chemistry and Molecular Biology, Am. Soc. Nephrology, Sigma Xi. Office: Univ Tenn Health Sci Ctr 800 Madison Ave Memphis TN 38163 Office Phone: 901-448-4374. Business E-Mail: lkraus@utmem.edu.

KRAUS, MARGERY, management consultant, communications company executive; b. Franklin, NJ, May 20, 1946; d. Soland Lily (Cvern) Rosen; m. Stephen Kraus, Sept. 4, 1966; children: Lisa, Evan, Mara. BA in Polit. Sci., Am. U., 1967, MA in Govt., 1970. With Close Up Found., Arlington, Va., 1971-84, v.p., 1976-84; exec. v.p. APCO, Inc., Washington, 1984—88; pres., CEO APCO Worldwide (formerly APCO, Inc.), Washington, 1988—. Bd. dirs. Internat. Mgmt. and Devel. Inst., Northwestern Mutual Govt'l Rels. Com., chair, Coun. of PR Firms, Pub. Affairs Coun., Catherine B. Reynolds Found., Inst. for Public Rels., Creative Coalition, Meridian Internat. Ctr.; cons., speaker in field; adv. bd. Kellogg Sch. Mgmt. Bd. dirs. Close Up Found. Named Washington Businesswoman of the Year, 1998, Pub. Rels. Profl. of Yr., Pub. Rels. Week, 1997, 2004, Internat. Pub. Rels. Profl. of Yr., 2001. Mem., Adv. Bd., Terry Sanford Inst. of Public Policy, Duke Univ, Coun. on Am. Politics, George Washington Univ. Grad. Sch. of Political Mgmt. Home: 9609 Whitecedar Ct Vienna VA 22181-5423 Office: APCO Worldwide 700 12th St NW Ste 800 Washington DC 20005 Business E-Mail: mkraus@apcoworldwide.com.

KRAUS, NAOMI, retired biochemistry professor; b. Budapest, Hungary, July 4, 1933; came to U.S., 1965; d. Jacob and Vilma (Schwartz) K.; (div.); 1 child, Daphna. MS, Hebrew U., Jerusalem, Israel, 1960; PhD, Hebrew U., 1966. Instr. U. Pa., Phila., 1968-74; asst. prof. U. Tex. Sch. Medicine, Houston, 1974-76, assoc. prof., 1976-86, prof., 1986—2000; ret., 2000. Editor: Hormonal Control of Gluconeogenesis, 1986. Pres. Assn. Women in Sci. (Gulf Coast chpt.), 1974-76, v.p., 1989-90. Recipient grants from NIH, NSF. Mem. AAAS, Am. Soc. Cell Biology. Achievements include pioneering experiments on role Ca 2+ plays in the transduction of hormonal signals. E-mail: naomik@mindspring.com.

KRAUS, NORMA JEAN, human resources executive; b. Pitts., Feb. 11, 1931; d. Edward Karl and Alli Alexandra (Hermanson) K. BA, U. Pitts., 1954; postgrad., NYU, 1959—61, Cornell U., 1969—70. Pers. mgr. for several cos., 1957-70; corp. dir. pers. TelePrompter Corp., NYC, 1970-73; exec. asst., speech writer to Lt. Gov. NY Office of Lt. Gov., Albany, 1974-79; exec. officer, v.p. human resources, labor rels. and stockholder rels. Volt Info. Scics., Inc., NYC, 1979—. Co-founder Manhattan Women's Polit. Caucus, 1971; co-founder NY State Women's Polit. Caucus, 1972, vice chair, 1978; bd. dirs. Ctr. for Women in Govt., 1977-79. Lt. (s.g.) USNR, 1954-57. Pa. State Senatorial Scholar, 1950-54. Democrat. Avocations: politics, women's rights. Office: Volt Info Scis Inc 560 Lexington Ave Fl 15 New York NY 10022-6828 Office Phone: 212-704-2423. E-mail: njkideas@optonline.net, nkraus@volt.com.

KRAUS, PETER STEVEN, diversified financial services company executive; b. Aug. 12, 1952; B in Economics, Trinity Coll., Hartford, Conn., 1974. Named ptnr. Goldman, Sachs & Co., NYC, 1994, co-head fin. institutions group, investment banking divsn., 1998—2001, co-head pvt. wealth mgmt., 2001, co-head investment mgmt. divsn., 2001—, also mng. dir. & mem. mgmt. com. Charter trustee Trinity Coll., 1998—; bd. overseers Calif. Inst. Arts; co-chair Friends of the Carnegie Internat.; commd. Kraus Campo garden for Carnegie Mellon U. campus, 2004. Named one of Top 200 Collectors, ARTnews mag., 2004. Avocation: Collector Contemporary Art. Office: Goldman, Sachs & Co 85 Broad St New York NY 10004*

KRAUS, ROBERT H., lawyer; b. Teaneck, NJ, May 10, 1939; s. Henry and Alice R. K.; m. Carol A. Gerry, June 10, 1961; children: William R., Karen B., Kathryn L. AB, Rutgers Coll., 1961, JD, 1964. Bar: N.J. 1965, D.C. 1965. Assoc. Lowenstein & Sandler, Newark, 1966—69, Johnstone & O'Dwyer, Westfield, NJ, 1968—70, Shear & Kraus, Scotch Plains, NJ, 1971, Leib, Kraus, Grispin & Roth, Scotch Plains, 1972—. Gen. ptnr. Woodland Estates Partnership, RVS/RHK Co., LLC, Scotch Plains, 1987—2001, Flemington Trade Ctr., LLC, Fanwood Plaza Ptnrs., LLC. Bd. dirs., trustee Fanwood Scotch Plains YMCA, 1976—; trustee Scotch Plains-Fanwood Scholarship Found., 1982-88, Fanwood Cmty. Found., 1998—; chmn. Rotary-Garbe Found., Inc., 1994—. Capt. U.S. Army, 1965-66. Recipient William D. Mason Disting. Svc. award Fanwood-Scotch Plains Jaycees, 1977. Mem. ABA, NJ Bar Assn., Union County Bar Assn., Scotch Plains-Fanwood Soccer Assn. (gen. mgr., coach 1977-83). Home: 96 Forest Rd Fanwood NJ 07023-1305 Office: Leib Kraus Grispin & Roth 328 Park Ave Scotch Plains NJ 07076-0310 Office Phone: 908-322-6200. E-mail: rkraus@lkgrlaw.com.

KRAUS, SONYA, artist; b. Waiblingen, Baden-Wuerttemberg, Germany, Nov. 12, 1970; d. Britt-Marie Nylund; m. Sebastian Matthias Mueller; children: Ian Lennart, Krister Maria, Lea Clarice. BA, Freiburg (Germany) U., 1995. Project coord. The Internat. Coun. for Local Environ. Initiatives, Freiburg, 1993—94; European liaison officer The Internat. Coun. for Local Environ. Initiatives, Brussels, 1994—96; asst. to sec. gen. European Textile Svcs. Assn., Brussels, 1996—97. Expert cons. YLE TV 1 Finnish TV, Helsinki, 1994; cons. Clearinghouse for Applied Futures/Wuppertal (Germany) Inst., 1995—96; lectr. Borgå (Finland) Folkhögskolan, 1997—98. Contbr. Book The European Partners for the Environment Workbook on Sustainable Development, 1996, articles to profl. jours. Mem., trainer Youth for Understanding, Hamburg, Germany, 1989—2001; vol. foster care reviewer DSS, Boston, 1999—2001; mem. Am. Jewish Com. German Jewish Dialogue Group, Boston, 1999—2001. Recipient Lang. award, Finnish-Swedish Soc., 1989. Mem.: Mus. for Women in the Arts. Avocations: feminist ethics, travel. Home: 675 VFW Pkwy #194 Chestnut Hill MA 02467-3656

KRAUSE, CHARLES JOSEPH, otolaryngologist; b. Des Moines, Apr. 21, 1937; s. William H. and Ruby I. (Hitz) Krause; m. Barbara Ann Steelman, June 14, 1962; children: Sharon, John, Ann. BA, State U. Iowa, 1959, MD, 1962. Diplomate Am. Bd. Otolaryngology. Intern Phila. Gen. Hosp., 1962—63; resident in surgery U. Iowa, 1965—66, resident in otolaryngology, 1966—69; fellow dept. plastic surgery Marien Hosp., Stuttgart, Germany, 1970; asst. prof. otolaryngology U. Iowa, 1969—72, asso. prof., 1972—75, vice chmn. dept. otolaryngology, 1973—77, prof., 1975—77; prof., chmn. dept. otolaryngology U. Mich. Med. Sch., Ann Arbor, 1977—92; pres. Am. Bd. Otolaryngology, Houston. Chief clin. affairs U. Mich. Hosps., Ann Arbor, 1986—89; asst. dean for clin. affairs U. Mich., 1986—89, sr. assoc. dean med. sch., 1992—96, chief clin. affairs, 1992—95, sr. assoc. hosp. dir., 1995—96, prof. dept. otolaryngology, 1996—; bd. dirs. Am. Bd. Otolaryngology, 1984—2002, pres., 1998—2000. Author: book in field; contbr. chapters to books, articles to profl. jours. Capt. USAF, 1963—65. Fellow: Am. Soc. Head and Neck Surgery (coun. 1980—83, chmn. rsch. com. 1980—83, pres. 1987—88); mem.: Am. Bd. Otolaryngology (bd. dirs. 1984—, exam. com. chair 1993—, pres.-elect 1996—98, pres. 1998—2000), Centurions of Deafness Rsch. Found., Am. Laryngol. Assn., Am. Laryngol., Rhinol. and Otol. Soc., Am. Cancer Soc. (med. adv. com. Washtenaw County unit), Walter P. Work Soc. (pres. 1987), Soc. United Otolaryngologists, Am. Acad. Depts. Otolaryngology, Mich. Otolaryngol. Soc., Mich. State Med. Soc., Washtenaw County Med. Soc. (exec. com. 1979—82), Assn. Rsch. in Otolaryngology, Am. Asssn. Cosmetic Surgeons, Assn. Head and Neck Oncologists, ACS (adv. coun. otolaryngology 1979—83), Am. Acad. Facial Plastic and Reconstructive Surgery (regional v.p. 1977—80, chmn. rsch. com. 1977—80, pres. 1981—82), Am. Acad. Otolaryngology Head and Neck Surgery (bd. dirs. 1987—93, sec.-treas. 1987—93, pres.-elect 1995, pres. 1996), AMA. Republican. Presbyterian. Home and Office: 880 Sea Dune Ln Marco Island FL 34145-1840 E-mail: cjkrause1@aol.com.

KRAUSE, CHESTER LEE, publishing executive; b. Iola, Wis., Dec. 16, 1923; s. Carl and Cora E. (Neil) K. Grad. high sch., Iola. Ind. contractor, 1946-52; chmn. bd. Krause Publs., Inc., Iola, 1952-95. Co-editor: Standard Catalog of World Coins. Chmn. bldg. fund drive Iola Hosp., 1975-80; active Village Bd., 1963-72, Assay Commn., 1961, Marshfield Clinic Nat. Adv. Coun., 1992-96. With AUS, 1943-46. Named Wis. Small Businessman of Yr. Wis. Small Bus. Adminstrn. Adv. Coun., 1990; Melvin Jones fellow, 1990; recipient Meguiar award, 1995, Friend of Automotive History award Soc. Automotive Historians, 1995, Marshfield Clinic Heritage Found. award, 2001. Mem. Soc. of Automobile Historians (Friends of Automobile Historians 1995), Am. Numis. Assn. (medal of merit, Farren Zerbe award, Hall of Fame, Lifetime Achievement award, Exemplary Svc. award 2005), Can. Numis. Assn Home: 290 E Iola St Iola WI 54945-9620 Office: 160 N Chet Krause Dr Iola WI 54945 Office Phone: 715-445-5570. E-mail: ckrause@ethenet.net. *To publish on time, all the time.*

KRAUSE, EDWARD CHARLES, priest, educator; b. Worcester, Mass., Sept. 11, 1940; s. Edward Krause and Elizabeth Linden. BA, Notre Dame U., 1963; STL, Gregorian U., Rome, 1967; PhD, Boston U., 1975. Priest Congregation of the Holy Cross. Prof., chaplain Stonehill Coll., North Easton, Mass., 1970—75, St. Mary's Coll., Notre Dame, Ind., 1975—80; prof., pastor Gannon U., Erie, Pa., 1980—. Mem. adv. bd. Scholars for Social Justice, St. Louis, Confraternity of Cath. Clergy. Author: (book) Democracy and J.C. Muray, 1975; contbr. essays to publs.; contbg. editor: Nat. Cath. Register Newspaper, Ency. Cath. Sch. Doctrine; contbg. editor Social Justice Rev.; author: (13-part series) Forming a Catholic Consience, Becoming Catholic: The RCIA. Med. moral advisor St. Mary's Nursing Home, Erie, 1980—, St. Vincent's Hosp., Erie, 1982—96, Diocese of Erie, 1986—. Recipient Pro Ecclesia award, The Vatican, 1994; fellow, NEH, 1987. Mem.: Am. Soc. Christian Ethics, Am. Acad. Religion, Fellowship of Cath. Scholars, Soc. Cath. Social Scientists (bd. dirs.). Achievements include numerous appearances and two 13-part series on EWTN, the Catholic TV/radio network. Office Phone: 814-871-7545.

KRAUSE, GLORIA ROSE, music educator; b. Milw., Oct. 30, 1922; d. Carl Fred and Rose (Bremeier) Runge; m. George Tanner Krause Jr., June 24, 1960; 1 child, George Henry. MusB, U. Rochester, 1946; MusM, Northwestern U., 1954. Music tchr. Livington Manor (N.Y.) Cen., 1946-59, Monticello (N.Y.) Cen. Sch., 1959-61, Liberty (N.Y.) Cen. Sch., 1966-67, Livingston Manor Sch., 1968-79, Narrowsburg (N.Y.) Ctrl. Sch., 1979-87. Dir. Ill. Winds Chamber Ensemble, Narrowsburg, N.Y., 1975—; gen. mgr. Delaware Valley Opera, Narrowsburg, 1986—. Music dir.: (operas) HMS Pinafore, Mikado, Pirates of Penzance, Princess Ida, Patience, Amahl and Night Visitors, The Medium, Gondoliers, Marriage of Figaro, Don Pasquale, Die Fledermaus, Gypsy Baron, The Beggars Opera, La Traviata, Madame Butterfly, La Boehme, The Medium, The Merry Widow, The Barber of Seville (Rossini), Student Prince, Orphans in the Underworld, Hansel and Gretel; bassoonist with Highland Symphony Orch., Middletown, NY, 1986-90, New Sussex Cmty. Orch., Sparta, NJ, 1984-90. Pres. Del. Valley Arts Alliance, 1980—; bd. dirs. Tusten-Cochecton Libr., Narrowsburg, 1988—. Recipient Svc. award Siddha Meditation Ashram Found., South Fallsburg, NY, 1990, Recognition award Alliance NY State Arts Coun., 1995; named Woman of Yr., Catskill Mountain Bus. and Profl. Women, 1995; Gloria R. Krause Recital Hall named in her honor Del. Valley Arts Alliance, 2002 Office: Del Valley Opera PO Box 188 Narrowsburg NY 12764-0188 E-mail: dvo@citlink.net.

KRAUSE, HARRY DIETER, law educator; b. Germany, 1932; naturalized, 1954; m. Eva Maria Disselnkötter, 1957; children: Philip Renatus, Thomas Walther, Peter Herbert. Student, Freie U., Berlin, 1950-51; BA, U. Mich., 1954, JD, 1958. Bar: Mich. 1959, D.C. 1959, Ill. 1963, U.S. Supreme Ct. 1963. With firm Covington & Burling, 1958-60; with Ford Motor Co., Dearborn, Mich., 1960-63; asst. prof. to prof. law U. Ill., Champaign, 1963-82, Alumni Disting. prof. law, 1982-89, Max L. Rowe prof. law, 1989-94, tchg. prof. emeritus, 1994—. Fulbright prof. U. Bonn, Germany 1976-77; vis. assoc. Ctr. Socio-Legal studies, 1977; vis. fellow Wolfson Coll. Oxford (Eng.) U., 1984; US Del. to Hague Conf. on Pvt. Internat. Law Treaty on Internat. Adoptions, 1990-93; commr. Uniform State Laws, Ill., 1991-97; reporter Uniform Parentage Act, 1969-73, Rev. Uniform Adoption Act, 1979-84, Uniform Putative Fathers Act, 1985, Nat. Conf. Commr. on Uniform State Laws; mem. Internat. Acad. Comparative Law Rapporteur US, Uppsala, 1966, Teheran, 1974, Budapest, 1978, Caracas, 1983, Sydney, 1986, Brisbane, 2002, gen. rep. Athens, 1994; cons. on family law and social legis. to fed. and state legis., jud. and exec. commns.; vis. prof. law U. Mich., 1981, U. Miami, 1987; Culverhouse prof. Stetson U., 1991. Author: Illegitimacy: Law and Social Policy, 1971, Family Law: Cases and Materials, 1976, 5th edit., (with Elrod, Garrison,Oldham), 2003, Kinship Relations, 1976, Family Law in a Nutshell, 1977, 4th edit. (with D. Meyer), 2003, Child Support in America: The Legal Perspective, 1981; law editor: (with R. Walker et. al.) Inclusion Probabilities in Parentage Testing, 1983, (with D. Meyer) Family Law (Thomson-West's Blackletter Series), 1988, 3d edit., 2004, International Library of Essays in Law and Legal Theory: Family Law I: Society and Family, 1992, Family Law II: Cohabitation, Marriage and Divorce, 1992, Child Law: Parent, Child and State, 1992; bd. editors Mich. Law Rev., 1957-58, Family Law Quar., 1971—, Jour. Legal Edn., 1988-91, Am. Jour. Comparative Law, 1991-2004, and others. With US Army, 1954-56. Recipient von Humboldt Found. rsch. prize, 1992, 2004; Guggenheim fellow, 1969-70; assoc. Ctr. Advanced Study U. Ill., 1970, 79; German Marshall Fund US fellow, 1977-78; Hewlett fellow, Australia, 1984; German Acad. Exch. Svc. fellow, 1985. Mem. ABA (past mem. coun. sect. family law, com. chmn.), Am. Law Inst. (life; adviser family law project 1990-2001), Ill. Bar Assn. (past mem. coun. sect. on family law, internat. law), Am. Assn. Comparative Study of Law (dir. 1980-2000), Internat. Soc. Family Law (v.p. 1973-77, exec. coun. 1977-97), Order of Coif. Office: U Ill Coll Law Champaign IL 61820

KRAUSE, HELEN FOX, retired otolaryngologist; b. Boston, Mar. 20, 1932; d. Nathan and Frances Lena (Rich) Fox; children: Merrick Eli, Beth Riva Harper, Kim Debra Codd. BS, U. Maine, 1954; MD, Tuft U., 1958. Diplomate Am. Bd. Otolaryngology. Intern Health Ctr. Hosps. Pitts., 1958-59; resident Eye & Ear Hosp., Children's Hosp., VA Hosp., 1959-62; pvt. practice Pitts., 1962—2003; ret., 2003. Mem. otolaryngology adv. bd. U.S. Pharmacopea, 1991-96, 2000—, chmn., 1995-2000; prof. U. Pitts. Sch. Medicine; vis. prof. Pan Hellenic Otorhinolaryngology Soc., Crete, Greece, 1993, Panama, Argentina, 1998, China, Hong Kong, 1999, Thailand, China, Taiwan, 2000, Pan Am. Oto Soc., 2000; pres., dir. 1st World Congress of Otorhinolaryngologic Allergy, Endoscopy and Laser Surgery, Athens, 1998, 2001; bd. dirs. Bayer Pharm. Women's Health Initiative; vis. prof. Thailand, Sigapore; lectr. 2nd World Congress Otolaryngology, Allergy and Immunology, 2001. Author, editor: Otolaryngic Allergy and Immunology, 1989; lectr., vis. prof. Singapore, Bangkok, Hong Kong (multiple tng. programs 1990); contbr. chpts. to books and articles to profl. jours. Pres. North Hills Jewish Community Ctr., Pitts., 1973-74; cons. North Allegheny Sch. Bd., Pitts., 1977; lectr. North Allegheny Sr. High Sch., Wexford, 1979-84; chmn. Desert Storm Project, North Hills Bus. and Profl. Women, 1991. Recipient Disting. Svc. award, Pa. Acad. Otolaryngology, 1993, Hon. Achievement award, Am. Acad. Otolaryngology Head and Neck Surgery, 1993, Bd. govs. Chair award, 2000, Recognition award, Panhellenic Soc. ORL-HNS, 2001, Bd. Govs. award, Practioner of Excellence, Am. Acad. Otolaryngology Head and Neck Surgery, 2003, Lifetime Achievement award, AAOA, 2002, Presdl. citation, Am. Acad. Otolaryngology Head and Neck Surgery, 2004, Volunteerism award, 2004; scholar Jackson Meml. Labs., Bar Harbor, Maine, 1954. Fellow ACS, Am. Acad. Otolaryngology Head and Neck Surgery (bd. govs. 1982-89, 90—, Practitioner Excellence award 2003, Presdl. citation 2004, Volunteerism award 2004), Am. Acad. Otolaryngolgic Allergy (pres. 2984-85, Lifetime Achievement award 2002,), Svc. award 1990, cert. appreciation 1991, Pres.'s award 1997, Spl. Achievement award 1997), Am. Acad. Facial Plastic and Rsch. Surgery; mem. Pa. Acad. Otolaryngology (pres. 1989-90), Internat. Soc. Otorhinolaryngic Allergy and Immunology (pres. 1995-98), Pitts. Otological Soc. (pres. 1983-85), Phi Beta Kappa, Phi Kappa Phi. Office: 1301 Aviara PL Gibsonia PA 15044-8042 Personal E-mail: hfk@zoominternet.net.

KRAUSE, JOHN L., retired optometrist; b. Portland, Oreg., Oct. 26, 1917; m. Nancy D., Sept. 30, 1942; children: Diana L., Karen L., Ronald L. OD, Ill. Coll. Optometry, 1947. Practice optometry, Niles, Ill., 1978—87; ret., 1987. USAF Med. Service liaison officer, Northwestern U. Med. Sch., Chgo., 1964-91. Author: Sight Check Your Child, 1961, Holiday Fax, 1991, Win-Win, Inc., 1994; contbr. articles to nat. mags.; patentee card holder, 1967. Bd. overseers S.E. Univ. Coll. Optometry, North Miami Beach, Fla., 1993; liaison to optometry Nat. Alliance Mental Health, 1993; mem. ins. coun. City Tamarac, Fla., 1995—, chmn., 2002—; ombudsman State of Fla., Broward County, 1996-2000. Served with U.S. Army, 1941-45, to lt. col. USAF, ret.,

1970. Decorated Bronze Star with cluster, Combat Medic badge; inductee Broward County Fla. Sr. Hall of Fame, 2000; nominee Internat. Health Prof. of Yr., England, 2002. Mem. Am. Optometric Assn., Ill. Optometric Assn., Fla. Optometric Assn. Armed Forces Optometric Soc. (Honor award 2002), Air Force Assn., Fla. Pub. Health Assn. (chmn.-elect vision sect. 1992), Fla. Ret. Optometrists Assn. (pres. 1993-95, editor 1995-), Kappa Phi Delta, Phi Theta Upsilon, Phi Mu Delta. Achievements include patents for eyedrop transport apparatus, 2002, 2004. Avocations: golf, stamp collecting/philately, autographs. Home: 7270 Fairfax Dr Tamarac FL 33321-4305 Personal E-mail: dockrause@webtv.net.

KRAUSE, MANFRED OTTO, physicist; b. Stuttgart, Germany, Mar. 11, 1931; came to U.S., 1960, naturalized, 1970; s. Friedrich Bernhard and Friedel Ernstine K.; m. Josephine Winifred Cammer, Dec. 26, 1963; m. C. Denise Caldwell, Sept. 15, 2001. BS, Technische Universitat Stuttgart, 1954, diploma in physics, 1957, PhD, 1960. Sr. physicist Wm. H. Johnston Labs., Inc., Balt., 1960-63; sr. scientist Oak Ridge Nat. Lab., 1963-95; exch. prof. U. Paris, 1975. Cons. Oak Ridge, 1995—, U. Ctrl. Fla. Contbr. articles on electron, charge and x-ray spectrometry to sci. publs., chpts. to books. Recipient Alexander von Humboldt award, 1975-76. Fellow Am. Phys. Soc.; mem. AAAS, Smithsonian Instn., Natural History Soc., Audubon Soc., Nature Conservancy. Achievements include discoverer of x-ray spectrometry based on photoelectric effect. Home: 125 Baltimore Dr Oak Ridge TN 37830-7837 Business E-Mail: mok@ornl.gov.

KRAUSE, MARCELLA ELIZABETH MASON (MRS. EUGENE FITCH KRAUSE), retired secondary education educator; b. Norfolk, Nebr.; d. James Haskell and Elizabeth (Vader) Mason; student Northeast C.C., 1928-30; B.S., U. Neb., 1934; M.A., Columbia, 1938; postgrad. summers U. Calif. at Berkeley, 1950, 51, 65, Stanford, 1964, Creighton U., 1966, Chico (Calif.) State U., 1967; m. Eugene Fitch Krause, June 1, 1945; 1 dau., Kathryn Elizabeth. Tchr., Royal (Nebr.) pub. schs., 1930-32, Hardy (Nebr.) pub. schs., 1933-35, Omaha pub. schs., 1935-37, Lincoln Sch. of Tchrs. Coll., Columbia, 1937-38, Florence (Ala.) State Tchrs. Coll., summer 1938, Tchrs. Coll., U. Nebr., 1938-42, Corpus Christi (Tex.) pub. schs., 1942-45, Oakland (Calif.) pub. schs., 1945-83. Bd. dirs. U. Nebr. Womens Faculty Club, 1940-42; mem. Nebr. State Tchrs. Conv. Panel, 1940—; mem. U. Nebr. Reading Inst., 1940; speaker Iowa State Tchrs. Conv., 1941; reading speaker Nebr. State Tchrs. conv., 1941; lectr. Johnson County Tchrs. Inst., 1942; chmn. Reading Survey Corpus Christi pub. schs., 1943; chmn. Inservice Reading Meetings Oakland pub. schs., 1948-57. Mem. Gov.'s Adv. Commn. on Status Women Conf., San Francisco, 1966; service worker ARC, Am. Cancer Soc., United Crusade, Oakland CD; Republican precinct capt., 1964-70; v.p. Oakland Fedn. Rep. Women. Ford Found. Fund for Advancement Edn. fellow, 1955-56; scholar Stanford, 1964; Calif. Congress PTA scholar U. Calif., 1965, Norfolk (Nebr.) Hall of Success Northeast C.C., 1990; recipient award of Excellence, U. Nebr. Tchrs. Coll., 1998. Mem. Nat. Council Women, AAUW (dir.), Calif. Tchrs. Assn., Oakland Mus. Assn., U. Nebr. Alumni Assn. (Alumni Achievement award 1984), Californians for Nebr., Ladies Grand Army Republic, 1960, 1986-87 Ruth Assn., Martha Assn. (pres. East Bay chpt. 1979), Sierra DAR (regent), Eastbay DAR Regents Assn. (pres.), Nebr. Alumni Assn. (life, alumni achievement award 1984), Grand Lake Bus. and Profl. Women, Internat. Platform Assn., Eastbay Past Matrons Assn., P.E.O., Pi Lambda Theta (pres. No. Calif. chpt.), Alpha Delta Kappa. Methodist. Mem. Order Eastern Star (past matron). Contbr. articles to profl. jours. Home: 5615 Estates Dr Oakland CA 94618-2725

KRAUSE, PAUL EDWARD, clergyman; b. Jersey City, May 13, 1956; s. Paul Edward and Helen (Daab) K.; m. Deborah Lyn Bone, June 10, 1978; children: Joshua Michael, Alexander Paul, Matthew Caleb. BS, King's Coll., Briarcliff Manor, N.Y., 1978; MDiv, Denver Conservative Bapt. Sem., 1981; DMin, Ea. Bapt. Theol. Sem., Phila., 1995. Ordained to ministry Evang. Free Ch. Am., 1991; cert. tchr. Evang. Tchr. Tng. Assn. Ch. planter, pastor Valley Evang. Free Ch., Kemmerer, Wyo., 1981-82, Trinity Evang. Free Ch., Port Jervis, N.Y., 1982-83; relief supr. Internat. Svc. Systems, Jersey City, 1982-84; mgr. Friendly Ice Cream Corp., Scotch Plains, N.J., 1984-86; devel. officer Christian Homes for Children, Hackensack, N.J., 1986-89; interim pastor Hoboken (N.J.) Evang. Free Ch., 1988-89, pastor, 1989—. Class bd. govs. King's Coll., 1987—; bd. dirs. Ea. Dist. Assn., vice chmn., 2000-2001, chmn., 2001-04. Rep. Avocations: photography, baseball, cooking, kayaking. Home: 209 Zabriskie St Jersey City NJ 07307-4319 Office: Hoboken Evang Free Ch 833 Clinton St Hoboken NJ 07030-2901 E-mail: hobokenefc@yahoo.com, paulekrause@yahoo.com. *It is often much better to be seen as a foolish man living for God, than a wise man without hope for tomorrow.*

KRAUSE, PETER, actor; b. Alexandria, Minn., Aug. 12, 1965; Student, Gustavus Adolphus Coll., St. Peter, Minn.; MFA, NYU. Actor: (films) Blood Harvest, 1987, LoveLife, 1997, Melting Pot, 1997, The Truman Show, 1998, My Engagement Party, 1998, It's a Shame About Ray, 2000, We Don't Live Here Anymore, 2004; (TV series) Carol & Company, 1990, Cybill, 1995, The Great Defender, 1995, If Not For You, 1995, Sports Night, 1998—2000, Six Feet Under, 2001—05; TV appearances include Seinfeld, 1992, Beverly Hills 90210, 1992, Party of Five, 1997. Office: c/o Creative Artists Agy 9830 Wilshire Blvd Beverly Hills CA 90212-1825*

KRAUSE, RICHARD MICHAEL, medical scientist, government official, educator, senior researcher; b. Marietta, Ohio, Jan. 4, 1925; s. Ellis L. and Jennie Mae (Waterman) Krause. BA, Marietta Coll., 1947, DSc (hon.), 1978; MD, Case Western Res. U., 1952; DSc (hon.), U. Rochester, 1979, Med. Coll. Ohio, Toledo, 1981, Hahnemann Med. Coll. and Hosp., 1982; LLD (hon.), Thomas Jefferson U., 1982. Rsch. fellow dept. preventive medicine Case Western Res. U., 1950—51; intern Ward Med. Svc., Barnes Hosp., St. Louis, 1952—53, asst. resident, 1953—54; asst. physician to hosp. Rockefeller Inst., 1954—57, asst. prof., assoc. physician to hosp., 1957—61; prof. epidemiology Sch. Medicine, Washington U., St. Louis, 1962—66, assoc. prof. medicine, 1962—65, prof. medicine, 1965—66; assoc. prof., physician to hosp. Rockefeller U., 1966—68, prof., sr. physician, 1968—75; dir. Rockefeller U. (Animal Rsch. Ctr.), 1974—75, Nat. Inst. Allergy and Infectious Diseases, NIH, HEW, Bethesda, Md., 1975—84; USPHS surgeon, 1975—77; asst. surgeon gen., 1977—84; dean Emory U. Sch. Medicine, Atlanta, 1984—89, Robert W. Woodruff prof. medicine, 1984—89; mem. program com. Inst. Medicine, 1986—87; sr. sci. adv. Fogarty Internat. Ctr. NIH, Bethesda, 1989—; sr. investigator NIAID NIH, Bethesda, 2000—. Bd. dirs. Mo.-St. Louis Heart Assn., 1962—66, mem. rsch. com., 1963—66; mem. exec. com. coun. on rheumatic fever and congenital heart disease Am. Heart Assn., 1963—66, chmn. coun. rsch. study com., 1963—66, mem. assn. rsch. com., 1963—66, mem. policy com., 1966—70; mem. commn. streptococcal and staphylococcal diseases U.S. Armed Forces Epidemiol. Bd., 1963—72, dep. dir., 1968—72; bd. dirs. N.Y. Heart Assn., 1967—73, chmn. adv. coun. on rsch., 1969—71, mem. dirs. coun., 1973—75; cons. WHO, 1967—, mem. coccal expert com., 1967—; mem. steering com. Biomed. Sci. Scientific Working Group, WHO, 1978; mem. infectious disease adv. com. Nat. Inst. Allergy and Infectious Disease, NIH, 1970—74; bd. dirs. Royal Soc. Medicine Found., Inc., 1971—77, treas., 1973—75; bd. dirs. Allergy and Asthma Found. Am., 1976—77, Lupus Found. Am., 1977—79. Assoc. editor: Jour. Immunology, 1963—71, sect. editor: Viral and Microbial Immunology, 1974—75; editor: Jour. Exptl. Medicine, 1973—75; adv. editor:, 1976—84; mem. editl. bd.: Bacteriological Revs., 1969—73, Infection and Immunity, 1970—78, Immunochemistry, 1973—80, Clin. Immunology and Immunopathology, 1976—78; contbr. articles to profl. jours. Served with U.S. Army, 1944—46. Decorated Gumhuria medal Egypt; recipient Disting. Svc. medal, HEW, 1979, C. William O'Neal Disting. Am. Svc. award, Robert Koch Medal in Gold, Berlin, 1985, Sr. U.S. Scientist award, Alexander Von Humboldt Found., Fed. Republic Germany, 1986. Mem.: AAAS, Am. Epidemiol. Soc., Practitioner's Soc. N.Y., Royal Soc. Medicine, Infectious Diseases Soc. Am., Am. Coll. Allergists, Harvey Soc., Am. Soc. Microbiology, Am. Assn. Immunologists, Am. Soc. Clin. Investigation, Am. Soc. Biol. Chemists, Am. Acad. Allergy, Assn. Am. Physicians, Inst. Medicine, U.S. Nat. Acad. Scis., Cosmos (Washington), Century Assn. (N.Y.C.). Achievements include research in pathogenesis and epidemiology of streptococcal diseases; immunochem. studies on streptococcal antigens; immunogenetics; recognition of rabbit antibodies with molecular uniformity, genetics of immune response. Home: 4000 Cathedral Ave NW Apt 413B Washington DC 20016-5268 Office: NIAID NIH Rm 202 16 Center Dr Bldg 16 Bethesda MD 20892-0001 E-mail: richard_krause@nih.gov.*

KRAUSE, ROY G., office staffing firm executive; BS in Acctg., Ohio State U.; MBA, Ga. State U. Acct. KPMG Peat Warwick, LLP, 1973—80; CFO HomeBanc Mortgage Corp., Atlanta, 1980—95; exec. v.p., CFO Spherion Corp., Ft. Lauderdale, Fla., 1995—2003, pres., 2003—, COO, 2003—04, CEO, 2004—. Office: Spherion Corp 2050 Spectrum Blvd Fort Lauderdale FL 33309*

KRAUSE, SANDRA LLOYD, academic administrator; b. Charlotte, NC, Feb. 27, 1959; d. William Jones Craven, Jr. and Jeanne Defosett Craven; m. Dirk Joseph Krause, July 25, 1998; 1 child, Benjamin Thomas Lloyd. BS in Printing Prodn. Mgmt., Appalachian State U., 1981, MA in Ednl. Media, 1985. Media technician Instnl. Tech. Ctr. Appalachian State U., Boone, NC, 1995—2001, mgr. grad programs office extension and distance edn., 2001—. Mem.: Adult Continuing Higher Edn., NC Adult Edn. Assn. Avocations: running, skiing, cooking. Office: Appalachian State U Office Extension and Distance Edn University Hall Boone NC 28608 Office Phone: 800-355-4084. Business E-Mail: krausesl@appstate.edu.

KRAUSE, SONJA, chemistry professor; b. St. Gall, Switzerland, Aug. 10, 1933; came to U.S., 1939; d. Friedrich and Rita (Maas) K.; m. Walter Walls Goodwin, Nov. 27, 1970 BS, Rensselaer Poly. Inst., 1954; PhD, U. Calif., Berkeley, 1957. Sr. phys. chemist Rohm & Haas Co., Phila., 1957-64; vol. U.S. Peace Corps, Nigeria, 1964-65; asst. lectr. Lagos U.; asst. prof. Gondar Health Coll. U.S. Peace Corps, Ethiopia, 1965-66; vis. asst. prof. U. So. Calif., L.A., 1966-67; chemistry faculty Rensselaer Poly. Inst., Troy, NY, 1967—, prof., 1978—2004, prof. emeritus, 2004—. Mem. coun. Gordon Rsch. Conf., 1981-83; mem. com. on polymers and engring. NRC, 1992-94; sabbatical Inst. Charles Sadron, Ctr. Rsch. on Macromolecules, Strasbourg, France, 1987. Author: (with others) Chemistry of Environment, 1978, 2d edit., 2002; editor: Molecular Electro-Optics, 1981; mem. editorial adv. bd. Macromolecules, 1982-84 Bd. dirs. Nat. Plastics Ctr. and Mus., Leominster, Mass., 1996-2000. Fellow Am. Phys. Soc. (coun. divsn. biol. physics 1980-93); mem. IUPAC (assoc.), Am. Chem. Soc. (chmn. ea. N.Y. sect. 1981-82, councillor 1991-95, adv. bd. petroleum rsch. fund 1979-81, assoc. mem. com. on edn. 1993-95, assoc. mem. internat. com. 1996), Biophys. Soc. (coun. 1977), N.Y. Acad. Scis., Sigma Xi (pres. Rensselaer Poly Inst. chpt. 1984-85). Office: Rensselaer Poly Inst Dept Chemistry Troy NY 12180 Office Phone: 518-276-8445. Business E-Mail: krauss@rpi.edu.

KRAUSE, THOMAS EVANS, record promotion and radio consultant; b. Mpls., Dec. 17, 1951; s. Donald Bernhard and Betty Ann (Nokleby) K.; m. Barbara Ann Kaufman, Aug. 17, 1974 (div. Apr. 1978); m. Nicole Michelle Purkerson, Aug. 13, 1988; children: Andrew Todd Evans, Allison Michelle. Student, Augsburg Coll., 1969-73; BA, Hastings Coll., 1975. Lic. 3d class with broadcast endorsement FCC. Air personality Sta. KHAS Radio, Hastings, Nebr., 1974-75; air personality, news dir. Sta. KWSL Radio, Sioux City, Iowa, 1975-76; asst. program dir. Sta. KISD Radio, Sioux Falls, S.D., 1976-78; music dir. Sta. KVOX Radio, Fargo, N.D., 1978; program dir. Sta. KPRQ Radio, Salt Lake City, 1978-79; air personality Sta. KIOA Radio, Des Moines, 1980; program dir., ops. mgr. Sta. KKSS Radio, Sioux Falls, 1981-83; program dir. Stas. KIYS/KBBK Radio, Boise, Idaho, 1983-87; program dir., ops. mgr. Sta. WSRZ AM/FM Radio, Sarasota, Fla., 1988-90; owner, cons. Tom Evans Mktg., Seattle, 1990—; editor., pub. Northwest Log, Seattle, 1991-96; mgr. neverMAN, 1994—. Co-founder Sta. KCMR Radio, Augsburg Coll., Mpls., 1973; TV show coord./host Z-106 Hottraxx, Sarasota, 1988-90; air personality/guest disc jockey various radio stas., Pacific N.W., 1990—; host Am. Music Report. Sta. KIX-106 Radio, Canberra, Australia, 1992; instr. Sta. KGRG-FM and KENU-AM, Green River Coll., Auburn, Wash., 1994—. Contbr. articles to profl. jours. and popular mags. Bd. judges Loyola U. Marconi Awards, Chgo., 1992-93; bd. dirs. Habitat for Humanity, Snohomish County, Wash., 1992-96, Martin Luther King Day Celebration, Sarasota County, Fla., 1989-90, Shoreline/So. County YMCA, 1992-95, Puget Sound Sr. Baseball League, 2001—; dist. coord. Carter for Pres., Nebr. 1st Dist., 1975-76; hon. chair March of Dimes Walk Am., Sioux Falls, 1977; head coach Seattle Beavers Baseball Club, 1999—; bd. dirs. Puget Sound Sr. Baseball League, 2001—; media vol., MC or spokesperson M.S. Soc., MDA, Am. Diabetes Assn., Human Soc., others; active Shoreline Covenant Ch. Avocations: sports, films, science fiction, photography, travel. Office: Tom Evans Mktg 16426 65th Ave W Lynnwood WA 98037-2710

KRAUSE, TIMOTHY GILBERT, web site manager; b. Chippewa Falls, Wis., July 17, 1969; s. Gregory Mitchem and Donna Mae (Ripienski) K.; m. Kimberly Catherine Taft, June 18, 1994. BS in Acctg., St. Johns U., 1991; MA in English, St. Cloud State U., 1993; postgrad., Purdue U., 1997. Acct. St. Johns U., Collegeville, Minn., 1988-97; pvt. practice West Lafayette, Ind., 1995-97; dir. web comm. Cargill, Inc., Mpls., 1997—99; mem. cmty. faculty Met. State U., 2003—; dir. web comm. Cargill, Inc., 2002—; dir. editl. ops. DirectAg.com., 1999—2001. Cons. Mpls. Pub. Libr.; instr. Princeton Rev., Chgo., 1994—96; educator St. Cloud (Minn.) State U., 1991—93, Purdue U., West Lafayette, Ind., 1993—97; lectr. Richard Hadley Profl. Devel., West Lafayette, 1996; presenter in field. Author: Wired Resumes; reviewer IEEE Profl. Comm., 1996—, Tech. Comm. Quar., 1997—; contbr. articles to profl. jours. Mem. MLA, Nat. Coun. Tchrs. English, Assn. for Bus. Comm. (book rev. editor 1997-98), Rhetoric Soc. Am., Conf. on Coll. Composition and Comm., Alliance for Computers & Writing, Phi Kappa Phi. Avocations: web design, fishing, marathon running. Home: 1110 Sunnyfield Rd N Minnetrista MN 55364 Office: PO Box 5625 Minneapolis MN 55440-5625 Personal E-mail: tkrause@concentric.net. Business E-Mail: tim_krause@cargill.com.

KRAUSE II, WILLIAM JOHN, medical educator, researcher; b. Glasgow, Mont., Mar. 24, 1942; s. William John and Hazel Ruby Krause; m. Winifred Alice Clark, Sept. 19, 1945; children: Phillip Roland Krause, Amanda Elisabeth Fletcher. PhD, U. of Mo., 1967—69. Lectr. in anatomy Monash U., Clayton, Australia, 1969—71; asst. prof. of anatomy U. of Mo., Columbia, Mo., 1971—76. Author: Excellence in Teaching with Technology, 2004, 20 books; contbr. over 180 articles to profl. jours. Recipient Jane Hickman Tchr. of the Yr., Mo. Med. Alumni Assn., 2002, Golden Apple awards, Am. Med. Students Assn., 2002, 2004. Office: University of Missouri M263 Med Sci Bldg Columbia MO 65212 Office Phone: 573-882-8912. E-mail: krausew@health.missouri.edu.

KRAUSEN, ANTHONY SHARNIK, plastic surgeon; b. Phila., Feb. 22, 1944; s. B. M. and Kay S. (Sharnik) Krausen; m. Susan Elizabeth Park, Sept. 6, 1970; children: Park, Allison. Student, Germantown Acad., 1949—61; BA, Princeton U., 1965; MD, U. Mich., 1969. Diplomate Am. Bd. Surgery. Intern Presbyn. Med. Ctr., Denver, 1969—70; resident St. Joseph Hosp., Denver, 1970—71, Barnes Hosp., St. Louis, 1972—76; with Milw. Med. Clinic, 1976—, head dept. facial plastic surgery, 1984—. Mem. staffs Columbia and St. Mary Hosp., Ozaukee. Pres. Contemporary Art Soc., Milw. Art Mus., 1983; bd. dirs. Friends of Art. With N.G. U.S. Army, 1970—76. Fellow: Am. Acad. Otalaryngology, Am. Acad. Facial Plastic and Reconstructive Surgery; mem.: Town Club (Milw.), Ivy Club (Princeton, N.J.). Office: 12203 N Corporate Pky Mequon WI 53092 Office Phone: 262-387-8202. E-mail: akraus@ah.com.

KRAUSER, ROBERT STANLEY, health care executive; b. NYC, Aug. 24, 1937; s. Benjamin and Eva (Ferester) K.; m. Mary Kay Edwards, June 12, 1977 (dec. May 1999); children: Robert Edwards, Kathryn Edwards. BA, U. Vt., 1958; MS, Columbia U. Grad. Sch. Bus., 1959. Rschr., portfolio analyst Merrill, Lynch, Pierce et al, NYC, 1961-63; dir. spl. situations rschr. Orvis Bros., NYC, 1964-66; dir. rsch. Amott, Baker, NYC, 1966-69; v.p. rsch. counsel Bruns, Nordemann & Rea, NYC, 1970-75; v.p. rsch. assoc. Rosenkrantz, Ehrenkrantz, NYC, 1976-77; investment banker Herzfeld & Stern, Stamford, Conn., 1978-82; chmn., pres. Viral Response Sys., Inc., Greenwich, Conn., 1983—. Patentee in field. With USAR, 1959. Recipient Cert. of Recognition Eli Whitney Mus., 1987. Mem. Nat. Assn. Chain Drug Stores, Am. Mensa (Philanthropic award 1987), Inventors Assn. Conn. (Inventor of Yr. 1988), U.S. Tennis Assn. (ranked 1995), The Wimbledon Soc., Landmark Club, East Hampton Tennis Club (mixed doubles champ 1972), Armonk Tennis Club, Grand Slam Tennis Club (singles champ 1977, 78), San Diego Tennis and Racquet Club, Balboa Tennis CLub. Avocations: tennis, skiing, swimming, travel, medical reading. Home and Office: 444 Taconic Rd Greenwich CT 06831-2850

KRAUSHAR, JONATHAN POLLACK, communications and media consultant; b. Kew Gardens, N.Y., Apr. 26, 1948; s. Leo and Evelyn (Pollack) K.; m. Linda Marie Pekarski, Apr. 20, 1980; children: Matthew, Elizabeth. BA in English, U. Wis., 1969; MBA in Mktg. and Internat. Bus., NYU, 1981. Reporter The Hudson Dispatch, Union City, N.J., 1970, The Record, Hackensack, N.J., 1970-72; assoc. prodr. Sta. WPIX-TV News, N.Y.C., 1973, Sta. WCBS-TV News, N.Y.C., 1974-76; spl. projects supr. Philip Morris Internat., N.Y.C., 1976-82; v.p. Ailes Comms., Inc., N.Y.C., 1982, sr. v.p., 1984, pres. corp. comms. group, 1990, pres., 1991-95, Jon Kraushar and Assocs., Inc., N.Y.C., 1996—. Freelance writer N.Y. Times, N.Y.C., 1972-76, Washington Post, Washington, 1972-76. Author: (with Roger Ailes) You Are the Message, 1988; inventor (video) Electronic Resume, 1982. Media adviser Reagan/Bush Campaign, N.Y.C., 1984, Bush/Quayle Campaign, N.Y.C., 1988, Forbes for Pres., 1996, 2000; debate coach Dick Cheney, 2000. Recipient Feature Writing award N.J. Press Assn., 1972; pub. affairs reporting fellow Washington Journalism Ctr., 1974; fed. grantee U. Wis. Dept. Behavioral Disabilities, 1969. Mem. Internat. Assn. Bus. Communicators (bd. dirs. N.Y. chpt., chmn. main event spkrs. program 1983-85), Econ. Club. Republican. Jewish. Avocations: in-line skating, swimming, water sports. Office: Jon Kraushar and Assocs Inc 10 E 40th St Ste 1308 New York NY 10016-0201

KRAUSMAN, FRANCES KAY, elementary educator, elementary science consultant; b. Dallas, Sept. 18, 1940; d. Mack H.and Gladys L. (Davis) R.; m. Edwin Paul, May 6, 1962; children: Charles C., Paul H., Karl M. BA, Calif. State U., Fullerton, 1975, MA, 1988. Rating clerk Farmers Ins. Regional Office, Santa Ana, Calif., 1960-61; lab. tech. quality control Laura Scudder Foods, Anaheim, Calif., 1961-62; elem. tchr. Fullerton Sch. Dist., Fullerton, Calif., 1975—. Tchr. trainer in Sci./Math Project AIMS, Fresno, Calif., 1985—. Fellowship Edwin Carr Fellowship Calif. State U., Fullerton, 1988; recipient Honorary and Continuing Svc. Awards, Fullerton Coun. PTA, 1974-80, Project Tomorrow Vision for Excellence award, 2004. Mem. AIMS Edn. Found., Nat. Sci. Tchrs., Orange County Math Coun., Adminstr. and Supr. Curriculum Devel. Assn. Republican. Lutheran.

KRAUSS, ALISON, country musician; b. Champaign, Ill., July 23, 1971; d. Fred and Louise Krauss; m. Pat bergeson, Nov. 8, 1997. Albums (with Union Sta.) So Long So Wrong, 1997, Too Late to Cry, 1987, Two Highways, 1989, I've Got That Old Feeling, 1990, Every Time You Say Goodbye, 1992, I Know Who Holds Tomorrow, 1994 (Grammy award Best Southern, Country or Bluegrass Gospel album), Now That I've Found You, 1995, Forget About It, 1999, New Favorite, 2001, Alison Krauss and Union Sta. Live, 2002, Lonely Runs Both Ways, 2002. Co-recipient with Brad Paisley, Music Video of Yr., "Whiskey Lullaby", Country Music Assoc., 2004, with Brad Paisley, Musical Event of Yr. "Whiskey Lullaby", 2004, with Brad Paisley, Video of Yr., Vocal Event of Yr., "Whiskey Lullaby", Acad. Country Music, 2005; named to Grand Ole Opry, 1993; recipient Female Vocalist of Yr. award, Internat. Bluegrass Music Assn., 1990—91, 1993, 1995, Entertainer of Yr. award, 1991, 1995, Rising Video Star of Yr.-Europe award Country Music TV, 1995, Single of Yr. award, Country Music Assn, 1995, Vocal Event of Yr., 1995, Horizon award, 1995, Female Vocalist of Yr., 1995, Best New Country Artist Tour award Pollstar, 1995, Americana Artist of Yr. award Gavin, 1995, Country Artist of Yr. Rolling Stone, 1995, Grammy award Best Bluegrass Recording, 1992, Grammy award Best Country Collaboration with Vocals, 1995, Grammy award Best Female Country Vocal Performance, 1996, Bluegrass/Old-Time Music Album award, 1996, Best Female Vocalist, 1996, Grammy award Best Country Instrumental Performance, 1998, Grammy award Best Bluegrass Album, 1998, Grammy award Best Country Performance by a Duo or Group with Vocals, 1998. Office: DS Management 2814 12th Ave S Ste 202 Nashville TN 37204-2513

KRAUSS, GEORGE, metallurgist; b. Phila., May 14, 1933; s. George and Berta (Reichelt) K.; m. Ruth A. Oeste, Sept. 10, 1960; children: Matthew, Jonathan, Benjamin, Thomas. BS in Metall. Engring., Lehigh U., 1955; MS, MIT, 1958, Sc.D., 1961. Registered profl. engr., Colo., Pa. Devel. metallurgist Superior Tube Co., Collegeville, Pa., 1955-56; prof. Lehigh U., Bethlehem, Pa., 1963-75, Colo. Sch. Mines, Golden, 1975—; dir. Advanced Steel Processing and Products Research Ctr., 1984-93; Amax Found. prof., 1975-90; prof. dept. metall. engring. Colo. Sch. Mines, Golden, 1990-92, John Henry Moore prof., 1992-97, Univ. prof. emeritus, metallurg. cons., 1997—. Author: Principles of Heat Treatment of Steel, 1980, Steels: Heat Treatment and Processing Principles, 1990, Tool Steels, 5th edit., 1998, Steels: Processing Structure and Performance, 2005; editor: Deformation Processing and Structure, 1984, Carburizing: Processing and Performance, 1989; editor Jour. Heat Treating, 1978-82; co-editor Fundamentals of Microalloying Forging Steels, 1987; contbr. articles profl. jours. NSF fellow Max Planck Inst. fur Eisenforschung, 1962-63; recipient Adolf Martens medal, Wiesbaden, 1990, Disting. Alumni award Lehigh U., 1993, George R. Brown Gold medal, 1998; named Outstanding Educator, Colo. Sch. Mines, 1990 Fellow ASM, The Metals Soc., Internat. Fedn. Heat Treatment and Surface Engring., Japan Soc. Promotion Sci.; mem. AIME, Iron and Steel Soc.-AIME (disting. mem. 1993, Howe lectr. 2003), Iron and Steel Inst. Japan (hon.), Am. Soc. Materials Internat. (hon.; trustee 1991-94, v.p. 1995-96, pres. 1996-97, C.S. Barrett silver medal 1998, Bodeen Heat Treating Achievement award 1999, A.E. White Disting. Tchr. award 1999, Campbell lectr. 2000), Internat. Fedn. Heat Treatment (pres. 1989-91), Materials Edn. Found. (trustee 2004-). Home: 3807 S Ridge Rd Evergreen CO 80439-8517 Office: Colo Sch Mines Dept Metall Engring Golden CO 80401 Office Phone: 303-674-0670. Business E-Mail: gkrauss@mines.edu.

KRAUSS, HENRY FREDERICK, JR., optometrist; b. Sewickley, Pa., Apr. 10, 1952; s. Henry Frederick and Mirella Anna (Guerrieri) K.; m. Sally Winston Miller, July5, 1975; children: Molly Anne, Henry Neil, Malinda Paige, Michael Winston. BS, Centre Coll., Ky., 1976; OD, U. Houston, 1980. Optometrist, owner Eye Care Assocs., Richardson, Tex., 1980—. V.p. ProComp Systems Inc., Albuquerque, 1983-86; ptnr. K-W Distbrs., Dallas, 1983-86, Summit Seminars, Richardson, 1985—; owner, operator Profl. Enhancement Strategies, 1997—; pres. Simplified Web Solutions, 2004-. Bd. dirs. Found. for Edn. and Rsch. in Vision, 1988-89, S.W. Vision Svc. Plan, 1982-84. Fellow Am. Acad. Optometry; mem. Am. Optometric Assn., Tex. Optometric Assn. (Young Optometrist of Yr. award 1985), North Tex. Optometric Assn. (pres. 1983-84), Am. Pub. Health Assn. (vision care sect.). Republican. Mem. Lds Ch. Avocations: golf, tennis, photography, horsemanship, sailing, scuba diving. Office: Eye Care Assocs 660 W Campbell Rd Richardson TX 75080-3301 Office Phone: 972-231-9595. E-mail: drkrauss@ecarichardson.com.

KRAUSS, HERBERT HARRIS, psychologist; b. Phila., June 13, 1940; s. Leon and Ethel Sarah (Cohen) K.; m. Beatrice Joy Osgood, Aug. 26, 1965; children: Michael Conal, Daniel Avram. BS, Pa. State U., 1961, MS, 1962; PhD, Northwestern U., 1966. Lic. psychologist, N.Y. Intern in med. psychology U. Oreg. Med. Sch., 1962-63; asst. prof. psychiatry, psychology U. Kans. Med. Sch., Kansas City, Kans., 1966-67; asst. prof. psychiatry, psychology, chief psychologist in child psychiatry Ohio State U. Coll. Medicine, Columbus, 1967-69; assoc. prof. psychology U. Ga., Athens, 1969-71; prof. psychology Hunter Coll., CUNY, N.Y.C., 1971-2001, chmn. dept. psychology, 1992-99; dir. rehab. rsch. and outcomes mgmt. Internat. Ctr. for the Disabled, N.Y.C., 1984—2002; prof., chmn. dept. psychology Pace U.,

N.Y.C., 2001—. Cons. Managed Health Network, N.Y.C., 1979-90, PhD Program, NYU, rehab. counselling, 1991—; adj. assoc. prof. psychiatry Cornell Med. Sch., N.Y.C., 1978—; assoc. attending psychologist Payne Whitney Clinic, N.Y. Hosp., 1978—; ptnr. Health Resources Mgmt. Co-author: Living with Anxiety and Depression, 1974; co-editor: Between Survival and Suicide, 1976, A Provider's Guide to Psychiatric Services in the General Hospital, 1986, The Aging Workforce: A Guide for University Administrators, 1992; co-editor Internat. Jour. Group Tensions, 1995-2000, assoc. editor, 2000—; cons. editor Jour. Individual Psychology, 1996—. Cons. Irvington, N.Y. Drug Coun., 1983; coach football and wrestling Irvington Sunnysiders, 1978-83, soccer Am. Youth Soccer Orgn., Houston, 1976-78. Named Outstanding Teacher Psychology, N.Y. Psychol. Assn., 1972. Mem. APA, N.Y. Acad. Scis., Ea. Psychol. Assn., Internat. Organ for Study of Group Tensions (v.p., co-pres. 1999—), Am. Coun. on Germany, Am. Evaluation Assn., Cornell Club, Sigma Xi. Home: 520 Grand Ave Newburgh NY 12550-1929 Office: Pace Univ Dept Psychology 41 Park Row Rm 1313 New York NY 10038-1598 Office Phone: 212-346-1434. Business E-Mail: hkrauss@pace.edu.

KRAUSS, JOHN LANDERS, public policy, urban affairs consultant, mediator, arbitrator; b. Orange, NJ, Oct. 20, 1948; s. George Howard Krauss Jr. and Shirley Krauss; m. M. Elizabeth Wood, May 23, 1976 (div. Sept. 1988); m. Eleanor C. Werbe, June 29, 1991. BA with honors in Polit. Sci., Colo. Coll., 1971; JD, Ind. U., Indpls., 1976. Bar: Ind. 1976, U.S. Dist. Ct. (so. dist.) Ind. 1976, U.S. Ct. Appeals (7th cir.) 1979, U.S. Supreme Ct. 1986, D.C. 1999, cert.: (mediator). Spl. asst. to gov. Office of Gov. of Ind., Indpls., 1971-72; dep. dir. Greater Indpls. Progress Com. Inc., Indpls., 1972-73, exec. dir., 1973-81; dir. dept. met. devel. City of Indpls., 1981-82, dep. mayor, 1982-91; sr. fellow Ind. U. Ctr. for Urban Policy and Environment, Indpls., 1991—2003; exec. dir. Gov.'s Gambling Impact Study Commn., 1998-99; dir. Ind. U. Ctr. for Urban Policy and the Environment, 2004—. Mediator Ind. Dept. Edn., 1998—, U.S. Postal Svc., 1998—; mediator and fact finder Ind. Edn. Employment Rels. Bd., 1991—; exec. dir. Ind. Adv. Commn. on Intergovtl. Rels., 1995—; assoc. Kettering Found., Dayton, Ohio, 1997—; cons. U.S. Govt. Projects, Ukraine, Morocco, Russia, Estonia, Turkey, South Africa; external mediator The World Bank, 2000—; adj. prof. law Ind. U. Sch. Law, Indpls., 2000—; clin. prof. Ind. U. Sch. Public and Environ. Affairs, 2003—; panel of arbitrators Nat. Arbitration Forum; vice-chmn., commr. Ind. Supreme Ct. Commn. on Continuing Legal Edn., 2003—; pub. arbitrator NASD Dispute Resolution, 2003—; mem. Roster of Neutrals Internal Rev. Office of Appeals, 2003—; spl. mediator Ind. Atty. Gen., 2003; mem. Nat. Roster Environ. Dispute Resolution Profls., U.S. Inst. Environ. Conflict, 2004—. V.p., bd. govs., trustee Indpls. Art Mus.; trustee emeritus Ptnrs. for Livable Cmtys., Washington; bd. govs. Orchard Sch., Indpls.; vice chmn. Tourism for Tomorrow, Inc., 2000—; past exec. com. organizing com. Pan Am. Games, 1987. Named Sagamore of the Wabash, State of Ind. Mem.: AIA (past bd. dirs. Indpls. chpt.), Am. Arbitration Assn. (comml. panel mediators and arbitrators 1998—), Assn. for Conflict Resolution, Dramatic Club, Pi Gamma Mu. Office: Ind U Ctr Urban Policy/Environment 342 N Senate Ave Indianapolis IN 46204-2630

KRAUSS, JUDITH BELLIVEAU, nursing educator; b. Malden, Mass., Apr. 11, 1947; d. Leo F. and Dorothy (Conners) Belliveau; m. Ronald L. Krauss, Sept. 5, 1970; children: Jennifer Leigh, Sarah Elizabeth. BS, Boston Coll., 1968; MSN, Yale U., 1970. RN, Conn. Clin. specialist Conn. Mental Health Ctr., New Haven, 1971-73; clin. instr. Yale Sch. Nursing, New Haven, 1971-73; asst. prof. rsch. Yale U. Sch. Nursing, New Haven, 1973-78, assoc. dean, 1978-85, prof., dean, 1985-98, prof., 1998—; master Yale U. Silliman Coll., 2000—. Cons. pharm. and pub. cons., sch., govt. agys. Author: The Chronically Ill Psychiatric Patient and the Community, 1982 (Am. Jour. Nursing Book of Yr. 1982); editor Archives of Psychiat. Nursing, 1986-2005; mem. editl. bd. Psychiat. Rehab., Psychiat. Svcs.; contbr. articles to profl. jours Trustee Boston Coll., 1991-99, trustee assoc., 2000—. Am. Nurses Found. scholar, 1978; recipient Chamberlain award Soc. Edn. and Rsch. in Nursing, 1994, Alumni Achievement award Boston Coll., 2004, medal Yale U. Sch. Nursing, 2005; named Disting. Alumna Yale Sch. Nursing, 1984; scholar Am. Acad. Nursing/Inst. Medicine, 1998-99. Mem. ANA (Disting. Contbn. to Psychiat. Nursing award 1992, Leadership citation 2002), Am. Acad. Nursing, Conn. Nurses Assn. (mem. cabinet on edn. 1987-89, bd. dirs. 1988-91, rep. to ANA house of dels. 1988-91, Josephine Dolan award 1989), Sigma Theta Tau (Disting. Lectr. award 1987), Delta Mu (Founders award 1987). Avocations: tennis, golf, hiking, skiing. Office: Yale U Sch Nursing Ste 200 100 Church St S New Haven CT 06536-0740 E-mail: judith.krauss@yale.edu.

KRAUSS, MARTY WYNGAARDEN, academic administrator; BA, U. Mich., 1974; PhD, Brandeis U., 1981. John Stein prof. disability rsch. Heller Sch. for Social Policy and Mgmt. Brandeis U., Waltham, Mass., provost, sr. v.p. for acad. affairs, 2003—. Chairperson Mass. Govs. Commn. on Mental Retardation, 1993—99; mem. com. on disability determination for mental retardation NRC, 2000—01. Author: numerous books; contbr. articles to profl. jours. Recipient Christian Pueschel Meml. Rsch. award, 2000, Disting. Rsch. award, 2001. Office: Brandeis Univ Office of Provost 415 South St MS 134 Waltham MA 02454 Office Phone: 781-736-2101.

KRAUSS, RONALD MAXWELL, research scientist, endocrinologist, educator; b. N.Y.C., May 12, 1943; s. Theodore Coloman Krauss and Lisbeth Hauser Rock; m. Sharon Anne Wald, May 11, 1969; children: Daniel Kalman, Jeffrey Aaron. AB magna cum laude, Harvard U., Cambridge, Mass., 1964; MD cum laude, Harvard Med. Sch., Boston, 1968. Lic. Am. Bd. of Endocrinology and Metabolism, 1977. Sr. investigator Nat. Heart and Lung Inst., Bethesda, Md., 1973—74; adj. prof., dept. nutritional scis. and toxicology U. Calif., Berkeley, 1993—, asst. clin. prof. medicine San Francisco, 1974—82, assoc. adj. prof. medicine, 1982—; assoc. dir. endocrine and metabolic svc. Alta Bates Hosp., Berkeley, Calif., 1976—85; sr. scientist and dir., atherosclerosis rsch. Children's Hosp. Oakland Rsch. Inst.; staff scientist Lawrence Berkeley Nat. Lab., Berkeley, Calif., 1976—84, sr. scientist, 1984—2003, head, molecular medicine rsch. program, 1989—92, head, dept. of molecular medicine, 1992—2003, co-director lipoprotein rsch. program, dep. dir. rsch. medicine and radiation biophysics divsn. Chmn. nutrition com. Am. Heart Assn., Dallas, nat. spokesperson panel, 1998—, founder and chmn. coun. on nutrition, phys. activity, and metabolism, 2000—; mem. bd. dir., 2004—; mem. macronutrient panel Food and Nutrition Bd. of Inst. of Medicine, Washington, 1999—2002; sr. sci. adviser Nat. Cholesterol Edn. Program, NIH, Bethesda, Md., 1999—2001; mem. steering com. Nat. Lipid Edn. Coun., N.Y.C., 1999—. Lead author: Am. Heart Assn Dietary Guidelines, 1996, 2000. Lt. comdr. U.S. Pub. Health Svc., 1970—74. Recipient Detur Prize, Harvard U., 1961, Spl. Recognition award, Am. Heart Assn. Coun. on Arteriosclerosis, Thrombosis, and Vascular Biology, 2001; grantee, NIH, 1976—. Fellow: Am. Heart Assn. (Disting. Achievement award 2001); mem.: Am. Fedn. Clin. Rsch., Fedn. of Am. Societies Exptl. Biology, Am. Soc. of Clin. Investigation, Alpha Omega Alpha, Phi Beta Kappa. Achievements include discovery of atherogenic lipoprotein phenotype as most common genetically influenced trait associated with premature heart disease risk; patents in field; first to demonstrate genetic influence on cholesterol and lipoprotein response to low fat diets; to demonstrate protection from atherosclerosis in genetically engineered mice. Avocations: jogging, singing, crossword puzzles. Office: Children's Hosp Oakland Rsch Inst 5700 Martin Luther King Jr Way Oakland CA 94609 Office Phone: 510-450-7908. E-mail: rkrauss@chori.org.

KRAUSZ, MICHAEL, philosopher, educator; b. Geneva, Sept. 13, 1942; s. Laszlo and Susan Beate (Strauss) K.; m. Constance Frances Costigan. BA, Rutgers U., 1965; spl. studies, London Sch. Econs., 1963; MA, Ind. U., 1966; PhD, U. Toronto, 1969; postgrad., Oxford U., 1969—70. Acting chmn. dept. Bryn Mawr Coll., Pa., 1983-84, chmn. dept., 1993—2003, Milton C. Nahm prof., 2003—. Vis. asst. prof. Am. U., Washington, 1973-74; vis. prof., lectr. Georgetown U., 1977-79, Hebrew U., Jerusalem, 1978, Swarthmore Coll., 1980-81, Haverford Coll., 1981-82, U. Nairobi, 1985; disting. vis. prof. Am. U., Cairo, 1980; spl. lectr. U. Oxford, 1987, 89; instr. Curtis Inst. Music, 2002, 04; chmn. external rev. com. dept. philosophy Swarthmore Coll., 1987, Smith Coll., 1990; rsch. assoc. to vice prin. Linacre Coll., Oxford U., 1988, vis. sr. mem., 1986-90; vis. sr. mem. Linacre Coll., 1986-90, 98, 99; vis. prof. Indian Inst. Advanced Studies, Shimla, India, 1992, U. Ulm, 1997; co-dir. Confs. on Philosophy of Human Studies, 1981-88, co-founder, chmn., 1988-94, Greater Phila. Philosophy Consortium; mem. emeritus fellowship selection panel, Andrew W. Mellon Found., 2003-04; overseas lectr. Indian Coun. Philos. Rsch., 2003. Referee: NEH, 1978, 1982, Jour. Aesthetics and Art Criticism, 1986, Nous, 1996; author: Rightness and Reasons: Interpretation in Cultural Practices, 1993, Limits of Rightness, 2000; co-author (with Rom Harré): Varieties of Relativism, 1995; editor: Critical Essays on the Philosophy of R. G. Collingwood, 1972, Relativism: Interpretation and Confrontation, 1989, The Interpretation of Music, 1993, Greater Phila. Philosophy Consortium Series, Philosophy in the Global Context, 1995, Is There a Single Right Interpretation?, 2002, Interpretation and Its Objects: Studies in the Philosophy of Michael Krausz, 2003, Andreea Ritivoi; co-editor: The Concept of Creativity in Science and Art, 1981, Relativism: Cognitive and Moral, 1982, Rationality, Relativism, and the Human Sciences, 1986, Jewish Identity, 1993, Interpretation, Relativism & the Metaphysics of Culture, 1999; editor: (series) Philosophy of History and Culture, E.J. Brill, 1986—; author: revs., papers. Bd. dirs. Solisti N.Y., 1987—88; founder, pres., assoc. artistic dir. Phila. Chamber Orch., 1984; guest condr. Pleven Philharm. Orch., Bulgaria, 1999, 2000, Vrasta Philharm., Bulgaria, 2001, Plovdiv Philharm., Bulgaria, 2002, 2004. Fellow Royal Soc. Arts, London, 1973—, Andrew Mellon, Aspen Inst. Humanistic Studies, 1977—78, Ossabaw Found., 1978, 1980, Ctr. for Study of Developing Soc., 1998—99; grantee Ford Found., 1971, Bryn Mawr Coll., 1973—74, 1976, 1985—86, 1989, Alfred Sloan Found., 1986; hon. fellow, Tata Energy Rsch. Inst., New Delhi. Fellow Ctr. Study Developing Soc.; mem. Am. Philos. Assn., Am. Soc. Aesthetics (program chmn. ea. divsn. 1987—, chmn. steering com. ea. divsn. 1989-90, program chmn. nat. divsn. 1991, mem. Am. steering com.), World Congress Philosophy. Jewish. Avocations: 20 solo national and international art shows, music (conducting). Office: Bryn Mawr Coll Dept Philosophy Bryn Mawr PA 19010 Office Phone: 610-526-5332. Personal E-mail: mkrausz@earthlink.net. Business E-Mail: mkrausz@brynmawr.edu.

KRAUTHAMMER, CHARLES, columnist, editor; b. N.Y.C., Mar. 13, 1950; s. Shulim and Thea K.; m. Robyn Trethewey; 1 child, Daniel. BA, McGill U., 1970; postgrad., Balliol Coll. Oxford U., 1970-71; MD, Harvard U., 1975. Diplomate Am. Bd. Psychiatry and Neurology. Resident in psychiatry Mass. Gen. Hosp., Boston, 1975-78; sci. advisor Dept. HHS, Washington, 1978-80; speech writer V.P. Walter Mondale, Washington, 1980-81; sr. editor The New Republic, Washington, 1981-88; essayist Time Mag., 1983—; syndicated columnist The Washington Post, 1984—. Author: Cutting Edges, 1985; contbr. sci. articles to psychiat. jours. Recipient Nat. Mag. award Am. Soc. Mag. Editors, 1984, Pulitzer prize for commentary, 1987, Bradley prize, 2003; Commonwealth scholar British Coun., Oxford, 1970-71.*

KRAVATH, RICHARD ELLIOT, retired pediatrician, educator; b. NYC, May 25, 1935; s. Reuben and Fannie Kravath; m. Pauline Sara Hauser, Aug. 27, 1960; children: Robert, Peter, Caroline. AB, Columbia U., 1956; MD, SUNY, Bklyn., 1960. Diplomate Am. Bd. Pediatrics. Intern Montefiore Med. Ctr., 1960-61, pediatric resident, chief resident, 1964-66, pediatric pulmonary fellowship, 1966-68; dir. div. intensive care pediatrics Albert Einstein Coll. Medicine, Bronx, 1981-82, prof. pediatrics, 1982; dir. in-patient pediatrics King's County Hosp. Ctr., Bklyn., 1982-2000; prof. clin. pediatrics SUNY, Bklyn., 1982-2000; ret., 2000. Author, co-author: Pediatrics: Pretest, 1987, 89, 92, 95; co-author: Water and Electrolytes in Pediatrics, 1982, 2d edit., 1993; contbr. articles to profl. jours. Capt. USAF, 1961-64. Mem. Alumni Assn. SUNY-Bklyn. (pres. 1992). Achievements include patents for monitoring of stress and a partitioning device for pools. Home: 6 Scott St Dobbs Ferry NY 10522-2614

KRAVEKA, JACQUELINE MARIA, pediatrician, oncologist; b. Velasco, Cuba, July 29, 1966; arrived in U.S., 1971, naturalized; d. Luis R. and Glenda J. Kraveka; m. Ernesto Mario Barros, July 17, 1999; children: Alejandro Mario Barros children: Emily Marie Barros. BA, Columbia U., 1989; DO, Nova Southeastern U., 1994. Diplomate Am. Bd. Pediat., Am. Bd. Pediat. Hematology-Oncology, Nat. Bd. Osteo. Med. Examiners. Resident in pediat. Miami (Fla.) Children's Hosp., 1994—97; fellow pediat. hematology oncology Med. U. SC, Charleston, 1997—2000, asst. prof. of pediat., 2000—, dir., pediatric bone marrow transplant program, 2002—. Study chmn. Children's Oncology Group. Contbr. articles to profl. publs. Recipient Pediatric Loan Repayment Program award, NIH, 2002—; grantee Mentored Career Devel. award, 2003—. Fellow: Am. Coll. Osteo. Pediatricians, Am. Acad. of Pediat.; mem.: AAAS, Am. Osteo. Assn., Am. Soc. Pediat. Hematology Oncology, Am. Soc. Hematology, Am. Soc. Clin. Oncology, Am. Assn. Cancer Rsch. (Minority Scholar award in cancer rsch. 2000, 2002), Children's Oncology Group. Office: Med U SC 135 Rutledge Ave PO Box 250558 Charleston SC 29425 E-mail: kravekjm@musc.edu.

KRAVETZ, KATHARINE, education educator; b. Houston, July 18, 1947; d. Frederick and Emily (Hollander) Kunreuther; m. Eric Stuart Kravetz, Aug. 25, 1974; children: Rachel, Daniel. BA, Harvard U., 1968; JD, Georgetown U., 1975. Bar: D.C. 1975, Md. 1981. Placement specialist TransCentury Corp., Washington, 1971—72; atty. Pub . Defender Svc. D.C., 1975—79, Law Offices of Katharine Kravetz, Washington, 1979—91; adj. prof. justice Am. U., Washington, 1979—82, 1988—91, asst. prof. justice, law and soc., 1991—94, academic dir. study abroad, 1994—98, asst. prof. justice, law and soc., 1998—. Mem. faculty senate Am. U., 2001—02, asst. prof. Transforming Communities, 2000—; mem. steering com. on ex-offenders D.C. Govt./Non-Profit Coalition, Washington, 2000—02. Contbr. articles to profl. jours. Vol. U.S. Peace Corps, Rezaiyeh, Iran, 1968—70; mem., study circles D.C. Prisoners Legal Svcs. Project, 2000. With US Peace Corps., 1968—70.

KRAVIS, HENRY R., venture capitalist; s. Raymond Kravis; m. Helene-Diane (Hedi) Shulman (div.); children: Robert S., Kimberly R., Harrison-(dec.); m. Carolyn Roehm (div.); m. Marie-Josée Drouin, 1994. BA in Economics, Claremont-McKenna Coll., 1967; MBA, Columbia U., 1969. Partner Bear Stearns; founding ptnr. Kohlberg Kravis Roberts, 1976—. Bd. dirs. PRIMEDIA Inc., 1991—. Bd. trustees Claremont-McKenna Coll., Met. Mus. Art, NYC, Mount Sinai Hosp., NYC. Named one of Top 200 Collectors, ARTnews mag., 2004. Mem.: Coun. Fgn. Rels. Achievements include historic billion dollar buyout of Wometco Companies in 1984; $25 billion RJR Nabisco buyout in 1989. Avocation: Collector Old Master drawings and paintings, Impressionist art, 20th-century art, French furniture. Office: Kohlberg Kravis Roberts & Co Ste 4200 9 W 57th St New York NY 10019*

KRAVIS, MARIE-JOSEE DROUIN, economist; b. Ottawa, Ont., Can., Sept. 11, 1949; d. Gaëtan and Anne Drouin; m. Henry R. Kravis, 1994. BA in Econs, U. Que., Montreal, 1970; MA, U. Ottawa, 1973; LLD (hon.), Univ. Windsor, Laurentian Univ., Canada. Fin. analyst Power Corp. Can. Ltd., 1969-70; spl. asst. to solicitor gen. Can., also to minister supply and services Govt. of Can., 1971-73; sr. economist Hudson Inst., 1973—76; exec. dir. Hudson Inst. Canada, Montreal, 1976—94; sr. fellow Hudson Inst., 1994—, bd. mem. & exec. com. mem. Mem. Canadian Council for Rsch. on Social Sci. & Humanities, 1982—86, Canadian Govt. Comm. Adv. Bd., 1982—89, Consultative Com. on Fin. Inst., Govt. Quebec, 1984—90; vice chmn. Royal Canadian Commn. on Nat. Passenger Transp., 1990—92; bd. dir. Ford Motor Co., 1995—, Vivendi Universal, 2001—, Interactive Corp., 2001—. Co-author: Canada HAS a Future, 1978, Quebec 1985, 1980, Western European Adjustment to Structural Economic Problems; contr. articles to profl. jours.; former weekly columnist for National Post, Canada; former host of weekly Canadian TV show on economics. Vice chmn. bd. trustees Mus. Modern Art, N.Y.C; trustee Inst. for Advanced Study, Princeton, NJ; chmn. Robin Hood Found. Named one of Top 200 Collectors, ARTnews Mag., 2004. Fellow: Council on Fgn. Rels.; mem.: Forest and Stream (Dorval, Que.) (sr. fellow). Avocation: collector of Old Masters, Impressionism, 20th century art & French furniture. Office: Hudson Institute Suite 300 1015 18th St NW Washington DC 20036 Office Phone: 202-223-7770. Office Fax: 202-223-8537.*

KRAVITCH, PHYLLIS A., federal judge; b. Savannah, Ga., Aug. 23, 1920; d. Aaron and Ella (Wiseman) K. BA, Goucher Coll., 1941; LLB, U. Pa., 1943; LLD (hon.) (hon.), Goucher Coll., 1981, Emory U., 1998. Bar: Ga. 1943, U.S. Dist. Ct. 1944, U.S. Supreme Ct. 1948, U.S. Ct. Appeals (5th cir.) 1962. Practice law, Savannah, 1944—76; judge Superior Ct., Eastern Jud. Circuit of Ga., 1977—79, U.S. Ct. Appeals (5th cir.), Atlanta, 1979—81, U.S. Ct. Appeals (11th cir.), 1981—, sr. judge, 1996—. Mem. Jud. Conf. Standing Com. on Rules, 1994—2000. Trustee Inst. Continuing Legal Edn. in Ga., 1979—82; mem. Bd. Edn., Chatham County, Ga., 1949—55; mem. coun. Law Sch., Emory U., Atlanta, 1985—; mem. vis. com. Law Sch., U. Chgo., 1990—93; bd. visitors Ga. State U. Law Sch., 1994—; mem. regional rev. panel Truman Scholarship Found., 1993—2000; mem. vis. com. Goucher Coll., 2000—. Recipient Hannah G. Solomon award, Nat. Coun. Jewish Women, 1978, Trailblazer award, Greater Atlanta Hadassah, 2000, James Wilson award, U. Pa. Law Alumni Soc., 1992, Kathleen Kessler award, Ga. Assn. Women Lawyers, 2001, Shining Star award, Atlanta Women's Found., 2002. Fellow: Am. Bar Found.; mem.: ABA (Margaret Brent award 1991), Nat. Assn. Women Lawyers (Arabella Babb Mansfield award 1999), U. Pa. Law Soc., Am. Law Inst., Am. Judicature Soc. (Devitt award com. 1998—99), State Bar Ga., Savannah Bar Assn. (pres. 1976). Office: US Ct Appeals 11th Cir 56 Forsyth St NW # 202 Atlanta GA 30303-2205 Office Phone: 404-335-6300.

KRAVITT, JASON HARRIS PAPERNO, lawyer; b. Chgo., Jan. 19, 1948; s. Jerome Julius and Shirley (Paperno) K.; m. Beverly Ray Niemeier, May 11, 1974; children: Nikola Wedding, Justin Taylor Paperno. AB, Johns Hopkins U., 1969; JD, Harvard U., 1972; diploma in comparative legal studies, Cambridge U., Eng., 1973. Bar: Ill. 1973, N.Y. 2002, U.S. Dist. Ct. (no. dist.) Ill. 1973, U.S. Dist. Ct. (so. dist.) N.Y. 2002. Assoc. Mayer, Brown Rowe & Maw (formerly Mayer, Brown & Platt), Chgo., 1973-78, ptnr., 1979—, co-chmn., 1998-2001. Adj. prof. law Northwestern U., Evanston, Ill., 1994—, adj. prof. fin. Kellogg Sch. Mgmt., 1998—. Editor: Securitization of Financial Assets, 2d edit., 1996. Bd. dirs. Chgo. Met. YMCA, 1998—2001, Mus. Contemporary Art, Chgo., 1974—75; dir., chmn. The Cameron Kravitt Found., 1984—; sec., chair legal, regulatory tax and acctg. com. Am. Securitization Forum, 2001—. Fellow Am. Coll. Comml. Lawyers; mem. ABA, Chgo. Coun. Lawyers, Chgo. Bar Assn., NY State Bar Assn., NYC Bar Assn., Econ. Club of Chgo., Execs. Club Chgo. Home: 250 Sheridan Rd Glencoe IL 60022-1948 Office: Mayer Brown Rowe & Maw 190 S La Salle St Ste 3100 Chicago IL 60603-3441 Office Phone: 212-506-2622. Business E-Mail: jkravitt@mayerbrown.com.

KRAVITZ, ELLEN KING, musicologist, educator; b. Fords, N.J., May 25, 1929; d. Walter J. and Frances M. (Prybylowski) Kokowicz; m. Hilard L. Kravitz, Jan. 9, 1972; children: Julie Frances, Heather Frances stepchildren: Kent, Kerry, Jay. BA, Georgian Ct. Coll., 1964; MM, U. So. Calif., 1966, PhD, 1970. Tchr. 7th and 8th grade music Mt. St. Mary Acad., North Plainfield, NJ, 1949-50; cloistered nun Carmelite Monastery, Lafayette, La., 1950-61; instr. Loyola U., L.A., 1967; asst. prof. music Calif. State U., L.A., 1967-71, assoc. prof., 1971-74, prof., 1974—99, emeritus prof., 1999—. Founder Friends of Music Calif. State U., L.A., 1976. Mem. editl. adv. bd.: Jour. Arnold Schoenberg Inst., 1977—87; editor: Jour. Arnold Schoenberg Inst., Vol. I, No. 3, 1977, Jour. Arnold Schoenberg Inst., Vol. II, No. 3, 1978; author (with others): Catalog of Schoenberg's Paintings, Drawings and Sketches; author: (book) Music in Our Culture, 1996. Guest lectr. Schoenberg Centennial Com., 1969—, mem., 1974. Mem.: Hist. Assn. L.A. Music Ctr., Am. Musicol. Soc., L.A. County Mus. Art, Pi Kappa Lambda, Mu Phi Epsilon.

KRAVITZ, LEE, editor; Degree, Yale U.; MA in Journalism, Columbia U. Editor React, 1995—2000; v.p. Parade Pubs., 1995—2000; editor Parade Magazine, N.Y.C., 2000—; sr. v.p. Parade Pubs., 2000—. Office: Parade 711 3rd Ave New York NY 10017-4014 Office Phone: 212-450-7000. Office Fax: 212-450-7023.*

KRAVITZ, LENNY, singer, guitarist; b. May 26, 1964; 1 child, Zoe. Singer, musician: albums Let Love Rule, 1989, Mama Said, 1991, Are You Gonna Go My Way, 1993 (2 Grammy nominations), Circus, 1995, 5, 1998 (Grammy award Best Male Rock Vocal Performance for song "Fly Away", 1998, Grammy award Best Male Rock Vocal Performance for song "American Woman", 1999), Greatest Hits, 2000 (Grammy award Best Male Rock Vocal Performance for song "Again", 2000), Lenny, 2001 (Grammy award Best Male Rock Vocal Performance for song "Dig In", 2001), Baptism, 2004; Soundtrack Cutting Edge, Waterboy, 1998, Twice Upon a Yesteryear, Austin Powers, The Spy Who Shagged Me, 1999, appeared (films) Lennon: A Tribute, 1991, Lenny Kravitz: Video Retrospective, 1992, (voice films) Rugrats: The Movie, 1999. Office: care CAA 9830 Wilshire Blvd Beverly Hills CA 90212-1804 also: Virgin Records 550 Madison Ave New York NY 10022-3211 also: 2100 Columbia Ave Santa Monica CA 90404

KRAVITZ, RICHARD L., medical educator, director; BS, Stanford Univ.; MD, Univ. Calif., San Francisco; MSPH in Epidemiology, Univ. Calif., LA. Faculty UCLA, 1988—93; prof. medicine Univ. Calif. Davis, 1993—; dir. Univ. Calif. Davis, Ctr. for Health Svcs. Rsch. in Primary Care, 1996—. Fellow Assn. for Health Svcs. Rsch. Named Picker/Commonwealth Faculty Scholar, 1993. Office: UC Davis Ctr Health Svcs Rsch in Primary Care 4150 V St Ste 2500 PSSB Sacramento CA 95817 Office Phone: 916-734-1248. Office Fax: 916-734-8731. Business E-Mail: rlkravitz@ucdavis.edu.*

KRAVTSOV, SERGEY V., oceanography educator, researcher; b. Moscow, June 28, 1971; s. Vyacheslav A. Kravtsov and Galina V. Kravtsova; m. Olga A. Lebedeva, Aug. 12, 1991; children: Maxim, Dmitriy, Maria, Ilya, Alexey. BSc in Physics and Math., Moscow Inst. Physics and Tech., 1991, MSc in Applied Math. and Physics, 1993; PhD in Phys. Oceanography, Fla. State U. Rsch. asst. Fla. State U., Tallahassee, 1993—98; postdoctoral rschr. IGPP UCLA, 1999—2001, asst. rschr., 2001—05; asst. prof. U. Wis., Milw., 2005—.

KRAW, GEORGE MARTIN, lawyer, writer; b. Oakland, Calif., June 17, 1949; s. George and Pauline Dorothy (Herceg) K.; m. Sarah Lee Kenyon, Sept. 3, 1983 (dec. Nov. 2001). BA, U. Calif., Santa Cruz, 1971; student, Lenin Inst., Moscow, 1971; MA, U. Calif., Berkeley, 1974, JD, 1976. Bar: Calif. 1976, U.S. Supreme Ct. 1980, D.C. 1992. Pvt. practice, 1976—; ptnr. Kraw & Kraw, San Jose, 1988—. Mem. adv. com. Pension Benefit Guaranty Corp., 2002—05. Mem. ABA, Internat. Soc. Cert. Employee Benefit Specialists, Nat. Assn. Health Lawyers, Inter-Am. Bar Assn. Office: Kraw & Kraw 333 W San Carlos St Ste 200 San Jose CA 95110-2735 Business E-Mail: gkraw@kraw.com.

KRAWCHECK, SALLIE L., finance company executive; b. Charleston, SC, 1966; BA, U. N.C., Chapel Hill, 1987; MBA, Columbia U., N.Y.C., 1992. Fin. analyst Salomon Brothers, Inc.; assoc. corp. fin. dept. Donaldson, Lufkin & Jenrette; sr. rsch. analyst Sanford C. Bernstein, 1994—98, dir. rsch., 1999—2001; exec. v.p. Alliance Capital Mgmt. L.P., 2001—02; chmn. and CEO Sanford C. Bernstein, 2001—02, Smith Barney, NYC, 2002—04; exec. v.p. fin., ops. & strategy, CFO Citigroup Inc., NYC, 2004—. Mem. Citigroup Mgmt. com., Citigroup Bus. Heads com. Bd. dirs. U. N.C. at Chapel Hill Foundations, Inc., Carnegie Hall; bd. overseers Columbia Bus. Sch. Named Most Influential Person Under the Age of 40, Fortune mag., 2003; named one of Global Business Influentials, Time mag., 2002, Most Powerful Women in Bus., Fortune mag., 2002, 2003, 2004, Most Powerful Women, Forbes mag., 2005. Office: Citigroup Inc 399 Park Ave New York NY 10022*

KRAWCZYK, EVA, information scientist, educator; b. Zgierz, Poland, Feb. 18, 1973; d. Tadeusz Ignacy and Stella Krawczyk. AS, Am. Acad. of Art, 1994; BA, Columbia Coll. of Chgo., 1996; MS in info. sci., Roosevelt U., 1998, MBA, 1999; PhD, Am. Coll. of Metaphysical Theology, 2002; DD, Trinity Coll. & U., 2002. Minister Minn., 2002. Mgr. Excel Mktg. and Comm., Inc., Chgo., 1999—; mergers & acquisitions bus. coord. Internat. Profit Assoc., Buffalo Grove, Ill., 1999—. Volunteering Mercy Home for Boys & Girls, Chgo., 2000—01. Author: (novel) The Investigation of Lived Experiences: From a Phenomenographic & Phenomenological Perspective in the Scope of a Metaphysical Aura and Knowledge Base, 2003, Addicted to a Degree, 2003, Eve's 365 Days of Christmas, 2003. Fund organizer Feed the Children, Chgo., 2000—02. Fellow Grad. Assistantship and fellowship, Walter E. Heller Coll. of Bus. Adminstrn., 1997—98. Mem.: IEEE (assoc.), Polish Am. Leadership Initiative PALI (assoc.), NAFE (assoc.), Nat. Hispanic Soc. (hon.). Independent Thinkers. Christian. Achievements include patents pending for doll and specific type of lamp. Avocations: art, reading, dance, animation, travel. Home: 5115 N Nagle Ave Chicago IL 60630-1816 Personal E-mail: globeeve@aol.com.

KRAWCZYNSKI, TONY EDWARD, music educator; b. Springfield, Mass., Jan. 14, 1974; s. Richard Michael and Dorothy Ellen Krawczynski. Grad., Berklee Coll. Music; MusB in Edn., U. Mass., 1999. Fla.Tchg. Cert. Fla. Dept. of Edn., 2001. Dir. bands Palm Harbor (Fla.) Mid. Sch., 1999—. Marching band asst. Dunedin (Fla.) H.S., 2000, 2003—. Mem. first no. region divsn. 9 USCG Aux., South Hadley, Mass., 1996. Grantee, Pinellas County Arts Coun., 2002. Mem.: Internat. Assn. Jazz Educators, Coll. Band Dir.'s Nat. Assn., Pinellas County Music Educator's Assn., Fla. Bandmaster's Assn., Music Educator's Nat. Conf. Independent. Roman Catholic. Avocation: baseball. Office: Palm Harbor Middle School 1800 Tampa Road Palm Harbor FL 34683 Office Phone: 727-669-1146. E-mail: tony_krawczynski@places.pcsb.org.

KRAWETZ, ARTHUR ALTSHULER, chemist, science administrator; b. Chgo., Oct. 30, 1932; s. John and Grace (Altshuler) K. BS in Chemistry, Northwestern U., 1952; MS in Phys. Chemistry, U. Chgo., 1953, PhD in Phys. Chemistry, 1955. Cert. chartered scientist Royal Soc. Chemistry, 2004, chartered chemist Royal Soc. Chemistry. V.p. Phoenix Chem. Lab., Inc., Chgo., 1950-73, tech. dir., 1958—, pres., 1974—. Contbr. articles to profl. jours. 1st Lt. USAF, 1956—58, capt. Res. USAF. Fellow Am. Inst. Chemists (life), Royal Soc. Chemistry (chartered chemist); mem. ASTM (chmn. sub-com. XI engring. scis., sub-com. N-VI fire resistance 1974-84, sub-com. IX-D oxidation 1974-81, task force on precautionary statements for hazardous material and lab. ops. 1976-84, com. mem.), Am. Chem. Soc., Instrument Soc. Am., Air & Waste Mgmt. Assn., Soc. for Applied Spectroscopy, Soc. Automotive Engrs., Soc. Tribologists and Lubrication Engrs., Nat. Lubricating Grease Inst., The Coblentz Soc., Nat. Fire Protection Assn. (com. on classification and properties of hazardous chemical data, phys. and chem. data consistency adv. com.), Chgo. Gas Chromatography Discussion Group, Internat. Assn. Stability and Handling Liquid Fuels,Phi Beta Kappa, Sigma Xi, Phi Lambda Upsilon, Pi Mu Epsilon Achievements include patents for temperature control apparatus and method, method of determining acid content of oil sample, automatic oxygen measuring system, viscometers, measurement of bulk modulus and pressure viscosity, corrosion rate evaluation procedures; registered copyrights for various software. Office: Phoenix Chem Lab Inc 3953 W Shakespeare Ave Chicago IL 60647-3497 Office Phone: 773-772-3577. Personal E-mail: pclinc@xnet.com.

KRAWETZ, STEPHEN ANDREW, molecular medicine and genetics scientist; b. Fort Frances, Ont., Can., Sept. 17, 1955; s. Stephen and Michaelene (Medynski) K.; m. Lorraine Ruth St. John, Aug. 19, 1977; children: Rhochelle Tairaesa, Alexandra Renée. BSc, U. Toronto, Ont., 1977, PhD, 1983. Tchr. Scarborough Bd. Edn., Ont., 1976-77; Alberta Heritage Found. Med. Rsch. postdoc. fellow U. Calgary, Alta., Can., 1983-89; asst. prof. rsch. ctr. for molecular biology Wayne State U., Detroit, 1989, asst. prof. molecular biology and genetics, 1989-92, asst. prof. obstetrics and gynecology and molecular biology and genetics, 1992-94, assoc. prof. ob/gyn. and molecular medicine and genetics, 1994-2000, prof. ob-gyn. and molecular medicine and genetics Inst. Sci. Computing, 2000-01, Charlotte B. Failing prof. ob-gyn. and molecular medicine and genetics and Inst. Sci. Computing, 2001—, dir. Bioinformatics Node Mich. Life Scis. Corridor, 2001—, dir. Ctr. of Excellence for Combating the Paternal Impact of Toxicol. Waste on the Next Generation. Biotech. cons., Calgary, 1985-89, Grosse Pointe Woods, Mich., 1989—; co-founder Genetic Imaging, Inc., 1988. Mem. editl. bd. BioTechniques, Ag Biotech News and Info., Cellular and Molecular Biology Letters, Gene Therapy and Molecular Biology; contbr. numerous articles to scholarly jours. Recipient B.C. Childrens Hosp. Rsch. award, Vancouver, 1984, Computer Applications in Molecular Biology award IntelliGenetics Inc., Mountain View, Calif., 1988, others, Bd. of Govs. award Wayne State U., 2004; named Outstanding Basic Scientist, C.S. Mott Ctr., 1999; Alta. Heritage Found. Med. Rsch. fellow, 1985-88. Mem. AAAS, Am. Soc. Human Genetics, Soc. for the Study of Reprodn. Achievements include development of a computer-based imaging system for biological data, of VPCS cloning vectors, of the basis of biological sequence alignment algorithm; one of the first to describe overlapping reading frames in eucaryotes; first detailed analysis of a mammalian protamine gene; first definition of sequence interpretation errors in the GenBank database; first to define a genic domain in human sperm; research in gene therapy targeted to the amelioration of human disease; showed that selective potentiation of our genome mediates cell-phenotype. Home: 590 S Brys Dr Grosse Pointe Woods MI 48236-1285 Office: Dept Ob-Gyn Ctr Molecular Med Genetics Detroit MI 48201 Office Phone: 313-577-6770. E-mail: steve@compbio.med.wayne.edu.

KRAYBILL, DONALD BRUBAKER, humanities educator, writer; b. Mt. Joy, Pa., Sept. 24, 1945; s. Wilmer Garber and Helen (Brubaker) K.; m. Frances Mellinger, Sept. 3, 1966; children: Sheila Lynn, Joy Louise. BA in Sociology and Religion, Ea. Mennonite U., Harrisonburg, Va., 1967; MA in Sociology, Temple U., 1972, PhD in Sociology, 1975. Prof. sociology Elizabethtown Coll., Pa., 1971-96, dir. Young Ctr., 1989—96, disting. prof., 2002—; provost Messiah Coll., Grantham, Pa., 1996—2002. Author: The Upside-Down Kingdom, 1978, 2003 (Nat. Religious Book award Religious Book Rev. 1979), The Riddle of Amish Culture, 2001, The Amish and the State, 2003(Outstanding Acad. Book award Choice 1994), Amish Enterprise, 1995, On the Backroad to Heaven, 2003, others. Sr. Rsch. fellow NEH, 1987. Office: The Young Ctr Elizabethtown Coll Elizabethtown PA 17022 Office Phone: 717-361-1469. Business E-Mail: kraybilld@etown.edu.

KRAYNAK, MARCELLE GEORGEANN, not-for-profit developer; b. N.Y.C., N.Y., Apr. 3, 1944; d. Richard A. and Bernice (Weinberg) Kane; m. Anthony Walter Kraynak, Sept. 27, 1989; children: Marylin Kotansky, Joseph Kossmann, Bobbi Dempsey, William Kossmann. AAS in Human Svcs. magna cum laude, Lackawanna Jr. Coll., Hazleton, Pa., 1996. LPN, Pa. Buyer cosmetics F. W. Woolworth, Jamaica, NY, 1964—65; asst. dir., group supr. YMCA/YWCA; staff nurse St. Joseph's Med. Ctr., Hazleton, 1989—90; dir. Children's Rainbow Found., Hazleton, 1990—92; founder, exec. dir. Silent Santa, Hazleton, 1992—. Co-chair Vietnam Relocation Com., Wilkes-Barre, Pa., 1974; v.p. Vine Manor Resident Coun., Hazleton, 1993—. Named Nurse of Hope, Am. Cancer Soc., 1989; recipient Sam-Son award, Sam-Son Prodns. Avocations: reading, writing. Home and Office: 320 W Mine St #204 Hazleton PA 18201

KRAYZELBURG, LENNY, Olympic athlete; b. Odessa, Ukraine, Sept. 28, 1975; arrived in U.S., 1989, 1995; s. Oleg and Yelena Krayzelburg. Student, UCLA. Recipient Gold medal 100-meter backstroke, 200-meter backstroke, 4 x 100-meter medley (team) Sydney Olympics, 2000, Summer Nats. Phillips Performance award, 1997-99, Gold medal 100-meter backstroke, Silver medal 200-meter backstroke U.S. Open Championships, San Antonio, 1999, Gold medal 100-meter backstroke, Silver medal 200-meter backstroke Janet Evans Invitational, L.A., 2000; named USA Swimming Swimmer of Yr., 1999; broke 3 world records 50-meter backstroke, 100-meter backstroke, 200-meter backstroke Pan Pacific Championships, 1999, ranked 1st in the world for 50m backstroke, 100m backstroke, 200m backstroke, 1999. Avocations: reading, computers, basketball. Office: USA Swimming 1 Olympic Plz Colorado Springs CO 80909-5746

KREAGER, EILEEN DAVIS, financial consultant; b. Caldwell, Ohio, Mar. 2, 1924; d. Fred Raymond and Esther (Farson) Davis. BBA, Ohio State U., 1945. With accounts receivable dept. M & R Dietetic, Columbus, Ohio, 1945—50; complete charge bookkeeper Magic Seal Paper Products, Columbus, 1950—53, A. Walt Runglin Co., L.A., 1953—54; office mgr. Roy C. Haddox and Son, Columbus, 1954—60; bursar Meth. Theol. Sch. Ohio, Delaware, 1961—86; adminstrv. cons. Fin. Ltd., 1986—. Ptnr. Coll. Adminstrv. Sci., Ohio State U., 1975-80; seminar participant Paperwork Systems and Computer Sci., 1965, Computer Systems, 1964, Griffith Found. Seminar Working Women, 1975; pres. Altrusa Club of Delaware, Ohio, 1972-73. Del. Altrusa Internat., Montreal, 1972, Altrusa Regional, Greenbrier, 1973. Fellow Am. Biog. Inst. (life); mem. AAUW, Assoc. Am. Inst. Mgmt. (exec. coun. of Inst. 1979), Am. Soc. Profl. Cons., Internat. Platform Assn., Ohio State U. Alumna Assn., Columbus Computer Soc., Air Force Assn., Fraternal Order of Police Ohio, Motts Mil. Mus., Innovation Alliance, Toastmasters Internat., Ohio State U. Faculty Club, Univ. Club Columbus, Capital Club, Delaware Country Club, Columbus Met. Club, Friends Hist. Costume & Textile Collection Ohio State U., Internat. Order Police Ohio, Inc., Kappa Delta Methodist. Home: PO Box 214 Columbus OH 43085-0214

KREAMER, CAROLYN LEE, nursing educator, community health nurse; b. Waynesboro, Pa., July 28, 1948; d. Martin Noah Kreamer and Manila Keturah Strausner Kreamer. Diploma in nursing, York (Pa.) Hosp. Sch. Nursing, 1969; BS, Pa. State U., U. Pk., Pa., 1975; MS, U. Md., Balt., 1980; PhD, U. Tex. at Austin, 1989. Staff nurse Milton S. Hershey Med. Ctr., Hershey, Pa., 1970—73, 1975; vis. nurse, pub. health status York Vis. Nurses Assn., Pa., 1975—76; assoc. instr. nursing York Hosp. Sch. Nursing, Pa., 1976—78; instr. nursing York Coll. of Pa., Pa., 1980—82, Pa. State U., Hershey, 1983—86; assoc. prof. nursing Messiah Coll., Grantham, Pa., 1986—, chairperson, 1986—. Treas. Pa. Higher Edn. Nursing Sch. Assn., Harrisburg, Pa., 2000—03; faculty adv. Lambda Kappa, Sigma Theta Tau Internat., Grantham, Pa., 2003—. Recipient Sci. award, York County Oilmen's Assn., 1969. Mem.: Am. Assn. Critical Care Nurses Assn., Am. Nurses Assn., Sigma Theta Tau. Democrat. Meth. Avocation: horseback riding. Home: 563 Fishing Creek Rd Lewisberry PA 17339 Office: Messiah College Dept Nursing PO Box 3031 One College Ave Grantham PA 17027 Office Phone: 717-691-6029.

KREBS, ARNO WILLIAM, JR., lawyer; b. Dallas, July 7, 1942; s. Arno W. and Lynette (Linnstaedter) K.; m. Peggy Sharon Stagg, Dec. 17, 1966; 1 child, Kirsten; m. Barbara Lyn Craig, Dec. 28, 1973 BA, Tex. A&M U., 1964; LL.B., U. Tex., 1967. Bar: Tex. 1967, U.S. Dist. Ct. (so. dist.) Tex. 1968, U.S. Ct. Appeals (5th cir.) 1971, U.S. Ct. Appeals (11th cir.) 1981, U.S. Dist. Ct. (we. and no. dists.) Tex. 1981, U.S. Supreme Ct. 1983, U.S. Dist. Ct. (ea. dist.) Tex. 1984. Assoc. Fulbright & Jaworski, Houston, 1967-75, ptnr., 1975—. Contbr. articles to profl. jours. Mem. Houston Bar Assn., Tex. Aggie Bar Assn. (pres. 1978-79), Tex. Bar Found., Houston Bar Found., Tex. A&M U. 12th Man Found. (pres. 1988), Houston Ctr. Club. Lutheran. Office: Fulbright & Jaworski 1301 Mckinney St Fl 51 Houston TX 77010-3031 Office Phone: 713-651-5522. Personal E-mail: akrebs@fulbright.com.

KREBS, CARL F., architectural firm executive; b. Phila., Aug. 27, 1959; AB, Harvard U., 1981; MARch, Columbia U., 1985. Ptnr. Davis Brody Bond, 1984—. Ptnr.-in-charge Health Scis. Learning Ctr., U. of Wis.; ptnr.-in-charge Sch. of Vet. Medicine, Cornell U., Lang. Resource Ctr., Columbia U. Recipient Arch. Record award, Bus. Week, 2000. Office: Davis Brody Bond LLP 315 Hudson St 9th Fl New York NY 10013

KREBS, EDWIN GERHARD, biochemistry educator; b. Lansing, Iowa, June 6, 1918; s. William Carl and Louise Helena (Stegeman) K.; m. Virginia Frech, Mar. 10, 1945; children: Sally, Robert, Martha. AB in Chemistry, U. Ill., 1940; MD, Washington U., St. Louis, 1943, DSc (hon.), 1995; DSc honoris causa, U. Geneva, 1979; hon. degree, Med. Coll. Ohio, 1993; DSc (hon.), U. Ind., 1993, U. Ill., 1995; D honoris causa, U. Nat. De Cuyo, 1993. Intern, asst. resident Barnes Hosp., St. Louis, 1944-45; rsch. fellow biol. chemistry Wash. U., St. Louis, 1946-48; prof., chmn. dept. biol. chemistry Sch. Medicine U. Calif., Davis, 1968-76; from asst. prof. to prof. biochemistry U. Wash., Seattle, 1948-66, prof., chmn. dept. pharmacology, 1977-83, prof. biochemistry and pharmacology, 1984-91, emeritus prof., biochemistry and pharmacology, 1991—; investigator, sr. investigator Howard Hughes Med. Inst., Seattle, 1983-90, sr. investigator emeritus, 1991—. Mem. Phys. Chemistry Study Sect. NIH, 1963-68, Biochemistry Test Com. Nat. Bd. Med. Examiners, 1968-71, rsch. com. Am. Heart Assn., 1970-74, bd. sci. counselors Nat. Inst. Arthritis, Metabolism and Digestive Diseases, NIH, 1979-84, Internat. Bd. Rev., Alberta Heritage Found. for Med. Rsch., 1986, external adv. com. Weis Ctr. for Rsch., 1987-91; mem. subgroup interconvertible enzymes IUB Spl. Interest Group Metabolic Regulation; internat. adv. bd. Advances in Second Messenger Phosphoprotein Rsch.; external adv. com. Cell Therapeutics Inc., Seattle; adv. bd. Kinetek, Vancouver, B.C. Mem. editorial bd. Jour. Biol. Chemistry, 1965-70; mem. editorial adv. bd. Biochemistry, 1971-76; mem. editorial and adv. bd. Molecular Pharmacology, 1972-77; assoc. editor Jour. Biol. Chemistry, 1971-93; mem. internat. adv. bd. Advances in Cyclic Nucleotide Rsch., 1972—; editorial advisor Molecular and Cellular Biochemistry, 1987—. Recipient Gairdner Found. award, Toronto, 1978, J.J. Berzelius lectureship, Karolinska Institutet, 1982, George W. Thorn award for sci. excellence, 1983, Sir Frederick Hopkins Meml. lectureship, London, 1984, Rsch. Achievement award Am. Heart Assn., Anaheim, Calif., 1987, 3M Life Scis. award FASEB, New Orleans, 1989, Albert Lasker Basic Med. Rsch. award, 1989, CIBA-GEIGY-Drew award Drew U., 1991, Steven C. Beering award, Ind. U., 1991, Welch award in chemistry Welch Found., 1991, Louisa Gross Horwitz award Columbia U., 1989, Alumni Achievement award Coll. Liberal Arts and Scis. U. Ill., 1992, Nobel prize in physiology or medicine, 1992, Kaul Found. award for excellence, 1996; John Simon Guggenheim fellow, 1959, 66. Mem. NAS, Am. Soc. Biol. Chemists (pres. 1986, edn l. affairs com. 1965-68, councillor 1975-78), Am. Acad. Arts and Scis., Am. Soc. Pharmacology and Exptl. Therapeutics. Achievements include life-long study of the protein phosphorylation process. Office: U Wash HSB K540E PO Box 357750 Seattle WA 98195-7750*

KREBS, KATHLEEN ELIZABETH PEELEN, artist, educator; b. L.A., July 7, 1944; d. Joseph Andrew and Mary Eve Peelen; m. Gary Fredrick Krebs, Aug. 19, 1972; 1 child, Matthew. BA, U. Calif., Berkeley, 1970; MA, U. Toronto, 1980. Rsch. asst. The Hosp. Sick Children, Toronto, 1977—81; tchr. City Coll., San Francisco, 1988—2003, Foothill Coll., Los Altos Hills, 1988—2003, Coll. San Mateo, 1988—2003; artist Berkeley, 1981—. Tchr. art Studio One, Oakland, Calif., 1989—2002, Albany Adult Sch., 1992—2003; tchr. reading resource Jefferson Elem. Sch., Berkeley, 1983—86; cons. and guest lectr. in field. Contbr. articles to profl. jours. Mem.: Bay Area Basket Makers (pres. 1997—99, publicity chair 2000—, internat. sales fiber vessels and baskets, art galleries, mus. 1989—), Am. Craft Coun. Avocations: travel, gardening, photography, basket weaving, writing.

KREBS, MARY, art educator; d. Andrew and Mary McCaffrey; m. Richard Krebs, May 11, 1980; 1 child, Michael. BS in Art Edn., SUNY, 1972; MBA in Mktg., Adelphi U., 1980; MEd in Elem. Edn., L.I. U., 1993. N.Y. State tchg. cert. elem. edn. (N-6), N.Y. State tchg. cert. art Eedn. (K-12). Buyer Bloomingdales, New York City, NY, 1973—80; dir. of customer svc. El Greco Leather (Candie's Shoes), Pt. Washington, NY, 1980—81; divisional mdse. mgr. Federated Dept. Stores, New York City, NY, 1981—83; graphic artist/sculptor Self Employed, Massapequa, NY, 1983—; tchr. - pre -sch. Cmty. Meth. Sch. & Our Lady of Assumption, Massapequa, NY, 1986—93; tchr. - elem. Massapequa Schools - Birch Ln./Unqua, Massapequa, NY, 1993—95; tchr. - art secondary Massapequa Schools - Berner Mid. Sch., Massapequa, NY, 1995—. Book, Rachel's Star of David. Bldg. rep. Massapequa Fedn. Tchrs., 2003. Named Outstanding Vol., YES Cmty. Counseling Ctr., 1996; named to Wall of Tolerance, Rosa Parks, Nat. Campaign for Tolerance, So. Poverty Law Ctr., Ala., 2003; recipient Cert. of Merit, Massapequa Bd. of Edn., 2002; M-TRACT and LINC-IT grants, NY Tchr. Ctr., Tech. Grants, 2000, 2001, Richard Gazzola Tchr. fellow, N.Y. State PTA, 2001. Mem.: Green County Coun. Arts, Massapequa S.D. (advisor 1993—), N.Y. State Art Tchr.'s Assn. (conf. presenter, spkr.'s bur. 1995—), N.Y. State PTA (life; chairperson 1985—2001, Hon. Life 2001), Massapequa PTA Coun. (life; mem. 1985—2001, Disting. Svc. 2001), Massapequa PTA (life; pres./mem. 1985—2001, tchr. rep. 1990, Hon. Life 1996). Avocations: sculpting, bowling, tennis. E-mail: mck_art@optonline.net.

KREBS, ROBERT DUNCAN, rail transportation company executive; b. Sacramento, May 2, 1942; s. Ward Carl and Eleanor Blauth (Duncan) K.; m. Anne Lindstrom, Sept. 11, 1971; children: Robert Ward, Elisabeth Lindstrom, Duncan Lindstrom. BA with distinction, Stanford U., 1964; MBA, Harvard U., 1966. Asst. gen. mgr. So. Pacific Transp. Co., Houston, 1974-75, asst. regional ops. mgr., 1975-76, asst. v.p. San Francisco, 1976-77, asst. to pres., 1977-79, gen. mgr., 1979, v.p. transp., 1979-80, v.p. ops., 1980-82, pres., 1982-83, also dir.; pres., chief operating officer Santa Fe So. Pacific Corp., 1983-88, pres., CEO, 1988-96; chmn., pres., CEO Burlington Northern Santa Fe Corp (merger Santa Fe So. Pacific Corp and Burlington Northern), 1997-99; chmn., CEO Burling No. Santa Fe Corp., 1999-2000, chmn., 2000—02; ret., 2002. Chmn. burlington Northern Santa Fe Corp., 2000—. Bd. dirs. Phelps Dodge Corp., Ft. Worth Symphony Orch. Assn., Tex. Christian U. Mem. Stanford U. Alumni Assn., Phi Beta Kappa, Kappa Sigma. Clubs: Onwentsia (Lake Forest, Ill.), Burlingame, Calif., Pacific Union, Bohemian, Chicago, City (Ft. Worth), Rivercrest Country (Ft. Worth). Office: Burlington Northern Santa Fe Corp PO Box 961052 Fort Worth TX 76161-0052

KREBS, WILLIAM HOYT, industrial hygienist, health science association administrator; b. Detroit, Apr. 6, 1938; s. William Thomas and Mary Louise (Hoyt) K.; m. Susan Kathryn Bartholomew, Aug. 8, 1964 (div. July 1976); children: Elizabeth Louise, William Thomas II; m. Jane Germer Meikle, June 18, 1983; stepchildren: David Andrew, Sarah Elizabeth. BS, U. Mich., 1960, MPH (IH), 1963, MS, 1965, PhD, 1970. Rsch. asst. U. Mich., Ann Arbor, 1962-63; indsl. hygienist Lumbermens Mut. Casualty Co., Chgo., 1963-64, GM Corp., Detroit, 1970-77, mgr. toxic materials control activity, 1977-81, dir. toxic materials control activity, 1981-90, dir. indsl. hygiene activity, 1990-93; v.p. Indsl. Health Scis., Inc., Grosse Pointe Park, Mich., 1993—94, pres., 2004—. Mem. asbestos adv. com. Mich. Occupational Health Standards Commn., Lansing, 1984—. Contbr. articles to profl. jours. Mem. Grosse Pointe Meml. Ch., Grosse Pointe Farms, 1954; mem. health and safety com. Detroit Area coun. Boy Scouts Am., 1980; mem. environment and energy com. Detroit Regional Chamber. Fellow Am. Indsl. Hygiene Assn. (hon. mem.; bd. dirs. 1976-79, v.p. 1986-87, pres. 1988-89); mem. AAAS, APHA, Mich. Indsl. Hygiene Soc. (pres. 1980-81), Brit. Occupational Hygiene Soc., Internat. Occupational Hygiene Assn. (v.p. 1990-91, pres. 1992-93), Internat. Commn. on Occpl. Health, Soc. Automotive Engrs. Presbyterian. Home: 1014 Bishop Rd Grosse Pointe Park MI 48230-1421 Office: Indsl Health Scis Inc 1014 Bishop Rd Grosse Pointe Park MI 48230-1421 Office Phone: 313-885-8225.

KREEK, MARY JEANNE, physician; b. Washington; d. Louis Francis and Esperance (Agee) K; m. Robert A. Schaefer, Jan. 24, 1970; children: Robert A., Esperance Anne. BA, Wellesley Coll., 1958; MD, Columbia U., Coll. Physicians and Surgeons, 1962; D honoris causa (hon.), Uppsala U., Sweden, 2000. Med. rschr. NIH, Bethesda, Md., 1957-62; intern, resident Cornell N.Y. Hosp. Med. Ctr., N.Y.C., 1962-65, fellow, 1965-67; instr. medicine Cornell Med. Coll., 1966-67; acad. medicine specializing in internal medicine, endocrinology, gastroenterology, hepatology, clin. pharmacology, neuroscience, molecular genetics NYC, 1966—. Mem. staff N.Y.-Presbyn. Hosp.-Weill Sch. Medicine of Cornell U., 1968—77, clin. asst. prof., asst. attending physician, now assoc. attending physician, adj. assoc. prof.; asst. prof. Rockefeller U., 1967—72, sr. rsch. assoc., physician, 1972—83, assoc. prof., physician, 1983—94, prof., sr. physician, head of lab., 1994—; head Ind. Lab. on Biology of Addictive Disease, 1975—94, head of lab., 1994—; sr. physician Rockefeller U. Hosp., 1994—; adj. prof. Beijing Med. U., 1996—2000, Peking U., 2000—, Karolinska Inst., 2001; mem. gen. medicine study sect. NIH, 1973—77; co-chmn. John E. Fogarty (NIH) Internat. Conf. Hepatotoxicity Due to Drugs and Chems., 1977, charter mem. peer rev. oversight group, 1996—2000; vis. prof. Pahlavi U., Shiraz, Iran, 1977; spl. adv. Nat. Inst. Drug Abuse, 1976—86, mem. nat. adv. coun., 1991—95, mem. molecular genetics consortium, 1999—; prin. investigator Rsch. Ctr. Biol. Basis Addictive Diseases, 1987—; mem. gastroenterology adv. com. FDA, 1975—79, 1992—96, NIH Gen. Clin.; mem. gen. rsch. ctr. study sect. NIH, 1979—83, chmn., 1982—83; mem. exec. com. Coll. Problems Drug Dependence, 1982—87, 1989—94, chmn. exec. com., 1985—87, chair sci. program com., 1991—96; fellow CPDD, 1992—; dir. NIH-Nat. Inst. Drug Abuse Rsch. Ctr., 1987—. Recipient Borden Rsch. award, 1962, Career Scientist award Health Rsch. Coun. City N.Y., 1974-75, Dole/Nyswander award, Rsch. Scientist award NIH Gen. Clin. sect., 1978—, Mentor of Mentors award Am. Soc. Addiction Medicine, 1995, Assn. for Med. Edn. and Rsch. in Substance Abuse-Betty Ford award for outstanding rsch., 1996, R. Brinkley Smithers Disting. Scholar award Am. Soc. Addiction Medicine, 1999, Nathan B. Eddy award, Lifetime Rsch. award Coll. on Problems of Drug Dependence, 1999, Gold Medal Lifetime Excellence award Columbia U. Coll. Physicians and Surgeons Alumni Assn., 2004, Marian Fischman award, Coll. Ptnrs., 2005, Founders award, Intenat. Narcotic Rsch. Conf., 2005. Fellow: ACP, Assn. Am. Physicians (coun. mem. 2004—), N.Y. Acad. Scis., Am. Coll. Neuropsychopharmacology, Am. Fedn. for Clin. Rsch.; mem.: Harvey Soc., Soc. on Neuroscis., Rsch. Soc. on Alcoholism, Coun. Fgn. Rels. (life), Internat. Narcotic Rsch. Conf. (exec. com. 1993—97, pres.-elect 2001—03, pres. 2003—), Internat. Assn. Study Liver, Am. Assn. Study Liver Diseases, Endocrine Soc., N.Y. Gastroent. Assn. (pres. 1987), Am. Gastroent. Assn., Shakespeare Soc. of Wellesley, Phi Beta Kappa, Sigma Xi. Office: Rockefeller U New York NY 10021

KREFTING, ROBERT J(OHN), publishing company executive; b. Peoria, Ill., Apr. 29, 1944; s. Walter and Rebecca Juliana K.; m. Sally Ann Kingsmill, Aug. 27, 1978; children: Matthew, Nicholas; children by previous marriage: Gordon, Melissa, Sarah. BA magna cum laude with honors in History, Williams Coll., 1966. Subscription sales mgr. Time, Inc., N.Y.C., 1966-71; assoc. pub. Psychology Today, Del Mar, Calif., 1971-74; with CBS Publs., N.Y.C., 1974-83, v.p., group pub. spl. interest mags., 1977-79, pres., 1979-83, City Home Pub., Houston, 1984-85; exec. v.p. McCall Pub. Co., 1985-87; pres. Park Ave. Pub., N.Y.C., 1987-90, Holly Hill Pub., Katanah, N.Y., 1991-98; sr. v.p. Reader's Digest Assn., Pleasantville, 1998—2001. Mem. Mag. Pubs. Assn., Young Presidents Orgn., Waccabuc Country Club, Sky Club, Phi Beta Kappa. Home: 4 Powder Hill Rd Waccabuc NY 10597-1004 E-mail: rkrefting@starband.net.

KREGEL, KEVIN R., astronaut; b. Amityville, N.Y., Sept. 16, 1956; s. Alfred H. and Frances T. Kregel. BS in Astronautical Engring., USAF Acad., Colo. Springs, Colo., 1978; MPA, Troy State U., 1988. Commd. 2d lt. USAF, 1978, student pilot Williams AFB, Ariz., 1978—79; exchange officer RAF, Lakenheath, England, 1980—83, USN, Whidbey Island Seattle, 1984—86; student USN Test Pilot Sch., Patuxent River, Md., 1987—88; test pilot Eglin AFB, Fla., 1988—90; resigned USAF, 1990; aerospace engr., instr. pilot NASA Shuttle Flights, 1990—92; astronaut trainee Johnson Space Ctr., Houston, 1992—93; space flight crew mem., 1995—. Recipient 4 Space Flight medals, NASA, Exceptional Svc. award. Achievements include 4 Space flights; 5000 flight hours in 30 different aircraft; 66 carrier landings. Office: Astronauts Office CB Johnson Space Ctr Houston TX 77058

KREGER, DAVID LAWRENCE, gastroenterologist; b. Portsmouth, Va., Feb. 8, 1946; s. H. Sol and Ruth S. (Silverman) K.; m. Ruth H., Mar. 31, 1974; children: Seth Adam, Senta Lauren. BA, Duke U., 1968; MD, Med. Coll. Va. Intern Med. Coll. Va. Hosp., Richmond, 1972-73, resident, 1973-75;

gastroenterologist Gastroen. Assocs. Tidewater, Norfolk, Va., 1978—. Gastroenterology fellow, Duke U. Med. Ctr., Durham, N.C., 1975—77. Office: Gastroen Assocs Tidewater 160 Kingsley Ln Ste 200 Norfolk VA 23505-4600 Office Phone: 757-889-6800.

KREGER, MELVIN JOSEPH, lawyer; b. Buffalo, Feb. 21, 1937; s. Philip and Bernice (Gerstman) K.; m. Patricia Anderson, July 1, 1955 (div. 1963), children: Beth Barbour, Arlene Roux; m. Renate Hochleitner, Aug. 15, 1975. JD, Mid-valley Coll. Law, 1978; LLM in Taxation, U. San Diego, 1988. Bar: Calif. 1978, U.S. Dist. Ct. (cen. dist.) Calif. 1979, U.S. Tax Ct. 1979, U.S. Supreme Ct. 1995; cert. specialist in probate law, trust law and estate planning law, taxation law, Calif. Life underwriter Met. Life Ins. Co., Buffalo, 1958-63; bus. mgr. M. Kreger Bus. Mgmt., Sherman Oaks, Calif., 1963-78, enrolled agt., 1971—; pvt. practice North Hollywood, Calif., 1978—. Mem. Nat. Assn. Enrolled Agts., Calif. Soc. Enrolled Agts., State Bar Calif., L.A. Bar Assn., San Fernando Valley Bar Assn. (probate sect., tax sect.). Jewish. Avocations: computers, travel. Office: 11424 Burbank Blvd North Hollywood CA 91601-2301 Office Phone: 818-506-4723. Business E-Mail: mel@meltaxlaw.com.

KREGG, JUDITH LYNNE, accountant; b. Miami, Fla., June 1, 1947; d. Edward and Vernon Margurite (Davis) Malm; m. Gene Robert Kregg, Dec. 11, 1971 (div. Mar. 1977). A in Bus., Miami-Dade C.C., 1980. Staff acct. SONY Corp., N.Y.C., 1968-72, First Mortgage Investment, Miami Beach, Fla., 1975-78; regional contr. Smith Barney, Miami, Fla., 1978; staff acct. Fininvest Internat., Key Biscayne, Fla., 1979; chief acct. Transway Internat., Coral Gables, Fla., 1980-81; constrn. acct. Senior Corp., Miami Beach, 1981-85; dir. acctg. The Continental Cos., Coconut Grove, Fla., 1985-90; contr. Ireland Cos., North Miami, Fla., 1990; comml. acctg. mgr. Harbour Realty, Bay Harbor, Fla., 1991-94; contr. divsn. Carnival Resorts and Casinos Grand Bay Resort & Residencies, Coconut Grove, Fla., 1994—. Editor The SandDollar, 1991-96. Bd. dirs., 2d v.p., community coun. WLRN, South Fla.'s Pub. Radio & TV Sta., Miami, 1992-94. Recipient Cert. of Appreciation, WLRN, 1993. Mem. Ctr. for Orangutan and Chimpanzee Conservation (asst. editor Primapes newsletter 1995-97), Inst. Mgmt. Accts.(pres. Miami chpt. 1993-94, bd. dirs. 1991-92, nat. dir., 1996—, cert. of appreciation 1995, 97), Am. Orchid Soc., Coral Gables Orchid Soc., PEO Sisterhood (Miami Lakes Chpt. treas. 1992-93, pres. 1995-96, 98-99). Avocations: orchid culture, victorian collectibles. Home: 2620 SW 23rd Ave Miami FL 33133-2322

KREHBIEL, FREDERICK AUGUST, II, electronics company executive; b. Chgo., June 2, 1941; s. John Hammond and Margaret Ann (Veeck) K.; m. Kay Kirby, Dec. 21, 1973; children: William Veeck, Jay Frederick. BA, Lake Forest Coll., 1963. Advt. and human resources mgr. Molex Inc., Lisle, Ill., 1965—67, export mgr., 1967—69; v.p. internat. Molex, Inc., Lisle, Ill., 1970—75; exec. v.p., dir. Molex Inc., Lisle, Ill., from 1976; vice chmn., CEO Molex Co., Lisle, Ill., 1988-93; chmn., CEO Molex, Inc., Lisle, Ill., 1993—98, co-chmn., CEO, 1998—2001, co-chmn., 2001—. Bd. dirs. Tellabs Inc., Molex, Inc., DeVry, Inc. Trustee Rush Med. Ctr., Chgo., Lyric Opera, Chgo., Chgo. Zool. Soc., Chgo. Hist. Soc., Mus. Sci. and Industry, Chgo., Chgo. Orch. Assn., Sch. of Art Inst., Chgo. Mem. Hinsdale (Ill.) Golf Club, Chgo. Club, Casino Club (Chgo.), Racquet Club Chgo., Everglades Club, Bath and Tennis Club Palm Beach. Home: 505 S County Line Rd Hinsdale IL 60521-4725 Office: Molex Inc 2222 Wellington Ave Lisle IL 60532-3820 Business E-Mail: fkrehbiel@molex.com.

KREIDER, CLEMENT HORST, JR., neurosurgeon; b. Annville, Pa., Oct. 14, 1932; s. Clement Horst and Eleanor Lucille (Etter) K.; m. Yvonne Maria Vignone, Mar. 6, 1983; children: Clement H. III, John William H., George E. Etter (dec. Jan. 2001); stepchildren: Michael A. Ketcham (dec. July 1997), David C. Ketcham. Student, Yale U., 1949-51, 53-54; BS, Bethany (W.Va.) Coll., 1957; MD, Temple U., 1963. Lic. physician, Pa., N.J. Intern Pa. Hosp., Phila., 1963-64; resident in gen. surgery Temple U. Hosp, Phila., 1964-65, resident in neurosurgery, 1965-69; pvt. practice neurosurgery Harrisburg, Pa., 1969-72, Ocean, N.J., 1972-99; chief sect. neurosurgery Jersey Shore Med. Ctr., Neptune, N.J., 1972-96, attending neurosurgeon, 1996-99, emeritus, 2000—. Sr. attending Monmouth Med. Ctr., Long Branch, N.J., 1972-99, emeritus attending, 2000—; full attending Riverview Med. Ctr., Red Bank, N.J., 1972-99, emeritus, 2000; cons. emeritus CentraState Med. Ctr., Freehold, N.J.; courtesy staff emeritus Med. Ctr. of Ocean County, Point Pleasant, N.J., Kimball Med. Ctr., Lakewood, N.J., Bayshore Cmty. Hosp., Holmdel, N.J.; clin. instr. surgery Hershey (Pa.) Med. Ctr., 1970-72, Hahnemann Med. Ctr., Phila., 1970-72. Contbr. articles to profl. jours.; mem. com. on pub. N.J. Medicine, Lawrenceville, 1985-99. With U.S. Army, 1951-53. Fellow Stroke Coun., Am. Heart Assn.; mem. Congress of Neurol. Surgeons, Am. Assn. Neurol. Surgeons Joint Sect. on Cerebrovasc. Surgery, Med. Soc. N.J., N.J. Neurosurg. Soc., Monmouth County Med. Soc., Acad. Medicine of N.J. Avocation: boating. Office Phone: 732-280-7374.

KREIDER, GARY P., lawyer; b. Newark, Ohio, June 7, 1938; s. Kenneth Kirby and Josephine (Stare) K.; m. Barbara B. Brown, Aug. 25, 1962; children— Kenneth, Katherine, Krista, Karen, Kimberly. B.A., U. Cin., 1960, M.A. in History, 1961, J.D., 1964. Bar: Ohio 1964, U.S. Dist. Ct. (so. dist.) Ohio 1964, U.S. Supreme Ct. 1971. Ptnr. Keating, Muething & Klekamp, Cin., 1963—; adj. prof. law securities regulation U. Cin., 1977-2005; lectr. in field. Contbr. articles to profl. jours. Pres. New Richmond Exempted Village Bd. Edn. Mem. Ohio State Bar Assn. (chmn. elect corp. law com.), ABA (mem. corp. counsel sect., chmn. securities subcom. real estate syndications and condominiums 1977-79), Cin. Bar Assn. (mem. corp. counsel sect., chmn. corp. and banking com. 1972-75, del.-at-large 1969-71), Nat. Assn. Securities Dealers, Inc. (arbitrator). Republican. Roman Catholic. Club: Univ. Avocations: fox hunting; farming. Office: Keating Muething & Klekamp 1 E 4th St Cincinnati OH 45202-3717 Office Phone: 513-579-6411.

KREIDER, JOHN WESLEY, medical educator; b. Phila., Mar. 24, 1937; s. Wesley Johnson and Angeline (Scafidi) K.; m. Kathleen Anne Porter, June 1, 1963; children: Eric, Ted. AB, LaSalle U., 1959; MD, U. Pa., 1963. Resident Yale U., New Haven, 1963-64; resident, postdoctoral fellow U. Pa., 1964-68; from asst. prof. to prof. Pa. State U., Hershey, 1968-98. Chief divsn. exptl. pathology, dir. Jake Gittlen Cancer Rsch. Inst. Hershey Med. Ctr.; cons. biotech. firms. Mem. AMA, Pa. Med. Soc. Avocations: model railroads, wood carving. Office: Hershey Med Ctr Exptl Pathology PO Box 850 Hershey PA 17033-0850

KREIDLER, CHARLES W(ILLIAM), linguist, educator; b. Frankfort, Ky., Aug. 5, 1924; s. Christopher George and Elizabeth Allen (Best) K.; m. Carol Jane Kardos, Aug. 15, 1959; children: James Christopher, Julia Frances Hickey. AB in Spanish, U. Cin., 1948; MA in Linguistics, U. Mich., 1951, PhD, 1957. Teaching fellow U. Mich., Ann Arbor, 1953-54, asst. prof. English, 1959-63; instr., then asst. prof. modern langs. St. Peter's Coll., Jersey City, 1954-58; Fulbright lectr. in English Ctrl. Univ. Ecuador and U. Guayaquil, Ecuador, 1958-59; assoc. prof., then prof. linguistics Georgetown U., Washington, 1963-93, prof. emeritus, 1993—; Fulbright Prof. U. Sao Paulo, Brazil, 1990, Cath. U. of Asuncion, Paraguay, 1994. Lectr. U. P.R., 1965, U. So. Calif., 1968; guest prof. U. Regensburg, Germany, 1975; cons. in field. Author: (with Allen Glatthorn and Ernest Heiman) The Dynamics of Language, 1971, The Pronunciation of English: A Course Book, 1989, 2d edit., 2003, Describing Spoken English, 1997, Introducing English Semantics, 1998; editor: Phonology: Critical Concepts, 2000; contbr. articles to profl. jours. With USNR, 1943-46. Home: 4512 Verplanck Pl NW Washington DC 20016-2432 E-mail: chak321@aol.com.

KREIDMAN, PERRY L., lawyer; b. Rockville Centre, NY, June 11, 1951; BA cum laude, Colgate U., 1973; JD, NYU, 1976. Bar: NY 1977, US Dist. Ct. Ea. Dist. NY, US Dist. Ct. So. Dist. NY. Ptnr. Wilson, Elser, Moskowitz, Edelman & Dicker LLP, NYC. Mem.: ABA (tort & ins. practice sect., litig. sect.), NY State Bar Assn. (ins. & negligence sect.), Phi Beta Kappa. Office: Wilson Elser Moskowitz Edelman & Dicker LLP 23rd Fl 150 E 42nd St New York NY 10017-5639 Office Phone: 212-490-3000 ext. 2226. Office Fax: 212-490-3038. Business E-Mail: kreidmanp@wemed.com.

KREIG, ANDREW THOMAS, trade association executive; b. Chgo., Feb. 28, 1949; s. Albert Arthur and Margaret Theresa (Baltzell) K. AB, Cornell U., 1970; MSL, Yale U., 1983; JD, U. Chgo., 1990. Bar: D.C. 1991, Mass. 1991, Ill. 1991. Writer, editor Hartford Courant, Conn., 1970—84; media dir. Conn. House Spkr., Hartford, 1994; freelance author, journalist, lectr. Hartford and Chgo., 1985—89; law clk. U.S. Dist. Judge Mark L. Wolf, Boston, 1990—91; assoc. Latham & Watkins, Washington, 1991—93; v.p., comm. dir. Wireless Comm. Assn. Internat., Inc., Washington, 1993—96, v.p., gen. counsel, 1996, pres., CEO, 1997—. Ethics com. Soc. Profl. Journalists, 1987-90. Author: Spiked: How Chain Management, 1987, 2d edit., 1988; editor Spectrum, 1994—; bd. editors Pvt. & Wireless Cable, 1994—, Wireless Internat., 1996—; contbr. articles to profl. jours. V.p. Residences Market Square, Washington, 1993-98; co-chair Fixed Wirless Com. Coalition, 2000—. Ford Found. fellow, Yale Law Sch., New Haven, 1982—83. Mem. Fed. Com. Bar Assn. (legis. com.). Home: PH8 701 Pennsylvania Ave NW Washington DC 20004-2608 Office: Wireless Comms Assn Ste 700 W 1333 H St NW Washington DC 20005 Office Phone: 202-452-7823. Business E-Mail: president@wcai.com.

KREIGER, BRUCE D., lawyer; b. Bronx, NY, Dec. 9, 1943; BA with honors, City U. NY, 1965; MBA, U. Calif., 1968, JD, 1971. Bar: Calif. 1972, U.S. Dist. Ct. Calif. (No. dist.) 1974, U.S. Ct. Appeals 1975, U.S. Supreme Ct. 2000. Atty. Dean Witter & Co., Nat. Assn. Securities Dealers; asst. gen. counsel, asst. atty. Shaklee Corp.; former spl. counsel U.S. Trade Reps. Exec. Office of the President, 1981; v.p., gen. counsel, sec. Colgate-Palmolive subsidiary, Blyth Industries, Inc., Greenwich, Conn. Adj. prof. Hastings Coll. Law, 1974—75. Contbr. articles to profl. jours. Mem.: ABA (mem. bus. law sect., bilateral investment treaty com.), Am. Corp. Counsel Assn. Office: Blyth Industries Inc One E Weaver St Greenwich CT 06831 Office Phone: 203-661-1926. Office Fax: 203-661-1969.

KREILING, JEAN LOUISE, music educator; b. Middletown, N.Y., Mar. 29, 1955; d. Robert Taylor and Mary Louise (Lucas) K. BA in English, The Coll. of William & Mary, 1976; MA in English, U. Va., 1978; BA in Musicology, U. N.C., Greensboro, 1981; MA in Musicology, U. N.C., 1983, PhD in Musicology, 1986. Instr. English Western Carolina Univ., Cullowhee, N.C., 1978-79; tchr., adminstr. South Shore Conservatory of Music, Hingham, Mass., 1986-87; asst. prof. to prof. music Bridgewater (Mass.) State Coll., 1987-97, prof. music, 1997—. Contbr. articles to James Joyce Quar., Beethoven Newsletter, and Bridgewater Review, (poetry) Exphrasis, The Formalist, Phoebe, SLANT. Fund raising vol. Nat. Public Radio, Chapel Hill, N.C., 1982-86, Boston, 1990; vol. tutor Mass. Coalition Adult Lit., Brockton, Mass., 1989-91; vol. Bridgewater Pub. Libr., 2000-03. Mem. Am. Musicological Soc., Coll. Music Soc., Am. Brahms Soc., Mass. State Coll. Assn. Office: Bridgewater State Coll Dept Of Music Bridgewater MA 02325-0001 E-mail: jkreiling@bridgew.edu.

KREIMER, MICHAEL WALTER, financial planner, investment company executive; b. N.Y.C., Aug. 29, 1963; s. Anthony Kreimer and Frieda (Göebel) Rath; m. Madeline Louise Lawler, Dec. 31, 1992; children: Jillian Marie, Maximilian Walter. BS cum laude, SUNY, Albany, 1985. Lic. ins. agt., N.Y.; CFP. Assoc. v.p. McLaughlin, Piven, Vogel Inc., Jericho, NY, 1985-88; fin. planner, br. mgr. A.G. Edwards & Sons, Smithtown, NY, 1988—. Agt. Ins. Dept. State of N.Y., 1989—. Cons. (newsletter) Investing, 1992—. Fundraiser Big Bros./Big Sisters Suffolk, Commack, N.Y., 1989; mem. Nat. Parks Conservation Assn., Washington, 1992; coach Bellport Girls Soccer, 2002-04, So. County Youth Soccer League, 2002-. Mem. Nat. Assn. Securities Dealers (lic.), Internat. Bd. Standards and Practices for CFPs (CFP mark 1993), Inst. CFPs (direct pub. awareness program 1994-97, L.I. chpt.), Southampton C. of C., Rotary Internat. (dir. 2003-2004, sec. 2004-2005, pres. 2005—). Republican. Roman Catholic. Avocations: tennis, skiing, golf, running. Home: 2 Abets Creek Path East Patchogue NY 11772-5400 Office: AG Edwards & Sons 760 Montauk Hwy Water Mill NY 11976-2624 Office Phone: 631-726-5100.

KREIMER, SETH F., law educator, lawyer; BA magna cum laude, Yale U., 1974, JD, 1977. Law clk. to Hon. Arlin M. Adams US Ct. Appeals, 1977—78; assoc. Fine, Kaplan & Black, Phila., 1978—81; asst. prof. U. Pa. Law Sch., Phila., 1981—85, assoc. prof., 1985—92, prof., 1992—2004, assoc. dean, 2002—04, Kenneth W. Gemmill prof., 2004—. Cons. ACLU, Planned Parenthood Fedn., Cmty. Legal Svcs., Lawyers Com. for Civil Rights under Law, Pub. Interest Law Ctr. of Phila., Phila. Mayor's Com. on Homeless, Phila. Human Rels. Commn., Disabilities Law Project, City of Phila., Juvenile Law Ctr., Women's Law. Office: U Pa Law Sch 3400 Chestnut St Philadelphia PA 19104 Office Phone: 215-898-7447. Office Fax: 215-573-2025. E-mail: skreimer@law.upenn.edu.*

KREIN, CATHERINE CECILIA, broadcast and journalism educator; b. NYC, July 2, 1935; d. Timothy T. and Catherine A. (Lavery) Mitchell; m. Robert Krein, Apr. 18, 1970; 1 child, Karyn Elise. BS, Fordham U., 1960; film cert., NYU, 1974; MA, Queens Coll., 1994. Various positions including prodr., editl. dir., writer CBS News, N.Y.C., 1963-86; chief spokesperson Bklyn. Dist. Atty., 1986-87; v.p. external affairs Molloy Coll., Rockville Centre, N.Y., 1987-99; adj. prof. Hofstra U., 1997—99, prof. journalism Hempstead, 1999—2004; adj. prof. journalism Monmouth U., West Long Br., NJ, 2004—. Mem.: IRTS, NATAS, L.I. Communicators Assn., L.I. Coalition Fair Broadcasting, Profl. Pub. Rels. of L.I., Soc. Profl. Journalists, Pub. Rels. Soc. Am., Radio TV News Dirs. Assn. Home: 904 Jersey Ave Spring Lake NJ 07762-1924

KREINDLER, MARLA J., lawyer; b. Cin., Feb. 20, 1963; Attended, London Sch. Econs., 1982; BA, U. Mich., 1984, JD, 1987. Bar: Ill. 1987. Ptnr., chair Employee Benefits and Exec. Compensation Dept., sr. mem. Corp. and Fin. Svcs. Dept. Katten Muchin Zavis Rosenman, Chgo. Mem.: WEB, Women in Financial Svcs. (founding mem. Chgo. chap.), Stable Value Investment Assn., Pension Real Estate Assn., Art Inst. Chgo. Office: Katten Muchin Zavis Rosenman 525 W Monroe St Chicago IL 60661 Office Phone: 312-902-5621. Office Fax: 312-577-8855. E-mail: marla.kreindler@kmzr.com.

KREINDLER, PETER MICHAEL, lawyer; b. Liberty, NY, Mar. 30, 1945; BA in Econ., Harvard U., 1967, JD magna cum laude, 1971. Bar: D.C. 1971, N.Y. 1989. Assoc. Hughes, Hubbard & Reed, 1975-77, ptnr., 1977-88; prin., assoc. gen. counsel Coopers & Lybrand, 1988—89; ptnr. Arnold & Porter, 1990-91; sr. v.p., gen. counsel and sec. AlliedSignal, Morristown, NJ, 1992—95; sr. v.p., gen. counsel Honeywell Internat., 1999—. Office: Honeywell Internat Inc 101 Columbia Rd Morristown NJ 07960-4640

KREINES, JOSEPH MELVIN, conductor; b. Chgo., Feb. 3, 1936; s. Leon David and Beatrice (Schoenbaum) Kreines. BA, U. Chgo., 1955, BA in Music, 1956; MusM, U. South Fla., 1977. Conductor U. Chgo. Symphony, 1957—59; assoc. conductor Fla. Symphony Orch., Orlando, 1961—65; conductor Brevard Symphony Orch., Cocoa, Fla., 1965—76; assoc. conductor Fla. Orch., Tampa, 1968—74; conductor Treasure Coast Symphony, Ft. Pierce, Fla., 2000—03. Cons. in field. Author: Music for Concert Band, 1989; composer American Song-Set. Mem.: Music Educators Nat. Conf., Fla. Orch. Assn. (assoc.), Fla. Bandmasters Assn. (assoc.). Avocations: movies, theater. Home and Office: 635 Auburn Ave Melbourne FL 32901

KREINHEDER, HAZEL FULLER, genealogist, historian; b. Northampton, Mass., Aug. 27, 1935; d. John Herbert and Hazel Gertrude Fuller; m. Robert Frederick Kreinheder, Nov. 14, 1959; children: John Frederick, Paul Robert. BA, U. Mass., 1957. Lab. asst. dept. chemistry Amherst (Mass.) Coll., 1952-57; rsch. analyst Dept. Def., Fort George G. Meade, Md., 1957-63; libr. staff mem. Columbia Hist. Soc., Washington, 1976-77; hist. rschr. Washington, 1977-81; staff genealogist DAR, Washington, 1981-85, corrections genealogist, 1985-2001, ethnic and minority genealogist, 1997—, asst. dir. genealogy divsn., 2001—. Hist./geneal. cons. Washington Perspectives, Inc., 1977—90. Co-author/author: 5 booklets. Mem. exec. bd. Capitol Hill Babysitting Coop., 1966—68; mem. Com. 100 Fed. City, 1978—, mem. hist. preservation com., 1978—81; vol. pre-sch. vision screening program Prevention Blindness Soc., 1969—72; mem. Oldest Inhabitants DC, 1999—, Bryan Sch. Neighborhood Assn., 1995—, Nat. Bldg. Mus., 1999—, Friends of Libr./U. Mass., Cir.-on-the-Hill, treas., 1964—65. Named Hon. Ky. Col., 2003; recipient Capitol Hill Citizen of the Yr., Capitol Hill Restoration Soc., 1970. Mem.: DAR (life; nat. vice chmn.'s assn., vice chair patriot index com. 1992—95, Mary Mattoon chpt. libr. 1996—, vice chair minority rsch. lineage rsch. com. 1998—, assoc. mem. Francis Duclos chpt. 2005), Assn. Profl. Genealogists, Soc. Genealogique Canadienne-Francaise, Soc. Genealogy Que., Nat. Geneal. Soc., Orgn. Am. Historians, Friends of Paul Revere, Capitol Hill Restoration Soc. (sec. 1967—68, treas. 1968—70, co-chmn. hist. preservation com. 1979—81, chmn. ho. com. 1979—81), Friends of Evergreens, Friends of Jones Libr., Nat. Assn. Rail Passengers, Nat. Mus. Am. Indian (charter mem.), Nat. Inst. Geneal. Rsch. Alumni Assn., Washington Humane Soc. Republican. Lutheran. Avocations: civic activities, reading. Home: 113 Kentucky Ave SE Washington DC 20003-1447 Office: Nat Soc DAR 1776 D St NW Washington DC 20006-5303 Office Phone: 202-879-3310. E-mail: hkreinheder@dar.org.

KREININ, MORDECHA ELIAHU, economics professor; b. Tel Aviv, Jan. 20, 1930; came to U.S., 1951, naturalized, 1960; m. Marlene Miller, Aug. 29, 1956; children: Tamara, Elana, Miriam. BA, U. Tel Aviv, 1951; MA, U. Mich., 1952, PhD, 1954. Asst. prof. econs. Mich. State U., East Lansing, 1957-59, assoc. prof., 1959-61, prof., 1961-90, univ. disting. prof. econs., 1990—. Vis. prof. econs. UCLA, 1969, UN, Geneva, 1971-73, NYU, 1975, 93, 96, U. Toronto, 1978, others; vis. scholar Inst. Internat. Econs. Studies, U. Stockholm, 1978-80, U. B.C., summer, 1983, Monash U., Melbourne, Australia, 1987-94, 2002, NYU, 1993, 96, Copenhagen Bus. Sch., Denmark, 1994-95, Kobe (Japan) U., 1997, Ctr. Southeast Asian Studies, U. Singapore, 1998, Johns Hopkins U., 2002; adj. rsch. assoc. East-West Ctr., Honolulu, 1990—; world lectr. tours on behalf of U.S. Info. Svc., 1974-96; cons. to Dept. Commerce, 1964-66, Dept. State, 1972-74, UN Coun. Fgn. Rels, N.Y.C., 1965-67, Brockings Instn., 1972-75, Ctrl. Am. Common Market, 1972-75, Internat. Monetary Fund, 1976, East-West Ctr., Honolulu, 1987—; mem. internat. econs. rev. bd. NSF, 1981, 85; bd. dirs. Internat. Trade and Fin. Assn., pres. 1993; sr. Fulbright specialist, 2001—. Author: Israel and Africa: A Study in Technical Cooperation, 1964, Alternative Commercial Policies*Their Effects on the American Economy, 1967, International Economics-A Policy Approach, 10th edit., 2005, Trade Relations of the EEC*An Empirical Investigation, 1974, International Commercial Policy: Issues for the 1990's, 1993, Contemporary Issues in Trade Policy, 1995, (with L. Officer) The Monetary Approach to the Balance of Payments: A Survey, 1978, Economics, 1983, 3d edit., 1999, 4th edit., 2003; co-author: Economic Integration on Asia, 2000, Economic Integration and Development, 2002; editor: Can Australia Adjust?, 1988, International Commercial Policy: Issues for the 90's, 1993, Contemporary Issues in Trade Policy, 1995, The U.S.-Canada Free Trade Agreement, 1999, Empirical Modeling in International Trade, 2005; co-editor: Asia-Pacific Economic Linkages, 1997; contbr. articles to profl. jours. NSF fellow, 1964-73, Ford Found. fellow, 1960-61; recipient Disting. Faculty award Mich. State U., 1968, State of Mich. Collegiate award, 1984, Whitefield Winslow Faculty award, 1994; Festschrift in his honor, Washington, 2003; essays pub. in his honor Empirical Models in International Trade, 2005 Mem. AAUP, Am. Econ. Assn., Midwest Econ. Assn., Western Econ. Assn., Royal Econ. Assn., Internat. Trade and Fin. Assn. (bd. dirs. 1991-94, pres. 1992). Jewish. Home: 1431 Sherwood Ave East Lansing MI 48823-1851 Office: Mich State U Dept Econs East Lansing MI 48824 E-mail: kreinin@msu.edu.

KREIPKE, MERRILL VINCENT, civil engineer, consultant; b. Evansville, Ind., Feb. 14, 1916; s. Charles Edwin and Ida Marguerite (Hufnagel) K.; m. Dorothy Louise Neu, July 17, 1937; children: Karen Jean Kreipke Walker, Jane Ann Kreipke Runyon. BSCE, Purdue U., 1936. Registered profl. engr., Ky., Ind., Va.; registered land surveyor, Ind. Various positions City Engr.'s Office, Evansville, 1936-39; from insp. to asst. engr. Louisville Dist. C.E., 1939-44, 46-51, chief soils and materials engring., 1951-56; civil engr. Chief of Engrs., Dept. Army, Washington, 1956-61; engr. geophys. scis. Chief of R&D, Dept. Army, Washington, 1961-69, chief geophys. scis., 1969-73, acting chief environ. scis., 1973-74; head mil. R&D C.E., Dept. Army, Washington, 1974-75; cons. Falls Church, Va., 1975—. Head U.S. del. NATO Sci. Studies, 1966, 68, 70. Mem. campsite devel. com. Girl Scouts of Am., No. Va., 1957-60; mem. retirement comty. task force Westminster at Lake Ridge, 1978-90, mem. integrated strategic plan com., 2003—; new site bldg. com., Covenant Presbyn. Ch., 2003—, mem. residents coun., 2004—, pres. residents coun., 2005-; bd. dirs. Westminster-Ingleside Found., 2004. Lt. (j.g.) USNR, 1944-46 Fellow ASCE; mem. NSPE, Internat. Soc. for Terrain-Vehicle Systems (founding), Va. Soc. Prof. Engrs. (Outstanding Svc. award 1979, No. Va. chpt. pres. 1978-79, Outstanding Svc. award 1988), Soc. Am. Mil. Engrs. Presbyterian. Home: Westminster at Lake Ridge 12191 Clipper Dr Apt 403 Woodbridge VA 22192-2240 E-mail: mukreipke@prodigy.net.

KREIS, JASON, professional soccer player; b. Omaha, Dec. 29, 1972; Student, Duke U. Midfielder Dallas Burn, 1998—, U.S. Nat. Team, 1999—. U.S. Nat. Soccer Team debut 1996; finished 9th in MLS scoring, 1996, scored goal in all-star game; 3-time All-Am., Duke U. Office: US Soccer Fedn 1801-1811 S Prairie Ave Chicago IL 60616 also: Dallas Burn 14800 Quorum Dr #300 Dallas TX 75254-7073

KREISBERG, JEFFREY I., medical educator, researcher; BS in Biology, SUNY, Albany, 1971; PhD in Exptl. Pathology, U. Md., 1975. Instr. dept. pathology Harvard Med. Sch., Boston, 1977-78, asst. prof. dept. pathology, 1978-80; asst. biologist dept. medicine Mass. Gen. Hosp., Boston, 1979-80; asst. prof. dept. pathology U. Tex. Health Sci. Ctr., San Antonio, 1980-83, assoc. prof. dept. medicine, 1983-89, assoc. prof. dept. pathology, 1983-89, prof. dept. medicine, prof. dept. pathology, 1989-2000, career scientist dept. VA dept. pathology, 1989-2000, prof. rsch. dept. surgery, 2000—. Mem. staff South Tex. VA Healthcare Sys., 1989—. Contbr. articles to profl. jours., chpts. to books. Recipient Rsch. award Am. Diabetes Assn., 1996. Office: U Tex Health Sci Ctr Dept Surgery 7703 Floyd Curl Dr San Antonio TX 78229-3901

KREISBERG, NEIL IVAN, advertising executive; b. N.Y.C., Feb. 1, 1945; s. Leo and Lucille (Levy) K.; children: Andrew Jay, Tracy Michelle (dec.); m. Linda Gering, Sept. 24, 1986; children: William Gering, James Gering. BS,BA, Rider Coll., Trenton, N.J., 1966. With Grey Worldwide, Inc., N.Y.C., 1966—, v.p., mgmt. supr., 1974-79, sr. v.p., account mgmt., 1979-85, exec. v.p., 1985-93, exec. v.p., group dir., 1993-99; group exec. v.p., exec. mng. dir. Grey Global Group, N.Y.C., 2000—. Mem.: Advt. Ednl. Found. (bd. dirs.), Brae Burn Country Club (bd. govs.). Jewish. Office: Grey Advt Inc 777 3rd Ave New York NY 10017-1401 Office Phone: 212-546-2683. E-mail: nkreisberg@grey.com.

KREISBERG, ROBERT A., dean, medical educator; Student, U. Ala., U. South Ala.; MD, Northwestern U., 1958. Vice chair dept. medicine U. Ala., Birmingham, prof.; interim dean Univ. of South Alabama Coll. of Med., 2000, dean, 2001—. Med. dir. Univ. Consortium Clin. Rsch. Fellow Am. Coll. Physicians (gov. Ala., regent, chair scientific program subcom., ednl. policy com., gen. chair, Disting. Tchr. award 1994); mem. Am. Fedn. Clin. Rsch. (pres. 1974-75). Office: Coll Med Univ South Ala 307 Univ Blvd 170 CSAB Mobile AL 36688

KREISER, FRANK DAVID, real estate executive; b. Sept. 20, 1928; s. Harry D. and Olive W. (Quist) K.; m. Patricia Williams, Aug. 23, 1973; children: Sally, Frank David, Susan, Paul, Mark, Patti, Richard. Student, U. Minn., 1950—51. Cert. residential broker. Real estate developer, 1960—. Founder, owner Frank Kreiser Real Estate, Inc., Mpls., 1966-89, pres., 1979—; owner F. & P.K. Properties, 1973—; membership chmn. RELO,

1987-88; br. mgr. Merrill Lynch Realty, 1989-90, br. mgr., v.p. Burnet Realty, 1990-97; broker Coldwell Banker, 1998—; ptnr., founder B & K Properties Co., Mpls., 1976-96; chmn. bd., founder Transfer Location Corp., Atlanta, 1979-84 . With U.S. Army, 1948-50, Korea. Mem. Nat. Assn. Realtors, Mpls. Bd. Realtors (dir. 1972), Minn. Assn. Realtors, Realtors Nat. Mktg. Inst., Minn. Multi Housing Assn., Edina C. of C., 50th France Bus. Assn. (pres. 2000-02), Edina Country Club. Lutheran. Address: 5036 France Ave S Minneapolis MN 55410-2033 E-mail: fkreiser@cbburnet.com.

KREISLE, WILLIAM ECKMAN, civil engineer, writer, surveyor, cartographer; b. Tell City, Ind., Oct. 13, 1924; s. John David and Ruth Ann (Eckman) K.; m. Marilyn Jane Ramsey, Aug. 26, 1950; childrne: Jonathan, Peter, Kristine (dec.). BS in Civil Engring., Purdue U., 1948; postgrad., U. Md. Ext., Paris, 1955; MA in Humanities, U. Louisville, 1971. Registered profl. engr., Ind.; registered land surveyor, Ind., Ohio, Ill., Ky. Structural and project engr. Maxon Constrn. Co., Inc., Dayton, Ohio, 1948-51, Tell City, 1948-51; design engr. Tex. Gas Transmission Co., Owensboro, Ky., 1951-52; chief engring. and planning sect. Dept. Army, Civilian Dist. Engr., Wuerzburg, Germany, 1953; chief planning Port Dist. Engrs., Bordeaux, France, 1954-55; arch. engr. North Dist. Joint Constrn. Agy., Paris, 1955-56; arch., engr. K & I Engring., Tell City, 1956-63, U.S. Army Corps of Engrs., Louisville, 1963-66, chief survey br., 1967-81; chief terrain analysis br. Def. Mapping Agy., Louisville, 1981-83; prin., chief engr. W.E. Kreisle and Assocs., Profl. Engrs. and Land Surveyors, 1983—. Asst. instr. Topo Command Seminar, Washington, 1973; vis. lectr. U. Cin., 1978-83; lectr. and spkr. in field. Co-author: Engr. Svy. Manual, including Hist. Engr. Surveying; contbr. articles to profl. jours., monographs on history and devel. of Ohio River for navigation. Cpl. USMC, 1942-45, WWII. Recipient citations Nuc. Power Commn., 1978, U.S. Supreme Ct. 1985, Atty. Gen. of the State Ind., 1985, Atty. Gen. of the State of Ill., 1994, U.S. Dist. Ct. (we. dist.) Ky.; cited for devising method for permanently location 560 mile-boundary line between four states (Ohio, Ind., Ill., Ky.) and supervising all field work involved. Mem. ASCE (life, past editor Jour. Surveying Engring.), Libr. Congress (assoc.), Ind. Hist. Soc., Tell City Hist. Soc. (v.p.), Sigma Chi (life). Avocation: history. Home and Office: 14450 S Alton Rd Leavenworth IN 47137

KREISLER, ROCHELLE, psychologist; b. Bklyn., June 13, 1956; d. Abe and Betty (Becker) Glass; children: Alanna, Adam. BA, Bklyn. Coll., 2000, postgrad., 2000—03, Yeshiva Univ., 2004—. Adv. cert. sch. psychology. Legal sec. Eric H. Green, Esq., N.Y.C., 1985—91, Zaslav & Auerbach, N.Y.C., 1993—97; summer sch. tchr. Bklyn. Pub. Schs., 2001; tchr. elem. and jr. h.s. Yeshiva Rambam, Bklyn., 1998—2002; intern sch. psychologist Youth Dares Offsite Ednl. Site, Bklyn., 2002—03; sch. psychologist Horizon Acad., Rikers Island, NY, 2003—. Author: (children's book) Johnny Compound, 2001. Mem.: Nat. Assn. Sch. Psychologists. Jewish. Avocations: reading, needlepoint, writing, swimming. Office: Horizon Acad Rikers Island Prison 15-15 Hazen St Queens NY Personal E-mail: RHKreisler@aol.com.

KREISMAN, ARTHUR, educational association administrator, consultant, humanities educator; b. Cambridge, Mass., June 7, 1918; s. Louis and Rose (Shechtell) K.; m. B. Evelyn Goulston, Apr. 20, 1940 (dec. July 1992); children: Peter Jon, Steven Alan, Richard Curt, James Bruce; m. Mamie Jewel Liles Tribble, July 17, 1994. AB, Brigham Young U., 1942; student, Harvard U., 1939; AM, Boston U., 1943, PhD, 1952; LittD (hon.), City U., 1988. Grad. asst. in English Boston U., 1942-43; with Signal Corps. U.S. Army, 1943-45, with Signal Corps. overseas, 1944-45; instr. U.S. Armed Forces Inst., 1945, So. Oreg. U., Ashland, 1946, asst. prof., 1947-51, assoc. prof., 1951-55, prof., 1955-81, chmn. dept. English, 1951-63, chmn. humanities div., 1955-69, dir. gen. studies, 1959-66, dean arts and scis., 1966-77, dir. curricular affairs, 1978-80, prof. emeritus, 1981—, appt. ofcl. univ. historian, 1985; co-founder with Evelyn Kreisman Edukon, Inc., 1982—. TV lectr. Network Ednl. TV, 1955-58; dir. Block Teaching Project, U.S. Office Edn., 1957-59, Nat. Def. Edn. Act Inst. for Advanced Study in English, 1966; cons. Fedn. Regional Accrediting Commns. in Higher Edn., 1974-75, Council on Postsecondary Accreditation, 1975-79, Chico (Calif.) State U., 1973-76, City U. Seattle, 1975-99, Lincoln Meml. U., 1976, Marylhurst Edn. Center, 1976, Oreg. Inst. Tech., 1977-79, Sheldon Jackson Coll., 1979-83, Council on Chiropractic Edn., 1982, 83, Griffin Coll., 1990-91; mem. Gov.'s Adv. Com. on Arts and Humanities, 1966-69, 71-76; mem. task force human services Oreg. Ednl. Coordinating Council, 1972; mem. steering com. Oreg. Joint Com. for Humanities, 1972-74; chmn. Seminar Coll. Evaluators NW Assn. Schs. and Colls., U. Wash., 1977-84; mem. nat. adv. bd. on quality assurance in experiental learning Council on Advancement Experiental Learning, 1978-80; team leader Danforth Found. Workshop on Liberal Arts Edn., Colo. Coll., 1972. Author: Correspondence Courses for State System, American Literature, 1955, World Literature, 1956, Contemporary Literature, 1961, Reader's Guide to the Classics, 1961, Remembering: The History of Southern Oregon University, 2002; editor: Oregon Centennial Anthology, 1959; Contbr. poetry and articles to periodicals. Active Ashland City Coun., 1950-54; co-founder Rogue Valley Unitarian Fellowship, 1953; bd. dirs. Comty. Chest, Inst. Renaissance Studies, 1956-64, Friends of Libr., 1991-96, pres., 1994-96; steering com. Learning in Retirement Program, 1993-94; chmn. bd. trustees Ashland Cmty. Hosp., 1960-64; bd. dirs. So. Calif. U. for Profl. Studies, 1997-99; chmn. bd. dirs. North Ctrl. U., 1998-99; emeritus bd. dirs. Ashland Cmty. Hosp. Found., 2005. Recipient Bicentennial anniversary prize in humanities Columbia U., 1954, Disting. Svc. award Ashland Cmty. Hosp. Found., 1998; prize for excellence in teaching, 1966, Outstanding Svc. award Indsl. Coll. Armed Forces, 1976, Disting. Svc. award Alumni Assn., 1977; Ford Found. fellow in Oriental philosophy and religion Harvard, 1954 Mem. AAUP (past pres. Oreg. coun.), Nat. Coun. Tchrs. English (past pres. Oreg. coun.), Commn. of Pacific Assn. of Schs. and Colls. (elected 1994-95), N.W. Assn. Schs. and Colls. (examiner 1958—, trustee 1976-80, mem. comm. colls. 1972-80), Am. Legion (past post comdr.), Lambda Iota Tau, Phi Kappa Phi, Tau Kappa Alpha. Office: 1880 Green Meadows Way Ashland OR 97520-3683

KREISSMAN, STARRETT, librarian; b. N.Y.C., Jan. 4, 1946; d. Bernard and Shirley (Relis) K.; m. David Dolan, Apr. 13, 1985; 1 child, Sonya. BA, Grinnell Coll., 1967; MLS, Columbia U., 1968. Asst. circulation libr. Columbia U., N.Y.C., 1968-70; sci. libr. N.Y. Pub. Libr., N.Y.C., 1970-71; outreach libr. Stanislaus County Free Libr., Modesto, Calif., 1971-73, Oakdale libr., 1974-79, acquisitions libr., 1979-85, br. supr., 1985-92, county libr., 1992—99; libr. dir. Ventura County Libr., 1999—. Writer book revs. Stanislaus County Commn. on Women. Mem. ALA, Pub. Libr. Assn., Calif. Libr. Assn. (legis. com. 1993-95, 2003—, Libr. of Yr. 1998), Rotary. Office: Ventura County Library 646 County Square Dr Ste 150 Ventura CA 93003 Office Phone: 805-477-7333.

KREITH, FRANK, research engineer, consultant; b. Vienna, Dec. 15, 1922; s. Fritz and Elsa (Klug) K.; m. Marion Finkels, Sept. 21, 1951; children: Michael, Marcia, Judith. BSME, U. Calif., Berkeley, 1945; MS in Engring., UCLA, 1946; DSc, U. Paris, 1964. Registered profl. engr., Calif., Colo. Rsch. engr. Jet Propulsion Lab. Calif. Inst. Tech., 1945-49; asst. prof. U. Calif., Berkeley, 1951-53; assoc. prof. mech. engring. Lehigh U., Bethlehem, Pa., 1953-59; prof. engring. U. Colo., 1959-77; chief solar thermal rsch. Solar Energy Rsch. Inst., Golden, Colo., 1977-87; sr. fellow Nat. Conf. State Legis., 1987—2001; pres. Environ. Cons. Svcs., 1974-77; cons. NATO, 1980-85, Nat. Renewable Energy Lab, 1990-98. Author: Principles of Heat Transfer, 1958, 2d edit., 1965, 3d edit., 1973, (with C. B. Wrenn) Nuclear Impact, 1975, (with J. F. Kreider) Principles of Solar Engineering, 1980; editor-in-chief Handbook of Energy Efficiency, 1996, Handbook of Mechanical Engineering, 1997, Handbook of Thermal Engineering, 2000. Mem. Human Rels. Commn., 1963-65, Energy Adv. Com., 1979-82. Guggenheim fellow, 1950; recipient medal ASME, 1998, Disting. Lectr., 2002—. Mem. ASME (heat transfer meml. award 1972, Edwin F. Church medal 2001), Internat. Solar Energy Soc., Sigma Xi (nat. lectr. 1980-81), Phi Tau Sigma. Office Phone: 303-443-1406.

KREITMAN, JAMES E., securities trader; Co-head, firm's equity derivatives and convertibles group, Europe Credit Suisse First Boston, co-head, European equities divsn., 2001—03, co-head, fixed income divsn., 2003—. Office: Credit Suisse First Boston Eleven Madison Ave New York NY 10010-3629 Office Phone: 212-325-2000.

KREITZ, PATRICIA ANN, information technology executive; b. Chgo., Sept. 8, 1949; d. Robert Charles and Mary Eileen Tronvig; m. Douglas Preston Kreitz, Dec. 1, 1985; children: Alexander Preston, Viktoria Ann. MA, U. Calif., Davis, 1975; MLS, U. Calif., Berkeley, 1978. Collection devel./reference libr. Doe Libr. U. Calif., Berkeley, 1979—86, head, gen. reference svcs., 1987—89; libr. mgr. Superconducting Super Collider Lab., Dallas, 1989—94; dir., tech. info. services Stanford (Calif.) Linear Accelerator Ctr., Stanford U., 1994—. Mem. editl. bd. Sci. and Tech. Librs., N.Y.C., 2002—. Contbr. articles to profl. jours.; designer websites in field. Grantee Gay and Lesbian Newspapers Microfilming Preservation Project grantee, U. Calif., 1988—90, Librs. Assn. U. Calif., 1983—85, Dept. of Energy Devel. Grant, 1995; Calif. State scholar, State of Calif., 1967—68, Chancellor's Grad. fellow, U. of Calif., Davis, 1973—74. Mem.: Assn. Coll. and Rsch. Librs. (bd. dirs. 2000—), Spl. Libr. Assn., ALA (chmn. various coms., sects. 1980—2004, divsn. bd. dirs.), Beta Phi Mu (life). Presbyterian. Avocations: international adoption advocate, cross country skiing. Office: Stanford Linear Accelerator Center 2575 Sand Hill Rd Menlo Park CA 94025-7090 Office Phone: 650-926-4385.

KREITZBURG, MARILYN JUNE, librarian; b. Rockford, Ill.; d. A.E. and Margaret Louise (Harvey) K.; student Rockford Coll. for Women, 1948-50; A.B. magna cum laude, Knox Coll., 1954; M.A., U. Va., 1956; degree in Philosophy U. Edinburgh (Scotland), 1960. Copywriter, broadcaster radio and TV, Black Hawk Broadcasting Co., Waterloo, Iowa, 1956-57; freelance promotion, N.Y.C., 1957; lectr. on Asia, women and fgn. affairs, Ill., Iowa, 1959-60; order librarian, asst. to coll. librarian Knox Coll., Ill., 1960-72; dir. libr. audio visual instrnl. svcs., 1972-1993; faculty librarian, asst. prof. U. Pitts. at Johnstown, 1972—75, reference librarian and head library instructional services, 1976—78, head instrn., ref. and rsch., 1989-93 . Faculty adv. Delta Zeta, 1980-83, Johnstown Venture Club; Pvt. music instr. 1946-48, 50-52; bd. dirs., actress Prairie Players Civic Theater, 1962-64; rescue vol. Richland Twp. Vol. Fire Dept., 1977, ARC Disaster Inquiry Service; mem. Inter-Service Club Council, 1976-80; leader Girl Scout Songsters, Rockford, Il., 1948-50; vol. Windbar Regional Hospice, Windebar Med. Ctr., 2002. Recipient medal DAR, 1948; Helen Lee Wessels fellow, 1954-55; Fulbright fellow at large, 1957-59. Mem. Women's Assn U. Pitts. (pres. 1978-79, exec. bd.), Assn. Coll. and Research Libraries, ALA, Johnstown Art League (pres. 2003, 04), Inter Nos, Phi Beta Kappa, Delta Kappa Gamma (chpt. v.p. 1986-88, pres. 89-91), Pi Sigma Alpha, Sigma Alpha Iota, Pi Beta Phi. Clubs: Soroptimists (pres. 1978-80, exec. bd.).

KREITZER, DAVID MARTIN, artist; b. Ord, Nebr., Oct. 23, 1942; s. David and Norma (Buls) K.; m. Ana Bueno, Apr. 1, 1972 (div. 1978); 1 child, Anatol Christian; m. Jacalyn Bower, Nov. 26, 1987; 1 child, Fredricka Jacalyn. BS, Concordia Coll., Seward, Nebr., 1965; MA, San Jose State U., 1967. Exhibited in group and one-man shows including Maxwell Gallery, San Francisco, 1968-72, Akrum Gallery, L.A., 1970-89, Adele M. Gallery, Dallas, 1972-90, Summa Gallery, N.Y.C., 1988-95, Stary-Sheets Gallery, L.A., 1991-95., Campanile Gallery, Chgo., 1995. Bd. dirs. Music and Arts for Youth, San Luis Obispo, Calif., 1983-85. Recipient Ciba-Geigy award 1971, Gold medal San Francisco Art Dirs. Club, 1970. Home: 1442 12th St Los Osos CA 93402-1711 Office Phone: 809-528-4999. Business E-Mail: jkreitze@calpoly.edu.

KREITZER, JACALYN BOWER, vocalist, voice educator; b. Silverton, Oreg., Feb. 16, 1956; d. Jack Allen and Coraliss Mae Bower; m. David M. Kreitzer, Nov. 26, 1987; children: Fredricka Jacalyn, Anatol. MusB, Univ. of Puget Sound, Tacoma, Wash.; MusM, Univ. of So. Calif., Los Angeles, Calif., 1982—85. Lead role Contessa/Andrea Chenier/San Francisco Opera, 1998, Erda/Das Rheingold/Deutsche Oper Berlin, 1991, Brangane/Tristan und Isolde/Teatro Liceu, Barcelona, 1989, Ericlea/Ritorno di Ulisse/San Francisco Opera, San Francisco, 1986, Urlich & Mahler 2/Prague Radio Symphony, Prague, Czech Republic, 1999, Rossweisse/Die Walkure/Metropolitan Opera, New York, NY, 1984—87; participant Mother/The Consul, Spoleto, Italy, Sosostris/Midsummer Marriage/New York City Opera, NYC, Waltraute/Die Walkure/Theatre Chatelet, Utrica/Un Ballo in Maschera/Dublin Grand Opera, Waltraute, Fricka/Die Walkure/Chgo. Lyric Opera, Chgo., Brangane/Tristan Und Isolde/LA Opera, Brangane/Tristan Und Isolde/Barcelona Opera, Erster Magd/Electra/Geneva Opera, Norns/Gotterdammerung/Artpark NY, NY, Norns, Waltraute, Fricka, Erda/Der Ring Des Nibelungen/Seattle Opera, Seattle. Prodr., Marilyn Horne/frederica von Stadoe recitals; voice-diction tchr. Cal Poly Music Dept., San Luis Obispo, 1999, prodr., master, 2001—03; lectr., prodr., dir. opera theater Cal Poly State U., San Luis Obispo; panelist Opera Am. Prodr.: Calif. Poly. State U. Opera, New Yorker. Received powerful reviews from: "Kansas City Star"; "Spandauer Volksblatt", Berlin; "Kreitzer"; "Newark News Star"; R. Pontizious, "San Francisco Examiner"; "Los Angeles Times"; and Phillip Collins, "San Jose Metro". Mem.: NATS, AGMA. Republican. Lutheran. Achievements include Master classes with Elizabeth Schwarzkopt, Birgitt Nielson. Avocation: Koi fish. Home: 1442 12th St Los Osos CA 93402 E-mail: jkreitze@calpoly.edu.

KREITZMAN, RALPH J., lawyer; b. N.Y.C., Nov. 11, 1945; s. Emanuel M. and Hannah G. (Steinhardt) K.; m. Wendy A. Karpel, Nov. 24, 1968; children: Susan Beth, Emily Meg. BS in Acctg., Rider U., 1967; JD cum laude, Bklyn. Law Sch., 1970. Bar: N.Y. 1971, U.S. Dist Ct. (so. dist.) N.Y. 1971, U.S. Dist. Ct. (ea. dist.) N.Y. 1973, U.S. Ct. of Appeals (2nd cir.) 1975, U.S. Supreme Ct. 1976. Assoc. Hughes Hubbard & Reed LLP, N.Y.C., 1970-80; sr. ptnr. real estate group Hughes Hubbard & Reed LLC, N.Y.C., 1980—. Trustee Village of Great Neck, 2001-, former chair planning bd., former mem. archtl. rev. com.; dep. mayor Village Great Neck, N.Y., 2003—. Served with U.S. Army Res., 1968-74. Mem. ABA (real property law sect. and com. on fgn. investment in U.S. real estate), N.Y. State Bar Assn. (real property law sect., com. on comml. leases and com. on financings), Assn. of Bar of City of N.Y. (com. on real property law, former chair leasing subcom.). Office: Hughes Hubbard & Reed LLP 1 Battery Park Plz New York NY 10004-1482 Office Phone: 212-837-6740. Business E-Mail: kreitzman@hugheshubbard.com.

KREIZINGER, LOREEN I., lawyer; b. Syracuse, N.Y., Apr. 16, 1959; d. David F. and Blanche L. (Heaney) Mosher; m. Kenneth R. Kreizinger, Aug. 30, 1985; children: Katelyn Rose, Hunter Robert. Grad. in nursing, Crouse-Irving Meml. Hosp., Syracuse, 1981; BS in Bus. with honors, Nova U., 1987, JD, 1990. Bar: Fla. 1990; RN, N.Y., Fla. Nurse ICU and infants neonatal unit, Syracuse, Ft. Lauderdale, Fla., 1979-86; med. malpractice cons. Krupnick, Campbell et al, Ft.Lauderdale, 1986-90, assoc., 1990-92, of counsel, 1992—; pvt. practice, Ft.Lauderdale, 1992—. Instr. adult intensive care Crouse-Irving Meml. Hosp., 1981-82; adj. prof. Nova U., Ft. Lauderdale, 1994—; seminar instr. legal aspects of nursing Fla. Bd. Nursing, 1990-92; guest spkr. TV talk show Med. Malpractice, 1991. Sec., bd. dirs. Shepherd Care Ministries, Hollywood, Fla., 1993, 94; mem. choir 1st Bapt. Ch. Ft. Lauderdale, 1994—. Mem. ABA (law and medicine com. 1990—), FBA, ATLA (spl. L-Trytophen com. 1991-94), Fla. Bar Assn., Fla. Assn. Women Lawyers, Fla. Acad. Trial Lawyers, Broward County Women Lawyers Assn., Broward County Trial Lawyers Assn., Phi Alpha Delta. Republican. Avocations: sailing, skiing, rollerblading. Office: 2601 E Oakland Park Blvd # 403 Fort Lauderdale FL 33306

KREJCI, ROBERT HARRY, not-for-profit developer, consultant; b. Chgo., June 4, 1913; s. John and Johanna (Tischer) K.; m. Marian Hallock, Mar. 28, 1941 (dec. Aug. 1986); 1 child, Susan Ann Krejci Stevens. BS in Forestry with honors, Mich. State U., 1940. Dist. exec. Boy Scouts Am., Chgo., 1940-48, asst. scout exec., 1948-50, scout exec. Herrin, Ill., Huntington, W.Va., 1950-65; devel. cons. The Cumerford Corp., Kansas City, 1965-73, dir. western divsn. Ft. Lauderdale, Fla., 1974-78; devel. cons. in pvt. practice, San Diego, 1978-90. Co-founder, pres. Philanthropy Coun., San Diego, 1987-93; dir. World War II Farm Labor Camp, State of Ill., 1942, 43. Author: How to Succeed in Fund Raising For Your Non-Profit Organization, 1989. Vol. organizer United Way, various cities, Ill., 1955, 56. Recipient George Washington medal Freedoms Found. at Valley Forge, 1953; named Vol. of Yr. Philanthropy Coun., 1996, Exemplar, Rancho Bernardo Rotary Found., 1995. Mem. Rotary Internat. (Paul Harris fellow). Avocations: travel, gardening, writing, collecting humor. Home: 16566 Casero Rd San Diego CA 92128-2743

KREJCI, ROBERT HENRY, aerospace engineer; b. Shenandoah, Iowa, Nov. 15, 1943; s. Henry and Marie Josephine (Kubicek) K.; m. Carolyn R. Meyer, Aug. 21, 1967; children: Christopher S., Ryan D. BS with honors in Aerospace Engring., Iowa State U., 1967, M in Aerospace Engring., 1971. Commd. 2d lt. USAF, 1968, advanced through grades to capt., 1978; dept. mgr. advanced Navy tech. programs ATK Thiokol Propulsion, Brigham City, Utah, 1978-84, mgr. space programs, 1984-85, mgr. Navy advanced programs, 1986—. Lt. col. USAFR. Fellow: AIAA (assoc.). Home: 885 North 300 East Brigham City UT 84302-1310 Office: ATK Thiokol Propulsion PO Box 707 Brigham City UT 84302-0707 E-mail: robert.krejci@atk.com.

KREMEN, RICHARD M., lawyer; b. Balt., 1945; BA with honors, Oberlin Coll., 1968; JD with honors, George Washington U., 1973. Bar: Md. 1973, D.C. 1974. Ptnr. Piper Marbury Rudnick & Wolfe, Balt., 1990—2004; ptnr., co-chmn. Bankruptcy & Bus. Reorganization practice group DLA Piper Rudnick Gray Cary, Balt., 2005—. Past. mem. Rules com., U.S. Bankruptcy Ct., Md. dist.; mem. Panel of Bankruptcy Trustees, Md. Chmn. emeritus Better Bus. Bureau of Greater Md.; bd. mem. Balt. Chamber Orch.; chmn. bd. trustees Beth Tfiloh Congregation. Fellow: Am. Coll. Bankruptcy; mem.: ABA (chmn. subcom. bankruptcy crimes and abuses), Am. Bankruptcy Inst., Turnaround Mgmt. Assn. (past pres., dir. Md. chpt.), Md. Bar Assn. (past chmn. subcom. creditors rights, bankruptcy and insolvency). Office: DLA Piper Rudnick Gray Cary 6225 Smith Ave Baltimore MD 21209-3600 Office Phone: 410-580-4191. Office Fax: 410-580-3001. Business E-Mail: richard.kremen@dlapiper.com.

KREMENTZ, JILL, photographer, author; b. N.Y.C., Feb. 19, 1940; d. Walter and Virginia (Hyde) Krementz; m. Kurt, Jr. Vonnegut, Nov. 1979; 1 child, Lily Vonnegut. Student, Drew U., 1958—59; attended Art Students League. With Harper's Bazaar mag., 1959—60, Glamour mag., 1960—61; pub. rels. staff Indian Industries Fair, New Delhi, 1961; reporter Show mag., 1962—64; staff photographer N.Y. Herald Tribune, 1964—65, staff photographer Vietnam, 1965—66; assoc. editor Status-Diplomat mag., 1966—67; contbg. editor N.Y. mag., 1967—68; corr. Time-Life Inc., 1969—70; contbg. photographer People mag., 1974—; chancellor, commr. Nat. Portrait Gallery, DC. Contbr. photography numerous U.S. and fgn. periodicals; one-woman shows include Madison (Wis.) Art Ctr., 1973, U. Mass., Boston, 1974, Nikon Gallery, N.Y.C., 1974, Del. Art Mus., Wilmington, 1975, Newark Mus., 1994, Staley-Wise Gallery, 1996, The Margaret Mitchell House, Atlanta, 1999, The Nat. Portrait Gallery, 2003—, The Mark Twain House, Hartford, Conn, 2004, Represented in permanent collections Mus. Modern Art, Libr. of Congress, The Face of South Vietnam (text by Dean Brelis), 1968, Words and Their Masters (text by Israel Shenker), 1974; author (photographer): Sweet Pea: A Black Girl Growing Up in the Rural South (foreword by Margaret Mead), 1969, A Very Young Dancer, 1976, A Very Young Rider, 1977, A Very Young Gymnast, 1978, A Very Young Circus Flyer, 1979, A Very Young Skater, 1979, The Writer's Image, 1980, How It Feels When a Parent Dies, 1981, How It Feels to be Adopted, 1982, How It Feels When Parents Divorce, 1984, The Fun of Cooking, 1985, Lily Goes to the Playground, 1986, Jack Goes to the Beach, 1986, Katherine Goes to Nursery School, 1986, Jamie Goes on an Airplane, 1986, Tanya Goes to the Dentist, 1986, Benjy Goes to a Restaurant, 1986, Holly's Farm Animals, 1986, Zachary Goes to the Zoo, 1986, A Visit to Washington, D.C., 1987, How It Feels to Fight for Your Life, 1989, A Very Young Skier, 1990, A Very Young Musician, 1990, A Very Young Gardener, 1990, A Very Young Actress, 1991, How It Feels to Live With a Physical Disability, 1992, The Writer's Desk, 1996, The Jewish Writer, 1998. Recipient Nonfiction award, Washington Post/Children's Book Guild, 1984, ACCH Joan Fassler Meml. Book award, 1990, Equality, Dignity, Independence award, Nat. Easter Seals, 1992. Mem.: PEN. Address: care Alfred A Knopf Inc 201 E 50th St New York NY 10022-7703

KREMER, HONOR FRANCES (NOREEN KREMER), real estate broker, small business owner; came to U.S., 1961; m. Manny Kremer; 1 child, Patrick David. BS, CUNY; MS, Baruch Coll. Group sec. Bentalls, Ltd.; office mgr. Aschner Assocs., N.Y.C., 1961-63; pub. rels. asst. McMaster U., Hamilton, 1963-64; office mgr. Packaging Components, N.Y.C., 1965-67; head acctg. Shaller Rubin Assocs., N.Y.C., 1967-72, v.p. fin. and adminstrn., 1979-82, sr. v.p., 1982—, sec.-treas. multi-media divsn., 1972-75. Pvt. practice bus. cons., 1986-89; sr. v.p., exec. v.p., fin. officer Lewis & Gace Med. Advt., N.Y.C., 1989-91; broker, owner Malone Kremer Realty, Leonia, N.J., 1991—; bus. cons., 1991—. Mem. Nat. Assn. Realtors, N.J. Assn. Realtors, Nat. Fedn. Bus. and Profl. Women (bd. dirs., v.p.), Advt. Fin. Mgmt. Group. Roman Catholic. Office Phone: 201-461-1100.

KREMER, MICHAEL, economist, educator; AB in Social Studies magna cum laude, Harvard U., 1985, PhD in Econs., 1992. Tchr., adminstr. Eshisiru Secondary Sch., Kakamega Dist., Kenya, 1985—86; exec. dir., founder WorldTeach, 1986—89; postdoctoral fellow MIT, 1992—93, asst. prof. econs., 1993—94, Pentti Kouri Career Devel. asst. prof. econs., 1994—96, Pentti Kouri Career Devel. assoc. prof. econs., 1996—98, prof. econs., 1998—99, Harvard U., 1999—. Vis. asst. prof. U. Chgo., 1993; faculty rsch. fellow Nat. Bur. Econ. Rsch., 1993—99, rsch. assoc., 1999—, Harvard Inst. Internat. Devel., 1997—2000; faculty fellow Ctr. Internat. Devel., 1998—; sr. fellow The Brookings Instn., 1998—; co-chair, co-founder Bur. Rsch. and Econ. Analysis of Devel., 2001—; cons. devel. econs. rsch. group The World Bank, 2001—; non-resident fellow Ctr. Global Devel., 2002—. Assoc. editor: Quarterly Jour. Econs., 1998—, Jour. Devel. Econs., 1999—; contbr. numerous articles to profl. jours. Recipient Presidential Early career award for Scientists and Engrs., 1996; fellow, Nat. Sci. Found., 1989—92; Nat. fellow, Hoover Instn., Stanford U., 1994—95, Health and Aging fellow, Nat. Bur. Econ. Rsch., 1996—97, MacArthur fellow, MacArthur Found., 1997. Fellow: Am. Acad. Arts and Scis. Office: Harvard U Dept Econs Littauer Ctr 207 Cambridge MA 02138

KREMINSKI, RICK, mathematics professor, academic administrator; b. Chgo., Jan. 22, 1961; s. Eugene and Wanda Kreminski; m. Anne Casey, Jan. 24, 1989; children: Benjamin, Christopher Gannon, Amelia. SB, MIT, 1981; MA, U. Md., 1990, PhD, 1994. Interim dean Coll. Arts and Scis. Tex. A&M U., Commerce, 2002—, head dept. math., 2003—. Author: Applied Abstract Algebra. Mem.: Am. Math. Soc., Math. Assn. Am., Sigma Xi. Home: 3007 Tanglewood Dr Commerce TX 75428 Office: Dept Math Tex A&M U Commerce TX 75429 Office Fax: 903-886-5145. Business E-Mail: Richard_Kreminski@tamu-commerce.edu.

KREMPASKY, ROBIN LEE, elementary school educator; b. Youngstown, Ohio, Apr. 1, 1963; d. Richard Frank and Hazel Irene (Weaver) Wakeman; m. Frank Andrew Krempasky, Apr. 1, 1989; children: April Elizabeth, Autumn Renae. BS in Edn. summa cum laude, Youngstown State U., 1984, MS in Edn., 1991. Cert. tchr., Ohio. Tchr. Austintown (Ohio) Local Schs., 1985—, math. and reading aide, 1984-85, pvt. tutor, 1984-87. Candy striper Youngstown Hosp. Assn., 1979. Recipient Irene Lewis Meml. scholarship Austintown Local Schs., 1981; grantee Youngstown Edn. Found., 1981-84, 89-91. Mem. Phi Kappa Phi. Democrat. Lutheran. Avocations: travel, reading, crafts. Home: 6606 Country Ridge Ave Youngstown OH 44515-5555

KREMPEL, ROGER ERNEST, public works management, retired consultant, conservationist; b. Oct. 8, 1926; s. Henry and Clara Krempel; m. Shirley Ann Gray, June 16, 1948; children: John, Sara, Peter. Student, Ripon Coll., 1944, Stanford U., 1945; BCE, U. Wis., Madison, 1950. Registered profl. engr., Wis., Colo.; registered land surveyor, Wis. Asst. city engr., Manitowoc,

Wis., 1950-51; city engr. dir. pub. works Janesville, Wis., 1951-75; dir. water utilities, pub. works Ft. Collins, Colo., 1975-84; dir. natural resources, streets and stormwater utilities, 1984-88; faculty affiliate Internat. Sch. for Water Resources Colo. State U., 1989—94; pub. works mgmt. cons., 1988—. Lectr. various univ., coll., nat. confs. and seminars. Contbr. numerous articles to profl. publs. Past pres. bd. Janesville YMCA. With U.S. Army, 1944-46. Recipient numerous tech. and profl. awards, Disting. Svc. citation U. Wis. Coll. Engring., 1989, Outstanding Leadership and Cmty. Devel. award Janesville C. of C., 1972. Fellow ASCE (life, Gov. Civil Engr. award 1984, Wis. Outstanding Civil Engring. Achievement award 1970); mem. NSPE, ASCE (Mgmt. award 1990), Am. Water Works Assn. (life), Am. Pub. Works Assn. (life mem., past pres. Colo. and Wis. chpts., past mem. rsch. found., Man of Yr. 1971, Nichols award 1984, Swearingen award 1988), Pub. Works Hist. Soc. (pres. 1993-95), Wis. Soc. Profl. Engrs. (past pres.), Am. Acad. Environ. Engrs. (diplomate 1982-91), Colo. Engrs. Coun. (pres. 1990-91, honor award 1989).

KREN, MARGO, artist, art educator; b. Houston; BS, U. Wis., 1966; MFA, U. Iowa, 1979. Instr. art Kans. State U., Manhattan, 1971-80, asst. prof., 1980-88, assoc. prof., 1988—95, prof., 1995—2003, prof. emeritus, 2003—, ret., 2003; prof. art Ji Lin Coll. Art, Changchun, China, 2005. Vis. artist Wichita (Kans.) State U., 1986, Kansas City Art Inst., 1987, Inst. Allende, San Miguel de Allende, Mexico, 2000, Inst. Allende, San Miguel de allende, Mexico, 2000, Deakin U., Melbourne, Australia, 2003, Charles Darwin U., Darwin, Australia, 2003, Coll. Art, Changchun, China, 2005 Represented Dennis Morgan Gallery, Kans. City, Mo., Olsen-Larson Gallery, Des Moines; critical review articles and artwork to New Art Examiner, others; one-person shows include U. Ctrl. Fla., Orlando, 1991, Swen Parson Gallery, De Kalb, Ill., 1983, South Bend (Ind.) Regional Mus. Art, 1985, Sacramento City Coll., Calif., 2003, Acad. Arts and Design Tsinghua U., Beijing, China, 2004, Coll. D'Enseignement Artistique et Artisanal, Kpalime, Togo, 2004; exhibited in group shows Downey Mus., LA, 1985, Spiva Art Ctr., Joplin, Mo., 1986, Karl Oskar Gallery, Kansas City, 1986, Deutsch-Amerikanishes Inst., Regensburg, Germany, 1988, U. Nebr., Lincoln, 1992, Port Elizabeth Technikon, Rep. of So. Africa, 1995, U. Durham, Westville, South Africa, 1995, U. SC, 1997, Yunnan Art Inst., China, 1997, New Harmony (Ind.) Gallery of Contemporary Art, 1998, No. Mich. U., 2000, Beach Mus. Art, Kans. State U., 2000, Iowa State U., 2001, Vanderbuilt U., Nashville, 2002, Waiting Room Gallery, New Orleans, 2002, Arts Ctr. of the Ozarks, Springdale, Ark., 2002, Jasper (Ind.) Art Ctr., 2002, Arts Ctr., Orange, Va., 2002; represented in permanent collections Acad. Art and Design Tsinghua U., Beijing, China, Jilin Coll. Art, Changchun, China, U. Va., Charlottesville, Maytag, West Des Moines, Iowa, NH Inst. Art, Manchester, NY Pub. Libr., print room, NYC, Pioneer Hi-Bred Internat., Des Moines, Va. Ctr. Creative Arts, Sweet Briar, Yunnan Art Inst., Kunming, Yunnan, China, Deakin U., Melbourne, McAllen (Tex.) Internat. Mus., South Bend Regional Mus. Art, Marianna Beach Mus. Art, Kans. State U., Monsanto Co., Ruhe Collection Aboriginal Art U. Va., Charlottesville, Va., Coll. D'Enseignment Artistique, Togo, Nelson Gallery/Atkins Mus., Kansas City, Mo., Springfield (Mo.) Art Mus., Nat. Mus. Women in the Arts, Washington, Topeka (Kans.) Pub. Libr., Yellow Freight Systems, Inc., Kansas City, Spencer Mus. Art, Lawrence, Kans., Mulvane Art Mus., Topeka, Sheldon Meml. Art Gallery, Lincoln, El Paso (Tex.) Mus. Art, Hosp. Trust Tower, Providence, Mut. Benefit Life Ins. Co., Kansas City, Nebr. Wesleyan U., Lincoln, Western Mich. U., Kalamazoo, Albrecht-Kemper Art Mus., St. Joseph, Mo., Wichita (Kans.) State U., Steel and Pipe Supply Co., Manhattan, Kans., Williston (ND) Arts Coun., Williston State U, Nelson Gallery/Atkins Mus., Kansas City, Mo., Nat. Mus. Women Artists, Washington, U. Spartansburg, SC, Kans. Arts Commn., Artist Fellowship award, 2000 Mid-Am. Visual Arts fellow panelist, 1992, Kans. Art Commn., 2002, 04; recipient Faculty Rsch. award Kans. State U., 1980, 85, 88, 89, Kans. Gov.'s Art award, 1989; grantee Kans. Arts Commn., 1992, NEA, 1981, others. Mem. Kans. Arts Commn. (visual artists panelist 1984-85, Artist in Edn. panelist 1984-87, 89), ARTS Midwest (visual artists panelist for NEA reg. fellowships 1988), Kansas City Artist Coalition (pres. 1982-83), Artist Colony, Ragdale Found., Va. Ctr. for the Creative Arts, Yaddo. Home: 2912 Tatarrax Dr Manhattan KS 66502-1978 Business E-Mail: mkren@ksu.edu.

KRENDEL, EZRA SIMON, systems and human factors engineering consultant; b. NYC, Mar. 5, 1925; s. Joseph and Tamara (Shapiro) K.; m. Elizabeth Spencer Malany, Aug. 20, 1950 (dec. Nov. 1983); children: David A., Tamara E. Krendel-Clark, Jennifer K. Hall; m. Janet Brownlee Allen, June 27, 1992. AB, Bklyn. Coll., 1945; Sc.M. in Physics, MIT, 1947; A.M. in Social Relations, Harvard, 1949; MA honoris causa, U. Pa., 1971. From research engr. to sr. staff engr. Franklin Inst. Research Labs., 1949-55, lab. mgr., 1955-63, tech. dir., 1963-66, sr. adviser, cons., 1961; dir. Mgmt. Sci. Ctr., Wharton Sch. U. Pa., Phila., 1967-69, prof. ops. research and stats., Wharton Sch., 1966-90, prof. emeritus, 1990—, prof. systems engring. Sch. Engring. and Applied Sci., 1983-93; prin. scientist Systems Tech., Inc., Hawthorne, Calif., 1987—89. Emeritus prof.; mem. rsch. adv. com. on control guidance and nav. NASA, 1964-65; various coms. Hwy. Rsch. Bd., NRC, 1964-74; vis. lectr. NATO, 1968, 71; mem. roster of arbitrators Fed. Mediation and Conciliation Svc.; cons. govt. agys., industry, legal profession. Author: Unionizing the Armed Forces, 1977; contbr. articles to profl. publs. Mem. Phila. Mayor's Sci. and Tech. Adv. Council. Recipient Louis E. Levy Gold medal Franklin Inst., 1960. Fellow IEEE, AAAS, APA, Am. Psychol. Soc., Human Factors Soc.; mem. Ergonomics Soc., Cosmos Club, Sigma Xi. Home: 211 Cornell Ave Swarthmore PA 19081-1933 Office Phone: 610-545-9107. Personal E-mail: ezra@krendel.org. Business E-Mail: krendel@wharton.upenn.edu.

KRENDL, CATHY STRICKLIN, lawyer; b. Paris, Tex., Mar. 14, 1945; d. Louis and Margaret Helen (Young) S.; m. James R. Krendl, July 5, 1969; children: Peggy, Susan, Anne. BA summa cum laude, North Tex. State U., 1967; JD cum laude, Harvard U., 1970. Bar: Alaska 1970, Colo. 1972. Atty. Hughes, Thorsness, Lowe Gantz & Clark, Anchorage, 1970-71; adj. prof. U. Colo. Denver Ctr., 1972-73; from asst. prof. to prof. law, dir. bus planning program U. Denver, 1973-83; ptnr. Krendl, Krendl, Sachnoff & Way, Denver, 1983—. Author: Colorado Business Corporation Act Deskbook, 2003—05; editor: Colorado Methods of Practice, 8 vols., 1983—2005, Closely Held Corporations in Colorado, vols. 1-3, 1981; contbr. articles to profl. jours. Named Disting. Alumna, North Tex. State U., 1985. Mem. Colo. Bar Assn. (bd. govs. 1982-86, 88-91, chmn. securities subsect. 1986, bus. law sect. 1988-89, Professionalism award), Denver Bar Assn. (pres. 1989-90). Avocation: reading. Home: 1551 Larimer St Apt 1101 Denver CO 80202-1630 Office Phone: 303-629-2600. E-mail: csk@krendl.com.

KRENDL, KATHY, dean; BA in english, Lawrence U., 1972; MA in journalism, Ohio St. U., 1977; PhD in comm., U. Mich., 1982. Dean Ind. U., Sch. of Continuing Studies, 1994—96, Ohio U. Coll. Comms., Athens, 1996—. Office: Ohio U Coll Comm RTVC 483B Athens OH 45701-2905

KRENEK, DEBBY, newspaper editor; b. Tex., Dec. 11, 1955; d. Ernest Reed and Elizabeth Pendleton (Brown) K.; m. James C. Roberts Jr., Feb. 28, 1987; children: Christine Elizabeth Roberts, Taylor James Roberts. BJ, Tex. A&M Univ., 1978. Copy editor Corpus Christi (Tex.) Caller-Times, 1978-81; copy editor to news editor Dallas Times Herald, 1981-85, asst. bus. editor, 1985-86, exec. news editor, 1986-87; dep. news editor NY Daily News, 1987-88, dep. mng. editor, 1988-91, mng. editor, 1991-93, exec. editor, 1993-97, editor-in-chief, 1997-2000; assoc. editor Newsday, 2001—03, cross-media editor, 2003—04, mng. editor, 2004—. Chief creative officer Petplace.com, 2000—01. Named to Acad. of Women Achievers YWCA, NY, 1992. Avocations: photography, tennis, home renovation. Office: Newsday 235 Pinelawn Rd Melville NY 11747-4250

KRENEK, MARY LOUISE, political scientist, researcher; b. Wharton, Tex., Dec. 8, 1951; d. George P., Jr. and Vlasta (Zahn) Krenek. AA, Wharton County Jr. Coll., 1972; BA, Tex. A&I U., 1974; MA in Polit. Sci., St. Mary's U., 1992; Czech lang. cert., Charles U., 1994. Cert. secondary and elem. tchr. Tex. Polygraph examiner, San Antonio, 1979—81; ind. contractor market, polit. and social rschr. San Antonio, Houston, 1982—. Substitute tchr., tchr. San Antonio Ind. Sch. Dist., 1981—82, Houston Ind. Sch. Dist., 1991—98, 2002—; instr. govt. Wharton County Jr. Coll., 1997—99; assoc. J.C. Penney Co., Inc., 1994—2000; with Am. Acad. Excellence, Houston. Sec. Egypt Plantation Mus., 2003; del. Tex. Dem. Conv., 1971—72. 1st lt. U.S. Army, 1975—78, lt. col. USAR, 1978—2003, ret. USAR, 2003. Mem.: AARP, Tex. Czech Heritage and Cultural Ctr., Am. Polit. Sci. Assn., Nat. Assn. Self-Employed, Point/Counterpoint (Houston chpt.), Res. Officers Assn. (sec.-treas. Alamo chpt., jr. v.p. Dept. Tex., sec. Greater Houston chpt., ROTC coord.), Wharton County Hist. Mus. Assn. (assoc.), Houston Czech Cultural Ctr., Women in Mil. Svc. Am. Meml. Found. (charter), St. Mary's U. Alumni Assn., Am. Legion, Pi Sigma Alpha. Roman Catholic. Avocations: reading, writing, travel. Home: 10502 Fountain Lake Dr Stafford TX 77477-3711 also: PO Box 310 Egypt TX 77436-0310 Personal E-mail: marykrenek01@aol.com.

KRENICKI, JOHN, JR., manufacturing executive; Joined GE, 1984; sales gen. mgr. for structured products GE Plastics; European comml. dir. GE Silicones; v.p. and gen. mgr. of the Americas GE Lighting, Cleve., 1999—2000; v.p. and gen mgr. of super abrasives GE, Worthington, Ohio, 2000; pres. CEO GE Trans. Sys., 2000—03, GE Plastics, Pittsfield, Mass., 2003—. Mem.: GE Elfun, GE Univ. Exec., U. Mich.

KRENS, THOMAS, museum director; b. N.Y.C., Dec. 26, 1946; BA in Polit. Economy with honors, Williams Coll., 1969; M in Art, SUNY, Albany, 1971; M in Pub. and Pvt. Mgmt., Yale U., 1984; HHD (hon.), SUNY, Albany, 1989. Asst. prof. art Williams Coll., Williamstown, Mass., 1972-80, asst. prof. history art grad. program, 1977-80, adj. prof.; dir. Mus. Art Williams Coll. Mus. Art, Williamstown, Mass., 1981-88; cons. Solomon R. Guggenheim Mus., N.Y.C., 1986-88; dir. Solomon R. Guggenheim Mus., Guggenheim Mus. SoHo, N.Y.C., 1988—, The Peggy Guggenheim Collection, Venice, Italy, 1988—; dir., trustee Solomon R. Guggenheim Found., 1988—. Adv. com. mus. project NEA and Am. Fedn. Arts, Washington; adj. prof. art history Williams Coll., 1988-91, dir. artist in residence program, 1976-80; lectr. in field. Mem. Aspen Inst. Italia (bd. dirs.), Soc. Kandinsky/Ctr. Georges Pompidou, Gesellschaft fur Moderne Kunst am Mus. Ludwig (adv. bd.), Coun. Fgn. Rels., Assn. Art Mus. Dirs. (assoc.), AFA (adv. com.), Yale Univ. Coun. (com. on the art gallery and Brit. Art Ctr). Office: Solomon R Guggenheim Mus 1071 5th Ave New York NY 10128-0112*

KRENSKY, ALAN MICHAEL, pediatrician, educator; b. Chgo., Oct. 12, 1951; s. Arthur Melvin and Joanne Hope (Phillips) K.; m. Carol Ann Clayberger, Oct. 14, 1979; children: Andrew, Matthew, Lauren. BA, U. Pa., 1973, MD, 1977. Diplomate Am. Bd. Pediat. Resident in pediat. Boston Children's Hosp., 1977-80, clin. fellow in nephrology, 1980-81; rsch. fellow in immunology Dana-Farber Cancer Inst., Boston, 1981-83; instr. pediat. Boston Children's Hosp./Harvard Med. Sch., 1983-84; from asst. prof. pediat. to assoc. prof. pediat. Stanford (Calif.) U., 1984-94, prof. pediat., 1994—, Shelagh Galligan prof. pediatrics, chief divsn. immunology. Chmn. exptl. immunology study sect. NIH, 1993-95. Contbr. more than 200 articles to profl. jours. Recipient Young Investigator award Am. Soc. Histocompatibility and Immunogenetics, 1985, Award for Rsch. Excellence Am. Acad. Pediatrics, 1993; Burroughs Wellcome scholar in exptl. therapeutics, 1994-99. Mem. Am. Assn. Immunologists, Am. Soc. Nephrology (Young Investigator award 1990), Am. Soc. Clin. Investigation, Am. Soc. Pediat. Nephrologists, Soc. Pediat. Rsch. (pres. 2002, Young Investigator award 1985), Transplantation Soc. Office: Stanford U Sch Med Dept Pediatrics Med Ctr Stanford CA 94305-5164 Office Phone: 650-498-6073. E-mail: krensky@stanford.edu.

KRENT, HAROLD J., dean, law educator; BA, Princeton U.; JD, NYU Sch. Law. Clerk for Hon. William H. Timbers Second Cir.; atty. Dept. Justice, Appellate Staff Civil Div.; prof. law Chgo.-Kent Coll. Law, Ill Inst. Tech., 1994—, assoc. dean, 1997—2002, interim dean, 2002—03, dean, 2003—. Cons. Adminstrn. Conf. of U.S. Author: Presidential Powers, 2004; contbr. articles to law jours. Office: Chgo-Kent Coll Law Ill Inst Tech 565 W Adams St Chicago IL 60661-3691 Office Phone: 312-906-5000. E-mail: hkrent@kentlaw.edu.

KRENTZIN, EARL, sculptor, silversmith; b. Detroit, Dec. 28, 1929; s. Harry and Anna (Kievski) K.; m. Lorraine Joan Wolstein, Aug. 15, 1954; 1 child, Alexander. BFA, Wayne State U., 1952; MFA, Cranbrook Acad., 1954; student, Royal Coll. Art, London, 1957-58. Instr. dept. art U. Wis., Madison, 1956-60; freelance sculptor, silversmith Detroit area, 1960—. Vis. prof. Kans. U., Lawrence, 1965-66; vis. lectr. Fla. State U., Talahassee, 1969. Metal work and sculpture exhibited in many regional, nat., and internat. exhbns., 1954—. Recipient L.C. Tiffany award, 1966, awards and prizes for works in numerous pvt. and pub. collections; Fulbright grantee, 1957-58. Avocation: collecting art and antiques. Home and Office: 412 Hillcrest Ave Grosse Pointe Farms MI 48236-2920

KREPPS, JERALD ANDREW, art educator; s. Cecil and Maxine Krepps; m. Kerry Lynn Krepps, Aug. 23, 1975; 1 child. Grad., U. Mo., 1968; AM, 1971; MFA, Ind. U., 1978. Instr. U. Mo., Columbia, 1973—74, Lancaster Coll., Pitts., 1974—75; assoc. prof. U. Minn., Mpls., 1978—. Bd. dirs. High Point Ctr. Printmaking, Mpls.; dir. Minn. Nat. Print Biennial, 1996—2003. Co-author: Printmaking: A Primary Form of Expression, 1992; Represented in permanent collections Academic Sinica, China, Manitoba Printmakers Assn., Winnipeg, Frederick R. Weisman Art Mus., Pratt Graphics Ctr., N.Y., Hunter Mus. Art, Silvermine Sch. Art, Mo. State Hist. Soc., Mpls. Inst. Arts, Oreg. Art Inst., The Pillsbury Collection, Visual Arts Ctr. Alaska, Miss. Mus. Art, So. Graphic Soc., Tyler Art Gallery, Timberwolves Corp., U. Dallas, Ind. U., Kans. State Coll., St. Johns U., U. Tenn. Sgt. U.S. Army, 1968—70, Vietnam. Mem.: Mpls. Inst. Arts (print & drawing coun. 2003—), So. Graphics Soc., Mid-Am. Print Coun. (v.p. 2004—). Avocation: prairie restoration. Home: 20 Wear Ln S Orono MN 55356 Office: U Minn Dept Art 402 21st Ave S Minneapolis MN 55455-0439

KRESA, KENT, retired aerospace executive; b. NYC, Mar. 24, 1938; s. Helmy and Marjorie (Boutelle) K.; m. Joyce Anne McBride, Nov. 4, 1961; 1 child, Kiren BSAA, MIT, 1959, MSAA, 1961, EAA, 1966. Sr. scientist rsch. and advanced devel. divsn. AVCO, Wilmington, Mass., 1959-61; staff mem. MIT Lincoln Lab., Lexington, Mass., 1961-68; dep. dir. strategic tech. office Def. Advanced Rsch. Projects Agy., Washington, 1968-73; dir. tactical tech. office Def. Advanced Rsch. Project Agy., Washington, 1973-75; v.p., mgr. Rsch. & Tech. Ctr. Northrop Corp., Hawthorne, Calif., 1975-76, v.p., gen. mgr. Ventura divsn. Newbury Park, Calif., 1976-82, group v.p. Aircraft Group L.A., 1982-86, sr. v.p. tech. devel. and planning, 1986-87, pres., COO, 1987-90; chmn. bd., pres., CEO Northrop Grumman Corp., L.A., 1990—2001, chmn. bd., CEO, 2001—03, now chmn. bd., 2003. Bd. dirs. Avery Dennison Corp., Fluor Corp., Eclipse Aviation Corp., Trust Co. of the W., Advanced Bionics. Bd. dirs. John Tracy Clinic for the Hearing-Impaired, W.M. Keck Found., L.A. World Affairs Coun.; bd. govs. L.A. Music Ctr.; bd. visitors Anderson Sch. Bus., UCLA; bd. trustees Calif. Inst. Tech. Recipient Henry Webb Salsbury award MIT, 1959, Arthur D. Flemming award, 1975, Calif. Industrialist of Yr. Calif. Mus. of Sci. and Industry and the Calif. Mus. Found., 1996, Bob Hope Disting. Citizen award Nat. Security Indsl. Assn., 1996; Sec. of Def. Meritorious Civilian Svc. medal, 1975, USN Meritorious Pub. Svc. citation, 1975, Exceptional Civilian Svc. award USAF, 1987. Fellow AIAA; mem. Aerospace Industries Assn. (past bd. govs.), Naval Aviation Mus. Found., Navy League U.S., Soc. Flight Test Engrs., Assn. U.S. Army, Nat. Space Club, Am. Def. Preparedness Assn., L.A. Country Club, NAE.

KRESGE, ALEXANDER JERRY, chemistry professor; b. Wilkes-Barre, Pa., July 17, 1926; married; 3 children. BA, Cornell U., 1949; PhD in Chemistry, U. Ill., 1953. Rsch. assoc. Purdue U., West Lafayette, Ind., 1954-55, MIT, 1955-57; assoc. chemist Brookhaven Nat. Lab., 1957-60; from asst. prof. to prof. chemistry Ill. Inst. Tech., Chgo., 1960-74, chmn. chem. group, 1974-78; prof. chemistry U. Toronto, Ont., Can., 1974-92, prof. emeritus, 1992—. Guest prof. MIT, 1965; vis. scientist Fritz Haber Inst., 1981, U. Goteborg, 1983; mem. Gordon Rsch. Conf. on Chemistry and Physics of Isotopes, vice chmn., 1967, chmn., 1968; lectr. in field. Mem. editorial adv. bd. Isotopes in Organic Chemistry, Jour. Phys. Organic Chemistry. Fulbright scholar U. London, 1953-54; NSF sr. fellow, 1964-65, Guggenheim fellow, 1964-65, Killam fellow, 1984-86, Yamada fellow, 1985; recipient Morley medal of Cleve. sect. Am. Chem. Soc., Syntex award Chem. Inst. Can. Fellow Royal Soc. Can., Chem. Inst. Can.; mem. AAAS, Am. Chem. Soc., Royal Soc. Chemistry (Ingold lectr. 1995), Argentinian Soc. Organic Chemistry (hon.). Achievements include research in reaction mechanisms, isotope effects, flash photolysis, acid-base catalysis and kinetics. Office: Dept Chemistry Univ Toronto Toronto ON Canada M5S 3H6 Office Phone: 416-978-7259. Business E-Mail: akresge@chem.utoronto.ca.

KRESGE, BRUCE ANDERSON, retired physician; b. Detroit, Dec. 20, 1931; s. Stanley Sebastian and Dorothy Eloise (McVittie) K.; m. Peggy Ann Sale, June 14, 1952; children: Deborah Kresge McDowell, Katherine Kresge Lutey, Susan Kresge Drewes, Cynthia Kresge Furlong, Stephen. BA, Albion Coll., 1953; MD, Wayne State U., 1956. Intern Detroit Receiving Hosp., 1956-57; resident U. Mich. Hosp., 1959-60; pvt. practice Rochester, Mich., 1960-90; mem. staff St. Joseph Mercy Hosp., Pontiac, Mich., also; Pontiac Gen. Hosp., 1960-67; Crittenton Hosp., Rochester, 1967—. Pres. Rochester br. YMCA, 1975-77; trustee Kresge Found., 1967—2003, Crittenton Hosp., 1993-99; hon. trustee Albion Coll., 1999—. With M.C., U.S. Army, 1957-59. Mem. AMA. Republican. Methodist. Home: 1071 N Lake Angelus Rd Lake Angelus MI 48326-1026

KRESH, J. YASHA, cardiovascular researcher, educator; b. Russia, July 13, 1948; came to U.S., 1967; m. Myrna Blickman. BSEE, N.J. Inst. Tech., 1971; MSBME, Rutgers U., 1973, PhD, 1976. Rsch. assoc. Beth Israel Med. Ctr., Newark, 1976-79; dir. rsch. Jefferson Med. Coll., Phila., 1979-86; prof. medicine, dir. cardiovascular biophysics and computing Cardiovascular Rsch. Ctr., Phila., 1986—; prof., dir. rsch. cardiothoracic surgery Drexel U. Coll. Medicine, Phila., 1986—. Prof. biomed. and mech. engring. Drexel U., 1984—. Author more than 175 publs. in physiol. cardiology and bioengring. jours.; patentee in field. Fellow Am. Coll. Cardiology, Am. Inst. Med. and Biol. Engring., IEEE, Biomed. Engring. Soc., Am. Inst. Med. Biol. Engr., Am. Heart Assn.; mem. Am. Soc. Artificial Internal Organs, Sigma Xi, Tau Beta Pi, Eta Kappa Nu. Avocations: fractal art, porsche-phile, theoretical biology, computing. Office: Drexel U Coll Medicine MS # 111 245 N 15th St Philadelphia PA 19102-1192 Office Phone: 215-762-1703. Business E-Mail: jkresh@drexelmed.edu.

KRESS, WILLIAM F., manufacturing executive; s. Jim Kress. Pres. Green Bay (Wis.) Packaging. Bd. dir., Shenandoah Energy Inc., 2000—. Office: Green Bay Packaging 1700 North Webster Ct Green Bay WI 54302-1166

KRESSE, WILLIAM JOSEPH, lawyer, educator, accountant; b. Evergreen Park, Ill., June 12, 1958; s. Robert Alvin and Ellenmary M. (Mulhall) K. BBA, U. Notre Dame, 1980; JD, U. Ill., 1985, MS, 1996, postgrad., 1997—. Bar: Ill. 1985, U.S. Dist. Ct. (no. dist.) Ill. 1985, U.S. Tax Ct. 1987, U.S. Ct. Appeals (7th cir.) 1989, U.S. Supreme Ct. 1989, U.S. Ct. Mil. Appeals 1990, U.S. Ct. Claims 1993. Acct. Deloitte, Haskins & Sells, Chgo., 1980-82; assoc. Hinshaw, Culbertson, Moelmann, Hoban & Fuller, Chgo., 1985-87; law clk. to sr. judge U.S. Dist. Ct. (no. dist.) Ill., Chgo., 1987-90; assoc. Ross & Hardies, Chgo., 1990, Gleason, McGuire & Shreffler, Chgo., 1991-92; pvt. practice, Chgo., 1992—. Corp. sec. Micro Records Co., Evergreen Park, Ill., 1987-2000, pres. 1995-2000; arbitrator arbitration program Cook County (Ill.) Cir. Ct., 1990—; mem. faculty St. Xavier U. Sch. Mgmt., Chgo., 1992-96, asst. prof., 1996—; lectr. U. Ill. Chgo., 1999—; election ctrl. atty. Chgo. Bd. Election Commrs. Author: (with others) Chicago Lawyer's Court Handbook, 1989, 92. Bd. dirs. St. John Fisher Sch. Bd., Chgo., 1988-94, pres., 1993-94; field adv. Met. Tribunal, Archdiocese of Chgo., 1994—; bd. dirs. Hist. Soc. U.S. Dist. Ct. for No. Dist. Ill., 1997—. Mem. ABA (mem. bus. law sect.), FBA, AICPA, Am. Acctg. Assn., Assn. Cert. Fraud Examiners (mem. higher edn. com. 2003—), Am. Bd. Forensic Acctg., Am. Coll. Forensic Examiners Inst., Chgo. Bar Assn. (co-chmn. young lawyer sect. bench/bar rels. com. 1988-89, bd. dirs. young lawyer sect. 1989-91, treas. young lawyer sect. 1991-93), Ill. Bar Assn., 7th Cir. Bar Assn., Hist. Soc. U.S. Dist. Ct. for No. Dist. Ill. (bd. dirs. 1997—), Ill. CPA Soc., Midwest Bus. Adminstrn. Acad., Nat. Lawyers Assn., KC, Elks, Delta Theta Phi. Roman Catholic. Avocations: current events, trivia, politics. Office: 10221 S California Ave Chicago IL 60655-1623 also: St Xavier U 3700 W 103rd St Chicago IL 60655-3105 Business E-Mail: kresse@sxu.edu.

KRESSEL, HENRY, venture capitalist; b. Vienna, Jan. 24, 1934; came to U.S., 1946, naturalized, 1955; s. Aaron and Hudi (Zauderer) K.; m. Bertha Horowitz, Sept. 16, 1956; children: Aron, Kim. BS magna cum laude, Yeshiva U., 1955; MS, Harvard U., 1956; MBA, U. Pa., 1959, PhD (David Sarnoff fellow), 1965. Engr. Solid State div. RCA, 1959-61, engring. leader, 1961-63, 65-66; mem. tech. staff RCA David Sarnoff Research Center, 1966-70, head semicondr. device research, 1970-78, dir. materials research lab., 1978-79, staff v.p. solid state research Princeton, N.J., 1979-83; sr. v.p. E.M. Warburg, Pincus & Co., N.Y.C., 1983-84, mng. dir., 1985—99, sr. mng. dir. N.Y.C., 2000—. Regents lectr. U. Calif., San Diego, 1978-79; bd. dirs. Yeshiva U. Rsch. Inst.; cons. solar energy U.S. ERDA, 1975, USAF; adv. com. engring. NSF, 1996-99; engring. adv. coun. N.C. State U., 1985-88; mem. bd. dirs. several high tech. companies. Author: Semiconductor Lasers and Heterojunction LED's, 1977; editor: Characterization of Epitaxial Semiconductor Films, 1976, Semiconductor Devices for Optical Communication, 1980; assoc. editor: IEEE Jour. Quantum Electronics, 1978-81; chmn. coordinating com. Jour. Lightware Tech., 1981-82; contbr. numerous articles to sci. jours.; patentee in field. Served with Fin. Corps U.S. Army, 1959. Recipient David Sarnoff award RCA, 1974, Revel award Yeshiva U., 1980 Fellow IEEE (pres. Lasers and Electro-optics Soc. 1978-79, Centennial award 1984, Millennium award 2000, Sarnoff award 1985, Leos Svc. award 1992), Am. Phys. Soc.; mem. AIME, Nat. Acad. Engring. Home: 1056 Fifth Ave New York NY 10028 Office: E M Warburg Pincus & Co 466 Lexington Ave Fl 10 New York NY 10017-3147 Business E-Mail: hkressel@warburgpincus.com.

KRESSEL, HERBERT YEHUDE, medical educator; b. Bklyn., Nov. 20, 1947; BA, Brandeis U., Waltham, Mass., 1968; MD, U. So. Calif., L.A., 1972. Diplomate Am. Bd. Radiology in diagnostic radiology; lic. physician, Calif., Pa., Wis., N.Y., N.J., Mass. Intern in medicine U. Wash. Hosp., Seattle, 1972-73; resident in radiology U. Calif., San Francisco, 1973-74, NIH fellow in diagnostic radiology, 1974-76, clin. instr. radiology, 1976-77, asst. prof., 1977-80, assoc. prof., 1980-85, prof., 1985-93; Miriam H. Stoneman prof. radiology Harvard Med. Sch., Boston, 1993—; attending physician GI radiology sect. dept. radiology Hosp. of U. Pa., 1977-82, dir. continung edn., 1979-93, attending physician, chief MRI sect., 1982-93; radiologist-in-chief Beth Israel Deaconess Med. Ctr., Boston, 1996—, pres., CEO, chief med. officer, 1998-2000, radiologist-in-chief, 2000—. Mem. plan devel. adv. task force on magnetic resonance for 1986 HealthSystems Plan-Health Systems Agy. Southeastern Pa., Inc., 1985-87; dir. R.I. Magnetic Resonance Imaging Network, Providence, 1988-93; mem. sci. adv. com. for rsch. grants Am. Cancer Soc., 1990-93; task force chmn. Com. on Studies Involving Human Beings, U. Pa., 1985-92; mem. coun. for continuing med. edn. U. Pa., 1990-93. Mem. editl. bds. Radiology, 1985-91, Magnetic Resonance in Medicine, 1987—; editor Magnetic Resonance Ann., 1985-88, Magnetic Resonance Quar., 1988-94; patentee in field. Mem. bd. dirs. Coregroup, 1996. Recipient Sylvia Sorkin Greenfield award Am. Assn. Physicists in Medicine, 1993. Fellow Am. Coll. Radiology (Commn. on Magnetic Resonance 1987-90, com. on pub. rels. 1987—, com. MR stds. and accreditation 1987—, chmn. com. on MR clin. applications 1987, Commn. on Govt. Rels. 1992—), Soc. Magnetic Resonance in Medicine (trustee 1987, sci. program com. chmn. 1989-90, pres.-elect 1990-91, pres. 1991-92, Crues Kressel award sect. magnetic resonance technologists 1991, Silver medal 1994), Radiol. Soc. N.Am. (refresher course com. 1992-93), Am. Roentgen Ray Soc., Soc. Gastrointestinal Radiologists, Soc. Computed Body Tomography (rsch. com.

1990-93), Mass. Radiol. Soc., New Eng. Roentgen Ray Soc. Office: Beth Israel Hosp Dept Radiology 330 Brookline Ave Rm Cc483B Boston MA 02215-5491 Office Phone: 617-667-2506. Business E-Mail: hkressel@bidmc.harvard.edu.

KRESSLEY, CARSON, television personality; b. Allentown, Pa., Nov. 11, 1969; B in Fin. and Fine Arts magna cum laude, Gettysburg Coll., 1991. Ind. stylist; stylist men's sportswear div. and nat. advt. campaign Polo Ralph Lauren, NYC; fashion specialist TV series Queer Eye for the Straight Guy, 2003—. Co-author: Queer Eye for the Straight Guy: The Fab 5's Guide to Looking Better, Cooking Better, Dressing Better, Behaving Better, and Living Better, 2004; author: (bi-weekly column) Us Weekly mag., 2003—; actor: (films) The Perfect Man, 2005. Avocation: nationally ranked equestrian (former mem. U.S. World Cup Equestrian Team). Office: ICM 8942 Wilshire Blvd Beverly Hills CA 90211-1934*

KRESTON, MARTIN HOWARD, advertising, marketing, public relations, and publishing executive; b. N.Y.C., May 27, 1931; s. Henry and Frances (Stoll) Kreizvogel; m. Audrey Elizabeth Muir, Aug. 20, 1960 (dec. Jan., 1992); children: Mark Bradley, Rebecca Sarah; m. Judith Kate Stern, Dec. 15, 1996. BS in Econs, Wharton Sch., U. Pa., 1953; postgrad., N.Y. U., Northwestern U. Asst. dept. mgr. R.H. Macy & Co., N.Y.C., 1953-54; mktg. supr., account exec. Edward H. Weiss & Co., Chgo., 1956-60; with Doyle Dane Bernbach Inc., N.Y.C., 1960-86, v.p., mgmt. supr., 1970-72, sr. v.p., mgmt. supr., 1972, group sr. v.p., 1972-86, exec. v.p., 1984-86, cons., 1986-88; exec. v.p. England & Co. Pub. Rels., 1988-89; pres., chief exec. officer Caggiano, Kreston & Siebel, N.Y.C., 1989-90; dir. mktg. optical group Jobson Pub. Corp., N.Y.C., 1990; N.E. sales dir. USA Today, N.Y.C., 1991-98; ret. With U.S. Army, 1954-56. Mem. Univ. Club, Met. Opera Club Republican. Jewish. Home: 930 Park Ave New York NY 10028-0209

KRETSCHMAN, KELLY, Olympic athlete; b. Aug. 26, 1979; BA in General Health studies, U. Alabama, 2002. Alternate U.S. Olympic Softball Team, Sydney Olympic Games, 2000; mem. U.S. Softball Team, Athens Olympic Games, 2004. Named First Team All-SEC, 2001, First Team NFCA All-Am., 1999—2001; named to All-Women's Coll. World Series Team, 2000, NCAA Regional All-Tournament Team, 2001. Achievements include led U. Alabama to Women's Coll. World Series, 2000; mem. Gold medal U.S. Elite Team, Canada Cup, 2003.

KRETSCHMAR, WILLIAM EDWARD, state legislator, lawyer; b. St. Paul, Aug. 21, 1933; s. William Emanuel and Frances Jane (Peterson) K. BS, Coll. St. Thomas, 1954; LLB, U. Minn., 1961. Bar: N.D. 1961, U.S. Dist. Ct. N.D. 1961. Pvt. practice Kretschmar Law Office, Ashley, ND, 1962—; mem. N.D. Ho. of Reps., Bismarck, 1972-98, speaker, 1988-90, 2000—. Mem. N.D. Commn. Uniform State Laws, 1987—; del. N.D. Constl. Conv., Bismarck, 1971-72. Mem. ABA, State Bar Assn. N.D., Lions (pres. local club 1972-73, 93-94), Elks. Republican. Roman Catholic. Avocations: hunting, swimming, hiking, bicycling, skiing. Home: 201 E 3d St Venturia ND 58413-4015 Office: Kretschmar Law Office 117 1st Ave NW Ashley ND 58413-7037

KRETSCHMER, FRANK FREDERICK, JR., electrical engineer, researcher, consultant; b. Phila., July 31, 1930; m. Shirley J. Kretschmer; children: Frank F. III, John, Diane, Linda, Thomas. BSEE, Pa. State U., 1957; MSEE, Drexel Inst. Tech., 1961; PhD, Johns Hopkins U., 1970. Asst. devel. engr. Burroughs Corp., Paoli, Pa., 1957-58; project engr. Bendix Radio Corp., Towson, Md., 1958-64; rsch. assoc. Johns Hopkins U., Balt., 1964-70; supervisory electronics engr. Naval Rsch. Lab., Washington, 1970-90, 90—. Cons. in field. Author: Aspects of Radar Signal Processing, 1986; contbr. over 30 articles to profl. jours. and confs. With USN, 1948-52. Fellow IEEE (life). Achievements include over 20 patents in field.

KRETSCHMER, KEITH HUGHES, investor; b. Omaha, Oct. 20, 1934; s. John G. and Mary (Hughes) K.; m. Adine Williams, Oct. 1, 1960; children: Hugh, Dara, Kurt. AA, Wentworth Acad., 1954; BS, U. Nebr., 1956; student, UCLA, 1968. With J.G. Kretschmer & Co., Omaha, 1958-60; gen. agt. Lincoln (Nebr.) Life & Casualty, 1960-62; exec. v.p., sec.-treas. Automated Mgmt. Systems, Kansas City, Mo., 1962-68; investment exec. Shearson, Hammill & Co., L.A., 1968-75; gen. ptnr. Bear Stearns & Co., L.A., 1975-85; sr. mng. dir. Bear Stearns & Co. Inc., Boston, 1985-91, spl. assoc. dir., 1991-92; mng. dir. Oppenheimer & Co., Inc., Boston, 1993-94, Oppenheimer Capital, 1995-2001; bd. dirs. Visiphor Corp. Mem. stockholders com. Tosco Corp., L.A., 1982; bd. dirs. Cogent Fin. Group dba Medi Credit. Author: Your Option, 1978. Advanceman Rep. Pres.'s Nixon and Ford, 1970-76; trustee Lighthouse Preservation Soc., 1986-88; founding dir. Option Soc. So. Calif, 1974-85; bd. dirs. Pacific Palisades-Malibu YMCA, 1976-86, chmn. bd. dirs., 1980; bd. dirs. South Shore Art Ctr., Cohasset, Mass., 1988-97, pres., 1991-93; bd. dirs. World Affairs Coun. Boston, 1989-96; mem. pres.'s coun. Accion Internat., 1992—. Served to maj. U.S. Army, Airborne Ranger, 1956-58. Mem. The Explorers Club, Aircraft Owners and Pilots Assn., Exptl. Aircraft Assn., Seaplane Pilots Assn., CEO Club, Angel Flight, AERO Club New Eng., Vintage Sports Car Club Am., Masons, Shriners. Congregationalist. Avocation: pilot since 1952. Office: 294 Sunshine Ave Sequim WA 98382 Home: 111 Lupine Dr Sequim WA 98382 Office Phone: 302-981-4382. Personal E-mail: kkretsc@aol.com.

KRETZSCHMAR, WILLIAM ADDISON, JR., language educator; b. Ann Arbor, Mich., Sept. 13, 1953; s. William Addison and Audrey June (Krauss) K.; m. Claudia Suzanne Miller. AB, U. Mich., 1975; MA in Medieval Studies, Yale U., 1976; PhD in English, U. Chgo., 1980. Instr. English Mundelein Coll., Chgo., 1977-82, dir. summer sch., 1979-81; asst. prof. English U. Wis., Whitewater, 1982-86, U. Ga., Athens, 1986-89, assoc. prof., 1989-95, prof., 1995—, dir. linguistics program, 1996-99, CHA Willson prof. in humanities, 2004—. Author: Introduction to Quantitative Analysis of Linguistic Survey Data, 1996; editor: Dialects in Culture (R.I. McDavid, Jr.), 1979, Handbook of the Linguistic Atlas of the Middle and South Atlantic States, 1993, Oxford Dictionary of Pronunciation for Current English, 2001; editor: Linguistic Atlas Middle and South Atlantic States, Linguistic Atlas North-Central States, 1984—; editor Jour. English Linguistics, 1983-99, Empirical Linguistic Series, 1996-99; contbr. articles to profl. jours. Mem. MLA (regional del. 1983-86), Am. Dialect Soc. (exec. com. 1999-2003, pres.-elect 2005—), Linguistic Soc. Am., Medieval Acad. Am., Assn. Computers Humanities (bd. dir. 1999-2003). Home: 125 Renfrew Dr Athens GA 30606-3936 Office: U Ga Dept English Athens GA 30602 Business E-Mail: kretzsch@uga.edu.

KREUTZ, ROBERT A., music educator, musician; b. Denver, July 5, 1961; s. Robert E. and Evelyn P. Kreutz; m. Lisa G. Kreutz, Aug. 3, 1985; children: Sara, Jeremy. B in Music Edn., Colo. State U., 1984; MusM in Orch. Conducting, U. Denver, 1998. Thcr. music, French Thompson Sch. Dist., Loveland, Colo., 1984—. Adv. bd. Colo. All State Orch., Denver, 1998—2001; guest conductor Lakewood Festival, 2002, Ft. Collins Festival, 2002, Longmount (Colo.) Festival, 2004, Boulder Festival, 2005. Musician (violinist): Loveland Chamber Orch., 1984—94, Cheyenne (Wyo.) Symphony Orch., 1984—86, Ft. Collins Symphony Orch., 1983—. Bd. dirs. Ft. Collins (Colo.) Symphony Orch., 1999—2000. Named Chamber Music Competition winner, U. Denver, 1997. Mem.: Colo. Educators Assn., Music Educators Nat. Conf. Avocations: fly fishing, camping, baseball. Office: Thompson Valley High Sch 1669 Eagle Dr Loveland CO 80537 Office Phone: 970-613-5456.

KREVANS, JULIUS RICHARD, academic administrator, internist; b. N.Y.C., May 1, 1924; s. Sol and Anita Krevans; m. Patricia N. Abrams, May 28, 1950; children: Nita, Julius R., Rachel, Sarah, Nora Kate. BS Arts and Scis, N.Y. U., 1943, MD, 1946. Diplomate: Am. Bd. Internal Med. Intern, then resident Johns Hopkins Med. Sch. Hosp., mem. faculty, until 1970, dean acad. affairs, 1969—70; physician in chief Balt. City Hosp., 1963—69; prof. medicine U. Calif., San Francisco, 1970—, dean Sch. Medicine, 1971—82, chancellor, 1982—93, chancellor emeritus, 1993—. Contbr. articles on hematology, internal med. profl. jours. Served with USMC, 1948—50, AUS. Mem. ACP, Assn. Am. Physicians. Address: 32 Birch Bay Dr Bar Harbor ME 04609 E-mail: krevansmaine@adelphia.net.

KREVANS, RACHEL, lawyer; b. Balt., June 15, 1957; d. Julius Richard and Patricia (Abrams) K. BA, Dartmouth Coll., 1979; JD, U. Calif., Davis, 1984. Law clk. hon. Robert Boochever U.S. Ct. Appeals for Ninth Cir., Juneau, Alaska, 1984-85; assoc. Morrison & Foerster LLP, San Francisco, 1985-90, mng. ptnr.-San Francisco office, 1991—. Office: Morrison & Foerster LLP 425 Market St San Francisco CA 94105-2482 Office Phone: 415-677-7178. Office Fax: 415-268-7522. Business E-Mail: rkrevans@mofo.com.

KREVSKY, MARGERY BROWN, talent agency executive; b. Phila., Oct. 24, 1944; d. John Lewis and Margery Jane (Moss) Brown; m. Joseph Langdon Stearns, Oct. 19, 1968 (div. Nov. 1979); 1 child, Joseph Leland Stearns; m. Seymour Krevsky, Feb. 11, 1981. BS in Elem. Edn., Lock Haven U., 1966; MFA in Retail Adminstrn., Tobe-Colburn, 1968. Tchr. 1st grade Yardley (Pa.) Sch. Sys., 1966-67; buyer Macy's Herald Sq., N.Y.C., 1968-69; asst. editor Glamour mag. Conde-Nast Publs., N.Y.C., 1969-71; mgr. fashion bur. Hudsons, Detroit, 1971-74; fashion merchandise mgr. Alvin's, Pontiac, Mich., 1974-81; pres., CEO Prodns. Plus, Birmingham, Mich., 1981—. Bd. dirs. Northwood U., Midland, Mich., Wayne State U., Detroit. Mem. Oakland Execs. Assn. (bd. dirs. 1990—), Adcrafters, Fashion Group, Women in Comm. Avocations: cooking, reading, aerobics. Office: Prodns Plus 30600 Telegraph Rd Ste 2156 Bingham Farms MI 48025-4532

KREWER, JULIE-ANN, scholar; b. N.Y.C., Oct. 21, 1951; d. Semyon Efimovitch and Elsa (Silberstein) K. BA, Harvard U., 1972; student, U. Pa. Scholar Univ. Pa., Phila., 1967—; rsch. asst. Hand Gym Inc., N.Y.C., 1967-85. A.A.S. candidate New Sch. Social Rsch., N.Y.C., 1995—. Mem. Congregation Beth Sholom, Long Beach, N.Y., 1996—. Félicitation Lycée-français de N.Y., 1958—. Mem. Pa. Club N.Y. Jewish. Avocations: crafts, piano, exhibiting artwork & photography. Office: Ben Franklin Scholar 240 S 33rd St 310 Hayden Hall Philadelphia PA 13103 Address: 645 Madison Ave 2004 New York NY 10022-1010

KREY, ROBERT DEAN, education educator emeritus; b. Prairie du Sac, Wis., Mar. 23, 1929; s. Oscar L. and Paula M. (Mueller) K.; 1 son, Thomas R. Student, Carroll Coll., Waukesha, Wis., 1946-47; diploma, Sauk County Normal Sch., Reedsburg, Wis., 1948; BS, Wis. State Coll., Platteville, 1958; MS, U. Wis., Madison, 1967; PhD, U. Wis., 1968. Rural sch. tchr., Sauk County, 1948-51; tchr. grade 7 and 8 Gays Mills, Wis., 1951-53; tchr. grade 7, boys phys. edn. and bsketball, jr. high sch. Black Earth, Wis., 1953-54; tchr. sci., math., reading Jr. High Sch., Lake Geneva, Wis., 1954-66; NDEA fellow dept. ednl. adminstrn. U. Wis., Madison, 1966-68, asst. dept. ednl. adminstrn., 1967-68, vis. assoc. prof., summer 1971, assoc. prof. ednl. adminstrn. Superior, 1968-74, prof., 1974-90, chmn. dept. ednl. adminstrn. and counseling, 1978-80, chmn. div. edn., 1981-89, emeritus, prof. ednl. adminstrn., 1990—. Co-author: Interdisciplinary Foundations of Supervision, 1970, (with Glen G. Eye and Lanore A. Netzer) Supervision of Instruction, 2d edit, 1971, A Design for Instructional Supervision, 1989, (with Peter J. Burke) Supervision: A Guide to Instructional Leadership, 2005. Bd. dirs. Wis. Sch. Adminstrn. Found., Inc., 1968-76. Mem. ASCD (bd. dirs. 1972-75), Wis. Assn. Supervision and Curriculum Devel. (pres. 1973-74), Wis. Assn. Sch. Dist. Adminstrs., U. Wis. Alumni Assn., U. Wis.-Platteville Alumni Assn., U. Wis.-Superior Alumni Assn., Wis. Assn. Colls. for Tchr. Edn. (pres. 1986-88), Phi Delta Kappa (chpt. pres. 1975, sec. 1982, faculty adviser 1986-90). Lutheran.

KREYCHE, GERALD FRANCIS, retired philosophy educator; b. Kenosha, Wis., June 19, 1927; s. Harold Joseph and Henrietta Fredericka (Oteman) K.; m. Eleanor Ann Okon, June 19, 1948. AB, DePaul U., 1949, AM, 1950; PhD cum laude, U. Ottawa, Can., 1958. Mem. faculty DePaul U., 1950-59, chmn. dept. philosophy, 1961-82, prof., 1965-89, prof. emeritus, 1989—; now also Danforth assoc. Aquinas lectr. Alverno Coll., Milw., 1963; vis. prof. St. Mary's Coll., Minn., 1977; bd. advisors Univ. Press Am. Condr.: radio programs What Do You Think?, What's the Big Idea?, 1960; frequent appearances ednl. and comml. TV, also radio, 1958—; Author: Perspectives on God, 1972, Thirteen Thinkers, Heroes of the American West; also articles religious publs.; Co-editor: Harbrace Philosophy series; Visions of the American West, 1988, Heroes of the American West, 2001; sr. editor: Am. Thought; sect. editor: U.S.A. Today; bd. advisors: Philos. Research and Analysis; former editor-in-chief Listening: A Journal of Religion and Culture; referee Archives of Philosophy With AUS, 1945-46. Recipient DePaul U. Distinguished Service award, 1969, Univ. award for excellence, 1984-85, Viam Sapientiae award, 1989 Mem. Am. Metaphys. Soc., Ill.-Ind. Am. Cath. Philos. Assn. (pres. 1960), Am. Cath. Philos. Assn. (pres. 1972-73), Chgo. Lit. Club (pres. 1986-87), Phi Kappa Theta, Phi Eta Sigma. Home: 15881 County Rd 28 Dolores CO 81323 E-mail: ellieok@fone.net.

KREYLING, EDWARD GEORGE, JR., retired railroad executive; b. St. Louis, June 1, 1923; s. Edward George and Mildred (Schroeder) K.; m. Mary Emily Gronemeyer, Sept. 4, 1943; children: Carol (Mrs. Robert D. Knight), Deborah Ann (Mrs. Hugh J. Risseeuw), Edward George III. BSBA, Washington U., St. Louis, 1947, MBA, 1954. Accountant Monsanto Chem. Co., 1947-50; chief statistician White Rodgers Elec. Co., St. Louis, 1950-54; dir. market research Laclede-Christy Co., St. Louis, 1954-55; with St. L.-S.F. Ry., 1955-69, dir. marketing, 1964-65, v.p. traffic and indsl. devel., 1965-69; v.p. traffic I.C. R.R., Chgo., 1969-70; exec. v.p. Penn Central Transp. Co., Phila., 1970-71; v.p. marketing So. Ry., 1971-79, sr. v.p. mktg. service, 1979-80, exec. v.p. mktg., 1981-82; v.p. mktg. services Norfolk So. Corp. (Va.), 1982-87, ret. Active Virginia Beach. Sch. Bd., 1992-94; dir. Seton House, 1995-98, Va. Christian Coalition, 1998-2001, v.p.; dir. Assist Crisis Pregnancy Ctr., 2001—. Served with AUS, 1943-45. Mem. Nat. Freight Traffic Assn. Home: 11307 Stones Throw Dr Reston VA 20194-1044 Personal E-mail: ekreyling@aol.com.

KRIBEL, ROBERT EDWARD, retired academic administrator, physicist; b. Pitts., Sept. 17, 1937; s. Joseph P. and Helen M. K.; m. Ruth Ann Gropelli; children— Robert E., Karen A., Mark P., Gary P. BS, U. Notre Dame, 1959; MS, U. Calif., San Diego, 1966, PhD in Physics, 1968. Research scientist Gen. Atomic, Inc., 1965-69; assoc. prof. physics Drake U., 1970-73; vis. assoc. prof. applied physics Cornell U., 1973-74; prof., head dept. physics James Madison U., 1974-78, Auburn (Ala.) U., 1978-87, acting dean scis. and math., 1985-87, prof. physics, 1987-88; v.p. acad. affairs Jacksonville (Ala.) State U., 1988-92, prof. physics, 1992-93; dean natural scis. and math. Mesa State Coll., 1993-99; pres. REK Enterprises, Auburn, Ala., 1999—; chief acad. officer Air U., 2000—02. Contbr. articles to profl. jours. Served with U.S. Navy, 1959-62. Mem. Am. Phys. Soc., IEEE, Am. Assn. Physics Tchrs., Sigma Xi, Phi Kappa Phi. Personal E-mail: bkribel@charter.net.

KRICKA, LARRY J., chemistry professor; b. Karlovy Vary, Czechoslovakia, Aug. 22, 1947; arrived in U.S., 1987; m. Barbara J. Kricka, July 25, 1970; children: Simon, Anna, Thomas. BA with honors, York (Eng.) U., 1968, DPhil, 1971. Rsch. asst. Liverpool (Eng.) U., 1971-73; from lectr. to sr. lectr. to reader Birmingham (Eng.) U., 1973-87; Med. Rsch. Coun. traveling fellow U. Calif., San Diego, 1981-82; prof. U. Pa., Phila., 1987—. Disting. vis. scholar Christ's Coll., Cambridge, England, 2002, Cambridge, 02. Author: (book) Ligand Binder Assays, 1985; editor: (book) Nonisotopic DNA Probe Techniques, 1992; co-author: (with J. Cheng) Biochip Technology, 2001; editor: Luminescence, 1983—; mem. editl. bd. Analytical Biochemistry, 1983—; contbr. articles to profl. jours. Recipient Rank prize for optoelectronics Rank Orgn., 1991. Fellow Royal Soc. Chemistry (SAC Silver medal 1981), Royal Coll. Pathologists, Nat. Acad. Clin. Biochemistry; mem. Assn. Clin. Biochemists, Am. Assn. Clin. Chemistry (pres. 2001, Kubasik Lectr. award Upstate N.Y. sect. 1997, Reimer award Capitol sect. 2000). Avocations: skiing, travel. Office: U Pa Med Ctr Dept Pathol/Lab Medicine 3400 Spruce St Philadelphia PA 19104 E-mail: kricka@mail.med.upenn.edu.

KRIDLER, JAMIE BRANAM, children's advocate, social psychologist; b. Newport, Tenn., Jan. 23, 1955; d. Floyd A. and Mary Leslie (Carlisle) Branam; m. Thomas Lee Kridler, Mar. 19, 1989; children: Brittani Audra, Houston Scott, Clark Eaton, Sabrina Morrow. BS, U. Tenn., 1976, MS, 1977; PhD, Ohio State U., 1985; cert. interior design, retailing, profl. modeling, Bauder Fashion Coll., Atlanta, 1973. Fashion coord. Bill's Wear House, Newport, Tenn., 1969-77; buyer Shane's Boutique, Gatlinburg, Tenn., 1977-78; instr. Miami U., Oxford, Ohio, 1978-81; asst. prof. U. Tenn., Knoxville, 1985-89; mktg. dir. Profitt's Dept. Stores, Alcoa, Tenn., 1989-90; mktg. cons. Kridler & Kridler Mktg., Newport, Tenn., 1990-93; children's advocate Safe Space, Newport, Tenn., 1993-95. Adj. faculty U. Tenn., Knoxville, 1990-94, Walters State Coll., Morristown, Tenn., 1990-96, Carson Newman Coll., Jefferson City, Tenn., 1993-99; prof. East Tenn. State U., 1996—, chmn. Dept. FACS, 1996-2004, woman's studies steering com.; founding mem. Cmty. House Coop., 1995—; mem., Tenn. evaluator Nation Funding Collaborative on Violence Prevention; participant Children's Def. Fund, Washington, 1992—; founding mem. Cmty. House Co-op; mem. Gov.'s Prevention Initiative and Family Needs Task Force. Costume designer Newport Theatre Guild: Guys and Dolls, Carousel, Fiddler on the Roof, Music Man, Crimes of the Heart, Rumors, Come Back to the Five and Dime, Jimmy Dean, Oliver, The Odd Couple, The Sunshine Boys, Harvey, Bus Stop, Miami U. Dance Theatre, Ice Show. Bd. dirs. Safe Space, 1991-92; v.p. Newport Theatre Guild, 1991-92, pres., 1992-96, bd. dirs., 1990-97; dir. Cast and Crew Youth Theatre; creator Looking Glass Players. Named Outstanding Tchr., Miami U., Oxford, 1981, Outstanding Educator, U. Tenn., Knoxville, 1989; recipient numerous grants from univ. and non-profit orgns. Mem. NAACP, Lioness Club, Kappa Omicron Nu. Democrat. Lutheran. Avocations: yogi exercise, fashion design, dance, family activities. Home: 112 Woodlawn Ave Newport TN 37821-3031 Office Phone: 423-439-7538. Business E-Mail: kridler@etsu.edu.

KRIEBEL, CHARLES HOSEY, management sciences educator; b. Tarrytown, N.Y., Nov. 6, 1933; s. Nelson Stearly and Elizabeth Grace (Hosey) K.; m. Jan Lilly McAuley, June 7, 1961; children: Paul Charles, Susan, James McAuley, Carl Nelson. BS in Econs., U. Pa., 1959, MA in Stats., 1961; PhD in Indsl. Mgmt., MIT, 1964. Instr. Wharton Sch. Fin., U. Pa., Phila., 1959-61; asst. prof. Sloan Sch., MIT, Cambridge, 1963-64, Grad. Sch. Indsl. Adminstrn., Carnegie-Mellon U., Pitts., 1964-67, assoc. prof., 1967-70, prof., 1970-2000, prof. emeritus Pitts., 2000—, head dept indsl. mgmt., 1981-86; dir. strategic tech. Met. Life, N.Y.C., 1987-88. Cons. McKinsey & Co., Inc., N.Y.C., Rand Corp., Santa Monica, Calif., Gulf Oil Corp., Pitts., Imperial Tobacco, Montreal, Que., Can., Mellon Bank (N.A.), Pitts., LTV STeel Co., Inc., Gen. Reins Corp., N.Y.C., Industrikonsulent I.K.O., Copenhagen, Westinghouse Electric Corp., Pitts., U.S. Steel Corp., Pitts., Rockwell Internat., Pitts., Am. Mgmt. Sys., Fairfax, Va., HAL Inst. Computer Tech., Osaka, Japan, other indsl. firms; rep. NAS; mem. adv. bd. NSF, 1985-88. Mem. editl. bd. Internat. Fedn. Info. Processing, 1971—; editl. cons. Prentice-Hall, Inc., 1967-80; contbr. more than 130 articles to profl. jours. With Signal Corps, U.S. Army, 1954-56. Fulbright-Hays advisor, 1965-79; Ford Found. fellow MIT, 1964. Fellow AAAS; mem. Assn. Computing Machinery (nat. lectr.), Inst. Mgmt. Scis. (dept. editor Mgmt. Sci.), Ops. Rsch. Soc. Am., Am. Econ. Assn., Am. Statis. Assn., Econometric Soc., N.Y. Acad. Scis., Info. Systems Rsch. (sr. editor bd.), Delta Kappa Epsilon (pres. 1959). Home: 108 Silent Run Rd Fox Chapel Pittsburgh PA 15238 Office: Carnegie-Mellon U Grad Sch Indsl Admin Pittsburgh PA 15213

KRIEG, KENNETH J., federal agency administrator; BA, Davidson Coll.; M in Public Policy, Harvard U. Various def. and foreign policy positions, Washington; various mktg. and sales positions including v.p. and gen. mgr. office and consumer papers divsn. Internat. Paper Co., Stamford, Conn., 1990—2001; exec. sec. sr. exec. coun. (SEC) US Dept. Def., Washington, 2001, spl. asst. to sec., dir. program analysis and evaluation, under sec. def. acquisition, tech. & logistics, 2005—. Office: US Dept Def 3010 Def Pentagon Rm 3E1006 Washington DC 20301-3010 Office Phone: 703-697-7021.*

KRIEG, NANCY KAY, social worker, poet, musician; b. Jefferson City, Mo., Oct. 11, 1954; d. Arlin Darrell and Doris Lee Basinger; m. Russell Hugh Krieg, Mar. 15, 1975 (div. Aug. 18, 1988). BA in Psychology, Columbia Coll., 1994. Co-owner The Melody Shop, Jefferson City, Mo., 1975—85; co-mgr. Premiere Video, Osage Beach, 1991—94; social worker Miller County Psychol. Svcs., Eldon, 1994—95; substitute tchr. Eldon Pub. Schs., 1995; tchg. counselor, supr. Overland Pk., Kans., 1995—96; substitute tchr. Oak Hill Day Sch., Gladstone, Mo., 1997—98; tchg. counselor Concerned Care, Inc., Kansas City, 1998—. Author poetry. Recipient Mo. Writers' Week award for Poetry, Mo. Writers Guild, 1994, 1995, 1996, 1997. Mem.: Am. Fedn. Musicians, Acad. Am. Poets, The Writers Pl. Avocations: jazz drummer/percussion, mandolin, guitar, songwriting, poetry. Home: 1236 E 25th Ave Kansas City MO 64116

KRIEGEL, JAY L., Olympic organizing committee executive, public relations executive; b. Bklyn., Oct. 10, 1940; s. I. Stanley and Charlotte (Karish) K.; (div.); children: Isabel, Connor. BA, Amherst Coll., 1962; LLB, Harvard U., 1965. Asst. to mayor, chief of staff City Hall, N.Y.C., 1966-73; dir. spl. projects Loews Corp., N.Y.C., 1975-78; co-founder and pub. The Am. Lawyer, N.Y.C., 1979-82; pres. Kriegel Communications, N.Y.C., 1983-87; sr. v.p. CBS, N.Y.C., 1988—93; counsellor Abernathy MacGregor Group, N.Y.C., 1994—; exec. dir. NYC2012, 1999—. Bd. dirs. Wildcat Svcs. Inc., N.Y.C. Pres. Bklyn. Jewish Hosp., 1979-87; bd. dirs. Cancer Rsch. Inst., N.Y.C., 1986—, Vera Inst. Justice, N.Y.C., 1978-88, Prep for Prep, 1990—, New Visions, The After School Corp., mktg. com., Museum of Modern Art. Office: Abernathy MacGregor Group 501 Madison Ave New York NY 10022 Office Phone: 212-371-5999. Office Fax: 212-371-7097.

KRIEGER, BRUCE PHILLIP, medical educator; b. Erie, Pa., May 31, 1952; s. Mortimer G. and Adele (Berger) K.; m. Deborah Ann Larson, Aug. 15, 1983; children: Jori, Ashley, Jonathan. BA in Philosophy, U. Mich., 1973; MD, U. Pitts., 1977. Diplomate Am. Bd. Internal Medicine with subspecialties in pulmonary disease and critical care medicine. Fellow in pulmonary medicine U. Calif., San Diego, 1980-84; asst. prof. medicine U. Miami, Fla., 1985-90, assoc. prof. medicine, 1990-95, prof. of medicine, 1996—. Mem. med. adv. bd. Fla. Medicare, Jacksonville, 1993-95; cons. Blue Cross/Blue Shield, Washington, 1996—; med. dir. respiratory therapy programs, Miami-Dade C.C., Miami, 1997—. Author: (books) Economics of Mechanical Ventilation, 1994, Non-invasive Respiratory Monitoring, 1989, Asthma in the Elderly, 1997. Bd. dirs. Colony Theater, Miami Beach, Fla., 1985-87. Recipient Armour Pharm. award Am. Respiratory Care Found., Dallas, 1986, Comty. Svc. award Am. Lung Found. of South Fla., Miami, 1987; named One to Watch, South Fla. Mag., Miami, 1987. Fellow Am. Coll. Chest Physicians (pres. Fla. chpt. 1991-94), Am. Thoracic Soc.; mem. Fla. Thoracic Soc. (treas. 1993-95, pres. elect 1997-99, pres. 2000-02), Fla. Soc. Critical Care Medicine (pres. 1992-93). Avocations: tennis, boating, music. Office: Critical Care Cons 3625 University Blvd South Jacksonville FL 32216

KRIEGER, IRVIN MITCHELL, retired chemistry professor; b. Cleve., May 14, 1923; s. William I. and Rose (Brodsky) K.; m. Theresa Melamed, June 9, 1965; 1 dau., Laura. BS, Case Inst. Tech., 1944, MS, 1948; PhD, Cornell, 1951. Rsch. asst. Case Inst. Tech., Cleve., 1946-47; teaching fellow Cornell U., Ithaca, N.Y., 1947-49; instr. Case Western Res. U., 1949-51, asst. prof., 1951-55, assoc. prof., 1955-68, prof., 1968-88, prof. emeritus, 1988—; dir. Center for Adhesives, Sealants and Coatings, 1983-88. Vis. prof. U. Bristol, 1977-78; cons. for chem. firms; prof. invité Ecole Nat. Supérieure de Chimie de Mulhouse, 1987, Louis Pasteur U., Strasbourg, France, 1989. Contbr. articles to profl. jours. With USNR, 1943—46. NSF fellow Université Libre De Bruxelles, 1959-60; sr. fellow Weizmann Inst., 1970 Mem. Am. Chem. Soc., Am. Inst. Chem. Engrs., AAUP, Soc. Rheology (pres. 1977-79, Bingham medalist 1989). Home: 3460 Green Rd Apt 101 Beachwood OH 44122-4076 Office Phone: 216-921-6133. Business E-Mail: imk@case.edu.

KRIEGER, MARCIA SMITH, federal judge; b. Denver, Mar. 3, 1954; d. Donald P. Jr. and Marjorie Craig (Gearhart) Smith; m. Michael S. Krieger, Aug. 26, 1976 (div. July 1988); children: Miriam Anna, Matthias Edward; m. Frank H. Roberts, Jr., Mar. 9, 1991; stepchildren: Melissa Noel Roberts, Kelly Suzanne Roberts, Heidi Marie Roberts. BA, Lewis & Clark Coll., 1975; JD, U. Colo., 1979. Bar: Colo. 1979, U.S. Dist. Ct. Colo. 1979, U.S. Ct. Appeals (10th cir.) 1979. Rotary grad. fellow U. Munich, Germany, 1975—76; assoc. Mason, Reuler & Peek, P.C., Denver, 1976-83, Smart, DeFurio Brooks, Eklund & McClure, Denver, 1983-84; ptnr. Brooks & Krieger, P.C., Denver, 1984-88, Wood, Ris & Hames, P.C., Denver, 1988-90; pvt. practice U.S. Bankruptcy Court, 10th Circuit, Denver, 1990-94; judge U.S. Bankruptcy Ct., 10th Circuit, Denver, 1994-2000; chief judge U.S. Bankruptcy Ct., Denver, 2000—02, U.S. Dist. Ct., 2002—. Lectr. U. Denver Grad. Tax Program, 1987—, Colo. Soc. CPA's, Denver, 1984-87, Colo. Continuing Legal Edn., Denver, 1980—, Colo. Trial Lawyers Assn., Denver, 1987—, U. Colo. Law Sch.; adj. instr. U. Colo. Sch. Law, 1999-2001; spkr. in field. Contbr. articles to profl. publs. Vestry person Good Shepherd Episcopal Ch., Englewood, 1986—, judge and coach for H.S. mock trial. Mem. Colo. Bar Assn. (past chair Com. Court Reform; past mem. Professionalism Com.), Arapahoe Bar Assn., Arraj Inn of Ct. (v.p.), Nat. Conf. Bankruptcy Judges (past chair Internat. Law Rels. Com, Ethics Com.; past mem. Newsletter Com., Program Com.), Littleton Adv. Coun. for Gifted and Talented education, Alfred A. Arraj Inn of Court (past pres.), Colo. Jud. Coordinating Coun., Kenya Children Found. (bd. dirs.). Republican. Avocations: international relations, travel, marksmanship. Office: US Dist Ct Dist Colo Alfred J Arraj US Courthouse 901 19th St A-941 Denver CO 80294

KRIEGER, MICHAEL JAY, writer; b. San Francisco, May 13, 1940; s. Alfred Paul and Nancy Snyder Krieger; m. Susan MacDonald Krieger, May 4, 1991. BA, U. Calif., Berkeley, 1963. Owner Internat. Bldg. Products, San Francisco, Singapore, 1964—69; European mgr. Cosco divsn. Consolidated Foods Corp., San Francisco, France, 1969—74; writer, journalist Wash., 1975—. Syndicated travel journalist Universal Press Syndicate, 1987. Author: Tramp, 1986 (Gov.'s award Wash. State, 1987), Conversations with the Cannibals, 1994, Where Rails Meet the Sea, 1998, All the Men in the Sea, 2002, paperback edit., 2003; contbr. articles to newspapers and mags. Founder, 1st pres. Friends of the San Juans, Wash., 1979. Served with U.S. Army N.G., 1963—69. Recipient Best Friend of the San Juans award, Friends of the San Juans, 1999.

KRIEGER, ROBERT LEE, JR., human resource/management consultant, educator, writer, travel/meeting planner, political analyst, internet marketing consultant; b. Louisville, Nov. 13, 1946; s. Robert Lee and June Elise (Waters) K. BBA, U. Memphis, 1968, MBA, 1969. Cert. pers. cons., travel planner, mgmt. cons. Adminstrv. asst. to mayor City of Memphis, 1969-72; dir. devel. programs U. Memphis, 1972-74; pvt. cons. practice, Memphis, 1974-76; exec. v.p. Randall Howard & Assocs., Memphis, 1976-95; pres. KR Internat. Inc., Memphis, 1995—. Mem. faculty U. Memphis Coll. Bus., 1984—; worldwide travel cons. and meeting planner, 1962—; keynote spkr. numerous profl. groups. Trustee, life mem. Rep. Presdl. Task Force, Washington, 1980—; mem. Rep. Nat. Adc. Com., Washington, 1972—, Rep. Regional Steering Com.; mem. US Olympic Soc., Boulder, Colo., 1968—. Recipient US Treasury award US Dept. Treasury, 1971, Nat. Presdl. Medal of Merit, Rep. Presdl. Task Force, 1984, Rep. Legion of Merit, Pres.'s award Memphis Cotton Carnival Assn., 1968-85. Mem. Data Processing Mgmt. Assn., Am. Mgmt. Assn., Soc. Profl. Journalists, Anm. Film Guild, Met. Opera Guild, US Navy League, Nat. Wildlife Fedn., U. Memphis Alumni Assn., Mensa, Alpha Delta Sigma. Episcopalian. Avocations: writing, bowling, movies, photography, travel. Home: 2948 Dalebrook St Memphis TN 38127-8316 E-mail: german711@hotmail.com.

KRIEGER, SANFORD, lawyer; b. N.Y.C., Nov. 4, 1943; s. Harry and Ruth Krieger; m. Carol B. Bachenheimer, Aug. 19, 1967; 1 child, Paul Matthew. BA cum laude, Cornell U., 1965; JD cum laude, Harvard U., 1968. Bar: N.Y. 1971, U.S. Dist. Ct. (so. dist.) N.Y., U.S. Supreme Ct. 1974.3. Legal adviser to Ethiopian Govt., 1968-70; assoc. Simpson Thacher & Bartlett, N.Y.C., 1970-73, Fried Frank Harris Shriver & Jacobson, London, 1973-75, ptnr. N.Y.C., 1977—; gen. counsel, mng. dir. AEA Investors LLC, N.Y.C., 2003—. Mem. ABA, Assn. Bar City N.Y. Office: Fried Frank Harris Shriver & Jacobson 1 New York Plz Fl 22 New York NY 10004-1980 also: AEA Investors LLC 65 East 55th St New York NY 10022 Office Phone: 212-859-8230. Business E-Mail: kriegsa@ffhsj.com.

KRIEGLER, ARNOLD MATTHEW, management consultant; b. Omaha, July 29, 1932; s. Matthew and Mildred Elsie (Svoboda) K.; m. Joan Willey, June 6, 1999; children: Kurt, Karen Davidenko; stepchildren: Sara Sharpe, Amy Druliner, Andrew Frost. BSc in Bus. and Engring. Adminstrn., U. Nebr., Omaha, 1955; postgrad., U. Iowa, 1957-58. Chief draftsman Ballantye Electronics, Omaha, 1948-55; various mgmt. positions Collins Radio div. Rockwell Internat., Cedar Rapids, Iowa, 1957-76, dir. mfg. electronics ops. Dallas, 1976-78, dir. prodn. ops. Collins Transmission Systems div., 1978-88; mgmt. cons. AMK Assocs., Frisco, 1988—. Mem. com. on computer aided mfg. NAS, Washington, 1978-81; mem. engring. scis. curriculum adv. com. U. Tex., Dallas, 1988—. Ret. 1st lt. USAF, 1955-57. Recipient Exec. of Yr. United Way, Cedar Rapids, 1973. Mem. Nat. Mgmt. Assn. (instr. 1977—, chpt. dir. 1978-79, Silver Knight Mgmt. 1989), Inst. Indsl. Engrs. (chpt. pres. 1973-74), Theta Chi (chpt. pres. 1954-55). Independent. Unitarian. Avocations: golf, music. Home and Office: 7918 Ruskin Cir Frisco TX 75034-5475 E-mail: amkriegler@comcast.net.

KRIEGSMAN, ALAN M., retired film critic; b. NYC, Feb. 28, 1928; s. Harry Pickel and May (Cohn) K.; m. Sali Ann Ribakove, Nov. 28, 1957. Student, MIT, 1945—46; BS, Columbia U., 1951, MA, 1953. Lectr. in music Columbia U., NYC, 1955-60; music and performing arts critic San Diego Union, 1960-65; asst. to the pres. Juilliard Sch., NYC, 1965-66; music and performing arts critic Washington Post, 1966-74, dance critic, 1974-96, critic emeritus, 1996—. Advisor-cons. vis. com. on arts and humanities, MIT, 1976-86; vis. lectr. Dance Critics Conf., Am. Dance Festival; adjudicator Pulitzer Prize juries in music, criticism, feature writing, 1980-94; bd. dirs. Choo-San Goh & H. Robert Magee Found., 1996—. Contbr. articles on performing arts to various publs. Mem. leadership group nat. dance/media project UCLA, 1999. With U.S. Army, 1946-47. Fulbright scholar U. Vienna, 1956-57; recipient Pulitzer prize in Criticism, 1976, Metro DC Dance awards, spl. citation for inestimable contbns., 2002, Trustees award Dance/USA, 2004. Mem. Dance Inst. Washington (bd. dirs. 1996—), Dance Critics Assn. (bd. dirs. 1996-98), Cunningham Dance Found. (bd. dirs. 1999—). Democrat. Jewish. Avocations: piano, mathematics, science. Home: 4701 Willard Ave Apt 1013 Chevy Chase MD 20815-4622 Office Phone: 301-657-3695. Personal E-mail: amkmike@verizon.net.

KRIEGSMAN, EDWARD MICHAEL, lawyer; b. Bridgeport, Conn., Oct. 29, 1965; s. Irving Martin and Marlene Sonya (Kates) K.; m. Meryl Gail Dennis, June 11, 1989; children: Barry Alan, David Jacob, Rachel Lynn. BS in Biology, MIT, 1986; JD, U. Pa., 1989. Bar: Pa. 1989, U.S. Patent and Trademark Office 1989, Mass. 1990, U.S. Ct. Appeals (Fed. cir.) 1990, U.S. Dist. Ct. Mass. 1992. Assoc. Finnegan, Henderson, Farabow, et al, Washington, 1989-90; ptnr. Kriegsman & Kriegsman, Framingham, Mass., 1990—. Mem. ABA, Am. Intellectual Property Law Assn., Mass. Bar Assn., Fed. Cir. Bar Assn., Boston Patent Law Assn., South Middlesex Bar Assn. Jewish. Avocations: reading, sports. Home: 103 Richard Rd Holliston MA 01746-1213 Office: Kriegsman & Kriegsman 665 Franklin St Framingham MA 01702 Office Phone: 508-879-3500. E-mail: edward.kriegsman@kriegsmanlaw.com.

KRIEGSMAN, SALI ANN, performing arts executive, consultant, writer; b. N.Y.C., Apr. 16, 1936; d. Aaron and Charlotte (Pomeranz) Ribakove; m. Alan M. Kriegsman, Nov. 28, 1957. MA, Goddard Coll., 1976. Rsch. assoc. Scripps Clinic and Rsch. Found., La Jolla, Calif., 1961-65; exec. editor Am. Film Inst., Washington, 1969-74; asst. prof. George Washington U., Washington, 1979-80; dance cons. Smithsonian Instn., Washington, 1979—84; dir. dance program NEA, Washington, 1986-95; exec. dir. Jacob's Pillow Dance Festival, Becket, Mass., 1995-98; chief investigator Digital Dance Library Feasibility Project, 2002—03. Writer An Evening of Dance, In Performance at the White House, Sta. WETA-TV, 1998; mem. arts acad. adv. com. Coll. Bd., 1996-97; mem. nat. dance and media project leadership group UCLA, 1996-2000; mem. steering com. Am. Assembly Art, Tech. and Intellectual Property, 2000-02; sr. advisor Digital Dance Libr., 2002-03. Author: Modern Dance in America: The Bennington Years, 1981; contbr.: Britannica Book Of The Year, 1984-86; contbg. author: International Encyclopedia of Dance, 1998. Bd. dirs. Mass. Mus. Contemporary Art, 1995-97, Meredith Monk/The House Found., 2001—; pres. Dance Heritage Coalition, 1999-2000. Recipient Flo-Bert award N.Y. Com. To Celebrate Nat. Tap Dance Day, 1997, Oklahoma City U. Preservation of Heritage Am. Dance award, 1999, Tap Preservation award, N.Y.C. Tap Festival, 2002; fellow Va. Ctr. for Creative Arts, 2003. E-mail: saliann@verizon.net.

KRIENS, SCOTT G., information technology executive; BA, Calif. State U., Hayward. Co-founder StrataCom, Inc., 1986—96; chmn., CEO Juniper Networks, Inc., Mountain View, Calif., 1996—. Dir. VeriSign, Inc., Equinox, Inc. Office: Juniper Networks Inc 1194 N Mathilda Ave Sunnyvale CA 94089-1206*

KRIER, ANN O., product designer, writer; d. Charles Albert Overslaugh and Carol Jane Dann; m. James T. Krier, Apr. 22, 1995; children: Brett James, Maggie Sue. BS, Muskingum Coll., 1984. V.p. Trimark/Foodcraft, Winston Salem, NC, 1999—2005; pres. Design One World, Inc., Lewisville, NC, 2004—. Author (designer): (book) Creative Beads from Paper and Fabric, 2005. Mem.: Craft and Hobby Assn., Associated Artists, Am. Sewing Guild, Soc. Creative Designers. Independent. Avocations: kayaking, camping, collage, fiber arts, repousse, art quilting. Home: 963 Ridge Gate Dr Lewisville NC 27023 Office: Design One World Inc PO Box 382 Lewisville NC 27023 Office Phone: 336-287-5361. Business E-Mail: akrier@designoneworld.com.

KRIER, JAMES EDWARD, law educator, writer; b. Milw., Oct. 19, 1939; s. Ambrose Edward and Genevieve Ida (Behling) Krier; m. Gayle Marian Grimsrud, Mar. 22, 1962 (div.); children: Jennifer, Amy; m. Wendy Louise Wilkes, Apr. 20, 1974; children: Andrew Wilkes-Krier, Patrick Wilkes-Krier. BS, U. Wis., 1961, JD, 1966. Bar: Wis. 1966, U.S. Ct. Claims 1968. Law clk. to chief justice Calif. Supreme Ct., San Francisco, 1966-67; assoc. Arnold & Porter, Washington, 1967-69; acting prof., then prof. law UCLA, 1969-78, 80-83; prof. law Stanford U., Calif., 1978-80, U. Mich. Law Sch., Ann Arbor, 1983—, Earl Warren DeLano prof., 1988—. Cons. Calif. Inst. Tech., EPA; mem. pesticide panel NAS, 1972—75, mem. com. energy and the environment, 1975—77. Author: (book) Environmental Law and Policy, 1971; author: (with Stewart) Environmental Law and Policy, 2d edit., 1978; author: (with Ursin) Pollution and Policy, 1977; author: (with Dukeminier) Property, 1981, Property, 5th edit., 2002; contbr. articles to profl. jours. Served to lt. U.S. Army, 1961—63. Mem.: Order of Coif, Artus, Phi Kappa Phi. Office: U Mich Law Sch 625 S State St Ann Arbor MI 48109-1215 Office Phone: 734-763-4701. Business E-Mail: jkrier@umich.edu.

KRIESBERG, IRVING, painter; b. Chgo., Mar. 13, 1919; s. Max and Bessie (Turner) K.; m. Ruth Miller, Apr. 5, 1921 (div. 1973); children: Nell, Matthias; m. Barbara Nimri Aziz, Dec. 2, 1974. BFA, Sch. of Art Inst. Chgo., 1941; MA, NYU, 1972. Tchr. Yale U. Grad. Sch., 1962-71; dir. state-wide honors studio program SUNY, 1972-77; tchr. painting Columbia U. Grad. Sch., 1977-79; tchr. painting and ceramics La. State U. Grad. Sch., 1980; Beaumont prof. painting Washington U., St. Louis, 1982; instr. terra-cotta, vis. artist Skidmore Coll., 1989; vis. artist painting Vt. Studio Sch., 1989; instr. sculpture Appalachian Ctr. for Crafts, 1992. Conductor lectrs. and workshops throughout the U.S. and India. Author: Looking at Pictures, 1955, Art, The Visual Experience, 1965, Working with Color, 1987; one-man shows at Guggenheim Mus., 1972, Fairweather-Hardin, Chgo., 1979, Dintenfass Gallery, N.Y.C., 1980-82, Everson Mus., Syracuse, N.Y., 1980, Rose Mus., Brandeis, 1980, Washington U. Art Mus., St. Louis, 1982, Graham Modern Gallery, N.Y.C., 1985, Montclair (N.J.) Art Mus., 1986; represented in permanent collections at Balt. Mus. Art, Cin. Mus. Art, Mus. Modern Art, N.Y.C., Whitney Mus., N.Y.C., Corcoran Gallery, Washington, Rose Mus., Brandeis, Nat. Gallery Am. Art, Washington, Rep. Peter Findlay Gall, N.Y.C. Recipient awards Ford Found., 1965, Fulbright, 1965-66, N.Y. State, 1974, 78, 91, NEA, 1984, Guggenheim, 1976. Mem. NAD (academician, 1994-)*

KRIESBERG, LOUIS, sociologist, educator; b. Chgo., July 30, 1926; s. Max and Bessie (Turner) K.; m. Lois Ablin, Aug. 23, 1959; children: Daniel A., Joseph A. PhB, U. Chgo., 1947, MA, 1950, PhD, 1953. Instr. sociology sch. gen. studies Columbia U., N.Y.C., 1953-56; Fulbright rsch. scholar U. Cologne, Germany, 1956-57; sr. fellow in law and behavior scis. U. Chgo., 1957-58; sr. study dir. Nat. Opinion Rsch. Ctr., 1958-62; assoc. prof. dept. sociology, 1962-67, Syracuse (N.Y.) U., 1962-67, prof., 1967-97, prof. emeritus, 1997—, dir. program on analysis and resolution conflicts, 1985-94, Maxwell prof. social conflict studies, 1994-97, Maxwell prof. emeritus social conflict studies, 1997—. Author: Mothers in Poverty, 1970, Social Inequality, 1979, Social Conflicts, 1973, rev. edit., 1982, International Conflict Resolution, 1992, Constructive Conflicts, 1998, 2nd edit., 2003; editor: Social Processes in International Relations, 1968, Research in Social Movements, Conflicts, and Change, vols. 1-14, 1978-92; co-editor: Intractable Conflicts and Their Transformation, 1989, Timing the De-escalation of International Conflicts, 1991. Cons., lectr. Syracuse Area Middle East Dialogue Group. Grantee U.S. Inst. Peace, MacArthur Found., Hewlett Found. Fellow Am. Sociol. Assn. (chair peace and war sect. 1990-91, award for Disting. Career 1993), Internat. Peace Rsch. Assn. (co-chair internat. conflict resolution 1989-94), Internat. Studies Assn. (chair peace studies sect. 1998-99), Internat. Sociol. Assn. (rsch. com. 1, exec. com. 1982-86), Internat. Soc. Polit. Psychology (governing coun. 1992-94), Soc. for Study Social Problems (pres. 1983-84, Lee Founders award 1990), Ea. Sociol. Soc. (exec. com. 1977-81), Peace Studies Assn. (ann. award 1995), N.Y. State Sociol. Assn. (Disting. Svc. award 1999). Jewish. Avocations: swimming, travel. Home: 164 Summerhaven Dr East Syracuse NY 13057-3115 Office: Conflicts Analysis Resolution Syracuse U Syracuse NY 13244-1090 Business E-Mail: lkriesbe@syr.edu.

KRIESBERG, SIMEON M., lawyer; b. Washington, June 4, 1951; s. Martin and Harriet M. K.; m. Martha L. Kahn, Jan. 9, 1994. AB, Harvard U., 1973; M in Pub. Affairs, Princeton U., 1977; JD, Yale U., 1977. Bar: D.C. 1977, U.S. Dist. Ct. D.C. 1978, U.S. Ct. Appeals (D.C. cir.) 1978, U.S. Ct. Internat. Trade 1979, U.S. Ct. Appeals (Fed. cir.) 1981, U.S. Supreme Ct. 1982. Assoc. Leva, Hawes, Symington, Martin & Oppenheimer, Washington, 1977—83; sr. counsel internat. trade Sears World Trade Inc., Washington, 1983—85, v.p., gen. counsel, 1985—87; ptnr. Mayer Brown Rowe & Maw LLP, Washington, 1987—. Professorial lectr. Nitze Sch. Advanced Internat. Studies, Johns Hopkins U., 1991-93; mem. binat. dispute resolution panel under U.S.-Can. Free Trade Agreement, 1990-92; guest scholar Brookings Inst., 1992-93; mem. roster of dispute resolution panelists under NAFTA, 1996-2004. Mem. editorial adv. com. Internat. Legal Materials, 1991-97; article and book rev. editor Yale Law Jour., 1976-77. Officer or dir. Washington Hebrew Congregation, 1980-94, Jewish Cmty. Rels. Coun. Greater Washington, 1986-94, Interfaith Conf. Met. Washington, 1989—, Wash. D.C. Jewish Cmty. Rels. Ctr., 1994—, Mid-Atlantic coun. Union Am. Hebrew Congregations, 1994-02. Recipient Pro Bono Svc. award Internat. Human Rights Law Group, 1991, Lawrence L. O'Connor medal Sears, Roebuck and Co., 1984. Mem. ABA, Am. Law Inst., Am. Soc. Internat. Law, D.C. Bar. Office: Mayer Brown Rowe & Maw LLP 1909 K St NW Washington DC 20006-1101 Business E-Mail: skriesberg@mayerbrownrowe.com.

KRIET, J. DAVID, medical educator; MD, U. of Okla., Oklahoma City, 1991; BS, U. of Okla., Norman, 1997. Diplomate Am. Bd. of Facial Plastic and Reconstructive Surgery, Am. Bd. of Otolaryngology. Clin. instr. dept. of otolaryngology/head and neck surgery Oreg. Health Scis. Ctr., Portland, 1997—98; asst. prof. dept. otolaryngology/head and neck surgery U. Kans. Sch. Medicine, Kansas City, 1998—2005, assoc. prof., 2005—; clin. asst. prof. divsn. of otolaryngology/head and neck surgery U. Mo.-Kansas City Sch. Medicine, Kansas City, 2000—05. Dir. divsn. of facial plastic and reconstructive surgery U. of Kans. Sch. of Medicine, Kansas City, Kans., 1998—. Photographic exhbn., U. Washington Med. Ctr. Art Collection. Overseer ops. Kans. U. MedWest Ambulatory Surgery Ctr., Shawnee, 2003—. Recipient Top Physician award, Kans. City, 2003. Fellow: ACS, Am. Acad. of Facial Plastic and Reconstructive Surgery. Office: U Kans Hosp MS 3010 3901 Rainbow Blvd Kansas City KS 66160 Office Phone: 913-588-6731. Business E-Mail: dkriet@kumc.edu.

KRIKALEV, SERGEI KONSTANTINOVICH, flight engineer, cosmonaut, researcher; b. Leningrad, Russia, Aug. 27, 1958; s. Konstantin Sergeevich and Nadia Ivanova Krikalev; m. Elena Yurl'vena Terekhina; 1 child, Olga Sergeevna Krikalyova. Degree in Mech. Engring., Leningrad Mech. Inst., 1981. Lab. asst. and sr. lab. asst. Leningrad Mech. Inst., 1980—97; aircraft technician on operation and repair of aircraft and engines All-Union Voluntary Soc. for Assistance to the Army, Air Force and Navy, 1981; with NPO Energia, Russia, 1981—85; cosmonaut Y.A. Gagarin Cosmonauts Tng. Ctr., Russia, 1985—, tng. for flight on Mir space sta., flight engr. Soyuz TM-7 mission, 1988—89, mem. backup crew Mir mission, 1990—92; flight engr. Soyuz TM-12, 1990—91, Soyuz TM-12 and Mir OS, 1991—92; tng. as flight expert of crew No 4 Discovery Orbiter under STS-60 program Johnson Space Ctr., 1992—94; prime mission specialist, mem. crew, STS-60 NASA Space Shuttle Mission, 1994; tng. as back-up cosmonaut of Titov, flight specialist of the Discovery crew-4 under the STS-63 program Johnson Space Ctr., 1994—95; back-up specialist Discovery Orbiter flight 4 under STS-63, 1995; flight engr. ISS-1, 1996; mem. crew STS-88 Endeavor Internat. Space Sta. assembly mission, 1998; mem. Expedition-1 crew, 2000—01; Soyuz and ISS comdr. Expedition 11, 2005—. Named Hero of the Soviet Union, Hero of the Russian Fedn., L'Officier de la L'egion d'Honneur (France); recipient Gold Star medal of the Hero of the Soviet Union, Order of Lenin, Order of Friendship of the Peoples, Gold Star medal of the Hero of the Russian Fedn., NASA Spaceflight medal, 1994, 1998, NASA Disting. Svc. medal, Order of Eagle First Class, Assn. of the Russian Manufactuers. Achievements include member of the Soviet and Russian National Aerobatic Flying Teams. Champion of Moscow in 1983 and Champion of the Soviet Union in 1986. Avocations: swimming, bicycling, aerobatic flying, amateur radio operations from space, skiing, windsurfing. Office: NASA Johnson Space Ctr c/o Astronaut Office/CB Houston TX 77058

KRIKORIAN, GREGORY H., academic administrator; b. Montreal, Can., Jan. 25, 1962; s. Art H. and Elsie G. Krikorian; m. Mary Krikorian, Aug. 18, 1990; children: Katie, Zack, Luy, Clare. BA in Criminal Justice, Niagara U., 1984; MA, Bowling Green State U., 1990. Dept. counselor West County Coun., Bowling Green, Ohio, 1988—90; dir. counseling Bethany (W.Va.) Coll., 1990—93, assoc. dean students, 1993—96; dir. resident life, asst. dean Hartwick Coll., Oneonta, NY, 1996—97, assoc. dean students, 1997—2002, dean students, 2002—04, v.p. student life, 2004—. Presenter in field. Bd. dirs. Oneonta Boys and Girls Club, 2004—05; coach Oneonta Youth Soccer Club, 1997—; basketball coach YMCA, Oneonta, 2003—. Named Adminstr. of Yr., Hartwick Coll., 2002—03. Mem.: Nat. Assn. Student Personnel Adminstrs., Am. Coll. Personnel Assn. Roman Catholic. Avocation: sports. Home: 67 West St Oneonta NY 13820 Office: Hartwick Coll Student Union Oneonta NY 13820

KRIKOS, GEORGE ALEXANDER, pathologist, educator; b. Old Phaleron, Greece, Sept. 17, 1922; came to U.S., 1946; s. Alexios and Helen (Spyropoulou) K.; m. Aspasia Manoni, June 22, 1949; children: Helen, Alexandra, Alexios. DDS, U. Pa., 1949; PhD, U. Rochester, 1959; PhD (hon.), U. Athens, Greece, 1981. Asst. prof. pathology U. Pa. Sch. Dentistry, 1958-61, assoc. prof., 1961-67, prof., 1967-68, chmn. dept., 1964-68; assoc. prof. oral pathology U. Pa. Grad. Sch., 1962-68, prof. oral pathology, 1968; prof. pathobiology Sch. Dentistry, U. Colo., Denver, 1968-75, chmn. dept. pathobiology, 1968-73, prof. oral biology, 1975-86, clin. prof. oral biology, 1986-91, prof. oral biology emeritus, 1991—, asst. dean basic sci. affairs, 1973-75, asso. dean oral biology affairs, 1975-76. Vis. prof. Sch. Dentistry, U. Athens, 1980-81; mem. dental study sect. NIH, 1966-70; mem. cancer com. Colo.-Wyo. Regional Med. Program, 1970-72; cons. oral pathology Denver VA Hosp., 1970-72 Served with AUS, 1949-54. Mem. Am. Soc. Investigative Pathology, Internat. Assn. Dental Rsch., Sigma Xi. Home: 350 Ivy St Denver CO 80220-5855

KRILL, KAY (KATHERINE LAWTHER KRILL), apparel executive; b. Wilmington, N.C., Mar. 27, 1955; d. James Wyatt and Katherine (King) L.; m. Charles Philip McEvoy III, Sept. 12, 1981 (div. Oct. 1985). BA in Psychology and Econ., Agnes Scott Coll., Decatur, Ga., 1977. From asst. buyer to buyer Macy's Dept. Store, Atlanta, 1977-81; buyer Talbot's, Hingham, Mass., 1981-84, dir. catalog merchandising, 1984-88; v.p. merchandising Mark Shale, Burr Ridge, Ill., 1988—90; exec. v.p. gen. merchandising mgr. women's operations Hartmarx Corp., 1990—92; pres. Carroll Reed, 1992—94; merchandising v.p. separates, dresses and petites Ann Taylor Stores Corp., 1994—96, sr. v.p. gen. merchandise mgr., Ann Taylor Loft, 1996—98, exec. v.p., Ann Taylor Loft, 1998—2001, pres., Ann Taylor Loft, 2001—04, pres., 2004—, bd. dirs., 2004—. Mem. Jr. League Atlanta, 1977-81, Boston, 1981-88, Chgo., 1988. Mem. Fashion Group Boston, Nat. Assn. Female Execs., Direct Mktg. Assn. Clubs: East Bank (Chgo.). Republican. Episcopalian. Avocations: tennis, aerobics, shopping. Office: Ann Taylor Stores Corp 1372 Broadway New York NY 10018*

KRIM, MATHILDE, medical educator; b. Como, Italy, July 9, 1926; came to U.S. BS, U. Geneva, Switzerland, 1948, PhD, 1953; DSc (hon.), Long Island U., 1987; LLD (hon.), Columbia U., 1988; DSc (hon.), Brandeis U., 1989; DHL (hon.), Southeastern Mass. U., 1990; DSc. (hon.), Tulane U., 1990; DHL (hon.), SUNY, Stonybrook, 1991; DSc(hon.), Columbia Coll., 1992; DSc (hon.), Dartmouth Coll., 2005. Asst. genetic sect., dept. exptl. biology Weizmann Inst. Sci., Rehovot, Israel, 1953-54, jr. scientist, 1954-57, rsch. assoc., 1957-59; rsch. assoc.divsn. virus rsch. Cornell Med. Coll., N.Y.C., 1959-62; rsch. assoc. Sloan Kettering Inst. Cancer Rsch., N.Y.C., 1962-68, assoc., 1968-75, assoc. mem., 1975-85, co-head interferon evaluation program, 1975-81, head interferon lab, 1981-85; assoc. rsch. scientist dept. pediatrics St. Luke's-Roosevelt Hosp. Ctr. and Columbia U., N.Y.C., 1986-90; adjunct prof. pub. health Columbia U., N.Y.C., 1990—; founding co-chair, chmn. bd., CEO Am. Found. for AIDS Rsch., N.Y.C. Bd. dirs. AIDSFILMS, Am. Com. for Weizmann Inst. Sci., Nat. Biomed. Rsch. Found.; trustee Scientists' Inst. for Pub. Information, Feinberg Grad. Sch. Weizmann Inst. Sci., African-Am. Inst.; mem. adv. panel on higher edn., New York, 1965, President's Com. on Mental Retardation, 1966-69, jury Albert D. Lasker Rsch. awards 1968-71, 78—, adv. bd. Health Profls. for Polit. Action, 1968-70, adv. com. to Sec. of HEW on Health Proteciton and Disease Prevention, 1969-70, Coun. NEH, 1969-73, Panel of Cons. on Cancer, Com. Labor and Pub. Welfare, U.S.Senate, 1970-71, adv. com. Nat. Colorectal Cancer Program NIH, 1971-73, working group develo. rsch. segment Virus Cancer Program NIH, 1971-74, review com. "A" Virus Cancer Program NIH, 1974-77, adv. com. Inst. Internat. Edn., 1974—, adv. com. Program of Sci., Tech., and Human Values NEH, 1974-78, U.S. Nat. Commn. for UNESCO, 1979-80, adv. com. World Rehabilitation Fund, 1978-82, Interferon Clin. Adv. Com. Schering-Plough Corp., 1980-85, Bristol Labs. Adv. Panel on Biological Response Modifiers, 1981-84, sci. adv. com. Am. Found. AIDS Rsch., 1985—, Com. of 100 for Nat. Health Ins., AIDS task force Am. Assn. Sex Educators, Counselors and Therapists, 1985—, rsch. adv. coun. Nat. Orgn. for Rare Disorders Inc., 1985—, AIDS Health Edn. Risk Reduction Consultation, Ctrs. for Disease Control, 1986, task force on Chemotherapeutics, Nat. Inst. of Allergy and Infectious Diseases, NIH, 1986, met. area adv. com. Lower Manhattan AIDS consortium, 1986—, scientific adv. bd. Nat. Coalition on Immune System Disorders, 1986—, adv. com. The Village Nursing Home, 1986—, sect. for the study of ethical, legal and social issues HIV Ctr. for Clin. and Behavioral Studies, 1987—, AIDS Rsch. Ctr., 1987—, bd. advisors Nat. Lawyers Guild AIDS Network, 1987—, AIDS adv. panel Planned Parenthood Fed. Am., 1988—, nat. adv. com. Nat. Communtiy AIDS Partnership, 1988—, adv. com. Women and AIDS Resource Network, 1988—; commr. Pres.'s

Commn. for the Study of Ethical Problems in Medicine and Biomedical and Behavioral Rsch., adv. bd. LOVE HEALS, 1989—, adv. bd. Internat. Alliance for Haiti, 1989—, adv. bd. AIDS-AUFKLARUNG, Frankfurt, Germany, 1990—, internat. com. Lottare Informare Formare Educare, Rome, Italy, 1990—, adv. coun. Columbia Sch. Pub. Health, 1990—, AIDS adv. panel, Med. Soc. State of New York, 1992—. Editor (with others) Mediation of Cellular Immunity in Cancer by Immune Modifiers: Progress in Cancer Research and Therapy, 1981;mem. editorial bd. The Aids Record; assoc. editor Cancer Investigation, Interferon Newsletter, Aids Care; contbr. articles to profl. jours. Bd. dirs. Nat. Med. Assn. Found., 1968-69, Inst. of Soc., Ethics, and the Life Scis. (The Hastings Ctr.), 1979-89; trustee Nat. Urban League, 1966-72, The Rockefeller Found., 1971-84, AIDS Med. Found. 1983-89, chairperson; vice chmn. Citizens Organized Against Drug Abuse, 1966; exec. sec. Am. Com for Assistance to Tunisia, 1968-69; dir. at large Am. Cancer Soc., 1970-72. Fellow NAS 1977; scholar, U. Geneva, 1947-52; recipient Spirit of Achievement award Nat. Women's Divsn. Albert Einstein Coll. Medicine, 1972, Humanitarian award Fund for Human Dignity, 1985, award for contbns. to civic life Women's City Club, 1986, John and Samuel Bard award in medicine and sci., 1986, Human Rights Campaign Fund award, 1986, Elizabeth Cutter Morrow award, City of New York YWCA, 1986, Jack Dempsey Humanitarian award St. Clare's Hosp. and Health Ctr., 1986, 10 Ams. Who've Made a Difference award Better Health and Living Mag., 1987, Eleanor Roosevelt Leadership award NOW, 1987, Achievement award Am. Assn. of Physicians for Human Rights, 1987, Humanist Disting. Svc. award Am. Humanist Assn., 1987, Hall of Fame award Internat. Women's Forum, 1987, Commitment to Life award, AIDS project L.A., 1987, Frontrunner award Sara Lee Corp., 1988, Exceptional achievement award, Women's Project and Prodns., 1988, Pres.'s award Am. Equity Assn., 1988, Medical award Hassadah, New York, 1988, award for Pioneering Achievements in Health and Higher Edn. Charles A. Dana Found., 1988, gold medal of honor Casita Maria, 1988, Caring award Stewart McKinney Found., 1988, Outstanding Mother award Nat. Mother's Day Com., 1989, Myrtle Wreath Humanitarian award Nat. Hassadah, 1991, Edwin C. Whitehead award Nat. Ctr. Health Edn., 1991, M. Carey Thomas award Bryn Mawr Coll., 1991, Scientic Freedom and Responsibility award AAAS, 1994; named Woman of Distinction Birmingham (Ala.) So. Coll., 1987, Dallas Cares Benefit honoree, 1989, 100 New York Women Barnard Coll., 1989. Mem. NAS, NAACP, Am. Assn. Advancement of Sci., Soc. Biological Therapy, Am. Soc. Microbiology, Internat. Soc. for Interferon Rsch., Am. Humanists Assn.

KRIMENDAHL, HERBERT FREDERICK, II, investment banker; b. Cin., Oct. 28, 1928; s. Herbert F. and Mary Bess (Christian) K.; m. Constance Kathryn McCown, Sept. 21, 1957 (dec. Sept. 1989); children: Elizabeth Knowles, Nancy Christian; m. Emilia Alice Saint-Amand, Feb. 4, 1999. BA, Ohio State U., 1950; MBA, Harvard U., 1952. Assoc. Goldman, Sachs & Co., N.Y.C., 1953-62, ptnr., 1963-87, ltd. ptnr., 1987-99, sr. dir., 1999—; chmn. Petrus Ptnrs. Ltd., N.Y.C., 1992—. Trustee Philharm. Symphony Soc. N.Y., 1977—, pres., 1989-96, The James Madison Coun. of Libr. of Congress, 1995—, Bridgehampton Chamber Music Assocs., 1997—; Ohio State U. Found., 1998—. Mem. River Club, Maidstone Club, The Brook, The Links, Jupiter Island Club, Deepdale Golf Club, The Everglades Club. Office: Petrus Ptnrs Ltd 1350 Ave of the Americas Ste 3000 New York NY 10019-4801 Office Phone: 212-977-3712. Business E-Mail: hfk@petruspartners.com.

KRIMIGIS, STAMATIOS MIKE, physicist, researcher, engineering executive, consultant; b. Chios, Greece, Sept. 10, 1938; s. Michael and Angeliki (Tsetseris) K.; m. Maria Anastasopoulou, 1990; children: Michael, John. BS, U. Minn., 1961; MS, U. Iowa, 1963, PhD, 1965. Research assoc. and asst. prof. physics U. Iowa, Iowa City, 1965-68; supr. space physics sect. Applied Physics Lab., Johns Hopkins U., Laurel, 1968-74, supr. space physics and instrumentation group, 1974-81, chief scientist space dept., 1980-90, head space dept., 1991—2004, head emeritus, 2004—; mem. Space Sci. Bd., Nat. Acad. Scis. NRC, 1983-86; chmn. com. on solar and space physics, 1983-86; cons. Mem. steering com. space sci. working group Assn. Am. Univs., 1983-85; mem. space sci. and applications adv. com., NASA, 1987-91, mem. solar sys. exploration subcom., 1998-01. Contbr. over 370 articles to sci. jours.; author book chpts. on solar, interplanetary and magnetospheric plasma physics, cosmic rays, magnetospheres of Earth, Jupiter, Saturn, Uranus and Neptune. Recipient Exceptional Sci. Achievement medal NASA, 1981, 86, Acad. prize Am. Hellenic Ednl. Progressive Assn., 1994, COSPAR Space Sci. award, 2002. Fellow AIAA (assoc.), Am. Geophys. Union, Am. Phys. Soc.; mem. AAAS, Internat. Acad. Astronautics (Space Sci. award 1994), Athens Acad. (corr.). Greek Orthodox. Home: 613 Cobblestone Ct Silver Spring MD 20905-5806 Office: Johns Hopkins U Applied Physics Lab Laurel MD 20723-6099 E-mail: tom.krimigis@jhuapl.edu.

KRIMM, SAMUEL, physicist, researcher; b. Morristown, NJ, Oct. 19, 1925; s. Irving and Ethel (Stein) K.; m. Marilyn Marcy Neveloff, June 26, 1949; children: David Robert, Daniel Joseph. BS, Poly. Inst. Bklyn., 1947; MA, Princeton U., 1949, PhD, 1950. Postdoctoral fellow U. Mich., Ann Arbor, 1950-52, mem. faculty, 1952—, prof. physics, 1963-2001, prof. emeritus, 2001—, mem. Macromolecular Rsch. Ctr., 1968—, mem. biophysics rsch. divsn., 1962—, chmn. biophysics rsch. div., 1976-86, dir. program in protein structure and design, 1985-94, assoc. dean research Coll. Lit., Sci. and Arts, 1972-75. Chmn. infrared spectroscopy Gordon Rsch. Conf., 1968; mem. NAS/NRC NBS Polymers divsn. Evaluation Panel, 1973-76, chmn., 1975-76; materials rsch. adv. com. NSF, 1981-86, chmn., 1984; mem. DOE Coun. on Material Scis., 1986-89; program adv. com. Internat. Conf. on Raman Spectroscopy, 1984-86, exec. com., 1988-90; Fraser Price Meml. lectr., 1988; disting. lectr. Inst. Materials Sci. U. Conn., 1995; com. on promoting rsch. collaboration NAS/IOM, 1987-89; cons. B.F. Goodrich, 1956-86, Allied 1963-93, Monsanto, 1987-92; vis. prof. U. Cambridge, 1962, Weizmann Inst., 1970, U. Mainz, 1983, U. Paris, 1991. Author papers on vibrational spectroscopy, x-ray diffraction studies of natural and synthetic polymers, potential energy function devel.; mem. editorial bd. Jour. Polymer Sci. Polymer Physics Edn., 1967-99; Biopolymers, 1973—; Macromolecules, 1968-71; Jour. Macromolecular Sci.-Rev. Macromolecular Chemistry, 1983-92. Served with USNR, 1944-46. Recipient Humboldt award, 1983; U. Mich. Disting. Faculty Achievement award, 1986; Textile Research Inst. fellow, 1947-50; NSF sr. postdoctoral fellow, 1962-63; sr. fellow U. Mich. Soc. Fellows, 1971-76 Fellow AAAS, Am. Phys. Soc. (High Polymer Physics prize 1977, chmn. div. biol. physics 1979, div. councilor 1981, exec. com. 1983, planning com. 1992); mem. Am. Chem. Soc., Biophys. Soc., Coblentz Soc. (hon., bd. mgr. 1967-70). Office: U Mich Biophysics Rsch Divsn 930 N University Ave Ann Arbor MI 48109 E-mail: skrimm@umich.edu.

KRING, CHARLES UDELL, retired civil engineer; b. Belle Rive, Ill., Aug. 31, 1910; s. Charles Harvey and Carolyn (Schoenmetzler) K.; m. Marguerite F. Kay, Aug. 25, 1945 (dec. Dec. 1999); children: Mary, Judith, Gary; m. Jeanne Millett, July 24, 2002. BSCE, U. Ill., 1932, MSCE, 1939, PhD in Civil Engring., 1948. Registered profl. engr., Calif. Field engr. San Francisco-Oakland Bay Bridge, 1934-35; engr. Golden Gate Bridge, 1936-37; supt. Ben Hur Constrn. Co., St. Louis and Indpls., 1937-38; bridge engr. Parsons, Brinkerhoff, Hall & Macdonald, N.Y., 1941-42; chief structural engr. Bermuda Architect-Engrs., 1942-43; cons. engr. Charles U. Kring Assocs., San Jose, Calif., 1946—; pres. Kring Constrn. Co., Inc., San Jose, 1948—; owner, mgr. Foxworthy Shopping Ctr., San Jose, Calif., 1956-84, Olympia Plaza Shopping Ctr., Seaside, Calif., 1966-77. Owner Kaydell Angus Farm, Los Gatos, Calif., 1959-96; lectr. Air U. Maxwell Field. Author: Selection of Weapons and Estimation of Force Requirements for Aerial Bombardment, 1947. Col. USAF, 1943-45, World War II. Decorated Medal of Freedom. Mem. ASCE, Commonwealth Club, San Jose Country Club, Tau Beta Pi. Republican. Avocations: photography, golf. Home: 7336 Via Laguna San Jose CA 95135-1332 Office: Kring Constrn Co Inc 1035 Minnesota Ave San Jose CA 95125-2431 Office Phone: 408-275-1065. E-mail: chaskring@aol.com.

KRINGEL, JEROME HOWARD, lawyer; b. Milw., Apr. 2, 1940; s. Lester E. and Irene A. (Kreutzer) K.; m. Mary Kathleen McAuliffe, Sept. 8, 1962; children: Anne, Mary Karen, Jennifer, Elisabeth, Katherine. AB, Marquette U., 1962; postgrad., U. Heidelberg, Germany, 1963; LLB, Yale U., 1966. Bar: Wis. 1966, U.S. Dist. Ct. (ea. dist.) Wis. 1966, U.S. Ct. Appeals (7th cir.) 1966. Ptnr., coord. bus. practice Michael, Best & Friedrich, Milw., 1966—. Trustee Shorewood (Wis.) Village Bd., 1974-80. Mem. ABA, Wis. Bar Assn. (chmn. bus. law sect. 1990-91), Milw. Bar Assn. Office: Michael Best & Friedrich LLP 100 E Wisconsin Ave Ste 3300 Milwaukee WI 53202-4108 Business E-Mail: jhkringel@michaelbest.com.

KRINGELIS, KURT, portfolio manager; b. Tucson, Sept. 14, 1970; s. Imants Kringelis and Gesche Gengelbach. BS in Fin., U. Ill., 1991, MBA, JD, U. Ill., 1995. Bar: Ill. 1995; CFA; CPA, Ill. Fin. analyst Equitable Investment Svcs., DesMoines, 1995-96, assoc. portfolio mgr., 1996-97; investment mgr. ING Investment Mgmt., Atlanta, 1998, dir. high yield bonds, 1999—. Mem. AICPA, ABA, Assn. for Investment Mgmt. and Rsch., Ill. State Bar Assn., Ill. CPA Soc., Atlanta Soc. CFA. Office: ING Investment Mgmt Ste 300 5780 Powers Ferry Rd NW Atlanta GA 30327

KRINSKY, CAROL HERSELLE, art historian, educator; b. NYC, June 2, 1937; d. David and Jane (Gartman) Herselle; m. Robert Daniel Krinsky, Jan. 25, 1959; 2 children. BA, Smith Coll., 1957; MA, NYU, 1960, PhD, 1965. Mem. faculty NYU, 1965—, assoc. prof. art history, 1973-78, prof., 1978—; Frederic Lindley Morgan prof. U. Louisville, 2001. Author: Vitruvius de Architectura, 1521. 1969, Rockefeller Center, 1978, Synagogues of Europe, 1985, rev. edit., 1996, Gordon Bunshaft of Skidmore, Owings & Merrill, 1988, Europas Synagogen, 1988, Contemporary Native American Architecture, 1996; contbr. articles to profl. jours. Bd. dirs. Internat. Survey Jewish Monuments, Syracuse, N.Y., 1981—, Soc. Archtl. Historians, 1978-80, 86-89, The Mac Dowell Colony, Inc., 1989—, Jewish Heritage Coun. World Monuments Fund; co-chair seminar on the city Columbia U., 1993-95. Am. Coun. Learned Socs. grantee, 1981, Nat. Endowment for the Arts grantee, 1993; recipient Arnold Brunner award N.Y.C. chpt. AIA, 1990. Fellow Soc. Archtl. Historians (pres. 1984-86, pres. NYC chpt. 1977-79); mem. Coll. Art Assn. (Disting. Tchg. of Art History award 2004), Planning History Group, Am. Urban History Assn., Internat. Ctr. Medieval Art, Women's City Club, Phi Beta Kappa. Office: NYU Dept Fine Arts 100 Washington Sq E New York NY 10003-6688 Office Phone: 212-998-8186. Business E-Mail: chk1@nyu.edu.

KRINSKY, DAVID A., lawyer; b. 1948; BA, U. So. Calif, 1969; MA, Rutgers U., 1970; JD, U. So. Calif., 1973. Bar: Calif. 1973. Ptnr., office head O'Melveny & Myers LLP, Menlo Park, Calif., ptnr. Newport Beach, Calif., mem. policy com. Mem. So. Calif. Law Review, 1972—73. Eagleton Fellowship. Office: O'Melveny & Myers LLP 2765 Sand Hill Rd Menlo Park CA 94025-7019 Address: O'Melveny & Myers LLP 610 Newport Center Dr 17th Fl Newport Beach CA 92660 Office Phone: 650-473-2626, 949-823-7902. Office Fax: 650-473-2601, 949-823-6994. Business E-Mail: dkrinsky@omm.com.

KRINSKY, ROBERT DANIEL, consulting firm executive; b. Bklyn., Jan. 24, 1937; s. Milton and Josephine E. (Bachrach) K.; m. Carol M. Herselle, Jan. 25, 1959; children: Alice E., John D. BA, Antioch Coll., 1957. Various actuarial positions The Segal Co., N.Y.C., 1954-65, v.p. to exec. v.p., 1966-82, pres., 1982-93, chmn., 1994—; bd. dirs. Wiss, Janney, Elster Assocs., Inc., 2003—. Mem. working com. Nat. Coordinating Com. for Multi-employer Pension Plans, Washington, 1982—. Trustee Antioch U., Yellow Springs, Ohio, 1983-2002, chmn., 1993-2002; trustee Moses L. Parshelsky Found., 1982—; bd. dirs. Harbor Festival Found., N.Y.C., 1983-87; chmn. Conf. Bd. Chmn. Small Liberal Arts Colls. and Univs., 2000-02; bd. dirs. Elderhostel, Inc., 2001-, vice chmn., 2003-2004, chmn., 2004—. Asst. health svc. officer USPHS, 1959-61. Fellow Conf. Actuaries in Pub. Practice; mem. Am. Acad. Actuaries, Soc. Actuaries (assoc.), Assn. Pvt. Pension and Welfare Plans (bd. dirs. 1982—, chmn. 1988-89), Nat. Dance Inst. (bd. dirs. 1987—, chmn. 1988-89, 93-2003), Musica Sacra (bd. dirs. 2003-), Century Assn. Office: The Segal Co 1 Park Ave New York NY 10016-5895 Personal E-mail: rdkactbird@aol.com. Business E-Mail: rKrinsky@segalco.com.

KRINSKY, SHARON FRANCES, editor, writer, librarian; b. Bronx, NY, June 5, 1945; d. Nathan and Dorothy (Rosen) K. BA, Queens Coll., 1966; MLS, Pratt Inst., 1993. Registration supr. New Sch. Social Rsch., NYC, 1975-78; ind. contractor editl. svs., 1980—; asst. editor H.W. Wilson Co., Bronx, 1993-98; libr. Mercy Coll, NYC, 1999—2000; reference libr. NY Inst. Tech., 2000—02, Channel Thirteen, WNET, 2002—03; asst. copy chief Disney Pub. Worldwide, 2004—. Author: The Ruddy Duck, 1995; contbr. Best American Poetry of 1992; contbr. poetry to jours.; contbg author: Twenty Stories by Eighteen Authors, 1996. Vol. Am. Coun. Arts Libr., 1990-91, Poets House, 1992. Mem. Internat. Women's Writing Guild, Assn. Coll. and Rsch. Librs., Am. Assn. Museums Avocations: multi-media artist, poetry performance. Office Phone: 212-727-4874. E-mail: sharon.krinsky@disney.com.

KRIPPNER, STANLEY CURTIS, psychologist; b. Edgerton, Wis., Oct. 4, 1932; s. Carroll Porter and Ruth Genevieve (Volenberg) Krippner; m. Lelie Anne Harris, June 25, 1966 (div. 2002). BS, U. Wis., 1954; MA, Northwestern U., 1957, PhD, 1961; PhD (hon.), U. Humanistic Studies, San Diego, 1982. Diplomate Am. Bd. Sexology. Speech therapist Warren Pub. Schs. (Ill.), 1954-55, Richmond Pub. Schs. (Va.), 1955-56; dir. Child Study Ctr. Kent (Ohio) State U., 1961-64; dir. dream lab. Maimonides Med. Ctr., Bklyn., 1964-73; prof. of psychology Saybrook Grad. Sch., San Francisco, 1973—. Adj. prof. psychology Calif. Inst. Human Sci., 1994—; vis. prof. U. P.R., 1972, Sonoma State U., 1972-73, U. Life Scis., Bogota, Colombia, 1974, Inst. for Psychodrama and Humanistic Psychology, Caracas, Venezuela, 1975, State U. West Ga., 1976, John F. Kennedy U., 1980-82, Inst. for Rsch. in Biopsychophysics, Curitiba, Brazil, 1990; adj. prof. Calif. Inst. Integral Studies, 1991-97; lectr. Acad. Pedagogical Scis., Moscow, 1971, Acad. Scis., Beijing, 1981, Minas Gerais U., Belo Horizonte, Brazil, 1986-87. Author: (with Montague Ullman) Dream Telepathy, 1973, rev. edit., 1989, Song of the Siren: A Parapsychological Odyssey, 1975, (with Alberto Villoldo) The Realms of Healing, 1976, rev. edit., 1987, 2003, Human Possibilities, 1980, (with Jerry Solfvin) La Science et les Pouvoirs Psychiques de l'Homme, 1986, (with Alberto Villoldo) Healing States, 1987, (with Joseph Dillard) Dreamworking, 1988, (with David Feinstein) Personal Mythology, 1988, (with Patrick Welch) Spiritual Dimensions of Healing, 1992, (with Dennis Thong and Bruce Carpenter) A Psychiatrist in Paradise, 1993, (with David Feinstein) The Mythic Path, 1997, (with Andre de Carvalho) Sonhos Exoticos, 1998, (with Fariba Bogzaron and Andre de Carvalho) Extraordinary Dreams and How to Work with Them, 2002, (with Stephen Kierulff) Becoming Psychic, 2004; editor: Advances in Parapsychological Research, Vol. 1, 1977, Vol. 2, 1978, Vol. 3, 1982, Vol. 4, 1984, Vol. 5, 1987, Vol. 6, 1990, Vol. 7, 1994, Vol. 8, 1997, Psychoenergetic Systems, 1979, Dreamtime and Dreamwork, 1990; co-editor: Galaxies of Life, 1973, The Kirlian Aura, 1974, The Energies of Consciousness, 1975, (with Susan Powers) Future Science, 1977, Broken Images, Broken Selves, 1997, (with Mark Waldman) Dreamscaping, 1999, (with Etzel Cardeña and Steven J. Lynn) Varieties of Anomalous Experience, 2000, (with Teresa McIntyre) The Psychological Effects of War Trauma on Civilians, 2003; mem. editl. bd. Alternative Therapies in Health and Medicine, Jour. Humanistic Psychology, Jour. Transpersonal Psychology, Jour. Indian Psychology, Dream Network, Humanistic Psychologist; contbr. 1000 articles to profl. jours Mem. Joseph Plan Found.; Bd. dirs., adv. bd. Acad. Religion and Phys. Rsch., Survival Rsch. Found., Hartley Film Found. Recipient Svc. to Youth award YMCA, 1959, Citation of Merit Nat. Assn. Creative Children and Adults, 1975, Cert. Recognition Office Gifted and Talented, U.S. Office Edn., 1976, Volker medal South Africa Soc. Psychical Rsch., 1980, Bicentennial medal U. Ga., 1985, Charlotte and Karl Bühler award, 1992, Dan Overlade Meml. award, 1994, Humanist of Yr. award Ch. of Humanism, 1996, Career Achievement award Parapsychol. Assn., 1998, J.B. Rhine Award, 2002, Ashley Montagu Peace prize, 2003; named to Wisdom Hall of Fame, 2001. Fellow APA (pres. divsn. 32, 1980, pres. divsn. 30, 1997, Disting. Contbns. to Profl. Hypnosis award 2002, Disting. Contbns. to Internat. Advancement of Psychology award 2002), Am. Soc. Clin. Hypnosis, Am. Psychol. Soc., Soc. Sci. Study Religion, Soc. Sci. Study Sexuality, Western Psychol. Assn.; mem. AAAS, ACA, Am. Soc. Psychical Rsch., Am. Ednl. Rsch. Assn., Internat. Coun. Psychologists, Assn. for Study of Dreams (pres. 1993-94), Soc. for the Anthropology Consciousness, Inter-Am. Psychol. Assn., Assn. Humanistic Psychology (pres. 1974-75), Assn. Transpersonal Psychology, Internat. Soc. Hypnosis, Internat. Soc. for Study of Dissociation, Nat. Assn. for Gifted Children, Sleep Rsch. Soc., Soc. Sci. Exploration, Biofeedback Soc. Am., Coun. Exceptional Children, Soc. Accelerative Learning and Tchg., Soc. Gen. Sys. Rsch., Swedish Soc. Clin. and Exptl. Hypnosis, Western Psychol. Assn., Internat. Soc. Gen. Semantics, Menninger Found., Nat. Soc. Study of Edn., Parapsychol. Assn. (pres. 1983), Soc. Clin. and Exptl. Hypnosis, World Future Soc. Office: Saybrook Grad Sch 747 Front St 3rd Fl San Francisco CA 94111 Business E-Mail: skrippner@saybrook.edu.

KRISCH, ALAN DAVID, physics professor; b. Phila., Apr. 19, 1939; s. Kube and Jeanne (Freiberg) K.; m. Jean Peck, Aug. 27, 1961; 1 child, Kathleen Susan. AB, U. Pa., 1960; PhD, Cornell U., 1964. Instr. Cornell U., 1964; mem. faculty U. Mich., Ann Arbor, 1964—, assoc. prof. high energy physics, 1966-68, prof., 1968—, dir. Spin Physics Ctr., 1994—. Vis. prof. Niels Bohr Inst., Copenhagen, 1975-76; trustee Argonne Nat. Lab., 1972-73, 80-82, chmn. zero gradient syncrotron users group, 1973-75, 78-79, chmn. internat. com. for high energy spin physics symposia, 1977-94, past chmn., 1995—, chmn. organizing com. conf. on particle and nuclear physics intersections, 1983-86, mem., 1987-91, hon. mem., 1994—; chmn.-elect, chmn. IUCF Users Group, 1997-2002; spokesperson NEPTUN-A Expt. at 400 GeV UNK accelerator in Russia, 1989-99, SPIN collaboration Fermilab, 1991-95, SPIN at HERA collaboration DESY in Germany, 1996-99, SPINatU-70 Exp. at 70 Gev IHEP accelerator in Protvino, Russia, 2000—, SPIN at COSY Expt. COSY accelerator, Jülich, Germany, 2002-, SPIN at J-PARC Collaboration, Tokai, Japan, 2003—. Trustee Ann Arbor Hands On Mus., 1999—. Fellow NSF, 1963, Guggenheim Found., 1971-72, Denmark Nat. Bank, 1975-76. Fellow Am. Phys. Soc.; mem. AAAS. Achievements include discovery of heavy elementary particles, of structure within the proton, of scaling in inclusive reactions, of spinning core within proton, of large spin forces in violent proton collisions, of precise confirmation of large spin forces; invention of inclusive reactions; development of first high energy spin-polarized proton beam, of first strong focusing spin-polarized proton beam; demonstration of "Siberian snake" technique for accelerating spin-polarized beams; first spin-flipping of polarized boson beam. Office: U Mich Randall Lab Ann Arbor MI 48109-1120

KRISE, THOMAS WARREN, academic administrator; b. Fort Sam Houston, Tex., Oct. 27, 1961; s. Edward Fisher and Elizabeth Ann (Bradt) K.; m. Patricia Lynn Love, Sept. 5, 1987. BS, USAF Acad., 1983; MSA, Cen. Mich. U., 1986; MA, U. Minn., 1989; PhD, U. Chgo., 1995. Commd. 2d lt. USAF, 1983, advanced through grades to lt. col.; dep. missile comdr. 742d Strategic Missile Squadron, Minot AFB, N.D., 1983-85, missile crew comdr., 1985-86, ICBM flight comdr., 1986-87; instr. English USAF Acad., Colorado Springs, 1989-91, asst. prof., 1991-92, 97-99, assoc. prof., 1999—2002, prof., 2002—05; prof. and chair dept. English U. Ctrl. Fla., 2005—. Sr. mil. fellow Inst. Nat. Strategic Studies, 1995—97; vice-dir. Nat. Def. U. Press, 1995—97; dir. English program USAF Acad., 1997—2000, dir. core lit. program, 1998—2000; dir. Air Force Humanities Inst., 1997—2005, pres. faculty forum, 2003—05; vis. prof. U. W.I., Mona, Jamaica, 1999; prof., chair dept. English U. of Ctrl. Fla., 2005—. Asst. editor: War, Lit. and the Arts, 1991—92, assoc. editor:, 1998—2003, mng. editor:, 2003—05, gen. editor: McNair Papers monograph series, 1995—97, Caribbeana: An Anthology of English Literature of the West Indies 1657-1777, 1999; contbr. articles to profl. jours. Adult literacy tutor Coalition for Adult Literacy, Colorado Springs, 1989-91, literacy tutor trainer, Adult Literacy Network, Colorado Springs, 1991-92 Recipient Pres.' Student Leadership award U. Minn., 1989; Summer Inst. grantee Nat. Endowment for the Humanities, 1990, Seiler Rsch. grantee F.J. Seiler Rsch. Lab., A.F. Systems Command, 1991, Faculty Rsch Com. grantee, 1998-2003, Salzburg Seminar grantee, 2003, Rsch. grant USAF Inst. Nat. Security Studies, 1998, 99, CBS Bicentennial Narrators scholar, 1994; Fulbright fellow, 1999. Mem.: MLA, SAR (Pikes Peak chpt. pres. 1991—92), Assn. Grads. USAF Acad. (bd. dirs. 1991—95, Chgo. chpt. pres. 1993—95), Mil. Officers Assn. Am., Royal United Svcs. Inst. Def. Studies, Soc. Early Americanists (exec. coord. 2003—05), Soc. 18th Century Am. Studies (sec.-treas. 1995—99), Am. Soc. 18th Century Studies (conf. dir. 2002), Colorado Springs Adult Literacy Network (pres. 1991—92), Royal Air Force Club (London), Army and Navy Club (Washington), Toastmasters Internat. (U. Minn. chpt. pres. 1988—89), Phi Kappa Phi. Episcopalian. Avocations: travel, sailing, skiing, hiking, scuba diving. Home: 2001 Cove Trl Winter Park FL 32789 Office: Dept English Univ Ctrl Florida Orlando FL 32816-1346 Office Phone: 407-823-1159. E-mail: tkrise@mail.ucf.edu, krisetw@hotmail.com.

KRISHER, BERNARD, foreign correspondent; b. Frankfurt, Germany, Aug. 9, 1931; s. Joseph and Fella (Solnica) K.; m. Akiko Yaginuma, May 1, 1960; children: Deborah, Joseph. BA, Queens Coll., 1953; postgrad., Columbia U., 1961-62. From staffwriter to asst. editor mag. N.Y. World-Telegram & Sun, 1955-61; corr. Newsweek, 1963—, bur. chief Tokyo, 1968-80; corr. Fortune, 1981-83; chief editl. advisor Focus Weekly Mag. Shincho-sha Pub. Co., Tokyo, 1981-97; editl. advisor Dohosha Pub. Co., Kyoto and Tokyo, 1984-98; editor at large Japan Avenue, 1991-94; editor at large Asia Wired mag., 1993-98; founder, pub. The Cambodia Daily, Phnom Penh, 1993—; editl. dir. Future Book series Tachibana Pub. Co., Tokyo, 1998—. Hon. rsch. assoc., vis. scholar East Asian Rsch. Ctr., Harvard U., 1978-79; Far East rep. The Media Lab. MIT, 1987—. Author: (with Alan Levy) Draftee's Confidential Guide, 1957, Interview, 1976, The Plus and Minuses of Being Japanese, 1978, Harvard Diary, 1979, How Harvard Sees Japan, 1979, We Who Lived in Japan, 1986; (with King Norodom Sihanouk) Charisma and Leadership, 1990, (with Cambodia Daily staff) A Vision for a New Asia, 2003. Founder, vol. chmn. Japan Relief for Cambodia, 1992—; vol. chmn. Am. Assistance for Cambodia, 1993—, Internet Appeal for N. Korean Flood Victims, 1995—; chmn. Sihanouk Hosp.- Ctr. of Hope, Phnom Penh, Cambodia, 1996—. Recipient Gleitsman Internat. Activist award, 2001, Iue Asia Pacific Culture prize, 2003. Mem Coun. Fgn. Rels. Home: 4-1-7-605 Hiroo Shibuya-ku Tokyo 150-0012 Japan Office Phone: 011-81-3-3486-4337. E-mail: bernie@krisher.com.

KRISHNA, KISHORE BELLAMKONDA, biomedical researcher, educator; b. Visakhapatnam, India, Aug. 2, 1953; s. Dharma Rao and Kamala Devi Bellamkonda; m. Ratnavathi Rolla, Feb. 24, 1989; children: Satya, Dharma. MBBS, Sri Venkateswara U., Tirupathi, India, 1975; MD, Banaras Hindu U., Varanasi, India, 1980; PhD in Biomed Scis., Cath. U. Louvain, Belgium, 1990. Med. registration Andhra Med. Coun., India, 1975. Asst. prof. pharmacology Cath. U. Louvain, Brussels, 1991-92; vis. fellow NLHBI/NIH, Bethesda, 1993-97; rsch. asst., prof. medicine divsn. nephrology and hypertension U. Cin. Med. Ctr., 1997-2001; rsch. assoc. prof. medicine nephrology and hypertension U. Utah Health Scis. Ctr., Salt Lake City, 2001—04. Mem. R&D com. Salt Lake City Healthcare System; ad hoc mem. study sect. NIH. Mem. editl. bd. Am. Jour. Physiology; contbr. articles. Fellow Japanese Ministry of Edn., Sci. and Culture, 1981-83, Internat. Inst. Cellular and Molecular Pathology, Belgium, 1987-89, Sci. Devel. Found. Cath. U. Louvain, 1989-91. Fellow: Am. Soc. Nephrology; mem.: AHA, Nat. Kidney Found., Am. Physiol. Soc., Internat. Soc. Nephrology, Inst. Biology (chartered biologist 1988), Smithsonian Inst. Hindu. Avocations: classical music, photography, philosophical reading. Office: U Utah Health Scis Ctr Rm 4R312 50 N Medical Dr Salt Lake City UT 84132 Office Fax: (801) 581-4343. E-mail: BK.Kishore@hsc.utah.edu.

KRISHNAKUMAR, AMBIKA, education educator; d. Ravndranathan and Vijaylakshmi Nayar. PhD, U. Tenn., 1992—97; BS with honors, Jadavpur U., 1984, MS in Child Devel., 1986. Contbr. articles to profl. jours.; manuscript rev. Jour. Develop. Psychology, Jour. Family Rels., Jour. Clin. Child Psychology, Jour. Child and Family Studies, Jour. Pediat. Psychology. Mem. YWCA bd., 2001. Recipient Chancellor's Citation for Extraordinary Profl. Promise, 1996, U. medal for standing first in the order of merit in child develop.,

Jadavpur U., 1987. Mem.: Soc. for Child Develop., Soc. for Rsch. on Adolescence, Nat. Coun. Family Rels. Office: Syracuse U 202 Slocum Hall Syracuse NY 13244 Office Phone: 315-443-4293.

KRISHNAMACHARI, BHASKAR, electrical engineer, educator; b. Sept. 10, 1977; BS in Elec. Engring., Cooper Union for Advancement of Sci. and Art, N.Y.C., 1998; MS in Elec. Engring., Cornell U., Ithaca, N.Y., 1999, PhD in Elec. Engring., 2002. Postdoctoral rschr. Sch. Elec. & Computer Engring., Cornell U., Ithaca, NY, 2002; asst. prof., dept. elec. engring. sys. U. So. Calif., L.A., 2002—. Contbr. articles to profl. jours., chapters to books. Grantee, NSF, 2003—, Bosch, 2003, Intel, 2003. Mem.: Eta Kappa Nu, Tau Beta Pi. Achievements include research in modeling, analysis, and design of wireless sensor networks; networked multi-agent systems. Office: Univ So Calif 3740 McClintock Ave Los Angeles CA 90089

KRISHNAMURTHY, RAMESH SALIGRAMA, environmental scientist, researcher; s. Saligrama RajaRao Krishnamurthy and K. G. Leelavathy; 1 child, Ravi James Cullop. BSc, Bangalore U., 1981—84; BS, Oreg. State U., Corvallis, 1989, MA, 1992, MS, 1994; Ph.D., U. Oreg., Eugene, 1999; MPH, UCLA, 2005. Rsch. asst. Indian Inst. Sci., Bangalore; radio prodr. Oreg. Pub. Broadcasting, Corvallis, Oreg., 1992—95; rsch. scientist Internat. Inst. Human Evolutionary Rsch., Bend, 1995—99; dir. Linus Pauling collection Oreg. State U., Corvallis; assoc. prof. and asst. dean U. Pacific, Stockton, Calif., 1999—2005; pub. health informatics scientist Ctrs. Disease Control & Prevention, Atlanta, 2005—. Health rsch. scientist and project dir. VA, L.A., Calif., 2005. Editor: Innovative Environmental Technology Evaluation and Commercialization. Technology, History of Atomic Energy Collection at Oregon State University: A Catalogue of Holdings, Linus Pauling on Peace, Pauling Symposium: A Discourse on the Art of Biography. Gov. UN Assn., N.Y.C., 1994—97; dir. and dep. permanent rep. to the UN Resource Ctr. for the UN, San Francisco, 1999—2004; dir. Ashoka Trust Rsch. in Ecology and the Environ., Boston, 1999—2003. Recipient Clara L. Simerville award, Oreg. State U., 1993, Recognition plaque, Coll. Pharmacy and the Linus Pauling Inst. Oreg. State U., 1998, Outstanding Tchr. of Yr., U. Pacific Sch. Internat. Studies, 2001—02; fellow Fulbright-Hays Seminar Abroad Program - Rwanda, U.S. Dept. Edn., 2004; Betsy Dana scholar, UN Office World Federalist Movement, 1993, Internat. Trade and Devel. Grad. fellow, Oreg. State Sys. Higher Edn., 1992, 1995. Mem.: APHA (assoc.; internat. health sect. 2005—), Hon. Order Ky. Cols. Achievements include research in health Informatics and international public health. Home: 1448 W Alpine Ave Stockton CA 95204 Office: Ctrs Disease Control & Prevention Atlanta GA

KRISHNAN, HEMA A., finance educator; b. Coimbatore, India, June 28, 1961; arrived in U.S., 1989; d. Ananthakrishnan Sekaripuram and Anandam Krishnan; m. Babu Viswanathan, June 24, 1993; 1 child, Naveen. MS, Indian Inst. Tech., New Delhi, 1982; MBA, Indian Inst. Mgmt., Bangalore, 1988; PhD, U. Tenn., 1993. Sales officer Hindustan Petroleum Corp., Madras, India, 1983—86, regional coord., 1988—89; grad. asst. U. Tenn., Knoxville, 1989—93; asst. prof. Xavier U., Cin., 1993—98, assoc. prof., 1998—. Contbr. articles to profl. jours. Mem.: Strategic Mgmt. Soc., Acad. Mgmt., Beta Gamma Sigma. Avocations: reading, music. Office: Xavier U 3800 Victory Pky Cincinnati OH 45207 E-mail: krishnan@xavier.edu.

KRISHNAN, USHA, pediatrician, cardiologist, educator; d. Mahadeva and Bhanumati Sundaram; m. Sankaran Krishnan; children: Sheila, Amit. MD, Seth Gordhandas Sunderdas Med. Coll., Bombay, 1985. Diplomate Am. Bd. Pediatric Cardiology. Chief pediat. cardiologist Inst. Cardiovasc. Diseases, Madras, 1997—2001; asst prof. N.Y. Med. Coll., Valhalla, 2001—. Contbr. multiple pubs. peer rev. jours., invited articles jours., books, and presentations internat. confs. Office: NY Med Coll 618 Munger Pavilion Valhalla NY 10595 Office Phone: 914-594-4370.

KRISHNASWAMY, DILIP, computer architect; s. N. and S. Krishnaswamy. BTech in Electronics and Comm., Indian Inst. Tech., Madras, 1991; MS in Computer Sci., Syracuse U., 1993; PhDEE, U. Ill., 1997. Vis. rschr. Ctr. Theoretical Studies, Indian Inst. Sci., Bangalore, 1990—90; vis. rschr. Thomas J Watson Rsch. Ctr. IBM, Yorktown Heights, NY, 1994; vis. rschr. Cadence Design Sys., San Jose, Calif., 1996; arch. Intel Corp., Folsom, Calif., 1997—; part-time tchg. faculty U. Calif., Davis, 1998—2005. Program com. mem. and session chair High Performace Computing Com., Calcutta, West Bengal, India, 1999; tech. program com. mem. Internat. MultiConf. Computer Sci. and Engring., Las Vegas, 2002—04; program com. mem. Systemics, Cybernetics and Informatics, Orlando, 2002—; vice-chair, design and developers forum, 48th ieee global comm. conf. IEEE Comm. Conf., New York, NY, 2005—; tech. program com. mem., 3G wireless conf. Delson Group, San Francisco, 2002—; session chair design and developers forum IEEE Globecom, San Francisco, 2003, session chair, design and developers forum, Dallas, 04; session chair, tech. program com. mem. IEEE MMNS, San Diego, 2004; tech. program com. mem. Internat. MultiConference in Computer Sci. and Engring., Las Vegas, 2002—04. Contbr. numerous articles to profl. jours., chapters to books. Fellow, Syracuse U., 1991—93. Mem.: IEEE (VLSI Test Symposium Com. Best Paper award 1998), IEEE Comm. Soc. (vice-chair tech. com. on design and devel. 2003—, session chair 56th vehicular tech. conf., co-chair, 49th global comm. conf. expo tech. program 2005—), IEEE Computer Soc. Achievements include design of Intel PXA800F cellular processor, presented at IEEE HotChips Conference at Stanford, 2003; patents pending for adaptive wireless networks and methods for communicating multimedia in a proactive enterprise; network aware cross-layer protocol methods and apparatus. Home: 406 Anacapa Dr Roseville CA 95678 Office: Intel Corp 1900 Prairie City Rd Folsom CA 95630 Office Phone: 916-356-2829.

KRISLOV, MARVIN, lawyer, educator; b. Balt., Aug. 24, 1960; s. Joseph and Evelyn (Moreida) K.; m. Amy Ruth Sheon, Aug. 25, 1993; children: Zachary Jacob, Jesse Harris, Eve Rose. BA in Econs. summa cum laude, Yale U., 1982; BA/MA in Modern History, Oxford (Eng.) U., 1985; JD, Yale U., 1988. Bar: Calif. 1988, D.C. 1989, Mich. 1999. Law clk to Judge Marilyn Hall Patel U.S. Dist. Ct. (no. dist.) Calif., San Francisco, 1988-89; trial atty. civil rights divsn. U.S. Dept. Justice, Washington, 1989-93; spl. asst. U.S. atty. U.S. Atty.'s Office, Washington, 1989-90; spl. counsel Office of Counsel to the Pres., Washington, 1993-94, asst. counsel, 1994, assoc. counsel, 1995-96; dep. solicitor U.S. Dept. Labor, Washington, 1996-98, acting solicitor, 1997-98; v.p., gen. counsel U. Mich., Ann Arbor, 1998—. Adj. prof. law, George Washington U. Law Sch., Washington, 1991-93; adj. prof. U. Mich. Law Sch., 2000—, U. Mich. polit. sci. dept., 2001—. Mem. New Haven Bd. Aldermen, 1982-83. Rhodes scholar, 1983. Mem. Phi Beta Kappa. Office: U Mich 4010 Fleming Adminstrn Bldg Ann Arbor MI 48109-1340

KRISS, GARY W(AYNE), priest; b. Balt., Dec. 29, 1946; s. Warren B. and Margaret L. (Austin) K. AB cum laude, Dartmouth Coll., 1968; MDiv, Yale U. Divinity Sch., 1972; postgrad. studies, The Gen. Theol. Sem., N.Y.C., 1972, St. George Coll., Jerusalem, 1978; DD, Nashotah House, 2001. Ordained to ministry Episcopal Ch. as deacon, 1972, as priest 1972. Chaplain to the congregation Cathedral Ch. of St. Paul, Burlington, Vt., 1972-74; coord. Rock Point (Vt.) Summer Confs., 1973-77; vicar St. Mark's, St. Luke's Parishes, Castleton and Fair Haven, Vt., 1974-78; asst. to dean The Cathedral of All Saints, Albany, N.Y., 1978-79, canon precentor, 1979-84, dir. inst. Christian studies, 1979-84; dean Cathedral of All Saints, Albany, 1984-91; dean and pres. Nashotah (Wis.) House, 1992—2001; interim rector St. Paul's Epis. Ch., Troy, NY, 2001—02, assoc. priest, 2002—04; vicar St. Paul's Ch., Salem, NY, 2003—. Bd. dirs. Brookhaven Home for Boys, Chelsea, Vt., 1975-79, Albany Collegiate Interfaith Ctr., 1982-90, pres. 1984-90; Episcopal campus priest, SUNY, Albany, 1980-84; bd. dirs. Capital Area Coun. of Chs., Albany, N.Y., 1989-91, chmn. of Faith and Learning Commn.; The Living Ch. Found., 1994—. Bd. dirs. Samaritan Shelters, Glenmont, N.Y., 1979-91, The Child's Hosp., Albany, 1986-90, Child's Nursing Home, Albany, 1987-91, pres. 1990-91. Episcopalian. Home and Office: PO Box 26 Cambridge NY 12816

KRISS, PATRICIA ANNE, health services executive; b. Syracuse, N.Y., Oct. 14, 1947; d. John Casimir and Annette Elizabeth (Burns) Miod; m. Gary Frederick Kriss, June 21, 1969. BA in Fine Arts and Edn., Coll. of New Rochelle, 1969. Psychiat. geriatric therapist N.Y. Hosp./Cornell U., White Plains, 1971-74; cmty. affairs coord. Assn. Vis. Nurse Svcs., White Plains, 1975-77; dir. pub. rels. and devel. St. Joseph's Med. Ctr., Yonkers, N.Y., 1977-82; chief devel. officer Lawrence Hosp., Bronxville, N.Y., 1982-90; devel. dir. Whitby Sch., Greenwich, Conn., 1990-94; asst. exec. dir. Stamford (Conn.) Orch., 1994; dir. cmty. affairs Vis. Nurse Svcs. of Conn., Bridgeport, 1994-98; found. exec. dir. Nursing & Home Care, Wilton, Conn., 1998—. Pres. Kristal Inkwell Cons., South Salem, N.Y., 1977—; lectr. in field. One woman show at Syracuse, 1975; exhibited in Second Ch., 1987; contbr. articles to Greenwich Mag., cartoons to Saturday Review. Organizer Afghanistan surgery effort Americares, Bronxville, N.Y., 1988; Stephen min. Second Congl. Ch., Greenwich, 1996—; chmn. conservation adv. coun. Town of Lewisboro, 1988-93; outreach chmn. Guatemala Heart Team, Greenwich, 1993; chmn. Conservation Adv. Coun., Lewisboro, 1988-93; mem. Wetlands Commn., Lewisboro, 1990-95. N.Y. Regents scholar, 1965; recipient Blue Ribbon Union Carbide Art Show, 1968; fellow Tchrs. Coll. Columbia U., 1969, Healthcare Mktg. award, 1996, 1997. Mem. St. Andrew's Soc., bd. dirs. Ridgefield Guild Artists. Avocations: birdwatching, conservation, bicycling, triathlon, antiques. Home: 169 Laurel Rdg South Salem NY 10590-2407 Office: Nursing Home Care Inc 180 School St PO Box 489 Wilton CT 06897-0489

KRISS, ROBERT J., lawyer; b. Cleve., Dec. 15, 1953; BA summa cum laude, Cornell U., 1975; JD cum laude, Harvard U., 1978. Bar: Ill. 1978, U.S. Dist. Ct. (no. dist.) Ill. 1978, U.S. Ct. Appeals (7th cir.) 1983, U.S. Dist. Ct. (no. dist. trial bar) Ill. 1982. Ptnr. Mayer, Brown, Rowe & Maw LLP, Chgo. Presenter in field; adj. prof. trial practice Northwestern U. Law Sch. Author: short story (semi-finalist Faukner Creative Writing Competition, 2004). Chmn. consent degree task force Chgo. Park Dist., 1986-87; bd. dirs. Chgo. Legal Assistance Found., 1996-2000, Victory Gardens Theater, 2003-04. Mem. Nat. Inst. Trial Advocacy (faculty midwest regional program 1988-91, 94), Winnetka Caucus (chmn. schs. candidate selection com. 1997). Avocation: writing. Office: Mayer Brown Rowe & Maw 190 S La Salle St Ste 3100 Chicago IL 60603-3441 Office Phone: 312-701-7165. Business E-Mail: rkriss@mayerbrown.com.

KRISTENSEN, DOUGLAS ALLAN, former state legislator; b. Kearney, Nebr., Jan. 4, 1955; s. Donald M. and Mary Lou (Martin) K.; m. Terri S. Harder; children: Morgan Claire, Paige Nicole. BA, U. Nebr., 1977; JD, Drake U., 1980. Ptnr. Lieske & Kristensen, 1981—; atty. Kearney County, 1982-88; mem. Nebr. Legislature from 37th dist., Lincoln, 1988—; chmn. transp. com. Nebr. Legislature, Lincoln, 1991-98, mem. intergovtl. coop. and revenue coms., mem. exec. bd., chair transp. com., 1991-97, speaker of the legislature, 1998—2002; chancellor U. Nebr., 2002—. Bd. dirs. young lawyers ssect. Nebr. Bar, 1984-88, Nebr. CLE Inc., 1986-90. Henry Toll fellow, 1991; recipient Pres.' award Nebr. Assn. County Ofcls., 1987. Mem. Nebr. Bar Assn., Iowa Bar Assn., Nebr. County Atty.'s Assn. (bd. dirs. 1985—), Rotary Internat., Optimists Club. Office: University of Nebraska at Kearney 905 W 25th St Lincoln NE 68849 Home: 219 N Brown Ave Minden NE 68959-1524

KRISTIANSEN, MAGNE, electrical engineer, educator; b. Elverum, Norway, Apr. 14, 1932; came to U.S., 1958, naturalized, 1967; s. Martin and Ella (Sobye) K.; m. Aud Bohn, July 6, 1957; children: Sonja Bohn, Eric Bohn. BS in Elec. Engring., U. Tex., Austin, 1961, PhD (Ford Found. fellow), 1967. Registered profl. engr., Tex. Rsch. engr. U. Tex., Austin, 1964-66; faculty Tex. Tech U., Lubbock, 1966—, prof., 1971—, dir. plasma lab., 1970—80; dir. pulsed power lab. Tex. Tech. U., 1980—2001, dir. Ctr. Pulsed Power and Power Electronics, 2001—; v.p. rsch. and engring. Enfitek, Inc., Lubbock, 1987-90; v.p. R & D Integrated Tech. Inc., Lubbock, 1990-98. Cons. def. products divsn. Varo, Inc., Garland, Tex., 1970-71; cons. Aerospace Corp., El Segundo, Calif., 1974-76, BDM Corp., Albuquerque, 1975-76, 85-87, Palisades Inst., N.Y. and NRC, 1977, Rockwell Internat., 1978, Maxwell Labs., 1979-83, LaJolla Inst., 1979, NASA, 1979, Norwegian Rsch. Coun., 1980, Sci. Applications, Inc., 1983-88, 91-92, Lawrence Livermore Nat. Lab., 1983-95, McDonnell Douglas, 1986, LTV Missiles and Electronics Group, 1987-89, NEA-Lindberg A/S, 1988, Physics Internat. Co., 1992-97, Rocket Rsch. Co., 1992, Swedish Def. Rsch. Inst., 1992-2000; Hazeltine Ocean Sys., 1995, Lockheed Martin, 1995-96, 2003, Integrated Technologies, Inc., 1998—; collaborator Los Alamos Nat. Lab., 1974-95, others; contractor DNA, 1986-97, NASA, 1990-2001, Wright Aeronautical Labs., 1994—. Co-author: An Introduction to Controlled Thermonuclear Fusion, 1977, Russian, Japanese, Chinese translations, 1980-81, Rotating Mirror Cameras, 1997; co-editor: Advances in Pulsed Power Technology, 1984—. Contbr. articles to profl. jours. Mem. USAF Sci. Adv. Bd., 1981-85. Served with Royal Norwegian Air Force, 1950-58. Recipient Meritorious Civilian Svc. award USAF, 1985, Excellence award Halliburton Found., 1994; grantee State of Tex., 1966-85, 88-94, NSF, 1967-87, AEC, 1968-71, Air Force Office Sci. Rsch., 1968—, Army Rsch. Lab., 1994-99, Dept. Energy, 1978-79; sr. fellow in sci. NATO, 1975, fellow Japan Soc. for Promotion Sci., 1979. Fellow IEEE (life, Pulsed Power Conf. Peter Haas award 1987, Nuc. and Plasma Sci. Soc. Merit award 1991, Millennium medal), Am. Phys. Soc.; mem. AAAS, Russian Acad. Scis. (fgn. mem., Ural sect.), Am. Soc. Engring. Edn., Sigma Xi, Tau Beta Pi, Eta Kappa Nu, Phi Kappa Phi. Home: 3105 78th St Lubbock TX 79423-1815 Office: Tex Tech U Dept Elec/Computer Engring Lubbock TX 79409-3102 Business E-Mail: m.kristiansen@ttu.edu.

KRISTIANSEN, UFFE STEEN, import/export company executive; b. Odense, Denmark, June 8, 1970; arrived in U.S., 2000; Export Engr., Bus. Sch., Denmark, 1996. Internal sales engr. Lachenmeier A/S, Sonderborg, Denmark, 1996—97; sales engr. Lachenmeier GmbH, Germany, 1997—99. Sales mgr. Maersk Industries, Denmark, 1999—2000; gen. mgr. Lachenmeier, Inc., Hollywood, Fla., 2000—; spkr. in field. Contbr. articles to profl. jours. Home: 1200 West Avenue PH6 Miami Beach FL 33139 Office: Lachenmeier Inc 3009 Greene Street Hollywood FL 33020 Office Phone: 954-925-0274. Office Fax: 954-925-0289.

KRISTIN, KAREN, artist; b. L.A., Aug. 27, 1943; d. Earle Barnard and Ann Maxine (Taylor) Immel; m. Richard Edward Amend, Aug. 21, 1976 (div. Aug. 1981); m. Gary Marchal Lloyd, Oct. 1, 1985 (div. Sept.1989). Student, Art Ctr. Coll. Design, 1961, Valley Jr. Coll., 1962, Pierce Jr. Coll., 1967, 68, UCLA, 1969, 70. Lectr. UCLA Ext. Program, 1973-76; scenic artist Hollywood, Calif., 1978-83; ptnr., designer, lead painter Sky Art Scenic Art Svcs., Hollywood, Calif., 1983-88; owner, pres., lead painter, designer Sky Art Karen Kristin, Inc., Englewood, Colo., 1989—. Spkr., lectr. in field. Co-author (under Karen Kristin Amend): Handwriting Analysis: The Complete Basic Book, 1980, Achieving Compatbility with Handwriting-Analysis, vol. I, Understanding Your Emotional Relationships, 1992, vol. II, Exploring Your Sexual Relationships, 1992; prin. murals include The Cirque Du Soleil Theater, Las Vegas, 1993, N.Mex. Mus. Natural History, 1989, 90, Forum Shops at Caesars, Las Vegas, 1992, 97, Kansas City Station Hotel and Casino, Kansas City, Mo., 1996, Sunset Station Hotel and Casino, Las Vegas, 1997, Venetian Hotel Grand Canal Shoppes, Las Vegas, 1998, Chaitanya Joti Mus., Puttaparthy, India, 2000, Hyatt Casino, Blackhawk, Colo., 2001, Argosy Casino, Kans. City, Mo., 2003, Rangeeli Mahal, Barsara, India, 2003, Boulder Sta. Casino, Las Vegas, 2004; sky art backdrops for numerous movies, commls., and TV. Mem. Am. Assn. Handwriting Analysts (spkr. 1991—), Am. Handwriting Analysis Found. (sprk. 1991—), Human Graphics Ctr., Graphex Internat. and Gold NIBS, Universal Soc. of Integral Why (mentor 1994—). Democrat. Avocations: photography, reading, travel, camping, fishing. Office: Sky Art Karen Kristin Inc 125 N Sligo Cortez CO 81321 Personal E-mail: skyartkk@aol.com.

KRISTOF, CINDY, librarian, educator; b. Lakewood, Ohio, Nov. 15, 1965; d. John J. and Ruth M. Kristof; m. R. Carmean, Sept. 29, 1990. BA in English, Ohio State U., 1989; MLS, Kent State U., 1995. Program asst. Eisenhower Nat. Clearinghouse, Columbus, Ohio, 1994-95, reference libr., 1995-96; assoc. prof. document delivery and distance learning libr. Kent (Ohio) State U., 1996—, head Access Svcs., 2005—. Author: (book) Electronic Reserve Operations in ARL Libraries: A SPEC Kit, 1999, (chpt.) The Role and the Impact of the Internet on Library and Information Services, 2001, (chpt.) Eletronic Reserves, Encyclopedia of Library and Information Science, 2003. Mem. ALA, AAUP, Assn. of Coll. and Rsch. Librs., Acad. Libr. Assn. Ohio (bd. dirs. 2000—), OCLC ILL and Illiad Users' Group, Beta Phi Mu. Office: Kent State U Librs PO Box 5190 Kent OH 44242 Office Phone: 330-672-1641. E-mail: ckristof@kent.edu.

KRISTOF, KATHY M., journalist; b. Burbank, Calif., Feb. 4, 1960; d. Joseph E. and Frances S. Kristof; m. Richard R. Magnuson, Jr., Jan. 4, 1986 (div.); 2 children. BA, U. So. Calif., L.A., 1983. Reporter L.A. Bus. Jour., 1984-88, Daily News, Woodland Hills, Calif., 1988-89, L.A. Times, 1989—; syndicated columnist L.A. Times Syndicate, 1991—. Author: Kathy Kristof's Complete Book of Dollars and Sense, 1997, Investing 101, 2000, Taming the Tuition Tiger, 2003; contbr. articles to mags. and profl. jours. Recipient John Hancock Fin. Svcs. award, 1992, Personal Fin. Writing award ICI/Am. U., 1994, Consumer Adv. of Yr., Calif. Alliance for Consumer Edn., 1998. Mem. Soc. Bus. Editors and Writers (pres. 2003), Calif. Newspapers Pubs. Assn. (2nd pl. Bus. and Fin. Story award 1999). Office: Los Angeles Times 202 W 1st St Los Angeles CA 90012 E-mail: kathy.kristof@latimes.com.

KRISTOF, LADIS KRIS DONABED, political scientist, writer; b. Cernauti, Romania, Nov. 26, 1918; came to U.S., 1952, naturalized, 1957; s. Witold and Maria (Zawadzki) Krzysztofowicz; m. Jane McWilliams, Dec. 29, 1956; 1 son, Nicholas. *My son, Nicholas D. Kristof, is a columnist for the New York Times; he has three children: Gregory (13), Geoffrey (11), and Caroline (7). They regularly spend vacations on our farm in Oregon.* Student, U. Poznan, Poland, 1937-39; BA, Reed Coll., Portland, Oreg., 1955; MA, U. Chgo., 1956, PhD, 1969. Regional exec. dir., Sovromlemn, Romania, 1948; sales mgr. Centre du Livre Suisse, Paris, France, 1951-52; lectr. U. Chgo., 1958-59; assoc. dir. Inter-Univ. Project History Menshevism, N.Y.C., 1959-62; mem. faculty dept. polit. sci. Temple U., 1962-64; research fellow Hoover Instn., Stanford U., 1964-67; faculty polit. sci. U. Santa Clara, 1967-68; asso. Studies Communist System, Stanford, 1968-69; mem. faculty polit. sci. U. Waterloo, Ont., Can., 1969-71; prof. polit. sci. Portland (Oreg.) State U., 1971-89, prof. emeritus, 1990—. Vis. prof. U. Wroclaw, Poland, 1990, U. Iasi, Romania, 1991, U. Punjab, India, 1992. *Now that I am retired, I regularly visit Romania - my country of origin - to give lectures and teach courses. I also visit my ancestral village of Karapchiv, now located in the Ukraine, where the old family home that was built by my grandfather serves as the village school, which I occasionally supply educational materials.* Author: The Nature of Frontiers and Boundaries, 1959, The Origins and Evolution of Geopolitics, 1960, The Russian Image of Russia, 1967, The Geopolitical Contours of the Post-Cold War World, 1992; also articles in Romania; co-author, co-editor: Revolution and Politics in Russia, 1972. Active Internat. YMCA Center, Paris, 1950-52, NAACP, Chgo., 1957-59, Amnesty Internat., Portland, 1975— . Served with Corps Engrs. Romanian Army, 1940-45. Fulbright scholar Romania, 1971, 84 Mem. Am. Polit. Sci. Assn., Assn. Am. Geographers, Am. Assn. for Advancement of Slavic Studies, Internat. Polit. Sci. Assn., Western Slavic Assn. (pres. 1988-90), Am.-Romanian Acad. Arts and Scis. (v.p. 1995-00). Home: 23050 NW Roosevelt Dr Yamhill OR 97148-8336 Office: Portland State Univ Dept Polit Sci Portland OR 97207 E-mail: kristofj@pdx.edu. *War, want and concentration camps, exile from home and homeland, these have made me hate strife among men, but they have not made me lose faith in the future of mankind. Personal experience, including my own unsteady progress through life, has taught me to beware of man's capacity for plain stupid, irrational, as well as consciously evil behavior, but it also has taught me that man has an even greater capacity for recovery from lapses. In a short thrust of planned, wisely guided activity he is able to climb to higher levels of material and intellectual achievement than he ever reached before. In short, I remain a rationalist and an optimist at a time when the prophets of doom have the floor. My query is, if man has been able to create the arts, the sciences and the material civilization we know in America, why should he be judged powerless to create justice, fraternity and peace.*

KRISTOF, NICHOLAS DONABET, journalist; b. Chgo., Apr. 27, 1959; s. Ladis K.D. and Jane (McWilliams) K.; m. Sheryl WuDunn; children: Gregory, Geoffrey, Caroline. BA, Harvard U., 1981; BA and MA in Law, U. Oxford, Eng., 1983; diploma in Arabic, Am. U. in Cairo, 1983-84; student, Taipei Lang. Inst., 1987-88. Econs. reporter N.Y. Times, N.Y.C., 1984-85, fin. corr. L.A. bur., 1985-86, chief Hong Kong bur., 1986-87, chief Beijing bur., 1988-93, chief Tokyo bur., 1995-99, sr. writer, 1993-2000, assoc. mng. editor, 2000—01, columnist, 2001—. Vis. fellow East-West Ctr., 1993; vis. scholar Linfield Coll., 1994, 99. Author: (with S. WuDunn) China Wakes: The Struggle for the Soul of a Rising Power, 1994, Thunder from the East: Portrait of a Rising Asia, 2000. Recipient Pulitzer prize for fgn. reporting, 1990, George Polk award for fgn. reporting L.I. U., N.Y., 1990, Hal Boyle award Overseas Press Club, 1990, Citations for Excellence, 1994, 96, 2000; Rhodes scholar, 1981-83. Avocations: travel, reading, running. Office: New York Times 229 W 43rd St New York NY 10036-3959

KRISTOFF, KARL W., lawyer; b. Buffalo, Mar. 31, 1942; BA, SUNY, Buffalo, 1965; JD, John Marshall Law Sch., 1968. Bar: Ill. 1968, U.S. Supreme Ct. 1974, N.Y. 1976. Ptnr., v.p. dipute resolution divsn., chair edn. law practice group Hodgson, Russ, LLP, Buffalo. Mem. editorial bd. The John Marshall Jour. Practice and Procedure, 1968, active, 1967. Mem. N.Y. Vets. Affairs Commn., 2002—. Maj. gen. ret. N.Y. Air N.G. Mem. Am. Arbitration Assn. (comml. panel arbitrators), Nat. Pub. Employer Labor Rels. Assn., Nat. Coun. Sch. Attys., N.Y. State Assn. Sch. Attys., N.Y. State Pub. Employer Labor Rels. Assn., Edn. Law Assn. Office: Hodgson Russ LLPr One M&T Plz Ste 2000 Buffalo NY 14203-2391 E-mail: kkristof@hodgsonruss.com.

KRISTOFFERSON, KRIS, singer, songwriter, actor; b. Brownsville, Tex., June 22, 1936; m. Fran Beir, 1960 (div. 1969), children: Tracy, Kris; m. Rita Coolidge, Aug. 19, 1973 (div.1980), 1 child, Casey.; m. Lisa Meyers, Feb. 19, 1983-, five children. BA in Creative Lit., Pomona Coll., 1958, D (hon.), 1974; Rhodes scholar, Oxford (Eng.) U., 1960. Worked at a variety of jobs in Nashville, including comml. helicopter pilot, 1965-69. Appeared at Newport (R.I.) Folk Festival, 1969, and on Johnny Cash TV program, 1970; concert and rec. artist, 1970—; albums recorded include Kristofferson, 1970, The Silver-Tongued Devil and I, 1971, Border Lord, Jesus Was a Capricorn, Spooky Lady's Sideshow, 1974, Big Sur Festival, Songs of Kristofferson, Who's to Bless and Who's to Blame, Easter Island, 1978, Shake Hands With the Devil, 1979, (with Rita Coolidge) Breakaway, Repossession, 1986, Third World Warrior, 1990, (with Highwaymen) Highwayman II, 1990, Singer, Songwriter, 1991, (with Willie Nelson, Rita Coolidge and Larry Gatlin) Live At The Philharmonic, 1992; actor (films): Cisco Pike, 1972, Pat Garrett and Billy the Kid, 1973, Blume in Love, 1973, Bring Me the Head of Alfredo Garcia, 1974, Alice Doesn't Live Here Anymore, 1974, The Sailor Who Fell From Grace With The Sea, 1976, A Star is Born, 1976, Vigilante Force, 1976, Semi-Tough, 1977, Convoy, 1978, Heaven's Gate, 1981, Rollover, 1981, Flashpoint, 1984, Songwriter, 1984, Trouble in Mind, 1985, Big Top Pee-Wee, 1988, Millennium, 1989, Welcome Home, 1989, Sandino, 1990, Night of the Cyclone, 1990, Knights, 1993, Paper Hearts, 1993, Lone Star, 1996, Fire Down Below, 1997, Girls Night, 1998, Blade, 1998, Dance with Me, 1998, Payback, 1999, The Joyriders, 1999, Planet of the Apes, 2001, Blade 2, 2002, Disappearances, 2004, Silver City, 2004, Blade Trinity, 2004, others; actor (TV Films): Freedom Road (miniseries), 1979, The Lost Honor of Kathryn Beck, 1984, Stagecoach, 1986, The Last Days of Frank and Jessie James, 1986, Blood and Orchids (miniseries), 1986, Amerika (miniseries), 1987, Miracle in the Wildnerness, 1991, Christmas in Connecticut, 1992, Bob Dylan 30th Anniversary Celebration, 1993, Tad 1995, America's Music: The Roots of Country Music (miniseries), 1996, Blue Rodeo, 1996, Dead Man's Gun, 1997, Two for Texas, 1998, Outlaw Justice, 1999, NetForce, 1999, Perfect Murder, Perfect Town: JonBenet and the City of Bolder, 2000, American Roots Music (miniseries), 2001, Lives of Saints (miniseries), 2003; performed (with Rita Coolidge) songs for soundtrack of The Last Movie,

1971; composer songs Sunday Morning Comin' Down, 1970 (Song of Year Country Music Assn.), Help Me Make It Through the Night, Me and Bobby McGee, (both nominated for Grammy award for Best Song 1971), Why Me, Lord, For the Good Times, Jody and the Kid, When I Loved Her. Capt. (helicopter pilot) U.S. Army, 1960—65. Named to Country Music Hall of Fame, Country Music Assn., 2004. Address: One Way 1 Prospect Ave PO Box 6429 Albany NY 12206-0429

KRISTY, JAMES E., financial consultant, consultant; b. Kenosha, Wis., Sept. 3, 1929; s. Eugene H. and Ann T. Kristy; m. Edith L. Reid, Feb. 19, 1955; children: James R., Ann E., Robert E. BS in Econs., U. Wis., 1951; MBA in Fin., U. So. Calif., 1964; postgrad., Claremont (Calif.) Grad. Sch.; PhD in Mgmt. and Edn., Columbia-Pacific U., 1981. V.p. Lloyds Bank Calif., L.A., 1969-71; chief treasury officer Computer Machinery Corp., L.A., 1971-75; sr. v.p., CFO Century Bank, L.A., 1979; vis. prof. Chapman U., 1995—. Cons., writer and lectr. in field; seminar leader Frost & Sullivan, London, CEL Ltd., Hong Kong, U. Calif., U. Hawaii, U. Colo., Temple U., Rutgers U., Tulane U. Author: Analyzing Financial Statements: Quick and Clean, 6th edit., 2003, Handbook of Budgeting, 1992; (with others) Finance Without Fear, 1983, Commercial Credit Matrix Software, 2002. 1st. lt. U.S. Army, 1951-53, Korea. Recipient Pub. Svc. award SBA, 1971. Address: PO Box 113 Buena Park CA 90621-0113 E-mail: edskrs@msn.com.

KRITCHEVSKY, DAVID, biochemist, educator; b. Kharkov, Russia, Jan. 25, 1920; arrived in U.S., 1923, naturalized, 1929; s. Jacob and Leah (Kritchevsky) K.; m. Evelyn Sholtes, Dec. 21, 1947; children: Barbara Ann, Janice Eileen, Stephen Bennett. BS, U. Chgo., 1939, MS, 1942; PhD, Northwestern U., 1948. Chemist Ninol Labs., Chgo., 1939-46; postdoctoral fellow Fed. Inst. Tech., Zurich, Switzerland, 1948-49; biochemist Radiation Lab., U. Calif., Berkeley, 1950-52, Lederle Lab., Pearl River, NY, 1952-57, Wistar Inst., Phila., 1957—; prof. biochemistry Sch. Vet. Medicine U. Pa., Phila., 1965—, prof. emeritus, 1992—, prof. biochemistry Sch. Medicine, 1970—81, chmn. grad. group molecular biology, 1972-84. Mem. USPHS study sect. Nat. Heart Inst., 1964-68, 72-76; chmn. rsch. com. Spl. Dairy Industry Bd., 1963-70; food and nutrition bd. NAS, 1976-82. Author: Cholesterol, 1958; Western Hemisphere editor Atherosclerosis, 1978-90, cons. editor, 1990—; contbr. articles to profl. jours. Recipient Rsch. Career award Nat. Heart Inst., 1962, Herman award Am. Soc. Clin. Nutrition, 1992, Disting. Svc. award U. N.C. Inst. Nutrition, 1993, Auenbrugger medal U. Graz, Austria, 1994, SUPELCO/AOCS award, 1996, Lifetime Achievement award Am. Inst. for Cancer Rsch., 1996; Caspar Wistar scholar, 1992. Fellow: AAAS, Am. Soc. Oil Chemists (chmn. methods com. 1963—64), Am. Coll. Nutrition (award 1978), Am. Inst. Nutrition (pres. 1979, Borden award 1974), Am. Oil Chemists Soc.; mem.: Am. Oil Chemistry Soc., Internat. Soc. Fat Rsch., Am. Heart Assn. (spl. recognition coun. on atherosclerosis 1993), Arteriosclerosis Coun., Soc. Exptl. Biology and Medicine (pres. 1985—87), Am. Chem. Soc. (award Phila. sect. 1977), Am. Soc. Biol. Chemists. Achievements include research on role vehicle when cholesterol and fat produces atherosclerosis in rabbits, effects of saturated and unsaturated fat, deposition of orally administered cholesterol in aorta of man and rabbit, caloric restriction and cancer. Home: 136 Lee Cir Bryn Mawr PA 19010-3724 Office Phone: 215-898-3213. Business E-Mail: kritchevsky@wistar.org.

KRITZER, PAUL ERIC, publishing executive, lawyer; b. Buffalo, May 5, 1942; s. James Cyril and Bessie May (Biddlecombe) K.; m. Frances Jean McCallum, June 20, 1970; children: Caroline Frances, Erica Hopkins. BA, Williams Coll., 1964; MS in Journalism, Columbia U., 1965; JD, Georgetown U., 1972. Bar: U.S. Supreme Ct. 1978, Wis. 1980. Reporter, copy editor Buffalo Evening News, 1964, 69, 70; instr. English Augusta (Ga.) Coll., 1968-69; law clk. Office of FCC Commr., Washington, 1971, MCI, Washington, 1972; counsel U.S. Ho. of Reps., Washington, 1972-77; assoc. counsel Des Moines Register & Tribune, 1977-80; editor, pub. Waukesha (Wis.) Freeman, 1980-83; legal v.p., sec. Jour. Communications Inc., Milw., 1983—. Trustee Carroll Co., Waukesha, 1981-89; producer Waukesha Film Festival, 1982; bd. dirs. Des Moines Metro Opera, Inc., 1979-80; bd. dirs. Milw. Youth Symphony Orch., 1992-2001, pres. 1994-97; bd. dirs. Milw. Symphony Orch., 1997-2004; bd. dirs. United Performing Arts Fund, 1994-97, Waukesha Landmarks Commn., 2005—. With U.S. Army, 1965—68. Presbyterian. Avocations: bridge, gardening. Home: 211 Oxford Rd Waukesha WI 53186-6263 Office: Jour Communications Inc 333 W State St PO Box 661 Milwaukee WI 53201-0661 Office Phone: 414-224-2374. Business E-Mail: pkritzer@journalcommunications.com.

KRITZMAN, LAWRENCE DAVID, humanities educator; b. N.Y.C. s. Melvin M. and Margy (Rosenstein) K.; m. Janie L. Kritzman; 1 child, Jeremy. BA, U. Wis., 1969; AM, Middlebury Coll., 1970; PhD, U. Mich., 1976. Lectr. Rutgers U., New Brunswick, N.J., 1976-77, asst. prof., 1977-82, assoc. prof., dir. grad. studies, 1982-87; prof. French civilization Ohio State U., Columbus, 1987-89; prof. French & comparative lit. Dartmouth Coll., Hanover, N.H., 1989—, Edward Tuck prof. French, 1994—, chair comparative lit. dept., 1992-95, Ted and Helen Geisel Third Century prof. in the humanities, 1995—2002, Pat and John Rosenwald rsch. prof. in Arts and Scis., 2002—. Chair Com. for Future of French Studies, French Embassy, N.Y., 1991—; vis. prof. U. Mich., Ann Arbor, 1991, 93, Duke NEH Inst., 1986, 90, Northwestern NEH Inst., assoc. dir., 1995; vis. prof. Stanford U., 1999, Harvard U., 2001, 2003, 2005; dir. Inst. French Cultural Studies, 1994— Author: Destruction/Découverte, 1980, Rhetoric of Sexuality and Literature fo French Renaissance, 1991, The Fabulous Imagination: The Mind's Eye in Montaigne's Essays, 2005; editor: Fragments, 1981, France Under Mitterand, 1984, Foucault: Politics, Philosophy, Culture, 1988, Le Signe et le Texte, 1989, Auschwitz & After: Race, Culture & The Jewish Question in France, 1995, Columbia History of 20th Century French Thought, 2005; mem. editl. bd.: Etudes Montaignistes, 1988, Montaigne Studies, Early Modern Culture, Studies in 20th Century Literature, Contemporary French Civilization Sites, French Forum, Sites, gen. editor: European Perspectives, 1989—, Columbia U. Press, mem. adv. bd.: French Politics and Society; contbr. numerous articles to profl. jours., numerous chpts. to books. Chair Com. Future of French Studies in U.S.; dir. Edward Morot-Inst. French Cultural Studies, 1994, 1997, 1999, 2001, 2003. Recipient Chevalier de l'Ordre des Palmes Academics, French Govt., 1991, Ordre de Merite Nat. by Pres. France, 2000; Officier des Palmes des Palmes Academics, 1994; sr. fellow Am. Coun. Learned Soc., 1989; Andrew W. Mellon Found. grant Duke U., 1980. Mem. MLA, Am. Coun. French Social and Cultural Affairs, Nat. Writer's Union, Am. Comparative Lit. Assn., Acad. Lit. Studies. Home: 24 Warwick Rd Brookline MA 02445 Office: Dept French Dartmouth Coll Hanover NH 03755

KRIVICICH, JOHN AUGUSTINE, lawyer; b. Chgo., Feb. 28, 1955; s. Anthony and Andriana K.; m. Ilona Mae Berry, July 28, 1984; children: James, Peter, Laura. BS in Journalism, Northwestern U., 1976; JD cum laude, U. Ill., 1980. Bar: Ill. 1980, U.S. Dist. Ct. (no. dist.) Ill. 1980, U.S. Ct. Appeals (7th cir.) 1981, U.S. Dist. Ct. (ctrl. dist.) Ill. 1993. Assoc. Reuben & Proctor, Chgo., 1980-84, Baker & McKenzie, Chgo., 1985-93, ptnr., 1993-96, Donohue, Brown, Mathewson & Smyth, Chgo., 1996—. Firefighter Western Springs (Ill.) Dept. Fire and EMS, 1994-96; mem. bd. appeals Zoning Bd. Western Springs, 1996—, chmn.—. Mem. ABA, Def. Rsch. Inst., Ill. Bar Assn. Office: Donohue Brown Mathewson & Smyth 140 S Dearborn St Chicago IL 60603-5202 Office Phone: 312-422-0972. E-mail: john.krivicich@dbmslaw.com, imbjak@sbcglobal.net.

KRIVKOVICH, PETER GEORGE, advertising executive; b. Bad Ischl, Austria, Oct. 25, 1946; came to U.S., 1953; s. George M. Krivkovich and Ada (Kalenkiewicz) Bajor; m. Linda J. Monken, Aug. 30, 1970; children: Peter A., Alexis C. BS, U. Ill., 1969; postgrad., Loyola U., Chgo., 1972-73. Advt. asst. Kemper Ins. Co., Chgo., 1969-71; account exec. Nader-Lief, Chgo., 1971-72; account mgr. Leo Burnett, Chgo., 1972-73; ptnr. Hackenberg, Normann, Krivkovich, Chgo., 1973-80; pres. Cramer-Krasselt, Chgo., 1981-86, pres., COO, 1987-98, pres., CEO, chmn. bd., 1999—; pres., CEO CKPR, 2002—. Mem. Nat. Advt. Rev. Bd. Bd. dirs. Avondale Bank, 1992—98, Manufacturers Bank/MB Fin., 1998—2004, Off The Street Club, Prentice Hosp., Chgo. Humanities Festival, 2002—03. Named One of 100 Best and Brightest Advt. Execs. of Yr. Advt. Age mag., 1986, Midwest Advt. Exec. of Yr. Adweek mag., 1987. Mem. Am. Assn. Advt. Agys. (chmn. Chgo. chpt. 1992, 93, regional bd. govs. 1996, 97, nat. bd. govs. 1998-2002), Direct Mktg. Assn., Chgo. Assn. Direct Mktg., Chgo. Advt. Club, Glenview (Ill.) C. of C., Tavern Club, Exec. Club. Office: Cramer-Krasselt 225 N Michigan Ave Ste 800 Chicago IL 60601-7690 E-mail: pkrivkov@c-k.com.

KRIVOSHIA, ELI, JR., lawyer; b. Midland, Pa., Apr. 20, 1935. BA, U. Pitts., 1957; LLB, Harvard U., 1960. Bar: 1961. Assoc., Throp, Reed & Armstrong, Pitts., 1960-69, ptnr., 1970-83; gen. Counsel Nat. Steel Corp., 1983-95, pvt. practice, Pitts., 1995—. Mem. Allegheny County Bar Assn., ABA, Pa. Bar Assn. Office Phone: 412-394-6810.

KRIVOVICHEV, SERGEY VLADIMIROVICH, science educator; b. Leningrad, Russia, Sept. 4, 1972; s. Vladimir Gerasimovich Krivovichev and Galina Leonidovna Starova; m. Irina Nikitichna Staritskaya, July 12, 1993; children: Ivan Sergeevich, Nikolay Sergeevich, Evfrasiya Sergeevna Krivovicheva, Vasilisa Sergeevna Krivovicheva, Alexey Sergeevich. DSc, St. Petersburg State U., Russia, 2001, PhD, 1994. Prof., chmn. St. Petersburg State U., Russia, 2005—. Author: (book) Crystal Chemistry of Minerals and Inorganic Compounds with Complexes of Anion-Centered Tetrahedra (European Mineral. Union Medal, 2002). Lt. Russian Mil. Recipient Young Scientist award, Russian Mineral. Soc., 1999, European Acad., 2004, Alferov Gold medal and award, Zh.I. Alferov Found., 2005; Postdoctoral fellowship in sci. and engring., NSF-NATO, 1999—2000, Rsch. fellowship, Alexander von Humboldt Found., 2002, Lise Meitner Rsch. fellowship, Austrian Sci. Fund, 2005. Mem.: Mineral. Soc. of Am., Russian Orthodox. Achievements include discovery of Uranium nanotubes. Home: Mayakovskogo 22 44 Saint Petersburg 191104 Russia Office: St Petersburg State Univ University Emb 7/9 Saint Petersburg 199034 Russia Office Phone: (812) 3289647. Personal E-mail: skrivovi@mail.ru.

KRIZ, GEORGE JAMES, retired agricultural studies educator, science association director, researcher; b. Brainard, Nebr., Sept. 20, 1936; s. George Jacob and Rose Agnes Kriz; m. Patricia Elizabeth Kelly (div. Feb. 1989); children: Rosalie Sue, Richard Patrick, Thomas George; m. Rhoda Mae Whitacre, June 23, 1989. BS in Agrl. Engring., Iowa State U., 1960, MS in Agrl. Engring., 1962; PhD, U. Calif., Davis, 1965. Lectr. U. Calif., Davis, 1965; asst. prof. agrl. engring. N.C. State U., Raleigh, 1965-68, assoc. prof., 1968-72, prof., 1972-99, assoc. dept. head, 1969-73, asst. rsch. dir., 1973-81, assoc. rsch. dir., 1981-99, prof. emeritus, 1999—. Operator bed and breakfast. Fellow Am. Soc. Agrl. Engring. (bd. dirs. 1983-85, found. trustee 1986-94, 96-97, pres. 1995-96, presdl. citation 1988, 91); mem. Coun. Agrl. Scis. and Tech. Avocations: gardening, walking. Office Phone: 540-450-0341. E-mail: house@visuallink.com.

KRIZANAC-BENGEZ, LJILJANA, medical educator, researcher; d. Dragica and Franjo Krizanac; m. Zdravko Bengez, May 3, 1986; 1 child, Lana Bengez. MD, U. Zagreb, Croatia, 1985, D of Med. Scis., 1992. Tchg. and rsch. asst. Rudjer Boskovic Inst., Zagreb, Croatia, 1986—92, sr. rsch. assoc., 1992—93; postdoctoral fellow Fred Hutchinson Cancer Rsch. Ctr., Seattle, 1993—96; asst. prof. Rudjer Boskovic Inst., Zagreb, Croatia, 1996—99; postdoctoral fellow Cleve. Clinic Found., 1999—2002, rsch. asst. prof., 2002—. Recipient Internat. Sci. and Tech. Collaboration award, Croatian State Fund, Manchester, 1990; grantee, Oncology Rsch. Faculty Devel. Program, Seattle, 1993—96; fellowship, Internat. Union Against Cancer, Manchester, 1989, Brit. Coun., Manchester, 1992. Mem.: Am. Heart Assn. (grant 2002—05), Neuroscience. Office Phone: 216-445-4307.

KRIZEK, EDWIN JOHN, marketing professional; b. N.Y.C., Dec. 28, 1954; s. Virginia Ruth and Edwin John Krizek; life ptnr. Caroline Leland. BA, U. Pa., 1975, MS, 1976; MBA, Columbia U., 1982, MPH, 1983. Pres. Krizek Mktg., Swarthmore, Pa., 1998—. Author: (chpt.) Threshold, 2002, (short story collection) Afterlife and Other Stories, 2004. Mem. Unitarian Universalist Ch. of Del. County, Media, Pa., 1994—2003. Home and Office: Krizek Mktg 801 Yale Ave #830 Swarthmore PA 19081 Office Phone: 610-328-7593. Personal E-mail: ekrizek@yahoo.com.

KRIZEK, RAYMOND JOHN, engineering educator, consultant; b. Balt., June 5, 1932; s. John James and Louise (Polak) K.; m. Claudia Stricker, Aug. 1964; children: Robert A., Kevin J. BE, Johns Hopkins U., 1954; MS, U. Md., 1961; PhD, Northwestern U., 1963; doctorate (hon.), U. Cantabria, Spain, 2003. Instr. U. Md., College Park, 1957-61; rsch. asst. civil engring. Northwestern U., Evanston, Ill., 1961-63, asst. prof. civil engring., 1963-66, assoc. prof. civil engring., 1966-70, prof. civil engring., 1970—, chmn. dept. civil engring., 1980-92, dir. Master of Project Mgmt. program, 1994—, Stanley F. Pepper chair prof., 1987—. Cons. to industry. Editor books; contbr. numerous articles to profl. jours. Served to lt. U.S. Army, 1955-57. Decorated Palmes Academiques (France), 1993; recipient Hogentogler award ASTM, 1970; named disting. vis. scholar NSF, 1972. Mem.: ASCE (pres. GEO Inst. 1997—98, Huber Rsch. prize 1971, Karl Terzaghi award 1997, Ill. sect. Civil Engr. of Yr. 1999, Hon. mem. 2002, Wallace Hayward Baker award Geo-Inst. 2003), Internat. Soc. Soil Mechanics and Geotech. Engring., Nat. Acad. Engring., Spanish Royal Acad. Engring. (corr.). Roman Catholic. Home: 1366 Sanford Ln Glenview IL 60025-3165 Office: Dept Civil Engring Northwestern U 2145 Sheridan Rd Evanston IL 60208-3109 Office Phone: 847-491-4040. Business E-Mail: rjkrizek@northwestern.edu.

KROCHALIS, RICHARD F., federal agency administrator; BS in Environ. Sys. Engring., Cornell U.; M in City and Regional Planning, Harvard U. Dir. dept. constrn. and land use City of Seattle, Seattle, 1992-99, dir. dept. design, constrn. and land use, 1999—2001; regional adminstr. Fed. Transit Adminstrn., 2002—. Examiner Wash. State Quality Award Bd., 1995-96. Past pres. Sustainable Seattle, 2002-03; mem. U. Wash. Capital Campaign Cabinet, 2003-; mem. coun. Cornell U., 1991-98. Mem. Urban Land Inst., Am. Planning Assn., Am. Inst. Cert. Planners, Wash. State City Planning Dir.'s Assn. (past pres.). Office: FederalTransit Adminstrn Ste 3142 915 Second Ave Seattle WA 98174-1002 Office Phone: 206-220-7954. E-mail: rick.krochalis@fta.dot.gov.

KROCK, CURTIS JOSSELYN, pulmonologist; b. Fort Smith, Ark., Oct. 11, 1935; s. Frederick Henry and Hazel Armiger (Josselyn) Krock; m. Ruth Leone Johnson, Apr. 27, 1968; children: Eric Gregory, Lynn Alyson. BA, Stanford U., 1957; MD, Johns Hopkins U. Sch. Medicine, 1961. Diplomate Am. Bd. Internal Medicine, Am. Bd. Pulmonary Medicine. Intern Barnes Hosp., St. Louis, 1961-62, resident in internal medicine, 1963-65; resident in pathology Johns Hopkins U. Sch. Medicine, Balt., 1962-63; pulmonary fellow Duke U., Durham, N.C., 1965-66; pvt. practice Holt-Krock Clinic, Ft. Smith, Ark., 1968-72, Carle Clinic, Urbana, Ill., 1972-2001, also bd. dirs., 1978-80, chief medicine dept., 1996-99; clin. asst. prof. U. Ill., Urbana, 1976-99, clin. assoc. prof., 2000—; interim chief of medicine UICOM-UC; chief of medicine Carle Found. Hosp., 2003—. Capt. U.S. Army, 1966—68. Fellow: ACP; mem.: Sierra Club, Sigma Xi. Avocations: violin, reading. Home: 2125 Lynwood Dr Champaign IL 61821-6606 Office: Carle Clin Edn Ctr Forum Bldg 611 W Park St Urbana IL 61801-2530 Office Phone: 217-383-4614. E-mail: curtis.krock@carle.com, ckrock1935@aol.com.

KROEBER, KARL, language educator; b. Oakland, Calif., Nov. 24, 1926; s. Alfred Louis and Theodora Quinn (Kracaw) K.; m. Jean Taylor, Mar. 21, 1953; children— Paul Demarest, Arthur Romeyn, Katharine. AA, Coll. of Pacific, Stockton, Calif., 1945; AB, U. Calif., Berkeley, 1947; MA, Columbia U., 1951, PhD, 1956. Asst. prof. U. Wis.-Madison, 1956-61, asso. prof., 1961-63, prof., 1963-70; asso. dean U. Wis.-Madison (Grad. Sch.), 1963-65; prof. English and comparative lit. Columbia U., N.Y.C., 1970—, chmn. dept. English and comparative lit., 1973-76, Mellon prof. humanities, 1987. Author: Romantic Narrative Art, 1960, The Artifice of Reality, 1964, Studying Poetry, 1965, Backgrounds to British Romantic Literature, 1968, Styles in Fictional Structure, 1971, Romantic Landscape Vision, 1975, Images of Romanticism, 1978, Traditional Literatures of the American Indian, 1981, rev. edit. 1997, Wordsworthian Scholarship and Criticism, 1973-84, 1986, British Romantic Art, 1986, Romantic Fantasy and Science Fiction, 1988, Retelling/Rereading, 1992, Romantic Poetry: Recent Revisionary Criticism, 1993, Native American Persistence and Resurgence, 1994, Ecological Literary Criticism, 1994, Artistry in Native American Myths, 1998, Ishi in Three Centuries, 2003, Native American Storytelling, 2004; emeritus editor Studies in American Indian Literatures; mem. editorial bd. The Wordsworth Circle, Native American Bibiliography Series, Studies in English Lit., Boundary 2, European Romantic Review. Served with USNR, 1944-46. Named Disting. Scholar, Keats-Shelley Assn., 1991; Fulbright Rsch. grantee Italy, 1960-61, U.S. Office Edn. Rsch. grantee, 1965-66; Guggenheim fellow, 1966-67; NEH fellow, 1991. Mem. MLA, Internat. Assn. Univ. Profs. English, N.Am. Soc. Study of Romanticism, Jane Austen Soc. N.Am., Acad. Lit. Studies, Byron Soc., Assn. for Study of Native Am. Lit., Keats-Shelley Assn. Home: 226 Saint Johns Pl Brooklyn NY 11217-3406 Office: Columbia U Dept English & Comparative Lit New York NY 10027 Business E-Mail: kk17@columbia.edu.

KROEGER, ARTHUR, retired academic administrator, retired federal official; b. Naco, Alta., Can., Sept. 7, 1932; s. Heinrich and Helena (Rempel) K.; m. Gabrielle Jane Sellers, May 7, 1966 (dec.); children: Alexandra, Kate. BA with honors, U. Alta., 1955; MA, Oxford U., Eng., 1958; LLD (hon.), U. Western Ontario, Can., 1991, U. Calgary, 1995, Carleton U., 2003, U. Alta., 2004. Fgn. service officer Can. Dept. External Affairs, 1958-71, treasury bd. secretariat, 1971-75, dep. minister Indian and No. affairs, 1975-79; dep. minister transport Can., Ottawa, Ont., 1979-83; sec. Ministry of State for Econ. Devel., Ottawa, Ont., 1983-84; spl. advisor to clk. Privy Council; dep. minister Regional Indsl. Expansion; dep. minister of Energy, Mines and Resources; dep. minister employment & immigration, 1988-92; chancellor Carleton U., Ottawa, Canada, 1993—2002. Vis. fellow Queen's U., Kingston, Ont., 1994-99; vis. prof. U. Toronto, 1993-94; chmn. Pub. Policy Forum, Ottawa, 1992-94. Program chmn. Gov. Gen.'s Study Conf., 1995; chmn. Can. Policy Rsch. Networks; bd. dirs. The Parliamentary Ctr.; chmn. Nat. Stats. Coun., chmn., 2005-; mem. Panel on Voluntary Sector Governance, 1997-99. Decorated companion Order of Can.; recipient Pub. Svc. Outstanding Achievement award, 1989, Disting. Alumnus award U. Alta.; Rhodes scholar, 1955; hon. fellow Pembroke Coll., Oxford. Mem. Can. Assn. Rhodes Scholars (exec. mem., pres. 1995-97). Clubs: Five Lakes Fishing. Home: 245 Springfield Rd Ottawa ON Canada K1M 0L1 E-mail: arthur.kroeger@sympatico.ca.

KROEHLER, BETH ANN, librarian; b. Freeport, Ill., Sept. 1, 1955; d. Ralph Senf and Marjorie Ann Kroehler. BE, U. Wisc., Whitewater, 1977; MA Libr. Sci., U. Wisc., Madison, 1981; MA Exec. Devel. for Pub. Svc., Ball State U., Muncie, Ind., 1987. Cert. Librarian II Ind., 1986. Libr./av Wild Rose and Pleasant View Elem. Sch., Wild Rose, Wis., 1977—80; h.s. libr. Northland Pines Sch. Dist., Eagle River, Wis., 1980—81, dist. audio-visual coord./lib. h.s., 1981—82; reference asst./young adult libr. Muncie (Ind.) Pub. Libr., 1983—87, spl. projects libr., 1987—93, coord. of circulation and computer services, 1993—95, asst. supr. tech. dept., 1995—. Presenter Pub. Libr. Assn. Conf., 1988, CODI Nat. Conf., 2000, 01. Contbr. articles to profl. jour.; co-editor: (booklet) Way to Go. Pres. and organizer Campus Girl Scouts U. Wisc.-Whitewater, Whitewater, Wis., 1973—74; organizer Laubach Literacy Coun., Eagle River, Wis., 1981, Whitewater City Laubach Literacy Coun., Whitewater, Wis., 1976—76; mem. LRC Adv. Com., Ind. Vocat. Tech. Coll., Muncie, Ind., 1983—85; treas. Ind. Literacy Coordinating Com., Ind., 1990—98; mem. Ctrl. Wis. Uniserv Coun., Wis., 1978—80; rec. sec. White Pines Cmty. Broadcasting Devel. Group, Wis., 1982—82; mem. Moore-Youse Hist. Mus., Muncie, Ind., 1985—87; trainer Laubach Literacy Action, 1982—90. Recipient Meritorious Svc. Award, Palatines to Am., 2003, Harvey Harsh award, 2005. Mem.: ALA, Ind. Libr. Fedn., Del. County Hist. Soc. (various positions 1984—2001), Ind. State Hist. Soc., Palatines to Am. (various positions 2000—, 2nd chpt., v.p. 1992—94, pres. 1994—98, nat. chpt., pres. 1996—2000), Phi Alpha Theta. Avocations: needlecrafts, travel, reading, post card collecting. Home: 301 W Charter Dr Muncie IN 47303 Office: Muncie Pub Libr 2005 S High St Muncie IN 47302 Personal E-mail: kroehler@juno.com.

KROEMER, HERBERT, electrical engineering educator; b. Weimar, Germany, Aug. 25, 1928; Diplom-Physiker, Gottingen U., Germany, 1951, Dr. rer. nat., 1952; Doctorate (hon.), Tech. U. Aachen, Germany, 1985, U. Lund, Sweden, 1998, U. Colo., 2001. Prof. elec., computer engring. U. Calif., Santa Barbara, faculty rsch. lectr., 1985—96, Donald W. Whittier chair in elec. engring., 1986—. Recipient Heinrich Welker medal Internat. Symposium on GaAs and related compounds, 1982, Alexander von Humboldt Rsch. award, 1994, NAE, 1997, Nobel Prize in physics, 2000, Order of merit, Germany, 2001. Mem. NAS, IEEE (J.J. Ebers award Electron Devices Group 1973, Nat. lectr. 1983, Jack Morton award 1986, Medal of Honor, 2002), Am. Phys. Soc. Office: Rm 4107 Elec-Computer Engring Dept Univ Calif Santa Barbara CA 93106-9560

KROENER, WILLIAM FREDERICK, III, lawyer; b. N.Y.C., Aug. 27, 1945; s. William Frederick Kroener Jr. and Barbara (Mitchell) Kroener; m. Evelyn Somerville Bibb, Sept. 3, 1966; children: William F. Kroener IV(dec.), Mary Elizabeth, Evangeline Alberta, James Mitchell. AB, Yale Coll., 1967; JD, MBA, Stanford (Calif.) U., 1971. Bar: Calif. 1972, N.Y. 1979, D.C. 1983. Assoc. Davis, Polk & Wardwell, N.Y.C., London, 1971-79, ptnr. N.Y.C., 1979-82, Washington, N.Y.C., 1982-94; gen. counsel FDIC, Washington, 1995—. Lectr. Stanford U. Law Sch., 1993—94, George Washington U. Law Sch., 1994—98, Washington Coll. Law, Am. U. Law Sch., Washington, 1996—; chmn. legal adv. group Fed. Fin. Instns. Exam. Coun., 2001—03. Pres. Kroener Family Found.; gov. bd. mem. St. Albans Sch., 1991—95; fin. com. mem. Protestant/Episcopal Cathedral Found.-Wash. Nat. Cathedral, 1992—95; mem. bd. visitors Stanford U. Law Sch., 1983—92, deans adv. coun., 1992—93; nat. chair Stanford Law Fund, 1990—92; dir., gen. counsel Kenwood Citizens Assn., Inc., 1993—94; governing bd. FDIC Corp. Univ. Mem.: ABA, N.Y. Law Inst., Assn. Bar City of N.Y., Am. Law Inst., Kenwood Golf Club, Yale Club. Republican. Episcopalian. Home: 6412 Brookside Dr Chevy Chase MD 20815-6649 Office: Fed Deposit Ins Corp 550 17th St NW Washington DC 20429-0001 Office Phone: 202-898-3680. Business E-Mail: wkroener@fdic.gov.

KROENERT, ROBERT MORGAN, retired lawyer; b. Kansas City, Mo., July 19, 1939; s. Robert Andrew and Marion Leona (Morgan) K.; m. Susan Aldrich, Aug. 18, 1962; children: Kathleen Susan, Ann Elizabeth, Robert Aldrich. BS, U. Kans., 1961; JD, U. Mich., 1964. Bar: Mo. 1964, U.S. Dist. Ct. (we. dist.) Mo. 1965, U.S. Ct. Appeals (8th cir.) 1984, U.S. Ct. Appeals (5th, 10th and D.C. cirs.) 1986, U.S. Supreme Ct. 1991. Assoc. Morrison & Hecker L.L.P., Kansas City, 1964-69; ptnr. Morrison & Hecker, Kansas City, 1969—2002. Bd. dirs. Guadalupe Ctr., Inc., Kansas City, 1978-87; mem. adv. bd. greater univ. fund, U. Kans., Lawrence, 1985-88; Mem. fin. com. Johnson County Rep. Com., 1987-90, Mo. Supreme Ct. Disciplinary Com. for Jackson County, 1992-2000, divsn. chair, 1995-97; mem. coun. Colonial Congregtional Ch., 1990-93, moderator, 1991-93. Mem.: Mo. Bar, Internat. Assn. Def. Counsel, Lawyers Assn. Kansas City (bd. dirs., pres. 1998—99, past. pres., past pres. found.), Mission Hills Country Club, Rotary. Avocation: golf.

KROENKE, E. STANLEY, real estate developer, professional sports team executive; b. Cole Camp, Mo. m. Ann (Walton) Kroenke; children: Whitney, Josh. Undergraduate degree in bus., U. Mo., MBA, 1973. Chmn., owner The Kroenke Group, Columbia, Mo.; chmn. THF Realty; owner Kroenke Sports Enterprises; vice chmn., co-owner St. Louis Rams, NFL, 1995—; owner Pepsi Ctr., Denver, 2000—, Denver Nuggets, NBA, 2000—, Colo. Avalanche, NHL, 2000—, Colo. Crush, Arena Football League, 2002—, Colo. Mammoth, Nat. Lacrosse League, 2002—, Colo. Rapids, MLS, 2003—. Bd. dirs. Cmty. Investment Partnership Funds I and II, St. Louis, Boone County Nat. Bank, Columbia, Ctrl. Bancompany, Jefferson City. Trustee Coll. of the Ozarks; mem. bd. Greater St. Louis Area Coun. Boy Scouts of Am., St. Louis Art Mus. Office: St Louis Rams 1 Rams Way Earth City MO 63045-1525*

KROEPPEL, WARREN, airport terminal executive; BS in Aeronautical Sci., Embry-Riddle Aeronautical U., 1976; MBA in Fin., Adelphi U., 1983. Cert. comml. pilot, flight instr. FAA. Comml. pilot; mgr. ops. planning redevel. program JFK Airport Port Authority, Flushing, NY, 1989—96, mgr. airport ops., security and svcs. LaGuardia Airport, 1996—99, dep. gen. mgr. John F. Kennedy Internat. Airport, 1999—2000, gen. mgr. LaGuardia Airport, 2000—. Office: LaGuardia Airport Hangar 7 Ctr 3rd Fl Flushing NY 11371 Business E-Mail: wkroeppel@panynj.gov.

KROESEN, FREDERICK JAMES, retired army officer, consultant; b. Phillipsburg, NJ, Feb. 11, 1923; s. Frederick James K. and Jean Ursula (Shillinger) Kroesen; m. Rowene Wilder McCray, Mar. 4, 1944; children: Karen McCray Kroesen Klare, Frederick J. III, Gretchen McCray Kroesen Tackaberry. BS in Agr., Rutgers U., 1944, LHD (hon.), 1983; BA in Internat. Affairs, George Washington U., 1962, MA in Internat. Affairs, 1966. Enlisted U.S. Army, 1942, commd. 2d lt., 1944, served with 63d Infantry div. WWII, advanced through grades to gen., 1976; served with 187th Airborne Regimental Combat Team, Korean War, 1953-55; instr. U.S. Army War Coll., 1962-65; mem. staff asst. chief of staff for force devel. U.S. Army, 1965-68, 70-71; served with Americal Div. Vietnam War, 1968 and 1971, comdr. Div., 1971; dep. comdr. XXIV Corps. U.S. Army, 1971-72, comdr. 1st Regn. Asst Command, VN, 1972, comdr. 82d Airborne Div., 1972-74, comdr. VII Corps in Europe., 1975-76, comdr. U.S. Army Forces Command, 1976-78, vice chief of staff U.S. Army, 1978-79; comdr.-in-chief U.S. Army, Europe, 1979-83; comdr. NATO Cen. Army Group Heidelberg, Germany, 1979-83; ret., 1983. Pvt. cons. in internat. security affairs; former mem. Army Sci. Bd. Decorated Def. D.S.M., Army D.S.M. with oak leaf cluster, Purple Heart with 2 oak leaf clusters, Silver Star with oak leaf cluster, Legion of Merit with 2 oak leaf clusters, D.F.C., Bronze Star with V and 2 oak leaf clusters, combat inf. badge with two stars; recipient Mil. Order of World War Disting. Svc. medal, 1985, Americanism award Am. Legion, 1993, State of N.J. Disting. Svc. medals, 1983, 95; named to Rutgers Hall Disting. Alumni, Rutgers Loyal Son, Cook Coll. Disting. Alumni award. Fellow Inst. Land Warfare (sr.), Assn. US Army (Creighton W. Abrams medal 2004); mem. US Army War Coll. Alumni Assn. (former pres.), US Army War Coll. Found. (past bd. dirs.), 63d Div. Assn., 82d Airborne Div. Assn., Amcl Div. Vets. Assn., Rakkasan Assn., Soc. French Legion of Honor, Soc. Rhin et Danube, Rutgers Cap & Skull, Delta Upsilon. Home: 1250 S Washington St # 223 Alexandria VA 22314-4455 Personal E-mail: fkroesen@earthlink.net.

KROFT, STEVE, news correspondent, editor; b. Kokomo, Ind., Aug. 22, 1945; s. Fred and Margaret Kroft; m. Jennet Conant, June 29, 1991; 1 child, John Conant. BS, Syracuse U., 1967; MS in Journalism, Columbia U., 1975; DHL (hon.), Ind. U., SUNY; DHL, LI U., 2005. Reporter Sta. WSYR-TV, Syracuse, NY, 1972—74; investigative reporter Sta. WJXT-TV, Jacksonville, Fla., 1975—77; reporter Sta. WPLG-TV, Miami, Fla., 1977—79, CBS News, N.Y.C., 1980—81, corr. S.W. bur. Dallas, 1981—83, corr. Cen. Am. bur. Miami, 1983—84, corr. London, 1984—86, prin. corr. W. 57th program N.Y.C., 1986—89, corr., co-editor 60 Minutes, 1989—. Trustee Syracuse U. Sgt. U.S. Army, 1970—71, Vietnam. Recipient Ohio State award, Ohio State U., 1979, 1992, 1994, Emmy awards, 1982, 1984, 1990, 1993, 1999, 2001, Lifetime Achievement Emmy award, 2003, Arents award, Syracuse U., 1992, George Foster Peabody award, 1992, 1998, 2003, Dupont award, Columbia U., 2003. Office: CBS News 60 Minutes 555 W 57th St New York NY 10019-2925

KROFT, STEVEN HOWARD, hematologist, medical educator; b. San Antonio, Tex., June 2, 1965; s. Arthur Ellis and Roslyn Ann Kroft; m. Laura Renee Field, June 17, 1989; children: Henry Oliver children: Maxwell Alexander, Charles William. BS, MIT, 1986; MD, U. Ill. Coll. of Medicine, 1991. Cert. anatomic and clinical pathology Am. Bd. Pathology, 1996, hematology Am. Bd. Pathology. Anatomic and clin. pathology residency McGaw Med. Ctr. Northwestern U., Chgo., 1991—96; hematopathology fellow U. Mich. Med. Sch., Ann Arbor, 1996—97; asst. prof. pathology U. Tex. Southwestern Med. Sch., Dallas, 1997—2002, assoc. prof. pathology, 2002—05, Med. Coll. Wis., 2005—; dir. hematopathology Dynacare Labs., Froedtert Hosp. and Med. Coll. of Wis., Milw., 2005—. Med. dir., hematology lab. Parkland Meml. Hosp., Dallas, 1997—2003; assoc. editor Clin. Cytometry, Chgo., 2002—; mem. editl. bd. Am. Jour. Clin. Pathology, Chgo., 2002—; assoc. editor Lab. Medicine, Chgo., 2004—; quality mgmt. hematopathology com. Am. Soc. Clin. Pathology, Chgo.; med. dir., clin. flow cytometry Veripath Labs. U. of Tex. Southwestern Med. Ctr., Dallas, 2003—; mem., med. adv. bd. Veripath Laboratories of U. of Tex. Southwestern Med. Ctr., Dallas, 2003—; mem., hematology and clin. microscopy resource committe Coll. Am. Pathologists, Chgo., 1998—2003, vice chair, hematology and clin. microscopy resource com., 2003—; sec., young pathologists sect. Tex. Soc. Pathologists, Austin, 2002—02, chair elect, young pathologists sect., 2002—02, chair, young pathologists sect., 2002—04, dir. at large, 2002—04. Editor: (textbook) Color Atlas of Hemoglobin Disorders; author: (over 60 journal articles) various journals, including Blood, Am. Jour. Clinical Pathology, British Jour. of Haematology, Modern Pathology, Am. Jour. Surg. Pathology, Leukemia, (book chpt.) Disorders of Bone Marrow, (book chapter) The Bone Marrow Manifestations of Hodgkin's and Non-Hodgkin Lymphomas and Lymphoma-Like Disorders. Named one of Best Doctors in Am., Best Doctors in Am., 2003-2004; recipient Outstanding Tchr. award, UT Southwestern, Sophomore Med. Sch. Class, 1999, Pathology Resident Tchg. award, Pathology Residents, UT Southwestern, 1999, 2000. Fellow: Am. Soc. Clin. Pathology, Coll. Am. Pathologists; mem.: Internat. Soc. Lab. Hematology, Soc. Hematopathology, U.S. and Can. Acad. Pathology, Tex. Soc. Pathologists (dir. at large 2002—04), Am. Soc. Hematology, Clin. Cytometry Soc. Office: MCW Dept Pathology 8701 Watertown Plank Rd Milwaukee WI 53226 Office Phone: 414-805-6966. Office Fax: 414-805-8444. E-mail: shkroft@alum.mit.edu.

KROGIUS, TRISTAN ERNST GUNNAR, marketing professional, consultant, lawyer; b. Tammerfors, Finland, Apr. 13, 1933; came to U.S., 1939; s. Helge Lorenz and Valborg Isolde (Antell) K.; m. Barbara Jane Brophy, Aug. 29, 1952; children— Ferril Anne, Lars Anthony, Karin Therese, Eric Lorenz, Marian Elaine, Rebecca Kristina BA, U. N.Mex., 1954; MA, Calif. State U.-Los Angeles, 1962; student Advanced Mgmt. Program, Harvard U., 1980; JD, Western State U., 1990. Bar: Calif. 1991. With Scott Paper Co., Phila., 1960-65, Hunt-Wesson Foods, Fullerton, Calif., 1965-75; pres. Hunt-Wesson Foods Can., Ltd., Toronto, Ont., 1969-71, pres. frozen and refrigerated foods div., 1971-75; pres., chief exec. officer Dalgety Foods, Salinas, Calif., 1975-78; v.p., gen. mgr. food div. Tenneco West, Inc., Bakersfield, Calif., 1978-80, pres., chief exec. officer, 1981-87; pres. Landmark Mgmt., Inc., 1987-88; ptnr. The Cons. Co., South Laguna, 1988-90, Internat. Mktg. Consultancy, 1990—; adj. prof. Western State U. Coll. of Law, 1992-97. Bd. dirs. South Coast Med. Ctr., Laguna Beach, Calif., 1969-74, pres., CEO, 1974; bd. dirs. South Sierra coun. Boy Scouts Am., 1981-87, Calif. State Coll. Found., Bakersfield, 1983-87, Found. for 21st Century, 1987-90; mgr. elder abuse program Pub. Law Ctr., 1992-93. Capt. USMC, 1954-60. Recipient World Food award Ariz. State U., Tempe, 1982 Republican. Episcopalian.

KROHN, BRETT DUANE, music educator; b. Denver, Colo., June 2, 1965; s. Bryce Duane and Patricia Ann Krohn; m. Melissa Jane Nelson, Jan. 2, 1988; children: Garrett Nathaniel, Elise Esther Kathryn. MusM, St. Cloud State U., 2005. Instrumental music instr. Cambridge Mid. Sch., Cambridge, MN, Minn., 1990—97; dir. of bands Robbinsdale Cooper H.S., New Hope, Minn., 1997—. Graduate student (transcription) A Transcription of Leonard Bernstein's Chichester Psalms for Wind Ensemble. Mem. Riverside Ch., Monticello, Minn., 1998—2005. Mem.: MENC. Conservative. Achievements include Excellence in Edn1. Leadership; Role Model award. Avocations: golf, music, sports. Office: Robbinsdale Cooper HS 8230 47th Ave N New Hope MN 55428 Office Phone: 763-504-8543. Office Fax: 763-504-8531. E-mail: brett_krohn@rdale.k12.mn.us.

KROHN, KENNETH ALBERT, radiology educator; b. Stevens Point, Wis., June 19, 1945; s. Albert William and Erma Belle (Cornwell) K.; 1 child, Galen. BA in Chemistry, Andrews U., 1966; PhD in Chemistry, U. Calif., 1971. Acting assoc. prof. U. Wash., Seattle, 1981-84, assoc. prof. radiology, 1984-86, prof. radiology and radiation oncology, 1986—, adj. prof. chemistry, 1986—. Guest scientist Donner Lab. Lawrence Berkeley (Calif.) Lab., 1980-81; radiochemist, VA Med. Ctr., Seattle, 1982—; affiliate investigator Fred Hutchinson Cancer Rsch. Ctr., 1997—. Contbr. articles to profl. jours.; patentee in field. Recipient Aebersold award, 1996; fellow, NDEA. Fellow AAAS; mem. Am. Assn. for Cancer Rsch., Am. Chem. Soc., Radiation Rsch. Soc., Soc. Nuclear Medicine, Acad. Coun., Sigma Xi. Home: 550 NE Lakeridge Dr Belfair WA 98528-8720 Office: U Washington Imaging Rsch Lab Box 356004 Seattle WA 98195-6004 Office Phone: 206-598-6245. Business E-Mail: kkrohn@u.washington.edu.

KROHNKE, DUANE W., retired lawyer; b. Keokuk, Iowa, June 29, 1939; s. Ward Glenn and Marian Frances (Brown) K.; m. Mary Alyce Luschen, June 25, 1963; children: Alan Duane, Brian Douglas. BA, Grinnell (Iowa) Coll., 1961, Oxford U., 1963, MA, 1970; JD, U. Chgo., 1966; DHL, Grinnell Coll., 1999. Bar: N.Y. 1967, Minn. 1970, U.S. Supreme Ct. 1970, U.S. Ct. Appeals (2d cir.) 1967, U.S. Ct. Appeals (8th cir.) 1970, U.S. Ct. Appeals (D.C.) 1974, U.S. Dist. Ct. (so., ea. dists.) N.Y. 1967, U.S. Dist. Ct. Minn. 1970. Assoc. atty. Cravath, Swaine, Moore, N.Y.C., 1966-70, Faegre & Benson, Mpls., 1970-73, ptnr., 1974-2000, of counsel, 2001; ret., 2001. Adj. prof. U. Minn. Law Sch., 2002—. Editl. bd.: U. Chgo. Lit. Rev., 1964—66. Co-chair Bicentennial com. U.S. Dist. Ct. Minn. dist., Mpls., 1986-88; elder Westminster Presbyn. Ch., Mpls., 1985-91; trustee United Theol. Seminary, New Brighton, Minn., 1988-98. Recipient Alumni award Grinnell Coll., 1982; Rhodes scholar Rhodes Trustees, Oxford, Eng., 1961-63; Mecham scholar U. Chgo., 1963-66. Mem. Minn. State Bar Assn. (co-chair antitrust sect. 1982-84, co-chair ethics/standards of practice com. of ADR sect. 1995-96, chair elect ADR sect. 1996-97, chair ADR sect. 1997-98), Minn. Human Rights Advocates (vol. award 1991, 99, 2002), Order of Coif, Phi Beta Kappa. Avocations: reading, cultural events, exercise.

KROL, DAVID MATTHEW, pediatrician, advocate; b. Oberlin, Ohio, Sept. 27, 1967; s. Andrew John and Therese Marie Krol; m. Christina Tobin, Nov. 13, 2004. BA, U. Toledo, 1990; MD, Yale U. Sch. Medicine, 1996; MPH, Columbia U. Mailman Sch. Pub. Health, 2004. Diplomate Am. Bd. Pediat., 2000. Profl. baseball player Minn. Twins, Kenosha, Wis. and Visalia, Calif., 1989—91; asst. prof. pediat. and health policy & mgmt. (in dentistry) Columbia U., N.Y.C., 2001—04, asst. prof. clin. pediat. and clin. health policy & mgmt. (in dentistry), 2004—; v.p., med. affairs The Children's Health Fund, N.Y.C., 2004—. Soros advocacy fellow Children's Dental Health Project, Wash., 2002—04, sr. policy rsch. cons., 2004—. Named to Varsity T Hall of Fame (baseball), U. Toledo, 2004; recipient Leadership award, AMA Found., 2001, Disting. Alumnus award, Elyria Cath. HS, 2003. Fellow: Am. Acad. Pediat. (chair, sect. on young physicians 2003—), N.Y. Acad. Medicine (assoc.); mem.: Acad. for Health Svcs. Rsch. and Health Policy, Ambulatory Pediat. Assn., Assn. of Clinicians for the Underserved, APHA. Achievements include 16th round draft choice of the Minnesota Twins, 1989. Office: The Children's Health Fund 317 E 64th St New York NY 10021

KROL, JOHN A., retired diversified chemicals executive; b. Gilbertsville, Mass., Oct. 16, 1936; m. Janet Ruth Valley, Sept. 12, 1938; children: Cynthia, Deborah. BS, MS in Chemistry, Tufts U., 1958, MS in Phys. Chemistry, 1959. With textile fibers sect. of DuPont Chestnut Run Rsch. Lab., Wilmington, Del., 1963-65, mktg. rep. Centre Rd. office, 1965-66, supr. indsl. tech. mktg. Centre Rd. office, 1966-69, mktg. mgr. N.Y.C., 1969-70, mktg. mgr. indsl. fibers Akron, Ohio, 1970-72; regional mktg. mgr. Textile Fibers, Wynnewood, Pa., 1972-73; product mgr. Dacron, Wilmington, 1973-75, mfg. supt. Old Hickory, Tenn., 1975-77; asst. plant mgr. mfg. DuPont, Old Hickory, Tenn., 1975-78; mktg. dir. DuPont Carpet Fibers and FIberfill divsn., Wilmington, 1978-80, dir., 1980-83; v.p. fibers DuPont DeNemours & Co., Wilmington, 1983-86, v.p. agrl. products dept., 1986-87, group v.p. agrl. products, 1987-90, sr. v.p. fibers, 1990-91, vice chmn., 1992—97, dir., CEO, pres., 1995-98, chmn., 1997-98. Bd. dirs. Ace Ltd., Tyco Ltd., MeadWestvaco Corp., Milliken & Co., Nat. Assn. Mfrs., Del. Art Mus.; bd. trustees Tufts Univ., Univ. Del., Elwyn Inst. Handicapped; corp. liaison bd. Am. Chem. Soc. Served to lt. USN, 1959-63. Mem. Nat. Agrl. Chems. Assn. (bd. dirs. 1987-90), Radley Run Country Club (West Chester, Pa., bd. govs.), Wilmington Country Club (dir.), Bonita Bay Country Club (Naples, Fla.), Olde Fla. Club (Naples). Republican. Roman Catholic. Avocations: golf, skiing, squash, tennis, boating. Office: DuPont 1007 N Market St Fl 2 Wilmington DE 19801-1229 E-mail: jkrol01@aol.com.

KROL, MARINA, computer scientist, researcher; b. Leningrad (St. Petersburg), Russia, June 25, 1948; d. Arnold Krol and Frida Tsauzner; m. Igor Tarnow, Aug. 10, 1981; children: George Arnold Tarnow, Michael Igmar Tarnow. BSEE with honors, Leningrad Electrotech. U., Russia, 1972; MS, Leningrad U., Russia, 1975; MPhil, CUNY, 1995, PhD, 1996. Analyst Phillips Bros., N.Y.C., 1986—89; asst. prof. Mt Sinai Sch. of Medicine, N.Y.C., 1996—, info. tech. dir., 2000—. Tech. program chair Computer Based Medical Sys., Washington, 2001, gen. chair, N.Y.C., 2003—; mem. spl. panel NIH Ctr. for Sci. Rev. Contbr. Grantee, NSF, 2000 - 2002; Tchg. fellowship, CUNY, 1994 - 1995. Mem.: IEEE (sr.; tech. com. on computational medicine 1999), Nat. Inst. Health (mem. spl. panel 2004), Am. Medical Informatics Assn. (Pres.'s Club 1997). Office: Mount Sinai Sch of Medicine 1 Gustave L Levy Pl Box 1010 New York NY 10029 Business E-Mail: marina.krol@mssm.edu.

KROLIK, JULIAN HENRY, astrophysicist, educator; b. Detroit, Apr. 4, 1950; m. Elaine F. Weiss, Oct. 9, 1983; children: Theodore, Abigail. BS, MIT, 1971; PhD, U. Calif., Berkeley, 1977. Mem. Inst. for Advanced Study, Princeton, N.J., 1977-79; postdoctoral scientist MIT, Cambridge, Mass., 1979-81; rsch. assoc. Harvard U., Cambridge, Mass., 1981-84; asst. prof. Johns Hopkins U., Balt., 1984-86, assoc. prof., 1986-91, prof., 1991—. Office: Johns Hopkins Univ Dept Of Physics Astron Baltimore MD 21218

KROLIKOWSKI, GARY E., social sciences educator; b. Warsaw, N.Y., May 14, 1953; s. Theodore Francis and Adela Kataryna (Wojtowicz) Krolikowski. BA, SUNY, 1974; MEd, St. Lawrence U., 1977; PhD, Northcentral U., 2003. Cert. counseling psychologist NY, Mass., 1997. Sr. mgr. Bayer Corp., Wilmington, Mass., 1983—90; cons. Boston, 1990—92; prof. psychology Rochester Inst. Tech., NY, 1992—; faculty Monroe C.C., Rochester, 1999—2003; prof. psychology SUNY, Genesco, 2001—; counselor County of St. Lawrence, NY, 1975; dir., tng. and devel. City of Somerville, Mass., 1978; adj. faculty Bunker Hill C.C., Mass., 1978; faculty Northeastern U., Mass., 1983. Mentor SUNY Empire Coll., faculty, 2004—. Contbr. articles various profl. jours. Recipient Nat. Merit Scholar, NYS Regents Scholar, Scholarship Merit award, Arion Found. award. Mem.: AFT, NYSUT, APA, ASTD, Assn. for Humanistic Psychology, Am. Psychol. Soc., United U. Profs., Dom Polski Assn., Silver Lake Assn., Polish Union Am., Kappa Delta Pi. Republican. Catholic. Avocations: reading, travel, camping, kayaking, cross country skiing. Home: 4380 Lakeshore Dr Castile NY 14427

KROLL, ARTHUR HERBERT, lawyer, educator, writer; b. N.Y.C., Dec. 2, 1939; s. Abraham and Sylvia Kroll; m. Lois Handmacher, June, 1964; children: Douglas, Pamela. BA, Cornell U., 1961; LLB cum laude, St. John's U., 1965; LLM in Taxation, NYU, 1969. Assoc. Patterson, Belknap, Webb & Tyler, N.Y.C., 1965-72, ptnr., 1972-90, Pryor, Cashman, Sherman & Flynn, N.Y.C., 1990-95; CEO KST Cons. Group, Inc. Adj. prof. U. Miami Sch. Law, NYU; lectr. numerous confs.; mem. adv. bd. Bur. Nat. Affairs Tax Mgmt., Inc., Practising Law Inst. Tax Adv. Bd., U. Miami Inst. Estate Planning, Bus. Laws, Inc.; mem. adv. com. NYU Ann. Inst. on Fed. Taxation. Author: Executive Compensation, 3 vols., Compensating Executives; monthly newsletter Family Bus. Profl.; mem. bd. contbg. editors and advisers Corporate Taxation; mem. editl. adv. bd. Jour. Compensation and Benefits. Office: KST Consulting Group Inc 250 E Hartsdale Ave Ste 30 Hartsdale NY 10530 Office Phone: 914-722-6330. Business E-Mail: kstconsultinggroup@worldnet.att.net.

KROLL, BARRY LEWIS, lawyer; b. Chgo., June 8, 1934; s. Harry M. and Hannah (Lewis) K.; m. Jayna Vivian Leibovitz, June 20, 1956; children: Steven Lee, Joan Lois Kroll Dolgin, Nancy Maxine Kroll Richardson. AB in Psychology with distinction, U. Mich., 1955, JD with distinction, 1958. Bar: Ill. 1958. Assoc. firm Jacobs & McKenna, Chgo., 1958-66, Epstein, Manilow & Sachnoff, Chgo., 1966-68, Schiff, Hardin, Waite Dorschel & Britton, Chgo., 1968-69; ptnr. Wolfberg & Kroll, Chgo., 1970-74, Kirshbaum & Kroll, Chgo., 1972-74; of counsel Jacobs, Williams & Montgomery, Ltd., Chgo., 1973-74; ptnr. Jacobs, Williams & Montgomery Ltd., Chgo., 1974-85, Williams & Montgomery Ltd., Chgo., 1985—2001; of counsel Williams Montgomery & John, Ltd., 2002—. Faculty John Marshall Law Sch., Chgo., 1969-73; atty. for petitioner in U.S. Supreme Ct. decision Escobedo vs Ill., 1964; mem. legal and legis. com. Internat. Franchise Assn., 1976-80 Asst. editor: Mich. Law Rev, 1957-58. Chmn. Park Forest Bd. Zoning Appeals, 1971-78. Served to capt. AUS, 1959-62. Named Outstanding Young Man, Park Forest Jr. C. of C., 1966. Mem. Ill. Bar Assn., Chgo. Bar Assn. (chmn. legis. com. 1974-75), Ill. Appellate Lawyers Assn. (treas. 1978-79, sec. 1979-80, pres. 1981-82), Bar Assn. 7th Fed. Circuit, Order of Coif, Tau Epsilon Rho, Alpha Epsilon Pi. Jewish (trustee congregation 1966-70, 72-75, 90—, pres. men's club 1965-66). Home: Apt 21B 1440 N State Pkwy Chicago IL 60610-6509 Personal E-mail: jaynabarry@msn.com, blk@willmont.com.

KROLL, BRIAN WALTER THOMAS, music educator; b. Mineola, NY, Mar. 29, 1974; s. Walter Albert Kroll and Lynda Alice Seelig; m. Mary Theresa Piekut, Dec. 23, 2000. BS in Edn., Hofstra U., 1997; Mus. M, Five Towns Coll., Dix Hills, NY, 2002. Cert. K-12 music tchr. NY. Vocal music tchr. Beach St. Mid. Sch., West Islip, NY, 1998—2000, Babylon Junior-Senior H.S., Babylon, NY, 2000—. Mem.: Music Educators Nat. Conf., Am. Choral Dirs. Assn., Suffolk County Music Educators Assn. (divsn. III east chorus chmn. 2001—04, asst. to v.p. for cen. divsn. 2004—05, ctrl. divsn. 2004—05), NY State Sch. Music Assn., Masons (sr. warden). Office: Babylon HS 50 Railroad Avenue Babylon NY 11702 Personal E-mail: bkroll@optonline.net.

KROLL, DENNIS EDWARDS, industrial engineering educator; b. Chgo., June 7, 1947; s. Witold Charles and Lillian Mary (Zwic) K.; m. Susan Ann Michalski, May 26, 1973 (div. Dec. 1979); children: Steven Edward, Brian Christopher; m. Karen Elizabeth Wood, Jan. 13, 1990 (div. Sept. 1994); m. Carolyn S. Clark, Nov. 25, 2000. BS in Indsl. Engring., Bradley U., 1970; MS in Indsl. Engring., U. Wis., 1973; PhD, U. Ill., 1989. Devel. engr. Western Electric Co., Chgo., 1970-74; plant mgr. Junis Mfg. Co., Franklin Park, Ill., 1974-75; sr. indsl. engr. Sunbeam Appliance Co., Chgo., 1975-76; sr. mfg. engr. Victor Comptometer, Chgo., 1976; indsl. engr. Methode Mfg., Rolling Meadows, Ill., 1976-77; planning engr. Western Electric div. AT&T Tech., Lisle, Ill., 1977-81; prof. indsl. and mfg. engring. Bradley U., Peoria, Ill., 1981—. Founding editor Jour. Indsl. Engring. Design, 1995—; contbr. articles to profl. jours., chpts. to books. Precinct committeeman Peoria Rep. Com., 1981-82; bd. dirs. West Peoria (Ill.) Street Light Dist., 1991-95; founding alderman City of West Peoria, 1993-2000; mem. Peoria Water Adv. Com., 1999-2000; mem. Eureka2000plus commn., 2001-04; precinct committeeman Woodford Rep. Com., 2002—; mem. liquor ordinance com. City of Eureka, 2005— Recipient lab. devel. award Soc. Mfg. Engrs., 1990, Simulation Lab. Devel. award St. Francis Med. Ctr., 1995, Bradley virtual course devel. award, 2001. Mem. Soc. Mfg. Engrs. (sr.), Inst. Indsl. Engrs. (sr.; cert. sys. integrator, chpt. pres. 1982-83, 94-95), Am. Legion, Am. Soc. for Engring. Edn. (IE Divsn. webmaster, sec., newsletter editor, chair) Roman Catholic. Avocations: fishing, gardening, cooking, history. Office: Bradley U IMET Morgan 110 1501 W Bradley Ave Peoria IL 61625-0003 Business E-Mail: dek@bradley.edu.

KROLL, JOHN HENNIG, classicist, numismatist; b. Washington, Feb. 12, 1938; s. John Henry and Ruth Waltner (Hennig) Kroll; m. Sandra Darin Puppel, Aug. 16, 1969 (div. Mar. 1999); children: Naomi, Jesse, Emily; m. Lisa Kallet, Dec. 18, 2003. BA, Oberlin Coll., 1959; MA, Harvard U., 1962, PhD, 1968. Jr. fellow Harvard U. Soc. Fellows, Cambridge, Mass., 1966—69; Agora rsch. fellow Agora Excavations, Athens, Greece, 1970—73; asst. prof., assoc. prof., prof. U. Tex.-Austin, 1974—. Lectr. Classics Harvard U., Cambridge, 1969; vis. prof. Am. Sch. Classical Studies, Athens, 2002—03. Author: Athenian Bronze Allotment Plates, 1973, Agora Excavation Greek Coins, 1992, Sylloge Nummorum-Munich-Athens, 2002; contbr. articles to profl. jours. Fellow, NEH, 1979—80, Am. Coun. Learned Socs., 1985—86, Inst. for Advanced Study, 1985—86. Mem.: Am. Numismatic Soc. (2nd v.p. 2000—), Am. Assn. Ancient Historians, Am. Philol. Assn., Archaeol. Inst. Am. Avocations: music, travel. Office: Dept Classics Univ Texas Austin TX 78712 Office Phone: 512-471-7890.

KROLL, MARK, music educator; b. Bklyn., N.Y., Sept. 13, 1946; s. Eugene and Frances Kroll; m. Carol Lieberman, July 9, 1975; 1 child, Ethan. BA cum laude, CUNY Bklyn., 1968; MusM, Yale U., 1971. Lectr. U. Calif. Santa Cruz, 1971—74, Emerson Coll., Boston, 1976—78; prof. Boston U., 1978—2002, prof. emeritus, 2002—. Vis. prof. Zagreb Music Acad., Croatia, 1989, Belgrade Music Acad., Yugoslavia, 1989, Wurzburg Conservatory, Germany, 1993; founder, program chair Boston Early Music Festival, 1981—83; harpsichordist Boston Symphony Orch., 1979—; bd. dirs. Brookline Music Libr. Assn., Brookline, Mass., 1978—90. Author: La Belle Execution, 2003, Playing the Harpsichord Expressively, 2004, The Beethoven Violin Sonatas, 2004, The Music Workbooks of Charles Avison, 2005; editor: J.N. Hummel: Arrangements, 2000, 2003; performer: numerous rec., 1974—. Recipient Solo Recitalist award, Nat. Endowment Arts, 1981, Rsch. award, DAAD, 1996, 2002; fellow, NEH, 2003. Avocation: Black Belt 1984. Home: 59 Naples Rd Brookline MA 02446

KROLL, ROBERT RONALD, music educator; b. Detroit, Aug. 30, 1960; s. Ronald M. Kroll; children: Lauren W., Robert A., Lindsay R. MusB in Performance, Ea. Mich. U., 1982; MusM in Composition, Northwestern U., 1983; MusB Edn., Ea. Mich. U., 1987. Music educator Grosse Pointe (Mich.) South H.S., 1984—87, West Mid. Sch., Rochester Hills, Mich., 1987—, Blue Lake Fine Arts Camp, Twin Lake, Mich., 1990—2004. Mem.: Music Educators Nat. Conf., Mich. Sch. Band and Orch. Assn. (dist. pres., 1st v.p., 2nd v.p., 3rd v.p., past pres. 1994—2005). Office Phone: 248-726-5000. Business E-Mail: bkroll@rochester.k12.mi.us.

KROLL, SOL, lawyer; b. Russia, Aug. 10, 1918; m. Ruth Saslow; children: Gerald, Judy, Elise, Elliott. LLB, St. John's U., 1942. Bar: N.Y. 1942, U.S. Supreme Ct. 1956. Former U.S. counsel Inst. London Underwriters; former U.S. counsel to Assn. Francaise des Socs. D'Assurances Transports; former mem. com. of interfraud task force N.Y. Ins. Dept.; sr. ins. counsel. County atty. Putnam County, N.Y. Contbr. articles on Am. ins. law to various ins. mags. Mem. ABA, Fed. Bar Assn., N.Y. State Bar Assn., N.Y.C. Bar Assn., Internat. Assn. Ins. Counsel, Industry Adv. Com. on Ins., Ins. Fedn. NY (bd. dirs.). Home: 600 Cantitoe St Bedford NY 10506-1107 Office: 1365 York Ave New York NY 10021 Fax: 212-980-7207. Office Phone: 212-750-4470. E-mail: skroll@solkroll.com.

KROLOPP, RUDOLPH WILLIAM, retired industrial designer, consultant; b. Chgo., June 7, 1930; s. Rudolph and Emma (Nice) K.; m. Dorcas S. Hall; children: Jacqueline, Mark, Joseph, Sharon, Lizabeth, John, Jennifer. BFA, U. Ill.-Champaign, 1956; postgrad., Lake Forest Coll., Ill., 1974-78. Staff designer Motorola Consumer Products, Chgo., 1956-59, chief designer, 1959-62, mgr. indsl. design communication div., 1962-82, dir. indsl. design, 1982-97, mem. patent com., 1981-97, chmn. corp. graphic standards council, 1983-97. Assoc. prof. indsl. design. U. Ill. Chgo. 1984; interviewed in CNN, MSMBC and Fox TV networks, and various publs., including Newsweek, Chgo. Sun Times, Reuters Am., others. Patentee in field. Instr. phys. fitness Oak Park YMCA, Ill., 1967; instr. cardiovascular health Buehler YMCA, Palatine, Ill., 1968—, bd. dirs., 1980—, chmn. program com., 1980—, sec. bd. dirs., 1983-84. Served with USMC, 1948-52. Recipient Master Design award Product Engring. Mag., 1961, Weson Design award Western Electronic Conv., 1970, Design Excellence award Indsl. Design Mag., 1972, Design

Engring. award Nat. Marine Electronics Assn., 1972, Good Design award Hannover Fair, Germany, 1978, Nekkei Design award, 1990, Internat. Design award, 1991, Corp. award for good design, 1992, Design Excellence award, 1996, Idea Design award, 1997, Good Design award Hannover Fair, 1997. Fellow Indsl. Designers Soc. Am. (chmn. fellowship awards com. 1996, program chmn., sec., regional v.p., chmn. nat. nominating com., Spl. award 1993). Clubs: Parkers SAC (Chgo.) (pres. 1962-65). Roman Catholic. Home: 103 Golfview Rd Lake Zurich IL 60047-1290

KROME, KARI MITCHELL, composer, singer; b. Lakewood, Calif., Aug. 1, 1961; d. Leo Andy Mitchell and Sandra Mae Cowan. Songwriter BMI, L.A., 1975—. Freelance recording artist, L.A., 1977—; freelance writer, L.A., 1976—; reporter In Style Mag., N.Y. Performer: The Runways, 1970; prodr.: High Weirdness; contbr. articles to websites. Recipient Gold Record award, Mercury Records, 1976. Avocation: music. Office: In Style Magazine c/o Time Life 1761 6th Ave 1803B New York NY 10020

KROMHOUT, ROBERT ANDREW, physics professor; b. Elgin, Ill., Oct. 23, 1923; s. Andrew and Sarah (Tiffany) K.; m. Ora Morlier, Dec. 21, 1950; children— Sharon, Brian, Ethan. BS, Kans. State U., 1947; MS, U. Ill., 1948, PhD, 1952. Asst. prof. U. Ill., 1952-56; asst. prof. Fla. State U., Tallahassee, 1956-58, assoc. prof., 1958-62, head dept. physics, 1959-62, prof. physics, 1962-92, prof. emeritus, 1992—; dir. Inst. for Cognitive Scis., 1985-92. Mem. Fla. Metric Coun., 1980-86 Served with AUS, 1943-46. Mem. Am. Phys. Soc., Am. Assn. Physics Tchrs., Sigma Xi, Phi Kappa Phi. Home: 206 Westminister Dr Tallahassee FL 32304-3519 E-mail: rkromhou@mailer.fsu.edu.

KROMINGA, LYNN, cosmetics executive, lawyer; b. L.A., May 16, 1950; d. Dale E. and Phyllis M. Krominga; m. Amnon Shiboleth, Apr. 9, 1992; 1 child, Karen Lee Shiboleth. BA in German, U. Minn., 1972, JD, 1974. Bar: Minn. 1974, N.Y. 1976. Assoc. firms in Mpls. and N.Y.C., 1974-77; assoc. counsel Am. Express Co., N.Y.C., 1977-80; sr. internat. counsel Revlon, Inc., N.Y.C., 1981-92, v.p. law, 1988-92, gen. counsel to exec. com., 1991-92, pres. licensing divsn., 1992-98, mem. exec. com., 1993-94, 97-99, exec. v.p. bus. devel., 1998-99; mem. bd. advisors MakeoverStudio.com, 1999—2001; bd. advisors Salonforce.com., 1999—2002; CEO Fashion Wire Daily, Inc., 2002; ptnr. KLS Mgmt. LLC, 2002—04, Krominga Holdings LLC, 2004—. Bd. dirs. StructuredWeb.com., 2000-02. Mem. ABA, Internat. Bar Assn. Cosmetic, Toiletry and Fragrance Assn. (vice chmn. govt. rels. com. 1991-92), Am. Arbitration Assn. (corp. counsel com. 1986-92, panel of arbitrators for large complex cases 1993-94, internat. panel of arbitrators 1997—), Phi Beta Kappa. Home: 180 Riverside Blvd Apt 21A New York NY 10069-0814 Office Phone: 917-270-4735. E-mail: lkrominga@aol.com.

KRONBERG, PHILIPP PAUL, physicist, educator; arrived in U.S., 2002; s. Philipp and Jean Stewart (Davidson) Kronberg; m. Roberta Secord Purdon, Aug. 3, 1963; children: Paul Andrew, Martin Thomas, Michael Philipp. BSc in Engring. Physics, Queen's U., Kingston, Ont., 1961, MSc in Physics, 1963; PhD in Physics, Manchester U., Eng., 1967, DSc, 1995. Lectr. U. Manchester, England, 1966—68; asst. to full prof. phys. scis. and astronomy U. Toronto, Canada, 1968—99, prof. emeritus dept. physics, 1999—2002; disting. Orson Anderson scholar Los Alamos Nat. Lab., N.Mex., 2002—03, vis. scholar, 2003—. Chmn. supercomputer user's group U. Toronto, Canada, 1968—88, chmn. Connaught phys. scis. and engring. rev. panel, 1982—85, mem. rsch. bd., 1985—88, 1988—89, mem. pres.' com. rev. Innovations Found., 1988, mem. provostial search com. dean sch. grad. studies, 89, project leader proposed collaboration with Calif. Tech. in millimetre astronomy, 1990—92; mem. VLA adv. com. Nat. Radio Astronomy Observatory, United States, 1978—80; chmn. VLA adv. com. Assoc. Univs. Inc., DC, 1979—80, mem. vis. com., 1979—82, chmn. vis. com., 1981—82; chmn. steering com. Algonquin Radio Observatory Millimetre Telescope NRC Canada, Ottawa, 1983—86, mem. governing coun., 1987—90, mem. assessment com., 1988—90, co-chmn. rev. com. divsn. physics, 1988—89; mem. Atlantic Coun., Toronto, 1985—90; mem. mgmt. bd. Ontario Ctr. Large Scale Computation, 1986—90, mem. Ontario Inter-Univ. adv. bd., 1986—90; mem. rev. panel nat. facility function of Assoc. Univs. Inc. and Nat. Radio Astronomy Observatory NSF, United States, 1987, mem. task force assess US radio astronomy facilities, 88, mem. rev. bd. design and constrn. Green Bank Telescope, 1989—90; chmn. and scientific organizer Internat. Astronomical Union Symposium No. 140, Heidelberg, Germany, 1988—90; chmn. scientific and tech. rev. com. Sudbury Neutrino Observatory NRC and NSERC, Canada, 1988; mem. bd. mgmt. Mont Mégantic Observatory U. Montreal/U. Laval, 1980—84; mem. Mgmt. Bd. James Clerk Maxwell Submillimeter Telescope, 1990—91; mem. mgmt. bd. ISOTRACE U. Toronto, 1990; Canadian rep. and scientific rev. com. Japan Inst. Space and Astronautical Scis./Canadian Space Agy. Very Long Baseline Interferometry Satellite, 1995—98; mem. scientific organizing com. summer workshop on cosmological magnetic fields Aspen Inst. Physics, Colo., 1996, co-organizer workshop on astrophysical dynamos, 2000. Bd. dirs. The Reserve at Santa Fe, 2005—. Recipient Humboldt award, Max Planck Inst., 1990, 1998; fellow, Guggenheim Found., 1985, Killiam Found., 1990; Humboldt awardee, Max Planck Inst., 1980. Mem.: Am. Astronomical Soc., Am. Phys. Soc., Boulevard Club (commodore), Sigma Xi (pres. Tornoto chpt.). Episcopalian. Avocations: sailing, tennis, history, international affairs. Home: Unit 1407 941 Calle Mejia Santa Fe NM 87501 Business E-Mail: kronberg@lanl.gov.

KRONE, CHERYL A., research scientist, consultant; b. Renton, Wa., May 25, 1948; d. Wilbur T. and Helen Faye K. BS, U. Washington, Seattle, 1978, MS, 1981, PhD, 1984. Vis. scientist U. Hawaii at Manoa, Honolulu, 1983; lectr. U. Washington, Seattle, 1983-84; rsch. chemist Nat. Oceanic and Atmospheric Adminstrn., Seattle, 1984-98; sr. rsch. scientist Applied Rsch. Inst., Seattle, 1998—. Deputy dir. Applied Rsch. Inst., Seattle, 1998—; cons. CK Consulting Svcs., Renton, Wa., 1998—. Author: (book chpt.) CRC Carcinogens and Mutagens in the Environment, 1982, over 30 articles in peer-reviewed med. sci. jours. Mem. Am. Chem. Soc., Inst. of Food Tech., New Zealand Assn. Scientists, Am. Physical Soc., Phi Beta Kappa, Sigma Xi. Avocations: bicycling, running, hiking. Office: Applied Rsch Inst PO Box 1969 Palmerston North 5301 New Zealand Fax: 64-6-353-1012. E-mail: cakrone@u.washington.edu.

KRONE, NORMAN BERNARD, real estate developer, lawyer; b. Memphis, Sept. 13, 1938; s. Irving and Eva (Sauer) K.; m. Norma Lee Moon; children: John, Christine, David. LLB, Stetson U., 1964. Bar: Fla. 1964, Ohio 1987, US Dist. Ct. (mid. dist.) Fla. 1965, US Ct. Appeals (7th cir.) 1968; lic. real estate broker, Ohio, Mich., Ala. Atty. Lifsey & Johnston, Tampa, Fla., 1964—65; pvt. practice Tampa, Fla., 1965—66; property mgmt. atty. Ford Motor Co., Dearborn, Mich., 1966—67; audit mgr. Montgomery Ward & Co., Chgo., 1967—68, corp. real estate mgr., 1968—75; exec. v.p. Montgomery Ward Properties Corp., Chgo., 1970—75; from v.p. to sr. v.p. Walgreen Co., Deerfield, Ill., 1975—85; pres., CEO The Hausman Co., Cleve., 1987—2001; sr. exec. v.p. Henry S. Miller, Grubb & Ellis Comml./Retail Svc., 1985—87; mng. prin. NK Devel. Ltd., 1996—2002; prin. NK Real Estate Adv. Ltd., 2002—; COO Olympia Devel. Group, 2004—. Trustee Internat. Coun. Shopping Ctr., NYC, 1976-79; dir. Myers Industries, Lincoln, Ill., 1976-83; instr. Intercoun. Shopping Ctr.-Inst. Profl. Devel.; dean U. Shopping Ctr. instructor - Law for Non-Lawyers, ednl. adv. com., small ctr. com., chmn. retail adv. com., 1975-76, cert. leasing specialist, 1995-; cons. Krone Group LLC, 2001-03; instr., spkr. in field, Law for Non-Lawyers. Author, editor: The Lease and Its Language, 1996, ICSC Study Lease, 2000, Anatomy of a Lease, 2001; contbr. articles to mags. Acting judge City of Tampa, 1964-66; bd. dir. Met. Housing and Planning Coun., Chgo., 1977-80, New City YMCA, 1976-78; mem. sch. bd. Palisades Cmty. Sch. Dist., 1968-69; mem. strategic planning com. Met. Chgo. YMCA, 1976-77; 1st pres. Cleve. Pops Orch.; bd. dir. Walgreen Hist. Found., 1984-87; co-founder, pres., mem. exec. com. Realty Resources (a network of comml. brokerage firms), 1987-2001. Named Entrepreneur of Yr. Operation Breadbasket, 1977. Mem. Cleve. Bar Assn., Real Estate Inst., Beachwood C. of C. (pres. 1996, exec. com. 1992-2001, life bd. dir.), Acacia Country Club (bd. dir. 1997-99, chmn. planning com. 1998-99, sec. 1998). Avocations: woodworking, golf. Office: Olympia Devel Group 1060 Keene Rd Dunedin FL 34698 Office Phone: 727-736-8622. Business E-Mail: norm-krone@olympia-group.com.

KRONENBERG, ANDREAS, nuclear chemist; b. Leipzig, Germany, Mar. 22, 1971; B in chemistry, Tech. U. of Dresden, Germany, 1993; M in chemistry, U. Marburg, Germany, 1997; PhD, U. Mainz, Germany, 2001. Rsch. assoc. Fla. State U., Tallahassee, 2001—02, Los Alamos Nat. Lab., N.Mex., 2003—04; stewardship rsch. assoc. Oak Ridge Assoc. Univs., Tenn., 2004—. Mem.: Radiochemistry Soc., Am. Soc. for Materials Internat. Material Info. Soc., Material Rsch. Soc., German Phys. Soc., German Nuc. Soc., German Chem. Soc., Am. Nuc. Soc., Am. Phys. Soc., Internat. Nuc. Target Devel. Soc., Am. Chem. Soc. Office: Oak Ridge Assoc Univs MS 6374 Bldg 6008 Oak Ridge TN 37831 Office Phone: 865-241-1514. Office Fax: 854-576-5780. Personal E-mail: kronenberg@nuc-tec-consult.com. E-mail: kronenberga@ornl.gov.

KRONENBERG, JANET LOIS, lawyer; b. Cleve., Jan. 13, 1948; d. Louis David and Shirley Evelyn (Weiskopf) K. Student, George Washington U., 1966-68; BA, NYU, 1970, MPA, 1976; JD, Cleve. State U., 1978. Bar: Ohio 1979, U.S. Dist. Ct. 1979, U.S. Ct. Appeals 1983, U.S. Supreme Ct. 1988. Rsch. asst. Cleve. State U., 1977-78, adj. lectr. law, 1980-91; dep. treas. Cuyahoga County, Cleve., 1977-78; ptnr. Kronenberg & Kronenberg, Cleve., 1979—2000; program officer Cuyahoga County Bd. Commrs., 2000—, atty., 2000—. Asst. to sr. v.p. Curtis Brown, Ltd., N.Y.C., 1970-75; presenter various continuing edn. programs; life del. 8th Jud. Conf., Cleve. Pres., trustee Ctr. for Prevention Domestic Violence, Cleve., 1981-89, N.E. Ohio Health Svcs., Cleve., 1992-95; trustee Womenspace, Cleve., 1989-91, N.E. Ohio Health Svcs., 1990-93; mem. citizens adv. bd. Broadview Devel. Ctr., Broadview Heights, Ohio, 1990-91; mem. Cuyahoga County Child Protection Coun., Cleve., 1993-95; mem. Cuyahoga County Women's Polit. Caucus. Named Vol. Lawyer of Yr., Legal Aid Soc., Cleve., 1987, honoree Coalition To End Domestic Violence, Cleve., 1989; recipient Legacy award Domestic Violence Ctr., Cleve., 2003. Mem. Ohio Bar Assn., Cuyahoga County Bar Assn. (trustee), Cuyahoga County Bar Found. (trustee). Avocation: travel. Home: 339 Claymore Blvd Richmond Hts OH 44143-1712 Office: 339 Claymore Blvd Cleveland OH 44143-1712

KRONENBERG, RICHARD SAMUEL, physician, educator; b. Chgo., Aug. 7, 1938; s. Frank Paul and Ruth Ida (Zaretzky) K.; m. Carole Marie Hurd, Oct. 11, 1963; children: Karen, Marilyn, Brenda. BA, Northwestern U., 1960, MD, 1963. Intern Parkland Meml. Hosp., Mpls., 1967-68, resident in internal medicine, 1968; rsch. fellow Cardiovascular Rsch. Inst. U. Calif., San Francisco, 1968-70; asst. prof. medicine U. Minn., 1970-74, assoc. prof., 1974-79, prof., dir. pulmonary div., 1979-84; prof. U. Tex. Health Sci. Ctr., Houston, 1984—2002; prof. medicine, exec. v.p. for clin. affairs U. Tex. Health Ctr., Tyler, 1984—2002; sr. v.p. Mother Frances Health Sys., 2002—. Reviewer subsplty. programs in internal medicine Accreditation Coun. Grad. Med. Edn., Chgo., 1985—. Mem. editorial rev. bd. The Asbestos Monitor, Nat. Asbestos Coun. Jour., 1990-93; contbr. chpts. to books. Capt. USAF, 1965-67. Recipient Rsch. Career Devel. award NIH, 1973-78. Fellow ACP, Am. Coll. Chest Physicians; mem. Nat. Asbestos Coun. (bd. dirs. 1990-93), Asbestos Disease Assn. (pres. 1990-93), Ctrl. Soc. Clin. Rsch. Avocation: bicycling. Home: 5615 Cedar Hill Cir Tyler TX 75703-3912 Office Phone: 903-531-5400. E-mail: richard.kronenberg@uthct.edu, kronenr@tmfhs.org.

KRONER, ARNOLD FRIEDRICH, financial consultant, economist; b. Gablonz, Czechoslovakia, May 16, 1939; came to U.S., 1962; s. Arnold and Anna Marie (Gramer) K.; m. Edith Ficklin Crammatte, Aug. 12, 1972; 1 child, Erik. MA, Cornell U., 1966, PhD, 1971. Asst. prof. econs. dept. U. Pitts., 1968-75, Columbia U., N.Y.C., 1973-74; asst. treas. Chase Manhattan Bank, N.Y.C., 1975-76; asst. v.p. Chem. Bank, N.Y.C., 1976-78; sr. v.p., treas. Nat. Australia Bank, N.Y.C., 1984-87; v.p. Algemene Bank Nederland, N.V., N.Y.C., 1978-84, 87-90; pres. Pegasus Econometric Group, Inc., Hoboken, N.J., 1991-92; v.p. ASLK-CGER Bank, N.Y.C., 1992-93; pres. Spectral Inc., White Plains, NY, 1993—. Cons. Intern. Banking Inst., St. Petersburg Russia, 1995-96; cons. to prime min. of Belarus, 1996-97. Editor Portfolio-Internat. Econ. Perspectives, 1972-75. V.p. Silver Lake Civic Assn., S.I., N.Y., 1979-82. Named Richardson fellow, 1960, UN fellow, 1961, U. N.C. fellow, 1962; recipient Andrew Clark fellowship Cornell U., 1966. Mem. Royal Econ. Soc., Am. Econ. Assn. Roman Catholic. Avocations: skiing, camping. Home and Office: PO Box 635 White Plains NY 10603-0635

KRONER, FRED L., journalist; b. Champaign, Ill., Nov. 16, 1955; s. James Carlton and Naomi Ruth Kroner; m. Dee Siddens, Aug. 21, 1976 (div. Nov. 1996); 1 child, Devin Richard; m. Emily Sue Moon, June 6, 1999. BS, U. Ill., 1978. Sportswriter Champaign Courier, 1974-78, Bloomington (Ill.) Pantagraph, 1978-81, Champaign News-Gazette, 1981—. Contbg. author: Cascade of Memories, 1998, Nature's Echoes, 2000, Enlightened Shadows, 2001; author: Citizen Pain, Brian Cardinal, 2001, booklets and newspaper series. Coach Little League Baseball, Champaign, 1982—86, Summer League Baseball, Sullivan, Ill., 1990—93; guest commentator WDAN Radio, Danville, Ill., 1995—. Named Newsman of the Yr., Ill. Wrestling Coaches Assn., 1984, 1988, 2000, Sportswriter of the Yr. for Ill., Nat. Sportscasters & Sportswriters Assn., 2001; recipient awards, AP, 1985, 1989. Mem.: Nat. Sportswriters and Sportscasters Assn., Ill. Press Assn., Soc. Profl. Journalists. Methodist. Avocations: gardening, poetry. Home: 105 S Division St # 778 Mahomet IL 61853-9237 Office: Champaign-Urbana News-Gazette PO Box 677 Champaign IL 61824-0677 E-mail: ItsFred586@aol.com.

KRONEY, ROBERT HARPER, lawyer; b. Dallas, May 16, 1939; s. Archie D. and Martha (Harper) K.; 1 child from a preivous marriage, Harper Paul; m. Susan K. Monaghan, Aug. 20, 1994. BS in Geol. Engring., U. Okla., 1962; LLB, U. Tex., Austin, 1964; LLM, So. Meth. U., 1972. Bar: U.S. Dist. Ct. (no. dist.) Tex. 1966. Ptnr. Strasburger & Pride, Dallas, 1966-73, Johnson & Swanson, Dallas, 1973-84, Kroney Mincey Inc., Dallas, 1984—. Adviser, continuing legal edn., So. Meth. U. Served to lt., USAR, 1962-66. Named Cooper Clinic Man of Yr., 2000. Fellow Am. Coll. Trust and Estate Counsel; mem. Dallas Estate Planning Coun. (bd. dirs. 1972, 84), State Bar Tex. (trust editor real estate, probate and trust law newsletter 1972-78), Am. Soc. CLUs (bd. dirs. Dallas chpt. 1976-83, pres. 1982), Tex. Bd. Legal Specialization (estate planning, probate law and tax law). Office: Kroney Mincey Inc 1210 Three Forest Plz 12221 Merit Dr Ste 1210 Dallas TX 75251-3287 Office Phone: 972-386-8500. Business E-Mail: bkroney@ksmdallas.com.

KRONFELD, EDWIN, natural gas company executive; m. Lydia Shepard Ballinger, Feb. 16, 1960; children: Nicholas, Alice, Alexander. Student, Harvard Coll., 1948—51; LLB, Harvard U., 1958; LLM, Georgetown U., 1962. Bar: N.Y., Washington, Okla. Staff atty. Securities & Exchange Commn., Washington, 1958-61; assoc. Lear & Scoutt, Washington, 1961-62; sole practice Washington, 1962-68; ptnr. Neal Siegler & Kronfeld, Washington, 1968-69, Morgan Lewis & Bockius, Washington, 1969-79, Thieman & Kronfeld, Tulsa, 1980-84, Kronfeld & Ribner, Tulsa, 1985-88; pres. Plymouth Resources Inc., Tulsa, 1982—. Lectr. Am. Law Inst.-ABA, Chgo., 1970-78; lectr. Practicing Law Inst., N.Y.C., 1970-78; adj. prof. law Georgetown U., Washington, 1971-78. Chmn. Tulsa Philharm., 1998 Mem. Okla. Ind. Petroleum Assn., Tulsa Assn. Petroleum Landmen, The Summit Club. Home: 2660 S Birmingham Pl Tulsa OK 74114 Office: Plymouth Resources Inc 15 W Sixth St Ste 2300 Tulsa OK 74119 Office Phone: 918-599-1812. E-mail: kronfeld@plymouthgas.com.

KRONFIELD, HARVEY S., lawyer; b. Wilmington, Del., June 28, 1929; s. Samuel Irving and Lena Arsht Kronfeld; m. Janet E. Lubowitz, Jan. 29, 1955; children: Linda Kronfeld, Andrew Kronfeld, Julia Kronfeld. BA with honors, U. Del., 1949; LLB cum laude, Harvard Law Sch., 1952. Bar: Pa. 1953, Del. 1962, Mich. 1967. Assoc. Wolf, Bloch, Schorr and Soes-Cohen, Phila., 1955, Morris, Nichols, Asht and Tunnel, Wilmington, Del., 1956—62; sr. atty. Ford Motor Co. Law Dept., Dearborn, Mich., 1962—67; ptnr. Mexisov, Gilman Jeffe and Levin, Phila., 1967—73; sr. ptnr., chmn. commercial lit. dept. Rawle and Henderson, Phila., 1980—85; sr. ptnr. Kromfeld and Newberg, Phila., 1985—89, Kromfeld, Newberg and Duggan, Phila., 1990—93; owner Harry S. Kronfield P.C. and Law Office, Govenors Sta., Pa., 1993—. Recipient Honors in Course Grad., U. of Del., 1949. Mem.: Phila. Bar Assn. Avocations: golf, travel, reading. Home: 403 Rockland Rd Merion Station PA 19066 Office: Law Office of Harvey S Kronfield 403 Rockland Rd Merion Station PA 19066

KRONGARD, HOWARD J., federal agency administrator, lawyer; b. Dec. 12, 1940; s. Raphael Harris and Rita (Keyser) K.; children: Kenneth, Mara Lynn. BA, Princeton U., 1961; JD, Harvard U., 1964; postgrad., Cambridge U., 1964-65. Bar: Md. 1965, N.Y. 1967, U.S. Dist. Ct. Md. 1965, U.S. Dist. Ct. (so. dist.) N.Y. 1967, U.S. Ct. Appeals (2d cir.) 1973, U.S. Ct. Appeals (8th cir.) 1980, U.S. Supreme Ct. 1991. Assoc. Piper & Marbury, Balt., 1964, Cravath, Swaine & Moore, N.Y.C., 1965, 66-73; law clk. to Hon. Kenneth B. Keating N.Y. Ct. Appeals, Albany, 1966; assoc., gen. counsel Peat, Marwick, Mitchell & Co., N.Y.C., 1973-86; gen. counsel Deloitte, Haskins & Sells, N.Y.C., 1986-89, Deloitte & Touche, LLP, N.Y.C., 1989-95; of counsel Freshfields Bruckhaus Deringer, London/N.Y.C., 1996—2005; insp. gen. US Dept. State, Washington, 2005—. Spkr. in field; bd. dirs. Lacrosse Found., Inc., Balt., 1981—, PCX Equities, Nat. Legal Ctr. Pub. Interest; U.S. rep. to Internat. Lacrosse Fedn.; pub. gov. Pacific Exch. Named Outstanding Player in U.S.A., U.S. Club Lacrosse Assn., 1968, 74; inducted into Lacrosse Hall of Fame, 1985, N.Y. Sports Hall of Fame, 1994; recipient Ames Briefwriting prize Harvard Law Sch., 1962; Frank Knox Meml. fellow, 1965. Mem. Assn. of Bar of City of N.Y., Harvard Club. Office: US Dept State 2121 Virginia Ave NW Rm 8100 Washington DC 20037

KRONIK, JOHN WILLIAM, language educator; b. Vienna, May 18, 1931; arrived in U.S., 1939, naturalized, 1944; s. Bernard and Melanie (Hollub) K.; m. Eva Kronik, Dec. 26, 1955; children: Theresa J., Geoffrey B. BA, Queens Coll., 1952; MA, U. Wis., 1953, PhD, 1960; DHL, Ill. Coll., 1979. Asst. prof. Romance lang. Hamilton Coll., Clinton, 1958-63; assoc. prof. Spanish, U. Ill., Urbana, 1963-66; prof. Romance studies Cornell U., Ithaca, N.Y., 1966-2000, prof. emeritus, 2001—. Vis. prof. Columbia U., 1968, Middlebury Coll., Vt., 1979, 80, 86, 91, Brigham Young U., 1982, U. Colo., 1989, U. Calif., Berkeley, 91, U. Calif., Irvine, 1994, U. Calif., L.A., 1999, 2000, U. Calif., Riverside, 2003; cons. NEH, 1973-92, Guggenheim Found., 1988—; corporator Internat. Inst. in Spain, Madrid, 1972—. Author: La farsa y el teatro espanol, 1971; co-editor: La familia de Pascual Duarte, 1961, Textos y Contextos de Galdos, 1994, Intertextual Pursuits: Literary Mediations in Modern Spanish Narrative, 1998; series editor Prentice-Hall, 1962-75; mem. editl. bd. MLA, N.Y.C., 1983-85; editor PMLA, 1985-92, Anales Galdosianos, 1986-90; contbr. articles to profl. jours. With U.S. Army, 1953—55. Fulbright fellow, 1960-61, 87-88; Rockefeller Found. rsch. resident, 1975; Guggenheim fellow, 1983-84; ACLS grantee, 1983-84. Mem. MLA, Internat. Assn. Hispanists, Internat. Galdos Assn. (pres.), Am. Assn. Tchrs. Spanish and Portuguese. Home: 1020 Highland Rd Ithaca NY 14850-1448 Office: Cornell U Dept Romance Studies Ithaca NY 14853-4701

KRONMAN, ANTHONY TOWNSEND, dean, law educator; b. 1945; m. Nancy I. Greenberg, 1982 BA, Williams Coll., 1968, PhD, 1972; JD, Yale U., 1975. Bar: Minn. 1975, N.Y. 1983. Assoc. prof. U. Minn., 1975-76; asst. prof. U. Chgo., 1976-79; vis. assoc. prof. Yale U. Law Sch., New Haven, 1978-79, prof., 1979—, Edward J. Phelps prof. law, 1985—2004, dean, 1994—2004, Sterling prof. law, 2004—. Editor: (with R. Posner) The Economics of Contract Law, 1979 (with F. Kessler and G. Gilmore) Cases and Materials on Contracts, 1986; past mem. editorial bd. Yale Law Jour.; author: Max Weber, 1983, The Lost Lawyer, 1993. Decorated comdr. Nat. Order Merit (France); Danforth Found. fellow, 1968-72. Fellow ABA, Am. Acad. Arts and Scis.; mem. Selden Soc., Conn. Bar Assn. (Cooper fellow), Coun. on Fgn. Rels. Office: Yale U Law Sch PO Box 208215 New Haven CT 06520-8215 Business E-Mail: anthony.kronman@yale.edu.

KRONMILLER, JAN E., academic administrator; BS in Chemistry, Ohio State U., DDS, 1978; PhD in biomedical sciences, U. Conn., 1991. Cert. pediatric dentistry and orthodontics. NIH rsch. fellow U. Conn. Health Ctr.; asst. prof. pediatric dentistry U. Pitts.; pvt. practice; head orthodontics section, Coll. Dentistry U. Ky.; prof. and chair. dept. orthodontics, Sch. Dentistry Oreg. Health Scis. U., prof., grad. program, Sch. Medicine; dean, Coll. Dentistry Ohio State U., 2001—. Recipient Nat. Rsch. Svc. award, NIH, Individual Physician Scientist award. Fellow: Internat. Coll. Dentists, Am. Coll. Dentists. Office: 305 W 12th Ave Columbus OH 43210

KRONOWITZ, PAMELA RENEE, music educator; b. Manhattan, N.Y., Dec. 3, 1954; d. Harold Arthur and Frieda (Kahn) Simmons; children: Lauren, Damon. BA, York Coll., 1976; MA, Queens Coll., 1978. Orch. tchr. Massapequa Pub. Schs., NY, 1994—. Coach Gemini Youth Orch., 1995—97; adjucator N.Y. State Sch. Music Assn. Home: 6 David Ave Hicksville NY 11801

KRONSCHNABEL, ROBERT JAMES, retired manufacturing company executive; b. Green Bay, Wis., Jan. 13, 1935; s. Cyril E. and Margaret (Bierman) K. m. Catherine G. Murray, June 27, 1959; children: Frederick, Nina, Erich, Lisel, Mara. BSME, Marquette U., 1958; MBA, Harvard U., 1963. Field svc. engr. A.C. Electronics div. GM, Milw., 1958-61; mgr. materials Clark Contr. div. A.O. Smith, Cleve. and Lancaster, S.C., 1963-65; v.p., sr. cons. MSI, Appleton, Wis., 1965-67; plant mgr. Allis Chalmers, Port Washington, Wis., 1967-77, Simplicity Mfg. Co., Lexington, S.C., 1970-73; dir. mfg. bearings div. TRW, Jamestown, N.Y., 1977-79; v.p. mfg. bldgs. div. Butler Mfg. Co., Kansas City, Mo., 1979-83, v.p. corp. mfg., 1983-88, pres. Skylight div. Garland, Tex., 1988-91; pres. grain sys. divsn. CTB, Inc., Kansas City, 1991-99, retired, 1999. Mem. prison industries bd. Mo. Dept. Corrections, Jefferson City, 1986-88. Chmn. bd. dirs. Prime Health, Kansas City, 1980-88; bd. regents Rockhurst U., Kansas City, 1985—2003; bd. dirs. Whatsoever Cmty. Ctr., Kansas City, 1997—. Mem. Harvard Bus. Sch. Club. Republican. Roman Catholic. Avocations: gardening, golf, fishing. E-mail: robertk916@wmconnect.com.

KROOT, JASON M., lawyer; b. St. Petersburg, Fla., Jan. 20, 1972; s. Jerry M. and Charlotte A. Kroot. Bsci. in Speech Comm., U. of Tex. at Austin, 1993—95; JD, Chicago-Kent Coll. of Law, Chgo., 1996—99. Bar: Ill. 1999, US Dist. Ct. (no. dist.) 1999, US Dist. Ct. (no. dist.) 2001. Law clk. Herbert F. Stride, Ltd. / Stride, Craddock, & Stride, Chgo., 1996—99; lawyer Sussman, Selig & Ross, Chgo., 1999—. Profl. harness racing driver, Chgo., 2004—. Profl. harness racing driver, Chgo., 2004—. Mem.: ABA (assoc.), Chgo. Bar Assn. (assoc.), Ill. Bar Assn. (assoc.), Ill. Trial Lawyers Assn. (assoc.), Am. Assn. of Trial Lawyers (assoc.). Office: Sussman Selig & Ross One E Wacker Drive Suite 2920 Chicago IL 60601 Office Phone: 312-977-4000. E-mail: jmk@ssrlaw.com.

KROP, LOIS PULVER, psychologist; b. Scranton, Pa., Dec. 24, 1930; d. Samuel Max and Esther Golden Pulver; m. Michael Morris Krop, June 14, 1953; children: Pamela Sue, Daniel Steven, Judith Mary, David Ralph. BA, Pa. State U., 1952; MSW, U. Pa., 1954; PhD, Nova Southeastern U., 1976. LCSW; lic. sch. psychologist Fla., cert. family ct. mediator Fla., lic. marriage and family therapist Fla., 1986, cert. clin. hypnotherapist, sports counselor, hypnotherapist 1995. Family therapist Alexandria Family Svcs., Va., 1954—58; treatment specialist Cath. Family Svcs., Miami, Fla., 1960—85; pvt. practice Marriage and Family Svcs., Inc., Aventura, Fla., 1985—; qualified supr. MFT-CSW and MHL, Tallahassee, 2000—. Prof. acad. lifelong learning Fla. Internat. U., Miami, Fla., 1998—; cons. Mgmt. Tng. Inst., Ft. Lauderdale, 1996—; lectr. Inst. for Ret. Profls., U. Miami, 2002—; prof. Univ. Miami Inst. for Ret. Profl., 2001—. Author: (book) Family Hour/Family Power, 2000; contbr. articles to profl. jours. Bd. trustees U. Pa. Dade Alumni, Miami, Fla., 1985—; pres. Majestic Towers, Bal Harbour, Fla., 1999—, Hadassah Chai Chpt., Miami, 1990—92. Mem.: NASW (pres. 1965), Barry U. Field Instrs. (pres. 1985—87), Assn. of Fla. Sch. Psychologists, Mensa (cert. sports instr. 1998—), Phi Beta Kappa, Mortar Bd., Phi Kappa Phi.

Avocations: tennis, scuba diving, bridge, reading, travel. Home: 9601 Collins Ave #1710 Bal Harbour FL 33154 Office: 19495 Biscayne Blvd #203 Aventura FL 33180 Office Phone: 305-937-4500. E-mail: drloiskrop@aol.com.

KROP, STEPHEN, retired pharmacologist; b. N.Y.C., Sept. 24, 1911; s. Dmetro Pantele Krop and Mary Badewko; m. Mary Lulick, July 28, 1934; children: Elaine, Marianne, Paul, Thomas. BS, George Washington U., 1939; MS, Georgetown U., 1940; PhD, Cornell U., 1942. Diplomate Fed. Exec. Inst., 1970. From asst. to instr. pharmacology Cornell U. Med. Coll., Ithaca, NY, 1939—44; chief pharmacology dept. reserach divsn. Ethicon Inc., 1957—63; chief drug pharmacology br. rsch. divsn. Bur. Sci. Rsch., 1963—79; cons. toxicologist EPA, others, Washington, 1979—85; from instr. to asst. prof. pharmacology Yale U. Sch. Medicine, 1944—46; chief pharmacology sect. med. divsn. CWS, U.S. Army, 1946—48; pres. Ethicon Rsch. Found., 1957—63; head pharmacodyamics dept. Squibb Inst. Med. Rsch., 1948—49; dir. pharmacology divsn. Warner Inst. Therapeutic Rsch., 1949—51; rsch. assoc. Chemical-Biological Coordination Ctr. NRC, 1951—52, asst. and acting dir., 1951—52; coord. physiology divsn. Med. Rsch. Labs., 1952—57; mil. chemicals rsch. and asst. chief divsn. physiology U.S. Army Chem. Warfare Med. Labs., 1952—57. Advisor grain infestation Nat. Grain Sanitation Conf., Kansas City, Kans., 1956—56; health edn. exch. scientist Polish Health Ministry, Poland, 1978—78; ret., 1979; ann. Stephen and Mary Krop lectr. Georgetown U. Med. Ctr. First editor Military Chemicals Safety Manual. Fellow: Wash. Acad. Scis., NY Acad. Sciences; mem.: Am. Indsl. Hygiene Assn., Am. Physiol. Soc., Am. Soc. Pharmacology and Exptl. Therapeutics, The Harvey Soc., Soc. Exptl. Biology and Medicine, Am. Assn. Advancement Sci., Cosmos Club (Washington), Soc. Sigma Xi. Catholic. Achievements include research in Treatment Of Nerve Gas Poison; Treatment Of Hexachlorophene Poisoning. Avocations: music, genealogy, memoirs, history.

KROPEWNICKI, THOMAS J., engineering manager; m. Cara M. Connor. BSChemE, U. of Notre Dame, 1994; PhD in Chem. Engring., Ga. Inst. of Tech., 1999; MSc in Tech. Commercialization, U. Tex.-Austin, 2003. Sr. process engr. Dielectric Etch divsn. Applied Materials, Inc., Sunnyvale, Calif., 1999—2003, sr. process engr. Condr. Etch divsn., 2004, engring. and tech. program mgr. Condr. Etch divsn., 2004—05; prin. staff scientist Freescale Semiconductor, Inc., Austin, Tex., 2005—. Author: (jour. article) Understanding the Evolution of Trench Profiles in the Via-First Dual Damascene Integration Scheme. Adult group leader for 9th grade confirmation class Our Lady of Angels Parish, Burlingame, Calif., 2003—05; v.p. Notre Dame Club of San Jose / Silicon Valley, 2004—05. Tex. Tech. Transfer Assn. scholarship, Tex. Tech. Transfer Assn., 2002. Mem.: Am. Vacuum Soc. Achievements include patents for substrate cleaning process, U.S. Patent #6, 440, 864. Avocations: travel, cooking, reading. Personal E-mail: tom.kropewnicki94@alumni.nd.edu.

KROPF, SUSAN J., cosmetics company executive; married. BA in English, St. John's U.; MBA in Fin., NYU. Adminstrv. asst. Avon Products, Inc., N.Y.C., 1970, various mgmt. positions, 1970-85, v.p. purchasing and package devel., 1985-90, v.p., sr. officer product devel., 1990-92, v.p. R&D and mfg., 1992-97, sr. v.p. global ops. and bus. devel., 1992-97, exec. v.p., 1998-99, COO N.Am. & Global Bus. Ops., 1999—, pres., 2001—. Bd. dirs. Green Point Savs. Bank. Mem.: Fashion Group Internat., Cosmetic Exec. Women. Office: Avon Products Inc Ste C2-04 1251 Avenue Of The Americas New York NY 10020-1196*

KROPP, EDWARD H., education educator, consultant; b. Reading, Pa., June 13, 1944; s. Karl Gustaf and Erna Mittag Kropp; m. Phyllis Ann Bauman, Nov. 5, 1966; children: Peter Alex, Julie Marie (Kropp) McKenzie. BA, Temple U., 1966; MA, George Mason U., 1994. Project mgmt. profl. George Washington U. Staff mgr. Chesapeake and Potomac Tel., Roanoke, Va., 1969—81; dist. mgr. A T & T, Basking Ridge, NJ, 1981—96; comml. bids dir. Sci. Application Internat. Corp., San Diego, 1996—2000; sr. mgr. KPMG Cons. (Bearing Point), McLean, Va., 2000—02; prof. Keller Grad. Sch. of Mgmt., McLean, 2002—. Pres. E. H. Kropp & Assoc., Vienna, 2002—. Author: (book) A Guide to Repair Svc. Bur. Analysis, 1971, (manual) Land Mine Warfare (USMC), 1983. Exec. bd. Nat. Capital Area Coun., BSA, Wash., DC, 1998—. Col. USMC, 1966—94. Mem.: Nat. Contact Mgmt. Assn. Avocations: ednl. leadership rsch., in-prison literacy instrn. Home: 8022 Kidwell Ct Vienna VA 22182 Office: Keller Grad Sch of Mgmt 1751 Pinnacle Dr Mc Lean VA 22102

KROPP, WILLIAM RUDOLPH, physicist; b. Chgo., Nov. 10, 1936; s. William R. Sr. and Nora J. (King) K.; divorced; children: Marianne, Kathryn; m. Christa McDonnell, Feb. 2, 2001. BS, DePaul U., 1958; PhD, Case Inst. Tech., 1964. Postdoctoral fellow Case Inst. Tech., Cleve., 1964-66, U. Calif., Irvine, 1966-68, asst. prof. physics, 1968-74, research physicist, 1974—. Co-recipient Bruno Rossi prize, Am. Astron. Soc., 1989. Mem. AAAS, Am. Phys. Soc. Home: 11711 Via Rancho Santa Ana CA 92705-3153

KROPSCHOT, RICHARD HENRY, retired physicist, lab administrator; b. Kalamazoo, May 25, 1927; s. Henry J. and Della (Burdorf) K.; m. Claire Mills, June 23, 1950; children: Susan, Anne. BS in Physics, Mich. State U., 1948, MS in Physics, 1950, PhD in Physics, 1958. Rsch. scientist N.Am. Aviation, Downey, Calif., 1950-51; physicist Nat. Bur. Standards, Boulder, Colo., 1951-79; dir. Office Basic Energy Scis., Dept. Energy, Washington, 1979-85; assoc. lab. dir. energy scis. Lawrence Berkeley (Calif.) Lab., 1985-90; liaison officer Office of Pres. U. Calif., Oakland, 1990-97, ret. Adj. prof. U. Colo., Boulder, 1969-79. Author: Technology of Liquid Helium, 1968; former editor Cryogenics, London, Rev. Sci. Instruments; contbr. articles to profl. jours. With USN, 1945-46, PTO, ETO. Recipient Gold medal U.S. Dept. Commerce, 1954, sci. fellow, 1976-77; recipient Disting. Svc. award U.S. Dept. Energy. Fellow Am. Phys. Soc. Presbyterian. Home: 341 Calle Loma Norte Santa Fe NM 87501-1256

KROPTAVICH, NATHAN PAUL, music educator, musician; b. Scranton, Pa., Aug. 16, 1980; s. Ronald John and Carol Joy Kroptavich; m. Stacy Leigh Appel, Aug. 7, 2004. MusB, Marywood U., Scranton, 2003. Tchrs.Cert. PA Dept. of Edn., 2003. Music tchr. Shohola Elem. Sch., Pa., 2003—. Ch. musician. Mem.: NEA, Pa. State Educators Assn., Delta Epsilon Sigma (life). Home: 1433 Luzerne St Scranton PA 18504 Office: Shohola Elem Sch 940 Twin Lakes Rd Shohola PA 18458 Office Phone: 570-296-3600.

KROSSER, HOWARD S., aerospace transportation executive; b. Bklyn., Dec. 2, 1936; s. Samuel and Celia (Wexler) K.; m. Roslyn Elaine Rosenthal, Apr. 30, 1939; children: Scott A., Barry I. BS in Engring., Rutgers Coll., 1959; MS in Indsl. Mgmt., Ga. Inst. Tech., 1970; postgrad., Harvard U., 1985. Engr., engring. supr. Picatinny Arsenal, Dover, N.J., 1959-66; br. mgr., engr. Prodn. Modernization Agy., Dover, 1966-73; divsn. engring. mgr. Army Prodn. Agy., Dover, 1973-78; program mgr. Army Tank Command, Warren, Mich., 1978-85; dir. lab. Army Armament R & D Ctr., Dover, 1985-86, tech. dir., 1986-88; v.p., gen. mgr. Hercules Aerospace, Wilmington, Del., 1988-89; pres. Hercules Def. Electronic Systems Inc., Wilmington, 1990-94; chmn. bd. dirs., pres. Alliant Def. Electronics Sys. Inc., Clearwater, Fla., 1994-96; v.p. smart weapons sys. Alliant Techsys., Inc., Mt. Arlington, N.J., 1996—. Mem. Army Sci. Bd., Washington, 1990-93. Recipient Meritorious Civilian Svc. award U.S. Army, 1986, Exceptional Civil Svc. award, 1988. Mem. Assn. of U.S. Army, Am. Def. Preparedness Assn. (Leslie Simon award 1988). Office: Alliant Techsys Inc PO Box 405 Wharton NJ 07885-0405

KROTINGER, MYRON NATHAN, lawyer; b. N.Y.C., Oct. 31, 1914; s. Benjamin A. and Anna M. (Perlo) K.; m. Ada S. Segal, Nov. 14, 1953; children: Andrew S., Jonathan H. BA, NYU, 1933; MA, Columbia U., 1935, LLB, 1937. Bar: N.Y. 1937, Ohio 1938, U.S. Dist. Ct. (no. dist.) Ohio 1944, U.S. Dist. Ct. (so. dist.) N.Y. 1948, U.S. Ct. Appeals (2d cir.) 1948, U.S. Ct. Appeals (4th and 6th cirs.) 1958, U.S. Supreme Ct. 1963. Assoc. Ulmer, Berne & Gordon, Cleve., 1937-39; atty. corp. reorgn. div., regional interpretive atty. SEC, Cleve., 1939-45; pvt. practice N.Y.C., 1945-48, Cleve., 1948-54; ptnr. Lane, Krotinger & Santora, Cleve., 1954-70, Van Aken, Withers and Webster and predecessor firm, Cleve., 1988—; of counsel Burke, Haber & Berick, Cleve., 1970-88. Instr. antitrust law and trade regulation Case Western Res. U., Cleve., 1951-70; panelist Practicing Law Inst., 1967-77. Contbr. articles to profl. publs. Trustee The Park Synagogue, Cleve., 1952—, Cleve. Inst. Art, 1986—; pres. Cleve. Art Assn., 1985-87. Mem. ABA, Fed. Bar Assn. (pres. 1978-79), Ohio State Bar Assn. (chmn. antitrust confs. 1973, 74), Cuyahoga County Bar Assn., Cleve. Bar Assn., Union Club, City Club, English Speaking Union. Avocation: fly fishing. Home: 2070 Cedar Rd Apt 328 Beachwood OH 44122 Office: Van Aken Withers & Webster 629 Euclid Ave Ste 1000 Cleveland OH 44114-3003

KROTKI, KAROL JOZEF, sociology educator, demographer; b. Cieszyn, Poland, May 15, 1922; emigrated to Can., 1964; s. Karol Stanislaw and Anna Elzbieta (Skrzywanek) K.; m. Joanna Patkowski, July 12, 1947; children—Karol Peter, Jan Jozef, Filip Karol. BA (hons.), Cambridge (Eng.) U., 1948, MA, 1952, Princeton U., 1959, PhD, 1960. Civil ser., Eng., 1948-49; dep. dir. stats. Sudan Govt., 1949-58; vis. fellow Princeton U., 1958-60; rsch. adviser Pakistan Inst. Devel. Econs., 1960-64; asst. dir. census rsch. Dominion Bur. Stats., Can., 1964-68; prof. sociology U. Alta., 1968-83, prof., 1983-91, prof. emeritus, 1991—. Vis. prof. U. Calif., Berkeley, 1967, U. N.C., 1970-73, U. Mich., 1975, U. Costa Rica, 1993; coord. program socio-econ. rsch. Province Alta., 1969-71; cons. in field. Author 14 books; contbr. articles to profl. jours. Served with Polish, French and Brit. Armed Forces, 1939-46. Decorated 10 wartime medals; recipient Achievement award Province of Alta, 1970, Commemorative medal for 125th Ann. of Can., 1992; hon. citizen Gizalki, Poland, 1994; grantee in field. Fellow Am. Statis Assn., Royal Soc. Can. (v.p. 1986-88), Acad. Humanities and Social Scis. (v.p. 1984-86, pres. 1986-88); mem. Fedn. Can. Demographers (v.p. 1977-82, pres. 1982-84), Can. Population Soc., Assn. des Demographes du Que., Soc. Edmonton Demographers (founder, pres. 1990-96, hon. advisor), Ctrl. and E. European Studies Soc. (pres. 1986-88), Population Assn. Am., Internat. Union Sci. Study Population, Assn. Internat. des Demographes de Langue Francaise, Internat. Statis. Inst., Royal Statis. Soc., Polish Culture Soc. (hon. mem.), Polish Soc. Arts & Scis. (London). Roman Catholic. Home: 10137 Clifton Pl Edmonton AB Canada T5N 3H9 Office: U Alta Dept Sociology Edmonton AB Canada T6G 2H4 Office Phone: 718-492-4377. E-mail: kkrotki@ualberta.ca.

KROTO, HAROLD WALTER, chemistry researcher, educator; b. Wisbech, Cambridgeshire, Oct. 7, 1939; s. Heinz and Edith K.; m. Margaret Henrietta Hunter, 1963; 2 children. BSc in Chemistry, U. Sheffield, 1961, PhD, 1964; PhDHC, U. Stockholm, 1992; DHC, U. Limburg, 1993, U. Sheffield, 1995, U. Kingston, 1995. Postdoctoral fellow NRCC, 1964-66; rsch. scientist Bell Tel. Labs., NJ, 1966-67; lectr. U. Sussex, Brighton Sussex, England, 1968-77, reader, 1977-85, prof. chemistry, 1985-91, Royal Soc. Rsch. prof., 1991—2004; prof. Fla. State U., Tallahassee, 2004—. Chmn. Vega Sci. Trust. Mem. editl. bd. Chem. Soc. Reviews, 1990—; contbr. over 280 articles to profl. jours. Created knight, 1996; recipient award Sunday Times Book Jacket Design Competition, 1964, Tilden lectr., 1981-82, Faraday lectr., 2002, medal 2002, Internat. New Materials prize Am. Phys. Soc., 1992, Italgas prize for innovation in chemistry, 1992, Longstaff medal Royal Soc. Chemistry, 1993, Hewlett Packard Europhysics prize, 1994, Science pour L'art prize Moet Hennessy Louis Vuitton, 1994, Copley medal, 2004; co-recipient Nobel prize in chemistry, 1996. Fellow: Royal Soc.; mem.: Academia Europea. Office: Fla State U Tallahassee FL 32301 E-mail: kroto@chem.fsu.edu.

KROTT, JOSEPH P., gas industry executive, comptroller; BS summa cum laude, U. Del., 1985. CPA. Formerly audit mgr. Coopers & Lybrand; comptr. Sunoco Inc., Phila., 1998—, joined, 1990, mgr. consolidation acctg. and spl. projects, 1990—, dir. compensation and benefits, 1998. Mem.: Pa. Inst. CPA, Am. Inst. Pub. Accts. Office: Sunoco Inc Ten Penn Ctr 1801 Market St Philadelphia PA 19103-1699*

KROUSE, GEORGE RAYMOND, JR., lawyer; b. Atlantic City, Sept. 30, 1945; s. George R. and Viola (Rogers) K.; m. Susan Naylor, Aug. 5, 1967; children: Geoffrey, Alison. AB cum laude, Brown U., 1967; JD with distinction, Duke U., 1970. Bar: N.Y. 1971, U.S. Ct. Mil. Appeals 1971, U.S. Dist. Ct. (so. and ea. dists.) N.Y. 1975. Assoc. Simpson Thacher & Bartlett, N.Y.C., 1970-71, 75-78, ptnr., 1978—, chmn. corp. dept., 1991—2002, sr. adminstrv. ptnr., 2002—, mem. exec. com. Articles editor Duke Law Jour. Mem. bd. visitors Sch. Law, Duke U., Durham, N.C., 1986-92, chmn., 1997-2001; mem. nat. devel. coun. Duke U., 1994-2000, dir. Global Capital Markets Ctr. Capt. USAF, 1971-75. Decorated Air Force Commendation medal, Meritorious Svc. medal. Mem. ABA, N.Y. State Bar Assn., Assn. of Bar of City of N.Y. (com. corps. 1985-88, com. art law 1990-93), Order of Coif, Montclair Golf Club, Cape Cod Nat. Golf Club, Bonita Bay Club. Avocation: golf. Office: Simpson Thacher & Bartlett LLP 425 Lexington Ave 18th Fl New York NY 10017-3954 Office Phone: 212-455-2730. Office Fax: 212-455-2502. Business E-Mail: gkrouse@stblaw.com.

KROUSE, HELENE JUNE, nursing educator; BS cum laude, SUNY, Bklyn., 1976; MS, U. Rochester, 1979; PhD, Boston Coll., 1984. Cert. adult nurse practitioner, cert. otorhinolaryngology nurse. Staff nurse Downstate Med. Ctr., Bklyn., 1976-77; instr. in nursing Hunter Coll.-Bellevue Sch. Nursing, N.Y.C., 1979-80; asst. prof., coord. med.-surg. nursing Emmanuel Coll., Boston, 1980-84; asst. prof. nursing Boston Coll., Chestnut Hill, Mass., 1984-89; adult nurse practitioner Mass. Eye and Ear Infirmary, Boston; adminstr., nurse practitioner to Ear, Nose, Throat, Sinus and Allergy practice, Ormond Beach, 1989—2001; assoc. prof. U. North Fla., Jacksonville, 1995-97, acting chairperson dept. nursing, 1996-97; assoc. prof. U. Fla., 1997-2001; masst. dean adult health Wayne State U., Detroit, 2001—04, prof., 2001—. Faculty fellow Boston Coll., 1988, rsch. fellow, 1987; bd. dirs. Nat. Certifying Bd. for Otorhinolaryngology and Head-Neck Nurses, 2000-2003. Mem. rev. panel Nursing Rsch., Jour. Advanced Nursing, Am. Jour. Nursing; feature editor ORL-Head and Neck Nursing; contbr. articles on otolaryngology and allergy, compliance and decision making to profl. jours., also chpts. to books. Bd. dirs. Ear, Nose, Throat Nursing Found., 2002—, pres.-elect, 2003, pres., 2004—. Recipient Ednl. award, ENT divsn. Smith and Nephew Inc., 1998, First Place in Ann. Videotape Contest, Soc. Otorhinolarygnology-Head and Neck Nurses, Sanders award for basic rsch., Am. Acad. Otolaryngic Allergy, 2001; grantee, U. Rochester Alumni Seed Found., 1978—79; scholar, So. Nursing Rsch. Soc./Am. Nurses Found., 1998; rsch. grantee, Am. Acad. Otolaryngic Allergy Found., 2004—. Fellow Am. Acad. Nursing; mem. Oncology Nurse Soc., So. Nursing Rsch. Soc. (awards com. 2000), Soc. Otorhinolaryngology and Head-Neck Nurses, Inc. (chair nat. rsch, com., bd. dirs. 2000-01, nat. cert. bd. 2001-02, pres.-elect 2003, pres. 2004-05), Sigma Theta Tau (Clin. Rsch. award 1986-87). Office: Wayne State U Coll Nursing 5557 Cass Ave Detroit MI 48202 Office Phone: 313-577-3911. E-mail: hjkrouse@wayne.edu.

KROUSE, JENNY LYNN, elementary school educator; b. Houston, Oct. 9, 1956; d. Thomas Raymond and Anna Margaret (Davis) K. BS, U. Houston, 1979, M Adminstrn., 2002. Cert. tchr., Tex. 4th grade tchr. Orange Grove Elem. Sch., Houston, 1979-86, pre-kindergarten tchr., 1986-88, 3rd grade tchr., 1988-89; 5th grade tchr. lang. arts Oleson Elem. Sch., Houston, 1989-93, pre-1st grade tchr., 1993-94, 4th grade tchr., 1994-95; 5th grade sci. tchr. Drew Magnet Sch. Acad. Math., Sci. and Arts, Houston, 1995-96, Title I coord., 1996-97, chair reading dept., 1997-98; skills specialist, assessment coord. Drew Magnet Sch., 1997—. Coop. learning facilitator Johns Hopkins U., Houston, 1993; GESA facilitator Gray Hill, Houston, 1995; mentor Region IV, Houston, 1996; critical friends group coach, Annenberg Initiative, 1998. Mem. Women's Action Coalition, Houston, 1992-95. Mem. ASCD, S.E. Tex. Legal Clin. (bd. dirs. 1998), Tex. PTA (life), Internat. Reading Assn., Tex. State Reading Assn. Avocations: camping, softball, cooking, travel, theater/movies. Home: 15421 Henry Rd Houston TX 77060-4542 Office: Drew Academy 1910 W Little York Rd Houston TX 77091-1914

KROVATIN, GERALD, lawyer; b. 1952; BA, Columbia U., 1974; JD, Rutgers U., 1977. Bar: N.J. 1977. Ptnr. Krovatin & Assocs. LLC, Newark. Adj. faculty crim. trial seminar Rutgers Sch. Law, Newark, 1987-90. Fellow Am. Coll. Trial Lawyers; mem. N.J. State Bar Assn., Assn. Criminal Def. Lawyers N.J. (trustee 1995-99). Office: Krovatin & Assocs LLC 744 Broad St Newark NJ 07102-3802 Office Phone: 973-424-9777. E-mail: gkrovatin@krovatin.com.

KROVVIDY, SRINIVAS, information technology manager; s. Krishna Murthy and Surya Kumari Krovvidy. BEngring. with Gold medal, Osmania U., Hyderabad, India, 1983; MTech, Indian Inst. Tech., Chennai, 1985; PhD, U. Cin., 1992. Cert. Java, WebLogic, Mgmt. Experience. Sr. knowledge engr. Inference Corp., McLean, Va., 1993—97; sr. rschr. Thomson Tech. Labs, Rockville, Md., 1998—99; sr. info. tech. devel. mgr. Fannie Mae, Herndon, Va., 2000—. Tech. reviewer Internat. Conf. on E-commerce, Sicily, Italy, 2003—; mem. program com. Internat. Workshops on Enabling Technologies: Infrastructure for Collaborative Enterprise, Modena, 2004—. Editor technical articles; tech. cons. (to profl. jours.); contbr. to profl. jours. Projects coord. team mem. Assn. for India's Devel., College Park, Md., 1988—; vol. Rejuvenate India Movement, Herndon, Va., 2002—; v.p. Country Walk Cluster, Reston, Va., 2004. Grad. Scholarship, U. Cin., 1986—92, Summer Rsch. fellowship, 1988—91. Mem.: Am. Assn. Artificial Intelligence, Assn. Computing Machinery. Achievements include first to develop and implement one of the early business rule specification language translators. Avocations: social develelopment work, politics. Home: 1676 Sierra Woods Ct Reston VA 20194 E-mail: srinivas.krovvidy@gmail.com.

KROWN, SUSAN ELLEN, physician, researcher; b. Bronx, N.Y., Sept. 8, 1946; d. Frederick B. and Paula (Hauser) K.; m. Roger E. Pitt, May 18, 1980 (div. 1988); 1 child, Catherine Krown Pitt. AB, Barnard Coll., 1967; MD, SUNY, Bklyn., 1971. Diplomate Am. Bd. Internal Medicine. Intern, then jr. and sr. resident in internal medicine Mt. Sinai Hosp., N.Y.C., 1971-74; with Meml. Sloan-Kettering Cancer Ctr., N.Y.C., 1974—, assoc. mem., 1984-94, mem., 1994—; clin. asst. Meml. Hosp., N.Y.C., 1977-78, asst. attending physician, 1978-82; assoc. attending physician Meml. Sloan-Kettering Cancer Ctr., N.Y.C., 1982-94, attending physician, 1994—; asst. prof. Med. Coll. Cornell U., N.Y.C., 1977-83; assoc. prof. Med. Coll. Cornell U., N.Y.C., 1983-94, prof., 1994—. Mem. oncologic drugs adv. com. FDA, Rockville, Md., 1986—90, cons., 1990—96; chair oncology com. AIDS Clin. Trials Group, Bethesda, Md., 1990—92, mem. exec. com., 1992—94; co-chair steering com. AIDS malignancy consortium NCI, Bethesda, 1995—99; chair Kaposi's sarcoma working group AIDS Malignancy Consortium, 2000—01; co-chair steering com. AIDS Malignancy Consortium NCI, 1995—99; chair task force on Kaposi's Sarcoma staging Am. Joint Com. on Cancer, Chgo., 1991—93. Mem. editorial bd. Jour. Interferon Rsch., 1985—, Jour. AIDS, 1988—; contbr. numerous articles to profl. jours. NIH Rsch. grantee; Am. Cancer Soc. Jr. Faculty fellow, 1978-81. Mem.: Internat. Soc. for Interferon Rsch. (coun. 1986—92, bd. dirs. 1995—96, Milstein award 1995), Alpha Omega Alpha. Office: Meml Sloan Kettering Ctr 1275 York Ave New York NY 10021-6094

KRSUL, JOHN ALOYSIUS, JR., lawyer; b. Highland Park, Mich., Mar. 24, 1938; s. John A. and Ann M. (Sepich) K.; m. Justine Oliver, Sept. 12, 1958; children: Ann Lisa, Mary Justine. BA, Albion Coll., 1959; JD, U. Mich., 1963. Bar: Mich. 1963. Assoc. Dickinson Wright PLLP, 1963-71, ptnr. Detroit, 1971-99, consulting ptnr., 2000—. Asst. editor: U. Mich. Law Rev, 1962-63. Recipient Disting. Alumnus award Albion Coll., 1984; Sloan scholar, 1958-59; Fulbright scholar, 1959-60; Ford. Found. grantee, 1964 Fellow: Am. Bar Found. (life; chmn. Mich. chpt. 1988—89); mem.: ABA (ho. of dels. 1979—2002, chmn. standing com. on membership 1983—89, exec. coun. 1984—91, chmn. sect. gen. practice 1989—90, tort and ins. practice sect., exec. coun. 1991—94, bd. govs. 1991—99, chmn. fin. com. 1993—94, exec. com. 1993—94, 1996—99, editl. bd. ABA Jour. 1996—99, treas. 1996—99, chmn. audit com. 2003—), Am. Bar Ins. Cons. Inc. (bd. dirs. sec. 1988—95), Am. Bar Endowment (bd. dirs. 1996—99), Nat. Conf. Bar Pres. (exec. coun. 1986—89), Am. Judicature Soc. (dir. 1971—79, exec. com. 1973—74), Fellows of Young Lawyers Am. Bar (bd. dirs. 1977—86, pres. 1983—84, chmn. bd. 1984—86), Mich. State Bar Found. (trustee 1982—83, 1985—99, chmn. fellows 1986—87), State Bar Mich. (commr. 1973—83, pres. 1982—83), Detroit Bar Assn. Found. (dir. 1971—84, pres. 1979—80), Detroit Bar Assn. (dir. 1971—80, pres. 1979—80), Am. Bar Retirement Assn. (bd. dirs. 1999—2005, sec. 2003—05, v.p. 2005—), Sixth Cir. Jud. Conf. (life), Detroit Club, Orchard Lake Country Club, Delta Tau Delta, Phi Eta Sigma, Omicron Delta Kappa, Phi Beta Kappa. Office: Dickinson Wright PLLC 500 Woodward Ave Ste 4000 Detroit MI 48226-3416 Home: 10048 Weko Dr Bridgman MI 49106

KRUCK, DONNA JEAN, special education educator, consultant; b. Peoria, Ill., Jan. 26, 1930; d. Walter George and Lois Irene (Newburn) Hagemeyer; m. Michael Roy Kruck Jr., June 27, 1948; children: Pamela Ann Kruck Hokanson, Michael Roy III, Quentin Robert; m. Somran Sirironrong, May 19, 1998. BS, Ill. State U., 1961; MEd, U. Ill., 1968. Cert. spl. edn. tchr. and adminstr., Ill. Tchr. New Lenox Dist. 122, Ill., 1956-61; tchr. spl. edn. Lincoln Way Area Joint Agreement, New Lenox, 1961-66; tchr. spl. edn., coord. Joliet Twp. High Sch. Dist. 204, Ill., 1966-86; pvt. practice cons. and diagnostician New Lenox, 1986-92. Child adv. New Lenox Dist. 122, 1986-88; instr. Chapel Christian U., 1994-96; LCMS missionary, ESL tchr., Bangkok, 1997—. Author: Let's Learn to Cook, 1971. Pres. Joliet Twp. Edn. Assn., 1971-76; donar Aurora Area Blood Bank, Joliet, 1974-90; v.p. Island Lakes Homeowners Assn., 1994-96; v.p. Luth. Women's Missionary League, 1993, pres., 1994-97; pres. Aid Assn. for Luths., 1995-97. Mem. AAUW, NEA (life), Nat. Ret. Tchr. Assn., Am. Assn. Ret. Persons, Am. Assn. Mental Retardation, Am. Bus. Women's Assn., Coun. Exceptional Children (life), Coun. Adminstrs. Spl. Edn., Christian Edn. Assn., Ill. Edn. Assn. (life), Ill. Div. Learning Disabilities, Coun. for Ednl. Diagnostic Svcs. (div. learning disabilities), Lutherans for Life, Brandywine Inst. Orthopedics (founder), Kappa Delta Pi, Delta Kappa Gamma. Lutheran. Avocations: travel, presenting travelogues. Office: Concordia Gospel Ministry 205/20 Soi Chairyakiat 1 Ngam Wong Wan Bangkok 10210 Thailand Office Phone: 011 662-589-6715. E-mail: Sirironrong@yahoo.com.

KRUCKEBERG, ARTHUR RICE, botanist, educator; b. L.A., Mar. 21, 1920; s. Arthur Woodbury and Ella Muriel K.; m. Mareen Schultz, Mar. 21, 1953; children— Arthur Leo, Enid Johanna; children by previous marriage—Janet Muriel, Patricia Elayne, Caroline. BA, Occidental Coll., Los Angeles, 1941; postgrad., Stanford U., 1941-42; PhD, U. Calif.-Berkeley, 1950. Instr. biology Occidental Coll., 1946; teaching asst. U. Calif.-Berkeley, 1946-50; mem. faculty U. Wash., Seattle, 1950—, prof. botany, 1964-88, emeritus, 1988—, chmn. dept., 1971-77. Cons. in field. Co-founder Wash. Natural Area Preserves system, 1966. Served with USNR, 1942-46. Mem. Wash. Native Plant Soc. (founder 1976), Calif. Bot. Soc. Rsch. edaphics of serpentines, flowering plants. Home: 20312 15th Ave NW Shoreline WA 98177-2166 Office: U Wash PO Box 351800 Seattle WA 98195-180o Office Phone: 206-543-1976. Business E-Mail: ark@u.washington.edu.

KRUCOFF, CAROLE, museum program director; b. Providence, R.I., Mar. 3, 1940; d. Bernard and Esther Sylvia Spector; m. Larry Stanley Krucoff, Apr. 14, 1963; children: Rachel Anna, Rebecca Miriam. BA magna cum laude, U. So. Calif., 1961; MA in Tchg. of History, U. Ill., 1988. Assoc. educator Chgo.(Ill.) Hist. Soc., 1972—88; dir. edn. Naper Settlement Mus. Village, Naperville, Ill., 1988—92; head of pub. and mus. edn. Oriental Inst., Chgo., 1992—. Grant reviewer Inst. Mus. and Libr. Svcs., Washington, 1996—, mem. panel, 1996—. Editor: Life in Ancient Egypt, Mesopotamia, and Nubia. Fellow, U. Ill., Chgo., 1986—88; grantee, Chgo. Cmty. Trust, 1996—97, Polk Bros. Found. of Chgo., Lloyd A. Fry Found. of Chgo., 1998—2004; scholar, State of Calif., 1957—61; Children's Theater at the Oriental Inst. grant, The Ill. Arts Coun., 1999. Mem.: Ill. Assn. Mus. (Superior Achievement award 1997, 2004), Mus. Edn. Roundtable, Am. Assn. Mus., Am. Assn. State and Local History, Ill. Coun. Social Studies, Archaeol. Inst. Am., Assn. Coll. and U. Mus., Assn. Midwest Mus., Am. Assn. Mus. (peer reviewer mus.

assessment program 1999—), The Expt. Internat. Living, Phi Beta Kappa, Phi Beta Kappa. Achievements include development of junior interpreter program at naper settlement museum village. Avocations: gardening, reading, travel, crossword puzzles, exercise. Home: 6821 South Euclid Avenue Chicago IL 60649 Office: Oriental Institute Museum 1155 East 58th Street Chicago IL 60637 Office Fax: 773-702-9853. E-mail: c-krucoff@uchicago.edu.

KRUECKEBERG, JOHN, education educator; s. Donald Allen and Lenore Spengler Krueckeberg; m. Mary Cornish. BA, Macalester Coll., 1989; PhD, U. Ariz., Tucson, Ariz., 1997. History prof. U. Ariz. South, Sierra Vista, Ariz., 1997—2001; assoc. prof. history Plymouth State U., NH, 2001—. Mem.: Orgn. of Am. Historians, Am. Hist. Assn. Office: Plymouth State Univ 17 High St MSC # 39 Plymouth NH 03264-1595 Office Phone: 603-535-2332. Office Fax: 603-535-2351. Business E-Mail: jkrueckeberg@plymouth.edu.

KRUEGER, ANNE O., international agency executive, economist; b. Endicott, NY; BA, Oberlin (Ohio) Coll., 1953; MS, U. Wis., 1956, PhD, 1958, Georgetown U., 1992; PhD (hon.), Hacettepe U., Ankara, Turkey, 1990, Monash U., 1995. Asst. prof. econs. U. Minn., Mpls., 1959-63, assoc. prof. econs., 1963-66, prof. econs., 1966-82; v.p. econs. and rsch. The World Bank, Washington, 1982-86; art and scis. prof. econs. Duke U., Durham, N.C., 1987-93; Herald and Caroline L. Ritch prof arts and scis. in econs. Stanford (Calif.) U., 1993—, dir. Ctr. Rsch. Econ. Devel. and Policy Reform, 1996-2001; 1st dep. mng. dir. IMF, 2001—, acting mng. dir., 2004—. Bd. dirs. Nordson Corp., Westlake, Ohio; mem. vis. com. Econs. Dept. Harvard U., 1990-98; sr. non-resident fellow Brookings Inst.; rsch. assoc. Nat. Bur. Econ. Rsch. Author: Trade Policies and Developing Nations, 1995, Economic Policies at Cross Purposes, 1993, Economic Policy Reform in Developing Countries, 1992, The Political Economy of Agricultural Pricing Policy, Vol. 5: A Synthesis of the Political Economy in Developing Countries, 1992, Economic Policy Reform: The Second Stage, 2000; co-author (with O. Aktan): Swimming Against the Tide: Turkish Trade Reform in the 1980s, 1992; editor: (with R.H. Bates) Political and Economic Interactions in Economic Policy Reform, 1993, The World Trade Organization as an International Institution, 1998, Economic Policy Reform: Second Stage, 2000, A New Approach to Sovereign Debt Restructuring, 2002, Economic Policy Reform and the Indian Economy, 2003, (with Jose Antonio Gonzales, Vittorio Corbo and Aaron Tornell) Latin American Macroeconomic Reform: The Second Stage, 2003, (with Sajjid Z. Chinoy) Reforming India's Economic, Financial and Fiscal Policies, 2003. Mem. N.Y. State Regents Commn. on Higher Edn., 1992-93. Recipient Robertson prize NAS, 1984, Bernhard Harms prize Inst. for World Economy, Kiel, 1990, Enterprise award Kenan Inst., 1990, Seidman prize, 1994. Fellow AAAS, Econometric Soc. (award 1984); mem. NAS, Am. Econ. Assn. (disting. fellow, chmn. com. rsch. 1988-92, chmn. commn. on grad. edn. in econs. 1989-90, v.p. 1977, pres.-elect 1995, pres. 1996, rep. to Internat. Econ. Assn. and mem. IEA exec. com. 1992-98, v.p. Internat. Econ. Assn. 1994-98). Office: Internat Monetary Fund 700 19th St NW Washington DC 20431

KRUEGER, ARLIN JAMES, physicist; b. Oct. 22, 1933; s. Rudolph August and Mathilda E. (Pooch) K.; m. Susan J. Peacock, Dec. 28, 1978; children: Sandra, Timothy, Terry. BA, U. Minn., 1955, postgrad., 1956—58, Colo. State U., 1976—78. Physicist Naval Weapons Ctr., China Lake, Calif., 1959-69; physicist-astrophysicist Goddard Space Flight Ctr., Greenbelt, Md., 1969-2000; W.H. Elkins prof. physics U. Md., Balt., 2000—01, rsch. prof., 2001—. Developer of rocket and satellite instruments: sensor sci. Nimbus-7 Total Ozone Mapping Spectrometer (TOMS), 1975—93, Rocoz Optical Rocket Ozonesonde, 1961—79, Volcanic Ash Mapper, 1998—2000; mem. com. ext. U.S. Std. Atmosphere; instrument scientist U.S.-USSR Meteor 3/TOMS mission, U.S. Earth Probe/TOMS mission; prin. investigator Japanese ADEOS/TOMS mission, NASA Earth Sys. Scis. Pathfinder, Volcanic Ash Monitor (VOLCAM) Satellite Program, NASA Airborne Antarctic Ozone Experiment/TOMS Real-Time Support, NASA Airborne Arctic Experiment/TOMS Real Time Support; co-investigator Earth Observing Sys. Volcanic Eruption Investigation, Rsch. on Antarctic Ozone Hole; adv. volcanic hazards panel Office Fed. Coord. of Meteorology; invited lectr. Nat. Inst. Polar Rsch., Tokyo, AT&T Bell Labs., U.S. Naval Acad., Goddard Space Flight Ctr. Engring. Colloquium, Gordon Rsch. Conf. on Volcano-Climate, Fermi Sch. Physics, Italy, Russian Acad. Scis., Moscow; Quaternary Rsch. lectr. U. Wash.; invited participant and spkr. sci. workshops and confs. Contbr. articles to profl. publs. Recipient Exceptional Sci. Achievement medal, NASA, Exceptional Svc. medal, 2001, Goddard rsch. and study fellow, Colo. State U., 1976—78. Mem. AAAS, Am. Meteorol. Soc., Internat. Assn. Meteorology and Atmospheric Physics (internat. ozone commn.), Am. Geophys. Union, Sigma Xi. Achievements include research on stratospheric ozone, remote sensing from satellites, volcanic eruptions, volcanic aviation hazards, atmosphere of Mars. Office Phone: 410-455-8906.

KRUEGER, BONNIE LEE, editor, writer; b. Chgo., Feb. 3, 1950; d. Harry Bernard and Lillian (Soyak) Krueger; m. James Lawrence Spurlock, Mar. 8, 1972. Student, Morraine Valley Coll., 1970. Adminstrv. asst. Carson Pirie Scott & Co., Chgo., 1969-72; traffic coord. Tatham Laird & Kudner, Chgo., 1973-74, J. Walter Thompson, Chgo., 1974-76, prodn. coord., 1976-78; editor-in-chief Assoc. Pubs., Chgo., 1978—, Sophisticate's Hairstyle Guide, 1978—, Sophisticate's Beauty Guide, 1978—, Complete Woman, 1981—; pub., editorial svcs. dir. Sophisticate's Black Hair Guide, 1983—, Sophisticate's Soap Star Styles, 1994-95. Active Statue of Liberty Restoration Com., NYC, 1983, Chgo. Architecture Found.; campaign worker Cook County State's Atty., Chgo., 1982; poll watcher Cook County Dem. Orgn., 1983. Recipient Exceptional Woman in Pub. award, Women in Periodical Pub., 2000, Communicator of Yr. award, Am. Health and Beauty Aids Inst. Mem. Soc. Profl. Journalists, Am. Health and Beauty Aids Inst. (assoc., Communicator of Yr. award), Lincoln Park Zool. Soc., Landmarks Preservation Coun. of Ill., Art Inst. Chgo., Chgo. Hist. Soc., Mus. Contemporary Art, Peta, Headline Club, Sigma Delta Chi. Lutheran. Office: Complete Woman 875 N Michigan Ave Chicago IL 60611-1803 Office Phone: 312-266-8680. Business E-Mail: krueger@associatedpub.com. *I approach my life like one would approach the climbing of a mountain— plenty of faith, determination, self criticism, hard work and the joy and knowledge that the top is there for everyone to reach, if you pursue it with a combination of fervor, patience and love.*

KRUEGER, DARRELL WILLIAM, academic administrator; b. Salt Lake City, Feb. 9, 1943; s. William T. and E. Marie (Nelson) K.; m. Verlene Terry, July 1, 1965 (dec. Jan., 1969); 1 child, William; m. Nancy Leane Jones, Sept. 2, 1969; children: Antonia, Amy, Susan. BA summa cum laude, So. Utah State Coll., 1967; MA in Govt., U. Ariz., 1969, PhD in Govt., 1971. Asst. prof. polit. sci. N.E. Mo. State U., Kirksville, 1971-73, v.p. acad. affairs, dean of instrn., 1973-89; pres. Winona State U., Minn., 1989—2005, pres. emeritus, 2005—. Facilitator The 7 Habits of Highly Effective People, 1993, Crucial Conservations, 2003; mem. adv. bd. U.S. Bank, Rochester, Minn., 1989—. Mem. Gamehaven Coun. Boy Scouts Am., 1989—. Recipient Outstanding Alumnus award, So. Utah State, 1992. Mem.: Am. Assn. Higher Edn., Am. Assn. State Colls. and Univs., Rotary, Phi Beta Kappa. Mem. Lds Ch. Avocations: running, golf. Home: 1411 Heights Blvd Winona MN 55987-2519 Office: Winona State U Somsen 201 8th & Johnson Winona MN 55987 Office Phone: 507-457-5003.

KRUEGER, DEBORAH A. BLAKE, school psychologist, consultant; b. Chgo., Aug. 22, 1954; d. Stanley Walter and Maryanne Lois Blake; m. Darrell George Krueger, May 31, 1986; children: Sarah, Joshua. BA, DePaul U., 1976, MEd, 1980; PhD, Loyola U., 1998. Lic. sch. psychologist Ill. Learning disabilities specialist Assocs. in Family Therapy, Lake Bluff, Ill., 1980-85; reading and learning disabilities specialist Proviso West H.S., Hillside, Ill., 1980-82; edn. therapist Hartgrove Hosp., Chgo., 1982-85; dir. spl. edn. Old Orchard Hosp., Skokie, Ill., 1985-87; program coord. One-to-One Learning Ctr., Northfield, Ill., 1995-98; sch. psychologist Winnetka (Ill.) Pub. Schs., 1997—. Cons. Naperville and Woodridge Schs., 1998—; lectr. Loyola U., Chgo., 1997—; pvt. practice, Northbrook, 2000—; third party cons. hartgrove Psychol. Hosp., Chgo., 1985—88, Old Orchard Psychol. Hosp., Skokie, 1987—89; co-founder Baby N'Me Mother-Infant Dyad Groups, 1991; spkr. Resolve Orgn., Good Samaritan Hosp., Downers Grove, Ill., 1991; global initiative del. partipant to Eastern Europe, 2004. Founder Living with Infertility and Experimentation, Evanston, Ill., 1990—96, mem. steering com., 1990—94. Grantee, Loyola U., 1996. Mem.: APA, Ill. Assn. Infant Mental Health, Ill. Sch. Psychol. Assn., Soc. Personality Assessment, Nat. Assn. Sch. Psychologists, Assn. Advancement Therapeutic Edn. Avocations: piano, exercise, reading, local school involvement. Home: 2434 Ridgeway Ave Evanston IL 60201-1858 Office: Winnetka Pub Schs 520 Glendale Ave Winnetka IL 60093-2135 also: 910 Skokie Blvd Northbrook IL 60062 Office Phone: 847-604-4160. Personal E-mail: DbKrueger@aol.com.

KRUEGER, EUGENE REX, academic program consultant; b. Grand Island, Nebr., Mar. 30, 1935; s. Rudolph F. and Alma K.; m. Karin Schubert, June 9, 1957; children: Eugene Eric, Richard Kevin, Kristina. Student, Kans. State U., 1952-53; BS in Physics, Rensselaer Poly. Inst., 1957, MS in Math, 1960, PhD in Applied Math, 1962. Research physicist IBM, 1957-58; research fellow Army Math. Research Center, U. Wis., 1962-63; prof. U. Colo., Boulder, 1965-74; vice chancellor, prof. Oreg. State System of Higher Edn., Eugene, 1974-82; exec. cons. Control Data Corp., 1982-85, v.p., 1985-89; exec. dir. tech.-based engring. edn. consortium William C. Norris Inst., 1989-96, v.p., 1996-97. Adj. prof. computer sci. U. Minn., 1989-94; adj. prof. Western Sem., 1997-01; chmn. seminar for dirs. of acad. computing facilities, 1969-82; pres. Krueger & Assocs., 1989—; cons. on computer graphics computing facility mgmt.; dir. various research grants and contracts; U.S. acad. cons. African Virtual U./World Bank, 1995-2001; interim pres. Christian Heritage Coll., 1998; interim exec. dir. WorldView/Internat. Inst. Christian Comm., 2004-05. Contbr. research papers in field to publs. Mem. Sigma Xi, Phi Kappa Phi. E-mail: rex@bendcable.com.

KRUEGER, GERALD PETER, psychologist; b. Evanston, Ill., Apr. 3, 1944; s. Albert August and Pauline Mary (Didier) K.; m. Jessica Ann Prendergast, Aug. 26, 1967; children: Michael G., Deborah L., Kevin A. BA in Psychology, U. Dayton, 1966; MA in Exptl. and Engring. Psychology, Johns Hopkins U., 1975, PhD in Exptl. Psychology, 1977; grad., U.S. Army Command and Gen. Staff Coll., 1980, U.S. Army War Coll., 1988. Cert. profl. ergonomist Bd. Certification Profl. Ergonomics. Rschr. engring. psychology Bunker-Ramo Corp., Wright-Patterson AFB, Ohio, 1966—69; human factors rsch. psychologist U.S. Army Human Engring. Lab., Aberdeen, Md., 1969—71; R & D coord. Def. Advanced Rsch. Projects Agy., Saigon, Vietnam, 1971—72; mil. police ops. officer U.S. Army, Ft. Meade, Md., 1972, aviation psychologist Aeromed. Rsch. Lab. Ft. Rucker, Ala., 1976—80; R & D programs staff officer U.S. Army Med. R & D Command, Ft. Detrick, Md., 1980—84; dep. chief dept. behavioral biology Walter Reed Army Inst. Rsch., Washington, 1984—88; dir. biomed. applications rsch. divsn. U.S. Army Aeromed. Rsch. Lab., Ft. Rucker, 1988—90; comdr., sci. tech. dir. U.S. Army Rsch. Inst. Environ. Medicine, Natick, Mass., 1990—94; ret. col. U.S. Army, 1994; v.p. ergonomics R & D svcs. Biomechanics Corp. Am., Melville, NY, 1994—95; prin. rsch. scientist, ergonomist Star Mountain, Inc., Alexandria, Va., 1995—98; pres. Krueger Ergonomics Cons., Inc., 1998—; prin. scientist, ergonomist Wexford Group Internat., Vienna, Va., 2000—. Tchr. U.S. Armed Forces Inst., Saigon, 1971, Johns Hopkins U., 1974-75, U. So. Calif., 1977-80; adj. asst. prof. med.-clin. psychology Uniformed Svcs. U. Health Scis., Bethesda, Md., 1997—; mem. sci. coun. to UTEK Corp., Plant City, Fla., 1999—; bd. dirs. Commonwealth Biotechnologies, Inc., Richmond, Va., 2004-. Book review editor Ergonomics in Design Mag., 1995—; assoc. editor Mil. Psychology, 1991-2003, mem. editl. bd., 2003—; guest editor jours. in field; contbr. articles to profl. jours. Recipient Richard M. Griffith Meml. award So. Soc. Philosophy and Psychology, 1978, Order of Mil. Med. merit for career contbns. Army Med. Dept., 1992, numerous mil. awards, medals and skill proficiency badges, including Legion of Merit, 1994, Bronze Star U.S. Army, 1972, Meritorious Svc. medals with 2 oak leaf clusters. Fellow APA (pres. divsn. mil. psychology 1995-96, pres. divsn. engring. psychologists 2001-02); mem. Soc. for Indsl. Orgnl. Psychologists, Am. Indsl. Hygiene Assn., Assn. U.S. Army, Nat. Def. Indsl. Assn., Ergonomics Soc., Human Factors and Ergonomics Soc. (pres. Potomac chpt. 2003), Aerospace Med. Assn., Aerospace Human Factors Assn., Soc. for Human Performance in Extreme Environments, Army War Coll. Alumni Assn., VFW, Am. Legion. Roman Catholic. Avocations: participating in running events, organizing community activities. Office: Krueger Ergonomics Consultants 4105 Komes Ct Alexandria VA 22306-1252 E-mail: jerrykrueg@aol.com. *Pick good mentors. Mine taught me to: 1) Try new things, welcome challenges. 2) Develop a high level of competence. 3) Know your customers' needs. 4) Always give them more than they expect.*

KRUEGER, JAMES A., lawyer; b. Sept. 21, 1943; s. A.A. and Margaret E. (Hurley) K.; m. Therese Eileen Connors, Aug. 2, 1968; 1 child, Colleen. BA cum laude, Gonzaga U., 1965; JD, Georgetown U., 1968; LLM, NYU, 1972. Bar: Wash. 1969, U.S. Supreme Ct. 1972, U.S. Tax Ct. 1972, U.S. Dist. Ct. (we. dist.) Wash. 1980, U.S. Ct. Appeals (9th cir.) 1982. Mem. staff U.S. senator from Wash., 1967-68; mem. Vandeberg, Johnson & Gandara (and predecessor firms), 1972—. Spl. dist. counsel Wash. State Bar Assn., 1984-94; adj. prof. law, U. of Puget Sound, 1974-76. Co-author: Representing the Close Corporation, 1979, Partnership Agreements, 1981, Planning for the Small Business Enterprise, 1982, The Partnership Handbook, 1984. Chmn. bd. Cath. Cmty. Svcs. of Pierce and Kitsap Counties, 1983-84; bd. dirs. United Way of Pierce County, 1973-82, 99—. Capt. U.S. Army, 1968-72. Decorated Bronze star. Mem. ABA, Wash. State Bar Assn., Tacoma-Pierce County Bar Assn. Roman Catholic. Office: 1201 Pacific Ave Ste 1900 Tacoma WA 98402-4315

KRUEGER, JAMES HARRY, chemistry educator; b. Milw., May 18, 1936; s. Clarence A. and Helen. K.; children: Melanie A., Diane M., Carolyn J. BS, U. Wis., 1958; PhD, U. Calif., Berkeley, 1961. Asst. prof. chemistry Oreg. State U., Corvallis, 1961-66, assoc. prof., 1966-73, prof., 1973—97, prof. emeritus, 1997—. Mem. Am. Chem. Soc. Office: Dept Chemistry Oreg State U Corvallis OR 97331-4003 Office Phone: 541-737-6710.

KRUEGER, JANICE MARIA, school librarian; b. Phila., Apr. 27, 1953; d. Francis Angelo and Jean Lembo; m. Frederick Richard Krueger, Sept. 25, 1982; children: Paula Diane, Frederick Phillip. BS, Duquesne U., 1977; MS, Drexel U., 1988. Tchr. Diocese of Stockton, Stockton, Calif., 1997—2000; libr. U. of the Pacific, Stockton, Calif., 2000—. Lt. USNR, 1982—90. Mem.: Internat. Reading Assn., Assn. for Supervision of Curriculum Devel., Am. Ednl. Rsch. Assn., Calif. Assn. of Rsch. Libraries, North Am. Serials Interest Group, Assn. of Coll. and Rsch. Libraries, ALA, Beta Phi Mu. Office: U of the Pacific 3601 Pacific Ave Stockton CA 95211 Office Phone: 209-946-3171.

KRUEGER, KATHLEEN SUSAN, special education administrator; b. Cape Girardeau, Mo., Jan. 21, 1951; d. Robert Settle and Myldred Frances (Jones) K. BS in Edn., Athens Coll., 1973; MEd, Ala. A&M U., 1980. Classroom tchr. Limestone County Schs., Athens, Ala., 1973-74; spl. edn. tchr. Huntsville (Ala.) City Schs., 1974-95, spl. edn. coord., 1995—. Mem. city-wide policy com. Huntsville City Schs., 1987-89, profl. devel. coord., 1986-95, dept. chair for spl. edn., 1993-95. Bd. dirs. H-Vote, Huntsville, 1989; vol. ARC, 1981-82; tchr. Sunday Sch., First United Meth. Ch., Huntsville, 1983-85, sec., 1985-86, mem. choir, 1985-89, hon. treas. for State of Ala., 1988. Mem. NEA (PAC), Ala. Edn. Assn., Huntsville Edn. Assn. (bldg. rep. 1992-95, treas. 1989, sec. 1992-93), Coun. for Exceptional Children, Ala. Coun. for Sch. Adminstrn. and Supervision, Phi Delta Kappa, Phi Mu (membership dir. 1970-71, treas. 1971-72). Home: 7801 Regent Pl SW Apt 8 Huntsville AL 35802-1471

KRUEGER, KENNETH JOHN, nutritionist, educator; b. L.A., Jan. 29, 1946; s. Charles Herbert and Adelaide Marie K.; m. Ellen Santucci, June 16, 1979 (div. 1989); children: Kenneth, Michael, Scott, David. BA in Humanities, U. So. Calif., 1968; MS in Edn. (Psychology), Mt. St. Mary's Coll., 1972. English tchr. Corcoran (Calif.) High Sch., 1968, Charter Oak High Sch., Covina, Calif., 1969-90; nutrition and exercise instr. Mt. San Antonio Coll., Walnut, Calif., 1974-90; pres. Mega Group, Ltd., 1990, The Krueger Group, Malibu, Calif., 1991—2000; exec. Overnite Express, L.A., Calif., 1993, Calif. Parcel Express, Encino, 1994-95; nutritionist Swiss Nat. Team, 1995-99; phys. edn. tchr. Hiram Johnson H.S., Sacramento, 1995-96. Adj. prof. phys. edn. Sierra Coll., Rocklin, Calif., 1996; health instr. L.A. City Coll., 1996-97, West L.A. Coll., 1998; swim coach Mt. San Antonio Coll., Walnut, Calif., 1974-77; coach, v.p. Trojan Swim Club, Newport Beach, Calif., 1978-90; bd. dirs. Nutrition and Exercise Cons., Tustin, Calif.; nutrition and exercise dir. Health Am., 1987-90; chmn., nutrition and fitness com. Internat. Eating Disorders Com., 1988; U.S. nat. team nutritionist for (FINA) World Cup 1988 Champions; recruiter Club Med, Paris, 1976-78; program coord. Pacific Am. Inst., San Francisco, 1983; asst. coach Vevey Natation, Switzerland, 1972-73; asst. swim coach Swiss Nat. Team, 1968, 85; chief marshall U.S. Olympic Swim Trials, Irvine, 1980, linguistics chmn. protocol U. So. Calif. Venue, L.A. Olympic Com., 1983-84; mem.-at-large long distance com. U.S. Swimming, Colorado Springs, 1987-91, coach So. Calif. Long Distance Swimming, 1987-89; del. chief, coach and swimmer So. Calif. Swimming for Internat. Crossing of Lake Geneva, sponsored by Internat. Olympic Com., Switzerland, 1987; meet dir. U.S. 25K Long Distance Swimming Championships/FINA World Cup Trials, Long Beach, Calif., 1988, U.S. 25K Swim Championships, Long Beach, 1989. Author: Reflections and Refractions, 1973; contbr. articles to internat. profl. nutrition and sport jours. Bd. dirs. U.S.A. Athletes Hall of Fame, 1991-92. Recipient NCAA All Am. award U. So. Calif., 1966, NCAA Nat. Champ award, 1966, U.S. Masters Swimming Champion, 1972 and annually 1974-81, Internat. Sr. Olympics Champion, 1972 and annually 1974-85; recipient commendations U.S. Congress, Calif. Senate, L.A. County Bd. Suprs; inducted into U.S.A. Athletes Hall of Fame. Mem. KC. Libertarian. Roman Catholic. Avocations: sports, reading. Mailing: 5435 Vesper Ave Sherman Oaks CA 91411

KRUEGER, RADIE LYNN, secondary school educator; b. Stuart, Fla., Nov. 14, 1962; d. Albert R. III and Martha Katherine (Brooks) Krueger; 1 child, Travis. AB, Ga. Wesleyan Coll., 1984; MS in Ednl. Leadership, Nova Southeastern U., 2004. Tchr. English Brevard County Sch. System, Melbourne, Fla., 1984-86; bank officer, tng. dir. First Nat. Bank and Trust, Stuart, 1987-90; dir. Christian edn. 1st Presbyn. Ch., Stuart, 1990-91; prof. English, Indian River Community Coll., Ft. Pierce, Fla., 1990-91; employment comm. cons. Curtis and Assocs., Grand Island, Nebr., 1992-93; exec. dir. Community HelpCenter, Grand Island, 1993, Martin County Literacy Coun., Stuart, Fla., 1993-94; mgr. ednl. svcs. The Palm Beach Post subs. Cox Enterprises, Inc., West Palm Beach, Fla., 1994-95; with audiotext advt./programming dept. The Stuart (Fla.) News, 1995-96; lang. arts tchr. Southport Middle Sch., Port St. Lucie, Fla., 1996—2002; h.s. English tchr. Lincoln Park Acad., Ft. Pierce, Fla., 2002—. Mem.: Fla. Reined Cow Horse. Republican. Episcopalian. Avocations: gardening, golf, bicycling, reined cow horse. Home: 1220 SE Ocean Blvd Stuart FL 34996 E-mail: writinggreyhounds@yahoo.com.

KRUEGER, RAYMOND ROBERT, lawyer; b. Portage, Wis., Aug. 29, 1947; s. Earl Andrew and Catherine Virginia (Klenert) K.; m. Barbara Bowen, June 21, 1969; children: Lindsey, Michael. BA in Econs., U. Wis., 1969, JD, 1972. Bar: Wis. 1972. Assoc. Charne, Glassner, Tehan, Clancy & Taitelman S.C., Milw., 1973-79, shareholder, 1979-91; ptnr. Charne Clancy Krueger Pollack & Corris S.C., Milw., 1991—92, Michael, Best & Friedrich LLP, Milw., 1992—. Chmn. Georgia O'Keeffe Found., Abiquiu, N.Mex., 1989—; trustee Village of Whitefish Bay, Wis., 1989—2003; mem. Milwaukee River Revitalization Coun., 1988—, vice chair, 1989—96, chair, 1996—; dir. River Revitalization Found., Inc., 1998—, chair, 2001—03; trustee Milw. Art Mus., 2003—, mem. bldg. com., 1996—; chair Whitefish Bay Cmty. Devel. Authority, 2002—. Capt. USAF, 1969—78. Mem. ABA (natural resources sect.), State Bar Wis. (environ. law sect.), Milw. Bar Assn. (environ. law sect.), Environ. Law Inst. Avocation: visual arts. Office: Michael Best & Friedrich LLP 100 E Wisconsin Ave Ste 3300 Milwaukee WI 53202-4108 Office Phone: 414-271-6560. E-mail: rrkrueger@mbf-law.com.

KRUEGER, ROBERT CHARLES, former ambassador, former congressman, former senator; b. New Braunfels, Tex., Sept. 19, 1935; s. Arlon E. and Faye (Leifeste) K.; m. Kathleen Tobin Krueger; children: Mariana, Sarah, Christian. BA, So. Meth. U., 1957; MA, Duke U., 1958; M.Litt., Oxford (Eng.) U., 1961, D.Phil., 1964; D.Litt. (hon.), U. St. Thomas; D.Pub.Service hon., Lycoming U., 2003. From instr. to assoc. prof. English Duke U., 1961-72; vice provost, dean Trinity Coll. Arts and Scis., Duke U., 1972-73; chmn. bd. Comal Hosiery Mills, 1973-75; ptnr. Krueger Brangus Ranch, 1974-86; mem. 94th-95th Congresses from 21st Tex. dist., 1975-79; U.S. ambassador-at-large, coord. for Mex. affairs, 1979-81; pres. Krueger Assocs., 1981-91; Bentsen prof. govt.-bus. rels. Lyndon B. Johnson Sch., U. Tex., 1985-86; Tsanoff prof. pub. affairs Rice U., 1986-88; Disting. lectr. So. Meth. U., 1991; commr. Tex. R.R. Commn., 1991—93; U.S. senator from Tex., 1993-94; amb. to Burundi, 1994-96; amb. to Botswana, 1996—2000; spl. rep. of sec. of state So. Africa Devel. Cmty., 1998—2000; rsch. fellow Merton Coll. Oxford (Eng.) U., 2000—01; cons. on nat. and internat. bus. and fgn. affairs, 2001—. Spkr. in field; mem. chancellor's bd. advisors U. Ill. Med. Ctr.; bd. dirs. Monagram Corp. Author: The Poems of Sir John Davies, 1975; contbr. over 300 articles to profl. jours. and newspapers. Mem. Tex. Philos. Soc. (pres. 1993), Blue Key, Phi Beta Kappa. Office: PO Box 311717 New Braunfels TX 78131-1717 Office Phone: 830-629-7347. E-mail: kruegerx@swbell.net.

KRUEGER, ROBERT EDWARD, mechanical engineer, manufacturing executive; b. L.A., Mar. 26, 1922; s. Edward Jr. and Ida Viola (Herren) K.; m. Elizabeth Westerfors, Sept. 10, 1949; children: Karen Elizabeth, Clarence Frederick (dec.), Roger Carl (dec.), Bruce Wayne, Glen Herren. Student, L.A. City Coll., 1939-40, Calif. Inst. Tech., 1940-43, 46-47, Yale U., Harvard U., MIT, Army Electronics Tng. Ctr., 1943-44; BSME, Stanford U., 1950, MBA, 1952. Lic. fed. firearms dealer and ammunition mfr. Bur. Alcohol, Tobacco and Firearms. Trainee Douglas Aircraft Co., Santa Monica, Calif., summers 1941-43; staff mem. Los Alamos (N.Mex.) Sci. Lab., 1947-49; chief engr. Rutishauser Corp., Pasadena, Calif., 1952-53; asst. to pres. Unitek Corp., El Monte, Calif., 1953-55; sales mgr. Donner Sci. Co., Concord, Calif., 1955-57, Shand & Jurs divsn. Gen. Precision Equipment Corp., Berkeley, 1957-58; v.p. sales Advanced Instruments, Richmond, Calif., 1958-60; sales mgr. Gilliland Instruments, Oakland, Calif., 1960-62; ptnr. Krueger & Smith, Berkeley, 1969-72; founder, pres. Tetra Valves, Inc., Berkeley, 1972-78; owner, propr. Krueger Mfg.-Engring., Lafayette, Calif., 1962—. Author or co-author books, manuals, other works; patentee in field. Donor portraits of U.S. Pres. George Bush and Barbara Bush, White Ho., Washington, 1995, portrait of U.S. Pres. George Bush, Nat. Portrait Gallery, Washington, 1995; v.p. Calif. Rep. Assembly, 1983-84. With USAAF, 1942-47; with USAFR, 1947-53. Recipient John Singleton Copley medal Nat. Portrait Gallery, 1999. Mem. IEEE (life), AAAS, ASTM, NRA (life, endowment), Am. Soc. for Metals Internat. (life), Am. Def. Indsl. Assn. (life), James Smithson Soc./Smithsonian Instn. (Patron award Benefactors Cir. 1991), Nat. Mus. Am. Indian (charter), Colonial Williamsburg Found., Raleigh Tavern Soc., USN League (life), Spencer Baird Soc., Calif. Rifle and Pistol Assn. (life), Calif. State Sheriffs Assn., Contra Costa County Sheriffs Posse. Pantheist. Avocations: U.S. national heritage, art collections, politics, travel, photography. Home: 1084 Via Roble Lafayette CA 94549-2925 Office: Krueger Mfg-Engring 1084 Via Roble Lafayette CA 94549-2925

KRUEGER, ROBERT J., music educator; s. Raymond Richard and Dorothy Augusta Krueger; m. Margaret J. Lenahan; children: Melissa Jane, Paul Robert, Anne Marie. BA in Music Edn., Calif. State U., Fullerton. Tchg. credential Calif. Band dir., music coord. Manteca (Calif.) Unified Sch. Dist., 1981—. Office: McParland Elem Sch 1601 Northgate St Manteca CA 95366 Office Phone: 209-825-3390. E-mail: rkrueger@sjcoe.net.

KRUEGER, STEPHANIE, music educator, consultant; b. Houston, May 24, 1975; d. H. Martin and Charlene Raye Krueger. B in Music Edn., E. Tex. Bapt. U., 1997; MA, U. Tex., Tyler, 1999. Cert. music tchr. K-12 Tex., Kodàly cert. Pvt. piano instr., Tyler, 1997—; keyboard cons. Mundt Music Co., Tyler,

1999—. Mem.: Nat. Guild Piano Tchrs., Tex. Music Tchrs. Assn., Music Tchrs. Nat. Assn., Suzuki Assn. Am. (cert. piano instr. 1B), E. Tex. Music Tchrs. Assn. (v.p. 2001—02), Nat. Guild Piano Tchrs. Conservative.

KRUEGER, WILMA HOIDT, artist; b. Effingham, Ill., Dec. 22, 1924; d. Ernest John and Vida Prather Hoidt; m. Raymond John Krueger, June 2, 1992; children: Rae, Karen, Cathy. Stenographer Vulcan Corp., Effingham, 1942—44, sec., 1944—45; bookkeeper Effingham (Ill.) Co-op, 1945—46, Allen Chevrolet, Effingham, 1946—52; prin., owner Motel Manor/Restaurant, Montrose, Ill., 1952—70; owner apartment Effingham, 1952—79; prin., owner 51 acre farm, Montrose, 1976—99, Wilhelmina Art Gallery, Effingham, 1997—2003. Adv. bd. Lakeland Coll. Bd., Ill. Represented in permanent collections Gov.'s Mansion, Ill., slides in Archives of Nat. Mus. Women in Arts, Washington, D.C., one-woman shows include First Nat. Bank, Effingham, Ill., 1976, Lake Land Coll., Mattoon, Ill., 1978—, Ramada Inn Conv. Ctr., Effingham, Ill., 1988, First Mid Ill. Bank, 1988, First Nat. Bank, 1990, The Master Khreaton Gallery, Paducah, Ky., 1993, exhibitions include Ft. Wayne (Ind.) Mus. Art, 1988 (Best of Show award, 1988), one-woman shows include Mo. Botanical Garden, St. Louis, Mo., 1998, exhibitions include Ill. State Mus. Gallery, Whittington, Ill., 1987—, The Strolling Gallery, St. Louis, Mo., Gallerie Frontenac, Bonutti Clinic Competition, 2003 (First Pl. award, 2003), numerous others. Republican. Luth. Avocations: swing dancing, painting, decorating, fashion. Home and Office: Wilhelmina Art Gallery 400 N Main St Effingham IL 62401

KRUG, DON L., secondary school educator, director; b. Crawfordsville, Ind., Mar. 19, 1948; s. Herbert L. and Geneva E. Krug; m. Diana Lynn Fountain, Aug. 20, 1972; children: Darren, Dyna. BS, Ind. State U., 1969; MA, Ball State U., 1974. Jr. high band dir. Knox (Ind.) Cmty. Sch., 1969—71, Southeastern Sch. Corp., Walton, Ind., 1971—94; band dir. Lewis Cass HS, Walton, 1994—2003, jr. high band dir., 2003—. Organist Main St. United Meth., Peru, Ind., 1972—. Mem.: Ind. State Tchr. Assn., Nat. Band Assn., Phi Beta Mu. Avocations: swimming, weightlifting, piano. Home: PO Box 271 107 W Grace Walton IN 46994 Office: Lewis Cass Jr Sr High Sch St Rd 218 Walton IN 46994

KRUG, EDWARD CHARLES, environmental scientist; b. New Brunswick, NJ, Aug. 24, 1947; s. Edward and Regina (Bartkoviak) K.; m. Nancy Wegner, July 19, 1988. BS in Environ. Sci with highest honors, Rutgers U., 1975, PhD in Soil Sci., 1981. cert. profl. soil scientist. Asst. scientist Conn. Agrl. Expt. Sta., New Haven, 1980-85; assoc. scientist Ill. State Water Survey U. Ill., Champaign, 1985-90; advisor Com. for a Constructive Tomorrow, Washington, 1989-90, dir. environ. projects, 1991-93; ind. environ. cons. Winona, Minn., 1993—. Sci. adv. com. Environ. Issues Coun., U.S.A., 1993—; adv. bd. Media Rsch. Ctr., Alexandria, Va., 1991—; adj. profl. scientist Ill. State Water Survey, U. Ill., Champaign, 1999—; biogeochemist Office of the Chief, Ill. State Water Survey, Champaign, 2000—; tech. adv. group, nutrient sci. com. Ill. EPA. Contbg. author: Encyclopedia for Earth System Science, 1992; contbr. articles to profl. jours. Mem. NJ Ad Hoc Water Quality Control Com., New Brunswick, 1972-73; reviewer, tech. advisor NJ Pub. Interact Rsch. Group, New Brunswick, 1972-75; chmn. ch. and soc. coms. United Meth. Ch., Winona, 1990-91, 2000—; mem. regional tech. adv. group U.S. Environ. Agy., 2001—. With USN, 1967-69. Recipient Frank G. Helyar award Rutgers U., 1973, Excellence in Rev. award Jour. Environ. Quality, 1991. Mem. Am. Geophys. Union, Soil Sci. Soc. Am., Internat. Union Soil Scientists, Ill. Soil Carbon Ptnrs. Working Group, Internat. Union Soil Scientists. Achievements include development of organic acid buffering theory; generalization of Rosenquist land-use theory to include naturally increased acidity of watershed from accelerated loss of bases; unified theory of acid/base biogeochemistry; generalization of nitrogen cycle to more comprehensively address internal cycling. Office: Ill State Water Survey 2204 Griffith Dr Champaign IL 61820 Office Phone: 217-244-0877. Business E-Mail: ekrug@uiuc.edu.

KRUG, JEFFREY ALAN, international business educator; b. Radford, Va., Jan. 21, 1959; s. Alan Sents and Elaine Myers Krug; m. Miriam Batista Siqueira; children: Viviane, Alan. BA, Pa. State U., 1982, MS, 1984; PhD, Ind. U., 1993. Fin. analyst Commerzbank, Duesseldorf, Germany, 1981; econ. analyst Austrian Postal Savings Bank, Vienna, 1982; instr., rsrch. asst. Pa. State U., 1983—84; fin. planning mgr. Tex. Instruments Inc., Dallas, 1984—88; mgr. of fin. PepsiCo, Inc., Louisville, 1988—89; instr. Ind. U., Bloomington, 1989—92; vis. prof. Coll. William & Mary, Williamsburg, Va., 1993—94; asst. prof. U. Memphis, Memphis, 1994—98, U. Ill., Champaign, 1998—2003; assoc. prof. Appalachian State U., Boone, NC, 2003—. Adj. prof. exec. MBA program U. Muenster, Germany, 2002—, U. Ill., 2003—. Lt. jg USNR, 1985—88. Mem.: So. Mgmt. Assn., Acad. of Mgmt., Strategic Mgmt. Soc., Delta Phi Alpha, Omicron Delta Epsilon, Beta Gamma Sigma. Methodist. Office: Appalachian State U Coll of Bus Adminstrn PO Box 32037 Boone NC 28608 Business E-Mail: Krugja@appstate.edu.

KRUG, JOHN CARLETON (TONY KRUG), academic administrator, library director, consultant; b. Evansville, Ind., Nov. 27, 1951; s. John Elmer and Mary Ellen K.; m. Anna Marie Waters, July 3, 1983. BA, Ind. State U., 1972, MLS, 1973; PhD, So. Ill. U., Carbondale, 1985. Lic. to ministry Bapt. Ch. Exec. dir. Olney (Ill.) Carnegie Pub. Libr., 1973-74; assoc. dean Wabash Valley Coll., Mt. Carmel, Ill., 1974-84; mem. Com. for U.S. Depository State Plan, Springfield, Ill., 1982-84; dir. librs. Maryville Coll., St. Louis, 1984-88; dir. info. svcs. Bethany (W.Va.) Coll., 1988-97; dean libr. svcs. Carson Newman Coll., Jefferson City, Tenn., 1997—2002; dir. ctrl. libr. Appalachian Coll. Assn., Berea, Ky., 2002—. Coord. libr. activities, Appalachian Coll. Assn., 1997-2002; sec. pro-tem Ill. Basin Coal Mining Manpower Council, Mt. Carmel, 1974-79; governing bd. exec. com. Higher Edn. Ctr. Cable TV, 1986-88; conf. speaker Kans. State U., 1982. Author: Libraries Using/Planning for Microcomputers, 1986; also computer programs. V.p. bd. dirs. Wabash Area Vocat. Enterprises, Mt. Carmel, 1978-81; bd. edn. Wabash Cmty. Unit, Mt. Carmel, 1980-83; exec. com. Cmty. Edn. and Arts Assn., Carbondale, 1983-84; visual arts adv. com. Ill. Arts Coun., Chgo., 1982-84; pastor Hopewell United Meth. Ch., Bridgeport, Ill., 1976-77; minister Terre Haute (Ind.) 1st Bapt. Ch., 1972—; elder Gateway Christian Ch., 1986-88; bd. dirs. Fair Haven Christian Sch., 1986-88; pres. T3-Tchrs., Tech., Tomorrow. Mem. Assn. Christian Librs. Office: Appalachian Coll Assn 210 Center St Berea KY 40403 Office Phone: 865-548-5450. Business E-Mail: tonyk@acaweb.org.

KRUGER, EHREN S., scriptwriter, film producer; b. Oct. 5, 1972; Former exec. asst. The Fox Network. Writer: (TV films) Killers in the House, 1998; (films) Arlington Road, 1999; New World Disorder, 1999; Scream 3, 2000; Reindeer Games, 2000; Impostor, 2002; The Ring, 2002; The Ring Two, 2005; The Skeleton Key, 2005; The Brothers Grimm, 2005.*

KRUGER, GUSTAV OTTO, JR., retired oral surgeon, educator, department chairman; b. N.Y.C., Sept. 28, 1916; s. Gustav Otto and Anna Charlotte (Mellquist) K.; m. Helyn E. Hollingsworth, Apr. 12, 1947; children: Deborah Ann (Mrs. M. Henry King III), Tristram Coffin, Abigail Hollingsworth Imus. BS, George Washington U., 1938, AM, 1939; DDS, Georgetown U., 1939, ScD (hon.), 1977. Diplomate Am. Bd. Oral and Maxillofacial Surgery (pres. 1964). Intern Johns Hopkins Hosp., 1939-40; fellow Mayo Found., 1940-42, 45-48; mem. faculty Georgetown U. Sch. Dentistry and Grad. Sch., 1948-87, prof. oral surgery, chmn. dept., 1948-87, prof. emeritus, 1987—, assoc. dean, 1966-82; ret. Chief dental dept. Georgetown U. Hosp., Washington, 1948-82; cons. VA hosps., Martinsburg, W.Va. and Washington, U.S. Naval Hosp., Bethesda, D.C. Gen. Hosp., Washington; cons. to Pres.'s physician, 1960-64; cons. Walter Reed Army Med. Ctr.; mem. cancer tng. com. Nat. Cancer Inst., USPHS, 1967-71, chmn., 1969-71. Author: Textbook of Oral and Maxillofacial Surgery, 1959, 6th edit., 1984; contbr. articles to profl. jours. Capt. Dental Corps AUS, 1942-45, CBI, PTO. Recipient Arnold K. Maislen award N.Y. U., 1970; Simon P. Hullihen award W.Va. Soc. Oral Surgeons and W.Va. Med. Ctr., 1980; named Man of Year Georgetown U. Alumni Assn., 1961, Disting. Svc. award, 1992. Fellow AAAS, Am. Coll. Dentists (chmn. D.C. sect. 1969-71, Disting. Svc. award 2002), Internat. Coll. Dentists (chmn. D.C. sect. 1967-70); mem. ADA (chmn. oral surgery sect. 1961, mem. rev. commn. on advanced edn. in oral surgery 1965-71, chmn. commn. 1969-71), D.C. Dental Soc. (pres. 1960, Sterling V. Mead award 1989), Am. Assn. Oral and Maxillofacial Surgeons (program chmn. 1961, 79th Ann. Meeting dedication 1997), Middle Atlantic Soc. Oral and Maxillofacial Surgeons (pres. 1952), Am. Assn. Dental Schs., Am. Acad. Oral Pathology, Am. Acad. Oral and Maxillofacial Radiology, Internat. Assn. Dental Research, Am. Coll. Oral and Maxillofacial Surgeons (Harry Archer award 1992), Wash. Dental Study Club (pres. 1993), Kiwanis (co-chmn. orthop. com. 1971-86), Xi Psi Phi, Sigma Gamma Epsilon, Omicron Kappa Upsilon. Home: 6806 Bradgrove Cir Bethesda MD 20817-3001

KRUGER, HARRY, retired conductor, retired music educator; b. Atlanta, July 20, 1929; s. Isaac and Sarah Kruger; m. Natalie Elizabeth Wyatt, Aug. 21, 1957; children: Rebecca, Anna, William. MusB, New Eng. Conservatory, Boston, 1953, MusM, 1955; Mus D, LaGrange Coll., Ga., 1991. Conductor Arlington Symphony, Mass., 1952—53; asst. conductor Atlanta Symphony, 1955—61; dir. orchestral activities Bowling Green State U., Ohio, 1961—65; conductor Columbus Symphony, Ga., 1965—87, Macon Symphony, Ga., 1977—83; conductor, dir. music LaGrange Symphony, 1989—2001, conductor emeritus, 2001—; ret. prof. music Columbus State U. Guest conductor Atlanta Symphony, 1983, 96, Birmingham Symphony, Ala., 1974, Tupelo Symphony, Miss., 1978, 79. Author: The Appreciation of Great Music, 2000. Conductor Atlanta Ballet Orch., 1956—61, Atlanta Cmty. Orch., 1957—61, So. Ballet Orch., Atlanta, 1958—61, Toledo Orch., 1961—65. Mem.: Am. Symphony Orch. League, Music Educators Nat. Conf., Ga. Music Educators Assn. (conductor ann. convs.). Democrat. Jewish. Avocations: swimming, travel, reading, camping, sports. Home: 4140 Oak Ferry Dr Kennesaw GA 30144

KRUGER, JEROME, materials science educator, consultant; b. Atlanta, Feb. 7, 1927; s. Isaac and Sarah (Stein) K.; m. Mollee Coppel, Feb. 20, 1955; children: Lennard, Joseph. BS, Ga. Inst. Tech., 1948, MS, 1949; PhD, U. Va., 1952. With Naval Rsch. Lab., Washington, 1952-55; with Nat. Bur. Standards, Commerce Dept., Washington, 1955-83, group leader Corrosion and Electrodeposition, 1966-83; prof. Johns Hopkins U., 1984-99, chmn. materials sci. and engring., 1986-88, prof. emeritus, 1999—. Cons. Argonne Nat. Lab., Lockheed, Balt. Gas & Electric, Teletech Thompson, Dalton & DeRose, Mueller Brass, S.W. Rsch. Inst., Dickenson, Wright, Moon, Van Dusen & Freeman, Haineness, Dickey & Pierce, W.O. Snead, H.M. Huber Co., DACCO Sci.; Jerome Kruger vis. scholar U. Va., 1998. Divisional editor Jour. Electrochem. Soc., 1966-83; subject area editor: Ency. of Materials Sci. and Engring.; also editor books; contbr. articles to tech. jours., chpts. to book. DuPont fellow U. Va., 1951-52; recipient Silver medal Commerce Dept., 1962, Gold medal, 1972; Blum award Nat. Capitol sect. Electrochem. Soc., 1966, Foley award, 1999; Samuel Wesley Stratton award Nat. Bur. Standards, 1982; Presdl. rank of Meritorious Exec. of Sr. Exec. Svc., 1982; U.R. Evans award Inst. Corrosion (U.K.), 1991, Hon. fellow, 1996; establishment of Jerome Kruger vis. scholar program at U. Va., 1998, 1st invited scholar, 1999. Fellow Electrochem. Soc. (treas. 1982-86, hon. mem. 1987, Outstanding Achievement award 1977, Olin Palladium medal 1995), fellow Nat. Assn. Corrosion Engrs. (bd. dirs. 1983-86, W.R. Whitney award 1976, Jerome Kruger award in corrosion sci., Balt.-Washington sect., 1997); mem. Am. Inst. Conservation, Internat. Corrosion Coun. (1st v.p. 1984-87, pres. 1987-90), Fedn. Materials Socs. (pres. 1977), Standards Alumni Assoc. (pres.) Nat. Inst. Stds. and Tech., Sigma Xi, Tau Beta Pi. Jewish. Home and Office: 619 Warfield Dr Rockville MD 20850-1921 E-mail: jk2727@aol.com.

KRUGER, KENNETH, architect; b. Newark, Aug. 13, 1928; s. Rudolph Robert and Clarise Estelle (Goldman) K.; m. Elinor Margaret Kane, July 22, 1978; children: Jonathan, Karen, Kai. BArch, MIT, 1951, MS, 1953, postgrad., 1964; MArch, Harvard U., 1952; postgrad., U. Rome, 1955. Registered arch., Mass., N.J., N.Y., profl. engr., Mass.; cert. Nat. Coun. Archtl. Registration Bds.; lic. constrn. supr., home inspector, real estate broker, title 5 sys. inspector, Mass. Archtl. designer Carl Koch & Assoc., Cambridge, Mass., 1953-54; structural designer Frank Grad, Paris, 1955; arch. Marcel Breuer & Assocs., N.Y.C., 1956-57; structural engr. Simpson & Stratta, San Francisco, 1959-60, Chin & Hensolt, San Francisco, 1961-62, Internat. Engring. Co., Rio de Janeiro, 1963; arch., engr. Kenneth Kruger, Boston, 1964-68, Kruger Kruger Albenberg Archs. & Engrs., Cambridge, 1969—. Instr. arch. MIT, Cambridge, 1952-53. Mem. Fresh Pond Adv. Bd., Cambridge, 2002, Mass. Designer Selection Bd., 2002—. Overseas fellow MIT, 1952, Rotch prize, 1951; Fulbright scholar, 1954-55. Fellow ASCE, AIA, Am. Soc. Home Inspectors (v.p. 1991, Pres.'s award 1991, exec. com. 1991-93, dir.-at-large 1988-90, 92-94, chmn. bylaws com. 1992-94; dir. New Eng. chpt. 1982), Boston Soc. Archs. (dir., commr. 1974-77), Boston Soc. Civil Engrs., Boston Assn. Structural Engrs., Constrn. Specification Inst., Sigma Xi, Alpha Epsilon Pi. Avocations: skiing, tennis, squash, backpacking, biking. Office: Kruger Kruger Albenberg 67 Grozier Rd Cambridge MA 02138-3314 Office Phone: 617-661-3812.

KRUGER, KENNETH CHARLES, architect; b. Santa Barbara, Calif., Aug. 19, 1930; s. Thomas Albin and Chleople (Gaines) K.; m. Patricia Kathryn Rasey, Aug. 21, 1955; children: David, Eric. BArch, U. So. Calif., 1953. Registered arch., Calif. Pres. Kruger Bensen Ziemer, Santa Barbara, 1960-90; part-time instr. architecture dept. Calif. Poly., San Luis Obispo, 1993-95; part-time arch., 1993—. Regent Calif. Archtl. Found., 1997-2003. Bd. dirs. United Boys and Girls Club, 2000-. Fellow AIA; mem. Archtl. Found. Santa Barbara (pres. 1987-89). Democrat. Home: 1255 Ferrelo Rd Santa Barbara CA 93103-2101

KRUGER, LEONDRA R., lawyer; AB magna cum laude, Harvard Univ., 1997; JD, Yale Univ., 2001. Bar: Calif. Law clk. U.S. Ct. Appeals (D.C. cir.), Washington, 2002—03; law clk. to Hon. John Paul Stevens U.S. Supreme Ct., Washington, 2003; assoc. Jenner & Block, Washington, Wilmer Cutler Pickering Hale & Dorr, Washington, 2004—. Editor-in-chief The Yale Law Joun. Mem.: Phi Beta Kappa. Office: Wilmer Cutler Pickering Hale & Dorr 2445 M St NW Washington DC 20037

KRUGER, MOLLEE COPPEL, writer; b. Bel Air, Md., Mar. 28, 1929; d. Benjamin and Mary Coppel; m. Jerome Kruger, Feb. 20, 1955; children: Lennard Gideon, Joseph Avrum. BA, U. Md., 1950. Columnist The Harford Gazette, Bel Air, Md., 1945-47; advt. copywriter Joseph Katz Co., Balt., 1951-55; TV scriptwriter Jewish Community Coun., Washington, 1960-72; columnist, feature writer various newspapers, Washington and N.Y.C., 1967-88; freelance writer various nat. publs., 1980—. Condr. writing workshop Montgomery County Cmty. Svcs., Rockville, Md., 1982; cons. Buddemeir Co., Balt., 1958-59; pres. Maryben Books, Rockville, 1970—; tchr. creative writing Jewish Cmty. Ctr., Rockville, 1974-78, cons. editor sr. adult publs., 1975, 76, 77; cons. editor Stds. Alumni Assn., 1992. Author: Unholy Writ, 1970, More Unholy Writ, 1973, Yankee Shoes, 1975 (Gold Ribbon Bicentennial award 1976), Daughters of Chutzpah, 1983, Admiral of the Mosquitoes, 1990, Ladies First, 1995 (mus. adaptation 1st prize Nat. Music Competition Nat. League Am. Pen Women), A Purse of Humorous Verse for Jewish Women, 2005; editor Std. newsletter Nat. Bur. Stds., 1978-80 (Excellence award 1979); performer one-woman show on Emma Lazarus, Jewish Cmty. Coun., Washington, 1976; playwright (one act plays) The Muted Note: A Pulpit Drama, 1965, Master of Dreams: S.Y. Agnon, 1968, President McKinley is Dead, 1977; playwright, prodr. hist. show for Md. 350 Com., Montgomery County, Rockville, 1982-84; contbr. articles to popular mags.; author numerous poems Founding mem. Humanities Commn. Montgomery County, 1984-91; judge Md. Writing Contest for Sr. Citizens, Annapolis, 1987-91, Montgomery County Bd. Elections,l 1990-92. Recipient Cert. of Recognition US Dept. Commerce, Washington, 1979, Alice Sherry Meml. award Poetry Soc. Va., Charlottesville, 1988, Courage award Dystonia Med. Found., 1997, Gov. Arts award Md. Citizens for the Arts Found., 2002, Lifetime Achievement recognition U. Md. Librs., 2003; named Outstanding Md. Woman Writer Md. State Dept. Edn., Md. Commn. for Women, Balt., 1989; Millenium poetry displayed in Montgomery County, Md. Govt. Bldg., 2000-; named Notable Montgomery County Author, Friends of the Libr., 2001. Mem. Nat. League Am. Pen Women (Md. state letters chmn. 1990-92, 1999-2001, br. pres.-elect, nat. letters bd. 1992-94, founding mem. Chesapeake Mag., 1993, chmn. nat. letters com., nat. membership chmn. 1994-95, nat. exec. bd. 1994-96, nat. pub. rels. chmn. 1996-98, writing awards 1983, 85, 87, 89, 1st prize Nat. Adult Short Story contest 1994, 1st prize Nat. Catherine Leach Poetry competition 1994, 1st prize Nat. Miriam S. Rogers letters contest, 1995, 2d prize Chesapeake Short Story contest 1996, 2d prize Md. Form Poetry 1999, centennial com. 1997, 1st pl. 1998, millenium planning com. 1999), Mortar Bd. Alumni Club (pres. 1977-78, 50th ann. recognition cert. 2000, 50th Class Reunion com. 2000, Comcast Humanities Achievement award, 2001). Democrat. Jewish. Avocations: walking, travel.

KRUGER, NANCY R., university program director, nurse; BS in Nursing, Skidmore Coll., 1967; MA in Parent-Child Health in Nursing, NYU, 1971; D of Sci. in Nursing, U. Pa., 1983. Staff nurse surgery SUNY Downstate Med. Ctr., Bklyn., 1967-68; staff nurse recovery room NYU Med. Ctr., 1968-70; clin. specialist, supr. critical care Mercer Med. Ctr., Trenton, N.J., 1971-81; clin. dir. U. Pa. Hosp., Dept. Med. Nursing and Emergency Svcs., Phila., 1981-84; asst. exec. dir., chief nursing officer Wills Eye Hosp., Phila., 1984-86; dir. nursing, chief nursing officer Pa. State U. Hershey Med. Ctr., Univ. Hosps., Hershey, Pa., 1986—, nurse practitioner cardiothoracic surgery, 1990-91; clin. instr. Sch. Nursing U. Pa., 1979-83; clin. prof. Coll. Allied Health Thomas Jefferson U., Sch. Nursing, Phila., 1985-89; adj. asst. prof. grad. faculty Pa. State U., Harrisburg, Pa., 1987—, co-dir. Quality Assurance Program, Grad. Pub. Adminstrn., 1987—. Various univ. com. memberships including clin. investigation com., 1986-89, strategic study group for nursing, 1987, planning com. for employee performance evaluation, 1993, search com. for chmn. pediatrics dept., 1989, others; cons. Commonwealth of Pa., Dept. Health, mem. application steering com. RWJ Found. Grant program, 1992. Contbr. articles to profl. jours. Bd. dirs. Harrisburg Opera Co., 1994-95; adv. com. Lion's Eye Bank of Ctrl. Pa., 1989—; mem. exec. com. Children's Miracle Network Telethon, 1986—. Mem. AACN, Am. Orgn. Nurse Execs., Nat. League for Nursing, Pa. Orgn. Nurse execs. (exec. com. 1988-92, chmn. nursing practice com. 1989, chmn. legis. com. 1992, pres. 1991, chmn. PONE nurse educators task force 1992—), South Ctrl. Orgn. Nurse Execs. (pres. 1989), Phila. Assn. Clin. Trials (human rsch. rev. bd. 1984-91), Coun. Health Profns. Edn. Hosp. Assn. Pa. (chmn. 1995), Am. Coun. Transplantation (bd. dirs. 1987-91), Sigma Theta Tau.

KRUGER, PAULA, telecommunications industry executive; b. Bklyn., July 31, 1950; d. Jean Jacques Kruger and Jo Campione; m. Lawrence C. Heller; children: Michael, Tracy, Jessica. BA, CW Post, 1972, MBA, 1976. V.p. customer rels. Cablevision, Woodbury, NY, 1994—97; corp. v.p. customer svc. Am. Express, N.Y.C., Citibank, N.Y.C., v.p. devel. divsn.; v.p. consumer svcs. group South Korea; v.p. teleservices Excel Comm., 1997—99, exec. v.p., customer and independent representative ops., 1999; gen. mgr. customer relationship mgmt. service line Electronic Data Systems Corp., 2002—03; exec. v.p. consumer markets group Qwest Comm., 2003—. Office: Qwest Comm Internat 1801 California St Denver CO 80202

KRUGMAN, PAUL ROBIN, economics professor; b. Albany, N.Y., Feb. 28, 1953; s. David Krugman and Anita Alman; m. Robin Wells. BA, Yale U., 1974; PhD, MIT, 1977. Asst. prof. Yale U., New Haven, 1977-80; assoc. prof. MIT, Cambridge, 1980-83, prof. econs., 1983—94, 1996—2000, Stanford, 1994—96; op-ed columnist N.Y. Times, 1999—; prof. internat. trade, internat. economics Princeton U., 2000—. Research assoc. Nat. Bur. Econ. Research, Cambridge, 1979—; economist internat. policy U.S. Council Econ. Advisers, Washington, 1982-83; mem. bd. economists L.A. Times. Author: Exchange Rate Instability, 1988, The Age of Diminished Expectations, 1990, Rethinking International Trade, 1990, Geography and Trade, 1991, Currencies and Crises, 1992, Peddling Prosperity, 1994, Development, Georgraphy, and Economic Theory, 1995, The Self-Organizing Economy, 1996, Pop Internationalism, 1996, The Accidental Theorist, 1998, The Return of Depression Economics, 1999, Fuzzy Math: The Essential Guide to the Bush Tax Plan, 2001, The Great Unraveling, 2003, over 200 jour. articles; co-author: Market Structure and Foreign Trade, 1985, International Economics: Theory and Policy, 1988, Market Structure and Trade Policy, 1989, Foreign Direst Investment in the United States, 1989, The Spatial Economy, 1999; editor: Strategic Trade Policy and The New International Economics, 1986, Exchange Rate Targets and Currency Bands, 1992, Trade with Japan: Has the Door Opened Wider?, 1994, Currency Crises, 2000; co-editor: Empirical Studies of Strategic Policy, 1994. Recipient John Bates Clark Medal, 1991, Eccles Prize for Excellence Econ. Writing, 1991, Adam Smith award, 1995, Nikkei Prize (with M. Fujita and A. Venables), 2001, Alonso Prize, Regional Sci. Assn., 2002. Fellow Econometric Soc., 1987-, Am. Acad. Arts and Sci., 1992-; mem. Group of Thirty, 1988-. Office: Princeton U Woodrow Wilson Sch 414 Robertson Hall Princeton NJ 08544*

KRUGMAN, RICHARD DAVID, pediatrician, academic administrator, educator; b. N.Y.C., Nov. 28, 1942; s. Saul and Sylvia (Stern) K.; m. Mary Elizabeth Kerber, July 9, 1966; children: Scott, Joshua, Todd, Jordan. AB, Princeton U., 1963; MD, NYU, 1968. Resident U. Colo. Sch. Medicine, Denver, 1968-71; staff assoc. Nat. Inst. Health, Bethesda, Md., 1971-73; asst. prof. U. Colo. Sch. Medicine, 1973-78, assoc. prof., 1978-87, prof. of pediatrics, 1988—, dean, 1992—. Author: The Battered Child, 5th edit., 1997; editor: (jour.) Child Abuse/Neglect, 1986-2001. Chmn. U.S. Adv. Bd. Child Abuse and Neglect, Washington, 1989-91; dir. Kempe Nat. Ctr. for Prevention and Treatment of Child Abuse and Neglect, Denver, 1981-92; trustee Princeton U., 2001—. Recipient C. Henry Kempe award Nat. Conf. on Child Abuse, 1989, St. Geme award U. Colo. Sch. Medicine, 1992, 98; Paul Harris fellow Rotary Internat., Sydney, Australia, 1992. Mem. Internat. Soc. Prevention of Child Abuse and Neglect (pres. 1992-94), Am. Acad. Pediatrics (Ray Helfer award 1995, Brandt Steele award 1996), Am. Pediatric Soc. Office: U Colo Sch Medicine 4200 E 9th Ave Denver CO 80262-0001

KRUGMAN, STANLEY LEE, international management consultant; b. N.Y.C., Mar. 2, 1925; s. Harry and Leah (Greenberg) K.; m. Helen Schorr, June 14, 1947; children: Vicky Lee, Thomas Paul; m. Carolyn Schambra, Sept. 17, 1966; children: David Andrew, Wendy Carol; m. Gail Jennings, Mar. 17, 1974. B Chem. Engring., Rensselaer Poly. Inst., 1947; postgrad., Poly. Inst. Bklyn., Columbia U., 1947-51. Process devel. engr. Merck & Co., Rahway, N.J., 1947-51; sr. process and project engr. C.F. Braun & Co., Alhambra, Calif., 1951-55; with Jacobs Engring. Co., Pasadena, Calif., 1955-76; from chief engr. to v.p. engring. and constrn. to v.p. gen. mgr. to exec. v.p. to pres., and dir.; exec. v.p., dir. Jacobs Engring. Group Inc., Pasadena, Calif., 1974-82; pres., dir. Jacobs Constructors of P.R., San Juan, 1970-82; pres. Jacobs Internat. Inc., 1971-82, Jacobs Internat. Ltd., Inc., Dublin, Ireland, 1974-82; dep. chmn. Jacobs LTA Engring., Ltd., Johannesburg, South Africa, 1981-82; pres. Krugman Assocs., 1982—; internat. mgmt. cons. Patentee in field. Served to lt. (j.g.) USNR, 1944-46, PTO. Mem.: Am. Chem. Soc., Am. Inst. Chem. Engrs., U.S. Naval Inst. Presbyterian. Home and Office: 3850 Rio RD Unit 40 Carmel CA 93923-8627 Business E-Mail: sno.3pws@earthlink.net.

KRUIDENIER, DAVID, retired newspaper executive; b. Des Moines, July 18, 1921; s. David S. and Florence (Cowles) K.; m. Elizabeth Stuart, Dec. 29, 1948; 1 child, Lisa. BA, Yale U., 1946; MBA, Harvard U., 1948; LLD, Buena Vista Coll., 1960, Simpson Coll., 1963; LittD, Luther Coll., 1990; DHL, Drake U., 1990. With Mpls. Star and Tribune, 1948-52; with Des Moines Register and Tribune, 1952-85, pres., pub., 1971-78, chief exec. officer, 1971-85, chmn., chief exec. officer, 1982-85; with Cowles Media Co., 1983-93, pres., chief exec. officer, 1983-84, chmn., chief exec. officer, 1984-85, chmn., 1985-97. Trustee Gardner and Florence Call Cowles Found., Drake U., Des Moines Art Ctr., Grinnell Coll. Greater Des Moines Found. With USAAF, 1942-45. Decorated Air medal with three clusters, D.F.C. Mem. Coun. on Fgn. Rels., Des Moines Club, Mpls. Club, Sigma Delta Chi, Beta Theta Pi, Beta Gamma Sigma. Home: 3409 Southern Hills Dr Des Moines IA 50321-1318

KRUK, BARBARA GUARINO, entrepreneur, public relations executive; d. Salvatore Ralph and Josephine Guarino; m. Kostanti Anthony Kruk, Oct. 3, 1971; children: Matthew, Kelly Marsella. BA, Long Island U., Southampton, NY, 1997—2000. Owner and pub. rels. dir. Roma Funeral Home, Shirley, NY, 1976—; owner and buyer I.M. Woman Custom Couture Boutique, Shirley, 1974—96; dir. of pub. rels. Svc. Corp. Internat., Houston, 1997—2001. Aftercare counselor/dir. of cmty. rels. Svc. Corp. Internat., Houston, 1996—2002. Author: (nonfiction novel) Connie's Story. Dir. of child and sr. awareness programs Svc. Corp. Internat., Houston, 1997—2002; contbg author South Shore Press, Moriches, NY, 1998—2003. Recipient Summa Cum Laude, Long Island U., 2000. R-Liberal. Roman Catholic. Achievements include introducing many cmty. programs including Child Safety; also brought programs to sr. centers throughout Long Island focusing on safety in the home as well as protection against financial scams. Avocations: writing, painting, architecture/design, travel, computers. Office: Roma Funeral Home 539 William Floyd Parkway Shirley NY 11967 Office Phone: 631-281-0800. Personal E-mail: kruk6187@aol.com.

KRUKOVA, ELIZAVETA, lawyer; Student, Moscow State Law U., 1997; M in law, Ind. U., 1998. Bar: N.Y. 2000, Md. 2002, U.S. Ct. Appeals (4th Cir.) 2004, U.S. Ct. Appeals, (9th Cir.) 2004, U.S. Ct. Appeals (3rd cir.) 2005. Legal asst. Steptoe & Johnson, Moscow, 1994—95; law clk. Skadden, Arps, Moscow, 1995—97; atty. Couder & Brothers, Washington, 1998—2001; atty., pres. Immigration Capital, Washington, 2002—; supr. atty. Office of Refugee Resettlement, Arlington, Va., 2002—. Mem.: Am. Immigration Lawyers Assn. Home: 6911 Highland St Springfield VA 22150 Office: Immigration Capital 701 W Broad St 202 Falls Church VA 22046 Office Phone: 703-534-5588.

KRUKOWSKI, Mrs. JAN See HARROW, NANCY

KRUKOWSKI, JAN, communications executive; b. Lodz, Poland, Nov. 18, 1930; arrived in U.S., 1941; s. Edward and Alice (Landau) K.; m. Nancy Harrow; children: Damon, Anton. BA, N.Y. U., 1952, MA, 1961. Writer Dem. Nat. Com., N.Y.C., 1952—56; account exec. Alfred Auerbach Assocs., 1957; v.p. Press Release, Inc., 1958; pres. Krukowski and Symington, Inc., 1959—63; exec. v.p. Barton-Gillet Co., 1964—80; pres. Jan Krukowski & Co., 1980—. Trustee Am. Symphony Orch., 2001—, chair trustees, 2005—; trustee Tchrs. Coll., Columbia U., 2002—; bd. dirs. Norman and Rosita Winston Found., 1997—. Mem.: Century Assn. Office: Jan Krukowski & Co 40 Wooster St New York NY 10013 E-mail: jkrukowski@jankrukowski.com.

KRULAK, CHARLES CHANDLER, bank executive; b. Quantico, Va., Mar. 4, 1942; s. Victor Harold and Amy (Chandler) K.; m. Zandra Lynn Meyers, June 27, 1964; children: David Chandler, Todd Cameron. BS, U.S. Naval Acad., 1964; MS, George Washington U., 1973; advanced mil. course, Amphib. War Sch., 1968, Army Command and Gen. Staff, Coll., 1976, Nat. War Coll., 1982. Commd. 2d lt. USMC, 1964, advanced through grades to gen., 1995, retired, 1999, rifle co. comdr., 1965-66, 69-70, bn. comdr., 1983-85; mil. asst. Asst. Sec. Def. for Command, Control, Comm. and Intelligence, Washington, 1986-87; dep. dir. White House Mil. Office, Washington, 1987-89; brigade comdr. and asst. divsn. comdr. USMC, N.C., 1989-91, force svc. support group comdr., 1989-90, force svc. support comdr., brigade comdr., 1990-91; dir. pers. mgmt., pers. procurement Hdqtrs. Marine Corps, 1991-92; comdg. gen. MCCDC, Quantico, Va., 1992-94; comdr. marine forces, Pacific and comdg. gen. Fleet Marine Forces, Pacific, Camp Smith, Hawaii, 1994-95; commandant USMC, 1995-99; sr. vice chmn. MBNA Am. Corp., Wilmington, Del., 1999—2001; chmn., CEO MBNA Europe Bank Ltd., 2001—; exec. vice chmn., chief adminstrv. officer MBNA Corp., 2004—. Contbr. articles to Marine Corps Gazette. Decorated D.S.M. (2), Def. D.S.M. (2), Silver Star, Bronze Star with combat V (3), Purple Heart (2). Avocations: running, reading. Office: MBNA Am 1100 N King St Wilmington DE 19884-0001*

KRULAK, VICTOR HAROLD, newspaper executive; b. Denver, Jan. 7, 1913; s. Morris and Besse M. (Ball) K.; m. Amy Chandler, June 1, 1936; children: Victor Harold Jr., William Morris, Charles Chandler. BS, U.S. Naval Acad., 1934; LL.D., U. San Diego. Commd. 2d lt. USMC, 1934; advanced through grades to lt. gen.; service in China, at sea, with USMC (Fleet Marine Forces), 1935-39; staff officer, also bn. regimental and divsn. comdr. World War II, World War II; chief staff (1st Marine Div. Korea); formerly comdg. gen. (Marine Corps Recruit Depot), San Diego; formerly spl asst. to dir., joint staff counterinsurgency and spl. activities (Office Joint Chiefs Staff); comdg. gen. Fleet Marine Force Pacific, Pacific, 1964-68; ret., 1968; v.p. Copley Newspaper Corp., 1968-79; pres. Words Ltd. Corp., San Diego. Trustee Zool. Soc. San Diego. Decorated D.S.M., Navy Cross, Legion of Merit with 3 oak leaf clusters, Bronze Star, Air medal, Purple Heart (2) U.S.; Cross of Gallantry; Medal of Merit Vietnam; Distinguished Service medal (Korea), Order of Cloud and Banner, Republic of China. Mem. U.S. Naval Inst., U.S. Marine Corps Assn., Am. Soc. Newspaper Editors, InterAm. Press Assn., U.S. Strategic Inst. (chmn.). Home: # 307 2404 Loring St San Diego CA 92109 Office: Words Ltd 2404 Loring St San Diego CA 92110-4827

KRULFELD, RUTH MARILYN, anthropologist, educator; m. Jacob Mendel Krulfeld, 1964; 1 child, Michael David. BA cum laude, Brandeis U., 1956; PhD, Yale U., 1974. Field rschr. micro-geog. rsch. farms, Singapore, Malaya, 1951-53; anthrop. rschr., Jamaica, 1957, Costa Rica, Nicaragua, Panama, 1958, Sasak of Lombok, Indonesia, 1960—63, 1993; anthrop. rschr. S.E. Asian refugees to U.S., 1981—; anthrop. rschr., Lombok, Indonesia and N.E. Thailand, 1993; asst. prof. anthropology, dir. grad. students George Washington U., Washington, 1964-72, 93-97, assoc. prof., 1973-76, prof., 1976-2000, chmn. dept. anthropology, 1984-87, founder spl. grad. program in internat. world devel., prof. anthropology, internat. affairs, prof. emeritus anthropology, human scis., internat. affairs, 2000—. Bd. dir. No. Va. Humanities Coun., Internat. Buddhist Com.; rschr. Laotian refugees in U.S., 1981—, also rschr. on culture change in villages in Indonesia; bd. dir.Newcomers Cmty. Svc. Ctr.; mem. bd. advisors Lao-Am. Women's Assn., Lao Cmty. Forum; mem. faculty Semester At Sea, 1999, 2003; bd. dir. Successful New Ams. Project of S.E. Asian Resource Action Ctr Co-author: Reconstructuring Lives, Recapturing Meaning: Refugee Identity, Gender and Culture Change, 1994, Beyond Boundaries: Selected papers on Refugees and Immigrants, 1997, Power, Ethics, and Human Rights: Anthropological Studies of Refugee Research and Action, 1998; contbr. articles to profl. jours.; editl. bd. com. on refugees and immigrants. Currier scholar Yale U., 1958; Ford fellow, 1960-62; grantee Found. for Study of Man, 1957, Am. Coun., 1963, Cotlow faculty rsch. grantee, 1992-93, faculty rsch. grantee George Washington U., 1992-93, rsch. grantee Va. Found. for Humanities and Pub. Policy, 1995-96; recipient Banneker award Ctr. for Washington Area Studies, 1996, George Washington U. award for Pedigogical Rsch. and Devel. in Edn., award for Outstanding Contributions to U. and Wider Soc., 2000. Mem. AAAS (com. on sci. freedom and responsibility), Anthrop. Soc. Washington, Am. Anthrop. Assn. (nominating com., com. on refugee issues gen. anthropology divsn., vice chair com. on refugee issues 1992-94, gen. anthropology divsn. 1993-94, exec. bd. com. on refugees and immigrants 1994-99, CORI editl. bd. 1998-99, CORI award for best paper on refugees issues 1992, Pedagogical Rsch. and Innovative Devel. in Edn. award 1994, award for leadership and contbn. to refugee studies com. on refugees and immigrants 2000). Office: George Washington U Dept Anthropology Washington DC 20052-0001 *Perhaps the major attitudes that have motivated my work have been a deep respect for my fellow human beings, and a need to learn from them, to experience their wondrous creativity, ability and diversity; as an anthropologist, to understand as much about human societies as I could, and as an educator, to ignite this enthusiasm and wonder in my students, to encourage them to go beyond our present understanding and abilities. As an advocate for human rights, I hope to instill in my students the wish to be involved in social action.*

KRULIA, STANLEY ANTHONY, school system administrator; s. Anthony and Maxine Krulia; m. Patricia Deely, Aug. 16, 1975; children: Katherine Ann Eschelbach, Timothy Anthony, Mary Susan. BS in Secondary Social Studies, Edinboro (Pa.) State Coll., 1974; MEd, Ohio U., 1977. Cert. local supt. Ohio, ednl. adminstrv. specialist Ohio, supr. Ohio, h.s. prin. Ohio, elem. prin. Ohio, spl. edn. K-12 Ohio, h.s. 7-12 comprehensive social studies Ohio. Spl. edn. tchr. 7-12 Gallipolis (Ohio) City Schs., 1974—78; spl. edn. supr. Fairfield County Ednl. Svc. Ctr., Lancaster, Ohio, 1978—97; dir. pupil pers. Lancaster City Schs., 1997—. Adj. prof. Ashland U., Columbus, Ohio, 2004—05; coord. Hocking County Coun. for Spl. Olympics, Lancaster, 1984—85. Named Adminstr. of Yr., Hocking Valley chpt. CEC, 1982; grantee Individuals with Disabilities Edn. Act, Fed. Govt., 1997—2005. Mem.: ASCD (assoc.), KC (assoc.; warden 2004—05, 4th Degree 2004). Democrat. Roman Catholic. Avocations: swimming, jogging, travel, birdwatching, golf. Home: 1915 Bunker Hill Ct Lancaster OH 43130 Office: Lancaster City Schs 111 S Broad St Lancaster OH 41330 Office Phone: 740-687-7360. E-mail: s_krulia@lancaster.k12.oh.us.

KRULIK, BARBARA S., art director, writer, curator; b. NYC, June 13, 1955; d. Herbert Arnold and Irene Sylvia K. BA in Art History, Pa. State U., 1976; MA in Museology, Reinwardt Acad., Amsterdam, The Netherlands, 2000. Asst. to dir. Nat. Acad. of Design, N.Y.C., 1976—78; acting dir. NAD, N.Y.C., 1977-78, coord. exhbns., 1978-83, asst. dir., 1983-89, interim dir., 1989-90, dep. dir., 1990-92; assoc. dir. Forum Gallery, N.Y.C., 1992-94; dir. Grad. Sch. Figurative Art New York Acad. Art, N.Y.C., 1994-97; owner, dir. KCCS (Krulik Cultural Cons. Svs.), 2001—; mgr. Magpie Music Dance Co., Amsterdam, Netherlands, 2003—; mem. steering com. Found. Exhibn. Man., Amsterdam, Netherlands, 2004—; prodn. mgr. No Apology, Amsterdam, Netherlands, 2004—05. Ind. curator, 1997—; cons., 1997—. Author, editor exhbn. catalogues. Mem. Am. Assn. Mus. (curators and registrars coms.), Internat. Coun. on Mus. Office Phone: +31 (0) 69242947. E-mail: b.krulik@chello.nl.

KRULITZ, LEO MORRION, financial planner, publishing executive, director; b. Wallace, Idaho, June 15, 1938; s. John Morrion and Myrtle (Parker) K.; m. Donna Eileen Ristau, June 18, 1960; children— Cynthia, Pamela. BA, Stanford U., 1960; JD cum laude, Harvard U., 1963; MBA, Stanford U., 1969. Bar: Idaho bar 1963, Ind. bar 1969, D.C. bar 1978, U.S. Supreme Ct. bar 1978. Ptnr. firm Moffatt, Thomas, Barrett & Blanton, Boise, Idaho, 1963-67; v.p., treas. Irwin Mgmt. Co., Columbus, Ind., 1969-77; solicitor Dept. of the Interior, Washington, 1977-79; gen. counsel Cummins Engine Co., Columbus, Ind., 1979-80, v.p., 1980-92; pres. Cummins Fin., Inc., 1984-92, Cummins Cash and Info. Svcs., Inc., 1988-92; pres., CEO Saunders, Inc., Birmingham, Ala., 1992-93; pres., CEO, dir. Parkland Mgmt. Co., Cleve., 1994—; endowment trustee Euclid Ave. Christian Ch., 1995-2001; dir. Horvitz Newspapers, Inc., Bellevue, Wash., 1994—. Trustee Lois U. Horvitz Found., 1998—; exec. dir. H.R.H. Family Found., 1994-98; treas. Irwin-Sweeney-Miller Found., Columbus, 1976-77; dir. L'Enfant Plaza Properties, Washington, 1974-77; mem. U.S. delegation Soviet Union Conf. on Environ. Law, 1978 Mem. Bartholomew Consol. Sch. Bd., 1982-88; trustee Wheelright Mus. of the Am. Indian, 2002—, Wheelright Mus. Endowment Fund, 2004—. Mem. Union Club (Cleve.). Democrat. Home: 20900 Colby Rd Shaker Heights OH 44122-1906 Office: 1001 Lakeside Ave E Ste 900 Cleveland OH 44114-1172

KRULL, JEFFREY ROBERT, library director; b. North Tonawanda, N.Y., Aug. 29, 1948; s. Robert George and Ruth Otilie (Fels) K.; m. Alice Marie Hart, Apr. 12, 1969; children: Robert, Marla. BA, Williams Coll., Williamstown, Mass., 1970; MLS, SUNY, Buffalo, 1974. Cert. profl. libr., N.Y., Ohio, Ind. Traffic mgr. New England Tel. Co., Burlington, Vt., 1970-71; tchr. Harrisburg (Pa.) Acad., 1971-72; reference libr. Buffalo and Erie County Pub. Libr., 1973-76; head libr. Ohio U., Chillicothe, 1976-78; dir. Mansfield-Richland County Pub. Libr., Ohio, 1978-86, Allen County Pub. Libr., Ft. Wayne, Ind., 1986—. Mem. exec. com. Ft. Wayne Area Libr. Svc. Authority, 1986-90, v.p., 1989; mem. exec. com. Ind. Coop. Libr. Svcs. Authority, 1992-96, pres., 1994-95; mem. Online Computer Libr. Ctr. Pub. Libr. Adv. Coun., 1994-97; pres. Ft. Wayne Area INFONET, 1995-2001. Pres. Three Rivers Literacy Alliance, 1997—99; trustee Ohionet, Columbus, 1984—86. Named Sagamore of the Wabash, Gov. Ind., 2001. Mem. ALA, Pub. Libr. Assn. (pres. met. librs. sect. 1990-91, statistical report adv. com.), Libr. Adminstrn. and Mgmt. Assn. (sec. libr. orgn. and mgmt. assn. 1996-97), Ohio Libr. Assn. (bd. dirs. 1985-86), Ind. Libr. Fedn. (vice chmn. legis. com. 1987—), Beta Phi Mu. Home: 3017 Oak Borough Run Fort Wayne IN 46804-7808 Office: Allen County Pub Libr PO Box 2270 Fort Wayne IN 46801-2270 Office Phone: 260-421-1201. E-mail: jkrull@acpl.lib.in.us.

KRULL, KATHLEEN, writer; b. Ft. Leonard Wood, Mo., July 29, 1952; d. Kenneth Owen and Helen (Folliard) K.; m. Loyal D. Cowles, Dec. 14, 1974 (div. May 1982); m. Paul W. Brewer, Oct. 31, 1989; stepchildren: Jacqui, Melanie. BA in English magna cum laude, Lawrence U., 1974. Editl. asst. Harper & Row, Evanston, Ill., 1973-74; assoc. editor Western Pub./Golden Books, Racine, Wis., 1974-79; mng. (acquiring) editor Raintree Pubs., Milw., 1979-82; sr. editor Harcourt Brace Jovanovich, San Diego, 1982-84; freelance writer and reviewer children's books, 1984—. Frequent speaker at confs., workshops and univs. Author: Golden Everything Workbook Series, 1979, Beginning To Learn (24 books transl. into 5 langs. 1979-82), Sometimes My Mom Drinks Too Much, 1980 (Outstanding Social Studies Trade Book award 1980), Trixie Belden and the Hudson River Mystery, 1979, Twelve Keys to Writing Books That Sell, 1989, Songs of Praise, 1989, Alex Fitzgerald, TV Star, 1990, Alex Fitzgerald's Cure for Nightmares, 1991, Gonna Sing My Head Off; American Folk Songs for Children, 1992, World of My Own (4 books 1994, 95), Lives of the Musicians: Good Times, Bad Times...And What the Neighbors Thought, 1993, Maria Molina and the Days of the Dead, 1994, Lives of the Writers: Comedies, Tragedies (And What the Neighbors Thought), 1995, V is for Victory: America Remembers World War II, 1995, Lives of the Artists, 1995, Wilma Unlimited, 1996, Wish You Were Here, 1997, Lives of the Athletes, 1997, Lives of the Presidents, 1998, Lives of the Musicians: Good Times, Bad Times: (And What the Neighbors Thought), 1998, Alex Fitzgerald's Cure for Nightmares, 1999, Gonna Sing My Head Off!: American Folk Songs for Children, 1999; also articles and revs. Recipient Celebrate Literacy award Greater San Diego Reading Assn., 1994, also numerous awards for writing, including Boston Globe/Horn Book honor award, PEN West children's lit. award, 1994, nonfiction award So. Calif. Coun. on Lit. for Children and Young People, ALA Notable Book awards, Tchrs.' Choice award Internat. Reading Assn., Best Book of 1993 award Pubs. Weekly. Mem. Soc. Children's Book Writers and Illustrators (bd. dirs. 1995—, Golden Kite honor award for nonfiction). Avocations: quilting, gardening, singing, playing piano, travel. Office: c/o Harcourt Brace & Co Childrens Books 525 B St Ste 1900 San Diego CA 92101-4495

KRULL, STEPHEN KEITH, lawyer; b. Peoria, Ill., Jan. 1965; m. Elizabeth A. Krull. BS, Ea. Ill. U., 1986; JD, Chgo.-Kent College Law, 1990. Atty. Sidley & Austin, Chgo.; v.p. Cop. Communications, 2002—; sr. v.p., gen. counsel, sec. Owens Corning, Toledo, 2003—. Office: Owens Corning 1 Owens Corning Pky Toledo OH 43659 Home: 7125 Oak Bluff Ln Maumee OH 43537-9418 Office Phone: 419-248-8000. Office Fax: 419-248-5337. Business E-Mail: stephen.k.krull@owenscorning.com.

KRUM, JACK KERN, food products executive; b. Kansas City, Mo., Mar. 17, 1922; s. Charles Jean Krum and Clara Louise Struble; m. Miriam Emily Siebert; children: Mark, Meredith, Eric, Andrew. BA, Hope Coll., 1940—44; MA, Mich. State U., 1946—48; PhD, U. Mass., 1949—51. Prof. food tech. U. of Tenn., 1950—52; dir. quality control, rsch. food tech. Oscar Mayer Inc., Madison, Wis., 1952—55; rsch. food tech. Nat. Biscuit Co., NYC, 1955—57; tech. dir. Sterwin Chem., NYC, 1956—68; v.p. tech. dir. Rt. French Co., 1972—80. Pres. Techniques, Inc., Kans. City., 1980—. Mem. Heartland Art Guild. Lt. USN, 1944—52. Fellow: Inst. Food Tech. Avocations: woodcarving, watercolors. Home: 16705 W 327 TH St Paola KS 66071

KRUMAN, MARC W., history professor, academic administrator; b. Bklyn., Dec. 13, 1949; s. Martin and Florence Kruman; m. Randie Schafer, Aug. 27, 1977; children: Sarah A. S., Elizabeth Molly, Benjamin Samuel. BS in Indsl. and Labor Rels., Cornell U., 1971; MPhil in History, MA in History, Yale U., 1973, PhD, 1978. Instr. history Wayne State U., Detroit, 1975—78, asst. prof. history, 1978—84, assoc. prof. history, 1984—95, prof. history, 1995—, chair dept. history, 1995—, dir. Ctr. for Study of Citizenship, 2002—; sr. lectr. Am. studies U. Rome, 1999. Author: Between Authority and Liberty: State Constitution Making in Revolutionary America, Parties and Politics in North Carolina, 1836-1865; contbg. author: Reader's Ency. of the Am. Presidency, Ency.of the Am. Legis. Sys.; contbr. articles to profl. jours. Coach Berkley (Mich.) Youth Soccer League, 1996—99, Huntington Woods (Mich.) Softball League, 1989—94; mem. Mich. Advanced Placement Adv. coun. Recipient Bd. of Governors Faculty Recognition award, Wayne State U., 1985, Pres.'s award for excellence in tchg., 1994, Bd. of Governors Faculty Recognition award, 1998, Best Article award, N.C. Hist. Rev., 1987, Jour. of the Early Republic, 1993; Andrew W. Mellon Faculty fellow in the humanities, Harvard U., 1980—81, sr. rsch. fellow, Nat. Endowment for the Humanities, 1985—86, Disting. Faculty fellow, Wayne State U., 2003—05, Fulbright Faculty fellow, Coun. for Internat. Exch. of Scholars, 1999. Mem.: Orgn. Am. Historians, Am. Hist. Assn. Avocations: swimming, weightlifting, travel. Office: Dept History Wayne State U 3094 Faculty Adminstrn Bldg Detroit MI 48202 Office Phone: 313-577-2525. Business E-Mail: m.kruman@wayne.edu.

KRUMBEIN, CHARLES HARVEY, lawyer; b. Ft. Benning, Ga., Dec. 15, 1944; s. Nathaniel and Amy (Meyers) K.; m. Cynthia J. Nerden, Dec. 17, 1967; children: Jason M., Laura R. BS, Pa. State U., 1966; JD, U. Ga., 1969. Bar: Va. 1970, U.S. Supreme Ct. 1975; cert. in consumer bankruptcy. Mgmt. trainee Heilig-Meyers Co., Richmond, Va., 1972-80, v.p., corp. counsel, 1980-89; prin. Krumbein and Assocs., 1990—. Mem. Va. adv. bd. U.S. Civil Rights, 1985-97; nat. commr. Anti-Defamation League of B'nai B'rith, 1986—; mem. Va. Commonwealth U. Dental Sch. Bd., 1999-2002. Served to capt. U.S. Army, 1970-72, Ger. Mem. So. Home Furnishing Assn. (dir. 1980-90, mem. exec. com. 1986-90), Richmond Retail Mchts. Assn. (pres. divsn. 1982-84), Fishing Bay Yacht Club (Deltaville, Va.). Office: Krumbein & Assocs 1650 Willow Lawn Dr Ste 300 Richmond VA 23230-3435

KRUMBOLTZ, JOHN DWIGHT, psychologist, educator; b. Cedar Rapids, Iowa, Oct. 21, 1928; s. Dwight John and Margaret (Jones) K.; m. Helen Brandhorst, Aug. 22, 1954 (div. Aug. 1986); children: Ann, Jennifer; m. Betty Lee Foster, Nov. 8, 1987. BA, Coe Coll., Cedar Rapids, 1950; MA, Columbia Tchrs. Coll., 1951; PhD, U. Minn., 1955; PhD (hon.), Pacific Grad. Sch. Psychology, 1991. Counselor, tchr. W. Waterloo (Iowa) H.S., 1951-53; from teaching asst. to instr. U. Minn., 1953-55; from asst. prof. ednl. psychology to assoc. prof. Mich. State U., 1957-61; faculty Stanford U. Sch. Edn., 1961-66, prof. edn. and psychology, 1966—. Vis. sr. research psychologist Ednl. Testing Service, 1972-73; fellow Ctr. for Advanced Study in Behavioral Scis., 1975-76, Advanced Study Ctr., Nat. Ctr. for Research in Vocat. Edn., Ohio State U., 1980-81; vis. colleague dept. psychology Inst. Psychiatry, U. London, 1983-84 Author: (with others) Learning to Study, 1960; (with Helen B. Krumboltz) Changing Children's Behavior, 1972; editor: Learning and the Educational Process, 1965, Revolution in Counseling, 1966; (with Carl E. Thoresen) Behavioral Counseling: Cases and Techniques, 1969, Counseling Methods, 1976; (with Anita M. Mitchell and G. Brian Jones) Social Learning and Career Decision Making, 1979; (with Daniel A. Hamel) Assessing Career Development, 1982; contbr. articles to profl. jours. With USAF, 1955-57. Recipient Eminent Career award Nat. Career Devel. Assn., 1994, Living Legend award Am. Counseling Assn., 2004; Guggenheim fellow, 1967-68. Mem. APA (pres. div. counseling psychology 1974-75, award for disting. profl. contbns. to knowledge 2002), Am. Ednl. Rsch. Assn. (v.p. div. E 1966-68), Am. Pers. and Guidance Assn. (Outstanding Rsch. award 1959, 66, 68, Disting. Profl. Svcs. award 1974, Leona Tyler award 1990). Home: 933 Valdez Pl Stanford CA 94305-1008

KRUMLAUF, ROBERT EUGENE, neuroscientist, educator; B in Chem. Engring., Vanderbilt U., 1970; PhD in Devel. Biology, Ohio State U., 1979. Chief chem. engr. Capital City Products Inc., Columbus, Ohio, 1970—75; fellow dept. biochemistry Ohio State U., 1975—79; postdoctoral fellow Dr A. Balmain Beatson Inst. Cancer Rsch., Glasgow, Scotland, 1979—82, Dr S. Tilghman Inst. Cancer Rsch., Phila., 1982—85; from group leader to adj. group leader NIMR, England, 1985—2000, adj. group leader, 2000; sci. dir. Stowers Inst. Med. Rsch., Kansas City, Mo., 2000—. Prof. oral biology Sch. Dentistry U. Mo., Kansas City, 2000—; prof. oral biology Dept. Anatomy and Cell Biology U. Kans. Med. Sch., Kansas City, 2001—; prof. neuroscience Graduate Program U. Kans., Kansas City, 2002—. Editor: Devel. Biology, 1995—; mem. editl. bd.: New Biologist, 1989—92, Mechanisms of Devel., 1990—, Nucleic Acids Rsch., 1992—, Current Biology, 1993—2000, Portland Press, 1994—2000, Devel., 1994—, Molecular and Cellular Neurobiology, 1995—, Human Molecular Genetics, 1996—98, Genes and Function, 1997—98, InScight, 1998—. Fellow: Acad. Med. Scis.; mem.: Am. Acad. Arts and Scis., Soc. Pathology and Teratology, Acad. Med. Scis. UK, The Genetical Soc., Am. Soc. Microbiology, Am. Assn. Anatomists, Soc. Devel. Biology, Brit. Soc. Devel. Biology, European Molecular Biology Org., European Devel. Biology Org. (sec. 1997—2001). Office: Stowers Inst 1000 E 50th St Kansas City MO 64110 Home: 5407 Mission Dr Mission Hills KS 66208 Office Phone: 816-926-4051. Business E-Mail: rek@stowers-institute.org.

KRUMMEL, DONALD WILLIAM, librarian, educator; b. Sioux City, Iowa, July 12, 1929; s. William and Leta Margarete (Fischer) K.; m. Marilyn Darlene Frederick, June 19, 1956; children: Karen Elisabeth, Matthew Frederick. Mus.B., U. Mich., 1951, Mus.M., 1953, MA in Library Sci, 1954, PhD, 1958. Instr. in music lit. U. Mich., 1952-56; reference librarian Library of Congress, Washington, 1956-61; head reference dept., asso. librarian Newberry Library, Chgo., 1962-69; asso. prof. library sci. U. Ill., 1970-71, prof. library sci. and music, 1971—, assoc. Center Advanced Study, 1974; univ. scholar, 1991; Centennial scholar, 1994. Middle mgmt. intern U.S. Civil Svc., 1960; scholar in residence Aspen Inst., 1969; mem. faculty Rare Book Sch. Columbia U., 1990-91, U. Va., 1993—; archival cons. Kneisel Hall, 1990-94. Author: Bibliotheca Bolduaniana, 1972, Guide for Dating Early Published Music, 1974, English Music Printing, 1553-1700, 1975, Bibliographical Inventory to the Early Music in the Newberry Library, 1977, Organizing the Library's Support, 1980, Resources of American Music History, 1981, Bibliographies, Their Aims and Methods, 1984, Bibliographical Handbook of American Music, 1987, The Memory of Sound, 1988, Grove-Norton Handbook of Music Printing and Publishing, 1990, The Literature of Music Bibliography, 1993, Fiat Lux, Fiat Latebra, 1999; contbr. numerous articles and revs. to profl. jours. Recipient awards Huntington Libr., 1965, Am. Coun. Learned Socs., 1966-77, Am. Philos. Soc., 1969, Coun. Libr. Resources, 1967; Newberry libr. travelling fellow, 1969-70; Univ. Coll. (London) hon. rsch. fellow, 1974-75; Guggenheim fellow, 1976-77. Mem. ALA (G.K. Hall award 1987, Beta Phi Mu award 1999), Music Libr. Assn. (pres. 1981-83, spl. citation award), Bibliog. Soc. (London), Bibliog. Soc. Am., Sonneck Soc. (Lowens award 1989), Am. Antiquarian Soc., Am. Printing Hist. Assn. (laureate 2004), Caxton Club (Chgo.), Grolier club. Home: 702 W Delaware Ave Urbana IL 61801-4807 Office: U Ill 501 E Daniel St Champaign IL 61820-6211 Office Phone: 217-333-3280. E-mail: donkay@uiuc.edu.

KRUMP, GARY JOSEPH, lawyer, judge; b. Breckenridge, Minn., June 27, 1946; m. Mary Kay Chermak; children: Adam, Jonathon. BA, N.D. State U., 1968; JD, U. Minn., 1971, postdoctoral, 1972; cert. in health care, So. Ill. U., Edwardsville, 1978, MBA, 1979; grad. cert., George Washington U., 1981; grad., Fed. Exec. Inst., 1988, U.S. Army Command & Gen. Staff Coll., 1989; grad. sr. mgrs. in govt. program, Harvard U., 1998. Bar: Minn. 1971, U.S. Ct. Mil. Appeals 1972, U.S. Supreme Ct. 1975, D.C. 1977. Commd. 2nd lt. U.S. Army, 1970, advanced through grades to capt., 1971, capt. with JAGC, 1972-76, chief internat. law-Japan, 1974-76; chief adminstrv. law Walter Reed Army Med. Ctr., 1976-77; sr. staff atty. office of gen. counsel VA, Washington, 1978-83, nat. coord. med. care recovery program, 1979, dep. asst. gen. counsel, 1983-87, assoc. dep., asst. sec. for acquisitions, 1988-89; v.p., gen. counsel JSA Healthcare Corp., 1989-91; dir., corp. sec. DKH Healthcare; dir. Office of Real Property Mgmt. Office Real Property Mgmt., U.S. Dept. VA, Washington, 1991-92, dep. asst. sec. acquisitions and material mgmt., 1992—2003, acting asst. sec. acquisitions and facilities, 1992-95; VA environ. exec., 1994—2003; chmn., chief adminstrv. judge VA Bd. Contract Appeals, 2003—; VA dispute resolution offcl., 2003—; fed. judge U.S. Dept. VA, Washington, 2003—. Mem. faculty Ctrl. Mich. U., U. Va.; apptd. to career Fed. Sr. Exec. Svc.; gen. counsel, dir. Soccerama Assn., Inc., 1987-93; sec. DKH Healthcare, Inc., 1990-91; prin., dir., gen. counsel ISG, Inc., 1991-97; dir., gen. counsel Am. Health Group, Inc., 1993-97; mem. Interagy. Com. on Supply Mgmt. Steering Group, Nat. Performance Rev. Com. on Reinventing VA; chair Interagy. Procurement Reform Working Group, 1993-95; chair interagy. contracts group GSA; mem. Interagy. Contracts Adv. Group; chair nat. conf. reinventing small bus. partnerships VA, 1993; chair interagy contracts group GSA, mem. adv. group; apptd. Pres.' Com. for Purchase from Blind and Other Severely Disabled, 1992-2003, chmn. fed. women's program, 1992-2003, mentoring program, 2003, chair, 1996-2000; com. chmn. Subcom. on Procurement Reform, 1996-97, pres. com. disting. svc. award, 2000, chmn. subcom. on governance, 2002-2003; mem. nat. adv. bd. Fed. Prison Industries, 1995-2003, chair subcom. administrn., 1994-2003; trustee Leadership VA, 1992-95; mem. Fed. Environ. Execs. Task Force, 1994-2003; mem. Interagy. Com. on Stds. Policy, 1995-2003, VA Stds. Exec., 1994-2003, VA Metrics Exec., 1994-2003; mem. Interagy. Electronic Commerce Task Force, 1994-2003; departmental co-chair Combined Fed. Campaign VA, 1994, departmental co-chair, campaign mgr., 1999; chair VA Departmental Environ. Adv. Group, 1994-2003; bd. dirs. VA Dept., 1992-95; chmn. bd. dirs. VA Supply Fund, 1993-2003; mem. Fed. Procurement Coun., 1991-97; mem. Procurement Execs. Coun., 1997-2003, vice chair, 2000-03, chair com. on electronic commerce, 1999-2003; mem. Interagy. e-Gov Task Force, Office Mgmt. & Budget, Exec. Office of Pres., 2000-2003; mem. VA e-Gov Steering com., 2000-2003; Creekmore lectr. on procurement law Judge Advs. Sch., Army, U. Va., 1997; mem. com. on ethics DC Bar, 2001-2003; judge VA Dispute Resolution Official, 2003; pres. com. leadership award, 2003; adv. bd. Fed. Procurement Conf., 2002-03; spkr. in field. Sec. Vets. Affairs Commendation, 1989, 95; mem. Ctr. for Pub. Resources Nat. Procurement Com., 1986-89, Adminstv. Conf. U.S. Alternative Disputes Resolution Symposium, 1988. Served to lt. col. JAGC, USAR, 1976-2000. Decorated U.S. Legion of Merit; recipient Fed. 100 Info. Tech. award, Fed. Procurement Coun., 1997, Presdl. Rank award, 1997, VA Meritorious Svc. award, 2000, Exceptional Svc. award, U.S. Army, P.R., 2000, Log. Chief award, USAF, 2002, VA Exceptional Svc. award, 2003, Exceptional Svc. award, Procurement Execs. Coun., 2003, U.S. Atty. Gen.'s Certificate, 2004. Fellow Nat. Contract Mgrs. Assn. (bd. advisors 1989-90, 93—, com. internat. contracting 1995-2003); mem. ABA (vice chair com. on healthcare contract law 1997-2003, com. on healthcare), VFW (life), Judge's Assn. (bd. contract appeals, 2003), Fed. Bar Assn. (nat. chmn. tort law com., health and human svcs. coun. chmn. 1980-81, chmn. Nat. Tort Conf. 1979, editor Tort Law Newsletter 1978-81, Superior Svc. awards 1979, 81), D.C. Bar Assn. (com. ethics), Nat. Forensic Ctr., Am. Coll.-Legal Medicine (assoc.), Internat. Soc. Mil. Law and Law of War, Internat. Legal Soc., Res. Officers Ass. (life), Mid-Atlantic Token Kai, Japanese Sword Soc. U.S., Fed. Acquisition Inst. Policy Bd., Fed. Procurement Coun., Contract Svcs. Assn. (procurement com. 1989-91), Interagency Med. Procurement Mgmt. Com., Govt. Procurement Tng. (adv. com.), Interagency Procurement Career Mgmt. Com., Fed. Real Property Execs. (interagy. adv. coun. 1991-93), Vets. of Am., Am. Legion (life), Bd. of Contract Appeals Judges Assn. (chmn. ethics seminar 2004), Bd. of Contract Appeals Bar Assn., VFW (life), Res. Officers Assn. (life), Rolls Royce Owners Club, Beta Gamma Sigma, Tau Kappa Epsilon. Home: 13812 Town Line Rd Silver Spring MD 20906-2112 Office: US Dept Vets Affairs Bd Contract Appeals 810 Vermont Ave NW Washington DC 20420-0001 Office Phone: 202-273-6743. E-mail: gary.krump@mail.va.gov.

KRUMP, PAUL J., insurance company executive; BA in bus. adminstrn., St. John's U. Underwriting trainee The Chubb Corp., 1982, exec. protection and internat. underwriter Dusseldorf, Germany, 1986, no. zone mgr. dept. fin. inst., U.S. underwriting mgr. dept. fin. inst., exec. v.p. Chubb & Son, 2000, COO Chubb Comml. Ins., 2000—. Attendee exec. edn. program IMD, Lausanne, Switzerland. Office: The Chubb Corp 15 Mountain View Rd PO Box 1615 Plainfield NJ 07061-1615

KRUPANSKY, BLANCHE ETHEL, retired judge; b. Cleve., Dec. 10, 1925; d. Frank and Anna K.; m. Frank W. Vargo, Apr. 30, 1960. AB, Flora Stone Mather Coll., 1943-47; JD, Case Western Res. U., 1948, LLM, 1966. Bar: Ohio 1949. Gen. practice law, 1949-61, 83-84; asst. atty. gen. State of Ohio; asst. chief counsel Ohio Bur. Workmen's Compensation; judge Cleve. Mcpl. Ct., 1961-69; judge Common Pleas Ct. Cuyahoga County, 1969-77, Ct. Appeals Ohio 8th Appellate Dist., 1977-81; justice Supreme Ct. Ohio, 1981-83; judge 8th Dist. Ct. Appeals, 1984—95, chief justice, 1991; ret., 1995. Vis. com. Case Western U. Law Sch., 1974-78, bd. govs., 1975-76; mem. adv. com. Akron State U., 1982-85, vis. com., 1982-86. Mem. adv. com. Akron State U., 1982—85, mem. vis. com., 1982—86. Recipient Outstanding Jud. Service award Supreme Ct. Ohio, 1972-76, Law Book scholar award Cuyahoga Women's Polit. Caucus, 1981, outstanding contbn. to law award Ohio Assn. Civil Trial Attys., 1982, Disting. Alumna award, 1982, Disting. Service award Women's Space, 1982, award Democratic Women's Caucus, 1983, award Women's Equity Action League Ohio, 1983; Personal Achievement and Community Svc. award Case We. Res. U., 1988, Margaret Ireland award Women's City Club, 1984; named Woman of Achievement Inter-Club Council Cleve., 1969; inducted into Ohio Women's Hall of Fame, 1981 Mem. Nat. Assn. Women Lawyers, Nat. Assn. Women Judges, Ohio Bar Assn. (Cronise Lutes award 1997), Bar Assn. Greater Cleve., Cuyahoga County Bar Assn., Cleve. Women Lawyers, LWV, Ohio Ctrs. of Appeals Assn., Ohio Assn. Attys. Gen., Ohio Appellate Judges Assn., Soc. of Benchers (chair 1994-95), SAR (Silver Medal award 1995). Republic. Roman Catholic. Club: Woman's City (Woman of Achievement award 1981) (Cleve.).

KRUPAT, KITTY WEISS, writer, educator; b. N.Y.C., Feb. 9, 1938; d. Paul and Magda (Neumann) Weiss; m. Arnold Krupat, Aug. 1962 (div. 1968). BA, NYU, 1961, Master's, 1998, postgrad., 1999—. Rsch. editor Esquire mag., N.Y.C., 1966-70; mng. editor pocket books Simon & Schuster, N.Y.C., 1970-74; organizer, edn. dir. dist. 65 UAW, N.Y.C., 1974-89; organizer grad. student organizing com. NYU, N.Y.C., 1996—; edn. dir. Internat. Ladies' Garment Workers Union, N.Y.C., 1989-95; instr. Cornell U., N.Y.C., 1997—; tchg. asst. NYU, 1995—2003; assoc. dir. Queen's Coll. Labor Resource Ctr. CUNY, 2002—. Instr. Queens Coll., CUNY. Co-editor (anthology) Out at Work: Building A Gay Labor Alliance, 2001; contbr. articles to profl. jours. Organizer No Sweat Coalition NYU, 1996—. Mem. MLA, Am. Studies Assn., Labor at the Crossroads (bd. dirs. 1989—), Wagner Labor Archives (bd. dirs. 1987—), United Assn. Labor Educators (bd. dirs. 1981—), Nat. Writers Union. Avocations: music, art, theater, gardening, movies.

KRUPCHAK, TAMARA, artist; b. Lake Station, Ind., Apr. 15, 1956; d. John Charles Krupchak and Rose Marie Maretich-Krupchak. BS, Ball State U., 1978. Artist, spkr., creativity coach Tamara Krupchak Fine Art, San Diego, 1988—. Group shows include San Diego Tijuana Yokohama Art Exchange, 1992, San Diego Mus. Art, 1994, 97, 98, 99; artist (book) Getting Exposure, 1995. Bd. dirs. artist guild San Diego Mus. Art, 1994-97, trustee, 1996-97; mem. nat. devel. com. Coll. Fine Arts, Ball State U., 2001. Recipient art commn. St. Mary's Health and Learning Ctr., Grand Rapids, Mich., 1998, Sunland Christian Sci. Healing Ctr., San Diego, 1998. Mem. Toastmasters Internat. (winner Area 21 Internat. Speech Contest 1998). Office: 1090 University Ave Ste 201A San Diego CA 92103-3362

KRUPER, JOHN GERALD (JACK KRUPER), sales and marketing executive; b. Carbondale, Pa., Feb. 10, 1949; s. John Joseph and Evelyn (Bernosky) K.; m. Renee Jane Shugg, Aug. 4, 1973; children: Kevin John, Melissa Lynn, Abbey Renee. BSBA in Acctg., U. Scranton, 1970; postgrad., SUNY, 1974, U. Scranton, 1985. Store mgr. Endicott Johnson Corp., schenectady, 1970-71; retail mdse. distbr. Endicott, 1971-72; asst. mdse. buyer, 1972-74; full line mdse. buyer, 1974-76; dir. corp. advt. and sales promotion, 1976-79; gen. sales mgr. Ranger divsn., 1979-81; v.p. merchandising, 1981-84; v.p. branded footwear divsn., 1984—86; v.p. Continental Mktg. Group, Inc., 1986-90, v.p. sales and mktg. Lehigh divsn., 1990-92, Iron Age divsn. Childs Corp., 1992-94; nat. sales dir. hy-test divsn. Florsheim Shoe Co., 1994—; nat. sales and prodn. devel. mgr. to gen. mgr. Florsheim Work Group, 1996-97, 96-97; brand gen. mgr. John Deere Footwear divsn., 1997-99, John Deere Internat. divsn., 1999—2001; v.p. sales and mktg. Tatra Mfg. Co., Cary, Ill., 2001—02; mng. dir., CEO Occupl. Footwear Co. Am., 2002—. Served with Corps Engrs., U.S. Army, 1970. E-mail: Jack.Kruper@florsheim.com. Office: 3307 South Rte 31 Prarie Grove IL 60012 Office Phone: 815-788-9314. Personal E-mail: jgkruper@aol.com.

KRUPKA, ROBERT GEORGE, lawyer; b. Rochester, NY, Oct. 21, 1949; s. Joseph Anton and Marjorie Clara (Meteyer) Krupka; m. Pamela Banner Krupka; children: Kristin Nicole, Kerry Melissa. BS, Georgetown U., 1971; JD, U. Chgo., 1974. Bar: Ill. 1974, Colo. 1991, D.C., 1991, Calif. 1998, U.S. Dist. Ct. (no. dist.) Ill. 1974, U.S. Dist. Ct. (ea. dist.) Wis. 1974, U.S. Ct. Appeals (7th cir.) 1976, U.S. Supreme Ct. 1978, U.S. Dist. Ct. (cen. dist.) Ill. 1980, U.S. Dist. Ct. (so. dist.) Ill. 1988, U.S. Dist. Ct. (no. dist.) Calif. 1980, U.S. Dist. Ct. (ctrl. and so. dists.) Calif. 1999, U.S. Dist. Ct. Ariz. 1998, U.S. Dist. Ct. Colo. 1998, U.S. Dist. Ct. Md. 2000, U.S. Ct. Appeals (4th and fed. cirs.) 1982, U.S. Ct. Appeals (6th cir.) 1985, U.S. Ct. Appeals (1st, 2d, 3d, 5th, 8th, 9th, 10th and 11th dists.) 1999. Assoc. Kirkland & Ellis LLP, Chgo., 1974-79, ptnr., 1979—. Author: Infringement Litigation Computer Software and Database, 1984, Computer Software, Semiconductor Design, Video Game and Database Protection and Enforcement, 1984. Mem. bd. trustees Francis W. Parker Sch., 1987-98, pres., 1994-97. Mem. ABA (chmn. sec. com. 1982-88, chmn. div. 1988-90, 98—, coun. 1994-97), Am. Intellectual Property Law Assn. (chmn. subcom. 1988—), Copyright Soc., Fed. Cir. Bar Assn., Internat. Bar Assn., Internat. Trademark Assn., ITC Trial Lawyers, Nat. Inst. for Trial Advocacy (trustee 2002—), Mid-Am. Club. Office: Kirkland & Ellis LLP 777 S Figueroa Ste 3700 Los Angeles CA 90017 Office Phone: 213-680-8400. E-mail: bkrupka@kirkland.com.

KRUPKAT, ANN KATHERINE, retired secondary school educator; b. River Falls, Wis., Feb. 25, 1926; d. Henry John and Emma (Gregerson) Laufenberg; m. Donald E. Krupkat, July 26, 1952; children: Constance Louise, Rachel Andrine. BS in Biology, U. Wis., River Falls, 1948; MS in Guidance and Counseling, U. Wis., Milw., 1973. Profl. counselor. Tchr. Manitowoc (Wis.) Bd. of Edn., 1948—52; tchr. sci. South Milw. Bd. of Edn., 1962—73, counselor, 1973—83, attendance and discipline adminstr., 1983—87. Dir. sr. outreach studies U. Wis., River Falls., 1988-2004. Mem. AAUW (past pres., Named Grant 1987). Home: 821 Oak Knoll Ave River Falls WI 54022-2646

KRUPMAN, WILLIAM ALLAN, lawyer; b. Cleve., Aug. 14, 1936; s. Joel and Betty (Button) K; m. Anne deLemos, June 19, 1960; children: Pamela, Theodore, Sally. BA, Amherst Coll., 1958; LLB, U. Mich., 1961; LLM in Labor Law, NYU, 1962. Bar: Ohio 1961, NY 1962. Ptnr. Jackson Lewis LLP, NYC, 1962-75, mng. ptnr., 1975—. Author: Winning NLRB Elections, 1997. Chmn. bd. dirs. Children's Village, Dobbs Ferry, NY Mem. NY State Bar Assn. Home: 2 Ponds Ln Purchase NY 10577 Office: Jackson Lewis LLP 59 Maiden Ln New York NY 10038-4502 Office Phone: 212-545-4002.

KRUPNICK, JANICE LEE, psychologist, psychotherapist, educator; b. Newark, Mar. 7, 1950; d. Jacob and Betty (Katz) K.; m. Richard Michael Suzman, July 21, 1976; children: Daniel, Jessica. AB, Oberlin Coll., 1972; MSW, U. Mich., 1974; MA, U. Calif., Berkeley, 1985, PhD, 1988. Lic. psychologist, Md., D.C. Social worker Long Beach (Calif.) Neuropsychol. Inst., 1974-75; fellow Mt. Zion Hosp./Med. Ctr., San Francisco, 1975-77; program analyst NIMH, Rockville, Md., 1980-81; asst. clin. prof. U. Calif., San Francisco, 1977-83; cons. NAS, Washington, 1983-84; asst. clin. prof. Georgetown U., Washington, 1984-90; asst. rsch. prof. George Washington U., Washington, 1988-91; assoc. clin. prof. Georgetown U., Washington, 1990-94, clin. prof., 1994—, rsch. prof., 2000—. Cons. NIMH, Bethesda, Md., 1990-91, Am. Psychiat. Assn., 1990-91; tchr. dynamic psychotherapy seminar for advanced psychiat. residents Georgetown U., lectr. interpersonal psychotherapy course. Co-author: Personality Styles and Brief Psychotherapy, 1984; contbr. articles to psychiat. and psychol. jours. Participant rallies for women's rights, Washington, 1986—. Clin. fellow NIMH, 1975-77, rsch. fellow NIMH, 1986-88. Mem. Am. Psychol. Assn., Soc. for Clin. Social Work, Soc. for Psychotherapy Rsch. Jewish. Avocations: reading, movies, travel, swimming. Home: 4100 Oliver St Chevy Chase MD 20815-7120 Office: 5480 Wisconsin Ave Ste 220 Chevy Chase MD 20815-3503 E-mail: krupnicj@georgetown.edu.

KRUPP, CLARENCE WILLIAM, lawyer, health facility administrator; b. Cleve., June 20, 1929; s. William Frederick and Mary Mae (Volchko) K.; m. Janice Margaret Heckman, June 28, 1952; children: Bruce, Carolyn. BBA cum laude, Cleve. State U., 1958, LL.B., 1959, LL.M., 1963; LL.D. (hon.), 1974. Bar: Wis. 1972. Dir. indsl. relations and indsl. engring. Buxbaum Co., Canton, Ohio, 1963-66; mgr. indsl. relations Trane Co., La Crosse, Wis., 1966-73; dir. personnel-labor relations environ. products div. ITT, Phila., 1973; v.p. indsl. relations, gen. counsel G. Heileman Brewing Co., La Crosse, 1973-76; atty., v.p. human resources-risk control, sec. Good Samaritan Hosp., Dayton, Ohio, 1976-80; mgr. compensation and benefits State of Ariz., Phoenix, 1980-83; personnel adminstr., law/land mgmt. divsn. agt. Salt River Project, 1983-94; Indian and sch. land specialist, 1992—; chmn., pres. C.W. Krupp P.C., 1986—. Cons. on labor rels., 1969, 81-83, 88—; elec. line land impact cons., western states, 2000—. Contbr. articles to profl. jours. Mcpl. arbitrator, La Crosse, 1976; pres., mem. La Crosse Bd. Edn., 1969-72; mem. Wis. Gov.'s Task Force on Edn., 1972-73, Ohio Little White House library del.; mem. Ariz. Spinal Injury Panel, 1984-2000. Served with U.S. Army, 1951-53. Named Outstanding Ariz. State Profl. Employee, 1982, Employee of Quarter, 1990, 91. Mem. Am. Bar Assn. (forum hosp. law, labor law sect.), Am. Corp. Counsel Assn., Nat. Notary Assn., Wis Bar Assn. (Continuing Edn. award 1972), Am. Assn. Hosp. Attys., Ariz. Assn. Industries (healthcare com. 1983-97, chmn. legis. subcom. 1983-97), Am. Soc. Law and Medicine, Dayton C. of C., Electric League of Ariz. (ins. advisor 1985-97), Internat. Right of Way Assn. (regional cons. Native Am. land rights 1998—), Harris, USA Today, Carol Wright Opinion Polls, 2003-. Clubs: Rotary. Democrat. Roman Catholic. Home and Office: 8701 E Via De La Gente Scottsdale AZ 85258-4040 Office Phone: 480-998-7653. Personal E-mail: clarewk@msn.com. *Understand and be tolerant of the views of others. With that insight your decisons will be respected and your judgment both honored and sought.*

KRUPP, EDWIN CHARLES, astronomer; b. Chgo., Nov. 18, 1944; s. Edwin Frederick and Florence Ann (Olander) K.; m. Robin Suzanne Rector, Dec. 31, 1968; 1 son, Ethan Hembree. BA, Pomona Coll., 1966; MA, UCLA, 1968, PhD (NDEA fellow, 1970-71), 1972. Astronomer Griffith Obs., Los Angeles Dept. Recreation and Parks, 1972—, dir., 1976—. Mem. faculty El Camino Coll., U. So. Calif., extension divs. U. Calif.; cons. in ednl. TV C.C. Consortium; host teleseries Project: Universe. Author: Echoes of the Ancient Skies, 1983, The Comet and You, 1986 (Best Sci. Writing award Am. Inst. Physics 1986), The Big Dipper and You, 1989, Beyond the Blue Horizon, 1991, The Moon and You, 1993, Skywatchers, Shamans & Kings, 1996, The Rainbow and You, 2000; editor, co-author: In Search of Ancient Astronomies, 1978 (Am. Inst. Physics-U.S. Steel Found. award for best sci. writing 1978), Archaeoastronomy and the Roots of Science; editor-in-chief Griffith Obs., 1984—; contbg. editor Sky & Telescope, 1993—. Mem. Am. Astron. Soc. (past chmn. hist. astronomy divsn., solar physics divsn. writing award 2002), Astron. Soc. Pacific (past dir., Klumpke-Roberts Outstanding Contbns. to the Public Understanding and Appreciation of Astronomy award 1989, G. Bruce Blair medal for contbns. to pub. astronomy 1996, Clifford W. Holmes award for contbns. to amateur astronomy 2002), Internat. Astron. Union, Explorers Club, Sigma Xi. Office: Griffith Observatory 2800 E Observatory Rd Los Angeles CA 90027-1255

KRUPP, FRED D., lawyer, environmental services administrator; b. Mineola, N.Y., Mar. 21, 1954; s. Arthur L. and Rosalind (Mehr) K.; m. Laurie Louise Devitt, Aug. 21, 1982; children: Alexander Mehr, Zachary Devitt, Jackson O'Connor. BS, Yale U., New Haven, 1975; JD, U. Mich., Ann Arbor, 1978. Ptnr. Albis & Krupp, New Haven, 1978-83; ptnr. Cooper, Whitney, Cochran & Krupp, New Haven, 1984; pres. Environ. Def., 1984—; gen. counsel Conn. Fund for the Environment, New Haven, 1978-84. Mem. Pres.'s Commn. on Environ. Quality, 1991-92; mem. Pres.'s Coun. on Sustainable Devel., 1993-99; mem. Pres.'s Adv. Com. Trade Policy and Negotiations, 1994-2002; bd. dirs. H. John Heinz III Ctr. for Sci., Econs. and Environment. Helen De Roy fellow U. Mich. Law Sch. 1986 Office: Environ Def 257 Park Ave S New York NY 10010-7304 Office Phone: 212-505-2100.

KRUPP, JAMES ARTHUR GUSTAVE, manufacturing executive, consultant; b. Naples, Italy, Oct. 27, 1944; arrived in U.S., 1945; s. Ralph Gustave and Lydia (Guerroni) Krupp; m. Joyce Ann Draffan, Nov. 5, 1966; children: James Michael Douglas, Matthew Ralph Alexander. Student, U.S. Naval Acad., 1963-66; BSME magna cum laude, U. New Haven, 1971, EMBA, 1981. Cert. fellow in prodn. and inventory. Prodn. control mgr. Sargent & Co., New Haven, 1966-72; prodn. scheduling mgr. Stanley Tools, New Britain, Conn., 1972-75; materials mgr. Whitney Blake, Hamden, Conn., 1975-76; materials control mgr. Burndy Corp., Norwalk, Conn., 1976-79; prodn. and inventory mgr. Picker Corp., Northford, Conn., 1979-81; materials mgr. Carlyle Johnson Machine Co., Manchester, Conn., 1981-84; dir. advanced planning systems ITT Sealectro, New Britain, 1984-89; v.p. materials Echlin Inc., Branford, Conn., 1989-99; dir. materials planning Stanadyne Corp., Windsor, Conn., 1999—. Mem. editl. bd. Prodn. and Inventory Mgmt. Jour., 1988—; contbr. articles to profl. jours. Chmn. bd. ethics, Wallingford, Conn., 1980—84; mem. Charter Revision Commn., Wallingford, 1988—89; councilman Town of Wallingford, 1984—85. With USN, 1963—67. Mem.: Assn. Internal Mgmt. Cons., Am. Prodn. and Inventory Control Soc. (Romey Everdell award 1998), Mensa. Democrat. Roman Catholic. Avocations: youth soccer and special olympics referee, fishing, chess. Office Phone: 860-683-4538. Business E-Mail: jkrupp@stanadyne.com. *Whether in life or business, there are 3 guiding principles whose attainment surpass all measures of success: 1) An unfaltering tradition of the highest sense of personal honor. 2) An absolute respect for the dignity of all those with whom one comes in contact. 3) An unwaivering commitment to excellence in all that one does.*

KRUSA-DOSSIN, MARY ANN, military officer; m. Paul F. Dossin; 1 child, Michael. BA in Psychology and Sociology, Tex. Christian U., 1974; MS in Human Rels., Golden Gate U., 1981; MS in Nat. Resource Planning, Nat. Def. U., 1995. Commd. 2d lt. USMC, 1975, advanced through grades to brig. gen., platoon comdr. security dept. MCAS El Toro, 1976—79, tng. and human affairs officer Aircraft Group 15, 1st Marine Aircraft Wing, 1979—81, ops. officer provost marshal's office Iwakuni, Japan, 1979—81, dir. family svc. ctr. Camp Lejeune, 1981—84, with provost marshal's office, 1984—85, provost marshal MCAS Yuma, Ariz., 1988—91, exec. offider Hdqrs. and svc. battalion MCB Camp Smedley D. Butler Okinawa, Japan, 1992—93, comdr., 1993—96, action officer joint staff J-7 operational plans and interoperability directorate Pentagon, 1996—98, comdr. security battalion MCB Camp Pendleton, 1998—2000, asst. chief of staff cmty. svcs. MCB Camp Pendleton, 2000—02, dep. dir. Marine Corps Pub. Affairs, 2002—03, dir. Marine Corps. Pub. Affairs, 2003—. Decorated Legion of Merit. Home: 1200 Crystal Dr Apt 412 Arlington VA 22202-4305

KRUSCHWITZ, WALTER HILLIS, physics educator; b. Edgerton, Ohio, July 20, 1920; s. Albin Gustav and Bertha Anna (Lehman) K.; m. Virginia Imogene Stone Kruschwitz, Feb. 13, 1926; children: Nancy Lynn, Sharon Leigh. BA, Taylor ., Upland, Ind., 1942; MA, Vanderbilt U., Nashville, 1948; PhD, U. Mich., Ann Arbor, 1961. Assoc. prof. physics and math. Cumberland U., Lebanon, Tenn., 1948-50; assoc. prof., prof. physics Union U., Jackson, Tenn., 1951-63; prof. physics Mobile (Ala.) Coll., 1963-67; assoc. prof. physics U. S. Fla., Tampa, 1967-90. 1st lt. USAF, 1942-45. Southern Baptist. Home: 3307 Korina Ln Tampa FL 33618-4215 E-mail: kruschwhk@aol.com.

KRUSE, ANN GRAY, computer programmer; b. Oklahoma City, Jan. 4, 1941; d. Floyd and Bernice Florence (Follansbee) Gray; m. Roy Edwin Kruse, Mar. 20, 1971 (dec.). AB, Randolph Macon Woman's Coll., 1963; MBA, U. Chgo., 1973. Programming mgr. Ind. Info. Controls, Valparaiso, Ind., 1966-67; systems programmer Am. Steel Foundries, Hammond, Ind., 1970-73; engr. applications programming Bell Helicopter Textron, Fort Worth, 1974-76; lead systems programmer Harris Data Communications, Dallas, 1976-81; sr. systems programmer Lone Star Gas Co., Dallas, 1981-82; sr. software specialist Raytheon, Dallas, 1982—. Republican. Episcopalian. Home: 6128 Black Berry Ln Dallas TX 75248-4909 Office: PO Box 660023 Dallas TX 75266-0023 E-mail: akruse@gsb.uchicago.edu.

KRUSE, F. MICHAEL, judge; Now chief justice High Ct. Am. Samoa, Pago Pago. Office: The High Ct Am Samoa Courthouse Chief Justice PO Box 309 Pago Pago AS 96799 Office Phone: 011-684-633-1401. Office Fax: 011-684-633-1318.*

KRUSE, JOHN ALPHONSE, lawyer; b. Detroit, Sept. 11, 1926; s. Frank R. and Ann (Nestor) K.; m. Mary Louise Dalton, July 14, 1951; children: Gerard, Mary Louise, Terence, Kathleen, Joanne, Francis, John, Patrick. BS, U. Detroit, 1950, JD cum laude, 1952. Bar: Mich. bar 1952. Ptnr. Alexander, Buchanan & Conklin, Detroit, 1952-69, Harvey, Kruse, PC, Detroit, 1969—. Guest lectr. U. Mich., U. Detroit, Inst. Continuing Legal Edn.; city atty. Allen Park, Mich., 1954-59; twp. atty., Van Buren Twp., Mich., 1959-61. Co-founder Detroit and Mich. Cath. Radio. Past pres. Palmer Woods Assn.; mem. pres.'s cabinet U. Detroit; bd. dirs. Providence Hosp. Found. Named one of 5 Outstanding Young Men in Mich., 1959, Outstanding Alumnus, U. Detroit Sch. Law, 1989, Humanitarian award Neuromuscular Inst. 1988. Mem. Detroit Bar Assn., State Bar Mich. (past chmn. negligence sect.), Assn. Def. Trial Counsel (bd. dirs. 1966-67), Am. Judicature Soc., Internat. Assn. Def. Counsel, Equestrian Order of the Holy Sepulchre. Clubs: Detroit Golf (past pres.). Roman Catholic. Home: 5569 Hunters Gate Dr Troy MI 48098-2342 Office: 1050 Wilshire Dr Ste 320 Troy MI 48084-1526 Office Phone: 248-649-7800. Personal E-mail: jakruse@comcast.net. Business E-Mail: jkruse@harveykruse.com. *Start each day with a simple petition - Lord help me to do your will today. End each day in thanks for his divine guidance. Prayer is to the soul as exercise is to the body. Neglect neither!.*

KRUSE, LAYNE E., lawyer; b. Emporia, Kans., Aug. 15, 1951; BA, Tex. A&M U., 1973; MSc, London Sch. Econs., 1974; JD, Yale U., 1977. Bar: Tex. 1978, cert.: Tex. Bd. Legal Specialization (civil trial law). Law clk. to Hon. John R. Brown U.S. Ct. Appeals (5th cir.); mem. Fulbright & Jaworski L.L.P., Houston. Past chair antitrust and bus. litigation sect. State Bar Tex. Mem.: ABA, Houston Bar Assn. Office: Fulbright & Jaworski LLP 1301 Mckinney St Ste 5100 Houston TX 77010-3031 Office Phone: 713-651-5194. Business E-Mail: lkruse@fulbright.com.

KRUSICK, MARGARET ANN, state legislator; b. Milw., Oct. 26, 1956; d. Ronald J. and Maxine C. K. BA, U. Wis., 1978; postgrad., U. Wis., Madison, 1979-82. Legal asst. Milw. Law Office, 1973-78; teaching asst. U. Wis., Milw., 1978-79; staff mem. Govs. Ombudsman Program for the Aging & Disabled, Madison, Wis., 1980; administrv. asst. Wis. Higher Edn. Aids Bd., Madison, 1981; legis. aide Wis. Assembly, Madison, 1982-83, state rep., 1983—. Author: Wisconsin Youth Suicide Prevention Act, 1985, Wisconsin Nursing Home Reform Act, 1987, Wisconsin Truancy Reform Act, 1988, Elder Abuse Fund, 1989, Stolen Goods Recovery Act, 1990, Fair Prescription Drug Pricing Act, 1994, Anti-Graffiti Act, 1996, Caregiver Criminal Background Checks and Abuse Prevention Act, 1997, Child Abuse Prosecution Act, 1998, Nursing Home Resident Protection Act, 1998, Seniorcare Prescription Drug Program, 2002, Criminal Background Checks for School Van and Bus Drivers, 2003, Child Protection and Clergy Abuse Reporting Act, 2004, Child Support Collection Act, 2004. Mem. St. Gregory Great Cath. Ch., Milw., 1960—, Dem. Party, Milw., 1980—; bd. dirs. Alzheimer's Assn., 1986-88. Named Legislator of Yr. award Wis. Sch. Counselors, Madison, 1986, Wis. County Constnl. Officers Legislator of Yr., 1999; recipient Sr. Citizen Appreciation Allied Coun. for Sr. Milw., 1987, Crime Prevention

...ice Dept., Milw., 1988, Cert. Appreciation, Milw. Pub. Sch., 1989, Friends of Homecare award, 1989, Environ. Decades' Clean 16 award, 1986-90, 95-96, Badger State Sheriff's Law and Order award, 1993, Appreciation award Coalition of Wis. Aging Groups, 1998, 2001. Mem. Jackson Park Neighborhood Assn.(Wis. Coun. Sr. Citizens award, 2003), U. Milw. Alumni Assn. (trustee 1986-90). Achievements include development of Alliance for attendance truancy abatement task force, which led to the Govenores state call to action to end child abuse and neglect. Office: Wis Assembly State Capitol Madison WI 53702-0001 Home: 128 N State Capital PO Box 8952 Madison WI 53708 Business E-Mail: rep.kusick@legis.state.wi.us.

KRUSKAL, MARTIN DAVID, mathematical physicist, astrophysicist; b. NYC, Sept. 28, 1925; married, 1950; 3 children. BS, U. Chgo., 1945; MS, NYU, 1948, PhD in Math., 1952. Rsch. scientist Plasma Phys. Lab., Princeton U., 1951—61, prof. astrophys. sci., 1961—, prof. math., 1981—89, emeritus, 1989—; David Hilbert prof. math. Rutgers U., New Brunswick, NJ, 1989—. Trustee Soc. for Indsl. & Applied Math., 1985—91, Math. Scis. Edn. Bd. of NRC, 1986—89; Ext. Adv. Com. Ctr. for Nonlinear Studies, Los Alamos Nat. Lab., 1980—. Recipient Dannie Heineman Math. Phys. prize, 1983, Potts Gold medal, Franklin Inst., 1986, Nat. medal Sci., NSF, 1993, John von Neumann Prize, Soc. Indsl. and Applied Math., 1994, James Clerk Maxwell Prize, Internat. Congress on Indsl. and Applied Math., 2003; fellow NSF (sr.), 1959—60, Weizmann Inst. Sci. (sr.), 1973—74, Japan Soc. Promotion Sci., 1979. Fellow: Am. Phys. Soc.; mem.: NAS (chmn. sect. of applied math. scis. 1990—93, award in Applied Math. and Numerical Analysis 1989), AAAS, Russian Acad. Nat. Scis., Royal Soc. London (fgn.), Math. Assn. Am., Am. Math. Soc. (Gibbs lectr. 1979). Home: PO Box 49 Arroyo Seco NM 87514-0049 Office: Rutgers U Dept Math Hill Ctr Busch Campus New Brunswick NJ 08903

KRUSZYNSKI, TIMOTHY EDWARD, retired protective services official, poet; b. Chgo., Sept. 21, 1949; s. Edward Michael and Dorothy Viola (Freske) K. BS in Psychology, DePaul U., 1971. Cert. Cook County Dep. Sheriff. Dishwasher Marshall Fields, Chgo., 1967-71; gen. duties clk. Continental Bank, Chgo., 1971-76; stockbroker, messenger Ernst & Co., Chgo., 1976-78; corrections officer Cook County, Chgo., 1978-99, sgt., 1992-99; ret., 1999. Author of poetry. Supporter Dem. Nat. Com., Washington, 1999-2000. Named Internat. Poet of Merit, Internat. Soc. Poets, Washington, 2000. Roman Catholic. Home: 14316 La Salle Riverdale IL 60827-2743

KRUTSICK, ROBERT STANLEY, retired science administrator; b. Lansford, Pa., Dec. 6, 1942; s. John Jacob and Mary Ann (Novak) K.; m. Charlotte Ann Harper, Feb. 18, 1977; children: Robert Steven, Laurie, Tracy, Andrew, Daniel. BS, Pa. State U., 1966; M in Local and State Govt., U. Pa., 1967. Sr. v.p., treas. Univ. City Sci. Ctr., Phila., 1978-88, acting pres., 1988-90, exec. v.p., 1988-97; ret., 1997. Supr. Upper Merion Twp., King of Prussia, Pa., 1989; pres. Upper Merion Park and Hist. Found., 1997—; bd. dirs. Upper Merion Area Sch. Dist.; chair Upper Merion Twp. Planning Commn.; pres. Lafayette Ambulance Squad, 2002; mem. joint oper. com. Ctr. for Tech. Studies; bd. dirs. Cradle of Liberty coun., Boy Scouts Am., Girl Scouts of Freedom Valley. Mem.: Upper Merion Area Edn. Found. (pres.), Optimist Club (past pres.). Republican. Roman Catholic. Avocations: tennis, golf, basketball. Home: 210 Cedar Pl Wayne PA 19087-2170 Personal E-mail: bkrutsick@aol.com.

KRUTTER, FORREST NATHAN, lawyer; b. Boston, Dec. 17, 1954; s. Irving and Shirley Krutter. BS in Econs., MS in Civil Enging., MIT, 1976; JD cum laude, Harvard U., 1978. Bar: Nebr. 1978, U.S. Supreme Ct. 1986, NY 1991. Antitrust counsel Union Pacific R.R., Omaha, 1978-86; sr. v.p. law, sec. Berkshire Hathaway Group, Omaha, 1986—; pres. Republic Ins., Dallas, 2000—. Co-author: Impact of Railroad Abandonments, 1976, Railroad Development in the Third World, 1978; author: Judicial Enforcement of Competition in Regulated Industries, 1979; contbr. articles Creighton Law Rev. Mem. ABA, Phi Beta Kappa, Sigma Xi. Office: Berkshire Hathaway Group 4016 Farnam St Omaha NE 68131-3016 Office Phone: 402-536-3214. Business E-Mail: fkrutter@berkre.com.

KRUTTSCHNITT, CANDACE MARIE, sociologist, educator; b. Glendale, Calif., June 9, 1951; d. Ernest Kruttschnitt and Lesley Maclerie; m. Thomas M. Hart IV, Dec. 16, 1977; children: Erica Hart, Lindsay Hart. BA in Criminology, U. Calif., Berkeley, 1973; MA in Sociology, Yale U., 1975, MPhil in Sociology, 1976, PhD in Sociology, 1979. Asst. prof. dept. criminal justice studies U. Minn., Mpls., 1979—80, asst. prof. dept. sociology, 1980—85, assoc. prof. dept. sociology, 1985—94, prof. dept. sociology, 1994—, interim assoc. dean Coll. Liberal Arts, 1996, chair dept. sociology, 1998—2001, 2005—06. Bd. dirs. Health Ptnrs., Bloomington, Minn. Author: Marking Time in the Golden State, 2005, Gender and Crime: Patterns in Victimizations Offending, 2005. Mem. girls study group Office Juvenile Justice and Deliquency Prevention, Washington, 2004—. Fellow, U. Helsinki, Dept. Social Policy, 1997, Inst. Criminology, Cambridge, England, 2004. Mem.: Am. Sociol. Assn. (sec. crime law and deviance sect. 1997—2000), Am. Soc. Criminology (v.p. 2002—03). Democrat. Office Phone: 612-624-1855.

KRY, ROBERT K., lawyer; B.Com., Queen's U., Toronto, 1997; JD with honors, Yale U., 2002. Bar: N.Y. 2004. Law clk. U.S. Ct. Appeals (9th cir.), Pasadena, Calif., 2002—03; law clk. to Hon. Antonin Scalia U.S. Supreme Ct., Washington, 2003—04; assoc. Baker Botts, Washington, 2004—. Editor (exec.): Yale Law Jour. Office: Baker Botts LLP The Warner 1299 Pennsylvania Ave NW Washington DC 20004-2400

KRYCH, MARGARET A., religious organization administrator, educator; b. Perth, Australia, Apr. 4, 1942; d. Ernest W and Hannah S Sanders; m. Arden L Krych, Sept. 4, 1971; children: Meredyth A. Krych Appelbaum, David A. BA, U. Western Australia, 1963; BD with honors, Melbourne Coll. of Div., Australia, 1965, ThM, 1970; PhD, Princeton Theol. Sem., 1985. Clergy Meth. Ch. Australasia, Perth, Australia, 1966—67, assoc. dir. dept. christian edn., 1968—70; editor Luth. Ch. Am., Phila., 1973—77; Charles Norton prof. of christian edn. and theology Luth. Theol. Sem., Phila., 1977—, assoc. dean grad. edn., 1997—. Cons. Ednl. Ministry with Youth Project, LTSP, Phila., 1999—; mem. ELCA Bd. of Augsburg Fortress Publ. House, Mpls., 2003—. Author: (non-fiction book) Teaching the Gospel Today, 1987, Teaching About Lutheranism, 1993, (non-fiction book, co-authored) Confirmation: Engaging Lutheran Foundations and Practices, 1999; co-author: (non-fiction book) Ministry of Children's Education, 2004; contbr. Named one of, Outstanding Young Women of Am., 1976, 1977; named to Women in Leadership in Theol. Edn. program, Assn. Theol. Schs., 2001; recipient JR Saunders prize in philosophy, U. Western Australia, 1960; grantee Wabash Ctr. for Teaching and Learning, 2005; scholar Hackett competitive scholarship, U. Western Australia, 1963, 1964; Tchg. and Learning grantee, Assn. Theol. Schs., 1999. Mem.: Assn. Profs. and Rschrs. in Religious Edn., Am. Acad. Religion, Assn. for Dr. of Ministry Edn. (steering com. 2001—04), Assn. Luth. Tchg. Theologians (discussion leader 2001—02), Soc. for Rsch. in Child Devel. Evangelical Lutheran. Avocations: music, travel. Office: Luth Theol Sem 7301 Germantown Ave Philadelphia PA 19119-1794 Office Phone: 215-248-6347. Business E-Mail: mkrych@ltsp.edu.

KRYGIER, ROMAN J., automotive executive; b. 1944; BME, Purdue Univ., 1964; MIT, 1974. Joined and held a variety of positions at the Chgo. Stamping Plant Ford Motor Co., 1964, named asst. plant ops. mgr. at the metal stamping division's gen. office, 1974, apptd. plant mgr. of the Buffalo stamping plant, 1977, held several mgmt. positions within the body and assembly ops., 1983—94; named exec. dir. of the advanced mfg. engring. and process leadership, Ford Automotive Ops., 1994; v.p. advanced mfg. engring. and process leadership Ford Motor Co., 1997—98; v.p. power train ops., Ford Automotive Ops., 1999—2001; group v.p. Mfg. and Quality Ford Motor Co., Dearborn, Mich., 2001—. Office: Ford Motor Co One American Rd Dearborn MI 48126-1899

KRYS, SHELDON JACK, retired diplomat, minister; b. NYC, June 15, 1934; s. Martin and Anna K.; m. Doris M., May 24, 1964; children— Wendy M., Madeleine S., Susan Jennifer. N.D., U. Md., College Park, 1955; grad., Nat. War Coll., Washington, 1977; PhD (hon.), St. John Fisher Coll., 1996. Newscaster Radio Sta. KRSD, Rapid City, SD, 1955-57; dir., prodr. Radio Sta. WWDC, Washington, 1957-59; prin. Chris Sheldon Pub. Rels., Washington, 1959-61; cons. to dir. FMCS, Washington, 1961-62; ednl. and cultural affairs officer, dir. reception ctrs. Dept. State, Washington, 1962-64, mgmt. officer London, 1965-66, spl. asst. to amb., 1966-69, dir. pers. Latin Am. Washington, 1969-74, adminstrv. counselor Belgrade, 1974-76, fgn. svc. insp. Washington, 1977-79, exec. dir. Bur. Near Eastern and South Asian Affairs, 1979-83, dep. dir. mgmt. ops., 1983-84, exec. asst. to under sec. for mgmt., 1984-85; amb. to Trinidad and Tobago, 1985-88; exec. sec. Laird Commn., 1987; asst. sec. state adminstrn. and info. mgmt., 1988-89; asst. sec. state diplomatic security, 1989-92; diplomat-in-residence George Washington U., Washington, 1992-93; cons. internat. and intergovtl. affairs Fletcher, Heald & Hildreth, P.L.C., Roslyn, Va., 1994—. Co-chmn. ambassadorial seminar Dept. of State, 1992—2003. Mem. bd. George Foster Peabody Awards, 1990-95, chmn. bd. 1993-95, chmn. emeritus 1996, chmn. editl. bd. Fgn. Svc. Jour., 1994-96; bd. dirs. Sr. Living Found., 1997—; bd. dirs., treas. Washington Inst. Fgn. Affairs, 1998—2004; trustee St. John Fisher Coll., 1997—. Recipient Meritorious Honor award, Dept. State, 1974, Disting. Honor award, 1981, Superior Honor award, 1983, Presdl. Meritorious Svc. award, 1983, Wilbur J. Carr award, 1994. Mem. Armed Forces Comm. and Electronics Assn. (bd. dirs. 1991-92), Nat. War Coll. Alumni Assn., Am. Fgn. Svc. Assn., Am. Broadcast Pioneers, Broadcast Found., City Tavern Club. Avocations: gardening, nature watching, tennis. Office: Fletcher Heald & Hildreth PLC 1300 North 17th St 11th Fl Arlington VA 22209-3801 Office Phone: 703-812-0400.

KRYSHTALOWYCH, HELEN ZWENYSLAWA, lawyer; b. Fed. Republic Germany, Nov. 27, 1945; came to U.S., 1950; d. Jaroslaw Gregory and Jaroslawa (Czorniak) K. BABS, Ohio State U., 1967; EdM, Kent State U., 1971; JD, Cleve. State U., 1980. Bar: Ohio 1980, U.S. Dist. Ct. (no. dist.) Ohio 1981, U.S. Ct. Appeals (6th cir.) 1981. Tchr. English East Tech. High Sch., Cleve., 1967-69; psychiat. social worker Fallsview Mental Health Ctr., Cuyahoga Falls, Ohio, 1971-73; counselor Chagrin Falls (Ohio) High Sch., 1973-80; assoc. Squire, Sanders & Dempsey, Cleve., 1980-89, ptnr., 1989—. Trustee Epilepsy Found. N.E. Ohio, Cleve., 1989; dir. Ukrainian-Mus. Archives, Cleve., 1991. Mem. ABA (internat. law and practice sect.), Ohio State Bar Assn. (employment law and sch. law coms.), Cleve. Bar Assn. (internat. law group), Ukrainian Am. Bar Assn. Avocation: languages. Office: Squire Sanders & Dempsey 4900 Society Ctr 127 Public Sq Ste 4900 Cleveland OH 44114-1304 E-mail: hkryshtalowych@ssd.com.

KRYSIAK, WILLIAM J., gas industry executive; b. Denver, 1960; Degree, Colo. State U., 1982. With Western Gas Resources, Inc., Denver, 1985—, contr., 1990—93, v.p. fin., 1993—2002, CFO, 2001—, exec. v.p., 2002—. Office: Western Gas Resources Inc 1099 18th St Ste 1200 Denver CO 80202

KRYTER, KARL DAVID, retired research scientist; b. Indpls., Oct. 13, 1914; s. George David and Mary Matilda (Christoph) K.; m. Grace Irene Brown, June 21, 1946; children: Dianne, Victoria (Mrs. Myron I. Liebhaber), Kathryn (Mrs. Richard A. Rendon). AB, Butler U., 1939; PhD, U. Rochester, 1942. Rsch. tchr. fellow Harvard U., Cambridge, Mass., 1942-46; asst. prof. Washington U., St. Louis, 1946-48; dir. human resources research labs. Air Force Cambridge Rsch. Ctr., 1948-57; head dept. psychoacoustics Bolt Beranek & Newman, Inc., Cambridge, Mass., 1957-65; dir. Sensory Scis. Rsch. Ctr., Menlo Park, Calif., 1965-76; staff scientist Stanford Rsch. Inst., Menlo Park, 1976-85. Adj. prof. San Diego State U., 1990—; tchr. Colby Coll., 1960—63, MIT, 1958—59; advisor U.S. Pres.'s Office for Sci. and Tech., 1968—70; mem. SST environ. study com. Dept. Interior, 1969; past chmn. coun. com. hearing and bioacoustics NAS/NRC, 1960. Author: The Effects of Noise on Man, 1970-85, Handbook of Hearing and the Effects of Noise, 1994. Recipient Disting. Svc. award in sci. Am. Speech and Hearing Assn., medal U. Liege, Belgium. Fellow APA (coun. reps. 1966-69), Soc. Engring. Psychologists (pres. 1965, Franklin V. Taylor award), Acoustical Soc. Am. (coun., pres. 1972). Home: 3969 Maricopa Dr Santa Barbara CA 93110 Personal E-mail: kdkryter@cox.net.

KRZYMINSKI, MARYANN MARIE, literature and language educator; b. Bay City, Mich., Nov. 14, 1964; d. Doris Marie North; m. Robert John Krzyminski; children: Robert John Jr., Johnathon James. BS in Secondary Edn., Ctrl. Mich. U., 1987. Tchr. West Branch (Mich.)-Rose City Area Schs., 1987—. Bldg. rep. West Branch-Rose City Edn. Assn., 1997—2001; Region 12 sec. Mich. Edn. Assn., 1998—2001. Home: 1522 W River Rd Auburn MI 48611 Office: Ogemaw Heights HS 960 South M-33 West Branch MI 48661 Office Phone: 989-343-2020. Personal E-mail: maryannkrzyminski@hotmail.com.

KRZYSZTOFOWICZ, ROMAN, systems engineering and statistical science educator, consultant; b. Cieszyn, Poland, Sept. 27, 1947; came to U.S., 1974; naturalized, 1985; s. Janusz and Irena (Rogozinska) K.; m. Liana Balayan, May 27, 1995; children: Arman, Nayiri. MS with highest distinction, Cracow (Poland) Tech. U., 1970; PhD, U. Ariz., 1978. Rsch. engr. Inst. for Meteorology and Water Resources, Cracow, 1970-72, head computer ctr., 1972-74; lectr. Chief Tech. Orgn., Cracow, 1973-74; asst. prof. systems engring. U. Ariz., Tucson, 1978-79; asst. prof. civil engring. MIT, Cambridge, Mass., 1979-82; assoc. prof. systems engring. U. Va., Charlottesville, Va., 1982-86, prof. systems engring., 1986—, dir. grad. program systems engring., 1984-89, assoc. dir. ctr. for risk mgmt. engring. systems, 1987-88, prof. statistics, 1995—. Vis. scientist Swiss Fed. Inst. Tech., Lausanne, 2002; lectr. George Washington U., 1982-83, NATO Advanced Study Inst., Tucson, 1985, Deauville, France, 1993, Coop. Program for Operational Meteorology, Edn. and Tng., Boulder, Colo., 1993-96; rep. NSF in coop. rsch. initiatives with Brazil and Poland, 1991; reviewer proposals NSF, 1980—, Natural Scis. and Engring. Rsch. Coun. Can., 1987—; rschr. Nat. Weather Svc., 1992, 1995; expert on flood forecasting, Commn. for Hydrology, World Meteorological Orgn., 1997-2000; mem. doctoral examination com. U. Que., 1997, 2000, U. Paris VI, 2002, École Nationale du Génie Rural des Eaux et des Forêts (ENGREF), Paris, 2004; reviewer articles for numerous jours. Editor Jour. of Hydrology, 1996—; mem. editl. bd. Stochastic Hydrology and Hydraulics, 1990-98, Control and Cybernetics, 1994—, Stochastic Environ. Rsch. and Risk Assessment, 1999—, Water Resources Monographs of the Polish Academy of Sciences, 2000—, Jour. Applied Meteorology, 2001—02; contbr. articles to profl. jours., chpts. to books, entries to Systems and Control Ency., Concise Ency. Environ. Systems, Ency. Ops. Rsch. and Mgmt. Sci., Ency. of Sci. and Tech. Recipient Prof. W. Wierzbicki award Polish Soc. Civil Engrs. and Technicians, 1970, Rsch. award NSF, 1978-99, Presdl. Young Investigator award Pres. of U.S., 1984. Mem. IEEE, Am. Statis. Assn., Soc. for Judgment and Decision Making, Internat. Inst. Forecasters, Inst. for Ops. Rsch. and the Mgmt. Scis., Am. Geophys. Union, Am. Water Resources Assn., Am. Meteorological Soc., Tau Beta Pi (Eminent Engr. award 1985). Republican. Armenian Catholic. Avocations: opera, theater, skiing, sailing, hiking. Office: U Va PO Box 400747 151 Engineer's Way Charlottesville VA 22904-4747 Business E-Mail: rk@virginia.edu. *Education is a launchpad to a rewarding life. Research demands passion and endurance. The challenge for me as an academician is to turn learners into thinkers, to bring about in students a transition from acquiring knowledge to creating new knowledge, to graduate scientists and engineers who not merely perpetuate today's technology but invent a better one. For it is the creative element that uplifts the individual and benefits mankind.*

KRZYZANOWSKI, EVE, video production company executive; b. N.Y.C., July 19, 1951; d. Ludwik and Janine (Malinowska) K.; m. Charles Richard Novitz, Feb. 11, 1988; 1 child, Alexandra Maris. BA with honors, Vassar Coll., 1972. Mgr. ABC News, N.Y.C., 1972-80, producer, 1978-80, NBC News, N.Y.C., 1980-82; sr. producer CBS News, N.Y.C., 1982; mng. producer Santa Fe Communications, L.A., 1984; sr. producer Fin. News Network, N.Y.C., 1985-87, v.p., news dir., 1987-90; exec. producer This Morning Bus., N.Y.C., 1988-90; producer Viacom, N.Y.C., 1990; v.p. devel. and programming BBC Worldwide Ams., N.Y.C., 1991-97; pres. EVE Video Enterprises, N.Y.C., 1997—; CEO, Branded Meida Corp., N.Y.C., 2005—. Exec. prodr. Eyewitness Nature Series, PBS, other series on cable networks. Recipient Parents' Choice award for Madison's Adventures, Growing Up Wild, 1995, NEA and Emmy award for Eyewitness, 1996. Mem. Soc. Profl. Journalists. Office: EVE Video Enterprises 160 West End Ave Ste 29C New York NY 10023-5616 also: Branded Media Corp 425 Maidson Ave Penthouse New York NY 10017 Office Phone: 212-230-1941. E-mail: evevideo@earthlink.net, evek@brandedmedia.com.

KRZYZANOWSKI, RICHARD L., lawyer; b. Warsaw, Mar. 25, 1932; came to U.S., 1967, naturalized, 1972; s. Andrew and Mary K.; children: Suzanne, Peter, Christine. BA, U. Warsaw, 1956; ML, U. Pa., 1960; PhD, U. Paris, 1962. Bar: Pa. With Crown Cork & Seal Co., Inc., Phila., 1967—, dir., exec. v.p. gen. counsel, 1990-2001. Counselor John Paul II Found., Vatican, Rome, Italy; exec. trustee, founder Krzyzanowski Found., Phila. Mem. Int. Bar Assn. (London). Home and Office: 466 Wyndmoor Ln Huntingdon Valley PA 19006

KRZYZEWSKI, MIKE, university athletic coach; b. Chgo., Feb. 13, 1947; m. Carol Mickie Marsh; children: Debbie Savarino, Linda Frasher, Jamie. BS, U.S. Mil. Acad., 1969. Capt. team, 1968—69; capt. second team All-NIT, 1969; capt. North-South game, 1969; head coach svc. teams, 1969—72; head coach U.S. Mil. Acad. Prep Sch., Ft. Belvoir, Va., 1972—74; grad. asst. Ind. U., 1974—75; head coach U.S. Mil. Acad., West Point, NY, 1975-80, Duke U. Blue Devils, Durham, NC, 1980—; head coach south team Nat. Sports Festival, 1983; instr. Olympic Trials, 1984. Chmn. Children's Miracle Network Telethon; bd. dirs. V Found.; with Comprehensive Cancer Ctr., NABC Coaches vs. Cancer; bd. dirs. K Lab Human Performance; fundraising leader Emily Krzyzewski Ctr. Immaculate Conception Cath. Ch., Durham, NC. Served U.S. Army, 1967—69, officer U.S. Army, 1969—74, ret. capt. U.S. Army, 1974. Named Met. N.Y. Basketball Writer's Coach of Yr., 1977, Coach of Yr., ACC, 1984, 1986, 1997, 1999, 2000, Nat. Coach of Yr., Basketball Times, 1997, CBS/Chevrolet, 1986, 2000, Naismith, 1989, 1992, 1999, Sporting News, 1992, UPI, 1986, Victor awards, 2001, Sportsman of Yr., Sporting News, 1992, Coach of Decade, NABC, 1990, Naismith Meml. Basketball Hall of Fame, 2001, America's Best Coach, Time/CNN, 2001, 3d Best Coach All Time, CBS show; recipient Wooden award, Legends of Coaching, 2000, GTE (now Verizon) Reads with the NABC Lit. Champion award, 2000. Mem.: NCAA (basketball issues com.), Nat. Assn. Basketball Coaches (pres. 1998—99, Dist. Coach of Yr. 1977, 1984, 1992, 1994, 1999, 2000, Nat. Coach of Yr. 1991, 1999). Achievements include coaching team to NCAA Divsn. I Championship, 1991, 92, 2001, 2nd place, 1986, 90, 94, 99, final four, 1986, 88, 89, 90, 91, 92, 94, 99, 2001, 2004; ranked first in the Big Apple NIT Champion, ACC Champion, NCAA Tournament Finalist, equal NCAA record for most victories in a season, 1986; ranked first, ACC Champion, NCAA Champion, team ranked number 1 from start to finish, a first repeat NCAA Champion since 1972-73; ranked first, NCAA Tournament Finalist, ACC regular season champion, ACC Champion, equal for most victories in a season, 1999; ranked first, NCAA Champion, ACC regular season co-champion, ACC Champion, TiVo Preseason NIT champion, 2001; ranked first, ACC Champion, NCAA Tournament Sweet 16, Maui Invitational champion, 2002; only 4th coach in NCAA history to earn 3 or more national championships along with John Wooden, Adolph Rupp, and Bob Knight. Office: Duke Univ Cameron Indoor Stadium Durham NC 27708-0556

KSANSNAK, JAMES EDWARD, diversified financial services company executive, accountant; b. Hazleton, Pa., Mar. 13, 1940; s. Edward J. and Helen (Holodick) K.; m. Valerie M. Anderson, June 9, 1962 (div. 1986); children: Keith, Janet, Linda; m. Suzanne M. Teefy, Feb. 21, 1987. BS magna cum laude in Acctg., St. Joseph's U., Phila., 1962. C.P.A. With Arthur Andersen & Co., Phila., 1962-86, sr. mem. staff, 1964-67, mgr., 1967-71, ptnr., 1971-79, mng. ptnr., 1979-86; sr. v.p. ARAMARK Corp. (formerly ARA Svcs., Inc.), Phila., 1986-87, sr. v.p., CFO, 1987-91, exec. v.p., CFO, 1991-97, vice chmn., 1997—2001. Bd. dirs. CSS Industries, Inc., Aramark Corp.; chmn. Tasty BakingCo., 2003—. Contbr. articles to profl. jours. Mem. Cmty. Leadership Seminar, 1972, trustee, bd. dirs., 1984; treas., bd. dirs. Ambler (Pa.) Youth Svcs., 1974-79; bd. dris., mem. exec. com. Phila. YMCA, 1974-94, chmn. fin. com., chmn. ann. meeting, city fundraising chmn., 1974-83, maj. gifts chmn., 1984-87, chmn. 1987-91; mem. exec. com. Phila. Urban Affairs Coalition, 1978-95; bd. dirs. Greater Phila. Internat. Network, 1980-86, INROADS-Phila., Inc., 1981-90, Am. Cancer Soc., 1994-96, Thomas Jefferson U., 1994—, Main Line Health Sys., 1996-98; mem. Mayor's Com. on Literacy, Phila., 1984-85; mem. fin. com., exec. com. Presbyn.-U. Pa. Med. Ctr., 1981-90, chmn. found., 1986; vice chmn. United Way, 1982; trustee Coll. Bus., St. Joseph's U., 1982-85. Recipient alumni award St. Joseph's U., 1980; named Profl. of Yr., Phi Chi Theta, 1981 Mem. AICPA, Pa. Inst. CPAs (chmn. tech. meetings 1970, chmn. coop. with attys. 1972, exec. comm. Phila. chpt. 1980-82), Planning Execs. Inst. (chmn. bd. 1981, Neil Denen award 1984), Union League, Sunnybrook Golf Club, Loxahatchee Golf Club, Knights of Malta. Republican. Roman Catholic. Home: 205 Echo Dr Jupiter FL 33458 Office: ARAMARK Corp 1101 Market St Philadelphia PA 19107-2988

KSIENSKI, AHARON ARTHUR, retired electrical engineer; b. Warsaw, June 23, 1924; came to U.S., 1951, naturalized, 1959; s. Isreal and Rebecca K.; married; children: David, Ruth. B.E. in Mech. Enging, Inst. Mech. Engring., London, 1947; M.Sc. in Elec. Engring, U. So. Calif., 1952, PhD, 1958. Sr. staff engr., head antenna dept. research staff Hughes Aircraft Co., Culver City, Calif., 1958-67; prof. elec. engring., tech. dir. communication systems electrosci. lab. Ohio State U., 1967-76, prof. elec. engring., chmn. communication and propagation com. electrosci. lab., 1976-87, prof. emeritus, 1987—; ret., 1987. Bd. dirs. Ohio State U. Research Found., 1975-79; cons. in field. Editor trans., revs. in field. Recipient Brabazon award Inst. Electronic and Radio Engrs., London, 1967, 76 Fellow IEEE; mem. Internat. Union Radio Sci. (chmn. commns. B and C 1972-75) Home: 1780 Lynnhaven Dr Columbus OH 43221-1410 Office: 1320 Kinnear Rd Columbus OH 43212-1156 Personal E-mail: a-arthur@worldnet.att.net.

KSYPKA, HELEN, organizational consultant; b. Boston, Jan. 30, 1952; d. Joseph and Agnes Ksypka; m. Peter V. Plachowicz (dec.). Asst. to hosp. adminstr. and orgnl. cons. Chelsea Meml. Hosp., Mass., 1969—71; orgnl. cons. to asst. v.p. Nat. Fire Protection Assn., 1972—76; singer/songwriter, 1977—78; performer classical roles WMBR FM Radio, 1979—80; on-camera prin. TV commls., indsl. films, 1981—89; drama instr., comm. coach, 1982—84; comm. cons., founder Born Organized, Cape Neddick, Maine, 2000—; performer classical roles WSCA FM Radio, 2005. Syndicated writer TV spots and ad copy, 1989—90; radio and voice over actress, 1989—90. Actor: (films) The Bostonians, The Verdict, Mr. North, Soul Man, Hanky Panky, 1981—89; (TV series) Cheers, St. Elsewhere, Miller's Court, The Law Works, The Law and Harry McGraw, Spenser for Hire, 1981—89; prodr.(dir., writer, actor): Basic Turmoil, 1980—85; author: Dave's Unhappy Teeth, 1991, Oh, Please, Not Opera...Learning La Boheme, 1991, The Determined Maiden, 1991, Booga the Caveman Discovers Oil, 1996, Quotes to the Rescue, 2004; contbr. articles to mags., quips and quotes and poetry to numerous pubs. Recipient award, Nickelodeon Fiml and Video Festival, 1983, 1st Place Plaque for best actress, Mass. Cable TV Commn., 1985, Cert. of Award, Nat. Fed. Local Cable Programmers, 1986. Mem.: SAG, AFTRA, Assn. of Profl. Comm. Cons. Avocations: ocean kayaking, forest trekking, flower arranging. Office: Born Organized (R) PO Box 435 Cape Neddick ME 03902 Business E-Mail: helen@bornorganized.com.

K-TURKEL, JUDITH LEAH ROSENTHAL (JUDI K-TURKEL), writer, editor, publisher; b. N.Y.C., Jan. 3, 1934; d. Samuel S. and Pauline (Turkel) Rosenthal; m. Franklynn Petersons; children: Joseph, Jeffrey Kesselman, David, Kevin Peterson. BA, Bklyn. Coll., 1955. Story and mng. editor Dell Publs., N.Y.C., 1955-58, 62-65; editor-in-chief Sterling, Stearn & KMR Publs., N.Y.C., 1959-62; sr. editor Macfadden-Bartell Publs., N.Y.C., 1966-68; freelance writer N.Y.C. and Wis., 1968-89; pres. P/K Assocs., Inc., Madison, Wis., 1977—. Instr. adult edn. Great Neck (N.Y.) Pub. Schs.,

1973-76, U. Wis., Madison, 1977-82; instr. journalism Madison Area Tech. Coll., 1984-87; lectr. nonfiction writing CW Post Ctr., L.I. U., Manhasset, N.Y., 1976-77; tchr.-in-residence Rhinelander (Wis.) Sch. Arts, 1984-86. Author: (writing as Judi Kesselman) Stopping Out, 1976, (writing as Judi Kesselman-Turkel with Franklynn Peterson) The Do-It-Yourself Custom Van Book, 1977, Vans, 1979, (with others) Eat Anything Exercise Diet, 1979, Snowmobile Maintenance and Repair, 1979, I Can Use Tools, 1981, (textbook) Good Writing, 1980, Test Taking Strategies, 1981, 2d edit., 2004, Study Smarts, 1981, 2004, Homeowner's Book of Lists, 1981, How to Improve Damn Near Everything Around Your Home, 1981, The Author's Handbook, 1982, rev., 1986, 2005, The Grammar Crammer, 1982, 2004, Research Shortcuts, 1982, 2004, Note-Taking Made Easy, 1982, rev. edit. 2004, The Vocabulary Builder, 1982, rev. edit. 2004, Getting it Down: How to Get Your Ideas on Paper, 1983, rev. edit.(as Secrets to Writing Great Papers), 2004, Spelling Simplified, 1983, 2004, The Magazine Writer's Handbook, 1983, rev. edit., 1986, 2005; syndicated computer newspaper columnist, 1983—; editor (newsletter) CPA Micro Report, 1985-92, CPA's PC Network Advisor, 1991-92; pub. CPA Computer Report, 1994—; contbr. articles to profl. jours. Chmn. non-partisan Citizens Nominating Com., Great Neck, 1972-75. Recipient Bus. Press. award, 1977, Nat. Press Club award, 1984, 85. Mem. Am. Soc. Journalists and Authors, Coun. Wis. Writers (pres. 1982-85), Authors Guild, Authors League. Avocations: travel, music. Office: P/K Assocs Inc 3006 Gregory St Madison WI 53711-1847 E-mail: info@booksthatteach.com.

KU, R. FASHUN, architect, urban development consultant; b. Meihsien, Kwontung, China, Feb. 16, 1951; s. Enfu and Gifung (Yeh) K. MS, U. Wis., 1972; MBA, U. Rochester, 1989. Registered architect, N.Y. Sr. city planner, Planning Bur. City of Rochester, N.Y., 1975-78, chief tech. services, Devel. Services Bur., 1979-81, dir. downtown devel. Econ. Devel. Dept., 1982-92, commr. econ. devel. dept., 1993—; prin. Ku and Assocs., Rochester, 1981—. Pres. Rochester Econ. Devel. Corp. Mem. Rochester Internat. Friendship Coun., 1985-86; bd. dirs. Rochester Health Assn. Recipient Good Neighbor award Corn Hill Neighbor Assn., 1982. Mem. AIA, N.Y. State Assn. Architects. Avocations: tennis, drawing, guitar, golf. Home: 877 Harvard St Rochester NY 14610-1528 Office: The City of Rochester 30 Church St Rm 205A Rochester NY 14614-1283

KUBALE, BERNARD STEPHEN, lawyer; b. Reedsville, Wis., Sept. 5, 1928; s. Joseph and Josephine (Novak) Kubale; m. Mary Thomas, Apr. 21, 1956 (dec. Jan. 13, 2001); children: Caroline, Catherine, Anne; m. Karen Robinson, Jan. 23, 2004. BBA, U. Wis., 1950, LLB, 1955; LLD (hon.), St. Norbert Coll., 1985. CPA Wis.; bar: Wis. 1955. Acct. John D. Morrison and Co., Marquette, Mich., 1950-51; atty., ptnr. Foley and Lardner, Milw., 1955—, chmn. mgmt. com., 1985-94. Bd. dirs. Green Bay Packers, Wis. E. R. Wagner Mfg. Co., Wausau Homes. Chmn. bd. dirs. St. Norbert Coll., DePere, Wis., 1980—84, Children's Hosp. Wis., Milw., 1982—91. 1st lt. USAF, 1951—53. Mem.: ABA, Milw. Bar Assn., Wis. Bar Assn., Wis. Inst. CPAs, Milw. Club, Milw. Country Club, Chenequa Country Club. Republican. Roman Catholic. Avocations: fishing, skiing. Home: 5935 Monclaire Rd Hartland WI 53029 Office: Foley & Lardner 1st Wisconsin Ctr 777 E Wisconsin Ave Ste 3800 Milwaukee WI 53202-5367

KUBAS, GREGORY JOSEPH, research chemist; b. Cleve., Mar. 12, 1945; s. Joseph Arthur and Esther Kubas; m. Chrystal Henry, Dec. 22, 1973; children: Kelly Richmond (dec. 1997), Sherry Lopez. BS, Case Inst. Tech., 1966; PhD, Northwestern U., 1970. Postdoctoral fellow Princeton (N.J.) U., 1971-72, Los Alamos (N.Mex.) Nat. Lab., 1972-74, mem. staff, 1974—; lab. fellow, 1987—. Author: Metal Dihydrogen And Sigma Complexes, 2001; contbr. articles to profl. jours. Recipient E.O. Lawrence Meml. award US Dept. Energy, 1994. Fellow AAAS; mem. Am. Chem. Soc. (Inorganic Chemistry award 1993). Achievements include patents in field. Office: Los Alamos Nat Lab # Ms-j514 Los Alamos NM 87545-0001 Home: 217 La Marta Ct Santa Fe NM 87501

KUBASIK, CHRISTOPHER E., aerospace transportation executive; b. Cheverly, Md., Mar. 26, 1961; BS in Acctg with honors, U. Md. Sch. Bus., 1983; attended exec. program, Northwestern U. Kellogg Sch. Bus., 1997. CPA. Ptnr. Ernst & Young, 1996; v.p., controller Lockheed Martin Corp., Bethesda, Md., 1999—2001, CFO, 2001—, exec. v.p., CFO, 2004—. Vice-chmn. Lockheed Martin Diversity Coun.; chmn., Ethics and Bus. Conduct Steering Com. Lockheed Martin; chmn. bd. dirs. Lockheed Martin Investment Mgmt. Co. Office: Lockheed Martin Corp 6801 Rockledge Dr Bethesda MD 20817-1877

KUBEK, GARY W., lawyer; b. June 4, 1954; BA summa cum laude, Yale U., 1975, JD, 1978. Bar: NY 1979. Law clerk to Judge J. Joseph Smith US Ct. Appeals, Second Cir., 1978—79; litig. ptnr. Debevoise & Plimpton LLP, NYC. Mem.: ABA (mem. Litig., Antitrust & Bus. Sect., vice chmn. distbn. and franchise com.), Assn. Bar of City NY (mem. Antitrust Com.). Office: Debevoise & Plimpton LLP 919 Third Ave New York NY 10022 Office Phone: 212-909-6267. Office Fax: 212-909-6836. E-mail: gwkubek@debevoise.com.

KUBIAK, ANDREA CELESTE, language educator; b. Orange, Calif., Aug. 14, 1975; d. Robert Joseph and Donna Jean Kubiak. AA, Coll. of the Desert, 1994; BA, U. of Calif., Riverside, Calif., 1996; MA, Ohio U., 2001. Tchg. asst. Ohio U., Athens, Ohio, 1999—2001; prof. of Spanish, French, and Italian Coll. of the Desert, Palm Desert, Calif., 2002—04, acad. advisor Indio, Calif., 2005—. Author: (films) Tosca Bartola, 2001. Vol. English tchr. Peace Corps., Kleczew, Poland, 1997—99; translator children's ministry and jail ministry Glory to God Ministries Internat., Cathedral City, Calif., 1993—2003. Recipient Alumni Assn. award, Coll. of the Desert, 1994, Dist. Writing award, Antioch Review, 2003; scholar Golf scholarship, Idaho State U., 1994—95, Tchg. scholar, Ohio U., 1999—2001. Democrat. Avocations: sports, travel, languages, books, music. Home: 326 W Santa Elena Rd Palm Springs CA 92262-2974 Office: Coll of the Desert Eastern Valley Ctr Acad Skills Ctr Monroe St Indio CA 92201 Office Phone: 760-347-2288. Personal E-mail: toscaria@yahoo.com. Business E-Mail: akubiak@collegeofthedesert.edu.

KUBIC, CHARLES RICHARD, naval officer; b. Greensburg, Pa., Dec. 7, 1950; s. William Louis and Josephine Roberta (Mologne) K.; m. Anne Renee Sheroda, July 29, 1972; children: Charles Brian, Kathryn Anne, Andrew William. BSCE, Lehigh U., 1972; MSCE, 1978. Registered profl. engr., Pa., Va. Commd. ensign CEC U.S. Navy, 1972, advanced through grades to rear admiral, 1998; asst. head constrn. dept. OICC, Thailand, Bangkok, 1973-75; co-comdr. NMCE Four, Port Hueneme, Calif., 1975-77; assignment officer Naval Mil. Pers. Command, Washington, 1978-80; asst. pub. works officer Nat. Naval Med. Ctr., Bethesda, Md., 1980-82; AOICC for design OICC Mediterranean, Madrid, 1982-85; White House fellow White House Office Policy Devel., 1985-86; dir. Strategic Programs Office Naval Facilities Engrng. Command, Alexandria, Va., 1986-89; comdg. officer NMCB Three, Port Hueneme, Calif., 1989-91; prodn. officer Navy Pub. Works Ctr., Norfolk, Va., 1991-94; vice comdr. Atlantic Divsn. Navfacengcom, Norfolk, 1994-97; com 22NCR Norfolk, 1997-98; vice comdr. Navfacengcom, 1998-99; comdr. Third Naval Constrn. Brigade and PACNAVFACENGCOM, 1999—2002, Com First Naval Constrn. Divsn., 2002—. Contbr. articles to profl. jours. Scoutmaster Boy Scouts Am., Bangkok, 1973-75, cubmaster, Madrid, 1984, Va., 1985-87, 92-94. Decorated 3 Legion of Merit medals, 4 Meritorious Service medals; CNO scholar, 1977-78. Fellow Soc. Am. Mil. engrs.; mem. NSPE, U.S. Naval Inst., Phi Beta Kappa, Tau Beta Pi, Sigma Phi Epsilon. Republican. Roman Catholic. Avocations: golf, skiing, scuba diving, running. Office: 501 Clark St Clarks Green PA 18411 E-mail: kubicfam@worldnet.att.net.

KUBIDA, WILLIAM JOSEPH, lawyer; b. Newark, Apr. 3, 1949; s. William and Catherine (Gilchrist) K.; m. Mary Jane Hamilton, Feb. 4, 1984; children: Sara Gilchrist, Kathleen Hamilton. BSEE, USAF Acad., 1971; JD, Wake Forest U., 1979. Bar: N.C. 1979, U.S. Patent Office 1979, Ind. 1980, U.S. Dist. Ct. (no. dist.) Ind. 1980, U.S. Dist. Ct. (so. dist.) Ind. 1980, U.S. Ct. Appeals (7th cir.) 1981, U.S. Dist. Ct. Ariz. 1982, U.S. Ct. Appeals (9th and fed. cirs.) 1982, Ariz. 1982, Colo. 1990, U.S. Dist. Ct. Colo. 1990, U.S. Ct. Appeals (10th cir.) 1990. Patent and trademark atty. Lundy and Assocs., Ft. Wayne, Ind., 1979-81; patent atty. Motorola, Inc., Phoenix, 1981-85; intellectual property counsel Nippon Motorola, Ltd., Tokyo, 1985-87; ptnr. Lisa & Kubida, Phoenix, 1987-89; engrng. law counsel Digital Equipment Corp., Colorado Springs, Colo., 1989-92; of counsel Holland & Hart, Denver, Colorado Springs, 1992-93, ptnr., chmn. intellectual property practice group, 1993-99; ptnr., dir. intellectual property practice group Hogan & Hartson LLP, Colorado Springs, 1999—. Bd. dirs. Colorado Springs Tech Incubator, Bd. dirs. Colorado Springs Tech. Incubator. 1st lt. USAF, 1971—76. Mem. Am. Intellectual Property Law Assn. (computer software sect.), Licensing Exec. Soc. (Pacific Rim subcom.), Country Club Colo., Mensa, Intertel, Federlist Soc., Aston Martin Owners Club, Phi Delta Phi. Republican. Mem. Christ Ch. Of Col. Springs. Office: Hogan & Hartson LLP Two N Cascade Ave Ste 1300 Colorado Springs CO 80903 Office Fax: 719-448-5909. Business E-Mail: wjkubida@hhlaw.com.

KUBIET, LEO LAWRENCE, advertising executive, consultant, marketing executive; b. Apr. 11, 1924; s. Joseph J. and Laura Agnes (Bucy) K.; m. Mary Jean Metz, Sept. 14, 1946; children: Lawrence Michael, Martin Alan. BA in Journalism and English, Fairmont State Coll., 1949; postgrad., U. Mich., 1950, Wayne State U., 1952, U. Detroit, 1953. With The News, Detroit, 1950-68; retail advt. mgr. St. Petersburg (Fla.) Times and Evening Ind., 1968-70, advt. mgr., 1970-75, advt. dir., 1975-76, corp. dir., 1976-89, v.p. advt., 1986-87, sr. v.p., 1987-89; dir. Modern Graphic Arts, Fla. Trend Mags., Inc. divsn. Semit Corp. Charter and hon. life mem. advt. adv. coun. U. Fla., 1978—, hon. life, 1995—; bd. dirs. U. Fla. Found., chmn. Embrace Excellence Campaign Fund, Coll. Journalism, 1989-93; bd. govs. St. Petersburg Area C. of C., 1979-83; bd. dirs. Fla. Orch., 1988-89, Hall of Fame Bowl, 1987-91; mem. fund raising com. St. Anthony's Hosp. Found., 1991-93; bd. dirs. Tampa Bay Coun., Nat. Assn. Investors Corp., 1995-2000. Mem. advt. agy. rev. com. Fla. Lottery Commn.; bd. dirs. Pt. Brittany Condo Two Corp., 1998—2003, v.p., 2000—01, treas., 2001—03. With Seabees USN, 1942—46. Mem.: Am. Newspaper Pubs. Assn. (plans com. 1975—89), Newspaper Advt. Bur., St. Petersburg Sales and Mktg. Execs. (pres. 1973—74), St. Petersburg Advt. Fedn. (bd. dirs., Silver medal 1977), Am. Press. Inst. (so. region adv. coun.), Internat. Newspaper Advt. and Mktg. Execs. (hon. life) (past pres.), Point Brittany Men's Round Table (v.p. 2004—, pres. 2005—, Man of Yr. 2004), Commerce Club Pinellas County (past pres.), Pt. Brittany Yacht Club (treas. 2001—03, commodore 2004—05, bd. govs. 2000—05), St. Petersburg Yacht Club. Roman Catholic. Avocations: golf, fishing, travel, computers, community service. Home: 5108 Brittany Dr S Apt 308 Saint Petersburg FL 33715-1525 E-mail: lejekub@tampabay.rr.com.

KUBISTAL, PATRICIA BERNICE, educational consultant; b. Chgo., Jan. 19, 1938; d. Edward John and Bernice Mildred (Lenz) Kubistal. AB cum laude, Loyola U., Chgo., 1959, AM, 1964, AM, 1965, PhD, 1968; postgrad., Chgo. State Coll., 1962, Ill. Inst. Tech., 1963, State U. Iowa, 1963, Nat. Coll. Edn., 1974-75. With Chgo. Bd. Edn., 1959-93, tchr., 1959-63, counselor, 1963-65, adminstrv. intern, 1965-66, asst. to dist. supt., 1966-69, prin. spl. edn. sch., 1969-75; prin. Simpson Sch., 1975-76, Brentano Sch., 1975-87, Roosevelt H.S., 1987, Haugan Sch., 1989; prin. Cook County Juvenile Temporary Detention Ctr. Sch. Jones Met. H.S. Bus. and Commerce, 1989-90, adminstr. dept. spl. edn., 1990-93; supr. Lake View Evening Sch., 1982-92, ednl. cons., 1993—. Lectr. Loyola U. Sch. Edn., Nat. Coll. Edn. Grad. Sch., Mundelein Coll., 1982-91, DePaul U., 1998-99; coord. Upper Bound Program of U. Ill. Circle Campus, 1966-68. Book rev. editor of Chgo. Prins. Jour., 1970-76, gen. editor, 1982-90. Active Crusade of Mercy; mem. com. Ill. Constnl. Conv., 1967-69; mem. Citizens Sch. Com., 1969-71; mem. edn. com. Field Mus., 1971; ednl. advisor North Side Chgo. PTA Region, 1975; gov. Loyola U., 1961-87; pres. St. Matthews Parish Coun., 1995-98. Recipient Outstanding Intern award Nat. Assn. Secondary Sch. Prins., 1966, Outstanding Prin. award Citizen's Sch. Com. of Chgo., 1986; named Outstanding History Tchr., Chgo. Pub. Schs., 1963, Oustanding Ill. Educator, 1970, one of Oustanding Women of Ill., 1970, St. Luke's Logan Sq. Cmty. Person of Yr., 1977; NDEA grantee, 1963, NSF grantee, 1965, HEW Region 5 grantee for drug edn., 1974, Chgo. Bd. Edn. Prins.' grantee for study robotics in elem. schs.; U. Chgo. adminstrv. fellow 1984. Mem. Ill. Personnel and Guidance Assn., NEA, Ill. Edn. Assn., Chgo. Edn. Assn., Am. Acad. Polit. and Social Sci., Chgo. Prins. and Adminstrs. Assn. (pres. aux.), Nat. Coun. Adminstrv. Women, Chgo. Coun. Exceptional Children, Loyal Christian Benevolent Assn., Kappa Gamma Pi, Pi Gamma Mu, Phi Delta Kappa, Delta Kappa Gamma (paliamentarian 1979-80, pres. Kappa chpt. 1988-90, Lambda state editor 1982-92, chmn. Lambda state comm. com. 1992, Internat. Golden Gift Fund award), Delta Sigma Rho, Phi Sigma Tau. Home and Office: 5111 N Oakley Ave Chicago IL 60625-1829

KUBLER, FRANK LAWRENCE, lawyer; b. Pensacola, Fla., July 4, 1957; s. Frank Martin and Esther Helen (Flora) K. AA, Miami-Dade Jr. Coll., 1978; BS in Mech. Engring., U. Miami, Coral Gables, Fla., 1981, BA in History, 1982, JD, 1986. Bar: Fla. 1986, U.S. Cir. Ct. (11th cir) 1988, U.S. Cir. Ct. (fed. cir.) 1989, U.S. Patent Office 1987. Assoc. Dominik, Stein, Saccocio, Reese, Colitz & Van der Wall, Miami Lakes, Fla., 1986-90; pres. Law Office of Frank L. Kubler, Miami Lakes, 1990—; cons. Oltman, Flynn & Kubler, Ft. Lauderdale, Fla., 1990-96, ptnr., 1996—. Mem. Inter-Am. Law Rev., 1985. Mem. Patent Law Assn. South Fla. (v.p. 1993-94, pres. 1994-95), Mensa, Rotary (dir. 1992-94, chmn. scholarship com. 1994-95), Tau Beta Pi. Office: 915 Middle River Dr Ste 415 Fort Lauderdale FL 33304-3561 Office Phone: 305-829-1869.

KÜBLER, FRIEDRICH KARL, law educator; b. Reutlingen, Fed. Republic Germany, Oct. 19, 1932; s. Wolfgang Eugen and Annemarie (Metzger) K.; m. Brigitte Christine Engels, Oct. 3, 1964; children: Dorothea, Florian, Johanna. PhD, U. Tübingen, Fed. Republic Germany, 1961, Habilitation, 1966; MA (hon.), U. Pa., 1984. Asst. U. Tübingen, 1960-62, 64-66, U. Paris, 1962-63; prof. law U. Giessen, Fed. Republic Germany, 1966-71; dean, prof. law U. Konstanz, Fed. Republic Germany, 1971-76; prf. law, dir. Banking Law Inst. U. Frankfurt, Fed. Republic Germany, 1976—; prof. law U. Pa., Phila., 1985—. Mem. Am. Law Inst. Office: U Pa Sch Law 3400 Chestnut St Philadelphia PA 19104-6204 Office Phone: 215-898-4935. Office Fax: 215-573-2025. E-mail: fkubler@law.upenn.edu.*

KUBO, EDWARD HACHIRO, JR., prosecutor; b. Honolulu, July 9, 1953; s. Edward H. and Rose M. (Coltes) K.; children: Diana K., Dawn M., Edward H. III. BA in Polit. Sci., U. Hawaii, 1976; JD, U. San Diego, 1979. Bar: Hawaii 1979. Legal asst. Legal Aid Soc. Hawaii, 1975-76; law clk. Kobayashi & Watanabe, Honolulu, 1979; dep. pros. atty. Honolulu City Prosecutor's Office, 1980-83, 85-90; assoc. Carlsmith & Dwyer, Honolulu, 1983-85; asst. U.S. atty. U.S. Dept. Justice, Honolulu, 1990—2001, US atty. Hawaii, 2001—. Instr. Honolulu Police Dept. Acad., Waipahu, Hawaii, 1986-89; lectr. U.S. Dept. Justice, Lincoln, Neb., 1997, Pearl Harbor Police Acad., 1995, Western State Vice Investigators Assn. Conf., Houston, 1997, Las Vegas, 1998; spkr. teleconf. U.S. Dept. Justice Violence Against Women Act, 1998, Hawaii Bar Assn. H.S. Mock trial adv., 1996-99. Co-author: Concurrent Jurisdiction for Civil RICO, 1987. Recipient Nat. Art medal (France), 1992, Cert. of Appreciation, U.S. Immigration and Naturalization Svc., 1992, Drug Enforcement Adminstrn., 1997, Plaque of Appreciation, U.S. Border Patrol, 1995, cert. appreciation Bureau Alcohol, Tobacco & Firearms, 1999. Mem. Hawaii Bar Assn., Order of Barristers.

KUBO, GARY MICHAEL, advertising executive; b. Chgo., Aug. 15, 1952; s. Robert S. and Hideko (Nishimura) Kubo; m. Harriet Davenport, June 14, 1975; children: Michael J., R. Scott. BS, Ill. State U., 1974. Rsch. project dir. Foote, Cone & Belding Comms., Chgo., 1974—76, account rsch. supr., 1976—79, rsch. mgr., 1979—80; assoc. rsch. dir. Young & Rubicam, Chgo., 1980—83; ptnr., group rsch. dir. Tatham, Laird & Kudner Advt., Chgo., 1983—89; v.p. dir. strategic planning and rsch./Midwest Bozell, Inc., Chgo., 1989—91, sr. v.p., dir. strategic planning and rsch./Midwe[illegible] v.p. dir. strategic planning rsch. Ogilvy & Mather, Chgo., 1993—95; prin. The KUBO Group, Ltd., Chgo., 1995—2001; exec. v.p. strategy rsch. 141 Worldwide, Chgo., 2001—. Bd. dirs. Chgo. Coun. Urban Affairs, 1992—, Prevent Child Abuse Am.-Chgo. Mem.: Am. Mktg. Assn. (speaker 1983—84, exec. bd.), Advt. Rsch. Found. Avocations: racquet sports, running, music. Home: 2129 Scarlet Oak Ln Lisle IL 60532-2855 Office: 54 W Hubbard St Chicago IL 60610

KUBOTA, MITSURU, chemistry educator; b. Eleele, Hawaii, Sept. 25, 1932; s. Giichi and Kiyono (Naskashima) K.; m. Jane Kinue Taketa, June 30, 1956; children: Lynne K., Keith N. BA, U. Hawaii, 1954; MS, U. Ill., 1957, PhD, 1960. Prof. chemistry Harvey Mudd Coll., Claremont, Calif., 1959-2000. Vis. prof. U. Venice, Italy, 1988, Cambridge (Eng.) U., 1989. 1st lt. U.S. Army, 1954-56. Faculty fellow NSF, 1966, career devel. award, 1981; Fulbright advanced rsch. fellow, Sussex, Eng., 1973, Spl. fellow NIH, 1974. Fellow Royal Soc. Chemistry, AAAS, Am. Chem. Soc. (rsch. award 1992); mem. Sigma Xi. Office: Harvey Mudd Coll 301 E 12th St Claremont CA 91711-5901 E-mail: kubota@hmc.edu.

KUBOTA, SHIGEKO, artist; b. Niigata, Japan, 1937; BA in Sculpture, Tokyo U. Edn., 1960; postgrad., NYU, 1965-66, New Sch. for Social Rsch., 1966-67, Art Sch. Bklyn. Mus., 1967-68. Vice chmn. Fluxus Orgn., N.Y.C., 1964; video curator anthology Film Archives, N.Y.C., 1974-82; tchr. video art Sch. Visual Arts, N.Y.C., 1978; video artist-in-residence Brown U., Providence, 1981. Video artist-in-residence Sch. Art Inst. Chgo., 1973, 81, 82, 84. Numerous one-woman shows, 1964—, including Sch. Art Inst. Chgo., 1973, Everson Mus. Art, Syracuse, N.Y., 1973, 75, 78, Art Gallery Ont., Toronto, Can., 1976, 77, Mus. Modern Art, N.Y.C., 1978, Mus. Contemporary Art, Chgo., 1981, D.A.A.D. Gallery, Berlin, 1981, Kunsthaus, Zurich, Switzerland, 1982, Am. Mus. Moving Image, Astoria, N.Y., 1991, Hara Mus. Contemporary Art, Tokyo, 1992, Stedelijk Mus., Amsterdam, The Netherlands, 1992, Kunstahlle in Kiel, Germany, 1993, Eric Fabre Gallery, Paris, 1996, Galerie de Paris, 1996, Whitney Mus. Am. Art, N.Y.C., 1996, Kamakura Gallery, Tokyo, 1998, Lance Fung Gallery, N.Y.C., 2000; exhibited in numerous group shows, 1962—, including Tokyo Mcpl. Mus., 1962, Mus. Modern Art, N.Y.C., 1974, 77, 88, Whitney Mus. Modern Art, 1975, 79, 83, 88, 95, Seibu Mus., Tokyo, 1981, Kennedy Ctr. for Performing Arts, Washington, 1982, Palais Beaux Art, Brussels, 1983, Stedelijk Mus., 1984, Tamayo Mus., Mexico City, 1985, Phila. Mus. Art, 1987, Houston Contemporary Art Mus., 1987, Aldrich Mus. Contemporary Art, Ridgefield, Conn., 1988, Art Space, Sydney, Australia, 1988, Nat. Mus. Art, Osaka, Japan, 1992, Walker Art Ctr., Mpls., 1993, Yokohoma (Japan) Mus., 1994, San Francisco Mus. Contemporary Art, 1995, Whitney Mus. Am. Art, 1995, Venice Biennale, 1995, Kwangju (Korea) Biennale, 1995, Jeu de Paume, Paris, 1996; work reviewed in numerous publs.; prodr. numerous videography, video sculpture and video installations. Recipient Indie award Assn. Ind. Video and Filmmakers, 1977, Maya Deren award Am. Film Inst., 1995; grantee Creative Artists Pub. Svc. Program, 1975, N.Y. Found. for Arts, 1985, visual arts grantee Nat. Endowment for Arts, 1988; fellow Nat. Endowment for Arts, 1975, 78, 80, Rockefeller fellow, 1979, German Acad. Exch. Svc., Berlin, 1979, Guggenheim fellow, 1987.

KUBRIN, CHARIS ELIZABETH, education educator; b. LA, Dec. 23, 1970; d. Stanley Herbert and Jane Julia Kubrin. BA cum laude, Smith Coll., 1989—93; MA, U. of Wash., 1993—95, PhD, 1995—2000. Asst. prof. George Wash. U., Washington, 2000—. Contbr. articles to profl. jours. Recipient, Smith Coll., 1993, Excellence in Tchg., U. of Wash., 1998, Jr. Scholar Incentive award, George Washington U., 2002, Urban Affairs Assn./Fannie Mae Found. Best Paper in Housing or Cmty. Devel. award, Urban Affairs Assn., 2005, others; fellow, George Washington U., 2003, 2005, George Washington Inst. Pub. Policy, 2003; grantee, Kosciuszko Found., 1999—2000, Assn. for Women in Sci. Ednl. Found., 2000, NSF, 2001—04, William Penn Found., 2002, Soros Found., 2002—03, Nat. Consortium on Violence Rsch., 2001—05, Am. Sociol. Assn., NSF, 2003—04, Smith Richardson Found., 2004—05; scholar, El Coll. Mex., 1995; Hewlett Found. fellow, George Washington U., 2002. Fellow: Inst. on Crime, Justice and Corrections; mem.: Am. Soc. of Criminology, Am. Sociol. Assn. Office: George Washington Univ 801 22nd St NW; Phillips Hall 409 Washington DC 20052 Office Phone: 202-994-6349. Office Fax: 202-994-3239. Personal E-mail: charisk@gwu.edu.

KUBY, RONALD LAWRENCE, lawyer; b. Cleve., July 31, 1956; s. Donald Joseph Kuby and Ruth Miller; m. Marilyn Vasta; 1 child, Emma Sojourner Vasta-Kuby. BA, U. Kans., 1979; JD magna cum laude, Cornell U., 1983. Bar: N.Y. 1984. Assoc. Kunstler & Kuby, N.Y.C., 1994—95, Law Office William M. Kunstler, N.Y.C., 1984—94; ptnr. Law Office Ronald L. Kuby, N.Y.C., 1996—2004, Kuby & Percz, LLP, 2004—. Contbr. articles to profl. jours. Mem. adv. bd. police misconduct task force N.Y. Civil Liberties Union, 1999—. Named Best Radio Talk Show Host, NY State Broadcasters Assn., 2005; recipient Thurgood Marshall award, N.Y. City Bar Assn., 1998, N.Y. Metro Achievement in Radio award for best talk show host, 2000, N.Y. Metro Achievement in Radio award for best talk show, 2001, award for excellence in 9/11 broadcasting, UFA/UFOA (N.Y. Firefighters), 2003, Radio and Rec. Industry award for best local talk show host in Am., 2004. Communist. Office: 119 W 23rd St New York NY 10011 E-mail: ronkuby@aol.com.

KUC, JOSEPH A., research scientist; b. N.Y.C., Nov. 24, 1929; s. Peter and Helen (Dubec) K.; m. Karola Ingrid Maywald, July 17, 1991; children: Paul D., Rebecca R., Miriam A. BS, Purdue U., 1951, MS, 1953, PhD, 1955. Asst. prof. Purdue U., West Lafayette, Ind., 1955—59, assoc. prof., 1959—63, prof., 1963—74, U. Ky., Lexington, 1974—95, prof. emeritus, 1995—. Contbr. numerous articles to profl. jours. Pres. Cen. Ky. ACLU, Lexington, 1977-79. Mem. Am. Chem. Soc., Am. Phytopathol. Soc., Am. Soc. Plant Physiologists, Am. Soc. for Biochemistry and Molecular Biology, N.Y. Acad. Sci., Phytochem. Soc., Ky. Acad. Sci., Sigma Xi. Avocations: hiking, gardening, conversation. Home and Office: 5502 Lorna St Torrance CA 90503

KUCERA, DANIEL WILLIAM, retired bishop; b. Chgo., May 7, 1923; s. Joseph F. and Lillian C. (Petrzelka) K. BA, St. Procopius Coll., 1945; MA, Catholic U. Am., 1950, PhD, 1954. Joined Order of St. Benedict, 1944, ordained priest Roman Cath. Ch., 1949. Registrar St. Procopius Coll. and Acad., Lisle, Ill., 1945—49, St. Procopius Coll., Lisle, Ill., 1954—56, acad. dean, head dept. edn., 1956—59, pres., 1959—65; abbot St. Procopius Abbey, Lisle, 1964—71; pres. Ill. Benedictine Coll. (formerly St. Procopius Coll.), Lisle, 1971—76, chmn. bd. trustees, 1976—78; aux. bishop Joliet, Ill., 1977—80; bishop of Salina Kans., 1980—83; archbishop of Dubuque, 1983—95; ret., 1995. Mem.: KC (4 degree). Roman Catholic. Personal E-mail: dwkucera@aol.com.

KUCERA, HENRY, linguistics educator; b. Trebarov, Czechoslovakia, Feb. 15, 1925; arrived in U.S., 1949, naturalized, 1953; s. Jindrich and Marie (Kral) K.; m. Jacqueline M. Fortin, Oct. 6, 1951; children: Thomas Henry, Edward James. MA, Charles U., Prague, Czechoslovakia, 1947, PhDr, 1991; PhD, Harvard U., 1952; MA ad eundem, Brown U., 1958; DSc (hon.), Bucknell U., 1984; PhilD (hon.), Masaryk U., Brno, Czechoslovakia, 1990. Asst. prof. fgn. langs. U. Fla., 1952-55; from mem. faculty to prof. Brown U., 1955—90, prof. emeritus, 1990—; mem. Ctr. for Cognitive Sci., 1977-85, exec. com., 1980-86; mem. Ctr. for Neural Studies, 1973-90, exec. com., 1977-90; dir. Inst. for Cognitive and Neural Research, 1981-88. Fellow Russian Rsch. Ctr., Harvard U., 1952, 79-87, rsch. assoc. Slavic dept., 1977-79; rsch assoc. MIT, 1960-63; vis. prof. U. Mich., 1967, U. Calif. at Berkeley, 1969; vis. scholar U. Vienna, 1968-69; pres. Lang. Software Systems, Inc., 1982-2001. Author: The Phonology of Czech, 1961, (with W.N. Francis) Computational Analysis of Present-Day American English, 1967, (with G. Monroe) A Comparative Quantitative Phonology of Russian, Czech and German, 1968, Computers in Linguistics and in Literary Studies, 1975, (with K. Trnka) Time in Language, 1975, (with W.N. Francis) Frequency Analysis of English Usage, 1982; also linguistic and lit. articles.;

Editor: American Contributions to the Sixth International Congress of Slavists, 1968. Bd. dirs. Internat. Inst. Providence, 1960-67; bd. adminstrn. Howard Found., 1977-95; mem. R.I. Com. for Humanities, 1986-90. Ford fellow, 1954-55; Howard Found. fellow, 1960-61; Guggenheim fellow, 1960-61; sr. fellow NEH, 1968-69; Am. Council Learned Socs. fellow, 1969-70 Hon. fellow Linguistic Soc. of Czech Acad. Scis.; mem. MLA, Linguistic Soc. Am., Czechoslovak Soc. Arts and Scis. in Am. (v.p. 1980-82), Prague Linguistic Circle (hon.), Phi Beta Kappa. Business E-Mail: henry_kucera@brown.edu.

KUCHARSKI, THOMAS EDWARD, secondary school educator; b. Chgo., Ill., Aug. 17, 1962; s. Chester and Anita Kucharski; m. Paula Walker, Oct. 11, 1986; children: Nicholas, Rachael. PhD, Loyola U., 2002. Cert. tchr. Ill. Tchr. Loyola U., Chgo., 1991—94, Loyola Acad., Wilmette, Ill., 1987—94, New Trier H.S., Winnetka, Ill., 1994—. Adviser New Trier H.S., Wilmette, 1995—2002, negotiator, Winnetka, 1996—2002; tour leader New Trier Ext., Winnetka, 1999—2002; pres. Loyola Acad. PA, Wilmette; presenter in field. Pres. New Trier Edn. Assn., 2004—. Recipient grant to study Mozart in Vienna, NEH, 1998, Spl. Recognition for Tchg., MIT, Charlton Coll., others. Mem.: New Trier Ednl. Assn. (pres. 2004—). Liberal. Avocations: travel, reading. Home: 1522 N Pine Arlington Heights IL 60004 Office: New Trier H S 385 Winnetka Ave Winnetka IL 60093 Personal E-mail: kucharst@newtrier.k12.il.us.

KUCHEMAN, CLARK ARTHUR, philosophy and religious studies educator; b. Akron, Ohio, Feb. 7, 1931; s. Merlin Carlyle and Lucile (Clark) K.; m. Melody Elaine Frazer, Nov. 15, 1986. BA, U. Akron, 1952; BD, Meadville Theol. Sch., 1955; MA in Econs., U. Chgo., 1959, PhD, 1965. Instr., then asst. prof. U. Chgo., 1961-67; prof. Claremont (Calif.) McKenna Coll., 1967—, Claremont Grad. Sch., 1967—. Co-author: Belief and Ethics, 1978, Creative Interchange, 1982, Economic Life, 1988; contbg. editor: The Life of Choice, 1978; contbr. articles to profl. jours. 1st lt. USAF, 1955—57. Mem. Am. Acad. Religion, Hegel Soc. Am., N.Am. Soc. for Social Philosophy. Democrat. Home: 10160 60th St Riverside CA 92509-4745 Office: Claremont McKenna Coll Dept Philosophy Religon Pitzer Hall 850 Columbia Ave Claremont CA 91711-6420 Office Phone: 909-607-7980. Business E-Mail: clark.kucheman@claremontmckenna.edu. *Education and life itself have the same purpose, and, borrowing words from G. W. F. Hegel, "...the final purpose of education is liberation and the struggle for a higher liberation still.".*

KUCHNER, EUGENE FREDERICK, neurosurgeon, educator, neuroscientist; b. N.Y.C., 1945; s. Morton H. and Edna Estelle Kuchner; m. Joan Ruth Freedman, Sept. 2, 1968; children: Marc Jason, Eric Benjamin. AB, Johns Hopkins U., 1967; MD, U. Chgo., 1971. Diplomate Am. Bd. Neurol. Surgery, Am. Bd. Med. Examiners. Resident in surgery Yale U. Sch. Medicine, New Haven, 1971-72; resident in neurosurgery Montreal (Que., Can.) Neurol. Inst., McGill U., 1972-76, spine fellow, 1976; neurosurgeon SUNY Downstate Sch. Medicine, Bklyn., 1976-79, SUNY Sch. Medicine, Stony Brook, 1979—, assoc. prof., 1983—; cons. neurosurgeon North Shore U. Hosp./NYU Sch. Medicine, 1997—. Mem. staff North Shore U. Hosp.-Cornell Med. Ctr., 1977—97, cons. surgeon, 1992—97; mem. neurosurgery attending staff Univ. Hosp., Stony Brook, 1979—97, Nassau County Med. Ctr., 1977—2000, St. John's Episcopal Hosp., 1976—99, Mt. Sinai-NYU Health Sys., 1997—, Nassau U. Med. Ctr., 2000—; clin. assoc. prof. surgery Cornell U. Coll. Medicine, NY, 1990—97. Contbr. articles to profl. publs.; specialist in microsurgery, magnetic resonance imaging, spinal trauma, pituitary surgery. Recipient K.G. McKenzie Meml. award, Royal Coll. Physicians and Surgeons Can., 1976, Open Scholarship award, John Hopkins U., yearly, 1963—66, Scholarship award, U. Chgo., yearly, 1967—70; fellow, NSF, Blackman-Hoffman Found., 1969—70, USPHS, Divsn. Epidemiology Columbia U. Sch. Pub. Health, N.Y.C., 1969; chemistry fellow, MIT, 1968. Mem. ACS, AMA, Am. Assn. Neurol. Surgeons, Congress Neurol. Surgeons, N.Y. Acad. Scis., L.I. Neurosci. Acad., Suffolk Acad. Medicine, Montreal Neurol. Ins. Fellows Soc., N.Y. State Neurosurg. Soc., N.Y. State Med. Soc., N.Y. State Soc. Surgeons, Am. Coll. Med. Quality, Healthcare Info. and Mgmt. Sys. Soc., Am. Epilepsy Soc., Am. Soc. Law Medicine and Ethics, Yale Surg. Soc., Yale Club N.Y.C., Sigma Xi. Office: Stony Brook Med Ctr PO Box 721 Stony Brook NY 11790-0721

KUCHTA, BEATRICE L. ESKEN, language educator; b. Pitts., Sept. 29, 1944; d. Christopher and Betty Beatrice (Gerhold) Esken; m. Kenneth K. Worton, Apr. 3, 1965; children: Eric J. Worton, Jill A. Worton Peters, Joi L. Worton Schwartz; m. Edward A. Kuchta, July 18, 1981. BS in Secondary Edn. English, California U. of Pa., 1966, MS in Counseling Edn., 1983. Cert. tchr., Pa.; lic. life ins., real estate agt., Pa. Tchr. art, phys. edn., English Munhall (Pa.) H.S., 1966-68; real estate salesperson, realtor Mt. Lebanon, Pa., 1970-76; sales assoc. J.C. Penney Co., Inc., Bridgeville, Pa., 1976-78; tchr. English Baldwin-Whitehall Sch. Dist., Pitts., 1979; tchr. English, econs., Japanese lang. and culture South Park (Pa.) Sch. Dist., Pa., 1980—. Amb. to Japan, Pa. Dept. Edn., Harrisburg, 1994, del. to Australia, 1997. Author, illustrator: Which Age Is Best?, 1995. Sunday sch. tchr. Jefferson Hills (Pa.) Bible Ch., 1995-99. Recipient Tchrs. Excellence award, 1999, 2000; name inscribed on Wall of Tolerance, 2005. Mem. NEA, Nat. Coun. English Tchrs., South Park Edn. Assn. (bldg. rep. 1997-), Pa. State Edn. Assn., Western Pa. Real Estate Investors Assn., Steel Valley Mother of Twins Club (charter). Avocations: travel, flower arranging, real estate, gourmet cooking, bowling. Home: 255 Coleen Dr Pittsburgh PA 15236-4308 Office: South Park Sch Dist 2005 Eagle Ridge Rd South Park PA 15129-8806 Office Phone: 412-655-3450. Personal E-mail: beakuchta@verizon.net.

KUCHTA, RONALD ANDREW, museum director, editor, curator; b. Lackawanna, N.Y., June 23, 1935; s. Andrew and Clara May (Barnes) K.; m. Sique Stoll, Oct. 1, 1970 (div. 1974). BA, Kenyon Coll., 1957; MA, Western Res. U., 1961; postgrad. in mgmt., Cornell U., 1979. Curator Chrysler Mus., Provincetown, Mass., 1961-68, Santa Barbara (Calif.) Mus. Art, (Calif.), 1968-74; dir. Everson Mus. Art, Syracuse, N.Y., 1974-95; editor Am. Ceramics mag., 1995; dir. Loveed Fine Arts, N.Y.C., 1995. Adj. prof. Syracuse U., 1974—95; trustee Fondo del Sol, Washington, 1974—, Nat. Conf. Educators of Ceramic Arts, 1986, Quarry Rd. Sculpture Pk., Cazenovia, NY; founding dir. Syracuse China Ctr. for Study of Am. Ceramics; chmn. Urban Arts Commn., Syracuse, 1992—93; juror Mino '89 Internat. Competition for Ceramics, Gifu, Japan, 1989, Concorso Internat. della Ceramica d'Arte, Faenza, Italy, 1990, Biennale Nat. de Ceramique, Trois Rivieres, Que., Canada, 1992, 2d Cairo Internat. Biennale Ceramics, 1994, Mainline Art Ctr., Phila., 1997, San Angelo (Tex.) Ceramic Nat., 1998, Ariz. Commn. on the Arts, 1999, 1st World Biennale for Ceramics, Ichon, Republic of Korea, 2001, 2d World Biennale for Ichon, 2003, No. Clay Ctr. McKnight Awards, Mpls., 2003; bd. dirs. Watershed Ctr., North Edgecomb, Maine, Longhouse Res., Easthampton, NY, Mus. Ceramic Art, N.Y.C., The Antonia and Vladimer Kulaev Cultural Heritage Fund Inc., L.A.; lectr. U. Regina, Sask., Canada, Mimar Sinan U., Istanbul, Turkey, Alta. Coll. Art, Calgary, Calif. Conf. Advancement of Ceramic Art, Davis, Nat. Mus. History, Taipei, Taiwan, 1993, Japan Soc., N.Y.C., 1994, Czech Ceramic Design Ctr., Cesky Krumlov, 1996, Internat. Acad. Ceramics, Nagoya, Japan, 1996, Nat. Arts Club, N.Y.C., Bard Coll., N.Y.C., 1997, Cleve. Mus. Art, Stetson U., DeLand, Fla., Washington U., St. Louis, 1997, Santa Barbara City Coll., 1998, Cotta Terra Symposium, Deruta, Italy, 1998, Konstfack U. Coll. Arts, Crafts and Design, Stockholm, 1998, Royal Coll. Art, London, 1998, Oslo (Norway) Internat. Ceramic Symposium, 2003, Arundal Coll., Anapolis, Md.; curator Enigmatic Visions/Sublime Forms Contemporary Japanese, 1998, Ceramic Longhouse Res., Easthampton; US commr. World Biennale for Ceramics, Republic of Korea, 2005; lectr. Anne Arundel Coll., Arnold, Md., 2005—. Author: Mayan Figurines, 1971, Interior Vision, 1971, Modern Mexican Art, 1972, Provincetown Painters, 1975, Batuz: Works in Paper, 1981, Robert Beauchamp: An American Expressionist, 1984, The Elegiac and the Primordial: Ceramics at the End of the Twentieth Century, 1997, Consuming Ceramics: Its Classification and Place in the U.S. Art Market, 2001, Norwegian Clay and the Possible Superiority of Ceramics, 2003, Elimination and Affirmation: The Potent Process of the Jury; pub.: A Century of Ceramics in the U.S., 1979, American Ceramics: Collection of Everson Museum of Art, 1989; translator: Pre-Hispanic Art: Time and Culture, 1997. Commr. 3d World CeramicBiennale, Republic of Korea, 2004—. With U.S. Army, 1958—60. Mem.: Assn. Art Mus. Dirs. (emeritus), Nat. Arts Club, Internat. Acad. Ceramics, Phi Kappa Sigma. Democrat. Episcopalian. Home: 60 Sutton Pl S New York NY 10022-4168 Office: Am Ceramics Mag 9 E 45th St New York NY 10017-2425 Office Phone: 212-661-4397, 212-605-0591.

KUCHYNSKI, MARIE, physician; b. Cleve., Sept. 23, 1964; d. Harry Gregory and Albina (Guarnera) K.; m. K. William Burdick; children: Nicole, Stephanie. BA, Case Western Reserve U., 1986, MD, 1990. Diplomate in internal medicine and in rheumatology Am. Bd. Internal Medicine. Intern U. Hosps. Cleve., 1990-91, resident, 1991-93; physician pvt. practice, Elyria, Ohio, 1995-98; pvt. practice Brunswick, Ohio, 1998—. Mem. utilization mgmt. com. Cleve. Health Network, 1996-98; med. advisor Tri-City Lupus Project, 1997-98. Rheumatology fellow U. Hosps. Cleve., 1993-95. Mem. AMA, Am. Coll. Physicians, Am. Coll. Rheumatology, Cleve. Soc. Rheumatology, Phi Beta Kappa. Democrat. Roman Catholic. Avocations: gardening, crafts, piano. Home: 21503 Brookfield Pl Strongsville OH 44149 Office: Univ Primary Care Practice 3812 Center Rd Brunswick OH 44212-3024 E-mail: mkuchynski@aol.com.

KUCIC, JOSEPH, management consultant, industrial engineer, network engineer, information security specialist; b. Mali Losinj, Croatia, Yugoslavia, Dec. 21, 1964; came to U.S., 1967, naturalized, 1974; s. Roman Kucic and Esterina (Karcic) Milevoj; m. Gia Michelle Bonavisa, Sept. 11, 1992; children: Ann Marie, Jillian Michelle. AAS, Coll. of Aeronautics, 1984; BS, Thomas A. Edison State Coll., 1986; B in Tech., N.Y. Inst. Tech., 1986; MBA, St. John's U., Jamaica, N.Y., 1989. Cert. info. sys. security profl., Microsoft, design assoc. CNCO, network assoc. Cisco. Workload planner Butler Aviation-Newark, Inc., Newark, 1984-85; tech. planner N.Y. Airlines, Flushing, NY, 1985-86; product support engr. United Techs.-Pratt & Whitney, East Hartford, Conn., 1986; indsl. engr. Montefiore Med. Ctr., Bronx, 1986-88; sr. work mgmt. analyst Bank Leumi Trust Co., N.Y.C., 1988-89; sr. methods analyst Salomon Bros., Inc., N.Y.C., 1989-92; mgmt. cons. United Mgmt. Techs., N.Y.C., 1992-93; sr. sys. analyst Met. Hosp. Ctr. N.Y.C. Health & Hosp. Corp. Metro. Hosp. Ctr., 1993; dir. info. svcs. N.Y.C. Health & Hosp. Corp. Bronx Mcpl. Hosp. Ctr., 1993-94; project mgr. Montefiore Med. Ctr., Bronx, 1994-96, ANS Comms., Inc., Elmsford, NY, 1996; mgr. infrastructure planning, divsn. of Am. Online ANS Comms., Inc., 1996-97; mgr. KPMG Peat Marwick, Hawthorne, NY, 1997-98; sr. mgr. KPMG LLP, N.Y.C., 1998-2000; dir. profl. svcs. Network Assocs., Inc., 1999; mng. dir. Pricewaterhouse Coopers, LLP, N.Y.C., 2000—02; cons. GM Asset Mgmt., N.Y.C., 2002—04; v.p. Computer Assocs. Internat., 2004—. Spkr. in field. Contbr. articles to profl. jours. Mem.: Internat. Info. Sys. Security Sys. Cert. Consortium, Info. Sys. Audit and Control Assn., Info. Sys. Security Assn., Asn. Computing Machinery Computer Security Inst., Coll. Aeronautics Alumni Asn. (pres. 1990-92), SAE (affiliate), AIAA, IEEE (assoc.), Inst. Indsl. Engr. (chpt. pres. 1988-89, chmn. bd. N.Y.C. chpt. 1989-90, bd. govs. 1988-92, Cert. of Recognition 1988) (sr.), St. John's Univ. Col. Bus. Admin. Alumni Asn. (bd. dir. 1991-93), Wings Club N.Y., Tau Alpha Pi. Republican. Roman Catholic. Avocation: tennis. Home: 42B Valley Rd Greenwich CT 06807 Office: 1351 Washington Blvd Ste 800 Stamford CT 06702 Personal E-mail: jkucic@mail.com.

KUCIJ, TIMOTHY MICHAEL, engineer, minister, musician; b. Whittier, Calif., Sept. 2, 1954; m. Paulina V. Jimenez, 1979. Studied with Frank Sanucci, Edward D. Berryman, Thurla Wallis, Kathreen Prout, Eddy L. Manson, Henry Charles Smith, Joseph P. Free, Ronald Gearman, 1965—78; student, Sherwood Music Conservatory, Chgo., 1965—68; BA in Music, Calif. State Poly. U., Pomona, 1978; ThM cum laude, Christian Bible Coll., 1983; grad. studies, Maranatha Bapt. Bible Coll., Ctrl. Bapt. Theol. Sem. Licensed minister Bapt. Ch., 1982. Tech. writer Honeywell Inc., West Covina (Calif.) and Mpls., 1977-84; hydromech. reliability engr. Advanced Systems divsn. Northrop Corp., Pico Rivera, Calif., 1984-86; sr. engr. quality and reliability Swedlow, Inc., Garden Grove, Calif., 1986-88, mgr., quality assurance, composites divsn., 1988-90, quality assurance staff specialist, 1990-92; div. quality assurance engr. Rexroth Corp. Piston Pump divsn., Fountain Inn, SC, 1992-94; sr. quality engr. Hi-Shear Corp., Torrance, Calif., 1996-98; sr. quality sys. mgr. TRW Automotive, Carson, Calif., 1998—2004; quality assurance mgr. Structural Composites Industries Harsco Corp., Pomona, Calif., 2004—. Lectr. tech. and engrng.; tchr. piano, organ and composition, 1971—81; active pulpit supply local Bapt. Chs., Calif., SC. Performer: (organ, piano) Debut, 1966; performer (pipe organ) Wiltern Theater, L.A., 1966—68, Busch-Reisinger Mus. Harvard U., Cambridge, Mass., 1972, 1973, 1974; composer: scores of original piano pieces including Persistence and The Storm, Purity, Remembrance, Your Song, Yearning, Compassion, A Little Jingle, A Familiar Song, Images, Paulina, Afterthought, Blue Fragrance, Sunset, Then, Piano Lesson # 1, Chase, Unrest, Nebulae, Distress, Retrograde, Frolic, The Happy Whistler, The Little Toy March, Hope, Teardrops, Reminisce, Wind Chimes, A Place Somewhere, Rainbows, The Bicentennial Rag, The Pulsar Rag, Dazzling Fingers, The Butterfly Rag, Serenity, first 25 original pieces written in honor of Am. bicentennial; music housed in numerous librs. including L.A. County Libr., Seattle Pub. Libr., Dallas Pub. Libr., Denver Pub. Libr., L.A. Pub. Libr., St. Louis Pub. Libr., Atlanta-Fulton County Libr., The Master's Coll. Libr., Calif. State Poly. U. Libr., Archive of Contemporary Music, N.Y.C., Phila. Free Libr., Juilliard Sch. Music Libr., Calif. Bapt. Coll. Libr., Biola U. Libr., N.Y. Pub. Libr., Cleve. Pub. Libr., Boston Pub. Libr., Harvard U. Libr., Chicago Pub. Libr., Univ. Kansas Gorton Music Libr.; musician: (recordings) KRC Records, 1993—, A Place Somewhere, 1993, 2003, LifeSongs, 1993, 2003; concertized nationally (piano, pipe organ), scored comprehensive piano arrangements Jesus Loves Me, Over the Rainbow, songwriter Jesus is the Answer, O Jesus; editor: The Golden State Baptist, 1995—96; contbr. articles to various periodicals. Asst. to local pastors Bapt. chs. in Tex., Ga., Wis., Minn., and Calif., 1978—82; pastor Victory Bapt. ch., Pine City, Minn., 1982—83; music dir., Bible tchr. Calvary Bapt. Ch., La Verne, Calif., 1988—92, mem. sch. bd., ch. coun., 1989—92; music dir., youth dir. Covina Bapt. Temple, 1985—87; pastor First Missionary Bapt. Ch., Gardena, Calif., 1994—96; bd. dirs. Garden Grove Symphony Orch., 1989—90. Named one of Outstanding Young Men in Am., U.S. Jaycees, 1980; recipient First prize, So. Calif. Organ Competition, 1966, Performer's cert., 1967, Disting. Alumnus award, Calif. State Poly. U., 1989. Mem.: Christian Fellowship Art Music Composers, Broadcast Music, Inc., Am. Symphony Orch. League, Am. Soc. Quality, Creation Rsch. Soc., Am. Composer's Forum. Republican. Baptist. Office: Structural Composites Industries 325 Enterprise Place Pomona CA 91768 E-mail: tkucij@comcast.net.

KUCINICH, DENNIS JOHN, congressman; b. Cleve., Oct. 8, 1946; m. Elizabeth Harper, Aug. 21, 2005. Student, Cleveland State U.; BA, Case Western Reserve U., 1973, MA. Pres. K Comm., Cleve.; v.p. sales & mktg. Town and Country Printing, Cleve.; councilman City of Cleve., 1969-73, clk. of mcpl. ct., 1975-77, mayor, 1977-79; senator OH State Senate, 1994—97; mem. U.S. Congress from 10th Ohio dist., 1997—; mem. edn. and the workforce, govt. reform coms.; chair. Congress. Prog. Caucus. Author: A Prayer for America, 2003. Recipient Outstanding Senator of the Year award Nat. Assn. of Social Workers, 1996, Green Thumb award, League of Conservation Voters, 1997 Charles Van Riper award, Nat. Coun. Communicative Disorders, 1998, Oak Tree award OH Parent-Teacher Assn., 1999, Congl. Appreciation award, Operation Lifesaver, 2000, Named Outstanding Pub. Official, Internat. Eagles. Democrat. Office: US Ho of Reps 1730 Longworth Ho Office Bldg Washington DC 20515-3510*

KUCK, JANE, librarian; b. Brimfield, Ill., Apr. 1, 1929; d. Carl and Betty Marie (Pulsipher) Gibbs; m. Joseph Russell Kuck, May 2, 1949; children: Sherida Laine, Joseph Russell III, Kayce Elizabeth. BS, Bradley U., 1968; MLS, George Peabody Coll. for Tchrs, Nashville, 1973. Libr. Farmington High Sch., Farmington, Ill., 1067—1991; ret. Pres. Elmwood (Ill.) Hist. Soc., 1988-89; mem. New England Hist. Genealogical Soc., Greene County (Ill.) Hist. and Genealogical Soc., Peoria County (Ill.) Genealogical Soc., Ross County (Ohio) Genealogical Soc., Tazewell County (Ill.) Genealogical Soc. Mem. Nat. Edn. Assn., Beta Phi Mu. Avocations: genealogy, travel. Home: 404 N Magnolia St Elmwood IL 61529-0697

KUCK, LEA HABER, lawyer; b. Lockport, N.Y., 1965; AB magna cum laude, Hamilton Coll., 1987; JD, NYU, 1990. Bar: N.Y. 1991, U.S. Dist. Ct. (ea. dist.) Mich. 1992. Law clk. HOn. Steven D. Pepe U.S. Dist. Ct. (ea. dist.) Mich., 1990—92; atty. Skadden, Arps, Slate, Meagher & Flom LLP, N.Y., 1992—98, ptnr., 1998—. Office: Skadden Arps Slate Meagher & Flom LLP Four Times Square New York NY 10036

KUCKUCK, ROBERT, physicist, science administrator; With Lawrence Livermore Nat. Lab., Calif., 1966—2001, dep. dir., 1994—2001; dep. adminstr., internal ops. and orgn. restructing Nat. Nuclear Security Adminstrn., Dept. Energy, 2001—03; sr. advisor, office of lab. mgmt. Univ. Calif.; interim dir. Los Alamos Nat. Lab., N.Mex., 2005—. Office: Los Alamos Nat Lab PO Box 1663 Los Alamos NM 87545

KUCZWARA, THOMAS PAUL, federal agency administrator, lawyer; b. Dec. 21, 1951; s. Stanley Leo and Eleanore (Pawelko) K.; m. Diana Lynn Rychtarczyk, Sept. 8, 1979; 1 child, Paul Stanley. BA, Loyola U., Chgo., 1973; JD, U. S.C., 1976. Bar: Ill. 1976, U.S. Dist. Ct. (no. dist.) Ill. 1982. Assoc. Doria Law Offices, Chgo., 1977-78; asst. corp. counsel City of Chgo., 1978-80; asst. city atty. City of Aurora, Ill., 1980-82; postal insp. U.S. Postal Inspection Svc., Salt Lake City, 1982-85, regional insp. atty. cen. region Chgo., 1985—. Mem. St. Bartholomew's Parish Coun., Chgo., 1978; vol. atty. Lawyers for Creative Arts, 1978. Ill. state scholar, 1969. Mem. Sierra Club, Pi Sigma Alpha. Roman Catholic. Office: US Postal Inspection Svc Chgo Divsn 433 W Harrison 6th Fl Chicago IL 60669-2201 Office Phone: 312-983-6227. E-mail: tpkuczwara@uspis.gov.

KUCZYNSKI, JOHN-MICHAEL MAXIME, humanities educator, writer; b. Washington, Aug. 21, 1972; s. Pedro-Pablo Godard Kuczynski. BA, UCLA, 1997. Author: Elements of Virtualism: A Study in the Philosophy of Perception, 2003; contbr. articles to profl. jours. Home and Office: PO Box 14163 Santa Barbara CA 93107 Office Phone: 805-967-6144. Personal E-mail: jsbach@jps.net.

KUCZYNSKI, PEDRO-PABLO, prime minister of Peru; b. Lima, Peru, Oct. 3, 1938; s. Maxime and Madeleine Louise (Godard) K.; married; 4 children. BA, Exeter Coll., Oxford (Eng.) U., 1959; M.P.A., Princeton U., 1961. Economist World Bank, 1961-67, sr. economist, 1971-73; dep. dir.-gen. Central Res. Bank Peru, 1967-69; sr. economist Internat. Monetary Fund, Washington, 1969-71; v.p., ptnr. Kuhn, Loeb & Co. Internat., N.Y.C., 1973-75; dir. dept. econs. Internat. Finance Corp., Washington, 1975-77; pres., chief exec. officer Halco Mining Inc., Pitts., 1977-80; chmn., mng. dir. First Boston Internat. Co., NYC, 1982-92; former pres., CEO Westfield Capital Ltd., Miami, Fla.; minister of energy and mines Peru, 1980-82; minister of economy and finance, 2001—02, 2004—05; Prime Minister, 2005—. Mem. Univ. Club (Washington), Pitts. Golf Club, Racquet and Tennis Club. Office: Presidencia del Consejo de Ministros Avenida 28 Julio 878 Miraflores Lima Peru

KUDELKA, JAMES, choreographer, artistic director; b. Newmarket, Ont., Can. Student, Nat. Ballet Sch., Toronto. Dancer Nat. Ballet of Can., Toronto, 1972-81, artist in residence, 1992-96; prin. dancer Les Grands Ballets Canadiens, Montreal, 1981-84, resident choreographer, 1984-90; works created for San Francisco and Joffrey Ballets, Am. Ballet Theatre, Birmingham Royal Ballet; artistic dir. Nat. Ballet Can., Toronto, 1995—2005, resident choreographer, 2005—. Choreographer (ballets) Sonata, Nat. Ballet of Can., 1973, Apples, 1974, A Party, 1976, Washington Square, 1977, 1979, Bach Pas de Deux, 1979, Windsor Pas de Deux, 1979, The Rape of Lucrece, 1980, Playhouse, 1980, All Night Wonder, 1981, Dido and Aeneas, 1982, Unfinished Business, 1984, Death of an Old Queen, 1985, Dracula, 1985, Collisions, 1986, Vers la Glace, 1986, The Heart of the Matter, 1986, Soudain d'Hiver Dernier, 1987, Signatures, 1988, In Camera, 1988, The Wakey Nights, 1989, Scheherazade, 1989, Divertissement Schumann, 1989, There, below, 1989, The Comfort Zone, 1989, Love Dracula, 1989, Pastorale, 1990, Violin Concerto, 1990, Romeo and Juliet Before Painting, 1990, Romance, 1990, Musings, 1991, Desir, 1991, Mixed Program, 1991, Mirror, 1991, This Isn't the End, 1991, The First Dance, 1992, The Miraculous Mandarin, 1993, Vittoria Pas De Deux, 1993, Ghosts, 1993, New York, 1993, Making Ballet, 1993, The Actress, 1994, Spring Awakening, 1994, Gluck Pas De Deux, 1994, Heroes, 1994, The Nutcracker, 1995, Solo for Rex, 1995, Missing, 1995, I'm a Stranger Here Myself, 1996, A Piece for Walter, 1996, Daisy's Dead, 1996, The Four Seasons, 1997, Les Chemins de L'Amour, 1998, Swan Lake, 1999, A Disembodied Voice, 1999, The Firebird, 2000, Nora's Tarantella, 2000, The Contract, Nat. Ballet Can., 2002, Chacony, 2004, Cinderella, 2004, An Italian Straw Hat, 2005, (ballets) Genesis, Les Grands Ballets Canadiens, 1982, In Paradisum, 1983, Alliances, 1984, Le Sacre du Printemps, 1987, La Salle des Pas Perdus, 1988, Concerto Grosso, 1988, Cruel World, Am. Ballet Theatre, 1994, Sin and Tonic, 2002, States of Grace, 1995, Dreams of Harmony, San Francisco Ballet, 1987, The End, 1992, Terra Firma, 1995, Some Women and Men, 1998, Le Baiser de la fée, Birmingham Royal Ballet, The Book of Alleged Dances, Australian Ballet, 1999, Fifteen Heterosexual Duets, Toronto Dance Theatre, Six Tableaus for the Sexually Challenged, Montreal Danse, Gazebo Dances, 2003, Cinderella, 2004, Passage, 1981, Intimate Letter, 1981, Hedda, 1983, Court of Miracles, 1983. Office: Walter Carsen Centre for The Nat Ballet of Can 470 Queens Quay W Toronto ON Canada M5V 3K4 E-mail: info@ballet.ca.*

KUDISH, DAVID J., financial executive; b. NYC, Aug. 10, 1943; s. L. Ben and Nellie D. (Kaufman) K.; m. Sheri K. Ross; children: Lisa, Seth, Debra. BS, U. Rochester, 1965; MS, U. Minn., 1967; postgrad., Harvard. U., 1996. With Dean Witter & Co., Inc., N.Y.C., 1968-73; with Oppenheimer & Co., N.Y.C., 1973-74; ptnr., dir. investment services Hewitt Assocs., Lincolnshire, Ill., 1974-82; pres., mng. dir. Stratford Adv. Group, Inc., Chgo., 1982—2001; pres. Stratford Investment Group, Inc., 1983-2000, Advocatae Investment Advisors, LLC (now called Advocate Asset Mgmt., LLC), Chgo., 2000—. Asset mgr. pension, endowment and charitable funds. Editor Benefits Quar. Mem. Mayor's Energy Task Force, City of Chgo.; gov. mem. Sustaining Fellows, Art Inst. Chgo., Contemporary Art Cir. of Mus. Contemporary Art; benefactor Lyric Opera of Chgo.; mem. gala com. Chgo. Abused Women's Coalition; bd. dirs. Com. for Accuracy in Mid. East Reporting in Am., Aspen Cmty. Campaign; mem. Jewish Cmty. Rels. Coun., Jewish Fedn. Met. Chgo.; mem. exec. bd. Chgo. chpt. Am. Jewish Com.; bd. govs. The Investigative Project; adv. bd. Middle East Forum; regent Ctr. Security Policy; lectr (Aspen, Chgo., Cleve.) Terrorism and the Media. With USAF, 1968, Air NG, 1968-73. Minn. Mining and Mgr. fellow U. Minn., 1967; NSF grantee, 1967 Mem. Tau Beta Pi, Sigma Alpha Mu. Clubs: Standard. Republican. Jewish. Office: Advocate Asset Mgmt LLC Ste 1510 10 S Riverside Plz Chicago IL 60606 Office Phone: 312-756-0074. Office Fax: 312-756-0084.

KUDO, EMIKO IWASHITA, former state official; b. Kona, Hawaii, June 5, 1923; d. Tetsuzo and Kuma (Koga) Iwashita; m. Thomas Mitsugi Kudo, Aug. 21, 1951; children: Guy J.T., Scott K., Candace F. BS, U. Hawaii, 1944; MS in Vocat. Edn., Pa. State U., 1950; postgrad., U. Hawaii, U. Oreg. Tchr. jr. & sr. h.s., Hawaii, 1945-51; instr. home econs. edn. U. Hawaii Tchrs. Coll., Honolulu, 1948-51, Pa. State U., State College, 1949-50; with Hawaii Dept. Edn., Honolulu, 1951-82, supr. sch. lunch svc., 1951-64, home econs. edn., 1964-68, adminstr. vocat.-tecy. edn., 1968-78; dep. supt. State Dept. Edn., Honolulu, 1978-82, cons. Am. Samoa vocat. edn. state plan devel., 1970-71; vocat. edn. U. Hawaii, 1986. Internat. secondary program devel. Ashiya Ednl. Sys., Japan, 1986-91; cons. to atty. gen. mental health svcs. for children and adolscents State of Hawaii, 1994; chief planner devel. State of Hawaii Children & Adolscents Mental Health Svcs. Implementation Plan, 1994-95; state coord. industry-labor-edn., 1972-76; mem. nat. task force edn. and tng. for minority bus. enterprise, 1972-73; mem. steering com. Career Info. Ctr. Project, 1973-78; co-dir. Hawaii Career Devel. Continuum project, 1971-74;

mem. Nat. Accreditation and Instl. Eligibility Adv. Coun., 1974-77, cons., 1977-78; mem. panel Internat. Conf. Vocat. Guidance, 1978, 80, 82, 86, 88; state commr. edn. commn. of the states, 1982-90; mem. Hawaii edn. coun., 1982-90. Author handbooks and pamphlets in field. Dir. Dept. Parks and Recreation, City and County of Honolulu, 1982-84; bd. dirs. Honolulu Neighborhood Housing Svcs., 1991—; exec. bd. Aloha coun. Boy Scouts Am., 1978-88; bd. trustees St. Louis H.S., 1988-95; mem. Gov.'s Commn. on Sesquicentennial Observance of Pub. Edn. in Hawaii, 1990-91; mem. Commn. State Rental Housing Trust Fund, 1992-98; mem. steering com. Hawaii Long Term Care Coalition, 1992—. Japan Found. Cultural grantee, 1977; Pa. State U. Alumni fellow, 1982; named to Konawaea H.S. Hall of Fame, 1997. Mem. ASCD, NEA, Am. Assn. Retired Persons (mem. state legis. com. 1990-92), Pa. State U. Disting. Alumni, Western Assn. Schs. and Colls. (accreditation team mem. Ch. Coll. of Hawaii 1972-73), Am. Vocat. Assn., Hawaii Vocat. Assn., Hawaii Edn. Assn. (trustee 1992—), Hawaii State Ednl. Officers Assn., Am. Family Consumer Sci. Assn., Hawaii Assn. Curriculum & Devel., Am. Tech. Edn. Assn., Hawaii Recreation and Park Assn., Omicron Nu, Pi Lambda Theta, Phi Delta Kappa, Delta Kappa Gamma. Home and Office: 217 Nenue St Honolulu HI 96821-1811

KUDRLE, ROBERT THOMAS, economist, educator; b. Sioux City, Iowa, Aug. 23, 1942; s. Chester John and Helen Marguerite (Crakes) K.; m. Venetia Hilary Mary Thomas, July 20, 1970; children: Paul John Reginald, Thomas David Chester. AB, Harvard U., 1964, AM, 1969, PhD, 1974; MPhil., U. Oxford, Eng., 1967. Grad. rsch. assoc. Ctr. Internat. Affairs Harvard U., Cambridge, Mass., 1969-71; instr. Tex. A & M Univ., College Station, 1971-72; asst., assoc. prof. Humphrey Inst. U. Minn., Mpls., 1972-83, asst., assoc. dir. Ctr. Internat. Studies, 1972-82, prof. Humphrey Inst., 1983—, dir. MA program pub. affairs, 1984-86, dir. Freeman Ctr. Internat. Econ. Policy, 1990-97, assoc. dean rsch. Humphrey Inst., 1992-96. Cons. U.S. Dept. Justice, U.S. AID, Urban Inst., UN Ctr. Transnat. Corps., Consumer and Corp. Affairs Can., WHO, others. Author: Agricultural Tractors: A World Industry Study, 1975; co-author State Evaluation of Foreign Sales Efforts, 1988; co-editor Reducing the Cost of Dental Care, 1983, The Industrial Future of the Pacific Basin, 1984, Jour. Internat. Studies Quarterly, 1980-84, 85; mem. editorial bd. Internat. Political Economy Yearbook, 1983—, Jour. Health Politics, Policy & Law, 1981-92; contbr. articles to profl. jours., chpts. to texts. 1st v.p. UN Assn. Minn., Mpls., 1976—78, mem. adv. coun., 1978—88. Graduate prize fellow Harvard U., 1967-69, Pew Faculty fellow in Internat. Affairs Harvard U., 1990-91; Nuffield Coll. studentship, Oxford, Eng., 1966-67; Rhodes scholar, Oxford, Eng., 1964-67. Mem. Assn. Pub. Policy Analysis and Mgmt. (instl. rep. 1988-97), Internat. Studies Assn. (v.p. 1998-99), Am. Econ. Assn., Harvard Club Minn. Avocations: running, gardening. Home: 4650 Fremont Ave S Minneapolis MN 55409-2263 Office: Humphrey Inst Pub Affairs 301 19th Ave S Ste 300 Minneapolis MN 55455-0429 Business E-Mail: bkudrle@hhh.umn.edu.

KUDRNA, JAMES, architecture educator; BArch, U. Nebr., 1974, MArch, 1979. Registered arch., Colo., 1976. Engrng. draftsman Omaha Pub. Power Dist., 1969—73; archtl. draftsman Glenn Stippich and Assocs., Nebr., 1974—76; asst. designer Henningson, Durham and Richardson, Nebr., 1976, project designer, 1977—79; asst. prof. U. Okla., Norman, 1977—85, assoc. prof. divsn. arch., 1985—, dir. arch., 1988—92, acting dean, 1994, dir. divsn. arch., 2000—. Cooperating ptnr. Studio "C", Norman, 1983—85. Recipient Disting. Lectureship award, U. Okl.a; Bd. Visitors fellow, U. Okla., 1991. Mem.: ACSA (accreditation team designate), AIA (ex-officio Okla. Coun. Archs. 1990—91, instr. Ctrl. Okla. chpt. 1988, Profl. award Nebr. chpt. 1976, hon. mention Edn. Honors Program 1990). Office: Univ Oka 319 Gould Hall Divsn Arch 830 Van Vleet Oval Norman OK 73019

KUDROW, LISA (LISA MARIE DIANE KUDROW), actress; b. Encino, Calif., July 30, 1963; d. Lee and Nedra Kudrow; m. Michael Stern, May 27, 1995; 1 child, Julian Murray. BS in Biology, Vassar Coll., Poughkeepsie, N.Y., 1985. Actress (TV series) Mad About You, 1991-99, Friends, 1994-2004 (Emmy award outstanding supporting actress, 1998, SAG award outstanding performance female, 2000, Am. Comedy award, 2000, Golden Satellite award best actress, 2000), Hopeless Pictures, 2005; (TV guest appearances) Cheers, 1989, Newhart, 1990, Life Goes On, 1990, Coach, 1993-94, Flying Blind, 1993, Hope & Gloria, 1996, The Simpsons (voice), 1998; (films) The Crazysitter, 1995, Romy and Michele's High School Reunion, 1997, Clockwatchers, 1997, The Opposite of Sex, 1998 (NY Film Critics Circle award, 2000), Hercules (voice) 1998, Analyze This, 1998, Hanging Up, 2000, All Over the Guy, 2001, Dr. Dolittle 2 (voice), 2001, Analyze That, 2002, Marci X, 2003, Wonderland, 2003, Happy Endings, 2005; exec. prodr.: (TV films) Picking Up and Dropping Off, 2003; actress, exec. prodr., writer (TV series) The Comeback, 2005; (music video) The Rembrandts I'll Be There For You, 1995. Named an 50 Most Beautiful People in World, People mag., 1997. Mem.: Groundlings Improv Group.*

KUDRYASHEVA, ALEKSANDRA A., microbiologist, nutritionist; b. Tula, Russia, Jan. 1, 1934; d. Andrew P. and Neonila K. (Volkonogova) Chernozhukov; m. Michael N. Kudryashev (dec.); m. Dan B. Chopyk, Dec. 19, 1990. BS in Biology, All-Union Inst. Food Industry, Moscow, 1965, DSc, 1969; PhD in Tech. Biol. Scis., Russia, 1983; PhD (hon.), Volgograd Tech. Inst., 1996. Technologist Glavkonserv Food Ministry, Govt. of USSR, Eisk, Krasnodar Region, 1954-61, head. of lab. irradiation microbiology Tula, 1962-71; from asst. prof. to prof. Russian Acad. Economy, Moscow, 1971-93, dean tech. and commodities, 1983-85, head dept. biotech., 1985-93; head food resources Inst. of Human Ecology, Moscow, 1993-97; pres. Internat. Ctr. Nutrition and Health Rehab., Toms River, N.J., 1997—; cons. UNO, 2001—03. V.p. radiology of food products, Russian Acad. Agr., Moscow, 1976-89; pres. Assn. of Commodities Specialists of USSR, 1985-91; chmn. cert. com. Coun. of Ministers of USSR, 1989-96; sec. commodities sect. Ministry of Edn., Govt. of USSR, 1978-85. Author: Humanity, Biodiversity and Environment (in Russian), 2004; contbr. more than 400 articles to sci. and profl. jours., books; holder more than 50 patents. Mem. Russian Acad. Natural Scis. (silver medal), Union of Concerned Scientists, N.Y. Acad. Scis., Internat. Info. Acad. (internat. prize 1996). Achievements include radiobiological and microbiological methods of food preservation; new technologies of manufacture and application of natural bio-correctors for food, medicine, agriculture and ecology. Avocations: travel, photography, ethnic cooking, poetry. Home and Office: 106 Guadeloupe Dr Toms River NJ 08757

KUDSK, KENNETH ALLAN, surgeon; b. Chgo., May 27, 1949; s. Kenneth and Hildegard Amanda (Toepel) K.; divorced. BA, U. Wis., 1971; MD, U. Ill., Chgo., 1975. Diplomate Am. Bd. Surgery, Am. Bd. Surg. Critical Care. Intern Ohio State U., Columbus, 1975-76, resident in surgery, 1977-79, 81-83; fellow in trauma San Francisco Gen. Hosp., 1979-81. Co. dir. trauma svcs. Ohio State U., 1983-87, dir. nutrition support svcs., 1984-87, asst. prof. surgery, 1983-87; staff Regional Med. Ctr., Memphis; assoc. prof. surgery U. Tenn., 1987-93, dir. surg. rsch., 1988-2001, assoc. prof. anesthesiology, 1989-2001, prof. surgery 1993-2001, prof. emergency medicine, 1994-2001; dir. nutrition support svcs. William F. Bowld Hosp., Memphis, 1995-2001; dir. surg. intensive care Regional Med. Ctr., Memphis, 1991-2001, nutrition support svcs.; prof. surgery, vice-chmn. surg. rsch. U. Wis., Madison, 2001—. Contbr. over 275 articles to profl. jours., chpts. to books. Fellow ACS; mem. Am. Surg. Assn., Am. Assn. for Surgery of Trauma, Am. Soc. for Parenteral and Enteral Nutrition, Assn. for Acad. Surgery, Shock Soc., Surg. Infection Soc., S.E. Surg. Congress, Soc. Internat. de Chirurgie, Ea. Assn. for the Surgery of Trauma, Soc. of Mucosal Immunology, Soc. Critical Care Medicine, Soc. for Surgery of Alimentary Tract, Soc. Univ. Surgeons, So. Surg. Assn. Lutheran. Home: 125 N Hamilton St 1404 Madison WI 53703 Office Phone: 608-262-2430. E-mail: kudsk@surgery.wisc.edu.

KUEBLER, CHRISTOPHER ALLEN, pharmaceutical executive; b. Hamilton, Ohio, Oct. 31, 1953; s. William E. and E. Dean (Morgan) K.; m. Susan Kuebler; children: Megan, Lauren, Samantha. BS, Fla. State U., 1975. Various sales and product mgmt. positions E.R. Squibb & Sons, Princeton, N.J., 1976-84; mgr. product devel. Monsanto Health Care, St. Louis, 1985-86; group product mgr. Abbott Pharms., Abbott Park, Ill., 1986-89, v.p. mktg. and sales, 1989-93; corp. v.p. European operation Abbott Internat., Abbott Park, 1993-95; CEO Covance Inc., Princeton, 1995—2004, chmn., 1995—. Bd. mem. Nat. Pharm. Coun., Washington, Inhale Therapeutic Systems, San Carlos, Calif.; mem. mktg. steering com. Pharm. & Rsch. Mfrs. Assn., Washington, 2001--. Office: Covance Inc 210 Carnegie Ctr Princeton NJ 08540-6233

KUECHLE, JOHN MERRILL, lawyer; b. Mpls., Dec. 18, 1951; s. Harry Bronson and Virginia (McClure) K.; m. Nancy Anderson, June 20, 1976; 1 child, David Michael. AB magna cum laude, Occidental Coll., 1974; JD cum laude, Harvard U., 1977. Bar: Calif. 1977. Assoc. Mitchell, Silberberg & Knupp, L.A., 1977-83, ptnr., 1983-2000, of counsel, 2001—. Mem. Phi Beta Kappa. Republican. Episcopalian. Avocations: masters track and field, orienteering, rock climbing. Home: 10733 Ranch Rd Culver City CA 90230-5458 Office: Mitchell Silberberg & Knupp 11377 W Olympic Blvd Los Angeles CA 90064-1625 Office Phone: 310-312-3139. Business E-Mail: jmk@post.harvard.edu.

KUEHL, HANS HENRY, electrical engineering educator; b. Detroit, Mar. 16, 1933; s. Henry Martin and Hilde (Schrader) K.; m. Anna Meidinger, July 25, 1965; children: Susan, Michael. BS, Princeton U., 1955; MS, Calif. Inst. Tech., 1956, PhD, 1959. Asst. prof. elec. engrng. U. So. Calif., 1960-63, assoc. prof., 1963-72, prof., 1972—2004, prof. emeritus, 2004—, chmn. dept. elec. engrng., electrophysics, 1987-98. Cons. Deutsch Co., L.A., 1973, Hughes Aircraft Co., Culver City, Calif., 1975. Contbr. articles to profl. jours. Recipient U. So. Calif. Teaching Excellence award, 1964, Haliburton award U. So. Calif., 1980. Fellow IEEE; mem. Am. Phys. Soc., Internat. Sci. Radio Union, Eta Kappa Nu (bd. dirs. 2000-02, Outstanding Faculty award 1977). Avocations: tennis, racquetball. Office: U So Calif Elec Engring Dept Phe 622 Mc 0271 Los Angeles CA 90089-0271 Business E-Mail: kuehl@usc.edu.

KUEHL, JEFFRY STEVEN (JEFF KEEL), art association administrator, actor; b. Elkader, Iowa, Oct. 12, 1962; s. Harvey James and Shirley Ann Kuehl; m. Julie Ann Westhafer, July 2, 1988; children: Kooper, Jillian, Spencer. BA in Theatre Arts, Winona State U., Minn., 1985. Sales Cellular Shop, Greensburg, Ind., 1997—99, WTRE Radio, Greensburg, 1999; actor Ind. Repertory, Indpls., 1998—; storyteller Children's Mus. of Indpls., 1998—; region 9 coord. Columbus (Ind,) Area Arts Coun., 2000—. Dir. Boar's Head and Yule Log Festival, Oldenburg, Ind., 2000—; grant evaluator Ind. Arts Commn., Indpls., 2001, 02, 04, mem. Gov.'s Arts Awards selection com., 03, 05. Actor: (films) Night Terror, 1989. Nominee Best Supporting Actor in a Drama, Backstage West Mag., 1995. Mem.: AFTRA, Actor's Equity, Decatur County Youth Soccer Club (pres. 2003—). Office: Columbus Area Arts Council 302 Washington Columbus IN 47201 Office Phone: 812-376-2539.

KUEHL, SHEILA JAMES, state legislator; b. Tulsa, Feb. 9, 1941; d. Arthur Joseph and Lillian Ruth (Krasner) K. BA, UCLA, 1962; JD, Harvard U., 1978. Actress, 1950-65; assoc. dean of students UCLA, 1969-75; pvt. practice L.A., 1978-85; law prof. Loyola U. of L.A., 1985-89; mng. atty. Calif. Women's Law Ctr., L.A., 1989-93; mem. Calif. State Assembly, Sacramento, 1995-2000, spkr. pro tem, 1997-99, chair jud. com., 1999-2000; mem. Calif. State Senate, 2001—, chmn. natural resources and water com., 2001—. Appeared in TV series Broadside, 1964-65, as Zelda Gilroy in Dobie Gillis, 1959-63, as Jackie Erwin in Trouble with Father, 1950-56. Mem. gender bias adv. com. Calif. Supreme Ct., 1985-91; bd. overseers Harvard U., 1997—. Named One of 20 Most Fascinating Women in Politics, George Mag., 1996, named One of 100 Most Influential Attys. in Calif., Calif. Law Bus., 1998; recipient Barry Goldwater Human Rights award, 1998, Legislator of Yr., Calif. Pks. and Recreation Soc., 1999, Pub. Svc. award UCLA Alumni Assn., 2000, Liberty award Lambda Legal Def. Edn. Fund, 2002, Women in Govt. award Good Housekeeping, 2003, Corageous Leader award, Women Against Gun Violence, 2005. Mem.: LA County Psychol. Assn. (Dinsting. Legislator 2004). Office: State Capitol Sacramento CA 95814-4906 Office Phone: 916-651-4023.

KUEHLING, ROBERT WARREN, lawyer, accountant; b. Madison, Wis., Aug. 31, 1952; s. Warren Ernest and Mary Alice (Jenkins) K.; m. Susan Mary O'Brien, July 8, 1978; children: Megan Ann, Jeffrey Robert. BBA, U. Wis., JD, 1976. Bar: Wis. 1977, U.S. Dist. Ct. (we. dist.) Wis. 1977, Fla. 2003; CPA. Ptnr. Kuehling & Kuehling, Madison, 1977—. Office: Kuehling & Kuehling 131 W Wilson St Ste 501 Madison WI 53703-3243 Office Phone: 608-257-1918. E-mail: kuehling@execpc.com.

KUEHN, BARBARA JEAN, lawyer; b. Frankfurt, Germany, May 10, 1952; parents U.S. citizens; d. Robert Adolf Kuehn and Lucy Elvira Miele; 1 child, Joanne Stephanik. AA, Coll. San Mateo, 1982; JD, San Francisco U., 1985. Bar: Calif. 1991. Family law atty. Anderlini, Guheen, Finkelstein & Emerick, 1991-92; pvt. practice San Mateo County, Calif., 1992—. Active Nat. Womens Polit. Caucus, 1992-96, v.p. San Mateo caucus, 1993. Mem. ABA, Calif. Women Lawyers (life, bd. govs. 1993-97, sec. 1994-95, 1st v.p. 1995-96, Pres. award 1994), State Bar Calif. (Wiley W. Manuel Pro Bono Legal Svcs. award 1994), Barristers San Mateo County Bar Assn. (pres. 1993, 94, Barrister of Yr. San Mateo County 1993, 94, 95), Delta Theta Phi (dean 1984-85). Democrat. Roman Catholic. Office: 630 N San Mateo Dr San Mateo CA 94401-2328 Fax: 650-373-2072. E-mail: bbqnesq@earthlink.net.

KUEHN, GEORGE E., lawyer; b. N.Y.C., June 19, 1946; m. Mary Kuehn; children: Kristin, Rob, Geoff. BBA, U. Mich., 1968, JD, 1973. Bar: Mich. 1974. Assoc. Hill, Lewis et al, Detroit, 1974-78; ptnr. Butzel, Long et al, Detroit, 1978-81; exec. v.p., gen. counsel, sec. The Stroh Brewery Co., Detroit, 1981-99—; shareholder Butzel Long, Detroit, 2000—. With U.S. Army, 1969-71. Office: Butzel Long 150 W Jefferson Ave Ste 100 Detroit MI 48226 Office Phone: 313-225-7058. E-mail: Kuehn@butzel.com.

KUEHN, JAMES MARSHALL, newspaper editor; b. Mobridge, S.D., May 23, 1926; s. Christ A. and Selma (Brandon) K.; m. Phyllis Yvonne Larson, Apr. 3, 1950; children— Douglas James, Deborah Kay, Diana Lisa. BA, U.S.D., 1949. State editor Rapid City (S.D.) Jour., 1949-54, wire editor, 1954-58, mng. editor, 1958-66, exec. editor, 1966-73, v.p.-editor, 1973-86. Vice pres. Rapid City Library Bd., 1969-73; dir. Mt. Rushmore Nat. Meml. Soc., 1991-2005. Served with C.E. AUS, 1945-46. Mem. Rapid City C. of C. (v.p. 1970-73), S.D. C. of C. (dir. 1978-81), Lambda Chi Alpha. Lodges: Kiwanis (pres. 1973-74). Republican. Lutheran. Personal E-mail: jmpykuehn@rushmore.com.

KUEHN, MICHAEL ROBERT, biomedical researcher; b. Chgo., Ill., July 25, 1953; PhD, Stony Brook, Stony Brook, N.Y., 1982. Asst. prof. U. Ill. Coll. of Medicine, Chgo., 1988—91; investigator Nat. Cancer Inst., Bethesda, Md., 1991—98, sr. investigator Frederick, Md., 1999—. Office: Natl Cancer Inst Bldg 560/Rm 12-90 NCI-Frederick Frederick MD 21702 Office Phone: 301-846-7451. Business E-Mail: mkuehn@mail.nih.gov.

KUEHN, RONALD L., JR., natural resources company executive; b. Bklyn., Apr. 6, 1935; m. Allison Spencer, June 7, 1986; children: Kathleen, Kelly, Erin, Coleen, Shannon, Caroline, Ronald L. III. BS, Fordham U., 1957, LL.B., 1964. Bar: N.Y. 1964. Assoc. Hughes, Hubbard & Reed, N.Y.C., 1964-68; exec. v.p., gen. counsel Allied Artists Pictures, N.Y.C., 1968-70; v.p., gen. counsel, sec. So. Natural Resources, Inc., Birmingham, Ala., 1970-79, exec. v.p., 1979-81; COO Sonat Inc., 1982-83, pres., CEO, 1984—99, chmn. bd., 1986-99, ret., 1999; non-exec. chmn. El Paso Corp., 1999—2000, consultant, 2001—03, lead dir., 2002—03, interim CEO, 2003, chmn., 2003—. Bd. dirs. Transocean Offshore, Inc., AmSouth Bancorp., Praxair Inc., The Dun & Bradstreet Corp.; trustee Tuskegee U. 1st lt. U.S. Army, 1958-59. Mem. ABA, N.Y. State Bar Assn., Assn. of Bar of City of N.Y., Fed. Energy Bar Assn., Newcomen Soc. of U.S., Bretton Woods Com. Roman Catholic. Office: El Paso Corporation 1001 Louisiana St Houston TX 77002

KUEHNE, MARTIN ERIC, chemist, educator; b. Floral Park, N.Y., May 29, 1931; s. Martin Ludwig and Ruth (Protze) K.; m. Hannelore E. Naumann, Aug. 15, 1953; 1 son, Stephen Eric. BA, Columbia, 1951, PhD, 1955; MA, Harvard, 1952. Sr. chemist Ciba Pharm. Co., Summit, N.J., 1955-61; mem. faculty U. Vt., Burlington, 1961—, asso. prof. chemistry, 1965-67, prof., 1967—, chmn. dept. chemistry, 1976-78. Boese fellow, 1954; Alfred P. Sloan Found. fellow, 1965-69 Mem. Am. Chem. Soc., Sigma Xi, Phi Lambda Upsilon. Research in new synthetic organic reactions; total syntheses of natural products; structure determinations of natural products; medicinal chems. Home: 169 S Cove Rd Burlington VT 05401-5443

KUEHNER, DENISE ANN, music educator, musician; b. Evanston, Ill., July 6, 1953; d. Alice Catherine Langan and Albert Edward Delgado; m. Eric Lee Kuehner, Oct. 26, 1954; children: Jeffrey Allen, Katherine Elizabeth. BME, Valparaiso U., 1977; MM in cello performance and lit., U. Notre Dame, 1984. Tchr., string specialist South Bend Cmty. Sch. Corp., Ind., 1984—; lectr./adj. faculty St. Mary's Coll., Notre Dame, Ind., 1986—. Sect. cellist NW Ind. Symphony, Gary, Ind., 1972—83; cellist Carlson String Quartet, South Bend, 1978—; sect. cellist SW Mich. Symphony, St. Joseph, Mich., 1979—84, South Bend Symphony Orch., Ind., 1981—; choir dir. St. Paul Luth. Ch., South Bend, Ind., 1984—; acad. youth orch. dir. Ind. U. at South Bend, South Bend, Ind., 1986—; guest condr. Ind. all-region orch. Am. String Tchrs. Assn., La Porte, Ind., 1987; sect. cellist/soloist Borderline Philharm. and Chamber Music Festival, Waubun, Minn., 1989—2003; cellist Whitewater String Trio, South Bend, 1996—; orch. guest condr. Gt. Lake Music Camp, Ind., 1998; orch. dir. Summer Symphonette, South Bend, Ind., 2000—; condr. SBCSC Firefly Prodns., South Bend, Ind., 2000—. Editor: (newsletter) Michiana Cello Society News of Note. Worship com. St. Paul Ch., South Bend, Ind., 1990—. Mem.: Nat. Educators Assn., Ind. Music Educators Assn., Nat. Sch. Orch. Assn., Am. String Tchrs. Assn., Sigma Alpha Iota (musical dir. 1975—76, Sword of Honor 1976). Lutheran (Ms). Avocations: reading, art appreciation, attending arts events (music/drama), dancing (in nutcracker ballet), singing for church, wedddings and parties. Home: 19576 Paxson Drive South South Bend IN 46637 Office: Clay High School 19131 Darden Rd South Bend IN 46637 Office Phone: 574-243-7037. E-mail: dkuehner@sbcsc.k12.in.us.

KUEHNLE, KENTON LEE, lawyer; b. Chgo., Nov. 10, 1945; s. Robert Louis and Mary Caroline (Recktenwald) K.; m. Sherry L. Esposito, June 6, 1970; children: Robert, Amanda, Matthew. BA, Augustana Coll., 1967; JD, Duke U., 1970. Bar: Ohio 1970, US Dist. Ct. (so. dist.) Ohio 1971. Assoc. Dunbar, Kienzle & Murphey, Columbus, Ohio, 1970-77; ptnr. Loveland, Callard & Clapham, Columbus, 1977-80, Scott, Walker & Kuehnle, Columbus, 1980-86, Thompson, Hine & Flory, Columbus, 1986—2001, Roetzel & Andress, Columbus, 2001—03, Allen, Kuehnle & Stovll, Columbus, 2003—. Instr. paralegal program Capital U. Law Sch., 1998-2001. Author: Ohio Real Estate Law, 3 vols., 2003, Ohio Condominium Law, 2005; co-author: Foreclosure Law, 1989-98, Title Insurance Endorsements, 1991-97, Commercial Leasing, 1994-97, Condominium Law, 1981-97, Use of Internet for Real Estate Lawyer, 1997, Ohio Condominium Law, 2005; contbr. articles to profl. jours. Mem. Augustana Coll. Alumni Bd., Rock Island, Ill., 1986-89; elder First Presbyn. Ch., Grove City, Ohio, 1990-93; pres. Computer Users Group, Columbus, 1985-86. Mem. ABA (sect. real property, probate and trust law 1973—, com. on condominium and coop. housing 1977—), Columbus Bar Assn. (chmn. real property com. 1976-78, chmn. micro computer subcom. 1986-87, 92-94, lectr. for bar assn. seminars), Ohio State Bar Assn. (bd. govs. real property sect. 1979-82, 90—, chmn. 1997-99, editor state real property sect. newsletter 1995-99, chmn. subcom. to rev. condominium statute 1980-81, mem. real property specialization bd. 2004—, lectr. continuing legal edn. programs), Am. Coll. Real Estate Lawyers (vice chair title ins. subcom., mem.condominium subcom.). Avocations: computer programming, baseball, theology. Home: 11325 Big Plain Circleville Rd Orient OH 43146-9301 Office: Allen Kuehnle & Stovall 21 West Borad St Ste 400 Columbus OH 43215 Office Phone: 614-221-8500. Business E-Mail: kkuehnle@prodigy.net. E-mail: kuehnle@akslaw.net.

KUELBS, JOHN THOMAS, lawyer; b. Springfield, Minn., Sept. 8, 1942; s. Alois Nicholas and Lucille Marie (Neudecker) K; m. J. Michele Norton; children: Susan, Thomas. BA, St. John's U., Collegeville, Minn., 1965; JD, Creighton U., 1973. Bar: Nebr. 1973, Calif. 1980, U.S. Ct. Claims, U.S. Ct. Appeals (9th circuit), U.S. Ct. Appeals (D.C. circuit), U.S. Supreme Ct. Sr. counsel Ford Aerospace, Newport Beach, Calif., 1976-78, divsn. counsel, 1978-81; group counsel Hughes Aircraft, El Segundo, Calif., 1981-86, staff v.p., asst. gen. counsel, 1986-88, v.p., assoc. gen. counsel L.A., 1988-94, sr. v.p., gen. counsel Arlington, Va., 1994-98; sr. v.p. legal Raytheon Sys. Co., Arlington, 1998-99, sr. v.p. acquisition policy, 1999. Col. (ret.) JAGC, U.S. Army, 1976. Mem. ABA (pub. contract law sect. coun. 1992-94, coun. officer 1994-96, sec. pub. contract law sect. chair 1996-97), FBA, Calif. Bar Assn., Nebr. Bar Assn.; fellow ABA Pub. Contract Law Assn., Nat. Contract Mgmt. Assn. Office: Raytheon Corp Ops 1100 Wilson Blvd Ste 1500 Arlington VA 22209-2297

KÜENG, CHRISTIAN ROULLAND, director; b. Pomona, Calif., Mar. 28, 1957; s. Robert and Margrith Küeng; adopted children: Tamerisa, John, Cody. AA, Chaffey Coll., Calif., 1977; BA, Calif. State U., 1980; MA, Azusa (Calif.) Pacific U., 1982; EdD, U. LaVerne (Calif.), 2003. Cert. single subject tchg., pupil personnel svcs., multiple subject tchg., profl. adminstrv. svcs. Asst. prin. Corona Norco (Calif.) Unified Sch. Dist., 1990—93; gate adminstr. Ontario (Calif.) and Montclair Sch. Dist., 1996—99, tchr. K, 2d, 4th-6th, 1993—97, project adminstr. intern program, 1997—99, asst. prin., 1999—2000, elem. prin., coord. performing arts and phys. edn., 2000—04; dir. curriculum and assessment Hemet Unified Sch. Dist., 2005—. Cons. pre-intern program Calif. Commn. on Tchr. Credentialing, Ontario, Calif., 1998—99. Mem. bd. trustees Mus. of History and Art, Ontario, Calif., 1999—; mem Ontario First Christian Ch., 1996—. Recipient Hon. Svc. award, Parent Tchr. Assn., 1998. Mem.: Assn. Calif. Sch. Adminstrs. Avocations: drawing, cartooning, writing children's stories, gardening, model trains. Home: 1341 N Euclid Ave Ontario CA 91762-1624

KUENN, MARJORIE ASP, music educator; b. Moorhead, Minn., Dec. 26, 1951; d. Robert Louis and Violet Rose Asp; m. Brent Jay Kuenn, Feb. 25, 1978 (div. Jan. 2001). *Grandparents Charles and Inga Asp and Lars and Hannah Foldoe were Swedish and Norwegian immigrants. They brought with them a strong work ethic and a desire for a better life. They believed that education and hard work were the means to accomplish their goals. Charles Asp became an educator. Her father Robert Asp was also an educator and a visionary. He built the Viking longship "Hjemkomst" that sailed from Duluth to Oslo Norway in 1982, and is now on display in Moorhead Minnesota. Robert and Rose Asp instilled in their children the belief that success is an attainable goal.* EdB in Violin, U. So. Miss., 1973, EdM, 1974. Violinist Fargo-Moorhead Symphony, 1967—69, Meridian (Miss.) Symphony, 1969—79, Jackson (Miss.) Symphony, 1969—79, Jackson Mini-Orch., 1969—79, Miss. Opera South, 1969—79, Miss. Opera, 1969—79, Gulfcoast (Miss.) Symphony, 1969—79, Miss. Ballet Orch., 1969—79, Mobile (Ala.) Opera, 1969—79, Tupelo (Miss.) Symphony, 1969—79, Greenville (Miss.) Symphony, 1969—79, Monroe (La.) Symphony, 1969—79, U. So. Miss. Symphony, Opera, Chamber & Ensemble, 1969—74; tchr. Jackson Symphony Orch., 1974—79; dir. orch. Hickman Mills Sch. Dist., Kansas City, Mo., 1979—; chair dept. music Smith-Hale Mid. Sch., Kansas city, 1990—. *Marjorie Kuenn has 23 years of experience working in the church music ministry. She has worked with instrumentalists and vocalists, and has taught vocal technique classes to choirs in several churches. She is currently teaching vocal techniques at Grace Baptist Church in Lee's Summit, Missouri.* Author: Vocal Techniques, vol. I, 1998, Vocal Techniques, vol. II, 2003, Choir Warm-up Exercises, 2002. Music scholar, U. So. Miss., 1969—73, Grad. Music Studies fellow, 1973—74. Mem.: U. So. Miss. Alumni Assn., Am. Fedn. Tchrs., Music Educators Nat. Conf., Mu Phi Epsilon, Alpha Lambda Delta. Avocations: sewing, reading, exercise. Office: Smith-Hale Mid Sch 8925 Longview Rd Kansas City MO 64134 Office Phone: 816-316-7663.

KUENNE, ROBERT EUGENE, economics professor; b. St. Louis, Jan. 29, 1924; s. Edward Sebastian and Margaret (Yochum) K.; m. Janet Lawrence Brown, Sept. 7, 1957; children: Christopher Brian, Carolyn Leigh Jeppsen. Student, Harris Jr. Coll., St. Louis, 1941-42; B.J., U. Mo., 1947; AB, Washington U., St. Louis, 1948, A.M., 1949, Harvard, 1951, PhD, 1953; PhD (hon.), Umea U., 1985. Asst. prof. econs. U. Va., 1955; mem. faculty Princeton (N.J.) U., 1956—, assoc. prof., 1960-69, prof. econs., 1969—. Cons. U.S. Naval War Coll., 1954, 55, Inst. Def. Analyses, Arlington, Va., 1968—2001, Inst. for Energy Analysis, Washington, 1978-82; vis. prof. mil. systems analysis U.S. Army War Coll., 1967-85; mem. sci. and mgmt. adv. com. U.S. Army Computer Systems Command. Author: The Theory of General Economic Equilibrium, 1963, The Attack Submarine: A Study in Strategy, 1965, The Polaris Missile Strike: A General Economic Systems Analysis, 1966, Monopolistic Competition Theory: Studies in Impact, 1967, Microeconomic Theory of the Market Mechanism, 1968, Eugen von Böhm-Bawerk, 1971, Rivalrous Consonance, 1986, Economics of Oligopolistic Competition, 1992, General Equilibrium Economics, 1991, Economic Justice in American Society, 1993, Price and Nonprice Rivalry in Oligopoly: The Integrated Battleground, 1999. Served with AUS, 1943-46. Named Oliver Ellsworth Bicentennial preceptor, 1975-60; fellow European Econs. and Fin. Ctr., 1992—; Fulbright fellow, 1991. Mem. Princeton Club (N.Y.C.). Home: 63 Bainbridge St Princeton NJ 08540-3901 Office: Princeton U Dept Econs Princeton NJ 08544-0001 Personal E-mail: kuenne@princeton.edu.

KUENNEN, THOMAS GERARD, journalist; b. St. Louis, June 30, 1953; s. George Glennon and Earline (Doherty) K.; m. Anne L. Gillette, Sept. 10, 1988; 1 child, Madeline Livingston. BJ, U. Mo., 1975. Copy editor Macon (Ga.) Telegraph & News, 1976-77; news editor Mascoutah (Ill.) Herald, and related newspapers, 1977-79; pub. rels. assoc. Booker Assocs., Inc., St. Louis, 1979-80, Fru Con Corp., St. Louis, 1980-81; assoc. editor Rock Products Mag., Chgo., 1981-84; editor Roads & Bridges Mag., Des Plaines, Ill., 1984-95; prin., editor Expresswaysonline.com, Wheeling, Ill., 1995—. Mem. editl. com. Am. Bus. Press, N.Y.C., 1984-85. Contbg. editor: Concrete Products, Better Roads, Constrn. Equipment. Recipient Jesse H. Neal award Am. Bus. Press, 1983, Svc. award La. Associated Gen. Contractors, 1990, Editl. Excellence award Am. Soc. Bus. Press Editors, 1998, finalist Jesse H. Neal award, 2005. Mem. Constrn. Writers Assn. (bd. dirs. 1985-86, 95-99, Robert F. Boger award 1985, 93, 95, 98, Hon. Mention 2003), The Rd. Info. Program (bd. dirs. 1999—), Road Gang, Nat. Asphalt Pavement Assn. (Hot Mix Hall of Fame), Women in Comm. (treas. 1983-84, Cub's Cup 1985). Roman Catholic. Office: Expresswaysonline.com 251 N Milwaukee Ave Ste 224B Buffalo Grove IL 60089

KUENSTER, JOHN JOSEPH, editor; b. Chgo., June 18, 1924; s. Roy Jacob and Katheryn (Holechek) Kuenster; m. Mary Virginia Maher, Feb. 15, 1947 (dec. Feb. 1983); m. Suely Brazão, July 1, 1995. Editor The Columbian, Chgo., 1948-57; staff writer Chgo. Daily News, Chgo., 1957-65; dir. devel. and pub. rels. Mercy Hosp., Chgo., 1965-66; sr. writer The Claretians, Chgo., 1966—; editor Baseball Digest, Evanston, Ill., 1969—; exec. editor Century Pub. Co., Evanston. Author: (book) Cobb to Catfish, Heartbreakers, At Home and Away, How St. Jude Came to Chicago, (booklet) The Police, Money, Mission in Guatemala, Honesty, Is it the Best Policy?; co-author: (book) To Sleep with the Angels. Mem.: Baseball Writers' Assn. Am. Roman Catholic. Office: Baseball Digest Century Publishing Co 990 Grove St Evanston IL 60201-6510 Office Phone: 847-491-6440. Business E-Mail: jkuenster@centurysports.net.

KUES, IRVIN WILLIAM, financial planner; b. Balt., Apr. 23, 1936; s. Harry Irvin and Theresa Frances (Seliga) K.; m. Mary Carolyn Gaff, Oct. 24, 1959; Pamela, Janet, Lynne, Leslie. BS in Engring. Sci., Johns Hopkins U., 1957, M in Bus. Sci., 1959. Cert. data processer. Rsch. analyst Am. Newspaper Rsch. Inst., Chgo., 1957-59; mgmt. analyst Western Elec. Co., Balt., 1959-61; asst. supt. E.D.P. Bethlehem (Pa.) Steel Co., 1961-66; v.p. data processing Comml. Credit Corp., Balt., 1966-74; CFO Johns Hopkins Hosp., Balt., 1974-86, Johns Hopkins Health System, Balt., 1986-94; chmn. provider reimbursement rev. bd. U.S. Dept. HHS, Balt., 1994—. Bd. dirs. Francis Scott Key Hosp., Balt., Med. Svcs. Corp., Balt., Dome Corp., Balt., Med. Ctr. Ins. Co., Bermuda; mem. fin. coun. Md. Hosp. Assn., Towson, 1984. Co-author: Yearbook of Healthcare Mgmt., 1991—. Advisor Villa Julie Coll., Stevenson, Md., 1991. Fellow Healthcare Fin. Mgmt. Assn.; mem. Healthcare Rate Coun., Ctr. Club. Avocations: tennis, golf, reading. Home: 1214 Brook Meadow Dr Towson MD 21286-1751 Office: Provider Reimbursement Rev Bd Ste L 2520 Lord Baltimore Dr Baltimore MD 21244-2670 Office Phone: 410-321-0109. Business E-Mail: ikues@cms.hhs.gov. E-mail: ikues@verizon.net.

KUESEL, THOMAS ROBERT, civil engineer; b. Richmond Hill, N.Y., July 30, 1926; s. Henry N. and Marie D. (Butt) K.; m. Lucia Elodia Fisher, Jan. 31, 1959; children— Robert Livingston, William Baldwin B. Engring. with highest honors, Yale U., 1946, M. Engring., 1947. With Parsons, Brinckerhoff, Quade & Douglas, 1947-90, project mgr. San Francisco, 1967-68, ptnr., sr. v.p. N.Y.C., 1968-83, chmn. bd., dir., 1983-90; cons. engr., 1990—; vice chmn. OECD Tunneling Conf., Washington, 1970; mem U.S. Nat. Com. on Tunneling Tech., 1972-74. Chmn. Geotech. bd. NRC, 1988-89. Contbr. 60 articles to profl. jours.; designer more than 120 bridges, 135 tunnels and numerous other structures in 36 states and 20 fgn. countries, most recent L.A. Metro, 1982-98, Geo Coleman Bridge Replacement, Yorktown, Va., 1991-95, Boston Ctrl. Artery and Harbor Tunnel, 1994—, Boston Ocean Outfall Tunnel, 1988-90, Cumberland Gap Tunnel, Ky. and Tenn., 1986-90, Jamuna River Bridge, Bangladesh, 1985-95, Trans Koolau Tunnel, Hawaii, 1985-90, Ft. McHenry Tunnel, Balt., 1978-85, Rogers Pass Rwy. Tunnel, B.C., 1981-85, Glenwood Canyon Tunnel, Colo., 1981-88, subways Boston, N.Y., Balt., Wash., Atlanta, Pitts., San Francisco, Seattle, L.A., Caracas, Singapore and Taipei. Fellow: ASCE; mem.: Nat. Acad. Engring., Yale Club N.Y.C., Yale Sci. and Engring. Assn., Am. Underground Constrn. Assn. (hon.), Wee Burn Club, The Moles, Tau Beta Pi.

KUFELDT, GEORGE, biblical educator; b. Chgo., Nov. 4, 1923; s. Henry and Lydia (Dorn) K.; m. Kathryn Rider, July 24, 1943 (dec. July 1956); children: Anita Kay Kufeldt Shelton, Kristina Sue Kufeldt Schmidt; m. Claudena Eller, June 21, 1957 (dec. Sept. 1978); m. Lydia Borgardt, Aug. 12, 1980. AB, Anderson Coll., Ind., 1945, ThB, 1946, MDiv, 1953; PhD, Dropsie U., 1974. Ordained to ministry Ch. of God, 1948. Pastor Ch. of God, Homestead, Fla., 1948-50, Cassopolis, Mich., 1954-57, Lansdale, Pa., 1957-61; prof. O.T. and Hebrew Anderson U., 1961-90, prof. emeritus O.T., 1990—. Contbr. to Wesleyan Bible Commentary, vol. II, 1968, Nelson's Expository Dictionary of the Old Testament, 1980, Educating for Service, 1984, The Genesis Debate, 1986, Listening to the Word of God, 1990. Author: The Book of Ezekiel Asbury Bible Commentary, 1992. Dropsie U. fellow, 1961, 63; Land of the Bible Workshop grantee NYU, 1966. Mem.: Am. Hist. Soc. Germans from Russia (life; bd. dirs. 1991—98). Home: 907 N Nursery Rd Anderson IN 46012-2721 Personal E-mail: gkufeldt@aol.com.

KUFFEL, EDMUND, electrical engineering educator; b. Poland, Oct. 28, 1924; s. Franciszek and Marta (Glodowska) K.; m. Alicja, Oct. 4, 1952; children: Anna, John, Richard, Peter. BSc, U. Coll., Dublin, 1953, MSc, 1954, PhD, 1959; DSc, U. Manchester, 1967. Rsch. engr. Met. Vickers Electric Co., Manchester, Eng., 1954-60; mem. faculty elec. engring. U. Manchester Inst. Sci. and Tech., 1960-68; head of elect. engring. U. Windsor, Ont., Can., 1970-78; prof. elec. engring. U. Man., Winnipeg, Can., 1968-70, head of elec. engring., 1978-79, dean of engring., 1979-89, prof. elec. engring., dean emeritus, 1989—. Cons. various mfrs. high voltage cables; bd. dirs. Man. Hydro Elec. Bd., 1978-96; cons. prof. Xi'an Jiaotong U., People's Rep. China, 1986—. Author or co-author 4 textbooks and more than 200 pub. tech. papers on high voltage engring. Fellow IEEE, Can. Acad. Engring. Home: 2661 Knowles Ave Winnipeg MB Canada R2G 2K7 Office: U Manitoba Fac Engring Winnipeg MB Canada R3T 2N2 E-mail: ekuffel@shaw.ca.

KUFUS, MARTIN W., homeland security specialist; b. Blackwell, Okla., Nov. 30, 1956; s. Wayne M. and Alberta L. (Ramsey) K.; m. Kim Gilbert, June, 2002; children: Josiah, Nathaniel. BS in Journalism, Okla. State U., 1980; MS in Journalism, Ohio U., 1991. Staff reporter Morning Jour. and Evening News, Daytona Beach, Fla., 1980-81; Russian-speaking paratrooper 5th Spl. Forces Group, Ft. Bragg, N.C., 1983-85; Russian linguist in signal intelligence U.S. Army Field Sta., Augsburg, West Germany, 1985-88; free-lance mag. writer, 1989—; constrn. safety officer BDM Constrn. Co., Columbus, Ohio, 1993-94; news editor, sr. reporter Wilson County News, Floresville, Tex., 1994—95, 1997—2002; asst. editor Soldier of Fortune mag., Boulder, Colo., 1995-97; security mgr. Bexar Met. Water Dist., San Antonio, 2002—. Fgn. correspondence intern AP, Jerusalem, 1989; guest lectr. journalism Ohio U., Ohio, 2001. Actor: (TV series, Discovery Channel docudrama) Critical Rescue, Swept Away episode, 2003. Vol. firefighter Wilson County, 1995, 1997—; flood rescue technician Wilson County Vol. Emergency Response Team, 1998—; mem. Wilson County Local Emergency Planning Com., 2003—, Wilson County assistance adv. com. ARC, 2001—02. Sgt. U.S. Army, 1981—88. Recipient 1st pl. award best original news story Tex. Cmty. Newspaper Assn., 1996, Watermark Media award Am. Water Works Assn., Tex., 2001. Mem.: Alamo Silver Wings Airborne Assn., State Firemen's and Fire Marshals' Assn. Tex., Spl. Forces Assn. Methodist. Avocations: fishing, cross country skiing, snorkeling. Office Phone: 210-354-6531. Business E-Mail: mwkufus@bexarmet.org.

KUH, CHARLOTTE VIRGINIA, economist; b. Apr. 13, 1944; d. Peter Greenebaum and Frederica Angela (Coerr) K.; m. Roy Radner, Jan. 22, 1978; children: Siobhan Frederica, Michael Edwin. BA magna cum laude, Radcliffe Coll., 1967; MPhil (Univ. fellow), Yale U., 1969, PhD (Dept. Labor grantee), 1976. Rec. sec.-treas. Econometric Soc., New Haven, 1970-75; acting asst. prof. engring. econ. systems Stanford U., 1974-76; asst. prof. Harvard U. Grad. Sch. Edn., 1976-79; staff mgr., dist. mgr. AT&T Corp., 1979-87; exec. dir. grad. records exams program Ednl. Testing Svc., 1987-95; exec. dir. Office of Sci. and Engring. Personnel Nat. Rsch. Coun., 1995—2001; dep. exec. dir. policy & global affairs divsn. Nat. Rsch. coun., Washington, 2001—. Mem. rev. panel NSF, 1979, 81, mem. adv. panel policy rsch. and sci. resource studies, 1983-87; mem. rev. panel Nat. Inst. Edn., 1978-85; mem. com. study nat. needs for biomed. and behavioral research pers. NRC, 1980-85, mem. adv. panel Office Sci. and Engring. Pers., 1983-90, mem. panel on stats. on supply and demand for precoll. sci. and math. tchrs., com. on nat. stats., 1986-89, mem. com. Women in Sci. and Engring. NRC, 1991-95, vice chair, 1993-95, mem. com. to study strategies to strengthen excellence of the N.I.H. Intramural Research Program, Inst. of Medicine, 1988; mem. exec. com. of dels. Am. Coun. Learned Socs., 1999—2002, chmn. 2001-02, treas., bd. dirs., 2002—; mem. adv. com. Bunting Inst., Radcliffe Coll., 1998—2001; cons. in field. Author articles in field. Grantee Carnegie Coun. Higher Edn., Ford Found., Spencer Found. Fellow Assn. Women in Sci.; mem. Am. Econ. Assn., Econometric Soc. Office: Natl Research Council 500 5th St Washington DC 20001 Office Phone: 202-334-2700. E-mail: ckuh@nas.edu, cvkuh@earthlink.net.

KUH, ERNEST SHIU-JEN, electrical engineering educator; b. Peking, China, Oct. 2, 1928; s. Zone Shung and Tsia (Chu) K.; m. Bettine Chow, Aug. 4, 1957; children: Anthony, Theodore. BS, U. Mich., 1949; MS, MIT, 1950; PhD, Stanford U., 1952; DEng (hon.), Hong Kong U. Sci. and Tech., 1997, Nat. Chiao Tung U., Taiwan, 1999. Mem. tech. staff Bell Tel. Labs., Murray Hill, NJ, 1952-56; assoc. prof. elec. engring. U. Calif., Berkeley, 1956-62, prof., 1962—, Miller rsch. prof., 1965-66, William S. Floyd Jr. prof. engring., 1990—, William S. Floyd Jr. prof. engring. emeritus, 1993—, chmn. dept. elec. engring. and computer sci., 1968-72, dean Coll. Engring., 1973-80. Cons. IBM Rsch. Lab., San Jose, Calif., 1957—62, NSF, 1975—84; mem. panel Nat. Bur. Stds., 1975—80; mem. vis. com. Gen. Motors Inst., 1975—79; mem. vis. com. dept. elec. engring. and computer scis. MIT, 1986—91; mem. adv. coun. elec. engring. dept. Princeton (NJ) U., 1986—98; mem. bd. councilors Sch. Engring. U. So. Calif., 1986—91; mem. sci. adv. bd. Mills Coll., 1976—80. Co-author: Principles of Circuit Synthesis, 1959, Basic Circuit Theory, 1967, Theory of Linear Active Network, 1967; Linear and Nonlinear Circuits, 1987. Recipient Alexander von Humboldt award, 1980, Lamme medal Am. Soc. Endring. Edn., 1981, U. Mich. Disting. Alumnus award, 1970, Berkeley citation, 1993, C & C prize Japanese Found. for Computers and Comm. Promotion, 1996, Phil Kaufman award EDAC, 1998; Brit. Soc. Engring. and Rsch. fellow, 1982. Fellow IEEE (Edn. medal 1981, Centennial medal 1984, Circuits and Systems Soc. award. 1988), AAAS; mem. NAE, Acad. Sinica, Chinese Acad. Scis. (fgn. mem.), Sigma Xi, Phi Kappa Phi. Office: U Calif Elec Engring & Computer Sci Berkeley CA 94720-0001 Office Phone: 510-642-2689. Business E-Mail: kuh@eecs.berkeley.edu.

KUH, RICHARD HENRY, lawyer; b. N.Y.C., Apr. 27, 1921; s. Joseph Hellmann and Fannie Mina (Rees) K.; m. Joyce Dattel, July 31, 1966; children: Michael Joseph, Jody Ellen. BA, Columbia Coll., 1941; LLB magna cum laude, Harvard U., 1948. Bar: N.Y. 1948, U.S. Dist. Ct. (so. dist.) N.Y. 1948, U.S. Dist. Ct. (ea. dist.) N.Y. 1967, U.S. Supreme Ct. 1968. Assoc. firm Cahill, Gordon & Reindel, 1948-53; asst. dist. atty. N.Y. County Dist. Attys. Office, 1953-64, dist. atty., 1974; pvt. practice law N.Y.C., 1966-71; ptnr. firm Kuh, Goldman, Cooperman & Levitt, N.Y.C., 1971-73, Kuh, Shapiro, Goldman, Cooperman & Levitt, P.C., N.Y.C., 1975-78, Warshaw Burstein Cohen Schlesinger & Kuh, N.Y.C., 1978—. Adj. prof. NYU Law Sch. Author: Foolish Figleaves, 1967; mem. bd. editors: Harvard Law Rev, 1947-48; mem. adv. bd.: Contemporary Drug Problems, 1975—, Criminal Law Bull, 1976—; contbr. articles to popular and profl. jours. Trustee Temple Israel, N.Y.C., 1975-84, Grace Ch. Sch., 1981-85. With U.S. Army, 1942-45, ETO. Walter E. Meyer Research and Writing grantee, 1964-65 Mem. ABA (chair criminal justice sect. 1983-84, chair spl. com. on evaluation jud. performance 1983-90, ho. dels. 1988-93, mem. jud. evaluation adv. com. Nat. Ctr. State Cts. 1990-91, chair 1st nat. conf. gun violence 1994), Assn. Bar City N.Y., Am. Bar Found., Harvard Law Sch. Assn. N.Y. (trustee 1989-92), Harvard Club (mem. admissions com. 1998-01), Phi Beta Kappa. Democrat. Jewish. Home: 14 Washington Pl New York NY 10003-6609 Office Phone: 212-984-7820.

KUHBACH, ROBERT GERDES, lawyer; b. New Haven, Conn., May 21, 1947; s. Arend Gerdes and Muriel Ruth (Dinger) K.; m. E. Sherrell Andrews, Nov. 5, 1977; children: Allison Meryl, Courtney Heather. BA in Econs., Yale U., 1969; JD, U. Mich., 1972. Bar: N.Y. 1974. Assoc. Breed, Abbott & Morgan, N.Y.C., 1973-79; atty., sr. atty., gen. counsel Gen. Host Corp., Stamford, Conn., 1980-89; sr. v.p., exec. v.p., dir., gen. counsel, sec. Sudbury, Inc., Cleve., 1989-92; v.p., gen. counsel, sec. Dover Corp., N.Y.C., 1993—. Capt. U.S. Army, 1971-78. Recipient S. Anthony Benton award U. Mich. Law Sch., Ann Arbor, 1972. Mem. ABA, Am. Soc. Corp. Secs., Am. Corp. Coun. Assn., Bar Assn. of City of N.Y. Office: Dover Corp 280 Park Ave New York NY 10017-1216 E-mail: rgk@doverc.com.

KUHI, LEONARD VELLO, astronomer, university administrator; b. Hamilton, Ont., Can., Oct. 22, 1936; came to U.S., 1958; s. John and Sinaida (Rose) K.; m. Patricia Suzanne Brown, Sept. 3, 1960 (div.); children: Alison Diane, Christopher Paul; m. Mary Ellen Murphy, July 15, 1989. BS, U. Toronto, 1958; PhD, U. Calif., Berkeley, 1964. Carnegie postdoctoral fellow Hale Obs., Pasadena, Calif., 1963-65; asst. prof. U. Calif., Berkeley, 1965-69, assoc. prof., 1969-74, prof., 1974-89, chmn. dept. astronomy, 1975-76, dean phys. scis. Coll. Letters and Sci., 1976-81, provost, 1983-89; sr. v.p. for acad. affairs, provost U. Minn., Mpls., 1989-91, prof. astronomy, 1989—, chmn. dept. astronomy, 1997—. Vis. prof. U. Colo., 1969, Coll. de France, Paris, 1972-73, U. Heidelberg, 1978, 80-81; bd. dirs. Am. Inst. Physics. Contbr. articles to profl. jours. Recipient Alexander von Humboldt Sr. Scientist award, 1980-81; NSF research grantee, 1966—. Fellow AAAS; mem. Am. Astron. Soc. (treas. 1987, 96—), Astron. Soc. Pacific (pres. 1978-80), Internat. Astron. Union, Assn. Univ. for Rsch. Astronomy (chair bd. dirs. 1998-2001). Office: U Minn Dept Astronomy 116 Church St SE Minneapolis MN 55455-0149 Office Phone: 612-624-7053. Business E-Mail: kuhi@astro.umn.edu.

KUHL, DAVID EDMUND, nuclear medicine physician, educator; b. St. Louis, Oct. 27, 1929; s. Robert Joseph and Caroline Bertha (Waldermeyer) Kuhl; m. Eleanor Dell Kasales, Aug. 7, 1954; 1 child, David Stephen. AB, Temple U., Phila., 1951; MD, U. Pa., 1955; LHD (hon.), Loyola U. Chgo., 1992. Diplomate Am. Bd. Radiology, Am. Bd. Nuc. Medicine (a founder; life trustee 1977-). Intern, then resident in radiology Sch. Medicine and Hosp. U. Pa., 1955—56, 1958—63, mem. faculty, 1963—76, chief div. nuc. medicine, 1963—76, prof. radiology, 1970—76, vice chmn. dept., 1975—76; prof. bioengring. Moore Sch. Electrical Engrng. U. Pa., 1974—76; prof. radiol. scis. UCLA Sch. Medicine and Hosp., 1976—86, chief div. nuc. medicine, 1976—84, vice-chmn. dept., 1977—86; prof. internal medicine and radiology U. Mich. Sch. Medicine, Ann Arbor, 1986—2000, chief divsn. nuc. medicine, dir. PET Ctr., 1986—2002, prof. radiology, 2000—. Disting. faculty lectr. in biomed. rsch. U. Mich. Med. Sch., 1992, Henry Russel lectr., 98; mem. adv. com. Dept. Energy, NIH, Internat. Commn. on Radiation Units and Measures, Max Planck Soc. Mem. editl. bd.: various jours.; contbr. articles to med. jours. Served as officer M.C. USNR, 1956—58. Recipient Rsch. Career Devel. award, USPHS, 1961—71, Ernst Jung prize for medicine, Jung Found., Hamburg, 1981, Emil H. Grubbe gold medal, Chgo. Med. Soc., 1983, Berman Found. award peaceful uses atomic energy, 1985, Steven C. Beering award for advancement med. sci., Ind. U., 1987, Disting. Grad. award, U. Pa. Sch. Medicine, 1988, William C. Menninger Meml. award, ACP, 1989, Javits Neurosci. Investigator award, NIH, 1989, Charles F. Kettering prize, GM Cancer Rsch. Found., 2001, Hon. Lifetime Mem. award, Einstein Soc., Nat. Atomic Mus. Found., 2001. Fellow: Nat. Inst. for Med. and Biol. Engring., Am. Coll. Nuc. Physicians, Am. Coll. Radiology; mem.: Inst. Medicine Nat. Aad. Scis., Am. Neurol. Assn. (Foster Elting Bennett Meml. lectr. 1981), Soc. Nuc. Medicine (ann. lectr. 1991, Nuc. Pioneer citation 1976, Disting. Scientist award 1981, Herman L. Blumgart, M.D. Pioneer award 1979, George Charles de Hevesy Nuc. Medicine Pioneer award 1995, Benedict Cassen prize for rsch. 1996), Radiol. Soc. N.Am. (ann. orator 1982, Outstanding Rschr. award 1996), Assn. Univ. Radiologists, Assn. Am. Physicians, Alpha Omega Alpha. Office: U Mich Hosp Divsn Nuc Medicine 1500 E Medical Center Dr Ann Arbor MI 48109-0005 Business E-Mail: dkuhl@umich.edu.

KUHL, JOHN R., JR., (RANDY KUHL), congressman, lawyer; b. Bath, NY, Apr. 19, 1943; s. John R. and Myrtle (Wombacker) K.; children: John R. III, Christopher, James Whitney. BS, Union Coll., 1966; JD, Syracuse U., 1969; DHL (hon.), Keuka Coll. Bar: NY 1970, US Supreme Ct. Formerly legal counsel Steuben County Social Svc. and Hwy. Dept.; formerly asst. atty. Steuben County, N.Y.; formerly county atty., village atty., Prattsburgh; formerly town atty. Rathbone and Pulteney; mem. N.Y. State Assembly, 1980-86, N.Y. State Senate, 1986—2004, chmn. agr. standing com., 1987-99, chmn. edn. com., 1999—2004; mem. U.S. Ho. Reps., 109th Congress, 29th Dist. NY, 2005—. Mem. adv. com. Five Rivers coun. Boy Scouts Am.; pres. bd. dir. Reginald Wood Scouting Mem.; past dir. Alliance for Mfg. & Tech. Recipient NYFB Disting. Svc. award. Mem. N.Y. Bar Assn., Steuben County Bar Assn., Rotary, Elks, Bath and Branchport Rod and Gun Club. Office: 1505 Longworth House Office Bldg Washington DC 20515-3229 Office Phone: 202-225-3161.*

KUHL, PATRICIA K., science educator; b. Mitchell, S.D., Nov. 5, 1946; d. Joseph John and Susan Mary (Schaeffer) K.; m. Andrew N. Meltzoff, Sept. 28, 1985; 1 child, Katherine. BA, St. Cloud (Minn.) State U., 1967; MA, U. Minn., 1971, PhD, 1973. Postdoctoral research assoc. Cen. Inst. for Deaf, St. Louis, 1973-76; from rsch. assoc. to prof. U. Wash., Seattle, 1976—82, prof., 1982—, William P. and Ruth Gerberding prof., 1997—, dept. chair, 1994—, dir. Inst. Learning and Brain Scis., 2003—. Gov. bd. Am. Inst. Physics, 1994-96; trustee Neurosci. Rsch. Found., 1994—; bd. dirs. Wash. Tech. Ctr., U. Wash., 1994-96; invited presenter White House Conf. on Early Learning and the Brain, 1997, Early Childhood Cognitive Devel., 2001. Editor Jour. Neurosci., 1989-96. Recipient Women in Research citation Kennedy Council, 1978, Virginia Merrill Bloedel Scholar award, 1992-94. Fellow AAAS, Am. Psychol. Soc., Acoustical Soc. Am. (assoc. editor Jour. 1988-92, chair medals and awards, 1992-94, v.p. 1997, Silver medal 1997, pres. 1999—); mem. Am. Acad. Arts and Scis. Office: Inst Learning and Brain Sci Dept Speech & Hearing Sciences 357988 Seattle WA 98105-6247 Office Phone: 206-685-1921. Business E-Mail: pkkuhl@u.washington.edu.

KUHL, PAUL BEACH, lawyer; b. Elizabeth, NJ, July 15, 1935; s. Paul Edmund and Charlotte (Hetche) K.; m. Janey Mae Stadheim, June 24, 1967; children: Alison Lyn, Todd Beach. BA, Cornell U., 1957; LLB, Stanford U., 1960. Assoc. Law Offices of Walter C. Kohn, San Francisco, 1961-63, Sedgwick, Detert, Moran & Arnold, San Francisco, 1963-73, ptnr., 1973-99, of counsel, 2000—. Pro tem judge, arbitrator San Francisco Superior Ct., 1989—. Served to lt. USCG, 1961. Recipient Def. Atty. of Yr. award, San Francisco (Calif.) Trial Lawyers Assn., 2001. Mem. ABA, Am. Coll. Trial Lawyers, Am. Bd. Trial Advocates, Def. Rsch. Inst., No. Calif. Assn. Def., Am. Platform Tennis Assn. (regional pres. and bd. dirs. 2003—), Mediation Soc., Tahoe Tavern Property Owners Assn. (sec. 1979-81, pres. 1981-83), Lagunitas Country Club (v.p. 1995-97). Avocations: tennis, reading. Home: PO Box 1434 Ross CA 94957-1434 Office: Sedgwick Detert Moran & Arnold 1 Embarcadero Ctr Ste 1600 San Francisco CA 94111-3716 Office Phone: 415-781-7900. Business E-Mail: beach.kuhl@sdma.com.

KUHLA, DONALD E., chemicals executive; b. Staten Island, N.Y., June 9, 1942; s. Robert Elliot and Dorothy (Ware) K.; m. Sandrra Cassellucci, June 19, 1965; children: Jennifer, Robert. BA in Chemistry, NYU, 1964; PhD in Organic Chemistry, Ohio State U., 1968. Rsch. chemist Pfizer, Groton, Conn., 1968-69, medicinal chemist, 1969-74, project leader, mgr., asst. dir., 1974-81; dir. medicinal chemistry, preclin. scis. Rorer Group, Ft. Washington, Pa., 1989-90, sr. v.p. ops., 1989-90; pres., chief. exec. officer Hybridon, Inc., Worcester, Mass., 1990—. Contbr. articles to profl. jours. Mem. AAAS, Am. Chem. Soc., N.Y. Acad. Scis., Internat. Soc. for the Study of Xenobiotics, Phila. Organic Chemists. Achievements include over 100 patents in field; rsch. on various aspects of organic synthesis. Office: Albany Molecular Research 21 Corporate Cir Albany NY 12212-5098

KUHLER, DEBORAH GAIL, grief therapist, retired state legislator; b. Moorhead, Minn., Oct. 12, 1952; d. Robert Edgar and Beverly Maxine (Buechler) Ecker; m. George Henry Kuhler, Dec. 28, 1973; children: Karen Elizabeth, Ellen Christine. BA, Dakota Wesleyan U., 1974; MA, U. N.D., 1977. Outpatient therapist Ctr. for Human Devel., Grand Forks, N.D., 1975-77; mental health counselor Community Counseling Services, Huron, S.D., 1978-88, 91-93; owner, dir. bereavement svcs. Kuhler Funeral Home, Huron, 1978—; adj. prof. Huron U., 1979—83, 1990—2002; mem. from dist. 23 S.D. Ho. Reps., Pierre, 1987-90; mem. House Judiciary com., chair House Health and Welfare Com., Pierre, 1990. Active First United Meth. Ch. Named Young Alumnus of the Yr., Dakota Wesleyan U., 1989, Bus. and Profl. Women, 1989. Mem. ACA, AAUW (Achievement in Politics award 1987), PEO, Am. Mental Health Counselors Assn., Assn. for Death Edn. and Counseling. Avocations: reading, breadmaking, sewing, piano.

KUHLER, RENALDO GILLET, retired museum director, medical illustrator; b. Teaneck, NJ, Nov. 21, 1931; s. Otto August and Simonne L. (Gillet) K.; 1 child, Anne Marie Cooper. BA, U. Colo., 1961. Curator of history, illustrator exhibit, miniature diorama preparator Ea. Wash. State Hist. Soc. Mus., Spokane, 1962-67; mus. illustrator NC State Mus. Natural History, Raleigh, 1969—2003, ret., 1999. Designer, executor of art work for sci. illustrations, awards, brochures, pamphlets and periodicals Dept. Agr. and Mus., NC, 1972-74; designer 36 illustrations for Handbook of Reptiles and Amphibians of Florida, Part 1 (Ray E. Ashton), 1981; contbr. many illustrations Atlas of Freshwater Fishes of North America (David Lee), Endangered Threatened and Rare Fauna of North Carolina (Ross, Rohde and Lindquist), Distribution Survey of North Carolina Mammals (Lee, Funderburg and Clark); Endangered Threatened and Rare Fauna of North Carolina, part 1 (Mary K. Clark), Potential Effect of Oil Spills on Seabirds, etc. (Lee and Socci), Poisonous Snakes of North Carolina (William M. Palmer), Reptiles of North Carolina (William M. Palmer and Alvin Braswell), Synopsis of North American Centipede (Rowland Shelley), 2002; gen.

illustrator: American Firearms and the Changing Frontier (Waldo E. Rosebush); also contbr. to jours. and bulls. including Then.C.Naturalist; currently working on skull illustrations for Mammals of North Carolina (Mary Kay Clark); calligrapher; creator wood handicrafts; violin maker, 1949. Appearance as sci. illustrator (TV) Nat. Geog., June 2001. Mem. Dem. Nat. Com.; life mem. Raleigh Rhinoceros Club, 2000—; vol. sci. illustrator NC State Mus. Natural History, 1999-. Mem. Nat. Trust Hist. Preservation, Nat. Smokers Alliance, Rails to Trails, East Coast Greenway Alliance, Raleigh Rhinoceros Club (life). Democrat. Avocations: experimenting with laminated paper and models of ships and trains, carburator fittings for smoking pipes, designer hiking and summer office suits. Home: Apt 3 510 Tilden St Raleigh NC 27605-1524 Office: NC State Mus Natural Scis 210 N Salisbury St Raleigh NC 27603-1358 Office Phone: 919-883-1067.

KUHLMAN, THOMAS ASHFORD, retired American studies educator, writer; b. Cleve., May 24, 1939; s. Orlyn Lee and Catherine Mary (Ashford) K.; m. Mary Louise Haynes, Aug. 22, 1964; children: John Christopher, Katherine Mary. Honors AB, Xavier U., 1961; AM, Brown U., 1963, PhD, 1967. Teaching fellow Brown U., 1963-64; instr. English Georgetown U., 1964-67; asst. prof. English Creighton U., 1967-70, assoc. prof., 1970—2005, coord. continuing edn., 1973-74; ret., 2005. Vis. scholar Am. Acad. in Rome, 1981; mem. faculty Inst. Jewish Studies, Omaha, 1974-75; regional dir. Nat. Bicentennial Youth Debates, 1975-76; dir. Copper Hollow Writers Workshop, 1977-78; regional humanist Nebr. Com. Humanities, 1976-78; reg. spkr. Joslyn Art Mus.; participant Attingham Study Tour of Brit. Country Houses, 2002. Playwright Each of These Landlords, 1976, Georgian Punch Bowl, Monteith Design, 1982, Idiots Delete, 1987, Hostages of the Court, 1993, Ambition in Exile, 1997, fiction in Prairie Schooner, Shadows; other literary jours.; author of numerous essays; editor The Beauty of Thy House: The History, Art, and Architecture of St. Cecilia Cathedral, Omaha, 2004. Mem. Omaha Symphony Coun., 1972-79, mem. exec. com., 1974-77; heritage chmn., bd. dirs. Omaha-Douglas County Bicentennial Commn., 1974-76; sec., bd. dirs. Met. Arts Coun., 1976-78; pres. Landmarks, Inc., 1987-88; bd. dirs. Florence Arts and Humanities Coun., 1979, pres. 1980; bd. dirs. Nebr. Archtl. Foun., 1992-99; mem. cmty. bd. Nebr. Shakespeare Festival, 1992-2004; mem. adv. bd. Joslyn Castle Inst. for Sustainable Cmtys.; v.p. Omaha chpt. Irish-Am. Cultural Inst.; bd. dirs. Irish ARts Coun., Omaha, 2004-; mem. pastoral coun. St. Cecilia Cathedral, Omaha; cons. Omaha Gold Coast Historic Preservation Assn. Woodrow Wilson fellow, 1961, Andrew W. Mellon fellow, U. Kans., 1984, NEH fellow U. N.C.-Chapel Hill, 1989; grantee Office of Edn. Humanities, 1968, Rsch. grantee Creighton U. Faculty, 1969, grantee Nebr. Arts Coun., 1978, grantee Can. Govt. Faculty Devel. Programme, 1979. Mem. Am. Studies Assn., Omaha Workshop Theater (pres. 1992-97), Nebr. Humanities Coun. (spkrs. bur. 1987-2005), Hist. Soc. Douglas County (dir. 1995-2001), Vasari Soc. (founding fellow), Alpha Sigma Nu. Republican. Roman Catholic. Home: 3650 Burt St Omaha NE 68131-1946

KUHLMAN, WALTER EGEL, artist, educator; b. St. Paul, Nov. 16, 1918; s. Peter and Marie (Jensen) K.; m. Nora McCants; 1 son, Christopher; m. Tulip Chestman, April 9, 1979. Student, St. Paul Sch. Art; BS, U. Minn., 1941; postgrad., Tulane U., Académie de la Grand Chaumière, Paris, Calif. Sch. Fine Arts. Mem. faculty Calif. Sch. Fine Arts Stanford, U. Mich., Santa Clara (Calif.) U., U. N. Mex., prof., Sonoma State U., Calif., 1969-89, prof. emeritus, 1989-. One person shows include U. N.Mex., Walker Art Center, Mpls., The Berkshire Museum, Mass., La Jolla Museum of Contemporary Art, Calif., Santa Barbara Mus. of Art, Calif., San Francisco Mus. of Modern Art, 1958, New Arts Gallery, Houston, 1959-61, Roswell Mus. Calif. Palace of the Legion of Honor, 1956, 64, De Saisset Gallery, Santa Clara U. 20-Year Retrospective, Jonson Gallery, U. N.Mex., 1963, 64, 65, Charles Campbell Gallery, San Francisco, 1981, 83, 85, The Carlson Gallery, San Francisco, Gump's Gallery, San Francisco, 1976, 1992, University Gallery, Sonoma State U. 40 Year Retrospective, Calif. Natsoulis Gallery, Davis, Calif., Albuquerque Mus. Fine Arts, George Krevsky Fine Arts, San Francisco, 1994, 96, 99, Robert Green Gallery, Mill Valley, Calif.; group shows include N.Y. World's Fair, St. Paul Gallery, WPA Exhibition, Lawson Galleries, San Francisco, A 1948 Portfolio: 16 Lithographs (Diebenkorn, Lobdell, Hultberg), All Annual Invitational Exhibitions, San Francisco Mus. Modern Art, 1948-58, Petit Palais Mus., Paris, San Francisco Mus. Modern Art, III Biennial of Sao Paulo, Museo de Arte Moderna, Brazil, L.A. County Mus., Mus. Modern Art, Rio de Janiero, San Francisco Mus. Modern Art, 1955, 57, 66, 76, 96, Graham Found., Chgo, L.A. County Mus., Calif. Palace of the Legion of Honor, Virginia Mus. Fine Arts, Richmond, Stanford U., Gallery, Roswell Mus., 1961, 62, Univ. Art Mus., Austin, Texas Santa Fe Mus. Fine Arts, NM, Ca. Palace of Legion of Honor, Richard L. Nelson Gallery, UC Davis, Natsoulis Gallery, Northern California Figuration Expositions Art USA, 1992, 93, 94, George Krevsky Fine Art, San Francisco, Art Mus. Santa Cruz, Calif., 1993, Pasquale Ianetti Art Galleries, San Francisco, 1994, Robert Green Fine Arts, Mill Valley, Calif. 1994, 95, Am. Acad. Arts and Letters, N.Y. 1995, Dark Avenue Armory Annual Internat. Fine Print Exhbn., N.Y., Va. Mus. Modern Art Am. Paintings, Petit Palais Mus., Paris, Mus. of Modern Art, Sao Paulo British Mus., London, Nat. Mus. Am. Art, Phillip Meml. Gallery, Washington, DC, Oakland Mus. Art, Calif., Laguna Mus. of Art, Calif., 1998, The Menil Collection, Houston, Cleve. Mus. Art, Mus. Modern Art, San Francisco Mus. Modern Art, Salander O'Reilly Gallery, N.Y.; permanent collections include: The Phillips Collection, Washington, Nat. Gallery Am. Art, Washington, Walker Art Ctr., Washington, San Francisco Mus. Modern Art, Brit. Mus., Met. Mus. Art, NAD, N.Y., others. Recipient Maestro award Calif. Arts Coun.; Outstanding Calif. Working Artist and Tchr. grantee; fellow Tiffany Found., Graham Found., Chgo., Cummington Found. Mem. Nat. Acad. Design N.Y. Studio: Indsl Ctr Bldg Studio 335 480 Gate 5 Rd Sausalito CA 94965-1461*

KUHLMANN, FRED MARK, lawyer; b. St. Louis, Apr. 9, 1948; s. Frederick Louis and Mildred (Southworth) K.; m. Barbara Jane Nierman, Dec. 30, 1970; children: F. Matthew, Sarah Ann Morgan. AB summa cum laude, Washington U., St. Louis, 1970; JD cum laude, Harvard U., 1973. Bar: Mo. 1973. Assoc. atty. Stolar, Heitzmann & Eder, St. Louis, 1973-75; from tax counsel to staff v.p. McDonnell Douglas Corp., St. Louis, 1975—87, sr. v.p., gen. counsel, 1991—97; exec. v.p. McDonnell Douglas Health Systems Co., 1987—89; pres. McDonnell Douglas Systems Integration Co., 1989—91; of counsel Bryan Cave, St. Louis, 1997-98; pres. Sys. Svc. Enterprises, St. Louis, 1998—2004, co-CEO, 2004—. Bd. dirs. Republic Health Corp., Dallas, 1988-90, Grace Place Retreats, 2005—; mem. governing bd. Luth. Med. Ctr., 1989-95, chmn., 1990-92. Bd. dirs. Luth. Charities Assn., 1982-91, sec. 1984-86, chmn. 1986-89; elder Luth. Ch. of Resurrection, 1977-80; mem. Regents Coun. Concordia Sem., 1981-84; chmn. cub scout pack 459 Boy Scouts Am., 1984-86; bd. dirs. Luth. H.S. Assn., 1978-84, 91-97, pres. 1992-97, long range planning com. 1990-92, chmn. alumni assn., 1981; chmn. North Star dist. Boy Scouts Am., 1990-93; bd. dirs. Mcpl. Theatre Assn., St. Louis, 1991—; chmn. long range planning com. St. Paul's Luth. Ch., 1988-91, 98-2001, pres., 1996-97, 2002-03; bd. dirs., mem. exec. com. United Way of Greater St. Louis, 1994-97, chmn. Vanguard divsn., 1994-97; mem. amb. coun. Luth. Family and Children's Svcs. of St. Louis, 1998—; bd. dirs. Luth. Found. St. Louis, 1998—, chmn., 2004-; mem. adv. bd. Webster U. Bus. and Tech. Sch., 1999-2001; mem. bd mgrs. worker benefit plans Luth. Ch.-Mo. Synod, 2001—; bd. dirs. Grace Place Retreats, 2005-. Recipient Disting. Leadership award Luth. Assn. for Higher Edn., 1981. Mem. ABA, Mo. Bar Assn., Bar Assn. Met. St. Louis, Bellerive Country Club, Phi Beta Kappa, Omicron Delta Kappa. Republican. Avocations: tennis, golf, racquetball. Home: 1711 Stone Ridge Trails Dr Saint Louis MO 63122-3546 Office: Sys Svc Enterprises 77 Westport Plz Ste 500 Saint Louis MO 63146-3126 Office Phone: 314-439-4702. Business E-Mail: fmkuhlmann@sseinc.com.

KUHLMANN-WILSDORF, DORIS, materials scientist, inventor, retired educator; b. Bremen, Germany, Feb. 15, 1922; came to U.S., 1956. d. A. Friedrich and Elsa S. (Dreyer) K.; m. Heinz G.F. Wilsdorf, Jan. 4, 1950; children: Gabriele, Michael. BS in Physics, U. Göttingen, Germany, 1944, MS, 1946, PhD in Materials Sci., 1947; DSc in Physics-Materials Sci., U. Witwatersrand, South Africa, 1954; DSc in Physics (hon.), U. Pretoria, South Africa, 2004. Postdoctoral fellow U. Göttingen, 1947-48; postdoctoral fellow in physics U. Bristol, Eng., 1949-50; lectr. physics U. Witwatersrand, Johannesburg, 1950-56; from assoc. prof. metall. engring. to prof. U. Pa., Phila., 1957-63; prof. engring. physics U. Va., Charlottesville, 1963-66, univ. prof. applied sci., 1966—2005; prof. emeritus, 2005; owner, pres. Kuhlmann-Wilsdorf Motors. Co-founder, co-owner HiPerCon; founder, owner KWM; inventor in field. Editor: 4 materials sci. books; contbr. articles to profl. jours. Recipient J. Shelton Horsley award Va. Acad. Sci., 1966, Americanism medal DAR, 1966, Heyn medal German Metall. Soc., 1988, Achievement award Soc. Women Engrs., 1989, Ragnar Holm Sci. Achievement award IEEE, 1991. Fellow Am. Soc. Materials Internat. (life, Edward DeMille Campbell Meml. lectr. 2002), Am. Phys. Soc.; mem. Am. Soc. Women Engrs. (life), Am. Soc. Engring. Edn. (medal for excellence 1965, 66), AIME Metall. Soc., Nat. Acad. Engring. Achievements include development of metal fiber brushes; invention of multipolar motors; patents in field. Business E-Mail: dw@virginia.edu.

KUHN, ALBERT JOSEPH, language educator; b. Dowell, Ill., Apr. 4, 1926; s. Albert and Elizabeth (Furjes) K.; m. Roberta Marshall, June 12, 1949 (dec. 1993); children— William, Frederick. BA, U. Ill., 1950; PhD, Johns Hopkins, 1954. Mem. faculty Ohio State U., 1954—, chmn. English dept., 1964-71, prof. English, 1965, provost, v.p. acad. affairs, 1971-79, dir. Univ. Honors, 1985-89, professor emeritus, 1989—. Contbr. to Romantic Bibliography, 1963, also articles.; editor: Three Sentimental Novels, 1970, Victorian Literature and Society, 1984 Mem. region VIII Woodrow Wilson Selection Com., 1961-68; mem. research bd. Children's Hosp., 1973-77; trustee Battelle Meml. Inst. Found., 1975-79. Served with USNR, 1944-46. Recipient Disting. Svc. award Ohio State U., 1991. Mem. MLA, North Cen. Assn. Colls. and Schs. (cons.-evaluator), Kit Kat Club (Columbus), Phi Beta Kappa, Phi Kappa Phi. Home: 35 Webster Park Ave Columbus OH 43214-3512

KUHN, BOWIE K., lawyer, former professional baseball commissioner, consultant; b. Takoma Park, Md., Oct. 28, 1926; m. Luisa Hegeler; four children. BA, Princeton, 1947; LL.B., U. Va., 1950. Bar: N.Y. 1951, U.S. Supreme Ct. 1972. With firm Willkie, Farr & Gallagher, N.Y.C.; legal counsel several baseball clients, 1950-69; rep. Maj. League club owners in negotiations with Maj. League Players Assn., 1968; commr. pro tempore of baseball, 1969; commr., 1969-84; of counsel Willkie, Farr & Gallagher, 1984-87; former ptnr. Myerson & Kuhn, N.Y.C., 1988-89; pres. The Kent Group Inc., Ponte Vedra Beach, Fla., 1990—, Sports Franchises, Inc., Milford, Conn., 1992—. Author: Hardball: The Education of a Baseball Commissioner, 1987. Office: The Kent Group Inc 136 Teal Pointe Ln Ponte Vedra Beach FL 32082-1935

KUHN, BRENT, advertising executive; BA in Comms., U. Ill. Account rep. Tatham, Laird & Rudner, Chgo.; with McCann Erickson; pres. Bennett Kuhn Varner Inc., Atlanta, 1989—. Office: Bennett Kuhn Varner Inc 2964 Peachtree Rd Ste 700 Atlanta GA 30305

KUHN, GARY D., speech educator; b. Portland, Jan. 21, 1956; s. Wayne Richard and Catherine Mildred Kuhn; m. Renee C. Lehr, Aug. 15, 1981; children: Khrizma Renee, Kory Gabriel, Kamila Rose. BS in Speech Comm., So. Oreg. U., 1978; MS in Edn., Capella U., 2002. Ter. mgr. Northrup King Co., Mpls., 1978—81; profl. sales rep. Ayerst Labs., NYC, 1982—84; employer svcs. rep. Clackamas County Employment, Tng. and Bus. Svcs., Marylhurst, Oreg., 1984—97; coop. work experience coord. Chemeketa C.C., Salem, 1997—. Adj. instr. speech comm. Chemeketa C.C., Salem, 1998—2005. Author: (website) Companion Website. Bd. mem. Children's Cancer Assn., Portland, 1995—98. Mem.: N.W. Career and Employers Assn. Avocations: photography, skiing. Home: 4000 Lancaster Dr NE Salem OR 97305 Home Fax: 503-399-7483. Personal E-mail: kuhg@chemeketa.edu.

KUHN, GRETCHEN, lawyer; b. San Antonio, June 11, 1951; d. Charles Louis and Evelyn (Patterson) K.; m. Dennis Norman Carnes, Oct. 29, 1977. BA, Rice U., Houston, 1973; JD, U. Tex., 1976. Bar: Colo. 1977. Land rep. Chevron U.S.A., Inc., Denver, 1976-80; atty, area landman Dome Petroleum Corp., Denver, 1980-81; atty., landman Hunt Oil Co., Denver and Dallas, 1981-87; ptnr. Kuhn & Carnes, Denver, 1987-91; shareholder Kuhn, Carnes & Anderson P.C., Denver, 1991—; pres. The Rockport-Essex Co., Denver, 1987—. V.p. H-3 USA for Poland, Denver. Mem. devel. com. Colo. Women's Found., Denver, 1987—; mem. Colo. Lawyers for Arts. Mem. ABA, Colo. Bar Assn., Denver Bar Assn., Colo. Petroleum Assn., Am. Assn. Petroleum Landmen, Rocky Mountain Mineral Law Found. (past trustee), Denver Art Mus. Democrat. Home: 766 Downing St Denver CO 80218-3429 Office: 1525 17th St Denver CO 80202-1201

KUHN, HOWARD ARTHUR, engineering executive, educator; b. Pitts., Dec. 6, 1940; s. Howard E. and Selma W. Kuhn; m. Beverly A. Burke, Dec. 23, 1961; children: Amy, Jeffrey, David, Stephen. BS, Carnegie-Mellon U., 1962, MS, 1963, PhD, 1966. Registered profl. engr., Pa., Fla., SC. Prof. engring. Drexel U., Phila., 1966-74, U. Pitts., 1975-89, adj. prof., 1989-2000, 2004—; v.p., CTO Scienda Bldg. Scis., 2000—02, cons. engr. Irwin, Pa., 2002—; dir. R & D The ExOne Co., 2002—. Dir. freshman engring. program, U. Pitts, 1981-88, indsl. adv. com.; cons. engr. Deformation Control Tech., Pitts., 1980-88; tech. dir. Concurrent Techs. Corp., 1988, tech. v.p., 1989-92, v.p., chief tech. officer, 1992-2000; bd. dirs. Pitts. Tech. Coun. Author: Powder Forging, 1990; editor: Powder Metallurgy Processing, 1978, ASM Handbook on Mechanical Testing, 2000; inventor powder metallurgy forging, aluminum plate rolling improvements. Pres. PTA, Gibsonia, Pa., 1976-77; mem. Civic Adv. Com., Gibsonia, 1978-82; chmn. Laurel Highlands Cancer Program, bd. dirs. Johnstown Chiefs Hockey Team, 1995-2000; dir. advanced tech. programs Cambria County Area C.C., 1994-96, bd. trustees C.C., 1996-2000; bd. dirs. Orangeburg-Calhoun Tech. Coll. Fellow Am. Soc. Materials Internat. (chmn. mfg. tech., nominating com., Pitts. chpt. exec. bd., Zay Jeffries award, Edgar C. Bain award, Campbell lecture selection com.); mem. ASME, Am. Powder Metallurgy Inst., Soc. Mfg. Engrs., Light Gage Steel Engrs. Assn., Richland Athletic Assn. (pres.). Democrat. Methodist. Home: 128 McCaffrey Ln Johnstown PA 15905 Office: 1 Industry Blvd Irwin PA 15642 Office Phone: 412-334-5520. Business E-Mail: howard.kuhn@exone.com.

KUHN, JAMES D., real estate company executive; BA in Fin., MA in Real Estate, Syracuse U.; postgrad., The Wharton Sch., Harvard U. Lender Met. Life Ins. Co.; owner, mgr. The Mendik Co., 1990; prin., pres., COO Newmark & Co. Real Estate Inc., N.Y.C., 1992—. Chmn. NYU Real Estate Inst.; trustee Nat. Jewish Med. and Rsch. Ctr. Recipient Nat. Jewish Humanitarian award, 1994. Mem.: Urban Land Inst. (corp. real estate coun.). Office: Newmark & Co Real Estate Inc 125 Park Ave New York NY 10017

KUHN, JAMES E., judge; b. Hammond, La., Oct. 31, 1946; s. Eton Percy and Mildred Louise (McDaniel) K.; m. Cheryl Aucoin, Dec. 27, 1969; children: James M., Jennifer L. BA, Southeastern La. U., 1968; JD, Loyola U. of South, 1973; attended, U.S. Army War Coll. Bar: La. 1973. Cert. 1995, U.S. Supreme Ct. 1978. Asst. dist. atty. 21st Jud. Dist., La., 1980-90, judge Livingston, St. Helena, Tangipahoa, 1990-95, Ct. Appeals (1st cir.), Baton Rouge, 1995—. Instr. history, and polit. sci. Southeastern La. U., Hammond, 1991—; past mem. appellate ct. performance and standards com. La. Supreme Ct.; past mem. La. State Bar Assn. com. on ins., negligence and worker's comp., 1983-90 Founder For Our Youth; past bd. dirs. La. Coun. Child Abuse, past sec.-treas. Conf. of Ct. Appeal Judges for State of La.; former mgr. La. Bar Assn. With Nat. Guard U.S. Army, 1969—74. Recipient Am. Jurisprudence award Loyola Law Sch. Mem. ABA, La. State Bar Assn. (Professionalism and Quality of Life com.), Colo. Bar Assn., 21st Jud. Bar Assn., Am. Judicature Soc., Am. Judges Assn., Fed. Cir. Bar Assn., New Orleans Bar Assn., Baton Rouge Bar Assn., Covington Bar Assn., Fla. Parishes Inns of Ct., Delta Theta Phi, Phi Kappa Phi Home: 253 W Oak St Ponchatoula LA 70454-3330

KUHN, JAMES PAUL, management consultant; b. Milw., July 11, 1937; s. Clarence George and Genevieve Mary K.; m. Josephine M. Keller, Dec. 27, 1958; children: Christine, Cynthia, George. BME, Marquette U., 1961; MBA, U. Chgo., 1972. Mfg. mgr. GE Co., Fairfield, Conn., 1961-65; prin. A.T. Kearney, Inc., Chgo., 1966-74, v.p., 1984—2001, Booz Allen & Hamilton, Inc., N.Y.C., 1975-77; pres. Case Mfg. Svcs., Chgo., 1978-83; dir. Case & Co., Inc., N.Y.C., 1980-83; CFO Timeless Designs, Inc., Chgo., 2001—; gen. mgr. AKN Properties LLC, Chgo., 2005—. Contbr. articles to profl. jours. Mem.: Marco Island Country Club.

KUHN, MATTHEW, retired engineering company executive; b. Sacalaz, Banat, Romania, Mar. 19, 1936; came to U.S., 1967; s. Peter and Katherine (Gerres) K.; m. Betty Jane Ritchie, Aug. 20, 1966; children: Andrew Jason, Andrea Suzanne. BASc in Engring. Physics, Queen's U., Kingston, Ont., Can., 1962; MASc, U. Waterloo, Ont., 1963, PhDEE, 1967, D of Engring. (hon.), 1985; postgrad., Brown U., 1967-68. Supr. MTS Bell Tel. Labs., Murray Hill, NJ, 1968—73; from mgr. adv. tech. to asst. v.p. BNR Ltd., Ottawa, Canada, 1973—85; asst. v.p. BNR Inc., Research Triangle Park, NC, 1985—89; pres. Microelectronics Ctr. of N.C., Research Triangle Park, 1989—94, EconTech Cons. & Rsch. Mgmt. Svcs., 1994—99, ret., 1999. Adj. prof. engring. mgmt. Duke U., 1997-2000; presenter numerous profl. meetings. Contbr. articles to profl. jours. Mem. N.C. Bd. Sci. & Tech., 1991-94; chmn. adv. coun. Queen's U., 1983-84; chmn. engring. adv. coun. Duke U., Durham, N.C., 1989-94. Fellow IEEE (editor spl. issue Electron Devices Jour. Optoelectronics 1975). Roman Catholic. Achievements include discovery of quasi-static method measurement technique for integrated circuit development; co-development first generation fiber optics technology. Home: 11 Piney Point Whispering Pines NC 28327 Personal E-mail: mkuhnet@charter.net. *It is sometimes necessary to disagree but never to be disagreeable.*

KUHN, MELANIE R., literature educator, consultant; d. Emma Gertrude and Raymond Joseph Kuhn; m. Jason Edward Chambers, Mar. 18, 2003. BA magna cum laude, Boston Coll., 1984; EdM, Harvard Grad. Sch. of Edn., Cambridge, MA, 1988; MPhil, Cambridge U., Eng., 1993; PhD, U. Ga., Athens, 2000. Clinician Ctr. Acad., London, 1989—92; asst. prof. literacy edn. Rutgers Grad. Sch. of Edn., New Brunswick, NJ, 2000—. Author: (chapter) Theoretical Models and Processes, 2004, Literacy: Major Themes in Education, 2004; contbr. articles to profl. jours. and books. Reviewer Am. Ednl. Rsch. Assn., 1997, Nat. Reading Conf., 1999—2003, Jour. of Ednl. Psychology, 2002, Internat. Reading Assn., Newark, Del., 2001—03; principle investigator Effectiveness of Recording for the Blind and Dyslexics Learning Through Listening Program; reviewer Jour. Literacy Rsch., 2001—; ad hoc reviewer Jour. of Spl. Edn., 2003. Recipient Finalist, Outstanding Dissertation of the Yr., Internat. Reading Assn., 2002, Finalist, Outstanding Student Rsch., Nat. Reading Conf., 2000; grantee full Grant for study at Cambridge U., ESRC, 1992-93, Eisenhower Grant for Profl. Devel. Across Districts, NJ. Dept. of Edn., 2001-03, RFB&D Learning Through Listening Study, 2004—05. Mem.: Assn. of Reading Grad. Students (assoc.; pres. 1995—96), Nat. Reading Conf. (assoc.), Am. Ednl. Rsch. Assn. (assoc.), Internat. Reading Assn. (assoc.), Alpha Upsilon Alpha (assoc.). Independent. Catholic. Achievements include research in IERI Grant The Development of Fluent and Automatic Reading: Precursor to Learning from Text. Avocations: swimming, travel, walking. Office: 144 Morris St #1 Jersey City NJ 07302 E-mail: melaniek@rci.rutgers.edu.

KUHN, PAUL HUBERT, JR., investment advisor; b. Chattanooga, Sept. 7, 1943; s. P. Hubert and Pauline Anna (Byrnes) Kuhn; m. Jeanne Bartlett Elmore, June 7, 1966 (dec. 1996); children: Katherine, Christopher. BA, Vanderbilt U., 1965; MBA, Ind. U., 1971. Chartered investment counselor. V.p., prin. Stein Roe & Farnham, Chgo., 1971-89; v.p. Stein Roe Spl. Fund, Chgo., 1983-89; mng. ptnr. Davidson Ptnrs. Investment Counsel, Nashville, 1989-2000; ptnr. J.C. Bradford & Co., Nashville, 1989-2000. Prin. Woodmont Investment Counsel, 2000—. Bd. dirs. Augustana Hosp., Chgo., 1980-83, USO of Chgo.; pres. Lincoln Park Renewal Corp., Chgo. Lt. USN, 1965-69. Mem. CFA Inst., CFA Soc. Nashville (bd. dirs. 1997-2001, pres. 2001-02), Nat. Orgn. Reform Marijuana Laws (bd. dirs. 1997—), Tavern Club (Chgo.) (bd. govs.), Woman's Athletic Club of Chgo. (hon.), Nashville City, Phi Beta Kappa, Omicron Delta Kappa. Republican. Roman Catholic. Office: Woodmont Investment Counsel Ste 600 102 Woodmont Blvd Nashville TN 37205 Office Phone: 615-297-0673. E-mail: paul@woodmontcounsel.com.

KUHN, WILLIAM ANDREW, music educator; b. North Tonawanda, NY, June 15, 1971; s. Frederick John and Marie Ann Kuhn; m. Rachelle Corpuz, May 25, 1994; children: Joshua Ryan, Victoria Lynn. AS, Villa Maria Coll., 1991; BMus, U. Ariz., 1994; MA, SUNY, Buffalo, 1999. Cert. tchr. NY. Music tchr. Baker Victory Sch., Lackawanna, NY, 1995—96, Kenmore Mid. Sch., Kenmore, NY, 1996—. Profl. jazz bassist, guitarist. Named Tchr. of Yr., Kenmore Mid. Sch., 2005; scholar Sch. of Music Jazz scholar, U. Ariz., 1991—94. Mem.: Erie County Music Educators Assn. (assoc.), NY State Sch. Music Assn. (assoc.; music performance adjudicator 2001—), Music Educators Nat. Conf. (assoc.), Kenmore Teachers Assn. (assoc.), NY State United Teachers (assoc.). Democrat. Home: 41 Stoneleigh Ave Buffalo NY 14223 Office: Kenmore Mid Sch 155 Delaware Rd Kenmore NY 14217 Office Phone: 716-874-8403. Office Fax: 716-874-8650. Personal E-mail: wakuhn1@yahoo.com. E-mail: william_kuhn@kenton.k12.ny.us.

KUHN, WILLIS EVAN, II, lawyer, mediator; b. Indpls., July 20, 1948; s. Theodore Roosevelt and Theresa Anne (Lupinacci) K.; m. Virginia Katherine Williams, Apr. 12, 1983; children: William Franklin, Virginia Anne. BA, Vanderbilt U., 1970; JD with honors, U. Tex., 1973. Bar: Tex. 1973; cert. mediator. Assoc. Johnson & Gibbs, Dallas, 1973-75, Moore & Peterson, Dallas, 1975-80; ptnr. Baker, Smith & Mills, Dallas, 1980-85, Kuhn & Fishman, Dallas, 1985-90, Hopkins & Sutter, Dallas, 1990-93; pvt. practice Dallas, 1993—. Mem. Dallas So. Meml. Assn., 1992—. Mem. State Bar Tex., Dallas Bar Assn., Dallas Athletic Club, Order of Coif, Phi Kappa Psi. Republican. Avocations: golf, history. Office: 15851 N Dallas Pkwy #600 Dallas TX 75001-6030 Home: 6062 Jereme Trl Dallas TX 75252-5130

KUHRAU, EDWARD W., lawyer; b. Caney, Kans., Apr. 19, 1935; s. Edward and Dolores (Hardman) Kuhrau; m. Janiece Christal (div. 1983); children: Quentin, Clayton; m. Sandy Shreve. BA, U. Tex., 1960; JD, U. So. Calif., 1965. Bar: Calif. 1966, Wash. 1968, Alaska 1977. With Perkins Coie (and predecessor firms), Seattle, 1968—, ptnr., 1973—. Editor-in-chief Wash. Real Property Deskbook; contbr. articles to profl. jours. With USAF, 1955—58. Mem. ABA, Wash. Bar Assn., Am. Coll. Real Estate Lawyers, Pacific Real Estate Inst. (pres., founding trustee), Order of Coif, Seattle Yacht Club. Office: Perkins Coie 1201 3rd Ave Fl 40 Seattle WA 98101-3029 E-mail: kuhre@perkinscoie.com.

KUHRMEYER, CARL ALBERT, manufacturing executive; b. St. Paul, May 12, 1928; s. Carl and Irma Luella (Lindeke) K.; m. Janet E. Pedersen, Oct. 31, 1953; children: Karen Graden, John, Paul. BSME, U. Minn., 1949. Registered profl. engr., Minn. Design engr. Magney, Tusler & Setter, St. Paul, 1950-51; with 3M Co., St. Paul, 1951-93, successively product devel. engr., machine devel. engr., project leader, copy machine prodn. supr., process engring. and contracting supr., process engring. mgr., project mgr., until 1964, tech. dir., 1964-66, div. v.p., 1967-70, corp. group v.p., 1970-80, corp. v.p., 1980-93. Bd. dirs., chmn. bd. Product Level Control, Eagan, Minn., 1995—. Patentee in field. Mem. nat. adv. coun. Nat. Multiple Sclerosis Soc., 1973—; trustee United Theol. Sem., St. Paul, 1986-2002; bd. dirs. Minn. Protestant Found., St. Paul, 1987—, pres., 1997—; bd. dirs. Minn. Pvt. Coll. Fund, St. Paul, 1986-95, St. Paul Winter Carnival Assn., 1987-93, chmn., dir., 1990-91; bd. dirs., v.p. Family Resources Devel. Inc., St. Paul. Mem. St. Paul C. of C. (bd. dirs. 1988-95, chmn. bd. 1993), Minn. Club (bd. dirs. 1994-2002), White Bear Yacht Club (bd. dirs. 1995-97), North Oaks Country Club (bd. dirs. 1981-83, pres. 1983), Osman Temple. Mem. United Church of Christ. Office: 3050 Minnesota World Trade Ctr 30 7th St E Saint Paul MN 55101-4914 E-mail: cakuhrmeyer@mmm.com .

KUIPER, RUTHANNE, medical educator; b. Sussex, N.J., July 16, 1955; d. Fred and Ruth Layne Kuiper. MN, UCLA, 1989; PhD in Nursing Philosophy, U. S.C., 2000. CCRN, AACN Calif., 1985. Faculty Presbyn. Hosp. Sch. of Nursing, Charlotte, NC, 1990—2000; asst. prof. Wintson-Salem State U., Winston-Salem, NC, 2000—02, U. NC, Wilmington, 2002—. Legal nurse cons. Self-employed, Wilmington, NC, 1995—, tutor, 1999—. Contbr. articles various profl. jours. Treas. Lambda Rho Chpt. of Sigma Theta Tau, Winston-Salem, NC, 2000—02; chpt. leader Nu Omega Chpt. of Sigma Theta Tau, Wilmington, NC, 2003—. Grantee monetary award, Nat. League for Nursing, 2001-2003, AACN, 2002-2004, monetary Innovations award, UNCW ITSD, 2003-2004. Mem.: Sigma Theta Tau Internat. (life; treas. and counselor 2000—). Achievements include research in clinical reasoning in nursing. Office: U NC Wilmington 601 S Coll Rd Wilmington NC 28403 Office Phone: 910-962-3343. Office Fax: 910-962-7656. E-mail: rakuiper@bellsouth.net, kuiperr@uncw.edu.

KUIRY, SURESH CHANDRA, materials engineer, researcher; arrived in U.S., 2001; s. Kailash Chandra and Chanchala Kuiry; m. Pritikana Prasad, June 27, 1997; 1 child, Shounak. BEngring in Metall. Engring., Regional Engring. Coll., Durgapur, 1986; MTech in Metall. and Materials Engring., Indian Inst. Tech., Kharagpur, India, 1991, PhD in Metall. and Materials Engring., 1996. Metall. engr. Tata Motors, Jamshedpur, India, 1986—89; asst. mgr. R&D Asea Brown Boveri Ltd., Vododara, India, 1996—96; mgr. R&D Mukand Ltd., Mumbai, India, 1996—2001; rsch. assoc. U. Ctrl. Fla., Orlando, 2001—04; sr. rsch. scientist Ctr. for Tribology, Inc., Campbell, Calif., 2004—. Contbr. articles to profl. jours. Recipient Nat. Young Metallurgist award, Ministry Steel and Mines, Govt. India, 1998, U. Gold medal, U. Burdwan, India, 1986; Nat. Merit scholar, Govt. West Bengal, India, 1979. Mem.: Electrochem. Soc., Am. Ceramic Soc., Materials Rsch. Soc., Indian Inst. Metals (life; hon. sec. 1998—2000). Achievements include research in development of nanomaterials for biological applications such as anti-aging, aleviation of free radical cell damage, treatment age-related problems in humans.

KUJALA, WALFRID EUGENE, musician, educator; b. Warren, Ohio, Feb. 19, 1925; s. Arvo August and Elsie Fannie (Ojajarvi) K.; m. Sherry Henry, Dec. 29, 1989; children by previous marriage: Stephen, Gwen, Daniel. MusB, Eastman Sch. Music, 1948, MusM, 1950. Flutist Rochester Philharm. Orch., 1948—54; soloist, flutist, piccoloist Chgo. Symphony Orch., 1954—2001; prof. flute Northwestern U., Evanston, Ill., 1962—. Vis. prof. of flute Shepherd Sch. Music, Rice U., 1995-97. Author: The Flutist's Progress, 1970, The Flutist's Vade Mecum of Scales, Arpeggios, Trills and Fingering Technique, 1995; consulting editor Flute Talk Mag., 1991—; contbr. articles to profl. jours.; performed world premiere of Concerto for Flute by Gunther Schuller with Chgo. Symphony Orch., conducted by Sir Georg Solti, 1988. Served with AUS, 1943-45, ETO, PTO. Recipient Exemplar of Music Tchg. award, Northwestern U., 1992. Mem.: Nat. Flute Assn. (past pres., Lifetime Achievement award 1997). Office: Sch Music Northwestern U Evanston IL 60208-2400 E-mail: walfridkujala@aol.com.

KUJAWA, SISTER ROSE MARIE, academic administrator; b. Detroit; d. Francis and Anne Kujawa. BS in math., Madonna U., Livonia, Mich., 1966; MS in edn. and math., Wayne State U., Detroit, 1971, PhD in higher edn. adminstrn., 1979. Dept. chair math. Bishop Borgess H.S.; asst. prin. and curriculum coord. Ladywood H.S.; prof. Madonna U., Livonia, Mich., 1975, academic dean, academic v.p., acting dean Coll. of Arts and Sci., pres., 2001—. Office: Madonna U 36600 Schoolcraft Rd Livonia MI 48150-1173

KUJAWA-HOLBROOK, SHERYL, theology studies educator, academic administrator; m. Paul BA, Marquette U.; MA, Sarah Lawrence Coll.; MTS, Harvard Div. Sch.; MDiv, Episcopal Div. Sch., 1983; EdD, Columbia U.; PhD, Boston Coll. & CUNY. Dir. ministries with young people Episcopal Ch. Ctr.; asst. Ch. Incarnation, NYC; youth missioner Diocese Mass.; asst. Cathedral Ch. of St. Paul, Boston; chaplain Dorchester Mental Health Ctr. & McLean Hosp., Mass.; assoc. prof. pastoral theology Episcopal Div. Sch., Cambridge, Mass., 1998—2004, Suzanne Radley Hiatt Chair in Feminist Pastoral Theology & Ch. History, 2004—, academic dean, 2005—. Chair anti-racism com. Episcopal Ch. Exec. Coun., 1998—. Author: A House of Prayer for All Peoples: Congregations Building Multiracial Community, By Grace Came Incarnation: A Social History of the Church of the Incarnation, Murray Hill, NY, 1952-2002; editor: A Documentary History of Women in the Episcopal Church; co-editor (with Fredrica Harris Thompsett): Deeper Joy: Lay Women and Vocation in the 20th Century Episcopal Church. Office: Episcopal Div Sch 99 Brattle St Cambridge MA 02138 E-mail: skujawa@eds.edu.*

KUJAWSKI, DANIEL, science educator; b. Bujenka, Poland, Feb. 23, 1948; came to U.S., 1996; s. Jan and Czeslawa Kujawska; m. Danuta Radziszewska, July 14, 1974; 1 child, Anna. MSc, Warsaw (Poland) Tech. U., 1973, DSc, 1992; PhD, Polish Acad. Scis., 1978. Lectr., sr. lectr. Warsaw Tech. U., 1975-89; lectr., sr. rsch. assoc. U. Alta., Edmonton, Can., 1989-96; from assoc. prof. to prof. Western Mich. U., Kalamazoo, 1996—. Co-chmn. low-cycle fatigue com. Polish Group Fracture, 1987-89. Author: (textbook) Fatigue Life of Metals, 1991, (book) Modeling of the Fatigue Life and Crack Propagation in Metals, 1991. Killam postdoctoral scholar U. Alta., Edmonton, 1983-85. Mem. ASME, SAE. Achievements include research in the mech. behavior of metals and composites, fatigue and fracture mechanics. Avocations: tennis, swimming, walking. Office: Western Mich U Mech and Aero Engring Kalamazoo MI 49008 Office Phone: 269-276-3428. Office Fax: 269-276-3421. Business E-Mail: daniel.kujawski@wmich.edu.

KUJAWSKI, ELIZABETH SZANCER, art curator, consultant; b. N.Y.C., Feb. 7, 1951; d. Henryk and Irene (Zilz) Szancer; children: Melissa, Stephanie. BA cum laude in Art History and Italian, Douglass Coll., 1972; MA in Art History, Queens Coll., 1975. Info. asst. Whitney Mus. Am. Art, N.Y.C., 1972-75; asst. curator Collection of Nelson A. Rockefeller, N.Y.C., 1975-79; asst. dir. SKT Galleries, Inc., N.Y.C., 1979-82; prin., art curator, cons. Elizabeth Szancer Kujawski Art Advisors, N.Y.C., 1982—. Mem. exhbn. com. Internat. Ctr. Photography, N.Y.C. Mem.: Art Table, Inc., Internat. Assn. Profl. Art Advisors (pres. 1998—2000, bd. dirs. 2000—05). Avocations: tennis, languages, travel. Office: 767 5th Ave Ste 4200 New York NY 10153-0023 Office Phone: 212-572-3867. Personal E-mail: eartsk@aol.com.

KUKES, PATRICK J., music educator; b. Billings, Mont., Jan. 22, 1952; s. Herman Dennis Kukes and Louise Reed; m. Cathy M. Dumas, July 10, 1992; children: Kiara Lenn, Kelly Ann. B in Music Edn., Mont. State U., 1974. Lic. profl. tchr. Wis. Orch. dir., youth symphony condr. Helena (Mont.) Sch. Dist., 1974—96; choral dir. Absarokee (Mont.) Sch. Dist., 1996—99; orch. dir. Aberdeen (S.D.) Sch. Dist., 1999—2001; mid. sch. choral dir. Ft. Lupton (Colo.) Sch. Dist., 2001—02; orch. dir. Greeley (Colo.) Sch. Dist. 6, 2002—04; string educator Madison (Wis.) Met. Sch. Dist., 2004—05; orch. dir. Natrona County H.S., Casper, Wis., 2005—. Studio musician, 1974—2005; condr. C.R. Anderson Orch. representing USA, Winter Olympics, 1988. Pres. Civitan Club Internat., Helena, 1982—84. Named Mont. State Fiddle Champion, 1974. Mem.: Music Educators Nat. Conf. (assoc.), Am. String Tchrs. Assn. (assoc.; state v.p. 1992—94). Avocations: fiddling, fishing, hiking, canoeing. Home: 1660 Clifton Ct Casper WY 82609 Office: 930 S Elm St Casper WY 82501 Office Phone: 307-577-6642. Personal E-mail: wolfzbear@aol.com.

KUKHTIN, ALEXANDER V., chemist; s. Victor A. Kukhtin and Gulnara T. Kukhtina; m. Nataliya N. Tikhonova, July 3, 1993. BS in Chemistry, Lomonosov Moscow State U., 1993, PhD in Chemistry, 1996. Chemist Engelhard Inst. Molecular Biology, Moscow, 1997—2000, Argonne (Ill.) Nat. Lab., 2000—. Soros Postgrad. scholar, Open Soc. Inst. (Soros Found.), 1994. Mem.: N.Y. Acad. Scis., Am. Chem. Soc. Achievements include patents for novel biochip reader; patents pending for novel substrate for protein biochip fabrication; research in use of biochips for rapid detection of pathogenic microorganisms. Office: Argonne Nat Lab 9700 S Cass Ave Argonne IL 60439

KUKIELKA, GILBERT LEON, physician; b. San Jose, Costa Rica, Jan. 28, 1959; came to U.S., 1987; s. Zelman Kukielka and Regina Hedrych; m. Morissa J. Ladinsky, Sept. 1, 1991; children: Andrew, Nicole. MD with highest honors, U. Costa Rica, 1983. Diplomate in internal medicine, cardiovasc. disease and interventional cardiology Am. Bd. Internal Medicine. Intern U. Costa Rica, San Jose, 1982-83, resident internal medicine, 1984-87, chief med. resident, 1986-87; resident internal medicine Baylor Coll. Medicine, Houston, 1988-90, fellow cardiovascular scis., 1990-94, rsch. asst. prof., 1992-95, asst. prof., 1995-96, adj. asst. prof., 1996—; fellow in cardiology Johns Hopkins U. Sch. Medicine, Balt., 1995-98, interventional cardiology fellow, 1998-99; peripheral vascular interventional fellow Lindner Ctr. Cardiovascular Clin. Rsch./Christ Hosp., Cin., 1999-2000; asst. prof., dir. peripheral vascular intervention Ohio State U., Columbus. Sci. reviewer Jour. Leukocyte Biology, 1993—, Circulation, 1994—, Gene, 1994—; contbr. articles to profl. jours. Recipient Outstanding Achievement award for basic rsch. Curaflex, 1992, Young Investigator award So. Soc. Pediat. Rsch., 1992, Virginia and Ernest Cocknell Jr. award The Meth. Hosp. Found., Houston, 1995, Outstanding Young Ams., 1988, Am. Coll. Cardiology/Bristol-Myers Squibb award, 1999; named one of Am.'s Top Physicians Consumers' Rsch. Coun. Am., 2003; Baylor Coll. Medicine grantee, 1994. Fellow ACP, Am. Coll. Cardiology, Soc. for Cardiovascular Angiography and Interventions; mem. AMA, Johns Hopkins Med. and Surg. Assn., Soc. Leukocyte Biology (Young Investigator award 1994). Office: Ohio State U Heart Ctr 473 West 12th St 200 HL RI Columbus OH 43210 E-mail: gkukielka@gmail.com.

KUKKADAPU, RAVI, research scientist; s. Harinath and Suguna Devi Kukkadapu; m. Prashanthi Debbad, Mar. 10, 1991; children: Mukthi Nath, Sai Nath. MS, Osmania U., 1979—81; PhD, Indian Inst. of Chem. Tech., 1981—86. Sr. rsch. scientist Pacific NW Nat. Lab., Richland, Wash., 2003—04, sr. rsch. scientist ii, 2005—. Mem.: Internat. EPR Soc., Clay Minerals Soc. of Am. Achievements include patents for. Office: Pacific Northwest Nat Lab Emsl Richland WA 99352 Office Fax: 509-376-3650.

KUKLA, EDWARD RICHARD, rare books & special collections librarian; b. Detroit, Jan. 31, 1941; s. Stanley Frank and ClaraBelle (Morton) K. BA, Wayne State U., 1962; MA, U. Mich., 1963, MLS, 1973. Asst. instr. Mich. State U., East Lansing, 1970-72; media mobile libr. State Libr. of Mich., 1972; asst. libr. rare books and manuscripts Greenfield Village and Henry Ford Mus., Dearborn, Mich., 1974-78; rare books and spl. collections libr. Wash. State U., Pullman, 1979-86; libr. Mpls. Athenaeum, 1987—2005; head spl. collections dept. Mpls. Pub. Libr., 1987—2003, spl. collections bibliographer, 2004—05. Educator, lectr. rare books, history of books and printing, book collecting; reviewer NEH. Author: Un estudio critico sobre Altazor de Vicente Huidobro, 1963, The Scholar and the Future of the Research Library Revisited, 1973, The Struggle and the Glory: A Special Bicentennial Exhibition, 1976. Recipient C. Allen Harlan scholarship, 1958, medal of distinction Fgn. Lang., 1958, Cert. of Appreciation, Mpls. Pub. Libr. Bd., 2004; tchg. fellow U. Mich, Ann Arbor, 1963-66. Mem. ALA, Assn. Coll. and Rsch. Librs. (rare books sect. 1990, local arrangements com.), U. Mich. Sch. Libr. Sci. Alumni Assn. (life), Am. Contract Bridge League, Am. Cut Glass Assn. (life), Am. Film Inst. (charter), English First (life), Haviland Collectors Internationale Found., Minn. Film Arts Founders Club, Pickard Collectors Club (charter), Walker Art Ctr., Mich. Jr. Acad. Sci., Art and Letters (jr. mem.), U. Mich. Union Club (life), Phi Beta Kappa, Sigma Delta Pi, Beta Phi Mu. Home: 2439 3rd Ave S Apt C-11 Minneapolis MN 55404-3518

KUKLIN, SUSAN BEVERLY, law librarian, lawyer; b. Chgo., Nov. 25, 1947; d. Albert and Marion (Waller) K. BA in English and History with honors, U. Ariz., 1969, JD, 1973; MLS, Ind. U., 1970; LLM in Taxation, DePaul U., 1981. Bar: Ariz. 1973, Ill. 1980, Calif. 1984, U.S. Dist. Ct. (no. dist.) Ill. 1980. Asst. city atty. City of Phoenix, 1974-75; dep. county atty. County of Pima, Ariz., 1975-76; polit. sci., law libr. asst. prof. law No. Ill. U., 1976-78; law libr., assoc. prof. U. S.D., 1978-79; dir. law libr., asst. prof. DePaul U., 1979-83; law libr. Santa Clara County, San Jose, Calif., 1983—. Sec. bd. trustees Law Library Santa Clara County. Mem. Am. Assn. Law Libr. (cert. law libr.), Coun. Calif. County Law Libr. (newsletter editor 1983-84), No. Calif. Assn. Law Libr., Phi Beta Kappa, Phi Kappa Phi, Alpha Lambda Delta, Phi Alpha Theta, Phi Delta Phi. Office: Santa Clara County Law Library 360 N 1st St San Jose CA 95113-1004 E-mail: sbkuklin@earthlink.net.

KUKLINSKI, JOAN LINDSEY, librarian; b. Lynn, Mass., Nov. 28, 1950; d. Richard Jay and M. Claire (Murphy) Card; m. Walter S. Kuklinski, June 17, 1972. BA cum laude, Mass. State Coll., Salem, 1972; MLS, U. R.I., 1976; CAGS in Pub. Adminstrn., Clark U., 2002. Classified librarian U. R.I. Extension Divsn. Libr., Providence, 1974-75, U. R.I. Cataloging Dept., Kingston, 1975-79; original cataloger Tex. A&M U. Libr., College Station, 1979-82; cataloger Goldfarb Libr., Braindeis U., Waltham, Mass., 1982-83, automation coord., 1983-85; exec. dir. Minuteman Libr. Network, Framingham, Mass., 1985-96, C/W Mars, Inc., Paxton, Mass., 1996—. Mem. Town of South Kingstown (R.I.) Women's Adv. Commn., 1977-79; trustee Princeton (Mass.) Pub. Libr., 1994—; mem. strategic planning com. for libr. svc. in yr. 2000 Mass. Bd. Libr. Commrs. Mem. ALA (resources and tech. svcs. divsn. 1980-85), Mass. Librs. Assn., New Eng. Libr. Assn., Libr. Info. Tech. Assn., Assn. Specialized Libr. and Coop. Groups (NELINET Bd. 1994—), Am. Contract Bridge League, Delta Tau Kappa. Office: C/W Mars Inc 1 Sunset Ln Paxton MA 01612-1105

KUKLOK, KEVIN B., career officer; b. Fargo, N.D., Dec. 20, 1946; m. Diana Lynn Roper; children: Nicole, Bryce. BS in Chem. Engring., U. N.D., 1968; MBA, U.S. Internat. U., San Diego; grad., Naval Aviation Flight Tng., Pensacola, Fla., 1969, Amphibious Warfare Sch., 1979. Commd. 2nd lt. USMC, 1968, advanced through grades to maj. gen., 1997; assigned to UH-1E helicopter transition HML-267, 1969; with HML-367, 1970-71; forward air contr. 2nd Bn. 7th Marines; with 4th Marine Aircraft Wing with HMA-773, Santa Ana, Calif., 1973-76; tng. officer CH-46 helicopter with HMM-766 Selfridge ANG Base, Mount Clemens, Mich.; with S-1 and maintenance dept. HMM-774, Norfolk, Va.; comdg. officer H&MS-41 Det B, 1986-88, HMM-764, 1988-92; dep. comdr., mobilization coord. MAG-46; dir. readiness and safety 4th Marine Aircraft Wing MARRESFOR, New Orleans; comdg. gen. Reserve Marine Air Ground Task Force East Command Element, Camp Lejeune, N.C., 4th Marine Aircraft Wing, New Orleans. Decorated Air medal with Numeral 66. Mailing: Hdqs Marine Corps Divsn Pub Affairs Washington DC 20380-0001

KUKOC, TONI, professional basketball player; b. Croatia, Sept. 18, 1968; Forward Chicago Bulls, 1993-99, Phila. 76ers, 1999—. Named European Player of the Yr.; recipient NBA Sixth Man of the Yr., 1995—96. Avocations: yachting, fishing, tennis, golf, movies. Office: Phila 76ers 1st Union Ctr Philadelphia PA 19148

KUKORA, JOHN STEVEN, surgeon; b. Detroit, Sept. 13, 1948; BS, U. Mich., MD, 1973. Intern U. Mich. Hosp., Ann Arbor, 1973-74, resident, 1974-79; sr. surgeon Abington (Pa.) Meml. Hosp., 1985—, chmn. surgery, 2004—; prof. surgery Temple U. Sch. Medicine, 1989—. Mem. Am. Assn. Endocrine Surgeons, Am. Coll. Surgeons, Am. Soc. Gastrointestinal Endoscopy, Soc. Am. Gastrointestinal Endoscopic Surgeons, Assn. Acad. Surgery, Am. Coll. Endocrinology. Office: 1245 Highland Ave Ste 604 Abington PA 19001-3714 Office Phone: 215-481-7464.

KUKSI, KRIS M., artist; b. Springfield, Mo., Mar. 2, 1973; s. Letha Mae and Vincent Clupny (Stepfather). MFA, Ft. Hays State U., 2002. Fine art, The Throne of Lucifer (First Pl. Artrom gallery Fantastic 2005 competition, 2005), one-man shows include The Strange and the Fantastic, The Great Passage, The Within, Toward the Within. Finalist 2d Pl. award, Impact Artists Gallery, 2002; recipient award of Merit, Williamsburg Art and Hist. Ctr., 2003, Publ., Slowart Productions, 2003. Mem.: Soc. for the Art of imagination (assoc.). Home: 717 1/2 Main B Hays KS 67601 Office: Kris Kuksi PO Box 1531 Hays KS 67601 Office Phone: 785-650-4990. Personal E-mail: kkuksi@hotmail.com.

KULAKOWSKY, BARRY L., elementary school educator; b. West Reading, Pa., Mar. 24, 1949; s. Stephen and Carolyn June Kulakowsky; m. Barbara N. Bowie, Nov. 23, 1974; children: Lisa Michelle, Peter Bruce. BS, Millersville U., Pa., 1971; Med, Lehigh U., Bethlehem, Pa., 1974. Cert. elem. prin. U. of Pa., 1980. Elem. tchr. Boyertown Area Sch. Dist., Boyertown, Pa., 1971—; interim prin. Pine Forge Elem. Sch., Pine Forge, Pa. Profl. edn. coun. rep. Boyertown Area Sch. Dist., Boyertown, Pa., 1996—. Cub master pack 597 Cub Scouts of Am., Amityville, Pa., 1987—90; boy scout merit badge counselor Boy Scouts of Am., Hawk Mountain Coun., Pa., 1980—2005; mem. and vice chmn. of amity township's recycling com. Amity Twp., Amityville, Pa.; adult Sun. sch. tchr. St. Paul's United Ch. of Christ, Amityville, Pa., 1987—2005, 250th anniversary com. chairperson, 1994—2003; mem., past pres. Parent -Teacher-Child Orgn., Pine Forge, Pa. Recipient Spl. Edn. award, Millersville U., 1969, 1970. Mem.: Boyertown Area Edn. Assn. (assoc.; exec. com. mem. & bldg. representative(various times)), NEA (life), Pa. State Edn. Assn. (life). United Church Of Christ. Avocations: walking, golf, travel, gardening, reading. Office: Pine Forge Elementary School 8 Glendale Rd Boyertown PA 19518 Office Phone: 610-323-7609. Office Fax: 610-323-8651. E-mail: bkulakowsky2@boyertownasd.org.

KULCINSKI, GERALD LAVERNE, nuclear engineer, educator, dean; b. La Crosse, Wis., Oct. 27, 1939; s. Harold Franklin and June Kramer K.; m. Janet Noreen Berg, Nov. 25, 1961; children: Kathryn, Brian, Karen. BS in Chem. Engring., U. Wis., 1961, MS in Nuclear Engring., 1962, PhD in Nuclear Engring., 1965. Rschr. Los Alamos (N.Mex.) Nuclear Lab., 1963; lectr. Ctr. Grad. Study, Richland, Wash., 1965-71; sr. rsch. sci. Battelle Northwest Lab., Richland, 1965-71; prof. U. Wis., Madison, 1972—, dir. Fusion Tech. Inst., 1973-75, 79—, Grainger Prof. Nuclear Engring., 1984—, assoc. dean coll. engring., 2001—. Vis. sci. Karlsruhe (Germany) Nuclear Rsch. Ctr., 1977, Bechtel Corp., San Francisco, 1989, 95; active Gov. Energy Policy Task Force, Wis., 1980; U.S. del. to Internat. Tokamak Reactor Project, Vienna, Austria, 1979-81; mem. adv. panel INTOR, 1987; mem. numerous review panels, including Los Alamos Nat. lab., Sandia Nat. Lab., Argonne Nat. Lab. Assoc. editor: Fusion Engring. and Design. Recipient Curtis W. McGraw Rsch. award Engring. Rsch. Com. Am. Assn. Engring. Edn., 1978, John Randle Grumman Achievement award Grumman Aircraft Corp., 1987, Leadership Fusion award Fusion Power Assocs., 1992, NASA Pub. Svc. medal, 1993, Disting. Faculty award Wis. Alumni Assn., 1994, Big 10 Centennial award, 1995. Fellow Am. Nuclear Soc. (sec. Richland sect. 1970, student advisor Wis. chpt. 1972-73, chmn. 2nd topical meeting on fusion tech. 1976, bd. dirs. 1987-90, chmn 16th topical meeting on fusion tech. 2004, Outstanding Achievement award 1980); mem. NAE. Home: 6013 Greentree Rd Madison WI 53711-3125 Office: U Wis 1500 Johnson Dr Madison WI 53706-1609 Business E-Mail: kulcinski@engr.wisc.edu.

KULENOVIC, DZAFER JEFF, bank executive, advocate; b. Dusseldorf, Germany, July 1, 1965; arrived in US, 1974; s. Nahid Kulenovic and Marijana Dezelic; m. Selma Kljako, June 21, 1992; 1 child, Jasmina. BBA with honors, Loyola U., Chgo., 1987; MBA, DePaul U., Chgo., 1990. Auditor River Forest Banc Corp, Chgo., 1987—92; loan rev. assoc. First Colonial Bankshares, Chgo., 1991—92; loan rev. officer Bank One Ill., Chgo., 1992—95; v.p. credit adminstrn. GreatBanc, Inc., Chgo., 1995—2005; dep. chief credit officer Bridgeview Bank, Chgo., 2005—. Radio commentator Voice of Croatia, Chgo., 1991—93, Voice of Bosniacs, 1993—94; dir. Bosnia United; v.p. and sec. Congress of North Am. Bosniacs, 2002—; mem. governing bd. Party Dem. Action, Sarajevo, Bosnia-Herzegovina, 2002—; bd. dirs. Chgo. Math. & Sci. Acad. Contbr. articles to Bosnian newspapers. Election judge, Chgo., 1998—99; pres. Islamic Cultural Ctr. Recipient Life Achievement award, Islamic Cultural Ctr., 1995. Mem.: Chgo. Math. & Sci. Acad., Risk Mgmt. Assn. (assoc.), Am. Croatian Soc. (corr.), Dem. Action Party Chgo. (corr.; pres. 1995—99, 2002—04, Life Time Achievement award 1997), Bosnian Am. Cultural Assn. (corr.; sec. 1995—2004, dir. 1992—2003, Appreciation award 2004), Mus. of Sci. & Industry (corr.). R-Conservative. Muslim. Avocations: travel, stamp collecting/philately, coin collecting/numismatics, swimming, golf. Office Phone: 773-989-5748. Personal E-mail: d.kulenovic@comcast.net.

KULESA, PATRICK, sociologist; b. Washington, May 13, 1971; s. Jerome John and Patricia Marie Kulesa. BS, Mt. St. Mary's U., 1993; MS, Purdue U., 1995; PhD, Northwestern U., 1999. Global rsch. dir. ISR, Chgo., 1999—. Cons. Symphony Orch. Inst., Evanston, Ill., 1997—99. Author: (column) Security Management; contbr. articles to profl. jours. Mem.: APA, Internat. Assn. Applied Psychology, Soc. for Psychol. Study of Social Issues, Am. Sociol. Assn. Roman Catholic. Avocations: travel, tennis, Tae Kwon Do. Office: LSR 303 E Ohio St Ste 2100 Chicago IL 60611 Office Phone: 312-828-9725. Personal E-mail: pkulesa@hotmail.com. E-mail: patrick.kulesa@isrinsight.com.

KULESZA, CHESTER STEPHEN (BUD KULESZA), financial executive; b. Elizabeth, NJ, Jan. 12, 1947; s. Chester S. and Mary Ellen (Sales) K.; m. Kathleen Marie Hickman, June 14, 1969; children: Kevin Michael, Marie Kathleen. AAS in Acctg., Middlesex County Coll., Edison, N.J., 1969; BS in Commerce, Rider U., 1973. Cert. mgmt. acct. Inst. Mgmt. Accts., cert. fin. mgmt. With fin./acctg. depts. Johnson & Johnson, New Brunswick, N.J., 1969-73; asst. contr. ITT Morton Frozen Foods, Charlottesville, Va., 1973—81; sr. fin. mgr. RJR Delmonte Frozen Foods, San Francisco, 1981-83; v.p., contr. ITT Bus. & Consumer Comm., Raleigh, NC, 1983—86; CFO, contr. ITT Electromech. Components, Fountain Valley, Calif., 1986—90; sr. v.p. fin. ITT Automotive-Worldwide, Auburn Hills, Mich., 1990—98. Presenter XV World Congress of Accountancy, 1997. Author of book foreword: The Practice Analysis of Management Accounting, 1996; contbr. articles to profl. jours. Chmn. acctg. and fin. adv. bd. Oakland U., Rochester, Mich., 1994—; bus. adv. curriculum com. Detroit Coll. of Bus., Dearborn, Mich., 1996—; acctg. accreditation com. Internat. Assn. Mgmt. Edn., St. Louis, 1997. With U.S. Army, 1964-67. Honoree Beta Gamma Sigma, 1997. Mem. Inst. Mgmt. Accts. (nat. pres. 1999-2000, bd. dirs.), Fin. Execs. Inst. (chair acad. rels. com. Detroit chpt. 1995—), Beta Alpha Psi (hon.). Republican. Avocations: accounting education, wine tasting, gourmet cooking, travel, choir. Home: 10301 Rhett Butler Dr Austin TX 78739-1674 Personal E-mail: bud.kulesza@att.net.

KULICKE, ROBERT M., artist; b. Phila., Mar. 9, 1924; Student, Phila. Coll. Art, Tyler Sch. Arts, Temple Univ., Academie Leger, Paris, 1949—51. Instr. Univ. Calif., 1964, 1970, Jewelry Arts Inst., NYC, 1964—74, dir., 1974—87, assoc., 1987; co-founder, co-dir. Kulicke-Stark Acad. Jewelry Art, NYC, 1974—88. One-man shows include Kornblee Gallery, NYC, 1970—73, Davis & Long, 1974—80, Mus. Art, Pa. State Univ., 1978, Davis & Langdale Co., NYC, 1981—2000, Columbia Mus. Art & Sci., So. Carolina, 1983, John C. Stoller & Co., Mpls., 1985, John F. Warren, Phila., 1988, Campbell-Thiebaud Gallery, San Francisco, 1991, 1994, Locks Gallery, Phila., 1992, Courtyard Gallery, Washington Studio Sch., 1993. Recipient Interior Design award, Am. Inst. Interior Designers, 1968. Mem.: NAD (academician 1994—).

KULIK, ROSALYN FRANTA, food company executive, consultant; b. Wilmington, Del., Aug. 29, 1951; d. William Alfred and Virginia Louise (Ellis) Franta. BS in Voc. Home Econs. Edn., Purdue U., 1972, MS in Foods and Nutrition, 1974; postgrad. in advanced mgmt. program, Harvard Bus. Sch., 1990. Registered dietitian. Home economist Kellogg Co., Battle Creek, Mich., 1974-75, nutrition and consumer specialist, 1975-77, mgr. advt. to children, 1977-79, corp. adminstrv. asst., 1979, dir. nutrition, 1979-82, dir. nutrition and analytical services, 1982, v.p. nutrition and chemistry, 1983, v.p.

quality and nutrition, 1983-87, v.p., asst. to chmn., 1987-88; exec. v.p., gen. mgr. Fearn Internat., Franklin Park, Ill., 1988-90; cons., 1991—. Adj. faculty U. Tampa, Fla., 2001—. Contbr. articles on food sci. and nutrition to profl. jours. Tampa Bay regional coord. Camp Invention, Inc., 2004—; mem. ch. coun. Grace Luth. Ch., Tampa, Fla., 2000—03, 2004—; bd. dirs. State Arthritis Found., County Vol. Ctr., Homeowners Property Assn. Avila, Neighborhood Property Owners Assn., 2002—. Recipient Ada Decker Malott Meml. scholarship, Purdue U., 1970, disting. alumna Purdue U. Sch. of Consumer and Family Sci. Fellow Am. Dietetic Assn. (cofounder, exec. officer nutrition in complementary care dietetic practice group 1998-2004, chair 2002-03); mem. Inst. Food Technologists (profl. mem.), Am. Dietetic Assn., Phi Kappa Phi, Gamma Sigma Delta, Omicron Nu, Alpha Omicron Pi. Republican. Lutheran. Avocations: music, church work, travel, jr. league volunteerism. Personal E-mail: kulikcon@msn.com.

KULIKOWSKI, CASIMIR ALEXANDER, computer scientist, engineer, educator; b. Hertford, Herts, Eng., May 4, 1944; arrived in U.S., 1961; s. Victor A. and Isabel S. (Tuckett) Kulikowski; m. Christine A. Wilk, May 31, 1969; children: Michael Edward, Victoria Anne. BE with honors, Yale U., 1965, MS, 1966; PhD, U. Hawaii, 1970. From asst. prof. to assoc. prof. Rutgers U., New Brunswick, NJ, 1970—77, prof., 1977—97, chmn. dept. computer sci., 1984—90, dir. Lab. Computer Sci. Rsch., 1985—96, bd. govs. prof., 1997—. Mem. bd. sci. counselors Nat. Libr. Medicine, Bethesda, Md., 1984—87; mem. biomed. libr. rev. com. NIH, 1994—99, chair, 1997—99; co-chair sci. program com. World Congress on Med. Informatics, 2004. Author: A Practical Guide to Designing Expert Systems, 1984, Computer Systems that Learn, 1992; editor: Artificial Intelligence Expert Systems and Languages in Modeling & Simulation, 1988; co-editor: Yearbook of Medical Informatics, 2001—; assoc. editor: Artificial Intelligence in Medicine Jour., 2001—; mem. editl. bd. Computers in Biology and Medicine, 1980—, Jour. Am. Med. Informatics Assn., 1993—98, Methods Info. in Medicine, 1999—, Iterations: An Interdisciplinary Jour. of Software History, 2001—. Pres. Highland Park (N.J.) Residents Assn., 1983—88. Fellow: IEEE, AAAS, Am. Inst. Med. and Biol. Engring., Am. Coll. Med. Informatics, Am. Assn. Artificial Intelligence; mem.: NAS Inst. Medicine. Office: Rutgers U Dept Computer Sci Hill Ctr Busch Campus New Brunswick NJ 08903 Office Phone: 732-445-2006.

KULKARNI, BIDY, reproductive endocrinologist, biomedical researcher, consultant; b. Janwa, Maharashtra, India, Apr. 18, 1930; arrived in U.S., 1961; s. Dhondu Y. Kulkarni and Sita Deshpande; m. Suman Sane, May 8, 1957; children: Neela, Bob. BS, Ferguson Coll., Poona, India, 1952; MS, U. Poona, 1956, PhD, 1962. Post doctoral fellow Clark U. and Worcester Found., Shrewsbury, Mass., 1961—64, Nat. Rsch. Coun., Ottawa, Canada, 1964—66; sect. chief dept. endocrinology S.W. Rsch. Found., San Antonio, 1967—70; asst. prof. ob-gyn. U. Chgo., 1970—73; dir. gynecol. endocrinology Michael Reese U., Chgo., 1970—72; dir. reproductive endocrinology Loyola U. Med. Ctr., Maywood, Ill., 1973—79, assoc. prof. ob-gyn., 1973—79; dir. reproductive endocrinology Cook County Hosp., Chgo., 1980—93; assoc. prof. ob-gyn. Chgo. Med. Sch., N. Chgo., 1981—93; pres. Rsch. and Edn. Svcs., Darien, Ill., 1991—. Cons. in field; dir. perinatal ctr. Loyola U. Med. Ctr., Maywood, 1975—77; hon. attending physician Cook County Hosp., Chgo., 1993—. Contbr. articles to profl. jours., chapters to books. Named Outstanding Citizen of Yr., Met. Chgo., 1973; grantee, Ctr. for Population Rsch., NIH, Agy. for Internat. Devel. Mem.: Internat. Fedn. Fertility Socs., Am. Fertility Soc., Nat. Acad. Biochemistry, Soc. for Study of Reprodn., Endocrine Soc., Chgo. Gynecol. Soc. (life), Chgo. Gynecol. Soc. (life Outstanding Scientist 2000), Soc. Reproductive Medicine (life). Democrat. Avocations: badminton, hiking, travel. Home: 9 S 155 Nantucket Darien IL 60561 Office: Rsch and Edn Svcs 9 S 155 Nantucket Darien IL 60561

KULKARNI, KISHORE GANESH, economics professor, consultant; b. Oct. 31, 1953; arrived in U.S., 1976; s. Ganesh Y. and Sindhu G. Dhekane; m. Jayu K., Aug. 17, 1980; children: Lina, Aditi. BA, U. Poona, India, 1974, MA, 1976, U. Pitts., 1978, PhD., 1982. Tchg. asst. U. Pitts., 1976—78, tchg. fellow, 1978—80, prof. semester at sea program, 1994, asst. prof. Johnstown, Pa., 1981—82, U. Ctrl. Ark., Conway, 1982—86; assoc. prof. U. La., Monroe, 1986—89, Met. State Coll., Denver, 1989—93, prof., 1993—, chmn. dept. econs., 1994—97. Author: Principles of Macro Monetary Theory, Modern Monetary Theory, Readings in International Economics; co-author: Understanding Microeconomics, Understanding Macroeconomics, Role of LIC in Economic Development of India; editor: Indian Jour. of Econs. and Bus., website; contbr. articles to profl. jours. Recipient 1st prize, Forum of Free Enterprise, Bombay, India, 1975, Rama Watumull Fund award, Honolulu, 1977, Disting. Svc. award, Faculty Senate Met. State Coll., Denver, 2004; fellow, Nat. Inst. Bank Mgmt., Pune, India, 1974, Winrock Internat., Morrilton, Ark., 1984—85. Mem.: Assn. Indian Econ. Studies, So. Econ. Assn., Southwestern Econ. Assn., Am. Econ. Assn., Golden Key Nat. Hon. Soc. (Outstanding Scholar/Rschr. 1997, Outstanding tchr. 2001). Avocation: tennis. Home: 2249 S Miller Ct Lakewood CO 80227 Office Phone: 303-556-2675. Business E-Mail: kulkarnk@mscd.edu.

KULKARNI, SHAILESH S., engineering educator; s. Manisha S Kulkarni; m. Rohini R Patankar, Dec. 21, 1997. B in Engring., U. Bombay, India, 1991; M in Mgmt. Studies, U. Bombay, 1994; MS, PhD, U. Cin., 1999. Structural design engr. Humphrey's and Glasgow Cons., Bombay, 1991—92; asst. prof. U. of North Tex., Denton, Tex., 1999—. Author: (journals) IIE Transactions; contbr. articles to profl. jours. Fellow PDI fellow, Profl. Devel. Inst., Univ. of North Tex., 2004—, George and Marion Plossl Doctoral Disseration (Hon. Mention) fellow, Am. Prodn. and Inventory Control Soc., 1998. Mem.: Decision Sciences Inst., Inst. for Ops. Rsch. and Mgmt. Sci., Prodn. and Ops. Mgmt. Soc. Achievements include development of new insights into strategic supply chain configuration decisions. Office: University of North Texas Box 305249 Denton TX 76203-5249 Office Phone: 940-565-4769. Office Fax: 940-565-4935. Business E-Mail: kulkarni@unt.edu.

KULL, BRYAN PAUL, information technology executive; b. Newark, Jan. 23, 1960; s. Paul and Joan Lorraine (Schell) K.; m. Lindsay Fairfield Patton, Nov. 26, 1983; children: Taylor Bryan, Kathryn. BS in Mgmt., Keene (N.H.) State Coll., 1982; MBA in Mktg., So. Ill. U., 1987. Sales rep. Warner-Lambert Co., Morris Plains, NJ, 1982—84; key account mgr. Clorox Co., Oakland, Calif., 1984—86; divsn. mgr. Alberto-Culver Co., Melrose Park, Ill., 1986—89; area mgr. Schering-Plough Corp., Memphis, 1989—90; nat. sales mgr. Shering-Plough Healthcare, Liberty Corner, NJ, 1991—94; v.p. spl. mkts. Sunshine Biscuits, Inc., Woodbridge, NJ, 1994—96; v.p. client svc. Info. Resources, Inc., Fairfield, NJ, 1997—2000; ptnr. Computer Sci. Corp., West Orange, NJ, 2000—01; client ptnr. Cambridge Technology Ptnrs., Mass., 2001—03; v.p. Intellinex LLC, N.Y.C., 2003—. Mem. Triathlon Fedn., Davis, Calif., 1988-89. Mem. Assn. MBA Execs., Nat. Assn. Chain Drug Stores (assoc.), Pres.'s Club at Schering-Plough. Republican. Presbyterian. Avocations: golf, tennis, skiing, bicycling, wine collecting.

KULL, MICHAEL D., management consultant; m. Rebecca A. Ward, Oct. 10, 2004. PhD, George Washington U., 2002. Prin. AMPLIFI, Arlington, Va., 1998—. Grantee, NSF, 1997. Mem.: Acad. Mgmt.

KULLAS, ALBERT JOHN, management consultant, systems engineer; b. Webster, Mass., May 5, 1917; s. Albert J. and Mary (Piechowiak) K.; m. Joyce M. Gladue, Jan. 31, 1942; children: Michael, Daniel, Mark, James. BS in Civil Engring., Worcester Poly. Inst., 1938; grad., Am. Mgmt. Assn., 1956; MS in Civil Engring., NYU, 1940; grad., Sloan Sch. Mgmt. Sr. Execs., MIT, 1973. Registered profl. engr. With Martin Marietta Corp., 1940-82, structures mgr. Balt., 1955-57, chief engr., 1957, design engring. mgr., 1957-59, tech. devel. mgr., 1959-60, Dyna Soar and Gemini Launch vehicle tech. dir., 1960-62, research and engring. dir. Denver, 1962-65, dir. tech. ops., 1965-66, dir. space sci., research, adv. tech., 1966-67, dir. Voyager program, 1967-68, dir. Planetary Systems, 1968, dir. Viking project, div. v.p., 1969-72, div. v.p. ops. rev., 1972-73, v.p. data systems, 1973-82; mgmt. and systems engring. cons. Littleton, Colo., 1982-98; pres. Albert J. Kullas, Inc. Rsch. and tech. panel space vehicles NASA, 1968-78; chmn. bd. Biax Corp., 1987-90; 1st v.p. Highlands, Inc., 1999-2004; bd. dirs. THI. Contbr. articles to profl. jours. Rsch. adv. coun. Colo. State U., 1971—; treas. Porter Hosp. Found., 1980-85, 1st v.p., 1986-88, pres., 1988-90, v.p., 1990-93, emeritus, 2003—; bd. dirs. Colo. Jud. Inst., 1980-91, chmn., 1984-86; exec. com. Rocky Mountain Sci. Coun., 1964-65; bd. dirs. MIT Alumni Colo., 1990-2002. Recipient Robert H. Goddard award Worcester Poly. Inst., 1962 Fellow AIAA (award 1967); Asso. fellow (chmn. honors and awards com. 1973-81); mem. ASCE, Sigma Xi, Tau Beta Pi. Home: 5088 W Maplewood Ave Littleton CO 80123-6729 *I believe that being thorough, consistent, and persistent in pursuing one's convictions are necessary ingredients for personal and managerial success.*

KULLBERG, DUANE REUBEN, accounting firm executive; b. Red Wing, Minn., Oct. 6, 1932; s. Carl Reuben and Hazel Norma (Swanson) K.; m. Sina Nell Turner, Oct. 19, 1958 (dec. Sept. 1989); children: Malissa Kullberg, Caroline Godellas; m. Susan Turley, Dec. 30, 1992; stepchildren: Betsy Lucas, Jane Holtzermann. BBA, U. Minn., 1954. With Arthur Andersen & Co., S.C., 1954-89, ptnr., 1967-89, mng. ptnr., Mpls., 1970-74, dep. mng. ptnr., Chgo., 1975-78, vice chmn. acctg. and audit practice worldwide, 1978-80, mng. ptnr., CEO, 1980-89, ret., 1989. Bd. dirs. Nuveen Investments, Inc., Carlson Cos., Inc., Chgo. Bd. Options Exch. Life trustee Northwestern U., Art Inst. Chgo., U. Minn. Found., chmn. bd. trustees, 1993-95; chair Swedish Coun. Am. Found., 1999-2001. With U.S. Army, 1956-58. Decorated comdr. Royal Order of Polar Star (Sweden), 1989; recipient Legend in Leadership award Emory U., 1992, Regents award U. Minn., 1995, Outstanding Achievement award U. Minn., 1990. Mem. Chgo. Club, Comml. Club, Mpls. Club. Home: 179 E Lake Shore Dr Apt 1001 Chicago IL 60611-1306 also: 6444 N 79th St Scottsdale AZ 85250-7919 Office Phone: 312-953-3083. Personal E-mail: drkchicago@mac.com.

KULLBERG, GARY WALTER, advertising agency executive; b. White Plains, NY, Dec. 15, 1941; s. Walter George and Neva Virginia (Franz) K.; m. Audrey Ellen Greenwald, June 20, 1976; 1 child, Eric Alan. BS, U. R.I., 1963. Contr. WCD, Inc., N.Y.C., 1963-66; v.p., mgmt. supr. Ogilvy & Mather, N.Y.C., 1966-77; sr. v.p., account group head Wells, Rich, Greene, N.Y.C., 1977-83; CEO, CFO, co-founder Fredericks Kullberg Amato Pisacane, Inc., 1983-88; pres. Kullberg Amato Pisacane/ABP, Inc., 1987-89; pres., COO PanCom Internat. Corp., 1989-91; CEO PanCom Comm. Corp., 1991-93, Kullberg Cons. Group LLC, 1993—. Spkr. in field. Chmn. Manhattan adv. bd., Greater NY adv. bd. pub. rels. com. Salvation Army. Mem.: Am. Mktg. Assn., West Point Soc. N.Y. (career adv. com.), U. R.I. Alumni Assn. (v.p., exec. com., govt. rels. com., mem. fin. com.), N.Y. Athletic Club, Phi Gamma Delta. Home and Office: Kullberg Cons Group LLC 171 Forge Rd North Kingstown RI 02852-1007 Office Phone: 401-886-5001. Business E-Mail: gary@kullbergconsultinggroup.com.

KULLGREN, JEFFREY TODD, health science association administrator, researcher; b. Colorado Springs, Colo., Nov. 2, 1977; s. Thomas Edward and Bonnie Mae Kullgren. BS with hon. in Sociology, Mich. State U. Honors Coll., 2000; MPH, U. Mich., 2002. Pub. policy intern AIDS Alliance for Children, Youth and Families, Washington, 1999, cons., 1999—2000; program analyst U.S. Agy.Healthcare Rsch. and Quality, Rockville, Md., 2000; adminstrv. extern Chgo. Health Outreach, Inc., Chicago, Ill., 2001; rsch. asst. Mich. State U., Ann Arbor, Mich., 2000—. Cons. AIDS Alliance for Children, Youth and Families, Washington, 1999—2000; co-chair U. Mich. Student Assn. Health Policy, Ann Arbor, Mich., 2001—02; referee Am. Jour. Pub. Health, Washington, 2001—, Jour. Health Care for the Poor and Underserved, Memphis, 2004—; med. scholar Mich. State U., East Lansing, Mich., 1996—; mem. Mich. State U. Coll. of Human Medicine Student Coun., East Lansing, Mich., 2002—03, Mich. State U. Coll. of Human Medicine Admissions Com., East Lansing, Mich., 2003—; student course dir. Mich. State U. Coll. of Human Medicine Cmty. Resource Elective, East Lansing, Mich., 2003—04. Contbr. scientific papers. Mem.: AcademyHealth, Am. Med. Student Assn., ACP, Soc. of Gen. Internal Medicine, AMA, Mich. State U. Order Omega (life), Sigma Phi Epsilon (life; chaplain 1998—2000). Roman Catholic. Avocations: running, reading, travel, fishing. Office: Mich State Univ 1000 Oakland Dr Kalamazoo MI 49008 Office Phone: 517-214-7366. Personal E-mail: kullgren@msu.edu.

KULOK, WILLIAM ALLAN, entrepreneur, venture capitalist; b. Mt. Vernon, N.Y., July 24, 1940; s. Sidney Alexander and Bertha (Lembeck) K.; m. Susan B. Glick, June 26, 1965; children: Jonathan, Brian, Stephanie. BS in Econs., U. Pa., 1962. CPA, N.Y. Acct. David Kulok Co., N.Y.C., 1962-67; asst. to pres. Syndicate Mags., N.Y.C., 1967-70; founder Kulok Capital Inc., N.Y.C., 1970, pres., 1970—. Bd. dir. Listcomp Corp., Mail Mgmt. Corp., Mag. Devel. Fund, Lazard Spl. Equities Fund, ASA Internat. Ltd., N.Y. Import/Export Ctr., Inc., Ctr. for Exec. Edn., Arts & Events, Inc., World Trade Ctr., Palm Beach; lectr. Wharton Sch., U. Chgo., NYU. Pres. N.Y. Soc. Ethical Culture, 1978-80; vice chmn. bd. Ethical Culture Schs., 1979, chmn., 1982-86. Mem. AICPA, Sleepy Hollow Country Club, Loxahatchee Club, Tryall Golf and Beach Club (Jamaica, W.I.). Home: 116 Echo Dr Jupiter FL 33458-7716 Personal E-mail: billkulok@hotmail.com.

KULONGOSKI, THEODORE RALPH, governor, former judge; b. Washington County, Mo., Nov. 5, 1940; married; 3 children. BA, U. Mo., 1967, JD, 1970. Bar: Oreg., Mo., U.S. Dist. Ct. Oreg., U.S. Ct. Appeals (9th cir.). Legal counsel Oreg. State Ho. of Reps., 1973-74; founding and sr. ptnr. Kulongoski, Durham, Drummonds & Colombo, Oreg., 1974-87; deputy dist. atty. Multnomah County, Oreg., 1992; atty. gen. State of Oreg., 1993-97; justice Oreg. Supreme Ct., 1997—2001; gov., State of Oreg., 2003—. State rep. Lane County (Oreg.), 1974-77, state senator, 1977-83; chmn. Juvenile Justice Task Force, 1994, Gov.'s Commn. Organized Crime; mem. Criminal Justice Coun.; exec. dir. Met. Family Svc., 1992; dir. Oreg. Dept. Ins. and Fin., 1987-91. Mem. Oreg State Bar Assn., Mo. Bar Assn. Democrat. Office: Gov's Office 254 Capitol Bldg 900 Court St NE Salem OR 97301*

KULSHRESTHA, PANKAJ, thoracic surgeon; b. New Delhi, Delhi, India, July 12, 1960; s. Dinesh Chandra and Snehlata Kulshrestha; m. Kunjamma George, Aug. 3, 1990; children: Sujay, Kevin. MD, All India Inst. Med. Scis., New Delhi, 1982, MCh, 1988. Cert. gen. surgery Am. Bd. Surgery, 2004. Sr. registrar cardiothoracic surgery All India Inst. Med. Scis. and Safderjung Hosp., New Delhi, 1989—90; clin. fellow cardiothoracic surgery Baylor Coll. Medicine, Houston, 1991, St. Vincent's Hosp., Portland, Oreg., 1991—93, Baystate Med. Ctr. Western Campus Tufts U. Sch. Medicine, Springfield, Mass., 1993—95, Baystate Med. Ctr. Western Campus Tufts U. Sch. Medicine, 1997—98, resident gen. surgery, 1998—2003; instr. dept. surgery U. Conn., Farmington, 1994—95; attending surgeon cardiothoracic surgery Medwin Hosp., Hyderabad, India, 1995—96, City Cardiac Rsch. Ctr., Vijaywada, 1996—97; clin. fellow cardiothoracic surgery Mt. Sinai Hosp., N.Y.C., 2003—. Contbr. articles to profl. jours. Avocations: travel, reading, publishing. Home: #6E 306 East 96th St New York NY 10128 Office: Mount Sinai Hosp 1190 Fifth Ave New York NY 10029 Personal E-mail: cor51@earthlink.net.

KULSKI, JULIAN EUGENIUSZ, architect, space designer, educator; b. Warsaw, Mar. 3, 1929; came to U.S., 1948, naturalized, 1950; s. Julian Spitoslav and Eugenia Helena (Solecka) K; children: Julian S., Stefan T.A. *Sir Julian E. Kulski joined the Underground Army when he was twelve and arrested by Gestapo, tortured, and sentenced to Auschwitz. After he was rescued, he joined the Commandos and fought in the Warsaw Uprising. He was captured, and sent to prisoner-of-war camp. After escaping, he went to Ireland. While at Portora Royal School, he won the Oxford and Cambridge certificate. His father, Julian S. Kulski, fought with Pilsudski Legions in World War I and 1920-21 Polish Soviet War. During World War II as Lord Mayor of Warsaw, he represented the Polish Government in Exile. He was a fierce protector of the Underground Army. His mother, Eugenia Solecka, descended from the King of Poland, Stanislaw Leszczynski, father-in-law of King of France Louis XV.* Student, Sch. Architecture Oxford (Eng.) U., 1947-48; BArch, Yale U., 1953, MArch, 1954; PhD, Warsaw Inst. Tech., 1966. Practice architecture, city planning, Conn., 1954-59, Washington, 1959—; prof. architecture U. Notre Dame, South Bend, Ind., 1960-65; prof., dir. urban and regional planning George Washington U., Washington, 1965-67; prof., dir. city and regional planning Howard U., 1967-90. Cons. World Bank, 1964-90; bd. dirs. Nat. Archtl. Accrediting Bd., 1971-76; chmn. accrediting com. Harvard U., 1972, 75, U. P.R., 1974, Pratt U., 1975, Carnegie-Mellon U., 1976, U. Va.1978. Author: Land of Urban Promise, 1967 (Book-of-Month award), Evolution of American Urban Systems, 1970, Architecture in a Revolutionary Era, 1971, Dying, We Live, 1979, Legacy of the White Eagle, 2004; contbr. numerous articles to profl. jours. Served with Polish Army, 1941-46. Decorated Home Army Cross, Army Cross (4), Combat medal (Poland); knight of Malta, Order St. John of Jerusalem; recipient cert. of achievement Nat. Archtl. Accrediting Bd., 1973, 76. Fellow AIA; mem. Am. Planning Assn., Am. Inst. Cert. Planners, AAUP. Office: 2022 Columbia RD NW Apt 203 Washington DC 20009 *My life has been guided by the following philosophy: It is hard to work for freedom, harder yet to die for it, and hardest of all to suffer for it.*

KULSTAD, GUY CHARLES, public works official; b. Feb. 28, 1930; s. John Marlyn and Anne Mildred (Boyd) Kulstad Ibison; m. Bonnie Jane Sherman, Aug. 28, 1955 (div. Aug. 1996); children: Anne Marie Kulstad Hurst, Mark, Alice Kulstad Krause. BS in Civil Engring., U. Calif., Berkeley, 1958. Registered profl. engr., Calif., Oreg., Wash., traffic engr., Calif., land surveyor, Oreg.; cert. c.c. instr., Calif. Engring. aid County Rd. Dept., L.A., 1951, asst. civil engr., 1953-58; dir. pub. wks. Benicia, Calif., 1958-59; dep. dir. pub. wks. Solano County, Calif., 1959-65; dir. pub. wks. Humboldt County, Calif., 1965-92; mgmt. cons., 1992—. Gen. mgr. Humboldt Bay Wastewater Authority 1975, 82-89. Mem. Employer support of N.G. and Res. With AUS, 1951-53. Recipient Outstanding Svc. award North Bay chpt. Calif. Soc. Profl. Engrs., 1964, Boss of the Yr. award Arcata Jaycees, Recognition award Humboldt Toastmaster, Meritorious Leadership award, Surveyor award Calif. Land Surveyors Assn., Illmars Lagzdin award for engring. contbns., Guy C. Kulstad award Humboldt County Dept. Pub. Wks. Fellow ASCE; NSPE, mem. Nat. Soc. County Engrs., Calif. County Engrs., County Engrs. Assn. Calif., Sons of Norway.

KULTERMANN, UDO, architectural and art historian, educator, writer; b. Stettin, Germany, Oct. 14, 1927; came to U.S., 1967, naturalized, 1981; s. Georg and Charlotte (Schultz) K.; m. Judith Danoff, May 10, 1975. Student, U. Greifswald, Germany, 1946—50; PhD magna cum laude, U. Muenster, Germany, 1953; PhD (hon.), Art Acad. Tallinn, Estonia, 2004. Curatorial asst. Kunsthalle, Bremen, Germany, 1954-55; art editor Bertelsmann Pubs., Guetersloh, Germany, 1955-56; program dir. Am. House, Bremen, Germany, 1956-59; dir. city art mus. Schloss Morsbroich, Leverkusen, Germany, 1959-64; dir. Morsbroicher Kunsttage, Leverkusen, 1961; prof. Washington U., St. Louis, 1967-94, prof. emeritus, 1994—. Ednl. leader study tours German architects to Japan, 1965, 67; arch. commn. Biennale Venice, 1979—82; ednl. leader Soviet-Am. Travelling Arch. Seminar, Russia, 1986—87; jury Nat. U., Al Ain, United Arab Emirates, 1987, Internat. Open Air Exhbn., Pistany, Czech Republic, 1969; ednl. leader Nat. Trust for Hist. Preservation, Cruise, Copenhagen, Amsterdam, Rouen, Mont St. Michel, Bordeaux, and Lisbon, 1989; lecture trips participant Beijing, Kuala Lumpur, Singapore, and Shanghai, 1999, Japan and China, 2001—02; participant in internat. confs. Author: Architecture of Today, 1958, Hans und Wassili Luckhardt-Bauten und Projekte, 1958, Dynamische Architektur, 1959, New Japanese Architecture, 1960, New Architecture in Africa, 1963, Junge deutsche Bildhauer, 1963, Der Schluessel zur Architektur von heute, 1963, New Architecture in the World, 1965, History of Art History, 1966, 2d edit., 2002, paperback edit., 1981, rev. edit., 1993, Japanese edit., 1996, Spanish edit., 1996, Italian edit., 1997, Korean edit., 1999, Croatian edit., 2001, The New Sculpture-Assemblage and Environments, 1967, Architektur der Gegenwart, 1967, Gabriel Grupello, 1968, The New Painting, 1969, rev. edit., 1978, New Directions in African Architecture, 1969, Art and Life: The Function of Intermedia, 1970, New Realism, 1972, Die Architektur im 20 Jahrhundert, 6th revised edit., 2003, Ernest Trova, 1978, I Contemporanei, Storia della Scultura nel Mondo, 1979, Architecture in the Seventies, 1980, Architects of the Third World, 1980, Zeitgenoessische Architektur in Osteuropa, 1985, Spanish edit., 1989, Kleine Geschichte der Kunsttheorie, 1987, Japanese edit., 1996, Korean edit., 1997, rev. 2d edit., 1998, Visible Cities-Invisible Cities-Urban Symbolism and Historical Continuity, 1988, Kunst und Wirklichkeit-Von Fiedler bis Derrida-Zehn Annaeherungen, 1991, Die Maxentius-Basilika.Ein Schluesselwerk spaetantiker Architektur, 1996, Contemporary Architecture in the Arab States-Renaissance of a Region, 1999, Thirty Years After-The Future of the Past, 2002, Architecture and Revolution-The Visions of Boullée and Ledoux, 2003; co-author (with Werner Hofmann): Modern Architecture in Color, 1970; editor: Kenzo Tange: Architecture and Urban Design, 1970, paperback edits., 1978, 1989, Architektur der Welt, Verlag und Datenbank fuer Geisteswissenschaften, Weimar, 1996—2005, St. James Modern Masterpieces: The Best of Art, Architecture, Photography and Design Since 1945, 1998, vol. VI Architecture in South and Central Africa in: World Architecture: A Critical Mosaic 1900-2000, 2000. Mem. Nat. Humanities Faculty, Atlanta, 1986—. Recipient Disting. Faculty award Washington U., 1985. Mem. Croatian Acad. Scis. and Arts (corr.). Personal E-mail: ukulter@rcn.com.

KULWIN, DWIGHT ROBERT, surgeon, educator; b. Rochester, Minn., Oct. 4, 1948; m. Elizabeth H. Brown, Dec. 13, 1981; children: Charles, Robert. BS, U. Ill., 1969; MD, U. Chgo., 1973. Diplomate Am. Bd. Ophthalmology. Prof. U. Cin. Coll. Medicine, 1979—. Author books, papers, and articles in field. Fellow ACS, Am. Soc. Ophthalmic Plastic and Reconstructive Surgery (Wendell Hughes lectr. 1996), Royal Jordanian Soc. Ophthalmology, Hellenic Ophthalmology Soc.; mem. Cosmos Club. Home: 260 Sunny Acres Dr Cincinnati OH 45255-3903 Office: 3219 Clifton Ave Ste 110 Cincinnati OH 45220 Office Phone: 513-618-3300.

KULYK, KAREN GAY, artist; b. Toronto, Can., July 19, 1950; d. Joseph and Natalie Melanie (Solowski) K. BFA with honors, York U., 1973. Founder, curator Seedlings Gallery, Toronto, 1973-75; established studios worldwide, 1975—. Tchr. various instns., Can., Thailand, Bermuda, Eng., Mexico. One-woman shows include Kitchener-Waterloo Art Gallery, 1994, Rodman Hall, St. Catharines, Ont., 1995, Harbinger Gallery, 1994—, Marianne Friedland Gallery, 1974-1996, Masterworks Found. Gallery, Hamilton, Bermuda, 1997, Henry Dyson Fine Art, London, 1996—, Carnegie Gallery, Dundas, Ont., Can., 1996, Nancy Poole's Studio, Toronto, 1996-99, Gallery on the Bay, Hamilton, Ont., 1997—, Wallack Gallery, Ottawa, Can., 1996—, Zwicker Gallery, Halifax, N.S., Can., 1999—, Nat. Gallery Thailand, Grey Coll. U. Durham, Eng., 2000; exhibited in group shows at Harbinger Gallery, Waterloo, Ont., Touchstone Gallery, Hong Kong, Marianne Friedland Gallery, Fla., Sotheby's, Toronto, Chgo. Internat. Art Exhbn., York U., U. Toronto, Offices of Gov. Gen. of Can., Carleton U. Art Gallery, numerous others; represented in collections at Kitchener-Waterloo Art Gallery, Wilfred Laurier U., Waterloo, Art Gallery of Hamilton, Carleton U., York U., Agnes Etherington Art Gallery, Nat. Gallery of Bermuda, Hartford Coll., Md., Can. Trust, Dominion Trust, Shell Can., Thai Airways Internat., Can. Airlines Internat., Dalhousie U., N.S., others, pvt. collections; illustration: Orff, 27 Dragons and a Snarkel, Dalhouseie U. Art Gallery, Halifax, Nova Scotia; subject of several newspaper articles. Recipient Grollo d'Oro, award Treviso Internat. Art Competition, 1983; grantee Sheila Hugh Mackay Found., 1996. Home and Office: 5270 Morris St Halifax NS Canada B3J 1B4 Personal E-mail: mgoodyear@dal.ca.

KULZICK, KEN STAFFORD, retired lawyer, writer; b. Milw., July 20, 1927; s. Earl Joseph and Claire Agnes (Blask) K.; m. Patricia Louise Siekert, June 19, 1949; 1 child, Kate Kulzick Stafford. PhB, Marquette U., Milw., 1950; JD, UCLA, 1956. Bar: Calif. 1956, U.S. Dist. Ct. (no. and cen. dists.) Calif. 1956, U.S. Ct. Appeals (9th cir.) 1956. Tchg. asst., rschr. UCLA, 1953—56; asst. U.S. atty. (honor grad program) Dept. Justice, L.A., San Francisco, 1956-58; ptnr. Lillick, McHose & Charles, L.A., 1958-86, Liebig & Kulzick, L.A., 1987-91, Gipson, Hoffman & Pancione, L.A., 1991-94; copyright lawyer, past pres. L.A. Copyright Soc. Media cons. specializing in dramatic documentaries, 1958—; media advisor League of Women Voters,

L.A., 1986, 90; lectr. UCLA, 1987—. Contbr. articles to L.A. Lawyer mag., EMMY mag., Entertainment Law Reporter, others; bd. editors UCLA Law Rev., 1954-56. Served to lt. USN, 1950-53; Korea Home (Winter): 1550 Scenic Dr Felton CA 95018-9642

KUMAKO, KUAMI MAWUNYO, agricultural scientist; b. Cotonou, Benin, Nov. 11, 1963; s. Martin Kouami Kumako and Felicia Kpogo. BS in Agrl. Sci. Engring., U. Bénin, Togo, 1995; MS in Agrl. Econs., U. Ky., 2000. Rsch. asst. devel. program UN, Lomé, Togo, 1994—95; rsch. asst. dept. agrl. econs. U. Ky., Lexington, 1998—2001. Rsch. cons. World Bank, Washington, 2000—01. Mem. Commité Action Renouveau, Togo, 1990—96. Achievements include discovery of principle of rainfall-based index contract application in insurance. Personal E-mail: kumako1@hotmail.com.

KUMANYIKA, SHIRIKI K., nutrition epidemiology researcher, educator; b. Balt., Mar. 16, 1945; m. Christiaan B. Morssink; children: Chenjerai, Annoesjka. BA, Syracuse U., 1965; MS in Social Work, Columbia U., 1969; PhD in Human Nutrition, Cornell U., 1978; MPH, Johns Hopkins U., 1984. Asst. prof. nutrition Cornell U., Ithaca, N.Y., 1977-84; from asst. prof. to assoc. prof. epidemiology Johns Hopkins U. Sch. Hygiene and Pub. Health, Balt., 1984-89, asst. prof. internat. health, 1984-89; assoc. prof. nutritional epidemiology Pa. State U., University Park, 1989-92, prof. epidemiology, 1993-96; assoc. dir. for epidemiology Pa. State U. Coll. Medicine, Hershey, 1992-96; prof. epidemiology, prof. human nutrition and dietetics U. Ill. at Chgo., 1996-99, head dept. human nutrition and dietetics, 1996-99; chief of svc. U. Ill. Hosp. Nutritional Svcs., 1996-99; prof. epidemiology U. Pa. Sch. Med., Phila., 1999—, assoc. dean health promotion and disease prevention, 1999—, dir., grad. program, pub. health studies. Adj. prof. epidemiology dept. health evaluation scis. Coll. Medicine, Pa. State U., Hershey, 1996-99; mem. adv. bd. Women's Health Alliance. Contbr. articles to profl. jours. Bd. dirs. Nat. Black Women's Health Project, 1994-99, Nat. Rural Ctr., 1978-82; active WHO. NIH grantee; recipient Bolton L. Corson medal Franklin Inst., 1997. Fellow Am. Coll. Epidemiology, Am. Coll. Nutrition; mem. AAUP, APHA, Am. Diabetes Assn., Am. Dietetic Assn., Am. Inst. Nutrition, Am. Soc. for Clin. Nutrition, Assn. Black Cardiologists, Internat. Soc. on Hypertension in Blacks, Nat. Med. Assn., N.Am. Assn. Study of Obesity, Soc. for Epidemiol. Rsch., Soc. for Nutrition Edn., Internat. Soc. and Fedn. Cardiology, Inst. Medicine, 2004. Office: Ctr Clin Epidemiology and Biostats U Pa Sch Med 8th Fl Blockley Hall 423 Guardian Dr Philadelphia PA 19104-4209

KUMAR, DILIP CHRISTOPHER, economics professor; s. Neelakanta and Grace Premachandra; m. Renuka P. Prem, June 23, 1982; children: Jonathan, Davina. BA, U. Mysore, 1969, MA, 1971, U. Akron, 1977. Prof. econs. Scottsdale C.C., Ariz., 1984—, chair social sciences dept., 1994—. Mem. Ariz. Town Hall, Phoenix, 2003; elder mem. Indo-Pak Christian Assn. Recipient Excellence Tchg. award, U. Tex., 2003. Mem.: Am. Econ. Assn., Gamma Beta Phi, Lambda Theta. Office: Scottsdale C C 9000 E Chaparral Scottsdale AZ 85256

KUMAR, FAITH, clinical professional counselor; b. South Haven, Mich., May 12, 1960; d. Norris Kendall and Verna Ann (Jeffries) Curtis BS, Western Mich. U., 1990, M Counseling Psychology, 1993. Lic. clin. profl. counselor, Ill. Nursery supr. Child Devel. Ctr., Kalamazoo, 1988-90; tchr. Kalamazoo Pub. Sch. Sys., 1990-93; supr. Victor C. Neuman, Chgo., 1993-94; mentor counselor IL Mentor, Schaumburg, Ill., 1994-97; pvt. practice Chgo., 1997—. Counselor Lakeside Boys and Girls Home, Kalamazoo, 1990-93; therapist Ctrl. Bapt. Family Svcs., Chgo., 1994; peer supr. for pvt. therapists, Chgo., 1998—. Author: (juvenile) Legend of Hun, 1986. Vol. Big Bros.-Big Sisters, Kalamazoo, 1989-93; vol. probation officer, Kalamazoo, 1989-92. Avocations: swimming, dance, travel, reading, stamp collecting/philately.

KUMAR, KAPLESH, materials scientist; b. Lucknow, India, Nov. 9, 1947; arrived in U.S.A., 1970. m. Savinder (Kaur), May 27, 1974; children: Priyadarshini, Ruchira. BS in engring., Indian Inst. Tech., 1969; MS, Stevens Inst. Tech., 1971; ScD, MIT, 1975; JD magna cum laude (hon.), New Eng. Sch. Law, 1997. Bar: Mass. 1998, U.S. Supreme Ct. 2004, registered: (patent atty.). Mem. tech. staff Charles Stark Draper Lab., Inc., Cambridge, Mass., 1975—80, chief materials devel. sect., 1980—88, chief materials sci. and tech. sect., 1988—91, prin. mem. tech. staff, tech. dir., 1992—. Vis. lectr. IIM-ASM Internat., 1989; chmn. workshop on super conductivity and its applications to nat. needs, 1991; session chmn. Structures, Dynamics, and Materials Conf., AIAA, 1996-97. Author: (with others) Plasma Spraying: Theory and Applications, 1993; patentee in materials processing; pub. Applied Physics Rev. monograph, 1988; opinion page columinist India New Eng., 2003-; contbr. articles to profl. jours. Recipient Patent Award Charles Stark Draper Lab., Inc., 1982, Outstanding Performance Award, 1994, Invention Disclosure Award NASA, 1983. Mem. ASM Internat. (mem. internat. materials revs. com. 1991—); AIAA (mem. materials tech. com. 1991-98); MIT Sangam Club for India Affairs (pres. 1972-73); India Assn. Greater Boston, Inc. (pres. 1995-97); IIT Soc. New Eng. (v.p. 1993-95); Indian Am. Forum for Polit. Edn. (pres. New Eng. chpt. 1998-2000, bd. trustees 2000—). Achievements include rsch. in intellectual property law; permanent and soft magnetic materials; structural materials; micromechanical devices, inertial instruments; sub-specialties include materials; ceramics.

KUMAR, KRISHNA, retired physics educator; b. Meerut, India, July 14, 1936; came to U.S., 1956, naturalized, 1966; s. Rangi and Susheila (Devi) Lal; m. Katharine Johnson, May 1, 1960; children: Jai Robert, Raj David. BSc in Physics, Chemistry and Math., Agra U., 1953, MSc in Physics, 1955; MS in Physics, Carnegie Mellon U., 1959, PhD in Physics, 1964. Rsch. assoc. Mich. State U., 1963-66, MIT, 1966-67; rsch. fellow Niels Bohr Inst., Copenhagen, 1967-69; physicist Oak Ridge (Tenn.) Nat. Lab., 1969-71; assoc. prof. Vanderbilt U., Nashville, 1971-77; fgn. collaborator AEC of France, Paris, 1977-79; Nordita prof. U. Bergen, Norway, 1979-80; prof. physics Tenn. Tech. U., Cookeville, 1980-83, univ. prof. physics, 1983-99, prof. physics emeritus, 1999—. Tax assoc. H&R Block, 2002—03; disting. hon. fellow Manibal Acad. Higher Edn., India, 2002—; lectr. in field; cons. various rsch. labs. Author: Nuclear Models and the Search for Unity in Nuclear Physics, 1984, Superheavy Elements, 1989, (with J.R. Kumar) The Redhead From Alpha Centauri, 2003; contbr. articles to profl. jours., books. Sec. India Assn., Pitts., 1958-59; faculty advisor, 1990-99, assoc. mem. Triangle Fraternity, 1990-99; deacon Presbyn. Ch., 1991-93, elder, 2000-02; faculty advisor Indian Assn. of Cookeville, 1994-95; mem. exec. com. Putnam County Dem. Party, 1999-2002; treas. Unity Ch., 2004—. Recipient Gold medal Agra U., 1955; NSF rsch. grantee, 1972-75; Paul Harris fellow Rotary Internat., 1995. Mem. Indian Phys. Soc., Am. Phys. Soc., Tenn. Acad. Scis., Internat. Cmty. Hospitality Assn. (pres. 1992-94), Planetary Soc., Phi Kappa Phi, Sigma Pi Sigma, Sigma Xi (bd. dirs. 1992-93, charter mem. chpt. installation 1994). Home: 718 W 12th St Cookeville TN 38501-7788 E-mail: kkaadmi_99@yahoo.com.

KUMAR, KRISHNA, chemistry professor; b. Madras, India, Nov. 1970; BS in Chemistry, St. Stephen's Coll., 1991; PhD in Organic Chemistry, Brown U., 1996. Skaggs rsch. fellow Scripps Rsch. Inst. & Skaggs Inst. for Chemical Biology, 1996—98; asst. prof. chemistry Tufts U., 1998—2002; assoc. mem. cancer ctr. Tufts Sch. Med. & New England Med. Ctr., 1999—; assoc. prof. chemistry Tufts U., 2003—. Named one of Top 100 Young Innovators, Tech. Review mag., 2003; recipient Career award, Nat. Sci. Found., 2002, DuPont Young Prof. award, E.I. du Pont de Nemours & Co., 2003. Office: Tufts U Chemistry Dept 62 Talbot Ave Medford MA 02155 Office Phone: 617-627-3441. Business E-Mail: krishna.kumar@tufts.edu.

KUMAR, KV, management consultant; s. M.V. and Saraswathi Krishna Murthy; m. Vijaya Srinivasa Murthy, Mar. 23, 1983; children: Sanjay, Vishnu Srinivas. Industrial & Production Engineering, Poly. Inst./India, 1967. CEO Bus. & Strategic Cons. Internat., Inc., Waldorf, Md., 2002—; pres. Kumar Enterprises LLC. Pres. & ceo Am. Systems Internat., Inc., Bethesda, Md., 2000—03; apptd. Nat. Adv. Coun., Small Bus. Adminstrn., 2005. Mem., bd. of governors Internat. Brain Injury Assn., Washington, 1995—2003; mem., round table, mbda U.S. Dept. of Commerce, Washington, 1992—93; mem., round table U.S. SBA, Washington, 1992—93; Ariz. local bd. mem. U.S. SSS, 1998—2004; mem., DC econ. devel. com. D.C. Govt., 1992—93; leader, help the sr. citizen group Sr. Citizen Group of Wash., D.C., 1973—78; coun. mem. Ariz. Governor's Coun. on Spinal & Head Injuries, 1998—2003, Ariz. State Rehab. Coun., 1998—2003; mem., nat. steering com. Bush-Cheney, 2004; nat. chmn. U.S. Indian Am. C. of C., Washington, 2003—05; nat. pres. Nat. Indian Am. C. of C., Washington, 1991—2003; founder/dir. First Liberty Bank Corp., Inc., Washington, 1987—91; mem., exec. bd. Red Means Stop Coalition, Phoenix, 2003—05; chmn, dist. appeals bd. U.S. SSS, Phoenix, 2004—05; mem., franchise alliance com. Internat. Franchise Assn., Washington, 1992—93. Recipient Millenium award, Brain Injury Assn. of USA, 2000, IBIA President's award for Outstanding Achievement, IBIA, Stockholm, Sweden, 2003, Meritorius Svc. award and Bronze medal, U.S. SSS, 2004, Honored Patriots award, U.S. Selective Svc. Svc. Sys., 2000, award for dedicated services to Minority Businesses, U.S. Hispanic C. of C., 1993, 1996, 1997. Mem.: Indian Inst. of Indsl. Engineers (hon.). R-Consevative. Hindu. Avocation: travel. Home: 7272 E Gainey Ranch Rd Unit # 103 Scottsdale AZ 85258 Office Phone: 480-368-5500. Home Fax: 480-607-9500; Office Fax: 480-607-9500. Personal E-mail: kvkumarusa@yahoo.com. E-mail: kvkumar@bscii.com.

KUMAR, MARTHA JOYNT, political science educator; b. Washington, July 4, 1941; d. John Howard and May Aberdeen (Lepley) Joynt; m. Vijayendra Kumar, June 12, 1970; 1 child, Zal Alexander. BA, Conn. Coll., 1963; MA, Columbia U., 1965, PhD, 1972. Rschr. NBC, News Dept., Election Unit, N.Y.C., 1965-66; instr. Tenn. State U., Nashville, 1967, U. Md., Balt., 1970-71, Towson State U., Balt., 1971-72, asst. prof., 1972-75, assoc. prof., 1975-81, prof., 1981—; sr. scholar Acad. Leadership, U. Md. Cons. in field; mem. adv. bd. series presdl. leadership Tex. A&M Press; bd. dirs. Ctr. Presdl. Studies, Tex. A&M U., Nat. Coordinating Com. for Promition of History; bd. regents U. system Md., 1998 (Regents Faculty award). Coauthor: Portraying the President: The White House and the News Media, 1981; co-editor: (jour.) Congress and the Presidency, 1996—; assoc. editor: Presdl. Studies Quar., 1986-89, co-chair editl. bd., 1994-96; contbr. articles to profl. jours. Mem. City Mgmt. Com., New Castle, Del., 1990-91; bd. regents U. Sys. of Md., 1998. Recipient Regents Faculty award for excellence in rsch./scholarship, 1998; Ford Found. grantee, 1978-80; consultancy grantee Pew Charitable Trusts, 1997; Joan Shorenstein Ctr. on the Pres., Politics and Pub. Policy fellow Harvard U., 1998. Mem. Am. Polit. Sci. Assn. (mem. Kirkpatrick fund bd. 1990-93), Presidency Rsch. Group (sec., treas. 1989-93, v.p. 1993-95, pres. 1995-97), Am. Polit. Sci. Assn. (rep. nat. archives), Phi Beta Kappa. Avocation: sculling. Office: Towson U Dept Polit Sci Baltimore MD 21204 Home: 1219 29th St NW Washington DC 20007

KUMAR, NANDA S., marketing educator; m. Bharti Tandon. BTech in Computer Sci., U Calcutta; MS in Computer Sci., U. Md.; PhD, U. Chgo., 1999. Asst. prof. mktg. Sch. Mgmt., U. Tex. at Dallas, Richardson, 1999—. Contbr. articles Mktg. Sci., Jour. Econ. Theory, and Jour. Retailing. Recipient Outstanding Grad. Tchg. award, Sch. Mgmt., Univ Tex. at Dallas, 2002—03; fellow, Grad. Sch. Bus., U. Chgo., 1994—97; Nat. Talent Search scholar, Nat. Coun. Ednl. Rsch. and Tng., India, 1983—90. Mem.: Inst. Ops. Rsch. and Mgmt. Scis. Office: U Texas at Dallas Sch Mgmt 2601 N Floyd Richardson TX 75083-0688 Office Phone: 972-883-6426. Office Fax: 972-883-6727. E-mail: nkumar@utdallas.edu.

KUMAR, PANGANAMALA RAMANA, electrical and computer engineering educator; b. Nagpur, Maharashtra, India, Apr. 21, 1952; arrived in U.S., 1973; s. Panganamala Bhavanarayana and Panganamala Kamala (Avasarala) Murthy; m. Devarakonda Jayashree Sundaram, Jan. 22, 1982; children: P. Ashwin, Shilpa P. BTech., Indian Inst. Tech., Madras, India, 1973; MS, Washington U., 1975, DSc, 1977. Asst. prof. dept. math. and computer sci. U. Md., Baltimore County, 1977-82, assoc. prof. dept. math. and computer sci., 1982-84; assoc. prof. dept. elec. and computer engring. and coordinated sci. lab. U. Ill., Urbana, 1985-87, prof. dept. elec. and computer engring., 1987—, rsch. prof. coordinated sci. lab., 1987—, Franklin Woeltge prof. elec. and computer engring., 2000—. Co-author: Stochastic Systems, 1986; assoc. editor: Systems and Control Letters, 1984-93, Math. of Control, Signals and Systems, 1986—2005, SIAM Jour. on Control and Optimization, 1989-93, Jour. of Discrete Event Dynamic Systems: Theory and Application, 1993-2004; mem. editl. bd. Jour. on Adaptive Control and Signal Processing, 1986-99, Math. Problems in Engring., 1995—, ACM Transactions on Sensor Networks, 2004—, Foundations and Trends in Networking, 2004—, IEEE Transactions on Mobile Computing, 2005—, ACM Transactions on Sensor Networks, 2005—; editor Info. and Sys., 1999—; assoc. editor IEEE Transactions on Automatic Control, 1982-83, assoc. editor at large, 1989-97; contbr. articles to profl. jours. Recipient Donald P. Eckman award, Am. Automatic Control Coun., 1985. Fellow IEEE (Control Systems award 2006). Avocation: ping pong/table tennis. Office: U Ill Coordinated Sci Lab 1308 W Main St Urbana IL 61801-2307 Business E-Mail: prkumar@uiuc.edu.

KUMAR, RAJ, psychologist; b. Dibai, India, Jan. 9, 1961; came to U.S., 1989; s. Dilbagh Rai and Laksmi Rani Kumar; m. Sunita M. Kumar, July 19, 1993; 1 child, Sapna. BA, Agra (India) Coll., 1981; MA, St. John's Coll., Agra, 1983; PhD, Agra U., 1987. Cert. hypnotist, Hawaii. Psychologist Dept. Health, Honolulu, 1989—. Author: From Darkness to Light, 2000, The Secrets of Health and Healing, The Spiritual Thoughts for the Day. Active Milan, Hawaii, 1999. Avocations: exercise, music, collecting books and antiques. Office: New Life Ctr 627 South St Honolulu HI 96813 E-mail: Raj@hgea.org.

KUMAR, RAJEEV, research scientist; b. Patna, India, Jan. 15, 1969; arrived in U.S., 1999; s. S. Gupta; m. R. Pallavi, Nov. 26, 2000; 1 child, Rishav. BS, Patna U., 1991; MS, U. Roorkee, 1993; MPhil, Jawaharlal Nehru U., 1995, PhD, 2000. Assoc. rsch. scientist McLaughlin Rsch. Isnt., Great Falls, Mont., 2003—. Recipient Career Transition award, Dept. Def., 2003; fellow, Con. Scientific Tech., India, 1995, SUNY, Stony Brook, N.Y., 1999, Cold Spring Harbor Lab., N.Y., 2001; grantee, 16th Sumposium Kallikrein-Kinin, 2002. Mem.: N.Y. Acad. Sci., Fedn. Am. Soc. Expt. Biosci., Am. Assn. Immunology. Achievements include inventor in field. Office: McLaughlin Rsch Inst 1520 23d St S Great Falls MT 59405

KUMAR, RAJENDRA, electrical engineering educator; b. Amroha, India, Aug. 22, 1948; arrived in US, 1980; s. Satya Pal Agarwal and Kailash Vati Agarwal; m. Pushpa Agarwal, Feb. 16, 1971; children: Anshu, Shipra. BS in Math. and Sci., Meerut Coll., 1964; BEE, Indian Inst. Tech., Kanpur, 1969, MEE, 1977; PhD, U. New Castle, NSW, Australia, 1981. Mem. tech. staff Electronis and Radar Devel., Bangalore, India, 1969-72; rsch. engr. Indian Inst. Tech., Kanpur, 1972-77; asst. prof. Calif. State U., Fullerton, 1981-83, Brown U., Providence, 1980-81; prof. Calif. State U., Long Beach, 1983—. Cons. Jet Propulsion Lab., Pasadena, Calif., 1984-91, Aerospace Corp., El Segundo, Calif., 1995—. Contbr. articles. Recipient Best Paper award Internat. Telemetering Conf., Las Vegas, 1986, 10 New Technology awards NASA, Washington, 1987-91. Mem.: AAUP, AIAA, NEA, IEEE (sr.), Inst. of Navigation, Calif. Faculty Assn., Inst. Navigation, Auto Club So. Calif. (Cerritos), Tau Beta Pi (eminent mem.), Sigma Xi, Eta Kappa Nu. Achievements include patents for efficient detections and signal parameter estimation with applications to hihg dynamic GPS receivers; multiusage estimation of received carrier signal parameters under very high dynamic conditions of the receiver; fast frequency acquisition via adaptive least squares algorithms; Kalman filter ionospheric delay estimator; method and apparatus for reducing multipath signal error using deconvolution; adaptive smoothing system for fading communication channels; others. Avocations: gardening, walking, hiking, reading. Home: 13910 Rose St Cerritos CA 90703-9043 Office: Calif State U 1250 N Bellflower Blvd Long Beach CA 90840-0001 Office Phone: 562-985-1556. Business E-Mail: kumar@csulb.edu.

KUMAR, RAMYA, academic administrator; d. Brinda Kumar. BA in Psychology, U. Mass., 2001, MS in Biol. Scis., 2003. Cert. rape aggression defense instr. Rape Aggression Defense Sys. Resident advisor U. Mass., Lowell, 1999—2000, asst. resident dir., 2000—02, resident dir., 2002—03, Mich. State U., East Lansing, Mich., 2003—04, assoc. dir. student affairs, Lyman Briggs Sch., 2003—04; hall dir. U. Ariz., Tucson, 2004—. Culture fest mktg. chair U. Mass., 2000—01, safety com., 2000—01, yearbook prodn. com., 2000—02; coord. residence hall orientation Mich. State U., 2003—04, advisor, Lyman Briggs ambassadors, 2003—04, com. mem. women's history banquet and conf., 2003—04; advisor, coalition Indian undergrad. students Mich. State U., East Lansing, Mich., 2003—04; regional conf. programming advisor affiliated coll. and univ. residence halls Inter Mountain, Tucson, 2004—04; freshman seminar instr. U. Ariz., Tucson, 2004—, advisor, residence hall coun., 2004—05, staff selection, tng. com., 2004—, acad. initiatives com., 2004—. Vol. tunnel of opression U. Ariz., 2004—, sexual assault awareness marathon organizer, 2004—; yound adult coord., tchr. children's spirituality class Sri Sathya Sai Baba Ctr. Tucson, 2005. Recipient Resident Advisor of Yr., U. Mass., 1999, Programmer of Yr., 1999, Psi Chi Inductee, Psi Chi Nat. Honors Soc. Psychology, 2001. Mem.: Assn. Internat. Mountain Affiliated Housing Ofcrs., Nat. Assn. Student Pers. Adminstrs., Am. Coll. Pers. Assn., Psi Chi. Achievements include research in Alzheimer's using mazes and diet patterns, published in the Journal of Neuromolecular Medicine.

KUMAR, ROMESH, chemical engineer; b. Rajpura, India, Oct. 18, 1944; arrived in U.S., 1966; s. Kundan Lal and Pushpa (Wati) Agarwal; m. Kumkum Khanna, Feb. 22, 1976. BS, Panjab U., India, 1965; MS, U. Calif., Berkeley, 1968, PhD, 1972. From postdoctoral appointee to sr. chem. engr. Argonne Nat. Lab., Ill., 1972—2004, sr. chem. engr., 2004—, head fuel cell dept. Chem. Engring. divsn. Tchr. fuel cell power sys. design and analysis for transp. applications. Contbr. to Weissberger's Techniques in Chemistry, 1975; patentee in field. Recipient Silver medal Panjab U., 1965, Medal for Disting. Performance U. Chgo., 2004. Hindu. Home: 1549 Ceals Ct Naperville IL 60565-6148 Office: 9700 Cass Ave Argonne IL 60439-4803 Office Phone: 630-252-4342. Business E-Mail: kumar@cmt.anl.gov.

KUMAR, SANDEEP, biophysicist, researcher; b. New Delhi, Nov. 13, 1968; arrived in U.S., 1997; s. Rajendra Pal Gupta, Lajwanti Gupta; m. Neeti Sinha; m. Neeti Sinha. BSc in Physics with honors, U. Delhi, New Delhi, 1989; MSc in Molecular Biology and Biotechnology, G. B. Pant U. Agr. and Tech., Pant Nagar, India, 1992; PhD in Molecular Biophysics, Indian Inst. Sci., Bangalore, 1998. Scientist Sci. Applications, Inc., Frederick, Md., 1998—99; vis. fellow lab. exptl. and computational biology Nat. Cancer Inst., Frederick, 1999—. Contbr. articles and sci. papers to profl. jours. Recipient Internat. Travel award, Coun. Sci. and Indsl. Rsch. (CSIR), India, 1996; fellow Jr. and Sr. Rsch., 1992-1994, 1994-1997. Office: NCI Frederick NIH Bldg 469, RM 151 Miller St Frederick MD 21702

KUMAR, SANJAY, professional sports team executive, former computer company executive; b. Colombo, Sri Lanka, 1962; came to the U.S., 1976; Dir. software devel. UCCEL Corp.; joined Computer Assocs. Internat., Inc., Islandia, NY, 1987, COO, 1994—2000, pres., 1994—2004, CEO, 2000—04, chmn., 2002—04, chief software arch., 2004; co-owner NY Islanders, 2000—.

KUMAR, SANJAYA, epidemiologist, biostatistician; arrived in US, 1998; m. Shalini Varma Kumar, Mar. 5, 1998. BSc&AH, G.B. Pant U. Agrl. & Tech., India, 1988; MS in Epidemiology, U. Guelph, Can., 1998; PhD, Hamilton U., 2001. Rsch. scientist N.Y. State Dept. Health, Troy, NY, 1999—. Fellow: Royal Statis. Soc.; mem.: NSHS, ACE, Sigma Xi. E-mail: sxk10@health.state.ny.us.

KUMAR, SHAILENDRA, urologist, educator; b. Patna, Bihar, India, Oct. 7, 1941; came to U.S., 1969; m. Singh Meera; children: Yash, Pratish, Priya. MD, Patna Med. Coll., 1964. Resident in surgery Worcester (Mass.) City Hosp., 1969-70; resident in urology Howard U., Washington, 1970-73; fellow dept. urology Meml. Sloan-Kettering Cancer Ctr., N.Y.C., 1973-74; clin. assoc. prof. urology/surgery Howard U., 1978—. Mem. Am. Urol. Assn., Montgomery County Med. Assn. Office: 6510 Kenilworth Ave Ste 2200 Riverdale MD 20737-1342

KUMAR, SRIKANTA PONNATHPUR, electrical engineer, researcher; b. Ponnathpur, India, Aug. 13, 1954; arrived in U.S.A., 1976; s. Ramaswamy and Padmamma Ponnathpur; m. Tara Vishwanath, Aug. 2, 1982; children: Shruti, Kumar. BSc with hons., Bangalore (India) U., 1971; BEE, Indian Inst. Sci., 1974, MEE, 1976; PhD, Yale U., 1981. Asst. prof. of elec. engring. Rennselaer Polytechnic Inst., Troy, NY, 1982—85, Northwestern U., Evanston, Ill., 1985—89, assoc. prof. of elec. engring., 1989—96, dir. masters program in info. tech., 1996—98; sr. tech. advisor Nat. Inst. Standards and Tech., Gaithersberg, Md., 1998—99; program mgr. Def. Advanced Rsch. Projects Agy., Arlington, Va., 1999—. Co-editor: Proceedings of IEEE, 2003; editor: Jour. High Speed Networks, 1994—, Mag. of Signal Processing: IEEE, —. Mem.: IEEE, Assn. Computing Machinery. Avocations: music, meditation, walking. Office: Defense Advanced Rsch Projects Agency 3701 N Fairfax Drive Arlington VA 22203 E-mail: skumar@darpa.mil.

KUMAR, SUBODHA, information scientist, educator; b. Pathargama, Bihar, India, Feb. 8, 1975; arrived in U.S., 1999; s. Shiva Kumar Tekriwal and Mira Devi; m. Susmita Sarawgi, Feb. 15, 2002. BSc in Engring., Bihar Inst. Tech., Sindri, India, 1994; M in Tech., Indian Inst. Tech., Kanpur, 1997; MBA, U. Tex., Dallas, 2000; PhD, U. Tex. Dallas, Richardson, 2001. Tchg. asst. Indian Inst. Tech., Kanpur, India, 1995—97; sr. engr. Tata Engring. and Locomotive Co., Janmshedpur, India, 1997—98; rsch. asst. U. Toronto, Canada, 1998—98; tchg. asst. U. Tex. at Dallas, Richardson, 1999—2000; rsch. asst. FSI Internat., Allen, Tex., 2000—01, rsch. scientist, 2001—01; asst. prof. U. Wash., Seattle, 2001—. Fellow, U. Toronto, 1998, U. Tex. at Dallas, 1999—2001; grantee, FSI Internat., 2000—01; Selden Leavell Merit Based scholar, U. Tex. at Dallas, 2000—01. Mem.: Assn. Info. Sys. Achievements include patents for robotic cell design. Office: Univ Wash Bus Sch 350 Mackienzie Box 353200 Seattle WA 98195 Office Phone: 206-543-4777. Business E-Mail: subodha@u.washington.edu.

KUMAR, VIKRAM SHEEL, information technology executive; BS in indsl. engring. and ops. rsch., Columbia U.; MD, Harvard Med. Sch. Pres., CEO Dimagi, Inc. Mem. adv. bd. Global Emerging Tech. Inst.; founding fellow Media Lab Asia. Named one of Top 100 Young Innovators, MIT Tech. Review, 2004; recipient Tech. in Svc. Humanity award, 2004, Paul and Daisy Soros New Am. Office: Dimagi Inc 390 Commonwealth Ave Ste 605 Boston MA 02215

KUMBLE, STEVEN JAY, lawyer; b. July 3, 1933; m. Barbara Kumble (div.); children: Charles Todd, Roger Glenn; m. Peggy Basten Vandervoort. BA, Yale U., 1954; JD, Harvard U., 1959; LLD (hon.), L.I. U., 1990. Bar: N.Y. 1960. Ptnr. Finley, Kumble, Wagner, Underberg, Manley & Casey, N.Y.C., 1968-87; of counsel Summit Rovins & Feldesman, N.Y.C., 1988-90; chmn. bd. dirs. Lincolnshire Mgmt., Inc., N.Y.C., 1985—. Vice chmn. bd. dirs. L.I. U., Greenvale, N.Y., 1984—, chm., 1982-94; trustee bd. Gov.'s Com. on Scholastic Achievement, N.Y.C., 1981—; mem. adv. bd. Inst. Civil Justice, Rand, 1999—. 1st lt. U.S. Army, 1955-57. Mem. Assn. of Bar of City of N.Y., Harvard Club, Salem Golf Club, Phi Beta Kappa, Yale Club. Avocations: skiing, golf.

KUMIN, LIBBY BARBARA, speech language pathologist, educator; b. Bklyn., Nov. 11, 1945; d. Herbert H. and Berniece (Shuch) K.; m. Martin J. Lazar, Jan. 18, 1969; 1 child, Jonathan Kumin Lazar. BA summa cum laude, LIU, 1965; MA, NYU, 1966, PhD, 1969. Lic. speech pathologist, pathology. Asst. prof. speech pathology U. Md., College Park, 1972-76, cons., 1976-80; assoc. prof. Loyola Coll., Balt., 1980-88, prof., 1988—, chmn. dept. speech and lang. pathology, 1993-99, dir. MS program, 1983—2003, dir. grad. programs, 1999—2003. Adj. prof. Loyola Coll., 1976-80; specialist in speech and language in Down Syndrome; mem. profl. adv. bd. Nat. Down Syndrome Cong.; leader of parent and profl. seminars; mem. Down Syndrome Med.

Interest Group. Author: Aphasia, 1978, Classroom Language Skills in Children with Down Syndrome, 2001, Early Communication Skills for Children with Down Syndrome, 2003; therapies editor: Down Syndrome Quar.; contbr. articles to profl. jours. Recipient Outstanding Individual of Yr. award Howard County Assn. Retarded Citizens, Nat. Meritorious Svc. award Nat. Down Syndrome Congress, 1987, Rsch. award Christian Pueschel Meml., 2004; grantee Loyola Coll., 1983, 91, 97, 99, 2002, 04, Aaron and Lillie Straus Found., 1983-89, 99-2005, Columbia Found., Joseph P. Kennedy Found., 1995, 2002, Shriver Ctr., 1996-98, 2002 Mem. Nat. Down Syndrome Soc. (Pres.'s award 2005), Nat. Down Syndrome Congress, Am. Speech/Lang./Hearing Assn. (cert.), Md. Speech and Hearing Assn., ARC, Sigma Tau Delta, Pi Lambda Theta. Office: Loyola Coll Dept Speech Pathology 4501 N Charles St Dept Speech Baltimore MD 21210-2601 Business E-Mail: lkumin@loyola.edu.

KUMIN, MAXINE WINOKUR, poet, writer; b. Phila., June 6, 1925; d. Peter and Doll (Simon) Winokur; m. Victor Montwid Kumin, June 29, 1946; children: Jane Simon, Judith Montwid, Daniel David. AB, Radcliffe Coll., 1946, MA, 1948; LHD (hon.), Centre Coll., 1976, Davis and Elkins Coll., 1977, Regis Coll., 1979, New England Coll., 1982, Claremont Grad. Sch., 1983, U. N.H., 1984, Bowdoin Coll., 2002. Instr. Tufts U., Medford, Mass., 1958-61, lectr. English, 1965-68. Scholar Radcliffe Inst. for Ind. Study, 1961-63; vis. lectr. U. Mass., Amherst, 1973, Princeton U., 1977, 79, 81-82; adj. prof. Columbia U., 1975; Fannie Hurst prof. of literature Brandeis U., 1975, Wash. U., St. Louis, 1977; Carolyn Wilkerson Bell vis. scholar Randolph-Macon Woman's Coll., 1978; poet in residence Bucknell U., 1983; vis. prof. MIT, 1984, U. Miami, 1995, Pitzer Coll., 1996; McGee prof. of writing Davidson Coll., 1997; writer in residence Fla. Internat. U., 1998-2000; master artist Atlantic Ctr. for Arts, New Smyrna Beach, Fla., 1984-2002; staff mem. Bread Loaf Writers' Conf., 1969-71, 73, 75, 77; poetry cons. Library of Congress, 1981-82; elector The Poet's Corner, The Cathedral of St. John the Divine, 1990-1996; mem. staff Sewanee Writer's Conf., 1993-94, Bucknell U. visiting poet, 2001. Author: (poetry) Halfway, 1961, The Privilege, 1965, The Nightmare Factory, 1970, Up Country: Poems of New England, 1972 (Pulitzer Prize for poetry 1973), House, Bridge, Fountain, Gate, 1975, The Retrieval System, 1978, Our Ground Time Here Will Be Brief, 1982, Closing the Ring, 1984, The Long Approach, 1985, Nurture, 1989, Looking for Luck, 1992 (Poets' Prize), Connecting the Dots, 1996, Selected Poems 1960-1990, 1997, The Long Marriage, 2001, Bringing Together, 2003, Jack and Other New Poems, 2005; (novels) Through Dooms of Love, 1965, The Passions of Uxport, 1968, The Abduction, 1971, The Designated Heir, 1974; (essays) To Make A Prairie: Essays on Poets, Poetry, and Country Living, 1980, In Deep: Country Essays, 1987, Women, Animals and Vegetables: Essays and Stories, 1994, Inside the Halo and Beyond, 2000, Always Beginning, 2000; (short stories) Why Can't We Live Together Like Civilized Human Beings?, 1982; (juvenile) Sebastian and the Dragon, 1960, Spring Things, 1961, A Summer Story, 1961, Follow the Fall, 1961, A Winter Friend, 1961, Mittens in May, 1962, No One Writes a Letter to the Snail, 1962, Archibald the Traveling Poodle, 1963, (with Sexton) Eggs of Things, 1963, (with Sexton) More Eggs of Things, 1964, Speedy Digs Downside Up, 1964, The Beach Before Breakfast, 1964, Paul Bunyan, 1966, Faraway Farm, 1967, The Wonderful Babies of 1809 and Other Years, 1968, When Grandmother Was Young, 1970, When Great-Grandmother Was Young, 1971, (with Sexton) Joey and the Birthday Present, 1971, (with Sexton) The Wizard's Tears, 1975, What Color Is Caesar?, 1978, The Microscope, 1984; contbr. poems to nat. mags. Recipient Lowell Mason Palmer award, 1960, William Marion Reedy award, 1968, Eunice Tietjens Meml. prize Poetry Mag., 1972, Borestone Mountain award, 1976, Radcliffe Coll. Alumnae Recognition award, 1978, Am. Acad. and Inst. Arts and Letters award for excellence in literature, 1980, Levinson award Poetry mag., 1987, The Poets' prize, 1994, Aiken Taylor Poetry prize, 1995, Centennial award Harvard Grad. Sch. Arts and Scis., 1996, NH Writers Project Lifetime Achievement award, 1998, Ruth Lilly Poetry Prize, 1999, Charity Randall award, 2000, Robert Frost award, Plymouth Coll., 2001, Harvard U. Arts medal, 2005; grantee Nat. Endowment for the Arts, 1966; fellow Nat. Coun. on Arts and Humanities, 1967-68; fellow Acad. Am. Poets, 1986-2002; fellow Woodrow Wilson, 1979-80, 91-93. Mem. Acad. Am. Poets (chancellor), Poetry Soc. Am., PEN Am., Authors Guild, The Writers Union.

KUMM, WILLIAM HOWARD, energy products company executive; b. Bahia, Brazil, Feb. 6, 1931; arrived in U.S., 1938, naturalized, 1949; s. Henry William and A. Joyce (Beale) Kumm; m. Anne K. Gibson, July 11, 1953; children: John H., Elizabeth A., Katharine L. BA, Amherst Coll., 1952; cert. bus. adminstrn., McCoy Coll., Johns Hopkins U., 1959. Registered profl. engr., Md. With Westinghouse Electric Corp., 1952—78, jr. engr. AirArm divsn. Balt., 1953—54, sr. engr., 1955—60; supervisory engr. Westinghouse Surface divsn., Balt., 1961—62, supervisory engr. Systems Ops. divsn., 1962—65; mgr. advanced concept engring. sect. Westinghouse Ocean Rsch. & Engring. Ctr., Annapolis, Md., 1965—69, subdivsn. mgr., 1969—71; presdl. interchange exec. Pres.'s Commn. on Pers. Interchange, assigned NOAA, 1971—72; staff Nat. Adv. Com. on Oceans and Atmosphere, Washington, 1972; program mgr. submarine transp. project U.S. Maritime Adminstrn., 1972—2019; mgr. marine programs Westinghouse Oceanic Divsn., 1973—78; pres., CEO Arctic Enterprises, Inc., 1978—, Arctic Energies Ltd., Trans Polar Shipping Co., Inc., Ottawa, Canada, 1981—; exec. v.p. Agua Solar SA de CV, Mexico, 1993—; pres. H2otec Corp., Irvine, Calif., 1994—, Marine Fuel Cells Ltd., 2002—. Participant NSF, 1987, NAS-NAE planning effort on Internat. Decade Ocean Exploration for Nat. Coun. on Marine Resources and Engring., 1968—69; partipant congl. office of Tech. Assessment Study of Marine Applications for Fuel Cell Tech., 1985. Contbr. (chpt.) Man Beneath the Sea, 1972, patentee in field. Del. County Coun. PTAs, 1970, 1971; treas. Cub Scout pack 332 Boy Scouts Am., Catonsville, Md., 1963—65; mem. Rural Area Devel. Bd., Carroll County, NH, 1964—65, Citizens Adv. Coun. on Edn., 1970—72. Mem.: Presdl. Interchange Exec. Assn., Soc. Naval Archs. and Marine Engrs. Home and Office: 511 Heavitree Ln Severna Park MD 21146-1010 Office Phone: 410-987-5454.

KUMMEROW, ARNOLD A., superintendent of schools; b. Framingham, Mass., Mar. 25, 1945; s. Arnold A. Sr. and Elizabeth Patricia (Westfield) K.; m. Constance Booth, July 10, 1971. BME, Eastern Mich. U., 1968, MA, 1975; PhD, U. Mich., 1989. Cert. adminstrn., Mich. Instrumental music dir. Vandercook Lake Pub. Schs., Jackson, Mich., 1968-74; instrumental music dir., asst. prin., prin. L'Anse Creuse Pub. Schs., Mt. Clemens, Mich., 1975-89; asst. supt. curriculum and pers. Lincoln Consol. Schs., Ypsilanti, Mich., 1989-91; asst. supt. Ypsilanti Pub. Schs., 1991-93; mem. curriculum devel. staff Mich. Dept. Edn., 1993-94; supt. Carsonville-Port Sanilac (Mich.) Schs., 1994-97, Armada (Mich.) Area Schs., 1997—. Named Exemplary Sch. Prin., Mich. Dept. Edn. and U.S. Dept. Edn. Mem. AASA, MASA, ASCD. Home: 17201 Knollwood Dr Clinton Township MI 48038-2833 Office: Armada Area Schs 74500 Burk St Armada MI 48005-3314

KUMMINGS, DONALD DALE, language educator; b. Lafayette, Ind., July 28, 1940; s. Herman Wilhelm and Estelle Catherine (Easterwood) K.; m. Gail Nadine Savage, Mar. 23, 1963 (div. Aug. 1978); children: Kevin Scott (dec.), Jeremy William; m. Patricia Finnelly Larson, Mar. 21, 1987. BA, Purdue U., 1962, MA, 1964; PhD, Ind. U., 1971. Tchg. assoc. Purdue U., West Lafayette, Ind., 1963—64; instr. English Adrian Coll., Adrian, Mich., 1964—66; assoc. instr. Ind. U., Bloomington, 1966—70; asst. prof. English U. Wis.-Parkside, Kenosha, 1970—75, assoc. prof. English, 1975—85, prof. English, 1985—, chair dept. English, 1974—76, 1991—94. Book rev. editor Rutgers U., Camden, N.J., 1983-90; panelist, reviewer NEH, Washington, 1992-2005; lectr. in field; book manuscript cons. Harcourt Brace Jovanovich, U. Tenn. Press, Susquehanna U. Press, U. Iowa Press, Houghton Mifflin, W.W. Norton, Oxford (Eng.) U. Press, Blackwell Pub., A.B. Longman, Bedford/St. Martin's. Author: Walt Whitman, 1940-1975: A Reference Guide, 1982, The Open Road Trip: Poems, 1989; editor: Approaches to Teaching Whitman's "Leaves of Grass," 1990; co-editor: Walt Whitman: An Encyclopedia, 1998; contbr. numerous articles to profl. jours. Mem. Honor Our Neighbors' Origins and Rights, 1991—. Named Wis. Prof. of Yr., Carnegie Found. for Advancement of Tchg., 1997. Mem. MLA (cons. reader 1993, 94), ACLU, Am. Lit. Assn., Acad. Am. Poets, Wis. Fellow of Poets, Walt Whitman Assn., Walt Whitman Birthplace Assn., Greenpeace. Avocations: travel, photography, jazz, racquetball. Office: U Wis-Parkside Dept English PO Box 2000 Kenosha WI 53141-2000 E-mail: kummings@uwp.edu.

KUMMLER, RALPH H., chemical engineer, educator, dean; b. Jersey City, Nov. 1, 1940; m. Jean Evelyn Helge, Aug. 25, 1962; children: Randolph Henry, Bradley Rolf, Jeffrey Ralf. BSChemE, Rensselaer Poly. Inst., 1962; PhD, Johns Hopkins U., 1966. Chem. engr. GE Space Scientist Lab., Valley Forge, Pa., 1965-69; assoc. prof. chem. engring. Wayne State U., Detroit, 1970-75, prof., 1975—, chmn. dept., 1974-93, dir. hazardous waste mgmt. programs, 1986—, assoc. dean rsch., 1997-2001, interim dean, 2001—04, dean, 2004—. Contbr. articles to publs. Bd. dirs., past pres. Kirkwood Lake Assn. Fellow: Engr. Soc. Detroit (Young Engr. of Yr. award 1975, Gold award 1990, Disting. Svc. award 1994, Horace Rackham Humanitarian award 1999, Disting. Svc. award 2004), Am. Inst. Chemists; mem.: AIChE (past pres. Detroit chpt.), Svc. award 1981, Chem. Engr. of Yr. award 1981), Mich. Air and Waste Mgmt. Assn. ((past pres.), Waste Mgmt. award 2002), Am. Chem. Soc., Tau Beta Pi, Sigma Xi. Achievements include co-patentee in chem. innovations. Office: Wayne State U Coll Engring Detroit MI 48202 Office Phone: 313-577-3775. Business E-Mail: rkummler@wayne.edu.

KUMP, WARREN LEE, retired radiologist; b. Jennings, Kans., June 30, 1926; s. Lee Robert and Hazel Jessie (Bobbitt) K.; m. Patricia Jeanne Burke, Oct. 16, 1950; children: Theresa, Lee, Mary, John. BA, U. Kans., 1947, MD, 1950. Diplomate Am. Bd. Radiology. Intern U. Ill., Chgo., 1950-51; med. officer USN/USMC, 1951-53; resident U. Minn., Mpls., 1953-56; staff radiologist North Meml. Med. Ctr., Mpls., 1957-96. Chief radiology North Meml. Med. Ctr., 1965-91, chief of staff, 1974-75, trustee, 1982-2001, chmn. bd. dirs., 1993-2000; pres. Mpls. Radiology Assocs., 1965-91. Bd. dirs. Newman Found., 1955-60, St. Therese Found., New Hope, Minn., 1962-94; pres. St. Therese Charitable Svcs., New Hope, 1991-94. Fellow Am. Coll. Radiology; mem. AMA, Radiol. Soc. N.Am., Am. Roentgen Ray Soc., Minn. Radiol. Soc. (pres. 1974-75), Minn. Med. Assn. Roman Catholic. Avocations: reading, travel, historical research. Office: Mpls Rad Assocs 604 Oakdale Med Bldg Minneapolis MN 55422 E-mail: Wlkump@aol.com.

KUMPFER, KAROL LINDA, research psychologist; b. Neptune, N.J., July 30, 1943; d. Beverly Donald and Mary Belle (Campbell) K.; m. Henry Overton Whiteside, Mar. 6, 1978; 1 child, Jane H. BA, Colo. Women's Coll., 1966; MA, U. Utah, 1970, PhD, 1972; postdoctoral, U. Minn., 1975. Lic. psychologist, Utah. Asst. prof. psychology Oberlin (Ohio) Coll., 1971-73; research assoc. Inst. Child Devel. U. Minn., Mpls., 1975-76; asst. prof. Colo. Women's Coll., Denver, 1976-78; psychologist Salt Lake County Mental Health Dept., 1979-80; dep. dir. State Div. Alcoholism and Drugs, Salt Lake City, 1980-84; vis. assoc. prof. Grad. Sch. Social Work U. Utah, Salt Lake City, 1983—88, asst. prof. pyschiatry, 1986—88, assoc. prof. dept. health promotion and edn., 1988—; dir. Ctr. Substance Abuse and Prevention, Washington, 1998—2000; author, dir. Strengthening Families Program, Salt Lake City, 1982—; coordinating scientist Center for Disease Control, 2000—03. Editor/author: Childhood and Chemical Abuse: Prevention and Intervention, 1986. Bd. dirs. Repetory Dance Theatre, Salt Lake City, 1983-87, Western Assn. Concerned Adoptive Parents, Salt Lake City, 1985-90, Utah Alliance for Mentally Ill, Salt Lake City, 1979-80, Utah Mental Health Assn., 2000-03, House of Hope, Salt Lake City, 1994-98; sec. bd. dirs., Utah Opera Guild, 1994-98; bd. dirs. Indian Walk-in Ctr., 2000—, chair-elect, 2004—; pres. U. Utah. Faculty Women's Club, 1974-75; mem. exec. com. Salt Lake City Mayor's Substance Abuse Prevention Coalition, 2000—. Grantee Utah Dept. Social Svcs., Salt Lake City, 1984-1986, Dept. Justice Office Juvenile Justice and Juvenile Delinquency Prevention, 1987-2003, Nat. Inst. on Drug Abuse, 1998-2004, Ctr. for Substance Abuse Prevention, 1997-2002; recipient SAMHSA/CSAP Model Prevention Program award, 2000, White House Office Nat. Drug Control Policy Dirs. award for Disting. Svc., 2000, Luther Terry Lectr. award U.S. Commd. Officers Assn., 2000. Mem.: APHA, AAAS, APA, Soc. for Prevention Rsch. (bd. dirs. 1995—2002, pres. 1997—99), Nat. Inst. Drug Abuse (spl. task force 1985—, grantee 1982—86, 1998—2004), Coun. on Social Work Edn., Nat. Inst. Alcoholism and Alcohol Abuse (spl. task force 1985—, grantee 1980, 2000—), Am. Acad. Child Psychiatry (spl. task force 1986—88), Utah Psychol. Assn. (bd. dirs. 1985—88), Nat. Coun. Social Work Edn., Am. Pub. Health Assn. (mem. 1996—), Utah Psychologists in Pvt. Practice Assn. (pres. 1985—90), Sigma Xi. Democrat. Unitarian Universalist. Avocations: skiing, sailing, travel. Office: Health Promotion Edn U Utah 250 S 1850 East Salt Lake City UT 84112-0920 Office Phone: 801-581-7718.

KUNC, KAREN, artist, educator; b. Omaha, Dec. 15, 1952; BFA, U. Nebr., Lincoln, 1975; MFA, Ohio State U., 1977. Assoc. prof. printmaking U. Nebr., Lincoln, 1983-97, full prof. printmaking, 1997—, gallery dir., 1988-91. Prof., art, Univ. Neb., 1983-, vis. asst. prof. U. Calif., Berkeley, 1987; vis. artist, instr. Carleton Coll., Northfield, Minn., 1989; rsch. fellow Kyoto Seika U., Japan, 1993; vis. artist Icelandic Coll. Arts & Crafts, Rekyavik, 1995. One-woman show Columbus (Ohio) Mus. Art, 1983, Sheldon Meml. Art Gallery, Lincoln, 1984, Mus. Art, U. Iowa, City, 1994, Joslyn Art Mus., Omaha, 1995, Gallery APA, Nagoya, Japan, 1995, Kutna Hora, Czech Republic, 1996, Galleria Harmonia, Jyvaskyla, Finland, 1996; exhibited in group shows San Francisco Mus. Modern Art, 1980, Honolulu Acad. Arts, 1985, Mednorodini Graficni Likovni Ctr., Ljubljana, Yugoslavia, 1987, Zimmerli Art Mus., Rutgers U., New Brusnwick, N.J., 1988, Greenville (S.C.) County Mus. Art, 1988, Calif. Palace Legion of Honor, San Francisco, 1989, Nat. Mus. Women in Arts, Washington, 1991, Elvehjem Mus. Art, U. Wis., Madison, 1993, 9th Seoul Internat. Print Biennale, 1994, Tama Art Mus., Japan, 1995, Graphicstudio Gallery, Tampa, Fla., 1996, Nat. Mus. Am. Art, Washington, 1997; represented in permanent collections Mus. of Modern Art, N.Y., Nat. Mus. Am. Art, Smithsonian Instn., Washington, Libr. Congress, Washington, Worcester (Mass.) Art Mus., Sheldon Meml. Art Gallery, U. Nebr., Nat. Art Libr., Victoria and Albert Mus., London, Mus. Modern Art, N.Y.C., Bklyn. Mus. Art, Fogg Art Mus. Harvard U.; commns. include woodcut print Madison Print Club, 1994, Benziger Winery Imagery Series, Glen Ellen, Calif., 1996, prints Zimmerli Art Mus., 1995, Rutgers Archives Printmaking Studios, 1995, artists book Nat. Mus. Women Arts, Washington, 1996; co-author, editor: Polish Prints: A Contemporary Graphic Tradition, 1989; author: Woodcut and the Contemporary Impressions, 1993; represented by Jane Haslem Gallery, Washington. Recipient 1st prize Graphica Atlaantica, Reykjavik, Iceland, 1987, purchase award U. Del., 1988, prize Machida City Mus. Graphic Art, Tokyo, 1993; fellow Nat. Endowment Arts, 1984, 96; Fulbright scholar, 1996. Mem. NAD (academician, 1994-), Mid-Am. Print Coun., Coll. Art Assn., Ctr. Book Arts, Calif. Soc. Printmakers, Boston Printmakers, Print Club. Office: Atrium Gallery 7638 Forsyth Blvd Saint Louis MO 63105-3404 also: Art & History 303B NCW Univ Nebraska Lincoln NE 68588-0114 Office Phone: 402-472-5541. E-mail: kkunc@unlserve.unl.edu.*

KUNCL, RALPH, provost; AB, Occidental Coll.; MD, PhD, U. Chgo. Former prof. neurology, pathology and grad. program in cellular and molecular medicine Johns Hopkins Med. Sch., Balt., former dir. Neuromuscular Lab.; former vice provost for undergrad. edn. Johns Hopkins U., Balt.; provost Bryn Mawr (Pa.) Coll. Fellow ACE, 2001. Office: Bryn Mawr Coll Office of Provost 101 N Merion Ave Bryn Mawr PA 19010-2899

KUNDEL, HAROLD LOUIS, radiologist, educator; b. N.Y.C., Aug. 15, 1933; s. John A. and Emma E. (Tolle) K.; m. Alice Marie Pape, Mar. 28, 1958; children: Jean, Catherine, Peter AB, Columbia U., 1955, MD, 1959; MS, Temple U., 1963; MA (hon.), U. Pa., 1980. Diplomate Am. Bd. Radiology. Asst. to assoc. prof. Temple U., Phila., 1967-73, prof. radiology, 1973-80; Matthew J. Wilson prof. research radiology U. Pa., Phila., 1980—2001, Matthew J. Wilson prof. emeritus radiology, 2001—. Dir. Pendergrass Diagnostic Imaging Labs. U. Pa., Phila., 1980—2001. Contbr. articles to profl. jours. Capt. USAF, 1963—65. Fellow: Am. Coll. Radiology; mem.: Soc. Thoracic Radiology, Am. Roentgen Ray Soc., Radiol. Soc. N.Am. (Honor award 1978), Assn. Univ. Radiologists (Meml. award 1963, Stauffer award 1982), Alpha Omega Alpha. Lutheran.

KUNDER, JAMES R., federal agency administrator; BS, Harvard U.; MS, Georgetown U. Founder, prin. Kunder/Reali Assocs., Arlington, Va.; dep asst. adminstr. bur. external affairs U.S. Agy. Internat. Devel., Washington, 1987—91, dir. office of U.S. fgn. disaster assistance, 1991—93, dir. for relief and reconstrn. in Afganistan, 2002, dep. asst. adminstr. bur. Asia and Near East, 2002—04, asst. adminstr. Bur. Asia and Near East, 2005—. Legis. dir. U.S. Ho. of Reps.; sr. transp. analyst Commonwealth of Pa.; dep. dir. Nat. Rep. Senatorial Com. Contbr. articles to profl. jours. V.p. program devel. Save the Children Fedn. Infantry platoon comdr. USMC, 1970—73. Office: US Agy Internat Devel Ronald Reagan Bldg 1300 Pennsylvania Ave NW Rm 409 034 Washington DC 20523-1000 Office Phone: 202-712-0200.*

KUNDTZ, JOHN ANDREW, lawyer; b. Cleve., June 23, 1933; s. Ewald E. and Elizabeth (O'Neill) K.; m. Helen Margaret Luckiesh, Aug. 31, 1957; children— John M., Helen E., Margaret L. BS in Social Studies, Georgetown U., 1955; JD, Case Western Reserve U., 1958. Bar: Ohio 1958, U.S. Dist. Ct. (no. dist.) Ohio 1961. Ptnr. Falsgraf, Kundtz, Reidy & Shoup, Cleve., 1961-69; ptnr. Thompson Hine and Flory, Cleve., 1970-90; pvt. practice Cleve., 1990—. Dir. Investment Advisors Internat., Inc., Cleve. Trustee Hathaway Brown Sch., Shaker Heights, Ohio, Chagrin River Land Conservancy, Chagrin Falls, Ohio, Cleve. Soc. for the Blind. 1st lt. USAF, 1958-60. Mem. Ohio State Bar Assn., Assn. Transp. Practitioners. Republican. Roman Catholic. Home: 32540 Creekside Dr Pepper Pike OH 44124-5224 Office: 3000 Aurura Rd Ste 250 Cleveland OH 44139

KUNDU, ARUN C., engineer; BSEE, Bangladesh U. of Engring. and Tech., 1989; Deng (hon.), Yamaguchi U., Japan, 1999. R&D engr. TDK Corp., Ichikawa, Japan, 1999—2001; sr. design engr. TDK R&D Corp., Phoenix, 2002—05. Author: (novels) Novel Filter Design for Communication (Submission for excellent Patent, 2001). Mem.: IEEE (sr.). Achievements include patents for novel bandpass filter design. Home: 4308 E REdwood Ln Phoenix AZ 85048 Office: TDK R&D Corp 4645 E Cotton Ctr Blvd Phoenix AZ 85040 Office Phone: 602-458-9014. Home Fax: 480-706-1723; Office Fax: 602-458-9055. Personal E-mail: ackundu@yahoo.com.

KUNDU, MUKUL RANJAN, physics professor, astronomy professor; b. Calcutta, India, Feb. 10, 1930; came to U.S., 1959; s. Makhan Lal and Monoroma K.; m. Sept. 9, 1958; children: Krishna, Rina, Sanjit. BS (with first class honors), U. Calcutta, India, 1949, MS, 1951; DSc, U. Paris, 1957. Assoc. prof. Cornell U., Ithaca, N.Y., 1962-65, Tata Inst. Fund Rsch., Bombay, India, 1965-68; prof. U. Md., College Park, 1968—, dir. astronomy, 1978-85. Editor: Radio Physics of the Sun, 1980, Unstable Current Systems and Plasma Instabilities in Astrophysics, 1984, Energetic Phenomena on the Sun, 1989; author: Solar Radio Astronomy, 1965; mem. editorial bd. Solar Physics, 1967—. Named Nat. Acad. Sci. fellow, 1967, 74-75, 86, U.S. Sr. Scientist awardee Humbolt Found., 1978, Am. Phys. Soc. fellow, 1989. Fellow Am. Phys. Soc.; mem. Am. Astron. Soc., Am. Geophys. Union, Internat. Astron. Union, Internat. Union Radio Sci. Office: U Md Dept Astronomy College Park MD 20742-0001 Office Phone: 301-405-1524. Business E-Mail: kundu@astro.umd.edu.

KUNDUR, DEEPA, electrical engineer, educator; b. Toronto, June 14, 1971; d. Prabha S. and Geetha Kundur; m. Takis Zournatos, June 18, 1995. BASc, U. Toronto, 1993, MASc, PhD, U. Toronto, 1995. Cert. profl. engr., Ont. Asst. prof. U. Toronto, Canada, 1999—2002, adj. asst. prof., 2003—; asst. prof. Tex. A&M U., College Station, 2003—. Bell Can. jr. chair-holder in multimedia U. Toronto, 1999—2002; assoc. Nortel Inst. for Telecom., Toronto, 1999—2001; dept. elec. engring. undergrad. rsch. coord. Tex. A&M U., College Station, 2003—. Contbr. articles to profl. jours. Grantee, Nortel Inst. for Telecom., 1999—2001, Natural Scis. and Engring. Rsch. Coun., 2000—04, Comm. and Info. Tech. Ont., 2000—02, Can. Found. for Innovation, 2001—05, Ont. Innovations Trust, 2001—05, Cannaught New Staff Mating, 2001—03, Bell U. Labs, 2002—04, NSF, 2004—; scholar, Govt. of Can., 1989—93, SCIEX, 1993, Natural Scis. and Engring. Rsch. Coun., 1993—95, 1995—97. Mem.: IEEE. Achievements include invention of Nonnegativity and Supports Constraints Inverse Filtering Algorithm for Blind Image Restoration Algorithm; first to have pioneered, analyzed and invented a number of digital image watermarking algorithms that make use of multiresolution wavelet analysis; research in lightweight strategies for securing multimedia information for digital rights management. Office: Texas A&M Univ 111D Zachry Engring Ctr College Station TX 77843-3128 Office Fax: 979-862-4630. E-mail: deepa@ee.tamu.edu.

KUNES, ELLEN, magazine executive; m. David Freeman; 2 children. Grad., U. NH, 1981. Cons. editor Mademoiselle Mag.; contbg. editor Omni Mag.; exec. editor Self Mag.; lifestyle dir. McCall's, 1991—94; exec. editor Redbook Mag., 1994—98, Cosmopolitan, 1998—99; editor O Mag., 1999; editor-in-chief Redbook Mag., 2001—04; with mag. devel. group Hearst Magazines, 2004—. Author: Living Well - Or Even Better - On Less, 1991. Office: Hearst Corp 959 8th Ave New York NY 10019-3795

KUNES, RICHARD W., cosmetics executive; MBA, Pace U. With Colgate-Palmolive Co.; internat. mfg. contr. internat. ops. group Estée Lauder Cos. Inc., N.Y.C., 1986, regional fin. officer Asia/Pacific markets, v.p., contr. global ops., v.p. ops. fin. worldwide, v.p. fin. adminstrn., corp. contr., 1998—2000, sr. v.p., CFO, 2001—. Office: Estée Lauder Co Inc 767 5th Ave New York NY 10153

KUNG, CANDIE, professional golfer; b. Kaohsiung, Taiwan, Aug. 8, 1981; Attended, U. So. Calif. Winner U.S. Pub. Links Championship, 2001, State Farm Classic, 2003; Wachovia LPGA Classic, 2003, LPGA Takefuji Classsic, 2003. Two-time NCAA All-Am.; winner Pac-10 Championships, 2000; three-time Am. Jr. Golf Assn. All-Am. Named Am. Jr. Golf Assn. Player of Yr., 1999. Office: c/o LPGA 100 International Golf Dr Daytona Beach FL 32124-1092

KUNG, GRACE C., cardiologist, educator; BA, Johns Hopkins U., 1989, MD, 1993. Cert. Am. Bd. Pediat. (specialization in pediatric cardiology). Asst. prof. Baylor Coll. of Medicine, Houston, 1999—2003, U. So. Calif., LA, 2003—. Fellow: Am. Coll. Cardiology. Office: Childrens Hospital Los Angeles 4650 Sunset Blvd Los Angeles CA 90027 Office Phone: 323-669-2461.

KUNG, PANG-JEN, materials scientist, electrical engineer; b. I-Lan, Taiwan, May 13, 1959; s. Ching-Yu and A-Se (Yu) K.; m. Tzyy-Yun Tzeng, May 18, 1986; children: Naihau, Naiwei. MSChemE, Nat. Tsing Hua U., 1983; MSEE, Auburn U., 1988; MMetE, Carnegie Mellon U., 1991, PhD in Materials Sci., 1993; MBA, U. Conn., 1998. Registered profl. engr. Jr. engr. Tatung Co., Taipei, Taiwan, 1979—80; tchg. asst. Nat. Tsing Hua U., Hsin-Chu, Taiwan, 1981—82, rsch. asst., 1982—83; assoc. scientist Indsl. Tech. Res. Inst., Hsin-Chu, 1985—86; tchg. and rsch. asst. Auburn U., Ala., 1986—89; rsch. asst. Carnegie Mellon U., Pitts., 1989—91; staff rsch. asst. Los Alamos Nat. Lab., N.Mex., 1991—92, rsch. fellow, 1993—94; sr. scientist Advanced Fuel Rsch., Inc., East Hartford, Conn., 1995—98; chmn. Pioneer Techs., Inc., West Hartford, Conn., 1996—99; cons. InfiMed, Inc., Liverpool, NY, 1998—2000; product devel. engr. JDS Uniphase, Research Triangle Park, NC, 2001—02; pres. Optotrack, Inc., Cary, NC, 2002—. Chmn. acad. affairs Tatung Inst. Tech., Taipei, 1979-80; tech. info. editor Indsl. Tech. Rsch. Inst., Hsin-Chu, 1985-86; translator tech. articles Super Tech. Books Co., Taipei, 1986; adj. prof. Strayer U., Cary, N.C., 2004—. Author, editor: Unit Operations in Chemical Engineering, 1986; contbr. articles to profl. jours. 2nd lt. Chinese Air Force, 1983-85. Recipient Editor's Choice award Nat. Poetry Assn., 1989, 90; Am.-Chinese Engr. scholar Am.-Chinese Assn. Engrs., 1980; Liang Ji-Duan fellow Carnegie Mellon U., 1991. Mem. AAAS, IEEE, SPIE, Materials Rsch. Soc., Am. Vacuum Soc.

(Tech. Paper award 1992), Acad. Am. Poets, Beta Gamma Sigma. Achievements include research in diamond thin films and high Tc superconductors; superconducting quantum interference devices and biomagnetic systems; surface characterization and microstructural analysis; ferroelectric devices, giant magnetoresistive sensors, high-speed microelectronics, epitaxial heterostructures, in-process monitors, pulsed laser deposition, thermal evaporation, sputtering; pyroelectric sensor arrays, gas sensors, plasma-enhanced chemical vapor deposition, x-ray imaging materials, digital radiography and fluoroscopy, microelectromechanical systems (MEMS); optical switches and waveguides; optical communication systems; nanotechnology, microfluidics, biol. and chem. assays. Office: Optotrack Inc PO Box 1242 Cary NC 27512 Office Phone: 919-363-2802. Business E-Mail: ckung@optotrack.com.

KUNG, PATRICK CHUNG-SHU, biotechnologist; b. Nanjing, China, July 10, 1947; came to U.S., 1969; s. Tao and Yuing (Li) K.; m. Yie Lu; children: Julia, Calvin, Charles Shen. BS, Fu Jen U., Taiwan, 1968; PhD, U. Calif., Berkeley, 1974. Rsch. fellow MIT, Cambridge, 1974-77; sr. rsch. fellow Ortho Pharm. Co., J & J, Raritan, NJ, 1978—81; v.p. rsch. Centocor Inc., Malvern, Pa., 1982-83; co-founder, exec. v.p., vice chmn. T Cell Sci., Inc./Avant Immunotherapies, Inc., Cambridge, 1984—98; bd. dirs. PhytoCeutica, Inc., New Haven. Exec. bd. Coll. Letters and Scis. U. Calif., Berkeley, 1989-91; bd. dirs. PhytoCeutica, Inc., pres., CEO, 1999-2003. Contbr. articles to profl. jours. Trustee Park Sch., Brookline, Mass., 1992-95. Recipient Philip Hoffman award Johnson & Johnson Co., 1979, Achievement award Chinese Inst. Engrs., 1988, Discoverers award U.S. Pharm. Mfrs. Rsch. Assn., 1991, Thomas Alva Edison award N.J. Rsch. Coun., 1991. Mem. Soc. Chinese Bioscientists in Am. (pres. bio/pharm. scis. divsn. 1994, 95). Personal E-mail: drpckung@aol.com.

KUNG, SHAIN-DOW, molecular biologist, academic administrator; b. China, Mar. 14, 1935; came to U.S., 1971, naturalized, 1977; s. Chao-tzen and Chih (Zhu) K. Grad., Chung-Hsing U., Taiwan, China, 1958; PhD, U. Toronto, Can., 1968. m. Helen C.C. Kung, Sept. 5, 1964; children: Grace, David, Andrew. Rsch. fellow Hosp. for Sick Children, Toronto, 1968-70; biologist UCLA, 1971-74; asst. prof. biology U. Md., Baltimore County, 1974-77, assoc. prof., 1977-82, prof., 1982-86, acting chmn. dept., 1982-84, assoc. dean arts and sci., 1985-86, prof. botany College Park, 1986-93; acting dir. U. Md. Ctr. for Agrl. Biotech., 1986-88, dir., 1988-93; acting provost Md. Biotech. Inst., 1989-91; dean sch. sci. Hong Kong U. Sci. and Tech., 1991-92, v.p. for acad. affairs, 1992-98, acting v.p. for acad. affairs, 2000; prof. emeritus U. Md., 1993—, Hong Kong U. Sci. and Tech., 2001—; pres. Shandong U., 2004—. Hon. prof. Fudan U., 1986, Beijing Agrl. U., 1987. Author 8 books; editor 14 books; contbr. chpts. to books, articles to profl. jours. Recipient Philip Morris award for disting. achievement in tobacco sci., 1979, Outstanding Alumni award, 1990, Outstanding Svc. award, 1990; named Disting. Scholar, Nat. Acad. Sci., 1981; Fulbright grantee, 1982-83, grantee NSF, NIH. Mem. AAAS, Am. Soc. Plant Physiologists. Office: Hong Kong U Sci and Tech Clear Water Bay Kowloon Hong Kong

KUNHARDT, ERICH ENRIQUE, physicist, researcher; b. Montecristy, Dominican Republic, May 31, 1949; came to U.S., 1961; s. Juan Enrique and Irma Mercedes (Grullon) K.; m. Christine Ann Koza, Oct. 23, 1976. BS, NYU, 1969; PhD, Poly. U., Bklyn., 1976. Asst. prof. Tex. Tech U., Lubbock, 1976-80, assoc. prof., 1980-83, prof., 1983-85, Poly. U., 1985-91; George Mead Bond prof. physics Stevens Inst. Tech., Hoboken, N.J., 1991—, Inst. prof., 1999—, dean Sch. Sci. and Humanities, 2000—, dean Sch. Sci. and Liberal Arts, 2001—. Dir. Weber Rsch. Inst., Poly. U., 1986-91. Editor: Breakdown and Discharges in Gases, 1983, The Liquid State and its Electrical Properties, 1985; mem. adv. bd. Jour. Transport Theory and Statis. Physics, 1984—; contbr. articles to profl. jours. Recipient Citation for Excellence in Rsch. Nassau County, 1988. Mem. IEEE, Am. Phys. Soc. Achievements include observation of plasma wavepacket bifurcation; research on kinetic behavior of a streamer, and on method for closure of fluid equations; patents for atmospheric pressure plasma sources. Office: Stevens Inst Tech Castle Point Hoboken NJ 07030

KUNIHOLM, BRUCE ROBELLET, university administrator; b. Washington, Oct. 4, 1942; s. Bertel Eric and Berthe Eugenie (Robellet) K.; m. Elizabeth Fairbank, June 29, 1968 (div. July 1987); children: Jonathan, Erin; m. Donna Slawson, Jan. 19, 2001. AB in English, Dartmouth Coll., 1964; MA in History, Duke U., 1972, MA in Pub. Policy Sci., PhD in History, Duke U., 1976. Instr. English Robert Acad./Robert Coll., Istanbul, Turkey, 1964-67; Coun. Fgn. Rels./NEH fellow Dept. State, Washington, 1979, internat. rels. officer policy planning staff, 1979-80; from instr. to prof. Duke U., Durham, NC, 1975—87, prof. pub. policy studies and history, 1987—, chmn. dept. public policy studies, 1989—94, 2005—, dir. Terry Sanford Inst. Pub. Policy, 1989-94, 2005—. Vis. prof. Internat. Rels. Koc U., Istanbul, Turkey, 1995-96, 2002; vice-provost for acad. and internat. affairs, Duke U., Durham, N.C., 1996—2001; chmn. acad. com.Can.-U.S. Fulbright Program, 2000—; dir. Ctr. for Internat. Studies, 1999—2001; guest scholar Woodrow Wilson Internat. Ctr. Scholars, 1982; cons. NEH, USMC, Dept. State, U.S. Army, United Tech. Corp.; invited lectr. numerous orgns., colls., univs., fgn. countries including U.S. Senate Fgn. Rels.Com., CIA, State Dept., Chase Manhattan Bank, Harvard U., Brown U., Dartmouth Coll., Yale U., Princeton U., France, Eng., Germany, Italy, Kuwait, Saudi Arabia, Sudan, Can., Turkey, also others. Author: Origins of the Cold War in the Near East, 1980 (Stuart L. Bernath prize 1981), The Persian Gulf and United States Policy, 1984, The Palestine Problem and United States Policy, 1986; contbr. articles to profl. jours.; contbr. chpts. books. Bd. dirs., chmn. acad. com. Found. for Ednl. Exch. between Can. and U.S., 2000—. Capt. USMC, 1967-71, Vietnam. Decorated Bronze Star with V device; recipient Disting. Teaching award Trinity Coll., Duke U., 1989; rsch. grantee Harry S. Truman Libr., 1984, Duke U. Rsch. Coun., 1985-86, Inst. Turkish Studies, 1986-87, travel grantee Ctr. Soviet and East European Studies, 1991; Fulbright sr. rsch. fellow, Turkey, 1986-87, Woodrow Wilson Internat. Ctr. Scholars fellow Smithsonian Instn., 1986-87, sr. fellow Nobel Inst., Oslo, 1994. Mem. Am. Hist. Assn., Fulbright Fellows, Coun. Fgn. Rels., Orgn. Am. Historians, Soc. Historians Am. Fgn. Rels., Middle East Inst., Middle East Studies Assn., Internat. Inst. Strategic Studies, Phi Beta Kappa. Democrat. Avocations: triathlons, bluegrass banjo, wine. Home: 613 Swift Ave Durham NC 27701 Office: Duke U Sanford Inst Public Policy Durham NC 27708 Office Phone: 919-613-7309. Business E-Mail: bruce.kuniholm@duke.edu.

KUNIN, MADELEINE MAY, former ambassador to Switzerland, former governor; b. Zurich, Switzerland, Sept. 28, 1933; came to U.S., 1940, naturalized, 1947; d. Ferdinand and Renee (Bloch) May; children: Julia, Peter, Adam, Daniel BA, U. Mass., 1956; MS, Columbia U., 1957; MA, U. Vt., 1967; numerous hon. degrees. Newspaper reporter Burlington Free Press, Vt., 1957-58; guide Brussels World's Fair, Belgium, 1958; TV asst. producer Sta. WCAX-TV, Burlington, 1960-61; freelance writer, instr. English Trinity Coll., Burlington, 1969-70; mem. Vt. Ho. of Reps., 1973-78; lt. gov. State of Vt., Montpelier, 1979-82, gov., 1985-91; disting. vis. in Pub. Policy Bunting Inst., Cambridge, Mass., 1991-92; Montgomery fellow Dartmouth Coll., Hanover, NH, 1992; dep. sec. edn. Dept. Edn., Washington, 1993-96; U.S. amb. to Switzerland, 1996-99; scholar in residence Middlebury Coll., 1999; disting. vis. prof. St.Michael's Coll. and U. Vt., 2003—. Fellow Inst. Politics, Kennedy Sch. Govt., Harvard U., 1983; lectr. Middlebury Coll., St. Michael's Coll., 1984; disting. pub. policy visitor Rockefeller Ctr., Dartmouth Coll., 1992; pub. policy fellow Bunting Inst., Radcliffe Coll., Harvard U., 1991-92; Vt. Joint Fiscal Com., 1977-78; mem. exec. com. Nat. Conf. Lt. Govs., 1979-80; founder, pres. Inst. Sustainable Cmtys., Montpelier, Vt., 1991—; mem. 3 person com. to recommend v.p. to Bill Clinton; mem. transition team, co-chair nat. com. Women for Clinton, 1992; scholar-in-residence Middlebury (Vt.) Coll., 1999-2003; disting visitor U. of Vt. and St. Michael's Coll., 2003—. Author: Living a Political Life: A Memoir, 1994, The Big Green Book, 1976; contbr. articles to profl. jours., mags. and newspapers. Commentator Vt. Pub. Radio. Scholar in residence Middlebury Coll., 1999—; Named Outstanding State Legislator, Eagleton Inst. Politics, Rutgers U., 1975; Montgomery fellow Dartmouth Coll., 1991. Fellow Am. Acad. Arts & Scis.; mem. Nat. Gov.'s Assn. (mem. exec. com.), Nat. Govs.' Conf. (chair com. on energy and the environ.), New Eng. Gov.'s Conf. (chairperson). Democrat. Office: Univ Vt Burlington VT 05401 Business E-Mail: madeleine.kunin@uvm.edu. E-mail: mkunin@smcvt.edu.

KUNKEL, DAVID NELSON, lawyer; b. Rochester, N.Y., Apr. 5, 1943; s. Frederick W. and Dorothy Jean (Smith) K.; m. Gayle Kellogg Van Dussen, Aug. 21, 1965; children: Jennifer Dawn, Nelson Charles. BA with high honors, U. Va., 1965; LLB, U. Pa., 1968. Bar: Pa. 1969, N.Y. 1972. Assoc. Montgomery, McCracken, Walker & Rhoads, Phila., 1968, Nixon, Hargrave, Devans & Doyle, Rochester, NY, 1971-78, ptnr., 1978-95, sr. counsel, 1995; vice chair, exec. v.p. PSINet, Inc., Ashburn, Va., 1995—2000; cons. internat. and tech. cos., 2000—02; pres., CEO Hopeman Bros. Marine Interiors LLC; pres., COO AWH Corp., 2002—03; cons. Internat. and Tech., 2003. Mem. Bd. Bloomfield Ctrl. Sch., East Bloomfield, N.Y., 1982-85. Lt. USNR, 1969-71. Mem. ABA. Home: 3244 Heathcote Ln Keswick VA 22947

KUNKEL, GEORGIE BRIGHT, freelance/self-employed writer, retired counseling administrator; b. Chehalis, Wash. d. George Riley and Myrtia (McLaughlin) Bright; m. Norman C. Kunkel, Apr. 25, 1946; children: N. Joseph D.C.(dec.), Stephen Gregory, Susan Ann, Kimberly Jane Waligorska. BA in Edn., Western Wash. U., 1944; MEd, U. Wash., 1968. Tchr. pub. schs., Vader, Centralia, Seattle, Wash., 1941-67; counselor Highline Pub. Schs., Seattle, 1967-82. Sch. counselor rep. State of Art Conf., Balt., 1980; spkr. on women's issues, humor, and the Holocaust. Author: You're Damn Right I Wear Purple! Color Me Feminist, 2000; editor: Women and Girls in Edn., 1972—75; columnist: West Seattle Herald and Northwest Prime Time; contbr. articles to profl. jours. Organizer Women and Girls in Edn., Wash. State, 1971; pres. Wash. State NOW, 1973; past pres. West Seattle Dem. Women's Club. Grantee Women Adminstrs. Wash. State, 1971, Edn. Svc. Dist., Seattle, 1980; recipient Woman of Achievement award Past Pres. Assembly, 2000; winner essay contest and appeared on Oprah show. Mem. NEA (sec. pub. rels.), ACA (pres. state br. 1982-83), Am. Sch. Counseling Assn. (pres. state divsn. 1980-81), Seattle Counselors Assn. (organizer, past pres. office exec., Counselor of Yr. award 1990). Unitarian Universalist. Avocation: singing with Raging Grannies. Home and Office: 3409 SW Trenton St Seattle WA 98126-3743

KUNKEL, JOE CARROLL, finance company executive; b. Killeen, Tex., Aug. 10, 1962; s. Melton Leroy and Carol Sue Kunkel. BBA, Howard Payne U., 1984. Sr. unit trainer SallieMae, Killeen, Tex., 1988—93; coord. loan servicing Brazos Higher Edn. Svc. Corp., Waco, Tex., 1993—97; compliance officer Academic Mgmt. Svcs., Swansea, Mass., 1997—2002; sr. v.p. edn. lending and mktg. NextStudent Inc., Phoenix, 2002—. Home: 3633 North 3rd Avenue 2089 Phoenix AZ 85013 Office: NextStudent Inc 11225 North 28th Drive Suite A-202 Phoenix AZ 85029-5607 Office Phone: 602-439-6070. Office Fax: 602-439-6069. E-mail: jkunkel@nextstudent.com.

KUNKEL, RICHARD LESTER, public radio executive; b. Syracuse, N.Y., Nov. 12, 1944; s. Lester DeLong Kunkel and Margaret Fanny Ralph; m. Mary Joan Goldsworthy, Aug. 10, 1968; children: Richard J., Charles J., Joseph B. BS, Syracuse U., 1967, MS, 1969. Lic. real estate broker, N.C. Program dir. Sta. WNBI, Northland Broadcasting, Park Falls, Wis., 1969-72; instr., prodn. dir. Sta. WMKY, Morehead (Ky.) State U., 1972-77; radio mgr. Maine Pub. Broadcasting Network, Orono, 1977-78; instr., sta. mgr. Sta. KNTU, U. North Tex., Denton, 1978-84; v.p., dean Southeastern Ctr. for Arts, Atlanta, 1985-88; pres., gen. mgr. Spokane (Wash.) Pub. Radio Inc., 1988—. Cons., 1978—. With Army N.g., 1968-74. Recipient Addy award 1975. Avocations: photography, computers. Office: KPBX/KIBX and KSFC Spokane Pub Radio 2319 N Monroe St Spokane WA 99205-4586 E-mail: rkunkel@kpbx.org.

KUNKEL, ROBERT ANTHONY, business educator; b. Spring Valley, Ill., Mar. 14, 1961; s. Joseph Conrad and Louise Thelma (Stenbeck) K.; m. Erin Elizabeth Coates, Dec. 30, 1989. BS in Agr., U. Ill., 1983; MBA, Western Ill. U., 1989; MA in Econs., U. Tenn., Knoxville, 1993, PhD in Fin., 1994. Asst. county supr. Farmers Home Adminstrn., USDA, western Ill., 1983-86, county supr. Macomb, Ill., 1986-88, asst. county supr. Carthage, Ill., 1988-90; grad. asst. U. Tenn., Knoxville, 1990-94; asst. prof. fin. Minot (N.D.) State U., 1994-95, Western Ill. U., Macomb, 1995-97, Ea. Ill. U., Charleston, 1997-99, U. Wis., Oshkosh, 1999—. Mem. fin. com. Sisters of St. Francis, Clinton, Iowa, 1996—; bd. dirs. Western Ill. Credit Union, Macomb, 1996-97. Contbr. articles to profl. jours. Mem. fin. com. N.D. Region II Child Care Svcs., Minot, 1994-95. Fin. Mgmt. ASsn. Knoxville grad. fellow, 1994. Mem. Fin. Mgmt. Assn., Eastern Fin. Assn., Midwest Bus. Adminstrn. Assn. Roman Catholic. Avocations: golf, travel, sports, movies. Home: 4000 Summerview Dr Oshkosh WI 54901-1287 Office: U Wis Coll Bus Adminstrn Oshkosh WI 54901 Office Phone: 920-424-7191.

KUNKLE, DAVID M., police chief; b. Nov. 13, 1950; BS, U. Tex., Arlington, 1976, MA, 1994. With Dallas Police Dept., 1972—82; police chief City of Grand Prairie, Tex., 1982—85, Arlington Police Dept., Tex., 1985—99, Dallas Police Dept., 2004—; dep. city mgr. City of Arlington, 1999—2004. Office: Dallas Police Dept 1400 S Lamar St Dallas TX 75215

KUNKLE, GARY K., JR., dental products executive; BS in Mktg., Univ. South Carolina, 1972. Pres. Johnson & Johnson Orthopaedics Inc.; pres., Vistakon Divsn. Johnson & Johnson, Jacksonville, Fla.; pres., COO Dentsply Internat., York, Pa., 1997—2004, vice chmn., 2004—05, CEO, 2004—, chmn., 2005—. Bd. dir. Dentsply, 2002—, Perrigo, 2002—05. Named a Disting. Alumni, Univ. South Carolina, 2000. Mem.: Dental Trade Alliance, Am. Dental Trade Assn. Office: Dentsply 570 W College Ave PO Box 872 York PA 17405-0872 Office Phone: 717-845-7511. Office Fax: 717-849-4762.*

KUNKLE, WILLIAM JOSEPH, judge, lawyer; b. Lakewood, Ohio, Sept. 3, 1941; s. William Joseph and Georgia (Howe) K.; m. Sarah Florence Nesti, July 11, 1964; children: Kathleen Margaret, Susan Mary. BA, Northwestern U., Evanston, Ill., 1963; Jd, Northwestern U., 1969. Bar: Ohio 1969, U.S. Dist. Ct. (no. dist.) Ill. 1969, Ill. 1969, U.S. Ct. Appeals (7th cir.) 1991, U.S. Supreme Ct. 1991. Process control engr. Union Carbide Corp., Cleve., 1964-65, prodn. supr. Greenville, S.C., 1965-66; assoc. Hauxhurst, Sharp, Mollison & Gallagher, Cleve., 1969-70; asst. pub. defender Cook County Pub. Defender, Chgo., 1970-73; asst. states atty. Cook County States Atty., Chgo., 1973-85; ptnr. Phelan, Cahill & Quinlan, Ltd., Chgo., 1985-96, Cahill, Christian & Kunkle, Ltd., Chgo., 1996—2002, Wildman, Harrold, Allen & Dixon, Chgo., 2002—04; judge Cir. Ct. Cook County, 2004—. Chmn. The Ill. Gaming Bd., 1990—93; dep. spl. outside counsel U.S. Ho. Reps., Washington, 1988—89; adj. prof. I.I.T. Chgo. Kent Sch. Law, 1980—84; instr. Nat. Inst. Trial Advocacy, 1978—82, 1986; lectr. Nat. Coll. Dist. Attys., 1978—85, Nat. Law Enforcement Inst., 1983—85; 1st asst. states atty. of Cook County, 1983—85; spl. state's atty. 18th Jud. Cir., DuPage County, 1995—99. Contbg. author: Punishment Prosecutor's Viewpoint, 1983, 1989, Trial Techniques Compendium, Nat. College of Dist. Attys. (2d, 3rd, 4th, 5th, 6th eds.). Recipient Disting. Faculty award Nat. Coll. Dist. Attys., 1980, Award for Prosecution Svc. Chgo. Assn. Commerce & Industry, 1981. Fellow Am. Coll. Trial Lawyers, ABA; mem. Internat. Soc. Barristers, Nat. Dist. Attys. Assn. (bd. dirs. 1984-85), Assn. Govt. Attys. in Capital Litigation (pres. 1983-84), Chgo. Bar Assn. (bd. mgrs. 1983-84), Ill. State Bar Assn. (LAWPAC trustee 1989-95), Internat. Assn. Gaming Attys., Chgo. Crime Commn. (bd. dirs.). Avocations: golf, softball, carpentry, motorcycling. Office Phone: 312-603-2600.

KUNKLER, ARNOLD WILLIAM, retired surgeon, educator; b. St. Anthony, Ind., Nov. 18, 1921; s. Edward J. and Selma (Hasenour) K.; m. Muriel Burns, 1954; m. Barbara McElroy, 2004; children: Lisa, Arnold William, Carolyn, Christine, Phillip, Kevin. AB, Ind. U., 1943, MD, 1949. Diplomate Am. Bd. Surgery. Intern Ind. U. Med. Ctr., Indpls., 1949-50, asst. resident in surgery, fellow vascular surg. research, 1950-54, resident in surgery, 1954-55, faculty, 1955—76, clin. prof. surgery, 1976-94; ret., 1994. Individual practice medicine specializing in gen. surgery, Terre Haute, Ind., 1955-94; dir. med. edn. Terre Haute Regional Hosp., 1970-79; staff Terre Haute Center Med. Edn.; chief of staff Terre Haute Regional Hosp., 1989-90. Contbr. articles to profl. jours. Pres. Terre Haute Med. Edn. Found., 1972-73, 78-81, bd. dirs., 1967-86; pres. cmty. adv. coun. Terre Haute Center Med. Edn., 1976-80; treas. Wabash Valley Cmty. Blood Program, 1974-78; trustee Terre Haute Regional Hosp., 1978-84, chmn. bd., 1981-84, Vigo County Bd. Health, 1990-97. With U.S. Army, 1943-46, ETO. Fellow ACS (pres. Ind. chpt. 1980-81); mem. Ind. State Med. Assn. (com. med. edn. 1986-92), Vigo County Med. Soc., Pam. Am. Med. Assn., Pan Pacific Surg. Assn., Midwest Surg. Assn., Aesculapian Soc. Wabash Valley, Ind. Soc. Chgo., Pres.'s Cir. Ind. U., Dean's Coun. Ind. U. Sch. Medicine, Rotary Club of Terre Haute, Sagamore of the Wabash, Skyline Club. Democrat. Roman Catholic. Home: 5300 W 96th St Indianapolis IN 46268 Personal E-mail: akunkler@msn.com. *Success and service are interdependent.*

KUNOS, GEORGE, pharmacologist; b. Budapest, Hungary, May 14, 1942; came to U.S., 1987; s. Istvan and Gabriella (Kalman) K.; m. Ildiko Vermes, June 11, 1967; children: Anne-Marie, Doreen. MD, Budapest Med. U., 1966; PhD, McGill U., Montreal, Can., 1973. Asst. prof. dept. pharmacology McGill U., 1974-79, assoc. prof., 1979-83, prof. dept. pharmacology and dept. of medicine, 1984-88; lab. chief Nat. Inst. Alcoholism, Bethesda, Md., 1987-92; prof., chmn. dept. pharmacology Va. Commonwealth U., Richmond, 1992—2000; scientific dir. Nat. Inst. Alcohol Abuse and Alocholism, Nat. Inst. Health, 2000—. Mem. pharmacology task force Nat. Bd. Med. Examiners, 1996-99. Editor monographs in field; contbr. over 150 sci. articles to profl. jours. Recipient Monat-Fraser Associateship award McGill U., 1981-87. Fellow Am. Heart Assn. (coun. on high blood pressure; mem. Am. Soc. Pharmacol. Exptl. Therapy, Am. Soc. Biochem. Molecular Biology, Soc. for Neurosci., Hungarian Acad. Scis. Achievements include identification of role of endogenous opioid peptides of the brain in regulation of blood pressure and in antihypertensive drug action, unique mechanisms in regulation of hormone receptors role of endogenous cannabinoids in cardiovascular appetite and body weight regulation. Office: Nat Inst Alcohol Abuse & Alcoholism Nat Inst Health PO Box 8413 Bethesda MD 20892-9413 Office Phone: 301-443-2069.

KUNOV, HANS, biomedical and electrical engineering educator; b. Copenhagen, Mar. 14, 1938; arrived in Can., 1967; s. Jens Christian and Ruth K.; m. Helle H.D. Jorgensen, Sept. 12, 1964 (div. 1972); children Mads Jacob, Niels Peter; m. D. Clare Lamb, Aug. 1, 1977. MASc, Tech. U. Denmark, Copenhagen, 1963, PhD, 1966. Registered profl. engr., Ont. Postdoctoral fellow Tech. U. Denmark, 1966-67; asst. prof. U. Toronto, Ont., 1967-73, assoc. prof., 1973-82, prof., 1982—, prof. emeritus, 2003—, dir. Inst. Biomed. Engring. Ont., Can., 1989-99. Dir. Elec. Engring. Consociates, Toronto, 1972—; pres. Artel Engring., 1975—; dir. rsch., co-founder Poul Madsen Med. Devices Ltd., Toronto, 1992—98; co-founder Electrobiologics Corp., 1995—, Vivosonics, Inc., 1999—; mem. grant selection com. Natural Scis. and Engring. Rsch. Coun., Ottawa, Ont., 1990—93. Contbr. numerous sci. papers and publs. Chmn. United Way, U. Toronto, 1991-92; mem. Big Bros. Met. Toronto, 1980—, dir., 1988-92. Recipient Big Brother of Yr. award, Big Bros. Met. Toronto, 1985, 1986, Irving Pomerantz award, 1989, 2002, Queen's Golden Jubilee award, 2003. Mem. IEEE (assoc. editor BME Trans. 1991-93), Acoustical Soc. Am., Can. Med. Biol. Engring. Soc., Danish Engring. Soc. Achievements include development of novel audiometric techniques, of accurate mechano-acoustic models of human hearing and speech apparatus. Home: 4 Princeton Rd Etobicoke ON Canada M8X 2E2 Office: U Toronto 4 Taddle Creek Rd Toronto ON Canada M5S 3G9 E-mail: H.Kunov@utoronto.ca.

KUNOWSKI, HERBERT PETER, lawyer; b. LA, Dec. 7, 1958; s. Samuel and Elizabeth (Koenig) K.; 1 child, Sredna A. AA with honors, El Camino Coll., 1984; BA magna cum laude, UCLA, 1987; JD, Pepperdine U., 1990. Bar: Calif. 1990; U.S. Dist. Ct. (so., ea., no. and cen. dists.) Calif. 1990; U.S. Ct. Appeals (9th cir.) 1990. With Office of City Atty., LA, 1989—90; assoc. Wilson, Elser, Moskovwitz, Edelman & Dicker LLP, LA, 1990, ptnr. Judicial arbitrator and mediator LA County Superior Ct., judge pro tem. Mem. Calif. State Bar, LA County Bar Assn., The Federalist Soc., Orange County Bar Assn. Office: Wilson, Elser, Moskowitz, Edelman & Dicker LLP Ste 2700 1055 W 77th St Los Angeles CA 90017 Office Phone: 213-624-3044 429. Office Fax: 213-624-8060. E-mail: kunowskih@wemed.com.

KUNSTADTER, GERALDINE SAPOLSKY, foundation executive; b. Boston, Jan. 6, 1928; d. Harry Herman and Nettie Sapolsky; m. John W. Kunstadter, Apr. 23, 1949; children: John W., Lisa, Christopher, Elizabeth Student, MIT, 1945-48. Draftsman U. Chgo. Cyclotron Project, 1948; engring. asst. Gen. Electric Corp., Lynn, Mass., 1948-49; pres. Capricorn Investments Corp., 1971—; chmn., pres., dir. A. Kunstadter Family Found., N.Y.C., 1966—. Host family program dir. N.Y.C. Commn. for UN, 1971-86; pres. Nat. Inst. Social Scis., 1979-81; adv. coun. hospitality com. UN Delegations. Mem. internat. hospitality com. Nat. Coun. Women; chmn. N.Y.-Beijing Sister City Com.; mem. Com. Mgmnt. of Network 20/20; bd. dirs. Bridge to Asia Found., Atlantic Coun. of U.S., Ballets Tech. Found., N.Y.C., Ctr. US.-China Arts Exch., Inst. World Affairs; bd. dirs Nat. Com. on US-China Rels. Recipient Windham award, 1970, Silver medal, Nat. Inst. Social Sci., 1981, Pres.'s medal, Archtl. Soc. China, 2001. Mem. Inst. Current World Affairs, Nat. Com. US-China Rels., Coun. on Fgn. Rels., Hurlingham Club, Lansdowne Club (London), Cosmopolitan Club N.Y.(Internat. com.).

KUNTZ, CAROL B., psychologist, educator; b. Dickinson, N.D., Oct. 13, 1952; d. John Nick Kuntz and Veronica Decker; divorced; children: Rick, Jess, Kristy. ADN, Dickinson State U., 1983; BS in Psychology, U. N.D., 1988; MA in Psychology, Ctrl. Mich. U., 1990, D in Psychology, 1993. Diplomate Am. Pyschotherapy Assn., cert. profl. qualification psychology Assn. State and Provincial Psychology Bd. RN St. Joseph's Hosp., Dickinson, ND, 1983, Minot, ND, 1983—86, United Hosp., Grand Forks, 1987—88, Ctrl. Mich. Hosp., Mt. Pleasant, 1988—92; rsch. asst. to Dr. David Stein U. N.D., Grand Forks, ND, 1987—88; psychologist Cath. Family Svcs., Mt. Pleasant, 1991—92; clin. psychologist Univ. Physicians, Sioux Falls, SD, 1993—2002, Avera McKennan Hosp., Univ. Health Ctr., Sioux Falls, 2002—. Cons. Healthy Solutions, Sioux Falls, 1992—93; asst. prof. U. S.D., Sioux Falls, 1994—, supr. psychiatry resident, 2002—; presenter in field. Mem.: APA, Am. Assn. Marriage and Family Therapy, Am. Psychol. Assn. Clin. Psychology, Am. Psychotherapy Assn., Am. Bd. Disability Analysts (diplomate), Internat. Neuropsychological Soc., Nat. Acad. Neuropsychology, S.D. Psychol. Assn., Clin. Neuropsychology, Psychology of Women, Nat. Register health SVc. Providers Psychology, Psi Chi. Roman Catholic. Avocations: ceramics, painting, poetry, bicycling, hiking. Office: Univ Psychiatry Assocs 1001 E 21st St Ste 2000 Sioux Falls SD 57105 Office Phone: 605-322-5700. Personal E-mail: drcbk52@aol.com.

KUNTZ, CHARLES, IV, neurosurgeon; b. Oct. 21, 1964; married; 2 children. BA in Chemistry magna cum laude, Holy Cross Coll., 1987; MD in Infectious Disease, Case Western Res. U., 1991. Intern, resident, fellow U. Washington Affiliated Hosps., Seattle, 1991-2000; assoc. prof., dir. spine and peripheral nerve surgery Mayfield Clinic and Spine Inst., U. Cin., 2000—. Contbr. articles to profl. jours. Mem. AMA, Am. Assn. of Neurol. Surgeons, Congress of Neurol. Surgeons, North Am. Spine Soc., Phi Beta Kappa, Alpha Omega Alpha. Office: Ste 3100 222 Piedmont Ave Cincinnati OH 45219 Office Phone: 513-558-4968. Fax: (513) 475-8033. E-mail: charlesKuntz@yahoo.com.

KUNTZ, EDWARD LAWRENCE, healthcare executive; b. Phila., Feb. 22, 1945; s. Samuel J. and Mary S. (Shulman) K.; m. Caroline L. Lessner, Aug. 3, 1969; m. Stuart M., David M., Beth. BA, Temple U., 1966, JD, 1969, ML, 1978. Pvt. practice, Phila., 1970-78; asst. gen. counsel ARA Svcs., Phila., 1978-79, sector counsel, 1979-84, assoc. gen. counsel, 1984-85; exec. v.p. ARA Living Ctrs., Houston, 1985-92; chmn., CEO Living Ctrs. Am., Houston, 1992-97, Vencor Inc. (now Kindred Healthcare), Louisville, 1999—2003; pres. Kindred Healthcare, Louisville, 1999—2002, chmn. of bd., 2004—. Dir. Alzheimer's Assn., Houston, 1993—; advisor Woodway

Fin. Group, Houston, 1994—; mem. com. Am. Health Care Assn., Washington, 1986—. Co-chmn. fundraising campaign United Way, Med. Ctr., Houston, 1993; bd. dirs. Alley Theater, 1994-97, mem. facilities com., 1994; bd. trustees, adminstrv. and pers. com. Enamu-El, 1996-97. Mem. Thyroid Soc. of Houston (bd. dirs., vice chmn. 1995—), Am. Health Care Assn. (chmn. multifacility steering com., bd. dirs., exec. com., long term financing task force 1997, former mem. numerous coms.), Alzheimer's Assn. (bd. dirs. 1992-97), Thyroid Soc. (vice chmn. bd. dirs., chmn. fund devel. 1996, chmn. bd. 1997), Anti-Defamation League (bd. dirs. 1996-97). Home: 8807 Stable Crest Blvd Houston TX 77024-7035 Office: Kindred Healthcare 680 S Fourth St Louisville KY 40202*

KUNTZ, HAL GOGGAN, petroleum exploration company executive, rancher; b. San Antonio, Dec. 29, 1937; s. Peter A. and Jean (Goggan) K.; children: Hal Goggan, Peter, Michael B., Vesta. BS in Engring., Princeton U., 1960; MBA, Oklahoma City U., 1972. Line, staff positions Mobil Oil Corp., Dallas, Oklahoma City, and New Orleans, 1963-74; co-founder, pres. CLK Corp., New Orleans and Houston, 1974—, IPEX Co., New Orleans, 1974—, CLK Investments I, II, III, and IV, 1979—; pres. Gulf Coast Exploration Co., New Orleans, 1979—, CLK Producing, CLK Oil and Gas Co., CLK Exploration Co., 1980—; rancher Tex. Bd. dirs. North Houston Bank. Mem. Mus. Fine Arts, Houston, 1978—; mem. condrs. cir. Houston Symphony, 1980; mem. governing bd. Houston Opera. With AUS, 1960-63. Mem. Am. Mgmt. Assn., Nat. Small Bus. Assn., Inter-Am. Soc., Soc. Exploration Geophysics, Am. Assn. Petroleum Geologists, Aircraft Owners and Pilots Assn., River Oaks C. of C., Petroleum Club, U. of Houston Club, Argyle Club, Order of Alamo, Coronado Club, Princeton Club, River Oaks Country Club, San Antonio Country Club. Republican. Roman Catholic. Avocations: golf, skiing, birdshooting. Office: CLK Co LLC 5 Post Oak Park Ste 2330 4400 Post Oak Pkwy Houston TX 77027 Office Phone: 713-871-0202. E-mail: Hal_Kuntz@sbcglobal.net.

KUNTZ, JAN MARIE, secondary school educator; d. Donald Henry and Jeannine Dotzel Steinle; m. Daniel Louis Kuntz, Oct. 10, 1981; children: Andrew Joshua, Emily Sara, Joseph Donald. BA, No. Ill. U., 1977, MA, 1987. Cert. tchr. Ill., 1977. Tchr. Genoa-Kingston (Ill.) H.S., 1977—80, Belvidere (Ill.) H.S., 1980—81, Indian Creek-Shabbona/Waterman (Ill.) Sch. Dist., 1981—. Coord. vacation ch. sch. Salem Luth. Ch., Sycamore, Ill., 1988—98. Dir.: (plays) Death of a Salesman, Joseph and the Amazing Technicolor Dreamcoat, Les Miserables. Sec. ch. coun. Salem Luth. Ch., 2000—02; coord. disciple formation Salem Luth. Chuch, Sycamore, Ill., 2001—02; bd. dirs. Stage Coach Players, DeKalb, Ill., 2004—. Named one of Those Who Make a Difference, Ill. Math and Sci. Acad., 1989; recipient Merit cert., State of Ill., 1989. Mem.: Indian Creek Edn. Assn. (corr.; pres. 1990—91). Avocations: theater, gardening. Office: Indian Creek High School 506 S Shabbona Road Shabbona IL 60550 Office Phone: 815-824-2197.

KUNTZ, JOEL DUBOIS, lawyer; b. Dennis, Mass., Feb. 5, 1946; s. Paul Grimley Kuntz and Harriette (Hunter) Ainsworth; m. Karan Judd, June 29, 1968; children: Matthew Christopher, Kristin Lara. BA, Haverford Coll., 1968; JD, Yale U., 1971; LLM in Taxation, NYU, 1980. Bar: Conn. 1972, Oreg. 1974. Assoc. Stoel, Rives, Boley, Jones & Grey, Portland, Oreg., 1974—79, ptnr., 1979—94; v.p., gen. counsel Entek Internat. LLC, Lebanon, Oreg., 1994—. Author (with James S. Eustice): Federal Income Taxation of S Corporations, 1982, 4th edit., 2001; author: (with James S. Eustice, Charles S. Lewis, Thomas P. Deering) Tax Reform Act of 1986: Analysis and Commentary, 1987; author: (with Robert J. Peroni) U.S. International Taxation, 1992. Capt. USMC, 1971-74. Mem. Am. Coll. Tax Counsel, Internat. Fiscal Assn. Democrat. Home: 3910 Lakeview Blvd Lake Oswego OR 97035-5549 Address: PO Box 39 Lebanon OR 97355-0039 Personal E-mail: jdkuntz@attglobal.net.

KUNTZ, LEE ALLAN, lawyer; b. Nashville, July 9, 1943; s. Irwin and Lucy (Kornman) K.; 1 child, Douglas. BA, Duke U., 1965; LLB, Columbia U., 1968. Bar: N.Y., 1968, U.S. Dist. Ct. (so. dist.) N.Y., 1973, U.S. Tax Ct., 1973. Assoc. Shearman Sterling LLP, N.Y.C., 1968—76, ptnr., 1976—, mng. ptnr., 1994—98, sr. ptnr. real estate group, 1988—93, 2004—. Mem. policy com. Shearman Sterling LLP, 1991—99. Contbr. articles to profl. jours. Bd. visitors Columbia Law Sch., 1998—; dir. Vol. Legal Svc., 2000—, Am. Coll. Real Estate Lawyers, 2002-. Mem. ABA, Assn. Bar City N.Y. Office: Shearman Sterling LLP 599 Lexington Ave Fl C2 New York NY 10022-6069 Office Phone: 212-848-7392.

KUNTZ, MARION LUCILE LEATHERS, classicist, educator, historian; b. Atlanta, Sept. 6, 1924; d. Otto Asa and Lucile (Parks) Leathers; m. Paul G. Kuntz, Nov. 26, 1970; children by previous marriage: Charles, Otto Alan (Daniels). BA, Agnes Scott Coll., 1945; MA, Emory U., 1964, PhD, 1969. Lectr. Latin Lovett Sch., Atlanta, 1963-66; from mem. faculty to prof. Ga. State U., 1966—75, Regents' Prof., 1975—, chmn. dept. fgn. langs., 1975-84, Fuller E. Callaway prof., 1984—, rsch. prof., 1984—. Author: Colloquium of the Seven About Secrets of the Sublime of Jean Bodin, 1975, Guillaume Postel, Prophet of the Restitution of All Things: His Life and Thought, 1981, Jacob's Ladder and the Tree of Life: Concepts of Hierarchy and the Great Chain of Being, 1987, Postello, Venezia e Il Suo Mondo, 1988, Venice, Myth and Utopian Thought, 1999, The Anointment of Dionisio: Prophecy and Politics in Renaissance Italy, 2002; also scholarly articles; mem. editl. bd. Library of Renaissance Humanism. V.p. acad. affairs Am.-Hellenic Found.; patron Atlanta Opera. Named Latin Tchr. of Yr. State Ga., 1965; Am. Classical League scholar, 1966, Gladys Krieble Delmas scholar, 1991; Am. Coun. Learned Socs. grantee, 1970, 73, 76, 81, 87, 90; recipient Alumni Disting. Prof. award Ga. State U., 1994, medal for excellence in Renaissance studies Pres. of Coun. Gen., Tours, France, 1995, Disting. Career Alumna award Agnes Scott Coll., 1995 Master: Soc. for Values in Higher Edn., Philosophy and Religion; mem.: Cath. Hist. Soc., Am. Cath. Hist. Soc., Classical Assn. Midwest and South (Semple award 1965), Am. Philol. Assn., Archaeol. Inst. Am., Soc. di Philosophique Medievale, Soc. Medieval and Renaissance Philosophy (exec. bd. 1988—90), Medieval Acad. Soc. de Culture Europèenne, Soc. des Seiziėmistes, Soc. Christian Philosophers (exec. bd. 1987—), Internat. Soc. Neo-Latin Studies, Internat. Soc. Neo-Platonic Studies, Am. Hist. Assn., Am. Soc. Ch. History, Am. Cath. Philos. Assn., Am. Soc. Aesthetics, Renaissance Soc. Am. (coun. 1994—97, trustee 2003—), The Atlanta Opera (patron), The Atlanta Symphony (patron), World Monuments Fund, Am. Acad. Rome (sec.-treas. 1970—74), Friends of the Warburg Inst., Atlanta Hist. Soc., Italian Cultural Soc., Amici di Querini-Stampalia Galleria e Biblioteca, Friends of the Vatican Libr., Italia Nostra, Fondazione Ambiente Italiana, Coun. Amici di Biblioteca Nazionale di San Marco, Nat. Trust Hist. Preservation, High Mus. of Art (patron), The Commerce Club, Omicron Delta Kappa, Phi Kappa Phi, Phi Beta Kappa. Roman Catholic. Home: Villa Veneziana 1655 Ponce De Leon Ave Atlanta GA 30307 also: Castello 6817 Venice Italy Business E-Mail: marion@gsu.edu.

KUNTZ, STUART MICHAEL, lawyer; b. Phila., Apr. 27, 1973; s. Caroline Lessner and Edward Lawrence Kuntz; m. Laurie Gail Abramson, June 27, 2004. BA, Emory U., 1995; JD, NYU, 1998. Assoc. Reed Smith LLP, Washington, 2002—04; assoc. counsel MCI, Inc., Ashburn, Va., 2004—. Mem. young leadership inst. Wash. Hebrew Congregation, Washington, 2004—05. Republican. Jewish. Office: MCI Inc 22001 Loudoun County Parkway Ashburn VA 20147 Office Phone: 703-886-1143. E-mail: stuart.kuntz@mci.com.

KUNTZ, WILLIAM FRANCIS, II, lawyer, educator; b. N.Y.C., June 24, 1950; s. William Francis I and Margaret Evelyn (Brown) K.; m. Alice Beal, May 20, 1978; children: William Thaddeus, Katharine Lowell, Elizabeth Anne. AB, Harvard U., 1972, AM, 1974, JD, 1977, PhD, 1979. Bar: N.Y. 1978. Assoc. Shearman & Sterling, N.Y.C., 1978-86; mem. Milgrim, Thomajan & Lee, N.Y.C., 1986-94; ptnr. Seward & Kissel, N.Y.C., 1994-2001, The Torys Law Firm, N.Y.C., 2001—04, Constantine Cannon, 2004—. Assoc. prof. Bklyn. Law Sch., 1987-2002. Author: Criminal Sentencing, 1988. Bd. dirs. MFY Legal Svcs., Inc., N.Y.C., 1984-90, Boys Brotherhood Republic, N.Y.C., 1986-90, Habitat for Humanity, N.Y.C., 1987-90; chmn. Resources for Children with Spl. Needs, N.Y.C., 1986-89; mem. N.Y. Civilian Complaint Rev. Bd., 1987—, chmn., 1994. Mem. ABA, N.Y. State Bar Assn., N.Y. County Lawyers Assn. (bd. dirs. 1991-96), Assn. of Bar of City of N.Y. (chmn. mcpl. affairs com. 1992-95, judiciary com., exec. com. 2002—, chmn. 2005—), Bklyn. Bar Assn. (judiciary com. 1995—), Met. Black Bar Assn. Democrat. Roman Catholic. Office: Constantine & Ptnrs 450 Lexington Ave New York NY 10017 Business E-Mail: wkuntz@constantinecannon.com.

KUNTZ, WILLIAM RICHARD, JR., lawyer; b. New Rochelle, NY, Oct. 6, 1949; s. William Richard and Mary Margaret (Kerkvliet) Kuntz. BSE, Princeton U., 1971; JD, U. So. Calif., 1974. Bar: Calif. 1974, US Dist. Ct. (cen. dist.) Calif. Assoc. McKenna & Fitting, LA, 1974—75, Stroock, Stroock & Lavan, LA, 1975—81, Hahn, Cazier & Leff, LA, 1981—82; ptnr. Hahn, Cazier & Smaltz, LA, 1982—87, Morgan, Lewis & Bockius, LA, 1987—88; from v.p., gen. coun. to exec. v.p., CFO Chart House Enterprises Inc., Solana Beach, Calif., 1988—97, exec. v.p., CFO, 1997; mng. dir. CB Richard Ellis, Inc., Newport Beach, Calif., 1997—99; of counsel Merrill, Schultz & Wolds, San Diego, 1999—2004; pvt. practice, 2004—. Mem.: ABA, State Bar Calif. Assn. Home: 13536 Kibbings Rd San Diego CA 92130-1242 Office: 12526 High Bluff Dr Ste 300 San Diego CA 92130 Business E-Mail: wkuntz@wrkuntzlaw.com.

KUNTZMAN, RONALD, research and development company executive; b. Bklyn., Sept. 17, 1933; s. Herman and Fanny Kuntzman; m. Bernice Russman, May 29, 1955; children: Fred, Gary. BS, Bklyn. Coll., 1955; MS, George Washington U., 1957, PhD in Biochemistry, 1962. Biochemist lab. chem. pharmacology Nat. Heart Inst., NIH, Bethesda, Md., 1955-62; sr. biochemist Wellcome Research Labs.-Burroughs Wellcome & Co. U.S.A. Inc., Tuckahoe, N.Y., 1962-66, dep. head biochem. pharmacology dept., 1967-70; assoc. dir. dept. biochemistry and drug metabolism Hoffmann-La Roche Inc., Nutley, N.J., 1970-71, assoc. dir. biol. research, 1972-73, dir. therapeutics research, 1973-79, asst. v.p., 1974-81, dir. pharm. R & D, 1980-81, v.p. pharm. R&D, 1981-84, v.p. R&D, 1984-92; adj. prof. dept. chem. biology and pharmacognosy Rutgers U. Coll. Pharmacy, Piscataway, N.J., 1990—; adj. mem. Roche Inst. Molecular Biology, Nutley, N.J., 1992-96. Mem. adv. coun. Nat. Orgn. for Rare Disorders, 1987-91; adj. prof. Rutgers U., 1990—. Mem. editl. bd. Biochem. Pharmacology, 1966-68, Neuropharmacology, 1970-78, Xenobiotica, 1970-84, Archives of Biochemistry and Biophysics, 1971-78, Life Scis., 1973-78; contbr. numerous articles to profl. jours. Mem. AAAS, Am. Soc. Pharmacology and Exptl. Therapeutics (editorial bd. jour. 1968-75, nominating com. 1972, chmn. div. nominating com. 1977, chmn. div. drug metabolism 1978-81, sec.-treas. 1981-83, coun. 1981-83, chmn. long-range planning com. 1987-92, exec. com. div. drug metabolism 1973-76, John Jacob Abel award 1969), Am. Soc. Biol. Chemists, Am. Coll. Neuropsychopharmacology, Soc. Toxicology, George Washington U. Alumni Assn. (Dist. Alumni Achievement award 1988), Roche Inst. of Molecular Biology (adj. 1992-96), Sigma Xi. Achievements include research on steroids and other normal body constituents which are metabolized by drug metabolizing enzymes; discovered P448, the hemoprotein inducible by hydrocarbon; demonstrated that DOPA-5HTP decarboxylase are the same enzyme. Address: 16 Reunion Rd Rye Brook NY 10573-1085 Personal E-mail: ronkfun@aol.com.

KUNZ, ALEXANDRA CAVITT, physician, anthropologist, researcher; b. Waukegan, Ill., Aug. 3, 1944; d. Howard Hamilton Cavitt and Evelyn Lucille (Becker) Goding; m. Louis William Kunz, Jan. 27, 1968 (div. July 1981); children: Jacob Alexander (dec.), Carmen Rachel. BS with Distinction, U. Nebr., 1966; MD, Ea. Va. Med. Sch., 1991; CPH, Harvard U., 1992, post-grad. Evolutionary Anthropology, 1995—2000. Registered dental hygienist. Mem U.S. Pub. Health Team, Hawaii, 1966; periodontal hygienist Nebr., Hawaii, Calif. Ariz., Mass., Va., 1966—91; med. rschr. Harvard U., Boston, 1992—. Rschr. Wampumpeag, Inc. Mem. AAAS, AMA, Am. Assn. Neurol. Surgeons Rsch. Found., Internat. Neurotrauma Soc., Physicians for Human Rights, Mass. Med. Soc., Physicians for Social Responsibility, Am. Found. AIDS Rsch., Women in Neurosurgery. Avocations: ice skating, cross country skiing, piano. E-mail: alexandrakunz@earthlink.net.

KUNZ, APRIL BRIMMER, state legislator, lawyer; b. Denver, Apr. 1, 1954; divorced. AA, Stephens Coll., 1974; BS, U. So. Calif., 1976; JD, U. Wyo., 1979. Bar: Wyo. Pres. K and R Enterprises; mem. Wyo. Ho. Reps., Cheyenne, 1985-86, 90-92, Wyo. Senate, Cheyenne, 1992—, chair jud. com., v.p., 1999—2000, majority floor leader, 2001—02, pres., 2003—04. Mem. Laramie County Rep. Women's Club. Mem. Wyo. State Bar Assn, Laramie County Bar Assn. Republican. Home: PO Box 285 Cheyenne WY 82003-0285 Office: Wyo Senate State Capitol Cheyenne WY 82002-0001

KUNZ, HEIDI, healthcare company executive; Grad., Georgetown U., 1977; MBA, Columbia U. Dir. overseas financing, asst. treas., then treas. GM Can.; treas. GM, White Plains, N.Y., 1993-95; exec. v.p., CFO ITT, 1995-99, Gap Inc., 1999—2003, Blue Shield Calif., San Francisco, 2003—. Bd. dirs. Agilent Technologies, Inc., 2000—. Office: Blue Shield 50 Beale St San Francisco CA 94105-1808

KUNZ, PHILLIP RAY, sociologist, educator; b. Bern, Idaho, July 19, 1936; s. Parley P. and Hilda Irene (Stoor) K.; m. Joyce Sheffield, Mar. 18, 1960; children: Jay, Jenifer, Jody, Johnathan, Jana. BS, Brigham Young U., 1961, MS cum laude, 1962; PhD (fellow), U. Mich., 1967. Instr. Eastern Mich. U., Ypsilanti, 1964, U. Mich., Ann Arbor, 1965-67; asst. prof. sociology U. Wyo., Laramie, 1967-68; prof. emeritus sociology Brigham Young U., Provo, Utah, 1968—, acting dept. chmn., 1973; dir. Inst. Geneal. Studies, 1972-74; cons. various ednl. and rsch. instns., 1968—. Missionary Ch. Jesus Christ LDS, Ga. and S.C., 1956-58, mem. high coun., 1969-70, bishop; mission pres. La. Baton Rouge Mission, 1990-93. Author: 10 Critical Keys for Highly Effective Families, other books; contbr. articles on social orgn., family rels. and deviant behavior to profl. jours. Housing commr. City of Provo, 1984— . Served with AUS, 1954-56. Recipient Karl G. Maeser rsch. award, 1977 Mem. Am. Sociol. Assn., Rocky Mountain Social Sci. Assn., Am. Coun. Family Rels., Rural Sociol. Soc., Am. Soc. Criminology, Soc. Sci. Study of Religion, Religious Rsch. Assn., Sigma Xi, Phi Kappa Phi, Alpha Kappa Delta (Alcuin award 1997). Democrat. Home: 3040 Navajo Ln Provo UT 84604-4820 Office: Brigham Young Univ Dept Sociology Provo UT 84602

KUNZE, GEORGE WILLIAM, retired soil scientist; b. Warda, Tex., Sept. 16, 1922; s. John Paul and Hermine (Moerbe) K.; m. Flora Mae Rothmann, July 11, 1947; children: Brenda Kay, Wayne Lester. BS, Tex. A&M U., 1948, MS, 1950; PhD, Pa. State U., 1952. Asst. prof. Tex. A&M U., 1952-56, assoc. prof., 1956-60, prof. soil mineralogy, 1960-84, asso. dean Grad. Sch., 1967-68, dean, 1968-84; ret., 1984. Cons. U. Alaska, 1963-66; cons. Bangladesh Agrl. U., 1970, Grad. Sch. Agrl. Scis., Castelar Argentina, 1972; mem. Fed. Adv. Com. on Affirmative Action in Employment Practices in Instns. of Higher Edn.; pres. Conf. So. Grad. Schs., 1980-81 Cons. editor Soil Science, 1958-84. With USAAF, 1943—45. Recipient Faculty Disting. Achievement award in research Tex. A&M U., 1966, in administration Tex. A.&M. U., 1984 Fellow: AAAS, Am. Soc. Agronomy, Mineral Soc. Am.; mem.: Clay Mineral Soc. Am. (councilor). Home: PO Box 107 Warda TX 78960-0107

KUNZE, OTTO ROBERT, retired agricultural engineering educator; b. Warda, Tex., May 27, 1925; s. John Paul and Hermine Amanda (Moerbe) K.; m. Alice Ruth Eifert, Aug. 5, 1951; children: Glenn, Allen, Charles, Karen. BS, Tex. A&M U., 1950; MS, Iowa State U., 1951; PhD, Mich. State U., 1964. Registered profl. engr., Tex. Agrl. and indsl. engr. Ctrl. Power and Light Co., San Benito, Tex., 1951-56; rsch. asst. agrl. engring. dept. Mich. State U., East Lansing, 1961-64; assoc. prof. agrl. engring. dept. Tex. A&M U., College Station, 1956-61, 64-69, prof. agrl. engring. dept., 1969-90, prof. emeritus agrl. engring. dept., 1990—. Vis. prof. Nanjing (China) Coll. Food, Grain and Oil Econs., 1993; lectr. Tsukuba U., Japan, 93; cons. and vis. prof. Nat. Chung Hsing U. in Taichung and Nat. Taiwan U. in Taipei, Taiwan, 1994; lectr., cons. Internat. Conf. on Grain Drying in Asia, Bangkok, Thailand, 1995; engring. cons. Advanced Dryer Sys., Inc., Alachua, 1997, Farmers Rice Coop., Sacramento, 1992, Post Harvest Process and Food Engring. Ctr., G.B. Pant U., Pantnagar, India, 1985, Rice Process Engring. Ctr., Indian Inst. Tech., Kharagpur, 1975, Rice Tec, Alvin, Tex., 1996; lectr. on rice harvesting Asian Productivity Orgn., Taichung, Taiwan, 1985, 87; lectr. U. PR, Mayaguez, 1990; keynote spkr. PR sect. Am. Soc. Agrl. Engrs., Añasco, 1990; publ. coord. Rice Tech. Working Group, 1976-90. Contbr. chpts. to 7 books, over 100 articles to profl. jours. Mem. A&M Consol. Bd. Equalization, College Station, 1969-71; mem. Tex. Air Control Bd., Austin, 1979-90; mem. pediatric scholarship com. M.D. Anderson Cancer Ctr., Houston, 1990—. With U.S. Army, 1944-46, ETO. Decorated 2 Bronze Stars; recipient Outstanding Svc. award Rice Tech. Working Group, 1990, Outstanding Agrl. Engring. achievement 20th Century, 2000; Faculty fellow NSF, 1961-62. Fellow Am. Soc. Agrl. Engrs. (tech. dir., numerous coms.), Am. Assn. Cereal Chemists (assoc. editor), Sigma Xi (sec. 1969-70, chmn. 1970-71), Phi Kappa Phi (pub. rels. officer 1984-85). Lutheran. Home: PO Box 3 Warda TX 78960-0003 Office: Tex A&M U Agrl Engring Dept College Station TX 77843-2117 Office Phone: 979-845-3931.

KUNZE, RALPH CARL, retired savings and loan association executive; b. Buffalo, Oct. 31, 1925; s. Bruno E. and Esther (Graubman) K.; m. Helen Hites Sutton, Apr. 1978; children by previous marriage: Bradley, Diane Kunze Cowgill, James. BBA, U. Cin., 1950, postgrad., 1962-63; grad., Ind. U. Grad. Sch. Savs. and Loan, 1956, U. Calif., 1973. With Mt. Lookout Savs. & Loan Co., Cin., 1951-63, sec., mng. officer, 1958-63; with Buckeye Fed. Savs. & Loan Assn., Columbus, Ohio, 1963-77, exec. v.p., sec., 1967-70, pres., sec., vice chmn. bd. dirs., 1970-77; pres., chief operating officer, dir. Gate City Savs. and Loan Assn., Fargo, N.D., 1977-81; chief exec. officer, dir. United Home Fed., Toledo, 1981-91, also chmn. bd. dirs., 1985-91; ret., 1991. Former trustee Ohio Savs. and Loan League, Toledo C. of C.; mem. investment adv. com. City of Toledo; mem. media contact group and legis. com. U.S. Savs. League. Mem. Toledo Com. 100, Toledo Zool. Soc., St. Vincent Hosp. Found.; past pres. Toledo Zoo; past pres. coun. Hope Luth. Ch.; pres. Toledo Neighborhood Housing Svcs., 1981-83; pres., chmn. pers. com. United Way Franklin County, Ohio; past pres. Ohio Soc. Prevention Blindness; bd. dirs. Revitalization Corp. Toledo, 1983-84, Bittersweet Farms, Autistic Cmty. of N.W. Ohio, Inc.; past mem., trustee Kidney Found. Northwestern Ohio and Luth. Social Svcs., Wesley Glen Retirement Meth. Ctr., Columbus, 1974-77. Served with USNR, 1944-45. Mem.: Lambda Chi Alpha. Home: 2606 Emmick Dr Toledo OH 43606-2701

KUNZLER, JOHN EUGENE, physicist; b. Willard, Utah, Apr. 25, 1923; s. John Jacob and Freida (Meier) K.; m. Lois McDonald, Dec. 29, 1950; children: Carol Kunzler Blaine, Marilyn Kunzler Barker, Bonnie Kunzler Stein, Kim Kunzler Tomeo. BS in Chem. Engring, U. Utah; PhD, U. Calif., Berkeley. With AT & T Bell Labs., Murray Hill, N.J., 1952—, dir. electronic materials lab., 1969-73, dir. electronic materials and device lab., 1973-79, dir. electronic materials, processes and devices lab., 1979-83, dir. magnetic bubble subsystems and common tech. support lab., 1983-85, dir. future devices study ctr., 1985-86; retired, 1986. Contbr. articles to profl. jours.; patentee in field. Recipient John Price Wetherill medal Franklin Inst., 1964; Internat. prize for new materials Am. Phys. Soc., 1979; Kamerlingh Onnes medal, 1979 Fellow Am. Phys. Soc.; mem. Am. Chem. Soc., Nat. Acad. Engring., Sigma Xi, Tau Beta Pi, Alpha Chi Sigma. Home: 80 Stephensburg Rd Port Murray NJ 07865-3204

KUO, CHUN-FANG FRANK, counselor, consultant; b. Taichung, Taiwan, July 25, 1963; arrived in U.S., 1990; s. Tung-Huan Samuel Kuo and I-Chung Esther Liu. BS in Psychology, Nat. Cheng-Chi U., 1986; MS in Counseling and Counselor Edn., Ind. U., 1993; PhD in Counseling Psychology, U. Mo., 2005. Adminstrv. asst. Chinese Army, Ping-Tung, Taiwan, 1986—88; staff counselor Lee-Ming Inst. Tech., Taipei, Taiwan, 1988—90; adminstrv. intern U. Mo., Kans. City, Mo., 1994—97, tchg. and rsch. asst., 1997—2002; cons. mental health ReStart Inc. Psychol. Svcs., Kans. City, 1997—2001; psychology intern U. Pitts., 2002—03; staff counselor Counseling Svcs. Truman State U., Kirksville, Mo., 2003—. Supr. Kans. City (Mo.) Family Ct., 2001—02; coord. Chinese Christian fellowship U. Mo., 1995—97; cons. in field. Author: Parent Education for Parents of Teenage Children, 1993, The Influence of Christian Belief on Perceptions of Counselor Empathy, Response Type, and Social Influence, Academic Procrastination and Anxiety of College Students. Active coll. outreach program Lake Rd. Chapel, Kirksville, 2003—; mem. visitation team Pitts. (Pa.) Chinese Christian Ch., 2002—03; co-worker evang. com. Emmanuel Chinese Bapt. Ch., Lenexa, Kans., 1994—96, mem. choir, 1994—2002, asst. prin. Sunday Sch., 1999—2001. Chancellor's Non-Resident fellow, U. Mo., 1994—2005, Alumni scholar, Taichung (Taiwan) Second H.S., 1979—81. Mem.: Am. Counseling Assn., Am. Psychol. Assn., Am. Coll. Personnel Assn. Avocations: tennis, ping pong/table tennis, bowling, volleyball, chinese calligraphy. Home: 1002 E Patterson St Apt 18 Kirksville MO 63501 Office: Truman State Univ Counseling Svcs 100 E Normal Kirksville MO 63501 Office Phone: 660-785-4014. Business E-Mail: fkuo@truman.edu.

KUO, FRANKLIN F., computer scientist, electrical engineer; b. Apr. 22, 1934; came to U.S., 1950, naturalized, 1961; s. Steven C. and Grace C. (Huang) K.; m. Dora Lee, Aug. 30, 1958; children: Jennifer, Douglas. BS, U. Ill., 1955, MS, 1956, PhD, 1958. Asst. prof. dept. elec. engring. Poly. Inst. Bklyn., 1958-60; mem. tech. staff Bell Telephone Labs., Murray Hill, N.J., 1960-66; prof. elec. engring. U. Hawaii, Honolulu, 1966-82; exec. dir. SRI Internat., Menlo Park, Calif., 1982-94; founder, v.p. GWcom, 1994-98; sr. adv. Mtone Wireless Inc., 1998—. Dir. info. systems Office Sec. of Def., 1976-77; liason scientist U.S. Office Naval Research, London, 1971-72; cons. prof. elec. engring. Stanford U., Calif., 1982—96; vis. prof. U. Mannheim, Germany, 1995-96, Nihon U. Global Bus. Sch., 1998-2002; mem. exec. panel Chief of Naval Ops., 1980-85; mentor, Stanford U. Grad. Sch. of Bus., 1999-; advisor China Vest, 2001-03. Author: Network Analysis and Synthesis, 1962, (2d edit.), 1966, Linear Circuits and Computations, 1973; co-author: System Analysis by Digital Computer, 1966, Computer Oriented Circuit Design, 1969, Computer Communications Networks, 1973, Protocols and Techniques in Data Communication Networks, 1981, Multimedia Communications, 1997; cons. editor, Prentice-Hall Inc., 1967—; mem. editorial bd. Future Generations Computer Systems; contbr. articles to profl. jours.; developer Alohanet packet broadcast radio network Mem. Pres. coun. U. Ill.; mem. adv. bd. Beckman Inst.; mem. dean's adv. bd. U. Calif. Santa Cruz, 2002—. Recipient Alexander von Humboldt Found. Rsch. award, 1994. Fellow IEEE; mem. The Internet Soc., Tau Beta Pi, Eta Kappa Nu Home: 824 La Mesa Dr Portola Valley CA 94028 E-mail: ffkuo@mindspring.com.

KUO, HSU-KO, geriatrician; b. Taipei, Taiwan; s. Keh and Chen Kuo. MD, MPH, Harvard U. Cert. of registration in medicine 2002, ECFMG 2002. House officer Nat. Taiwan U. Hosp., Taipei, 1997—2000, chief resident, 2000—01; geriatrics fellow Harvard Med. Sch., Boston, 2002—. Tchr. Nat. Taiwan U. Hosp., 1997—2001, cons., 2000—01, adminstrn., 2000—01; tchr. Harvard Med. Sch., 2002—03, rsch. investigator, 2003—. Author: (article) Jour. Am. Geriatric Soc. (New Investigator award, 2004), (Jour. Gerontology series) A Medical Sciences and Biological Sciences; contbr. (exhbn.) Annual Meeting Gerontol. Soc. Am., Annual Meeting Geriatric Soc., 2004. Contbr. Park St. Ch., Boston, 2001—04. Recipient rsch. fellowship, Men's Assocs. Hebrew Rehabilitation Ctr. for Aged, travel award, First Dementia Congress. Mem.: Am. Geriatric Soc., Divsn. Aging Harvard Med. Sch. Office: Hebrew Rehabilitation Ctr for Aged 1200 Centre St Boston MA 02131 E-mail: hkuo@post.harvard.edu.

KUO, JOHN TSUNGFEN, geophysicist, educator, researcher; b. Hangchow, Chejiang, China, Apr. 1, 1922; came to U.S., 1949; naturalized, 1967; s. Lee Kuo; m. Marilyn Dunlap, Apr. 14, 1957; children: Ping Andrea, Sonya Sue, J. David. BS in Geology with Physics and Math., U. Redlands, 1952, ScD (hon.), 1978; MS in Geophysics, Cal. Inst. Tech., 1954; PhD in Geophysics, Stanford U., 1958. Asst. prof. San Jose (Calif.) St. Coll., 1957-60; rsch. assoc. Stanford U., 1958-60; rsch. scientist Columbia U.,

N.Y.C., 1960-64, assoc. prof., 1964-67, prof., 1967-83, Vinton prof., 1983-85, Ewing and Worzel prof., 1985-92, Ewing and Worzel prof. emeritus, 1992—. Participant DEEPSCAN, 1963; dir. Aldridge Lab. Applied Geophysics, 1964-92, Lamont-Doherty's Underground Geophys. Obs., Ogdensburg, N.J., 1967-77, Columbia U., Project Migration, Inversion, Diffraction and Scattering, 1979-89; disting. sr. vis. scholar U. Cambridge, Eng., 1970-71; vis. prof. U. Tex., Austin, 1977-78, Cornell U., N.Y., 1978, 92-97, Tech. U. Clausthal, Fed. Rep. of Germany, 1987; adj. prof. Cornell U., 1992-98; Columbia U. del. People's Republic of China, 1979; tech. adv. 20th Dist. Congressman, 1983—; hon. prof, co-dir. integrated basin studies Chengdu U. Tech., People's Republic of China, 1986; hon. prof. Acad. Sinica, 1979—, China U. Geoscis., Beijing, 1992; hon. sr. rschr. Inst. Geophysics, China Seismological Bur., People's Republic of China, 1995—; expert World Bank, 1982. Mem. editl. bd. Bollettino di Geofisica, Italy, 1985-89; contbr. over 120 articles to profl. jours. Danforth Tchg. fellow, 1957—, Sr. Postdoctoral fellow NSF, 1970; Rsch. grantee NSF, NASA, U.S. Geol. Survey, Office Naval Rsch., Air Force Office Sci. Rsch., Air Force Geophysics, U.S. Bur. Mines; recipient Alexander von Humboldt award for disting. U.S. sr. scientist, Fed. Republic Germany, 1986, Hon. Knight for Life award Knights Round Table Internat., 1993, Alumni Career Achievement award U. Redlands, 2002. Fellow Geol. Soc. Am. (sr.), Royal Astron. Soc. U.K.; mem. Internat. Union Geodesy and Geophysics (fellow Assn. Geodesy, pres. permanent commn. for Earth tides 1979-87), Am. Geophys. Union (life, assoc. editor Geophysics Rev.), Soc. Exploration Geophysicists (rep.-at-large, com. mem., chmn. com.), Seismol. Soc. Am., Petroleum Exploration Soc. NY, Round Table Internat. (hon. life), China Geophys. Soc. (fgn. corr.), Sigma Xi. Home: 11 Hoffman Ln Blauvelt NY 10913-1707 Office: Columbia U New York NY 10027 Business E-Mail: kuojt@ldeo.columbia.edu.

KUO, LIH, medical educator; b. Taipei, Taiwan, Aug. 28, 1957; came to U.S., 1983; BS in Biology, Tunghai Univ., Taichung, Taiwan, 1979; MS in Physiology, Nat. Taiwan U., 1983; DPhil, Med. Coll. Va., 1987. Rsch. asst. Dept. Physiology & Biophysics Nat. Def. Med. Ctr., 1979-81; tchg. asst. Dept. Physiology Nat. Taiwan U., 1981-83, Med. Coll. Va., Richmond, 1985-87; postdoctoral rsch. assoc. Dept. Med. Physiology Tex. A&M U., 1990-91; asst. prof. Tex. A&M U. Health Ctr., 1992-98, assoc. prof., 1998-2001, prof., 2001—, Kruse Centennial chair, 2003, dir. Ophthalmic Vascular Rsch. Program, 2003. Mem. exptl. cardiovascular scis. study sect. NIH, 1994-98; spkr. in field. Contbr. articles to profl. jours. Dr. Sun Yet Sen Sci. scholar Tunghai U., 1977-79, Ministry Edn. scholar Outstanding Student Coll. Medicine Nat. Taiwan U., 1981-83; A.D. Williams award Postdoctoral fellow Med. Coll. Va., 1983-85, Med. Coll. Va. Grad. fellow, 1985-87. Fellow Am. Heart Assn. (mem. basic cardiovasc. scis.), Am. Physiol. Soc. (cardiovasc. sect.); mem. Chinese Physiol. Soc., Microcirculatory Soc. (Grega-Zacharkow Young Investigator award 1990), Phi Kappa Phi. Office: Tex A&M U Dept Med Physiology Med Rsch Bldg 702 SW HK Dodgen Loop Temple TX 76504

KUO, MICHELLE CHEN (CHOU-HSIA CHEN), musician, educator; d. Shin-Yang and Yu-Shou Chen; m. Cheng Kuo, Aug. 12, 1983; children: Anthony Charles, Christopher Michael. B, U. Rochester, 1984; M, The Juilliard Sch., 1986. Lic. The Royal Schs. of Music, London. Pvt. tchr., Morris Plains, NJ, 1974—. Pianist numerous concert performances and competitions. Mem.: Montclair Music Club Assn., N.Y. State Music Tchrs. Assn. (assoc.), Nat. Guild Piano Tchrs. (assoc.), Music Educators Assn. (assoc.; v.p. 2002—).

KUO, WINSTON PATRICK, biomedical researcher; s. Chien and Helen Kuo. BS in Biology, SUNY, Albany; DDS, Columbia U., 1993; MS in Med. Informatics, MIT, 2001; PhD, Harvard Med. Sch., 2005. Resident Catholic Med. Ctr., Brooklyn, 1993—95; resident, pediatric dentistry U. So. Calif. & Rancho Los Amigos Med. Ctr.; dental fellowships Harvard Sch. of Dental Medicine; now biomedical informatics rsch. fellow Hardard Med. Sch. Recipient Brazil/US Internat. Training in Med. Informatics Fellowship award, 2003. Mem.: Internat. Soc. for Computational Biology, Am. Med. Informatics Assn., Am. Acad. of Oral Medicine (Lester W. Burket award 2003, Robert I. Schattner award 2002), Am. Acad. of Pediatric Dentistry, Am. Dental Assn. Office: Harvard Med Sch 77 Ave Louis Pasteur Boston MA 02115*

KUPCHELLA, CHARLES EDWARD, academic administrator, author, educator; b. Nanty Glo, Pa., July 7, 1942; s. Charles Francis and Margaret (Bouite) K.; m. R. Adele Kiel, July 20, 1963; children: Richard Charles, Michele Louise, Jason Charles. BS in Edn., Indiana U. of Pa., 1964; PhD, St. Bonaventure U., 1968. Asst. prof. Bellarmine Coll., Louisville, 1968-72, assoc. prof., 1972-73; assoc. dir. cancer rsch. ctr. Sch. of Medicine, assoc. prof. U. Louisville, 1973-79; prof., chmn. dept. biology Murray (Ky.) State U., 1979-85; dean Ogden Coll. Western Ky. U., Bowling Green, 1985-93; provost S. E. Mo. State U., Cape Girardeau, 1993—99; pres. U. N.D., 1999—. Author: Sights/Sounds: Special Senses, 1976, Environmental Science, 1986, 3rd rev. edit., 1993, Dimensions of Cancer, 1987; contbr. chpts. to books, over 50 articles to profl. jours. Bd. dirs. Ky. Ctr. for Pub. Issues, Lexington, 1990-93; mem. cancer edn. rev. com. NIH/Nat. Cancer Inst., 1993-97; mem. inst. rsch. grant rev. com. Am. Cancer Soc., 1993-96. NDEA fellow, 1964-68. Mem. AAAS (nominating com. sect. on sci. and engring. 1995-97), Ky. Acad. Sci. (pres. 1977), Ky. Sci. and Tech. Coun. (sec., treas. Lexington 1988-93), Am. Assn. Cancer Edn. (chair fin. com. 1990-93, treas. 1993-96, pres. 1999-2000, exec. coun.). Office: U of North Dakota Office of Pres Grand Forks ND 58202

KUPCHYNSKY, JERRY MARKIAN, orchestra conductor, educator; b. Stryj, Ukraine, Sept. 12, 1928; arrived in U.S.A., 1946; s. Jaroslav and Cecilia Elizabeth (Jurkiv) K.; m. Jean Estelle (Brown), June 29, 1957 (dec.); children: Melanie Jean, Stephanie Joy; m. Joan M. (Rear), Sept. 13, 1997. B in Music Edn., Murray State U., 1951, MA in Edn., 1952; MEd, Rutgers U., 1961. Cert. tchr., supr., N.J. Tchr. music Pub. Sch., Shawneetown, Ill., 1954—57, East Brunswick, NJ, 1957—68, supr. music, 1968—95; guest condr. youth orch. various Eastern states, 1965—. Founder, condr. Middlesex Youth Symphony Orch., 1961, Imperial Symphony Orch., 1979; founder, dir. Summer Conf. String Teachers, 1964—; founder, chair East Brunswick Young Musicians Project, 1985—. Contbr. articles to profl. publications. Bd. dir. East Brunswick Arts Commn., 1979; N.J. Teen Arts Festival, 1976; Alliance Arts Edn., 1977. Served in U.S. Army, 1952-54, Korea. Recipient N.J. Governors's Award Arts Edn. for Disting. Leadership Music Edn., 1989; Cert. of Merit, N.J. Coun. on Arts, 1970; Fay S. Mathewson Award Friends of Recreation, Parks, and Conservation, 2003; named to Order Ky. Col., Commonwealth of Ky., 1978; selected for Wall of Honor, Brunswick Bd. Edn., 1998. Mem. N.J. String Teachers Assn. (Disting. Svc. Award 1974, 78, 84, 89), Music Educators Nat. Conf., N.J. Music Educators Assn. (dir. Disting. Svc. Award 1986), Am. String Teachrs Assn. (nat. pres. 1976-78, Disting. Leadership Award 1980), Nat. Sch. Orch. Assn. (nat. pres. 1984-86, Disting. Leadership Award 1987, Merle J. Isaac Lifetime Achievement Award 1994); N.J. Principals and Supervisors Assn. Home: 38 Mason Ave East Brunswick NJ 08816-4837 Personal E-mail: kupchynsky@aol.com.

KUPEL, FREDERICK JOHN, business services executive; b. Burbank, Calif., Apr. 22, 1929; s. Martin Charles and Lorene (Murray) K.; m. Nancy Kathryn Eubank, 1952 (div. 1979); children: James Frederick, Douglas Edward; m. Karen J. Jensen, 1980 (div. 1992); 1 stepchild, John Robert Jensen, Jr.; m. Beverly A. Blom, 2004. Student, Claremont McKenna Coll., 1948-50; BA in Econs., U. Calif., Berkeley, 1951; MA in Psychology, Sonoma State U., 1980. Lic. profl. counselor. Acctg., fin. and mgmt. positions, 1951-66; acctg. and ops. exec. Evans Products Co., Portland, Oreg., 1967-71; v.p. fin. Columbia Corp., Portland, 1971-77, Plantronics, Inc., Santa Cruz, Calif., 1977-78; counselor Yellow Brick Rd. Program, Portland, 1975-76; cons., 1978-84; dir. bus. devel. and acquisitions ITT Communication Services, Inc., 1985-87; v.p. fin., chief fin. officer Bohemia, Inc., Eugene, Oreg., 1987-89; pres. Bus. Devel. Corp., Lake Oswego, Oreg., 1989-93; bus. owner, 1994—2000; CEO, Kupel & Co., Portland, 2000—. With AUS, 1946-47. Office: 3735 SE Ogden St Portland OR 97202 Office Phone: 503-774-0885. E-mail: fred@kupel.com.

KUPER, ADAM JONATHAN, anthropologist, educator; b. Johannesburg, Republic of South Africa, Dec. 29, 1941; s. Simon Meyer and Gerty (Hesselson) K.; m. Jessica Sue Cohen, Dec. 16, 1966; children: Simon, Jeremy, Hannah. BA, U. Witwatersrand, Johannesburg, 1961; PhD, U. Cambridge, Eng., 1966; D (hons.), U. Gothenburg, Sweden, 1978. Lectr. in social anthropology Makerere U., Kampala, Uganda, 1967-70; lectr. in anthropology Univ. Coll. U. London, 1970-76; prof. African anthropology and sociology U. Leiden, Netherlands, 1976-85; prof. social anthropology, head human scis. dept. Brunel U., Middlesex, England, 1985—. Mem. Inst. for Advanced Study, Princeton, N.J., 1994-95. Author: Kalahari Village Politics: An African Democracy, 1970, Anthropologists and Anthropology: The British School, 1922-72, 1973, 2d rev. ed. 1983, 3rd rev. ed. 1996, Changing Jamaica, 1976, Regionaal Vergelijkend Onderzoek in Afrika, 1977, Wives for Cattle: Bridewealth and Marriage in Southern Africa, 1982, South Africa and the Anthropologist, 1987, The Invention of Primitive Society: Transformations of an Illusion, 1988; editor: The Social Anthropology of Radcliffe-Brown, 1982, The Social Science Encyclopedia, 2004, 3d edit., 1996, Current Anthropology, 1985-93, Conceptualizing Society, 1992, The Chosen Primate, 1994, Culture: The Anthropologist' Account, 1999, Among the Anthropologists, 1999; contbr. more than 90 articles to profl. jours. Fellow British Acad.; mem. Acad. Europe. Avocation: golf. Home: 16 Muswell Rd London N10 2BG England Business E-Mail: adan.kuper@brunel.ac.uk.

KUPERMAN, ROBERT IAN, retired advertising agency executive; b. Bklyn., Dec. 31, 1941; s. Morris and Gertrude Kuperman; m. Colette Chestnut, Aug. 22, 2004; 1 stepchild, John. BFA, Pratt Inst., 1963. Vice pres., sr. art dir. Doyle Dane Bernbach, N.Y.C., 1963-71; v.p., creative dir. Della Femina Travisano & Ptnrs., N.Y.C., 1971-73; sr. v.p., creative dir. Wells, Rich & Greene, N.Y.C. and Los Angeles, 1973-80, BBDO/West, Los Angeles, 1980-82; exec. v.p., exec. creative dir. DDB, LA, 1982—87; exec. v.p., creative dir. chiat/Day, LA, 1987—98, pres., CEO, 1998—2001; chmn. DDB New York, 2001—03, pres., CEO, 2001—05; cons. DDB Worldwide, 2005—. Instr. Sch. Visual Arts, N.Y.C., 1968-74, Pratt Inst., Bklyn., 1966-68, Art Ctr., LA, 1975-79; adv. Jackson Lab. Art dir. TV comml. 1949 Auto Show, 1970 (Clio Hall of Fame award 1979), Volkswagen advertisements, (now in Smithsonian Mus. Art), other TV commls. Recipient Gold medals N.Y. Art Dirs. Show, 1969, 71, Andy award Advt. Club N.Y., 1970, Clio awards for excellence in worldwide advt., 1970, 72, 74, 78, 83; Ellis Island Medal of Honor. Mem. Los Angeles Creative Club (co-founder, chmn. bd. dirs.), Los Angeles Advt. Club (bd. dirs. 1979). Office: DDB Worldwide 437 Madison Ave New York NY 10022 Office Phone: 212-415-2525.

KUPERS, TERRY ALLEN, psychiatrist, educator; b. Phila., Oct. 14, 1943; s. Edward Carlton and Frances Shirley (Praissman) K.; m. Ruth Kupers, June 1968 (div. 1978); children: Eric, Jesse; m. Arlene Marilyn Shmaeff, Jan. 16, 1983; 1 adopted child, Jake. BA, Stanford U., 1964; MD, UCLA, 1968, M in social psychiatry, 1974. Diplomate Am. Bd. Psychiatry and Neurology. Intern Kings County Hosp., Brooklyn, 1968-69; resident in psychiatry UCLA, 1969-72, fellow in social and cmty. psychiatry, 1972-74; asst. prof. Martin L. King, Jr. Hosp., L.A., 1974-77; staff psychiatrist Richmond (Calif.) Cmty. Mental Health Ctr., 1977-81; pvt. practice Oakland, Ca., 1977—; psychology prof. Wright Inst., Berkeley, Ca., 1980—. Author: Public Therapy: The Practice of Psychotherapy in the Public Mental Health Clinic, 1981, Ending Therapy: The Meaning of Termination, 1988, Revisioning Men's Lives: Gender, Intimacy and Power, 1993, Prison Madness: The Mental Health Crisis Behind Bars, 1999; editor: Using Psychodynamic Principles in Public Mental Health, 1990; co-editor: Prison Masculinities, 2002; contbr. articles to profl. jours. Fellow. Am. Psychiat. Assn. (disting.), Am. Orthopsychiat. Assn.; mem. Physicians Social Responsibility, Alpha Omega Alpha. Democrat. Jewish. Avocations: tennis, jazz, writing. Office: 8 Wildwood Ave Oakland CA 94610-1044 Office Phone: 510-654-8333.

KUPERSMITH, JOEL, internist, medical school dean; b. Nov. 26, 1939; s. Charles Douglas and Sally K.; m. Judith Freidman, June 15, 1969; children: David, Rebecca, Adam. BS, Union Coll., Schenectady, 1960; MD, N.Y. Med. Coll., 1964. Prof., chief clin. pharmacology Mt. Sinai Sch. Medicine, NYC, 1974-86; chief cardiology divsn. Beth Israel Med. Ctr., NYC, 1985-86; prof., chief cardiology divsn. U. Louisville Sch. Medicine, East Lansing, 1986-91, V.V. Cooke prof. medicine Lubbock, 1987-91; prof., chair medicine Mich. State U., East Lansing, 1991-97; dean Sch. Medicine, dean Sch. Biomed. Sci. Tex. Tech U. Sch. Medicine, Lubbock, 1997—2001, v.p. clin. affairs, 1997—2001, prof. internal med., 1997—; chief br. devel. office Dept. Vets. Affairs, Washington, 2005—. Chief cardiac arrhythmia clinic Mt. Sinai Med. Ctr., 1977—85, assoc. prof. pharmacology, 1979—84; scholar-in-residence Inst. Medicine, Assn. Am. Med. Coll., 2003—. Author: Clinical Manual of Electrophysiology, 1997, The Pharmacologic Management of Heart Disease, 1993. Recipient Affirmative Action award U. Louisville, 1988, Alumni Assn. Disting. Achievement award N.Y. Med. Coll. Med. Sch., Coun. Deans, 1992. Mem.: AMA (med. sch. sect., governing coun.), Assn. Am. Med. Coll. (Petersdorf scholar-in-residence 2003—05, task force on fraud/abuse), Am. Heart Assn. (exec. com. Coun. on Clin. Cardiology 1991—94), Assn. Profs. Medicine (program com. 1994), Am. Soc. Clin. Investigation (sr.). Office: Dept Veterans Affairs 810 Vermont Ave NW Washington DC 20402 Personal E-mail: joel.kupersmith@va.gov.

KUPETS, COURTNEY, Olympic athlete; b. Bedford, Tex., July 27, 1986; Mem. U.S. Nat. Gymnastics Team, 1999—; gymnast Team USA, Athens Olympic Games, 2004—. Named TOPs Athlete of the Yr., 2002. Achievements include World Champion, Uneven Bars, World Gymnastics Championships, Hungary, 2002; U.S. Champion, All-Around, U.S. Nat. Championships, 2003; mem. U.S. World Championships Gold medal team, 2003; U.S. co-champion, All-Around, U.S. Nat. Championships, 2004. Avocations: reading, shopping, diving. Office: c/o USOC One Olympic Plz Colorado Springs CO 80909

KUPFER, DAVID J., psychiatry educator; b. N.Y.C., Feb. 14, 1941; s. Alex and Muriel (Greenfield) Kupferstein; m. Barbara Stern Burstin, June 1963 (div. Mar. 1975); m. Ellen Frank, June 1975; children: Andrea, Jeffrey, Deborah, Nancy, Erica, Tonia. BA magna cum laude, Yale U., 1961, MD, 1965. Diplomate Am. Bd. Psychiatry and Neurology. Med. intern Montefiore Hosp. Ctr., N.Y.C., 1965—66; clin. fellow in psychiatry Yale U. Sch. Medicine, New Haven, 1966—67; postdoctoral fellow, chief resident in psychiatry Dana Psychiat. Clinic, Yale-New Haven Hosp., 1969—70; asst. prof. Yale U. Sch. Medicine, New Haven, 1970—73; assoc. prof. psychiatry U. Pitts., 1973—75, prof., 1975—, chmn. dept., 1983—; dir. rsch. Western Psychiat. Inst. and Clinic Western Psychiat. Inst. and Clinic, Pitts., 1973—. Thomas Detre prof., chmn. dept. psychiatry, 1994—. Office: U Pitts Western Psychiat Inst & Clinic 3811 Ohara St Pittsburgh PA 15213-2593

KUPIETZKY, MOSHE J., lawyer; b. NYC, May 17, 1944; s. Jacob Harry and Fanny (Dresner) K.; m. Arlene Debra Usdan, June 22, 1966; children: Jay, Jeff, Jacob. BBA cum laude, CCNY, 1965; LLB magna cum laude, Harvard U., 1968. Bar: NY 1969, Calif. 1970. Law clerk to Hon. William B. Herlands U.S. Dist. Ct., NYC, 1968-69; assoc. Mitchell Silberberg & Knupp, LA, 1969-74, ptnr., 1974-80; ptnr., prin. Hayutin Rubinroit Praw & Kupietzky, LA, 1980-87; ptnr. Sidley, Austin, Brown & Wood, LA, 1987—, mng. partner, LA office and head, corp. and fin. practice group, mem. exec. com. Editor: Harvard Law Rev., 1967—68. Bd. dirs. Nat. Inst. Jewish Hospice, Beverly Hills, Calif., 1986-98, LA Econ. Devel. Corp.; bd. advisors Graziadio Sch. Bus. and Mgmt. Pepperdine U., LA, 1996-98. Mem. ABA, Beverly Hills Bar Assn., LA County Bar Assn., Calif. State Bar (vice-chair opinions com. 2004-05.). Office: Sidley Austin Brown & Wood 555 W 5th St Ste 4000 Los Angeles CA 90013-3000 Office Phone: 213-896-6000. E-mail: mkupietzky@sidley.com.

KUPPER, KETTI, artist; b. L.A., Oct. 14, 1951; d. Charles Parnell Kupper and Donna Corrine Callen; m. Steven Robert Ford Feb. 9, 1978 (div. Mar. 1994); children: Ashley Elizabeth, Kimberly Brianna. BS, Brigham Young, 1974; student, Acad. Art, San Francisco, 1974-76; MFA in Visual Art, Norwich U., 1994. Freelance painter, illustrator, 1980—; prin., co-owner Fordesign Mktg., Wilton, Conn., 1990-93; chmn. of art U. Bridgeport, 1991-96; ind. cons. Milford, Conn., 1994-98; mentor, tchr. Conn. Commn. Arts, Hartford, Conn., 1996-98; non resident studio tchr. Vt. Coll., Monpelier, 1998—; pres. Ketti Kupper's Art & Design Inc., L.A. Featured garden designer Beverly Hills Garden and Design Showcase, Hist. Greystone Mansion, 2004. Commd. paintings include portrait Clint Murchison for Dallas Times Herald Mag., 1984, Am. Express Olympiadas Barcelona for commercial, 1992, portrait U. Bridgeport Pres. Edwin Eigel, 1995; collections include: Nestle Corp., Ptnrs. Nat. Health Plans, Tex. Instruments; designer, Romantic Backyard Getaway (winning designer, HGTV Landscaper's Challenge); art pub. in Times, Newsweek, Conn. Mag., Dallas Life Mag., Readers Digest. Curator Focus on Environ. U. Bridgeport Coll.; cmty. environ. activist Bridgeport Area Arts Coun.; dir. contest Smithsonian Nat. Mus. Am. Indian, N.Y.C., 1994; grantwriter, mural dir. Conn. commn. Arts, 1995; bd. dirs. Women's Caucus for Art, L.A. Recipient Addy 14th Dist. Region award Am. Adv. Fedn., 1984, Painting award The Discovery Mus., 1995, Painting award Silvermine Artists Guild, 1996, Painting award Artworks Gallery, 1997, One of 10 Landscape Designers Beverly Hills Hist. Greystone Estate Garden & Design Showcase. Mem. AIA, Coll. Art Assn., Women's Caucus for Arts (chpt. pres. 1996-98), N.Y. Soc. Illustrators, Calif. Lawyers for Arts, Nat. Art Educators Assn., Assn. Profl. Landscape Designers. Democrat. Avocations: writing, gardening, remodeling, construction design. Office: 4208 1/2 Camero Ave Los Angeles CA 90027-4519 Office Phone: 323-660-7756. E-mail: info@kettikupper.com.

KUPPER, WILLIAM P., JR., publishing executive; Mgr. advtsg. sales Sports Illustrated Time, Inc., advtsg. dir. Life mag., internat. advtsg. dir. Time mag.; pub. Health mag., 1992—95; sr. v.p. U.S. advtsg. sales Bus. Week Mc-Graw Hill Cos., New York, 1995-99, pub. Bus. Week, 1999-2000, pres. Bus. Week Group, 2000—. Office: The McGraw Hill Cos Inc McGraw Hill Bldg 43rd Fl 1221 Ave of the Americas New York NY 10020-1093 Office Phone: 212-512-6945. E-mail: bill_kupper@businessweek.com.*

KUPPERSMITH, JUDITH CAROLYN, psychology educator; b. Bklyn., Feb. 12, 1942; d. Herman H. and Grace R. (Rubenstein) K.; 1 child, Anya Gabriela. BA, Bard Coll., 1963; MA, New Sch. for Social Rsch., 1968; PhD, Union Grad. Sch., 1974; cert., U. Film Study Inst., 1978. Cert. psychoanalytic psychotherapist. Rsch. asst. Bur. Applied Social Rsch., Columbia U., N.Y.C., 1962-63, Inst. for Devel. Studies, NYU, N.Y.C., 1963-66, Child Devel. Ctr., Jewish Bd. Guardians, N.Y.C., 1966-68; lectr. Borough of Manhattan C.C., CUNY, N.Y.C., 1968-70; assoc. prof. Coll. S.I., CUNY, 1970—. Field faculty Goddard Grad. Sch., Vt., 1979-82; co-dir. grad. program in cmty. mental health Richmond Coll., CUNY, 1984-86, mentoring and psychol. devel. program undergrad. mentoring adolescent girls in lock-up Coll. S.I., 1991—; grant evaluator Profl. Staff Congress-CUNY Rsch. Fund, 1988—; pvt. practice psychotherapy, Bklyn., 1970-00, Manhattan, 2000—. Prodr., dir. (documentary videos) A Struggle for Identity: The Emerging Ethnic Working Class Woman, 1977, Girls: Moving Beyond Myth, 2004; contbr. articles to profl. jours Vol., cons. N.Y. State Divsn. for Youth, N.Y.C., 1995—, sexual harassment educator, Coll. SI CUNY, 1999—. Grantee NSF, London, 1972, Am. Jewish Com., N.Y.C., 1977, Coll. S.I., N.Y., 1995, Profl. Staff Congress/CUNY, 1997—. Mem. APA (com. mem., cons. editor Jour. Profl. Psychology, 1976-84), Nat. Assn. for the Advancement Psychoanalysis. Avocations: travel, gardening, knitting. Office: Coll SI CUNY 2800 Victory Blvd Staten Island NY 10314-6609 Office Phone: 718-982-3795. Personal E-mail: jcksmith@prodigy.net. Business E-Mail: kuppersmith@mail.csi.cuny.edu.

KUPPUSWAMY, CARTHY, telecommunications industry executive; b. Madras, TamilNadu, India, Oct. 16, 1977; s. Kuppuswamy Sundaraman and Lalitha Kuppuswamy. B in Mech. Engring., U. Madras, 1999; MS in Indsl. Engring., Okla. State U., 2001. Rsch. asst. Okla. State U., Stillwater, 2000—01, tchg. asst., 2001—01; network engr. Sprint, Overland Park, Kans., 2002—04, bus. and reporting analyst, 2004—. Scholar, Okla. State U., 2000—01. Mem.: INFORMS (hon.; pres. 2001—01). Achievements include research in VPN and Data Security; Industrial Enginnering Research for FAA; design of and implementation of a performance plan for Sprint customer service operations; found ways to measure work loads when none existed; currently challenged with developing and automating actionable metrics for Sprint Cor. security. Avocations: travel, learning, computers, volleyball. Home: 11212 W 108 th St Overland Park KS 66210 Office: Sprint 6480 Sprint Pkwy Overland Park KS 66251 Business E-Mail: carthy.kuppuswamy@mail.sprint.com.

KURAHARA, TED NAOMI, artist, educator; b. Seattle, July 16, 1925; s. Kyotaro and Miyuki (Yonemura) K.; m. Joan Vennum, Apr. 24, 1954; children: Mie, Thomas, Leon. BFA, Washington U., St. Louis, 1951; MA, Bradley U., 1952. Dir. Springfield (Ill.) Art Assn., 1953-56; instr. art Iowa State Tchrs. Coll., Cedar Falls, 1956-60, Bklyn. Coll., 1962-63; specialist NYU, N.Y.C., 1965; asst. prof. Hofstra U., Hempstead, N.Y., 1965-70, dir. Emily Lowe Gallery, 1967-70; prof. art Pratt Inst., Bklyn., 1970—, chmn. fine arts dept., 1981-84; prof. grad. program in fine arts, 1984—. Coord. program devel. City of N.Y., 1961-67; producer Career Films, N.Y.C., 1965-69; resident Yaddo Found., Saratoga, N.Y., 1978. One-man shows at Woodside-Braseth Gallery, 1982, Anders Tornberg Gallery, Sweden, 1981, 84, 90, 98, Leif Stahle Gallery, Paris, 1987, Kiyo Higashi Gallery, L.A., 1995-97, 99-2002, Robert Pardo Gallery, NYC., 2001, Milan, 2004; exhibited in group show Anita Shapolsky Gallery, NYC, 1987, Andre Zarre, NYC, 2002. Sgt. AUS, 1944-47, ETO. Guggenheim fellow, 1984, Nat. Endowment Arts fellow, 1985. Studio: 78 Greene St New York NY 10012-5100 Office Phone: 212-966-2336.

KURASZ, RICHARD MICHAEL, music educator; b. Villa Park, Ill., Nov. 1, 1971; s. Richard and Barbara Ann Kurasz; m. Diana Lynn Butler, July 10, 1999. MusB, U. Ill., 1994, postgrad., 1998—; MusM, U. Akron, 1996. Asst. prof. music Idaho State U., Pocatello, 2000—01, Western Ill. U., Macomb, 2002—. Arranger: musical composition Soca Tutie, 1996, Sa Sa Yea, 1997; author: Meditations on an African Groove, 1999. Mem.: Coll. Music Soc., Ill. Music Educators Assn., Percussive Arts Soc. (treas. Ill. chpt. 2004—, performer internat. conv. 2004). Office: Western Ill Univ 1 University Cir Macomb IL 61455

KURATA, PHILLIP CEDOMIR, journalist; b. Coaldale, Pa., Oct. 28, 1946; s. Fred and Virginia May (Mefford) Kurata; m. Chialing Chang, July 5, 1980 (div. Apr. 1995); 1 child, Shana Rebecca. BA, Kans. U., 1968, MA, 1982. Tchr. English Peace Corps, Tunis, Tunisia, 1968—70; tchr. pub. health Project Hope, Tunis, 1970—71; corr. Far Ea. Econ. Rev., Taiwan, 1979—81, 1979—81, UPI, Hong Kong, 1981—82; editor/translator Agence France-Presse, Paris, 1982—85; journalist Voice of Am., Tokyo, Beijing and Washington, 1985—98; writer U.S. State Dept., Washington, 1998—. Profl. boxer All-Japan Kickboxing Assn., Tokyo, 1972—74. Author: (novels) The Reluctant Agent, 2000 (Fiction prize, Washington Writers' Pub. House, 2000). Recipient Superior Hon. award, State Dept., 2004. Bahai. Home: 3409 Pendleton Dr Silver Spring MD 20902 Office Phone: 202-453-8258. E-mail: kuratapc@hotmail.com.

KURATKO, DONALD F., entrepreneur, educator, consultant; b. Chgo., Aug. 27, 1952; s. Donald W. and Margaret M. (Browne) K.; m. Deborah Ann Doyle, Dec. 28, 1979; children: Christina Diane, Kellie Margaret. BA in Econs., John Carroll U., 1974; MS in Mortuary Sci. and Adminstrn., Worsham Coll., 1975; MBA in Mktg.-Mgmt., Benedictine U., 1979; DBA in Entrepreneurship, Nova Southea. U., 1984. Lic. funeral dir., Ill. Funeral dir. Kuratko Funeral Home, North Riverside, Ill., 1975-83; prof. bus. Benedictine U., Lisle, 1979-83; prof., exec. dir. entrepreneurship program Ball State U., Muncie, Ind., 1983—2004, disting. prof., 1990—2004; Jack M. Gill chair entrepreneurship, prof. entrepreneurship, exec. dir. Johnson Ctr. for Entrepreneurship and Innovation, Kelley Sch. Bus., Ind. U., Bloomington, 2005—. Cons. Kendon Assocs., Riverside, 1983-88, Intrapreneurial Group, 1989—, Acordia, AT&T, GTE, United Techs., Ameritech, Union Carbide Corp.; dir. Pathologists Assocs., Acordia Ctrl. Ind., Ind. monument advisors, Beacon Venture Capital; developed entrepreneurship program Ball State U., Ind. U.

Author: Management, 1988, 3rd edit., 1991, Effective Small Business Management, 1986, 7th edit., 2001, Entrepreneurship, 1989, 6th edit., 2004, Entrepreneurship and Innovation in the Corporation, 1987; Entrepreneurial Strategy, 1994, The Entrepreneurial Decision, 1997, The Breakthrough Experience, 1998, Strategic Entrepreneurial Growth, 2001, 2d edit., 2004, Human Resource Function in Emerging Enterprises, 2002, Corporate Entrepreneurship, 2002, FrontLine HR, 2005, Innovation Acceleration, 2005; editor: Jour. Small Bus. Mgmt.; mem. editl. bd. Mid-Am. Bus. Jour., 1985-95, Jour. Bus. Venturing; cons. editor Entrepreneurship Theory & Practice Jour.; contbr. over 150 articles to profl. jours. Named Outstanding Young Hoosier, Ind. Jaycees, 1985, one of Outstanding Young Men of Am., 1983-84, #1 Entrepreneurship Program Dir. in USA, Entrepreneur Mag., 2003, #2 Entrepreneurship Program Dir. in USA, 2004-05, Disting. Tchg. Professorship, 1990, Stoops Disting Prof. Bus., 1990, Outstanding Univ. Prof., 1996, Entrepreneur of Yr. in Ind., Ernst & Young, Inc. Mag. and Merrill Lynch, 1990; 21st Century Entrepreneurship Rsch. fellow; Disting. scholar U.S. Assn. for Small Bus. and Entrepreneurship, 2003; recipient George Washington medal of honor, 1987, Leavey Found., 1988, Excellence award N.F.I.B. Found., 1993, Nat. Outstanding Entrepreneurship Educator of Yr. award, 1993, Kauffman Found. Entrepreneurship Educator award, 1994, Entrepreneural World of Differences award, 1998, Thomas W. Binford Meml. award, 2000, Outstanding Rschr. award, 1999; Top 20 Business Week, Top 25 Success Mag., Top 5 Entrepreneur Mag., Top 19 U.S. News and World Report, Nat. Innovative Pedagogy award, 2001, Outstanding Educator award Ind. Distance Learning Assn., 2004. Mem. US Assn. Small Bus. and Entrepreneurship (pres. 1993-94), Nat. Acad. Mgmt., Internat. Coun. Small Bus., Midwest Bus. Adminstrn. Assn. (pres. entrepreneurship divsn. 1992-93), Nat. Consortium Entrepreneurship Ctrs. (exec. dir. 2000—). Roman Catholic. Avocations: weightlifting, jogging. Office: Ind Univ Kelley Sch Bus Bloomington IN 47405-1703 Home: 3223 Acadia Ct Bloomington IN 47401 Business E-Mail: dkuratko@indiana.edu.

KUREHA, TOSHINARI, software engineer; b. Yokohama, Japan, Mar. 29, 1977; s. Tomonari Wu and Shinko (Pao) K. BS with honors, Princeton (N.J.) U., 1999. Software developer Formal Systems, Princeton, 1998; software engr. Oracle Corp., Redwood Shores, Calif., 1999—. Tchg. asst. Princeton U., 1997-98. Mem. Sigma Xi. Avocations: tennis, piano, reading mystery/detective novels, scuba diving, travel. Home: 410 Barnegat Ln Redwood City CA 94065 Office: Oracle Corp 500 Oracle Pky 1op 655 Redwood City CA 94065

KURER, CHERYL C., pediatric cardiologist; d. Berthold and Cynthia L. Kuerer; m. Daniel R. Berg. AB, Vassar Coll., 1976—79; MD, Mt. Sinai Sch. Medicine, N.Y.C., 1979—83. Diplomate Nat. Bd. Med. Examiners, 1984, Am. Bd. Pediat., 1987, Am. Bd. Pediat., Sub-bd. Pediatric Cardiology, 1991. Attending, pediatric cardiologist Children's Hosp. of Phila., 1989—90, Schneider Children's Hosp., New Hyde Park, NY, 1990—98, Hackensack U. Med. Ctr., NJ, 1998—2004; chief pediat. cardiologist St. Peter's Univ. Hosp., New Brunswick, NJ, 2004—. Named Top Dr., N.Y. Met. Area, Castle Connolly, 2003, 2004; recipient Phi Beta Kappa Award, Valedictorian, Vassar Coll., 1979; fellow Eloise Ellery Fellowship for post baccalaureate study, 1980—81, James Ryland & Ga. A. Kendrick Fellowship f, 1981—82. Fellow: Am. Coll. Cardiology, Am. Acad. Pediat.; mem.: Pediatric Electrophysiologic Soc., Pediatric Cardiology Soc. of Greater N.Y. (exec. com. 2003—04), Am. Heart Assn. Office: Chief Pediat Cardiology St Peters Univ Hosp 254 Easton Ave New Brunswick NJ 08901 Office Phone: 732-846-2855. Business E-Mail: kurer@email.chop.edu.

KURFEHS, HAROLD CHARLES, real estate executive; b. Jersey City, Dec. 10, 1939; s. Harold Charles and Matilda Gertrude (Ruschman) Kurfehs; m. Linda Roberta Lepis, Aug. 1, 1964; children: Harold Charles III, Diane E., Robert C. BS (Oaklawn Found. scholar), St. Peter's Coll., 1962; MBA, Wharton Sch. U. Pa., 1964. Product mgr. Am. Brands, Inc., N.Y.C., 1958-62, 64-66; account exec. Benton & Bowles, N.Y.C., 1966-68; account mgr. Wells, Rich, Greene, Inc., N.Y.C., 1968-69; v.p., dir. mktg. Meta-Language Products, Inc., N.Y.C., 1969-70; sr. acct. exec. McCaffrey & McCall, Inc., N.Y.C., 1970-71; dir. advt. Ethan Allen, Inc., N.Y.C., Danbury, Conn., 1971-75; v.p., gen. mgr. retail/franchise divsn. N.Am. Ops. Reed Ltd., Toronto, 1975-76; v.p., gen. mgr. fabric divsn. Reed Nat. Drapery Co. and Sanderson Fabrics, Toronto, 1975-76; pres. Fairfield Book Co., Inc., Harlin House, Ltd., Brookfield, Conn., 1977-83; dir. advt. and pub. rels., bd. dirs., mem. mktg. planning bd. Ethan Allen, Inc., Danbury, Conn., 1983-85; sr. comml. investment broker William Raveis Comml. Investment Real Estate, Danbury, Conn., 1985-96; sr. comml. broker Century 21, Scalzo Realty, Inc., Bethel, Conn., 1996—2002; v.p. Coldwell Banker Comml., Scalzo Group, 2002—. Lectr. We. Conn. State U., 1985—86; chmn. Real Estate United Way No. Fairfield County, Conn., 1990, 91, account exec., bus. and industry divsn., 2001; mem. policies and procedures com. lead mgmt. Conn. Econ. Resource Ctr., 1995—96; alt. mem. Brookfield Planning Commn., 1997, 98, elected mem., 1999—, vice chmn., 2002—; mem. Brookfield Econ. Devel. Commn., 2004—05. Contbr. articles to profl. jours. Del. Rep. State Conv., 2004. Named Top Prodr., State of Conn., 1988, 1989, Broker of Month, Conn. Real Estate Jour., 1990, Broker of Yr., Scalzo Comml., 1998, Listing Agt. of Yr., 2001, Broker of Yr., Coldwell Banker Comml., 2002—03. Mem.: NRA (life), Internat. Coun. Shopping Ctrs., Conn. Assn. Realtors (regl. treas. 1992, state dir. 1993, regional pres. 1995—96, state dir. 1993—94, state sec. 1994, state v.p. 1995, regional pres. 1995—96, state pres.-elect 1996), Wharton Grad. Club N.Y., Pi Sigma Phi. Home: 42 Obtuse Rd N Brookfield CT 06804-3140 Office: 6 Stony Hill Rd Bethel CT 06801-1028 Office Phone: 203-205-7665. Business E-Mail: kurfehs@coldwellbankerscalzo.com.

KURFIRST, LEONARD STANLEY, lawyer; b. Chgo., Oct. 10, 1959; s. Leonard Richard and Margaret Josephine Kurfirst; m. Sally Gordon, Sept. 26, 1987; children: Kyle, Kelsy. BA, Stanford U., 1981; JD cum laude, Ind. U., 1984. Bar: Ill. 1984, U.S. Dist. Ct. (no. dist.) Ill. 1984. Assoc. Hinshaw & Culbertson, Chgo., 1984-86, Wildman, Harrold, Allen & Dixon, Chgo., 1986-92, ptnr., 1992-95, Hickey, Driscoll, Kurfirst, Patterson & Melia, Chgo., 1995—. Editor De Paul Jour. Health Care Law, 1998. Commr. Traffic and Safety Commn., Village of Western Springs, Ill., 1993—; coach Am. Youth Soccer Orgn., Western Springs, 1998. Mem. ABA, Ill. Bar Assn., Chgo. Bar Assn. (chmn. med./legal rels. com. 1995-96). Avocations: softball, basketball, coaching. Office: Hickey Driscoll Kurfirst Patterson & Melia 77 W Washington St Ste 800 Chicago IL 60602-2804

KURIAN, GEORGE THOMAS, publisher; b. Changanacherry, Kerala, India, Aug. 4, 1931; came to U.S., 1968; s. Thomas Kurian and Mary (Abraham) George; m. Annie Cyriack, Aug. 22, 1966; 1 child, Sarah Claudine. MA, Madras (India) Christian Coll., 1951. Dir. Indian Univs. Press, Madras, 1960-68; editor Clarence L. Barnhart, Bronxville, N.Y., 1968-71, Macmillan Inc., N.Y.C., 1971-72; pres. George Kurian Reference Books, Baldwin Place, N.Y., 1972—. Bd. dirs. Fgn. Affairs Info. Svc., Baldwin Place, 1982—. Editor: Ency. of Third World, 1978 (ALA award 1978), World Press Ency., 1982, World Edn. ency., 1988 (ALA award 1988), Ency. of First World, 1990, Ency. of the Future, 1995, World Christian Encyclopedia, 2000, also 12 other encys. and 18 books. Mem. The Encyclopedists: Internat. Ency. Soc. (pres. 1990—), World Future Soc. Republican. Avocation: carpentry. Home: 3689 Campbell Ct Yorktown Heights NY 10598-1808 Office: George Kurian Reference Books PO Box 519 Baldwin Place NY 10505-0519 Office Phone: 914-962-3287. E-mail: gtkurian@aol.com.

KURIANSKY, JUDY, television personality, radio personality, reporter, clinical psychologist, writer, educator; b. NYC, Jan. 31, 1947; d. Abraham and Sylvia (Feld) Brodsky; m. Edward Kuriansky, Aug. 24, 1969. BA, Smith Coll., 1968; EdM, Boston U., 1970; PhD, NYU, 1980. Diplomate Am. Bd. Sexology, 2003. Reporter Sta. WABC-TV, N.Y.C., 1980-82, Sta. WBZ-TV, Boston, 1981-82, Sta. WCBS-TV, N.Y.C., 1982-86, N.Y.C., 1986-88, Sta. WPIX-TV, N.Y.C., 1987-89, Sta. CNBC-TV, Ft. Lee, NJ, 1989-93; host Total Wellness for Women program Sta. WDBB-TV, Birmingham, Ala., 1988-89; program host Sta. WABC-AM, N.Y.C., 1980-87, Sta. WOR-AM, 1987-88; temp. program host ABC Talk Radio, N.Y.C., 1988-90; host Modern Satellite Network, 1981; TV host J.C. Penney Golden Rule Network, Dallas, 1988-90; feature contbr. Attitudes Show LifeTime, 1992-94; host Love Phones, nat. syndicated Premiere Radio Networks, N.Y.C., 1992-97; host Dr. Judy Show, Winstar Radio, 1998-99. Spokesperson Universal Studios Fla., 1993—94, Church and Dwight, 2000—01; cons. Lily of France, Charles of the Ritz, The Rolland Co., Taylor-Gordon Arons Advt., Clairol, Durex, London Internat., 1995, Organon, 1999—, Ky. Married for Life Survey, 2003—; tchr. Columbia U. Med. Sch., 1974—79, Inst. for Health and Religion, 1980—82; adj. prof. clin. psychology NYU, 1993—95; adj. prof. psychology Columbia U. Tchrs. Coll., 2001—; vis. prof. Beijing U. Health Sci. Ctr., 2002—; judge Most Unforgettable Women contest Revlon, 1990; judge Close-Up N Roll Contest, 1993, Cooney Waters P.R., Herpes Awareness Contest, 1996; therapy coord. Nat. Inst. for Psychotherapists, 1977—79; therapist Ctr. for Marital and Family Therapy, 1986—; cons. Shanghai Inst. Reproductive Health Instrn., China, 1999—; trainer marital cons. China Sexology Assn., 2000—; v.p. Quezon Corp., 1978—79; sr. rsch. scientist N.Y. State Psychiat. Inst., 1970—78; lectr. Blanton Peale Inst., 1979—81; mem. adv. bd. Single Living mag., 1997—98, Lane Bryant, 1997—98; adj. prof. psychology Yeshiva Univ., 2003—; asst. clin. prof. psychiatry Columbia Med. Ctr., 2003—; vis. prof Peking U. Health Sci. Ctr.; instr. dept. psychiatry Hong Kong U. Author: Sex, Now That I've Got Your Attention, Let Me Answer Your Questions, 1984, How to Love a Nice Guy, 1990, Italian and Japanese transls., Generation Sex, 1995, The Complete Idiots Guide to Dating, 1996, 2d edit., 1999, 3rd edit., 2003, The Complete Idiots Guide to a Healthy Relationship, 1997, 2d edit., 2001, The Complete Idiots Guide to Tantric Sex, 2001, 2d edit., 2004, China Reproductive Health Hotline Professionals Solve Problems on Sex and Emotions, 2001; columnist Family Circle mag., 1984—89, Whole Life Times, 1986—87, King Features Newspaper, 1984—86, N.Y. and L.I. Newsday, 1993—2000, Penthouse mag., 1995—, Soap Opera Update, 1995—96, Telluride Daily Planet, 1995—98, Cosmo Girl mag., 2001—03, Singapore Straits Times, 2002—, N.Y. Daily News website, 2004—; columnist: China Trends Health mag., 2004—; writer New Woman, Ad Age, Boardroom Reports, Am. Advt. Fedn. mag., Chgo. Tribune Woman News, South China Morning Post, 2001—; contbg. editor: Beauty Mag., 1989—90; guest editor Ladies Home Jour., 1993, AOL On-Line Show, Keyword: Dr. Judy, 1996—97, www.cameraplanet.com, 2001—02, www.matureamerica-.com, 2002—03, mem. adv. bd. Single Living mag., 1997—99; author: Goodbye My Troubles, Hello My Happiness, 1997. UN del. Internat. Assn. Applied Psychology and World Coun. for Psychotherapy, 2004—; bd. dirs. Scientists Com. for Pub. Info., 1977—79; mem. adv. bd. N.Y. City Self Help Orgn., 1983—85; mem. benefits com. Mental Health Svcs. for Deaf, 1980—82; bd. advisors Planned Parenthood, 1998—. Recipient Civilian Commendation, N.Y.C. Police Dept., 1984, Cert. for Unique Pub. Svc. AWRT, 1984, Star award for individual achievement in radio, 1997, Sabo Media Programming Visionary award, 1984, Maggie award Planned Parenthood, 1985, 93, Freedoms Found. award Children for a Better Soc., 1986, Olive award Coun. of Chs., 1986, Mercury award Larimi Comm., 1987, Lifetime Achievement in Sexology medal, AACS, 2004. Fellow APA; mem. Am. Women in Radio and TV (pres. N.Y. chpt. 1988-89, nat. found. vice chair 1988-90, nat. bd. treas. 1995-98, Internat. Outreach award 2003), Soc. Sex Therapy and Rsch. (charter), Am. Assn. Sex, Educators, Counselors and Therapists (exec. bd. 2004-05), TV Acad. of N.Y. (gov. 1987-91), Friars Club. Office Phone: 212-445-3995. E-mail: apollack@premiereradio.com.

KURIE, EDITH JOAN, librarian, writer; b. Charlotte, NC, Oct. 17, 1955; d. John Forsythe and Edith Joan (Rodgers) Kurie; m. Lunsford Richardson Smith, Dec. 29, 1976 (div. July 1982); 1 child, William Richardson. BA in English, Guilford Coll., 1978; MLIS, U. N.C., 2001. Dir. pub. rels. The Webb Sch., Bell Buckle, Tenn., 1979; co-pub. The Mecklenburg Times, Charlotte, 1982-87; legal asst. Law Offices of M.S. Shulimson, Charlotte, 1986; travel agt., tour wholesaler CCI Travel/GoGo Tours, Charlotte, 1987-89; vet. asst. Pineville Animal Hosp., Charlotte, 1989; substitute tchr. Charlotte Mecklenburg Schs., 1990-91; test evaluator Measurements, Inc., Charlotte, 1996; libr. assoc. Pub. Libr. Charlotte and Mecklenburg County, 1996, libr. asst. level I, 1996-98, libr. asst. level III, 1998—; libr. Jacksonville Pub. Libr., 2003—05; youth svc. libr. Broward County Pub. Libr., Ft. Lauderdale, 2005—. Contbg. poet: Songs on the Wind, 1994, Celebrating Excellence, 1995 (Pres.'s award 1995). Pres. Women's Rep. Club, Bedford County, Tenn., 1981; mem. Queen City Civitan, Charlotte, 1983. Recipient Blue Ribbon award So. Poetry Assn., Pass Christian, Miss., 1994. Mem. Legal and Bus. Pubs. (bd. dirs. 1985X), Fla. Libr. Assn., ALA, PLA. Republican. Presbyterian. Avocations: reading, walking, needlecrafts, bicycling. Office: Carrollton Sch of the Sacred Heart 3747 Main Hwy Miami FL 33133 Home: 21701 SW 99 Ave Miami FL 33190 Office Phone: 954-492-1802. Personal E-mail: billsmom02@yahoo.com.

KURIN, RICHARD, museum program director; b. Bronx, NY, Nov. 27, 1950; m. Allyn Bland; children: Danielle, Jaclyn. BA, SUNY, 1972; MA in Anthropology, U. Chgo., 1974; cert. in Urdu lang., U. Calif., Berkeley, 1974; PhD in Anthropology, U. Chgo., 1981. Vis. asst. prof. dept. anthropology So. Ill. U., Carbondale, 1981-84, asst. prof., 1984-85; program coord., curator, cons. Festival of India, Aditi & Mela Exhbns., Smithsonian Instn., Washington, 1984-85; chair 150th Anniversary Program Com. Smithsonian Instn., Washington, 1993—, dep. dir. Ctr. for Folklife and Cultural Heritage, 1985—87, acting dir., 1987-90, dir., 1990—2004, acting dir. Nat. Programs, 2004—; professorial lectr. Johns Hopkins U., Paul Nitze Sch. Adv. Internat. Studies, 1985-95. Collector Am. Mus. Natural History, Punjabi Indian village artifacts, 1970; vis. instr. cmty. devel. program So. Ill. U., Carbondale, 1979-81; program coord. Indian Puppetry Program, Smithsonian Instn., 1980; cons. anthropologist Harza Engring. Co., UNDP and World Bank, Indus Basin Master Planning Project, 1977; ethnic tours mgr. divsn. performing arts On-Tour India Program, Pakistan Program, Smithsonian Instn., 1976; adv. bd. Coun. Overseas Rsch. Ctrs., 1989; adj. prof. George Washington U., 1999; internat. jury UNESCO Masterpieces Intangible Cultural Heritage, 2000-04; commr. U.S. Nat. Commn. UNESCO. Author: Aditi: The Living Arts of India, 1986, Reflections of a Culture Broker: A View From the Smithsonian, 1997, Smithsonian Folklife Festival: Culture Of, By, and For the People, 1998; (film) Aditi: The Living Arts of India, 1986; lead writer, organizer: Iowa Folklife: Our People, Traditions and Communities, 1996-97; advisor film: Jerusalem: Gateways to the City, 1995, Hosay: Muslim Transnationalism in Trinidad, 1994—, White House Workers, 1994; edtl. advisor film Kathputli: An Indian Puppetry Tradition, 1986—; recs. Smithsonian Folkways Records, 1986—. Trustee Smithsonian Sec.'s Rep., Libr. of Congress, Am. Folklore Ctr., 1989—, Am. Pakistan Rsch. Orgn., 1989—, U.S. Nat. Commn. for UNESCO, 2004—; mem. Fairfax County Citizen Assn. Edn. Com., 1991—; pres. Bailey's Elem. Sch. P.T.A., 1989-91. Fellow NDEA, Title VI, 1973, Fulbright-Hayes, HEW, 1976, Social Sci. Rsch. Coun., 1976, 83, Am. Inst. Pakistan Studies, 1983, Sec.'s Gold medal for exceptional svc. Smithsonian Instn., 1996; grantee Smithsonian Instn., 1979, 86, 89-90, 92, 95-96, NEH, 1982, 1991—, Nat. Endowment Arts, 1987. Fellow Soc. Applied Anthropology; mem. Am. Folklore Soc. (Benjamin Botkin lifetime achievement award 1999), Am. Ethnological Soc., Assn. Asian Studies, Am. Anthropol. Assn. Office: Ctr Folklife & Cultural Heritage Smithsonian Instn Washington DC 20560-0953 Business E-Mail: kurin@folklife.si.edu.

KURISH, JAMES BRIAN, finance executive; b. Amherst, Ohio, May 18, 1955; s. Andrew Stefan and Betty Louise (Bryner) K.; m. Mary Lyn Valkenburg, Dec. 23, 1988; 1 child: Andrew Stefan. BA, The Coll. of Wooster, Ohio, 1977; MS, U. Ill., Champaign, 1980; PhD, 1983; MBA, Yale U., New Haven, 1989. Mktg. analyst J.M. Smucker Co., Orrville, Ohio, 1976; researcher Dept. Energy, Oak Ridge, Tenn., 1976-79; asst. prof. Econ. U. Hartford, West Hartford, Conn., 1981-84; dir. grad. studies, 1984-85; asst. dean, exec. dir. Paris, 1985-87; assoc. The First Boston Corp., Chgo., 1989-92; dir. Govt. Fin. Officers Assn., Chgo., 1992-94; pres. J.B. Kurish & Assocs., Chgo., 1994-95; exec. dir. Mcpl. Issuer Rsch. and Analysis Ctr., Chgo., 1995-99; dir. Ctr. Fin. Rsch. and Svcs., Chgo., 1999—. Author: Debt Issuance, 1993, Pricing Bonds in a Negotiated Sale, 1994; contbr. articles to profl. jours. Mem. Govt. Fin. Officers Assn., Am. Econ. Assn. Home: 10th Fl 2120 N Lincoln Park West Chicago IL 60614 Office: U Ill Coll Bus Adminstrn Dept Fin M/C 168 601 S Morgan St Chicago IL 60607-7100 E-mail: jbkurish@uic.edu.

KURIT, NEIL, lawyer; b. Cleve., Aug. 31, 1940; s. Jay and Rose (Rainin) K.; m. Doris Tannenbaum, Aug. 9, 1964 (div.); m. Donna Chernin, Aug. 24, 1986. BS, Miami U., Oxford, Ohio, 1961; JD, Case Western Res. U., 1964. Bar: Ohio 1964. Prin. Kahn, Kleinman, Yanowitz & Arnson Co., L.P.A., Cleve., 1964—. Co-author Handbook for Attys. and Accts., Jewish Cmty. Fedn. Endowment Fund. Trustee, v.p. Montefiore Home, 1983-87; trustee Jewish Cmty. Fedn. Cleve., 1983-86, 90-95. Mem. ABA, Ohio State Bar Assn. Home: 2870 Courtland Blvd Cleveland OH 44122-2802 Office: Kahn Kleinman Co LPA 2600 Tower at Erieview Cleveland OH 44114 Office Phone: 216-736-3352. E-mail: nkurit@kahnkleinman.com.

KURITA, DEBRA LYNN, city official; b. Salt Lake City, Nov. 30, 1954; d. Ikuya and Rosemary (Baer) K.; m. Keene N. Wilson, Oct. 1, 1983; children: Skyler E., Wyatt F. Ba in Polit. Sci., U. Calif., Davis, 1976; MPA, U. So. Calif., 1981. Adminstrv. intern small bus. L.A. Mayor's Office, 1979-80; with mcpl. svcs. dept. City of Lawndale, Calif., 1980-81; adminstrv. specialist fin. dept. City of Torrance, Calif., 1981-84; adminstrv. asst. I and II community devel. agy City of Santa Ana, Calif., 1984-86, mgr. adminstrv. svcs., 1986-89, asst. city mgr., 1989—. Mem. Am. Soc. Pub. Adminstrn., Mcpl. Mgmt. Assts. So. Calif. (treas. 1984-85). Office: City of Santa Ana PO Box 1988 Santa Ana CA 92702-1988

KURITZKES, MICHAEL S., gas industry executive, lawyer; b. Tarrytown, NY, Oct. 30, 1960; BS in indsl./labor rels., Cornell U., 1982; JD, U. Pa., 1985. Bar: NY 1987, Calif. 1994, Pa. 1998. Assoc. Kaye, Scholer, Fierman, Hays & Handler, NYC, 1985—87, Battle Fowler, NYC, 1987—91; corp. counsel Am. Ultramar Ltd., Greenwich, Conn., 1991—93; v.p., gen. counsel Ultramar, Long Beach, Calif., 1993—97; gen. atty. Sunoco, Inc., Phila., 1997—2000, v.p., gen. counsel, 2000—03, sr. v.p., gen. counsel, 2003—. Chmn. bd. overseers Annenberg Ctr., U. Pa. Office: Sunoco Inc Ten Penn Ctr 1801 Market St Philadelphia PA 19103-1699

KURK, KATHERINE CHENAULT, education educator; d. Victor John Kurk and Elizabeth Dean Guy. BA, U. of Ky., 1968—72, MA, 1972—74, PhD, 1974—79. Asst. prof. Drury Coll., Springfield, Mo., 1979—84; dir. Le Village Francais, Springfield, Mo., 1980—84; assoc. prof. Drury Coll., Springfield, Mo., 1983—84; asst. prof. No. Ky. U., Highland Heights, 1986—90, assoc. prof., 1990—97; vis. assoc. prof. Davidson Coll., NC, 1994, U. of Ky., Lexington; french ap and ib prof. Holmes H.S., Covington, Ky., 2002; prof. of modern languages No. Ky. U., Highland Heights, 1997—. Asst. editor French Forum, Inc., 1984—2000; editor Ky. Philol. Rev., 1990—. Mem.: Ky. Philol Assn. (exec. com., editor 1990—), Am. Assn. of Teachers of French Nat. Fgn. Languages in the Elem. Sch. Commn. (assoc.). Independent. Avocation: gardening. Office: Northern Kentucky University Dept of Lit & Language Highland Heights KY 41099

KURKUL, WENYI WANG, musician, educator, administrator; b. Taipei, Taiwan, Oct. 30, 1964; arrived in U.S., 1986; d. Shih-Ming and Hsieh-Chu Wang. MusM, Ohio U., 1988; MusD, U. Mo., 1995; D in Music Edn., Ind. U., 2000. Prof., adminstr. Sch. Music Tainan (Taiwan) Woman's Coll. Arts & Tech., 1989—92; prof. Nat. Taiwan Acad. Arts, 1989—92, Nat Sun Yat-Sen U., Kaohsiung, Taiwan, 1990-92; vis. faculty Sch. Music Ind. U., Bloomington, 1999—2000; prof. dept. music George Mason U., 2000—03, dir. music edn. dept. music Coll. Visual and Performing Arts, 2001—03, exec. dir. Orff Schulwerk Tchr. Tng. and Cert. Program, 2001—03; prof. dept. music Montgomery Coll., 2004—, also music dir., condr. symphony orch.; founder, exec. dir. Empowered to Excel program Montgomery Coll and Montgomery County Pub. Schs. Symphony Orch. Partnership Program, 2005—. Music dir., condr. Montgomery Coll. Symphony Orch. Soloist-in-residence Nat. Chiang Kai Shek Cultural Ctr., Taipei, 1991-94; flutist Asian Composers League, Taipei, 1990-92; asst. prin. flutist Taiwan Symphony Orch., Taichung, 1984-86; founder, dir. Empowered to Excel, Montgomery Coll. and Montgomery Pub. Schs. Symphony Orch. Partnership Program, 2005—; contbr. articles to profl. publs. Nat. Art and Sci. Coun. scholar, Taiwan, 1989-92; Nat. rsch. grantee Ministry of Edn., Taiwan, 1989-92; named New Performing Star of Yr. Nat. Theatre and Concert Hall Planning and Mgmt. Coun., Taiwan, 1991. Mem.: APA, AAUP, Nat. Assn. Student Personnel Adminstrs., Nat. Assn. Student Affairs Profls., Internat. Soc. Philosophy Music Edn. (founding), Pub. Rels. Soc. Am., Am. Edn'l. Rsch. Assn., Am. Orff-Schulwerk Assn., Internat. Soc. for Music Edn. (Eng.), European Recorder Tchrs. Assn., Soc. for Rsch. in Music Edn., Music Edn. Nat. Conf., Coll. Music Soc., Nat. Flute Assn. (life), Am. Symphony Orch. League, Phi Kappa Lambda. Home: 403 Misty Knoll Dr Rockville MD 20850-2879 Personal E-mail: wenyi.kurkul@verizon.net. Business E-Mail: Wen.Kurkul@montgomerycollege.edu.

KURLAN, MARVIN ZEFT, retired surgeon; b. Wilkes-Barre, Pa., Feb. 20, 1934; s. Ephraigm Joseph and Fannye Lillian Kurlancheek; m. Eleanor Frank, June 21, 1964; 1 child, Todd. BA, Wilkes Coll., 1957; MS, U. Ill., 1958; MD, SUNY, Buffalo, 1964. Diplomate Nat. Bd. Med. Examiners, Am. Bd. Surgery. Intern then resident in surgery Millard Fillmore Hosp., Buffalo, 1964-69, dir. trauma svcs., 1974-82, sr. attending surgeon, 1984-95; surgeon emeritus, 1995—; plant surgeon Bethlehem (Pa.) Steel Corp., 1969-74; med. dir. Bros. of Mercy Health Facilities, Clarence, N.Y., 1974-82. Assoc. examiner Am. Bd. Surgery, Phila., 1987-95; chmn. James Platt White Soc., Sch. Medicine and Biomed. Scis., SUNY, Buffalo, 1992-94 (Dean's adv. coun., 1995-97); cons. in surgery Walter Reed Army Med. Ctr., Washington. Contbr. articles to profl. jours. Vol. Empire State Games, Buffalo, 1986; mem. Jack Kemp Forum, Buffalo, 1985-91; bd. dirs. Jewish Fedn. Allentown, Pa., 1972-74. Served AUS (res.) to lt. col. Med. Corps, 1965-91, active duty operation Desert Shield and Desert Storm. Decorated Army Svc. medal with Oak Leaf Cluster, Army Achievement medal; named Top One Hundred Health Profls., Internat. Biographical Ctr., Cambridge, Eng., 2005. Fellow Am. Coll. Gastroenterology, Am. Trauma Soc. (founder), N.Y. Acad. Scis.; mem. ACS (life fellow leadership soc.), Assn. Mil. Surgeons U.S., Hastings on Hudson Bioethics Ctr., Buffalo Surg. Soc. (sec. 1986-88, v.p. 1988-89, pres. 1989-90), SUNY at Buffalo Found. (pres.'s assoc.), Grand Coun. World Parliament, Confedn. Chivalry, Knight of Humanity, Order White Cross Internat. (dist. comdr. N.Y., U.S.), Chevalier Grand Cross, Ordre Soverain et Militaire de Milice du St. Sepulcre, Phi Lambda Kappa (nat. pres. 1993), Nu Sigma Nu, Sci. Progress Rsch. Club (Buffalo) (v.p. 1983-84), Equality Club, Masons Lodge, Shriners Lodge. Republican. Jewish. Avocations: world travel, genealogy. Home and Office: 413 Dan Troy Dr Buffalo NY 14221-3558 Personal E-mail: mkurlan@adelphia.net.

KURLAN, ROGER, neurologist, educator; m. Cathy Morris; children: Melissa, Matthew. BA, U. Rochester, 1974; MD, Wash. U., St. Louis, 1974—78. Cert. neurologist Am. Bd. Psychiatry and Neurology, 1984. Intern, resident in medicine Jewish Hosp., St. Louis, 1978—80; resident in neurology Sch. Medicine U. Rochester, NY, 1980—83, fellow in neurology Sch. Medicine, 1983, fellow in movement disorders and clin. neuropharmacology Sch. Medicine, 1983—84, 1984—88, assoc prof., neurology Sch. Medicine, 1988—92, prof., neurology Sch. Medicine, 1992—. Mem.: Movement Disorder Soc., Am. Acad. Neurology, Am. Neuropsychaitric Assn., Am. Neurol. Assn., Phi Beta Kappa. Office: Univ Rochester Med Ctr 1351 Mt Hope Ave Ste 100 Rochester NY 14620 Office Phone: 585-341-7500. Office Fax: 585-473-4678. Business E-Mail: roger_kurlan@urmc.rochester.edu.

KURLAND, HAROLD ARTHUR, lawyer; b. N.Y.C., Jan. 20, 1952; s. Jordan Emil and Anita (Siegel) K.; m. Christine Rogers, June 28, 1975; children: Thomas Philip, Andrew Rogers. AB, Dartmouth Coll., 1973; JD, Cornell U., 1976. Bar: N.Y. 1977, D.C. 1977, U.S. Dist. Ct. (we. dist.) N.Y. 1977, U.S. Dist. Ct. (no. dist.) N.Y. 1983, U.S. Dist. Ct. (no. dist.) Tex. 1981, U.S. Ct. Appeals (2d cir.) 1980, U.S. Dist. Ct. (D.C. dist.) 1986, U.S. Ct. Appeals (D.C. cir.) 1986, U.S Ct. Appeals (3d cir.) 1988, U.S. Dist. Ct. (mid. dist.) Pa. 1988, U.S. Dist. Ct. (ea. and so. dists.) N.Y. 1991, U.S. Supreme Ct. 1980. Assoc. Nixon, Hargrave, Devans & Doyle LLP (now Nixon Peabody LLP), Rochester, N.Y., 1976-84, ptnr., 1985-2000; founding ptnr. Ward Norris Heller & Reidy LLP, Rochester, 2000—. Mediator, arbitrator Am. Arbitration Assn.; mem. adv. com. on civil practice N.Y. Office Ct. Adminstrn. Past chmn.

bd. dirs. Rochester Philharm. Orch.; bd. dirs. Vol. Legal Svcs. Project. Mem. ABA, Am. Bar Found., Am. Bd. Trial Advs. (assoc.), N.Y. State Bar Assn., D.C. Bar Assn., Monroe County Bar Assn. (past chair judicary com., cts. com., fed. ct. com., exec. com., trustee), Rochester Inn of Ct. (past. pres., master). Democrat. Home: 154 Council Rock Ave Rochester NY 14610-3335 Office: Ward Norris Heller & Reidy LLP 300 State St Rochester NY 14614 Office Phone: 585-454-0700. Business E-Mail: hak@wnhr.com.

KURLAND, STUART M., English language educator; b. Greensboro, N.C., 1955; s. Jordan E. and Anita Kurland; m. Donna L. Ringle, Sept. 23, 1989; children: Michael, Alex. AB, Dartmouth Coll., 1977; MA, U. Chgo., 1978, PhD, 1984. Vis. asst. prof. Hamilton Coll., Clinton, N.Y., 1984-85, Emory U., Atlanta, 1985-86, Coll. William and Mary, Williamsburg, Va., 1986-87, St. John's U., Collegeville, Minn., 1987-88; asst. prof. English, Duquesne U., Pitts., 1988-93, assoc. prof., 1993—. Contbr. articles, revs. to profl. jours. Mem. Edgewood Vol. Fire Dept., 1989-92, Mt. Lebanon Vol. Fire Dept., 1993—. Office: Duquesne U English Dept 600 Forbes Ave Pittsburgh PA 15282-0001

KURLANDER, ERIC A., history professor; b. Evanston, Ill., Jan. 4, 1973; s. Clyde and Michele Kurlander; m. Monika Aleksandra Walusiak, Mar. 25, 2000. BA, Bowdoin Coll., 1994; MA, Harvard U., 1997, PhD, 2001. Law clk. Lindenbaum, Coffman, Chgo., 1994—95; tchg. fellow Harvard U., Cambridge, Mass., 1997—2001; asst. prof. Stetson U., Deland, Fla., 2001—. Mem. various coms. Stetson U., 2002—. Author: Let's Go Germany, 1998, Let's Go Europe, 1998; contbr. articles to profl. jours. Recipient James Bowdoin Book prize, 1992; fellow, Dudley House, 1996, Social Sci. Rsch. Coun., 1998, Fulbright Found., 1998, Krupp Found., 1998, Harvard U., 1999; grantee, Krupp Found., 1997, DAAD, 1997; Tng. grant, 1996, Harvard Merit scholar, 1998, Sheldon Travelling fellowship, 1998. Mem.: Am. Hist. Assn., German Studies Assn., So. Hist. Assn., Modern Lang. Assn., Harvard Ctr. European Studies (assoc.). Office: Stetson Univ Dept History 421 North Woodland Blvd Deland FL 32724 Office Phone: 386-822-7578.

KURLI, MADHAVI, ophthalmologist; b. Madanapalli, Andhra Pradesh, India, Mar. 9, 1974; d. Parthasarathy and Janaki Devi Katukota; m. Vineel Kurli, Jan. 22, 1999. MB, BS, Chennai Med. Coll., India, 1998. Diplomate Royal Coll. of Ophthalmologists, London, 2002. Ho. officer in internal medicine Hull Royal Infirmary, Hull, England, 1999—2000; extern in ophthalmology St. James' U. Hosp., Leeds, England, 2000; sr. ho. officer in ophthalmology Stepping Hill Hosp., Stockport, England, 2000—01, Wolverhampton and Midland Counties Eye Infirmary, England, 2001—03; rsch. fellow in ophthalmic oncology N.Y. Eye Cancer Ctr., N.Y.C., 2003—. Author: (book chapt.) Ophthalmology Clinics of North America, 2005, Progress in Kidney Cancer Research, 2005; presenter: in field; contbr. articles to profl. jours. Mem.: Royal Coll. of Ophthalmologists, London, N.Y. Acad. Scis., Assn. for Rsch. in Vision and Ophthalmology, Am. Acad. of Ophthalmology. Home: 812 E 92d St Apt 2A New York NY 10128 Office: NY Eye Cancer Ctr 115 E 61st St New York NY 10021 Personal E-mail: mkurli@hotmail.com. Business E-Mail: mkurli@eyecancer.com. E-mail: mkurli@gmail.com.

KURLINSKI, JOHN PARKER, physician; b. Buchanon, W.Va., Jan. 17, 1948; s. John Peter and Jean (Holloway) K.; m. Claire Sawyer, June 12, 1971; children: Joshua John, Ryan Edward, Seth Parker. AB cum laude, Williams Coll., 1970; MD, Johns Hopkins Sch. Medicine, 1974. Intern, then resident Johns Hopkins Hosp., Balt., 1974-77; fellowship neonatal/perinatal medicine U. Calif., San Diego, 1977-79; chief resident pediatrician Johns Hopkins Hosp., 1979-80; pediatrician, co-dir. neonatology S.W. Regional Neonatal Ctr. at Sunrise Hosp. and Med. Ctr., Las Vegas, 1980-93; vice chief pediat. Sunrise Children's Hosp., Las Vegas, 1983-90, vice chief of staff, 1989-90, chief of staff, 1990-95, dir. NICU, 1994—2002; clin. assoc. prof. pediatrics U. Nev. Sch. Medicine, Reno, 1994—. Bd. dirs. S.W. Regional Neonatal Ctr. Edn. Found.; chmn. bd. dirs. Sunrise Children's Hosp. Found.; mem. Med.-Legal Screening Panel, Nev., 1986—; many hosp. coms., 1980—. Bd. dirs. So Nev. chpt. March of Dimes, Las. Vegas, 1984—. Mem. AMA, Am. Acad. Pediatrics (v.p. Nev. chpt. 1987-90, pres. 1990-93, coun. mem. dist. VIII sect. on perinatal pediatrics), Clark County Med. Soc., Las Vegas Pediatric Soc. (founding), Phi Beta Kappa. Avocations: rugby, skiing, hiking, camping. Home: 3322 Beam Dr Las Vegas NV 89139-5902 Office: Sunrise Childrens Hosp 3186 S Maryland Pky Las Vegas NV 89109-2317 Office Phone: 702-731-8240. E-mail: kurli@cox.net.

KURN, NEAL, lawyer; b. Springfield, Mass., July 19, 1934; s. Samuel and Jane Etta (Freeman) K.; m. Barbara Agron, June 9, 1957; children: Jeffrey Howard, Sharon Ilene Marcus-Kurn, Jennifer Rose Endsley. BSBA with high honors, U. Ariz., 1956, JD with honors, 1963. Bar: Ariz. 1963; cert. specialist tax and estate and trust law, Ariz.; CPA, Ariz. Staff mem. Price Waterhouse & Co., San Francisco, L.A. and Phoenix, 1956, 58-60; assoc., ptnr. Moore, Romley, Kaplan, Robbins & Green, Phoenix, 1963-71; ptnr. Powers, Ehrenreich, Boutell & Kurn, Phoenix, 1971-82; ptnr., also bd. dirs. Fennemore Craig, Phoenix, 1982—. Adj. prof. law Ariz. State U., 1980-82. Editor-in-chief Ariz. Law Rev., 1962-63. Past chmn. tax adv. commn. Ariz. State Bd. Legal Specialization; bd. dirs. Ariz. Cmty. Found., 1986—, chmn. 1994-96; bd. dirs. Ariz. Bar Found., 1983-89, chmn., 1988; bd. dirs. Jewish Fedn. Greater Phoenix, pres., 1977-79; bd. dirs. U. Ariz. Found., 1998-2004; bd. visitors U. Ariz. Law Sch.; v.p. coun. Jewish Fedn., 1988-90; chmn. Jewish Cmty. Found. Greater Phoenix, 1998-2001; bd. dirs. Trust for Jewish Philanthropy, 2000-2003; chmn. adv. bd. Leave a Legacy, State of Ariz., 2001-2005. With U.S. Army, 1956-58. Fellow Am. Coll. Tax Counsel, Am. Bar Found., Am. Coll. Trust and Estate Counsel; mem. ABA, State Bar Ariz. (past chmn. taxation sect., bd. govs. 1991-93), Maricopa County Bar Assn., Phi Kappa Phi, Beta Gamma Sigma. Democrat. Jewish. Office: Fennemore Craig 3003 N Central Ave Ste 2600 Phoenix AZ 85012-2913 Office Phone: 602-916-5485. Business E-Mail: nkurn@fclaw.com.

KURNICK, NATHANIEL BERTRAND, retired oncologist, hematologist; b. Bklyn., Nov. 8, 1917; s. Jacob and Celia (Levine) K.; m. Dorothy Manheimer, Oct. 4, 1940 (dec. Dec. 1985); children: John E., Katherine(dec.), James T.; m. Sally Ann Kreeger, June 23, 1989. BA, Harvard U., 1936, MD, 1940. Diplomate Am. Bd. Internal Medicine, Am. Bd. Med. Oncology, Am. Bd. Hematology, Am. Bd. Med. Examiners. Intern Mt. Sinai Hosp., N.Y.C., 1941-42, chief resident internal medicine, 1946; asst. prof. medicine Tulane U. Med. Sch., New Orleans, 1949-54; chief hematology svc. VA Hosp., Long Beach, Calif., 1954-59, cons., 1959—; assoc. clin. prof. medicine U. Calif., L.A., 1954-64, clin. prof. medicine Irvine, 1964-99; pvt. practice Long Beach, 1959-83; dir. Bixby Hematology-Oncology Lab. Long Beach Cmty. Med. Ctr., 1982—99. Chmn. cancer activities, 1968—90; chmn. dept. medicine, 1966—68; chmn. dept. med. oncology and hematology, 1982—87; pres. Long Beach Soc. Internal Medicine, 1971; chmn. Franklin Bank of Calif., Orange, Calif., 1988—2004. Contbr. over 150 articles to jours. in field. Trustee Garden Grove, Calif. Union High Sch.Dist., 1960-64. Capt. U.S. Army Med. Corps., 1942—46, Pacific Ocean area. Am. Cancer Soc./NRC fellow, 1946-47, Rockefeller Inst., 1946-47, Nobel Inst., 1947-49; NIH/Am. Cancer Soc. grantee, 1949-1972; Henry Hunter Workman rsch. fellow Harvard Med. Sch./Mass. Gen. Hosp., 1940-41. Fellow ACP; mem. Intern. Soc. Exptl. Hematology, Am. Soc. Hematology, Western Soc. Clin. Rsch., Cen. Soc. Clin. Rsch., Sigma Xi (fellow 1951). Democrat. Jewish. Avocations: sailing, skiing, travel. Business E-Mail: nbkurnick@post.harvard.edu.

KURNICK, ROBERT H., JR., automotive executive, lawyer; b. 1961; BA, Mich. State U.; JD, U. Notre Dame. Ptnr. Honigman Miller Schwartz and Cohn, Detroit, 1986—95; asst. gen. counsel Penske Corp., 1995—99; sr. v.p., gen. counsel Penske Auto Ctrs., Inc., 1995—2001, Penske Motorsports, Inc., 1996—99; exec. v.p., gen. counsel United Auto Group, Inc., 2000—; pres. Penske Corp., 2002—. Office: Penske Corp 2550 Telegraph Rd Bloomfield Hills MI 48302

KURNOW, ERNEST, statistician, educator; b. Bklyn., Oct. 21, 1912; s. Harry and Sarah Malka (Shagaloff) K.; m. Joyce Litzky, Oct. 6, 1938; children: Ruth (Mrs. Jeffrey Jarrett), Susan Carol (Mrs. Leonard Weistrop), Alice Rose (Mrs. Claude Morin). BS cum laude, CCNY, 1932, MS in Edn, 1933; PhD, NYU, 1951. Tchr. N.Y.C. Bd. Edn., 1935-40, statistician, 1941-48; mathematician ordnance div. War Dept., 1940-41; mem. faculty NYU, 1948—, prof. econs., 1960-63, prof. bus. stats., chmn. dept., 1963-86, prof. emeritus bus. stats., adj. prof. bus. stats., 1986—, chmn. dept., 1963-76; chmn. doctoral program N.Y. U., 1976-85, dir. Careers in Bus. program, 1979-88. Cons. N.Y. State Tax Structure Study Commn., 1959-64, Mayor N.Y.C. Com. Mgmt. Survey, 1950-51, Turkish Ministry Finance, 1955-56; cons. temporary commn. Revision N.Y. State Constn., 1958; temporary commn. fiscal affairs N.Y. State Govt., 1953-54; cons. Tri-State Transp. Commn., 1964-66, 73-75; participant Brazilian capital markets program, 1968; study dir. Govs.' Spl. Commn. on Financing Mass Transp., 1970-71; cons. Commn. on Charter Revision, City of N.Y., 1973-74, Temporary Commn. on City Finances, 1975-76 Author: The Turkish Budgetary Process, 1956; also articles. Statistics for Business Decisions, 1959, Theory and Measurement of Land Rent, 1961. Recipient Gt. Tchr. award NYU Alumni Assn., 1974; named Tchr. of Yr., 1999-2000; Fulbright grantee to Greece, 1966-67; Kurnow Classroom established in his honor, NYU, 1993; Ernest Kurnow doctoral fellowship established in his honor, 2003. Fellow Am. Statis. Assn.; mem. Internat. Statis. Inst. (elected), Am. Econ. Assn., Econometric Soc., Inst. Mgmt. Scis., Nat. Tax Assn., Am. Soc. Quality Control, Sphinx, Beta Gamma Sigma, Sigma Eta Phi, Delta Pi Sigma, Alpha Phi Sigma, Delta Sigma Pi. Jewish. Home: 3 Washington Square Vlg Apt 17I New York NY 10012-1810 Office: New York Univ Dept Stats Washington Sq N New York NY 10003-6635 Business E-Mail: ekurnow@stern.nyu.edu.

KURODA, YASUMASA, political science professor, researcher; b. Tokyo, Apr. 28, 1931; arrived in U.S., 1951; s. Shohei and Take (Ishii) Kuroda; m. Alice Kassis, Mar. 21, 1961 (div. Mar. 1995); children: Kamilla, Kamil; m. Miyoko Otaguro, Aug. 14, 1998. Student, Waseda U., 1951; BA, U. Oreg., 1956, MA, 1958, PhD, 1962. From instr. to asst. prof. polit. sci. Mont. State U., Bozeman, 1960-64; asst. prof. polit. sci. U. So. Calif., LA, 1964-66; assoc. program officer advanced projects East-West Ctr., Honolulu, 1967-69; assoc. prof. U. Hawaii-Manoa, Honolulu, 1969—71, prof. polit. sci., 1971—2002, prof. emeritus, 2002—; lectr. Japan-Am. Inst. Mgmt. Sci., Honolulu, 1973-90; pres. Election Svcs. Hawaii, Inc., 1996—2001; exch. rschr. Waseda U., Tokyo, 2002—03; rsch. assoc. Inst. for Japanese Culture and Classics, Kokugakuin U., 2004—. V.p. Minerva Rsch., Inc., Honolulu, 1981-96. Author: Reed Town, Japan, 1974, Chiho Toshi no Kenryokukozo, 1976, (with others) Palestinians Without Palestine, 1978; co-editor: Studies in Political Socialization in the Arab States, 1987, Japan in a New World Order: Contributing to the Arab-Israeli Peace Process, 1994, Japanese Culture in Comparative Perspective, 1997, The Core of Japanese Democracy: Interparty Relations Politics, 2005. Bd. of govs. Japanese Cultural Ctr. Hawaii, Honolulu, 1988-2000, program com., 1988-2000. Recipient Disting. Vis. Lectr. award SUNY, 1994; Rockefeller Found. grantee, 1963-64, Social Sci. Rsch. Coun. grantee, 1966-67, Toyota Found. grantee, 1984-87, 87-90; vis. rsch. fellow Harry S. Truman Rsch. Inst. of the Advancement of Peace, Hebrew U., 1992, Inst. Legal Studies, Kansai U., 1994. Mem. Am. Polit. Sci. Assn., Internat. Polit. Sci. Assn., Internat. Assn. Mid. Ea. States (coll. of fellows 1986—). Democrat. Avocation: stamp collecting/philately. Home: Garden Associe I-208 3-45 Kasama Sakae-ku Yokohama 247-0006 Japan E-mail: ykuroda@hawaii.edu, ykuroda@hh.e-mansion.com.

KUROGI, YASUHISA, chemist; b. Kawasaki, Japan, Oct. 8, 1964; s. Hisashi Kurogi, Junko Kurogi; m. Satoko Kurogi; children: Fumika, Takafumi. PhD, Hiroshima U., 1992. Med. chemist Otsuka Pharm. Factory, Inc., Naruto, Japan, 1992—2000, mgr., 2001—02, Otsuka Pharm. Co. Ltd., Tokushima, Japan, 2002—03; dir. Cambridge Isotope Labs. Inc., Andover, Mass., 2003—. Vis. lectr. Tohoku U., Sendai, Miyagi, Japan, 2000. Editor: SAR News, 2001—, Letters in Drug Design and Discovery, 2004—. Com. mem. Structure-Activity Relationship Soc. Japan, Tokyo, 2001—; chief sec. MSI Japan User Group, Urayasu, Japan, 1999—2001; com. mem. EMIL project, Osaka, Japan, 1994—2002; co-organizer Third Australia-Japan Joint Symposium Drug Design, Naruto, Japan, 1998. Mem.: Pharm. Soc. Japan (organizer bioinformatics symposium 1999, Lecture award 1998). Avocation: travel. Office: Cambridge Isotope Laboratories Inc 50 Frontage Rd Andover MA 01810-5413 Personal E-mail: yasukisakurogi@yahoo.com. Business E-Mail: kurogi@isotope.com.

KURPAKUS WHEATER, MICHELLE, cell biologist, educator; b. Arcadia, Calif., June 8, 1959; d. Paul and Magdalene Kurpakus; m. Bryan David Wheater, Mar. 16, 1999; 1 child, Ryan David Wheater. BS, Ind. Univ. Pa., 1982; PhD, Iowa State U., 1988. Post doctoral fellow Northwestern U. Med. Sch., Chgo., 1987—91; assoc. prof. Sch Medicine Wayne State U., Detroit, 1991—2004; assoc. prof. Mercy Sch. Dentistry U. Detroit, 2004—. Dir. grad. recruitment Sch. Medicine Wayne State U., Detroit, 2000—04. Recipient Med. tchg. awards, Wayne State U. Sch. Medicine, Dental tchg. award, U. Detroit Mercy Sch. Dentistry; grantee, Nat. Eye Inst./NIH. Mem.: Am. Dental Edn. Assn., Assn. Rsch. in Vision and Ophthalmology, Am. Soc. Cell Biology. Avocations: travel, animal rescue. Office: Univ Detroit Mercy Sch Dentistry 8200 W Outer Dr Detroit MI 48219 Office Phone: 313-494-6634. Office Fax: 313-494-6643. E-mail: wheatemi@udmercy.edu.

KURSUN, VOLKAN, engineering educator, researcher; b. Ankara, Turkey, June 5, 1974; s. Rifat Kursun and Nazen Aksoy. PhD, U. Rochester, N.Y., 1999—2004. Rschr. U. Rochester, NY, 1999—2004; prof. U. Wis., Madison, 2004—. Contbr. articles to profl. jours. Mem.: IEEE. Achievements include patents for monolithic power supplies, low voltage DC-DC converters, sleep switch dual threshold voltage domino logic, domino logic with variable threshold voltage keeper. Office Phone: 608-698-1565.

KURT, JOHNNY THOMAS, music educator; s. Thomas James Kurt and Sandra Sue Abel-Kurt. MusB, U. Nebr., Omaha, 1991; Med in Ednl. Adminstrn., U. Nebr., Lincoln, 1995; Endorsement in Gifted/Talented Edn., U. Iowa, 2002. Cert. tchr., adminstr. Iowa, Nebr., jazz edn. Internat. Assn. Jazz Educators, jazz pedogogy tchr. Baker U. and Internat. Assn. Jazz Educators, 2004. Grad. tchg. asst. Baylor U., Waco, Tex., 1991; substitute tchr. Omaha Pub. Sch. Dist., 1992—95; instrumental music instr. Lewis Ctrl. Pub. Sch. Dist., Council Bluffs, Iowa, 1995—. Instr. in gifted/talented summer programs Creighton U., Omaha, 2001—. Contbr. articles to profl. publs., procs. in field. (Publ., 1991). Vol. Nebr. Humane Soc., Omaha, 1998. Nominee Disney Tchr. award, 2000, All Tchr. Team, USA Today, 2001; named one of Outstanding Young Ams., 1992, 1996, 1997, 1998; Belin-Blank Gifted/Talented Educator fellowship, U. Iowa, 2000, 2001. Mem.: NEA, Iowa Bandmasters Assn. (mem. R&D state bd. 1997—99), Iowa H.S. Music Assn. (adjudicator 1998—), Omicron Delta Kappa, Phi Delta Kappa. Office: Lewis Ctrl Sch Dist 1600 East South Omaha Bridge Rd Council Bluffs IA 51503 Business E-Mail: jkurt@lewiscentral.k12.ia.us.

KURTH, LIESELOTTE, foreign language educator; b. Wuppertal, Germany; came to U.S., 1951; s. Otto and Emmi (Klammer) Voigt. MA, Johns Hopkins U., 1960, PhD, 1963. Asst. prof. German Johns Hopkins U., Balt., 1964-68, assoc. prof., 1968-73, prof., 1973-89, chmn. dept., 1980-87, prof. emerita, 1989—. Author: Die Zweite Wirklichkeit, 1969, Perspectives and Points of View, 1974, Continued Existence, Reincarnation, and the Power of Sympathy in Classical Weimar, 1999; contbr. articles top profl. jours. and yearbooks; editor collections and edits. Gilman fellow, 1958-62; Gail fellow, 1962-63 Mem. MLA (mem. exec. com. South Atlantic br. 1982-84, pres. br. 1985-86), Lessing Soc., Goethe Soc. of N.Am., Phi Beta Kappa. Home: 800 Southerly Rd Apt 914 Towson MD 21286-8409 Office: Johns Hopkins U Dept German 34th and Charles Sts Baltimore MD 21218 Personal E-mail: lkurth@verizon.net.

KURTH, RONALD JAMES, retired academic administrator, retired military officer; b. Madison, Wis., July 1, 1931; s. Peter James and Celia (Kuehn) K.; m. Esther Charlene Schaefer, Dec. 21, 1954; children: Steven, Audrey, John, Douglas. BS, U.S. Naval Acad., 1954; MPA, Harvard U., 1961, PhD, 1970. Commd. ensign U.S. Navy, 1954, advanced through grades to rear adm., 1981; U.S. naval attache Moscow, 1975-77; comdg. officer NAS, Memphis at Millington, Tenn., 1977-79; mil. fellow Council Fgn. Relations, N.Y.C., 1979-80; exec. asst. to dep. chief naval ops. Dept. Navy, Washington, 1980-81, dir. Pol-Mil Policy and Current Plans, 1981-83, dir. Long Range Planning Group, 1983-84; U.S. def. attache Moscow, 1985-87; pres. U.S. Naval War Coll., Newport, R.I., 1987-90, Murray (Ky.) State U., 1990-94; dean acad. affairs Air War Coll., Maxwell AFB, Ala., 1994-98; pres. St. John's Northwestern Mil. Acad., Delafield, Wis., 1998—2004, pres. emeritus, 2004—. Teaching fellow Harvard U., Cambridge, Mass., 1969-70. Author: The Politics of Technological Innovation in the Navy, 1970. Mem. nat. adv. bd. Boy Scouts Am. Decorated Def. D.S.M., Navy D.S.M., Legion of Merit with 2 gold stars, Meritorious Svc. medal with gold star. Mem. U.S. Naval Inst. (life), Naval War Coll. Found. (life), U.S. Naval Acad. Alumni, Harvard U. Alumni, Rotary. Episcopalian. Home: 8106 Ainsworth Ave Springfield VA 22152 Personal E-mail: randckurth@aol.com. *Among those who know you, ponder whose respect you have and whose you do not. It will provide you with a measure of your worth.*

KURTH, SUZANNE M., criminalist; d. William A. Glaser and Wilma Smith; m. James L. Kurth, Sept. 19, 1998. BA, U. Hawaii, 1981; MA, U. Denver, 1983, PhD, 2001. Cert. law enforcement thermographer Law Enforcement Thermographers Assn., 2002, advanced POST (Peace Officers' Standards and Training) cert. Colo., 1988, cert. field tng. officer Kaminsky and Assocs., 2001, Peace Officer Colo., 1984, level I accident investigator Rocky Mountain Inst. for Transp. Safety, 2001. Police officer Arvada (Colo.) Police Dept., 1984—2004, criminalist Crime Lab., 2004—. Sec. U.S. Police Canine Assn., Region 14, Colo., 1990—95, Fraternal Order Police-Lodge 29, Arvada, 1992—97; adj. prof. dept. sociology/criminology U. Denver, 1998—2004. Named Police Officer of Yr., Arvada Masonic Lodge, 2004; recipient Certification of Appreciation, Colo. Assn. of Robbery Investigators, 1999, Cert. of Appreciation, Parker, CO Police Dept., 2004, Police Chief's Citation, Arvada, CO Police Dept., 2004, Police Chief's Commendation, Arvada Police Dept., 1992; Beth Haynes Meml. scholar, Colo. Women in Criminal Justice, 2000. Mem.: Assn. Crime Scene Reconstruction, Internat. Assn. Women Police, Internat. Assn. for Identification (Rocky Mountain divsn.), Am. Sociol. Assn., Rocky Mountain Assn. Bloodstain Pattern Analysts (assoc.), Internat. Assn. Bloodstain Pattern Analysts (assoc.), Fraternal Order of Police - Lodge 29. Avocations: skiing, dog training, running, reading, weightlifting. Office: Arvada Police Dept - Crime Lab 8101 Ralston Rd Arvada CO 80002 Office Phone: 720-898-6714. Business E-Mail: skurth@ci.arvada.co.us.

KURTYKA, BRENDA CHIMILESKI, middle school educator; b. Passaic, N.J., Mar. 13, 1948; d. Benjamin and Louella (Rankin) C.; m. Martin John Kurtyka, Dec. 23, 1978; 1 child, Karen Marie. BA, Montclair State Coll., 1970; MA, NYU, 1975. Cert. tchr. phys. edn. and health. Tchr. phys. edn. health, dance Woodrow Wilson Jr. High Sch., Clifton, N.J., 1970-75, Clifton Sr. High Sch., 1975-87, Clifton Elem. Schs., 1989-92; tchr. phys. edn., health, dance Woodrow Wilson Mid. Sch., Clifton, 1992—. Recipient N.J. Gov.'s Arts Edn. award, 1986. Mem. NEA, AAPERD (ea. dist., v.p. N.J. chpt. 1985-86, Dance Merit award 1987, rep. dance Coun. Svcs. 1985-87, Dance award 1985), N.J. Edn. Assn., Passaic County Educators Assn., Clifton Tchrs. Assn. (Educator of Yr. 1985-86). Home: 78 Seminole Ave Wayne NJ 07470-4437 Office: Clifton Bd Edn 745 Clifton Ave Clifton NJ 07013-1838

KURTZ, ALFRED BERNARD, radiologist; b. Albany, NY, May 1, 1944; s. Leonard David and Esther (Lederman) K.; m. Barbara Ellen, July 3, 1973; children: Dana, Liza, Amy. BA, NYU, 1966; MD, Stanford U., 1972. Diplomate Am. Bd. Radiology. Internal medicine intern Montefiore Hosp. and Med. Ctr., Bronx, N.Y., 1972-73, resident in internal medicine, 1973-74, resident in diagnostic radiology, 1974-77; from fellow in ultrasound and body CT to prof. Jefferson Med. Coll. Thomas Jefferson Univ. Hosp., Phila., 1977—85; prof. ob-gyn. Jefferson Med. Coll. Thomas Jefferson U. Hosp., Phila., 1985—, vice chmn. dept. radiology Jefferson Med. Coll., 1989—2002, dir. med. student edn. Dept. Radiology, 2004—. Examiner oral bds. in ultrasound category Am. Bd. Radiology, 1985—; med. advisor Blue Shield of Pa., Phila., 1983—; mem. adv. com. Ctr. of Excellence in Biomed. Imaging, Phila., 1987—. Author: Ultrasound: The Requisites, 1995, 2d edit., 2003, Obstetrical Measurements in Ultrasound: A Reference Manual, 1988; editor: Atlas of Ultrasound Measurements, 1990; assoc. editor Radiology; contbr. articles to profl. jours. Grantee Nat. Cancer Inst., NIH, 1993-96. Fellow Am. Inst. Ultrasound in Medicine (bd. govs. 1990-92, sec. 1993-97, pres.-elect 1999-2001, pres. 2001-03, immediate past pres., 2003-05), Am. Coll. Radiology (chmn. com. on edn. and tng. of commn. 1987-93, commn. on ultrasound 1987-93), Soc. Radiologists in Ultrasound (pres. 1991-93), Coll. Physicians Phila. Achievements include rsch. in ultrasound to establish an accurate fetal age; ultrasound patterns for analysis of diffuse liver disease; ultrasound in evaluation of obstetrical and gynecologic problems including intravaginal scanning and cross sectional imaging evaluation for ovarian cancer. Home: 1050 Indian Creek Rd Wynnewood PA 19096-3407 Office: Thomas Jefferson U Hosp 111 S 11th St Philadelphia PA 19107-5084 Office Phone: 215-955-6343.

KURTZ, ALICE KAUFMAN, elementary school educator; b. NYC, Oct. 31, 1946; d. Samuel and Miriam (Newman) Kaufman; m. Sheldon Francis Kurtz, June 22, 1968; children: Andrea, Emily. BA in Liberal Arts, BA in Edn., Syracuse U., 1968; MA, U. Iowa, 1987. Cert. tchr., Iowa. Tchr. Midland Park (N.J.) Pub. Schs., 1968-70; tchr. gifted-talented Iowa City Community Schs., 1984—; instr. adult edn. Kirkwood Community Coll., 1974-77. Instr. Coll. Edn. U. Iowa, 1995—96; reviewer Multimedia Sch. Mag. Author: Learning at Lunch in the Gifted Child Today, 1988, Lou Henry Hoover, Independent Girl: A Curriculum Guide, 1993; contbr. articles to profl. jours. Sec. bd. dirs. Friends Hist. Preservation. Recipient Recognition award, Connie Belin Ctr. for Gifted Edn., 1993, 1999, 2002, 2003, Irving B. Weber award, Johnson County Hist. Soc., 1996. Mem.: Phi Lambda Theta (sec.). Avocations: swimming, reading, piano. Home: 6 Glendale Ter Iowa City IA 52245-3222 Office: Iowa City Community Schs 509 S Dubuque St Iowa City IA 52240-4228 Personal E-mail: alikur@aol.com. Business E-Mail: kurtz.alice@iccsd.k12.la.us.

KURTZ, ANTHONY DAVID, physicist; b. N.Y.C., May 3, 1929; s. Jacob Kurtz and Claire Juscow; m. Nora Morcos, May 27, 1985; 1 child, Sandria; m. Margery Geilich, Apr. 3, 1955 (div. May 1985); children: Jennifer Kurtz Unger, John. BS in Physics, MIT, 1951, MS in Physics, 1952, ScD in Phys. Metallurgy, 1955. Staff mem. semiconductor physics Lincoln Lab., 1952—55; project mgr. diffused device rsch. Clevite Transistor Products, 1955—56; dir. semiconductor applied rsch. Mpls.-Honeywell Regulatory Co., 1956—59; dir. R&D, sr. scientist, CEO Kulite Semiconductor Products, Inc., Leonia, NJ, 1959—. Adj. prof. dept. mech. engring. Columbia U., N.Y.C., 2002—. Contbr. articles to profl. jours. Named to N.J. Inventors Congress and Hall of Fame, State N.J., 1991; recipient I R 100 for miniature semiconductor pressure transducer, Indsl. Rsch. Inc., 1968, Si Fluor Tech. award, Instrument Soc. Am., 1978. Achievements include patents in field; invention of MEMS technology. Home: 136 E Saddle River Rd Saddle River NJ 07458 Office: Kulite Semiconductor Products Inc 1 Willow Tree Rd Leonia NJ 07605 Office Phone: 201-461-0900. E-mail: drkurtz@kulite.com.

KURTZ, CHARLES JEWETT, III, lawyer; b. Columbus, Ohio, May 13, 1940; s. Charles Jewett, Jr. and Elizabeth Virginia (Gill) K.; m. Linda Rhoads, Mar. 18, 1983. BA, Williams Coll., 1962; JD, Ohio State U., 1965. Bar: Ohio 1965, D.C. 1967, U.S. Dist. Ct. (so. dist.) Ohio 1967, U.S. Dist. Ct. (no. dist.) Ohio 1976, U.S. Ct. Appeals (6th cir.) 1992. Law clk. to justice Ohio State Supreme Ct., Columbus, 1965-67; assoc. Porter, Wright, Morris & Arthur, Columbus, 1967-71, ptnr., 1972—, mng. ptnr. litigation dept., 1988-91, mem. directing ptnrs. com., 1988-89. Mem. faculty Ohio Legal Ctr. Inst. Trustee Ballet Met., Columbus, 1990-94; mem. vestry St. Albans Episcopal Ch., 1986-89. Mem. ABA, Am. Arbitration Assn. (mem. panel comml. arbitrators), Columbus Bar Assn. (common pleas ct. com.), Columbus Bar Found.,

Columbus Def. Assn. (pres. 1976), Athletic Club, Columbus Country Club, Capital Club. Office: Porter Wright Morris & Arthur 41 S High St Ste 2900 Columbus OH 43215-6194 E-mail: Ckurtz@porterwright.com.

KURTZ, EUGENE ALLEN, composer, educator, consultant; b. Atlanta, Dec. 27, 1923; s. Wilbur George and Annie Laurie (Fuller) K. BA in Mus., U. Rochester, 1947; MA in Mus., Eastman Sch. Mus., 1949; studied with Arthur Honegger and Darius Milhaud, Ecole Normale de Musique, Paris, 1949-51; studied with Max Deutsch, Paris, 1953-57. Guest prof. composition U. Mich., Ann Arbor, 1967-68, 70-71, 73-74, 80-81, 88, Eastman Sch. Mus., Rochester, N.Y., 1975, U. Ill., Urbana, 1976, U. Tex., Austin, 1977-78, 85-86, Hartt Sch. Mus., Hartford, Conn., 1989; cons. Editions Jobert, Paris, 1972—; lectr. in field. Compositions include The Solitary Walker, 1964, Conversations for 12 Players, 1966, Ca...Diagramme Pour Orchestre, 1972, The Last Contrabass in Las Vegas, 1974, Mècanique, 1975, Logo, 1979, Five-Sixteen for piano, 1982, World Enough and Time, 1982, String Trio, Time and Again, 1984-85, From Time to Time for violin and piano, 1986-87, The Broken World for string quartet, 1993-94, Shadows on the Wind for 17 players, 1995-96, Icare for solo flute, 1997, also film scores and incidental music for radio, theatre and TV; commd. by U. Mich., 1958, Am. Cultural Ctr., Paris, 1966, Ministère de la Culture Français, 1972, 82, U. Nev., 1974, Radio France, 1975, 79, 85, Musical Arts Assn., Cleve., 1976. Sgt. inf. U.S. Army, 1942-46, ETO. NEA grantee, 1982-83; recipient Am. Acad. Inst. Arts and Letters award, 1992, French Acad. des Beaux-Arts award, 1997. Mem. Société des Auteurs, Compositeurs et Editeurs de Musique. Office: 6 Rue Boulitte 75014 Paris France

KURTZ, HAROLD PAUL, foundation executive; b. Milw., May 21, 1936; s. Henry John and Minnie Christina (Olson) K.; m. Grace Jahn, June 16, 1963; children: Steven, David. BA, Wartburg Coll., 1958; MS, U. Wis., 1961. Journalist Post-Crescent, Appleton, Wis., 1961-63; dir. pub. rels. Luth. Gen. Hosp., Park Ridge, Ill., 1963-73, Med. Coll. Wis., Milw., 1973-77; v.p. Children's Hosp., St. Paul, 1977-90; dir. devel. U. Minn., 1990-95; exec. dir. Lyngblomsten Found., 1995—2002; pres. Wright-Berglund Found., 2002—. Author: Public Relations for Hospitals, 1969; Public Relations and Fund Raising for Hospitals, 1981; (with M. Burrows) Effective Use of Volunteers, 1971; editor: Toward a Creative Chaplaincy, 1973, Fly the Banner High, 1991, Hardly a Silent Night, 2004. Bd. dirs. Bd. Edn., Dist. 621, Mounds View, 1985-95; bd. dirs. Spl. Intermediate Sch. Dist. 916, 1986-95; bd. dirs. Wright-Berglund Found., 1980—. Recipient Community Svc. citation Wartburg Coll., 1970; named Boss of Yr., Internat. Assn. Bus. Comms. Mem. Chgo. Hosp. Pub. Rels. Soc. (pres. 1971-72), Wartburg Coll. Alumni Assn. (bd. dirs. 1962-66). Lutheran. Home: 1465 17th Ave NW Saint Paul MN 55112-5524

KURTZ, HARVEY A., lawyer; BA, U. Wis., 1972; JD, U. Chgo., 1975. Bar: Wis. 1975, U.S. Dist. Ct. (ea. dist.) Wis. 1980. Ptnr. Foley & Lardner LLP, Milw., 1989—. Mem. ABA, State Bar of Wis. Assn., Milw. Bar Assn. (chmn. employee benefits sect. 1993-94), Greater Milw. Employee Benefit Coun., Wis. Retirement Plan Profls. (pres. 1987-88), Internat. Pension and Employee Benefits Lawyers Assn., Kiwanis, Phi Beta Kappa. Home: 3927 N Stowell Ave Milwaukee WI 53211-2461 Office: Foley & Lardner LLP Ste 3800 777 E Wisc Ave Milwaukee WI 53202-5306 Office Phone: 414-297-5819. E-mail: hkurtz@foley.com.

KURTZ, JEROME, lawyer, educator; b. Phila., May 19, 1931; s. Morris and Renee (Cooper) K.; m. Elaine Kahn, July 28, 1956; children: Madeleine, Nettie Kurtz Greenstein. BS with honors, Temple U., 1952; LLB magna cum laude, Harvard U., 1955. Bar: Pa. 1956, N.Y. 1981, D.C. 1982; CPA, Pa. Assoc. Wolf, Block, Schorr & Solis-Cohen, Phila., 1955-56, 57-63, ptnr., 1963-66, 68-77; tax legis. counsel Dept. Treasury, Washington, 1966-68; commr. IRS, 1977-80; ptnr. Paul, Weiss, Rifkind, Wharton & Garrison, 1980-90; prof. law NYU, 1991-2001, dir. grad. tax program, 1995-98. Instr. Villanova Law Sch., 1964-65, U. Pa., 1969-74; vis. prof. law Harvard U., 1975-76; mem. adv. group to commr. IRS, 1976. Editor: Harvard Law Rev. 1953-55; contbr. numerous articles to profl. jours. Pres. Ctr. Inter-Am. Tax Adminstrn., 1980; bd. dirs. Common Cause, 1984-90, chmn. fin. com., 1985-88; bd. dirs. Nat. Capitol Area ACLU, 1990-91; mem. adv. bd. NYU Tax Inst., 1988-97, Little, Brown Tax Practice Series, 1994-96. Recipient Exceptional Service award Dept. Treasury, 1968, Alexander Hamilton award, 1980 Mem. ABA (chmn. tax shelter com. 1982-84), N.Y. Bar Assn. (exec. com. tax sect. 1981-82), Pa. Bar Assn., Phila. Bar Assn. (chmn. tax sect. 1975-76), Assn. of the Bar of the City of N.Y. (chmn. tax coun. 1993-95), Am. Law Inst. (cons. fed. inc. tax project taxation of pass through entities), Am. Coll. Tax Counsel, Beta Gamma Sigma. Home: 17 E 16th St New York NY 10003-3116 E-mail: jeromekurtz2@aol.com.

KURTZ, JOEL, construction company executive; b. Paterson, N.J., June 13, 1940; Student, Paul Smith Coll., 1961-63. Lumbering contractor JK Forest Products, N.Y, Pa., 1965-67; v.p., owner Martin Hermann Lumber Co., Callicoon, N.Y., 1968-75; pres., owner Transea Rsch. & Devel., Callicoon, 1976—. Inventor, patentee split keel system for sailboats. Served in U.S. Army, 1963-65. Mem. Soc. Naval Architects & Marine Engrs., Cocheton Men's Club. Republican. Avocations: art, science, travel, sailing. Home: 24 Hortonville-main St Callicoon NY 12723-5616 Office Phone: 914-887-4489.

KURTZ, MATTHEW, psychologist, researcher; s. Seymour I. and Ruth M. Kurtz. BA, Reed Coll., 1989; PhD, Princeton U., 1995. Cert. clin. neuropsychology CUNY. Postdoctoral fellow U. Pa., 2000; asst. clin. prof. psychiatry Yale Sch. Medicine, New Haven, 2000—; neuropsychologist schizophrenia rehab. program Inst. Living, Hartford, Conn., 2004—05, rsch. scientist Olin Neuropsychiatry Ctr., 2005—. Contbr. articles to profl. jours. NRSA Postdoctoral fellow, NIMH, 1993, B/START grantee, 2001, Young Investigator grantee, NARSAD, 2002, Mentored Clin. Scientist Devel. grantee, NIMH, 2005. Avocations: reading, jazz, travel. Office: Inst Living 200 Retreat Ave Hartford CT 06106 Office Phone: 860-545-7304. Business E-Mail: mkurtz@harthosp.org.

KURTZ, MELVIN H., lawyer, cosmetics executive; b. N.Y.C., Mar. 31, 1936; s. Philip and Sadie (Brandt) K.; m. Sandra Koss, Dec. 21, 1958; children: Lisa Dawn, Glenn Michael, Jill Meredith. B in Chem. Engring., CCNY, 1959; JD, Fordham U., N.Y.C., 1963. Bar: N.Y. 1963, U.S. Patent and Trademark Office 1965, U.S. Ct. Appeals (3d cir.) 1967, U.S. Supreme Ct. 1967, U.S. Dist. Ct. (so. dist.) N.Y. 1976, U.S. Ct. Appeals (Fed. cir.) 1982. Assoc. Eyre, Mann & Lucas, N.Y.C., 1959-68; asst. gen. counsel Lever Bros. Co., N.Y.C., 1968-82; patent and trademark counsel Chesebrough-Pond's Inc., Greenwich, Conn., 1982-87, gen. counsel, v.p., sec., 1987—, also bd. dirs. Mem. trademark affairs pub. adv. com. Patent and Trademark Office. Bd. dirs. Stamford (Conn.) Symphony Orch., Greenwich YMCA. Mem. ABA, Internat. Patent and Trademark Assn., N.Y. State Bar Assn., N.Y. Patent Law Assn. Home: 93 Walworth Ave Scarsdale NY 10583-1140 Office: 33 Benedict Pl Greenwich CT 06830-5339 E-mail: mel.kurtz@unilever.com.

KURTZ, MICHAEL JULIAN, astronomer, computer scientist; b. Glen Ridge, N.J., Oct. 20, 1947; s. Warren Bachup and Katherine M. Kurtz; m. Gabriele Maria Germann, Jan. 5, 1979 (div. Sept. 14, 1994); children: Wilhelm Julian, Johannes Michael, Rita Gabriele; m. Ruth Elizabeth Scheiber, June 20, 1998. BA, San Francisco State U., 1977; PhD, Dartmouth Coll., Hanover, N.H., 1977—82. Astronomer Smithsonian Astrophys. Obs., Cambridge, Mass., 1982—, computer scientist, 1984—; lectr. Harvard U., Cambridge, 1983—84. Dir. Wolbach Image Processing Lab., Cambridge, 1984—92. Recipient Citation Rsch. award, Am. Soc. Info. Sci. and Tech., 2000. Mem.: Internat. Astron. Union, Am. Astron. Soc. (George Van Biesbroeck Award 2001). Achievements include design of NASA Astrophysics Data System. Office: Harvard-Smithsonian Ctr for Astrophys 60 Garden St Cambridge MA 02138 Office Phone: 617-495-7434. E-mail: kurtz@cfa.harvard.edu.

KURTZ, MYERS RICHARD, hospital administrator; b. Schaefferstown, Pa., June 18, 1924; m. Linda Bewan, Dec. 26, 1988; 1 child, Ronald Hayden; 1 stepchild, Erin B. Brown. BS, U. Md., 1958; MBA, Ind. U., 1963. Served as enlisted man U.S. Army, 1942-51, commd. 2d lt., 1951; advanced through grades to lt. col. Med. Svc. Corps, 1965; mem. staff Army Surgeon Gen., Washington, 1963-67; ret., 1967; affiliation adminstr. NYU Med. Ctr., N.Y.C., 1967-69; exec. dir. Ephrata Community Hosp., Pa., 1969-76; supt. Longview State Hosp., Cin., 1976-79; asst. dir. Ohio Dept. Mental Health and Mental Retardation, Columbus, 1979-81, dir., 1981-82; sr. v.p. Cleve. Met. Gen. Hosp., 1982-83; supt., CEO Ctrl. State Hosp., Milledgeville, Ga., 1983-93; adminstr., CEO G. Pierce Wood Meml. Hosp., Arcadia, Fla., 1995-98. Adj. asst. prof. dept. psychiatry U. Cin., 1977-83. V.p., bd. dirs. Coordinated Home Care Agy., Inc., Lancaster County; pres. Lancaster County Hosp. Coun.; bd. dirs. Pa. Hosp. Assn., Baldwin County United Way, 1986-91, Baldwin County Salvation Army; mem. adv. bd. Youth Devel. Ctr., 1984-91. Decorated Legion of Merit, Army Commendation medal with oak leaf cluster, Soldiers medal. Fellow Royal Soc. Health; mem. Am. Coll. Hosp. Adminstrs. (life diplomate), Am. Acad. Med. Adminstrs., Am. Hosp. Assn., Milledgeville-Baldwin County C. of C. (bd. dirs. 1984-87, exec. com. 1986—, treas. 1987—), Nassau County Vol. Ctr. (bd. dirs., 1998-, pres. 2002-2003), Sigma Iota Epsilon, Rotary Internat. Home: 95485 Captains Way Fernandina Beach FL 32034-4346 E-mail: LmKurtz@bellsouth.net.

KURTZ, PAUL, philosopher, educator, writer, publisher; b. Newark, Dec. 21, 1925; s. Martin and Sara (Lasser) K.; m. Claudine C. Vial, Oct. 6, 1960; children: Valerie L., Patricia A., Jonathan, Anne BA, NYU, 1948; MA, Columbia U., 1949, PhD, 1952. Instr. Queens Coll., 1950—52; instr. philosophy Trinity Coll., Hartford, Conn., 1952—55, asst. prof., 1955—58, assoc. prof., 1958—59, Vassar Coll., Poughkeepsie, NY, 1960—61; vis. prof. New Sch. Social Rsch., N.Y.C., 1960—65; assoc. prof. Union Coll., Schenectady, 1961—64, prof., 1964—65; vis. prof. U. Besancon, France, 1965; prof. philosophy SUNY, Buffalo, 1965—91, prof. emeritus, 1992—. Moderator TV series Author (with Rollo Handy): A Current Appraisal of the Behavioral Sciences, 1964; author: Decision and the Condition of Man, 1965, The Fullness of Life, 1974, Exuberance, 1977, In Defense of Secular Humanism, 1983, A Skeptics Handbook of Parapsychology, 1985, The Transcendental Temptation, 1986, Forbidden Fruit, 1988, Eupraxophy, 1989, Philosphical Essays in Pragmatic Naturalism, 1990, The New Skepticism, 1992, Toward a New Enlightenment, 1994, The Courage to Become, 1997, Humanist Manifesto 2000, 1999, Embracing the Power of Humanism, 2000, Skepticism and Humanism: The New Paradigm, 2001, Affirmations, 2004; editor: American Thought Before 1900, 1966, American Philosophy in the Twentieth Century, 1966, Sidney Hook and the Contemporary World, 1968, Moral Problems in Contemporary Society, 1969; co-editor: International Directory of Philosophy and Philosophers, 4th edit., 1978—81, Tolerance and Revolution, 1970, Language and Human Nature, 1971, A Catholic/Humanist Dialogue, 1972, The Humanist Alternative, 1973, Idea of a Modern University, 1974, The Philosophy of the Curriculum, 1975, The Ethics of Teaching and Scientific Research, 1977, University and State, 1978, Sidney Hook: Philosopher of Democracy and Humanism, 1983, Building a World Community, 1989, Challenges to the Enlightenment, 1994, Skeptical Odysseys, 2001; author, co-editor Science and Religion, 2003; editor: The Humanist, 1967—78; mem. editl. bd. The Humanist, 1964—78, Philosophers Index, 1969—85, Question, 1969—81, The Skeptical Inquirer, 1976—, pres. Prometheus Books, 1970—, editor-in-chief Free Inquiry Mag., 1980—, pub. The Sci. Rev. of Alternative Medicine, 1998—; pub.: Sci. Rev. Mental Health Practice, 2002—. Chmn. Coun. for Secular Humanism, 1980—, Coun. on Internat. Studies and World Affairs, 1966-69, Ctr. for Inquiry, 1995—; trustee Behavioral Rsch. Coun., Great Barrington, Mass.; bd. dirs. U.S. Bibliography of Philosophy, 1958-70, Univ. Ctrs. for Rational Alternatives, 1969-96, Internat. Humanist and Ethical Union, 1968-2000, co-chmn., 1986-94; chmn. Com. for Sci. Investigation Claims of Paranormal, 1976—. With AUS, 1944-46 Behavioral Rsch. Coun. fellow, 1962-63, French Govt. fellow, 1965, John Dewey fellow, 1986-87; recipient Bertrand Russell Soc. award, 1988, Internat. Humanist award, 1999, Chancellor Charles Norton award, 2001 Fellow: AAAS; mem.: U.K. Rationalists Press Assn. (v.p. 1990—), Acad. Humanism (Laureate, pres. 1983—). Office: Prometheus Books Inc 59 John Glenn Dr Amherst NY 14228-2197 Personal E-mail: paulkurtz@aol.com. *Two passions have dominated my intellectual and professional life: (1) a commitment to critical intelligence-I am skeptical of the false beliefs and mythologies that have motivated other men and women; and (2) a belief in the importance of human courage, particularly in defending reason in society and in attempting to reconstruct ethical values so that they are more democratic and humane.*

KURTZ, PAUL MICHAEL, law educator; b. Bronx, NY, Sept. 22, 1946; s. Louis and Helen (Mechanic) K. m. Carol Porter, June 6, 1971; 1 child, Benjamin. BA, Vanderbilt U., 1968, JD, 1972; LLM, Harvard U., 1974. Bar: Tenn. 1972, U.S. Ct. Appeals (6th cir.) 1973, U.S. Ct. Appeals (5th cir.) 1977, U.S. Supreme Ct. 1978. Law clk. to chief judge U.S. Ct. Appeals (6th cir.), 1972-73; instr. Boston U. Law Sch., 1973-74, Boston Coll. Law Sch., 1974-75; asst. prof. law U. Ga., Athens, 1975-78, assoc. prof., 1978-83, prof., 1983-94, assoc. dean, 1991—, J. Alton Hosch prof., 1994—. Vis. prof. U. Mo. Law Sch., 1982, Mercer Law Sch., 1984, U. Tex., 1986, Vanderbilt U., 1987; commr. on Uniform State Laws, 2001—; reporter Nat. Conf. Commrs. on Uniform State Laws, Com. on Interstate Child Support Enforcement, Com. on Status of Children of Aided Conception; reporter Ga. Supreme Ct. Com. on Indigent Def. Reform, 2000-03; mem. Ga. Pub. Defender Stds. Coun., 2003—; mem. Ga. Pub. Defender Standards Coun., 2003—. Author: Criminal Offenses in Georgia, 1980, Family Law: Cases, Text, Problems, 1986, 4th edit., 2004; contbr. articles to profl. jours.; mem. editl. bd. Family Law Quar., 1983—. Mem. Am. Assn. Law Schs. (chmn. sect. family and juvenile law), ACLU, Am. Humane Assn. (bd. dirs. 1998-2004), Common Cause, Soc. Am. Law Tchrs., Am. Law Inst. (reporter 1995-96), Supreme Ct. Hist. Soc., Order of Coif, B'nai B'rith (Ga. state sec., pres. Athens lodge). Democrat. Avocations: reading, travel, bowling, politics. Home: 362 W Cloverhurst Ave Athens GA 30606-4212 Office: U Ga Law Sch Athens GA 30602 E-mail: pmkurtz@uga.edu.

KURTZ, SHELDON FRANCIS, lawyer, educator; b. Syracuse, N.Y., May 18, 1943; s. Abraham Kurtz and Rosalyn (Bronstein) Stern; m. Alice Kaufman, June 22, 1968; children: Andrea, Emily. AB, Syracuse U., 1964, JD, 1967. Bar: N.Y. 1967, Iowa 1973. Assoc. Nixon, Mudge, Guthrie, Alexander & Mitchell, N.Y.C., 1967-69, Cleary, Gottlieb, Steen & Hamilton, N.Y.C., 1970-73; prof. U. Iowa Coll. Law, Iowa City, 1973-89, U. Va. Sch. Law, Charlottesville, 1979-80; dean Coll. Law, Fla. State U., Tallahassee, 1989-91; prof. Coll. Law U. Iowa, Iowa City, 1991—, prof. Coll. Med. Author: Kurtz on Iowa Estates, 3 vols., 1981, 2d edit., 2 vols., 1989, Problems, Cases and Materials on Family Estate Planning, 1983, (with Hood and Shors) Estate Planning for Shareholders of a Closely Held Corporation, 2 vols. and supplement, 1986, (with Hovenkamp) American Property Law, 1987, 3d edit., 1999, (with McGovern) Wills, Trusts and Estates, 3d edit., 2004, (with Hovenkamp) The Law of Property, 2001 (with Moynihan) Introduction to the Law of Real Property, 3d edit., 2002; also articles. Recipient Burlington No. tchg. award U. Iowa, 1987, Michael J. Brody Disting. Svc. award, 2001. Mem. Iowa Bar Assn. (commr. Uniform State Laws), Am. Law Inst. Avocations: cooking, hiking. Office: U Iowa Coll Law Rm 446 Iowa City IA 52242 Office Phone: 319-335-9069. Business E-Mail: sheldon-kurtz@uiowa.edu.

KURTZ, SWOOSIE, actress; b. Omaha, Sept. 6, 1944; d. Frank and Margo (Rogers) K. Student, Acad. Music and Dramatic Art, London, U. So. Calif. Appeared on TV series As the World Turns, 1956, Mary, 1978, Love, Sidney, 1981-83 (nominated Best Actress in Comedy Series 1982-83), Sisters, 1991-96 (Emmy nominee Lead Actress in Drama 1993, 94, SAG award nominee 1995), Suddenly Susan, 1996, 97, Touched by an Angel, 1997, ER, 1998, Love and Money. 1999; (TV films) Ah, Wilderness!, 1976, Walking Through the Fire, 1979, Uncommon Women and Others, 1979, Marriage is Alive and Well, 1980, The Mating Season, 1980, Fifth of July, 1982, A Caribbean Mystery, 1983, Guilty Conscience, 1985, A Time to Live, 1985, The House of Blue Leaves, 1987, Baja Oklahoma, 1988 (Golden Globe nominee 1987), Terror on Track 9, 1992, The Image (Emmy nominee, Ace award nominee), 1990, The Positively True Adventures of the Alleged Texas Cheerleader-Murdering Mom, 1993, And the Band Played On, 1993 (Emmy award nominee 1994, Ace award nominee), One Christmas, 1994, Betrayed: A Story of Three Women, 1995, A Promise to Carolyn, 1996, Little Girls in Pretty Boxes, 1997, More Tales of the City, 1998, My Own Country, 1998, Harvey, 1999, The Wilde Girls, 2001; TV guest appearances on Kojak, Carol and Co. (Emmy award); (films) Slap Shot, 1977, The World According to Garp, 1982, Against All Odds, 1984, Wild Cats, 1986, True Stories, 1986, Vice Versa, 1988, Bright Lights, Big City, 1988, Dangerous Liaisons, 1988, Stanley and Iris, 1989, A Shock to the System, 1990, Reality Bites, 1994, Citizen Ruth, 1996, Liar, Liar, 1997, Outside Ozona, 1999, Cruel Intentions, 1999, The White River Kid, 2000, Sleep Easy, Hutch Rimes, 2000, Get Over It, 2001, Bubble Boy, 2001, The Rules of Attraction, 2002, Duplex, 2003; (theater) Ah Wilderness!, 1975, Children, 1976, Tartuffe, 1977 (Tony award nominee), A History of the American Film, 1978 (Drama Desk award), Uncommon Women and Others, 1978 (Obie award, Drama Desk award), Who's Afraid of Virginia Woolf, 1980, Summer, 1980, Fifth of July, 1980-82 (Tony award, Drama Desk award, Outer Critics Circle award), Michael Bennett's Scandal, 1985, Beach House, 1986, The House of Blue Leaves, 1986-87 (Tony award, Obie award), Hunting Cockroaches, 1987 (Drama Logue award nominee), Love Letters, 1989-90, Six Degrees of Separation, 1990, Lips Together, Teeth Apart, 1991, The Mineola Twins, 1999 (Obie award, Drama Desk award nominee, Outer Critics Circle nominee), The Vagina Monologues, 2000, Imaginary Friends, 2002-03, Frozen, 2004 (Tony award nominee, Best Actress in a Play).

KURTZ, THOMAS EUGENE, retired mathematics professor; b. Oak Park, Ill., Feb. 22, 1928; s. Oscar Christ and Helen (Bell) K.; m. Patricia Anne Barr, June 13, 1953 (div. Aug. 1973); children— Daniel Barr, Timothy David, Beth Louise; m. Agnes Seelye Bixler, June 10, 1974. BA, Knox Coll., Galesburg, Ill., 1950; PhD, Princeton, 1956; DSc, Knox Coll., 1985. Mem. faculty Dartmouth U., 1956-93, prof. math. and computer sci., 1966-93, chmn. Program in Computer and Info. Sci., 1984—88, dir. Kiewit Computation Ctr., 1959-75; dir. Office Acad. Computing, 1975-78; ret., 1993. Author: Basic Statistics, 1963, (with J.G. Kemeny) Basic Programming, 1967, 2d edit., 1971, 3d edit., 1980, (with J.G. Kemeny) Structured Basic Programming, 1987. Trustee, chmn. coun. EDUCOM, 1974-78; chmn., bd. dirs. NERComp, Inc., 1970-78; trustee, vice chmn. Dartmouth Time Sharing Sys., Inc., 1972-78; chmn. X3J2 sub. com. Am. Nat. Standards Inst., 1974-84, convenor WG8 Internat. Standards Orgn. Basic Com., 1987-94; bd. dirs., vice chmn. True Basic, Inc., 1983-2003; mem. panel uses of computers in edn. Pres.'s Sci. Adv. Com., 1965-66. Democrat. Mem. United Ch. Christ. Achievements include co-designing BASIC computer lang. and Dartmouth time sharing system. Home: 3 Lakeview Dr Hanover NH 03755-3407

KURTZ, THOMAS GORDON, mathematics professor; b. Kansas City, Mo., July 14, 1941; s. Paul Stanton and Ruth Corine (Kreikenbaum) K.; m. Carolyn Sue Neville, Aug. 24, 1963; children: Marcia Ann, Kevin Michael. BA, U. Mo., 1963; MS, Stanford U., 1965, PhD, 1967. Vis. lectr. U. Wis., Madison, 1967-69, from asst. prof. to assoc. prof., 1969-75, prof. math., 1975—, prof. stats., 1985—, Paul Levy prof., 1996—, chmn. dept., 1985-88, dir. Ctr. Math. Scis., 1990-96. Vis. prof. U. Strasbourg, France, 1977-78. Author: Approximation of Population Processes, 1981, Markov Processes: Characterization and Convergence, 1986; contbr. numerous articles to profl. jours. Mem. supervisory bd. Dane County, Madison, 1974-75; chmn. parking utility com. City of Madison, 1976-77. Romnes fellow U. Wis., 1976; NSF research grantee, 1968—. Fellow Inst. Math. Stats.; mem. Am. Math. Soc., Soc. Indsl. and Applied Math., Bernouli Soc., Ops. Research Soc. Am., Internat. Statis.Inst. Democrat. Presbyterian. Avocations: singing, canoeing. Home: 117 N Oak Grove Dr Madison WI 53717-1196 Office: U Wis Dept of Math 480 Lincoln Dr Madison WI 53706-1325

KURTZBERG, JOANNE, pediatrics educator; b. N.Y.C., Nov. 18, 1950; d. Lawrence Kurtzberg; m. Henry S. Friedman; children: Joshua, Sara. BA, Sarah Lawrence Coll., 1972; MD, N.Y. Med. Coll., 1976. Intern in pediats. Dartmouth Med. Ctr., Hanover, NH, 1976—77; resident in pediats. Upstate Med. Ctr., Syracuse, NY, 1977—79, clin. rsch. fellow in pediat. hematology/oncology, 1979—80; mem. faculty Duke Comprehensive Cancer Ctr., Durham, NC, 1983—; sr. rsch. fellow in pediat. hematology/oncology Duke U. Med. Ctr., Durham, NC, 1980—86, asst. prof., assoc. prof. pediat., 1983—88, prof. pediat., 1993—, dir. pediatric bone marrow lab., 1989—, dir. pediat. blood and marrow transplant program, 1989—2004, mem. grad. faculty Grad. Sch. pathology dept., 1993—, assoc. prof. pathology, 1991—2003, prof. pathology, 2003—, dir. Carolinas cord blood bank, 1996—, chief divsn. pediatric blood and marrow transplant, 2004—. Recipient R. Wayne Rundles award for excellence in cancer rsch., 1993, Basil O'Connor Starter Scholar Rsch. award, 1985-87. Fellow Leukemia Soc. Am. (spl. fellow, scholar 1986-89); mem. Internat. Soc. for Hematotherapy and Graft Engring., Am. Soc. for Blood & Marros & Transplantation, Am. Soc. Pediat. Hematology/Oncology, Am. Soc. Hematology, Soc. for Pediat. Rsch., Pediat. Oncology Group, Alpha Omega Alpha. Home: 1808 Faison Rd Durham NC 27705-2439 Office: Duke U Med Ctr PO Box 3350 Durham NC 27702-3350 Office Phone: 919-668-1119.

KURTZER, DANIEL C., former ambassador; b. Elizabeth, NJ; m. Sheila Kurtzer; 3 children. BA, Yeshiva U., 1971; MA, MA, Columbia, PhD, 1976. Dean Yeshiva Coll., Yeshiva U., N.Y.C., until 1979; joined Fgn. Svc., US Dept. State, Washington, 1976, from 1979, with Bur. Internat. Orgn. Affairs, from 1976; 2d sec. for polit. affairs Am. Embassy, Cairo, 1979-82, 1st sec. for polit. affairs Tel Aviv, 1982-86; dep. dir. for Egyptian affairs US Dept. State, 1986—87, speechwriter, mem. sec.'s policy planning staff, 1987—89, dep. asst. sec. for Nr. Ea. Affairs, 1989-94, prin. dep. asst. sec. for intelligence and rsch. Washington, 1994-97, acting asst. sec., 1997, U.S. amb. to Egypt, Cairo, 1997—2001, U.S. amb. to Israel Tel Aviv, 2001—05.*

KURTZKE, JOHN FRANCIS, SR., neurologist, epidemiologist; b. Bklyn., Sept. 14, 1926; s. John Ambrose and Teresa Rose (Knipper) K.; m. Margaret Mary Nevin, June 30, 1950; children: John Francis Jr., Catherine Kurtzke Brown, Elizabeth Kurtzke Siebert, Joan Kurtzke Brennan, Robert, James, Christine Kurtzke Hughes. BS summa cum laude, St. John's U., 1948; MD, Cornell U., 1952; MD (hon.), U. Ferrara, Italy, 2000. Diplomate in neurology Am. Bd. Psychiatry and Neurology (asst. examiner, then examiner and sr. examiner in neurology 1964-96, cert. appreciation 1969, 90). Intern Kings County Hosp., Bklyn., 1952-53; resident in neurology VA Hosp., Bronx, N.Y., 1953-56, chief neurology svc. Coatesville, Pa., 1956—63, Washington, 1963—95; chief neuroepidemiology sect. VA Med. Ctr., Washington, 1995—2002, cons. in neurology, 1995—, cons. in neuroepidemiology, 2002—. Mem. faculty Jefferson Med. Coll., Phila., 1958-63, asst. prof. clin. neurology, 1963; mem. faculty Georgetown Med. Sch., Washington, 1963—, prof. neurology, 1968-2000, prof. emeritus, 2000—, vice chmn. dept. neurology, 1976-95, prof. cmty. and family medicine, 1968-95; Disting. prof. neurology uniformed svcs. U. Health Scis., Bethesda, 1992—, USN med. student liaison officer, 1979-85; vis. prof. neurology and neuroepidemiology Temple U. Sch. Medicine, 1984-89; cons. neurology Nat. Naval Med. Ctr., Bethesda, 1966-2000, Surgeon Gen. Navy, 1970-97; mem. med. adv. bd. Nat. Multiple Sclerosis Soc., 1966-94, hon. mem., 1995—, mem. working group on design of clin. studies in multiple sclerosis, 1976-84, mem. exec. com., 1981-83; med. adv. bd. Internat. Fedn. Multiple Sclerosis Socs., 1972—, hon. mem., 1998—; mem. com. multiple sclerosis World Fedn. Neurology, 1967—, com. neuroepidemiology, 1977—; chmn. epidemiology sect. NIH Epilepsy Adv. Com., 1973-76; med. rsch. program specialist for neurology and neurobiology VA Rsch. Svc., 1977-80; chmn. work group epidemiology HEW Comm. Control of Huntington's Disease, 1976-78; mem. naval exam. bd. Naval Med. Command, 1980-83; mem. Residency Rev. Com. Neurology, 1983-88, vice chmn., 1985-86, chmn., 1987-88; chmn. U.S. Naval Res. Med. Flag Coun., 1985-86; mem. instnl. rev. bd. Nat. Inst. Neurol. Diseases and Stroke, 1989-98; established investigator Nat. Multiple Sclerosis Soc., 1987—; mem. spl. panel Inst. Medicine, 1990; mem. Am. Com. Treatment and Rsch. in Multiple Sclerosis, L.Am. Com. on Treatment and Rsch. in Multiple Sclerosis, Consortium of Multiple Sclerosis Ctrs. Author, co-author: Epidemiology of Multiple Sclerosis, 1968, Epidemiology of Cerebrovascular Disease, 1969, Epidemiology of Neurologic and Sense Organ Disorders, 1973, Neuroepidemiology, 1998, Psychiatry/Neurology, 1998, Practice Questions. Book One, 1998, Psychiatry Neurology, 1998, Book Two, 1998, Encyclopedia of the Neurological Disorders (Neuroepidemiology), 2003; mem. editl. bd. Neuroepidemiology, 1980—, Neurology, 1984-92, Stroke, 1986-2000, Jour. Clin. Epidemiology, 1988-2005, Jour. Neurol. Sci., 1990-96, Acta Neurologica Scandinavica, 1990-97; contbr. over 480 articles to profl. jours., chpts. to books. Served with USN, 1944-46; rear adm. M.C., USNR, 1946-86, ret. 1986. Decorated Legion of Merit (2), Navy Commendation medal, Armed Forces Res. medal with gold hourglass, others; recipient cert. of merit, Surgeon Gen. Navy, 1969, Gold Bicennial medal, Georgetown U., 1982, Sec.'s Disting. Career award, Dept. Vets. Affairs, 1998, Charcot award, Internat. Fedn. MS Socs., 1999, Lifetime Achievement award, Consortium of MS Ctr., 2003, others. Fellow: ACP, AAAS (life), Pan Am. Med. Assn. (coun. neurology sect.), Am. Coll. Preventive Medicine, Am. Coll. Epidemiology, Am. Acad. Neurology (chmn. sect. on neuro-epidemiology 1971—75, chmn. com. nat. needs in neurology 1981—85, subcom. nat. needs in neurology 1985—86, mem. work force task force 1997, John Jay Dystel prize for mulitple sclerosis rsch. 1997), N.Y. Acad. Sci., Am. Heart Assn. (stroke coun. 1991—2000); mem.: AMA, AAUP, Consortium Multiple Sclerosis Ctrs. (Lifetime Achievement award 2003), Lat. Am. Com. Treatment and Rsch. in Multiple Sclerosis, Am. Com. Treatment and Rsch. in Multiple Sclerosis, Soc. Med. Cons. to Armed Forces (com. on res. affairs 1980—83, com. on manpower 1984—98), Sr. Stroke Soc., Res. Officers Assn. (life), Naval Inst. (life), Fleet Res. Assn. (life), Naval Officers Assn. Am. (life), Am. Neurol. Assn. (hon.; chmn. bylaws ad hoc com. 1990—91), Danish Neurol. Soc. (hon.), French Soc. Neurology (hon.; fgn.), Assn. Nicoló Copernico (hon.), German Soc. Neurology (hon.), Assn. Mil. Surgeons (life), Naval Res. Assn. (life), Naval Order U.S. (life), Internat. Stroke Soc., Am. Soc. Microbiology, Am. Epilepsy Soc., Assn. Rsch. in Nervous and Metal Disease, Internat. Epidemiol. Assn., Am. Epidemiol. Soc., So. Med. Assn., Navy League (life). Home: 7509 Salem Rd Falls Church VA 22043-3240 Office: 7509 Salem Rd Falls Church VA 22043-3240 Office Phone: 703-560-6016, 703-560-6490. Business E-Mail: kurtzke2@aol.com. *To be a physician demands recognition of the intrinsic value and dignity of human life while pursuing the goal of relieving pain and impairment due to disease or injury.*

KURTZMAN, CLETUS PAUL, microbiologist, researcher; b. Mansfield, Ohio, July 19, 1938; s. Paul A. and Marjorie M. (Gartner) K.; m. Mary Ann Dombrink, Aug. 4, 1962; children: Mary, Mark, Michael. BS, Ohio U., 1960; MS, Purdue U., 1962; PhD, W.Va. U., 1967. Microbiologist Nat. Ctr. Agrl. Utilization Rsch./USDA, Peoria, Ill., 1967-85, rsch. leader, 1985—. U.S. rep. Internat. Commn. on Yeasts, 1980—, World Fedn. Culture Collections, 1988—2000. Editor: Yeasts in Biotechnology, 1988, The Yeasts, A Taxonomic Study, 4th edit., 1998; contbr. papers to sci. jours. 1st lt. U.S. Army, 1962-64. Named Midwest Area Outstanding Scientist USDA, 1986; recipient Medal of Merit award Ohio U., 1992. Fellow AAAS, Am. Acad. Microbiology; mem. Internat. Mycol. Assn. (sec.-gen. 1990-94, v.p. 1994-2002), Mycol. Soc. Am., Am. Soc. Microbiology (divsn. chair 1991-92, J. Roger Porter award 1990), U.S. Fedn. Culture Collections (pres. 1976-78), Soc. Gen. Microbiology. Achievements include patent for xylose fermentation in yeasts; research in the correlation of DNA relatedness and fertility in yeasts, correlation of ribosomal RNA divergence. Office: Nat Ctr Agrl Utilization Rsch 1815 N University St Peoria IL 61604-3902 Business E-Mail: kurtzman@ncaur.usda.gov.

KURTZMAN, JOEL ALLAN, economist; b. LA, June 25, 1947; s. Samuel Michael and Roselle (Rosencranz) K.; m. Susan Leslie Kurtzman, Dec. 28, 1969; 1 child, Eli. AB, U. Calif., Berkeley, 1969; MS, U. Houston, 1976. Cons. United Nations, various locations worldwide, 1970; economist UN, NYC, 1978; editor devel. bus. World Bank, NYC, 1984; former exec. editor Harvard Business Review; former bus. columnist NY Times; founding editor-in-chief Strategy and Business mag.; former global lead ptnr., thought leadership and innovation PricewaterhouseCoopers; chmn. Kurtzman Group LLC, Concord, Mass., 1995—; also sr. fellow, pub., Milken Inst. Rev. Milken Inst., Santa Monica, Calif. Bd. dirs. Medtec Internat., Beverly Hills, Calif., Orbit Prodns., Washington, Soc. for Trial Peoples, Bombay. Author: Crown of Flowers, 1970 (Eisner Prize 1970), Sweet Bobby, 1976, No More Dying, 1976, Futurecasting, 1980, Decline and Crash of the American Economy, 1988, The Death of Money, 1993, Thought Leaders, 1997, How the Markets Really Work, 2002, Startups That Work, 2005; Co-author: Radical E: From GE to Enron Lessons on How to Rule the Web, 2001, MBA in a Box, 2004, co-editor New International Economic Order Library, 1978-82, editor: Thought Leaders, 1997; editl. bd Sloan Mgmt. Rev, MIT; lectr. in field. Grantee Moody Found., 1976, Govt. Italy, 1980, Govt. the Netherlands, 1982. Avocation: jogging. Office: Milken Inst Rev 1250 Fourth St Santa Monica CA 90401 also: Kurtzman Group LLC 94 Lowell Rd Concord MA 01742-5513 Office Phone: 310-570-4600, 978-369-6661. Office Fax: 310-570-4601. Business E-Mail: joel.kurtzman@kurtzmangroup.com.*

KURTZMAN, NEIL A., medical educator; b. Bklyn., June 18, 1936; s. Louis S. and Roselie (Yegla) K.; m. Sandra Sabatini, Feb. 14, 1976; children from previous marriage: Jonathan, Laura. BA with honors, Williams Coll., 1957; MD, N.Y. Med. Coll., 1961. Intern Robert Packer Hosp., Sayre, Pa., 1961-62; resident Ohio State U. Hosp., Columbus, 1962-63; asst. chief med. services Nobel Army Hosp., Ft. McClellan, Ala., 1963-64; med. resident William Beaumont Gen. Hosp., El Paso, Tex., 1964-65, chief med. resident, 1965-66; fellow in nephrology U. Tex. Southwestern Med. Sch., Dallas, 1966-68; chief renal div. Brooke Army Med. Ctr., Ft. Sam Houston, Tex., 1969-72; prof., chief nephrology sect. U. Ill. Coll. Medicine, Chgo., 1972-84; from prof. to Grover E. Murray prof. Health Scis. Ctr. Tex. Tech U., Lubbock, Tex., 1985—2004, Grover E. Murray prof. Health Scis. Ctr., 2004—. Mem. gen. medicine B study sect. Nat. Inst. Arthritis, Metabolic and Digestive Diseases, Bethesda, Md., 1978-83; mem. merit rev. bd. VA, Washington, 1979-82, chmn., 1981-82; mem. sci. adv. bd. Nat. Kidney Found., N.Y.C., 1981-92, chmn., 1988-90, v.p., 1990-92, pres., 1992-94; prin. investigator regulation urinary acidification NIH, Bethesda, 1978—. Author: Handbook of Urinalysis and Urinary Sediment, 1974, Pathophysiology of the Kidney, 1977, Doing Nothing, 2000; also more than 300 sci. papers, more than 600 sci. presentations; editor-in-chief Seminars in Nephrology, 1981—, Am. Jour. Kidney Diseases, 1997-2002; assoc. editor Am. Jour. Nephrology; mem. editorial bd. 7 sci. jours.; referee 16 sci. jours. Faculty advisor Alpha Omega Alpha, U. Ill., 1977-84, Tex. Tech U. Health Sci. Ctr., 1985-2002. lt. col. U.S. Army, 1963-72. Decorated U.S. Army Meritorious Svc. award; recipient Pres.'s award Nat. Kidney Found., 1990, Outstanding Acad. Achievement award N.Y. Med. Coll., 1993, So. Soc. for Clin. Investigation's Founder's award, 1996, Tex. chpt. Am. Coll. Physicians Laureate award, 1996, David M. Hume award Nat. Kidney Found., 1999, Headliner award, 2003, medal IV Giovanni Alfonso Borelli Conf., 2004 Fellow AAAS; mem. Am. Physiol. Soc., Am. Soc. Clin. Investigation, Assn. Am. Physicians, Ctrl. Soc. Clin. Research, So. Soc. Clin. Investigation, Alpha Omega Alpha. Office: Dept Int Med TTUHSC 3601 4th St Lubbock TX 79430-0001 Business E-Mail: neil.kurtzman@ttuhsc.edu.

KURTZMAN, RALPH HAROLD, JR., biochemist, researcher, consultant; b. Mpls., Feb. 21, 1933; s. Ralph Harold, Sr. and Susie Marie (Elwell) K.; m. Nancy Virginia (Leussler), Aug. 27, 1955; children: Steven Paul, Sue. BS, U. Minn., 1955; MS, U. Wis., 1958, PhD, 1959. Asst. prof. U. R.I., Kingston, 1959—62, U. Minn., Morris, 1962—65; biochemist U.S. Dept. Agriculture, Albany, Calif., 1965—97; ret., 1997. Instr. U. Calif., Berkeley, 1981-82; cons. Bliss Valley Farms, Twin Falls, Idaho, 1983-84, Kodik Farm, Lida, Belarus, 2003, Small Farms, Manazales, Colombia, 2004, VostokAgrabaza, Ust Kamenogorsk, Kazakstan 2004, Gusev Farm, Melenki, Russia 2005, Irzem Co. Batyrevo, 2005; pres. Santa Clara Valley Tex. Instrument PC Users' Group, 1991-92, editor, 1993-97; cons. and spkr. in field. Author Oyster Mushroom Cultivation, 2004; editor Internat. Jour. Mushroom Sci., 1995-2000; co-editor Micologia Aplicada Internat., 2001—; editor, pub. Solliday/Sallade Family of Bucks County, Pa., 1999; mem. editl. bd. Pakistan Jour. Phytopathology, 2001—; inventor mushroom substrate (compost) preparation, decaffeination of beverages; contbr. articles to profl. jours. Chmn. Berkeley YMCA Camp Program Com., 1971-72; official Amateur Athletic Union (swimming), San Francisco, 1973-80; treas. Calif. Native Plant Soc., 1970; docent Oakland Mus. Calif., 2001—. Mem. Am. Mushroom Inst., Mycological Soc. Am. (organizer symposium mushroom cultivation in Am. tropics 1998), Mycological Soc. Japan, Sigma Xi. Avocations: computers, woodworking, photography, clock making. Home and Office: 445 Vassar Ave Berkeley CA 94708-1215 Personal E-mail: kurtzmanr@earthlink.net.

KURY, BERNARD EDWARD, lawyer; b. Sunbury, Pa., Sept. 11, 1938; AB, Princeton U., 1960; LLB, U. Pa., 1963. Bar: NY 1964. Assoc. Dewey, Ballantine, Bushby, Palmer & Wood, NYC, 1963-71, ptnr., 1971—2004; v.p., gen. counsel Guidant Corp., Indpls., 2004—. Contbg. editor Ency. of Venture Capital. Mem.: NY State Bar Assn., Assn. of the Bar of the City of NY, ABA. Office: Guidant Corp 111 Monument Cir 29th Fl Indianapolis IN 46204

KURZ, DAVID BRYAN, web site designer; s. Thomas Willard Kurz and Verna Carolyn Bryan; m. Helen Jean Gawthrop; m. Cheryl Lee Decker (div.); 1 child, Rosalee. BS in Botany, Ohio U., 1983, MS in Botany, 1990; MSLS, Case Western Res. U., 1984. Dir. Herbert Wescoat Meml. Libr., McArthur, Ohio, 1988—93, Wash. County Pub. Libr., Marietta, Ohio, 1993—95; sr. web developer Ohio U., Athens, Ohio, 1996—. Cons. Nat. Cancer Inst., Bethesda, Md., 1992—93. Prodr.(creator): (multimedia web site) Wired for Books, wiredforbooks.org (Streamers WebSage Award - Real Networks -San Francisco, 1999), (radio show) Talking about Science, A Christmas Carol (Hon. Mention - Arts - Ohio Pub. Radio, 2002). Co-founder, incorporator Athens Food Coop, Athens, Ohio, 1975—90; pres. Friends of the Athens Pub. Libr., Athens, Ohio, 1995—98, Friends of Ohio U. Libr., Athens, Ohio, 2001—02. Mem.: Am. Soc. for Info. Sci. and Tech. Avocations: bicycling, boating, gardening. Office: Ohio U Telecommunications Ctr Athens OH 45701 Office Phone: 740-593-4789. E-mail: kurz@ohio.edu.

KURZ, MARY ELIZABETH, lawyer; b. Scranton, Pa., May 13, 1944; m. William H. Bright III. Student, U. Paris, Sorbonne, summer 1965; BA in French magna cum laude, Marywood Coll., 1966; postgrad., U. Md., 1966-67, U. N.C., 1967, U. Wis., 1969; JD with honors, U. Md., 1971. Bar: Md. 1972, D.C. 1978, Mont. 1982, Mich. 1988, Tex. 1994, N.C. 1996, U.S. Dist. Ct. (we. dist.) Mich., U.S. Supreme Ct., U.S. Ct. Appeals (4th, 6th, D.C. cirs.), U.S. Dist. Ct. Mont. Law clk. to presiding justice Ct. Spl. Appeals Md., 1971-72; asst. atty. gen. criminal div. State of Md., 1972-74, asst. legis. officer to gov., 1974-75, asst. atty. gen. representing U. Md. College Park, 1975-82; legal counsel U. Mont., Missoula, 1982-87; gen. counsel, v.p. legal affairs Mich. State U., East Lansing, 1987-94; vice chancellor and gen. counsel Tex. A&M U. System, 1994-96; vice chancellor, gen. coun. N.C. State U., Raleigh, 1996—. Speaker numerous confs. and profl. meetings; mem. Commn. to Study Sovereign Immunity, 1975. Mem. staff Md. Law Rev. Reginald Heber Smith fellow, 1969. Mem. ABA, Nat. Assn. Coll. and Univ. Attys. (mem. numerous coms., chmn. com. site selection 1985-86, chmn. com. continuing legal edn. 1986-89, bd. dirs. 1985-88, 2d v.p. 1989-90, 1st v.p. 1990-91, pres.-elect 1991-92, pres. 1992-93) Home: 102 King George Loop Cary NC 27511-6334 Office: NC State U 3rd Fl Holladay Hall Raleigh NC 27695

KURZ, MITCHELL HOWARD, marketing communications executive; b. N.Y.C., Nov. 5, 1951; s. Robert Sydney and Lorraine Ruth (Wolosky) K.; m. Sandy Mitchell, Aug. 25, 1979; children: Zachary, Maxwell. BA, Dartmouth Coll., 1973; MBA, Harvard U., 1975. Acct. exec. Young & Rubicam, N.Y.C., 1976-77, v.p., account supr., 1978-80, sr. v.p., 1980-87, corp. sr. v.p., 1987-90; chmn. N.Am. Wunderman Worldwide, N.Y.C., 1990-91; pres., CEO worldwide Wunderman Cato Johnson, N.Y.C., 1992-97; pres., COO Young & Rubicam Advt., N.Y.C., 1997-98, chair client svcs., 1998-99; chmn., CEO Kurz and Friends, Westport, Conn., 1998—. Bd. dirs. Young and Rubicam. Trustee Rheedlen Ctrs. for Children and Families, Town Sch., 1994—; bd. dirs. New Visions for Pub. Schs., 1994—, Teach for Am., 1996. Rufus Choate Scholar, Dartmouth Coll., 1971, 72, 73. Mem. Am. Mgmt. Assn., Pequot Runners, Phi Beta Kappa. Avocation: marathon running. Home: 95 Old Rd Westport CT 06880-4145 Office: Kurz and Friends 191 Post Rd W Westport CT 06880-4625

KURZ, MORDECAI, economics professor; b. Natanya, Israel, Nov. 29, 1934; came to U.S., 1957, naturalized, 1973; s. Moshe and Sarah (Kraus) K.; m. Lillian Rivlin, Aug. 4, 1963 (div. Mar. 1967); m 2d Linda Alice Cahn, Dec. 2, 1979. BA in Econs. and Polit. Sci., Hebrew U., Jerusalem, 1957; MA in Econs., Yale U., 1958, PhD in Econs., 1962; MS in Stats., Stanford U., 1960. Asst. prof. econs. Stanford U., 1962-63, assoc. prof., 1966-68, prof., 1969—, Joan Kenney prof. econs., 1997—, dir. econs. sect. Inst. for Math. Studies, 1971-89; sr. lectr. in econs. Hebrew U., 1963-66. Cons. econs. SRI Internat., Menlo Park, Calif., 1963-78; spl. econ. advisor Can. health and Welfare Ministry, Ottawa, Ont., 1976-78; spl. econ. advisor Pres.'s Commn. on Pension, Washington, 1979-81; rsch. assoc. Nat. Bur. Econ. Rsch., 1979-82; Lady Davis vis. prof. Hebrew U., Jerusalem, 1993; prin. investigator Smith Richardson Found., 2001—; mem. adv. bd. Annals of Fin., 2004—. Author: (with Kenneth J. Arrow) Public Investment, The Rate of Return and Optimal Fiscal Policy,1970, Endogenous Economic Fluctuations: Studies in the Theory of Rational Beliefs, 1997; co-editor Econ. Theory, 1997—. Bd. dirs. Ben-Gurion U. of the Negev, Israel, 1998—. Ford Found. faculty fellow Stanford U., 1973; Guggenheim Found. fellow Stanford U., Harvard U., Jerusalem, 1977-78; Inst. Advanced Studies fellow Hebrew U., Mt. Scopus, Jerusalem, 1979-80; prin. investigator NSF, 1969-93, Smith-Richardson Found., 2001—. Fellow Econometric Soc. (assoc. editor Jour. Econ. Theory 1976-90); mem. Am. Econ. Assn. Democrat. Jewish. Office: Stanford U Econs Dept Serra St at Galvez Stanford CA 94305-6702 Office Phone: 650-723-2220. Business E-Mail: mordecai@stanford.edu.

KURZ, RAYMOND A., lawyer; b. Aug. 6, 1957; BA magna cum laude, SUNY Albany, 1978; JD, George Washington U. Law Ctr., 1981. Bar: D.C. 1981, U.S. Dist. Ct., D.C. 1982, U.S. Ct. Appeals D.C. Cir. 1985, U.S. Ct. Appeals Fed. Cir. 1986, U.S. Supreme Ct. 1989. Ptnr. Hogan & Hartson LLP, Washington, dir. intellectual property practice group. Co-chmn. & lectr. Internet & Law Conf., Washington, 1998; editor & prin. author Internet & Law: Legal Fundaments Internet User, 1996. Contbr. articles to profl. jour. Mem.: Intellectual Property Owners Assn., Am. Intellectual Property Law Assn., Internat. Trademark Assn., ABA (Intellectual Property Law Sect.), D.C. Bar (Patent, Trademark & Copyright Law Sect.). Office: Hogan & Hartson LLP Columbia Sq 555 Thirteenth St NW Washington DC 20004-1109 Office Phone: 202-637-5683. Office Fax: 202-637-5910. Business E-Mail: rakurz@hhlaw.com.

KURZ, WILLIAM CHARLES FREDERICK, lawyer; b. Baton Rouge, Aug. 26, 1942; s. William Charles Frederick Jr. and Helen Mae (Lafrantz) K. AB, Harvard U., 1964, LLB, 1967. Bar: N.Y. 1968, U.S. Dist. Ct. (so. dist.) N.Y. 1972, U.S. Supreme Ct. 1971. Assoc. Winthrop, Stimson, Putnam & Roberts, NYC, 1968-74, ptnr., 1975—2001; (Winthrop, Stimson, Putnam & Roberts merged with Pillsbury Madison & Sutro, 2001); ptnr., fin. & vice chair professional responsibility com. Pillsbury Winthrop LLP, NYC, 2001—05; (Pillsbury Winthrop LLP merged with Shaw Pittman LLP, 2005); ptnr., fin. Pillsbury Winthrop Shaw Pittman LLP, NYC, 2005—. Lectr. Sch. Law Columbia U., N.Y.C., 1987-92. Editorial advisor Internat. Fin. Law Rev., London, 1982—; contbr. articles to profl. jours. Mem. ABA, Assn. of Bar of City of N.Y., Down Town Assn., Harvard Club. Avocation: opera. Office: Pillsbury Winthrop Shaw Pittman LLP 1540 Broadway New York NY 10036 Office Phone: 212-858-1242. Office Fax: 212-858-1500. Business E-Mail: william.kurz@pillsburylaw.com.

KURZER, MARTIN JOEL, lawyer, consultant; b. May 6, 1938; s. Louis and Clare (Steinberg) K.; m. Karen Sue Zinn, Sept. 17, 1945; children: Sandra Lois, Jody Renee (dec.). BBA, U. Wis., Milw., 1960; JD cum laude, Marquette U., 1968; LLM in Taxation, U. Miami, 1971. Bar: Wis. 1968, Fla. 1968; CPA, Wis.; cert. master practitioner neuro linguistic programming. Assoc. Blackwell, Walker, Fascell & Hoehl, Miami, Fla., 1968-72, jr. ptnr., 1973-77, gen. ptnr., 1978-90; of counsel Matzner, Ziskind, Hermelee & Jaffe, 1990-91; pvt. practice, 1991—; litigation comm. cons., 1996—. Dir. legal svcs. Miami Heart Rsch. Inst., 1992-96; adj. pof. law, grad. tax dept. U. Mami, 1976-80; lectr. seminars and orgns. Author monthly column Health Notes, 1986; contbr. articles to profl. jours. Sales com. Elizabeth Arden Golf Classic Am. Cancer Soc., Miami, 1984-86. Capt. USAR, 1960-69. Mem. Greater Miami Tax Inst. (sec. 1979, treas. 1980, 1st v.p. 1981, pres. 1982), Am. Assn. Atty.-CPAs (dir. 1978—, treas. 1981-82, sec. 1982-83, v.p. 1983-84, 1st v.p. 1984-85, pres.-elect 1986-87, pres. 1987-88), Am. Soc. Trial Cons., Fla. Assn. Atty.-CPAs (dir. 1975—, v.p. 1975-81, exec. v.p. 1981-87, 92—), South Fla. Employee Benefits Coun. (sec. 1979-80), Fla. Bar Assn. (chmn. com. on rels. with Fla. Inst. CPAs 1981-82, health law com., chmn. travel programs com. 1986), State Bar Wis., The Fla. Bar, Miami Club, Miami Shores Country Club (adminstrn. bd. 1976), Westview Country Club. Jewish. Avocations: golf, travel, collecting 1950's music. Home and Office: 1951 NE 191st Dr Miami FL 33179-4353

KURZER, MINDY SUSAN, adult education educator; b. N.Y.C., Sept. 18, 1951; d. Herbert and Leonore Gottlieb K. BA, SUNY, Buffalo, 1974; MS, U. Calif., Berkeley, 1979, PhD, 1984. Asst. prof. U. Minn., St. Paul, 1989-95, assoc. prof., 1995—. Recipient Future Leader award Inst. Life Scis.-Nutrition Found., Washington, 1992-93. Avocations: canoeing, backpacking, reading. Office: U Minn 1334 Eckles Ave Saint Paul MN 55108-1038 Fax: 612-625-5272.

KURZWEG, ULRICH HERMANN, engineering science educator; b. Jena, Germany, Sept. 16, 1936; came to U.S., 1947, naturalized, 1952; s. Hermann Herbert and Erna Herta (Michaelis) K.; m. Sophia Speth, Dec. 21, 1963; 1 dau., Tina. BS, U. Md., 1958; MA (Woodrow Wilson fellow 1958-59), Princeton U., 1959, PhD in Physics, 1961. Sr. theoretical physicist United Tech. Rsch. Labs., East Hartford, Conn., 1962-68; adj. assoc. prof. math. Hartford (Conn.) Grad. Ctr., Rensselaer Poly. Inst., 1964-68; mem. faculty U. Fla., Gainesville, 1968—, prof. mech. and aerospace engring., 1968—2004, prof. emeritus, 2004—. Contbr. numerous articles to sci. and tech. publs. Fulbright grantee, 1961-62; recipient Cert. of Recognition, NASA, 1984, award for excellence in undergrad. teaching U. Fla., 1991. Mem. AAAS, Sigma Xi. Home: 3742 SW 86th St Gainesville FL 32608-7900 Office: U Fla Dept Mech and Aerospace Engring Gainesville FL 32607 E-mail: uhk@mae.ufl.edu.

KURZWEIL, EDITH, sociology educator, editor; b. Vienna; d. Ernest W. and Wilhelmine M. (Fischer) Weiss; m. Charles H. Schmidt, June 24, 1945 (div. 1958); children: Ronald J., Vivien A.; m. Aug. 2, 1958 (widowed 1966); 1 child, Allen J. BA, Queens Coll., CUNY, 1967; MA, New Sch. Social Rsch., 1969, PhD, 1973. Asst. prof. sociology Hunter Coll., N.Y.C., 1972-75, Montclair State Coll., Upper Monclair, NJ, 1973-78; assoc. prof. sociology Rutgers U., Newark, 1979-85, prof. sociology, chmn., 1985-92; Disting. Olin. Prof. Adelphi U., 1993, univ. prof., 1994—2001, univ. prof. emeritus, 2001—. Vis. prof. Goethe U., 1984. Author: The Age of Structuralism, 1980, Italian Entrepreneurs, 1983, The Freudians: A Comparative Perspective, 1989, Freudians and Feminists, 1995, Briefe aus Wien: Nazi Laws & Jewish Lives, 1999, English Lang. edit., 2005, The Partisan Century: 60 Years of Partisan Review, 1996, (with others) Literature and Psychoanalysis, 1983, Writers and Politics, 1983, Cultural Analysis, 1984; exec. editor Partisan Rev., Boston, 1978-94, editor, 1994-2003; mem. editl. bd. Psyche, 1990—, Psychoanalytic Books, 1990-2000; series editor Psychiatry and Psychology Transaction, 1995—. Bd. govs. New Sch. Univ., 1999—; adv. bd. N.Y. Civil Rights Coalition, 2001—. Recipient Nat. Humanities medal, 2003; Rockefeller Humanities fellow, 1982-83, NEH fellow, 1987-88; NEH grantee, 1989-90, 91-92; NYCH grantee, 1995. Mem. Am. Sociol. Assn., Tocqueville Soc., Internat. Assn. History of Psychoanalysis, Internat. Sociol. Assn., Women's Freedom Network (bd. dirs. 1994—), PEN. Home: 1 Lincoln Plz New York NY 10023-7129 Personal E-mail: ekurzweil@rcn.com.

KURZWEIL, HARVEY, lawyer; b. Bklyn., Mar. 23, 1945; s. Martin E. Kurzweil and Muriel (Krause) Kanow; m. Barbara Kramer, Aug. 17, 1969; children: David, Paul (dec.), Emily, Elizabeth. AB, Columbia Coll., 1966, JD, 1969. Bar: N.Y. 1970, D.C. 1977, U.S. Dist. Ct. (ea. & so. dist. N.Y.), U.S. Ct. Appeals (2d, 3d, 5th, 7th, 8th, 9th, Fed. & D.C. cir.). Assoc. Dewey, Ballantine, Bushby, Palmer & Wood, N.Y.C., 1969-77, ptnr., 1977-90, Dewey Ballantine LLP, N.Y.C., 1990—, co-chmn. litig. dept. Mem. mgmt. com. Dewey Ballantine LLP, 1990—. Contbr. chapters to books. Bd. dirs. Volunteer Lawyers for the Arts 1994-1999, Menningee Found., 1997-; trustee Menninger Found.1997-; bd. visitors Columbia Law Sch 2000-. Fellow Am. Bar Found., Internat. Acad. Trial Lawyers; mem. ABA, N.Y. State Bar Assn., D.C. Bar Assn., Assn. of Bar of City of N.Y. (trade regulation com. 1982-85), Fed. Bar Council, D.C. Bar Assn., Univ. Club. Jewish. Avocations: sports cars, reading, gardening, sports. Home: 1025 5th Ave New York NY 10028 Office: Dewey Ballantine LLP 1301 Avenue Of The Americas New York NY 10019-6092 also: PO Box 370 Saddle River NJ 07458-0389 Office Phone: 212-259-8300. Office Fax: 212-259-6333. Business E-Mail: hkurzweil@dbllp.com.

KURZWEIL, JEFFREY, lawyer; b. NYC, Feb. 4, 1950; AB cum laude, Duke Univ., 1972; JD, Vanderbilt Univ., 1975. Bar: NC 1975, DC 1980. Law clerk, Hon. Naomi E. Morris NC Ct. Appeals, 1975—76; spl. asst. to gen. counsel US Dept. Commerce, Washington, 1978—79; ptnr., legis., govt. affairs Venable LLP, Washington. Bd. dir., exec. com., treas. Best Friends Found. Office: Venable LLP 575 Seventh St NW Washington DC 20004 Office Phone: 202-344-4678. Office Fax: 202-344-8300. Business E-Mail: jkurzweil@venable.com.

KURZWEIL, RAYMOND C., computer scientist, entrepreneur; b. NYC, Feb. 12, 1948; s. Fredric and Hannah Kurzweil; m. Sonya Rosenwald, Aug. 3, 1975; 2 children. BS in Computer sci. and Lit., MIT, 1970; DHL (hon.), Hofstra U., 1982, Misericordia Coll., 1989; D of Music (hon.), Berklee Coll. Music, 1987; DSc (hon.), Renssalaer Polytech. Inst., 1988, Northeastern U., 1988, NJ Inst. Tech., 1990, Queens Coll., CUNY, 1991, Dominican Coll., 1993, Worcester Polytechnic Inst.; D of Engring. (hon.), Merrimack Coll., 1989; LHD (hon.), Misericordia Coll., 1989, Lnadmark Coll., 2002; D in Sci. and Humanities (hon.), Mich. State U., 2000. Founder, former CEO Kurzweil Computer Products, Inc. (now Xeroc Imaging Systems), Cambridge, Mass., 1974—80; chmn., former CEO (sold to Young Chang) Kurzweil Music Systems, Inc., Waltham, Mass., 1982—90; founder, former CEO Kurzweil Applied Intelligence, Inc. (acquired by Lernout & Hauspie), Waltham, Mass., 1982—97; founder, chmn., CEO Kurzweil Technologies Inc., 1995—; founder, former CEO Kurzweil Ednl. Systems Inc. (acquired by Lernout & Hauspie), 1996—98; founder, pres., CEO Med. Learning Co. Inc. and FamilyPractice.com, 1997—; founder, chmn., CEO FAT KAT Inc., 1999—, Kurzweil Cyber Art Technolgies, Inc., 2000; founder, CEO, and editor-in-chief KurzweilAI.net, 2001; co-founder, chmn., co-CEO Ray & Terry's Longevity Products, Inc., 2003. Chmn. exhbn. bd. Age of Intelligent Machines Exhbn. Mus. of Sci., Boston, 1985—; bd. dirs. Wang Labs., Med. Mgr. Corp., United Therapeutics, Inforte; lectr. in field. Author: The Age of Intelligent Machines, 1990 (Best Computer Sci. Book, 1990), The 10% Solution for a Healthy Life, 1993, The Age of Spiritual Machines, When Computers Exceed Human Intelligence, 1999 (Literary Lights prize, 1999), Fantastic Voyage: Live Long Enough to Live Forever, 2004, The Singularity Is Near: When Humans Transcend Biology, 2005, (collection of essays) The Ray Kurzweil Reader, (series of articles) "The Futurecast", Library Journal, 1991—93; contbr.; co-author (with Terry Grossman): Fantastic Voyage: The Science Behind Radical Life Extension, 2004; contbr. numerous articles to profl. jours., chapters to books; prodr.: (films) The Age of Intelligent Machines, 1987 (The Chris Plaque, 1987, Creative Excellence award, 1987, Gold Medal-Sci. Edu., 1987, CINE Golden Eagle award, 1987, Technology Culture award, 1988, Prize of the Pres. of the Festival, Internat. Film Festival of Czechoslovakia, 1988). Former mem. tech. adv. com. Nat. Ctr. Adult Literacy U. Pa.; chmn., founder The Kurzweil Found.; trustee Beth Israel Hosp.; overseer New. Eng. Conservatory of Music; incorporator Boston Mus.

Sci.; mem. vis. com. MIT Sch. Music and MIT. Sch. Humanities; overseer, bd. overseers New England Conservatory Music; former dir. Boston Computer Soc.; chmn. Robots and Beyond: The Age of Intelligent Machines Exhbn. Named Hon. Chmn. for Innovation, White House Conf. on Small Bus., 1986, New Eng. Inventor of Yr., 1988; named to Computer Design Hall of Fame, Computer Design Mag., 1982, Nat. Inventors Hall of Fame, US Patent office, 2002; recipient First prize, Electronics and Comm., Internat. Sci. Fair, 1965, Gov.'s award, Mass. Gov. Michael Dukakis, 1977, Personal Computing to Aid the Handicapped Nat. award, Johns Hopkins U., 1981, Computer Sci. award, 1982, Francis Joseph Campbell award, Am. Libr. Assn., 1983, Best of the New Generation award, Esquire Mag., 1984, Disting. Inventor award, Intellectual Property Owners, 1986, Entrepreneurial Excellence award, White Ho. Conf. on Small Bus., 1986, Founders award, MIT, 1989, Engr. of Yr. award, Design News mag., 1990, Louis Braille award, Associated Svcs. for the Blind, 1991, Mass. Quincentennial award for innovation and discovery, 1992, Gordon Winston award, Can. Nat. Inst. Blind, 1994, Dickson prize, Carnegie Mellon U., 1994, Software Industry Achievement award, Mass. Software Coun., 1996, Access prize, Am. Found. Blind, 1995, Pres.'s award, Assn. Higher Edn. and Disability, 1997, Vision award, Stevie Wonder/SAP, 1998, Nat. Medal of Tech., 1999, Lemelson-MIT prize, 2000, Am. Composers Orchestra award, 2001, Migel Lay/Volunteer award, Am. Found. for the Blind, 2004. Fellow: Boston Computer Soc. (former bd. dirs.), Assn. Computing Machinery (Grace Murray Hopper Outstanding Young Computer Scientist of Yr. 1978). Achievements include patents in field; principal developer of the first omni-font Optical Character Recognition, the first print to speech reading machine for the blind, the first CCD flat-bed scanner, the first text-to-speech synthesizer; the first music synthesizer capable of recreating the grand piano and other orchestral instruments; the first commerically marketed large-vocabulary speech recognition; the first knowledge base system for creating medical reports; the first speech recognition dictation system for Windows; the first Continous Speech Natural Language Command and Control Software; the first print-to-speech reading system for persons with reading disabilities that reads from a displayed image of the page; the first virtual performing and recording artist (Ramona) to perform in front of a live audience with a live band; first host/hostess Avatar on the Web to combine a lifelike photo realistic, moving and speaking facial image with a conversational engine. Avocation: music. Office: Kurzweil Technologies Inc PMB 193 733 Turnpike St North Andover MA 01845 Office Phone: 781-263-0000. Office Fax: 781-263-9999. Business E-Mail: ray@kurzweiltech.com.*

KUSAMA, YAYOI, sculptor, painter; b. Matsumoto-shi, Japan, Mar. 22, 1929; came to U.S., 1957, naturalized, 1963; Student, Kyoto (Japan) Arts and Crafts Sch., 1948-49. Pres. Japan Edn. Co., 1977—. Author: Manhattan Suicide Addict, 1978, Christopher Homosexual Brothel, 1983, Lost in Swapland, 1992, others; contbr. articles to mags. and newspapers; one-man shows include Aggregation One Thousand Boats, N.Y.C., 1963, Driving Image show, N.Y.C., 1964, Chrysler Mus., Provincetown, 1965, Castellane Gallery, N.Y.C., 1965, 66, Naviglio Gallery, Milan, Italy, 1966, 82 Thelen Gallery, Essen, Germany, 1966, Fillmore East Theatre Happening, 1968, Mus. Modern Art, N.Y.C., 1969, Fashion show Venice, Italy, 1971, The Haag, The Netherlands, 1971, Am. Ctr., Tokyo, 1980, Fuji Television Gallery, Tokyo, 1982, 84, 86, 88, 91, 94, Galerie Christian Cheaneau, Paris, 1986, Musée des Beaux-Art, Calais, 1986, Kitakyushu Mcpl. Mus., 1987, Musée Mcpl., Dôle, France, 1987, (retrospective) Ctr. for Internat. Contemporary Arts, N.Y.C., 1989, Mus. Modern Art, Oxford, London, 1989, Sogetsu Mus. Art, Tokyo, 1992, Niigata City Art Mus., 1992, Japan Pavilion Venezia Biennale, 1993, Galleria Valentina Moncada, Rome, 1993, Naviglio Venezia, 1993, Paula Cooper Gallery, N.Y.C., 1996, Robert Miller Gallery, N.Y.C., 1996, Baumgertner Galleries, Inc., Washington, 1997; group shows include Bklyn. Mus., 1955, 58, De Cordova Mus., Boston, 1960, 65, Riverside Mus., N.Y.C., 1960, Städtisches Mus., Schloss Morsbroish, Leverkusen, Germany, 1960, 61, Whitney Mus. Am. Art, N.Y.C., 1961, 62, Pitts. Mus., 1961, City Mus., Städtisches Mus., Trier, Germany, 1961, Nul Stedelijk Mus., Amsterdam, 1962, Inst. Contemporary Art, 1964, 65, Modern Art Gallery, Washington, 1965, Chrysler Mus., Provincetown, Mass., 1965, Mus. Modern Art, Stockholm, Sweden, 1966, Met. Mus., Tokyo, 1965, Mus. Modern Art, N.Y.C., 1966, Woman's Work-Am. Art, Phila., 1974, Improbable Furniture, U. Pa., 1977, Neich und Plastisch-Soft Art, Zurich, 1979, Nat. Mus. Art, Osaka, 1980, Nat. Mus. Modern Art, Tokyo, 1981, Yokohama City Gallery, 1982, Landmark Tower, Yokohama, 1993, Guggenheim Mus., 1994, Scream Against the Sky, San Francisco Mus. Modern Art, 1995, Otis Gallery, L.A., 1995, Ars 95, Helsinki, 1995, Louisiana Mus., Denmark, 1995, L.A. County Mus. Art, Mus. Modern Art, N.Y., Walker Art Ctr., 1998, Taipei Biennale, Taipei Art Fair, 1998, many others; represented in permanent collections Chrysler Mus., Stedelijk Mus., Amsterdam; organized, presented happenings worldwide. Invented infinity mirror room. Address: 1008 Ushigome Heim 30-2 chome Haramachi Shinjuku-ku Tokyo Japan E-mail: yayoi@super.win.ne.jp.*

KUSHAR, KENT, information technology executive; BS, Univ. Montana; student, Advanced Bus. and Tech. Program, Harvard Bus. Sch., Kellogg Sch. at Northwestern, Chgo. Dir. IBM Consulting; gen. mgr. IBM-ROLM subs., Calif.; co-founder EDP Industries; tech. v.p. Citicorp; mng. prin. Unisys Cons.; v.p. & chief info. officer E&J Gallo Winery, Modesto, Calif. Nat. bd. advisors Univ. Ariz.; bus. advisory bd. Calif. State Univ., Stanislaus; bd. of advisors Info. Tech. Rsch. Ctr. Named one of top tech. innovators, Info. Week mag., 2004. Avocation: motorcycling. Office: VP & CIO E&J Gallo Winery PO Box 1130 Modesto CA 95353

KUSHEN, ALLAN STANFORD, retired lawyer; b. Chgo., Oct. 5, 1929; s. Barney and Ethel (Friedman) K.; m. Betty Cohen, Sept. 2, 1951 (dec. Jan. 2000); children: Annette Joyce, Robert Allan; m. Natalie Best, June 1, 2001. BBA cum laude, LLB cum laude, U. Miami, Fla., 1952; LLM, NYU, 1955. Bar: Fla. 1952, N.Y. 1956. Atty. Schering Corp., Bloomfield, N.J., 1955-67, atty. counsel labs. divsn., 1967-69, atty. domestic ops. divsn., 1969-73; v.p., gen. counsel Schering-Plough Corp., Kenilworth, N.J., 1973-80, sr. v.p. pub. affairs Madison, N.J., 1980-94; ret., 1994. Adj. counsel Am. Allendale Ins. Co., N.Y., 1986-94; lectr. in field. Trustee Food and Drug Law Inst., 1972-94, trustee emeritus, 1994—; trustee Art Coun. Morris Area, 1983-93, 2005-, pres., 1989-93; trustee Montclair Art Mus., 2000-05, Friends of Florham, 2005, Food and Drug Law Inst. fellow NYU, 1955. Mem. Phi Delta Phi, Omicron Delta Kappa, Iron Arrow. Home: 58 Millbrook Rd New Vernon NJ 07976

KUSHINSKY, JEANNE ALICE, humanities educator; b. Reading, Pa, Jan. 12, 1937; d. Otis Jacob and Alice Elizabeth (Kurtz) Rothenberger; m. Sheldon Melvin Wallerstein, May 9, 1959 (div. July 1978); children: Seth, Gail Wallerstein Melichar; m. David Lazar Kushinsky, Apr. 11, 1987. BS, Cedar Crest Coll., 1958; postgrad., Kean U. N.J., 1978—92, Rutgers U., 1993. Tchr. East Orange Bd. Edn., NJ, 1958—60; editor Dept. Testing and Assessment State Dept. Edn., Trenton, NJ, 1974—76; tchr. Edison Township Bd. Edn., NJ, 1974—2000; pvt. tutor SAT verbal sect. Edison, NJ, 1980—. Mem. Citizen's Adv. Coun. Edn., Edison, NJ, 1991—93. Fashion show com. Rahway Hosp. Found., 2002—; chairperson gala Edison Arts Soc., 2003—, bd. trustees, 2000—; active Dist. VIII Middlesex County Bd. Atty. Ethics, Trenton, NJ, 2000—. Grantee grant, N.J. Coun. for Humanities, 1996. Mem.: Brandeis Univ. Nat. Women's Comm., NJ Edn. Assn., NEA, Metuchen-Edison Hist. Soc., Proprietary House, Nat. Trust for Hist. Preservation, Borough Improvement League. Democrat. Jewish. Avocations: historic preservation architecture, feminist issues, mentoring young people, film studies, reading. Home: 119 Turner Ave Edison NJ 08820

KUSHLAN, JAMES A., biology educator, science administrator; b. Cleve., Oct. 11, 1947; BS in Biology and Chemistry cum laude, U. Miami, 1969, MS in Biology, 1972, PhD in Biology, 1974; DSc (hon.), Thiel Coll., Greenville, Pa., John Cabot U., Rome, Italy. Rsch. biologist U.S. Dept. of Interior, 1975-84; assoc. prof. biology Tex. A&M U., Commerce, 1984—87, prof. biology, 1987-88, dir. ctr. water resources studies, 1986-88; prof. biology U. Miss., 1988-98, chmn. dept. biology, 1988—95; dir. Patuxent Wildlife Rsch. Ctr., 1995-2001; sr. sci. advisor U.S. Geol. Survey, 2001—02; sr. rsch. assoc. Smithsonian Inst., 2001—05. Author: The Herons Handbook, 1984, Freshwater Fishes of Southern Florida, 1987, Storks, Ibises and Spoonbills of the World, 1992, Heron Conservation, 2000, The Herons, 2005; contbr. to Dictionary of Birds, 1985, Encyclopedia of Birds, 1985, Ecosystems of Florida, 1990, The Rivers of Florida, 1991; editor Fla. Field Naturalist, 1981-86, Colonial Waterbirds, 1985-88; mem. editl. bd. Wetlands, 1982, assoc. editor, 1993-95; author 200 papers, revs., commentaries; contbr. articles to profl. jours. Mem. United Way Planning Coun., Oxford, Miss., 1991-92; bd. dirs. Miss. Nature Conservancy, 1991-95; bd. dirs. John Cabot U., Am. Bird Conservancy, N.Am. Bird Conservation, Hawk Mountain Sanctuary, Waterbird Conservation for Ams.; chair Bird Conservation Alliance, 2002-; chair Herons Specialist Group, 1985-97, 2003-; mem. sci bd. Station Biology de la Tour du Valat. Recipient Citizen award WIOD Radio, Miami, 1980; Paul Harris fellow Rotary Internat., 1989. Fellow Am. Ornithologists' Union (life, mem. coun., v.p. 1998-99, pres. 2004—), mem. Soc. Wetland Scientist (life, assoc. editor), Waterbird Soc. (bd. dirs., pres. 1996-98, Lindahl award for internat. conservation 2003), Am. Ornithologists' Union (pres. 2004—), Rotary (chpt. pres. 1987-88), Sigma Xi (chpt. pres. 1983-84). Achievements include research in ornithology, wetland sciences, international wetland and biodiversity conservation, and waterbirds. Office: PO Box 2008 Key Biscayne FL 33149 Office Phone: 305-365-0306. Personal E-mail: jkushlan@earthlink.net.

KUSHLAN, SAMUEL DANIEL, internist, educator, hospital administrator; b. New Britain, Conn., Feb. 17, 1912; s. H. David and Bessie M. K.; m. Ethel Ross, June 24, 1934; children: Nancy Kushlan Wanger, David Ross. BS, Yale U., 1932, MD, 1935. Diplomate: Am. Bd. Internal Medicine with subsplty in gastroenterology. Intern New Haven Hosp., 1935-36, asst. resident, 1937; vol. research fellow Mass. Gen. Hosp., 1938; assoc. physician-in-chief Yale-New Haven Hosp., 1967-82, cons. to chief staff, 1982—; clin. prof. medicine Yale U., 1967—. Contbr. numerous articles to profl. jours. Mem. bequest and endowment program Yale Med. Sch. Alumni Fund, 1977—; cons. to office of alumni affairs Yale Med. Sch., 1990—. Named Physician of Yr. Conn. Digestive Disease Soc., 1975 Mem. AMA, Am. Gastroenterol. Assn., Am. Soc. Gastrointestinal Endoscopy, Conn. State Med. Soc., New Haven Med. Assn., Conn. Regional Soc. for Gastrointestinal Endoscopy, World Med. Assn., Assn. Yale Alumni in Medicine (pres. 1957-59), Yale Alumni Fund (bd. dirs. 1986-91), ACP (Lifetime Achievement award Conn. chpt. 2003), Sigma Xi, Alpha Omega Alpha. Office: Suite 1063 CB Yale-New Haven Hosp New Haven CT 06504 Office Phone: 203-688-2604. *Life must have Meaning.*

KUSHMEIDER, ROSE MARIE, economist; b. Washington, Sept. 26, 1956; d. Albert Nicholas and Elizabeth Anne (Mangum) Kushmeider. BA, U. Md., 1978, MA, 1980. Teaching asst., instr. U. Md., College Park, 1978-84; economist, cons. Cornell, Pelcovits & Brenner, Economists Inc., Washington, 1984-86; rsch. assoc. Am. Enterprise Inst. Pub. Policy Rsch., Washington, 1986-88; sr. fin. economist U.S. GAO, Washington, 1989-97, FDIC, Washington, 1997—. Co-author, co-editor: Restructuring Banking and Financial Services in America, 1988. Mem.: Com. Status Women in Econ. Profession, Western Economic Assn., Women in Housing and Fin., Am. Econ. Assn., Phi Beta Kappa, Phi Kappa Phi. Democrat. Methodist. Avocations: reading, gardening, cooking. Home: 602 Whitcliff Ct Gaithersburg MD 20878-2751 Office: FDIC Rm 2124 550 17th St NW Washington DC 20429-0001 Business E-Mail: rkushmeider@fdic.gov.

KUSHNER, DAVID ZAKERI, musicologist; b. Ellenville, N.Y., Dec. 22, 1935; s. Nathan and Rita (Forgatsh) K.; m. Rebecca Ann Stefan, Dec. 20, 1964 (div. Nov. 1979); children: Jonathan Moses (dec.), Joshua Sanford, Jeremy Avram, Jason Daniel; m. Leslie Cheryl Dack, Dec. 4, 1985. MusB, Boston U., 1957; MusM, U. Cin., 1958; PhD, U. Mich., 1967. Asst. prof. music Miss. U. For Women, Columbus, 1964—66; from assoc. prof. to prof. music Radford U., Va., 1966—69; coord. musicology studies U. Fla., Gainesville, 1969—, head musicology/music history. Vis. prof. music Florence (Italy) Study Center, 1975; charter mem., program annotator Pro Arte Musica of Gainesville, 1970-75; host, commentator on Music from Fla., weekly radio program over WRUF-FM, 1969-75; mem. People-to-People del. Nat. Music Coun., Austria, Germany, Hungary, Poland and Czechoslovakia, 1977, Oxford, Eng., 1997, Lisbon, Portugal, 1999; pre-concert lectr. Fla. Orch., Clearwater, Tampa, St. Petersburg, 1986-88, Internat. Congress on Arts and Comm., Nairobi, Kenya, 1990, Edinburgh, Scotland, 1994, U. Fla. Ctr. Performing Arts, 1995—; vis. prof. Mus. Conservatory A. Steffani, Castelfranco-Veneto, Italy, 1996, vis. prof. musicology Hebrew U., Jerusalem, 1998; adjudicator Fla. Music Tchrs. Assn., Chopin Competition; performer ann. Recitals in Schs. series; lectr., presenter in field. Author: Ernest Bloch and His Symphonic Works, 1967, Ernest Bloch and His Music, 1973, Ernest Bloch: A Guide to Research, 1988, Ernest Bloch Companion, 2002; contbr. articles to profl. jours.; book reviewer: Am. Music Tchr. mag. Mem. arts in edn. com. Arts Coun. Alachua County; pres., chmn. adv. bd. Sta. WUFT-FM, Gainesville, 1987-89; v.p. Found. for Promotion Music, 1990-91, 92-94. Javits fellow Gainesville Music Tchrs. Assn.; recipient Pro Mundi Beneficio medal Brazilian Acad. Humanities, 1975; rsch. grantee U. Calif., Berkeley, NEH, 1986, Jaromir Weinberger Archives, Jerusalem, 1987, U. Fla., Tchg. Excellence award State of Fla., 1994-95, Professorial Excellence award State of Fla., 1996-97, Profl. Incentive award, 1998-99; named Tchr. of Yr. Coll. Fine Arts, U. Fla., 1988-89, 2004-05, Fine Arts Scholarship Enhancement Fund award, 1998-99, Musician of Yr., Found. for Promotion of Music, 1991-92. Mem. Am. Liszt Soc. (co-founder, bd. dirs., pres. chpt. 1984—, charter life), Coll. Music Soc. (chmn. So. chpt. 1985-87, musicology bd. dirs.), Am. Musicological Soc. (chmn. So. chpt. 1971-74), Fla. Music Tchrs. Assn. (1st. pres. collegiate artist competitions 1972-73, hon. mem. com), Music Tchrs. Nat. Assn. (life, master tchrs. cert. in music history and lit. 1984), Fla. State Music Tchrs. Assn., Membership Inc., Pi Kappa Lambda (charter, pres. U. Fla. chpt. 1970-76, 94-97), Phi Mu Alpha Sinfonia (life), Sigma Alpha Iota (nat. arts assoc.), 19th Century Studies Assn. (bd. dirs.), Phi Kappa Phi, Phi Beta Delta (pres. Pi chpt. 1988-89). Democrat. Jewish. Avocations: travel, record and cd collecting. Home: 3518 NW 136th St Gainesville FL 32606-4764 Office: U Fla School of Music Gainesville FL 32611 *It has been my credo to establish goals that are attainable and consistent with standards of personal and professional conduct that I view as honorable. One must be true to himself and measure his own being by the same criteria he would apply to others. Real success is adjudged not by the perceptions of society, but by one's own sense of self-worth.*

KUSHNER, EVA, academic administrator, educator, author; b. Prague, Czechoslovakia, June 18, 1929; d. Josef and Anna (Kafkova) Dubsky; m. Donn Jean Kushner, Sept. 15, 1949 (dec. 2001); children: Daniel Peter, Roland Joseph, Paul Joel. PhB, Coll. Marie de France, Montreal, 1946; BA, McGill U., 1948, MA, 1950, PhD in French Lit., 1956; D (hon.), Acadia U., 1988, United Theol. Coll., 1992, St Michael's U., 1993, U. Western Ont., 1996, U. Szeged, 1997. Lectr. French McGill U., Montreal, 1952-55, instr. French, 1956, 58, 61-62, 67-69, prof. French lang. and lit., 1976-87, chair dept. French, 1976-80; pres., vice chancellor Victoria U. U. Toronto, 1987-94, dir. ctr. comparative lit., 1994-95; vis. prof. Princeton U., 2000; Mary Rowell Jackman and Mary Coyne Rowell prof. Victoria Coll., 2001—. Sessional lectr. philosophy Sir George Williams U., 1952-53; lectr. U. Coll., London, 1958-59; lectr. Carleton U., 1961; asst. prof. French & comparative lit., 1963, assoc. prof., 1965, prof., 1969-76, chmn. comparative lit., 1965-69, 70-72, 75-76, adj. prof. lit., 1976-79; mem. exec. com. Can. Coun., 1975-81; v.p. Social Scis. & Humanities Rsch. Coun. Can., 1983-86; mem. adv. bd. Nat. Libr. Can.; pres. Humanities Rsch. Coun. Can. 1970-72; vice-chmn. George R. Gardiner Mus. Ceramic Arts, 1990-94. Author: Patrice de La Tour de Pin, 1961; Le Mythe d'Orphée dans la Littérature Française Contemporaine, 1961; Chants de Bohême, 1963; Rina Lasnier, Collection Ecrivains Canadiens d'Aujourd'hui, 1964; Poètes d'Aujourd'hui, 1969; Saint-Denys Garneau, 1967; François Mauriac, 1972, Japanese transl., 1976; co-author anthology Que. poetry, transl. into Hungarian, 1978, Polish, 1985, The Living Prism. Itineraries in Comparative Literature, 2001, Pontus de Tyard et son oeuvre poétique, 2001, Le dialogue à la Renaissance Histoire et poétique, 2004; editor Renewals in the Theory of Literary History; co-editor/co-author: L'Avènement de l'Esprit Nouveau (1400-80), 1988, Crises et essors nouveaux (1560-1610), 2000, Théorie Littéraire: Problèmes et Perspectives, 1989, Histoire des Poétiques, 1997; editor, co-author La Problématique du Sujet chez Montaigne, 1995; co-dir. rsch. Renaissance vols. Histoire Comparée des Littératures de Langues Européennes; dir. critical edit. Complete Works of Pontus de Tyard, Vol. 1, Oeuvres Poetiques, 2004; mem. editl. com. Can. Comparative Lit. Rev., Dalhousie French Studies, Etudes Montaignistes; mem. internat. adv. bd. Synthesis, Lit. Rsch., 1990-95; contbr. articles to profl. publs. Named Officer Order of Can., 1997. Fellow Royal Soc. Can. (v.p. 1980-82); mem. Académie Européenne des Lettres, des Sciences et des Arts, Am. Comparative Lit. Assn. (adv. bd.), Internat. Comparative Lit. Assn. (pres. 1979-82, co-editor proc. 7th and 9th ICLA Congress, 11th Congress, vols. IV-V, 1991, VI, 1992, VII-VIII, 1993, IX, 1994, X, 1995), Internat. Fedn. for Modern Langs. and Lits. (v.p. 1987-93, pres. 1996-99), MLA (del. assembly, chmn. 16th century French lit. divsn., mem. exec. coun. 1983-86, nominating com. 1986-88), Assn. Internat. des Études Françaises, Assn. Canadienne de Littérature Comparée (v.p. 1969-71), Internat. Assn. Neo-Latin Studies, Soc. Canadienne d'Études de la Renaissance, Assn. des Littératures Canadienne et Québecoise, Renaissance Soc. Am., Assn. des Professeurs de Français des Universités Canadiennes, Renaissance Soc. Am. (discipline rep. for French studies 1996-99), Can. Pensioners Concerned (mem. Ont. bd.), Ont. Coalition Sr. Citizens Orgns. (co-chair 2003-2004). Office: Victoria Coll 73 Queen's Park Toronto ON Canada M5S 1K7 Business E-Mail: eva.kushner@utoronto.ca.

KUSHNER, FREDERICK GARY, cardiologist, medical educator; b. NYC, May 20, 1948; s. Jack and Gloria Kushner; m. Ivy Erica Sommerstein, May 8, 1977; children: Adam Benjamin, Jared Scott. BA, Columbia U., 1970, MD, 1974. Med. intern, resident Harvard Beth Israel, Boston, 1974—76; cardiology fellow U. Pa., Phila., 1976—78, Mass. Gen. Hosp., Boston, 1978—79; clin. assoc. prof. medicine Tulane U. Sch. Medicine, New Orleans, 1993—; med. dir. Heart Clinic La., Marrero, 1995—. Chmn. credentials com. Leadership Com. of the Coun. on Clin. Cardiology of the Am. Heart Assn., Dallas, 1999—2001; com. mem. Guidelines Com. for mgmt. of ST Elevation MI of the Am. Heart Assn. and Am. Coll. of Cardiology, Washington, 2001—. Exhibitions include World Trade Ctr., New Orleans Acad. Fine Arts, others. Pres. The New Orleans Friends Music, 2000—03; bd. mem. Touro Synagogue, New Orleans, 2002—, Columbia Coll. Alumni Assn., N.Y.C., 1996—; alumni coun. bd. mem. Columbia Coll. Physicians and Surgeons, N.Y.C., 1996—. Fellow: ACP (licentiate), Am. Heart Assn., Soc. Cardiac Angiography and Interventions (licentiate), Soc. Nuc. Cardiology (licentiate), Am. Coll. Cardiology (licentiate; v.p. La. chpt. 1990); mem.: Alpha Omega Alpha (Vol. Clin. Faculty Tchg. award 1999). Achievements include research in nuclear cardiology and perfusion scanning. Avocations: painting, sailing, travel, reading, golf. Home: 6026 St Charles Ave New Orleans LA 70118 Office: Heart Clinic La Suite 613 Physicians Center North Marrero LA 70072 Office Phone: 504-349-2010. Personal E-mail: fjakush@aol.com.

KUSHNER, GARY JAY, lawyer; b. Bronx, NY, Mar. 17, 1950; s. Israel Sol and Shyrle Renee (Mervish) K.; m. Gail Barbara Kline, June 27, 1981; children: Aaron, Jamie, Stuart. AB, U. Mich.; JD, Georgetown U. Bar: Md. 1975, D.C. 1976, U.S. Dist. Ct. D.C., 1976, U.S. Ct. Appeals (D.C. cir.) 1978, U.S. Ct. Appeals (fed. cir.) 1991, U.S. Ct. Appeals (5th cir.) 1992, U.S. Ct. Appeals (9th cir.) 1994, U.S. Ct. Appeals (11th cir.) 2004, U.S. Supreme Ct. 1984. Law clk. to judge Superior Ct., Washington, 1975-76; staff counsel Grocery Mfrs. Am., Washington, 1976-78; assoc. Leighton, Conklin & Lemov, Washington, 1978-80, Collier, Shannon, Rill & Scott, Washington, 1980-82, ptnr., 1985-89; v.p., gen. counsel Am. Meat Inst., Washington, 1982-85; ptnr. Hogan & Hartson LLP, Washington, 1989—, food drug & medical device practice group dir. Adv. bd. USDA Grad. Sch., 1989—; bd. dirs. Seed Programs, Inc.; adj. fellow Ctr. for Food and Nutrition Policy Va. Poly. Inst. Contbr. articles to profl. jours. Mem. adv. bd. Food Safety Letter, 1983-88, bd. govs., exec. com., nat. commn. nat. commn. Anti-Defamation League, Washington, 1995; pro bono counsel Second Harvest, Chgo., 1989-95; bd. dirs. D.C. Hunger Action, 1995, 2000, Advocates for Better Children's Diets, Washington, 1994—2000. Mem. ABA, Fed. Bar Assn. (coun. chair 1975-95), Am. Agrl. Law Assn., Inst. Food Technologists, Am. Soc. Assn. Execs., City Club Washington (bd. dirs. 1995), Disting. Order Zerocrats. Avocations: running, tennis, golf. Office: Hogan & Hartson LLP 555 13th St NW Ste 7W Washington DC 20004-1161 Office Phone: 202-637-5856. Office Fax: 202-637-5910. Business E-Mail: gjkushner@hhlaw.com.

KUSHNER, HAROLD JOSEPH, mathematics professor; b. NYC, July 29, 1933; s. Hyman and Harriet Kushner; m. Linda Rosen, Sept. 20, 1960; children: Diana, Nina. BA, CCNY, 1955; MS, U. Wis., 1956, PhD, 1958. Mem. staff Lincoln Lab., Lexington, Mass., 1955-63, Rias, Balt., 1963-64; prof. applied math. Brown U., Providence, 1964—, dir. Lefschtez Ctr. Dynamical Systems, 1980-87, 95-99, chmn. divsn. applied math., 1988-91. Cons. numerous govt. agys. and cos., 1964—. Author: Stochastic Stability and Control, 1967, Introduction to Stochastic Control Theory, 1972, Probability Methods for Approximations in Stochastic Control, 1977, Stochastic Approximation, 1978, Weak Convergence Methods and Applications to Stochastic Systems, 1984, Weak Convergence Methods and Singularly Perturbed Stochastic Control and Filtering Problems, 1991, Numerical Methods for Stochastic Control Problems in Continuous Time, 1992, 2d edit. 2001, Stochastic Approximation Algorithms and Applications, 1997, 2d edit. 2003, Heavy Traffic Analysis of Controlled Queuing and Communication Networks, 2001. Recipient Louis E. Levy award, Franklin Inst., 1994, Bellman Heritage award, Am. Automatic Control Coun., 2004; grantee, U.S. govt. agys., 1964—. Fellow IEEE (life, Control Systems Field award 1992); mem. Inst. Math. Stats., Soc. Indsl. and Applied Math. (W.T. and Idalia Reid prize 2003), Ops. Rsch. Soc. Am., Inst. Mgmt. Sci. Home: 560 Lloyd Ave Providence RI 02906-5427 Office: Brown U Divsn Applied Math Providence RI 02912-0001 Business E-Mail: hjk@dam.brown.edu.

KUSHNER, HARVEY DAVID, management consultant; b. N.Y.C., Dec. 28, 1930; s. Morris K. and Hilda Kushner; m. Rose Rehert, Jan. 14, 1951 (dec. 1990); children: Gantt A., Todd R., Lesley K.; m. Patricia E. Sacks, Jan. 1992. BS in Engring., Johns Hopkins U., 1951. Assoc. engr. U.S. Navy Bur. Ships, 1951-53; mem. tech. staff Melpar Inc., 1953-54; with ORI Inc., 1955-88, pres., 1969-83; chmn. bd., CEO ORI, Inc., 1977-88; chmn. bd., pres. The ORI Group, Inc., 1985-88; v.p. Reliance Group Inc. (parent co. of ORI, Inc.), 1970-77; pres. Disclosure Inc., 1972-77; group pres., sr. v.p. Atlantic Rsch. Corp. parent co. of ORI Group, Inc., 1987-88; pres. Kushner Mgmt. Planning Corp., Bethesda, Md., 1988—; chmn. bd. trustees Maryland Venture Capital Trust, 1990-2001. Cons. in bus. and tech. devel., mgmt. and orgn.; bd. dirs. Computer Tech. Assocs., 1988-01, MRJ Tech., Inc., 1988-00, Naviant Tech., Inc., 1998-00, Stamet, Inc., 1994—, Hyperspace Comms., Inc., 2002-05. Pub. Rose Kushner's If You've Thought About Breast Cancer. Chmn. Commn. Higher Edn. in Sci. and Tech., Montgomery County, Md., 1984-85, Md. Govs. High Tech. Roundtable, Annapolis, Md., 1983-86, United Way Campaign, Montgomery County, 1980, mem. exec. bd., 1981-85; bd. dirs. Montgomery County High Tech. Coun., 1986-96, chmn. 1986-1991; chmn. bd. dirs. Rose Kushner Breast Cancer Adv. Ctr., 1990—; mem. nat. subcom. on breast cancer detection and control Am. Cancer Soc., 1991-95; mem. bd. vis. Sch. Pub. Affairs, U. Md., 1988-93, chmn., 1991-92; mem. nat. adv. coun. Sch. Engring. Johns Hopkins U., 1987—, mem. adv. bd. Info. Security Inst., 2004—; mem. bd. visitors U. Md. Biotech. Inst., 1993—. Recipient Superior Pub. Svc. medal Dept. of Navy, 1988. Fellow AAAS, N.Y. Acad. Scis.; mem. ASME, IEEE (sr.), Nat. Security Indsl. Assn. (chmn. exec. com. 1987-88, chmn. anti-submarine warfare com. 1986-88, mem. bd. trustees 1982-97, vice-chmn. bd. trustees 1987-88, chmn. bd. 1988-89, Vice-Adm. Charles E. Weakley award 1991), Profl. Svcs. Coun. (bd. dirs. 1974-2002, v.p. 1983-88, chmn. bd. dirs. 1991-92), Inst. for Ops. Rsch. and the Mgmt. Scis., Am. Inst. Aerospace Sci., Nat. Def. Industry Assn. (trustee 1997-2001), (assoc.) Sigma Xi, Cosmos Club. E-mail: harveydk@aol.com.

KUSHNER, HOWARD I., public health and history of medicine educator; s. Samuel N. Kushner and Gertrude N. Slotnikoff; m. Carol R. Rubin, Mar. 5, 1976; 1 child, Peter Eavan. AB, Rutgers U., 1965; MA, Cornell U., 1968,

PhD, 1970. Prof. history of medicine San Diego State U., 1979—2000; Robertson disting. prof Emory U., Atlanta, 2000—; assoc. dir. Ctr. for Health, Culture & Soc. Emory Univ. Author: A Cursing Brain?: The Histories of Tourtte Syndrome, 1999, Self-Destruction on the Promised Land: A Psychocultural Biology of Suicide, 1991; mem. editl. bd. Bull. of History of Medicine, 2003—, History of Neurosci.; contbr. articles to profl. jours. Recipient award for outstanding faculty contbns., San Diego State U. Alumni Assn., 1995. Office: Emory U Sch Pub Health 1518 Clifton Rd NE Atlanta GA 30322 E-mail: hkushne@emory.edu.

KUSHNER, JACK, retired physician; b. Montgomery, Ala., Dec. 5, 1939; s. Louis Harry and Rose (Feldman) K.; m. Annetta Esther Horwitz, June 21, 1964; children: Reyna, Eve. Student, U. Sheffield, 1959—60; BA in History, Tulane, 1960; MD, U. Ala., 1964; M in Fin., U. Md., 1990. Diplomate Am. Bd. Neurosurgery, 1976, cert. in Neurosurgery Wake Forest U., 1972. Intern George Washington U. Hosp., Washington, 1964-65; resident in surgery U. Mich., Ann Arbor, 1965-66; resident in neurosurgery Bowman Gray Sch. Medicine Wake Forest U., Winston-Salem, N.C., 1968-72; pvt. practice neurosurgery, Annapolis, Md., 1972-95; clin. asst. prof. neurosurgery George Washington U., 1976—80; pres., CEO, Futuristic Instruments, Annapolis, 1995-98; chmn., bd. dirs. Telehealth, 1999; ret., 2000; cons. in field. Bd. mgrs. Anne Arundel Med. Ctr., Annapolis, Md., 1978-80; mem. Mil. Leadership Coun., U. Md., 2003—; bd. dirs. E-Global Telehealth, 1999—; chmn., CEO Am. Opportunity Portal, Annapolis, 2003—; cons. Artemis Strategy Fund.; lectr. UMUC-Graduate Sch. Bus Author: Preparing To Tack: When Physicians Change Careers, 1995; contbr. articles to profl. jours. With U.S Army, 1966-68, combat surgeon, Vietnam; founding mem. 1902 Soc. Decorated Bronze Star; recipient Most Disting. Alumnus award U. Md., 2001, Man of Yr. Am. Biographical Inst., 2004; named one of Top 100 Healthcare Profls. Internat. Biographical Ctr., 2005. Fellow Am. Coll. of Surgeons (emerging tech. and edn. com.), Internat. Coll. of Surgeons; mem. Am. Assoc. Neurol. Surgeons, Congress of Neurol. Surgeons, So. Neurosurgical Soc., Pan Pacific Neurosurgical, Tulane U. Alumni Assn. (bd. dirs., u. coll. dir.-at-large), US Naval Acad. Golf Assn.(sr. men's tournament dir.). Republican. Jewish. Avocations: golf, yacht racing. Home: Ferry Farms 2030 Homewood Rd Annapolis MD 21402-5970 Office Phone: 410-757-3754. E-mail: jkaoportal@comcast.net.

KUSHNER, JEFFREY L., manufacturing executive; b. Wilmington, Del., Apr. 7, 1948; s. William and Selma (Kreger) K.; m. Carolyn Patricia Hypes, May 2, 1975; children: Tawnya Lynne. BBA summa cum laude, U. Hawaii, 1970; MBA, Columbia U., 1972. Sr. fin. analyst Black & Decker, Towson, Md., 1972-73, div. controller Solon, Ohio, 1973-74; asst. div. controller Rockwell Internat., Pitts., 1974-75; div. contr. Carborundum Corp., Niagara Falls, N.Y., 1975-77; mgr. fin. planning United Techs. Corp., Hartford, Conn., 1977-80, corp. v.p. fin. planning, 1986-88, corp. v.p. asset mgmt., 1989-92; asst. contr. Sikorsky Aircraft, Stratford, Conn., 1980-82, div. controller, 1982-83, v.p. fin., chief fin. officer, 1983-85; v.p. fin. and adminstrn. MasterBrand Industries Inc., Deerfield, Ill., 1993-98; sr. v.p. fin. and CFO Lorillard Tobacco Co., 1998; exec. v.p., CFO Cookson Electronics, 1999—2005; ret., 2005. Bd. dirs. ACR, Hartford. 1987-88. Recipient Bronfman Found. fellowship, 1970-71. Mem. Conf. Bd. (coun. 1987-88), Fin. Execs. Inst. Home: 195 Woodland Rd Westwood MA 02090-2631 Business E-Mail: jlk95@columbia.edu.

KUSHNER, LAWRENCE MAURICE, physical chemist, consultant; b. N.Y.C., Sept. 20, 1924; s. Hyman Tobias and Mary (Malkin) K.; children: Robb Adam, Leslie Meryl; m. Shirley Gayle Brown, June 24, 1972. BS, Queens Coll., 1945; A.M., Princeton U., 1947, PhD, 1949. Teaching asst. Princeton U., 1947-48; with Nat. Bur. Standards, 1948-73, chief, metal physics sect., 1956-61, chief, metallurgy div., 1961-66; dep. dir. Inst. Applied Tech., 1966-68, dir., 1968, dep. dir. bur., 1969-73, acting dir. bur., 1972-73; commr. Consumer Product Safety Commn., Washington, 1973-77; policy devel. Nat. Bur. Standards, 1977-80; mem. div. staff Mitre Corp., McLean, Va., 1980-85, cons. scientist, 1985-89; adj. prof. engring. and public policy Carnegie-Mellon U., 1981-91. Lectr. chemistry Am. U., 1952-60; spl. asst. for legis. to asst. sec. of commerce for sci. and tech., 1964-65; mem. ad hoc internat. group metal physics OECD, 1961 Recipient Superior Accomplishment award Dept. Commerce, 1954, gold medal, 1968; Meritorious Svc. award Am. Nat. Standards Inst., 1973. Mem. Am. Phys. Soc., AAAS, Fed. Profl. Assn., Am. Chem. Soc., Washington Acad. Scis., ASTM (hon.), Sigma Xi (nat. pres. 1976, bd. dirs.) Achievements include spl. rsch. crystal properties, surface phenomena in chemistry and metallurgy, materials sci., product safety and environ. regulation, sci. and tech. policy, technol. innovation. Home: 20506 Beaver Ridge Rd Montgomery Village MD 20886 E-mail: lskush@comcast.net.

KUSHNER, MICHAEL JAMES, neurologist, consultant, educator; b. Hackensack, N.J., July 18, 1951; s. Samuel and Ruth Ellen (Paul) K.; m. Sarah Joan Warden, Aug. 14, 1976; children: Hunter Paul, Paul Macrae (dec.). BA in Physics, Yale U., 1973; MD, NYU, 1977. Diplomate Am. Bd. Psychiatry, Am. Bd. Neurology, Am. Bd. Med. Examiners; cert. Am. Bd. Electrodiagnostic Medicine, Am. Bd. Pain Medicine. Intern Parkland Meml. Hosp., U. Tex., Dallas, 1977-78; resident in neurology Neurol. Inst., Columbia-Presbyn. Med. Ctr., N.Y.C., 1978-81; rsch. assoc. U. Pa., Phila., 1981-83, asst. prof. neurology, 1983-90; attending physician Hosp. of U. Pa., Phila., 1983-90; with Wilson (N.C.) Neurology Ctr., 1992—; clin. asst. prof. East. Carolina U. Sch. Medicine, 1997—. Dir. SPECT facility Hosp. of U. Pa., 1986-90, asst. dir. neurovascular lab., 1987-90; mem. sensory disorders and lang. study sect. NIH, Bethesda, Md., 1988-90; cons. Dupont Med. Products Div., Billerica, Mass., 1987—; staff neurologist Wilson (N.C.) Orthop. Surgery Neurology Ctr.; legal medicine cons.; neurology physician advisor N.C. Blue Cross/Blue Shield; asst. prof. East Carolina U. Sch. Medicine; dir. Wilson Regional MRI Ctr. Contbr. numerous articles to profl. jours. Interviewer alumni schs. com. Yale U., Phila., 1984—. Fellow Am. Acad. Neurology, Am. Heart Assn. (stroke coun.); mem. AMA, Internat. Soc. for Blood Flow and Metabolism, N.C. Neurol. Soc. (pres. 1995-97), Yale of N.Y.C., Yale of Cen. N.C., Yale of N.C. Republican. Episcopalian. Avocations: oenology, travel, personal fitness, art. Home: 1110 Salem St NW Wilson NC 27893-2137 Office: Wilson Neurology Ctr PO Box 3148 Wilson NC 27895-3148 Office Phone: 252-243-9629.

KUSHNER, TODD ROGER, computer scientist, application developer; b. Bethesda, Md., June 18, 1956; s. Harvey David and Rose Molly (Rehert) K.; m. Lea Louise Friedman, Nov. 11, 1990; children: Joshua Philip, Daniel Stuart. BS in Life Scis., MIT, 1976; MS in Computer Sci., U. Md., 1980, PhD in Computer Sci., 1982. Rsch. technician NIH, Bethesda, 1976-77; programmer Tech. Mgmt. Inc., Washington, 1977-78, GTE-Telenet, McLean, Va., 1978-79; grad. rsch. asst. U. Md., College Park, 1980-82, mem. rsch. staff, 1985-88; computer scientist SRI Internat., Menlo Park, Calif., 1982-83; sr. software engr. Vicom Sys. Inc., San Jose, 1983-85; sr. engr. Stanford Telecoms., Reston, Va., 1988-89; adv. programmer IBM Corp., Gaithersburg, Md., 1989-93; sr. scientist CTA Inc., Rockville, 1993-96; mem. sr. software staff Lockheed Martin Fed. Systems, Denver, 1996-99; mem. tech. staff Lucent Techs., 1999—2002; sr. programmer CSG Systems, Inc., 2002—04; tech. lead Jeppesen Corp., Englewood, 2004—. Adj. lectr. U. Santa Clara, Calif., 1983, U. Md., Gaithersburg, 1989-90, Johns Hopkins U., Gaithersburg, 1989-93; participant Software Process Interchange Network, McLean, 1993. Contbr. articles to profl. publs. Fellow Grad. fellow, Air Force Office Sci. Rsch., 1980. Mem. IEEE Computer Soc., Assn. Computer Machinery. Democrat. Jewish. Avocations: swimming, racquetball, skiing, golf.

KUSHNER, TONY, playwright; b. 1956; Student, Columbia U., NYU. Assoc. artistic dir. N.Y. Theatre Workshop, 1987; guest artist, grad. theater program Yale U., NYU & Princeton U., 1989—; dir. literary services Theatre Comm. Group, NYC, 1990—91; playwright-in-residence Juilliard Sch. of Drama, 1990—92. Author: (plays) A Bright Room Called Day, 1990, Angels in America: A Gay Fantasia on National Themes Part I "Millenium Approaches", 1992 (Pulitzer Prize for drama, 1993, Tony award best play, 1993), Part II "Perestroika", 1993 (Tony award best play, 1994), Slavs!, 1994, Thinking about the Longstanding Problems of Virtue and Happiness, 1995 (Lambda Literary award, 1996), Dybbuk and Other Tales of the Supernatural, 1997, Death and Taxes, 2000, Homebody/Kabul, 2001, Caroline, or Change, 2003 (Tony nom. best book of a musical, 2004, Obie award, 2004), Only We Who Guard the Mystery Shall Be Unhappy, 2004; adaptor The Illusion (Pierre Corneille), 1988, dir., author Yes Yes No No: The Solice of Solstice, Apogee/Perigee, Bestial/Celestial Holiday Show, 1985, In Great Eliza's Golden Time, 1986; author: (TV miniseries) Angels in America, 2003 (Emmy award, Outstanding Writing for a Miniseries, Movie or a Dramatic Series, 2004). Recipient Princess Grace award, 1986, John Whiting award, Arts Council of Great Britain, 1990, Kesserling award, Nat. Arts Club, 1992, Will Glickman playwriting prize, 1992, London Evening Standard award, 1992, AAAL award, 1994; grantee NEA, 1985, 1987, 1993. Mem.: AAAL.

KUSHNIR, ANDREI, artist, consultant; b. Regensberg, Germany, Aug. 30, 1947; BA, U. Ill., Chgo., 1969; MA, Georgetown U., 1971; JD, Howard U., 1975. Bar: D.C., Ill. Atty. FAA, Washington, 1975—81; assoc. counsel Dept. Navy, Office Gen. Counsel, Washington, 1981—97; artist Taylor & Sons Fine Art, Washington, 1999—2001; owner Andrei Kushnir/Michele Taylor, LLC, Ellicott City, Md., 2002—04, N.Y.C., 2004—. Guest instr. outdoor painting workshop South Fla. Coll., Sebring, 2002; ofcl. artist USCG. Book, My River, 1999, American Light, 2001, Painted History, 2004, Represented in permanent collections USCG, D.C. Commn. of Arts and Humanities, Univ. Club, Washington, Mus. of Fla. Art and Culture, Avon, Va. Hist. Soc., Richmond, exhibitions include Mus. Fla. Art & Culture, Sebring, Fla., 1998, Capital Hill Art League, Wash., 1998, Univ. Club, 1999, Taylor & Sons Fine Art, 1999, 2001, Rehoboth Art League, Rehoboth Beach, Del., 2003, Va. Hist. Soc., 2004, paintings included in, Along the Potomac, Philip Ogilvie, Arcadia Pub., Rock Creek Park, Gail Silsbury, Johns Hopkins Press, exhibited in group shows at Holter Mus. Art, Helena, MT, 1998, Art Inst. & Gallery, Salisbury, Md., 1998, Mus. Contemporary Art, Wash., 1999, Nat. Parks Acad. Arts, 2001—03, Alexandria Art League, Va., 1991—98, Arts Coun., Md., 1995, Blue Ridge Arts Coun., Front Royal, Va., 1995—2002, Foundry Gallery, Wash., 1995, Touchstone Gallery, 1996, Capitol Hill Art League, Howard County, Md., 1998, 2000, Artists Atelier, Atlanta, Ga., 1996, Serendipity Gallery, Boca Grande, Fla., 1997—2003, Coun. for the Arts, Chambersburg, PA, 1998, Nagano Olympics Ofcl. Art Exhbn., Japan, 1998, Spectrum Gallery, Washington, 1999, Hudson Valley Art Assn., NY, 1999, Period Gallery, Omaha, 2000, Nat. Oil & Acrylic Painters Soc., 2000, 2001, 2003, Schoharie County Arts Coun., Cobleskill, NY, 2001—02, Crane Collection, Wellesley, Mass., 2002—04, Alexander Gallery, NY, 2002, Mill Atelier, Santa Fe, N.Mex., 2003—04. Recipient First place oils, Casper Artist Guild, Wyo., 2002, Award of Excellence, Period Gallery, Omaha, 2000, Best in Show, Blueridge Arts Coun., Front Royal, Va., 2000. Mem.: Nat. Oil and Acrylic Painters Soc., Miniature Painters, Gravers and Sculptors Soc. (v.p. 1999—2001), Washington Soc. Landscape Painters, Salmagundi Club N.Y. Office: Andrei Kushnir/Michele Taylor LLC 208 E 6th St New York NY 10003 Office Phone: 212-254-2628. Personal E-mail: artgallery@verizon.net.

KUSIK, CHARLES LEMBIT, chemical engineer; b. Apr. 24, 1934; s. Charles and Mary (Jackson) K. BS, MIT, 1956, MS, 1958; ScD, N.Y. U., 1961. Registered profl. engr., Mass. Scientist ops. rsch. group MIT, Cambridge, 1961-62; project officer U.S. Army, Aberdeen, Md., 1962—63; engr. Avco Corp., Wilmington, Mass., 1963-64; mem. profl. staff Arthur D. Little, Inc., Cambridge, Mass., 1964—2002, mgr. metals and energy mgmt., 1980-89, dir., 1989—98; with ICF Consulting, Cambridge, 2002—03; pvt. practice cons. Lincoln, Mass., 2003—. Author: (with Kenahan) Energy Use Patterns for Metal Recycling, 1978, (with Makar and Mounier) Availability of Critical Scrap Metals Containing Chromium in the United States, 1980; contbr. articles to profl. jours. Mem. Metall. Soc., Am. Inst. Chem. Engrs., Assn. for Iron and Steel Tech. Office: 209 Lincoln Rd Lincoln MA 01773-5100 E-mail: kusik773@alum.mit.edu.

KUSIN, GARY M., consumer products company executive; b. Texarkana, Tex. married; 4 children. BA, U. Tex., Austin; MBA, Harvard U. V.p., gen. mgr. Sanger-Harris divsn. Federated Dept. Stores; pres., co-founder Babbage's Inc., Dallas, 1983—95; co-founder Laura Mercier Cosmetics, Dallas, 1995—98; pres., CEO OmniOffices, Inc. (later HQ Global Workplaces), 1998—99; CEO HQ Global Workplaces, 1999—2001; pres., CEO FedEx Kinko's Inc., Dallas, 2001—. Bd. dirs. Electronic Arts, Inc. Bd. trustees St. Mark's Sch. Tex.; chmn. Dallas Young Pres.' Orgn.; mem. Dallas Citizen's Coun. Named Entrepreneur of Yr., Inc. Mag. Mem.: Dallas C. of C. (bd. dirs.). Office: Fed Ex Kinko s Inc Three Galleria Tower 13155 Noel Rd Ste 1600 Dallas TX 75240*

KUSMIERZ, ANN MARIE DOROTHY, elementary school educator; b. Pittston, Pa., July 26, 1944; d. Anthony Francis and Dorothy Eleanor (Lukasik) Ferretti; m. Michael J. Kusmierz, Sr., June 26, 1965; children: Michelle, Marie, Michael, Anthony, Mary, Melissa, Marleah, Allyn, Andrew, Adam, Aaron, Alexander, Mark. BS in Edn., Pa. State U., University Park, 1965. Third grade tchr. N.E. Bradford Sch. Dist., LeRaysville, Pa., 1965—68; sub. tchr. Wyalusing Area Sch. Dist., Pa., 1968—72, third grade tchr., 1975—76, sixth grade tchr., 1976—88, kindergarten tchr., 1988—, G.E.D. tchr., 1990—92, wrestling cheerleader advisor, 1983—; daycare supervisor Bradford County Day Care, Towanda, Pa., 1972—75. Religious edn. tchr. St. Mary's Ch., Wyalusing, 1970—, coord. confraternity Christian Doctrine, 1975—95. Mem.: NEA, Local Assn. Union (pres. 1983—84, mem. rep. coun. 1970—), Pa. State Edn. Assn. Democrat. Roman Catholic. Home: RR 2 Box 288 Wyalusing PA 18853 Office: Wyalusing Elem Sch RR 4 Box 4008 Wyalusing PA 18853

KUSPIT, DONALD BURTON, art historian, critic, educator; b. N.Y.C., Mar. 26, 1935; s. Morris and Celia (Schmukler) Kuspit Sigmund; m. Judith Clements Price, Mar. 22, 1962. BA in Philosophy with distinction, Columbia U., 1955; MA in Philosophy, Yale U., 1957; DPhil magna cum laude, U. Frankfort, 1960; PhD in Art History, U. Mich., 1971; DFA (hon.), Davidson Coll., 1993; DFA, San Francisco Art Inst., 1996; LHD (hon.), U. Ill., 1998. Asst. prof. Pa. State U., State College, 1960-66; assoc. prof. U. Windsor, Ont., Can., 1966-70; prof. U. N.C., Chapel Hill, 1970-78; Univ. Disting. prof. Rutgers U., New Brunswick, N.J., 1982-83; prof. art, chmn. dept. art SUNY-Stony Brook, 1978-83; editorial cons. UMI Rsch. Press, Ann Arbor, Mich., 1980-90; Andrew Dixon White prof. at large Cornell U., Ithaca, N.Y., 1991-97. Editl. cons. Cambridge U. Press, 1991—, Ency. Brit. European Art 1900-1950, Art Criticism and Theory; mem. overview com. visual arts sect. NEA, Washington, 1983-85. Author: Clement Greenberg, ARt Critic, 1979, the Critiic as Artist: The Intentionality of Art, 1984, Leon Golub: Existentialist/Activist Painter, 1985, Idiosyncratic Indentities: Artists at the End of Avant-Garde, 1986, The New Subjectivism: Art of the 1980's, 1988, Eric Fischl, 1988, Louise Bourgeois, 1989, Alex Katz: Night Paintings, The Dialectic of Decandence, 1993, Alex Katz: Night Paintings, The Dialectic of Decandence, reprinted, 2000, The Cult of the Avant-Garde Artist, 1993, Signs of Psyche in Modern and Post-Modern Art, 1993, Albert Renger-Patzch, 1993, Primordial Prosences: The Sculpture of Karel Appel, 1994, Health and Happiness in Twentieth Century Avant-Garde Art, 1996, Dale Chihuly, 1997, Jamali, 1997, Joseph Raffael, 1998, The Rebirth of Painting in the Late 20th Century, 2000, Psychostrategies of Avant-Garde Art, 2000, Redeeming Art: Critical Reveries, 2000, Don Eddy, 2001, Steve Tobin, 2003, The End of Art, 2004, April Gornas, 2005; editor: Art Criticism, 1984—; contbg. editor: Art in Am., 1978—92, Contemporanea, 1988—90, ArtForum, 1982—, Sculpture Mag., 1992—, New Art Examiner, 1993—. Recipient award for disting. contbn. to the visual arts Nat. Assn. Schs. Art and Design, 1997; Younger humanist fellow NEH, 1973, critic fellow Nat. Endowment for Arts, 1977, Guggenheim fellow, 1977. Fellow Asian Cultural Coun.; mem. PEN, Coll. Art Assn. (Frank Jewett Mather award 1983), Am. Soc. Aesthetics, Internat. Assn. Art Critics (v.p. Am. sect. 1982-84), Am. Psychoanalytic Assn. Home: 38 W 26th St New York NY 10010-2012 Office: SUNY Dept Art Stony Brook NY 11794-5400 Office Phone: 631-632-7270.

KUSSART, DANIEL, accountant, writer; s. Walter and Gertrude Kussart; m. Bonnie Wirth. BA, Lakeland Coll., Sheboygan, Wis., 1996. Author: (novel) Regarding The Clouds, 2002, The Clock Shop, 2004. Pres. St. Mark Luth. Ch., Sheboygan, Wis., 1995—98. Home: 2403 South 16th St Sheboygan WI 53081 Personal E-mail: wirkus@bytehead.com.

KUSSEROW, JAMES, music educator; b. Susanville, Calif., July 18, 1958; s. Vernon James Teel and Maxine Eylner Baker; m. Kellie Kusserow, May 20, 1989; children: Kaylan, Michael, Christopher. AA, Porterville (Calif.) C.C., 1978; BA in Music With Distinction, San Jose (Calif.) State U., 1980; MA in Pub. Sch. Adminstrn., Calif. State U., Bakersfield, 1991. Tchg. credential Calif. Band dir. Mulcahy Mid. Sch., Tulare, Calif., 1981—88, Live Oak Mid. Sch., Tulare, 1989—90, Porterville H.S. and C.C., 1990—. Musician H.S. Band Dir. of Yr., 1991; musician, condr. concert J.F. Kennedy Ctr. for the Performing Arts, 1994. Pres. Tulare-Kings Music Educators Assn., 1984—85; prin. trumpet Tulare County Symphony, 1981—89; mem. Fabulous Studio Band. Named Nat. H.S. Band Dir. of Yr., Nat. Hall of Fame, 1990. Mem.: NBA, CMEA, MENC, IAJE, Internat. Trumpet Guild. Home: 3102 W Howard Ave Visalia CA 93277 Office: Porterville HS Panther Band 465 W Olive Ave Porterville CA 93257 Personal E-mail: jazzer31@hotmail.com. E-mail: kussband@porterville.k12.ca.us.

KUSSEROW, RICHARD PHILLIP, federal agency administrator, corporate financial executive; b. San Jose, Calif., Dec. 9, 1940; s. Roger Berthold and Eve W. (Larson) K.; m. Rebecca Hatchell, Sept. 14, 1985; 1 child, Carrie Elizabeth. BA in Polit. Sci, UCLA, 1963; MA in Govt., Calif. State U., L.A., 1964; postgrad., So. Meth. U., 1965, John Marshall Sch. Law, 1972, Harvard U., 1984. Cert. internal auditor, cert. govt. auditor; cert. govt. fin. mgr., cert. fraud examiner. Lectr. Calif. State U., L.A., 1963, 64; case officer CIA, 1968-69; spl. agt. supr. in white collar and organized crime FBI, 1969-81; Insp. Gen., U.S. Dept. HHS, 1981-92; mem. Pres.'s Coun. on Integrity and Efficiency, 1981-92, vice chmn., 1986-89, chmn. legislation com., 1982-85, 89-92; mem. Pres.' Council on Mgmt. Improvement, 1986-89, 91-92; chair Nat. Task Force of Implementation of Chief Fin. Officers Act, 1990-91; chmn. Chief Fin. Officers Task Force, 1991; pres., CEO Strategic Mgmt. Sys., Inc., 1992—; ptnr. O.K. Real Estate, 1993—; pres. Govt. Mgmt. Sys., Inc., 1995—2002; pres., CEO, chmn. bd. Nat. Hotline Svcs., Inc., 1995—; CEO Corp. Compliance Svcs., Inc., 1995—2002. Presdl. appointee to Nat. Adv. Commn. on Law Enforcement, 1989; mem. CFOs Coun., 1990-92, Def. Procurement Round Table, 1993—; lectr. white collar crime, asset protection, health care, fraud and abuse, internal controls, corporate compliance programs, others; mem. Atty. Gen.'s Econ. Crime Coun., 1988-90; nat. chmn. Am. Compliance Inst., 1995. Author: Principles of Investigative Targeting, 1974, Management Principles for Asset Protection, 1995, Corporate Compliance Policies & Procedures: Guide to Assessment and Development, 2000, Compliance Training Manual, 2001, Sarbanes-Oxley: Best Practices for Private and Non Profit Health Care Entities, 2003, Ultimat Hotline Resources Manual, 2005; contbr. articles on corp. compliance investigations, auditing and mgmt. to profl. jours. Pres. Nat. Honor Svc., 1996—. Capt. USMCR, 1964-68. Recipient Sec.'s Bronze medal for good govt., 1983, Outstanding Leadership award Pres. Coun. on Mgmt. Improvement, 1988, Cert. of Svc. Appreciation, Pres. of U.S., 1989, Donald L. Scantlebury award for fin. mgmt. excellence Assn. Govt. Accts., 1992; H. Horton Rontree Disting. lectr. in health law, 1990. Mem. Assn. Fed. Investigators (nat. pres. 1984-85, chmn. awards com. 1986-87), Soc. Former FBI Agts., Assn. Govt. Accts. (nat. task force on fed. fin. mgmt. 1983-88, pres. Balt. chpt. 1987, chmn. nat. profl. devel. conf. 1989, nat. pres. 1990, nat. leadership awards Boston chpt. 1985, No. Va. chpt., Washington chpt., D.C. chpt. 1985, Nat. Assn. 1987), Am. Health Lawyers Assn., Nat. Health Care Anti-Fraud Assn. (pub. svc. award 1989), Inst. Internal Auditors (cert.), Am. Compliance Inst. (governing bd. 1996-2001), Army-Navy Club. Presbyterian. Avocations: reading, travel, tennis. also: 620 Kenmore Ave ste B Fredericksburg VA 22401-5759 Office Phone: 703-535-1431. Business E-Mail: rkusserow@strategicm.com.

KUSSMAUL, DONALD, academic administrator; Bachelor's degree, Master's degree, So. Ill. U.; Doctorate, Loyola U. Supt. East Dubuque (Ill.) Unit Sch. Dist. 119, 1983—. Mem. adv. com. to state supt. Ill.; dir. ext. svcs. East Dubuque campus Hillside C.C.; dir. Family T.I.E.S. Early Childhood At Risk Program. Co-author: (book) Preparing Schools and School Systems for the 21st Century. Active Greater Dubuque Area Red Cross, Jr. Achievement Orgn. Mem.: Ill. Assn. Sch. Adminstrs., Am. Assn. Sch. Adminstrs. (pres.-elect 2003—, exec. bd. 2000—, former chmn. rural/small schs. com.), Horace Mann League, Lions. Office: East Dubuque Sch Dist 119 200 Park Lane Dr East Dubuque IL 61025-9568

KUSSROW, NANCY ESTHER, educational association administrator; BA, Valparaiso U., 1952; MA, U. N.C., 1954. Exec. dir. Nat. Assn. prins. of Schs. for Girls; ret., 1996.

KUSTERER, THOMAS, science administrator; b. Balt., July 9, 1946; s. Edward Thomas and Anne Thelma (Ekas) K.; m. Janet Elizabeth Polunas, Sept. 16, 1972; children: David, Robert. BS, Loyola Coll., 1968, MBA, 1982; MS, Rutgers U., 1972. Instr. Balt. C.C., 1968-69; tchg. asst. Rutgers U., 1969—71; cons. Benedict (Md.) Estuarine Lab., 1971-72; planner Harford County (Md.) Govt., Bel Air, Md., 1972-84; natural resources mgr. Md. Dept. of the Environment, Balt., 1984-89; program mgr. Montgomery County Govt., Rockville, Md., 1989—. Mem. Md. Coastal Resources Adv. Com., 1984-88, Govs. Solid Waste Mgmt. Task Force, 1987, Md. Acid Deposition Adv. Com., 1984-88, nat. round table on unit pricing for solid waste collection and disposal U.S. EPA, 1992, nat. round table on full cost acctg. for solid waste mgmt. systems, 1994. Contbg. author/advisor: Pay As You Throw: Lessons Learned about Unit Pricing, 1994; contbg. author Developing Agreements on the Siting of Waste Management Facilties, 1994, Innovative Approaches to Siting Solid Waste Management Facilities, 1992; editor (newsletter) Md. Environ., 1986, 87; contbr. articles to profl. jours. Mgr. youth sports teams Parks and Recreation Depts., Howard and Balt. Counties, 1983-97; officer Md. Save Our Streams, Annapolis, 1973-76. Mem. Baltimore Mus. Art, Cent. Pk. Conservancy, Guggenheim Mus., Hist. Ellicott City, Inc. (officer), Lower East Side Tenement Mus., Sierra Club, Nature Conservancy, Walters Art Mus., Whitney Mus. Am. Art. Home: 3796 Dorsey Search Cir Ellicott City MD 21042-3753 Office: Montgomery County Recycling Ctr 16105 Frederick Rd Derwood MD 20855 Office Phone: 301-840-2701. Personal E-mail: kuzcomms@comcast.net.

KUSTIN, KENNETH, chemist; b. Bronx, N.Y., Jan. 6, 1934; s. Alex and Mae (Marvisch) K.; m. Myrna May Jacobson, June 24, 1956; children: Brenda Jayne, Franklin Daniel, Michael Thorpe. BSc, Queens Coll., Flushing, N.Y., 1955; PhD, U. Minn., 1959. Postdoctoral fellow Max Planck Inst. for Phys. Chemistry, Göttingen, Germany, 1959-61; asst. prof. chemistry Brandeis U., Waltham, Mass., 1961-66, assoc. prof., 1966-72, prof., 1972-97, prof. emeritus, 1997—, chmn. dept. chemistry, 1974-77. Vis. prof. pharmacology Harvard U. Med. Sch., 1977-78; Fulbright-Hays lectr., 1978; program dir. NSF, 1985-86; adj. rsch. scientist U.S. Army, Natick RD&E Ctr., 1991—. Editor: Fast Reactions, vol. 16 of Methods in Enzymology, 1969; bd. editors Internat. Jour. Chem. Kinetics, 1983-90, Inorganic Chemistry, 1993-95; rsch. and publs. in field. Mem. AAAS, Am. Chem. Soc. (councilor 1983-85), Phi Beta Kappa. E-mail: kmkustin@ix.netcom.com.

KUSUKAWA, AKIRA, demographer, educator; b. Fukuoka, Kyushu, Japan, May 13, 1925; s. Tokuzo Tanaka and Ko Kusukawa; m. Emiko Fujita, June 3, 1952. BS, Yamaguchi Coll., 1944; MPH, Johns Hopkins U., 1953; MD, Kyushu U., 1948, D of Med. Sci., 1956. Tech. advisor to Coun. of Mins. Govt. of Sudan, 1959—60; sec. UN Population Commn., N.Y.C., 1964—74; spl. asst. UN Population Fund, N.Y.C., 1974—77, dir., 1977—86; ret., 1986. Prof. Moscow State U., Russia, 1988, N.Y. Med. Coll., 1986—2004, L.I. U., N.Y.C., 1986—, UN Demographic Centre, India, 1963—64. Author: Cardiovascular Epidemiology, 1956; co-author: Ageing Research, 1999; contbr. UN Documents on Population, 1973—86. Recipient Medal of Peace, State Coun. Bulgaria, 1986, Golden Order Labor, Presdl. Coun. Hungary, 1986. Mem.: APHA, N.Y. Acad. Scis., Japanese Med. Soc. Am. (dir.), Population Assn.

Am., Internat. Union Sci. Study Population. Avocations: swimming, music, painting. Home: 214 Harriman Dr #2023 Goshen NY 10924-2425 Office: Long Island Univ Hoxie Hall 720 Northern Blvd Brookville NY 11548-1300

KUTANOGLU, ERHAN, engineering educator, researcher; b. Amasya, Turkey, Mar. 14, 1970; s. Isa and Hadiye Kutanoglu; m. Oya Kutanoglu; children: Selin, Erin. BS in Indsl. Engring., Bilkent U., Ankara, Turkey, 1992; MS in Indsl. Engring., Bilkent U., 1995; PhD in Indsl. Engring., Lehigh U., 1999. Rsch. asst. Bilkent U., 1995-99; rsch. and tchg. asst. Lehigh U., Bethlehem, Pa.; ops. rsch. analyst, devel. engr. IBM Global Svcs., Mechanicsburg, Pa., 1999; asst. prof. U. Ark., Fayetteville, 1999—. Cons. IBM, Tyson Foods, Fayetteville, 1999—. Mem. Inst. Ops. Rsch. and Mgmt. Scis., Inst. Indsl. Engrs., Am. Soc. Engring. Edn., Turkish Operational Rsch. and Indsl. Engring. Soc. Office: U Ark 4207 Bell Engineering Ctr Fayetteville AR 72701 Fax: (501) 575-8431. E-mail: erhank@uark.edu.

KUTCHER, ASHTON (CHRISTOPHER ASHTON KUTCHER), actor; b. Cedar Rapids, Iowa, Feb. 7, 1978; Actor: (TV series) That '70s Show, 1998—2005; (films) Coming Soon, 1999, Down to You, 2000, Reindeer Games, 2000, Dude, Where's My Car?, 2000, Texas Rangers, 2001, Just Married, 2003, Cheaper by the Dozen, 2003, A Lot Like Love, 2005; actor, co-prodr.: (films) My Boss's Daughter, 2003; co-creator, exec. prodr.: (TV series) Punk'd, 2003—; actor, exec. prodr.: (films) The Butterfly Effect, 2004; actor, prodr. Guess Who, 2005; exec. prodr.: (TV series) You've Got a Friend, 2004—. Mailing: c/o Endeavor Talent Agy 10th Fl 9701 Wilshire Blvd Beverly Hills CA 90212*

KUTCHER, KENNETH E., manufacturing executive; b. N.J. BS in Acctg., Seton Hall U. Staff acct. Coopers & Lybrand; CFO Celanese Chems. and Trevira; CFO, sec. Grief Bros. Corp.; exec. v.p., CFO Springs Industries, Ft. Mill, SC, 2001—. Office: Spring Industries 205 N White St PO Box 70 Fort Mill SC 29715

KUTCHI, JUDITH ANN, elementary school educator; b. Hazelton, Pa., Oct. 20, 1942; d. Nicholas I and Elizabeth Veronica Bachman; m. Robert John Kutchi, Aug. 10, 1963; children: S Robert, Steven N, Nicholas A, Elizabeth A(dec.). BE, Bloomsburg State U., 1963, MEd, 1967. Tchr. Prince George County Bd. of Edn., Upper Marlboro, Md., 1963—67, resource tchr., 1967—69, tchr., 1969—92, St. Mary Star of the Sea, Indian Head, Md., 1992—2001; reading specialist Prince George's County Bd. Edn., 2001—. Mem.: Internat. Reading Assn., Delta Kappa Gamma Soc. (pres. Alpha Epsilon Chpt.). Avocations: reading, quilting, sewing, travel. Home: 2951 Bannock Rd Bryans Road MD 20616 Office: Henry G Ferguson Elem Berry Rd Bryans Road MD 20616

KUTEMEYER, PETER MARTIN, industrial engineering executive; b. Freiburg, West Germany, Nov. 19, 1938; came to U.S., 1954, naturalized, 1956; s. Martin Henry and Gertrude Barbara (Buechel) K.; m. Fresquez, June 25, 1961 (div. Aug. 1986); children: Michael, Kristina. BME with distinction, Ariz. State U., 1968, MS in Engring. Mechanics, 1969; MBA, U. Utah, 1977. Enlisted USAF, 1958, commd. 2d lt., 1967, advanced through grades to capt., 1970, aero. engr., 1969-71, sys. devel. engr., 1971-74, tech. liaison officer to W. German Fed. Govt., 1974-78; indsl. mgr. Mining Progress, Inc., Highland Mills, N.Y., 1978-79, prodn. mgr., 1979-81; gen. mgr. Bischoff Environ. Sys. divsn. Intertech Inc., Highland Mills, N.Y., 1981-89, v.p., gen. mgr., 1989—92; pres. PMK Enterprises, Inc., Wilmington, Del., 1989—. Mem.: AIAA, ASME, Nat. Assn. Realtors. Home: 5225 Pooks Hill Rd Apt 1020S Bethesda MD 20814-6718 Office Phone: 301-493-4149. Personal E-mail: p.kutemeyer@verizon.net.

KUTER, KAY E., writer, actor; b. L.A., Apr. 25, 1925; s. Leo E. and Evelyn Belle (Edler) K. Student, Pomona Coll., 1943, UCLA, 1944; BFA in Drama, Carnegie Inst. Tech., 1949. Radio actor NBC, 1944; actor, 1944—. Actor in 198 musicals, off-Broadway, stock, repertory, touring, and Shakespearean stage prodns.; 51 feature films; more than 435 TV shows including 7 yrs. as a series regular (Newt Kiley) in Green Acres and Petticoat Junction; voiceover actor for cartoon series Aladdin, The Little Mermaid, Prince Valiant, Biker Mice From Mars, Fantastic Four, Julius and Friends; in cartoon spls. Olympic Mascot Izzy, Annabelle's Wish, The Jungle Book: Mowgli's Story, The Little Mermaid II; in CD-ROMS The Beast Within, Ultima 9, Grim Fandango, The Curse of Monkey Island, Heretic II, Emperor Dune, Arcanum; in radio prodns. Getting Married, Treasure Island, Macbeth, Satanic Verses, Heartbreak House; author: Carmen Incarnate, 1946, Ships That Never Sailed, 1994, Hollywood Houdini, Picture Perfect World, 1995; voiceover spokesman Hershey's Kisses, 1989—; editor: The Jester, 1956-60, The Jester 35th Anniversary, 1960, 50th Anniversary, 1976; contbr. to Nat. Libr. Poetry anthologies, 1995, 96, 97, 99, 2000 (Editor's Choice award); dir. more than 50 stage prodns. including Steve Allen's The Wake. Bd. dirs. Family Svc. of L.A., 1950-70. Mem. SAG (bd. dirs. 1970-73), AEA, AFTRA, ADA, ACLU, NOW, NARAL, UNICEF, UN Assn. U.S., Nat. Trust Hist. Preservation, Smithsonian, Carnegie Mellon U. Westcoast Drama Alumni Clan (founding mem., officer, bd. dirs. 1968-80), Ephebian Soc., Internat. Soc. Poets (disting. mem.), Albert C. May Soc., Acad. Am. Poets, Andrew Carnegie Soc., Pacific Pioneer Broadcasters, Carnegie Mellon U. Alumni Assn. (regional v.p. 1976-79, Svc. award 1979), Van Nuys H.S. Alumni Assn., Interfaith Alliance, Libr. Found. L.A., Nat. Audubon Soc., Hist Soc. So. Calif., L.A. Conservancy, Nat. Trust Pub. Edn., Theatre 40, Calif. Artists Radio Theatre, Am. Film Inst., Libr. Congress Assocs., Ams. United, Masquers Club (bd. dirs. 1953-75, rec. sec. 1956-70, corr. sec. 1957-69. v.p. 1971-75), Actors' Fund of Am. (life mem.), others. Democrat. Avocations: composing, piano. Home: 6207 Satsuma Ave North Hollywood CA 91606-3819

KUTKA, NICHOLAS, nuclear medicine physician; b. Czechoslovakia, Dec. 17, 1926; s. Vladimir and Agatha (Flenko) Kutka; m. Anna Cizmar, Apr. 14, 1965 (dec. Oct. 1996); children: Andrew, Gregory; m. Veronika Filova, Apr. 28, 2001. MD, Comenius U., Slovakia, 1951; PhD, Slovak Acad. Scis., 1962. Diplomate in internal medicine Postgrad. Edn. of Physicians; diplomate Am. Bd. Nuc. Medicine, Am. Bd. Disability Analysts. Asst. prof. Inst. Physiology Comenius U., Bratislava, 1951; intern, resident in internal medicine Mil. Hosp., Bratislava, 1952-55; chief dept. radioisotopes Inst. Endocrinology, Slovak Acad. Scis., Bratislava, 1956-69; tech. asst. IAEA, Bogota, Colombia, 1969-70; resident in nuc. medicine Duke U., 1971-73; asst. prof. radiology Baylor Coll. Medicine, Houston, 1973-95, assoc. prof. radiology, 1995—; dir. nuc. medicine Ben Taub Gen. Hosp., Houston, 1978-81; chief nuc. medicine svc. VA Med. Ctr., Houston, 1982-96, staff physician, 1996—2001, chief nuc. medicine sect., 2001—. Mem. med. staff univ. affiliated hosps. Houston, faculty Sch. Nuc. Medicine Tech.; fellow IAEA, Rome, 1962-63. Contbr. numerous articles to profl. jours; mem. editl. bd. Endocrinologia Experimentalis. Served with Health Svc. Czechoslovak Army, 1952-54. Recipient prize in nuc. medicine J.E. Purkyne, 1965. Mem.: Houston Radiol. Soc., Am. Soc. Nuc. Cardiology, Soc. Nuc. Medicine, Tex. Med. Assn., Harris County Med. Soc. Address: VA Med Ctr #115 2002 Holcombe Blvd PO Box 20183 Houston TX 77225-0183 Office Phone: 713-794-7077. Business E-Mail: kutka.nicholas@med.va.gov. E-mail: nkutka@aol.com.

KUTLAR, FERDANE, genetics educator, researcher; b. Turkey, Apr. 15, 1945; came to U.S., 1984; d. Mehmet and Sidika Tanrikulu; m. Abdullah Kutlar, Feb. 7, 1975. MD, Istanbul (Turkey) Med. Sch., 1971. Bd. cert in internal medicine, Turkey, 1976. Resident in internal medicine Istanbul U. Sch. Medicine, 1972-76; chief resident dept. medicine Istanbul Hosp., 1977-81; rsch. fellow Med. Coll. Ga., Augusta, 1982; hematology fellow Istanbul U. Sch. Medicine, 1983; rsch. fellow Med. Coll. Ga., Augusta, 1984, asst. prof., 1985-99, assoc. prof. medicine, 1999—. Dir. DNA lab. Med. Coll. Ga., Augusta, 1994—; presenter in field. Contbr. articles to profl. jours. Mem. Am. Soc. Hematology, Am. Soc. Human Genetics, Med. Coll. Ga. Pres.'s Club. Avocations: painting, gardening, decorating, chess. Home: 623 Sawgrass Dr Martinez GA 30907-9137 Office: Med Coll Ga Dept Medicine 15th St AC-1000 Augusta GA 30912-2100 Office Phone: 706-721-9768. Business E-Mail: fkutlar@mail.mcg.edu.

KUTLER, ALISON L., lawyer; d. Stuart and Sandy Kutler. BA in Govt., cum laude, Georgetown U., 1993; JD, Stanford U., 1999. Bar: DC, Nebr. 1999. Mem. staff US Rep. Peter Hoagland, 1991—93; various positions with Clinton Adminstrn., 1993—96; asst. to US Sec. Commerce Ron Brown; Congl. affairs specialist US Dept. Commerce Bur Export Adminstrn., Small Bus. Adminstrn.; dep. chief of staff to Hadassah Lieberman Gore-Lieberman Presdl. Campaign, 2000; assoc. Arent Fox Kinter Plotkin & Kahn, Washington; assoc., pub. law & policy strategies group Sonnenschein Nath & Rosenthal LLP, Washington, 2002—. Office: Sonnenschein Nath & Rosenthal LLP Ste 600, E Tower 1301 K St NW Washington DC 20005 Office Phone: 202-408-9142. Office Fax: 202-408-6399. Business E-Mail: akutler@sonnenschein.com.

KUTLER, STANLEY IRA, historian, lawyer, educator; b. Cleve., Aug. 10, 1934; s. Robert P. and Zelda R. (Coffman) K.; m. Sandra J. Sachs, June 24, 1956; children: Jeffrey, David, Susan, Andrew. BA, Bowling Green State U., 1956; PhD, Ohio State U., 1960. Instr. history Pa. State U., State College, 1960-62; asst. prof. San Diego State U., 1962-64; from asst. prof. to prof. U. Wis., Madison, 1964-80, E. Gordon Fox prof. Am. instns., law and history, 1980—. Disting. exchange scholar to China Nat. Acad. Scis., 1982; Kenneth Keating lectr. Tel Aviv U., 1984; sr. Fulbright lectr. to Japan, 1977, to Israel, 1985, China, 1986; disting. vis. Fulbright scholar, Peru, 1987; Bicentennial prof. Tel Aviv U., 1985; cons. NEH, 1975—, The Constitution Project, 1985—; disting. chair Polit. Sci., U. Bologna, 1991; hist. cons. BBC/Discovery series Watergate, 1994. Author: Judicial Power and Reconstruction, 1968, Privilege and Creative Destruction, 1971, 2d edit., 1990, The American Inquisition, 1983, The Wars of Watergate: The Last Crisis of Richard Nixon, 1990, 92, Abuse of Power: The New Nixon Tapes, 1997; editor: Supreme Court and the Constitution, 1969, 3d edit., 1984, Looking for America, 1975, 80, The Encyclopedia of the Vietnam War, 1995, Encyclopedia of 20th Century America, 1995, American Perspectives: Historians on Historians, 1996, Watergate: The Fall of Richards Nixon, 1996, Dictionary of American History, 10 vols., 1996—; founding editor Rev. in Am. History, 1972-97; mem. adv. editor Greenwood Pub., 1968-73, Johns Hopkins U. Press, 1982—. Recipient Silver Gavel award ABA; fellow Sage Found., 1967-68, Emmy award, 1994, Peabody award, 1994, Best Reference Work award, Am. Assn. Pubs., 1996; fellow Guggenheim Found., 1971-72, Rockefeller Found., 1979-80. Jewish. Office: U Wis Dept History Madison WI 53706 Business E-Mail: sikutler@wisc.edu.

KUTNER, JANET, art critic, book reviewer; b. Dallas, Sept. 20, 1937; m. Jonathan D. Kutner, Jan. 15, 1961. Student, Stanford U., 1955-57; BA in English, So. Meth. U., 1959. Asst. dir. Dallas Mus. Contemporary Arts, 1959-61; art critic, book reviewer Dallas Morning News, 1970—; Dallas/Ft. Worth corr. ARTnews Mag., 1975—. Mem. arts adv. panel Dallas Mcpl. Libr., 1981-91; mem. adv. bd. Arts Magnet H.S. of Dallas, 1980-92; mem. adv. com. Sch. Architecture and Environ. Design, U. Tex., Arlington, 1985-87; mem. long range planning com. Dallas Mus. Art, 1985-86; mem. visual arts and architecture adv. panel Tex. Com. on Arts, 1980-82. Contbr. articles to profl. jours.; juror various art exhbns. Bd. trustees Greenhill Sch., Dallas, 1980-81. Art critic's grantee Nat. Endowment for Arts, 1976-77, art critic's fellow Nat. Gallery Art, 1991—; recipient Legend award, Dallas Ctr. Contemporary Art, 2005. Mem. Am. Assn. Museums, Dallas Mus. Art, Internat. Coun. Museums, ArtTable, Dallas Press Club (Critics award 1997). Office: Dallas Morning News PO Box 655237 Dallas TX 75265-5237

KUTNER, LAWRENCE ALAN, television producer, columnist; b. N.Y.C., Feb. 29, 1952; s. Michael and Mary (Viener) K.; m. Cheryl Kay Olson, Oct. 1988. AB, Oberlin Coll., 1974; PhD, U. Minn., 1978. Lic. consulting psychologist, Minn., N.Y. Psychologist Mayo Clinic, Rochester, N.Y., 1977-78; sci. producer Sta. WNET-TV, N.Y.C., 1978-79; ind. producer Westport, Conn., 1979-81; producer, reporter Sta. WCCO-TV, Mpls., 1981-84; pres. Health and Sci. Communications, Inc., Mpls., 1984—. Clin. assoc. prof. U. Minn.; bd. dirs. Walk-In Counseling Ctr., Mpls. Columnist: N.Y. Times, 1987—; co-producer TV program Project Abuse, 1984, Emmy award 1985; producer numerous TV programs which have received nat. and internat. awards. Psychology fellow Mayo Clinic, 1977; communications fellow AAAS, 1976. Home and Office: 54 Trowbridge St # F Cambridge MA 02138-4113

KUTOSH, SUE, artist; b. Elizabeth, N.J., Dec. 25, 1947; d. Stephen and Irene (Ribecky) K. BFA, Carnegie-Mellon U., 1971; MA, Kent State U., 1973. One-woman shows include Keane Mason Gallery, N.Y.C., 1978, West Broadway Gallery, N.Y.C., 1981, Kristen Richards Gallery, N.Y.C., 1983, Mussavi Arts Gallery, N.Y.C., 1987, N.Y. Bot. Garden, Bronx, 1992, Montserrat Gallery, N.Y.C., 1996, Pleiades Gallery, N.Y.C., 1997; art included in books: The Films of Jane Fonda, 1981, Hispanic Hollywood, 1990, The Lavender Screen, 1993, Hollywood Babble On, 1994, New Art Internat., 1998-2000, Direct Art mag., 2005; scenic art contbns. Sesame Street Recipient Daytime Emmy for Seseame Street, 1993-94. Mem. United Scenic Artists, Local 829, Catharine Lorillard Wolfe Art Club, N.Y. Artists Equity, Nat. Assn. Women Artists. Avocation: photography. Home: 200 E 16th St Apt 2-d New York NY 10003-3708

KUTRZEBA, JOSEPH S., theater producer, director; b. Lodz, Poland, Oct. 11, 1927; came to U.S., 1950; s. Israel and Malka (Hakman) Fajwiszys; m. Valerie M. Hageman, Sept. 1955 (div. 1959); 1 child, Karen Janina; m. Michaela Lacher, Jan. 14, 1979; children: Marcus, Claudia Nina. BA, U. Munich, 1950; MFA, Yale U., 1956; PhD, NYU, 1974. Rschr., prodn. coord., dir., stage mgr. CBS-TV, N.Y.C., 1956-73; prodr., dir., writer, narrator UN Radio, N.Y.C., 1959-69; dir., mem. Actors Studio, N.Y.C., 1960-62; founder, prodr., artistic dir. Queens Playhouse, Flushing Meadows, NY, 1972-74, also mem. bd. dirs., pres.; mem. faculty New Sch. for Social Rsch., N.Y.C., 1975-77. Interpreter, translator U.S. Cts.; tchr. English. Prodr., dir. documentary film Children in the Holocaust, 1980, (English and Polish versions) Helena: the Emigrant Queen, 1996 at La Mama and Kosciuszko Found.; dir. 7 stage plays, N.Y.C., 1995-2004; presented Shakespeare's Sonnets at St. Peter's Ch. with Sam Waterston and Jan Englert. Mem. citizens com. Study N.Y. Theater, 1971-72; aux. mounted officer N.Y.C. Police Dept., 1974-77; founder Warsaw Ghetto Resistance Orgn.; exec. sec., dep. presiding officer Hidden Child Found. Lt. U.S. Army, 1950-52, Korea. Recipient Tony award, Drama Desk award nominations for prodr. Best Broadway musical The Lieutenant, 1975; recipient bronze award Internat. Film and TV Festival N.Y. for Children in the Holocaust with Liv Ullman, 1980; MacDowell Colony fellow, 1973. Mem. Dirs. Guild Am., Yale U. Alumni Assn. Avocations: tennis, skiing, horseback riding. Office Phone: 718-760-0863.

KUTSCHER, MARTIN L., pediatrician, neurologist; BA, Columbia Coll., 1977, MD, 1981. Diplomate Am. Bd. Pediats., 1986, cert. child neurologist Am. Bd. Pediats., 1986. Resident in pediats. St. Christopher Hosp. Children, Phila., 1981—84; fellow in child neurology Albert Einstein Coll. Medicine, Bronx, NY, 1984—87; physician Pediat. Neurol. Assocs., White Plains, NY, 1987—. Asst. prof. N.Y. Med. Coll., Valhalle, NY, 1987—. Contbr. articles to internet site; author: Adnobook: Living Right Now!, 2002, Special Nees Kids, 2003, Childhood Services, 2003. Bd. trustees Found. Thactology, N.Y., 1988—, Jewish Family Congregation, South Salem, NY, 2000—, Soundview Prep. Sch., Mt. Kises, NY, 2002—. Named Top Doctor Child Neurology, N.Y. Metro Area Connelly Guide, 2002—04, Westchester (N.Y.) Mag., 2002—04, N.Y. Mag., 2004. Fellow: Am. Acad. Neurology, Am. Acad. Pediatrics; mem.: Child Neurology Soc. Office: Pediatric Neurological Assoc 125 S Broadway White Plains NY 10605

KUTSCHER, RONALD EARL, retired federal agency administrator; b. Hebron, Nebr., Apr. 18, 1932; s. Earl Harvey and Doris Lillian (Zong) K.; m. Elizabeth Elin Granholm, Dec. 28, 1963; children: Laura Ingrid, Steven Ronald. BA, Doane Coll., 1955; postgrad., U. Ill., 1955-56. Economist Bur. Labor Stats., Washington, 1957-68, asst. chief for rsch. divsn. of econ. growth, 1968-76, asst. commr., 1976-82, assoc. commr., 1982-96. Contbr. articles to profl. jours. With U.S. Army, 1952—54. Mem. Am. Statis. Assn. (chair com. on coms. 1989-91, chair program com. 1985, Pres Best Econ. Forecast 1973). Lutheran. Avocations: photography, golf. E-mail: brekutsch@aol.com.

KUTSIN, LEONID, engineering educator, researcher; b. Belaya Tserkov, Ukraine, Jan. 12, 1935; arrived in U.S., 1993; s. Kutsin and Mitnitsky; m. Genya Vishnevetsky, Nov. 11, 1961; children: Igor Vishnevetsky, Renata Dielman. MS in Mechanics, Petrozavodsk (Russia) State U., 1957; Candidate in Tech. Scis., Kuban State Agrointstitut, Krasnodar, Russia, 1967; D in Tech. Scis., Rostov (Russia) State Inst. Machinery, 1982. Sr. rschr., dept. head State Rsch., Tech. and Design Inst. for Mechanization Livestock Farms, Kiev, Ukraine, 1960—87; prof., head mech. engring. dept. Saratov (Russia) State Agroengineering U., 1987—93; cons. Bion Techs., Inc., Amherst, NY, 1998; prof. Erie Coll., Amherst, 1998—99; cons. N.Am. Acad. Info. Scis., Toronto, Canada, 2000—03. Cons. Pan-Am. Environmental, Inc., Buffalo, 1999—2000. Author: (textbook) Distribution of Furage, 1971; contbr. articles to profl. jours. Mem.: N.Y. Acad. Scis., Am. Assn. Agrl. Engring., Internat. Info. Acad. Jewish. Achievements include patents in field. Home: 420 Old Falls Blvd North Tonawanda NY 14120 Office: SEAM Inc Director of Technologies 1576 Sweet Home Rd Amherst NY 14228 Office Phone: 716-694-9553. Personal E-mail: leonidkutsin2@yahoo.com.

KUTTER, CATHERINE JANE, psychologist; d. David Allen and Elizabeth Anne Kutter; m. John Kyle Walker. PhD, U. Kans., 2001. Lic. psychologist Mass., 2003, Health Service Provider Mass., 2003. Postdoctoral trainee Nat. Ctr. PTSD, VA Boston Healthcare Sys., Boston, 1999—2004; psychologist VA Med. Ctr., White River Junction, Vt., 2004—. Contbr. articles to profl. jours., chpts. to books. Mem.: Internat. Soc. Traumatic Stress Studies. Office: VA Med Ctr (116A) 215 N Main St White River Junction VT 05009 Office Phone: 802-295-9363 5687. E-mail: catherine.kutter@med.va.gov.

KUTTLER, CARL MARTIN, JR., academic administrator; b. Daytona Beach, Fla., Jan. 31, 1940; s. Carl M. and Winona (Ellis) K.; m. Evelyn Flathmann, June 29, 1963; children: Cindy, Carl Martin III, Erika. AA, St. Petersburg Jr. Coll., 1960; BS in Mgmt., Fla. State U., Tallahassee, 1962; JD, Stetson U., 1965. Bar: Fla. 1965. Rsch. aide 2d Dist. Ct. Appeals, Lakeland, Fla., 1965-66; instr. St. Petersburg (Fla.) Jr. Coll. (now St. Petersburg Coll.), 1965-76; asst. to v.p. for adminstrn. St. Petersburg (Fla.) Jr. Coll., 1966-67, dean. adminstrv. affairs, 1967-78, pres., 1978—. Adj. instr., cons. grad. edn. program U. Tex., Austin; judge Templeton Prize in Religion. Co-author: 1,001 Exemplary Practices in America's Two-Year Colleges, 1994. Mem. pres.'s Coun. Divsn. Cmty. Colls., 1978—; candidate for Fla. Commr. Edn., 1974; mem. judging panel selecting outstanding high schs. in Am. for U.S. Sec. Edn.; apptd. by Pres. U.S. Nat. Adv. Coun. Ednl. Rsch. and Improvement; apptd. by U.S. Sec. VA to Adminstr.'s Ednl. Assistance Adv. Com. Named Most Disting. Alumnus, Stetson U. Alumni Assn., 1978, 1988, Hon. Father of C.C. Sys. in Russia, Assn. Edn. for Everybody, 1994, Outstanding C.C. Pres. in Am., Assn. of C.C. Trustees, 1998; recipient Disting. Floridian award, Phi Theta Kappa, 1986, Nat. Disting. Coll. Pres. award, 1991, Internat. Leadership award, 1990, vis. scholar award, 1987, master tchr. award, 1988, 1992, 1993, U. Tex. Disting. Pres.'s award, PTK Fla., 1991, Alumnus award, Fla. State U., 1981, 1988, Liberty Bell award, St. Petersburg Bar Assn., 1992, Werner Kubsch award for outstanding achievement in internat. edn., C.C. for Internat. Devel., Inc., 1997, top Phi Theta Kappa chpt. award of 1200 cmty. colls., 2001, Chmn.'s award, St. Petersburg C. of C., 2001, C.W. Bill Young Pinellas Pinnacle award, Dept. Econ. Devel., 2002, Pres. award Profl. Excellence, Fla. Assn. C.C., 2002. Mem.: Fla. Bar Assn., Fla. Assn. C.C.s (Pres.'s award for profl. excellence 2002), Am. Assn. C.C.s, Nat. Assn. Coll. and Univ. Attys. Republican. Presbyterian. Home: 8336 40th Ave N Saint Petersburg FL 33709-3935 Office: St Petersburg Coll PO Box 13489 Saint Petersburg FL 33733-3489 Office Phone: 727-341-3245. Business E-Mail: kuttlerc@spcollege.edu.

KUTTNER, BERNARD A., retired judge, lawyer; b. Berlin, Jan. 13, 1934; arrived in U.S., 1939; s. Frank B. and Vera (Knopfmacher) Kuttner; children: Karen M. Capato, Robert D., Stacey M. Gilby. AB cum laude, Dartmouth Coll., 1955; postgrad., U. Va. Law Sch., 1956; JD, Seton Hall U., 1959; postgrad., N.Y. U., 1960. Bar: N.J. 1960, U.S. Supreme Ct. 1964, U.S. Ct. Mil. Appeals 1967, N.Y. 1982, DC 1982, cert.: N.J. (civil trial lawyer). Assoc. Toner, Crowley, Woelper & Vanderbilt, 1959-62; pvt. practice Newark, 1962-75; corp. counsel Irvington, 1963-66; judge N.J. State Divsn. Tax Appeals, 1977-79; instr. civil litigation Montclair State Coll., 1979-82. Del. Jud. Conf. N.J. Supreme Ct., 1974—81; vice chmn. dist. ethics com. Supreme Ct. N.J., 1984—85, chmn., 1985—86, apptd. bd. trial atty. cert., NJ, 1986—90. Contbr. articles to profl. jours. Founding mem. Cesar E. Chavez Found.; commr. Essex County (N.J.) Pk. Commn., 1973—79. To lt. comdr. USNR, 1964—74. Mem.: ATLA (com. ethical conduct 2000—), ABA (chmn. trial techniques com. 1988—89, co-editor trial techniques newsletter sect. tort and ins. practice, mem. sect. litig.), Am. Counsel Assn., Essex County Bar Assn. (trial and appellate litig., jud. com. 1972—75, chmn. 1973—75, treas. 1975—79, pres. 1980—81, products liability com. 1981—), Irvington Bar Assn. (pres. 1968—70), DC Bar Assn., Inst. Ethical Behavior (pres. 1985—). Jewish. Office: Kuttner Law Offices 24 Lackawanna Pl Millburn NJ 07041-1618 Office Phone: 973-467-9132. Personal E-mail: kuttnerbuck@aol.com.

KUTTNER, ROBERT LOUIS, editor, writer, columnist; b. N.Y.C., Apr. 17, 1943; s. Arthur Paul Kuttner and Pauline M. Levy; m. Sharland Grace Trotter, Dec. 19, 1971 (dec. Nov. 1997); children: Gabriel A., Jessica A.; m. Joan Fitzgerald, May 7, 2000. AB, Oberlin Coll., 1965; MA, U. Calif., Berkeley, 1966; cert., London Sch. Econs., 1963-64; LLD (hon.), Swarthmore Coll., 1999. Asst. to I.F. Stone, Washington, 1966; legis. asst. to Congressman W.F. Ryan, 1967-68; corr. program dir. Pacifica Radio, N.Y.C., 1968-71; editor The Village Voice, Washington, 1971-73; staff writer Washington Post, 1974-75; chief investigator Senate Banking Com., Washington, 1975-78; editor Working Papers, Mass., 1980-83; econs. writer, editor The New Republic, 1983-91; columnist Bus. Week, 1984—, Boston Globe and Washington Post Syndicate, 1985—; co-editor The Am. Prospect, 1989—. Contbr. editor More Mag., Washington, 1973-78; lectr. Boston U., 1980-82, W. Colston Leigh Bur., N.J., 1987—; vis. prof. U. Mass., 1987-88, Brandeis U., Mass., 1991-92, 2003—. Author: Revolt of the Haves, 1980, The Economic Illusion, 1984, The Life of the Party, 1987, The End of Laissez-Faire, 1991, Everything for Sale, 1997, Family Reunion, 2002; nat. policy corr.: New Eng. Jour. Medicine, 1996—2000. Exec. dir. Nat. Commn. on Neighborhoods, Washington, 1978; bd. dirs. Econ. Policy Inst. Washington, 1986—, Families USA, Boston, 1989-96, Florence Fund, 1999-2004. Recipient Jack London award, United Steelworkers Am., 1982, John Hancock award, John Hancock Co., 1988, Paul Hoffman award UN Devel. Program, 1996, Sidney Hillman award Sidney Hillman Found., 1998; Woodrow Wilson fellow U. Calif., 1965-66, Kennedy fellow, Harvard U., 1979, fellow John Guggenheim Meml. Found., 1988, McCormack Inst, 1987-88, Radcliffe Pub. Pollicy Ctr., 1998-2000. Mem. Nat. Acad. Social Ins. Avocations: tennis, photography, poetry. Office: Am Prospect 11 Beacon St Boston MA 02108 Office Phone: 617-570-8030.

KUTYNA, DONALD JOSEPH, air force officer; b. Chgo., Dec. 6, 1933; s. Frank A. and Isabel E. (Kmiec) K.; m. Lucille Mae Moellering, June 5, 1957; children: Dale J., Douglas J. Student, U. Iowa, 1951-53; BS, U.S. Mil. Acad., 1957; MS in Aero./Astronautics, MIT, 1965. Commd. 2d lt. USAF, 1957, advanced through grades to 4 star gen., 1990; pilot trainee Vance AFB, Enid, Okla., 1958; comdr. B-47 crew March AFB, Riverside, Calif., 1958; test pilot Edwards AFB, Calif., 1965-69; pilot 44th Tactical Fighter Squadron, Royal Takhli AFB, Thailand, 1969-70; planner R&D Pentagon, Washington, 1971-72; exec. officer Undersec. of Air Force, Washington, 1973-76; program mgr. Air Force Electronics Systems Div., Bedford, Mass., 1976-82; mgr. Dept. Def. Space Launch Program, L.A., 1982-84; dir. space systems Pentagon, Washington, 1984-86; vice comdr. Space Div., L.A., 1986-87; comdr. USAF Space Command, Peterson AFB, Colo., 1987-90; comdr.-in-chief N.Am. Aerospace Def. Command, U.S. Space Command, Peterson AFB, 1990-92; v.p. advanced space systems Lockheed Martin Corp. (formerly Loral Corp.), N.Y.C., 1993-99; v.p. space tech. Loral Space & Comm. Corp., N.Y.C.,

1999—2004; ret., 2004. Recipient Space award Nat. Geog. Soc., 1987, James V. Hartinger award Nat. Security Indsl. Assn., 1990, Heritage award Polish Am. Congress, 1990. Mem. Air Force Assn. (Schriever award 1991). Avocations: skiing, surfing, fishing, hunting, antique cars.

KUTZ, ALEXANDRA ELLEN, prosecutor; b. Oceanside, NY, June 18, 1974; d. DiAnne Tiley and Allan Morris Kutz. BA in Polit. Sci., BA in Psychology, BA in Philosophy, U. Rochester, 1996; JD, Am. U., 1999. Bar: Md. 1999, DC 2000, Calif. 2004. Intern US Dist. Ct. for the DC, Washington, 1998; dean's fellow Am. U., Wash. Coll. Law, 1997—98; law clk. US Attorney's Office, Dist. of Md., So. Divsn., Greenbelt, Md., 1998—98; dean's fellow Am. U., Wash. Coll. Law, Washington, 1998—99, student atty., criminal justice clinic, 1998—99; asst. atty. gen. appellate divsn. Office Atty. Gen. for DC, 1999—2000, asst. atty. gen., gen. crimes sect., 2000—00, asst. atty. gen. juvenile sect., 2000—03, asst. atty. gen. sex offense unit of the juvenile sect., 2003—. Intern coord. for the juvenile sect. Office Atty. Gen. for DC, Juvenile Sect., Washington, 2003—. Scholar Xerox award, U. Rochester, 1992—96. Mem.: ABA. Office: Office Attorney Gen DC 441 4th St NW Ste 450N Washington DC 20001

KUVSHINOFF, BORIS WILLIAM, surgical oncologist, educator; b. Balt., Jan. 30, 1960; s. Boris William and Hrisa Kazaras Kuvshinoff; m. Barbara Elizabeth Naff, Feb. 17, 1985; children: Christina, Alexander. BS, U. Md., Princess Anne, 1982; MD, U. Md., Balt., 1986. Diplomate Am. Bd. Surgery. Intern in surgery U. Cin., 1986—87, resident in surgery, 1987—93; fellow in surg. oncology Meml. Sloan-Kettering, N.Y.C., 1993—95; asst. prof. surgery U. Mo., Columbia, 1995—2001, assoc. prof. surgery, 2001—02, SUNY, Buffalo, 2002—05; surg. dir. operating rm. Roswell Pk. Cancer Inst., Buffalo, 2003—. Interim chief surg. oncology U. Mo., Columbia, 2001—02. Contbr. articles to profl. jours.; editor: Mont Reid Surgical Handbook, 1996. Fellow: ACS; mem.: Am. Hepatipanc-biliary Soc., Am. Coll. Physician Execs., Ctrl. Surg. Soc., Soc. Surg. Oncology. Eastern Orthodox. Avocations: tennis, softball, skiing, golf. Office: Roswell Pk Cancer Inst Elm & Carlton Buffalo NY 14263 Office Phone: 716-845-5807. Business E-Mail: boris.kuvshinoff@roswellpark.org.

KUWABARA, JAMES SHIGERU, research hydrologist; b. Honolulu, Apr. 26, 1953; s. Donald Shigeyuki and Setsue (Ogawa) K.; m. Rie Rita Kimura, June 6, 1982; children: Sara Mie, Annie Mako. BSCE, U. Hawaii, 1975; MS in Environ. Engring., Calif. Inst. Tech., 1976, PhD in Environ. Engring., 1980. Computer operator Computer Info. Svcs., Honolulu, 1971; engring. rschr. U. Hawaii, Honolulu, 1971-73; aquacultural rschr. Sea Grants Program, Honolulu, 1973-75; grad. rsch. fellow NSF, Pasadena, Calif., 1975-78; grad. rsch. asst. Calif. Inst. Tech., Pasadena, Calif., 1978-80; postdoctoral rsch. fellow Nat. Rsch. Coun., Menlo Park, Calif., 1980-82; rsch. hydrologist U.S. Geol. Survey, Menlo Park, Calif., 1982—. Conf. chmn. West Coast Water Chem. Workshop, Stanford, 1986; final rev. panel Water Res. Rsch. Grants, Reston, Va., 1988-89; session organizer Estuarine Rsch. Conf., San Francisco, 1991; session moderator Am. Chem. Soc., Washington, 1992; coord. San Francisco Bay Toxic Substances Hydrology Program, 1994—. Editor Estuaries, 1993; assoc. editor Water Resources Rsch., 2001, dep. editor, 2003; contbr. chpts. to books, numerous articles to Geochimica et Cosmochimica Acta, Limnology and Oceanography, Sci., other profl. jours. Mem. Eagle Scout rev. bd. Boy Scouts Am., Honolulu, 1974-75. Hawaii State Acad. scholar U. Hawaii, 1972; NSF Grad. fellow Calif. Inst. Tech., 1975; Nat. Rsch. Coun. postdoctoral rsch. assoc. U.S. Geol. Survey, 1980. Mem. ASCE, Am. Inst. Chemists, Estuarine Rsch. Fedn., Phycological Soc. Am. Achievements include development of a larval culturing system of State of Hawaii's prawn industry; optimization of gametophytic culturing of giant kelp for biomass conversion program; design of toxicant introduction device, process-interdependent solute transport modeling; modeling benthic flux of contaminants. Office: US Geol Survey Water Resources Discipline 345 Middlefield Rd # MS439 Menlo Park CA 94025-3591 Business E-Mail: kuwabara@usgs.gov.

KUWAHARA, KULDIP KAUR, literature and language professor; b. Amritsar, June 5, 1947; arrived in U.S., 1981; m. Kazuhide Kuwahara; 1 child, Rita Kaur. MA in English, Panjab U., Chandigarh, India, 1968; diploma in Eng. Lang. and Lit., U. Edinburgh, 1975; PhD, U. N.C., 1990. Assoc. prof. english N.C. Ctrl. U., Durham, NC, 1999—. Fellow U. Calif., Santa Barbara, Calif., 1993; asst. prof. of english Alma (Mich.) Coll., 1997—99; svc. learning fellow Campus Compact U. N.C., 2003—. Author: Jane Austen at Play, 1993. Scholar, Edinburgh U., 1975. Mem.: MLA (assoc.). Democrat. Sikh. Avocations: writing, travel, tatting, painting. Home: 401 Wellingham Drive Durham NC 27713 Office: North Carolina Central University 1801 Fayetteville Street Durham NC Office Phone: 919-530-7114. Home Fax: 919-530-7991. Personal E-mail: kkuwahara@nccu.edu.

KUWAYAMA, S. PAUL, physician, immunologist, allergist; b. Sapporo, Hokkaido, Japan, Nov. 8, 1932; s. Satoru and Chiyoko (Nishikawa) K.; m. Barbara Ann Dresback, June 29, 1974; children: David, Steven, Jason. BS, Hokkaido U., Sapporo, 1955, MD, 1959. Diplomate Am. Bd. Pediatrics, 1965, Am. Bd. Allergy & Immunology, 1972, Am. Bd. Pediatric Allergy, 1970; lic. Nat. Bd. Med. Examiners of Japan, 1960, Wis. State Bd. Med. Examiners, 1968, Ariz. State Bd. Med. Examiners, 1987, N.Mex. State Bd. Med. Examiners, 1987, Tenn. State Bd. Med. Examiners, 1992. Intern U.S. Naval Hosp., Yokosuka, 1959-60, St. Mary's Hosp., Milw., 1960-61; jr. resident in pediatrics Temple U. Sch. of Medicine, Phila., 1961-62; chief pediat. resident W.Va. U. Sch. of Medicine, Morgantown, 1962-63; postdoctoral fellow in immunology, jr. fellow in pediatric allergy The Children's Mercy Hosp.-U. Kans. Sch. of Medicine, Kansas City, 1964-65; staff pediatrician Atomic Bomb Casualty Commn. in Hiroshima, U.S. Nat. Acad. of Scis.-U.S. Atomic Energy Commn., 1966-67; sr. pediatric allergist, dept. immunobiology U. Kans. Sch. of Medicine, 1967-68. Asst. clin. prof. pediatric allergy and immunology Med. Coll. Wis., Milw., 1970—. Contbg. author texts and forward to books. Fulbright scholar, 1960-63. Fellow Am. Acad. Pediatrics (sect. on allergy and immunology), Am. Coll. Allergy, Am. Assn. Cert. Allergists, Am. Acad. Allergy, Asthma and Immunology, Am. Assn. Clin. Immunology and Allergy; mem. AMA, Fulbright Scholarship Grantee Alumni Assn., State Med. Soc. of Wis., Milw. Pediatric Soc. Office: 11035 W Forest Home Ave Hales Corners WI 53130-2541

KUYKENDALL, CRYSTAL ARLENE, educational consultant, lawyer; b. Chgo., Dec. 11, 1949; d. Cleophus Avant and Ellen (Campbell) Logan; m. Roosevelt Kuykendall, Apr. 10, 1969 (dec. Aug. 1972); children: Kahlil, Rasheki, Kashif. BA, Southern Ill. U., 1970; MA, Montclair State U., 1972; EdD, Atlanta U., 1975; JD, Georgetown U., 1982; LHD (hon.), Lewis and Clark Coll., Portland, 2002; MDiv, Va. Union U., 2005. Bar: D.C. 1988. Instr. Seton Hall U., South Orange, N.J., 1971-73; adminstrn. intern D.C. Pub. Schs., 1974-75; dir. citizens tng. inst. Nat. Com. for Citizens in Edn., Washington, 1975-77; dir. urban and minorities rels. dept. Nat. Sch. Bd. Assn., Washington, 1977-79; edn. dir. PSI Assocs., Inc., Washington, 1979-80; exec. dir. Nat. Alliance of Black Sch. Educators, Washington, 1980-81; dir. mktg. Roy Littlejohn Assoc., Inc., Washington, 1983—; pres., gen. counsel K.I.R.K., Inc. (Kreative and Innovative Resources for Kids), Washington, 1981—. Cons. to Ministry of Sport and Recreation, Western Australia Govt., 1990; chmn. U.S. Pres. Nat. Adv. Coun. on Continuing Edn., Washington, 1978-81; cons. U. Pitts. Race Desegregation Assistance Ctr., 1982-87, J.H. Lowry Assn., Chgo., 1982, U.S. Dept. of Edn. Transition Team, Washington, 1980. Author: Developing Leadership for Parent/Citizen Groups, 1975, You & Yours: Making the Most of this School Year, 1987, Improving Black Student Achievement by Enhancing Self Image, 1989, From Rage to Hope: Strategies for Reclaiming Black and Hispanic Students, 1992, 2d edit., 2004, Dreaming of a PHAT Century, 2000, 2nd edit., 2003, 2005 Mem. adv. bd. Inst. of the Black World, Atlanta, 1975-81; mem. steering com. Nat Conf. on Parental Involvement, Denver, 1977-78; mem. edn. task force Martin Luther King Jr. Ctr. for Social Change, Atlanta, 1978-80; mem. bd. dirs. Health Power, Inc., 1995-2001; chairperson, bd. dirs. Henry C. Gregory III Family Life Ctr. Found. of Shiloh Bapt. Ch. of Washington, 2003—, bd. mem., 1996—. Named Honorary Citizen of New Orleans, Mayor's Office, 1976; Ford found. fellow, 1973-74; Honorary Ky Colonel award, 1993, 99, 2002; Cert. Congl. Recognition, 2001. Mem. Nat. Bar Assn., Nat. Alliance of Black Sch. Edn., Alpha Kappa Alpha. Democrat. Baptist. Avocations: poetry writing, card playing, swimming, jogging, skiing. Office: KIRK Inc PO Box 60115 Potomac MD 20859-0115 Office Phone: 301-299-4189. Personal E-mail: ckuykendal@aol.com.

KUYKENDALL, GREGORY JOHN, lawyer; b. Denver, Jan. 13, 1961; s. Louis George and Mary (Spragins) K. BA, U. Colo., 1983; MA, Tulane U., 1985; JD, Northwestern U., 1988. Bar: Ariz. 1989, U.S. Dist. Ct. Ariz. 1989, U.S. Ct. Appeals (9th cir.) 1989, U.S. Dist. Ct. Mich. (Ea. Dist.) 1990, Colo. 1991, U.S. Dist. Ct. (Ctrl. Dist. Ill.) 1996, U.S. Supreme Ct. 2003, cert. specialist criminal law: Ariz. Bd. Legal Specialization. Atty. O'Connor, Cavanagh, Tucson, 1988-92, Butler & Stein, Tucson, 1992—94; pvt. practice Tucson, 1994—. Lectr. in field. Mem.: Ariz. Attys. Criminal Justice, State Bar Ariz., Fed. Bar Assn., Colo. Bar Assn., NACDL (life), Phi Beta Kappa. Democrat. Avocations: skiing, running, bicycling. Office: Gregory J Kuykendall PC 145 S 6th Ave Tucson AZ 85701 Office Phone: 520-792-8033. Office Fax: 520-792-0113.

KUYKENDALL, JOHN WELLS, academic administrator, educator; b. Charlotte, N.C., May 8, 1938; s. James Bell and Emily Jones (Frazer) K.; m. Nancy Adams Moore, July 15, 1961; children— Timothy Moore, James Frazer BA cum laude, Davidson Coll., 1959; BD cum laude, Union Sem., Richmond, Va., 1964; STM, Yale U., 1965; MA, Princeton U., 1972, PhD, 1975; DD (hon.), Hanover Coll., 1999; LHD (hon.), Wofford Coll., 1999. Ordained to ministry Presbyterian Ch., 1965. Campus minister Presbyn. Ch., Auburn, Ala., 1965-70; faculty Auburn U., 1973-84; pres. Davidson (N.C.) Coll., 1984—97, pres. emeritus, prof. religion, 1997—2003. Author: (with others) Presbyterians: Their History and Beliefs, 1978, Southern Enterprize: The Work of Evangelical Societies in the Antebellum South, 1982; contbr. articles to profl. jours. Recipient Algernon Sydney Sullivan award Auburn U., 1982 Mem. Am. Soc. Ch. History, Phi Beta Kappa, Omicron Delta Kappa, Phi Kappa Phi. Democrat.

KUYPER, JOAN CAROLYN, foundation administrator; b. Balt., Oct. 22, 1941; d. Irving Charles and Ethel Mae (Pritchett) O'Connor; m. William Kuyper, Dec. 20, 1964; children: Susan Carol, Edward Philip. BA in Edn., Salisbury State U., 1963; postgrad., Columbia U., 1978; MA in Arts Mgmt. and Bus., NYU, 1988. Elem. sch. tchr. Prince Georges County Schs., Md., 1963—68; freelance singer, opera, oratorio, chamber music Amato Opera, N.Y.C., 1967—80; owner, mgr. Privette Artists' Registry, Placement for Svc. for Singers, Teaneck, NJ, 1969—78; exec. dir. Teaneck Artists Perform-Chamber Music Series, 1975—80; bd. dirs. Pro Arte Chorale and adv. bd. on arts, Teaneck, 1976—81; program dir. Vols. in Arts & Humanities Vol. Bur. Bergen County, NJ, 1978—81; dir. Bergen Mus. Art and Sci., 1981—83; cons. Am. Soc. Prevention Cruelty to Animals, 1984, Am. Coun. for Arts, 1987; dir. ops. Isabel O'Neil Found. and Studio, 1984—85; dir. vol. svcs. March of Dimes Birth Defects Found. of Greater N.Y., 1985—88; dir. chpt. devel. Huntington's Disease Soc. Am., 1988—91; mgmt. cons. Girl Scouts Am., 1992—2000; dep. dir. for orgnl. advancement Soc. Women Engrs., 2000—03; CEO, exec. dir. The Netherland-Am. Found., 2003—. Sr. counsel The Forbes Group. Mem.: PEO, Exec. Women in Golf Assn., SearchNet, Orgnl. Devel. Network, Nat. Soc. Fund Raising Execs., Assn. for Vol. Adminstrn. (author handbook), Am. Mktg. Assn. (bd. dirs. 1990—96), Mus. Coun. N.J., Assn. Mus., Am. Soc. Assn. Execs. (cert.), N.Y. Soc. Assn. Execs. (membership com. 1991—94, Cert. Assn. Execs. chair 1995—96, program planning com. 1996—98, chmn. profl. devel. com. 1998—), Altrusa Club (bd. dirs. 1984—86, pres. 1986—88, bd. dirs. 1990—93, 1996—), Phi Alpha Theta. Democrat. Presbyterian. Home: 345 W 58th St Apt 14X New York NY 10019-1142 also: 1275 Pebble Beach Rd Tobyhanna PA 18466-9119 E-mail: joankuyper@aol.com.

KUZAN, KATHLEEN, speech pathology services professional, educator; b. East Orange, N.J., July 2, 1955; d. James and Angela (Poeta) Massotto; m. Roman Michael Kuzan, Aug. 14, 1977; children: Larissa Marie, Michael Nicholas. BA, Montclair U., Upper Montclair, N.J., 1977, MA, 1983. Cert. speech lang. pathologist, speech lang. specialist, tchr. of the handicapped, reading tchr., CCC. Supplemental speech correctionist Bd. of Edn., Union, NJ, 1977—78, reading tchr. Irvington, 1978—80, speech cons. pre-sch. summer screening Union Twp., 1978—90; adj. prof. Kean U., Union, 1990—94; speech - lang. pathologist Bd. of Edn., Union Twp., NJ, 1980—. Supr. clin. fellowship yr. ASHA - Union Twp. Schs., 2001—02; speech lang. pathologist pvt. practice, 1985—. Mem. Holy Spirit Ch., Union, religion tchr., 1996—. Mem.: N.J. Edn. Assn., Am. Speech Lang. Hearing Assn., Alpha Delta Kappa (epsilon chpt.) (sec. 1998—), Phi Kappa Phi. Achievements include development of k-12 curriculum guide for speech and language svcs; program integrating speech and lang. svcs. in self-contained and regular classrooms. Avocations: reading, needlepoint, soccer mom. Office: Union Twp Bd of Edn Wash Sch Washington Ave Union NJ 07083

KUZAT, HANAN S, education educator; d. Said M Qazait and Rasha M Shaladan. MSc, Tenn. State U., 1994—97. Tchg. asst. Tenn. State U., 1994—97; instr. Nashville State Tech. C.C., 1997—98, Tenn. State U., 1998—. Tcap test monitor Hull Jackson Montossorri Sch., Nashville, 2004—05. Mem.: Math. Assn. of Am. (corr.). Achievements include design of Math Website. Office: Tenn State Univ 3500 John Merittee BLVD Nashville TN 37209 Office Phone: 615-963-1575. E-mail: hkuzat@tnstate.edu.

KUZMA, GEORGE MARTIN, retired bishop; b. Windber, Pa., July 24, 1925; s. Ambrose and Anne (Marton) K. Student, Benedictine Coll., Lisle, Ill.; BA, postgrad., Duquesne U., U. Mich.; grad., SS Cyril and Methodius Byzantine Cath. Sem. Ordained priest Byzantine Cath. Ch., 1955. Asst. pastor SS Peter and Paul Ch., Braddock, Pa., 1955—57; pastor Holy Ghost Ch., Charleroi, Pa., 1957—65, St. Michael Ch., Flint, Mich., 1965—70, St. Eugene Ch., Bedford, Ohio, 1970—72, Annunciation Ch., Anaheim, Calif., 1970—86; rev. monsignor Byzantine Cath. Ch., 1984, titular bishop, 1986, consecrated bishop, 1987; aux. bishop Byzantine Cath. Diocese of Passaic, NJ, 1987—90; bishop Van Nuys, Calif., 1991—2000; ret., 2000. Judge matrimonial tribunal, mem. religious edn. commn., mem. commn. orthodox rels. Diocese of Pitts., 1955—69; judge matrimonial tribunal, vicar for religious Diocese of Parma, 1969—82; treas., bd. dirs., chmn. liturgical commn., mem. clergy & seminarian rev. bd., liaison to ea. Cath. dirs. religious edn., bd. dirs. Diocese of Van Nuys, 1982—86, diocesan credit un, chmn. diocesan heritage bd., chmn. diocesan ecumenical commn., 1982—86; vicar gen. Diocese of Passaic; Episcopal vicar for Ea. Pa.; chmn. Diocesan Retirement Plan Bd.; pres. Father Walter Cizsek Prayer League; chaplain Byzantine Carmelite Monastery, Sugarloaf, Pa. Assoc. editor: Byzantine Cath. World; editor: The Apostle. With USN, 1943—46, PTO. Office: Byzantine Cath Eparchy of Van Nuys 8131 N 16th St Phoenix AZ 85020-3901*

KUZMA, JOHN JOSEPH, church musician; b. Cin., Ohio, Mar. 16, 1946; s. John Joseph and Martha Mary (Byrne) Kuzma; m. Bess Jeannette Kuzma. MusB, Eastman Sch. Music, 1968; MusM, U. Ill., 1971. Music dir. St. Paul's Cathedral, San Diego, 1971—75; music faculty U. Calif., Santa Barbara, Calif., 1975—79; music dir. San Diego Chamber Orch., San Diego, 1980—82, Am. Boychoir, Princeton, NJ, 1982—85, Montview Presbyn. Ch., Denver, 1989—. Composer: (Operas) An Island of Sand, 1996, musician (organist). Recipient Fulbright scholarship, U. Copenhagen, 1969, Internat. Inst. of Edn., 1969; Music Composition fellow, Colo. Arts Coun., 0199. Mem.: Am. Guild of Organists. Avocations: cooking, classical languages. Office: Montview Presbyn Ch 1980 Dahlia St Denver CO 80220 Office Phone: 303-322-4607. Office Fax: 303-355-8816. E-mail: johnkuzma@aol.com.

KUZMANOVIC, JANE VIOLET, academic administrator; b. Akron, Ohio, Apr. 9, 1962; d. Ljubomir Emanuel and Viorika Violet Bodjanac; m. Dragan Kuzmanovic, May 1, 1983; children: Miriam Violeta Tomek, Lorraine Ljubica, Michael Miroslav, Daniel Branislav, Thomas Dragoslav, Stefanie Adela, Julianne Jovana, Melanie Dragana. BS in Bus. Mgmt., U. of Phoenix, 2004. Publications prodn. coord. Hughes Aircraft Co., El Segundo, Calif., 1984—93; dept. sec. Norstan Cabling Svcs., Van Nuys, Calif., 1995; exec. asst. AVEX, Inc., Camarillo, Calif., 1995—97; faculty and curriculum coord. Kennedy-Western U., Thousand Oaks, Calif., 1997—2000, sr. faculty and curriculum coord., 2000—02, faculty and curriculum mgr., 2002—04, sr. faculty and curriculum mgr., 2004—. Translator, office asst. Star Upholstering, Beverlywood, Calif., 1976—98; tchr., Sunday sch. Apostolic Christian Ch., Nazarean, Lawndale, Calif., 1989—. Singer (alto): Apostolic Christian Ch. Choir; dir.: (children's Sunday sch. choir) Apostolic Christian Ch., Nazarean. Grantee Pell, NAFSA, 2003. Avocations: gardening, travel, cooking, canning. Office: Kennedy-Western U 30301 Agoura Rd Agoura Hills CA 91301 E-mail: jkuzmanovic@kw.edu.

KUZNETSOV, VLADIMIR A., biomedical researcher, computational biologist; s. Andrey D. and Mariya M. (Zazulina) K.; m. Anna V. Ivshina, May 12, 1981; 1 child, Andrey. Ms. Sci., Kyrghyz State U., Russia, 1966—71; Ph. D., Moscow State U., Moscow, Russia, 1984—84. Dr. of Physical and Matematical Sciences Scietific&Technical Union, Russian Acad. of Sciences, St.-Peterburg, 1992. Head of lab. The Inst. of Chem. Physics, Russian Acad. of Sciences, Moscow, 1992—98, sr. rschr., 1982—91, Moscow Acad. of Vet. Medicine, Moscow, 1981—82; rschr. Rsch. Inst. of Oncology & Radiology, Frunze, 1972—81; sr. group leader Dept. Info. and Math. Sci., Genome Inst. of Singapore, 2004—; sr. mem. profl. staff Systems Rsch. and Applications Internat. Inc., Fairfax, Va., 2004; sr. rsch. fellow Nat. Inst. of Child Health and Human Devel., Nat. Inst. Health, 1999—2004; chief scientist Civilized Software, Inc., 1998—99. Rsch. scholar Ctr. for Biol. Evaluation&Research, FDA USA, Bethesda, Md., 1995—97. Author: Dynamics of Immune Processes During Tumor Growth, 1992; editl. bd. book series: Advances in Math for Applied Science, 1994. Recipient Medal, Russian acad. Natural Sci., 1994; am. Cancer Soc. grantee, 1995-97; Nat. Cancer Inst./NIH grantee, 1997-98. Fellow Russian Acad. Natural Scis.; mem. Am. Math. Soc., Am. Assn. Cancer Rsch. (corr.), London Math. Soc. Achievements include research in Computational & Systems Biology, Statistical Genomics And Evolution, Mathematical Immunology, Cancer Biology, Infectious Diseases; discovery of Mathematical theory of cancer immunobiology; development of Probability models of gene expression and molecular evolution; Voting prediction methods in clinical trials based on limited data; contributions to substantiation & development of basic mathematical models of tumor & immune system internations; leadership in mathematical immunology of cancer and computational clinical immunology; inventor of the statistically weighted syndromes methods for prognosis of fuzzy systems; inventor of a family of scale dependent and time dependent skewed statistical distributions associated with evolution of conserved sequences encoded in the genomes; inventor of a basic mathematical theory of the Serial Analysis Gene Expression method; inventor of the probablistic theory of evolution of the conserved biological sequences (genes, transcripts, motifs, domains, protein families) named the Binomial Difference Distribution Model; and generalized hypergeometric model of evolution. Avocations: archaeology, tourism, swimming. Office: Genome Inst of Singapore 60 Biopolis Str #02-01 138672 Singapore Singapore Personal E-mail: vk28u@nih.gov. E-mail: kuznetsov@gis.a.star-edu.sg.

KUZNETSOVA, SVETLANA, professional tennis player; b. St. Petersburg, Russia, June 27, 1985; d. Alexandr Kuznetsov and Galina Tsareva. Profl. tennis player WTA Tour, 2001—. Named WTA Tour Newcomer of Yr., 2002. Achievements include Winner 5 WTA Tour singles titles: Helsinki, 2002, Bali, 2002, 2004, US Open, 2004, Eastbourne, 2004; Winner 10 WTA Tour doubles titles: (with Likhovtseva) Doha, 2004, Gold Coast, 2004, (with Navratilova) Leipzig, 2003, Canadian Open, 2003, Dubai, 2003, Gold Coast; (with Sanchez-Vicario) Tokyo, 2002, Helsinki, 2002, Sopot, 2002; Member Russian Olympic Team, 2004. Office: c/o WTA Tour Corp Hdqs One Progess Plz Ste 1500 Saint Petersburg FL 33701

KUZNIECKY, RUBEN ITAMAR, neurologist, educator; b. Panama, Republic of Panama, Aug. 18, 1957; came to U.S., 1988; s. Salem and Sara Kuzniecky; m. Yvonne Zelenka, Dec. 11, 1983; children: Avi, Hannah, Joel. BS, David Wolfshon, Buenos Aires, 1975; MD, U. Buenos Aires, 1981. Diplomate Am. Bd. Psychiatry and Neurology. Intern CSS, Panama, 1981-83; resident McGill U., Montreal, Can., 1983-86, fellow in epilepsy, 1986-88; asst. prof. neurology U. Ala., Birmingham, 1988-92, assoc. prof., 1992-97, prof., 1997—. Dir. Epilepsy Ctr., U. Ala., 1995—. Author: MR in Epilepsy, 1995. Avocations: classic music, opera. Office: U Ala Dept Neurology UAB Station Birmingham AL 35294

KUZUHARA, LOREN WYATT, management consultant, educator; b. Evanston, Ill., Nov. 15, 1962; s. Daniel Kei Kuzuhara, Toyoko Teresa Kuzuhara; m. Lavina Mohanlal Harjani, Dec. 28, 1990; children: Daniel, Carolyn. PhD, U. Wis.-Madison, 1994, MBA, 1993; BS, U. Ill.-Champaign-Urbana, 1985. Prof. Sch. Bus. U. Wis.-Madison, 1998—2002; strategic rschr. Am. Family Ins., Madison, 1995—98; mgmt. cons. Orgnl. R&D, MADISON, 2001—. Trustee Madison Country Day Sch., 1996—. Author: Organizational Behavior and Management: An Integrated Skills Approach, 2002, Applied Organizational Behavior, 2003. Recipient Dr. Brenda Pfaehler award of excellence, Trio Student Support Svcs. Program, U. Wis.-Madison, 2001, Dean's Acad. Staff Excellence in Tchg. award, Sch. of Bus., U. Wis.-Madison, 2001, Reggie Tate Excellence in Tchg. award, Sch. Bus., U. Wis.-Madison, 1989, Svc. award, Madison Country Day Sch., 2002. Mem.: ASTD, Soc. Human Resource Mgmt., Acad. Mgmt. Avocation: travel, movies, auto racing, reading. Home: 9 Apostle Island Madison WI 53719 Office: Sch Bus Univ Wis-Madison 975 University Ave Madison WI 53706-1323 Office Phone: 608-262-4453. Home Fax: 608-262-8773; Office Fax: 608-262-8773.

KVALEBERG, ERIK, oceanographer, researcher; b. Stavanger, Rogaland, Norway, Nov. 22, 1974; s. Kjell and Ingerid Solvig Kvaleberg. PhD, Fla. State U., 2001. Rsch. asst. Ctr. Ocean-atmospheric Prediction Studies, Fla. State U., Tallahassee, 2001—04; post-doctoral rsch. fellow dept. earth and planetary scis. Johns Hopkins U., Balt., 2004—. Rsch. asst. Saclant, NATO, La Spezia, Italy, 2002—02. Recipient Cert. of Appreciation, Nat. Oceanic and Atmospheric Adminstrn., 2001. Mem.: Am. Geophys. Union. Office: Johns Hopkins University Olin Bldg 34th and N Charles St Baltimore MD 21218 Office Phone: 410-516-8241. Business E-Mail: kvaleberg@jhu.edu.

KVALSETH, TARALD ODDVAR, mechanical engineer, educator; b. Brunkeberg, Telemark, Norway, Nov. 7, 1938; married; 3 children. BS, U. Durham, King's Coll., Eng., 1963; MS, U. Calif.-Berkeley, 1966, PhD, 1971. Research asst. engring. expt. sta. U. Colo., Boulder, 1963-64, teaching asst. dept. mech. engring.; mech. engr. Williams & Lane Inc., Berkeley, Calif., 1964-65; research asst. dept. indsl. engring. and ops. research U. Calif., Berkeley, 1965-71, research fellow, 1973; asst. prof. Sch. Indsl. and Systems Engring. Ga. Inst. Tech., Atlanta, 1971-74; sr. lectr. indsl. mgmt. div. Norwegian Inst. Tech. U. Trondheim, 1974-79, head indsl. mgmt. div., 1975-79; assoc. prof. dept. mech. engring. U. Minn., Mpls., 1979-82, prof., 1982—2005, prof. emeritus, 2005—. Guest worker NASA Ames Research Ctr., Calif., 1973; mem. organizing com. 1st Berkeley-Monterey Conf. Timespan, Pay and Discretionary Capacity, 1973; mem. steering com. Internat. Conf. Human Factors in Design and Op. Ships, Gothenburg, Sweden, 1977; mem. bd. Norwegian Ergonomics Com., 1977-80; gen. session chmn. Conf. Work Place Design and Work Environ. Problems, Trondheim, 1978 Author book chpts., articles, presentations, reports in field; editor text books; mem. editl. bd., reviewer for numerous profl. jours., patentee in field. Fellow AAAS; mem. IEEE, Inst. Indsl. Engrs. (sr.), Human Factors and Ergonomics Soc. (pres. upper Midwest chpt.), Nordic Ergonomics Soc. (coun. 1977-80), Internat. Ergonomics Assn. (gen. coun. 1977-80, v.p. 1982-85), Ergonomics Soc., Psychonomic Soc., Am. Psychol. Soc., Am. Statis. Assn., Math. Assn. Am., Sigma Xi. Lutheran. Home: 4980 Shady Island Cir Mound MN 55364 Office: U Minn Dept Mech Engring Minneapolis MN 55455 Office Phone: 612-625-5051. Business E-Mail: kvals001@umn.edu.

KVAMME, MARK D., marketing professional; BA in French, Econs. and Lit., U. Calif., Berkeley. Programmer Apple Computer; founding mem., then internat. product mgr. in U.S. Apple France; founder, pres., CEO Internat. Solutions, 1984-86; dir. internat. mktg. Wyse Tech., 1986-89; ptnr. CKS Group, Cupertino, Calif., 1989-91, chair, CEO, 1991-98; chair USWEB/CKS, Cupertino, Calif., 1998—99; ptnr. Sequoia Capital, Menlo Park, Calif., 1999—. Office: Sequoia Capital 3000 Sand Hill Rd Bldg 4 Menlo Park CA 94025-7113

KVANVIG, JONATHAN LEE, philosophy educator; b. Dickinson, N.D., Dec. 7, 1954; s. Kenneth George and Alice Mae K., Edith Mae Kvanvig (Stepmother); m. Carol Dobbs Dobbs, June 9, 1958; children: Jared Daniel, Brittany Mae. BA, Evangel Coll., Springfield, Mo., 1977; MA, U. of Mo., Columbia, 1979; PhD, U. of Notre Dame, South Bend, Ind., 1982. Philosophy prof. Tex. A&M U., College Station, Mo., 1983—2001, U. Mo., Columbia, Mo., 2001—, dept. chair, 2001. Bd. govs. Clarendon Found., Washington, 1991—2003. Fellow, NEH, 1986, summer fellow, 1991. Mem.: Southwestern Philos. Soc. (sec.-treas. 1995—98), Soc. Christian Philosophers (exec. com. 1999—2001), Am. Philos. Assn. Avocations: bicycling, coaching, umpiring. Home: 4705 Newcastle Dr Columbia MO 65203 Office: U Mo 436 Gcb Columbia MO 65211 Office Phone: 573-882-2764. Business E-Mail: kvanvigj@missouri.edu.

KVETKO, COLLEEN M., bank executive; m. Kirk Kvetko. From nat. comml. lender to pres. Fifth Third Bank, Fla., Naples, Fla., 1987—2002, pres., 2002—05. Bd. dir. NCH Found. Chmn. YMCA Collier County, Econ. Devel. Coun. Collier County; campaign chmn. United Way Collier County. Named 10th Most Powerful Woman in Banking, U.S. Bankers Mag., Vol. of Yr., YMCA Collier County, 1998, Businesswoman of Yr., Gulfshore Bus. Mag. Mem.: Fla. Bankers Assn. (bd. dir.), Naples C. of C. Office: Fifth Third Bank Fla Po Box 413021 Naples FL 34101-3021

KVETON, KYLE, lawyer; b. Huntington, N.Y., Jan. 7, 1959; s. Frank and Jean Kveton; m. Karen Renee Palmersheim, Apr. 3, 2004; children: Eric Matthew, Mark Bradley. BA, SUNY, Binghamton, 1980; JD, U. So. Calif., L.A., 1983. Bar: Calif. 1983. Atty. Texaco Inc., L.A., 1983—86; mem. Robie & Matthai, L.A., 1987—. Mem.: ABA, Def. Rsch. Inst., L.A. County Bar Assn. Office: Robie & Matthai 500 S Grand Ave #1500 Los Angeles CA 90071 Office Phone: 213-624-3062. Office Fax: 213-624-2563. Business E-Mail: kkveton@romalaw.com.

KVINT, VLADIMIR LEV, economist, mining engineer, finance educator; b. Krasnoyarsk, Siberia, Russia, Feb. 21, 1949; s. Lev V. Kvint and Lidia E. Adamskaya; children: Liza, Valeria. MS in Mining Engring., Inst. Non-Ferrous Metals and Gold, Krasnoyarsk, 1972; PhD in Managerial Econs., Inst. Nat. Economy, Moscow, 1975; D of Econs., Inst. Econs., Acad. Scis., Moscow, 1988; HHD, U. Bridgeport, 1997; D (hon.), Acad. of Pub. Adminstrn. of Pres. of Russia, 2004, Vlora Tech. U., Albania, 2004. Asst. prof. Inst. of Non-Ferrous Metals, 1972; chief dept. mining-metallurgical co., Norilsk, Russia, 1975—76; dep. chair, chief economist Automation of non-ferrous metals com., 1976—78; chief dept. sci.-tech. progress Siberian br. Acad. of Scis., Novosibirsk, 1978—82; part-time prof. various Russian univs., 1976—89; leading rschr., fellow Inst. Econs., Acad. Scis., Moscow, 1982—89; econ. adviser Govt. of Albania, 2002—; chmn. expert econ. coun. Fed. Com. for Sport and Tourism, Russia, 2002—. Cons. GE, N.Y.C., 1989—94, Cable & Wireless, London, 1989—97; vis. prof. Vienna (Austria) Econ. U., 1989—90; disting. prof. econ. Babson Coll. Bus., Mass., 1990; mng. dir. emerging markets Arthur Andersen, 1992—97; prof. internat. bus. Stern Grad. Sch. Bus., N.Y. U., 1995—2000; prof. Fordham U. Grad. Sch. Bus., N.Y.C., 1990—2004; econ. adviser King of Bulgaria, 1996—2001, Pres. of UN, 1997—98; dir. for govtl. affairs Metromedia Internat. Telecom. Inc., 1997—2000; chmn. Kogod Sch. Bus. Am. U., Washington, 2004—, prof. internat. bus. Kogod Sch. Bus., 2004—. Author: The Acceleration of Technological Development of Production, 1976, The Introduction and Use of Automation Systems, 1981, The Krasnoyarsk Experiment, 1982, Management of Scientific-Technical Progress, 1986, The Economic and Scientific-Technical Information, 1987, Development of Economy of Daghestan, 1988, The Barefoot Shoemaker: Capitalizing on the New Russia, 1993, A Different Perspective on Emerging Markets, 1995, Incorporating Global Risk Management in the Strategic Decision Making Process, 1997, The Global Emerging Market in Transition, 1999, 2d edit. 2004; co-author: Creating and Managing International Joint Ventures, 1996, International M&A, Joint Ventures and Beyond, 1998, 2d edit., 2002, Investing Under Fire: Winning Strategies, 2003; editor-in-chief: Emerging Market of Russia: Sourcebook for Investment and Trade, 1998; contbr. articles to CNN, Forbes, Harvard Bus. Rev., others. Bd. dirs. USSR Exporters Assn., Moscow, 1988-90; mem. internat. com. Muhlenberg Coll., Allentown, Pa., 1992-99; chmn. Summits Instl. Investors & Global Risk Management, World Econ. Devel. Congress, Washington, 1995-97. Recipient Silver medal for achievements in nat. economy, USSR Main Nat. Com., Moscow, 1986, GLOBE Ann. award, Fordham U., 2002, Gold medal Hon. Lawyer of Russia, 2003, Vernadskiy Silver medal, Russian Acad. Natural Scis., 2004; US Fulbright scholar, 2001. Fellow: Wexner Heritage Found. (N.Y.C.), New Eng. Ctr. for Internat. and Regional Studies (hon.); mem.: Bus. Coun. Internat. Understanding (BCIU) (sr. advisor 2001—), Internat. Acad. Emerging Markets (pres.), Bretton Woods Com. (Washington), Internat. Acad. Regional Devel. (life), Russian Acad. Natural Scis. (life), Internat. Informatization Acad. of UN (hon.), Am. Econ. Assn., Philos. Soc., N.Y. Acad. Scis., World Jewish Acad. Scis. (pres.). Achievements include devel. of theory of regionalization of scientific tech. progress; evaluation of role of scientific-technical strategy in devel. of regional economy; devel. of regional programs, developed a theory of global emerging market, developed a system of optimization models of business strategies in new emerging markets, economic solutions to poverty. Office: Am Univ Sch Bus 4400 Massachusetts Ave NW Washington DC 20016-8044 Office Phone: 202-885-3908. Business E-Mail: kvint@american.edu. *Terrorism is a social manifestation of evil and requires complete extermination. Terrorists interpret kindness as weakness—such methodologies will not solve their malevolence. Compromising with them only prolongs their ability to wage war against humanity and creates an ocean of grief and extended poverty as the existence of this plague diverts badly needed funds from the war on hunger. Just as barbarians destroyed Rome and plunged mankind into darkness, terrorists with modern weapons can bring a global catastrophe to civilization.*

KVINTA, CHARLES J., lawyer; b. Hallettsville, Tex., Feb. 16, 1932; s. John F. and Emily (Strauss) K.; m. Margie N. Brenek, Oct. 9, 1954; children: Charles, Sherri, Kenneth, Christopher. BA in Govt., U. Tex., 1954, LLB, 1959. Bar: Tex. 1959. Atty. Tex. Hwy. Dept., Yoakum, 1959-61; ptnr. Gaus & Kvinta, Yoakum, 1962-67, Kvinta, Young & Frietsch, Yoakum, 1975—, Kvinta & Kvinta Attys., Yoakum, 1986—. Exec. v.p. First State Bank, Yoakum, 1968-74, atty., 1975—; city atty. City of Yoakum, 1980—. Co-founder Bluebonnet Youth Ranch, Yoakum, 1968, bd. trustees, bd. dirs., pres. Yoakum Ind. Sch. Dist.; judge Lavaca County. 1st lt. U.S. Army, 1954-56. Recipient Outstanding Cmty. Svc. award Sons of Hrman, 1984, Outstanding Svc. award Bluebonnet Youth Ranch, 1975, Yoakum Little League, 1982, Yoakum Lions, 1982, Paul Gustwick Outstanding Cmty. Svc. award, 1986, Tex. Rd. Hand award for outstanding support Tex. Hwy. Tex. Dept. Transp. Mem. Tex. Bar Assn., Am. Legion. Roman Catholic. Home: 713 Coke St Yoakum TX 77995-4415 Office: Kvinta & Kvinta Attys 403 W Grand Ave Yoakum TX 77995-2617

KWAAN, JACK HAU MING, retired physician; b. Hong Kong, Apr. 9, 1928; came to U.S., 1953; s. Y.K. and Rose W. Kwaan; m. Min K. Ho, Feb. 11, 1973; children: Mary, Peter, Rebecca, Nicholas. MD, U. Hong Kong, 1952. Diplomate Am. Bd. Radiology, Am. Bd. Surgery, Am. Bd. Thoracic Surgery. Resident in radiology Roswell Park Meml. Inst., 1955-56; chief resident Peter Bent Brigham Hosp., 1956-57; rsch. fellow in radiology Harvard Med. Sch., Boston, 1956-57; sr. cancer rsch. radiol. therapist Roswell Park Meml. Inst., Buffalo, 1958-59; asst. prof. radiology U. Ky., Lexington, 1963-65; resident in surgery U. Calif., Irvine, 1965-68; rsch. fellow oncologic surgery M.D. Anderson Hosp., Houston, 1968-69; resident in thoracic U. Calif., Irvine, 1969-71, chief resident thoracic surgery, 1970, asst. prof. surgery, 1972-73; chief vascular surgery sect., co-dir. vascular surgery tng. program U. Calif. Irvine/Long Beach VA Med. Ctr., 1974-87; prof. surgery U. Calif., Irvine, 1983-87; sr. resident in thoracic surgery U. So. Calif./L.A. County Med. Ctr., 1971; staff thoracic cardiovasc. surgeon Long Beach VA Hosp., 1972-73; asst. chief dept. surgery Valley Med. Ctr., Fresno, Calif., 1973-74; prof. surgery U. Okla., Tulsa, 1987-93; ret., 1993. Chief dept. surgery Valley Med. Ctr., Fresno, Calif., 1973-74; chief vascular surgery sect. Long Beach VA Med. Ctr., 1974-87; surgical cons. Kaiser Permanente Hosp. Contbr. articles to profl. jours. Fellow Am. Coll. Surgeons; mem. Brit. Med. Assn., Gen. Med. Coun. London (registrant), Assn. Mil. Surgeons of U.S. (life), Assn. VA Surgeons, Internat. Cardiovascular Soc. Home: PO Box 50183 Long Beach CA 90815-6183

KWAK, SANGSHIN, research scientist; b. Daegu, Republic of Korea, Aug. 16, 1973; s. Tae-Joon Kwak and Sang-Hee Do; m. Won-Young Kim, Dec. 7, 1976. PhD, Tex. A&M U., Tex., 2005. Rsch. engr. LG Elec. Corp., Chang-Won, Republic of Korea, 1999—2000; lectr. Ui-Duk U., Kyung-Ju, Republic of Korea, 2001—01; intern Whirlpool Corp. R&D Ctr., Benton Harbor, Mich., 2004—04; tchg. asst. Tex. A&M U., Coll. Sta., Tex., 2002, rsch. asst., 2001—. Student mem. IEEE, 2001—; reviewer IEEE Transactions on Energy Conversion, 2003—, IEEE Applied Power Electronics Conf., Austin, Tex., 2005, IEEE Internat. Electric Machine Dr. Conf., San Antonio, 2005. Author: CRC Press; contbr. articles pub. to profl. jour. Scholar Electric Power and Power Electronics Inst. Scholarship, Tex. A&M U., 2001, 2002, 2003, Elec. Engring. Dept. Scholarship, 2001. Achievements include patents pending for Current source inverter with simple commutation method and apparatus. Home: 309 Ball St #2003 College Station TX 77840 Office: Tex A&M Univ 111A Zachry Engring Bldg College Station TX 77843-3128 Mailing: 102 1803 Hyundae Apt Bo Ra Ri 564 Gi Heung Eup Young In Si Kyung Gi Do Republic of Korea 449 904 Office Phone: 979-845-1171. Personal E-mail: sskwak01@gmail.com. Business E-Mail: sskwak@ee.tamu.edu.

KWAK, SEUNG-KEON, research scientist; b. Seoul, Republic of Korea, Feb. 2, 1967; arrived in U.S., 1992; s. Sebom Kwak, Kyungja Lim; m. Jeong-Eun Rhee; 1 child, Bethia. BS, Hankook Aviation U., Kyunggi, Korea, 1989; MS, W.Va. U., 1994; PhD, Ohio State U., 1999. Postdoctoral rschr. Ohio State U., Columbus, 1999—2001; dir. rsch. and devel. Quality Rsch., Devel. and Cons., Inc., Chaska, Minn., 2001—04; CEO SenAnTech, Inc., 2004—. Tech. reviewer IEEE Trans. on Automatic Control, IEEE Conf. on Decision and Control, Am. Control Conf. Contbr. articles to profl. jours. Lt. Republic of Korea Air Force, 1989—92. Mem.: ASME (mem. organizing com. 2000 Conf. 1999—2000, tech. reviewer ASME Internat. Mech. Engring. Congress and Exposition). Home: 121 Radcliffe Ave Port Washington NY 11050 Office: SenAnTech Inc Ste 6 125 Columbia Ct Chaska MN 55318 Business E-Mail: skwak@senantech.com.

KWAK, YOUNG HOON, management science educator; s. Soo-Il Kwak and Chungkyu Choi; m. Heekyung (Kay) Han; children: Jason Seungho, Kevin Jeongho. PhD, U. Calif., Berkeley, 1997. Prof. George Washington U., Washington, 1999—. Contbr. articles to profl. jours., chapters to books. Office: George Washington U Dept Mgmt Sci Washington DC 20052

KWAME, GUY ALLEN, protective services official; s. Guy and Annie Mae Jackson Allen; m. Lagaya Allen Hester, Oct. 3, 1995; children: Konshawnia Jacinda Allen, Aisha-Safiya Allen, Ebuni Qubilah Allen, Keira Akilah Allen, Khabira Amilah Allen, Tarik Reaves, T'Aaron Reaves, Tyrese Allen, Marcus Fowles. AA in Social Scis., Miami-Dade C.C., 1978, AS in Supervision and Mgmt., 1981; BA in Anthropology, Fla. Internat. U., 1980. Cert. in law enforcement Fla. Inventory mgmt. staff USAF, Homestead AFB, Fla., 1973—77; pub. safety ofcl. City of Miami, 1982—2003. Active youth sports activitites, Miami, 1982—; asst. QUE Taekwondo, Miami, 1990—. Avocations: fitness and nutrition, sports excercise.

KWAN, BENJAMIN CHING KEE, ophthalmologist; b. Hong Kong, July 12, 1940; came to U.S., 1959; s. Shun Ming and Lurk Ming (Lai) K.; m. Catherine Ning, Aug. 29, 1964; children: Susan San, David Daiwai. MD, Wash. U., St. Louis, 1967. Diplomate Am. Bd. Ophthalmology. Ptnr. So. Calif. Permanente Med. Ctr., Harbor City, 1976—, chief of svc. ophthalmology, 1976-88; clin. prof. dept. ophthalmology UCLA, 1995—. Chmn. winter blossom ball Chinese Am. Debutante's Guild, 1993. Capt. U.S. Army, 1969-71. Recipient Svc. award Asian Am. Sr. Citizens Svc. Ctr., 1993, Proclamation award Calif. Sec. of State, 1993, Svc. award East L.A. Chinese Everspring Sr. Assn., 1994. Fellow Am. Acad. Ophthalmology; mem. Chinese Am. Ophthal. Soc. (pres. elect 1997-99, pres. 1999-00, Svc. award 1994), Chinese Physician's Soc. So. Calif. (bd. dirs., pres. 1983, Svc. award 1983, 89), Orgn. Chinese Ams. (pres. L.A. chpt. 1986-87). Roman Catholic. Avocations: ballroom dancing, singing, skiing. Home: 6327 Tarragon Rd Rancho Palos Verdes CA 90275-5834 E-mail: benckwan@hotmail.com.

KWAN, MICHELLE WING, professional figure skater; b. Torrance, Calif., July 7, 1980; d. Danny and Estella Kwan. Attends, UCLA. Nat. spokesperson, Champions Across Am. Children's Miracle Network, 1996—, co-chair, ProKid's Program; founder Chevrolet/Michelle Kwan R.E.W.A.R.D.S. scholarship program. Recipient Skating Mag. Readers' Choice award for figure skater of yr., 1993-94, U.S. Figure Skating Skater of Yr. award, 1994-96, 98, 99, 2001-03, Dial award, 1997, Sullivan award for top amateur athlete in Am., 2001, Kids' Choice award, 2002, 03, Teen Choice award, 2002, Skating Mag. Reader's Choice award, 2003; named Female Athlete of Yr. U.S. Olympic Com., 1996, 98-2001, 2003, Women's Sports Found. Sportswoman of Yr., 2003, CosmoGirl of Yr., 2002. Achievements include being the youngest World Champion in US history; most decorated figure skater in US history; third youngest World Champion; received 50 perfect 6.0 marks in major competitions; victories include: World Junior Championships, 1994, 96, Nations cup, 1995, U.S. Postal Svc. Challenge, 1995, State Farm U.S. Championships, 1996, 1999, 2001, 2003, Champions Series Final, 1996, Japan Open, 1997, 1999, Skate Am., 1995, 1997, 1999, 2000, Skate Can., 1995, 1997, 1999, US Championships, 1996, 1998-2004, World Championships, 1998, 1999, 2000, 2001, 2003, Goodwill Games, 1998, 1998 Ultimate Four, 1998, Grand Slam Figure Skating, 1998, US Pro Classic, 1998, Masters of Figure Skating, 1998, 1999, 2000, Silver Medal, Olympics, 1998, Bronze Medal, 2002; Michelle Kwan Trophy named in her honor, 2004. Office: US Figure Skating Assn 20 1st St Colorado Springs CO 80906-3624 Mailing: Proper Marketing Assoc c/o Shep Goldberg 44450 Pinetree Dr Ste 103 Plymouth MI 48170*

KWARTLER, JED ARYEH, otolaryngologist; b. St. Louis, Feb. 4, 1958; s. Irwin E. and Shirley (Platt) K.; m. Carol L. Barash, Mar. 11, 1984; children: Zachary, Talia, Eliana. BS, Brown U., 1979; MD, U. Medicine Dentistry N.J., 1983. Diplomate Am. Bd. Otolaryngology, Nat. Bd. Med. Examiners. Intern dept. surgery U. Medicine Dentistry N.J., 1983-84, resident, 1984-85, 85-88, clin. asst. prof., 1990-95, clin. assoc. prof., 1995—; fellow in otology/neurotology House Ear Clinic and Inst., L.A., 1989-90. Dir. neurotology, attending dept. otolaryngology, dir. temporal bone anatomy lab United Hosp., Newark; cons. otology/neurotology East Orange (N.J.) VA Hosp., attending otolaryngology Univ. Hosp., Newark, Overlook Hosp., Summit, N.J., St. Barnabas Med. Ctr., Livington, N.J.; cons. neurosurgery Morristown (N.J.) Meml. Hosp.; mem. numerous profl. coms.; lectr. in field; peer rev. Med. Interinsurance Exch., 1994; regional rep. ins. reimbursement task force Cochlear Implant Club Internat., 1992—. Contbr. articles to numerous profl. jours.; mem. editl. rev. bd. Archives in Otolaryngology, Head and Neck Surgery Jour., 1990—. Trustee Summit Speech Sch., 1990-96, chmn. ednl. policy com., 1992-93; mem. long range planning task force Oheb Shalom Congregation, South Orange, N.J., 1992. Recipient Ciba Geigy Cmty. Svc. award, 1980, Resident Travel award NIH-Assn. for Rsch. in Otolaryngology, 1988, Disting. Clin. Svc. award NJSHA, 1993. Mem. Am. Acad. Otolaryngology-Head and Neck Surgery (award of honor 1996), Am. Soc. Evoked Potential Monitoring, Am. Auditory Soc., Am. Neurotology Soc., N.Am. Skull Base Surgery Soc., William F. House Soc., Soc. Univ. Otolaryngologists, N.J. Hearing and Speech Assn., N.J. Acad. Otolaryngology (at-large mem. bd. govs. 1991-92, sec. 1992-93, v.p. 1993-94, pres. 1996), Sigma Xi. Avocations: sailing, tennis, skiing, woodworking. Office: Ear Splty Group 55 Morris Ave Ste 304 Springfield NJ 07081-1422

KWASNICK, PAUL JACK, retail executive; b. N.Y.C., Apr. 8, 1925; s. Joseph and Dorothy (Ginsberg) K.; m. Selma Marcus, Sept. 7, 1947; children: Raymond, Diane, Robert. BBA, CCNY, 1947, MBA, 1957. Fin. exec. M.H. Fishman Co., Inc., N.Y.C., 1947-61; asst. sec.-treas. Zayre Corp., Natick, Mass., 1961-66, v.p., asst. sec.-treas., 1966-68, v.p., treas., 1968-72, sr. v.p., treas., 1972-73; exec. v.p., gen. mgr. Kings Dept. Stores, Inc., Newton, Mass., 1973-75, pres., chief operating officer, 1975-78, pres. retail div., chief operating officer, dir., mem. exec. com., 1981; chmn., pres., chief exec. officer, dir., mem. exec. com. Mars Stores, Inc., North Dighton, Mass., 1982-89; pres., chief exec. officer Landmark Advisors, Inc., Boston, 1989—. Pres., chief exec. officer, chmn. Data Printer Corp., Malden, Mass., 1978-80, bd. dirs., 1967-83; regional dir., bd. dirs. Shawmut Community Bank, Framingham, Mass. Bd. dirs., asst. treas. Mass. Easter Seal Soc., 1986-88, treas., 1988-89, vice chmn., 1989-91, chmn. 1991-93; trustee Combined Jewish Philanthropies of Greater Boston, 1977—. The West Suburban YMCA, Newton, 1984-2000, chmn., 1991-2000; dir. Mass. Coun. Compulsive Gambling, 1990-91. With AUS, 1943-46. Mem. Internat. Mass Retail Assn. (bd. dris. 1981-89, treas. 1986-89). Jewish.

KWASTENIET, JAMES GERALD, secondary school educator, coach; b. Blue Island, Ill., Apr. 3, 1950; s. Jan Kwasteniet; m. Nancy Jo Batts, June 3, 1972; children: Ross Mitchell, Gwen Janine Vogelzang, Kyle James. BA, Calvin Coll., Grand Rapids, Mich., 1972; MA, Chgo. State U., 1982. Cert. tchr. Ill. State Bd. Edn., 1972. Tchr. and coach Chgo. Christian H.S., Palos Heights, Ill., 1981—. Recipient Track Coach of Yr., Ill. Track and Field Coaches Assn., 1990, 1991, 1992. Home: 7129 W 113th St Worth IL 60482 Office: Chicago Christian HS 12001 S Oak Park Ave Palos Heights IL 60463 Home Fax: 708-388-0154; Office Fax: 708-388-0154. Personal E-mail: jkwasteniet@swchristian.org.

KWEMBE, TOR ANTHONY, mathematics professor, researcher; b. Gboko, Nigeria, Nov. 23, 1955; came to U.S., 1981; s. Peter Wundu and Adzuai Margerite K.; m. Azungwe Isabel Kwembe, July 15, 1980; children: Terfa, Fanen, Wundu. BS, U. Calabar, Nigeria, 1980; MS, U. Ill., 1983, PhD, 1989. Acad. coord. U. Ill. Engring., Chgo., 1985-88, postdoctoral rsch. assoc., 1988-90; asst. lectr. U. Sokoto, Nigeria, 1980-81; asst. prof. Chgo. State U., 1990-93, assoc. prof., 1993-98, prof., 1998—. Chairperson dept. math. Chgo. State U., 1994, chair faculty senate, 1997-98; coord. minority engring. program U. Ill., Chgo., 1987-90. Contbr. articles to profl. jours. Dwight E. Eisenhower grant Ill. Bd. of Higher Edn., 1993. Mem. Math. Assn. of Am., Soc. for Math. Biology, Internat. Fedn. of Non Linear Analyst, U. Profls. of Ill. (chpt. treas. 1996-98). Avocations: travel, ping pong/table tennis, lawn tennis, music. Home: 4100 Poplar Ave Richton Park IL 60471 Office: Dept Math Chgo State U 9501 S King Dr Chicago IL 60628 Office Phone: 773-995-3813. E-mail: tkwembe@csu.edu, kwembe@sbcglobal.net.

KWIAT, DAVID MARK, performing arts educator, actor; b. Mpls., May 9, 1951; s. Joseph J. and Charlotte (Adler) K. BA summa cum laude, U. Minn., 1974; MFA, Fla. State U., 1976. Actor, dir. Actors Theatre of St. Paul, Minn., 1978-80, 81-89; actor Ariz. Theatre Co., Tucson, 1980-81; prof. New World Sch. of the Arts, Miami, Fla., 1989—. Author: (play) John Barrymore: Confessions of an Actor, 1976, (collection of poetry) Travelers in Residence, 1999. Endowed tchg. chair, Miami-Dade Coll., 1996; named Best Supporting Actor, Miami New Times, 2003, Best Actor, 2004; recipient Bill Hindman award for Disting. Svc., 2003; Carbonell award for Best Supporting Actor, 2003, Best Actor, 2004. Mem. Actors' Equity Assn., S. Fla. Theatre League, Fla. Assn. for Theater Edn. (bd. dirs. 1991-96), voting mem. Carbonell awards S. Fla. Entertainments Writers Assn., Miami, 1992-95, Phi Beta Kappa. Home: 11207 SW 114th Lane Cir Miami FL 33176-3863 Office: New World Sch of the Arts 300 NE 2d Ave Miami FL 33132 Office Phone: 305-237-3075. Business E-Mail: dkwiat@mdc.edu.

KWIK-KOSTEK, CHRISTINE IRENE, physician, retired military officer, public health service officer; b. Lvov, Poland, Sept. 12, 1939; d. Karol Stanislaus and Leonarda Fryderica (Seniuk) Kostek; widowed; children: Christine and Catherine. Grad. summa cum laude, Med. Acad. Cracow, Poland, 1956-62; grad. primary flight medicine, Brooks AFB, Tex., 1985; completed chief of profl. staff, Sheppard AFB, Tex., 1988. Diplomate Am. Bd. Emergency Medicine, Am. Bd. Internal Medicine, Poland; cert. Ednl. Coun. Fgn. Med. Grad.; re-cert. Extended Allergy Care Provider. Intern. Med. Acad., Cracow, Poland, 1962-63; residency internal medicine II Clinic Internal Diseases, Cracow, Poland, 1963-66; staff II Clinic of Internal Diseases, Cracow, Poland, 1966-69; gen. med. officer Gen. Hosp., Sokoto, Nigeria, 1969-72; intern. Frankford Hosp., Phila., 1972-73; house physician Holy Redeemer Hosp., Meadowbrook, Pa., 1973-74; emergency room physician John F. Kennedy Hosp., Phila., 1974-76, Emergency Rm. dir., 1976-78; commd. capt. USAF Med. Corp, 1978, advanced through grades to colonel, 1993; primary care physician USAF Clinic Emergency Rm., Ramstein, Germany, 1978-81; officer in charge Emergency Rm. and Gen. Practice Clinic, Peterson Field, Colo., 1981-84; primary care physician Malcolm Grow Med. Ctr., Andrews AFB, Md., 1984-88; chief clinic svc. 63d Med. Group/SGH, Norton AFB, Calif., 1988-93; staff physician 60h Med. Group, Travis AFB, Calif., 1993-96, Occupl. and Environ. Health and Safety Svc., Ft. George Meade, Md., 1996-99; ret. USAF, 1999—; regional med. officer Dept. of State. Asst. tchr., sr. asst. tchr. Inst. Descriptive Anatomy, Cracow, Poland 1963-69; emergency physician on call First Aid Sta., Cracow, Poland 1966-69. Fellow: Am. Coll. Emergency Physicians; mem.: AMA, World Med. Assn. Avocations: photography, travel, gourmet cooking. Business E-Mail: kwikci@state.gov. E-mail: kwika@yahoo.com.

KWIRAM, ALVIN L., physical chemistry professor, university official; b. Riverhills, Man., Can., Apr. 28, 1937; came to U.S., 1954; s. Rudolf and Wilhelmina A. (Bilske) K.; m. Verla Rae Michel, Aug. 9, 1964; children: Andrew Brandt, Sidney Marguerite. BS in Chemistry, BA in Physics, Walla Walla (Wash.) Coll., 1958; PhD in Chemistry, Calif. Inst. Tech., 1963; DS (hon.), Andrews U., 1995. Alfred A. Noyes instr. Calif. Inst. Tech., Pasadena, 1962-63; research asso. physics dept. Stanford (Calif.) U., 1963-64; instr. chemistry Harvard U., Cambridge, Mass., 1964-67, lectr., 1967-70; assoc. prof. chemistry U. Wash., Seattle, 1970-75, prof., 1975—, chmn. dept. chemistry, 1977-87, vice provost, 1987-88, sr. vice provost, 1988-90, vice provost for rsch., 1990—2002. Bd. dirs. Seattle Biomed. Rsch. Inst.; mem. divsn. rev. com. Pacific N.W. Nat. Lab., Environ. and Health Scis. Divsn., 1998—2001; mem. adv. com. Pacific N.W. Nat. Lab., 2000—; exec. dir. NSF Ctr. Materials and Devices Info. Tech. Rsch., 2002—. Contbr. numerous articles to sci. jours. Bd. dirs. Seattle Econ. Devel. Commn., 1988-92, Wash. Rsch. Found., 1989-94, Seattle-King County Econ. Devel. Coun., 1989-98, Helen R. Whiteley Found., 1997-, Lumera Corp., 2001-03; mem. vis. com. divsn. chemistry and chem. engring. Calif. Inst. Tech., 1991-96; chmn. adv. bd. Sch. Engring., Walla Walla Coll., 1992—. Recipient Eastman-Kodak Sci. award, 1962, Univ.-Industry Rels/ award Coun. for Chem. Rsch., 1986; Woodrow Wilson fellow, 1958; Alfred P. Sloan fellow, 1968-70; Guggenheim Meml. Found. fellow, 1977-78. Fellow: AAAS (chmn.-elect, chmn., past chmn. sect. on chemistry 1991—94, program com. 1994—98), Am. Phys. Soc.; mem.: Nat. Acad. Sci. (com. on advanced rsch. instrumentation, com. sci. and pub. policy), Worldwide Univ. Network (acad. adv. bd. 2002—, U.S. liaison 2003—), Coun. Chem. Rsch. (bd. dirs. 1980—84, chmn. 1982—83), Am. Chem. Soc. (sec.-treas. divsn. phys. chemistry 1976—86, divsn. councilor 1986—, com. on sci., chmn. subcom. on fed. funding for rsch. 1990—94, adv. bd. for grad. edn. 2000—, chair 2005—), Nat. Assn. State Univs. and Land Grant Colls. (chmn.-elect, chmn., past chmn. 2000—03, exec. com., coun. rsch. policy and grad. edn.), Sigma Xi. Office: Univ Wash Dept Chem Seattle WA 98195-1700 Office Phone: 206-543-4020. Business E-Mail: kwiram@u.washington.edu.

KWITEK, BENJAMIN JOSEPH, entrepreneur, consultant; s. Donald Joseph and Frances Ann Kwitek. BA with honors, Colo. State U., Pueblo, 1995; MPA, U. Colo., 1997. Pres. InterForm Inc., Colorado Springs, 1998—. Rsch. assoc. Independence Inst., Golden, Colo., 1994—95; trademark designer. Author: Colorado In The Balance, 1995; contbr. articles to periodicals. Bd. dirs. United Way, Colo., 1994—95. Presdl. scholar, Colo. State U., 1993—95. Achievements include patents in field; patents pending in field; invention of laptop GellyFish product. Avocations: travel, performance driving, writing.

KWOCK, ROYAL, architect; b. San Bernardino, Calif.; s. Eddie Sing and Jeanie K.; m. Irene L. Leau, June 26, 1983. BArch, Calif. Poly. U., 1972. Registered architect, Calif. Draftsman Martinskis & Prodis, San Jose, Calif., 1973-74; intern architect, staff architect, assoc. Hawley, Stowers & Assoc., San Jose, 1974-83; project architect Winston & May, Santa Clara, Calif., 1983-86; prin. May & Kwock, Santa Clara, 1986-98, Ahearn & Kwock Archs., San Jose, 1998—. Bd. dirs. Youth Sci. Inst. Santa Clara Valley, 1985-95; mem. Nat. Trust Hist. Preservation, San Jose, 1984. Corp. mem. AIA (corr. mem. Interiors Commn. 1982-83), Kiwanis Club of West San Jose (bd. dirs. 1993, 98). Office: Ahearn & Kwock Archs 600 N 3rd St San Jose CA 95112-5119

KWOK, WINGCHI EDMUND, radiologist, educator; b. Hong Kong, Feb. 6, 1962; s. Alice Lee. PhD, Rensselaer Poly. Inst., 1990. Cert. radiologic physics diagnostician Am. Bd. Radiology. Assoc. prof. dept. radiology U. Rochester, NY, 1990—2004. Presenter in field. Contbr. articles to profl. jours.; rev.: various profl. jours. Fellow, Intermagnetics Gen. Corp., 1986—89; grantee, NIH, 2003—; scholar, Hong Kong Bapt. Coll., 1985. Mem.: Am. Phys. Soc., Internat. Soc. Magnetic Resonance in Medicine, Radiol. Soc. N.Am. (assoc. grantee 1995). Achievements include patents and patents pending for magnetic resonance imaging. Office: U Rochester Dept Radiology 601 Elmwood Ave Rochester NY 14642 Office Phone: 585-275-6506. Office Fax: 585-273-1033. E-mail: edmund_kwok@urmc.rochester.edu.

KWOLEK, STEPHANIE LOUISE, chemist, researcher; b. New Kensington, Pa., July 31, 1923; d. John and Nellie (Zajdel) Kwolek. BS, Carnegie-Mellon U., 1946; DSc (hon.), Worcester Poly. Inst., 1981, Clarkson U., 1997, Carnegie Mellon U., 2001. Chemist E.I. duPont de Nemours & Co., Inc., Wilmington, Del., 1946—59, rsch. chemist, 1959—67, sr. rsch. chemist, 1967—74, rsch. assoc., 1974—86, cons. in polymer chemistry, 1986—. Contbr. articles to profl. jours.; prodr.:. Named a Women in Tech. Internat., 1996; named to U. Akron Polymer Processing Hall of Fame, 1985, Dayton, Ohio Engring. and Sci. Hall of Fame, 1992, Nat. Inventors Hall of Fame, 1995; recipient award for contbns. to Kevlar, Am. Soc. Metals, 1978, Engring./Tech. award, Soc. Plastics Engrs., 1985, Harold deWitt Smith award, ASTM, 1988, George Lubin Meml. award, SAMPE, 1991, Medal of Excellence in composite materials, U. Del., 1992, Jack Kilby award, Kilby Awards Found., 1994, Am. Innovation award, Patent and Trademark Office, 1995, Achievement award, Indsl. Rsch. Inst., Inc., 1996, Nat. Medal of Tech. award, U.S. Dept. of Commerce Tech. Adminstrn., 1996, Perkin medal, Soc. Chem. Industry, 1997, Commonwealth award, Commonwealth Trust and PNC Bank, 1998, Lemelson-MIT Lifetime Achievement award, 1999, Henry E. Millson award, AATCC, 2001. Mem.: Phi Kappa Phi, Franklin Inst. Phila. (Howard N. Potts medal 1976), Nat. Acad. Engring., Am. Inst. Chemists (Chem. Pioneer award 1980), Am. Chem. Soc. (award for creative invention 1980), Carnegie Mellon U. Alumni Assn. (Merit award 1983, Disting. Achievement award 1998), DuPont Country Club, Phi Beta Kappa, Sigma Xi. discovered the fiber that led to the development of Kevlar, a bulletproof material five times stronger than steel. Home and Office: 312 Spalding Rd Wilmington DE 19803-2422

KWON, CHUL SOO, psychiatrist; b. Seoul, Korea, Sept. 10, 1948; m. Sung Hee Chung, Apr. 6, 1974; 1 child, Soon Jeong (Susan). MD, Seoul Nat. U., Korea, 1974. Diplomate Am. Bd. Psychiatry and Neurology. Intern Washington Hosp. Ctr., 1975—76, resident in gen. surgery, 1976—77; resident in psychiatry Johns Hopkins Hosp., Balt., 1977—80; fellow in behavioral sci. Johns Hopkins U., Balt., 1977—80, asst. in psychiatry, 1980—86; dir. partial hospitalization program North Charles Genl. Hosp., Balt., 1981—88; med. dir. partial hospitalization program Homewood Hosp. Ctr., Balt., 1988—91; med. dir. psychiat. partial hospitalization program Union Meml. Hosp., Balt., 1991—; physician St. Joseph Med. Ctr., Towson, Md., 1991—, Church Hosp., Balt., 1991—99, Md. Gen. Hosp. (U. Md. Med. System), Balt., 1991—98, 2000—, Taylor Manor, Ellicott City, Md., 1987—98; mgmt. mem. EHP Group Practice, 1993—; physician JL Kernan Hosp., Balt., 1995—, Sheppard-Enoch Pratt Hosp., 1998—; physician, subinvestigator Ctr. for Behavioral Health, 1999—. Instr. psychiatry Johns Hopkins U., 1986—96; physician, sub-investigator Ctr. Behavioral Health, 1999—; psychiat. cons. U. Splty. Hosp. (U. Md. Med. System), 2001—; psychiatrist-in-charge, cons. Harbor Hosp. (Medstar Health Sys.), Balt., 2001—. Mem.: AMA, Internat. Neuropsychiat. Assn., Korean Am. Med. Assn., Internat. Psychogeriatric Assn., Am. Soc. Clin. Psychopharmacology (cert.), Am. Acad. Clin. Psychiatrists, Md. Psychiat. Soc., Johns Hopkins Med. and Surg. Assn., Am. Neuropsychiat. Assn. Home: 2908 Chainita Ct Ellicott City MD 21042-7625 Office: Union Meml Hosp Dept Psychiat 201 E University Pkwy Baltimore MD 21218-2829 Fax: 410-313-9641, 410-554-6603. Business E-Mail: cskwon@jhu.edu.

KWON, NAHYUN, library and information scientist, educator; Ph. D., U. Wis., Madison, 2002. Asst. prof. U. South Fla., Tampa, 2002—. Mem.: The Am. Soc. for Info. Sci. and Tech. Office: University of South Florida 4202 E Fowler Ave CIS 2031 Tampa FL 33620 Office Phone: 831-974-6846. Office Fax: 813-974-6840.

KWON, O-MUN, electrical engineer, researcher; BSEE, MSEE, Hanyang U., 1992; PhD, Rensselaer Poly. Inst., 2003. Rsch. engr. Hyosung Corp., Seoul, 1992—99; post doctorall fellow Rensselaer Poly. Inst., Troy, NY, 2003—. Decan Shalom Korean Ch., Albany, 2002—04. Office Phone: 518-276-8708. E-mail: omkwan@hotmail.com.

KWON, TAEK, Internet company executive; V.p., engring. & ops. Hotwire, San Francisco; exec. v.p. product & tech. Citysearch.com, LA, 2003—05; CEO Friendstar, Inc., Mountain View, Calif., 2005—. Office: Friendster Inc 1380 Villa St Mountain View CA 94041 Office Phone: 650-618-2527.

KWONG, EVA, artist, educator; b. Hong Kong, 1954; came to the U.S., 1967; d. Tony and Ivory Kwong; m. Kirk Mangus, 1976; children: Una, Jasper. BFA, RISD, 1975; MFA, Tyler Sch. Art/Temple U., Phila., 1977. Vis. artist, 1977—; vis. faculty Cleve. Inst. Art, 1982-83; part-time faculty U. Akron, Ohio, 1987, 89, 95, Kent (Ohio) State U., 1990—. Lectr. in field. Works in over 300 exhbns. Visual Arts Regional fellow Arts Midwest, Mpls., 1987, Visual Arts fellow Nat. Endowment for the Arts, Washington, 1988, Ohio Arts Coun., Columbus, 1988, 94, 99, 2004, Ohio Arts Coun. fellow in visual arts, 2004; recipient Internat. award China NCECA, 2003. Mem. Nat. Coun. on Edn. for the Ceramic Arts (dir.-at-large 1995-97).

KWUON, JANET HEJAE, lawyer; BA in Polit. Sci., U. Calif., Berkeley; JD, U. of the Pacific, 1989. Bar: U.S. Dist. Ct. (ctrl. dist.) Calif. 1989, U.S. Dist. Ct. (so. dist.) Calif. 1990, U.S. Dist. Ct. (no. dist.) Calif. 1990, D.C. 1990. Assoc. Crosby, Heafey, Roach and May, L.A., 1992—93, ptnr., 1997—2003; practice group leader Crosby Heafey Roach and May, L.A., 2001—02; dep. dist. atty. L.A. County Dist. Atty., L.A., 1993—94; mng. ptnr. L.A. Office Reed Smith, L.A., 2002—03, ptnr., 2003—. Named one of So. California's Top Lawyers, L.A. Mag., 2004, 2005. Office: Reed Smith 355 South Grand Ave Los Angeles CA 90071 Office Phone: 213-457-8013. Office Fax: 213-457-8080. Business E-Mail: jkwuon@reedsmith.com.

KYBAL, ELBA GOMEZ DEL REY, economist, non-profit organization executive; b. Santa Fe, Argentina, Apr. 1, 1915; came to U.S., 1942; d. J. Ignacio and Concepción (del Rey) Gómez; m. Milic Kybal, July 16, 1950 (dec. July 1977); children: Cynthia, Alexander. BA in Internat. Rels., U. Litoral, Rosario, Argentina, 1940; MA in Econs., Harvard U., 1945, PhD in Econs., 1946. Economist Fed. Res. Bank, N.Y.C., 1946-47; economist, polit. affairs officer UN, N.Y.C., 1947-56, sr. economist; head specialized conf., chief L.Am. econ. integration Orgn. Am. States, Washington, dir. under secretariat for econ. and social affairs, 1956—80. Advisor InterAm. com. of women OAS, Washington, 1960—80; vol. cons. Pan Am. Devel. Found., Washington, 1980—82; vol. Argentine, Ecuadorian and Peruvian Found., Washington, 1988—90; pres. Pan Am. Roundtable, Washington, 1999—, Pan Am. Liaison Com. of Women's Orgns., 1999—2005, Retirees Assn. Orgn. Am. States, Washington, 2001—; bd. dirs. Gala Hispanic Theatre, Washington, 1997—2005. Named Vol. of the Yr., Pan Am. Devel. Found., 1981, Bus. and Profl. Women's Club, 1984. Mem.: Phi Beta Kappa. Roman Catholic. Avocation: travel. Home: Watergate South # 801 700 New Hampshire Ave NW Washington DC 20037-2406

KYDLAND, FINN E., economics professor; b. Norway, 1943; BS, Norwegian School of Economics and Business Admin., 1968; PhD, Carnegie Mellon U., 1973. Prof. econ. Carnegie Mellon, Tepper Sch. of Bus. Recipient John Stauffer National Fellowship Award, Hoover Institution, 1982—83, Nobel Prize in Econ., 2004. Fellow: Econometric Society. Office: Carnegie Mellon Unversity 5000 Forbes Avenue Pittsburgh PA 15213

KYGER, EDGAR ROSS, surgeon, educator; b. Kansas City, Mo., June 23, 1941; m. Mary K.; children: Caroline Boone, Christopher Boone, E. Ross IV. BS, Washington and Lee U., 1963; MD, U. Pa., 1967. Lic. surgeon, Tex., 1969. Intern Hosp. U. Pa., 1967-68, resident, 1968-73, St. Luke's Episcopal Hosp., 1973-74; attending surgeon Tex. Heart Inst., 1974-78; from asst. prof. to assoc. prof. surgery U. Tex. Med. Sch., Houston, 1974-78, clin. assoc. prof. surgery, 1978—; chief, thoracic, cardiovascular surgery Hermann Hosp., Houston, 1977-78, Woodland Hts. Hosp., Lufkin, Tex., Nacogdoches (Tex.) Meml. Hosp.; chief thoracic and cardiovasc. surgery St. Joseph's Hosp., Houston, 1978-88, 88-93. Bd. dirs. Lufkin Nat. Bank, 1994—; med. dir. and bd. dirs. Hospice in the Pines, 1995—. Pres. Houston chpt. Am. Heart Assn., 1980; pres. bd. dirs., Tex. Affiliate of Am. Heart Assn., 1988-89; mem. corp. bd. Boys and Girls Clubs. Fellow ACS, Am. Coll. Cardiology; mem. AMA, Tex. Med. Assn., Tex. Surg. Soc. (v.p. 2002), Harris County Med. Soc., Denton A. Cooley Cardiovascular Surgery Soc., Assn. Acad. Surgery, Ravdin-Rhoads Surg. Soc. E-mail: Drerk3@aol.com.

KYL, JON L., senator; b. Oakland, Nebr., Apr. 25, 1942; s. John and Arlene (Griffith) K.; m. Caryll Louise Collins, June 5, 1964; children: Kristine Kyl Gavin, John Jeffry. BA, U. Ariz., 1964, LLB, 1966. Atty. Jennings, Strouss & Salmon, Phoenix, 1966-86; mem. U.S. Ho. Reps. 100th-103rd Congresses from 4th Ariz. dist., 1987-94; U.S. senator from Ariz., 1994—. Mem. Fin. Com., Jud. Com. Chmn. Rep. Policy Com.; founding dir. Crime Victim Found. Mem. Ariz. State Bar Assn. Republican. Presbyn. Office: US Senate 730 Hart Senate Bldg Washington DC 20510-0001 Office Fax: 202-224-2207.

KYLE, CORINNE SILVERMAN, management consultant; b. N.Y.C., Jan. 4, 1930; d. Nathan and Janno (Harra) Silverman; m. Alec Kyle, Aug. 29, 1959 (div. Feb. 1969); children: Joshua, Perry (dec.), Julia. BA, Bennington Coll., 1950; MA, Harvard U., 1953. Assoc. editor Inter-Univ. Case Program, N.Y.C., 1956-60; co-founder, chief editor Financial Index, N.Y.C., 1960-63; rsch. analyst McKinsey & Co., N.Y.C., 1963-64; sr. rsch. assoc. Mktg. Sci. Inst., Phila., 1964-67; founding ptnr. Phila. Group, 1967-70; sr. assoc. Govt. Studies and Systems, Phila., 1970-72, cons. program planning and control, 1972-78; sr. assoc. Periodical Studies Svc., 1978-81; v.p., dir. rsch. Total Rsch. Corp., Princeton, N.J., 1981-82; mgr. social rsch. The Gallup Orgn., Princeton, 1982-86; v.p. Response Analysis Corp., 1986-91; dir. rsch. Gallup Internat. Inst., 1991-97; assoc. Krog & Ptnrs., Inc., 1997-99; survey rsch. cons., 1999—. Lectr. rsch. methods Temple U., 1981-82; vis. prof. Fairleigh Dickinson U., 1990-91, 93; dir. Verbena Corp., N.Y.C. Contbr. numerous articles to profl. publs. Mem. adv. coun. to 8th Dist. city councilman, Phila., 1971-79; mem. 22nd Ward Dem. Exec. Com., 1971-78, State Dem. Com., 1974-76; mem. Pa. Gov.'s Council on Nutrition, 1974-76; v.p. Miquon Upper Sch. Bd., Phila., 1977-78; trustee Princeton Regional Scholarship Found., 1982-85, pres., 1984-85; mem. bd. edn. Princeton Regional Sch. Dist., 1984-93, pres. 1987, 89; mem. exec. bd. Mercer County (N.J.) Sch. Bds. Assn., 1987-92, v.p., 1991-92; mem. exec. com. Princeton Community Dem. Orgn., 1992-97; mem. Princeton Regional Planning Bd., 1994-99, chair, 1997-99, Princeton Environ. Commn., 1994-97; chair Princeton Borough task force on consolidation, 1995; chair One Princeton, 1996-97; mem. West Orange Bd. Edn., 2002-, pres., 2004-05. Mem.: West Orange Advocates. Home: 32 Randolph Pl West Orange NJ 07052-4808

KYLE, DAVID L., gas industry executive; b. Wichita, Kans. BS in Indsl. Engring. and Mgmt., Okla. State U., 1974; MBA, U. Tulsa, 1987; grad. advanced mgmt. program, Harvard U., 1992. Joined ONEOK, Inc., Tulsa, 1974, pres. ONG, 1995, pres., COO, 1997, chmn., CEO, 2000—, also bd. dirs. Office: ONEOK Inc 100 W Fifth St Tulsa OK 74103

KYLE, GENE MAGERL, merchandise presentation artist; b. Phila., Oct. 11, 1919; d. Elmer Langham and Muriel Helen (Magerl) Kyle. Student, Ctr. for Creative Studies, Detroit, 1938—45. Mdse. presentation artist D.J. Healy Shops, Detroit, 1946—50, Saks Fifth Ave., Detroit, 1950—58, J.L. Hudson Co., Detroit, 1958—84, Grosse Point, Mich., 1989—95; freeland mdse. presentations for windows Grosse Point, 1989—. Papercraft Detroit Artists Mkt. Holiday Shows, 1997—2003; tchr. workshop classes. Exhibited in group shows at Mich. Watercolor Soc., 1944, 1953, 1974, Mich. Artists Exhbn., 1962, 1964, Scarab Club, 1948—49, 1952, Detroit Artist Mkt., 1946—97, Mich. Gallery, 1989—92, Coach House Gallery, 1980, 1990, Cmty. House, Birmingham, Mich., 1993—94, First Fed. Mich. Bank, 1994, 1995, Swann Gallery, 1996—97, Detroit Artists Mkt., 1997—2000. Vol. presentation work. Recipient various art awards. Mem.: Grosse Pointe Artists Assn., Windsor Art Gallery, Mich. Watercolor Soc., Detroit Inst. Arts Founders Soc.

KYLE, JOHN EMERY, mission executive; b. San Diego, July 7, 1926; s. John E. and Agnes (McDaniel) K.; m. Lois Ellen Rowland, June 8, 1947; children: Arlette Marie, Jayson Duane, Marcus Justin, Darlene Patricia. BS in Agriculture, Oreg. State U., 1950; BDiv, Columbia Theol. Sem., 1961, MDiv, 1971; D in Ministry (hon.), Belhaven Coll., 1999. Ordained to ministry Presbyn. Ch. in U.S., 1961. Sr. buyer Eastwest Produce Co.-Safeway Stores Inc., San Francisco, 1951-57; pastor Presbyn. Ch. in U.S., Hazard, Ky., 1961-63; adminstr. Wycliffe Bible Translators, Manila, Philippines, 1964-73; coord. Mission to the World, Presbyn. Ch. in Am., Decatur, Ga., 1974-77, Wycliffe Bible Translators, Washington, 1977-79; missions dir., v.p. Intervarsity Christian Fellowship, Madison, Wis., 1979-88; exec. dir. Mission to World Presbyn. Ch. in Am., Atlanta, 1988-94; sr. v.p. Evang. Fellowship of Mission Agys., Norcross, Ga., 1994—. Trustee Columbia Bible Coll. and Sem., 1982—86, Concerts of Prayer Internat., 1988—99, Berkeley Hts., NJ, Overseas Missionary Fellowship, Robesonia, Pa., 1982—86, A.D. 2000 Movement, Colorado Springs, Colo., 1989—2000, Co mission, 1992—98, World Relief Bd., 1997—, Christ's Coll., Taipei, Taiwan, 1992—98; dir. World Student Mission Convention, 1979, 81, 84, 87, Urbana, Ill. Author: Now This Generation, 1990; editor: The Unfinished Task, 1982, Finishing the Task, 1987, Urban Missions, 1988; contbr. chpts. to books. Midshipman USNR, 1944-45. Recipient Presdl. Merit medal Pres. of Philippines. Mem. Evang. Fgn. Missions Assn. (trustee 1989-94), Nat. Assn. Evang., Assn. Ch. Missions Com., World Evang. Fellowship, Concerts of Prayer Internat. Presbyterian. Office: 2343-A Granville Place Monroe NC 28110- Business E-Mail: john-lois_kyle@wbt.org.

KYLE, NICHOLAS SCOTT, art educator, artist; b. Ft. Worth, Tex., Aug. 17, 1942; s. Chester Scott and Desolee Mcmanus Kyle; m. Rose Gayle Allison, Dec. 1, 1979; m. Jerolyn Joan Fowler, Feb. 1, 1963 (div. May 24, 1979); 1 child, Christian Scott. MA, Purdue U., West Lafayette, Ind., 1970—71; BA, U. of Ctrl. Okla., Edmond, Okla., 1964—65. Cert. K-12 Teaching - Visual Art Okla., 1965. Art instr. South Jr. H.S., Joplin, Mo., 1965—67; art instr. and chair, practical arts dept. Western Oaks Jr. H.S., Okla. City, Okla., 1972—77; art instr. Putnam City West H.S., Okla. City, Okla., 1977—80; art instr. and chair, fine arts dept. Putnam City H.S., Okla. City, Okla., 1980—97; adj. art instr. Okla. City C.C., Okla. City, Okla., 1972—82; assoc. prof. art, head art dept. Mo. So. State U., Joplin, 1997—. One-man shows include Three Rivers C.C., Pine Bluff, Mo., Bartlesville (Okla.) Ctr., Kirkpatrick Mus. Complex, Oklahoma City, Firehouse Art Ctr., Norman, Okla. Art Ctr. Annex, Oklahoma City, Mus. Art, U. Ctrl. Okla., John Porter Gallery, Oklahoma City, Governor's Gallery Okla. State Capitol, Labette C.C., Parsons, Kans., Spiva Gallery Mo. So. State U., Coty Coll., Nevada, Mo., Locus Gallery, St. Louis, M.A. Doran Gallery, Tulsa, Okla., Gallery 219, Tubac, Ariz., Ascencio Design Gallery, Tucson, Ariz., exhibited in group shows at Individual Artists of Okla., Phoenix, City Arts Ctr., Oklahoma City, Donna Nigh Gallery, U. Ctrl. Okla., Edmond, Md. Mansion, Ponca City, Okla., Individual Artists of Okla. Gallery, Oklahoma City, Arts Pl. II Gallery, Keyes Gallery, Springfield, Mo., Ponca City (Okla.) Art Gallery, Back Door Gallery, Dallas, Fred Jones Mus. Art, U. Okla., Norman, Lafayette Art Ctr., West Lafayette, Ind., Tar Box Gallery, San Diego, Calif., Stephen F. forte Gallery, Shreveport, La., Norick Art Ctr., Okla. City U., Spiva Art Mus., Joplin, Mo., Untitled Gallery, Oklahoma City, Mullsjo Folkhogskola, Sweden, East Gallery, Okla. State Capitol, Oklahoma City, U. Ctrl. Okla., Edmond, Represented in permanent collections Nestle Purina Corp., St. Louis, Tinnin Mus. Three Rivers C.C., PIne Bluff, Mo., Okla. State Art Collection, Oklahoma City, Kirkpatrick Ctr. Mus., Maybee-Gerrer Mus. Art, Shawnee, Okla.; appeared on PBS Can Johnny Think, 1992, subject (video prodn.) Creative Expression; one-man shows include Gallery 100 Southeast Mo. Arts Coun., Cape Girardeau, Mo., exhibited in group shows at Gallery 219, Chgo. Okla. city arts festival edn. com. and opening night new years eve celebration com. Arts Coun. of Okla., Okla. City, Okla., 1990—97; project assistance and artist in residence selection committees State Arts Coun. of Okla., Okla. City, Okla., 1986—97; final selection com. Disney Am. Tchr. Awards, Calif., 2004; pres. 2000-2002, dir. of exhibits 1998-2003 George Spiva Ctr. for the Arts Regional Mus., Joplin, Mo., 1998—2003; representing the visual art edn. members Okla. Alliance for Arts Edn., Okla. City, Okla., 1986—97; alumni dir. Okla. Arts Inst., Okla. City, Okla., 1990—2003; founding bd. mem., treas., v.p. Okla. Visual Arts Coalition, Okla. City, Okla., 1988—97. Recipient Tchr. of the Yr., Western Oaks Jr. H.S., Okla. City, Okla., Putnam City Sch. Dist. and the Okla. Edn. Assn., Okla. City, Okla., 1976, Tchr. of the Yr., Putnam City H.S., Okla. City, Okla., 1983, Tchr. of the Yr., 1983, Okla. County Tchr. of the Yr., Okla. State Dept. of Edn., 1983, Nat. Visual Art Tchr. of the Yr., Disney Am. Tchr. Awards, LA, Calif., 1991, Okla. Art Educator of the Yr., Okla. Art Edn. Assn. and the Nat. Art Edn. Assn., 1991, Award of Excellence, Okla. Edn. Assn., 1992, Mayor Ron Norick and Okla. City Coun., 1992, Medal of Excellence in Tchg., Okla. Found. for Excellence, 1992, The Governor's Art Award, Okla. State Arts Coun., 1992, Judge - Arts Festival Okla., Okla. City C.C., 1992, Judge - Ctrl. Art Assn. Arts Festival, Okla. City, Okla., Ctrl. Art Assn., 1995 and 1996, Judge - El Reno Arts Festival, El Reno, Okla., El Reno Arts and Humanities Coun., 1996, Judge - Okla. Sculpture Soc. Ann. Exhbn., Okla. City, Okla., Okla. Sculpture Soc., 1997, Judge - Ponca City Arts Festival, Ponca City, Okla., Ponca City Arts Coun., 1997; grantee Nat. Arts Edn. Rsch. Ctr. Visual Arts Rsch. Grant, NY U., NY, NY, Nat. Arts Edn. Rsch. Ctr. funded by Nat. Endowment for the Arts and U.S. Dept. of Edn., 1988. Mem.: AAUP, Coll. Art Assn., NEA, Okla. Edn. Assn., Putnam City Assn. of Classroom Teachers (exec. bd. mem. 1996—97), Mo. Art Edn. Assn., Nat. Art Edn. Assn. (western region secondary dir. 1996—97), Okla. Art Edn. Assn. (pres. 1986—88, Okla. Art Educator of the Yr. 1991), Kappa Delta Pi, Internat. Honor Soc. in Edn. Home: 9805 County Lane 185 Carthage MO 64836 Office: Mo So State Univ 3950 East Newman Rd Joplin MO 64801-1595 Office Phone: 417-625-3045. E-mail: kyle-n@mssu.edu.

KYLE, PENELOPE WARD, academic administrator; b. Hampton, Va., Aug. 6, 1947; d. Lanny Astor and Penelope (Ward) K.; m. Charles L. Menges, Oct. 10, 1981; children: Kyle Ward, Penelope Whitley, Patricia Lee. BA, Guilford Coll., 1969; postgrad., So. Meth. U., 1969-71; JD, U. Va., 1979; MBA, Coll. William and Mary, 1987. Bar: Va. 1979, U.S. Ct. Appeals (4th cir.) 1979. Asst prof. Thomas Nelson C.C., Hampton, 1970-76; assoc. McGuire, Woods Battle & Boothe, Richmond, Va., 1979-81; assoc. counsel CSX Realty, Inc., Richmond, 1981-83, asst. v.p., asst. to pres., 1987-89, v.p., 1989-92; asst. corp. sec. CSX Corp., Richmond, 1983-87, v.p., 1993-94; exec. dir. Va. Lottery, Richmond, 1994—2005; pres. Radford U., Va., 2005—. Mem. exec. com. N.Am. Assn. State and Provincial Lotteries, 1997—, treas., 1998—. Trustee Hist. Richmond Found., 1983-94, 1st v.p., 1987-89, pres., 1989-91, chmn., 1991-93; mem. bd. visitors James Madison U., Harrisburg, Va., 1984-92; mem. Port of Richmond Commn., 1985-94; bd. dirs. Ctrl. Richmond Assn., 1988-96, vice-chair, 1991-93, chair, 1993-96; mem. Indsl. Devel. Authority City of Richmond, 1990-94, vice-chair, 1991-93, chair, 1993-94, bd. dirs. Richmond Childrens Mus., 1992-96, sec., 1995-96; bd. dirs. Cornerstone Realty Income Trust, Inc., Apple Residential Income Trust, Inc., Maymont Found., 1996—; commr. Richmond Redevel. and Housing Authority, 1994—; trustee Richmond United Way, 1996-97, exec. com. 1996-97; trustee Va. Commonwealth U. Found., 1994—; mem. U. Val. Law Sch. Alumni Coun., 1998—. Mem. ABA, Va. Bar Assn. (pres. young lawyers conf. 1984-85, mem. coun. 1984-85), Richmond Bar Assn., Jr. League Richmond, Greater Richmond C. of C. (bd. dirs. 1998—), Bear and Bull Club (bd. dirs. 1986-89, sec. 1987-88), The Country Club of Va. Home: 4706 Charmian Rd Richmond VA 23226-1706 Office: Radford U Office of Pres PO Box 6890 Radford VA 24142 Office Phone: 540-831-5401.

KYLE, RICHARD GRANVILLE, history professor, religion educator; b. Abington, Pa., July 22, 1938; s. Frank Shutt and Evelyn Mary (McBride) K.; m. Joyce Lynn Kinkel, June 8, 1968; children: Bryan, Brent. BS, Kutztown (Pa.) U., 1961; MA, Temple U., Phila., 1965; MDiv, Denver Sem., 1968; ThM, Princeton Sem., 1980; PhD, U. N.Mex., 1972. Tchr. Paulsboro (N.J.) Schs., 1961; tchr., coach Morrisville (Pa.) Schs., 1961-63; tchr. Phila. Schs., 1964-65; counselor Lookout Mountain Sch., Golden, Colo., 1965-68; teaching asst. U. N.Mex., Albuquerque, 1971-72; prof. history and religion Tabor Coll., Hillsboro, Kans., 1972—. Divsn. chair Tabor Coll., Hillsboro, 1978-89, travel tour dir., 1975—; spkr. in field Author: The Mind of John Knox, 1984, From Sect to Denomination, 1985, Religious Fringe, 1993, The New Age Movement in American Culture, 1995, The Last Days are Here Again, 1998, Awaiting the Millennium, 1998, The Ministry of John Knox: Pastor, Preacher and Prophet, 2002; assoc. editor Direction, 1984—, book rev. editor, 1985—; contbr. articles and book revs. to profl. jours. Com. mem. Hillsboro Mennonite Brethren Ch., 1976-81. Cpl. USMCR, 1956-62. Named to Athletic Hall of Fame Kutztown U., 1992, Hatboro Horsham H.S. Hall of Fame, 2003; Fulbright scholar, 1999-2000; Richard G. Kyle faculty lectr. named in his honor, 2004; recipient Rothermel Disting. Alumna aaward Kutztown U., 2004 Mem. Am. Hist. Assn., Am. Soc. Ch. History, Conf. on Faith and History (exec. com. 1991—), Sixteenth Century Studies Conf., Kans. History Tchrs. Assn. (exec. com. 1987-90, 93-96), Soc. for Reformation Rsch. Republican. Avocations: travel, weightlifting, jogging, football. Home: 412 Briarwood Ln Hillsboro KS 67063-1930 Business E-Mail: richard@talor.edu.

KYLE, RICHARD HOUSE, federal judge; b. St. Paul, Apr. 30, 1937; s. Richard E. and Geraldine (House) K.; m. Jane Foley, Dec. 22, 1959; children: Richard H. Jr., Michael F., D'Arcy, Patrick G., Kathleen. BA, U. Minn., 1959, LLB, 1962. Bar: Minn. 1962, U.S. Dist. Ct. Minn. 1992. Atty. Briggs & Morgan, St. Paul, 1963-68, 1970-92; solicitor gen. Minn. Atty. Gen. Office, St. Paul, 1968-70; judge U.S. Dist. Ct., St. Paul, 1992—. Pres. Minn. Law Rev., Mpls., 1962. Mem. Minn. State Bar Assn., Ramsey County Bar Assn. Republican. Episcopal. Office: US Dist Ct Federal Courts Bldg 316 Robert St N Saint Paul MN 55101-1495

KYLE, ROBERT ARTHUR, medical educator, oncologist; b. Bottineau, N.D., Mar. 17, 1928; s. Arthur Nichol and Mabel Caroline (Crandall) K.; m. Charlene Mae Showalter, Sept. 11, 1954; children: John, Mary, Barbara, Jean.

AA, N.D Sch. Forestry, 1946; BS, U. N.D., 1948; MD, Northwestern U., 1952; MS, U. Minn., 1958. Diplomate Am. Bd. Internal Medicine; subsplty. Hematology. Fellow Mayo Grad. Sch., Rochester, Minn., 1953-59; clin. asst. Tufts U. Sch. Medicine, Boston, 1960-61; cons. internal medicine Mayo Clinic, Rochester, 1961—; prof. medicine and lab. medicine Mayo Med. Sch., Rochester, 1975—. Pres. med. subjects unit Am. Topical Assn., Johnstown, Pa., 1976-81; chmn. standards, ethics and peer rev. orgn. Cancer & Acute Leukemia Group B, Scarsdale, N.Y., 1978-82; Robert A. Hettig lectr. in hematology Baylor U. Coll. of Medicine, Houston, 1984; Waldenström lectr., Stockholm, 1988; Redlich Meml. lectr Cedars-Sinai Med. Ctr., U. Calif., L.A.; vis. prof. St. Elizabeth's Med. Ctr., Tufts U. Sch. Medicine, Boston, 1998. Author: The Monoclonal Gammopathies, 1976, Medicine and Stamps, vols. 1 and 2, 1980; author/editor: Neoplastic Disease of the Blood, 4th edit., Myeloma: Biology and Management, 1995, 2nd edit. 1998. Chmn. bd. trustees First Presbyn. Ch., Rochester, Minn., 1967; chmn. Rochester Med. Ctr. Ministry, 1979-86; chmn. adv. bd. Internat. Waldenstrom's Macroglobulinemia Found. Capt. USAF, 1955-57. Named Disting. Topicl Philatelest, Am. Topical Soc., 1982; Recipient Waldenström award Internat. Workshop for Myeloma, Italy, 1991, Henry S. Plummer Distinguished Internist award Mayo Clin., 1995, Mayo Distinguished Clinician award 1996, Sioux award U. N.D., 1998; Bruce Wiseman lectr. Ohio State U., 1991, Kauffman Meml. lectr. Meml. Sloan Kettering Med. Ctr., N.Y.C., 1997; Clement Finch prof. U. Wash., 1993. Master ACP; mem. Royal Coll. Pathologists (hon.), N.Y. Acad. Scis., Am. Soc. Hematology, Internat. Soc. Hematology (sec.-gen. Inter-Am. divsn. 1990), Am. Assn. Cancer Rsch., Internat. Myeloma Found. (chmn. sci. adv. bd. 1995), Internat. Soc. Amyloidosis (pres. 2001-), Phi Beta Kappa. Republican. Avocation: stamp collecting/philately. Home: 1207 6th St SW Rochester MN 55902-1918 Office: Mayo Clinic 200 1st St SW Rochester MN 55905-0002 also: 920 Hilton Rochester MN 55905-0001 Office Phone: 507-284-3039. Business E-Mail: kyle.robert@mayo.edu.

KYLE, ROBERT CAMPBELL, II, publishing executive; b. Cleve., Jan. 6, 1935; s. Charles Donald and Mary Alice (King) K.; children: Peter F., Kit C., Scott G. BS, U. Colo., 1956; MA, Case Western Res. U., 1958; MBA, Harvard U., 1963, DBA, 1966. Ptnr. McLagan & Co., Chgo., 1966-67; founder, pres. Devel. Sys. Corp. (subs. Longman Group USA), Chgo., 1967-82; pres. Longman Group USA, Chgo., 1982-89; chmn., CEO Dearborn Pub. Group, Inc. (formerly Longman Group USA), 1989-98. Chmn. CTS Fin. Pub., 1997-2000. Author: Property Management, 1979; co-author: Modern Real Estate Practice, 1967, How to Profit From Real Estate, 1988 (Chgo. Book Clinic Lifetime Achievement award 1998). Mem. dean's adv. coun. Coll. Bus. U. Colo., 1992-98, Ctr. for Entrepreneurship Adv. Bd., U. Colo., 1996-2002; trustee Mystic Seaport Mus., 1989—2004, exec. com., 1999—2004, vice chair, 2001—2004; dir. Chgo. Maritime Soc., pres. 1999-2000; trustee The Burnham Inst., 2002—, San Diego Maritime Mus., 2002—, exec. com., 2003—, chair audit com., 2003—. Mem. Real Estate Educators Assn. (pres. 1981), Internat. Assn. Fin. Planning, Chgo. Book Clinic (dir.), Harvard Club N.Y., Chgo. Econs. Club, San Diego Yacht Club (chair history com. 2004—), N.Y. Yacht Club, Explorers Club. Avocations: yacht racing, tennis. Home: 2910 Owens St San Diego CA 92106 E-mail: rckyle@aol.com.

KYLEN, HELENE, writer, educator; b. N.Y.C., May 26, 1933; d. Louis and Harriet (Baruch) Klein; m. Seymour Weintraub, Sept. 10, 1960; children: Lisa Beth Swan, Karen Cooper. BA, NYU, 1955. Instr. creative writing Midchester Ctr. for Active Retirement, 1988-91; adj. faculty Baruch Coll. CUNY, 1988-96; freelance writer, editor, rschr., 1988—. Pub. rels. dir. N.Y.C. Coalition for Women's Mental Health, 1987-99; advisor N.Y.C. Dept. Probation, 1992, 93; judge nat. essay contest Job Action Corps, Washington, 1993—; spkr. in field. Editor: The American Press and the Rise of Hitler 1923-1933, 1997; editor Tng. Manual on Domestic Violence, 1992, (chpt.) Gender in Transition, 1989; editl. reviewer Jour. Vol. Adminstrn., 1994-96; contbr. articles to profl. jours. Mem. Internat. Women's Writing Guild. Avocations: theater, piano, tennis, gardening, grandchildren. Office: 111 Barrow St New York NY 10014-2869

KYLER, ARLENE, advertising executive; b. N.Y.C., Apr. 21, 1944; d. Abraham S. and Evelyn Estrin Hoberman; m. Jerry Kyler, June 20, 1964; children: Elizabeth Amy, Alison Eve. BA, Bklyn. Coll., 1964. Cert. tchr. common branches subjects SUNY-State Edn. Dept. Elem. sch. tchr. Pub. Sch. 216K, Bklyn., 1964—67; pres. Parties Unlimited Entertainment, Inc., East Rockaway, NY, 1974—86, Take My Card, Inc., East Rockaway, 1985—. Founder PTA's 1st Pub. Pre-Sch. Program, Oceanside, NY, 1973—79; pre-sch. chairperson Nassau Dist. PTA, L.I., NY, 1976—79; initiator PTA's Pre-Sch. Hearing Screening, L.I., NY, 1976; legis. co-chairperson PTA Coun., Oceanside, 1978—79; trustee Temple Avodah Sisterhood, Oceanside, NY, 1976—80; co-founder Free Sons and Daughters Investment Club, L.I., NY, 2000. Recipient United Jewish Appeal award Honoring Free Sons of Israel, Chai Lodge Long Is., N.Y., 1994. Mem.: Workmen's Benefit Fund of the U.S.A. (charter sec.-treas. br. #849), N.Y. Soc. for Profl. Inventors (trustee 1995—99), Free Sons of Israel Inc. (dist. dep. 1984, founder Chai Singles' Lodge #230 1992, 2nd dep. grand master 1993—96, 1st dep. grand master 1996—99, U.S. Grand Master 1999—2002). Achievements include patents for card display stands; card display apparatus; display and dispensing apparatus. Avocations: theater, travel, watersports, cats and medical studies, music. Office: Take My Card Inc 3445 Park Ave Oceanside NY 11572

KYLES, CEDRIC ANTONIO (CEDRIC THE ENTERTAINER), comedian, actor; b. Jefferson City, Mo., Apr. 24, 1964; s. Rosetta Kyles; m. Lorna Wells, Sept. 3, 1999; children: Croix, Lucky Rose; 1 child from previous marriage, Tiara. Bachelor's in Mass Comm., S.E. Mo. State U., 1991. Actor: (films) Ride, 1998, Big Momma's House, 2000, The Smoker, 2000, Kingdom Come, 2001, Barbershop, 2002, Serving Sara, 2002, Intolerable Cruelty, 2003, Barbershop 2: Back in Bus., 2004, Lemony Snicket's A Series of Unfortunate Events, 2004, Man of the House, 2005, Be Cool, 2005, The Honeymooners, 2005; voice actor: Ice Age, 2002; Dr. Dolittle 2, 2001; Madagascar, 2005; actor: (TV series) The Steve Harvey Show, 1996—2002 (Image award for outstanding supporting actor comedy series, 1999, 2000, 2001, 2002); voice actor: The Proud Family, 2001 (Image award for outstanding supporting actor comedy series, 2003); host Black Entertainment TV's Comicview, 1993—94; creator, writer, prodr., actor, host Cedric the Entertainer Presents, 2002—03; exec. prodr. and comedian: (TV spl.) Cedric the Entertainer: Starting Lineup, 2002; prodr. and actor: (films) Johnson Family Vacation, 2004; performer: Kings of Comedy tour, 1997—2000. Co-founder CTE Charitable Found. Inc., 1995—. Named Richard Pryor Comic of Yr., Black Entertainment TV. Office: care of Marla Winston Entertainment Enterprises 401 Le Doux Rd Ste 401 Los Angeles CA 90048*

KYLLONEN, FRANCES THOMPSON, retired educator; b. Omaha, Oct. 24, 1915; d. Jacob S. and Effie Anna (Robinson) Thompson; m. Toimi E. Kyllonen, Dec. 31, 1940 (dec.); children: Roger L. (dec.), Julie F. Rose. AA, Stephens Coll., 1936; BA, U. Mo., 1941, MA, 1946, MEd, 1968. Cert. tchr. social studies and art, Mo. Secondary art instr., art coord. kindergarten-12th grades Columbia (Mo.) Pub. Schs. Recipient award for outstanding contbns. to the profession of art edn. Mo. Art Edn. Assn., 1982. Mem. Nat. Art Edn. Assn. (chair retired art educator affiliate 1991-93), Pi Lambda Theta, Delta Kappa Gamma. Home: 604 Westmount Ave Columbia MO 65203-3471

KYLLONEN ROSE, JULIE FRANCES, college program administrator; b. Columbia, Mo., Mar. 18, 1943; d. Toimi Enoch Kyllonen and Frances Aileen Thompson; m. Charles Lincoln Rose, Mar. 17, 1972 (div. 1974). AA in Liberal Arts, Stephens Coll., 1963; AB in Polit. Sci., U. Mo., Columbia, 1965; MS in Fgn. Svc., Georgetown U., 1968. Clk.-typist US Peace Corps, Washington, 1965-67; jr. profl. Fgn. Census Rsch. Br. of U.S. Census Bur., Washington, 1967-68; office mgr. Teknekron Inc., Washington, 1968; archivist Eisenhower Presdl. Libr. Nat. Archives, Washington and Abilene, Kans., 1968-72; dir. admissions ELS Lang. Ctr., Oakland, Calif., 1974-78; program coord. for Sponsored Students Iowa State U., Ames, 1978-88; dir. internat. student/scholar/faculty svcs. Western Ill. U., Macomb, 1988—. Cons. Macomb Area Indsl. Devel. Corp., 1989-98; presenter and spk. in field, in U.S. and internationally. Fulbright-Hays fellow U.S. Dept. of Edn., Egypt, 1988, Malone fellow Nat. Coun. U.S.-Arab Rels., Saudi Arabia, 1996; scholar Rotary Internat. Group Study Exch. program, Korea, 1994, scholar NAFSA, China, 1989. Mem.: SIETAR-U.S.A., Soc. for Intercultural Edn., Tng. and Rsch. Internat., NAFSA: Assn. Internat. Educators (coord. Nigerian Student Concerns 1980—85, chmn. Mid-East spl. interest group 2000—03, Region IV newsletter editor), Macomb Area C. of C., Univ. Women's Club (2d v.p. 1994—96), Altrusa Internat. (bd. dirs. 1993—95), Delta Kappa Gamma. Avocations: artwear designer, fiber artist, weaver, mysteries. Office: Western Ill U Office Internat Edn One Univ Cir Macomb IL 61455 E-mail: J-Rose@wiu.edu.

KYLSTRA, JOHANNES ARNOLD, physician; b. Manado, Indonesia, Nov. 30, 1925; s. Jan Arnold and Johanna Leonore (Van Praag) K.; m. Carol S. Rous (dec.); children: Jan Andrew, Kimberly; m. Yvonne C. Alden. MD, U. Leiden, 1952, PhD, 1958. Asst. prof. physiology U. Leiden, 1961-63; vis. asst. prof. physiology SUNY, Buffalo, 1963-65; asst. prof. medicine and physiology Duke U., Durham, N.C., 1965-66, assoc. prof. medicine, 1966-72, prof. medicine, 1972-89, prof. emeritus medicine, 1989—, assoc. prof. physiology, 1972-89; TB control physician N.C. Dept. Environ., Health & Natural Resources, 1989-98. Contbr. numerous articles on respiratory physiology, liquid breathing and lung lavage to profl. jours. Served with Royal Netherlands Navy, 1955-58. Recipient Lockheed award Marine Technology Soc., 1970, Disting. Research award Sigma Xi, 1974, Stover-Link award Undersea Med. Soc., 1979 Home: 3615 Ocean Dr Corpus Christi TX 78411-1342

KYNCL, JOHN JAROSLAV, pharmacologist; b. Prague, Czechoslovakia, Aug. 16, 1936; arrived in US, 1971; s. Jan Petr and Marie (Mikesova) K.; m. Mila Marie Tomaides, Mar. 4, 1961; children: Marketa Kyncl Leisure, John Anthony. PhD, Komensky U., Bratislava, 1963; ScC, Czech. Acad. Sci., 1967. Pharmacologist Rsch. Inst. for Biochemistry & Pharmacy, Prague, 1963-68; A. von. Humboldt fellow U. Heidelberg, Ger., 1968-71; rsch. fellow Cleveland Clinic Found., 1971-72; E. Volwiler rsch. fellow Abbott Labs., North Chicago, Ill., 1972—. Contbr. over 100 articles to profl. jours. Fellow Coun. for High Blood Pressure Rsch. Am. Heart Assn., Am. Soc. Exptl. Biology; mem. Am. Hypertension Soc., Am. Endocrine Soc., Internat. Hypertension Soc. (Paris). Achievements include invention of invention of terazosin (Hytrin) and terlipressin (Glypressin); patents in field. Home: 800 Green Bay Rd Lake Bluff IL 60044-1829 Personal E-mail: kynclj@comcast.net.

KYRA, artist, educator; b. Harbin, China (parents Am. citizens); BFA, Ariz. State U., 1973; MFA, Fla. State U., 1975. Mem. faculty Broward Community Coll., Pembroke Pines, Fla., 1975—, dept. chmn. humanities, 1981-83, gallery dir., 1981—; mem. faculty Miami-Dade Community Coll., 1975, Barry U., Miami, Fla., 1981-82; lectr. and cons. in field; one-woman shows Artful Dodger Gallery, Tallahassee, 1975, Bainbridge Jr. Coll., 1975, The Gallery, Fla. State U., 1975, William D. Pawley Creative Arts Ctr., 1976, Womanart Gallery, N.Y.C., 1977, 78, An Alternative Gallery, Miami, 1979, A.I.R. Gallery, N.Y.C., 1979, Art and Culture Ctr. Hollywood, 1980, Fla. Atlantic U. Library, Boca Raton, 1981, Broward Community Coll., 1982, Fine Arts Gallery, Broward Community Coll., 1977, 1982, 84, 85, 86, The Gallery, Bailey Hall, 1983, Met. Mus. and Art Ctr., 1985; exhibited in group shows Gallery 741, 1975, Burdines Gallery, 1975, Boca Raton Ctr. for Arts, 1976, Grove House, 1976, 81, Lowe Art Mus., 1976, U. Miami, 1977, Avery Fisher Hall, Lincoln Ctr., 1977, Soho 20 Gallery, 1977, Womanart Gallery, 1977, An Alternative Gallery, 1978, Grove House South Gallery, 1978, Jeanne Taylor Gallery, 1978, Long Galleries, 1978, Womanart Galleries, 1978, Broward Art Guild, 1979, Hanson Galleries, 1980, Aventura Libary, 1980, Lowe-Levinson Gallery, 1980, Alain Bilhaud Gallery, 1981, Barry U., 1981, Nova U., 1982, Mus. Art, Ft. Lauderdale, 1982, Continuum Gallery, 1982, Broward Community Coll., 1983, Art and Culture Ctr. of Hollywood, 1983, Union Art Gallery, U. Wis., Madison, 1984, numerous others. Fla. Art Council fellow 1982-83; Broward Art in Pub. Places Commn. for So. Regional Courthouse, Hollywood, 1981; named Outstanding Artist of S.E., Am. Art/S.E., 1978; Gene Segal award Sta. WPBT-TV, 1981, Ltd. Edit. award, 1980, 1st Nationwide Savs. award, 1982, numerous juried arts awards. Mem. Women's Caucus for Art (dir. Fla. chpt., nat. dir.), Coalition Women's Art Orgns. (nat. dir., v.p.), Fla. Assn. Community Colls., AAUP (dir. Fla. chpt.), Coll. Art Assn. Am., Democrat. Contbr. articles to profl. jours., books. Home: PO Box 6735 Hollywood FL 33081 Office: Broward Community Coll 7200 Hollywood Blvd Hollywood FL 33024-7225

KYRIAKIDES, TASSOS CONSTANTINO, biostatistician; b. Nicosia, Cyprus, Mar. 2, 1969; s. Constantinos and Nina Kyriakides; m. Kristen Rachele Aversa, Oct. 9, 1999; children: Siena Christina children: Tassos Andreas. BSc, UCLA, 1993; MPhil, Yale U., New Haven, 1996; PhD, Yale U., 1999. Epidemiologist/biostatistician VACSPCC, West Haven, Conn., 1999—; assoc. rsch. scientist Yale AIDS Program, New Haven, Conn., 2002—. Cyprus del. UN, 2001; mem. clin. trials com. Can. Inst. Health Rsch., 2001—04. Fellow Berlex fellow, Berlex/Yale U. Sch. of Pub. Health, 1996; grantee John F. Enders Rsch. grantee, Yale U., 1997; scholar Fulbright scholar, AMIDEAST/AID, 1989—93. Office: VACSPCC West Haven 950 Campbell West Haven CT 06516 E-mail: tassos@aya.yale.edu.

KYRIAKOU, LINDA GRACE, communications executive; b. N.Y.C. d. Frank T. and Dolores Helen Lagamma; m. Konstantinos G. Kyriakou, 1 child, Christina Elena. BA, Hunter Coll. Acct. exec., dir. rsch. Booke and Co., N.Y.C., 1969-75; mgr. pub. rels. CIT Fin. Corp., N.Y.C., 1975-79; dir. corp. comm. Sequa Corp., N.Y.C., 1979-88, v.p. corp. comm., 1988—. Recipient Twin award, 1985. Mem. Pub. Rels. Soc. Am., Nat. Investor Rels. Inst. (bd. dirs. 1981-82, Sr. Roundtable), Women's Bond Club N.Y. (bd. govs. 1978-80). Office: Sequa Corp 200 Park Ave Rm 4401 New York NY 10166-4400 Business E-Mail: Linda_Kyriakou@sequa.com.

KYRIAZIS, ARTHUR JOHN (ATHANASIOS IOANNIS KYRIAZIS), lawyer, biotechnologist; b. Thessaloniki, Greece, Nov. 2, 1958; came to U.S., 1960; s. George A. and Elpis (Halkedis) K.; m. Maria M. Zissimos, Aug. 31, 1986; children: Cassandra Hope, Michael John, George Athanasios II. AB, Harvard U., 1981; postgrad., Pepperdine U., 1982—83; JD cum laude, Temple U., 1985; student in Biotechnology, U. Pa., 1998—. Bar: Pa. 1985, U.S. Dist. Ct. (ea. dist.) Pa. 1985, U.S. Bankruptcy Ct. (ea. dist.) Pa. 1985, U.S. Bankruptcy Ct. NJ, 1986, Calif. 1987, U.S. Dist. Ct. (ea. dist.) Calif. 1988, U.S. Ct. Appeals (3d cir.) 1991, U.S. Supreme Ct. 1994. Vol. Med. Coll. Hahneman U., Pa., 1974—76, lab. rsch. technician mouse mammers tumor virus project Coll. Medicine, 1977—78; assoc. Cardillo & Corbett, NYC, 1983; law clk. to Hon. Norma J. Shapiro U.S. Dist. Ct. (ea. dist.) Pa., 1984; assoc. Needleman Needleman Caney Stein & Kratzer, 1984—85; law clk. to Hon. James Gardner Colins Commonwealth Ct. Pa., Phila., Harrisburg, 1985—86; assoc. Rawle & Henderson, Phila. and Marlton, NJ, 1987—88, Lesser & Kaplin and predecessor firm, Phila., Blue Bell, Pa. and Marlton, 1988—89; prin. Kyriazis & Assocs., Springfield, 1989—92; intellectual property coord. ESI, 1992—93, React red, Inc., 1993—. Arbitrator Phila. Ct. Common Pleas, 1988—, Delaware County Ct. Common Pleas, 1993—; pro bono counsel Am. Assn. Univ. Students, 1989—; solicitor to Register of Wills, Montgomery County, Pa., 2000; law clk. Registrar Wills Del. County, 2002; rsch. assoc. U. Pa. Hosp., 1999—2000; tutor chemistry U. Pa., 1994—2000, clin. rsch. assoc. hosp. emergency rm., 2000—01; presenter in field. Contbr. articles to profl. jours. Pa. co-coord. Dukakis for Pres., 1987-88; del. Nat. Fin. Com., Dem. Conv., Atlanta, 1988; mem. Hellenic Am. for Dukakis, Pa., 1987-88; founder Am. Assn. Univ. Students, Cambridge, Mass. and Phila., 1978-79; v.p. Hercules-Spartan Phila. chpt. 26 Am. Hellenic Progressive Edn. Assn., 1989-90, pres., 1990-91, bd. govs., 1987-93; alumni assn. bd. trustees Haverford Sch., 1999—; mem. alumni bd. The Haverford Sch., 1998—, fin. com.; vol. rschr. Emergency Room Rsch. Project U. Pa. Hosp., 2000-01. Mem. ATLA, ABA (young lawyers divsn., litig. and bus. law sect., bus., real estate sects.), Am. Hellenic Lawyers Assn. (founder, treas. 1992-94), Phila. Bar Assn. (exec. com. young lawyers sect. 1988-90, fin. sec. exec. com. 1990, sec. exec. com. 1989, co-chmn. law related edn. com. 1988—, bar edn. found. com. 1988—, mem. Bill Rights 200 coms., fed. cts. 200 com., chmn. debate com. and mock trial 1987—, debate dir. fed. cts. 200 nat. high sch. debate tournament 1990—), Pa. Bar Assn. (litig., young lawyers jud. adminstrn.), Pa. Trial Lawyers Assn., Am. Arbitration Assn. (comml. arbitrator 1988—), Pa. Bar Assn., State Bar Calif. (litig., intellectual property, entertainment), Am. Assn. Univ. Students (legal counsel 1989—), Coll. Admissions Inst. Am. (adv. bd. 1992—), Hellenic Univ. Club (bd. trustees 1996-98), Harvard Club, Penn Club, Maxwell Football Club, Nat. Press Club, Harvard-Radcliffe Club (schs. com., chmn. Del. county schs. com.), Penn Faculty Club. Republican. Greek Orthodox. Office: 336 Bay Ave Unit 503 Ocean City NJ also: Kyriazis & Associates 491 Baltimore Pike #217 Springfield PA 19064-3810 Office Phone: 610-543-6453. Personal E-mail: akyriazis@msn.com.

KYSOR, DANIEL FRANCIS, psychologist; b. Corry, Pa., Aug. 3, 1956; s. Darrell Francis and Louise Mary (Col) K.; m. Kate Galbraith Morrison, Sept. 7, 1991; children: Kenneth Jon Kron, Samuel Morrison, Charles Col. BS, Edinboro U., 1980; MS in Ednl. Psychology, Edinboro U., Pa., 1988; MEd in Secondary Sch. Adminstrn., Edinboro U., 1994; postgrad., Miss. State U., 1991—. Cert. elem. edn., guidance, elem. and secondary adminstr., sch. psychologist; lic. psychologist, Pa. Tchr. Calhoun County Schs., Grantsville, W.Va., 1982; counselor, tchr. Bradford (Pa.) Children's Home, Pa., 1983; residential program counselor Assn. for Retarded Citizens, Meadville, Pa., 1984-86; resident hall dir. Edinboro (Pa.) U., 1984-86, counselor Edinboro Summer Acad. for the Gifted, 1985-96; guidance counselor Cranberry Sch. Dist., Seneca, Pa., 1986; dropout prevention counselor Erie (Pa.) Sch. Dist., 1988; sch. psychologist Seneca Highlands IU #9, Coudersport, Pa., 1989—. Pvt. practice Addis & Assocs., Bradford, Pa., 1994-97; CEO, dir. psychol. svc. Por t Psychol. Svcs., Inc., 1996—. Pa. Rural Leadership Program scholar Pa. State U., 1989; Rsch. grantee St. Bonaventure (N.Y.) U.; recipient citations Pa. House of Reps., 1991, 93, 95. Mem. ACA (life), NASP, Am. Sch. Counselor Assn., Nat. Fedn. Interscholastic Ofcls. Assns., Pa. Interscholastic Athletic Assn., Ea. Wrestling League, Ea. Ind. Officials Wrestling Assn., Nat. Wrestling Officials Assn., Clowns of Am. Internat., Inc./POCO Clowns. Democrat. Presbyterian. Avocations: wrestling officiating, reading, biking, backpacking. Home: 109 Chestnut St Port Allegany PA 16743-1248 Office: Seneca Highlands IU #9 306 N Main St Coudersport PA 16915-1626 E-mail: kysor@adelphia.net.

KYTE, SHANNAN DYAN, multimedia designer; BS in Info. Sci., Christopher Newport U., 1997. Tech. comm. coord. Thomas Jefferson Nat. Accelerator Facility, Newport News, Va., 1998—2000, electronic media mgr., 2000—. Mem.: Phi Mu Frat. (philanthropic chair 1997—99, alumnae pres. 1999—2003). Office: Jefferson Lab 12000 Jefferson Ave Newport News VA 23606

LAANE, JAAN, chemistry professor; b. Paide, Estonia, June 20, 1942; came to US, 1949. s. Robert Freidrich and Linda (Treufeldt) L.; m. Tiiu Virkhaus, Sept. 3, 1966; children: Christina J., Lisa A. BS in Chemistry, U. Ill., 1964; PhD in Chemistry, MIT, 1967; Doctorate (hon.), U. Tartu, Estonia, 2000. Asst. prof. of chemistry Tufts U., Medford, Mass., 1967-68; asst. prof. of chem. Tex. A&M U., Coll. Sta., 1968-72, assoc. prof. of chem., 1972-76, prof. of chemistry, 1976—, chmn. div. of phys. and nuc. chemistry, 1977-87, 93-94, dir. Inst. for Pacific Asia, 1987-90, assoc. dean sci., 1994-97; dep. exec. dir., sr. policy advisor Tex. A&M U./Koriyama, Coll. Sta., 1990-94; editor Jour. Molecular Structure, 1994—. Reviewer numerous profl. jour. and grant agys., 1968—; cons. indsl. and govt. orgn., 1970—; vis. prof. U. Bayreuth, Fed. Republic Germany, 1979-80; speaker Tex. A&M Faculty Senate, College Station, 1985-86; dir. NATO Advanced Rsch. Workshop, Ulm, Germany, 1992. Contbr. numerous articles to profl. jour.; lectr. numerous sci. presentations. Pres., founder Coll. Sta. Assn. for Gifted and Talented, 1982-83. Recipient 11 rsch. grants Robert A. Welch Found., 1970-97, 10 rsch. grants NSF, 1976-2001, US Sr. Sci. award Alex Von Humboldt Found., Fed. Republic Germany, 1979, Disting. Tchg. award Tex. A&M Assn. Former Students; elected to Estonian Acad. Sci., 1995, Lippincott award for molecular spectroscopy, 2005; Robert A. Welch Found. lectr., 1998-99. Fellow Am. Inst. Chemists, Am. Phys. Soc.; mem. Am. Chem. Soc. (sect. pres. 1977-78), Soc. for Applied Spectroscopy, Alexander von Humboldt Assn. Am. (bd. dir. 2003-06, pres. Tex. chpt. 2001-02), Coblentz Soc. (bd. dir., treas. 1986-89), Tex. A&M Faculty Club (pres. 1987-88), Phi Beta Delta (pres. 1990-91). Achievements include rsch. in molecular spectroscopy and vibrational potential energy functions of molecules, laser Raman spectroscopy, laser induced fluorescence spectroscopy, ft-infrared spectroscopy. Home: 1906 Comal Cir College Station TX 77840-4818 Office: Tex A&M U Chemistry Dept College Station TX 77843-0001 Fax: 979-845-3154. Office Phone: 979-845-3352. Business E-Mail: laane@mail.chem.tamu.edu.

LAATSCH, GARY KENNETH, lawyer; b. Chgo., Oct. 7, 1954; BA cum laude, Augustana Coll., 1976; JD, Loyola U., Chgo., 1979. Bar: Ill. 1979, U.S. Dist. Ct. (no. dist.) Ill. 1979. Ptnr. Pavalon, Gifford, Laatsch & Marino, Chgo., 1979—. Office: Pavalon Gifford Et Al 2 N Lasalle St Chicago IL 60602-3702 Office Phone: 312-419-7400. E-mail: laatsch@pglmlaw.com.

LAB, CHARLES EDWARD, lawyer; b. Findlay, Ohio, Dec. 21, 1952; s. Eugene G. and Estella E. L.; m. Cynthia A. Bank, June 4, 1977; children; Stephanie J., Ashley V. BA, Purdue U., 1975; JD, Ill. Inst. Tech., 1979. Bar: Ill. 1979, U.S. Dist. Ct. (no. dist.) Ill. 1979. Assoc. James L. Elsesser & Assocs., Chgo., 1979-81; Galowich & Galowich, Joliet, Ill., 1981; atty. pvt. practice, Minooka, Ill., 1982—. Trustee Village of Shorewood (Ill.), 1985-89; deacon St. John Luth. Ch., Joliet. Mem. Ill. State Bar Assn. Republican. Lutheran. Avocations: music, golf, martial arts. Office: PO Box 911 Minooka IL 60447-0911

LABA, MARVIN, management consultant; b. Newark, Mar. 17, 1928; s. Joseph Abraham and Jean Cecil (Saunders) L.; m. Sandra Seltzer, Apr. 16, 1961 (div. May 1974); children: Stuart Michael, Jonathan Todd; m. Elizabeth Luger, June 11, 1974 (div. 1979). BBA, Ind. U., 1951. Buyer Bamberger's (Macy's N.J.), Newark, 1951-67; v.p., mdse. adminstr. Macy's N.Y., 1967-73; v.p., gen. mdse. mgr. Howland/Steinback, White Plains, N.Y., 1973-75, Pomeroy's, Levittown, Pa., 1975-76; v.p., gen. mdse. mgr., sr. v.p., exec. v.p. May Co. Calif., North Hollywood, 1976-79; pres., chief exec. officer G. Fox & Co. (div. of the May dept. stores), Hartford, Conn., 1979-82; pres. Richard Theobald & Assocs., L.A., 1983; pres., chief exec. officer Marvin Laba & Assocs., L.A., 1983—. With U.S. Army, 1946-48. Avocations: coins, tennis, theater, travel. Office: Marvin Laba & Assoc 4433 Whitsett Ave Ste 5 Studio City CA 91604 Office Phone: 818-762-2122. E-mail: mcaddy444@hotmail.com.

LABADIE, BERNARD, performing company executive; b. Quebec, Can., 1963; Grad., Ecole de musique de l'Universite Laval. Founder Les Violons du Roy, 1984, La Chapelle de Quebec, 1985; condr. over 100 performances globally, 1988—; artistic dir. Opéra Que., 1994—2003, Opéra Montreal, 2002—. Named Personality of Yr., Que., 1997—98, Officer Order of Can., 2005; recipient Raymond Blais medal, Universite Laval, 1992, Rayonnement Internat. prize, Conseil de la Culture de Quebec, 1996. Office: L'Opera de Montreal 260 de Maisonneuve Blvd W Montreal PQ H2X 1Y9 Canada Office Phone: 514-985-2222. Business E-Mail: mbarretti@operademontreal.com.

LA BAGNARA, JAMES, JR., otolaryngologist, educator; b. Paterson, N.J., Dec. 5, 1946; MD, U. Medicine N.J., 1974. Diplomate Am. Bd. Otolarngology. Surgery resident CMDNJ-Newark Affiliate Hosps., 1974-75, resident in otolaryngology, 1975-78, Newark Eye & Ear Infirmary, 1979-81; staff St. Joseph's Hosp. Med. Ctr., Paterson, NJ; active staff Valley Hosp., Ridgewood, N.J., St. Josephs Wayne (N.J.) Hosp., 2004—. Clin. assoc. prof. N.J. Med. Sch., 1992—, Seton Hall Sch. Grad. Med. Edn., 1991—. Fellow ACS; mem. AMA, Am. Acad. Otolaryngology-Head and Neck Surgery, Am. Acad. Facial Plastic and Reconstructive Surgery, Am. Soc. Head and Neck Surgery. Office Phone: 973-942-1300.

LABAN, MYRON MILES, physician, hospital administrator; b. Detroit, Mar. 9, 1936; s. Larry Max and Mary Marsha (Harris) LaBan; m. Rita Joyce Hochman, Aug. 17, 1958; children: Terry, Amy, Craig. BA, U. Mich., Ann Arbor, 1957, MD, 1967; M.Med. Sci., Ohio State U., Columbus, 1965. Diplomate Am. Bd. Phys. Medicine and Rehab. Intern Sinai Hosp., Detroit, 1961-62; resident Ohio State U. Hosp., 1962-65; assoc. dir. phys. medicine and rehab. Letterman Gen. Hosp., San Francisco, 1965-67; dir. phys. medicine and rehab. William Beaumont Hosp., Royal Oak, Mich., 1967—; Licht lectr. Ohio State U., 1986, clin. prof., 1993. Bd. dirs. Oakland County Med. Bd., Birmingham, Mich., 1982—87; clin. prof. Oakland U., Rochester, Mich., 1983, Wayne State U., Detroit, 1990, Ohio State U., Columbus, 1992; rep. to Commn. Phys. Medicine and Rehab. Mich. State Med. Soc. Contbr. chapters to books, articles to profl. jours. Med. dir. Oakland County March of Dimes, Mich., 1969—83; pres. Bloomfield Art Ctr., 2003—. Served to capt. U.S. Army, 1965—67. Fellow: Am. Acad. Phys. Medicine and Rehab. (bd. dirs. 1980, pres. 1985—86, Bernard Baruch Rsch. award 1961, R. Rosenthal Rsch. award 1982, Zeiter lectureship, Disting. Clinician award 1991, Top Doc PM& R Detroit Monthly 1993, 1996, Frank H. Krusen award 1997); mem.: AMA, Mich. Acad. Phys. Med. and Rehab. (pres. 1982—84, jud. commr. 1991—95, mem. editl. bd. Jour. Phys. Med. and Rehab.), Mich. State Med. Soc., Oakland County Med. Soc. (treas. 1983, pres.-elect 1987, pres. 1988—89), Am. Assn. Electromyography adn Electrodiagnosis (program dir. 1972), Am. Congress Rehab. Medicine. Republican. Jewish. Avocations: gardening, ship modeling. Office: LMT Rehabilitation Assocs 3535 W 13 Mile Rd Rm 703 Royal Oak MI 48073-6710 Office Phone: 248-288-2243. Personal E-mail: myjoy@comcast.net.

LABAREE, BENJAMIN W., JR., history educator; b. Boston, Oct. 10, 1960; s. Benjamin Woods and Linda Prichard Labaree; m. Alison C. Snow, Sept. 25, 1999. BA, Williams Coll., 1982; PhD, U. Wis., 1996. History instr. St. Albans Sch., Washington, 1995—99, chair, dept. history, 1999—. Recipient John F. McCune Tchg. award, St. Albans Sch., 1998; fellow Lubin-Winant Rsch. fellow, Franklin D. Roosevelt Inst., 1992. Mem.: Am. Hist. Assn., Orgn. of Am. Historians. Office: St Albans Sch 3665 Massachusetts Avenue Washington DC 20016 Office Phone: 202-537-6675.

LABARGE, CHRISTOPHER W., priest; b. Pittsfield, Mass., May 9, 1953; s. Paul Willson LaB. and Nanette Marie Passier. BA in Sacred Theology, St. Francis de Sales Coll., Milw., 1979; BS in Theology, MDiv, St. Mary's Sem. and U., Balt., 1985; Lic. in Sacred Theology, St. Mary's Sem. and Univ., Balt., 1986. Ordained priest Roman Cath. Ch., 1985. Assoc. pastor Our Lady of Fatima, New Castle, Del., 1985—88, St. Elizabeth's, Wilmington, Del., 1988—92, Holy Cross, Dover, Del., 1992—95; adminstr. Immaculate Conception, Marydel, Md., 1995—96, pastor, 1996—. Chaplain Wilmington Fire Dept., 1989—92; leadership W.W. Marriage Encounter, Wilmington, 1992—95. Bd. dirs. Choptank Cmty. Health, Denton, Md., 2000—, Social Svcs. Adv. Bd., Denton, 1998—2005. Mem.: Mid Shore Regional Coun. (rep. 2003—), Gov.'s Commn. Hispanic Affairs (commr. 2003—), KC (friar 4th degree 1993—, Del. state chaplain 1998—2000, dean of the diocese 2002—). Home: 517 Main St PO Box 411 Marydel MD 21649 Office: Immaculate Conception PO Box 399 Marydel MD 21649

LABARGE, MARGARET WADE, medieval history professor, historian, writer; b. NYC, July 18, 1916; arrived in Can., 1940; d. Alfred Byers and Helena (Mein) Wade; m. Raymond C. Labarge, June 20, 1940 (dec. May 1972); children: Claire Labarge Morris, Suzanne, Charles, Paul. BA, Radcliffe Coll., 1937; LittB, Oxford (Eng.) U., 1939; LittD (hon.), Carleton U., Ottawa, Ont., Can., 1976; LLD (hon.), U. Waterloo, Ont., Can., 1993; HHD (hon.), Mount St Vincent U., Halifax, N.S., 2003. Lectr. history U. Ottawa, Carleton U., 1950-62; adj. prof. history Carleton U., Ottawa, 1983—2005. Author: Simon de Montfort, 1962, A Baronial Household, 1965, Gascony, 1980, A Small Sound of the Trumpet, 1987, A Medieval Miscellany, 1997, others; contbr. articles to profl. jours. Bd. dirs. St. Vincent's Hosp., Ottawa, 1969-81; chmn. 1977-79; pub. rep. bd. dirs. Can. Nurses Assn., 1980-83; bd. dirs. Carleton U., 1984-93, Coun. on Aging, 1986-93 (pres., 1989-91). Recipient Alumnae Recognition award Radcliffe Coll., 1987, Founders award, Carleton U., 2001 Fellow Royal Soc. Can.; mem. Medieval Acad., Soc. of Can. Medievalists (pres. 1993-94), Order of Can., Phi Beta Kappa. Roman Catholic. Avocations: travel, reading, walking. Home and Office: 402-555 Wilbrod St Ottawa ON Canada K1N 5R4 E-mail: mwlabarge@sympatico.ca.

LABARRE, CARL ANTHONY, retired federal agency administrator; b. Sherwood, N.D., July 16, 1918; s. William Paul and Josephine K. LaB.; m. Persis Wester, Sept. 9, 1941; 1 son, William Paul, II. Student, U. Mont., 1936-40; postgrad., Naval Acad. Postgrad. Sch., 1945-46; grad., Naval War Coll., 1958-59, Advanced Mgmt. Program, Harvard U. Commd. ensign U.S. Navy, 1941, advanced through grades to capt., 1971; served in various fin., inventory control systems and purchasing assignments, to 1971; insp. gen. (Naval Supply Systems Command), to 1971; ret., 1971; dep. dir. materials mgmt. service GPO, Washington, 1971-75, dir. materials mgmt. service, 1975, asst. public printer, supt. documents, 1975-82. Decorated Navy Commendation medal with V, Joint Service commendation medal, Legion of Merit with gold star; recipient Public Printers Disting. Service award, 1977, 81 Mem.: Harvard Bus. Sch. (Washington).

LABARRE, DENNIS W., lawyer; b. Binghamton, NY, Dec. 27, 1942; BA, Northwestern U., 1965; LLB, U. Va., 1968. Bar: Ohio 1978. Ptnr. Jones, Day, Reavis & Pogue, NYC; now ptnr.-in-charge NYC office Jones Day. Office: Jones Day 222 E 41st St New York NY 10017-6702 Office Phone: 212-326-3600. Office Fax: 212-755-7306. Business E-Mail: dwlabarre@jonesday.com.

LABBE, MICHELLE ANN, art educator; d. Richard Lucien and Ann Labbe. BA Studio Art, Mary Washington Coll., Fredricksburg, Va., 1996; postgrad. studies Art Edn., Va. Commonwealth U., Richmond, 1997—. Cert. Tchr.k-12 Va., 1999. Elem. art tchr. Fairfax County Pub. Schs., Sringfield, Va., 1999—2003, Indian River Sch. Dist., Selbyville, Del., 2003—. Mem. student art show com. Rehobeth Art League, Rehobeth Beach, Del., 2004—. Fellow Nat. Art Edn. Assn. Inst., 2001. Mem.: NEA, Indian River Sch. Dist.Art Tchr. Assn. (facilitator), Del. Edn. Assn., Nat. Art Edn. Assn., Greater Reston Art Ctr., Smithsonian Instn., Kappa Delta Pi. Avocations: painting, reading, sculpting, fitness. Office: Indian River Sch Dist 31 Hooster Rd Selbyville DE 19975 Office Phone: 302-732-3808. E-mail: mlabbe@irsd.k12.de.us.

LABBETT, JOHN EDGAR, financial analyst; b. Chesham, Buckinghamshire, Eng., June 19, 1950; came to U.S., 1987; s. Gordon F. and Sylvia (Dalton) L.; m. Mary McGagh, Jan. 30, 1976; children: Jennifer F., Alexander T. Audit clk. White Withers and Co., Bexhill, England, 1966—71; auditor Peat Marwick Mitchell, London, 1971—73; chief acct. Guild S&V Ltd., London, 1973—74; from fin. analyst to contr. Roneo Vickers Ltd., London, 1974—81; fin. contr. Cambridge (Eng.) Instruments Ltd., 1981—82; fin. dir. Linfood C&C Ltd. subs. Dee Corp., Milton Keynes, England, 1982—85; fin. controller Dee Corp., Milton Keynes, 1985—87; exec. v.p., CFO Hermans Sporting Goods, Inc., Carteret, NJ, 1987—93; v.p., CFO The Petfood Giant, Inc., 1994—95; exec. v.p., CFO House of Fabrics, Inc., Sherman Oaks, Calif., 1995—98, Egghead.com, Inc., Menlo Park, Calif., 1998—2001; ind. fin. cons. Bell Canyon, Calif., 2001—03; CFO, Oversee.net, L.A., 2004—. Fellow Inst. Chartered Accts. Eng. and Wales. Mem. Ch. Eng. Home: 80 Stagecoach Rd Bell Canyon CA 91307-1042 Personal E-mail: jlabbett@earthlink.net.

LABE, ROBERT BRIAN, lawyer; b. Detroit, Sept. 2, 1959; s. Benjamin Mitchell and Gloria Florence (Wright) L.; m. Mary Lou Budman, Nov. 12, 1989; two children: Bridget and Katherine. BA with high honors, Mich. State U., 1981; JD, Wayne State U., 1984; LLM, Boston U., 1985. Bar: Mich. 1984, U.S. Dist. Ct. Mich. 1985, U.S. Tax Ct. 1985. Assoc. Weingarden & Hauer, P.C., Bingham Farms, Mich., 1988-92, shareholder, 1992-94, Williams, Williams, Ruby & Plunkett, P.C., Birmingham, Mich., 2002—, Robert B. Labe, P.C., Southfield, Mich., 1994—2002. Adj. prof. taxation and estate planning Walsh Coll., Troy, Mich., 1990-92; adv. bd. Inst. Continuing Legal Edn. U. Mich., 1993—; lectr. and presenter in field. Author: Research Edge-Taxation Guide, 1994, Bus. Succession Planning, 1996, Family Limited Liability Cos. and Limited Partnerships, 1998, Business Planning and Estate Planning After EGTRA Tax Act, 2004; contbr. articles to profl. jours. Bd. dirs. Oakland County Bar Found. Avocations: tennis, spectator sports. Office: Williams Williams Ruby & Plunkett Ste 300 380 N Woodward Ave Birmingham MI 48009 Office Phone: 248-642-0333. Business E-Mail: rbl@wwrplaw.com.

LABELLE, PATTI (PATRICIA LOUISE HOLTE), singer, entertainer; b. Phila., May 24, 1944; d. Henry and Bertha Holte; m. Armstead Edwards, 1969 (div. 2000); 5 children. PhD (hon.), Berkeley Sch. Music, 1996, Cambridge U., Drexel U. Singer Patti LaBelle and the BlueBelles, 1961—70; lead singer musical group LaBelle, 1970-76; solo performer, 1977—; entrepreneur Patti LaBelle's Fragrances & Cosmetics, 1995. Established clothing line Patti LaBelle Clothing, 2003—. Albums (with the BlueBelles) Sweethearts of the Apollo, 1963, Over the Rainbow, 1967, (with LaBelle) LaBelle, 1971, Moon Shadows, 1972, Pressure Cookin', 1973, Nightbirds, 1974, Phoenix, 1975, Chameleon, 1976, (solo) Patti LaBelle, 1977, Live at the Apollo, 1980, Gonna Take A Miracle-The Spirit's in It, 1981, I'm in Love Again, 1983, Winner in You, 1986, The Best of Patti LaBelle, 1987, Patti, 1985, Be Yourself, 1989, Burnin', 1991 (Grammy award best r&b vocalist, 1991), Live (Apollo Theater), 1992, Gems, 1994, Live! One Night Only, 1998 (Grammy award best trad. r&b vocal perf., 1998), Greatest Hits, 1996, Flame, 1997, When a Woman Loves, 2000, Timeless Journey, 2004, Patti Labelle: Classic Moment, 2005; actress (films) A Soldier's Story, 1984, Sing, 1989; (TV movies) For Colored Girls Who Have Considered Suicide, 1982, Working, 1982, Unnatural Causes, 1986, Fire and Rain, 1989, Parker Kane, 1990, Santa Baby! (voice), 2001, My Life in Idlewild, 2005; (TV series) A Different World, 1990-93, Out All Night, 1992; (guest appearances) Dolly, 1987, The Nanny, 1994, Cosby, 1997, All of Us, 2004; (TV specials) Live Aid, 1985, The Patti LaBelle Show, 1985, Sisters in the Name of Love, 1986 (CableACE award best perf. music special, 1987) Motown 30: What's Goin' On!, 1990, Sinatra Duets, 1994, The Remarkable Journey, 2000, Born to Diva, 2003, Nina Simone: A Tribute, 2003, VH1 Divas Live, 2004, (plays) Your Arms Too Short to Box with God (revival), 1980; author Don't Block the Blessings: Revelations of a Lifetime, 1997, LaBelle Cuisine: Recipes to Sing About, 1999, Patti's Pearls: Lessons in Living Genuinely, Joyfully & Generously, 2001, Patti LaBelle's Lite Cuisine; host (TV show) Living It Up with Patti LaBelle, 2004—. Spokesperson Am. Diabetic Assn., Nat. Minority AIDS Council, Nat. Cancer Inst., founder The Patti LaBelle Med. Ed. Scholarship Fund. Recipient award of Merit, Phila. Art Alliance, 1987, Soul Train Lifetime Achievement award, 1997, Walk of Fame honoree Black Entertainment TV, 2000; Entertainer of Yr. Image award NAACP, 1992. Office: Def Soul Classics 825 8th Ave 29th Fl New York NY 10019

LABELLE, THOMAS JEFFREY, academic administrator; b. Owen, Wis., Sept. 21, 1941; s. Wendell Allen and Katherine (Dolan) LaB.; m. Nancy Reik, June 16, 1966 (dec. 1981); children: Katherine Anne, Jeanette Marie AA, Pierce Coll., Woodland Hills, Calif., 1962; BA, Calif. State U., Northridge, 1964; MA, U. N.Mex., Albuquerque, 1967, PhD, 1969. Prof. UCLA, 1969-86, asst. dean edn., 1971-79, assoc. dean grad. div., 1980-86; prof. comparative and internat. edn. U. Pitts., 1986-90, dean Sch. Edn., 1986-90; v.p. acad. programs, provost Ga. State U., Atlanta, 1990-93; provost, v.p. acad. affairs and rsch. W.Va. U., Morgantown, 1993-96; provost v.p. acad. affairs San Francisco State U., 1996—2002; exec. dir. internat. and area studies U. Calif., Berkeley, Calif., 2002—. Cons. InterAm. Found., U.S. AID, Ford Found., CBS, Acad. Ednl. Devel., Juarez and Assocs. Author: Education and Development in Latin America, 1972, Nonformal Education in Latin America and the Caribbean, 1986, Stability, Reform or Revolution, 1986, Education and Intergroup Relations, 1985, Multiculturalism and Education, 1994, Ethnic Studies and Multiculturalism, 1996. Vol. Peace Corps, Colombia, 1964-66. Grantee Fulbright Found., 1983, 96, InterAm. Found., Latin America, 1984; recipient Andres Bello award 1st Class, Venezuela, 1987. Fellow Soc. Applied Anthropology; mem. Comparative and Internat. Edn. Soc. (pres. 1981), Coun. on Anthropology and Edn. (bd. dirs. 1977), Inter-Am. Found. (chmn. learning fellowship on social change), Golden Key, Omicron Delta Kappa, Phi Kappa Phi. Democrat. Office: U California IAS 360 Stephens Hall Berkeley CA 94720-2300 Office Phone: 510-642-5284. Business E-Mail: tlabelle@berkeley.edu.

LABENSKY, SARAH ROSS, culinary educator; b. Murray, Ky., Mar. 16, 1958; d. James Mason and Lucille Thomson Ross; m. Steven Jay Labensky, Oct. 14, 1983 (div. May 1995); m. Louis David Moline, Sept. 3, 1995 (dec. Aug. 2003) BS, Murray (Ky.) State U., 1980; JD, Vanderbilt U., 1983; cert., Scottsdale C.C., 1986. Atty. Hocker and Axford, Tempe, Ariz., 1983-85; cook/chef Phoenix, 1985-90; prof. Scottsdale C.C., 1990-98; dir. Miss. U. for Women Culinary Arts Inst., Columbus, 1998—. Author: On Cooking, 1995, 3d edit., 2003, Webster's N.W. Dictionary of Culinary Arts, 1997, 2d edit., 2000, Applied Math for Food Service, 1998, Complete Idiot's Guide to Cooking Techniques and Science, 2002, On Baking, 2004. Mem.: Internat. Assn. Culinary Profls. (cert., bd. dirs. 1999—, sec.-treas. 2002, v.p. 2003, pres. 2004), Am. Culinary Fedn. Office: FRP 2451 Atrium Way Nashville TN 37214 Office Phone: 662-241-7472. Business E-Mail: slabensk@muw.edu.

LABENZ-HOUGH, MARLENE, mediator; b. St. Edward, Nebr., May 25, 1954; d. Ralph Labenz and Lorene (Laudenklos); m. Jeff Hough, Mar. 5, 1983. Assocs., Platte Coll., 1974; BS in Social Work magna cum laude, U. Nebr., 1976; MA in Clin. Psychology, Trinity U., 1980. Adminstrv. asst., mgmt. analyst II City of San Antonio Dept. Human Resources and Svcs., 1980, adminstrv. asst. II, 1980-82, casework supr., Victims of Crime Program, 1982-89, program coord., Children's Resources Divsn., 1989-90; asst. dir. Bexar County Dispute Resolution Ctr., San Antonio, 1990-92, dir., 1992—. Bd. dirs. KidShare, 1993-96, YWCA, 1990-93; mem. ADR sect. coun. State Bar Tex., 1996-99. Recipient Liberty Bell award, San Antonio Young Lawyers Assn., 2003, Recognition award, San Antonio Bar Found., 2004, Appreciation award, 2005, Recognition award for leadership. Mem.: ABA (chmn. conf. com. ADR sect. 2002), Tex. Bar Assn. (ADR sect.), Assn. Family and Conciliation Cts., Tex. Mediators Credentialing Assn., Alamo Area Mediators Assn., Tex. Dispute Resolution Ctrs. Dirs. Coun., Tex. Mediation Trainers' Roundtable, Assn. Conflict Resolution, Conflict Resolution and Peer Mediation Coun., Nat. Assn. Cmty. Mediation (founding dir.), Soc. Profls. in Dispute Resolution (co-chair S.W. region chpt. 1993, co-chair nat. conf. 1995, Profl. Dedication award 1994), Acad. Family Mediators, Tex. Assn. Mediators (chair conf. 1998, bd. dirs. 1998—2001), Alpha Xi Delta. Home: 2518 Ashton Village Dr San Antonio TX 78248-2200

LABINER, GERALD WILK, physician, medical educator; b. N.Y.C., Nov. 7, 1923; s. Benjamin and Mollie (Wilk) L.; m. Suzanne Solov, May 3, 1953; children: Caroline Moser, Charles. BS, Rutgers U., 1944; MD, Ind. U., 1949. Intern. Phila. Gen. Hosp., 1949-51, resident, 1951-52; sr. asst. surgeon USPHS, Washington, 1951-53; fellow Lahey Clinic, Boston, 1953-55; pvt. practice Beverly Hills, Calif., 1955-98, L.A., 1998—. Lt. j.g., USN, 1944-45; with USPHS, 1951-53. Fellow ACP, Am. Geriat. Soc., Contemporary Art Soc.; mem. Aescolapi Assn., Far Eastern Coun. (pres. 1964-65), Alpha Omega Alpha. Avocation: art. Office: 1125 S Beverly Dr Ste 710 Los Angeles CA 90035-1180 Office Phone: 310-201-9898. E-mail: holmby@earthlink.net.

LABINGER, LYNETTE, lawyer; m. Ross A. Eadie, Jan. 21, 1972; 1 child, Loren Labinger Eadie. AB magna cum laude, Mt. Holyoke Coll., 1971; JD cum laude, NYU, 1974. Bar: Mass. 1974, R.I. 1975, U.S. Dist. Ct. R.I. 1975, U.S. Ct. Appeals (1st Cir.) 1978, U.S. Supreme Ct. 1980. Law clk. U.S. Dist. Ct. R.I., Providence, 1974—76; assoc. Abedon, Michaelson, Stanzler, Biener, Skolnik & Lipsey, Providence, 1976—82; ptnr. Roney & Labinger LLP, Providence, 1983—. Mem. U.S. Dist. Ct. Bar Examiners, 1981—2004, Commn. on Jud. Tenure and Discipline, 1983—86; assoc. justice part-time term appointment Housing Ct. of City of Providence, 2004—. Bd. dirs., vol. atty. R.I. affiliate ACLU, 1978—; bd. dirs. R.I. Legal Svcs. Inc., 1980-83. Recipient Vol. Atty. award ACLU, 1982, Charles Potter award Planned Parenthood R.I., 1982, NYU Prize, 1974, Alumnae Key award NYU Law Sch., 1974, Sorrentino award Nat. Women's Polit. Caucus, 1988, Civil Libertarian of Yr. award R.I. ACLU, 1989; Root-Tilden scholar, 1971-74. Fellow Am. Coll. Trial Lawyers, R.I. Bar Found. (bd. dirs.); mem. R.I. Bar Assn., Order of Coif, Phi Beta Kappa. Democrat. Office: Roney & Labinger LLP 344 Wickenden St Providence RI 02903-4469 Office Phone: 401-421-9794. E-mail: office@roney-labinger.com.

LA BLANC, ROBERT EDMUND, information technology executive; b. NYC, Mar. 21, 1934; s. Charles Wesley and Anne R. (Dobson) La B.; m. Elizabeth Lammers, 1962; children: Elizabeth, Robert, Jeanne Marie, Paul, Michelle. B.E.E., Manhattan Coll., 1956; DHL honoris causa (hon.), Manhattan Coll., 1997; MBA, NYU, 1962. With Bell System, 1956-69; mem. tech. staff Bell Telephone Labs., 1961-62; seminar leader AT&T Long Lines, Cooperstown, NY, 1965-67; mktg. supr. AT&T Hdqrs., NYC, 1967-68; planning engr. N.Y. Telephone, 1968-69; mgr. Salomon Bros., NYC, 1969-73, v.p., 1973-75, gen. partner, 1975-79; vice chmn. Continental Telephone Corp., NYC, 1979-81; pres. Robert E. LaBlanc Assocs., Inc., 1981—. Bd. dirs. Chartered Semicondr. Mfg. Ltd., Singapore, Computer Assocs. Internat., Inc., Titan Corp., Fibernet Telecom Group, Inc.; dir., trustee Prudential/Jennison/Dreyden Mutual Funds. Vice chmn. bd. trustees Manhattan Coll., 1987-93, trustee, 1994—. Served to 1st lt. USAF, 1956-59. Named Wall St. Leading Analyst Instl. Investor Mag., 1973-78 Fellow: Fin. Analysts Fedn.; mem.: Assn. for Computing Machinery, NY Soc. Security Analysts (sr.), Econ. Club, Univ. Club, Equestrian Order Holy Sepulchre of Jerusalem (knight). Republican. Roman Catholic. Office Phone: 201-445-0195. Personal E-mail: rlablanc@aol.com.

LABODA, GERALD, oral and maxillofacial surgeon; b. Phila., Aug. 15, 1936; s. Lewis and Rose (Waldman) L.; m. Sheila Lois Plasky, Aug. 2, 1956; children: Amy, Michèle, Alane, Bruce. Student, Temple U., 1954-56, DMD, 1960; postgrad., U. Pa., 1960-61. Diplomate Am. Bd. Oral and Maxillofacial Surgery. Resident physician in oral and maxillofacial surgery Jefferson U. Hosp., Phila., 1961-63; pvt. practice oral and maxillofacial surgery S.W. Fla. Oral and Facial Surgery Assocs., Ft. Myers, 1965—. Bd. dirs Nationsbank, S.W. Fla., 1974-99; chmn. bd. trustees S.W. Fla. Regional Med. Ctr., Ft. Myers, 1989-94, sec. bd. trustees, 1974-89; med. dir. S.W. Fla. divsn. Columbia/HCA Healthcare Corp., 1994-99; trustee Gulf Coast Hosp., Ft. Myers; v.p. Flordeco, Inc.; chmn. bd. dirs. Procraft Industries, L.L.C. Contbr. articles to profl. jours. Pres. YMCA of Lee County, 1976; pres., bd. dirs. Found. for Lee County Pub. Schs., Ft. Myers, Fla., 1991, Fla. Gulf Coast Univ. Found.; vice chmn. Downtown Redevel. Agy., Ft. Myers, 1985—93; chmn., 1993—; bd. dirs. United Way of Lee County, 1981, Fla. Repertory Theater, 1999—, chmn., 2001—, Oral and Maxillofacial Surgery Found., 1990—2000; mem. bd. dentistry State of Fla., 1999—2003, chmn., 2002—. Fellow Am. Assn. Oral and Maxillofacial Surgeons (trustee Dist. III 1984-87, v.p. 1987-88, pres. 1989-90); mem. Fla. Soc. Oral and Maxillofacial Surgeons (pres. 1980-81), Fla. Dental Soc. of Anesthesiology (pres. 1978-79), S.W. Fla. Dental Soc. (pres. 1974), Southeastern Soc. Oral and Maxillofacial Surgery Found. (bd. dirs. 1993—, vice chmn. 1997, chmn. 1998-2000). Republican. Jewish. Avocations: flying, skiing, scuba diving, white water rafting. Office: SW Fla Oral Facial Surg Assocs Summerlin Med Park 5285 Summerlin Rd Fort Myers FL 33919-7602 Home: 9904 Bellagio Ct Fort Myers FL 33913-7041 Office Phone: 239-936-8151. Business E-Mail: Splaboda@comcast.net.

LABOON, LAWRENCE JOSEPH, human resources specialist, consultant; b. St. Louis, Aug. 4, 1938; s. Joseph Warren and Ruth (Aab) LaBoon; m. Glynys M. Brown, Sept. 16, 1989; children: Lawrence Bradley, Meredith Ashley;children from previous marriage: Lindsey Beth, Allison Ruth. BS magna cum laude, Tex. Wesleyan U., 1962. Cert. pers. cons., staffing profl. Oper. mgr. Firestone Tire & Rubber Co., Akron, Ohio, 1962—66; pres., CEO, Met. Pers., Inc., Phila., 1966—, chmn., 2000—; pres. Metro Tech, Valley Forge, Pa., 1977—, Metro Temps, Valley Forge, 1978—, Transport Tng. Corp., Valley Forge, 1993—, Metro Med., Valley Forge, 2001—; dir. Alpha-Indian Rock Savs. and Loan Assn., chmn. compensation com., 1986—90; chmn. pvt. employment agy. adv. coun. Pa. Dept. Labor and Industry, 1973—82. Guest lectr. Drexel U., 1976—91; human resources del. to USSR Citizen Amb. Program, 1991. Mem. People to People Internat. Mission to Vietnam and Asia, 1993; pres. Sunwood Farm Homeowners Assn., 2002—03; mem., pres. exec. bd. Valley Forge Profl. Ctr., 2001—, pres., 2005—. With USAF, 1954—60. Mem.: Am. Staffing Assn. (staffing profl.), Exec. Riders Ltd. (pres. 1986—88), Nat. Assn. Profl. Employers, TEMPNET (bd. dirs. 1986—88), Mid-Atlantic Assn. Temporary Svcs. (pres. 1983—84), Am. Soc. Pers. Adminstrn., Nat. Assn. Pers. Cons., Pa. Assn. Pers. Svcs. (pres. 1971—72, Blanchet Meml. award 1973), Nat. Employment Assn. (state certification bd. chmn. 1969—71, bd. dirs. 1972—74, chmn. bd. regents 1973, cert.), Glenhardle Condominium Assn. (non-resident exec. bd. 1989—91), Phoenixville Country Club, Alpha Chi. Republican. Home: 255 Country Ln Phoenixville PA 19460-1708 Office: 1260 Valley Forge Rd Valley Forge PA 19482-0641 Business E-Mail: ljl@metpersnl.com.

LABOON, ROBERT BRUCE, lawyer; b. St. Louis, June 14, 1941; s. Joseph Warren LaBoon and Ruth (Aab) LaBoon Freling; m. Ramona Ann Hudgins, Aug. 24, 1963; children: John Andrew, Robert Steven. BSc, Tex. Christian U., 1963; LLB cum laude, So. Meth. U., 1965. Bar: Tex. 1965. Sr. ptnr. Locke Liddell & Sapp LLP, Houston, 1965-86, 88—; vice chmn. and gen. counsel Tex. Commerce Bancshares, Inc., 1986-88. Bd. dirs. Tex. Med. Ctr., Tex. Children's Hosp. Bd. dirs. The Greater Houston Partnership, Bio-Houston, Inc., Tex. Environl. Rsch. Consortium; bd. visitors M.D. Anderson Cancer Ctr.-U. Cancer Found.; bd. govs. Am. Red Cross. Fellow Tex. Bar Found., Am. Coll. of Trust and Estate Counsel; mem. ABA, Am. Law Inst., Tex. Assn. of Bank Counsel, Houston Bar Assn., State Bar Tex., Houston Club, River Oaks Country Club. Office: Locke Liddell & Sapp LLP 600 Travis St Ste 3500 Houston TX 77002-3095 Office Phone: 713-226-1330. E-mail: laboon@lockeliddell.com.

LABOR, EARLE GENE, literature and language professor; b. Tuskahoma, Okla., Mar. 3, 1928; s. Earle Labor and Sylvia Kirkpatrick Steger; m. Betty Garrett, Sept. 21, 1952 (dec. Aug. 1989); children: Royce, Kirk, Kyle, Isabel; m. Gayle Johnson, May 25, 1996; 1 child, Andrea. AB, So. Meth. U., Dallas, 1949, MA, 1952; PhD, U. Wis., Madison, 1961. Instr. English So. Meth. U., Dallas, 1950-52; asst. sales mgr. Haggar Co., Dallas, 1954-55; instr. English Centenary Coll., Shreveport, La., 1955-56, asst. prof. English, 1959-62, George A. Wilson prof. Am. Lit., 1966—; tchg. asst. U. Wis., Madison, 1956-59; head dept. English, chmn. dept. Humanities Adrian (Mich.) Coll., 1962-66. Adv. bd. Jack London Found., Glen Ellen, Calif., 1973—. Author: Jack London, 1974, 2d edit.,94; co-author: A Handbook of Critical Approaches to Literature, 1966, 5th edit., 2005; co-editor: The Letters of Jack London, 1988, The Complete Short Stories of Jack London, 1993; editor: Viking Portable Jack London, 1994. Fulbright prof., Denmark, 1973-74; named Jack London Man of Yr. Jack London Found., 1975, Humanist of Yr. La. Endowment for Humanities, 1991. Mem. MLA, Coll. English Assn. (editor 1967-75, pres. 1977-79, Disting. Svc. award 1983, Lifetime Membership award 1990), Internat. Assn. Univ. Profs. of English, Jack London Soc. (bd. dirs. 1990—), Nat. Assn. Scholars and Critics. Avocation: photography. Personal E-mail: elabor@centenary.edu.

LABORDE, ENRIQUE, retired communications engineer; b. Madrid, July 15, 1939; s. Francisco Laborde and Victoria Torrecilla; m. Clara Laborde; children: Enrique, Maria, Beatriz, Gonzalo, Ana. Ingenius Superior de Telecommunicacion, U. Madrid, Spain, 1966; MS in computer sys., U. Md., 1989. Tech. staff ITT Labs. of Spain, Madrid, 1966—72, asst. mgr. space divsn., 1972—74, mgr. transmission and space divsn., 1974—79, mgr. data comm. divsn., 1979—82; sr. sys. engr. Hughes Network Sys., Germantown, Md., 1982—88, adv. engr., 1988—95, chief scientist, 1995—2004; ret., 2004. Contbr. articles various profl. jours. Recipient Outstanding Achiev. award, Standards Com. Telecomm., 1997. Mem.: Inst. Electrical and Electronics Engrs. Democrat. Cath. E-mail: elaborde@comcast.net.

LABORIE, MARIE-PIERRE GENEVIÈVE, education educator; b. Montpelllier, France, June 23, 1972; d. Jean-Michel and Marie-José Laborie. Engring. Degree of Wood Sci. and Tech., Ecole Nationale Superieure des Sciences et Technologies du Bois (ENSTIB), Epinal, France, 1996; PhD, Va. Poly. Inst. and State U., Blacksburg, Va., 2002. Grad. rsch. asst. Va. Poly. Inst. and State U., Blacksburg, Va., 1997—2002; asst. prof. of civil and environ. engring. Wash. State U., Pullman, Wash., 2002—. Affiliate prof. in the sch. mech. and materials engring. Wash. State U., Pullman, Wash., 2003—, adj. prof. of materials sci. Recipient Best Paper, 6th Pacific Rim Bio-based Composites Symposium, Portland, Oreg., 2002, Young Faculty Recognition, Coll. of Engring. and Arch., Wash. State U., 2003-2004; fellow, Ctr. for Adhesive and Sealant Sci., Va. Poly. Inst. and State U., 1998-2001; grantee Fundamental Investigations and Design of Bio-based Composites, US Depts. of Def., Agr. and Energy, 2002-2005. Mem.: Forest Products Soc. (chair of the tech. interest goup in adhesives 2003—), Adhesion Soc., Am. Chem. Soc., Soc. of Wood Sci. and Tech., North Am. Thermal Analysis Soc. (symposium chair of wood materials at the 58th ann. meeting 2004). Achievements include research in Fundamental understanding of Polymer Interactions in Bio-Based Composites and Devel. of Bio-Based Composites; development of Polymer/Composite Graduate Curriculum at Wash. State Univ. Office: Wash State Univ WMEL 1445 Terre View Dr Pullman WA 99164 Office Phone: 509-335-8722. Office Fax: 509-335-5077.

LABOUFF, JACKIE PEARSON, personal care industry executive, educator; b. Wilmington, Calif., June 26, 1936; d. Maurice Emerson and Juanita Armstrong Pearson; m. John Robert LaBouff, Oct. 5, 1957; children: Margaret C., Mark J., Thomas F., Joan. BA, Calif. State U., Domingez Hills, 1972, MA, 1987. Tchg. credential Calif., 1982, counseling credential Calif., 1987. Flight attendant Am. Airlines, LA, 1956—57; pre-sch. tchr. Hickory Tree, Torrance, Calif., 1972—77; adult edn. tchr. Torrance (Calif.) Unified Sch Dist., 1977—84, Calif. State U., Domingez Hills, 1984—94; grant dir. Lawndale (Calif.) Sch. Dist., 1991—95; exec. dir. Project Touch, Hermosa Beach, Calif., 1996—2005. Adult edn. anger mgmt. tchr. Beach Cities Health Dist., Redondo Beach, Calif., 2000—05; sch. bd. candidate Torrance (Calif.) Unified Sch. Dist., 1995. Commr. Cmty. Svcs. Commn., Torrance, Calif., 1991—99. Recipient Magnificent Woman, Carson Coord. Co., 2003. Mem.: Am. Assn. Univ. Women (pres. 1991—94, Ednl. Found. Honor award 1994). Democrat. Roman Catholic. Avocations: travel, knitting, crocheting, needlecrafts. Home: 3810 W 173 St Torrance CA 90504 Office: Project Touch 710 Pier Ave Hermosa Beach CA 90254 E-mail: sticher61@hotmail.com.

LABOVITZ, DANIEL LOCKETT, neurologist; b. N.Y.C., Jan. 12, 1965; s. Jeffrey Niles Labovitz and Ann Elizabeth Lockett; m. Laura Shaw Boylan, May 27, 1994; 1 child, Nora Sonia Valencia-Boylan. AB, Harvard U., 1987; MD, Columbia U., 1994, MS, 2001. Diplomate Am. Bd. Psychiatry and Neurology. Intern in medicine St. Vincent's Hosp., N.Y.C., 1994—95; resident in neurology Neurol. Inst., N.Y. Presbyn. Hosp., N.Y.C., 1995—98, stroke fellow, 1998—2000; asst. attending neurologist St. Luke's-Roosevelt Hosp. Ctr., N.Y.C., 2000—. Contbr. articles to profl. jours. Mem.: Am. Acad. Neurology. Office: St Luke's-Roosevelt Stroke Ctr 1111 Amsterdam Ave New York NY 10025

LABRECQUE, RICHARD JOSEPH, retired industrial executive; b. Lawrence, Mass., Dec. 19, 1938; s. Eugene N. and Ludivine M. (Roy) L.; m. Janet Marie Michaud, July 16, 1960; children: David R., Lisa M., Susan M. BSEE, Tufts U., 1962; MS in Indsl. Adminstrn., Union U., 1971. Mgr. mfg. engring. GE Aircraft Engine Group, Lynn, Mass., 1962-68; with Colt Industries, 1969-81; pres. FM Pump divsn., Kansas City, Kans., 1973-78, Quincy (Ill.) Compressor divsn., 1979-81; with ITT Industries, Inc., 1982-2000, pres. fluid handling divsn., 1982-95, sr. v.p., 1996-98; pres., CEO ITT Fluid Tech. Corp., Upper Saddle River, NJ, 1996-2000; exec. v.p. ITT Industries, 1998-2000, ret., 2000. Bd. dirs. Big Machines Inc., PeopleFlo Mfg. Inc. Campaign chmn. United Way Wyandotte County, Kansas City, 1979. Mem. Hydraulic Inst. (bd. dirs. 1976—, pres. 1979, 96, chmn. 1997), Oro Valley(Ariz.) Country Club (treas. 2002-03).

LABREE, ROSANNE, librarian, consultant; b. Lewiston, Maine, Jan. 6, 1948; d. Carroll Albion Jr. and Evelyn Jean (Hecimovich) L.; m. Richard Carl Coursen Jr., Aug. 20, 1988; 1 child, Catherine. BA, U. Maine, 1970; MLS, Simmons Grad. Sch. Libr. Sci., 1972. Instr. Simmons Coll. Grad. Sch. Libr. and Info., 1980-83; intern Widener Libr. Harvard U., Cambridge, Mass., 1970-72; reference libr. Countway Libr. Medicine Harvard Med. Sch., Boston, 1972-84; dir. Mental Health Sci. Libr. McLean Hosp., Belmont, Mass., 1984-94, lib. cons., 1995—; founder Lib. and Info. Svcs., 1995—. Contbr. articles to profl. jours. Nat. Libr. Medicine fellow med. informatics, 1992; Nat. Libr. Medicine grantee, 1993, NSF grantee, 1993, Connection to Internet grantee, 1993. Mem. Med. Libr. Assn. (mem. coms. 1979-83, 89-93, nominating com. 1990, chpt. coun. chmn., 1986-89, bd. dirs. 1986-89), Acad. Health Info. Profls., North Atlantic Health Scis. Librs., Spl. Libr. Assn. Office: Lib and Info Svcs 61 Washington St Belmont MA 02478-2844 Office Phone: 617-489-3595. Personal E-mail: rosanne.labree@gmail.com.

LABROCCA, RONALD JOSEPH, mathematics educator; b. Flushing, NY, Jan. 11, 1949; m. Elaine Frances Labrocca, July 11, 1974; children: Dawn Marie Rinaldi, Aaron James, Jennifer Claire. BS with honors in Math., Mich. State U., 1971; MS in Math., Adelphi U., 1974; cert. in advanced study ednl. adminstrn., Hofstra U., 1979. Cert. adminstr. NY. Dist. math. coord. Manhasset (N.Y.) Pub. Sch., 2000—. SAT testing coord. Manhasset Pub. Sch., 2002—; SAT math. instr. Manhasset Cmty. Ctr., 2002—; prin. summer sch., Manhasset, 2004. Home: 2 Edi Ave Plainview NY 11803-2106 Office: Manhasset Pub Schs 200 Memorial Pl Manhasset NY 11030 Office Phone: 516-267-7570. Home Fax: 516-349-0832. Personal E-mail: ronlab@earthlink.net. E-mail: rlabrocc@manhasset.k12.ny.us.

LABRY, EDWARD A., III, finance company executive; BS, Cumberland U., PhD (hon.), 2003. From salesman to pres. Concord EFS, Inc., Memphis, 1985—2001, pres., 2001—. Bd. dir. Concord EFS, Inc., Link2Gov Corp., Polar Wrap LLC. Bd. dirs. Children's Mus. Memphis, The Dixon Gallery and Gardens, Hutchison Sch., Cumberland U. Recipient Award of the Phoenix, Cumberland U., 2002, First Annual Movers and Shakers award, Transaction World, 2003. Office: Concord EFS Inc 2525 Horizon Lake Dr Ste 120 Memphis TN 38133

LABUDDE, ROY CHRISTIAN, lawyer; b. Milw., July 21, 1921; s. Roy Lewis and Thea (Otteson) LaB.; m. Anne P. Held, June 7, 1952; children: Jack, Peter, Michael, Susan, Sarah. AB, Carleton Coll., 1943; JD, Harvard U., 1949. Bar: Wis. 1949, U.S. Dist. Ct. (ea. and we. dists.) Wis. 1950, U.S. Ct. Appeals (7th cir.) 1950, U.S. Supreme Ct. 1957. Assoc. Michael, Best & Friedrich, Milw., 1949-57, ptnr., 1958—. Dir. DEC-Inter, Inc., Milw. Western Bank, Western Bancshares, Inc., Superior Die Set Corp., Aunt Nellie's Farm Kitchens, Inc. Bd. dirs. Wis. Hist. Soc. Found.; chmn., bd. dirs. Milw. div. Am. Cancer Soc. Served to lt. j.g. USNR, 1943-46. Mem. Milw. Estate Planning Coun. (past pres.), Wis. Bar Assn., Wis. State Bar Attys. (chmn. tax sch., bd. dirs. taxation sect.), Univ. Club, Milw. Club, Milw. Country Club. Republican. Episcopalian. Home: 4201 W Stonefield Rd Mequon WI 53092-2771 Office: Michael Best & Friedrich 100 E Wisconsin Ave Ste 3300 Milwaukee WI 53202-4108

LABUDOVIC, MARKO, research scientist, consultant; b. Podgorica, Yugoslavia, Sept. 7, 1967; came to U.S., 1998; s. Saleta and Stanislava Labudovic; m. Natasa Labudovic. BSc, U. Montenegro, Podgorica, 1992, MSc, 1995, PhD in Metallurgy & Materials Sci., 1998; PhD in Mech. Engring., So. Meth. U., 2001. Asst. lectr. U. Montenegro, 1992-96, 97-98; rsch. scientist Brunel U., London, 1996-97, So. Meth. U., Dallas, 1998-2000; rsch. devel. Corning Lasertron, Bedford, 2000—. Contbr. articles to Metall. Transactions, Jour. Mfg. Sci., Math. Sci. & Tech. Recipient 19 Dec. award County of Podgorica, 1990, LUCA award, 1986, Univ. award, 1992, British Sch. Trust, 1996, Grad. Assistance in Areas of Nat. Needs, 1998, Frederik E. Terman award, 2000. Office: 11 Oak Park M/S L2-727 Bedford MA 01730 Home: 26 Beacon St Apt 6C Burlington MA 01803-3804

LABUNSKI, STEPHEN BRONISLAW, professional society administrator; b. Jordanow, Poland, Sept. 24, 1924; came to U.S., 1928, naturalized, 1943; s. Wiktor and Wanda (Mlynarski) L.; m. Betty E. Marley, Oct. 2, 1947 (div. June 1963); children: Linda, Richard, Roger; m. Jeralyn LeBrun, Aug. 28, 1967. Student, U. Kansas City, Mo., 1946-49, George Washington U., 1950. Adminstrv. asst. to U.S. Congressman Richard W. Bolling, 1949-51; with Storz Broadcasting Co., 1954-57; v.p. ABC radio network, 1957; head broadcast div. Crowell Collier Pub. Co., 1958; v.p., gen. mgr. WMCA Radio/Straus Broadcasting Group, N.Y.C., 1958-65; pres. radio div. NBC, 1965-69; mng. dir. WMCA Radio, 1969-71; v.p., partner Chuck Blore Creative Services, 1971-75; exec. v.p. Merv Griffin Group Radio, 1975-77; exec. dir. Internat. Radio and TV Soc., N.Y.C., 1978-94, Circles Spl. Events, N.Y.C., 1994-98; dir. spl. events Cahners Bus. Info., N.Y.C., 1998—. Bd. dirs. Radio Advt. Bur., 1965-69, Nat. Assn. Broadcasters, 1965-67 Chmn. adv. com. Voice of Am., 1987-89; Democratic candidate for Mo. Legislature, 1948. With AUS and USAAF, 1943-46. Mem. Advt. Council. Home: 30 E 37th St New York NY 10016-3019 Office Phone: 212-889-6716.

LABUTTI, RONALD S., orthopedist; b. Tacoma, Oct. 12, 1965; s. Ronald Justin and Judith Ann LaButti; m. Robin Michelle Ford, Sept. 2, 2001. BA, Providence Coll., 1987; DO, U. New England Coll. Osteopathic Medicine, 1994. Cert. Am. Osteo. Bd. of Orthop. Surgery. Orthop. surgery resident Okla. State U. Coll. Osteo. Medicine, Tulsa, 1995—99; lower extremity and joint reconstruction fellow SUNY, Buffalo, 1999—2000; asst. clin. prof. Okla. State U. Coll. Osteo. Medicine, 2002—, asst. program dir. orthop. surgery residency, 2003—. Contbr. articles various profl. jours. Chmn. Osteo. Founders Found. Winterset Ball Benefit, Tulsa, 2003—04. Mem.: Am. Osteo. Acad. Orthop. Surgery, Am. Osteo. Assn. (Psi Sigma Alpha 1994). Office: Ctrl States Orthop Specialists Inc 6585 S Yale Ste 200 Tulsa OK 74136 Office Phone: 918-481-2767. E-mail: ronlabutti@cox.net.

LACAGNINA, MICHAEL ANTHONY, judge; b. Rochester, N.Y., July 6, 1932; s. Frank and Josephine (LoMaglio) L.; m. Mary Laura Mantle, June 8, 1952; children: John Michael, Gina Laura, Frank Anthony. BS in Bus. Adminstrn, U. Ariz., 1955, LL.B., 1957. Bar: Ariz. 1957. Asst. U.S. atty., Tucson, 1958-60; partner firm Bilby, Shoenhair, Warnock & Dolph, Tucson, 1960-83, of counsel, 1983-84; judge divsn. II Ariz. Ct. Appeals, 1984-95; vice chief judge Div. II, Ariz. Ct. Appeals, 1985-87, chief judge, 1987-89. Served with USMCR, 1950-52. Fellow Am. Coll. Trial Attys., Ariz. Bar Found. (chmn. fellows 1986-87); mem. ABA, Ariz. Bar Assn., Pima County Bar Assn. (pres. 1981), Nat. Assn. R.R. Trial Attys., Am. Bd. Trial Advs. (nat. exec. com., nat. sec. 1981, nat. pres. 1983), Ariz. Judges Assn. (exec. com. 1985-95), Tucson Def. Attys. (pres.), Los Charros del Desierto, Phi Delta Phi, Alpha Kappa Psi. Democrat. Episcopalian. Home: 7100 E River Canyon Rd Tucson AZ 85750-2110

LACALANDRA, TERESA FICO, music educator; b. Bayonne, N.J., June 19, 1955; d. Antonio and Maria Fico; m. Joseph Anthony Lacalandra, June 26, 1982 (dec. Feb. 18, 2000); children: Anthony, Joseph. BA in Music Edn., N.J. City U., Jersey City, 1977. Cert. Music Edn. K-12, Elem. Edn. K-8 N.J. Gen. music/choir educator Woodbridge Bd. of Edn., Avenel, NJ, 1978—81, vocal music educator Colonia, NJ, 1981—85; gen. music/choir dir. St. Vincent DePaul Elem. Sch., Bayonne, NJ, 1985—92; organist/choir dir. St. Aloysius Roman Cath. Ch., Jersey City, 1992—95; gen. music/vocal/2d grade reading Barneget (N.J.) Bd. Edn., 1995—98; h.s. choir dir. Lacey Twp. Bd. Edn., Lanoka Harbor, NJ, 1998—; organist/choir dir. St. Elizabeth Ann Seton, Whiting, NJ, 2000—. Republican. Roman Catholic. Avocations: cooking, boating. Home: 1110 Laurel Blvd Lanoka Harbor NJ 08734 Office: Lacey Twp High Sch PO Box 206 Haines St Lanoka Harbor NJ 08734

LACAPRA, DOMINICK CHARLES, historian, educator; b. NYC, July 13, 1939; s. Joseph and Mildred (Sciascia) LaC.; m. Anne-Marie Hlasny, June 15, 1965 (div.); 1 dau., Veronique. BA, Cornell U., 1961; PhD, Harvard U., 1970. Tutor Harvard U., Cambridge, Mass., 1967-69; asst. prof. history Cornell U., Ithaca, NY, 1969-74, assoc. prof., 1974-79, prof. history, 1979—, Goldwin Smith prof. European intellectual history, 1985-92, Bryce and Edith M. Bowmar prof. humanistic studies, 1992—. Assoc. dir. Sch. of Criticism and Theory Cornell U., 1997-2000; dir. Sch. Criticism and Theory, 2000—. Author: Emile Durkheim, 1972, A Preface to Sartre, 1978, "Madame Bovary" on Trial, 1982, Rethinking Intellectual History, 1983, History and Criticism, 1985, History, Politics and the Novel, 1987, Soundings in Critical Theory, 1989, Representing the Holocaust, 1994, History and Memory after Auschwitz, 1998, History and Reading: Tocqueville, Foucault, French Studies, 2000, Writing History, Writing Trauma, 2001, History in Transit, 2004. Fulbright fellow France, 1961-62, Woodrow Wilson fellow Harvard U., 1962-63, sr. fellow NEH, 1979, Sch. Criticism and Theory; recipient Disting. Tchg. award Coll. Arts and Sci. Cornell U., 1979. Mem. MLA, Am. Hist. Assn., Internat. Assn. Philosophy and Lit., Soc. Phenomenological and Existential Philosophy, Am. Comparative Lit. Assn., Soc. for the Humanities (dir.1993-2003). Home: 624 Highland Rd Ithaca NY 14850 Office: Cornell U History Dept McGraw Hall Ithaca NY 14853 Business E-Mail: dominick.lacapra@cornell.edu.

LACCAVOLE, DENNIS MARK, lawyer; b. Bridgeport, Conn., Feb. 5, 1953; s. Louis Andrew and Jean (Knapik) L.; m. Judith J. Steckler, June 10, 1979; 1 child, Michael B. BS, Fairfield U., 1975; JD, St. John's U., 1978. Bar: Conn. 1978, N.Y. 1979, U.S. Dist. Ct. Conn. 1979, U.S. Cir. Ct. Appeals (2d cir.) 1980, U.S. Supreme Ct. 1981. Ptnr. Bai, Pollock & Dunnigan, Bridgeport, Conn., 1979-87; founding ptnr. Murphy, Laccavole & Karpie, Bridgeport, Conn., 1987-92; ptnr. Goldstein and Peck, P.C., Bridgeport, Conn., 1993—. Seminar lectr. New Haven, Conn., 1990-91. Mem. ABA, Conn. Bar Assn., Conn. Trial Lawyers Assn., Conn. Def. Lawyers Assn., Def. Rsch. Inst., Easton, Conn. Exch. Club. Democrat. Roman Catholic. Office: Goldstein and Peck PC 1087 Broad St Ste 2 Bridgeport CT 06604-4241 Business E-Mail: laccavod@goldsteinandpeck.com.

LACER, ALFRED ANTONIO, lawyer, educator; b. Hammonton, NJ, Feb. 14, 1952; s. Vincent and Carmen (Savall) Lacer; m. Kathleen Visser, June 15, 1974; children: Margaret, James, Matthew. BA in Polit. Sci., Gordon Coll., 1974; JD, Cath. U. Am., 1977. Law clk. to Honorable Joseph A. Mattingly, Sr. Cir. Ct. St. Mary's County, Leonardtown, Md., 1977-78; ptnr. Lacer, Sparling, Densford & Reynolds PA and predecessors, Lexington Park, Md., 1978-99; county atty. St. Mary's County, Md., 1999-2000, CEO, county adminstr., 2000—03; atty. in pvt. practice, 2003—. Adj. prof. bus. law Fla. Inst. Tech., Patuxent, Md., 1989—92, 1995—99; vis. instr. St. Mary's Coll. Md., 1988, 91, 2004—05; bd. dirs. Pro Bono Resource Ctr. Md. Mem. inquiry panel Atty. Grievance Commn. Md., 1984—90; mem. bd. edn. St. Mary's County Pub. Schs., Md., 1989—94, pres., 1991—92; bd. dirs. So. Md. Cmty. Action, Inc., Hughsville, 1982—84, St. Mary's County Tech. Coun., 1997—99, St. Mary's Hosp., Leonardtown, 1982—88, v.p., 1985—88. Excellence Local Governance fellow, U. Md., 2001. Mem.: ABA, St. Mary's County Bar Assn. (v.p. 1979—80, pres. 1980—81), Md. Bar Assn. (mem. com. jud. appointments 1982—85). Office Phone: 301-475-9600. Personal E-mail: al.lacer@alfredalacer.com.

LACEY, AARON MICHAEL, actor, director, film producer, scriptwriter; b. Washington, May 26, 1969; Advanced cert., Nat. Conservatory Drama Arts, 1993. CEO AML Productions, Washington, 1987—. Appearances include: (tv series) In Our Lives, 1987-94, (tv primetime spls.) Running Out of Time, 1989, Fatal Mix, 1990, (films) Major League II, 1993, Twelve Monkeys, 1995, Shadow Conspiracy, 1996; assoc. prodr., story writer, screenwriter, Edge, 1997; exec. prodr., story writer, screen writer, dir. Sync, 2000; screen plays include: (tv) (In Our Lives) Gangs, 1993, (films) Crimson Road, 1989, Cumulus Nine, 1990, Mind Walker, 1991. Supporter Anti Defamation League, People for Ethical Treatment of Animals, MADD, Wash. Regional Alcohol Program. Recipient Capital Region Emmy awards NATAS, 1991. Mem. Screen Actors Guild, Actors Equity Assn., Am. Fedn. TV Radio Artists. Avocation: karate (first-degree black belt). Home: 21034 Thoreau Ct Sterling VA 20164-2436 E-mail: amlfilms@aol.com.

LACEY, CLOYD EUGENE, retired insurance company executive; b. New Lexington, Ohio, Mar. 12, 1918; s. Russell Anderson and Freda (Bahr) L.; m. Jane Linn Williams, Sept. 12, 1941; children: Thomas, Melinda Lacey Houfek, Janene Lacey Paulus. BS in Bus. Adminstrn., Ohio State U., 1941. Acct., asst. treas. Pioneer Mut. Causualty Co., Columbus, Ohio, 1945-51; various corp. fin. positions Nationwide Ins. Cos., Columbus, 1951-73, v.p., asst. controller, 1973-75, v.p., corp. controller, 1975-78, v.p. Office of Treas., controller, 1978-81, sr. v.p. fin., 1981-82, ret., 1982. Served with U.S. Army, 1943-45. Republican. Methodist. *I believe in God and put my trust in him. I believe in treating other people fairly and in giving them credit for accomplishments. I believe in maintaining a high degree of integrity. I believe in diligence and determination in performing a task. I believe in striving for excellence.*

LACEY, DOROTHY ELLEN, theology studies educator, religious organization administrator; b. Urbancrest, Ohio, Feb. 24, 1931; d. Charles Franklin Nesbitt and Clifford (Dickerson); m. Joseph W. Lacey; 1 child, Michael Clifford. B in Christian Edn., M in Christian Edn., Grace Internat. Coll., 1996, ThD, D in Christian Edn., Adminstrn. and Org., Grace Internat. Coll., 2002. Ednl. dir. Emmanuel Tempe Ch. of Rochester N.Y., Inc., 1962—, adminstr., 1985—. Women's ministry evangelistic seminar tchr. Pentecostal Assemblies of the World, Indpls., 1960—; pres., founder Lacey's Travel Agy., Rochester, 1983—88; pres. women's ministry N.Y. Coun., 1990—96; bd. trustees Grace Internat. Coll., 2003—; dean of ministries Grace Coll., 2000. Pres. of trustee bd. Emmanuel Temple Ch. of Rochester, N.Y., 1962—. Mem.: NAACP, Profl. Bus. Women, Urban League. Pentecostal Assemblies. Avocations: singing, playing musical instruments. Home: 3500 Brown Rd PO Box 148 Caledonia NY 14423 Office: Emmanuel Temple Ch Rochester 1 Seneca Pkwy Rochester NY 14613

LACEY, JOHN IRVING, psychologist, physiologist, educator; b. Chgo., Apr. 11, 1915; s. David and Cecelia (Burnstein) L.; m. Beatrice Lucile Cates, Apr. 16, 1938; children— Robert Arnold, Carolyn Ellen. AB, Cornell U., 1937, PhD, 1941. Instr. Queen's Coll., Flushing, N.Y., 1941-42; mem. faculty Antioch Coll., 1946-77, prof. psychophysiology, 1956-77; mem. staff Fels Research Inst., Yellow Springs, Ohio, 1946-82, chief sect. behavioral physiology, 1946-82; Fels prof. psychiatry Wright State U. Med. Sch., 1977-82, prof. emeritus, 1982—. Cons. USPHS, 1957-82, FDA, 1977-82; mem. bd. sci. counselors Nat. Inst. Aging, NIH, 1977-80 Cons. editor Jour. Comparative and Physiol. Psychology, 1953-69, Jour. Psychosomatic Medicine, 1962-65, Jour. Psychophysiology, 1964-69, Jour. Physiol. Psychology; contbr. articles to profl. jours. Served to capt. USAAF, 1942-46 Centennial scholar Johns Hopkins U., 1976; recipient Psychol. Sci. Gold medal Am. Psychol. Found., 1985. Fellow Am. Psychol. Soc. (William James fellow 1989); mem. Soc. Psychophysiol. Research (award for disting. contbns. 1970, pres. 1961-62, dir. 1965-68), Am. Psychosomatic Soc. (bd. dirs. 1959-62), Soc. Exptl. Psychologists, Am. Psychol. Assn. (pres. div. physiol. and comparative psychology 1969-70, mem. council 1964-68, 70-73, 78-79, bd. dirs. 1974-77, Disting. Sci. Contbn. award 1976), AAAS (chmn. sect. 1985-86), Psychonomic Soc., Soc. for Neurosci., Acad. Behavioral Medicine Rsch., Internat. Brain Rsch. Orgn., Nat. Acad. Scis. (chair com. new techs. in cognitive psychophysiology with NRC 1988), Sigma Xi, Phi Kappa Phi. Home: 70-260 Mottle Cir Rancho Mirage CA 92270 E-mail: jilacey@aol.com.

LACEY, PEELER GRAYSON, diagnostic radiologist; b. Kosciusko, Miss., June 16, 1954; s. Dick Grayson and Beatrice (Peeler) L.; m. Holley Anne Westbrook, July 8, 1978; children: Peeler Grayson Jr., Lauren Elizabeth. BA in Chemistry, Emory U., 1975; MD, U. Miss., 1979. Diplomate Am. Bd. Radiology. Intern U. Miss Med. Ctr., Jackson, 1979-80, resident in diagnostic radiology, 1980-83; diagnostic radiologist South Cen. Regional Med. Ctr., Laurel, Miss., 1983—, Jasper Gen. Hosp., Bay Springs, Miss., 1983—. V.p., ptnr. Radiology Assocs., Laurel, 1983— Past asst. scoutmaster Troop 32, exec. bd. mem. Pine Burr Area coun. Boy Scouts Am.; chmn. Chickasawhay dist. Boy Scouts Am.; Sun. sch. tchr., deacon. First Bapt. Ch., Laurel. Named one of Outstanding Young Men of Am., 1987; recipient Silver Beaver award Boy Scouts Am. Mem. AMA, NRA (life), Radiol. Soc. N.Am., So. Radiology Soc., Am. Coll. Radiology, Am. Heart Assn., Miss. State Med. Assn., Miss. Radiol. Soc., South Miss. Med. Soc. (pres. 1992), South Cen. Regional Med. Ctr. (pres. 1994), Roentgen Ray Soc., Miss. Bowhunters Assn. (life), Found. N.Am. Wild Sheep, Nat. Eagle Scout Assn. (life, past chmn. Pine Burr area coun.), Cum Laude Soc., Safari Club Internat. (life), Boone and Crockett Club (life assoc.), FND NA. Wild Sheep (life), Grand Slam club, Sigma Chi (life loyal Sig.). Avocations: hunting, fishing, reading. Home: 2432 Ridgewood Dr Laurel MS 39440-2147 Office: Radiology Assocs 235 S 12th Ave # 2427 Laurel MS 39440-4324

LACEY, TRUDI, professional athletics coach; Grad., N.C. State U., 1981. Asst. coach Manhattan Coll., 1981, James Madison Coll., 1982, N.C. State U., 1983—84; head coach Francis Marion Coll., SC, 1987—88, U. South Fla., 1989—96; asst. coach U. Md., 1996—97; asst. dir. women's program USA Basketball, 1997—2003; head coach, asst. gen. mgr. Charlotte Sting, NC, 2003—. Mem. women's player selection com. USA Basketball, 1993—96; asst. coach R. William Jones Cub team, 1995, Olympic Festival East team, 1994; participant USA Select Team, 1978, World U. Games team, 1981, USA Nat. eam, 1982, USA World U. Games Team, 1983; profl. player, Italy, 1985—87; founding pres. Life Coach Designs, LLC; analyst ESPN, FoxSportsNet. Named Sun Belt Conf. Coach of the Yr., 1989; recipient All-ACC honoree. Office: Charlotte Sting 100 Hive Dr Charlotte NC 28217*

LACH, ALMA ELIZABETH, food and cooking writer, consultant; b. Petersburg, Ill. d. John H. and Clara E. Satorius; m. Donald F. Lach; 1 child, Sandra Judith. Diplome de Cordon Bleu, Paris, 1956. Feature writer Children's Activities mag., 1954-55; creator, performer childrens cooking TV show Let's Cook, 1955; food editor Chgo. Daily Sun-Times, 1957-65; hostess weekly food program on CBS, 1962-66; pres. Alma Lach Kitchens, Inc., Chgo., 1966—; performer TV show Over Easy, PBS, 1977-78. Dir. Alma Lach Cooking Sch., Chgo.; lectr. U. Chgo. Downtown Coll., Gourmet Inst., U. Md., 1963, Modesto (Calif.) Coll., 1978, U. Chgo., 1981; resident master Shoreland Hall, U. Chgo., 1978-81; food cons. Food Bus. Mag., 1964-66, Chgo.'s New Pump Room, Lettuce Entertain You, Bitter End Resort, Brit. V.I., Midway Airlines, Flying Food Fare, Inc., Berghoff Restaurant, Hans' Bavarian Lodge, Unocal '76, Univ. Club Chgo. Author: A Child's First Cookbook, 1950, The Campbell Kids at Home, 1953, Let's Cook, 1956, Candlelight Cookbook, 1959, Cooking a la Cordon Bleu, 1970, Alma's Almanac, 1972, Hows and Whys of French Cooking, 1974, reprint, 1998; contbr. to World Book Yearbook, 1961-75, Grolier Soc. Yearbook, 1962; columnist Modern Packaging, 1967-68, Travel & Camera, 1969, Venture, 1970, Chicago mag., 1978, Bon Appetit, 1980, Tribune Syndicate, 1982; inventor: Curly-Dog Cutting Bd., 1995, Alma's Walker Tray, 1996; one woman show: 50 pixellist art pictures, 1999, Tavern Club, Chgo., 2002-2004. Recipient Pillsbury award, 1958, Grocery Mfrs. Am. Trophy award, 1959, certificate of Honor, 1961, Chevalier du Tastevin, 1962, Commanderie de l'Ordre des Anysetiers du Roy, 1963, Confrerie de la Chaine des Rotisseurs, 1964, Les Dames D'Escoffier, 1982, Culinary Historians of Chgo., 1993. Mem. Am. Assn. Food Editors (chmn. 1959), Tavern Club, Quadrangle Club (Chgo.). Home and Office: 5750 S Kenwood Ave Chicago IL 60637-1744 Fax: 773-363-2875. Office Phone: 773-684-4906. E-mail: alma@almalach.com. *The art of cooking rests upon one's ability to taste, to reproduce taste, and to create taste. To achieve distinction the cook must taste everything, study cookbooks of all kinds, and experiment constantly in the kitchen. I stress in my writing and teaching the logic of food preparation, for the cook who possesses logic, knows how to create dishes rather than being content merely to duplicate the recipes of others.*

LACH, JOSEPH ANDREW, lawyer; b. Wilkes-Barre, Pa., Oct. 26, 1949; s. Joseph and Catherine (Pavelko) L.; m. Barbara Jean Lach, July 29, 1972; children: Elizabeth Ann, Joseph Robert. BA in Psychology, Lafayette Coll., 1971; JD, Pa. State U., 1977. Bar: Pa. 1977, U.S. Dist. Ct. (mid. dist.) Pa., U.S. Ct. Appeals (3d cir.), U.S. Supreme Ct. Assoc. Lenahan & Dempsey, Scranton, Pa., 1977-81; prin. Hourigan, Klugerr & Quinn, Wilkes-Barre, 1981-94, mng. prin., 1994—. Mem. ethics com. Good Samaritan Regional Med. Ctr., Pottsville, Pa., 1988—, Mercy Hosp., Wilkes-Barre, 1991—; pres. bd. dirs. Wyoming Valley Montessori Sch., Kingston, Pa., 1994—; trustee Mercy Health Care Ctr., Nanticoke, Pa., 1991-95; bd. dirs. Little Flower Manor, Wilkes-Barre, 1996—. Mem. ABA, Pa. Bar Assn. (mem. ho. of dels. 1991—), Psi Chi. Democrat. Roman Catholic.

LACH, JOSEPH THEODORE, physicist; b. Chgo., May 12, 1934; s. Joseph and Kate (Ziemba) L.; m. Barbara Ryan, June 26, 1965; children—Michael, Elizabeth AB, U. Chgo., 1953, MS, 1956; PhD, U. Calif.-Berkeley, 1963. Rsch. assoc. in physics Yale U., Hew Haven, 1963-65, asst. prof. physics, 1966-69; physicist Fermi Nat. Accelerator Lab., Batavia, Ill, 1969—, chmn. dept. physics, 1974-75; chmn. Gordon Rsch. Conf. in Elem. Particle Physics, 1975. Mem. joint rsch. program with USSR and People's Republic of China. Fellow Am. Phys. Soc., Physicians for Social Responsibility, Ill. Geol. Survey (rsch. affiliate). Home: 28w364 Indian Knoll Trl West Chicago IL 60185-3013 Office: Fermilab PO Box 500 Batavia IL 60510-0500 E-mail: lach@fnal.gov.

LACH, PETER, humanities educator; b. Indpls., Aug. 14, 1944; s. Theodore and Madge Marie Lach; life ptnr. Bruce F. Betts (dec.). BA, DePauw U., Greencastle, Ind., 1966, MA, 1968; MFA, U. Iowa, 1973. Dean Sch. Fine Arts, Fairmont State Coll., W.Va., 2002—; chair, theatre arts dept. U. of the Pacific, Stockton, Calif., 1995—2002; asst. prof. theatre Shaw U., Raleigh, NC, 1993—95; assoc. dean and prof. Calif. State U., Dominguez Hills, Carson, 1974—83; instr. Calif. State U., Chico, 1973—74, Elmira Coll., NY, 1968—71. Cons., audience bldg. strategies Calif. State U., Hayward, 1996—97; presenter in field. Designer (play) The Moon Over Buffalo (Willie Award, 2002), The First Jewish Boy in the Ku Klux Klan, (outdoor pageant, weber point stockton) Stockton, The Dream Lives On, (play, New 42nd St. Theatre, New York) Bridges, (play, Asian American Repertory Theatre) Maiden Voyages. Artistic dir. Stockton Opera Assn., Calif., 1996—2001. Achievements include published production photographs. Avocations: travel, theater, theater, theater. Home: 112 David Daniels Dr Fairmont WV 26554 Office: Fairmont State U 1201 Locust Ave Fairmont WV 26554 Office Phone: 304-367-4219. Personal E-mail: plach@fairmountstate.edu.

LACH, SUSAN MARIE, lawyer; b. Mpls., Aug. 4, 1948; d. Edward T. and Delores T. (Baillargeon) L. BA summa cum laude, U. Minn., 1970; JD magna cum laude, U. Ga., 1975. Ptnr. Lach & Elliott PC, Ft. Collins, Colo., 1976-82; owner Susan M. Lach PC, Ft. Collins, Colo., 1982-86; ptnr. Frey, Lach & Michaels PC, Ft. Collins, Colo., 1986-93; assoc. Lang, Pauley, Gregerson & Rosow, Ltd., Mpls., 1992-96; shareholder Messerli & Kramer P.A., Mpls., 1996—. Contbr. chpt. to book. Bd. dirs. U. Minn., YMCA, Mpls., 1995-2000. Fellow Am. Acad Matrimonial Lawyers (chair Minn. chpt. 2001-02, bd. mgrs. Minn. chpt. 1996—); mem. ATLA (chair family law sect. 1994-95), Colo. Bar Assn. (exec. coun. 1982-93), Hennepin County Bar Assn. (exec. coun. family law sect. 1995—, co-chair 1998-99), Order of Coif, Phi Kappa Phi. Democrat. Roman Catholic. Office: Messerli & Kramer PA 1800 5th St Towers 150 S 5th St Ste 1800 Minneapolis MN 55402-4218 Office Phone: 612-672-3730. Fax: 612-672-3777. E-mail: slach@mandklaw.com.

LACHANCE, JANICE RACHEL, educational association administrator, former federal agency administrator, lawyer; b. Biddeford, Maine, June 17, 1953; d. Ralph L. and Rachel A. (Desnoyers) L. BA, Manhattanville Coll., 1974; JD, Tulane U., 1978. Bar: Maine 1978, D.C. 1982, U.S. Supreme Ct. 1999. Staff dir. subcom. on antitrust Ho. of Reps., Washington, 1982-83; adminstrv. asst. Congresswoman Katie Hall, 1983-84; asst. pres. sec. Mondale-Ferraro Campaign, Washington, 1984; press sec. Congressman Tom Daschle, 1985; ptnr. Lachance and Assocs., Washington, 1985-87; dir. communications and polit. action Am. Fedn. Govt. Employees (AFL-CIO), Washington, 1987-93; dir. policy and communications U.S. Office Pers. Mgmt., Washington, 1993-96, chief of staff, 1996-97, dep. dir., 1997, dir., 1997—2001; mgmt. consultant Analytica Inc., Alexandria, Va., 2001; exec. dir. Spl. Libraries Assn., Washington, 2003—. Vis. scholar Cornell U., 1972-73. Editor newsletter Govt. Standard, 1987-93. Mem. Delta Delta Delta, Phi Alpha Delta; fellow Nat. Acad. Pub. Admin. Democrat. Roman Catholic. Office: Spl Libraries Assn 1700 Eighteenth St NW Washington DC 20009-2514

LACHANCE, PAUL ALBERT, food science educator, clergyman; b. St. Johnsbury, Vt., June 5, 1933; s. Raymond John and Lucienne (Landry) Lachance; m. Therese Cecile Cote; children: Michael P, Peter A, M-Andre, Susan A. BS, St. Michael's Coll., 1955; postgrad., U. Vt., 1955-57; PhD, U. Ottawa, 1960; cert. in pastoral counseling, N.Y. Theol. Sem., 1981; DSc (hon.), St. Michael's Coll., 1982. Ordained deacon Roman Cath. Ch., 1977. Assigned to St. Paul's Ch., Princeton, N.J.; aerospace biologist Aeromed. Research Labs., Wright-Patterson AFB, Ohio, 1960-63; lectr. dept. biology U. Dayton, Ohio, 1963; flight food and nutrition coordinator NASA Manned Spacecraft Center, Houston, 1963-67; assoc. prof. dept. food sci. Rutgers U., New Brunswick, N.J., 1967-72, dir. Sch. Feeding effectiveness research project, 1969-72, prof., 1972—2004, prof. emeritus, 2005—, faculty rep. to bd. trustees, 1988-90, dir. grad. program food sci., 1988-91, chmn. food sci. dept., 1991-97, chmn. univ. senate, 1990-93, faculty rep. to bd. govs., 1990-94, dir. The Nutraceuticals Inst., 1997—. Consult Nutritional Aspects Food Processing, Nutraceuticals; mem nutrition adv comt Whitehall-Robins/Centrum Consumer div, 1989—2000; mem sci adv bd Roche chem div Hoffmann La Roche Co, 1976—88; mem nutrition policy comt Beatrice Food Co, 1979—86; trustee religious ministries comt Princeton Med Ctr; bd dirs J R Short Milling Co; mem. Cert. Bd. Nutritional Scis. Mem. editl. adv. bd.: Nutrition Reports Internat., 1963—83, Sch. Food Svc. Rsch. Rev., 1977—82, Profl. Nutritionist, 1977—80, mem. editl. adv bd.: Jour. Med. Consultation, 1985—2002, Jour. Medicinal Foods, 1998—, Food and Chem. Toxicology, 2000—, Jour. Nutraceuticals Functional & Health Foods, 2000—05; contbr. articles to profl. jours. Served to capt USAF, 1960—63. Named to Academic Hall of Fame, St. Michael's Coll., 2002; recipient Endel Karmas award for excellence in tchg. food sci., 1988. Fellow: Am. Soc. Nutritional Sci., Am. Coll. Nutrition, Inst Food Technologists (William Cruess award for excellence in tchg. 1991, Babcock-Hart award 2001); mem.: APHA, AAAS, Soc. for Free Radical Biology and Medicine, Nat. Assn. Cath. Chaplains, Soc. Nutrition Edn., Am. Dietetic Assn., NY Acad. Sci., Am. Soc. Clin. Nutrition, NY Inst Food Technologists (chmn 1977—78), Am. Assn. Cereal Chemists, Sigma Xi, Delta Epsilon Sigma. Home: 34 Taylor Rd Princeton NJ 08540-9521 Office: Rutgers U Food Sci 65 Dudley Rd New Brunswick NJ 08901-8520 Business E-Mail: lachance@aesop.rutgers.edu.

LACHANCE, PHILIP ROLAND, music educator; b. Fall River, Mass., Jan. 8, 1961; s. Honore Jr. A and Diane Lachance; m. Diana Montanaro, July 1, 1984; children: James D, Sara E, Kathryn A, Zachary D. MusB, U. R.I., Kingston, 1983. Cert. tchr. R.I. Dept. of Edn., 1983. Head of MIS Illumination Concepts and Engring., N. Kingston, RI, 1985—86; tchr. of music Taunton Pub. Schools, Mass., 1986—91, Cranston Pub. Schools, RI, 1991—. Dir. of liturgical music St. Clements Cath. Ch., Warwick, RI, 1977—87, Our Lady, Queen of Martyrs Cath. Ch., Woonsocket, RI, 1987—98; choral singer Immaculate Conception Cath. Ch., Cranston, RI, 2004—. Named Wal-Mart #1873 Tchr. of the Yr., Wal-Mart, 2002; recipient Disney Award nominee, Disney Learning, 2001. Mem.: R.I. Music Educators Assn. Roman Catholic. Avocation: youth baseball coach. Office: Hugh B Bain Middle School 135 Gansett Ave Cranston RI 02910 Office Phone: 401-270-8010.

LACHAPELLE, CLEO EDWARD, retired real estate broker; b. West Warwick, R.I., Aug. 16, 1925; s. Wilfrid Maxim and Alice (Michaud) L.; m. Ann Wilcox, July 17, 1954; children: Linda, Susan. BA in Sociology, St. Bonaventure U., 1950. Real estate broker, R.I.; lic. clin. social worker, 1962-97. Probation officer R.I. Dept. Social Welfare, Cranston, 1951-53; prevention coord. R.I. Juvenile and Family Cts., Providence, 1953-63; asst. dir. Providence Youth Progress Bd., Inc., 1963-64, exec. dir., 1965-67, Progress for Providence, Inc., 1967-70; adminstr. Marathon House, Inc., Providence, 1970-77; dir. Washingtonian Hosp. and Ctr. for Addictions, Boston, 1977-80; state refugee coord. R.I. Office Refugee Resettlement, Cranston, 1980-85; broker, owner C.E. Lachapelle Real Estate Agy., Warwick, 1986—2004. Organizer, advisor Roger Williams Parent's Assn., 1954-62; organizer, chair So. Providence Youth Bd., 1961-64, supr. SPYB Brown U. Youth Guidance Student Mentors, 1961-64, Miami U. and Nat. Inst. Mental Health Souteast Drug Abuse Tng. Ctr., Coral Gables, Fla., 1972, ret. social svcs. cons. VA Hosp., 1971-72, Nat. Ctr. Urban Ethnic Affairs, Washington, 1974-76, City of Providence, 1976-77, HHS, 1985, NIMH, 1985, and others; part-time detached youth worker Providence Recreation Dept., 1953-63; mem. mayor's adv. bd. City of Providence Model Cities Program, 1968-70; mem. adv. panel Nat. Inst. Drug Abuse, Rockville, Md., 1978; mem. Harvard Sch. Public Health Cmty. Diagnostic Workshop, 1979-80; chair gov.'s study com. spl. needs population State of R.I., 1982-85; chair refugee policy Northeastern Regional Consultations, Boston, 1983; active U.S. Refugee Coodinators Policy Adv. Group, Washington, 1983, guest lectr. universities, profl. orgn. and cmty. interest groups 1954-, and others. Sgt. USAF, 1943-46, PTO. Named to Athletic Hall of Fame, West Warwick HS, 1997. Mem. Redwood libr. (Newport), Audubon Soc. (life) Roman Catholic. Avocations: reading, golf, gardening.

LACHAR, BARBARA LEESER, psychologist, educator; b. Columbus, Ohio, Sept. 7, 1946; d. David Oscar and Marilyn Bachman Leeser; m. David Lachar, June 23, 1968; children: Ruth Lachar Wintz, Gregory Samuel. BA, U. Mich., Ann Arbor, 1968; MA, U. Minn., Mpls., 1970; PhD, Wayne State U., Detroit, 1979. Registered health svc. provider in psychology Nat. Register. Mgr. pers. rsch. unit AAA Mich., Dearborn, 1981—85; cons. Psychol. Assessment Svcs., Inc., Scottsdale, Ariz. and Sugar Land, Tex., 1986—88; instr. dept. psychology Houston C.C. Sys., 1987—91; asst. prof. psychology and behavioral scis. Baylor Coll. of Medicine, Houston, 1992—96; pvt. practice Tarnow Ctr. for Self Mgmt., Houston, 1997—98; prof. psychology Houston C.C. S.W., 1997—. Instr. dept. psychology Wayne State U., Detroit, 1975, lectr. dept. psychology, 1977—78; mgr. pers. rsch. unit AAA Mich., Dearborn, 1981—85; adj. asst. prof. dept. psychology Ariz. State U., Tempe, 1986—87; clin. dir. behavioral medicine program St. Luke's Episcopal Hosp., Houston, 1992—96. Contbr. articles to profl. jours. Mem.: Am. Psychol. Assn. Office: Ste 330 11000 Richmond Ave Houston TX 77042 also: Houston CC SW 10141 Cash Rd Stafford TX 77477 Office Phone: 713-337-2880. Business E-Mail: Barbara.Lachar@hccs.edu.

LACHMANN, ELISABETH AMANDA, physician; b. Middletown, N.Y., Sept. 12, 1961; d. Erich Frederick and Christa Luise Lachmann; m. Kevin Charles Hunt, July 11, 1992; children: Lars Christian Hunt, Elisabeth Alexandra Hunt. AB, Bryn Mawr (Pa.) Coll., 1983; MD, Med. Coll. Pa., 1987. Intern in internal medicine North Shore U. Hosp., Manhasset, N.Y., 1987-88; resident in phys. medicine and rehab. N.Y. Hosp.-Cornell Med. Ctr., 1988-91; attending physiatrist N.Y. Presbyn. Hosp., 1991—, assoc. attending physiatrist, 1999—; assoc. prof. Weill Medical Coll. Cornell Univ., N.Y.C., 1991—2001, clin. assoc. prof., 2001—; pvt. practice, 2001—. Program dir. Dept. Rehab. Medicine N.Y. Presbyn. Hosp., 1991-99, quality assurance rep., 1991-2001; advisor Weill Med. Coll. of Cornell U., 1995—. Author: (with others) Clinical Oncology, 1995, 00, Principles/Practice Supportive Oncology, 1998, 2001, Physical Medicine and Rehabiliation, The Complete Approach, 1999. Recipient Conrad Jobst Found award Am. Congress of Rehab. Medicine, 1990. Mem. AMA, Am. Acad. of Phys. Medicine and Rehab. (mem. spl. interest group cancer rehab.), Office of Women in Medicine (sr. advisor). Republican. Lutheran. Home: 17 Hungerford Rd Briarcliff Manor NY 10510-1308 Office: 115 E 64st St 1st Fl New York NY 10021 Office Phone: 212-535-3005.

LACINA-GIFFORD, LORNA J., education educator; m. Russell Gifford, Aug. 0, 1991; children: James R. Gifford, Lauren Gifford. AA in Math., Blinn Coll., 1973; BS in Ednl. Curriculum and Instrn., Secondary Edn.-Math., Tex. A&M U., 1975, MS in Ednl. Psychology, 1976, EdD in ednl. curriculum and instruction, 1984. Asst. prof. Loras Coll., Dubuque, Iowa, 1984—89; coll. prof. Northwestern State U., Coll. of Edn., Natchitoches, La., 1989—. Parent vol. Northwestern State U. Elem. Lab. Sch., Natchitoches, 1999—2005. Recipient Excellence in Tchg. award, Northwestern State U., 2003. Mem.: Phi Delta Kappa (chpt. pres. 1986—89), Nat. Assn. Alt. Certification, Am. Edn. Rsch. Assn. Avocation: tennis. Office: Northwestern State U Coll Edn Natchitoches LA 71497 Office Phone: 318-357-5521.

LACITIS, ERIK, journalist; b. Buenos Aires, Dec. 10, 1949; came to U.S., 1960, naturalized, 1965; s. Erik and Irene Z. L.; m. Malorie Nelson, Aug. 30, 1976. Student, Coll. Forest Resources, U. Wash., 1967-71. Editor U. Wash. Daily, 1970; pub. New Times Jour., 1970-71; reporter, pop-music cons. Seattle Post Intelligencer, 1972—; reporter, columnist Seattle Times, 1974—; v.p., treas. Malorie Nelson, Inc., 1980—. Bd. mem. Wash. News Coun., 2005. Recipient numerous awards from Wash. State chpt. Sigma Delta Chi; Nat. Headliners Club award, 1978; winner gen. interest competition Nat. Soc. Newspaper Columnists, 1987, 2003, Best of the West Journalism contest, 2000. Lutheran. Office: Fairview Ave N And John St PO Box 7070 Seattle WA 98133-2070 E-mail: lacitis@prodigy.net.

LACK, ANDREW R., music company executive; b. NYC, May 16, 1947; m. Betsy Kenny; children: Andrew, Sam. BFA, Boston U., 1968. Sr. exec. prodr. CBS Reports, 1978—85; exec. v.p. West 57th, 1985—89; pres. NBC News, 1993—2001; pres., COO NBC, Inc., 2001—03; chmn., CEO Sony Music Entertainment, 2003—04; CEO Sony BMG Music Entertainment, 2004—. Office: Sony BMG Music Entertainment 550 Madison Ave New York NY 10022

LACK, LEON, pharmacology and biochemistry educator; b. Bklyn., Jan. 7, 1922; s. Jacob and Yetta (Wolf) L.; m. Pauline Kaplan, Feb. 14, 1948; children: Elias David, Joshua Morris, Johanna Elaine, Adina Roberta, Evonne Clara. BA, Bklyn. Coll., 1943; MS, Mich. State Coll., 1948; PhD, Columbia U., 1953; postgrad., Duke U., 1954—55. Instr. in pharmacology and exptl. therapeutics Johns Hopkins U. Sch. Medicine, 1955-59, asst. prof. pharmacology and exptl. therapeutics, 1959-63; asst. prof. physiology and pharmacology Duke U. Med. Ctr., 1964-66, prof. pharmacology, 1966-92, prof. emeritus pharmacology, 1992—, chief biochemist to clin. rsch., 1966-70. Cons. E.I. DuPont de Nemours and Co., 1990-91, Monsanto, 1992-93. Contbr. numerous articles to profl. publs. Served with USAAF, 1943-46, PTO. Univ. postdoctoral fellow Duke U., 1954-55; grantee NIH, 1960-90, OSHA, Ctr. for Disease Control, 1991-93. Mem. Am. Soc. Biol. Chemists, Am. Soc. Pharmacology and Exptl. Therapeutics. Jewish. Achievements include research in pharmacology of cholesterol and lipids, pharmacology of intestinal bile salt transport, enzyme inhibitors relevant to prostatic cancer. Home: 2936 Welcome Dr Durham NC 27705-5556 Office: Duke U Med Ctr PO Box 3185 Durham NC 27715-3185 Office Phone: 919-684-2141.

LACK, PATRICIA ANN, drilling and pumping company executive, consultant; b. Phoenix, Oct. 15, 1946; d. J.V. and Vivian Margaret Henry; m. Ronald Lee Jackson, Mar. 6, 1964 (div. May 1969); 1 child, Vicki Marie Snyder; m. Larry Henry Lack, Aug. 19, 1978. Student, Glendale (Ariz.) C.C., 1985—86. Enlisted USAF, 1973, advanced through grades to E-6, 1978—; equipment mgr. Supply Squadron, Eglin AFB, Fla., 1973-74; supr. inventory mgmt. 3d Supply Squadron, Clark Air Base, Philippines, 1974-77; chief supply sr. advisor 443d Supply Squadron, Altus AFB, Okla., 1977-79; instr., br. chief curriculum devel. SAC Non-Commd. Officers Acad., Barksdale AFB, La., 1979-84; resigned, 1984; pres. Lack Industries, Inc., Phoenix, 1984-90; chmn. bd. Stellar Innovations, LLC, Phoenix, 1996—. Freelance cons. and trainer, Phoenix, 1984-90; sexual discrimination recognition, protection, prevention trainer Glendale C.C. and to cos., Phoenix, 1984-90; cons. on career motivation enhancement to bus., Phoenix, 1984-95; counselor sexual assault recovery workshops, Phoenix, 1993—. Author: (novel) Willowman, 1993, (screenplay) Willowman, Means and Ends. Pub. spkr. to various women's groups and bus., Phoenix, 1990—. Mem. DAV (life), NRA (life), NRA Inst. for Legis. Action (life, honor roll 1995), Women Entrepreneurs Ariz. Republican. Avocations: flying, scuba diving, sport shooting, reading, camping. Office: Stellar Innovations LLC PO Box 7632 Phoenix AZ 85011-7632 Home: 4317 W Waltann Ln Glendale AZ 85306-2709 Office Phone: 602-866-1707. Business E-Mail: stellarinvestigations@msn.com.

LACK, ROBERT JOEL, lawyer; b. Glen Ridge, N.J., Mar. 7, 1955; s. Walter and Carolyn Lack; m. Colleen Phyllis Kelly, June 9, 1979; children: Kelly Ann, Jonathan Andrew. AB, Princeton U., 1977, M in Pub. Affairs, 1978; JD, Harvard U., 1981. Bar: N.Y. 1982, N.J. 1990, U.S. Dist. Ct. (so. and ea. dist.) N.Y. 1982, U.S. Ct. Appeals (3d cir.) 1982, U.S. Ct. Appeals (1st cir.) 1984, U.S. Ct. Appeals (2d cir.) 1985, U.S. Supreme Ct. 1986, U.S. Ct. Appeals (7th cir.) 1987, U.S. Ct. Appeals (D.C. and 9th cirs.) 1988, U.S. Dist. Ct. (no. dist.) Calif. 1988, U.S. Dist. Ct. N.J. 1991. Law clk. to judge U.S. Ct. Appeals (3d cir.), Newark, 1981-82; assoc. Sullivan & Cromwell, N.Y.C., 1982-90; ptnr. Friedman Kaplan Seiler & Adelman LLP, N.Y.C., 1991—. Editor Harvard Law Rev. 1979-81. Recipient Whitney North Seymour medal Columbia U. Law Sch., 1981. Mem. ABA, N.Y. State Bar Assn. (mem. com. on civil rights 1984-90, mem. securities litigation com. 1998—), N.Y.C. Bar Assn. (sec. com. on lectures and continuing edn. 1984-86, mem. com. on antitrust and trade regulation 1991-94, mem. com. on fed. cts. 1998-2001), Fed. Bar Coun. Office: Friedman Kaplan Seiler & Adelman LLP 1633 Broadway New York NY 10019-6708 Office Phone: 212-833-1108.

LACKENMIER, JAMES RICHARD, academic administrator, priest; b. Lackawanna, N.Y., May 15, 1938; s. Harold and Margaret (Murphy) L. AB, Stonehill Coll., 1961; STL, Pontifical Gregorian U., Rome, 1965; AM, U.N.C., 1968; MA, U. Chgo., 1970. Ordained priest, Roman Catholic Ch. Tchr. English Notre Dame High Sch., Bridgeport, Conn., 1965-66, St. Peter's High Sch., Gloucester, Mass., 1966-68; chaplain St. Xavier Coll., Chgo., 1969-71; dir. collegiate formation Moreau Sem., Notre Dame, Ind., 1971-73; dir. campus ministry King's Coll., Wilkes-Barre, Pa., 1974-75, dir. devel., 1975-81, pres., 1981-99. Program dir. U. Portland Ctr., Salzburg, Austria, 1999-2001; treas. Congregaton of Holy Cross, Eastern Province, 2000—. Bd. regents U. Portland, 1993-99, 2002—; bd. trustees Mercy Hosp., 1989-95; bd. dirs. Pa. Ednl. Telecom. Exch. Network, 1994-99, Com. on Econ. Growth, Earth Conservancy, 1992-99, Pa. Ind. Coll. and Univ. Rsch. Ctr., 1995-99, Ctr. for Agile Pa. Edn., 1994-99, Greater Wilkes-Barre Partnership, Inc.; mem. United Way Campaign Cabinet, 1995-99; adv. bd. Pa. Mountains coun. Boy Scouts Am., Tuition Acct. Program, Office of Gov., Commonwealth Pa., 1992-96, 97-99; chmn. United Way Wyoming Valley, 1986; corp. mem. Holy Cross Family Ministries, bd. dirs., 2001—; bd. dirs. Pius XII Youth and Family Svcs., 2001—. Mem. Rotary Internat. Lodges: Rotary Internat.; K.C. Democrat. E-mail: jlack@hcep.com.

LACKEY, KAYLE DIANN, elementary school educator; b. Willard, Ill., Oct. 22, 1937; d. Lon Edward and Eldora Grace (Pecord) Ogborn; m. Joseph Donald Lackey, Nov. 29, 1958; 1 child, Dana Lyn Embree. BA in History, Asbury Coll., Wilmore, Ky., 1958; MA with honors, Webster U., 1975, cert. reading specialist, 1977; cert. gifted and talented educator, So. Ill. U., Edwardsville, 1990. Ltd. cert. elem. edn., Ill; cert. pub. sch. tchr. (life), Mo.; cert. reading specialist, Mo.; registered profl. real estate salesperson, Mo. Tchr. kindergarten Dist. # 196, Dupo, Ill., 1959—63, reading specialist, 1973—79, tchr. 2d grade, 1979—84, tchr. 4th grade, 1985—93, tchr. gifted and talented, 1990—92; tchr. 1st grade Mehlville R-9 Dist., St. Louis, 1963—65, substitute tchr., 1965—72, 1993—. Clin. coop. tchr. So. Ill. U., Edwardsville, 1989; salesperson Coldwell Banker Real Estate, St. Louis, 1985-2000. Rep. for tchrs. Am. Fedn. Tchrs., Dupo, 1975-77, negotiation com., 1981; tchr. U.S. Divsn. Laubach Lit. Internat., St. Louis, 1987-89; author, tchr. gifted and talented enrichment summer program, 1991; participant Asbury Coll. travel seminar on Near-Ea. studies, 1985; rep. ecumenical com. Cmty. Resource Svcs., 1986-89, trustee 2000-02; chmn. bd. edn. presch. Zion United Meth., St. Louis, 1987-88, 2000-02, trustee, 1986-90, adminstrv. bd. religion and race, ch. and soc., 1989-93, fin. sec., 1999, bd. dirs., 2000; active Ill. Tchrs. Retirement Sys., 1993—, Met. Congregations United of St. Louis, 2001—, Gephardt for Congress, St. Louis, 1993-95; vol. Am. Cancer Soc., 2000, 2004. Recipient Appreciation for Tchg. Excellence award Bd. Edn., Dupo, 1993, Ill. Math. and Sci. Acad. award of Excellence, 1999, Senatorial Inner Circle Honoree Mo., 2005, Outstanding Intellectual of 21st Century award Internat. Biographical Ctr., England, 2004 Mem.: St. Louis Art Mus., Mo. Bot. Soc., St. Louis Zoo Soc. Avocations: piano, travel, writing, reading, political campaign volunteerism. Home: 6511 Towne Woods Dr Saint Louis MO 63129-4521

LACKEY, MICHAEL E., JR., lawyer, educator; b. Hopkinsville, Ky., May 3, 1961; s. Michael E. Lackey, Sr. and Linda L. Sterling; m. Cynthia L. Sheppard, May 23, 1987; children: Michael E. III, Ashleigh L. BS in Aero. and Astronautical Engring., MIT, 1983; JD with high honors, George Washington U., 1993. Bar: Fla. 1993, DC 1994, U.S. Supreme Ct. 1999. Assoc. atty. Arnold & Porter, Washington, 1993—94, Mayer, Brown & Platt, Washington, 1995—97, 1998—2001; law clk. to Hon. Jacques L. Wiener U.S. Ct. Appeals, Shreveport, La., 1994—95; assoc. ind. counsel Office David Barrett Ind. Counsel, Washington, 1997—98; ptnr. Mayer, Brown, Rowe & Maw LLP, Washington, 2002—. Adj. prof. George Washington U. Law Sch., Washington, 1995—. Contbr. articles to profl. jours.; guest commentator (TV series) Supreme Court Watch with Fred Graham. Lt., naval aviator USN, 1983—90. Named Top Gun, USN, 1987; Nat. Merit scholar. Mem.: Fed. Bar Assn. (chmn. antitrust and trade regulation 2001—). Episcopalian. Avocations: golf, running, coaching children's sports teams. Office: Mayer Brown Rowe and Maw LLP 1909 K St NW Washington DC 20006 Office Phone: 202-263-3000. Business E-Mail: mlackey@mayerbrown.com.

LACKEY, SUSAN BAKER, middle school educator; b. Lexington, Ky., Aug. 13, 1951; d. Clarence Ray Baker and Barbara Frances Smith; children from previous marriage: Tabitha Lyndsay Roberts, Bethany Danette Roberts; m. Leroy Lackey, July 19, 2003. AA, Somerset (Ky.) C.C., 1971; BS, Cumberland Coll., 1978, postgrad., 1986. Cert. tchr., Ky. Tchr. art, English, drama Monticello (Ky.) Ind. Sch., 1978-88; art tchr. Drakes Creek Mid. Sch., Bowling Green, Ky., 1988—; art tchr. camp gifted adolescents Western Ky. U., Bowling Green, 1990—. Site coord. Ky. Arts Coun., Monticello, 1983-88; tchr.-advisor Arts in Edn., Bowling Green, 1989-93; mem. exec. com. Ky. Young Woman of Yr., Bowling Green, 1990-95, adv. bds. Scholastic Arts Awards South-Ctrl. Ky., Bowling Green, 1990-93. Mem. NEA, Nat. Art Edn. Assn., Nat. Mid Sch. Assn., Ky. Edn. Assn., Ky. Art Edn. Assn. (state sec. 1993-95, Middle Sch. Art Tchr. of Yr. 2004) Democrat. Avocations: pottery, watercolor, reading, sewing, beading. Home: 2128 Plano Rd Bowling Green KY 42104-0315 Office: Drakes Creek Mid Sch 704 Cypress Wood Ln Bowling Green KY 42104-0301

LACKIE, ROBERT JONATHAN, university librarian, educator, consultant; b. Wilmington, Del., Dec. 24, 1966; s. William R. and Geraldine F. Lackie; m. Cynthia Renee Steele, Aug. 11, 1990; 1 child, Christon Robert. BS, U. State NY, 1992; M in Libr. and Info. Sci., U. SC, 1996; MA, Rider U., NJ, 2000. Tactical aircraft maintenance specialist, dedicated crew chief USAF, Upper Heyford, England, 1984—89, profl. mil. edn. instr. Sumter, SC, 1990—92; adj. instr. of English Trident Tech. Coll., North Charleston, SC, 1993—94; libr. tech. asst. iii Charleston So. U., North Charleston, 1994—96, asst. libr. in ref., instr. libr. sci., 1996—98; instrn. and reference libr., assoc. prof. libr. sci. Rider U., Lawrenceville, NJ, 1998—. Instr., evaluator NJ Train-the-Trainer, Freehold, NJ, 1998—; presenter in field. Co-editor (course book) New Jersey Train-the-Trainer: Training Techniques for Library Staff: Course Book; author: (website) Sci-Math World, 2000, Those Dark, Hiding Places: The 'Invisible Web' Revealed, 2001 (USA Today's "Hot Site" award, 2001, Bangkok Post's "Internet Site of the Week" award, 2005); co-author: (book chpts.) The Plagiarism Plague: A Resource Guide and CD-Rom Tutorial for Educators and Librarians; contbr. articles to profl. jours.; featured U. Oxford's Internat. Summer Sch. Brit. Lit. E-5 staff sgt. USAF, 1984—92, Eng., SC. Decorated Humanitarian Svc. award USAF, Achievement medal,

Commendation medal, Gen. Leo Marquez Maintenance Technician Yr. award; recipient Acad. Achievement award, Tactile Air Command Non-commd. Officer Leadership Sch., Shaw AFB, SC, 1989, Disting. Grad. award, 1989, Communicative Skills award, 1989, Non-commd. Officer Assn. Esprit de Corps, 1989, Ann. Grad. award curriculum, instrn. and supervision, Rider U., 2000, Grad. Student award, Phi Delta Kappa, 2000, Disting. Tchg. award, Rider U., 2004; Kenneth E. Toombs fellow, U. SC, Coll. Libr. and Info. Sci., 1996. Mem.: NJ Acad. Libr. Leadership, Phi Delta Kappa Internat. (exec. bd. Trenton-area chpt. program co v.p., found. rep., rsch. rep. 2003—), Ctrl. Jersey Regional Libr. Coop. (exec. bd., acad. libr. rep. 2003—), Tri-state Coll. Libr. Coop., Continuing Edn. Coun. (chair 2004—), NJ Libr. Assn., User Edn. Com. (chair 2002—03, NJ Libr. of Yr. 2004), Beta Phi Mu, The Libr. and Info. Sci. Honor Soc. Home: 20 Fairway Ct Lawrenceville NJ 08648 Office: Rider Univ 2083 Lawrenceville Rd Lawrenceville NJ 08648 Office Phone: 609-895-5626. Office Fax: 609-896-8029. Business E-Mail: rlackie@rider.edu.

LACKLAND, JOHN, lawyer; b. Parma, Idaho, Aug. 29, 1939; AB, Stanford U., 1962; JD, U. Wash., 1964; Master Gardener, Colo. State U., 1996. Bar: Wash. 1965, U.S. Dist. Ct. (we. dist.) Wash. 1965, (ea. dist.) Wash. 1973, U.S. Ct. Appeals (9th cir.) 1965, Conn. 1981, U.S. Dist. Ct. Conn. 1983, U.S. Supreme Ct. 1973, U.S. Dist. Ct. (so. dist.) N.Y. 1988; cert. Profl. Nurseyman, Idaho, 2005; cert. nurseryman, Idaho. Assoc. firm Lane Powell Moss & Miller, Seattle, 1965-69; asst. atty. gen. State of Wash., Seattle, 1969-72, asst. chief U. Wash. divsn., 1969-72; v.p., sec., gen. counsel Western Farmers Assn., Seattle, 1972-76, Fotomat Corp., Stamford, Conn., 1976-80; ptnr. Leepson & Lackland, 1981-88, Lackland and Nalewaik, 1988-92; pvt. practices Westport, Conn., 1992-94; prin. Lackland Assocs., Grand Junction, Colo., 1994—2002. Profl. nurseryman, 1996—; nursery mgr. Boutique Nursery, Twin Falls, Idaho, 2005—. Bd. dirs. Mercer Island (Wash.) Congl. Ch., 1967-70, pres. bd. dirs., 1970; mem. land use plan steering com. City of Mercer Island, 1970-72; bd. dirs. Mercer Island Sch. Dist., 1970-73, v.p. bd. dirs., 1972, pres. 1973; trustee Mid-Fairfield Child Guidance Ctr., 1982-84, Norfield Congl. Ch., 1982-84; bd. dirs. Grand Junction Symphony Orch., 1995-99.

LACKLAND, THEODORE HOWARD, lawyer; b. Chgo., Dec. 4, 1943; s. Richard and Cora Lee (Sanders) L.; m. Dorothy Ann Gerald, Jan. 2, 1970; 1 child, Jennifer Noel. BS, Loyola U., Chgo., 1965; MA, Howard U., 1967; JD, Columbia U., 1975; grad., U.S. Army Ranger Sch., 1968. Bar: N.J. 1975, U.S. Dist. Ct. N.J. 1975, Ga. 1982, U.S. Tax Ct. 1983, U.S. Supreme Ct. 1979, U.S. Dist. Ct. (no. dist.) Ga. 1982, U.S. Dist. Ct. (mid. dist.) Ga. 1985, U.S. Dist. Ct. (so. dist.) Ga. 2003. Assoc. Dewey, Ballantine, Bushby, Palmer & Wood, N.Y.C., 1975-78; asst. U.S. atty. Dist. N.J., Newark, 1978-81; ptnr. Arnall Golden & Gregory, Atlanta, 1981-93, Lackland & Assoc., Atlanta, 1993-95, Lackland & Heyward, Atlanta, 1995-2000, Lackland & Assocs., LLC, Atlanta, 2000—. Adj. prof. law Ga. State U. Law Sch., 1989-99. Assoc. editor Columbia Human Rights Law Rev., 1974-75; contbr. articles to profl. jours. Adv. dir. Atlanta Bus. Devel. Ctr., Minority Bus. Devel. Coun., Atlanta, 1983-91; mem. exec. com. Leadership Atlanta, 1986, 1990-91. Capt. U.S. Army, 1967-71. Decorated Bronze Star with 1 oak leaf cluster, Purple Heart, Air medal. Mem.: Atlanta Bar Assn., Gate City Bar Assn., Fed. Bar Assn., Ga. Bar Assn., ABA. Democrat. Roman Catholic. Home: 4400 Oak Ln Marietta GA 30062-6355 Office: Lackland & Assocs LLC 230 Peachtree St NW Atlanta GA 30303-1562 Office Phone: 404-522-8155. Business E-Mail: tlackland@e-lacklaw.com.

LACKNER, JAMES ROBERT, aerospace medicine educator; b. Virginia, Minn., Nov. 11, 1940; s. William and Lillian Mae (Galbraith) L.; m. Ann Martin Graybiel, Aug. 26, 1970. BSc, MIT, 1966, PhD, 1970. Asst. prof. psychology Brandeis U., Waltham, Mass., 1970-74, assoc. prof. psychology, 1974-79, Riklis prof. physiology dept. psychology, 1977—, chmn. dept. psychology, 1975-83, provost, dean faculty, 1986-89, dir. Ashton Graybiel Spatial Orientation Lab., 1982—. Research assoc. dept. psychology and clin. research ctr. MIT, Cambridge, 1970-80; sci. adv. bd. Space Biomed. Research Inst., Houston, 1982—, Aphasia Research Ctr. Boston U. Sch. Med., 1977-82, Eunice Kennedy Shriver Ctr. Harvard U. Med. Sch., Cambridge, 1980-90; sci. adv. panel astronaut longitudinal health program Johnson Space Ctr., NASA, 1983, exec. sec. space adaptation syndrome steering com., 1982-84, pre-adaption trainer working group, 1986—, artificial gravity working group, 1987—; fabricant com. life scis. experiments for a space sta., 1982; space scis. bd. sensory motor panel NAS, 1984-86; com. on hearing, bioacoustics and biomechanics NRC, 1985-89, com. on vision, 1987-92, com. on space, biology and medicine, 1991-99, mem. com. virtual reality rsch. and devel., 1992-95. Mem. editorial bd. Presence, 1992—, Jour. Vestibular Rsch., 1991-2001, Jour. Neurophysiology, 1995—, Exptl. Brain Rsch., 1997—, Jour. Exptl. Psychology, 2001—; contbr. more than 200 articles to sci. jours. Mem. Am. Soc. for Gravitational and Space Biology, Aerospace Med. Assn. (Arnold B. Tuttle award), Soc. for Neurosci., Psychonomics Soc., Internat. Brain Research Orgn., Barany Soc. (hon.), Internat. Acad. Astronautics (hon.). Achievements include research in human sensory-motor coordination and spatial orientation. Home: Boyce Farm Rd Lincoln MA 01773-4813 Office: Brandeis U Ashton Graybiel Lab 415 South St Waltham MA 02453-2728

LACKNER, KLAUS STEPHAN, physicist; b. Bad Neuenahr, Fed. Republic of Germany, Sept. 15, 1952; came to U.S., 1979; m. Margaret S. Black, July 31, 1982; children: Claire, Audrey, Maureen. MS, U. Heidelberg, 1976, PhD, 1978. Fellow Calif. Inst. Tech., Pasadena, 1979—82; rschr. Stanford (Calif.) Linear Accelerator Ctr., 1982—83; staff Los Alamos (N.Mex.) Nat. Lab., 1983—2001; Ewing Worzel prof. earth and environ. engring. Columbia U., 2001—.

LACOMBE, JACQUES, conductor, music director; Student, Conservatoire de musique du Québec, Trois-Rivières, Montreal; grad. in Choral and Orchestral Conducting, Hochschule für Musik und darstellende Kunst; studied with Vaclav Neumann, Peter Eötvös, Karl Österreicher, Raffi Armenian. Assoc. condr. Amati Ensemble, 1987-94; prof. music theory and conducting Univ. Québec, Trois-Rivières, Can., 1989-94; music dir., condr. Les Grands Ballets Canadiens, Montréal, 1992—; asst. condr., chorus master L'Opera de Montréal, Montréal, 1992—98; asst. condr. L'Orchestre symphonique de Montreal, Montréal, 1994—98; music dir., prin. conductor Les Grands Ballets Canadiens de Montéal, Montréal, 2003—. Condr. orchs. including Philharm. Orchs. of Slovakia and Savaria, Hungarian Radio TV Orch., Budapest Symphony Orch., L'orchestre métropolitan, CBC Vancouver Orch., L'Orchestre symphonique de Montréal, L'Orchestre symphonique de Québec; also numerous recs. Can. Arts Coun. grantee; recipient Joseph S. Stauffer award, 1988. Office: Montreal Symphony Orch 2d Fl 260 de Maisonneuve Blvd W Montreal PQ H2X1Y9 Canada*

LACOSTE, ALAN DANIEL, physician, educator, medical company executive; b. New Orleans, Aug. 25, 1943; s. Charles and Viola Lacoste; 1 child, Natasha. BA, Loyola U., New Orleans, 1971; MD, La. State U., New Orleans, 1975. Cert. Am. Bd. in Opthalmology. CEO The Eye Clinic, Lake Charles, La., 1979—; clin. prof. opthalmology La. State U. Sch. Medicine, 1997—. Physician, surgeon Benevolent Missions Internat., Africa, 1986—, 1986—. Office: The Eye Clinic 1717 Oak Park Blvd Lake Charles LA 70601 Office Phone: 337-478-3810. Office Fax: 337-478-6360.

LACOSTE, PAUL, law educator, academic administrator; b. Montreal, Que., Can., Apr. 24, 1923; s. Emile and Juliette (Boucher) L.; m. Louise Marcil, Aug. 31, 1973 (div.); children: Helene, Paul-André, Anne-Marie. BA, U. Montreal, 1943, MA, 1944, Licenciate in Philosophy, 1946, Licenciate in Law, 1960; postgrad., U. Chgo., 1946-47; Docteur de l'Universite, U. Paris, 1948; LLD (hon.), McGill U., 1975, U. Toronto, 1978; D Univ. (hon.), Laval U., 1986. Bar: Que., Can. 1960. Prof. philosophy U. Montreal, 1946-86, prof. law, 1960-68, 1985-87, vice rector, 1966-68, exec. vice rector, 1968-75, rector, 1975-85, prof. emeritus, 1987—. Moderator, commentator CBC, 1956-63; mem. firm Lalande, Brière, Reeves, Lacoste et Paquette, Montreal, 1964-66; mem. Royal Commn. on Bilingualism and Biculturism, 1963-71, Que. Superior Coun. Edn., 1964-68, Que. Conf. Univs., 1969-77; mem. Conf. Rectors and Prins. Que. Univs., 1967-85, pres. 1977-79; chmn. Fed. Commn. and Coms. for Environ. Projects, 1991-98. Author: (with others) La crise de l'enseignement au Canada Francais, 1961, Justice et Paix scolaire, 1962, A Place of Liberty, 1964, Le Canada au seuil du siecle de l'abondance, 1969, Education permanente et potentiel universitaire, 1977; contbr. articles to profl. jours. Mem. Corp. de l'Ecole des Hautes Etudes Commerciales, 1975-85, Ecole Polytechnique, 1975-85, Corp. du Coll. Marie de France; bd. dirs. Clin. Rsch. Inst. of Montreal, 1975-85; pres. Assn. des universités partiellement ou entièrement de langue française, 1978-81. Mem. Assn. Univs. and Colls. of Can. (mem. com. of pres. 1975-85, v.p. 1977, pres. 1978-79), Assn. Commonwealth Univs. (dir. 1977-80) Home: 60 Willowdale Montreal PQ Canada H3T 2A3 Office: Univ Montréal CP 6128 Pavillon 2910 bur 127 Montreal PQ Canada H3C 3J7 Office Phone: 514-343-7727.

LA COUR, LOUIS BERNARD, retired lawyer; b. Columbus, Ohio, Aug. 12, 1926; s. Louis and Cleo (Carter) La C.; m. Jane Lee McFarland, Mar. 24, 1950; children: Lynne Denise, Avril Rose, Cheryl Celeste. BA, Ohio State U., 1951; LLB, Franklin U., 1961; JD, Capital U., Columbus, 1967. Bar: Ohio 1962. Land commr. U.S. Dist. Ct. (so. dist.) Ohio, Columbus, 1981, spl. master, 1983-87; spl. counsel City of Columbus Atty.'s Office, 1986—. Contbr. articles to profl. jours. Cons. NAACP, N.Y.C., 1975-80; mem. Greater Columbus Arts Coun., Model State Legis. Com.; sec. Mid-Ohio Regional Planning Commn., Columbus, 1978; vice-chmn. Columbus Civic Ctr. Commn., 1979; mem. rural zoning commn. Franklin County, 1994; mem. Ohio Elected Ofcls. Commn.; mem. Franklin Soil and Water Conservation Dist. Mem. ABA, Franklin County Rural Zoning Commn., Columbus Bar Assn., Am. Planning Assn. (task force), Ohio Elected Ofcls. Commn., New Albany C.C., Franklin Soil and Water Conservation, Sigma Pi Phi, Lambda Boulé. Democrat. Roman Catholic. Avocations: tennis, cooking, theater, jazz. Home: 1809 N Cassady Ave Columbus OH 43219-1520 Office: 500 S Front St Ste 1140 Columbus OH 43215-7628

LACOUR, NAT, labor union administrator; b. New Orleans; BS, MS, So. U., Baton Rouge. Pres. United Tchrs. New Orleans, 1996—99; v.p. exec. coun. Am. Fedn. Tchrs., Washington, 1997—99, exec. v.p., 1999—. Founding mem. Nat. Bd. Profl. Tchg. Stds.; bd. mem. Albert Shanker Inst., Nat. Dem. Inst., Learning First Alliance, The Thurgood Marshall Scholarship Fund; nat. bd. mem. A. Philip Randolph Inst., Coalition Black Trade Unionists; mem. White House Commn. on Presdl. Scholars, 1993—2000. Office: Am Fedn Tchrs 555 New Jersey Ave NW Washington DC 20001

LACOVARA, CHRISTOPHER, venture capitalist; AB, Harvard Coll.; BEES, Hofstra U.; MS, Columbia U. Fin. analyst corp. fin. dept. Goldman, Sachs & Co.; assoc. mergers and acquisitions dept. Lazard Frères & Co., 1987—88; joined Kohlberg & Co., 1988, prin., 1995. Bd. dirs. Allied Aerospace Engring., Inc., Applied Graphics Tech., Inc., CUSA Busways, LLC, Holley Performance Products, Inc., Innotek, INc., Katy Industries, Inc., Nancy's Specialty Foods, Inc., Orion Food Sys., LLC, Redaelli Tecna, S.p.A., Simplicity Mfg., Inc., KTTI Holding Co., Inc., Tinnerman Palnut Engineered Products, LLC; mem. mgmt. com. Katonah Capital LLC. Office: Kohlberg & Co 111 Radio Cir Mount Kisco NY 10549 Office Phone: 914-241-7430. Office Fax: 914-241-7476.

LACOVARA, MICHAEL, lawyer; b. Bklyn., Oct. 21, 1963; s. Philip Allen and Madeline Estelle (Papio) L.; m. Carla J. Foran, Sept. 9, 1989; children: Claire Elizabeth, Edward Christopher. BA, U. Pa., 1984; MPhil, Cambridge (U.K.) U., 1985; JD, Harvard U., 1988. Law clk. Hon. Stephen Reinhardt, L.A., 1988-89; assoc. Sullivan & Cromwell, N.Y.C., 1989-96, ptnr., 1997—2001, Palo Alto, Calif., 2000—04; prin., gen counsel Sandler O'Neill & Ptnrs., LP, N.Y.C. and San Francisco, 2004—. Bd. dirs. Lower Manhattan Cultural Coun., N.Y.C., 1995-2002, chair, 1998; trustee Cambridge U. in Am., 2000— Thouron Found. fellow, 1984. Mem. ABA, Assn. of Bar of City of N.Y., San Francisco Bar Assn., Phi Beta Kappa. Democrat. Roman Catholic. Home: 3383 Washington St San Francisco CA 94118 Office: Sandler O'Neill & Ptnrs LP 455 Market St San Francisco CA 94105 Office Phone: 415-978-5055. Business E-Mail: mlacovara@sandleroneill.com.

LACOVARA, PHILIP ALLEN, lawyer; b. N.Y.C., July 11, 1943; s. P. Philip and Elvira Lacovara; m. Madeline E. Papio, Oct. 14, 1961; children: Philip, Michael, Christopher, Elizabeth, Karen, Daniel, Andrew. AB magna cum laude, Georgetown U., 1963; JD summa cum laude, Columbia U., 1966. Bar: N.Y. 1967, D.C. 1974, U.S. Supreme Ct. 1970. Law clk. to presiding justice U.S. Ct. Appeals D.C. Cir., 1966-67; asst. to solicitor gen. U.S. Washington, 1967-69; assoc. Hughes Hubbard & Reed, N.Y.C., 1969-71, ptnr. N.Y.C. and Washington, 1974-88; v.p., sr. counsel GE, Fairfield, Conn., 1988-90; mng. dir, gen. counsel Morgen Stanley & Co., N.Y.C., 1990-93; ptnr. Mayer, Brown & Platt, N.Y.C. and Washington, 1993—2003; sr. counsel Mayer Brown Rowe & Maw LLP, 2004—; attaché Permanent Observer Mission Sovereign Mil. Order of Malta to UN, 2005—. Spl. counsel to N.Y.C. Police Commr., 1971-72; dep. solicitor gen. U.S. Dept. Justice, Washington, 1972-73; counsel to spl. prosecutor Watergate Spl. Prosecution Force, 1973-74; lectr. law Columbia U.; adj. prof. Georgetown U. Law Ctr.; vis. lectr. various colls., univs.; mem. Jud. Conf. D.C. Circuit, 1973—; chmn. commn. on admissions and grievances U.S. Ct. Appeals for D.C. Circuit, 1980-86; spl. counsel U.S. Ho. of Reps. Com. on Standards Ofcl. Conduct, 1976-77; chmn. bd. trustees Public Defender Service for D.C., 1976-81; sec. exec. com. bd. visitors Columbia U. Sch. Law; pres. Columbia U. Sch. Law Alumni Assn., 1986-88; bd. govs. D.C. Bar, 1981-84, gen. counsel, 1985-87, pres., 1988-89, mem. legal ethics com., 1976-81, chmn. code subcom., 1977-81; panel arbitrator JAMS, The Resolution Experts, 2004—. Contbr. articles to profl. jours. Co-chair, Washington Lawyers Com. for Civil Rights Under Law, 1982-84; mem. D.C. Jud. Nomination Commn., 1981-86; bd. dirs. Legal Aid Soc. of N.Y.C., 1992—. Fellow Am. Coll. Trial Lawyers; mem. ABA (ho. of dels. 1978-89, vice-chmn. sect. individual rights and responsibilities 1985-87, 89-91, chmn. 1991-92), Am. Law Inst., Practicing Law Inst. (trustee), Cath. Interracial Coun. N.Y., Lawyers Com. for Human Rights (trustee 1991—), Legal Aid Soc. N.Y.C. (bd. dirs. 1992-98), London Ct. of Internat. Arbitration, Lotos Club, Knights of Malta. Roman Catholic. Home: 1137 Smith Ridge Rd New Canaan CT 06840-2333 Office: 1675 Broadway New York NY 10019-5820

LACROIX, CHRISTIAN MARIE MARC, fashion designer; b. Arles, Bouches du Rhône, France, May 16, 1951; s. Maxime and Jeannette (Bergier) L. Grad., U. Valery, Montpelier, France, 1973. Asst. Hermes Co., Paris, 1978-79, Guy Paulin Co., Paris, 1980-81; chief designer Jean Patou Co., Paris, 1982-87; prin. Christian Lacroix Co., Paris, 1987—; creative dir. Emilio Pucci, 2002. Author: Pieces of a Pattern, 1992, The Diary of a Collection, 1996; illustrator: Style d'aujourd hui, 1995. Recipient Golden Thimble award, 1986, 88, Coun. Fashion Designer Am. award, 1987, Prix Balzac, 1989, Das Goldene Spinnrad award Kreffeld, Germany, 1990, Molière Best Costumes award for Phédre, 1996; decorated Comdr. de L'Order des Arts et des Lettres, 1996, Chevalier de la Legion d'honneur, 2002. Roman Catholic. Office: Christian Lacroix 73 Faubourg Saint-Honoré 75008 Paris France Office Phone: 0142687800.

LACROIX, JEFFREY WILLIAM, management consultant; b. Cocoa Beach, Fla., May 17, 1968; s. Sidney Gilbert LaCroix and Jean Elizabeth Black-Hummel; m. Deidra Jeanice Bardin, Apr. 14, 2001. BSME, U. Fla., 1990. Cert. energy manager, Assn. Energy Engrs., 1994. Logistics mgr. Union Carbide Corp., Houston, 1991—2001; energy mgmt. cons. self-employed, 2001—. Dir. Houston Gator Club, 2002—02. Mem.: Assn. Energy Engrs. Independent-Republican. Avocations: riding personal watercraft, travel, sports. Home: 14502 Markhurst Dr Cypress TX 77429 Personal E-mail: jlacroix@comwerx.net.

LACY, ALAN JASPER, retail executive; b. Cleveland, Tenn., Oct. 19, 1953; BSIM, Ga. Inst. Tech., 1975; MBA, Emory U., 1977. CFA. Fin. analyst Holiday Inns, Inc., Memphis, 1977-79; mgr. investor rels. Tiger Internat., L.A., 1979-80, Dart Industries, L.A., 1980-81; dir. corp. fin. Dart & Kraft, Northbrook, Ill., 1981-82, asst. treas., 1982-83, treas., v.p., 1984-86, v.p. fin. and adminstrn. internat., 1987-88; v.p., treas., CFO Minnetonka Corp., Bloomington, Minn., 1988-89; sr. v.p. strategy and devel. Kraft Gen. Foods, Glenview, Ill., 1989-90, sr. v.p. fin., 1990-92, sr. v.p. fin., strategy, sys., 1992-93; v.p. fin. svcs. and sys. Philip Morris Cos., Glenview, Ill., 1993-95; exec. v.p., CFO Sears, Roebuck & Co., 1995-97, pres., credit svcs., 1997-99, pres., CEO, chmn., 2000—. Mem. Econ. Club (Chgo.). Office: Sears Roebuck & Co 3333 Beverly Rd Hoffman Estates IL 60179

LACY, ALEXANDER SHELTON, retired lawyer; b. South Boston, Va., Aug. 18, 1921; s. Cecil Baker and Lura Elizabeth (Byram) L.; m. Carol Jemison, Aug. 8, 1952; children: John Blakeway, Joan Elizabeth Chancey, Alexander Shelton. BS in Chemistry, U. Ala., 1943; LL.B., U. Va., 1949. Bar: Ala. 1949, U.S. Ct. Appeals (5th, 11th and D.C. cirs.) 1981, U.S. Supreme Ct. 1979. Assoc. Bradley, Arant, Rose & White, Birmingham, Ala., 1949-54; with Ala. Gas Corp., Birmingham, 1954-86; v.p., asst. sec., atty. Ala. Gas Corp./Energen Corp., 1969-86; v.p., sec., atty. Ala. Gas Corp., 1974-86; with Patrick and Lacy, Birmingham, 1986-96, ret., 1996. Pres., chmn. bd. Birmingham Symphony Assn., 1964-67; chmn. Birmingham-Jefferson Civic Center Authority, 1965-71. Served with USN, 1943-46. Mem. ABA, Ala. Bar Assn. (chmn. energy law com. 1984-86), Birmingham Bar Assn., Am. Gas Assn. (chmn. legal sect. 1983-85), Fed. Energy Bar Assn., Fed. Bar Assn., Am. Judicature Soc., Mountain Brook Club, Phi Gamma Delta, Phi Delta Phi. Episcopalian. Home: 3730 Montrose Rd Birmingham AL 35213-3824

LACY, ANDRE BALZ, industrial executive; b. Indpls., Sept. 12, 1939; s. Howard J. Lacy II and Edna B. (Balz) Lacy; m. Julia Lello, Feb. 23, 1963; children: Mark William, Peter Lello, John Andre. BA Econs., Denison U.; DEng (hon.), Rose-Hulman Inst. Various mgmt. positions U.S. Corrugated, Indpls., 1961-69, exec. v.p., 1969-72; exec. v.p., chief ops. officer Lacy Diversified Industries, Indpls., 1972-78, chmn. bd. subs., 1973-78, pres., chief ops. officer, 1978-83; pres., chief exec. officer Lacy Diversified Industries, now LDI, Ltd., Indpls., 1983—, chmn., 1992. Bd. dirs. Herff Jones, Inc., Indpls., Patterson Dental Co., Mpls., Finish Master, Inc.; bd. dirs. Nat. Bank Indpls. Chmn. United Way Greater Indpls., 1989—91; Mem. bd. mgrs. Rose-Hulman Inst., Terre Haute, Ind.; pres. Indpls. Bd. Sch. Commn., Indpls., 1985—86; hon. mem. 500 Festival Assocs., Inc., Indpls.; bd. dirs. Hudson Inst., Indpls. Conv. and Visitors Assn., 1996; dir. Ctrl. Ind. Corp. Partnership, Indpls. Downtown, Inc. Mem.: Nat. Assn. Wholesaler Distbrs. (dir.), Ind. Pres. Orgn., Kiwanis Club of Indpls., Young Pres. Orgn., Ind. C. of C. (bd. dirs. 1989), Columbia Club, Meridian Hills Golf and Country Club (Indpls.), Lost Tree Club. Republican. Episcopalian. Avocation: sailing. Home: 450 E Vermont St Indianapolis IN 46202-3680 Office: LDI Ltd 54 Monument Cir Ste 800 Indianapolis IN 46204-2928

LACY, BILL, academic administrator, architect; b. Madill, Okla., Apr. 16, 1933; s. Leon and Eunice L.; m. Susan Cavert Butler, Dec. 27, 1992; children: Jan, Kate, Shawn, Ross, Jessica. BArch, Okla. State U., 1955, MArch, 1958; DFA (hon.), Miami U., Oxford, Ohio, 1985. Design architect Caudill, Rowlett, Scott, Houston, 1958-61; prof., assoc. chmn. dept. architecture Rice U., Houston, 1961-65; prof., dean sch. architecture U. Tenn., Knoxville, 1965-70; v.p. Omniplan, Dallas, 1970-71; dir. architecture and environ. arts Nat. Endowment Arts, Washington, 1971-77, dir. fed. design program, 1972-77; pres. Am. Acad. in Rome, N.Y.C., 1977-80, The Cooper Union, N.Y.C., 1980-88; pres. Purchase Coll. SUNY, 1993—. Archtl. cons. Fgn. Bldgs. Ops., Dept. State Author: 100 Contemporary Architects, 1991, Angels and Franciscans, 1992; contbr. articles, designs to profl. jours. Bd. dirs. Internat. Design Conf. Aspen, 1973-92; bd. dirs. Tiffany Found., Am. Archtl. Found.; cons. Rothschild Found., J. Paul Getty Trust; exec. dir. Pritzker Architecture Prize. With U.S. Army, 1955-57. Loeb fellow Harvard U., 1973; Getty scholar, 1991. Fellow AIA; mem. Univ. Club. Office: 735 Anderson Hill Rd Purchase NY 10577-1402 E-mail: lacy@purchase.edu.

LACY, CLIFTON R., internist, commissioner; MD, U. Medicine and Dentistry N.J., 1979. Diplomate Am. Bd. Internal Medicine, Am. Bd. Cardiovasc. Disease. Intern in internal medicine U. Medicine and Dentistry N.J., New Brunswick, NJ, 1979—80, resident, 1980—82, fellow in cardiovasc. disease, 1982—84; physician Robert Wood Johnson U. Med. Group, New Brunswick, St. Peters Univ. Hosp.; v.p., med. affairs, chief staff Robert Wood Johnson U. Hosp.; commr. N.J. Dept. Health and Sr. Svcs., 2002—. Assoc. prof. Robert Wood Johnson Med. Sch. Fellow: ACP, Am. Coll. Cardiology; mem.: Alpha Omega Alpha. Office: Clin Acad Bldg Ste 5200 125 Paterson St New Brunswick NJ 08901-1977 Business E-Mail: lacycr@umdnj.edu.

LACY, ELIZABETH BERMINGHAM, state supreme court justice; b. 1945; BA cum laude, St. Mary's Coll., Notre Dame, Ind., 1966; JD, U. Tex., 1969; LLM, U. Va., 1992. Bar: Tex. 1969, Va. 1977. Staff atty. Tex. Legis. Coun., Austin, 1969-72; atty. Office of Atty. Gen., State of Tex., Austin, 1973-76; legis. aide Va. Del. Carrington Williams, Richmond, 1976-77; dep. atty. gen. jud. affairs div. Va. Office Atty. Gen., Richmond, 1982-85; mem. Va. State Corp. Commn., Richmond, 1985-89; justice va. Supreme Ct., Richmond, 1989—. Office: Va Supreme Ct PO Box 1315 Richmond VA 02321-1315

LACY, HERMAN EDGAR, management consultant; b. Chgo., June 21, 1935; s. Herman E. and Florence L.; m. Mary C. Lacy; children: Frederick H., Carlton E., Douglas H., Jennifer S., Victoria J., Rebecca M. BS in Indsl. Engring., Bradley U., 1957; MBA, U. Chgo., 1966. Cert. mgmt. cons. Plant mgr., indsl. engring. supr. Hammond Organ Co., Chgo., 1961-66; mgr. corp. indsl. engring. Consol. Packaging Corp., Chgo., 1966-68; mgr. mgmt. cons. Peat, Marwick, Mitchell & Co., Chgo., 1968-70; dir. ops. Wilton Enterprises, Inc., Chgo., 1970-77; v.p., gen. mgr. Intercraft Industries Corp., Chgo., 1978-79; pres. Helmco Cons. Assocs., Fountain Hills, Ariz., 1979—. Instr. Roosevelt U., Oakton Coll., Harper Coll. Served to capt. USAF, 1957-61. Mem. Inst. Indsl. Engrs. (past pres., founder north suburban Ill. chpt.), Am. Mgmt. Assn., Nat. Coun. Phys. Distbn. Mgmt., Soc. Mfg. Engrs., Inst. Mgmt. Cons.(past pres. Pnoenix chpt.). Office: Helmco Cons Assocs 17030 Rand Dr Ste 100 Fountain Hills AZ 85268-5029 Home: 17030 Rand Dr Fountain Hills AZ 85268 Office Phone: 480-846-3595.

LACY, JOHN FORD, retired lawyer; b. Dallas, Sept. 11, 1944; s. John Alexander and Glenda Arcenia (Ford) L.; m. Cece Smith, Apr. 22, 1978. BA, Baylor U., 1965; JD, Harvard U., 1968. Bar: Tex. 1968. Atty. Akin, Gump, Strauss, Hauer & Feld, Dallas, 1968—99; ret., 1999. Co-founder, pres., chmn. rsch. coun. U. Tex. Southwestern Med. Ctr., Dallas, 1985-91; bd. dirs. Vis. Nurse Assn. Tex., 1994-2001, 1st vice chmn., 2000-01. With USAR, 1968-74. Home: 3710 Shenandoah St Dallas TX 75205-2121 Personal E-mail: jofola@charter.net.

LACY, JOHN ROBERT, lawyer; b. Dallas, Dec. 15, 1942; BS, San Diego State U., 1966; MS, U. So. Calif., 1971; JD, U. Calif., 1973. Bar: Calif. 1973, Hawaii 1974. Atty. Goodsill Anderson Quinn & Stifel, Honolulu. Arbitrator Ct. Annexed Arbitration Program, 1986—. Comment editor Hastings Law Jour., 1972-73. Mem. ABA, Hawaii Bar Assn., State Bar Calif., Am. Bd. Trial Advs., Maritime Law Assn. U.S., Thurston Soc., Order of Coif. Office: Goodsill Anderson Quinn & Stifel PO Box 3196 1800 Alii Pl 1099 Alakea St Honolulu HI 96813-4511 Office Phone: 808-547-5600. Business E-Mail: jlacy@goodsill.com.

LACY, JOHN RUSSELL, retired state government administrator, public affairs counselor; b. Trenton, N.J., June 12, 1938; s. J(ohn) Russell and Mary Grey (Snedeker) L.; m. Joanne Ida Fitzpatrick, Apr. 20, 1963; 1 child, Shannon Rae. BA, Rutgers U., 1961; MA, St. Regis U., 2000. Pers. technician N.J. Dept. Civil Svc., Trenton, 1962-63; pub. info. dir. Internat. Hdqrs. Babe Ruth Baseball, Trenton, 1963-68; comms. mgr. Univac Divsn.-Sperry Rand Corp., Blue Bell, Pa., 1968-69; dir. membership rels. N.J. Taxpayers Assn., Trenton, 1969-71; exec. asst. to state treas. N.J. Dept. Treasury, Trenton, 1971-73; exec. v.p. N.J. Retail Mechts. Assn., Trenton, 1973; owner Lacy

Comms., J.R. Lacy Assocs., Hamilton, NJ, 1973—; pub. Mercer Messenger, Hamilton, 1983-88; dep. dir. N.J. State Lottery Commn., Trenton, 1988-90; dir. spl. projects/alumni affairs Mercer County C.C., Trenton, 1990-99; dir. N.J. Human Resource Devel. Inst., Trenton, 1999—2002. Mem. Hamilton Twp. Coun., Hamilton, 1976-99, N.J. League of Municipalities, Elected Ofcls. Hall of Fame; pres. Hamilton YMCA, 1974-75; chmn. Hamilton Twp. Econ. Devel. Commn., 1973-75; pres. Mercer County League Municipalities, Hamilton, 1995-99; bd. dirs. Project Freedom, Inc.; pres. Hamilton Little Bigger League Grads., Inc., 2002--. Named Humanitarian of Yr., Animals in Distress, Inc., 1990, Outstanding Chpt. Pres. in Mercer County, N.J. Jaycees, 1971. Mem. Hamilton Twp. Optimist Club (charter mem.), Ancient Order of Hibernians, VFW (hon.), DAV (life), Tau Kappa Epsilon. Republican. Methodist. Avocations: team sports, historical fiction and biographies, restoring antique furniture. Home: 9 Compton Way Hamilton NJ 08690-3920 Office: JR Lacy Assocs PO Box 3489 Hamilton NJ 08619 Personal E-mail: Jrlacy@aol.com.

LACY, ROBINSON BURRELL, lawyer; b. Boston, May 7, 1952; s. Benjamin Hammett and Jane (Burrell) L. AB, U. Calif., Berkeley, 1974; JD, Harvard U., 1977. Bar: NY 1978, US Dist. Ct. (so. and ea. dists.) NY 1979, US Dist. Ct. (we. dist.) NY 1992, US Ct. Appeals (2d cir.) 1983, US Ct. Appeals (10th cir.) 1990, US Ct. Appeals (3d cir.) 2002, US Supreme Ct. 1986. Law clk. to judge US Dist. Ct. (so. dist.) NY, NYC, 1977-78; law clk. to chief justice Warren Burger US Supreme Ct., Washington, 1978-79; assoc. Sullivan & Cromwell, NYC, 1979-85, ptnr., 1985—, and coord. reorganization/bankruptcy practice area. Mem.: ABA, NY State Bar Assn., Assn. of Bar of City of NY. Office: Sullivan & Cromwell 125 Broad St Fl 28 New York NY 10004-2489 Business E-Mail: lacyr@sullcrom.com.

LACY, STEPHEN M., broadcast and publishing executive; m. Cathy Lacy; 2 children. B in acctg., Kans. State U., 1976, M in acctg., 1977. CPA. Sr. audit mgr. Deloitte & Touche, Des Moines, Kansas City, Mo.; v.p., CFO Commtron Corp., Des Moines, 1986—92; with Johnson & Higgins/Kirke-Van Orsdel Inc., Des Moines, 1992—98, v.p., CFO, exec. v.p., pres.; v.p., CFO Meredith Corp., Des Moines, 1998—2000, pres. mktg. group, 2000, COO, pres. publ. group, 2004—. Bd. dirs. Advt. Coun. Chair bd. dirs. United Way Cent. Iowa; bd. dirs. Am. Red Cross, Jr. Achievement Cent. Iowa. Named Publ. Exec. Yr., Advt. Age, 2003. Mem.: Direct Mktg. Assn. (bd. dirs., exec. com., treas.). Office: Meredith Corp 1716 Locust St Des Moines IA 50309-3023

LACY, TERRI, lawyer; b. Dillon, Mont., 1953; BA with highest honors, So. Meth. U., 1975, JD, 1978. Bar: Tex. 1978. Ptnr., Estates & Estates Planning Andrews & Kurth LLP, Houston. Mng. editor Southwestern Law Jour., 1977—78. Mem.: Houston Estate & Fin. Forum, Houston Bus. & Estate Planning Coun., Houston Bar Assn., State Bar Tex., ABA, Order of Coif. Office: Andrews Kurth LLP 600 Travis St Ste 4200 Houston TX 77002-3090 Office Phone: 713-220-4482. Office Fax: 713-238-7220. Business E-Mail: tlacy@andrewskurth.com.

LACY-PENDLETON, STEVIE, editor; BA in Polit. sci., Case Western Res. U.; postgrad., John Jay Coll. Criminal Justice, N.Y.C. Tchr. Cleve. Urban Learning Ctr., 1974—75; gen. assignment reporter, columnist Xenia (Ohio) Daily Gazette, 1975—78; coord. student recruitment Ctrl. State U., Wilberforce, Ohio, 1978—79; consumer rschr., reporter Dayton (Ohio) Jour. Herald, 1979—80; gen. assignment reporter, real estate editor, TV mag. editor, nat. news editor, world news editor Staten Island (N.Y.) Advance, 1981—95, Sunday Perspective editor, dep. editl. page editor, sr. advance columnist, 1995—2002, mem. editl. bd., 1999—. Spkr. in field. Chmn. bd. trustees Soc. Children and Families, Staten Island; mem. N.Y. Pres.'s Cmty. Adv. Coun., Coll. of Staten Island, mem. SEEK adv. com.; former soup kitchen vol. Trinity Luth. Ch.; founder, sponsor cash scholarships Staten Island schs.; founder, pres. Ebony Elves. Recipient awards, AP, 1981, 1999, 2000, Stevie Lacy-Pendleton Day named in her honor, Staten Island Borough Pres., 1981, Leadership award, United Negro Coll. Fund, Inc., 1993, Cmty. Svc. award, The African-Am. Polit. Action Assn., 1995, awards, N.Y.C. Deadline Club of Soc. Profl. Journalists, 1996, Front Page award, Newswomen's Club of N.Y., 1996, 1997, The Black Am. Achievement award, Staten Island Borough Pres. Guy V. Molinari, 1997, Cmty. Svc. award, Staten Island North Shore Rotary Club, 1997, James Josey Meml. Cmty. Harmony award, 1997, Caring Cmty. award recognition of excellence, Schs. Chancellor Rudolph F. Crew, 1997, 1st pl. award for commentary, Nat. Assn. Black Journalists, 1999, 1st pl. award for columns, N.Y. State AP, 2000, Cmty. Svc. award, Staten Island chpt. Nat. Coun. Negro Women, 2001, award of excellence, N.Y. Newspapers Editors and Pubs., 2001, Cmty. Svc. award, Brown Bombers, 2002, 1st pl. for columns, N.Y. Assn. Black Journalists, 2002, Cmty. Svc. award, Staten Island sect. Nat. Negro Coll. Fund, Svc. award, WEEM, Camelot Drug Counseling Ctrs., Cmty. Svc. award, Staten Island Tech. H.S., Edn. award, Port Richmond H.S., Pub. Svc. award, Amethyst Ho. and Staten Island Coun. on Alcoholism, Cmty. Svc. award, New Brighton Local Devel. Corp., First Ctrl. Bapt. Ch. Avocations: photography, skydiving, collecting African and African-American artwork. Home: 10 Bay St Landing Apt A2H Staten Island NY 10301 Office: Staten Island Advance 950 Fingerboard Rd Staten Island NY 10306 Office Phone: 718-981-1234. Office Fax: 718-981-5679. Business E-Mail: lacy@siadvance.com.

LACZHAZY, ROBERT STEPHEN, registrar, data processing system consultant; b. Long Island, N.Y., Mar. 8, 1968; BS in Mgmt., Pa. State U., 1990. Rsch. asst. Pa. State U., University Park, 1988-90; computer technical asst. Warren County C.C., Washington, N.J., 1990, registrar, 1990—. Chmn. acad. & student devel. com. Warren County C.C., Washington, N.J., 1991-92, instl. rsch. cons., 1992-93, mem. Mgmt. Info. Sys. com., 1992—. Chpt. adviser Phi Theta Kappa, Washington, N.J., 1991—. Mem. Middle States Assn. of Collegiate Registrars and Officers of Admission, Am. Assn. of Collegiate Registrars and Officers of Admission, Assn. for Computing Machinery, C.C. Computer Consortium. Republican. Roman Catholic. Avocations: desktop pub., tennis, music, electronics, sportfishing. Office: Warren County CC Rte 57 W Washington NJ 07882

LADANYI, BRANKO, civil engineer, educator; b. Zagreb, Croatia, Dec. 14, 1922; emigrated to Can., 1962, naturalized, 1967; s. Adalbert and Zora (Kniewald) L.; m. Nevenka Zilic, Dec. 14, 1946; children: Branka, Thomas, Marc. BCE, U. Zagreb, 1947; PhD in Soil Mechanics, U. Louvain, Belgium, 1959. Design engr. Dept. Transp., Zagreb, 1947-52; teaching asst. U. Zagreb, 1952-58; research engr. Belgian Geotech. Inst., Ghent, 1958-62; asso. prof., then prof. civil engring. Laval U., Quebec, Can., 1962-67; prof. civil engring. Ecole Poly., U. Montreal, 1967-94, prof. emeritus, 1994—, dir. North Engring. Centre, 1972—. Author papers in geotech. field, chpts. in books. Recipient Que. sci. award Que. Ministry Edn., 1974, De Beer Geotech. award Belgian Geotech. Soc., 1986, North Sci. award Govt. of Can., 1996. Fellow ASCE (Amity award 1995, Harold R. Peyton award 2003, Elbert F. Rice Meml. award 1991), Royal Soc. Can., Can. Acad. Engring., Engring. Inst. Can., Can. Soc. Civil Engring.; mem. ASTM, Order Engrs. Que., Can. Geotech. Soc. (R.F. Legget Geotech. award 1981, Roger J.E. Brown Meml. award 1993), Can. Inst. Mining and Metallurgy. Office: Ecole Polytech Box 6079 Succ Centre-Ville Montreal PQ Canada H3C3A7 E-mail: bladanyi@polymtl.ca. *There is no end to learning.*

LADAR, JERROLD MORTON, retired lawyer; b. San Francisco, Aug. 2, 1933; AB, U. Wash., 1956; LLB, U. Calif., Berkeley, 1960. Bar: Calif. 1961, U.S. Supreme Ct. 1967. Law clk. to judge U.S. Dist. Ct. (no. dist.) Calif., 1960-61; asst. U.S. atty. San Francisco, 1961-70; chief criminal div., 1968—71; mem. firm MacInnis & Donner, San Francisco, 1971—73; prof. criminal law and procedure U. San Francisco Law Sch., 1962-83; pvt. practice San Francisco., 1971—; ptnr. Ladar & Ladar, San Francisco, 1994—2002; ret., 2002. Lectr. Hastings Coll. Law, Civil and Criminal Advocacy Programs, 1985-2002; chair pvt. defender panel U.S. Dist. Ct. (no. dist.) Calif., 1980-90; ct. apptd. chair stats. and tech. subcom. Fed. Civil Justice Reform Act Com. (no. dist.) Calif., 1990-95; ct. apptd. mem. Fed. Ct. Civil Local Rules Revision Com. (no. dist.) Calif., 1994—; ct. apptd. chmn. Criminal Local Rules Revision Com. (no. dist.) Calif., 1991-99; mem. continuing edn. of bar criminal law adv. com. U. Calif., Berkeley, 1978-83, 89-2001; panelist, mem. nat. planning com. ABA Nat. Ann. White Collar Crime Inst., 1996—; ct. apptd. mem. Local Disciplinary Rule Draft com., 1998-99 Author: (with others) Selected Trial Motions, Grand Jury Practice, Asset Forfeiture, (6 edits., California Criminal Law and Procedure Practice, 3d edit. 4th edit., 5th edit., 6th edit., 2002, Collateral Effects of Federal Convictions, 1997, Insult Added to Injury: The Fallout From Tax Conviction, 1997, Give Me A Break-Finding Federal Misdemeanors, 1998, The Court: We're Here to Seek the Truth; Defense Counsel: Excuse Me, That's Not My Job, 1999, A Day At The Grand Jury, 2000, The Art of Direct Examination, 2002. Trustee Tamalpais Union High Sch. Dist., 1968-77, chmn. bd., 1973-74; mem. adv. com. Nat. PTA Assn., 1972-78; apptd. mem. criminal justice act com. U.S. Ct. Appeals (9th cir.) Fellow Am. Bd. Criminal Lawyers; mem. ABA, San Francisco Bar Assn. (editor in Re 1974-76), State Bar Calif. (pro-tem disciplinary referee 1976-78, vice chmn. pub. interest and edn. com. criminal law sect., mem. exec. com. criminal law sect. 1980-87, editor Criminal Law Sect. News 1981-87, chmn. exec. com. 1983-84), Am. Inns. of Ct. (exec. com. 1994-97), Fed. Bar Assn. (panelist), Nat. Sentencing Inst. (contbr.) Office: 1916 Vallejo St San Francisco CA 94123-4918

LADAU, ROBERT FRANCIS, architect, planner; b. N.Y.C., Jan. 31, 1940; s. A. Ralph and Marguerite Louise (de ValoisVignand) L.; m. Anne Horton, May 30, 1970. AB, Columbia U., 1961, BArch, MArch, 1965. Registered architct, N.Y., N.J., Del., D.C., Conn. Chmn. bd. dirs., CEO, Environers Inc., N.Y.C., 1964-66, dir., 1966-73; assoc. Rogers, Butler & Burgun, Architects, N.Y.C., 1966-69; prin. Robert F. Ladau, AIA Architect/Planner, N.Y.C., 1969-70, pres., 1973—. Ptnr. Metcalf & Assocs. Architects and Engrs., Washington and N.Y.C.; founder, ptnr. Sir Robert Matthew, Metcalf & Ptnrs., London and Edinburgh, 1970-73; v.p. architecture A.M. Kinney Affiliation Architects & Engrs., Cin., N.Y.C., Chgo., Denver, L.A., San Juan and Basel, Switzerland, 1975-80; sr. v.p. Welton Becket Assocs., N.Y.C., 1980-84; pres., CEO, The Miller Orgn., 1984-90; pres. Emergy Roth & Sons Interior Design/Facilities Mgmt., 1990—; lectr. on planning, design of health facilities; mem. nat. panel Am. Arbitration Assn; prin. AHSC Arch., 2002—. Co-author: Color in Interior Design and Architecture, 1988; contbr. articles to profl. jours.; designer numerous office and comml., health, ednl., urban, recreational, residential and indsl. facilities. Mem. bd. fellows Frick Collection; chmn. long range planning com. bd. govs. Columbia U. Club N.Y.; mem. Bedford (N.Y.) Conservation Bd., 1975-78. Recipient Group Exhibit award Rockefeller Found., 1964; design awards Rockefeller Found., 1962, N.Y. Soc. Architects, 1966, Internat. Conf. Med. Primatology, 1974, Carnegie Heroism medal, 1989; William Kinne Fellows traveling fellow, 1965. Mem. AIA, N.Y. Soc. Architects, N.Y. State Assn. Architects, Nat. Coun. Archtl. Registration Bds. (cert.), Humane Soc. N.Y. (bd. advisors 1992-93, trustee 1993—), Princeton Club, Mashomack Club, Quaker Hill Club. Home: Mooney Hill Rd Patterson NY 12563 Office: 777 Old Sawmill River Rd Tarrytown NY 10591-6721

LADD, ALAN PRESTON, pediatrician, surgeon; s. Barry Lewis and Gwendolyn Ann Ladd; m. Tonya Ann Ladd, Nov. 6, 1993; 1 child, Benjamin Thomas. BS, Ind. U., 1990, MD, 1994. Attending surgeon Riley Hosp. Children, Indpls., 2002—. Asst. prof. Ind. U. Sch. Medicine, Indpls., 2002—. Mem.: Am. Pediatric Surg. Assn., AM. Acad. Pediatrics, Am. Coll. Surgeons. Avocations: golf, sailing. Office: Riley Hosp Children 702 Barnhill Dr Ste 2500 Indianapolis IN 46202

LADD, CHARLES CUSHING, III, civil engineer, educator; b. Bklyn., Nov. 23, 1932; s. Charles Cushing and Elizabeth (Swan) Ladd; m. Carol Lee Ballou, June 11, 1954; children: Melissa, Charles IV, Ruth, Matthew. AB, Bowdoin Coll., 1955; SB, MIT, 1955, SM, 1957, ScD, 1961. Asst. prof. MIT, Cambridge, 1961-64, assoc. prof., 1964-70, prof., 1970-94, dir. Ctr. Sci. Excellence Offshore Engring., 1983-94, Edmund K. Turner prof., 1994-2001, Edmund K. Turner prof. emeritus, 2001—. Gen. reporter 9th Internat. Conf. Soil Mechanics and Found. Engring., Tokyo, 1977; co-gen. reporter 11th Internat. Conf. Soil Mechanics and Found. Engring., San Francisco, 1985; mem. geotech. bd. NRC, 1992—94; casagrande lectr. 12th Pan-Am. Conf. Soil Mechanics and Geotech. Engring., Cambridge, Mass., 2003. Contbr. articles to profl. jours. Commr. Concord Dept. Pub. Works, 1965—78, chmn., 1972—74; mem. Concord Rep. Town Com., 1968—82. Fellow: ASCE (hon.; Terzaghi lectr. 1986, mem. exec. com. geotechnical engring. divsn. 1989—96, chmn. 1993—94, Geo-Inst. bd. govs. 1996—98, Rsch. prize 1969, Croes medal 1973, Norman medal 1976, Middlebrooks award 1996, Karl Terzaghi award 1999, Middlebrooks award 2002); mem.: AAUP, NSPE, ASTM (Hogentogler award 1990), NAE, Can. Geotech. Soc., Brit. Geotech. Soc., Assn. Engring. Firms Practicing Geosci., Am. Soc. Engring. Edn., Internat. Soc. Soil Mechanics and Geotech. Engring., Transp. Rsch. Bd., Boston Soc. Civil Engr. (bd. govs. 1972—81, pres. 1977—78, Arthur Casagrande meml. lectr. 2000). Home: 7 Thornton Ln Concord MA 01742-4107 Office: MIT Dept Civil & Environ Engrng Cambridge MA 02139 Office Phone: 978-369-3886. Business E-Mail: ccladd@mit.edu.

LADD, CULVER SPROGLE, secondary school educator; b. Bismarck, N.D., Nov. 15, 1929; s. Culver Sprogle and Eleanor (Pearson) Ladd. BS, U. Md., 1953; MA, Am. U., 1963, PhD, 1984; postgrad., Harvard U., summer 1963, Oxford (Eng.) U., 1975-76; cert. by correspondence, Nat. Def. U., Thailand, 1972. Clk.-photographer Dept. Justice, FBI, Washington, 1946-54; intercept controller Dept. of Def., USAF, 1954-56; asst. office mgr. Covington & Burling, Lawyers, Washington, 1956-62; tchr. Internat. Sch. Bangkok, Thailand, 1964-66; lectr. U. Md., Thailand, 1966-67, 71-74; project dir. Bus. Rsch. Ltd., Thailand, 1966-67, 72-74; spl. lectr. Payap U., Chiang Mai, Thailand, 1974-75, 2000-2001; tchr. D.C. Pub. Schs., 1978-2000. Cons. USAID, Thailand, 1973—74; vis. scientist Brookhaven Nat. Labs., L.I., 1988; master tchr. Woodrow Wilson Fellowship Found., 1989; bd. dirs. Chesapeake Water Assn., 2002—. Pub.: Pure Food Crusader, Edwin Fremont Ladd, 1859-1925. Rep. candidate Md. Senate 29th Legis. Dist., 1998. Capt. USAFR, 1953—72. Recipient Appreciation award, Payap U., 1987. Mem.: Mid. States Coun. Social Studies, Nat. Coun. Tchrs. Math., Nat. Capital Area Polit. Sci. Assn., Mid-Atlantic Region Assn. Asian Studies, Exptl. Aviation Assn., Aircraft Owners and Pilots Assn., Pi Sigma Alpha, Omicron Delta Kappa. Republican. Presbyterian. Avocations: gardening, flying. Office: POACRE Airfield 845 Crystal Rock Rd PO Box 2084 Lusby MD 20657-1884 Office Phone: 410-326-2282. E-mail: csladd@juno.com.

LADD, DAVID SCOTT, music educator; b. Milw., Wis., Feb. 7, 1962; s. Donald Alfie and Marilyn Bender Ladd; m. Katherine Lynne Condit-Ladd. MusB, U. Wis., 1985; MusM, Northeastern Ill. U., 1999. Cert. tchr. State of Ill. Music tchr. Waukesha Pub. Schs., Waukesha, Wis., 1986; choral music tchr. Deerfield HS, Deerfield, Ill., 1994—95, Mundelein HS, Mundelein, Ill., 1994—96, New Trier HS, Winnetka, Ill., 1996—2002, choral music tchr., music dept. chair, 2002—. Audition host Ill. Music Educators Assn., Winnetka, Ill., 2002, participating judge, 1994—2004. Author: Musical Theatre as Career Choice, 2004. Profl. actor, 1985—94; singing mem. Coriolis. Recipient Signature Sch. Gold, The Grammy Found., 2000, Grammy award, 2000. Mem.: Actor's Equity Assn., Am. Choral Dirs. Assn., Nat. Edn. Assn. Avocations: travel, golf, home renovation. Office: New Trier HS 385 Winnetka Ave Winnetka IL 60093 Office Phone: 847-784-6696. Office Fax: 847-784-6690. E-mail: laddd@newtrier.k12.il.us.

LADD, JEFFREY RAYMOND, lawyer; b. Mpls., Apr. 10, 1941; s. Jasper Raymond and Florence Marguerite (DeMarce) L.; m. Kathleen Anne Crosby, Aug. 24, 1963; children: Jeffrey Raymond, John Henry, Mark Jasper, Matthew Crosby. Student, U. Vienna, Austria; BA, Loras Coll.; postgrad., U. Denver; JD, Ill. Inst. Tech. Bar: Ill. 1973, U.S. Dist. Ct. 1973. V.p. mktg. Ladd Enterprises, Des Plaines, Ill., 1963-66, v.p. mktg. and fin. Crystal Lake, Ill., 1966-70; ptnr. Ross & Hardies, Chgo., 1973-81, Boodell, Sears, et al., 1981-86, Bell, Boyd & Lloyd, Chgo., 1986—. Spl. asst. atty. gen. for condemnation State of Ill., 1977-82; chmn. Metra, 1984—. Mem., chmn. Ill. Bd. Govs. of State Colls. and Univs., 1972—75; mem. bd. regents Loras Coll., 2003—; del. 6th Ill. Constnl. Conv., 1969—70. Recipient W. Graham Claytor, Jr. award for disting. svc. to passenger transp., 1995, Disting. Svc. award IIT/Chgo.-Kent Law Sch., 1997; named Citizen of Yr., Chgo. City Club, 1995. Mem. ABA, Chgo. Bar Assn., Nat. Assn. Bond Lawyers, Ill. Assn. Hosp. Attys., Am. Acad. Hosp. Attys., Crystal Lake Jaycees (Disting. Svc. award), Crystal Lake C. of C. (past pres.), Econ. Club, Legal Club, Union League Club, Bull Valley Golf Club, Woodstock Country Club, Alpha Lambda. Roman Catholic. Avocations: golf, hunting, fishing, tennis, skiing. Office: Bell Boyd & Lloyd 3 First National Pla 70 W Madison St Ste 3100 Chicago IL 60602-4284

LADD, JOSEPH CARROLL, retired insurance company executive; b. Chgo., Jan. 26, 1927; s. Stephen C. and Laura (McBride) L.; m. Barbara Virginia Carter, June 5, 1965; children: Carroll, Joseph Carroll, Barbara, Virginia, William. BA, Ohio Wesleyan U., 1950; CLU, Am. Coll., Bryn Mawr; D in Bus. Adminstrn. (hon.), Spring Garden Coll., 1985. Agt. Conn. Gen. Life Ins. Co., Chgo., 1950-53, staff asst., 1953-54, mgr. Evanston (Ill.) br. office, 1954-60, dir. agys., 1960-62, mgr. Los Angeles br. office, 1963; v.p. sales Fidelity Mut. Life Ins. Co., Phila., 1964-67, sr. v.p. sales, 1968, exec. v.p., 1969-71, pres., chief exec. officer, dir., 1971-84, chmn., chief exec. officer, dir., 1984-89, chmn., dir., 1989-91; ret. Bd. dirs. Corestates Fin., Phila. Suburban Corp., Phila. Electric Co. Trustee Bryn Mawr Hosp.; trustee United Way of S.E. Pa.; trustee Phila. United Way, also gen. chmn. 1978 campaign; bd. dirs. Phila. YMCA. Served with USNR, 1945-46. Recipient Civic Achievement award Am. Jewish Com., 1978, Achiever's award WHEELS Med. and Specialized Transp., 1978, Ohio Wesleyan U. Life Achievement award Delta Tau Delta, 1982, William Penn award, Greater Phila. C. ofC. and PENJERDEL Coun., 1988, Robert Morris Citizenship award Valley Forge Coun. Boy Scouts Am., 1988; named YMCA Man of Yr., 1979, William Penn Found. Disting. Pennsylvanian, 1980. Mem. Greater Phila. C. of C. (dir., chmn. 1979, 83-84), Phila. Country Club, Union League Club (Phila.), Summer Beach (Fla.) Country Club.

LADD, MARCIA LEE, medical products executive; b. Bryn Mawr, Pa., July 22, 1950; d. Edward Wingate and Virginia Lee (McGinnes) Mullinix; m. Leroy D. Werley, III, Aug. 5, 2000; children from previous marriage: Joshua Wingate, McGinnes Lee. BA, U. Pa., 1972; MEd, U. Va., 1973; MA, Emory U., 1979. Rsch. assoc. N.C. Tng. and Standards Coun., Raleigh, 1973-75; dir. counseling svc. N.C. State Youth Svcs. Agy., Raleigh, 1975-76; acad. dean Duke U., Durham, N.C., 1976-77; prin. Ladd & Assocs. Mgmt. Cons., Chapel Hill, N.C., 1979-88; v.p. adminstrn. CompuChem Corp., Research Triangle Park, N.C., 1988-91; v.p. mktg. Prentke Romich Co., Wooster, Ohio, 1991-94; v.p. ops. Exec. Staffing Svcs., Inc., Cary, N.C., 1994; pres., CEO, owner Triangle Aftercare, Durham, N.C., 1994—. Bd. dirs. Home Med. Svcs., 1997—; mem. N.C. Bd. Pharmacy, 2004—. Bd. dirs. Oackwood Hist. Soc., Raleigh, 1981—84; mem. bd. vis. Carolina Friends Sch., Durham, 1986—89; bd. dirs. Orange Enterprises, 2000—; Stephen min. Univ. Presbyn. Ch., Chapel Hill, 1994—97, 2003—, youth group leader, 1995—97, 2000—02, trustee, 1998—2000; bd. dirs. Wayne County Arts Coun., Wooster, 1992, Stoneridge/Sedgefield Swim/Racquet Club, Chapel Hill, 1985—88. Decorated Order of Long Leaf Pine Gov. of N.C.; named one of Impact 100 Most Influential People, Research Triangle, N.C., 1997. Office: Triangle Aftercare 105 W NC Hwy 54 Ste 267 Durham NC 27713

LADD, NATHANIEL FAIRBANKS, JR., secondary school educator; b. Brookline, Mass., Nov. 9, 1965; s. Nathaniel Fairbanks and Linda Louise Ladd; m. Kimberly Ann Condon, Feb. 5, 1999; children: Piper Louise, Alexandra Louise. BS in Journalism, Northeastern U., 1988; MEd, Cambridge Coll., 2000. Lic. tchr. Commonwealth of Mass., 1996. Tchr. Concord Assabet Sch., Lexington, Mass., 1996—98, Walker Sch., Needham, 1998—99; tchr. English Melrose H.S., Melrose, 1999—2000, Greater Lawrence Tech Sch., Andover, 2000—03, Lawrence H.S., Lawrence, 2003—04; tchr. spl. edn. Burlington H.S., 2004—. Mem.: NEA, Mass. Teachers Assoc. Office: Burlington High Sch Cambridge St Burlington MA 01803 Office Phone: 339-234-0509. Personal E-mail: riz1165@comcast.net.

LADD, ROSE DIANE, actress; b. Meridian, Miss., Nov. 29, 1942; m. Bruce Dern (div.); 1 child, Laura; m. William Shea, Jr. (div.); m. Robert C. Hunter, Feb. 14, 1999; step-children: Brandon Hunter, Amy Oleson, Emily Hunter. Grad., St. Aloysius Acad. Appearances include (films) The Wild Angels, 1966, The Reivers, 1969, Macho Callahan, 1970, Rebel Rousers, 1970, WUSA, 1970, White Lightning, 1973, Alice Doesn't Live Here Anymore, 1974, Chinatown, 1974, Embryo, 1976, The November Plan, 1976, All Night Long, 1981, Something Wicked This Way Comes, 1983, Black Widow, 1987, Plain Clothes, 1988, National Lampoon's Christmas Vacation, 1989, Wild at Heart, 1990, A Kiss Before Dying, 1991, Rambling Rose, 1991, Cemetery Club, 1992, Hold Me, Thrill Me, Kiss Me, 1992, Code Name: Chaos, 1992, Carnosaur, 1993, Father Hood, 1993, Spirit Realm, 1993, Obsession, 1994, Mrs. Munck (also dir., writer, co-prodr.), 1994, The Haunted Heart, 1995, Raging Angels, 1995, Ghosts of Mississippi, 1996, Mother (also exec. prodr.), 1996, Citizen Ruth, 1996, James Dean: Race With Destiny, 1997, Primary Colors, 1998, Daddy N Them, 1999, 28 Days, 2001, Rain, 2001, Law of Enclosures, 2001, Charlies War, 2002; (TV series) Alice, 1980-81; (TV movies) The Devil's Daughter, 1973, Thaddeus Rose and Eddie, 1978, Black Beauty, 1978, Willa, 1979, Guyana Tragedy: The Story of Jim Jones, 1980, Desperate Lives, 1982, Grace Kelly, 1983, I Married a Centerfold, 1984, Crime of Innocence, 1985, Celebration Family, 1987, Bluegrass, 1988, The Lookalike, 1990, Rock Hudson, 1990, Shadow of a Doubt, 1991, Hush Little Baby, 1994, Ruby Ridge: An American Tragedy, 1996, Breach of Faith: Family of Cops II, 1997, The Waiting Game, 1997, The Staircase, 1998; (TV mini-series) Cold Lazarus, 1996, Aftermath, 2001, Damage Care, 2001, Kristy, James Van Praag Story, (15 hour TV spl.) Stephen King's Kingdom Hospital, ABC, 2003. Recipient award Brit. Acad., Spirit award, Golden Globe award, 3 Acad. award nominations, 4 Golden Globe nominations, 3 Emmy nominations for Guest Actress in a Series (Grace Under Fire), 1994, Dr. Quinn, Medicine Woman, Touched by an Angel; named Woman of Yr. City of Hope, 1992; recipient Achievement award Women in Film, 1992, PATH Angel award, 1992, Dist. Artist award L.A. Music Ctr., 1994, Hollywood Legacy award, 1994, 1st Time Dir. award Dla. Film Festival, 1996, Tribuate award Newport Festival, 1996.

LADDON, MICHAEL M, retail executive; Group v.p., CIO Ralphs Grocery Co., 1995—99; exec. v.p., CIO Produceline.com, 2000—01; exec. v.p. Brix Software, 2001—02; CIO, sr. v.p. Longs Drug Stores Corp., 2003—. Office: Longs Drug Stores PO Box 5222 Walnut Creek CA 94596

LADEMACHER, HARTMUT, computer software and services company executive; With IBM, Germany, 1073-90, mgr. project mktg., until 1990; a founder, chmn. bd., CEO, LHS Group Inc., Atlanta, 1990—. Office: LHS Group Inc 3000 Mill Creek Ave #100 Alpharetta GA 30022-1555

LADEN, BEN ELLIS, economist, writer; b. Savannah, Ga., Mar. 4, 1942; s. Bernard and Fannie Rachel (Cooper) L.; m. Susan Sherman, Aug. 16, 1964; children: Francine, Jonathan, Paul. AB, Princeton U., 1963; PhD, Johns Hopkins U., 1969. Asst. prof. econs. Ohio State U., 1967-71; economist Fed. Res. Bd., 1971-74; v.p., chief economist T. Rowe Price Assocs., Balt., 1974-87; dir. fin. instns. regulation staff HUD, Washington, 1990-94; pres. Bel Assocs., Washington, 1994—. Sr. adjunct scholar Hudson Inst., 2001. Author: Economic Trend, 1974-87; also articles. Fellow Nat. Assn. Bus. Economists (dir. 1981-87, pres. 1984-85); mem. Am. Econs. Assn. Jewish. Home: 3111 Rittenhouse St NW Washington DC 20015-1614 Personal E-mail: benladen@prodigy.net. *Each person has to find his own unique formula for success. My greatest achievements have come from the following elements. 1. A clear concept of priorities with persistent concentration on the highest priority. 2. Building structures which will continue to payoff in the future, rather than trying for immediate results. 3. Identifying those areas where my contribution could be the greatest and could be unique. 4. Always striving for the highest quality in my work. 5. Most important, learning from the experience of others and respecting the individual ways of other people.*

LADENDORFF, LINDA HARDIN-REED, early childhood education educator; b. Gunnison, Colo., Nov. 21, 1941; d. L. Douglas and Gertrud (Helmecke) Hardin; m. Robert Henry Ladendorff, dec. 20, 1964; children: Noma Ladendorff Collins, Lisa Wordelman. BA in Elem. Edn., U. Ariz., 1964; MA in Reading and Learning Disabilities, No. Ariz. U., 1986. Cert. in elem. edn., pre-sch., spl. edn. and adult edn., also cert. reading specialist, Ariz. Kindergarten tchr. St. Johns (Ariz.) Unified Schs., 1977-84; tchr., dir. Escuela Para Los Ninas Pre-Sch., St. Johns/Springerville, Ariz., 1985-88; instructional specialist Inst. for Human Devel./No. Ariz. U., Flagstaff, 1989, Alcohol Misuse Prevention Project/U. Mich., Ann Arbor, 1990; tchr. 1st grade Miami (Ariz.) Area Schs., 1991—. Bd. dirs., sec. Apache County Guidance Clinic, St. Johns, 1981; mem. spl. edn. adv. com. Ariz. Dept. Edn., Phoenix, 1986, 87, 88. Mem. adv. com. to City Coun., Victoria, Tex., 1974-75; membership sec. Fine Arts Assn., Victoria, 1973-75; sec. Cmty. Action Com., Victoria, 1974. U.S. Dept. Edn. spl. edn. grantee, 1984, 85, 86, other grants. Mem. TESOL, Ariz. Reading Assn. (bd. dirs.), Gila County Reading Assn. (pres.), Ariz. Assn. Lifelong Learners, Internat. Reading Assn., Delta Kappa Gamma. Methodist. Avocations: needlecrafts, gardening, travel. Home: 1308 Crestwood Dr Globe AZ 85501-1517 Office: Inspiration Addition Sch 929 Rose Rd Miami AZ 85539-1160

LADENHEIM, JULES CALVIN, neurosurgeon; b. Union Hill, NJ, Apr. 21, 1923; s. Solomon and Miriam (Preminger) L.; m. Janet Bloom, Feb. 15, 1959; children: Eric, Fred (dec.), Karen. AB, Harvard U., 1944; MD, NY Med. Coll., 1947. Diplomate Am. Bd. Surgery, Am. Bd. Neurologic Surgery. Intern Queens Gen. Hosp., NYC, 1947-48; resident gen. surgery NY Med. Coll., 1948-50, Pitts. Med. Ctr., 1952-53, Mt. Sinai, Cleve., 1953-54; resident neurosurgery Serafimer Hosp., Stockholm, 1954-56, Med. Coll. Va., Richmond, 1956-57; resident in neurosurgery Neurology Inst. NY, 1957-58; resident neurosurgery Mary Hitchcock, Hanover, NH, 1958-60; pvt. practice Hackensack, NJ, 1960—. Staff neurosurgeon Hackensack U. Hosp., 1960—, Holy Name Hosp., Teaneck, NJ, 1960—, Meadowland Hosp., Secaucus, NJ, 1987—, St. Mary Hosp., Hoboken, 1987—. Co-author: Arteriovenous Aneurysm, 1956; author: Intraventric Meningiomas, 1961, Leonard Bertapaglia, 1991, Firearms and Ballistics, 1996, Alien Horseman, 2003. Lt. USNR, 1950—52. Decorated Navy and Marine Corps medal. Mem. Am. Assn. Neurologic Surgeons, Congress of Neurosurgery, Nordiska Neurokirugiska Forening, Abraham Lincoln Soc. (pres. 1993-94), USS Columbus Vets. Assn., Harvard Club NY. Office: 664 River Rd Teaneck NJ 07666-1642 E-mail: julescalvin@aol.com.

LADENSON, MARK LAWRENCE, economist, educator; b. Chgo., Dec. 12, 1941; s. Alex and Inez (Sher) L.; m. Joyce Ruddel, Aug. 14, 1971; 1 child, Sharon. BA, U. Wis., 1963; MBA, U. Chgo., 1965; PhD, Northwestern U., 1970. Asst. prof., then assoc. prof. econs. Mich. State U., East Lansing, 1970-84, prof. econs., 1984—2000, prof. emeritus, 2000—. Vis. scholar Ga. State U., Atlanta, 1975-76; faculty fellow, supervising economist U.S. GAO, Washington, 1978-80. Book rev. bd. editors Atlantic Econ. Jour., Edwardsville, Ill., 1986—; contbr. numerous articles to profl. jours. Mem. Atlantic Econ. Assn., Internat. Assn. Jazz Record Collectors (best article award 1988), Jazz Photographers Assn. Home: 230 Oxford Rd East Lansing MI 48823-2627 Office: Mich State Univ Dept Econs East Lansing MI 48824 Office Phone: 517-355-7583. E-mail: ladenso1@msu.edu.

LADER, MALCOLM HAROLD, pharmaceutical consultant; b. Liverpool, England, Feb. 27, 1936; s. Abe and Minnie (Sholl) L.; m. Susan Ruth Packer, Apr. 16, 1961; children: Deborah, Vicki, Charlotte. BSc, U. Liverpool, 1956, MB, ChB, 1959, MD, 1964; PhD, U. London, 1963, DSc, 1978. Rsch. staff MRC, England, 1966—2001. Cons. Maudsley Hosp., 1970-2001; prof. clin. psychopharmacology, U. London, 1978-2001, emeritus prof., 2001—; advisor WHO, trustee Psychiatry Rsch. Trust. Author: Biological Treatments in Psychiatry, 1996; contbr. articles to profl. jours. Decorated Order of Brit. Empire. Fellow: Acad. Med. Scis., Royal Soc. Psychiatrists, Soc. for Study of Addiction (hon.), Am. Coll. Psychiatry (hon.), Brit. Assn. Psychopharmacology (hon.). Avocations: antiques, paintings. Home: 16 Kelsey Park Mansion 78 Wickham Rd Beckenham Kent BR3 6QH England Office Phone: 44-207-848-0372. E-mail: m.lader@iop.kcl.ac.uk.

LADER, PHILIP, lawyer, academic administrator, diplomat; b. Jackson Heights, N.Y., Mar. 17, 1946; BA, Duke U., 1966; MA, U. Mich., 1967, Oxford (Eng.) U., 1968; JD, Harvard U., 1972. Bar: Fla. 1972, D.C. 1973, S.C. 1979. Atty. Sullivan & Cromwell, N.Y.C., 1972; law clk. to U.S. cir. judge, 1973; pres. Sea Pines Co., Hilton Head Island, SC, 1979-83, Winthrop U., Rock Hill, SC, 1983-85; exec. v.p. Sir James Goldsmith's US Holding Co., 1986-88; pres. Bus. Execs. for Nat. Security, Washington, 1990—91; pres., vice chancellor Bond U., Queensland, Australia, 1991-93; adminstr. SBA, Washington, 1994-97; mem. President's Cabinet, Washington, 1994-97; U.S. amb. to Ct. of St. James, 1997-2001; chmn. WPP plc, 2001—; sr. advisor Morgan Stanley, 2001—; ptnr. Nelson Mullins Riley & Scarborough, 2001—. Dep. dir. for mgmt. Office Mgmt. and Budget, Exec. Office Pres., 1993; dep. chief of staff White House, asst. to Pres., 1993-94; chmn. Pres.'s Coun. on Integrity and Efficiency, 1993, chmn. Pres.'s Mgmt. Coun.; chmn. policy com. Nat. Performance Rev., 1993; candidate for gov. S.C., 1986; bd. dirs Marathon Oil, AES Corp, RAND Corp. Founder Renaissance Inst.; trustee Brit. Mus., Brit-Am. Bus. Coun., St. Paul's Cathedral Found., Windsor Leadership Trust, Found. for the 21st Century; chmn., Am. assoc. Royal Acad. Art., 2001—04; mem. vis. com. Harvard Law Sch.; chmn. bd. visitors Duke U. Sanford Inst. Pub. Policy, 1999—2001; bd. dirs. ARC, 1996—97; mem. adv. bd. Prince of Wales Trust; mem. coun. Lloyd's of London, 2004—. Hon. fellow Pembroke Coll., Oxford U., London Bus. Sch., John Moores U.; hon. bencher Mid. Temple. Mem.: World Pres.'s Orgn., Chief Execs. Orgn., Coun. Fgn. Rels., Royal Soc. Arts, Mfrs. and Sci. (Benjamin Franklin medal 2001), Soc. Internat. Bus. Fellows, Harvard Club N.Y.C., D.C. Met. Club, Phi Beta Kappa. Episcopalian. Achievements include 14 hon. doctorates from Brit. and Am. univs. Office: Liberty Ctr 151 Meeting St Ste 600 Charleston SC 29401

LADERMAN, GABRIEL, artist; b. Bklyn., Dec. 26, 1929; s. Isidore and Leah (Stock) L.; m. Carol Ciavati, Feb. 12, 1953; children— Raphael, Michael. BA, Bklyn. Coll., 1952; M.F.A., Cornell U., 1957. Faculty State U. N.Y., New Paltz, 1957-59, Pratt Inst., 1959-66, Queens Coll., Flushing, N.Y., 1966-96, chmn., 1979-83; ret., 1996. Vis. prof. La. State U., Baton Rouge, 1966-67, Yale U., 1968, 81, 83, 89, 91, Viterbo Coll., 1969, 80, Art Students League, 1972-81, Boston U., 1973, N.Y. Studio Sch., Am. U., 1994—; dir. G.-T. Mus., 1980-84, Caumsett Summer Landscape Painting Program, 1980, 81; vis. critic, lectr. Yale U., Syracuse U., Bennington Coll., Vassar Coll., Rutgers U., Princeton, Cooper-Union, Phila. Coll. Art, Mus. Fine Arts, Boston, Md. Inst. Art, Swain Sch., Boston U., Boston Mus. Sch., Ind. U., Bard Coll., Kansas City Art Inst., Fla. State U., SUNY at New Paltz, Amherst Coll., Skowhegan Sch., Yale-Norfolk Sch., New York Studio Sch., Pratt Inst., N.Y. Inst. Tech., Boston Mus., Tyler Sch. of Temple U., U. R.I., U. N.H., Artists for Environment, Iowa State U., Hobart Coll., U. Wis., 1980, Md. Art Inst., 1980, Royal Sch. Art, Bangkok, Thailand, 1976, Nat. Art Sch., Jakarta, Indonesia, 1975, Art Sch., Surabaya, Indonesia, 1975, Victorian Coll. Art, Melbourne, Australia, 1975, Coll. Art, Ballarat, Australia, 1975, Prahran Coll., Melbourne, 1975, U. Minn., 1987, Yale U., 1987, State U. Calif. Arts seminars San Luis Obispo, 1986, Stanford U., 1987, 91, U. Calif., Santa Barbara, 1987, Calif. State U., Long Beach, 1987, Pa. Acad., 1988, Chautauqua Art Program, N.Y. Acad. Art, numerous others; USIS lectr., Japan, 1975; vis. lectr., critic Long Beach State Coll., 1987, Parsons Sch., 1991, Ox Bow Sch., 1991, N.Y. Acad., 1987, 91; vis. critic Chautauqua Art Sch., 1993; critic, lectr. Stanford U. Chautaugua Art Program, Bard Coll., Pa. Acad.; Disting. vis. prof. Am. Univ., Washington, 1994. Contbr. articles to profl. jours.; one man shows at Schoelkopf Gallery, 1964, 67, 70, 72, 74, 77, 86, 90, Hobart Coll., 1968, R.I. U., 1969, Temple U., 1971, La. State U., 1967, Bennington Coll., Ithaca Coll., R.I. U., So. U., Dart Gallery, Chgo., 1977, Savage Gallery, Boston, 1976, Meade Mus., Amherst Coll., 1983, Contemporary Realists Gallery, San Francisco, 1987, 90, Jessica Darraby Gallery, Los Angeles, 1987, Peter Tattistcheff Gallery, N.Y., 1994, 97; exhibited in group shows at Whitney Mus., 1971, Mus. Modern Art, 1974, Corcoran Gallery, 1972, 76, Boston Mus., 1974, 75, Bklyn. Mus., 1952, 57, 59, 61, Library of Congress, 1957, 59, Gallery of Modern Art, 1972, N.Y. Cultural Center, 1972, Phila. Mus., 1970, Wadsworth Atheneum, 1976, Fogg Mus., 1976, Mpls. Inst. Arts, 1976, Milw. Art Center, 1977, Ft. Worth Art Mus., 1977, High Mus., 1977, San Francisco Mus. Modern Art, 1977, Pa. Acad., 1981, traveling shows sponsored by A.F.A., Smithsonian Instn., Library of Congress, Pa. Acad. Arts; represented in permanent collections Witherspoon Mus., Cleve. Mus., Mus. Fine Arts, Boston, Brandeis U. Art Mus., Chase-Manhattan Bank, A.D. White Mus. Cornell U., Nat. Gallery Art, Muzium Negara, Kuala Lumpur, Mead Mus. Amherst Coll., Glen S. Janss Collection Boise Art Mus., FMC Corp. Chgo., Archdiocese of Baton Rouge, Fidelity Bank Collection, Phila., Sierra Club; curator of juried exhbn. Bowery Gallery, 1996, "Poetic Dimensions in the Modern Still Life," Emily Lowe Gallery, Hofstra Mus., 2005. Recipient Rsch. award CUNY, 1970-71, 75-76, 82, 86-87, 88-89, Fed. Govt. Commn., through Interior Dept. for Bicentennial, 1974, award Rockefeller Found. at Bellagio, 1989, Altman Figure Painting prize Nat. Acad. Biennial, 1995; asst. Cornell U., 1955-57; L.C. Tiffany grantee, 1959; Fulbright fellow to Italy, 1962-63; Yaddo fellow, 1960, 62; Ingram Merrill fellow, 1975-76, 84, 90; J.S. Guggenheim fellow, 1989-90; NEA sr. grantee, 1983, 87-88; juror NEA, 1984, N.Y. State Coun. on Arts, 1985; Altman prize for Figure Painting 170th Annual Exhbn. of Nat. Acad., 1995, vis. Artist U. Pa., 1997, juror Bowery Gallery Exhbn., 1996, vis. disting. prof. Am. U., 1994-95, Washington. Mem. NAD (Proctor Portrait Prize Biennial Exhbn. 1993, academician, 1994-). Office Fax: 212-855-4806.*

LADERMAN, KATHLEEN ANN, magazine publisher; b. Inglewood, Calif; d. Allan and Brenda Ann Laderman. BA, Pomona Coll., 1985; MA, U. So. Calif., 1987. Assoc. McAnally Publs., La Canada, Calif., 1987-92; pres., pub., editor-in-chief KAL Publs., Inc., Anaheim, Calif., 1992—. Editl. adviser novel Into the Deep, 1998. Editor Automotive Booster mag., Oil and Automotive Mktg. News. Com. mem. Mt. Wilson Vista coun. Girl Scouts U.S.A., 1985-95; decorator La Canada Tournament of Roses Assn., 1977—; bd. dirs. So. Calif. Petroleum Industry Charity Assn., Anaheim Hills, Calif., 1995—; mem., event chmn. Verdugo Hills Chorus, 1996-2001, Herbolites Chorus, 2001—, Odyssey Quartet, 1998—. Mem. Automotive Booster Club L.A. (bd. dirs. 1990—, Mem. of Yr. award 1991). Avocations: photography, barbershop singing, travel. Office: KAL Publs Inc 559 S Harbor Blvd Ste A Anaheim CA 92805-4525

LADHA-KARMALI, SHAINOOR, lawyer; arrived in U.S., 1982; d. Akbarali Fazal Ladha and Zaibunisha Ladha Nanji; m. Sulaiman Karmali, Aug. 30, 1991. BS in Psychology cum laude, U. Wash., 1991; JD cum laude, Seattle U., 1998. Bar: Fla. 1998. Staff atty. Adventist Health System, Winter Park, Fla., 1999—. Mem. med. ethics. com. Fla. Hosp., Orange City. Mediator Shia Imamli Ismaili Reconciliation and Arbitration Bd., Orlando, Fla., 2002—05; search and rescue Cert. Emergency Response Team, Orlando, 2002—04. Mem.: Ctrl. Fla. Assn. Women Lawyers. Democrat. Muslim. Avocations: outdoor activities, going to beach, hiking. Office: Adventist Health System 111 N Orlando Ave Winter Park FL 32789 Office Fax: 407-975-1414. Business E-Mail: shainoor.ladha-karmali@ahss.org.

LADIK, STEVEN M., lawyer; b. Chgo., Mar. 15, 1953; m. A. Robin Ridgeway, Nov. 3, 2001. BA, North Tex. State U., 1977; JD, So. Meth. U., 1983. Bar: Tex. 1983, US Dist. Ct. No. Dist. Tex. 1983, US Ct. Appeals 5th Cir. 1983. Ptnr. Gardere & Wynne, Dallas; shareholder Jenkens & Gilchrist, P.C., Dallas, 2000—, firm leader immigration practice group. Mem.: Am. Immigration Law Found. (pres. 2004—), Am. Immigration Lawyers Assn. (pres. 2001—02, past chair Tex. chpt.), State Bar Tex. Office: Jenkens & Gilchrist PC Ste 3200 1445 Ross Ave Dallas TX 75202-2799 Office Phone: 214-855-4117. Office Fax: 214-855-4300. Business E-Mail: sladik@jenkens.com.

LADIN, EUGENE, communications company executive; b. N.Y.C., Oct. 26, 1927; s. Nat and Mae (Cohen) L.; m. Millicent Dolly Frankel, June 27, 1948; children: Leslie Hope, Stephanie Joy. BBA, Pace U., 1956; MBA, Air Force Inst. Tech., 1959; postgrad., George Washington U., 1966—69. Cost engr. Rand Corp., Santa Monica, Calif., 1960—62; mgr. cost and econ. analysis Northrop Corp., Hawthorne, Calif., 1962—66; dir. fin. planning Comm. Satellite Corp., Washington, 1966—70; treas., chief fin. and adminstrv. officer Landis & Gyr, Inc., Elmsford, NY, 1970—76; v.p., treas., comptr. P.R. Telephone Co., San Juan, 1976—77; v.p. fin. Comtech Telecomm. Corp., Smithtown, NY, 1977—; acting pres. Comtech Antenna Corp., St. Cloud, Fla., 1978—80; chmn., CEO Telephone Interconnect Enterprises/Sunshine Telephone Co., Balt., Md. and Orlando, 1980—82; pres. Ladin and Assocs., Cons. and Commodity Traders, Maitland, Fla., 1982—84; pres., CFO Braintech Inc., South Plainfield, NJ, 1984; sr. v.p. fin., CFO Teltec Savs. Comm. Co., Miami, Fla., 1984—88; CFO Hurwitz Group Inc., North Miami Beach, Fla., 1988—91; cons. pvt. practice, 1991—98; v.p., CFO Ginsite Materials, Inc., Plantation, Fla., 1998—99. Assoc. prof. acctg. So. Ill. U., East St. Louis, 1960; assoc. prof. bus. U. Md., 1969-70; adj. prof. George Washington U., 1969-70; vis. prof. acctg. Pace U., 1970; cons. E. Ladin, Pembroke Pines, Fla., 1999—. Served to capt. USAF, 1951-60. Decorated Air Force Commendation medal; recipient Air Force Outstanding Unit award. Avocations: golf, sailing. Home and Office: 13355 SW 16th Ct Apt 401E Hollywood FL 33027-2429 Office Phone: 954-437-4886. *An individual must have sufficient self esteem to sustain the courage of his convictions, a high degree of professional integrity, and his individual character. Society has adopted a philosophy of "walk the middle road".*

LADISCH, MICHAEL R., engineering educator; b. Upper Darby, Pa., Jan. 15, 1950; s. Rolf Karl and Brigitte M. L.; m. Christine Schmitz, July 26, 1975; children: Sarah, Mark. BSChemE, Drexel U., Phila., 1973; MSChemE, Purdue U., 1974, PhD in Chem. Engring., 1977. Rsch. engr. Lab. Renewable Resources Engring. and dept. chem. engring. Purdue U., West Lafayette, Ind., 1977-78, asst. prof. food and agrl. engring., 1978-81, assoc. prof., 1981-85, prof., 1985-2000, disting. prof., 2000—. Dir. Lab Renewable Resources, Eng., 1999—. Contbr. articles to profl. jours.; patentee in field. Chmn. com. on bioprocess engring. Nat. Rsch. Coun., 1991—92. Recipient U.S. Presdl. Young Investigator award NSF, 1984, Johnson Rsch. award ACS, 2002. Fellow Am. Inst. Med. and Biol. Engrs., U.S. Nat. Acad. Engring; mem. AIChE (Food, Pharm., and Bioengring. Rsch. award 2001), Am. Chem. Soc. (librarian 1982-84, chmn.-elect 1985—86, program chmn. 1985-86, past chmn. 1986—87, coord. long range program 1990—94, Van Lanen award BIOT div. 1990, W.H. Peterson award Microbiol. div. 1977, Agrl. Rsch. award from Purdue U. 1985), Am. Soc. Agrl. Engrs. Office: Purdue U LORRE 500 Central Dr West Lafayette IN 47907 Office Phone: 765-494-7022. Business E-Mail: ladisch@purdue.edu.

LADJEVARDI, HABIB, historian; b. Tehran, Iran, May 28, 1938; came to U.S., 1950; s. Seyed Mahmoud and Tahereh (Kashani) L.; m. Mina Nassirzadeh, Aug. 3, 1962 (div. June 1979); children: Mahmoud, Mariam, Leila. BS, Yale U., 1961; MBA, Harvard U., 1963; DPhil, Oxford U., 1981. Personnel dir. Behshahr Ind. Group, Tehran, 1963-65, mktg. dir., 1966-69; pres. Paxan Corp., Tehran, 1969-70; chmn. bd. dirs. Container Corp. of Iran, 1969-79; founder, v.p. Iran Ctr. Mgmt. Studies, Tehran, 1970-79; sr. rsch. assoc. Harvard U. Bus. Sch., Cambridge, Mass., 1980-81; rsch. assoc. Harvard U. Ctr. for Middle Eastern Studies, 1981—, assoc. prof., 1981-87, dir. Iranian oral history project, 1981—. Mem. acceptance coms. Tehran Stock Exch., 1973-76; lectr. Iran Ctr. for Mgmt. Studies, 1975-79; vis. fellow Oxford (Eng.) Ctr. Mgmt. Studies, 1976-79; v.p. exec. coun. Harvard U. Bus. Sch., 1978-79; exec. sec. Soc. for Iranian Studies, Cambridge, 1982-87; chmn. Iranian Studies Harvard U. Ctr. for Middle Eastern Studies, 1990—, chmn. pubs. com., 1990—. Author: Labor Unions and Autocracy in Iran, 1985, Guide to the Iranian Oral History Collection, 1993, Memoirs of Hamid Kadjar, 1996, Memoirs of M.E. Amirteymour, 1997, Memoirs of Abdolmajid Madjidi, 1998, Memoirs of Fatemeh Pakravan, 1998, Memoirs of Jafar Sharif-Emami, 1999, Memoirs of M.A. Modjtahedi, 2000, Memoirs of Mehdi Hairi-Yazdi, 2001, Memoirs of Mahmoud Foroughi, 2003; contbr. articles to profl. jours., chapters to books. Mem. coun. of state Adminstrv. and Employment Affairs of Iran, 1972-76; dir. devel. and investment Bank of Iran, 1972-79; mem. ctrl. coun. Pres. of Univs. and Colls. of Iran, 1971-78; pres. Tahereh Found., Cambridge, Mass., 1982—. NEH grantee, 1984-87. Mem. Am. Hist. Assn., Young Presidents Orgn., Acad. Polit. Sci., N.Y. Acad. Scis., Iranian Assn. of Boston (founder, pres. 1988-91), Yale U. Class Coun., Yale Club of N.Y. Democrat. Avocations: skiing, grandchildren, gardening.

LADJEVARDI, HAMID, portfolio manager; b. Tehran, Iran, June 11, 1948; arrived in U.S., 1948; s. Ahmad and Banoo (Barzin) Ladjevardi; children: Adella, Lilly. BA in Econs., BA in Polit. Sci., U. Calif., Berkeley, 1971; MBA, Harvard U., 1973. Dep. mng. dir. Behshahr Indsl. Group, Tehran, 1974-79; vice-chmn., fin. dir. Akam Group of Cos., Tehran, 1975-79; investment mgr., v.p. Morgan Stanley & Co., N.Y.C., 1980-92; mgr. Baltic Fund 1 LLC, NY, 1994—2002, Am. Baltic Investments, 2002—. Instr. Fairleigh Dickinson U., Rutherford, NJ, 1984. Co-chmn. U.S. Baltic Found.; trustee Zimmerli Art Mus. Mem.: Carnegie Coun. Ethics and Internat. Affairs, Fgn. Policy Assn., Nat. Arts Club, Harvard Club, U.S. Senatorial Club. Home: 284 Lafayette St Apt #5D New York NY 10012 Office Phone: 0113717222275. E-mail: hamid@americanbaltic.com.

LADNER, BENJAMIN, academic administrator; b. Mobile, Ala. m. Nancy Bullard Ladner; 4 children. BA, Baylor U.; BD, Southern Seminary; PhD, Duke U.; D (hon.), Elizabethtown (Pa.) Coll., SookMyung Women's U., South Korea. Prof. dept. philosophy and religious studies U. N.C., Greensboro; pres. Nat. Faculty of Humanities, Arts & Scis., Atlanta, Am. U., Washington, 1994—. Bd. dir. chair Patriot League Coun. of Presidents; chair, bd. trustee Consortium of Universities of the Washington Met. Area; mem. Com. for Econ. Develop. Bd., Nat. Assn. for Independent Coll. and U., NCAA Divsn. I. Achievements include leading Am. U. team by providing leadership in the design, establishment, and operation of the Am. U. of Sharjah (AUS) in United Emirates since its inception in 1997. Office: Am Univ 4400 Massachusetts Ave NW Washington DC 20016-8060

LADOW, C. STUART, financial consultant; b. Warren, Pa., Apr. 21, 1925; s. Clyde and Glendine (Bentley) LaD.; m. Donna Elizabeth Miller, Aug. 21, 1993; 1 child, Paul Stuart. BA, Cornell U., 1947. With Gen. Electric Co., 1947-50; mgr. N.Y. region Gen. Electric Credit Corp., N.Y.C., 1950-80, v.p. Stamford, Conn., 1971-80; pres. GECC Fin. Services, 1975-78, Color Tyme TV Rental div. Curtis Mathes Corp., Athens, Tex., 1980; sr. v.p. Yegen Assocs., Inc., Paramus, N.J., 1981-85, exec. v.p., 1985-87; pres. Yegen Equity Loan Corp., Paramus, N.J., 1987; fin. svcs. cons. Allison Park, Pa., 1988-99; dir. Nat. Capital Holdings, Allison Park, Pa., 1997-98; ret., 1999. Bd. dirs. Puritan Life Ins. Co., Providence. V.p., bd. dirs. Jr. Achievement of Stamford, Inc., 1973-80; exec. budget com., chmn. budget panel United Way of Stamford, 1973-80; chmn. Stamford chpt. Am. Cancer Soc., 1977; pres. Spring Meadow Condominium Assn., Wyckoff, N.J., 1983, trustee, 1983-88; moderator Emmanuel Bapt. Ch., Ridgewood, N.J., 1985-86; trustee North Hills Community Baptist Ch., 1988-91; dir. Hampton Twsp. Mcpl. Authority, Allison Park, Pa., 1991-97, dir., treas. Baptist Homes of Western Pa., 1992-98, pres. Arbors Homeowners Assn., Allison Park, 1992-93; pres. Cornell U. Class of 1947, 1992-97. Recipient Cmty. Svc. award Gen. Electric Credit Corp., 1976. Mem. Nat. Second Mortgage Assn. (pres. 1987-88, Outstanding Service award, Meritorious Svc. award 1989), Nat. Consumer Finance Assn. (certificate of appreciation), Masons, Shriners, Cornell Club of Pitts. Republican. Baptist. Home and Office: 4211 Latour Ct Allison Park PA 15101-2968 *Ours is a great country that deserves the devotion and strong support of those who call it home. There can be few satisfactions in life greater than assisting in the moral, spiritual and career growth of those whom we have the opportunity to know and possibly influence.*

LADUE, FERNE, retired education educator; b. NYC; d. Irving Harold and Sylvia Newman Spielman; children: Margaret LaDue McGonigle, David. BA in lit., U. Mich., 1944—46; MA in english, Lehman Coll., 1972—76. Copywriter JC Penney, NYC, 1950—52; ex dir. Riverdale Cmty. Coll., 1972—2003; adj. instr. Bronx Cmty. Coll., 1972—92. Bd. dirs. PS 81 After Sch. Ctr., 1985—86; mem. Cmty. Bd. Bronx, 1985—2003. Recipient Avery Hopwood award for poetry, Ann Arbor, Mich., 1945; Mabel Louise Robinson fellowship, 1968. Personal E-mail: ferneladue@yahoo.com.

LADWIG, HAROLD ALLEN, neurologist; b. Manilla, Iowa, May 11, 1922; s. Ernest and Iva Marie (Allen) L.; m. Marjorie Lois Foster, June 26, 1946; children: Stephen H., Rosemary A. BA, U. Iowa, 1942, MD, 1947. Intern St. Joseph Hosp., Sioux City, Iowa, 1947-48; pvt. practice U. Minn., 1948-49, resident, 1949-50; pvt. practice Nebr., 1954-83, 1983—; pres. Omaha Neurol. Clinic, 1972-83. Contbr. articles to profl. jours. Bd. dirs. Boys and Girls Club, Wilson, NC, 1995—, Salvation Army, Wilson, 1996-, Country Drs. Mus., Bailey, NC, 1995-2002, Mental Health Bd., Wilson, 1995—. Comdr. USNR, 1950-52. Fellow ACP, Am. Acad. Neurology; mem. AMA, Am. Assn. Electrodiagnostic Medicine, Am. Soc. Electroencephalography and Neurophysiology, Wilson County Med. Soc. (sec. 1993, v.p. 1994, pres. 1995), Wilson Meml. Hosp. Found. (pres. 1993—), Douglas County Med. Soc. (exec. bd. 1960-63), Kiwanis (pres. Wilson chpt. 1995, Kiwanian of Yr. award 1992-93), Phi Beta Kappa, Beta Beta Beta. Methodist. Avocation: computers. Home: PO Box 3164 Wilson NC 27895-3164 E-mail: hladwig@nc.rr.com.

LAESSIG, ROBERT H., artist; b. West N.Y., N.J., Nov. 15, 1913; s. Ernest and Martha (Weigert) L.; m. Isolde Helene Grosser, June 6, 1942; children: Thomas, Constance. B.F.A., Textile Sch., Pauen, Germany; postgrad., Art Students League, N.Y.C. Sr. art cons. Am. Greetings, Inc.; painting represented in collections Norfolk Mus. Art, Cleve. Mus. Art, Springfield Inst. Fine Art, Denver Mus. Art; designer personal Christmas cards Pres. Lyndon B. Johnson, 1964-66, Gov. Celeste, Ohio, 1983-90; works exhibited 100th anniversary Met. Mus., N.Y.C.; combat artist 13th Air Force; illustrator From the Fijis Through the Philippines; instr. condr. seminars. Pub. of prints Art Beats, Salt Lake City; assoc. with Gallery One, Mentor, Ohio. Served with USAAF, 1942-46. Recipient award Am. Watercolor Soc., 1979, 81, 82, 83, award Ky. Watercolor Soc., 1984, Adirondack Nat. Show, Old Forge, N.Y., 1982, 83, Ohio Watercolor Soc., 1979-85, Pitts Watercolor Soc., 1981, award Mainstreams Marietta, Ohio, 1983, Lifetime Achievement award, Fairmount Ctr., Ohio, 2003. Mem. NAD (assoc. 1964-94, academician, 1994-), Am. Watercolor Soc., Ohio Watercolor Soc. (Gold medal 1987, 88, other awards 1979-87), Dolphin Club. Lutheran.*

LAESSIG, RONALD HAROLD, preventive medicine and pathology educator, state official; b. Marshfield, Wis., Apr. 4, 1940; s. Harold John and Ella Louise L.; m. Joan Margaret Spreda, Jan. 29, 1966; 1 child, Elizabeth Susan. BS, U. Wis., Stevens Point, 1962; PhD, U. Wis., 1965. Cert. chem. chemist Nat. Registry Cert. Chemists, 1968. Jr. faculty Princeton (N.J.) U., 1966; chief clin. chemistry Wis. State Lab. Hygiene, Madison, 1966-80, dir., 1980—; asst. prof. preventive medicine U. Wis., Madison, 1966-72, assoc. prof., 1972-76, prof., 1976—, prof. pathology, 1980—. Cons. Ctr. Disease Control, Atlanta; dir. Nat. Com. for Clin. Lab. Stds., Villanova, Pa., 1977-80; chmn. invitro diagnostic products adv. com. FDA, 1974-75; mem. rev. com. Nat. Bur. Stds., 1983-86; bd. sci. counselors Nat. Ctr. Environ. Health COC Ga., 2004-; legis. coun., State of Wis., 2003-04; Chan Pub. Health Advisory Com., Wis., 2003-, mem. 1998-. Mem. editl. bd. Med. Electronics, 1970—, Analytical Chemistry, 1970-76, Health Lab. Sci., 1970—; contbr. articles to profl. jours. Mem. State of Wis. Tech. Com. Alcohol and Traffic Safety, 1970-88. Recipient Excellence in Advocacy award, March of Dimes, 2001; Sloan Found. grantee, 1966; recipient numerous grants. Mem. CDC, APHA (Difco award 1974), Am. Assn. Clin. Chemistry (chmn. safety com. 1984-86, bd. dirs. 1986-89, Natelson award 1989, Contbns. Svc. to Profession award 1990, Reiner award 1998, Eiler award 1999), Am. Soc. for Med. Tech., Nat. Com. Clin. Lab. Stds. (pres. 1980-82, bd. dirs. 1984-87), Assn. of Pub. Health Labs. (chmn. environ. health com. 2001-04, Gold Std. Pub. Health Excellence award), Nat. Ctr. Environ. Health (bd. counselors 2004-), Sigma Xi. Avocation: woodworking. Office: State Lab Hygiene 465 Henry Mall Madison WI 53706-1578 Business E-Mail: rhl@mail.slh.wisc.edu. *If you are doing something you really enjoy and it affords you the opportunity to really help your fellow man--you're really blessed (like I am).*

LAETTNER, CHRISTIAN DONALD, professional basketball player; b. Angola, N.Y., Aug. 17, 1969; Student, Duke U. Basketball player Minn. Timberwolves, 1992-1995, Atlanta Hawks, 1995-98, Detroit Pistons, 1998-99, Dallas Mavericks, 2000—01, Wash. Wizards, 2001—04, Dallas Mavericks, 2004—. Named Most Outstanding Player in NCAA Divsn. 1A Tournament, 1991, Sporting News Coll. Player of Yr., 1992, Naismith award, 1992, Wooden award, 1992; mem. Gold medal Winning Olympic Team, Barcelona, Spain, 1992. mem. NCAA Nat. I Championship Team, 1991, 1992. Office: c/o Dallas Mavericks The Pavillion 2909 Taylor St Dallas TX 75226

LA FALCE, JOHN JOSEPH, former congressman, lawyer; b. Buffalo, N.Y., Oct. 6, 1939; s. Dominic E. and Catherine M. (Stasio) La F.; m. Patricia Fisher, 1979. BS, Canisius Coll., 1961; JD, Villanova U., 1964; LLD (hon.), Niagara U., 1979, St. Johns U., 1989; LHD (hon.), Canisius Coll., 1990; LLD (hon.), Villanova U., 1991. Bar: N.Y. 1964. Mem. N.Y. State Senate, 1971—72, N.Y. State Assembly, 1973—74, 94th-107th Congresses representing 29 dist. N.Y., 1975—2003; ranking minority mem. House Banking & Fin. Svcs. Com., Washington. Capt. adj. gen. corps U.S. Army, 1965—67. Democrat.

LAFARGE, ALBERT, literary agent; s. W.E.R. and Ann LaFarge. MA, Columbia U., 1992. Prin. Albert LaFarge Lit. Agy., Boston, 2003—. Editor: (anthology) The Essential William H. Whyte. Office: Albert LaFarge Literary Agency E-mail: a.lafarge@netzero.com.

LA FARGE, TIMOTHY, retired plant geneticist; b. N.Y.C., Mar. 14, 1930; s. Louis Bancel and Hester Alida (Emmet) La F.; m. Anne Blackstone, Oct. 16, 1960 (div. Mar. 1964); m. Frances Madelyne Holst, Aug. 6, 1966 (dec. 1992); 1 child, Jason Emmet; m. Nkem R. Salako, Dec. 4, 1993 (div. Oct. 1998); m. Frances W. Stott, Sept. 5, 2002. BA in Dance, Black Mountain Coll., 1952; BSc in Forestry, U. Maine, 1964; M in Forestry, Yale U., 1965; PhD, Mich. State U., 1971. Forestry aid Forest Svc., Orono, Maine, 1962-64; lab. technician geology dept. Yale U., New Haven, 1965; rsch. forester USDA Forest Svc., Macon, Ga., 1965-69, plant geneticist Southea. Sta., 1970-82, plant geneticist Nat. Forest Sys. Atlanta, 1982-2000; consulting assoc. Daniels and Assocs., Inc., Forest Genetics Cons., 2000. Contbr. articles to profl. jours, rsch. papers in field. Recipient Certs. of Merit, USDA Forest Svc., Atlanta, 1986, 88. Mem. AAAS, Soc. Am. Foresters (chair Bay area chpt. 2003-2004). Republican. Achievements include demonstration that back-crossing and hybridization between shortleaf pine and loblolly pine can effectively produce fast-growing back-cross hybrids that are resistant to fusiform rust; application of Best Linear Prediction to analysis of unbalanced or messy progeny test data. Home: 863 Foerster St San Francisco CA 94127-2307 Office Phone: 415-337-0304. Personal E-mail: timlaf@comcast.net.

LAFARGUE, MELBA FAYE FULMER, credit manager, realtor; b. Baton Rouge, July 13, 1937; d. Harry Geon and Alice (Peters) Fulmer; m. Leo Wallace LaFargue, Aug. 13, 1953 (div. Aug. 1983). BS in Acctg., La. State U., 1959; postgrad., Am. Sch. Banking, 1962. Cert. fin. mgr., realtor. Co-owner Newspaper Crossroads, Kinder, La., 1958-74; loan officer Great So. Mktg. and Loan, 1959-60; office mgr. Savant Constrn. Co., Kinder, 1960-74; cons. Baton Rouge Recreation and Park Commn., 1975-77; realtor Sherwood Realty, Inc., Baton Rouge, 1974—; service mgr. Campus Fed. Credit Union, Baton Rouge, 1980—. Fin. counselor Displaced Homemakers, Baton Rouge, 1983. Mem. Women in Politics, Baton Rouge; cons. fin. Cath. Daus. Am., 1960—. Mem. Nat. Assn. of Bank Women, Nat. Assn. Realtors, Am. Mgmt. Assn., Investors Assn. Democrat. Roman Catholic. Office: AmSouth Investment Svcs Inc 201 NW Railroad Ave Hammond LA 70401-3249 Home: 6323 Westridge Dr Baton Rouge LA 70817-3452

LAFAVORE, MICHAEL J., editor-in-chief; b. Portland, Maine, Apr. 28, 1952; s. Joseph T. and Marion (Brown) L.; m. Trieste A. Kennedy; children: Nico, Alec. BA in English, U. Maine, 1975. Reporter Jour. Tribune, Biddeford, Maine, 1975-79; sr. editor Organic Gardening, Emmaus, Pa., 1979-84, Practical Homeowner, Emmaus, Pa., 1984-88; exec. editor Men's Health, Emmaus, Pa., 1988-96, editor-in-chief, 1996—2000, TV Guide, NYC, 2003—04. Screening com. Nat. Mag. Awards, NYC, 1994; cons. in the field. Author: The Home Gym, 1978, Radon: The Invisible Threat, 1985; editor: Men's Health Advisor, 1992-93. Recipient Mont award Photo Design Mag., 1989, Mental Health Media award Nat. Mental Health Assn., 1991, Award for Excellence, Men's Fashion Assn., 1992, 95; named Editor of Yr., Advertising Age, 1995, Internat. Editor of Yr., Fgn. Press, 1998.

LAFAYE, TERI KIRKHAM, literature and language educator, writer; b. Ruston, La., July 24, 1960; d. Kenneth Calvin and Christene Marie Piker; m. Kenneth Barron Kirkham, Aug. 27, 1986. Student, La. Tech U., 1990—92; BA, Cumberland U., 1996; instr. cert., Stephen F. Austin U., 2000. Cert. Tex. State Bd. Edn., 2000. English, spl. edn. tchr. West Sabine Indep. Sch. Dist., Pineland, Tex., 1998—99; English tchr. Colmesneil (Tex.) Indep. Sch. Dist., 2000—. Tchr.'s aide Brookeland (Tex.) Indep. Sch. Dist., 1996—98. Author: (children's book) Tattle Tom, (poetry) Inferences (Best Poem award, Internat. Libr. Poetry, 2003), Thankfulness in Aftermath (1st pl. award, 14th Annual Azalea Festival, 2003), A Positive (2d pl. award, 2003), Yesterday's Rose (3d pl. award, 14th Annual Azalea Festival, 2003), 911 (Celebration of Poets award, Creative Comm. Inc., 2003), Orchestrated Serenade (Best Poems award, Internat. Libr. Poets, 1996); lyricist: On & On; author: (poetry) Acknowledgement (Best Poems award, 1990). Scholar, Stephen F. Austin U., 1999—2000. Mem.: Irlen Inst. (licentiate; screener 2001—), BMI (life), Omicron Kappa Delta (life). Democrat-Npl. Avocations: drawing, writing, guitar. Office: Colmesneil Indep Sch Dist PO Box 37 FM Hwy 256W Colmesneil TX 75938 Office Phone: 409-837-5272. Personal E-mail: parfaye@sabinenet.com. E-mail: tkirkham_1@hotmail.com.

LAFEBER, WALTER FREDERICK, historian, educator, writer; b. Walkerton, Ind., Aug. 30, 1933; s. Ralph N. and Helen (Lidecker) LaF.; m. Sandra Gould, Sept. 11, 1955; children: Scott Nichols, Suzanne Margaret Kahl. BA, Hanover Coll., 1955; MA, Stanford, 1956; PhD, U. Wis., 1959. Asst. prof. history Cornell U., 1959-63, assoc. prof., 1963-67, prof., 1967—. Mem. adv. com. hist. div. State Dept., 1971-75; lectr. in field. Author: The New Empire...1860-1898, 1963, 2d edit., 1998, America, Russia and the Cold War, 1966, 9th edit., 2002, The Panama Canal, The Crisis in Historical Perspective, 1978, expanded edit., 1979, 2d edit., 1989, Inevitable Revolutions: The U.S. in Central America, 1983, 2d edit., 1992, The American Age...1750 to the Present, 1989, 2d edit., 1994, The American Search for Opportunity, 1865-1913, 1993, The Clash: U.S. Japanese Relations Throughout History, 1997, Michael Jordan and the New Globalism Capitalism, 1999, 2d edit., 2002, The Deadly Bet: LBJ, Vietnam, and the 1968 Election, 2005; co-author: The American Century, 5th edit., 1997, America in Vietnam, 1985; editor: John Quincy Adams and American Continental Empire, 1965, America in the Cold War, 1969, also others; co-editor: Behind the Throne, Essays in Honor of Fred Harvey Harrington, 1993; mem. editorial adv. bd.: Polit. Sci. Quar.; cons., appeared on PBS programs on Theodore Roosevelt, Harry Truman, 1900, War of 1898 and others. Recipient Gustavus Myers prize, 1985, Bancroft prize, 1998; Guggenheim fellow, 1990. Mem.: Soc. Historians of Am. Fgn. Rels. (pres. 1999—2000), Am. Acad. Arts and Scis., The Hist. Soc., Am. Hist. Assn. (Albert Beveridge prize 1962), Orgn. Am. Historians (Hawley prize 1998). Office: Cornell U Dept History McGraw Hall Ithaca NY 14853-4601 Business E-Mail: WFL3@cornell.edu.

LAFER, FRED SEYMOUR, data processing company executive; b. Passaic, N.J., Mar. 17, 1929; s. Abraham David and Pauline (Braer) L.; m. Barbara Bernstein, Apr. 4, 1954; children: Deborah, Gordon, Diana. BIE, NYU, 1950, JD, 1961; LHD (hon.), William Paterson Coll., 1987. Bar: N.J. 1961. Sec. to Justice Hayden Proctor, N.J. Supreme Ct., 1961-62; partner firm Hoffman Humphreys Lafer, Wayne, N.J., 1962-67; sec., gen. counsel Automatic Data Processing, Inc., Clifton, N.J., 1967-97, v.p., 1968-81, sr. v.p., 1981-96; pres. N.J. Nets Profl. Basketball Team, 1984. Pres. Taub Found., 1996—. Chmn. United Jewish Appeal Fedn. North Jersey, 1973-74; pres. Jewish Fedn. North Jersey, 1976-77; v.p. N.J. Bd. Edn., 1967-68; bd. dirs. Chilton Meml. Hosp., Pompton Plains, N.J., 1970-72; trustee William Paterson Coll., 1974—, vice-chmn. bd., 1977, chmn. bd., 1978-80; pres. Am. Friends of Hebrew U., 1985-89; exec. com. Washington Inst. Near East Policy, sec.-treas., 1993-99, pres., 2000—. Served to lt. USAF, 1951-52. Recipient honorary doctorate Hebrew U. Jerusalem, 1995. Mem. Computer Law Assn. (pres. 1972-74), Assn. Data Processing Service Orgns. (chmn. 1983), ABA Office: c/o Taub Found 300 Frank M Burr Blvd Teaneck NJ 07666

LA FERLE, CARRIE, advertising executive, educator; BA in Sociology, U. Western Ont., London, 1989; MA in Advt., Mich. State U., 1990; PhD in Advt., U. of Tex., 1998. Diploma in mktg. comms. Internat. Advt. Assn. With account svcs. TBWA/Chiat Day, Toronto, 1990—92; fgn. corr. JCM Enterprise, Tokyo, 1992—95; grad. asst. U. of Texas, Austin, 1995—97, lectr., 1997—98; asst. prof. Mich. State U., East Lansing, 1999—. Consulting faculty mem. Women and Internat. Devel. Program, East Lansing, 2003—. Contbr. articles to profl. jours. Grantee, Intramural Rsch. Grant Program, Mich. State U., 2002—03. Mem.: Internat. Advt. Assn., Am. Mktg. Assn., Soc. for Consumer Psychology, Am. Acad. of Advt. (sec. exec. com. 2003—, editor newsletter 1999—2002, rsch. fellow 2001—02), Phi Kappa Phi. Office: Mich State U Dept Advt East Lansing MI 48824 E-mail: laferlec@msu.edu.

LAFERNEY, MICHAEL C., mental health nurse, mental health counselor; b. St. Louis, Mo., Jan. 5, 1954; s. Clyde M and Shirley M (Carney) LaFerney; m. Carolyn A. Sukus, Feb. 14, 1978; children: Michael S, Adam P. CAGS, Bridgewater State Coll., 1983—89. Registered Naturopath Wash. DC, 2002; RN, Ma., 1987, APRN, BC Clinical Specialist in Adult Psychiatric and Mental Health, ANCC, 1987; Licensed Mental Health Counselor Mass., 1993. Clin. nurse specialist Arbour Sr. Care, Rockland, Mass., 1999—; exec. don services Bridgewater State Hosp., Mass., 2002. Dir. of partial hosp. programs St. Joseph's Health Svc. of RI, Providence, 1995—98; adj. faculty Bay State Coll., 2002, 03; adj. faculty psychology Quincy Coll., 2003—05. Contbr. articles to profl. jours. E-4 USAF, 1973—77, Lackland AFB, TX, nurse officer, capt. USAR, 1982—96. Recipient Listing-A Values -Based Program For Aging and Chronically Ill Adults, Cath. Health Assn. of the U.S, 1998, Profl. Devel. award, Fed. Emergency Mgmt. Agy., Mass. Emergency Mgmt. Agy., 2003. Mem.: Henry George Inst. (corr. Grad. of Inst. in Polit. Economy 2003). Independent. Roman Catholic. Achievements include showed that Geriatric patients graduate at same rate dispelling myth that older patients don't complete treatment (awarded for study). Avocations: music, travel. Home: 88 Pickens St Lakeville MA 02347 Office: Arbour Senior Care 100 Ledgewood Pl Ste 202 Rockland MA Personal E-mail: laferney@hotmail.com.

LAFEVER, HOWARD NELSON, botanist, educator, geneticist; b. Wayne County, Ind., May 13, 1938; s. Samuel L. and Flossie B. (Ellis) L.; m. Kay M. Schutz, Aug. 30, 1958; children: Julie, Jeff BS, Purdue U., 1959, MS, 1961, PhD, 1963. Instr. Wis. State U., LaCrosse, 1963; assoc. prof. Purdue U., West Lafayette, Ind., 1963; research geneticist USDA-Agrl. Research Service, Starkville, Miss., 1963-65; plant breeder, prof. agronomy Ohio State U., Ohio Agr. Research and Devel. Ctr., Wooster, 1965-91; owner Sunbeam Extract Co., 1991—. Patentee Becker, Cardinal, Dynasty, Freedom Hopewell, Bravo and Daisy wheats and developer of 40 other small grain varieties; contbr. numerous articles to profl. jours. Fellow Am. Soc. Agronomy (bd. dirs. 1982-84, assoc. editor 1982-85); mem. Assn. Ofcl. Seed Certifying Agys., Ohio Seed Improvement Assn. (dir. 1968-83, grantee 1975-91). Presbyterian. Avocations: woodworking, golf. E-mail: hnlafever@aol.com.

LAFFERTY, JOYCE G. ZVONAR, retired elementary school educator; b. Balt., July 9, 1931; d. George S. and Carolyn M. (Bothe) Greener; children: Barbara Z. Gunter, John G. Zvonar, David A. Zvonar. BS, Towson State U., 1963; M equivalent, Md. Inst. Coll. Art, 1978. Cert. tchr., Md. Tchr., dept. chmn. Hampstead Hill Jr. High Annex, Balt.; tchr. Forest Park Sr. High, Balt.; tchr., dept. chmn. Roland Park Mid. Sch., Balt. Mem. Nat. Art Edn. Assn., Internat. Soc. Artists, Balt. Tchrs. Union. Home: 1225 Tetbury Ln Austin TX 78748

LAFFERTY, RICHARD THOMAS, architect; b. Allentown, Pa., Dec. 12, 1932; s. Arthur M. and Emily (May) L.; m. Janece Fiore, Apr. 28, 1962; children: Alicia, Hope. BArch, Syracuse U., 1956. Registered architect, N.Y. Draftsman Sweeney-Burden, Architects, Syracuse, 1954-56, Gordon P. Schopfer, AIA, Syracuse, 1959-63; job capt. Sargent, Webster, Crenshaw & Folley, Syracuse, 1963-75, assoc., chief estimator, 1975-88; project architect V.I.P. Archtl. Assocs., Syracuse, 1988-90, assoc., 1989-90; project architect Schopfer Architects, 1990-93; architect Richard T. Lafferty, 1993-94, Fuligni-Fragola Architects, 1994—. Instr. drafting Onondaga Community Coll., Syracuse, 1968-70, instr. codes, 1972-76, curriculum adviser archtl. tech., 1986—; curriculum adviser archtl. tech. SUNY, Delhi, 1984—; mem. N.Y. State Bd. Architecture, 1990-2000, chmn., 1995-96; sec. region II NCARB, 1995-97, mem. code com., 1996-97, A.R.E. com., 1997—. Adv. mem. Onondaga County Plumbi Bd., Syracuse, 1978—; curriculum adviser Nat. Tech. Inst. for Deaf, Rochester, N.Y., 1984—, mem. Uniform Code Syracuse/Watertown Bd. Rev., 1984—; mem. Capitol Dist. Bd. of Rev., 1997—. Served to capt. USAF, 1956-59. Recipient Matthew W. Del Gaudio award, 1983. Mem. AIA (energy com. 1981-85, profl. devel. com. 1981-85), Central N.Y. AIA (treas. 1978-79, pres. 1981, sec. 1989-94, editor newsletter 1978—, chmn. code com. 1983-84, 1989—), N.Y. State Assn. Architects (dir. 1980-84, mem. handicap com. 1983-84, pres. 1987, past pres. 1988, Pres. Medal 1991), N.Y. State Assns. of Professions (pres. 1991). Republican. Roman Catholic. Home and Office: Limeledge and Glover Rds Marcellus NY 13108

LAFFERTY, WILLIAM MICHAEL, lawyer; b. Springfield, Pa., July 4, 1963; s. John Jacob and Joan (Paynter) L.; m. Melissa Suzanne Grubb, Dec. 23, 1995. BSBA, U. Del., 1985; JD, Dickinson Sch. Law, 1989. Bar: Del. 1989, Pa. 1990, U.S. Dist. Ct. Del. Jud. law clk. Del. Ct. of Chancery, Dover, 1989-90; assoc. Morris, Nichols, Arsht & Tunnell, Wilmington, Del., 1990-96, ptnr., 1997—. Republican. Roman Catholic. Office: Morris Nichols Arsht & Tunnell 1201 N Market St Wilmington DE 19801-1147 E-mail: wlafferty@mnat.com.

LAFLEUR, CHRISTOPHER J., ambassador; BA, Oberlin Coll. Diplomat U.S. Embassy, Paris, U.S. Mission to UN, NYC, Am. Inst., Taiwan, 1993—97; mission dep. chief U.S. Embassy, Tokyo, 1997—2001; dir. Indochina affairs US Dept. State, Washington, 1991—93, prin. dep. asst. sec. East Asia and Pacific affairs, 2001—03; Cyrus Vance fellow in diplomatic studies Coun. on Fgn. Rels., Washington, 2003—04; U.S. amb. to Malaysia US Dept. State, Kuala Lampur, 2004—. Office: 4210 Kuala Lumpur Pl Washington DC 20521*

LAFLEUR, KENNETH CHARLES, ophthalmologist; b. Lawtell, La., Aug. 22, 1941; s. Abram George and Mary Irene (Olivier) L.; m. Patricia Ione McNamara, Aug. 3, 1963; children: James Mathew, Suzanne Annette, Caroline Marie. BS, U. So. La., 1963; MD, Tulane U., 1966. Diplomate Am. Bd. Ophthalmology. Intern Hermann Hosp., Houston, 1966-67; ophthalmology resident U. Tex., 1967-70; practice medicine specializing in ophthalmology Opelousas, La., 1972—. Clin. asst. prof. La. State U. Eye Ctr., New Orleans, 1983—. Trustee St. Landry Roman Cath. Ch., Opelousas, 1979-99. Maj. M.C., U.S. Army, 1970-72. Fellow Am. Acad. Ophthalmology, Soc. Mil. Ophthalmologists; mem. Am. Intraocular Implant Soc., Elks, K.C. (Knight of Yr. award 1984). Avocation: fishing. Office: 1110 Dr AC Terrence Blvd Opelousas LA 70570 Office Phone: 337-942-3613. Personal E-mail: klafleur@earthlink.net.

LAFLEY, ALAN G., consumer products company executive; b. Keene, N.H., June 13, 1947; AB, Hamilton Coll., 1969; MBA, Harvard Bus. Sch., 1977. Brand asst. Joy The Proctor & Gamble Co., 1977-78, sales tng. Denver Sales Dist., 1978-80, asst. brand mgr. Tide, 1978-80, brand mgr. Dawn & Ivory Snow, 1980-81, brand mgr. spl. assignment and Ivory Snow, 1981-82, brand mgr. Cheer, 1982-83, assoc. advt. mgr. PS&D Divsn. to advt. mgr., 1983-86, 86-88, gen. mgr. laundry products PS&D Divsn., 1988-91, v.p. laundry & cleaning products, 1991-92, group v.p., pres. laundry and cleaning products, 1992-94, group v.p., pres. Far East Divsn., 1994-95, exec. v.p., pres. Asia Divsn., 1995-98, exec. v.p., pres. N.Am. Divsn., 1998-99, pres. Global Beauty Care & North Am., 1999-2000, pres., CEO, 2000—, chmn., 2002—. Trustee Hamilton Coll., Cin. Playhouse in the Park, Cin. Symphony Orchestra, Cin. Inst. of Fine Arts, The Seven Hills Sch.; past mem. Am. C. of C. in Japan, adv. coun. Schulich Sch. of Bus., York U., Toronto. With USN, 1970-75. Mem. Hamilton Club of So. Ohio, Harvard Club of Cin., Met. Club, Commonwealth Club of Cin. Office: The Proctor & Gamble Co 1 Procter & Gamble Plz Cincinnati OH 45202-3315

LA FOLLETTE, DOUGLAS J., state official; b. Des Moines, June 6, 1940; s. Joseph Henry and Frances (Van der Wilt) LaF. BS, Marietta Coll., 1963; MS, Stanford U., 1964; PhD, Columbia U., 1967. Asst. prof. chemistry and ecology U. Wis.-Parkside, 1969-72; mem. Wis. Senate, 1973-75; sec. state State of Wis., Madison, 1975-79, 83—. Author: Wisconsin's Survival Handbook, 1971, The Survival Handbook, 1991. Mem. Council Econ. Priorities; mem. Lake Michigan Fed., Wis. Environ. Decade, 1971, S.E. Wis. Coalition for Clean Air, Dem. candidate for U.S. Congress, 1970, for Wis. lt. gov., 1978, for U.S. Senate, 1988. Recipient Environ. Quality EPA, 1976, Fulbright Disting. Am. scholar, 2003. Mem. Am. Fedn. Tchrs., Fedn. Am. Scientists, Phi Beta Kappa, Sierra Club (nat. bd. mem.). Democrat. Office: Office Sec State of Wis 30 West Mifflin St PO Box 7848 Madison WI 53707-7848

LA FORCE, JAMES CLAYBURN, JR., economist, educator; b. San Diego, Dec. 28, 1928; s. James Clayburn and Beatrice Maureen (Boyd) La F.; m. Barbara Lea Latham, Sept. 23, 1952; children: Jessica, Allison, Joseph. BA, San Diego State Coll., 1951; MA, UCLA, 1958, PhD, 1962. Asst. prof. econs. UCLA, 1962-66, assoc. prof., 1967-70, prof., 1971-93, prof. emeritus, 1993—, chmn. dept. econs., 1969-78, dean Anderson Sch. Mgmt., 1978-93; acting dean Hong Kong U. Sci. & Tech., 1991-93. Bd. dirs. Arena Pharms., The Black Rock Funds, Payden & Rygel Investment Trust; adv. Series Trust, Cancavax; chmn. adv. com. Calif. Workmen's Compensation. Author: The Development of the Spanish Textile Industry 1750-1800, 1965, (with Warren C. Scoville) The Economic Development of Western Europe, vols. 1-5, 1969-70. Bd. dirs. Nat. Bur. Econ. Rsch., 1975-88, Found. Francisco Marroquin, Lynde and Harry Bradley Found., Pacific Legal Found., 1981-86; trustee Found. for Rsch. in Econs. and Edn., 1970—, chmn., 1977—; mem. bd. overseers Hoover Inst. on War, Revolution and Peace, 1979-85, 86-93; mem. nat. coun. on humanities NEH, 1981-88; chmn. Pres.'s Task Force on Food Assistance, 1983-84. Social Sci. Research Council research tng. fellow, 1958-60; Fulbright sr. research grantee, 1965-66; Am. Philos. Soc. grantee, 1965-66 Mem.: Mont Pelerin Soc., Econ. History Assn., Phi Beta Kappa. Office: UCLA Anderson Grad Sch Mgmt 405 Hilgard Ave Los Angeles CA 90095-9000

LAFORGIA, JEANNE ELLEN, performing arts educator; b. Ho-Ho-Kus, NJ; d. Jerry and Eileen LaForgia; m. James Joseph Zambuto. High Honors, Phillips Exeter Acad., 1988; BA in English and Drama with honors, Dartmouth Coll., 1992; MM in Vocal Performance, Boston U., 1995; vocal studies with Metropolitan Opera soprano Phyllis Curtin. Stage dir. and voice tchr. BU Tanglewood Inst., Lenox, Mass., 1994—97; head of drama Convent of the Sacred Heart, Greenwich, Conn., 1996—99; head of performing arts Boston U. Acad., 1999—. Singer: (cd recording) Night at the Moulin Rouge (Boston Globe Calendar Pick), Our Kinda Guys: the Music of Sinatra, Chevalier, and Montand (Boston Globe Critics Choice), (Operas) Aspen Music Festival, Tanglewood Music Ctr., Manhattan Sch. Music, Moscow Art Theater Sch. Dramatic Studies. Recipient Excellence in Tchg. prize, Harvard U., 2004. Roman Catholic. Home: 8 Wellington Rd Winchester MA 01890 Office: Boston U Acad 1 University Rd Boston MA 02115 Office Phone: 617-353-9000.

LA FORGIA, ROBERT M., hotel executive; BA in Acctg. summa cum laude, Providence Coll.; MBA, UCLA. With Hilton Hotels Corp., Beverly Hills, Calif., 1981—, v.p., corp. contr., 1994—96, sr. v.p., contr., 1996—2004, sr. v.p., CFO, 2004—. Mem.: Contr. Coun. Conf. Bd., Fin. Execs. Inst. Office: Hilton Hotels Corp 9336 Civic Center Dr Beverly Hills CA 90210

LAFORTUNE, BILL, mayor; State asst. atty. gen. City of Tulsa, 1990—93; spl. judge State of Okla. for 14th Judicial Dist., 1993; dist. atty. Tulsa County, 1995; mayor City of Tulsa, Okla., 2002—. Dir. Gilcrease Mus. Assn., Child Abuse Network, Inc. Mem.: Tulsa County Bar Assn. Office: City Hall 200 Civic Ctr Tulsa OK 74103*

LAFRANCE, WILLIAM CURT PHILLIP, JR., neuropsychiatrist, educator, medical researcher; b. Monroe, La., Feb. 6, 1969; s. William C. and Emily F. LaFrance; m. Lori Anne Smith, Sept. 10, 1994; 1 child, William Curt Phillip III. BA, Wake Forest U., 1991; MD, Med. Coll. Ga., 1995. Diplomate in neurology and in psychiatry Am. Bd. Psychiatry and Neurology. Intern internal medicine Brown U. Sch. Medicine, Providence, 1995—96, resident neurology and psychiatry, 1996—2001, fellow clin. rsch., 2001—03, asst. prof. psychiatry and neurology rsch., 2003—; chief resident neuropsychiatry Butler Hosp., Providence, 2000—01; chief resident neurology R.I. Hosp., Providence, 1998—99, dir. neuropsychiatry, 2003—. Asst. instr. clin. neuroscis. Brown U., Divsn. Biology and Medicine, Providence, 1998—99; lectr. in field. Contbr. articles to profl. jours. Team leader Gainesville (Ga.) Aid Project, 1994, Summer Med. Inst., Phila., 1997; hosp. vol. Maua (Kenya) Meth. Hosp., 1991. Recipient Instl. Nat. Rsch. Svc. award, NIH, 2001—03, Mentored Patient-oriented Rsch. Career Devel. award, Nat. Inst. Neurol. Disorders and Stroke, 2003—; Readers Digest Internat. fellow, Siriraj Hosp. Med. Assistance Program Internat., Bangkok, 1995. Mem.: Am Epilepsy Soc, Christian Med. and Dental Assns., Am. Acad. Neurology, Am. Psychiat. Assn., Am. Neuropsychiat. Assn. (rsch. com. 1997, Career Devel. award 2003). Independent. Achievements include research in treatments for nonepileptic seizures. Avocations: skiing, fishing, tennis. Office: RI Hosp Divsn Neuropsychiatry 593 Eddy St Potter 3 Providence RI 02903 Office Phone: 401-444-3534. E-mail: william_lafrance_jr@brown.edu.

LAFRENIERE-DAJC, JODIE E., contracting officer; d. Andrew and Shirley LaFreniere; m. David Dajc, Apr. 25, 1998. BA, BSBA, U. Mo.-Columbia, 1996, MBA, 1998; postgrad. certificate, Am. U., 2002. Contract specialist USN, Wash., 1998—2004, contracting officer, 2004—. Sec. Va. Hills Citizens Assn., Alexandria, 2000—; pres. Ladies Aux. to VFW Post 3150, Arlington, Va., 2003—. Recipient Certificate of Excellence in Acquisition Reform, USN, 2000. Mem.: Am. Soc. Pub. Adminstrn., Acad. Polit. Sci.

LAFUZE, WILLIAM L., lawyer; b. Washington, Feb. 21, 1946; children: Molly, Betsy, William Jr. BS in physics, U. Tex., Austin, 1969, JD, 1973; MS in applied sci., So. Meth. U., 1971; postgrad., U. London, 1973. Bar: Tex. 1973, US Patent and Trademark Office, US Supreme Ct., US Ct. Appeals Fed. Cir. Rsch. scientist Ctr. for Nuclear Studies, Austin, 1966-69; instr. computer sci. U. Tex., Austin, 1968-69, 71-73; assoc. Vinson & Elkins LLP, Houston, 1973-80, ptnr., 1980—, co-head Intellectual Property / Technical Litig. Sect. Mem. Bush Cheney Transition Team for Dept. Commerce, Patent and Trademark Office matters, 2000—01; mem. patent pub. adv. com. US Patent and Trademark Office, Dept. Commerce, 2002—04; mem. adv. bd. Houston Tech. Ctr. Speechwriter; contbr. articles to profl. jours. Fellow: Am. Intellectual Property Law Assn. (bd. dirs. 1983—94, chmn. amicus brief com. 1986—88, pres. 1992—93), Houston Bar Found., Greater Houston Partnership (life), ABA (life; intellectual property law sect. coun. 1998—, chmn. 2004—, chair sectionof intellectual property 2004—05), Texas Bar Found. (life); mem.: MIT Enterprise Forum of Tex. (past bd. dirs.), Licensing Executives Soc., Nat. Coun. Patent Law Associations (del. 1982—, bd. dirs. 1987—90, past pres.), US Trademark Assn. (bd. editors Trademark Reporter 1976—78), Houston Bar Assn., State Bar Tex. (intellectual property law sect.

coun. 1979—83, consumer law sect. coun. 1981—88, chmn. 1984—85, computer sect. coun. 1990—97), Houston Intellectual Property Law Assn. (past pres.), Nat. Inventors Hall of Fame (bd. dirs. 1987—, pres. 1994—95). Office: Vinsin & Elkins First City Tower 1001 Fannin St Ste 2300 Houston TX 77002-6760 Office Phone: 713-758-2595. Business E-Mail: wlafuze@velaw.com.

LAGACE, PAUL ALFRED, aeronautical engineering educator; b. Lewiston, Maine, July 27, 1957; s. Lucien Alfred and Claire (Malo) L.; m. Robin Lea Pare, July 9, 1983. SB, MIT, 1978, SM, 1979, PhD, 1982. Rsch. fellow MIT, Cambridge, 1978-82, Draper asst. prof., 1982-86, assoc. prof. aeronautics and astronautics, 1986-91, prof., dir. Tech. Lab. for Advanced Composites, 1986—, exec. officer dept. aeronautics and astronautics, 1990-92, MacVicar faculty fellow, 1995—, assoc. dir. engring. sys. divsn., 1999-2001. Cons. Foster-Miller, Inc., Waltham, Mass., 1983-95, McClellan AFB, Sacramento, Calif., 1983-90, Raytheon, Mass., 1985—; co-dir. Leaders Mfg. Program and Sys. Desing and Mgmt. Program, 1998-2003. Editor Jour. Composites Tech. and Rsch., 1990-91; contbr. articles to profl. jours. Hertz Found. fellow, 1978. Fellow AIAA (sr.); mem. ASTM (Wayne W. Stinchcomb award 2001), Internat. Com. on Composite Materials (pres. 1993-99; world fellow), Soc. for Advancement of Material and Process Engring., Am. Soc. for Composites, Am. Composite Tech. Assn. (chmn. sci. adv. bd. 1987-95), Sigma Xi, Tau Beta Pi, Sigma Gamma Tau. Avocations: football officiating, softball. Home: 10 Wilton Dr Wilmington MA 01887-2216 Office: 77 Massachusetts Ave Cambridge MA 02139-4301 Office Phone: 617-253-3628. Business E-Mail: pal@mit.edu.

LAGALLY, MAX GUNTER, physics professor; b. Darmstadt, Germany, May 23, 1942; came to U.S., 1953, naturalized, 1960; s. Paul and Herta (Rudow) L.; m. Shelley Meserow, Feb. 15, 1969; children: Eric, Douglas, Karsten BS in Physics, Pa. State U., 1963; MS in Physics, U. Wis.-Madison, 1965, PhD in Physics, 1968. Registered profl. engr., Wis. Instr. physics U. Wis., Madison, 1970-71, asst. prof. materials sci., 1971-74, assoc. prof., 1974-77, prof. materials sci. and physics, 1977—, dir. thin-film deposition and applications ctr., 1982-93, John Bascom Prof. materials sci., 1986—, E.W. Mueller Prof. materials sci. and physics, 1993—. Gordon Godfrey vis. prof. physics, U. New South Wales, Sydney, Australia, 1987; cons. in thin films, 1977—; vis. scientist Sandia Nat. Lab., Albuquerque, 1975; founder, pres. Piezomax Techs., Inc. (now nPoint, Inc.), 1997—, now chmn., chief sci. officer; founder, chmn., chief sci. officer Sonoplot, Inc., 2003—. Editor: Kinetics of Ordering and Growth at Surfaces, 1990, (with others) Methods of Experimental Physics, 1985, Evolution of Surface and Thin-Film Microstructure, 1993, Morphological Organization in Epitaxial Growth and Removal, 1998; mem. editl. bd., also editor spl. issue Jour. Vacuum Sci. and Tech., 1978-81; prin. editor Jour. Materials Rsch., 1990-93; mem. editl. bd. Surface Sci., 1994-2001, Revs. Sci. Instruments, 1997-2000, Diffusion and Defect Data, 1997-2002, Jour. Phys. D, 2004—. Applied Physics, 2004—; contbr. articles to profl. jours.; patentee in field. Max Planck Gesellschaft fellow, 1968, Alfred P. Sloan Found. fellow, 1972, H.I. Romnes fellow, 1976, Humboldt Sr. Rsch. fellow, 1992, 93; grantee fed. agys. and industry; recipient Outstanding Sci. Alumnus award Pa. State U., 1996, Tibbetts award U.S. SBA, 2002. Fellow AAAS, Am. Phys. Soc. (D. Adler award 1994, Davisson-Germer prize 1995), Australian Inst. Physics, Am. Vacuum Soc. (M.W. Welch prize 1991, trustee 1995-97); mem. Materials Rsch. Soc. (medal 1994), Leopoldina-German Acad. Scis., Nat. Acad. Engring. Home: 5110 Juneau Rd Madison WI 53705-4744 Office: U Wis Materials Sci & Engring 1509 University Ave Madison WI 53706-1538 Office Phone: 608-263-2078. Personal E-mail: max.lagally@npoint.com. Business E-Mail: lagally@engr.wisc.edu. E-mail: lagally@sonoplot.com.

LA GAMMA, EDMUND FRANCIS, pediatrician; b. N.Y.C., June 28, 1952; s. Armando Monte and Theresa (Carbone) La G.; m. Kalliope Spanondis, June 13, 1976; children: Armando Michael, Nicholas Alexander. BS, CCNY, 1973; MD, N.Y. Med. Coll., 1976. Intern, N.Y. Hosp.-Cornell U., N.Y.C., 1976-77, resident, 1977-78, neonatal fellow, 1978-80; practice medicine specializing in neonatal-perinatal medicine and pediatrics, N.Y.C., 1981—; postdoctoral scholar U. Calif.-San Francisco Cardiovascular Rsch. Inst., 1980-81; asst. prof. pediatrics N.Y. Hosp.-Cornell U., 1980-86, assoc. prof. pediatrics, perinatal medicine in ob-gyn, 1986, instr. neurology, 1983-84, asst. prof. neurology, 1984-86; assoc. prof. pediatrics and neurobiology and behavior SUNY-StonyBrook, 1986-94, prof., 1994, dir. divsn. newborn medicine; mem. staff SUNY Hosp., N.Y. Hosp., Lenox Hill Hosp., Jamaica Hosp., U. Hosp. StonyBrook. Contbr., investigator Proc. Nat. Acad. Sci., Jour. Sci., Jour. Circulation Rsch., Jour. Pediatric Rsch., Am. Jour. Ob Gyn, Advances in Pediatrics. Recipient Clin. Investigator award NIH, 1980-85; Basil O'Connor award March of Dimes, 1985-87; Am. Heart Assn. grantee, 1985-88, NSF grantee, 1988-91. Fellow Am. Acad. Pediatrics (Young Investigators award 1985); mem. AAAS, N.Y. Acad. Sci., AMA, Med. Soc. State N.Y., Soc. Pediatric Rsch.(council mem. 1992-95), Soc. Neurosci., N.Y. Perinatal Soc. (pres. 1986-89). Roman Catholic. Office: SUNY Dept Pediatrics and Neurobiology Behavior Stony Brook NY 11794-0001

LAGAN, GREGORY J., language and history educator; s. Alfred A. and Joan P. Lagan; m. Maria Mercedes Herrera, July 25, 1998; children: Samuel, Isabella, Gabriella. BA in History, St. Michaels Coll., Colchester, Vt., 1990; MA in Internat. Edn., Columbia U., 1997. Cert. ESL tchr. Tchr. history Colegio Bennett, Cali, Colombia, 1993—95; tchr. English Javeriana U., Cali, 1994—95; tchr. English as 2d lang. Cathedral H.S., Boston, 1997—98; tchr. history and English as 2d lang. Framingham (Mass.) H.S., 1998—. Presenter in field. Mem.: ASCD.

LAGANI, DANIEL, publishing executive; married; 2 children. BA, SUNY, Oneonta, 1985. Ea. advt. mgr. & group advt. mgr. Better Homes and Gardens and Country Home mag. Meredith Corp., 1988—94; pub. George mag.; assoc. pub. New Woman mag. Primedia, 1994—96; assoc. pub. Traveler mag. Condé Nast, 1997—99; v.p., pub. Ladies Home Jour. Meredith Corp., 2001—02, v.p., pub. Better Homes & Gardens NYC, 2002—05; v.p., pub. Bride's mag. Fairchild Bridal Group, 2005—. Office: Fairchild Bridal Group 750 Third Ave 4th Floor New York NY 10017 Office Phone: 212-630-4020. E-mail: Daniel.Lagani@fairchildpub.com.*

LAGANI, JOSEPH A., publishing executive; b. Yonkers, N.Y., Dec. 3, 1957; s. Salvatore Joseph and Joanne (D'Elia) L. BA in Psychology, SUNY, Albany, 1979. Media planner Nadler & Lariner, N.Y.C., 1980-81; assoc. media dir. Benton & Bowles, N.Y.C., 1981-85; acct. mgr. Woman's Day mag., N.Y.C., 1985—88; eastern sales mgr. Ladies Home Jour. (Meredith Pub.), N.Y.C., 1988—89, adv. dir.; pub. Country Home mag., N.Y.C., 1992—95; pub. dir. Meredith Pub., N.Y.C., 1995—99, v.p., pub. group, 1999—2004; v.p., pub. House & Garden mag. (Conde Nast Pub.), N.Y.C., 2004—. Office: VP & Publisher House & Garden 8th Fl 4 Times Square New York NY 10036 Office Phone: 212-286-2191. Office Fax: 212-286-4549.*

LAGARDE, CHRISTINE, French government official, lawyer; b. Paris, Jan. 1, 1956; d. Lallouette Robert and Carre Nicole; m. Wilfrid Lagarde, June 17, 1982 (div. Apr. 1992); children: Pierre-Henri, Thomas. BA, U. Avignon, France, 1979; M of Law, U. Paris, 1979; M Polit. Scientist, Polit. Scis. Inst., 1977. Assoc. Baker McKenzie, Paris, 1981-87, ptnr., 1987-91, mng. ptnr., 1991-95, chmn. exec. com. Chgo., 1999—2004, chmn. policy com., 2004—05; minister delegate for fgn. trade Govt. of France, Paris, 2005—. Author: Breaking New Ground, 1991, Into France, 1993. Mem. French Prime Min. Adv. Bd. on Attractivity of France; mem. internat. bus. leaders adv. coun. Mayor of Beijing; mem. supervisory bd. ING Group. Decorated chevalier de la Legion d'Honneur; named one of 100 Most Powerful Women in World, Forbes mag., 2005. Mem. Cercle Foch (Paris), Athenaeum Club (London), Exec. Club (Chgo.). Office: Minister Delegate for Foreign Trade 139 rue de Bercy 75572 Paris France*

LAGARDERE, ARNAUD, publishing executive; CEO Grolier, Inc., Danbury, Conn. Office: Grolier Inc 90 Sherman Tpke Danbury CT 06816-0002

LAGASSE, BRUCE KENNETH, retired structural engineer; b. Bklyn., Feb. 1, 1940; s. Joseph F. Lagasse and Dora S. Gould. BSME, U. Calif., Berkeley, 1964. Structures engr. Rockwell Internat., Canoga Park, Calif., 1964-69; tech. staff Hughes Aircraft Co., L.A., 1969-70; scientist, engr. Hughes Aircraft Co. (now Raytheon Sys. Co.), El Segundo, Calif., 1972-97; sr. engr. Litton Ship Sys., L.A., 1971-72; prin. mech. engr. Raytheon Sys. Co., El Segundo, 1997-2000; ret., 2000. Lectr., tech. edn. class coord. Hughes Aircraft Co., El Segundo, 1980—97; state chmn. Calif. Libertarian Party, 1978—79; cons. in field. Mem. Libertarian Nat. Com., Washington, DC, 1979—81; chair Calif. Libertarian Jud. Com., 1996—2000. Mem.: ASME (life). Avocations: reading, symphonic music. Home: 1029 Ringneck Way Sparks NV 89436 Personal E-mail: bklagasse@aol.com.

LAGASSE, EMERIL, chef, restaurant owner, television show host; b. Fall River, Mass., Oct. 15, 1959; s. John and Hilda Lagasse; children: Jessica, Jillian. BS in Culinary Arts, D. Johnson & Wales U., Providence, R.I.; studied culinary arts, France. Owner, chef Emeril's restaurant, New Orleans, 1990—, Nola restaurant, New Orleans, 1992—, Emeril's New Orleans Fish House restaurant, Las Vegas, 1995—, Delmonico Restaurant and Bar, New Orleans, 1998—, Emeril's restaurant, Orlando, Fla., 1999—, Delmonico Steakhouse restaurant, Las Vegas, 1999—, Tchoup Chop restaurant, Orlando, Fla., 2002—; host cooking show Essence of Emeril (The Food Network), 1994—, Emeril Live (The Food Network), 1997—; food corr. Good Morning Am., ABC, 1998—. Author: (cookbook) New Orleans Cooking, 1993, Louisiana Real and Rustic, 1996, Emeril's Creole Christmas, 1997, Emeril's TV Dinners, 1998, Every Day's a Party, 1999, There's a Chef in My Soup, 2002, Emeril's Potluck: Comfort Food with a Kicked-Up Attitude, 2004; actor: (TV series) Emeril, 2001. Established Emeril Lagasse Found., 2002. Named Chef of Yr., GQ Mag., 1998, Exec. of the Yr., Restaurants & Institutions mag., 2004; named one of Most Intriguing People of Yr., People Mag., 1998; named to Am. Express for Fine Dining Hall of Fame, 1994; recipient Esquire award for Restaurant of Yr., 1991, Food and Wine award for one of Am.'s Top 25 New Chefs, 1991, James Beard award for Best S.E. Chef, 1991, Best Esquire award for restaurant of yr., 1993, Ivy award for restaurants and instns., 1994, Cable ACE award for best informational show, 1997, Salute to Excellence award, Nat. Restaurant Assn., 1998, Grand award, Wine Spectator Mag., 1999. Office: Food Network 5757 Wilshire Blvd Los Angeles CA 90036*

LAGASSE, THOMAS JOSEPH, language educator; b. Bristol, Conn., Jan. 28, 1964; s. Joseph A.W. and Yolanda (Beardsley) L. BA in Mass Communication, Bonaventure U., 1986; MA in English, Trinity Coll., Hartford, Conn., 1992. Claim rep. Cigna Corp., Kansas City, Mo., 1986-87, sr. claim rep. Sherman, Tex., 1987-88; admissions counselor St. Bonaventure (N.Y.) U., 1988-89; researcher ESPN, Bristol, Conn., 1991-92; instr. Tunxis Community Coll., 1992—. Home: 24 Briarwood Rd Bristol CT 06010-7205

LAGEMANN, ELLEN CONDLIFFE, history and education educator, former dean; b. N.Y.C., Dec. 20, 1945; d. John Charles and Jane Grace (Rosenthal); m. Jonathan Kord Lagemann, June 28, 1969; 1 child, Nicholas Kord. AB cum laude, Smith Coll., 1967; MA, Columbia U., 1968, PhD with distinction, 1978. Tchr. Roslyn H.S., Roslyn, NY, 1967-69; exec. dir. WMCA: Call for Action, N.Y.C., 1969-71; asst. dir. Bank Street Sch. for Children, N.Y.C., 1971-72; tching. and rsch. asst. Inst. Phil. and Politics of Edn., Tchrs. Coll. Columbia U., N.Y.C., 1974-78; asst. prof., then assoc. prof. Tchrs. Coll. Columbia U. Dept. Hist., N.Y.C., 1978-87, prof. history and edn., 1987-94, NYU, N.Y.C., 1994—2000; pres. Spencer Found., 2000—02; dean Harvard Grad. Sch. Edn., Cambridge, Mass., 2002—05, Charles Warren prof. history of Am. edn., 2002—. Trustee Concord (Mass.) Acad.; bd. dirs. Jobs for the Future, Boston, Oasis Children's Svcs., N.Y.C. Author: A Generation of Women: Education in the Lives of Progressive Reformers, 1979, Private Power for the Public Good (Outstanding Book award), 1983, The Politics of Knowledge, 1989, An Elusive Science: The Troubling History of Education Research, 2000; editor: Nursing History: New Perspectives, New Possibilities, 1983, Jane Addams on Education, 1985, Teachers College Record, 1990-95, Brown v. Bd. of Education: The Challenge for Today's Schools, 1996, Philanthropic Foundations: New Scholarship, New Possibilities, 1999, Issues in Educational Research, Problems and Possibilities, 1999; many articles and book chpts. Grantee Carnegie Corp., Spencer Found, Carnegie Found. for Advancement of Teaching, Kettering Found., Lilly Endowment, fellow Ctr. for Advanced Study in Behavioral Scis. Mem. Nat. Acad. Edn. (pres. 1998-2001), History of Edn. Soc. (pres. 1987-88), Am. Hist. Assn., Orgn. Am. Historians, Am. Ednl. Rsch. Assn., Century Assn., Cosmopolitan Club. Office: Harvard Grad Sch Edn Dean's Office Appian Way Cambridge MA 02138 Office Phone: 617-495-3401. E-mail: ellen_lagemann@harvard.edu.

LAGIN, NEIL, landscape designer, consultant; b. Bronx, Jan. 10, 1942; s. Barney and Helen (Goldberg) L. Cert. Xeriscape instr. South Fla. Water Mgmt. Buyer Alexanders, N.Y.C., 1961-69; sales mgr. Halldon, Ltd., N.Y.C., 1969-79; mgr., ptnr. in concession Michele Craig, Westbury, N.Y., 1979-85; ptnr. ALW Trading, "9", N.Y.C., 1985-87; owner, operator Accent Foliage, Delray Beach, Fla., 1987-89; pres. Neil Lagin Property Mgmt., Neil's Landscape Svc., Boca Raton, Fla., 1988—97; landscape dir. Am. Heritage Sch., Boca Raton; ptnr. All Star Landscaping, 1997-99; landscape mgmt. cons., 1999-2001; landscape dir. Every Bloomin' Thing Ltd., Cayman Islands, 2001—02; landscape cons. Vero Beach, Fla., 2002—05, Sebastian, Fla., 2005—. Cable TV host Five Minutes with Dr. Neil. Author numerous poems; exhibited in group shows at Ward Nasse Gallery-Salon, 1975-79, Timothy Blackburn Gallery, 1978, Washington Art Show, others. Nursery adv. bd. Habilitation Ctr. for the Handicapped, Boca Raton, 1991—; overall adv. com. Palm Beach County Ext., 1992—, sec., chair program rev. com.; bd. dirs. Greater Palm Beach Area Alzheimers Assn., 1993; mem. Environ. Resource Landscape Team; mem. Boca Raton Postal Customer Adv. Coun., 1994-96; bd. dirs. Pheasant Walk Homeowners Assoc., 1996-97; adv. coun. Plant the Planet TV series, 1997; mem. Sebastian Vol. Police; mem. Sebastian Tree and Landscape Adv. Bd. Named Fla. Master Gardener, Inst. Food and Agrl. Scis., U. Fla., 1989, Best Landscaper in Boca Raton, South Fla. Newspaper Network, 1991, Best Local Vol. in Boca Raton, 1994, Outstanding Master Gardener, State of Fla., 1995, Gold award Best Landscaping Indian River County, 2004. Mem. Internat. Palm Soc. (Palm Beach chpt.), Rare Fruit Coun. Internat. (Palm Beach chpt.), Boca Raton C. of C. (grad. leadership program 1991). Home and Office: c/o Neil's Landscape Svc 838 Wentworth St Sebastian FL 32958 Office Phone: 772-589-4312. E-mail: doctorneil9@yahoo.com.

LAGNESE, JOSEPH F., environmental engineer; b. Pittsburgh, P.A., USA, May 20, 1929; s. Joseph F. Lagnese and Mary Mannella; m. Patricia Adams Lagnese, June 23, 1951; children: Les, John, David, Keith, Joseph III, Paul. B.S. Civil Engr., U. of Pittsburgh, 1947—51; M.S. San. Engr., Johns Hopkins U., 1952—53. Project engr. Gannet Fleming Engrs., Pittsburgh, Pa., 1956—58; found. ptnr. Duncan Lagnese and Assoc., Pittsburgh, Pa., 1958—81; pvt. cons. Pittsburgh, Pa., 1981—; adj. asst. prof. Civil Engring. Dept. U. of Pittsburgh, Pittsburgh, Pa., 1981—. Author: (tech. articles) Jour. and Tech Publications; editor: (Manual of Practice) Water Environ. Fedn., 1992. Pres. Pa. Water Pollution Control Assn., 1965, dir., 1962—69. 1st lt. USAF, 1951—56. Mem.: Pa. Soc. Profl. Engrs., Am. Soc. Civil Engr. (pres.), Am. Acad. of Environ. Engr. (pres. 1991—92), Water Environ. Fedn. (pres. 1972). Catholic. Avocations: music, painting, gardening. Home: 3066 Woodland Rd Allison Park PA 15101 E-mail: jlagnese@aol.com.

LAGOMASINO, MARIA ELENA, bank executive; b. Havana, Cuba, 1949; B in French Lit., Manhattanville Coll.; MLS, Columbia U.; MBA, Fordham U. Joined Citibank, 1976, v.p., 1977—83; mgr., divsn. exec. Chase Pvt. Banking Internat., 1983—89, mgr. Western Hemisphere ops., 1989—94, mktg. exec. Ams. region, 1994—97; sr. mng. dir. Chase Manhattan Pvt. Bank, 1997—2000; chmn., CEO J.P. Morgan Pvt. Bank, N.Y.C., 2001—. Bd. dirs. Philips-Van Heusen, Avon Products, Coca-Cola, 2003—; trustee Synergos Inst. Mem. dean's coun. John F. Kennedy Sch. Govt., Harvard U. Named one of 25 Women to Watch, US Banker Mag., 2003; named to 2004 Hispanic Bus. Corp. Elite, Hispanic Bus. Mag., 2004. Mem.: Com. of 200, Coun. on Fgn. Rels. Office: JP Morgan Pvt Bank 345 Park Ave New York NY 10154-1002

LAGONIA, SALVATORE ANTHONY, lawyer; b. Bronx, N.Y., Mar. 23, 1952; s. Salvatore Gene and Julie T. (Motta) L.; children: Salvatore A. III, Dena Lynn. BS, Mercy Coll., 1987; JD, Pace U., 1991. Bar: N.Y. 1991, U.S. Supreme Ct. 1998, U.S. Fed. Ct. 1999. Police officer New Castle Police Dept., Chappaqua, N.Y., 1980-2000; pvt. practice Yorktown, N.Y., 1992—; gen. counsel legal and bus. affairs JKBD Prodns., Pound Ridge, N.Y., 1994—. Gen. counsel Yorktown Fire Dept., 1992—; gen. counsel Yorktown Parks and Recreation, 1995, commr., 1997—. Capt. Yorktown Fire Dept., 1995—. Mem. Yorktown Bar Assn. (pres. 1995-96, 2001—). Republican. Roman Catholic. Office: PO Box 571 Yorktown Heights NY 10598-0571 E-mail: slagonia@aol.com.

LAGORIA, GEORGIANNA MARIE, curator, writer, editor, visual art consultant; b. Oakland, Calif., Nov. 3, 1953; d. Charles Wilson and Margaret Claire (Vella) L.; m. David Joseph de la Torre, May 15, 1982; 1 child, Mateo Joseph. BA in Philosophy, Santa Clara U., 1975; MA in Museology, U. San Francisco, 1978. Exhbn. coord. Allrich Gallery, San Francisco, 1977-78; asst. registrar Fine Arts Mus., San Francisco, 1978-79; gallery coord. de Saisset Mus., Santa Clara, Calif., 1979-80, asst. dir., 1980-83, dir., 1983-86, Palo Alto (Calif.) Cultural Ctr., 1986-91; ind. writer, editor and cons. mus. and visual arts orgns., Hawaii, 1991-95; dir. The Contemporary Mus., Honolulu, 1995—. V.p. Non-Profit Gallery Assn., San Francisco, 1980-82; bd. dirs. Fiberworks, Berkeley, Calif., 1981-85; field grant reviewer Inst. Mus. Svcs., Washington, 1984, 85, 97, 98; adv. bd. Hearst Art Gallery, Moraga, Calif., 1986-89, Womens Caucus for Art, San Francisco, 1987—; mem. adv. bd. Weigand Art Gallery, Notre Dame Coll., Belmont, Calif. Curator exhbns. The Candy Store Gallery, 1980, Fiber '81, 1981; curator, author exhbn. catalogue Contemporary Hand Colored Photographs, 1981, Northern Calif. Art of the Sixties, 1982, The Artist and the Machine: 1910-1940, 1986; author catalogue, guide Persis Collection of Contemporary Art at Honolulu Advertiser, 1993; co-author: The Little Hawaiian Cookbook, 1994; coord. exhbn. selections Laila and Thurston Twigg-Smith Collection and Toshiko Takaezu ceramics for Hui No'eau Visual Arts Ctr., Maui, 1993; editor Nuhou (newsletter Hawaii State Mus. Assn.), 1991-94; spl. exhbn. coord. Honolulu Acad. Arts, 1995; dir. The Contemporary Mus., Honolulu, 1995—. Mem. Arts Adv. Alliance, Santa Clara County Arts Coun., 1985-86; grant panelist Santa Clara County Arts Coun., 1987; mem. art adv. bd. Kapiolani C.C., 1994—. Exhbn. grantee Ahmanson Found., 1981, NEA, 1984, Calif. Arts Coun., 1985-89 Mem. Am. Assn. Mus., ArtTable, 1983—, Calif. Assn. Mus. (bd. dirs. 1987-89), Assn. Art Mus. Dirs., Hawaiian Craftsmen (bd. dirs. 1994-95), Honolulu Jr. League, Key Project (bd. dirs. 1993-94). Democrat. Roman Catholic. Avocations: dance, fiction writing. Home and Office: 47-665 Mapele Rd Kaneohe HI 96744-4918

LAGOS, JAMES HARRY, lawyer; b. Springfield, Ohio, Mar. 14, 1951; s. Harry Thomas and Eugenia (Papas) Lagos; m. Nike Daphne Pavlatos, July 3, 1976. BA cum laude, Wittenberg U., 1970; JD, Ohio State U., 1972. Bar: Ohio 1973, U.S. Dist. Ct. (so. dist.) Ohio 1973, U.S. Tax Ct. 1975, U.S. Supreme Ct. 1976, U.S. Ct. Appeals (6th cir.) 1979. Asst. pros. atty. Clark County, Ohio, 1972-75; with Lagos & Lagos, Springfield, 1975—. Mem. Springfield Small Bus. Coun., 1977—, past chmn.; mem. Ohio Small Bus. Coun., 1980—, past chmn., vice chmn.; past pres., v.p. Nat. Small Bus. United, 1982—; del., resource person regulatory and licensing reform com. Small Bus. Nat. Issues Conf., 1984. Chmn. Ohio del. White Ho. Conf. Small Bus., 1985—86, del., 1995; past chmn. Clark County Child Protection Team, 1974—82; mem. Clark County WORKPLUS Bd., 1999—, v.p., pres.; mem. Clark County Young Rep. Club, past pres., sec., treas., 1968—76; bd. dirs., past pres. Greek Orthodox Ch., 1974—; mem. coun. Greek Orthodox Diocese of Detroit, 1985—86. Staff sgt. Ohio Air N.G., 1970—76. Named Small Bus. Advocate of Yr., U.S. SBA, 1991; named one of Outstanding Young Men of Am., 1978; recipient Disting. Svc. award, Springfield-Clark County, 1977, medal of St. Paul the Apostle, Greek Orthodox Archdiocese N.Am. and S.Am., 1985. Mem.: W. Ctrl. Ohio Hearing and Speech Assn. (bd. dirs., pres., v.p. 1973—84, Dr. Melvin Emanuel award 1983), Clark County Bar Assn. (past sec., mem. exec. com. 1973—), Ohio State Bar Assn., Rsch. Inst. Small and Emerging Bus. (bd. dirs. 1993—), Am. Hellenic Ednl. Progressive Assn. (pres., past treas.), Jaycees (past chmn. several coms. 1973—89, Spoke award 1974), Am. Hellenic Inst. (pub. affairs com. 1979—, bd. dirs.), C. of C. (chmn., bd. dirs., vice-chmn., treas.), Pi Sigma Alpha, Tau Pi Phi, Phi Eta Sigma, Alpha Alpha Kappa. Home: 2023 Audubon Park Dr Springfield OH 45504-1113 Office: Lagos & Lagos 1 S Limestone St Ste 1000 Springfield OH 45502-1294 E-mail: jameshlagos@yahoo.com.

LAGOW, RICHARD JAMES, chemistry professor; b. Albuquerque, Aug. 16, 1945; BA, Rice U., 1967, PhD, 1969. Instr. dept. chemistry Rice U., Houston, 1967-69; from asst. to assoc. prof. dept. chemistry MIT, Cambridge, Mass., 1969-76; assoc. prof. dept. chemistry U. Tex., Austin, 1976-80, prof. dept. chemistry, 1980-94, L.N. Vauquelin Regents prof. chemistry dept. chemistry, 1994—. Recipient Alexander von Humboldt award, 1992, award for creative work in fluorine chemistry Am. Chem. Soc., 1997; Alfred P. Sloan fellow, 1974-75. Fellow AAAS. Office: Dept Chemistry Univ Tex Austin TX 78712

LAGOWSKI, BARBARA JEAN, writer, editor; b. Adams, Mass., Nov. 9, 1955; d. Frank Louis and Jeanette (Wanat) L.; m. Richard Dietrich Mumma III, Oct. 11, 1980; 1 child, Adam Dietrich. BA, U. South Fla., 1977; MA, Johns Hopkins U., 1978. Asst. editor Fred Jordan Books Grossett and Dunlap Pubs., N.Y.C., 1978-80; mng. editor Methuen Inc., N.Y.C., 1980-81; mng. assoc., sr. editor Bobb-Merrill Co Inc., N.Y.C., 1981-84; editor New Am. Libr., N.Y.C., 1984-85. Poet-in-the-schs. Hillsborough County Arts Council, Tampa., Fla., 1976-77; poet-in-residence Cloisters Children's Mus., Balt., 1977-78 Author: Silver Skates series, 1988—89; co-author: Good Spirits, 1986, Teen Terminators, 1989, How to Get the Best Public School Education for Your Child, 1991, The Sports Curmudgeon, 1993, How to Attract Anyone, Anytime, Anyplace, 1993, Daily Negotiations: A Malcontent's Book of Meditations for Every Interminable Day of the Year, 1996, 101 Ways to Flirt: How to Get More Dates and Meet Your Mate, 1997, Cyberflirt: How to Attract Anyone, Anywhere on the World Wide Web, 1999; singer: Angel Signs: A Celestial Guide to the Powers of Your Own Guardian Angel, 2002. Mem. Authors Guild, Phi Kappa Phi Home: 237 Lenox Ave Long Branch NJ 07740-5022 Office Phone: 732-610-1569. Personal E-mail: blagowski@aol.com.

LAGRAND, JAMES, JR., minister; b. Grand Rapids, Mich., Apr. 24, 1941; s. James and Katherine Tornga LaGrand; m. Virginia Ann VanderMeer, June 5, 1963; children: David, John Patrick, Paul Damien, Peter. AM, U. Mich., 1968; MDiv, Yale U., 1968; ThD, Basel (Switzerland) U., 1989. Ordained to ministry Christian Reformed Ch. N.Am., 1969. English master St. Paul's Coll., Zaria, Nigeria, 1963-65; lectr. Grand Valley State U., Allendale, Mich., 1965-66; min. Garfield Ch., Chgo., 1969-74, All Nations Ch., Halifax, N.S., Can., 1977-87, Beacon Light Ch., Gary, Ind., 1993—; ecumenical scholar Brit. Coun. of Chs., Sheffield, Eng., 1974-76; lectr., supr. (semester) Chgo. Metro Ctr., 1991-92. Founding pres. Chgo. Westside Christian Sch., 1970-71; chair faith and order Halifax-Dartmouth Coun., 1978-85; exec. com. Christian Reformed World Missions, Grand Rapids, 1980-85; cons. in urban ministry, Chgo., 1990-93. Author: To Mysterion, 1976, Earliest Christian Mission, 1995. Bd. dirs. Westside Cmty. Orgn., Chgo., 1970-74; Christian spokesman Muslim-Christian Dialogue, Halifax, 1980-82; organizer Anti-Apartheid Coalition, Halifax, 1980-85; mem. Interfaith Clergy Coun., Gary, 1993-2005. Centennial missions scholar, 1975-76; grantee Kampen Theologische Hog. Kampen, 1976, Tyndale fellow, 1976-77; recipient Outstanding Svc. award Calvin Coll., 1986. Fellow Inst. for Bibl. Rsch.; mem. Am. Soc. Ch. History, Soc. Bibl. Lit., Tyndale Fellowship of Bibl. Rsch., Chgo. Soc. Bibl. Rsch.,

Urban Mission Bd. Avocations: urban silvaculture, church history, linguistics, city politics. Home: 3745 Keck Pl Gary IN 46408-1243 Office: Beacon Light Ch 3770 Burr St Gary IN 46408-1231 Office Phone: 219-838-0586. E-mail: LaGrand@aya.yale.edu.

LAGRANGE, CLAIRE MAE, librarian; b. Tarkio, Mo., Oct. 11, 1937; d. Floyd Gerald and Phyllis Geneva (Wilson) McElfish; m. Irving Joseph LaGrange, May 20, 1955; children: Raymond, Robert, Rhonda, Roger. BA, U. Southwestern La., 1983; MEd, Northwestern State U., 1990. Cert. English, spl. edn., K-12 mild and moderate, assessment tchr., libr. sci., La. Tchr.'s aide St. Martin Parish Sch. Bd., Cecilia, La., 1979-82; tchr. English Florien (La.) High Sch., 1984-86; tchr. Zwolle (La.) High Sch., 1986-90, Cecilia (La.) Jr. High Sch., 1990-92, Cecilia High Sch., 1992-96; libr. Teche Elem. Sch., Breaux, La., 1996—99, St. Martin Parish Librs., Cecilia and Arnaudville, La., 1999—2001; br. mgr. Arnaudville (La.) Libr., 2001—. Den mother Cub Scouts-Boy Scouts Am., Spokane, Wash., 1967-69; Sunday sch. tchr. First Friends Ch., Spokane, 1968-69. Fellow U. La. Alumni Assn., Northwestern State U. Alumni Assn.; mem. NEA, ALA, Nat. English Honor Soc., La. Assn. Educators, St. Martin Assn. Educators. Avocations: sketching, reading, writing, crossword puzzles, studying the Bible. Home: 1052 Charles Marks Rd Arnaudville LA 70512-3820

LAGRECA, THOMAS RICHARD, consumer products company executive, lawyer; b. N.Y.C., Dec. 16, 1957; s. Jack Charles and Gloria LaG.; m. Joanne Baio, Nov. 25, 1989; children: Jack, Jessica, Joseph. BA, Pa. State U., 1979; JD, St. John's U., 1983. Atty. Dewey Ballatine, N.Y.C., 1983-85, Nynex Corp., N.Y.C., 1985-90; prin. Concourse Floors, Inc., Bklyn., 1990-97, Spectrum Flooring, Ltd., Bklyn., 1997—. Editor-in-chief St. John's Law Rev., 1982-83; contbr. poetry and short stories to profl. publs. Mem. Tau Kappa Epsilon. Avocations: reading, music. Home: 788 Winding Way Rivervale NJ 07675

LAGRUTTA, JANICE A., literature and language professor; b. Paterson, NJ, Jan. 28, 1945; d. Robert Edward McCoobery and Margaret Eileen Grish-McCoobery; m. Robert LaGrutta, Dec. 28, 1969; children: Margaret, Thomas, Elizabeth, Joseph. BA in English, French, Caldwell Coll., 1966; MA in edn. k-12, Seton Hall U., 1996. English tchr. DePaul HS, Wayne, NJ, 1966—93, Lakeland HS, Wanague, NJ, 1993—. Mem.: NJEA, NEA. Home: 21 Rolling Views Dr Little Falls NJ 07424 Office: Lakeland Regional HS 205 Conklintown Rd Wanaque NJ 07465 Office Phone: 973-835-1900. E-mail: jlagrutta@lakeland.k12.nj.us.

LAGUARDIA, CHERYL M., school librarian, writer; b. Sidney, N.Y., July 07; d. Enrico Donato and Leta M. LaGuardia. MLS, SUNY Albany; BS in Lit., SUNY Oneonta. Public Library certification NY State. Head of interlibrary loan Schaffer Libr., Union Coll., Schenectady, NY, 1981—86; asst. head reference Davidson Libr., U. Calif., Santa Barbara, Calif., 1986—94; head of instrnl. svc. coll. libr. Harvard U., Cambridge, Mass., 1994—. Editor R. R. Bowker, Chanlon, NJ, 2000—; editor-in-chief Neal-Schuman Pub. Inc., New York, 1994—. Author: (book) Teaching the New Library, 1996; co-author: Becoming a Library Teacher, 2000; editor: Finding Common Ground: Creating the Library of the Future Without Diminishing the Library of the Past, 1998, Recreating the Academic Library: Breaking Virtual Ground, 1998; author: (reviewing) E-Views and Reviews (Libr. Jour. E-Media Reviewer Yr., 2000), (column) (RASD/Louis Shores Reviewer Yr. Award, 1996). Mem.: Reference Svc. Rev. Editl. Bd. Office: Widener Libr Harvard Coll Libr Harvard University Cambridge MA 02138 Office Phone: 617-496-4226. Business E-Mail: claguard@fas.harvard.edu.

LAGUEUX, RONALD RENE, federal judge; b. Lewiston, Maine, June 30, 1931; s. Arthur Charles and Laurette Irene (Turcotte) L.; m. Denise Rosemarie Boudreau, June 30, 1956; children: Michelle Simone, Gregory Charles, Barrett James. AB, Bowdoin Coll., 1953; LLB, Harvard U., 1956. Assoc. then ptnr. Edwards and Angell Law Firm, Providence, R.I., 1956-68; assoc. justice Superior Ct. State of R.I., Providence, 1968-86; judge U.S. Dist. Ct., Providence, 1986—; chief judge, 1992-99. Exec. counsel to Gov. Chafee, R.I., 1963-65. Rep. candidate for U.S. Senate, 1964; corporator R.I. Hosp., Providence, 1965-01; solicitor Southeastern New Eng. Province United Way, 1957-68. Mem. Bowdoin Coll. Alumni Council (past v.p., pres.), Am.-French Geneal. Soc. Home: 90 Greenwood Ave Rumford RI 02916-1934 Office: US Dist Ct 1 Exchange Ter Providence RI 02903-1744

LAGUNA, MARIELLA, artist; b. N.Y.C. d. I. Maurice and Bertha (Keats) Fenichel; m. Lawrence Laguna; children; Kenneth, Sanford. B.Arch., N.Y. U.; student, New Sch., Adelphi U., Pratt Graphic Ctr. Archtl. draftsperson Foster Wheeler, York, 1st Nat. Bank, NYU; dir. arts and crafts Oceanside Sch. Dist., N.Y.; tchr. art Valley Stream Community Arts Council, N.Y., Art Sch. Lincoln Ctr., N.Y.C., St. Margarete Sch., Tappahannock, Va.; artist in residence Oceanside Baldwin Rockville Ctr., Saratoga, N.Y. One woman shows Morris Gallery, N.Y.C., Hofstra U., Hempstead, N.Y., Post Coll., Westbury, N.Y., Bklyn. Coll., Cone Gallery, N.Y.C., Gallery Artemis, Cedarhurst, L.I., Merrick Gallery, L.I.; exhibited in group shows Naples and Florence, Italy, Pitts., Ga., Ind., Ark., Baylor U., Waco, Tex., Norfolk Mus. Art, Va., Nat. Acad. Fine Arts, N.Y.C., Pa. Acad. Fine Arts, Phila., Silvermine Guild Ann., Sweet Briar Coll., Va.; represented in permanent collections. Resident fellow MacDowell Colony, 1965, 79, 71, 73, 76, Ossobow Project, 1969, Helene Wurlitzer Found., 1971, Montalvo Ctr. for Arts, 1977, Yaddo, 1973, 76, 78, Hambidge Ctr., Rabun Gap, Ga., 1985, Va. Ctr. for Creative Arts, 1973, 76, 78, 93, 94; recipient Gold medal 1st prize Hofstra competition, 1963, 1st prize Friend's Acad. N.Y., Grace F. Lee Meml. prize and medal of honor Nat. Assn. Women Arts, 1967, Seligson Meml. award, 1976, ann. award Am. Soc. Contemporary Artists, 1983, 89. Home: 324 Christopher St Oceanside NY 11572-3424

LAGUZZI, CARINA, lawyer; d. Heraldo Olter Ricardo and Felinda Cristina Laguzzi. JD, Boston U., 2001. Bar: Pa. 2001. With dist. atty. office, Phila., 2001—03; assoc. Britt, Hankins, Schiable & Maughen, Phila., 2003—04; assoc., owner Laguzzi & Assocs., P.C., Phila., 2004—. Mem.: Hispanic Bar Assn. (officer legal edn. fund), Pa. Bar Assn., ABA. Avocations: skiing, writing fictional works. Office: Laguzzi & Assocs PC 1500 JFK Blvd Ste 200 Philadelphia PA 19102 Office Phone: 215-854-4027. Business E-Mail: claguzzi@comcast.net.

LAHAIE, L. SCOT, theater educator; b. Tulsa, Okla., Jan. 10, 1961; s. Arley R. and Joyce Lahaie; m. Ute S. Klappenecker, Jan. 25, 1985; children: Michele, Isabelle. BFA in Drama, Sam Houston State U., 1983; MA in Theater History, Dramatic Criticism, Baylor U., 1995—96, MFA in Stage Directing, 2000. Theater dir. US Army Entertainment Program, Europe, Giessen, Germany, 1983—89, entertainment dir., 1989—93; lectr. theater arts Baylor U., Waco, Tex., 2000—02; asst. prof. and dir. of theater Gardner-Webb U., Boiling Springs, NC, 2003—. Entertainment coord. Muenzenberg Renaissance Faire, Muenzenberg, Hessen, Germany, 1986—93; project officer for the ann. european tournament of plays US Army Entertainment Program, Giessen, Hessen, Germany, 1990—92; faculty rsch. fellow Oral History Inst., Baylor U., Waco, Tex., 2001—01; v.p. The Horton Foote Soc., Waco, Tex., 2002—; artistic dir., found. new plays festival Gardner-Webb U., Boiling Springs, NC, 2003—. Editor: (plays) New Plays Festival, Volume One: New One-Act Plays by Emerging American Playwright, vol. two, 2004, The Best of 24 Hours: New Ten-Minute Plays, 2005; author The Cattleman's Suite: A Comedy in Two Acts; translator (from German to English) The Beloved by Heinz Coubier; dir.: (plays) Tartuffe by Moliere (Best Dir. Play, European Tournament of Plays, 1988); lighting designer: The Mousetrap by Agatha Christie (Best Lighting for a Play (in the European Tournament of Plays), 1992); editor: Horton Foote Review, Volume One: The Journal of the Horton Foote Society, 2005. Mem.: The Internat. Christian Studies Assn., The Inst. Interdisciplinary Rsch., N.C. Theater Conf., The Horton Foote Soc. (founding v.p. 2002—), Theatre Comm. Group. Office: Gardner-Webb U Main St Boiling Springs NC 28017 Office Phone: 704-406-4371. Business E-Mail: scot@scotlahaie.com.

LAHANN, JOERG, chemist; BSc in chemistry, U. Saarland, 1993; MS in chemistry, RWTH Aachen, 1995; PhD in macromolecular chemistry, RWTH Achen, 1998; postdoctoral rsch., MIT, 1999—2003, Harvard U., 1999—2003. Asst. prof. dept. chemical engring. U. Mich., 2003—. Contbr. articles to profl. jour. Named one of Top 100 Young Innovators, MIT Tech. Review, 2004. Mem.: Sigma Xi. Office: U Mich Dept Chemical Engring 2300 Hayward St Ann Arbor MI 48109-2136 Business E-Mail: lahann@umich.edu.

LAHAYE, BEVERLY, cultural organization administrator; m. Tim LaHaye; 4 children. Founder, chmn. Concerned Women for Am., Washington, 1979—; founder, radio talk show host Beverly LaHaye Live (now Concerned Women Today). Author: The Spirit Controlled Woman, The Desires of A Woman's Heart, Who Will Save Our Children?; co-author (with Dr. Janice Crouse): The Strength of a Godly Woman, 2001; co-author: (with Terry Blackstock) (fiction series) Seasons Under Heaven. Bd. dirs. Internat. Right to Life Fed., Liberty U., Childcare Internat. Recipient Christian Woman of the Year, 1984, Church Woman of the Year, 1988, Religious Freedom Award, S. Baptist Convention, 1991, Thomas Jefferson award, 2001.

LAHEY, JOSEPH PATRICK, engineering executive; b. Pitts., Apr. 3, 1947; s. Michael Patrick and Henrietta (Szczesny) L.; m. Diane Ruth Lapp, July 24, 1971; children: Brendan, Meghan. BSME magna cum laude, U. Pitts., 1973, MBA, 1978. Registered profl. engr., Pa. Engring., mktg. Dravo Corp., Pitts., 1973-81; dir. mktg. M.W. Kellogg, Houston, 1981-83; v.p., gen. mgr. Combustion Engring., Stamford, Conn., 1985-88; pres., CEO Barnard & Burk Group, Inc., Baton Rouge, 1988—94; sr. exec. positions with various firms, 1994—96; pres., CEO Worldwide, Inc., Dallas, 1996—2002; co-founder Pluris Capital Advisors Co., 2002—04; pres., CEO Corrpro Cos., Inc., Medina, Ohio, 2004—. Mem. Am. Soc. Mech. Engrs., Soc. Petroleum Engrs., Constrn. Industry Inst. (bd. dirs.), Constrn. Industry Pres.'s Forum, Omicron Delta Kappa, Tau Beta Pi. Republican. Roman Catholic. Avocations: golf, fishing, jogging. Office: Corrpro Cos Inc 1090 Enterprise Dr Medina OH 44256*

LAHEY, RICHARD THOMAS, JR., nuclear engineer, fluid mechanics engineer; b. St. Petersburg, Fla., Feb. 20, 1939; married, 1961; 3 children. BS, U.S. Mcht. Marine Acad., 1961; MS, Rensselaer Poly. Inst., 1964; ME, Columbia U., 1966; PhD in Mech. Engring., Stanford U., 1971. Engr. Knolls Atomic Power Lab., 1961-64; rsch. assoc. Columbia U., N.Y.C., 1964-66; mgr. core & safety devel. nuc. energy divsn. GE, 1966-75; chmn. dept. nuc. engring. Rensselaer Poly. Inst., Troy, NY, 1975-87, prof. nuc. engring. and engring. physics, 1987—, prof. dept. chem. engring., 1987—, Edward E. Hood, Jr. prof. engring., 1989—, dir. ctr. multiphase rsch., 1991-94, dean engring., 1994-98. Bd. mem. PJM Interconnect LLC, 1997-; mem. sci. adv. com. EG&G Idaho, Inc., 1976-83; mem. Advanced Code Rev. Group & LOFT Rev. Group U.S. Nuc. Regulatory Commn., 1976-84; commr. Engring. Manpower Commn., 1981-84; pres. R.T. Lahey, Inc., 1981-83; vis. prof. U. Pisa, Italy and Claude Bernard U., France, 1987; Alexander von Humboldt Sr. scientist fellow, 1994-95. Editor: Jour. Nuc. Engring. & Design, 1983-94. Recipient Arthur Holly Compton award, 1989, Glenn T. Seaborg medal, 1992, E. O. Lawrence Meml. award U.S. Dept. Energy, 1988; Fulbright fellow Magdalen Coll., Oxford U., 1983-84. Fellow ASME, Am. Nuc. Soc. (Tech. Achievement award 1985), N.Y. Acad. Scis., Am. Soc. Engring. Edn. (Glen Murphy award 1985), Sigma Xi; mem. NAE, Russian Acad. Sci. (fgn. mem. Bashkorstan, Russia). Achievements include research in two-phase flow and boiling heat transfer technology; nuclear reactor thermal-hydraulics and safety, bubble fusion technology. Office: Rensselaer Poly Inst Jonsson Engring Ctr 110 8th St Troy NY 12180-3522 Office Phone: 518-276-6614. Business E-Mail: laheyr@rpi.edu.

LAHIRI, JHUMPA, writer; b. London, Eng., July 1967; BA in English Lit., Barnard Coll.; MA in English, MA in Creative Writing, MA in Comparative Lit., PhD in Renaissance studies, Boston U. Author: (short stories) The New Yorker, 1998, (collection of short stories) Interpreter of Maladies, 1999 (O. Henry award, Pulitzer prize for fiction, 2000), (photography collection) India Holy Song, 2000, The Namesake: A Novel, 2003. Office: c/o Houghton Mifflin 222 Berkeley St Boston MA 02116

LAHOOD, JULIE ANN, small business owner; b. Martins Ferry, Ohio, May 31; d. Joseph Noah LaHood and Thelma Marie Rafful LaHood. *Father, Joseph Noah (b. 1903), was born in Saint John, New Brunswick, Canada. My father and grandfather were in business together as merchants, and eventually came to Wheeling, West Virginia to continue the Grandfather Noah, and Son business. Mother, Thelma Marie Rafful La Hood (b. 1905), was a school teacher in Toledo, Ohio. Both of my parents were talented singers. I was awarded Miss Toledo runner up at the age of seventeen. At the age of 10, I received the Tri State piano award. I have played in recitals that were heard on the local radio for the tri-state area of West Virginia, Virginia, and Ohio.* Student, Ray Coll. Design, Chgo., 1954—55, Loyola U., 1974—79. Jr. exec. Bonwit Teller, Chgo., 1959—62; asst. dept. mgr. Saks Fifth Ave., Chgo., 1962; owner Historic Properties, Monroe, Mich., Julie's Trading Post, Monroe, St. Charles, Ill. Author: numerous poems. Mem Monroe County Hist. Soc., Mich., Nat. ProLife Alliance, Washington, 2004—; humane amb. Neglected Animals, St. Charles, 1999. Recipient Best Poems and Poets, Internat. Soc. Poets, 2002, 2003. Mem.: Internat. Bio. Ctr. (Bus. award 2005), US Navy League, Nat. Trust for Historic Preservation, Chgo. Hist. Soc. Republican. Roman Catholic. Avocations: gardening, cooking, poetry, music. Home: 707 Monroe Ave Saint Charles IL 60174

LAHOOD, MARVIN JOHN, language educator; b. Auburn, NY, Mar. 21, 1933; s. Salem and Anna (Mahfoud) L.; m. Marjorie Braun, Aug. 22, 1959; children: John, Melissa, Mark. BS, Boston Coll., 1954; MA in English, U. Notre Dame, 1958, PhD in English, 1962. Instr. Niagara U., 1960-61, assoc. prof., 1962-64, Buffalo (N.Y.) State Coll., 1964-67, prof., 1967-71, prof. ind. study, 1968-69, prof., assoc. for acad. devel., 1969-71, prof., 1978-95, Disting. tchg. prof., 1995—2005; prof., acad. dean Coll. Misericordia, 1971-72, Salem State Coll., 1972-75; prof., dean faculty D'Youville Coll., 1975-78; ret., 2005. Chair Burchfield Poets and Writers Com., 1985—; manuscript reviewer Prentice Hall, 1986-88, book reviewer Buffalo News, 2000-; lectr. U. Dortmund, Germany, 1986, Lille U., France, Cath. U. Lille, 1991; chair senate ops. com. SUNY, 1994-97, chair undergrad com., 1999-2002, chair awards com., 2002-05; mem. SUNY Task Force on Distance Learning, 1994-95, Gen. Edn., 1998-99, Faculty Devel., 2002. Author: Conrad Richter's America, 1974, State University College at Buffalo, A History: 1946-1972, 1980; editor: Latvian Literature, 1964, Tender Is the Night: Essays in Criticism, 1969, Stories of Tragedy and Triumph, 1997; contbr. Grad. Degrees column Notre Dame Mag., 1996--; contbr. articles to prof. jours. Pres. Mt. St. Mary Acad. Bd. Trustees, 1990-94. SUNY Faculty Rsch. fellow, 1967-68, USOE fellow Inst. on Ednl. Media, 1967, SUNY fellow Inst. for Devel. Black Studies, 1969; SUNY Faculty Exch. scholar, 1969—; recipient SUNY Chancellor's award, 1985, Boston Coll. Alumni award, 1997, Tchr. of Yr. award Buffalo State Coll. United Student Govt., 1999. Mem. F. Scott Fitzgerald Soc. (bd. dirs. 1999—). Office Phone: 716-878-5404. Business E-Mail: lahoodmj@buffalostate.edu.

LAHOOD, MARY ANNE, real estate investor; b. Grosse Pointe Farms, Mich., Aug. 23, 1947; d. Tom and Melinia (Simon) LaHood; children: Lila, Michael. BA, Wayne State U., 1972. Ptnr. LaHood Lanes, Inc., St. Clair Shores, Mich., 1972-89, LaHood Properties, Grosse Pointe Shores, Mich., 1972—. Patron Detroit Inst. of Arts, Grosse Pointe Yacht Club; sec. environ. group NYCE, Detroit Hist. Soc. Avocations: fiction writing, art collecting, long distance walking, sailing, tennis. Home: 20 Stillmeadow Ln Grosse Pointe Shores MI 48236-1118 Business E-Mail: lahood@alumni.wayne.edu.

LAHOOD, RAY H., congressman; b. Peoria, Ill., Dec. 6, 1945; m. Kathleen (Kathy) Dunk LaHood; children: Darin, Amy, Sam, Sara. Student, Canton Jr. Coll., Ill.; BS in Edn. and Sociology, Bradley U., 1971. Tchr. Catholic and pub. jr. high schs., 1971-77; dist. administrv. asst. to congressman Tom Railsback, 1977; mem. Ill. Ho. of Reps., 1982—83; Chief of Staff to Congressman Bob Michels Ho. of Reps., 1993—94; mem. U.S. Congress from 18th Ill. dist., 1995—. Mem. Intelligence Com., Appropriations Com. Bd. dirs. Economic Devel. Coun.; pres. sch. bd. Spalding and Notre Dame H.Schs., Bradley U. Nat. Alumni Bd.; svc. to Children's Hosp. Bd., Peoria Area Retarded Citizens Bd.; dir. Rock Island County Youth Svcs. Bur., 1972-74. Mem. ITOO Soc., Downtown Rotary Club, Holy Family Ch. (Peoria), Peoria Area C. of C. Republican. Roman Catholic. Office: US House Reps 1424 Longworth HOB Washington DC 20515-1318 also: 100 NE Monroe St Ste 100 Peoria IL 61602-1003*

LAHTI, CHRISTINE, actress; b. Detroit, Apr. 5, 1950; d. Paul Theodore and Elizabeth Margaret (Tabar) L.; m. Thomas Schlamme, Sept. 4, 1983; 1 child, Wilson Lahti. BA in Speech, U. Mich., 1972; postgrad., Fla. State U., 1972-73; studies with William Esper, Uta Hagen, Herbert Berghof Studios. Actress: (stage prodns.) The Woods, 1978 (Theater World award 1979), Division Street, 1980, Loose Ends, 1981, Present Laughter, 1983, Landscape of the Body, 1984, The Country Girl, 1984, Cat on a Hot Tin Roof, 1985, Little Murders, 1987, The Heidi Chronicles, 1989, Three Hotels, 1993; regular mem. cast (TV series) Dr. Scorpion, 1978, The Harvey Korman Show, 1978, Chicago Hope, 1995-1999, (TV films) The Last Tenant, 1978, The Henderson Monster, 1980, The Executioner's Song, 1982, Single Bars, Single Women, 1984, Love Lives On, 1985, Amerika, 1987, No Place Like Home, 1989, Crazy from the Heart, 1991, The Fear Inside, 1992, The Good Fight, 1985, The Four Diamonds, 1995, Subway Stories: Tales from the Underground, 1997, Hope, 1997, An American Daughter, 2000, The Pilot's Wife, 2002, Out of the Ashes, 2003 (feature films) And Justice For All, 1979, Whose Life Is It, Anyway?, 1981, Swing Shift, 1984 (N.Y. Film Critics Circle award for best supporting actress 1985, Acad. award nominee 1985, Golden Globe award nominee 1985), Ladies and Gentlemen: The Fabulous Stains, 1985, Just Between Friends, 1986, Housekeeping, 1987, Season of Dreams, 1987, Stacking, 1988, Running on Empty, 1988, Gross Anatomy, 1989, Miss Firecracker, 1989, Funny About Love, 1990, The Doctor, 1991, Leaving Normal, 1992, Hideaway, 1995, Pie in the Sky, 1995, A Weekend in the Country, 1996; prodr. short action film, actress: Lieberman in Love, 1995 (Acad. award nominee for best live action short film 1996). Recipient Golden Globe award for Best Actress in a Miniseries or Motion picture Made for TV. Office: ICM c/o Toni Howard 8942 Wilshire Blvd Beverly Hills CA 90211-1934

LAI, ERIC PONG SHING, family physician, educator; b. Kowloon, Hong Kong, May 20, 1946; s. Man Hoi and Lai Ming (Chiu) L.; m. Mimi Maria Mak Lai, Sept. 11, 1972; children: Gordon, Jennifer. BSc, Acadia U., Wolfville, Nova Scotia, 1971; MB, B CH, LRCS, LLMRCP, U. Ireland, Dublin, 1977; DFM, Chinese U. Hong Kong, 1989. Med. diplomate, Ireland, UK, Hong Kong. Rsch. fellow Med. Sch. McGill U., Montreal, Can., 1971; resident in medicine Chesterton Hosp. Cambridge (Eng.) U., 1977; resident New Addenbrooke Hosp., Cambridge, 1978; resident in gynecology Princess Margaret Hosp., Kowloon, Hong Kong, 1979-81; pvt. practice family physician Hong Kong, 1981-2001. Bd. dirs. First Med. Mgmt. Ltd., Calgary, Alta., Can., 1989; found. dir. Chinese Recreation Assn., Calgary; lectr. Hong Kong U., 1986-92, Chinese U. Hong Kong, 1986-92; facilitator Hong Kong Coll. Gen. Practitioners, 1986-92; internat. dir. World Orgn. Health Promotion, 1993-2002; cons. G-Way Holdings Internat. Inc., 1993-2002; internat. med. dir. G-Way Health Centre, Can., 1995-2002. Mem. Hong Kong Dem. Found., 1990-92, Hong Kong Bd. Edn. Coll. Gen. Practitioners, 1986-92, chmn., 1991-92, com. chmn. refresher course, 1991-92; vice chmn. found. Kidney Ctr. Precious Blood Hosp., 1991; adviser S.E. Asia Rsch. Inst., 1992; mem. Pub. Edn. Com., 1993-95; med. cons. World Orgn. Health Promotion, Can., 1993-2002. Named Henry Burton De Wolfe scholar to McGill U., 1971. Mem. Internat. Lions Club (v.p. Mt. Cameron chpt. 1986-90, pres. 1990-91, zone chmn. Internat. Club 1991-92, Melvin Jones fellow 1991-2002). Democrat. Avocations: reading, meditation, poetry, walking, boxing.

LAI, FENG-QI, designing educator; b. Shanghai, Mar. 25, 1948; arrived in U.S., 1992; d. Zheng-Zhong Lai and Yao-Zhang Zhu; m. Qun Zhang, Oct. 22, 1984. *Both parents were lawyers in the late 1930s and early 1940s. Father Zheng-Zhong Lai was also an educator. He started a high school named Wu Xian Nu Zhong in Suzhow, China. Mother Yao-Zhang Zhu was a top student. She was awarded a gold medal upon her graduation from Fudan University, Shanghai, China in 1935. Grandniece Jia-Ying Lai, born in 1996, won five awards at the Chinese National Children's Drawing competitions for the three consecutive years from 2000 to 2002. Of the five awards, two were silver, one bronze, and two were honorable mention.* BA, Changsha (China) Railway Inst., 1982; MS, Purdue U., 1994, PhD, 1997. Asst. lectr. Shanghai Tiedao U., 1982-86, lectr., assoc. dir., 1986-91; instrnl. designer Nat. Edn. Tng. Group, Naperville, Ill., 1998; sr. instr., dir. tng. Advanced Tech. Support, Inc., Schaumburg, Ill., 1998-2000; sr. instrnl. designer, project mgr. Cognitive Concepts, Inc., Evanston, Ill., 2000—02; asst. prof. Ind. State U., Terre Haute, Ind., 2002—. Transl.: Writing Scientific Papers in English, 1983; co-author: Applied Cryptography, 1999, Fundamental Computer Skills, 2004. Mem.: Phi Kappa Phi. Avocations: music, reading, Chinese poetry, photography, crafts. Business E-Mail: eslai@isugw.indstate.edu.

LAI, JUEY HONG, chemical engineer; b. Taipei, Taiwan, Dec. 4, 1936; arrived in U.S., 1961, naturalized, 1976; s. Kwo-Wang and Chin-Fong L.; m. Li-Huey Chang, June 30, 1968; children: Eric Yo-Ping, Bruce Yo-Sheng. BSChemE, Nat. Taiwan U., 1959; MSChemE, U. Wash., 1963, PhD in Phys. Chemistry, 1969. Rsch. specialist dept. chemistry U. Minn., 1969-73; prin. rsch. scientist Honeywell Phys. Scis. Ctr., Honeywell, Inc., Bloomington, 1973-78, sr. prin. rsch. scientist, 1978-83; staff scientist Honeywell Tech. Ctr., Honeywell, Inc., 1983-87; pres. Lai Labs., Inc., Burnsville, 1988—. Mem. spl. emphasis rev. panel Nat. Inst. Dental and Craniofacial Rsch./NIH, 2000—04; lectr. in field. Author, editor: Polymers for Electronic Applications, 1989; contbr. articles on solid state chemistry, polymer chemistry and dental materials to tech. jours.; rschr. on polymer materials for electronics, gas removal tech., solid state chemistry and dental materials; holder 9 patents in electronic and dental materials. Bd. dirs. Chinese Am. Assn. Minn., 1977-79, Minn. Taiwanese Assn., 1995-97, 1998-2001. Recipient H.W. Sweatt Tech. award, Honeywell, Inc., 1980, Small Bus. Innovation Rsch. award, Dept. Health and Human Svcs., 1990, 1993—94, 1995, 1996—98, 1997, 1999—2001; grantee, Minn. Tech. Inc., 1991. Fellow: Acad. of Dental Materials, Am. Inst. Chemists; mem.: Am. Chem. Soc., Am. Assn. Dental Rsch., Phi Lambda Upsilon, Sigma Xi. Office: Lai Labs Inc 14617 White Oak Dr Burnsville MN 55337-2982 E-mail: jlai@aol.com.

LAI, LIWEN, b. Taipei, Taiwan, 1957; d. Kwan-Long Lai. BS, Nat. Taiwan U., 1980; MS, U. Calif., San Francisco, 1983; PhD, U. Tex., Dallas, 1987. Diplomate Am. Coll. Med. Genetics. Postdoctoral fellow NIH, Bethesda, Md., 1987-89; asst. rsch. sci. U. Ariz., Tuscon, 1990-94, asst. dir. Molecular Diagnostic Lab., 1992—, rsch. asst. prof., 1995-97; rsch. assoc. prof., 1997—2003; rsch. prof., 2003—. Rsch. grantee Elks, 1994-96, Dialysis Clinic Inc., 1994-96, So. Ariz. Found., 1996—, NIH, 1997—. Mem. Am. Soc. Human Genetics, Am. Soc. Gene Therapy, Am. Soc. Nephrology, Am. Soc. Cell Biology. Office: U Ariz Dept Medicine 1501 N Campbell Ave Tucson AZ 85724-0001

LAI, TZE LEUNG, mathematician, educator; b. Hong Kong, China, June 28, 1945; s. Chi Yau Lai and Wai Chun Cheng; m. Letitia Chow, June 23, 1975; children: Peter, David. PhD, Columbia U., 1971. Prof., chair of stats. Stanford U., Calif., 1987—; prof. math. stats. Columbia U., New York, 1977—87. Adv. bd. mem. Academia Sinica, Taipei, Taiwan, 1991—. Author books and jour. articles. Recipient Guggenheim Fellowship, Guggenheim Found., 1983—84. Fellow: Am. Statis. Assn. (COPSS Award 1983). Office: Stanford Univ Sequoia Hall Serra Mall Stanford CA 94305-4065 Office Phone: 650-7232622. Business E-Mail: lait@stat.stanford.edu.

LAI, W(EI) MICHAEL, mechanical engineer, educator; b. Amoy, Fukien, China, Nov. 29, 1930; naturalized U.S. citizen, 1967; m. Linda Yu-ling Chu, Dec. 21, 1963. BSCE, Nat. Taiwan U., 1953; MS in Engring. Mech., U. Mich., 1959, PhD, 1962. Asst. prof. mechanics Renssalaer Poly. Inst., Troy,

N.Y., 1961-66, assoc. prof., 1967-77, prof., 1978-87, acting dept. chmn., 1986-87; prof. mech. engring. and orthopaedic bioengring. Columbia U., N.Y.C., 1987—2004, prof. emeritus, 2004—, acting chmn. dept. mech. engring., 1995-96, chmn. dept. mech. engring., 1996—2002. Author: Elements of Elasticity, 1965, Introduction to Continuum Mechanics, 1974, 3rd edit., 1993, Fundamentals of Surface Mechanics, 2002. Fellow: ASME (chmn. bioengring. divsn. 1996—97, Melville medal for best paper 1982, Best Paper award bioengring. divsn. 1991, Lissner medal for outstanding achievement in bioengring. 2001), Am. Inst. Med. and Biol. Engring. (founding); mem.: AAAS, Orthopaedic Rsch. Soc., Am. Soc. Biomechanics. Home: 215 W 95th St Apt 9H New York NY 10025-6355 Office: Columbia U Dept Mech Engring W 120th St Mail Code 4703 New York NY 10027 E-mail: WML1@columbia.edu.

LAI, ZHENNAN, research scientist; s. Shuzhen Lai and Wenju Deng; m. May Jumei Zhang; children: Anny, Sharon. PhD, U. Uppsala, 1994; BS in Biol. Sci., Guangzhou U., China. M. Sc. Pharmacology Faculty of Pharmacy, 1990. Rsch. scholar dept. pharm. biosci. Biomedical Ctr., Uppsala, Sweden, 1988—94; postdoctoral molecular genetist dept. med. and molecular genetics Ind. U. Sch. Medicine, Ind., 1996—97; rsch. fellow Devel. and Metabolic Neurology Br., Nat. Inst. Neurol. Disorders and Stroke NIH, Bethesda, Md., 1997—2000; Outstanding (0-1) scientist, supr. DMNB-NIH postdoctoral fellows, summer students NIH, 2000—. Guest prof. Guangzhou U., 2002; sci. adv. bd. Precision Sys. Sci. Co. Ltd., Japan. NIH Rsch. fellowship, NIH, 1997. Mem.: Fedn. of Am. Soc. for Exptl. Biology, Soc. for Devel. Biology, Soc. for Am. Gene Therapy, Soc. for Neuroscience. Achievements include invention of a lentiviral two-gene vector expressing VP22 fusion protein; lentiviral-based gene trap vector; therapeutic uses of a defective HIV-1 lentiviral vector lacking the nef gene; preparative zone electrophoresis in a muti-buffer syst with purified protein retaining biological activity; discovery of hGH and hPRL receptors in human brain. Office: DMNB-NINDS Nat Inst of Health Bethesda MD 20892 E-mail: laiz@ninds.nih.gov.

LAIBMAN, DAVID, economist, educator; b. N.Y.C., Dec. 25, 1942; s. Erwin Milton Laibman, Beatrice Rosenberg Laibman; m. Marcia Elaine Klugman; children: Anthony Klugman, Leslie, Raquel Klugman. BA in Econ., Antioch Coll., 1965; PhD in Econ., New Sch. for Social Rsch., 1973. Prof. of econ. CUNY, N.Y.C., 1982—. Author: Value, Technical Change and Crisis: Explorations in Marxist Economic Theory, 1992, Capitalist Macrodynamics: A Systematic Introduction, 1997; editor: Science & Society, 1991—. Recipient Edith Henry Johnson Meml. award in Econ., New Sch. for Social Rsch., 1973. Mem.: Union for Radical Polit. Econ. Avocation: Acoustic guitar (ragtime); folk music. Home: 50 Plaza Street E #2C Brooklyn NY 11238 Office: Graduate School CUNY 365 Fifth Avenue New York NY 10016 Personal E-mail: dlaibman@jjay.cuny.edu.

LAIDLAW, ANDREW R., lawyer; b. Durham, NC, Aug. 28, 1946; BA, Northwestern U., 1969; JD, U. NC, 1972. Bar: Ill. 1972. Ptnr. Seyfarth Shaw LLP, Chgo., mem. exec. com., head Contracts Practice Area, head Litig. Practice Area. Contbr. articles to profl. jour. Mem.: Barristers, ABA (securities law com. 1982—, antitrust com.). Office: Seyfarth Shaw LLP Mid Continental Plz 55 E Monroe St Ste 4200 Chicago IL 60603-5863 Office Phone: 312-269-8823. Office Fax: 312-269-8869. Business E-Mail: alaidlaw@seyfarth.com.*

LAIDLAW, ROBERT RICHARD, publishing company executive; b. Berwyn, Ill., Mar. 25, 1923; s. John and Mabel Josephine (Howard) L.; m. Evangeline Rene Harrelson, Aug. 12, 1944; children— Andrew Robert, Kimberly, Lisa; m. Marilyn C. Carlson, Sept. 7, 1998. Student, Dartmouth Coll., 1941-42; AB, U. N.C., 1947, JD, 1950. Sales rep. Laidlaw Bros. (textbook pubs.), River Forest, Ill., 1950-58, sales mgr., 1958-60, exec. v.p., 1960-68, pres., 1968-85. Served with USNR, 1942-45. Congregationalist.

LAIDLAW, SAUNDRA See WESTON, SAUNDRA

LAIDLAW, WILLIAM SAMUEL HUGH, oil company executive; b. London, Jan. 3, 1956; s. Christopher Charles Fraser and Nina Laidlaw; m. Debbie Laidlaw, 4 children. MA, Cambridge U., 1977; MBA, Insead, France, 1981. Solicitor Macfarlanes, London, 1977-79; corp. planner Société Françaises Pétroles B.P., Paris, 1979-80; mgr. corp. planning Amerada Hess Corp., N.Y.C., 1981-83; v.p. Amerada Hess Ltd., London, 1983-85, mng. dir., 1986—95, chmn., 1995; exec. v.p. Amerada Hess Corp., 1993—95, pres., COO London, 1996—2001; CEO Enterprise Oil plc, 2001—02; exec. v.p., bus. devel. ChevronTexaco Corp., San Ramon, Calif., 2003—. Mem. Inst. Petroleum (v.p.), U.K. Offshore Operators Assn (pres. 1991-92), P.S.T.I. (chmn.), N.E.L. (dir.). Office: ChevronTexaco Corp 6001 Bollinger Canyon Rd San Ramon CA 94583

LAIDLER, DAVID ERNEST WILLIAM, economics professor; b. Tynemouth, Northumberland, Eng., Aug. 12, 1938; s. John Alphonse and Leonora (Gosman) L.; m. Antje Charlotte Breitwisch, Jan. 29, 1965; 1 dau., Nicole Joanna; m. Frances Joan Hutner, Aug. 1960 (div. 1964). B.Sc., London Sch. Econs., 1959; MA, U. Syracuse, 1960; PhD, U. Chgo., 1964; MA, U. Manchester, Eng., 1973. Temporary asst. lectr. London Sch. Econs., 1961-62; asst. prof. U. Calif.-Berkeley, 1963-66; lectr. econs. U. Essex, Colchester, Eng., 1966-69; prof. econs. U. Manchester, 1969-75; vis. prof. econs. Brown U., Providence, 1973; prof. econs. U. Western Ont., London, Canada, 1975—2004, prof. emeritus, 2004—. Chair Bank of Montreal, 2000-05; econ. adv. panel to Marc Lalonde, minister fin., Ottawa, Ont., 1982-84; rsch. coord. Macdonald Royal Commn., 1984-85; scholar in residence C.D. Howe Inst., 1990—; Canadian Bankers' Assn. scholar, 2000-03; mem. econs. com. Social Sci. Rsch. Coun., Gt. Britain, 1972-75; program adv. com. Carnegie-Rochester Pub. Policy Conf. Series, Rochester, Pitts., 1978-79; Lister lectr. Brit. Assn. Advancement Sci., 1972; spl. advisor Bank of Can., 1998-99. Author: The Demand for Money - Theories and Evidence, 1969, Introduction to Microeconomics, 1974, Essays on Money and Inflation, 1975, Monetarist Perspectives, 1982, Taking Money Seriously, 1990, The Golden Age of the Quantity Theory, 1991; (with W. Robson) The Great Canadian Disinflation, 1993, Money and Macroeconomics, Selected Essays, 1997, Fabricating the Keynesian Revolution, 1999, Two Percent Target, 2004; mem. editl. bd. Rev. Econ. Studies, 1970-75, Am. Econ. Rev., 1976-78, Can. Jour. Econs., 1977-79, Jour. Econ. Lit., 1978-91; assoc. editor: Jour. Money, Credit and Banking, 1979—. Rsch. grantee NSF, 1964-66, Social Sci. Rsch. Coun., 1971-76, Social Scis. and Humanities Rsch. Coun. Can., 1977-81, 94-99, 94—, Bradley Found., 1991-96. Fellow Royal Soc. Can., mem. Am. Econ. Assn., Can. Econ. Assn. (exec. com. 1980-83, pres. 1987-88, Douglas Purvis Meml. prize 1994). Home: 345 Grangeover Ave London ON Canada N69 4K8 Office: U Western Ont Dept Econs London ON Canada N6A 5C2 Office Phone: 519-661-3400. Business E-Mail: laidler@uwo.ca.

LAIKIN, ROBERT J., electronics company executive; V.p. Centruy Cellular Network, 1986-87, pres., 1988—93; v.p., treas. Brightpoint, Inc., Indpls., 1989-92, pres., 1992—96, chmn., CEO, 1994—. Office: Brightpoint Inc 501 Airtech Pkwy Plainfield IN 46168-7408*

LAIN, DAVID CORNELIUS, health scientist, researcher; b. Savannah, Ga., May 17, 1955; s. Marion Cornelius and Sandra (Weatherly) L.; m. Brenda Kay Gastin, May 24, 1980; children: Candace, Heather. BS, MS, Columbia Pacific U., 1985, PhD, 1987; JD, Newport U., 1996. Diplomate Am. Bd. Forensic Examiners, Am. Bd. Forensic Medicine; lic. respiratory care practitioner. Instr. dept. continuing edn. Ga. So. U., Statesboro, 1983; rsch. devel. coord. Meml. Med. Ctr. Inc., Savannah, Ga., 1983-87; rsch. coord., asst. prof. dept. allied health sci. Med. Coll. Ga., Augusta, 1987—; clin. mgr. Ohmeda Respiratory Care, Columba, Md., 1990—95; clin. mgr., v.p. clin. and program devel. Respironics, Inc., Murrysville, Pa., 1995-2001; pres. Lain Med. Consultants, Inc., Kennesaw, Ga., 1997-2000; pres., CEO Nationwide Sleep Cons., Inc., Murrysville, Cleve., 2001—04; sleep specialist S.W. Cleve. Sleep Ctr., 2002—04; v.p. clin. devel. Vapotherm, Stevensville, Md. Bd. dirs. Ga. Soc. Cardiopulmonary Tech., Atlanta, 1987; mem. Respiratory Therapy Adv. Com., Augusta, 1987-90; cons. Aero-Med. Internat., 1987; rsch. affiliate Siemen Elem., Schaumburg, Ill., 1986; manuscript reviewer Am. Assn. Respiration Therapy, Dallas, 1988, Am. Col. Chest Disease, 1990. Contbr. articles to profl. jours. Recipient Appreciation award Am. Heart Assn., 1985, Outstanding Achievement award Calif. Coll. Health Sci., 1986. Mem. AAAS, So. Med. Assn., N.Y. Acad. Sci., Am. Assn. Respiratory Care, Nat. Bd. Respiratory Care (registered respiratory therapist). Democrat. Achievements include 9 inventions; research on reduction of peak inspiratory pressure during acute lung injury to reduce latrogenic progression of lung pathology; diagnosis and treatment of newborn jaundice. Office: 198Log Canoe Cir Stevensville MD 21666

LAINE, CHRISTINE E., poet; b. El Paso, Tex., Nov. 30, 1968; d. Robert John Worden and Shirley Rae Walsh; m. John Patrick Lennon, June 20, 1988 (div. Feb. 2002); children: Jesse Alexander, Corey Christopher. Lic. realtor Va. Dept. Profl. Occupl. Regulation, 2002. Web designer Artisan Studio Design, Falls Church, Va., 1999—. Editor Little Poem Press & VLQ, Falls Church, Va., 2000—. Author: Allegory, 2002, The Weight of Dust, 2003, Postcards From A Summer Girl, 2004. Pub. info. officer Nat. Capitol Squadron of the Commemorative Air Force, Culpeper, Va., 2001—. With U.S. Army, 1992—96. Nominee Pushcart prize, 2004, 2005; recipient Favorite Individual Poet's Page, Poetry Super Hwy., 2001, Favorite Featured Poet - Hon. Mention, 2000. Mem.: No. Va. Assn. of Realtors (licentiate), Aircraft Owners and Pilots Assn., Commemorative Air Force (pub. info. officer 2001—), Ninety Nines. Avocations: aviation, art/photography, music, antiques, travel. Office: Artisan Studio Design PO Box 185 Falls Church VA 22040-0185 Home Fax: 703-852-3906. Personal E-mail: poet@celaine.com.

LAINE, IRIS RUTH, minister, advertising executive, public relations executive; b. Aurora, Ill., Feb. 8, 1925; d. Herman Carl Butke and Ella Stallman; m. Steven Laine, Nov. 4, 1970; 1 child, Leah Reich; stepchildren: Karen McGivney, David, Mark. BA, Fla. Atlantic U., 1981; postgrad., Harvard Div. Sch., 1983, St. Vincent de Paul Sem., 1985-86; MDiv, Luth. Sem., 1988. Ordained to ministry Evangelical Luth. Ch., 1988. Advt. writer, prodr. Chgo. Advt. Agys. and Sears Roebuck & Co., Chgo., 1950—61; promotion copy chief Chgo. Sun-Times/Daily News, 1962—65; trade rels. dir. Smith, Bucklin & Assocs., Inc., Chgo., 1966—78; v.p., treas. Stirco, Inc., Boca Raton, 1979—82; pastor, preacher Evang. Luth. Ch. in Am., Fla., 1987—95. Author: Getting to Know God, 2001; co-author: Promotion in Foodservice, 1972. Mem. Cmty. Interfaith Coalition, Boca Raton, 1992-94, Women in Ministry, Boca Raton, 1988-90, Tradewinds Conf. Mins., Palm Beach/Martin counties, Fla., 1987-92, Synodical Coun., Evang. Luth. Ch. in Am., Fla., 1989-90; dir. Coun. on Hotel, Restaurant and Instnl. Edn., 1969; dir., sec. Internat. Food Editl. Coun., Nat. Orgn., 1968; vol. Rep. Orgns., Palm Beach County, 1996—. Recipient Award Art Dirs. Club of Chgo., 1964; named Top Ten in TV Pharms. award Am. TV Commls. Festival, 1960. Mem. Rotary Internat., Phi Kappa Phi, Alpha Sigma Lambda. Avocations: writing, social service. Home: 500 S Ocean Blvd Apt 904 Boca Raton FL 33432 Fax: 561-392-4822. E-mail: irislaine@aol.com.

LAING, JAMES THOMAS, retired not-for-profit developer; b. Charleston, W.Va., Jan. 2, 1934; s. James Tamplin and Claire (Lenila) Laing; m. Patricia Ann Boehmer, June 25, 1955 (div. Mar. 1976); children: Michael Thomas, Susan Kay; m. Barbara Jean Crossman, Apr. 11, 1981. AB, Kent State U., 1955, MA, 1956. Asst. exec. dir. United Cmty. Svcs., Lorain, Ohio, 1959-64; assoc. exec. sec. United Fund, Canton, Ohio, 1964-69, exec. dir. St. Joseph, Mo., 1969-73, United Way, South Bend, Ind., 1973-76, United Way Oakland County, Pontiac, Mich., 1976-97, pres., 1997-99; ret., 1999. Instr. sociology Kent State U., St. Mary's Coll., South Bend, Oakland U., Rochester, Mich., 1959—80; field cons. United Health Founds., N.Y.C., 1967—71; mem. profl. adv. com. United Way Am., Alexandria, Va., 1979—84; mem. profl. adv. bd. United Way Internat., 1981—96. Bd. dirs. United Way Nat. Retiree Assn., 1998—, v.p., 2000—02; bd. dirs. Internat. Bluegrass Music Mus., Owensboro, Ky., 1994—2004, treas. bd., 1999—2001; bd. dirs. United Way Mich., 1999—2000. Mem.: Blue Key, Rotary (past pres.), Pi Gamma Mu, Alpha Kappa Delta, Phi Sigma Kappa. Methodist. Avocations: bluegrass music, golf, photography. Home: 3254 Angelus Dr Waterford MI 48329-2512 E-mail: frippster@copper.net.

LAING, KAREL ANN, magazine publishing executive; b. Mpls., July 5, 1939; d. Edward Francis and Elizabeth Jane Karel (Templeton) Hannon; m. G. R. Cheesebrough, Dec. 19, 1959 (div. 1969); 1 child, Jennifer Read; m. Ronald Harris Laing, Jan. 6, 1973; 1 child, Christopher Harris Grad., U. Minn., 1960. With Guthrie Symphony Opera Program, Mpls., 1969-71; account supr. Colle & McVoy Advt. Agy., Richfield, Minn., 1971-74; owner The Cottage, Edina, Minn., 1974-75; salespromotion rep. Robert Meyers & Assocs., St. Louis Park, Minn., 1975-76; cons. Webb Co., St. Paul, 1976-77, custom pub. dir., 1977-89; pres. K.L. Publs., Inc., Bloomington, Minn., 1989—. Contbr. articles to profl. jours. Community vol. Am. Heart Assn., Am. Cancer Soc., Edina PTA; charter sponsor Walk Around Am., St. Paul, 1985 Mem. Bank Mktg. Assn., Fin. Instn. Mktg. Assn., Advt. Fedn. Am., Am. Bankers Assn., Direct Mail Mktg. Assn., Minn. Mag. Pub. Assn. (founder, bd. govs.), St. Andrews Soc. Republican. Presbyterian. Avocations: painting, gardening, reading, travel. Office: KL Publs 2001 Killebrew Dr Minneapolis MN 55425-1865

LAINGEN, LOWELL BRUCE, diplomat; b. Odin Twp., Minn., Aug. 6, 1922; s. Palmer K. and Ida Mabel (Eng) L.; m. Penelope Babcock, June 1, 1957; children: William Bruce, Charles Winslow, James Palmer. BA cum laude, St. Olaf Coll., 1947; MA in Internat. Relations, U. Minn., 1949, LLD honoris causa, 2005. Internat. rels. officer State Dept., 1949-50; joined U.S. Fgn. Svc., 1950; vice consul Hamburg, Germany, 1951-53; 3d sec. embassy Teheran, Iran, 1953-54; consul Meshed, Iran, 1954-55; asst., then officer chargé Greek affairs State Dept., 1956-60; 2d sec., then 1st sec. embassy Karachi, Pakistan, 1960-64; with Pakistan/Afghanistan affairs bur. State Dept., 1964-67; assigned Nat. War Coll., 1967-68; dep. chief mission to Afghanistan Kabul, 1968-71; country dir. Pakistan, Afghanistan and Bangladesh, State Dept., 1971-73, 1973-74, acting dep. asst. sec. state for Near Eastern and South Asian affairs, 1974-75, dep. asst. sec. state for European affairs, 1975-76; ambassador to Malta, 1977-79; chargé d'affaires Am. Embassy, Teheran, Iran, 1979; held hostage by Iranian student militants, 1979-81; v.p. Nat. Def. U., Ft. McNair, Washington, 1981-86; exec. dir. Nat. Commn. Pub. Service, Washington, 1987-90; pres. Am. Acad. Diplomacy, 1991—. Lectr. Security Overseas Seminar, Fgn. Svc. Inst., 1995-2000; Sol Linowitz chair in internat. rels. Hamilton Coll., 1998; ex officio mem. NAt. Commn. Pub. Svc., 2002—. Recipient Fgn. Svc. cup, 1998. Home: 5627 Old Chester Rd Bethesda MD 20814-1035 E-mail: bplaingen@aol.com.

LAIOU, ANGELIKI EVANGELOS, history professor; b. Athens, Greece, Apr. 6, 1941; came to U.S., 1959; d. Evangelos K. and Virginia I. (Apostolides) Laios; m. Stavros B. Thomadakis, July 14, 1973; 1 son, Vassili N. BA, Brandeis U., 1961; MA, Harvard U., 1962, PhD, 1966. Asst. prof. history Harvard U., Cambridge, Mass., 1969-72, Dumbarton Oaks prof. Byzantine history, 1981—; assoc. prof. Brandeis U., Waltham, 1972-75; prof. Rutgers U., New Brunswick, N.J., 1975-79, disting. prof., 1979-81; chmn. Gennadeion com. (Am. Sch. Classical Studies), Athens, Greece, 1981-84; dir. Dumbarton Oaks, 1989-98; prof. history Harvard U., Cambridge, 1998—. Mem. Greek Parliament, 2000-2002; dep. min. fgn. affairs, Greece, 2000. Author: Constantinople and the Latins, 1972, Peasant Society in the Late Byzantine Empire, 1977, Mariage, amour et parenté à Byzance, XIe-XIIIe siècles, 1992, Gender, Society and Economic Life in Byzantium, 1992, The Economic History of Byzantium, 2002. Guggenheim Found. fellow, 1971-72, 79-80, Dumbarton Oaks sr. fellow, 1983—, Am. Coun. Learned Socs. fellow, 1988-89. Fellow: Acad. des Inscriptions et Balles Lettres, Am. Acad. Arts and Scis., Acad. Athens, Medieval Acad.; mem.: Am. Hist. Assn., Medieval Acad. Am., Greek Com. Study of South Eastern Europe. Office: Harvard U Dept History Cambridge MA 02138 Office Phone: 617-495-5108. E-mail: laiou@fas.harvard.edu.

LAIRD, DAVID, humanities educator emeritus; b. Marshfield, Wis., Oct. 17, 1927; s. Melvin Robert and Helen Melissa (Connor) L.; m. Helen Astrid Lauritzen, Sept. 10, 1955; 1 child, Vanessa Ann. PhB, U. Chgo., 1947; BA with highest honor, U. Wis., 1950, MA, 1951, PhD, 1955; postgrad., Courtauld Inst., 1953. Instr. to asst. prof. Oberlin Coll., 1955-58; mem. faculty Calif. State U., L.A., 1958—, chmn. dept. English, 1969-73, chmn. dept. Am. studies, 1977-79. Nat. Humanities Inst. fellow U. Chgo., 1978-79; sr. Fulbright lectr. U. Tunis, Tunisia, 1979-80; fellow Folger Shakespeare Libr., 1982; Fulbright lectr. Odense U. (Denmark), 1983-84; vis. prof. U. Ottawa, 1984-85; cons. to Choice. Mem. editorial bd. Jour. Forest History; contbr. articles on Shakespeare, Am. lit. and cultural history to profl. jours. Mem. Western Shakespeare Seminar, Friends of Huntington Libr. Recipient Outstanding Prof. award Calif. State U., 1987, Nat. Endowment for the Humanities Summer Seminar award Northwestern U., 1989; Uhrig Found. grantee, 1964-65; Fulbright fellow, 1953-54. Mem. MLA, Malone Soc., Am. Studies Assn., Phi Beta Kappa. Home: 208 S Cherry Ave Marshfield WI 54449-3732 Office: Calif State U Humanities Dept Los Angeles CA 90032

LAIRD, DORIS ANNE MARLEY, retired humanities educator, musician; b. Charlotte, N.C., Jan. 15, 1931; d. Eugene Harris and Coleen (Bethea) Marley; m. William Everette Laird Jr., Mar. 13, 1964; children: William Everette III, Andrew Marley, Glen Howard. MusB, Converse Coll., Spartanburg, S.C., 1951; opera cert., New Eng. Conservatory, Boston, 1956; MusM, Boston U., 1956; PhD, Fla. State U., 1980. Leading soprano roles S.C. Opera Co., Columbia, 1951-53, Plymouth Rock Ctr. of Music and Art, Duxbury, Mass., 1953-56; soprano Pro Musica, Boston, 1956, New Eng. Opera Co., Boston, 1956; instr. Stratford Coll., Danville, Va., 1956-58, Sch. Music Fla. State U., Tallahassee, 1958-60, dept. humanities, 1960-68; tchr. Fla. State U., 1973-79; asst. prof. Fla. A&M U., Tallahassee, 1979-89, assoc. prof., 1990—2002; ret., 2002. Vis. scholar Cornell U., 1988; participant So. Conf. on Afro-Am. Studies, Inc. Author: Colin Morris: Modern Missionary, 1980; contbr. articles to profl. jours. Soprano Washington St. Meth. Ch., Columbia, S.C., 1951-53, Copley Meth. Ch., Boston, 1953-56; soloist Trinity United Meth. Ch., Tallahassee, 1983—; mem. Saint Andrews Soc., Tallahassee, 1986—; judge Brain Bowl, Tallahassee, 1981-84; mem. alumnae bd. Converse Coll., 2004—. Named subject of article, Glamour mag., 2001, Self mag., 2003; recipient NEH award, 1988, Disting. Alumna award, Converse Coll., 2001; scholar Phi Sigma Tau, 1960. Mem. AAUP, AAUW, Nat. Art Educators Assn., Tallahassee Music Tchrs. Assn., Tallahassee Music Guild, Am. Guild of Organists, DAR (mus. rep. 1984-85, registrar 2005-), Colonial Dames of 17th Century (music dir. 1984-85), Nat. Assn. Humanities Edn., U. Wyo. Women's Club, Woman's Club Tallahassee (v.p. 2004), Converse Coll. Alumni (bd. dirs. 2003—) Republican. Achievements include subject of article Self Magazine, 2004. Avocations: travel, dance, music. Home: 1125 Mercer Dr Tallahassee FL 32312-2833 Business E-Mail: wlaird@garnet.acns.fsu.edu.

LAIRD, MARY See WOOD, LARRY

LAIRD, SHIRLEY EDER, small business owner, communication company executive; b. Ridley Park, Pa. d. Charles E. and Wilhelmina F. Eder; married; children: Craig, Holly Alison, Heather Anne. BA, Cedar Crest Coll. Dir. publs. The Kling Ptnrship, 1966-70, 71-77; assoc. Weld Coxe Mgmt. Cons., 1970-71; editor living sect. Today's Post, King of Prussia, Pa., 1970-71; pub. affairs counsel to pres. Hahnemann Med. Coll. and Hosp., Phila., 1977; owner Laird Unltd., Haverford, Pa., 1977—. Columnist Montgomery Pub. Co., 1967-81; contbr. to mags. Chmn. 12:12 Forum YMCA, Phila., 1970, vice chmn., 1978-80; adv. bd. Villanova U. Theatre, 1983-87; bd. mem. COLLAB fund raising group for Phila. Mus. of Art; mem. Phila. Orch. com. Mem. Phila. Pub. Rels. Assn., Nat. League Am. Pen Women, Soc. Profl. Journalists, Victorian Soc. Am., Athenaeum. Democrat. Episcopalian. Home and Office: 523 Montgomery Ave Haverford PA 19041-1601

LAIRD, WILLIAM EVERETTE, JR., economics professor; b. Hattiesburg, Miss., Feb. 4, 1934; s. William Everette and Mildred Alvah (Howard) L.; m. Doris Anne Marley, Mar. 13, 1964; children: William Everette III, Andrew Marley, Glen Howard. BS, Stetson U., 1956; MA, George Washington U., 1958; PhD, U. Va., 1962. Asst. prof. Fla. State U., Tallahassee, 1960-66, assoc. prof., 1966-71, prof., 1971—, chmn. dept. econs., 1974-97, SERVICE prof., 1997—2002, prof. emeritus, 2002—. Contbr. articles to profl. jours. DuPont fellow, 1959-60; recipient awards Fla. State U. Grad. Research Council, 1965, 66, Faculty Devel. awards Fla. State U., 1971 Mem. Am. Econs. Assn., So. Econ. Assn., Plantagenet Soc. Magna Charta Barons, Jamestowne Soc., St. Andrew Soc., Order of First Families of Va., Econ. Club of Fla. Methodist. Home: 1125 Mercer Dr Tallahassee FL 32312-2833 Business E-Mail: wlaird@garnet.acns.fsu.edu.

LAIRES, FERNANDO, concert piano educator; b. Lisbon, Portugal, Jan. 3, 1925; came to U.S., 1956; s. Joaquim Augusto and Clementina (Belfo) L.; m. Nelita True, Dec. 24, 1971. Artist diploma, Nat. Conservatory Music, Lisbon, 1945. Prof. piano Nat. Conservatory Music, Lisbon, 1949-56; asst. prof. U. Tex., Austin, 1956-61; artist-in-residence, prof. piano Okla. Coll. Liberal Arts, Chickasha, 1961-68; artist-in-residence, chmn. piano dept. Interlochen (Mich.) Arts Acad., Interlochen, 1968-72; prof. piano Peabody Conservatory, Balt., 1972-87; adj. prof. piano Cath. U. Am., Washington, 1978-92; artist faculty Eastman Sch. Music, Rochester, N.Y., 1992-95, prof. piano, artist faculty, 1999—2004. Permanent guest prof. piano performance Shenyang (People's Republic of China) Conservatory of Music, 1989—; juror Tchaikowsky Internat. Piano Competition, Moscow, 1982, Van Cliburn Internat. Piano Competition, Ft. Worth, 1973, Gina Bachauer Internat. Piano Competition, Salt Lake City, 1978, 80, U. Md. Internat. Piano Competition, College Park, 1975, 77, 86, Franz Liszt Internat. Piano Competition, Budapest, 1996; dir. U. Md. Internat. Piano Festival, 1979-81. Performed in cycle the 32 piano sonatas of Beethoven, 1944; dir.-founder 20-record Anthology Portuguese classical music, 1972-82; co-founder Pro-Arte Concert Soc., Portugal, 1949, The Am. Liszt Soc., 1964; contbr. articles to Clavier, The Piano Quar., Am. Music Tchr. Decorated comdr. Order of Price Henry the Navigator (Portugal); recipient Beethoven medal Harriet Cohen Internat. Music Awards, London, 1956, Franz Liszt medal Liszt Soc. Hungary, Budapest, 1984, Liszt medal for excellence Am. Liszt Soc., Inc., 1985, Liszt Commemorative medal Hungarian People's Republic, 1986. Mem. European Piano Tchrs. Assn., Am. Liszt Soc., Inc (pres. 1976-85, 89-99), Music Tchrs. Nat. Assn., Am. Liszt Soc. (pres.) Avocations: travel, reading, writing. Home: 210 Devonshire Dr Rochester NY 14625-1905 Office Phone: 585-586-9922.

LAITIN, DAVID DENNIS, political science professor; b. Bklyn., June 4, 1945; s. Daniel and Frances (Blumenkranz) L.; m. Delia Fortune; children: Marc Oliver, Anna Elizabeth. BA, Swarthmore Coll., 1967; PhD, U. Calif., Berkeley, 1974. Instr. Nat. Tchr. Edn. Ctr., Afgoy, Somalia, 1969; master Grenada Boys' Secondary Sch., West Indies, 1970-71; asst. prof. dept. polit. sci. U. Calif.-San Diego, La Jolla, 1975-79, prof., 1984-87, chmn., 1986-87; reader dept. polit. sci. U. Ife, Nigeria, 1979-80; prof. polit. sci., dir. Wilder House Ctr. for Study Politics, History and Culture U. Chgo., 1987-99, William R. Kenan, Jr. prof., 1992—99; prof. polit. sci. Stanford (Calif.) U., 1999—, James T. Watkins and Elise V. Watkins prof. polit. sci., 2005—. Expert witness fgn. affairs subcom. U.S. Ho. Reps., 1981; resident Rockefeller Found., Bellagio Ctr., Sept. 1996. Author: Politics, Language and Thought: The Somali Expeirience, 1977, Hegemony and Culture: Politics and Religious Change Among the Yoruba, 1986, Somalia: A Nation in Search of a State, 1987, Language Repertoires and State Construction in Africa, 1992, (with James Fearon) Explaining Ethnic Cooperation, 1996, Identity in Formation: The Russian-Speaking Populations of the Near Abroad, 1998, (with James Fearon) Ethnicity, Insurgency and Civil War, 2003, (with Alan B. Kruger) Misunderestimating Terrorism, 2004. Fellow NEH, 1979-80, Howard Found., 1984-85, German Marshall Fund, 1984-85, John Simon Guggenheim Found., 1995-96, Harry F. Guggenheim Found., 1997—, Ctr. for Advanced Study in Behavioral Scis., 1989-2000, Russell Sage Found., 2003-2004; co-prin. investigator award NSF, 1993-95, 2002—; recipient award Am. Assn. for the Advancement of Slavic Studies, Dogan award Soc. for Comparative

Rsch.; co-prin. investigator award Carnegie Found., 2000-01. Mem. Am. Polit. Sci. Assn. (2 awards), Am. Acad. Arts and Scis., Coun. Am. Polit. Sci. Assn. Office: Stanford U Dept Polit Sci Stanford CA 94305 Business E-Mail: dlaitin@stanford.edu.

LAJE, ZILIA L., writer, publisher, translator; b. Havana, Cuba, Feb. 1, 1941; came to U.S., 1961; d. Luis B. Laje and Zilia Isabel Bello; divorced; 1 child, Alberto Luis Dominguez. Comml. acct., Escuela Profl. de Comercio, Havana, 1959-61; AA in Bus. Adminstrn., Miami-Dade C.C., 1989. Export documentation clk. Pittsburgh Plate Glass Internat., Havana, 1959-60; agy. sec. Occidental Life Ins. Co., Miami, 1962-67; sec. to v.p./br. mgr. Chgo. Title Ins. Co., Miami, 1972-76; corp. banking asst. S.E. Bank, N.A., Miami Springs, Fla., 1978-90; writer, transl. Miami, 1991—. Exhibitor Miami Book Fair Internat., 1995—. Author: (novels) La Cortina de Bagazo, 1995, The Sugar Cane Curtain, 2000, Cartas Son Cartas, 2001, Love Letters in the Sand, 2002, Divagaciones, 2003, 100 Recetas de Cocina Tradicionales, 2004. Mem.: PEN Com. for Writers in Exile, Writers, N.Y., Cuban Writers in Miami (founder, assoc.), Women's Nat. Book Assn. (corr.), Cuban Geneal. Soc., Alliance Française de Miami. Republican. Roman Catholic. Avocations: needlepoint, photography, travel, genealogy. Office: Escritores Cubanos de Miami PO Box 45-1732 Miami FL 33245-1732 E-mail: guarinapub@juno.com.

LAJOHN, LAWRENCE ANTHONY, research scientist; b. Jamestown, N.Y., Apr. 23, 1949; s. Anthony Raymond and Anne Theresa La John. BA, Ohio No. U., 1971; MS, George Washington U., 1976, Clarkson U., 1988, PhD, 1990. Chemist NIH, Bethesda, Md., 1972-76; rsch. asst. Miles Labs., Elkhart, Ind., 1976-77; U. Notre Dame, South Bend, Ind., 1977-78; So. Ill. U., Carbondale, 1978-82; Queen's U., Can., 1982-84; Clarkson U., 1985-90; postdoctoral fellow Dept. Applied Math., U. Western Ont., London, Ont., 1990-93; rsch. scientist dept. physics & astronomy U. Pitts., Pa., 1993—. Physics instr. U. Pitts., Carnegie Mellon U., Duquesne U. Contbr. articles to profl. jours. Mem. AAAS, Am. Chem. Soc., Am. Math. Soc., Am. Phys. Soc., Math. Assn. Am., N.Y. Acad. Sci., Sigma Xi. Avocations: weightlifting, baseball, bowling. Office: Dept Physics & Astronomy Univ Pitts Pittsburgh PA 15260 Office Phone: 412-624-9050. Business E-Mail: lajohn@stribor.phyast.pitt.edu.

LAJOIE, THOMAS PRESTON, music educator; b. Charlotte, NC, Sept. 12, 1970; s. Thomas Preston and Ann B. LaJoie; m. Heather Kathryn MacAlister, Dec. 28, 1996; 1 child, Kathryn Ann. MusB, Winthrop Coll., Rock Hill, SC, 1992; BA in Music Edn., U NC, Charlotte, 2000. Dir. orchs. Myers Pk. and Butler HS, Charlotte, 1993—. Composer: (arrangement) Symphony No. 29. Named Outstanding Educator, Coca-Cola Found., 2003. Mem.: Music Educators Nat. Conf. Democrat. Avocations: computer programming, composing, arranging. Home: 3024 Old Ironside Dr Charlotte NC 28213 Office: Myers Park HS 2400 Colony Rd Charlotte NC 28209 Office Phone: 980-343-5800. Office Fax: 980-343-5800. Personal E-mail: tlajoie@carolina.rr.com. E-mail: thomas.lajoie@cms.k12.nc.us.

LAJOUX, ALEXANDRA REED, editor, educator; b. Washington, Mar. 4, 1950; d. Stanley Foster and Stella Swingle Reed; m. Bernard Jacques Lajoux, Aug. 14, 1982; 1 child, Franklin Alberto; stepchildren: Valerie Corinne, Sylvia Patricia. BA, Bennington Coll., 1972; MA, Princeton U., 1974, PhD, 1978; MBA, Loyola Coll., Balt., 1981. Asst. prof. French lang. and lit. SUNY Coll. Oswego, N.Y., 1977-78; sr. editor Dirs. and Bds. Info. for Industry, McLean, Va., 1978-80; editor Mergers and Acquisitions The Hay Group, Phila., 1980-83; editor Export Today Export Info. Group, Washington, 1983-87; editor-in-chief Nat. Assn. Corp. Dirs., Washington, 1987—2004, dir. rsch. and publs., 1992-2000, sr. rsch. analyst, 2001—04, chief knowledge officer, 2005—. Pres. Alexis & Co., Arlington, Va., 1987—; Washington bur. co-chief N.E. Internat. Bus., Washington, 1987-90; dir. M&A rsch. E-Know, Inc., Arlington, 2000-01; mem. Nat. Infrastructure Adv. Coun. - Risk Mgmt. Study Group, 2005; mem. adv. bd. E-Know, Inc., Arlington, 2005—. Author: The Art of M&A Integration, 1997; co-author (with J.F. Weston): The Art of M&A Financing and Refinancing, 1999; co-author: (with S.F. Reed) The Art of M&A: A Merger/Acquisition/Buyout Guide, 3d edit., 1999; co-author: (with C.M. Elson) The Art of M&A Due Diligence, 2000; co-author: (with H.P. Nesvold) The Art of M & A Structuring, 2004; editor-in-chief: HR Dir.: The Arthur Andersen Guide to Human Capital, 1998, 1999, 2000, 2001; contbr. articles to profl. jours. Co-dir. Gunston Mid. Sch. Chorus, 2000; drama and music tchr. Commonwealth Acad., Falls Church, Va., 2000—02, music tchr., spring, 2003; music tchr. Lab Sch., Washington, 2003—04; cantor, children's music asst. St. Ann Cath. Ch., Arlington, 1988—, catechist, 1999—2001; alto sect. leader St. James Ch., Falls Church, 2001—; bd. dirs. Arlington Little League, 1992—94. Princeton fellow, 1972-74, French Govt. fellow, 1975-76, Mrs. Giles Whiting fellow, 1976-77. Mem. Toastmasters Internat. (v.p. local club membership 1999-2000), Assn. Princeton Grad. Alumni (trustee 1999-2002), Nat. Assn. Pastoral Musicians, Songwriters Assn. Washington. Republican. Roman Catholic. Avocations: singing and composing music, organizing musical performances, writing poetry and fiction, learning foreign languages, teaching youth. Home: 2256 N Nottingham St Arlington VA 22205-3344 Office: Nat Assn Corp Dirs Ste 700 1133 21st St NW Washington DC 20036 Office Phone: 202-775-0509. Business E-Mail: arlajoux@nacdonline.org. E-mail: arlajoux@aol.com.

LAJTHA, ABEL, biochemist; b. Budapest, Hungary, Sept. 22, 1922; naturalized; married; 2 children. PhD in Chemistry, Eotvos Lorand U., Budapest, 1945; MD (hon.), U. Padua. Asst. prof. biochemistry Eotvos Lorand U., 1945-47; asst. prof. Inst. Muscle Rsch., Mass., 1949-50; sr. rsch. scientist N.Y. State Psychiat. Inst., 1950-57, assoc. rsch. scientist, 1957-62, prin. rsch. scientist, 1962-66; dir. N.Y. State Rsch. Inst. Neurochemistry, 1966—; prof. exptl. psychiatry Sch. Medicine NYU, 1971—; now dir. Ctr. for Neurochemistry Nathan S. Kline Inst., Orangeburg, NY. Asst. prof. Coll. Physicians & Surgeons, Columbia U., 1956-69. Zoology Station fellow Italy, 1947-48, Rsch. fellow Royal Inst. Great Britain, 1948-49. Mem. Armenian, Hungarian, Slovenian Acad. Sci., Internat. Brain Rsch. Orgn., Am. Soc. Biol. Chemists, Am. Acad. Neurology, Am. Coll. Neuropsychopharmacology, Internat. Soc. Neurochemistry (pres.), Am. Chem. Soc., Am. Soc. Neurochemistry (pres.). Achievements include rsch. in neurochemistry, amino acid and protein metabolism of the brain and the brain barrier system. Office: Nathan S Kline Inst 140 Old Orangeburg Rd Orangeburg NY 10962 Office Phone: 845-398-5530. Business E-Mail: lajtha@wki.rfma.org.

LAKAH, JACQUELINE RABBAT, political scientist, consultant; b. Cairo, Apr. 14, 1933; arrived in U.S., 1969, naturalized, 1975; d. Victor Boutros and Alice (Mounayer) Rabbat; m. Antoine K. Lakah, Apr. 8, 1951; children: Micheline, Mireille, Caroline. BA, Am. U. Beirut, 1968; MPh, Columbia U., 1974; cert., Mid. East Inst., 1975, PhD, 1978. Adj. asst. prof. polit. sci. and world affairs Fashion Inst. Tech., N.Y.C., 1978-88, asst. prof., 1988-93, assoc. prof., 1993-97, prof., 1997—, asst. chair dept. social scis., 1989-95, chair dept. social scis., 1995-97, acting dean liberal arts, 1998-2000. Asst. prof. grad. faculty polit. sci. Columbia U., N.Y.C., summer 1979, vis. scholar, 1982-83, also mem. seminar on Mid. East, 1978—; guest faculty Sarah Lawrence Coll., 1981-82; cons. on Mid. East; faculty rsch. fellow SUNY, summer 1982. Columbia Faculty fellow, 1970-73, NDEA Title IV fellow, 1971-72; Mid. East Inst. scholar, 1976; Rockefeller Found. scholar, 1967-69. Home: 41-15 94th St Flushing NY 11373-1745 Personal E-mail: jlakah@nyc.rr.com.

LAKE, ANTHONY (W. ANTHONY LAKE), former national security advisor; b. NYC, Apr. 2, 1939; married; 3 children. AB magna cum laude, Harvard U., 1961; PhD, Princeton U., 1974. Joined Fgn. Svc., US Dept. State, Washington, 1962, U.S. vice consul Saigon, Vietnam, 1963, Hue, Vietnam, 1964-65, spl. asst. to Pres. for nat. security affairs Washington, 1969-70; polit. coord. Muskie Election Campaign, 1971—72; exec. dir. Internat. Vol. Svcs., 1973—77; policy planning for US Dept. State, Washington, 1977-81; prof. Amherst Coll., 1981—84; Five Coll. Prof. Internat. Rels. Mount Holyoke Coll., 1984—92; sr. fgn. policy analyst Clinton-Gore Campaign, 1991—92; asst. to Pres. for nat. security affairs Nat. Security Coun., Washington, 1993—97; dist. prof. diplomacy, Edmund A. Walsh Sch. Foreign Affairs Georgetown U., 1997—. Author: 'The Tar Baby Option': American Policy Toward Southern Rhodesia, 1976,Third World Radical Regimes: U.S. Policy Under Carter and Reagan, 1985 Somoza Falling: A Case Study of Washington at Work, 1989, 6 Nightmares, 2000; co-author: Our Own Worst Enemy: The Unmaking of American Foreign Policy, 1984; editor: After the Wars, 1990; contbg. editor: Legacy of Vietnam: The War, American Society, and the Future of U.S. Foreign Policy, 1976, After the Wars, 1990, Six Nightmares, 2000. Office: Georgetown U Bldg ICC Room 507 Washington DC 20057 Business E-Mail: lakea@georgetown.edu.

LAKE, BRUCE MENO, applied physicist; b. LA, Nov. 22, 1941; s. Meno Truman and Jean Ivy (Hancock)_ L. BS in Engring., Princeton U., 1963; MS, Calif. Inst. Tech., 1965, PhD, 1969. Mem. tech. staff advanced instrumentation dept. TRW Corp., Redondo Beach, Calif., 1969-73, head exptl. hydrodynamics sect., 1973-81, asst. mgr. dept. fluid mechanics, 1977-81, mgr. dept. fluid mechanics, 1981-96, mgr. computational physics bus. area, 1996-2000; pvt. cons., 2000—. Contbr. articles to profl. jours. and books. Ford Found. fellow, 1964-65, TRW tech. fellow. Mem. Am. Phys. Soc., Nat. Acad. Engring. Office: 41650 Calle Pino Murrieta CA 92562 Business E-Mail: blake@alumni.princeton.edu.

LAKE, CAROL LEE, anesthesiologist, physician, educator; b. Altoona, Pa., July 14, 1944; d. Samuel Lindsay and Edna Winifred (McMahon) L. BS, Juniata Coll., 1966; MD, Med. Coll. Pa., 1970; MBA, U. Calif., Irvine, 1997; MPH, U. Mich., 2000. Intern Mercy Hosp., Pitts., 1970-71, resident in anesthesiology, 1971-73; staff anesthesiologist Pitts. Anesthesia Assocs., 1973-75; asst. prof. anesthesiology U. Va., Charlottesville, 1975-80, assoc. prof., 1980-89, prof. anesthesiology, 1989-94; prof. anesthesiology, chair U. Calif., Davis, 1994-95, prof. clin. anesthesiology, 1996; chief of staff Roudebush VA Med. Ctr., 1997-99; asst. dean, prof. anesthesia Ind. U., Indpls., 1997-99; prof. anesthesiology, chair U. Louisville, 1999—2004, assoc. dean for continuing med. edn., 1999—2004, asst. v.p. for health affairs/continuing edn., 2002—04; CEO Verefi Techs., Inc., Elizabethtown, Pa., 2005—. Sr. assoc. examiner Am. Bd. Anesthesiology, 1981—. Author: Cardiovascular Anesthesia, 1985; editor: Pediatric Cardiac Anesthesia, 1988, 4th edit., 2004; Clinical Monitoring, 1990, 2d edit., 2000; editor Seminars in Cardiothoracic and Vascular Anesthesia, 1999—; co-editor: Blood: Hemostasis, Transfusion and Alternatives in the Perioperative Period, 1995; editor Advances in Anesthesia, 1993—. Fellow Am. Coll. Cardiology; mem. Assn. Cardiac Anesthesiologists (pres. 1987-88), Soc. Cardiovascular Anesthesiologists (bd. dirs. 1988-92), Assn. Univ. Anesthesiologists, Am Coll. Physician Execs., Alpha Omega Alpha. Presbyterian. Avocations: music, entomology, gardening. E-mail: carol.lake@verefi.com.

LAKE, I. BEVERLY, JR., state supreme court justice; b. Raleigh, NC, 1934; s. I. Beverly, Sr. and Gertrude L.; m. Susan Deichmann Smith; children: Lynn Elizabeth, Guy, Laura Ann, I. Beverly III. Student, Mars Hill Coll., 1951; BS, Wake Forest U., 1955, JD, 1960. Bar: N.C. Pvt. practice, 1960-69, 76-85; asst. atty. gen. State of NC, 1969-74, dep. atty. gen., 1974-76; Gov.'s legis. liason, chief lobbyist, 1985; judge Superior Ct., 1985-91; assoc. justice NC Supreme Ct., 1992—2000, chief justice Raleigh, 2001—. Chmn. bd. trustees Ridge Rd. Bapt. Ch., 1968-69; mem. N.C. Senate, 1976-80, chmn. Senate Judiciary Com.; Rep. nominee Gov. N.C., 1979-80; del. Rep. Nat. Convention, 1980; Rep. state fin. chmn., mem. ctr. com., mem. exec. com., 1980-82; N.C. eastern chmn. Reagan-Bush Campaign, 1984; bd. visitors Wake Forest U. Sch. Law, 1995—; bd. vis. Southeastern Bapt. Theol. Sem. Military intelligence staff officer USAR, 1958—68, captain USAR, 1958—68, colonel, state staff judge advocate NC State Militia, 1989—92. Mem. AMVETS, N.C. Bar Assn., Wake County Bar Assn., Assn. Interstate Commerce Commn. Practitioners, Navy League, Am. Legion, Masons, Shriners, Phi Alpha Delta. Office: NC Supreme Ct PO Box 2170 Raleigh NC 27602-2170*

LAKE, JOSEPH EDWARD, ambassador; b. Jacksonville, Tex., Oct. 18, 1941; s. Lloyd Euel and Marion Marie (Allen) L.; m. Sarah Ann Bryant (div.); children: Joseph Edward, Mary Elizabeth; m. Jo Ann Kessler, June 12, 1971; 1 child, Michael Allen. BA summa cum laude, Tex. Christian U., 1962, MA, 1967. 3rd sec. U.S. Embassy, Taipei, Taiwan, 1963-65, Bur. of European Affairs Dept. State, 1966-67; second sec. U.S. Embassy, Cotonou, Dahomey, 1967-69; with bur. intelligence and rsch. Dept. State, 1969-71; second sec. U.S. Embassy, Taipei, Taiwan, 1971-76; with office Philippine affairs Dept. State, 1976-77; second sec. U.S. Embassy, Lagos, Nigeria, 1977-78; prin. officer and consul U.S. Consulate, Kaduna, Nigeria, 1978-81; with Fgn. Svc. Inst., Washington, 1981-82; first sec. U.S. Embassy, Sofia, Bulgaria, 1982-84, charge d'affaires, 1984, counselor, dep. chief mission, 1984-85; dep. dir. regional affairs, bur. East Asian and Pacific Affairs Dept. State, 1985-86; advisor U.S. delegation 41st UN Gen. Assembly, 1986; dir. ops. ctr. Dept. State, Washington, 1987-90; amb. to Rep. of Mongolia, Ulaanbaatar, 1990-93, Rep. of Albania, Tirana, 1994-96; dep. asst. sec. of state for info. mgmt. Dept. State, Washington, 1996-97, chair com. on messaging and interagy. collaboration, 2002—05; dir. internat. affairs City of Dallas, 1997—2002; rsch. assoc. Tower Ctr. So. Meth. U. Mem. adv. bd. Asian studies program So. Meth. U. Contbr. articles to profl. jours. Bd. dirs. Dallas Coun. on World Affairs; mem. Dallas Com. on Fgn. Rels.; mem. exec. edn. adv. coun. U. Tex., Sch. Mgmt., Dallas. Mem.: Am. Fgn. Svc. Assn. Home: 6145 Highgate Ln Dallas TX 75214-2155 Personal E-mail: joelake@hotmail.com.

LAKE, KATHLEEN COOPER, lawyer; b. San Antonio, Jan. 11, 1955; d. Herschel Taliaferro and Virginia Mae (Hylton) Cooper; m. Randall Brent Lake, Apr. 9, 1977; 1 child, Ethan Taliaferro. AB in Polit. Sci. magna cum laude, Middlebury Coll., 1977; JD with high honors, U. Tex., 1980. Bar: Tex. 1980, U.S. Ct. Appeals (5th cir.) 1981, U.S. Ct. Appeals (D.C. and 3rd cirs.) 1984. Assoc. atty. Vinson & Elkins, Houston, 1980-88; ptnr. Vinson & Elkins, LLP, Houston, 1989—. Bd. advisors, columnist Utilities, Y2K Advisor, 1998-99. Adult leader, com. mem. Sam Houston Area Coun.-Golden Arrow dist. Boy Scouts Am., 1993—, chair troop com., 1998-2001. Recipient Unit Svc. award Sam Houston Area Coun.-Golden Arrow dist. Boy Scouts Am., 1996, 98. Fellow Tex. Bar Found. (life), Houston Bar Found.; mem. ABA (vice-chair com. 1997-99), Energy Bar Assn., Electric Coop. Bar Assn., State Bar Tex., Coll. State Bar Tex., Tex. Law Rev. Assn. (life), Houston Bar Assn., Middlebury Coll. Alumni Assn. (com. mem. 1980-2000, Houston com. chair 2001—), Order of Coif, Phi Beta Kappa, Phi Kappa Phi. Office: Vinson & Elkins LLP 2300 First City Tower 1001 Fannin St Houston TX 77002-6760 Office Phone: 713-758-3826. E-mail: klake@velaw.com.

LAKE, KEVIN BRUCE, medical association administrator; b. Seattle, Jan. 25, 1937; s. Winston Richard and Vera Emma (Davis) L.; m. Suzanne Roto, Oct. 25, 1986; children from previous marriage: Laura, Kendrick, Wesley. BS, Portland State U., 1960; MD, U. Oreg., 1964. Intern Marion County Gen. Hosp. and Ind. Med. Ctr., Indpls., 1964-65; resident U. Oreg. Hosps. and Clinics, 1968-70, fellow in infectious and pulmonary diseases, 1970-71; fellow in pulmonary diseases U. So. Calif., 1971-72, instr. medicine, 1972-75, asst. clin. prof., 1975-79, assoc. clin. prof., 1979-84, clin. prof., 1986—. Dir. med. edn. and research La Vina Hosp., 1972-75; dir. respiratory therapy Methodist Hosp., Arcadia, Calif., 1975—; mem. staff Los Angeles County/U. So. Calif. Med. Center, Santa Teresita Hosp., Duarte, Calif., Huntington Meml. Hosp., Pasadena, Calif.; attending physician, mem. med. adv. bd. Foothill Free Clinic, Pasadena. Contbr. articles to profl. jours. Mem. exec. com. Profl. Staff Assn. U. So. Calif. Sch. Medicine; 2d v.p. bd. mgmt. Palm St. br. YMCA, Pasadena, 1974, 1st v.p., 1975, chmn., 1976-78, met. bd. dirs., 1976-84; bd. dirs. Mendenhall Ministries, La Vie Holistic Ministries, Hospice of Pasadena, Hastings Found. co-pres. PTA, Allendale Grade Sch., Pasadena, 1975-76. Served to lt. U.S. Navy, 1965-68. NIH grantee, 1971-72. Fellow ACP, Am. Coll. Chest Physicians; mem. Am. Thoracic Soc., Calif. Thoracic Soc. Home: 875 S Madison Ave Pasadena CA 91106-4404 Office: 444 N Altadena Dr Pasadena CA 91107-2501 Office Phone: 626-795-5118. Personal E-mail: kblmd@aol.com.

LAKE, PABLO, health products executive; b. Santiago, Chile, July 8, 1962; arrived in U.S., 1970; s. William B. and Adriana B. Lake; m. Eileen V. Tomaselli, June 13, 1987; children: Christopher, Nicolas, Isabel, Sofia. BA, U. Va., 1984; MBA, U. Pa., 1989. Analyst Actuarial Rsch. Group, Annandale, Va., 1984—87; bus. svcs. dir. Children's Hosp., Phila., 1989—97; billing dir. SmithKline Beecham, Phila., 1997—99; revenue svcs. dir. Quest Diagnostics, Teterboro, NJ, 1999—. Mem.: Am. Soc. Quality, Healthcare Fin. Mgmt. Assn. Roman Catholic. Avocations: travel, soccer. Office: Quest Diagnostics 2750 Monroe Blvd Norristown PA 19403

LAKE, RANDALL ALAN, forensic specialist, educator; b. Fairmont, Minn., Apr. 21, 1953; s. C. Vernon Lake and June Margaret Bergman; m. Colleen Marie Keough, July 14, 1984. BA, Ottawa U., 1974; MA, U. Kans., 1978, PhD, 1982. Instr. U. Wis., Eau Claire, 1979—81; asst. prof. U. So. Calif., L.A., 1981—87, assoc. prof., 1987—. Asst. dir. forensics U. Wis., Eau Claire, 1979—80, dir. forensics, 1980—81; dir. debate Annenberg Sch. for Comm., L.A., 1981—90, dir. forensics, 1990—94, dir. doctoral studies, 1997—2003. Contbr. articles to profl. jours., chapters to books, scientific papers. Recipient Disting. Coach Award, U. Utah, 1989. Mem.: Kenneth Burke Soc., We. Forensics Assn. (vice-president 1988—90, pres. 1990—92), Am. Soc. for History Rhetoric, Internat. Soc. for Study Argumentation, We. States Comm. Assn., Nat. Comm. Assn. (Golden Anniversary Monograph award 1998, Golden Anniversary Prize Fund award 1982), Am. Forensic Assn. (editor Argumentation and Advocacy: Jour. Am. Forensic Assn. 2004—, Daniel Rohrer Rsch. award 1998), Pi Kappa Delta. Avocation: dogs. Office: Univ Southern California 3502 Watt Way Los Angeles CA 90089-0281

LAKE, SHELLEY, artist; BFA, RI Sch. Design, 1976; MS, MIT, 1979; D of chiropractic, Cleve. Chiropractic Coll. Teacher, aesthetics, Northampton, Mass.; and profl. photographer. Tech. dir.: (films) The Last Starfighter. Recipient three CLIO awards, Nicograph award, Japan, first place, AT&T Image Competition; grantee, Ctr. for Advanced Visual Studies. Office: 116 Pleasant St #1114 Easthampton MA 01027 Office Phone: 413-527-5350. Business E-Mail: drshelleylake@aol.com.

LAKE, SIM, federal judge; b. Chgo., July 4, 1944; BA, Tex. A&M, 1966; JD, U. Tex., 1969. Bar: Tex. 1969, U.S. Dist. Ct. (so. dist.) Tex. 1969, U.S. Ct. Appeals (5th cir.) 1969, U.S. Supreme Ct. 1976. From assoc. to ptnr. Fulbright & Jaworski, Houston, 1969-70, 72-88; judge U.S. Dist. Ct. (so. dist.) Tex., Houston, 1988—. Past editor Houston Lawyer. Capt. U.S. Army., 1970-71. Fellow Tex. Bar Found., Houston Bar Assn., State Bar Tex., Am. Law Inst. (mem. jud. conf. com. on criminal law 1999—, chair conf. com. on criminal law 2003—). Office: US Courthouse 515 Rusk Ave Rm 9535 Houston TX 77002-2605

LAKE, SUZANNE, singer, music educator; b. Palisade, N.J., June 26, 1929; d. Mayhew Lester and Suzanne Louise (Robin) Lake; m. George A. De Vos, Nov. 19, 1974. Pvt. tchr., Oakland, Calif., 1976-86, univ. extension U. Calif., Sacramento State U., 1981-84. Featured roles opera, N.Y.C., 1948-51; appeared in Broadway plays The King and I, 1951-54, History of Musical Comedy with Leonard Bernstein, 1957, Flower Drum Song, 1960-61; featured singer with Guy Lombardo, 1964, 65, Experiencing Music, Expressing Culture, Oxford U. Press; concert and supper club appearances in U.S., Can., Carribbean, Japan, Korea, Taiwan and Europe, 1955-91, recs. include the Soul of Chanson, Potpourri, others; also TV appearances. Mem. Actors Equity, AFTRA, Am. Guild Mus. Artists, Am. Guild Variety Artists. Home: 2835 Morley Dr Oakland CA 94611-2547

LAKE, TINA SELANDERS, artist, educator; b. London, Sept. 12, 1953; came to U.S., 1956; d. Leslie Martin Selanders and Doris Kirk; m. Paul Saunders Lake III, Dec. 30, 1971; children: Rachel, Alexander. BS, Towson State U., 1977; MFA, San Francisco Art Inst., 1980; postgrad., Ark. Arts Ctr., 1985. Teaching asst. Towson State U., Balt., 1977; grad. teaching asst. San Francisco Art Inst., 1979; instr. drawing and painting, summer arts camp, adult drawing Ark. River Valley Art Ctr., Russellville, 1986, instr. beginning drawing for children, painting and drawing, 1991. Vis. instr. U. Ozarks, 1987, Ark. Tech. U., Russellville, 1987; part-time instr. Ark. Tech. U., 1986, vis. lectr., 1982, 83; guest speaker 3d Ann. Young Author's Conf., Ark. Tech. U., 1991; pub. rels. asst. San Francisco Art Inst., 1980; lectr. Berkeley (Calif.) Art Ctr., 1981, Ark. Arts Ctr., 1992. Exhibited in group shows at Holtzman Gallery, Balt., 1976, Balt. Arts Festival, 1977, San Francisco Art Inst., 1979, The Woman's Bldg., L.A., 1980, The Goodman Bldg., San Francisco, 1981, Ark. River Valley Arts Ctr., Russellville, 1981, 91, Ark. Arts Ctr., Little Rock, 1985, 86, 89, 91, 92, 93, 94, U. Ark. Fine Arts Ctr. Gallery, Fayetteville, 1986, Ark. Tech. U., 1991, Ark. Territorial Restoration Exhbn., Little Rock, 1992, 93, Russell Fine Arts Ctr., Henderson State U., Arkadelphia, Ark., 1992, 94, Treishmann Gallery Hendrix Coll., Conway, Ark., 1993, Springfield (Mo.) Art Mus., 1994, Ark. Art Ctr., Little Rock, 1995 (Jungkind Photographic Art Material award), Ft. Smith (Ark.) Art Ctr., 1996 (hon. mention); represented in Ctrl. Ark. Libr. Sys., and numerous pvt. collections; graphic designer: (design and layout literary mag.) Occident, 1980-81; art adv. (literary mag.) Nebo, 1984-86. Recipient numerous Best of Show awards and Purchase awards. Home: 2802 Honeysuckle Ln Russellville AR 72801-5520

LAKE, VICTOR HUGO, former manufacturing company executive; b. Quincy, Mass., Nov. 11, 1919; s. Victor Hugo and Edna Beatrice (Blott) L.; m. Jeannette Elzena Stewart, Apr. 26, 1942; children: Victor Stewart, Valerie Jean; m. 2d, Jacqueline Rose Davis, July 4, 1975. Student, Lawrence Inst. Tech., 1939—42, U. Maine, 1943. Asst. supt. Taylor Winfield Corp., Detroit, 1938—43; mgr. prodn. control Fed. Machine & Welder Co., Warren, Ohio, 1944—49; with Am. Welding & Mfg. Co., Warren, 1949—82, mgr. materials, 1969—82; ret., 1982. Served with AUS, 1943-44. Mem. Am. Soc. Metals, Trumbull County Indsl. Mgmt. Assn. (pres. 1972-73). Republican. Methodist. Home: 9042 Tiara Ct New Port Richey FL 34655-1532 Personal E-mail: victorlake@msn.com.

LAKE, WESLEY WAYNE, JR., internist, allergist, medical educator; b. New Orleans, Oct. 11, 1937; s. Wesley Wayne and Mary McGehee (Snowden) L.; m. Abby F. Arnold, Aug. 1959 (div. 1974); children: Courtenay B., Corinne A., Jane S.; married Melissa Bowman, Mar. 1999. AB in Chemistry, Princeton U., 1959; MD, Tulane U., 1963. Diplomate Am. Bd. Internal Medicine, Am. Bd. Allergy and Immunology. Intern Charity Hosp. of La., New Orleans, 1963-64, resident internal medicine, 1966-69; NIH fellow allergy and immunology La. State U. Med. Ctr., 1969-70; instr. dept. medicine Tulane U., New Orleans, 1967-69; fellow dept. medicine La. State U., New Orleans, 1969-70, instr. dept. medicine, 1970-73, asst. clin. prof. medicine, 1973-77; chief allergy clinic La. State U. Svc. Charity Hosp. La., New Orleans, 1970-77; assoc. clin. prof. medicine Tulane U., 1978—93. Temp. staff positions various hosps., 1963-70, including Baton Rouge Gen. Hosp., Our Lady of the Lake Hosp., Glenwood Hosp., St. Francis Hosp., Monroe, La., Lallie Kemp Charity Hosp., Independence, La., Huey P. Long Hosp., Pineville, La.; gen. med. officer outpatient clinic Hunter AFB, Savannah, Ga., 1964-65, gen. med. officer internal medicine svc., 1965-66; cons. physician Seventh Ward Gen. Hosp., Hammond, La., 1971-77, Slidell (La.) Meml. Hosp., 1971-89, St. Tammany Parish Hosp., Covington, La., 1977-85; cons. physician East Jefferson Hosp., Metairie, La., 1971-77, staff physician, 1990—; asst. vis. physician Charity Hosp. New Orleans, 1970-75, staff physician, 1975-77, vis. phys. Tulane divsn., 1979-93; assoc. physician So. Bapt. Hosp., New Orleans, 1970-75, chmn. dept. medicine, chmn. internal medicine com., 1982-84, chmn. pharmacy and therapeutics, 1980-82, mem. investigative rev. com., 1984-85, mem. internal medicine quality assurance com., 1989-94; staff physician Kenner (La.) Regional Med. Ctr. (formerly St. Jude Med. Ctr.), 1985-99, chmn. quality assurance com., 1987-89; staff physician Drs. Hosp. of Jefferson, 1988—; mem. pharmacy and therapeutics com. and continuing med. edn. com. East Jefferson Gen. Hosp., 1997—. Author: (with others) Infiltrative Hypersensitivity Chest Diseases, 1975; contbr. articles to profl. jours. including Jour. Immunology, Internat. Archives Allergy and Applied Immunology, Jour. Allergy and Clin. Immunology; also chpts. in books concerning chest diseases. Fellow ACP, Am. Coll. Allergy, Sigma Xi; mem. New Orleans Acad. Internal Medicine, Musser-Burch Soc., S.E. Allergy Soc., La. Allergy Soc. (sec. 1975-76, v.p. 1976-77, pres.

1977-78). Republican. Episcopalian. Home: 4636 Perrier St New Orleans LA 70115-3920 Office: 4224 Houma Blvd Ste 250 Metairie LA 70006-2935 Home: 1850 Gause Blvd Slidell LA 70461 Office Phone: 504-456-5111. E-mail: lakejrmd@aol.com.

LAKE, WILLIAM TRUMAN, lawyer; b. Henderson, Nev., Nov. 13, 1943; s. Meno Truman and Jean Ivy (Hancock) L.; m. Dorothy Ann Diehl, Nov. 26, 1965 (div. 1973); 1 child, Alison; m. Morgan Day Hodgson, Jan. 18, 1975; children: Devon, Spencer, Eve, Braden. BA, Yale U., 1965; LLB, Stanford U., 1968. Bar: Calif. 1969, DC 1972, US Dist. Ct. DC, 1972, US Ct. Appeals (DC cir.) 1973, US Ct. Appeals (2d cir.) 1975, US Ct. Appeals (5th cir.) 1979, US Ct. Appeals (11th cir.) 1981, US Ct. Appeals (9th cir.) 1987, US Ct. Appeals (8th cir.) 1996, US Ct. Appeals (10th cir.) 1997, US Ct. Appeals (6th cir.) 2005, US Ct. Fed. Claims 1996, US Supreme Ct. 1973. Law clk. to judge U.S. Ct. Appeals, N.Y., 1968-69; law clk. to Justice John M. Harlan U.S. Supreme Ct., Washington, 1969-70; counsel U.S. Coun. on Environ. Quality, Washington, 1970-73; assoc. Wilmer, Cutler & Pickering, Washington, 1973-76, ptnr., 1976-80; dep. legal adviser U.S. Dept. State, Washington, 1980-81; ptnr. Wilmer, Cutler & Pickering, Washington, 1981—2004; ptnr., Comm. dept., mem. mgmt. com. Wilmer Cutler Pickering Hale & Dorr, Washington, 2004—. Contbr. articles to profl. jours. Governing bd. Beauvoir Sch., Washington, 1987-93; bd. dirs. Little Folks Sch., Washington, 1981-89, Global Rights, Washington, 1982—, World Wildlife Fund, Washington, 1992— Mem. ABA, Calif. Bar Assn., DC Bar Assn., Fed. Communications Bar Assn., US Coun. Internat. Bus Episcopalian. Mailing: Wilmer Cutler Pickering Hale & Dorr 2445 M St NW Washington DC 20037-1487 Office: Wilmer Cutler Pickering Hale & Dorr 1801 Pennsylvania Ave Washington DC 20006 Office Phone: 202-663-6725. Office Fax: 202-663-6363. Business E-Mail: william.lake@wilmerhale.com.

LAKEFIELD, BRUCE R., air transportation executive; b. Jan. 29, 1944; m. Bernadine J. Lakefield; 2 children. BS, US Naval Acad., 1967. With Lehman Bros. Inc., 1974—99; chmn., CEO Lehman Bros. Internat., 1995—99; mng. dir. Lehman Bros. Inc., 1996—99, COO, 1999; non.-exec. dir. Constellation Corp., PLC, 2000—04; pres., CEO US Airways, Inc., 2004—, US Airways Group, Inc., 2004—. Sr. adv. investment policy com. HGK Asset Mgmt., 2000—04; mem. bd. dirs. US Airways Group, 2003—; non-exec. dir. Constellation Corp. PLC. With USN, 1968—71, with USNR, 1971—90, ret. as comdr., 1990. Office: US Airways Group Inc 2345 Crystal Dr Arlington VA 22227*

LAKES, DIANA MARY, artist; b. Sussex, N.J., Aug. 12, 1948; d. Renato and Lillian Vezzetti; m. Roderic S. Lakes, Aug. 14, 1971. BA, Russell Sage Coll., 1970. Artist Gallerie Je Reviens, Westport, Conn., 1996-2001. Juried mem. Wis. Watercolor Soc., 2003. Exhibitions include Swen Parson Gallery, Dekalb, Ill., 1987, Wright Mus. Art, Beloit, Wis., 1987, Tarble Arts Ctr., Charleston, Ill., 1988, Purdue U. Galleries, West Lafayette, Ind., 1988, Midwest Mus. Am. Art, Elkhart, Ind., 1988, Yolanda Fine Arts, Chgo., 1989, McCormick Place, 1990, Sonje Mus. Contemporary Art, Kyongju, Korea, 1992, China World Trade Ctr., Beijing, 1995, Chgo. Ctr. Self-Taught, 1996, U.S. Embassy, Montevideo, Uruguay, 1998—2001, Pittori Naifs a Guiglia 5th Salone Internazionale, Modena, Italy, 1999, The Naive Painters in Castelvetro, Italy, 2001, Cedar Rapids Mus. of Art, Iowa, 2002—03, Leigh Yawkey Woodson Art Mus., Wausau, Wis., 2005, Represented in permanent collections Musee d'Art Naif Max Fourny, Paris, Daryl Hannah, Musee Internat. d'Art Naif Yvon-M. Diagle, Que., others. Home: 1225 Edgehill Dr Madison WI 53705-1414

LAKEW, DEJENIE ALEMAYEHU, mathematician; b. Debre-Tabor, Gondar, Ethiopia, Dec. 12, 1963; s. Alemayehu Lakew and Chekolech Dessie; m. Melete Tesfamichael Gebrehiwot, Aug. 18, 1964; 1 child, Tewodros Dejenie Alemayehu. BSc, Addis Ababa U., 1984, MSc, 1988, U. Alberta, 1996; PhD, U. Ark., 2000. Asst. lectr. Asmara U., Ethiopia, 1984—86, math. lectr., 1988—90, Addis Ababa U., Ethiopia, 1990—92, sr. lectr., 1992—94; tchg. asst. U. Ark., Fayetteville, 1996—2000. Asst. prof. U. Ark., Pine Bluff, 2000—. Contbr. articles pub. to profl. jour. Mem.: Math. Assn. Am., Am. Math. Soc. Office: U Ark at Pine Bluff 1200 N University Dr Pine Bluff AR 71601 Office Phone: 870-575-8766.

LAKIN, JAMES DENNIS, allergist, immunologist, director; b. Harvey, Ill., Oct. 4, 1945; s. Ora Austin and Annie Pitranella (Johnson) L.; m. Sally A. Stuteville, July 22, 1972 (dec. July 25, 2002); children: Tracey A., Margaret K., Matthew A., Christian J., Anne E.; m. Debra J. Franz, May 29, 2004. PhD, Northwestern U., 1968, MD, 1969; MBA in Med. Group Mgmt., U. St. Thomas, 1996. Diplomate Am. Bd. Internal Medicine, Am. Bd. Allergy and Immunology; cert. comml. pilot FAA, cert. flight instr., aviation med. examiner. Dir. allergy rsch. Naval Med. Rsch. Inst., Bethesda, Md., 1974-76; clin. prof. U. Okla., Oklahoma City, 1976-89; dir. lab., chmn. allergy and immunology dept. Oxboro Clinics, Bloomington, Minn., 1989—2001; dir. Fairview Allergy and Asthma Svcs., Bloomington, 1995-2001; mng. ptnr. Minn. Allergy and Asthma Consultants, LLP, 2001—. Bd. dirs. Okla. Med. Rsch. Found., Oklahoma City, 1980-89; regional cons. Diver Alert Network, Duke U., Chapel Hill, N.C., 1987—; cert. diving med. officer NOAA, 1988. Co-author: Allergic Diseases, 1971, 3d edit., 1986; contbr. articles, revs. to profl. publs. Councilperson Our Lord's Luth. Ch., Oklahoma City, 1978-88, Faith Luth. Ch., Lakeville, Minn., 1990-91. Lt. comdr. USN, 1970—76, Vietnam, ret. Fellow ACP, Am. Acad. Allergy and Immunology, Am. Coll. Chest Physicians, Am. Coll. Med. Practice Execs. (E.B. Stevens Article of Yr. award 1998); mem. Am. Assn. Immunologists, Med. Group Mgmt. Assn. (bd. dirs. 2002—, E.B. Stevens Article of Yr. award, 1998), Am. Coll. Physician Execs. Achievements include research in characterization of the immunoglobulin system of the rhesus monkey, alterations in allergic reactivity during immunosuppression. Office: 303 E Nicollet Ave # 362 Burnsville MN 55337-4559 Office Phone: 952-223-3040. Business E-Mail: jdlakin@minnesotaallergy.com.

LAKSHMAN, MAHESH KUMAR, chemist; b. Poona, India, Mar. 14, 1963; BS in Chemistry, U. Bombay, 1982, MS in Organic Chemistry, 1984, U. Okla., 1987, PhD in Organic Chemistry, 1989. Vis. fellow NIH, Bethesda, Md., 1989-94; sr. scientist Chemsyn Sci. Labs., Lenexa, Kans., 1994-97; asst. prof. dept. chemistry U. N.D., Grand Forks, 1998—2000, City Coll. and City U., NY, 2000—04, assoc. prof. dept. chemistry, 2004—. Presenter in field. Contbr. articles and revs. to profl. jours. Karcher fellow U. Okla., 1986-87, Fogarty fellow NIH, 1989-94, Cleo Cross Internat. Student fellow, 1988-89. Mem. Am. Chem. Soc., N.Y. Acad. Scis., Sigma Xi, Phi Lambda Upsilon. Office Phone: 212-650-7835.

LAKSHMANA, VISWANATH, information technology executive; b. Trivandrum, Kerala, India, Mar. 3, 1958; arrived in U.S., 1980; s. Lakshmana and Lakshmy L.; m. Rukmani, July 15, 1985; children: Avinash, Abiram. MS in Computer Sci., Iowa State U., 1987; MS in Meteorology, S.D. Sch. Mines and Tech., 1982; MS in counseling psychology, Tex. A&M Internat. U., 2000. Contract programmer Iowa State U., 1984-87, software cons., 1984-87; coord. academic computing SUNY, Cortland, N.Y., 1987-91; dir. computer and info. systems Pa. State U., Harrisburg, 1991-95; dir. computer and telecomm. svcs. Texas A&M Internat. U., 1995—. Contbr. articles to profl. jours. Office: TAMIU 5201 University Blvd Laredo TX 78041-1920 Home: 2009 Manzanares Dr Laredo TX 78045-6308

LAKSHMIKANTHAM, VANGIPURAM, mathematics professor; b. Hyderabad, India, Aug. 8, 1926; arrived in US, 1960, naturalized, 1966; s. Soroja Bukkapatnam, Feb. 22, 1942; children: Sreekantham, Neerada, Nirupama. MA, Osmania U., Hyderabad, 1955, PhD, 1958. Mem. faculty UCLA, 1960-61, Math. Rsch. Ctr., U. Wis., Madison, 1961-62; mem. Rsch. Inst. Advanced Studies, Balt., 1962-63; assoc. prof. U. Alta., Calgary, Can., 1963-64; prof., chmn. dept. math. Marathwada U., Aurangabad, India, 1964-66, U. R.I., Kingston, 1966-73, U. Tex., Arlington, 1973-88; prof., head dept. math. scis. Fla. Inst. Tech., Melbourne, 1989—. Author 38 books; founder, editor: Jour. Nonlinear Analysis, A-Series and B-Series, Nonlinear Studies, Stochastic Analysis and Applications, Mathematical Problems in Engrng., Hybrid Systems and Applications; assoc. editor other jours.; contbr. over 400 rsch. articles to profl. publs. Mem. Am. Math. Soc., Indian Math. Soc., Soc. Indsl. and Aplied Math., Nat. Acad. Sci. India, Internat. Fedn. Nonlinear Analysts (founder). Office: Fla Inst Tech Dept Math Scis 150 W University Blvd Melbourne FL 32901-6975 Office Phone: 321-674-8091. Business E-Mail: lakshmik@fit.edu.

LAL, ANIL, health facility administrator; s. Sudhamo Lal and Kamla Devi; m. Mona Ahuja, May 26, 2000; 1 child, Arun. MB BChir, U. of Karachi, 1992—97; M in healthcare adminstr., U. M in healthcare adminstr., MBS, MBA, U. Minn., 2002. Adminstr. U. of Chgo., 2002—. State rep. Assn. of Otolaryngology Administrators, 2004—05. Office: Univ of Chgo 5841 S Maryland Ave Chicago IL 60637 Office Phone: 773-702-1862. Office Fax: 773-702-6809. E-mail: alal@uchicago.edu.

LAL, DEVENDRA, nuclear geophysics educator; b. Varanasi, India, Feb. 14, 1929; s. Radhe Krishna and Sita Devi L.; m. Aruna Damany, May 17, 1955 (dec. July 1993). BS, Banaras Hindu U., Varanasi, 1947, MS, 1949, DSc (hon. causa), 1984; PhD, Bombay U., 1960. Research student Tata Inst. of Fundamental Research, Bombay, 1949-60, research fellow, fellow, assoc. prof., 1960-63, prof., 1963-70, sr. prof., 1970-72; dir. Phys. Research Lab., Ahmedabad, India, 1972-83, sr. prof., 1983-89; vis. prof. UCLA, 1965-66, 83-84; prof. Scripps Instn. Oceanography, La Jolla, Calif., 1967—. Editor: Early Solar System Processes and the Present Solar System, 1980, Biogeochemistry of the Arabian Sea, 1995. Recipient K.S. Krishnan Gold medal Indian Geophys. Union, 1965, S.S. Bhatnagar award for Physics, Govt. of India, 1971, award for Excellence in Sci. and Tech., Gedn. of Indian Chamber Com., 1974, Pandit Jawaharlal Nehru award for Scis., 1986, Group Achievement award NASA, 1986, Raman Birth Centenary award, 1996, V.M. Goldschmidt medal, 1997. Fellow AAAS, Royal Soc. London, Indian Nat. Sci. Acad., Indian Acad. Scis., Geol. Soc. India (hon.), Phys. Rsch. Lab. Ahmedabad, Tata Inst. Fundamental Rsch., Geochem. Soc. USA, Am. Geophys. Union; mem. NAS U.S.A. (fgn. assoc.), Third World Acad. Scis. (founding mem.), Indian Geophys. Union, NAS India, Royal Astron. Soc. (assoc.), Internat. Acad. Aeronautics, Internat. Union of Geodesy and Geophysics (pres. 1984-87), Am. Acad. Arts and Scis. (fgn., hon. mem.), Internat. Assn. Phys. Sci. of Ocean (hon. mem., pres. 1979-83). Hindu. Avocations: chess, photography, painting, puzzles. Office: U Calif Scripps Inst Oceanography GRD-0244 La Jolla CA 92093-0244 Fax: (858) 822-3310. Office Phone: 858-534-2134. E-mail: dlal@ucsd.edu.

LAL, DHANANJAY, information technology executive, researcher; b. New Delhi, Delhi, India, July 6, 1977; s. Krishna B. and Bela Lal. BS, Indian Inst. Tech. Roorkee, 1999; PhD, U. Cin., 2004. Grad. rsch. asst. U. Cin., 1999—2004; postdoctoral fellow UCLA, 2004—05; wireless sys. engr. Rsch. and Tech. Ctr. N.Am. Robert Bosch Corp., Palo Alto, Calif., 2005—. Mem. rsch. staff WINMEC, L.A., Calif., 2004—05. Author (innovative rsch.): (transactions) Performance Evaluation of Medium Access Control with Multiple Beam Smart Antennas in Wireless LANs. Pres. Grad. Students' Assn., Cincinnati, Ohio, 2004. Scholar Grad. Rsch. Assistantship, U. Cin., 1999—2004; Postdoctoral Fellowship, UCLA, 2004, Inst. Merit Scholarship, Indian Inst. Tech. Roorkee, 1995—99, Nat. Talent Scholarship, Govt. of India, 1994—95, Jr. Sci. Talent Scholarship, Govt. of Delhi, India, 1993. Mem.: IEEE. Achievements include patents pending for A Novel Scheme for Space Division Multiple Access in Wireless Ad Hoc Networks; A Scheme for Exploiting Spatial Parallelism at an Access Point with Multiple Beam Antennas. Avocations: drummer (percussion), travel, tennis, golf. Office: Robert Bosch Corp Rsch and Tech Ctr 4009 Miranda Ave Palo Alto CA 94304 Office Phone: 650-320-2970. Office Fax: 650-320-2999. E-mail: dhananjay.lal@rtc.bosch.com.

LALA, DOMINICK JOSEPH, manufacturing executive; b. NYC, June 2, 1928; s. Joseph and Mary Lala; m. Nancy Lala, Nov. 30, 1957; children: John, Steven, James, Thomas, Patrice. BS, NYU, 1951. Mem. staff BDO/Seidman (CPAs), N.Y.C., 1951-62; v.p., contr. Universal Am. Corp., N.Y.C., 1962-68; sr. v.p. fin. Paramount Pictures Corp., 1968-70; exec. v.p. Gould Paper Corp., N.Y.C., 1970—2002. With AUS, 1946-47. Mem. AICPA, N.Y. State Soc. CPAs.

LALA, JAYNARAYAN HOTCHAND, computer engineer; b. Hyderabad, Sind, Pakistan, Jan. 12, 1951; came to U.S., 1971; s. Hotchand Menghraj and Jamuna (Gandhi) L.; m. Michele Simone Breton, Sept. 2, 1977. SB in Aero. Engrng., Indian Inst. Tech., Bombay, 1971; SM in Aeros.-Astronautics, MIT, 1973, ScD in Instrumentation, 1976. Mem. tech. staff Charles Stark Draper Lab., Inc., Cambridge, Mass., 1976-83, chief systems architecture sect. NASA dept., 1983-85, div. leader fault tolerant systems div., 1985-91, leader advanced computer architectures group, 1991-93, prin. mem. tech. staff, 1993—99. Advisor USN Combat System Architecture Adv. Panel, 1985-86; session chmn. 8th Digital Avionics Systems Conf., San Jose, Calif., 1988, Workshop on Fault Tolerance in Parallel and Distributed Computing, 1987, Conf. on Dependable Computing for Critical Applications, 1989; mem. program com. 20th Internat. Symposium on Fault Tolerant Computing, 1990, 21st Internat. Symposium, 1991, tech. program chmn. 22nd Internat. Symposium, 1992; mem. program com. 2nd Conf. on Dependable Computing for Critical Applications, Tucson, 1991, program com. 3d Conf., Sicily, Italy, 1992, program com. Internat. Conf. on Recent Advances in Intrusion Detection, Zurich, Switzerland, 2002, program com. Internat. Conf. on Dependable Systems and Networks, San Francisco, 2003, Florence, Italy, 2004; mem. battle mgmt. panel Strategic Def. Initiative, 1992; tech. dir. Bosnia Command and Control Augmentation Program, 1996; chief architect NASA X-38 Crew Return Vehicle Avionics and Flight Critical Computers, 1998-99; program mgr. Intrusion Tolerant Sys. Def. Advanced Rsch. Projects Agy. U.S. Dept. Def., 1999-2003; engrng. fellow Raytheon Co., 2003—, govt. advisor to 2000 Def. Sci. bd. on Defensive Info. Ops., gen. chair Internat. Conf. on Dependable Systems and Networks, Washington, 2002; del. on bilateral agreements countering cyber terrorism India, U.S. Govt., New Delhi, India, 2002; vice-chmn. IEEE Tech. Com. Fault Tolerant Computing, 2003-04, chmn. 2005-. Producer, dir., writer tech. documentary Advanced Information Processing System, 1989; contbr. articles to profl. jours., chpts. to books; patentee fault tolerant computer designs. Recipient Best Paper award C.S. Draper Lab., 1989, 94, Best Patent award, 1990; Draper fellow, 1972-76; scholar Indian Sci. Talent Bd., 1966, Indian Inst. Tech., 1967-71. Fellow AIAA (assoc., chmn. digital avionics tech. subcom. 1987-91), IEEE; mem. Internat. Fedn. Info. Processing (working group on dependable computing and fault tolerance 1988—), Indian Inst. Tech. Soc. New Eng. (v.p. 1995-97). Hindu. Avocations: flying, chess, tennis, piano. Home: 10103 Walker Lake Dr Great Falls VA 22066-3501 Office: Raytheon Co Crystal Ctr 2 2461 S Clark St Ste 1000 Arlington VA 22202 Office Phone: 703-419-1401. Business E-Mail: jay_lala@raytheon.com.

LALA, PEEYUSH KANTI, research scientist, educator; b. Chittagong, Bengal, India, Nov. 1, 1934; came to U.S., 1963, to Can., 1967. s. Sudhangshu Bimal and Nani Bala (Chaudhuri) L.; m. Arati Roy-Burman, July 7, 1962 (dec.); children: Probal, Prasun; m. Shipra Bhattachareya, Nov. 6, 1992. MB, BS, Calcutta (India) U., 1957, PhD in Med. Biophysics, 1961, MD, 1962. Demonstrator, lectr. in pathology Calcutta Med. Coll., 1959-60, NRS Med. Coll., Calcutta, 1961-62; resident rsch. assoc. biol. and med. rsch. divsn. Argonne (Ill.) Nat. Lab., 1963-64; rsch. scientist, asst. prof. Lab. Radiobiology U. Calif. Med. Ctr., San Francisco, 1964-66; rsch. scientist Biol. and Health Physics divsn. Chalk River (Ont., Can.) Nuc. Lab., 1967-68; from asst. prof. to assoc. prof. to prof. dept. anatomy McGill U., Montreal, Canada, 1968—83; prof. dept. anatomy and cell biology U. Western Ont., London, 1983-2000, chmn. dept. anatomy and cell biology, 1983-93, prof. dept. oncology, 1990-2000, prof. emeritus dept. anatomy and cell biology, dept. oncology, microbiology and immunology, 2000—. Mem. grants panel MRC Can., Can. Inst. Health Rsch., Ottawa, Ont., 1983-87, 93-96, NIH U.S.A., Bethesda, Md., 1977-01, Nat. Cancer Inst. Can., Toronto, 1987-90, Cancer Rsch. Soc., Montreal, 1987-90; mem. Cannaught Com., Toronto, 1990-91; vis. prof. Walter and Eliza Hall Inst. Med. Rsch., U. Melbourne, Australia, 1977-78. Mem. editl. bd.: Exptl. Hematology, 1974—77, Leukemia Rsch., 1977—86, Am. Jour. Reproductive Immunology, 1989—93, Early Pregnancy: Biology and Medicine, 1995—, Placenta, 1996—2001, Biology of Reproduction, 2001—04, assoc. editor: Am. Jour. Anatomy, 1987—90, guest editor: Cancer and Metastasis Revs., Vol. 17, 1998; contbr. 12 chapters to books, 200 articles to profl. jours. Chmn. Bengali Cultural Ctr., Montreal, 1978-83. Recipient Faculty of Medicine Rsch. award, U. Western Ont., 1996; fellow, Fulbright Found., 1962; grantee, MRC Can. (now CIHR), 1968—, NCI Can., 1968—, NIH, 1976—79, Cancer Rsch. Soc., 1978—96, U.S. Army Med. Rsch., 1996—2001, Breast Cancer Soc. Can., 1999—, Can. Breast Cancer Rsch. Alliance, 2001—05, Can. Breast Cancer Found., 2005—. Mem. Am. Assn. Cancer Rsch., Am. Assn. Anatomists, Can. Assn. Anatomists, Cell Biologists and Neurobiologists (chmn. awards com. 1987-89, v.p. and pres.-elect 1989-90, pres. 1991-93, J.C.B. Grant award 1990), Internat. Soc. Exptl. Hematology, Soc. Leukocyte Biology, Am. Assn. Immunologists, Can. Soc. Immunologists, Internat. Soc. Reproductive Immunology (councillor 1986-89), Am. Soc. Reproductive Immunology (v.p. 1985-86), Soc. Study Reproduction. Achievements include discovery of a new mode of cancer immunotherapy resulting in a successful phase two human trial; of mode of treatment of interleukin-2 therapy-induced side effects of capillary leakage; of mechanism responsible for nitric oxide-mediated stimulation of breast cancer progression; production of normal, precancerous and cancerous trophoblast cell lines from first trimester human placentae; identification control mechanisms in the protection of the uterus from placental overinvasion of the uterus; international symposium held as a tribute at Queen's University, Kingston in 2001. Office: U Western Ont Dept Anatomy and Cell Biology London ON Canada N6A 5C1 Office Phone: 519-661-3015. Business E-Mail: pklala@uwo.ca.

LALANNE, JACK (FRANÇOIS HENRI LALANNE), physical fitness specialist, entrepreneur; b. San Francisco, Calif., Sept. 26, 1914; m. Elaine LaLane, 1959; children: Jon Allen, Yvonne, Janet (dec.). Opened first gym Jack LaLanne's Physical Culture Studio, Oakland, Calif., 1936; host The Jack LaLanne Show, 1956-70, Jack LaLanne and You, 1981-83; spokesperson Jack LaLanne Juicing products. Released Jack LaLanne's Glamour Stretcher Time (album), 1959, Jack LaLalanne's Low Impact Plus Workout Featuring Kim Scott (video), 1988; books inlclude: The Jack LaLanne Way to Vibrant Good Health, 1960, Foods for Glamour, 1961, For Men Only, with a Thirty-Day Guide to Looking Better and Feeling Younger, 1973, Revitalize Your Health: Improve Your Health, Your Sex Life & Your Look after Age Fifty, 1995, Revitalize Your Life, Total Juicing; DVDs and Videoes include: The Jack LaLanne Way, The Jack LaLanne Show Commemorative Special, Hydronastics Exercises, Back to Basics Chair Exercises, Forever Young and Face-a-Tonic. Office: Befit Enterprises Inc PMB 151 430 Quintana Rd Morro Bay CA 93442

LALE, CISSY STEWART (LLOYD LALE), freelance writer; b. Port Arthur, Tex., Jan. 15, 1924; d. Lloyd M. and May (Cowart) Stewart; m. Max Sims Lale, Oct. 9, 1983. BJ, U. Tex., 1945. Reporter Record-News, Wichita Falls, Tex., 1945, News-Messenger, Marshall, Tex., 1945-47; editor Times-Rev., Cleburne, Tex., 1947-49; women's editor, columnist Star-Telegram, Ft. Worth, 1949-87; freelance writer Children's Promise mag., Health-Scope mag., Ft. Worth, 1987-89. Author: Sweetie Ladd's Historic Fort Worth, 1999. Bd. dirs. Trinity Ter. Retirement Cmty., 1991-94. Recipient Ballard Heritage award North Tex. Hist. Soc.; Cissy Stewart Day proclaimed by Ft. Worth City Coun., 1987, portrayed in outdoor mural City of Ft. Worth, 1987. Mem. Women in Comm., Inc. (nat. pres. 1968-71), Tex. State Hist. Assn. (pres. 1996-97), East Tex. Hist. Assn. (pres. 1994), Tex. Heritage, Inc. (bd. dirs. Ft. Worth chpt. 1990), Womans Club Ft. Worth, Ft. Worth Garden Club (v.p. 1995-96). Episcopalian. Home: # 101 3900 White Settlement Rd Fort Worth TX 76107-7822 E-mail: cissymay@aol.com.

LALIBERTE, ANDREA SABINA, biologist; b. Hofheim, Taunus, Germany, Jan. 24, 1959; arrived in US, 1998; d. Fritz and Rosmarie Balke; m. Marc Andre Laliberte, May 31, 1984. B in Natural Resource Sci., U. Coll. Cariboo, Kamloops, B.C., Can., 1997; MS, Oreg. State U., 2000, PhD, 2003. Grad. rsch. fellow Dept. Forest Resources Oreg. State U., Corvallis, Oreg., 2000—03; remote sensing scientist ARS Jornada Exptl. Range USDA, Las Cruces, N.Mex., 2003—. Contbr. articles to profl. jours. Schutz Family Edn. Fund fellowship, Coll. Forestry, Oreg. State U., 2002, Richardson Family Grad. Rsch. fellowship, 2000. Mem.: BC Inst. of Agrologists, Am. Soc. for Photogrammetry and Remote Sensing (dir. Rio Grande chpt. 2003—), Soc. for Range Mgmt. (assoc.), Gamma Sigma Delta. Avocations: horseback riding, hiking, gardening. Office Phone: 505-646-4144.

LALIBERTE, CATHERINE ELAINE, elementary school educator; b. Nashua, N.H., June 8, 1954; d. Leopold Antoine and Jeannette Simone Dupont; children: Sara Emily, Rebecca Ellen. BS, Rivier Coll., 1976, MEd, 1980. 1st grade tchr. City of Nashua Sch. Dist., NH, 1976—82, 6th grade tchr., 1992—2000, 3d grade tchr., 2000—03, reading specialist, 2003—. Recipient Sister Mary Jane Benoit Outstanding Educator of Yr. award, Rivier Coll., 2003. Mem.: Alpha Delta Kappa. Avocations: reading, needlecrafts, walking.

LALIME, PATRICK, professional hockey player; b. St. Bonaventure, PQ, Can., July 7, 1974; Goaltender Pitts. Penguins, 1996—97, Ottawa Senators, 1999—2004; goaltender St. Louis Blues, 2004—. Named to NHL All-Star game, 2003. Office: c/o St Louis Blues Savvis Center 1401 Clark Ave Saint Louis MO 63103

LALKAKA, RUSTAM, chemist, engineer, technology consultant; b. Nagpur, India, Sept. 5, 1928; came to U.S., 1979; s. Darab Rustam and Nargis R.; m. Phiroza Billimoria; 1 child, Dinyar BSc in Chemistry, Nagpur U., 1949; BS in Metallurgy, Stanford U., 1950, MS in Metall. Engring., 1951. Founder, bd. dirs. M.N. Dastur & Co., Ltd., Calcutta, India, 1955—68; chief Dastur Engrng. Internat., Gmbh, Dusseldorf, Germany, 1969—72; regional adviser on tech. transfer UN Indsl. Devel. Orgn., Bangkok, 1972—76; chief indsl. devel. adviser UNIDO, Anakara, Turkey, 1976—79; dir. UN Fund for Sci. and Tech., N.Y.C., 1980—89; pres. Bus. and Tech. Devel. Strategies, Internat. Cons., N.Y.C., 1990—. Chmn. bd. govs. Found. for Internat. Tng., Toronto, Can., 1988—; past adj. prof. Asian Inst. Tech., Bangkok; assoc. Inst. for Internat. Entrepreneurship, Northwestern U., Evanston; sr. advisor to private sector devel. program UN Devel. Program, N.Y; cons. to private sectors and govts. in China, Korea, India, Thailand, Turkey, Egypt, Syria, Nigeria, Brazil, Chile, Uruguay, Mexico and others. Co-author: (with others) Guidelines for Technological Development in Asia and the Pacific, 1976; (with Wu Ming Yu) Managing Science Policy and Technology Acquisition: Strategies for China and a Changing World, 1984, (with D. Bishop) Business Incubators in Economic Development, 1996; contbr. over 80 articles to profl. internat. jours. Recipient scroll of honor The Iron and Steel Inst., London, 1964 Mem. World Assn. Indsl. and Tech. Rsch. Orgs., (exec. bd., award of honor 1992), Indian Inst. of Metals (hon. sec.), Latin Am. Iron and Steel Inst. (hon. mem.) Home: 1441 3rd Ave Apt 5A New York NY 10028-1975 Office Phone: 212-452-1678. E-mail: rlalkaka@btels.biz.

L'ALLIER, JAMES JOSEPH, communications executive, graphics designer, educator; b. St. Paul, June 24, 1945; s. Charlemagne Joseph and Mildred Marie (LeVasseur) L'A.; m. Susan Kay Margulies, Apr. 28, 1973. BS magna cum laude, U. Wis., River Falls, 1969, MS, 1973; PhD, U. Minn., 1980. Instr. English, multimedia specialist River Falls Sr. High Sch., 1969-71; instr. English Stillwater (Minn.) Sr. High Sch., 1971-80; mgr. computer assisted instrn. Wilson Learning Corp., Mpls., 1980-83, dir. R&D, 1983-86; v.p. R&D Wilson Learning Interactive Tech. Group, Santa Fe, 1986-89; v.p. product devel. Nippon Wilson Learning, Tokyo, 1989-90; v.p. instructional design Whole Systems International, Cambridge, Mass., 1990-93; v.p. product devel. NETg, A Thomson Learning Co., Naperville, 1993-98; v.p. R&D NETg, A Harcourt Brace Co., Naperville, Ill., 1998-2000; chief learning officer, v.p. R&D NETg, A Thomson Learning Co., 2000—. Expert witness Universal Tng., Chgo., 1989-91; bd. dirs. Info. Tech. Tng. Assn., chair standards com. 2000—. Author: (video prodns.) Who Shot the Terminal?,

1984, The Tenth Woman, 1987, Working Toward the Future, 1991, America's Workforce: A Vision for the Future, 1992; mem. editorial bd. Learning Age, Mpls., 1987-89, CLO Mag., Chgo., 2002-; product reviewer Ednl. Tech., N.Y.C., 1981-83; assoc. editor Performance and Instrn., Washington, 1983-85; inventor Interactive Learning System-Skill Builder; holder 240 copyrights; inventor, patent for interactive learning sys. Skill Builder; inventor, patent holder Precision Skilling. Curriculum chair Total Info. Ednl. Systems, St. Paul, 1971-76; fund raiser U. Minn. Alliance, Mpls., 1983-89; contbr. Am. Cancer Soc., Washington, 1987—; mem. pub. svc. com. Instructional Systems Assn., Sunset Beach, Calif., 1988—; reviewer William H. Donner Found., Inc., N.Y.C., 1993—; mem. ednl. tech. adv. bd. Utah State U., Logan. U. Minn. Grad. Sch. Edn. sr. fellow, 1984; U.S. Dept. Labor grantee, 1991. Mem. U. Wis. Alumni Assn., Instructional Systems Assn. (conf. chair 1980, 84), U. Minn. Alumni Assn., Boston Computer Soc., Ednl. Tech. Adv. Bd., Utah Sate U., Pres.'s Club U. Minn., Heritage Soc. U. Wis. Avocations: reading, photography, music. Office: Thomson NETg 1751 W Diehl Rd Naperville IL 60563-1840

LALLY, JOHN PATRICK, investment company executive; b. Newark, Mar. 17, 1951; s. John James and Rita Margaret L.; m. Ann Bierbower, May 2, 1987; children: John B., Mark B. BS, Boston Coll., 1973; MBA, Columbia U., 1975. Staff acct. Coopers & Lybrand, Boston, 1975-78; v.p. Goldman, Sachs & Co., N.Y.C., 1978-86; mng. dir. Bankers Trust Co., N.Y.C., Atlanta, 1986-90; pres. Lally Percival & Co., Atlanta, 1991-95, Resurgens Capital Ptnrs., Atlanta, 1996—2002, Europe Capital Ptnrs., 2003—. Bd. dirs. Integrated Energy Svcs., Inc., Atlanta, EquipMD, Atlanta, Response Mktg. Group, LLC, Richmond. Avocations: reading, outdoor activities, sports.

LALLY, MICHAEL DAVID, writer, actor; b. Orange, N.J., May 25, 1942; s. James A. and Irene I. (Dempsey) L.; m. Lee Fischer, 1964 (dec. 1986); children: Caitlin Maeve, Miles Aaron; m. Jaina Flynn, 1997; 1 child, Flynn Albert James. BA, U. Iowa, 1968, MFA, 1969. Instr. Trinity Coll., Washington, 1969-74; book reviewer Washington Post, 1974-77; editor Franklin Library div. Franklin Mint, 1976-79; editor, pub. various newspapers and presses including Iowa Defender, Some of Us Press, The Washington Review of the Arts, 1966-80, Venice mag., 1988-91, The Hollywood Rev., 1991. Bd. dirs. The Print Center, Bklyn., 1972-75, Washington Film Classroom, 1970-72 Actor: (films) Last Rites, 1980, The Nesting, 1981, White Fang, 1991, Cool World, 1992, Basic Instinct, 1992, Not Again, 1996, The Technical Writer, 2003, Last Grave, 2005, (stage) The Heroes, 1981, Balm in Gilead, 1983, The Rhythm of Torn Stars, 1988-89, Short Eyes, 1994, (TV) Cagney and Lacey, 1984, Berrengers, 1985, Hardcastle and McCormick, 1986, L.A. Law, 1989, Father Dowling's Mysteries, 1991, Caught in the Act, 1993, Diagnosis Murder, 1994, NYPD Blue, 1995, 97, 99, Brooklyn South, 1997, JAG, 1997, 98, Law and Order, 2000, Ed, 2001, Deadwood, 2004; freelance writer, reviewer, actor, N.Y.C., 1975-82; screenwriter, actor, L.A., 1982-99, screenwriter, actor, N.Y.C., 1999—; author 20 books including Rocky Dies Yellow, 1974, German edit., 1982, Dues, 1974, Catch My Breath, 1976, 95, Just Let Me Do It, 1978, Attitude, 1982, Hollywood Magic, 1982, Cant Be Wrong, 1996, Of, 1999, It's Not Nostalgia, 1999, It Takes One to Know One, 2001, March 18, 2003, 2004; author, dir. (one-act play) Four Grown Men, N.Y.C., 1982, Hollywood Magic, L.A., 1983; co-author (play) The Rhythm of Torn Stars, 1988-89, (film) Fogbound, 2003; 3 short plays, 1995; recorded poems on CD, What You Find There, 1994; contbr. articles and poetry to profl. jours., newspapers, mags. Served with USAF, 1962-66. Nat. Endowment for Arts fellow, 1974, 81; recipient Discovery award N.Y. Poetry Ctr., 1972, award Poets Found., 1974, Lit. Prize award Pacificus Found., 1996, Am. Book award, 2000. Mem. SAG, AFTRA, Writers Guild Am., P.E.N. (Oakland Josephine Miles award for excellence in lit. 1997). Home: 43 Dunnel Rd Maplewood NJ 07040 Personal E-mail: lallyjmf@comcast.net.

LALLY, NORMA ROSS, retired federal agency administrator; b. Crawford, Nebr., Aug. 10, 1932; d. Roy Anderson and Alma Leona (Barber) Lively; m. Robert Edward Lally, Dec. 4, 1953 (div. Mar. 1986); children: Robyn Carol Murch, Jeffrey Alan, Gregory Roy. BA, Boise (Idaho) State U., 1974, MA, 1976; postgrad., Columbia Pacific U., 1988—. With grad. admissions Boise State U., 1971-74; with officer programs USN Recruiting, Boise, 1974; pub. affairs officer IRS, Boise and Las Vegas, 1975-94; ret., 1994. Speaker in field, Boise and Las Vegas, 1977—. Contbr. articles to newspapers. Mem. task force Clark County Sch. Dist., Las Vegas, 1986-96, Las Vegas Art Mus. Staff sgt. USAF, 1950-54. Mem.: NAFE, Women in Mil. Svc. Am. (charter), Mensa, Marine's Meml. Club (life), Am. Legion (life). Avocations: writing, music, swimming, travel. Home: 3013 Hawksdale Dr Las Vegas NV 89134-8967 Personal E-mail: norlally@aol.com.

LALLY, VINCENT EDWARD, atmospheric scientist; b. Brookline, Mass., Oct. 13, 1922; s. Michael James and Ellen Teresa (Dolan) L.; m. Marguerite Mary Tibert, June 5, 1949; children: Dennis V., Marianne Baugh, Stephen J. BS in Meteorology, U. Chgo., 1944; BSEE, MIT, 1948, MS in Engring. Adminstrn., 1949. Engr. Bendix-Friez, Balt., 1949-51; chief metall. equip. devel. Air Force Cambridge Rsch. Labs., Bedford, Mass., 1951-58; rsch. dir. Teledynamics, Phila., 1958-61; dir. Nat. Sci. Balloon Facility Nat. Ctr. for Atmospheric Rsch., Boulder, Colo., 1961-66, sr. scientist, 1966-91, sr. scientist emeritus, 1991—. Contbr. articles to sci. jours., chpt. to handbook in field. 1st lt. USAAC, 1942-46. Fellow Am. Meteorol. Soc. (Cleveland Abbe award 1990); mem. Inst. Navigation, Sigma Xi. Achievements include 7 patents for space inflatables, superpressure balloons, rocket instruments, communications techniques; made first balloon flight around the world, longest balloon flight; pioneered technology in measurements from radiosondes, aircraft and rockets. Home: 4875 Sioux Dr Apt 304 Boulder CO 80303-3765 Office: Nat Ctr Atmospheric Rsch PO Box 3000 Boulder CO 80307-3000 Personal E-mail: lallyvincent@qwest.net.

LALONDE, BERNARD JOSEPH, finance educator; b. Detroit, June 3, 1933; s. John Bernard and Fannie (Napier) LaL.; m. Barbara Elaine Eggenberger, Sept. 6, 1958; children— Lisa Renee, Michell Ann, Christopher John. AB, U. Notre Dame, 1955; MBA, U. Detroit, 1957; PhD, Mich. State U., 1961. Asst. prof. mktg. U. Colo., Boulder, 1961-65; assoc. prof. Mich. State U., East Lansing, 1965-69; James R. Riley prof. mktg. and logistics Ohio State U., Columbus, 1969-85, Raymond E. Mason prof. transp. and logistics, 1985-95, prof. emeritus, 1995. Author: Physical Distribution Management, 2d edit, 1968, Customer Service: A Management Perspective, 1988; Editor: Jour. Bus. Logistics; Jour. book and monographs editor, Am. Mktg. Assn.; Contbr. articles to profl. jours. Pres. Transp. Research Found. Recipient John Drury Sheehan award, 1976; Formerly Ford scholar; Gen. Electric fellow. Mem. Am. Marketing Assn., Regional Sci. Assn., Council Logistic Mgmt., Soc. Logistics Engrs., Beta Gamma Sigma, Alpha Kappa Psi. Roman Catholic. Home: 8538 Pitlochry Ct Dublin OH 43017-9770 Office: Ohio State U Coll Bus Supply Chain Mgmt Rsch Grp 351 Fisher Hall 2100 Neil Ave Columbus OH 43210

LALONDE, MARC, lawyer, former Canadian government official; b. Ile Perrot, Que., Can., July 26, 1929; s. J. Albert and Nora (St-Aubin) L.; m. Claire Tetreau, Sept. 8, 1955; children: Marie, Luc, Paul, Catherine. BA, Coll. St. Laurent, Montreal, 1950; LLB, U. Montreal, 1964, LLM, 1955; MA in Econs. and Polit. Sci., Oxford (Eng.) U., 1957; PhD honoris causa, Limburg U., The Netherlands, 1989; PhD, Univ. Western Ontario, Can., 2005. Bar: Que. 1955, Queen's Coun. 1971, Order of Can, 1988. Prof. bus. law and econs. U. Montreal, 1957-59; spl. asst. to Minister of Justice, Ottawa, Ont., Can., 1959-60; partner firm Gelinas, Bourque, Lalonde & Benoit, Montreal, 1960-68; policy adviser to Prime Minister Lester B. Pearson, Ottawa, 1967-68; prin. sec. to Prime Minister Pierre E. Trudeau, Ottawa, 1968-72; elected to House of Commons for Montreal-Outremont, 1972; minister of nat. health and welfare, 1972-77; minister of state for fed.-provincial relations, 1977-78; minister responsible for status of women, 1975-78; minister of justice and atty. gen. Can., 1978-79; minister of energy, mines and resources, 1980-82; minister of finance, 1982-84; sr. counsel Stikeman, Elliott, Montreal. Bd. dirs. Citibank of Can., O&Y Properties, Inc., Sherritt Internat. Corp., Oxbow Equities Corp.; ad hoc judge Internat. Ct. Justice, 1995—. Decorated officer Order of Can.; Queen's Counsel; recipient Dana award APHA, 1978; named to Can. Med. Hall of Fame, 2004. Mem. Internat. Coun. on Comml. Arbitration, Am. Arbitration Assn., London Ct. Internat. Arbitration, Privy Coun. Can. Mem. Liberal Party. Home: 1477 boul Perrot Ile Perrot PQ Canada J7V 7P2 Office Phone: 514-397-3080. E-mail: mlalonde@stikeman.com.

LALWANI, ANIL KUMAR, otolaryngologist; b. Sept. 17, 1960; MD, U. Mich., 1985. Diplomate Am. Bd. Otolaryngology. Intern Duke U., Durham, N.C., 1985-86, resident in gen. & thoracic surgery, 1986-87; resident in otolaryngology & head & neck surgery U. Calif., San Francisco, 1987-91, fellow in otolaryngology skull base surgery, 1987-91; sr. staff fellow NIH, 1992-94; staff U. Calif., San Francisco, 1994—; now Mendik Found. prof. otolaryngology NYU Sch. of Medicine, chmn., prof. physiology & neuroscience; surgeon NYU Cochlear Implant Center. Mem. Am. Acad. Otolaryngology & Head & Neck Surgery, Am. Coll. Surgeons. Office: NYU Sch of Medicine 550 First Ave New York NY 10016

LAM, BYRON L., ophthalmologist; MD, Boston U., 1986. Diplomate Am. Bd. Ophthalmology, 1991. Asst. prof. Jones Eye Inst., Little Rock, Ark., 1992—95; prof. Bascom Palmer Eye Inst., Miami, Fla., 1995—. Author: (textbook) Electrophysiology of Vision: Clinical Testing and Applications. Recipient Achievement award, Am. Acad. Ophthalmology, 2003. Fellow: N.Am. Neuro-Ophthalmology Soc. (edn. com. mem. 2002—03); mem.: Internat. Soc. Clin. Electrophysiology of Vision, Soc. Heed Fellows, Alpha Omega Alpha. Office: Bascom Palmer Eye Inst 900 NW 17th St Miami FL 33136 Office Phone: 305-326-6021.

LAM, CAROL C., prosecutor, lawyer; b. N.Y. m. Mark Burnett; 4 children. BA in Philosophy, Yale U., 1981; JD, Stanford U., 1985. Law clk. to Hon. Irving R. Kaufman US Ct. Appeals (2nd cir.), 1985—86; asst. US atty. (so. dist.) Calif. US Dept Justice, 1986—90; chief, major fraud sect. US Dept. Justice, 1997—2000, interim US atty. (so. dist.) Calif., 2002, US atty. (so. dist.) Calif., 2002—; judge Calif. Superior Ct., San Diego, 2000—02. Recipient Spl. Achievement award, US Dept. Justice, 1990—94, 1997—99, Dir.'s award for Superior Performance as an Asst. US Atty., 1994, Health & Human Svc. Inspector Gen.'s Integrity award, 1995, Atty. Gen.'s award for Disting. Svc., 1997, Health & Human Svc. Inspector Gen.'s award for Exceptional Achievement, 1997. Mem.: Stanford Law Sch. bd. visitors, Stanford Alumni Assn. Office: US Atty Office 880 Front St Rm 6293 San Diego CA 92101-8893

LAM, FAT CHEUNG, mathematician, educator; b. Canton, China, July 17, 1946; came to U.S., 1968; m. Kay Ho, Aug. 16, 1975. BA, Gallaudet U., 1971; MA, George Washington U., 1974; PhD, U. Mont., 1987. Prof. math. Gallaudet U., Washington, 1981—. Mem. Math. Assn. Am., Sigma Xi. Achievements include being the first deaf Chinese to obtain a PhD. Office: Gallaudet Univ Mathematics Dept 800 Florida Ave NE Washington DC 20002-3660

LAM, GALEN KA-RON, electrical engineer; b. Winnipeg, Man., Can., May 18, 1969; s. Peter Kuen-Yui and Sau-Yin (Ng) Lam; m. Mamiko Nishiguchi, Mar. 25, 1997. BSc in Elec. Engring., U. Calgary, Alta., Can., 1991. Sys. planning engr., overseas plant engring. dept. NEWJEC, Inc., Osaka, Japan, 1993-97; facilities planning, power sys. engr. TransAlta Utilities Corp., Calgary, 1997—98; transmission adminstr., tech. svcs. group ESB Internat., Calgary, 1998—2002; sys. planning engr. Transmission Adminstr. Alta. Ltd., Calgary, 2002—03; sr. tech. specialist, sys. planning Alta. Elec. Sys. Operator, Calgary, 2003—. Mem.: IEEE, Geologists and Geophysicists Alta., Assn. Profl. Engrs. Achievements include numerous pre-feasibility and feasibility studies on coal thermal, hydro and combined cycle plants, pumped storage, and nuclear power projects in numerous countries. Avocations: bicycling, music, reading, tennis. Home: 2948-5 Tannowa Misaki-cho Osaka 599-0301 Japan Office: Alta Elec Sys Operator 2500 330 5th Ave SW Calgary AB Canada Personal E-mail: galen.lam@shaw.ca. Business E-Mail: galen.lam@aeso.ca.

LAM, PAULINE POHA, library director; b. Hong Kong, Oct. 21, 1950; came to U.S., 1971; d. Cheung and Kam-Chun (Mo) Li; m. Frank Sung-Lun Lam, Nov. 28, 1973; children: Candace See-Win Lam, Megan See-Kay Lam. BA, U. B.C., 1977; MLS, U. Tex., 1980; cert. City Mgmt. Acad., Austin C.C., 1994; grad., Cedar Park Leadership Class, 2004. Libr. dir. City of Cedar Park (Tex.). Bd. dirs. Cedar Park Pub. Libr. Found., 1994—. Mem. Work Force Literacy Com. Literacy Coun. of Williamson County, 1995, Cedar Park Leadership Class 2004, Williamson County Children's Advocacy Ctr. Bd., 2003; bd. dirs. ARC of Ctrl. Tex., Austin, 1995—97, Williamson County Children's Advocacy Ctr., 2003. Mem. ALA, Tex. Libr. Assn., Tex. Mcpl. League Libr. Dir. Assn. Avocations: reading, crocheting, painting. Office: Cedar Park Pub Libr 550 Discovery Blvd Cedar Park TX 78613-2200

LAM, SIMON SHIN-SING, computer science educator; b. Macao, July 31, 1947; arrived in US, 1966; s. Chak Han and Kit Ying (Tang) Lam; m. Amy Leung, Mar. 29, 1971; 1 child, Eric. BSE.E. with distinction, Wash. State U., 1969; MS in Engring., UCLA, 1970, PhD, 1974. Research engr. ARPA Network Measurement Ctr., UCLA, Los Angeles, 1971-74; research staff mem. IBM Watson Research Ctr, Yorktown Heights, N.Y., 1974-77; asst. prof. U. Tex.-Austin, Austin, 1977-79, assoc. prof., 1979-83, prof. computer sci., 1983—; David S. Bruton Centennial prof. U. Tex., Austin, 1985-88, anonymous prof., 1988-2001, chmn. dept. computer sci., 1992-94, regents chair computer sci., 2001—. Editor-in-chief IEEE/ACM Transactions on Networking, 1995-99; editor: Principles of Communication and Networking Protocols; contbr. articles to profl. jours. Recipient William R. Bennett prize, 2001, Software System award, 2004; grantee, NSF, 1978—; Chancellor's Tchg. fellow, UCLA, 1969—73. Fellow IEEE (Leonard G. Abraham prize 1975, William R. Bennett prize 2001, W.Wallace McDowell award 2004), Assn. for Computing Machinery (program chmn. symposium 1983, SIGCOMM award 2004, Software Sys. award 2004). Avocations: tennis, swimming, skiing, travel. Office: Univ Tex 1 U Station CO500 Austin TX 78712

LAM, SIUWA MONICA, education educator, consultant; arrived in U.S., 1986; d. Pui Lam and Shuk Wah Chan. BS, Chinese U. of Hong Kong, 1984; MS, Tex. A & M U., 1988; PhD, U. Wis., 1994. Assoc. of acctg. technologist, Soc. of Mgmt. Accountants, Canada, 1991. Exec. officer Chinese U. of Hong Kong, 1984—86, asst. lectr., 1988—90; assoc. prof. Calif. State U., Sacramento, 1994—2000, prof., 2000—. Cons. Access Health, Rancho Cordova, Calif., 1996—97, Calif. State Dept. Parks and Recreation, Sacramento, 1999—2000; internship Wells Fargo Bank, San Francisco, 2000. Author: Accounting Information System Cases, 2002 (Prentice Hall award), Integrated Systems: The Accountant in the 21st Century, 2005; contbr. articles to profl. jours. Summer fellow, Calif. State U., Sacramento, 1998, 2000, Assigned Time grantee, 1997—98, MIS Tech. grantee, 2001. Mem.: Soc. Mgmt. Accountants, Can., Decision Sci. Inst., Informs, Assn. of Info. Sys. Achievements include copyright of program for rule extraction for neural networks. Office: Calif State Univ 6000 J St Sacramento CA 95819 Office Phone: 916-278-7037. E-mail: lamsm@csus.edu.

LAMACH, BERNARD D., county commissioner; b. Big Timber, Mont., Oct. 10, 1934; m. Deborah Lamach; 6 children. BS, BA, Colo. U., 1975; student, Internat. Corr. Sch., 1958. Owner retail store, Bradford, N.H.; cons. engr.; mem. N.H. Ho. of Reps., 1994-98; commr. Merrimack County, 1998—2003. Mem. Bradford budget com., solid waste com., bus. assn. Kearsarge regional sch. dist. budget com. N.H. Ho. of Reps., sci. tech. and energy com. Mem. Bradford Hist. Soc., Lake Massasecum Improvement Assn. Republican. Address: 5309 Shalley CIR Fort Myers FL 33919-2211

LAMAGNA, CARLO M., art educator; BA in English, Coll. Holy Cross; MA in art history, U. Mass. Prof. & chmn. art dept. NYU. Office: New York U 82 Washington Sq East New York NY 10003 Office Phone: 212-998-5700. Office Fax: 212-995-4320. E-mail: carlo.lamagna@nyu.edu.*

LAMALFA, JAMES THOMAS, art educator, consultant; b. Milw., Nov. 30, 1937; s. Anthony and Beulah Marie LaMalfa; children: Lawrence James, Brenda Louise Stolz, Anthony Edward, Leah Elizabeth. MFA, U. Wis., 1962. Prof. U. Wis., Eau Claire, 1963—66, Marinette, 1969—, Wittenberg U., Springfield, Ohio, 1966—69. Prin. works include sculpture Weaver Chapel; artist other pub. and outdoor sculptures. Alderman City of Marinette, 1970—2002. Mem.: Coalition Active Sculpture Tchrs. (sec. 1991—92, pres. 1992—94). Avocations: model railroad collector, art. Office: U Wis 750 West Bay Shore Rd Marinette WI 54143 Office Phone: 715-735-4300. Business E-Mail: jlamalfa@uwc.edu.

LAMALIE, ROBERT EUGENE, retired executive search company executive; b. Fremont, Ohio, June 3, 1931; s. Glennis and Mildred M. (Hetrick) L.; m. Dorothy M. Zilles, June 20, 1953; children: Deborah, Dawn, Elaine. BA, Capital U., Columbus, Ohio, 1954; postgrad., Case Western Res. U. Asst. dir. recruiting Xerox Corp., 1959-62; mgr. orgn. planning and profl. recruiting Glidden Co., 1962-65; search cons. Booz, Allen & Hamilton, Inc., Cleve., 1965-67; pres., chief exec. officer Lamalie Assocs., Inc., Tampa, Fla., 1967-84, chmn. bd. dirs., chief exec. officer, 1984-87, chmn. bd. dirs., 1987-88; pres. Robert Lamalie, Inc., Marco Island, Fla., 1988-90, ret., 1990. Served with U.S. Army, 1954-56, Korea.

LAMANTIA, CHARLES ROBERT, management consulting company executive; b. NYC, June 12, 1939; s. Joseph Ferdinand and Catherine (Perniciaro) LaM.; m. Ann Christine Carmody, Sept. 16, 1961; children: Elise, Matthew. BA, Columbia U., 1960, BS, 1961, MS, 1962, ScD, 1965; grad. advanced mgmt. program, Harvard Bus. Sch., 1979. Cons. staff Arthur D. Little, Inc., Cambridge, Mass., 1967-77, v.p., 1977-81, pres., COO, 1987-88, pres., CEO, 1988-98, chmn., CEO, 1998-99, also bd. dirs.; pres., CEO Koch Process Sys., Westboro, Mass., 1981-86. Mem. adv. coun. Sch. Engring. Columbia U., 1990-98; mem. adv. bd. Sch. Mgmt. Boston Coll., 1995—; bd. dirs. State St. Corp., 1994—, Marathon Techs., 2001-02, Neurometrics, Inc., 2004-; trustee Meml. Dr. Trust, 1988-99; bd. govs. New Eng. Med. Ctr., 1989-95; bd. advisors StoneGate Ptnrs., 2000-01, Intellect-Exchange.com, 2000—03. Mem. Corp. Woods Hole Oceanog. Inst., 1996-2004; mem. bd. overseers Mus. Sci., Boston, 1988-94, Sta. WGBH-TV, 1990-2004, mem. Conf. Bd., 1989-99; mem. Mass. Gov.'s Coun., Mass. Bus. Roundtable, 1992-99, bd. dirs. 1998-99; bd. dirs. Boston Pub. Libr. Found., 1997-2001. Lt. USN, 1965-67. Sloan Found. fellow, 1962, NSF fellow, 1965. Mem. AIChE.

LAMAR, HOWARD ROBERTS, academic administrator, historian; b. Tuskegee, Ala., Nov. 18, 1923; s. John Howard and Elma (Roberts) L.; m. Doris Shirley White, Sept. 3, 1959; children: Susan Kent, Sarah Howard. BA, Emory U., 1944; MA, Yale U., 1945, PhD, 1951; LHD (hon.), Emory U., 1975; LLD (hon.), Yale U., 1993; LittD (hon.), U. Nebr., 1994. Instr. U. Mass., 1945-46, Wesleyan U., Middletown, Conn., 1948-49; mem. faculty Yale U., 1949-94, prof. Am. History and history Am. West, 1964-94, W.R. Coe prof. Am. history, 1979-87, Sterling prof. history, 1987—, chmn. history dept., 1962-63, 67-70, dir. history grad. studies, 1964-67, fellow Ezra Stiles Coll., 1961-94, dean, 1979-85, pres., 1992-93, Sterling prof. history emeritus, 1994—. Author: Dakota Territory, 1861-1889, 1956, 97, The Far Southwest, 1846-1912, A Territorial History, 1966, 2d edit., 2000; also articles, reviews.; Editor: (Joseph Downey) Cruise of the Portsmouth, 1958, Western Americana Series, 1961—, New Encyclopedia of the American West, 1998, Gold Seeker: Adventures of A Belgian Argonaut in California, 1985, paperback 1998; co-author, co-editor The Frontier in History: North America and Southern Africa Compared, 1981, History of the American Frontier Series, 1976—. Alderman, New Haven, 1951-53. Mem. Orgn. Am. Historians, Western History Assn. (pres. 1971-72), Am. Antiquarian Soc., Elihu Soc., Conn. Acad. of Arts and Scis., Phi Beta Kappa. Democrat. Home: 1747 Hartford Tpke North Haven CT 06473-1249 Office: Yale U Dept History New Haven CT 06520

LAMAR, MARTHA LEE, chaplain; b. Birmingham, Jan. 2, 1935; d. Alco L. and Anne Lee (Morris) Lee; m. William Fred Lamar, Jr., June 7, 1986; children: Barbara Gayle Martin, Owen Parker Jr. BS, Auburn U., 1955; MA, Christian Theol. Sem., Indpls., 1992. From adminstv. asst. to rsch. coord. Ala. Affiliate Am. Heart Assn., Birmingham, 1977-86; adminstrv. asst. alumni office De Pauw U., Greencastle, Ind., 1986-89; nursing home chaplain Heritage House Health and Rehab. Ctr., Greencastle, 1989-98. Nursing home chaplain Garfield Park Health Facility, Indpls., 1992-94, Heritage House Health and Rehab. Ctr., Martinsville, Ind., 1992-95; chaplain cons. Oakwood Corp., Indpls., 1991-97. Vol. chaplain's office De Pauw U., 1986-97, community work for homeless, Greencastle, 1986-98, Fountain Sq. Devel. Corp., Indpls., 1992. Mem. Am. Soc. on Aging, Forum on Religion, Spirituality and Aging, Acad. Sr. Profls. at Eckerd Coll. (assoc.). Methodist. Avocations: travel, hiking, reading, entertaining, volunteering.

LAMAR, WILLIAM FRED, chaplain, educator; b. Birmingham, Ala., Jan. 4, 1934; s. William Fred Sr. and Everette (Kelley) L.; m. Roberta Anton, Sept. 17, 1955 (dec.); 1 child, Jonathan Frederick; m. Martha Anne Lee, June 7, 1986. BA, U. Ala., 1954; BD, Vanderbilt U., 1957; PhD, St. Louis U., 1972; D Min., Eden Theol. Sem., 1974; grad., Spanish Lang. Sch., Antigua, Guatemala, 1993. Minister United Meth. Ch., Bynum, Ala., 1959-61, Fultondale, Ala., 1961-65; campus minister U. Mo., Rolla, 1965-74; chaplain, prof., dir. overseas missions DePauw U., Greencastle, Ind., 1974-97; dir. United Meth. Com. on Relief Vol. Programs, Travnik, Bosnia, 1996-98. Advisor overseas vol. program United Meth. Ch. Ind., Indpls., 1980-88; mem. Eli Lilly Found. study on the future of the ministry, 1989-91; cons. internat. vol. programs United Theol. Sem., Vanderbilt U. Div. Sch. and Westminster Coll., Oxford U., 1989-93; bd. dirs. Ecumenical Ventures, The Philippines, China; adj. prof. Eckerd Coll., 2001-02; adj. prof. Eckerd Coll. Author: (book) Role of the College Chaplain at the Church-Related College, 1984; designer electric utility computer programs, 1979-85. Vice chmn. County Welfare Bd., Rolla; bd. dirs. Sr. Vol. Program Action, Greencastle, 1977-80. Served to 1st lt. U.S. Army, 1957-59. Recipient Award of Honor, Ind. Gov.'s. Voluntary Action, 1976, Cross of Jerusalem, Episcopal Diocese of Guatemala, 1979, Cross of St. Francis, Inst. de Asuntos Culturales del Peru, 1982, 587th Point of Light award Pres. George Bush, 1991, Vol. award Ind. Nature Conservancy, 1993; Danforth fellow, 1971-72. Fellow Ctr. Spiritual Life, Eckerd Coll.; mem. Nat. Campus Ministry Assn. (chmn. sci. and ethics network), Nat. Assn. Coll. Chaplains, Assn. Religion in Intellectual Life, Assn. Coll. and U. Religious Advisors (nat. program chair 1993; bd. dirs. Ind. office campus ministry 1988-98), Acad. Sr. Profls. (Eckerd Coll.). Home and Office: 5565 Escondida Blvd S Saint Petersburg FL 33715-1454 E-mail: fwlamar@eckerd.edu.

LAMARRE, BERNARD, engineering executive; b. Chicoutimi, Que., Can., Aug. 6, 1931; s. Emile J. and Blanche M. (Gagnon) L.; m. Louise Lalonde, Aug. 30, 1952 (dec. Dec. 2002); children: Jean, Christine, Lucie, Monique, Michèle, Philippe, Mireille. BSc, Ecole Poly., Montreal, Que., Can., 1952; MSc, Imperial Coll., U. London, 1955; LLD, St. Francis Xavier U., N.S., Can., 1980; DEng (hon.), U. Waterloo, Ont., 1984; LLD (hon.), U. Concordia, Montreal, 1985; DEng (hon.), U. Montreal, 1985; D in Applied Sci. (hon.), U. Sherbrooke, Que., 1986; D in Bus. Adminstrn. (hon.), U. Chicoutimi, Que., 1987; DSc (hon.), Queen's U., Kingston, Ont., 1987; DEng (hon.), U. Ottawa, Ont., 1988, Tech. U. N.S., 1989, Royal Mil. Coll., Kingston, 1990; PhD in Sci. (hon.), McGill U., 2001. Structural and founds. engr. Lalonde-Valois, Montreal, 1955-60, chief engr., 1960-62; ptnr., gen. mgr., pres. Lalonde, Valois, Lamarre, Valois, Montreal, 1962-72; chmn., CEO Lavalin Group, 1972-91; sr. advisor SNC-Lavalin Inc., 1991-99. Chmn. Soc. du Vieux Port de Montreal, Bellechasse Santè, Ecole Polytechnique de Montreal; bd. dirs. Design Inst. Chmn. Montreal (Can.) Mus. Fine Arts. Decorated officer Ordre nat. du Québec, Order of Can.; Athlone fellow, 1952. Fellow Engring. Inst. Can., Can. Soc. Civil Engring.; mem. ASCE, Order Engrs. Que., Mont-Royal Club, St. Denis Club. Roman Catholic. Home: 4850 Cedar Crescent Montreal PQ Canada H3W 2H9 Personal E-mail: bernard.lamarre@bellnet.ca.

LAMAS, GERVASIO ANTONIO, cardiologist, educator; b. Jan. 10, 1952; BA, Harvard U., 1974; MD, NYU, 1978. Diplomate Am. Bd. Cardiology. Fellow Harvard/Brigham Hosp., 1978-84; asst. prof. Harvard U., Cambridge, Mass., 1987-93; assoc. prof. U. Miami, Miami Beach, Fla., 1993—. Hon. prof., Argentina; dir. cardiovasc. rsch. Mt. Sinai Med. Ctr., Miami, 1999. Contbr. articles to profl. jours. Grantee to study chelation therapy. Mem.: Am. Coll. Cardiology (dist. rep. 1995—98), Am. Heart Assn. (bd. dirs. 1999—, pres. Miami Dade 2000—01). Office: Cardiovasc Assocs Miami 4300 Alton Rd Ste 207 Miami Beach FL 33140-2800 E-mail: glamas@msmc.com.

LAMB, BRIAN P., broadcast executive; b. 1941; Asst. mgr. Sta. WLFI, Lafayette, Ind., 1968—69; press sec. to congressman Peter Dominich Ho. of Reps., Denver, 1969—71, asst. to dir. office telecomm. policy, 1971—74; pres. Media Rsch., Inc., Denver, 1974—76; Washington bur. chief Titsch Pub. Co., Denver, 1976—78; chmn., CEO C-span, Washington, 1978—. With USN, 1962—67. Office: C-Span 400 N Capitol St NW Ste 650 Washington DC 20001-1550*

LAMB, CARL VERNON, writer, retired engineer; b. Jacksonville, Ark., Nov. 30, 1928; s. Fred Norman Lamb and Minnie Louise Anderson; m. Nancy J. Shields, July 30, 1950; children: Lisa, Mark, Carl II, Michael. Diploma in Mech. Engring., Internat. Corre Sch. ICS, Scranton, Pa., 1960. H.V.A.C. engr. Bechtel Inc., Ann Arbor, Mich., 1981, Gulf Chem. Co., Marietta, Ohio, 1981, Union Carbide, Charleston, W.Va., 1981—82; with Lambs Machine Shop, Boswell, Pa., 1982—83; facilities engr. IBM, Indicott, NY, 1983—84; project engr. MTI Corp., St. Albans, W.Va., 1984; facilities engr. Nissan Motors, Smyrna, Tenn., 1984—85; project engr. cons. Union Carbide, Charleston, W.Va., 1986—91; H.V.A.C. engr. Salem Tech. Svc., Coeur d' Alene, Idaho, 1991—92; self-employed land developer Scott Depot, W.Va., 1992—98; mech. engr. cons. Washington, 1993; self-employed writer Scott Depot, W.Va., 1998—. Author: (book) The Last Parade, 1999. Staff sgt. USMC, 1945—52. Republican. Avocation: poker. Office: Anderson Pub PO Box 611 Teays WV 25569 Office Phone: 304-755-1159.

LAMB, CHARLES F., retired minister, retired educator; b. Maryville, Tenn., Dec. 18, 1934; s. C. Fred and Sadie Ellen (Tedder) L.; children: Elizabeth Susan, Linda Louise, Jennifer Janet; m. Betty Jane Zimmerman, Dec. 29, 1979. BA, Maryville Coll., 1956; MDiv, Grad. Sem. of Phillips U., 1961; D in Ministry, N.Y. Theol. Sem., 1990. Ordained to ministry Christian Ch., 1961. Pastor East Aurora Christian Ch., N.Y., 1961-71; assoc. regional min. Christian Ch., Disciples of Christ, Northeastern Region, Buffalo, N.Y., 1971-75, regional min., 1975-99; ret., 1999. Mem. orgns. clergy and coun. of chs. Trustee Village of East Aurora, 1968-73; active environ. groups Conf. Mayors and Village Ofcls. N.Y., 1968-73; adj. prof. Niagara U., 1998-2005; asst. to the minister First Presbyn. Ch., Youngstown, N.Y., 1999—; interim conf. regional minister N.Y. Conf. United Ch. of Christ, 2004; bd. dirs. Residents for Responsible Govt., 2002—. Author: Doc's Diary, 1996, More Meanderings from Doc's Diary, 2000. Pres. Coll. Regional Mins., 1997-99; mem. adminstrv. com. Gen. Bd. of Christian Ch., Disciples of Christ, 1997-99. Mem. Conf. Regional Ministers and Moderators of the Disciples of Christ (pres. 1997-99), Sierra Club (mem. exec. com. Niagara group 2001-). Democrat. Mem. Christian Ch. Home: 335 Walnut Ln Youngstown NY 14174-1348 E-mail: clamb0@prodigy.net.

LAMB, CHARLES MOODY, political scientist, educator; b. Mar. 1, 1945; s. Edward Clay and Opal Irene Lamb. BS, Mid. Tenn. State U., 1967; MA, U. Ala., 1970, PhD, 1974. Adminstrv. specialist NASA, Washington, 1971; rsch. scientist George Washington U., Washington, 1973—75; equal opportunity specialist U.S. Commn. on Civil Rights, Washington, 1975—77; asst. prof. polit. sci. SUNY-Buffalo, 1977—84, assoc. prof., 1984—. Vis. assoc. prof. U. Wis., Madison, 1990—91; cons. U.S. Congress Office Tech. Assessment, Washington, 1974—75, Washington, 1984. Co-editor, contbg. author: Supreme Court Activism and Restraint, 1982 (Choice Outstanding Acad. Book award, 1983), Implementation of Civil Rights Policy, 1984, Judicial Conflict and Consensus, 1986, The Burger Court: Political and Judicial Profiles, 1991; author: Housing Segregation in Suburban America Since 1960: Presidential and Judicial Politics, 2005. 1st lt. U.S. Army, 1972. Recipient awards in field; grantee, NSF, 1974—75, Office Tech. Assessment, 1974—75, SUNY Rsch. Found., 1982, Lyndon Baines Johnson Found., 1996, Gerald R. Ford Found., 1997. Mem.: Midwest Polit. Sci. Assn., Leadership Conf. on Civil Rights, Law and Soc. Assn., N.E. Polit. Sci. Assn., Am. Polit. Sci. Assn. (exec. com. sect. on law cts. and jud. process 1984—86, 1992—94), NY State Polit. Sci. Assn. (pres. 1985—86), Common Cause, Pi Sigma Beta, Pi Gamma Mu, Phi Sigma Alpha. Democrat. Presbyterian. Avocations: tennis, swimming. Home: 6331 Lakemont Ct East Amherst NY 14051-2055 Office: SUNY Dept Polit Sci 520 Park Hall Buffalo NY 14221-5013 Business E-Mail: clamb@buffalo.edu.

LAMB, DARLIS CAROL, sculptor; b. Wausa, Nebr. d. Lindor Soren and June Berniece (Skalberg) Nelson; m. James Robert Lamb; children: Sherry Lamb Sobh, Michael, Mitchell. BA in Fine Arts, Columbia Pacific U., San Rafael, Calif., 1988, MA in Fine Arts, 1989. Exhibitions include Nat. Arts Club, N.Y.C., 1983 (Catherine Lorillard Wolfe award sculpture, 1983, 1997, C.L. Wolfe Horse's Head award, 1994, Anna Hyatt Huntington cash award, 1995, honorable mention, 1996, medal of honor, 1998, Anna Hyatt Huntington bronze medal, 2000, Paul Manship Meml. award, 2001, Harriet W. Frishmuth Meml. Sculpture award, 2002), 1985, 1989, 1991—93, 1995—97, 1998, 2000—05, 2001, N.Am. Sculpture Exhibit, Foothills Art Ctr., Golden, Colo., 1983—84 (Pub. Svc. Co. of Colo. sculpture award, 1990), 1986—87, 1990—91, Nat. Acad. of Design, 1986, Nat. Sculpture Soc., 1985 (C. Percival Dietch Sculpture prize, 1991), 1991, 1995, 1997, 2003—05, exhibitions include Loveland Mus. and Gallery, 1990—91, Audubon Artists, 1991, Allied Artists Am., 1992, 1995, Pen and Brush, 1993 (Roman Bronze award, 1995), 1995—97, 1999, 2000, 2001, Colorado Springs Fine Arts Mus., 1996 (Award of Merit), 1998, 2000, All Colo. Exhibit, 2001 (1st prize sculpture), Represented in permanent collections Nebr. Hist. Soc., Am. Lung Assn. of Colo., Benson Park Sculpture Garden, Loveland, U.S. Space Found., Colorado Springs Osteo. Found., Thomas Jefferson H.S., Council Bluffs, Iowa (Hall of Fame, 2004), one-woman shows include Curtis Arts & Humanities Ctr., Greenwood Village, Colo., 2002. Named to Hall of Fame, Thomas Jefferson H.S., 2004. Mem. Catherine Lorillard Wolfe Art Club, N.Am. Sculpture Soc. Office: PO Box 9043 Englewood CO 80111-8000 Office Phone: 303-779-4527. Personal E-mail: dlambsculpture@usa.net.

LAMB, GORDON HOWARD, music educator; b. Eldora, Iowa, Nov. 6, 1934; s. Capp and Ethel (Hayden) L; m. Nancy Ann Painter; children: Kirk, Jon, Phillip. B in Music Edn., Simpson Coll., 1956; M of Music, U. Nebr., 1962; PhD, U. Iowa, 1973. Choral dir. Iowa pub. schs., Tama/Paullina, Sac City, 1957-68; asst. prof. music U. Wis., Stevens Point, 1969-70, U. Tex., Austin, 1970-74, prof., dir. divsn. music San Antonio, 1974-79, prof., v.p. acad. affairs, 1979-86; pres. Northeastern Ill. U., Chgo., 1986-95, pres. emeritus, 1996—; sr. v.p. EFL Assocs./TranSearch, Overland Park, Kans., 2000—. Vis. prof. music dept. Western Ill. U., 1996-97; interim chancellor U. Wis., Parkside, 1997-98, U. Mo., Kansas City Author: Choral Techniques, 1974, 3d edit. 1988; editor: Guide for the Beginning Choral Director; contbr. articles to scholarly and profl. jours.; composer numerous pieces choral music. Served with U.S. Army, 1957-58. Recipient Most Supportive Pres. or Chancellor award Am. Assn. Colls. for Tchr. Edn., 1992. Mem. Am. Assn. Higher Edn., Am. Assn. State Colls. and Univs., Am. Choral Dirs. Assn. (life, chmn. nat. com. 1970-72). Office: EFL Assocs/TranSearch 7101 College Blvd Ste 550 Overland Park KS 66210

LAMB, IRENE HENDRICKS, medical researcher; b. Ky., May 9, 1940; d. Daily P. and Bertha (Hendricks) Lamb. Diploma in nursing, Ky. Bapt. Hosp.; student, Berea Coll., Calif. State U. L.A. RN, Ky. Charge nurse, head nurse acute medicine, med. ICU, surgical ICU, emergency room various med. ctrs., 1963—67; staff nurse rsch. CCU U. So. Calif./L.A. County Med. Ctr., 1968, nurse mgr. clin. rsch. ctr., 1969—74; sr. rsch. nurse cardiology Stanford U. Sch. Medicine, Calif., 1974—85, rsch. coord. pvt. clin., 1988; dir. clin. rsch. San Diego Cardiac Ctr., 1989—92; sr. cmty. health nurse Madison County Health Dept., Berea, Ky., 1993—97; sr. clin. rsch. mgr. stroke program U. Ky. Coll. Medicine, Lexington, 1997—2001. Co-contbr. numerous articles to med. jours.; contbr. articles to nursing jours., chpts. to med. books. Bd. dirs. Ky. Stroke Assn., 1998—2000. Mem.: Am. Heart Assn. Home: 107 Lorraine Ct Berea KY 40403-1317 Personal E-mail: imeadows@alltel.net.

LAMB, ISABELLE SMITH, manufacturing executive; b. Charteris, Que., Can., Dec. 14, 1922; arrived in U.S., 1948; d. Gordon R. and Beatrice L. (Dale) Smith; married, Oct. 2, 1948 (dec.); 1 child, David E. Student, Gowling Bus. Coll., Ottawa, Ont., 1939, Carleton U., 1940—42. Sec. Gatineau Power, Ottawa, 1942; sec. to city treas. Ottawa, 1943; sec. Can. Internat. Paper, Gatineau, 1943-48; adminstrv. asst. to C/B Enterprises Internat., Inc., Hoquiam, Wash., 1948-84, pres., 1984—2000, br. chmn., 2001—. Bd. dirs. U.S. Bank Washington, Seattle, Export Assistance Ctr. Wash., Seattle, N.W. Burn Found., Seattle, Wash. Coun. for Econ. Edn., Seattle, Ind. Colls. of Wash., Seattle. Participant spl. gifts United Way, Aberdeen, Wash., 1988—; active scholarships and philanthropic causes E.K. and Lillian Bishop Found., Seattle, 1985—. Avocations: reading, horseback riding. Office: Enterprises Internat Inc Blaine And Firman St Hoquiam WA 98550

LAMB, JAMIE PARKER, JR., retired mechanical engineer; b. Boligee, Ala., Sept. 21, 1933; s. Jamie Parker and Cletus (Hixson) Lamb; m. Nancy Catherine Flaherty, June 11, 1955; children: David Parker, Stephen Patrick. BS, Auburn U., 1954; MS, U. Ill., 1958, PhD, 1961. Asst. prof. engring. mechanics N.C. State U., Raleigh, 1961-63; mem. faculty dept. mech. engring. U. Tex., Austin, 1963-2001, prof., 1970-2001, prof. faculty aerospace engring., 1981-88, Ernest Cockrell Jr. Meml. prof., 1981-2001, prof. emeritus, 2001—, chmn. dept., 1970—76, 1981-88, 1996—2001, assoc. dean engring., 1976-81; dir. engring. program U. Tex.-Pan Am., 1993-94. Cons. LTV Aerospace Corp., Dallas, Marshall Space Flight Ctr., Huntsville, Ala., Tracor, Inc., Austin, Rocketdyne, McGregor, Tex., ARO, Inc., Tullahoma, Tenn., Tex. Gas Transport Co., Austin, Mobil Oil Corp., Dallas, Gilbarco, Inc., Greensboro, NC; spl. cons. U. São Paulo, Brazil, 1974; mem. rev. panel postdoctoral assoc. NRC, 1981—95; mem. U.S. nat. com. theoretical and applied mechanics, 1985—89; chmn. 10th U.S. Nat. Congress Applied Mechanics, 1986. Assoc. tech. editor: Jour. Fluids Engring., 1976—79; contbr. articles to profl. jours. Served to 1st lt. USAF, 1955—57. Recipient Joe J. King Profl. Engring. Achievement award, U. Tex., Austin, 1984, Disting. Alumnus award, U. Ill. Dept. Mech. and Indsl. Engring., 1986. Fellow: ASME (chmn. fluid mechanics tech. com. 1982—84, Founder's award Ctrl. Tex. sect. 1975, Leadership award 1976, 1981, Centennial award 1980), AIAA (assoc.); mem.: NSPE, Am. Soc. Engring. Edn. (chmn. summer faculty programs com. 1978—80, chmn. mech. engring. divsn. 1979—80, bd. dirs. profl. interest coun. I 1981—82), Sigma Xi, Sigma Gamma Tau, Tau Beta Pi, Pi Tau Sigma. Baptist. Home: 2605 Pinewood Ter Austin TX 78757-2136 Business E-Mail: jplamb@mail.utexas.edu.

LAMB, KEVIN THOMAS, lawyer; b. Quincy, Mass., Nov. 14, 1956; s. John Phillip and Kathleen Elaine (O'Brien) L. BA, Washington and Lee U., 1978, JD, 1982. Bar: Va. 1982, D.C. 1988, Mass. 1990. Law clk. to presiding justice U.S. Bankruptcy Ct. (we. dist.) Va., Lynchburg, 1982-84; atty. U.S. Dept. Justice, Los Angeles, 1984-85; assoc. Jones, Day, Reavis & Pogue, Los Angeles, 1985-86, Ballard, Spahr, Andrews & Ingersoll, Washington, 1986-89, Testa, Hurwitz & Thibeault, L.L.P., Boston, 1989-91, ptnr., 1992—2005, Gunster, Yoakley & Stewart PA, West Palm Beach, Fla., 2005—. Mem. ABA (com. on bus. bankruptcy), Am. Bankruptcy Inst. (com. on legis.), Comml. Law League Am. Office: Gunster Yoakley & Stewart PA Ste 500 East 777 S Flagler Dr West Palm Beach FL 33401 Office Phone: 561-650-0657. Business E-Mail: klamb@gunster.com.

LAMB, MICHAEL JOHN, librarian, consultant; b. Joliet, Ill., May 31, 1960; s. John Michael and Louise (Erdman) L.; m. Holly Ward, Sept. 14, 1997. BA in Econs., Lewis U., Romeoville, Ill., 1984, MBA, 1990; MS in Econs., Ind. State U., Terre Haute, 1986; MLS, Wayne State U., 1994. Rsch. asst. Wayne State U., Detroit, 1990-94; libr. Downtown Libr./Detroit Pub. Libr., 1994-95; asst. mgr. Conely br. Detroit Pub. Libr., 1995—; dir. DeWitt Pub. Libr. Contbr. articles to profl. jours. Mem. ALA, Mich. Libr. Assn. Home: 1535 Spencer St Lansing MI 48915-1269

LAMB, RICHARD COMPTON, physicist, researcher; b. Lexington, Ky., Sept. 8, 1933; s. Jennings Chalmer and Neolia Frances (Roberts) L.; m. Jane Oldham, Aug. 29, 1959; children: Chery Leigh, Richard Compton Jr., David Robert, Wayne Eagleheart. BS, MIT, 1955; PhD, U. Ky., Lexington, 1963. Rsch. assoc. Argonne (Ill.) Nat. Lab., 1963-64, asst. scientist, 1964-67; assoc. prof. Iowa State U., Ames, 1967-72, prof., 1972-96, emeritus prof., 1996—. Cons. Los Alamos (N.Mex.) Nat. Lab., 1990-96; vis. assoc. Caltech, 1996—. Contbr. more than 150 articles to scholarly and profl. jours. With U.S. Army, 1955-57. NRC-Jet Propulsion Lab. sr. rsch. assoc., 1982-83; honor lectr. Mid-Am. State U., 1988-89; recipient Coll. Rsch. award, 1993; prin. investigator U.S. Dept. Energy, Iowa State U., 1980-96. Fellow Am. Phys. Soc. (nominating com. High Energy Astrophysics div. 1985); mem. Am. Astron. Soc., Internat. Astron. Union. Mem. Evangelical Free Ch. Achievements include co-discovery of high energy gamma rays from the Crab Nebula; co-development of a sensitive detector of very high energy cosmic gamma rays. Office: Caltech 220-47 Space Radiation Lab Pasadena CA 91125

LAMB, ROBERT, industrial relations specialist, consultant; b. Glasgow, Scotland, Oct. 10, 1936; s. Robert and May L.; m. Virginia Mary Lamb, Oct. 5, 1963; children: Iain Robert, Margaret Sheila, Rodgreik Charles. BS, Royal Scottish Coll., 1954-59; MSC in indsl. mgmt., Glasgow U., 1960-62. Design engr. Vickers and Bookers, Glasgow, 1959-61, John Brown Engr., Clyolbank, Scotland, 1961-62; power engr. Being-Manning, Waterville, N.Y., 1962-66; systems gen. mgr. G.E. & IASE, Scheetady, N.Y., 1966-69; sales mgr. G.E. & Indsl. Turbings Div., Fitchburg, Mass., 1969-72; marine engr. supt. G.E. & I.A.S.G., San Francisco, 1972-72; mgr. marine sales G.E. M.& I. Turbings, Geneva, 1979-82; mgr. A/C engring. sales G.E. A/C Engring., Cin., 1982-85; mgr. mktg. and sales A/C Comml. Engring. G.E. Cent Engring., Toulouse, France, 1985-94; gen. mgr. ops. Lockhead Martin, Toulouse, France, 1994-96; cons. arro and marine industry Dalriaoa Cons. Precision, Oak Bluffs, Mass., 1996—. Youth soccer coach, Morasa, Lafpeite and Orioa Soccer Club, Morosa, 1972-79, Montgomery/Cin. Soccer Club, Montgomery, Ohio, 1982-85. Mem. Am. Soc. Naval Engrs., Soc. Naval Archs. Marine Engr., U.S. Naval Instit., Royal Arronautical Engr. Soc. Toulouse (dir.), New England Steamship Found., Natl. Maritime Hist. Soc. Democrat. Roman Catholic. Avocations: marine and naval history, sailing, golf, scottish history, bagpipes. Home: 48 Puritan Dr Oak Bluffs MA 02557 Office: Dalriaoa Cons 48 Puritan Dr Oak Bluffs MA 02557

LAMB, ROBERT BOYDEN, finance and management educator; b. Washington, June 19, 1941; s. Robert Keen Lamb and Helen Elizabeth (Boyden) Lamb Lamont; m. Rosemarie Lamb (div.); m. Nancy Axelrod, June 31, 1975; children: Corinna, Robert, Roland, Helena. BA, U. Chgo., 1963; PhD, London Sch. Econs., 1970; MBA, Columbia U., 1976. Asst. prof. Columbia U., N.Y.C., 1971-75; spl. lectr. Wharton Sch., U. Pa., Phila., 1976-78; prof. fin. and mgmt. Stern Sch. Bus., NYU, 1978—. Dir. Middleby Corp., bond holders Commn. Group, assoc. editor Fortune mag., N.Y.C., 1976-77; bd. dirs. Eagle Clothes Corp., N.Y.C. Author 18 books on mcpl. bonds and mgmt.; editor-in-chief Jour. Bus. Strategy, 1980—. Founding mem. Starndard and Poors' Academic Counsel. Mem.: Century, N.Y. Athletic (N.Y.C.); Waccabuc Country (N.Y.). Democrat. Mem. Soc. Of Friends. Office: NYU Stern Sch Business KMC 7-53 44 W Fourth St New York NY 10012 Home: Parsons Field 8 Cantitoe St Katonah NY 10536 E-mail: rlamb@stern.nyu.edu.

LAMB, ROBERT C., finance company executive; BS, Westpoint Mil. Acad.; MBA, L.I. U. Contr. Fleet Svcs. Corp., 1986—90; sr. v.p., CFO Recoll Mgmt. Corp., 1991; sr. v.p., dir. Corp. Acctg. Ops., 1992; exec. v.p., corp. contr. FleetBoston, 1993—2000; exec. v.p., CFO BearingPoint, 2000—02. Named one of Top 25 Most Influential Cons., Cons. Mag., 2002. Office: Fleet Boston Fin Corp 100 Federal St Boston MA 02110

LAMB, ROBERT EDWARD, retired diplomat, professional society administrator; b. Atlanta, Nov. 17, 1936; s. T. E. and Lois (Harris) Lamb; m. Lucille Trujillo, Jan. 13, 1962; children: Robert Edward, Anne Gretchen, Michael David. BA in Internat. Rels., U. Pa., 1962. Joined Fgn. Svc. Dept. State, Washington, 1963, dir. fin. services, 1975-77, dir. passport office, 1977-79; adminstrv. counsellor U.S. Embassy, Bonn, Germany, 1979-83; asst. sec. of state for adminstrn. Dept. State, Washington, 1983-85; asst. sec. of state Diplomatic Security, Washington, 1985-89; U.S. Amb. to Cyprus Cyprus, 1990-93; spl. Cyprus coord., 1993-94; exec. dir Am. Philatelic Soc., State Coll., Pa., 1994—. Pub.: Index of American Philatelic Literature, 1999—2001. With USMC, 1958—61. Mem.: Am. Fgn. Svc. Assn. (governing bd. 1999—2001), Bellefonte C. of C. (b. dirs.). Home: 1340 Oak Ridge Ave State College PA 16801 Office: 100 Match Factory Pl Bellefonte PA 16823 Office Phone: 814-933-3803. E-mail: relamb@stamps.org.

LAMB, RONALD M., convenience stores executive; Store mgr. Casey' Gen. Stores, Inc., v.p., 1976-88, pres., CEO Ankeny, Iowa, 1988—, chmn. Office: Casey's Gen Stores Inc 1 Convenience Blvd Ankeny IA 50021-8045*

LAMB, SYDNEY MACDONALD, linguistics and cognitive science educator; b. Denver, May 4, 1929; s. Sydney Bishop and Jean Louisa (MacDonald) L.; m. Sharon Reese Rowell, June 17, 1956 (div. 1971); children: Christina, Sarah, Nancy; m. Susan Ellen Jones, May 15, 1977. BA, Yale U., 1951; PhD, U. Calif., Berkeley, 1958. From asst. to assoc. prof. linguistics U. Calif., Berkeley, 1958-64; from assoc. to prof. Yale U., New Haven, 1964-77; mng. ptnr. Semionics Assocs., Houston, 1977-93; prof. Rice U., Houston, 1980—. Fellow Ctr. for Advanced Study in Behavioral Scis., Stanford, Calif., 1973-74. Author: Outline of Stratificational Grammar, 1966, (with others) Sprung from Some Common Source, 1991, Pathways of the Brain: The Neurocognitive Basis of Language, 1999, Language and Reality, 2004; inventor associative computer memory, 1977, 80, 4 patents; contbr. articles to profl. jours. NSF grantee, 1959-64, 66-70; Am. Council of Learned Soc. grantee, 1973-74. Mem. Linguistic Soc. Am. (exec. com. 1966-68), Linguistics Assn. of Can. and U.S. (pres. 1983-84, chmn. bd. dirs. 1995—), Houston Philos. Soc. (pres. 1992-93). Avocations: singing, songwriting, flying trapeze. Office: Rice U Dept Linguistics Houston TX 77251 Business E-Mail: lamb@rice.edu.

LAMB, WALLY, writer; b. Norwich, Conn., Oct. 17, 1950; BA in Edn., U. Conn., 1972, MA in Edn., 1977; MFA in Writing, Vt. Coll., 1984. English tchr. Norwich (Conn.) Free Acad., 1972—88, writing ctr. dir., 1988—97; dir. creative writing U. Conn., 1997—99. Author: (poetry textbook) Always Begin Where You Are, 1979, Couldn't Keep It to Myself: Testimonies from Our Imprisoned Sisters, 2003, (novels) She's Come Undone, 1992, I Know This Much Is True, 1998. Recipient Govs. Arts award, Conn., 1998, William Peden award, Mo. Rev. Office: c/o Darhansoff Verrill Feldman Lit Agys 226 W 26th St New York NY 10001

LAMB, WILLIAM H., lawyer, former state supreme court justice; b. Bryn Mawr, Pa., 1940; m. Patricia Kelly Lamb; children: Amanda, Joshua, Kate. BA (hon.), Duke U., 1962; JD (hon.), U. Pa., 1965. Bar: Pa. 1965, U.S. Dist. Ct. (3d cir.) 1966, Superior Ct. Pa. 1968, U.S. Tax Ct. 1972, U.S. Ct. Appeals (3d cir.) 1966, U.S. Supreme Ct. 1974. Law clk. to presiding justice Pa. Supreme Ct., 1965-66; asst. dist. atty. Chester County, 1967-72, dist. atty., 1972-80; ptnr. Lamb McErlane P.C., West Chester, Pa., 1967—2003, chmn., 2004—; justice Pa. Supreme Ct., Pa., 2003—04; judge Pa. Ct. of Jud. Discipline, 2004—05. Mem. Supreme Ct. Fund for Client Security; bd. dir. Jefferson Bank, Downingtown, Pa. Solicitor Reps. of Chester County, campaign chmn. 1966; campaign mgr. congressman John H. Ware, 1968; chmn. Chester County Reps., 1983—; del. Rep. Nat. Conv., 1984, 88, 92; former chmn. Upper Main Line Young Reps.; former vice chmn. Chester County Fedn. Young Reps.; mem. Rep. Exec. Com. Chester County; pres. Little People's Nursery Sch., Paoli, Pa.; past bd. dirs. Chester Valley Little League, Upper Main Line Red Cross; bd. dirs. St. Davids Ch. Nursery Sch., Devon, Pa., lay server St. David's Episcopal Ch., Devon; vice chmn., trustee bd. Alumni mgrs. Episc. Acad. Recipient Citizen of the Yr., Chester County Chamber of Bus. & Industry, 2003. Fellow Am. Coll. Trial Lawyers; mem. ABA, Pa. Bar Assn., Chester County Bar Assn., Pa. Bar Inst. (lectr.), Pa. Trial Lawyers Assn. (lectr.). Lodges: Lions. Office: Box 565 24 E Market St West Chester PA 19381-0565 Office Phone: 610-430-8000. Business E-Mail: wlamb@chescolaw.com.

LAMB, WILLIS EUGENE, JR., physicist, researcher; b. LA, July 12, 1913; s. Willis Eugene and Marie Helen (Metcalf) Lamb; m. Ursula Schaefer, June 5, 1939 (dec. Aug. 1996); m. Bruria Kaufman, Nov. 29, 1996. BS, U. Calif., 1934, PhD, 1938; DSc (hon.), U. Pa., 1953, Gustavus Adolphus Coll., 1975, Columbia U., 1990; MA, Oxford (Eng.) U., 1956; MA (hon.), Yale U., 1961; LHD (hon.), Yeshiva U., 1965; Dr.rer.nat. (hon.), U. Ulm., Germany, 1997. Mem. faculty Columbia U., 1938—52, prof. physics, 1948—52, Stanford U., 1951—56; Wykeham prof. physics and fellow New Coll., Oxford U., 1956—62; Henry Ford 2d prof. physics Yale U., 1962—72, J. Willard Gibbs prof. physics, 1972—74; prof. physics and optical scis. U. Ariz., Tucson, 1974—, Regents prof., 1990—2003, Regents prof. emeritus, 2003—; prof. emeritus Ariz. Rsch. Lab., 2003—, Optical Sci. Ctr. and Dept. Physics, 2003—. Morris Loeb lectr. Harvard U., 1953—54; Gordon Shrum lectr. Simon Fraser U., 1972; cons. Philips Labs., Bell Telephone Labs., Perkin-Elmer, NASA; vis. com. Brookhaven Nat. Lab. Recipient Rumford premium, Am. Acad. Arts and Scis., 1953, award, Rsch. Corp., 1954, (with P. Kusch) Nobel prize in Physics, 1955, Yeshiva award, 1962, Einstein Medal, Soc. for Optical & Quantum Electronics, 1992, Nat. medal of Sci., 2000, Gian Carlo Wick Gold Medal, World Fedn. of Scientists, 2002; fellow Guggenheim, 1960—61, sr. Alexander von Humboldt, 1992—94. Fellow: Royal Sci. Edinburgh, N.Y. Acad. Scis., Optical Soc. Am., Am. Phys. Soc., Inst. Physics and Phys. Soc. (hon. Guthrie lectr. 1958); mem.: NAS, Sigma Xi, Phi Beta Kappa. Achievements include discoveries concerning the fine structure of the hydrogen spectrum. Office: U Ariz Optical Scis Ctr Meinel Bldg 1630 E University Blvd Tucson AZ 85721-0094 E-mail: willis@primus.optsci.arizona.edu.*

LAMBE, JAMES PATRICK, lawyer; b. Washington, June 4, 1952; s. John Joseph and Patricia Ann (Job) Lambe; m. Marie Barbara Giardino, May 21, 1977; children: Katherine Mary, Joseph Patrick. AB with distinction, U. Mich., 1974; JD, U. Ill., 1977. Bar: Calif. 1977, U.S. Dist. Ct. (ea. dist.) Calif. 1977, U.S. Ct. Appeals (9th cir.) 1978, U.S. Supreme Ct. 1981, U.S. Dist. Ct. (ctrl. dist.) Calif. 1983, DC 1985, cert.: State Bar Calif. Bd. Legal Specialization (specialist in criminal law), Nat. Bd. Trial Advocacy (specialist in criminal trial advocacy). Assoc. Wagner & Wagner, Fresno, Calif., 1978-79, Parichan, Renberg & Crossman, Fresno, 1979; claims atty. CIGNA Corp., Fresno, 1979-85; dep. city atty. City of Fresno, 1985-86; dep. pub. defender County of Fresno, 1986—2005, sr. dep. pub. defender, 2005—. Cons., author Continuing Edn. Bar, U. Calif./State Bar Calif., Oakland, 1992—; judge pro tem Fresno County Superior Ct., 2000—; instr. Summer Trial Skills Inst., San Diego, 2001—. Cons. (book) California Criminal Law Procedure and Practice, update, 1992, 3d edit., 1996, California Criminal Law Forms Manual, 1995, rev., 2001; co-author: (book) California Criminal Law Procedure and Practice, 8th edit., 2005. Mem.: Nat. Assn. Criminal Def. Lawyers, State Bar Calif. (conf. of dels. 1996—99, criminal law sect. exec. com. 2001—), Calif. Pub. Defenders Assn., Calif. Attys. for Criminal Justice (bd. govs. 2002—), D.C. Bar, Fresno County Bar Assn. (bd. dirs. 1998—99), Am. Mensa, Phi Alpha Delta. Democrat. Avocation: running. Office: Fresno County Pub Defenders Office 2220 Tulare St Ste 300 Fresno CA 93721-2130

LAMBERG-KARLOVSKY, CLIFFORD CHARLES, anthropologist, archaeologist; b. Prague, Czechoslovakia, Oct. 2, 1937; came to U.S., 1939; s. Carl Othmar von Lamberg and Bellina Karlovsky; m. Martha Louise Veale,

Sept. 12, 1959; children: Karl Emil Othmar, Christopher William. AB, Dartmouth Coll., 1959; MA (Wenner-Gren fellow), U. Pa., 1964, PhD, 1965; MA (hon.), Harvard U., 1970; DS (hon.), Russian Acad. Scis., 2002. Asst. prof. sociology and anthropology Franklin and Marshall Coll., 1964-65; asst. prof. anthropology Harvard U., 1965-69, prof., 1969-90, Stephen Phillips prof. archaeology, 1991—; curator Near Eastern archaeology Peabody Museum Archaeology and Ethnology, 1969—, mus. dir., 1977-90. Assoc. Columbia U., 1969—; trustee Am. Inst. Iranian Studies, 1968-98, Am. Inst. Yemeni Studies, 1976-77; dir. rsch. Am. Sch. Prehist. Rsch., 1974-79, 94—, Centro di Richerche Ligabue, 1984; Reckitt archaeol. surveys in Syria, 1965, excavation projects at Tepe Yahya, Iran, 1967-75, Sarazm, Tadjikistan, USSR, 1985, archaeol. surveys in Saudi Arabia, 1977-80, USSR, 1990-91; dir. survey and excavations Anau, Turkmenistan, 1992-97; corr. fellow Inst. Medio and Extremo Orient, Italy; mem. UNESCO com. for sci. study of mankind, 1989-97. Author: (with J. Sabloff) Ancient Civilizations: The Near East and Mesoamerica, 1979; editor: (with J. Sabloff) The Rise and Fall of Civilizations, 1973, Ancient Civilizations and Trade, 1975, Hunters, Farmers and Civilization, 1979, Archaeological Thought in America, 1988, Beyond the Tigris and Euphrates, 1996; author, gen. editor: Tepe Yahya: The Early Periods, 1986, Tepe Yahta: The Third Millenium, 2004, Tepe Yahya, The Iron Age, 2005. Recipient medal Iran-Am. Soc., 1972; NSF grantee, 1966-75, 78-80, 93, Nat. Endowment for Arts grantee, 1977—, NEH grantee, 1977—. Fellow AAAS (chmn. USA/USSR archaeol. exch. program), Am. Acad. Arts and Scis., Soc. Antiquaries Gt. Britain and Ireland (sec. N.Am. chpt. 1985-93), Am. Anthrop. Assn., N.Y. Acad. Sci., USSR Acad. Sci., Soc. Am. Archaeology, Archeol. Inst. Am.; mem. German Archaeol. Inst., Danish Archaeol. Inst., Brit. Archaeol. Inst., Tavern Club (Boston). Office: Peabody Mus Archaeology & Ethnology 11 Divinity Ave Cambridge MA 02138-2019 Office Phone: 617-496-8162. Business E-Mail: karlovsk@fas.harvard.edu.

LAMBERSON, JOHN ROGER, insurance company executive; b. Aurora, Mo., Aug. 16, 1933; s. John Oral Lamberson and Golda May (Caldwell) Tidwell; m. Virginia Lee, Aug. 10, 1957; 1 child, John Clinton. BA, U. Calif., Berkeley, 1954. Coach, tchr. Thousand Palms (Calif.) Sch., 1954-55; underwriter trainee Fireman's Fund Ins. Co., San Francisco, 1955; surety mgr. Safeco Ins. Co. (formerly Gen. Ins. Co.), San Francisco and Sacramento, Calif., 1957-61; pres., COO Willis Corroon Corp., N.Y.C., 1966-92, also bd. dirs., chmn. constrn. industry div., mem. exec. com., aquisition com.; pres., chmn., CEO Lamberson Consulting LLC, San Francisco, 1992—. Bd. dirs. Willis Cornoon Group PLC, London, Consumers Benefit Life Ins. Co., Constrn. Inst., FMI Corp., Griffith Co., Webcor, Rosendin Electric, Sheedy Drayage Co., Valentine Corp. Mem. ASCE (bd. dirs. Construction Institute), Nat. Assn. Heavy Engring. Constructors (bd. dirs. 1985—, Golden Beavers award for outstanding svc. to industry), Constrn. Fin. Mgmt. Assn. (bd. dirs. 1987-91, exec. com.), Assoc. Gen. Contractors Am. (membership devel. com., past chmn. bd. dirs. nat. assoc. mems. coun.), Assoc. Gen. Contractors Calif. (bd. dirs. 1976), Nat. Acad. Constrn., Consulting Contractors Coun. Am., Bldg. Futures Coun. (bd. dirs.), Nat. Assn. Surety Bond Prodrs. (past nat. pres., regional v.p.), Am. Inst. Contractors, Soc. Am. Mil. Engrs., The Moles-Heavy Engring. Constrn. Soc., Young Pres. Orgn. (sem. leader), Bankers Club, Sharon Heights Golf and Country Club, Bermuda Dunes Country Club, Rockaway Hunting Club, Villa Taverna Club. Home: 85 Greenoaks Dr Atherton CA 94027-2160 Office: Lamberson Consulting LLC 580 California St Ste 500 San Francisco CA 94104-1000 Office Phone: 415-439-4822. E-mail: jrlamberson@mindspring.com.

LAMBERT, CHRISTINA, telecommunications executive; b. Panama; m. Jim Lambert; children: Bill, Christine, Monica. BA in bus. mgmt., Ind. U.; M in bus. adminstrn., Ind. Wesleyan U. Joined Contel (merged with GTE in 1991), 1974; asst. v.p. process planning GTE, asst. v.p. customer care; v.p., gen. mgr. wireline svcs. PR Telephone, 1999—2003, pres., CEO, 2003—. Office: Telecommunicaciones de Puerto Rico Inc 1515 FD Roosevelt Ave Guaynabo PR 00968 Office Phone: 787-793-1818. Business E-Mail: clambert@prtcmail.prtc.net.

LAMBERT, DAVID, lawyer; b. Cleve., Nov. 9, 1965; m. Julie H. Beamish. BA, Duke U., 1988; JD, N.C. Ctrl. U., 1993; LLM, NYU, 1995. Bar: NC 1993. Law clk. N.C. Ct. Appeals, Raleigh, 1993—94, U.S. Bankruptcy Ct. (ea. dist.) N.C., Raleigh, 1995—96; ptnr. Kirkland & Ellis, Washington, 2001—. Contbr. articles to law jours. Office: Kirkland & Ellis 655 15th St NW Ste 1200 Washington DC 20005

LAMBERT, DEBORAH CUYLER, secondary school educator; b. Amsterdam, N.Y., Jan. 31, 1953; d. Louis Edward and Evelyn Fraker (Pearce) Cuyler; m. Michael Allan Lambert (div.). BA, U. San Diego, Calif., 1974; MEd, U. Nev., Las Vegas, 1986; M Pastoral Studies, Loyola U., New Orleans, 1997. Lic. tchr. Nev. Choral instr. Rialto Jr. H.S., Calif., 1975—78, Boulder City H.S., Nev., 1978—84; biology inst. Las Vegas H.S., Nev., 1985—90; dean of students Rancho H.S., Las Vegas, Nev., 1990—98; chair sci. dept., tchr. biology Las Vegas Acad. Performing Arts, 1998—. Cantor and music dir. Christ the King Cath. Cmty., Las Vegas, Nev., 1987—. Named Tchr. of Yr., Clark County, Nev., 2002, 2004. Mem.: Nat. Assn. Pastoral Musicians. Avocations: fountain pen collector, needlepoint.

LAMBERT, DELORES ELAINE, secondary school educator; b. Fairmont, W.Va., Dec. 16, 1947; d. William Beuglas and Grace Marie (Dillon) Fletcher; m. Paul Edward Lambert, Aug. 20, 1966; children: Christopher, Abigail. BA in Edn., Fairmont (W.Va.) State Coll., 1980; MA, W.Va. U., 1989, postgrad., 1989—. H.s. English instr. Bd. Edn. Marion County, Fairmont, 1983—2000, chmn. dept. English, 1995—2000; h.s. English instr. Bd. Edn. Berkeley County, Martinsburg, W.Va., 2000—. Mem. NCTE, Alpha Delta Kappa. Avocations: reading, needlecrafts. Home: 164 La Costa Blvd Martinsburg WV 25401 Office: Musselman High Sch 126 Excellence Way Inwood WV 25428

LAMBERT, ETHEL GIBSON CLARK, secondary school educator; b. Atlanta, Apr. 18, 1943; d. Robert Harold and Ethel (Gibson) Clark; m. Hugh Felder Lambert, June 27, 1964 (div. Nov. 3, 1988); children: Courtney, Elizabeth, Hugh Jr. BA, Oglethorpe U., Atlanta, 1965; MEd, Kennesaw State U., Marietta, Ga., 1992; EdS, State U. West Ga., Carrollton, 1997. Lic. tchr. T-6 Ga. Tchr. Clayton County Bd. Edn., Jonesboro, Ga., 1965-66, tchr. remedial edn. program Riverdale HS, 1990—2004, tchr. English spkrs. other langs. Sequoyah Mid. Sch., 2005—; tchr. Fulton County Bd. Edn., Atlanta, 1866—67; tchr. pre-sch. weekday program First Bapt. Ch., Gainesville, Ga., 1984-88. Author: The Impact of Geography on the Campaigns of the Civil War Fought in Georgia, 1993, The Utilization of Georgia Historical Sites as Teaching Methodology in Middle Grades Education, 1993, Obnoxious Bill, 1993, Research on Academic Motivation of Elementary, Middle and Secondary School Students in America, 1993, Reading Strategies that Address the Reluctant Reader in America's Public Middle and High Schools, 1995, Mathematics: Tying Together the World of School and the World of Work, 1996, A Martin Family History: An Interview of Aunt Clyde: "I Look Back..., 1999. Den leader Cub Scouts Am., Gainesville, 1980—83; mem. Christian Businessmen's Prayer Breakfast, Atlanta, 1990—95, 1996. Mem.: College Park Hist. Soc., Profl. Assn. Ga. Educators, College Park Women's Club, Order Eastern Star, Pi Lambda Theta. Baptist. Avocations: swimming, water-skiing, reading, walking, genealogy. Home: 1881 Myrtle Dr SW Apt 711 Atlanta GA 30311-4919 Office: Babb Mid Sch 5500 Reynolds Rd Forest Park GA 30297-4048 Business E-Mail: elambert@clayton.k12.ga.us.

LAMBERT, FREDERICK WILLIAM, lawyer, educator; b. Millburn, N.J., Feb. 12, 1943; m. Barbara E. Fogell, Aug. 13, 1965; children: Elisabeth, Mark. BA, U. Mich., 1965, JD, 1969. Bar: Ohio 1969, Fla. 1973, Calif. 1973, U.S. Supreme Ct. 1975. Law clk. to Stanley N. Barnes, U.S. Cir. Judge U.S. Cir. Ct., L.A., 1969-70; atty. advisor Office Legal Counsel U.S. Dept. Justice, Washington, 1970-71; law clk. to Justice William H. Rehnquist U.S. Supreme Ct., Washington, 1971-72; pvt. practice L.A., 1973-90; acting gen. counsel Itel Corp., San Francisco, 1981-82; ptnr. Adams, Duque & Hazeltine, L.A., 1985-90, chmn. bus. law dept., 1989-90; assoc. prof. Hastings Coll. Law, U. Calif., San Francisco, 1993-99, prof. law, 1999—. Vis. prof. U. Mich. Law Sch., Ann Arbor, 1990-91, Duke Law Sch., Durham, N.C., 1992-93. Mem. Am. Law Inst., Am. Law and Econs. Assn., Econ. Round Table of L.A., Calif. State Bar Assn., Half Moon Bay Yacht Club. Home: 1100 Pilarcitos Ave Half Moon Bay CA 94019-1459

LAMBERT, GEORGE H., pediatrician, educator; MD, U. Ill., Chgo., 1972. Diplomate in pediats. and neonatal-perinatal medicine Am. Bd. Pediatrics. Intern Johns Hopkins Hosp., Balt., 1972—73, resident in pediats., 1973—74; rsch. assoc. molecular teratology NIH, Bethesda, 1974—76; fellow in neonatal pharmacology Children's Hosp. Phila., 1976—77; physician dept. pediats. Robert Wood Johnson Med. Sch., New Brunswick, NJ, 1987—; dir. pediat. clin. rsch. ctr. and divsn. pediat. pharmacology and toxicology EPA/NIH, New Brunswick, NJ; dir. NIH Ctr. Childhood Neurotoxicology and Exposure Assessment Rutgers U., 2001—, Robert Wood Johnson Med. Sch., 2001—. Assoc. prof. pediatrics Robert Wood Johnson U. Hosp., New Brunswick, NJ, 1984—. Office: Robert Wood Johnson Med Sch One Robert Wood Johnson Pl New Brunswick NJ 08901 Office Phone: 732-235-7900. Business E-Mail: glambert@umdnj.edu.

LAMBERT, GEORGE ROBERT, lawyer, realtor; b. Muncie, Ind., Feb. 21, 1933; s. George Russell and Velma Lou (Jones) L.; m. Mary Virginia Alling, June 16, 1956; children: Robert Allen, Ann Holt, James William. BS, Ind. U., Bloomington, 1955; JD, Chgo.-Kent Coll. Law, 1962. Bar: Ill. 1962, U.S. Dist. Ct. (no. dist.) Ill. 1962, Iowa 1984, Pa. 1988, Ind. 1999. V.p., gen. counsel, sec. Washington Nat. Ins. Co., Evanston, Ill., 1970-82; v.p., gen. counsel Washington Nat. Corp., Evanston, 1979-82; sr. v.p., sec., gen. counsel Life Investors Inc., Cedar Rapids, Iowa, 1982-88; v.p., gen. counsel Provident Mut. Life Ins. Co., Phila., 1988-95; pres. Lambert Legal Consulting, Inc., Wilmington, Del., 1995—2002; realtor Coldwell Banker, North Palm Beach, Fla., 1996—2001, Cressy and Everett GMAC Real Estate, South Bend, Ind., 1999-2000; ind. real estate broker Granger, 2001—03; realtor Martinique II Realty Inc., Port St. Lucie, Fla., 2002—; ind. real estate broker Bloomington, Ind., 2004—. Alderman Evanston City Coun., 1980-82; mem. bd. edn. Lake Bluff (Ill.) Elementary Sch. Dist., 1970-71. Served to lt. USAF, 1955-57. Mem.: Assn. of Life Ins. Counsel (past pres.). Home: 7958 Poppy Hills Ln Port Saint Lucie FL 34986 Home (Summer): 9411 Harbour Pointe Dr Bloomington IN 47401 Personal E-mail: glamb10100@aol.com.

LAMBERT, JEREMIAH DANIEL, lawyer, educator; b. N.Y.C., Sept. 11, 1934; s. Noah D. and Clara (Ravage) L.; m. Vicki Anne Asher, July 25, 1959 (div.); children: Nicole Stirling, Alix Stewart, Leigh Asher; m. Sanda Kayden, Dec. 3, 1983; children: Clare Kayden, Hilary Kayden. AB magna cum laude, Princeton U., 1955; LL.B., Yale U., 1959. Bar: N.Y. 1960, D.C. 1964, U.S. Ct. Appeals (5th cir.) 1964, U.S. Supreme Ct. 1964. Assoc. Cravath, Swaine & Moore, N.Y.C., 1959-63; sr. ptnr. Peabody, Lambert & Meyers, Washington, 1969-84; ptnr. Shook, Hardy & Bacon, Washington, 1997—2002; co-chmn. bd. dirs. Global Crossing, Ltd., 2002—03, mem. exec. com., 2003—; chmn. bd. dirs. Asia Global Crossing, Ltd., 2002—03. Adj. prof. law Georgetown U., Washington, 1978-79; trustee Internat. Law Inst., Washington, 1983-88; mem. adv. com. on Electricity Futures Contracts, N.Y. Merc. Exch., 1994-95; mem. bd. editors Yale Law Jour., 1958-59. Author: Creating Competitive Markets: The PJM Model, 2001; author, editor (with Fereidun Fesharaki): Economic and Political Incentives to Petroleum Development, 1990; co-author (with Lawrence White): Handbook of Modern Construction Law, 1982; mem. editl. adv. bd., contbr. The Impact of Competition, 2000; contbr. articles to legal publs. 1st lt. USAR, 1963-66. Fulbright scholar U. Copenhagen, 1955-56. Mem. ABA, Am. Soc. Internat. Law, D.C Bar Assn., Assn. Bar City N.Y., Cosmos Club, Princeton Club, Yale Club, Chevy Chase Club, Nassau Club, Phi Beta Kappa. Office: Law Offices of Jeremiah D Lambert 1350 I St NW Ste 510 Washington DC 20005 Office Phone: 202-872-5291. Business E-Mail: jlambert@lambertlaw.net.

LAMBERT, JOHN BOYD, chemical engineer, consultant; b. Billings, Mont., July 5, 1929; s. Jean Arthur and Gail (Boyd) L.; m. Jean Wilson Bullard, June 20, 1953 (dec. 1958); children: William, Thomas, Patricia, Cathy, Karen; m. Ilse Crager, Sept. 20, 1980 (dec. 1995). BS in Engring., Princeton U., 1951; PhD, U. Wis., 1956. Rsch. engr. E.I. DuPont de Nemours Co., Wilmington, Del., 1956-69; sr. rsch. engr. Fansteel, Inc., Balt., 1969, mktg. mgr., plant mgr. North Chicago, Ill., 1970-73, mgr. mfg. engring. Waukegan, Ill., 1974-80, corp. tech. dir. North Chicago, 1980-86, gen. mgr. metals, 1987-90, v.p., corp. tech. dir., 1990-91. IESC vol., Brazil, 1995; ind. cons., Lake Forest, Ill., 1991—. Contbr. articles to profl. jours. Recipient Charles Hatchett medal Inst. Metals, London, 1986. Mem. AIChE, Am. Chem. Soc., Am. Soc. Metals, Sigma Xi. Episcopalian. Achievements include patents in field of dispersion-strengthened metals, refractory metals, chemical vapor deposition, both products and processes. Home and Office: 617 Greenbriar Ln Lake Forest IL 60045-3214 Fax: 847-234-7649. Office Phone: 847-234-7645. E-mail: drjbl@aol.com.

LAMBERT, JOHN WALTON, music educator; s. James Alfred and Samaria Mercedes Lambert. B in Music Edn., Troy State U., 1973. Cert. tchr. Ala. Band dir. Dallas County HS, Plantersville, Ala., 1973—75, Escambia County Middle Sch., Atmore, 1976—77, Escambia County HS, Atmore, 1977—2000, Monroe Acad., Monroeville, 2001—05, Flomaton (Ala.) HS, 2005—. Freelance band dir., cons., 1993—; mem. Music Educators Nat. Conf., 1973—. Mem. Atmore Fine Arts Coun., 1996—2000. Staff sgt. Nat. Guard U.S. Army, 1995—2002. Recipient Army Achievement medal, Army Nat. Guard, 1990, 1992. Mem.: Phi Mu Alpha (pres. 1973). Avocations: nature, history.

LAMBERT, JOSEPH BUCKLEY, chemistry professor; b. Ft. Sheridan, Ill., July 4, 1940; s. Joseph Idus and Elizabeth Dorothy (Kirwan) L.; m. Mary Wakefield Pulliam, June 27, 1967; children: Laura Kirwan, Alice Pulliam, Joseph Cannon. BS, Yale U., 1962; PhD (Woodrow Wilson fellow 1962-63, NSF fellow 1962-65), Calif. Inst. Tech., 1965. Asst. prof. chemistry Northwestern U., Evanston, Ill., 1965-69, assoc. prof., 1969-74, prof. chemistry, 1974-91, Clare Hamilton Hall prof. chemistry, 1991—, Charles Deering McCormick prof., 1999—2002, chmn. dept., 1986-89, dir. integrated sci. program, 1982-85. Vis. assoc. Brit. Mus., 1973, Polish Acad. Scis., 1981, Chinese Acad. Scis., 1988. Author: Organic Structural Analysis, 1976, Physical Organic Chemistry through Solved Problems, 1978, The Multinuclear Approach to NMR Spectroscopy, 1983, Archaeological Chemistry III, 1984, Introduction to Organic Spectroscopy, 1987, Recent Advances in Organic NMR Spectroscopy, 1987, Acyclic Organonitrogen Stereodynamics, 1992, Cyclic Organonitrogen Stereodynamics, 1992, Prehistoric Human Bone, 1993, Traces of the Past, 1997, Organic Structural Spectroscopy, 1998, Nuclear Magnetic Resonance Spectroscopy, 2004; audio course Intermediate NMR Spectroscopy, 1973; editor in chief Journal of Physical Organic Chemistry; contbr. articles to sci. jours. Recipient Nat. Fresenius award, 1976, James Flack Norris award, 1987, Fryxell award, 1989, Nat. Catalyst award, 1993, Mosher award, 2003; Alfred P. Sloan fellow, 1968-70, Guggenheim fellow, 1973, Interacad. exch. fellow (U.S.-Poland), 1985, Air Force Office sci. rsch. fellow, 1990. Fellow AAAS, Japan Soc. for Promotion of Sci., Brit. Interplanetary Soc., Ill. Acad. Sci. (life); mem. Am. Chem. Soc. (chmn. history of chemistry divsn., 1996, F.S. Kipping award 1998, S.M. Edelstein award 2004), Royal Soc. Chemistry, Soc. Archaeol. Scis. (pres. 1986-87), Phi Beta Kappa, Sigma Xi (hon. lectr. 1997-98). Home: 1956 Linneman St Glenview IL 60025-4264 Office: Northwestern University Dept of Chemistry 2145 Sheridan Rd Evanston IL 60208-3113

LAMBERT, JOSEPH EARL, state supreme court chief justice; b. Berea, Ky., May 23, 1948; s. James Wheeler and Ruth (Hilton) L.; m. Debra Hembree, June 25, 1983; children: Joseph Patrick, John Ryan. BS in Bus. and Econs., Georgetown Coll., 1970; JD, U. Louisville, 1974; PhD (hon.), Eastern Ky. U., 1999, Georgetown Coll., 1999, Northern Ky. U., 2002. Bar: Ky. 1974. Staff Sen. John Sherman Cooper U.S. Senate, Washington, 1970-71; law clk. to judge Rhodes Bratcher U.S. Dist. Ct., Louisville, 1974-75; ptnr. Lambert & Lambert, Mt. Vernon, Ky., 1975-87; justice Supreme Ct. Ky., Frankfort, 1987-98, chief justice, 1998—. Chmn. Appellate Rules Commn., 1989-91, Civil Rules Com., 1991-93, Criminal Rules Com., 1996-97, Jud. Form Retirement Commn., 1996-; mem. bd. directors Ctr. for Rural Devel., 1996-, Nat. Assn. Drug Ct. Professionals, 2001-, Conference of Chief Justices, 2001-03. Mem. Bd. Regents Eastern Ky. U., Richmond, 1988-92. Recipient Disting. Alumni award U. Louisville Sch. Law, 1988; named Outstanding Judge of Ky., 2000, Leadership award Nat. Assn. Drug Ct. Professionals, Ky. Public Advocate award, 2001. Fellow: Ky. Bar Foundation; mem.: ABA, Ky. Bar Assn. Republican. Baptist. Office: Ky Supreme Ct Rm 231 700 Capitol Ave Frankfort KY 40601 Business E-Mail: cjlambert@kycourts.net.

LAMBERT, JUDY LANIER, computer scientist, educator; b. Goldsboro, N.C., Oct. 26, 1954; d. Rayford Roy and Eloise Potts Lanier; m. Parker Lee Lambert, July 30, 1983; children: Jennifer Lynn Portanova, Timothy. BS, Fayetteville (N.C.) State U., 1994; MEd, N.C. State U., 1999, PhD, 2004. Cert. tchr. N.C. Dept. Pub. Instrn., 1994. Asst. prof. The U. Toledo, 2004—. Adj. faculty N.C. State U., Raleigh, NC, 2000—04, grad. rsch. asst., 2000—04; tech. coord., tchr. Erwin (N.C.) Mid. Sch., 1994—99; adj. faculty Barton Coll., Wilson, NC, 2002—03. C.I. Brown scholarship, Fayetteville State U., 1992. Mem.: Internat. Soc. Tech. in Edn., Am. Ednl. Rsch. Assn., Assn. Advancement Computing in Edn., Kappa Delta Pi, Phi Kappa Phi. Office: The University of Toledo 2801 W Bancroft Toledo OH 43606 Office Phone: 419-530-2064. Office Fax: 419-530-2466. E-mail: judy.lambert@utoledo.edu.

LAMBERT, KIRSTEN SCHNOOR, public relations executive, writer; b. Chgo., Dec. 26, 1963; d. Walter Karl and Irmgard Schnoor; m. Christopher Jay Lambert, May 25, 1996; 1 child, Evan BA in Liberal Arts, DePaul U., 1995. Editl. and prodn. asst. Kraft Inc., Glenview, Ill., 1986-89; comm. assoc. Budget Rent A Car, Chgo., 1989-91; spl. events asst. Chgo. Sun-Times, 1992-94; editl. asst. Chgo. Reader, 1994-95; freelancer DonTech Corp., Chgo., 1995-96; comm. mgr. The Sherwood Group, Inc., Northbrook, Ill., 1996-00; mktg. and comm. mgr. Am. Orthopaedic Assn., Rosemont, Ill., 2000—02; pres. Watermark Comm., Chgo., 2002—. Author: Chicago '96 Democratic National Convention Visitors' Guide, 1996; editor newsletter Interactions, 1999 (Circle of Excellence award Am. Soc. Assn. Execs, 1999). Support mgr. Howard Brown Meml. Clinic, Chgo., 1987-91. Mem. Internat. Assn. Bus. Communicators (chpt. membership com. 1989-91). Avocations: writing, music, dance. Office: Watermark Comm Inc 1934 W Belle Plaine Ave Chicago IL 60613 Office Phone: 773-472-1969. Business E-Mail: kirsten@watermark-communications.com.

LAMBERT, LECLAIR GRIER, writer, lecturer, consultant, former state government public information administrator; b. Miami, Fla. s. George F. and Maggie (Grier) L. BS, Hampton Inst., 1959; postgrad., Harvard U., 1959, U. Munich, 1965-66. Rschr., copy reader Time-Life Books, 1961-64; tchr. biology and Eng. lit., secondary level U.S. Dependent's Schs. Overseas, Tripoli, Libya, 1964-65; biology editor H.S. textbooks Holt, Rinehart & Winston, N.Y.C., 1966-69; biology editor and writer Ency. Britannica, N.Y.C., 1969; copy editor Russian sci. monographs The Faraday Press, N.Y.C., 1970-71; writer Med. World News, N.Y.C., 1971; pub. rels. writer Nat. Found./March of Dimes, White Plains, N.Y., 1972. Lectr. cmty. and human rels. Black Cultural heritage at local schs. and colls., 1977-87; guest lectr. Liberty Sq. (Fla.) 50th Anniversary, 1986, Black History Month Minn. Ho. of Reps., 1987-96, creator and coord. student spkr. Ho. of Reps. Youth Forum, 1992; radio commentator Sta. KEEY, 1975-80; reporter Twin Cities Courier, Mpls., 1976-86. Author: Reflections of Life--Poems, Prose and Essays, 1981, A Learning Journey Through Black History, 1982; editor, writer: Minnesota's Black Community, 1977; editor: Art in Development: A Nigerian Perspective, 1983; freelance writer and designer of brochures and pamphlets, 1974—; contbr. articles to profl. jours. Dir. comm. St. Paul Urban League, 1972-80, asst. to exec. dir., 1985-86, bd. dirs., 1992—, sec. bd., 1999—, co-chair 75th and 80th Anniversary Celebrations; mem. adv. bd. Archie Givens Found. for African Am. Lit. Rare Books Collection, U. Minn., 1988—; exec. dir. African Am. Mus. Art and History, 1980-86; info. officer Mpls. Urban League, 1978-79; co-founder, bd. dirs. Summit-Univ. Free Press, 1974-79, U. Minn. Black Learning Resource Ctr., 1980-83; past mem. Roy Wilkins Meml., Com. Civic Ctr., St. Paul, 1985; mem. state meml. com. Martin Luther King Celebration Com., 1987-96; mem. Ethiopian Famine Relief Com.; mem. rev. com. Twin Cities Mayors' Pub. Art Awards, 1981; co-founder W. Suburban Annual Black History Month Celebration Com., 1983-86; mem. St. Paul Civic Ctr. Authority Bd., 1985-97, vice chair, 1991-97, bd. rep. pub. art, bldg. expansion com., bd. rep. "Am.'s Smithsonian" exhbn.; mem. St. Paul City Art Plan Com., 1987-88, Minn. Mus. Am. Art orgn. exhibits plan coms., 1989-91, trustee, 1991-96, v.p., 1992-93, pres., 1993-94, chair, 1994-95; adv. bd. YMCA Youth in Govt., 1997-2003; sgt-at-arms, officer Minn. Ho. of Reps., 1987-96, coord. edl. programs, mem. cultural diversity tng. task force, 1992-93, dir. pub. info., 1996-2003; pub. weekly column Reflections, Session Weekly; trustee Coll. Visual Arts, governance com., new mem. orientation chair, 1997—; mem. St. Paul-Mpls. com. on fgn. rels., 1998-2000; cons. ARD/USAID staff tng. Palestinian Legis. Coun., Curr. tng. plan for Birzeit U., West Bank, 1997; bd. dirs. Minn. Landmarks, 2001-2002; commr., St. Paul Human Rights Commn., 1999—2004; bd. dirs. St. Paul Visitors and Conv. Bur., 1990-93. Served to 1st lt., Chem. Corps., U.S. Army, 1959-61. Recipient Cmty. Martin Luther King Comm. award, 1978, Spl. Recognition award Mpls. St. Acad., 1983, Spl. Achievement award Roosevelt H.S., 1985, Spl. Recognition award Twin Cities African Am. Mus., 1985, Liberty Sq. Tenants' Spl. Recognition award, 1986, Vol. Svc. award St. Paul Urban League, 1988, Spl. Recognition award Palestine Journalists Assn., 1997, Outstanding Achievement award Minn. Coun. Black Minnesotans, 2003, Info. Staff award Nat. Conf. State Legislatures, 2003, Hubert H. Humphrey Inst. Internat. Fellows award, 1998, 2000, Spl. Recognition award, Minn. Ho. of Reps., 2003; named Nat. Outstanding Info. and Media Staff Mem., Nat. Conf. State Legislatures, 2003; LeClair Lambert Day proclaimed by City of St. Paul, 1997. Mem. Pub. Rels. Soc. Am., African-Am. Mus. Assn. (mem. nat. legis. edn. com. 1983, exec. coun., Midwest region rep. 1984-89, Achievement award 1985). Office Phone: 651-647-9508.

LAMBERT, LLOYD LAVERNE, minister; b. Augusta, Ill., June 5, 1925; s. Charles N. Sr. and Lena (Johnson) L.; m. Dorothy Mae Spaar, June 22, 1946; children: Rebecca, Toby, Michael, Corey. Student, Millikin U., 1948-49, Anderson (Ind.) Coll., 1953-54, student, 1956-57. Ordained to ministry Ch. of God (Anderson, Ind.), 1955. Founder, exec. dir. The Christian Ctr., Anderson, 1956—. Chaplain Madison County Detention Ctr. Bd. dirs. Habitat for Humanity, Anderson, Recovery in Christ, Sowers of Seeds, Inc., Counselors for Alcohol and Other Drug Abuses; past chmn. Nursing Home Ministries; past pres. Madison County Svcs. Coun.; past dep. sheriff Madison County Sheriff's Dept.; mem. adv. bd. for drug abuse St. John's Hosp.; chmn. Human Rels. Commn., City of Anderson, 1981-84; founder Home for Alcoholics, Anderson. With F.A., U.S. Army, 1943-46; PTO. Recipient spl. recognition Exchange Club Anderson, 1971, recognition Ind. Dept. Corrections, 1972, Liberty Bell award ABA, 1973, Outstanding Citizenship award Ind. Elks, 1973-74, Svc. to Mankind award Sertoma Club, 1980, 98, 99, Chief Anderson award, 1986, Elmo A. Funk Ideal of Svc. award, 1990, Anderson/Madison County Homeless Task Force award, 2003; named as one of top people of the century Anderson Newspaper and Madison County, 1999, Sagamore of the Wabash Gov. State Ind. Frank O'Bannon; Rev. Lloyd Lambert Homeless Svc. award named in his honor. Mem. Anderson Ministerial Assn., Internat. Union Gospel Missions (past pres., sec.-treas. midwestern dist.), Rotary (past sergeant-at-arms and sec., pres. Anderson club 1975-76, Community Image award 1973, 80, Internat. Paul Harris fellow 1983). Home: 603 Main St Anderson IN 46016 Office: The Christian Ctr 625 Main St PO Box 743 Anderson IN 46015-0743

LAMBERT, LYN DEE, law librarian; b. Fitchburg, Mass., Jan. 5, 1954; m. Paul Frederick Lambert, Aug. 11, 1979; children: Gregory John, Emily Jayne, Nicholas James. BA in History, Fitchburg State Coll., 1976, MEd in History, 1979; JD, Franklin Pierce Law Ct., 1983; MLS, Simmons Coll., 1986. Law libr. Fitchburg Law Libr., Mass. Trial Ct., 1985-96; media specialist libr. Samoset Sch., Leominster, Mass., 1996—. Instr. paralegal studies courses Fisher Coll., Fitchburg, 1989-94, Anna Maria Coll., Paxton, Mass., 1995—, Atlantic Union Coll., Lancaster, Mass., 1995—, pre-law coll. courses Fitchburg State Coll., 1995—; tech. com. City of Leominster Shc., Net Day Participant and trainer/leader, Leominster H.S., Northwest, Johnny Appleseed, Fall Brook, Southeast and Samoset. Mem. Am. Legion Band, Fitchburg, 1959—, Westminster (Mass.) Town Band, 1965—, Townsend Town Band, 1999—; appt. to Mass. Strategic Plan Com. for delivery of libr. svcs. among multi-type librs. within the commonwealth; mem. Patrick S. Gilmore Cmty. Honor Band, Hatch Shell, Boston, 2000—02; mem. cmty. theatre Theatre at the Mount Mount Wachusett Cmty. Coll., Gardner, Mass., 2002—, Greater Gardner Cmty. Choir, 2004—. Recipient Community Leadership award Xi Psi chpt. Kappa Delta Pi-Fitchburg State Coll. chpt., 1993. Mem. ALA, Am. Assn. Law Librarians (copyright com. 1987-89, publs. rev. com. 1990-92, state, ct. and county law librs. spl. interest sect. publicity com. 1993—), Law Librarians New Eng. (conf. com. 1988), Mass. Libr. Assn. (edn. chair 1991-93, freedom of info. com., legislation com.), Mass. Computer Using Educators, Mass. Sch. Media Libr. Assn., New Eng. Libr. Assn., New Eng. Microcomputer Users Group (profl. assoc.), North Cen. Mass. Libr. Alliance (newsletter editor 1990—), Spl. Libr. Assn., Beta Phi Mu, Phi Alpha Delta, Phi Delta Kappa (newsletter editor Montachusett chpt. 1998-2000, pres. Montachusett chpt. 2000-02). Avocations: singing, guitar, clarinet, hiking, camping. Office: Samoset Libr Media Ctr 100 DeCicco Dr Leominster MA 01453-5161

LAMBERT, MARIANNE T., retired elementary school educator, retired military officer; d. Roger and Ruth (Kustush) Lambert. BS in physical edn., So. Ill. U., 1980, MS in physical edn., motor learning and control, 1989. Cert. P.E. Elem. & Secondary, English as a Second Lang., first aid instr., HIV/AIDS instr. Commd. lt. USN, 1969, advanced through grades to, ret., 2005; sales Fuller Brush, Berkeley, Ill., 1967; keypunch operator, verifier,teletype operator, receptionist Montgomery Ward, Berkeley, Ill., 1967; keypunch operator Jewell Food Co., Melrose Pk., Ill., 1968—69; pitter, sorter Libby and McNeil Food Co., Selma, Calif., 1969; machinist McCullough Chain Saws, Lake Havasu City, Ariz., 1969; seam, recruit transfers divsn. Bainbridge (Md.) Naval Tng. Ctr. USN, 1970, record's vault clerk Naval Tng. Ctr., 1971, chaplain's asst. Naval Tng. Ctr., 1971, master at arms, security clerk Naval Tng. Ctr., 1971—72, detailer Bur. of Naval Personnel Arlington, Va., 1972—74, various positions Bur. of Naval Personnel, 1972—76, congressional dept. HQ Navy Recruiting Commd., 1974—76; sec., receptionist J. Hugh Shelnutt, CPA, Carbondale, Ill., 1976—77; tchr. State Ill. U., Carbondale, 1978; photographer Ctr. for Electron Microscopy So. Ill. U., Carbondale, 1979, sec. Dept. Analytical Chemistry, 1979; basketball coach Unity Point Sch. Dist. #140, Carbondale, 1979—90, bus driver, 1979—2005, physical edn., health educator, track coach, 1980—99, physical edn., health educator, 2000—01, ESL tchr., 2001—02, health educator, 2002—03, physical edn. tchr., 2004—05, ret., 2005. Pres., southern dist. IAHPER, Ill., 1977—79; com. mem. Ill. Heart Assn., 1978—81; health and safety dir. Am. Red Cross, Carbondale, Ill., 1990—92; track and field athlete St. Domitilla's Sch., Hillside, Ill., 1963—64; tennis player Naval Tng. Ctr. USN, Bainbridge, 1971—72, umpire, judge, official various sports, 1971—72, 1977—85. Author: Bible Study Methods, 1983, Godliness and Contentment is a Great Gain, 1989. Mem.: Am. Red Cross. Avocations: chess, travel, cooking, bible study, table tennis. Home: Erling Gospel Ctr 381 Hanmin Rd 10F Hsiaokang Dist Kaohsiung Taiwan Office: 3999 S Illinois Ave Carbondale IL 62903 Personal E-mail: xiaoyangjer911@yahoo.com.

LAMBERT, MEG STRINGER, construction executive, architect, interior designer; b. Selma, Ala., Aug. 10, 1941; d. John Bryant and Margaret Vandiver (Clark) Stringer; m. George Edward Buchner, June 30, 1962 (div. 1972); children: Susan Mayo Buchner, George Bryant Buchner, Robert Carson Buchner; m. Joseph Smith Lambert, June 20, 1975. BS, Auburn U., 1961, postgrad., 1972-73. Lic. real estate broker Ala., home builder Ala., master builder cert. Nat. Assn. Home Builders, cert. constrn. assoc. Nat. Assn. Women in Constrn. Math tchr. Selma (Ala.) Pub. Sch., 1961-62, Oscoda (Mich.) Pub. Sch., 1963-64; real estate sales Stower's Gallery of Homes, Montgomery, Ala., 1974-75; constrn. mgr. Lambert Constrn. Co., Inc., Montgomery, 1975-80, home builder, designer Prattville, Ala., 1984—; sec. estimating dept. Aesco Steel Co., Montgomery, 1981-82; steel bridge estimator and sales assoc. Trinity Industries, Montgomery, 1983-84; pres. Home Touch Builders, Inc., 2000—. Chmn. parade homes Prattville/Millbrook chpt. Home Builders, 1985—87, program chmn., 1985—90; masonry adv. bd. Prattville Vocat. Sch., Prattville, 1994—2001. Author: (book) A History of the Pleasant Hill Baptist Church (1840-1990), 1990. Vice-chmn. Prattville Planning Commn., 1992—95; mem. land use com. City Comprehensive Plan, Prattville, 1994—95; mem. leadership steering com. Autagua County, 1995—98, bd. equalization, 1995—99; chmn. health and welfare com. 1st United Meth. Ch., 1993; mem. beautificiation com. Prattville C. of C., 1992—95; pres. Pleasant Hill Cemetary Assn., 1990—98, 2000—02, South Dallas Hist. Preservation Assn., 2002—. Named Woman of the Yr., Montgomery chpt. Nat. Women in Constrn., 1990. Mem.: Greater Montgomery Home Builders Assn. (mem. longe range planning com. 1986, bd. dirs., exec. com. 2001, Named Builder of the Yr. 1989), Autauga County Heritage Assn. (pres. 1992). Republican. Avocations: genealogy, painting, historical preservation activities, working in political campaigns. Home: 394 Kingston Ridge Rd Prattville AL 36067-1725 Office: Lambert Construction Co Inc PO Box 680656 Prattville AL 36068-0656

LAMBERT, MICHAEL CANUTE, psychologist, educator; b. Norwich District, Portland, Jamaica, Oct. 1, 1954; s. Canute Emanuel and Leonora Lambert; m. Barbara Smith, 1974 (div. 1984); children: Michael Christopher, Donna-Maria Patricia; m. Karen Adrienne Smith, Oct. 18, 1993; children: Adrienne Michelle, Mikhaila Marie Kelso. BS in Mental Health Tech., Hahnemann Med. Coll., 1980; MS in Clin. Social Work, Bryn Mawr Coll., 1982; MA in Clin. Psychology, U. NC, 1986, PhD in Clin. Psychology, 1988. Lic. psychologist Mich. Asst. prof. U. Miss., Oxford, 1988—92; assoc. prof. Mich. State U., East Lansing, 1992—2001; Millsap prof. U. Mo., Columbia, 2001—. Pvt. forensic psychol. cons., Oxford, 1991—92; pvt. practice psychologist, East Lansing, 1993—2001; cons. psychologist State of Mich. Disability Rev., Lansing, 1994—2001. Cons. editor: editl. rev. Psychol. Assessment, 1995—, Jor. Clin. Psychology, 2001—. Mem. Sudanese refugee study group Mich. State U. and Refugee Svcs., Lansing, 2000—. Named Outstanding Scientist of 20th Century, Century Internat. Biog. Ctr., Cambridge, England, 2000. Mem.: APA, Am. Psychol. Soc. Avocations: weight training, cardiovascular exercise. Office: U Mo Dept Human Devel 314 Gentry Hall Columbia MO 65211 Home: 2009 Rainwood Dr Columbia MO 65203-0867 Business E-Mail: lambertm@missouri.com.

LAMBERT, NADINE MURPHY, psychologist, educator; b. Ephraim, Utah; m. Robert E. Lambert, 1956; children: Laura Allan, Jeffrey. PhD in Psychology, U. So. Calif., 1965. Diplomate Am. Bd. Profl. Psychology, Am. Bd. Sch. Psychology. Sch. psychologist Los Nietos Sch. Dist., Whittier, Calif., 1952-53, Bellflower (Calif.) Unified Sch. Dist., 1953-58; research cons. Calif. Dept. Edn., Los Angeles, 1958-64; dir. sch. psychology tng. program U. Calif., Berkeley, 1964—, assoc. prof. edn., 1964-70, assoc. prof., 1970-76, prof., 1976—, grad. prof., 1994—, assoc. dean for student svcs. Berkeley, 1988-94. Mem. Joint Com. Mental Health of Children, 1967-68; cons. state depts. edn., Calif., Ga., Fla.; cons. Calif. Dept. Justice; mem. panel on testing handicapped people Nat. Acad. Scis., 1978-81. Author: School Version of the AAMD Adaptive Behavior Scale, 3d edit., 1993; co-author: (with Wilcox and Gleason) Educationally Retarded Child: Comprehensive Assessment and Planning for the EMR and Slow-Learning Child, 1974, (with Hartsough and Bower) Process for Assessment of Effective Functioning, 1981, (with Windmiller and Turiel) Moral Development and Socialization -- Three Perspectives, 1979; assoc. editor Am. Jour. Orthopsychiatry, 1975-81, Am. Jour. Mental Deficiency, 1977-80, (with McCombs) How Students Learn-Reforming Schools Through Learner-Centered Education, 1998, (with Hylander and Sanoval) Consultee-Centered Consultation, 2004, others. With Hartsough and Sandoval Children's Attention and Adjustment Survey, 1990. Recipient Dorothy Hughes award for outstanding contbn. to ednl. and sch. psychology NYU, 1990, Tobacco Disease Related Rsch. award U. Calif., 1990-94, 1994-2001; grantee NIMH, 1965-87, Calif. State Dept. Edn., 1-72, 76-78, NHSTE Dept. Transp., 1995. Fellow APA (coun. reps. divsn. sch. psychologists, bd. dirs. 1984-87, mem. bd. profl. affairs 1981-83, bd. ednl. affairs 1991-94, chmn. 1992-94, exec. com. divsn. sch. psychology 1994-96, mem. commn. for recognition of specialities in psychology 1993-97, 2004—, Disting. Svc. award 1980, award for disting. profl. contbns. 1986, award for disting. career contbns. of applications of psychology to edn. and tng. 1999, Div. Sch. Psychologists sr. scientist award 2005), Nat. Assn. Sch. Psychologists (hon.; Legend in Sch. Psychology 1998), Am. Orthopsychiat. Assn.; mem. NEA, Calif. Assn. Sch. Psychologists (pres. 1962-63, Sandra Goff award 1985). Office: U Calif Grad Sch Berkeley CA 94720-1670 Business E-Mail: nlambert@socrates.berkeley.edu.

LAMBERT, RICHARD BOWLES, JR., freelance writer; b. Clinton, Mass., Apr. 20, 1939; s. Richard Bowles and Dorothy Elisabeth (Peck) L.; m. Sherrill Faye Smith, July 4, 1964; 1 child, Lisa Beth Lauren. AB in Physics, Lehigh U., 1961; ScM in Physics, Brown U., 1964, PhD in Physics, 1966; postgrad., Goethe Inst., Germany, 1966, NATO Internat. Sch., 1966, Max Planck Inst. for Physics & Astrophysics, 1966. Fulbright fellow Inst. for Stromungsmechanik Tech. Hochschule, Munich, 1966-67; asst. prof. U. R.I. Grad. Sch. Oceanography, 1968-74, assoc. prof., 1974; program dir. physical oceanography program NSF, Washington, 1975-77; rsch. oceanographer Sci. Applications Internat. Corp., 1977-79, mgr. ocean physics divsn., 1979-83, asst. v.p., 1980-83, sr. rsch. oceanographer, 1983-84; assoc. program dir. physical oceanography program NSF, Washington, 1984-91, program dir. physical oceanography program, 1991-99; dir. ops. Master Works Festival, 1997—2003. Adv. com. NOAA; assoc. dir. U.S. TOGA Project Office 1985-91; delegate Intergovernmental TOGA Bd., 1985-91; delegation head Intergovernmental WOCE Panel; co-investigator, chief scientist on oceanographic rsch. cruises, 1971-74. Interim editor Jour. Geophys. Rsch.-Oceans, 1999-2000; contbr. articles to profl. jours. including Jour. Fluid Mech. Bd. dirs. Christian Performing Artist's Fellowship, Winona Lake, Ind., 1998—; adminstr. MW Festival, 1997-2003; elder 4th Presbyn. Ch., 2005—. Mem. Am. Geophys. Union (Ocean Scis. award 1999), The Oceanography Soc. (life), Am. Sci. Affiliation, Phi Beta Kappa, Sigma Xi. Independent. Presbyterian. E-mail: rblambert@cavtel.net.

LAMBERT, RICHARD WILLIAM, retired mathematics professor; b. Gettysburg, Pa., May 1, 1928; s. Allen Clay and Orpha Rose (Hoppert) L.; m. Phyllis Jean Bain, Sept. 2, 1949 (div. May 1982); children: James Harold, Dean Richard; m. Kathleen Ann Waring, Aug. 30, 1982; stepchildren: Gregory Scott Gibbs, LeAnn Marie Gibbs. BS, Oreg. State U., 1952; MA in Teaching Math., Reed Coll., 1962. Instr. Siuslaw High Sch., Florence, Oreg., 1954-55, David Douglas High Sch., Portland, Oreg., 1955-67, Mt. Hood Community Coll., Gresham, Oreg., 1967-87, ret., 1987. NSF grantee, 1959, 60, 62. Mem. Nat. Coun. Tchr. Math., Am. Math Soc., Math. Assn. Am., Am. Math. Assn. of Two Yr. Colls., Oreg. Coun. Tchrs. Math. Democrat. Methodist. Avocations: travel, camping, home improvements, reading. Home: 11621 SE Lexington St Portland OR 97266-5933

LAMBERT, ROBERT FRANK, electrical engineer, consultant; b. Warroad, Minn., Mar. 14, 1924; s. Fred Joseph and Nutah (Gibson) L.; m. June Darlene Flatten, June 30, 1951; children: Cynthia Marie, Susan Ann, Katherine Cheryl. B.E.E., U. Minn., 1948, MS in Elec. Engring, 1949, PhD, 1953. Asst. prof. U. Minn. Inst. Tech., Mpls., 1953-54, assoc. prof., 1955-59, prof. elec. engring., 1959-94, prof. emeritus, 1994; dir. propagation research lab. U. Minn., 1968-87; assoc. dean U. Minn. (Inst. Tech.), 1967-68; asst. prof. Mass. Inst. Tech., 1954-55. Cons. elec. engr., also in acoustics, 1953—; guest scientist Third Phys. Inst., Göttingen, Fed. Republic Germany, 1964; vis. scientist NASA, Hampton, Va., 1979; dir. Inst. Noise Control Engring., Washington, 1972-75 Contbr. numerous articles to tech. jours. Served with USNR, 1943-46. Fellow IEEE, Acoustical Soc. Am. (assoc. editor jour. 1985-93); mem. Am. Soc. Engring. Edn., Am. Soc. Engring. Sci., AAAS, Inst. Noise Control Engring. (dir., John C. Johnson Meml. award), Sigma Xi, Tau Beta Pi, Eta Kappa Nu, Gamma Alpha. Lutheran. Achievements include rsch. in acoustics, communication tech. random vibrations. Home: 2503 Snelling Curv N Saint Paul MN 55113 Office: U Minn Inst Tech Dept Elec Engring Minneapolis MN 55455

LAMBERT, SAMUEL WALDRON, III, foundation executive; b. N.Y.C., Jan. 12, 1938; s. Samuel W. and Mary (Hamill) L.; children: Louisa Kelly, Samuel William, Sarah Hamill. BA, Yale U., 1960; LLB, Harvard U., 1963. Bar: N.J. 1964, U.S. Tax Ct. 1975. Assoc. Albridge C. Smith III, Princeton, N.J., 1964-67; ptnr. Smith, Cook, Lambert & Miller, and predecessors, Princeton, 1967-80; officer, dir. Smith, Lambert, Hicks & Miller, P.C., Princeton, 1981-87; ptnr. in charge of office Drinker, Biddle & Reath, 1988-2000, mng. ptnr., 1994-96; chmn. Windham Found., 1997—; ptnr. Drinker, Biddle & Reath, LLP, Princeton, 1988—2003, chair personal law dept., 2001—03, bd. dirs. Bd. dirs. Winslow Found., Bunbury Co., Curtis W. McGraw Found.; capt. Princeton Republican County Com., 1967-69. With USAR, 163-69. Mem. ABA, N.J. Bar Assn., Princeton Bar Assn. (pres. 1976-77). Business E-Mail: lambersw@aol.com.

LAMBERT, STEVEN CHARLES, lawyer; b. Kingsport, Tenn., Aug. 22, 1947; s. M. Charles and Janet (Sultner) L.; m. Barbara Marshall-Lambert; children: Shelley Elizabeth, Charles Burnette. BA, Duke U., 1969; JD, Georgetown U., 1974. Bar: D.C. 1975, U.S. Ct. Fed. Claims, U.S. Ct. Appeals (fed. cir.), U.S. Tax Ct. Law clk. to Chief Judge Wilson Cowen, U.S. Ct. Claims, Washington, 1974-75; assoc. Wilkinson, Cragun & Barker, Washington, 1975-80, ptnr., 1980-82, Hamel & Park, Washington, 1982-88, Hopkins & Sutter, Washington, 1988-2001, Foley & Lardner, Washington, 2001—. Chmn. adv. coun. U.S. Ct. Claims, 1982-86, mem. adv. coun., 1986—, chmn. bicentennial commn., 1987-91. Co-author: Tax Ideas Desk Book, 1980; contbr. articles to profl. jours. Chmn. bd. trustees Ferrum Coll.; pres. bd. pensions United Meth. Ch.; mem. bd. govs., Wesley Sem., 2000—. With U.S. Army, 1970-72. Fellow Am. Bar Found.; mem. ABA (sec. litigation and natural resources), Am. Arbitration Assn., Claims Ct. Bar Assn. (pres. 1990-91, bd. dirs. 1999—), Fed. Cir. Bar Assn. (bd. dirs. 1986-88, 99-2002), Bar Assn. D.C. (bd. dirs. 1981-83). Methodist. Avocations: boating, fishing, tennis. Office: Foley & Lardner 3000 K St NW Ste 500 Washington DC 20007-5143 Home: 7830 Brink Rd Laytonsville MD Office Phone: 202-295-4067. Business E-Mail: slambert@foley.com.

LAMBERT, VICKIE ANN, retired dean, nursing consultant; b. Hastings, Nebr., Oct. 28, 1943; d. Victor E. and Edna M. (Hein) Wagner; m. Clinton E. Lambert, Jr., June 30, 1974; 1 child, Alexandra. Diploma, Mary Lanning Sch. Nursing, 1964; BSN, U. Iowa, 1966; MSN, Case Western Res. U., 1973; DNSc, U. Calif., San Francisco, 1981. RN, Ga. Acting chair dept. nursing adminstrn. Med. Coll. Ga., Augusta, 1982-84, coord. doctoral program nursing, 1984-85, George Mason U., Fairfax, Va., 1986-88; assoc. dean Case Western Res. U., Cleve., 1989-90; dean Sch. Nursing Med. Coll. Ga., Augusta, 1990-2001. Contbr. articles to profl. jours. Fellow Am. Acad. Nursing; mem. ANA, Sigma Theta Tau, Sigma Xi. Home: 8608 Wandering Fox Trail Unit 403 Odenton MD 21113 E-mail: Vlambert@mcg.edu.

LAMBERT, WILLIE LEE BELL, mobile equipment company owner, educator; b. Texas City, Tex., Oct. 23, 1929; d. William Henry and Una Oda (Stafford) Bell; m. Eddie Roy Lambert, July 2, 1949; (dec. Mar. 1980); children: Sondra Kay Lambert Bradford, Eddie Lee. Degree in bus., Met. Bus. Coll., 1950; AAS, Coll. of Mainland, 1971; BS, Sam Houston U., 1976. Cert. hand and foot reflexologist, Hatha Yoga instr. Sec. Judges Reddell & Hopkins, Texas City, 1945-47, Union Carbide Chemicals, Texas City, 1947-48, John Powers Modeling, 1948—49, Charles Martin Petroleum, Texas City, 1948-50; acct. Goodyear Co., La Marque, Tex., 1968-70; instr. Coll. of the Mainland, Texas City, 1970—, serials libr., 1970-77, instr., 1970; exec. dir., office mgr. Mobile Air Conditioning, La Marque, 1977-80; owner Kivert, Inc., La Marque, 1982—; ptnr., exec. dir. A/C Mobile Equipment Corp., La Marque, 1988—94. Owner Star Bell Ranch, 1985—. Vol. Union Carbide Chems., Texas City, 1970—, Carbide Retiree Corp., Inc., Texas City, 1980—, Hospice, Galveston, Tex., 1985—, various polit. campaigns, Texas City, 1951-62, MD Anderson Cancer Inst., U. Tex., 1995—; v.p. Coalition on Aging Galveston County, Tex. City, 1990-92; vol. Baylor Coll. Medicine, Houston, 1990—; mem. adv. coun. bd. Galveston County Sr. Citizens, Galveston, 1990—; mem. planning bd. Heart Fund and Cancer Fund, Texas City, 1953-62, Santa Fe (Tex.) St. Citizens, 1990—; benefactor mem. Mainland Mus., Texas City, Tex., 1994—; sec. YMCA, 1947-55; sec. Ladies VFW, 1950-59; leader Girl Scouts Am., 1958-65; v.p. PTA, 1957-60; counselor Bapt. Ch. Camp, 1960-64; v.p. Santa Fe Booster Club, 1963-67; mem. Internat. Platform Assn., 1995—. Named Vol. of Yr., Heights Elem. Sch., Texas City Sch. Dist., 1959, Most Glamorous Grandmother, 1985, Mother of Yr., Texas City/La Marque C. of C., 1990, Unsung Hero award Texas City, 1995, 96, 97, 99, 2001-04; named to Tex. Women's Hall of Fame, 1984. Mem. Internat. Platform Assn. Republican. Baptist. Avocations: making porcelain dolls and soft sculpture dolls, painting china portraits, sewing, needlecrafts, volunteer work. Home: PO Box 1253 Santa Fe TX 77510-1253

LAMBERTA, GAIL CAROL, recreational therapist, physical education educator; d. Gaspare and Yolanda Lamberta. AAS, SUNY, 1980; BS cum laude, St. Joseph's Coll., 1982; MA, Adelphi U., 1984; PhD, Walden U., 2005. Sr. program dir. Huntington (N.Y.) Township YMCA, 1976—83; dir. sports and fitness YMCA Greater N.Y., Bellrose, NY, 1986—87; metro dir. program and svcs. YMCA L.I., Huntington, 1987—93; assoc. prof. St. Joseph's Coll., Patchogue, NY, 1988—; exec. dir. Smithtown (N.Y.) YMCA, 1993—96, Brookhaven ROC, Smithtown, NY, 1993—96, Holtzville, NY, 1996—2000. Team reviewer Nat. Program Collegiate Sports, Albany, NY, 1998—; bd. dir. L.I. (N.Y.) Leisure Svc. Assn., Garden City, NY; mem. task force youth sports N.Y. State Recreation and Pks. Soc., Saratoga, NY, 2004—; cons. Village Great Neck (N.Y.) Estates, 2004—. Author: Confidence Plus, 1988 (Discovery award YMCA, 88). Mem.: Therapeutic Recreation Assn. Suffolk County, L.I. (N.Y.) Leisure Svcs. Assn., Assn. Profl. Dirs., Am. Alliance Health Phys. Edn., Recreation, Dance, Soc. Parkland Recreation Educators, Nat. State Recreation and Pks. Soc., N.Y. State Recreation and Pks. Soc. (program com., chmn. annual conf., award Met. chpt. 2004), Nat. Alliance Youth Sports. Avocations: golf, walking, weightlifting, hiking. Office: St Josephs College 155 W Roe Blvd Patchogue NY 11772 Office Phone: 631-447-3313.

LAMBERTH, JAMES A., lawyer; b. Coleman, Tex., 1961; BA, George Washington Univ., 1984, JD with honors, 1987. Bar: Ga. 1987, DC 1989. Assoc. Troutman Sanders LLP, 1987—92, 1993—94, ptnr., intellectual property, spl. investigations Atlanta, 1995—, and practice group leader, media and entertainment; atty. Howrey & Simon, Washington, 1992—93. Named a Super Lawyer, Atlanta Mag., 2004. Mem.: ABA, State Bar Ga. Office: Troutman Sanders LLP One Logan Sq Ste 5200 600 Peachtree St NE Atlanta GA 30308-2261 Office Phone: 404-885-3362. Office Fax: 404-962-6611. Business E-Mail: james.lamberth@troutmansanders.com.

LAMBERTI, MARJORIE, retired social studies educator; b. New Haven, Sept. 30, 1937; d. James and Anna (Vanacore) L. BA, Smith Coll., 1959; MA, Yale U., 1960, PhD, 1965. Prof. history Middlebury Coll., Vt., 1964—84, Charles A. Dana prof., 1984—2002, ret., 2002, full-time scholar, 2002—. Author: Jewish Activism in Imperial Germany, 1978, State, Society and the Elementary School in Imperial Germany, 1989, The Politics of Education: Teachers and School Reform in Weimar Germany, 2002; mem. editl. bd.: History of Edn. Quar., 1992—94; contbr. articles to profl. jours. Mem. exec. com. Friends of Smith Coll. Librs., 1995—2001. NEH fellow, 1968-69, 81-82, Inst. for Advanced Study, Princeton, 1992-93, The Woodrow Wilson Ctr., Washington, 1997-98; German Acad. Exch. Svc. rsch. grantee, 1988, Rockefeller Archive Ctr. rsch. grantee, 2003. Mem. Am. Hist. Assn., Conf. Group for Ctrl. European History, Leo Baeck Inst., Phi Beta Kappa. Home: 8 S Gorham Ln Middlebury VT 05753-1002 Office: Middlebury Coll Library Middlebury VT 05753 E-mail: Lamberti@middlebury.edu.

LAMBERTON, JACQUELYN E., psychotherapist; b. Dover, N.H., July 15, 1924; d. Guy Ordway and Marjorie Gladys (Cheney) Edmunds; m. Bruce Alexander Lamberton, July 5, 1947 (dec. Mar. 9, 1988); children: Karen-(dec.), Christopher J., Andrew B, Valerie A.; m. George Louis Frigie, Dec. 17, 1994. BS, Simmons Coll., Boston, 1947; Grad., Gestalt Inst., Cleve. Lic. ind. chem. dependency counselor. Therapist United Meth. Ch. Orgn., Berea, Ohio, 1980—85; therapist outpatient family program Glenbeigh Hosp., Cleve., 1985—87; dir. assessment, svcs. Glenbeigh Outpatient Family Program, 1987—89, dir., 1989—92; therapist chem. dependency Taylor, Dean, Masci, Inc., Broadview Heights, Ohio, 1992—95; addictions therapist Mosaics Integrated Health, Independence, Ohio, 1995—99; pvt. practice therapy Independence, Ohio, 1999—, Pepper Pike, 2003—. Instr. 4-week pub. edn. intervention program Glenbeigh of Rock Creek, Ohio, 2000. Author: Intervention - Why?...Why Not?... Alcohol is a Drug, and Drugs Kill...That's Why, 2004—05. Citizen advocate for C.D. prevention Ohio Citizen Advocates, Columbus, 2001—; Vestry woman St. Thomas Episcopal Ch., Berea, Ohio, 1997—2003; co-chair commn. on alcoholism Episcopal Diocese of Cleve., 1990—91. Mem.: Nat. Assn. Alcohol and Drug Abuse Counselors. Episcopalian. Avocations: music, pianist. Home: 8889 Barton DR Strongsville OH 44149

LAMBERTSEN, CHRISTIAN JAMES, environmental physiologist, physician, educator; b. Westfield, N.J., May 15, 1917; s. Christian and Ellen (Stevens) Lambertsen; m. Naomi Helen Hill, Feb. 5, 1944; children: Christian James, David Lee, Richard Hill, Bradley Stevens. BS, Rutgers U., 1939; MD, U. Pa., 1943; DSc, Northwestern U., 1977. Prof. pharmacology and exptl. therapeutics, prof. medicine U. Pa. Sch. Medicine, 1946—87, Markle scholar in med. sci., 1948—53; founding dir. Inst. for Environ. Medicine, U. Pa. Med. Ctr., 1968—, disting. prof. environ. medicine, 1985—; mem. adv. panel on med. scis. Office of Asst. Sec. Defense, 1954—61; sec. basic scis. Nat. Bd. Med. Examiners, 1955—71; mem. Pres.'s Space Panel, 1967—70; mem. oceanographic adv. bd. Office of Asst. Sec. of Navy for R & D, 1968—77; mem. marine bd. Nat. Acad. Engring., 1973—77. Dir. Environ. Biomed. Stress Data Ctr., 1992—; adviser Office of Marine Resources, NOAA, 1972—76; med. adviser Ocean Sys. Inc., Houston, 1960—83; med. dir. SubSea Intern, 1984—; chmn. com. Man in Space; with Space Sci. Bd., NAS, 1960—62; chmn. life scis. adv. bd. McDonnell-Douglas Aircraft Corp., St. Louis, 1960—67; sr. life scis. adviser Union Carbide Corp., Buffalo, Westinghouse Elec. Corp., Annapolis, Md., 1972—74, Air Products and Chems. Corp., Allentown, Pa., 1983—87; pres. Ecosystems, Inc., Phila., 1972—. Editor: Underwater Physiology Symposium, II, III, IV, V, 1963—76; mem. editl. bd.: Marine Tech. Soc. Jour., 1977—85; contbr. articles to med. and sci. jours. Maj. AUS, OSS, 1944—46. Decorated Legion of Merit U.S. Army; recipient Lindback award for disting. tchg., 1967, Tuttle award, Aerospace Med. Assn., 1970, Undersea Med. Behnke award, 1970, Dept. Def. Disting. Pub. Svc. medal, 1972, Marine Tech. Soc. award in Ocean Sci. and Engring., 1972, Dept. Navy Commendation Adv. Svc., 1972, award in environ. scis., N.Y. Acad. Scis., 1974, Disting. Pub. Svc. award, USCG, 1976, Disting. Med. Grad. award, U. Pa., 1989, Lifetime Achievement award, UDT-Seal Assn., 1995, Spl. Forces Green Beret award, U.S. Army, 1996, Pioneer award, Hist. Diving Soc., 2001, Socom medal, U.S. Spl. Ops. Command, 2001, Lifetime Achievement award, Undersea and Hyperbaric Med. Soc., 2002; grantee, NIH, USN, USAF, NASA, NOAA. Fellow: Aerospace Med. Assn. (v.p. 1968); mem.: NAE, Phila. Maritime Mus., U.S. Army Spl. Forces Regiment One, Pa. Med. Soc., Phila. County Med. Soc., Undersea Med. Soc. (founding pres.), Peripatetic Med. Soc., Marine Tech. Soc., USN UDT/Seal Assn. (hon. life mem.), John Morgan Med. Rsch. Soc., Internat. Union Physiol. Scis., Internat. Astronautic Fedn., Internat. Acad. Astronautics, Phila. Coll. Physicians, Assn. Am. Med. Colls., Am. Soc. Clin. Investigation, Am. Physiol. Soc., Am. Soc. Pharmacology and Exptl. Therapeutics, Am. Coll. Clin. Pharmacology and Chemotherapy, Cosmos Club (Washington), Sigma Xi. Home: 3500 W Chester Pike # 129 Newtown Square PA 19073-4101 Office: U PA Med Ctr Inst Envrion Medicine 1 John Morgan Bldg Philadelphia PA 19104-6068

LAMB-FAFFELBERGER, MARGARETE BARBARA, foreign language educator; b. Amstetten, Austria, Sept. 6, 1954; came to U.S., 1968; d. Othmar and Margarete Faffelberger; m. Walter James Lamb, Apr. 2, 1980; children: Thomas, Christina, Nikolas. BEd, Tchr's. Acad., Vienna, Austria, 1977,

Tchr's. Acad., Baden, Austria, 1979; MA, Rice U., 1981, PhD in German, 1991. Tchr. secondary sch. Hauptschule, Ybbs, Austria, 1978-79; teaching asst. U. Ill., Urbana, 1979-81, Rice U., Houston, 1981-83, 87-91, postdoctoral fellow, 1991—92; prof. of German Lafayette Coll., Pa., 1992—, head, dept. fgn. langs. and lit. Editor: Austrian Culture Series, Peter Lang Pub., 2001—. Office: Lafayette Coll Pardee Hall 433 Easton PA 18042 also: Peter Long Publishing USA 275 Seventh AVe 28th Fl New York NY 10001 Office Phone: 610-330-5255. Business E-Mail: lambfafm@lafayette.edu.

LAMBORN, LEROY LESLIE, law educator; b. Marion, Ohio, May 12, 1937; s. LeRoy Leslie and Lola Fern (Grant) Lamborn. AB, Oberlin Coll., 1959; LLB, Western Res. U., 1962; LLM, Yale U., 1963; JSD, Columbia U., 1973. Bar: N.Y. 1965, Mich. 1974. Asst. prof. law U. Fla., 1965-69; prof. Wayne State U., Detroit, 1970-97, prof. emeritus, 1997—. Vis. prof. State U., Utrecht, 1981. Author: (book) Legal Ethics and Professional Responsibility, 1963; contbr. articles on victimology to profl. jours. Mem.: World Soc. Victimology (exec. com. 1982—94), Nat. Orgn. Victim Assistance (bd. dirs. 1979—88, 1990—91), Am. Law Inst. Home: Apt 2502 1300 E Lafayette St Detroit MI 48207-2924

LAMBRIGHT, STEPHEN KIRK, brewing company executive, lawyer; b. Kansas City, Mo., Dec. 3, 1942; s. Ray B. and Janet Lambright; m. Gail T. Tabler; children: Stephen K. Jr., James H., Sarah E., Catherine L. BS in Acctg., U. Mo., 1965; JD cum laude, St. Louis U., 1968, MBA in Fin., 1977. Bar: Mo., 1968, Va. 1979, D.C. 1979; CPA, Mo. Tax acct. Arthur Andersen & Co., 1965-69; atty. Lashly, Caruthers, Thies, Rava & Hamel, 1970-77; asst. gen. counsel Anheuser-Busch Cos., St. Louis, 1977-78, exec. asst. chmn. bd., 1978-79, v.p., nat. affairs Washington, 1979-81, v.p., industry and govt. affairs St. Louis, 1981-83, mem. corp. policy com., 1981—, v.p. group exec., 1983—, group v.p., gen. counsel. Mem. Shriner's Hosp. for Crippled Children, Keep Am. Beautiful. Mem. C. of C. of U.S. Presbyterian. Office: Anheuser-Busch Cos Inc 1 Busch Pl Saint Louis MO 63118-1852 Home: 7 Bonhomme Grove Ct Chesterfield MO 63017-6053

LAMBRO, DONALD JOSEPH, columnist; b. Wellesley, Mass., July 24, 1940; s. Pascal and Mary (Lapery) L.; m. Jacquelyn Mae Killmon, Oct. 6, 1968; 1 son, Jason Phillip. BS, Boston U., 1963. Reporter, Boston Herald-Traveler, 1963; freelance writer Washington, 1965-67; statehouse reporter UPI, Hartford, Conn., 1968-70, reporter Washington, 1970-80; columnist United Feature Syndicate, Washington, 1981—; commentator AP Radio Network, 1982-83, Nat. Pub. Radio, 1984-85. Writer, host TV documentary Star Spangled Spenders, 1982; host, co-writer PBS TV documentary Inside the Republican Revolution, 1995; nat. editor Washington Times, 1987-88; chief polit. corr. Washington Times, 1988—. Author: The Federal Rathole, 1975; The Conscience of a Young Conservative, 1976; Fat City: How Washington Wastes Your Taxes, 1980; Washington-City of Scandals, 1984; Land of Opportunity, 1986. Recipient Warren Brookes award for Excellence in Journalism, Am. Legis. Exch. Coun., 1995. Albanian Orthodox. Office: The Washington Times 3600 New York Ave NE Washington DC 20002-1996 also: United Media Syndicate 4th Fl 200 Madison Ave New York NY 10166 Business E-Mail: dlambro@washingtontimes.com.

LAMEL, LINDA HELEN, professional society executive, retired insurance company executive, retired college president, lawyer; b. N.Y.C., Sept. 10, 1943; d. Maurice and Sylvia (Abrams) Treppel; 1 child, Diana Ruth Sands. BA magna cum laude, Queens Coll., 1964; MA, NYU, 1968; JD., Bklyn. Law Sch., 1976. Bar: N.Y. 1977, U.S. Dist. Ct. (3d dist.) N.Y. 1977. Secondary sch. tchr. Farmingdale Pub. Sch., NY, 1965-73; curriculum specialist Yonkers Bd. Edn., Yonkers, 1973-75; program dir. Office of Lt. Gov., Albany, 1975-77; dep. supt. N.Y. State Ins. Dept., N.Y.C., 1977-83; pres. CEO Coll. of Ins., 1983-88; v.p. Tchr.'s Ins. and Annuity Assn., 1988-96; exec. dir. Risk and Ins. Mgmt. Soc., 1997-2000; CEO Claims on Line, Inc., 2000—02; adj. assoc. prof. Bklyn. Law Sch., 2005—. Contbr. articles to profl. jours. Campaign mgr. lt. gov.'s primary race, N.Y. State, 1974; v.p. Ednl. Found., 1997-2000. Mem. ABA (tort and ins. sect. com. chmn. 1985-86), N.Y. State Bar Assn. (exec. com. ins. sect. 1984-88), Assn. of Bar of City of N.Y. (chmn. med. malpractice com. 1989-91, ins. law com. 1997-98), Am. Mgmt. Assn. (ins. and risk mgmt. coun.), Am. Soc. Workers Compensation Profls. (bd. dirs. 1999—), Fin. Women's Assn., Assn. Profl. Ins. Women (bd. dirs. 2002—04, Woman of Yr. 1988), Bklyn. Law Sch. Alumni Assn. (pres.), Phi Beta Kappa Assocs. (bd. dirs. 1992—2002). Office Phone: 212-371-8257. Personal E-mail: artemisbeach@yahoo.com.

LAMENDOLA, WALTER FRANKLIN, technology educator, technology business executive; b. Donora, Pa., Jan. 29, 1943; BA in English, St. Vincent Coll., 1964; MSW in Cmty. Orgn., U. Pitts., 1966; diploma in Sociology and Social Welfare, U. Stockholm, 1970; PhD in Social Work, U. Minn., 1976. Cmty. svcs. dir. Ariz. tng. programs State Dept. Mental Retardation, Tucson, 1970-73; assoc. prof. social welfare adminstrn. Fla. State U., 1976-77; pres., CEO Minn. Rsch. and Tech., Inc., 1977-81; assoc. prof., dir. Allied Health Computer Lab. East Carolina U., 1981-84; prof., dir. info. tech. ctr. Grad. Sch. Social Work U. Denver, 1984-87, 99—, cons. info. tech., rsch. human svcs., 1987-90; v.p. rsch. Colo. Trust, Denver, 1990-93, info. tech. and rsch. cons., 1993—. Cons. European Network Info. Tech. and Human Svcs.; mem. rebuilding cmtys. initiative PODER project Casey Found., 1996-97; mem. adv. bd. ctr. Computers in Tchg. Initiative, U. Southampton, Brit. Rsch. Coun. Univs., Human Svc. Info. Tech. Applications, CREON Found., Netherlands; lectr. conf., symposia, univs. U.S., Europe; mem. nat. adv. bd. Native Elder Health Resource Ctr., 1994-96; co-founder Denver Free Net, 1993; adj. prof. U. Colo. Health Scis. Ctr., 1996—; dir. tech. GSSU, U. Denver, 1998—; info. tech. cons. Healthy Nations Program Robert Wood Johnson Found, 1993-96; evaluator Nat. Libr. Rsch. Program, Access Colo. grant, 1994, Nat. Info. Infrastructure grant Colo. State Libr.; cons. set up on the Internet for U.S. Cts.-Ct. for Mental Health Svcs., NIH, Frontier Mental Health Svcs. Network grant; collaborating investigator SBIR award Computerized Advance Directives, tech. plan San Mateo County and Seattle Dist. Cts.; keynote spkr. conf. Human Svc. Info. Tech. Applications, Finland, 1996; adj. prof. U. Colo., 1997-98; dir. tech., adj. prof. U. Denver, 1997-98; adj. prof. informatics U. Colo. Health Scis. Ctr., 1998, 2003-; mem. nat. adv. coun. Ctr. Substance Abuse Prevention Dept. HHS, 1998, co-chair prevention decision support sys. steering group, 1999; pres. ActiveGuide, L.L.C.; mem. nat. design team Decision Support Sys., U.S. Dept. HHS, 1998—, mem. nat. adv. bd. Data Coord. Ctr., 1999—; prin. investigator bridge project Cmty. Tech. Ctr., U.S. Dept. Edn., 2000-03; prin. investigator, The Bridge Cmty. Tech. Ctr. Dept. Edn., 2000-03; mem. external steering com. Date Coord. Ctr., Ctr. for Substance Abuse Prevention, 2003—. Co-author: Choices for Colorado's Future, 1993, The Integrity of Intelligence: A Bill of Rights for the Information Age, 1992, Choices for Colorado's Future: Executive Summary, 1991, Choices for Colorado's Future: Regional Summaries, 1991; co-editor: A Casebook of Computer Applications in Health and Social Services, 1989; contbr. numerous articles to profl. jours. Capt. U.S. Army, 1966-69. Recipient Innovative Computer Application award Internat. Fedn. Info. Processing Socs., 1979; Nat. Lib. Rsch. Evaluator grantee, Colo., 1994—, Nat. Info. Infrastructure grantee Dept. Edn., State Libr. and Adult Literacy, 1994-95; Funds & Couns. Tng. scholar United Way Am., 1964-66, Donaldson Fund scholar, 1965-66, NIMH scholar, 1964-66, 73-76, St. Vincent Coll. Benedictine Soc. scholar, 1963-64; vis. fellow U. Southampton, 1992-95. Office: GSSW Univ Denver 2148 South High St Denver CO 80208 also: ActiveGuide LLC PO Box 24994 Denver CO 80224-4994 Business E-Mail: wlamendo@du.edu.

LAMENSDORF, HUGH, urologist, educator; b. Greenville, Miss., July 20, 1936; s. Jerome Hugh and Rosann (Mundt) Lamensdorf; m. Louise Faye Doernberg, July 6, 1958; children: Jerome Stewart, Marilyn Elizabeth, Bradley Hugh, Jonathan Louis. BS, Tulane U., 1958, MD, 1961. Diplomate Am. Bd. Urology. Intern U. Miss. Hosp., Jackson, 1961—62; resident in urology Ochsner Found. Hosp., New Orleans, 1962—66; mem. staff Urology Clinics of N. Tex., Ft. Worth, 1966—2002. Chief staff Med. Plaza Hosp., Ft. Worth; prof. surgery Southwestern Med. Sch., Dallas. Bd. dirs. Ft. Worth Opera, 2002—; bd. trustees Presbyn. Night Shelter, 2005—. Served to capt. USAF, 1966—68. Mem.: AMA (pres. forum for med. affairs 2002, del. from Tex., vice chmn.), ACS, Pan Am. Med. Assn. (coun.), Tarrant County Med. Assn. (pres. 1986), Tex. Med. Assn. (pres. 1996—97), Tex. Urol. Soc. (pres. 1975), Societe Urologie Internat., Tex. Surg. Soc., Am. Acad. Pediat., Soc. for Pediatric Urology, Am. Fertility Soc., Am. Assn. Clin. Urologists, Am. Urol. Assn. (del. to AMA 2002—), Ft. Worth C. of C. (bd. dirs.). Republican. Home: 1424 Shady Oaks Ln Fort Worth TX 76107-3538

LAMIA, THOMAS ROGER, lawyer; b. Santa Monica, Calif., May 31, 1938; s. Vincent Robert II and Maureen (Green) L.; m. Susan Elena Brown, Jan. 10, 1969; children: Nicholas, Katja, Jenna, Tatiana, Carlyn, Mignon. Student, U. So. Calif., 1956, BS, 1961; student, U. Miss., 1957-58; JD, Harvard U., 1964. Bar: Calif. 1965, D.C. 1980, N.Y. 1990, U.S. Dist. Ct. (ctrl. dist.) Calif. 1965, U.S. Dist. Ct. D.C. 1980, U.S. Tax Ct. 1982. Assoc. McCutchen, Black, Verleger & Shea, L.A., 1964-66; lectr. in law U. Ife, Ile-Ife, Nigeria, 1966-67, U. Zambia, Lusaka, 1967-68; assoc. Paul, Hastings, Janofsky & Walker, 1968-72, ptnr., 1972-99, mem. exec. com., 1976-80, mng. ptnr. Washington office, 1980-83; pvt. practice N.Y.C., 1999—. Office: 54 Charles St New York NY 10014-2750 Office Phone: 212-206-9290. Business E-Mail: trlamia@lamialaw.com.

LAMID, SOFJAN, physician, educator; b. Pangkalan, West Sumatra, Indonesia, June 30, 1929; came to the U.S., 1969; naturalized, 1981. s. Datuk Besar and Zamrud (Muhamad) L.; m. Burlini Tamin, Feb. 4, 1962; children: Dicky Sofwandi, Rudy Sofriza. MD, U. Indonesia, Jakarta, 1960; MSc in Pharmacology, U. Calif., San Francisco, U.S.A., 1962. Diplomate Am. Bd. Phys. Medicine and Rehab. Chmn. dept. pharmacology U. Indonesia, Jakarta, Indonesia, 1960-68; residency in internal medicine, fellow in clin. pharmacology Southwestern Med. Sch., U. Tex., 1969-70; fellow in clin. pharmacology George Washington U., Washington, 1970-72; residency in anesthesiology Washington Hosp. Ctr., 1972-73; staff physician, clin. pharmacology Wood VA Med. Ctr., Milw., 1973-77, staff physican, spinal cord injury svc., 1977-84, acting chief, spinal cord injury svc., 1983-84; asst. adj. prof. pharmacology Med. Coll. Wis., Milw., 1975-77, asst. prof. physical medicine and rehab., 1978-84; residency in physical medicine and rehab. Medical Coll. Wis., Milw., 1978-91; assoc. prof. medicine and rehab. LSU Med. Ctr., New Orleans, 1984-87; assoc. dir. La. Rehab. Inst., New Orleans, 1984-87; pvt. practice New Orleans, 1987—; mem. staff Hotel Dieu Hosp., New Orleans, Jo Ellen Smith Med. Ctr., New Orleans, F. Edward Hebert Hosp., New Orleans. Vis. prof. pharmacology U. Tex., Dallas, 1969-70; pres. QRS Lamid Enterprises, Inc., Indonesian Am. Found., Inc. Mem. editorial bd. The Jour. Am. Paraplegia Soc., 1982—; manuscript reviewer Archives of Physical Medicine and Rehab., 1980—. Pres. Indonesian Am. Found., Inc.; past pres. Indonesian Am. Cmty. Assn. Grantee Travenol Labs., 1984; grantee (with Richard Crout) Vitamin Drug Co., 1969-70, (with Raymond Jenkins) Beecham Massengil Pharmacology, 1970-72. Fellow Am. Acad. Phys. Medicine and Rehab.; mem. Am. Soc. Clin. Pharmacology and Therapeutics, Am. Paraplegia Soc., Am. Congress Rehab. Medicine (program com. 1982-84, rehab. practice com. 1983—), Assn. Academic Physiatrists, Dutch New Am. Club. Home: 3837 Sue Ker Dr Harvey LA 70058-1604

LAMIS, LEROY, artist, retired art educator; b. Eddyville, Iowa, Sept. 27, 1925; s. Leo and Blanche (Bennett) L.; m. Esther Sackler, Aug. 13, 1954; children: Alexander, Jonas. BA, N.Mex. Highlands U., 1953; MA, Columbia U., 1956. Mem. faculty dept. art Ind. State U., 1961—, prof., 1972-89, retired 1989; artist-in-residence Dartmouth Coll., 1970; founder PC ART, 1983, milliondollarart.com, 2000. One-man sculpture exhbns. include Staempfli Gallery, N.Y.C., 1966, 69, 73, Gillman Gallery, Chgo., 1967, Tacoma Mus., 1970, Ft. Wayne Art Mus., 1968, Des Moines Art Ctr., 1970, La Jolla Mus., 1970, Ind. State U., 1976, Sheldon Swope Art Mus., Terre Haute, Ind., 1979; kinetic computer art exhbns. at Ben Shahn Gallery, William Patterson Coll., N.J., Ind. State U., 1985, Bronx Mus. Art, 1986, 55 Mercer Gallery, 1990, Indpls. Art Mus., 1992, Evansville Mus. Sci. and Art, 1994, Swope Art Mus., Terre Haute, 1996-97, Fifth Annual N.Y. Digital Salon Sch. Visual Arts, N.Y.C., 1997, Seventh Annual N.Y. Digital Salon Sch. Visual Arts, 99; represented in permanent collections Albright-Knox Mus., Des Moines Art Ctr., Mus. Fine Arts, Boston, Whitney Mus. Am. Art, Joseph H. Hirshorn Collection, Washington, Indpls. Mus., J.B. Speed Mus., Louisville; author: (computer program) Eighty 5, 1985; creator, prodr. various computer software. Served with AUS, 1943. Recipient Award Commn. N.Y. State Coun. of the Arts, 1970. Address: 640 Wabash Ave Apt 307 Terre Haute IN 47807 E-mail: arlamis@isugw.indstate.edu.

LAMKIN, FLETCHER M., JR., academic administrator; b. Lakehurst, N.J., Apr. 2, 1942; married; 3 daus. BS, U.S. Mil. Acad., 1964; MS in Engring., U. Calif., Berkeley; DPhil, U. Wash.; grad., Army Command Gen. Staff Coll., Naval War Coll. Commd. 2d lt. U.S. Army, 1964; early assignments include battery exec. officer 7th bn., 11th field arty., Republic South Vietnam, bn. fire support officer, battery comdr., 1966-67; comdr. 1st spl. tng. co. Ft. Gordon, Ga., 1967-68; bn. ops. officer 1st bn., 38th field arty., Korea, 1975-76; bn. exec. officer, tng. officer, dep. ops. officer 9th infantry divsn., Ft. Lewis, Wash., 1976-80; inspections team chief, Office of Inspector Gen. U.S. Army Europe, Heidelberg, Germany, 1980—81; bn. comdr. 4th bn., 77th field arty., Babenhausen, Germany, 1981—83; instr., asst. prof. dep. mechs. U.S. Mil. Acad., West Pt., NY, 1971-74, assoc. prof. dept. engring., 1987-89, prof., dep. head dept. civil and mech. engring., 1989-92, vice dean acad. bd., 1993-94, prof., head dept. civil and mech. engirng., 1994-95, dean acad. bd., 1995—2000; pres. Westminster Coll., Fulton, Mo., 2000—. Office: Office of the President Westminster College 501 Westminster Ave Fulton MO 65251-1299

LAMM, CAROLYN BETH, lawyer; b. Buffalo, Aug. 22, 1948; d. Daniel John and Helen Barbara Lamm; m. Peter Edward Halle, Aug. 12, 1972; children: Alexander P., Daniel E. BS, SUNY Coll. at Buffalo, 1970; JD, U. Miami (Fla.), 1973. Bar: Fla., 1973, D.C., 1976, N.Y. 1983. Trial atty. frauds sect. civil div. U.S. Dept. Justice, Washington, 1973-78, asst. chief comml. litigation sect. civil div., 1978, asst. dir., 1978-80; assoc. White & Case, Washington, 1980-84, ptnr., 1984—. Mem. Sec. State's Adv. Com. Pvt. Internat. law, 1987—, Secs. Study Com. on Proposal Hague Conv. on Jurisdiction and the Enforcement of Judgements, 1992—; arbitrator US Panel of Arbitrators, Internat. Ctr. Settlement Investment Disputes, 1994-02, Uzbekistan, 2003-; mem. com. on pvt. dispute resolution NAFTA Mem. editl. adv. bd. Inside Litigation; contbg. editor: Internat. Arbitration Law Rev., 1997—; contbr. articles to legal publs. Mem. Holy Trinity Parish Coun., 1998—2001. Fellow Am. Bar Found., Am. Coll. Trial Lawyers; mem. ABA (chmn. young lawyers divsn. 1982-83, bd. govs. 2002-, chair opers. com., exec. com., rules and calendar com., chmn. house membership com., chmn. assembly resolution com., sec. 1984-85, chmn. internat. litigation com. coun. 1991-94, sect. litigation, ho. dels. 1982—, nomination com. 1984-87, chair 1995-96, D.C. Cir. mem. 1992-95, standing com. fed. judiciary 1992-95, chmn. com. scope and correlation of work 1996-97, commn. on multidisciplinary practice, bd. govs. 2002-), Am. Arbitration Assn. (bd., arbitrator, adv. com. internat. arbitration, exec. com.), Fed. Bar Assn. (chmn. sect. on antitrust and trade regulation), Bar Assn. D.C. (bd. dirs., sec., found. bd.), D.C. Bar (pres. 1997-98, bd. govs. 1987-93, steering com. litigation sect., found. bd. 2001—), Am. Law Inst. (coun.), Women's Bar Assn. D.C. (Woman Lawyer of Yr. 2002), Am. Soc. Internat. Law (chair Interest Group Dispute Resolution), Am. Indonesian C. of C. (bd. dirs.), Am. Uzbekistan C. of C. (bd. dirs., v.p., gen. counsel), Am. Turkish Friendship Coun. (bd. dirs.), Women's Forum, Columbia Country Club, Manchester Country Club, Stratton Mountain Club. Democrat. Office: White and Case 701 13th St NW Washington DC 20005-3807 Office Phone: 202-626-3600. Business E-Mail: clamm@whitecase.com.

LAMM, DONALD STEPHEN, literary agent; b. N.Y.C., May 31, 1931; s. Lawrence William and Aleen Antonia (Lassner) L.; m. Jean Stewart Nicol, Sept. 27, 1958; children: Douglas William, Robert Lawrence, Wendy Nicol. BA with honors, Yale, 1953; postgrad., Oxford (Eng.) U., 1956. With W.W. Norton & Co., Inc., N.Y.C., 1956-2000, from v.p. to pres., 1968-94, chmn., 1984-2000, also dir. Also dir. New Directions Pub. Corp.; assoc. Fletcher & Parry, N.Y.C.; guest fellow Yale U., 1980, 85, Phi Beta Kappa lectr. 1994; Ida Beam disting. vis. prof. U. Iowa, 1987-88; guest fellow Woodrow Wilson Ctr., 1996; regents lectr. U. Calif., Berkeley, 1998-99; pres. Yale U. Press, 1985-2000; mem. bd. advisors Yale Rev., mem. bd. trustees U. Calif. Press; fellow Ctr. for Advanced Study in the Behavioral Scis., 1998-99; trustee Sch. Am. Rsch., Santa Fe; mem. editl. bd. Am. Scholar. Author: (with others) The Spread of Economic Ideas, 1989, Beyond Literacy, 1990, Book Publishing in the United States Today, 1997, Perception, Cognition, and Language, 2000. With Counter Intelligence Corps U.S. Army, 1953—55. Fellow Branford Coll., Yale U. Fellow Am. Acad. Arts and Scis.; mem. Manuscript Soc., Century Assn., Elizabethan Club. Phi Beta Kappa (senator 1990—, exec. com. 1998—, v.p. 2003-). Home: 741 Calle Picacho Santa Fe NM 87505 Office: Fletcher & Parry 121 E 17th St New York NY 10003 Personal E-mail: donlamm@earthlink.net.

LAMM, MICHAEL EMANUEL, pathologist, immunologist, educator; b. Bklyn., May 19, 1934; s. Stanley S. and Rose (Lieberman) L.; m. Ruth Audrey Kumin, Dec. 16, 1961; children: Jocelyn, Margaret. Student, Amherst Coll., 1951-54; MD, U. Rochester, 1959; MS in Chemistry, Western Res. U., 1962. Diplomate Am. Bd. Pathology. Intern, asst. resident in pathology Inst. Pathology Western Res. U. and Univ. Hosps. of Cleve., 1959-62; research assoc. NIMH, Bethesda, Md., 1962-64; asst. prof. pathology NYU Sch. Medicine, N.Y.C., 1964-68, assoc. prof., 1968-73, prof., 1973-81; prof. dept. pathology Case We. Res. U. Sch. Medicine, 1981—; chmn. dept. Case Western Res. U. Sch. Medicine, 1981-2001. Vis. sci. dept. biochemistry U. Oxford, 1968; vis. prof. dept. pathology U. Geneva, 1976-77; mem. cancer spl. program adv. com. Nat. Cancer Inst., Bethesda, 1976-79, mem. bd. sci. counselors divsn. cancer biology, diagnosis and ctrs., 1993-95; mem. sci. adv. com. Damon Runyon-Walter Winchell Cancer Fund, N.Y.C., 1978-82; mem. immunol. sci. study sect. NIH, Bethesda, 1988-92; mem. immunotoxicology subcom. NRC, 1989-90; mem. toxin peer rev. panel Am. Inst. Biol. Sci., 1990—; bd. dirs. Univ. Associated for Rsch. and Edn. Pathology. Mem. editl. bd. Procs. Soc. Exptl. Biology and Medicine, 1973-82, Molecular Immunology, 1979-83, Jour. Immunol. Methods, 1980—, Jour. Immunology, 1981-85, Am. Jour. Pathology, 1982-92, Regional Immunology, 1988-95, Modern Pathology, 1989-96; contbr. articles to profl. jours. Recipient Excellence in Tchg. award NYU Sch. Medicine, 1974, Gold-Headed Cane award Am. Soc. for Investigative Pathology, 2004; named Career Scientist Health Rsch. Coun., City of NY, 1966-75; NIH grantee 1965—. Fellow AAAS, N.Y. Acad. Scis.; mem. Am. Assn. Pathologists (councilor 1986-88, sec. treas. 1988-90, v.p. 1990-91, pres. 1991-92), Am. Assn. Immunologists, Am. Soc. Biochemistry and Molecular Biology, Coll. Am. Pathologists, U.S. and Can. Acad. Pathology, Soc. for Exptl. Biol. Medicine, Clin. Immunology Soc., Soc. Mucosal Immunology, Am. Soc. Clin. Pathologists, Harvey Soc., Sigma Xi, Alpha Omega Alpha. Home: Apt 6B 13515 Shaker Blvd Cleveland OH 44120-5602 Business E-Mail: mel6@case.edu.

LAMM, NORMAN, academic administrator, rabbi; b. Bklyn., Dec. 19, 1927; s. Samuel and Pearl (Baumol) L.; m. Mindella Mehler, Feb. 23, 1954; children: Chaye Lamm Warburg, Joshua B., Shalom E., Sara Rebecca Lamm Dratch. BA summa cum laude, Yeshiva Coll., 1949; PhD, Bernard Revel Grad. Sch., 1966; Dr. of Hebrew Letters (hon.), Hebrew Theol. Coll., 1977, Gratz Coll., 1999. Cert. Ordained rabbi 1951. Ordained rabbi, 1951; asst. rabbi Congregation Kehilath Jeshurun, N.Y.C., 1952—53; rabbi Congregation Kodimoh, Springfield, Mass., 1954—58, Jewish Center, N.Y.C., 1958—76; Erna and Jakob Michael prof. Jewish philosophy Yeshiva U., N.Y.C., 1966—, pres., 1976—2002, Rabbi Isaac Elchanan Theol. Sem., N.Y.C., 1976—; chancellor Yeshiva U., 2002—. Vis. prof. Judaic studies Bklyn. Coll., 1974-75; dir. Union Orthodox Jewish Congregations Am. Author: A Hedge of Roses, 1966, The Royal Reach, 1970, Faith and Doubt, 1971, Torah Lishmah, 1972 (rev. English edition 1989), The Good Society, 1974, Halakot ve'Halikhot: Essays on Jewish Law, 1990, Torah Umadda: The Encounter of Religious Learning and Worldly Knowledge in the Jewish Tradition, 1990, The Shema: Spirituality and Law in Judaism, 1998, The Religious Thought of Hasidism: Text and Commentary, 1999 (Nat. Jewish Book awrd); editor: Library of Jewish Law and Ethics, 1975—; co-editor: The Leo Jung Jubilee Volume, 1962, A Treasury of Tradition, 1967, The Joseph B. Soloveitchik Jubilee Vol., 1984, Halakhot ve'Halikhot (Heb.): Essays on Jewish Law, 1990, Torah Umadda: The Encounter of Religious Learning and Worldly Knowledge in the Jewish Tradition, 1990. Trustee-at-large Fedn. Jewish Philanthropies, N.Y.; mem. exec. com. Assn. for a Better N.Y.; bd. dirs. Am. Friends-Alliance Israelite Universelle; mem. Pres.'s Commn. on the Holocaust, 1978-89; chmn. N.Y. Conf. on Soviet Jewry, 1970; mem. Halakhah Commn., Rabbinical Council Am. Recipient Abramowitz Zeitlin award, 1972 Mem. Assn. Orthodox Jewish Scientists (charter; bd. govs.) Office: Yeshiva U Office of Pres 500 W 185th St New York NY 10033-3201 also: Rabbi Isaac Elchanan Theol Sem 2540 Amsterdam Ave New York NY 10033-2807*

LAMMERS, LAURA BEA, writer, communications executive; b. San Diego, Nov. 22, 1963; d. Lennis Larry and Beatrice Mearlyn Lammers. Student, U. Tulsa, 1981-82; A sum cum laude, Ocean County Coll., 1993; postgrad., Stockton U., 1994-95. Tech. writer SpaceCom, Gaithersburg, Md., 1984-85; computer tng. cons. Portsmouth, NH, 1985-89; actress, model Foster Fell Agy., NYC, 1989-92; tech. writer Preferred Behavioral Health, Lakewood, NJ, 1992-96, Zellweger Uster, Knoxville, Tenn., 1997-2001, Hampton-Tilley Assocs., Knoxville, 1999-2000; dir. content, bus. devel. Webcortex, Inc., Queens, 2000—. Pres., founder CyberNuts, Inc., Knoxville, 1998—; cons. Maximus, Washington, 1997; German translator Learning Co., Knoxville, 1998; trade show salesperson, NYC, 1989-92. Author, editor: A Hero Borne, Tribute to John Glenn, 1999, Poetry of the Web, 2000; artist works includes restoration of Embassy of Kuwait, Washington, 1983; adminstr. editor Alliance for Women in History, 1990-97. Vol. CMC Hosp., Toms River, NJ, 1992-96; fundraiser Hurricane David and Kobe Earthquake Relief; sci. officer region 9 Star Trek Orgon, Toms River, 1994-97; host Barnes & Noble Women's Poetry Group, 1998-99. Recipient Poetry award, Am. Collegiate Poets, 1981, 1st pl. French Extemporaneous award, Clemson U., 1979. Mem.: Nat. Soc. DAR, AITP, NAFE, AAUW, Knoxville Assn. Women Execs., Peoria Tribe Okla., Soc. Tech. Comm., Info. Tech. Bus. Assn., Knoxville Assn. Women Execs. (bd. dirs.), Padi Scuba (cert. mem.), Phi Theta Kappa. Avocations: poetry, art, scuba, piano, travel. Office: CyberNuts Inc DBA APoetBorn Com PO Box 24238 Knoxville TN 37933-2238

LAMMIE, JAMES LOUIS, engineering executive, retired military officer; b. 1931; BS, U.S. Mil. Acad., 1953; MSE, Purdue U., 1957; MSBA, George Washington U., 1969. Commd. to lt. U.S. Army Corps of Engrs., 1953; advanced through grades to col. U.S. Army, 1972, ret., 1953—74; with Atlanta Transit Sys. Parsons Brinckerhoff, Inc., N.Y.C., 1975—82, COO, 1982—90, dir., 1983—2000, CEO, 1990—96, sr. exec., 2000—. Office: Parsons Brinckerhoff Inc One Penn Plz Fl 4 New York NY 10119-0061 Office Phone: 212-465-5006. Business E-Mail: lammie@pbworld.com.

LAMMON, MARTIN DEAN, literature educator, writer; b. Wilmington, Ohio, June 19, 1958; s. Stanley Howard Lammon and Linda Lou Lichtenwald; m. Frances Elizabeth Davis, Aug. 17, 1996. BA, Wittenberg U., Springfield, Ohio, 1980; MA, Ohio U., Athens, 1982, PhD, 1991. Tchr. assoc. Ohio U., Athens, 1980—85; lectr. Pa. State U., 1986—88; vis. instr. English Juniata Coll., Huntingdon, Pa., 1988—91; asst. prof. English Fairmont State Coll., W.Va., 1991—97; Flannery O'Conner chair prof. English Ga. Coll. and State U., Milledgeville, 1997—. Co-founder, co-editor Kestrel Jour. Lit. and Art in the New World, Fairmont, W.Va., 1993—97; founder, editor Arts and Letters Jour. of Contemporary Culture, Milledgeville, Ga., 1997—. Editor: (Book) Written in Water Written in Stone: 20 years of Poets on Poetry, 1996; author: News from Where I Live: Poems, 1998; contbr. poems and essays to literary jours. Recipient Pablo Neruda Poetry prize, Nimrod Internat. Jour., Tulsa, Okla., 1997, Non-Fiction prize, Chatahoochee Rev., Atlanta, 2003; fellow, W. Va. Commn. on Arts, Charleston, 1994. Mem.: Assn. Writers and Writing Programs (bd. dirs. 1998—2003, v.p. 1998—2000, pres. 2000—02). Office: Ga Coll and State U Campus Box 44 Milledgeville GA 31061 Office Phone: 478-445-3508. Business E-Mail: martin.lamon@gcsu.edu.

LAMON, HARRY VINCENT, JR., lawyer, director; b. Macon, Ga., Sept. 29, 1932; s. Harry Vincent and Helen (Bewley) Lamon; m. Ada Healey Morris, June 17, 1954; children: Hollis Morris, Kathryn Gurley. BS cum laude, Davidson Coll., 1954; JD with distinction, Emory U., 1958. Bar: Ga. 1958, DC 1965. Of counsel Troutman Sanders LLP, Atlanta, 1995—. Adj. prof. law Emory U., 1960—79. Contbr. articles to profl. jours. Pension and benefits reporter adv. bd. Bur. Nat. Affairs, 1972—2003; adv. coun. employee welfare and pension benefit plans U.S. Dept. Labor, 1975—79; mem. nat. adv. bd. Salvation Army, Atlanta, 1976—96, chmn., 1991—93, emeritus mem., 1996—; founding trustee, pres. So. Fed. Tax Inst., Inc., 1965—, emeritus, 2000—; bd. visitors Davidson Coll., 1979—89; trustee Am. Tax Policy Inst., Inc., 1989—96, Embry-Riddle Aero. U., 1989—2001, Cathedral St. Philip Endowment Fund, Atlanta, 1989—. 1st lt. U.S. Army, 1954—56. Named Atlanta Centennial honoree, Salvation Army, 1990; recipient Others award, 1979. Fellow: Am. Coll. Employee Benefits Counsel, Internat. Acad. Estate and Trust Law, Am. Coll. Tax Counsel, Am. Coll. Trust and Estate Counsel, Am. Bar Found. (life), Ga. Bar Found. (life), Phi Beta Kappa (life; fellow); mem.: ABA, Practicing Law Inst., So. Employee Benefits Conf. (hon.; pres. 1972, Hazelhurst Lamon outstanding achievement award named in his honor), Atlanta Bar Assn. (life), Am. Law Inst. (life), Atlanta Tax Forum, Am. Judicature Soc., State Bar Ga. (chmn. sect. taxation 1969—70, vice chmn. comm. continuing lawyer competency 1982—89, emeritus 2002), Am. Employee Benefits Conf., Nat. Emory U. Law Sch. Alumni Assn. (pres. 1967), Am. Bar Retirement Assn. (bd. dirs. 1989—96, pres. 1994—95), Group, Inc. (hon.), Cosmos Club (Washington), Atlanta Coffee House Club, Lawyers Club Atlanta, Capital City Club (life), Peachtree Racket Club (pres. 1986), Kiwanis (hon.; pres. Atlanta 1974), Phi Delta Theta (chmn. nat. cmty. svc. day 1969—72, legal commr. 1973—76, province pres. 1976—79, Golden Legion 2001), Phi Delta Phi, Omicron Delta Kappa. Episcopalian. Home: 4415 Paces Battle NW Atlanta GA 30327-3023 Office: Lamon & Sherman Consulting LLC 1950 N Park Pl Ste 125 Atlanta GA 30339 Office Phone: 770-933-0060. E-mail: harry.lamon@Lamonsherman.com.

LAMONT, BRUCE THOMAS, management educator; b. Pitts., Aug. 29, 1955; s. Stanley and Ruth Lamont; m. Lametria DeAlma Cliatt, Apr. 20, 2002; children: Jodeci Richards, Marcel Hodge, Kai Tameron, Case Devlin. PhD in Bus. Adminstrn., U. NC. Vis. asst. prof. Temple U., Phila., 1985—86, Tex. A&M U., College Station, 1986—88; from asst. to assoc. to full prof. Fla. State U., Tallahassee, 1989—2003, prof., chmn. Exec. com. BPS divsn. Acad. Mgmt., rsch. com. BPS divsn.; mem. editl. rev. bd. Jour. Mgmt. Mem.: So. Mgmt. Assn. (bd. govs., chair jr. faculty consortium). Office: Fla State U Coll Bus Tallahassee FL 32306-1110 Office Phone: 850-644-9846. E-mail: blamont@fsu.edu.

LAMONT, GENE, professional baseball coach, former professional baseball team manager; b. Rockford, Ill., Dec. 25, 1946; m. Melody; children: Melissa, Wade. Student, No. Ill. U., Western Ill. U. Player various minor league teams Detroit Tigers, 1965-73, 75-77; mgr. minor league team Kansas City Royals, Fort Myers, Fla., 1977-79, Jacksonville, Fla., 1979-84; coach Pitts. Pirates, 1986-91; mgr. Chgo. White Sox, 1991-95, Pittsburgh Pirates, 1995—2001; coach Houston Astros, 2001—. Named Southern League Mgr. of Yr., 1982. Office: Houston Astros PO Box 288 Houston TX 77001

LAMONT, LANSING, journalist, writer; b. N.Y.C., Mar. 13, 1930; s. Thomas Stilwell and Elinor (Miner) L.; m. Ada Jung, Sept. 18, 1954; children: Douglas Ranlet, Elisabeth Jung Lamont Wolcott, Virginia Alden Lamont Cazedessus, Thomas Stilwell II. AB, Harvard U., 1952; MS in Journalism with honors, Columbia U., 1958. Reporter Washington Star, 1958-59; Washington corr. Worcester (Mass.) Gazette, also other New Eng. papers, 1959-60; sci. reporter Washington bur. Time mag., 1961-63, polit. reporter, 1964-68, corr., dep. chief London bur., 1969-71, chief Can. corr., chief Ottawa bur., 1971-73; chief corr. UN bur. Time mag., N.Y.C., 1973-74; v.p., mng. dir. Can. Affairs The Americas Soc., 1981-91, sr. fellow, 1991-94. Author: Day of Trinity (alt. selection Lit. Guild Am.), 1965, Campus Shock, 1979, Journey to the Last Empire: The Soviet Union in Transition, 1991, Breakup: The Coming End of Canada and the Stakes for America, 1994 (Notable Books of Yr., N.Y. Times), Sand and Glitter: Exploring the Ancient Middle East, 1994-95, In the Land of Sangria and Sorrows: Spain, 1997, No Twilight About Me: A Life in Letters, 1999; co-editor Private Letters of John Masefield, 1979, Friends So Different: Essays on Canada and U.S. in the 1980's, 1989. Mem. alumni bd. dirs. Harvard U., also chmn. nominating com. for overseers; trustee Milton Acad., 1976-88, Am. Mus. Natural History, N.Y.C., Nat. Inst. for Music Theatre; pres. Am. Trust for the Brit. Libr.; pres. Century Assn. Archives Found., 1998-2004; mem. Can.-Am. Com., 1984-94, Coun. Fgn. Rels. 1985—, Carnegie Coun. on Ethics and Internat. affairs. Served to 1st lt., inf. U.S. Army, 1954-57. William Cullen Bryant fellow Met. Mus. Art, 1984-. Mem. Century Assn. (N.Y.C.), Harvard Club (N.Y.C.). Episcopalian. Office: 133 E 80th St New York NY 10021-0317 Office Phone: 212-772-6581.

LAMONT, LEE, music company executive, communications executive; b. Queens, N.Y. m. August Tagliamonte, Apr. 30, 1951; 1 child, Leslie Lamont. With Nat. Concerts & Artists Corp., N.Y.C., 1955-58; asst. Sol Hurok Concerts, N.Y.C., 1958-67; person rep. for concerts, rec. and TV Isaac Stern, N.Y.C., 1968-76; v.p. ICM Artists Ltd., N.Y.C., 1976-85; pres. ICM Artists Ltd. and ICM Artists (London) Ltd., N.Y.C., 1985-95, chmn. bd. dirs., 1995—2002, chmn. emeritus, 2002—. Former mem. adv. com. Hannover (Germany) Internat. Violin Competition. Former mem. bd. overseers Curtis Inst. Music. Mem. Ams. for the Arts, Japan Soc., Asia Soc., Am. Symphony Orch. League (bd. dirs.), Bohemian Club. Avocations: painting, sculpture. E-mail: llamont@icmtalent.com.

LAMONT, ROSETTE CLEMENTINE, language educator, journalist, translator; b. Paris; arrived in US, 1941, naturalized, 1946; d. Alexandre and Loudmilla (Lamont) L. BA, Hunter Coll., 1947; MA, Yale U., 1948, PhD, 1954. Tutor Romance langs. Queens Coll., CUNY, 1950-54, instr., 1954-61, asst. prof., 1961-64, assoc. prof., 1965-67, prof., 1967-96; mem. doctoral faculties, comparative lit., theatre, French and women's studies cert. program CUNY, 1968-96, prof. emeritus PhD program in theater, 1996—. State Dept. envoy Scholar Exch. Program, USSR, 1974; rsch. fellow, 1976; lectr. Alliance Francaise, Maison Francaise of NYU; vis. prof. Sorbonne, Paris, 1985-86; vis. prof. theatre Sarah Lawrence Coll., 1994—. Author: The Life and Works of Boris Pasternak, 1964, De Vive Voix, 1971, Ionesco, 1973, The Two Faces of Ionesco, 1978, Ionesco's Imperatives: The Politics of Culture, 1993, Women on the Verge, 1993; translator: Days and Memory, 1990, Auschwitz and After, 1995 (ALTA prize), Brazen, 1996, The Storm, 1999; also contbr. to various books; author, guest editor The Metaphysical Farce issue Collages and Bricolages, 1996-97; mem. editl. bd. Western European Stages, also contbg. editor; European corr. Theatre Week: Columbia Dictionary of Modern European Literature; fgn. corr. Stages; reviewer France-Amérique-Le Figaro. Decorated chevalier, then officier des Palmes Academiques, officier des Arts et Lettres (France); named to Hunter Coll. Hall of Fame, 1991; Guggenheim fellow, 1973-74; Rockefeller Found. humanities fellow, 1983-84. Mem. PEN, MLA, Am. Soc. Theatre Research, Internat. Brecht Soc., Drama Desk (voting mem.), Internat. Assn. Theatre Critics, Phi Beta Kappa, Sigma Tau Delta, Pi Delta Phi. Clubs: Yale. Mailing: 683 Main St PO Box 568 Falmouth MA 02541-0568 *An educator does not merely impart knowledge: he or she communicates an attitude, a way of looking at the world. So does the writer. Through each creative mind the world is born anew.*

LAMONTAGNE, DONALD A., career officer; b. Sanford, Maine; BS in Engring., Cath. U. Am., 1969; student basic meteorology tng., Tex. A&M U., 1969-70; student pilot tng., Air Tng. Command, Reese AFB, Tex., 1972-73; student, Squadron Officer Sch., 1975; student basic fighter tng., 474th Tactical Fighter Wing, Nellis AFB, Nev., 1976-77; MS in Aero. Sci., Embry-Riddle Aero. U., 1980; disting. grad., Air Command and Staff Coll., 1982; student, Nat. War Coll., 1990, U. Ill., 1993. Commd. 2d lt. USAF, 1969, advanced through grades to maj. gen., 1998; weather officer oper. location-A Hdqs. Air Weather Svc. Buckley Air NG bur., Colo., 1970-72; various positions 35th Flying Tng. Squadron, Reese AFB, 1973-76; aircraft comdr., instr. pilot and chief consolidated tng. 20th Tactical Fighter Wing, RAF Upper Heyford, Eng., 1977-81; stationed at Hdqs. Tactical Air Command, Langley AFB, Va., 1982-85; instr. pilot and ops. officer 495th Tactical Fighter Squadron, RAF Lakenheath, Eng., 1985-86; comdr. 492d Tactical Fighter Squadron, RAF Lakenheath, 1986-87; dir. assignments, dep. chief staff personnel Hdqs. USAF Europe, Ramstein Air Base, W. Germany, 1987-89; vice comdr. then comdr. 27th Tactical Fighter Wing, Cannon AFB, N.Mex., 1990-93; chief forces div., directorate force structure, resources assessment Joint Staff, Pentagon, Washington, 1993-94, spl. asst. roles and missions, directorate strategic plans and policy, 1994-96; comdg. gen. Combined Task Force Operation Provide Comfort U.S. European Command, Incirlik Air Base, Turkey, 1996, comdg. gen. Combined Task Force Operation No. Watch, 1997-98; comdr. Air Force Personnel Ctr., Randolph AFB, Tex., 1998—. Decorated Air medal with two oak leaf clusters. Office: AFPC/CC 550 C St W Ste 1 Randolph Afb TX 78150-4703

LAMONT-HAVERS, RONALD WILLIAM, retired physician, retired medical association administrator; b. Wymondham, Norfolk, Eng., Mar. 6, 1920; came to U.S., 1955, naturalized, 1964; m. Gabrielson, Oct. 16, 1965; children: Wendy, Melinda, Ian. BA, U. B.C., 1942; MD, U. Toronto, 1946; diploma in internal medicine, McGill U., 1953. Intern Vancouver (B.C., Can.) Gen. Hosp., 1946-48; resident in internal medicine Queen Mary Vets. Hosp., Montreal, Canada, 1949-51; Can. Arthritis and Rheumatism Soc. fellow Columbia Presbyterian Hosp., Coll. Physicians and Surgeons, Columbia U., N.Y.C., 1951-53; med. dir. Can. Arthritis and Rheumatism Soc., B.C. divsn., Vancouver, 1953-55, Arthritis and Rheumatism Found., N.Y.C., 1955-64; instr. in medicine Coll. Physicians and Surgeons, Columbia U., 1955-64; assoc. dir. extramural programs NIAMD, Bethesda, Md., 1964-68, dep. dir., 1972-74; assoc. dir. extramural programs NIH, Bethesda, 1968-72, acting dir., dep. dir., 1974-76, acting dir., 1975, dep. dir., 1974-76; dep. to gen. dir. for rsch. policy and adminstrn. Mass. Gen. Hosp., Boston, 1976-87, v.p. rsch. and tech. affairs, 1987-90, sr. cons. for rsch., 1990-99; dep. dir. Cutaneous Biology Rsch. Ctr. Mass. Gen. Hosp. and Harvard U., 1990—99, sr. advisor, 1999—2005; ret., 2005. Del. USSR-Arthritis Exch. Program, 1964; U.S. coord. U.S.-USSR Coop. Program in Arthritis, 1973-75. Served with M.C. Royal Can. Army, 1944-46. Recipient Superior Svc. award HEW, 1973; Spl. citation Sec. HEW, 1975. Fellow Royal Coll. Physicians (Can.); mem. Am. Coll. Rheumatology (dir. Met. Washington sect. 1964-66), N.Y. Rheumatism Assn. (pres. 1960), Arthritis Found. (dir., governing mem. 1966-80, pres. Mass. chpt. 1987-89), Alpha Omega Alpha. Office: Mass Gen Hosp 13th St Bldg 149 Charlestown MA 02129-2000 Office Phone: 617-726-7531. Personal E-mail: rwlh@att.net. Business E-Mail: rlh@chrc2.mgh.harvard.edu.

LAMOREAUX, PHILIP ELMER, geologist, hydrologist, consultant; b. Chardon, Ohio, May 12, 1920; s. Elmer I. and Gladys (Rhodes) L.; m. Ura Mae Munro, Nov. 11, 1943; children: Philip E Jr., James W., Karen L. BA, Denison U., 1943, PhD (hon.), 1972; MS, U. Ala., 1949. Registered profl. geologist, Ga., Tenn., Ind., Ariz., Fla., Pa., Mo., Ala. Geologist U.S. Geol. Survey, Tuscaloosa, Ala., 1943-45, dist. geologist Groundwater Office, 1945-57, divsn. hydrologist water resources programs, 1957-59, chief ground water br. Washington, 1959-61; state geologist, oil and gas supr. Ala. Geol. Survey, Tuscaloosa, 1961-76; pres. P.E. LaMoreaux & Assocs. Inc., Tuscaloosa, 1976-87, chmn. bd. dirs., 1987-90, sr. hydrologist, 1990—. Lectr. Am. Geol. Inst. Coll. Program, 1969-71, Am. Geophys. Union Coll. Program, 1961—, NSF, Ala. Acad. Sci. H.S. Program, 1961—, No. Engring. and Testing, Salt Lake City, 1985, Ga. State U., Fla. State U., Vanderbilt U., Denison U., Auburn U., U. of Montpellier, France, U. Christ Church, New Zealand, U. Praetoria, South Africa; hydrogeology cons. to 30 fgn. countries. Editor in chief Jour. Environ. Geology, 1982—; editor in chief: Annotated Bibliography Carbonate Rocks, vols. 1-5; contbr. articles to profl. jours. Active Nat. Drinking Water Adv. Coun. EPA, 1984-88; tech. rev. group Oak Ridge Nat. Lab., 1984-88; trustee Denison U.; adv. Boy Scouts Am. Black Warrior Coun., 1993—. Recipient Comdrs. medal C.E., 1990. Mem.: AAAS, NAS (nat. rsch. coun. geotech. bd. 1990—92, water sci. and tech. bd. 1990—97, bd. earth scis. and resources 1992—97, earth resources com. 1995—97, nat. landslide hazard mitigation strategy com. 2001—02), AIME, ASTM, NAE, Ala. C. of C. (Pres.'s adv. com., Rep. of Energy 1980), Southeastern Geol. Soc., Soil Conservation Soc. Am., Soc. Econ. Paleontologists and Mineralogists, Soc. Econ. Geologists, Nat. Ground Water Assn. (group 2020 2001—), Nat. Water Well Assn., Nat. Water Resources Assn., Nat. Speleological Soc., Nat. Rivers and Harbors Congress, Nat. Assn. Geology Tchrs., Miss. Geol. Soc., Interstate Oil Compact Commn. (vice chmn. 1963, chmn. rsch. com.), Internat. Water Resources Assn. (Karst Commn. 1961—), Internat. Assn. Hydrogeologists (pres. 1977—80, v.p. 1973—77, com. on water rsch. 1978—80, chmn. hydrology hazardous waste commn. 1983—91, mem. com. thermal and mineral waters 1994—, adv. to pres. 1995—), Geol. Soc. London, Geol. Soc. Am. (1st. chmn. hydrogeology group 1963, chmn. O.E. Meinzer award com. 1965, cons. membership S.E. sect. 1967—68, chmn. nominating com., bd. dirs., bd. trustees, publs. com., chmn.), Assn. Am. State Geologists (statistician 1966—69), Am. Inst. Profl. Geologists (chmn. com. on rels. with govtl. agencies 1967—70, bd. dirs. 1969—70, chmn. liaison com. fed. agencies 1968—70, pres.), Am. Inst. Hydrology, Am. Geophys. Union, Am. Geol. Inst. (chmn. com. on publs. 1968—70, pres. 1971—72, chmn. environ. geosci. adv. com. 1994—, mem. AGI Found., bd. trustees, Ian Campbell award 1990, William B. Heroy award 1995), Am. Assn. Petroleum Geologists (acad. liaison com., Ho. of Dels. 1970—72, com. preservation samples and cores 1998—, chmn. divsn. geosci. hydrogeology com., mem. pubs. com. 1998—), Ala. Geol. Soc., Ala. Acad. Sci. Republican. Presbyterian. Avocations: photography, stamp collecting/philately, coin collecting/numismatics, gardening. Office: PE LaMoreaux PO Box 2310 Tuscaloosa AL 35403 Office Phone: 205-758-4634. Business E-Mail: pel@dbtech.net.

LAMORIELLO, LOUIS ANTHONY, professional sports team executive; b. Providence, Oct. 21, 1942; s. Nicholas Schiano and Rose (Ventura) Lamoriello; m. Patricia A. Renaldo, Aug. 9, 1970; children: Christopher, Heidi, Timothy. BA in Math. and Econs., Providence Coll., 1963. Hockey coach Providence Coll., 1968—82, athletic dir., 1982—87; CEO, pres., gen. mgr. NJ Devils, East Rutherford, 1987—; CEO NJ Nets, 2002—04. Commr. Hockey East Assn., Providence, 1984—87; mem. hockey com. U.S. Olympics, 1984, 88; pres. Am. Hockey Coaches Assn., 1982—83. Named to Hall of Fame, Providence Coll. Athletic Dept., 1982, I.T.L.U.-Am. Hall of Fame, 1986, R.I. Hall of Fame, 1987. Mem.: Nat. Collegiate Athletic Assn. (profl. devel. com. 1984—87). Office: NJ Devils Continental Airlines Arena PO Box 504 East Rutherford NJ 07073-0504*

LAMOTTE, JANET ALLISON, retired management consultant; b. Norfolk, Va., Mar. 3, 1942; d. Charles Nelson Jr. and Geneva Elizabeth (Baird) Johnson; m. Larry LaMotte, Aug. 30, 1964 (div. Aug. 1979); children: Lisa Renee LaMotte Buchholz, Lori Louise. AA, Rose State Coll., 1982; BA, U. Ctrl. Okla., 1984; MA in Human Rels., U. Okla., 1986. Clk./typist U.S. Army, Washington, 1960, Fort Belvoir, Va., 1961, Dallas, 1961, IRS, Dallas, 1962, Richmond, Va., 1962—63, sec., 1963—64; pers. asst. State Bd. Control, Austin, Tex., 1964—65; procurement clk. FAA, Oklahoma City, 1965—66; clk./typist DLA, Alexandria, Va., 1978, IRS, Oklahoma City, 1978—79, Tinker AFB, 1979; acctg. clk., 1980—81; clk./stenographer, 1980—81; sec., 1981—82; supply specialist, 1982—87; worldwide inventory mgmt. specialist, 1987—98. Safety chmn. Kensler Elem. Sch. PTA, Wichita, 1974-75; vol. CONTACT Crisis Helpline, 1986-89. Federally Employed Women scholar, 1984. Mem.: AARP, AAUW, Tinker Mgmt. Assn. (membership, ticket monitor 1994—98, scholar 1981—85), Okla. Air Force Assn. (v.p. comm. 1995—97, exec. sec. 1996—97, Okla. Mem. of Yr. 1996, Nat. Exceptional Svc. award 1996), Air Force Assn. (v.p. pub. rels. Gerrity chpt. 1994, v.p. comm. 1995—98, Nat. medal of Merit 1995, Nat. Exceptional Svc. award 1996, Chpt. Exceptional Svc. award 1998), Nat. Assn. Ret. Fed. Employees, Am. Bus. Women's Assn. (v.p. membership downtown reflections chpt. 1992—93), Nat. Air Force Meml. (charter), Wythe County Hist. and Gen. Assn., Okla. Geneal. Soc., Nat. WWII Meml. (charter), Okla. Hist. Soc., Toastmasters (edn. v.p. 1988, pres. Tinker chpt. 1989, area gov. 1991—92, area editor K-3 Newsletter 1992—93, awards), Rural Retreat Hist. Soc., Morrow County Geneal. Soc., Pulaski County Hist. Soc., Nat. Trust for Hist. Preservation. Methodist. Avocations: history, writing, genealogy, computer, reading. Home: 9525 Ridgeview Dr Oklahoma City OK 73120-3419 Personal E-mail: jlamott99@msn.com.

LAMOUREUX, GERARD WILLIAM, container manufacturing company executive; b. Chgo., July 27, 1946; s. Donald Benjamin and Anna Rita (Williamson) L.; m. Gloria Jean Kempa, Feb. 13, 1971; children: Gerard Joseph, Jennifer Ann, Brian Gerard. BS in Mech. Engring. Tech., Purdue U., 1970; AAS in Mech. Tech., Thornton C.C., 1968. Design draftsman Whiting Corp., Harvey, Ill., 1967-69; plant engr. DeSoto, Inc., Chicago Heights, Ill., 1970-74; maintenance mgr. Panduit Corp., Tinley Park, Ill., 1974-75; plant engr., plant supt. Container Corp. Am., Dolton, Ill., 1975-79, plant engr. Anderson, Ind., 1979-84, regional staff engr. Carol Stream, Ill., 1984-86; project engr. Jefferson Smurfit Corp. and Container Corp. Am., Carol Stream, 1986-89, sr. staff engr., 1989-91, mgr. mfg. engring. Mo., 1991-95, mgr. engring. and environment Chesterfield, Mo., 1995-98; corp. mgr. environ. svcs. Smurfit Stone Container Corp., Mo., 1998—2001, dir. environ. svcs. Clayton, Mo., 2001—. Mem. mech. adv. bd. Thornton C.C., South Holland, Ill., 1975-79; mem. South Holland United Fund-Crusade of Mercy Com., 1976-78; bd. dirs. Madison County Jr. Achievement, 1980-83. Mem. Technical Assn. Pulp Paper Industry (exec. com. Chgo. sect. 1987—), Nat. Assn. for Environ. Mgmt., Am. Inst. Plant Engrs., Madison County Mgmt. Club (v.p. 1984), Fibre Box Assn. (chmn. environ. com. 1999—), Purdue U. Alumni Assn, Nat. Assn. for Environ. Mgmt. Roman Catholic. Home: 16746 Chesterfield Farms Dr Chesterfield MO 63005-1656 Office: Smurfit Stone Container Corp 8182 Maryland Ave Clayton MO 63105 Office Phone: 314-746-1241. Business E-Mail: glamoureux@smurfit.com.

LAMP, BENSON J., tractor company executive; b. Cardington, Ohio, Oct. 7, 1925; m. Martha Jane Motz, Aug. 21, 1948; children: Elaine, Marlene, Linda, David. BS in Agr. and B in Agrl. Engring., Ohio State U., 1949, MS in Agrl. Engring., 1952; PhD in Agrl. Engring., Mich. State U., 1960. Registered profl. engr., Ohio. Prof. agrl. engring. Ohio State U., Columbus, 1949-61, 87-91, prof. emeritus, 1991—; product mgr. Massey Ferguson Ltd., Toronto, Can., 1961-66; product planning mgr. Ford Tractor Ops. div. Ford Motor Co., Troy, Mich., 1966-71, mktg. mgr., 1971-76, bus. planning mgr., 1978-87; v.p. mktg. and devel. Ford Aerospace div. Ford Motor Co., Dearborn, Mich., 1976-78. Author: Corn Harvesting, 1962. Served to 2d lt. USAF, 1943-45. Fellow Am. Soc. Agrl. Engrs. (pres. 1985-86, Gold medal 1993); mem. Nat. Acad. Engring., Country Club at Muirfield Village (Dublin, Ohio). Avocations: golf, tennis, bridge. Office: BJM Company Inc 6128 Inverurie Dr E Dublin OH 43017-9472 Office Phone: 614-761-9745. E-mail: blamp2@aol.com.

LAMPARD-NACCARI, CATHERINE ANN, lawyer; b. New Orleans, Feb. 9, 1951; d. Robert Emmett and Catherine Rita (Hand) L.; m. Bruce E. Naccari, Dec. 8, 1984; children: Paolo Atilio, Paz Catherine. BA in Anthropology, Newcomb Coll. of Tulane U., 1971, U. of Ams., Cholula, Puebla, Mex., 1972; postgrad., U. Rafael Landivar, Guatemala City, Guatemala, 1979, Escuela Libre de Derecho, Mexico City, 1979; JD, Loyola U., New Orleans, 1982. Bar: La. 1982. Grants planning officer Office Health Svcs.-Environ. Quality La. Dept. Health and Human Resources, New Orleans, 1979-83; with Hand & Lampard, Metairie, La., 1982—97; adj. prof. clin. law Tulane Immigration Law Clin., 1986—2002. Law clk. 24th Jud. Dist. Ct., Gretna, La., 1983; dir., staff atty. Ecumenical Immigration Svcs., Inc., New Orleans, 1983-89; spkr. in field Recipient Pro Bono award La. Bar Assn., 1986, 1996, svc. award Latin Am. Apostolate of Archdiocese of New Orleans, 1989; Loyola Law Clinic award, 1982. Mem. ABA, Internat. Bar Assn., Am. Immigration Lawyers Assn. (treas. La. chpt. 1989-92), Rotary Democrat. Roman Catholic. Avocations: reading, film, photography, watercolor. Office: 210 Baronne St Ste 1800 New Orleans LA 70112-5732 Office Phone: 504-525-4361. Business E-Mail: lampard@nola-law.com.

LAMPASSO, JUDITH DORISCA, orthodontist, researcher; d. Jean Lamartine and Jeanette Marie Dorisca; m. James Gerald Lampasso, Nov. 8, 1988; children: Christian James, Cullen Scot. DDS, PhD, U. Buffalo, 2001. Asst. prof. U. Buffalo, 2002—. Rsch. grantee, NIH, 2003—05, Orthodontic Faculty Devel. fellow, 2004. Mem.: Am. Assn. Orthodontist (assoc.). Office: Univ Buffalo 3435 Main St 140 Squire Hall Buffalo NY 14214 Office Phone: 716-829-2845. Office Fax: 716-829-2572. E-mail: lampasso@acsu.buffalo.edu.

LAMPE, KRISTEN ANNE, mathematics professor; d. James Peter and Patricia Ann Toft; m. Peter Hartnell Lampe, July 27, 1996; children: Kaitlyn, Megan. BA, U. Dayton, 1993; MA, Washington U., St. Louis, 1995, PhD, 1999. Asst. prof. U. Wis., Whitewater, 1999—2000, Carroll Coll., Waukesha, 2000—05, assoc. prof., 2005—. Mem.: Math. Assn. Am. (Wis. sect. state contest coord. 2003—). Office: Carroll Coll 100 N East Ave Waukesha WI 53186

LAMPEN, RICHARD JAY, lawyer, investment banker; b. New Brunswick, N.J., Nov. 12, 1953; s. J. Oliver and Miriam (Walsh) L.; m. Susan Matson, June 8, 1975; children: Katharine, Caroline. BA, Johns Hopkins U., 1975; JD, Columbia U., 1978. Bar: Fla. 1978, U.S. Dist. Ct. (so. dist.) Fla. 1978. From assoc. to ptnr. Steel Hector & Davis, Miami, Fla., 1978-86, co-chmn. corp. dept., 1992-95; mng. dir. Salomon Bros. Inc., N.Y.C., 1986-92; exec. v.p., gen. counsel New Valley Corp., Miami, Fla., 1995—; exec. v.p. Vector Group Ltd., 1996—. Bd. dirs. New Valley Corp., CDSI Holdings Inc., Ladenburg Thalmann Fin. Svcs. Inc., Douglas Elliman Realty, LLC. Pres. Miami Children's Mus.; chmn. Ransom-Everglades Sch. Mem. Fla. Bar Assn. (chmn. securities law com. 1985-86), City Club, Riviera Club. Office: New Valley Corp 100 SE 2nd St Fl 32 Miami FL 33131-2158 Office Phone: 305-579-8000. E-mail: rlampen@vectorgroupltd.com.

LAMPERT, EDWARD, investment company executive; b. Roslyn, NY, July 19, 1962; s. Floyd and Dolores Lampert; m. Kinga Lampert; 2 children. BS in econ., Yale U., 1984. With Goldman Sachs Group Inc., 1984—88; founder, chmn. ESL Investments, Inc., Greenwich, Conn., 1988—. Bd. mem. Auto-Nation, Inc., AutoZone, Inc., 1999—; chmn. bd. Kmart Holding Corp., Troy, Mich., 2003—; corp. chmn. Sears Holdings Corp. Mem.: Phi Beta Kappa. Achievements include ranked by Forbes as one of the Worlds Richest People, 2004. Office: ESL Investments Inc 200 Greenwich Ave Greenwich CT 06830 Office Phone: 203-861-4600.*

LAMPERT, ELEANOR VERNA, retired human resources specialist; b. Porterville, Calif., Mar. 23; d. Ernest Samuel and Violet Edna (Watkins) Wilson; m. Robert Mathew Lampert, Aug. 23, 1935; children: Sally Lu Winton, Lary Lampert, Carol R. John. Student in bus. fin., Porterville Jr. Coll., 1977-78; grad., Anthony Real Estate Sch., 1971; student, Laguna Sch. of Art., 1972, U. Calif., Santa Cruz, 1981. Bookkeeper Porterville (Calif.) Hos., 1956-71; real estate sales staff Ray Realty, Porterville, 1973; sec. Employment Devel. Dept. State of Calif., Porterville, 1973-83; orientation and tng specialist CETA employees, 1976-80; ret. sec. Employer Adv. Group, 1973-80, 81—. Author: Black Bloomers and Han-Ga-Ber, 1986. Mem. U.S. Senatorial Business Adv. Bd., 1981-84, Rep. Nat. congl. Com., 1982-88, Sierra View Hosp. Vol. League, 1988-89 (pres.); charter mem. Presdl. Republican Task Force, 1981—, Republican National Committee; vol. Calif Hosp. Assn., 1983-89, Calif. Spl. Olympics Spirit Team, Sonora Cmty. Hospital Oak Plus League, Special Olympics Northern Calif. partner. Recipient Merit Cert., Gov. Pat Brown, State of Calif., 1968. Mem. Lindsay Olive Growers, Sunkist Orange Growers, Am. Kennel Club, Internat. Assn. Personnel in Employment Security, Calif. State Employes Assn. (emeritus Nat. Wildlife Fedn., NRA, Friends of Porterville Library, Heritage Found., DAR (Kaweah chpt. rec. sec. 1988—), Internat. Platform Assn., Dist. Fedn. Women's Clubs (recording sec. Calif. chpt. 1988—), Ky. Hist. Soc., Women's Club of Calif. (pres. Porterville chpt. 1988-89, dist. rec. sec. 1987-89), Mo.

Rep. Women of Taney County, Internat. Sporting and Leisure Club. Ladies Aux, VFW (No. 5168 Forsyth,Mo.), Ozark Walkers League, Women of the Moose Lodge, Humane Soc. U.S. Republican.

LAMPERT, JAMES B., lawyer; b. Montpelier, Vt., June 26, 1938; s. James Benjamin Lampert and Margery Frances (Mitchell) Lampert-Dudley; m. Mary Elizabeth Shugrue; children: Nicholas, Michael, Stephen. BSME, MIT, 1961; JD magna cum laude, Harvard U., 1964. Bar: Mass. 1964, U.S. Dist. Ct. Mass., U.S. Ct. Appeals (1st cir.) 1967, U.S. Patent and Trademark Office 1967, U.S. Ct. Appeals (fed. cir.) 1985. Sr. ptnr. Fish & Richardson, Boston, 1964-85; adj. prof. law Boston U., 1972-87; sr. ptnr. Hale and Dorr, Boston, 1985—2004; ptnr., chmn. Intellectual Property dept., mem. Litigation dept. & Corp. dept. Wilmer Cutler Pickering Hale & Dorr, Boston, 2004—. Capt. U.S. Army Corps of Engineers, 1964-66. Named a Mass. Super Lawyer, Boston Mag., 2004. Mem. Mass Bar Assn., Boston Patent Law Assn., Tau Beta Pi, Pi Tau Sigma, Sigma Xi. Avocations: sailing, skiing, swimming. Home: 148 Washington St Duxbury MA 02332-4523 Office: Wilmer Cutler Pickering Hale & Dorr 60 State St Boston MA 02109-1816 Office Phone: 617-526-6456. Office Fax: 617-526-5000. Business E-Mail: james.lampert@wilmerhale.com.

LAMPERT, S. HENRY, retired dentist; b. Bklyn., Mar. 10, 1929; s. Joseph and Sadie (Bass) L.; m. Jacqueline Adler, Mar. 27, 1955; children: Karen Ann, Beth Robin, Judith Ellen. BA, U. Ill., 1950; DDS, NYU, 1954. Intern in dentistry Mt. Sinai Hosp., N.Y.C., 1954-55; gen. practice dentistry Essex Junction, Vt., 1957-95; ret., 1995. Dir. Temporo Mandibular Joint Program, Med. Ctr. Hosp. Vt., Burlington, 1970-76, attending staff 1957-92, peer rev. com., 1978-92; mem. staff Fanny Allen Hosp., Winooski, Vt., 1961-89; assoc. prof. Sch. Allied Health Scis., U. Vt., Burlington, 1963-73, clin. instr. Coll. Medicine, 1974-75, clin. instr. dept. oral surgery, 1986-96. Sec., Vt. Bd. Dental Examiners, 1973-76, pres., 1976-77; instr. photography Church St. Ctr. for Cmty. Edn., U. Vt., until 1998; mem. N.E. Regional Bd. Dental Examiners, 1973-84, 96-98, cons. and examiner; CPR instr. Vt. Heart Assn., 1977-2000; photographer Essex (Vt.) Reporter, 1997—02; instr. photography Essex Town Parks and Recreation Dept., 1999—; lectr. in field Contbr. articles to profl. jours., photographs pub. in numerous mags. and jours. Capt. AUS, 1955-57, USAR, 1957-60; col. Vt. State Guard, 2005. Fellow Internat. Coll. Dentists; mem. ADA (standard setting com. of coun. on nat. bd. exams. 1978-81), Champlain Valley (pres. 1961-62), Acad. Operative Dentistry, Vt. Dental Soc., Masons, Rotary, Alpha Omega. Jewish (bd. govs. synagogue 1967-70, 72-73, chmn. bd. edn.). Home: PO Box 667 Essex Junction VT 05453-0667 Personal E-mail: jackieejvt@aol.com.

LAMPERTI, JOHN WILLIAMS, mathematician, educator; b. Montclair, N.J., Dec. 20, 1932; s. Frank A. and Louise (Williams) L.; m. Claudia Jane McKay, Aug. 17, 1957; children— Matthew, Steven, Aaron, Noelle. BS, Haverford Coll., 1953; PhD, Calif. Inst. Tech., 1957. Instr., then asst. prof. math. Stanford (Calif.) U., 1957-62; rsch. assoc. Rockefeller Inst., 1962-63; faculty Dartmouth Coll., Hanover, N.H., 1963-98, prof. math., 1968-98, prof. emeritus, 1998—. Sci. exch. visitor to USSR, 1970; vis. prof. U. Aarhus, Denmark, 1972-73, Nicaraguan Nat. U., 1990; cons. Am. Friends Svc. Com., 1980, 85, 91. Author: Probability: A Survey of the Mathematical Theory, 1966, 2d edit., 1996, Stochastic Processes: A survey of the Mathematical Theory, 1977, What Are We Afraid Of? An Assessment of the "Communist Threat" in Central America, 1988. Fellow Inst. Math. Stats.; mem. ACLU, War Resisters League, Peace Action, Amnesty Internat., Fedn. Am. Scientists. Home: Upper Loveland Rd Norwich VT 05055 Office: Dartmouth Coll Dept Math Hanover NH 03755 Office Phone: 603-646-2866. Business E-Mail: j.lamperti@dartmouth.edu.

LAMPHERE, LEIGH ANN, elementary school educator, music educator; b. Montpelier, Vt., Oct. 28, 1960; d. Robert Ivan Lamphere and Marjorie Louise Pillsbury; m. Brian Charles Allaire, July 7, 1990; children: Phillip Lamphere Allaire, Nathan Lamphere Allaire. B of Music Edn., SUNY, Potsdam, 1982; MEd, St. Michaels Coll., 1994. Tchr. music Union Elem. Sch., Montpelier, Vt., 1982—84, Morristown Elem. Sch., Morrisville, 1985—. Instr. Morrisville Ski Program, Stowe, 2001—; bd. dirs. Lamoille County Mental Health, Morrisville. Mem.: NEA, Vt. Music Educators Assn., Music Educators Nat. Conf. Democrat. Avocations: theater, reading, bell choir. Home: 88 Red Pine Estate Morrisville VT 05661 Office: Morristown Elem Sch 548 Park St Morrisville VT 05661

LAMPINEN, JOHN A., newspaper editor; b. Waukegan, Ill., Nov. 26, 1951; s. Walter Valentine and Patricia Mae Irene (Pruess) L.; m. Belinda Walter, Oct. 20, 1973; children: Amanda Michelle, Heidi Elizabeth. BS in Comm., U. Ill., 1973. Staff writer Paddock Cir. Newspapers, Libertyville, Ill., 1973-75; regional editor The Jour., New Ulm, Minn., 1975-76; various positions Daily Herald, Arlington Heights, Ill., 1976-90, asst. v.p., mng. editor, 1990—97, asst. v.p., exec. editor, 1997—99, v.p., exec. editor, 1999—2001, sr. v.p., editor, 2001—. Adj. prof. Medill Sch. Journalism, Northwestern U., Evanston, Ill., 1995-98. Mem. Assoc. Press Mng. Editors, Soc. Profl. Journalists, Am. Soc. Newspaper Editors. Avocations: baseball, long-distance running, coaching girls softball, sports memorabilia. Office: Daily Herald 155 E Algonquin Rd Arlington Heights IL 60005-4617

LAMPING, KATHRYN G., medical educator, medical researcher; BS in Biology, U. Ill., 1976; MS in Pharmacology, Med. Coll. Wis., 1982, PhD in Pharmacology, 1983. Postdoctoral rsch. fellow Dept. Internal Medicine, U. Iowa, Iowa City, 1983-86, asst. rsch. scientist, 1986-89, adj. asst. prof., 1989-95, asst. prof., 1995—. Contbr. articles to profl. jours. Mem. Am. Heart Assn. (Established Investigator award 1995), Am. Physiol. Soc., Microcirculatory Soc. Office: U Iowa Ctr on Agin 2159 Westlawn S Iowa City IA 52242-1100

LAMPL, PEGGY ANN, public information officer; b. N.Y.C., Dec. 12, 1930; d. Joseph and Alice L. BA, Bennington Coll., 1952. Dir. program devel. dept. mental health AMA, Chgo., 1962-66; spl. asst. NIMH, HEW, Washington, 1967-69; public relations dir. LWV, Washington, 1969—73, exec. dir., 1973—78; dep. asst. Sec. of State for congressional relations Dept. State, Washington, 1978-81; dep. dir. Iris Systems Devel., 1982-83; exec. dir. Children's Def. Fund, Washington, 1984-89, LWV, Washington, 1989—90; project mgr. Crimes of War, W.W. Norton, 1999; founder Project Vote Smart, Washington, 1993—; bd. dirs. Crimes of War Project, Washington, 1998—. Home: 2500 Q St NW Washington DC 20007-4373

LAMPMAN, GARY MARSHALL, chemistry educator; b. Southgate, Calif., Oct. 8, 1937; s. Carlton Webster and Ruth Nina (Barrett) L.; m. Marian Shulze, Sept. 17, 1971; children: Elizabeth, Karl. BS, UCLA, 1955-59; postgrad., U. Wash., 1959-62, PhD, 1964; postgrad., Yale U., 1962-64. Asst. prof. chemistry We. Wash. U., Bellingham, 1964-68, assoc. prof., 1968-73, prof., 1973—. Hon. research fellow U. Coll. U. London, 1978-79, 81, 83, 86-87. Author: Introduction to Spectroscopy, 2000, Organic Techniques, 1998, 3d edit., 1999; contbr. articles to profl. jours. Recipient Outstanding Tchr. award We. Wash. U., 1976. Mem. Am. Chem. Soc., Sigma Xi. (pres. 1977-78). Episcopalian. Avocations: hiking, travel, swimming. Office: Western Wash U Dept Chemistry Bellingham WA 98225

LAMPMAN, RICHARD H. (DICK LAMPMAN), computer company executive; BSEE, MSEE, Carnegie Mellon U. With Hewlett-Packard, 1971—, with HP labs., 1981—86, dir. measurement sys. lab., 1986—88, dir. computer sys. lab., 1988—92, dir. worldwide Computer Rsch. Ctr., 1992—99, dir. HP Labs. Palo Alto, Calif., 1999—, sr. v.p. research, 2001—. Mem. adv. bd. Carnegie Inst. Tech., Internet Soc. Adv. Coun., Corp. Exec. bd.; represent HP on the adv. bd. Bay Area Sci. Infrastructure Consortium, Computer Systems Policy Project CTO. Mem.: IEEE (sr.), Assn. Computing Machinery, Computing Rsch. Assn., Silicon Valley Computer Sci. Rsch. Dirs., Math. Scis. Rsch. Inst. (mem. adv. bd.), Internet Soc. (mem. adv. coun.). Office: Hewlett-Packard Co 3000 Hanover St Palo Alto CA 94304

LAMPORT, ANTHONY MATTHEW, venture capitalist; b. N.Y.C., Dec. 8, 1935; s. Harold and Golden (Siwek) L.; m. Cynthia Hullinger, 1961; children: Sarah, Aaron. BA, Harvard U., 1957, MBA, 1959. With Drexel Burnham Lambert, N.Y.C., 1959-90; pres. Lambda Fund, Mgmt., N.Y.C., 1990—. Bd. dirs. Super Shuttle Internat., Prophesy Software, Sr. Bridge Family Cos., Paladin, Inc. Trustee Found. for Investor Edn., N.Y.C., 1976—. Office: Lambda Fund Mgmt Inc 147 E 48th St New York NY 10017 Office Phone: 212-230-9835.

LAMPRECHT, ELIZABETH ANN, mathematics professor; b. Buffalo, Sept. 7, 1966; d. James Alois and Christine Ann Lamprecht; m. James Joseph Carson, Aug. 13, 1988; children: Christopher Michael Lamprecht-Carson, Alexandra Maria Lamprecht-Carson, Gregory James Lamprecht-Carson, Daniel Peter Lamprecht-Carson, Andrew Stephen Lamprecht-Carson, Philip Anthony Lamprecht-Carson. BS magna cum laude, SUNY, Buffalo, 1988; MA, SUNY, Binghamton, 1990, PhD, 1994. Rsch. project asst. GE, Johnson City, NY, 1991—92; assoc. prof., chair math. dept. Adrian Coll., Mich., 1995—. Vis. asst. prof. SUNY, Oswego, 1993—95. Contbr. text reviews Statistics Teacher Network. Recipient Tchg. award, Mortar Bd. Soc., 1999. Mem.: Am. Statis. Assn., Assn. Women Math., Math. Assn. Am. Avocations: piano, reading, cooking. Office: Adrian Coll 110 South Madison St Adrian MI 49221 Office Phone: 517-264-3936. Personal E-mail: lampcar@aol.com. Business E-Mail: elamprecht@adrian.edu.

LAMPSON, BUTLER WRIGHT, computer scientist; b. Washington, Dec. 23, 1943; s. Edward Tudor and Mary Caroline (Wright) L.; m. Lois Helen Alterman, Sept. 23, 1967; children: Michael Alterman, David Wright AB, Harvard U., 1964; PhD, U. Calif.-Berkeley, 1967; D.Sc. (hon.), Eidgenossiche Technische Hochschule, Zurich, 1986; D in Info. (hon.), U. Bologna, 1996. Asst. prof. U. Calif.-Berkeley, 1967-70, assoc. prof., 1970-71; dir. system devel. Berkeley Computer Corp., 1969-71; prin. scientist Xerox Research Ctr., Palo Alto, Calif., 1971-75, sr. research fellow, 1975-84; sr. cons. engr. Digital Equipment Corp., Palo Alto, 1984-86, corp. cons. engr., 1986-93, sr. corp. cons. engr., 1993-95; arch. Microsoft Corp., Cambridge, Mass., 1995—, disting. engr., 2000—. Adj. prof. elec. engring. and computer sci. MIT, 1987—. Contbr. articles to profl. jours. Patentee in field Recipient IEEE Computer Pioneer award, 1996, Nat. Computer Sys. Security award NIST/NSA, 1998, von Neumann medal IEEE, 2001, Charles Stark Draper prize NAE 2004. Fellow AAAS, Assn. Computing Machinery (Software System award 1984, A.M. Turing award 1992); mem. NAE, Nat. Acad. Scis. Office Phone: 425-703-5925. E-mail: blampson@microsoft.com.

LAMPSON, NICHOLAS V., former congressman; b. Beaumont, Tex., Feb. 14, 1945; m. Susan Lampson; children: Hillary, Stephanie. BA, Lamar U., 1968, MA, 1974. Biology tchr. Beaumont Pub. Schs.; tax assessor-collector Jefferson County, 1977—95; mem. U.S. Congress from 9th Tex. dist., 1997—2005, mem. sci., transp. and infrastructure coms., chmn., founder congl. missing and exploited children's caucus. Del. White Ho. Conf. Aging, 1995; dir. Area Agy. Aging; active Am. Heart Assn., Land Manor, Young Men's Bus. Assn.; chair Bishop's Faith Appeal St. Jude Cath. Ch., 1995. Named Outstanding Young Man of Beaumont Tex. Jaycees, 1978. Democrat.

LAMPTON, DUNN O., prosecutor; b. Oskya, Miss. married; 2 children. AA, SW Miss. Jr. Coll.; BE, U. Miss., JD, 1975. Bar: Miss. 1975. Ptnr. Phillips, Regan & Lampton, 1976—80; dist. atty. 14th Cir. Ct. Dist., 1976—2001; U.S. atty. so. dist. Miss. U.S. Dept. Justice, Jackson, 2001—. Staff judge adv. to col. USNG, 1980—. Office: So Dist Miss 188 E Capital St Ste 500 Jackson MS 39201

LAMSON, ROBERT WOODROW, retired school system administrator; b. LA, Dec. 28, 1917; s. Ernest K. and Mabel (Mahoney) L.; m. Jeannette Juett, July 22, 1949; children: Robert Woodrow Jr., Nancy Virginia, Kathleen Patricia. BA, Occidental Coll., 1940; MA, U. So. Calif., 1955. Cert. tchr., prin., supt., Calif. Tchr. El Monte (Calif.) Sch. Dist., 1940-43, L.A. City Sch. Dist., 1945—78, prin., 1949-55, supr., 1955-57, adminstrv. asst., 1957-59, area supt., 1959-78; ret., 1978; agt. Keilholtz Realtors, La Canada, Calif. Instr. various colls. and univs. so. Calif.; co-founder, v.p. U.S. Acad. Decathlon, Cerritos, Calif., 1981-86 Bd. dirs. 10th Dist. PTA, LA, 1965-70; chmn. Scout-O-Rama, Gt. Western coun. Boy Scouts Am., 1980. Lt. comdr. USNR, 1943-46, mem. Res. ret. Mem. Am. Assn. Sch. Adminstrs., Assn. Adminstrs. L.A., Alumni Occidental Coll. in Edn. (a founder, past pres., bd. dirs.), Town Hall, Nat. PTA (hon. life), Calif. PTA (hon. life, bd. dirs. 1978-80), 31st Dist. PTA (hon. life, bd. dirs. 1965-78, auditorium named in his honor 1978), Phi Beta Kappa, Alpha Tau Omega. Republican. Avocations: gardening, reading. Home: 4911 Vineta Ave La Canada Flintridge CA 91011-2624 Office: Richard Keilholtz Realtors 727 Foothill Blvd La Canada Flintridge CA 91011-3405

LAMSTEIN, SARAH ZAVELLE, writer; b. Boston, July 28, 1943; d. Milton Selig and Lenore Marjorie Marwil; m. Joel Harvey Lamstein, June 25, 1966; children: Josh, Emily, Abby. BA, U. Mich., Ann Arbor, 1965, MA, 1966; MLS, Simmons Coll., Boston, 1985; MFA, Vt. Coll., Montpelier, 2003. Tchr. English Lynbrook Jr. H.S., NY, 1966—77, Arlington H.S., Mass., 1967—69; libr. Milton Acad., 1985—88, Roxbury Latin Sch., Boston, 1988—92; libr. cons. Mather Sch., 1992—97; puppeteer, 1975—; writer children's books, 1997—. Poet in residence Hawthorne Youth Cmty. Ctr., Boston, 1987—88. Author: Annie's Shabbat, 1997 (Top Ten Religion Books Youth, Booklist, 1998), From the Mango Tree, 1997, I Like Your Buttons!, 1999 (Best Children's Books of Yr., Bank St. Coll. of Edn., 2000), Hunger Moon, 2004. Founder Newton Peace Vigil, Mass., 1991; bd. mem. Temple Emanuel Social Action Com., Newton, 1980—2000; bd. dirs. Puppet Showplace Theatre, Brookline, Mass., 2004—. Mem.: Soc. of Children's Book Writers and Illustrators, Puppeteers of Am., Boston Area Guild of Puppetry (bd. mem. 1975—, sec. 1975—). Democrat. Jewish. Avocations: reading, gardening, painting furniture, walking.

LAMSTER, IRA BARRY, academic administrator; b. N.Y.C., Mar. 6, 1950; s. Nathan and Mollie (Garber) L.; m. Gail Maxine Marcovitz, Aug. 28, 1971; children: Rachel Amy, Stephanie Anne. BA, CUNY, 1971; SM, U. Chgo., 1972; DDS, SUNY, Stony Brook, 1977; M.M.Sc., Harvard U., 1980; grad. splty. training in periodontology and oral medicine, Harvard U. Sch. Dental Medicine. Diplomate Am. Bd. Periodontology, Am. Bd. Oral Medicine. Assoc. prof., dir. rsch. ctr. Coll. Dental Medicine Fairleigh Dickinson U., Hackensack, N.J., 1980-88; dir. divsn. periodontics Columbia U. Sch. Dental and Oral Surgery, NYC, 1988—98, vice dean, 1998—2001, dean, 2001—. Cons. VA, various oral health care companies. Inventor in field; contbr. chpts. to books and articles to profl. jours. Recipient Young Investigator Rsch. award Pub. Health Svc., 1982-85, Individual Rsch. award 1985-89, 2002-, prin. Investigator Program Project 1991-97. Fellow: Am. Coll. Dentists. Mem.: AAAS, ADA, Am. Acad. Periodontology (editorial bd.), Am. Assn. Dental Rsch., Am. Acad. Oral Medicine, N.Y. Acad. Scis., Northeastern Soc. Periodontists (contbg. editor). Avocations: golf, tennis, reading. Office: Columbia U Sch Dental and Oral Surgery Dean's Office Box 20 630 W 168th St New York NY 10032

LAMY, M. REBECCA (MARY REBECCA LAMY), consultant, land developer, government official; b. Ft. Bragg, N.C., Nov. 21, 1929; d. Charles Joseph and Sarah Esther (Koonce) Lamy. BA, U. N.C., Greensboro, 1952. Procurement analyst Air Force Mil. Interdept. Purchase Request Mgmt. Office, Washington, 1958-60, procurement and fiscal officer, 1960-68; budget analyst Naval Air Sys. Command, Washington, 1968-69, indsl. specialist, 1969-71, Armament Devel. and Test Ctr., Eglin AFB, Fla., 1971-74, Def. Logistics Agy., Alexandria, Va., 1974-81; logistics mgmt. specialist Strategic Sys. Project Office, Dept. Navy, Washington, 1981-82; procurement analyst Hdqrs. Dept. Army, Washington, 1982-85. Emeritus mem. Onslow Mus. Found. Bd., Richlands, NC, Onslow Meml. Hosp. Aux., Jacksonville, NC, 1985—91. Recipient Outstanding Performance awards USAF, 1956, 65, 72, 73, Quality award Def. Logistics Agy., 1979, Outstanding Performance award, 1978, 79, Exceptional Svc. award, 1983, 84, 85, Comdr.'s award Hdqrs. Dept. Army, 1985, others. Mem. U. N.C. at Greensboro Alumni Assn. Harriet Elliott Soc., Unbroken Band.

LAN, DONALD PAUL, JR., lawyer; b. Orange, N.J., July 19, 1952; s. Donald Paul and Hannah Paula (Resnik) L.; m. Deborah Sue Rothenberg, Aug. 20, 1978; children: Jennifer Robyn, Adam Christopher, Eric Jacob. BS in Acctg., U. R.I., 1974; JD, Rutger U., 1977; LLM in Taxation, Georgetown U., 1982. Bar: N.J. 1977, D.C. 1978, Tex. 1983, U.S. Dist. Ct. N.J. 1977, U.S. Dist. Ct. (no., so., we. and ea. dists.) Tex. 1983, U.S. Ct. Claims 1978, U.S. Tax Ct. 1977, U.S. Ct. Appeals (fed. cir.) 1978, U.S. Ct. Appeals (5th cir.) 1984, U.S. Ct. Appeals (8th cir.) 1997. Clk. to spl. trial judge U.S. Tax Ct., Washington, 1977-78; trial atty. tax div. U.S. Dept. Justice, Washington, 1978-82; assoc., ptnr. Shank, Irwin & Conant, Dallas, 1982-87; ptnr. Finley, Kumble Wagner et al, Dallas, 1987, Strasburger & Price, Dallas, 1988-96; shareholder Kroney, Mincey, Inc., Dallas, 1996—. Adj. prof. law So. Meth. U., 1990—; lectr. on tax controversy and litigation, 1983—. Named Outstanding Atty. tax div. U.S. Dept. Justice, 1980. Fellow: Am. Coll. Trust and Estate Counsel; mem.: ABA (ct. procedures com. tax sect. 1987—, stds. in tax practice com. tax sect. 1992—, chmn. 2001—03), D.C. Bar Assn., Dallas Bar Assn., State Bar Tex. (chmn. ct. procedures com. tax sect. 1995—97, coun. mem. 1997—2000), Beta Gamma Sigma, Beta Alpha Psi, Phi Kappa Phi. Jewish. Avocation: all sports. Office: Kroney Mincey 12221 Merit Dr Ste 1210 Dallas TX 75251-2244 Office Phone: 972-386-8500. Business E-Mail: dlan@ksmdallas.com.

LAN, XUEKUI, engineer; arrived in US, 1991; BS, Xi'an (China) Jiaotong U., 1983, MS, 1986; PhD, Auburn U., 1995. Tchg. asst. Xi'an Jiaotong U., 1986-88, lectr., 1988-91; R&D engr. R&D Ctr. Beloit Corp., Rockton, Ill., 1995-98, product engr. R&D Ctr., 1998-2000; sr. project engr. ICEM CFD Engring., Livonia, Mich., 2000—. Contbr. articles to profl. jours. Mem.: Soc. Automotive Engrs., ASME (assoc.). Achievements include inventor of method and apparatus for coating a traveling paper web. Home: 5181 Allison Dr Troy MI 48085-3469

LANAHAN, DANIEL JOSEPH, lawyer; b. Bklyn., Jan. 13, 1940; Attended, L.I. U., Temple U.; JD, San Francisco Law Sch., 1969. Bar: Calif. 1970. Dir. Ropers, Majeski, Kohn & Bentley, P.C., Santa Rosa, Calif., 1970-96; mng. ptnr. Lanahan & Reilley L.L.P., Santa Rosa, 1997—. Mem. State Bar Calif., Sonoma County Bar Assn., Internat. Assn. Def. Counsel, Assn. Def. Counsel. Office: Lanahan & Reilley LLP 3558 Round Barn Blvd Ste 300 Santa Rosa CA 95403-0992 E-mail: dlanahan@lanahan.com.

LANAM, LINDA LEE, lawyer; b. Ft. Lauderdale, Fla., Nov. 21, 1948; d. Carl Edward and Evelyn (Bolton) L. BS, Ind. U., 1970, JD, 1975. Bar: Ind. 1975, Pa. 1979, U.S. Dist. Ct. (no. and so. dists.) Ind. 1975, U.S. Supreme Ct. 1982, Va. 1990. Atty., asst. counsel Lincoln Nat. Life Ins. Co., Ft. Wayne, Ind., 1975-76, 76-78; atty., mng. atty. Ins. Co. of N.Am., Phila., 1978-79, 80-81; legis. liaison Pa. Ins. Dept., Harrisburg, 1981-82, dep. ins. commr., 1982-84; exec. dir., Washington rep. Blue Cross and Blue Shield Assn., Washington, 1984-86; v.p. and sr. counsel Union Fidelity Life Ins. Co., Am. Patriot Health Ins. Co., etc., Trevose, Pa., 1986-89; v.p., gen. counsel, corp. sec. The Life Ins. Co. Va., Richmond, 1989-97, sr. v.p., gen. counsel, corp. sec., 1997-98, also bd. dirs.; v.p., dep. gen. counsel Am. Coun. Life Insurers, Washington, 1999—. Chmn. adv. com. health care legis. Nat. Assn. Ins. Commrs., 1985-87, chmn. long term care, 1986-87, mem. tech. resource com. on cost disclosure and genetic testing, 1993-98; mem. tech. adv. com. Health Ins. Assn. Am., 1986-89; mem. legis. com. Am. Coun. Life Ins., 1994-96, mem. market conduct com., 1997-98. Contbr. articles to profl. jours. Pres. Phila. Women's Network, 1980—81; chmn. city housing code bd. appeals Harrisburg, 1985—86; bd. dirs. Shakespeare Theatre Guild, 2001—. Mem. ABA, Richmond Bar Assn. Republican. Presbyterian.

LANCASTER, CARROLL TOWNES, JR., manufacturing executive; b. Waco, Tex., Mar. 14, 1929; s. Carroll T. and Beatrice L.; m. Catherine Virginia Frommel, May 29, 1954; children: Loren Thomas, Barbara, Beverly, John Tracy. Student, U. Tex., 1948-51, 52-53. Sales coord. Union Tank div. Butler Mfg. Co., Houston, 1954-56, sales rep. New Orleans, 1956-57, br. mgr., 1957-60; asst. to exec. v.p. Maloney-Crawford Mfg. Co., Tulsa, 1960-62; mktg. cons., sr. assoc. Market/Product Facts, Tulsa, 1962-63; market devel. asst. Norriseal Controls divsn. Dover Corp., Houston, 1963-66; area dir. Arthritis Found., Houston, 1966-69, regional dir., 1969-71; exec. dir. United Cerebral Palsy, Tex. Gulf Coast, 1971-74, Leukemia Soc. Am., Gulf Coast, 1974-76, Lancaster & Assocs., 1976—. Christian edn. tchr., 1970, supr. 1971, asst. youth football coach, Bellaire, 1967-68, 70-71; mem. Houston-Galveston Area Health Commn. Study Group, 1972-76, co-chmn. 1976; dir. essayist Tex. Low Vision Coun., 1976-79, sec.-treas., 1978-81, pres. 1981-85; pres. Bellaire Civic Action Club, 1987-88, del. Houston Interfaith Sponsoring Com., 1979-81; bd. dirs. Coun. Chs. Greater Houston, 1966-68, v.p. 1968. With USNR, 1946-48, 51-52. Recipient award for securing free blood for indigent Harris County Hosp. Dist., 1968. Mem. Am. Mktg. Assn., Huguenot Soc., Military Order of Stars and Bars, San Marcos Acad., Ex-Students Assn. (pres. 1982-84), SAR, Delta Sigma Phi. Episcopalian (vestryman 1975-78). Home: 6900 County Road 261 Zephyr TX 76890-3779

LANCASTER, H(AROLD) MARTIN, congressman, academic administrator; b. Patetown Community, N.C., Mar. 24, 1943; s. Harold Wright and Eva (Pate) L.; m. Alice Matheny; children: Ashley Elizabeth, Mary Martin. AB, U. N.C., 1965, JD, 1967; doctorate (hon.), U. Ulster, 2005. Asst. staff judge adv. 12th Naval Dist., San Francisco, 1968; staff judge adv. USN, USS Hancock, 1968-70; ptnr. Baddour, Lancaster, Parker, Hine & Keller P.A., Goldsboro, N.C., 1970-86; rep. N.C. Gen. Assembly, Raleigh, 1978-86; mem. 100th-103rd Congresses from 3d N.C. dist., Washington, D.C., 1987-94; spl. advisor to the President on chem. weapons, 1995; asst. sec. of the Army, 1996-97; pres. N.C. Cmty. Coll. Sys., 1997—. Mem. armed svcs. com., readiness subcom., mil. pers. subcom.; chmn. morale, welfare and recreation panel; small bus. com. Mcht. Marine and Fisheries com.; chmn. judiciary com. N.C. Ho. of Reps., 1983-86; chmn. hwy. safety com., 1981-83; chmn. congrl. study group on Germany, 1994, North Atlantic Assembly, 1989-94; former mem. numerous other coms.; bd. dirs. Nat. Ctr. Family Literacy, 1998—, Global Transpark Auth., 1997—, N.C. Global Ctr., N.C. Pub. Sch. Forum, 1997—. Chmn. N.C. Arts Coun., 1977-81, Goldsboro Wayne Bicentennial Commn., 1975-76; pres. Community Arts Coun., 1973-74, Wayne Community Concert Assn., 1972-73; chmn. bd. trustees Wayne County Pub. Libr., 1979-80; chmn. Wayne chpt. ARC, 1978-79; mem. adv. bd. Z. Smith Reynolds Found.; deacon First Presbyn. Ch., 1972-75, elder, 1980-86; elder White Meml. Presbyn. Ch., 2002—, chmn. worship com., 2002—. Recipient Disting. Svc. award Goldsboro Jaycees, 1977, N.C. Crime and Justice award Gov.'s Crime Commn., 1984, Spl. award Gov.'s Adv. Coun. for Persons with Disabilities, 1985, Valand award Mental Health Assn. N.C., 1985, Outstanding Legislators awards Neuse River Coun. Govts., N.C. Assn. Sch. Counselors, Nat. Security Leadership award, 1987, 89, 90, 91, 92, Sound Dollar award, 1988, 89, 90, Spirit of Enterprise award U.S. C. of C., 1989, 92, 93, Doer of Deeds award House Leadership, 1989, Pub. Health Svc. award N.C. Primary Care Assn., 1991, Charles Dick Medal of Merit, U.S. Nat. Guard Assn., 1992, Tad Davis Meml. award, U.S. Mil. Sports Assn., 1992, Lifetime Achievement award Y-H, 2004; named N.C. and U.S. Alumnus of Yr., 4-H, 1987, Knight Comdr. of the Ct. of Honor, 1994, 33 degree Mason Scottish Rite, 1997, Silver Order of the de Fleuriers (Corps of Engrs.), 1997, Tar Heel of the Week, Raleigh News and Observer, 2000, Outstanding Alumnus U. NC Sch. of Law, 2002. Mem. ABA, Assn. Trial Lawyers Am., N.C. Bar Assn. (bd. govs.), Eighth Jud. Dist. Bar Assn., N.C. Acad. Trial Lawyers (Outstanding Legislator award), Wayne County Hist. Soc. Lodges: Masons (33d degree), Shriners, Elks. Office: NC Cmty Coll Sys 200 W Jones St Raleigh NC 27603-1378 Office Phone: 919-807-6950. Personal E-mail: martinl@ncccs.cc.nc.us.

LANCASTER, JEANETTE (BARBARA LANCASTER), dean, nursing educator; BSN, U. Tenn.; MSN, Case Western Res. U.; PhD, U. Okla. Staff nurse U. Tenn.; nurse clinician Univ. Hosps. of Cleve.; assoc. prof. psychiat.

nursing Tex. Christian U.; coord. cmty. health nursing U. Ala., Birmingham, chair master's degree program Sch. Nursing; dean, prof. Sch. Nursing Wright State U., Dayton, Ohio; now dean, prof. nursing U. Va., Charlottesville; assoc. dir. patient care svcs. U. Va. Health Scis. Ctr., Charlottesville. Former chmn. bd. dirs. Va. Statewide Area Health Edn. Ctr.; former pres. Charlottesville and Albemarle divsn. Am. Heart Assn.; presenter in field. Author: Community and Public Health Nursing: Nursing Issues in Leading and Managing Change; editor: Family and Cmty. Health; contbr. Bd. dirs. U. Va. Women's Ctr., Hospice of the Piedmont. Recipient Disting. Alumni award Frances Payne Bolton Sch. Nursing, Case We. Res. U., 1984, Outstanding Alumni award, U. Tenn. Coll. Nursing, 1985, honored with establishment of Jeanette Lancaster Professorship in Nursing, 1999. Fellow: Am. Acad. Nursing; mem.: Am. Assn. Colls. Nursing (pres. elect). E-mail: lancaster@virginia.edu.

LANCASTER, JOAN ERICKSEN, judge; b. 1954; BA magna cum laude, St. Olaf Coll., Northfield, Minn., 1977; spl. diploma in social studies, Oxford U., 1976; JD cum laude, U. Minn., 1981. Atty. LeFevere, Lefler, Kennedy, O'Brien & Drawz, Mpls., 1981-83; asst. U.S. atty. Dist. Minn., Mpls., 1983-93; shareholder Leonard, Street and Deinard, Mpls., 1993-95; dist. ct. judge 4th Jud. Dist., Mpls., 1995-98; assoc. justice Minn. Supreme Ct., 1998—2002; judge U.S. Dist. Ct., St. Paul, 2002—. Office: US District Court 316 N Robert St Saint Paul MN 55101*

LANCASTER, JOHN LYNCH, III, lawyer; b. Dallas, Nov. 10, 1936; s. John Lynch Jr. and Loretta Charlotte (Delaney) L.; m. Jane Frances Riddle, Sept. 5, 1959; children: Delaney, John, Jim. Student, Washington and Lee U., 1954-56; BA, U. Tex., 1958, LLB, 1960. Bar: Tex. 1960; diplomate Am. Bd. Trial Advs. Ptnr. Jackson Walker, L.L.P., Dallas, 1962—. Mayor Town of Highland Park, Tex., 1984-86. Fellow Am. Coll. Trial Lawyers; mem. Inn of Ct. (master). Office: Jackson Walker LLP 901 Main St Ste 6000 Dallas TX 75202-3797

LANCASTER, KARINE R., city health department administrator; b. Australia; MPH, U. Tex. Health Sci. Ctr., Houston, 1994. Pvt. practice, pediatrician, Dallas, 1978—; med. dir., health authority Dallas Co. Dept. Health and Human Svcs., Dallas, 1997—. Office: Dallas Co Dept Health and Human Svcs 2377 N Stemmons Fwy Dallas TX 75207-2710

LANCASTER, LIANE KAY, daycare administrator, elementary school educator; b. Grand Rapids, Mich., Feb. 10, 1960; d. Dale Gordon and Lorraine Beatrice (Erickson) Lancaster; children from previous marriage: Nicholas Antonio Lancaster Ruberto, Anthony Michael Lancaster Ruberto. AA, Grand Rapids C. C., 2002. Nationally registered paramedic Life Ambulance, Grand Rapids, Mich., 1982—91; client coord. Houston County Group Home, La Cresent, Minn., 1991—93; daycare provider self employed, Champlin, Minn., 1993—96; ednl. asst. Oxbow Creek Elem., Champlin, Minn., 1996—. Targeted svcs. asst. Oxbow Creek Elem., Champlin, Minn., 2002—. Coach Spl. Olympics, Grand Rapids, Mich., 1979; facilitator, talent devel. Oxbow Creek Elem., 2000—01, coord., arts and academics expo., 2001—02; instr. Kids Coll., North Hennepin Cmty., Brooklyn Park, 2001—03. Recipient Ednl. award, Am. Corp., 2004—05. Mem.: Paraprofl. Assn. Avocations: running, reading, bicycling, rock climbing, swimming. Home: 11832 Jersey Ave N Champlin MN 55316 Office: Oxbow Creek Elem Sch 6050 109th Ave Champlin MN 55316 Office Phone: 763-506-3889. Office Fax: 763-506-3803. Business E-Mail: liane.lancaster@anoka.k12.mn.us.

LANCASTER, PETER M., lawyer; b. 1954; AB, Princeton Univ., 1976; JD, Yale Univ., 1980. Bar: DC 1981, Minn. 1984. Ptnr., intellectual property litig. group Dorsey & Whitney LLP, Mpls., and mem., policy com. Mem.: Minn. Intellectual Property Law Assn., Am. Intellectual Property Law Assn. Office: Dorsey & Whitney LLP Ste 1500 50 S Sixth St Minneapolis MN 55402-1498 Office Phone: 612-340-7811. Office Fax: 612-340-2868. Business E-Mail: lancaster.peter@dorsey.com.

LANCASTER, RALPH IVAN, JR., lawyer; b. Bangor, Maine, May 9, 1930; s. Ralph I. and Mary Bridget (Kelleher) L.; m. Mary Lou Pooler, Aug. 21, 1954; children: Mary Lancaster Miller, Anne, Elizabeth Peoples, Christopher, John, Martin. AB, Coll. Holy Cross, 1952; LLB, Harvard U., 1955; LLD (hon.), St. Joseph's Coll., 1991. Bar: Maine 1955, Mass. 1955. Law clk. U.S. Dist. Ct. Dist. Maine, 1957-59; ptnr. firm Pierce Atwood, Portland, Maine, 1961—, mng. ptnr., 1993-96; ind. counsel In Re Herman apptd. by spl. divsn. D.C. Ct. Appeals, 1998—2001. Condr. trial advocacy seminar Harvard U.; lectr. U. Maine; chmn. merit selection panel U.S. Magistrate for Dist. of Maine, 1982, 88; bd. visitors U. Maine Sch. Law, 1991-96, chair, 1991-93; spl. master by appointment U.S. Supreme Ct. in State of N.J. vs. State of Nev. et al, 1987-88; mem. 1st Ctr. Adv. Com. on Rules, 1991-96, legal adv. bd. Martindale Hubbell, Lexis Nexis, 1990—; represented U.S. in Gulf of Maine in World Ct. at The Hague, 1984; U.S. Supreme Ct. apptd. spl. master Commonwealth of Va. vs. State of Md., 2000-03, chmn. bd. trustees, Davis Family Found., 2000-; chmn. Maine Lawyers Assistance Program, 2002-2003; nat. membership chair, Supreme Ct. Hist. Soc., 2002-2003. Former mem. Diocese of Portland Bur. Edn., mem. Cath. Found. of Maine (chair governance com., 2003). With U.S. Army, 1955-57. Mem. Maine Jud. Coun., Am Coll. Trial Lawyers (chmn. Maine 1974-79, bd. regents 1982-87, treas. 1985-87, pres. 1989-90), Maine Bar Assn. (pres. 1982), Cumberland County Bar Assn., Canadian Bar Assn. (hon.). Republican. Roman Catholic. Home: 162 Woodville Rd Falmouth ME 04105-1120 Office: 1 Monument Sq Portland ME 04101-4033 Office Phone: 207-791-1260. Business E-Mail: RLancaster@PierceAtwood.com.

LANCE, ALAN GEORGE, federal judge, former state attorney general; b. McComb, Ohio, Apr. 27, 1949; s. Cloyce Lowell and Clara Rose (Wilhelm) Lance; m. Sheryl C. Holden, May 31, 1969; children: Lisa, Alan Jr., Luke. BA, S.D. State U., 1971; JD, U. Toledo, 1973. Bar: Ohio 1974, U.S. Dist. Ct. (no. dist.) Ohio 1974, U.S. Ct. Mil. Appeals 1974, Idaho 1978, U.S. Supreme Ct. 1996. Asst. pros. atty. Fulton County, Wauseon, Ohio, 1973—74; ptnr. Foley and Lance, Chartered, Meridian, Idaho, 1978—90; prin. Alan G. Lance, Meridian, 1990—94; rep. Idaho Ho. of Reps., Boise, 1990—94, majority caucus chmn., 1992—94; atty. gen. State of ID, 1995—2003; prin. Lance, Elia & Assocs. PLLC, Boise, 2004; judge US Ct. Appeals Vets. Claims, Washington, 2004—. Capt. U.S. Army, 1974—78. Mem.: Idaho Trial Lawyers Assn., Idaho Bar Assn., Ohio Bar Assn., Nat. Assn. Attys. Gen. (vice-chmn. conf. western attys. gen. 1998, chmn. 1999), Meridian C. of C. (pres. 1983), Elks, Am. Legion (judge adv. 1981—90, state comdr. 1988—89, alt. nat. exec. com. 1992—94, nat. exec. com. 1994—96, chmn. nat. fgn. rels. commn. 1996—97, ex-officio mem. nat. POW/MIA com. 1996—99, nat. comdr. 1999—2000, chmn. nat. adv. com. 2000—01). Republican. Avocation: fishing. Office: US Ct Appeals Vets Claims 625 Indiana Ave Ste 900 Washington DC 20004 Office Phone: 202-501-5887.

LANCE, HOWARD L., communications executive, industrial engineer; BS in Indsl. Engring., Bradley U.; MS in Mgmt., Purdue U. With Sales and Mktg. Dept. Scott-Fetzer Co., Caterpillar Inc.; from mem. staff to exec. v.p. Emerson Electric Co., 1984—2000, exec. v.p. Electronics and Telecom., 2000—01; co-pres., COO Retail and Fin. Group NCR Corp., 2001—02; pres. Harris Corp., Melbourne, Fla., 2003—, CEO, 2003—, chmn. bd. Bd. govs. Aerospace Industries Assn.; exec. com. bd. trustees Mfrs. Alliance; bd. trustees Fla. Inst. Tech. Bd. dirs. United Way Brevard County. Mem.: Fla. Coun. 100. Office: Harris Corp 1025 W NASA Blvd Melbourne FL 32919

LANCE, LEONARD, state legislator; b. Easton, Pa., June 25, 1952; s. Wesley L. and Anne (Anderson) L.; m. Heidi A. Rohrbach. BA, Lehigh U., 1974; JD, Vanderbilt U., 1977; MPA, Princeton U., 1982. Law clk. to judges Warren County Ct., Belvidere, N.J., 1977-78; asst. counsel Office of Gov., State of N.J., Trenton, N.J., 1983-90; mem. N.J. Gen. Assembly, Trenton, 1991—2002, N.J. State Senate, 2002—, minority leader, 2004—. Mem. Grandin Libr. Bd., Clinton, N.J., 1990-2000, N.J. Coun. for Humanities, Trenton, 1994—; trustee Newark Mus., 1995—, Centenary Coll., Hackettstown, N.J., 1998—, McCarter Theatre, 1998—. Mem. Princeton Club N.Y., Phi Beta Kappa. Republican. Home: PO Box 5240 Clinton NJ 08809-0240 Office: NJ State Senate 119 Main St Flemington NJ 08822-1615

LANCHNER, BERTRAND MARTIN, lawyer, advertising executive; b. Boston, Oct. 3, 1929; s. Abraham Joseph and Mina (Grossman) L.; m. Nancy Nelson, Apr. 26, 1979; 1 son by previous marriage, David; 1 stepdau., Renate. BA, Stanford U., 1951; postgrad., Columbia U. Grad. Sch. Bus., 1951-52, U. Vienna, Austria, summer 1955; JD, Harvard U., 1955. Bar: N.Y. bar 1956. Asso. firm Sage, Gray, Todd & Sims, N.Y.C., 1955-57; atty. Warner Bros. Pictures, N.Y.C., 1957-59; asst. gen. counsel Dancer-Fitzgerald-Sample, N.Y.C., 1959-62; gen. counsel Lawrence C. Gumbinner Advt. Agy., N.Y.C., 1962-63; dir. bus. affairs and sports contract negotiations CBS-TV, N.Y.C., 1963-69; gen. counsel, exec. v.p. Videorecord Corp. Am., Westport, Conn., 1969-73; sr. v.p., sec., gen. counsel N.W. Ayer, Inc., N.Y.C., 1973-97, also bd. dirs.; with Lanchner Law Firm, 1997—. Bd. dirs. 170 E. 79th St. Corp., Advt. Info. Services Inc., N.Y.C.; guest lectr. Yale U. Law Sch. Mem. adv. bd.: Communications and the Law. Mem. ABA, N.Y. State Bar Assn., Assn. of Bar of City of N.Y. (chmn. subcom. advt. agy. 1981-83), Copyright Soc. U.S., Am. Assn. Advt. Agys. (chmn. legal com. 1986-89, 95-97), Am. Corp. Counsel Assn. (chair advt. com. 1996—), Am. Advt. Fedn. (mem. legal com.), Harvard Club N.Y.C., East Hampton Tennis Club, Tennisport Club., Green Hollow Tennis Club. Office: Lanchner Law Firm 170 E 79th St New York NY 10021-0436 Office Phone: 917-855-7949.

LANCI, JANET MEAD, academic administrator, educator; b. Derby, Conn., Apr. 24, 1960; d. Wesley John and Sandra Lee Mead; m. James David Lanci, July 17, 1992; m. Edward Lawrence Lanci, June 0, 1979 (div. Aug. 0, 1982); children: Christopher James, Edward Lawrence Tatro Jr., Alexandra Lynn. AS in Human Svcs., Housatonic C.C., Bridgeport, Conn., 1988; BS in Devel. Psychology, Liberty U., Lynchburg, Va., 1994; MS in counseling/Human Resources, U. of Bridgeport, 1999. Lic. profl. counselor in pub. health Conn., battered women's counselor Conn. Woman's adv. Domestic Violence Services of Greater New Haven, 1989—92; master resource specialist Housatonic C.C., 1992—2000, asst. dir. of the acad. support ctr., 2000—. Co-facilitator workshop for new faculty Conn. Distance Consortium Faculty Inst., New Britain, 2002; co-facilitator - critical incident tng. Housatonic C.C., Bridgeport, 2002; facilitator domestic violence workshop Bridgeport Family Resource Ctr., 2002; adj. prof. Teikyo Post U., Waterbury, 2000—, U. Bridgeport, 2003—, Houstatonic C.C., Bridgeport, 1999—. Counselor CT-1 Disaster Med. Assistance Team, Hartford, 2002, Ctr. for Trauma Response/Recovery and Preparedness, Hartford, Conn., 2002. Recipient Award of Excellence, Nat. Instn. for Staff and Orgnl. Devel., 2002. Mem.: Soc. for the Psychology of Women, Conn. Counselors U. and C.C. Assn. (assoc.), Adminstrv. Syst. Adv. Com. (assoc.; recorder 2003), Nat. Academic Advising Assn. (assoc.), Conn. Counselors Assn. (assoc.), Conn. C.C. Couselors Assn. (assoc.; recorder/treas. 2002). Independent. Methodist. Avocations: camping, swimming, reading, crafting, counted cross-stitch. Home: 161 Pine Bridge Rd Beacon Falls CT 06403 Office: Housatonic C C 900 Lafayette Blvd Bridgeport CT 06604

LAND, GEORGE A., philosopher, consultant, writer; b. Hot Springs, Ark., Feb. 27, 1933; s. George Thomas Lock and Mary Elizabeth Land; m. Jo A. Gunn, 1957 (dec. 1969); children— Robert E., Thomas G., Patrick A.; m. Beth Smith Jarman, 1987. Student, Millsaps Coll., 1952-54, U. Veracruz, Mexico, 1957-59; numerous hon. degrees U.S. and abroad. Program dir. Woodall TV Stas. of Ga., Columbus, 1951-52; ops. mgr. Lamar Broadcasting, Jackson, Miss., 1952-54; anthrop. research Cora, Huichole and Yaqui tribes, Latin Am. Mexico, 1955-60; dir. gen. Television del Norte (NBC), Mexico, 1960-62; v.p. Roman Corp., St. Louis, 1962-64; chmn. Transolve Inc., Cambridge, Mass., and St. Petersburg, Fla., 1964-68; chief exec., chmn. Innotek Corp., N.Y.C.; also pres. Hal Roach Studios, Los Angeles and N.Y.C., 1969-71; chmn. emeritus Turtle Bay Inst., N.Y.C., 1971-80, Farsight Group, N.Y.C., 1971—80; vice chmn. Wilson Learning Corp., Mpls., 1980-86; chmn., CEO Leadership 2000 The Farsight Group, Phoenix, 1986—; prof. Mankato State U., 1973-74; sr. fellow U. Minn., 1982—; chmn. Global Alliance for Creative Peace. Cons.-in-residence Synplex Inc., N.Y.C., AT&T, Forest Hosp., Des Plaines, Social Systems Inc., Chapel Hill, N.C., Children's Hosp., Nat. Med. Ctr., Washington, Herman Miller Inc., Arthur Anderson & Co., strategy cons. Intermedics Orthopedics; mem. Nat. Action Com. on Drug Edn., 1974-75, sr. exec. svc. U.S. Govt. 2001-2002, Assn. Non-profit mgmt., 1999, The Congerence Bd. 1999, 2000, Ctr. for Disease Control, 2002, The Concours Group, 2002, Global Fourm Ctr., 2002, CEO, 2002; co-chmn. Syncon Conf., So. Ill. U., 1972-74; keynoter Emerging Trends in Edn. Conf., Minn., 1974, 75, Bicentennial Conf. on Limits to Growth, So. Ill. U., 1976, No. States Power Conf., 1975, U.S. Office Edn., Nat. Conf. Improvements in Edn., 1979, World Conf. on Gifted, 1977, S.W. Conf. on Arts, 1977, World Symposium on Humanity, 1979, Internat. Conf. Internal Auditors, 1977, Four Corners Conf. on Arts, 1977, Chautaugua Inst., 1977, 78, Conf. Am. Art Tchrs. Assn., 1979, Internat. Conf. on Gifted, 1982, Japan Mgmt. Assn., Nat. Conf. Art Curators, Chgo., 1985, others; keynoter, Nat. Conf. on Econ. Devel., Mex., 1988, Credit Union Roundtable, Tampa, Fla., 1988, Internat. Bihai Conf., Princeton, N.J., 1982, co-chmn. com. on society World Conf. Peace and Poverty, St. Joseph's U., Phila., 1968, Internat. Bahai Conf. Princeton U., 1987, Gov.'s Trade Corridor Conf., Phoenix, 1994, Cath. Hosp. Assn., Phila, 1994, Am. Assn. Adminstrs., 1994, Inst. Pub. Execs., 1994, Fed. Conf. Quality, Washington, 1994, MAC IS Nat. Conf., Ont., 1994, Innovative Thinking Conf., 1994, Ventana Groupware Conf., 1994, Assn. Non-Profit Orgs., 1998, The Conf. Bd., 1999, 2000, Strategic Innovation Conf., 1999, Tng. Dirs. Forum, 1999, Young Pres.' Orgn., Cannes, 1993, Assn. Convn. and Visitors Bureau, Phoenix, 1993, Profession Conv. Mgmt. Assn., Atlanta, Internat. Assn. Law Enforcement, 1995, Cath. Health Assn., 1995, Excellence in Govt. Fellows, 1996, U.S. Govt. Sr. Exec. Svc., 2000, 01, Chautauqua Instn., 2001, PEMEX, 2002, Coca-Cola, 2002, U.S. Fish and Wildlife Svc., 2003, Innovation Convergence, Mpls., 2003, Internat. Conference Energy, Geneva, 2003, Am. Med. Systems, France, 2003, Adv. Innovation, Zurich, Switzerland, 2003, Mex. Petroleum Inst., Mexico City, 2004, Ctr. for Competitiveness, Belfast, No. Ireland, 2004, Creative Edn. Found., Buffalo, 2004, Congress Innovation and Quality Pub. Adminstrn., Mex. DF, 2005, Internat. Petroleum Conf., Venacruz, Mex., 2005, any others; mem. Nat. Security Sem., U.S. Dept. Def., 1975; cons. keynoter corp. policy strategic sems. The Bell System, AT&T, 1978—; mem. faculty Edison Electric Grad. Mgmt. Inst., 1972-78; lectr., seminarian in transformation theory, strategic planning and interdisciplinary rsch. Menninger Found., U. Ga., Emory U., Waterloo (Can.), Office of Sec. HEW, Jamestown (N.Y.) Coll., Hofstra U., U.S. Office Edn., Calif. Dept. Edn., St. Louis U., Coll. William and Mary, Webster Coll., St. Louis, Wash. State Dept. Edn., U. Ky., So. Ill. U., St. John's U., Harvard U., U. South Fla., MIT, U. Veracruz, Children's Hosp. D.C., Gov.'s Sch. N.C., Scottsdale (Ariz.) Ctr. Arts, Humbolt U., East Berlin, AAAS, others; advanced faculty Creative Problem SolvingInst., SUNY, 1965—, S, Conn. Coll.; disting. lectr. Northwestern State U., La., SUNY, Coll. of the Lakes, Ill.; cons. govt., industry and instrns. in U.S. and abroad including AT&T, IBM, Dow Chem, Dow Corning, DuPont, Hughes, TRW, 3Mm OAS, Fed. Quality Inst., U.S. Dept. Commerce, U.S. Dept. Agr., Office Patent & Trademarks, U.S. Gen. Svc. Adminstrn., Gen Mills, GM, Moore Corp., Branch Corp., Credit Union Nat. Assn., USDA, Excellence in Govt. Fed. Quality Cons. Group, U.S. Dept. Energy, Lockheed Martin, Dept. Housing and Urban Devel., Wescorp, PEMEX, Petroleos de Venezuela, Am. Medicas Sys., Def. Evaluation and Rsch. Agy (U.K.)., Stanford U., Pricewaterhouse Coopers, others. Author: Innovation Systems, 1967, Innovation Technology, 1968, Four Faces of Poverty, 1968, (as George T.L. Land) Grow or Die: The Unifying Principle of Transformation, 1973, Creative Alternatives and Decision Making, 1974, The Opportunity Book, 1980, (with Vaune E. Ainsworth), Breakpoint and Beyond, 1994, (with Beth Jarman) New Paradigm in Business, 1994, Community Building in Business, 1995, Forward to Basics; contbr. to profl. jours. and gen. mags. Sr. fellow U. Mich. Fellow: World Bus. Acad., NY Acad. Scis.; mem.: Authors League Am., Authors Guild, Com. for Future (colleague), World Future Soc., Am. Soc. Value Engrs. (past dir.), Creative Edn. Found. (trustee, Lifetime Achievement award 1993), Am. Soc. Cybernetics (past v.p.), Soc. Gen. Sys. Rsch. Achievements include research on interdisciplinary unification, orginated transformation theory. Inventor computer-assisted group creative thinking processes, "The Innovator," "CoNexus," "TeamWare," "Synnovas" and others. Home: 7470 E San Miguel Ave Scottsdale AZ 85250-6446 Office: Leadership 2000 The Farsight Group 6619 N Scottsdale Rd Scottsdale AZ 85250 *I was fortunate enough in my youth to experience and learn what has been the most important idea and principle in my life, the natural law of enrichment through diversity. This concept means that change and growth come about more by combining differentnesses than by adding likenesses. As in the biological world, where such behavior produces the vitality of hybrids, and as in chemistry, where the co-valent bonds of carbon make life possible, in human life we can also benefit immeasurably from using our differences as a creative way to grow anew. Thus, we can evolve beyond polarizations such as nationalism, racism, sexism, institutionalism and other obstacles that separate us and stunt our ability to realize the full community of Man.*

LAND, H. BRUCE, III, electronics engineer, aerospace engineer; s. H. B. Land, Jr and Evelyn J. Land; m. Sharon Lee Land; children: Cynthia D. Nickel, Janette E. Lovell, Joel B. BEE, Johns Hopkins U., Balt., 1984. Data contr. Goddard Space Flight Ctr., Greenbelt, Md., 1967—67; sr. electronics technician JHU/APL, Laurel, Md., 1967—73, engring. asst., 1973—76, engring. staff assoc., 1976—87, sect. supr., 1987—97; program mgr. Johns Hopkins U. Applied Physics Lab., Laurel, Md., 1991—, systems engr., 1991—2003. Assoc. dir. Instrument Soc. of Am., Research Triangle Park, NC, 1988—; chmn. of com. on symposiums Internat. Instrumentation Symposium, Instrument Soc. of Am., Research Triangle Park, NC, 1999—, registration chmn., 2000—; newsletter editor Aerospace Industries Divsn., ISA, Research Triangle Park, NC, 2003—; expert witness Before the Nat. Transp. Safety Bd., Washington, 2000. Contbr. articles to profl. jours. Chmn., vice chair, sec. 1st Bapt. Ch. of Laurel, Md., 1980—; pres., treas. Northgate Woods Cmty. Assn., Laurel, Md., 1997—. Recipient Letter of Commendation, Rear Adm. R. B. Horne, Jr, 1990. Fellow: Instrumentation Systems and Automation Soc. (assoc. dir. aerospace industries divsn. 1988—). Southern Baptist. Achievements include patents for Thermal Ionization Detector; patents pending for Pulsed Plasma Thruster; development of Arc Fault Detector System for Switchboards; Continuous Thermal Monitoring for Switchboards; System to protect nuclear power plants from electrical fires. Home: 9426 Northgate Rd Laurel MD 20723 Office: Johns Hopkins Univ Applied Physics 11100 Johns Hopkins Rd Laurel MD 20723 Office Phone: 240-228-6083.

LAND, HENRY BRUCE, III, electronics engineer, researcher; s. Henry Bruce Land, Jr. and Evelyn Janette Land; m. Sharon Lee Headley, June 5, 1971; children: Cynthia Land Nickel, Janette Elizabeth Lovell, Joel Bruce. AAEE, Catonsville C.C., Catonsville, Md., 1979; BEE, Johns Hopkins U., Balt., 1984. Electronics technician Sperry Piedmont divsn. Sperry Rand, Charlottesville, Va., 1965—67; launch data contr. Goddard Space Flight Ctr., Greenbelt, Md., 1967; sr. electro-chem. technician Johns Hopkins U. Applied Physics Lab, Laurel, Md., 1967—73, engring. asst., 1973—76, engring. staff, 1976—87, sect. supr., 1987—97, systems engr., 1988—, program mgr., 1991—. Chmn. Com. on Symposiums ISA, Research Triangle Park, NC, 1999—; chmn. of com. on symposiums Internat. Instrumentation Symposium, Research Triangle Park, NC, 1999—, registration chmn., 1999—; expert witness arcing faults Nat. Transp. Safety Bd., Washington, 2000. Contbr. articles to profl. .jours. Chmn., vice chair, sec., of trustees First Bapt. Ch. of Laurel, Laurel, Md., 1980—2005; treas., pres. Northgate Woods Cmty. Assoc, Laurel, Md., 1997—2005. Recipient Letter of Commendation, Rear Adm. R. B. Horne, Jr, 1990, Commendation, Asst. Dep. Under Sec., Dept. of the Navy, 1993. Fellow: ISA (assoc. dir. 1988—2005, newsletter editor Aerospace Industries divsn. 2003—); mem.: AIAA. Southern Baptist. Achievements include patents for Detector for prediction of electrical fires; development of System to protect electrical switchboards from fires; System to protect nuclear power plants from electrical fires; System for Continuous Thermal Monitoring of electrical switchboards; invention of Means of locating impacts on a surface; development of Arc Fault Detector System to protect Switchboards; patents pending for Pulsed Plasma Thrusters; Unattended spaces monitoring system; development of System to protect nuclear power plants from electrical fires; patents pending for Enhanced sampling device for SPME Sampling; Micro Pulsed Plasma Thrusters; High temperature fiber optic connector. Avocations: teaching sunday school, handyman. Home: 9426 Northgate Rd Laurel MD 20723 Office: Johns Hopkins Univ Applied Physics Lab 11100 Johns Hopkins Rd Building 10 Laurel MD 20723 Office Phone: 240-228-6083. Personal E-mail: bland3@mindspring.com. E-mail: bruce.land@jhuapl.edu.

LAND, IRENE STOKVIS, marketing executive; b. N.Y.C., Sept. 29, 1939; d. Joseph William and Beatrice Winifred (Turetsky) Stokvis; m. Paul Ivan Land, Nov. 5, 1965; 1 child, Jonathan Brock. BA, CUNY, Queens, 1961. Assoc. book rev. editor Library Jour., N.Y.C., 1961-76; mgr. advt. and promotion Elsevier Sci. Pub. Co., N.Y.C., 1980-86; mgr. promotion Springer-Verlag, N.Y.C., 1986-88; freelance personal mgr. for actors, 1988-92; freelance mktg. and media comm., 1992—. Avocations: painting, piano, writing. Home: 401 E 34th St Apt N5B New York NY 10016-4921

LAND, JOHN CALHOUN, III, lawyer, state senator; b. Manning, S.C., Jan. 25, 1941; s. John Calhoun, Jr. and Anna Abbott (Weisiger) L.; m. Marie Mercogliano, Oct. 23, 1965; children— John Calhoun IV, Frances Ricci, William Ceth. Student vocat. forestry U. Fla., 1960-62; B.S., U. S.C., 1965, J.D., 1968. Bar: S.C. 1968. Mem. Land, Parker and Welch, P.A., Manning, 1968—; mem. S.C. Ho. of Reps., 1975-76, mem. S.C. Senate, 1977— . Sec. Clarendon County Democratic Com., 1968-70; commr. S.C. Hwys. and Pub. Transp., 1971-74. Mem. ABA, Clarendon County Bar Assn., S.C. Bar Assn., S.C. Trial Lawyers Assn. Avocations: hunting; fishing. Office: 504 Gressette Bldg Columbia SC 29202 Office Phone: 803-435-8894.

LAND, KENNETH CARL, sociologist, educator, demographer; b. Llano, Tex., Aug. 19, 1942; s. Otto Carl and Tillie (Lindemann) L.; m. Jacqueline Yvette Apere, Mar. 22, 1969; 1 child, Kristoffer Carl. BA, Tex. Luth. Coll., 1964; MA, U. Tex., 1966, PhD, 1969. Staff assoc. Russell Sage Found., N.Y.C., 1969-73; lectr. Columbia U., N.Y.C., 1970-73; assoc. prof. U. Ill., Urbana, 1973-76, prof., 1976-81; prof. sociology U. Tex., Austin, 1981-86; prof., chmn. dept. sociology Duke U., Durham, N.C., 1986-97, John Franklin Crowell prof. sociology, 1990—. Editor: Social Indicator Models, 1975, Social Accounting Systems, 1981, Multidimensional Mathematical Demography, 1982, Forecasting in the Social and Natural Sciences, 1987; contbr. articles to profl. jours.; co-author: Criminal Circumstance, 2003. Fellow AAAS, Am. Statis. Assn., Internat. Soc. Quality Life Studies; mem. Sociol. Rsch. Assn., Am. Sociol. Assn. (Paul F. Lazersfeld award methodology sect. 1997), Population Assn. Am., Am. Soc. Criminology. Lutheran. Office: Duke U Dept Sociology Durham NC 27708-0088 Business E-Mail: kland@soc.duke.edu.

LAND, REGINALD BRIAN, library administrator; b. Niagara Falls, Ont., Can., July 29, 1927; s. Allan Reginald and Beatrice Beryl (Boyle) L.; m. Edith Wyndham Eddis, Aug. 29, 1953; children— Mary Beatrice, John Robert Eddis. BA, U. Toronto, Ont., Can., 1949, BLS, 1953, MLS, 1956, MA, 1963. Catalogue copy editor T. Eaton Co. Ltd., Toronto, 1950-51; reference librarian Toronto Pub. Library, 1953-55; cataloguer U. Toronto Library, 1955-56, asst. librarian, 1959-63, assoc. librarian, 1963; head div. bus. and industry Windsor Pub. Library, Ont., Can., 1956-57; asst. editor Canadian Bus. Mag., Montreal, Que., Can., 1957-58, assoc. editor, 1958-59; exec. asst. to Minister Fin. of Can., Ottawa, Ont., 1963-64; prof. library sci. U. Toronto, 1964-78, part-time prof., 1978-93, prof. emeritus, 1993—, dean Faculty Library Sci., 1964-72; exec. dir. Ont. Legis. Library, Toronto, 1978-93. Author: Sources of Information for Canadian Business, 1962, 4th rev. edit., 1985, Eglinton: The Election Study of a Federal Constituency, 1965; founder, gen. editor: Directory of Associations in Canada, 1974, 18th rev. edit., 1997. Mem. Canadian Radio-TV and Telecommunications Commn., 1973-78, Ont. Hist. Soc. Decorated Knight Hospitaller Order of St. John of Jerusalem; recipient Kenneth R. Wilson Meml. award Bus. Newspapers Assn. Can., 1959, Disting. Achievement award Ont. Library Trustees Assn., 1968, Queen Elizabeth IIs

Silver Jubilee medal, 1977, Spl. Librarianship award Can. Assn. for Spl. Librs. and Info. Svcs., 1991, 125th Anniversary Confederation Can. medal, 1992, Alumni Jubilee award U. Toronto Libr. & Info. Sci. Alumni Assn., 1994. Mem. ALA (chmn. com. on accreditation 1973-74), Assn. Parliamentary Librs. in Can. (pres. 1982-84), Can. Libr. Assn. (pres. 1975-76), Ont. Libr. Assn. (1st v.p. 1962-63), Ont. Govt. Librs. Coun. (chmn. 1984-85), Assn. for Libr. and Info. Sci. Edn. (pres. 1973-74), Can. Assn. for Grad. Edn. in Libr. Archival and Info. Studies (pres. 1966-67), Can. Coun. Libr. Schs. (chmn. 1971-72), Ex Libris Assn. (bd. dirs. 1994-99, pres. 1998), Inst. Profl. Librs. Ont. (pres. 1961-62), Ont. Coun. Libr. Schs. (chmn. 1968-72), Spl. Librs. Assn. (Mem. of Yr. award Toronto chpt. 1986), Ont. Geneal. Soc., Ont. Coll. and Univ. Librs. Assn. (merit award 1992), Ont. Hist. Soc., United Empire Loyalists' Assn. Can. Mem. Anglican Ch. Home: 9 Wild Rose Court Guelph ON Canada N1G 4X7

LAND, RICHARD DALE, minister, religious organization administrator; b. Houston, Nov. 6, 1946; s. Leggette Sloan and Marilee (Welch) L.; m. Rebekah Ruth Van Hooser, May 29, 1971; children: Jennifer, Richard Jr., Rachel. BA, Princeton U., 1969; ThM, New Orleans Bapt. Theol. Sem., 1972; D.Phil., U. Oxford, Eng., 1980. Ordained to ministry So. Bapt. Conv., 1969. Pastor S. Oxford Bapt. Ch., Oxford, Eng., 1972-75; prof. theology and ch. history Criswell Coll., Dallas, 1975-76, acad. dean, 1976-80, v.p. for acad. affairs, 1980-88; pres. ethics and religious liberty commn. So. Bapt. Conv., Nashville, 1988—. Mem. exec. com. Nat. Coalition against Pornography, Cin., 1989—; bd. dirs. Bapt. Joint Com. Pub. Affairs, Washington, 1987-91, Nat. Pro-Life Religious Coun., Washington; host nationally syndicated daily radio program For Faith & Family, 1998—, daily radio commentary 1999—; host weekly call-in talk show Richard Land Live, 2002—; appointed by Pres. George W. Bush to U.S. Comn. on Internat. Religious Freedom, 2000—. Cons. editor Criswell Study Bible, 1979. Mem. Gov.'s Task Force on Welfare Reform, Austin, Tex., 1988, Pres.'s Campaign for a Drug-Free Soc., Washington, 1991—; bd. dirs. Nat. Law Ctr., Arlington, Va., 1991—. Recipient Disting. Alumnus award New Orleans Bapt. Theol. Sem., 1997. Mem. Bapt. World Alliance (spl. com. on racism 1992, gen. bd. 1993, v. chmn. christian ethics com. 1995—). Office: Ethics & Religious Liberty Commn 901 Commerce St Ste 550 Nashville TN 37203-3600

LAND, TERRI LYNN, state official; m. Dan Hibma; children: Jessica Hibma, Nicholas Hibma. BA in Political Sci., Hope Coll., Holland, MI. Clerk Kent County, 1992—2000; sec. of state State of Mich., 2003—. Atty. Grievance Commn., 1999—2002; sec. Atty. Grievance Commn., 2001—02; mem. Secchia Millennium Commn., 2000, Cmty. Archives & Rsch. Ctr., 1997—, 54 Jefferson Study Com., 1997—. Mem. Grandville Rotary, 1990—99; mem. bd. dirs. Am. Heart Assn., 1995—99, Junior Achivement Alumni Bd., 1997—99, Project Rehab Found., 1997—98. Mem.: Mich. Supreme Ct. Hist. Soc., US Supreme Ct. Hist. Soc., Women's Resource Ctr. (v.p., bd. of dirs. 2001—02), Grand Rapids Pub. Mus. Found. Bd., Grand Rapids Rotary, Grand Rapids Early Morning Riser's Club, Friends of John Ball Zoological Park, Byron Ctr. Fine Arts Found. (pres. 1999—), Friends of Van Andel Mus., Frederick Meijer Gardens, Grand Rapids C. of C., Byron Ctr. Hist. Soc. (pres. 1990—92), Byron Ctr. Cmty. Fine Arts Coun., Potters House Found. (mem., bd. dirs. 1997—). Office: Treasury Bldg 430 West Allegan St 1st Fl Lansing MI 48918

LANDA, HOWARD MARTIN, lawyer, management consultant; b. Bklyn., Oct. 12, 1943; s. George and Lilli (Skolnik) L.; m. Nori Neinstein, Mar. 14, 1971; children— Alyson, David. BA (N.Y. State Regents scholar), Bklyn. Coll., 1964; JD (tuition scholar), U. Chgo., 1967. Bar: N.Y. 1968. Pvt. practice, N.Y.C., 1968-69; assoc. Garfield, Solomon & Mainzer, N.Y.C., 1969-70, Szold, Brandwen, Meyers & Altman, N.Y.C., 1970-74; v.p., sec., gen. counsel IPCO Corp., White Plains, N.Y., 1974-90, also bd. dirs.; pres., mng. dir. Martin Hand Assocs., Inc., Greenwich, Conn., 1990-92, also bd. dirs.; owner Law Offices of Howard M. Landa, N.Y.C., 1990-94; counsel Rand Rosenzweig Smith Radley & Gordon LLP, N.Y.C., 1994—. Lectr. Dental Lab. Conf., 1977. Contbr. articles to profl. jours. Mem. Mayor N.Y.C. Panel to Study Dept. Gen. Services' Div. Mcpl. Supplies, 1978-79; vice-chmn. So. N.Y. chpt. Nat. Multiple Sclerosis Soc., 1984-86, bd. dirs., 1984-2003. Mem.: ABA, Bus. Network Internat. (chpt. pres. 1998—2000, 2003—04). Office: 605 3rd Ave New York NY 10158-0180 Office Phone: 212-687-7070. E-mail: hlanda@randrose.com.

LANDAETA, RAFAEL ERNESTO, industrial engineer, researcher; b. Valencia, Carabobo, Venezuela, Dec. 4, 1969; s. Juan Ernesto Landaeta and Magaly Feo de Landaeta; m. Maria Gabriela Gonzalez; 1 child, Gabriel Ernesto. PhD in Indsl. Engring., Mgmt. Sys., U. Ctrl. Fla., 2003. Tech. auditor Polar Enterprises, Valencia, Venezuela, 1996—98; rschr. constructability lab. U. Ctrl. Fla., Orlando, 1999—2000, rschr. mgmt. sys. performance lab., 2000—. Fellow Merit fellow, U. Ctrl. Fla., 2003—04, Enhancement and Merit fellow, 2000. Mem.: Acad. Mgmt. (assoc.). Achievements include research in theory of knowledge management across projects. Office: Industrial Engineering and Management 4000 Central Florida Blvd Orlando FL 32816 Business E-Mail: rlandaet@mail.ucf.edu.

LANDAN, HENRY SINCLAIR, business consultant, financial consultant; b. Chgo., Aug. 4, 1943; BS, DePaul U., 1965, JD, 1969; LLM in Taxation, NYU, 1970. Bar: Ill. 1969-97, N.Y. 1971-97, U.S. Supreme Ct. 1976-97. Assoc. Altman, Kurlander & Weiss, Chgo., 1969-70, Roberts & Holland, N.Y.C., 1970-72; sr. ptnr. Kamensky & Landan and predecessor, Chgo., 1972—85, Law Offices of Henry S. Landan, Chgo, 1985—88; of counsel Keck, Mahin & Cate, Chgo., 1988-90, ptnr., 1990-96. Counsel Caribbean Hotel Assn., Santurce, P.R., 1975-83. Contbg. author: Tax Planning for Professionals; contbr. articles to profl. jours. Mem. exec. com., bd. dirs. Jewish Coun. for Youth Svcs., 1972-77, predecessor; mem. exec. com., bd. dirs. Men's Coun., Mus. Contemporary Art Chgo., 1977-84, pres., 1980-82; bd. dirs. Mus. Contemporary Art, Chgo., 1980-82; bd. dirs. Little City, Chgo., 1977-82; bd. dirs., mem. exec. com. Renaissance Soc. U. Chgo., 1984-96, v.p., 1988-95; mem. Soc. Contemporary Art, Art Inst. Chgo., 1982-95; mem. Contemporary Arts Coun., Chgo., 1994-96; mem. bd. mgrs. Henry Horner Boys and Girls Club, 1992-95, James Jordan Boys and Girls Club, 1995-96; bd. dirs., mem. exec. com. Randolph St. Gallery, Chgo., 1983-88, mem. adv. bd., 1988-96. Named Life Dir., Young Men's Jewish Coun., 1980, Man of Yr., 1985. Office: 225 W Washington St Ste 2200 Chicago IL 60603 Personal E-mail: hslandan@scbglobal.net. Business E-Mail: hslandan@lsichicago.com.

LANDAU, ANNETTE HENKIN, writer, librarian; b. N.Y.C., Apr. 7, 1921; d. Bernard and Bessie (Diamond) Henkin; m. Philip Landau (dec.); children— Harriette, Robert, Jessica (dec.). B.A., Queens Coll., 1941; M.A., Columbia U., 1943, M.Phil., 1973; M.S., C.W. Post Coll., 1969. Tchr. English, Queens Coll., N.Y.C., 1943-48; libr. E.M. Pub. Library, East Meadow, N.Y., 1969-83; libr. The Klein Libr. Stephen Wise Free Synagogue, N.Y.C., 1988-95, Nat. Coun. Jewish Women N.Y. Sect. Libr., 1997—. Author short stories various mags.; contbr. articles to profl. jours. Mem. Poets and Writers, Internat. Women's Writing Guild, NOW, Nat. Coun. Jewish Women. Home: 301 E 66th St New York NY 10021-6205 Office Phone: 212-687-5030 ext. 33. E-mail: alandau@ncjwny.org.

LANDAU, BERNARD ROBERT, biochemist, educator, internist; b. Newark, N.J., June 24, 1926; s. Morris Harry and Estelle (Kirsch) L.; m. Lucille Slosberg, Jan. 11, 1956; children: Steven Brian, Deborah Louise (dec.), Rodger Martin. S.B., MIT, 1947; PhD, Harvard U., 1950, MD, 1954; MD (hon.), Karolinska Inst., 1993. Diplomate: Am. Bd. Internal Medicine. Intern Peter Bent Brigham Hosp., Boston, 1954-55; clin. assoc. Nat. Cancer Inst., Bethesda, Md., 1955-57; fellow in biochemistry Harvard U., 1957-58; sr. resident Peter Bent Brigham Hosp., 1958-59; asst. prof. medicine Case Western Res. U., 1959-62, assoc. prof., 1962-67, prof., 1969—, prof. biochemistry, 1979—, physician Univ. Hosps., 1969—. Dir. dept. biochemistry Merck and Co., Rahway, N.J., 1967-69 Contbr. articles to profl. jours. Fellow Commonwealth fund 1965-66, Fogarty Sr. Internat. fellow 1986-87, 93-94, Nobel fellow Karolinska Inst., 1996-97; grantee Am. Heart Assn., 1959-64; recipient William B. Peck Postgrad. Research award, 1961 Fellow AAAS; mem. Am. Fedn. Clin. Research, Am. Soc. Clin. Investigation, Assn. Am. Physicians, Am. soc. Biol. Chemists, Am. Physiol. Soc., Endocrine Soc., Central Soc. Clin. Research, Am. Diabetes Assn., Sigma Xi, Alpha Omega Alpha Home: 19501 S Woodland Rd Cleveland OH 44122-2834 Office: Case Western Res U 10900 Euclid Ave Cleveland OH 44106-4951 Office Phone: 216-368-6129. E-mail: brl@cwru.edu.

LANDAU, DAVID H., lawyer; b. NYC, July 26, 1962; BS cum laude, U. Pa., 1984; JD, NYU, 1987. Bar: NY 1988. Ptnr. Katten Muchin Zavis Rosenman, NYC. Mem.: ABA. Office: Katten Muchin Zavis Rosenman 575 Madison Ave New York NY 10022 Office Phone: 212-940-6608. Office Fax: 212-940-8776. E-mail: david.landau@kmzr.com.

LANDAU, DAVID PAUL, physics educator; b. St. Louis, June 22, 1941; s. Bernard Israel and Selma (Goldstein) L.; m. Heidi Humpert, Aug. 28, 1966; children: Ladina Aviva, Anya Karina. BA, Princeton U., 1963; MS, Yale U., 1965, PhD, 1967. Chargé de recherche CNRS, Grenoble, France, 1967-68; lectr. Yale U., New Haven, 1968-69; asst. prof. physics U. Ga., Athens, 1969-73, assoc. prof., 1973-78, prof., 1978-84, rsch. prof., 1984—, dir. Ctr. for Simulational Physics, 1986—. Editor books; author more than 300 sci. publs. Recipient Creative Rsch. medal U. Ga., 1981, sr. U.S. scientist prize Alexander von Humboldt Found., 1988, Aneesur Rahman award, 2002, Lamar Dodd award, 2003. Fellow Am. Phys. Soc. (Jesse Beams award 1987). Jewish. Office: U Ga Ctr Simulational Physics Athens GA 30602

LANDAU, ELLIS, hotel executive; b. Phila., Feb. 24, 1944; s. Manfred and Ruth (Fischer) L.; m. Kathy Suzanne Thomas, May 19, 1968 (div.); children: Rachel, David; m. Yvette Ehr Cohen, Nov. 1, 1992. BA in Econs., Brandeis U., 1965; MBA, Columbia U., 1967. Fin. analyst SEC, Washington, 1968-69; asst. treas. U-Haul Internat., Phoenix, 1969-71; v.p., treas. Ramada, Inc., Phoenix, 1971-90; CFO Boyd Gaming Corp., Las Vegas, Nev., 1990—. Home: 7571 Silver Meadow Ct Las Vegas NV 89117-2986 Office: Boyd Gaming Corp 2950 Industrial Rd Las Vegas NV 89109-1100 Office Phone: 702-792-7210. Personal E-mail: ellislandau@boydgaming.com.

LANDAU, EMANUEL, epidemiologist; b. NYC, Nov. 28, 1919; s. Meyer and Annie (Heller) L.; m. Davetta Goldberg, Sept. 5, 1948; children: Melanie (dec.), Elizabeth. BA, CCNY, 1939; Phd, Am. U., 1966. Supervisory analytical statistician Calif. Dept. Public Health, 1957-59, chief biometry sect., divsn. air pollution, 1959-62; head lab. and clin. trials sect. Nat. Cancer Inst., 1962-65; statis. adviser Nat. Air Pollution Control Administrn., 1965-69; epidemiologist Environ. Health Svc., 1969-71; chief epidemiologic studies br. Bur. Radiol. Health, 1971-74; project dir., sci. cons. Am. Pub. Health Assn., Washington, 1975—. Cons., adv. WHO adv. on air quality criteria, Geneva, 1967, Karolinska Inst., Stockholm, 1968, others. Contbr. articles to profl. jours. Vol. White House Health Care Reform Corr. With AUS, 1942-46, capt. USPHS Res. Decorated Belgian Fourragere; recipient Superior Svc. award HEW, 1963. Fellow Am. Pub. Health Assn., Royal Soc. Health; mem. Soc. Epidemiologic Rsch., Am. Statis. Assn. (chmn. com. on stats. and environ.), Cosmos Club. Democrat. Jewish. Home: 4601 N Park Ave Apt 208 Chevy Chase MD 20815-4575 Office: Am Pub Health Assn 800 I Street NW Washington DC 20001-3710 Office Phone: 202-777-2424.

LANDAU, EMILY FISHER, art collector, foundation administrator; b. Glen Falls, N.Y., Aug. 23; d. Samuel and Cecelia (Greene) Lanzner; m. Martin A. Fisher (dec.); children: Richard L. Fisher, M. Anthony Fisher (dec.), Candia Fisher; m. Sheldon Landau. Ptnr. Fisher Bros., N.Y.C.; prs. Fisher Landau Found., N.Y.C., 1984—; founder Fisher Landau Ctr. Art, Long Island City, 1991; PhD (hon.) Yeshiva U., 1998—. Trustee Whitney Mus. Am. Art, N.Y.C., 1987—, co-chmn. contemporary com., 1994—; mem. chmn.'s coun. Mus. Modern Art, N.Y.C., 1992—, mem. com. on painting and sculpture, 1997—, mem. com. on prints and illustrated books, 1985—; bd. dirs. The Georgia O'Keeffe Mus., Santa Fe, 1996; adv. dir. Met. Opera Assn., N.Y.C., 1986-88, mng. dir., 1988—; sponsor Emily Fisher Landau professorship of neurology Harvard Med. Sch., Cambridge, Mass., 1995—; founder Fisher Landau Ctr. for Treatment of Learning Disabilities, Albert Einstein Coll. Medicine/Yeshiva U., N.Y.C., 1997—; founding mem. Nat. Mus. Women in the Arts, 1987; charter mem. U.S. Holocaust Meml. Mus., 1992; bd. dirs. Site Santa Fe, 1994. Pub. exhbn. catalog Jasper Johns: The Screenprints, 1996; Mishoo Cosmopolitan Cat (children's storybook), 2000. Vice chmn. Anti-Defamation League of B'nai B'rith, N.Y.C.; sec. Anti-Defamation Found., N.Y.C.; sponsor Music Outreach, West End Symphony Pub. Sch. Project, N.Y.C. Decorated Chevalier Order Arts and Letters (France); named one of Top 200 Collectors, ARTnews mag., 2004. Mem. Met. Club, Doubles, Palm Beach Country Club. Avocation: collector of contemporary Am. art.*

LANDAU, JOEL, health services administrator; b. Goshen, NY, Aug. 22, 1980; s. Joseph Landau; m. Rachel Stein; children: Judah, Rebecca. Master's, UTA, 2000. Rabbi diplomat 1999. CEO E-ZBILL, LLC, Bklyn., 2002—. Advisor Yetev Lev, Bklyn., 2001—03. Mem.: Bus. Advisory Coun. Office: E-ZBILL, LLC 199 Lee Ave #182 Brooklyn NY 11211 Office Phone: 718-858-4944. Office Fax: 718-504-5339. Business E-Mail: joe@e-zbill.com.

LANDAU, JON, music producer, manager; m. Barbara Landau. Grad., Brandeis U., 1968. Rock critic Crawdaddy!, Boston Phoenix, Rolling Stone, The Real Paper; founder, co-owner Jon Landau Mgmt.; former mgr. for Shania Twain, Natalie Merchant; mgr. for Bruce Springsteen, Train, Patti Scialfa; has produced albums for MC5, Livingston Taylor, Jackson Brown, Bruce Springsteen. Author: It's Too Late to Stop Now: A Rock and Roll Jour., 1972. Named one of Top 200 Collectors, ARTnews mag., 2004. Achievements include Famous for line "I saw rock and roll future and its name is Bruce Springsteen", which appeared in his article for The Real Paper on May 22, 1974. Avocation: Collector Old Master painting and sculpture, 19th-century French painting, Am. modernist art. Office: Jon Landau Mgmt 80 Mason St Greenwich CT 06830*

LANDAU, LAURI BETH, accountant, consultant; b. Bklyn., July 21, 1952; d. Jack and Audrey Carolyn (Zuckernick) L. BA, Skidmore Coll., 1973; postgrad., Pace U., 1977-79. CPA, N.Y. Mem. staff Audrey Z. Landau, CPA, Suffern, N.Y., 1976-78, Ernst & Whinney, N.Y.C., 1979-80, mem. sr. staff, 1980-82, supr., 1982-84; mgr. Arthur Young & Co., N.Y.C., 1984-87, prin., 1987-89; sr. mgr. Ernst & Young, N.Y.C., 1989-92; ptnr. Landau & Landau, Pomona, N.Y., 1992—. Ptnr. Audrey Z. Landau & Co., Wilmington, Vt., 1995—; spkr. World Trade Inst., N.Y.C., 1987—, Nat. Fgn. Trade Coun., N.Y.C., 1989—. Composer songs. Career counselor Skidmore Coll., Saratoga Springs, N.Y., 1977—; mem. leadership com. Class of 1973, 83-85, pres., 1985-93, fund chmn., 1987-88, mem. planned gift com., 1989—. N.Y. State Regents scholar, 1970. Mem. Nat. Conf. CPA Practitioners, N.Y. State Soc. CPAs, Rockland Bus. Assn., Skidmore Coll. Alumni Assn. (mem. nominating com. 1989-92). Skidmore Alumni Club. Democrat. Avocations: music, ballet, photography, sports. Office: 26 Firemans Memorial Dr Pomona NY 10970-3553 Business E-Mail: lauri@landauandlandau.com.

LANDAU, MICHAEL B., law educator; b. Wilkes-Barre, Pa., July 3, 1953; s. Jack Landau and Florence (Rabitz) Simon. BA, Pa. State U., 1975; JD, U. Pa., 1988. Vis. prof. law Dickinson Sch. Law, Pa. State U., Carlisle; assoc. Cravath, Swaine and Moore, N.Y.C., 1988-90, Skadden, Arps, N.Y.C., 1990-92; assoc. prof. Coll. Law Ga. State U., Atlanta, 1992-99, prof. law, 1999—, dir. intellectual property, tech. and media law program. Vis. prof. law U. Ga. Law Sch., 1998; guest lectr. Johannes Kepler U., Linz, Austria, summer 1994, 95, 96; vis. scholar Univ. Amsterdam, 2000, U. Helsinki, Finland, 2005 Contbr. articles to law jours. on copyright, art, patent, entertainment law. Scholar, Fulbright Found., 2005. Mem. ABA, N.Y. State Bar Assn., Internat. Bar Assn., Vol. Lawyers for Arts, Am. Fedn. Musicians, Am. Intellectual Property Law Assn., Copyright Soc. U.S. Am., Phi Kappa Phi, Omicron Delta Epsilon. Democrat. Avocations: photography, jazz guitar, jazz piano. Office: Ga State U Coll Law University Pla Atlanta GA 30303 Office Phone: 404-651-2084. Business E-Mail: mlandau@gsu.edu.

LANDAU, NORMA BEATRICE, historian, educator; b. Toronto, Ont., Can., Sept. 13, 1942; d. Julius and Anne L. BA, U. Toronto, 1964, MA, 1965; PhD, U. Calif., Berkeley, 1974. Lectr. Duke U., Durham, N.C., 1972-74; lectr. UCLA, 1975-76; prof. U. Calif., Davis, 1976—. Author: The Justices of the Peace, 1984; contbr. articles profl. jours. Mem. Pacific Coast Conf. on Brit. Studies, North Am. Conf. on Brit. Studies. Office: History Dept U Calif Davis CA 95616

LANDAU, PETER EDWARD, editor; b. N.Y.C., July 16, 1933; s. Edward and Charlotte (Schmidt) L. AB, Duke U., 1955; MS in Econs., Columbia U., 1959. Editl. asst. Newsweek mag., N.Y.C., 1955-57, asst. editor, 1958-61, assoc. editor, 1962-67; v.p. Tiderock Corp., 1967; sr. editor Instl. Investor, N.Y.C., 1968, mng. editor, 1968-70, editor, 1971-91, editor-at-large, 1991-97; historian St. Andrew's Golf Club, 1993—. Co-author: Presidential Lies: The Illustrated History of White House Golf, 1996. Home: 10 Old Jackson Ave Unit 11 Hastings On Hudson NY 10706

LANDAU, SIDNEY IVAN, lexicographer; b. N.Y.C., Apr. 11, 1933; s. Emanuel and Sadie Mildred (Halpern) L.; m. Sarah Gaston Bradford, June 19, 1959; children: Paul, Amy. BA in English, Queens Coll., 1954; MFA in Creative Writing, U. Iowa, 1959. Instr. English Miami U., Oxford, Ohio, 1959-61; editor, then editor-in-chief dictionaries Funk & Wagnalls, N.Y.C., 1961-70; editor-in-chief Doubleday Dictionary, Doubleday Roget's Thesaurus Doubleday & Co., N.Y.C., 1975-77; editor-in-chief Internat. Dictionary of Medicine and Biology, John Wiley & Sons, N.Y.C., 1977-88, mgr. med. jours., 1982-84, exec. editor medicine, 1985-87, pub. chemistry and life scis. sci.-tech. div., 1987-88; editl. dir. N.Am. br. Cambridge U. Press, N.Y.C., 1988-93; editor-in-chief Cambridge Dictionary of Am. English, 2000. Author: Dictionaries: The Art and Craft of Lexicography, 1984, 2d edit., 2001; contbr. numerous articles to profl. jours. With U.S. Army, 1954-56. Fellow: Dictionary Soc. N.Am. (pres. 1993—95). Home: 50 W 96th St Apt 2A New York NY 10025-6527

LANDAU-CRAWFORD, DOROTHY RUTH, retired social services administrator; b. Staten Island, NY, Oct. 5, 1957; d. Robert August and Dorothy Faith (Schaut) Landau; m. John W. Crawford, Oct. 21, 1989; 1 child, Jacqueline Lauren. AS, SUNY, Farmingdale, 1977; BS in Biology, Wagner Coll., 1979. Sci. tchr. Bais Yaakov, S.I., 1979-81; dental asst. Dr. Marvin Freeman, S.I., 1981-82; office mgr. Dr. Bennett C. Fidlow, S.I., 1982-85; polit. aide to S.I. Borough Pres. S.I. Borough Pres., 1985-89; exec. dir. Richmond Sr. Svcs. Project Share, 1990—2000; ret., 2000. V.p. N.J. Shared Housing Assn., regional dir. Nat. Shared Housing Resouces Ctr., 1995—; environ. chmn. S.I. League for Better Govt., 1984—; pres. Tottenville Improvement Council Inc., Staten Island, 1985—. Dem. candidate N.Y State Assembly 60th Dist., 1986, dist. leader; dir. cmty. bds. S.I. Borough Pres.'s Office; founder, pres. environ. group S.I.L.E.N.T., S.I., 1985; 1st v.p. 123d Cmty. Coun., L.I., 1986; social chmn. South Shore Dem. Club; founding mem. Friends of Clay Pit Pond Park; active Protectors of Pine Oak Woods Inc., Roserio Alliotta Dem. Club, Dem. Orgn. Richmond; trustee S.I. Bd. Leukemia Soc. Am., 1988—, chair Celebrity Waiters Luncheon; spl. election candidate for 51st Councilmatic Dist., 1994. Recipient Cmty. Activist award Office of pres. S.I. Borough, 1987. Mem. NAFE, Bus. and Profl. Women (young careerist for S.I.). Avocations: photography, sports, ceramics, youth programs. Home: 370 Jackson Mills Rd Jackson NJ 08527-4446 Personal E-mail: bsa65@aol.com.

LANDAUER, ELVIE ANN WHITNEY, humanities educator, writer; b. Detroit, Dec. 10, 1937; d. Augustus and Leona (Green) Moore; m. Thomas Whitney, 1963 (div. 1978); m. Ernest Landauer, Dec. 31, 1987. BA, Calif. State U., L.A., 1978; MA, San Francisco State U., 1989; postgrad., U. N.Mex. Dep. dir. Calif. Arts Coun., Sacramento, 1976-79; exec. dir. Mothers Emergency Svc., Sacramento, 1979-82; assoc. dir. San Francisco Cmty. Bds., 1982-83; adminstr. San Francisco Rsch. Project, 1983-86; exec. dir. East Bay Ctr. for Performing Arts, Richmond, Calif., 1987-89; instr. English Calif. C.C.s, Pittsburg, Fremont & Hayward, 1990-93; instr. Am. studies U. N.Mex., Alburg, 1993-94; instr. humanities New Coll., San Francisco, 1994-95. Rschr. LA Cmty. Arts Alliance, 1972; bus. owner, pres., pub. Academics of Course, Inc., Vallejo, Calif., 1997—. Author: (drama anthology) The Disinherited, 1971, The Uptown Mrs. Carrie, 1989; prodr.: Meat Theater Co., 1970—72. Bd. dirs. Richmond (Calif.) Arts Coun., 1986-89; workshop coord. L.A. Writers Workshop, 1966-69, Sacramento Civic Theater, 1980; project coord. City Spirit Project, Pasadena, Calif., 1972-75. With USN, 1958-61. Recipient Woman of Yr. award Iota Phi Lambda, Sacramento, 1981. Office: Academics of Course Inc PO Box 9010 Vallejo CA 94591 Office Phone: 707-642-4703.

LANDAW, STEPHEN ARTHUR, physician, educator; b. Paterson, NJ, June 20, 1936; s. Louis and Ida (Machowsky) L.; children: Jared Lawrence, Nicole Renee. BS, U. Wis., 1955; MD, George Washington U., 1959; PhD, U. Calif., Berkeley, 1969. Intern Mt. Sinai Hosp., N.Y.C., 1959-60, resident in internal medicine, 1960-61; fellow in hematology Med. Coll. Va., 1962-63; fellow in nuclear medicine Donner Lab., U. Calif., 1963-69, asst. physician, 1970-73; chief isotope lab. Highland-Alameda County Hosp., Oakland, Calif., 1970-73; asso. prof. SUNY, Syracuse, 1973-78, prof., 1978-99; assoc. chief staff research and devel. VA Med. Center, Syracuse, 1973-94; chief, hematology VA Med. Ctr., Syracuse, 1997-99; vis. prof. Rockefeller U., N.Y.C., 1988; vis. physician Rockefeller U. Hosp., N.Y.C., 1988; dep. editor, hematology Uptodate, Inc., Wellesley, Mass., 1999—; attending physician hematology-oncology Beth Israel Deaconess Med. Ctr., Boston, 2003—. Pres. Ctrl. NY Rsch. Corp., 1989—94; clin. instr. medicine Harvard Med. Sch., Boston, 2003—. Contbr. in field. Served with U.S. Army, 1961-62. VA grantee, 1973-93; NASA grantee, 1976-82; recipient NASA Kosmos Achievement awards, 1975, 77 Fellow ACP; mem. Am. Soc. Hematology, Am. Fedn. Clin. Rsch., Soc. Pediat. Rsch., Soc. Exptl. Biology and Medicine, N.Y. Acad. Sci., Sigma Xi, Alpha Omega Alpha. Jewish. Home: 241 Perkins St Apt C105 Jamaica Plain MA 02130-4058 Office: Uptodate Inc 34 Washington St Ste 200 Wellesley MA 02481-1903 Office Phone: 781-416-3221. Personal E-mail: slandaw@uptodate.com.

LANDE, JAMES AVRA, retired lawyer; b. Chgo., Oct. 2, 1930; s. S. Theodore and Helen C. (Hamburger) L.; m. Ann Mari Gustavsson, Feb. 21, 1959; children: Rebecca Susanne, Sylvia Diane. BA, Swarthmore Coll., 1952; JD, Columbia U., 1955. Bar: N.Y. 1958, Calif. 1967. Assoc. Rein, Mound & Cotton, N.Y.C., 1957-59; atty. VA, Seattle, 1959-61, Weyerhaeuser Co., Tacoma, 1961-63, Lande Assocs., San Francisco, 1963-67, NASA, Ames Rsch. Ctr., Moffett Field, Calif., 1967-70; house counsel Syntex Corp., Palo Alto, Calif., 1970-73; dir. contracts dept. Electric Power Rsch. Inst., Palo Alto, Calif., 1973-81; corp. atty., dir. contracts Lurgi Corp., Belmont, Calif., 1981-82; contracts mgr. Bechtel Corp., San Francisco, 1982-92; sr. contract mgr. Bay Area Rapid Transit Dist., Millbrae, Calif., 1992—2004; ret. Adj. prof. U. San Francisco Sch. Law, 1972-73; lectr. law U. Santa Clara Sch. Law, 1968-82; pres. Syntex Fed. Credit Union, 1971-72. Served with U.S. Army, 1955-57. Mem. Calif. Bar Assn., Nat. Contract Mgmt. Assn. (past pres., dir. Golden Gate chpt.), Lawyers Club San Francisco. Home: 1330 33rd Ave San Francisco CA 94122-1305

LANDECK, CARL, corporate financial executive; CPA. V.p. fin., chief acctg. and fin. officer Herman's Sporting Goods, Inc.; CFO Nobody Beats the Wiz, Carteret, NJ; exec. v.p. Cablevision Electronics Investments Inc., Edison, NJ, 1998; CFO, chief adminstrv. officer Levitz Home Furnishings Inc.; CFO Bally's Total Fitness, Chgo., 2005—. Office: Bally Total Fitness 8700 W Bryn Mawr Ave Chicago IL 60631

LANDEFELD, STEWART M., lawyer; b. Cleve., Mar. 13, 1954; BA, Yale U., 1976; JD, U. Chgo., 1980. Bar: Wash. 1980, US Ct. Appeals (9th Cir.). Ptnr., Corp. Fin .& Securities Practice Area Perkins Coie LLP, Seattle. Co-author: Washington Corporate Law: Corporations and LLCs, 1991—. Vice chmn. bd. trustees Seattle Found.; chmn. bd. trustees Henry Art Gallery; mem. Pike Place Market Preservation and Devel. Authority. Named a Wash.

Super Lawyer, Wash. Law & Polit. Office: Perkins Coie LLP 1201 3rd Ave Fl 40 Seattle WA 98101-3029 Office Phone: 206-359-8430. Office Fax: 206-359-9430. Business E-Mail: slandefeld@perkinscoie.com.

LANDEL, MICHEL, food service and management company executive; b. 1952; MBA, European Bus. Sch., Paris; student, France, U.K., Germany. With acctg. and control dept. for Europe, Chase Manhattan Bank, France, founder, country ops. mgr.; gen. mgr. Poliet Group, mfrs. and distbrs. bldg. materials, France, 1980-84; chief operating mgr. for Ea. Africa, Libya and Algeria, Sodexho, 1984-86, pres. remote site ops. in Africa, 1986-89; pres., CEO, Sodexho N.Am. (merger with Marriott Mgmt. Svcs.), 1989-98; exec. v.p., pres. corp. svcs. divsn. Sodexho Marriott Svcs., Inc., Gaithersburg, Md., 1998-99, pres., CEO, 1999—, group pres., COO, 2003—, also chmn. bd. dirs. Gaithersburg, Md. Recipient Golden Chain award Multi-Unit Food Svc. Operators, 1997, Ivy award Restaurant & Instns., 1998. Office: Sodexho Marriott Svcs Inc 9801 Washington Blvd Gaithersburg MD 20878*

LANDEN, ROBERT GERAN, retired historian, academic administrator; b. Boston, July 13, 1930; s. Harry James and Evelyn Gertrude (Geran) L.; m. Patricia Kizzia, July 19, 1958; children— Michael Geran, Robert Kizzia, Jill Arnett, Amy Patricia. AB, Coll. of William and Mary, 1952; MA, U. Mich., 1953; A.M., Princeton U., 1958, PhD (Ford Found. fellow), 1961. Asst. prof. social sci. Ball State U., Muncie, Ind., 1959-60; asst. prof. near eastern studies U. Mich., Ann Arbor, 1960-61; asst. prof. history Dartmouth, Hanover, N.H., 1961-66, asst. dean of freshmen, 1963-64, asso. prof. history, 1966-67; prof., head dept. history Va. Poly. Inst. and State U., Blacksburg, 1967-69; prof. history U. S.C., Columbia, 1969-75, asso. vice provost, 1971-72, asso. provost, 1972-73; dean U. S.C. (Coll. of Social and Behavioral Scis.), 1972-75; prof. history U. Tex. at Arlington, 1975-77; dean U. Tex. at Arlington (Coll. Liberal Arts), 1975-77; prof. history U. Tenn., Knoxville, 1977-86; dean Coll. Liberal Arts, 1977-85; prof. history, v.p. acad. affairs, provost U. Montevallo, 1986-88; prof. history and humanities, dir. programs in the humanities Va. Poly Inst. and State U., Blacksburg, 1988-95, prof. emeritus history and humanities, 1995—. Author: Oman Since 1856, 1967, The Emergence of the Modern Middle East, 1970, (with Abid Al-Marayati) The Middle East, Its Governments and Politics, 1972; contbr. articles to profl. jours. and book revs. to hist. publs. Served with AUS, 1953-55. Am. Coun. Learned Socs. fellow, 1965-66, Comparative Studies Ctr. Faculty fellow, 1965-66, Malone fellow, 1988. Fellow Middle East Studies Assn. of N. Am.; mem. Theta Delta Chi, Phi Kappa Phi. Roman Catholic. Home: 108 Edgewood Ln Williamsburg VA 23185-3213

LANDER, ERIC STEVEN, geneticist, molecular biologist, mathematician; b. Bklyn., Feb. 3, 1957; BA in Math. with hons., Princeton U., 1978; DPhil in Math., Oxford (Eng.) U., 1981. Asst. prof. Grad. Sch. Bus., Harvard U., 1981-86, assoc. prof., 1987-90; Whitehead fellow MIT, Cambridge, 1986, vis. scientist, 1984-89, assoc. prof., 1989-93, prof. dept. biology, 1993—, mem. Whitehead Inst. Biomed. Rsch., 1989—, founder, dir. Whitehead Ctr. Genome Rsch., 1990—, founding dir., Broad Inst., 1990—. Med. geneticist Mass. Genl. Hosp., Boston, 1993—; Ralph R. Braund disting. vis. prod. U. Tenn., 1994; mem. U.S. Presdl. Commn. Nat. Medal Sci., 1995-97; mem. genetics working group NIMH, 1997—; Christian A. Herter disting. lectr. NYU, 1993; Gladstone disting. lectr. Gladstone Inst., 1994; Herbert Boyer lectr. genetics U. Calif., San Francisco, 1995. Contbr. articles to profl. jours. Named Millennium Lectr., The White House, 1999, Scientist of Year, Nat. Disease Rsch. Interchange, 2003, R&D Mag., 2003; recipient Beckman prize for lab automation, Chiron prize in biotechnology, Woodrow Wilson prize for pub. svc., Princeton U., Dickson prize in cancer, Rhodes prize in cancer, Gairdner award, Gairdner Found., 2002, Pub. Understanding of Sci. and Tech. award; fellow MacArthur fellow, 1987; scholar Rhodes scholar, 1978. Fellow AAAS; mem. NAS (mem. math. and molecular biology com. 1989-90), Human Genome Orgn., Genetics Soc. Am., Am. Soc. Human Genetics, Math. Assn. Am., Am. Acad. Forensic Sci., Am. Assn. Cancer Rsch, Inst. Medicine Achievements include founding the center which is the leading contributor to the Human Genome Project. Address: MIT 77 Massachusetts Ave Cambridge MA 02139-4307 Office: Whitehead Inst/MIT 9 Cambridge Center Cambridge MA 02142-1479 Office Phone: 617-252-1906. Office Fax: 617-258-0903.

LANDER, HOWARD, entertainment newspaper publisher; b. N.Y.C., Oct. 25, 1950; s. Leo T. and Doris (Davis) L.; m. Gail Melanie Ravitz, Sept. 6, 1976; children: Aimee, Jared. BA, Rutgers U., Newark, 1972. Sportswriter Buffalo Courier-Express, 1973; reporter Amusement Bus., N.Y.C., 1973-76, sales rep., 1976-79, pub. Nashville, 1981-88; advt. mgr. Residential Interiors mag., N.Y.C., 1980; v.p., group pub. BPI Comm., 1988-90; pub. Billboard Mag., N.Y.C., 1990-91; sr. v.p. BPI Comm., 1991-92, exec. v.p., 1993—; pres., pub. Billboard Music Group, 1994—, Billboard Literary Group, 1994—; COO, VNU Bus. Media, 2004—. Recipient Spirit of Life award City of Hope, 1998. Avocations: sports, literature, music.

LANDER, JAMES ALBERT, retired military officer, controller; b. Abbeville, S.C., Apr. 9, 1930; s. William Jones and Annie (Cheatham) L.; m. Jolene Patricia Smith, June 8, 1952; children: Theresa (dec.), Britt, Leslie, Victoria (dec.), Gail, Jean, David. BS, Lander Coll., 1986; LLD (hon.), Lander U., 2000. Technician S.C. Nat. Guard, Abbeville, 1952-53; life ins. salesman Gulf Life Pilot, Met., Anderson, S.C., 1953-66; maj. U.S. Army, 1966-71; plans and ops. officer, chief of staff S.C. Army N.G., Columbia, 1971-85, maj. gen. mil., 1988-91; mem. S.C. Senate, Columbia, 1993-99; elected state comptr. State of S.C., Columbia, 1999—2003. Chmn. RSVP Adv. Com., 1991—, Newberry County Literacy Assn., 1991-93; deacon Newberry 1st Bapt. Ch.; past chmn. Boy Scouts Am., Newberry. Decorated Bronze Star, Legion of Merit; recipient Arc Legis. award, 1999, Order of Palmetto State of S.C., 1985, Palmetto Cross, 1991, Silver Beaver award Boy Scouts Am., 1990; named Legislator of Yr. S.C. Assn. Counties and S.C. Assn. Deaf, 1994. Mem.: AARP (pres.), VFW, Mil. Officers Assn. Am., C. of C. Newberry, Assn. U.S. Army, Mil. Order World Wars, Vietnam Vets. Assn., Exch. Club (pres.), Rotary, Masons, Shriners, Am. Legion. Democrat. Baptist. Avocations: reading, gardening. Home: 2029 Main St Newberry SC 29108-3521 Personal E-mail: jalander@bellsouth.net.

LANDER, JOYCE ANN, retired nursing educator, retired medical/surgical nurse; b. Benton Harbor, Mich, July 27, 1942; d. James E. and Anna Mae Remus LPN, Kalamazoo Practical Nursing, Ctr., 1967; AAS, Kalamazoo Valley C.C., 1981, Grad. Massage Therapy Program, 1995. LPN-RN Bronson Meth. Hosp., Kalamazoo, 1972-82; RN med./surg. unit Borgess Med. Ctr., Kalamazoo, 1982-84; RN pediat. Upjohn Home Health Care, Kalamazoo, 1984-88; supr. nursing lab Kalamazoo Valley Comm. Coll., 1982—2005, ret., 2005. Therapeutic massage therapist in client homes with Business Kneading Peace Therapeutic Massage, Kalamazoo, 1995—; nursing asst., instr. State of Mich. Observer, 1990-96. Author: What Is A Nurse, 1980. Address: 3300 Woodstone Dr E Apt 108 Kalamazoo MI 49008-2548

LANDER, RUTH A., medical group and association administrator; b. Fitchburg, Mass., Dec. 13, 1948; d. H. Allison and Violet K. (Erickson) Linné; m. C. Stephen Lander, June 28, 1968; children: Timothy, Mary. BA, Ohio State U., 1978; postgrad., Kennedy-Western U., 1995—. Dir. fin. Luth. Svc. Assn. New England, Natick, Mass., 1973—76; gen. mgr. Logos, Columbus, Ohio, 1976—87; practice adminstr. Columbus Oncology Assocs., Inc., 1987—. Sec., treas. Adminstrs. Oncology Hematology Assembly, Englewood, Colo., 1994-95, legis. liaison, 1994-95, pres.-elect, 1995-96, pres., 1996-97; spkr. med. group mgmt. issues. Editor Administrs. in Oncology Hematology Assembly News, 1994-95; mem. editl. bd. Oncology Issues Mag., 1998-2000; mem. editl. adv. bd. for coding and reimbursement Oncology & Hematology, 2001; contbr. articles to profl. jours. Mem. task force Cmty. Oncology Alliance, 2004-05. Fellow Med. Group Mgmt. Assn., Am. Coll. Med. Practice Execs. (nat. chair membership devel. com. 1999, nat. bd. dirs. 2004—); mem. Am. Soc. Clin. Oncology (assoc.), Nat. Oncology Soc. Network, Ctrl.-Ohio Med. Group Mgmt. Assn. (pres. 1993-94, sec. 1992-93, program dir. 1991-92, exec. com. 1990-97), Assn. Cmty. Cancer Ctr. (editl. bd. mag. 1998-2000), Ohio Med. Group Mgmt. Assn. (exec. com. 1994-2001, sec. 1995-96, pres. 1998, rep. to Medicare PCOM adv. group 2003—, grass roots legis. group 1994—), Ohio Oncology Med. Group Mgmt. Assn. (pres. 1997), Ohio State Med. Assn. (assoc.; group practice task force 2000—), Columbus Med. Assn. (group practice mgrs. task force 2002—). Republican. Avocations: reading, computers, crafts, knitting, bible study. Office: Columbus Oncology Assocs 810 Jasonway Ave Ste A Columbus OH 43214-2329

LANDERS, AUDREY, actress, singer; d. Ruth Landers. BA, Barnard Coll. Records singles and albums with sister Judy Landers. Appeared in (films) A Chorus Line, 1985, Getting Even, 1986, (TV) The Merv Griffin Show, The Secret Storm, Somerset, Dallas; singer U.S., European tours. Office: care Jo-Ann Geffen & Assocs 3151 Cahuenga Blvd W Ste 235 Los Angeles CA 90068-1749

LANDERS, PATRICIA GLOVER, language educator; b. Pine Bluff, Ark., Nov. 15, 1945; d. Maurice Alexander Glover and Ruth Wells-Glover Wimberly; 1 child, Wendolynn. BS in Edn., Ark. State U., 1967; MS in Edn., OBU, 1976; postgrad., U. Ark., 1980—81, U. Ariz., 1980—81, Ariz. State U., 1983—88, U. Phoenix, 1988—89. Cert. tchr. English, reading specialist K-12 Ariz., C.C., English, lang. arts, composition Ariz. Elem. music supr. Greene County Tech. Schs., Paragould, Ark., 1967—68; band & choir dir. Naylor (Mo.) Schs., 1968—70; elem. tchr. Poughkeepsie (Ark.) Schs., 1970—72; reading specialist Sheridan (Ariz.) Schs., 1975—82, Casa Grande Union High Sch., Casa Grande, Ariz., 1982—; assoc. prof. Pima C.C., Tucson, 1982—94, Centra Ariz. Coll., Coolidge, Ariz., 1983—93; English tchr. Casa Granda Regional Med. Ctr. Alternative, Casa Grande, 1994—2001; owner Landers' Tutoring Svc., Casa Grande, 2001—. Test supr. SAT, ACT Testing Svcs., Casa Grande, 1997—. Author: Making English Make Sense, 1996. Invited rep. U.S. to China People to People Amb. Program, 2000; French hornist CAC Cmty. Concert Band, Coolidge, Ariz., 1984—2000; organist North Trekell Bapt. Ch., Casa Grande, 1996—, founder instrumental music founds. group, 2001; chair babysitting com. Casa Grand Regionl Med. Ctr., Casa Grande, 1995—98. Mem.: NEA, Ark. Reading Coun., Ctrl. Ariz. Reading Coun., Ariz. Reading Coun., Ariz. Edn. Assn., Casa Grande Edn. Assn. (pres. 1985—86, Outstanding Svc. award 1985—86), Sheridan Ednl. Assoc. (pres. 1978—79), Internat. Reading Assoc., CGRMC Aux. (com. chairperson 1995—98, Vol. of Month 1995). Democrat. Baptist. Avocations: reading, jogging, musical instruments. Home: PO Box 589 Arizona City AZ 85223 Office: CGUHS 2730 N Trekell Rd Casa Grande AZ 85222 Office Phone: 520-466-5747, 520-836-8500 4179. Personal E-mail: langders@egmailbox.com. Business E-Mail: planders@cguhs.org. E-mail: landers@egmailbox.com.

LANDERS, THOMAS LEE, dean, educator; b. Dumas, Tex., May 7, 1950; s. Sidney Wayne and Murriel K. Landers; m. Patti Sue Stone, Aug. 19, 1972; children: Stephen Thomas, David Wayne, Andrew Stone. BS in Indsl. Engring., Tex. Tech. U., 1972, MS in Indsl. Engring., 1973, PhD, 1985. Registered profl. engr., Okla., Ark. Rsch. asst. dept. indsl. engring. Tex. Tech. U., Lubbock, 1972—73, lectr., rsch. asst. dept. indsl. engring., 1984—85; reliability and maintainability engr. divsn. aero. sys. Wright-Patterson AFB, Dayton, Ohio, 1973—77; devel. engr. Tex. Instruments Inc., Lubbock, 1978; mgr. Arthur Young and Company, Dallas, 1979—83; engr., cons. project engr., warranty mgr. Lone Star Mfg. Co., Ft. Worth, 1983; from asst. prof. to prof. dept. indsl. engring. U. Ark., Fayetteville, 1985—98; dir. U. Okla. Sch. Indsl. Engring., Norman, 1998—2001; assoc. dean for rsch. and grad. programs U. Okla. Coll. Engring., Norman, 2001—. Rsch. program leader Material Handling Rsch. Ctr., 1992—95; dir. Logistics Inst., 1995—98, Inst. for Okla. Tech. Applications, Norman, 2004—; co-dir. Ctr. for Aircraft and Sys. support Infrastructure, Okla., 1999—2001, dir., Okla., 2001—03; co-dir. Okla. Transp. Ctr., 2001—, exec. dir., 2003—; co-dir. Ctr. for Engring. Logistics and Distribution, 2001—; presenter, cons. in field. Co-author (with T. Landers, W. Brown, E. Fant, E. Malstrom, N. Schmitt): Electronics Manufacturing Processes, 1994, Instructors' Manual, Electronics Manufacturing Processes, 1994; contbr. articles to profl. jours. Capt. USAF, 1970—77. Named Outstanding Tchr., Halliburton, 1986—87, 1992—93, Outstanding Rschr., 1988—90, Tex. Instruments, 1995—97, Outstanding Prof., Phillips Petroleum Co., 1992; recipient Outstanding Svc. award, ASME, 2000; grantee, NSF, 1994—98, 2001—03, Global Concepts, 1999, Trane Co., 1999—2000, USAF, 2000—02, FAA, 2000—02, Okla. Dept. Transp., 2001—02, US Dept. Transp., 2002, 2004, Fed. Transit Adminstrn., 2004, others. Mem.: AAAS, Soc. Am. Mil. Engrs., Am. Soc. Engring. Edn., Coun. Logistics Mgmt., Coll. Industry Coun. on Material Handling Edn., Inst. Indsl. Engrs. (sr.), Phi Kappa Phi, Alpha Pi Mu, Tau Beta Pi, Sigma Xi. Home: 4408 12th Ave NE Norman OK 73071 Office: Univ Okla 202 W Boyd CEC 107 Norman OK 73019 Fax: 405-325-7805. Business E-Mail: landers@ou.edu.

LANDES, GEORGE MILLER, biblical studies educator; b. Kansas City, Mo., Aug. 2, 1928; s. George Y. and Margaret B. (Fizzell) L.; m. Carol Marie Dee, Aug. 30, 1953; children: George Miller Jr., Margaret Dee, John Christopher. AB, U. Mo., 1949; M.Div., McCormick Theol. Sem., 1952; PhD, Johns Hopkins U., 1956. Minister to youth Second Presbyn. Ch., Balt., 1952-53, Govans Presbyn. Ch., Balt., 1953-56; instr. Old Testament Union Theol. Sem., N.Y.C., 1956-58, asst. prof. Old Testament, 1958-62, assoc. prof., 1962-70, prof., 1970-95, prof. emeritus, 1995—. Ann. prof. Am. Sch. Oriental Rsch., Jerusalem, Israel, 1967-68 Author: Building Your Biblical Hebrew Vocabulary, 2001; author, editor: Report on Archaeological Work, 1975. Nettie F. McCormick fellow, 1952-54; Am. Council Learned Socs. fellow, 1967-68 Mem. Soc. Bibl. Lit., Amman Ctr. Archaeol. Rsch. (v.p. 1969-79), Am. Schs. Oriental Rsch. (sec. 1972-94), Phi Beta Kappa. Personal E-mail: g.m.landes@att.net.

LANDES, WILLIAM M., law educator; b. 1939; AB, Columbia U., 1960, PhD in Economics, 1966. Asst. prof. economics Stanford U., 1965—66, U. Chgo., 1966—69; assoc. prof. Columbia U., 1969—72, CUNY Grad. Ctr., 1972—74; prof. economics U. Chgo. Law Sch., 1974—80, Clifton R. Musser prof. economics, 1980—92, Clifton R. Musser prof. law & economics, 1992—; founder, chmn. Lexecon, Inc., 1977—98, chmn. emeritus, 1998—; mem. bd. examiners GRE in Econs., ETS, 1967—74. Author (with Richard Posner): The Economic Structure of Tort Law, 1987; editor (with Gary Becker): Essays in the Economics of Crime and Punishment, 1974; editor: Jour. Law and Econs., 1975—91, Jour. Legal Studies, 1991—. Mem.: Am. Law and Econ. Assn. (v.p. 1991—92, pres. 1992—93), Am. Econ. Assn., Mont Pelerin Soc. Office: U Chgo Sch Law 1111 E 60th St Chicago IL 60637-2776 also: Lexecon Inc 332 S Michigan Ave Ste 1300 Chicago IL 60604-4406

LANDES, WILLIAM-ALAN, publishing executive; b. Bronx, NY, Apr. 27, 1945; s. Sidney H. and June Dorothy (Heal-Gordon) L.; m. Sharon, Dec. 14, 1991 (div. Apr. 1995); children: William, Paula, Wendy. BA, BS, Hunter Lehman Coll., 1968; MS, NYU, 1969; MA, Calif. State U., 1972; PhD, UCLA, 1976. Mgr. Jay's, N.Y.C., 1967-69; assoc. producer New World Prodns., Hollywood, Calif., 1971-72; entertainment editor Showcase Mag., Hollywood, Calif., 1972-75; artistic dir., dir. theatre Players U.S.A., San Gabriel, Calif., 1975-78; artistic dir. Merrick Studios, Hollywood, 1978-79; producer, dir. Empire Entertainment, Studio City, Calif., 1979—; chmn. Players Press, Inc., Studio City, Calif., 1980—97; mng. dir. Empire Publishing Svc., England, 1998—. Capt. USAF, 1962-67. Mem. SAG, AFTRA, AEA, DGA, SSDC, Writers Guild. Avocations: writing, painting.

LANDESMAN, HOWARD M., academic administrator; b. Bklyn., N.Y., 1938; m. Lynne Landesman; 1 child, Lori. BS, UCLA, 1958; DDS, U. So. Calif., 1962, MS in Edn., 1971. Named co-dir., grad. prosthodontics program U. So. Calif. Sch. Dentistry, 1973, chair, dept. restorative dentistry, assoc. dean academic and faculty affairs, exec. assoc. dean, dean, 1991—99; dean. Sch. Dentistry U. Colo., 1999—. Mem.: Acad. Prosthodontics. Office: 4200 E 9th Ave Box C284 Denver CO 80262

LANDESS, FRED STONE, retired lawyer; b. Memphis, Jan. 27, 1933; s. Sterling Stone and Beulah Elizabeth (Melton) L.; m. Catherine Sue Lee, Dec. 27, 1953; children— Susan Elinor, Charles Barton, Catherine Elizabeth Student, Wake Forest Coll., 1951-53; AB, George Washington U., 1955; LL.B., U. Va., 1958. Bar: Va. 1958. Enforcement atty. NLRB, Washington, 1958-60; assoc., then ptnr. McGuire, Woods, Battle & Boothe LLP, Charlottesville, VA., 1960-99, ret., 1999. Sec. Bd. Zoning Appeals, City of Charlottesville, Va., 1967-69; bd. dirs. YMCA, Charlottesville, 1975, Westminister Child Care Ctr., Charlottesville, 1978 Fellow Am. Coll. Real Estate Lawyers; mem. Charlottesville-Albemarle Bar Assn. (pres. 1983-84), Va. Bar Assn. (real estate com.), Va. State Bar (7th dist. disciplinary com. 1986-88, sec. 1987, chmn. 1987-88), Charlottesville-Albemarle Bd. Realtors (assoc.), Blue Ridge Homebuilders Assn. (assoc.). Clubs: Boar's Head Sports (Charlottesville). Democrat. Presbyterian. Avocations: tennis, sailing, gardening. Home: 515 Wiley Dr Charlottesville VA 22903-4650

LANDESS, MIKE (MALCOLM LEE LANDESS III), television news anchorman; b. Houston, June 20, 1946; s. Malcolm Lee Jr. Landess and Joyce Ardis (Halley) Quitter; children: Kristen and Jennifer. Grad., Robert E. Lee H.S., Tyler, Tex. Radio reporter WFAA-AM, Dallas, 1969-70; TV reporter WFAA-TV, Dallas, 70-72, KTRK-TV, Houston, 1972-73; noon anchor, reporter KYW-TV, Phila., 1973-74; NBC news anchor WKYC-TV, Cleve., 1974-77; news anchor KUSA-TV, Denver, 1977-93; Gannett anchor WXIA-TV, Atlanta, 1993—. Anchor, reporter, producer: (TV documentary) Wednesday's Child, 1978, Fight of His Life, 1982; anchor, reporter (TV spl.) Say "NO" to Strangers, 1979. Bd. dirs. Am. Cancer Soc., Denver, 1982-86, Colo. Head Injury Assn., Denver, 1990-93, Brain Injury Assn Ga., Atlanta, 1994—. Recipient numerous Emmy awards: Outstanding Achievement Anchor, 1988, 91, Outstanding Achievement Children's Programming, 1983, TV Programming Excellence, 1995, Outstanding Achievement award Luth. Social Svcs., Am. Cancer Soc. Mem. NATAS, Radio & TV News Dir. Assn., Atlanta Press Club, Sigma Delta Chi. Baptist. Avocations: vintage guitars, motorsports. Office: WXIA-TV 1611 W Peachtree St NE Atlanta GA 30309-2664

LANDGRAF, KURT M., educational association administrator; b. Oct. 12, 1946; m. Barbara Landraf. B in Econs. and Bus. Adminstrn., Wagner Coll.; M in Econs., Pa. State U.; M in Adminstrn., Rutgers U.; M in Sociology, Western Mich. U.; grad. advanced mgmt. program, Harvard U., 1992. Mergers and acquistions intern Kidder Peabody, Inc., NYC; sales rep., brand mgr. Johnson & Johnson, Inc., New Brunswick, NJ; assoc. dir. Ednl. Testing Svc., Princeton, NJ; with The Upjohn Co., 1974-80; mgr. worldwide mktg. svcs. DuPont, 1980-83, mktg. dir. pharms. for Europe, Middle East and Africa Frankfurt, Germany, 1983-85, dir. pharms. for Europe, Middle East and Africa, 1985-86, planning mgr. corp. plans dept. Wilmington, Del., 1986-87, dir. bus. devel. and internat. divsn. pharms. divsn. dir., 1987-88, dir. pharms. divsn., 1988-89, dir. pharms. and imaging agts. divsn., 1989; with DuPont Merck, 1991—95; CFO DuPont, 1996, exec. v.p., 1997; chmn., ceo DuPont Pharmaceuticals, 2000; chmn., CEO Ednl. Testing Svc., 2000—. Co-chair bd. dirs. DuPont Merck Pharm. Co.; bd. dirs. DuPont Can., DuPont Dow Elastomers, Nat. Pharm. Coun.; instr. econs., sociology and labor rels. various colls. Bd. dirs. United Way Del., Del. Assn. for Rights of Citizens with Mental Retardation, Wilmington Med. Ctr. Found., Biotech. Industry Orgn., Nat. Alliance Bus., U. Del. Rsh. Found., Wilmingotn Grand Opera House; trustee Goldey-Beacom Coll., Wagner Coll. Mem. Pharm. Rsch. and Mfrs. Am. Mem. Del. State C. of C. (vice chmn. Mfg. Assn.). Office: Ednl Testing Svc Rosedale Rd Princeton NJ 08541*

LANDGREBE, DAVID ALLEN, electrical engineer; b. Huntingburg, Ind., Apr. 12, 1934; s. Albert E. and Sarah A. L.; m. Margaret Ann Swank, June 7, 1959; children: James David, Carole Ann, Mary Jane. BSEE, Purdue U., 1956, MSEE, 1958, PhD, 1962. Mem. tech. staff Bell Telephone Labs., Murray Hill, N.J., 1956; electronics engr. Interstate Electronics Corp., Anaheim, Calif., 1958, 59, 62; mem. faculty Purdue U., West Lafayette, Ind., 1962—, dir. lab. for applications of remote sensing, 1969-81, prof. elec. engring., 1970—2002, assoc. dean engring., 1981-84, acting head sch. elec. and computer engring. West Lafayette, 1995-96, prof. emeritus of elec. and computer engring., 2002—. Rsch. scientist Douglas Aircraft Co., Newport Beach, Calif., 1964; dir. Univ. Space Rsch. Assn., 1975-78. Author: Signal Theory Methods in Multispectral Remote Sensing, 2003, (with others) Remote Sensing: The Quantitative Approach, 1978. Recipient medal for exceptional sci. achievement NASA, 1973, William T. Pecora award NASA/U.S. Dept. Interior, 1990. Fellow IEEE (pres. Geosci. and Remote Sensing Soc. 1986-87, Exceptional Svc. award 1988, Sci. Achievement award 1992, Edn. award 2003), AAAS, Am. Soc. Photogrammetry and Remote Sensing; mem. NAE, Am. Soc. for Engring. Edn., Sigma Xi, Tau Beta Pi, Eta Kappa Nu. Office: Purdue U Dept Elec Engring West Lafayette IN 47907-1285 Business E-Mail: landgreb@ecn.purdue.edu.

LANDGREBE, JOHN ALLAN, chemistry professor; b. San Francisco, May 6, 1937; s. Herbert Frederick and Janet Miller (Allan) L.; m. Carolyn Jean Thomson, Dec. 23, 1961; children— Carolyn Janet, John Frederick BS, U. Calif.-Berkeley, 1959; PhD, U. Ill., 1962. Asst. prof. U. Kans., Lawrence, 1962—67, assoc. prof., 1967—71, prof., 1971—2002, prof. emeritus, 2002—, dept. chmn., 1970—80. Vis. prof. U. Calif.-Berkeley, 1974 Author: Theory and Practice in the Organic Laboratory, 1973, 5th edit., 2005. NSF fellow, 1960-62; E. Watkins Faculty fellow U. Kans., 1963; recipient Career Tchg. award Chancellors Club, 1999. Mem. Am. Chem. Soc., Royal Soc. of Chemistry, Phi Lambda Upsilon. Republican. Lutheran. Avocations: shade and water gardening, camping, hiking. Home: 1125 Highland Dr Lawrence KS 66044-4523 Office: U Kansas Dept Chemistry Lawrence KS 66045-0001

LANDIN, DAVID CRAIG, lawyer; b. Jamestown, N.Y., Aug. 1, 1946; s. David Carl and Rita L.; m. Susan Ann Gregory, July 11, 1970; children: Mary Stuart, Alexander Craig, David Reed. BA, U. Va., 1968, JD, 1972. Bar: Va. 1972, Pa. 1991, Tex. 1992, U.S. Supreme Ct. 1979. Ptnr. McGuire, Woods & Battle, Richmond, Va., 1972-95, mgr. of product liability and litigation mgmt. group, 1987-95; gen. counsel Va. Assn. Ind. Schs., 1989—, Coun. for Religion in Ind. Schs., 1990—95; ptnr., litig., intellectual property, antitrust Hunton & Williams LLP, Richmond, Va., 1995—, and co-chair recruitment com., 2001—05. Pres. The Landin Cos., 1994—. Chmn. ctrl. Va. chpt. Nat. Multiple Sclerosis Soc., 1995-96; chair standing com. on fed. jud. improvements ABA, 2003-. With USAR, 1968-74. Fellow: Va. Law Found. (pres. 1987—88, DRI Exceptional Performance award 1988); mem.: Greater Richmond C. of C. (bd. dirs. 1998—2000), Va. Assn. Def. Attys. (pres. 1987—88), Va. Bar Assn. (chmn. young lawyers sect. 1979—80, pres. 1999—2000). Roman Catholic. Avocations: squash, tennis, golf. Home: 310 Oak Ln Richmond VA 23226-1639 Office: Hunton & Williams Riverfront Plaza East Tower PO Box 1535 Richmond VA 23218-1535 Office Phone: 804-788-8387.

LANDIS, DONNA, retired elementary school educator; b. Howard County, Ind., Apr. 1, 1939; d. Don Raymond and Annis (Wyrick) Barker; m. G. Mason Landis Jr., Dec. 22, 1961. BS in Elem. Edn., Marion Coll., 1961; MA, Ball State U., 1968. Tchr. kindergarten through 4th grade various schs.; primary tchr. Marion (Ind.) Cmty. Schs.; tchr. 4th grade Madison-Grant United Sch. Corp., Fairmount, Ind.; ret. Mem. Ind. Ret. Tchrs. Assn. Address: 1317 W 55th St Marion IN 46953-5753

LANDIS, DONNA MARIE, nursing administrator, women's health nurse; b. Lebanon, Pa., Sept. 5, 1944; d. James O.A. and Helen Joan (Fritz) Muench; m. David J. Landis, Feb. 4, 1967 (div. Jan. 1985); children: Danielle M. Landis Barry, David J., Derek J.; m. John C. Broderick, May 8, 1990 (div. Jan. 1995). RN, St. Joseph's Hosp. Sch. Nursing, Reading, Pa., 1965. RN 1993, cert. densitometry technologist. Head nurse med.-surg. unit HUP, 1965-67; nurse various hosps. and physician's offices, 1968—84; clin. dir., clin. rsch. coord., DXA technologist Osteoporosis Diagnostic and Monitoring Ctr., Laurel, Md., 1985-95, owner, 1995—; clin. dir., clin. rsch. coord. Osteoporosis Assessment Ctr., Wheaton, Md., 1985-95; owner, clin. dir., clin. rsch. coord. Women's Health Rsch. Ctr., Laurel, Md., 1996—. Nurses adv. bd. NPS Pharms., 2005—; cons. in field. Mem. task force on osteoporosis State of Md., 1996—. Named one of MD's Top 100 Women in Bus., 2002. Mem.: Nat. Osteoporosis Risk Assessment Project (specialist practice and lead technologist trainer 1997—98), Allied Health Profls./Arthritis Found. (pub. policy contact), Nat. Osteoporosis Found. (pub. policy contact), Internat. Soc. Clin. Densitometry (steering com. 1993—94, contbg. editor SCAN newsletter 1994—2002, cert. and credentialing com. technologists and physicians 1995—2000, sci. adv. com. 1996—2003, trustee 1999—2002, technologist edn. subcom. 2000—03, accreditation coun. 2004), St. Joseph's Hosp. Alumni Assn., Balt. Bone Club, Washington Met. Bone Club (steering com. 1996, bd. dirs. 1999—2001, sec. 1999—2001), Kiwanis Internat. (bd. dirs. 1997—2002, pres. Prince George's County 2000—01, Capital dist. lt. gov. 2003—04). Office: 14201 Laurel Park Dr Laurel MD 20707-5203 Office Phone: 301-725-6786. Personal E-mail: dmlandis@verizon.net.

LANDIS, EDGAR DAVID, business consultant; b. Myerstown, Pa., Jan. 7, 1932; s. Edgar Michael and Anna Irene (Dubble) L.; m. Patricia Ann Leininger, June 13, 1953; children: Susan, Jean. BS, Lebanon Valley Coll., 1953; MBA, U. Pa., 1957. CPA. Acct., audit supr. Peat, Marwick, Mitchell & Co. (now KPMG), Phila., 1957-64; corp. contr., divsn. exec. v.p. Carlisle Corp., Pa., 1964-73; v.p., sr. v.p., exec. v.p. CDI Corp., Phila., 1973-97, also dir.; dir. affiliates in U.S. and Europe; dir., vice chmn., co-chmn. Allegiance Bank of N.A., Bala Cynwyd, Pa., 1998—. Cons. to CDI Corp., Phila., 1998-2001. Bd. dirs. Carlisle Sch. Dist., 1967-71, YMCA, Ardmore, Pa., 1981-87, chmn., 1984-86, YMCA, Phila., 1988-97, vice chmn. 1991-97, YMCA, Sarasota, Fla., 1998—, Capital U. Integrative Medicine, Washington, 2002-. With U.S. Army, 1954-56, Japan. Mem. Lebanon Valley Coll. Alumni Assocs. (regional chmn. 1977-82). Republican. Methodist. Home: 988 Blvd Of The Arts #511 Sarasota FL 34236-4872

LANDIS, GREGORY P., lawyer; b. 1951; BA magna cum laude, Yale U., 1973; JD cum laude, Harvard U., 1978. Bar: Calif. 1978. Ptnr. McCutchen, Doyle, Brown & Enerson, San Francisco; joined AT&T Wireless Svcs., Inc., Redmond, Wash., 1996, sr. v.p., gen. counsel, exec. v.p., gen. counsel. Chmn. bd. dirs. Equal Justice Works, 2001—03, treas., bd. dirs., 2003—; adv. bd. CoroporateProBono.Org. Recipient Corp. Pro Bono award, Am. Corp. Counsel Assn., 2000. Mem.: Cellular Telecom. Industry Assn. (bd. dirs.). Office: AT&T Wireless Svcs Inc NE Bldg 1 7277 164th Ave Redmond WA 98052

LANDIS, JOHN WILLIAM, engineering executive, consultant, government advisor; b. Kutztown, Pa., Oct. 10, 1917; s. Edwin Charles and Estella Juliabelle (Barto) L.; m. Muriel Trayes Souders, July 5, 1941; children: Maureen Lucille, Marcia Millicent BS in Engring. Physics summa cum laude, Lafayette Coll., Easton, Pa., 1939, ScD (hon.), 1960. Registered profl. engr., Calif. Research engr. Eastman Kodak Co., Rochester, N.Y., 1939-43; cons. Navy Dept., Washington, 1946-50; head sci. and engring. dept. Ednl. Testing Service, Princeton, N.J., 1948-50; reactor engr. AEC, Washington, 1950-53; dir. customer relations atomic energy div. Babcock & Wilcox Co., N.Y.C., 1953-55, asst. mgr. atomic energy div. Lynchburg, Va., 1955-62, mgr. atomic energy div., 1962-65, gen. mgr. Washington ops., 1965-68; regional v.p. Gulf Gen. Atomic Co., Washington, 1968-69, group v.p. LaJolla, Calif., 1969-70, pres., dir. subs., 1970-74; pres. Power Systems Co., Gen. Atomic Partnership, LaJolla, Calif., 1974-75; sr. v.p., dir., pres. subs. Stone & Webster Engring. Corp., Boston, 1975-92, pvt. cons., 1992—. Founding dir. Cen. Fidelity Banks, Inc., Richmond, Va.; founding gov. Nat. Materials Property Data Network, Inc., Phila.; chmn. adv. com. isotopes and radiation devel. and four other adv. coms. AEC, Washington, 1957-70; chmn. coms., co. rep. Atomic Indsl. Forum (now U.S. Nuclear Energy Inst.), Washington, 1953-95; mem. N.Y. State Adv. Com. on Atomic Energy, 1956-59, Va. State Adv. Com. on Nuclear Energy, 1959-68; vice chmn. mgmt. com. Nat. Environ. Studies Project, Washington, 1974-89; dir., v.p., pres., chmn. bds. and coms., trustee Internat. Fund, Am. Nat. Standards Inst., N.Y.C., 1957—; vice chmn. ISO-9000 Registration Com.; dir., chmn. Fusion Power Assocs., Gaithersburg, Md., 1981-98; chmn. U.S. Fusion Industry Coun., Internat. Thermonuclear Exptl. Reactor Industry Coun., 1994-98; chmn. com. on energy-related atmospheric pollution World Energy Conf., London, 1984-90, N.Am. coord. global energy study, 1989-93; dir., chmn. com. on protection of environ. U.S. Energy Assn., Washington, 1981-98; fusion adv. panel U.S. Ho. Reps., Washington, 1979-87; charter mem. magnetic fusion adv. com. U.S. Dept. Energy, Washington, 1982-84, chmn. internat. R&D panel, chmn. civilian nuclear power panel, vice chmn., chmn. energy rsch. advisory bd., 1984-90; mem. adv. bd. Sec. of Energy, 1990-93, fusion energy adv. com., 1994-99; advisor Carnegie-Mellon U., Pitts., 1971-73, Pa. State U., State College, 1980-83, U. Calif. San Diego, 1974-82, U. Fla., Gainesville, 1984—; vis. and sustaining fellow MIT, Cambridge, 1971-90; chmn. bus. administrn. adv. bd. U. San Diego, 1972-75; chmn. engnring. adv. com. Lafayette Coll., 1988-98. Co-author: six books; contbr. articles to profl. and trade jours. Trustee, chmn. Randolph-Macon Woman's Coll., Lynchburg, Va., 1963—; trustee Lafayette Coll., Easton, Pa., 1962—, Va. Poly. Inst. and State U., Blacksburg, 1966-70; bd. dirs. Va. Poly. Inst. Ednl. Found., Blacksburg, 1968-80; mem. U. Calif. Pres.'s Coun. on the Nat. Labs., 1993-99; chmn. MIT Reactor Com., 1995—; mem. Sr. Rev. Group, Amarillo Nat. Resource Ctr. for Plutonium, 1994-99; mem. Va. Adv. Bd. on Indsl. Devel. and Planning, Richmond, 1962-72; bd. dirs. Va. Engring. Found., Charlottesville, 1962-65; trustee Seven Hills Sch., Lynchburg, Va., 1960-65; dir. Harvard U. Ctr. for Blood Rsch., 1992-99; mem. Mayor's Com. on Energy, San Diego, 1973-75; chmn., mem. six coms. Nat. Rsch. Coun., 1976-96. Served to lt. USN, 1943-46, ETO. Decorated Letter of Commendation, two battle stars; recipient Gen. of Industry award State of Okla., 1971, George Washington Kidd award, Joseph E. Bell award Lafayette Coll., Lehigh Valley Favorite Son award State of Pa., 1976, Dwight D. Eisenhower Award of Honor, 1990, Winston Churchill Medal of Wisdom, 1988, Disting. Career award Fusion Power Assocs., 1991, Howard Coonley medal Am. Nat. Standards Inst., 1991, Exceptional Pub. Svc. award U.S. Dept. Energy, 1992, Henry DeWolf Smyth Nuclear Statesman award Am. Nuclear Soc. and Nuclear Energy Inst., 1996; named Hon. Citizen City of Dallas, 1973, Alumni fellow Lafayette Coll., 1984, Internat. Scientist of Yr., 2004; elected to Soc. d'Honneur Lafayette Coll., 1989; named to Wisdom Hall of Fame, 1987 Fellow ASME, Am. Nuclear Soc. (pres. 1971-72, v.p. 1970-71, treas. 1964-68, chmn. coms. 1956—, bd. dirs. 1956-74), Am. Soc. Macro-Engring. (pres. 1985-88, chancellor 1988—, charter bd. dirs. 1983—); mem. NAE, Internat. Assn. Macro-Engring. Socs. (founding dir. 1987—, treas. 1989—, pres. 1999—), San Diego Hall Sci. (life), Phi Beta Kappa, Sigma Xi, Tau Beta Pi, Pi Delta Epsilon, Omicron Delta Kappa. Avocations: photography, landscaping, book-collecting, hiking. Home: 2131 Chestnut Oak Ct SW Roanoke VA 24018-2118 Office Phone: 540-774-0987. Personal E-mail: jwlandis@cox.net.

LANDIS, KEVIN, diversified financial services company executive; BSEE, U. Calif., Berkeley, Calif.; MBA, Santa Clara (Calif.) U. With S-MOS Sys., Dataquest; co-founder Firsthand Capital Mgmt., San Jose, Calif., 1993—, CIO, 1993—. Office: Firsthand Capital Management 125 S Market St Ste 1200 San Jose CA 95113-2206

LANDIS, LARRY SEABROOK, state agency administrator; b. Princeton, NJ, Nov. 2, 1945; s. Donald Edward and Caroline Ann (Magalhaes) L.; m. Carol Louise Butz, Sept. 28, 1974; 1 child, Christopher Seabrook. AB cum laude, Wabash Coll., 1967; postgrad., U. N.C., 1967-68, Ind. U., 1969-70. Asst. to mayor Richard G. Lugar (now U.S. Senator, R-Ind.), Indpls., 1969-71; press sec. to Otis R. Bowen (Rep. candidate for gov., Ind.) Indpls., 1972; dir. mktg. svcs. Garrison, Jasper Rose & Co., Indpls., 1972-76; v.p. mktg. and media services Hickman & Assoc., Indpls., 1976—80; v.p. corp. advt. Am. Fletcher Nat. Bank (Bank One Indpls., N.A.), Indpls., 1980-84; dir. comm. PALLM, Inc., Indpls., 1984—85; v.p., dir. acct. planning Handley & Miller, Inc., Indpls., 1985—91; pres. Marketrends, Inc., Indpls., 1991—2003; mng. ptnr., COO Am. Grassroots, LLC, Indpls., 2000—03; commr. Ind. Utility Regulatory Commn., 2003—. Lectr. polit. sci. Ind. U./Purdue U., Indpls., 1969-71. Co-author: How To, 1974; contbr. articles to profl. jours. Active gov.-elect Ad Hoc Com. on Ednl. Fin., Indpls., 1972-73, campaign mgr. Salin for Congress Com., Ft. Wayne, Ind., 1971-72; exec. com. statewide Rep. legis. campaign Victory '90, Ind., 1989-90; mktg. com. United Way Ctrl. Ind., 1992-93; mktg. adv. com. Indpls. Symphony Orch., 1992-97; bd. dirs. USCO Adult Edn. Program, Indpls., 1975-82, pres., 1980-82, Citizens Environ. Coun., Inc., Zionsville, Ind., 1984-86, v.p., 1986-96, bd. Vis. Nurse Svc. Found, Inc., 2003-; rsch. dir. Ruckelshaus for U.S. Senate, 1968; exec. com. Blankenbaker for Congress, 1995-98; gov.'s adv. panel Children's Health Ins. Program, 1998-99. With U.S. Army, 1968-69. Mem. Am. Mktg. Assn., Am. Water Works Assn., Soc. Healthcare Strategy and Market Devel., Greater Wabash Found., Indpls. Assn. Wabash Men (bd. dirs.), Indpls. C. of C., Indpls. Advt. Club, Ind. Hist. Soc. (life, trustee 1995-2004, exec. com. 1996-2000, 2002-04), Indpls. Press Club, Columbia Club, Econ. Club, Indsl. Computing Soc. (founding) Nature Conservancy, TechPoint, Intercarrier Compensation Task Force, Pi Delta Epsilon, Delta Sigma Rho/Tau Kappa Alpha, Phi Kappa Psi. Republican. Methodist. Avocations: photography, woodworking, gardening. Office: Ind Utility Regulatory Commn 302 W Washington St Ste E306 Indianapolis IN 46204 E-mail: llandis@urc.state.in.us.

LANDIS, ROBERT KUMLER, III, investment banker, lawyer; b. Dayton, Ohio, June 20, 1953; s. Robert Kumler Landis Jr. and Rebecca Baird; m. Robin Lee Taylor, June 2, 1979; children: Robert Kumler IV, Taylor McCall, Samuel Tufts. AB, Princeton (N.J.) U., 1975; JD, Harvard U., 1978. Bar: N.Y. 1978. Assoc. Simpson Thacher & Bartlett, N.Y.C., 1978-83; dir. Merrill Lynch & Co., N.Y.C., 1984-94; mng. dir. Schooner Capital Internat., Boston, 1994-96; pres. Northern Lights Investors, LLC, 1996—. Dir. Western Quebec Mines, Inc., Montreal.

LANDIS, STORY C., federal agency administrator, neurobiologist; BA, Wellesley Coll., 1967, MA, 1970; PhD, Harvard U., 1973. Former faculty mem. in neurobiology Harvard Med. Sch.; faculty Dept. Pharmacology Case Western Res. U. Sch. of Medicine, Cleve., 1985—90, chair Dept. Neuroscis., 1990—95; sci. dir. of intramural program Nat. Inst. of Neurological Disorders and Stroke, NIH, 1995—2003, dir., 2003—. Contbr. articles to profl. jours. Fellow: AAAS, Acad. of Arts and Scis.; mem.: Soc. of Neuroscience (pres.-elect 2002). Achievements include research in the study of the developmental interactions required for the formation of functional synapses. Office: Office of Dir Nat Inst Neurological Disorders and Stroke Bldg 31 Rm 8A52 36 Convent Dr MSC 4150 Bethesda MD 20892-4150

LANDO, JEROME BURTON, macromolecular science educator; b. Bklyn., May 23, 1932; s. Irving and Ruth (Schwartz) L.; m. Geula Ahroni, Dec. 2, 1962; children: Jeffrey, Daniel, Avital. AB, Cornell U., 1953; PhD, Poly. Inst. Bklyn., 1963. Chemist Camille Dreyfus Lab., Research Triangle Inst., Durham, N.C., 1963-65; asst. prof. macromolecular sci. Case Western Res. U., Cleve., 1965—68, assoc. prof., 1968—74, prof., 1974—2005, prof. emeritus, 2005—; pres., CEO Edison Polymer Inovation Corp., 2000—. Dept. chmn. Case Western Res. U., Cleve., 1978—85; Erna and Jakob Michael vis. prof. Weizmann Inst. Sci., Rehovot, Israel, 1987; Lady Davis vis. prof. Technion, Haifa, Israel, 1992—93. Author: (with S. Maron) Fundamentals of Physical Chemistry, 1974; mem. editl. adv. bd. Polymers for Advanced Techs. Served to lt. U.S. Army, 1953-55. Named Alexander Von Humboldt Sr. Am. Scientist U. Mainz, Germany, 1974, disting. alumnus Poly. U., 1990. Fellow Am. Phys. Soc.; mem. Am. Chem. Soc., Am. Crystallographic Assn., Soc. Plastics Engrs. (rsch. award 1994, edn. award 1999), Sigma Xi. Jewish. Home: 21925 Byron Rd Cleveland OH 44122-2942 Office: Case Western Res U Dept Macromolecular Sci Kent Hale Smith Bldg 321 Cleveland OH 44106 Office Phone: 216-368-6366. E-mail: jblr@case.edu.

LANDON, JAMES HENRY, lawyer; b. Atlanta, Oct. 24, 1945; s. Ralph Henry and Gertrude Leola (Rew) L. BA, Vanderbilt U., 1967; JD, Harvard U., 1970. Bar: Ga. 1971, U.S. Dist. Ct. (no. dist.) Ga. 1971, U.S. Ct. Claims 1972, U.S. Supreme Ct. 1976, U.S. Tax Ct. 1980. Assoc. Hansell & Post, Atlanta, 1971-76, ptnr., 1976-89, Jones Day, Atlanta, 1989—. Adj. prof. Emory Law Sch., Atlanta, 1983—84; dir. TRC Staffing Svc., Inc., Atlanta, 1987—; mem. steering com. So. Pension Conf., Atlanta, 1985—88; mem. Atlanta Adv. Com. Asset Mgmt. Advisors; mem. adv. coun. Ga. Asset Mgmt. Assocs., 2004—. Co-author: Transportation Politics in Atlanta, 1970; contbr. article to profl. jour. Dir. Atlanta Symphony Orch., 1981-87, 89-92; trustee Atlanta Hist. Soc., 1983-98, 99—, Ctr. for Puppetry Arts, Inc., 1995-2001, Atlanta Bot. Garden, 1998-2004; mem. cmty. adv. bd. Jr. League of Atlanta, 1987-90; gen. counsel Woodruff Arts Ctr., Inc., 1993—; trustee Atlanta Med. Heritage, Inc., 1993—, pres., 1996-97; trustee The Hambidge Ctr., 1994-99, chmn. 1998-99; trustee Cherokee Garden Libr., 2000-03, 04—. Mem. ABA, Ga. Bar Assoc., Atlanta Bar Assoc., Explorers Club of N.Y.C., Phi Beta Kappa. Presbyterian. Avocations: mountain climbing, hiking. Home: 1327 Peachtree St NE Apt 503 Atlanta GA 30309-3254 Office: Jones Day Ste 800 1420 Peachtree St Atlanta GA 30309-3053 Office Phone: 404-581-8907.

LANDON, JANE KEYTE, music educator; b. Montoursville, Pa., Feb. 6, 1934; d. M. Robb Keyte Sr. and Frances Helen Entz; m. Eugene Earl Landon, Aug. 22, 1955; 1 child, Benjamin Eugene. BA cum laude, Lycoming Coll., 1955. Instr. piano Lycoming Coll., Williamsport, Pa., 1956-62; music tchr. Montoursville H.S., 1962-64; min. of music Bethany Luth. Ch., Montoursville, 1964-71; pvt. piano instr. Montoursville, 1962—. Adjudicator Pa. Fedn. Music Clubs. Mem. Messiah Luth. Ch., sanctuary choir mem., mem. Madrigal Singers, dir. men's quartet. Mem. Music Tchrs. Nat. Assn., Nat. Guild Piano Tchrs. (chmn. Williamsport 1965—), Pa. Music Tchrs. Assn. (pres. Williamsport local 1970—), Williamsport Music Club (past pres.), The Clio Club (corr. sec. 1997—), DAR. Republican. Avocations: concerts, antiques, gardening, cooking. Home: 144 Quaker State Rd Montoursville PA 17754-7608

LANDON, JOHN CAMPBELL, research and development company executive; b. Hornell, N.Y., Jan. 3, 1937; s. Earl Shephard and Eleanor (Crane) Landon; m. Nancy Ann Bachenheimer, Aug. 24, 1958; children: David Bachenheimer, Martha Susan, Katherine Ellen, Peter Crane. BA in Biology, Alfred (N.Y.) U., 1959; MS in Biology, George Washington U., Washington, 1962, PhD in Biology, 1967. Biologist Nat. Cancer Inst., NIH, Bethesda, Md., 1960-65; from virologist to dir. sci. Frederick Cancer Rsch. Ctr., Litton Bionetics, Kensington, Md., 1965-75; pres., dir. EG&G Mason Rsch. Inst., Worcester, Mass., 1975-82; pres., CEO Bioqual, Inc., Rockville, Md., 1982—; founder, v.p., co-owner Brewster (Mass.) Book Store, Inc., Brewster, Mass, 1982—; pres., CEO Sema, Inc., Rockville, 1986-91; pres. BIOQUAL Inc. (formerly Diagnon Corp.), Rockville, 1986—, also chmn. bd. dirs.; founder, pres., CEO Enhanced Therapeutics, Inc., Rockville, 1994—. Cons. EG&G, Worcester, Mass., 1982—85; reviewer ad hoc com. NIH, Bethesda, Md., 1981—; mem. nat. coun. arts and scis. George Washington U., 1996—2005; mem. credit com. Potomac Cmty. Fed. Credit Union, 1982—85. Contbr. articles to profl. jours. Bd. dirs. Found. Comparative and Conservation Biology, 1999—, Peirce Warwick Adoption Svc., Washington, 1970—79, pres., 1972—75; bd. dirs. Venture Expeditionary, Washington, 1979—83, pres., 1981—83. Mem.: AAAS, N.Y. Acad. Scis., Am. Soc. Microbiology, Am. Soc. Cell Biology, NIH Alumni Assn. (bd. dirs. 2002—), Sigma Xi. Office: Bioqual Inc 9600 Medical Center Dr Rockville MD 20850-3336 also: Brewster Bookstore 2648 Main St Brewster MA 02631-1958 E-mail: jlandon@bioqual.com.

LANDON, JOHN WILLIAM, retired minister, social worker, educator; b. Marlette, Mich., Mar. 24, 1937; s. Norman A. and Merle Irene (Lawrason) L. BA, Taylor U., 1959; MDiv, Northwestern U., Christian Theol. Sem., 1962; MSW, Ind. U., 1966; PhD in Social Sci., Ball State U., 1972. Regional supr. Iowa Dept. Social Welfare, Des Moines, 1965-67; acting chmn. dept. sociology Ind. Wesleyan U., Marion, 1967—69; asst. prof. sociology and social work Ball State U., Muncie, Ind., 1969-71; asst. prof. social work, coord. base courses Coll. Social Work U. Ky., Lexington, 1971-73, assoc. prof., coord. Undergrad. Program in Social Work, 1974-85, prof., assoc. dean, 1985—98, prof. emeritus, 1998—. Dir. social work edn. Taylor U., Upland, Ind., 1973-74. Author: From These Men, 1966, Jesse Crawford, Poet of the Organ, Wizard of the Mighty Wurlitzer, 1974, Behold the Mighty Wurlitzer, The History of the Theatre Pipe Organ, 1983, The Development of Social Welfare, 1986. Mem. AAUP, Coun. on Social Work Edn., Nat. Assn. Social Workers, Am. Guild Organists. Home: 13419 Mcintosh St Dade City FL 33525-5182 Personal E-mail: landon.jw@verizon.net.

LANDON, MICHAEL DE LAVAL, retired history professor; b. St. John, NB, Can., Oct. 8, 1935; arrived in U.S., 1960; s. Arthur Henry Whittington and Elizabeth Worthington (Fair) Landon; m. Doris Lee Clay, Dec. 31, 1959 (div. May 1980); children: Clay de Laval, Letitia Elizabeth; m. Carole Marie Prather, Feb. 28, 1981. BA, Oxford (Eng.) U., 1958, MA, 1961, U. Wis., 1962, PhD, 1966. Asst. master Manor House Sch., Horsham, England, 1957, Dalhousie Sch., Ladybank, Scotland, 1958, Lakefield (Can.) Coll. Sch., 1958-60; asst. prof. history U. Miss., Oxford, 1964-67, assoc. prof., 1967-72, prof., 1972-2000, prof. emeritus, 2000—, acting dir. librs., 1986-87, acting chair modern langs., 1996-99. Author: The Triumph of the Lawyers, 1970, The Honor and Dignity of the Profession, 1979, Erin and Britannia, 1980, The Challenge of Service, 1995. Commr. City Housing Authority, Oxford, 1983—, chmn., 1993—; lay Eucharistic min. Episcopal Ch. Am. Am. Philos. Soc. Rsch. grantee, 1967, 1974. Fellow: Royal Hist. Soc. (Eng.); mem.: Am. Soc. Legal History (sec.-treas. 1988—97), Pi Delta Phi, Phi Alpha Theta, Eta Sigma Phi, Phi Kappa Phi. Avocation: bird feeding. Home: 219 Bramlett Blvd Oxford MS 38655-3434 Business E-Mail: hslandon@olemiss.edu.

LANDON, ROBERT GRAY, retired manufacturing company executive; b. Portsmouth, Ohio, Dec. 22, 1928; s. Herman Robert and Hazel Ruth Landon; m. Carole A. Beaumont, Aug. 30, 2001; children: Geoffrey, Suzanne. Student, Cornell U., 1947-49; BA in Econs., U. Pa., 1955; grad. advanced mgmt. program, Harvard Sch. Bus., 1978. Loan officer Nat. City Bank, Cleve., 1955-60; SEC adminstr. Smith Kline Corp., 1960-64; controller, treas. Grumman Allied Industries, Inc., Garden City, N.Y., 1964-76, v.p., 1977-82; v.p. investment mgmt. Grumman Corp., Bethpage, N.Y., 1978-79; pres. Grumman Ohio Corp., Worthington, Ohio, 1979-88. Served with AC, USN, 1949-53. Mem. The Oaks Club.

LANDON, ROBERT KIRKWOOD, volunteer; b. N.Y.C., Apr. 27, 1929; s. Kirk A. and Edith (Ungar) L.; children: Chris, Kathleen Landon Staley, Kellyann Landon Spears. Student, U. Va., 1946-48; BS, Ga. Inst. Tech., 1950. With Am. Bankers Life Assurance Co., Miami, Fla., 1952-99, pres., 1960-74, 95, chmn., chief exec. officer, 1974-99; chmn. bd., CEO Am. Bankers Ins. Group Inc., Miami, 1980-95, chmn. bd., 1980-99; pres. Landon Corp., Dover, Del., 1971-99; charter mem. advisory bd. Fla. Internat. U., 1972-74. Trustee Kirk A. and Dorothy P. Landon Found., 1969—. Barry U. Lt. (j.g.) USNR, 1950-53. Mem. World Bus. Coun., Scabbard and Blade, Phi Gamma Delta. Republican. Congregationalist. Home: 10 Edgewater Dr Apt 16E Coral Gables FL 33133-6969 Office: The Kirk Found 255 Alhambra Cir Ste 820 Coral Gables FL 33134-7412 E-mail: kirk_landon@assurant.com.

LANDON, SUSAN MELINDA, petroleum geologist; b. Mattoon, Ill., July 2, 1950; d. Albert Leroy and Nancy (Wallace) L.; m. Richard D. Dietz, Jan. 24, 1993. BA, Knox Coll., 1972; MA, SUNY, Binghamton, 1975. Cert. profl. geologist; cert. petroleum geologist. Petroleum geologist Amoco Prodn. Co., Denver, 1974—87; mgr. exploration tng. Amoco, Houston, 1987—89; ind. petroleum geologist Denver, 1990—. Editor: Interior Rift Basins, 1993. Mem., chmn. Colo. Geol. Survey Adv. Com., Denver, 1991-98; mem. Bd. on Earth Sci. and Resources-NRC, 1992-97, chair com. on earth resources, 1998-2003; mem. Nat. Coop. Geologic Mapping Program Fed. Adv. Com., 1997—. Recipient Disting. Alumni award Knox Coll., 1986. Mem. Am. Assn. Petroleum Geologists (hon., treas., Disting. Svc. award 1995), Am. Inst. Profl. Geologists (pres. 1990, Martin Van Couvering award 1991, Ben H. Parker medal 2001), Am. Geol. Inst. (pres. 1998), Rocky Mountain Assn. Geologists (pres. 2000, Disting. Svc. award 1986, Disting. Pub. Svc. to Earth Sci. award 1995). Achievements include frontier exploration for hydrocarbons in U.S. Home: 780 Ballantine Rd Golden CO 80401-9503 Office: Thomasson Ptnr Assocs 1410 High St Denver CO 80218-2609 Office Phone: 303-436-1930. Personal E-mail: susanlandon@att.net.

LANDON, WILLIAM J., retired intelligence officer; b. Menno, SD, June 23, 1939; s. Helmuth Samuel and Violet A. (McPherson) Neuharth. LLB, Blackstone Sch. Law, 1962, JD, 1968; AA in Bus. Mgmt., Coastline C.C., 1984; postgrad., Am. Mil. U., 2001—; degree in criminal justice, Ashworth Coll., 2003. Criminal investigator Internat. Acad. Police Sci., Oklahoma City, Southwestern Inst. Criminology, Lawton, Okla.; criminal investigator, intelligence officer ASI divsn. Internat. Investigators and Police, St. John, Canada, 1964-94; intelligence officer, analyst Internat. Investigators & Police, Rapid City, SD, 1990—2001, ret., 2001. Sponsor Robin Anne Syperda Benedict meml. scholarship Calif. State U., Fullerton, 1990—. With USMC, 1957-65. Mem.: Marine Corps Intelligence Assn., Nat. Mil. Intelligence Assn., Assn. Former Intelligence Officers, Internat. Investigators Police Assn. Avocations: martial arts, classical music, fencing. Personal E-mail: nmiaafio@aol.com.

LANDOW-ESSER, JANINE MARISE, lawyer; b. Omaha, Sept. 23, 1951; d. Erwin Landow and Beatrice (Hart) Appel; m. Jeffrey L. Esser, June 2, 1974; children: Erica, Caroline. BA, U. Wis., 1973; JD with honors, George Washington U., 1976. Bar: Va. 1976, DC 1977, Ill. 1985. Atty. U.S. Dept. Energy, Washington, 1976-83, Bell, Boyd & Lloyd, Chgo., 1985-86, Seyfarth, Shaw, Fairweather & Geraldson, Chgo., 1986-88, Holleb & Coff, Chgo., 1988-2000, Quarles & Brady, Chgo., 2000—. Contbr. articles to profl. jours. Bd. dirs. Bernard Zell Anshe Emet Day Sch. Parent-Tchr. Orgn., 1991-95. Mem. ABA, Chgo. Bar Assn. (vice chmn. environ. law com. 1990-91, chmn. 1991-92), Am. Jewish Congress (bd. dirs., pres. Midwest Region 2001-04). Office: Quarles & Brady 500 W Madison St Ste 3700 Chicago IL 60661-2592 Office Phone: 312-715-5055. Business E-Mail: je3@quarles.com.

LANDRETH, KATHRYN E., lawyer; U.S. atty. Dept. Justice, Las Vegas, 1993—2001; chief of policy and planning Met. Police Dept., Las Vegas, Nev., 2001—02; metro counsel Las Vegas, 2003—. Office: Las Vegas Metro Police Dept 400 E Stewart Ave Las Vegas NV 89101

LANDRIEU, MARY L., senator; b. Arlington, Virginia, Nov. 23, 1955; m. E. Frank Snellings. BA, La. State U., 1977. Real estate agt.; La. state rep. from dist. 90, 1980—88; La. state treas., 1988—96; U.S. senator from La., 1997—; mem. small business com.; mem. energy and natural resources com.; mem. appropriations com. Del., Dem. Nat. Conv., 1980 Author: (novels) Nine and Counting: The Women of the Senate, 2000. Mem. LWV, Women Execs. in State Govt., Fedn. Dem. Women, Delta Gamma. Democrat. Roman Catholic. Office: 724 Hart Senate Off Bldg Washington DC 20510-0001*

LANDRIEU, MITCHELL JOSEPH, lieutenant governor; b. Aug. 16, 1960; m. Cheryl P. Quirk; children: Grace, Emily, Matthew, Benjamin, William. BA, Catholic U.; JD, Loyola U., New Orleans. Mem. La. State Ho. of Reps., Baton Rouge, 1988—2003; lt. gov. State of La., Baton Rouge, 2004—. Adj. prof. Loyola U. Law Sch., New Orleans; pres. Internat. Mediation and Arbitration, Ltd. Recipient Friends of the Parishes award, La. Police Jury Assn., 1988, Bus. Champion award, C. of C., 2001, 2002, Legislator of Yr. award, Alliance for Good Govt., 2002, Orleans Parish Med. Soc., 2002, Outstanding Legislator award, Victims and Citizens Against Crime, 2002. Democrat. Mailing: Office of Lt Gov PO Box 44243 Baton Rouge LA 70804-4243

LANDRIGAN, PHILIP JOHN, epidemiologist; b. Boston, June 14, 1942; s. John Joseph and Frances Joan (Conlin) Landrigan; m. Mary Florence Magee, Aug. 27, 1966; children: Mary Frances, Christopher Paul, Elizabeth Marie. AB, Boston Coll., 1963; MD, Harvard U., 1967; MS, DIH, London Sch. Hygiene and Tropical Medicine, 1977. Diplomate Am. Bd. Pediat., Am. Bd. Preventive Medicine, Am. Bd. Occupl. Medicine, Am. Coll. Epidemiology. Intern Cleve. Met. Gen. Hosp., 1967—68; resident in pediatrics Children's Hosp. Med. Ctr., Boston, 1968—70; fellow in pediatrics Harvard U. Med. Sch., Boston, 1969—70; clin. instr. pediatrics Emory U. Sch. Medicine, Atlanta, 1970—71; epidemic intelligence service officer Ctrs. for Disease Control, Atlanta, 1970—73, dir. research and devel. smallpox eradication program, 1973—74, chief environ. hazards activity, 1974—79; dir. div. Surveillance, Hazard Evaluations and Field Studies Nat. Inst. for Occupational Safety and Health, Cin., 1979—85; prof. community medicine and pediatrics Mt. Sinai Sch. Medicine, N.Y.C., 1985—, dir. div. environ. and occupational medicine, 1985—90; prof., chmn. dept. community and preventative medicine, 1990—. Mem. bd. on toxicology and environ. health hazards NAS, Washington, vice chmn., 1981—86, chmn. com. on pesticides in the diets of infants and children, 1988—93; sr. advisor to adminstr. on children's health and environment U.S. EPA, Washington, 1997—98; clin. prof. environ. health Sch. Pub. Health U. Wash., Seattle, 1983—. Contbr. numerous articles to prlfl. jours.; cons. editor: Archives of Environ. Health, 1982—, Am. Jour. Indsl. Medicine, 1979—, editor-in-chief: Environ. Rsch., 1987—. Recipient Vol. award, Dept. HEW, 1973, Pub. Health Svc. Career Devel. award, 1975, group citation as mem. of Ctr. for Disease Control beryllium rev. panel, 1978, Meritorious Svc. medal, USPHS, 1985. Fellow: Royal Soc. Medicine; mem.: AAAS, APHA, Soc. for Epidemiologic Rsch., Am. Epidemiol. Soc., Inst. of Medicine Internat. Commn. on Occupl. Health. Home: 915 Stuart Ave Mamaroneck NY 10543-4124 Office: Mt Sinai Sch Medicine Dept Community Medicine 1 Gustave L Levy Pl # 1057 New York NY 10029-6500 E-mail: phil.landrigan@nasa.gov.

LANDRY, ABBIE VESTAL, librarian; b. Martinsville, Va., Oct. 29, 1954; d. Samuel Raynor and Grace Loraine (Cochrane) Vestal; m. Michael Ray Landry, Aug. 4, 1979. Assoc. Gen. Edn., Patrick Henry C.C., Martinsville, Va., 1975; BA in History, Longwood Coll., Farmville, Va., 1977; M in Libr. and Info. Sci., U. Tenn., Knoxville, 1981. Grad. asst. history dept. U. Tenn., Knoxville, 1977-78, grad. teaching asst., 1978-80, grad. asst. libr. and info. sci., 1980-81; reference libr., coord. online svcs., coord. biog. instrn. Watson Libr., Northwestern State U., Natchitoches, La., 1981-87, head reference divsn., supr. reference, 1987—, interim dir., 2000—01. Adv. bd. Bowker Publ. Topical Reference Books, Princeton, N.J., 1988-89; sec. La. Assn. for Acad. Competition, 1991—; chmn. faculty-staff devel. com. Watson Libr,. 1983-88, chmn. devel. com. collection, 1988-89, chmn. quiz bowl com., 1989—, automated circulation sys. com., 1984-85, centennial com. 1983-84, chmn. libr. evaluation com., 1997—; cons. Best Books for Academic Librs. Vol. 4, American History. Contbg, author: Booktalking the Award Winners, Vols. 1, 2, 3; mem. editl. bd. Alumni Reviewer for Reference Books Bull., 1991—; co-editor newsletter Libr. Users Edn., 1991-92; editor Online Svcs. Interest Group Newsletter, 1986-87; editor Watson Libr. Newsletter Ex Libris, 1983-93; contbr. articles to profl. jours. Mem. Assn. for Preservation Historic Natchitoches, 1985—, Natchitoches Humane Soc., 1983—. Recipient Sigma Xi award, Natchitoches, 1986. Mem. ALA, La. Libr. Assn. (vice chair acad. sect. 1988-89, chair 1989-90, mem. exec. bd. 1988-90, coord. online svcs. interest group 1985-86), Southeastern Libr. Assn., Phi Kappa Phi, Beta Phi Mu, Phi Alpha Theta. Episcopalian. Avocations: reading, needlecrafts, travel. Office Phone: 318-357-4574.

LANDRY, BROCK R., lawyer; b. Detroit, Sept. 15, 1947; BA cum laude, Yale Univ., 1970; JD, Univ. Mich., 1974. Bar: Ill. 1974, DC 1982. Ptnr., trade assn. law, mgr., govt., regulatory affairs divsn. Venable LLP, Washington. Exec. com., dir., treas. Cancer Rsch. Found. Mem.: ABA, DC Bar Assn. Office: Venable LLP 575 Seventh St NW Washington DC 20004 Office Phone: 202-344-4877. Office Fax: 202-344-8300. Business E-Mail: brlandry@venable.com.

LANDRY, CLAUDEA D., music educator; b. New Orleans, Mar. 30, 1955; d. Edward C. and Olga D. Dugas; m. Paul S. Landry, Jan. 7, 1978; children: Samantha E., Meghan L. B of Music Edn., Southeastern La. U., 1977, MusM, 1981. Cert. tchr. La., 1977. Tchr. gen. music Walker Lower Elem., La., 1977—78; band dir. Jackson H.S., 1978—79, Walker H.S., 1979—94, Ponchatoula Jr. H.S., 1994—. Recipient Outstanding Young Women Am., 1984. Mem.: NEA (assoc.), Am. Fedn. Tchrs. (assoc.), La. Music Educators' Assn. (assoc.; exofficio bd. mem., superior ratings, dist.and state band festivals), La. Bandmasters' Assn. (assoc.; pres., exec. sec.). Democrat. Roman Catholic. Avocations: music, computers, crafts. Home: 14235 Hwy 22 Ponchatoula LA 70454 Office: Ponchatoula Jr High Sch 315 East Oak St Ponchatoula LA 70454 E-mail: claudea.landry@tangischools.org.

LANDRY, JANE LORENZ, architect; b. San Antonio, Feb. 12, 1936; d. John Henry and Lulie Amanda (Sample) L.; m. Duane Eugene Landry, Sept. 8, 1956; children: Rachel, Claire, Ellyn, Jean. Student, U. Tex., 1952-55, Yale U., 1955-56; BArch, U. Pa., 1957. Registered arch., Tex. Project arch. O'Neil Ford & Assoc., San Antonio, 1959-65; prin. Duane Landry, Arch., San Antonio, 1965-68, Dallas, 1968-76; ptnr. Landry & Landry, Archs. & Planners, Dallas, 1976—, Meyer, Landry & Landry, Archs. & Planners, Dallas, 1977-80. Instr. San Antonio Coll., 1965. Dir. at large Interfaith Forum on Religion, Art and Architecture, 1991—; mem. Liturgical Commn. Diocese of Dallas, 1978-90. Recipient design awards Interfaith Forum on Religion, Art and Architecture, 1985, 89, 90, 97, 98, 2000, 2003. Fellow AIA (mem. hist. resources com., design awards Dallas chpt. 1970, 75, 76, 77, 80); mem. Tex. Soc. Architects (design award 1969, 81), The Liturgical Design Consultancy. Roman Catholic. Office: Landry & Landry Archs & Planners 6319 Meadow Rd Dallas TX 75230-5140 Office Phone: 214-265-8398.

LANDRY, JOSEPH L., JR., retired affirmative action specialist; b. Woodlawn, La., Dec. 23, 1940; s. Joseph L. Landry and Clara Desmairis; widowed; children: Alan Joseph, Kevin Dale. Student, Northwestern State U. La., 1959-61, McNeese State U., 1961-62, Hosp. Corps. Sch., Great Lakes, Ill., 1962, Cardiopulmonary Technique Sch., Bethesda, Md., 1964, Instr. Tng. Sch., Norfolk, Va., 1968, Pers. Adminstrn. & Career Counseling Sch., San Diego, 1973, Disease Vector Ecology Control Ctr. Sch., Jacksonville, Fla., 1974; AA, Prince George's C.C., Largo, Md., 1975. Gas meter reader Tex. La. Gas Co., Alexandria, La., 1959; hosp. orderly Lake Charles (La.) Meml. Hosp., 1961-62; staff hosp. corpsman Charleston (S.C.) Naval Hosp., 1962-63; staff instr. Cardiopulmonary Technique Sch., U.S. Naval Hosp., Bethesda, Md., 1964-66, chief respiratory therapy dept., 1967-70; staff pulmonary technologist VA Hosp., Washington, 1966-67, staff cardiopulmonary technologist, 1970-74; clin. instr. Respiratory Therapy Sch., Washington Technical Inst., D.C. U., 1970-74; cardiopulmonary technologist divsn. coal mine workers' compensation U.S. Dept. Labor, Washington, 1974-82; program analyst Office Fed. Contract Compliance Programs, 1982-84, equal opportunity specialist, 1984-96; ret., 1996. Co-writer guidelines for Freedom of Info. Act and Privacy Act; cons. Peopleclick, New Orleans, 1996—; lectr. in field. Acting chair citizens adv. com. Reston Police Dist., 1986; past pres., bd. dirs. Deepwood Homeowners' Assn.; bd. dirs., "F" lic. coach Reston Soccer Assn.; mem. PTA and Booster Club of South Lakes High Sch.; bd. dirs., past v.p. amateur divsn. La. Soccer Assn.; past asst. dist. dir., past dist. dir. Boy Scouts Am., St. Tammany Parish.; cert. referee USSF Region III. With USN, 1962-66, USNR, 1966-89, ret. 1989. Mem. Nat. Active and Ret. Fed. Employees (past pres. chpt. 1428, past v.p. dist. IV, LA fedn. chpts., 2d v.p. La. fedn. chpts.), Am. Legion (adj. post 415 Mandeville), Mil. Officers Assn. Am. (pres. Ozone chpt.), Am. Heart Assn. Democrat. Roman Catholic. Home: PO Box 8823 Mandeville LA 70470-8823 Office Phone: 985-630-9573. E-mail: landry_joseph@bellsouth.net.

LANDRY, MARK EDWARD, podiatrist, researcher; b. Washington, May 24, 1950; s. John Edward and Daphne (Fay) L.; m. Mary Ann Kotey, Sept. 7, 1974; children: John Ryan, Christopher John, Jessica Marie. D in Podiatry, Ohio Coll. Podiatric Medicine, 1975; MS in Edn., U. Kans., 1982. Diplomate Am. Bd. Podiatric Surgery, Am. Bd. Podiatric Orthopedics and Primary Podiatric Medicine; cert. NAUI, 2000, RADI scuba diver, 2004. Gen. practice podiatry, Kansas City, Mo., 1977—, Overland Park, Kans., 1980—; clin. asst. prof. U. Health Scis., Kansas City, 1985-98; clin. assoc. prof. Coll. Podiatric Medicine and Surgery U. Osteo. Medicine and Health Scis., Des Moines, 1985-92; clin. instr. Sch. Medicine U. Mo., Kansas City, 1987-95. Founder, bd. dirs. Kansas City Podiatric Residency Program, Kansas City, 1982-91; adv. bd. Rockport Shoe Co., 1988-89; chmn. podiatry dept. Park Lane Med. Ctr., Kansas City, Mo., 1995-97; dir. continuing edn. Kans. Podiatric Med. Assn., 1997—. Contbr. articles to profl. jours. Cons. Mid-Am. Track and Field Assn., Lenexa, Kans., 1978-88; com. chmn. Boy Scouts Am., Overland Park, Kans., 1986; coach Johnson County Soccer League, 1987-90; head coach 6th and 7th grade girls' Cath. Youth Orgn. Basketball, 1995-96, 97; sponsor 8 & 11 Baseball League, 1987-90. 1st lt. USAF, 1975-77. Recipient Pres.'s award Ohio Sch. Podiatric Medicine, 1975; USAF scholar Armed Forces Health Professions, 1973-75. Fellow Am. Coll. Foot and Ankle Surgeons, Acad. Podiatric Sports Medicine; mem. Kans. Podiatric Med Assn. (bd. dirs. 1997—), Brit. Podiatry Assn. (hon.), Am. Bd. Primary Podiatric Medicine (founding dir., bd. examiner 1994-2000), Holy Cross Social Club (pres. 1983-84), Prairie Life Club, Leukemia Assn. of Am. (team in tng. 1997-2000, 2005, team capt. 1999, K.C. corp. challenge participant 1997-99), K.C. (4th degree 1995—, chancellor 1998, 99), KC Ski Club (trip capt. 1999), Fifty States Marathon Club, 50 State Marathon Group, D.C. Marathon Group. Republican. Roman Catholic. Avocations: triathlon training, skiing. Office: 10550 Quivira Rd Ste 260 Overland Park KS 66215-2375 Office Phone: 913-438-9898.

LANDRY, PAUL LEONARD, lawyer; b. Mpls., Nov. 23, 1950; s. LeRoy Robert Landry and Alice Ruth (Swain) Stephens; m. Lisa Yvonne Yeo, Dec. 13, 1984; children: Marc, Lauren, Matthew. BA, Macalester Coll., 1974; postgrad., Georgetown U., 1976-77; JD, Boston U., 1977. Bar: Va. 1977, D.C. 1978, Minn. 1984, U.S. Dist. Ct. D.C., U.S. Dsit. Ct. Va., U.S. Dist. Ct. Minn., U.S. Ct. Appeals (D.C., 2d, 4th and 8th cirs.). Dancer Dance Theater Harlem, N.Y.C., 1971-72; prin. dancer Dance Theatre Boston, 1972-75; atty. EPA, Washington, 1976-77; assoc. Reed, Smith, Shaw & McClay, Washington, 1977-83; officer, shareholder Fredrikson & Byron, P.A., Mpls., 1984—. Adj. prof. law William Mitchell Coll. Law, St. Paul, 1985-89. Bd. dirs. Ind. Sch. Dist. 284, Wayzata, Minn., 1989-96, 2002-, chmn., 1992-93; bd. dirs. Walker Art Ctr., Mpls., 1992—; bd. dirs., vice chair Greater Twin Cities Youth Symphonies, 1999-2001; advisor Kevin McCary Scholarship Fund. Mem. ABA (conf. of minority ptnrs. adv. com.), Nat. Bar Assn., Minn. State Bar Assn. (art and entertainment sect., labor and employment sect.), D.C. Bar, Hennepin Conty Bar Assn., Black Entertainment and Sports Lawyers Assn., Barristers. Avocations: golf, music, basketball. Office: Fredrickson & Byron 200 S 6th St Ste 4000 Minneapolis MN 55402-1425 E-mail: plandry@fredlaw.com.

LANDRY, SARA GRIFFIN, social worker; b. Thomaston, Ga., Sept. 17, 1920; d. John Carl and Mary Thelmå (Abercrombie) Griffin; m. Thomas Leonard Perkins, Dec. 22, 1939 (dec. Jan. 27, 1945); 1 child, Thomas Leonard Perkins Jr.; m. George Kimball Landry, Dec. 19, 1949 (dec. Aug. 30, 1971). AB in Social Work magna cum laude, Wesleyan Coll., 1980; MS in Family Counseling, Mercer U., 1981. Receptionist Social Security Adminstrn., Macon, Ga., 1945—50, clerical, 1960—65, svc. rep., 1965—78; dir., organizer Bibb County Foster Grandparent Program, Macon, Ga., 1981—84; coord. rsch. project Med. Ctr. of Ctrl. Ga., Macon, Ga., 1986—87; social worker, bd. dirs. Bibb County Sr. Citizens Inc., Macon, Ga., 1984—; sec. bd. dirs. Bibb County Sr. Citizens, Inc., Macon, Ga., 1989—90, pres. bd. dirs., 1990—91. Bd. dirs. grant chmn. Family Counseling Ctr., Macon, 1986-92, 94-97. Contbr. articles, poems and various short stories to profl. jours. Bd. dirs., v.p., com. chmn. Am. Cancer Soc., Macon, 1956—, hon. life mem., 1993—; sec., com. chmn. Dem. Women Bibb County, 1979—; mem., sec. Civic Woman's Club, Macon, 1955-61; mem. Coun. Cath. Women, St. Joseph's Parish, pres., 1956-58; mem., bd. dirs. Savannah Diocesan Coun. Cath. Women, 1957-59; bd. dirs. Macon Little Theatre, 1994-96. Recipient Disting. Alumnae award for cmty. svc. Wesleyan Coll., 1996, Svc. to Mankind award Sertoma Club of Macon, 1995, Spl. Recognition award Foster Grandparent Program Adv. Coun., 2004; named Vol. of Yr., Bibb County Sr. Citizens, Inc., 1988, Am. Cancer Soc., 1987-88, Cherry Blossom Sr. Queen for Cmty. Svc., 1986; Fundraiser honoree Am. Cancer Soc., 1991; Sara Landry Day proclaimed in her honor Mayor of Macon, 1991. Mem. LWV, AAUW (pres. 1991-93, Vol. of Yr. Macon br. 2004), Wesleyan Coll. Alumnae Assn. (Sara Griffin Perkins Landry scholarship established for non-traditional age students 1994, Disting. Alumnae award for cmty. svc. 1996), Nat. Honor Soc., Macon Little Theatre. Democrat. Roman Catholic. Avocations: reading, swimming, travel, theater. Home: 3807 Drury Dr Macon GA 31204-1313

LANDSBERG, GERALD, social sciences educator, consultant; b. N.Y.C., July 15, 1942; s. Louis and Sadie L.; m. Claire Warga Landsberg, Mar. 24, 1974; 1 child, Joshua. MSW, NYU, 1967, MPA, 1979; DSW, CUNY, 1979. Dir. rsch. Maimonides Hosp. CMHC, Bklyn., 1968-79; commr. Ulstor County Mental Health Svcs., Kingston, N.Y., 1979-87; assoc. commr. N.Y.C. Dept. Mental Health, 1987-91; prof. chair social policy NYU Sch. of Social Work, 1991—. Editor: Forensic Mental Health, 2001, Interional Forensic, 2001, (newsletter) Community Mental Health Report, 2000. Mem. N.Y. Nat. Assn. of Social Workers (v.p. 1999-2001). Office: NYU Sch of Social Work One Washington Sq N New York NY 10003

LANDSBERG, LEWIS, dean, endocrinologist, medical researcher; b. N.Y.C., Nov. 23, 1938; AB, Williams Coll., 1960; MD, Yale U., 1964. Intern Yale-New Haven Hosp., 1964—65, resident in internal medicine, 1965—66, 1968—69; fellow in endocrinology NIH, 1966—68; from instr. to asst. prof. medicine Sch. Medicine Yale U., 1969-72; from asst. prof. to assoc. prof. Harvard Med. Sch., 1972-77, from assoc. prof. to prof., 1977-86; Irving S. Cutter prof., chmn. dept. medicine Northwestern U. Feinberg Sch. Medicine, Chgo., 1990—2000, dir. Ctr. Endocrinology, Metabolism & Nutrition, 1990-93, dean, v.p. for medical affairs, 2000—. Assoc. physician Yale-New Haven Hosp., 1969-71, attending physician, 1971-72, Beth Israel Hosp., 1974-79, physician, 1979-88, sr. physician, 1988-90; attending physician West Haven VA Hosp., 1970-72; assisting physician Boston City Hosp., 1972-73, assoc. vis. physician, 1973-74; physician-in-chief dept. medicine Northwestern Meml. Hosp., 1990—. Fellow ACP, AAAS; mem. Am. Fedn. Clin. Rsch., Endocrine Soc., N.Y. Acad. Scis., AHA, Am. Soc. Pharmacology and Exptl. Therapeutics, Am. Physiology Soc., Am. Soc. Clin. Investigators, Am. Clin. and Climatological Assn., Assn. Am. Physicians. Achievements include rsch. in catecholamines and the sympathoadrendal system, nutrition and the sympathetic nervous system, obesity and hypertension. Office: Northwestern Univ Med Sch Morton 4-656 310 East Superior St Chicago IL 60611-2958

LANDSBERG, MICHELE, retired journalist; b. Toronto, July 12, 1939; d. Jack and Naomi Leah Landsberg; m. Stephen Lewis, May 30, 1963; children: Ilana Naomi, Avram David, Jenny Leah. BA, U. Toronto, 1962. Reporter Globe & Mail, Toronto, 1962-65, columnist, 1985-89; freelancer, 1965-71; editor, feature writer Chatelaine, 1971-78; columnist Globe and Mail, Toronto, 1985-88, The Toronto Star, 1978—84, 1989—2003; ret., 2003. Author: Women & Children First, 1982, Reading for the Love of It, 1986, This is New York, Honey! A Homage to Manhattan in Love & Rage, 1989. Recipient Nat. Newspaper award (columns), 1980, (feature writing) 1981, Gov.-Gen.'s Persons' awrd, 2002; co-recipient Florence Bird award, 1997. Office: Toronto Star 1 Yonge St Toronto ON Canada M5E 1E6

LANDSBERGER, JOSEPH FRANK, academic administrator; b. St. Paul, May 6, 1945; s. Claude Edward and Blanche Evelyn (Dvorak) L. MA, U. Minn., 1981; M in Internat. Mgmt., U. St. Thomas, 1990. Mgr. learning ctr. U. St. Thomas, St. Paul, 1976—2002. Vol. educator U.S. Peace Corps, Soutouboua, Togo, 1968-71. Author: Study Guides and Strategies. Vol. park developer Dept. Parks & Recreation, St. Paul, 1995—. Mem. Assn. Edn., Comm. & Technology. Mem. Soc. Friends. Avocations: garden design, ednl. website development, international travel. Office: U St Thomas 2115 Summit Ave Saint Paul MN 55105 E-mail: jflandsberge@stthomas.edu.

LANDSMAN, MIRIAM JOY, social worker, educator, researcher; d. Jerome Joel and Estelle Franklin Landsman; m. Steven Paul Horowitz, Jan. 18, 1976; children: Veronica Landsman Horowitz, Jacob Landsman Horowitz, Jordan Landsman Horowitz. BA, U. Del., 1976; MSW, U. Iowa, 1982, PhD, 2000. Rsch. assoc. Nat. Resource Ctr. for Family Centered Practice, Iowa City, 1983—93, exec. dir./rsch. dir., 1994—2000; asst. prof. social work U. Iowa, Iowa City, 2000—. Co-author (with Kristine Nelson): (non-fiction book) Alternative Models of Family Preservation: Family Based Services in Context, 1992; mem. editl. bd.: Family Preservation Jour.; contbr. articles to profl. jours. Grantee, Iowa Dept. Edn., 1997—99, Iowa Dept. Human Svcs., 1997—98, 1998—2003, Iowa Dept. Human Rights, 2003—, Iowa Dept. Pub. Health, 1998—2005; numerous grants, U.S. Dept. Health and Human Svcs., 1988—. Mem.: Alpha Kappa Delta, Phi Beta Kappa. Office: Univ Iowa Sch Social Work 351 North Hall Iowa City IA 52242 Office Phone: 319-335-4934. E-mail: miriam-landsman@uiowa.edu.

LANDSMAN, RICHARD, investment company executive, finance educator; b. N.Y.C., Oct. 31, 1949; s. Irving and Shirley (Siegel) L.; m. Wendy Benfield, Apr. 18, 1988; 1 child, Nerys. BS, Queens Coll., 1970, MS, 1971; MSW, Hunter Coll., 1977; MBA, Pace U., 1982. Exec. dir. CoPay Inc., Great Neck, N.Y., 1972-84; sr. v.p. Smith Barney Inc., N.Y.C., 1984-89, 92-96, Shearson Lehman Inc., N.Y.C., 1989—92, Prudential Securities, Garden City, N.Y., 1996; pres. Nottinghill Capital Mgmt. Inc., Roslyn, NY, 1997—. Prof. Grad. Sch. Bus. Columbia U., N.Y.C., 1996—; disting. prof. St. Johns U. Grad. Sch. Bus., N.Y.C., 1999—. Author numerous articles on security analysis and equity valuation; featured in publs.; subject of feature article: Sunday Bus. edit. of Newsday, 2002; featured in front page article Rising Young Star of Wall St., Crains News, 1984. Office Phone: 516-621-6080. E-mail: nhillcap@aol.com.

LANDSMARK, TED, academic administrator; BS, JD, Yale U.; PhD in Am. Studies, Boston U. Asst. prof. MIT, U. Mass., Boston; adminstr. Harvard U.; dean Grad. and Continuing Edn. Mass. Coll. Art; pres., CEO Boston Archtl. Ctr., 1997—. Spl. asst. Mayor of Boston; dir. Office of Cmty. Partnerships. Contbr. Maine Antique Digest, editl. bd. mem. Architecture Boston, Jour. Early So. Decorative Arts. Trustee Mus. Fine Arts, Boston, New England Found. for Arts, Boston Fund for Arts. Fellow Winterthur Mus., Mus. of Early So. Decorative Arts, Winston-Salem, NSF. Office: Boston Architectural Ctr 320 Newbury St Boston MA 02115 Office Phone: 617-262-5000.*

LANDSTROM, ELSIE HAYES, retired editor; b. Kuling, Kiangsi, China, June 22, 1923; came to the U.S., 1935; d. Paul Goodman and Helen Mae (Wolf) Hayes; m. Victor Norman Landstrom, Jan. 21, 1953 (dec. Oct. 1989); children: Peter S., Ruth H. BA magna cum laude, Hamline U., 1945. Writer, editor adminstrv. staff Am. Friends Svc. Com., Phila., 1946-52, MIT, Cambridge, Mass., 1952-53; mem. editl. bd. Approach Mag., Phila. and Needham, 1947-67; sr. editor Word Guild, 1976-82; freelance writer and editor Conway, Mass., 1976-98; ret., 1998. Author: Closing the Circle—An American Family in China, 1998; editor: Propaganda and Aesthetics, 1979, Taoism and Chinese Religion, 1981, Hyla Doc in China 1924-1949, 1991, Hyla Doc in Africa 1950-1961, 1994; exhibited Chinese paintings, 1996, 97. Newsletter editor, draft resisters support com. Wellesley (Mass.) Friends Meeting; chair Fair Housing Com., Needham. Avocations: birding, reading, painting. Home: 86 Kendal Dr Kennett Square PA 19348-2327

LAND-WEBER, ELLEN, photography professor; b. Rochester, N.Y., Mar. 16, 1943; d. David and Florence Epstein; 1 child, Julia. BA, U. Iowa, 1965, MFA, 1968. Faculty mem. UCLA Extension, 1970-74, Orange Coast Coll., Costa Mesa, Calif., 1973, U. Nebr., Lincoln, 1974; asst. prof. photography Humboldt State U., Arcata, Calif., 1974-79, assoc. prof., 1979-83, prof., 1983—. Photographer Seagram's Bicentennial Courthouse Project, 1976-77, Nat. Trust for Hist. Preservation/Soc. Photographic Edn., 1987. Author: The Passionate Collector, 1980, To Save a Life: Stories of Holocaust Rescue, 2000; contbr. sects. to books; photographs pub. in numerous books and jours. Named Humboldt State U. Scholar of Yr., 2004-2005; Nat. Endowment for Arts fellow, 1974, 79, 82; Artist's support grantee Unicolor Corp., 1982, Polaroid 20X24 Artist's support grantee, 1990, 91, 93, 94; Fulbright sr. fellow, 1993-94. Mem. Soc. for Photog. Edn. (exec. bd. 1979-82, treas. 1979-81, sec. 1981-83) Avocation: weaving. Office: Humboldt State U Art Dept Arcata CA 95521

LANDWEHR, AMY MARIE, lawyer; b. Des Moines, Iowa, Jan. 18, 1974; d. Michael Alan and Susan Kay Landwehr; m. Jeremy Benjamine Andrews Feitelson, July 8, 2000; 1 child, Adrik Feitelson. BA in Psychology, U. Ctrl. Fla., 1996; JD, U. Louisville, 2001. Bar: Iowa 2001. Atty. Davis, Brown, Koehn, Shors & Roberts, PC, Des Moines, 2001—. Mem. exec. bd. dirs. Iowa chpt. Lupus Found. Am., Des Moines, 2002—. Mem.: Am. Immigration Lawyers Assn. Office: Davis Brown Koehn Shors Roberts 666 Walnut St 2500 Des Moines IA 50309 Office Phone: 515-288-2500. Office Fax: 515-243-0654. Business E-Mail: amy.landwehr@lawiowa.com.

LANDY, BURTON AARON, lawyer; b. Chgo., Aug. 16, 1929; s. Louis J. and Clara (Ernstein) L.; m. Eleonora M. Simmel, Aug. 4, 1957; children: Michael Simmel, Alisa Anne. Student, Nat. U. Mex., 1948; BS, Northwestern U., 1950; postgrad. scholar, U. Havana, 1951; JD, U. Miami, 1952; postgrad. fellow, Inter-Am. Acad. Comparative Law, Havana, Cuba, 1955-56. Bar: Fla. 1952. Practice law in internat. field, Miami, 1955—; ptnr. firm Ammerman & Landy, 1957-63, Paul, Landy, Beiley & Harper, P.A. and predecessor firm, 1964-94, Steel Hector & Davis, 1994-97; ptnr. firm, chmn. emeritus Internat. Practice Group Akerman, Senterfitt & Eidson, P.A., 1997—. Lectr. Latin Am. bus. law U. Miami Sch. Law, 1972-75; also internat. law confs. in U.S. and abroad; mem. Nat. Conf. on Fgn. Aspects of U.S. Nat. Security, Washington, 1958; mem. organizing com. Miami regional conf. Com. for Internat. Econ. Growth, 1958; mem. U.S. Dept. Commerce Regional Export Expansion Council, 1969-74, mem. Dist. Export Council, 1978—; mem. U.S. Sec. State Adv. Com. on Pvt. Internat. Law; dir. Fla. Council Internat. Devel., 1977—, chmn. 1986-87, 99; mem. U. Miami Citizens Bd., 1977—; chmn. Fla. del. S.E. U.S.-Japan Assn., 1980-82; mem. adv. com. 1st Miami Trade Fair of Ams., 1978; dir., v.p. Greater Miami Fgn. Trade Zone, Inc., 1978—; mem. organizing com., lectr. 4 Inter-Am. Aviation Law Confs.; bd. dirs. Inter-Am. Bar Legal Found., VIII FTAA Ministerial, Am. Bus. Forum; participant Aquaculture Symposium Sci. and Man in the Ams., Mexico City, Fla. Gov's Econ. Mission to Japan and Hong Kong, 1978; mem. bd. exec. advisors Law and Econs. Ctr.; mem. vis. com., internat. adv. bd. U. Miami Sch. Bus.; mem. internat. fin. council Office Comptroller of Fla.; founding chmn. Fla.-Korea Econ. Coop. Com., 1982—, Southeast U.S.-Korea Econ. Com., 1985—; chmn. Expo 500 Fla.-Columbus Soc., 1985-87; founding co-chmn. So. Fla. Roundtable-Georgetown U. Ctr. for Strategic and Internat. Studies, 1982-85; chmn. Fla. Gov.'s Conf. on World Trade, 1984—; founding gen. counsel Fla. Internat. Bankers Assn.; dir., former gen. counsel Fla. Internat. Ins. and Reins. Assn., chmn. Latin Am. Carribbean Bus. Promotion Adv. Counc. to U.S. Sec. of Commerce and Aid Adminstr; appointee Fla. Internat. Trade and Investment Coun.; mem. steering com. Summit of Ams., 1994—, co-chair post summit planning com.; strategic planning com. Mayor Miami Dade County Internat. Trade Commn. Contbg. editor Econs. Devel. Lawyers of the Ams., 1969-74; contbr. numerous articles to legal jours. in U.S. and fgn. countries. Chmn. City of Miami Internat. Trade and Devel. Com., 1984-86; chmn. internat. task force Beacon Coun. of Dade County, Fla., 1985, dir., chmn., 1991—; bd. dirs., exec. com. Internat. Comml. Dispute Resolution Ctr., Miami Internat. Arbitration and Mediation Inst.; chmn. Comml. Dispute Resolution Ctr. for the Ams., Miami, 1995—; apptd. by Gov. of Fla. to Internat. Currency and Barter Commn., 1986; lectr. U. Miami Inter-Ban course for Latin Am. bankers; steering com. Summit of the Americas, Miami, 1994, co-chair post Summit Planning Com., 1994; co-chair mayor Miami-Dade County Strategic Planning for Internat. Trade, 1998—; co-chair strategic planning com. Mayor of Miami Dade County Internat. Trade Commn.; bd. dirs. Trade Mission Ctr. Am., 2000—, Internat. Trade Coun. Miami-Dade County, Fla., Fla. Free Trade Area Agreement, Inc.; mem. internat. adv. com. Enterprise Fla., 2000—; bd. trustee Fla. Free Trade Area of the Americas; bd. dirs. Fla. Free Trade AGreement Ams., Inc. With JACGC, USAF, 1952-54, Korea; to maj. Res. Recipient Pan Am. Informatica Comunicaciones Expo award, 1983, Lawyer of Americas award U. Miami, 1984, Heung-in medal (Order of Diplomatic Service), 1986, Ministerial Citation, Min. of Fgn. Affairs, 1988, Richard L. McLaughlin award Fla. Econ. Devel. Coun., 1993, Order of the Rising Sun Golden Rays with Garnet medal, Emperor of Japan, 2004; named Internat. Trader of Yr., Fla. Council Internat. Devel., 1980, Bus. Person of Yr., 1986, hon. consul gen. Republic of Korea, Miami, 1983-88, State of Fla., 99—; apptd. Hon. consul Ft. Lauderdale, Fla., 1991-98; apptd. Hon. consul gen. State of Fla., 1999—. Fellow ABA Found. (chmn. com. arrangements internat. and comparative law sect. 1964-65, com. on Inter-Am. affairs of ABA 1985-87); mem. Inter-Am. Bar Assn. (asst. sec.-gen. 1957-59, treas. 11th conf. 1959, co-chmn. jr. bar sect. 1963-65, mem council 1969—, exec. com. 1975—, pres. 1982-84, Diploma de Honor 1987, William Roy Vallance award 1989), Spanish Am. Bar Assn., Fla. Bar Assn. (vice chmn. adminstrv. law com. 1965, vice chmn. internat. and comparative law com. 1967-68, chmn. aero. law com. 1968-69), Dade County Bar Assn. (chmn. fgn. laws and lang. com. 1964-65), Internat. Ctr. Fla. (World Trade Ctr., pres. 1981-82), World Peace Through Law Ctr., Miami Com. Fgn. Rels., Inst. Ibero Am. Derecho Aero., Am. Soc. Internat. Law, Coun. Internat. Visitors, Am. Fgn. Law Assn. (pres. Miami 1958), appointed to Nat. and Internat. panels of Arbitrators of the Am. Arbitration Assn., 2003-, Bar of South Korea (hon. mem.), Greater Miami C. of C. (bd. gov. 1986—), Colombian-Am. C. of C. (bd. dirs. 1986—), Peruvian-Am. C. of C. (bd. dir.), Norwegian Am. C. of C. (bd. dir.), Phi Alpha Delta. Home: 605 Almeria Ave Coral Gables FL 33134-5602 Office: One SE Third Ave 28th Flr Miami FL 33131 Business E-Mail: blandy@akerman.com.

LANDY, LISA ANNE, lawyer; b. Miami, Fla., Apr. 20, 1963; d. Burton Aaron and Eleonora Maria (Simmel) L. BA, Brown U., 1985; JD cum laude, U. Miami, 1988. Bar: Fla. 1988, U.S. Dist. Ct. (so. dist.) Fla. 1988. Atty. Paul, Landy, Beiley & Harper, P.A., Miami, Fla., 1988-94, Steel Hector & Davis, Miami, Fla., 1994-97, ptnr., 1996-97; shareholder Akerman Senterfitt & Eidson P.A., Miami, 1997—. Bd. dirs. Miami City Ballet, 1992-97, pres., 1996; bd. dirs. Women in Internat. Trade, Miami, 1992—, pres., 1995; bd. dirs. Orgn. Women in Internat. Trade, 1994—, v.p., 1997, 98, pres. 1998-2000; bd. dirs. Women in Tech. Internat. South Fla, chmn. The Next Step Youth Cmty. Ctr., Inc., 200-02, IT Women, Inc., 2002— dir., Commonwealth Inst. of So. Fla., Women of interlaw, 2004—. Mem. ABA, Inter-Am. Bar Assn. (asst. sec. 1997-2000). Avocations: sports, arts, languages.

LANDY, RICARDO LOPEZ, humanities educator; b. Guatemala City, Guatemala, Sept. 17, 1949; came to U.S., 1963; s. Lino and Mercedes (Villaverde) L. BA, U. Tex. El Paso, 1970; MA, U. Tex. Austin, 1972, PhD, 1976. Cert. tchr., Tex. Instr. U. Tex., Austin, 1970-76; asst. prof. Tex. A&M U., College Station, 1976-77, Harvard U., Cambridge, Mass., 1977-82; lectr. Spanish UCLA, 1983-84; asst. prof. Grambling (La.) State U., 1992-93; coord. Spanish Tarleton State U., Stephenville, Tex., 1994-95; dir., cons. Pacific Basin Internat., El Paso, Tex., 1995—. Spl. vis. faculty agr., pedagogy in Spanish, Calif. State U., Stanislaus, 1999-2000. Author: El espacio Novelesco en Galdós, 1984, Journey to Montserrat, 1996, (play) La chamaca brava, 1988, El gran magnate, (novel), 1998. Mem. Sigma Delta Pi. Avocations: painting, photography. Office: Pacific Basin Internat 304 Carnival Dr El Paso TX 79912-5704 Office Phone: 915-584-4407. Business E-Mail: rlvirgoyorix@wmconnect.com.

LANDZBERG, JOEL SERGE, cardiologist; b. N.Y.C., Dec. 20, 1958; s. Sol and Marilyn Joy (Aboff) L.; m. Barbare Eugene Ross, May 1, 1983; children: Rebecca, Elizabeth. BA summa cum laude, Columbia Coll., 1979; MD, Columbia U., 1983. Resident medicine Vanderbilt U., Nashville, 1983-86, chief resident medicine, 1987-88; rsch. fellow cardiology U. Calif. San Francisco, Cardiovascular Rsch. Inst., 1986-87; cardiology fellow Brigham & Woman's Hosp., Boston, 1988-90; instr. medicine Harvard U., Boston, 1990-91; pvt. practice cardiology Westwood, N.J., 1991—. Fellow Am. Coll. Cardiology; mem. AMA, Am. Med. Athletic Assn., Phi Beta Kappa. Office: Westwood Cardiology 333 Old Hook Rd Ste 200 Westwood NJ 07675-3267

LANE, ALFRED THOMAS, medical educator; b. Dayton, Ohio, July 17, 1947; BS, U. Dayton, 1969; MD, Ohio State U., 1973. Diplomate Am. Bd. Pediatrics, Am. Bd. Dermatology; lic. physician, Calif. Intern, resident pediatrics Children's Hosp. L.A., 1973-76; pvt. practice Pleasant Valley Pediatric Med. Group, Camarillo, Calif., 1976-79; resident dermatology U. Colo. Sch. Medicine, Denver, 1979-82; asst. prof. dermatology and pediatrics U. Rochester (N.Y.) Med. Ctr., 1982-88; attending physician Strong Meml. Hosp., 1982-90; staff dermatologist Rochester Gen. Hosp., 1985-90; dir. Dermatology Clinic VA, Rochester, 1985-90; assoc. prof. dermatology and pediatrics U. Rochester Med. Ctr., 1988-90; staff physician in dermatology and pediatrics Stanford (Calif.) U. Med. Ctr., Stanford Children's Hosp., 1990—, dir. pediatric dermatology, 1990—; assoc. prof. dermatology and pediatrics Stanford U. Med. Ctr., 1990-96; prof. dermatology Stanford (Calif.) U. Med. Ctr., 1996—; acting chmn. dept. dermatology Stanford U. Med. Ctr., 1995-96, chmn. dermatology, 1996—; chief dermatology svc. Stanford U. Med. Ctr., Stanford Health Svcs., 1995—. Author: with W.L. Weston) Color Textbook of Pediatric Dermatology, 1991, 3d edit. 2002; (with W.L. Weston and J.G. Morelli) Color Textbook of Pediatric Dermatology, 1995; contbr. articles to profl. jours. Recipient Buswell fellowship U. Rochester, 1982-83, Clin. Investigator award NIH, 1983-88. Fellow Am. Acad. Pediatrics, Am. Acad. Dermatology (mem. task force on pediatric dermatology 1987-92, mem. adv. coun. 1988-90, mem. Presdl. Commn. on Melanoma/Skin Cancer 1988-92, mem. task force on youth edn. 1989-94); mem. Soc. Pediatric Dermatology (bd. dirs. 1986-93, pres. elect 1990-91, pres. 1991-92), Soc. Investigative Dermatology (com. on pub. rels. 1990-94, com. on govt. and pub. rels. 1992-94), Soc. Pediatric Rsch., Am. Dermatol. Assn. Office: Stanford U Med Ctr Dept Dermatology 900 Blake Wilbur Dr Dept W71 Palo Alto CA 94304-2201

LANE, ALVIN HUEY, JR., management consultant; b. Dallas, May 2, 1942; s. Alvin Huey and Marianne (Halsell) L.; m. Melanie Kadane, June 21, 1963; children— Alvin Huey, III, Michael, Lance, Marianne. BA, Rice U., Houston, 1964, BS, 1965. Mgmt. positions with Procter & Gamble Mfg. Co., 1965-68; mgmt. cons. Ernst & Young, CPA's, Dallas, 1968-69; v.p. fin., sec. Balanced Investment Dynamics Co., Dallas, 1969-72, Dr Pepper Co., Dallas, 1972-80, sr. v.p. fin., sec., 1980-83; pres. Lane & Assocs., Dallas, 1983—. Chmn. bd. dirs., CEO Love Bottling Co., Muskogee, Okla.; vice chmn. bd. dirs. Marketplace Christian Network, Dallas. Western Electric scholar Rice U., 1964, J. Venn Leeds scholar, 1964. Mem. Lakewood Country Club, Muskogee Country Club. Home: 3415 Colgate Ave Dallas TX 75225-4830 Office: Lane and Assocs 10440 N Central Expy Ste 610 Dallas TX 75231-2227 Office Phone: 214-363-6173. E-mail: alane@laneassociates.net.

LANE, ALVIN S., lawyer; b. Englewood, NJ, June 17, 1918; s. Martin Lane and Nettie (Gans) Daniels; m. Terese P. Lyons, Apr. 24, 1949; children: Mary-Jo, Judith Lyons. Ph.B., U. Wis., 1940; LL.B., Harvard U., 1943. Bar: N.Y. 1947. Sr. ptnr. Wien, Lane & Malkin, 1954-83; chmn. Rapidata, Inc., 1967-82; Mem. adv. bd. to N.Y. atty. gen. on art legis., 1966-71. Contbr. articles to art publs. and legal jours. Mem. bd. mgmt. Henry Ittleson Rsch. Ctr. Disturbed Children, Riverdale, N.Y., 1961-70; fellow Brandeis U., 1966—, nat. adv. coun. 20th Century Art Soc. High Mus. of Art, 1986-95; sec., trustee Aldrich Mus. Contemporary Art, Inc., 1969-76; trustee Lexington Sch. Deaf, 1971; v.p., trustee Soho Ctr. Visual Artists, Inc., 1974-83; dir. Creative Artists Pub. Svc. Program, Inc., 1982-84; mem. drawing com. Whitney Mus. Am Art, 1991-93; mem. The Elvehjem Mus. Art Coun., 1992—. Served as lt. USNR, 1942-46. Mem. Assn. of Bar of City of N.Y. (chmn. com. art 1963-65), N.Y. Artists Equity Assn. (dir. 1982-84) Clubs: Harvard (N.Y.C.), Riverdale Yacht. Office: 35 E 38th St New York NY 10016-2529 Address: 80 Lyme Rd Apt 221 Hanover NH 03755-1231 Office Phone: 212-682-1957.

LANE, ANN JUDITH, history and women's studies educator; b. N.Y.C., July 27, 1931; d. Harry A. and Elizabeth (Brown) Lane; children: Leslie Patricia, Joni Alexandra. BA, Bklyn. Coll., 1952; MA, NYU, 1958; PhD, Columbia U., 1968. Mng. editor Challenge Mag., NYU, 1953-56; asst. prof. Douglass Coll., Rutgers U., New Brunswick, N.J., 1968-71; prof. John Jay Coll., SUNY, 1971-83; vis. prof. Wheaton Coll., Norton, Mass., 1981-82; prof. history, dir. women's studies Colgate U., Hamilton, N.Y., 1983-90, U. Va., Charlottesville, 1990—. Author: To Herland and Beyond, 1990, Mary Ritter Beard: A Sourcebook, 1977, 2d edit., 1988, The Brownsville Affair, 1971; editor: Charlotte Perkins Gilman Reader, 1980, Herland: A Lost Utopian Novel, 1979. Chair Com. on Status of Women in the Profession, Orgn. of Am. Historians, 1992-95; dir. History Tchr. Inst., N.Y. Coun. for Humanities, summer 1985; mem. historians adv. com. Nat. Women's Hall of Fame, 1986—; bd. dirs. Louis M. Rabinowitz Found., 1972-76. Recipient Va. Soc. Sci. Outstanding History scholar, 2005; fellow, Berkshire Conf. Women Historians, 1988, Ford Found., 1981—82, Nat. Endowment for Humanities, 1980—81, Lilly Endowment, Inc., 1977—79, AAUW, 1959—60. Mem. AAUP (mem. com. on women 1987—), Orgn. Am. Historians (mem. Frederick Jackson Turner prize com. 1979), Women in Hist. Profession (exec. bd., coordinating com. 1971-74). Home: 2603 Jefferson Park Cir Charlottesville VA 22903-4133 Office Phone: 434-982-2961. E-mail: annlane@virginia.edu.

LANE, ARTHUR ALAN, lawyer; b. NYC, Dec. 2, 1945; s. George and Delys L.; m. Jane Ficocella, Dec. 30, 1972; 1 child, Eva B. BA, Yale U., 1967; JD, Columbia U., 1970, MBA, 1971. Bar: N.Y. 1971. Assoc. Webster, Sheffield, Fleischmann, Hitchcock & Brookfield, N.Y.C., 1971-72; asst. to divsn. counsel Liggett & Myers, Inc., N.Y.C., 1973; assoc. Wickes, Riddell, Bloomer, Jacobi & McGuire, N.Y.C., 1974-78, Morgan, Lewis & Bockius, N.Y.C., 1979; ptnr. Eaton & Van Winkle, N.Y.C., 1980—94, DeForest & Duer, N.Y.C., 1994-99, Lamb & Barnosky, Melville, 1999—. Mem. ABA, Assn. of Bar of City of N.Y. Avocation: gardening. Home: 103 Brooksite Dr Smithtown NY 11787-4456 Office: Lamb & Barnosky 534 Broadhollow Rd Melville NY 11747 Office Phone: 631-694-2300. Business E-Mail: aal@lambbarnosky.com.

LANE, BARBARA MILLER (BARBARA MILLER-LANE), humanities educator; b. N.Y.C., Nov. 1, 1934; d. George Ross Rede and Gertrude Miller; m. Jonathan Lane, Jan. 28, 1956; children: Steven Gregory, Eleanor. BA, U. Chgo., 1953, Barnard Coll., 1956; MA, Radcliffe Coll., 1957; PhD, Harvard U., 1962. Tutor history and lit. Harvard U., Cambridge, Mass., 1960-61; lectr. to prof. history Bryn Mawr (Pa.) Coll., 1962-75, dir. Growth and Structure of Cities Program, 1971-89, Andrew W. Mellon prof. humanities, 1981-99, Katherine McBride prof., 1999—, dir. grad. group in archaeology, classics and history of art, 2004. Vis. prof. architecture Columbia U., 1989; cons. NEH sr. fellowships, Washington, 1971-73, Time-Life Books, N.Y.C., 1975; advisor Macmillan Ency. of Architects, N.Y.C., 1979-82; vis. examiner U. Helsinki, 1991; vis. lectr. Technische Universität, Berlin, 1991, Royal Inst. Tech., Stockholm, 2002. Author: (books) Architecture and Politics in Germany, 1968, 1985, National Romanticism and Modern Architecture in Germany and the Scandinavian Countries, 2000; co-author: Nazi Ideology Before 1933, 1978; contbg. author: books Growth and Transformation of the Modern City, 1979; author (contbg.): Macmillan Encyclopedia of Architects, 1982, Urbanisierung im 19. und 20. Jahrhundert, 1983, Perspectives in American History, 1984, The Evidence of Art: Images and Meaning in History, 1986, Art and History, 1988, Nationalism in the Visual Arts, 1991, Moderne Architektur in Deutschland: Expressionismus und Neue Sachlichkeit, 1994, Ultra terminum vagari: Scritti in onore di Carl Nylander, 1997; contbg. editor: Urbanism Past and Present, 1980—85; bd. editors Archtl. History Found., 1988—, (journal) Ctrl. European History, 1992—97; contbr. articles to profl. jours. Co-founder, dir., chmn. bd. dirs. New Gulph Child Care Ctr., Bryn Mawr, 1971-75; mem. Mid. Atlantic Regional Com., Mellon Fellowships in the Humanities, 1985-87; mem. vis. com. Harvard U. Dept. History, 1986-92, Berlin Stadtforum (adv. coun. to Senator for Urban Devel. and Environment), 1991-96; mem. nat. screening com. Inst. Internat. Edn., 1999-2004; mem. com. NEH sr. fellowships, 2002. Recipient Lindback award for excellence in tchg., 1988, medal of honor U. Helsinki, 1996; fellow AAUW, 1959-60, Fels Found., 1961-62, Am. Coun. Learned Socs., 1967-68, Guggenheim Found., 1977-78, sr. fellow Ctr. for Advanced Study in Visual Arts, Nat. Gallery Art, Washington, 1983; Am. Scandinavian Found. fellow, 1989, Wissenschaftskolleg zu Berlin fellow, 1990-91; NEH grantee, summer 1989; NEH sr. fellow, 1998; emeritus fellow Mellon Found., 2005—. Mem. Soc. Archtl. Historians (bd. dirs. 1977-80, Alice Davis Hitchcock award 1968, chmn. awards coms. 1976, 82, chmn. jour. com. 1982-83), Conf. Group on Ctrl. European History (bd. dirs. 1977-79, chmn. awards com. 1987), Am. Hist. Assn. (mem. coun. 1979-82, chmn. com. on Popular Mag. of History 1982), Coll. Art Assn., Phi Beta Kappa. Office: Bryn Mawr Coll Bryn Mawr PA 19010

LANE, BRUCE STUART, lawyer; b. New London, Conn., May 15, 1932; s. Stanley S. and Frances M. (Antis) L.; m. Ann Elizabeth Steinberg, Aug. 10, 1958; children: Sue Ellen, Charles M., Richard I. Student, Boston U., 1948-49; AB magna cum laude, Harvard U., 1952, JD, 1955. Bar: Ohio 1955, D.C. 1966, U.S. Ct. Claims 1960, U.S. Tax Ct. 1961, U.S. Supreme Ct. 1961. Assoc. Squire, Sanders & Dempsey, Cleve., 1955-59; sr. trial atty. tax div. Dept. Justice, Washington, 1959-61; tax atty. Dinsmore, Shohl, Barrett, Coates & Deupree, Cin., 1961-65; sec., asst. gen. counsel corp. and tax matters Communications Satellite Corp., Washington, 1965-69; v.p., gen. counsel Nat. Corp. Housing Partnerships, Washington, 1969-70; pres. Lane and Edson P.C., Washington, 1970-89; ptnr. Kelley Drye & Warren, Washington, 1989-93, Peabody & Brown, Washington, 1993-99, Nixon Peabody LLP, Washington, 1999-2000, sr. counsel, 2001—. Co-editor-in-chief Housing and Devel. Reporter; author publs. and articles on tax, partnership and real estate. Prin., All About Wine, LLC 2000-; incorporator, bd. dirs., past pres. D.C. Inst. Mental Health; past chmn. citizens Com. sect. 5 Chevy Chase, Md.; past mem. Montgomery County Hist. Preservation Commn., Md.; mem. nat. coun. Smithsonian Nat. Mus. of the Am. Indian; trustee The Round House Theatre, Bethesda, Md.; mem. chmn. coun. Crow Canyon Archaeol. Ctr., Cortez, Colo. Maj. JAG, USAR, 1952-68. Mem.: ABA, Anglo-Am. Real Property Inst., Am. Coll. Real Estate Lawyers (pres. 1986—87), Am. Law Inst., Phi Beta Kappa. Home: 5630 Wisconsin Ave #1003 Chevy Chase MD 20815 Office: Nixon Peabody LLP 401 9th St NW Ste 900 Washington DC 20004-2134 Office Phone: 202-585-8777.

LANE, CARRIE BELLE (HAIRSTON), retired music educator; b. Columbus, Ohio, Nov. 12, 1936; d. Samuel Arthur and Carrie Belle Hairston; m. LeRoy Elsworth Lane, June 27, 1964; children: Peter Kevin, Samuel Elsworth, Todd Lucien. BS in Edn., Ohio State U., 1960. Cert. music tchr. Ohio, Wash., N.J., 1960. Music tchr. Ctrl. Local Schs., Farmer, Ohio, 1961—64, Cleve. Pub. Schs., 1964—66, Clover Pk. Pub. Schs., Tacoma, 1969, Columbus Pub. Schs., 1968—69, Mt. Laurel Pub. Schs., NJ, 1967, Pemberton Twp. Schs., NJ, 1974—77, Willingboro Pub. Schs., NJ. Pvt. voice and piano tchr., Willingboro, 1977—2002, Delanco, NJ, 2004—. Charter mem. and sec., v.pres. Willingboro Chpt. NAACP, 1977—88; v.p. Willingboro Dem. Com., 1982; pres. Willingboro Zoning Bd. of Adjust., 1978—94; committeewoman dist. 26 Willingboro Dem. Club, 1992—94; sr. choir soloist and dir. Willingboro Presbyn. Ch., 1977—90; soloist and asst. dir. Christ Bapt. Ch. Sr. Choir, Burlington, NJ, 1991—. Recipient Cmty. and Edn. award, Willingboro NAACP, 1982, Ft. Dix Mil. Wife of the Yr., Ft. Dix Post Comdr. and Cmty., 1974, Edn. award, Nat. Orgn. Black Law Enforcement, Camden, NJ, 1992, Edn. plaque, Camden/Phila. chpt. The Hairston Clan, Inc., 2002, Edn. and Cmty. award, Nothing But the Word Deliverance Ch., Florence, NJ, 2002, Retirement cert., NJ Senate and Assembly, WEA, Willingboro Bd. Edn., 2002. Mem.: N.J. Ret. Edn. Assn., NEA Ret. Tchrs. (assoc.), N.J. Edn. Assn. (assoc.; union rep. jr. hs 2001—02), Alpha Kappa Alpha (assoc.; charter mem. treas. 1978—, corres. sec., asst. sec., parliamentarian). Democrat-Npl. Baptist. Avocations: reading, travel, singing, teaching, directing. Home: 11 Shipps Way Delanco NJ 08075 Personal E-mail: chlane29@comcast.net.

LANE, COLETTE MARIE, writer; b. Cambridge, Eng., Aug. 14, 1958; arrived in U.S., 1960; d. George V. and Sheila V. Lane; 1 child, Jessica Ann. Student, Fullerton (Calif.) Jr. Coll. Quality control insp. ACT Connector, Anaheim, Calif., Acra Aerospace, Anaheim, North Auto Wheel Divsn., Fullerton. Author: Tribute to the Redwoods Poem, 2001, California Sunset Photo, 2001, Northern Lights, 2003. Avocations: music, writing, poetry, painting, psychic reading. Home: 23953 Cherrywood Ln Chiloquin OR 97624

LANE, DAVID OLIVER, retired librarian; b. Flint, Mich., Oct. 17, 1931; s. Clinton Ellis and Mary Ailene (Sanders) L. BA, U. Mich., 1958, A.M. in L.S, 1959; doctoral fellow, U. Chgo., 1968. Various library assignments, 1959-63; asst. dir. libraries Boston U., 1963-67; asst. univ. librarian U. Calif., San Diego, 1968-69; chief librarian, prof., dept. chmn. Hunter Coll., N.Y.C., 1969-90. Dir. NSF funded study of library acquisitions, 1967-68; chmn. Council Chief Librarians, City U. N.Y., 1972-75; trustee N.Y. Met. Reference Library Agy., 1978-87. Author: Study of the Decision Making Procedures for the Acquisition of Science Library Materials, 1968. Mem. A.L.A. (life), Assn. Coll. and Research Libraries, Beta Phi Mu. Home: 27D E Hill Dr Somers NY 10589

LANE, DIANE, actress; b. N.Y.C., Jan. 22, 1965; d. Burt Lane and Colleen Farrington; m. Christopher Lambert, Oct. 1988 (div. Mar. 1994); 1 child, Eleanor; m. Josh Brolin, 2004. Actress: (stage prodns.) Medea, 1972, Agamemnon, 1977, The Cherry Orchard, 1977, Runaways, 1978, Electra, The Trojan Woman, As You Like it, The Good Woman of Setzuan, (feature films) A Little Romance, 1979 (Young Artist Award for best juvenile actress motion picture, 1980), Cattle Annie and Little Britches, 1981, National Lampoon Goes to the Movies, 1981, Six Pack, 1982, Ladies and Gentlemen, The Fabulous Stains, 1982, The Outsiders, 1983, Rumble Fish, 1983, The Cotton Club, 1984, Streets of Fire, 1984, Lady Beware, 1987, The Big Town, 1987, Vital Signs, 1990, Chaplin, 1992, Knight Moves, 1992, Indian Summer, 1993, Wild Bill, 1995, Judge Dredd, 1995, Jack, 1996, Mad Dog Time, 1996, The Only Thrill, 1997, Murder at 1600, 1997, Over the Moon, 1998, GunShy, 1998, A Walk on the Moon, 1999, The Setting Sun, 1999, My Dog Skip, 1999, The Perfect Storm, 2000, Hard Ball, 2001, The Glass House, 2001, Unfaithful, 2002 (Acad. Award nomination for best actress, 2003, Golden Satellite award for best actress, 2003, Nat. Soc. of Film Critics award for best actress, 2003, NY Film Critics Circle award for best actress, 2003), Under the Tuscan Sun, 2003, Fierce People, 2004, Must Love Dogs, 2005; (TV movies) Child Bride of Short Creek, 1981, Miss All-America Beauty, 1982; appeared in TV miniseries, Lonesome Dove, 1989, The World's Oldest Living Confederate Widow Tells All, 1994, A Streetcar Named Desire, 1995, Grace and Glorie, 1998. Named Actress of Yr., Hollywood Film Festival, 2003. Mem. Actors' Equity Assn., AFTRA.*

LANE, DOROTHY SPIEGEL, preventive medicine physician; b. Bklyn., Feb. 17, 1940; d. Milton Barton and Rosalie (Jacobson) Spiegel; m. Bernard Paul Lane, Aug. 5, 1962; children: Erika, Andrew, Matthew. BA, Vassar Coll., 1961; MD, Columbia U., 1965, MPH, 1968. Diplomate Am. Bd. Preventive Medicine, Am. Bd. Family Practice. Resident in preventive medicine N.Y.C. Dept. Health Dist., 1966-68, project dir. children and youth project Title V, HHS Rockaway, 1968-69; med. cons. Maternal and Child Health Svc. HHS, Rockville, Md., 1970-71; asst. prof. preventive medicine Sch. Medicine SUNY, Stony Brook, 1971-76, assoc. prof., 1976-92, prof., 1992—2002, Disting. Svc. prof., 2002—, assoc. dean, 1986—; chair dept. cmty. medicine, dir. med. edn. Brookhaven Meml. Hosp. Med. Ctr., Patchogue, N.Y., 1972-86. Contbr. articles to profl. jours. Exec. com. L.I. divsn. Am. Cancer Soc., 1975—96, pres. L.I. divsn., 1982, mem. nat. assembly, 1996—2001, nat. bd. dir., 1994—96; corp. mem. Nassau Suffolk Health Sys. Agy, 1977—97; bd. dir. Cmty. Health Plan Suffolk, Hauppauge, NY, 1986—91. Grantee, HHS-USPHS, 1977—2002, 2004—, Nat. Cancer Inst., 1987—, 2004—. Fellow: APHA, Am. Bd. Preventive Medicine (trustee 1991—2000, chair 1998—2000), NY Acad. Medicine, Am. Acad. Family Physicians, Am. Coll. Preventive Medicine (regent 1988—96, sec.-treas. 1994—96, pres.-elect 1998—2001, pres. 2001—03, immediate past pres. 2003—05), Assn. Tchrs. Preventive Medicine (pres. 1996—98); mem.: Accreditation Coun. for Continuing Med. Edn. (bd. dirs. 2002—). Office: SUNY at Stony Brook Sch Medicine Health Scis Ctr L 4 Stony Brook NY 11794-0001 Office Phone: 631-444-2094. Business E-Mail: dorothy.lane@stonybrook.edu.

LANE, ELEANOR SYLVIA, music educator, organist; b. Cheyenne, Wyo., Jan. 21, 1947; d. Richard Frederick and Virginia Rose Bivens; m. John Everett Lane, Sept. 20, 1969; children: Michael Douglas, Jason Andrew, Susan Christine. MusB of Piano Performance, U. Wyo., 1969. Permanent Professional Certification in Piano and Music Theory Music Teachers Nat. Assn., 1980. Tchr. piano Ln. Piano Studio, Cheyenne, Wyo., 1969—; prin. organist First Presbyn. Ch., 2002—04. Musician numerous piano performances. Worship and music ministry mem. First Presbyn. Ch., Cheyenne, Wyo., 1992—2005. Named Music Tchr. of Yr., Wyo. Music Tchrs. Assn., 2001. Mem.: Music Tchrs. Nat. Assn. (local pres. 2000—02). Presbyterian. Home: 920 Foyer Ave Cheyenne WY 82001 Office: Lane Piano Studio 920 Foyer Ave Cheyenne WY 82001 Office Phone: 307-638-6348. Personal E-mail: esblane@worldnet.att.net.

LANE, ELIZABETH ANN, genealogist, researcher; b. Horton, Kans., Mar. 9, 1957; d. Dale D. Sheets and Marlene E. Kletchka; m. Rex L. Lane; children: Laura, Catherine. BSW, U. Kans., 1983. Dir. CASA, Atchison, Kans., 1997—98; asst. dir. Juvenile Intake and Assessment, Oskaloosa, Kans., 1998—2001. Mem.: AAUW, Atchison Preservation Alliance (bd. dirs. 1999—2001, treas., bd. dirs. 2004—), Friends Atchison Libr. (pres. 2001—03), Atchison County Hist. Soc. (bd. dirs. 1998—2002, pres. 2001—02). Avocations: gardening, reading, music, travel. Home: EA Lane Rsch Svcs 841 S Fourth St Atchison KS 66002-2904 Office Phone: 913-367-0391. Personal E-mail: llane1@charter.net.

LANE, FIELDING H., lawyer; b. Kansas City, Mo., May 6, 1926; s. Ralph Fielding and Nancy Lee (Greene) L.; m. Patricia Cecil Parkhurst, Jan. 25, 1980 BS in Bus. Adminstrn., U. Mo.-Columbia, 1948; LL.B. cum laude, Harvard U., 1951. Bar: Mo. 1951, Calif. 1956. Assoc. Watson Ess Marshall & Enggas, Kansas City, Mo., 1951-55; assoc. Thelen Marrin Johnson & Bridges, San Francisco, 1955-66, ptnr., 1967-95, of counsel, 1996—. Served with USN, 1944-46; PTO; lt. comdr. Res. (ret.) Home: PO Box 1495 Aptos CA 95001-1495 Office: Thelen Reid & Priest LLP 101 2d St Ste 1800 San Francisco CA 94105 Office Phone: 415-371-1200. Business E-Mail: fhlane@thelenreid.com.

LANE, FRANK JOSEPH, JR., lawyer; b. St. Louis, May 10, 1934; s. Frank Joseph and Virginia Laurette (Hausman) L.; m. Margaret Ann Dwyer, Mar. 2, 1957; children: Mary, Stephen, Thomas, Michael. BS in Commerce, JD, St. Louis U., 1956; LLM, Georgetown U., 1960; grad. Parker Sch. Internat. Law, Columbia U., 1970; cert., Coll. Fin. Planning, Denver, 1988. Bar: Mo. 1956, U.S. Dist. Ct. (ea. dist.) Mo. 1956, U.S. Ct. Appeals (8th cir.) 1960, U.S. Supreme Ct. 1959, U.S. Ct. Mil. Appeals, 1957. Ptnr. Goldenhersh, Goldenhersh, Fredericks, Newman & Lane, St. Louis, 1960-64, Lane & Leadlove, St. Louis, 1964-66, Dill & Lane, St. Louis, 1978-79; counsel Ralston Purina Co., St. Louis, 1966-78, mem. pres.'s adv. bd., 1967-69; of counsel Petrolite Corp., St. Louis, 1979-83; v.p., trust officer Gravois Bank, St. Louis, 1983-85; regional v.p., trust officer Merc Bank N.A., St. Louis, 1985-89; of counsel Dill, Wamser, Bamvakais & Newsham PC, St. Louis, 1989—. Instr. internat. law St. Louis U., 1979. Bd. dirs. Met. St. Louis Sewer Dist., 1965-73, chmn., 1968-69; bd. dirs. Webster Groves KC Home Assn., 1999-01; mem. St. Louis Regional Commerce & Growth Assn. environ. com., 1978-82; mem. planned giving com. Am. Heart Assn., St. Louis, 1986-88, St. Louis Soc. for Crippled Children, 1991; bd. dirs. Midwestern Braille Vols., Inc., chmn., 1995—; atty. St. Louis Geneal. Soc., 1996—; pres. Ozark Cmties. Coun. St. Louis County, 1964-65. Capt. U.S. Army JAGC, Pentagon, 1957-60. Mem. Mo. Bar Assn., Met. St. Louis Bar Assn. (chmn. rels. with law schs. com. 1961-62, enrollment com. 1962-63, chmn. office practice com. 1963-64, elected admissions com. 1967), Estate Planning Coun. St. Louis, Rotary (bd. dirs. Crestwood, Mo. chpt. 1988-89), KC (grand knight 1964-66, adv. West County 1983-90, Webster Groves 1991-2001). Republican. Roman Catholic. Avocations: painting, golf, travel, investment analysis. Home: 520 Lering Dr Ballwin MO 63011-1588 Office: 9939 Gravois Rd Saint Louis MO 63123-4211 E-mail: fjlane@sbcglobal.net.

LANE, GARY MATTHEW, lawyer; b. Fairfield, Iowa, Oct. 12, 1944; m. Gerda C. Murra; children: Matthew P., Stephen W. BA, U. Iowa, 1967, JD with distinction, 1969. Bar: Iowa 1969, U.S. Dist. Ct. (so. dist.) Iowa 1969, U.S. Dist. Ct. (no. dist.) Iowa 1977. Asst. county atty. Scott County, Davenport, Iowa, 1969-78; ptnr. Wehr, Berger, Lane & Stevens and predecessors, Davenport, Iowa, 1969—. Bd. dirs., pres. HELP, Legal Svcs. Corp., Davenport, Iowa, 1972—; founding dir., past pres. Legal Svcs. Corp. Iowa, Des Moines, 1977-93. Pres. Davenport Diocesan Lay Coun., Iowa, 1980-82; trustee Quad City Symphony Orch., Davenport, 1980-89; pres. Marriage and Family Counseling Svc., Davenport, 1985-87; chmn. Davenport Neighborhood Task Force, 1991; pres. bd. Assumption H.S., 1994-96. Fellow Iowa Acad. Trial Lawyers; mem. ATLA (Disting. Mem. award 1989), Iowa Trial Lawyers Assn. (bd. govs. 1980-88, Outstanding Key Mem. 1988), Iowa Bar Assn., Scott County Bar Assn., Outstanding Lawyers of America. Office: Wehr Berger Lane & Stevens Ste 900 Kahl Bldg 326 W 3d St Davenport IA 52801 Office Phone: 563-326-1000. Business E-Mail: garylane@wblslaw.com.

LANE, GLORIA JULIAN, foundation administrator; b. Chgo., Oct. 6, 1932; d. Coy Berry and Katherine (McDowell) Julian; m. William Gordon Lane (div. Oct. 1958); 1 child, Julie Kay Rosewood. BS in Edn., Cen. Mo. State U., 1958; MA, Bowling Green State U., 1959; PhD, No. Ill. U., 1972. Cert. tchr. Assoc. prof. William Jewell Coll., Liberty, Mo., 1959-60; chair forensic div. Coral Gables (Fla.) High Sch., 1960-64; assoc. prof. No. Ill. U., DeKalb, 1964-70; prof. Elgin (Ill.) Community Coll., 1970-72; owner, pub. Lane and Assocs, Inc., San Diego, 1972-78; prof. Nat. U., San Diego, 1978-90; pres., chief exec. officer Women's Internat. Ctr., San Diego, 1982—. Founder, dir. Living Legacy Awards, San Diego, 1984—. Author: Project Text for Effective Communications, 1972, Project Text for Executive Communication, 1980, Positive Concepts for Success, 1983; editor Who's Who Among San Diego Women, 1984, 85, 86, 90—, Systems and Structure, 1984. Named Woman of Accomplishment, Soroptimist Internat., 1985, Pres.'s Coun. San Diego, 1986, Center City Assn., 1986, Bus. and Profl. Women, San Diego, 1991, Woman of Yr., Girls' Clubs San Diego, 1986, Woman of Vision, Women's Internat. Ctr., 1990, Wonderwoman 2000 Women's Times Newspaper, 1991; recipient Angel in Action award, 1999, Independence award Ctr. for Disabled, 1986, Founder's award Children's Hosp. Internat., Washington, 1986, Making Difference for Women award, Soroptimist Internat., 1998, Women Who Mean Business Courage Award San Diego Bus. Jour., 1998. Avocations: computers, painting, writing. Home and Office: 6202 Friars Rd Unit 311 San Diego CA 92108-5000 Office Phone: 619-295-6446. E-mail: gloria311@aol.com.

LANE, HANA UMLAUF, editor; b. Stockholm, Mar. 14, 1946; came to U.S., 1951, naturalized, 1957; d. Karel Hugo Antonin and Anatolia (Spitel) Umlauf; m. John Richard Lane, Feb. 16, 1980; 1 stepchild, Matthew John AB magna cum laude, Vassar Coll., 1968; AM in Russian and East European Studies, Yale U., 1970. Asst. to exec. editor Newspaper Enterprise Assn., N.Y.C., 1970-72, sr. asst., asst. editor World Almanac divsn., 1972-75, assoc. editor World Almanac, 1975-80, spl. project editor, 1977-80; editor World Almanac and World Almanac Publs., N.Y.C., 1980-85; editor in chief Pharos Books, N.Y.C., 1984-91, sr. editor, 1991-93, John Wiley & Sons, 1993—. Editor: World Almanac Book of Who, 1980, World Almanac and Book of Facts, 1981-85; editor: (with others) The Woman's Almanac, 1977. Democrat. Home: 140 Fairview Ave Stamford CT 06902-8040 Business E-Mail: hlane@wiley.com.

LANE, HOLLY DIANA, artist; b. Cleve., Sept. 13, 1954; d. Edwin Joseph and Ursula Anna (Neustadt) Selyem; m. L.A. Lane, Apr. 20, 1975. AA in 2-Dimensional Art, Cuesta Coll., San Luis Obispo, Calif., 1982; BFA with great distinction, San Jose State U., 1986, MFA in Pictorial Art, 1988. One-woman shows include Ivory/Kimpton Gallery, San Francisco, 1989, Rutgers Barclay Gallery, Santa Fe, 1990, Bingham Kurts Gallery, Memphis, 1992, (solo survey show with catalog) Art Mus. S.E. Tex., Beaumont, 1995, Natalie & James Thompson Gallery, San Jose State U., 2001, Yellowstone Art Museum, 2001, Lyman Allyn Mus. Art, 2001, Schmidt Bingham Gallery, NYC, 1991, 93, 95, 97, 99, 2001, Forum Gallery, NYC, 2003; exhibited in group shows at Eiteljorg Mus., Indpls., 1995, 2000, Yerba Buena Ctr. for the Arts, San Francisco, 1994, Knoxville (Tenn.) Mus. Art, 1993-94, Fine Arts Ctr. U. RI, Kingston, 1992, Contemporary Mus., Honolulu, 1993, 2002, Boise (Idaho) Art Mus., 1994, Castle Gallery-Coll. New Rochelle, NY, 1996, Kennedy Mus. Am. Art, Athens, Ohio, 1996, Calif. Ctr. for the Arts Escondido Mus., 1996, Samuel P. Harn Mus., U. Fla., Gainesville, 1996, Whitney Mus. Am. Art, Champion, Conn., 1997-98, Arnot Art Mus., Elmira, NY, 1997-98, Susan H. Arnold Art Gallery Lebanon Valley Coll., Anneville, Pa., 1997-98, Pelham (NY) Art Ctr, 1998, Art Mus. Western Va., 1999-2000, San Jose Mus. Art, 1999-2000, Art Mus. Western Va., 1999-2000, Santa Cruz Art Mus., 2000, Brevard Mus. Art and Sci., Melbourne, Fla., 2000, Gallery of Contemporary Art, Sacred Heart U., Fairfield, Conn., 2002, NJ Ctr. For Visual Arts, Summit, 2002, Jarvic Ctr., NYC, 2002, Forum Gallery, NYC, 2002, 04, Internat. Art and Design Fair, NYC, 2004, San Francisco Internat. Art Exposition, 2005, others; represented in permanent collections Art Mus. S.E. Tex., Contemporary Mus., Honolulu, A.R.A. Svcs., Phila., Dow Jones & Co., NYC, Detroit Zool. Gardens, Prin. Fin. Group, Des Moines, IDS, Mpls., Memphis Cancer Ctr., Seven Bridges Found., Greenwich, Conn.; works reproduced in books, mags., calendars, jours., including ARTNews, Art in America, NY Times, Art Papers, Art & Antiques, New Yorker Mag., Artweek, Christian Sci. Monitor, Pvt. Arts, Forensic Examiner, NYarts Mag., The Wilson Quar., Review Mag., NYC, 1999, Women Artists calendar 1996-98, San Raphael, Calif., The Sciences, NY Acad. Scis., 1992-93, (textbook) Artist and Audience, (London) 1996, Dreams 1900-2000, NY Sun, 2003, CAA News, 2003: Sci., Art and the Unconscious Mind (book), 1999, Wilson Quarterly, 1998, Rev. Mag., 1999, Dreamworks: Twentieth-Century Artistic and Psychological Perspectives, 1999, N.Y. Sun, 2003; works presented in TV documentaries including Welcome to Nocturnia, 1993, Women in Art, Time-Warner, Manhattan Cable, NYC, 1993-94; in books accompanying TV show Bill Moyers Genesis, A Living Tradition, PBS, 1996, Healing and the Mind, 1993. Named Alumna of Yr., Cuesta Coll., 1992; pres.'s scholar San Jose State U., 1986, Johanna Rietz scholar Art Assn. of Morro Bay, Calif., 1981. Mem. Coll. Art Assn. Avocations: nature walks, contemplation, reading. Home: 182 Brian Ln Santa Clara CA 95051-6704 Address: care Forum Gallery 745 Fifth Ave 5th Fl New York NY 10151 Office Phone: 408-248-6995. Personal E-mail: hlane42@earthlink.net.

LANE, IRIS MARY, retired educator; b. Kellogg, Idaho, June 24, 1934; d. Ivan John and Dorothy Vivian (McKinney) Green; m. C. Clayton, Dec. 19, 1959 (div. 1962); 1 child, Mark Andrew. AA, N. Idaho Jr. Coll., 1955; BS, U. Idaho, Moscow, 1964; postgrad., Whitworth Coll., Spokane, 1967, Eastern Wash. U., Cheney, 1967. Tchr. Sch. Dist. 391, Kellogg, Idaho, 1955-57, Sch. Dist. 81, Spokane, Wash., 1958-93; ret., 1993. Master tchr. Local Colls., Spokane, 1962-85. Vol. Am. Heart Assn., Spokane, 1988-93, orphan and foster children assns., illiteracy improvement programs; mem. PTA Recipient Golden Acorn award Garfield Parent Tchrs. Assn., Spokane, 1978. Mem. NEA, Wash. Edn. Assn., Spokane Edn. Assn., Alpha Delta Kappa Honorary, Alpha Delta Kappa. Republican. Lutheran. Avocation: church activities. Home: 3405 W Francis Ave Spokane WA 99205-7427 Office Phone: 509-328-6894.

LANE, JAMES MCCONKEY, retired investment banker; b. Pitts., July 9, 1929; s. Mortimer Bliss and Mary (Knapp) L.; m. Arlyne Ruth Nelson, Dec. 16, 1950; children: James, Theodore, Thomas, Karen, David. BA, Wheaton Coll., 1952; MBA, U. Chgo., 1953; postgrad., NYU, 1956, U. Buffalo, 1960. Credit corr. John Plain & Co., Chgo., 1951; trainee Chase Manhattan Bank, N.Y.C., 1953-55, account mgr. investment adv. divsn., 1955-59, investment officer, 1959-62, 2d v.p., 1962-64, v.p., mgr. corp. pension trust investments, 1964-66, v.p. divsn. exec. pension trust investment divsn., 1966-68, chmn. investment policy com., 1968-78, sr. v.p., investment group exec., 1968-70, exec. v.p. fiduciary investment dept., 1970-78; pres., dir. Chase Investors Mgmt. Corp., N.Y.C., 1972-78; mng. dir. Cyrus J. Lawrence Inc., N.Y.C., 1978-82; sr. v.p., chief investment officer, head trust investment divsn. NBD Bank N.A., Detroit, 1982-94, sr. mgmt., 1984-94; ret., 1994. Bd. dirs. NAIC Growth Fund, Inc., Christian Camps Inc., 1978-, Baseball Chapel Inc., 1994-. Trustee Wheaton Coll., 1971—; chmn. Wheaton Coll. Trust Co., 2000—. Mem. Stone Harbor Golf Club, Boca Raton Resort and Club, Premier Club. Home and Office: 3700 S Ocean Blvd Unit 1006 Highland Beach FL 33487 also: 2 86th St Stone Harbor NJ 08247-1607

LANE, JEFFREY H., lawyer; b. NYC, Apr. 14, 1949; AB, Columbia U., 1970; JD cum laude, Boston U., 1975. Bar: Wis. 1975. With Foley & Lardner, Milw., 1975—96, ptnr.; sr. v.p., gen. counsel, sec. MGIC Investment Corp., 1996—. Mem. ABA, State Bar Wis. Office: MGIC Investment Corp MGIC Plz 250 E Kilbourn Ave PO Box 488 Milwaukee WI 53201-0488 Office Phone: 414-347-6406. Office Fax: 414-347-6696.

LANE, JEREMY SCOTT, music educator; b. Albuquerque, May 7, 1969; s. Al and Terry Lane. PhD in Music Edn., La. State U., 2003. Asst. prof. U. SC., Columbia, SC, 2003—. Home: 4117 Spring Hill Columbia SC 29204 Office: Univ SC School of Music Columbia SC 29208 Office Phone: 803-777-1501.

LANE, JOAN FLETCHER, academic administrator; b. San Francisco, May 7, 1928; d. Howard French and Kathryn Elizabeth (Kraft) Fletcher; m. Melvin Bell Lane, Feb. 15, 1953; children: Whitney Lane-Miller, Julie Lane-Gay. AB, Smith Coll., 1949. Staff World Affairs Coun. No. Calif., San Francisco, 1949-51, Inst. Internat. Edn., Stanford, Calif., 1952; spl. asst., dean Sch. H&S Stanford U., 1982-93, spl. asst. bd. trustees, 1993—. Bd. dirs. McClatchy Newspapers, Sacramento; dir. The James Irvine Found., San Francisco, 1990-02. Trustee San Francisco Found., 1984-92; trustee Smith Coll., Northampton, Mass., 1978-85, chmn. bd. trustees, 1982-85, v.p. alumnae assn., 1975-78; bd. dirs. Internat. House, U. Calif., Berkeley, 1971-80; pres., assoc. coun. Mills Coll., Oakland, Calif., 1974-78. Recipient John M. Greene award, Smith Coll., 1988, Gold Spike award, Stanford U., 2005. Avocations: hiking, gardening. Home: 99 Tallwood Ct Atherton CA 94027-6431

LANE, JOHN DENNIS, lawyer; b. Norwalk, Conn. s. John J. and Theresa A. (Donnelly) L.; m. Elizabeth J. Galliher, Apr. 28, 1949; children: Elizabeth J., John Dennis, Margaret A., Robert E., Paul G. BS, Georgetown U., 1943, JD, 1948. Bar: D.C. 1948, Conn. 1950. Atty. Office Chief Counsel, Bur. Internal Revenue, Washington, 1948-49; exec. sec. to U.S. Senator Brien McMahon, 1949-50; adminstrv. asst., 1950-52; pvt. practice Washington and Norwalk, 1953-2001; ptnr. Hedrick & Lane, 1954— 82, Wilkes, Artis, Hedrick & Lane, 1982-2000, Wilkes Artis, 2000-2001. Mem. coun. Adminstrv. Conf. U.S., 1961; bd. regents Georgetown U., 1979—. Served to capt. USMCR, 1943-45. Recipient Citation of Merit. Fellow Am. Bar Found.; mem. ABA (chmn. standing com. unauthorized practice of law 1971-73, chmn. standing com. nat. conf. groups 1973-75, D.C. cir. mem. standing com. on fed. judiciary 1984-86, Fed. cir. mem. 1987-90), Fed. Commn. Bar Assn. (pres.-elect 1990, pres. 1991-92, alt. rep. to UN 1997-99), Am. Law Inst., Met. Club, Columbia Country Club (Chevy Chase, Md.). Home: 5045 Van Ness St NW Washington DC 20016-1960 Office: 8th Fl 1200 New Hampshire Ave NW Washington DC 20036-6802

LANE, JOHN EDWARD, multimedia and theater educator; b. Topeka, Sept. 19, 1962; s. Larwence Joseph and Virginia Mary Lane; m. Kelly E. Hart, Apr. 8, 1961; 1 child, Jacob N. Hart-Lane. MSE, U. of Kans., 1996. Cert. tchr. English and theater Kans. Tchr. English and theater Ctr. Sch. Dist. Unified Sch. Dist. 58, Kansas City, Mo., 1986—92, Olathe (Kans.) Sch. Dist. Unified Sch. Dist. 233, 1992—2005, tchr. broadcast and multimedia, 2000—. Tchr. St. Pauls Parish, Olathe, 1995—98. Named McDonalds Tchr. of the Month, 1994. Mem.: NEA, Theater Educators Assn. Roman Catholic. Office Phone: 913-780-7140. Personal E-mail: jlaneon@olatheschools.com.

LANE, JOHN RODGER, museum director; b. Evanston, Ill., Feb. 28, 1944; s. John Crandall Lane and Jeanne Marie (Rodger) L. Moritz; m. Inge-Lise Eckmann, 1992. BA, Williams Coll., 1966; MBA, U. Chgo., 1971; AM, Harvard U., 1973, PhD, 1976; DFA (hon.), San Francisco Art Inst., 1995. Asst. dir. Fogg Art Mus., Cambridge, Mass., 1974; exec. asst. to dir., adminstr. curatorial affairs, asst. dir. curatorial affairs Bklyn. Mus., N.Y.C., 1975-80; dir. Carnegie Mus. Art, Pitts., 1980-86, San Francisco Mus. Modern Art, 1987-97; Eugene McDermott dir. Dallas Mus. Art, 1999—. Vis. com. Williams Coll. Mus. Art, 1998—. Author: Stuart Davis: Art and Art Theory, 1978; co-editor: Abstract Painting and Sculpture in America, 1927-1944, 1983, Carnegie International, 1985, Dallas Mus. Art 100 Years, 2003, Sigmar Polke: The History of Everything, Paintings, and Drawings, 1998-2003m Gerhard Richerter, 1965-2004, Lothar Baumgartern: Carbon, 2004; exec. editor: The Making of a Modern Museum/SFMOMA, 1995. Trustee Fountain Valley Sch., Colorado Springs, 1999—. Served to lt. USNR, 1966-69. Nat. Endowment Arts Mus. fellow, 1974-75 Mem. Assn. Art Mus. Dirs. (trustee 2000—02), Am. Assn. Museums. Office: Dallas Mus Art 1717 N Harwood St Dallas TX 75201-2398 Office Phone: 214-922-1304. Business E-Mail: jlane@DallasMuseumofArt.org.*

LANE, KATHLEEN MARGARET, refrigeration company official; b. Mpls., Oct. 25, 1946; d. Bernard Melvin and Margaret (Beck) Aanerud; m. Kenneth LeRoy Lane, Sept. 1, 1979; 1 child, Dennis Leon. Cost acct. Honeywell, Mpls., 1964-66; bookkeeper Columbia Heights State Bank, Minn., 1968-71; mgr. inventory control Hodes Optical Inc., Torrance, Calif., 1972-75, office mgr., 1975-79; lens supr. Coburn Optical Industries, inc., Carson, Calif., 1979-85, br. mgr. St. Paul, 1985-93; office mgr. J.M. Refrigeration, St. Croix Falls, Wis., 1993—99; owner, mgr. Lanes Portable Bandsaw Mill, 2000—. With customer rels. dept. Opti Fair, Aneheim, Calif., 1978-83. Mem. Am. Inst. Banking, NAFE. Avocations: restoring old furniture, camping, knitting. E-mail: kklane@tds.net.

LANE, KATHY S., information technology executive, consumer products company executive; Dir. tech. svcs. Pepsi Cola Internat., 1997—98; mgr. corp. initiatives group Gen. Electric Co., 1998—99, sr. v.p. and chief info. officer, vendor fin. svcs., 1999—2000; gen. mgr. e- bus. and info. tech. Gen. Electric Oil & Gas, 2000—02; sr. v.p. corp. info. tech. and applications Gillette Co., Boston, 2002—, chief info. officer, 2002—. Office: The Gillette Co Prudential Tower Boston MA 02199-8004

LANE, KENNETH ROBERT, producer, distributor; b. N.Y.C., N.Y., Dec. 3, 1942; s. Carl Lane and Freda Rosalind; m. Marjory Horowitz, Dec. 1965 (div. 1967); m. Nicole Sloan Helguero (div.); m. Yolanda Natalia Bianco, Mar. 1990; 1 child, Jonathan. BA, CUNY, 1965. Cert. engr. Prodn. mgr. Saul Bass & Assocs., Los Angeles, 1968-70; cameraman, prodn. mgr. Nat. Film Bd. Can., Vancouver, 1970-71; producer, distbr. Troma Inc., N.Y.C., 1976-77; prin. Ken Lane Films, N.Y.C., 1976—; producer, prodn. mgr. Platinum Prodns./Platinum Pictures, N.Y.C., 1977-78, Ganymede Prodns., N.Y.C., 1978-80; cameraman, audio mixer Madison Sq. Garden Network, N.Y.C., 1981-82; tech. dir. Sta. WNET Channel 13 (PBS), N.Y.C., 1983; cameraman Fox Broadcasting Co., Sta. WNYW, N.Y.C., 1981—; audio mixer, engr. ABC, N.Y.C., 1982—, CBS, N.Y.C., 1988—, NBC, N.Y.C., 1991—. Producer/distbr.: (motion pictures) Delora, 1977, Legacy of Horror, 1981, The Navy vs. the Night Monsters, 1981, Women of the Prehistoric Planet, 1981. Treas. Washington Market Community Park, N.Y.C., 1985-86. Mem.: Nat. Ct. Reporters Assn. (cert. legal video specialist), Internat. Brotherhood Elec. Workers, Internat. Brotherhood Elec. Workers, Nat. Assn. Broadcast Engrs. Technicians, Internat. Alliance Theatrical and Stage Employees. Jewish. Avocations: tennis, baseball, golf, art collecting. Office: 80 N Moore St Apt 26G New York NY 10013-2734 Office Phone: 917-833-7977. Business E-Mail: kenlaneproductions@earthlink.net.

LANE, LAURENCE WILLIAM, JR., retired ambassador, publisher; b. Des Moines, Nov. 7, 1919; s. Laurence William and Ruth (Bell) L.; m. Donna Jean Gimbel, Apr. 16, 1955; children: Sharon Louise, Robert Laurence, Brenda Ruth. Student, Pomona Coll., 1938-40, LLD (hon.), 1976; BJ, Stanford U., 1942; DHL (hon.), Hawaii Loa Coll., 1991. Chmn. bd. Lane Pub. Co.; pub. Sunset Mag., Sunset Books and Sunset Films; U.S. amb. to Australia and Nauru, 1985-89; ret., 1990. Bd. dirs. Calif. Water Svc. Co., Crown Zellerbach Corp., Pacific Gas and Electric Co.; bd. dirs. Time Inc.; bd. dirs. Oreg. Coast Aquarium, Internat. Bd. Advice, ANZ Bank; U.S. amb. and commr. Gen. Worlds Fair, Japan, 1975-76; hon. fellow Coll. Notre Dame, 1974. Former mem. adv. bd. Sec. Interior's Bd. Nat. Parks; mem. adv. coun. Grad. Sch. Bus., Stanford U., SRI; mem. Pres.'s Nat. Productivity Adv. Com.; mem. Pacific Basin Econ. Coun.; former bd. dirs. Pacific Forum, CSI, Nat. Parks Found.; vol. The Nat. Ctr.; mem. bd. overseers Hoover Instn. War, Revolution and Peace; mem. exec. com. Ctr. for Australian Studies, U. Tex., Austin. Lt. USNR, World War II, PTO. Decorated officer Order of Australia; recipient Conservation Svc. award Sec. Interior; Theodore and Conrad Wirth award NPF, 1994; Wiliam Penn Mott Jr. Conservationist of Yr. award NPCA, 1995; named hon. prof. journalism Stanford U. Mem. Newcomen Soc. N.Am., Pacific Asia Travel Assn. (life mem., chmn. 1980-81), Coun. of Am. Ambs., Los Rancheros Vistadores, Advt. Club San Francisco, No. Calif. Alumni Assn., Bohemian Club, Pacific Union, Men's Garden Club L.A., Alpha Delta Sigma. Republican. Presbyterian. Office: 3000 Sand Hill Rd Bldg 215 Menlo Park CA 94025-7113

LANE, LAWRENCE JUBIN, retired electrical engineer, consultant; b. Morganton, N.C., Feb. 19, 1927; s. Lawrence and Sarah Virginia (Jubin) Lane; m. Gladys Verna Lee Hock, Dec. 25, 1947 (dec. 1975); children: Priscilla Gayle, Richard Jubin; m. Helen Elizabeth Sollazzo, Dec. 19, 1975. B.E.E., N.C. State Coll., 1950; MSE.E., U. Va., 1972. Lic. profl. engr., Va. Engr. GE, Schenectady, N.Y., 1950-54, class supr. Phila., 1954-55, devel. engr. Waynesboro, Va., 1955-63, sr. devel. engr., 1963-78, sr. systems design engr. Roanoke, Va., 1978-83, cons. engr., 1983-95; ret., 1995. Patentee in field. Pres. Stuarts Draft PTA, Va., 1960, 61. Served as petty officer USN, 1944-46, 50-51. Recipient Managerial award Gen. Electric Co., 1965 Fellow IEEE (chpt. chmn. 1982-83); mem. Eta Kappa Nu, Tau Beta Pi, Phi Eta Sigma, Phi Kappa Phi Methodist. Home: 1601 Chatham Rd Waynesboro VA 22980-3203 Office Phone: 540-943-7502. E-mail: juhelane@cfw.com. *Since my occupational accomplishments have been judged to be noteworthy, I am indeed fortunate. I thank God and Jesus Christ for my abilities and for the opportunities for such accomplishments.*

LANE, LOUIS, musician, conductor; b. Eagle Pass, Tex., Dec. 25, 1923; s. William Bartlett and Virginia (Gardner) L. B.Mus., U. Tex., 1943; Mus.M., Eastman Sch. Music, 1947; Mus.D. (hon.), Akron U., 1973, Cleve. State U., 1974, Kent State U., 1988, Cleve. Inst. Music, 1995, Oberlin Coll., 2000. Adj. prof. music Akron U., 1969-82; vis. prof. music U. Cin., 1973-75, Oberlin Coll., 1995-98; artistic advisor, condr. Cleve. Inst. Music, 1982—; sr. lectr. music U. Tex., 1989-91. Mem., Cleve. Orch., 1947-73, assoc. condr., 1960-70, resident condr., 1970-73; condr., Akron (Ohio) Symphony Orch., 1959-83, co-condr., Altanta Symphony Orch., 1977-83, prin. guest condr., Atlanta Symphony Orch., 1983-88, prin. condr., SABC Symphony Orch., Johannesburg South Africa, 1984-85, prin. guest condr., Dallas Symphony Orch., 1973-78, guest condr. in, Chgo., Seattle, St. Louis, Detroit, Houston, San Antonio, Vancouver, B.C., Can., Montevideo, Uruguay, Warsaw, Poland, Johannesburg, S.Africa, Helsinki, Finland, mus. dir., Lake Erie Opera Theatre, Cleve., 1964-72; co-dir., Blossom Festival Sch. of Cleve. Orch. and Kent State U., 1969-73; rec. artist for Columbia Records, Telarc Records. Served with F.A. AUS, 1943-46. Decorated chevalier l'Ordre des Arts et des Lettres de France; recipient Mahler medal, 1971, Ditson award Columbia, 1972, Grammy award for best orch. rec., 1989. Office: Herbert Barrett Management Fl 20 266 W 37th St New York NY 10018-6648 Home: 1 Bratenahl Pl Apt 1504 Cleveland OH 44108-1156

LANE, MARGARET BEYNON TAYLOR, librarian; b. St. Louis, Feb. 6, 1919; d. Archer and Alice (Jones) Taylor; m. Horace C. Lane, Jan. 6, 1945; children: Margaret Elizabeth, Thomas Archer. BA, La. State U., 1939, JD, 1942; BS in Libr. Sci., Columbia U., 1941. Reference and circulation asst. Columbia Law Libr., N.Y.C., 1942-44; law libr., asst. prof. U. Conn. Sch. Law, Hartford, 1944-46; law libr. La. State U. Law Sch., Baton Rouge, 1946-48; recorder documents La. Sec. of State's Office, Baton Rouge, 1949-75; law libr. Lane Fertitta, Lane Janney & Thomas, 1976-96. Mem. depository libr. coun. to Pub. Printer, 1972-77; mem. plan devel. com. La. Fed. Depository Libr., 1982-83. Author: State Publications and Depository Libraries, 1981, Selecting and Organizing State Government Publications, 1987. Treas. Delta Iota House Bd. of Kappa Kappa Gamma, 1965-68; mem. La. Adv. Coun. State Documents Depository Program, 1991—. Inductee La. State U. Law Ctr. Hall of Fame, 1987. Mem.: ALA (interdivisional com. pub. documents 1967—74, chmn. 1967—70, govt. documents round table, state and local documents task force 1972—, coord. 1980—82, James Bennett Childs award 1981, anniversary honor roll 1996, Hoduski Founders award 1997), Baton Rouge Bar Assn., La. Bar Assn., La. Libr. Assn. (Essae M. Culver Disting. Svc. award 1976, Lucy B. Foote award 1986, Margaret T. Lane award named in her honor 1994), Mortar Bd., Baton Rouge Libr. Club, Kappa Kappa Gamma, Phi Delta Delta. Home: 333 Lee Dr Apt 274 Baton Rouge LA 70808 Personal E-mail: mtlane@cox.net.

LANE, MARIE IRENE, retired librarian; b. East Stroudsberg, Pa., Mar. 5, 1944; d. Robert Fulton and Margureite Irene (Melhin) Chamberlain; m. John Marcus Lane, Jan. 23, 1965; 1 child, Jennifer Marie. Student, U. Fla., 1962-64; BA, U. Hawaii, 1968, MLS, 1971. Asst. br. libr. Fairfax County (Va.) Pub. Libr., 1971-78; asst. libr. George Mason U. Sch. Law Libr., 1978-82; media specialist Fairfax Hosp., 1990. Vol. Camelot Nursing Home, Arlington, Va., 1984-90, Manor Care, 2003-, Arlington Ministering to Emergency Meals, 1984-90, Hope Counseling for Women, Falls Church, Va., 1989-90; asst. ch. libr. Clarendon United Meth. Ch., Arlington, 1982-90; mem. libr. adv. com. Arlington Sch. Bd., 1987, adv. com. home econs., 1989-90. Recipient Scribner Sons award, N.Y., 1972. Mem. DAR, Bibl. Storyteller. Republican. Christian. Avocations: writing, crewel embroidery, research, oil painting. Home: 3730 N Pershing Dr Arlington VA 22203-3519

LANE, MARK, lawyer, educator, writer; b. N.Y.C., Feb. 24, 1927; s. Harry Arnold and Elizabeth Lane; m. Patricia Ruth Erdner, 1987; children: Anne-Marie, Christina. LLB, Bklyn. Law Sch., 1951. Bar: N.Y. 1951, D.C. 1995. Mng. mem. The Lane Law Firm, LLC, Greenwich, NJ, pvt. practice, 1952—; founder Mid-Harlem Community Parish Narcotics Clinic, 1953, East Harlem Reform Dem. Club, 1959; prof. law Cath. U., Washington, 1975—76. Founder and dir. Citizens Commn. Inquiry; founder Wounded Knee Legal Def.-Offense Com., 1973, The Covered Wagon, Mountain Home, Idaho, 1971. Author: (books) Rush to Judgment, 1966, A Citizen's Dissent, 1968, Chicago Eye-Witness, 1969, Arcadia, 1970, Conversations with Americans, 1970, Executive Action, 1973, (with Dick Gregory) Code Name Zorro, 1977, The Strongest Poison, 1980, Plausible Denial, 1991, Murder in Memphis, 1993; prodr. films Rush to Judgment, 1967, Two Men in Dallas, 1987, 92; writer, prodr. plays Trial of James Earl Ray, 1978, Plausible Denial, 1992, Winds of Doctrine, 1994; writer, prodr. screenplays, Arcadia, 1992, Slay the Dreamer, 1992, Plausible Denial, 1993; founder publs. Citizens Quar., 1975, Helping Hand, 1971. Mem. N.Y. State Assembly, 1960-62. With AUS, 1945-47. Home and Office: 272 Tindall Island Rd Greenwich NJ 08323 Office Phone: 856-459-3999. *I do not believe that our fate is pre-ordained. I do believe that women and men, working together, can determine their own destiny and that the people write their own history. What moves me most directly into action is the fact that I hate bullies. What concerns me the most in contemporary America is the influence of the police and spy organizations with the national news media. Together these are bullies to contemplate and oppose.*

LANE, MARY B., education educator, writer; b. Edwardsville, Mich., Mar. 7, 1911; d. Hugh Dunning Beauchamp and Carrie Scott; m. Howard Lane, July 16, 1958 (dec.); children: Jay Howard, Mary Kelley. BS, Kirksville State U., 1930; MA, Northwestern U., 1945; EdD, N.Y. Coll., 1950. Lifetime cert. tchr. Calif. Tchr., LaPlata, Mo., 1930—39, Webster Groves, Mo., 1939—45; adminstrv. asst. Pub. Sch. Bd. Edn., Webster Groves, 1945—48, Mpls., 1948—50; asst. to supt. pub. sch. Pasadena, Calif., 1950—53; prof. U. Fla., N.Y. U., U. Calif. & San Francisco State U., 1950—72, San Francisco State U., 1999; dir. Head Start, Oakland, Calif., 2002. Spkr. in field, Can., South Africa; dir. bay area Head Start, 1966, nat. cons., 1967—75; project dir. nurseries NIMH, 1965—70; dir. Oakland Parent Child Ctr., 1977—87. Co-author (with Howard Lane): Human Relations in Teaching, 1955, Understanding Human Development, 1959; editor: On Educating Human Beings, 1964; contbr. articles to profl. jours. Home: 984 Dolores St San Francisco CA 94110

LANE, MARY WINSTON, secondary school educator; b. Middlesboro, Ky., Oct. 10, 1923; d. Shelton and Rena (Ward) Evans; m. Richard Alan Lane, Aug. 15, 1965 (Dec.); children: Barbara Ann Lane Partin', John Brian. BS,

Ea. Ky. U., 1944, cert. tchr., 1961; MS in Chemistry, U. Mo., Rolla, 1966; postgrad., Ohio State U., 1971-73. Cert. secondary chemistry, math. and physics tchr., Ohio, Ky., gifted and talented tchr., Ky. Chemist med. physics rsch. Donner Lab., U. Calif., Berkeley, 1944—59; tchr., head dept. Bell County High Sch., Pineville, Ky., 1959-66; tchr. Ottiville (Ohio) Schs., 1969-71, Bath High Sch., Lima, Ohio, 1974-79, Middlesboro (Ky.) High Sch., 1979-99; retired. Prof. Lincoln Meml. U., summers 1988-89, 91; organizer, dir. Southeastern Regional Sci. Fair, 1962-66; organizer Southeastern Alliance Sci. Tchrs., 1991; workshop presenter Chem 93; presenter Woodrow Wilson Workshop, 1993. Recipient Award of Excellence in Tchg. Chemistry for Ky., Am. Chem. Soc., 1995; named Tandy tchr., 1992, 93. Mem. NEA, Nat. Sci. Tchrs. Assn., Middlesboro Edn. Assn., Ky. Sci. Tchrs. Assn. (state bd. dirs., Disting. Svc. award 1994), Alliance 5th Dist. Sci. and Math. Tchrs. (co-dir. 1989—), Delta Kappa Gamma. Democrat. Baptist. Avocations: gardening, designing and building geo solar home. Home: RR 1 Box 519A Rose Hill VA 24281-9720

LANE, MAUREEN ANNE, elementary school educator; b. Flint, Mich., June 20, 1960; d. D. Jack and Margaret Irene Kildee; m. Enoch Edward Lane II, Apr. 4, 1987; children: Kevin Alexander, Brianne Colleen, Erin Brenna, Kyle Edward. BA in Elem. Edn., U. Mich., Flint, 1992; MA in the Art of Tchg., Marygrove Coll., Detroit, 2005. First grade tchr. Flint Cmty. Schs., Flint, Mich., 1992—. Home: 9522 W Hill Rd Swartz Creek MI 48473 Office: Bryant Elem Sch of Fine Arts 201 E Pierson Rd Flint MI 48505 Business E-Mail: mlane@flintschools.org.

LANE, NANCY, advocate, editor; b. N.Y.C., Dec. 20, 1938; d. Morton and Lillian (Gelb) L. AB in Am. Civilization, Barnard Coll., 1960. Mem. staff N.Y. Times, 1959-61; from asst. to assoc. editor Polit. Sci. Quar. and Procs. Acad. Polit. Sci., Columbia U., N.Y.C., 1962-70; from assoc. editor to mng. editor Am. Hist. Rev. Am. Hist. Assn., 1970-74; from sr. editor to exec. editor Oxford U. Press, N.Y.C., 1974-97; cons., 1997—98. Vol. Bellevue-NYU Program for Survivors of Torture, 1998-99. Mem.: ACLU, Ams. United for Separation of Ch. and State, Amnesty Internat. U.S.A. (vol. 1995—, torture-abolition coord. for USA Group 11, mem. Turkey Regional Action Network Group 11). Home: 45 W 10th St New York NY 10011-8731

LANE, NATHAN (JOSEPH LANE), actor; b. Jersey City, N.J., Feb. 3, 1956; Appeared in plays (off-Broadway) A Midsummer Night's Dream, Dedication or the Stuff of Dreams, 2005; Present Laughter, Merlin, The Wind in the Willows, Some Americans Abroad, On Borrowed Time, Guys and Dolls (Tony nomination, Drama Desk and Outer Critics Circle awards), Laughter on the 23rd Floor, A Funny Thing Happened... (Tony, Drama Desk and Outer Critics Circle awards), Love, Valour, Compassion (Drama Desk and Outer Critics Circle awards, Obie award), Love, N.Y.C., 1984, Raving, N.Y.C., 1984, She Stoops to Conquer, N.Y.C., 1984, The Common Pursuit, 1984-85, A Backer's Audition, N.Y.C., 1985, Wind in the Willows, 1985, The Common Pursuit, 1986-87, Claptrap, N.Y.C., 1987, Uncounted Blessings, 1988, The Film Society, 1988, The Lisbon Traviata, 1989 (Drama Desk award best actor 1989), A Pig's Valise, 1989, Some Americans Abroad, 1990, Bad Habits, 1990, Lips Together, Teeth Apart, 1991, On Borrowed Time, 1991, Guys and Dolls, 1992, Laughter on the 23rd Floor, 1993-94, Love! Valor! Compassion!, 1995, A Funny Thing Happened On The Way To The Forum, 1996 (Tony award best actor in a musical, 1996), The Man Who Came to Dinner, The Producers, 2001-02, 2003 (Tony award best actor in a musical, 2001), Trumbo Red White and Blacklisted, 2003, The Frogs, 2004; (TV series) Charlie Lawrence, 2003; (TV miniseries) Valley of the Dolls, 1981, One of the Boys, 1982, host the 50th anniversary Tony awards show, 1996, Encore!Encore!, 1998-99, Charlie Lawrence, 2003; (films) Ironweed, 1987, The Lemon Sisters, 1990, Joe Versus the Volcano, 1990, He Said, She Said, 1991, Frankie and Johnny, 1991, Life With Mikey, 1993, Addams Family Values, 1993, The Lion King (voice), 1994, The Birdcage, 1996 (SAG and Am. Comedy awards, Golden Globe nomination), The Boys Next Door, 1996, Mouse Hunt, 1997, Merry Christmas, George Bailey, 1997, At First Sight, 1999, Isn't She Great?, 2000, Love's Labour's Lost, 1999, Trixie, 2000,(voice) Stuart Little, 1999, (voice) Titan A.E., 2000, Man Who Came to Dinner, 2000, Laughter on the 23rd Floor, 2001, Nicholas Nickelby, 2002, Stuart Little 2, 2002, Austin Powers in Goldmember, 2002, Teacher's Pet (voice), 2004, Win a Date with Tad Hamilton!, 2004. Office: Creative Artists Agy 9830 Wilshire Blvd Beverly Hills CA 90212-1825*

LANE, NATHAN, III, lawyer; b. Phila., 1946; AB, Duke U., 1968; JD cum laude, U. Pa., 1971. Bar: Calif. 1972, registered: US Dist. Ct. (No. Dist.) Calif. 1972, US Ct. Appeals (9th cir.) 1972, US Dist. Ct. (So. Dist.) Calif. 1976, US Dist. Ct. (Ctrl. Dist.) Calif. 1980, US Ct. Appeals (10th cir.) 1985, US Dist. Ct. (Ea. Dist.) Calif. 1987, US Ct. Appeals (8th cir.) 1991, US Tax Ct. 1992, US Ct. Appeals (Fed. Cir.) 1997, US Patent & Trademark Office 1999. Ptnr. Graham & James, San Francisco, Squire, Sanders & Dempsey LLP, San Francisco, chmn., Intellectual Property Practice Group. Editl. bd. U. Pa. Law Rev., 1969—71; author: Discovery in Other Nations, 1988. Bd. dir. Legal Aid Soc., San Francisco, 1986—91. Mem.: Bar Assn. San Francisco (chmn. Antitrust Sect. 1988), ABA (Antitrust Sect., Intellectual Property Sect., Internat. Law Sect., Litig. Sect.), Order of Coif. Office: Squire Sanders & Dempsey LLP One Maritime Plaza Ste 300 San Francisco CA 94111-3492 Office Phone: 415-954-0249. Office Fax: 415-393-9887. Business E-Mail: nlane@ssd.com.

LANE, PATRICE ELLEN, music educator; d. Frederick William and Helen Stella Ebmeier; m. Robert Joseph Lane, Jan. 8, 1977; children: Timothy, Matthew. BA in Edn., Concordia U., 1975; MA in Edn., U. Mo., 1993. Tchr. St. Paul Elem. Sch., St. Louis, 1976—78, St. Augustine Elem. Sch., Belleville, Ill., 1978—81; music tchr. St. Matthias Elem. Sch., St. Louis, 1984—89; band dir., music tchr. Fox C-6 Sch. Dist., Arnold, Miss., 1991—2005. Mem.: Delta Kappa Gamma (pres. local chpt. 2001—02). Avocations: piano, travel.

LANE, RANDY JAMES, education educator, consultant; s. Clyde Columbus Lane and Margaret Kathyrn Lane-McCumsey; m. Linda Jean Shirley, Sept. 5, 1970; children: Rebecca Judith Walker, Brenda Katherine. AA, Shasta Coll., Redding, Calif., 1970; BA in History and Lit., U. Nev., Reno, 1973; MA in Edn., Simpson Coll., Redding, 1998; EDs, Samford U., Birmingham, 1999; PhD, U. Ala., Tuscaloosa, 2003. Lic. tchr. K-8 Calif., 1998, Ala., 1998. Sr. account agt. Allstate Ins. Co., Reno, 1973—95; grad. rsch. asst. U. Ala., Tuscaloosa, 1999—2003, adj. prof., 2003—04; asst. prof. Fayetteville (NC) State U., 2004—. Cons. Madison City Sch. Dist., Ala., 2000—01, Mobile County, Ala., 2002, Ala. Sch. Math. and Sci., Mobile, 2004—, Gadsden City Schs. Dist., Ala., 2001—02, Greene County Sch. Dist., Eutaw, Ala., 2002—, Hale County Sch. Dist., Greensboro, Ala., 2002—, Sumter County Sch. Dist., Livingston, Ala., 2002—, Tuscaloosa City Sch. Dist., Ala., 2003—, Tuscaloosa County Sch. Dist., 2003—04, Selma City Sch. Dist., Ala., 2003—04, Autauga County Sch. Dist., Prattville, Ala., 2001—02, Randolph County Sch. Dist., Roanoke, Ala., 2002—02. Contbr. articles to profl. jours. With U.S. Army, 1964—68. Decorated Vietnam Svc. Medal, Vietnam Campaign Medal, Good Conduct Medal, Expert Rifle M-14, Meritorious Unit Citation award, Nat. Def. Svc. Medal US Army; recipient Outstanding Grad. Student for Cmty. Svc. award, U. Ala., 2002, US Nat. Collegiate award, US Achievement Acad., 2002; grantee U. Ala. Superintendency Acad., State of Ala., 2002—, Tuscaloosa City Schs. Sch. Leadership program, U.S. Dept. Edn., 2002—. Mem.: Phi Delta Kappa (assoc.). Avocations: travel, bird hunting, fishing, writing, scuba diving. Home: 2438 Caithness Dr Fayetteville NC 28306 Office: Fayetteville State Univ 1200 Murchison Rd Fayetteville NC 28301 Office Phone: 910-672-1725. Personal E-mail: rlane@uncfsu.edu.

LANE, RICHARD ALLAN, preventive medicine physician, educator; b. Camp LeJuene, NC, Feb. 5, 1956; s. Howard Allan and Elizabeth Jane (Fischer) L.; m. Cynthia Diane Gastineau, Jan. 7, 1978; children: Tiffany Marie, Laurel Christina. BS, U. Md., 1978, MD, 1982; MPH in Tropical Medicine, Tulane U., 1986. Diplomate Am. Bd. Preventive Medicine. Intern Md. Gen. Hosp., Balt., 1982-83; squadron flight surgeon, 363rd Tactical Fighter Wing USAF, Shaw AFB, 1983-85, resident in aerospace medicine Brooks AFB, 1986-87, advanced through grades to maj., 1983-87; chief aeromed. svcs. Warner Robins Air Logistics Ctr., Robins AFB, 1987-89; staff physician, microbiology instr. Liberty U., Lynchburg, Va., 1989-91, assoc. prof. health scis., 1991—. Cons., spkr. Liberty Godparent Home, Lynchburg, 1989—; mem. residency adv. bd. Meharry Med. Coll., Nashville, Tenn., 1987-89; adj. faculty health sci. Internat. Health Honduras project James Madison U., Harrisonburg, Va., 1993-2000; adj. clin. prof. nurse practitioner program Old Dominion U., 1997-2000. Contbr. articles to profl. jours. Bd. dirs. Network for Women in Crisis, Lynchburg, 1990-91; exec. bd. Lynchburg chpt. ARC, 1991-93; founder Emmanuel Bapt. Ch., chpt. AWANA, Warner Robins, Ga., 1987-89; trainer Youth at the Crossraods Internat. AIDS Prevention Program, 1996—; med. cons. World Help. Fellow Am. Coll. Preventive Medicine; mem. Gideons Internat. (camp treas. 1988-89), Am. Soc. Tropical Medicine and Hygiene, Aerospace Med. Assn. Republican. Evang.

LANE, ROBERT W., farm equipment manufacturing executive; b. Washington D.C. BA (high honors), Wheaton (Ill.) Coll., 1972; MBA, U. Chgo. Grad. Sch. Bus., 1974. First Nat. Bank Chgo., Europe; various positions Deere & Co., Moline, Ill., 1982—, CFO, sr. v.p. fin./tax/acctg., 1996—98, sr. v.p., mng. dir. mfg. mktg. Europe, Africa, Middle East, 1998—99, pres. worldwide agrl. equip. divn., 1999, COO, pres., 2000, chmn. bd., CEO, 2000—. Mem. bd. dirs. Verizon Communications Inc.; Trustee Committee for Econ. Devel.; mem. Bus. Roundtable, Bus. Coun. Mem. Nat. Adv. Coun. Figge Art Mus., Iowa. Mem.: Lyric Opera bd. in Chgo. Office: Deere & Co 1 John Deere Rd Moline IL 61265-8098*

LANE, ROBIN, lawyer; b. Kerrville, Tex., Nov. 28, 1947; d. Rowland and Gloria (Benson) Richards; m. Stanley Lane, Aug. 22, 1971 (div.); 1 child, Joshua; m. Anthony W. Cunningham, Nov. 22, 1980; 1 child, Alexandra Cunningham. BA in Econs. with honors, U. Fla., 1969; MA, George Washington U., 1971; JD, Stetson U., 1978. Bar: Fla. 1979, U.S. Ct. Appeals (11th cir.) 1981, U.S. Supreme Ct. 1986, U.S. Ct. Appeals (D.C. cir.) 1992, U.S. Ct. Appeals (3d cir.) 1993. Mgmt. trainee internat. banking Gulf Western Industries, N.Y.C.; internat. rsch. specialist Ryder Systems, Inc., Miami, 1973, project mgr., 1974; assoc. Wagner, Cunningham, Vaughan & McLaughlin, Tampa, Fla., 1979—85; pvt. practice law, 1985—. Guest lectr. med. jurisprudence Stetson U. Coll. Law, 1982—91, also mem. exec. coun. law alumni bd. Contbr. articles to various revs. Recipient Am. Jurisprudcne award-torts, Lawyers Co-op. Fla., 1979; Scottish Rite fellow, 1968—69. Mem.: ATLA, ABA, Fla. Bar Assn., Acad. Fla. Trial Lawyers (mem. com. 1983—84), Fla. Women's Alliance, Omicron Delta Epsilon. Office: PO Box 10155 Tampa FL 33679-0155 Home: 880 5th Ave #15C New York NY 10021 Office: 345 Bayshore Blvd P5 Tampa FL 33606 Office Phone: 917-312-6773. Personal E-mail: RRL1128@aol.com.

LANE, RONALD ALAN, lawyer; b. Ames, Iowa, July 15, 1950; s. Raymond Oscar and Beverly (Burdge) L.; m. Eileen Smietana, June 17, 1972; children: Andrew, Audrey. AB, Miami U., Oxford, Ohio, 1972; JD, Northwestern U., 1975; MBA, U. Chgo., 1987. Bar: U.S. Dist. Ct. (no. dist.) Ill. 1975, U.S. Ct. Appeals (7th cir.) 1975, U.S. Supreme Ct. 1980. Atty. Atchison, Topeka & Santa Fe Ry. Co., Chgo., 1975-78; from asst. gen. atty. to gen. atty. Santa Fe So. Pacific Corp., Chgo., 1979-86, gen. corp. atty., 1986-87; asst. v.p. pers. and labor rels. Atchison, Topeka & Santa Fe Ry. Co., 1987-90; v.p., gen. counsel Ill. Ctrl. R.R. Co., Chgo., 1990-99; of counsel Franczek Sullivan, P.C., 1999—2000; ptnr. Fletcher & Sippel, LLC, 2001—. Dir. Chgo. Ctrl. Area Com., 1995-99, Transp. Tech. Ctr., Inc., 1997-99; mem. railroad shipper trans. adv. coun. Surface Transp. Bd., 1996-99. Office: Fletcher & Sippel LLC 29 N Wacker Blvd Ste 920 Chicago IL 60606

LANE, SARAH MARIE CLARK, elementary school educator; b. Conneaut, Ohio, July 27, 1946; d. Robert George and Julia Ellen (Sanford) Clark; m. Ralph Donaldson Lane, May 28, 1977; children: Richard, Laura. BS in Edn., Kent State U., 1977; MS in Edn., Coll. Mt. St. Joseph, 1988. Cert. tchr., Ohio. Coord. newspaper in edn. Tribune Chronicle, Warren, Ohio, 1986-89; tutor MacArthur Found. Project, Warren, Ohio, 1988-89; tchr. chpt. I Lakeview Local Schs., Cortland, Ohio, 1989—. Freelance writer newspaper Conn. News Herald, 1963-64, Tribune Chronicle, 1980-89; contbr. articles to profl. jours.; author: A Walk Through Historic Cortland, 1994, B is for Bazetta, C is for Cortland. V.p. Bazetta Cortland Hist. Soc., 1983-85; chmn. com. local history project Lakeview Schs., Cortland, 1992—; mem. Trumbull County Bicentennial Commn., 1996—. George Record Found. scholar, 1964-66. Mem. Internat. Reading Assn. (Ohio coun.), Cortland Community Concert Band (pres. 1991-92), Mem. Christian Ch. (Disciples Of Christ). Avocations: writing, historical research, genealogy, reading. Home: 298 Corriedale Dr Cortland OH 44410-1622 Office: Cortland Elem Sch 264 Park Ave Cortland OH 44410-1098

LANE, SYLVIA, economist, educator; b. N.Y.C. m. Benjamin Lane, Sept. 2, 1939; children: Leonard, Reese, Nancy. AB, U. Calif., Berkeley, 1934, MA, 1936; postgrad., Columbia U., 1937; PhD, U. So. Calif., 1957. Lectr., asst. prof. U. So. Calif., 1947—60; assoc. prof. econs. San Diego State U., 1961-65; assoc. prof. finance, assoc. dir. Ctr. for Econ. Edn. Calif. State U., Fullerton, 1965-69, chmn. dept. fin., 1967-69; prof. agrl. econs. U. Calif., Davis, 1969-82, prof. emerita, 1982—; prof. emerita and economist Giannini Found., U. Calif.-Berkeley, 1982—; vis. scholar Stanford U., 1975-76. Cons. Calif. Adv. Commn. Tax Reform, 1963, Adv. Office Consumer Affairs, Exec. Office of Pres., 1972-77, FAO, UN, 1983, Consumer food Subsidiaries Project, 1993. Author: (with E. Bryant Phillips) Personal Finance, 1963, rev. edit., 1979, The Insurance Tax, 1965, California's Income Tax Conformity and Withholding, 1968, (with Irma Adelman) The Balance Between Industry and Agriculture in Economic Development, 1989; author video: Women in Agriculture - Africa, 1994; editl. bd. Agrl. Econs., 1986-92; also articles, reports in field. Project economist Los Angeles County Welfare Planning Coun., 1956-59; del. White House Conf. on Food and Nutrition, 1969, Pres.'s Summit Con. on Inflation, 1974; mem. adv. com. Ctr. for Bldg. Tech., Nat. Bur. Stds., 1975-79; bd. dirs. Am. Coun. Consumer Interests, 1972-74; exec. bd. Am. Agr. Econ. Assn. 1976-79. Ford Found. fellow UCLA, 1963; Ford Found. fellow U. Chgo., 1965; fellow U. Chgo., 1968; fellow Am. Agrl. Econ. Assn., 1984; fellow Sylvia Lane Fellowship Fund, 1993. Mem. Am. Econ. Assn., Am. Coun. Consumer Interests, Omicron Delta Epsilon (pres. 1973-75, trustee 1975-83, chmn. bd. trustees 1982-84). Home and Office: Pacific Regent - La Jolla 3890 Nobel Dr #1508 San Diego CA 92122 Office Phone: 858-625-8713. *Select goals carefully ...*

LANE, TED A., music educator, musician; s. Clifford A. and Evelyne Lane. MusB, The Juilliard Sch., 1975, MusM, 1977. Cert. music edn. tchr. Tex., 1998. Prof. music Fla. State U., Tallahassee, 1979—81, Calif. State U., Sacramento, 1984—92, U. Nebr., Omaha, U. Tex., Brownsville, 2000—; music tchr. Alamo Ind. Sch. Dist., San Juan, Tex., 1987—; prof. clarinet Wichita State U., Kans., 1994—95; head testing & quality control The Leblanc Corp., Kenosha, Wis.; prin. clarinetist South Tex. Symphony, Edinburg, Am. Sinfonietta, Bellingham, Wash. Prin. clarinetist La Bienalle, Venice, 1975—76; clarinetist NY Philharm., NYC, 1975—77; bd. mem. Sacramento Chamber Music Soc., Sacramento, 1986—91; owner Alvin Ltd., Mission, Tex., 2000—; founder Kansa Winds, Mission. Recipient First Prize award, Naftzger Competition, 1976, First Place award, Internat. Clarinet Competition, 1983, Most Meritorious Tchg. award, 1985; scholar Full Music Scholarship to study at Juilliard, Naumberg, 1975-1977. Mem.: Internat. Clarinet Congress (assoc.). Achievements include design of a clarinet mouthpiece. E-mail: tlane@rgv.rr.com.

LANE, WILLIAM W., electronics executive; b. Roanoke, Va., Feb. 25, 1934; s. Melvin V. and Cecile (Lane); m. Ronnie G Lane, Sept. 14, 1978; children: Jonathan D., Drew H., Craig M. BA, Bklyn. Coll., 1956; MBA, Cornell U., 1958. V.p. Major Electronics Corp., 1959-70, chmn., dir., 1970; v.p., dir. Internat. Transistor Corp., Burbank, Calif., 1971-73; vice chmn., dir. Internat. Chia Hsin, Taipai, Taiwan, 1973-76; chmn., dir. Emerson (H.K. Ltd.), Hong Kong, from 1976; chmn., CEO, dir. Emerson Radio Corp., North Bergen, N.J., 1974-91; officer, bd. dirs. Star Light Electronics, Ridgefield, NJ. Pres. Majorette Enterprises, from 1961; chmn. MAJ EXCO Imports Inc., 1977-85, Emerson Computer Corp., 1989-91, H.H. Scott, Inc. Cardiac Resuscitator Corp., Portland, Oreg., Emerson Italy, Emerson Spain, Atlantic Shore 400 Cons. Corp., Emerson Investment Corp., Major Realty Corp., Emteck Tech. (U.K.) Ltd.; pres. W. Lane & Assocs. Inc., 1992—. Served with AUS, 1958-59. Mem. bus. adv. bd. U.S. Senate.

LANER, RICHARD WARREN, lawyer; b. Chgo., July 12, 1933; s. Jack E. and Esther G. (Cohon) L.; m. Barbara Lee Shless, Aug. 15, 1954 (dec. Oct. 1997); children: Lynn, Kenneth; m. Daryl Lynn Homer, Sept. 17, 1998. Student, U. Ill., 1951-54; BS, Northwestern U., 1955, LLB, 1956. Bar: Ill. 1956. Assoc. Laner, Muchin, Dombrow, Becker, Levin & Tominberg, Ltd., Chgo., 1956-62, ptnr., 1962-99, of counsel, 1999. Editor Northwestern Law Rev., 1954-56; contbr. articles to profl. jours. Mem. Chgo. Bar Assn. (chmn. com. labor law 1972-73), Chgo. Assn. Commerce and Industry, Order of Coif. Home: 161 E Chicago Ave Unit 41de Chicago IL 60611-2601 Office: Laner Muchin Dombrow Becker Levin & Tominberg Ltd 515 N State St Fl 28 Chicago IL 60610-4325 Office Phone: 312-467-9800. Business E-Mail: rlaner@lanermuchin.com.

LANE STONE, NANCY ANN, elementary school educator; b. Montague, Mass., Oct. 23, 1945; d. John Henry Adams and Helen Ann (Yez) Lane; m. Richard F. Koscinski, June 8, 1968 (dec. June 1980); children: Todd Lane Koscinski, Michael Lane Koscinski; m. David Lewis Stone, Feb. 26, 1984. BA, U. Mass., 1981; M in Human Svcs., Keene State Coll., 1990, Cert. in Ednl. Adminstrn., 1999. Cert. tchr., Mass.; cert. experienced educator, N.H. Substitute tchr. Montague Pub. Schs., 1981-84, Keene (N.H.) Pub. Schs., 1985-96; v.p. Beck Mfg., Keene, 1986—; dir. Good Mourning Children, Keene, 1988-98; dir. children's svcs. Hospice of Monadnock Region, Keene, 1992-94; elem. sch. tchr. Marlborough (N.H.) Sch. Dist., 1997—. Cons. to staff adv. com. Franklin County Tech. Sch., Turners Falls, Mass., 1977-84; intern, vol. Hospice of Cheshire County, Keene, 1989-90; mem. adj. clin. faculty Antioch New Eng. Grad. Sch., 1993-94; mem. adj. faculty Keene State Coll., 1999—, site supr. for student tchrs., 1999—. Dir. Big Bros./Big Sister Orgn. Recipient Sch. Vol. award Symonds Sch., Keene, 1984-85. Mem. AAUW, Assn. for Death Edn. and Counseling, Keene Woman's Club (v.p. 1986-88), Keene Bus. and Profl. Women's Club, N.H. Hospice Orgn., Children's Hospice Internat. Roman Catholic. Avocations: macrophotography, travel, reading, speed walking. Office: Good Morning Children Program 54 Blackberry Ln Keene NH 03431-2120

LANEVE, MARK R., automotive executive; b. Beaver Falls, Pa., Mar. 8, 1959; m. Paula LaNeve; children: Jake, Drew. Bachelor in bus. comm., Univ. Va. Sales & mktg. positions GM, 1981—95, brand mgr., Pontiac Bonneville, 1995—97; v.p. mktg. Volvo Cars No. Am., 1997—2000, pres. & CEO, 2000—01; gen. mgr. Cadillac GM, 2001—04, v.p. mktg. & advt., GM No. Am., 2004—05, v.p. vehicle sales, svc. & mktg., GM N Am., 2005—. Trustee Judson Ctr. Named Grand Marketer of the Year, Brandweek mag., 2003. Office: General Motors Corp 300 Renaissance Ctr Detroit MI 48265-3000*

LANEY, BEVERLY JOYCE, music educator; b. Southington, Conn., July 3, 1968; d. Edward S. and Dolores Jean Ann Topol; m. Kenneth Wayne Laney, Dec. 26, 1992; children: Kenneth Wayne II, Jessica Lauren. B of Music Edn., Appalachian State U., 1990; M of Music Edn., Winthrop U., 2001. Choral dir. Parkwood High Sch., Monroe, NC, 1991—92, Sullivan Mid. Sch., Rock Hill, 1999—2005, South Pointe High Sch., 2005—. Entertainment dir. S.C. Mid. Sch. Assn., 2004—05. Artsin Ednl. grantee, S.C. Dept. Edn., Columbia, 2000. Mem.: S.C. Music Educators Assn. (mem. jr. high com. 2005), Music Educators Nat. Conf., Am. Choral Dirs. Assn., Sigma Alpha Iota. Avocations: swimming, walking, camping. Home: 10015 Mini Ranch Rd Waxhaw NC 28173 Office: South Pointe High Sch Rock Hill SC

LANEY, JAMES THOMAS, former ambassador, educator; b. Wilson, Ark., Dec. 24, 1927; s. Thomas Mann and Mary (Hughey) L.; m. Berta Joan Radford, Dec. 20, 1949; children: Berta Joan Vaughan, James T., Arthur Radford, Mary Ruth Laney Reilly, Susan Elizabeth Castle. BA, Yale U., 1950, BD, 1954, PhD, 1966; DD (hon.), Fla. So. Coll., 1977, Wofford Coll., 1986, Emory U., 1994, Yonsei U., Korea, 1997, Kwansei Gakuin U., Japan, 2000; DD (hon.), Africa U., Zimbabwe, 2004; LHD (hon.), Rhodes Coll., 1979, Millsaps Coll., 1988, Austin Coll., 1990, W.Va. Wesleyan Coll., 1990, Yale U., 1993, U. S.C., 1997, Queens Coll., 1998, LaGrange Coll., 2000; LHD (hon.), Nebr. Wesleyan U., 2004; LHD (hon.), U. Richmond, 2001; HHD (hon.), Mercer U., 1980; LLD (hon.), DePauw U., 1985, U. St. Andrews, Scotland, 1994, Alaska Pacific U., 1994; LLD (hon.), Piedmont Coll., 1999, Africa U. Zimbabwe, 2004; D in Internat. Affairs, Am. U., 1998. Chaplain Choate Sch., Wallingford, Conn., 1953-55; ordained to ministry Meth. Ch., 1955; asst. lectr. Yale Div. Sch., 1954-55; pastor St. Paul Meth. Ch., Cin., 1955-58; sec. student Christian movement, prof. Yonsei U., Seoul, Korea, 1959-64; asst. prof. Christian ethics Vanderbilt U. Div. Sch., 1966-69; dean Candler Sch. Theology, Emory U., 1969-77, pres. univ., 1977-93, pres. emeritus, 1993—; US amb. to Republic of Korea, 1993-97. Vis. prof. Harvard Div. Sch., 1974. Author: The Education of the Heart, 1994; (with J.M. Gustafson) On Being Responsible, 1968; contbr. columns NY Times, Washington Post, LA Times. Fgn. Affairs pres. Nashville Cmty. Rels. Coun., 1968-69; mem. Yale Coun. Com., 1972-77; bd. dir. Fund Theol. Edn.; chmn. United Bd. Christian Higher Edn. in Asia, 1990-93; bd. dir. Atlanta Symphony, 1979-91; chmn. bd. overseers com. to visit Harvard Div. Sch., 1980-85; mem. Yale U. Exec. Com., 1990-93, 97-2003; mem. Carnegie Endowment Nat. Commn. on Am. and the New World; mem. adv. com. Atlanta Project; chmn. so. dist. Rhodes Scholarship Com., 1980-90; bd. dir. Atlantic Coun., 1987-93. Henry Luce Found., 1990—; mem. tercentenary steering com. Yale U., 1998-01; co-chmn. Faith & City, Atlanta, Ga.; trustee Carter Ctr., 1997—. With AUS, 1946-48. Selected for Leadership Atlanta, 1970-71; recipient Disting. Alumnus award Yale U. Div. Sch., 1979, 93, Kellogg award for leadership in higher edn., 1983, Wilbur Cross medal Yale Grad. Sch., 1996, James Van Fleet award, Korean Soc., 1996, Kangwa medal for disting. diplomatic svc., Rep. Korea, 1997, Dept. Defense medal for disting. pub. svc., U.S. Govt., 1997, 1st Internat. Human Rights award Inst. Human Rights, Korea, 1998; D.C. Macintosh fellow Yale U., 1965-66. Mem. Soc. Values Higher Edn. (pres. 1987-91), Coun. on Fgn. Rels. (co-chair task force on Korean Peninsula 1997-2002), Pilgrim Soc., Atlanta C. of C., Commerce Club, Atlanta Rotary Club, Phi Beta Kappa, Omicron Delta Kappa, Elihu Soc. (hon).

LANEY, JOHN THOMAS, III, federal judge; b. Columbus, Ga., Mar. 27, 1942; s. John Thomas Jr. and Leila (Davis) L.; m. Louise Pierce, Nov. 23, 1974; children: Thomas Whitfield, Elizabeth Davis. AB, Mercer U., 1964, JD magna cum laude, 1966. Bar: Ga. 1965, U.S. Dist. Ct. (mid. dist.) Ga. 1966, U.S. Ct. Appeals (5th cir.) 1966, U.S. Ct. Mil. Appeals 1967, U.S. Ct. Appeals (11th cir.) 1981. Assoc. Swift, Pease, Davidson & Chapman, Columbus, 1970-73; ptnr. Page, Scrantom, Harris & Chapman, Columbus, 1973-86; judge mid. dist. Ga. U.S. Bankruptcy Ct., Columbus, 1986—. Co-editor-in-chief Mercer Law Rev., 1965—66; contbr. articles to profl. jours. Former pres., dir. Metro. Boys Club of Columbus. Capt. U.S. Army, 1966-70. Mem. ABA (judge adminstrv. divsn. Nat. Conf. Fed. Trial Judges), State Bar Ga. (chmn. gen. practice and trial sect. 1983-84, chmn. state disciplinary bd. 1984-85), Am. Judicature Soc., Nat. Conf. Bankruptcy Judges, Columbus Bar Assn., Inc. (pres. 1985-86), Rotary. Presbyterian. Office: US Bankruptcy Ct 1 Arsenal Pl 901 Front Ave Ste 309 Columbus GA 31901-2797 Office Phone: 706-649-7840. E-mail: k4bai@worldnet.att.net.

LANEY, MICHAEL L., manufacturing executive; b. Los Angeles, Sept. 10, 1945; s. Roy and Wanda Laney; m. Marti Miller, Dec. 31, 1964; children: Tynna, Kristen. BS with honors, Calif. State U., Northridge, 1967; MBA, UCLA, 1969. CPA, Calif. Sr. tax acct. Haskins-Sells, Los Angeles, 1967-69; asst. prof. acctg. Calif. State U., Northridge, 1969-72; tax prin. M. Klaiman Acctg. Corp., Beverly Hills, Calif., 1972-75; pvt. practice Beverly Hills, 1975-80; v.p., controller Ducommun, Inc., Los Angeles, 1980-87; sr. v.p., fin. and adminstrn. Monarch Mirror Door Co. Inc., Chatsworth, Calif., 1987-92; v.p. ops. feature animation Walt Disney Pictures and TV (part of The Walt

Disney Co.), Glendale, Calif., 1992-93; sr. v.p. ops. Warner Bros., Glendale, Calif., 1994-96; pres. Children's Wonderland, Agoura, Calif., 1996-97; CFO Dacor, Pasadena, Calif., 1997-2001; pres., CEO Cool Roof of Calif., Inc., Calabasas, 2001—; pres. Laney & Assocs., Calabasas, 2002—04; CFO Energy Trust Oreg., Inc., 2004—. Mem. Fin. Execs. Inst., Tax Execs. Inst., Am. Inst. CPA's, Calif. Soc. CPA's; Assn. for Corp. Growth., Am. Sch. Counselors Assn., Soc. Human Resources (practioner). Office Phone: 503-445-7604. Personal E-mail: mlaneyassoc@yahoo.com.

LANEY, ROBERT LOUIS, JR., academic administrator; b. Connay, SC; s. Robert Louis and Thillian Hamot; 1 child, Christian. BA, SC State U, 1976; MBA, Atlanta U., 1979; EdD, Clark Atlanta U., 1990. Adminstrv. officer, asst. dir. Ga. Inst. Tech., Atlanta, 1984—92; dir. admissions La. State U., Baton Rouge, 1992—96, Lincoln U., 1996—2004; v.p., dir. admissions and enrollment mgmt. Tuskegee U., Ala., 2004—. Reader cons. UNCF, Va., 2000—. Methodist. Home: PO Box 830471 Tuskegee Institute AL 36088 Office: Tuckegee U Old Admission Bldg Rm 102 Tuskegee Institute AL 36088 Office Phone: 334-727-8500. Business E-Mail: rlaney@tuckegee.edu.

LANEY, SANDRA EILEEN, chemicals executive; b. Cin., Sept. 17, 1943; d. Raymond Oliver and Henrietta Rose (Huber) H.; m. Dennis Michael Laney, Sept. 30, 1968; children: Geoffrey Michael, Melissa Ann. AS in Bus. Adminstrn., Thomas More Coll., 1988, BA in Bus. Adminstrn., 1993. Adminstrv. asst. to chief exec. officer Chemed Corp., Cin., 1982, asst. v.p., 1982-84, v.p., 1984-91, v.p., chief adminstrv. officer, 1991-93, sr. v.p., chief adminstrv. officer, 1993-2001, bd. dirs., 1986—, exec. v.p. chief adminstrn. officer, 2001—02; CEO, chmn. Cadre Computer Resources Co., 2001—. Bd. dirs. Omnicare Inc., Covington, Ky. Mem. bd. advisors Sch. Nursing U. Cin., 1992—; bd. overseers Cin. Symphony Orch., 1998; trustee Lower Price Hill Cmty. Sch., Cmty. Land Coop. of Cin. Mem. AAUW, NOW, Internat. Platform Assn., Amnesty Internat., World Affairs Coun., Women's Action Coun. Roman Catholic. Office: Cadre Computer Resources Co 1200 Chemed Ctr 255 E 5th St Cincinnati OH 45202-4700

LANFORD, LUKE DEAN, retired electronics company executive; b. Greer, S.C., Aug. 4, 1922; s. John D. and Ethel W. (Ballenger) L.; m. Donna Marie Cellar, Dec. 20, 1945 (dec. Apr. 29, 1984); 1 dau., Cynthia Lea Lanford Brown; m. Jacquelyn Sue Carr Bussell, Feb. 14, 1986 BSE.E., Va. Poly. Inst., 1943. With Western Electric Co., Inc., 1946-78, asst. mgr. tng. N.Y.C., 1957-60, mgr. engring. Kansas City, 1960-63, asst. works mgr. Allentown, Pa., 1963-65; plant mgr. Reading, Pa., 1965-69; gen. mgr. Indpls., 1969-78. Dir. Met. Indpls. Television Assn., Inc., Sta. WFYI-TV, 1970—, pres., 1975-79 Served with U.S. Army, 1943-46. Mem. IEEE, Telephone Pioneers Am., Jacaranda West Country Club, Eta Kappa Nu, Tau Beta Pi, Phi Kappa Phi. Republican. Roman Catholic. Home: 1935 Pebble Beach Ct Venice FL 34293-3830

LANG, CATHERINE LOU, small business owner; b. Hugo, Okla., June 12, 1946; d. John Wilburn Sr. and Velma Lou (Evans) Freeman; m. Laurence Larry Lang, Nov. 20, 1974; children: Tana Louise, Henry Nathan, Gina Elise; 1 stepchild, Michael. BA in Sociology and Econs., Northeastern State U., 1970. Co-owner C&L Jewelry, Waterford, Mich., 1980—. Landlord of rental home, Novi, Mich., 1977-93. Active Northwest Child Rescue Women Jr. League, 1975—, League of Women of Detroit; mem. PTA Mercy Sch. for Girls, Farmington, Mich., 1990-94, Walled Lake Mich. Schs., 1981—; mem. Great Decisions, active in leadership, 1988; team parent Team Elan Skating Team, 1991-92; mem. Lakes Assn., Novi, 1992; mem. Covenant Bapt. Ch., 1977—, Am. Bapt. Women, Novi PTSA Parent Assn., 1999, Evergreen Coll. Parent Assn., 1998—; chairperson Great Decisions, 2004—; mem. Dem. Party, 2005—. Recipient (with son) Arrow of Light pin Cub Scouts. Mem. AAUW (charter, Novi-Northville br., membership/diversity v.p. 1998—, dist. VIII co-chair 1999), MADD, Internat. Fedn. Univ. Women, Nat. Assn. Investors Corp., Detroit Skating Club, Top Stock Stock Club, Lioness of Mich. Democrat. Avocations: ceramic and porcelain dolls, ice skating team supporter, nat. vol. work. Home: 1369 E Lake Dr Novi MI 48377-1442 Office: C&L Jewelry 924 W Huron St Waterford MI 48328-3726

LANG, CHERYL A., library director; b. Kansas City, Mo., May 12, 1959; d. Louis A. and JoAnn (Nash) Lang; m. Steven E. Meyer, Jan. 6, 1979 (div. 1993); m. J. Randall Noble, Oct. 14, 1994 (div. 1999); children: Steven N., Cameron A., Cara D., Eric M., Laura E. AA in Office Mgmt., Longview C.C., Lee's Summit, Mo., 1986; BBA, Webster U., St. Louis, 1994; MLS, Emporia (Kans.) State U., 1999. Corp. sec. Charles Paint Rsch., Inc., Kansas City, 1976-89; exec. asst. St. Luke's Health Sys., Kansas City, 1989-96; dir. Carnegie Pub. Libr., Albany, Mo., 1997—. Troop leader Girl Scouts U.S., Albany, 1996-99, Overland Park, Kans., 1990-96. Mem. ALA, Mo. Libr. Assn., Pub. Libr. Assn., Mo. Pub. Libr. Dirs. Assn., Assn. Rural and Small Librs. Avocations: family camping, genealogy. Home: 101 Fourth St Darlington MO 64438-9700 Office: Carnegie Public Libr 101 W Clay St Albany MO 64402-1601 Business E-Mail: cheryl@carneige.lib.mo.us.

LANG, DANIEL S., artist; b. Tulsa, Mar. 17, 1935; s. Irving and Dorothy D. (Lauterer) L. B.F.A., Tulsa U., 1953; M.F.A., Iowa U., 1959. Asst. prof. art SUNY, Fredonia, 1959-60, Art Inst. Chgo., 1962-64, Washington U., St. Louis, 1964-65; vis. artist Ohio State U., 1968-69, U. South Fla., 1971, U. Utah, spring 1984. Adj. prof. U. Utah, 1984— One-man shows include Boston Mus. Fine Arts, 1961, Arthur Tooth & Sons, London, 1970, 74, Alexandra Monett Gallery, Brussels, Belgium, 1973, 78, Fairweather Hardin Gallery, Chgo., 1971, 77, 80, Il Gabbiano Gallery, Rome, 1975, DM Gallery, London, 1975, Gimpel & Weitzenhofer, N.Y.C., 1976, Fischbach Gallery, N.Y.C., 1977, 79, Graphik Internat. GMBH, Stuttgart, Germany, 1979, Richard Demarco Gallery, Edinburgh, Scotland, 1981, 83, Watson/Willour Gallery, Houston, 1981, David Findlay Gallery, N.Y.C., 1981, 83, Sherry French Gallery, N.Y.C., 1984, Meredith Long Gallery, Houston, 1984, Washington Gallery, Glasgow, 1986, Phillips Gallery, Salt Lake City, 1988, Gilcrease Mus., Tulsa, 1989, Am. Stock Exch., N.Y.C., 1991, Galleria Civica, Seregno, Italy, 1991, The Hokin Gallery, Palm Beach, Fla., 1991, Taylor's Contemporary Gallery, Hot Springs, Ark., 1992, Galleria Delle Art, Cittá di Castello, Italy, 1992, William Hardie Gallery, Glasgow, Scotland, 1992, Civic Gallery, Urbino, Italy, 1992, London Art Fair, 1994, Elliot Smith Gallery, St. Louis, 1994, Alexandre Gallery U. Tulsa, 1995, Galerie Hertz, Louisville, Ky., 1996, Bridgewater/Lustberg Gallery, N.Y., 1997, MD Modern Gallery, Houston, 1999; group shows include Am. Fedn. of Arts travelling exhbn., 1968-69, U. Pa. Inst. Contemporary Art, 1970, Moore Coll. Art, 1971, Boston U., 1972, Joslyn Art Mus., Omaha and Sheldon Meml. Art Galleries, Lincoln, Nebr., 1973-74, Sherry French Gallery, 1983, 85, 86, Ruth Siegel Gallery, N.Y.C., 1989, Antarctica 2-man show sponsored by NSF, organized by Smithsonian Instn., 1976-79, America 1976 travelling exhbn., 1976-78, including stops at Fogg Art Mus. Harvard U., Wadsworth Atheneum, Hartford, Conn. and, Corcoran Gallery Art, Washington, Watson/de Nagy Gallery of Houston travelling exhbn., 1978-79, Hirschl & Adler Gallery, N.Y.C., 1980, Gerald Peters Gallery, 1993, Landfall Press, Chgo., 1993, Cline Fine Art Gallery, Sante Fe, 1994, U. Tulsa, 1994, London Art Fair, 1997, Glasgow Art Fair, 1997, MD Modern Gallery, 1998, MB Modern Gallery, N.Y., 1998, Stewart & Stewart Pubs., N.Y., 1998, Waterman Fine Art Ltd., London, 1998, M.A. Doran Gallery, Tulsa, Okla., 1999; represented in permanent collections including Bklyn. Mus. High Mus. Art, Atlanta, Denver Art Mus., Mus. Modern Art, N.Y.C., Art Inst. Chgo., Library of Congress, Boston Public Library, Calif. Palace Legion of Honor, Nelson Rockefeller Collection, N.Y.C., Victoria and Albert Mus., London, Hunterian Art Gallery, U. Glasgow, Smithsonian Institution: Am. Art Mus., Elliot Smith Gallery, St. Louis, 1994, The Cline Fine Art Gallery, Santa Fe, 1994, R. Duane Reed, St. Louis, 1996, Galerie Hertz, Louisville, Ky., 1996, Bridgewater, Lustberg, N.Y., 1999, MB Modern Gallery, N.Y., 2000, Rocca di Umbertide Centro per L'Arte Contemporanea, Italy, 2003, Bisonte Galleria, Florence, 2004, other pub. and pvt. collections; designer sets for Orfeo, Kent Opera Co., Eng., later filmed by BBC, 1976. Served with U.S. Army, 1954-56. Home: 38 W 56th St New York NY 10019-3814 also: Montone (PG) 06014 Montone Italy

LANG, DANNY ROBERT, planning consultant; b. St. Louis, June 4, 1955; s. George Robert and V. Arlene (Underwood) L.; m. Diane Marie Martin, Aug. 14, 1976; children: Douglas Gerald, Derek Robert, Darin Kenneth. BS, U. Mo., 1977. Dir. lakes and pks. Lake Saint Louis (Mo.) Cmty. Assn., 1977-80; environ. planner Harland Bartholomew & Assoc., St. Louis, 1980-81, Booker Assocs., St. Louis, 1981—87; dir. cmty. devel. City of St. Peters, Mo., 1987-95; dir. city devel. City of St. Charles, Mo., 1995—2001; sr. planner Horner & Shifrin, St. Louis, 2001—. Dir. deanery planning St. Charles Deanery-St. Louis Archdiocese. Recipient Eagle Scout Boy Scouts Am., 1972. Mem. Am. Planning Assn. (past pres. Mo. chpt. 1992-97, Excellence in Planning award 1985, 87, 91, 96, 2002), Mo. Tax Increment Fin. Assn. (bd. dirs. 1995-97). Roman Catholic. Avocations: coaching little league baseball, stamp collecting/philately. Office: Horner & Shifrin Inc 5200 Oakland Ave Saint Louis MO 63110

LANG, DAVID PAUL, mathematics professor; b. Framingham, Mass., Oct. 27, 1950; s. Earl Francis and Josephine Marie Lang. AB, Stonehill Coll., 1972; PhD in Philosophy, Boston Coll., 1993; PhD in Math., Northeastern U., 1997. Instr. philosophy Oblates of Virgin Mary Sem. Coll., Boston, 1988—93, St. Paul House of Studies, Jamaica Plain, Mass., 1989—96; prof. math. Assumption Coll., Worcester, Mass., 1997—99, Wentworth Inst. Tech., Boston, 2000—01; math. instr. Boston Coll., Chestnut Hill, Mass., 2000—01. Author: Why Matter Matters, 2002, Short Circuit to God: The Story of Frank Kelly, 2003; contbr. articles to profl. jours. Mem. respect life com. St. Mary's Parish, Franklin, Mass., 1987—. Mem.: Math. Assn. Am. Mem. Constitution Party. Roman Catholic. Avocation: piano. Office: Wentworth Inst Tech 550 Huntington Ave Boston MA 02115

LANG, DOUGLAS STEWART, judge; b. St. Louis, July 25, 1947; s. Ervin Jacob and Jacqueline Helen (Kratky) L.; m. Martha Kay Taylor, Aug. 25, 1973; children: Brian Chester and Christopher John (twins), Stewart Taylor. BSBA, Drake U., 1969; JD, U. Mo., Columbia, 1972. Bar: Mo. 1972, Tex. 1973, U.S. Dist. Ct. (no. dist.) Tex. 1973, U.S. Ct. Appeals (5th cir.) 1977, U.S. Dist. Ct. (ea. dist.) Tex. 1992, U.S. Dist. Ct. (we. dist.) Tex. 1993. Law clk. to Hon. Fred L. Henley Mo. Supreme Ct., St. Louis, 1972—75; assoc. Weber, Baker & Allums, Dallas, 1975—78; ptnr. Gardere, Porter & DeHay, Dallas, 1978-79, Gardere Wynne Sewell LLP, Dallas, 1979—2002; judge Ct. Appeals 5th Dist., Dallas, 2002—. Bd. dirs. Legal Svcs. of North Tex., Inc., 1997—, vice chair, 1998, chair, 1999-2000; spkr. in field. Chalice bearer and lay reader Ch. of Incarnation, Dallas, 1984—, vestry mem. 1990-95; campaign chmn.; troop com. Boy Scout Troop 72, Dallas, 1989-97, asst. scoutmaster, 1992-97; v.p. Park Cities Ctrl. Dads' Club, Dallas, 1990-91; pres. Univ. Park Grade Sch. Dad's Club, 1990-91; bd. trustees Drake U., 2002—; bd. councillors U. Dallas, 1991-93; bd. dirs. Com. for Qualified Judiciary, 1999-2002; bd. trustees, vice chmn. chair long range planning com., exec. com. Anglican Sch. Theology, 2000-2005; exec. coun. Episcopal Diocese of Dallas, 2002-2004. Recipient Outstanding Svc. awd. Legal Svcs. North Tex., Dallas, 1991, Alumni Achievement award, Drake U., Des Moines, Iowa, 1992, Double D award Drake U., 1993. Fellow Tex. Bar Found. (sustaining, life, trustee 1997-2000), Am. Bar Found., Dallas Bar Found (trustee 1991—, sec.-treas. 1994-96, vice chair 1996-98, chair 1998-2001); mem. ABA (litigat. sect. 1974—, exec. coun. Nat. Conf. of Bar Pres. 1995-98, pres., 2004-2005, exec. com. Met. Bar Caucus 1991-97, sec.-treas. 1992-93, pres.-elect 1993-94, pres. 1994-95, ho. of dels. 1996-2000), State Bar Tex. (bd. dirs. 1992-95, exec. com. 1994-95, Outstanding Third Yr. Dir. award 1995, Presdl. Citation 1999), Dallas Bar Assn. (bd. dirs. 1976-78, 80-2000, pres. 1991), Dallas Assn. Young Lawyers (bd. dirs. 1975, v.p. 1976, treas. 1975, pres. 1977, Outstanding Young Lawyer in Dallas 1981), Tex. Young Lawyers Assn. (bd. dirs. 1976-78), Am. Law Inst., Tex. Assn. Bank Coun. (bd. dirs. 1990-93, v.p. 1994-95, pres. 1996-97), Am. Inn of Ct. (membership chmn. 1991-95, exec. com. 1991-99, counselor 1995-96, pres. 1997-99), Salesmanship Club of Dallas, Tex. Ctr. for Ethics and Professionalism (chair 1999-2002), Drake U. Nat. Alumni Assn. (bd. dirs. 1998—, v.p. programming 2000-2002, v.p. 2000-2002, pres. 2002-04). Republican. Episcopalian. Avocations: golf, hiking, rafting, camping. Office: Tex Ct Appeals 5th Dist 2d Fl 600 Commerce St Dallas TX 75202

LANG, ENID ASHER, psychiatrist; b. LA, Aug. 28, 1944; d. Alvin Melville and Inez (Silverberg) Asher; m. Norton Lang; children: Eugenie, Aaron. BA, Harvard U., 1966; MD, U. So. Calif., 1975; MPH in Pub. Health, Columbia U., N.Y.C., 1975. Intern Beth Israel Hosp., N.Y.C., 1971-72; resident in psychiatry Columbia Psychiat. Inst., N.Y.C., 1972-75; fellow Columbia Health Svc., N.Y.C., 1974-75; asst. clin. prof. psychiatry Mt. Sinai Med. Sch., NYC, 1976—. Lectr. psychiatry and lit. for faculty, Mt Sinai Dept. Psychiatry, NYC, 1983-97. Co-author (Dr. E. Ackerman) Study of Health in Rural France, 1978; (with D. Halperin) Group Psychotherapy, 1983. Bd. govs. Harvard-Radcliffe Club of Westchester County, NY, 1993-98. Milbank fellow Barrio Health Care, LA, 1970-71. Mem.: Am. Psychiat. Assn. Jewish. Avocations: literature, cello, judging high school debates. Office: 1158 5th Ave New York NY 10029-6917

LANG, EVERETT FRANCIS, JR., brokerage house executive; b. Providence, Sept. 27, 1942; s. Everett Francis and Catherine Mary (Cuddigan) L.; m. Margaret Letitia McKenna; 1 child, Joseph; m. Frances Marie Biasi. BS, Boston U., 1965; MEd, U. Va., 1972, EdD, 1976. Lic. security broker. Elem. sch. tchr. Henrico County Sch. Systems, Highland Springs, Va., 1970-71, middle sch. tchr., 1971-72; asst. regional dir. Sch. Continuing Edn. U. Va., Charlottesville, 1972-76; assoc. dir. human resources Met Property & Liability Ins. Co., Warwick, R.I., 1976-79; human resources cons. Colonial Penn Group, Phila., 1979-81; v.p. Bankers Trust Co., N.Y.C., 1981-86; v.p. sales BT Brokerage Corp., N.Y.C., 1986-90; chmn., pres., chief exec. officer Bankers Trust Brokerage Corp., N.Y.C., 1990-92; pres. Nat. Discount Brokers, N.Y.C., 1993-95, pres., CEO, 1995-98; pres. of Digital Trading facility Soundview Tech., N.Y.C., 1999-2000; exec. v.p. Fleet Securities, 2001—. Capt. USAF, 1965-69, Vietnam. Decorated with Bronze Star, Army Commendation medal. Mem. Phi Delta Kappa, Kappa Delta Pi, Sigma Alpha Epsilon. Avocation: golf. Home: 5 Michele Ct Allendale NJ 07401-1013 Office: Fleet Securities 26 Broadway New York NY 10004

LANG, GARY, artist, educator; b. LA, Mar. 13, 1950; s. Ray and Shirley Lang; m. Ruth Koren Pastine; children: Chance Ray, Sage Raybeka. BFA, Chouinard Art Inst., 1970, Whitney Ind. Study Program, 1971, Calif. Inst. Arts, Valencia, 1972; MFA, Yale U., 1974. One-man shows include Yale U. Art Gallery, New Haven, 1974, Inst. Am. Studies, 1975, Ulrike Kantor Gallery, LA, 1980, Todd Gallery, Phoenix, 1981, Quint Gallery, San Diego, 1982, Mark Quint Gallery, 1983, 1986, Kirk de Gooyer Gallery, 1983, 1984, Paris/NY Kent Gallery, Conn., 1986, Madison Art Ctr., Wis., 1987, Julian Pretto/Berland Hall, NYC, 1988, Annina Nosei Gallery, 1989, NYC, 1990, 1991, Michael Klein Inc., NYC, 1992, 1994, Brian Gloss Fine Art, San Francisco, 1993, 1994, 1999, 2001, Galerie Zurcher, Paris, 1995, 1999, 2004, Haags Gemeentemus., The Hague, Netherlands, 1996, 2004, Sordoni Art Gallery, Wilkes U., Wilkes-Barre, Pa., 1997, Claremont Grad. U., Calif., 1998, Stark Gallery, 1999, 2001, Internat. Studio, NYC, 2000, Galerie Trabant, Vienna, 2001, 2003, Flower Fields, Pub. Garden Commn., Carlsbad, Calif., 2001, 2002, Gallery K, Kurashiki, Japan, 2002, Quint Contemporary Art, La Jolla, Calif., 2002, 2003, Mus. Contemporary Art, 2004, exhibited in group shows at Shasta Col. Art Gallery, Shasta Coll. Dept. Art, Redding, Calif., 2001, Oceanside Mus. Art, Calif., 2001, Kruglak Gallery, Oceanside, 2001, Boehm Gallery, 2001, Parks Exhbn. Ctr., Idyllwill, Calif., 2002, Haags Gemeentemus., 2002, Peggy Phelps Gallery, 2003, Claremont Grad. U., 2003, Domestic Settings Gallery, LA, 2004, Mus. Contemporary Art San Diego, La Jolla, 2004. Fulbright/Hayes Travel grant, Barcelona, Spain, 1974—75. Home: 11225 Creek Rd Ojai CA 93023 Personal E-mail: glang13@earthlink.net.

LANG, GEORGE, restaurateur; b. Székesfehérvár, Hungary, July 13, 1924; arrived in U.S., 1946, naturalized, 1950; s. Simon and Ilona (Deutsch) Lang; m. Jenifer Lang; children: Andrea, Brian, Simon John, Georgina Kathlyn Attended, U. Szeged, Hungary, 1945, Mozarteum, Salzburg, Austria, 1945-46, U. Stranieri, Perugia, Italy, 1950-51; LHD (hon.), Ind. U., 1994, U. Johnson and Wales, 2004. Asst. banquet mgr. Waldorf-Astoria, 1953-58; v.p. sales and mktg. Brass Rail Orgn., 1958-60; v.p. Restaurant Assocs., 1960-71; pres. George Lang Corp., N.Y.C., 1971-83; co-owner Gundel's Restaurant, Budapest, Hungary, 1990—2004, Café des Artistes Restaurant, N.Y.C., 1975—. Author: The Cuisine of Hungary, 1971, Lang's Compendium of Culinary Nonsense and Trivia, 1980, The Café des Artistes Cookbook, 1984, Nobody Knows the Truffles I've Seen, A Memoir, 1998; co-author: Gundel Album, 1993; cons. editor Time-Life Book div. Foods of the World series, 1966-70; contbg. editor Town and Country mag.; contbr. to Ency. Brit., 1974, also various columnist mag. Pub. mem. Am. Revolution Bicentennial Commn., 1969-, mem. exec. com., chmn. Festival U.S.A. coordinating art, internat. exchange and spl. events for Bicentennial celebrations. Recipient James Beard Lifetime Achievement Award, 2002. Address: 33 W 67th St New York NY 10023-6224 Office Phone: 212-721-3100. E-mail: glang@cafenyc.com. *In the great recipe of life, salt is the passion and the spice is enthusiasm.*

LANG, GERHARD, psychology educator; b. Germany, Mar. 19, 1925; came to U.S., 1940; s. Bertold and Else Lang; m. Adell Lang, Dec. 27, 1951; children: Kenneth, Judith Lang Knutsen. BS in Psychology, CCNY, 1952, MA in Sch. Psychology, 1954; PhD in Devel. and Ednl. Psychology, Columbia U., 1958. Cert. psychologist, N.Y.; lic. psychology, N.J. Tchg. fellow, rsch. asst., cons., lectr. CCNY, 1954-60; instr., asst. prof. psychology Fairleigh Dickinson U., Rutherford, N.J., 1958-63, assoc. prof., 1963-64; assoc. prof. psychology and edn. Montclair State U., Upper Montclair, NJ, 1966-70, prof., 1970—2001, prof. emeritus, 2001—, chmn. dept. ednl. rsch. and evaluation, 1970-73, team leader, 1973-94. Cons. N.Y.C. Bd. Edn., 1966-90, rsch. assoc. bd. examiners, 1964-66; cons. Jewish Edn. Svc. N.Am., N.Y.C., 1960-84, Title I reading project Dist. 29, Queens, N.Y., 1973-77, Twp. of Montclair, 1991—; pvt. practice, 1971—. Author: A Practical Guide to Statistics for Research and Measurements, 6th edit., 1998, A Practical Guide to Research Methods, 6th edit., 1998; contbr. articles to profl. jours., also chpts. and pamphlets. Grantee James McKeen Cattel Fund, 1957, U.S. Dept. Edn., 1962-64, 65-67. Mem.: APA. Avocations: playing piano, tennis, reading, eating. Home: 4-39 Lyncrest Ave Fair Lawn NJ 07410-1634 Office: Montclair State U Dept Psychology Montclair NJ 07043 Office Phone: 201-796-8782.

LANG, GORDON, JR., retired lawyer; b. Evanston, Ill., July 27, 1933; s. Gordon and Harriet Kendig Lang; m. Clara Bates Van Derzee, Sept. 26, 1970; children: Elizabeth K., Gordon III, Harriet B. BA, Yale U., 1954; MA in History, U. Ariz., 1958; LLB, Harvard U., 1960. Bar: Ill. 1960. Assoc. Gardner, Carton & Douglas, Chgo., 1960-67, ptnr., 1967-98, ret., 1998. Cons. in field. Dir. North Side Boys' Clubs, Chgo., 1961-67, Yale Scholarship Trust Ill., 1966-69, pres., 1967; mem. Assocs. Rush-Presbyn.-St. Luke's Med. Ctr., Chgo., 1962-2003, Assocs. Northwestern U., Evanston, 1970—; dir. Chgo. Youth Ctrs., 1967—, pres., 1982-84; trustee Chgo. Latin Sch. Found., 1978—, pres., 1995-2003; trustee Groton (Mass.) Sch., 1982-93; dir. United Way of Chgo., 1984-90, United Way/Crusade of Mercy (Met. Chgo.), 1989-95; apptd. Bush/Cheney elector 2000 presdl. election. 1st lt. USAF, 1955-57. Mem. ABA (sect. bus. law), Ill. State Bar Assn., Chgo. Bar Assn. (mem. Corp. Law Com. 1975-98, mem. Fin. Instns. Com. 1985-98), Chgo. Club (former dir. and sec.), Econ. Club Chgo. (former dir. and sec.), Onwentsia Club, Racquet Club Chgo., Chgo. Commonwealth Club, Yale Club Chgo. (former dir., past pres.). Republican. Episcopalian. Avocations: golf, skiing, hiking. Home: 1520 N Astor St Chicago IL 60610-1610 Office: Gardner Carton & Douglas 191 N Wacker Dr Ste 3700 Chicago IL 60606-1698 Office Phone: 312-569-1084. E-mail: glang@gcd.com.

LANG, HOWARD LAWRENCE, electrical engineer; b. St. Louis, Nov. 16, 1958; s. William and Hermine L.; m. Karen Friedman, June 26, 1988; children: Arielle Ilyssa, Emily Danielle. BS in Biophysics with high distinction, U. Ill., 1981; MSEE, Cert. Biomed. Engring., Washington U., St. Louis, 1984; MSE in Computer and Info. Sci., U. Pa., 1990. Registered profl. engr., Pa., NJ, NY. Biomed. engr. Midwest Rsch. Inst., Kansas City, Mo., 1983; sr. engr. AT&T Bell Labs., Holmdel, NJ, 1984—. Contbr. articles to profl. jours.; designer fiber optic comm. sys. Chmn. AT&T Magic Club, Holmdel, 1985-88, Illini Emergency Med. Svcs., Urbana, 1979-81. Mem. IEEE (sr., sec. Computer Soc. NJ coast sect. 1998-99, Svc. award 1984), NSPE, NJ Soc. Profl. Engrs., Tau Beta Pi, Phi Eta Sigma. Achievements include patents in field. Avocations: magic, bicycling. Home: PO Box 200 Holmdel NJ 07733-0200

LANG, JACKIE ANN, nursing consultant; b. Cin., Oct. 10, 1960; d. John Harvey and Sallie Joan (Ralston) Kegley; m. James Edward Lang, Nov. 19, 1988; children: Rachel, Victoria, Rebecca, Stephanie, Michael. BSN, U. Cin., 1983, MSN, 1988. RN, Ohio; cert. quality mgmt. Staff and charge nurse med.-surg. Univ. Hosp., Cin., 1983-86, critical care staff nurse, 1986-88; med.-surg. instr. nursing sch. Good Samaritan Hosp., Cin., 1987-89; med.-surg. clin. nurse specialist The Jewish Hosp., Cin., 1989-91; cons. Greater Cin. Internal Medicine, 1990—. Contbr. nursing newsletters. Mem. aux. The Jewish Hosp. of Cin., 1993—2001, Parks and REcreation Commn., Montgomery, 2001—; mem. N.E. Cmty. Challenge Coalition, 2001—; parent assn. leader Cin. Children's Choir, 2004—05; first v.p. All Saints PTO, 2000—01, 2005—, pres., 2001—02, first v.p., 2005—; chair silent auction Usuline Acad., 2004—05. Univ. grad. scholar U. Cin., 1985-86. Mem.: ANA, Southwestern Ohio Nurses Assn., Ohio Nurses Assn., Montgomery Women's Club (Sunshine chmn. 1996—97, arts dept. chmn. 1997—98, rec. sec. 1998—2000, 2nd v.p. 2000—01, Conservation Chairman), Ohio Fedn. Women's Clubs, Gen. Fedn. Women's Clubs, Sigma Theta Tau, Alpha Chi Omega (pledge pres. 1979—80, 3d v.p. 1981—82, chpt. pres. 1982—83, alumni sec. 1984—86, alumni mem. co-chmn. 1995—99). Roman Catholic. Home: 8884 Castleford Ln Cincinnati OH 45242-6351

LANG, JAMES DEVORE, JR., ministry executive; b. Ft. Lewis, Wash., Apr. 29, 1941; s. James Devore and Margaret Lang; m. Barbara Jo Drury, July 3, 1965; children: Kathrena, Teresa, Christina, Angela. BS, USAF Acad., 1963; postgrad., Pepperdine U., 1977-79. Commd. 2d lt. USAF, 1963, advanced through grades to capt., resigned, 1969; regional dir., v.p. Lorraine L. Blair, Inc., San Francisco, 1969-71; v.p. Capital Planning Assn., San Rafael, Calif., 1971-73; pres. Delger Corp., Novato, Calif., 1973-76; chmn., CEO Delger Fin. Corp., Novato, 1976-83; pres., chmn., CEO Alternate Energy Corp., Novato, 1978-81; pres., CEO Shiloh Resources, Novato, 1980-83; sales rep., engr., v.p. Aztec Bldg., Inc., Norman, Okla., 1985-90; pres., CEO Amerex Corp., Norman, 1990-93; v.p., exec. dir. Bill Glass Prison Ministries, Inc., Dallas, 1994-99, exec. v.p., 1996—98, pres., 1999-2001; exec. dir. Prison Ministry, Dallas, 2001—02; exec. v.p. Bill Glass/Champions for Life, 2001—04; COO Performance Consulting Group LLC, 2004—. Elder, pastor Trinity Bapt. Ch., Norman, 1990-93. Author: Real Estate Investment Trusts in Financial Planning, 1973; contbr. numerous articles to profl. publs. Regent Coll. for Fin. Planning, 1974-76; exec. dir. Christian Fellowship Internat. Decorated Air medal with 7 oak leaf clusters, Air Force Commendation medal; Paul Harris fellow Rotary Internat., 1978; recipient Golden Bull award Bank of Marin, 1977. Mem. Internat. Assn. Fin. Planning (nat. pres. 1973-74, chmn. 1974-75). Avocations: ministry, family, sports, flying. Home: 910 Fairway Dr Duncanville TX 75137-4612 Office: Champions for Life PO Box 761101 Dallas TX 75376-1101 Office Phone: 405-447-2977. E-mail: jimlang41@aol.com.

LANG, JAMES PATRICK, priest; b. Syracuse, N.Y., Feb. 14, 1949; s. Eugene Adolph and Rita James Lang. BA, Wadhams Hall Seminary Coll., 1971; MDiv, St. Mary's Sem. and Univ., Balt., 1974. Deacon Cathedral of the Immaculate Conception, Syracuse, NY, 1974—75; assoc. pastor Our Lady of Lourdes Ch., Utica, NY, 1975—77, St. Mary of the Assumption Ch., Rome, NY, 1977—81; chaplain and dir. of Hall Newman Ctr. & Chapel of Lady of the Holy Spirit at SUNY, Oswego, 1981—91; chaplain and dir. Alibrandi Cath. Ctr. and Thomas More Chapel at Syracuse U., 1991—98; diocesan dir. Office of Pastoral Planning, Diocese of Syracuse, 1999—; diocesan vicar for parishes Diocese of Syracuse, 2000—. Mem. faculty Formation for Minisry Program, Diocese of Syracuse, 1984—91; mem. Senate of Priests, Diocese of

Syracuse, 1984—, mem. exec. com., 1985—98, vice chair exec. com., 1989—93, chair exec. com., 1993—97; mem. Diocesan Pastoral Coun., Syracuse, 1984—; vice chair Diocesan Pastoral Coun, 1992—94; mem. Priests' Coun. State of N.Y., 1986—98; treas., 1987—91; pres., 1991—95; observer Nat. Coun. Cath. Bishops, 1991—95; mem. Diocesan Coll. Consultors, 1996—; other related appointments; cons. in field, 1996—. Chmn. adv. com. Phi chpt. Syracuse U. Alpha Phi Omega Nat. Co-Ed Svc. Fraternity, 1991—, chmn. adv. com. Epsilon Nu Chpt. Syracuse U., 1991—; Bd. dirs. Hiawatha Coun. BSA, 1993—99; mem. faculty Nat. Camping Sch. BSA, 1992—, chaplain, 1992—, program instr., 1996—; chair N.E. Region BSA Outdoor Program Seminar, 1998—; v.p. Hiawathy Seaway coun. Boy Scouts Am., 1999—; bd. dirs. Oneida County Comty. Action, Inc., Utica, NY, 1976—81, fin. chmn., 1980—81, treas., 1981; Bd. dirs. Cath. Charities of Onondaga County, 1993—. Recipient Robert E. Hall award, Oswego (N.Y.) Newman Found.,Inc., 1991, Key to the City, Mayor's Office City of Oswego, 1991, St. George award, Cath. Com. on Scouting, Diocese of Syracuse, 1992, Silver Beaver award, Hiawatha Coun. BSA, Syracuse, 1998, Silver Antelope award, Northeast Region BSA, 2001, Disting. Svc. Key, Alpha Phi Omega, Phi chpt. Syracuse U., 1998, Chancellor's award for pub. svc., Syracuse U., 1998. Mem.: Nat. Assn. Ch. Personnel Adminstrs., Conf. on Pastoral Planning and Coun. Devel., Theta Alpha Kappa, Theta Chi Beta. Republican. Home: 4845 S Salina St Syracuse NY 13205 Office: Vicar for Parishes Diocese of Syrcuse 240 E Onondaga St PO Box 511 Syracuse NY 13205 E-mail: jplang@aol.com.

LANG, JAMES RICHARD, education consultant; b. Cleve., Feb. 7, 1945; s. Francis H. and Rachel L. (Boyce) L.; m. Marilyn F. Hosken, July 1, 1967; children: Christopher Charles, James Walter. Salesman Stas. WOHI-AM/WRTS-FM, East Liverpool, Ohio, 1967-68; gen. mgr. Sta. WEIR-AM, Weirion, W.Va., 1969-76; v.p. sales Paperwork Systems, Inc., Bellingham, Wash., 1976-78; v.p. market devel. Sta. Bus. Systems div. Control Date Corp., Greenwich, Conn., 1978-85; mgr. Eaglestone div. Siber Hegner N.Am., Inc., Milford, Conn., 1986-89; dir. mktg. MacMillan/McGraw-Hill, Avon, Conn., 1990-93; pres. Imagination Works, Trumbull, 1993—. With USN, 1968—69. Recipient Outstanding Service to Cmty. award Italian Sons and Dads Am., 1970. Mem. Instrument Soc. Am., Direct Mtkg. Assn., Jaycees (Cmty. Svc. award 1975), Internat. Brotherhood of Magicians (Wizard award 2003), Rotary (pres. 1996-97, area rep. 1997-98, asst. gov. dist. 7980, 1999-2001, dist. gov. 2002-2003, bequest soc. mem., Man of Yr. 1975, Paul Harris fellow dist. 1980, Norm Parsells award 2000, Rotary Found. Cert. Meritorious Svc. 2005), Fellowship of Rotary Magicians. Methodist. Office: Imagination Works 24 Primrose Dr Trumbull CT 06611-5043

LANG, JOHN DENTON, electronics executive; b. N.Y.C., Aug. 19, 1953; s. William Denton Jr. and Marion C. (Andren) L.; m. Patricia Ann Beck, Aug. 7, 1976; children: Diane, William, Jonrobert, Kevin. BS in Acctg., Villanova U., 1975. CPA, Calif. Staff acct. ITT, J.C. Carter Co., Costa Mesa, Calif., 1975-77; mgr. acctg. Dennys Inc., Winchells, LaMirada, Calif., 1977-81; mgr. mgmt. cons. svcs. Coopers & Lybrand, L.A., 1981-87; exec. v.p. Epson Am., Inc., Long Beach, Calif., 1987—, pres., CEO. Mem. bd. mgrs. YMCA, Torrance. Mem. Inst. Mgmt. Accts., Calif. Soc. CPAs, Nat. Assn. Accts. (CMA). Office: Epson Am Inc 3840 Kilroy Airport Way Long Beach CA 90806 Office Phone: 562-981-3840. Office Fax: 562-290-5220.

LANG, JOSEPH HAGEDORN, lawyer; b. Cleve., Sept. 30, 1937; s. Carl Frederick and Martha Clotilda (Hagedorn) L.; m. Elsie A. O'Berry, Aug. 8, 1965; children: Joseph H. Jr., Robert Warren, James O'Berry. AA, St. Petersburg Jr. Coll., 1959; BA, Duke U., 1961; JD, U. Fla., 1963. Bar: Fla. 1964, U.S. Dist. Ct. (mid. dist.) Fla. 1965, U.S. Ct. Appeals (5th cir.) 1965, U.S. Supreme Ct. 1975. Assoc. Baynard McLeod & Overton, St. Petersburg, Fla., 1964-69; ptnr. Baynard McLeod & Lang, St. Petersburg, 1969-80; pres. Baynard McLeod & Lang, P.C., St. Petersburg, 1980—. Charter mem., chmn. Police Cmty. Coun., Cmty. Alliance; chmn. bd. dirs. St. Petersburg Jr. Coll., Pinellas County, 1983-97, trustee, 1977-97, chmn., 1982-89, 92-96, chmn. emeritus, 1997—; mem. State Bd. C.C.'s, 1997-2001, vice chmn. 1998-99, chmn., 1999-2000. Named Sch. Adv. Com. Mem. of Yr.; recipient Trustee of Yr. award Fla. Assn. Cmty. Coll., 1993, Bob Graham C.C. Disting. Svc. award, 1994, Trustee Leadership award So. Region, ACCT, 1994, Alumni award St. Petersburg Jr. Coll., 1990, Disting. Alumni award LeRoy Collins C.C., 2002, Leadership Cmty. Svc. award, 2002. Mem. Fla. Bar Assn., St. Petersburg Bar Assn., St. Petersburg C. of C. (Outstanding Mem. award 1990), Suncoasters Club, Dragon Club, Phi Theta Kappa (Disting. Alumni award 1978). Democrat. Roman Catholic. Office: Baynard McLeod & Lang 669 1st Ave N Saint Petersburg FL 33701-3696 Office Phone: 727-894-0676.

LANG, K. D. (KATHERINE DAWN LANG), country music singer, composer; b. Consort, Alta., Can., Feb. 11, 1961; d. Adam and Audrey L. Lang. Mem. Tex. swing fiddle band, 1982—; formed band The Reclines. Albums include A Truly Western Experience, 1984, Angel with a Lariat, 1986, Shadowland, 1988, Absolute Torch and Twang, 1990 (Can. Country Music Awards album of the yr.), Ingenue, 1992, Even Cowgirls Get the Blues (soundtrack), 1993, Drag, 1997, Australian Tour, 1997, Invincible Summer, 2000, Live By Request, 2001; (with others) All You Can Eat, 1995; actress (film) Salmonberries, 1991; Teresa's Tattoo, 1994, The Last Don, 1997, TV guest appearance Ellen, 1997, Eye of The Beholder, 1999. Recipient Can. Country Music awards, including Entertainer of Yr., 1989, Grammy award, 1990, 1993, Best Pop Female Vocal for Constant Craving, Grammy nomination Best Pop Female Vocal for Miss Chatelaine, 1994, William Harold Moon award Soc. of Composers, Authors and Music Publishers of Can., 1994. Office: Warner Bros Records Inc 3300 Warner Blvd Burbank CA 91505-4694

LANG, LILLIAN OWEN, retired accountant; b. Yorkville, Tenn., Oct. 8, 1915; d. Hugh Preston and Susan (Davis) Owen; m. John H.C. Lang, 1936 (div. 1956); 1 child, John Sanford Lang. Student, U. Tenn. Extension, 1956-62, Memphis State U., 1963-64, Memphis Acad. Arts, 1965-66. CPA, Tenn. Shipping clk. Buckeye Cellulose Corp., 1943-46; x-ray technician Memphis and Shelby County Health Dept., 1948-56; acctg. clk. Purex Corp., 1957-59; bookkeeper Electrolock, Inc., 1959-62; sec.-treas. Allied Bruce Terminix Cos., Inc., Mobile, Ala., 1962-80, v.p., 1980-86; also dir.; pvt. practice acctg. Memphis, 1986-2000; ret., 2000. Mem. DAR, Am. Soc. Women Accts. (pres. Mobile chpt. 1977-78, dir. SE area 1979-81). Mem. Christian Ch. (Disciples Of Christ). Home and Office: 5799 Whale Point Ln Rock Hall MD 21661

LANG, LINDA A., food service executive; B in Fin., U. Calif., Berkeley; MBA, San Diego State U. Joined Jack in the Box Inc., 1985, divsn. v.p. new products and promotions, 1994—96, v.p. products, promotions and consumer rsch., 1996—99, v.p. mktg., 1999—2001, sr. v.p. mktg., 2001—02, exec. v.p. mktg. and ops., human resources, restaurant devel., quality assurance and logistics, 2002—03, pres., COO San Diego, 2003—, also bd. dirs. Office: Jack in the Box Inc 9330 Balboa Ave San Diego CA 92123

LANG, LINDA KAY, music educator; b. Scott City, Kans., Mar. 20, 1952; d. Eugene F. and Blanche (Slivey) Carver; m. Paul Lang, Aug. 5, 1978; children: Jenny, Stacy. BMus, Ft. Hays State U., 1974, M. in Elem. Edn., 1980; Orff tchg. cert., Hamline U. Vocal music tchr. Unified Sch. Dist., Grainfield, Kans., 1974-75, Garden City, Kans., 1975-78, Hays, Kans., 1980—. Mem. Hays Symphony, Ft. Hays State U., 1997—. Adjudicator Jr. High Music Festivals, 1988—; organist Immaculate Heart Mary Parish, Hays, 1985—, religion tchr., 1989-2000. Mem. Kans. Nat. Edn. Assn. (bldg. rep. 1993-94, 2002—), Kans. Music Tchrs. Assn. (pres. dist. IV 1994-95), Kans. Music Edn. Assn. (dist. IV elem. choir chmn., dist. IV Outstanding Elem. Music Tchr. 1999-2000). Avocations: sewing, crocheting, cooking, music. Home: 1601 E 27th Street Ter Hays KS 67601-2114 Office: Lincoln Sch 1906 Ash St Hays KS 67601-3297

LANG, LINDA MARIE, music educator; Student, Concordia Coll., 1969—70; BA, Augustana Coll., 1972; postgrad., Ariz. State U., 1979—81. Tchr. music Patrick Henry Jr. High Sch., Sioux Falls, SD, 1972—79; tchr. voice Augustana Coll., 1976—79, dir. Women's choir, 1976—79; organist, tchr., dir. various musical, schs. churches and chorus', L.A., 1980—89, writer, performer HATS, 1989—93; organist, choir dir., 1993—2001; dir. choir organist, bell choir, tchr. voice Akiba Temple/Grace Luth., Culver City, Calif., 2001—05. Composer (actress, singer): (children's video) Mother Goose Workout, 1991. Pres., bd. mem. Food Coop., Venice, Calif., 1985—2002. Olsen scholar, Augustana Coll., 1970—72. Mem.: Am. Guild Organists, Mu Phi Epsilon (dist. advisor 1977—79). Avocations: piano, pipe organ, singing, music, puppetry.

LANG, MABEL LOUISE, classics educator; b. Utica, N.Y., Nov. 12, 1917; d. Louis Bernard and Katherine (Werdge) L. BA, Cornell U., 1939; MA, Bryn Mawr Coll., 1940, PhD, 1943; Litt.D., Coll. Holy Cross, 1975, Colgate U., 1978; L.H.D., Hamilton Coll. Mem. faculty Bryn Mawr Coll., 1943-91, successively instr., asst. prof., 1943-50, assoc. prof., 1950-59, prof. Greek, 1959-88, chmn. dept., 1960-88, acting dean coll. 2d semester, 1958-59, 60-61; chmn. mng. com. Am. Sch. Classical Studies, Athens, 1975-80, chmn. admissions and fellowship com., 1966-72; Blegen disting. rsch. prof. semester I Vassar Coll., 1976-77; Martin classical lectr. Oberlin Coll., 1982. Co-author: Athenian Agora Measures and Tokens; author: Palace of Nestor Frescoes, 1969, Athenian Agora Graffiti and Dipinti, 1976; Herodotean Narrative and Discourse, 1984, Athenian Agor Ostraka, 1990; contbr. articles profl. jours. Guggenheim fellow, 1953-54; Fulbright fellow Greece, 1959-60 Mem. Am. Philos. Soc., Am. Acad. Arts and Scis., German Archaeol. Inst., Am. Philol. Assn., Soc. Promotion Hellenic Studies (Eng.), Classical Assn. (Eng.). Home: 905 New Gulph Rd Bryn Mawr PA 19010-2941 Office: Dept Greek Bryn Mawr Coll Bryn Mawr PA 19010

LANG, MARGO TERZIAN, artist; b. Fresno, Calif. d. Nishan and Araxie (Kazarosian) Terzian; m. Nov. 29, 1942; children: Sandra J. (Mrs. Ronald L. Carr), Roger Mark, Timothy Scott. Student, Fresno State U., 1939-42, Stanford U., 1948-50, Prado Mus., Madrid, 1957-59, Ariz. State U., 1960-61; workshops with, Dong Kingman, Ed Whitney, Rex Brandt, Millard Sheets, George Post. Maj. exhbns. include, Guadalajara, Mex., Brussels, N.Y.C., San Francisco, Chgo., Phoenix, Corcoran Gallery Art, Washington, internat. watercolor exhbn., Los Angeles, Bicentennial shows, Hammer Galleries, N.Y.C., spl. exhbn. aboard, S.S. France, others, over 80 paintings in various Am. embassies throughout world; represented in permanent collections, Nat. Collection Fine Arts Mus., Smithsonian Instn.; lectr., juror art shows; condr. workshops.; interviews and broadcasts on Radio Liberty, Voice of Am. Bd. dirs. Phoenix Symphony Assn., 1965-69, Phoenix Musical Theater, 1965-69. Recipient award for spl. achievements Symphony Assn., 1966, 67, 68, 72, spl. awards State of Ariz., silver medal of excellence Internat. Platform Assn., 1971; honoree U.S. Dept. State celebration of 25 yrs. of exhbn. of paintings in embassies worldwide, 1989. Mem. Internat. Platform Assn., Ariz. Watercolor Assn., Nat. Soc. Arts and Letters (nat. dir. 1971-72, nat. art chmn. 1974-76), Nat. Soc. Lit. and Arts, Phoenix Art Mus., Friends of Mexican Art, Am. Artists Profl. League, English-Speaking Union, Musical Theater Guild, Ariz. Costume Inst., Phoenix Art Mus., Scottsdale Art Ctr., Ariz. Arts Commn. (fine arts panel 1990-91), Friends of Art and Preservation in Embassies. Home: 6127 E Calle Del Paisano Scottsdale AZ 85251-4212 *As a romantic impressionist I feel a tremendous exhilaration at being able to communicate my philosophy through my paintings. I look for God's beauty and mystery in all things, and as an artist, I feel very fortunate that I can eliminate the ugliness and the negatives and concentrate on the wonders of the universe around us.*

LANG, MATTHEW, music educator; b. Belleville, Ill., Apr. 7, 1973; s. David and Linda Lang. BS in Music Edn., U. Ill., 1995. Cert. tchr. K-12 Ill. Asst. band dir. O'Fallon (Ill.) Twp. H.S., 1998—2001, dir. of bands, music dept. chmn., 2001—. Mem.: Ill. Music Educators Assn., Music Educators Nat. Conf., Internat. Double Reed Soc. Office: O'Fallon Twp HS 600 S Smiley St O Fallon IL 62269 Office Phone: 618-632-3507. Office Fax: 618-632-6484. E-mail: mattl@oths.k12.il.us.

LANG, NICHOLAS PAUL, surgeon; b. Jonesboro, Ark., Apr. 11, 1947; s. Paul Alexandra and Lula (Cornish) L.; m. Carol Ann Holl, Aug. 1968 (div. May 1978); 1 child, Christopher; m. Helen Felecia Haley, July 25, 1979; children: Patrick, Courtney. Student, U. Ark., 1969; MD, U. Ark. Med. Scis., 1973. Diplomate Am. Bd. Surgery. Resident in surgery U. Ark. Med. Scis., Little Rock, 1973-77, assoc. prof. surgery, 1977-84, 1984-90, prof. surgery, 1990—; rsch. fellow Nat. Cancer Inst., Bethesda, Md., 1977-79; staff surgeon Little Rock VA Hosp. (now Ctrl. Ark. Vets. Healthcare Sys.), 1979-95, chief of surgery, 1995—2002, chief of staff, 2001—, acting medical ctr. dir., 2004—. Contbr. articles to profl. publs. Mem. nat. bd. Am. Cancer Soc., Atlanta, 1989-96; bd. dirs. CARTI, Little Rock, 1994—. Grantee Nat. Cancer Inst., 1995-2000, EPA, 1996-99, NIA, 1997-2003. Fellow ACS, Southwestern Surg. Congress (councillor 1989-95, pres. 2000-2001); mem. AMA, So. Surg. Assn., Assn. for Surg. Edn. (pres. 2000-2001), Am. Assn. Cancer Rsch. Baptist. Avocations: woodworking, gardening. Home: 1323 White Rd Little Rock AR 72211-4019 Office: Ctrl Ark Vets Healthcare Sys # 11-LR 4300 W 7th St Little Rock AR 72205-5446 Office Phone: 501-257-5300. Business E-Mail: nick.lang@med.va.gov.

LANG, NORTON DAVID, physicist; b. Chgo., July 5, 1940; s. Charles and Sadelle Lang; m. Enid Asher, June 8, 1969; children: Eugenie, Aaron. AB summa cum laude, Harvard U., 1962, A.M., 1965, PhD, 1968; postgrad. (Knox fellow), London Sch. Economics, 1962-63. Asst. research physicist, lectr. U. Calif., San Diego, 1967—69; mem. staff IBM Rsch. Ctr., Yorktown Heights, NY, 1969—. Erwin W. Mueller meml. lectr., Pa. State U., 1992; adj. prof. elec. engring. Columbia U., 2005— Contbr. articles on theoretical physics to profl. jours.; asso. editor: Phys. Rev. Letters, 1980-83. Fellow N.Y. Acad. Scis., Am. Phys. Soc. (chmn. fellowship com. divsn. condensed matter physics 1985-87, Davisson-Germer prize 1977, chmn. Davisson-Germer Prize com. 1990); mem. IEEE (sr.), Am. Chem. Soc., Phi Beta Kappa. Office: IBM Rsch Ctr Yorktown Heights NY 10598 Business E-Mail: LangN@us.ibm.com.

LANG, PEARL, dancer, choreographer; b. Chgo., May 1922; d. Jacob and Frieda (Feder) Lack; m. Joseph Wiseman, Nov. 22, 1963. Student, Wright Jr. Coll., U. Chgo.; DFA (hon.), Juilliard Sch. Music, 1995; PhD (hon.), DFA, Juilliard Sch., 1995. Formed own co., 1953; faculty Yale, 1954-68; tchr., lectr. Juilliard, 1953-69, Jacobs Pillow, Conn. Coll., Neighborhood Playhouse, 1963-68. Founder Pearl Lang Dance Found.; mem. Boston Symphony, Tanglewood Fest. Soloist, Martha Graham Dance Co., 1944-54; featured roles on Broadway include Carousel, 1945-47, Finian's Rainbow, 1947-48, Danced Martha Graham's roles in Appalachian Spring, 1974-76, El Pentitente, 1954, Primitive Mysteries, 1978-79, Diversion of Angels, 1948-70, Herodiade, 1977-79; role of Solvieg opposite John Garfield Broadway include, ANTA Peer Gynt; choreographer: TV shows CBC Folio; co-dir. T.S. Eliot's Murder in the Cathedral, Stratford, Conn., Direction, 1964-66, 67, Lamp Unto Your Feet, 158, Look Up and Live TV, 1957; co-dir., choreographer: full length prodn. Dybbuk for CBC; dir. numerous Israel Bond programs; assumed roles Emily Dickinson: Letter to the World, 1970; Clytemnestra, 1973; Jocasta in: Night Journey, 1974, for Martha Graham Dance Co.; choreographer: dance works Song of Deborah, 1952, Moonsung and Windsung, 1952, Legend, 1953, Rites, 1953, And Joy Is My Witness, 1954, Nightflight, 1954, Sky Chant, 1957, Persephone, 1958, Black Marigolds, 1959, Shirah, 1960, Apasionada, 1961, Broken Dialogues, 1962, Shore Bourne, 1964, Dismembered Fable, 1965, Pray for Dark Birds, 1966, Tongues of Fire, 1967, Piece for Brass, 1969, Moonways and Dark Tides, 1970, Sharjuhm, 1971, At That Point in Place and Time, 1973, The Possessed, 1995, Prairie Steps, 1975, Bach Rondelays, 1977, I Never Saw Another Butterfly, 1977, A Seder Night, 1977, Kaddish, 1977, Icarus, 1978, Cantigas Ladino, (10 sephardic songs), 1978, Notturno, 1980, Gypsy Ballad, 1981, Hanele The Orphan, 1981, The Tailor's Megilleh, 1981, Bridal Veil, 1982, Stravinsky's opera Oedipus Rex, 1982, Song of Songs, 1983, Shiru L'adonay, 1983, Tehillim, 1983, Sephardic Romance and Tfila, 1989, Koros, 1990, Eyn Keloheynu, 1991, Schubert Quartetsatz No. 12, 1993, Schubert Quartet 15 1st Mov., 1994, And Again a Begining, 1994, Dream Voyages, 1996, Memories and Dreams of Isaac the Blind, 1997, A Bouquet of Love Song Waltzes, 1998, Song of Azerbaijan, 1999, Icarus, 1999, The Time Is Out of Joint, 2000, Dance Panel #7, 2000, Cityscape, 2000. Recipient 2 Guggenheim fellowships; recipient Goldfadden award Congress for Jewish Culture, Achievement award Artists and Writers for Peace in the Middle East, Cultural award Workmen's Circle, Queens Coll. award, 1991, Jewish Cultural achievement award Nat. Found. for Jewish Culture, 1992; named to Hall of Fame, Internat. Com. for the Dance Libr. of Israel, 1997. Mem. Am. Guild Mus. Artists. Home and Office: Dance Foundation Inc 382 Central Park W New York NY 10025-6054 Office Phone: 212-866-2680.

LANG, PHILIP DAVID, retired state legislator, insurance company executive; b. Portland, Oreg., Dec. 16, 1929; s. Henry W. and Vera (Kern) L.; m. Marcia Jean Smith, May 29, 1952 (div. Oct. 1979); 1 son, Philip David, III; m. Virginia Ann Wolf, Feb. 16, 1980. Student, Lewis and Clark Coll., 1951-53, Northwestern Coll. Law, 1956. Police officer Oreg. Dept. State Police, Salem, 1953-55; claims adjuster Glenns Falls Ins. Co., Portland, 1955-57, Oreg. Automobile Ins. Co., Portland, 1959-61; adminstrv. asst. to mayor City of Portland, 1957-58; spl. agt., underwriter North Pacific Ins. Co., Portland, 1961-63, mgr., 1963-65, asst. v.p., 1965-80, v.p., 1980-95; ret., 1995; asst. v.p. Oreg. Automobile Ins. Co., 1965-80, v.p., 1980-95; ret., 1995; appt. chmn. Oreg. Liquor Control Commn., 1998—. Mem. Oreg. Ho. of Reps., 1960-79, speaker, 1975-79; Div. leader Multnomah County (Oreg.) Democratic Com., 1956-60, precinct com., 1956—. With USAF, 1947-50. Mem. Oreg. Ins. Underwriters Assn., Nat. Alcoholic Beverage Control Assn. (mem. bd. 2001, pres. elect 2005), VFW, Masons, DeMolay (Legion Honor), Theta Chi. Roman Catholic. Home: 5769 SW Huddleson St Portland OR 97219-6645 Fax: 503-245-2452. E-mail: pdavidlang@msn.com. *Success is achieved through commitment to, and perserverance in, all that is undertaken; balanced with tolerance and understanding of all persons.*

LANG, ROBERT MAYS, JR., manufacturing executive; s. Robert Mays Lang and Mary Elizabeth Davis Lang Mannweiler, Gordon Banatynne Mannweiler (Stepfather); m. Janice Ruth Mooney, Sept. 23, 1978; m. Sarah N. McIntyre, Aug. 21, 1965 (div. Nov. 15, 1974). AB in Econs., Miami U., Oxford, Ohio, 1965. Sales rep., various locations, 1972—82; pres. Reach for the Stars Inc., Cross River, NY, 1982—94, Imagination Group Ltd., Cross River, NY, 1990—; sec., treas., exec. dir. Mannweiler Found. Inc., Naugatuck, Conn., 2001—; CEO Fabrique Cosmetique Inc., Cross River, NY, 1992—. Rep. Creative Packaging Inc., 1965—68, Arkay Packaging Inc., 1968—72; pvt. practice, 1972—82; bd. dirs. The Mannweiler Found., Naugatuck, Conn., 2001—. Contbr. articles to profl. jours. and trade mags. Treas. Pound Ridge (NY) Cmty. Ch., Pound Ridge, 1984—87; fin. com. Katonah (NY) Meth. Ch., 1997—99. Recipient Cosmetic Innovator Yr. award, Ind. Cosmetic Mfr. and Distbr. Assn., 2004. Mem.: Nat. Assn. Watch Clock Collectors (pres. chpt. 84 2003—), Various Sq. Dance Clubs (pres. 1998—99). Independent. Methodist. Achievements include development of custom blended cosmetic sys., cosmetic filling equipment and unique forumlations. Avocations: book collecting, clock collecting & repair, gardening, woodworking, square dancing. Home: PO Box 362 Cross River NY 10518 Office: Fabrique Cosmetique Inc PO Box 361 Cross River NY 10518

LANG, SCOTT M., music educator; b. Buffalo, Aug. 24, 1967; s. John Lang and Sheila Donatelle. MS in Ednl. Supv., Ariz. State U., 1989. Dir. bands, asst. prin. Tempe H.S., Ariz., 1991—2000; dir. bands Marcos de Niza, 2000—03. Dir. Synergy Leadership Endeavors, Tempe, 1992—2003. Recipient Governing Bd. award Excellence, Tempe Union H.S. Dist., 1995. Mem.: Ariz. Music Educators Assn. (assoc.; sec. 2001—03). Office: Marcos de Niza High Sch 6000 S Lakeshore Dr Tempe AZ 85283 Personal E-mail: slang.mdn@tuhsd.k12.az.us.

LANG, SUSAN MARIE, minister; b. Trenton, N.J., Sept. 2, 1956; d. William Gustav and Ruth Dolores Cook; m. Thomas Michael Lang, May 30, 1981; children: Mary Michele, Kristina Marie. AB, Goucher Coll., 1978; MDiv, Luth. Theol. Sem., Gettysburg, Pa., 1983. Ordained min. Luth. Ch. in Am., 1983. Archivist I Md. Hall of Records, Annapolis, 1978—79; pastor Manor Luth. Parish, Adamstown, Md., 1983—87; campus pastor Luth. Campus Ministry at Indiana U. of Pa., 1987—94; intentional interim pastor Jerusalem Luth. Ch., Sellersville, Pa., 1997—98, Christ Luth. Ch., Trumbauersville, Pa., 1999, St. Lukes Luth. Ch., Ferndale, Pa., 2000—02; author, spkr., cons. Perkasie, Pa., 2002—. Part-time chaplain Luth. Cmty. at Telford, Pa., 2002—03; cons. in leadership Southeastern Pa. Synod, Evangelical Luth. Ch. in Am., 2004—; dir. Annual Rev. Writers Conf., Sellersville, Pa., 2003—; owner Revwriter Resources Cons., 2004—. Author: Our Community: Dealing with Conflict in Our Congregation, 2002, Campus Ministry Communications Brochure, 1995, Who Is My Neighbor? The Stories of Ruth and Jonah, 2003; co-author: Welcome Forward: A Field Guide for Global Travelers, 2005; editor: (electronic newsletter) The RevWriter Resource, 2002—; contbr. chapters to books. Mem. pub. rels. com. New Growth Arts Festival, Indiana, 1994—95; newsletter editor Habitat for Humanity, Indiana, 1993—94; mem. resource and devel. com. Interim Ministry Network, Balt., 2001—02; local coord. for global mission event Evang. Luth. Ch. in Am., Indiana, 1992, del. to nat. ch. assembly Chgo., 1989; mem. synodical women's orgn. N.W. Pa. Synod, Oil City, 1994—96, chairperson leadership support com., 1989—90; pres. Interfaith Coun. at Indiana U. of Pa., 1991—93; mem. social ministry resource team Va. Synod. Luth. Ch. Am., Roanoke, 1981—83. Mem.: Soc. for Advancement of Continuing Edn. in Ministry, Soc. Advancement Contg. Edn., Del. Valley Assn. Psychol. Type, Assn. Psychol. Type, Interim Ministry Network, Pennwriters, The Alban Inst. Avocations: reading, writing, photography, gardening. Office: RevWriter PO Box 81 Perkasie PA 18944 Business E-Mail: sue@revwriter.com.

LANG, THOMPSON HUGHES, publishing company executive; b. Albuquerque, Dec. 12, 1946; s. Cornelius Thompson and Margaret Miller (Hughes) L. Student, U. N.Mex., 1965-68, U. Americas, Mexico City, 1968-69. Advt. salesman Albuquerque Pub. Co., 1969-70, pres., 1971—; pub., pres., treas., dir. Jour. Pub. Co., 1971—; pres., dir. Masthead, Internat., 1971—; pres. Magnum Systems, Inc., 1973—; pres., treas., dir. Jour. Ctr. Corp., 1979—; chmn. bd., dir. Starline Printing, Inc., 1985—. Chmn. bd. dirs. Corp. Security and Investigation, Inc., 1986—; pres., bd. dirs. Eagle Systems, Inc., 1986—. Mem. HOW Orgn., Sigma Delta Chi. Home: 8643 Rio Grande Blvd NW Albuquerque NM 87114-1301 Office: Albuquerque Pub Co PO Drawer JT 87103 7777 Jefferson St NE Albuquerque NM 87109-4343

LANG, WILLIAM CHARLES, retail executive; b. Bronx, N.Y., Jan. 29, 1944; s. Harold C. and Katherine L. (Pratt) L.; m. Marilyn Warshow, June 27, 1965 (dec.); children: Kenneth William, Pamela Sue. BS magna cum laude, Lehigh U., 1965. C.P.A. Accounting supr. Peat, Marwick, Mitchell & Co., 1965-69; contr. Pueblo Internat., Inc., N.Y.C., 1970-72, v.p. fin., 1972-77; exec. v.p. adminstrn. and fin. Kenyon & Eckhardt, Inc., 1977-85; exec. mng. dir. Finley, Kumble, Wagner, Heine, Underberg, Manley, Myerson & Casey, 1985-88; pres., CO, Furr's Inc., Lubbock, Tex., 1989-92; exec. v.p. fin. and adminstrn., chief fin. officer Duane Reade, N.Y.C., 1993-96, chief adminstrv. officer, 1993-96; exec. v.p. fin, CFO, CAO GAF Materials Corp., Wayne, N.J., 1997-2001; prof. acctg., law and taxation Montclair (N.J.) State U., 2001—03. Mem. AICPA, Fin. Execs. Inst., Am. Acctg. Assn., N.Y. State Soc. CPAs, Beta Gamma Sigma, Sigma Phi. E-mail: wlang9@optonline.net.

LANG, WILLIAM WARNER, physicist; b. Boston, Aug. 9, 1926; s. William Warner and Lilla Gertrude (Wheeler) L.; m. Asta Ingard, Aug. 31, 1954; 1 son, Robert. BS, Iowa State U., 1946, PhD, 1958; MS, MIT, 1949. Acoustical engr. Bolt Beranek and Newman, Inc., Cambridge, Mass., 1949-51; instr. in physics U.S. Naval Postgrad. Sch., Monterey, Calif., 1951-55; cons. engr. E.I. du Pont de Nemours & Co., Wilmington, Del., 1955-57; mem. research staff MIT, 1958; physicist IBM, Poughkeepsie, N.Y., 1958-92, program mgr. acoustics tech., 1976-90, mem. sr. tech. staff, 1990-92; pres. Internat. Inst. Noise Control Engring., Leuven, Belgium, 1988—99. Editor: Designing for Noise Control, 1978. Pres. Noise Control Found., Poughkeepsie, 1975-92, 1994—; adj. prof. physics Vassar Coll., 1979-96; chmn. working group Internat. Orgn. Standardization, 1969—; chmn. tech. com. 29

Internat. Electrotech. Commn., 1975-84. Served with USN, 1944-47, 52. Decorated Meritorious Svc. medal; recipient Pro Silentio medal, Hungarian Optical, Acoutstical and Film Tech. Soc., 1989. Fellow AAAS, IEEE (Audio and Electroacoustics Achievement award 1970, dir. 1970-71, Centennial medal 1984), Audio Engring. Soc., Acoustical Soc. Am. (Silver medal 1984, treas. 1994-98), Inst. Acoustics (U.K.) (hon. fellow); mem. Nat. Acad. Engring., Inst. Noise Control Engring./U.S.A. (pres. 1978, chair study team on nat. noise policy 2000—, Disting. Noise Control Engr. award 2002), Rotary (pres. local club 1975-76). Episcopalian. Home and Office: 29 Hornbeck Rdg Poughkeepsie NY 12603-4205 Business E-Mail: langww@noisecontrolfoundation.org.

LANGACKER, PAUL GEORGE, physics professor; b. Evanston, Ill., July 14, 1946; s. George Rollo and Florence (Hinesley) L.; m. Irmgard Sieker, June 25, 1983. BS, MIT, 1968; PhD, U. Calif., Berkeley, 1972; MA, U. Pa., 1981. Postdoctoral assoc. Rockefeller U., N.Y.C., 1972-74, U. Pa., Phila., 1974-75, asst. prof. physics, 1975-81, assoc. prof. physics, 1981-85, prof. physics, 1985-93, 98—, William Smith Term prof. physics, 1993-98, chair, dept. physics and astronomy, 1996-2001. Exec. com. Divsn. Particles & Fields of Am. Phys. Soc., Washington, 1989-91; mem. editorial bd. Phys. Rev., 1986-88, 91-93; sci. dir. Theoretical Advanced Study Inst., Boulder, Colo., 1990, 98. Editor: Testing the Standard Model, 1991, Precision Tests of the Standard Electroweak Model, 1995; divsnl. assoc. editor Phys. Rev. Letters, 1998-2004. Recipient Humboldt award A.V. Humboldt Soc., 1987-88. Fellow Am. Phys. Soc., AAAS. Office: U of Pa Dept of Physics 2N10 David Rittenhouse Lab Philadelphia PA 19104 E-mail: pgl@electroweak.hep.upenn.edu.

LANGACKER, RONALD WAYNE, linguistics educator; b. Fond du Lac, Wis., Dec. 27, 1942; s. George Rollo and Florence (Hinesley) L.; m. Margaret G. Fullick, June 5, 1966 (dec.); m. Sheila M. Pickwell, Mar. 28, 1998. AB in French, U. Ill., 1963, A.M. in Linguistics, 1964, PhD, 1966. Asst. prof. U. Calif. at San Diego, La Jolla, 1966-70, asso. prof., 1970-75, prof. linguistics, 1975—2003; ret. Author: Language and its Structure, 1968, Fundamentals of Linguistic Analysis, 1972, Non-Distinct Arguments in Uto-Aztecan, 1976, An Overview of Uto-Aztecan Grammar, 1977, Foundations of Cognitive Grammar I, 1987, Concept, Image and Symbol, 1990, Foundations of Cognitive Grammar II, 1991, Grammar and Conceptualization, 1999; assoc. editor: Lang, 1971-77, Cognitive Linguistics, 1989—; contbr. articles in field to profl. jours. Guggenheim fellow, 1978 Mem. Linguistic Soc. Am., Cognitive Sci. Soc., Soc. for Study Indigenous Langs. of Ams., Internat. Cognitive Linguistics Assn. (pres. 1997-99), ACLU. Home: 7381 Rue Michael La Jolla CA 92037-3915 Office: U Calif San Diego Dept Linguistics 0108 La Jolla CA 92093 E-mail: rlangacker@ucsd.edu.

LANGAN, KENNETH J., lawyer; b. Sept. 14, 1955; BSFS cum laude, Sch. Fgn Svc., Georgetown Univ., 1977; JD, Columbia Univ., 1980. Bar: N.Y. 1981, Calif. 1993, England & Wales (solicitor) 1998. Ptnr., Project Fin. Practice Group Arnold & Porter, LA. Mem.: Phi Beta Kappa. Office: Arnold & Porter 777 S Figueroa St Los Angeles CA 90017-2513 Office Phone: 213-243-4114. Office Fax: 213-243-4199. Business E-Mail: kenneth.langan@aporter.com.

LANGAN, MARIE-NOELLE SUZANNE, cardiologist, educator; b. White Plains, N.Y., Aug. 4, 1960; Grad., U. Toronto, Can., 1980, MD, 1984. Diplomate Am. Bd. Internal Medicine, Am. Bd. Cardiology, Am. Bd. Clin. Electrophysiology. Intern St. Mary's Hosp./ McGill U., Montreal, Can., 1984-85; resident U. Toronto/ St. Michael's Hosp., 1985-87; cardiology fellow Phila. Heart Inst./ U. Pa. Med. Ctr., 1988-90, 1990-91; clin. instr. medicine Sch. Medicine U. Pa., 1988-89, fellow dept. medicine, 1990-91; asst. prof. medicine, dir. electrophysiology lab. George Washington U., Washington, 1991-93; asst. prof. medicine Mt. Sinai Med. Ctr., N.Y.C. Contbr. chpts. to books and articles to profl. jours. Fellow Am. Coll. Cardiology, Royal Coll. Physicians and Surgeons Can.; mem. N.Am. Soc. Pacing and Electrophysiology, Am. Heart Assn. (Clinician Scientist award 1996), Coll. Physicians and Surgeons Can. Office: Mt Sinai Med Ctr 1 Gustave L Levy Pl Box 1054 New York NY 10028-0007

LANGAN, RICHARD F., JR., lawyer; b. Darby, Pa., 1955; BA magna cum laude, Fordham U., 1977; JD, George Washington U., 1980. Ptnr., chair Bus. & Fin. Dept. Nixon Peabody LLP, NYC. Dir. Minetta Brook. Mem.: ABA, Assn. Bar of City NY (mem. securities regulations com. 2001—05, fin. reporting com. 2005—), Phi Beta Kappa. Office: Nixon Peabody LLP 437 Madison Ave New York NY 10022-7001 Office Phone: 212-940-3140. Office Fax: 866-947-2436. Business E-Mail: rlangan@nixonpeabody.com.

LANGBAUM, ROBERT WOODROW, language educator; b. NYC, Feb. 23, 1924; s. Murray and Nettie (Moskowitz) L.; m. Francesca Levi Vidale, Nov. 5, 1950; 1 child, Donata Emily. AB, Cornell U., 1947; MA, Columbia U., 1949, PhD, 1954. Instr. English Cornell U., 1950-55, asst. prof., 1955-60; assoc. prof. U. Va., Charlottesville, 1960-63, prof. English, 1963—99, James Branch Cabell prof. English and Am. lit., prof. emeritus, 1999—. Vis. prof. Columbia U., summer 1960, 65-66, Harvard U., summer 1965; mem. supervising com. English Inst., 1970-71, chmn., 1972; mem. Christian Gauss Book Award Com., 1984-86; U.S. Info. Svc. lectr. Japan, Taiwan, Hong Kong, 1988. Author: The Poetry of Experience: The Dramatic Monologue in Modern Literary Tradition, 1957 (Spanish trans. 1996), The Gayety of Vision: A Study of Isak Dinesen's Art (Danish trans. 1964), 1964, The Modern Spirit: Essays on the Continuity of Nineteenth and Twentieth Century Literature, 1970, The Mysteries of Identity: A Theme in Modern Literature, 1977, The Word From Below: Essays on Modern Literature and Culture, 1987, Thomas Hardy in Our Time, 1995; editor: The Tempest (Shakespeare), 1964; anthology The Victorian Age: Essays in History and in Social and Literary Criticism, 1967; mem. editl. bd. Victorian Poetry, 1963—, New Lit. History, 1969—, Bull. Rsch. in Humanities, 1977—, Studies in English Lit., 1978—, So. Humanities Rev., 1979—, Studies in Browning and His Circle, 1987—, Victorian Lit. and Culture, 1991—, Symbiosis, 1995—. Served to 1st lt. M.I. AUS, 1942-46. Ford Found. fellow Center for Advanced Study, Stanford, Calif., 1961-62; Guggenheim fellow, 1969-70, Sr. fellow Nat. Endowment for Humanities, 1972-73; Am. Council Learned Socs. grantee, 1961, 75-76; fellow Clare Hall, Cambridge U., Eng., 1978; U. Va. Ctr. Advanced Study fellow, 1982; resident scholar Bellagio Study and Conf. Ctr. Rockefeller Found., Italy, 1987. Mem. MLA (del. assembly 1979-81), AAUP, PEN, Assn. Lit. Scholars and Critics, Phi Beta Kappa. Home: 223 Montvue Dr Charlottesville VA 22901-2022 Business E-Mail: rwl8v@virginia.edu.

LANGBEIN, JOHN HARRISS, lawyer, educator; b. Washington, Nov. 17, 1941; s. I. L. and M. V. (Harriss) L.; m. Kirsti M. Hiekka, June 24, 1973; children: Christopher, Julia, Anne. AB, Columbia U., 1964; LLB, Harvard U., 1968, Cambridge U., 1969, PhD, 1971; MA (hon.), Yale U., 1990. Bar: D.C. 1969, Fla. 1970; barrister-at-law Inner Temple, Eng., 1970. Asst. prof. law U. Chgo., 1971-73, assoc. prof., 1973-74, prof., 1974-80, Max Pam prof. Am. and fgn. law, 1980-90; Goodhart Prof. Legal Sci. Cambridge Univ., 1997-98, Chancellor Kent prof., 1990—2001; Sterling prof. law and legal history Yale U., New Haven, 2001—. Commr. Nat. Conf. Commrs. on Uniform State Laws, 1984—; reporter Uniform Prudent Investor Act; assoc. reporter Am. Law Inst., Restatement of Property (3d): Wills and Other Donative Transfers, 1990—. Author: Prosecuting Crime in the Renaissance, 1974, Torture and the Law of Proof: Europe and England in the Ancient Regime, 1977, Comparative Criminal Procedure, 1977, The Origins of Adversary Criminal Trial, 2003; author: (with L. Waggoner) Uniform Trusts and Estate Statutes, rev. edit., 2005; author: (with R. Helmholz et al.) The Privilege Against Self-Incrimination, 1997; author: (with B. Wolk) Pension and Employee Benefit Law, 1990, 1995, 2000; contbr. articles to profl. jours. Fellow Trinity Hall Cambridge U. (hon.); mem. ABA, Am. Acad. Arts. and Scis., Am. Coll. Trust and Estate Counsel, Am. Law Inst., Am. Soc. Legal History, Am. Hist. Assn., Selden Soc., Gesellschaft fuer Rechtsvergleichung, Internat. Acad. Estate and Trust Law, Internat. Acad. Comparative Law. Republican. Episcopalian. Office: Yale Univ Sch Law PO Box 208215 127 Wall St New Haven CT 06520-8215 Office Phone: 203-432-7299. Business E-Mail: john.langbein@yale.edu.

LANGBERG, BARRY BENSON, lawyer; b. Balt., Nov. 24, 1942; s. Nathan and Marion (Cohen) L.; m. Vickie Williams, Mar. 27, 1978 (div. 1987); children: Mitchell, Marie, Elena. BA, U. San Francisco, 1964, JD, 1968. Bar: Calif. 1971, U.S. Dist. Ct. (cen. dist.) Calif. 1971, U.S. Supreme Ct. 1974, U.S. Tax Ct. 1976. Dep. pub. defender Los Angeles County, 1971-72; assoc. Trope & Trope, L.A., 1972-74, Hayes & Hume, Beverly Hills, Calif., 1974-85; pres. David Jamison Carlyle Corp., L.A., 1979-84; ptnr. Hayes, Hume, Petas & Langberg, L.A., 1985-89; atty. Barry B. Langberg & Assocs., L.A., 1989-97; ptnr. Bronson, Bronson & McKinnon, L.A., 1997—2000; mng. ptnr., LA office, entertainment law practice area Stroock & Stroock & Lavan LLP, L.A., 2000—. Prof. Mid-Valley Coll. Law, L.A., 1972-82; lectr. U. So. Calif., 1980. Mem. ABA. Democrat. Avocations: sailing, baseball. Office: Stroock & Strook & Lavan LLP 2029 Century Pk E Los Angeles CA 90067-3086 Office Phone: 310-556-5861. Office Fax: 310-556-5959. Business E-Mail: blangberg@stroock.com.

LANGBO, ARNOLD GORDON, former food company executive; b. Richmond, B.C., Can., Apr. 13, 1937; s. Osbjourn and Laura Marie (Hagen) Langbo; m. Martha Marie Miller, May 30, 1959; children: Sharon Anne, Maureen Bernice, Susan Colleen, Roderick Arnold, Robert Wayne, Gary Thomas, Craig Peter, Keith Edward. Student, U. B.C. Retail salesman Kellogg Co., Vancouver, 1956-57, dist. mgr. Prince George, B.C., 1957-60, supermarket salesman Vancouver, 1960, dist mgr. Winnipeg, Man., 1964-65; acct. mgr. Kellog Co. of Can., Ltd., Toronto, 1965-67; sales staff asst. Kellogg Co., Battle Creek, Mich., 1967-69, adminstrv. asst. to pres., 1969; exec. v.p. Kellogg Co. of Can. Ltd., London, Ont., 1970; v.p. sales and mktg. Kellogg Salada Can. Ltd., Toronto, 1971-74, sr. v.p. sales and mktg., 1974-76, pres., CEO, 1976-78; pres. food products divsn. Kellogg U.S., Battle Creek, 1978-81; group exec. v.p. Kellogg Co., Battle Creek, 1983-86, exec. v.p., 1986—; pres. Mrs. Smith's Frozen Foods Co. subs. Kellogg Co., Battle Creek, 1983-85, chmn., CEO, 1985—86; pres. Kellogg Internat., 1986—90, pres., COO, internat. bd. dirs., 1990-99; chmn., CEO, pres. Kellogg Co., Battle Creek, 1992-99, also bd. dirs., retired, 1999. Bd. dirs. Johnson & Johnson, 1991—, Whirlpool Corp., 1994—, Weyerhaeuser Co., 1999—, Atlantic Richfield Co.; chmn. Grocery Mfrs. Am. Co-trustee W.K. Kellogg Found. Trust; chmn. trustees Albion Coll. Bd.; bd. dirs. Internat. Youth Found., America's Promise; mem. adv. bd. J.K. Kellogg Grad. Sch. of Mgmt., Northwestern U. Mem.: Bus. Roundtable.

LANGBORT, POLLY, retired advertising executive; b. N.Y.C. d. Julius and Nettie (Berman) L. BA, Adelphi U. Sec. Young & Rubicam, Inc., N.Y.C., media buyer, media planner, 1960-65, planning supr., 1965-70, v.p. group supr., 1970-75, v.p. dir. planning devel., 1975-80, sr. v.p., dir. planning, 1980-85, sr. v.p. direct mktg. and media services Wunderman, Worldwide div., 1985-86, exec. v.p. dir. mktg. & media services, 1986-90; assoc. pub. Lear's Mag., N.Y.C., 1990-91; ret., 1991. Author: DMA Factbook, 1986; contbr. articles to profl. jours. Spl. gifts chairperson Am. Cancer Soc., N.Y.C., 1985-90. Mem. Boca Raton Resort and Club, Boca Pointe Country Club. Avocations: classical music, outdoor activities, bridge. Home: 7614 La Corniche Cir Boca Raton FL 33433-6055 Personal E-mail: pollylang@aol.com.

LANGDALE, EMORY LAWRENCE, retired physician; b. Walterboro, S.C., Oct. 14, 1919; s. Clint May and Lillian Blanch (Reddish) L.; m. Maggie Lee Herndon (dec. 1971); children: Fred Emory, Betty Marlene, Thomas Wayne, Emory Lawrence, Jr.; m. Annie Newell Smith, Feb. 17, 1973. BS, Coll. Charleston, 1949; MD, Med. U. S.C., 1953. Diplomate Am. Acad. Phys. Medicine and Rehab. Resident VA Hosp., Richmond, Va., 1963-66; chief rehab. medicine VA Med. Ctr., Hampton, Va., 1966-69; asst. prof. physical medicine and rehab. Med. Coll. Va., Richmond, 1969-74; med. officer Charleston (S.C.) Regional Naval Hosp., 1974-76; chief rehab. medicine VA Med. Ctr., Augusta, Ga., 1974-81; assoc. prof. Med. U. S.C., 1981-85; med. dir. Rehab. Svc. Colleton Rsch. Hosp., Walterboro, SC, 1987-91; pvt. practice North Charleston, SC, 1989—2004; ret., 2003. With Coast Guard, 1942-45, ATO, PTO. Fellow Am. Acad. Phys. Medicine and Rehab.; mem. AMA (Physician's Recognition award 1980), Med. Soc. Va., S.C. Med. Assn., So. Soc. Phys. Medicine and Rehab., Charleston County Med. Soc. Republican. Baptist. Avocations: hunting, fishing. Home: 1064 Stonehenge Dr Charleston SC 29406-2417 Office: 1064 Stonehenge Dr Hanahan SC 29406-2417

LANGDALE, NOAH NOEL, JR., retired education educator, retired academic administrator; b. Valdosta, Ga., Mar. 29, 1920; s. Noah N. and Jessie Katharine (Catledge) Langdale; m. Alice Elizabeth Cabaniss, Jan. 8, 1944; 1 child, Noah Michael. AB, U. Ala., 1941, LLD, 1959; LLB, Harvard U., 1948, MBA, 1950. Bar: Ga. 1951. Asst. football coach U. Ala., 1942; pvt. practice law Valdosta, 1951-57; from instr. to asst. prof. econs. and social studies, chmn. dept. acctg., econs., bus. adminstrn. Valdosta State Coll., 1954-57; pres. Ga. State U., Atlanta, 1957-88, Disting. univ. rsch. prof., 1988-89, pres. emeritus, disting. rsch. prof. emeritus, 1989—; ret., 1989. Past mem. U.S. Adv. Comm. Ednl. Exch.; former mem. Pres.'s Commn. NCAA. Served to lt. (s.g.) USNR, 1942—46. Recipient 1st Georgian of the Yr. award, Ga. Assn. Broadcasters, 1962, Silver Anniversary All-Am. award, Sports Illustrated, 1966, Myrtle Wreath award, Hadassah, 1970, Salesman of the Yr. award, Sales and Mktg. Execs. Atlanta, 1975, Silver Knight of Mgmt. award, Lockheed-Ga. chpt. Nat. Mgmt. Assn., 1978, Humanitarian award, Nat. Jewish Hosp. and Rsch. Ctr./Nat. Asthma Ctr., 1980, Robert T. Jones award, Boy Scouts Am. Mem.: SAR (past v.p. Ga.), ABA, Ga. Assn. Colls. (pres. 1962—63), Ga. Bar Assn., Ga. Bar Found. (life), Rotary, Gridiron Soc., Phi Beta Kappa, Phi Kappa Phi, Delta Chi, Omicron Delta Kappa. Methodist.

LANGDON, JAMES C., JR., lawyer; b. LA, Sept. 20, 1945; BBA, U. Tex., 1967, JD, 1970. Bar: Tex. 1970, D.C. 1976. Assoc. adminstr. Fed. Energy Office, Washington, 1972-73, Fed. Energy Adminstrn., Washington, 1973-74; dir. Office Comml. Affairs Dept. Treasury, Washington, 1974-75; mem. Akin Gump Strauss Hauer & Feld LLP, Washington, 1975—, now sr. exec. ptnr. energy-related issues and mem. mgmt. com. Washington, Texas, Moscow; and prin. AG Global Solutions (joint venture of Akin Gump and First Internat. Resources). Mem. ABA, State Bar Tex., DC Bar. Office: Akin Gump Strauss Hauer & Feld LLP Ste 400 1333 New Hampshire Ave NW Washington DC 20036-1564 Office Phone: 202-887-4044. Office Fax: 202-955-7758. Business E-Mail: jlangdon@akingump.com.

LANGE, ANDREW E., astrophysicist; BA, Princeton U., 1980; PhD, U. Calif., Berkeley, 1987. Vis. assoc. Calif. Inst. Tech., 1993—94, prof., 1994—2001, Marvin L. Goldberger prof. physics, Observational Cosmology Group, 2001—. Named Calif. Scientist Yr., Calif. Sci. Ctr., 2003. Mem.: Nat. Acad. Scis. Achievements include expert in structure and geometry of very early universe and in measurement of irregularities in cosmic microwave background radiation. Office: Calif Inst Tech m/C 59-33 Pasadena CA 91125 Business E-Mail: ael@astro.caltech.edu.

LANGE, CARL JAMES, retired psychology professor; b. Seneca, Pa., June 1, 1925; s. Otto Carl and Rose Marie (Jetter) L.; m. Veronica Szelypecz, Jan. 14, 1950; children: David Carl, Veronica Jean. BS, Duke U., 1945; MS, U. Pitts., 1948, PhD, 1951. Lic. psychologist, Va. Project dir. Human Resources Research Office, George Washington U., 1953-60, dir. research, planning, 1960-69; asst. v.p. research George Washington U., 1969-75, v.p. adminstrn., research, prof. psychology, 1975-88, v.p. rsch., prof. psychology, 1988-89, prof. emeritus, 1989—. Cons. NSF, Ford Found.; bd. dirs. Sch. for Contemporary Edn., Nat. Lab. Higher Edn., Eric Clearinghouse for Higher Edn., Southeastern Univs. Rsch. Assn. Contbr. articles in field to profl. jours.; bd. editors: Research in Higher Education. Served with USN, 1943-45. Fellow Am. Psychol. Assn.; mem. AAAS, Sigma Xi. Home: 7 Clarendon Ct Williamsburg VA 23188-1513

LANGE, CHRISTOPHER STEPHEN, radiation biophysics educator; b. Chgo., Feb. 11, 1940; s. Oscar Richard and Irene Alice (Oderfeld) L.; m. Kathleen Gale Johnson, June 24, 1964 (div. Nov. 1971); 1 child, Tamara Alice Merry; m. Eleanor Esther Gitlin, Sept. 21, 1973; 1 child, Theodore Oskar. BS in Physics, MIT, 1961; DPhil, Oxford U., 1968. MRC rsch. asst. radiobiology lab. Churchill Hosp., Headington, England, 1961—62; NHS rsch. officer Christie Hosp. and Holt Radium Inst., Manchester, England, 1962—68, NHS sr. rsch. officer, 1968—69; asst. prof. radiology, radiation biology and biophysics U. Rochester Sch. of Medicine and Dentistry, NY, 1969—80; prof., dir. radiobiol. div. dept. radiation oncology SUNY Health Sci. Ctr., Bklyn., 1980—, prof. molecular and cell biology, Sch. Grad. Studies, 1992—. Guest scientist Brookhaven Nat. Lab., Upton, N.Y., 1983-; mem. translational rsch. and path. coms. radiation therapy oncology group NCI/NIH, Phila., 1988-; mem. scholarship adv. com. Koscuiszko Found., N.Y.C., 1989-; mem. NIH/DRG Spl. Rev. Sect. 2, 1993; mem. bd. dirs. Sigma Xi Internat. Sci. Rsch. Soc., 1995-2005, mem. exec. com., 2002-05. Contbr. over 100 rsch. articles to Internat. Jour. Radiation Biology, Radiation Rsch., Biopolymers, Exptl. Cell Rsch., others, also chpts. to books. Zone chmn. Manhasset (N.Y.) Zone Dem. Party, 1987—; mem. exec. com. Town of North Hempstead (N.Y.) Dem. Party, 1988—, Nassau County (N.Y.) Dem. Party, 1988—. Decorated knight's cross Order of Service to the Republic of Poland, 2004; grantee NIH/Nat. Cancer Inst./Nat. Inst. Gen. Med. Scis., NSF, Mather's Found., Royal Soc. London, U.S. Dept. of Energy, 1966—; recipient Presdl. cert. of gratitude, U. Hirosaki, Japan, 1979, Rsch. Career Devel. award HEW, 1972-77. Mem. AAAS, N.Y. Acad. Scis., Radiation Rsch. Soc., Biophys. Soc., Sigma Xi (chpt. treas. 1993—), Omicron Delta Epsilon. Mem. Soc. Of Friends. Achievements include research in cellular basis of organismal radiation lethality, cellular theory of aging, demonstration of DNA double-strand break repair in mammalian cells, demonstration of shoulder of survival curve for reproductive integrity as being due to repair processes; measurement of size and shape of mammalian chromosomal DNA molecules; demonstration of mammalian interphase chromosome conformation as a chain of loop cluster; demonstration that cell survival occurs predictable from DNA double-strand brake rejoining kinetics. Office: SUNY Downstate Med Ctr Dept Radiation Oncology 450 Clarkson Ave # 1212 Brooklyn NY 11203-2056 Office Phone: 718-270-1050. Business E-Mail: clange@downstate.edu.

LANGE, CLIFFORD E., librarian; b. Fond du Lac, Wis., Dec. 29, 1935; s. Elmer H. and Dorothy Brick (Smithers) L.; m. Janet M. LeMieux, June 6, 1959; children: Paul, Laura, Ruth. Student, St. Norbert Coll., 1954-57; BS, Wis. State U., 1959; MSL.S. (Library Services Act scholar), U. Wis., 1960, PhD (Higher Edn. Act fellow), 1972. Head extension dept. Oshkosh (Wis.) Pub. Libr., 1960-62, head reference dept., 1962-63; asst. dir. Jervis Libr., Rome, 1962; dir. Eau Claire (Wis.) Pub. Libr., 1963-66; asst. dir. Lake County Pub. Libr., Griffith, Ind., 1966-68; asst. prof. Sch. Libr. Sci., U. Iowa, 1971-73; dir. Wauwatosa (Wis.) Pub. Libr., 1973-75; asst. prof. U. So. Calif., 1975-78; state libr. N.Mex. State Libr., Santa Fe, 1978-82; dir. Carlsbad City Libr., Calif., 1982—2005. Served with U.S. Army, 1958. Mem. ALA, Calif. Libr. Assn. Home: 3575 Ridge Rd Oceanside CA 92056-4952 Office: 1775 Dove Ln Carlsbad CA 92009-4048 Office Phone: 760-602-2010. Business E-Mail: clang@ci.carlsbad.ca.us.

LANGE, DALE LOWELL, language educator, researcher; b. Granite Falls, Minn., Nov. 4, 1934; m. Estella Marie Gahala, Apr. 18, 1998; m. Sylvia Ann Martinsen, Apr. 30, 1957 (div. Apr. 23, 1981); m. Linda Marie Crawford, July 11, 1981 (div. Mar. 20, 1992); children: Bryan Andre, Stefan Peter, Erik David, Kevin Mark, Kristofer Brent, Sara Stephanie, Heather Ann. BS, U. Minn., 1958, MA, 1963, PhD, 1966. Tchg. asst. German dept., NDEA Inst. Stanford (Calif.) U., 1960, instr. German dept., NDEA Inst., 1961; instr. U. H.S., Coll. Edn., U. Minn., Mpls., 1958—65, lectr., 1965—66; asst. prof. dept. secondary edn. Coll. Edn. U. Minn.-Twin Cities, Mpls., 1966—69, assoc. prof. dept. secondary edn. Coll. Edn., 1969—72, prof. dept. curriculum and instrn. Coll. Edn., 1972—99, assoc. dean for academic affairs Coll. Edn., 1989—94, dir. Ctr. for Advanced Rsch. on Lang. Acquistion, 1994—95, prof. emeritus Coll. Edn. and Human Devel., 1999—. Presenter in field. Co-editor: Foreign Language Learning Today and Tomorrow: Essays in Honor of Emma M. Birkmaier, 1979, Culture as the Core: Perspectives on Culture in Second Language Learning, 2003; contbr. articles to profl. publs. Docent Albuquerque Mus. Art and History, 1996—2000; bd. mem., v.p., sec./treas. Art in the Sch., Inc, Albuquerque, 2001—05. Recipient Emma Birkmaier award for Svc. to Fgn. Lang. in the State of Minn., Minn. Coun. on the Tchg. Fgn. Langs. and Cultures, 1981; scholar NDEA Inst., U. Texas,Austin, 1959, Stanford U., 1960. Mem.: MLA, Am. Assn. Tchrs. French, Am. Assn. Tchrs. German, Am. Edn. Rsch. Assn., Am. Coun. on the Tchg. Fgn. Langs. (bibliographer 1969—73, pres. 1980—80). Dfl. Avocations: genealogy, art collecting, gardening, music. Home: 2315 Madre Drive NE Albuquerque NM 87112-2503 Office Phone: 505-298-9138. Home Fax: 505-298-9138; Office Fax: 505-298-0307. Personal E-mail: dalelange@aol.com.

LANGE, ELIZABETH ANN, retired librarian; b. Webster, S.D., Sept. 20, 1938; d. Martin Gustave and Mabelle Emma Lou (Reich) L. BS, No. State U., Aberdeen, S.D., 1960; MA, U. Minn., 1970. Cataloger Iowa State U. Library, Ames, 1961-68, head catalog dept., 1968-72; head catalog div. U. Minn. Libraries, Mpls., 1972-79; asst. dir. tech. services U. S.C. Libraries, Columbia, 1979-89; dean libr. Winona (Minn.) State U., 1989—93; ret., 1993. Mem. ALA (chmn. elect catalog norms discussion group 1976). Home: 1914 Waterford Pl SW Rochester MN 55902-4281

LANGE, FREDERICK EDWARD, JR., computer information systems architect; b. Johnstown, Pa., Oct. 21, 1946; s. Frederick Edward and Jean Louise (Huebner) L.; m. Karen Ann Mawson, Mar. 15, 1975; 1 child, Sharon Ann. BA in Social Scis., Cleve. State U., 1969, MA in Econs., 1978. Cert. secondary tchr., Ohio. Vol. Peace Corps, Liberia and Micronesia, 1969-73; tchr. Cleve. Pub. Schs., 1973-74; dir. Westside Inst. Tech., Cleve., 1974-81; systems analyst Case Western Res. U., Cleve., 1982-83; systems engr. Profl. Support, Inc., Brecksville, Ohio, 1983-91; analyst Setpoint, Brecksville, 1991-93; prin. cons. Cap Gemini Am., Beechwood, Ohio, 1994-96; sr. prin. cons. Oracle Corp., Cleve., 1996—2001; info. arch. Nat. City Corp., Highland Hills, Ohio, 2001—03, Key Corp., Cleve., 2004—, Key Bank, Cleve., 2005—; cons., 2003—04; ind. cons. in field. Bd. dirs. Zoe, Inc., Cleve., Fast Refund Svc. Editor: Fuel Efficiency and Safety, 1979; contbr. Data Mgmt. Rev. Mem. Richmond Heights (Ohio) Civic League, 1986, Northeast Ohio Returned Vol. Assn. (Beyond War award 1987), Cleve., 1978—, Nat. Peace Corps Assn.; judge Internat. Sci. and Engring. Fair Grand Awards, 2003. Mem. Am. Econs. Assn., Data Processing Mgmt. Assn., Assn. Computing Machinery, Instument Soc. Am. (Dedicated Svc. award 1980), Javelin Class Assn. (fleet capt. 1982-83, sec. 1987-88, commodore 1989-91), Forest City Yacht Club. Avocations: sailing, gardening, genealogy. E-mail: fredklange@aol.com, fred_lange@keybank.com.

LANGE, JESSICA PHYLLIS, actress; b. Cloquet, Minn., Apr. 20, 1949; d. Al and Dorothy Lange; m. Paco Grande, 1970 (div. 1981); 1 child with Mikhail Baryshnikov, Alexandra; children with Sam Shepard: Hannah Jane, Samuel Walker Student, U. Minn.; student mime, with Etienne DeCroux, Paris. Dancer Opera Comique, Paris; model Wilhelmina Agy., N.Y.C. Film appearances include King Kong, 1976, All That Jazz, 1979, How to Beat the High Cost of Living, 1980, The Postman Always Rings Twice, 1981, Frances, 1982 (Acad. award nominee 1982), Tootsie, 1982 (Acad. award 1983), Country, 1984, Sweet Dreams, 1985, Crimes of the Heart, 1986 (Acad. award nominee 1987), Everybody's All American, 1988, Far North, 1988, Music Box, 1989 (Acad. award nominee 1990), Men Don't Leave, 1990, Cape Fear, 1991, Night and the City, 1992, Blue Sky, 1994 (Golden Globe award Best Actress in a Drama 1995, Acad. award for Best Actress 1995), Losing Isaiah, 1995, Rob Roy, 1995, A Thousand Acres, 1997, Hush, 1998, Cousin Bette, 1998, Titus, 1999, Big Fish, 2003, Broken Flowers, 2005, Don't Come Knocking, 2005; TV movies: Cat on a Hot Tin Roof, 1984, O' Pioneers!, 1992, A Streetcar Named Desire, 1995 (Golden Globe award 1996), Prozac Nation, 2001, Normal, 2003; in summer stock prodn. Angel on My Shoulder,

N.C., 1980, A Streetcar Named Desire, 1992; prodr. Country, 1984; TV guest appearance Inside the Actors Studio, 1994; theatre: The Glass Menagerie, 2005. Mailing: c/o Barrymore Theatre 243 West 47th St New York NY 10036*

LANGE, LESTER HENRY, mathematics professor; b. Concordia, Mo., Jan. 2, 1924; s. Harry William Christopher and Ella Martha (Alewel) L.; m. Anne Marie Pelikan, Aug. 17, 1947 (div. Oct. 1960); children: Christopher, Nicholas, Philip, Alexander; m. Beverly Jane Brown, Feb. 4, 1962; 1 son, Andrew. Student, U. Calif., Berkeley, 1943-44; BA in Math, Valparaiso U., 1948; MS in Math, Stanford, 1950; PhD in Math, U. Notre Dame, 1960. Instr., then asst. prof. math. Valparaiso U., 1950-56; instr. math. U. Notre Dame, 1956-57, 59-60. Mem. faculty San Jose State U., Calif., 1960—, prof. math., head dept., 1961-70, dean Sch. Natural Scis. and Math., 1970—, dean Sch. Sci., 1972-88, emeritus prof. math., emeritus dean, 1988—; founder Soc. Archimedes at San Jose State U., 1982; now spl. asst. to dir. Moss Landing (Calif.) Marine Labs.; founding bd. dirs. Friends of MLML, Inc. Author text on linear algebra; sr. editor Calif. Math, 1981-84; contbr. to profl. jours. Served with inf. AUS, 1943-46, ETO. Decorated Combat Infantryman's Badge and Bronze Star; Danforth fellow, 1957-58; NSF faculty fellow, 1958-59. Fellow Calif. Acad. Scis.; mem. Math. Assn. Am. (bd. govs., L.R. Ford Sr. award 1972, George Polya award 1993, Meritorious Svc. award 2003), Calif. Math. Coun., London Math. Soc., Fibonacci Assn. (bd. dirs. 1987-97). Home: 308 Escalona Dr Capitola CA 95010-3419 Office: Moss Landing Marine Labs Moss Landing CA 95039 E-mail: lange@cruzio.com.

LANGE, LIZ STEINBERG, apparel designer and executive; b. N.Y. m. Jeffrey Lange; 2 children. BA in Comparative Lit., Brown U., 1988. Asst. editor Vogue; fashion designer Stephen DiGeronimo; founder Liz Lange Maternity Clothing Line, N.Y.C., 1997—. Office: Liz Lange Maternity Corp Office 2nd Fl 347 W 36th St New York NY 10018

LANGE, PETER, academic administrator; BA, Oberlin Coll., 1967; PhD in Polit. Sci., MIT, 1975. Assoc. prof. Duke U., Durham, NC, 1982—89, prof., 1989—, spl. asst. to the provost for internat. affairs, 1993—94, vice provost for acad. and internat. affairs, 1994—96, chair dept. polit. sci., 1996—99, provost, 1999—. Woodrow Wilson fellow, 1967, Fulbright Rsch. scholar, Milan, 1986. Office: Duke Univ Office of the Provost Box 90005 Durham NC 27708

LANGE, PHIL C., retired education educator; b. North Freedom, Wis., Feb. 26, 1914; s. Richard Samuel and Martha (Grosinske) L.; m. Irene Oyen, June 8, 1940; children— Dena Rae, Richard (dec.). BA, U. Wis., 1934, MA, 1936, PhD, 1941. Tchr. Reeseville (Wis.) Pub. Sch., 1935-37; chmn. English dept. Wayland Jr. Coll. and Acad., Beaver Dam, Wis., 1937-39; instr. English, student teaching supr. Beloit (Wis.) High Sch., 1939-40; asst. instr. U. Wis., Madison, 1940-41, summers 1938, 39; chmn. psychology dept., dean men. Ariz. State Coll., Flagstaff, 1941-42; chmn. edn. dept. SUNY, Fredonia, 1942-50; prof. edn., coordinator student teaching Tchrs. Coll., Columbia U., 1950—. Cons., expert for Dept. State, UNESCO, AID, 1948, Korea, 1958-59, Chile, 1970, India, Pakistan, 1972-73, Afghanistan. Author, editor curriculum materials. Coord. Issues and Ideas program Cmty. Ch. Coll. Served with USNR, 1943-46. Recipient Filmstrip award Graphic Arts, 1966; Communication award Nat. Soc. Programmed Instrn., 1968; award Ednl. Press Assn. Am., 1969 Home: Lake Towers Apt 764 101 Trinity Lakes Dr Sun City Center FL 33573-5755 Office: Tchrs Coll Columbia Univ New York NY 10027

LANGE, RON Q., music educator; b. Waco, Tex., July 18, 1955; s. Leo Clarence and Ouida Joy Lange; m. Sharolyn K. Adams, Sept. 19, 1961; children: Casey, Samantha. B in Music Edn., U. Tex., El Paso, 1979. Tchg. cert. Alaska, Tex. Choral dir. Grand Prairie (Tex.) H.S., 1985—91, Plainview (Tex.) H.S., 1992—94, Chugiak H.S., Eagle River, Alaska, 1995—. Mem. music curriculum com. Anchorage Sch. Dist., 1999—2002; member music book adoption com. Ysleta Ind. Sch. Dist., El Paso, 1981—82; choral dir. First Presbyn. Ch., Anchorage, 2000—02, Joy Luth., Eagle River, 1994—96; commr. Arts Adv. Commn., Anchorage, 2000—02. Named Alaska Tchr. of the Year 1st Alt., Dept. Edn. State of Alaksa, 2001, Tchr. of Excellence, British Petroleum, 1999; recipient CREATE award, Municipality of Anchorage, 1998. Mem.: NEA, Am. Choral Dirs. Assn., Music Educators Nat. Conf., Anchorage Educators Assn., Alaska Choral Dirs. Assn. (president elect 2002—), Alaska Music Educators Assn. (region rep. 2000—02). Home: 17470 Beaujolais Cr Eagle River AK 99577 Office: Chugiak HS S Birchwood Exit Eagle River AK 99577 Personal E-mail: lange@gci.net.

LANGE, WILLIAM MICHAEL, lawyer; b. Hammond, Ind., Oct. 9, 1946; s. William Frederick L.; m. Nancy A. White, 1 child, William Robert. BA, Ind. U., 1968; JD, George Washington U., 1974. Bar: D.C. 1975, Colo. 1977, U.S. Ct. Appeals (D.C. cir.) 1975, U.S. Ct. Appeals (10th cir.) 1977, U.S. Ct. Appeals (5th cir.) 1984, U.S. Supreme Ct. 1982, U.S. Ct. Appeals (3d cir.) 1988, U.S. Ct. Appeals (7th cir.) 1989, U.S. Ct. Appeals (6th cir.) 1989, U.S. Ct. Appeals (2d cir.) 1997. Assoc. Wolf & Case, Washington, 1974-75, J.R. Wolf, Washington, 1975-76; atty. Colo. Interstate Gas Co., Colorado Springs, 1976-79, sr. atty., 1979-82, gen. atty., 1982-84, asst. gen. counsel, 1984-87, The Coastal Corp., 1985—87; assoc. gen. counsel ANR Pipeline Co., 1986-87; pvt. practice, 1987; asst. gen. counsel Consumers Energy Co.; gen. coun. Mich. Gas Storage Co., 1987—2002; asst. gen. coun. CMS Enterprises, 2001—02, asst. gen. counsel, 2001—02; of counsel Pillsbury Winthrop LLP, Washington, 2002—04. Lt. (j.g.) USN, 1968-71, Vietnam. Independent. Episcopalian. E-mail: wmlange@bellsouth.net.

LANGEJANS, CALVIN PAUL, music educator; b. Holland, Mich., Dec. 17, 1936; s. John and Esther Langejans; m. Yvonne Carol Tubergen, Oct. 18, 1956; children: Thomas Jay, William Jon, Susan Joy, Mary Jo, Robert James. BA, Hope Coll., 1958; M in Music Edn., U. Mich., 1959. Avocations: tennis, model building, walking, gardening, gardening. Home: 3290 Hollywood Dr Holland MI 49424 Office: Evergreen Commons 480 State St Holland MI 49423 Office Phone: 616-355-5158. E-mail: calvon@wmol.co=m.

LANGELLA, FRANK, actor; b. Bayonne, N.J., Jan. 1, 1940; m. Ruth Weil, Nov. 1977. Student, Syracuse U.; studies with Seymour Falk. Apprenticed Pocono Playhouse, Mountain Home, Pa., appeared Erie (Pa.) Playhouse, 1960, mem. original, Lincoln Center repertory tng. co., 1963; actor (Broadway shows) Yerma, 1966, Seascape, 1974-75 (Tony award best featured actor, 1975, Drama Desk award, 1975), A Cry of Players, 1968 (Drama Desk award, 1968), Dracula, 1977-80 (Drama League award, 1978, Tony nom. best actor in a play, 1978), Passion, 1983, Design for Living, 1984, Hurlyburly, 1985, Sherlock's Last Case, 1987, The Father, 1996, Present Laughter, 1996-97, Fortune's Fool, 2002, Match, 2004 (Tony nom. best actor in a play, 2004); other stage appearances include: The Immoralist, 1963, Benito Cereno, 1964, The Old Glory, 1964-65 (Obie award, 1965), Good Day, 1965-66 (Obie award, 1966), The White Devil, 1965-66 (Obie award, 1966), Long Day's Journey Into Night, The Skin of Our Teeth, The Cretan Woman, all 1966, The Devils, Iphigenia at Aulis, all 1967, Cyrano de Bergerac, 1971, A Midsummer Night's Dream, 1972, The Relapse, The Tooth of Crime, 1972, The Taming of the Shrew, 1973, The Seagull, 1974, Ring Round the Moon, 1975, After the Fall, 1984, Booth, 1994, The Prince of Hamburg, Cleve. Playhouse Co., 1967-68, L.I. Festival repertory, 1968, Les Liaisons Dangereuses; stage directing debut in John and Abigail, 1969; (films) Diary of a Mad Housewife, 1970 (Nat. Soc. Film Critics award, 1970), The Twelve Chairs, 1970, The Deadly Trap, 1972, The Wrath of God, 1972, Dracula, 1979, Those Lips Those Eyes, 1980, Sphinx, 1981, The Men's Club, 1986, Masters of the Universe, 1987, And God Created Woman, 1988, True Identity, 1991, 1492: Conquest of Paradise, 1992, Dave, 1993, Body of Evidence, 1993, Brainscan, 1994, Junior, 1994, Bad Company, 1995, Cutthroat Island, 1995, Eddie, 1996, Lolita, 1997, I'm Losing You, 1998, Alegría, 1998, Small Soldiers, 1998, The Ninth Gate, 1999, Stardom, 2000, Sweet November, 2001, House of D, 2004; (TV movies) appearances include: Benito Cereno, 1965, Good Day, 1967, The Mark of Zorro, 1974, The Ambassador, 1974, The Seagull, 1975, The American Woman: Portraits of Courage, 1976, Eccentricities of a Nightingale, 1976, Sherlock Holmes, 1981, I, Leonardo: A Journey of the Mind, 1983 (Emmy nom. best actor, 1983), Liberty, 1986, The Doomsday Gun, 1994, Moses, 1996, Kilroy, 1999, Jason and the Argonauts, 2000, Cry Baby Lane, 2000. Bd. dirs. Berkshire Festival. Mem. Actors Equity, Screen Actors Guild. Office: Special Artists Agency Inc 345 N Maple Dr Ste 302 Beverly Hills CA 90210-3860

LANGENBACHER, ERIC ANTON, humanities educator; b. Vancouver, Can., Dec. 9, 1972; s. Wolfgang Gerhard and Linda Hoyer Langenbacher; m. Kayoko Hashimoto, Aug. 7, 1993; children: Adam Toru, Maximilian Takuji. BA, Carleton U., Can., 1994; MA, U. of Toronto, 1995; PhD, Georgetown U., 2002. Vis. asst. prof. Georgetown U., Washington, 2002—. Author: (book chpt.) The Allies in World War Two: The Anglo- American Bombardment of German Cities. Recipient Bronze medal for Outstanding Academic Achievement, Gov. Gen. of Can., 1990; Dissertation Rsch. Grant, U.S.-German Fulbright Commn., 1999—2000, Ernst-Reuter Scholarship, Ernst-Reuter Soc./Free U. of Berlin, 1999—2000, Hopper Meml. Fellowship, Georgetown U., Dept. of Govt., 2000—01. Mem.: German Studies Assn., Am. Polit. Sci. Assn. Avocations: travel, gardening, bicycling, tennis. Office: Georgetown U 37th and O Streets NW Washington DC Office Phone: 202-687-6130. Personal E-mail: langenbe@georgetown.edu.

LANGENBERG, DONALD NEWTON, retired academic administrator, physicist; b. Devils Lake, N.D., Mar. 17, 1932; s. Ernest George and Fern (Newton) L.; m. Patricia Ann Warrington, June 20, 1953; children: Karen Kaye, Julia Ann, John Newton, Amy Paris. BS, Iowa State U., 1953; MS, UCLA, 1955; PhD (NSF fellow), U. Calif. at Berkeley, 1959; D.Sc. (hon.), U. Pa., 1985, MA (hon.), 1971; DSc (hon.), SUNY, 1998. Electronics engr. Hughes Research Labs., Culver City, Calif., 1953-55; acting instr. U. Calif. at Berkeley, 1958-59; mem. faculty U. Pa., Phila., 1960-83, prof., 1967-83; dir. Lab. for Research on Structure of Matter, 1972-74; vice provost for grad. studies and research, 1974-79; chancellor U. Ill.-Chgo., 1983-90, U. Sys. Md., Adelphi, 1990—2002. Maitre de conference associe Ecole Normale Superieure, Paris, France, 1966-67; vis. prof. Calif. Inst. Tech., Pasadena, 1971; guest researcher Zentralinstitut für Tieftemperaturforschung der Bayerische Akademie der Wissenschaften and Technische Universität München, 1974; dep. dir. Nat. Sci. Found., 1980-82 Rschr., contbr. to publs. on solid state and low temperature physics including electronic band structure in metals and semiconductors, quantum phase coherence and nonequilibrium effects in superconductors, sci. and edn. policy and rsch. adminstrn. Recipient John Price Wetherill medal Franklin Inst., 1975, Disting. Contribution to Research Adminstrn. award Soc. Research Adminstrs., 1983, Disting. Achievement Citation, Iowa State Alumni Assn., 1984, Significant Sig award Sigma Chi, 1985; fellow NSF, 1959-60, Alfred P. Sloan Found., 1962-64; Guggenheim Found., 1966-67 Fellow AAAS (pres. 1990), Am. Phys. Soc. (pres. 1993), Sigma Xi. Address: 130 Chancellor Ln Queenstown MD 21658-1347 Office: Univ Md Dept Physics College Park MD 20742-4111 Office Phone: 301-405-9983. E-mail: dnl@usmd.edu.

LANGENBERG, FREDERICK CHARLES, manufacturing executive; b. N.Y.C., July 1, 1927; s. Frederick C. and Margaret (McLaughlin) L.; m. Jane Anderson Bartholomew, May 16, 1953; children: Frederick C., Susan Jane; m. Marguerite Cardone, Apr. 13, 1996. BS, Lehigh U., 1950, MS, 1951; PhD, Pa. State U., 1955; postgrad. execs. program, Carnegie-Mellon U., 1962. With U.S. Steel Corp., 1951-53; vis. fellow MIT, 1955-56; with Crucible Steel Corp., Pitts., 1956-68, v.p. research and engring., 1966-68; pres. Trent Tube div. Colt Industries, Milw., 1968-70; exec. v.p. Jessop Steel Co., Washington, Pa., 1970, pres., 1970-75; pres., bd. dirs. Am. Iron and Steel Inst., Washington, 1975-78; pres. Interlake Corp., Oak Brook, Ill., 1979-81, pres., chmn, chief exec. officer, 1981-91, also bd. dirs.; chmn. Langand Corp., Pitts., 1991—. Contbr. articles to tech. jours.; patentee in field. Served with USNR, 1944—45. Named Oak Brook Bus. Leader of the Yr., 1986, Disting. Bus. Leader, DuPage County, 1988; Alumni fellow Pa. State U., 1977; recipient Disting. Alumni award, Pa. State U., 1989, Lehigh U., 1990. Fellow Am. Soc. Metals (disting. life mem. 1982, trustee, Pitts. Nite lectr. 1970, Andrew Carnegie lectr. 1976; David Ford McFarland award Penn State chpt. 1973); mem. AIME, Am. Soc. Metals, Metals Powder Industry Fedn., Phi Beta Kappa, Sigma Xi, Tau Beta Pi. Clubs: Duquesne, St. Clair Country (Pitts.), Congl., Burning Tree, Chgo. Golf, Chgo., Laurel Valley, Rolling Rock (Ligonier, Pa.), Belleair County Club (Fla.). Office: Langand Corp PO Box 1286 Mc Murray PA 15317 Office Phone: 724-941-1914. E-mail: peggycl15241@yahoo.com.

LANGENBRUNNER, JAMIE, professional hockey player; b. Duluth, Minn., July 24, 1975; Left wing Dallas Stars, 1994—2002, New Jersey Devils, 2002—. Mem. U.S. Olympic Hockey Team, Nagano, Japan, 1998, Team U.S.A, World Cup of Hockey, 2004. Achievements include mem. Stanley Cup Champion Dallas Stars, 1999, New Jersey Devils, 2003. Office: c/o New Jersey Devils 50 rte 120 N East Rutherford NJ 07073

LANGENHEIM, JEAN HARMON, biologist, educator; b. Homer, La., Sept. 5, 1925; d. Vergil Wilson and Jeanette (Smith) Harmon; m. Ralph Louis Langenheim, Dec. 1946 (div. Mar. 1962). BS, U. Tulsa, 1946; MS, U. Minn., 1949, PhD, 1953. Rsch. assoc. botany U. Calif., Berkeley, 1954-59, U. Ill., Urbana, 1959-61; rsch. fellow biology Harvard U., Cambridge, Mass., 1962-66; asst. prof. biology U. Calif., Santa Cruz, 1966-68, assoc. prof. biology, 1968-73, prof. biology, 1973-93, prof. biology emerita, 1993—, rsch. prof. ecol. and evolution biology, 2001—. Acad. v.p. Orgn. Tropical Studies, San Jose, Costa Rica, 1975—78; chmn. com. humid tropics U.S. Nat. Acad. Nat. Rsch. Coun., 1975—77; mem. com. floral inventory Amazon NSF, Washington, 1975—87; mem. sci. adv. bd. EPA, Washington, 1977—81. Author: (Book) Botany-Plant-Biology in Relation to Human Affairs, Plant Resins: Chemistry, Evolution, Ecology and Ethnobotany, 2003 (Klinger Best Ethnobotany Book award, Soc. Economic Botany, 2004); contbr. articles to profl. jours. Recipient Disting. Alumni award, U. Tulsa, 1979; grantee, NSF, 1966—88. Fellow: AAUW, AAAS, Bunting Inst., Calif. Acad. Scis.; mem.: Soc. Econ. Botany (pres. 1993—94), Assn. Tropical Biology (pres. 1985—86), Internat. Soc. Chem. Ecology (pres. 1986—87), Ecol. Soc. Am. (pres. 1986—87), Bot. Soc. Am. Home: 191 Palo Verde Ter Santa Cruz CA 95060-3214 Office: U Calif Dept Ecol and Evolutionary Biology Earth and Marine Scis Bldg Santa Cruz CA 95064 Office Phone: 831-459-2918. Business E-Mail: lang@darwin.ucsc.edu.

LANGENKAMP, R. DOBIE, law educator, lawyer; b. Tulsa, Aug. 14, 1936; BA, Stanford Univ., 1958; JD, Harvard Univ., 1961. Bar: D.C. 1962, Okla. 1964, U.S. Supreme Ct. 1968. Assoc. Steadman Collier & Shannon, Washington, 1962—64; ptnr. Doerner Stuart Saunders Daniel & Langenkamp, Tulsa, 1964—77; dep. asst. sec. U.S. Dept. Energy, Washington, 1977—81; pres. & owner Cherokee Operating Co., Okla., 1981—96; adj. prof. Tulsa Univ. Law Sch., 1981—89, Chapman disting. vis. prof., 1989—91; dep. asst. sec. U.S. Dept. Energy, Washington, 1996—97; cons. in Kazakhstan & Georgia USAID, 1997—2000; owner Petroleum Associates Internat., 1997—2000; prof. Univ. Tulsa Law Sch., 2000—; dep. dir. Nat. Energy-Environ. Law & Policy Inst., Univ. Tulsa, 1989—91, dir., 2000—. Trustee Okla. Sch. Sci. & Math., 1994—99; regent Rogers Univ., 1996—98; trustee & regent Univ. Ctr. Tulsa, 1992—96, chmn., 1992—93; trustee Okla. Ordnance Works Authority, 1998—2002, chmn., 2002—; trustee Okla. Nature Conservancy, 2001—. Recipient Patriotism in Energy award, Internat. Soc. Energy Adv., 1998. Mem.: Phi Beta Kappa. Office: NELPI University of Tulsa 3120 E 4th Pl Tulsa OK 74104

LANGENKAMP, SANDRA CARROLL, retired human services administrator; b. St. Joseph, Mo., Feb. 10, 1939; d. William Harry Minger and Beverly (Carroll) Lee; m. R. Hayden Downie, June 1, 1963 (div. Feb. 1979); children: Whitney Downie, Timothy Downie, Allyson Downie; m. R. Dobie Langenkamp, Aug. 1993. BS, Tex. Women's U., 1960. Adjunctive therapist Menninger Meml. Hosp., Topeka, 1960-66; asst. adminstr. Hillcrest Med. Ctr., Tulsa, 1977-82; dir. Vol. Action Agy., Tulsa, 1982-83; exec. dir. Tulsa Bus. Health Group, 1983-95; v.p. Met. Tulsa C. of C., 1985-95; exec. dir. Tulsa Program Affordable Health Care, 1986-96; ret., 1996. Cons. mem. Okla. Employment Security Commn., Oklahoma City, 1988—; exec. dir. Tulsa Cmty. Found. Indigent Health Care, 1986—96, Long-Term Car Authority, 1999—; officer State of Okla. Basic Health Benefits Bd., 1985—96, chmn., 1992—93; mem. health benefit com. Okla. Ins. Commn., 1994—; mem. Gov.'s Com. Health Care, 1993; bd. dirs. Exec. Svc. Corps Tulsa, Associated Ctrs. Therapy. Editl. columnist: Point of View, 1985—, Tulsa Mag., 1985—. Count commn. appointee Tulsa Met. Area Planning Commn., 1973—81; mayor's appointee Tulsa Housing Authority, 1985—88; vol. Police Svc. Homicide Divsn., Police Svc. Detective Divsn., 1999—; exec. dir. Tulsa Met. Literacy Coalition, 1998—; apptd. mem. Okla. Health Care Auth., 2005—; pres. Tulsa Met. Ministry, 1980—83; bd. dirs. ARC, Tulsa, 1971—73, 1984—85, Okla. Arts Inst., 1995—, Simon Estes Found., 2000—, Tylsa Philharm., Inc., 2000—, City of Tulsa Arts Commn., 2003—. Mem.: Met. Tulsa C. of C. (v.p. 1983—95), Am. C. of C. (exec. dir. Okla. chpt.), Tulsa Tennis Club. Democrat. Roman Catholic. Avocations: reading, gardening, knitting, drawing, pottery, painting.

LANGER, ALOIS, communications executive; b. Pitts. BSEE, MIT, 1967; PhDEE, Carnegie Mellon U., 1973. Project engr., chief scientist Madrad/Intec, 1973—91; founder, pres. Cardiac Telecom Corp., Pitts., 1991—. Named to National Inventors Hall of Fame, 2002. Achievements include invention of Telemetry @ Home; design of of automatic implantable cardioverter defibrillator. Home: 111 Saddlebrook Dr Harrison City PA 15636-1413 E-mail: a.a.langer@gmx.net.

LANGER, BERNARD, medical association administrator; Head divsn. gen. surgery, chmn. dept. surgery Toronto Gen. Hosp./U. Toronto, 1982—92; pres. The Royal Coll. Physicians and Surgeons of Can., 1992—2003. Fellow: Royal Coll. Surgeons Can.; mem.: ACS (bd. regents), Soc. Surgery of the Alimentary Tract (pres.), Can. Assn. Gen. Surgeons (pres.), Med. Rsch. Coun. of Can. (coun. mem.). Office: Toronto Gen Hosp 200 Elizabeth St Toronto ON Canada M5G 2C4

LANGER, BERNARD, professional golfer; b. Anhausen, Germany, Aug. 27, 1957; m. Vikki Langer; children: Jackie Carol, Stefan Bernhard, Christina Joy, Jason D. Winner Masters, 1985, 1993; 58 internat. tournament victories, 12 German Open Championships, 1974—92. Mem. European Ryder Cup team, 2004; rep. Germany Hennesy Cognac Cup, Nissan Cup, Asashi Glass Four Tours, Dunhill Cup. Winner 7 German Nat. Opens and 2 German Nat. PGAs, over 65 internat. tournaments including Dunlop Masters, 1980, Colombian Open, 1980, German Open, 1981, 82, 85, 86, Bob Hope Brit. Classic, 1981, Italian Open, 1983, Glasgow Classic, 1983, Johnnie Walker Tournament, 1983, Caslo World, 1983, Irish Open, 1984, 87, Dutch Open, 1984, French Open, 1984, Spanish Open, 1984, Australian Masters, 1985, European Open, 1985, Sun City Challenge, 1985, PGA Championship Eng., 1987, Belgian Classic, 1987, European Epson Match Play, 1988, Peugeot Spanish Open, 1989, German Masters, 1989, Madrid Open, 1990, Benson & Hedges Open, 1991, Heineken Dutch Open, 1992, Honda Open, 1992, Volvo PGA Championship, 1993, European Open, Volvo PGA, 1995, Dunhill Asian Masters, 1996, Italian Open, Benson & Hedges Internat. Czech Open, Linde German Masters, Argentine Masters, 1997; winner Lancome Trophy, 1986, TNT Dutch Open, 2001, Linde German Masters, 2001, Volvo Masters, 2002; leader European Order of Merit, 1981, 84; tour victories include Masters, 1985, 93, Sea Pines Heritage Classic, 1985. Achievements include finishing 2003 with a career high ranking of No. 4. Avocations: skiing, football, tennis, cycling. Office: c/o PGA Tour 112 PGA Tour Blvd Ponte Vedra Beach FL 32082

LANGER, DENNIS HENRY, pharmaceutical company executive; b. NYC, Sept. 8, 1951; s. Nathan and Mira (Kenig) L.; m. Susan D. Follett, Jan. 21, 1980; children: William, Thomas. BA, Columbia U., 1971; MD, Georgetown U., 1975; JD cum laude, Harvard U., 1983. Diplomate Am. Bd. Psychiatry. Intern, resident, chief resident Yale U. Sch. Medicine, New Haven, 1975-78; clin. assoc. Nat. Inst. Mental Health, Bethesda, Md., 1978-80; clin. fellow Harvard Med. Sch., Boston, 1980-82, instr., 1982-83; assoc. clin. investigator Eli Lilly and Co., Indpls., 1983-84; assoc. med. dir. Abbott Lab., North Chicago, 1984-86; product mgr. Abbott Lab, North Chicago, 1986-87, sr. product mgr., 1987-88; sr. group product dir. G.D. Searle and Co., Skokie, Ill., 1988-89, sr. dir. mktg., 1989-91; pres., CEO, dir. Neose Technols. Inc., Horsham, Pa., 1991-94; v.p. bus. strategy-U.S. SmithKline Beecham Pharm., Phila., 1994-96, v.p. health mgmt. svcs., 1996-98; sr. v.p. rsch. and devel. SmithKline Beecham Healthcare Svcs., Phila., 1998-99; sr. v.p. product devel. strategy, rsch. and devel. SmithKline Beecham Pharmaceuticals, 1999-2000; sr. v.p. project mgmt. and rsch. and devel. strategy Glaxo SmithKline, King of Prussia, Pa., 2000—04; pres. N.Am. Dr. Reddy's Labs., 2004—05; mng. ptnr. Phoenix IP Ventures, Phila., 2005—. Cons. Food and Drug Adminstrn., Rockville 1980-82, clin. assoc. prof. Ind. U. Sch. Medicine, Indpls. 1983-84, U. Health Scis. Chgo. Med. Sch., 1984-91; clin. prof. Georgetown U., Sch. Medicine, 2003-. Contbr. articles to profl. jour. Bd. dirs. Epilepsy Svcs. Northeast Ill., 1985-91, v.p., 1986-89, SmithKline Beecham Found., 1996-2000; bd. vis. Georgetown U. Sch. medicine, 1998—; bd. regents Georgetown U., 2000—; dir. Myriad Genetics, Inc., 2004—, Cytogen, 2005—, Transkaryotic Therapies, Inc., 2003-05. Mem. Am. Acad. Child and Adolescent Psychiatry (Com. On Rights and Legal Matters), Am. Psychiatric Assn., Am. Soc. Law and Medicine. Office Phone: 267-765-3223. Business E-Mail: dennis@phoenixipv.com.

LANGER, ELLEN JANE, psychologist, educator, writer, artist; b. N.Y.C., Mar. 25, 1947; d. Norman and Sylvia (Tobias) L. BA, NYU, 1970; PhD, Yale U., 1974. Cert. clin. psychologist. Asst. prof. psychology The Grad. Ctr. CUNY, 1974-77; assoc. prof. psychology Harvard U., Cambridge, Mass., 1977-81, prof., 1981—. Cons. NAS, 1979-81, NASA; mem. div. on aging Harvard U. Med. Sch., 1979—, mem. psychiat. epidemiology steering com., 1982-90; chair social psychology program Harvard U., 1982-94, chair Faculty Arts and Scis. Com. of Women, 1984-88. Author: Personal Politics, 1973, Psychology of Control, 1983, Mindfulness, 1989, The Power of Mindful Learning, 1997, On Becoming an Artist: Reinventing Yourself Through Mindful Creativity, 2005; editor: (with Charles Alexander) Higher Stages of Human Development, 1990, (with Roger Schank) Beliefs, Reasoning and Decision-Making, 1994; contbr. articles to profl. and scholarly jours.; exhibits at Julie Hellery Gallery, Provincetown, Mass., J&W Gallery, New Hope, Pa. Guggenheim fellow; grantee NIMH, NSF, Soc. for Psychol. Study of Social Issues, Milton Fund, Sloan Found., 1982; recipient Disting. Contbn. of Basic to Applied Psychology award APS, 1995. Fellow Computers and Soc. Inst., Am. Psychol. Assn. (Disting. Contributions to Psychology in Public Interest award 1988, Disting. Contributions of Basic Sci. to Applied Psychology 1995); mem. Soc. Exptl. Social Psychology, Phi Beta Kappa, Sigma Xi. Democrat. Jewish. Avocations: tennis, horseback riding. Office: Harvard U Dept Psychology 33 Kirkland St Cambridge MA 02138-2044 Business E-Mail: langer@wjh.harvard.edu.

LANGER, GLENN ARTHUR, cellular physiologist, educator; b. Nyack, N.Y., May 5, 1928; s. Adolph Arthur and Marie Catherine (Doscher) L.; m. Beverly Joyce Brawley, June 5, 1954 (dec. Nov. 1976); 1 child, Andrea; m. Marianne Phister, Oct. 12, 1977. BA, Colgate U., 1950; MD, Columbia U., N.Y.C., 1954. Diplomate Am. Bd. Internal Medicine. Asst. prof. medicine Columbia U. Coll. Physicians and Surgeons, N.Y.C., 1963-66; assoc. prof. medicine and physiology UCLA Sch. Medicine, 1966-69, prof., 1969-97, Castera prof. cardiology, 1978-97, assoc. dean rsch., 1986-91, dir. cardiovascular rsch. lab., 1987-97, emeritus prof., 1997—. Griffith vis. prof. Am. Heart Assn., L.A., 1979; cons. Acad. Press, N.Y.C., 1989-97; founder, dir. Partnership Scholars Program, 1996—. Author: Understanding Disease, 1999; editor: The Mammalian Myocardium, 1974, 2d edit., 1997, Calcium and the Heart, 1990; mem. editl. bd. Circulation Rsch., 1971-76, Am. Jour. Physiology, 1971-76, Jour. Molecular Cell Cardiology, 1974-97; contbr. more than 200 articles to profl. jours. Co-pres., dir., founder Partnership Scholars Program for disadvantaged youth, 1996—. Capt. U.S. Army, 1955-57. Recipient Disting. Achievement award Am. Heart Assn. Sci. Coun., 1982, Heart of Gold award, 1984, Cybulski medal Polish Physiol. Soc., Krakow, 1990, Pasarow

Found. award for Cardiovascular Sci., 1993, Outstanding Acad. Title citation Choice mag., 2001; Macy scholar Josiah Macy Found., 1979-80. Fellow AAAS, Am. Coll. Cardiology, Internat. Soc. for Heart Rsch.; mem. Am. Soc. Clin. Investigation, Am. Assn. Physicians. Achievements include research on control of cardiac contraction. Business E-Mail: glang@mcn.org.

LANGER, JAMES STEPHEN, physicist, researcher; b. Pitts., Sept. 21, 1934; s. Bernard F. and Liviette (Roth) L.; m. Elinor Goldmark Aaron, Dec. 21, 1958; children: Ruth, Stephen, David. BS, Carnegie Inst. Tech., 1955; PhD, U. Birmingham, Eng., 1958. Prof. physics Carnegie-Mellon U., Pitts., 1958-82, assoc. dean, 1971-74; prof. physics U. Calif., Santa Barbara, 1982—, dir. Inst. for Theoretical Physics, 1989-95. Contbr. articles to profl. jours. Guggenheim fellow, 1974-75; Marshall scholar, 1955-57 Fellow AAAS, Am. Acad. Arts and Scis., Am. Phys. Soc. (chair divsn. condensed matter physics 1997-98, pres.-elect 1999, pres. 2000, Oliver E. Buckley Condensed-Matter Physics prize 1997); mem. NAS (v.p. 2001-05). Democrat. Home: 1130 Las Canoas Ln Santa Barbara CA 93105-2331 Office: U Calif Dept Physics Santa Barbara CA 93106 Business E-Mail: langer@physics.ucsb.edu.

LANGER, JUDITH ANN, language educator; b. N.Y.C. BA, CUNY, 1962, MSEd, 1965; PhD, Hofstra U., 1978; PhD (hon.), U. Uppsala, Sweden, 2005. Asst. prof. L.I. U., 1973-78; asst. prof. dept. ednl. psychology NYU, 1978-80; sr. rschr. lang. behavior rsch. lab. U. Calif., Berkeley, 1980-84; assoc. prof. sch. of edn. Stanford U., 1984-87; prof. SUNY, Albany, 1987—, disting. prof., 2001—. Dir. Albany Inst. for Rsch. in Edn., Nat. Rsch. Ctr. on English Learning & Achievement; co-dir. Nat. Rsch. Ctr. Lit. Tchg. and Learning; trustee Rsch. Found.; task force mem. Nat. Commn. on Edn. Stds. and Testing; adv. com. New Stds. in Edn. Project, Literacy Unit, LRDC and Nat. Ctr. on Edn. and the Economy; adv. bd. Nat. Coun. of Chief State Sch. Officers, Nat. Objective in Reading, Nat. Assessment of Ednl. Progress, Reading and Writing Assessments, 1980—; cons. Calif. Assessment Program, N.C. English Lang. Arts Standards, Calif. State Dept. Edn., Ctr. for Lang. Edn. and Rsch., Ctr. for the Study of Writing, Rev. of Rsch. on Reading and Writing Relationships, Mich. State Edn. Dept. Author: Reader Meets Author/Bridging the Gap, 1982, Understanding Reading and Writing Research, 1985, Children Reading and Writing: Structures and Strategies, 1986, Language, Literacy, and Culture, 1987, Issues of Society and Schooling, How Writing Shapes Thinking: Studies of Teaching and Learning, 1987, Literature Instruction: A Focus on Student Response, 1992, Literature Instruction: Practice & Policy, 1994, Envisioning Literature, 1995, Effective Literacy Instruction: Building Successful Reading and Writing Programs, 2002, Getting To Excellent: How to Create Better Schools, 2004; contbr. articles to profl. jours.; editor: Research in the Teaching of English, 1984-92; editl. bd. English Internat., Jour. of Reading Behavior, Newsletter, Lab. of Comparative Human Cognition, Jour. of Reading and Writing, Internat. Jour. of Reading and Writing; reviewer in field. Recipient numerous grants, Presdl. award for lifetime achievement, Hofstra U., 1992, Chancellor's award for Exemplary Contbns. to Rsch., 2001, Albert J. Harris award, 2003; fellow, Rockefeller Found.; Benton fellow, U. Chgo., 1997. Fellow Am. Psychol. Assn., Nat. Conf. on Rsch. in English; mem. MLA, Am. Ednl. Rsch. Assn., Am. Psychol. Soc., Conf. on Coll. Composition and Comm., Internat. Reading Assn., Nat. Reading Conf., Nat. Coun. of Tchrs. of English (trustee), Soc. for Rsch. in Child Devel., Soc. for Text and Discourse, Kappa Delta Pi. Office: Univ at Albany 1400 Washington Ave Albany NY 12222-0100

LANGER, LAWRENCE LEE, language educator, writer; b. N.Y.C., June 20, 1929; s. Irving and Esther (Strauss) L.; m. Sondra Weinstein, Feb. 21, 1951; children: Andrew, Ellen. BA, CCNY, 1951; AM, Harvard U., 1952, PhD, 1961. Teaching fellow Harvard U., Cambridge, Mass., 1954-57; instr. English U. Conn., Storrs, 1957-58, Simmons Coll., Boston, 1958-61, asst. prof., 1961-66, assoc. prof., 1966-72, prof., 1972-76, Alumnae prof., 1976-92, Alumnae prof. emeritus, 1992—. Fulbright prof. Am. Lit. U. Graz, Austria, 1963-64. Author: The Holocaust and The Literary Imagination, 1975, The Age of Atrocity, 1978, Versions of Survival, 1982, Holocaust Testimonies, 1991 (Nat. Book Critics Cr. award for Criticism 1991), Art From the Ashes: A Holocaust Anthology, 1995, Admitting the Holocaust: Collected Essays, 1995, Landscapes of Jewish Experience: Paintings of Samuel Bak, 1997, Preempting the Holocaust, 1998, The Game Continues: Chess in the Art of Samuel Bak, 1999, In a Different Light: The Book of Genesis in the Art of Samuel Bak, 2001. Sr. rsch. fellow NEH, 1978-79, 89-90, Koerner fellow for study of the Holocaust, Ctr. for Hebrew and Jewish Studies, Oxford, Eng., 1997; Shapiro Sr. scholar-in-residence Rsch. Inst. U.S. Holocaust Meml. Mus., 1996, Strassler disting. vis. prof. Ctr. for Holocaust and Genocide Studies, Clark U., 2002; resident scholar Rockefeller Found. Study and Conf. Ctr., Bellagio, Italy, 2003. Mem. MLA, PEN. Office: care Yale Univ Press Authors Mail PO Box 209040 New Haven CT 06520-9040 E-mail: llanger@world.std.com.

LANGER, PATRICIA ADELA, elementary school educator; b. Putnam, Conn., Sept. 8, 1954; d. Frank and Isabel (Lazur) L. BS, Cen. Conn. State U., 1976; 6th yr. cert., postgrad., 1988; MA, U. Conn., 1981. Cert. Orff-Schulwerk. Music educator Univ. of Conn., Storrs, Hartt Sch., West Hartford, Conn.; music tchr. The Learning Lab, Norwich, Conn., Ellington Bd. of Edn., Ellington, Conn., Woodstock Pub. Schs. Mem. NCSA, ACDA, MENC, CMEA, ASCD, Phi Delta Kappa. Home: 337 W Quasset Rd Woodstock CT 06281

LANGER, RALPH ERNEST, journalist, retired editor; b. Benton Harbor, Mich., July 30, 1937; s. Ralph L. and Mary (Skuda) L.; m. Katherine B. McGuire, June 25, 1960; children: Terri B., Tammi L. Student, Central Mich. U., 1955-57; BA in Journalism, U. Mich., 1957-59. Telegraph editor, reporter Grand Haven (Mich.) Daily Tribune, 1959-60; mng. editor Port Angeles (Wash.) Evening News, 1962-66; copy desk Detroit Free Press, 1966-68; asst. mng. editor Dayton Jour. Herald, 1968, mng. editor, 1968-75; editor Everett (Wash.) Herald, 1975-81; mng. editor Dallas Morning News, 1981-83, exec. editor, 1983-86, v.p., 1986-91, sr. v.p., exec. editor, 1991-96, exec. v.p., editor, 1997-98; ret., 1999; exec.-in-residence So. Meth. U., 1999—2002. Pres. Freedom of Info. Found. Tex., 1985-89; founding pres. Nat. Freedom of Info. Coalition, 1989-93, Coun. of Presidents, 1991-92. 1st lt. U.S. Army, 1960-62. Named to Journalism Hall of Fame, Ctrl. Mich. U., 2003. Mem. Am. Soc. Newspaper Editors (bd. dirs. 1997—99), Press Club Dallas (pres. 1985-86), A.P. Mng. Editors Assn. (bd. dirs. 1980—, sec. 1989, v.p. 1990, pres. 1990-91), Coun. of Pres.'s (founding pres. 1992-93), AP Mng. Editors Assn. Found. (pres. 1991-92), Scabbard and Blade, Alpha Phi Gamma, Sigma Phi Epsilon. Personal E-mail: ralphlanger@sbcglobal.net.

LANGER, RAY FRITZ, retired insurance executive; b. Manchester, N.H., Apr. 29, 1921; s. Fritz Bruno and Clara (Lindh) L.; m. Myrtle Elaine Sargent, May 23, 1942; 1 child, Barry Frederick. Cert., U. N.H., 1940. Chief statistician N.H. Ins. Co., Manchester, 1942-71; chief statistician, asst. sec. N.H. & Am. Internat. Group, Manchester, 1972-84, asst. sec., 1984-91; cons. N.H. Group, Manchester. Dir. Suncook Bank, 1979—83. Selectman Town of Hooksett, N.H., 1970-78, councilor, 1988-91, state rep., 1993-05; pres. Hooksett-ites Sr. Citizens, 1993-97; vol. VA Hosp., 2005-. Capt. USAF, 1943-46, PTO, 1955-57, Korea, ret. 1981. Mem. Soc. Ins. Accts. (past pres.), Am. Legion. Republican. Methodist. Avocations: hunting, fly fishing, painting.

LANGER, RICHARD CHARLES, minister; b. Chgo., Sept. 23, 1957; s. Gerhard and Ann Mae L.; m. Shari Lynn Langer, June 19, 1982; children: Crystal, Mark. BS, Colo. State U., 1979; MDiv, Talbot Sch. Theology, La Mirada, Calif., 1985; MA, U. Calif., Riverside, 1987, PhD, 1990. Ordained to ministry Evang. Free Ch. of Am. Pastor Trinity Ch., Redlands, Calif., 1985—; lectr. U. Calif., Riverside, 1990—; bio-ethicist Smart Practice, Phoenix, Ariz., 1994-96. Mem. instnl. rev. bd. Loma Linda (Calif.) U., 1993-98, southwest dist. bd. Evang. Free Ch. of Am., Mpls., 1996—-98 Contbr. articles to profl. jours. Active Bldg. a Generation task force United Way, Redlands, 1995—. Mem. Am. Philos. Assn., Soc. Christian Philosophers, Ministerial Assn. Evang. Free Ch. Avocations: photography, camping, sports. Office: Trinity Ch 1551 Reservoir Rd Redlands CA 92374-6463

LANGER, RICHARD J., lawyer; b. Rockford, Ill., June 10, 1944; s. John W. and Dorothy E. (Brunn) Langrehr; m. Audrey A. Russo, Jan. 28, 1967; children: Kathleen M., Michael R. BS, U. Ill., 1967; JD, U. Wis., 1974. Bar: Wis. 1974, U.S. Dist. Ct. (we. dist.) Wis. 1974. Assoc. Ela, Esch, Hart & Clark, Madison, Wis., 1974-76; ptnr. Stolper, Koritzinsky, Brewster & Neider, Madison, 1976-91, Michael, Best & Friedrich, Madison, 1991—. Pres. Hospice Care Found., Inc. Author: The Marital Property Classification Handbook, 1986, 2d edit., 1998, Workbook For Wisconsin Estate Planners, 1997, Family Estate Planning in Wisconsin, 1996, Conservation Easements: An Important Estate Planning Tool, 2002; contbr. articles to profl. jours. Named Outstanding Vol. Fund Raiser, Hospice Care Found., Inc., 2002. Fellow Am. Coll. Trust and Estate Coun.; mem. ABA, State Bar Wis., Madison Estate Coun. Avocations: scuba diving, travel, bicycling. Home: 1502 Windfield Way Madison WI 53562-3808 Office: Michael Best & Friedrich 1 S Pinckney St Madison WI 53703-2892 Office Phone: 608-283-2248. Business E-Mail: rjlanger@michaelbest.com.

LANGER, ROBERT MARTIN, retired chemical engineering company executive, consultant; b. Boston, May 29, 1925; s. Samuel Morton and Ethel (Shlivek) L. B.Engring., Yale U., 1945, D.Engring., 1952; S.M., MIT, 1948. Sales mgr. The Badger Co., Inc., Cambridge, Mass., 1968-70; dep. mng. dir. Badger B.V., The Hague, The Netherlands, 1970-74, mng. dir., 1974-78; v.p., project adminstrn. The Badger Co., Inc., Cambridge, 1978-80; sr. v.p. Badger Am., Inc., Cambridge, 1981-83; v.p., treas. The Badger Co., Inc., Cambridge, 1983-87. Served to lt. j.g. USNR, 1945-46 Mem. AIChE. Home: 280 Commonwealth Ave Boston MA 02116-2422

LANGER, ROBERT SAMUEL, chemical, biomedical engineering educator; b. Albany, N.Y., Aug. 29, 1948; s. Robert Samuel Sr. and Mary (Swartz) L.; m. Laura Feigenbaum, July 31, 1988; children: Michael David, Susan Katherine, Samuel Alexander. BS, Cornell U., 1970; ScD, MIT, 1974; PhD (hon.), ETH, Switzerland, 1996, Technion U., Israel, 1997, U. Catholique Louvain, Brussels, Hebrew U., U. Liverpool, U. Uppsala, 2005, Pa. State U., 2005, U. Nottingham, 2005. Rsch. assoc. Children's Hosp. Med. Ctr., Boston, 1974—; asst. prof. chem. and biomed. engring. MIT, Cambridge, Mass., 1978-81, assoc. prof., 1981-85, prof., 1985-89, Germeshausen prof., 1989—. Bd. dirs. Alkermes, Cambridge, Acusphere, Cambridge, Focal, Lexington; tchr. Group Sch., Lexington, 1971—73; endowed lectr. U. P.R., 1983, Case Western Res. U., 1986, U. Mich., 1987, U. Wash., 1988, U. Kans., 1989, U. Calif., San Francisco, 1991, U. Wis., 1991, Ga. Inst. Tech., 1991, Ohio State U., 1991, U. Pitts., 1992, Purdue U., 1992, U. Del., 1993, Pa. State U., 1993, Beth Israel Hosp., 1994, Cornell U., 1994, Calif. Inst. Tech., 1995, Ill. Inst. Tech., 1995, Ohio State Med. Sch., 1995, U. Calif., 1996, U. Tenn., 1996, U. N.C., 1997, 97, U. Pa., 1998, Wash. U., 1998, U. Tex., San Antonio, 1998, U. MIch., 1998, U. Calif., Berkeley, 1999, U. Notre Dame, 1999, U. Liverpool, 2000, Brown U., 2001, Stanford U., 2001, Cornell U., 2001, U. Pa., 2002, U. Louisville, 2002; cons. Genentech, San Francisco, 1981—, Merck Sharpe and Dohme, 1981—85; others; sci. advisor Cygnus, Redwood City, Calif., 1987—97, Opta Foods, Bedford, Mass., 1991—; mem. FDA Sci. Bd., 1995—2002, chmn., 1999—2002. Author: (with D. Cincotta and K. Cole) Group School Chemistry Curriculum, 1972, (with W. Thilly) Laboratory in Applied Biology, 1978, Analaytical Practices in Biochemistry, 1979, (with W. Hrusheysky and F. Theeuwes) Temporal Control of Drug Delivery, 1991; editor: (with M. Chasin) Biodegradable Polymers in Drug Deliveryy, 1990, (with D. Wise) Medical Applications on Control Release, Vols. I and II, 1984, (with R. Steiner and P. Weisz) Angiogenesis, 1992; contbr. over 700 articles to sci. jours.; patentee in field. Recipient John W. Hyatt Svc. to Mankind award Soc. Plastics Engrs., 1995, Internat. award, 1996, Ebert Prize, Am. Pharm. Assn., 1995, 96, 99, Rsch. award Am. Diabetes Assn., 1996, internat. award Gairdner Found., 1996, Wiley medal FDA, 1997, Killian award MIT, 1997, Lemelson-MIT prize for invention, 1998, Nagai Found. Internat. award, 1998; Charles Stark Draper prize, Nat. Acad. of Engring, 2002, Dickson prize for Sci., 2002, Heinz award for Tech., Economy and Employment, 2003, Harvey prize, 2003, John Fritz award, 2003, Gen. Motors Kettering award fo Cancer Rsch., 2004; Union Oil fellow, 1970-71, Chevron fellow, 1971-72; cited for Outstanding Patent in Mass., Intellectual Property Owners Inc., 1989; named one of the 25 most important individuals in biotech. by Bio World mag, 1990 and Forbes mag., 1999, Discovery mag, 2002; selected by Forbes mag. as one of 15 innovators worldwide who will reinvent the future, 2002; named one of six heroes whose rsch. may save your life, Parade mag., 2004. Fellow: Am. Inst. Med. and Biol. Engrs. (founding fellow), Am. Assn. Pharm. Scis. (Disting. Pharm Sci. award 1993), Soc. Biomaterials (Clemson award 1990); mem.: NAE, NAS, AIChE (Food, Pharm. and Bioengring. award 1986, Profl. Progress award 1990, Charles M. Stine Materials Sci. and Engring. award 1991, William Walker award 1996), Controlled Release Soc. (bd. govs. 1981—85, chmn. regulatory affairs com. 1985—89, pres. 1991—92, Founders award 1989, Outstanding Pharm. Paper award 1990, 1992, Millerial Pharm. award 2000, Glaxo Wellcome award 2000), Internat. Soc. Artificial Internal Organs, Am. Soc. Artificial Internal Organs (mem. program com. 1984—87), Biomed. Engring. Soc. (bd. dirs. 1991—94, Whitaker lectr. 1994), Internat. Soc. Artificial Internal Organs (Organon-Teknika award 1991), Am. Chem. Soc. (Creative Polymer award 1989, Phillips Applied Polymer Sci. award 1992, Pearlman Meml. Lectr. award 1992, Polymer Chemistry award 1999), Am. Acad. Arts and Scis., Inst. Medicine of NAS. Avocations: magic, jogging. Office: MIT Dept Chem Engring 77 Mass Ave Rm 342 Cambridge MA 02139-4307

LANGER, STANLEY HAROLD, chemical engineer, educator; b. New Orleans; s. Julius Mark and Leah Langer. BS in Chemistry, La. State U.; PhD in Phys. Chemistry, Northwestern U.; PhD (hon.), U. Oviedo, Spain, 1996. Supervisory phys. chemist U.S. Bur. Mines, Bruceton, Pa.; group leader, Am. Cyanamid fellow U. Cambridge, England; prof. chem. engring. U. Wis., Madison, 1967—97. Cons. in field. Contbr., articles to profl. jours. With USN. Fellow, Guggenheim Found., 1959. Mem.: AIChE, Metall. Soc., Chromatography Soc., Electrochem. Soc., Am. Chem. Soc. Achievements include patents for first commercial fuel cell electrodes; first to use trimethylsilyl derivatives for chromatography and mass spectral analysis. Avocations: reading, walking. Office: U Wis Dept Chem amd Biol Engring 1415 Engineering Dr Madison WI 53706 Office Phone: 608-262-1190. Business E-Mail: langer@engr.wisc.edu.

LANGER, STEVEN, personnel director, psychologist; b. NYC, June 4, 1926; s. Israel and Anna (Glaisner) L.; m. Jacqueline White, Oct. 11, 1954 (dec. Dec. 1969); children: Bruce, Diana, Geoffrey; m. Elaine Catherine Brewer, Dec. 29, 1979 (dec. Feb. 1992). BA in Psychology, Calif. State U., Sacramento, 1950; MS in Pers. Svcs., U. Colo., 1958; PhD, Walden U., 1972. Lic. psychologist, Ill. Asst. to pers. dir. City and County of Denver, 1956-59; pers. dir. City of Pueblo (Colo.), 1959-60; pers. cons. J.L. JAcobs & Co., Chgo., 1961-64, adminstrv. mgr., 1966-67; sales selection mgr. Reuben H. Donnelly Corp., Chgo., 1964-66; pres. Abbott, Langer & Assocs., Crete, Ill., 1967—. Vis. prof. mgmt. Loyola U., Chgo., 1969-71; community prof. behavioral scis. Purdue U., Calumet campus, Hammond, Ind., 1973-75. Contbr. articles on indsl. psychology and human resources mgmt. to profl. publs. Mem. Ill. Psychol. Assn. (chmn. sect. indsl. psychologists 1971-72), Chgo. Psychol. Assn. (pres. 1974-75, 94-95), Chgo. Indsl./Orgnl. Psychologists, Soc. Human Resources Mgmt. (accredited, chmn. rsch. award com. 1966-69), World at Work, Chgo. Compensation Assn. (sec. 1976-77), Mensa (pres. Chgo. chpt. 1972-74). Unitarian Universalist. Home: 309 Herndon St Park Forest IL 60466-1132 Office: Abbott Langer & Assoc 548 1st St Crete IL 60417-2199 Office Phone: 708-672-4200. Business E-Mail: slanger@abbott-langer.com.

LANGERAK, ESLEY OREN, retired research chemist; b. Pella, Iowa, Oct. 28, 1920; s. William Henry and Grace Dena (Vander Linden) L.; m. Elizabeth Jane Rhodes (dec.), Nov. 18, 1944; children— Kristin, Lisbeth, Peter; m. Marian Sawin Stauffer, May 22, 1999. BS in Chemistry, Central Coll., Iowa, 1941; MS, U. Del., 1947, PhD in Organic Chemistry, 1949. High sch. tchr. Garden Grove Consol. Sch., Iowa, 1941-42; research chemist, supr., lab mgr. DuPont Co., Wilmington, Del., 1949-81, compensation mgr. chems. and pigments dept., 1981-85; ret., 1985. Contbr. articles to profl. jours.; patentee in field (3). Served with Ordnance, U.S. Army, 1942-46, PTO. Mem.: DuPont Country. Republican. Presbyterian.

LANGERMANN, JOHN W. R., financial services company executive; b. N.Y.C., Aug. 14, 1943; BA with highest honors, Lehigh U., 1965. Ptnr., sales mgr. L.F. Rothschild, Unterberg, Towbin, Boston, 1977-87; sr. v.p. County Nat. West Securities, Boston, 1987-90; mng. dir. instl. sales Ladenburg, Thalmann & Co., Inc., Boston, 1994-96; mgr. Brown Bros. Harriman & Co., Boston, 1996-99; ptnr. Blue River Fin. Consulting Group, 2001—, pres.; dir. Whitman and Co., 2001—. Avocations: vintage sports car racing, wu shu. Address: PO Box 410250 Cambridge MA 02141

LANGEVIN, JAMES R., congressman, former state official; b. Providence, Apr. 22, 1964; s. Richard Raymond and June Katherine (Barrett) L. B Arts and Scis., R.I. Coll., 1990; MPA, Harvard U., 1994. State rep. City of Warwick, R.I., 1988-94; sec. of state State of R.I., Providence, 1995-2001; mem. U.S. Congress from 2d R.I. dist., 2001—; mem. armed svcs. com., small bus. com., homeland sec. com. Bd. mem. Am. Red Cross, Pawtucket, R.I., 1993—, Tech Access, Providence, 1995, R.I. State House Restoration Com., 1995, March of Dimes, Warwick Shelter, Naval War Coll. Found., Pari Independent Living. Mem. Save the Bay R.I., K.C. Democrat. Roman Catholic. Avocations: reading, public speaking, community involvement. Office: 109 Cannon House Office Bldg Washington DC 20515*

LANGEVIN, THOMAS HARVEY, educational association administrator, consultant; b. St. Paul, Mar. 20, 1922; s. Thomas E. and Myrtle (Damsgard) L.; m. Pearl E. Mattfeld, Aug. 29, 1942; children: Dennis, Timothy. BS, Concordia Tchrs. Coll., Seward, Neb., 1947; MA, U. Neb., 1949, PhD, 1951. Quarantine insp. USPHS, 1943-45; grad. asst., asst. instr. U. Neb., 1947-51; prof. Concordia Tchrs. Coll., 1951-63, dean coll., 1961-63, acting pres., 1961-63; dir. long-range planning project Luth. Ch.-Mo. Synod, 1964-65; also cons. Bd. Higher Edn.; acad. v.p. Pacific Luth. U., 1965-69; pres. Capital U., Columbus, Ohio, 1969-79, pres. emeritus, 1979—; pres. Thomas H. Langevin Assoc., LadyLake, Fla., 1979—. Prin. Registry for Coll. and Univ. Pres., 1992—; chmn. Luth. Edn. Conf. N.Am., 1980-87; cons. Battelle Inst., 1979-87; cons., vis. fellow Battelle Seattle Rsch. Ctr., 1976. Co-chmn. Tacoma Area Urban Coalition Edn. Task Force, 1967-69; mem., past chmn. Ohio Com. Pub. Programs in Humanities; former exec. com. Fedn. Pub. Programs in Humanities; former mem. Ohio Higher Edn. Facilities Commn.; former mem. Commn. on Future Lutheran Edn., Luth Edn. Conf. N.Am., pres., 1977-78; bd. dirs. Nat. Urban League, 1979-83; mem. Columbus Urban League; former mem. Met. Columbus Sch. Com.; bd. dirs. Tacoma Citizens Com. Pub. TV, 1967-69, Design for Progress Tacoma, 1969, Tacoma Area Urban Coalition, 1967-69; bd. rev. Air U.; former adv. com. Center Sci. and Industry, Columbus; assoc. in urban affairs Nat. Inst. Pub. Affairs; bd. control Concordia Coll., Portland, Oreg., 1965-69; bd. overseers Acad. Contemporary Problems, Columbus, 1972-75; trustee Columbus Symphony Orch., pres., 1979-81; past trustee Columbus Sch. Girls, Columbus Met. Area Community Action; hon. trustee Internat. Council of Mid-Ohio; past bd. govs. Goodwill Industries Central Ohio, Salesian Inner City Boys' Club; past bd. dirs., pres. Blue Cross Central Ohio; bd. dirs. Options, Learning Connections, Franklin County Heart Br., Columbus Area Mental Health Center; bd. dirs. Battelle Meml. Inst. Found., chmn., 1977-78; mem. bd. dirs. Nationwide Corp. Served with USCGR, 1943-45. Recipient Carnegie grant, postdoctoral fellow Center for Study Higher Edn., U. Mich., 1963-64 Mem. Assn. Ind. Colls. and Univs. Ohio (chmn. 1971-74), Orgn. Am. Historians, Nebr., Ohio hist. socs., Am. Assn. Higher Edn., Newcomen Soc. N.Am., Navy League U.S. (past dir. Columbus council), Columbus Area C. of C. (dir. 1971-74) Clubs: Columbus Rotary (dir.). Lutheran. Home: 441 San Pedro Dr Lady Lake FL 32159-8664 Office Phone: 352-753-1488. E-mail: thlangevin@aol.com.

LANGFELD, PATRICIA ANN, trade association administrator; b. Washington, Nov. 4, 1942; d. Charles Edwards and Kathryn Marie (Griffin) Junkin; m. Stanley Chaitt Langfeld, May 1, 1981. Cert. in orgn. mgmt. U.S. C. of C. Mgr. adminstrv. svcs. Nat Stone Assn., Washington, 1966-76; dir. comm. Nat. Ice Assn., Bethesda, Md., 1976-77; dir. mem. svcs. Optical Labs. Assn., Bethesda, 1977-82; v.p. confs. and edn. Internat. Franchise Asn., Washington, 1982-94; dir. profl. edn. svc. Congl. Quar. Inc., Washington, 1994-98; dir. meetings and exhibits Nat. Assn. Life Underwriters, Washington, 1998-2000; v.p. mktg. and devel. Competitive Telecom. Assn., Washington, 2000—02; dir. mktg. and bus. devel. Nat. Parking Assn., Washington, 2002—. Mem. coun. advisors Walt Disney World, Orlando, Fla., 1992-94; mem. bd. advisors Greenbrier Resort, White Sulphur Springs, W.Va., 2001—. Editor, contbr. monthly newsletters Stone News, 1974-76, Ice News, 1976-77, OLA News, 1977-82; contbr. writer Franchising World, 1982-94. Mem. ball exec. com. Nat. Symphony Orch., Washington, 1995—, com. chmn., 1997—, mem. com. for wine tasting and silent auction benefit, 1993-96; mem. campaign leadership bd. Salvation Army Turning Point Ctr. for Homeless Women and Children, Washington, 1996—; mem. fall benefit com. Woodrow Wilson House Armistice Day Event, Washington, 1998—; mem. benefit com. Woodrow Wilson Princeton Centennial Celebration, 2002. Mem. Am. Soc. Assn. Execs., Profl. Conv. Mgmt. Assn., Greater Washington Soc. Assn. Execs. (innovate adv. coun. 1997-98, Springtime in Park adv. coun. 1998-2000, profl. women's forum 1998-2000). Republican. Jewish. Avocations: collecting oriental art, classical music, deep sea fishing, travel adventures, interior decorating. Home: 5300 Camberley Ave Bethesda MD 20814 Office: Nat Parking Assn Ste 300 1112 16th St NW Washington DC 20036 Office Phone: 202-296-4336. E-mail: plangfeld@npapark.org.

LANGFELD, STANLEY CHAITT, government executive; b. Harrisburg, Pa., Jan. 10, 1945; s. Millard Ash Jr. and Bessie Chaitt; m. Patricia Ann Junkin, May 1, 1981. BA in History, U. Md., 1968; MS in Real Estate and Urban Devel. Plng., Am. U., 1971. Market analyst The Rouse Co., Columbia, Md., 1971-72; dir. residential and recreational devel. couns. Urban Land Inst., Washington, 1972-74; realty specialist U.S. Gen. Svcs. Adminstrn., Washington, 1975-78, sr. realty specialist, 1978-81, program control officer, 1981-83, dep. dir. Office of Program Control, 1983-85, spl. asst. to asst. commr. Office Real Property Mgmt./Safety, 1985-88, spl. asst. to asst. commr. for real property devel., 1988-90, dep. dir. Office Real Estate Pub. Bldgs. Svc., 1990-91, dir. real estate policy divsn. Office Real Estate, 1991-95, dir. real property policy div. Office Government-wide Policy, 1995—. Mem. bd. editors: Pub. Mgr. Quart. Mag., 1998—; author: (publs.) The Balanced and Orderly Development of a Site in Close Proximity to a Metro Station as a Contributor to a More Viable Urban Environment in the Washington Metropolitan Area, 1971, Federal Real Property Asset Management Principles, 1996, Project Reference Files, Urban Land Institute, 1973. Mem. com. for wine tasting and silent auction benefit Nat. Symphony Orch., Washington, 1993—96; mem. exec. com. Nat. Symphony Orch. Ball, 2000—01; advisor to bd. Salvation Army's Turning Point Ctr. for Homeless Women and Children, Washington, 1996—; mem. benefit com. Woodrow Wilson Princeton Centennial Celebration, 2002; mem. fall benefit com. Woodrow Wilson House Armistice Day Event, 1998—. Recipient Morris Cafritz Meml. scholar, Am. U., 1970, Dean's scholar, 1970, Hammer award, Nat. Partnership for Reinventing Govt., 1999, Disting. Svc. award, U.S. Govt., 2001; fellow, Urban Transp. Ctr., Urban Mass Transit Adminstrn., U.S. Dept. Transp., 1971. Mem.: Fed. Exec. Inst. Alumni Assn. (bd. dirs., exec. sec., treas., chair 2000—02), Cosmos Club (new mem. orientation com. 2000—02, mem. house com. 2002—04, mem. fin. com. 2005—). Republican. Jewish. Avocations: reading, travel, walking, collecting fine arts and Oriental carpets. Home: 5300 Camberley Ave Bethesda MD 20814 Office: US Gen Svcs Adminstrn 1800 F St NW Washington DC 20405 Office Fax: 202 219 0104. E-mail: stanley.langfeld@gsa.gov.

LANGFORD, CHAD, music educator, composer; b. Dallas, Tex., Aug. 20, 1973; s. Thad and Terry Langford; life ptnr. Masako Negayama. B in Music Edn., Mont. State U., 2000. Co-owner Jeni Fleming Acoustic Trio, Bozeman,

2002—; adj. prof. double bass Mont. State U., Bozeman, 2003—; prin. Hitori Unltd., Hitori Internat. Press, Bozeman, 2003—. Guest clinician, lectr. in field, 2002—; presenter undergrad. scholars conf. Mont. State U., 1998, 99. Musician (producer): (performing ensemble) Jeni Fleming Acoustic Trio (Performing Ensemble); composer: Speak You Too, for violin and orch., 2003, Tanabata, for four flutes, 2003, Point Counter Point, for string orchestra, 2004, Traveling/Looking, for marimba and piano, 2004; musician, composer (recording project) Springhill. Educator, clinician Bozeman Pub. Schs., Bozeman, Mont., 2002—05. Named Most Outstanding Performer, Mont. State U. Music Dept., 2000. Mem.: ASCAP, Western Arts Alliance, Arts NW, Am. Music Ctr., Am. Composers Forum. Avocations: music history, tennis, travel. Home: 620 S Sixth Ave Apt 3 Bozeman MT 59715 Office: Hitori Unltd 620 S Sixth Ave #3 Bozeman MT 59715 Home Fax: 406-587-2308; Office Fax: 406-587-2308. Personal E-mail: chad@chadlangford.com.

LANGFORD, CHARLES DOUGLAS, lawyer; b. Montgomery, Ala., Dec. 9, 1922; s. Nathan G. and Lucy B. (Brown) Langford. BS, Tenn. State U., 1948; LLB, Cath. U. Am., 1952, JD, 1967. Bar: Ala. 1953, U.S. Dist. Ct. (mid. dist.) Ala. 1954, U.S. Ct. Appeals (5th cir.) 1969, U.S. Supreme Ct. 1976, U.S. Ct. Appeals (11th cir.) 1982. Ptnr. Gray, Langford, Sapp, McGowan, Gray & Nathanson, Montgomery, Ala., 1968—; mem. Ala. State Senate, Montgomery, 1983—2002. Officer St. John A.ME. Ch. With U.S. Army, 1943—46. Mem.: Elks (past exalter ruler So. Pride lodge), Alpha Phi Alpha. Democrat. Office: 400 S Union St Ste 205 Montgomery AL 36104-4316 Home: 1019 E Washington Ave Montgomery AL 36104-4738 Office Phone: 334-269-2563.

LANGFORD, DEAN TED, lighting and precision materials company executive; b. Princeton, Ill., June 19, 1939; s. Claude Robert and Dorothy Alene (Tuckerman) L.; m. Nancy Hirsch; children: Douglas T., John P. BS in Math. and Aero. Engring., U. Ill., 1962; LHD (hon.), Salem State Coll., 1990. Regional sales mgr. N.E. region IBM, Westport, Conn., 1980-81, corp. dir. mgmt. devel. Armonk, NY, 1981-82, group dir. comm. Ryebrook, NY, 1982-83; v.p. mktg. GTE Comm. Sys., Stamford, Conn., 1983-84; pres. GTE Elec. Products, Danvers, Mass., 1984-93; pres., CEO, Osram Sylvania Inc., Danvers, 1993—2002; ret., 2002. Bd. dirs. Osram Sylvania Inc., 2001—. Mem. bd. advisers U. Ill. Sch. Engring., Chgo., 1984-92; mem. adv. bd. Northeastern U., Boston, 1984-1998; trustee Civic Edn. Found. Lincoln-Filene Ctr., Tufts U.; mem. corp. bd. Mass. Gen. Hosp.; bd. dirs. Nat. Park Found., 2002—. Mem. NAM, Nat. Elec. Mfg. Assn. (bd. dirs.), Alliance To Save Energy (co-chmn., 1992—), U. Ill. Alumni Assn. (bd. dirs.), Salem Country Club, Las Campanas Country Club, Sawgrass Country Club, Marsh Landing Country Club. Avocations: biking, golf, cross country skiing.

LANGFORD, GEORGE MALCOLM, cell biology educator; b. Halifax, N.C., Aug. 26, 1944; s. Maynard and Lillie Virginia (Grant) L.; m. Sylvia Audrey Tyler, June 8, 1968; children: George II, Joy, Grant. BS in Biology, Fayetteville State U., 1966; MS, Ill. Inst. Tech., Chgo., 1969; PhD, Ill. Inst. Tech., 1971. Postdoctoral fellow U. Pa., Phila., 1971-73; asst. prof. U. Mass., Boston, 1973-77, Howard U., Washington, 1977-79; from assoc. prof. to full prof. physiology U. N.C., Chapel Hill, 1979—91; program dir. cell biology program NSF, 1988—89; Ernest Everett Just prof. biol. scis. and physiology Dartmouth Coll. and Dartmouth Med. Sch., Hanover, NH, 1991—. Dir. cell biology program NSF, Washington, 1988-89. Editorial bd. Biol. Bulls., 1987-91; contbr. articles to profl. jours. Trustee Marine Biol. Lab., Woods Hole, Mass., 1984-92. Fellow NIH, 1971-73, Marine Biol. Lab, 1972-78; grantee NIH, 1978-86, NSF, 1986-91, NATO, 1986-90. Mem. Am. Soc. Cell Biology (chair minorities affairs com. 1986-90), Sigma Xi. Achievements include research in dynamic instability of native microtubules from squid axous, gliding and vesicle transport. Office: Dartmouth Coll Dept Biol Scis Rm 416 6044 Gilman Lab Hanover NH 03755

LANGFORD, JAMES JERRY, lawyer; b. Birmingham, Ala., May 19, 1933; S. N.B. and Margaret Elizabeth (Fuller) L.; m. Mary Elizabeth Fryant, Mar. 21, 1958; children: Jan Carol Langford Hammett, Joel Fryant L. BS, U. So. Miss., 1955; JD, U. Miss., 1970. Bar: Miss. 1970, U.S. Dist. Ct. (no. and so. dists.) Miss. 1970, U.S. Ct. Appeals (5th cir.) 1971, U.S. Ct. Appeals (11th cir.). Agt. Met. Life Ins. Co., Jackson, Miss., 1957—58; sales rep. Employers Mut. of Wausau, Jackson, 1958—64; v.p. Reid-McGee Ins. Co., Jackson, 1964—67; from assoc. to sr. ptnr., mng. ptnr. Wells Marble & Hurst, Jackson, 1970—97, sr. ptnr., 1997—. Editor-in-chief Miss. Law Jour., 1969-70. 1st lt. U.S. Army, 1955-57. Fellow. Miss. Bar Found.; mem. ABA, Fed. Bar Assn. (pres. Miss. chpt. 1981-82), Fedn. Def. and Corp. Counsel, Nat. Assn. RR Trial Counsel, Miss. Bar Assn. (mem. ethics com. 1998-2004), Miss. Def. Lawyers Assn. (pres. 1992-93), Country Club Jackson, Phi Delta Phi, Omicron Delta Kappa, Pi Kappa Alpha. Presbyterian. Avocations: military history, baseball. Home: 12 Plum Tree Ln Madison MS 39110-9620 Office: Wells Marble & Hurst PO Box 131 Jackson MS 39205-0131 Personal E-mail: jlangfordesq@aol.com. *People respect honesty, trustworthiness, hard work and sincerity. Do what you truly want to do for your vocation, for that is the secret of happiness in a business career.*

LANGFORD, LAURA SUE, corporate financial executive; b. Evansville, Ind., Sept. 28, 1961; d. Lee Denmar Miller and Susan E. (Morton) Reitz; m. John E. Langford, May 15, 1992; 1 child, Rowan Diane. BFA in Drama, U. So. Calif., L.A., 1983; MBA in Fin. & Pub./Non-Profit, Columbia U., 1992. Credit mgr. Super-Freeze Co., Inc., Burbank, Calif., 1984-86; asst. Salomon Bros. Inc., L.A., 1986-87; rsch. analyst Bank of Calif., N.A., L.A., 1987, pub. fin. officer, 1988-90; intern Citizens Budget Commn., N.Y.C., 1991; analyst Standard & Poor's Ratings Group, N.Y.C., 1992-93, assoc., 1993-94, assoc. dir., 1994-95, dir., 1996-98; v.p. Duff & Phelps Credit Rating Co., N.Y.C., 1998—2000; dir. HypoVereinsbank, N.Y.C., 2000—; CFO HVB Global Assests Co., 2003—. Contbr. to periodical Standard & Poor's Credit Week, 1993—98, Duff & Phelps Credit Rating Co. Issues Update, 1998—2000. Fellow Divsn. Rsch. Assn. Student Officer fellow, Columbia U., 1991—92; scholar Pres.'s scholar, U. Evansville, 1979—81. Avocations: skiing, roller-coaster riding, science fiction. Office: HVB Group 150 E 42nd St New York NY 10017 Office Phone: 212-672-5614. Business E-Mail: Laura_Langford@HVBAMERICAS.com.

LANGFORD, LINDA KOSMIN, library consultant; b. Phila., Nov. 7, 1939; d. Edward I. and Ruth (Blumfield) K.; m. Jonathan P. Meyerson, Aug. 7, 1960 (div.); m. George Langford, Oct. 31, 2000. BA, U. Pa., 1961; MSLS, Drexel U., 1966, MS in Environ. Sci., 1974. Chemistry instr. U. Md., College Park, 1961-63; libr. sci. instr., engring. libr. Drexel U., Phila., 1963-78; dep. dir. biomed. libr. U. Pa., Phila., 1979-80; libr. sect. supr. applied physics lab. The Johns Hopkins U., Laurel, Md., 1980-94; sec. mgr. libr./archives/records NASA Jet Propulsion Lab., Pasadena, Calif., 1994—2000; libr. cons., 2001—. Contbg. editor (author): (Quarterly Jour.) IEEE Engring. Mgmt. Rev., 1999—. Nat. sec. Friends of Danilo Dolci, Inc., Phila., 1971-72, bd. dirs., Short Hills, N.J., 1972-73. Recipient Exceptional Achievement medal NASA, 1998. Mem. IEEE (PCS adminstrv. com. 1995-96, EMS bd. govs. 1998-2003), Spl. Librs. Assn. (v.p., pres.-elect Phila. chpt. 1968-69). Avocation: painting. Home: 32 Bodine Rd Berwyn PA 19312-1237 E-mail: l.kosmin@ieee.org.

LANGFORD, MARGARET SULLIVAN, French professor, consultant; b. Chgo., Feb. 2, 1935; d. James Kelso and Margaret Euphemia (Murdoch) Sullivan; m. Robert Frank Langford, June 12, 1970. BA summa cum laude, U. Calif., Fresno, 1956; PhD in Comparative Lit., U. Wash., Seattle, 1974. With U. Wash., 1958-62; instr. U. Calif., Sacramento, 1962-67; asst. prof. U. N.H., Durham, 1967-70; prof. Keene (N.H.) State Coll., 1970—. Freelance lang. cons., N.H., 1987—. Author: (with R. Perreau) American Dictionary of Figurative and Idiomatic Language, 1972. Jasper-Whiting Found. grantee, 1984. Mem. Assn. Assn. Tchrs. French, N.H. Assn. Tchrs. French (pres. 1988—), N.H. Tchrs. Fgn. Langs. (pres. elect 1988, pres. 1989—). Democrat. Avocation: automatic writing.

LANGFORD, ROLAND EVERETT, environmental scientist, safety engineer, writer; b. Owensboro, Ky., Apr. 11, 1945; s. John Roland and Mary Helen (Cockriel) L.; m. Son-Hee Shin, Dec. 18, 1971; children: John Everett, Lee Shin. AA, Armstrong State Coll., 1965; BS, Ga. So. Coll., 1967; MS, U. Ga., 1971, PhD, 1974, U. N.C., 1996. Cert. profl. environ. auditor, indsl. hygienist, safety profl., registered hazardous substances profl., sanitarian, State of Ariz., Nat. Environ. Health Assn.; diplomate Am. Acad. Sanitarians. Instr. Savannah (Ga.) Sci. Mus., 1971-72, Bainbridge (Ga.) Jr. Coll., 1973-74; asst. prof. chemistry Ga. Mil. Coll., Milledgeville, 1975-77; asst. prof. Ga. So. Coll., Statesboro, 1977-78; commd. capt. U.S. Army, 1978, advanced through grades to lt. col., 1992; chief chemistry sect. U.S. Army Acad. Health Scis., Ft. Sam Houston, Tex., 1978-79; sanitary engr. U.S. Army Environ. Hygiene Agy., Aberdeen Proving Ground, Md., 1979-81; comdr. environ. sanitation detachment Taegu, Republic of Korea, 1981-83; environ. sci. officer Ft. Huachuca, Ariz., 1984-88; chief occupl. health rsch. U.S. Army Biomed. R&D Lab., Ft. Detrick, Md., 1991-92; comdr. med. rsch. detachment Walter Reed Army Inst. Rsch., Wright-Patterson AFB, Ohio, 1992-98; preventive medicine officer NATO/IFOR, Zagreb, Croatia, Sarajevo, Bosnia-Herzegovina, 1996-97; chief abiotic processes br. Robert S. Kerr Lab. of U.S. EPA, Ada, Okla., 1998; supt. health and safety Huntsman Corp. Jefferson County Ops., Port Neches, Tex., 1998-2000; mgr. indsl. hygiene and product stewardship Huntsman Corp., Houston, 2000—04; EHSS mgr. Shanghai Lianheng Isocyanate Co. Ltd., 2004—. Mem. panel Comprehensive Assistance to Undergrad. Sci. Edn., NSF, 1975-77; mem. emergency response planning guidelines com. panel Am. Indsl. Hygiene Assn., 1999—; judge Internat. Sci. Fair, San Antonio, 1979; mem. sci. rev. panel NIH, 1986—; adj. faculty St. Leo's Coll., San Antonio, 1978-79, U. Md., Taegu and Pusan, Korea, 1981-83, AFIT, 1993-98, Purdue U., 1995—; mem. submarine atmosphere health assessment U.S. Navy, 2000—. Author: International Book of Units and Measurement Systems, 1999, Introduction to Weapons of Mass Destruction, 2004; co-author: Hazardous Materials Training Program for International Union of Operating Engineers, 1988, Fundamentals of Hazardous Materials Incidents, 1990, Substance Abuse in the Workplace, 1994, Introduction to Weapons of Mass Destruction, 2004; contbr. articles to profl. jours. Active Boy Scouts Am., Ft. Sam Houston, 1978-79; mem. parish coun., lay minister Holy Family Parish, Ft. Huachuca, 1985-88, lay min., lector 1985-88; advisor Med. Explorer Post, Ft. Huachuca, 1986-88; lay minister St. Thomas More Ch., 1988-91, WPAFB Chapel, 1992-98. Fellow Am. Inst. Chemists; mem. AIChE, Am. Soc. Safety Engrs., Am. Acad. Indsl. Hygiene (cert.), Am. Chem. Soc., Nat. Environ. Health Assn. (cert. hazardous materials profl.), Korean Chem. Soc., Royal Asiatic Soc. (bd. dirs. 1982-83), Assn. Mil. Surgeons U.S., Am. Acad. Sanitarians (cert.), Health Physics Soc., Am. Indsl. Hygiene Assn., Am. Acad. Health Physics (assoc.). Republican. Roman Catholic. Avocations: amateur radio, asian studies, photography. Office: Shanghai Lianheng Isocyanate Co Ltd Shanghai Chem Indsl Pk No 127 Shengong Rd Shanghai 201507 China Office Phone: 86-21-6712-1122 ext. 2003. E-mail: langfoe@slic.com.cn.

LANGGOOD, JUDITH ANN, secondary level art educator; b. Buffalo, Feb. 2, 1950; d. Alfred Victor Canetti and Irma Frances (Oakes) Reitz. BA, Geneseo (N.Y.) State Coll., 1972; MS in Edn., SUNY, Buffalo, 2000. Cert. elem. and secondary sch. art tchr., N.Y. H.S. art tchr., Holland, 1995—2002, Christian Home & Bible Sch., Mount Dora, Fla., 2002—. Dir. art Camp Agape, Buffalo, 1978-80; cons. art activities Camp Fresh Horizons, Buffalo, 1995. Freelance jewelry designer and fabricator, 1975—; exhibited paintings in area art shows, 1977—. Mem. Nat. Art Edn. Assn., N.Y. State Art Tchrs. Assn., Fla. Art Edn. Assn., Buffalo Fine Arts Acad., Kappa Delta Pi, Alpha Sigma Lambda. Avocations: painting, ceramics, jewelry design, music, literature. Home: 613 Chautauqua Dr Mount Dora FL 32757-6348

LANGGUTH, ARTHUR JOHN, journalist, educator, writer; b. Mpls, July 11, 1933; s. Arthur John and Doris Elizabeth (Turnquist) Langguth. BA cum laude, Harvard U., 1955. Corr. Cowles Newsletter, 1959; mem. bur. Look Mag. Bur., Washington, 1959; polit. corr. for Presdl. election Valley Times Cowles Publ., San Fernando Valley, Calif., 1960, corr. Calif. gubernatorial election, 1962; reporter NY Times, Dallas, 1963, NC, 1963, corr. S.E. Asia, 1964, bur. chief Saigon (Vietnam), 1965; spl. assignment NY Times Mag., 1968, 70; reporter NY Times, Miss., 1963, 1963. Prof. emeritus Annenberg Sch. of Journalism, USC. Fellow Shaw traveling fellow, Harvard Coll., 1955—56, John Simon Guggenheim Meml. Found., 1976—77. Mem.: Author's Guild. Home: 1922 Whitley Ave Los Angeles CA 90068-3233 E-mail: langguth@usc.edu.

LANGHAMMER, FRED H., cosmetics company executive; b. Germany, 1944; Gen. mgr. Dodwell Japan subs. Inchcape, Brit. trading com.; pres. Estee Lauder Japan, Tokyo, 1975-82; mng. dir. Estee Lauder Germany, 1982-85; exec. v.p., COO, Estee Lauder Cos., Inc., N.Y.C., 1985, in-charge rsch. and quality control, 1991-95, pres., COO, 1995—2000, CEO, 2000—04, chmn. global affairs, 2004—. Bd. dirs. RJR Nabisco Holdings Corp.; ind. dir. The Walt Disney Co., 2004—. Bd. dirs. Johns Hopkins U. Am. Inst. for Contemporary German Studies. Mem.: Mem. Cosmetic, Toiletry and Fragrance Assn. (bd. dirs.). Office: Estee Lauder Cos Inc 767 5th Ave New York NY 10153-0003

LANGHANS, EDWARD ALLEN, drama and theater educator; b. Warren, Pa., Mar. 11, 1923; s. Allen Milton and Frances Allen L. BA, U. Rochester, 1948, MA in English, 1949; MA in Theatre, U. Hawaii, 1951; PhD in Theatre, Yale U., 1955. Asst. prof. drama U. Tex., Austin, 1955-57; asst. prof. drama and theatre U. Hawaii, Honolulu, 1957-64, assoc., 1964-71, prof., chmn. dept., 1971-85, assoc. dean arts and humanities, 1987, prof. emeritus, 1988—. Vis. prof. Tufts U., 1967-68; rsch. prof. George Washington U., 1975-76. Author: (with Philip Highfill and Kalman Burnim) A Biographical Dictionary of Actors, Actresses, Musicians, Dancers, Managers and Other Stage Personnel in London 1660-1800, 16 vols., 1973-93, Five Restoration Theatrical Adaptations, 1980, Restoration Promptbooks, 1981, Eighteenth-Century British and Irish Promptbooks, 1987; co-author: An International Dictionary of Theater Language, 1985; contbr. chpt. to book and articles to The New Grove Dictionary of Opera, 4 vols., 1992, International Dictionary of Theatre: Actors, Directors and Designers, 1996, Cambridge and Blackwell Companions to Restoration Drama, 2000, 01, Brief Lives, 2003; dir., designer numerous plays. Bd. dirs. Honolulu Theatre for Youth, 1958-63, Hawaii Theatre Council, 1965-70, Hawaii Theatre Festival, 1978-82. Served with USAAF, 1942-47. Decorated Air medal, D.F.C.; Nat. Endowment for Humanities grantee, 1975-76, 85-86; Folger Shakespeare Library fellow, 1970-73 Mem. Am. Assn for Theatre in Higher Edn., Soc. Theatre Research, Am. Soc. Theatre Research. Home: 1212 Punahou St Apt 3402 Honolulu HI 96826-1026

LANGHINRICHS, RUTH IMLER, playwright, writer; b. Chgo., Oct. 30, 1922; d. Roy Franklin Imler and Susan Martha Smith; m. Richard Alan Langhinrichs, May 31, 1958 (dec. July 31, 1990); children: Julia Marie Lewis-Langhinrichs, Jennifer Florence Langhinrichsen-Rohling. BS cum laude, Northwestern U., Evanston, IL, 1944. Rsch. asst. LOOK Mag., N.Y.C., 1944—46; asst. editor Sci. Illus., N.Y.C., 1946—49; asst. feature editor Scholastic Mag., N.Y.C., 1949—51; assoc. editor Ladies Home Jour., Phila., 1951—58; faculty Purdue U., Fort Wayne, Ind., 1966—76; instr. Channing Sch. for Girls, London, 1974—75; writer Fort Wayne Fine Arts Found., Ind., 1977—79; pub. rels. Pk. Ctr., Fort Wayne, Ind., 1979—84; writing cons. Ind.-Purdue U. a, Fort Wayne, Ind., 1998—. Facilitator: memoir writing workshops Friends of the Libr., Fort Wayne, Ind., 1998—. Playwright (play) Feathers, The Heart of the Limberlost: Gene Stratton-Porter, Mermaids in the Basement; author: (book) Boy Dates Girl, You're Asking Me?, (novel) The Maiden and the Crone; playwright (play) A Night on Walden Pond. Charter mem. Fort Wayne Civic Youtheatre, Ind., 1973—77; bd. mem. Martin Luther King Montessori Sch., Fort Wayne, Ind., 1975—78; founding mem. Cinema Ctr., Fort Wayne, Ind., 1976—80; bd. mem. Citizen's Cable, Fort Wayne, Ind., 1981—84; pres. Aging and In Home Svcs. of N.E. Ind., Fort Wayne, Ind., 1976—2001; bd. mem. Ft. Wayne Women's Bur., Ind., 1991—97, N.E. Ind. Coun. of Tchrs. of English, Fort Wayne, Ind., 1969—73. Recipient Four-year scholarship, Chgo. Women's Ideal Club, 1940, Woman of the Yr. award, Ft. Wayne Women's Bur., 2001, Summit award, Zonta Club Internat., 2003. Mem.: Internat. Assn. of Bus. Communicators (charter mem. 1978—79), Zonta Club Internat. (v.p. 2003), Fortnightly Club, Delta Delta Delta (life). Unitarian Universalist. Avocations: gardener, artist, commissioned clown. Home: 4422 S Wayne Ave Fort Wayne IN 46807 Personal E-mail: ruthlangx@aol.com.

LANGLAND, HAROLD REED (TUCK), sculptor, educator; b. Mpls., Oct. 6, 1939; BA in Art, U. Minn., 1961, MFA in Sculpture, 1964. Asst. lectr. Carlisle Coll. Art, Eng., 1964-65, Sheffield Coll. Art, Eng., 1965-67; asst. prof. Murray State U., Ky., 1967-71; assoc. prof. Ind. U. at South Bend, 1971-77, prof., 1978—. Vis. prof. N. Staffordshire Poly., Stoke-on-Trent, Eng., 1977-78. One man shows include Midwest Mus. Am. Art, 1984, South Bend Regional Mus. of Art, 1987, Filli Gallery, Chgo., 1997, Hillsdale Coll., Mich., 1996, Krasl Art Ctr., St. Joseph, Minn., 1999, S.W. Mich. Coll., Dowagiac, Mich., 1999, Hoosier Salon Show, Indpls., 1980, 82, 84, 85, 86 (Outstanding Work in Sculpture awards), collections include: Midwest Mus. Am. Art, Elkhart, Ind., Calhoun St. Pedestrian Mall, Ft. Wayne, Ind., Beatrice Foods, Chgo., Morris Civic Auditorium, South Bend, U. Minn., Mpls., Ind. U. at South Bend, Notre Dame U., South Bend, Minn. Mus. Art, St. Paul; nat. exhbns. include: NAD, N.Y.C., 1982, 83, 99, Salmagundi Club, N.Y.C., 1982, 83, 99, Terrace Gallery Show (Honorable Mention award), Palenville, N.Y., 1982, Audobon Artists, N.Y.C., 1984, Nat. Sculpture Soc. (Liskin Prize 1986), N.Y.C., 1985; invitational exhbns. include: Royal Festival Hall, London, 1980, Promega, Madison, Wis., 1996, Lyme Acad., Conn., 1997, Chesterwood, Mass., 1997. Recipient grants Ind. Arts Commn., 1980, U.S. Ednl. Found. India, 1982, USIA to Uganda, 1992. Mem. NAD (academician, 1995-), Nat. Sculptors Guild. Avocations: choral singing, swimming. Office Phone: 219-272-2708. Personal E-mail: tuckandjan@aol.com.

LANGLANDS, ROBERT PHELAN, mathematician, educator; b. New Westminster, Can., Oct. 6, 1936; came to U.S., 1960; s. Robert and Kathleen (Phelan) L.; m. Charlotte Lorraine Cheverie, Aug. 13, 1956; children: William, Sarah, Robert, Thomasin. BA, U. B.C., 1957, MA, 1958, DS honoris causa, 1985; PhD, Yale U., 1960; DSc (hon.), McMaster U., 1985, CUNY, 1985; D in Math. (hon.), U. Waterloo, 1988; DSc (hon.), U. Paris, 1989, McGill U., 1991, Toronto U., 1993, U. Montréal, 1997, U. Laval, 2002. From instr. to assoc. prof. Princeton (N.J.) U., 1960-67; prof. math. Yale U., New Haven, 1968-72, Inst. Advanced Study, Princeton, 1972—. Author: Euler Products, 1971, (with H. Jacquet) Automorphic Forms on GL (2), 1970, On the Functional Equations Satisfied by Eisenstein Series, 1976, Base Change for GL (2), 1980, Les Débuts d'une Formule des Traces Stable, 1983. Recipient Wilbur Lucius Cross medal Yale U., 1975, Common Wealth award Sigma Xi, 1984, Mathematics award Nat. Acad. Sci., 1988, Wolf prize in math. Wolf Found., 1995-96, la Grande Médaille d'Or de l'Académie des Scis., 2000. Fellow Royal Soc. London, Royal Soc. Can.; mem. NAS, Am. Math Soc. (Cole prize 1982, Steele prize 2005), Can. Math. Soc. Office: Inst Advanced Study Sch Math Olden Ln Princeton NJ 08540

LANGLEY, DONNA, film company executive; Sr. v.p. prodn. New Line Cinema, 1994—2001, Universal Pictures, 2001—03, exec. v.p. prodn., 2003—05, pres. prodn., 2005—. Exec. prodr.: (films) Austin Powers: The Spy Who Shagged Me, 1999, Drop Dead Gorgeous, 1999, The Astronaut's Wife, 1999, The Bachelor, 1999, The Cell, 2000, Lost Souls, 2000, Highway, 2002. Office: Universal Pictures 100 Universal City Plz Universal City CA 91608*

LANGLEY, GEORGE ROSS, medical educator; b. Sydney, N.S., Can., Oct. 6, 1931; s. John Goerge Elmer and Freda Catherine (Ross) L.; m. Jean Marie Ballantyne, June 22, 1957; children: Joanne Marie, Mark Ross, Richard Graham. BA, Mt. Allison U., 1952; MD, Dalhousie U., 1957. Intern Victoria Gen. Hosp., Halifax, N.S., 1957, resident, 1958, Toronto (Ont.) Gen. Hosp., 1960, U. Melbourne, Australia, 1961, U. Rochester, N.Y., 1962; John and Mary Markle scholar in acad. medicine Dalhousie U., Halifax, 1963-68, from lectr. to prof. medicine, 1963-69, prof., chmn. dept. medicine, 1974-82; chief of service medicine Camp Hill Hosp., Halifax, 1969-74; head dept. medicine Victoria Gen. Hosp., 1974-82; prof. medicine Dalhousie U., Queen Elizabeth II Health. Sci. Ctr., 1982—2002; exec. dir. Strategic Hlth. Svcs. Dept. Hlth. Provinces, Nova Scotia, Canada, 1998-2000, prof. emeritus, 2002—, Dalhousie U., 2002—. Chmn. clin. investigation grants com. Med. Research Council, 1976-78; chmn. clin. and epidemiol. research adv. com., bd. dirs. Nat. Cancer Inst. Can., 1978-86 Contbr. articles to profl. jours. Recipient Queen's Silver Jubilee medal, 1977, Queen's Golden Jubilee medal, 2002, Dalhousie Med. Alumnus of Yr., 2003. Fellow Internat. Soc. Hematology, Royal Coll. Physicians and Surgeons (v.p., coun., Wightman vis. prof. 1990), ACP (bd. govs. 1973-78, laureate Atlantic region 1996), Royal Coll. Physicians (Edinburgh); mem. Can. Hematology Soc. (pres. 1976-78), Can. Soc. Clin. Investigation, Am. Soc. Hematology, Can. Soc. Oncology, Alpha Omega Alpha. Mem. United Ch. Can. Home: 6025 Oakland Rd Halifax NS Canada B3H 1N9 Office: Victoria Gen Hosp Ste 8-024 Halifax NS Canada B3H 2Y9 Office Phone: 902-473-7538. Business E-Mail: ross.langley@dal.ca.

LANGLEY, PATRICIA ANN, lobbyist; b. Butler, Pa., Feb. 13, 1938; d. F.J. and Ella (Serafine) Piccola; m. Harold D. Langley, June 12, 1965; children: Erika, David. BA, U. Pitts., 1961; postgrad., Georgetown U., 1967, Cath. U. Am., 1985, George Mason U., 1990—. Legis. staff U.S. Congress, Washington, 1961-63; dir. social studies Am. Polit. Sci. Assn., Washington, 1963-65; legis. specialist U.S. Congress, Washington, 1965-67, caseworker, 1967-68; polit. staff Dem. Study Group U.S. Congress, Washington, 1969; Washington rep. Family Services Am., 1975-82, dir. Washington hdqrs., 1989-92, v.p. for govt. rels., 1992; pres. Policy Directions, Arlington, Va., 1992—. Vis. lectr. in sociology George Mason U., Fairfax, Va., 1994; bd. dirs. Coalition for Children and Youth, Washington, 1977-78; chmn. steering com. for the Coalition on White House Conf. on Families, 1979-80, Ad Hoc Coalition on A.F.D.C., 1981-82; co-founder Ptnrs. in Change Group, 1996. Active Donaldson Run Civic Assn., Arlington, Va., 1980—; bd. dirs. Va. Chamber Orch.; vol. docent Hillwood Mus., Washington, 1995—. Recipient Service Recognition award, U.S. Dept. Health and Human Svcs., 1980. Mem.: Nat. Coun. Family Rels., Women in Govt. Rels., Am. Soc. Assn. Execs., Arnova, Groves Conf., N. Va. Assn. Female Execs. Roman Catholic. Avocations: gardening, reading, old movies, community organizing. Home and Office: 2515 N Utah St Arlington VA 22207-4031 Business E-Mail: plangley@aol.com.

LANGLEY, RHONDA HOOD, reading specialist; b. Chgo., Ill., June 15, 1965; d. Delmer H. and Marian L. Hood; m. Mike L. Langley, Apr. 29, 1988; children: Kaydi Lynn, Noah Lee. BS in Early Childhood Edn., U. Ala., 1987; MA in Early Childhood Edn., West. Ala. U., 1991; adminstrn. cert., U. Ala., 2000; reading specialist cert., Ala. A&M U., 2004. Tchr. K-1 Martin Luther King Jr. Elem., Tuscaloosa, Ala., 1987—91; parent involvement Winston County Schs., Double Springs, Ala., 1991—92; tchr. K-1 Double Springs (Ala.) Elem., 1992—2000, reading specialist, 2000—02, Addison (Ala.) Elem., 2002—. Named Tchr. of Yr., Double Springs Elem., 2002. Mem.: Ala. Reading Assn., Internat. Reading Assn. Republican. Baptist. Avocations: scrapbooks, reading. Home: 6 County Rd 3728 Addison AL 35540

LANGLEY, RICKY LEE, occupational medicine physician; b. Fountain, NC, Aug. 31, 1957; s. Ernest Lee and Janie Ruth (Fulford) L.; m. Sandra Jane Ward, June 7, 1980; children: Patrick, Nicholas, Megan. BS magna cum laude, NC State U., 1979; MD, Bowman Grey Sch. Medicine, 1983; MPH, U. NC, 1988. Diplomate Am. Bd. Internal Medicine, Am. Bd. Preventive Medicine. Intern East Carolina Sch. Medicine, Greenville, NC, 1983-84, resident, 1984-86; asst. prof. dept. preventive medicine and health policy East Carolina U., Greenville, 1989-91, adj. asst. prof. dept. family medicine, 1989-91, adj. asst. prof. dept. environ. health, 1989-98, asst. prof. dept. internal medicine, 1991; fellow Sch. Medicine Duke U., Durham, NC, 1986-88, asst. cons. prof. in occupl. medicine, 1989-90, asst. clin. prof. dept. cmty. and family medicine, 1991-96; pvt. practice occupl. medicine Health and Hygiene, Inc., Greensboro, NC, 1988-89; med. dir. Mebane (NC) Med. Ctr., 1996-98, Kernodle Clinic, Inc., 1998; pub. health physician Occupl. and Environ. Epidemiology, Dept. Health & Human Svc., Raleigh, NC, 1998—. Adj. asst. prof. dept. biol. and agrl. engring. NC State U., 1996—99; cons. in field; mem. planning com. on agrl. safety NC State Fair, 1991; mem. task force Agri-Bus. for Gov.'s Commn. on Reduction of Infant Morality, 1992; mem. NC State Task Force on Blood-Borne Pathogens NC Occupl. Health and Safety Adminstrn., 1991—92; presenter in field.; mem. Nat. Pork Procedures Coun. Task Force on Worker Health and Safety, 1995; occupl. medicine residency program evaluator for NIOSH, 1992—96, mem. spl. emphasis panel, 1996—; mem. agrl. safety and health coun. NC Dept. Labor, 1996—; mem. NC Pesticide Bd., 1998—; occupl. medicine residency adv. com. Duke U., 1998—; mem. bd. collaborators NC Inst. Health and Safety in Agr., Forestry & Fisheries, 2001—. Author: Sex and Gender Differences in Health and Disease, 2003; editor: Safety and Health in Agriculture, Forestry and Fisheries, 1997, (textbook) Animal Handlers; guest editor NC Med. Jour., 1992, 93, 95, mem. editl. bd., 1999—; mem. editl. bd. Jour. Agromedicine, 2004—; co-editor Environmental Health Secrets, 2001; contbr. articles to profl. jours. Vol. Greenville Cmty. Shelter, 1990, Health Hotline, WITN, 1990, 91, State Employee Wellness Day 1989, Adopt-A-Hwy. Project, 1989; Dr. of the Day, NC State Legislature, 1991; doctor on call blood drive ARC, Greensboro, 1989; vol. Freemont Peoples Clinic, 1993; pub. affairs officer, mem. USCG Aux., 1996-99, flotilla 18-11, 1995-98; hunting safety educator, NC, 1996—; mem. Alamance County (NC) Bd. Adjustment, 1997-99. Lloyd T. Weeks scholar, 1978, Benjamin Elloit Ibie and Benjamin Elliot Ibie Jr. Meml. scholar, 1976. Fellow ACP, Am. Coll. Occupl. and Environ. Medicine (del. 1995-98), Am. Coll. Preventive Medicine; mem. AMA, NC Med. Soc. (environ. health subcom. 1991—, vice chair 1999-2000, chair 2000-01), Am. Occupl. Med. Assn. (mem. med. ctr. occupl. health com. 1990-97), Carolinas Occupl. Med. Assn. (sec.-treas. 1991-92, pres-elect 1992-93, pres. 1993-94, del. 1995-98), NC Archeol. Soc. (exec. bd. 1998-2000), Tarheel Archaeology Soc. (edn. chair 1996-2000), Found. for Advanced Lithics Studies (sec.-treas. 2000—), Jour. Agromedicine (editl. bd. mem., 2004-05, Sigma Xi, Phi Kappa Phi, Phi Eta Sigma, Gamma Sigma Delta, Alpha Epsilon Delta. Avocations: astronomy, archeology. Home: 1506 Miles Chapel Rd Mebane NC 27302-9008 Office: Mebane Med Clinic Mebane NC 27302 Office Phone: 919-773-3410. E-mail: rick.langley@ncmail.net.

LANGLEY, ROLLAND AMENT, JR., engineering and management consultant; b. San Francisco, Aug. 22, 1931; s. Rolland Ament and Kathryn Lee (Beals) L.; m. Pamela Winston, May 15, 1954 (div. 1978); children: Owen C., Cynthia, James R.; m. Chiara Bini-Sexton, Apr. 12, 1978. BS in Engring. and Physics, U. Calif., Berkeley, 1953; MME, U. Pitts., 1961; MBA, Golden Gate U., 1973. Engr. Bettis Atomic Power Lab. of Westinghouse Electric Corp., Pitts., 1957-62; with Bechtel Corp., San Francisco, 1962-71; mgr. refinery and chem. nuclear fuel ops. Bechtel Inc., San Francisco, 1977-78; mgr. projects nuclear fuel ops. Bechtel Nat. Inc., San Francisco, 1979-80, mgr. decontamination and restoration nuclear fuel ops., 1980-81, v.p., mgr. nuclear fuels ops. Oak Ridge, Tenn., 1981-84, sr. v.p., mgr. div. ops., R & D ops. San Francisco, 1985-89; dep. mgr. Uranium Enrichment Assocs., San Francisco, 1972-76; v.p. Uranium Enrichment Tech. Inc., San Francisco, 1976-77; pres., dir. Bechtel Systems Mgmt. Inc., 1988-90; pres., CEO BNFL Inc., 1990-97, 98-99, also bd. dirs., 1994-2000; exec. v.p. Project Time & Cost, Inc., 2005—. Bd. dirs. 21st Century Coatings, Plato Sys., GmbH; trustee, pres. World Mem. Fund-U.S.A., 1993-98; chmn., Pajarito Sci. Corp., 1995-97, bd. dirs.; pres. Pacific Nuclear Coun., 1998-2000; mem. Nat. Acad. Sci. panel on nuclear separation and transmutation, 1992-95; counsellor Atlantic Coun. U.S., 2003—; adv. dir. European Inst., 2000—. Contbr. articles to profl. jours. Trustee Environ. Sci. and Tech. Inst., 1995-98. Capt. USNR. Recipient Bausch and Lomb Sci. award, 1948. Mem. Naval Res Assn. (past pres. Golden Gate chpt.), Brit.-Am. Bus. Assn. (bd. dirs. 1997—). Achievements include patents in nuclear fuel and reactor systems design; research on uranium enrichment, nuclear waste disposal, fast breeder reactors, and engineering management. Home: PO Box 208 Middleburg VA 20118-0208 Office Phone: 540-687-4137. E-mail: ralangley@earthlink.net.

LANGMEAD, JOSEPH MICHAEL, accountant, consultant, educator; b. Balt., Nov. 5, 1944; s. Richard James and Dorothy Kathleen (DeCarlo) L.; m. Judy Kay Kearney, June 26, 1969; children: Maureen Langmead Cochran, Gregory, Benjamin. BSBA, Loyola Coll., 1968, MBA, 1973; postgrad., St. Mary's Sem. and Univ., Balt., 2000—. CPA, Md. Acct. Kushnick & Waldman, Balt., 1965—68; auditor KPMG, Balt., 1968—76, ptnr. NYC, 1976—2000. SEC reviewing ptnr. KPMG, London, 1994—2000; exec. in residence, adj. prof. acctg. and fin. Sellinger Sch. Bus. and Mgmt., Loyola Coll., 2002—; cons. in field. Pres. bd. trustees Ctr. Stage, Balt., 1981-88, chmn. capital campaign, 1988-91; chmn. bd. trustees Loyola H.S., Towson, Md., 1983-87; bd. fin. City of Balt., 1988-92; trustee Roland Pk. Country Sch., Balt., 1990-93, Md. State Arts Coun., Balt., 1991-94; chmn. Balt. Arts Stabilization Project Com., 1991-94; bd. dirs. Nat. Arts Stabilization, Balt., 1991-2001, chmn., 2000-2001; bd. dirs. Md. chpt. Nat. Multiple Sclerosis Soc., 2002-04, vice chmn., 2003-04. With U.S. Army, 1968-70 Mem. AICPA, Md. Assn. CPA (bd. dirs. 1990-93), Mensa. Democrat. Roman Catholic. Avocations: opera, music, theology, history. Home: 102 Witherspoon Rd Baltimore MD 21212 Office Phone: 410-435-8333. Personal E-mail: joseph.langmead@verizon.net.

LANG-MIERS, ELIZABETH ANN, judge; b. Mpls., Nov. 26, 1950; BA, U. Mo., 1972, JD, 1975. Bar: Mo. 1975, Tex. 1977, U.S. Ct. Appeals (5th cir.), U.S. Supreme Ct. Law clk. to presiding justice Mo. Supreme Ct., Jefferson City, 1975-76; ptnr. Locke Liddell & Sapp, LLP, Dallas, 1976—2003; judge Ct. Appeals, 5th Dist. Bd. dirs. Tex. Bar. Mem. Dallas County Med. Soc. Aux., bd. dirs. Met. YWCA; bd. dirs., chairperson adv. bd. Women's Resource Ctr. Leadership Dallas, Leadership Tex., Leadership Am. Recipient Am. Jurisprudence awards 1973, 74. Fellow Am. Bar Found., Tex. Bar Found. (trustee), Dallas Bar Found. (trustee, chair); mem. ABA (mem. ho. dels), Am. Law Inst., Dallas Bar Assn. (v.p. adminstrn., v.p. activities, sec.-treas., chair, vice chair bd. dirs., pres. 1998), Dallas Found. (vice chair bd. govs.), Tex. Young Lawyers Assn. (com. chair), Dallas Assn. Young Lawyers (com. chair), State Bar (bd. dirs., com. chair, Pres.'s citation 1996, 98, Woman of Excellence award, 1998, Louise Raggio award 1998, Judge Sam Williams Leadership award). Office: Ct of Appeals 600 Commerce Ste 200 Dallas TX 75201 Office Phone: 214-712-3403.

LANGONE, KENNETH, investment company executive; married; 3 children. BA, Bucknell U., 1957; MBA, NYU Stern Sch. of Bus. Exec. v.p. R.W. Pressprich & Co.; founder, chmn., mng. dir., CEO and pres. Invemed Assocs., NYC, 1974—, dir., 1999; co-founder, dir., mem. exec. com. Home Depot Inc., 1978. Bd. dirs. Choicepoint, Inc., GE, 1999—, Yum Brands, Inc., 1997—, Unifi, Inc., NY Stock Exch., Home Depot, 1978—, TRICON Global Restaurants, AutoFinance, Inc., InterWorld Corp., DBT Online, Inc., US Satellite Broadcasting of Minn. Vice-chmn. bd. overseers Stern Sch. Bus.; chmn. bd. trustees NYU Med. Sch.; trustee, chmn. nominating com., chmn. endowment com., mem. exec. com. Bucknell U.; contbr., advisor, transformation team Mayor Rudolph Giuliani, 1993; chmn., NY State Sen. Bob Dole, presidential election, 1996; trustee, chmn. nominating com., chmn. endowment com., mem. exec. com. NY Philharm., Children's Oncology Soc. (Ronald McDonald House), Robin Hood Found.; trustee, mem. exec. com. NYU; bd. dirs., vice-chmn. bd. develop. Damon Runyon-Walter Winchell Found.; trustee Ctr. for Strategic & Internat. Studies (CSIS). Office: Invemed Assocs 375 Park Ave Ste 2205 New York NY 10152 Address: Damon Runyon Cancer Rsch Found 675 Third Ave New York NY 10017

LANGRAN, ROBERT WILLIAMS, political scientist, educator; b. N.Y.C., Feb. 15, 1935; s. Robert Joseph and Leona Gertrude (Williams) L.; m. Eleanor Victoria Groh, Dec. 26, 1959; children: Irene, Elizabeth, Thomas. BS with honors, Loyola U., Chgo., 1956; MA, Fordham U., 1959; PhD, Bryn Mawr Coll., 1965. Prof. polit. sci. Villanova U., Pa., 1959—. Author: The United States Supreme Court: An Historical and Political Analysis, 1989, 5th edit. 2004, The Supreme Court: A Concise History, 2004; co-author: Government, Business, and the American Economy, 2001; contbr. articles to profl. publs. Served to 1st lt. U.S. Army, 1956-58. Mem. Am. Polit. Sci. Assn., Supreme Ct. Hist. Soc. Office: Villanova Univ Political Sci Dept Villanova PA 19085 Office Phone: 610-519-4734. Business E-Mail: robert.langran@villanova.edu.

LANGRIDGE, ROBERT, biophysicist, educator, computational biologist; b. Essex, Eng., Oct. 26, 1933; came to U.S., 1957; naturalized, 1987. s. Charles and Winifred (Lister) L.; m. Ruth Gottlieb, June 26, 1960; children: Elizabeth, Catherine, Suzanne. BSc in Physics (1st class honours), U. London, Eng., 1954, PhD in Crystallography, 1957. Vis. research fellow biophysics Yale, 1957-59; research assoc. biophysics M.I.T., 1959-61; research assoc. pathology Children's Cancer Research Found., Boston; research assoc. biophysics, lectr. biophysics, also tutor biochem. scis. Harvard, 1961-66; research assoc. Project MAC, Lab. for Computer Sci., M.I.T., 1964-66; prof. biophysics and info. scis. U. Chgo., 1966-68; prof. chemistry and biochem. scis. Princeton, 1968-76; prof. pharm. chemistry, biochemistry and biophysics, dir. Computer Graphics Lab. U. Calif., San Francisco, 1976-94, prof. emeritus, 1994—, mem. adv. com. resource for biocomputing visualization and informatics, 1998—2004. Vis. prof. computer sci. Stanford U., 1983-84; vis. prof. biochem., biophys. Oreg. State U., 1995-97; mem. computer and biomath. rsch. study sect. NIH, USPHS, 1968-72, chmn., 1975-77, mem. nat. adv. rsch. resources coun., 1992-96, mem. adv. com. to dir., 1993-95, mem. biomed. informatics expert panel, 2004—; mem: vis. com. biology dept. Brookhaven Nat. Lab., 1977-80, mem. adv. com. neutron diffraction, biology dept., 1980-83; mem. sci. and ednl. adv. com. Lawrence Berkeley Labs., 1988-92; chair U. Calif. Berkeley/U. Calif. San Francisco Grad. Group in Bioengring., 1991-93; mem. computer sci. and telecomm. bd. NRC, NAS, 1988-91. Guggenheim fellow, 1983-84 Fellow AAAS; mem. NAS, Inst. of Medicine. Home: 60 The Crescent Berkeley CA 94708-1702 E-mail: rl@cgl.ucsf.edu.

LANGROCK, KARL FREDERICK, writer, retired academic administrator; b. Toeterville, Iowa, Jan. 26, 1927; s. Lee Henry and Alice Dora (Grube) L.; m. Rose Marie Meyer, June 4, 1950; children: Laura Sue, Charles Alan. BA, U. No. Iowa, 1949; MA, U. Iowa, 1951; MDiv, Luth. Sch. Theology, Chgo., 1955; LittD (hon.), Grand View Coll., 1989. Pastor Lake Park Luth. Ch., Milw., 1955-57, Resurrection Luth. Ch., Franklin Park, Ill., 1957-62, Luth. Ch. of the Holy Spirit, Deerfield, Ill., 1962-69; asst. to pres. Berea (Ky.) Coll., 1969-72; pres. Grand View Coll., Des Moines, 1972-88; free-lance writer, 1988—. Mem. Iowa Coll. Aid Commn., Des Moines, 1980-84, Luth. Social Services of Ill., Chgo., 1962-70, pres., 1968-70. Served in USN, 1945-46. Mem. Iowa Assn. Independent Colls. and Univs. (bd. dirs. 1972-87, chmn. 1986-87), Council of Luth. Ch. in Am. Colls. (pres. 1978), Phi Eta Sigma. Lutheran. Address: 6665 W Burnside Rd Apt 456 Portland OR 97210-6669

LANGSLEY, PAULINE ROYAL, psychiatrist; b. Lincoln, Nebr., July 2, 1927; d. Paul Ambrose and Dorothy (Sibley) Royal; m. Donald G. Langsley, Sept. 9, 1955; children: Karen Jean, Dorothy Ruth Langsley Runman, Susan Louise. BA, Mills Coll., 1949; MD, U. Nebr., 1953. Cert. psychiatrist, Am. Bd. Psychiatry and Neurology. Intern Mt. Zion Hosp., San Francisco, 1954; resident U. Calif., San Francisco, 1954-57, student health psychiatrist Berkeley, 1957-61, U. Colo., Boulder, 1961-68; assoc. clin. prof. psychiatry U. Calif. Med. Sch., Davis, 1968-76; student health psychiatrist U. Calif., Davis, 1968-76; assoc. clin. prof. psychiatry U. Cin., 1976-82; pvt. practice psychiatry Cin., 1976-82; cons. psychiatrist Federated States of Micronesia, Pohnpei, 1984-87; fellow in geriatric psychiatry Rush-Presbyn./St. Luke Hosp., Chgo., 1989-91. Mem. accreditation rev. com. Accreditation Coun. for Continuing Med. Edn., 1996-98. Trustee Mills Coll., Oakland, 1974-78, 2001—; bd. dirs. Evanston Women's Club. Fellow Am. Psychiat. Assn. (chair continuing med. edn. 1990-96); mem. AMA, Am. Med. Womens Assn., Ohio State Med. Assn., Ill. Psychiat. Soc. (sec. 1993-95, pres.-elect 1995-96, pres. 1996-97, accreditation coun. 1996-98). Home and Office: 9445 Monticello Ave Evanston IL 60203-1117

LANGSNER, ALAN MICHAEL, pediatric cardiologist; b. N.Y.C., Dec. 21, 1948; s. Herman and Celeste (Prince) L.; m. Hilary Schmidt, Dec. 19, 1971. BA in Psychology, Fairleigh Dickinson U., 1970; MD, U. Autonomia Guadalajara, Jalisco, Mex., 1977; postgrad., NYU, 1977-78. Cert. Am. Bd. Pediat. and Pediat. Cardiology. Resident in pediatrics N.Y. Med. Coll./Met. Hosp. Ctr., N.Y.C., 1978-79, resident in pediatrics-primary care tng. program, 1979-80, chief resident in pediatrics-primary care tng. program, 1980-81; pvt. practice pediatric cardiology N.Y.C., 1983—; attending pediatrics, sr. cons. pediatric cardiology St. Barnabas Med. Ctr., Livingston, N.J., 1983—; assoc. cons. pediatric cardiology St. Vincent's Med. Ctr., S.I., N.Y., 1983—; chief dept. pediatric cardiology Children's Hosp. of N.J. at Newark Beth Israel Hosp., 1999—2004. Cons. pediatric cardiology, assoc. prof. pediatrics NYU Sch. Medicine, N.Y.C., 1983—, S.I. U. Hosp., 1985—; mem. perinatal rev. com., med. bd. St. Barnabas Med. Ctr.; presenter in field Contbr. articles to profl. jours. Fellow Am. Coll. Cardiology, Am. Acad. Pediatrics; mem. AMA, Essex County Med. Soc. Office: 405 Northfield Ave West Orange NJ 07052-3023 Office Phone: 973-736-9997.

LANGSTAFF, JOHN MEREDITH, musician; b. Bklyn., Dec. 24, 1920; s. Bridgewater Meredith and Esther Knox (Boardman) Langstaff; m. Diane Guggenheim; 1 child, Carol; m. Nancy Graydon Woodbridge, Apr. 3, 1948; children: John Elliot, Peter Gerry, Deborah Graydon. Student, Curtis Inst. Music, Juilliard Sch. Music, Columbia U. Founder, dir. emeritus Revels, Inc., Watertown, Mass. Mem. faculty Simmons Coll., Boston, 1970—86, Wheelock Coll., Boston, 1974—79, Mass. Coll. Art, 1977, Boston Coll., 1979, U. Conn., 1977—79, Lesley Coll., 1978—99; artistic dir. Young Audiences Mass., 1972—81, adv. bd. mem., 1981—; lectr. in field. Author: Frog Went a-Courtin', 1955, Over in the Meadow, 1957, On Christmas Day in the Morning, 1959, The Swapping Boy, 1960, Ol' Dan Tucker, 1963, Hi! Ho! The Rattlin' Bog, 1969, Jim Along, Josie, 1970, Gather My Gold Together, 1971, The Golden Vanity, 1971, Soldier, Soldier, Won't You Marry Me?, 1972, The Two Magicians, 1973, Shimmy, Shimmy Coke-a-pop!, 1973, St. George and the Dragon, 1973, A-Hunting We Will go, 1974, A Season for Singing, 1974, Sweetly Sings the Donkey, 1976, Hot Cross Buns, 1978, The Christmas Revels Songbook, 1985, Sally Go Round the Moon, 1986, What a Morning!, 1987, Climbing Jacob's Ladder, 1991, I Have a Song to Sing-O, 1994; author: (foreword) Old Christmas, 1996; co-author: Celebrate the Spring, 1998, Celebrate the Winter, 2001, Making Music, 2003; co-author: (film) The Lively Art of Picture Books; recitals: rec.: Odeon-Capital, Jupiter, RCA-Victor, Nixa, Renaissance, CRI, Tradiiton, HMV, Desto, Weston Woods, Revels Records, Minstrel Records; soloist: Cantata Singers, N.Y. Philharmonic, Nat. Symphony, Montreal Symphony Orch., Little Orch. soc., N.Y. Oratorio Soc., Collegium Musicum, Stratford Shakespeare Festival, Mpls. Symphony Orch.; video: Making Music in the Classroom, 1995; Let's Sing!, Let's Keep on Singing!, 1997; Making Music with Children, 1999; dir.(music dept.): Potomac Sch., 1953—68, Shady Hill Sch., 1969—72. 1st lt. inf. AUS, WWII. Recipient Hope S. Dean Meml. award, Found. for Children's Books, 1991, citation, Boston Theater, 1996, award, Kodaly Music Inst., 2001, Country Dance and Song award, 2005. Mem.: English Folk Song Soc. (founder, dir. Christmas Revels 1956, 1957, 1966, 1970—2000, dir. Spring Revels 1972—97, dir. Sea Revels 1983—94), Actors Equity, Internat. Folk Music Coun. Office: Revels Inc 80 Mount Auburn St Watertown MA 02472-3930 E-mail: john.nancylangstaff@juno.com.

LANGSTON, JAMES LELAND, electronics engineer; b. Atlanta, Tex., July 26, 1942; s. Paul T. and Vernie D. (Bridges) Langston; m. Alice Jean Evans, 1985; 1 child, Brent Leland. BSEE, So. Meth. U., 1966, postgrad., 1966-67. Registered profl. engr., Tex. Technician Collins Radio, Richardson, Tex., 1961-65, design engr., 1965-67, lead engr., 1967-70, sr. engr., 1970-71, Tex. Instruments, Dallas, 1971-73, project engr., 1973-75, sys. engr., 1975-78, mem. tech. staff, 1978-82, sr. mem. tech. staff, 1982-98, disting. mem. tech. staff, 1998-99, engring. fellow, 1999—, program mgr. com. and signal processing, 1986-92, chief engring. comm. and electronic sys., 1992-96; chief tech. officer Crosspan divsn. Raytheon, 1998-2000, mgr. sys. engring. Colorado Springs, Colo., 2000—. Contbr. articles pub. to profl. jours. Recipient Group Achievement award, NASA, 1976, Pub. Svc. Award medal, 1981. Mem.: AIAA, ASCE, AAS, IEEE (sr.), Nat. Soc. Profl. Engr. Achievements include patents in field. Personal E-mail: leland_Langston@msn.com. Business E-Mail: j-langston2@raytheon.com.

LANGSTON, NANCY SUE FRIEDRICH, dean; b. Little Rock, Dec. 14, 1944; BSN cum laude, U. Ark., 1966; M in Surg. Nursing, Emory U., 1972; PhD in Edn., Ga. State U., 1977. RN, Va. Staff RN U. Ark. Med. Ctr., Little Rock, 1966-67, Doctor's Hosp., Shreveport, La., 1967; instr. Confederate Meml. Med. Ctr. Sch. Nursing, Shreveport, La., 1967-70, Northwestern State U. Sch. Nursing, Shreveport, La., 1970-71, Emory U. Sch. Nursing, Atlanta, 1972-73; adminstrv. intern U. Tex. Sys. Sch. Nursing, Austin, 1974-75, rsch. assoc., 1975-76; assoc. prof., assoc. dean undergrad. programs U. Nebr. Med. Coll. Nursing, Lincoln, 1976-85; prof., dean U. N.C. at Charlotte Coll. Nursing, 1985-91, Va. Commonwealth U. Sch. of Nursing, Richmond, 1991—. Nurse-cons. Goodwill Industries of Atlanta, Inc., 1973-74; adj. assoc. prof. U. Nebr. at Lincoln Tchrs. Coll., 1983-85 Contbr. articles to profl. jours., chpts. to books; presenter in field. Mem. bd. Fan Free Clinic, strategic planning com., 1994, med. svcs. com, 1994—, chmn. 1995; mem. Richmond Rotary, med. svcs. com. 1993—, chmn. 1994; mem. adv. bd. Here's To Your Health; bd. dirs. Hospice of Charlotte, 1988-91, chair profl. adv. com., 1989-91; mem. Civitan Charlotte, 1989-91, at-large 1991—; bd. dirs. Lincoln Lancaster Commn. on Status of Women, 1983-85, edn. com. 1981-85; bd. dirs. Southeast Nebr. Health Systems Agy., 1981-82; pub. issues com. Nebr. Cancer Soc., 1978-80; adv. bd. geriat. Atlanta Regional Commn., 1973; chair nursing sect., Shreveport chpt. ARC, 1969-71. Recipient award of honor Alumni Assn. Nell Hodgson Woodruff Sch. Nursing, Emory U., 1989; Am. Nurses' Found. scholar 1972, Rockefeller scholar 1962-64. Mem. ANA, Nat. League for Nursing, So. Nursing Rsch. Coun., Phi Kappa Phi, Phi Theta Kappa, Sigma Theta Tau. Office: Va Commonwealth U Sch Nursing PO Box 980567 Richmond VA 23298-0567

LANGSTON, PAUL T., dean, composer, music educator; b. Marianna, Fla., Sept. 15, 1928; s. Howard McGhee and Rosa (Jeffries) L.; m. Esther Howard, Aug. 12, 1950; children: Claire Beth, Erin, Howard. Pvt. study with Nadia Boulanger, 1962, 63; diploma, Conservatoire Americaine, France; BA, U. Fla., 1950; MS in Music, So. Bapt. Theol. Sem., 1953; SMD, Union Theol. Sem., 1963; DMus (hon.), Stetson U., 1985. Organist-choirmaster St. John's Bapt. Ch., Charlotte, N.C., 1953-60; instr. music theory Davidson Coll., 1959-60; mem. faculty Stetson U., De Land, Fla., 1960-93, dean Sch. Music, 1963-85, William Kenan Jr. prof. music, 1985-93, prof. and dean music emeritus, 1993—; assoc. condr. Charlotte Oratorio Singers, 1954-60. Dir. Fla. Internat. Music Festival, Fla. Internat. Music Festival Inst.; research fellow Inst. Sacred Music, Yale U., 1985 Composer organ, choral works.; oratorio Petros (premier Nov. 1983). Recipient Hand award for outstanding rsch., 1993; NEH fellow, U. N.C., Chapel Hill, 1978. Mem.: Assn. Anglican Musicians, Am. Guild Organists (McEniry award for tchg. excellence 1991), Delta Tau Delta, Pi Kappa Lambda, Omicron Delta Kappa. Home: 313 N Salisbury Ave Deland FL 32720-4054 E-mail: plangsto@dnet.net.

LANGSTON, SUE H., elementary school educator, director; d. George C. and Lucy S. Hays; m. Marvin G. Langston; children: William, Austin, Scott. BA in Bus. Edn., St. Andrews Presbyn. Coll., 1968. Tchr., sponsor Crystal Lake Jr. High, Lakeland, Fla., 1968—71; bus. edn. tchr., sponsor Lafayette HS, Ballwin, Mo., 1971—75; tchr. Moody Meth. Pre-Sch., Galveston, Tex., 1979—80; tchr., coord., sponsor Trinity Episcopal Sch., Galveston, 1980—. Cookbook chair, nominating com. Jr. League Galveston County, Galveston. Named Tchr. of Yr., Trinity Episcopal Sch. Republican. Episcopalian. Avocations: gardening, sports. Office: Trinity Episcopal Sch 720 Tremont St Galveston TX 77550

LANGSTON, THOMAS SAMUEL, political science professor; b. Louisville, Nov. 25, 1960; s. John Harold and Patricia Marie Langston; m. Mary Anne Sprague, May 15, 1982; children: Jessica, Taylor. Student, Duke U., 1980; BA cum laude, U. Tex., 1982; PhD, MIT, 1989. Tchr. Keystone Sch., San Antonio, 1982—83; vis. instr. SUNY, Geneseo, 1988—89; asst. prof. dept. polit. sci. Tulane U., New Orleans, 1989—95, assoc. prof., 1995—2002, prof., 2003—, dept. chmn., 1999—2002, 2005—. Author: Ideologues and Presidents, 1992, With Reverence and Contempt, 1995, Lyndon Baines Johnson, 2002, Uneasy Balance, 2003, George Washington, 2003. Vestry mem. St. George's Episcopal Ch., New Orleans, 1995-98, 2001-03. Moody grantee Lyndon Johnson Presdl. Libr. Found., 1987, O'Donnell grantee George Bush Presdl. Libr. Found., 2000; John M. Olin fellow Boston U. Inst. for Study of Econ. Culture, 1990-91. Mem. Am. Polit. Sci. Assn. (bd. dirs. Presidency Rsch. Group 2000-05, editor Presidency Rsch. Group Report 2000-05), Thackeray Soc. Episcopalian. Avocations: triathlon, marathons, photography. Home: 4616 Prytania St New Orleans LA 70115 Office: Dept Polit Sci Tulane U New Orleans LA 70118 E-mail: langston@tulane.edu.

LANGTON, CLEVE SWANSON, advertising executive; b. N.Y.C., Sept. 1, 1950; s. Raymond Benedict and Viola (Swanson) L.; m. Patricia Scott, July 16, 1976; children: Elizabeth Renwick, Cleve., Jr. BA, NYU, 1972; MBA, Columbia U., 1974. Product mgr. Gen. Foods Corp., White Plains, N.Y., 1974-76; account supr. Dancer Fitzgerald Sample, N.Y.C., 1976-79; v.p. account dir. D'Arcy MacManus Masius, N.Y.C., 1979-83; corp. v.p. bus. devel. worldwide DMB&B, 1983-89; corp. sr. v.p. DDB Needham Worldwide, 1990-92, corp. exec., v.p., dir. bus. devel. worldwide, 1993—. Bd. dirs. Weissman Ctr. Internat. Bus. CUNY, Helen Keller Worldwide. Mem. Met. Club. Office: DDB Worldwide Inc 437 Madison Ave New York NY 10022-7001

LANGTON, JANE GILLSON, writer, illustrator; b. Boston, Dec. 30, 1922; d. Joseph Lincoln and Grace Irene (Brown) Gillson; m. William Gale Langton, June 10, 1943 (dec. Apr. 1997); children: Christopher, David, Andrew. BS, U. Mich., 1944, MA, 1945, Radcliffe Coll., 1948. Author: The Transcendental Murder, 1964, Dark Nantucket Noon, 1975, The Memorial Hall Murder, 1978, Natural Enemy, 1982, Emily Dickinson is Dead, 1984, Good and Dead, 1986, Murder at the Gardner, 1989, The Dante Game, 1991, God in Concord, 1992, Divine Inspiration, 1993, The Shortest Day, 1995, Dead as a Dodo, 1996, The Face on the Wall, 1998, The Thief of Venice, 1999, Murder at Monticello, 2001, The Escher Twist, 2002, The Deserter, Murder at Gettysburg, 2003, Steeplechase, 2005; (children's books) Her Majesty, Grace Jones, 1961, The Boyhood of Grace Jones, Paper Chains, The Diamond in the Window, The Swing in the Summerhouse, The Astonishing Stereoscope, The Fledgling (Newbery Honor book 1980), The Fragile Flag, 1984, The Time Bike, 2000, The Mysterious Circus, 2005. Home: 9 Baker Farm Rd Lincoln MA 01773-3005 E-mail: janelangton@earthlink.net.

LANGUM, DAVID JOHN, law educator; b. Oakland, Calif., Oct. 24, 1940; s. John Kenneth and Virginia Anne (deMattos) Langum; m. Frances M. Short, 1996; children: Virginia Eileen, John David, David John Jr., Audrey Leora Kari, Anna Louisa Kari. AB, Dartmouth Coll., 1962; JD, Stanford U., 1965; MA in History, San Jose State U., 1976; LLM in Legal History, U. Mich., 1981, SJD in Legal History, 1985. Bar: Calif. 1966, Mich. 1981, Ala. 2003, U.S. Supreme Ct. 1972. Rsch. clk. Calif. Ct. Appeals, San Francisco, 1965-66; assoc. Dunne, Phelps & Mills, San Francisco, 1966-68; ptnr. Christenson, Hedemark, Langum & O'Keefe, San Jose, Calif., 1968-78; adj. prof. Lincoln U. Sch. Law, 1968-78; prof. law Detroit Coll. Law, 1978-83; prof. Old Coll. Sch. Law, Reno, Nev., 1983-85, dean, 1983-84; prof. Cumberland Sch. Law Samford U., Birmingham, 1985—. Editor: Law in the West, 1985; author: Law and Community on the Mexican California Frontier, 1987 (Hurst prize, 1988); author: (with Harlan Hague) Thomas O. Larkin: A Life of Patriotism and Profit in Old California, 1990 (Caroline Bancroft prize, 1991), Crossing Over the Line: Legislating Morality and the Mann Act, 1994; author: (with Howard Walthall) From Maverick to Mainstream: Cumberland School of Law, 8947-1997, 1997, William M. Kunstler: The Most Hated Lawyer in America, 1999; contbr. articles to profl. jours. Mem. House of Flag, pro bono litigation, San Francisco, 1973-76; past pres. Victorian Preservation Assn., Santa Clara County, Calif.; bd. dirs. ACLU of Ala., 1999—, pres., 2000-02. Mem.: Western History Assn. (Bolton award 1978), Am. History Assn., Am. Soc. for Legal History (bd. dirs. 1992—95). Office: Samford U Cumberland Sch Law 800 Lakeshore Dr Birmingham AL 35229-0002 Office Phone: 205-726-2424. Business E-Mail: djlangum@samford.edu.

LANGWIG, JOHN EDWARD, retired wood science educator; b. Albany, N.Y., Mar. 5, 1924; s. Frank Irving and Arlene Stone (Dugan) L.; m. Margaret Jacquelyn Kirk, Aug. 31, 1946; 1 dau., Nancy Ann Langwig Davis. BS, U. Mich., 1948; MS, Coll. of Forestry, SUNY, Syracuse, 1968, PhD, 1971. Asst. to supt. Widdicomb Furniture Co., Grand Rapids, Mich., 1948-50; salesman John B. Hauf Furniture, Inc., Albany, N.Y., 1950-51; asst. mgr. furniture dept. Montgomery Ward Co., Menands, N.Y., 1951-52; office mgr. U.S. Plywood Corp., Syracuse, 1952-65; instr. wood products engring. SUNY Coll. Forestry, Syracuse, 1969-70; asst. prof. wood sci. Okla. State U., Stillwater, 1971-74, prof., head dept. forestry, 1974-81, prof. wood sci., wood products extension specialist, 1982-86, mem. faculty council, 1983-86; mem. Gov.'s Com. on Forest Practices, 1975-77. Contbr. articles to profl. jours. Served with AUS, 1943-45. NSF fellow, 1966-68 Mem. Soc. Am. Foresters, TAPPI, Forest Products Research Soc. (regional bd. dirs. 1983-89, regional rep. to nat. exec. bd. 1983-86), Soc. Wood Sci. and Tech., Okla. Acad. Sci., Okla. Forestry Assn. (bd. dirs. 1982-83), Council Forestry Sch. Execs., Sigma Xi, Xi Sigma Pi., Gamma Sigma Delta, Alpha Zeta, Phi Kappa Phi. Episcopalian. Home: 33 Liberty Cir Stillwater OK 74075-2015 Office: Okla State U Dept Forestry Stillwater OK 74078-0001 *My graduate education began after a seventeen year career in the forest products industry. This additional education broadened my life, and opened up a rich new world of experience beyond my greatest expectations. I commend to all young people the pursuit of a maximum education, as one of life's most worthy efforts.*

LANGWORTHY, EVERETT WALTER, professional society administrator, natural gas exploration company executive; b. West Springfield, Mass., Aug. 17, 1918; s. Walter Carr and Lucy Anne (Laurent) L.; m. Mary Jane Mateer, Nov. 30, 1946 (dec. Oct. 1966); children: John Alan, Jo Ann Langworthy Sears, Robert Carr; m. Joan E. Scott, Feb. 27, 1982; stepchildren: Russell, Michael, Gregory BA, U. Mass., 1940; MA, George Washington U., 1964; grad., Nat. War Coll., 1964. Commd. 2d lt. U.S. Army, 1943; commd. capt. U.S. Air Force, 1947; advanced through grades to col., 1963; ret., 1972; v.p. ops. Meteor Aero Inc., Gaithersburg, Md., 1972-76; sec. contest and record bd. Nat. Aero. Assn., Washington, 1976-80, exec. v.p., 1980—. V.p. LABCO Inc., Martinsburg, W.Va., 1974—; gen. ptnr. M&E Assocs., Gaithersburg, 1976—; dir. Acad. Model Aeronautics, Reston, Va.; cons. FBI, 1992—; cons. FBI; cons., expert witness, 1995—. Contbr. articles and columns on aerospace activities to profl. pubs. U.S. rep. Fedn. Aeronautique Internat., Paris, 1980—. Decorated DFC, Air medal African Campaign award, Berlin Air Life medal; recipient Paul Tissandier diploma Fedn. Aeronautique Internationale, 1987. Mem. Nat. Aviation Club (elder statesman aviation 1990), Aero Club Washington, Air Force Assn., Ret. Officers Assn., Soaring Soc. Am. (bd. dirs. 1980—), U.S. Hang Gliding Assn. (bd. dirs. 1980—), VFW. Clubs: Lakewood Country (Rockville, Md.). Republican. Avocations: golf, writing. Home: 610 Gunston Ln Wilmington NC 28405-5317 Office: Nat Aeronautic Assn 1815 Ft Myer Dr Arlington VA 22209-1805 Office Fax: 910-256-0480. Personal E-mail: ewlang@earthlink.net.

LANGWORTHY, ROBERT BURTON, lawyer; b. Kansas City, Mo., Dec. 24, 1918; s. Herman Moore and Minnie (Leach) L.; m. Elizabeth Ann Miles, Jan. 2, 1942; children: David Robert, Joan Elizabeth Langworthy Tomek, Mark Burton. AB, Princeton U., 1940; JD magna cum laude, Harvard U., 1943. Bar: Mo. 1943, U.S. Supreme Ct. 1960. Practiced in, Kansas City, 1943—; assoc., then mem. and v.p. Linde, Thomson, Langworthy, Kohn & Van Dyke, P.C., 1943—91; pres., mng. shareholder Blackwood, Langworthy & Schmelzer, P.C., Kansas City, Mo., 1991—96; mng. mem. Blackwood, Langworthy & Tyson, L.C., and predecessor, Kansas City, Mo., 1996—. Lectr. on probate, law sch. CLE courses U. Mo., Kansas City. Mem. bd. editors Harvard Law Rev., 1941-43; contbr. chpts. to Guardian and Trust, Powers, Conservatorships and Nonprobate Desk Books of Mo. Bar. Mem. edn. appeal bd. U.S. Dept. Edn., 1982-86; commr. Housing Authority Kansas City, 1963-71, chmn., 1969-71; chmn. Bd. Election Commrs. Kansas City, 1973-77; chmn. bd. West Ctrl. area YMCA, 1969-95; bd. dirs. Mid-Am. region YMCA, 1970-83, vice chmn., 1970-73, chmn., 1973-78; pres. Met. Bd. Kansas City (Mo.) YMCA (now YMCA Greater Kansas City), 1965, bd. dirs., 1965—2004, nat. bd. 1971-78, 79-83; bd. dirs. YMCA Found. Kansas City, 2004—; bd. dirs. YMCA of the Rockies, 1974-2003, bd. sec., 1994-99, adv. dir., 2004—; trustee Sioux Indian YMCAs, 1983-2002, chmn. bd. trustees, 1983-2002, chmn. hon. trustees, 2003—; bd. dirs. Armed Svcs. YMCA, 1984-85; pres. Met. Area Citizens Edn., 1969-72; chmn. Citizens Assn. Kansas City (Mo.), 1967, bd. dirs., 1995-96; bd. dirs. Project Equality Kans.-Mo., 1967-80, pres., 1970-72, treas., 1972-73, sec., 1973-76; 1st v.p. Human Resources Corp. Kansas City, 1969-73, bd. dirs., 1965-73; hon. v.p. Am. Sunday Sch. Union (now Am. Missionary Fellowship), 1965—; vice chmn. bd. trustees Kemper Mil. Sch., 1966-73; U.S. del. YMCA World Coun., Buenos Aires, 1977, Estes Park, Colo., 1981, Nyborg, Denmark, 1985; bd. dirs. Mo. Rep. Club, 1960—; del., platform com. Rep. Nat. Conv., 1960; Rep. nominee for U.S. Congress, 1964; mem. gen. assembly Com. on Representation Presbyn., 1991-97, moderator, 1993-94; commr. to gen. assembly Presbyn. Ch., 1984, gen. assembly com. on location of hdqrs. 1984-87; moderator Heartland Presbytery, 1984. Lt. (j.g.) USNR, 1943-46, capt. Res. ret. Mem.: ABA, Harvard Law Sch. Assn. Mo. (v.p. 1973—74, pres. 1974—75, 1985—87), Lawyers Assn. Kansas City, Mo. State Bar (chmn. probate and trust com. 1983—85, chmn. sr. lawyers com. 1991—93), Kansas City Met. Bar Assn. (chmn. probate law com. 1988—90, 1999—2000, living will com. 1989—91), Kansas City Club. Presbyterian (Elder). Home: Claridge Ct Apt 305 8101 Mission Rd Prairie Village KS 66208-5238 Office: 1220 Washington St Ste 300 Kansas City MO 64105-1439 Office Phone: 816-474-6200. Business E-Mail: robert.langworthy@blackwoodlaw.com.

LANGWORTHY, ROBERT H., law educator; MS, SUNY Albany, PhD, 1983. Prof. Univ. Cincinnati, 1987—97; mem. Cmty. Oriented Policing project, Nat Inst. Justice, 1995—96; prof. Univ. Alaska, Anchorage, 1997—; dir. Justice Ctr., Univ. Alaska, Anchorage. Author: The Structure of Police Organizations, Policing in America; contbr. articles to prof. jour. Office: University of Alaska Justice Center 3211 Providence Dr Anchorage AK 99508

LANGWORTHY, WILLIAM CLAYTON, college official; b. Watertown, N.Y., Sept. 3, 1936; s. Harold Greene and Carolyn (Peach) L.; m. Margaret Joan Amos, Sept. 6, 1958; children: Kenneth, Geneva. BS magna cum laude, Tufts U., 1958; PhD, U. Calif.-Berkeley, 1962. Asst. prof. Alaska Meth. U., Anchorage, 1962-65; asst. prof. chemistry Calif. State U.-Fullerton, 1965-67, assoc. prof., 1967-72, prof., 1972-73, assoc. dean Sch. Letters Arts and Scis., 1970-73; prof. chemistry Calif. Poly. State U., San Luis Obispo, 1973-76, head dept. chemistry, 1973-76; dean Sch. Sci. and Math Calif. Poly State U., San Luis Obispo, 1976-83; v.p. acad. affairs Ft. Lewis Coll., Durango, Colo., 1983-95, prof., 1995-2000. Author: monograph Environmental Education, 1971; contbr. articles to profl. jours. Treas. Coun. Concerned Citizens, Inc., Arroyo Grande, Calif., 1976—83; mem. Clean Air Coalition, San Luis Obispo, 1978—83; active Mozart Festival, 1981—82; mem. Jacksonville Boosters, 2001—, treas., 2002—04, pres., 2004—05; mem. Rogue Valley Harmonizers, 2001—05; mem. forestry com. City of Jacksonville, Oreg., 2002—05; bd. dirs. Durango Choral Soc., 1984—93, San Juan Symphony League, pres, 1997—2000; bd. dirs. Durango Repertory Theatre Co., 1990—96, pres., 1992—94. Mem. AAAS, AAHE, Am. Chem. Soc., Coun. Colls. Arts and Scis. (bd. dirs. 1982), Sierra Club, Phi Beta Kappa, Sigma Xi, Kappa Mu Epsilon, Phi Kappa Phi. Home: 4954 SW Hollyhock Cir Corvallis OR 97333 E-mail: hillsidebill@aol.com.

LANHAM, PAUL C., information technology executive; B, Univ. Tex. Sys. analyst, merchandise analyst, distbr. and store mgr. Gap; asst. dir., merchandise planning Home Front Stores; distrbn. mgr. and regional merchandise mgr. Payless Shoe Source; dir. inventory Brookstone; v.p. planning and allocation Ames Dept. Stores, Conn., 1994—95, sr. v.p.-merchandise info. sys., 1995—98, sr. v.p. & CIO, 1998—2000; sr. v.p. & CTO Jones Apparel Group, Bristol, Pa., 2000—. Named one of top tech. innovators, Info. Week mag., 2004. Office: SVP & CTO Jones Apparel Corp 250 Rittenhouse Cir Bristol PA 19007

LANHAM, SALLIE CLAY, artist, educator; b. Louisville, Dec. 15, 1939; d. Watson and Virginia Murphy (Alexander) Clay; m. Jame Forrest Thompson, Aug. 25, 1962 (div. Sept. 1985); children: James Clay, Forrest Clay; m. Charles Robert Lanham Jr., Dec. 27, 1986. Grad., Cin. Art Acad., 1964. Artist Stone Advt. Studio, Lexington, Ky., 1964-65; artist tours dept. Commonwealth of Ky., Frankfort, 1965-70; artist educator Capital Day Sch., Frankfort, 1970-84; adult art tchr. Ky. State U., Frankfort, 1972-74; art dir. Assn. Publs., Inc., Louisville, 1984-88; artist, art dir. Lanham Media Svc., Frankfort & Crystal Lake, Ill., 1988—. One woman show at Ctrl. Bank Gallery, Lexington; exhibited in group shows at Loudoun House, Lexington, Frankfort Arta Art Guild, Ky. Watercolor Soc., Louisville, Ctrl. Ky. Art Guild, Elizabethtown, Ky., Lexington Arts and Cultural Coun., 1998, Arts Pl. Gallery, Lexington, Masterpieces of Maturity, Lexington, 1998, Indpls. Mus. Art Rental Gallery, Totally Transparent, Louisville, Ky. Visions, Frankfort and Somerset, 1998. 1st v.p. Frankfort Arts Found., 1986-87; chmn. County Rep. Party, Franklin County, Ky., 1987—; bd. dirs. King Ctr., Frankfort Arts Found.; 3d v.p. Off Broadway Theater, Frankfort Presbyn. Ch.; pres. Northland Area Art League; bd. dirs., treas. Civic Ctr. Authority, Crystal Lake; mem. steering com. Women's Network. Fellow Va. Ctr. for Creative Arts, 1998; recipient Ky. visions award Project Art Tchr. prize Ky. Art Edn. Assn., Ky. Arts Coun., 1998, 1st pl. award several juried art fairs, Ill.; Arts Showcase grante Frankfort Arts Found., 1999. Mem. Frankfort Area Art Guild (v.p. 1999-2000, bd. dirs. 1986—, chmn. student art show 1987-2000), Ky. Watercolor Soc. (3d pl. award 1988), Lexington Art League, Ctrl. Ky. Art Guild, Colonial Dames Am. (3d v.p. Ky. chpg. 1987—). Presbyterian. Avocation: water sports. Office: Lanham Media Svc 8 Justice Ln Frankfort KY 40601-9495 E-mail: lanham@dcr.net.

LANIER, DEBRA, secondary school educator, retired counseling administrator; b. Hamilton, Ohio, Dec. 13, 1950; d. William T. and Jeraleen E. (Ruff) Hensley; m. Paul W. Lanier, Dec. 15, 1973 (div. Oct. 1986); children: Stacey Marie, Scott Ryan. BS, Ea. Ky. U., 1973; MEd, Xavier U., Cin., 1984. Tchr. health and phys. edn. Fairfield (Ohio) City Schs., 1973—94; varsity soccer coach Fairfield High Sch., 1990—94. Group facilitator Aring Inst. Beechmont Acres, Cin., 1991-1993; rape crisis counselor Oxford (Ohio) Crisis Ctr., 1991-1994. Recipient Amb. award Fairfield City Schs., 1991, 92, Coach of Yr. and Metro Coach of Yr. award, Cin. Enquirer, 1992, Coach of Yr. award Greater Miami Conf., 1992, Fairfield High Sch. Athletic Hall of Fame, 2000. Mem. AAHPERD (conv. speaker 1991), Ohio Alliance Health, Phys. Edn., Recreation and Dance (membership com. 1991—), Fairfield Classroom Tchrs. Asns., Delta Psi Kappa, Chi Omega. Republican. Avocations: racquetball, softball, volleyball, poetry. Home: 5276 Sioux Dr Fairfield OH 45014-3345

LANIER, ELIZABETH K., lawyer; m. Addison Lanier; 3 children. BA with honors, Smith Coll.; JD, Columbia U.; Degree (hon.), Cin. State Tech. C.C., Coll. Mt. St. Joseph. Assoc. Davis Polk & Wardell, N.Y.C.; assoc., ptnr. Frost & Jacobs (now Frost Brown Todd LLC), Cin.; gen. counsel S.W. Ohio Regional Transit Authority; dir. Star Gas Corp.; v.p., chief of staff Cinergy Corp., 1996—98; v.p., gen. counsel GE Power Sys., 1998—2002; sr. v.p., gen. counsel Trizec Properties, 2002; exec. v.p., corp. affairs and gen. counsel US Airways Group, Inc. US Airways, Inc., Arlington, Va., 2003—, corp. sec., 2004—. Bd. dirs. Patina Oil & Gas Corp. Chmn. Aronoff Ctr.; vice chmn. Cin. Arts Assn.; mem. adv. bd. Civic Forum; bd. dirs. Ohio Bd. Regents, 1990, sec. of the bd., 1994, 1995, chmn., 1996; bd. dirs. Cin. Parks Found., Greater Cin. Conv. and Visitors Bur., Lighthouse Youth Svcs., World Affairs Coun., Children's Svcs. Levy Com. Harlan Fiske Stone scholar, Columbia U. Sch. Law. Office: US Airways 2345 Crystal Dr Arlington VA 22227

LANIER, GREGORY WARREN, theater educator; b. Denver, Colo., Nov. 5, 1956; s. Sidney Joseph and Norma Elise Lanier; m. Lorraine Susan Schnapp, July 3, 1989; children: Keith, Kathryn. BA, U. Colo., 1979; MA, U. Mich., 1981, PhD, 1986. Asst. prof. U. West Fla., Pensacola, Fla., 1986—92, assoc. prof., 1992—, chmn. Dept. Theater, 2002—, head Fine and Performing Arts Divsn., 2003—. Dir. U. Honors Program U. West Fla., 1999—; pres. Fla. Collegiate Honors Coun., 2002—03; faculty rep. Nat. Collegiate Honors Coun., 2003—. Contbr. articles to profl. jours. Bd. dirs. Pensacola (Fla.) Little Theatre, 2003—. Avocations: model railroads, woodworking. Office: Univ West Fla Honors Bldg 50 11000 Univ Pkwy Pensacola FL 32514 Office Phone: 850-474-2934. E-mail: glanier@umt.edu.

LANIER, RICHARD SANDERS, foundation administrator; s. Calvin Dent and Ann Lee Lanier; m. Mary Stewart, May 25, 1968; 1 child, Marie Denise. BA, Tulane U., 1965; MA, Inst. of Fine Arts, N.Y. U., 1967. Acting asst. prof. art dept. U. Calif., Santa Barbara, 1970—71; asst. prof. dept. art history Johns Hopkins U., Balt., 1971—72, dir. mus. tng. program, 1971—72; asst. to dir. Asian Cultural Program JDR 3d Fund, N.Y.C., 1972—73, assoc. Asian cultural program, 1973—75, dir. Asian cultural program, 1975—80; pres. Asian Cultural Coun., 1980—; dir. Trust for Mut. Understanding, 1984—. Trustee Asian Cultural Coun., N.Y.C., 1980—, Trust for Mut. Understanding, 1984—; bd. dir. Chinese Internat. Sch. Found., Hong Kong, Japan Soc., N.Y.C., Tibetan Bibliographic Resource Ctr.; mem. bd. advisors Gallery Assn. of N.Y., 1982—84; mem. art adv. com. Japan Ho. Gallery, 1986—2004; trustee Laura Dean Dance Found., 1980—86, Isamu Noguchi Found., 1984—, Washington Sq. Fund, 1980—86, JDR 3d Fund, 1988—95; mem. Pres.'s cultural prperty adv. com. U.S. Dept. of State, Washington, 1998—2003; vis. com. dept. Asian Arts Metro. Mus. Art, N.Y.C. Mem.: Century Assn., Internat. Coun. of Mus., Am. Assn. of Mus., Coll. Art Assn. Office: Trust for Mut Understanding Rm 5600 30 Rockefeller Plz New York NY 10112 Fax: 212-632-3409. E-mail: tmu@tmuny.org.

LANIER, ROBERT C. (BOB LANIER), real estate owner, real estate developer, former mayor; b. Baytown, Tex., 1925; Student, Lee Coll., Univ. N.Mex.; grad. in law with hons., U. Tex., 1949. Former reporter The Baytown Sun and The Austin Am.-Statesman.; law assoc. Baker & Botts; then pvt. practice; mayor Houston, 1991-97. Chmn. Tex. Highway and Pub. Transp. Commn., Houston Met. Transit Authority; founder Houston Community Coll.; founder, chmn. bd. Hope Ctr. Wilderness Camp. Office: Ste 3210 909 Fannin St Houston TX 77010-1015

LANIER, W. MARK, lawyer; b. Dallas, Oct. 20, 1960; m. Becky Lanier; 5 children. BA, David Lipscomb Coll., 1981; JD, Tex. Tech. U., 1984. Bar: Tex. 1985, U.S. Dist. Ct. (so. and ea. dists.) Tex. 1985, U.S. Ct. Appeals (5th cir.) 1985, U.S. Supreme Ct. 1985, U.S. Dist. Ct. (no. dist.) Tex. 1995, cert.: Tex. Bd. Legal Specialization (personal injury trial law). With Fulbright & Jaworski, Houston, 1983—89; founder The Lanier Law Firm, P.C., Houston, 1990—. Named Tex. Super Lawyer, Tex. Monthly Mag., 2003; named one of Top 40 Attys. Under the Age of 40 in U.S., Nat. Law Jour., 1995, Top 10 Trial Lawyers in Am., 1998, Top 5 Personal Injury Lawyers, Tex. Lawyer Go-To-Guide, 2002, Top 45 Lawyers Under the Age of 45, Am. Lawyer, 2003. Mem.: ABA, Tex. Trial Lawyers Assn., Houston (Tex.) Bar Assn., Order of Barristers. Office: The Lanier Law Firm PC 6810 FM 1960 West Houston TX 77069 Office Phone: 713-659-5200. Business E-Mail: wml@lanierlawfirm.com.

LANIER, WILLIAM LOVEL, JR., anesthesiologist, educator; b. Statesboro, Ga., June 8, 1955; s. William Lovel Sr. and Nancy (Jones) L.; m. Mary Duckworth, July 15, 1978; children: Elizabeth Brooke, William Hudson. BS, U. Ga., 1976; MD, Med. Coll. of Ga., 1980. Diplomate Am. Bd. Anesthesiology (examiner 1994—, cert. of recertification 2001-). Resident in anesthesiology Wake Forest U. Med. Ctr., Bowman Gray Sch. Medicine, Winston-Salem, N.C., 1980-83; fellow in neurosurg. anesthesia Mayo Grad. Sch. Medicine, Rochester, Minn., 1983-84; cons. in anesthesiology Mayo Clinic, Rochester, Minn., 1984—; prof. anesthesiology Mayo Clinic Coll. Medicine, Rochester, Minn., 1995—. Aitken Meml. lectr. U. Western Ont., London, 1993; Marshall Meml. lectr. U. Toronto, 2000. Sect. editor: Jour. Neurosurg. Anesthesiology, 1988—92, editor-in-chief: Mayo Clinic Procs., 1999—; contbr. numerous articles and editls. to profl. publs, chapters to books. Grantee, NIH, 1999—2004. Mem.: Coun. Sci. Editors, Am. Diabetes Assn., Assn. of Univ. Anesthesiologists (mem. sci. adv. bd. 1998—2001), Soc. Neurosurg. Anesthesiology and Critical Care (pres. 1993—94), Am. Soc. Anesthesiologists, First Families of Ga., Phi Kappa Phi, Phi Beta Kappa. Roman Catholic. Avocations: fishing, hunting, reading, boating. Office: Mayo Clinic 200 1st St SW Rochester MN 55905-0002 Office Phone: 507-255-4235. Business E-Mail: lanier.william@mayo.edu.

LANIGAN, RICHARD LEO, JR., humanities educator, writer, editor; b. Santa Fe, Dec. 31, 1943; s. Richard Leo Lanigan, Sr. and Margaret Alcy Kendall; m. Rui-hong Guo, Sept. 14, 1990 (div. Jan. 1, 2001); children: James Guo, Robert Guo. BA, U. N.Mex, 1967, MA, 1968; PhD in Communicology, So. Ill. U., 1969. Cert. English lang. examiner Sichuan U., China, 1996. Rsch. assoc. Dundee (Scotland) U. and St. Andrews U., Joint Postgraduate Program in Philosophy, 1970—72; founding chair philosophy comm. divsn. Internat. Comm. Assn., Berlin, 1977; rsch. assoc. East-West Ctr., Honolulu, 1980—81; Andrew Mellon fellow in linguistics Vanderbilt U., Nashville, 1981—82, Andrew Mellon fellow in philosophy, 1984—85; rsch. assoc. U. Calif., Berkeley, 1982—83; pres. Semiotic Soc. Am., Houston, 1994—95, editor Am. Jour. Semiotics, 1996—; fellow Internat. Acad. for Intercultural Rsch., University, Miss., 1998—; dir. and fellow Internat. Communicology Inst., Carbondale, Ill., 2000—. Author: (book) The Human Science of Communicology, Phenomenology of Communication (Transl. into Korean, 1997), Semiotic Phenomenology of Rhetoric, Speech Act Phenomenology, Speaking and Semiology (2nd edit., 1991); mem. editl. bd.: Critical Studies in Mass Comm., 1986—89, Signifying Behavior, 1993—98, TEXT: An Interdisciplinary Jour. for the Study of Discourse, 1997—, guest editor: Semiotica Vol. 41, 1982. Chpt. pres. So. Ill. U. AAUP, Carbondale, 1984—87. Scholar, Nat. Comm. Assn., 1995. Mem.: NEA, Internat. Assn. Semiotic Studies (v.p. 2004—), Ill. Edn. Assn., Am. Philos. Assn., Tau Kappa Alpha, Phi Sigma Tau. Democrat. Roman Catholic. Avocations: writing, reading, travel, swimming. Home: 335 May Apple Ln Carbondale IL 62903-7695 Office: Southern Illinois Univesity Spcm 6605 Carbondale IL 62901-6605 Office Phone: 618-453-1894. Business E-Mail: rlanigan@siu.edu.

LANIGAN, SUSAN S., lawyer; b. May 1962; BA, U. Ga.; JD, U. Ga. Law Sch. Assoc. gen. counsel Zale Corp., Irving, Tex., 1996—97, sr. v.p., gen. counsel, sec., 1997—2002; v.p., gen. counsel, corp. sec. Dollar Gen. Corp., Goodlettsville, Tenn., 2002—03, sr. v.p., gen. counsel, corp sec., 2003—. Office: Dollar General Corp 100 Mission Ridge Goodlettsville TN 37072

LANING, ROBERT COMEGYS, retired physician, retired military officer; b. Haiti, Sept. 20, 1922; s. Richard Henry and Marguerite C. (Boyer) L.; m. Alice Teresa Lech, Sept. 9, 1961; 1 dau., Maria Laning LeBerre. MD, Jefferson Med. Coll., 1948; BA, U. Va., 1986; MA, Ohio State U., 1988; PhD in Edn., George Mason U., 1997. Diplomate: Nat. Bd. Med. Examiners, Am. Bd. Surgery. Intern Jefferson Hosp., Phila., 1948-50; enlisted USN, 1950, advanced through grades to rear adm., 1973, mem. astronaut recovery teams, 1960-66; chief of surgery Naval Hosp., San Diego, 1967-71, Portsmouth, NH, 1963—66, Chelsea, Mass., 1966—67, med. dir. Yokosuka, Japan, 1972-73; med. officer Pacific Fleet, 1973-75; asst. chief Bur. Medicine and Surgery for Operational Med. Support, Washington, 1975-77; dep. dir. surg. service Cen. Office, VA, Washington, 1977-79, dir. surg. service, 1979-87. Fellow ACS (gov. 1984-87); mem. AMA, KC (4th degree), Am. Assn. Mil. Surgeons, Soc. Med. Cons. to Armed Forces (pres. 1988-89, bd. dirs.), Ret. Officers Assn. Roman Catholic. Home: 6532 Sunny Hill Ct Mc Lean VA 22101-1639

LANITIS, TONY ANDREW, market researcher; b. Port Said, Egypt, May 29, 1926; came to U.S., 1929; s. Christopher and Helen (Joanides) L.; m. Anne Mortimer, Feb. 4, 1947 (div. 1951); 1 son, Philip; m. Gertrude Lettese, June 14, 1959; 1 dau., Melissa. BS in Econs., NYU, 1950, MA, 1951. Assoc. research dir. Morey, Humm & Warwick, N.Y.C., 1954-55; sr. group supr. Colgate-Palmolive Co., N.Y.C., 1955-60; sr. v.p. SSC & B: Lintas Worldwide, Inc., N.Y.C., 1960-89, dir. rsch., 1960-87, dir. market planning and rsch., 1987-89; market planning and rsch. cons. N.Y.C., 1989—; instr. Ulster County C.C., 1993—. Guest lectr. NYU, 1970-72, Pace Coll., 1970-73, L.I. U., 1968-70; lectr. in field Cons. editor Psychology and Mktg. Jour., 1983—; editor: Bio-Etheric Healing—A Breakthrough in Alternative Therapies, 1999; contbr. articles to profl. jours. Bd. dirs. Port Chester (N.Y.) Coun. Arts, 1981-89, Unison Art and Learning Ctr., New Paltz, N.Y., 1990-92; chmn. mktg. and publicity chpt. 533 SCORE, 1991-97. Named Marketer of Month Kansas City, Am. Mktg. Assn, 1972. Mem. Am. Mktg. Assn., Advt. Research Found., Advt. Agy. Research Dirs. Council, Am. Psychol. Assn., Inst. Mgmt. Sci., Market Research Council, Communications Research Council. Clubs: Commerce. Home: 6287 Bahia Del Mar Cir Apt 506 Saint Petersburg FL 33715-1067

LANK, EDITH HANDLEMAN, journalist, educator; b. Boston, Feb. 27, 1926; m. Norman Lank; children: Avrum, David, Anna. BA magna cum laude, Syracuse U. Columnist L.A. Times Syndicate, 1976—2000; TV host Sta. WOKR-TV, Rochester, N.Y., 1983-84; radio host Sta. WBBF-AM, Rochester, 1984-85; columnist Tribune Media Svcs., 2000—02, Creators Syndicate, 2003—. Lectr. St. John Fisher Coll., Rochester, 1977-89; commentator Sta. WXXI-FM, Rochester, 1977—; guest Pub. Radio Internat., St. Paul, 1987—; speaker in field. Author: Home Buying, 1981, Selling Your Home, 1982, Modern Real Estate Practice in New York, 1983, rev. 9th edit., 2004, The Home Seller's Kit, 1988, rev. 4th edit. 1997, The Complete Home Buyer's Kit, 1989, rev. 4th edit., 1997, Dear Edith, 1990, Essentials of New Jersey Real Estate, rev. 7th edit., 2004, 201 Questions Every Homebuyer and Seller Must Ask, 1996, Jane Austen speaks to Women, 2000; co-author: Your Home as a Tax Shelter, 1993; contbr. articles to Time, New Yorker, McCall's, Real Estate Today, Persuasions, Modern Maturity, others. Recipient media award Bar Assn. Monroe County, 1982, Matrix award Women in Ommunications, 1984, Woman of Distinction award Gov. Mario Cumo, N.Y., 1985; named Communicator of Yr., SUNY, Brockport, 1986. Mem. Real Estate Educators Assn. (bd. dirs., Consumer Edn. award 1982, 83, 86, 96, Real Estate Educator of Yr. 1984), Nat. Assn. Real Estate Editors (bd. dirs), Jane Austen Soc. N.Am. (dir.), Phi Beta Kappa. Avocation: scuba diving. Home and Office: 240 Hemingway Dr Rochester NY 14620-3316 E-mail: edithlank@aol.com.

LANKFORD, JAMES E., food service executive; Grad., U. Md., 1974. Sales mgr. S.E. Lankford Jr. Produce Co., 1974—81; v.p. sales S.E. Lankford Jr. Produce Co. (now Sysco Corp.), 1981—86; sr. v.p. Sysco Corp., 1986—91, exec. v.p., CEO Harrisburg, Pa., 1991, pres., CEO, 1991—95, Phila., 1995—98, San Francisco, 1998—2001, sr. v.p. food svc. ops. Fremont, 2000—. Office: Sysco Corp 5900 Stewart Ave Fremont CA 94538

LANKOWSKY, ZENON P., lawyer, retail executive; BA, Univ. Syracuse, 1976; JD, Western New England Coll. Sch. of Law, 1980. V.p., gen. counsel, sec. CVS Corp., Woonsocket, R.I. Mem.: Am. Corp. Counsel Assn. Office: CVS Corp One CVS Dr Woonsocket RI 02895

LANNAMANN, RICHARD STUART, executive search consultant; b. Cin., Sept. 4, 1947; s. Frank E. and Grace I. (Tomlinson) L.; m. Katharine Tinkham Scheffler, Sept. 5, 1998; children by previous marriage: Thomas Cleveland, Edward Payne, John Stewart. AB in Econs., Yale U., 1969; MBA, Harvard U., 1973. Investment analyst U.S. Trust Co. N.Y., N.Y.C., 1969-71; rsch. analyst Smith, Barney & Co., N.Y.C., 1973-75, 2d v.p., 1975-77; v.p. successor firm Smith Barney, Harris Upham & Co., N.Y.C., 1977-78, Russell Reynolds Assocs., Inc., N.Y.C., 1978-83; sr.v.p. Mgmt. Asset Corp., Westport, Conn., 1986-87; mng. dir. Russell Reynolds Assocs., N.Y.C., 1983—86, 1987—2002; vice chmn. Spencer Stuart & Assocs., N.Y.C., 2002—. Corp. mem. The Jackson Lab., Bar Harbor, Maine. Trustee Orpheus Chamber Orch. Fellow: Foreign Policy Assn.; mem.: Chartered Fin. Analyst Inst., N.Y. Soc. Security Analysts, The Oaks Club, Links Club, Yale Club of N.Y., Riverside Yacht Club. Home: 21 Willowmere Cir Riverside CT 06878-2503 Office: 277 Park Ave New York NY 10172-2998 Office Phone: 212-336-0320.

LANNAN, MAURA ANNE KELLY, reporter; b. Bridgeport, Conn., Apr. 2, 1971; d. Richard Francis and Margaret Mary Kelly. BA, Boston Coll., 1993; MS in Journalism, Northwestern U., 1994. Intern The Patriot Ledger, Quincy, Mass., 1993; corr. Conn. Post, Bridgeport, 1993; reporter Naugatuck bur.

Waterbury (Conn.) Rep.-Am., 1994—95, edn. reporter, 1995, city hall reporter, 1995—96, state capitol reporter, 1996-99; reporter Chgo. Tribune, 2000—01, Associated Press, 2001—. Mem. reporters' roundtable discussion Conn. Jour. on Conn. Pub. TV, Hartford, 1998-99 and WFSB's CT '97, CT '98, Ct '99 in Hartford. Co-recipient Explanatory Reporting-Team Coverage, Pulitzer Prize, 2001. Mem. Soc. Profl. Journalists (Reporting awards Conn. chpt. 1998, 99, 2000, co-recipient Peter Lisagor award for deadline reporting, Headline Club chpt. 2003), Investigative Reporters and Editors, Boston Coll. Alumni Assn., Northwestern U. Alumni Club Conn. Roman Catholic. Avocations: photography, travel, skiing, tennis, swimming. Home: 2506 N Bosworth Ave Chicago IL 60614 Office: Associated Press Ste 2500 10 S Wacker Dr Chicago IL 60606 Personal E-mail: makelly42@hotmail.com.

LANNERT, ROBERT CORNELIUS, manufacturing executive; b. Chgo., Mar. 14, 1940; s. Robert Carl and Anna Martha (Cornelius) L.; children: Jacqueline, Krista, Kevin, Meredith. BS in Indsl. Mgmt., Purdue U., 1963; MBA, Northwestern U., 1967; grad. Advanced Mgmt. Program, Harvard U., 1978. With Navistar Internat. Corp. (formerly Internat. Harvester), Chgo., 1963—; staff asst. overseas fin. Navistar Internat. Transp. Corp. (formerly Internat. Harvester), Chgo., 1967-70; asst. mgr., treas. and contr. IH Finanz AG, Zurich, Switzerland, 1970-72; mgr. overseas fin. corp. hdqrs. Internat. Truck & Engine Co., Chgo., 1972—76, asst. treas., 1976—79, v.p., treas., 1979—90; exec. v.p., chief fin. officer Navistar Internat. Corp., Chgo., 1990—2002, vice chmn., CFO, 2002—, also bd. dirs. Bd. dirs. Internat. Truck and Engine Co., Harbour Assurance Co., Bermuda, Navistar Fin. Corp., Chgo. Home: 904 Kenmare Dr Burr Ridge IL 60527 Office: Navistar Internat Corp 4201 Winfield Rd PO Box 1488 Warrenville IL 60555

LANNES, WILLIAM JOSEPH, III, electrical engineer; b. New Orleans, Oct. 12, 1937; s. William Joseph Jr. and Rhea Helen (Simon) L.; m. Patricia Anne Didier, Jan. 17, 1961; children: David Mark, Kenneth John, Jennifer Anne. BEE, Tulane U., 1959; MEE, U.S. Naval Postgrad. Sch., 1966. Registered profl. engr., La. Commd. 2d lt. U.S. Marine Corps, 1959, advanced through grades to maj., 1967, served as electronics officer, ops. officer, 1967-70; substation engr. La. Power & Light, New Orleans, 1970-71, utility engr., 1971-76, systems relay engr., 1976-77, systems substation engr., 1977-79, engring. supr. for substation, 1979-83, substation engring. mgr., 1983-86, dir. systems engring., 1986—, v.p. systems engring., 1986-88, with ctrl. engring., 1988-89; sr. v.p. Energy Supply Fossil, 1989-91; v.p. svc. and support Entergy Corp., 1991-92; assoc. dean rsch. and grad. studies Coll. Engring. U. New Orleans, 1992-97. Dir. U. New Orleans EPRI Cmty. Initiative Ctr., 1993-95; assoc. dir. Ctr. Energy Resources Mgmt., 1993-96, dir. Ctr. Energy Resources Mgmt., 1996-2002; dir. Engring. Mgmt. Program, 1995-2002, chmn. engring. mgmt. dept., 2002—; instr. Delgado Jr. Coll., 1973-74; instr. elec. engring. U. New Orleans, 1979-80; dir. 5th Dist. Savs. and Loan, 1982—; spkr. profl. confs. Contbr. articles to profl. jours. Committeeman New Orleans Area Coun., Boy Scouts Am., 1972-76; vol. United Way 1975, 76, 81; treas. PTA, 1971; vol. tchr. Confraternity of Christian Doctrine, 1972; mem. bus. adv. coun. Our Lady of Holy Cross Coll., 1981-86; chmn. engring. adv. coun. U. New Orleans; bd. dirs. New Life in La.; vol. coach New Orleans Recreation Dept., 1973; mem. La. Employees Com. on Polit. Action, Tulane Univ. Engring. Coun., New Orleans Archdiocesan Pastoral Coun., 1988-91; mem. adv. bd. Bridge House, 1992-95. Decorated Bronze Star; Cross of Gallantry Republic S. Vietnam; recipient Cert. of Merit Mayor New Orleans, 1964. Fellow IEEE (profl. mem. 1996, Outstanding Svc. award 1976, chmn. New Orleans sect. 1981-82, Edward Freitag award 1988, Region 3 Outstanding Engr. award 1991); mem. Electric Power Rsch. Inst. (industry advisor), Edison Electric Inst. (systems and equipment com.), Soc. Power Rsch. and Implementation (chmn. 1987-94), Southeastern Electric Exch. (substation com. 1977-85), Power Engring. Soc. (Prize Paper award 1988), Sigma Xi, Eta Kappa Nu. Republican. Roman Catholic. Office: Coll Engring U New Orleans New Orleans LA 70148-0001 Office Phone: 504-280-7122. Business E-Mail: wlannes@uno.edu.

LANNI, TERRY (JOSEPH TERRENCE LANNI), hotel corporation executive; b. Los Angeles, Mar. 14, 1943; s. Anthony Warren and Mary Lucille (Leahy) L. BS, U. So. Calif., 1965, MBA, 1967. Vice pres. Intervest, Inc., Los Angeles, 1967-69; treas. Republic Corp., L.A., 1969-76; treas., chief fin. officer Caesars World Inc., L.A., 1977-78, sr. v.p., 1978-79, exec. v.p., 1979-81, pres., chief oper. officer, dir., 1981—95, Caesars N.J., Inc., 1981—95; pres. MGM Mirage, 1995, chmn., 1995—, CEO, 1995—99, 2001—. Author: Anthology of Poetry, 1965. Trustee St. John's Hosp. and Med. Ctr., Archdiocese of L.A. Edn. Found., Loyola Marymount U.; bd. councillors U. So. Calif. Sch. Bus. Adminstrn. Mem. Calif. C. of C. (bd. dirs.), Commerce Assocs., Regency Club, Rep. Senatorial Inner Circle, Clermont Club (London), Annabel's (London. Clubs: Bachelors; Crockfords (London), Beach (London). Office: MGM Mirage 3600 Las Vegas Blvd Las Vegas NV 89109

LANNIE, PAUL ANTHONY, lawyer; b. Hayti, Mo., Feb. 21, 1954; m. Donna Dean; children: Heather, Anthony. BA magna cum laude, Vanderbilt U., 1974, JD, 1978. Bar: Tex. 1978. Assoc. Johnson & Swanson, Dallas, 1978-83; exec. v.p. BusLease Inc., Dallas, 1983-87, GLI Holding Co., Dallas, 1987—91, Greyhound Lines Inc., Dallas, 1987-91; v.p., gen. counsel, sec. Baroid Corp., Houston, 1991-94; sr. v.p., gen. counsel Tejas Gas Corp., Houston, 1994—98, Coral Energy, Houston, 1995—99; pres. Coral Energy Can., 1999, Kinder Morgan Power Co., Houston, 2000—03; v.p., gen. counsel Apache Corp., Houston, 2003—04, sr. v.p., gen. counsel, 2004—. Bd. dirs. Dallas Indsl. Devel. Corp., 1985-87; exec. mem. Ctrl. Dallas Assn., 1990. Mem. Order Coif, Phi Beta Kappa. Office: Apache Corp 2000 Post Oak Blvd Ste 100 Houston TX 77056-4400

LANNIGAN, JAMES WILLIAM, voluntary service officer; b. Rochester, N.Y., Mar. 2, 1944; s. Clarence Lannigan and Catherine Weber; m. Margaret E. McLeod, May 19, 1984. Bachelor's degree, Empire State Coll., 1984; MBA, Wichita State U., 1998. News/sports editor Sta. WBTA, Batavia (N.Y.) Broadcasting Inc., 1968-84; therapeutic recreation therapist Lyons (N.J.) VA Med. Ctr., 1984-88; asst. vol. chief Hines (Ill.) VA Hosp., 1988-90; vol. svc. officer Kansas City (Mo.) VA Med. Ctr., 1990—. Mem. com. on profl. devel. and stds. Am. Soc. Vol. Svcs./Am. Hosp. Assn., Chgo., 1991, mem. com. on continuous quality improvement, 1993; mem. task force on disabilities Heart of Am. United Way, Kansas City, Mo., 1994; com. chmn. policies and procedures Mo. Assn. Dir.'s of Vol. Svcs., Jefferson City, 1997. Bd. dirs. Heart of Am. Stand Down Com., Kansas City, Mo., 1994—; adv. bd. S.E. Med. Professions H.S., Kansas City, Mo., 1994—; mem. gov. vol. support network adv. com. Points of Light Found. With USAF, 1963-67. Office: VA Med Ctr 4801 E Linwood Blvd Kansas City MO 64128-2226

LANNING, JAMES W., retail executive; Grad., Western Carolina U., 1980. Joined Ingles Markets Inc., Black Mountain, NC, 1976, mgr. various stores, dist. mgr. Ga., 1995—2003, pres., COO Black Mountain, NC, 2003—, also bd. dirs. Office: Ingles Markets Inc 1560 US Hwy 70 Black Mountain NC 28711

LANNING, YVONNE BRADSHAW, elementary school educator; b. Smithville, Mo., Mar. 12, 1956; d. Arbeth McKinley and Frances Valjean (Whelan) Bradshaw. AA, Kansas City (Kans.) C.C., 1976; BS, St. Mary Coll., Leavenworth, Kans., 1985; MS, Kans. State U., 2002; PhD, St. Regis U., 2003. Cert. tchr., Kans., Kans. Assn. for Edn. Young Children. Paraprofl. St. Peter's Cathedral Sch., Kansas City; elem. and kindergarten tchr. Holy Family Sch., Kansas City; tchr. kindergarten Unified Sch. Dist. 500, Kansas City, Kansas City (Mo.) Sch. Dist. Pres. Mid-County Dem. Club, 1988; mem. Kans. Fedn. Dem. Women, Southside Dem. Club. Mem. Cath. Edn. Assn., Kans. Edn. Assn. (chmn. polit. action commn. 1988-89), Quill and Scroll, Southside Ladies Club, Women of the Moose (chpt. 1562), Am. Legion (aux. post #327), Ladies Aux. VFW (post #111), Slavic Am. Citizens Club.

LANNOM, JULIE CONWAY HUDSON, secondary school educator; b. Knoxville, Tenn., Dec. 8, 1950; d. Julius F. and Rhema Y. (Smith) Hudson; m. David C. Lannom, Oct. 7, 1972; children: Marcus David, Michael Franklin. BS, U. Tenn., 1972, MS, 1976. Tchr. Roane County Schs., Kingston, Tenn., 1975—. Mem.: Nat. Coun. Tchrs. Maths. Avocations: quilting, reading, cooking. Office: Roane County High Sch 540 W Cumberland St Kingston TN 37763

L'ANNUNZIATA, MICHAEL FRANK, chemist, consultant, nuclear scientist; s. Michael Peter and Irene M. L'Annunziata; m. Maria del Carmen; children: Michael O., Helen, Frank E. BS, St. Edward's U., Austin, Tex., 1965; MS, U. Ariz., 1967, PhD, 1970. Rsch. chemist Amchem Products, Inc., Ambler, Pa., 1971—72; rsch. assoc. U. Ariz., Tucson, 1972—73; prof., sect. head U. Chapingo, Mexico, 1973—75; rsch. scientist Nat. Inst. Nuc. Rsch., Mexico City, 1975—77; assoc. officer IAEA, Vienna, 1977—80, 2d officer, 1980—83, 1st officer, head sci. visits program, 1983—86, sr. officer, head fellowships and tng. sect., 1986—91; mng. dir. LMS Internat. Tech. Svcs., Ltd., Coronado, Calif., 1992—95; dir. WorldTech Internat. Tech. Svcs., Oceanside, Calif., 1995—99; pres. Montague Group, 1999—. Bd. dirs. internat. sci. programs Uppsala (Sweden) U.; internat. IAEA cons.; cons., lectr. Forestry Rsch. Inst., Ibadan, Nigeria, 1994-95, Ministry Edn., Jakarta, Indonesia, 1995, Internat. Sales, Mktg., Tng., Packard BioScis. Co., Meriden, Conn., 1995-2002, PerkinElmer Life and Analytical Scis., Downers Grove, Ill., 2003—, Canberra Industries, Inc., Meriden, Conn., 2003, Egypt Atomic Energy Authority, Cairo, 1995-96, Gezira Rsch. Sta., Wad Medani, Sudan, 1995, Ethopian Sci. and Tech. Commn., Addis Ababa, 1996, Nat. Radiation Commn., Arusha, Tanzania, 1996; vis. lectr. Advanced Sch. Tropical Agriculture, Cardenas, Mexico, 1973, Atomic Energy Commn. of Ecuador, Quito, 1978, Timiryazev Agrl. Acad., Moscow, 1980, 81, Nuc. Rsch. Inst. in Vet. Medicine, Lalahan, Turkey, 1981, IAEA Seilbersdorf Labs., Seibersdorf, Austria, 1978-82, U. Guanajuato, Mex., 1981, Coll. Montecillo, Chapingo, Mex., 1989, Korea Atomic Energy Rsch. Inst., Seoul, 1991, Nat. Atomic Energy Agy., Jakarta, 1991-94, Zhejiang U., Hangzhou, China, 1992, Ctrl. Nuc. "La Reina", Santiago, Chile, 1992, Internat. Atomic Energy Agy., Vienna, 1993-2005, Mt. Makulu Ctrl. Rsch. Sta., Lusaka, Zambia, 1994, Office Atomic Energy Peace, Bangkok, 1995, Swedish Radiation Protection Inst., Stockholm, 1996, CIEMAT, Madrid, 1996, Laguna Verde Nuc. Power Plant, Vera Cruz, Mex., 1996, Oak Ridge (Tenn.) Nat. Labs., 1998, Min. Water and Irrigation, Amman, Jordan, 1998, Wyeth-Ayerst, Pearl River, NY, 1998, Chem. Industry Inst. Toxicology, Rsch. Triangle Park, NC, 1998, Los Alamos Nat. Labs., N.Mex., 2000, U.S. Dept. Energy Idaho Nat. Engring. and Environ. Labs., Idaho Falls, 2000, China Atomic Energy Auth, Beijing, 2004. Author: (textbooks) Radiotracers in Agricultural Chemistry, 1979, Radionuclide Tracers, Their Detection and Measurement, 1987; author, editor (with J.O. Legg) Isotopes and Radiation in Agricultural Sciences, Vol. 1, 1984, Vol. 2, 1984, Handbook of Radioactivity Analysis, 1998, 2d edit., 2003; contbr. articles to profl. jours. Recipient hon. tchg. diploma, silver plaque Ctrl. U., Ecuador, Quito, 1978; hon. prof. Zhejiang U., 1992. Mem. AAAS, N.Y. Acad. Scis., Am. Nuc. Soc., Sigma Xi, Phi Lambda Upsilon, Gamma Sigma Delta. Achievements include discovery of molecular D-chiro-inositol phosphate in soil/plant systems; determination of a biochemical pathway involved in the formation of soil chiro-inositol phosphate; discovered microbial epimerization as origin of inositol phosphate isomers in soil; elucidated mechanisms of soil organic phosphorus fixation; separation of the radioactive nuclides Sr-90 from soil surfaces after nuclear fallout; first separation of radioactive nuclides Sr-90 and Y-90 by electrophoresis; execution of over 80 fact-finding, planning, and implementation missions to over 50 countries of Asia, Africa, Europe, Latin America, North America, and the Middle East for United Nations, International Atomic Energy Agy. from 1978 to the present; development of several chemical and instrumental techniques for the analysis of radioactive nuclides. Office: The Montague Group Sorrento Towers North 5355 Mira Sorrento Pl Ste 100 San Diego CA 92121 Mailing: PO Box 5033 Oceanside CA 92052-5033 Personal E-mail: montague-group@cox.net.

LANO, CHARLES JACK, retired finance company executive; b. Port Clinton, Ohio, Apr. 17, 1922; s. Charles Herbin and Antoinette (Schmitt) L.; m. Beatrice Irene Spees, June 16, 1946 (dec. 1995); children: Douglas Cloyd, Charles Lewis. BS in Bus. Adminstrn. summa cum laude, Ohio State U., 1949. C.P.A., Okla. With U.S. Gypsum Co., 1941-46, Ottawa Paper Stock Co., 1946-47; accountant Arthur Young & Co. (C.P.A.'s), Tulsa, 1949-51; controller Lima div. Ex-Cell-O Corp., 1951-59, electronics div. AVCO Corp., 1959-61, Servomation Corp., 1961; asst. comptroller Scovill Mfg. Co., Waterbury, Conn., 1961-62, comptroller, 1962-67; controller CF&I Steel Corp., Denver, 1967-69, v.p., controller, 1969-70; controller Pacific Lighting Corp., 1970-76; exec. v.p. Arts-Way Mfg. Co., Armstrong, Iowa, 1976-85; mgmt. auditor City of Anaheim, Calif., 1985-96; ret., 1996. *Undefeated in World, Pan-American, and USA Masters Weightlifting competitions since 1975.* Served with USMCR, 1942-45. Mem. Am. Inst. C.P.A.'s, Calif. Soc. C.P.A.'s, Inst. Internal Auditors. Home: 6274 E Calle Jaime Anaheim CA 92807-4005

LANOU, ROBERT EUGENE, JR., physicist, researcher; b. Colchester, Vt., Feb. 13, 1928; s. Robert E. and Flora G. (Goyette) L.; m. Cornelia Rockwell Wheeler, May 14, 1960; children: Katharine, Gregory, Elizabeth, Steven. BS, Worcester Poly. Inst., 1952; PhD, Yale U., 1957. Physicist Lawrence Berkeley (Calif.) Lab., 1956-59; asst. prof. physicist Brown U., Providence, 1960-63, assoc. prof., 1963-67, prof., 1967—, chair dept. physics, 1986-92, prof. rsch., 2001—, prof. emeritus, 2001—. Cons. Brookhaven Nat. Lab., Upton, N.Y., Los Alamos (N.Mex.) Nat. Lab.; sci. advisor Gov. State of R.I., Providence, 1986-88. Contbr. articles to profl. jours. With USN, 1946-48, ETO. Grantee Dept. Energy, 1960—, NSF, 1995—2000. Fellow AAAS, Am. Phys. Soc.; mem. Sigma Xi, Tau Beta Pi. Achievements include research in experimental particle physics and astrophysics. Home: 90 Keene St Providence RI 02906-1508 Office: Brown U Dept Physics Providence RI 02906 Office Phone: 401-863-2632.

LA NOUE, TERENCE DAVID, artist, educator; b. Hammond, Ind., Dec. 4, 1941; s. George David and Lois (Lish) L.; children: Daniel, Alexandra. BFA, Ohio Wesleyan U., 1964; Fulbright meister student, Hochschule fur Bildenden Kunste, West Berlin, 1964-65; MFA, Cornell U., 1967; DFA, Ohio Wesleyan U., 1994. Prof. Trinity Coll., Hartford, Conn., 1967-72, CUNY, N.Y.C., 1972-85, NYU, 1987. Works represented in various museums, including Whitney Mus., Guggenheim Mus., Bklyn. Mus., Albright-Knox Mus., Corcoran Gallery Art, Carnegie Inst., Power Inst. Fine Arts, Sydney, Australia, Musé d'Art et Archeologie, Toulon, France, Musée de Strasbourg, France, Mus. Contemporary Art, Teheran, Iran, Mus. Modern Art, N.Y.C., Tate Mus., London, (retrospective) Tucson Mus. Art, 2003, Metropolitan Mus. of Art, N.Y., Singapore Mus. Art; monograph, Terence La Noue, Ashton Dore, 1992. Grantee Fulbright Found., Berlin, 1964-65, NEA, 1972-73, 83-84, Guggenheim Found., 1982-83. Address: PO Box 22 Patagonia AZ 85624 Office Phone: 520-287-3066. E-mail: terencedlanoue@aol.com.

LANOUETTE, NICOLE MARIE, psychiatrist; b. Washington, Sept. 8, 1975; d. William John and JoAnne Marie Lanouette. BA cum laude, Cornell U., 1997; MD with distinction, Mt. Sinai Sch. Medicine, 2003. Rsch. asst. Sloan Kettering Cancer Ctr., N.Y.C., 1997—99; resident UCLA Med. Ctr., L.A., 2003—. Mem.: APA, Alpha Omega Alpha. Office: UCLA Neuropsychiat Inst 760 Westwood Plz Los Angeles CA 90024

LANPHER, BEN EVERT, psychologist, researcher; b. Cape Girardeau, Mo., July 15, 1958; s. Paul Gene and Mildred Wanda Lanpher; m. Kerri Lynn Seabaugh, Oct. 20, 1984; children: Lindsey Michelle (Lanpher) McClelland, Levi Lemual, Harry D. BS, S.E. Mo. State U., 1988, MA, 1992; PhD, U. Akron, 1999. Lic. psychologist Mo., social worker Mo., cert. health svc. provider Mo. Cottage supr. Cottonwood Residential Treatment Ctr., Cape Girardeau, Mo., 1988—89; cmty. support worker Beetheel Counseling Svc., Dexter, Mo., 1989—92, psychotherapist, 1992—93; rsch. asst. U. Akron, Ohio, 1993—96; intern in psychology The Guidance Ctr., Murfreesboro, Tenn., 1996—97, Cmty. Counsing Ctr., Cape Girardeau, Mo., 1997—99; psychologist Advance, Mo., 1999—. Rschr. People of the Trail Rsch. Project, Advance, Mo., 2003—. Sec. sch. bd. Advance R-IV Sch. Dist., Mo., 2002—; pk. bd. dirs. City of Advance, Mo., 2000—; mental health bd. dirs. Stoddard County Mental Health, Bloomfield, Mo., 2003—. Mem.: APA. Democrat. Avocations: backpacking, tennis, fishing, camping. Home: 19103 State Hwy C Advance MO 63730

LANPHER, KATHERINE, radio personality, columnist; b. May 27, 1959; BA, Northwestern U.; MA in Am. Cultural History, U. Chgo. Columnist St. Paul Pioneer-Press, Minn.; host Weeknights with Katherine Lanpher, KSTP-AM 1500, Mpls., 1995—96, Midmorning, Minn. Pub. Radio, 1988—2004, Talking Volumes; co-host The Al Franken Show, Air Am. Radio, NYC, 2004—. Guest host Talk of the Nation, Nat. Pub. Radio, 1999; commentator CNN, MSNBC, CNBC. Office: Air Am Radio 3 Park Ave New York NY 10016*

LANQUETOT, E. ROXANNE, retired special education educator; b. Kansas City, Nov. 29, 1933; d. Myron Lewis and Bonnie (Goldberg) Leiser; m. Guy Alfred Lanquetot, Oct. 3, 1958; 1 child, Serge Normand. Student, Stanford U., 1951-53; cert. in French Pronunciation, Inst. de Phonetique, Sorbonne, Paris, 1954; BS, Columbia U., 1956, MA, 1957, CCNY, 1976; postgrad., CUNY, 1980-83. Asst. tchr. English Lycee Fenelon, Paris, 1960-62; tchr. kindergarten Lycee Francais N.Y., N.Y.C., 1964-65; dir. nursery & kindergarten Lyceum Francais, N.Y.C., 1965-66; tchr. 2d grade Pub. Sch. 113 M, N.Y.C., 1966-69; tchr., jr. guidance counselor Pub. Sch. 87 M, N.Y.C., 1969-71; tchr. emotionally handicapped Pub. Sch. 106, Bellevue Hosp., N.Y.C., 1971-99; ret., 1999. Contbr. articles to profl. publs., Newsday, Wall St. Jour., France-Amerique, others. Fellow Am. Orthophyschiatric Assn.; mem. Nat. Alliance for Rsch. on Schizophrenia and Depression (mem. leadership coun.). Avocations: classical music, theater, creative writing, travel, ballet, classical music, theater. Home and Office: 315 W 106th St New York NY 10025-3445 E-mail: rglanquetot@yahoo.com.

LANS, CARL GUSTAV, architect, economist; b. Gothenburg, Sweden, Oct. 19, 1907; came to U.S., 1916; s. Carl and Ida Carolina (Schon) L.; m. Gwynne Iris Meyer, Dec. 21, 1935; children: Douglas C., C. Randolph. Student, CCNY, 1925-26, Sch. Architecture, Columbia U., 1926-30. Registered architect, Calif. Architect with Harry T. Lindeberg, N.Y.C., 1930-32; architect Borgia Bros. Ecclesiastical Marble, N.Y.C., 1932-34; with architects Paist & Stewart, Miami, Fla., 1934-35; chief engr. insp. Dept. Agr., 1936-38; asst. tech. dir. FHA, 1938-48; tech. dir. Nat. Assn. Home Builders, Washington, 1948-52; with Earl W. Smith Orgn., Berkeley, Calif., 1952-56; architect, economist Huntington Beach, Calif., 1956—; ptnr. John Hans Graham & Assocs. Architects, Washington, 1947-55. Spl. adviser Pres. Rhee, Republic of Korea, 1955-56; guest lectr. various univs., 1949-52. Author: Earthquake Construction, 1954. Chmn. bd. edn. adv. com., Arlington, Va., 1948. Recipient Outstanding and Meritorious Svcs. citation Republic of Korea, 1956. Mem. AIA (citation), Nat. Acad. Scis. (bldg. rsch. adv. bd. dirs.), S.W. Rsch. Inst., Seismol. Soc. Am., Prestressed Concrete Inst., Urban Land Inst., Nat. Press Club. Home and Office: 21821 Fairlane Cir Huntington Beach CA 92646-7902

LANS, DEBORAH EISNER, lawyer; b. NYC, Oct. 26, 1949; d. Asher Bob and Barbara (Eisner) L. AB magna cum laude, Smith Coll., 1971; JD cum laude, Boston U., 1974. Bar: NY 1975, U.S. Dist. Ct. (so. and ea. dists.) NY 1975, U.S. Ct. Appeals (2d cir.) 1975, U.S. Supreme Ct. 1983. Assoc. Lans, Feinberg & Cohen, NYC, 1975-80, ptnr., 1980-84, Morrison Cohen Singer & Weinstein, NYC, 1984-2000; counsel Morrison Cohen Singer & Weinstein LLP, NYC, 2000—01, Wasserman Grubin & Rogers LLP, 2001—03; mng. ptnr. Cohen Lans LLP, NYC, 2003—. Exec. dir. Mentoring USA, 2000-02; mem. Supreme Ct. appellate divsn. first dept. disciplinary com., 2000-04; bd. dirs. St. Jean Baptiste Sch., Mark and Helene Eisner Found. Mem. ABA (bd. editors comml. banking litig. sects. 1998-2000), Nat. Arbitration Forum (comml. panel arbitrators), Assn. Bar City of NY (chmn. young lawyers com. 1981-83, joint com. fee disputes, 1982, judiciary com. 1984-85, exec. com. 1985-89, spl. com. bioethical issues, 1992-94, coun. on jud. adminstrn. 1996—), NY State Bar Assn. (ho. of dels. 1984-87, comml. and fed. litig. sect. com. on judiciary, alternative dispute resolution 1992—, environ. law sect. 1995—, family law sect., co-chair women in cts. com. 1994—), NY Bar Found. Office: Cohen Lans LLP 885 Third Ave New York NY 10022 Office Phone: 212-326-1704. Business E-Mail: dlans@cohenlans.com.

LANSAW, CHARLES RAY, rendering industry executive; b. Middletown, Ohio, Mar. 5, 1927; s. Edward Curtis and Lura (Tyra) L.; m. Joan Betty Kalbaugh, July 4, 1949; children: Charles E., Gail D., Leslie J., Kristi L. Student, Miami U., Oxford, Ohio, 1947-48; student engring., U. Cin., 1949-51. Chief engr., sales mgr. Dupps Co., Germantown, Ohio, 1950-85; pres. C.R. Lansaw, Inc., Germantown, 1985—. Past mem. Germantown Planing Commn.; past bd. dirs. Germantown Pub. libr., 1991-2001; served with VOCA at Saratov and Volgograd, Russia, 1996, Internat. Exec. Svc. Corps, Alexandria, Egypt, 1993. With USNR, 1944-46. Mem. Rotary (pres. Germantown 1987-88, Paul Harris fellow). Avocations: sailing, woodworking, tennis. Home and Office: 73 Sue Dr Germantown OH 45327-1628 E-mail: clansaw@woh.rr.com.

LANSBURY, ANGELA BRIGID, actress; b. London, Oct. 16, 1925; came to U.S., 1940; d. Edgar and Moyna (Macgill) L.; m. Peter Shaw, Aug. 12, 1949 (dec. 2003); children: Anthony, Deirdre. Student, Webber-Douglas Sch. Drama, London, 1939-40, Feagin Sch. Drama, N.Y.C., 1940-42; LHD (hon.), Boston U., 1990. Host 41st-43d Ann. Tony Awards, 45th Ann. Emmy Awards. Actress with Metro-Goldwyn-Mayer, 1943-50; films include: Gaslight, 1944 (Acad. award nomination), National Velvet, 1944, The Picture of Dorian Gray, 1944 (Golden Globe award, Acad. award nomination), The Harvey Girls, 1946, The Hoodlum Saint, 1946, Till the Clouds Roll By, 1946, The Private Affairs of Bel Ami, 1947, If Winter Comes, 1948, Tenth Avenue Angel, 1948, State of the Union, 1948, The Three Musketeers, 1948, The Red Danube, 1949, Samson and Delilah, 1949, Kind Lady, 1951, Mutiny, 1952, Remains to be Seen, 1953, A Life at Stake, 1955, The Purple Mask, 1956, A Lawless Street, 1956, Please Murder Me, 1956, The Court Jester, 1956, The Long Hot Summer, 1958, Reluctant Debutante, 1958, A Breath of Scandal, 1960, Dark at the Top of the Stairs, 1960, Season of Passion, 1961, Blue Hawaii, 1961, All Fall Down, 1962, Manchurian Candidate, 1962 (Golden Globe award, Acad. award nomination), In the Cool of the Day, 1963, Dear Heart, 1964, The World of Henry Orient, 1964, The Greatest Story Ever Told, 1965, Harlow, 1965, The Amorous Adventures of Moll Flanders, 1965, Mister Buddwing, 1966, Something for Everyone, 1970, Bedknobs and Broomsticks, 1971, Death on the Nile, 1978, The Lady Vanishes, 1980, The Mirror Crack'd, 1980, The Pirates of Penzance, 1982, The Company of Wolves, 1983, Beauty and the Beast, 1991, Your Studio and You, 1995, Beauty & the Beast: Enchanted Christmas (vioce), 1997, Anastasia (Voice), 1997; star TV series Murder, She Wrote, 1984-96 (Golden Globe awards 1984, 86, 91, 92, 12 Emmy nominations, Lead Actress - Drama), Murder, She Wrote: A Story to Die For, 2000, Murder, She Wrote: The Last Free Man, 2001, Murder, She Wrote: The Celtic Riddle, 2003; appeared in TV mini-series Little Gloria, Happy at Last, 1982, Lace, 1984, Rage of Angels, part II, 1986; other TV movies include: The First Olympics-Athens 1896, A Talent for Murder, Gift of Love, 1982, Shootdown, 1988, The Shell Seekers, 1989, The Love She Sought, 1990, Mrs. 'Arris Goes to Paris, 1992, (musical) Mrs. Santa Claus, 1996; appeared in plays Hotel Paradiso, 1957, A Taste of Honey, 1960, Anyone Can Whistle, 1964, Mame (on Broadway), 1966, 83 (Tony award for Best Mus. Actress 1966), Dear World, 1968 (Tony award for Best Mus. Actress 1969), All Over (London Royal Shakespeare Co.), 1971, Prettybelle, 1971, Gypsy, 1974 (Tony award for Best Mus. Actress 1975, Sarah Siddons award), The King and I, 1978, Sweeney Todd, 1979 (Tony award for Best Mus. Actress 1979, Sarah Siddons award), Hamlet, Nat. Theatre, London, 1976, A Little Family Business, 1983; TV appearances Law & Order: SVU, 2005. Named Woman of Yr., Harvard Hasty Pudding Theatricals, 1968, Comdr. of British Empire by Queen Elizabeth II, 1994; named to Theatre Hall of Fame, 1982, TV Hall of Fame, 1996; recipient British Acad. award, 1991, Silver Mask Lifetime Ach. Award, British Acad. Film and TV Arts, 1992, Lifetime Achievement award, Screen Actors' Guild, Hollywood, 1997, 16

Emmy Award Nominations, 8 Golden Globe Nominations; Won 6 Golden Glode Awards; received Nat. medal of the Arts from President Clinton, 1997. Office: c/o William Morris Agy 151 El Camino Dr Beverly Hills CA 90212*

LANSBURY, EDGAR GEORGE, theatrical producer; b. London, Jan. 12, 1930; came to U.S., 1941, naturalized, 1953; s. Edgar Isaac and Charlotte Lillian (McIldowie) L.; m. Rose Anthony Kean, Aug. 12, 1955; children: James, Michael, David, George, Brian, Kate. Ed., UCLA. Designer stock and off-Broadway prodns., 1953-55; art dir. ABC-TV, 1955, CBS-TV, 1955-62, Channel 13, N.Y.C., 1962-63; motion picture art dir., 1963-64; formed Edgar Lansbury Prodns. Inc., for ind. prodn. in theatre and films, 1964—; chmn. The Acting Co. Bd. dirs. drama dept. Story Line Press; chair Russian Mus. Arts Soc. Am. Producer Broadway plays: First One Asleep Whistle, 1966, The Subject Was Roses, (Critics Circle award, Antoinette Perry award, Pulitzer Prize) 1964, That Summer-That Fall, 1967, The Only Game in Town, 1968, Promenade, 1970, Look to the Lilies, 1970, Engagement Baby, 1971, Godspell, 1971, Elizabeth I, 1972, The Night That Made America Famous, 1974, The Magic Show, 1974, Gypsy, 1975, American Buffalo, 1977, Broadway Follies, 1981, O, Pioneer!, 1989, Club XII, 1990, Amphigorey, 1992, Any Given Day, 1993, Curtains, Grace and Glorie, 1996, In Circles, 1997, As Bees in Honey Drown, 1997, June Moon, 1998, Lennon, 2005; films The Subject was Roses, 1968, Godspell, 1973, The Wild Party, 1974, Squirm, 1976, Blue Sunshine, 1978, He Knows You're Alone, 1980, The Clairvoyant, 1982, Summer Girl, 1983, A Stranger Waits, 1986, Advice from a Caterpillar, 1999, Gypsy "83", 2001; dir. Without Apologies, 1989, All the Queen's Men, 1989, Advice from a Caterpillar, 1990. The Country Club, 1992. Pres. Agni Yoga Soc., Nicholas Roerich Mus., N.Y.C.; bd. govs. League N.Y. Theatres and Prodrs.; chmn. Russian Chamber Chorus, N.Y.C., The Acting Co., N.Y.C. Served with U.S. Army, 1951—53. Recipient N.Y. Art Dirs. award for best comml. film, 1963; N.Y. Outer Critics Circle award, 1965; N.Y. Critics Circle award, 1965; Antoinette Perry award for best produced play, 1965; nomination for Antoinette Perry award for best mus. play, 1977; N.Y. Critics Circle award for best drama, 1977 Office: Edgar Lansbury Prodns 630 9th Ave Ste 214 New York NY 10036-3708 Home: 15 W 81st St #8c New York NY 10024-6022

LANSDALE, H. PARKER, minister, historian, non-profit administrator; b. Worcester, Mass., Mar. 18, 1923; s. Herbert P. Jr. and Marjorie M. (McKay) L.; m. Elizabeth Ann MacCollum, Feb. 25, 1945 (div. Jan. 1976); children: Ann T., Kirk M., Todd A.; m. Dorothy Phillips Deschamps, May 26, 1976; children: Thomas A. Deschamps, Margaret D. Sticklen, Brian P. Deschamps, Patricia S. Deschamps. AB, Oberlin Coll., 1944; BD, Yale Div. Sch., 1950; MA, Yale Grad. Sch., 1953, PhD, 1956. Ordained to ministry Presbyn. Ch. (USA), 1950. Boys work sec. YMCA, New Haven, 1948-56; mem. faculty Yale Div. Sch., 1948-56; assoc. gen. sec. YMCA, Wilmington, Del., 1956-59; program dir. YMCA Greater N.Y., N.Y.C., 1959-61; gen. sec. YMCA of Greater Bridgeport, Conn., 1961-69; dir. (on loan from YMCA) Higher Edn. Ctr. for Urban Studies, Bridgeport, 1968-77; cmty. liaison (on loan) Bridgeport Area Found.-United Way, Bridgeport, 1977-83; ret., 1983; hon. rsch. assoc. YMCA U.S.A., 1990—. Exec. dir. (on loan) Action for Bridgeport Cmty. Devel., 1964—65; health care organizer, pres. Conn. Health Plan, 1973—80; mem. Conn. State Bd. Mental Health, 1975—83; urban cons. U. Bridgeport Nursing Sch. Planning com., 1973—78; courtesy historian in residence Sarasota-Manatee Campus, U. South Fla., 1996—2004; pastoral assoc. 1st Presbyn. Ch., Sarasota; bd. advisors. Sr. Acad. U. South Fla, Sarasota, 1998—2003; lectr. in field. Author: History of the Work of the YMCA with Boys (1900-25), 1992; co-editor: There is a Tide, 2000; contbr. articles to profl. jours. Mem. Peace River Presbyn. Ch.; ARC, 1963—70; Bridgeport Model Cities, 1969—74; Park City Hosp., 1970—83; Conn. Health Plan, 1972—80; sr. bd. advi. nd. sr. acad., lectr. NSF Sarasota. With USMC, 1942—46. Recipient Cmty Ptnr. in Edn., U. South Fla., 1997, F. William Stahl award, N. Am. Fellowship of YMCA Retirees, 2000. Fellow N.Am. Fellowship YMCA Retirees, World Fellowship YMCA Retirees. Democrat. Avocations: history, writing, volunteer service.

LANSDOWNE, WILLIAM M., police chief; b. May 10, 1944; s. Leonard M. and Grace (Dabuque) L.; m. Sharon L. Young, June 12, 1994; children: Greg, Erik. BS in Law Enforcement, San Jose State U., 1971. Asst. chief San Jose (Calif.) Police Dept., 1966-94; chief Richmond (Calif.) Police Dept., 1994—98; chief of police San Jose Police Dept., Calif., 1998—2003, San Diego Police Dept., Calif., 2003—. Mem. Internat. Assn. Chiefs of Police, Calif. Police Chiefs Assn., Police Exec. Rsch. Forum, Calif. Homeland Security Pub. Safety Adv. Com. Office: San Diego Police Dept 1401 Broadway San Diego CA 92101-5729 Office Phone: 619-531-2000.

LANSFORD, EDWIN GAINES, accountant; b. Chattanooga, Aug. 20, 1924; s. Frederick Duke Lansford and Edwina (Gaines) Lansford Stone; m. Sue Ann Kemmer, May 29, 1954, remarried, Apr. 27, 2005; children: Virginia Nan, Sue Ann, Edwin Gaines, Jr., James Robert, Frederick Scott. BBA, U. Chattanooga, 1948; LLB, McKenzie Coll., 1958. Bar: Tenn. Cost acct. Cavalier Corp., Chattanooga, 1948-52; staff acct. O.T. Draewell and H.L. Oakes, Chattanooga, 1952-54; pvt. practice Crossville & Chattanooga, 1954-98; v.p. Lansford Kawasaki, Inc., Crossville, 1978—; of counsel Lansford & Stephens, CPAs, Pikeville and Crossville, Tenn., 1999—. Bd. dirs. Rotary Found. of Cumberland County, 2001—, sec.-treas., 2003—; scoutmaster Cherokee Area coun. Boy Scouts Am., 1947-52. With U.S. Army, 1943-46, ETO. Mem.: NRA, AICPA (hon.), Tenn. Bar Assn., Cumberland County C. of C. (bd. dirs. 1976—79), Tenn. Shooting Sports Assn. (H.P. Rifle Team 1963—64, pres. 1969—71), Nat. Assn. Tax Profls. (bd. dirs. Tenn. chpt. 1996—, treas. 1998—2001), Tenn. Soc. CPAs (life; pres. Chattanooga chpt. 1962—63, 1st pres., co-founder Upper Cumberland chpt. 1978—79, sec., various coms.), Elks, Rotary (all offices and bd. dirs. Crossville noon chpt. 1983—, Paul Harris fellow), Lions (treas. Signal Mountain club 1974—75). Methodist. Avocations: hunting, hiking. Office: 92 Rockwood Ave Crossville TN 38555-4610 E-mail: lansford@multipro.com.

LANSFORD, JAMES LOWELL, technologist; b. Huntland, Tenn., June 9, 1957; BS, Auburn (Ala.) U., 1980; MS, Ga. Tech, 1982; PhD, Okla. State U., Stillwater, 1988. Sr. mem. tech staff Ga. Tech Rsch. Inst., Atlanta, 1987—90; asst. prof. U. of Colo., Colorado Springs, 1990—95; chief tech. officer Momentum Microsys., Colorado Springs, 1994—96; sr. staff Intel Corp., Hillsboro, Oreg., 1996—2000; chief tech. officer, vp bus. devel. Mobilian, Portland, Oreg., 2000—03; chief tech. officer Alereon, Inc., Austin, Tex., 2003—. Pres. Mobile Data Sys., Colorado Springs, 1993—96. Bd. dirs., pres.-elect Unitarian-Universalist Ch., Stillwater, 2000—04. Mem.: IEEE. Unitarian. Achievements include patents in field; patents pending for. Avocation: travel. Office: Alereon Inc 7600V N Capital of Texas Hwy Suite TX 78731 Office Phone: +1 512 345 4200 x2166. Office Fax: +1 206 337 1703. E-mail: jim.lansford@ieee.org.

LANSFORD, RAYMOND WILLIAM, retired finance educator; b. Linn, Mo. s. August Franklin and Annie Louise (Miller) L.; m. Beuna Alma Ridenhour, May 25, 1945. BS, S.W. Mo. State U., 1947; MBA, Northwestern U., 1948; PhD, NYU, 1954. Prof. Ctrl. Mo. State U., Warrensburg, 1949—57, U. Mo., Columbia, 1957—85, asst. dean Coll. Bus., 1961—75, ednl. dir., 1975—85, prof. emeritus, 1985—, disting. prof., 1992; CEO Analytical Biochemistry Corp., Columbia, 1993—94. Author: Real Estate Contracts, 1967, Real Estate Closing Guide, 1968, (booklet) Renting Property, 1971, Appraisal Primer, 1973. Mem. ch. county com. Boone County Reorgn., Columbia, 1967-68; v.p. U. Children's Hosp., 1987-88. Decorated Air medal with five oak leaf clusters; named Realtor of Yr., Mo. Assn. Realtors, 1976. Mem. Kiwanis (gov. 1974-75, trustee 1977-84, v.p. 1982-83, bd. dirs. 1992-93, internat. pres. 1984-85, Disting. Leader award, Tablet of Honor, Hixson Fellow), Heritage Soc. Avocation: antique tool collecting. Home: 2 Springer Dr Columbia MO 65201-5425 Office Phone: 573-442-6943.

LANSING, MARTHA HEMPEL, internist; b. New Haven, Conn., 1942; Degree in music, Houghton Coll.; MD, U. Okla., 1982. Diplomate Am. Bd. Family Practice, cert. psychoanalytic psychotherapist. Resident in family practice U. Tenn., 1982—84, Williamsport (Pa.) Hosp.-U. Pa., 1984—85; group family practice physician, 1985—95; dir. family practice residency program U. Medicine and Dentistry N.J., 1997—, program dir., dir. family health ctr., assoc. prof. Staff physician Capital Health Sys.-Fuld Campus. Author (with Carol D. Goodheart): Treating People with Chronic Disease: A Psychological Guide, 1996; contbr. chpt. to book. Named one of Top Drs. 2002, Castle Connolly and N.J. Monthly Mag., Top Drs. 2003. Fellow: Nat. Inst. Program Dir. Devel. Office: Family Health Ctr 666 Plainsboro Rd # 640 Plainsboro NJ 08536-3019 Office Phone: 609-275-0487.

LANSING, SHERRY LEE (HEIMANN), former film company executive; b. Chgo., July 31, 1944; d. Norton and Margo L.; m. William Friedkin, July 6, 1991. BS summa cum laude in Theatre, Northwestern U., 1966. High sch. tchr. math., L.A., 1966-69; model TV commls. Max Factor Co., 1969-70, Alberto-Culver Co., 1969-70; story editor Wagner Internat. Prodn. Co., 1972-74, dir. west coast devel., 1974-75; story editor MGM, 1975-77, v.p. creative affairs, 1977; senior v.p. prodn. Columbia Pictures, 1977-80; pres. studio 20th Century Fox Prodns., Hollywood, 1980-82; founder Jaffee-Lansing Prodns., 1983—92; pres. Paramount Communications, 1990—2005; chmn. Paramount Motion Pictures Group, L.A., 1992—2005; CEO The Sherry Lansing Found., 2005—. Bd. dirs. Rand Corp. Appeared in movies Loving, 1970, Rio Lobo, 1970; (TV apparances) Ironside, 1971, Frasier, 1996; ind. producer., Jaffe-Lansing Prodns.; exec. prodr. Racing With the Moon, 1984, Firstborn, 1984; prodr. Fatal Attraction, 1987, The Accused, 1988, Black Rain, 1989, School Ties, 1992, Indecent Proposal, 1993; exec. prodr. (TV movies) When the Time Comes, 1987, Mistress, 1992. Bd. dirs. ARC; bd. regents U. Calif., 1991—; bd. trustees The Carter Center, 2005—, Am. Assn. Cancer Rsch. Named one of 100 Most Powerful Women in Entertainment, Hollywood Reporter, 2003, 2004; recipient Producers Guild of Am. Milestone award, 2000, Horatio Alger award, 2004.

LANSNER, RUTH L., lawyer; b. NYC, June 29, 1950; BA cum laude, Yale U., 1971; JD, NYU Sch. Law, 1974. Bar: NY 1975. Practiced Gilbert, Segall and Young LLP (joined Holland & Knight), 1974—2001; ptnr. Holland & Knight LLP, NY, 2001—, mem. dir. com., dep. sect. leader bus. law sect. Mem. def. adv. com. on women in the svcs. (DACOWITS) US Dept. Def., 1998—2000; lectr. in field. Mem. bd. editors Leader's Equipment Leasing Newsletter, 1986, newsletter editor Aeronautical Law Com.; contbr. articles to profl. jours. Nat. commr. Anti-Defamation League, chmn., Nat. Legal Affairs Com., 1990—98; mem. Nat. Exec. Com.; vice-chair Nat. Religious Freedom Task Force. Fellow: ABA (vice-chair women's interest network sect. on internat. law & practice 1999—, rep. to UN econ. and social coun. for NY 2000—01, mem. sect. internat. law and practice, reg. coord. for NY women's interest network's); mem.: Inst. of Trade Mark Attys. (UK), Internat. Trademark Assn., Am. Fgn. Law Assn. (v.p. 1997—2000), Am. Fgn. Lawyers Assn. (dir. 2001—03), NY County Lawyers Assn. (dir. 1997—2000), Internat. Bar Assn. (co-chair of a panel "Sale of a Bus. Using an Auction Process" 2002, vice-chair 2002—, former chmn. subcommittee on the sale contract, former chmn. com. on internat. sales & related comml. transactions), Assn. Bar City NY (mem. com. on aeronautics 1978—81, sec. 1981—83, chair 1983—86, mem. com. on aeronautics 1983—86). Office: Holland & Knight LLP 195 Broadway 24th Fl New York NY 10007 Office Phone: 212-513-3440. Business E-Mail: rlansner@hklaw.com.

LANTER, LANORE, writer, educator; b. Argenta, Ill., Apr. 30, 1928; d. Floyd Depin Lanter and Goldie May Elkins; m. Andrew Kasparian, Oct. 17, 1948 (div. July 1976); children: Andra Kay, Dana Lee, Mark Scott, David Andrew. BA in English, Fresno State Coll., 1969. Cert. std. elem. tchr., 1972, early childhood, 1972, registered Calif., 1972. Tutor lang. skills Fresno County, Calif., 1972; co-dir. curriculum N.W. Ch. Day Care, Fresno, 1972—73; writer curriculum, head tchr. First Presbyn. Ch., Fresno, 1973—74; owner, tchr., writer curriculum Children's Corner Presch., Fresno, 1977—83; educator (older adults writing) Clovis Adult Edn./Clovis Unified Sch. Dist., Calif., 1995—; columnist Wryte Rite Tips Win Win Writing Orgn., Fresno, 2001—05. Editor, cons. San Joaquin Valley Sr. Writers, Fresno, 1994—. Author: (textbook) You Can Wryte Rite Series, 1994; editor: (6 book anthologies) Inklings, 1994, 1995, 1996, We Remember When, 1997, Flights of Fantasy, 2000, Poemscapes, 2005. Vol. tchr., writing educator (55 yrs. and older) St. Agnes Hosp. Club 55 Plus, Herndon, Fresno, 1994—; mem. task force Muscular Dystrophy Assn., Shaw, Fresno, 1994; vol. Win Win Writers Orgn., 2002—05. Named Highest Achiever with muscle disease, Muscular Dystrophy, Shaw, Fresno, 1995; recipient Best Tchr. plaque, San Joaquin Valley Sr. Writers, 1997, Tolerance award, So. Poverty Law Ctr., Mont., Ala., 2003, First Pl. Srs. of William Saroyan Writing Contest, 1992, Cert. of Recognition for Outstanding Contbn., Muscular Dystrophy Assn., Calif. Legis. Assembly, 1995. Independent. Protestant. Avocations: reading, flower arranging, painting, poetry writing. Home: 2934 E Ashlan Ave Fresno CA 93726-3304 Office Phone: 559-243-1156. Office Fax: 559-243-1156. Personal E-mail: lanore22@aol.com.

LANTER, ROBERT B., osteopath; s. Bernard Lanter and Dorothy Statman; m. Wendy Lanter, Jan. 11, 1964; children: Sophie, Charley. BA in Biology, Clark U., 1982; DO, N.Y. Coll., 1988; cert. in acupuncture, UCLA, 2001. Diplomate Am. Bd. Phys. Medicine. Resident rehab. medicine Met. Hosp. Ctr., Valhalla, 1988—89; intern Westchester County Med. Ctr., Valhalla, 1989—90, resident rehab. medicine, 1990—91; chief resident Lincoln Hosp., Bronx, 1991—92; fellow sports medicine Hosp. Joint Disease, Orthop. Inst., N.Y.C., 1992—93; pvt. practice, 1993—94. Team physician varsity athletic program Queens Coll., 1992—; team physician U.S. Tennis Open, 1992, Empire State Games, 1992; covering physician Madison Sq. Garden Events, 1992; team physician Freeport H.S., 1993—95; attending physician supr. residents Hosp. Joint Disease, 1993—; staff Franklin Hosp. Med. Ctr., 1993—, Peninsula Hosp. Med. Ctr., 1993—; attending physician in charge of metro sports rehab. medicine program Meth. Hosp. Mem.: Am. Acad. Electrodiagnostic Medicine, Am. Acad. Phys. Med. & Rehab., N.Y. Soc. Phys. Medicine & Rehab. Avocations: basketball, ice skating. Office: 131 Main St Ste 4 East Rockaway NY 11518 also: 371 Doughtery Blvd Inwood NY 11096 also: 431 Beach 1w9 St Belle Harbor NY 11694 Office Phone: 516-766-5495. E-mail: RobertLanterDo@aol.com.

LANTHIER, RONALD ROSS, retired manufacturing company executive; b. Montreal, Que., Can., May 2, 1926; s. Emile Edgar and Edith (Martin) L.; m. Jacqueline Barbara Dyment; children: April Carolyn, Bonnie Alice, Ronald Dyment, Andrea Elizabeth, John Elliott. Chartered Accountant, McGill U., 1952. Pub. accountant, 1944-51; chief accountant St. Lawrence Flour Co., 1951-52; controller Canadian Underwriters Assn., 1952-54; div. controller Canadian Aviation Electronics Co., 1954-56; treas. Webb & Knapp, Can., 1956-62; dir. adminstrn., mem. exec. com. Greenshields, Inc. (investment dealers), 1962-67; v.p. finance, treas., mem. exec. com. Canadian Marconi Co., 1967-72; v.p. finance, dir., mem. exec. com. Macdonald Tobacco, Inc., 1972-75; pres. Lanco Mgmt. Ltd., 1975-98; v.p. finance MacDonald Stewart Textiles, 1976-77; v.p. fin., mem. exec. com. Electrolux Can., 1978-79; pres. Robert R. Bramhall & Assos. (Can.) Ltd., 1980-81; sr. v.p. Camflo Mines Ltd., 1981-84; v.p. fin. Starnav Corp., 1984-86; v.p. VR Fin. Svcs., 1987-95. Mem. Inst. Chartered Accts. Que. and Ont., Phi Kappa Pi. Anglican. Home: 100 Westview Dr Aurora ON Canada L4G 7C9 Personal E-mail: jarba@interhop.net.

LANTIS, DONNA LEA, retired banker, artist, art educator; b. Medford, Oreg., Oct. 12, 1931; d. James Warren Fader and Amy Bell (Crump) Fader-Snyder; m. Victor Earl Lantis, July 9, 1950 (div. Apr. 1975); children: Deborah Ann Hayes, Diana Lorraine Keaton. BS, So. Oreg. U., 1966; postgrad., Otis Art Inst., L.A., 1969; 5th yr. cert., U. Oreg., 1974. Art tchr., Oreg., Tenn., Ky.; cert. banker Am. Inst. Banking. Banker First Nat. Bank, Ashland, Oreg., 1951-62; tchr. art, history Klamath County Sch. Dist., Klamath Falls, Oreg., 1966-68; tchr. art Ashland Sch. Dist., 1968-75; banker First Interstate Bank, Medford, Oreg., 1979-92. Supr. student tchrs. So. Oreg. U., Ashland, 1968-75, work with traumatized children, 1968-69. Author illustrated poetry; exhbns. include Oreg. State Fair, So. Oreg. U., Portland, Monmouth Rogue Art Gallery, Medford, Oreg., banks, librs.; dollmaker. Asst. founder lupus support group, Ashland, Oreg., 1977, 78, 79. Elks scholar, 1950, John Dickey Art scholar So. Oreg. U., 1966; recipient Voice of Democracy 1st Place Hon. Mention Broadcasters and Radio Dealers of Am. KWIN, 1949. Mem. AAUW, So. Oreg. Alumni Assn., Libr. of Congress, Women in Arts. Avocations: music, history, writing, gardening, dolls, glass-blowing.

LANTOS, THOMAS PETER, congressman; b. Budapest, Hungary, Feb. 1, 1928; m. Annette Tillemann; children: Annette, Katrina. BA, U. Wash., 1949, MA, 1950; PhD, U. Calif., Berkeley, 1953. Faculty U. Wash., San Francisco State U., 1950-83; TV news analyst, commentator; sr. econ. and fgn. policy adviser to several U.S. senators; mem. Presdl. Task Force on Def. and Fgn. Policy, U.S. Congresses from 12th Calif. Dist., 1981—; ranking minority mem., internat. rels. com., mem. govt. reform com. Founder study abroad program Calif. State U. and Coll. Sys. Mem. Millbrae Bd. Edn., 1950-66; co-founder, co-chair Congl. Human Rights Caucus. Democrat. Office: US Ho of Reps 2413 Rayburn Ho Office Bldg Washington DC 20515-0512*

LANTZ, DELANO MERLIN, lawyer; b. St. Paul, Sept. 21, 1943; s. Wallace Arthur and Martha Cecila (Frestedt) L.; m. Donore Noe James, Jan. 4, 1969; children: Chandra, Carl, Cristin. BS, U. Minn., 1968; postgrad., Pa. State U., 1968-69; JD, Dickinson Sch. of Law, 1975. Bar: Pa. 1975, U.S. Dist. Ct. (mid. dist.) Pa. 1976, U.S. dist. Ct. (e.d. dist.) Pa. 1979, U.S. Ct. Appeals (3rd cir.). Math. tchr. Virginia (Minn.) Sch. Dist., 1967; assoc. McNees, Wallace & Nurick, Harrisburg, Pa., 1972-81, ptnr., 1982—. Trustee Second Presbyn. Ch., Carlisle, Pa., 1997. With USAF, 1968-72. Abel Klau scholar, 1971. Mem. ABA, Pa. Bar Assn., Pa. Def. Inst., PHi Kappa Phi, Chi Epsilon Pi. Democrat. Avocation: woodworking. Office: McNees Wallace & Nurick 100 Pine St PO Box 1166 Harrisburg PA 17108-1166 Office Phone: 717-237-5348. Business E-Mail: dlantz@mwn.com.

LANTZ, JOANNE BALDWIN, retired academic administrator; b. Defiance, Ohio, Jan. 26, 1932; d. Hiram J. and Ethel A. (Smith) Baldwin; m. Wayne E. Lantz. BS in Physics and Math., U. Indpls., 1953; MS in Counseling and Guidance, Ind. U., 1957; PhD in Counseling and Psychology, Mich. State U., 1969; LittD (hon.), U. Indpls., 1985; LHD (hon.), Purdue U., 1994; LLD (hon.), Manchester Coll., 1994. Tchr. physics and math. Arcola (Ind.) High Sch., 1953-57; guidance dir. New Haven (Ind.) Sr. High Sch., 1957-65; with Ind. U.-Purdue U., Fort Wayne, 1965—, interim chancellor, 1988-89, chancellor, 1989-94, chancellor emeritus, 1994—. Bd. dirs., hon. dir. Ft. Wayne Nat. Corp.; bd. dirs. Foellinger Found. Contbr. articles to profl. jours. Mem. Ft. Wayne Econ. Devel. Adv. Bd. and Task Force, 1988-91, Corp. Coun., 1988-94; bd. advisors Leadership Ft. Wayne, 1988-94; mem. adv. bd. Ind. Sml. Bus. Devel. Ctr., 1988-90; trustee Ancilla System, Inc., 1984-89, chmn. human resources com., 1985-89, exec. com., 1985-89; trustee St. Joseph's Med. Ctr., 1983-84, pers. adv. com. to bd. dirs., 1978-84, chmn., 1980-84; bd. dirs. United Way Allen County, sec., 1979-80; bd. dirs. Anthony Wayne Vocat. Rehab. Ctr., 1969-75. Mem.: AAUW (Am. women fellowship com. 1978—83, program com. 1981—83, chmn. 1981—83, internat. fellowship com. 1986—88, trust rsch. grantee 1980), APA, Southeastern Psychol. Assn. (referee conv. papers 1987, 1988), Ft. Wayne Ind.-Purdue Alumni Soc. (hon. mem. 1987), Ind. Sch. Women's Club (v.p. program chair 1979—81), Delta Kappa Gamma (leadership devel. com. 1978—82, dir. N.E. region 1982—84, adminstrv. bd. 1982—84, exec. bd. 1982—84, gen. chair conv. 1985—86, editl. bd. 1986—88, bd. trustees ednl. found. 1996—2002, nominating com. 2002—), Sigma Xi, Pi Lambda Theta. Avocations: swimming, reading, knitting, boating. E-mail: joalantz@aol.com.

LANTZ, KENNETH EUGENE, consulting firm executive; b. Altoona, Pa., Mar. 9, 1934; s. William Martin and Alice Lucretia (Glass) L.; m. D. Arlene Yocum, Nov. 28, 1959; children: Antonia Marie, Theresa Antoinette. BS cum laude, Fordham U., 1956. Cons. Sutherland Co., 1960-62; spl. rep. IBM, L.A., 1962-67; dir. info. svcs. Loyola-Marymount U., L.A., 1967-70; pres. CBIS, L.A., 1970-72; mgr. fin. sys. Occidental Life Ins., L.A., 1973-77; pres. Kenneth Lantz Assocs., L.A., 1977-82; dir. sys. Sayre & Toso, L.A., 1982-83; prin. Atwater, Lantz, Hunter & Co., L.A., 1983—. Lectr. computing topics Technology Transfer Inst., 1987-88. Author: The Prototyping Methodology, 1984; contbr. articles to profl. jours. 1st lt. USAF, 1957-60. Mem. Future of Automation Roundtable (dir. 1983—), Ins. Acctg. and Sys. Assn. (nat. Merit award 1984). Republican. Roman Catholic. Office: Atwater Lantz Hunter & Co PO Box 572366 Tarzana CA 91357-2366 E-mail: kel@manageknowledge.com.

LANTZ, PHILLIP EDWARD, security firm executive, consultant; b. Laramie, Wyo., Sept. 21, 1938; s. Everett Delmer and Elizabeth Mary (Stratton) L.; m. Paula Bogel, June 16, 1962; children: Kirk Edward, Eric William. BA in Math., U. Colo., 1960; MA in Math., U. Wyo., 1966; MS in Ops. Rsch., Johns Hopkins U., 1972. Grad. teaching asst. U. Wyo., Laramie, 1964-65; sr. engr. Applied Physics Lab. Johns Hopkins U., Silver Spring, Md., 1965-70; v.p. Ops. Rsch. Inc., Silver Spring, Md., 1970-72; dir. Tetra Tech. Inc., Arlington, Va., 1972-74; pres., chief exec. officer Systems Planning and Analysis, Inc., Alexandria, Va., 1974—, also bd. dirs. Lt. USN, 1960-64. Home: 2911 Eddington Ter Alexandria VA 22302-3503 Office: Systems Planning and Analysis Inc Ste 400 2000 N Beauregard St Alexandria VA 22311-1712

LANTZER, JASON SCOTT, historian, educator; b. Goshen, Ind., Feb. 13, 1975; s. Jack Douglas and Juanita Lantzer; m. Erin Heuer, July 24, 1999. BA, Ind. U., 1997, MA, 1999, PhD, 2005. Vis. lectr. in history Ind. U. Columbus, Columbus, Ind., 2002—03, Franklin Coll., Franklin, Ind., 2002—05, Ind. U., Indpls., 2003—05, lectr. history Bloomington, 2005—. Rschr. Conner Prairie Living History Mus., Fishers, Ind., 2000—02, The Polis Ctr., Indpls., 1997—99. Contbr. articles to profl. jours., chapters to books. Recipient essay award, South Conf. Ind. United Meth. Ch., 2001; Wiseman Family fellow, 2002, Hoover Presdl. Lib. Travel Grantee, Cushwa Ctr. grantee, U. Notre Dame. Mem.: Hist. Soc., Ind. Hist. Soc., Orgn. Am. Historians, United Meth. Ch. Hist. Soc., Hist. Soc. Episcopal Ch. Methodist. Personal E-mail: jlantzer@indiana.edu.

LANYON, E. JEAN, artist, poet; b. Wilmington, Del., July 1, 1935; d. John Milton Lanyon Sr. and Mabel (Howard) Miller; 1 child, Stephanie Irene. Student, Chouinard Art Inst., L.A., 1956—58; BA, Goddard Coll., Plainfield, Vt., 1974; postgrad., Md. Inst. Coll. of Art, Balt., 1978—80, Vermont Coll., Montpellier, 1983. Owner, artist, instr. Lanyon Studio and Gallery, Wilmington, Del., 1961—; instr. Del. Coll. Art and Design, Wilmington, 1998—, Wilmington Coll., New Castle, Del., 2004—, Del. Art Mus., Wilmington, 1951—98. Archtl. drafter and designer various archtl. firms; poetry readings various univs., clubs, bars; Poet Laureate State of Del., 1979—2001; architect-in-residence Kate Millet's Art Colony, Poughkeepsie, NY, 1979, 91. Author, illustrator The Rose Bush, 2003, The Myrno Bird, 1970 (FSW Prize Pub.); author: (poetry) People Garden, 1976; illustrator, poet Palingenesis, 2002; Ornament for White House Christmas Tree, 2002, exhibitions include Deines Cultural Ctr., Russell, Kans., 2003. Bd. dirs. Ctr. for Creative Arts, Yorklyn, Del., 1990—99. Recipient Gov.'s Award for the Arts in poetry and painting, 2000; grantee Established Artist grantee, Del. Divsn. of the Arts, NEA, 1996. Mem.: Del. Found. for Visual Arts (libr., adv. bd. 1993—), First State Writers (pres. 1991—), Phila. Watercolor Soc. Avocation: miniature scale furniture. Home and Office: 8 Winston Ave Wilmington DE 19804 Office Phone: 302-654-6236.

LANYON, ELLEN (MRS. ROLAND GINZEL), artist, educator; b. Chgo., Dec. 21, 1926; d. Howard Wesley and Ellen (Aspinwall) L.; m. Roland Ginzel, Sept. 4, 1948; children: Andrew, Lisa. BFA, Art Inst. Chgo., 1948; MFA, U. Iowa, 1950; Fulbright fellow, Courtauld Inst., U. London, 1950-51. Tchr. jr. sch. Art Inst. Chgo., 1952-54; past tchr. day sch., tchr. Rockford Coll., summer 1953, Oxbow Summer Sch. Painting, Saugatuck, Mich., 1961-62, 67-70, 71-72, 78, 88, 94, U. Ill., Chgo., 1970, U. Wis. Extension, 1971-72, Pa. State U., 1974, U. Calif., 1974, Sacramento State U., 1974, Stanford U., 1974, Boston U., 1975, Kans. State U., 1976, U. Mo., 1976, U. Houston, 1977; assoc. prof. Cooper Union, N.Y.C., 1980-93; ret., 1993. Founder, sec.-treas.

Chgo. Graphic Workshop, 1952-55; participant Yaddo, 1973, 75, 76, Ossobow Island Project, 1976; adj. vis. prof. So. Ill. U., 1978, No. Ill. U., 1978, SUNY, Purchase, 1978, Cooper Union, N.Y.C., 1978-79, Parsons Sch. Design, N.Y.C., 1979; disting. vis. prof. U. S.D., 1980, U. Calif. Davis, 1980, Sch. Visual Arts, N.Y.C., 1980-83; vis. artist U. N.Mex., 1981, So. Ill. U., 1984, Sch. Art Inst., Chgo., 1985, U. Tenn., Md. Inst., Northwestern Grad. Sch., 1988, U. Pa., U. Iowa, 1991, 92; instr. workshops Anderson Ranch Workshop, Snow Mass, Colo., 1994, 96, Aspen Design Conf., 1994; vis. prof. U. Iowa, 1991-92; bd. dirs. Oxbow Summer Sch. Painting, 1972-82, emeritus, 1982—, instr., 1960, 72-82, 88, 94,2005; vis. artist, instr. workshops Vt. Studio Sch., 1996, 97, 2001, 2005, Oxbow, 2005, Vt. Studio, 2005, U. Costa Rica, San Pedro and San Ramon, 1995; instr. Interlaken Sch. of Art, 1996; tchr. master class Nat. Acad. Design, 1999, Nat. Acad. Abbey Mural Workshops, 2001-2005. One woman shows, Superior St. Gallery, Chgo., 1960, Stewart Richart Gallery, San Antonio, 1962, 65, Fairweather Hardin Gallery, Chgo., 1962, Zabriskie Gallery, N.Y.C., 1962, 64, 69, 72, B.C. Holland Gallery, Chgo., 1965, 68, Ft. Wayne Art Mus., 1967, Richard Gray Gallery, Chgo., 1970, 73, 76, 79, 82, 85, Madison Art Center, 1972, Nat. Collection at Smithsonian Instn., 1972, Odyssia Gallery, Rome, 1975, Krannert Performing Arts Center, 1976, Oshkosh Pub. Mus., 1976, U. Mo., 1976, Harcus Krakow, Boston, 1977—, Fendrick Gallery, Washington, 1978, Ky. State U., 1979, Ill. Wesleyan U., 1979, U. Calif., Davis, 1980, Odyssia Gallery, N.Y., 1980, Landfall Press, 1980, Alverno Coll., Milw., 1981, Susan Caldwell, Inc., N.Y.C., 1983, N.A.M.E. Gallery, Chgo., 1983, Printworks, Ltd., Chgo., 1989, 93, 99, 2002, Printworks, 2003, Pretto Berland Hall, N.Y.C., 1989, Struve Gallery, Chgo., 1990, 93, Berland Hall Gallery, N.Y.C., 1992, Sioux City Art Mus., Iowa, 1992, U. Iowa Mus. Art, 1994, Andre Zarre Gallery, N.Y.C., 1994-97, TBA, Chgo., 1996, Centrocultural Costarricense Norteamericano, San Jose, Costa Rica, 1997, Jean Albano Gallery, 1997, 99, 2001, Albano, 2001, Jan Abrams Fine Arts, N.Y.C., 2005, Valerie Carberry Gallery, Chgo., 2005; retrospective exhibitions, Krannert Art Mus., McNay Art Mus., Chgo. Cultural Ctr., Stamford Mus., U. Tenn., Nat. Mus. for Women in the Arts, 1999; exhibited group shows, 1946—, including numerous traveling exhbns., Am. Fedn. Arts, 1946-48, 50, 53, 57, 65, 66, 69; Art Inst. Chgo., 1946-47, 51-53, 55, 57-58, 60-62, 64, 66-69, 71, 73, Corcoran Gallery Art, 1961, 76, Denver Art Mus., 1950, 52, Exhbn. Momentum, Chgo., 1948, 50, 52, 54, 56, Libr. Congress, 1950, 52, Met. Mus. Art, 1952, Mus. Modern Art, 1953, 62, Phila. Mus. Art, 1946, 47, 50, 54, San Francisco Mus. Art, 1946, 50, U. Ill., 1953, 54, 57, Drawing Soc., 1965-66, Mus. Contemporary Art, Chgo., 1969, Graham Gallery, N.Y.C., 1969-71; Ill. Arts Council, 1968-71; HMH Publs. Europe, 1971, Chgo. Imagists, 1972, Chgo. Sch, 1972, Am. Women, 1972, Artists Books, 1973; Downtown Whitney, N.Y.C., 1978—, Queens Mus., 1978, Dayton Art Inst., 1978, Odyssia Gallery, N.Y.C., 1979, Chgo. Cultural Center, 1979, Aldrich Mus. Contemporary Art, 1980, Bklyn. Mus., 1980, Walker Art Ctr., 1981, also Lisbon, Venice biennales, Voorhees Mus. Rutgers U., Mus. Contemporary Art, Chgo., Milw. Art. Mus., Berkeley Art Mus., 1987, Cooper Union, 1989, Randall Gallery, St. Louis, 1991, Printworks Ltd., Chgo., 1989-96, 97-98, 99, 2003, Berland Hall, N.Y.C., 1991, The Cultural Ctr., Chgo., 1992, Matnan Locks Gallery, Phila., 1992, Art Inst. Chgo., 1992, Nat. Mus. Women in Arts, Washington, 1994-97, Wadsworth Atheneum, Hartford, Conn., 1996, Mus. Contemporary Art, 1996, Block Gallery, Northwestern U., 1996, Rockford Art Mus., Ill. State Mus., 1997; represented in permanent collections Art Inst. Chgo., Denver Art Mus., Libr. Congress, Inst. Internat. Edn., London, Finch Coll., N.Y., Krannert Mus., U. Ill., U. Mass., N.J. State Mus., Ill. State Mus., Bklyn. Mus., Mus. Contemporary Art, Chgo., Nat. Coll. Fine Arts, Walker Art Ctr., Mpls., Boston Pub. Libr., Des Moines Art Ctr., Albion Coll., Met. Mus., McNay Art Inst., Albion Coll., Kans. State U., U. Dallas, U. Houston, Cornell U., CUNY, 1997, Neuberger Mus. Art, 1999, Nat. Acad. Bienwines, N.Y., 1999, 2001, 2003, 2005, Am. Acad. Arts and Letters, N.Y., 2004; also numerous pvt. collections-; mural paintings: Working Men's Coop. Bank Boston, 1979, Boston Pub. Libr., 2000, State of Ill. Bldg., Chgo., 1985, State Capitol, Springfield, Ill., 1989, City of Miami Beach, Art in Public Places project, Police and Court Facility, 1993; also commns.: City Of Chicago, 1999, Riverwalk Gateway Project, 1999, St. Patrick's Ch., Chgo, 1999, Hiawatha-LRT, Mpls., 2004; published: Wonder Production Vol. I, 1971, Jataka Tales, 1975, Transformations, 1976, Transformations II (Endangered), 1983, Index, 2003; editorial bd.: Coll. Art Jour., 1982-92; illustrator:The Wandering Tattler, 1975, Perishible Press, 1976—, Red Ozier Press, 1980—. Recipient Armstrong prize Art Inst. Chgo., 1946, 55, 77, Town and Country purchase prize, 1947, Purchase prize Denver Art Mus., 1950, Purchase prize Libr. of Congress, 1950, Blair prize, 1958, Chan prize, 1961, Palmer prize, 1962, 64, Vielehr prize, 1967, Cassandra Found. award, 1970, Logan prize, 1981; grantee NEA, 1974, 87, Herewood Lester Cook Found., 1981, Florsheim Found., 1999, Purchase prize Am. Acad. Arts and Letters, 2004; named to Nat. Acad., 1997. Mem. Nat. Acad. (mem. coun. 2002-2005, chair exhbn. com. 2004-2005, elected treas. 2005), Coll. Art Assn. (dir., exec. com. 1977-80), Century Club (elected), Delta Phi Delta. Address: 138 Prince St New York NY 10012-3135

LANZA, FRANK C., electronics executive; b. 1931; BS, Heralds Engring. Coll., 1956. Project engr. Philco Western Devel. Labs., 1957-59; v.p. Textron Corp., Providence, 1960-72; with Loral Corp., N.Y.C., 1972-97, v.p., 1973-79, exec. v.p., 1979-81, corp. pres., chief operating officer, 1981-97, also bd. dirs.; chmn., chief exec. ofcr. L-3 Communications, N.Y.C., 1997—, bd. dirs., 1998—. Served with USCG, 1953-55. Office: L-3 Communications 600 3rd Ave Fl 36 New York NY 10016-2001

LANZA, FRANK LEO, gastroenterologist, researcher; b. Trenton, N.J., Oct. 4, 1932; s. Leo Michael and Jennie (Petrino) Lanza; m. Alice Folz, Apr. 7, 1956; children: Joseph, Frank Jr., Jeanne, Alicia, Leo Michael II. BS, U. Md., 1954; MA, MD, U. Tex., Galveston, 1962. Diplomate Am. Bd. Internal Medicine, Am. Bd. Gastroenterology. Intern USPHS Hosp., Staten Island, NY, 1962—63; resident Baylor U. Coll. Medicine Affiliated Hosps., Houston, 1963—65; fellow in gastroenterology U. Tex. M.D. Anderson Hosp. and Tumor Inst., Houston, 1965—66, clin. asst. internist, 1966—70; attending physician, digestive diseases Meth. Hosp., Houston, 1966—70; chief, endoscopic tng. program Ben Taub Hosp., Houston, 1970—88, chief emeritus, 1988—; med. staff Sharpstown Gen. Hosp., 1966—92, Rosewood Med. Ctr., 1992—2000, Meml. Hosp. Southwest, 1966—. Clin. asst. to assoc. prof. medicine, dept. gastroenterology Baylor U. Coll. Medicine, Houston, 1970—80, clin. prof. medicine, 1981—; chief of medicine Bellaire (Tex.) Gen. Hosp., 1970—73, Sharpstown Gen. Hosp., Houston, 1976—78; chief of gastroenterology Meml. Hosp., Houston, 1982—84; dir., prin. investigator Houston Inst. Clin. Rsch., 1985—; mem. internat. scientific bd. Argomenti di Gastroenterologia Clinica, 1991—; cons. editor in gastroenterology Jour. Musculoskeletal Medicine, 1991—; editl. com. Gastroprotection news; cons. med. staff Hermann Hosp., 1992—, St. Luke's Hosp., 1995—; reviewer numerous profl. jours., including Gastrointestinal Endoscopy, Jour. Rheumatology, Digestive Disease and Scis., Archives Internal Medicine, New Eng. Jour. Medicine, others. Contbr. articles to profl. jours. Team physician, internal medicine Houston Rockets and NBA, 1972—93; pres. bd. Discovery Dance Group, Houston, 1989—96. Specialist 3d class (x-ray technician) U.S. Army, 1954—57, Brooke Army Hosp., San Antonio. Fellow: ACP, Am. Coll. Gastroenterology (rsch. com. 1982—83, gov. 1983—90, ad hoc com. medico-legal affairs 1986—88, credentials com. 1986—89, nominating com. 1988—89, constn. and bylaws com. 1989—90, ACT practice affairs ad hoc com. 1989—90, ad hoc com. practice parameters 1990—93, bd. trustees 1992—97, rsch. com. 1993—95, chmn. membership com. 1993—97, ad hoc com. indusry rels. 1995—98, treas. 1997—2000, practice affairs com. 1997—, task force on future GI pvt. practice 1997—, bd. dirs. Inst. Clin. Rsch. and Edn. 1998—, chmn. ad hoc com. industry rels. 1998—, v.p. 2000—01, pres.-elect 2001—02, pres. 2002—); mem.: AMA, Am. Soc. Clin. Pharmacology and Therapeutics, Tex. Soc. Gastroenterology and Endoscopy (Tex. rep. 1980—83, sec. 1983—85, pres. 1985—87, sec. 1990—), Houston Gastroenterol. Soc., Houston Soc. Internal Medicine, So. Med. Assn., Harris County Med. Soc. (chmn. med. adjudication com. 1978—79), Am. Gastroenterol. Soc., Tex. Medicine Assn., Am. Soc. Gastrointestinal Endoscopy (sec. treas. coun. regional endoscopic socs. 1980—82, med. scientific com. 1980—84), Am. Numismatic Assn., Alpha Omega Alpha, Sigma Xi. Office: Houston Inst Clin Rsch 7777 Southwest Freeway Ste 720 Houston TX 77074

LANZA, JOHN FRANCIS, JR., artist, educator; b. Weymouth, Mass., Dec. 31, 1948; s. John Francis and Sadie (Rizzotto) L.; m. Kathy Louise McGill, Aug. 1, 1976; children: Rebecca Elizabeth, Maria Melanie. BA cum laude, Amherst Coll., 1971; MFA, Boston U., 1975. Painting conservator Iso Papo, Brookline, Mass., 1974-86; prof. Art Inst. of Boston, Lesley U., 1978—, coord. drawing and sculpture, 1981-99, acting dept. chair illustration, 1989, acting dept. chair found. dept., 1998. Instr. anatomy Cambridge Ctr. Adult Edn., 1977-85; instr. anatomy and painting South Shore Art Ctr., Cohasset, Mass., 1979-81; instr. Boston Visual Sch., Trieste, Italy, 1988-91, Viterbo, Italy, 1994, Montserrat Coll. Art, Viterbo, 1997; sec., clk. Boston Visual Sch., Dorchester, Mass., 1991-95; jurist South Shore Art Ctr., 1981—; chair curriculum com. Art Inst. of Boston, Lesley Coll., 1985-88, sec., 1988-95, ad hoc faculty com., sec. faculty/staff senate and coun., 1990-99, rep., 1980-88, chair faculty affairs and acad. policies com., 1999-2002. Illustrator: Heritage Collection, The Bragging Tortoise, Theme Books, 1989; one-man show at Helen Bumpus Gallery, 1996, James Libr. and Ctr. for Arts, 2000, The Gallery, Porter Exchg., 2002, Landmark Bldg. Boston, 2005; exhibited in group shows at Art Inst. Boston, 1979-2004, South Shore Art Ctr., 1979-88 (Best Realist award 1988, 2d pl. award for oils 1987), 2004, Art Inst. Boston Show, 1980, 84, 90, Boston Visual Sch. Exhibits, 1989, 90, 91, U.S. Extemporaneous Show, 1994, U.S. Extemporaneous Show, Vitorchiano, Italy, 1994, Attleboro Mus., 1998, South Shore Conservatory, 2004, Helen Bumpus Gallery, 2005 Libr. vol. Plymouth River Sch., Hingham, Mass., 1988—; worship commn. St. John the Evangelist Ch., Hingham, 1991-99. Recipient Disting. Svc. award, Plymouth River Sch., 1998; fellow Amherst Coll. 1969, Boston U., 1973. Avocations: reading, traveling abroad. Home: 152 Summer St Hingham MA 02043-1062

LANZEROTTI, LOUIS JOHN, physicist; b. Carlinville, Ill., Apr. 16, 1938; s. Emanuel Louis and Mary Pauline (Orienti) L.; m. Mary Yvonne DeWolf, June 19, 1965; children: Mary Yvonne, Louis DeWolf. BS, U. Ill., 1960; MA, Harvard U., 1963, PhD, 1965. Postdoctoral fellow Lucent Techs. Bell Labs., Murray Hill, NJ, 1965-67; mem. tech. staff AT&T Bell Labs., Murray Hill, N.J., 1967-82, Disting. mem. tech. staff, 1982—2002; Disting. rsch. prof. N.J. Inst. Tech., Newark, 2002—; physics cons. Lucent Techs., 2002—. Adj. prof. U. Fla., Gainesville, 1978-97; mem. polar rsch. bd. NRC, Washington, 1982-91, mem. space sci. bd., 1980-84, chmn. space studies bd., 1988-94, mem. ocean studies bd., 1995-99, chmn. bd. rev. Army Rsch. Lab., 1996-2000, report rev. com., 2000—, chmn. survey com. solar space physics rsch., 2001—; mem. phys. sci. com. NASA, Washington, 1975-79, chmn. space and earth adv. commn., 1984-88, mem. adv. coun., 1984-94; mem. adv. com. on future U.S. space program, 1990, mem. v.p.'s space policy adv. bd., 1992-93, v.p. blue ribbon adv. com. on redesign of space sta., 1993-94; mem. corp. Woods Hole Oceanographic Instn., 1993-2001; mem. governing bd. Am. Inst. Physics, 1997—, mem. exec. com. of governing bd., 2002--; mem. Nat. Sci. Bd., NSF, 2004-. Co-author: Particle Diffusion in Rad. Belts, 1974; co-editor 3 books related to space physics, 1977, 79, 2004; contbr. more than 500 tech. papers to profl. jours. V.p. Harding Twp. (N.J.) Sch. Bd., 1982-90, com., 1993—, dep. mayor, 1999—. Recipient Antarctic Svc. medal U.S., 1979, Disting. Pub. Svc. award NASA, 1988, 94, Disting. Sci. medal NASA, 1998, Achievement award Blackburn Coll. Alumni Assn., 1993, COSPAR William Nordberg medal, 2004; mountain named in his honor in Antarctica; minor planet 5504 named in his honor. Fellow AIAA, IEEE, Am. Phys. Soc., Am. Geophys. Union, AAAS; mem. NAE, Internat. Acad. Astronautics. Office: Dept Physics NJ Inst Tech Newark NJ 07102

LANZEROTTI, MARY YVONNE, physicist, researcher; AB in Physics, Harvard-Radcliffe Colls., Cambridge, Mass., 1989; MPhil in Physics, U. Cambridge, England, 1990; MS, PhD in Physics, Cornell U., Ithaca, N.Y., 1996. Rsch. staff mem. T. J. Watson Rsch. Ctr. IBM, Yorktown Heights, NY, 1996—. Assoc. editor IEEE-Lasers and Electo-Optics Soc. newsletter, Piscataway, NJ, 1995—2000; exec. editor IEEE-Lasers and Electro-Optics Soc. newsletter, Piscataway, NJ, 2000—; mem. bd. gov. IEEE-Lasers and Electro-Optics Soc., Piscataway, NJ, 2003—. Recipient Detur prize, Harvard-Radcliffe Colls., 1986, Jr. Sci. prize, 1988, IBM Rsch. Divsn. Outstanding Contbn. award, 1998; fellow, NSF, 1990—93; grantee, AT&T, 1990—96; scholar, Fed. Employee Edn. and Assistance, Wash., 1988, The Winston Churchill Found. U.S., 1989—90; John Harvard scholarship, Harvard Coll., 1986—88, Elizabeth Cary Agassiz scholarship, Radcliffe Coll., 1987—88, Andrew Dickson White fellow, Cornell U., 1990—91, Spencer T. and Ann W. Olin Found. Grad. fellow, 1991—95. Achievements include patents for digital instant camera with printer. Office: IBM T J Watson Rsch Ctr Route 134 1101 Kitchawan Rd Yorktown Heights NY 10598 Office Fax: 914-945-1358. E-mail: myl@us.ibm.com.

LANZILLOTTO, ANN RACHELE, performance artist, writer; b. Bronx, NY, June 1, 1963; d. Joseph Rocco and Rachel Claire (Petruzzelli) Lanzillotto. Student, Am. U. Cairo, 1985; BA with honors, Brown U., 1986; MFA, Sarah Lawrence Coll., 1990. Tchr. Sing-Sing, Bedford Hills correctional facilities through Mercy Coll., NY, 1989—92; literacy coord. Housing Works, 1992—93; curator Opera Vindaloo at Dixon Pl., N.Y.C., 1994—96; guest editor Movement Rsch. Performance Jour., N.Y.C., 1995; dir. Opera Stand, Arthur Ave. Retail Market, Bronx, 1996—97; curator The Kitchen, N.Y.C., 1998—2000, guest artist in schs., 1988—; vol tutor Arab-Am Family Svcs. Ctr., Bklyn., 2004. Dir.: (cmty. art performance) A Schapett!, 1996—97; author, actor, dir. (solo show) Confessions of a Bronx Tomboy, 1993; author, actor, dir How to Wake Up a Marine in a Foxhole, 1998; performance artist at Smithsonian Folklife Festival: A Stickball Memoir, 2001. Cmty. organizer Belmont Small Bus. Assn., Bronx, 2000. Grantee, Franklin Furnace, 1994, Dancing in the Streets, N.Y.C., 1996; prodn. arts prodn. grantee, Rockefeller Found., 1996, multidisciplinary arts fellow, NY State Found. for Arts, 1999, Rockefeller Found. fellow, Next Generation Leadership Program, 2000. Mem.: Italian Am. Writers Assn., Malia Collective of Italian Am. Women. Avocation: flying. Home: 133 7th Ave Brooklyn NY 11215 Personal E-mail: lanzillotto@gmail.com.

LANZINGER, JUDITH ANN, state supreme court justice; b. Toledo, Ohio, Apr. 2, 1946; m. Robert C. Lanzinger, Jr., 1967; 2 children. BA in Ed., U. Toledo, 1968; JD, U. Toledo Coll. of Law, 1977; Ms of Jud. Studies, Nat. Jud. Coll. & U. Nev., 1992. Bar: Ohio, U.S. Supreme Ct., U.S. Dist. Ct. for Northern Dist. of Ohio, U.S. Dist. Ct. for Eastern Dist. of Mich., Sixth Circuit Ct. of Appeals. Atty. environmental law Toledo Edison Co., 1978—81; atty. employment law and litigation Shumaker, Loop and Kendrick, 1981—85; judge Toledo Municipal Ct., 1985—88, Lucas County Common Pleas Ct., 1989—2003, Ohio Sixth Dist. Ct. of Appeals, 2003—04; justice Ohio Supreme Ct., 2005—. Adjunct prof. U. Toledo Coll. of Law, 1988—; prof. Nat. Jud. Coll., 1990—; mem. Ohio Criminal Sentencing Commn., 1991—97; co-chair Public Ed. and Awareness Task Force Ohio Cts. Futures Commn., 1996—2000; chair Ohio Jud. Coll., 2000—01; former mem. Ohio Supreme Ct. Bd. of Grievances and Discipline. Recipient Superior Jud. Service award, Ohio Supreme Ct., 1985, Arabella Babb Mansfield award, Toledo Women's Bar Assn., 1995, Service to Judicial Ed. award, Ohio Jud. Coll., 2002, Golden Gavel award, Ohio Common Pleas Judges' Assn., 2002. Fellow: Ohio Bar Found.; mem.: Thurgood Marshall Assn., Am. Judicature Soc., Nat. Assn. of Women Judges, Am. Judges Assn., Ohio Bar Assn., Morrison R. Waite Am. Inn of Ct. (pres. 2000—02). Office: Ohio Supreme Ct 65 S Front St Columbus OH 43215-3431 Office Phone: 614-387-9090.

LANZINGER, KLAUS, language educator; b. Woergl, Tyrol, Austria, Feb. 16, 1928; arrived in U.S., 1971, naturalized, 1979; m. Aida Schuessl, June, 1954; children: Franz, Christine. BA, Bowdoin Coll., 1951; PhD, U. Innsbruck, Austria, 1952. Rsch. asst. U. Innsbruck, 1957-67; assoc. prof. modern langs. U. Notre Dame, Ind., 1967-77, prof., 1977-97, prof. emeritus, 1997—. Resident dir. fgn. study program, Innsbruck, 1969-71, 76-78, 82-85; acting chmn. dept. Modern and Classical Langs., U. Notre Dame, fall 1987, chmn. dept. German and Russian, 1989-96. Author: Epik im amerikanischen Roman, 1965, Jason's Voyage: The Search for the Old World in Am. Lit., 1989, (online) Amerika-Europa: Ein transatlantisches Tagebuch 1961-1989, 2003; editor: Americana-Austriaca, 5 vols., 1966-83; contbr. numerous articles to profl. jours. Bowdoin Coll. fgn. student scholar, 1950-51; Fulbright rsch. grantee U. Pa., 1961; U. Notre Dame summer rsch. grantee Houghton Libr., Harvard U., 1975, 81; named to Internat. Order of Merit, 2001. Mem. MLA, Deutsche Gesellschaft für Amerikastudien, Thomas Wolfe Soc. (Zelda Gitlin Lit. prize 1993). Home: 52703 Helvie Dr South Bend IN 46635-1215 Office: Dept German Russian Langs & Lits U Notre Dame Notre Dame IN 46556

LANZINO, GIUSEPPE, physician; b. Cosenza, Italy, Jan. 6, 1965; came to U.S., 1992; MD, U. Bologna, Italy, 1989. Rsch. fellow dept. neurosurgery U. Pitts., 1990—91, U. Va., Charlottesville, 1992—94, resident dept. neurosurgery, 1994—97; endovascular fellow dept. neurosurgery U. Buffalo, 1997—99; sr. registrar dept. neurosurgery Plymouth (Eng.) Hosp., 1999—2000; chief resident dept. neurosurgery U. Va., Charlottesville, 2000—01; cerebrovascular fellow Barrow Neurol. Inst., 2001—02; assoc. prof. dept. neurosurgery U. Ill. Coll. Medicine, Peoria, 2002—. Fellow Am. Coll. Angiology; mem. Soc. Critical Care, Am. Heart Assn., N.Y. Acad. Scis. Avocations: history of medicine, history of neurosurgery, soccer. Home: 1324 Independence Ct Metamora IL 61548 Office: Ill Neurol Inst Dept Neurosurgery 530 NE Glen Oak Ave Peoria IL 61637-0001 Office Phone: 309-624-9448. Business E-Mail: lanzino@uic.edu.

LANZKOWSKY, PHILIP, physician; b. Cape Town, S. Africa, Mar. 17, 1932; came to U.S., 1965, naturalized, 1974; m. Rhona Chiat, Dec. 4, 1955; children— Shelley, David Roy, Leora, Jonathan, Marc. M.B., Ch.B., U. Cape Town, 1954, MD, 1959. Diplomate Child Health Eng. Intern Groote Schuur Hosp., U. Cape Town, 1955-56; resident Red Cross Children's Hosp., U. Cape Town, 1957-60; fellow in pediatric hematology Duke U., 1961-62, U. Utah, Salt Lake City, 1962-63; dir. pediatric hematology N.Y. Hosp.-Cornell U. Med. Center, 1965-70; asst. prof., then assoc. prof. pediatrics Cornell U. Med. Sch., 1965-70; chmn. pediatrics L.I. Jewish Med. Center, New Hyde Park, N.Y., 1970—; prof. pediatrics SUNY Med. Sch., Stony Brook, 1970-89; chief of staff Schneider Children's Hosp., 1983—; prof. pediatrics Albert Einstein coll. Medicine, 1989—; chief pediatric hematology-oncology Schneider Children's Hosp., L.I. Jewish Med. Ctr., 1992—. Con. pediatrics Nassau County Med. Ctr., East Meadows, NY, 1970—, Cath. Med. Ctr., Queens, NY, Peninsula Hosp. Ctr., Far Rockaway, NY, Jamaica Hosp., Queens, St. John's Episcopal Hosp., Far Rockaway, NY; v.p. Children's Health Network, NS-LIJ Health Sys., 1998—; exec. dir. Schneider Children's Hosp., 2002—. Author: Manual of Pediatric Hematology-Oncology: A Treatise for the Clinician, 4th edit.; Pediatric Oncology; contbr. to med. jours. Mem. med. adv. bd. L.I. chpt. Leukemia Soc. Am.; med. dir., bd. trustees Ronald McDonald House, L.I. Cecil John Adams Meml. traveling fellow, 1960; Hill-Pattison-Sruthers burser, 1960; Nutrition Found. grantee, 1968 Fellow Royal Coll. Physicians Edinburgh, Am. Acad. Pediat.; mem. Soc. Pediatric Rsch., Am. Pediatric Soc., Harvey Soc., Am. Hematology Soc., Am. Soc. Clin. Oncology, Am. Assn. Cancer Rsch., Am. Council Emigres in the Professions, trustee No. Shore Long Is. Jewish Health Sys., 2003-. Home: 159 W Shore Rd Great Neck NY 11024-1730 Office: Schneider Children's Hosp New Hyde Park NY 11040

LANZNAR, HOWARD S., lawyer; b. Champaign, Ill., Aug. 15, 1955; BA, Amherst Coll., 1977; JD, U. Chgo., 1983. Bar: Ill. 1983. Ptnr. Katten Muchin Zavis Rosenman, Chgo. Mem.: ABA, Chgo. Bar Assn., Lincoln Park Zoological Soc. Office: Katten Muchin Zavis Rosenman 525 W Monroe St Chicago IL 60661 Office Phone: 312-902-5696, 312-577-8798. E-mail: howard.lanznar@kmzr.com.

LAO, JOSEPH R., education educator, researcher; b. Bay Shore, NY, Sept. 29, 1955; s. Mary and Israel Lao; m. Deborah E Bynoe-Lao, Feb. 19, 2000; 1 child, Asa K. BA, LI U., 1973—78; MA, Columbia Univeristy, 1979—85; PhD, Columbia U., 1992—99. Adj. assoc. prof. of psychology and edn. Teachers Coll., Columbia U., N.Y.C, 2003—; adj. asst. prof. Hunter Coll., N.Y.C, NY, 2002—. Pres. Internat. Ctr. Accelerated Devel., 2004—. Membership reviewer United Way of N.Y., 1999—2002; bd. mem. Lincoln Sq. Neighborhood Ctr., Inc., 2004—. Mem.: Am. Ednl. Rsch. Assn., N.Y. Acad. Scis. (life). Buddhist. Avocations: horseback riding, chess. E-mail: jrl19@columbia.edu.

LAO, LANG LI, nuclear fusion research physicist; b. Hai Duong, Vietnam, Jan. 28, 1954; came to U.S., 1972; s. Thich Cuong and Boi Phan (Loi) L.; m. Ngan Hua, Dec. 22, 1979; children: Bert J., Brian J. BS, MS, Calif. Inst. Tech., 1976; MS, U. Wis., 1977, PhD, 1979. Staff scientist Oak Ridge (Tenn.) Nat. Lab., 1979-81, TRW, Redondo Beach, Calif., 1981-82; mgr. integrated modeling br. Gen. Atomics, San Diego, 1982—. Contbr. articles to sci. jours. Recipient award for Excellence in Plasma Physics Rsch. Am. Physical Society, 1994 Fellow Am. Phys. Soc. (co-recipient excellence in plasma physics rsch. award 1994). Achievements include being world leader in equilibrium analysis of magnetic fusion plasma physics experiments; developed a widely used computer code essential for successful operation and interpretation of tokamak fusion experiments. Office: General Atomics 3550 General Atomics Ct San Diego CA 92121-1122

LAPAGLIA, ANTHONY, actor; b. Adelaide, Australia, Jan. 31, 1959; m. Gia Carides, 1998; 1 child. Actor: (films) Cold Steel, 1987, God's Payroll (Phone Calls), 1988, Slaves of New York, 1989, Mortal Sins, 1990, Betsy's Wedding, 1990, Criminal Justice, 1990, He Said, She Said, 1991, One Good Cop, 1991, 29th Street, 1991, Keeper of the City, 1992, Whispers in the Dark, 1992, Innocent Blood, 1992, The Custodian, 1993, So I Married an Axe Murderer, 1993, Killer, 1994, Lucky Break, 1994, The Client, 1994, Mixed Nuts, 1994, Empire Records, 1995, Chameleon, 1995, Commandments, 1996, Brilliant Lies, 1996, Trees Lounge, 1996, Phoenix, 1998, The Repair Shop, 1998, Summer of Sam, 1999, Sweet and Lowdown, 1999, Company Man, 2000, Looking for Alibrandi, 2000, The House of Mirth, 2000, Autumn in New York, 2000, Jack the Dog, 2001, Lantana, 2001, The Bank, 2001, The Salton Sea, 2002, Dead Heat, 2002, I'm With Lucy, 2002, The Guys, 2002, Manhood, 2003, Happy Hour, 2003, Spinning Boris, 2003; (plays) A View From the Bridge (Tony award for Best Performance Male in a Drama, 1998); (TV miniseries) Murder One: Diary of a Serial Killer, 1997; (TV films) Police Story: Gladiator School, 1988, Frank Nitti: The Enforcer, 1988, The Brotherhood, 1991, Black Magic, 1992, Past Tense, 1994, Never Give Up: The Jimmy V. Story, 1996, Garden of Redemption, 1997, Black and Blue, 1999, Lansky, 1999, The Other Side, 2001; (TV series) Normal, Ohio, 2000, Frasier, 2000, 2002, Without a Trace, 2002— (Gloden Globe award for best actor in a dramatic series, 2004). Office: Internat Creative Mgmt 8942 Wilshire Blvd Beverly Hills CA 90211-1934

LA PAGLIA, UMBERTO, retired secondary education educator; b. Phila., Feb. 1, 1927; s. Ignazio and Concetta La P. BSEd, Temple U., 1952, MA in History, 1956. High sch. tchr. Sch. Dist. of Phila., 1952-90. Exch. tchr. Fitzmaurice Grammar Sch., Bradford-on-Avon, Eng., 1961-62. Author: Exploring World Cultures, 1974. With U.S. Army, 1946-47, Korea. Mem. Orgn. Am. History. Avocation: travel. Home: 216 Uxbridge Cherry Hill NJ 08034-3731

LAPALOMBARA, JOSEPH, political science educator, industrial management educator; b. Chgo., May 18, 1925; s. Louis and Helen (Teutonico) LaP.; m. Lyda Mae Ecke, June 22, 1947 (div.); children— Richard, David, Susan; m. Constance Ada Bezer, June, 1971. AB, U. Ill., 1947, AM, 1950; AM (Charlotte Elizabeth Proctor fellow), Princeton U., 1952, PhD, 1954; student, U. Rome (Italy), 1952-53; MA (hon.), Yale U., 1964. Instr., then asst. prof. polit. sci. Oreg. State Coll., 1947-50; instr. politics Princeton U., 1952; mem. faculty Mich. State U., 1953-64, prof. polit. sci., 1958-64, head dept., 1958-63; prof. polit. sci. Yale U., 1964-96, prof. polit. sci. and mgmt., 1996—2001, Arnold Wolfers prof., 1969—2001, Arnold Wolfers prof. polit. sci. and mgmt. emeritus, 2001—, chmn. dept. polit. sci., 1974-78, 82-85, prof. Sch. Orgn. and Mgmt., 1979—84, 1997—2001; sr. rsch. scholar Yale Ctr. for Comparative Rsch., 2001—; dir. Instn. for Social and Policy Studies, 1987-92; chmn. Coun. Comparative and European Studies, 1966-71; cultural attache, first sec. U.S. embassy, Rome, 1980-81. Vis. prof. U. Florence, Italy,

1957-58, U. Calif.-Berkeley, 1962, Columbia U., 1966-67, U. Turin, 1974, U. Catania, 1974, John Cabot U., 2003, LUISS, Rome, 2003, John Cabot U., Rome, 2003; cons. FCDA, 1956, Carnegie Corp., 1959, Brookings Instn., 1962, Ford Found., 1965-76, Twentieth Century Fund, 1965-69, AID, 1967-68, Fgn. Svc. Inst., 1968-72, 74-76, Ednl. Testing Svc., 1970-75, Alcoa, 1978-80, Rohm & Haas, 1975-76, GE, 1978-80, Union Carbide, 1981-92, Montedison, 1984-85, Ente Nazionale Idrocarburi, 1983-93, Guardian Industries, 1990-93, Praxair, 1992—, Swiss Bank Corp., 1994-99, Athena, 1994-95, Richard Medley Advisors, 1995-2001, Telecom Italia, 1996-99, S.I.A.D., 1999—; sr. rsch. assoc. Conf. Bd. N.Y., 1976-81; pres. Italian-Am. Multimedia Corp. N.Y., 1988—; bd. dirs. Transparency Internat.-U.S.A., 1994—. Author: The Initiative and Referendum in Oregon, 1950, The Italian Labor Movement: Problems and Prospects, 1957, Guide to Michigan Politics, rev. edit, 1960, (with Alberto Spreafico) Elezioni e Comportamento Politico in Italia, 1963, Bureaucracy and Political Development, 1963, Interest Groups in Italian Politics, 1964, Italy: The Politics of Planning, 1966, (with Myron Weiner) Political Parties and Political Development, 1966, Clientela e Parentela, 1967, Burocracia y desarrolo politico, 1970, Crises and Sequences of Political Development, (with others), 1972, Politics Within Nations, 1974, Multinational Corporations and National Elites: A Study in Tensions, 1975, (with Stephen Blank) Multinational Corporations in Comparative Perspective, 1976, Multinational Corporations and Developing Countries, 1979, A Politica nos Interior das Nações, 1982, Democracy, Italian Style, 1987, Democrazia all'italiana, 1988, Die Italiener: oder Demokratie als Lebenskunst, 1988, Democratie à l'italienne, 1990, SIAD at Seventy Five, 2002; bd. editors Midwest Jour. Polit. Sci, 1956-57, Yale U. Press, 1965-72, 73-76, ABC-CL10, 1976—, Global Perspectives, 1983-2000; mem. editorial bd. Comparative Politics, 1968—, Jour. Comparative and European Studies, 1969—, Am. Jour. Polit. Sci, 1976-80, Italian Jour., 1988, Yale Rev., 1993—; editor series comparative politics Prentice-Hall Co., 1971-85; editor Jour. Internat. Bus. Edn., 2001-; mem. editorial adv. bd. Jour. Comparative Adminstrn, 1970-74, Adminstrn. and Soc, 1974—; adv. bd. ABC Polit. Sci; N.Am. editor: Mediterranean Observer, 1981-86; editor in chief Italy, Italy, 1988—; contbr. articles to profl. jours. Mem. exec. com. Inter Univ. Consortium Polit. Rsch., 1966-70; mem. staff Social Sci. Rsch. Coun., 1966-73; chmn. West European fgn. area fellowship program Social Sci. Rsch. Coun.-Am. Coun. Learned Socs., 1972-74; bd. dirs. Mich. Citizenship Clearing House, 1955; mem. internat. coun. Ctr. for Strategic and Internat. Studies, 1990—; mem. Coun. on Fgn. Rels.; U.S. com. Am. Fgn. Policy, 1996—. Decorated knight comdr. Order of Merit, Republic of Italy; Fulbright scholar, 1952-53, 57-58, Penfield scholar U. Pa., 1953; fellow Social Sci. Rsch. Coun., 1952-53, Ctr. Advanced Study Behavioral Scis., 1961-62, Rockefeller Found., 1963-64, Ford Found., 1969, Guggenheim Found., 1971-72, European U. Inst., 1996, Wissenschaftszentrum Berlin, 1996; recipient Guido Dorso prize, Italy, 1984, Medal of Honor, Italian Constitutional Ct., 1993, Presidency of Italian Republic, 1993, Disting. Alumni Achievement award U. Ill., 2003. Mem. Am. Acad. Arts and Scis., Conn. Acad. Arts and Scis., Am. Acad. in Rome (trustee 1984-90), Social Sci. Rsch. Coun. (com. comparative politics 1958-72), Am. Polit. Sci. Assn. (exec. coun. 1963-65, exec. com. 1967-68, v.p. 1979-80, mem. conf. group on Italian politics and soc. 1978, conf. pres. 1984-85), Am. Acad. Polit. and Social Sci., Soc. for Italian Hist. Studies, Società Italiana di Studi Elettorali, Consiglio Italiano di Scienze Sociali, Phi Beta Kappa, Phi Kappa Phi, Phi Eta Sigma, Yale Club of N.Y., Elizabethan Club, Morys Assn., Pot and Kettle Club (Maine). Home: 50 Huntington St New Haven CT 06511-1333 Business E-Mail: joseph.lapalombara@yale.edu.

LAPCHICK, RICHARD EDWARD, educator, civil rights specialist; b. Yonkers, N.Y., July 16, 1945; s. Joseph Bohumiel and Elizabeth (Sarubbi) L.; children: Joseph Michael, Elisa Chamy; m. Ann Lavaughann Pasnak, Feb. 18, 1989; 1 child, Emily. BA in Polit. Sci., St. John's U., 1967; MA in Internat. Studies, U. Denver, 1970, PhD African Studies/Internat. Race Rels., 1973; D (hon.), Bridgewater State Coll., 1994, U. Nev., 1994, Northeastern U., 1994, U. Dist. Columbia, 1996, Newbury Coll., 2000. Assoc. prof. polit. sci. Va. Wesleyan Coll., 1970-78; sr. liaison officer UN Ctr. Against Apartheid, N.Y.C., 1978-80, World Conf. for UN Decade for Women, N.Y.C., 1980-81, Internat. Conf. on the Mid. East, N.Y.C., 1982-83; dir. Ctr. for the Study of Sport in Soc. Northeastern U., Boston, 1984—. Author: The Politics of Race and International Sport: The Case of South Africa, 1975, Resisting Oppression: The Saga of Women in Southern Africa, 1982, Broken Promises: Racism in American Sport, 1984, On the Mark: Putting the Student Back in the Student-Athlete, 1986, Fractured Focus: Sport As A Reflection of Society, The Rules of the Game: Ethics in College Sports 1989, Five Minutes to Midnight: Race and Sport in the 1990s, 1991, Sport in Society: Equal Opportunity of Business As Usual?, 1995, Never Before, Never Again: The Autobiography of Eddie Robinson, 1999; editor Jour. Sport & Social Issues, 1975-78, World Conf. of UN Decade for Women, 1981; mem. editorial bd. various refereed jours.; columnist The Sporting News, The Sports Business Jour.; contbr. over 150 articles to profl. jours. Nat. chair ACCESS, Boston, 1976—; exec. dir. ARENA, The Inst. for Sport and Social Analysis, Boston, 1974-94, exec. bd. dirs. Am. Com. on Africa, N.Y., 1978-86, Phelps-Stokes Fund, 1992-98; exec. dir. PRIDE, Denver, 1968-70. Recipient Humanitarian of Yr. award United Meth. Ch. Fedn., N.Y., 1978, Tenn. Coalition Against Racism and Apartheid, 1978, Kenneth Kuanda Humanism award Kenneth Kuanda Assn., N.Y., 1987, Ralphe Bunche Internat. Peace award Anti-Defamation League, Boston, 1988, World of Difference award, 1991, Campus of Difference award, 1992, Dryslongo award for Combatting Racism Community Exch., 1991, Man of Yr. award Nat. Invitation Tournament, 1992, In the Spirit of Crazy Horse award, 1993, Dist. Am. in Svc. To Our Children award, Dist. Alumni award Univ. of Denver, 1993, Arthur Ashe Voice of Conscience award, 1997, Pres. award Women's Sports Found., 1997, Man of Yr. award Boston Celtics, 1998, Hero Among Us award Boston Celtics, 1999, Jean Mayer Global Citizenship award Tufts U., 2000; name to Commonwealth Sports Hall of Fame as humanitarian, 2000; Martin Luther King fellow Ford Foun., 1969. Mem. Am. Polit. Sci. Assn., African Studies Assn., N.Am. Soc. for Sport Sociology. Office: U Central Fla Devos Sport Bus Mgnt PO Box Boston MA 02115-5000

LAPE, ROBERT CABLE, broadcast journalist; b. Akron, Ohio; s. C. Robert and Mary Elizabeth (Cable) L.; m. Marcia Giesy, 1954 (div. 1969); children: Debra, Robert S., Alida, Douglas; m. Eve Bergman, Feb. 14, 1982 (dec. 2002); m. Joanna Pruess, Sept. 19, 2004. BS in Journalism and Radio Speech, Kent State U., 1955. Reporter, asst. news dir. WCUE Radio, Akron, 1954-56; news dir. WICE Radio, Providence, 1956-61; corr., news dir. WBZ Radio, Boston, 1961-68, WABC-TV, N.Y.C., 1968-82; critic, writer on food and travel, lectr. WABC, WCBS, Crain's N.Y. Bus., N.Y. Law Jour., Agenda N.Y., N.Y.C., 1983—2002, LaCucina Italiana, N.Y. Pocket Guide, The Record (N.J.), Foodwinetravel.com, 1999—. Bd. dirs. Internat. Food Media Conf., N.Am., 1986—; anchor The CPA Report, 1999-2000. Author: Epicurean Rendezvous, 1990-96, Bob Lape's Restaurant Index, 1987-91. Nat. judge food March of Dimes, 1991—; spkr., M.C. Crohn's and Colitis Found., N.Y., Nat. Cancer Soc.; judge James Beard Found. Awards. Decorated chevalier d'honneur Swiss Ordre du Channe, 2004; Recipient Emmy award for TV News Coverage, 1980, 1st Ann. Lifetime Achievement award N.Y. State Restaurant Assn., 1998. Mem. SAG, AFTRA, N.Y. Press. Club, Broadcasters' Found., Broadcasters' Hall of Fame, Assn. Italian Sommeliers, Commanderie de Cordon Bleu de France, Compagnons de Beaujolais, Friars Club, Lambs Club. Avocations: travel, reading. Office Phone: 718-694-2050. E-mail: foodbob@aol.com.

LAPHAM, LEWIS HENRY, editor, television personality, writer; b. San Francisco, Jan. 8, 1935; s. Lewis Abbot and Jane (Foster) L.; m. Joan Brooke Reeves, Aug. 10, 1972; children: Lewis Andrew, Elizabeth Delphina, Winston Peale. Grad., Hotchkiss Sch., 1952; BA, Yale U., 1956; postgrad., Cambridge U., 1956—57; LLD, Hampden-Sydney Coll., Va. Reporter San Francisco Examiner, 1957-60, N.Y. Herald Tribune, 1960-62; author, editor USA-1, N.Y.C., 1962, Saturday Evening Post, N.Y.C., 1963-67; writer Life mag., Harper's, N.Y.C., 1968-70; mng. editor Harper's, N.Y.C., 1971-75, editor, 1975-81, 83—. TV host weekly series Bookmark, PBS, also host, author documentary series America's Century. Author: (essays) Fortune's Child, 1980, Money and Class in America, 1988, Imperial Masquerade, 1989, The Wish for Kings, 1993, Hotel America, 1995, Waiting for the Barbarians, 1997, The Agony of Mammon, 1999, Lapham's Rules of Influence, 1999, Lights, Camera, Democracy!, 2001, Theater of War, 2002, 30 Satires, 2003, Gag Rule: On the Stifling of Dissent and the Suppression of Democracy, 2004. Bd. dirs. Americans for Libraries Coun., The Harry Frank Guggenheim Found. Mem. Coun. on Fgn. Rels., Century Assn., The Blind Book Club, Inc. Office: Harper's Mag 666 Broadway Fl 11 New York NY 10012-2394 Office Phone: 212-420-5731.

LAPHAM, LOWELL WINSHIP, physician educator, researcher; b. New Hampton, Iowa, Mar. 20, 1922; s. Percy Charles and Altha Theresa (Dygert) L.; m. Miriam Amanda Sellers, June 22, 1945 (div. 1982); children: Joan, Steven, Judith, Jennifer. BA, Oberlin Coll., 1943; MD cum laude, Harvard U., 1948. Diplomate Am. Bd. Pathology in neuropathology, Am. Bd. Psychiatry and Neurology in neurology. Instr. Case Western Res. U. Sch. Medicine, Cleve., 1955-57, asst. prof., 1957-64, assoc. prof., 1964, U. Rochester (N.Y.) Sch. Medicine, 1964-69, prof., 1969-92; prof. emeritus, 1992—. Cons. neuropathology Cleve. Met. Gen. Hosp., 1957-64, Cleve. VA Hosp., 1957-64, Genesee Hosp., Rochester, 1966-92, Rochester Gen. Hosp., 1966-92. Contbr. numerous articles to profl. jours. 1st lt. USAR, 1951-53. Fellow Nat. Multiple Sclerosis Soc., 1957-59; rsch. grantee NIH, USPHS. Mem. Am. Assn. Neuropathologists. Unitarian Universalist. Avocations: music, travel. Home: 121 Kendal Dr Oberlin OH 44074-1905

LA PIANA, WILLIAM PAUL, law educator; b. Buffalo, Mar. 7, 1952; s. William Anthony and Mary Dolores (DiFonzo) LaP. AB summa cum laude, Harvard Coll., 1974, AM in History, 1975; JD cum laude, Harvard U., 1978, PhD in History, 1987. Bar: N.Y. 1980. Assoc. Davis Polk and Wardwell, N.Y.C., 1979-83; asst. prof. law U. Pitts., 1983-87; assoc. prof. law The N.Y. Law Sch., N.Y.C., 1987-92, prof. law, 1992—, Rita and Joseph Solomon prof. law of wills, trusts, estates, 1993—. Seminar, conf. speaker Author: Logic and Experience: The Origin of Modern American Legal Education, 1994; contbg. editor: Will Manual Svc., co-editor, N.Y. edit.; contbr. chpts. to books, numerous articles to profl. jours. Fellow Am. Coll. Trust and Estate Counsel (mem. coun. real probate and trust sect.); mem. ABA (real property prorate and trust section, coun., mem.), Am. Law Inst., Am. Hist. Assn., Am. Soc. Legal History (bd. dirs.), N.Y. State Bar Assn. (Trusts and Estates Law sect.), Lesbian and Gay Law Assn. Greater N.Y., Phi Beta Kappa. Democrat. Roman Catholic. Avocations: motorcycling, weightlifting, reading. Office: NY Law Sch 57 Worth St New York NY 10013-2959 Office Phone: 212-431-2883. Business E-Mail: wlapiana@nyls.edu.

LAPIDUS, ARNOLD, mathematician, educator; b. Bklyn., Nov. 6, 1933; s. Morris and Mollie L. m. Nancy Beatrice Latner, Aug. 9, 1952 BS, Bklyn. Coll., 1956; MS, PhD, N.Y. U., 1967. Research scientist Courant Inst., N.Y.C., 1956-68; computer application math. analyst Goddard Inst. for Space Studies, N.Y.C., 1968-70, math. analyst programming methods, 1970-71, sr. mem. tech. staff computer scis., 1971-73; assoc. prof. quantitative analysis Fairleigh Dickinson U., Teaneck, N.J., 1973-83, prof., chair dept. computer and decision systems, 1983-85; sr. engr. Singer Electronic Systems Corp., Little Falls, N.J., 1986-87; owner Advanced Math. Co., Englewood, 1987—2000; pvt. practice Englewood, 1987—. Vol. mathematician UMDNJ, Newark, 1998-2001 Contbr. articles to profl. publs. Mem. AAAS, AAUP, Math. Assn. Am., Am. Math. Soc., Soc. Indsl. and Applied Math. Home and Office: 401 Fergus Way Tobyhanna PA 18466-4068

LAPIDUS, JULES BENJAMIN, educational association administrator; b. Chgo., May 1, 1931; s. Leo R. and Lillian D. LaPidus; m. Anne Marie Liebman, June 8, 1970; children: Steven, Amy, Mark, Marilyn. BS, U. Ill., 1954; MS, U. Wis., 1957, PhD, 1958. Prof. medicinal and pharm. chemistry Ohio State U., 1958-84; assoc. dean Grad. Sch., 1972-74; dean Grad. Sch., 1974-84; vice provost for research, 1974-82; pres. Council Grad. Schs., 1984-2000. Mem. pharmacology and toxicology tng. com. NIH, 1965-67, pharmacology program com., 1971-74; mem. Grad. Record Exam. Bd., 1982-2000.

LAPIDUS, KEVIN S., lawyer; b. Queens, NY; m. Nancy Lapidus; 2 children. Grad., Washington U., 1992, Harvard U., 1997. With Wilmer, Cutler, Pickering, Hale, & Dorr, Hogan & Hartson; sr. v.p., gen. counsel OneMain-.com, 1999—2000, YellowBrix, Inc., Alexandria, Va., 2000—. Spkr. in field. Contbr. articles to profl. jours. Mem.: Assn. Corp. Counsel (bd. dirs. WMACCA chpt.). Avocations: tennis, bicycling. Office: YellowBrix Inc 44 Canal Ctr Plaza Ste 110 Alexandria VA 22314 E-mail: klapidus@yellowbrix.com.

LAPIERRE, DOMINIQUE, writer, historian; b. Chatelaillon, France, July 30, 1931; s. Jean and Luce (Andreota) L.; m. Dominique Conchon, Apr. 5, 1980. Student (Fulbright Exchange scholar), U. Polit. Sci., Paris, 1950-51; BA, Lafayette Coll., Easton, Pa., 1952, LittD (hon.), 1982. Sr. editor Paris Match News mag., 1955-67. Author: The City of Joy, 1985, Beyond Love, 1990, A Thousand Suns, 1999, Five Past Midnight in Bhopal, 2002; co-author: Is Paris Burning?, 1964, ...Or I'll Dress You In Mourning, 1967, O Jerusalem, 1971, Freedom at Midnight, 1975, The Fifth Horseman, 1980, Is New York Burning?, 2004. Founder, pres. Action Aid for Lepers' Children of Calcutta. Decorated comdr. Order of Tastevin, grand cross Civil Order of Social Solidarity (Spain), chevalier Legion of Honor (France); recipient Gold medal of the City of Calcutta for humanitarian action, 1987, Rainbow Internat. award UN, 1999; Internat. Prize for Peace Vatican, 1999, Christopher award, U.S., 1986, 2002. Home: 37 rue Charles-Laffitte 92200 Neuilly-sur-Seine France Office: care Morton Janklow Lit Agy 445 Park Ave New York NY 10022-2606 E-mail: d.lapierre@wanadoo.fr.

LAPIERRE, WAYNE R., JR., lobbyist; b. Schenectady, NY, Nov. 8, 1949; BA, Siena Coll.; MA, Boston Coll., in Govt. & Politics. State liaison NRA, Fairfax, Va., 1978—79, dir. state & local affairs, 1979—80, exec. dir. Inst. for Legis. Action, 1986—91, exec. v.p., CEO, 1991—. Mem. bd. dirs. Am. Assn. of Political Consultants. Author: Guns, Crime, and freedom, 1994, Guns, Freedom, and Terrorism, 2003; co-author (with James Jay Baker): Shooting Straight: Telling the Truth About Guns in America, 2002. Roman Catholic. Office: NRA 11250 Waples Mill Rd Fairfax VA 22030

LAPIN, HARVEY I., lawyer; b. St. Louis, Nov. 23, 1937; s. Lazarus L. and Lillie L. Lapin; m. Cheryl A. Lapin; children: Jeffrey, Gregg. BS, Northwestern U., 1960, JD, 1963. CPA Ill.; bar: Ill. 1963, Fla. 1980, Wis. 1985, cert.: Fla. (tax lawyer). Atty. Office Chief Counsel, IRS, Washington, 1963-65; trial atty. Office Regional Counsel, IRS, Washington, 1965-68; from assoc. to ptnr. Fiffer & D'Angelo, Chgo., 1968-75; pres. Harvey I. Lapin, P.C., Chgo., 1975-83; mng. ptnr. Lapin, Hoff, Spangler & Greenberg, Chgo., 1983-88, Lapin, Hoff, Slaw & Laffey, Chgo., 1989-91; ptnr. Gottlieb and Schwartz, Chgo., 1992-93; prin. Harvey I. Lapin & Assocs., P.C., Northbrook, Ill., 1993—2003, Harvey I. Lapin, P.C. (formerly Harvey I. Lapin & Assocs., P.C.), Northbrook, 2004—. Instr. John Marshall Law Sch., 1969—; facility adv. lawyers asst. program Roosevelt U., Chgo.; mem. cemetery adv. bd. Ill. Comptr., 1974—96, 1999—; mem. IRS Gt. Lakes TE/EO Coun., 2001—. Asst. editor: Fed. Bar Jour., 1965—67; contbg. editor: (book) Cemetery and Funeral Service Business and Legal Guide; contbr. articles to profl. jours. Mem.: ABA, Chgo. Bar Assn., Ill. Bar Assn., Wis. Bar Assn., Fla. Bar Assn. Jewish. Office: Harvey I Lapin PC PO Box 1327 Northbrook IL 60065-1327 Office Phone: 847-509-0501.

LAPIN, SHARON JOYCE VAUGHN, interior designer; b. Lagrange, Mo., July 28, 1938; d. John Nolan and Wilma Emma (Huebotter) Vaughn; m. Byron Richard Lapin, Oct. 14, 1972. BA summa cum laude, U. Wash., Seattle, 1960. Appeared in various Broadway shows, TV commls. and TV shows, 1962—72; mgr. arts and crafts divsn. Convenience Products Clayton Corp., Fenton, Mo. Bd. dirs. St. Louis Conservatory and Schs. for Arts, 1977—92, v.p., 1982—87; chmn. bd. Studio Set, 1978—81, pres., 1975—78, bd. dirs., 1975—83, Friends of Sci. Mus., 1980—90, v.p., 1984—85; pres. assocs. bd. dirs. St. Louis Sci. Ctr., Inc., 1986-87, 1986—87; bd. dirs. Jr. divsn. St. Louis Symphony Women's Assn., 1973—75; bd. dirs. Women's Assn. St. Louis Symphony, 1988—90. Mem. AFTRA, SAG, AEA, ASID, Phi Beta Phi, Mu Phi Epsilon.

LAPINE, JAMES ELLIOT, playwright, director; b. Mansfield, Ohio, Jan. 10, 1949; s. David Sanford and Lillian (Feld) L.; m. Sarah Marshall Kernochan, Feb. 24, 1985; 1 child, Phoebe BA, Franklin and Marshall Coll., Lancaster, Pa.; hon. degree, Franklin and Marshall Coll., 1994; MFA, Calif. Inst. of Arts, Valencia. Author, dir.: (plays) Photograph, 1977 (Obie award 1977), Table Settings, 1980 (George Oppenheimer/Newsday award), Twelve Dreams, 1983, Sunday in the Park with George, 1984 (N.Y. Drama Critics' Circle award 1984, Pulitzer prize for drama 1984), Into the Woods, 1987 (Tony award 1988, N.Y. Drama Critics' Circle award 1988, Drama Desk award 1988), Falsettoland, 1990 (2 Tony awards 1992), Luck, Pluck and Virtue (La Jolla Playhouse), 1993, Passion, 1994 (Tony award 1994); dir.: March of the Falsettos, 1982, Merrily We Roll Along (La Jolla Playhouse), A Midsummer Night's Dream, A Winter's Tale, 1988, Golden Child, (Broadway revival) The Diary of Anne Frank, Earthly Possessions, 1999, (films) Impromptu, Passion, 1990, Life with Mikey, 1993, The 25th Annual Putnam County Spelling Bee, 2005 (Drama Desk award, outstanding director of a musical, 2005). Recipient 4 Drama Desk awards, Outer Critics Circle award, Evening Standard award, Olivier award; Guggenheim fellow Mem. Dramatists Guild. Office: c/o Shubert Orgn 234 W 44th St New York NY 10036-3909*

LAPINSKI, TADEUSZ ANDREW, artist, educator; b. Rawamazowiecka, Poland, June 20, 1928; s. Tadeusz Alexander and Valentina (Kwiatkowska) L. MFA, Acad. Fine Arts, Warsaw, Poland, 1955. Prof. U. Md., College Park, 1973—. One-man shows include Mus. Modern Art, N.Y.C., also mus. in Washington, São Paulo and Rio de Janeiro, Brazil, Turin, Italy, Belgrade, Yugoslavia and Vienna, Austria, Regional Mus. of Torun, Poland, 1992, Plock Mus. and Libr., Poland, 1993, Regional Mus. of Zyrardow, Poland, 1994, Sci. Soc. Plock, 1993, Dist. Mus. City of Zyrardow, Poland, 1994, Zyrardow Mus. of Art, Poland, 1994, Gallery Esta Gliwice, Poland, 2003, Pulaski Museum, Warka, Poland, 2003, RAWA Mazowiecka Museum, Poland, 2003, Omisali, Croatia, 2003; group shows include Nat. Royal Acad., London, biennial exhbns. in Venice, Italy, Paris, Buenos Aires, Argentina, John Guggenheim Gallery Exhbn., Coral Gables, Fla., 1988, numerous others; retrospective exhbn. Nat. Mus. Torun, Poland, 1956-92; represented in permanent collections Mus. Modern Art, N.Y.C., Libr. of Congress, Washington, Nat. Mus. Am. Art, Washington, Nat. Gallery of Art, 2002, mus. in São Paulo, Warsaw and Cracow, Poland, others. Recipient Gold medal Print Festival, Vienna, 1979, Silver medal World Print '80, Paris, medal City of Zamosc, Poland, 1980, UNESCO prize Paris, Statue of Victory 85 World prize, Italy, Achievement award Prince George's County, 1989, Cultural Achievement award Am. Polish Art award U. Md., 1991, Am. Polish Arts Assn. award, 1991, medal Am. Inst. Polish Culture, 1996, medal City of Konin, Poland, 1999, medal of honor City of Gliwice, Poland, medal of highest merit City of Grodzisk Mazowiecki, others; T. Lapinski day proclaimed by mayor of Washington, 1981; named Man of Yr. Md. Perspectives Mag., 1984, Internat. Man of Yr. Intern., Art award City Plock, Poland, 1994, Tadeusz Lapinski Hall of Fame in the Arts, Internat. Biographical Ctr., Cambridge, England, 2002, Educator of Yr. Internat. Biographical Ctr., Cambridge, England, 2003. Mem. Soc. Graphic Art, Painters and Sculptors Soc. N.J. Office: U Md Dept Art College Park MD 20742-0001 Office Phone: 301-405-1454.

LAPINSKY, JOSEPH F., manufacturing executive; married; 2 daughters. MS in Indsl. Rels., W.Va. U., 1973; MBA in Mgmt., Youngstown State U., 1984. Early career positions include conditioning foreman Copperweld Steel Co., then ops., mgr. human resources, v.p. human resources, 1974-91, also exec. v.p.; ind. industry cons., 1991-95; gen. mgr. hot rolled bar ops. Republic Techs. Internat., Akron, Ohio, 1995-97, pres. Hot Rolled Bar divsn., 1997-98; pres., COO Republic Engineered Steels and Bar Techs., Akron, 1998—99; COO Republic Techs. Internat., Akron, 1999—2002; CEO, pres. Republic Engineered Products (formerly Republic Techs. Internat.), 2002—.

LAPOINTE, LUCIE, paper company executive, Canadian government official; b. Valleyfield, Que., Can., Dec. 23, 1954; d. Paul and Jeannette (Gagné) Lapointe; m. Clive Willis, Apr. 13, 1996; 1 child, Lauren Lapointe-Shaw. BSc in Biol. Scis., McGill U., 1977; MBA, U. Ottawa, Ont., Can., 1982. Tech. officer divsn. biol. scis. NRC, Ottawa, 1977-80, program officer program svcs. secretariat, 1982-84, exec. mgr. pub. rels. and info. svcs., 1984-87, dir. mgmt. svcs. br., 1987-89, sec. gen., 1989—2001; v.p. adminstrn., sec.-treas. Pulp and Paper Rsch. Inst. Can., Pointe-Claire, 2001—; exec. mem. Internat. Coun. for Sci. Office: PAPRICAN 570 boul St-Jean Pointe-Claire PQ Canada H9R 3J9 Office Phone: 514-630-4103. Business E-Mail: llapointe@paprican.ca.

LAPOLT, MARGARET, librarian; b. Austin, Pa., June 9, 1931; d. Thomas Wilbur and Frances Leona (Smith) Bennett; m. Sanford Howard LaPolt, Apr. 14, 1957 (dec. Nov. 1996); children: Cheryl Lynn LaPolt Remson, Mark Alan LaPolt. BSEd, Mansfield (Pa.) U., 1953; MSEd, Western Conn. State U., Danbury, 1963; MSLS, So. Conn. State U., New Haven, 1973. Tchr. 5th grade Bd. Edn., Clearfield, Pa., 1953-54; tchr. 6th grade Emporium (Pa.) Bd. Edn., 1954-58; tchr. 5th grade Darien (Conn.) Bd. Edn., 1958-64; tchr. 3d grade Stratford (Conn.) Bd. Edn., 1965-69, libr., 1969-70, Norwalk (Conn.) Bd. Edn., 1973-92, part-time libr., 1993—2005, ret., 2002. Singer, Norwalk Cmty. Chorus, 1961-73; singer Cmty. Bapt. Ch., Norwalk, 1958—, bd. deacons, 1993-99, trustee, 1981-87. Computer grantee, Norwalk Bd. Edn., 1985. Mem. ALA, Kappa Delta Phi, Kappa Pi. Avocations: knitting, embroidery, travel, walking.

LAPONCE, JEAN ANTOINE, political scientist, educator; b. Decize, France, Nov. 1925; s. Fernand and Fernande (Ramond) L.; m. Joyce Price, July, 1950; children: Jean-Antoine, Marc, Patrice; m. Iza Fiszhaut, Apr. 10, 1972; 1 child, Danielle. Diploma, Inst. d'études politiques, Paris, 1947; PhD, UCLA, 1955; LLD (hon.), U. B.C., Can., 2003. Instr. U. Santa Clara, 1956; asst. prof. polit. sci. U. B.C., Can., Vancouver, 1956-61, assoc. prof., 1961-66, prof., 1966—; dir. Inst. Interethnic Rels. U. Ottawa, 1993-2001. Mem. grad. faculty Aichi Shukutoku U., 1994-97. Author: The Protection of Minorities, 1961, The government of France under the Fifth Republic, 1962, People vs Politics, 1970, Left and Right, 1981, Langue et territoire, 1984, Languages and Their Territories, 1987. Fellow Royal Soc. Can. (pres. Acad. Humanities and Social Scis. 1988-91); mem. Can. Polit. Sci. Assn. (pres. 1972-73), Am. Polit. Sci. Assn., French Polit. Sci. Assn., Internat. Polit. Sci. Assn. (pres. 1973-76) Office: U BC Dept Polit Sci Vancouver BC Canada V6T 1Z1 Office Phone: 604-822-2832. Business E-Mail: jlaponce@interchange.ubc.ca.

LAPORTA, SARA, retail executive; Grad, U. Sussex; PhD, Kings Coll. U. London; grad, Mass. Inst. Tech. V.p. Boston Cons. Group, 1986—2002; sr. v.p. chief strategy officer Sears, Roebuck and Co., 2002—. Office: Sears Roebuck and Co 3333 Beverly Rd Hoffman Estates IL 60179

LA PORTA, TINA RITA, artist; b. Chgo., Sept. 26, 1967; d. Louis Francis LaPorta and Christina Marie (Koenigsaecker) Smith. BA, Columbia Coll., 1989; MFA, Sch. Visual Arts, 1994. Prof. Parsons Sch. Design, N.Y.C., 1996-97, Cooper Union, N.Y.C., 1998, Pratt, N.Y.C., 1998—, N.Y.U., 2001—03. Mem. Women's Caucus for Art, N.Y.C., 1993-94; artist-in-residence Exptl. TV Ctr., N.Y., 1996, Ars Electronica Futurelab, Linz, Austria, 1997-98, Gumosluk Acad., Turkey, 2002, Momenta Art, N.Y.C., 2003. One-woman shows include Whitebox, N.Y.C., 2003, Universal Concepts Unlimited, N.Y.C., 2002, Soros Ctr. Contemporary Art, Skopje, Mecedonia, 1998, Leonardo's Electronic Gallery, Mass., 1998, U.N. 4th World Conf. Women, Beijing, 1998; group shows include Karsai Sanat Galerisi, Turkey, Museu da Imagem e do som, Brazil, Espaif, Barcelona, 2003, Inst. Contemporary Art, London, 2003, Riva Gallery, N.Y.C., 2002, Nikolai Fine Art, N.Y.C., 2002, Acad. Media Arts, Cologne, Germany, 2001, New Konst Mus., Switzerland, 2001, San Francisco Art Inst., 2001, Centre Cultural de la

Fundacio, Spain, 2000, others; other exhbns. include Total Screen, 2003, Voyeur_web, 2002, The Kitchen, N.Y.C., 1996, Harvestworks, N.Y.C., 1998, Studio XX, Montreal, Can., 1998, Mus. of Contemporary Art Tokyo, 2000, Boston Photographic Resource Ctr., 2000, candy factory: Kanagawa, Japan, 2000, others; artistic dir. (videos/installations) 28 Days and Less Then 60 Seconds, 1993, Translate Expression, 1994, Cyber Femme Remix, 1995; artistic dir. (video) Camera Work, 1996; prodr. Cyberfemme TV, 1996-97; contbr. articles to various mags.; commn. "Turbulence.org", NEA, N.Y., 1999, Whitney Mus. Am. Art, 2002; works on worldwide web, 1997-2000; archivist YWCA 125th Ann. Catalogue, Nat. Mus. for Wome in the Arts, D.C., 1993; rsch. asst. History of Women Photographers, 1993. Photographer NOW, Chgo., 1991-92, Nat. Abortion Rights Action League, N.Y.C., 1995, Emergency Clinic Def. Task Force, N.Y.C., 1995. Semi-finalist: Global Info. Infrastructure award in arts and culture, 1999. E-mail: laporta@interport.net.

LAPORTE, ADRIENNE AROXIE, nursing administrator; b. Oceanside, NY, Sept. 29, 1938; d. Leonide and Grace (Ajamian) LaP. Diploma in nursing, St. John's Episc. Hosp., 1960; BA in Behavioral Scis., Lesley Coll., 1986; MA in Counseling, Liberty U., 1994. RN, NY, Fla., Mass., La., Ala.; cert. psychiat., mental health nurse Am. Nurses Credentialing Bd.; cert. legal nurse cons.; lic. alcohol and drug counselor I. Supr. Creedmoor State Hosp., Queens Village, NY, 1960-66, Taunton (Mass.) State Hosp., 1985-87, Mental Health Resources, Jacksonville, Fla., 1990-92, Staff Builders Home Health Agy., New Bedford, Mass., 1996-99; supr. psychiat. unit Univ. Hosp. of Jacksonville, 1977-79, Parkwood Hosp., New Bedford, 1980-84; dir. nursing Care Unit of Jacksonville Beach, Fla., 1987-90, Bradford Adult & Adolescent, Pelham, Ala., 1992-93, 94-95; program dir. Bowling Green Hosp., Mandeville, La., 1993; nurse mgr., therapist Ctr. for Health and Human Svcs., Inc., New Bedford, 1999—. Nurse cons. Seven Hills Found., 1996—. Lt. col. Nurse Corps U.S. Army, 1966-87, Vietnam. Decorated Bronze Star, Legion of Merit, Armed Forces Res. medal, Army Commendation medal, Combat Readiness medal, Meritorious Svc. medal, Presdl. and Unit citation, Republic of Vietnam Campaign medal, Vietnam Svc. medal. Mem. ACA, VFW, Internat. Nurses Soc. on Addictions, Fla. Nurses Assn., Am. Legion, Vietnam Vets. Am., Internat. Soc. Psychiat.-Mental Health Nurses, Internat. Nurses Soc. on Addictions. Home: 47 Little Oak Rd New Bedford MA 02745-2021 Office Phone: 508-999-3126 ext 209.

LAPORTE, CLOYD, JR., retired lawyer, retired manufacturing executive; b. N.Y.C., June 8, 1925; s. Cloyd and Marguerite (Raeder) L.; m. Caroline E. Berry, Jan. 22, 1949; children— Elizabeth, Marguerite, Cloyd III. AB, Harvard U., 1946, JD, 1949. Bar: N.Y. 1949. Assoc. mem. firm Cravath, Swaine & Moore, N.Y.C., 1949-56; dir. adminstrn. Metals div. Olin Corp., N.Y.C., 1957-66; legal counsel Dover Corp., N.Y.C., 1966-93, sec., 1971-93. Dir. Putnam Hosp. Ctr., 2000—. 2d lt. A.C. AUS, WWII. Mem. Harvard Club (N.Y.C.). Home: Gipsy Trail Club Carmel NY 10512

LAPORTE, GERALD JOSEPH SYLVESTRE, lawyer; b. Windsor, Ont., Can., Oct. 16, 1946; came to U.S., 1948, naturalized, 1954; s. Rosaire Joseph and Catherine Rose (Sylvestre) L. BA, Sacred Heart Sem. Coll., 1968; STB, St. Paul U., Ottawa, Ont., 1971; BTh, U. Ottawa, 1971; MA, Georgetown U., 1974; JD, George Washington U., 1976. Bar: Mich. 1976, D.C. 1977. Legis. asst. to U.S. Congressman William J. Randall, Washington, 1971-75; law clk. to Judge U.S. Dist. Ct., Washington, 1976-77; assoc. Wilmer, Cutler & Pickering, Washington, 1977-82; spl. counsel Office Gen. Counsel, SEC, Washington, 1982—84, sr. spl. counsel, 1984—85, counsel to commr., 1985-87; assoc. Nutter, McClennen & Fish, Washington, 1987—88; assoc., then ptnr. Patton Boggs, LLP, Washington, 1988-96; counsel Hogan & Hartson LLP, Washington, 1996—2002; chief Office of Small Bus. Policy, SEC, Washington, 2002—. Chmn. steering com. sect. corp., fin. and securities law D.C. Bar, 1997-98; vice chmn. securities law & disclosure com., Nat. Assn. Bond lawyers, 1994-96. Mng. editor George Washington Law Rev., 1975-76. Mem. Arlington County Hist. Affairs and Landmark Rev. Bd., 2001—. Mem. ABA (sect. on bus. law, fed. regulation of securities com.), Arlington Hist. Soc. Inc. (bd. dirs. 1997—, pres. 2001-03, 05—). Democrat. Roman Catholic. Home: 3154 Key Blvd Arlington VA 22201-5037 Office: SEC 100 F St NE Washington DC 20549-3628 Personal E-mail: g.laporte@verizon.net. Business E-Mail: LaporteG@SEC.gov.

LAPORTE, LEO FREDERIC, geologist, educator, paleontologist; b. Englewood, N.J., July 30, 1933; s. Leo Frederic and Edea (Giacobbe) L.; married, 1956 (div. 1983); children: Leo G., Eva R.; m. Margaret Liniecki, 1985; 1 child, Noel A. Student, Fordham Coll., 1951-53; AB, Columbia U., 1956, PhD, 1960. From instr. to prof. dept. geol. scis. Brown U., Providence, 1959-71; prof. dept. earth scis. U. Calif.-Santa Cruz, 1971-94, prof. emeritus, 1994, chmn., 1972-75, dean div. natural scis., 1975-76, provost Crown Coll., 1993-98, assoc. vice chancellor for undergrad. edn., 1994-98. Vis. prof. Yale U., 1964; geologist N.Y. State Geol. Survey, 1962-64; petroleum rsch. cons.; mem. com. geol. scis. Nat. Acad. Sci.-NRC, 1970-72; sec. U.S. Nat. Commn. on the History of Geology, 1991-93, chair, 1994-96; mem. Internat. Commn. on the History of Geology, 1994—; docent Jasper Ridge Biol. Preserve, Stanford U., 2004—. Author: Ancient Environments, 1968, 79, 89, Encounter with the Earth, 1975, George Gaylord Simpson-Paleontologist and Evolutionist, 2000; prin. author: The Earth and Human Affairs, 1972; editor: Reefs in Time and Space, 1974, Evolution and the Fossil Record, 1978, Simple Curiosity: Family Letters of George G. Simpson, 1987, Establishment of a Geologic Framework for Paleoanthropology, 1990; contbr. articles to profl. jours. Recipient President's award Am. Assn. Petroleum Geologists, 1969; U. Calif. Santa Cruz Alumni Disting. Tchg. award, 1980 Fellow: AAAS, Calif. Acad. Sci., Geol. Soc. Am.; mem.: Soc. Econ. Mineralogists and Paleontologists (chmn. rsch. com., paleontology councilor, editor PALAIOS 1984—89, pres. 1995—96, Hon. Mem. award 1999), History of Earth Scis. Soc. (pres. 1994). E-mail: laporte@ucsc.edu.

LAPOSATA, JOSEPH SAMUEL, army officer; b. Johnstown, Pa., Oct. 3, 1938; s. Joseph Thomas and Mary Marie (Coco) L.; m. Anita Louise Sabo, Aug. 12, 1961; children: Joseph S. Jr., David G., Matthew M. BS, Indiana U. Pa., 1960; MS, Cornell U., 1968; grad., Command and Gen. Staff Coll., Leavenworth, Kans., 1971, Indsl. Coll. Armed Forces, Washington, 1980. Commd. 2d lt. U.S. Army, 1960, advanced through grades to lt. gen., 1991; asst. chief of staff for logistics 5th Inf. Div., Ft. Polk, La., 1978-79; chief war res. div. Office Dep. Chief of Staff for Logistics, Hdqrs. Dept. Army, Washington, 1980-81; comdr. 8th Support Group, U.S. Army So. European Task Force, Livorno, Italy, 1981-84, dep. comdr., chief of staff Vicenza, Italy, 1984; exec. to dep. chief of staff for logistics Hdqrs. Dept. Army, Washington, 1984-86, dir. plans and ops., dep. chief of staff for logistics, 1986-88; comdg. gen. U.S. Army Material Command-Europe, Heidelberg, Fed. Republic Germany, 1988-89; dep. chief of staff for logistics U.S. Army Europe and 7th Army, Heidelberg, 1989-91; chief of staff Allied Forces So. Europe, Naples, Italy, 1991-93; Presdl. appointee as sec. Am. Battle Monuments Commn., Washington, 1994-95; ret. Apptd. diplomatic post as dep. gen. mgr. and dir. logistics ops. and programs NATO Maintenance and Supply Agy., Luxembourg; now ret. Decorated Def. DDSM, DSM (2), Legion of Merit (3), Bronze Star (2); knight comdr. Republic of Italy; recipient Man of Yr. award Interclub Coun., Johnstown, Pa., 1990, Disting. Alumnus award Ind. U. of Pa., 1992, medal for meritorious svc. Am. Battle Monuments Commn., medal for disting. svc., NATO Maint. and Supply Agy., 1999; inducted into Quartermaster Hall of Fame, 1994; named Col. Emeritus, U.S. Army Q.M. Rgt. Mem. Assn. U.S. Army (pres. European dept. 1989-91), Quartermaster Found. (bd. dirs.), Rotary, Phi Kappa Phi, Tau Kappa Epsilon. Roman Catholic. Avocation: golf. Address: 1823 Freedom Dr Melbourne FL 32940-6875 Office Phone: 321-751-9586. Personal E-mail: jlaposata@cs.com.

LAPOSKY, JAMES EDWARD, pastor; b. Huron, S.D., Jan. 5, 1956; s. Russell Gale and Eleanor Jean L.; m. Elaine Hazel Sessler, Oct. 25, 1980; children: Josiah, Benjamin, Adam, Christopher. BS, S.D. State U., 1979. Rsch. asst. U. Nebr., Omaha, 1980-83; dir. Youth for Christ, Sandstone, Minn., 1983-87; pvt. practice ServiceMaster Pine County, Askov, Minn., 1987-96; pastor Cmty. Worship Ctr., Sandstone, 1989—; dir. Ctr. Hope Ministries, Sandstone, 1997—. Chmn. Pine County Reps., 1993—; vice chair Minn. 8th Congl. Dist. Rep., 1997—. Republican. Home: 3534 E Bregnedalgade St Askov MN 55704 Office: Ctr Hope Ministries 312 Main St Sandstone MN 55072 E-mail: coh@scicable.net.

LAPP, CHARLES WARREN, internist, pediatrician; b. Bklyn., June 10, 1947; s. Warren Anthony and Katherine Emma (Beard) L.; m. Darie Eleanor Conners, Aug. 28, 1971; children: Lauren Michelle, Warren Rutherford. BS, Rensselaer Poly. Inst., 1969, MBME, 1970; MD, Albany Coll. Medicine, 1974. Diplomate Am. Bd. Internal Medicine, Am. Bd. Pediat., Am. Bd. Ind. Med. Examiners. Intern U. N.C., Chapel Hill, 1974-75, resident, 1975-78, assoc. clin. prof., 1978-91; med. dir. Hill Haven and Blue Ridge Nursing, Raleigh, NC, 1978-91; assoc. clin. prof. Duke. U. Med. Ctr., 1982—; founder and pres. Piedmont Med. Assn., Raleigh, 1978-95; med. dir. Cheney Clinic, Charlotte, NC, 1991-95; pres. Hunter-Hopkins Ctr., P.A., Charlotte, 1995—. Cons. TASA Tech. Adviser, Phoenix, 1979—2001; adv. bd. Raleigh Employee Assistance Plan, 1987—89, Health Plus, 1987—89; med. cons. CFIDS Assn. of Am., Charlotte, 1991—. Contbr. articles to profl. jours. including Jour. AMA and Lancet; presenter exhibits to sci. assemblies. Pres. Muscular Dystrophy Assn., 1982-84. Named Richard T. Beebe Scholar in Medicine Albany (N.Y.) Med. Coll., 1974, named Man of Yr. Jaycees, Raleigh, 1983. Fellow Am. Acad. Family Physicians, Am. Acad. Pediat., Am. Assn. Disability Evaluating Physicians; mem. AMA, N.C. Med. Soc., Am. Assn. for Chronic Fatigue Syndrome (bd. dirs.), Am. Pain Soc. Presbyterian. Avocations: boating, hiking, travel. Office: 10344 Park Rd Ste 300 Charlotte NC 28210-8401 Office Phone: 704-543-9692. E-mail: cwlapp@cs.com.

LAPP, DOUGLAS MARTIN, museum director; b. Dec. 20, 1938; BS in Engring. Physics, U. Ill., 1960; MS in Biophysics, U. Washington, Seattle, 1962; EdD in Sci. Edn., Harvard U., 1968. Rsch. and teaching asst. U. Washington Med. Sch., Seattle, 1960-62; tchr. math., physics, chemistry Peace Corps Vol. Sasse Coll., Cameroon I Project, W. Africa, 1962-65; instr. physics dept. Cornell U., Ithaca, N.Y.; rsch. asst. physics project Harvard U., Cambridge, Mass., 1965-67; dir. African Primary Sci. Program Makerere U. Ctr., Nat. Inst. Edn. (USAID Project), Kampala, Uganda, 1967-70; sci. curriculum coord., dir. program devel. Fairfax (Va.) County Pub. Schs., 1970-85; exec. dir. Nat. Sci. Resources Ctr. Smithsonian Instn.-Nat. Acad. Scis., Washington, 1985—. Sci. edn. cons. to White House Office of Sci. Tech. Pol., also to Nat. Sci. Fedn.; mem. bd. Rockefeller African Forum Childrens Literacy in Sci. & Tech., CASE/Carnegie Inst. Wash., Caltech Precoll. Sci. Initiative. Contbr. articles to profl. jours., papers to edn. and sci. confs. Fellow AAAS; mem. Phi Kappa Phi, Tau Beta Pi.

LAPP, JAMES MERRILL, minister; b. Lansdale, Pa., July 20, 1937; s. John E. and Edith (Nyce) L.; m. Nancy Swartzentruber, Aug. 13, 1960 (dec. Dec. 1998); children: Cynthia Ann, J. Michael, Philip A.; m. Miriam F. Book, Dec. 23, 2000. BA, Eastern Mennonite Coll., 1960; B.D., Goshen Bibl. Sem., 1963; D.Min., Drew U., 1981. Ordained to ministry Mennonite Ch., 1963. Pastor Belmont Mennonite Ch., Elkhart, Ind., 1961-63; tchr. Christopher Dock Mennonite High Sch., Lansdale, Pa., 1963-70; paster Perkasie Mennonite Ch., Pa., 1963-72, Albany Mennonite Ch., Oreg., 1972-81; dir. campus ministries Goshen Coll., Ind., 1981-87; gen. sec., gen. bd. Mennonite Ch., Elkhart, 1987-95; conf. pastor Franconia Mennonite Conf., Souderton, Pa., 1996—. Moderator Pacific Coast Conf. on Mennonite Ch., Oreg., 1977-79, Mennonite Gen. Assembly, Lombard, Ill., 1985-87. Contbr. articles to Mennonite Ch. publs. Democrat. Avocations: gardening, baking, walking. Home: 443 Penn Oak Ct Harleysville PA 19438 Office: Franconia Mennonite Conf 771 Route 113 Souderton PA 18964-1000

LAPP, KATHRYN S., social studies educator; b. Port Clinton, Ohio, July 12, 1941; d. Norton Carl and Emma Katherine (Fisher) Rosentreter; m. Conrad Lee Lapp, Jan. 1, 1969; 1 child, Aaron Carl. BS, U. Colo., 1963; Peace Corps cert. (hon.), Columbia U., 1963; MA, NYU, 1968. Peace Corps vol. Kaduna (Nigeria) Govt. Coll., 1964-66; secondary sch. tchr. N.Y.C. Pub. Schs., 1966-69, Sch. Dist. II, Colorado Springs, Colo., 1969-89, instrnl. specialist, 1989-98, grant coord., 1997-2001; instr. tchg. methods U. Colo., Colorado Springs, 1999—2003, Colo. Coll., 2003—05. Tchr. cons. Nat. Geog. Soc., Washington and Colo., 1989-99; cons., instr. for Japan studies Colo. Coll. Summer Program, Colorado Springs, 1991-92; mem. writing task force Colo. geog. stds. Colo. Dept. Edn., Denver, 1994-95. Contbr. author: Geographic Inquiry into Global Issues, 1992; contbr. articles to profl. jours. Coord. Washington and Colo. Close Up, Colorado Springs, 1990-98; coord. Colo. congl. dist. 5, U.S. Congress and Ctr. for Civic Edn., Calabasas, Calif., 1990-2001; mem. steering com. Kids Voting, Colorado Springs, 1995-2001; active Womens Edn. Soc., Colo. Coll., 1999—; mem. Nat. Geog. Soc. adv. com. Colo. Geography Edn. Fund, 2000—05. Mem.: Colo. and Colorado Springs Assn. Sch. Execs. (Educator of Yr. 1998), Colo. Coun. for the Social Studies (pres. 1998—99), Nat. Coun. for the Social Studies (Outstanding Svc. award 2004), Nat. Coun. for Geog. Edn., Nat. Coun. for Hist. Edn., Colo. Geog. Alliance (steering com. 1988—99, Contbn. to Geog. Edn. award 1998), Alpha Delta Kappa (pres. 1984—85). E-mail: lappkc@earthlink.net.

LAPPAS, SPERO THOMAS, lawyer; b. Danbury, Conn., Oct. 20, 1952; s. Tom John and Alexandria (Manolakes) L.; m. Josephine Wahrendorf, Nov. 8, 1981 (div. 1986); 1 child, Thom Spero; m. Julie Marie Waugh, July 12, 1986 (div. 1995); 1 child, Alexandria Julia. BA cum laude, Allegheny Coll., Meadville, Pa., 1974; JD cum laude, Dickinson Sch. Law, Carlisle, Pa., 1977. Bar: Pa. 1977, U.S. Dist. Ct. (mid. dist.) Pa. 1977, U.S. Ct. Appeals (3rd cir.) 1980, U.S. Supreme Ct. 1991, U.S. Dist. Ct. (we. dist.) Pa., 2002. Assoc. Law Office of Arthur Kusic, Harrisburg, Pa., 1977-79; atty. Kusic & Lappas, P.C., Harrisburg, 1979-84; pvt. practice Harrisburg, 1984-85; ptnr. Stefanon & Lappas, Harrisburg, 1985-88; prin. Law Offices Spero T. Lappas, Harrisburg, 1988—2002; mem. Serratelli, Schiffman, Brown & Calhoon P.C., Harrisburg, 2002—. Mem. Pa. Bar Assn., Dauphin County Bar Assn., Nat. Assn. Criminal Def. Lawyers, Pa. Assn. Criminal Def. Lawyers, Mensa, Am. Hellenic Ednl. and Progressive Assn., U.S. Fencing Assn. Office: 2080 Linglestown Rd Ste 201 Harrisburg PA 17110 E-mail: slappas@ssbc-law.com.

LAPPEN, CHESTER I., lawyer; b. Des Moines, May 4, 1919; s. Robert C. and Anna (Sideman) L.; m. Jon Tyroler Irmas, June 29, 1941; children— Jonathan Bailey, Timothy, Andrea L., Sally Morris. AB with highest honors in Econs, U. Calif., 1940; LL.B. magna cum laude (Faye diploma), Harvard, 1943. Bar: Calif. bar 1943. Practice in, Los Angeles, 1946—; sr. partner firm Mitchell, Silberberg & Knupp, 1949—; advisory bd. Bank Am., 1962-65; chmn. bd., dir. Zenith Nat. Ins. Corp., 1975-77. Bd. dirs. Arden Group, Inc. (chmn. exec. com. 1978), 1963-91, Data Products Corp. (chmn. fin. com.), 1965-93, City Nat. Bank Corp., 1967-92; trustee, pres. Citinat, Devel. Trust; bd. dirs., chmn. bd. Pacific Rim Holding Corp., 1987-94. Editor-in-chief: Harvard Law Rev, 1942-43. Chmn. bd. trustees Immaculate Heart Coll., 1981-88; trustee UCLA Found.; v.p., dir. Ctr. for Childhood. Spl. agt., counter intelligence U.S. Army, 1943—46. Named to Artus Econs. Honor Soc., U. Calif., 1939. Mem. ABA, Los Angeles Bar Assn. (dir. 1953), Los Angeles Jr. Bar Assn. (pres. 1953), Beverly Hills (Calif.) Bar Assn., Harvard Law Sch. Alumni Assn. So. Calif. (pres. 1973-82). Republican. Office: Mitchell Silberberg & Knupp 11377 W Olympic Blvd Los Angeles CA 90064-1625

LAPPENBUSCH, RICHARD W., software company official; b. Bellingham, Wash., Apr. 4, 1968; s. Charles F. and Sylvia (Sullivan) L.; m. Brittany Abbott; children: Vivian Mary, Amelia Jayne. BSBA, U. Redlands, 1990; MPS in Interactive Telecom., NYU, 1993. Program mgr. Continuum Prodns., Bellevue, Wash., 1993; dir. strategic planning Microsaft, Redmond, Wash., 1993—. Office: Microsoft One Microsoft Way Redmond WA 98052 Fax: 425-936-7329. E-mail: richlap@microsoft.com, richlap@hotmail.com.

LAPPIN, HARLEY G., federal agency administrator; BA in Forensic Studies, Ind. U., 1978; MA in Criminal Justice and Correctional Adminstrn., Kent State U., 1985. Case mgr. to ctrl. inmate monitoring adminstr. Fed. Correctional Instn. Fed. Bur. Prisons, Texarkana, Tex., 1985—89, camp adminstr. Fed. Correctional Instn. Jesup, Ga., 1989—91, assoc. warden Fed. Med. Ctr. Carville, La., 1991, br. adminstr. program rev. divsn. Wash., 1993—96, warden, dir. habilitation program Fed. Correctional Instn. Butner, NC, 1996—98, warden, founder spl. confinement unit U.S. Penitentiary Terre Haute, Ind., 1998—2001, regional dir. Mid-Atlantic Region, 2001—03, dir., 2003—. Chmn. Mgmt. Reengineering Team Fed. Bur. Prisons, chmn. Forward Thinking Workgroup; mem. Am. Correctional Assn. Standards Com. Office: Fed Bur Prisons 320 First St NW Washington DC 20534

LAPPIN, LAUREN, Olympic athlete; b. June 26, 1984; d. Dean and Kelly. Student, Stanford U., 2002—. Mem. U.S. Women's Softball Team, Athens Olympic Games, 2004. Named Top Defensive Player, Canada Cup, 2003; named to WCWS All-Tournament Team selection, 2003. Achievements include mem. Gold medal U.S. Elite Team, Canada Cup, 2003.

LAPSLEY, JAMES NORVELL, JR., minister, educator; b. Clarksville, Tenn., Mar. 16, 1930; s. James Norvell and Evangeline (Winn) L.; m. Brenda Ann Weakley, June 4, 1953 (dec. May 1989); children: Joseph William, Jacqueline Evangeline; m. Helen Joan Winter, Feb. 24, 1990. BA, Rhodes Coll., 1952; BD, Union Theol. Sem., 1955; PhD (Div. Sch. fellow, Rockefeller fellow), U. Chgo., 1961. Ordained to ministry Presbyn. Ch., 1955; asst. min. Gentilly Presbyn. Ch., New Orleans, 1955-57; instr. Princeton (N.J.) Theol. Sem., 1961-63, asst. prof., 1963-67, assoc. prof., 1967-76, prof. pastoral theology, 1976-80, Carl and Helen Egner prof. pastoral theology, 1980-92, acad. dean, 1984-89, prof. emeritus, 1992—. V.p. N.W. Maricopa UN Assn., 1995-96, pres., 1997-98; pres. Critical Issues Coun. of Sun Cities, 1996-97; sec. Sun City Orch., 1999-2001, pres. 2001-2003. Editor: The Concept of Willing, 1967, Salvation and Health, 1972, Renewal in Late Life Through Pastoral Counseling, 1992, (with B.H. Childs, D.W. Waanders), Festschrift: The Treasure of Earthen Vessels, 1994; chmn. editl. bd. Pastoral Psychology Jour., 1975-84; mem. editl. bd. Jour. Pastoral Care, 1966-69, 91—. Bd. dirs. Westminster Found., Princeton U., 1970-76. Danforth fellow Menninger Found., 1960-61 Mem.: Soc. for Pastoral Theology (co-founder 1985), Phi Beta Kappa. Presbyterian. Home: 6024 Mountain Oaks Dr Flagstaff AZ 86004 E-mail: jlapsley@infomagic.com.

LAQUEUR, WALTER, history professor; b. Breslau, Germany, May 26, 1921; s. Fritz and Else (Berliner) L.; m. Barbara Koch, May 29, 1941 (dec.); children: Sylvia, Shlomit; m. Christa Susi Wichmann, 1996. Grad., Johannesgymnasium, Breslau, 1938; student, Hebrew (Jerusalem) U., 1938-39; HHD (hon.), Hebrew Union Coll., 1988, Adelphi U., 1993, Brandeis U., 1994. Agrl. worker, Palestine, 1940-44; newspaper corr., free-lance author, 1944-55; founder, editor Survey, London, Eng., 1955-67; vis. prof. Johns Hopkins, 1957, U. Chgo., 1958, Harvard, 1977; dir. Inst. Contemporary History, Wiener Library, London, 1964-92; prof. history ideas and politics Brandeis U., Waltham, Mass., 1967-72; prof. history U. Tel Aviv, 1970-80; chmn. internat. rsch. coun. Ctr. Strategic and Internat. Studies, Washington, 1973—2001; univ. prof. govt. Ctr. Strategic and Internat. Studies Georgetown U., Washington, 1977-91. Author: Communism and Nationalism in the Middle East, 1956, The Soviet Union and the Middle East, 1959, Young Germany, 1962, Russia and Germany, 1966, The Fate of the Revolution, 1967, The Road to War, 1967, The Struggle for the Middle East, 1969, Europe Since Hitler, 1970, Out of the Ruins of Europe, 1971, Confrontation: The Middle East and World Politics, 1974, A History of Zionism, 1972, Weimar, 1975, Guerrilla, 1976, Terrorism, 1977, Guerrilla Reader, 1977, Terrorism Reader, 1978, A Continent Astray, 1979, The Missing Years, 1980, Political Psychology of Appeasement, 1980, Farewell to Europe, 1981, The Terrible Secret, 1981, America, Europe, and the Soviet Union, 1983, Germany Today, 1985, A World of Secrets, 1985, The Age of Terrorism, 1987, The Long Road to Freedom: Russia and Glasnost, 1989, Stalin, 1991, Thursday's Child Has Far to Go, 1992, Black Hundred, 1993, The Dream That Failed, 1994, Generation Exodus, 2001; editor: The Holocaust Encyclopedia, 2001; co-editor, founder: Jour. Contemporary History, 1966-2005; founder Washington Papers, 1972—. Recipient 1st Distinguished Writer's award Center Strategic and Internat. Studies, 1969, Inter Nationes award, 1985-05, Grand Cross of Merit German Fed. Republic, 1987. Personal E-mail: walter@laqueur.net.

LARACH, MARILYN GREEN, physician; b. Phila., Apr. 7, 1952; d. Philip and Freda (Rubin) Green; m. David Ross Larach, Aug. 8, 1976; 1 child, Daniel Benjamin. AB, Princeton U., 1973; MD, NYU, 1978. Diplomate Nat. Bd. Med. Examiners, Am. Bd. Anesthesiology, Am. Bd. Pediat. Resident in pediat. Jacobi Hosp-Albert Einstein Coll. Medicine, Bronx, 1978—80; intern in pediat. Bronx Mcpl. Hosp. Ctr., Phila., 1978—79, resident in pediat., 1979—80; resident in anesthesia Hosp. of U. Pa., 1980—83; fellow in anesthesiology Children's Hosp. Phila., 1982—83; chief of anesthesia svc. U. Hosp. for Rehab., Elizabethtown, Pa., 1983—90. Asst. prof. anesthesiology Pa. State U., Hershey, 1983-92, assoc. prof., 1992—; dir. N. Am. Malignant Hyperthermia Registry, Hershey, 1988-97, sr. rsch. assoc., 1997—. Contbr. articles to profl. jours. Mem. Princeton U. Schs. and Scholarship Com., Ctrl. Pa., 1985—. Named Woodrow Wilson scholar, Princeton U., 1973; recipient McConnell fellowship, Princeton U., 1972. Mem. Malignant Hyperthermia Assn. U.S. (profl. adv. coun. 1989—), Am. Acad. Pediat., Am. Soc. Anesthesiologists. Office: Dept Anesthesia PO Box 850 Hershey PA 17033-0850 Office Phone: 717-531-6597. E-mail: mlarach@alumni.princeton.edu.

LARAGH, JOHN HENRY, cardiologist, surgeon, educator; b. Yonkers, N.Y., Nov. 18, 1924; s. Harry Joseph and Grace Catherine (Coyne) L.; m. Adonia Kennedy, Apr. 28, 1949; children: John Coyne, Peter Christian, Robert Sealey; m. Jean E. Sealey, Sept. 22, 1974. MD, Cornell U., 1948. Intern Presbyn. Hosp., N.Y.C., 1948-49, asst. resident, 1949-50; cardiology trainee Nat. Heart Inst., 1950-51; rsch. fellow N.Y. Heart Assn., 1951-52; asst. physician Presbyn. Hosp., 1950-55, asst. attending, 1954-61, assoc. attending, 1961-69, attending physician, 1969-75, pres. elect med. bd., 1972-74; faculty Coll. Physicians and Surgeons Columbia U., 1950-75, prof. clin. medicine, 1967-75, spokesman exec. com. faculty coun., 1971-73; vice-chmn. bd. trustees for profl. and sci. affairs Presbyn. Hosp., 1974-75; dir. Hypertension Ctr., chief nephrology divsn. Columbia-Presbyn. Med. Ctr., 1975—76; Master prof. medicine, dir. Hypertension and Cardiovascular Ctr., N.Y. Hosp.-Cornell Med. Ctr., 1975—96, chief cardiology divsn., 1975—96. Cons. USPHS, 1964—. Editor-in-chief Am. Jour. Hypertension, 1985—, Cardiovascular Reviews and Reports, 1980—; Editor: Hypertension Manual, 1974, Topics in Hypertension, 1980, Frontiers in Hypertension Rsch., 1981; editor Hypertension: Pathophysiology, Diagnosis, and Management, 1990, 1995; editorial bd.: Am. Jour. Medicine, Am. Jour. Cardiology, Kidney Internat., Jour. Clin. Endocrinology and Metabolism, Hypertension, Jour. Hypertension, Circulation, Am. Heart Jour., Procs. of Soc. Exptl. Biology and Medicine. Mem. policy adv. bd. hypertension detection and follow-up program Nat. Heart and Lung Inst., 1971, bd. sci. counselor, 1974-79; chmn. U.S.A.-USSR Joint Program in Hypertension, 1977-93. With U.S. Army, 1943-46. Recipient Stouffer prize Med. Rsch., 1969, J.K. Lattimer award Am. Urol. Assn., 1989, Robert Tigerstedt award Am. Soc. Hypertension, 1990, John P. Peters award Am. Soc. Nephrology, 1990, Lifetime Achievement in Medicine award N.Y. Acad. Medicine, 1993, Disting. Alumnus award Cornell U. Med. Coll., 1993, Bristol Myers Squibb award for disting. achievement cardiovalcular rsch., 1996, Disting. Achievement award Coun. for High Blood Pressure Rsch., Am. Heart Assn., 1999, Stevo Julius awrd for edn. in hypertension Internat. Soc. Hypertension, 2002; subject of Time Mag. cover story, 1975; Most Frequently Cited Scientist: Top Ten Advances in Cardiopulmonary Medicine, 1946-75. Fellow Am. Coll. Cardiology; mem. ACP (Master), Am. Heart Assn. (chmn. med. adv. bd. coun. high blood pressure rsch. 1968-72), Am. Soc. Clin. Investigation, Assn. Am. Physicians, Assn. Univ. Cardiologists, Endocrine Soc., Am. Soc. Nephrology, Am. Soc. Hypertension (founder, 1st pres. 1986-88), Internat. Soc. Hypertension (pres. 1986-88), Harvey Soc., Kappa Sigma, Nu Sigma Nu, Alpha Omega Alpha, Country Club of Fla., Shinnecock Hills Golf Club (Southampton, N.Y.). Achievements include discovery of renin-angiotensin-aldosterone hormonal control system and the causal roles of its overactivity in malignant and in most essential hypertension. Home: 5 Sandpiper Dr Village Of Golf FL 33436-5621 Office: NY Hosp-Cornell Med Ctr 525 E 68th St New York NY 10021-4885 Office Phone: 212-746-2206. E-mail: jhlaragh@aol.com. *In my research, a key resource has been the ability to perceive everyday clinical phenomena differently, to recognize and* *develop new ideas and experiments about human physiology and the causes of hypertension and major cardiovascular diseases. These perceptions enable hypotheses and experiments for creation and synthesis of new knowledge that redirects medical thinking.*

LARAYA-CUASAY, LOURDES REDUBLO, pediatrician, pulmonologist, educator; b. Baguio, Philippines, Dec. 8, 1941; came to U.S., 1966; d. Jose Marquez and Lolita (Redublo) Laraya; m. Ramon Serrano Cuasay, Aug. 7, 1965; children: Raymond Peter, Catherine Anne, Margaret Rose, Joseph Paul. AA, U. Santo Tomas, Manila, Philippines, 1958, MD cum laude, 1963. Diplomate Am. Bd. Pediatrics. Resident in pediatrics U. Santo Tomas Hosp., 1963-65, Children's Hosp. Louisville, 1966-67, Charity Hosp. New Orleans-Tulane U., 1967-68; fellow child growth and devel. Children's Hosp. Phila., 1968-69; fellow pediatric pulmonary and cystic fibrosis programs St. Christopher's Hosp. for Children, Phila., 1969-71, rsch. assoc., 1971-72; clin. instr. Tulane U., New Orleans, 1967-68; asst. prof. pediatrics Temple Health Scis. Ctr., Phila., 1972-77; assoc. prof. pediatrics Thomas Jefferson Med. Sch., Phila., 1977-79, U. Medicine & Dentistry N. J., Robert Wood Johnson Med. Sch., New Brunswick, 1980-85, prof. clin. pediatrics, 1985-98, prof. pediat., 1998—. Dir. pediatric pulmonary medicine and cystic fibrosis ctr. U. Medicine and Dentistry, Robert Wood Johnson Med. Sch., New Brunswick, 1981—. Co-editor: Interstitial Lung Diseases in Children, 1988. Recipient Pediatric Rsch. award Mead Johnson Pharm. Co., Manila, 1965. Fellow Am. Coll. Chest Physicians (steering com., chmn. cardiopulmonary diseases in children 1976—), Airways Network, Am. Acad. Pediatrics (tobacco free generation rep. 1986-92); mem. Am. Ambulatory Pediatric Soc., Am. Thoracic Soc., Am. Sleep Disorder Assn., N.J. Thoracic Soc. (chmn. pediatric pulmonary com. 1986-91, governing coun. mem. 1981-94), European Respiratory Soc. Avocation: pianist. Home: 100 Mercer Ave Spring Lake NJ 07762-1208 Office: UMDNJ Robert Wood Johnson Med Sch One RWJ Place New Brunswick NJ 08903 Office Phone: 732-235-7899. E-mail: larayacuasay@yahoo.com.

LARBERG, JOHN FREDERICK, wine consultant, educator; b. Kansas City, Mo., Jan. 21, 1930; s. Herman Alvin and Ann (Sabrowsky) L. AA, Kansas City Jr. Coll., 1948; AB cum laude, U. Mo., 1950, postgrad., 1955-56; MSW, Bryn Mawr Coll., 1961. Cert. social worker. With Westinghouse Electric Corp., 1953-56; dir. House of Industry Settlement House, Phila., 1957-61; asst. to exec. dir. Health and Welfare Coun., Inc., Phila., 1961-66; sr. staff cons., 1966-73, dir. Washington office, 1971-72, Nat. Assembly for Social Policy and Devel., Inc., N.Y.C.; nat. dir. community and patient services Nat. Multiple Sclerosis Soc., N.Y.C., 1974-81, nat. dir. spl. projects, 1981-82; adminstrv. v.p. Fedn. Protestant Welfare Agys. N.Y., 1982-86; sr. advisor, 1986-87; exec. dir. Am. Assn. State Social Work Bds., 1987-89; cons. The Wine Aficionado, N.Y., 1990—. Cons. exec. com. Commn. on Vol. Svc. and Action, 1967-76, cons. Met. N.Y. Project Equality, 1968-73, Encampment for Citizenship, 1973-74, Symphony for UN, 1974-77, Lower Eastside Fam. Union, 1984—, Wielenga Psych. Svc., 1993—, Malignant Hyperthermia Assn. U.S., 1994—, Internat. Fedn. Multiple Sclerosis Socs., 1995—, Nat. Multiple Sclerosis Soc., 1997—; bd. dirs. Health Systems Agy. of N.Y., 1984-86; trustee The Riverside Ch., N.Y.C., 1985-89, worship commn., 1992-94, ordination com., 1993—, chmn., 1996—; bd. dirs., mem. exec. com. Metro Assn. United Ch. of Christ, N.Y., 1993—, dir. N.Y. state coun., 1995—, nat. del. Gen. Synod, 1997; mem. Disciples of Christ/United Ch. of Christ N.Y. State Joint Task Force, 1996—; nat. dir. Coun. Soc. Wk. Edn., 1985-86. Served with AUS, 1951-53. Mem. Acad. Cert. Social Workers (charter), Nat. Assn. Social Workers (chpt. legis. com. 1968-70, nat. publs. com. 1968-71, nat. legal regulation com. 1987-89), Internat. Coun. Social Welfare (internat. com. of reps. 1980-84, U.S. com. for Internat. Coun. Social Welfare, bd. dirs. 1983-90, exec. com. 1983-90), Internat. Fedn. Multiple Sclerosis Socs. (vice chmn. patient services com. 1976-81, chmn. 1981-84, mem. individual and family services com. 1984-97, non-govtl. rep. to UN, 1990-96, rep. to Rehab. Internat. Med. Commn. 1976-81), Nat. Conf. Social Welfare (program com. 1966-73, chmn. combined assoc. groups 1969-70, nat. dir. 1971-73, 83-87), Fedn. of Assns. Regulatory Bds. (nat. dir. 1988-89), Malignant Hyperthermia Assn. U.S. (nat. dir. 1984-93, nat. pres. 1985-89, rep. 10th Quad. World Congr. Anesth. Hague 1992), Am. Acad. Polit. and Social Sci., Nat. Urban League (nat. trustee-at-large 1968), Hawk Mountain Sanctuary Assn., Bryn Mawr Social Work Alumni Assn. (pres. 1963-65), Am. Mus. Natural History, N.Y.C. Citizens Union, N.Y. Mcpl. Art Soc., Phi Beta Kappa Assn. N.Y. (pres. 1980-82), Omicron Delta Kappa, QEBH, Alpha Phi Omega, Alpha Pi Zeta, Pi Sigma Alpha, Alpha Kappa Psi. Home and Office: 400 E 58th St Apt 2F New York NY 10022-2333

LARDENT, ESTHER FERSTER, lawyer, consultant; b. Linz, Austria, Apr. 23, 1947; arrived in US, 1951; d. William and Rose (Seidweber) Ferster; m. Dennis Robert Lardent, July 27, 1969 (div. Dec. 1981). BA, Brown U., 1968; JD, U. Chgo., 1971. Bar: Ill. 1972, Mass. 1975, admitted to practice: US Dist. Ct. (Ill.) 1972, US Dist. Ct. (Mass.) 1975. Civil rights specialist Office of Civil Rights U.S. HEW, Chgo., 1971-72; staff dir. individual rights ABA, Chgo., 1972-74; staff atty., supr. Cambridge (Mass.) Problem Ctr., 1975-76; exec. dir. Vol. Lawyers Project Boston Bar Assn., 1977-85; legal and policy cons. Santa Fe and Washington, 1985—; ind. legal and policy cons. Ford Found., Washington, 1990—96; pres. and CEO Pro Bono Inst., 1996—. Vis. prof. U. N.Mex. Sch. Law, Albuquerque, 1985; cons. Nat. Vets. Legal Svcs. Program, Washington, 1991—; vis. scholar ethics program Boston U. Sch. Law, 1991—92; reporter ABA/Tulane Law Sch., New Orleans, 1988—90; adj. prof. law Georgetown U., Washington. Contbr. Vis. com. U. Chgo. Law Sch., 1992—. Recipient Founder Award, Phila. Bar Assn., 1991, Outstanding Pub. Interest Adv. Award, Nat. Assn. Pub. Interest Law, 1992, Exemplar Award, Nat. Legal Aid and Defender Assn., William Reece Smith Jr. Award, Nat. Assn. Pro Bono Coordinators. Mem.: DC Bar (spl. adv. pub. svc. activities rev. com. 1990—), Nat. Legal Aid and Defenders Assn. (bd. dirs. 1990—), ABA (Ho. of Dels. 1991—, cons. 1974—76, legal cons. postconviction death penalty 1987—96, legal cons. law firm pro bono project 1989—96, bd. gov. 1996—99). Office: Pro Bono Institute at Georgetown Univ Law Ctr 600 New Jersey Ave NW Washington DC 20001

LARDNER, GEORGE, JR., journalist, writer; b. NYC, Aug. 10, 1934; s. George Edmund and Rosetta (Russo) Lardner; m. Rosemary Schalk, July 6, 1957; children: Helen, Edmund, Richard, Charles, Kristin(dec.). AB in Journalism summa cum laude, Marquette U., 1956, MA, 1962. Reporter The Worcester (Mass.) Telegram, 1957—59, The Miami (Fla.) Herald, 1959—63, The Washington Post, 1963—64, 1966—2004, columnist, 1964—65; Pub. Policy fellow Woodrow Wilson Internat. Ctr. for Scholars, 2005. Chmn. bd. Fund for Investigative Journalism, Washington, 1997—. Author: The Stalking of Kristin, 1995; contbg. author Deadlock: The Inside Story of America's Closest Election, 2001. Recipient Byline award, Marquette U., 1967, Front-page Nat. News award, Washington-Balt. Newspaper Guild, 1984, 1986, Pulitzer Prize for feature writing, 1993. Roman Catholic. Home: 5604 32nd St NW Washington DC 20015-1623

LARDNER, HENRY PETERSEN (PETER LARDNER), insurance company executive; b. Davenport, Iowa, Apr. 5, 1932; s. James Francis and Mary Catharine (Decker) L.; m. Marion Cleaveland White, Dec. 28, 1954; children: Elisabeth, Emily, David, Peter, Sarah (dec.). BSE. (Indsl. Engring.), U. Mich., 1954; MA, Augustana Coll., 1982. C.P.C.U. Indsl. engr. Cutler-Hammer, Milw., 1954; Agt. H.H. Cleaveland Agy., Rock Island, Ill., 1956-60; with Bituminous Ins. Cos., Rock Island, 1960—2001, exec. v.p., 1968-72, pres., 1972-95, chmn. and CEO, 1984-2000, chmn., 2000—01; pres. Bitco Corp., Rock Island, 1973-95, chmn. bd. dirs., 1973—2001. Bd. dirs. Old Republic Internat., 1985—; trustee Underwriters Lab., Inc., 1997-2004. Bd. govs. State Colls. and Univs., 1971-80; trustee Black Hawk Coll., 1964-72; mem. Ill. Bd. Higher Edn., 1976-77; chmn. Ill. State Scholarship, 1982-85. Served with AUS, 1954-56. Home: 3227 29th Ave Rock Island IL 61201-5568 E-mail: peter.lardner@verizon.net.

LARDY, HENRY A. (HENRY ARNOLD LARDY), biochemistry professor; b. Roslyn, S.D., Aug. 19, 1917; s. Nicholas and Elizabeth (Gebetsreiter) L.; m. Annrita Dresselhuys, Jan. 21, 1943; children; Nicholas, Diana, Jeffrey, Michael. BS, S.D. State U., 1939, DSc (hon.), 1979; MS, U. Wis., 1941, PhD, 1943. Asst. prof. U. Wis., Madison, 1945-47, assoc. prof., 1947-50, prof., 1950-88, Vilas prof. biol. sci., 1966-88, prof. emeritus, 1988—. Henry Lardy annual lectr. S.D. State U., Brookings, 1985. Edtl. bd. Archives Biochemistry and Biophysics, 1957-60, Jour. Biol. Chemistry, 1958-64, 80-85, Biochem. Preparations, Methods of Biochem. Analysis, Biochemistry, 1962-73, 75-81; contbr. over 450 articles to profl. jours. Pres. Citizens vs McCarthy, Wis., 1950. Recipient Neuberg medal Am. Soc. European Chemists, 1956, Wolf Found. award in Agr., 1981, Nat. award Agrl. Excellence, 1982. Fellow Wis. Acad. Arts and Scis.; mem. Am. Chem. Soc. (chmn. biol. divsn. 1958, Paul-Lewis Labs. award 1949), Am. Soc. Biol. Chemists (pres. 1964, William Rose award 1988), Am. Acad. Arts and Scis. (Amory prize 1984), Am. Philos. Soc., Am. Diabetes Assn., Nat. Acad. Scis., Biochem. Soc. Great Britain, Harvey Soc., Soc. for Study of Reprodn. (Carl Hartman award 1984), The Endocrine Soc., Japanese Biochem. Soc. (hon.), Golden Retriever Club Am. (pres. 1964). Democrat. Achievements include patents for steroid compounds and lab. apparatus. Home: 1829 Thorstrand Rd Madison WI 53705-1052 Office: U Wis 1710 University Ave Madison WI 53726-4087 E-mail: halardy@wisc.edu.

LARDY, NICHOLAS RICHARD, economist, educator; b. Madison, Wis., Apr. 8, 1946; s. Henry Arnold and Annrita (Dresselhuys) Lardy; m. Barbara Jean Dawe, Aug. 29, 1970; children: Elizabeth Brooke, Lillian Henry. BA, U. Wis., 1968; MA, U. Mich., 1972, PhD, 1975. Asst. prof. Yale U., New Haven, 1975-79, assoc. prof., 1979-83, asst. dir. econ. growth ctr., 1979-82, Frederick Frank adj. prof. in internat. trade and fin. Sch. Mgmt., 1997-2000; assoc. prof. U. Wash., Seattle, 1983-85, chair China program, 1984-89, prof., 1985-95, dir. The Henry M. Jackson Sch. Internat. Studies, 1991-95; sr. fellow Brookings Instn., Washington, 1995—2003, Inst. Internat. Econs., Washington, 2003—. Bd. dirs. Nat. Com. U.S.-China Rels., N.Y.C., 1986—, Comm. Internat. Rels. Studies with China, 1989—92, Program Internat. Studies in Asia, 1993—95; chmn. Com. Advanced Study in China; vice chmn. com. scholarly comm. China NAS, Washington, 1991—95; bd. mgrs. Blakemore Found., 1993—95; founding mem. Pacific Coun. Internat. Policy, 1995—; mem. Coun. Fgn. Rels. Author: (book) Economic Growth and Distribution in China, 1978, Agriculture in China's Modern Economic Development, 1983, Foreign Trade and Economic Reform in China, 1978-1990, 1992, China in the World Economy, 1994, China's Unfinished Economic Revolution, 1998, Integrating China into the Global Economy, 2002, (policy study) Economic Policy Toward China in the Post-Reagan Era, 1989; co-author: Prospects for a US-Taiwan Free Trade Agreement, 2004; mem. editl. bd.: The China Quar. (London), China Econ. Rev., Jour. Asian Bus., Jour. Contemporary China. Rsch. fellow, Am. Coun. Learned Socs., 1976, 1978—79, 1989—90, Henry Luce Found., Inc., 1980—82, Faculty Rsch. grantee, Yale U., 1976, 1978. Mem.: Assn. Comparative Econ. Studies (mem. exec. com. 1986—88), Assn. Asian Studies (mem. nominating com. 1986—87), Am. Econ. Assn. Avocations: skiing, squash, tennis, sailing. Home: 2811 Albemarle St NW Washington DC 20008-1037 Office: Inst for Internat Econs 1750 Massachusetts Ave NW Washington DC 20036-1903 Office Phone: 202-328-9000. Business E-Mail: nlardy@iie.com.

LARET, MARK R., school system administrator, health facility executive; BS, regents in Polit. sci., UCLA; M, Haynes in Polit. sci., U. Southern Calif. Asst. dir. UCLA Med. Ctr., 1985, assoc. dir. marketing and planning, 1990, dep. dir., 1994; CEO UCLA Med. Group, 1994, Univ. Calif. Irvine Med. Ctr., Orange, Calif., 1995—2000, exec. dir., 1995; CEO Univ. Calif. San Francisco (UCSF) Med. Ctr., 2000—, Univ. Calif. San Francisco (UCSF) Children's Hosp., 2000—. Exec. com. bd. Univ. Healthcare Consortium; bd. dir. CaloPTIMA, 1997, AAMC Coun of Teaching Hosp. and Health Systems (COTH), 2003—04. Named Orange County Manager of Year, Soc. for Advancement of Mgmt., 1999. Office: Med Ctr Adminstrn Univ Calif San Francisco Box 0296 500 Parnassus Ave MU 509E San Francisco CA 94143-0296 Office Phone: 415-353-2733. Office Fax: 415-353-2765. Business E-Mail: mark.laret@ussfmedctr.org.

LARGE, JOHN ANDREW, library and information service professor; b. Mexborough, Yorkshire, Eng., Mar. 27, 1947; arrived in Can., 1989; s. Gordon and Winifred Mary L.; m. Valerie Merle Wilson, Aug. 30, 1972; children: Amanda Fiona, Kirsty Jane. BSc in Econs., London U., 1968, diploma in libr., 1973; PhD, Glasgow U., Scotland, 1973. Asst. libr. Glasgow U. Libr., 1973-74; libr. Inst. Soviet and East European Studies, Glasgow U., 1974-78; prin. lectr. Coll. Librarianship Wales, Aberystwyth, 1978-89; prof., dir. Grad. Sch. Libr. and Info. Studies McGill U., Montreal, Que., Can., 1989-98, CN-Pratt-Grinstad prof. of info. studies, 1998—. Vice chmn. U.K. Online User Group, London, 1987-89; chmn. Can. Coun. Libr. Schs., 1991-93, 97-98; external examiner U. W.I., 1991-99, U. Ibadan, Nigeria, 1992-95; bd.d irs. Atwater Libr. and Computer Ctr., 1999-2002. Author: The Foreign-Language Barrier, 1983, The Artificial Language Movement, 1985, Japanese edit., 1995, A Modular Curriculum for Information Studies, 1987; co-author: Online Searching: Principles and Practice, 1990, Information Seeking in the Online Age, 1999, Digital Libraries, 2005; editor: Manual of Online Search Strategies, 1988, 3d edit., 2001, CD-ROM Information Products: An Evaluative Guide vol. 1, 1990, vol. 2, 1991, vol. 3, 1992, World Info. Report, 1997, ICT for Library and Information Professionals: A Training Package-Modules 1-6, 2001-02; mem. editl. bd. Jour. Librarianship and Info. Sci., 1992—, Jour. Universal Lang., 2000—, South African Jour. Librs. and Info. Sci., 2002—, Can. Jour. Info. and Libr. Sci., 2003—; editor jour. Edn. for Info., 1983—, Treasures of Islam, 1999, CD-ROM Info. Products, 1993. Rsch. grantee Brit. Libr. R&D Dept., 1981-82, 85-86, European Space Agy., 1983-85, Nat. Libr. Can., 2002; IBM Acad. Info. Exch. fellow, 1991-92, Social Sci. and Humanities Rsch. Coun. fellow, 1991-94, 96-98, 98-99, 2002-05, 2004—; recipient Commemorative medal for 125th Anniversary Confedn. Can., 1992. Avocation: music listening and playing. Office: McGill U Grad Sch Libr and Info Studies 3459 McTavish Montreal PQ Canada H3A 1Y1 E-mail: andrew.large@mcgill.ca.

LARGEN, JOSEPH, retail executive, purchasing agent; b. Union, N.J., June 13, 1940; s. Fred and Wilma Largen; children: Lori, Lisa. BS in Econs, U. Mo., 1963. Mgmt. trainee R.R. Donnelly Corp., Chgo., 1964-67; distbn. mgr., material control and distbn. Warwick Electronic Co., Niles, Ill., 1967-69; with Brodart, Inc., 1969—, v.p. prodn. Williamsport, Pa., 1973-75, exec. v.p., 1975-78, pres., 1978—. Served with USCG, 1963-64. Home: 2000 1st Ave Apt 2602 Seattle WA 98121-2172 Office: Brodart Co 500 Arch St Williamsport PA 17701-7809

LARGENT, STEVEN MICHAEL, telecommunications industry executive, former congressman, former professional football player; b. Tulsa, Sept. 28, 1954; m. Terry Largent; children: Kyle, Kelly, Kramer, Casie BS in biology, U. Tulsa, 1976. Wide receiver Seattle Seahawks, NFL, Kirkland, Wash., 1976-89; player Pro Bowl, 1979, 80, 82, 85-88; mktg. cons. Sara Lee Corp., 1991-94; mem. 103rd-106th Congresses from 1st Okla. dist., Washington, 1995—2002, mem. budget com., mem. health care task force, mem. sci. com., mem. energy & environ. and space & aeronautics subcoms., mem. commerce com.; candidate for Governor, Okla., 2002; pres., CEO Cellular Telecom. & Internet Assn., Washington, 2003—. Mem. commerce com., energy and power subcom., telecomms., trade and consumer protection com., fin. and hazardous materials subcom. Holder NFL record for passes caught in consecutive games, also for career receiving yardage, receptions; named to NFL Hall of Fame, 1995. Republican. Office: Cellular Telecom & Internet Assoc 1250 Connecticut Ave NW Ste 800 Washington DC 20036-2603

LARIONOV, IGOR, professional hockey player; b. Voskresensk, Russia, Dec. 3, 1960; married; 3 children. Left wing Vancouver Canucks, 1985-88, 90-92, Lugano, Switzerland, San Jose Sharks, 1994-96, Detroit Red Wings, 1996-00; center Florida Panthers, 2000—03, New Jersey Devils, 2003—. Mem. Team Russia World Cup of Hockey, 1996; player NHL All-Star Game. Named Soviet Player of Yr., 1987—88; named to 5 All-Star Teams, Ctrl. Red Army. Avocations: travel, tennis, soccer. Office: c/o Florida Panthers One Panther Pkwy Sunrise FL 33323*

LARIVIERE, RICHARD WILFRED, academic administrator, educator; b. Chgo., Jan. 27, 1950; s. Wilfred Francis and Esther Irene Lariviere; m. Janis Anne Worcester, June 5, 1971; 1 child, Anne Elizabeth. BA, U. Iowa, 1972; PhD, U. Pa., 1978. Lectr. U. Pa., Phila., 1978-79; asst. prof. U. Iowa, Iowa City, 1980-82; prof. U. Tex., Austin, 1982—, Ralph B. Thomas Regents prof. Asian studies, 1993—, assoc. v.p., 1995-99, dean Coll. Liberal Arts, 1999—2003. Dir. Sinha & Lariviere Ltd., Austin; founder Doing Bus. in India seminar; cons. Perot Sys. Corp., Dallas, 1993—; bd. dirs. eMR Tech. Ventures; chmn. Coun. Am. Overseas Rsch. Ctrs., Washington; Mossiker chair in humanities, 2003-. Author: Ordeals in Hindu Law, 1981, Narada Smrti, 2003; gen. editor Studies in South Asia. Fellow NEH, 1979-83. Fellow Royal Asiatic Soc.; mem. Am. Oriental Soc., Am. Inst. Indian Studies (sr.fellow 1989, 95, v.p. 1990), Assn. Asian Studies. Lutheran. Home: 3415 Cactus Wren Way Austin TX 78746-6636

LARKAM, BEVERLEY MCCOSHAM, social worker, marriage and family therapist; b. Vancouver, Can., Mar. 3, 1928; arrived in U.S., 1951; d. William Howard and Marjorie Isobel (Jerome) McCosham; children: Elizabeth, Charles, Daphne, Peter, John. A Royal Conservatory of Mus., U. Toronto, Toronto, 1948; BA, U. B.C., Can., 1949; BSW, U. B.C., 1950, MSW, 1951. Bd. cert. diplomate in clin. social work; LCSW; lic. marriage and family therapist, Tex. Psychiat. social worker Brackenridge Hosp., 1952-54; chmn. dept. sr. high. sch. Univ. Presbyn. Ch., Austin, Tex., 1952-55, mem. Christian edn. com., 1961-67, bd. dirs. developing and organizing nursery sch., 1967-70; social worker Counseling-Psychol. Svcs. Ctr., U. Tex., 1971-72; psychiat. social worker, chief supr. Adult, Children's Mental Health Human-Devel. Ctr.-South, Austin, Tex., 1972-79; pvt. practice marriage and family therapy, sex therapy and individual and group psychotherapy Austin, Tex., 1975—. Field supr. Sch. Social Work U. Tex.; cons. in field. Mem. cmty. orgn. to establish classes for mentally retarded children, 1966-68; active City of Austin Commn. for Women, 1978—, chmn., 1982-84, emeritus, 1985—; organizer Austin Assn. for Marriage and Family Therapy, 1980-82, bd. dirs. Tex. Assn. for Marriage and Family Therapy, 1980-82, Nat. Assn. Commns. for Women, 1985-88; vol. usher Austin Symphony Orch. Soc., 1972—; mem. Heritage Soc. Austin, Georgetown Heritage Soc., Women's Symphony League of Austin, Austin Art Mus.; mem. Dean Sch. Social Work, profl. linkage com., 1993—. Mem. NASW, Am. Assn. Marriage and Family Therapy (approved supr., com. on racial, ethnic and cultural diversity 1992-95), Am. Group Psychotherapy Assn. (cert. group psychotherapist), Southwestern Group Psychotherapy Soc. (sr. faculty), Austin Group Psychotherapy Soc., Am. Assn. Sex Educators, Counselors and Therapists (cert. sex therapist, supr.), Acad. Cert. Social Workers, Register Clin. Social Workers, Diplomate Internat. Conf. Advancement of Pvt. Practice of Clin. Social Work, Tex. Soc. for Clin. Social Work (bd. dirs. 1990—, pres. 1997-99), Clin. Social Work Fedn. (fin. chmn. 1998-2000), PEO Sisterhood, Austin Woman's Forum (pres. 1994-95, 2002-03). Presbyterian (elder, session of Univ. Presbyterian Ch. 1997—). Home and Office: 2112 Raleigh Ave Austin TX 78703-2128 also: 207 E 9th St Georgetown TX 78626-5908 Office Phone: 512-476-4182.

LARKIN, BARRY LOUIS, professional baseball player; b. Cin., Apr. 28, 1964; m. Lisa Davis. Student, U. Mich., 1982—85. Baseball player Cin. Reds, 1986—. Named Most Valuable Player, Nat. League, 1995, Rookie of Yr., 1988—95; named to Nat. League All-Star Team, 1988—91, 1993—97, 1999—2000, 2004; recipient Nat. League Gold Glove Award, 1994—96, Silver Slugger Award, 1988—91, 1995—96, 1998—99. Achievements include being first baseball player twice named most valuable player of Big Ten Athletic Conf; receiving two-time All-Am. honors; being a mem. of U.S. Olympic Baseball Team, 1984; being a mem. of World Series Team, 1990. Office: Cin Reds 100 Cinergy Fld Cincinnati OH 45202-3543

LARKIN, CHARLES, political science professor, academic administrator; b. Bayonne, N.J., Apr. 20, 1925; s. Alexander Paul Larkin and Alease Salina Jones; m. Blanche Alvina; children: Sheela, Thomas, Anthony. BA in Arts and Scis., NYU, 1953; MA, Jersey City U., 1967; PhD, Fordham U., 1996. Tchr. Jersey City Schs., 1955—67, Essex County Coll., Newark, 1968—91. Cpl. U.S. Army, 1943—45, Europe. Fellow: Acad. Polit. Sci.; mem.: Essex County Coll. Faculty Assn. (pres. 1983—). Democrat. Avocations: reading, tennis, fishing. Home: 106 Wood St Rutherford NJ 07070 Office Phone: 973-877-3013. E-mail: larkin@essex.edu.

LARKIN, CHARLES BYRNE, neuropsychiatrist; b. Madison, Wis., June 6, 1924; s. Edwin Newcomb and Genevieve (Byrne) L.; m. Irene Louise Schneider, Aug. 30, 1947; children— Lucy J., Charles J., Mary E., Lawrence S., Patrick E., Elizabeth L., Laura J. B.S. in Med. Sci., U. Wis.-Madison, 1947, M.D., 1949. Diplomate Am. Bd. Psychiatry and Neurology (examiner 1976—). Intern Madison Gen. Hosp., 1949-50; resident St. Mary's Hosp., Madison, 1955-57, VA Hosp., Madison, 1957-58, Patton Hosp., San Bernardino, Calif., 1966-69, U. So. Calif./Los Angeles County Med. Ctr., 1969-71; gen. practice medicine, Madison, 1952-55; practice medicine specializing in internal medicine, Madison, 1958-61; physician cons. Calif. Dept. Mental Health, San Bernardino, 1961-72; dir. behavioral sci. San Bernardino Gen. Med. Ctr., 1972-78; physician cons. in neuropsychiatry VA Hosp., Loma Linda, Calif., 1978-82, VA Med. Ctr., Reno, Nev., 1982-85, ret., 1987; assoc. prof. neuropsychiatry Loma Linda U., 1972-78, U. Nev., Reno, 1982-85. Served with USN, 1943-46, capt. USAF, 1950-52, col. USAFR ret. Fellow Am. Psychiat. Assn.; mem. Am. Acad. Neurology, ACP. Roman Catholic. Home: PO Box 5000 Solana Beach CA 92075-5000

LARKIN, EUGENE DAVID, artist, educator; b. Mpls., June 27, 1921; s. John Peter and Martha Lavinia (Vandevere) L.; m. Audrey Jean Krueger, Jan. 29, 1947; children: Andrew, Alan. BA, U. Minn., 1946, MA, 1949. Mem. faculty dept. art Kans. State Coll., Pittsburg, 1949-54; head printmaking dept., chmn. divsn. fine arts Mpls. Sch. Art, 1954-69; prof. design dept. U. Minn., St. Paul, 1969—, prof. emeritus design, housing and apparel, 1991—. One man exhbns. include, Mpls. Inst. Arts, 1957, 60, 68, Syracuse U., 1962, Walker Art Center, Mpls., 1967, New Forms Gallery, Athens, Greece, 1967, U. Kans., 1972, Macalester Coll., 1974, U. Minn., St. Paul, 1973, 78, 87, 91; group exhbns. include, Phila. Printmakers Club, 1966, 20 American Artists, Geneva, Switzerland, 1964, Big Prints, N.Y. U., 1968, Midwestern Printmakers, Walker Art Center, 1973, Cabo Frio Internat. Print Biennial, Brazil, 1983, Nat. Works on Paper, Minot State Coll., 1986, 17th Annual Works on Paper SW State U., San Marcos, Tex., 4th Annual North Coast Coll. Soc. Exhbn., Hiram Coll., Hudson, Ohio, 1988, 20th Annual Works on Paper Dulin Nat. Knoxville, Knoxville Mus. Art, 1988, Paepcke Meml. Bldg. Gallery, 1993, Aspen Inst. and Music Assoc. of Aspen, 1993, U. St. Thomas, Mpls./St. Paul, 1999; represented in permanent collections, Mus. Modern Art, N.Y.C., Nat. Mus. S.Africa, Capetown, Library Congress, Chgo. Art Inst., Mpls. Inst. Arts, U. Minn. Gallery, Des Moines Art Center, U. Tenn., Kans. State Tchrs. Coll., Minn. Mus. Art, Nat. Collection Fine Arts, Smithsonian Instn; author: Design: The Search for Unity, 1988. Recipient juror's award Rockford Internat. Print and Drawing Biennale, 1983 Mem.: Coll. Art Assn. Am. Home: 1010 W Washington South Bend IN 46601 Office Phone: 612-377-2189.

LARKIN, JOAN, poet, literature and language educator; b. Boston, Apr. 16, 1939; d. George Joseph and Celia Gertrude (Rosenberg) Moffitt; m. James A. Larkin, Dec. 23, 1966 (div. 1969); 1 child, Kate. BA, Swarthmore Coll., 1960; MA, U. Ariz., 1969; MFA, Bklyn. Coll., 2005. Asst. prof. English CUNY-Bklyn. Coll., 1969—94, ret., 1994, adj. faculty MFA program, 1997—98; assoc. faculty MFA program Goddard Coll., 1994—96, 2002. Mem. guest faculty poetry writing Sarah Lawrence Coll., Bronxville, NY, 1984—86, 1988, 1997—; mem. core faculty MFA program New Eng. Coll., 2002—. Author: (poems) Housework, 1975, A Long Sound, 1986, Cold River, 1997, (rec. poetry reading) A Sign I Was Not Alone, 1980, (prose) If You Want What We Have, 1998, Glad Day, 1998; co-editor: Gay and Lesbian Poetry in Our Time: An Anthology, 1988 (Lambda Lit. award 1988), Amazon Poetry, 1975, Lesbian Poetry, 1981; editor: A Woman Like That, 1999; co-translator: Sor Juana's Love Poems, 1997; contbr. poems to periodicals including Am. Poetry Rev., Conditions, Ms., Paris Rev., Sinister Wisdom, The Village Voice, Aphra, Endymion, The Lamp in the Spine, Global City Rev., Am. Rev., Genesis West, Sojourner, Margie, Hanging Loose. NEA fellow in poetry,

1987-88, 96, N.Y. Found. for Arts fellow in poetry, 1987-88; Creative Artists Pub. Svc. Program grantee N.Y. State Coun. Arts, 1976, 80; Mass. Cultural Coun. grantee in playwriting, 1995. Personal E-mail: larkin7@earthlink.net.

LARKIN, JOAN See JETT, JOAN

LARKIN, JOHN EDWARD, JR., orthopedic surgeon; b. St. Paul, Nov. 8, 1930; s. John E. and Ann G. (Wedebrand) L.; m. Colles Baxter, June 16, 1981. BS, U. Minn., 1953, MD, 1960. Intern Detroit Receiving Hosp., 1960-61; resident Harvard Surgery Svc./Boston City Hosp., 1961-62, Children's Hosp., Boston, 1963-66, Mass. Gen. Hosp., Boston, 1963-66; pvt. practice St. Paul, 1966-98; emeritus asst. prof. orthopedic surgery U. Minn., 1998—. Pres. Orthop. Surgery, P.A., St. Paul, 1966-98. Bd. dirs. Minn. Coun. for Quality Edn., 1970-79, Minn. Opera, 1974-79, Minn. Mus. Art, St. Paul, 1971-86, 94-95, Irish Am. Cultural Inst., 1974—, U. Minn. Arboretum, 1998—, James Ford Bell Libr., 2000—; trustee Mpls. Inst. of Art, 1980-89; mem. accessions com. Mpls. Inst. Art, 1979—. With U.S. Army, 1953-55. Fellow Am. Bd. Orthop. Surgery; mem. AMA, N.Am. Spine Soc., Minn. State Med. Assn., Minn. Orthop. Soc., Ramsey County Med. Soc., Min-Da-Mann Orthop. Soc., Irish Am. Orthop. Soc., Twin City Orthop. Soc., New Eng. Orthop. Soc. (hon.), Irish Orthop. Soc. (hon.).

LARKIN, LEE ROY, retired lawyer; b. Oklahoma City, Aug. 11, 1928; s. William Patrick and Agnes (Matthis) L.; m. Mary Jane Langston, Apr. 17, 1965; children— James William, John Patrick (dec.). BS, Oklahoma A&M U., Stillwater, 1950; MA, Vanderbilt U., 1952; LLB, William Mitchell U., St. Paul, 1959. Bar: Minn. 1959, Tex. 1963, D.C. 1963. Economist U.S. Dept. Agr., Washington, 1953; economist, lawyer Pillsbury, Mpls., 1953-62; ptnr. Harris & Larkin, Houston, 1963-65; sr. ptnr. Andrews & Kurth, Houston, 1966-93; retired, 1994. Speaker Continuing Legal Edn. Officer Sharpstown Civic Assn., Houston, 1966-94; elder St. Philip Presbyn. Ch., Houston; moderator Presbytery of New Covenant, Houston, 1980. Served to capt. USAR, 1951-58. Fellow Tex. Bar Found., Houston Bar Found.; mem. ABA, State Bar Tex., Houston Bar Assn., Riverbend Country Club, Rotary (pres. 1978-79), Delta Theta Phi. Avocations: golf, tennis, travel. Home: 3725 Wickersham Ln Houston TX 77027-4013

LARKIN, MICHAEL JOHN, editor, journalist; b. Boston, Sept. 27, 1950; s. Alfred Sinnott and Lillian Louise L.; m. Sarah Jane Wood, July 6, 1970 (div. 1985); children— Jonathan Michael, Joshua Stuart; m. Alison Rose Biggs, June 1, 1986. BA in English, U. Mass., 1973. News copy editor Boston Globe, 1974-76, sports copy editor, 1976-80, asst. bus. editor, 1980-82, Sunday editor, 1982, mag. editor, 1982-85, living/arts editor, 1985-89, sr. asst. met. editor zoned editions, 1989-92, Sunday editor, 1992-95, asst. mng. editor, 1995-2000, dep. mng. editor/news ops., 2001—. Contbr. BBC, 1997-99. Mem., editl. com., New England Newspaper Assn., 1998—. Office: Boston Globe PO Box 2378 Boston MA 02107-2378

LARKIN, THOMAS ERNEST, JR., investment management company executive; b. Wilkes-Barre, Pa., Sept. 29, 1939; s. Thomas Ernest and Margaret (Gorman) L.; m. Margaret Givan, Nov. 2, 1979; 1 child, Thomas Ernest III. BA in Econs., U. Notre Dame, 1961; postgrad., Grad. Sch. Bus., NYU, 1962-66. New bus. rep. Mfrs. Hanover Trust Co., 1963-66; mgr. pension dept. Eastman Dillon, Union Securities, 1966-69; v.p. Shearson Hayden Stone, Inc., N.Y.C., 1969-75; sr. v.p. Bernstein Macaulay Inc., N.Y.C., 1969-75, Crocker Investment Mgmt. Corp., San Francisco, 1975-77, Trust Co. of the West, L.A., 1977, mng. dir., 1982—, pres., COO, 1989-2000; vice chmn. The TCW Group, Inc., 2000—. Trustee U. Notre Dame, Loyola Marymount U., Mt. St. Mary's Coll., Childrens Hosp. L.A., Orthopaedic Hosp. Found., Amateur Athletic Found. of LA, Heart and Lung Surgery Found., Town Hall LA. With U.S. Army, 1961-63. Mem. Assn. Investment Mgmt. Sales Execs., Investment Counsel Assn. Am., Calif. Club, Jonathan Club, Wilshire Country Club, Regency Club, Olympic Club, N.Y. Athletic Club, Westchester Country Club, LA Country Club. Republican. Roman Catholic. Office: TCW Group 865 S Figueroa St Ste 1800 Los Angeles CA 90017-2593

LARKIN, WILLIAM VINCENT, JR., corporate financial executive; b. NYC, July 19, 1953; s. William Vincent and Gloria Ann (Stone) L.; m. Margaret Catherine Gunn, Nov. 12, 1988; children: William Vincent III, Jeremy Stone. AB cum laude, Harvard U., 1976; MBA, Yale U., 1980. Intern White House, 1975; staff acct. Price Waterhouse & Co., N.Y.C., 1976-78; mktg. asst. AMF Ben Hogan Co., Ft. Worth, 1980-81; asst. to pres. AMF Biol. & Diagnostic Co., Seguin, Tex., 1981-82; mktg. mgr. AMF Tuboscope, Houston, 1982-83, mgr. mill divsn., 1983-84; v.p. Tuboscope Inc., Houston, 1984-91; pres., COO Tuboscope Vetco Internat., Houston, 1991-93, pres., CEO, 1993-96; pres., COO Galtney Group, Inc., Houston, 1996-98; pres., CEO Travis Internat., Inc., Houston, 1999—2002; pres. The Six Stars Club, Houston, 2003—. Bd. dirs. Family Svcs. Greater Houston; trustee Groton Sch., 2000-02, Young Pres. Orgn., 1992-2004. Mem. World Pres.' Orgn., Yale Sch. Mgmt. Alumni Assn. (chmn. nominating com. 1980-82), A.D. Club (Cambridge, Mass.), Harvard Club (NYC), Yale Club (NYC), River Oaks Country Club. Republican. Episcopalian. Avocations: woodworking, golf, tennis. Home: 369 Pineypoint Rd Houston TX 77024 Office Phone: 713-333-7827. E-mail: wvlarkin@sixstarsclub.com.

LARLEE, CHRISTOPHER, quality assurance professional; Cert. in Automatic Sprinkler Systems, Nat. Fire Protection Assn.; studied NYC Fire Suppression Codes and Installations, Troise Vocat. Sch. Master Fire Suppression Contractors Lic. NYC, Fire Suppression Lic. State of NJ, cert. fire protection specialist Nat. Fire Protection Assn., EPA cert., Plumbers' Apprentice cert. TBPE, Electricians' Apprentice Cert. TDLR. Facilities/contract mgr. various major retail stores, Staten Island, NY, 1979—86; project supervisor The Main Connection, Inc., Staten Island, 1986—99; adminstr., owner Main Connection NY, Inc., Howell, NJ, 1999—2005; purchasing/project support Comml. Consol. Inc., Georgetown, Tex., 2005—. Mem.: Soc. Fire Protection Engrs., Nat. Fire Protection Assn. (participating mem. in healthcare and bldg. fire safety systems sections), Internat. Code Coun.

LARO, DAVID, federal judge; b. Flint, Mich., Mar. 3, 1942; s. Samuel and Florence (Chereton) L.; m. Nancy Lynn Wolf, June 18, 1967; children: Rachel Lynn, Marlene Ellen. BA, U. Mich., 1964; JD, U. Ill., 1967; LLM, NYU, 1970 Bar: Mich. 1968, U.S. Dist. Ct. (ea. dist.) Mich. 1968, U.S. Tax Ct. 1971. Ptnr. Winegarden Booth Shedd and Laro, Flint, Mich., 1970-75; sr. ptnr. Laro and Borgerson, Flint, 1975-86; prin. David Laro, P.C., Flint, 1986-92; judge U.S. Tax Ct., Washington, 1992—. Of counsel Dykema Gossett, Ann Arbor, Mich., 1989-90; pres., CEO, Durakon Industries, Inc., Ann Arbor, 1989-91, chmn., Lapeer, Mich., 1991—; chmn. Republic Bank, 1986—, vice chmn. Republic Bancorp, Inc., Flint, 1986—; instr. Nat. Inst. Trial Advocacy, vis. prof. U. San Diego Law Sch., adj. prof. law Georgetown Law Sch., 1994—; cons. lectr. on tax reform and litigation in Moscow Harvard U., 1997, Ga. State U., 1998. Regent U. Mich., Ann Arbor, 1975-81; mem. Mich. State Bd. Edn., 1982-83; chmn. Mich. State Tenure Commn., 1972-75; commr. Civil Svc. Commn., Flint, 1984—. Mem. Am. Coll. Tax Counsel, State Bar Mich., Phi Delta Phi. Republican. Office: US Tax Ct 400 2nd St NW Rm 217 Washington DC 20217-0002

LA ROCCA, ISABELLA, artist, educator; b. El Paso, Apr. 14, 1960; d. Remo and Alicia Estela (Gonzalez) La Rocca. BA, U. Pa., 1984; MFA, Ind. U., 1993. Freelance photographer, N.Y.C., 1986—90; assoc. instr. Ind. U., Bloomington, 1991—93; instr. Herron Sch. Art, Indpls., 1992; vis. asst. prof. Ind. U., 1994—; asst. prof. DePauw U., Greencastle, Ind., 1994—95; vis. asst. prof. Bloomsburg (Pa.) U., 1995—96; freelance photographer, designer, animator San Francisco, 1996—. Instr. art Vista C.C., 1998—, Coll. of Marin, 1999—2000, Calif. State U., Hayward, 1999—2001, City Coll. San Francisco, 2000—. One-woman shows include Haas Gallery, Bloomsburg, 1996, Ctr. Photography Woodstock, N.Y., Moore Coll., Pa., 1994, Emison Art Ctr., Greencastle, 1996, exhibited in group shows at 494 Gallery, N.Y.C., 1993, Kala Art Inst., Berkeley, Calif., 2000; prodr., dir.: (films) Mariana of the Universe, 2004. Ind. U. CIC Minority fellow, 1990-91; Jewish Found. Edn. Women scholar, 1990; recipient Friends of Photography Ferguson award, 1993, Serpent Source Grant for Women Artists, 1998. Personal E-mail: ilr@isabellalarocca.com.

LA ROCCA, PHILLIP R., lawyer, educator; b. Newark, Sept. 25, 1934; s. Raymond O. La Rocca and Susan Kauchek; m. Teresa Louise Garcia, Aug. 11; children: Lisa, Dominic. JD, Southwestern U. Law, L.A., 1965. Assoc. prof. law Chapman U., Palm Desert, 1988—; legal liaison to Azerbaijan ABA, 1999—2000. With USN, 1951—55, Europe. Named Judge of Yr., Riverside County Bar Assn., 1978, Inland Empire Bar Assn., 1978, Desert Bar Assn., Coachella Valley, Calif., 1980—81. Avocations: reading, golf. Office: 44489 Town Center Way Palm Desert CA 92260 E-mail: judgel@aol.com.

LA ROCCO, ANTHONY P., lawyer; BA magna cum laude, Rutgers Univ., 1979; JD, Seton Hall Univ., 1982. Bar: N.J. 1982, N.Y. 1983, US Dist. Ct. (N.J., so. & ea. N.Y.), US Ct. Appeals (3d cir.). Adminstrv. ptnr. & mem. mgmt. com. Kirkpatrick & Lockhart Nicholson Graham LLP, Newark. Mem.: ABA, Def. Rsch. Inst., N.J. State Bar Assn., Nat. Diocesan Attorneys Assn., Essex County Bar Assn., Assn. Knights & Ladies of Equestrian Order of Holy Sepulchre of Jerusalem, Phi Beta Kappa, Phi Alpha Theta. Office: Kirkpatrick & Lockhart Nicholson Graham LLP 10th Fl One Newark Ctr Newark NJ 07102-5252 Office Phone: 973-848-4014. Office Fax: 973-848-4001. Business E-Mail: alarocco@klng.com.

LAROCHE, LYNDA, artist, educator; Asst. prof. Indiana U. of Pa., 1997—. Exhibitions include include Contemporary Arts Ctr., Cin., 1991, exhibitions include Am. Craft Mus., N.Y.C., 1991, Swidler Gallery, Royal Oak, Mich., 1991—92, Nat. Ornamental Metal Mus., Memphis, 1992, 1993, 1997, Aaron Faber Gallery, N.Y.C., 1993, Artifacts Gallery, Indpls., 1993, Fine Arts Gallery, Bloomington, 1993, Arrowmont Sch. Arts and Crafts, Gatlinburg, Tenn., 1994—96, Renwick Gallery/Mus. Shop, Washington, 1994, Montgomery Coll. Art Gallery, Rockville, Md., 1996, Shipley Gallery, Gateshead, Eng., 1996, Cleve. Craft Ctr., Middlesborough, Eng., 1997, Seafirst Gallery, Seattle, 1998, numerous others. Fellow Visual Artist fellow, Nat. Endowment Arts, 1988—89, Master Summer fellow, Ind. Arts Com. and Nat. Endowment Arts, 1984, 1987, Visual Artists fellow, S.D. Arts Coun. and Nat. Endowment Arts, 1993. Mem.: Soc. N.A. Goldsmiths, Coll. Arts Assn., Soc. Am. Silversmiths (Disting. mem.). Office: Indiana U Pa Dept Art 324 Sprowls Hall 470 S 11th St Indiana PA 15705-1044

LAROCHELLE, PATRICIA ANNE, technologist; b. Bath, Maine, Apr. 21, 1952; d. Oliver George and Minnie V. (Dinsmore) Wass; m. Marc Joseph Larochelle, Feb. 23, 1974; children: Meghan Joy Larochelle Melville, Robert Oliver. BA in Med. Tech., U. Maine, 1976. Med. technologist chemistry Maine Med. Ctr., Portland, 1976—80, asst. chemistry supr., 1980—83; supr. Park Ave. lab. Oncology, Hematology Assocs., Portland, 1983—85; med. technologist Diamed/Diaexport, Windham, Maine, 1987—90, Westbrook (Maine) Cmty. Hosp., 1990—99; sr. med. technologist Mercy Westbrook Lab., Mercy Hosp., 1999—. Sec. Maine chpt. Am. Soc. Med. Technologists, 1981—83, del. Maine to nat. convs., 1981—82; fund-raiser, mem. Windham Youth Football, 1999—2003; videographer Windham H.S. Football, 2000—; bd. dirs. Little Sebago Lake Assn., Maine, 1996—97. Mem.: Am. Soc. Clin. Pathologists (registrant). Avocations: gardening, kayaking, shopping, walking. Office: Mercy Westbrook Lab 40 Park Rd Westbrook ME 04092 E-mail: larochellep@mercyme.com.

LA ROCQUE, EUGENE PHILIPPE, bishop emeritus; b. Windsor, Ont., Can., Mar. 27, 1927; s. Eugene Joseph and Angeline Marie (Monforton) LaR. BA, U. Western Ont., 1948; MA, Laval U., 1956. Ordained priest Roman Cath. Ch., 1952, consecrated bishop 1974. Asst. parish priest Ste. Therese Ch., Windsor, 1952-54; registrar, then dean men, lectr. Christ The King Coll., U. Western Ont., 1956-64; asst. spiritual dir. St. Peter's Sem., 1964-65; prin., dean King's Coll., 1965-68; pastor St. Joseph's Ch., Rivière-aux-Canards, Canada, 1968-70, Ste. Anne's Ch., Tecumseh, 1970-74; bishop of Alexandria-Cornwall, Canada, 1974—2002; bishop emeritus, 2002—. Dean Essex County, 1970-73; trustee Essex County Roman Cath. Separate Sch. Bd., 1972-74; 1st chmn. liaison com. Can. Jewish Congress Can. Coun. Chs. and Can. Cath. Conf. Bishops, 1977-84, mem. pro-life com., 1992-94; pres. Ont. Conf. Cath. Bishops, 1992-96; pres. Fedn. Couns. Priests of Can., 1973-74. Mem. KC (3d degree, chaplain Ont. 1977-87). Roman Catholic. Address: St Joseph Parish 9399 Townline Rd Windsor ON Canada N9J 2W6 E-mail: stjosephrc@rcec.london.on.ca. *Belief in God, who creates my unique human life and has a loving plan and concern for each of his children, sustains me amidst the strains, challenges and turmoils of life.*

LAROCQUE, LINDA LOU, interior designer, educator, playwright; b. Lake Odessa, Mich., May 10, 1944; d. Emory Eugene and Lillian Martha Blakslee; m. Robert Bonte, Feb. 29, 1980 (div. May 15, 1989); 1 child, Timothy; m. Raymond John LaRocque, 1960 (div. 1977). Interior design educator Kalamazoo Valley Coll., Kalamazoo, Mich., 1973—77; interior designer Jacobson Store Home, Kalamazoo, Mich., 1974—76; owner, operator Linda LaRocque Interiors, Kalamazoo, Mich., 1976—99; interior design educator Civic and Art Groups throughout Mich. and Fla., 1973—. Author: (play) Aint Tina Turner Classical Music (Second Pl., 1998), Revival at Possum Creek Community Church (Second Pl., 99), Joyce's Choices (First Pl., 2000); contbr. short stories to various publs. including Guideposts, Signs of the Times, Chicken Soup for the Soul and others. Active Ministry Cmty., Kalamazoo, Mich., 1991—97, Mich. Maritime Mus., South Haven, Mich., 1994—99. Recipient Writer of the Yr., Am. Christian Writers Assn., 1997, Second Pl. Prodn., Mich. Play Festival, 1997, Third Pl. Prodn., 2001, 1st pl. playwriting award, Nat. League Am. Pen Women Ark. Writers Conf., 2005. Mem.: South Haven Ctr. Arts, Douglas Writers Club, Cmty. Theatre Assn. Mich., Am. Pen Women, Scott Club Writers Group. R-Consevative. Roman Catholic. Avocations: rehabilitating distressed real estate, gardening, cooking, music, theater. Home: 118 Superior Street South Haven MI 49090 Address: 3610 S Ocean Blvd Palm Beach FL 33480 Office Phone: 269-637-3416, 561-202-9919.

LAROIA, RAJIV, communications executive; B in EE, Indian Inst. Tech., 1985; MS, U. Md., College Park, 1989, PhD, 1992. With Mathematical Scis. Rsch. Ctr. Lucent Technologies Bell Laboratories, 1992, head Bell Labs' Digital Comm. Rsch. Dept., Wireless Rsch. Ctr., 1997; founder, CTO Flarion Technologies, Inc., Bedminster, NJ, 2000—. Lectr. in the field. Assoc. editor: IEEE Transactions on Information Theory; contbr. to numerous publs. Fellow: IEEE. Generated over 35 patents (granted and applied); Flarion's FLASH-OFDM® technology which originated in Bell Labs under his leadership and his wireless team in early 1998. Flarion was created to commercialize that technology. Office: Flarion Technologies Inc Bedminster One 135 Rt 202/206 S Bedminster NJ 07921

LA ROSA, FRANCISCO GUILLERMO, pathologist, researcher, educator; b. Lima, Peru, Jan. 17, 1949; came to U.S., 1981; s. Anibal and Carmen (de la Pascua) La R.; m. Clara Ann Duffiey, May 21, 1989; children: David, Anamaria, Joseph, MarieCarmen. MD, U. Nacional Federico Villarreal, Lima, 1975. cert. (AP/CP), 1995. Instr. U. Nacional Federico Villarreal, Lima, 1973-79, asst. prof., 1979-81; resident in clin. pathology U. de San Marcos, Lima, 1977-79; postdoctoral fellow in immunology U. Colo., Denver, 1981-85, instr., 1985-87, asst. prof., 1987—92, resident in pathology, 1992-95, fellow in lung pathology, 1995-96; lab. dir. Miners Colfax Med. Ctr., Raton, N.Mex., 1996—2000; clin. asst. prof. dept path., immunology U. Colo. Health Sci. Ctr., 1996—2002, asst. prof. prostate cancer rsch. lab, dept. pathology, 2002—. Pathologist Sterling Regional Med. Ctr., 1996-2000, Longmont (Colo.) United Hosp., 2002-03; pres. Pathology Cons., PC, 1995—, Telepathology Cons., PC, 1996—; cons. Ortho Pharm., Lima, 1979-81, Reaads Med. Products, Inc., Denver, 1991; bd. dirs. comm. Christian Life Movement, Denver; webmaster U. Colo. Health Sci. Ctr., Dept. Pathology, 2005—. Contbr. chpts. to books, revs. and articles to profl. jours. Krock Found. fellow, 1985-86, Juvenile Diabetes Found. fellow, 1985-86; NIH grantee, 1988-91; recipient award Diabetes Rsch. and Edn. Found., 1987-88; hon. prof. U. Nat. Federico Villareal, 2003. Mem. Coll. Am. Pathologists, Transplantation Soc., Soc. Española Immunologia, Am. Assn. Immunologists, Am. Soc. Clin. Pathologists, Am. Telemedicine Assn., Peruvian Soc. Clin. Pathology, Peruvian Soc. Immunology and Allergy, Colo Med. Soc. Roman Catholic. Avocations: photography, videotaping, web page design, telepathology. Home: 2663 S Nelson Ct Lakewood CO 80227-2767 Office: U Colo HSC Fitzsimmons Porstate Cacncer Rsch Lab Stop 8104 PO Box 6511 Aurora CO 80045-0508 Office Phone: 303-724-3782. Business E-Mail: francisco.larosa@uchsc.edu. E-mail: flarosa@telepathology.com.

LAROSE, KATHERINE STENCEL, music educator; b. Croswell, Mich., Oct. 3, 1945; d. Jacob Stanley and Catherine Marie Stencel; m. Alan Roger La Rose; children: Renee Catherine, Alan Gregory. MusB, We. Mich. U., 1969; MusM, U. Massn., 1971. Tchg. asst. U. Mass., Amherst, Mass., 1969—71, lectr. piano, 1972—80; pvt. piano tchr. San Lorenzo, Calif., 1981—87, Fremont, Calif., 1987—. Dir., organist St. Christopher's Episc. Ch., San Lorenzo, 1993—2000; dir. music St. Barnabas Ch., Alameda, Calif., 2000—. Musician: numerous recitals, 1963—, Isabella Stewart Gardner Mus., 1974—. Mem.: Music Tchrs. Assn. Calif. (coord. theory site, bd. dirs. 1984—2004), Am. Guild Organists. Home: 4265 Jacinto Dr Fremont CA 94536 Office: St Barnabas Church 1427 Sixth St Alameda CA 94501

LAROSE, LAWRENCE ALFRED, lawyer; b. Lowell, Mass., Oct. 26, 1958; s. Alfred M. and Rita B. (Plunkett) L.; m. Janet G. Yedwab, Aug. 12, 1984. BA summa cum laude, Tufts U., 1980; JD magna cum laude, Georgetown U., 1983. Bar: N.Y. 1984. Assoc. Sullivan & Cromwell, N.Y.C., 1983-85, 87-90, Melbourne, Australia, 1985-87, Cadwalader, Wickersham & Taft, N.Y.C., 1990-92, ptnr., 1993-2001; ptnr., co=head fin. restructuring group King & Spalding, N.Y.C., 2001—. Vis. fellow Faculty of Law, U. Melbourne, 1986-87. Co-author: Public Companies, 2002; contbr. articles to profl. publs. Mem. adv. bd. NAD, N.Y.C. Mem. ABA, N.Y. State Bar Assn., N.Y. County Lawyers Assn., Assn. Bar City N.Y., Am. Soc. Internat. Law, Georgetown U. Nat. Law Alumni Bd. (exec. com., sec.), Down Town Assn. in City of N.Y., Union League Club, Phi Beta Kappa. Avocations: art collecting, art history. Office: King & Spalding 1185 Ave of the Americas New York NY 10036-4003

LAROSE, MELBA LEE, performing company executive, actress, playwright, theater director; d. Kenneth Lee and Melba Lauren LaRose; m. Elson Jose de Faria, July 14, 1987. AAS in Bus. Mgmt., SUNY, Cobleskill, 1962; at, HB Studios, N.Y.C., 1963—65, Free U. of L.A., 1972—74; pvt. tng., Acting, Dance, Voice, N.Y.C., 1977—90. Freelance actress, playwright, dir., N.Y.C., 1965—; actress, playwright and dir. Group Repertory Theatre, L.A., 1972—76; adminstrv. asst., fundraiser and actress N.Y. St. Theatre Caravan, N.Y.C., 1990—96; adminstrv. asst. The Actors Studio, N.Y.C., 1992—94; founder, artistic and adminstrv. dir. N.Y. Artists Unlimited, Inc., N.Y.C., 1982—, Downeast Arts Ctr., 2004—. Panelist A.R.T. New York, Lower Manhattan Cultural Coun., Theatre Resources Unlimited, N.Y.C., 2000—; fulbright sr. specialist roster candidate Coun. for Internat. Exch. of Scholars, Washington, 2002—. Playwright-director: (plays) Rime Ice; Who's There?; Voices of the Town - A Vaudeville Salute; Song of the Simple Truth; actor, playwright, dir.: (3 one-act plays) Cityscapes 3; (plays) Little Red - Girl from the Hood; actor, playwright A Builder of Dreams, based on the poems & life of Myrtle Evelyn Lawrence (1893-1963); Tables I Have Danced On; actor: La Ronde, The Love of Don Perlimplin & Belisa in the Garden, Glamour, Glory & Gold (the Life & Legend of Nola Noonan, Goddess & Star), Blues in Rags, The Grand Inquisitor; (films) Eyes of a Blue Dog (Best Actress - Town Hall's First Run Film Festival, 1994), Dadetown, Working Girl; (plays) Lucky Wonderful, Sganarelle, The Fugitives, The Adding Machine; dir.: The Prince & The Moon. Recipient Disting. Alumnus award, SUNY, 1987; grantee, Fund for Creative Cmtys., Lower Manhattan Cultural Coun., 1998—, Nancy Quinn Fund, 1998—, N.Y.C. Dept. of Cultural Affairs, 1999—, Puffin Found., 1999—, N.Y. Coun. for Humanities, 1999—, NEA, 2003, Gannett Found., 2004—. Mem.: AFTRA, SAG, Actors' Equity Assn., Dramatists Guild of Am., Drama League, Theatre Resources Unlimited, Alliance of Resident Theatres N.Y., Phi Theta Kappa. Avocation: travel. Office: NY Artists Unlimited Inc Ste #2A 212 W 14 Street New York NY 10011 Office Phone: 212-228-2886. E-mail: nyartunltd@aol.com.

LAROUCHE, LYNDON H., JR., economist; b. Rochester, NH, Sept. 8, 1922; s. Lyndon H. Sr. and Jesse (Weir) LaRouche; m. Helga Zepp, 1977; 1 child, Daniel Vincent. Student, Northeastern U., 1940—42, Student, 1946—47. Mgmt. cons., 1947—48, 1952—72; founder, contbg. editor Exec. Intelligence Rev., 1974—; co-founder Fusion Energy Found., 1975—87, bd. dirs., 1981—87; chmn. adv. com. Nat. Dem. Policy Com., 1980-83; founder Lyndon LaRouche Polit. Action Com., 2004—. Host weekly news and info. TV program The LaRouche Connection; presdl. candidate US Labor Party, 1976, Dem. Party, 1980, 84, 88, 92, 96, 2000, 04; candidate for US Repr 10th Congl. Dist Va., 1990. Author: (books) Dialectical Economics, 1975, Power of Reason: A Kind of Autobiography, 1979, How to Defeat Liberalism and William F. Buckley, 1979, Will the Soviets Rule in the 1980s?, 1979, Basic Economics for Conservative Democrats, 1980, What Every Conservative Should Know About Communism, 1980, Why Revival of "SALT" Won't Stop War, 1980, The Ugly Truth About Milton Friedman, 1980, There Are No Limits to Growth, 1983, Imperialism: The Final Stage of Bolshevism, 1984, So, You Wish To Learn All About Economics?, 1984, Power of Reason- 1988: An Autobiography, 1987, In Defense of Common Sense, 1989, The Science of Christian Economy, 1991, Now, Are You Ready to Learn Economics?, 2000, The Economics of Noösphere, 2001, others, numerous pamphlets and articles. Served U.S. Army, WWII, Myitkyina, Burma & Calcutta, India. Mem.: Universal Ecol. Acad., Moscow, Internat. Club of Life, Schiller Inst. Office: care Exec Intelligence Rev PO Box 17390 Washington DC 20041-0390*

LAROUNIS, GEORGE PHILIP, manufacturing executive, director; b. Bklyn., Mar. 19, 1928; s. Philip John and Helen (Cormentelou) L.; m. Mary G. Efthymiatou, Jan. 13, 1958; 1 child, Daphne H. B.E.E., U. Mich., 1950, postgrad. in Law; JD, N.Y. U., 1954. Electronics engr. in research and devel. Columbia U. Electronics Research Lab., 1952-54; assoc. firm Pennie, Edmonds, Morton, Barrows & Taylor, N.Y.C., 1954-58; fgn. patent atty. Western Electric Co., N.Y.C., 1958-60; asst. dir. Bendix Internat., Paris, 1960, dir. licensing and indsl. property rights, to 1974; v.p. staff ops. Bendix Europe, 1974-77; v.p. Bendix Internat. Fin. Corp.; v.p. Europe, Middle East and Africa Bendix Corp., Paris, 1977-82; pres. Bendix Internat. Cons. Corp., 1974-86; v.p., group exec. Allied Automotive, 1982-85; pres. Allied-Signal Fibers Europe S.A.; v.p. Allied-Signal Internat., 1985-93. Bd. dirs. Hellenic Link, Inc., CopyTele, Inc., Delphi Soc., Am. Farm Sch., Greece. With U.S. Army, 1946-47. Decorated chevalier Legion of Honor (France). Mem. N.Y. Patent Bar Assn., Fed. Patent Bar Assn., Licensing Execs. Soc., Am. C. of C. in France and Greece (dir., pres., exec. com. European Coun.), PanHellenic Sci.-Culture Union, Polo Club de Paris, Papagou Tennis Club (Athens), Tau Beta Pi, Eta Kappa Nu. Home: 15-17 A Tsoha St Athens 11521 Greece E-mail: mglar@otenet.gr.

LARPENTEUR, JAMES ALBERT, JR., lawyer; b. Seattle, Aug. 6, 1935; s. James Albert and Mary Louise (Coffey) L.; m. Hazel Marie Arntson, Apr. 23, 1965 (div. 1983); children: Eric James, Jason Clifford; 1 adopted child, Brenda Mon Fong; m. Katherine Annette Bingham, Nov. 8, 1986. BS in Bus., U. Oreg., 1957, LLB, 1961. Bar: Oreg. 1961, U.S. Dist. Ct. Oreg. 1961, U.S. Tax Ct. 1962, U.S. Ct. Appeals (9th cir.) 1962, U.S. Supreme Ct. 1965. Assoc. Schwabe Williamson & Wyatt, Portland, Oreg., 1961-69, ptnr., 1969-82, sr. ptnr., 1982—2002, mem. exec. com., 1989—93, ret., 2003. Dir. exec. com. Portland Rose Festival Assn., 1975—2004, pres., 1987; ex-officio dir. Portland Visitors Assn., 1981—; bd. dirs., mem. exec. com. Providence Child Ctr. Found., 1983—94, chmn. exec. com., 1986—87; bd. dirs. Willamette Light Brigade, 1987—, Cath. Charities Portland, 1989—92, Albertina Kerr Ctrs., 1996—2003, Japanese Garden Soc., 2000—. Mem.: Oreg. Bar Assn. (chmn. bus. law sect. 1986—87, editor, writer, spkr. numerous continuing legal edn. programs, real estate, alternate dispute resolution, securities regulation sects), Thunderbird Country Club of Rancho Mirage, City Club of Portland, Waverley Country Club, Univ. Club of Portland, Multnomah Athletic Club (pres. 1984). Avocation: golf. Office: Schwabe Williamson & Wyatt 1211 SW 5th Ave Ste 1800 Portland OR 97204-3713 Office Phone: 503-796-2920.

LARR, PETER, retired bank executive; b. Indpls., Jan. 17, 1939; s. David and Marjorie Kathleen (Hearne) L.; m. Rosamond Holmes Woodfield, July 7, 1962; children— Alexia Aisha, Diana Kirsten, David Hearne BA, Princeton U., 1960. Asst. mgr. London and Beirut brs. Chase Manhattan Bank, 1961-67, v.p., div. exec. land transp., 1976-78, v.p., group exec. credit tng. and devel., 1978-80, v.p., div. exec. commodity fin., 1980-83; sr. v.p., bus. exec. nat. corr. banking Chase Manhattan Bank, N.Y.C., 1983-85, sr. v.p., exec. domestic instl. banking, 1985-90, sr. v.p., risk asset rev. exec., 1990-97, sr. v.p. sr. credit and porfolio mgmt. exec. Asia Hong Kong, 1997—; mgr. dir. group credit officer Global Bank, 1997-2000; ret., 2000—. Assoc. vestry Christ Ch., Rye, N.Y., 1983-85; planning commr., City of Rye, 1992-94, 97—, human rights commr., 2001—. Mem. Assn. Res. City Bankers (assoc., bank pay sys. com. 1984-90), Am. Bankers Assn. (chmn. corp. banking divsn. 1988-94), Robert Morris Assn. N.Y. (pres. 1994), Am. Yacht Club, Apawamis Club. Avocations: tennis, golf, geneaological rsch.

LARRABEE, BARBARA PRINCELAU, retired intelligence officer; b. Oakland, Calif., Sept. 21, 1923; d. Paul and Mary Emilie (Rueger) Princelau; m. John Joseph Boyle, Oct. 21, 1950 (dec.); m. Donald Richard Larrabee, Nov. 2, 1996. BA, U. Calif., Berkeley, 1948. Intelligence officer CIA, Langley, Va., 1954-82. Bd. dirs. The Thift Shop, Washington, 1988-92; mem. Women's Bd. Columbia Hosp. for Women, Washington, 1986-2001, mem. exec. com., 1989-91, 96-98; mem. com. Washington Antiques Show, 1989—; active Rep. Womens Fed. Forum, Washington, League of Rep. Women of D.C., Inc. Recipient Cert. of Distinction CIA, 1982. Mem.: Assn. Former Intelligence Officers (bd. dirs. 1993—99, v.p. 1997—99, exec. com. 1997—99), Ctrl. Intelligence Retiree Assn., Evergreen Garden Club (v.p. 2001—02), Sulgrave Club, Nat. Press Club, U. Calif. Berkeley Alumni Club of Washington (rec. sec. 1976—77, v.p. 1984—86), Sigma Kappa (v.p. No. Va. alumnae 1992—95, devel. com. Sigma Kappa Found., Inc. 1993—95). Episcopalian. Avocations: aerobics, needlecrafts, travel. Home: 4956 Sentinel Dr Apt 304 Bethesda MD 20816-3562

LARRABEE, DONALD RICHARD, publishing company executive; b. Portland, Maine, Aug. 8, 1923; s. Henry Carpenter and Marion (Clapp) L.; m. Mary Elizabeth Rolfs, Oct. 9, 1948 (dec. Feb. 1996); children: Donna Louise (Mrs. John Palmer), Robert Rolfs; m. Barbara Princelau Boyle, Nov. 2, 1996. Student, Syracuse U., 1941-43. Reporter Portland Press Herald, 1941-43, Syracuse Post Standard, 1943; reporter Griffin-Larrabee News Bur., Washington, 1946-54, mng. editor, 1954-67, bur. chief, 1967-69, owner, 1969-78; dir. Washington office, State of Maine, 1978-89. Dir. Nat. Press Bldg. Corp., 1973-85 Bd. dirs. Nat. Press Found., 1978— . Served with USAAF, 1943-45. Mem.: Assn. Former Intelligence Officers (bd. dirs. 1999—2002), Corrs. for Congl. Press Galleries, Maine Soc. Washington (pres. 1950—53), Chevy Chase Club, Nat. Press Club (Washington) (sec. 1953—54, treas. 1966—67, chmn. bd. 1969, pres. 1973), Gridiron Club (Washington). Episcopalian. Home and Office: 4956 Sentinel Dr #304 Bethesda MD 20816-3562

LARRABEE, MATTHEW L., lawyer; b. Palo Alto, Calif., July 7, 1955; AB, U. Calif., Davis, 1977; JD, U. Calif., San Francisco, 1980. Bar: Calif. 1980. Atty. Heller, Ehrman, White & McAuliffe, San Francisco, 1990—, Co-Chair, San Francisco Litigation Dept., 1995—97, San Francisco Managing Ptnr., 1997—99, Firmwide Practice Chair, Litigation, 1999—2005, chmn., 2005—. Mem. ABA, Am. Law Inst., Order of Coif. Office: Heller Ehrman White & McAuliffe 333 Bush St San Francisco CA 94104-2806

LARRABEE, WAYNE FOX, JR., facial plastic surgeon; b. Ft. Benning, Ga., May 10, 1945; s. Wayne Fox and Ruth (Truex) L.; m. Tane; children: Shane, Sascha, Kai, Spencer, Gregory. BS in Math., Midland Coll., 1967; postgrad., U. Edinburgh, 1965-66; MD, MPH in Epidemiology, Tulan U., 1971. Diplomate Am. Bd. Otolaryngology; lic. MD, Wash. Intern Letterman Gen. Hosp., San Francisco, 1971-72; resident in surgery Tulane U. Svc. Charity Hosp., New Orleans, 1975-76, resident in otolaryngology and maxillofacial surgery, 1976-79; head sect. reconstructive and aesthetic plastic surgery Va. Mason Med. Ctr., Seattle, 1986-88, head sect. otolaryngology, 1985-88. Instr. dept. surgery Tulane Med. Sch., 1975-79, instr. dept. otolaryngology, 1976-79; clin. assoc. prof. U. Wash., 1979-88; clin. prof., U. Wash., 1988-2001; pres. med. bd. Virginia Mason Rsch. Ctr., 1985-88; observations fellowship Moorfields Eye Hosp., London, 1988; presenter in field; pres. Am. Bd. Facial Plastic Surgery, 2000-03. Author: Surgical Anatomy of the Face, 1993, Principles of Facial Reconstruction, 1995, Roslyn A Town's Portrait, 2d edit., 1999; mem. editl. bd. JAMA, 1999—; editor Archives of Facial Plastic Surgery, 1999—. Maj. U.S. Army Med. Corps, 1972-75, Panama Canal Zone. Fellow ACS, Am. Acad. Facial Plastic and Reconstructive Surgery (pres. 1996), Am. Soc. Head and Neck Surgery, Triological Soc., Am. Bd. Otolaryngology (bd. dirs., ps. 2002—); mem. King County Med. Soc., Am. Acad. Otolaryngology-Head and Neck Surgery. Avocations: photography, poetry. Office: Ctr for Facial Plastic Surgery 600 Broadway # 280 Seattle WA 98122 Office Phone: 206-386-3550. Business E-Mail: info@larrabeecenter.com.

LARRICK, PAMELA MAPHIS, marketing executive; married; 1 stepchild. Various positions Ogilvy Mather, 1978—92; gen. mgr. O&M Direct, 1992—94; joined as mng. dir. MRM (then McCann Direct), NYC, 1994; reg. dir., N. Am. MRM; COO MRM Worldwide; pres., CEO MRM, NYC, 2001; chmn. MRM Ptnrs. (McCann customer rels. mktg.), NYC; chmn., CEO Foot Cone & Belding Worldwide, customer rels. mktg. (FCBi), NYC, 2005—. Named one of 25 Women Leaders of Advt. Industry, Ad Age, 1997, Global Power 100, 2002; recipient Emerson Lifetime Achievement award for Innovation in and Svc. to direct mktg., John Caples awards orgn. Office: FCBi 100 W 33rd New York NY 10001 Office Phone: 212-885-3000. Office Fax: 212-885-2903.*

LARRIMORE, RANDALL WALTER, retired wholesale company executive; b. Lewes, Del., Apr. 27, 1947; s. Randall A. and Irene Larrimore; m. Judith Cutright, Aug. 29, 1970; children: Jacob, Alex. BS, Swarthmore (Pa.) Coll., 1969; MBA, Harvard U., 1971. Product mgr. Richardson-Vick, Wilton, Conn., 1971-75; sr. engagement mgr. McKinsey & Co., N.Y.C., 1975-80; pres. Pepsi-Cola Italia, Rome, 1980-83, Beatrice Home Specialties, Inc. (later acquired by Am. Brands), Skokie, Ill., 1983-87; pres., CEO, MasterBrand Industries, Inc. (subs. of Am. Brands, Inc.), 1988-97; v.p. Am. Brands, Inc., 1988-95; chmn. Moen Inc., 1990-97, chief exec. officer, 1990-94; chmn., chief exec. officer Master Lock Co., 1996-97; pres., CEO United Stationers, Des Plaines, Ill., 1997—2002. Bd. dirs. Olin Corp., 1998—, chmn., 2003—; bd. dirs. Campbell Soup Co., 2003—. Trustee Winnetka Congl. Ch., 1989-90; exec. com. hardware/home improvement coun. City of Hope, 1991-97, pres. 1991-93; exec. com. office products coun. City of Hope, 1997-2002, pres., 2000-02; commr. Landmark Preservation Coun., Winnetka, 1992-98; bd. dirs. Evanston Hosp. Corp., 1996—, Students In Free Enterprise, 1998-2002; trustee Lake Forest Acad., 2000—. Capt. USAR, 1971-79. Named Exec. of Yr., Office Products Internat., 1999. Mem.: Plumbing Mfg. Inst. (bd. dirs. 1991—93).

LARROCA, RAYMOND G., lawyer; b. Jan. 5, 1930; s. Raymond Gil and Elsa Maria (Morales) L.; m. Barbara Jean Strand, June 21, 1952 (div. 1974); children: Denise Ann Sheehan, Gail Ellen, Raymond Gil, Mark Talbot, Jeffrey William. BSS, Georgetown U., 1952; JD, 1957. Bar: Dc. 1957, U.S. Supreme Ct. 1960. Assoc. Kirkland, Fleming, Green, Martin & Ellis, Washington, 1957-64; ptnr. Kirkland, Ellis, Hodson, Chaffetz & Masters, Washington, 1964-67, Miller, Cassidy, Larroca & Lewin, Washington, 1967-2000, Baker Botts, Washington, 2000—. Served with arty. U.S. Army, 1948-49, to 1st lt., inf., 1952-54. Mem. ABA, D.C. Bar, Bar Assn. D.C., The Barristers. Republican. Roman Catholic. Club: Congl. Country (Potomac, Md.). Office: Baker Botts LLP 1299 Pennsylvania Ave NW Washington DC 20004-2400 E-mail: ray.larroca@bakerbotts.com.

LARROWE, CHARLES PATRICK, economist, educator; b. Portland, Oreg., May 1, 1916; s. Albertus and Helen (Maginnis) L.; 1 child, Peter (dec.). BA, U. Wash., Seattle, 1946, MA, 1948; PhD, Yale U., 1952. Asst. instr. econs. U. Wash., 1946-49, Yale U., 1949-52; assoc. prof. U. Utah, 1952-56; mem. faculty Mich. State U., East Lansing, 1956-89, prof. econs., 1961-89, faculty grievance ofcl., 1976-80, 88-89. Cons. to govt. Author: Shape-Up and Hiring Hall, 1955, Harry Bridges, 2d edit., 1977, Lashing Out, 1982. Served with Am. Field Service, 1942-43; Served with AUS, 1943-45. Decorated Silver Star, Purple Heart with oak leaf cluster, Combat Infantryman's badge; grantee Rabinowitz Found., 1962 Mem. ACLU, NAACP, Amnesty Internat., Rolls-Royce Owners' Club. Democrat. Home: 537 Gunson St East Lansing MI 48823-3525 Office: Mich State Univ Dept Econs East Lansing MI 48824

LARRY, R. HEATH, lawyer, director; b. Huntingdon, Pa., Feb. 24, 1914; s. Ralph E. and Mabel (Heath) L.; m. Eleanor Ketler, Sept. 10, 1938; children: David Heath, Dennis Ketler, Thomas Richard. AB, Grove City Coll., 1934, LL.D., 1964; JD, U. Pitts., 1937. Bar: Pa. 1937, D.C. 1937. Pvt. practice, 1937-38; atty. Nat. Tube Co., 1938-44, sec., dir., 1944-48; gen. atty. U.S. Steel Corp., Pitts., 1948-52, asst. gen. solicitor, 1952-58, adminstrv. v.p. labor relations, 1958-66, exec. v.p., asst. to chmn., 1966—76, vice chmn. bd., 1976—77; pres. N.A.M., 1977-80; of counsel Reed Smith Shaw & McClay, Washington, 1980—. Dir. emeritus Textron, Inc. Trustee emeritus Grove City Coll.; former trustee Conf. Bd. Mem. Am. Iron and Steel Inst. Clubs: Met. (Washington); Economic (N.Y.C.); Gulf Stream Golf, Delray Beach Yacht, Gulf Stream Bath and Tennis, Little. Presbyterian. Home: 4333 N Ocean Blvd Apt A53 Delray Beach FL 33483-7559 E-mail: heathlarry@aol.com.

LARSDOTTER, ANNA-LISA, retired translator, artist; b. Uddevalla, Bohus Län, Sweden, May 12, 1932; d. Lars Helge Svensson and Signe Ingeborg Jacobsson-Svensson; m. Erich S. Weibel, Aug. 17, 1956 (div. 1962). Student, Tchrs. Coll. for Women, Stockholm, 1951—52, Art Student's League, N.Y.C., 1953—55, New Sch. for Social Rsch., 1963—66, Summit Art Ctr., N.J., 1964—68, Academie des Beaux-Arts, Lausanne, Switzerland, 1960—62. Sec., translator internat. program Mus. Modern Art, N.Y.C., 1956; archivist Lawrence-Myden Collection, N.Y.C., 1963—64; archivist, translator Frederick Kiesler Catalogue, N.Y.C., 1979; freelance translator Data Profls. Inc., Ft. Lauderdale, Fla., 1986—97. Mem. exec. com. Summit Art Ctr., 1967—69. Contbr. articles to profl. jours.; performer: (dances) Byrd Hoffman Sch., 1969—75; appeared in: (films) Strong Medicine, 1984; (plays) Life and Times of Sigmund Freud, 1969—74; Life and Times of Joseph Stalin, 1973; Attic Clouds, 1973; A Letter for Queen Victoria, 1974; Festival d'Automne, 1974; Overture in N.Y.C., 1972; actor: (tour) Theatre des Nations, 1973; organizer: (exhbns.) with Summit Art Ctr. and Bell Tel. Labs., 1964—69; preparer: catalogue pvt. collection of composer Jack Lawrence and Walter Myden, 1963. Lutheran. Avocations: art, music, history, genealogy. Personal E-mail: allarsdotter@yahoo.com.

LARSEN, ANITA DONICE, writer, consultant; b. Hastings, Nebr., Dec. 29, 1942; d. Donald S. and Zelda L. L.; m. Brian L. Gustafson, Aug. 25, 1963 (div. Nov. 1984). BA, Buena Vista Coll., 1967; MA, Drake U., 1973. Tchr. Alta (Iowa) H.S., 1967—68; lectr. Drake U., Des Moines, 1972—74; copywriter CMF& Z Adv. Agy., Des Moines, 1983; writer, editor Larsen Assocs., Des Moines, 1980-95, St. Paul, 1985-91, Taos, N.Mex., 1991-94, Albuquerque, 1994-99, Mpls., 1999—. Speechwriter What's Cookin': Pillsbury Study of Trends in American Eating Behaviors, 1988, others. Author: Psychic Sleuths, 1994, The Magus Doll, 1993 (Best Children's novel Southwestern Writers 1993), True Crimes and How They Were Solved, 1993, Lost.and Never Found I, 1984, II, 1991, Guilty or Innocent, (screenplays) The Frog Never Knows When to Scream, Done Deal, Ghost Sister; author, packager, editor: History's Mysteries Series, 1992; playwright: Felix Culpa, 1973, Hungerbear, 1974, Fish of April, 1974, Tale of the Mouse, 1976, adaptation The Velveteen Rabbit, 2003, musical version, 2005; author: (CD ROM on tape and book) Some Feet Have Noses, 1983, George Lucas, 1999, others; contbr. articles to profl. jours. Organizer St. Paul Pub. Libr. Youth Svcs. Dept. Event, 1988. Prodn. grantee Iowa State Art Coun. Fox Boy's Night Vision, 1982. Mem. Iowa Scriptwriters Alliance, Wis. Screenwriters Forum, Sigma Tau Delta, Alpha Psi Omega.

LARSEN, EINAR V., electrical and systems engineer, consultant; b. Feb. 14, 1951; BSEE, Calif. Poly. Inst., 1973; MS in Elec. Power Engring., Rensselaer Poly. Inst., 1974. Sr. cons. engr. GE. Fellow IEEE (region 1 awad 1980, chmn. Schenectady sect. Power Engring. soc. 1977, mem. edn. sys. working group, HVDC harmonics working group, HVDC control working group, chmn. FACTS working group). Office: General Electric Co 1 River Rd # 2-605 Schenectady NY 12345-6789

LARSEN, ERIK, art history educator; b. Vienna, Oct. 10, 1911; arrived in U.S., 1947, naturalized, 1953; s. Richard and Adrienne (Schapringer de Csepreg) L.; m. Lucy Roman, Oct. 4, 1932 (dec. 1981); children: Sigurd-Yves, Annik-Eve., Erik-Claude (dec.); m. Anna Gallup Moses, May 8, 1982 (div. Sept. 1986); m. Katharina Ehling, Oct. 21, 1989. Candidate, Institut Superieur d'Histoire de l'Art et d'Archéologie, Brussels, 1931; Licentiate, Louvain (Belgium) U., 1941; Docteur en Archéologie et Histoire de l'Art, 1959; D. honoris causa, Janus Pannonius U., Pécs, Hungary, 1992. Dir., editor-in-chief on semi-ofcl. cultural mission for Belgian Govt. Pictura, art. mag., Brussels, Rio de Janeiro, Brazil, 1946-47; research prof. art Manhattanville Coll. of Sacred Heart, 1947-55; instr. CCNY, 1948-55; lectr, then vis. prof. Georgetown U., 1955-58, assoc. prof. fine arts, 1958-63, prof., 1963-67, head dept. fine arts, 1960-67; prof. history of art U. Kans., 1967-80, prof. emeritus, 1980—. Dir. Center for Flemish Art and Culture, 1970-80; cons. old masters' paintings, guest-prof. U. Salzburg, Austria, 1988. Author: books, the most recent being La Vie, Les Ouvrages et Les Eleves de Van Dyck, 1975, Calvinistic Economy and 17th Century Dutch Art, 1979, rev. edit., 1999, Anton van Dyck, 1980, Rembrandt, Peintre de Paysages: Une Vision Nouvelle, 1983, Japanese edit., 1992; Seventeenth Century Flemish Painting, 1985, The Paintings of Anthony van Dyck, 2 vols., 1988, Jan Vermeer. Catalogo completo, 1996 (Am. edit., 1998), Hieronymus Bosch, Catalogo completo, 1998 (Am. edit., 1998); contbr. numerous articles, revs. to profl. publs., newspapers. Mem. Kans. Cultural Arts Commn., 1971-73; mem. Kans. Cultural Arts Adv. Council, 1973-79. Served with Belgian Underground, 1942-45. Decorated knight's cross Order Leopold, knight's cross Order of Crown, officer Order Leopold (Belgium); officer Order of Rio Branco (Brazil), Knight's Cross Mex. Order of Law, Culture, and Peace (Mex.); recipient Medal Marques de Olinda for Univ. Merit, Fed. U. of Pernambuco, Brazil, 2001, prix Thorlet, Laureate Inst. France, Académie des sciences morales et politiques, 1962; Internat. Hon. Citizen, New Orleans, 1989; named hon. Ky. col., 1977. Fellow Soc. Antiquaries of Scotland; mem. Appraisers Assn. Am., Association des Diplomés en Histoire de l'Art et Archéologie de L'Université Catholique de Louvain, Académie d'Aix-en Provence (France) (corr.), Académie de Mâcon (France) (assoc.), Académie d'Alsace (France) (hon.), Comité Cultural Argentino (hon.), Schweizerisches Institut fuer Kunstwissenschaft (Zurich, Switzerland), Academia di Belle Arti Pietro Vanucci (Perugia, Italy) (hon.), Royal Soc. Arts (London) (Benjamin Franklin fellow); correspondent-academician Real Academia de Bellas Artes de San Telmo (Malága, Spain), Real Academia de Bellas Artes de San Jorge (Barcelona, Spain), Accademia Tiberina (Rome), Académie Royale D'Archéologie de Belgique (fgn. assoc.). Home: 511 S Washington St Beverly Hills FL 34465-4312 Office Phone: 352-527-0619.

LARSEN, GARY LOY, physician, researcher; b. Wahoo, Nebr., Jan. 10, 1945; s. Allan Edward and Dorothy Mae (Hengen) L.; m. Letitia Leah Hoyt, Dec. 22, 1967; children: Kari Lyn, Amy Marie. BS, U. Nebr., 1967; MD, Columbia U., 1971. Diplomate Am. Bd. Pediat., Am. Bd. Pediatric Pulmonology (chmn. 1990-92). Pediatric pulmonologist Nat. Jewish Med. and Rsch. Ctr., Denver, 1978—2003, head divsn. pediatric pulmonary medicine, 1989—; mem. faculty U. Colo. Sch. Medicine, Denver, 1978—, dir. sect. pediatric pulmonary medicine, 1987—2003, prof. pediat., 1990—; head dept. respiratory medicine The Children's Hosp., Denver, 2002—03. Assoc. editor: Jour. Allergy and Clin. Immunology; editl. councillor: Pediatric Pulmonology; contbr. articles to prof. jours. Mem. sci. adv. panel Nat. Urban Air Toxics Rsch. Ctr., 1998—. Maj. M.C., U.S. Army, 1974-76. Med. rsch. grantee NIH, 1981—. Mem. Am. Thoracic Soc. (chmn. pediatric assembly 1987-88), Soc. Pediatric Rsch., N.Y. Acad. Scis., Chilean Respiratory Soc. (hon.), Western Soc. Pediat. Rsch., Phi Beta Kappa, Alpha Omega Alpha. Lutheran. Office: Nat Jewish Med & Rsch Ctr 1400 Jackson St Denver CO 80206-2761 Business E-Mail: larseng@njc.org.

LARSEN, JOHN ALEXANDER, music educator; b. Jacksonville, Fla., Mar. 21; s. John T. and Gloria R. Larsen (Stepmother). B in Music Edn., Jacksonville U., 1986. Cert. tchr. Fla. Choral dir. duPont Jr. H.S., Jacksonville, 1987—90; music tchr. Hyde Grove Elem. Sch., Jacksonville, 1990—91; choral dir. First Coast H.S., Jacksonville, 1991—; dir. music ministries Ortega United Meth. Ch., Jacksonville, 1997—. Chmn. Dist. 4 Fla. Vocal Assn., Jacksonville, 1995—97. Mem. Springfield Preservation and Restoration Coun., Jacksonville, 1990—2005. Named Tchr. of Yr., First Coast H.S., 1995, 2000. Mem.: Fla. Vocal Assn., Fla. Music Educators Assn., Music Educators Nat. Conf., Am. Choral Dirs. Assn. Office: First Coast HS 590 Duval Station Rd Jacksonville FL 32218-1869 Office Phone: 904-757-0080 x 137. Office Fax: 904-696-8721. E-mail: larsenj@educationcentral.org.

LARSEN, JONATHAN ZERBE, journalist; b. N.Y.C., Jan. 6, 1940; s. Roy Edward and Margaret (Zerbe) L.; m. Katharine Wilder, May 28, 1966; m. Jane Amsterdam, Aug. 31, 1985 (div. 2000); 1 child, Edward Roy. BA, Harvard U., 1961, MAT, 1963; DHL, Cambridge Coll., 1997. Contbg. editor Time mag., N.Y.C., 1965-66, corr. Chgo., 1966-68, Los Angeles, 1968-70, bur. chief Saigon, Vietnam, 1970-71, asso. editor, 1972-73; editor New Times mag., N.Y.C., 1974-79; Nieman fellow Harvard U., 1979-80; news editor Life mag., 1980-81, sr. editor, 1981-82; editor-in-chief The Village Voice, N.Y.C., 1989-94; free-lance writer, 1982—. Chmn. editl. bd. OnEarth Mag., 1982-2005. Trustee Natural Resources De. Coun., 1982—2005; bd. dirs. Larsen Fund, mem. panel of judges John B. Oakes award; chmn. bd. Cambridge Coll. Recipient Clarion award, 1986. Home: 565 West End Ave New York NY 10024

LARSEN, LOUISE EDITH, elementary school educator, researcher, retired bookstore manager; b. Alton, Ill., Feb. 23, 1918; d. Anson Andrew and Irma Margaret Lampert; m. David Robert Larsen, Oct. 16, 1940 (dec.); children: David, Edith, Nancy. AB, Washington U., 1939. With Howard Letter Improvement Co., St. Louis, 1939—41; tchr. English and Latin Webster Groves H.S., 1956—69, Affton H.S., 1972—76; 5th grade tchr. St. Justin the Marytr, 1969—76; bookstore mgr. Christ Ch. Cathedral, 1976—86; ret., 1986. Vol. tutor Edgar Rd. Sch., Webster Groves, Mo., 2001—05; part time tchr. English and Latin Kirkwood H.S., St. Louis. Contbr. articles and stories to mags. Vol. aerobics instr. YMCA, 1972—2004; Bible study leader. Recipient 1st place essay, Sr. Cir. Newspaper, 2003, People's Choice award for essays, 2003—04, 1st place contest award, The Silver Quill Soc., 2004, 5-Yr. Tutor award, Kirkwood H.S., 2005. Mem.: Oasis Writers Orgn., Delta Gamma. Home: 604 Deerhurst Dr Saint Louis MO 63119-5320

LARSEN, LYNN BECK, lawyer; b. Salt Lake City, Feb. 26, 1945; BA in Math. magna cum laude, U. Utah, 1969; MS in Engring., U. Wash., 1971; JD with honors, George Washington U., 1975. Bar: Va. 1975, U.S. Dist. Ct. (ea. dist.) Va. 1975, D.C. 1976, U.S. Dist. Ct. D.C. 1976, U.S. Ct. Appeals (4th and D.C. cirs.) 1976, U.S. Claim Ct. 1977, Calif. 1978, U.S. Dist. Ct. (cen. dist.) Calif. 1978, U.S. Dist. Ct. (so. dist.) Calif. 1979, U.S. Ct. Appeals (9th cir.) 1979, Utah 1983, U.S. Dist. Ct. Utah 1983, U.S. Ct. Appeals (fed. cir.) 1983, U.S. Ct. Appeals (10th cir.) 1988. Engr. Boeing Co., Seattle, 1969-70; engring analyst CIA, Washington, 1971-73, contracting officer, 1973-74; ptnr. Wickwire Gavin, P.C., Washington, Los Angeles and Salt Lake City, 1974-86, Larsen & Wilkins, Salt Lake City, 1986—88, Larsen & Stewart, 1988—94, McKay, Burton & Thurman, 1995-2000, Project Analysts, Salt Lake City, 2000—. Chmn. legal adv. com. Associated Gen. Contractors Calif. 1983, Associated Gen. Contractors Utah. Contbr. articles to profl. jours. Mem. Phi Beta Kappa. Mem. Lds Ch. Office: Project Analysts 505 E 200 S Ste 400 Salt Lake City UT 84102-2818 E-mail: lynn@projan.com.

LARSEN, MARSHALL O., corporate financial executive; b. ND; BS, U.S. Mil. Acad., West Point, 1970; MS, Purdue Univ. Op. analyst and fin. mgr. Goodrich Corp., Charlotte, NC, 1977—81, dir. of planning and analysis, dir. of product mktg., 1981—86, asst. to the pres., gen. mgr., 1986—94, v.p., 1994—95, exec. v.p., 1995—2002, pres., COO, 2002—03, pres., CEO, 2003—, chmn., 2004—. Lt. U.S. Army, 1970—76. Office: Goodrich Corp Four Coliseum Ctr 2730 W Tyvola Rd Charlotte NC 28217-4578*

LARSEN, POUL STEEN, library educator; b. Copenhagen, Jan. 30, 1940; s. Kaj Poul and Inger Elise (Seligmann) L.; m. Marianne Pugdahl, July 27, 1963; children: Maria, Anne. Exam.Phil., U. Copenhagen, 1961. Lectr. Copenhagen Coll. Engring., 1961-73, Royal Sch. Librarianship, Denmark, 1971-73, libr., 1972, asst. dept. head, assoc. prof., 1973-76, head dept. info. media, prof., 1976—, chmn. faculty, 1992-99. Chmn. Danish Best Books of Yr. Com., 1982-89, Danish Standards Com. Phys. Characteristics of Media, 1988-2001; vice-chmn. ISO com. Terminology of Info. and Documentation, 1993-2001; convenor ISO Expert Group Standardization of Graphic Materials, 1991-2001; vis. prof. UCLA, 1983. Author: Contemporary Danish Book Art, 1986, 2nd edit., 1989; co-author: Informationsordbogen (Danish Standards Dictionary of Information Terms), 1991, 3d edit., 2002; contbg. author: Danish Dictionary of National Biography, 1978-85, Danish Handbook of Cultural History, 1991, Danish National Ency., 1993-2000, ISO 5127 Information and Documentation-Vocabulary, 2001; contbr. articles to profl. jours.; editor, book designer, designer typefaces for digital typesetting: LIBER, 1993, MEGA, 1996, COLONNA, 1996; mem. editl. bd. The Libr. Quar., U. Chgo., 1999-2004. Recipient Prize of Distinction, Soc. for Bookcrafts, 2003; Yale U. fellow, 1984. Home: Vasevej 85 DK-3460 Birkerod Denmark also: Kirkebyen 11 DK 3790 Hasle, Isle of Bornholm Denmark Office: Royal Sch Libr/Info Sci 6 Birketinget DK-2300 Copenhagen Denmark E-mail: psl@psl.dk.

LARSEN, RALPH IRVING, environmental research engineer; b. Corvallis, Oreg., Nov. 26, 1928; s. Walter Winfred and Nellie Lyle (Gellatly) L.; m. Betty Lois Garner, Oct. 14, 1950 (dec. Feb. 1989); children: Karen Larsen Cleeton, Eric, Kristine Larsen Burns, Jan Alan; m. Annie Harmon King, Aug. 3, 1991; children: Vikki King Ball, Terri King Blankenship, Cindi King King (dec.). BSCE, Oreg. State U., 1950; MS, Harvard U., 1955, PhD in Air Pollution and Indsl. Hygiene, 1957. San. engr. divsn. water pollution control USPHS, Washington, 1950-54; chief tech. svc. state and cmty. svc. sect. Nat. Air Pollution Control Adminstrn., Cin., 1957-61; with EPA and Nat. Air Pollution Control Adminstrn., 1961—; environ. rsch. engr. Nat. Exposure Rsch. Lab., Rsch. Triangle Park, N.C., 1971—. Air pollution cons. to Poland, 1973, 75, Brazil, 1978; condr. seminars for air pollution researchers, Paris, Vienna and Milan, 1975; adj. lectr. Inst. Air Pollution Tng., 1969—; Falls of Neuse cmty. rep. City of Raleigh (N.C.), 1974—. Contbr. more than 55 articles to profl. jours. Elder Christian and Missionary Alliance Ch. Recipient Commendation medal USPHS, 1979; named to Engring. Hall of Fame at Oreg. State U., 2001. Mem. Air and Waste Mgmt. Assn. (mem. editl. bd. jour. 1971-88), Conf. Fed. Environ. Engrs., USPHS Commd. Officers Assn. (past br. pres.), Sigma Xi. Republican. Home: 4012 Colby Dr Raleigh NC 27609-6045 *God issued me a 1928-model body. It works best, for others and me, as I read a chapter of the Owner's Manual (The Holy Bible) first thing each morning.*

LARSEN, RALPH S(TANLEY), retired pharmaceutical executive; b. Bklyn., Nov. 19, 1938; s. Andrew and Gurine (Henningsen) L.; m. Dorothy M. Zeitfuss, Aug. 19, 1961; children: Karen, Kristen, Garret. BBA, Hofstra U., 1962. Mfg. trainee, then supr. prodn. and dir. mfg. Johnson & Johnson, New

Brunswick, NJ, 1962—77; v.p. ops., v.p. mktg. McNeil Consumer Products Co. div. Johnson & Johnson, Ft. Washington, Pa., 1977—81; pres. Becton Dickenson Consumer Products, Paramus, NJ, 1981—83; pres. Chicopee divsn. Johnson & Johnson, New Brunswick, NJ, 1983—85, co. group chmn., 1985—86, vice chmn., exec. com., bd. dirs., 1986—89, chmn. bd., pres., CEO, 1989—2002, bd. dirs., mem. exec. com. Bd. dirs. Xerox Corp., GE. Trustee Robert Wood Johnson Found. Mem. Bus. Coun. Republican. Avocations: skiing, boating, art. Office: 100 Albany St Ste 200 New Brunswick NJ 08901

LARSEN, RICHARD GARY, accounting firm executive; b. Tampa, Fla., Nov. 28, 1948; s. Dagfinn T. Larsen and Elizabeth M. (Koch) Thompson; m. Harriet Taylor Jones, Dec. 19, 1970; children— Jonathan Daniel, Alice Taylor BBA in Acctg., George Washington U., 1971, JD, 1974; postgrad., Columbia U., 1985. Bar: Va. 1974; CPA, D.C., Va. Mem. staff U.S. Senate, Washington, 1967-73; ptnr. Ernst & Young, Washington, 1973—; adj. prof. U. Md., College Park, 1976-78, Am. U., Washington, 1977-78. Mem. ABA, Va. Bar Assn., AICPAs, Md. Soc. CPAs, Univ. Club (Washington), Coral Beach and Tennis Club (Bermuda), Chatham Beach and Tennis Club, Eastward Ho Country Club (Chatham), Columbia Country Club (Chevy Chase), Belle Haven Country Club. Home: 319 S St Asaph St Alexandria VA 22314-3745 Office: Ernst & Young 1225 Connecticut Ave NW Washington DC 20036-2621 E-mail: richard.larsen@ey.com.

LARSEN, RICHARD LEE, city manager, consultant, retired mayor, arbitrator; b. Jackson, Miss., Apr. 16, 1934; s. Homer Thorsten and Mae Cordelia (Amidon) L.; m. Virginia Fay Alley, June 25, 1955; children: Karla, Daniel, Thomas (dec.), Krista, Lisa. BS in Econs. and Bus. Adminstrn, Westminster Coll., Fulton, Mo., 1959; postgrad., U. Kans., 1959-61. Fin. dir. Village of Northbrook, Ill., 1961-63; city mgr. Munising, Mich., 1963-66, Sault Ste. Marie, Mich., 1966-72, Ogden, Utah, 1972-77, Billings, Mont., 1977-79; mcpl. cons., 1979—2003; pub./pvt. sector labor rels. cons., arbitrator, 1979—2003; ret., 2003. Mayor City of Billings, Mont., 1990-95; dep. gen. chmn. Greater Mich. Found., 1968. Bd. dir. Ctrl. Weber Sewer Dist., 1972-77; chmn. labor com. Utah League Cities and Towns, 1973-77, Mont. League Cities and Towns, 1977-79; bd. dir., coach Ogden Hockey Assn., 1972-77, Weber Sheltered Workshop, 1974-77, Billings YMCA, 1980-86, Rimrock Found., 1980-86; chmn. cmty. rels. coun. Weber Basin Job Corps Ctr., 1973-77; bishop LDS Ch.; missionary LDS Ch., Portland, Oreg., 2003-05. With USCG, 1953-57. Recipient Cmty. Devel. Disting. Achievement awards Munising, 1964, Cmty. Devel. Disting. Achievement awards Sault Ste. Marie, 1966-70, Citizen award Dept. of Interior, 1977, Alumni Achievement award Westminster Coll., 1990, Dist. award of merit Boy Scouts Am., 1993, Silver Beaver award Boy Scouts Am., 1994; named Utah Adminstr. of Yr., 1976. Mem. Utah City Mgrs. Assn. (pres. 1972-74), Greater Ogden C. of C. (dir.), Rotary (pres. Billings 1997-98), Phi Gamma Delta. Home and Office: 1733 Parkhill Dr Billings MT 59102-2358 Office Phone: 406-248-4252. Business E-Mail: rllarsen@bresnan.net.

LARSEN, RICHARD R., congressman; b. Arlington, Wash., June 15, 1965; m. Tiia; children: Robert, Per. BA, Pacific Luth. U.; MPA, U. Minn. Dir. public affairs Wash. State Dental Assn.; econ. devel. official Port of Everett; councilman Snohomish County, Wash., County Coun. chair, 1999; mem. Ho. Reps. from 2nd Wash. dist., 2001—. Mem. Congressional coms. Transportation and Infrastructure com., aviation subcom., hwys., transit and pipelines subcom.; Agriculture com., Livestock and horticulture subcom., gen. farm commodities and risk mgmt. subcom.; Armed Svcs. Com., terrorism, unconventional threats and capabilities subcom., readiness subcom. Democrat. Office: 1529 Longworth House Office Bldg Washington DC 20515-4702*

LARSEN, ROBERT LEROY, artistic director; b. Walnut, Iowa, Nov. 28, 1934; s. George Dewey and Maine M. (Mickel) L. MusB, Simpson Coll., Indianola, Iowa, 1956; MusM, U. Mich., 1958; MusD, Ind. U., 1972. Music prof. Simpson Coll., 1957—, chmn. music dept., 1965-99. Founder, artistic dir. Des Moines Met. Opera, 1973—, mus. and stage dir. over 100 prodns., 1973—. Mus. coach Tanglewood, Lenox, Mass., 1963, Oglebay Pk. (W.Va.) Opera, 1965, Chgo., N.Y. studios; condr., stage dir. Simpson Coll., Des Moines Met. Opera, Miss. Opera, U. Ariz.; solo pianist, song recital coach and accompanist; adjudicator Met. auditions and competitions, Mpls., Chgo., Kansas City, Mo., Tulsa, San Antonio; stage dir., condr. operas, Simpson Coll., Des Moines Met. Opera, 1973—; editor Opera Anthologies by G. Schirmer; piano rec. artist for G. Schirmer Libr. Recipient Gov's. award State of Iowa, 1974, Iowa Arts award for long term commitment to excellence in the arts, 1998. Mem. Am. Choral Dir. Assn., Nat. Opera Assn., Music Tchrs. Nat. Assn., Pi Kappa Lambda, Phi Kappa Phi, Phi Mu Alpha Sinfonia (faculty advisor). Presbyterian. Avocations: reading, theater, coaching students. Office: Des Moines Metro Opera 106 W Boston Ave Indianola IA 50125-1836 Office Phone: 515-961-1571.

LARSEN, SYLVIA B., state legislator; b. Troy, Ohio, July 1949; m. Robert M. Larsen; 2 children. Student, Briarcliff Coll., 1968-69; BA, U. Wis., 1972. Past pres., bd. dirs. Bancroft Products, Concord, N.H., 1984-2000; cons. pub. rels. Concord; mem. Concord City Coun., 1989-98; mem. Dist. 15 N.H. Senate, Concord, 1994—, vice chmn. pub. affairs com., mem. edn. com., intrnal affirs com. Named Servant of Yr. Pineconia Grange, 1992, Legislator of Yr., N.H. Grange, 2001. Democrat. Address: 23 Kensington Rd Concord NH 03301-2528

LARSEN, TERRANCE A., retired bank holding company executive; b. 1946; BA, U. Dallas, 1968; PhD, Tex. A&M U., 1971. With Phila. Nat. Bank, from 1977, sr. v.p., 1980-83, exec. v.p., from 1983, Corestates Fin. Corp. (parent), Phila., 1983-86, pres., 1986-88, COO, 1986-87, chmn., CEO, 1988-99, also bd. dirs. Home: 75 Bryn Mawr Ave Lansdowne PA 19050-1911

LARSEN, WILLIAM LAWRENCE, engineering educator; b. Crookston, Minn., July 16, 1926; s. Clarence M. and Luverne (Carlisle) L.; m. Gracie Lee Richey, June 19, 1954; children— Eric W., Thomas R. B.M.E., Marquette U., 1948; MS, Ohio State U., 1950, PhD, 1956; postgrad., U. Chgo., 1950-51. Registered profl. engr., Iowa. Research assoc. Ohio State U., Columbus, 1951-56; research metallurgist E. I. duPont de Nemours & Co., Wilmington, Del., 1956-58; metallurgist Ames Lab., AEC, Iowa, 1958-73; assoc. prof. Iowa State U., Ames, 1958-73, prof. materials sci. and engring., 1973-93; prof. emeritus, 1993—. Cons. metallurgical engring., 1960— Contbr. articles to profl. jours. Served with USNR, 1944-46 Mem.: NSPE, NACE Internat., ASTM, ASM Internat. (life). Home and Office: 2332 Hamilton Dr Ames IA 50014-8201

LARSON, ALAN PHILIP, former federal agency administrator; b. Osage, Iowa, July 19, 1949; s. Philip Harold and Marilyn (Lack) L.; m. Nancy Ruth Naden, June 3, 1972; children: Nathan Christopher, Lara Marie, Philip Gardner. BA, U. Iowa, 1971, MA, 1978, PhD, 1982. Econ. officer U.S. Embassy US Dept. State, Kinshasa, 1975-77, dep. dir. Washington, 1978-82, counselor for econ. and comml. affairs U.S. Embassy Kingston, Jamaica, 1982-84, exec. asst. to under sec. Washington, 1984-86, dep. asst. sec. for internat. energy, 1986-87, prin. dep. asst. sec. for econs. and bus., 1987-90, U.S. amb. to OECD Paris, 1990-94, dep. asst. sec. for internat. fin. and devel. Washington, 1994-96, asst. sec. econ. & bus. affairs, 1996-99, under sec. econ., bus. & agrl. affairs, 1999—2005.

LARSON, ALLAN LOUIS, political scientist, educator, lay worker; b. Chetek, Wis., Mar. 31, 1932; s. Leonard Andrew and Mabel (Marek) L. BA magna cum laude, U. Wis., Eau Claire, 1954; PhD, Northwestern U., 1964. Instr. Evanston Twp. (Ill.) High Sch., 1958-61; asst. prof. polit. sci. U. Wis., 1963-64; asst. prof. Loyola U., Chgo., 1964-68, assoc. prof., 1968-74, prof., 1974—. Author: Comparative Political Analysis, 1980, Soviet Society in Historical Perspective: Polity, Ideology and Economy, 2000, (essay) The Human Triad: An Introductory Essay on Politics, Society, and Culture, 1988; (with others) Progress and the Crisis of Man, 1976; contbr. articles to profl. jours. Assoc. mem. Paul Galvin Chapel, Evanston, Ill. Norman Wait Harris fellow in polit. sci. Northwestern U., 1954-56 Mem. AAAS, ASPCA, AAUP, Humane Soc. U.S., Northwestern U. Alumni Assn., Am. Polit. Sci. Assn., Am. Acad. Polit. and Social Sci., Acad. Polit. Sci., Midwest Polit. Sci. Assn., Nat. Assn. Scholars, Spiritual Life Inst., Anti-Cruelty Soc., Nat. Wildlife Fedn., N.Am. Butterfly Assn., Acad. of Am. Poets (assoc.), Policy Studies Orgn., Noetic Scis. Inst., Nat. Assn. Scholars, Humane Soc. U.S., Kappa Delta Pi, Pi Sigma Epsilon, Pi Sigma Alpha. Roman Catholic. Home: 11152 43d Ave Chippewa Falls WI 54729-6626 Office: Loyola U 6525 N Sheridan Rd Damen Hall Rm 915 Chicago IL 60626 *We are each of us mysteries to ourselves. We are on a life-long search for meaning: questions about where we have come from, what we are doing and where we are going. The deepest desires of a person embody the spiritual quest. The Kingdom of God tells us where to place our priorities. Life is short. No one is untouched by tragedy. We are reminded every day of our finiteness. We care because it is our nature to care. Christianity teaches a reverence for life that urges us to transcend narcissism and selfishness.*

LARSON, ANDREW LLOYD, conductor, voice educator; b. Idaho Falls, Idaho, Dec. 30, 1973; s. Larry Lee and Arlene Griffin Larson; m. Carol Geneva Richins, Sept. 3, 1978; children: Aria Jane, Maxwell Glen, Simon Boyd. MusB, Utah State U., 1998; MusM, Brigham Young U., 2000; Dr. in Mus. Arts, U. Ill., 2002. Instr. Brigham Young U., Provo, Utah, 1998—2000; asst. prof. music Stetson U., DeLand, Fla., 2002—. Composer: (choral composition) Hodie Christus natus est, Magnificat, Exultate Deo, Haec Dies, O quam gloriosum, Tenebrae factae sunt. Jr. leader trainer Boy Scouts Am., Richmond, Utah, 1990—93; full-time missionary Ch. of Jesus Christ LDS, Bucuresti, Romania, 1992—94; young men pres. DeLand LDS Stake, 2003—05. Howard Choral scholar, Utah State U., 1997-1998, Performance scholar, Brigham Young U. Sch. Music, 1998-2000. Mem.: Nat. Assn. Tchrs. Singing, Am. Choral Dir.s' Assn., Pi Kappa Lambda. Mem. Lds Ch. Avocations: skiing, jogging, racquetball, basketball, golf. Home: 903 East Michigan Ave Deland FL 32724 Office: Stetson U 421 N Woodland Blvd Unit 8399 DeLand FL 32723 Office Phone: 386-822-8971. Home Fax: 386-822-8948. Personal E-mail: alarson@stetson.edu.

LARSON, ANNE M., hepatologist; b. Grand Forks, ND, Sept. 1, 1957; BS, U. Wash., 1987, MD, 1991. Diplomate Am. Bd. Internal Medicine, 1994, Am. Bd. Gastroenterology, 1997. Resident internal medicine U. Wash., Seattle, 1991—94, acting instr. medicine, 1997—2000, asst. prof. medicine, 2000—, dir. hepatology clinic, 2000—. Sr. Hepatology fellow, U. Wash., 1996—97. Mem.: Am. Liver Found. (bd. dirs. 1999—2003, med. adv. com. 1999—2003), Pacific N.W. Gastroenterology Soc. (pres. 2002), Am. Assn. Study Liver Diseases, Alpha Omega Alpha. Office: Univ Wash Box 356174 1959 NE Pacific St Seattle WA 98195-6174

LARSON, ARVID GUNNAR, electrical engineer; b. July 26, 1937; s. Arvid G. and Marion Edith (Parker) L.; m. Gladys Lorraine Anderson, June 6, 1959 (dec. 1987); 1 child, Gregory Monte; m. Nicole Sours, Aug. 26, 1989. BSEE, Ill. Inst. Tech., Chgo., 1959; MSEE, Stanford (Calif.) U., 1966, PhD in Elec. Engring., 1973. Registered profl. engr., Calif., Va. Rsch. engr. Stanford Rsch. Inst., Menlo Park, Calif., 1964-74; mgr. advanced rsch. Planning Rsch. Corp., McLean, Va., 1974-78; project mgr. Sys. Planning Corp., Arlington, Va., 1978-80; mgr. Washington divsn. Advanced Rsch. and Applications Corp., Vienna, Va., 1980-85; v.p. Analytical Disciplines Inc., Vienna, 1985-86; prin. Booz, Allen and Hamilton, Inc., 1986-90; sr. v.p. JJH Inc., Arlington, 1990-91; chmn. Nicole Larson Assocs., McLean, 1991—. Rsch. prof. George Mason U., Fairfax, Va., 1991-93; chmn. bd. dirs. Electronics and Aerospace Sys. Conf., 1982-84; bd. dirs. Rsch. Inst. in Info. Scis. and Engring., 1978-99; chmn. 3d NATO Advanced Study Inst. in Info. Scis., 1978. Author: Information Science in Action: System Design, 1983; contbr. articles to profl. jours. Lt. USN, 1959-63. Fellow IEEE (chmn. def. R&D com. 1985-86, chmn. No. Va. sect. 1986-87, vice-chmn. tech. activities com. 1986-87, chmn. new tech. issues com. 1987-89, chmn. fed. govt. activities 1989-90, gen. chmn. U.S. Tech. Policy Conf., 1988, 89, inst. editl. bd. 1986-88, editl. bd. jour. Spectrum 1988-91, Centennial medal 1984, Profl. Achievement award 1987, chmn. U.S. activities 1992, v.p. 1992, bd. dirs. 1992, chmn. govt. fellow com. 1997-98); mem. Am. Assn. Engring. Socs. (chmn. R&D task force 1996-99), Armed Forces Comms. and Electronics Assn., U.S. Naval Inst., Sigma Xi, Cosmos Club (chmn. fin. com. 1993-96, treas. 1997-00, mem. bd. mgmt. 1997-00), Shady Oaks Yacht Club (commodore 1991-93). Home: PO Box 83130 San Diego CA 92138-3130 Office Phone: 858-274-6160. Personal E-mail: larsons@n2.net.

LARSON, BENNETT CHARLES, solid state physicist, researcher; b. Buffalo, N.D., Oct. 9, 1941; s. Floyd Everet and Gladys May (Hogen) L.; m. Piola Anne Taliaferro, June 6, 1969; children: Christopher Charles, Andrea Kay BA in Physics, Concordia Coll., Moorhead, Minn., 1963; MS in Physics, U. N.D., 1965; PhD in Physics, U. Mo., 1970. Rsch. physicist, group leader x-ray diffraction Oak Ridge Nat. Lab., Tenn., 1969—, corp. fellow, condensed matter scis. divsn., 1969—. Contbr. numerous articles to profl. jours. Recipient Sidhu award Pitts. Diffraction Soc., 1974 Fellow Am. Phys. Soc.; mem. Am. Crystallographic Assn. (Bertram E. Warren Diffraction Physics award 1985), Materials Research Soc. Office: Oak Ridge Nat Lab Solid State Divsn PO Box 2008 Oak Ridge TN 37831-2008 Business E-Mail: larsonbc@ornl.gov.

LARSON, BETHANY ANN, theater educator, actress; b. Iowa City, Jan. 8, 1965; d. Lowell Vernon and Nancy Ann Larson; m. David Grant Walker, July 6, 1991; children: Dalton Eli Lowell Walker, Beatrice Ella Mae Walker. BFA in Theatre, Tex. Tech U., 1986; MA in Drama, U. Ark., 1989; PhD in Theatre and Film, U. Kans., 1999. Asst. bus. mgr. U. Theatre, Tex. Tech U., Lubbock, 1986; dir. children's theatre Sherman Cmty. Players, 1986; costume shop mistress U. Theatre, U. Ark., Fayetteville, 1987—89; receptionist Smile Ctr., Springdale, Ark., 1989; theatre grad. tchg. asst. dept. theatre and film Univ. Kans., Lawrence, 1989—93, asst. box office mgr. U. Theatre, 1990—93; receptionist Theodore Wiklund, D.D.S., Lawrence, Kans., 1993—94; on air announcer KAYL Radio AM & FM, Storm Lake, Iowa, 1994—95; dir. Acad. and Cultural Events Series Buena Vista U., Storm Lake, Iowa, 1996—2002, dir. svc. learning, 2001—02, asst. prof. theatre, 2003—. Actress Mt. Sequoyah New Play Retreat, Fayetteville, Ark., 1988—96, Playwrights Theatre NJ, 1997, Copenhagen Buena Vista U., Storm Lake, Iowa, 2005; prodr., actress Door Mats No More Prodns., Storm Lake, Iowa, 2002—. Actor: (museum performance) Nellie McGarry, (liturgical performance) Women of the Bible; (films) Cora Unashamed; dir.: (theatrical/media performance) Radio Daze, (musical production) Quilters, (radio production) The House that Death Built; (plays) Grease, The Merchant of Venice, Stepping Out, How I Learned to Drive, Emma's Child, (acting coach): (theat. prodn.) Much Ado About Nothing, Galileo. County conv. del. Buena Vista County Republican Party, Storm Lake, Iowa, 2000; creativity, drama cons. Storm Lake United Meth. Ch., Storm Lake, Iowa, 1996—2005; mem. bd. higher edn. and campus ministries Iowa Ann. Conf. U. Meth. Ch.; mem. bd. Harker Found., Storm Lake, Iowa, 1995—2005. Instl. Renewal grantee, Rhodes Consultation Future Ch. Related Coll., 2001-2003, Nat. Dance Project grantee, New Eng. Found. Arts, 2000. Mem.: Mid Am. Theatre Conf., Theatre Comm. Group, Assn. Theatre Higher Edn., Kappa Alpha Theta, P.E.O. (treas. 1994—96). Meth. Achievements include first to use multiple media forms, combined with digital delivery technology to make live performances accessible to regional audiences. Avocations: quilting, reading, playing piano, gardening, home improvement. Office: Buena Vista U 610 W Fourth St Storm Lake IA 50588 Office Phone: 712-749-2129. Business E-Mail: larsonb@bvu.edu.

LARSON, BRYAN ALAN, lawyer; s. Byron Ancedus and Betty Marilyn Larson; m. Kathy Stevenett; children: Aaron, Adam, Conor, Kaden, Sara, Aubrey. BA, Brigham Young U., 1980, JD, 1983. Bar: Utah 1983. Assoc. Christensen, Jensen & Powell, Salt Lake City, 1983-86, McKay, Burton & Thurman, Salt Lake City, 1986-91; ptnr. Larson, Jenkins & Halliday, Salt Lake City, 1991-95, Larson, Kirkham & Turner, Salt Lake City, 1995-99, Larson, Turner, Fairbanks and Dalby, Salt Lake City, 1999—. Editor: Backtalk Newsletter, 1995—, Utah Auto Body Watch Dawg, 2002—. Mem. ATLA (mem. polit. action com. 1991—), Utah Bar Assn. (com. chmn. 1990-92), Utah Trial Lawyers Assn. (exec. bd., treas., bd. govs.), Spkrs. Bur., Order of Barristers. Mem. Lds Ch. Avocations: boating, skiing. Office: Larson Turner Dalby & Ethington 1218 W South Jordan Pkwy Ste B South Jordan UT 84095 Office Phone: 801-446-6464. E-mail: larson@bestattorneys.com.

LARSON, CAROLE ALLIS, library and information scientist, educator; b. Dayton, Ohio, Aug. 31, 1945; d. Harold Arthur and Myra Barbara Larson; m. Lowell Wilson Eyer, Jr., Nov. 16, 1985. BA in Sociology, Carleton Coll., 1967; MA in Edn., Washington U., 1968; MA in Asian Studies, U. Oregon, 1975; MA in Libr. Sci., U. Denver, 1977. Reference libr. instrnl. svcs. U. Nebr., Kearney, 1978-80; campus libr. Met. Comty. Coll., Omaha, 1980-81; asst. prof. social scis., reference libr. U. Nebr., Omaha, 1981-85, assoc. prof., 1985—2001, ret., 2001. Cons. Bellevue Coll. Libr., Omaha, 1982-83 Contbr. articles to profl. jours. Co-recipient Reference Svc. Press award ALA Reference and Adult Svcs. Divsn., 1995; Washington U. fellow. Mem.: ALA, Nebr. Libr. Assn. Democrat. E-mail: researchercl@yahoo.com.

LARSON, CHARLES FRED, management consultant; b. Gary, Ind., Nov. 27, 1936; s. Charles F. and Margaret J. (Taylor) Larson; m. Joan Ruth Grupe, Aug. 22, 1959; children: Gregory Paul, Laura Ann. BSME, Purdue U., 1958; MBA summa cum laude, Fairleigh Dickinson U., 1973. Registered profl. engr., N.J. Project engr. Combustion Engring., Inc., East Chicago, Ind., 1958-60; sec. Welding Rsch. Council, N.Y.C., 1960-70, asst. dir., 1970-75; exec. dir. Indsl. Rsch. Inst., Inc., Washington, 1975-99, pres., 1999—2001, Innovation Rsch. Internat., Washington, 2001—. Mem. mech. engring. adv. bd. Purdue U.; mem. selection com. Nat. Inventors Hall of Fame. Assoc. editor: Jour. Pressure Vessel Tech., 1973—75, mem. bd. advisors: Who's Who in Am. Mem. Wyckoff (N.J.) Bd. Edn., 1973—78, pres., 1976—77; reader In Touch Networks, Inc., N.Y.C., 1979—89; chmn. 43d Nat. Conf. Advancement Rsch. Fellow: ASME, AAAS; mem.: Burning Tree Club, Kenwood Club, Univ. Club. Republican. Methodist.

LARSON, CHARLES ROBERT, naval officer; b. Sioux Falls, S.D., Nov. 20, 1936; s. Eldred Charles and Gertrude Edythe (Jensen) L.; m. Sarah Elizabeth Craig, Aug. 19, 1961; children: Sigrid Anne, Erica Lynn, Kirsten Elizabeth. BS in Marine Engring., U.S. Naval Acad., 1958. Commd. ensign USN, 1958, advanced through grades to adm., 1990; naval aviator, attack pilot, 1958-63; nuclear power, submarine tng., 1963-64; assigned nuclear subs., 1964-76; naval aide to the Pres., 1969-71; comdg. officer USS Halibut, 1973-76; comdr. submarine devel. group one, head operational deep submergence program, 1976-78; chief naval ops. staff Strategic Submarine Programs, 1978-79; dir. long range planning group Washington, 1978-82; comdr. submarines, Mediterranean, 1982-83; supt. U.S. Naval Acad. Annapolis, Md., 1983-86; comdr. 2d Fleet, 1986-88; dir. plans, policies and ops. DCNO, 1988-90; comdr. U.S. Pacific Fleet, 1990-91, U.S. Pacific Command, Hawaii, 1991-94; supt. U.S. Naval Acad., 1994-98; v.p. U.S. Naval Inst., 1994-98; sr. fellow The CNA Corp., Alexandria, Va., 1998—. Bd. dirs. Northrop Grumman. Mem. USO Coun., Honolulu, 1990-92; mem. Honolulu area coun. Boy Scouts Am., 1990-94. Decorated Def. D.S.M., Navy D.S.M. (7), Legion of Merit (3), Bronze Star, others; White House fellow, 1968-69. Mem. NAS (com. on internat. security and arms control), Coun. on Fgn. Rels. Home: 591 Coover Rd Annapolis MD 21401-6921 Office: The CNA Corp 4825 Mark Ctr Dr Alexandria VA 22311-1850

LARSON, CHARLES W., prosecutor; m. Ellen Larson; 2 children. Grad., Kans. State U., U. Iowa Sch. Law, U.S. Army War Coll., U.S. Army Command and Gen. Staff Coll. Magistrate Iowa 5th Judicial Ct., 1973; commr. Iowa Dept. Public Safety, 1973—79; mgr. law enforcement Sanders and Assocs., Kingdom of Saudi Arabia, 1979—82; ptnr. Walker, Larson and Billingsley, Newton, Iowa, 1982—86; U.S. atty. no. dist IA US Dept. Justice, Cedar Rapids, 1986—93, 2001—; dir. Iowa Office Drug Control, 1993—98; chmn. Iowa Bd. Parole, 1998—2001. Office: PO Box 74950 Cedar Rapids IA 52407-4950

LARSON, DAVID ALLEN, law educator; b. Libertyville, Ill., Nov. 5, 1954; s. Allen John and Mary Jane (Williams) L.; m. Patricia Pierman. BA magna cum laude, DePauw U., Greencastle, Ind., 1976; JD, U. Ill., 1979; LLM, U. Pa., Phila., 1987. Bar: Minn. 1979, U.S. Dist Ct. Minn. 1980, U.S. Ct. Appeals (8th cir.) 1980, Ill. 1982, U.S. Dist. Ct. (no. dist.) Ill. 1982, Nebr. 1989, U.S. Supreme Ct. 1990. Assoc. Meagher & Geer, Mpls., 1979-81; asst. prof. Loyola U. Chgo. Sch. Bus. Adminstrn., 1981-83; assoc. prof. Millsaps Coll. Sch. Mgmt., Jackson, Miss., 1983-87; prof. Creighton U. Sch. Law, Omaha, 1987-90, 91-99; prof.-in-residence appellate div. EEOC, Washington, 1990-91; dir. Dispute Resolution Inst., 1999—2001, sr. fellow, 2000—; prof. law Hamline U., St. Paul, 1999—. Hearing examiner Nebr. EEOC, 1997-2000; vis. scholar Macalester Coll., Sch. Law Hamline U., St. Paul, 1997-98; arbitrator, mediator, expert witness, editor-in-chief Jour. of Alternative Dispute Resolution in Employment. Contbr. articles to profl. jours. Rsch. scholar Lund (Sweden) U. Law Sch., 1985, 88, 89. Mem. ABA (past vice chmn. sect. on internat. law and practice, employment law com., vice-chmn. dispute resolution sect., legal edn. com.), Phi Beta Kappa. Avocations: classical music, theater, films, sports, fishing. Office: Hamline Univ Sch Law 1536 Hewitt Ave Saint Paul MN 55104-1205 Office Phone: 651-523-2128. Office Fax: 651-523-2236. Business E-Mail: dlarson@hamline.edu.

LARSON, DAVID ELI, lawyer; b. Dayton, Ohio, Feb. 9, 1945; s. Eli Christian and Myrtle Lorene (Heeren) L.; m. Beverly Jean Farlow, June 17, 1967 (div.); m. Roberta Elizabeth Longfellow, Aug. 25, 1979; children: Jessica Deane Longfellow, Christian David Longfellow. BA, Wittenberg U., 1967; MPA, U. N.C., 1974; JD, Ohio State U., 1979. Bar: Ohio 1979, U.S. Dist. Ct. (so. dist.) Ohio 1980. Cmty. devel. rep. HUD, Columbus, Ohio, 1970-73, multifamily housing rep., 1975-76; cmty. devel. dir. City of Miamisburg, Ohio, 1973-75; assoc. Law Clinic of D.W. Bench, Dayton, 1980-83; ptnr. Certo and Larson, Kettering, Ohio, 1983—98, Altick & Corwin, Kettering, Ohio, 1998—. Vol. Peace Corps, Turkey, 1968; active Grace United Meth. Ch., Dayton, 1981. Wittenberg alumni scholar Wittenberg U., 1963; study fellow for internat. devel. U. N.C., Chapel Hill, 1969. Mem. Am. Immigration Lawyers Assn., Am. Bankruptcy Law Forum, Ohio State Bar Assn., Dayton Bar Assn. Democrat. Home: 836 Belmonte Park N Dayton OH 45405-4406 Office: Altick & Corwin 1700 One Dayton Ctr One S Main St Dayton OH 45402-2026 Office Phone: 937-223-1201. E-mail: larsons836@earthlink.net, larsond@altickcorwin.com.

LARSON, DAVID LEE, surgeon; b. Kansas City, Mo., Dec. 9, 1943; s. Leonard Nathaniel and Mary Elizabeth (Stuck) L.; m. Sherrill Ankli, Apr. 16, 1977; children: Jeffrey David, Dawn Elizabeth, Bradley Jesse. BS, Bowling Green State U., 1965; MD, La. State U., 1969. Diplomate Am. Bd. Plastic Surgery (bd. dirs. 1996—, sec.-treas. 1998—). Intern Charity Hosp. of La., New Orleans, 1969-70; resident otolaryngology Baylor Coll. Medicine, Houston, 1972-76; plastic surgery resident Ind. U., Indpls., 1976-78; surgeon M.D. Anderson Cancer Ctr., Houston, 1978-85; prof., chmn. dept. plastic and reconstructive surgery Med. Coll Wis., Milw., 1986—. Alano J. Ballantyne prof. in head and neck surgery, M.D. Anderson Cancer Ctr., Houston, 1985; sec.-treas. Am. Bd. Plastic Surgery, 1996-2002. Editor: Cancer in the Neck, 1987, Essentials of Head and Neck Oncology, 1998. Capt. USNR, 1991—. Mem. Am. Assn. Plastic Surgeons, Nat. Inst. Healthcare Rsch. (chmn. bd. dirs. 1995-2000), Plastic Surgery Ednl. Found. (pres. 2001—). Avocations: reading, exercise. Home: 13510 Braemar Dr Elm Grove WI 53122-2509 Office: Med Coll Wis 8700 Watertown Plank Rd Milwaukee WI 53226-3522 E-mail: dlarson@mcw.edu.

LARSON, DONALD CLAYTON, physics professor, consultant; b. Wadena, Minn., Jan. 29, 1934; s. Clyde Melvin and Selma (Wilson) L.; m. Susan Dunnet, July 17, 1960; children: Tor Frederick, Jun Dunnet (dec.), Erika Rose. BS, U. Wash., 1956; SM, Harvard U., 1957, PhD, 1962. Asst. prof. U. Va., Charlottesville, 1962-67; assoc. prof. Drexel U., Phila., 1967-83, full prof., 1983—. Vis. prof. Univ. Chile, Santiago, 1969, 73, Tel-Aviv (Israel) U., 1984, 92; vis. scientist Naval Air Devel., Warminster, Pa., summers 1981-91; cons. NIST, Gaithersburg, Md., 1984-95. Author: Physics of Thin Films, vol.

VI, 1971, Experimental Methods in Preparation and Measurement of Thin Films, vol. II, 1974. Mem. Optical Soc. Am., Phi Beta Kappa, Tau Beta Pi, Sigma Xi. Home: 409 Drew Ave Swarthmore PA 19081-2407 Office: Drexel U Physics Philadelphia PA 19104 Office Phone: 215-895-2724. Business E-Mail: donlarson@drexel.edu.

LARSON, DOROTHY ANN, business educator; b. Nekoosa, Wis., Feb. 27, 1934; d. Edwin E. and Ruby E. (Burch) Larson; children: Jean Marie Harkey, Kenneth Lee Fitz, Cynthia Ann Anderson. BS with high distinction in Bus. and English, No. Ariz. U., 1969, MA in English, 1971; EdD in Bus., Ariz. State U., 1980. Tchr. English Cottonwood Oak Creek Elem. Sch., Ariz., 1969—70; tchr. bus. and English Mingus Union HS, Cottonwood, 1970—79, dir. vocat. edn., 1976—79; mem. facultydept. bus. adminstrn. Yavapai Coll., 1979—81, chairperson bus. divsn., 1981—86, tech. prep. coord., 1994—95. Cons. Ariz. Dept. Edn.; curriculum specialist Northern Ariz. U., 1995—98. Editor: Ariz. Bus. Edn. Newsletter, 1972—74. Mem. adv. coun. Gov.'s Coun. Practitioners. Mem.: Nat. Tech. Prep. Network, NEA, Ariz. Edn. Assn., Am. Vocat. Assn., Nat. Bus. Edn. Assn., Ariz. Bus. Edn. Assn. (pres. 1980—81), Phi Delta Kappa, Alpha Delta Kappa, Phi Kappa Phi, Delta Pi Epsilon, Pi Omega Pi. Republican. E-mail: dalarson@qwest.net.

LARSON, EDWARD, retired state supreme court justice; m. Mary Loretta Thompson; children: Sarah, John, Mary Elizabeth. BS, Kans. State U., 1954; JD, Kans. U., 1960. Pvt. practice, Hays, Kans., 1960—87; judge Kans. Ct. Appeals, 1987—95; justice Kans. Supreme Ct., Topeka, 1995—2003; ret., 2003. Mcpl. judge City of Hays, 1965—72. 2nd lt. USAF. Home: 2761 SW Plass Ave Topeka KS 66611

LARSON, EDWARD JOHN, historian; b. Mansfield, Ohio, Sept. 21, 1953; s. Rex and Jean (Uncapher) Larson; m. Lucy Marie Kaiser, July 28, 1990; children: Sarah Marie, Luke Anders. BA, Williams, 1974; MA, U. Wis., 1976, PhD, 1985; JD, Harvard U., 1979; DHL (hon.), Ohio State U., 2004. Bar: Wash. 1979, U.S. Dist. Ct. (we. dist.) Wash. 1979, U.S. Ct. Appeals (9th cir.) 1979, U.S. Tax Ct. 1981, U.S. Supreme Ct. 1984. Atty. Davis, Wright & Tremaine, Seattle, 1979—82; assoc. counsel U.S. House Com. on Edn. and Labor, Washington, 1983—86; counsel U.S. Office Edn. Rsch. and Improvement, Washington, 1986—87; Richard B. Russell prof. history and Talmadge prof. law Univ. Ga., Athens, 1987—, chair history dept., 2001—. Panelist human genome project NIH, Washington, 1990—2004; adv. U.S. Dept. Edn., Washington, 1987—93; vis. prof. Univ. Jean Moulin, Lyon, France, 1996; John Adams chair Fulbright program U. Leiden, The Netherlands, 2000—01; participant Antarctic Artists and Writers Program, NSF, 2003—04; Straus disting. vis. prof. Pepperdine Law Sch., 2005. Author: Trial & Error, 1985, Sex, Race & Science, 1995, Summer for the Gods, 1997, A Different Death, 1998, Evolution's Workshop, 2001, Evolution, 2004, Constitutional Convention, 2005. Counsel Wash. State House Reps., Olympia, 1981—82; analyst Wis. State Senate, Madison, 1974—76. Recipient Pulitzer prize for history, 1998, Templeton Found. Article prize, 1997, George Sarton award, AAAS, 2000, James Livingood award, Conf. on So. Lit., 2003; scholar, Rockefeller Found., 1996. Mem.: Forum History Sci. Am. (exec. com. chair 1992—94), History Sci. Soc. (com. chair 1994—97), Wash. State Bar Assn. Avocations: travel, hiking, bicycling, birdwatching. Home: 253 Cobb St Athens GA 30601-2407 Office: Univ Ga LeConte Hall Athens GA 30602 Office Phone: 706-542-2660. Business E-Mail: edlarson@uga.edu.

LARSON, EDYTHE K., science educator; b. N.Y.C., Mar. 23, 1922; d. George Vincent and Catherine Schultes Kershaw; m. Carl W. Larson, June 15, 1969. BSc, Wagner Coll., 1944; MA, NYU, 1946, PhD, 1957. Cert. clin. lab. dir. N.Y.C. Dept. Health, 1984. Assoc. dir. Colosi Clin. Lab., N.Y.C., 1944—84; prof. Wagner Coll., S.I., NY, 1944—84, chmn. dept. bacteriology and health scis., 1960—84, prof. emeritus, 1984—. Recipient Life Achievement award, NCC br., 1988. Mem.: Royal Soc. Health (award 1963), Am. Soc. Microbiology (Lifetime Achievement award 1988). Home: 15B Turtle Creek Dr Tequesta FL 33469 E-mail: larsonteq@aol.com.

LARSON, ERIC B., medical educator, director; BA in History, Stanford Univ., Stanford, Calif, 1969; MD, Harvard Med. Sch., 1973; MPH, U. Wash. Sch. Pub. Health, Seattle, Wash., 1977. Diplomate Am. Bd. of Internal Medicine, 1977. Assoc. diener, dept. pathology Children's Hosp., Boston, 1969—71; intern in medicine Beth Israel Hosp., Harvard Med. Sch., Boston, 1973—74, asst. resident in medicine, 1974—75; internist Harborview Med. Ctr., Seattle, 1975—77; rsch. assoc. Va. Mason Hosp./Rsch. Found., Seattle, 1975—77; chief resident, medicine U. Hosp., Seattle, 1977—78, attending physician, 1977—; Robert Wood Johnson Clin. scholar, sr. fellow, dept. medicine U. Wash., Seattle, 1975—77, assoc. dean clin. affairs; med dir. U. Wash. Med. Ctr., 1989—2002; dir. group health coop. Ctr. for Health Studies, Seattle, 2002—. Instructor, medicine Harvard Med. Sch., Boston, 1973—75; acting instructor, medicine U. Wash. Sch. of Medicine, Seattle, 1977—78; asst. prof., medicine U. Wash., Seattle, 1978—82; adj. asst. prof., cmty. medicine Sch. Pub. Health, Seattle, 1979—82; adj. assoc. prof., health services & cmty. medicine U. Wash. Sch. of Public Health, Seattle, 1982—88, adj. prof., health services & cmty. medicine, 1988—; prof. medicine U. Wash., Seattle, 1988—; sect. head, gen. internal medicine U. Hosp., Seattle, 1988—89; assoc. dean for clin. affairs U. Wash., Sch. of Medicine, Seattle, 1989—2002; sr. investigator and dir. Ctr. for Health Studies, Group Health Coop., 2002. Contbr. articles to profl. jours.; assoc. editor: Jour. of Gen. Internal Medicine, 1989—94, editl. bd.: Annals of Internal Medicine, 1992—95, Health Services Rsch., 1994—, Am. Jour. of Medicine, 1997—, Primary Care Case Reviews, 1988—, editl. adv. bd.: Rsch. and Practice, 1998—. Nat. reviewer, abstract selection Soc. of Gen. Internal Medicine (SGIM), 1984, co-chmn., NW regional mtg., 1983, chmn., NW regional mtg., 1986, regional rep., 1986—87, coun., 1986—89, pres., 1994—95; commr. Joint Commn. on Accreditation of Healthcare Orgns., 2003; nat. reviewer Am. Fedn. for Clin. Rsch.-Clin. Epidemiology-Health Care Rsch., 1983—88, western regional reviewer, 1985, chmn., abstract selection, 1990 Nat. Mtg., 1989—90; DHHS Adv. Panel on Alzheimer's Disease Office of Tech. Assessment, 1987—89, chmn., 1993—98. Fellow: ACP (regent 1998—, chmn. publications comm. 2000—03, chair-elect 2003); mem.: ACP Jour. Club (editl. adv. bd. 1990—), Wash. State Medical Soc., King County Med. Soc. (editl. adv. bd. 1987—90), Am . Fedn. for Med. Rsch., Seattle Acad. of Medicine, Soc. of Gen. Internal Medicine, AMA, Am. Clin. and Climatological Assn., Am. Soc. Clin. Investigation, Am. Geriatrics Soc. (editl. bd. 1988—91, Service award 1992), Assn. Am. Physicians, Phi Beta Kappa. Office: Ctr for Health Studies Ste 1600 1730 Minor Ave Seattle WA 98101-1448 Business E-Mail: larson.e@ghc.org. E-mail: ebl@u.washington.edu.

LARSON, ERIK, writer; m. Christine Gleason; children: Kristin, Lauren, Erin. BA in Russian history summa cum laude, U. Pa., 1976; MA, Columbia Grad. Sch. of Journalism, 1978. Author: (book) The Naked Consumer: How Our Private Lives Become Public Commodities, 1992, Lethal Passage: The Story of a Gun, 1994, Isaac's Storm: A Man, a Time ad the DeadliestHurrican in History, 1999 (Pacific Northwest booksellers award), The Devil in the White City: Murder Magic and Madness at the Fair that Changed America, 2003 (Nat. Book award nominee).

LARSON, GARY ARTHUR, farmer, financial consultant; b. Madison, Minn., Dec. 16, 1959; s. Alvin J. and Leona L.; m. Ingrid Carol Bellows, Aug. 9, 1986; children: Brent, Sonja. BS in Agrl. Bus., S.D. State U., 1982. Farmer Gary A. Larson Farm, Canby, Minn., 1981—; loan officer, computer programmer Farm Credit Svcs., Canby and Madison, Minn., 1983-85, credit analyst, computer programmer Wilmar and Marshall, Minn., 1986-91, computer sys. coord. Wilmar, 1992-93. Fin., computer cons. Larson Cons., Canby, 1993—; cons. Small Bus. Adminstr., Brookings, S.D., 1982. Inventor windpower model/report, 1978; patent for planting toolbar. Chmn. parish coun. St. James Ch., Dawson, Minn., 1995-99; mem., worker PTA, Dawson, 1997-2002; mem., telethon worker Pioneer Pub. TV, Appleton, Minn., 1988-2001. Finalist Top 100 Best Managed Farms, Farm Futures Mag., 2002; named one of, 1993—2002; recipient 1st place for wheat yield, Nat. Assn. Wheat Growers, 1990. Mem. Corn Growers Assn., Wheat Growers Assn., Soybean Growers Assn., Lac Qui Parle County Soybean Growers Bd., Mortar Bd., Alpha Zeta (vice chmn. 1981-82). Avocations: restoring classic cars and tractors, hunting, reading. Home and Office: Gary A Larson Farm 2282 130th St N Canby MN 56220

LARSON, GEORGE CHARLES, magazine editor, writer; b. Mar. 31, 1942; s. George Lester and Mildred Caroline (Frehner) L.; m. Valarie Ann Thompson, Aug. 20, 1946; children: Evan Richard; Alice Lynn and Keely Mae (twins). BA, Harvard U., 1964. Staff writer Scholastic Mag., N.Y.C., 1971; regional editor, mng. editor Flying Mag., N.Y.C., 1972-78; tech. editor Bus. & Comml. Aviation Mag., White Plains, N.Y., 1980-85; editor Air & Space/Smithsonian Mag., Washington, 1985—. Author: Fly on Instruments, The Blimp Book. Served with U.S. Army, 1966-70, Vietnam. Office: Air & Space Mag PO Box 37012 MRC 951 Washington DC 20013-7012 Office Phone: 202-275-1230. Business E-Mail: glarson@si.edu.

LARSON, JAMES R., retired oil industry executive; BBA, U. Iowa, 1972. CPA. Joined Ea. Pipe Line Co. (former parent of Anadarko Petroleum Corp.), The Woodlands, Tex., 1981; asst. dir., taxes Ea. Pipe Line Co., 1981—82, dir., taxes, 1982, asst. contr., 1983—86, contr., 1986—2002, v.p., contr., 1995—2002, sr. v.p., 2002—05. Mem.: AICPA, Fin. Execs. Inst., Tax Execs. Inst. Office: Anadarko Petroleum 1201 Lake Robbins Dr The Woodlands TX 77380-1046

LARSON, JANE WARREN, ceramist; b. San Francisco, June 2, 1922; d. Stafford Leak and Viola (Lockhart) Warren; m. Clarence Ernest Larson, Apr. 21, 1957; children: Lawrence Ernest, Lance Stafford, Robert Edward. Student, Swarthmore Coll., 1939—41; BA with honors, U. Rochester, 1943; MFA in Ceramics, Antioch Coll., 1972. Sci. reporter, tech. editor Tenn. Eastman Corp., Oak Ridge, 1943-46; chief Tech. Info. Ctr. Carbide & Carbon Chem. Corp., Oak Ridge, 1946-51; tech. editor physics div. Rand Corp., Santa Monica, Calif., 1954-55, tech. libr. Washington, 1955-57; ceramist Janeware, Santa Monica, 1953-55; pres., bldg. founder Oak Ridge Cmty. Art Ctr., 1963-66, ceramic tchr., 1965-69; ceramic tchr. Inst. Learning in Retirement Am. U., Washington, 1985-88, 94. One-person shows at AAAS, Washington, 1990, Studio Gallery, Washington, 1992, 95, Cosmos Club, Washington, 1998, others 1973—, Creative Ptnrs. Gallery, Bethesda, Md., 1996; group shows at Bader Gallery and others, 1971—, Internat. Sculpture Conf., Washington, 1990, U. Md. Sculpture Show, 1994-95; vanishing diversity murals with water Guest Quarters Hotel gardens, Bethesda, Md., 1987, Oak Ridge Com. Art Ctr. garden, energy and life murals, 1992, Fed. City Shelter, Washington, 1988, U. Md. Chemistry Bldg., 1997; columns: Johns Hopkins Ctr. Internat. Studies, Washington, 1990, NAE, Beckman Ctr., Irvine, Calif., 1990, Asia Nora Restaurant, Washington, 1994; permanent collections include U. Md., College Park, (sculpture) AAAS, Am. Ctr. Physics, College Park, Renwick Gallery Nat. Mus. Am. Art; commns. include 4 murals 20 vases Germaines Restaurant, Washington, 1978, East Wind Restaurant, Alexandria, Va., 1980; lobby murals Nat. Milk Producers Assn., Rosslyn, Va., 1983, U. Md. Chem. Bldg., 10 Molecules that Shaped the World, 1997, 10 Molecules that Matter to Medicine, 1998, NIH Libr. Medicine, The Arrow of Time, 1999, Arlington County Libr., Ubby Blake H.S., 2000, ORNL Reborn, 2003-04; contbr. articles to profl. jours. including Cosmos 2000, It Is Time for Durable Records. Commr. Cable TV Commn., Montgomery County, Rockville, Md., 1989-90. Recipient Tile Heritage award, Tile Heritage Found., 2001, Pin with Diamond prize, ORNL, 2003. Mem. Ind. Agy. Women (pres. 1964-65), Kiln Club Washington (1st prize ann. show 1993), Achievement Rewards Coll. Sci., Inc. (v.p. 1980-81), Artists Equity, Internat. Sculpture Ctr., Bethesda Ceramic Guild (1st prize ann. show 1994, 95), Cosmos Club Washington, Phi Beta Kappa. Avocation: poetry. Home and Office: Apt 1420 9707 Old Georgetown Rd Bethesda MD 20814-1751

LARSON, JANICE TALLEY, computer science programmer; b. Houston, Sept. 29, 1948; d. Hiram Peak Talley and Jennie Edna Donahoo; m. Harold Vernon Larson, Apr. 8, 1977; children: Randall Neil, Christopher Lee. AA in Computers, San Jacinto Coll., 1981; BA in Computer Info. Systems, U. Houston, Clear Lake, 1984, MA in Computer Info. Systems, 1988; EdD in Instrnl. Tech., U. Houston, 1999. Programmer Control Applications, Houston, 1985-86, Tex. Eastern Pipeline, Houston, 1988-90; instr. computer sci. San Jacinto Coll., Houston, 1990-94; computer sci. reader Ednl. Testing Svc., Houston, 1996—2000; programmer for shuttle cockpit avionics upgrade United Space Alliance, 2000—02; programmer Creative Process Cons., League City, Tex., 2003—. Adj. instr. U. Houston, Clear Lake, Tex., 1996, 99, 2003-05; sponsor Computer Sci. Club, Houston, 1992-94. Mem.: AIAA, IEEE (assoc.), U. Houston Clear Lake Alumni Assn., U. Houston Alumni Assn., Kappa Delta Pi, Phi Delta Kappa. Personal E-mail: burnwuffie@aol.com.

LARSON, JEANETTE CAROLYN, librarian; b. Ft. Dix, N.J., Sept. 16, 1952; d. Wilbur Arthur and Carolyn Linda (Baker) Pawson; m. James Warren Larson, Jan. 31, 1975. BA, U. N.Mex., 1974; MS in Libr. Sci., U. So. Calif., 1979. Libr. Anaheim (Calif.) Pub. Libr., 1977-79; children's libr. Irving (Tex.) Pub. Libr., 1979-80, Mesquite (Tex.) Pub. Libr., 1980-85, supr. pub. svc., 1985-91; mgr. continuing edn. and cons. Tex. State Libr., Austin, 1991—98, dir. libr. devel. divsn., 1998—2000; youth svcs. mgr. Austin Pub. Libr., 2000—. Cons. Author Promotions, Austin, 1991—. Author: Animal Antics, 1987, Secret Code is READ, 1990; co-author: Model Policies for Small and Medium-Sized Public Libraries, 1996, Color Your World...Read!, 2004, Bringing Mysteries Alive, 2004; reviewer: Booklist, 1985—, Mostly Murder, Sch. Libr. Jour.; contbr. articles to libr. jours.; mem. editl. bd.: Book Links, 2003—, National Geographic, 2004—, book rev. editor: Parentwise, 2005—. Active nat. adv. bd. Grolier Pub., 1996—; v.p. bd. dirs. Connections Resources Ctr., Austin, 1998—2001; bd. dirs., prodrs. Vols. for USA, Film Fest Dallas, 1989—91; vol. Reading is Fundamental, Austin, 1992—, Humane Soc., Austin, 1991—93; mem. Tex. Book Festival, 1996—2004; adv. bd. Nat. Geog. Pub., 2004—. Mem.: ALA (Shirley Olofson award 1982), U. N.Mex. Alumni Assn. (pres. Austin chpt. 1994—95), Dallas County Libr. Assn. (pres. 1985—86), Tex. Libr. Assn. (Outstanding New Libr. award 1987, Libr. of Yr. 1998, Siddie Joe Johnson award 2002), Beta Phi Mu. Avocations: counted cross-stitch, animation art, animal welfare, films, travel. Home: 7300 Geneva Dr Austin TX 78723-1515 Office: Austin Pub Libr 800 Guadalupe Austin TX 78701 Office Phone: 512-974-7405. Personal E-mail: larsonlibrary@yahoo.com.

LARSON, JERRY LEROY, state supreme court justice; b. Harlan, Iowa, May 17, 1936; s. Gerald L. and Mary Eleanor (Patterson) L.; m. Debra L. Christensen; children: Rebecca, Jeffrey, Susan, David. BA, State U. Iowa, 1958, JD, 1960. Bar: Iowa. Partner firm Larson & Larson, 1961-75; dist. judge 4th Jud. Dist. Ct. of Iowa, 1975-78; justice Iowa Supreme Ct., 1978—. Office: Supreme Ct Iowa PO Box 109 Des Moines IA 50319-0001*

LARSON, JOAN ISBELL, musician, educator; b. Seattle, Wash., May 14, 1934; d. Robert Lyle and Lillian Darnall (Soward) Isbell; m. Carl Frithiof Larson, May 31, 1956; children: Dale James, Linda Darleen, Brian Carlyle, Mark Edward. BA magna cum laude Edn with music major, U. Ariz., Tucson, 1956, postgrad. studies, 1965—69; master counseling courses, Liberty U., Lynchburg, Va. Cafeteria food server Yellowstone Nat. Park, Wyo., 1955; tchr. 3d grade Lineweaver Sch., Tucson, 1956—57; substitute tchr. Owego-Appalachian Schs., 1966—69; saleswoman Worldbook-Childcraft, Field Entrpises, Owego, NY. Accompanist, performer religious services Chs. of Many Christian Denominations and charity events, 1985—; ch. pianist and singer Nichols United Meth. Ch., NY, 1978—; private music tchr. self-employed, Owego, NY, 1959—. Contbr. poetry to Poetic Voices of Am. Trainee to be mediator and emergency responder Broome and Tioga Counties, NY, 2005—; peformer with comty. groups and local bands, 1995—; spiritual dir. and guide Candlehouse Teen Challenge, Owego, NY, 1996—, edn. dir., 1995—2003. Recipient Gold Ring award, Sherwood Music Sch., Chgo., 1952; scholar summer session, 1951. Mem.: Am. Coll. Musicians (Internat. Piano Recording Competition, 6th place Tchr. Divsn. 1986, Paderewski medal 1996), Nat. Guild of Piano Tchrs. (adjudicator), Am. Assn. Christian Counselors., Phi Kappa Phi, Pi Lambda Theta, Sigma Alpha Iota. Avocations: art, gardening, dance.

LARSON, JOHN BARRY, congressman, insurance executive; b. Hartford, Conn., July 22, 1948; s. Raymond and Pauline (Nolan) L.; m. Leslie Best, Sept. 20, 1981; children: Carolyn, Laura, Raymond. BS, Cen. Ct. State U., 1971. HS teacher, 1972—77; ptnr. Larson & Lysik Ins., 1977—90; mem. Conn. Senate, 1983—94, pres. Pro Tempore, 1987—94; mem. U.S. Congress from 1st Conn. dist., 1998—; mem. ways and means com. Mem. East Hartford Town Coun., 1979—83, East Hartford Bd. of Edn., 1978—79. Recipient Outstanding Alumni award East Hartford High Sch. Nat. Honor Soc., 1985, Legis. Leadership award Conn. Assn. Human Svcs., 1987, Disting. Alumni award Cen. Conn. State U., 1987; Legislator of Yr. award Jr. League Conn., 1988, Conn. Valley Girl Scouts, 1989, Cath. Charities/Cath. Family Svcs., 1989; Man of Yr. award United Irish Socs., 1990, Champion for Children award Conn. Commn. on Children, 1990, recognition award Alzheimer's Assn. Greater Hartford, 1991, appreciation award Conn. AIDS Consortium/United Way Conn., 1991, Child Advocacy Legis. Leadership award Conn. Coalition for Children, 1991, sr. fellow, Yale Bush Ctr. for Child Devel., others. Mem. Hartford Club. Democrat. Roman Catholic. Achievements include creator/chmn. ConneCT96 Project, 1996. Office: Ho of Reps 1005 Longworth Hob Washington DC 20515-0001 also: 221 Main Street, 2nd Floor Hartford CT 06106

LARSON, JOHN DAVID, insurance company executive, lawyer; b. Madison, Wis., July 6, 1941; s. Lawrence John and Anna Mathilda (Furseth) Larson; m. Evelyn Vie Smith, Jan. 22, 1966 (div. Apr. 1980); children: Eric John, Karen Annette; m. Nancy With Jay, Nov. 29, 1980 (div. Dec. 1998); stepchildren: Andrew Zachary Jay, Anne Elizabeth Jay, Christopher Allen Jay; m. Sherri Ann Sturtz Kliczak, July 12, 2002; 1 stepchild, Cristopher Howard Kliczak. BBA, U. Wis., 1964, JD, 1965, MBA, 1966. CPA Wis.; CLU; bar: Wis. 1965, U.S. Ct. Mil. Appeals 1966; chartered fin. cons. With Nat. Guardian Life Ins. Co., Madison, 1969—, exec. v.p., treas., 1973, pres., dir., 1974—, pres., CEO, 1989—2004, chmn., pres., CEO, 2004—. Bd. advisors U.S. Bank, Madison; bd. dirs. TV Wis., Inc., KELAB, Inc. Chmn. Madison chpt. ARC, 1974—75; pres. United Way Dane County, Wis., 1975, Wis. N.G. Assn., 1992—96; trustee Village of Maple Bluff, Wis., 1997—2003, pres., 2003—. With U.S. Army, 1966—69, brig. gen. Wis. Army N.G., 1998. Named Disting. Bus. Alumnus, U. Wis.-Madison, 1996; recipient Know Your Madisonian award, Wis. State Jour., 1973. Mem.: ABA, Am. Soc. Fin. Svc. Profls., State Bar Wis., U. Wis. Bus. Alumni (bd. dirs. 1986—90), Madison C. of C. (dir. 1976—80), Maple Bluff Club (bd. dirs. 1974—80), Rotary. Lutheran. Home: 401 New Castle Way Madison WI 53704-6070 Office: PO Box 1191 Madison WI 53701-1191 Business E-Mail: jdlarson@nglic.com.

LARSON, JOHN HYDE, retired utilities executive; b. Phila., Sept. 15, 1930; s. Roy Frank and Olive (Alden) L.; m. Priscilla Hibbs Beane; children: Michael Alden, Christopher Hibbs, Cynthia Ann. BA, Trinity Coll., 1953; M City Planning, MIT, 1955. Vice-pres. The Potomac Edison Co., Hagerstown, Md., 1969-72; treas. Allegheny Power System, Inc., N.Y.C., 1973-79; v.p. fin. Conn. Energy Corp., Bridgeport, Conn., 1980-85, pres., chief exec. officer, 1985-89; exec. v.p., chief operating officer So. Conn. Gas. Co., Bridgeport, Conn., 1981-85, pres., chief exec. officer, 1985-89; acting dir. fin. City of Bridgeport, 1989-90, chmn. mgmt. adv. com., 1990—93; chmn. selectman's com. on ops. improvement Westport, Conn., 1991; chmn. oversight and audit com., pres. trustees Epis Diocese, Vt., 1998—. Mem. Internat. Exec. Svc. Corps., Vladimir, Russia, 1996. Vice chmn. Bridgeport Hosp., 1991-93; chmn. Nova Med. Corp., 1991-95; hon. chmn. capital funds drive Family Svcs. Woodfield, 1988; treas. Christ Episcopal Ch., Bethel, Vt., 1995-98, 2003; trustee Clara Martin Ctr.; pres. Barnard Edn. Found., Inc., 2000—. Lt. (SC) USNR. Recipient Corp. Leadership award MIT, 1987, Century Svc. award Bridgeport Boys and Girls Club, 1991, Richard P. Bodine Community Leadership award, 1993. Mem. New Eng. Gas Assn. (chmn. 1988-89). Home: PO Box 185 Barnard VT 05031 Personal E-mail: vtlars@aol.com.

LARSON, JOHN M., educational consultant; BS in Bus. Adminstrn., U. Calif., Berkeley, Calif.; diploma in Exec. Mgmt. Program, Stanford U., 2000. With Mktg. Dept. DeVry Inc.; v.p. mktg. Nat. Edn. Ctrs., Inc., 1980—89; sr. v.p. ops. Geneva Cos., 1989; sr. v.p. Coll. Ops. Phillips Colls., Inc., 1989—93; ea. regional operating mgr. Ednl. Med., Inc., 1993; cons. Heller Equity Capital Corp., 1993—94; pres. Career Edn. Corp., Hoffman Estates, Ill., 1994—, CEO, 1994—, chmn. bd., 2000—. Named Entrepreneur of Yr. Ill. and N.W. Ind. Region, Ernst & Young. Office: Career Education Corp 2895 Greenspoint Pkwy Ste 600 Hoffman Estates IL 60195*

LARSON, JOHN WILLIAM, lawyer; b. Detroit, June 24, 1935; s. William and Sara Eleanor (Yeatman) L.; m. Pamela Jane Wren, Sept. 16, 1959; 1 dau., Jennifer Wren. BA with distinction, honors in Economics, Stanford, 1957; LLB, Stanford U., 1962. Bar: Calif. 1962. Assoc. Brobeck, Phleger & Harrison, San Francisco, 1962-68, ptnr., 1968—71, 1973—2003, CEO, 1988—96; asst. sec. Dept. Interior, Washington, 1971-73; exec. dir. Natural Resources Com., Washington, 1973; counsellor to chmn. Cost of Living Coun., Washington, 1973; ptnr. Morgan, Lewis & Backius LLP, 2003—. Faculty Practising Law Inst.; bd. dirs. Sangamo Bio Scis., Inc. Mem. 1st U.S.-USSR Joint Com. on Environment; mem. bd. visitors Stanford U. Law Sch., 1974-77, 85-87, 95-96; pres. bd. trustees The Katherine Branson Sch., 1980-83. With AUS, 1957-59. Mem. ABA, Calif. Bar Assn., San Francisco C. of C. (bd. dirs., chmn. 1996), Bay Area Coun., Calif. Acad. Sci., Order of Coif, Pacific Union Club, Burlingame Country Club, Bohemian Club, Lagunitas Country Club. Home: PO Box 349 Ross CA 94957-0349 Office: Brobeck Phleger & Harrison Spear St Tower 1 Market Plz San Francisco CA 94105-1420

LARSON, JOSEPH STANLEY, environmentalist, educator; b. Stoneham, Mass., June 23, 1933; s. Gustave Adolph and Marian (Kelly) Larson; m. Wendy Nichols, Nov. 23, 1958; children: Marion Elizabeth, Sandra Frances. BS, U. Mass., 1956, MS, 1958; PhD, Va. Poly. Inst., 1966. Exec. sec. Wildlife Conservation, Inc., Boston, 1958-59; state ornithologist Mass. Divsn. Fisheries and Wildlife, Boston, 1959-60; head conservation edn. divsn. Natural Resources Inst., U. Md., Annapolis, 1960-62; rsch. asst. prof. LaVale, 1965-67; wildlife rsch. biologist U.S. Fish and Wildlife Svc., Amherst, Mass., 1967-69; prof., dir. The Environ. Inst., U. Mass., Amherst, 1969-2000, prof. emeritus natural resources conservation, 2000—. Cons. in field. Contbr. articles to profl. jours. Apptd. by gov. Mass. Fisheries and Wildlife Bd., 2000—; mem. adv. com. Mass. Natural Heritage, 2000—. Named Conservationalist of the Yr., Mass. Wildlife Fedn., 1997; recipient Chevron Conservation award, 1990, Dir.'s award, N.E. Sci. Ctr., Nat. Marine Fisheries Svc., 2000; grantee, in field. Mem.: AAAS, AAUP (pres. Mass. chpt. 1976—77), Internat. Union Conservation Nature and Natural Resources (commn. ecosystem mgmt. Switzerland), Soc. Wetland Scientists (profl. wetland scientist), Am. Assn. Mammalogists, Ecol. Soc. Am. (cert. sr. ecologist), Wildlife Soc. (cert. wildlife biologist), Cosmos Club, Faculty Univ. Club, Xi Sigma Pi, Phi Sigma, Sigma Xi. Congregationalist. Home: 27 Arnold Rd Pelham MA 01002-9757 Office: U Mass Environ Inst Blaisdell House Amherst MA 01003-0820 Office Phone: 413-545-2842. E-mail: larson@tei.umass.edu.

LARSON, JUDY L., museum director, curator; b. Glendale, Calif., Mar. 9, 1952; d. John Arthur and Lorraine V. Larson. BA, UCLA, 1974, MA, 1978; PhD, Emory U., 1998. Acting asst. curator Los Angeles County Mus. Art, L.A., 1978; sr. cataloguer Am. Antiquarian Soc., Worcester, Mass., 1978-85; curator High Mus. Art, Atlanta, 1985—98; exec. dir. Art Museum of W. Va., W.Va., 1998—2002; dir. Nat. Museum of Women in the Arts, Washington, 2002—. Author: (catalogue) Am. Illustration 1890-1925, 1986; co-author: (catalogue) Am. Paintings at High Mus. Art, 1994; editor: Graphic Arts and the South, 1993. Office: Nat Museum of Women in the Arts 1250 New York Ave NW Washington DC 20005*

LARSON, KERMIT DEAN, finance educator; b. Algona, Iowa, Apr. 7, 1939; s. Loren L. and Hansena Laurena (Andersen) L.; m. Nancy Lynne Weber, June 17, 1961; children: Julie Renee, Timothy Dean, Cynthia Lynne. AA, Ft. Dodge Jr. Coll., 1960; BBA, U. Iowa, 1962, MBA, 1963; PhD, U. Colo., 1966. CPA Tex. Faculty U. Tex., Austin, 1966-94, Arthur Andersen & Co. Alumni prof. emeritus, 1994—, chmn. dept. acctg., 1971-75. Vis. assoc. prof. Tulane U., New Orleans, 1970-71; cons. sales tax audit litig., pvt. anti-trust litig., expropriation ins. arbitration. Author: (with John Wild and Barbara Chiappetta) Fundamental Accounting Principles, 1978, 17th edit., 2005, Financial Accounting, 7th edit., 1997, (with Charlene Spoede and Paul Miller) Fundamentals of Financial and Managerial Accounting, 1994; contbr. articles to profl. jours. Mem. AICPA, Am. Acctg. Assn. (v.p. 1978-79), Beta Gamma Sigma, Beta Alpha Psi. Home: 1310 Falcon Ledge Dr Austin TX 78746-5120

LARSON, L. JEAN, educational administrator; b. Sioux City, Iowa, Jan. 27, 1934; d. Marion A. and Lola J. (Willenborg) Robey; m. Herbert L. Larson, June 25, 1955; 1 child, Joan Irene. BA with honors, U. No. Iowa, 1954; MEd, U. Ariz., 1959. Cert. adminstr., elem. tchr., Ariz., cert. speech therapist, K-12 tchr., Iowa. Tchr. Tucson Unified Sch. Dist., counselor, prin.; dir. Tucson Hebrew Acad. Dir. Children's Ministries. Mem. Internat. Reading Assn., Ariz. Reading Assn., Tucson Reading Assn., ASCD, PTA, NEA, NAFE, Altrusa, Delta Kappa Gamma, Kappa Delta, Delta Sigma Rho, Kappa Delta Pi (Purple Arrow award). Home: 7041 E Hawthorne St Tucson AZ 85710-1232

LARSON, LARRY, retired librarian; b. El Dorado, Ark., July 18, 1940; s. Willie Lee and Myrtle Elizabeth (McMaster) L.; m. Dorothy Ann Bing, Apr 23, 1966; 1 child, Larisa Ann. BS, Ouachita Baptist U., 1962; MLS, George Peabody Coll., 1967. Asst. librarian, media specialist Hall High Sch., Little Rock, 1962—65; asst. librarian, circulation Ark. Tech. U., Russellville, 1965—67; asst librarian reference Hendrix Coll., Conway, Ark., 1967—73; head librarian U. Ark., Monticello, 1973—75; librarian, dir. N. Ark. Regional Library, Harrison, 1975—85, Ft. Smith (Ark.) Pub. Library, 1985—2004. Mem. adv. bd. Sparks Regional Med. Ctr., 1998—2001. Bd. dirs. Ft. Smith Hist. Soc., 1986—90, Info. Network Ark., 1997—2001; treas. bd. dirs. Pub. Awareness Com., Ft. Smith, Ark., 1986—2004. Mem.: ALA, Ark. Adminstrs. Pub. Librs. (chair 1988—89, del. Ark. govs. conf. on librs. 1990), Ark. Libr. Devel. Dist. (chair 1985—87), Ark. Libr. Assn. (vice chair membership com. 1968, chair pub. libr. divsn. 1993, Disting. Svc. award 1985), Info. Network Ark. (bd. dirs. 1997—2001). Democrat. Baptist. Avocations: gardening, woodworking.

LARSON, MARILYN J., retired elementary music educator; b. Lindstrom, Minn., July 20, 1933; d. Reuben and Dorothy (Holm) L.; m. Harold P. Cohen, Aug. 4, 1957 (div. Dec. 1975); children: Paul, Morrie, Robert. BS with distinction, U. Minn., 1955, MA with honors, 1957. Nat. cert. tchr. music; cert. tchr., Minn.; lic. realtor. Tchr. U. Minn., Mpls., 1955-57, Mpls. Jr. High Sch., 1957-60; piano tchr. pvt. studio, Fridley, Minn.; tchr. Mpls. Pub. Schs., 1976-78, St. Paul Pub. Schs., 1978-97. Designed music curriculum Mpls. Pub. Schs.; mem. INS Roundtable, 2000-04; accompanist Adult Day Care, St. Mary's Home, 2001-04; piano music for vets., 2000-03. Accompanist U. Minn. Chorus, 1953-56, Berkshire Music Ctr. at Tanglewood, Mass., 1953. Mem. Music Tchrs. Nat. Assn., Fedn. for Am. Immigration Reform, Minnesotans for Immigration Reform (founder, exec. dir. 1999—). Independent. Luth. Avocations: reading, music. Home: 5890 Stinson Blvd Fridley MN 55432-6002 E-mail: marilynmusic@webtv.net.

LARSON, MARK DEVIN, communications executive; b. Rockford, Ill., Aug. 6, 1955; s. Burdette D. Larson and Inga Mae Sandberg; m. Marcia L. Sutton, Feb. 14, 1976; children: Jeffrey, Brandon, Kristin. Grad. high sch., Rockford, 1973. Announcer WRWC Radio, Rockton, Ill., 1971-72; announcer, asst. prodn. dir. WRRR-AM, Rockford, 1972-73; prodn. dir., afternoon host WROK-AM, Rockford, 1973-76; announcer KFMB-AM, San Diego, 1976-77, asst. program dir., 1977-78, program and ops. mgr., afternoon personality, 1978-94; gen. mgr. KPRZ-AM Radio, San Diego, 1994—2002, Sta. KPRZ-AM Sta. KCBQ-AM Radio, San Diego, 1999—2002; talk show host Sta. KCBQ and KPRZ, 1995—2004, mgr., program cons., 2002—04; guest host for Michael Medved, Dennis Prager and Hugh Hewitt Network Radio Talk Shows, 2000—04; talk show host KOGO-AM, San Diego, 2004—; founder ML Spkrs. Group, 2003—; talkshow host KOGO-AM, San Diego, 2004—. Co-founder The Program Group, San Diego, 1984-94; co-owner, cons. KISN AM/FM, Salt Lake City, 1985-95; founder, pres. Mark Larson Media Svcs. Inc., El Cajon, Calif., 1985—; nat. program dir./radio Midwest TV, 1988-93; morning talk show host Sta. KRLA-AM, L.A., 2002-03, Sta. KCBQ-AM, San Diego, 2000-04. Creator (audio seminar series) Personal Program Power, 1985-93; host (TV show) KTTY-TV, 1993-94 (Emmy award 1993); columnist Daily Californian, 1995-2000. Chmn., co-founder Family Heritage Found., 1988—, FHF chmn., 1994—, Prison Fellowship, San Diego, 1990-96; vice chair Arts Ctr. Found., 2003—; comm. chmn. San Diego County Rep., 1995; active San Diego Youth for Christ, 1987-97; nat. bd. dirs., mem. global leadership coun. Heart to Heart Internat., 2002—; charter mem. Salem Comm. Polit. Action Com. Named Citizen of Yr., San Diego City Club and Jaycees, 1995, Best Talk Show Host, Achievement in Radio awards, 2002. Mem. Media Fellowship Internat. (chmn. 1998—2003), San Diego Radio Broadcasters Assn. (pres. 1998—2004), San Diego Aerospace Mus. (bd. dirs.), City Club San Diego. Avocations: collecting rare books, collecting political autographs and memorabilia. Office: Mark Larson Media Svc Inc 4370 La Jolla Village Dr #400 San Diego CA 92122 Office Phone: 858-546-4855. E-mail: mark@marklarson.com.

LARSON, MARK EDWARD, JR., lawyer, educator, financial planner; b. Oak Park, Ill., Dec. 16, 1947; s. Mark Edward and Lois Vivian (Benson) L.; m. Patricia Jo Jekerle, Apr. 14, 1973; children: Adam Douglas, Peter Joseph, Alex Edward, Gretchen Elizabeth. BS in Acctg., U. Ill., 1969; JD, Northwestern U., 1972; LLM in Taxation, NYU, 1977. Bar: Ill. 1973, N.Y. 1975, D.C. 1976, Minn, 1982, Tex. 1984, U.S. Dist. Ct. (no. dist.) Ill. 1973, U.S. Dist. Ct. (so. dist.) N.Y. 1975, U.S. Ct. Appeals (2d cir.) 1975, U.S. Ct. Appeals (7th cir.) 1976, U.S. Dist. Ct. D.C. 1977, U.S. Ct. Appeals (D.C. cir.) 1977, U.S. Dist. Ct. Minn. 1982, U.S. Ct. Appeals (8th cir.) 1982, U.S. Tax Ct. 1976, U.S. Supreme Ct. 1976; CPA, Ill. Acct. Deloitte & Touche (formerly Haskins & Sells), N.Y.C., 1973—76, Chgo., 1978—81; atty., ptnr. Larson, Perry & Ward, P.C. and former firms, Chgo., 1983—; prin. Winfield Fin. Svcs. and affiliates, Houston, Austin and Chgo., 1986—. Adj. faculty U. Minn., Mpls., 1982—83, Aurora (Ill.) U., 1990—98, St. Xavier U., Chgo., 2000—; exec. dir. united fin. group ins. for profl. edn. Marquette U., Milw., 1996—; bd. dirs. Rush-Wood Imaging Ptnrs., Ltd. Contbr. articles to profl. jours. Mem.: AICPA, ABA, Am. Acctg. Assn., Acad. Fin. Svcs., Acad. Molecular Imaging, Am. Assn. Atty.-CPAs, Am. Hosp. Lawyers Assn. Office: 1212 S Naper Blvd Ste 119-131 Naperville IL 60540-7349 Office Phone: 630-369-3340. Personal E-mail: larsgen@usa.net. E-mail: larson@attorney-cpa.com.

LARSON, MELORA, physicist; b. Los Alamos, N.Mex. married. B in Physics with honors, Stanford U.; PhD, U. Calif., Santa Barbara. Postdoctoral NASA Jet Propulsion Lab., Pasadena, Calif., mem. tech. staff, cognizant cryogenic engr. Confined Helium Expt., prin. investigator EXACT. Office: NASA Jet Propulsion Lab 4800 Oak Grove Dr MS 79-24 Pasadena CA 91109 Business E-Mail: melora.e.larson@jpl.nasa.gov.

LARSON, MICHAEL LEN, newspaper editor, hospital administrator, publishing executive; b. St. James, Minn., Feb. 3, 1944; s. Leonard O. and Lois O. (Holte) L.; m. Kay M. Monahan, June 18, 1966; children: Christopher, David, Molly. BA, U. Minn., 1966; MBA, Mankato State U., 1986. Mng. editor Paddock Circle Inc., Libertyville, Ill., 1972-74, New Ulm (Minn.) Journal, 1974-76, Republican-Eagle, Red Wing, Minn., 1976-79, Mankato (Minn.) Free Press, 1979-84, editor, 1984-95, editor of editl. page, 1995-97; editor Minot (N.D.) Daily News, 1997-2000; bus. editor St. Cloud (Minn.) Times, 2000—01; asst. adminstr. Melrose Area Hosp. Complex, 2001—03; pres., pub. Red Hat Enterprises, Bloomington, Minn., 2003—. Bd. dirs. Minot Area Devel. Corp. Bd. dirs. Valley Indsl. Devel. Corp., Mankato, 1985-95, treas.; adv. bd. Mankato State U. Bus. Sch.; bd. dirs. Sartell Planning Commn., 2003—. With U.S. Army, 1966-68, Vietnam. Recipient First Place award for investigative reporting Minn. Newspaper Assn., 1969, 71, 72, 76, 78, First Place award for feature writing, Suburban Newspapers Am., 1974. Mem. Minn. AP (pres. 1988—), Kiwanis. Roman Catholic. Avocation: bicycling. Home: 1808 N Eighth St Sartell MN 56377-1697 Office: Red Hat Enterprises 11025 Irwin Ave S Bloomington MN 55437

LARSON, NANCY CELESTE, information technology manager; b. Chgo., July 17, 1951; d. Melvin Ellsworth and Ruth Margaret (Carlson) L. BS in Music Ed., U. Ill., 1973, MS in Music Edn., 1976; postgrad., Purdue U., 1982—86. Vocal music educator Consol. Sch. Dist., Gilman, Ill., 1975-77; elem. vocal music tchr. Sch. Dist. 161, Flossmoor, 1977-87; instr. Vander Cook Coll., Chgo., 1980-88; systems programmer analyst Sears, Roebuck & Co., 1987-92, tech. instr., 1989-90, project leader, 1990-91, sr. systems analyst, 1991-92, Trans Union LLC, 1992-94, mgr., 1994—. Tchr. adult computer edn. Homewood-Flossmoor HS, 1986—90. Chmn. Faith Luth. Ch., 1982-87, pres. bd., 1988-91, vocal soloist and voice-over performer. Mem. Ill. Music Educators Assn., Music Educators Nat. Conf., Ill. Educators Assn., Nat. Educators Assn., Am. ORFF Schulwerk Assn., Flossmoor Edn. Assn. (negotiator 1983-86). Republican. Avocations: swimming, reading, antiques. Home: Apt 904 1960 N Lincoln Park W Chicago IL 60614-5440 Office: Trans Union LLC 555 W Adams St Fl 4 Chicago IL 60661-3696

LARSON, PAUL MARTIN, lawyer; b. Tacoma, June 8, 1949; s. Charles Philip and Margeret (Kobervig) L.; m. Kristina Simonson, June 19, 1971; children: Kristin Ilene, Paul Philip, Erika Louise. AB, Stanford U., 1971; JD, Gonzaga U., 1974. Bar: Wash. 1975, U.S. Dist. Ct. (we. dist.) Wash. 1975, U.S. Dist. Ct. (ea. dist.) Wash. 1978, U.S. Ct. Appeals (9th cir.) 1981. Assoc. Hoff & Cross, Tacoma, 1975-76; ptnr., prin. Brooks & Larson, P.S., Yakima, Wash., 1976-87; ptnr. Bogle & Gates, Yakima, 1987-93, Larson & Perkins, 1994—. Author: (with others) Commercial Law Deskbook, 1981 Pres. Cardio & Pulmonary Inst., Yakima, 1981; bd. dirs. Yakima YMCA, 1981-98, pres.-elect bd. dirs. 2000, pres., 2001-2003; bd. dirs. Yakima Youth Commn., 1989-93, Yakima Valley chpt. ARC, 1990-93; bd. dirs. Sisters of Providence Med. Ctr.-Yakima Found., 1986-96, pres., 1992-93, Area Svc. bd. mem., 2000—; bd. dirs. Yakima Schs. Found., 1993-2000, pres., 2000; bd. dirs. EPIC, 2003-. Fellow ABA (standing com. lawyer's responsibility for client protection 1984-89); mem. Wash. State Bar Assn. (spl. dist. counsel, 1985-96, pres. corp. bus. and banking sect. 1987-88, chmn. unauthorized practice of law task force 1995-96), Yakima Estate Planning Coun. (pres. 1981), Rotary (pres. 2005—). Avocations: tennis, fishing. Office: Larson & Perkins PO Box 550 Yakima WA 98907-0550 Office Phone: 509-457-1515. Business E-Mail: paul@lplaw.com.

LARSON, PAUL WILLIAM, public relations executive; b. Wilmington, NC, May 28, 1956; s. Robert William and Helen Joyce (Hillen) L. BA, U. Calif., Berkeley, 1981; MS in Journalism Medill Sch. of Journalism, Northwestern U., Evanston, Ill., 1991. Reporter Turlock (Calif.) Daily Jour., 1982-84; writer, editor Paul Larson Commns., Modesto, Calif., 1984-90, Evanston, Ill., 2002—; dir. external affairs and publs. Medill Sch. Journalism, Northwestern U., Evanston, 1991-96; mgr. strategic com. AMA, Chgo., 1996-98, dir. membership com., 1998-2000, v.p. mem. and bus. comms., 2000—02; prin. Paul Larson Comms., 2002—. Bd. dirs. Housing Options for Mentally Ill, Evanston, 1993-2000, chmn. comm. com. 1995-2000; docent Evanston Hist. Soc., 1992-95. Recipient Rotary Group Study Exchg. award Rotary Internat., 1986, Rotary Found. Dist. Svc. award, 1995, Leadership Evanston Evanston Cmty. Rels., 1995-96, Vol. of the Yr. award Evanston McGaw YMCA, 1995. Mem. Rotary (bd. dirs. Evanston 1991-95). Home: 1017 Greenleaf St Evanston IL 60202-1235

LARSON, PETER N., manufacturing executive; b. 1939; BS, Oreg. State U.; JD, Seton Hall U. With Johnson & Johnson, N.J., 1967-78, 91-95, Kimberly Clark; chmn. bd., CEO Brunswick Corp., Lake Forest, Ill., 1995—. Office: Brunswick Corp One Northfield Ct Lake Forest IL 60045

LARSON, PHILIP C., lawyer; b. Clarinda, Iowa, June 14, 1946; BS, Iowa State U., 1968; JD with honors, Duke U., 1971. Bar: D.C. 1971, U.S. Supreme Ct. 1975. Ptnr. Hogan & Hartson L.L.P., Washington, dir. antitrust practice group. Article editor Duke Law Jour., 1970-71; contbr. articles to profl. jours. Mem. ABA (antitrust law sect., litigation sect.), D.C. Bar, Order of Coif. Office: Hogan & Hartson LLP Columbia Square 555 13th St NW Ste 800E Washington DC 20004-1161 Office Phone: 202-637-5738. Office Fax: 202-637-5910. Business E-Mail: pclarson@hhlaw.com.

LARSON, PHYLLIS SHEPHERD, librarian; b. Winston-Salem, NC, Sept. 19, 1933; d. John Ervin and Annie Jay (Walters) Shepherd; m. Carl Erik Larson, Jr., June 14, 1958; children: Douglas Alan, Brian Edward. AB in Chemistry, U. N.C., 1955, BSLS, 1956. Librarian Am. Cyanamid Co., various cities, 1956-60. Chmn. Citizens for Librs., Delaware County, Pa., 1974-76; mem. dist. adv. com. Phila. Free Libr., 1974-77; mem. libr. svcs. task force Delaware County Planning Commn., 1975; chmn. Del. County delegation to Gov.'s Conf. on Librs. and Info. Svcs., Harrisburg, 1977; pres. Delaware County Bd. Libr. Dirs., 1980-88; mem. steering com. White House Conf. on Librs. and Info. Svcs. Task Force, 1985-1991; mem. Pa. Gov.'s Adv. Coun. on Libr. Devel./Fed. Adv. Coun., Harrisburg, 1986-1993; del., Pa. Gov's conf. on librs. and info. svcs., Harrisburg, 1990; del. White House Conf. on Libr. and Info. Svcs, 1991. Named Woman of Achievement Dela. County Girl Scouts, 1989. Mem. ALA, Pa. Libr. Assn. (cert. of merit 1977, Disting. Svc. award 1992), Delta Phi Alpha, Beta Phi Mu. Republican. Methodist. Avocations: sailing, travel, music. Address: 216 Versailles Dr Cary NC 27511-6018

LARSON, REED EUGENE, foundation administrator; b. Smith County, Kans., Sept. 27, 1922; s. George Christian and Edith Hazel (Whitney) L.; m. Marjorie Jeanne Hess, Aug. 31, 1947; children: Patricia Kay Larson Sween, Barbara Ann Larson Finnegan, Marcia Lynn Larson Craig. Student, Kans. Wesleyan U., 1940-41, Ohio State U., 1943-44; BS in E.E, Kans. State U., 1947. Design engr. Stein Labs., Atchison, Kans., 1947-48; processing engr. Coleman Co., Wichita, Kans., 1948-54; exec. v.p. Kansans for the Right to Work, Wichita, 1954-58; from exec. v.p. to chmn. exec. com. Nat. Right-to-Work Com., Washington, 1959—2003; chmn. exec. com. Nat. Right-to-Work Legal Def. Found., 2003—. Chmn. Hallmark Bank & Trust, 1984-96; vice chmn. F&M Bank-No. Va., 1996-99. Served with AUS, 1943-46. Recipient Seldon Waldo award U.S. Jaycees, 1956; Silver Anvil award Pub. Rels. Soc. Am., 1966; James J. Kilpatrick award Internat. Platform Assn., 1980; Awarded Doctor of Laws Campbell U., 1988. Mem. Mont Pelerin Soc., Phila. Soc., Eta Kappa Nu, Tau Beta Pi. Clubs: Kansas Jaycees (pres. 1953-54), Rotary, Am. Legion. Baptist. Office: 8001 Braddock Rd Springfield VA 22160-0001 Home: 3013 Downing St Williamsburg VA 23185 Office Phone: 703-321-9820. Business E-Mail: larson@nrtw.org.

LARSON, RICHARD EVERETT, lab administrator; b. New London, Conn. s. Everett Richard and Rachel (Amendola) L. BS, U. Conn., Storrs, 1977, MS, 1981; student, U. R.I., Kingston, 1982-83. With USCG, 1990—. Episcopalian. Avocations: golf, fishing. Office: US Coast Guard Acad 27 Mohegan Ave New London CT 06320-8101 E-mail: RLarson@cga.uscg.mil.

LARSON, RICHARD SMITH, pathologist, researcher; b. Ithaca, N.Y., Aug. 27, 1962; s. Richard Ingwald and Judith Ann (Larsen) Larson; m. Blaire Martin, June 4, 1989. AB in Chemistry summa cum laude, U. N.C., 1984; MD, PhD, Harvard U., 1990. Diplomate Am. Bd. Pathology. Resident Barnes Hosp., St. Louis, 1990-93; hematopathology fellow Vanderbilt U., Nashville, 1993-96; from assoc. prof., divsn. chief to prof., sr. assoc. dean U. N.Mex., 1996—. Co-founder Cancer Svcs. N.Mex.; bd. dirs. Tricore Corp., Lit. Coun. Contbr. over 100 articles to profl. jours., chapters to books. Named designated investigator, Am. Cancer Soc. Coaches Against Cancer, Hoops for Lymphoma; recipient Lansky award, UNM Regents' Lectureship; grantee, Am. Cancer Soc., Am. Heart Assn., NIH, NSF. Mem.: Pediat. Oncology Group, Am. Soc. Hematology, Coll. Am. Pathologists, Phi Beta Kappa. Achievements include patents in field.

LARSON, ROBERT WILLIAM, education educator, consultant; b. Iowa City, Feb. 8, 1935; s. Robert William and Mary Alice (Scannell) Larson; m. Linda Louise Carolan, Nov. 30, 2002. BS, U. Wyo., Laramie; MA, EdD, U. N. Colo., Greeley. Pres. Media, Inc., 1967—72; dir. Title 1 and fed. programs Greeley Sch., Colo., 1972—74; advt., pub. rels. dir. Blue Cross/Blue Shield, Cheyenne, Wyo., 1976—83; mktg. cons. Stress Mgmt. Inst., Cheyenne, Wyo., 1983—86; asst. prof. Minn. State U., Moorhead, 1986—90; mktg. cons. Ad Pro, Duluth, Ga., 1990—92; assoc. prof. Breneau U., Gainesville, Ga., 1990—92; asst. prof. Pitts. State U., 1992—98, Northwestern Okla. State, 1998—2002; adj. assoc. prof. Washburn U., Topeka, 2002—, Kansas City (Kans.) C.C., 2003—. Contbr. Wild Horses, 1963. Dir. Joplin (Mo.) AdFedn., 1996-98; county coord. Sally Thompson Senate, Pittsburg, Kans., 1996; states coord., Kathy Karpan Sec. of State, Cheyenne, Wyo., 1986. Maj. USMC, 1958-62, USMCR, 1963-85. Mem. Pittsburg C. of C., Moorhead C. of C. Democrat. Methodist. Avocations: triathlons, waterskiing, basketball, tennis, woodworking. Office Phone: 785-670-1807. Personal E-mail: blarson83@aol.com.

LARSON, ROGER KEITH, physician, writer; b. Cadillac, Mich., Apr. 27, 1924; s. William E. and Ethel Lydia (Rose) Larson; m. Frances Ann Appel, July 1, 1949; children: Ronald Allen, John William, Joan Elizabeth, Sharon Ruth. BS, N.W. Univ. Wheaton Coll., 1944; MD, Univ. Ill. Coll. of Medicine, Chgo., 1947. Cert. Am. Bd. of Internal Medicine, 1956, in subspeciality of Pumonary Disease 1978. Internship Cook County Hosp., Chgo., 1947—49; residency Kern Gen. Hosp., 1949—52; pvt. practice, 1957—61; chief of medicine Univ. Med. Ctr., Fresno, Calif., 1961—90; dir. HRSA and NIMH AIDS Profl. Edn. and Trng. Grant, Calif., Oregon, Nevada, Ariz., 1990—93. Instr. UCLA Sch. of Medicine, 1955—76; clin. prof. UCSF, 1976—93, prof. emeritus, 1993—; clin. prof. UCD, 1990—93. Contbr. chapters to books, articles to profl. jour. Cpt. U.S. Army, 1952—54, Korea, Japan. Recipient Disting. Svc. award, AHA, 1969, Henry E. Randel award, Ctrl. Calif. Lung Assn., 1980, Kasier award, USCF, 1981, Award for Outstanding Cmty. Svc, Fresno Med. Soc., 1991, Laureate award of the Calif. Chptr. of Am. Coll. of physicians, 1992. Achievements include first to establish the relationship of smoking to chronic lung disease; major contbr. to the understanding of the disease pulmonary alveolar proteinosis; first to devel. major acad. med. program in Calif. San Joaquin Valley. Faculty grew from one time person to approx. fifty and from non-Univ. affiliated to full UCSF affiliation. Avocations: music, history.

LARSON, ROLAND ELMER, health facility administrator; b. Chgo., Jan. 21, 1939; s. Elmer Gustav and Anna (Alphida) L.; children: Eric R., Jennifer L., Melissa K. BA, Augustana Coll., 1961; MHA, U. Iowa, 1963; postgrad., Harvard U., 1978. Adminstrv. asst. U. Vt. Med. Ctr., Burlington, 1962-64; assoc. adminstr. Roger Williams Hosp., Providence, 1964-73; v.p. adminstrn. Norwalk (Conn.) Hosp., 1973-81; pres., chief exec. officer Nashoba Community Hosp., Ayer, Mass., 1981-88; v.p. Charles River Assn., Boston, 1988-90; cons. Charles River Assocs., Boston, 1990-93; ind. healthcare cons. Harvard, Mass., 1990—. Chmn. Harvard (Mass.) Coalition Against Drugs and Alcohol, Opportunities, Inc., Providence, 1966-68, Greater Norwalk Community Coun., 1980; bd. dirs. Nat. Arthritis Found., N.Y.C., 1967-71, Am. Cancer Soc., Stamford, Conn., 1978-81. Fellow Am. Coll. Healthcare Execs.; mem. Cen. Mass. Hosp. Coun. (chmn. 1987-88), Rotary. Avocations: sailing, bicycling, golf, squash, woodworking. Home and Office: Larson & Assocs PO Box 602 Boylston MA 01505-0602

LARSON, ROY, journalist, publishing executive; b. Moline, Ill., July 27, 1929; s. Roy W. and Jane (Beall) L.; m. Dorothy Jennisch, June 7, 1950; children: Mark, Bruce, Jodie, Bradley. AB, Augustana Coll., Rock Island, Ill., 1951; M.Div., Garrett Theol. Sem., 1955. Ordained to ministry Methodist Ch., 1956; min. Covenant United Meth. Ch., Evanston, Ill., 1963-68, First United Meth. Ch., Elmhurst, Ill., 1968-69; religion editor Chgo. Sun-Times, 1969-85; pub. The Chgo. Reporter, 1985-94; exec. dir. Garrett-Medill Ctr. for Religion and News Media, Evanston, Ill., 1995—2002; dir. comm. Chgo. Temple, 2003—. Home: 1508 Hinman Ave Evanston IL 60201-4664 Office: Chgo Temple 77 W Washington Chicago IL 60602 Office Phone: 312-336-4548. E-mail: drlarson29@aol.com.

LARSON, SANDRA PAULINE, music educator; b. Milw., Jan. 27, 1944; d. Arthur Herman and Pauline Frances (Schneck) Voss; m. Dale Edwin Larson, Jan. 20, 1968; children: Eric Dale, Stephan Harold, Jonathan Arthur. MusB, Cardinal Stritch Coll., 1966; MusM, Southeastern La. U., 1992. Cert. Am. Coll. Musicians. Pvt. piano tchr., Slidell, La., 1974—; adj. faculty Delgado C.C. Slidell Learning Ctr. Piano adjudicator Am. Coll. Musicians Nat. Guild, 1994—. Piano accompanist Slidell Little Theater, 1994, 2002, 2003, 2005. Named to Order of St. Louis, Archdiocese of New Orleans, 1989. Mem. Music Tchrs. Nat. Assn. (nat. cert., piano adjudicator 1990—), Nat. Guild of Piano Tchrs. (local chair 1993-2003), La. Music Tchrs. Assn. (state cert., piano adjudicator 1990—, chmn. electronic music 1994-97), North Shore Music Tchrs. Assn. (pres. 1993-96), La. Fedn. of Music Clubs (local co-chmn. 1996-2004). Roman Catholic. Avocations: sewing, crafts, reading. Home and Office: 1130 Rue La Tour Slidell LA 70458-2220

LARSON, VERN L., state agency administrator; b. Pierre, SD, Oct. 25, 1948; BS in Polit. Sci. and English, No. State U., 1970. Aide to Rep. Jim Abdnor, SD, 1974—78; state auditor State of S.D., Pierre, 1979—2002, state treas., 2003—. Republican. Achievements include being the longest running constitutional officer in South Dakota history. Office: Office of State Treasurer Capitol Bldg 2d Fl 500 E Capitol Pierre SD 57501-5070

LARSON, VERNON DALE, audiologist, researcher; b. Sioux Falls, S.D., May 10, 1941; s. Leonard Gehard and Agnes E. Larson; m. Janice C. Haugen, Aug. 25, 1962; children: Tamara Lyn Whittemore, Kristen Eve Kidd, Jamie Durant. BA, Augustana Coll., Sioux Falls, S.D., 1965; MS, Colo. State U., 1966; PhD, Okla. U. Health Scis. Ctr., 1973. Lic. Calif. Chief audiology and speech pathology VA Med. Ctr., Augusta, Ga., 1979—94; prof., chair dept. speech and hearing George Wash. U., Washington, 1996—2000; mgr. dept. audiology Howard Leight/Bacou-Dalloz Safety, San Diego, 2002—. Mem. career scientist rev. panel Rehab. R&D, Vets. Affairs, Washington. Contbr. articles to profl. jours.; reviewer: Am. Jour. Audiology, Ear and Hearing, Jour. Speech Lang. and Hearing Rsch., Jour. Rehab. R&D. With U.S. Army. Recipient rsch. grant, NIH NIDCD, 1995—99, Deafness Rsch. Found., 1987—88, VA Rehab. Rsch., 1983—95. Fellow: Am. Acad. of Audiology; mem.: Nat. Hearing Conservation Assn., Am. Auditory Soc., Acoustical Soc. of Am., Am. Speech-Lang. (CCC 1968), Am. Legion, Sons of Norway. Office: Howard Leight/Bacou-Dalloz Safety 7828 Waterville Rd San Diego CA 92154 Home: 204 Berry Pl Mc Cormick SC 29835-2712 E-mail: vlarson@bacou-dalloz.com.

LARSON, VICKI LORD, communication disorders educator; b. Prentice, Wis., Sept. 21, 1944; d. Edward A. and Stella Mae (Hilton) Lord; m. James Roy Larson, Sept. 3, 1966. BSEd, U. Wis., Madison, 1966, MS, 1968, PhD, 1974. Speech-lang. pathologist Coop. Ednl. Svc. Agy. 2, Minoqua, Wis., 1967—69; instr. U. Wis., Whitewater, 1969—71, rsch. asst. Madison, 1971—73, asst. prof. Eau Claire, 1973-77, assoc. prof., 1977—81, prof. communication disorders, 1981—91, dept. chair, 1978—83, asst. dean grad. studies and univ. rsch., 1984—89, assoc. dean grad. studies and univ. rsch., 1989—91, interim chancellor, 2005—, prof. comm. Oshkosh, 1991—2000, dean Grad. Sch. Rsch., 1991—94, provost, vice chancellor acad. affairs, 1994—2000. Acquistions editor Thinking Publs., Eau Claire, 2001—04, acquistions mgr., 2004—. Author: Adolescents: Communication Development and Disorder, 1983, Communication Assessment and Intervention Strategies for Adolescents, 1987; contbr. Handbook of Speech-Language Pathology and Audiology, 1988, Language Disorders in Older Students, 1995,

Working Out With Listening, 2002, Communication Solutions for Older Students, 2003, S-MAPs curriculum-based assessment, 2004, Aspergers Syndrome: Strategies for Solving the Social Puzzle, 2005. Fellow: Am. Speech, Lang., Hearing Assn. (councilor); mem.: Wis. Speech, Lang., Hearing Assn. (pres. 1976, honors 1991, pres. found. 2000—04), Phi Kappa Phi, Omicron Delta Kappa. Avocations: travel, quilting, reading. Office Phone: 800-225-4769. E-mail: vicki@thinkingpublications.com.

LARSON, WANDA Z., writer, poet; b. Cle Elum, Wash., Aug. 26, 1926; d. Stanley Aloysius and Anele (Valente) Zackovich; m. Glen B. Larson, Nov. 18, 1950 (div. Mar. 1967); children: Karen Holk, Margot Huffman, Lisa Larson Landrey (dec. 1998). BA, U. Wash., 1949. Columnist North Bend Herald, Snoqualmie, Wash., 1955-61, Goldendale (Wash.) Sentinel, 1962-67; news editor West Seattle Herald, 1950-51; editor employee newsletter Alaska Steamship Co., Seattle, 1951; editl. asst. Associated Publs., Portland, Oreg., 1970-72, staff writer, 1974-78; pub. Blue Unicorn Press Inc., Portland, 1990—; poet Sta. KOPB, Portland, 1991—. Author: Portlandia, 1991, Miracle at Blowing Rock, 1992, Elisabeth: A Biography, 1997, 2nd edit., 2002, Our Flag - Born Through Valor, 1999, Bird Woman/Mojave (Sacajawea), 2001, Always, 2005, The Legend of Something More (King Arthur), 2005, Byzantium the Bridge, 2005. Co-recipient 2nd pl. award Poetry Forum Quar., 1990; hon. mention Still Water Press, 1990. Avocations: humanitarian interests, history. Home and Office: PO Box 40300 Portland OR 97240-0300

LARSSON, WILLIAM DEAN, manufacturing executive; b. Newberg, Oreg., June 8, 1945; s. Richard A. and Beverly L. (Phillips) Larsson; m. Debra T. Moore, Apr. 19, 1986; children: Amy, Alexander, Anna. BS in Econs., U. Oreg., 1967, BS in Math., 1968; MBA, Calif. State U., 1970. Supr. fin. analysis Ford Motor Co., Dearborn, Mich., 1968—75; v.p., contr. Wheel Horse Products, South Bend, Ind., 1975—79; v.p. fin. Whiting Corp., Chgo., 1979—80, Precision Castparts Corp., Portland, Oreg., 1980—. Home: 1210 Chandler Rd Lake Oswego OR 97034-2806 Office: Precision Castparts Corp 4600 SE Harney Dr Portland OR 97206-0825

LA RUE, CARL FORMAN, lawyer; b. Ann Arbor, Mich., Aug. 4, 1929; s. Carl D. and Evelina F. La R.; children: Steven, Edward; m. Ann Williams Lindbloom, June 28, 1971; stepchildren: Eric, Sarah Relyea. AB, Harvard U., 1952; LL.B., U. Mich., 1957. Bar: Ohio 1957, Ill. 1964, Calif. 1969. Assoc. firm Fuller & Henry, Toledo, 1957-59; asst. U.S. atty. for Northwestern Ohio, Dept. Justice, 1959-61; staff atty. Aeroquip-Vickers, Inc. (then Libbey-Owens-Ford Co., now part of Eaton Corp.), Toledo, 1961-64; sr. atty. Armour and Co., Chgo., 1964-68; asst. gen. counsel Rockwell Internat., L.A., 1968-78; v.p., gen. counsel, sec. Aeroquip-Vickers, Inc. (then Trinova Corp.), Toledo, 1978-87; of counsel Marshall & Melhorn, Toledo, 1988-96. With U.S. Army, 1952-54. Mem.: Toledo Tennis Club, Toledo Club. Home: 3553 Brookside Rd Toledo OH 43606-2610

LARUE, PAUL HUBERT, retired lawyer; b. Somerville, Mass., Nov. 16, 1922; s. Lucien H. and Germaine (Choquet) LaR.; m. Helen Finnegan, July 20, 1946; children: Paul Hubert, Patricia Fell, Mary Hogan. PhB, U. Wis., 1947, JD, 1949. Bar: Ill. 1955, Wis. 1949, U.S. Supreme Ct. 1972. Grad. asst. instr. polit. sci. dept. U. Wis., 1947-48; mem. staff Wis. Atty. Gen., 1949-50; trial atty., legal advisor to commr. FTC, 1950-55; pvt. practice Chgo.; mem. Chadwell & Kayser, Ltd., 1958-90; ptnr. Vedder, Price, Kaufman & Kammholz, 1990-93; of counsel, 1993-99; ret., 1999. Spkr. profl. meetings; mem. Com. Modern Cts. in Ill., 1964; mem. Com. for Constl. Conv. Ill., 1968, Better Govt. Assn., 1966-70 Contbr. articles to profl. jours. Mem. lawyers com. Met. Crusade of Mercy, 1967-68, United Settlement Appeal, 1966-68; apptd. pub. mem. Ill. Conflict of Interest Laws Commn., 1965-67. With AUS, 1943-45, ETO; capt. JAGC, USAFR, 1950-55. Fellow Ill. Bar Found. (life); mem. ABA (mem. coun. sect. antitrust law 1980-83, chmn. Robinson-Patman Act com. 1975-78), Ill. State Bar Assn., Chgo. Bar Assn. (chmn. antitrust com. 1970-71), Wis. State Bar (emeritus mem.), Rotary. Roman Catholic. Home: 250 Cuttriss St Park Ridge IL 60068 Personal E-mail: phlarue@aol.com.

LARUE, PETER JAMES, music educator; b. Lancaster, Ohio, Mar. 22, 1957; s. Patrick Lewis and Elsie LaRue. MusB, Capital U. Conservatory Music, Ohio, 1979; MS, U. Ill., Urbana-Champaign, 1980, EdD, 1986. Dir. of bands Bloom-Carroll Local Sch. Dist., Caroll, Ohio, 1980—84, Mars Hill Coll., NC, 1986—93; dir. of bands, prof. of music Georgetown Coll., Ky., 1993—. Music dir. & condr. Ctrl. Ky. Concert Band, Lexington, Ky., 1994—; dir. - summer programs & camps Georgetown Coll., Ky., 1995—. Contbr. articles to profl. jours. Recipient John WAlker Manning Disting. Mentor & Tchr. award, Georgetown Coll., 1998, Rollie Graves Tech. award, 2000. Methodist. Home: 303 Shenandoah Trl W Georgetown KY 40324 Office: Georgetown Coll 400 E College St Georgetown KY 40324 Office Phone: 502-863-8054. Personal E-mail: plarue123@aol.com.

LA RUSSA, TONY, JR., (ANTHONY LA RUSSA JR.), professional baseball manager; b. Tampa, Fla., Oct. 4, 1944; m. Elaine Coker, Dec. 31, 1973; 2 daus.: Bianca, Devon. Student, U. Tampa; BA, U. So. Fla., 1969; LLB, Fla. State U., 1978. Bar: Fla., 1979. Player numerous major league and minor league baseball teams, 1962-77; coach St. Louis Cardinals orgn., 1977; mgr. minor league team Knoxville, 1978, Iowa, 1979; coach Chgo. White Sox, 1978, mgr., 1979-86, Oakland A's, 1986-95, St. Louis Cardinals, 1996—. Mgr. A.L. champion Oakland A's, 1988, 89, 90, World champions, 1989; mgr. All-Star team, 1988, coach, 1984, 87. Named Am. League Mgr. of Yr. Baseball Writers' Assn. Am., 1983, 88, 92, AP, 1983, Sporting News, 1983, Am. League Mgr. of Yr., 1988, 92. Achievements include coach Nat.League All-star Team, 2005. Office: St Louis Cardinals Busch Stadium 250 Stadium Plz Saint Louis MO 63102-1722*

LARUSSO, NICHOLAS F., gastroenterologist, educator, scientist; Prof., chmn. dept. internal medicine Mayo Med. Sch. Clin. & Found., Rochester, Minn., 1977—, dir. Ctr. Basic Rsch. Digestive Disorders, 1977—. Office: Mayo Clinic Ctr Basic Rsch Digestive Disease Guggenheim 17 Rochester MN 55905-0001 Office Phone: 507-284-3725. Business E-Mail: larusso.nicholas@mayo.edu.

LARWOOD, LAURIE, psychologist; b. NY, 1941; PhD, Tulane U., 1974. Pres. Davis Instruments Corp., San Leandro, Calif., 1966—71; cons., 1969—; asst. prof. orgnl. behavior SUNY, Binghamton, 1974—76; assoc. prof., chair dept. psychology Claremont (Calif.) McKenna Coll., 1976—83, assoc. prof. bus. adminstrn., 1976—83, Claremont Grad. Sch., 1976—85; prof., head dept. mgmt. U. Ill., Chgo., 1983—87; dean sch. bus. SUNY, Albany, 1987—90; dean Coll. Bus. Adminstrn. U. Nev., Reno, 1990—92, prof., 1990—2003, prof. emerita, 2003—; dir. Inst. Strategic Bus. Issues, 1992—2003. Western regional adv. coun. SBA, 1976-81; dir. Mgmt. Team; pres. Mystic Games, Inc.; mng. ptnr. Quail Lane Studios, 2003-. Author: (with M.M. Wood) Women in Management, 1977, Organizational Behavior and Management, 1984, Women's Career Development, 1987, Strategies-Successes-Senior Executives Speak Out, 1988, Women's Careers, 1988, Managing Technological Development, 1988, Impact Analysis, 1999; mem. editl. bd. Sex Roles, 1979-2003, Consultation, 1986-91, Jour. Orgnl. Behavior, 1987-2003, Jour. Vocat. Behavior, 1999-, Group and Orgn. Mgmt., 1982-84, editor, 1986-91; founding editor Women and Work, 1983, Jour. Mgmt. Case Studies, 1983-87; contbr. articles to profl. jours. Mem. Acad. Mgmt. (editl. rev. bd. Rev. 1977-82, past chmn. women in mgmt. divsn., managerial consultation divsn., tech. and innovation mgmt. divsn.), Am. Psychol. Assn., Assn. Women in Psychology. Office: Quail Ln Studios 10225 N Quail Ln Tucson AZ 85742 Mailing: Box 89789 Tucson AZ 85752 Office Phone: 520-579-9773. E-mail: larwood@earthlink.net.

LARWOOD, SUSAN ELIZABETH, elementary school educator; d. Edward Wayne and Marianna Larwood. AA in Human Svcs., Golden West Jr. Coll., Huntington Beach, Calif., 1979; BA, Calif. State U., Long Beach, 1984; MA, U.S. Internat. U., San Diego, 1990. Lic. psychol. nurse, Calif.; Calif. State Tchg. Credential. Educator Del Obispo Elem. Sch., San Juan Capistrano, Calif., 1986—89, George White Elem. Sch., Laguna Niguel, Calif., 1989—2001, Don Juan Avila Elem. Sch., Aliso Viejo, Calif., 2001—. Mem. various coms., curriculum leader and exercise path designer Capistrano Unified Sch. Dist.; yearbook advisor George White Sch., 1991—2001, student coun. advisor, 1986—. Recipient Tchr. of Yr., Capistrano Unified Edn. Assn., 1995, hon. svc. award, PTA, 1995, Star Fish award, 2001. Mem.: Calif. Tchrs. Assn. (corr.). Office: Capistrano Unified Sch Dist San Juan Capistrano CA 92675 Personal E-mail: suelarwood@cox.net.

LARZELERE, KATHY LYNN HECKLER, paralegal; b. Sellersville, Pa., Dec. 4, 1955; d. Harold Tyson and Hannah Ruth (Wile) Heckler; m. Lawrence Sollanek, Nov. 1984 (div.); m. Loel Harry Larzelere, Aug. 29, 1992; 1 stepdaughter, Lindsie M. AAS magna cum laude, Columbus State C.C., 1991. From sales person to dept. mgr. Macy's New York, North Wales, Pa., 1977-83; dept. mgr. Macys, Christiana, Del., 1983; store mgr. Bathtique, Wilmington, Del., Towson, Md., 1983-86; customer svc. person Marshall Fields, Chgo., 1987; word processor Franklin County Children Svcs., Columbus, Ohio, 1988-89; legal sec., paralegal M. Cohen and Assocs., Columbus, 1989-94; paralegal Calig and Handelman LPA, Columbus, 1994-97, Weltman, Weinberg & Reis, Columbus, 1997—2004; co-owner BeKa Kostuming & Embroidery, Inc., 2004—; freelance comml. artist, 1973—77. History mus. interpreter Ohio Hist. Soc., 2005—. Author: numerous poems. Ward coord. Amelia Salerno for City Coun., Columbus, 1993; co-chmn. home amb. com. Rebuilding Together, Columbus, also mem. materials and in-kind donations com., chmn. in-kind donations com., 2003—; vol. Ohio Bicentennial Commn.; mem, interpretive program vol. Ohio Hist. Soc. Mem. award Phi Theta Kappa, award Nat. Honor Soc. Mem. Paralegal Assn. Ctrl. Ohio (writer newsletter The Citator, co-chair student outreach com. 1994-95, chair 1995-97, 1st v.p. 1995-97, 2000-2001, pres. 1997-99, mem. adv. bd. 1999-2000, chair student outreach com. 1999-2000), Columbus Bar Assn. (assoc.), Ohio Sticher's Group, Nat. Fedn. Paralegal Assns, Ohio Costumer's Group, Phi Theta Kappa. Lutheran. Avocations: handcrafts, reading, walking, watercolor painting, counted cross-stitch. Personal E-mail: klarzele@columbus.rr.com.

LARZELERE, ROBERT EARL, psychologist, researcher; b. Greensburg, Pa., Apr. 3, 1945; s. John H. and Mary Alice (Mark) L.; m. Rosalie B. Ash, Dec. 16, 1972; children: Lisa M. Fleming, William A. BA, Wabash Coll., 1967; MS, Ga. Inst. Tech., 1975; PhD, Pa. State U., 1979. Tchr. math. Josey High Sch., Augusta, Ga., 1971-72; dept. chair Bryan Coll., Dayton, Tenn., 1977-79; asst. prof. psychology Western Bapt. Sem., Portland, Oreg., 1980-82; assoc. prof. Biola U., La Mirada, Calif., 1982-90; dir. residential rsch. Father Flanagan's Boys' Home, Boys Town, Nebr., 1990—2002; assoc. prof. U. Nebr. Med. Ctr., 1998—. Contbr. articles to profl. jours. With U.S. Army, 1968-71, Korea. NIMH fellow, 1976-77, 79-80, 88-89. Mem. Am. Psychol. Assn., Nat. Coun. Family Rels., Soc. Rsch. in Child Devel. Republican. Avocations: camping, sports. Business E-Mail: rlarzelere@unmc.edu.

LA SALLE, ARTHUR EDWARD, historic foundation executive; b. Aug. 9, 1930; s. Rene Charles and Jeanne Matilda (Senac) La Salle; children: Carl Alan, Adam David, Jeanne Ambre Victoria. Student, Jesus Holy Name of Jesus Coll. Founder, pres. R.R. Equipment Assn., Asheville, NC, 1960—; founder Trains of Yesterday Mus., Hilliard, Fla., 1964—73; owner, restorer Brush Hill mansion, Irwin, Pa., 1973—77; lessee, restorer Springfield mansion, Fayette, Miss., 1977—; founder, pres. Hist. Springfield Found., Fayette, 1977—. Cons. Smithsonian Instn., 1959, 75, Japanese Nat. Rys., Tokyo, 1968, Henry Ford Mus., 1975, City of Natchez, Miss., 1985, Old South Soc., Church Hill, Miss., 1985—; cons., lectr. in field. Author: The Marriage of Andrew Jackson at Springfield Plantation, 1987; contbr. articles to profl. jours. Mem.: U.S. Naval Inst., Natchez Hist. Soc., Nat. Trust for Hist. Preservation, Ry. and Locomotive Hist. Soc. Avocations: historic preservation and study, writing, painting. Home and Office: Springfield Plantation 8733 River Rd 553 South Fayette MS 39069-9527 Office Phone: 601-786-3802.

LASALLE, ERIQ, actor, film director; b. Hartford, Conn., July 23, 1962; Student, Julliard Sch.; BFA, NYU, 1984. Founder Humble Journey Films. TV appearances include: (series) Mariah, ABC, 1987, The Human Factor, CBS, 1992, ER, NBC, 1994-2001, The Twilight Zone (also writer), 2002; (TV movies) Out of the Darkness, 1985, What Price Victory, 1988, When We Were Young, 1989, Winner Takes All episode B.L. Stryker: The ABC Saturday Mystery, 1990, Eyes of a Witness, CBS, 1991, Empty Cradle, ABC, 1993; (spls.) Teen Father, ABC Aftersch. Spl., 1986, Vietnam War Story, HBO, 1987, 47th Ann. Primetime Emmy Awards, Fox, 1995, host Life in the Fat Lane II, NBC, 1995; (pilot) Hammer, Slammer, and Slade, ABC, 1990; film appearances include: Coming to America, 1988, DROP Squad, 1994, One Hour Photo, 2002, Inside Out, 2004; prodr., actor: Crazy as Hell, 2002; prodr. The Salton Sea, 2002; appeared in Two Rains Running, Goodman Theatre, Chgo., 1992-93; actor, dir. (TV show) Rebound: The Legend of Earl 'The Goat' Manigault, 1996, Mind Prey, 1999, ER. Recipient SAG awards, 1998, 99, Image awards, 1999, 2000.

LASANSKY, LEONARDO, artist, educator; b. Iowa City, Mar. 29, 1946; s. Mauricio Lasansky and Emilia Barragan; 1 child, Amadeo Galgo. B of Gen. Studies, U. Iowa, 1971, MA, MFA, U. Iowa, 1972. Prof. art Hamline U., St. Paul, 1972—, chair fine arts divsn., 1981—85; artist-in-resident Dartmouth Coll., Hanover, NH, 1982—82; dir. exhbns. Hamline U., St. Paul, 1995—, chair dept. studio arts and art history, 1995—; artist-in-resident Hamline U. Coll. of Liberal Arts, St. Paul, 2004—. Mem. adv. panel Minn. State Arts Bd., St. Paul, 1988—90; academitian Nat. Acad., N.Y.C., 1994—. Curator (exhibitions) Espana: The Legacy of War: Works by Francisco Goya (Best Curated Exhbn. in the Twin Cities, Mpls. Star Tribune, 1998), Mus. African Art, N.Y.C., Star Tribune, Mary Abbe; exhibitions include Intergrafia '94, Prague, Czechoslovakia, Augsburg, Germany, Krakow and Torun, Poland, Nat. Acad. and Mus., N.Y.C., Heard Mus., Phoenix, Internat. Print Triennial, Krakow, Poland, Mus. Modern Art, Wakayoma, Japan, Prefectural Mus. of Art, Fukuoka, Japan, Jane Haslem Gallery, Washington, Am. Printmaking, Belgrade, Yugoslavia, Grabado Latinoamericano, San Juan, Puerto Rico, Premio Internazional Biella, Italy, Internat. Triennial of Coloured Graphic Prints, Grenchen, Switzerland, Bklyn. Mus., Figura 3, IBA, Leipzig, Germany, Intergrafic '80, Berlin, Germany, AAAL, N.Y.C. (Spl. Purchase Award, 1979), Norfolk (Va.) Mus. of Arts and Scis., Grabado Latinoamericano, San Juan, Puerto Rico, Ball State Univ. Mus. of Art, rep. in numerous permanent collections. Mem.: Nat. Acad. Office: Hamline Univ Dept Studio Arts and Art History 1536 Hewitt Ave Saint Paul MN 55104 Office Phone: 651-523-2386. Office Fax: 651-523-3057. E-mail: llasansky@hamline.edu.

LASANSKY, MAURICIO, artist; b. Buenos Aires, 1914; arrived in U.S., 1943, naturalized, 1952; m. Emilia Lasansky; 6 children. Attended, Superior Sch. Fine Arts, Argentina; DFA (hon.), Iowa Wesleyan Coll., 1959, Pacific Lutheran Univ., 1969; HHD (hon.), Associated Colls. Twin Cities, 1977; DFA (hon.), Carleton Coll., 1979, Coe Coll., 1985. Dir. Free Fine Arts Sch., Cordoba, Argentina, 1936—39, Taller Manualidades, Cordoba, Argentina, 1939—45; prof. Univ. Iowa, 1945—67, Virgil M. Hancher disting. prof., 1967—84, Virgil M. Hancher prof. emeritus, 1984—. Exhibitions include over 250 one-man shows in the U.S. and other countries; represented in collections of over 140 museums. Recipient 2 Eyre Medals, Pa. Acad. Fine Art, 1957—59, Posada award, Primera Exposicion Bienal Interamericana, Mexico City, 1959, Accadamico Onorario, Classe de Incisione, Accademia della Arti del Designo, Florence Italy, 1965, Arts award, Dickinson Coll., 1974, Disting. Svc. citation, Nat. Assn. Sch. Art, 1978, Honored Artist award, Fourth Latin Am. Bienal Graphic Arts, 1979, Disting. Tchg. Art award, Coll. Art Assn. Am., 1980, Honorary award, Arts & Humanities Commn. for the Aging, Iowa, 1983, Iowa Arts Council, 1990, Cert. of Recognition for Disting. Svc., State of Iowa, 1991, Iowa award, 1999, 14th Recipient of State of Iowa Highest Honor award, Gov. Iowa, 2000, Hon. Artist Mem. LA Soc. Printmakers, 2001; grantee 5 Guggenheim Fellowships, 1943—63. Fellow: Inst. Advanced Study, Indiana Univ.; mem.: L.A. Soc. Printmakers (Honorary Artist 2001), NAD (academician 1990). Best known for series of Nazi Drawings, 1961-66. Office: Lasansky Corporation 216 E Washington St Iowa City IA 52240 Office Phone: 319-337-9336. Business E-Mail: info@lasanskyart.com.

LASAROW, MARILYN DORIS, artist, educator; b. Seattle, Oct. 23, 1928; d. Samuel Irving and Molly Pearl Powell; m. William Julius Lasarow, Feb. 4, 1951; children: Richard Michael, Elisabeth Hollins Lasarow Tozzi. BA cum laude in Philosophy, Stanford U., 1950. Pvt. art tchr., L.A., 1968—2003. One-woman shows include Feigen Palmer Gallery, L.A., 1967, exhibited in group shows at Purdue U., Ind., 1965, L.A. County Mus. Art, 1966, Feigen Palmer Gallery, L.A., 1966, Occidental Coll., Eagle Rock, Calif., 1967, Lytton Gallery, L.A., 1968, featured, in L.A. Times, Art Forum and Art in Am., work appeared on cover, Home Sect., L.A. Times, 1967. Mem.: AAUW, Nat. Mus. Women in Arts, L.A. Mus. Contemporary Art, L.A. County Mus. Art (award 1966—67), Cap and Gown, Phi Beta Kappa. Avocations: gardening, tennis, photography, filmmaking. Home: 11623 Canton Pl Studio City CA 91604 E-mail: wlasarow@mindspring.com.

LASATER, W(ILLIAM) ROBERT, JR., lawyer; b. El Dorado, Kans., Oct. 31, 1944; s. W. Robert and Marguerite Lasater; children: W. Robert III, Alisa Linn. BA, Kans. U., 1966, JD, 1969. Bar: Kans. 1969, U.S. Ct. Mil. Appeals 1972, N.Mex. 1974, U.S. Supreme Ct. 1976. Legal aid Wyandotte Co., Kansas City, Kans., 1969; forensic medicine cons. USAF, 1971-74; assoc. Rodey, Dickason, Sloan, Akin & Robb, Albuquerque, 1974-78, ptnr., 1978—. Bd. dirs. Bernalillo County (N.Mex.) chpt. Am. Cancer Soc., 1984. Capt. JAG, USAF, 1969-71. Named one of best lawyers in Am., 2003—04. Fellow Am. Acad. Health Care Attys.; mem. ABA, N.Mex. State Bar Assn.(chmn. Dental-Legal Panel 1981-1990, chmn. Health Law Sect. 1988-1989, Med. Legal Liaison Com. 1991-, Med. Rev. Com. 1989-), Am. Bd. Trial Advs., Am. Coll. Trial Lawyers, Kans. Bar Assn., Albuquerque Bar Assn., N. Mex Health Lawyers Assn., Am. Arbitration Assn. (panel neutrals), Phi Delta Phi. Republican. Methodist. Office: Rodey Dickason Sloan Akin & Robb PO Box 1888 Albuquerque NM 87103-1888 Office Phone: 505-768-7287. Business E-Mail: rlasater@rodey.com.

LASCELLES, SUSAN, artist; b. Chgo., Jan. 29, 1958; d. Robert John and Donna Lee (Hjorth) L.; m. David Linn Hekelnkaemper, Apr. 17, 1998; children: Michael Lascelles DiCenzo, Max Lascelles Hekelnkaemper. Student, Ohio State U., 1984-87; BA, Empire State Coll., 1990. Artist, painter, photographer, stained glass, animator (film) Uncut, 1981; group shows include The Little Gallery, Springfield, Ohio, 1981, Millennium, N.Y.C., 1981, Rosenmarkt, Zurich, Switzerland, 1982, Upper Arlington Pub. Libr., Columbus, Ohio, 1987, The Dance Circle, Ithaca, N.Y., 1989, Dodajk Internation, Tucson, 1990, New Doors of the Arts, Tucson, 1993, Orts Theatre of Dance, Tucson, 1995, 96, 97, 98, Urban Picnic and Art Auction, Tucson, 1998, Daturo Studios and Gallery, Tucson, 1999, The 14th, 15th Annual Jerome Beillard Festival for Life for So. Ariz. Aids Found., 2002, 2003, El Pollo De Tucson, The Alamo Gallery, 2003, The Drawing Studio, Tucson, 2004, Solar Culture Gallery, Tucson, 2004, others; represented in permanent collections Corning Mus. Glass Film Libr., Empire State Coll., Färber Hüsli, Hallau, Switzerland, Fred and Pat Crain, Mechanicsburg, Ohio. Acad. merit scholar Scarlet and Gray, Ohio State U., Columbus, 1985, 87; grantee Changes Inc., N.Y.C., 1993. Avocations: gardening, pets, music, alternative healing, gemology. Home: 7151 S Sandpiper Ave Tucson AZ 85746-6531 Office Phone: 520-270-6835.

LASCH, PAT, artist, educator; b. N.Y.C., Nov. 20, 1944; d. Fred and Helen Lasch; 1 child, Melinda. BA, Queens Coll., 1970; FAAR, Am. Acad. in Rome, 1983; MFA, Ga. State U., Atlanta, 1990. Mem. found. faculty Parsons Sch. of Design, N.Y.C., 1979-88; asst. prof. R.I. Sch. of Design, Providence, 1988-89; assoc. prof. U. Mass., Amherst, 1990-97, prof., 1997—. Artist: solo exhibits include A.I.R. Gallery, N.Y.C., 1973, 77, 79, 80, 94, Zabrskie Gallery, N.Y.C., 1975, Galleriet, Lund, Sweden, 1980, Galerie Ahlner, Stockholm, 1980, Kathryn Markel Gallery, N.Y.C., 1981, 84, 85, Albright Knox Gallery, Members' Gallery, Buffalo, 1977-84, Thomas Segal Gallery, Boston, 1988, Sculpture Ctr., N.Y.C., 1993, Herter Gallery, U. Mass., Amherst, 1993; group shows inclde Inst. Contemporary Art, Phila., Street Scenes, 1981, Malmo (Sweden) Konsthall, Food, 1984, San Francisco Internat. Airport, The Right Foot Show, 1987, Thomas Segal Gallery, The Raw and the Cooked, Boston, The New Mus., N.Y.C., Bad Girls, 1994; spl. exhibition The Mus. of Modern Art (50th Anniversary), Homage 1929-79; represented in permanent collections Met. Mus. Art, N.Y.C., Mus. Modern Art, N.Y.C., Nat. Acad. Design, N.Y.C., Woman's Mus., Washington, Oberlin Mus., Queen's Coll. Recipient Yaddo, 1978, 80, 94, 98, Rome prize, 1982-83, Lilly fellowship, 1993-94, NEA-MCC fellowship, 1995-96; grantee: C.A.P.S., 1980, NEA, 1980-81, N.Y. State Coun. for the Arts, 1984-85, Ariana Found., 1987-88, Pollock-Krasner, 1987-88. Fellow Soc. of Fellows Am. Acad. in Rome; mem. Nat. Acad. Design (life). Democrat. Roman Catholic. Home: 463 West St Apt 228 G New York NY 10014-2030 Office: Univ Mass Fine Arts Ctr Amherst MA 01002

LASCHER, ALAN ALFRED, lawyer; b. N.Y.C., Dec. 8, 1941; s. Morris Julius and Sadie Lillian (Chassen) L.; m. C. Amy Weingarten, July 12, 1969; children: David, Lauren, Alexandra, Carlyn. BS, Union Coll., 1963; LLB, Bklyn. Law Sch., 1967. Bar: N.Y. 1967. Assoc. Kramer, Leven et al, N.Y.C., 1969-75; ptnr. real estate dept. Weil, Gotshal & Manges, N.Y.C., 1975—. Mem. law com. N.Y. Real Estate Bd., N.Y.C., 1981—; bd. advisors Chgo. Title Ins. Co., 1995—. Served to sgt. USAF, 1968-69. Named Real Estate Lawyer of Yr. Am. Lawyer, 1982. Mem. Am. Coll. Real Estate Lawyers (mem. resolution trust corp., bankruptcy and housing coms.). Office: Weil Gotshal & Manges 767 Fifth Ave New York NY 10153-0119

LASCOLA, RUSSELL A., philosophy educator; b. Buffalo, Oct. 29, 1939; s. August and Grace LaScola; m. Esperanza Boubion LaScola, Nov. 3, 1962; children: Therese, Annette, Russell, Christopher, Gregory. BA, Calif. State U., L.A., 1963; MA, U. So. Calif., 1964, PhD, 1970. Instr. Mt. St. Mary's Coll., L.A., 1966—70, L.A. City Coll., 1966—70, Glendale (Calif.) Coll., 1966—70; prof. Calif. Poly. State U., San Luis Obispo, 1970—. Chair philosophy dept. Calif. Poly. State U., 1977—79. Contbr. articles to profl. jours. Mem.: Calif. Assn. Scholars, Nat. Assn. Scholars, Internat. Berkeley Soc. Avocations: curing olives, hiking, studying Italian language. Office: Calif Poly State U Philosophy Dept San Luis Obispo CA 93407 Business E-Mail: rlascola@calpoly.edu.

LASEE, MARK EDWARD, lawyer; b. Burbank, Calif., Mar. 12, 1957; m. Jean A. Lasee, July 24, 1982. BSBA, U. Wis., 1979; JD, Hamline U., 1983. Bar: Minn. 1983, U.S. Dist. Ct. Minn. 1983, Ariz. 1986, U.S. Dist. Ct. Ariz. 1986. Assoc. Thomsen Nybeck Johnson Bouquet and Van Valkenburg, Edina, Minn., 1983-86; ptnr. Shull, Rolle, Watland & Kalyna, Phoenix, 1986-92, Watland, Allen & Lasee PLLC, Phoenix, 1992—. Mem. Kiwanis (pres. Metroctr. chpt. 1994-95). Avocation: sailing. Office: Watland Allen & Lasee PLLC 393 E Palm Ln Phoenix AZ 85004-1532 E-mail: mark.lasee@azbar.org.

LASER, CHARLES, JR., oil company executive; b. Redford Twp., Mich., July 8, 1933; s. J.C. and Gertrude L.; m. Glenda Johnson, Sept. 27, 1972; 1 child, Susan Faye. Student, Mich. Tech. U., 1952-54, Ctrl. Mich. U., 1959-60; DD (hon.), Palm Beach Theol. Sem. Coll., 1991; LLD (hon.), Northwood U., 2000. With Retail Credit Co., 1958-60; exec. dir. Saginaw County Rep. Com., 1960-65, Rep. Com. D.C., 1967; fin. dir. San Joaquin Rep. Party, Stockton, Calif., 1968; owner Laser Advt., Bay City, Mich., 1969-75; exec. v.p. Vindell Petroleum, Inc., Midland, Mich., 1972-75, Geo Spectra Corp., Ann Arbor, Mich., 1977-86; pres. Laser Exploration Inc., Deerfield Beach, Fla. Task force Domestic Violence Gov. Jeb Bush, 1999—; adv. bd. Union Bank, Boca Raton, Fla.; sr. cons. Peking U. Resource Coll., China, 2004. Chmn. Genesee County Rep. Com., 1981-82, mem. Broward County Rep. Exec. Com., 1987-88, indsl. bond screening com. Deerfield Beach, 1992; chmn. U.S. Senator Connie Mack Palm Beach County Round Table; bd. dirs. Palm Beach County

Libr. Found., Shepherd Care Ministries, Hollywood, Foa., 1991—; adv. com. Tall Pines coun. Boy Scouts Am., mem. adv. bd. Gulf Stream Coun., 1980; mem. gov. prevention adv. com. Juvenile Justice Deliquency, Fla., 1988-96; mem. adv. bd. Humanitarian Soc., 1989—; bd. dirs., life mem. Large Freedoms Found., Valley Forge Broward County, Fla. chpt., 1995—; bd. govs. Northwood U., West Palm Beach, Fla., 1997; chmn. emeritus Fla. Symphonic Pops Orch., 1998; apptd. mem. Task Froce on Domestic Violence. With U.S. Army, 1954-58. Decorated Knight Order of St. John of Jerusalem Knights Hospitallier. Mem. Deerfield Beach C. of C. (v.p.), World Trade Coun. (Palm Beach, Fla. chpt.), Detroit Econ. Club, Bankers Club (Boca Raton), Humanitarian Soc. (adv. bd.), Rep. Men's Club (past pres., v.p. Boca Raton chpt.), Gold Coast Venture Capital Club (Delray Beach chpt.), Palm Beach Roundtable (bd. dirs., chmn. exec. com., sec. 1994-2002), Hillsboro Cove Condominium Assn. (pres. 1994), Rotary, Elks. Home: PO Box 8604 1523 E Hillsboro Blvd Apt 131 Deerfield Beach FL 33441-4301

LASH, STEPHEN SYCLE, auction company executive; b. Boston, Feb. 10, 1940; s. Samuel George and Carolyn Virginia (Sycle) L.; m. Wendy Lehman, Oct. 29, 1967; children: Abigail Sycle, William Lehman. BA, Yale U., 1962; MBA, Columbia U., 1966. V.p. Bali Footwear, Inc., Marlborough, Mass., 1962-64, 66-68, S.G. Warburg and Co., London, N.Y.C., 1968-76, Christies, N.Y.C., 1976-80, sr. v.p., 1980-84, exec. v.p., 1984-93, vice chmn., 1993-2000, chmn., 2000—; also bd. dirs. Christies Internat. PLC & Christies Fine Art Ltd. Vis. prof. residential coll. seminar Yale U., 2004. Co-author: A Vision of Paradise: Robertson Ward and the Mill Reef Club. Mem. coun. Nat. Trust for Historic Preservation, 2002—; founder, pres. Ocean Liner Mus., 1983—88, co-chmn., 1988—96; commr. N.Y.C. Landmarks Preservation Commn., 1973—76; bd. dirs. N.Y. Landmarks Conservancy, 1975—95, 1997—, chmn., 1992—95; bd. dirs. Nat. Bldg. Mus., Washington, 2001—, Mus. City N.Y., 2003—, Avon Old Farms Sch., 2004—; bd. overseers Peabody-Essex Mus., Salem, Mass., 2000—. Pan Am. Union fellow, 1965. Mem. Yale U. Alumni Assn. Metro N.Y. (pres. 1987-90), River Club, Mill Reef Club, Century Assn., Wadawanuck Club (Stonington, Conn.). Home: 151 E 79th St New York NY 10021-0417 Office: Christies 20 Rockefeller Plz New York NY 10020-1902 Office Phone: 212-636-2905. Business E-Mail: slash@christies.com.

LASHBROOKE, ELVIN CARROLL, JR., law educator, consultant; b. Dec. 14, 1939; s. Elvin Carroll Sr. and Lois Lenora (Weger) L.; m. Margaret Ann Jones, Dec. 19, 1964; children: Michelle Ann, David C. BA, U. Tex., 1967, MA, 1968, JD, 1972, LLM, 1977; PhD, Mich. State U., 1993. Bar: Tex. 1972, Fla. 1973. Legis. counsel Tex. Legis. Coun., Austin, 1972-75; pvt. practice law, 1975-77; asst. prof. coll. of law DePaul U., Chgo., 1977-79, Stetson U., St. Petersburg, Fla., 1979-80; assoc. prof. sch. law Notre Dame, South Bend, Ind., 1981-85; prof., chmn. bus. law dept. Mich. State U., East Lansing, 1985-95; assoc. dean adminstrn. Eli Broad Coll. Bus., East Lansing, 1993-97; pvt. practice cons., 1986-97; dean Coll. Bus. U. Nev., Las Vegas, 1997-99; assoc. dean Broad Grad. Sch. of Mgmt. Mich. State U., East Lansing, 1999—2001, dir. study abroad and e-learning initiatives, 2001—03, dir. edn., 2003—04, assoc. dean emeritus, 2004—; exec. mem. Lashbrooke of Barrowfield, LLC, 2004—. Instr. St. Edward's U., Austin, 1975-76. Author: Tax Exempt Organizations, 1985, The Legal Handbook of Business Transactions, 1987; contbr. articles to profl. jours. Mem. Tex. Bar Assn., Fla. Bar Assn. Avocation: computers. Home: 6204 E Golfridge Dr East Lansing MI 48823 Office: Mich State Univ Broad Grad Sch of Mgmt East Lansing MI 48824-1122 Office Phone: 517-353-4336. Business E-Mail: lashbrooke@bus.msu.edu.

LASHER, CRAIG RICHARD, policy analyst; b. Newfane, N.Y., Jan. 21, 1959; s. Keith Arlen and Charlotte Marie (Cash) L. AB, Hamilton Coll., 1981; MA, Am. U., 1986. Policy analyst, legis. asst. Population Action Internat., Washington, 1983-89, sr. policy analyst, 1989—. Bd. dirs. U.S. Global Leadership Campaign, 1998—, mem. polit. adv. com. League of Conservation Voters, 1998-. Grad. fellow United Meth. Ch., 1982; named All-Am. Swimmer Coll. Swimming Coaches Assn. Am., 1978, Eagle Scout Boy Scouts Am., 1974. Mem. SAR, Masons (33 degree), Shriners, Scottish Rite, York Rite, Delta Upsilon. Methodist. Office: Population Action Internat 1300 19th St NW Fl 2 Washington DC 20036-1609 E-mail: clasher@popact.org.

LASHER, ESTHER LU, minister; b. Denver, June 1, 1923; d. Lindley Aubrey and Irma Jane (Rust) Pim; m. Donald T. Lasher, Apr. 9, 1950 (dec. Mar. 1982); children: Patricia Sue Becker, Donald T., Keith Alan, Jennifer Luanne Oliver. A of Fine Arts, Colo. Women's Coll., 1943; BA, Denver U., 1945, MA, 1967; MA in Religious Edn., Ea. Bapt. Sem., 1948; grad., Jerusalem Ctr. for Bibl. Studies, 1995. Ordained to ministry Bapt. Ch., 1988. Christian edn. dir. 1st Bapt. Ch., Evansville, Ind., 1948-52; min. Perrysburg Bapt. Ch., Macy, Ind., 1988-95; min.-at-large Am. Baptist Conv./USA, 1996—; interim pastor United Bapt. Ch., Lewiston, Maine, 1997-98. Libr. Peru (Ind.) Pub. Schs., 1990—91; sec. Ind. Ministerial Coun., Indpls., 1990—92; chairperson Women in Ministry, Indpls., 1988—93; min. Kairos Ministry to Women in Prison, 2002; chmn. Fellowship Mission Circle, Rochester, Ind., 1988—93; mem. Partnership in Ministry, Indpls., 1990—94; bd. mgrs. Am. Bapts./Ind., 1991—93; asst. dir. Greenwood Pub. Libr., 1978—84; dir. Fulton County Pub. Libr., 1984—90; ch. & cmty. chair Am. Bapt. Conv. of Maine, 2002—; caregiver Edge Nursing Home, Damariscotta, Maine, 2002—. Mem. Evansville Symphonic Orch., 1948—55, Denver Civic Orch., 1955—65, Augusta Symphony Orch., 1998—, Midcoast Cmty. Orch., 1999—; founder Fulton County Literacy Coalition, Rochester, 1989—90; tutor/trainer Peru Literacy Coalition of Peru Pub. Libr., 1994—95; active CASA Lincoln Co., Maine, 1996—; vol. libr. Rutherford Libr., South Bristol, Maine, 1996—, So. Bristol Libr., Lincoln Retirement Home; mem. Sea Coast Cmty. Orch., 1999—; chair for ch. and cmty. ABC of Maine, 2002—; chmn. diaconate bd. Damariscotta Bapt. Ch., 2004—; tutor Literacy of Lincoln County, 2005—; sec.-treas. North Miami County Mins. Fellowship, 1993—95; chmn. Christian Edn. Bd. and ch. planter, Denver, 1953—59, Colorado Springs, 1959—68; chaplain vol. Miles Hosp., 1997—; prayer advisor Christian Women's Club Damariscotta Bapt. Ch., 1997—, hostess, 1995—97, exec. bd., 1995—, chair missions com., 1997—; pres. Women's Mission Cir., Damariscotta Bapt. Assn., 1997—; chaplain-on-call Miles Meml. Hosp.; sec. Lincoln County Clergy, 1998—; ch. planter Indpls. and Zionsville, 1970—82; bd. dirs. Manitau Tng. Ctr., Rochester, 1988—90, Peru Civic Ctr., 1995; pres. Toastmasters, Rochester, 1984—90, 1995, edn. v.p., 1992—93; v.p. Mental Health Ctr., Rochester, 1987—90; sec. Northwest Area ABC/IN, 1994—95. Named Outstanding Libr., Biog. Inst., 1989, Profl. Woman of Year, 2005. Mem. Leadership Acad. (bd. dirs., sec.), Bus. and Profl. Women (pres. Greenwood, Ind. chpt. 1984-86), Rochester Women's Club (pres. 1989-92), Fulton County Mins. Assn. (treas. 1993-95), Logansport Assn. Bapt. Women, Peru Lit. Club (v.p.-elect 1995), CASA Miami County, Rotary, Sigma Alpha Iota (adv.), Christian Edn. (chmn. 1996-98), Damariscotta Assn. Women (pres. 1998—, mem. small ch. com. 1998—, chmn. diaconate bd. 2001—), Christian Women's Club (prayer group 1999—); Success 6 Reader Program, 2004-. Republican. Home and Office: 2063 State Route 129 South Bristol ME 04568-4317 *Wisdom is a powerful tool, without knowledge, it can entice or terrify an individual, all depending on how it is used with much forethought.*

LASHER, HIRAM NELSON, entrepreneur, consultant; b. Catskill, N.Y., Feb. 8, 1920; s. Nelson Frederick and Elizabeth Esther (Palmer) L.; m. Bertha Mae Van Vlierden, Dec. 12, 1948; children: Steven Hiram (dec.), Douglas Nelson, Sandra Elizabeth, Hiram Dennis, Denise Helen, Michael Clark, Michele Betty. Studied, Hougton Coll., 1938; DVM, Cornell U., 1942; AAS, Del. Tech. C.C., 1978. Hon. diplomate Am. Coll. Poultry Vets.; lic. vet., Del., N.Y. Pvt. practice, Catskill, 1942-48; poultry pathologist State Bd. Agr., Millsboro and Frankford, Del., 1948-50; founder, pres. Del. Poultry Labs./Sterwin Labs., 1950-79, Inter-Continental Biologics, Inc. (Intervet Am.), Millsboro, 1979-82, Lasher Assocs., Inc., Millsboro, 1982—. With Del. State Bd. Edn., 1962, v.p., 1963—70; found. founder Del. Tech. and Cmty. Coll., 1965—98. Lasher Dining Hall named in his honor Boy Scouts Am., Wilmington, 2000, Lasher Lab., U. Del. named in his honor, 1997; recipient Disting. Citizen award Delmarva Poultry Industry, Inc., 2000, Svc. to Agr. award U. Del., 1999, Order of 1st State, Del. Gov. Tom Carper, 1994, Disting. Leadership award U. Del., 1993, Medal of Achievement, Delmarva Poultry Industry, Inc., 1998, Health Care award Beebe Med. Ctr., 1989, Spl. Svc. award U. Ga., 2001; founder Caswell S. Eidson Eminent scholar program U. Ga. Coll. Vet. Medicine, 2001. Mem.: NY Acad. Scis., Poultry Sci. Assn., Am. Assn. Avian Pathologists (charter mem.) (Spl. Svc. award 2001, Am. Poultry Hall of Fame 2004). Republican. United Methodist. Avocations: philanthropic activities, capital campaigns and scholarships. Office: Lasher Assocs Inc DuPont Hwy Millsboro DE 19966 Office Phone: 302-934-8700. Office Fax: 302-934-8745. Business E-Mail: lasherinc@mchsi.com.

LASHER, JON-MICHAEL, music educator; b. Brookhaven, NY, Jan. 9, 1974; s. John Joseph and Lucille Prudence Lasher; m. Susan Jane Fry, July 31, 1999; 1 child, Margaret. MusB, SUNY, Potsdam, 1996; MusM, Duquesne U., 1998; diploma in ednl. leadership and adminstrn., LI U., 2004. Cert. tchr., sch. adminstr. NY. Music tchr. Sewanhaka HS, Floral Park, NY, 1998—99, Mid. Country Sch. Dist., Selden, NY, 1999—2004, Connetquot HS, Bohemra, NY, 2004—. Mem.: NY State Band Dirs. Assn., Music Educators Nat. Conf., NY State Sch. Music Assn. Roman Catholic. Home: 213 Fairview Cir Middle Island NY 11953 Office: Connetquot High Sch 190 7th St Bohemia NY 11716

LASHER, LORI L., lawyer; b. June 16, 1960; BA in polit. sci. magna cum laude, Westminster Coll., 1981; JD cum laude, Dickinson Sch. Law, 1984. With Reed Smith LLP, Phila., 1994—, mem. exec. com., head mergers & acquisitions/gen. corp. practice group. Mem. exec. bd. Homeless Advocacy Project. Mem.: Phila. Bar Assn., Pa. Bar Assn., ABA. Office: Reed Smith LLP 2500 One Liberty Pl 1650 Market St Philadelphia PA 19103-7301 Office Phone: 215-851-8136. Office Fax: 215-851-1420. Business E-Mail: llasher@reedsmith.com.

LASHINGER, GENROSE MULLEN, retired elementary school music educator; b. Jackson, Miss., Oct. 25, 1945; d. John DeWitte and Nelle Sue (Fly) Mullen; m. Donald R. Lashinger, July 10, 1976. BA in Music Edn. and Voice, Millsaps Coll., 1967; MA in Elem. Edn., Coll. William and Mary, 1974. Cert pre-K-12 music tchr., Va. Tchr. music Matthew Whaley Sch., Williamsburg, Va., 1967—2001. Assoc. choirmaster Bruton Parish Ch., Williamsburg, 1982-92; lectr. music Coll. William and Mary, Williamsburg, 1984-89; founding dir. Rainbow Connection, Williamsburg, 1987-2001; music coord. Williamsburg-James City County Schs., 1989-93; mem. del. to study music and dance to China and Commonwealth Ind. States, 1988, 90, 92. Performer with Robert Shaw Workshop Choir at Mostly Mozart Festival, N.Y.C., St. Cere Music Festival, France. Named Tchr. of Yr., Daily Press, 1993, Music Educator of Yr., Va. Music Educators Assn., 1992. Mem. Am. Choral Dirs. Assn., Music Educators Nat. Conf. (state chmn. 1984-86), Soc. for Gen. Music (chmn. 1990-94), Va. Music Educators Assn. (elem. pres. 1984-86). Episcopalian. Avocations: travel, gardening. Home: 2513 Campbell Close Williamsburg VA 23185-8072

LASHLEY, CURTIS DALE, lawyer; b. Urbana, Ill., Nov. 3, 1956; s. Jack Dale and Janice Elaine (Holman) L.; m. Tamara Dawn Yahnig, June 14, 1986. BA, U. Mo., Kansas City, 1978, JD, 1981. Bar: Mo. 1981, U.S. Dist. Ct. (we. dist.) Mo. 1981, U.S. Tax Ct. 1982, U.S. Ct. Appeals (8th cir.) 1992. Assoc. Melvin Heller, Inc., Creve Coeur, Mo., 1982; ptnr. Domjan & Lashley, Harrisonville, Mo., 1983—86; asst. gen. counsel Mo. Dept. Revenue, Independence, 1986—89, assoc. gen. counsel, 1989—92, sr. counsel, 1992—, adminstrv. hearing officer, 1995—; spl asst. atty. gen., 1986—; spl. asst. prosecutor Jackson County, Mo., 1990—. City atty., Adrian and Strasburg, Mo., 1985-86. V.p. Cass County Young Reps., Harrisonville, 1985. Recipient honor Senate Resolution 830 and Mo. Ho. Resolution 2314, 2001, Cert. of Appreciation, Kansas City Bd. Police Commrs., 2001, Legis. Resolution honor, Jackson County Mo., 2001. Mem. ABA, NRA, Federalist Soc., Kiwanis (treas. Harrisonville chpt. 1985-86, Harrisonville Disting. Svc. award 1985), Phi Alpha Delta. Republican. Presbyterian. Office: Mo Dept Revenue 16647 E 23rd St S Independence MO 64055-1922 E-mail: curtisl752@excite.com.

LASHLEY, FELISSA R., dean, nursing educator, researcher; b. N.Y.C., Apr. 6, 1941; d. Jack and Ruth (Dorbin) Lashley; divorced; children: Peter, Heather, Neal. BS, Adelphi Coll., 1961; MA, NYU, 1965; PhD, Ill. State U., 1973. Cert. Am. Bd. Med. Genetics., Am. Coll. Med. Genetics. Dean Coll. Nursing, Rutgers U., Newark, 2002—. Author: Clinical Genetics in Nursing Practice, 1998 (book of yr. award); editor: The Person with AIDS: Nursing Perspectives, 1987 (Book of Yr. award), Tuberculosis: A Sourcebook for Nursing Practice and Women, Children and HIV/AIDS (Book of Yr. award, 1993), Emerging Infectious Diseases: Trends and Issues, 2002, The Person with HIV/AIDS: Nursing Perspectives, 2000. Mem.: AAAS, ANA (coun. nurse researchers), Am. Coll. Med. Genetics, Ill. Nurses Assn., Midwest Nursing Rsch. Soc., Nat. League Nursing, Am. Acad. Nursing, Am. Soc. Human Genetics. Office Phone: 973-353-5293 x 647. Business E-Mail: lashley@nightingale.rutgers.edu.

LASHLEY, VIRGINIA STEPHENSON HUGHES, retired computer science educator; b. Wichita, Kans., Nov. 12, 1924; d. Herman H. and Edith M. (Wayland) Stephenson; m. Kenneth W. Hughes, June 4, 1946 (dec.); children: Kenneth W. Jr., Linda; m. Richard H. Lashley, Aug. 19, 1954; children: Robert H., Lisa Lashley Van Amberg, Diane Lashley Tan. BA, U. Kans., 1945; MA, Occidental Coll., 1966; PhD, U. So. Calif., 1983. Cert. info. processor, tchr. secondary and community coll., Calif. Tchr. math. La Canada (Calif.) High Sch., 1966-69; from instr. to prof. Glendale (Calif.) Coll., 1970-92, chmn. bus. div., 1977-81, coord. instructional computing, 1974-92, prof. emeritus, 1992—; sec., treas., dir. Victory Montessori Schs., Inc., Pasadena, Calif., 1980—; pres. The Computer Sch., Pasadena, 1983-92, ret., 1992—. Real estate investor, 1992—; pres. San Gabriel Valley Data Processing Mgmt. Assn., 1977-79, San Gabriel Valley Assn. for Systems Mgmt., 1979-80; chair Western Ednl. Computing Conf., 1980, 84. Editor Jour. Calif. Ednl. Computing, 1980. Grantee NSF, 1967-69, EDUCARE scholar U. So. Calif., 1980-82; John Randolph and Dora Haynes fellow, Occidental Coll., 1964-66; named student computer ctr. in her honor Dr. Virginia S. Lashley Ctr., 1992. Mem. AAUP, AAUW, DAR (scholarship chair, 1994-2002, vice regent 2002—), Calif. Edn. Computing Consortium (bd. dirs. 1979—, v.p. 1983-84, pres. 1985-87), Orgn. Am. Historians, San Marino Women's Club, Colonial Dames, XVII Century (scholarship chair, 1997-99), Nat. Geneal. Soc., New Eng. Hist. Geneal. Soc. (life mem.), Town Hall, World Affairs Coun., Trojan Guild, Phi Beta Kappa, Pi Mu Epsilon, Phi Alpha Theta, Phi Delta Kappa, Delta Phi Upsilon, Gamma Phi Beta. Republican. Congregationalist. Home: 1240 S San Marino Ave San Marino CA 91108-1227 Personal E-mail: vslash@aol.com.

LASHLEY, WILLIAM BARTHOLOMEW, county official; b. Dayton, Ohio, Jan. 2, 1952; s. William Bartholomew and Reta Carolyn (Reicken) L.; m. Loukia Simopoulos, June 30, 1973; children: Nichole E., Felicite D. BA in Econs., Wright State U., 1976; opthomol. sci. degree, Regis U., 1982. Asst. mgr. First Nat. Bank, Dayton, Ohio, 1973-77; mgr. store Kroger Co., Dayton, 1977-80; cashier Frontier Bank, Denver, 1980-82; asst. v.p. Empire Savs., Denver, 1982-85; mgr. investor acctg. Security Pacific Mortgage Corp., Denver, 1985-88; corp. acct. investors Crossland Mortgage Corp., Salt Lake City, 1988-89; dir. fin. and adminstrv. svcs. Montgomery County Cts., Dayton, 1989—. Mem. Montgomery County Fiscal Task Force, Dayton, 1990—. Mem. ABA (assoc.), Am. Bankers Assn., Govt. Fin. Officers Assn. (mem. select review com.), Mortgage Bankers Assn., Ohio State Bar Assn. (assoc.). Home: 3307 Waltham Ave Kettering OH 45429-3529 Office: Montgomery County Cts 41 N Perry St Dayton OH 45402-1431

LASHMAN, L. EDWARD, arbitrator, mediator, consultant; b. New Orleans, June 6, 1924; s. L. Edward and Edith Ruth (Deutsch) L.; m. Elizabeth Gitt Fichman, June 6, 1948 (dec. Aug. 1984); children: Deborah, Rebekah, David W. (dec. Feb. 1993), Judith; m. Joyce Blicher Schwartz, July 25, 1987. Student, U. N.C., 1940-42, Tulane U., 1942-43. Ptnr. Caire Assocs., New Orleans, 1946-51; with CIO and AFL-CIO, 1951-67; asst. to sec., dir. cong. liason HUD, Washington, 1967-69; mng. ptnr. Urban Housing Assocs., Denver, 1969-70; v.p. U. Mass., 1970-75; dir. external affairs, sr. planning counselor Harvard U., Cambridge, Mass., 1975-89; sec. adminstrn. and fin. Commonwealth of Mass., Boston, 1989-91, chmn. Mass. bd. regents pub. higher edn., 1986-88; chmn. Commonwealth Land Bank, Boston, 1975-77, Mass. Housing Fin. Agy., Boston, 1977-79; ret., 1991. Acting exec. dir. (pro bono) Mass. State Lotterty, 1999; contract mediator U.S. Equal Employment Opportunity Commn.; contract arbitrator U.S. Postal Svc. Exec. com. Denver County Dem. Party, 1952-64; chmn. Colo. Urban League, Denver, 1961-63; acting COO (pro bono) Judge Baker Children's Ctr., Boston, 1993-94; dir. Nat. Housing Conf., Washington, 1969-75; v.p. Handel & Haydn Soc., Boston, 1982-84. With U.S. Army, 1943-46, ETO. Mem. Am. Arbitration Assn., Mass. Assn. Mediation Programs, Norfolk and Suffolk County Superior Ct. Mediation Panels, Joint Labor Mgmt. Com. Mediation Panel. Avocations: fly fishing, cooking, photography. Home and Office: 236 Conant Rd Weston MA 02493-1654

LASHMAN, SHELLEY BORTIN, retired judge; b. Camden, NJ, Aug. 18, 1917; s. William Mitchell and Anna (Bortin) L.; m. Ruth Horn, Jan. 3, 1959; children: Karen E. Lashman Hall, Gail A. McBride, Mitchell A., Christopher R. BS, William and Mary Coll., 1938; postgrad., Columbia U., 1938, 39; JD, U. Mich., 1946. Bar: N.Y. 1947, N.J. 1968. Judge NJ Workers Compensation, 1981—2001; ret., 2001. With USNR, 1940—70. Mem. Atlantic County Bar Assn., Am. Judges Assn., Atlantic County Hist. Soc., Am. Judicature Soc., U.S. Navy League, Mil. Officers Assn. Am., VFW, Fleet Res. Assn., USS Yorktown CV-5 Club, Mil. Order World Wars, N.J. Workers' Compensation Inns of Ct. Republican. Home: 1209 Old Zion Rd Egg Harbor Township NJ 08234-7667 Home Fax: 608-653-6686.

LASHNER, WILLIAM MARK, writer; b. Phila., July 16, 1957; s. Melvin and Marilyn (Auerbach) L.; m. Pam Ellen Stern, June 11, 1989; children: Nora, Jack, Michael. BA, Swarthmore Coll., 1979; JD, NYU, 1983; MFA in Creative Writing, U. Iowa, 1991. Bar: Pa. Clk. Hon. James B. Moran, Chgo., 1983-85; trial atty. U.S. Dept. Justice, Criminal Divsn., Washington, 1985-86; ptnr. Lashner & Lashner, Phila., 1987-95; writer Harper, Collins, NYC, 1995—. Bd. dirs. B.F. Healthcare, Phila. Author: Hostile Witness, 1995, Bitter Truth, 1997, Fatal Flaw, 2003, Past Due, 2004, Falls the Shadow, 2005. Mem. Authors Guild. Address: c/o Wendy Sherman Ste 3400 450 Seventh Ave New York NY 10123*

LASHOF, JOYCE COHEN, public health service officer, educator; b. Phila. d. Harry and Rose (Brodsky) Cohen; m. Richard K. Lashof, June 11, 1950; children: Judith, Carol, Dan. AB, Duke U., 1946; MD, Women's Med. Coll., 1950; DSc (hon.), Med. Coll. Pa., 1983. Dir. Ill. State Dept. Pub. Health, 1973—77; dep. asst. sec. for health programs and population affairs Dept. Health, Edn., and Welfare, Washington, 1977—78; sr. scholar in residence IOM, Washington, 1978; asst. dir. office of tech. assessment U.S. Congress, Washington, 1978—81; dean sch. pub. health U. Calif., Berkeley, 1981—91; prof. pub. health U. Calif. Sch. Pub. Health, Berkeley, 1981—94, prof. emeritus, 1994—. Co-chair Commn. on Am. after Roe vs. Wade, 1991—92; mem. Sec.'s Coun. Health Promotion and Disease Prevention, 1988—91; chair Pres.'s Adv. Com. on Gulf War Vets. Illnesses, 1995—97. Mem. editl. bd.: Wellness Letter, 1993—, Ann. Rev. of Pub. Health, 1987—90. Recipient Alumni Achievement award, Med. Coll. Pa., 1975, Sedgewick Meml. medal, APHA, 1995. Avocation: hiking. Home: 601 Euclid Ave Berkeley CA 94708-1331 Office: U Calif Sch Pub Health 140 Earl Warren Hl Berkeley CA 94720-7360 Office Phone: 510-642-2493. Business E-Mail: jlashof@berkeley.edu.

LASHUTKA, GREGORY S., mayor, lawyer; b. New York City, 1944; m. Catherine (Adams); children: Nicholas, Lara, Stephanie, Michael. BS, Ohio State U., 1967; JD, Capital U., 1974. Bar: Ohio, 1974, Fla. and D.C., 1975. Ptnr. Squire, Sanders, and Dempsey, Columbus, Ohio; elected mayor City of Columbus, Ohio, 1991—99; former Columbus City Atty., Ohio; sr. v.p. corp. rels. Nationwide, Columbus, Ohio, 2000—. Past chmn. Columbus Area Sports Devel. Corp.; pres. Nat. League of Cities; comentator of the Ohio State U. Football Color, 1983-90; active civic and charitable orgn.; bd. dir. Simon Kenton, coun. Boy Scouts Am.; bd. dir. Cath. Social Svc., lt., USN. Named Mcpl. Leader of the Yr., Am. City and County mag., 1993. Mem. Nat. Acad. Pub. Adminstr. Office: Nationwide One Nationwide Plz Columbus OH 43215-2220

LASICH, VIVIAN ESTHER LAYNE, secondary school educator; b. Hopewell Twp., Pa., Dec. 17, 1935; d. Charles McClung and Harriette Law (George) Layne; m. William G. Lasich, Apr. 10, 1958; children: C. Laurence, Celeste M., Michelle R. AB, Geneva Coll., 1956; MA in Edn., No. Mich. U., 1970, postgrad. Secondary tchr. Freedom (Pa.) High Sch., 1956-57; elem. educator Gilbert Elem. Sch., Gwinn, Mich., 1967-69; lang. arts educator Gwinn Mid. Sch., 1970-99; ret., 1999. Adv. bd. panel Mich. Dept. Edn./Arts, 1976-79; mem. sch. improvement team, 1988-91, 93-94, co-chair, 1995-98; mid sch. concept team, 1992-98, mid sch. at-risk coord. dist. curriculum coord. coun., 1995-96; dist. curriculum strategy action team, 1993-94; dist. profl. devel. strategy action team, 1993-94; mem. sounding bd. Mid. Sch., 1994-98, dist. sch. improvement team, 1994-98; lang. arts curriculum design com., 1997-98; rep. Gwinn Edn. Assn. Mid. Sch., 1995-98. Author: Prophets Without Honor: Teachers, Students, & Trust, 1991. V.p. Marquette (Mich.) Community Theatre, 1962-63 bd. dirs. 1963-74, mem. 1961-92; pres. Marquette Arts Coun. 1973-74, v.p. 1972-73, bd. dirs. 1970-78, mem. 1970-84; pres. Upper Peninsula Arts Coordinating Bd. 1976-78, v.p. 1974-76, bd. dirs. 1978-84; bd. dirs. Mich. Community Theatre Assn. 1972-73; bd. dirs. Mich Community Arts Agys., 1976-79. Recipient Committment to Excellence award Marquette Community Theatre, 1965. Devotion to Arts Development award Upper Peninsula (Mich.) Arts Coord. Bd. 1979. Mem. ASCD, NEA, AAUW, Mich. Edn. Assn., Phi Delta Kappa. Presbyterian. Avocations: writing, theater, music. Home: 508 Pine St Marquette MI 49855-3838 Office: Gwinn Area Community Schs Gwinn MI 49841

LASKER, JONATHAN LEWIS, artist; b. Jersey City, July 30, 1948; s. Lester and Henrietta Selma (Gross) L. Student, Sch. Visual Arts, N.Y.C., 1975-77, Calif. Inst. Arts, 1977. One-man shows include Landmark Gallery, NY, Gunnar Kaldeway, Dusseldorf, Fed. Republic Germany, 1981, Annette Gmeiner, Kirchzarten, Fed. Republic Germany, 1984, Tibor de Nagy, NYC, 1984, 1986, Michael Werner, Cologne, Fed. Republic Germany, 1986, 1987, 1990, Massimo Audiello, NYC, 1986, 1988, 1989, Anders Tornberg, Lund, Sweden, 1987, 1990, Gian Enzo Sperone, Rome, 1988, 1991, Sperone Westwater Gallery, NYC, 1991, 1993, 1996, 1999, 2002, 2003, Lars Bohman, Stockholm, 1991, 1994, 2001, Inst. Contemporary Art U. Pa., Phila., 1992, Thaddaeus Ropac Gallery, Paris, 1992, 1997, 2000, Witte de With Ctr. Contemporary Art, Rotterdam, 1993, Rhona Hoffman Gallery, Chgo., 1993, Soledad Lorenzo, Madrid, 1995, 1998, L.A. Louver Gallery, 1995, Kunsthalle Bielefeld, Germany, 1997, Stedelijk Mus., Amsterdam, Holland, 1998, Kunstverein St. Gallen, Switzerland, 1998, Timothy Taylor, London, England, 1998, 2004, Forum for Contemporary Art, St. Louis, Mo., The Power Plant Contemporary Art Gallery, Toronto, Canada, 1999, Rose Art Mus. Brandeis U., Waltham, Mass., 2000, Thomas Schulte, Berlin, 2002, 2003, K-20 Kunstsammlung Nord-Rhein-Westfalen, Düsseldorf, Germany, 2003, Museo Nacional Centro de Arte Reina Sofia, Madrid, 2003, Kunstallen Brandts Klaedefabrik, Odense, Denmark, 2005, Galleria Cardi & Co., Milan, 2005, numerous others, exhibited in group shows at Mus. Ludwig, Cologne, Wacoal Art Ctr., Tokyo, 1985, Rose Art Mus. Brandeis U., Waltham, Mass., 1986, 1999, Corcoran Gallery Art, Washington, 1987, Roos Mus., Malmo, Sweden, U. N. Tex., Denton, J.B. Speed Mus., Louisville, Alta. Coll. Art, Edmonton, Can., Contemporary Arts Ctr., Cin., Santa Fe Community Coll., Gainesville, Fla., Met. Mus. Art, NYC, 1988, Stedelijk Mus., Amsterdam, The Netherlands, 1989, Marc Richards Gallery, LA, Thaddaeus Ropac, Salzburg, Austria, 1989, 2001, 2003, 2004, Paris, 1992, 1999, Scott Hansen Gallery, N.Y.C., 1990, Pace Gallery, 1990, Sperone Westwater Gallery, 1991, 1994, 1995, 1996, 1997, 1998, 2001, Gallery Modern Art, Bologna, Italy, 1991, Hirshhorn Mus. and Sculpture Garden, Washington, 1991, 2004, Mus. Contemporary Art of Dayton Art Inst., 1992, Documenta IX, Kassel,

Germany, Gallerie Nächst Sankt Stephan, Vienna, 1992, Ruth Bloom Gallery, L.A., 1993, Hayward Gallery, London, 1994, Ctr. for the Fine Arts, Miami, 1994, Va. Mus. Fine Arts, Richmond, 1995, Mus. Contemporary Art, Helsinki, Folkwang Mus., Essen, Germany, 1995, Mus. Reina Sofia, Madrid, 1996, Kunsthalle Zurich, Switzerland, 1996, Musée D'Art Modern Centre, St. Etienne France, 1997, Mus. Am. Art of Pa. Acad. Fine Arts, Phila., 1998, Malmø Konsthall, Sweden, 1998, Menil Collection, Houston, 1999, Aargauer Kunsthaus, Aarau, Switzerland, 2000, Palazzo Cavour, Turin, Italy, 2000, Michael Hue-Williams, London, England, 2000, Rudolfinum Ctr for Contemporary Art, Prague, Czech Republic, 2001, Kunstverein St. Gallen in Kunstmuseum, Switzerland, 2001, Yale U. Art Gallery, New Haven, Conn., 2002, Mus. Morsbroich, Leverkusen, Germany, 2003, Orlando Mus. Art, Fla., 2004, Samuel Dorsky Mus. Art, New Platz, N.Y., 2005, Chelsea Mus. Art, NYC, 2005, BA-CA Kunstforum, Vienna, Austria, 2005, numerous others, Represented in permanent collections Corcoran Gallery, Hirshhorn Mus. and Sculpture Garden, Washington, Mus. Ludwig, Cologne, Wacoal Art Ctr., Tokyo, Whitney Mus. Am. Art, NYC, Moderna Museet, Stockholm, Fond. Nat. d'Art Contemporain, Paris, High Mus., Atlanta, Museo de Arte Contemporaneo, Seville, Spain, La Fundacion Caja De Pensiones, Barcelona, Albright Knox Art Gallery, Buffalo, NY, Los Angeles County Mus. Art, Calif., Museo Nacional Centro de Arte Reina Sofia, Madrid, Musée Nat. D'Art Modern Centre Pompidov, Paris, Birmingham Mus. Art, Ala.; critic (numerous art books, catalogs, mags. including) Beyond Boundaries: New York's New Art (Jerry Saltz), N.Y. Art Now, The Saatchi Collection (Dan Cameron), The Silent Baroque (Christian Leigh editor), Interpreting Contemporary Art (Rainer Crone and David Moos), Art at the End of the Social (Collins and Milazzo), Art Since Mid-Century: 1945 to the Present (Daniel Wheeler), Jonathan Lasker, Telling the Tales of Painting (Rainer Crone and David Moos), The 20th Century Art Book (Tony Godfrey, Melissa Larner, et al), Hist. Modern Art (H.H. Arnason and Marla Prather) 4th edit., Hist. Modern Art (H.H. Arnason and Peter Kalb) 5th edit., Art of the 20th Century (Ingo Walther, editor) Taschen Verlag, Modern Art (Sam Hunter, John Jacobus, Daniel Wheeler) 3d rev. edit., Caravaggio on the Beach: Essays on Art in the 1990's (Richard Milazzo), Art News (Feb. 1990, Apr. 1992, Feb. 2004), Le Monde (June 1992), Art in America, (Apr. 1995), Contemporary Visual Arts (Apr.-May 2000), Frankfurter Allgemeine Zeitung (Oct. 2003), New Yorker, Peter Schjeldahl (Dec. 2003). NEA fellow, 1987, 89. Office: care Sperone Westwater Gallery 415 W 13th St New York NY 10014

LASKER, JOSEPH L., artist, illustrator; b. N.Y.C., June 26, 1919; s. Isidore and Rachel (Strollowitz) L.; m. Mildred Jaspen, Nov. 28, 1948; children: David Raymond, Laura, Evan. Student, Cooper Union Art Sch., evenings 1936-39, Escuela Universitaria de Bellas Artes, Mexico, 1948. Tchr. Coll. City N.Y., 1947; vis. assoc. prof. art U. Ill., 1953-54. Exhibited one-man shows Kraushaar Galleries, N.Y.C., most recently 2003; works represented in permanent collections Whitney Mus., Cal. Palace Legion of Honor, Phila., Springfield Mus., Mass., Joseph Hirschorn Collection, Balt. Mus., Munson-Williams Proctor Inst., Phila. Mus. Art; murals in Calumet (Mich.) P.O., Millbury, Mass., Henry Street Settlement Play House, N.Y.C.; author, illustrator juvenile books: Mothers Can Do Anything, 1972, He's My Brother, 1974, Tales of a Seadog Family, 1974, Merry Ever After (best illustrated children's book, N.Y. Times, 1976, Notable Bk. of Yr. Am. Library Assn. 1977), 1976, The Strange Voyage of Neptune's Car, 1977, Lentil Soup, 1977, Nick Joins In, 1980, The Do-Something Day, 1982, The Great Alexander the Great, 1983, Tournament of Knights, 1986; illustrator numerous other children's Books. Served with U.S. Army, 1941-45. Abbey Meml. scholar, 1946, 47; Prix de Rome fellow, 1950, 51; Guggenheim fellow, 1954; Benjamin Altman prize (figure) Nat. Acad. Design, 1958, 80; grantee Nat. Inst. Arts and Letters, 1968 Mem. NAD (academician, 1965-) Office: care Kraushaar Galleries 724 5th Ave New York NY 10019-4106*

LASKER, MORRIS E., judge; b. Hartsdale, N.Y., July 17, 1917; m. Helen M. Schubach; 4 children. BA magna cum laude, Harvard U., 1938; LLB, JD, Yale U., 1941. Bar: N.Y. 1941. Atty. Nat. Def. Com., U.S. Senate, 1941-42, Battle, Fowler, Jaffin & Kheel, 1946-68; fed. judge U.S. Dist. Ct. (so. dist.) N.Y., 1968-94, U.S. Dist. Ct., Boston, 1994—. Contbr. articles to profl. jours. Hon. trustee, bd. dirs. Vera Inst. Justice. Maj. U.S. Army, 1942-46. Recipient Learned Hand medal Fed. Bar Coun., Edward Weinfeld award N.Y. County Lawyers Assn. Mem. ABA, Assn. of Bar of City of N.Y. (exec. com. 1985-89). Avocations: gardening, reading, history, english and american literature. Office: US Dist Ct US Courthouse 1 Courthouse Way Boston MA 02210-3002

LASKI, JOHN N., finance educator; b. Passaic, N.J., Jan. 14, 1954; m. Priscilla Laski; children: Alicia, Michelle, Veronica, Michael, Jonathan. AS in Criminal Justice, Salve Regina U.; BS in Orgn. Mgmt., Nyack Coll.; MBA in Fin., St. Thomas Aquinas Coll.; PhD in Fin., Nova Southeastern U. Nat. sales mgr. UVA Machine Co., Bromma, Sweden; fin. cons. Merrill Lynch, Wayne, NJ; investment mgr. Citicorp, L.I., NY; asst. v.p. Jaron Equities, Hicksville, NY; asst. v.p. investments N.E. Securities, N.Y.C.; assoc. prof. fin., dir. MBA program Nyack (N.Y.) Coll., N.Y.C. Commr. Passaic County Planning Bd., Paterson, NJ; bn. chief UGL Vol. Fire Co., Hewitt, NJ; asst. arson investigator Tiverton (R.I.) Fire Dept. With USN, 1973—80. Recipient medal of honor, Passaic County Bd. Freeholders, Paterson, N.J. Mem.: Masons. Avocations: boating, golf, target shooting, photography. Office: Nyack Coll 1 South Blvd Nyack NY 10960

LASKIN, BARBARA VIRGINIA, management analyst; b. Chgo., July 2, 1939; d. Cyril Krieps and Gertrude Katherine (Kujawa) Szymanski; children: Dawn Katherine Potthoff, Amy Lynn Anderson. BA, U. Ill., Chgo., 1967; MA, Am. U. Beirut, 1978, Georgetown U., 1985. Asst. buyer Carson, Pirie, Scott & Co., Chgo., 1967-69; fgn. svc. officer Dept. State, Washington, 1969-79; mgr. gift shops Marriott Hotels, Washington, 1979-81; office mgr. Robt Schwinn & Assoc., Bethesda, Md., 1983-85; exec. dir. Internat. Acad. Trial Lawyers, San Jose, Calif., 1985-97; mktg. mgr. convention and destination mgmt. svcs. San Jose Conv. and Vis. Bur., 1998-99; mgmt. analyst Santa Clara County, San Jose, Calif., 2002—. Fellow Rotary Club San Jose; mem. AAUW (v.p. 1987), Am. Soc. Assn. Execs., Meeting Planners Internat., Internat. Spl. Events Soc. (v.p. membership 1996), Internat. Spl. Events Found. (dir.), Profl. Conservation Mgrs. Assn. Roman Catholic. Office: Santa Clara County East Wing 70 W Hedding St 7th Fl San Jose CA 95110 Office Phone: 408-299-5703. E-mail: barbara.laskin@pln.sccgov.org.

LASKIN, DANIEL M., oral and maxillofacial surgeon, educator; b. Ellenville, NY, Sept. 3, 1924; s. Nathan and Flora (Kaplan) L.; m. Eve Pauline Mohel, Aug. 25, 1945; children: Jeffrey, Gary, Marla. Student, NYU, 1941—42; BS, Ind. U., 1947; MS, U. Ill., 1951; DSc (hon.), Ind. U., 2001. Diplomate Am. Bd. Oral and Maxillofacial Surgery, Am. Dental Bd. Anesthesiology. Faculty U. Ill., Chgo., 1949-84, prof. dept. oral and maxillofacial surgery, 1960-84, head dept., 1973-84, clin. prof. surgery, 1961-84, dir. temporomandibular joint and facial pain research center, 1963-84; prof., chmn. dept. oral and maxillofacial surgery Med. Coll. Va., Richmond, 1984—2002, chmn. emeritus, 2003, dir. temporomandibular joint and facial pain rsch. ctr., 1984—2002; affiliate clin. prof., dept. psychology Va. Commonwealth U.; head dept. dentistry MCV Hosp., Richmond, 1986—2002; former attending oral surgeon Edgewater, Swedish Covenant, Ill. Masonic, Skokie Valley Cmty. hosps., Chgo.; former chmn. dept. oral surgery Cook County Hosp., Chgo. Cons. oral surgery to Surgeon Gen. Navy, 1977-83; dental products panel FDA, 1988-92, cons., 1993-95; Francis J. Reichmann Lectr., 1971, Cordwainer lectr., London, 1980, Donald B. Osborn Meml. lectr., 1999. Author: Oral and Maxillofacial Surgery, Vol. I, 1980, Vol. II, 1985; contbr. articles to profl. jours.; editor-in-chief: Jour. Oral and Maxillofacial Surgery, 1972-2002; mem. editl. bd. Internat. Jour. Oral and Maxillofacial Surgery, 1978-88, Topics in Pain Mgmt., Densat, Internat. Jour. Oral and Maxillofacial Implants, Quintessence Internat., Revista Latino America Cirugia Traumatologia Maxilofacial, Va. Dental Jour., Jour. Dental Rsch.; mem. internat. editl. bd. Headache Quar.; mem. editl. bd. Greek Jour. Oral and Maxillofacial Surgery, Electronic Jour. Dentistry; assoc. editor Odontology; mem. internat. adv. bd. Asian Jour. Oral and Maxillofacial Surgery; OMFS editor Jewish Med. Jour. Nat. hon. chmn. peer campaign A.A.O.M.S. Edn. and Rsch. Found., 1990; bd. dirs. Internat. Assn. Oral and Maxillofacial Surgeons Found.; chmn. Nat. Acad. Dentistry, 1997-99; pres.-elect Nat. Acad. of Practice, 1999, pres., 2002—04. Recipient Disting. Alumni Svc. award, Ind. U., 1975, William J. Gies editl. award 1st prize, 1978—79, 1984, 1987, 1989, 1992, 1996, 2001, Simon P. Hullihen Meml. award, 1976, Arnold K. Maislen Meml. award, 1977, Thomas P. Hinman medallion, 1980, W. Harry Archer Achievement award for rsch., 1981, Heidbrink award, 1983, Disting. Alumnus award, Ind. U. Sch. Dentistry, 1984, U. Ill. Coll. Dentistry, 2003, Rene Lefort medal, 1985, Semmelweis medallion, Semmelweis Med. U., 1985, Golden Scroll award, Internat. Coll. Dentists, 1986, Internat. award, Friends Sch. Dental Med., U. Conn. Health Ctr., Donald B. Osbon award, 1991, Achievement medal, Alpha Omega, 1992, Norton M. Ross Excellence in Clin. Rsch. award, 1993, Va. Commonwealth U. Faculty award of excellence, 1994, named Zendium Lectr., 1989, Edward C. Hinds Lectr., 1990, Disting. Practitioner Nat. Acads. Practice, 1992, Hon. Diplomate Am. Soc. Osseointegration, 1992, Silver Scroll award, Internat. Coll. Dentists, 2004; fellow in dental surgery, Royal Coll. Surgeons Eng.; grantee, Glasgow Royal Coll. Physicians and Surgeons (hon.). Fellow: AAAS, Am. Acad. Implant Prosthodontists (academia), Internat. Coll. Dentists (Spl. Editl. citation 1999, Silver Scroll award 2004), Am. Coll. Dentists, Acad. Internat. Dental Studies (hon.), Internat. Assn. Oral and Maxillofacial Surgeons (hon.; exc. com. 1980—95, pres. 1983—86, sec. gen. 1989—95, exec. dir. 1995—99, gen. chmn. 14th Internat. Conf. on Oral and Maxillofacial Surg. 1999, found. cons.); mem.: ADA (adv. com. advanced edn. in oral surgery 1968—75, cons. Coun. on Dental Edn. 1968—82, mem. Commn. on Accreditation 1975—76), Hungarian Assn. Oral and Maxillofacial Surgeons, Odontographic Soc., William F. Harrigan Soc., Nat. Chronic Pain Outreach Assn. (adv. bd.), Am. Dental Bd. Anesthesiology (pres. 1983—92), Scandinavian Assn. Oral and Maxillofacial Surgeons (hon.), Hellenic Assn. Oral Surgery (hon.), Sadi Fontaine Acad. (hon.), Internat. Congress Oral Implantologists (hon.), Soc. Maxillofacial and Oral Surgeons South Africa (hon.), Japanese Soc. for Temporomandibular Joint (hon.), Am. Soc. Laser in Dentistry (hon.), Internat. Study Group for Advancement of TMJ Arthroscopy (hon.), Can. Assn. Oral and Maxillofacial Surgeons (hon.), Japanese Soc. Oral and Maxillofacial Surgeons (hon.), Brazilian Coll. Oral and Maxillofacial Surgery and Traumatology (hon.), Chilean Soc. Oral and Maxillofacial Surgery (hon.), Royal Soc. Medicine, Am. Assn. Dental Editors, Am. Soc. Exptl. Pathology, Am. Dental Soc. Anesthesiology (pres. 1976—78), Internat. Assn. Dental Rsch., Am. Assn. Oral and Maxillofacial Surgeons (editor Forum 1965—96, pres. 1976—77, editor AAOMS Today 1996—, Disting. Svc. award 1972, rsch. recognition award 1978, William J. Gies award 1979, dedication 73d ann. meeting and sci. sessions 1991), Ill. Splty. Bd. Oral Surgery, Sigma Xi, Omicron Kappa Upsilon. Rsch. and publs. on connective tissue physiology and pathology, particularly cartilage and bone metabolism, craniofacial growth, oral maxillofacial surgery, and pathology of temporomandibular joint. Office: Va Commonwealth U Dept Oral/Maxillofac Surg PO Box 980566 Richmond VA 23298-0566 Office Phone: 804-828-3547. Business E-Mail: dmlaskin@vcu.edu.

LASKIN, LEE B., judge, state senator; b. Atlantic City, June 30, 1936; m. Andrea Solomon; 1 dau., Shari. Student, Am. U., Temple U., Rutgers U., 1960. Bar: NJ. Asst. U.S. atty., NJ, 1964-68; mem. NJ Gen. Assembly, NJ, 1968-70, Camden County Bd. Chosen Freeholders, NJ, 1970-73, NJ Senate, NJ, 1977-92; judge NJ Superior Ct., NJ, 1994—. Mcpl. atty. Audubon, Berlin Borough, Berlin Twp., Clementon, Laurel Springs, Mt. Ephraim and Waterford, NJ, and Winslow Twp.; counsel Bellmawr Bd. Edn., Berlin Zoning Bd., Camden County Welfare Bd., Non-Resident Taxpayers Assn., Animal Welfare Assn., Brith Sholom Fed. Credit Union, Camden Hebrew Fed. Credit Union, Union Fed. Savs. and Loan Assn., Div. 880 Amalgamated Transit Union, Local 18 of Am. Fed. Tech. Engrs., Camden Fire Officers Assn., Am. Postal Workers Union, Fuel Mchts. Assn., Shamong Twp. Bd. Edn., Cherry Hill Zoning Bd.; field counsel Fed. Nat. Mortgage Assn.; founder, 1st chmn. Glendale Nat. Bank. Del. Rep. Nat. Conv., 1984. With USMC, 1957-64, USMCR. Office: Camden County Hall Justice 5th and Mickle Blvd Camden NJ 08103-4001 Office Phone: 856-379-2314. E-mail: gerrymander3010@aol.com.

LASKIN, RICHARD SHELDON, orthopedic surgeon; b. Bklyn., July 13, 1940; s. Herman Myron and Gertrude (Klein) L.; m. Joyce Sparrow, Mar. 3, 1991; children: Joanthan, Andrew. AB, Hofstra U., 1960; MD, NYU, 1964. Diplomate Am. Bd. Orthopedic Surgery. Intern, resident Albert Einstein Coll. Medicine Affiliated Hosps., N.Y.C., 1964-66, resident, 1968-70, Nassau County Med. Ctr., 1970-71; chmn. dept. orthopedic surgery L.I. Jewish Med. Ctr., 1980-91; prof. SUNY, Stony Brook, 1984-89, Albert Einstein Coll. Medicine, 1989-91, Cornell U., 1991—. Mem. N.Y. Hosp.; chief knee svc. Hosp. for Spl. Surgery. Author: Replacement of Knee Joint, Total Knee Replacement, Controversies in Total Knee Replacement; editor: The Knee; dep. editor: Clinical Orthopaedics and Related Research; contbr. clin. rsch. articles to orthopedic surgery to profl. jours., also papers in Amsterdam, Milan, Jerusalem, Athens, Copenhagen, Oslo, Paris, London, Mex., U.S., Madrid, Barcelina, Sweden, Australia, Japan, China, Berlin. With MS, AUS, 1966-68, col. MC USAR, 1989-91. Decorated Bronze Star, Combat Med. Badge, Air medal. Mem. ACS, Am. Acad. Orthopedic Surgeons, Am. Orthopaedic Assn., Internat. Arthroscopy Assn., N.Y. Acad. Medicine, Knee Soc., Ea. Orthopedic Soc., N.Y. State Orthopedic Surgeons, N.Y. Stqte Med. Soc., Internat. Knee Soc., Orthopedic Rsch. Soc., Norwegian Orthopedic Assn., Spanish Orthopedic Soc., Soc. Mil. Orthopedic Surgery, SICOT, SIROT, Assn. Bone & Joint Surgeons. Office: The Hosp for Spl Surgery 535 E 70th St New York NY 10021-4898

LASKO, ALLEN HOWARD, pharmacist; b. Chgo., Oct. 27, 1941; s. Sidney P. and Sara (Hoffman) L.; m. Janice Marilynn Chess, Dec. 24, 1968 (div. Aug. 1993); children: Stephanie Paige, Michael Benjamin. BS, U. Ill., 1964. Staff pharmacist Michael Reese Hosp. and Med. Ctr., Chgo., 1964-68; clin. pharmacist City of Hope Med Ctr., Duarte, Calif., 1968-73; chief pharmacist Monrovia (Calif.) Cmty. Hosp. 1973-74, Santa Fe Meml. Hosp., L.A., 1974-77; pvt. investor, 1977-93; clin. pharmacist Foothill Presbyn. Hosp., Glendora, Calif., 1993—. Author: Diabetes Study Guide, 1972, A Clinical Approach to Lipid Abnormalities Study Guide, 1973, Jet Injection Tested As an Aid in Physiologic Delivery of Insulin, 1973. Mem. Magic Castle. Recipient Roche-Hosp. Pharmacy rsch. award, 1972-73; James scholar U. Ill. Mem. Mensa (life), Rho Pi Phi. Jewish. Home: 376 Hill St Monrovia CA 91016-2340 Office: Foothill Presbyn Hosp 250 S Grand Ave Glendora CA 91741-4218 E-mail: allenlasko@aol.com.

LASKO, JOEL, marketing executive; b. N.Y.C., Nov. 1, 1932; s. Max Lasko and Charlotte Parker; m. Mary Anne Thune, Dec. 19, 1973; children: Elizabeth, Andrew. BS in Mktg., Syracuse U., 1955; MBA in Mktg. Mgmt., CCNY, 1957. Br. mgr. Olivetti Corp., Washington, 1958—70; pres. Washington Photocopy, Washington, 1970—. Recipient Mktg. medal Am. Mktg. Assn., 1957. Avocations: tennis, skiing. Office: Washington Photocopy 4380 Macarthur Blvd NW Washington DC 20007-2594 Office Phone: 202-333-4585.

LASKO, NATASHA B., psychologist; b. St. Petersburg, Russia, Feb. 12, 1946; d. Boris Mendelevich Golzberg and Zoya Mitrofanovna Andreeva; m. Mark Vladimir Lasko, Mar. 24, 1972; 1 child, Dennis Mark. MA in Clin. Psychology, St. Petersburg U., Russia, 1969, PhD in Clin. Psychology, 1978. Clin. psychologist Bekhterev Psychoneurol. Inst., St. Petersburg, 1969-80; instr. psychology Harvard Med. Sch., Boston, 1990—2001, asst. prof. psychology, 2001—; asst. rsch. Mass. Gen. Hosp., Boston, 1998—; psychodiagnostician VA Rsch. Svc., Manchester, N.H., 1989—. Cons. in field. Mem. APA, N.Y. Acad. Scis., Mass. Mental Health Counselors Assn., Russian Soc. Traumatic Stress Studies, Internat. Soc. Traumatic Stress Studies Republican. Avocation: travel. Office: PTSD Research Lab MGH Bldg 149 13th Street Charlestown MA 02129 Office Phone: 603-624-4366 6818. Business E-Mail: natasha_lasko@hms.harvard.edu.

LASKOWSKI, LEONARD FRANCIS, JR., microbiologist; b. Milw., Nov. 16, 1919; s. Leonard Francis and Frances (Cyborowski) L.; m. Frances Bielinski, June 1, 1946; children— Leonard Francis III, James, Thomas. BS, Marquette U., 1941, MS, 1948; PhD, St. Louis U., 1951. Diplomate: Am. Bd. Microbiology. Instr. bacteriology Marquette U., 1946-48; mem. faculty St. Louis U., 1951—, prof. pathology and internal medicine, Div. Infectious Diseases, 1969-90, prof. emeritus, 1990—, assoc. prof. internal medicine, 1977-90—. Dir. clin. microbiology sect. St. Louis U. Hosps. Labs., 1965—; cons. clin microbiology Firmin Desloge Hosp., St. Louis U. Group Hosps., St. Marys Group Hosps.; cons. bacteriology VA Hosp.; asst. dept. chief Pub. Health Lab., St. Louis Civil Def., 1958—; cons. St. Elizabeths Hosp., St. Louis County Hosp., St. Francis Hosp. Contbr. articles to profl. jours. Health and tech. tng. coordinator for Latin Am. projects Peace Corps, 1962-66. Served with M.C. AUS, 1942-46. Fellow Am. Acad. Microbiology; mem. Soc. Am. Bacteriologists, N.Y. Acad. Scis., Am., Mo. pub. health assns., AAUP, Med. Mycol. Soc. Am., Alpha Omega Alpha. Office: 1402 S Grand Blvd Saint Louis MO 63104-1004 Home: 505 Cedar Summit Ln Villa Ridge MO 63089

LASKY, DAVID, lawyer; b. N.Y.C., Nov. 12, 1932; s. Benjamin and Rebecca (Malumed) L.; m. Phyllis Beryl Sumper, Apr. 14, 1957; children— Jennifer Lee, Robert Barry. BA, Bklyn. Coll., 1954; LLB, Columbia U., 1957. Bar: N.Y. 1957. Atty. N.Y.C. R.R. Co., 1957-62; with Curtiss-Wright Corp., N.Y.C., 1962—, corp. counsel, 1966-67, gen. counsel, 1967-93, v.p., 1972-80, sr. v.p., 1980-93, sec., 1989-93, pres., 1993-99, chmn., 1995-2000, bd. dirs., 1993—. Bd. dirs. Primex Technologies, Inc. Chmn. zoning bd. appeals, Ramapo, N.Y., 1968-72; dir., v.p. Oak Trail Homeowners Assn., 1987-90. Mem. ABA (chmn. com. corp. gen. counsel 1992-93), Phi Beta Kappa.

LASKY, RICHARD DONALD, psychoanalyst, educator; b. N.Y.C., Jan. 22, 1943; s. Sidney Lasky and Alice Presser; m. Judith Faye Sherman. PhD in Psychology, NYU, 1970, postdoctoral cert., 1974. Lic. psychologist, N.Y.; diplomate Am. Bd. Profl. Psychology. Jr. rsch. scientist Rsch. Found. State N.Y., Downstate Med. Ctr., SUNY, Bklyn., 1964-68; asst. prof. L.I. Univ., Greenvale, N.Y., 1969-74; clin. assoc., supr. psychologist doctoral program psychology CUNY, N.Y.C., 1975—; chmn. of faculty Inst. for Psychoanalytic Tng. and Rsch., N.Y.C., 1985-2000; clin. prof. psychology postdoctoral program NYU, 1990—. Author: Multiple Personality and the Related Dissociative Disorders, 1984, Dynamics of Development and the Therapeutic Process, 1993; editor: Symbolization and Desymbolization: Essays in Honor of Norbert Freedman, 2002. Rsch. fellow VA, 1968, NIMH fellow, 1969-71. Fellow Acad. of Psychoanalysis; mem. APA, Internat. Psycho-Analytical Assn., Am. Psychoanalytic Assn., Nat. Register of Health Care Providers in Psychology. Office Phone: 212-595-0442. E-mail: richardlasky@nyc.rr.com.

LASLEY, THOMAS J., II, education educator; b. Delaware, Ohio, July 23, 1947; s. Thomas J. and Anna F. (Cooper) L.; m. Janet L. Olney, Apr. 21, 1973; children: Julianne Marie, Elizabeth Ann. BS, Ohio State U., 1969, MA, 1972, PhD, 1978. Cert. tchr. and adminstr. Ohio. Tchr. Upper Arlington, Ohio, 1969-75; rsch. assoc. Ohio State U., 1975-77. Cons. Ohio Dept. Edn., 1977-80, asst. dir. tchr. edn. and cert., 1980-83; prof. U. Dayton (Ohio), 1983—, chmn. dept., 1983-92, dean Sch. Edn., 1998—; cons. on sch. research and disruptive student behavior. Author: Issues in Teacher Education, 1986, Dynamics of Change in Teacher Education, 1986, Teaching Peace, 1994, Strategies for Teaching in a Diverse Society: Instructional Models, 2002, Strategies for Effective Teaching, 2004, Secondary and Middle School Methods, 2005; contbr. articles to profl. jours. Mem. Am. Ednl. Rsch. Assn., Phi Delta Kappa. Office: U Dayton Chaminade Hall Dayton OH 45469 Office Phone: 937-229-3327. Business E-Mail: thomas.lasley@notes.udayton.edu.

LASLO, ANN REICHARD, artist, writer; b. N.J., Aug. 2, 1951; BA, MA, PhD. Chief graphic designer Metropolitan Arts & Antiques; graphic designer Nat. Keyboard Arts, Princeton, NJ; author interview series to newspapers; feature writer; poet. Cultural advisor Gt. Plains Devel. Bd.; editl. commentator Opinion Shaper; cons. Diligence Cottage & Barclay Hall, New Hope, Pa., 2001. Author: Selected Views of Random Days, All the People; exhibitions include May Show, The Mansfield Art Ctr., 1972, McCarter Theatre, Princeton, NJ, Trenton City Mus. at Ellarslie, 1979, NJ. Artists Ann., 1979, Abstract Naturalists Invitational Exhbn., Mansfield Art Ctr., Ohio, 1987, Lambertville & Surrounding Area Ann. Exhbn., 2003, one-woman shows include Ohio State U. Mansfield Campus, 1973, Eye for Art Gallery, Princeton, N.J., 1978. Achievements include first woman commentator U. Cin. Radio. Home: PO Box 353 Holmdel NJ 07733-0353 Office Phone: 215-862-3160. Personal E-mail: mzlaslo@yahoo.com.

LASORDA, THOMAS CHARLES (TOMMY LASORDA), professional baseball team manager; b. Norristown, Pa., Sept. 22, 1927; s. Sam and Carmella (Covatto) Lasorda; m. Joan Miller Lasorda, Apr. 14, 1950; children: Laura, Tom Charles. Student pub. schs., Norristown. Pitcher Bklyn. Dodgers, 1954—55, Kansas City A's, 1956; with L.A. Dodgers, 1956—, mgr. minor league clubs Pocatello, Idaho, Ogden, Utah, Spokane, Albuquerque, 1965—73, coach, 1973—76, mgr., 1976—96, v.p. fin., 1996—98, gen. mgr., 1998—, sr. v.p., 1998—. Author (with David Fisher): autobiography The Artful Dodger, 1985. With U.S. Army, 1945—47. Named Pitcher of Yr., Internat. League, 1958, L.A. Dodgers winner, Nat. League pennant, 1977, 1978, 1981, 1988, 2d Nat. League mgr. to win pennant first two yrs. as mgr., Nat. League Mgr. Yr., UPI, 1977, AP, 1977, Baseball Writers' Assn. Am., 1988, Sporting News, 1988, Baseball Writers Assn. Am., 1983, 1988, coach, Nat. League All-Star team, 1977, 1983—84, 1986, 1993; named to Baseball Hall of Fame, 1997; recipient World Championship, 1981, 1988, Milton Richman Meml. award, Assn. Profl. Baseball Players Am. Mem.: Profl. Baseball Players Am., Variety Club of Calif. (v.p.). Roman Catholic. Office: c/o Los Angeles Dodgers 1000 Elysian Park Ave Los Angeles CA 90012-1112*

LASPA, JUDE, engineering company executive; m. Eileen Laspa. Grad., Harvey Mudd Coll., 1965. Mgr. bus. devel. Bechtel, gen. mgr. Bechtel/KWU alliance, mng. dir. Bechtel Enterprises, pres. Bechtel Sys. and Infrastructure Inc., sr. v.p. enging. and constrn., exec. v.p., dep. COO San Francisco, 1997—. Office: Bechtel 50 Beale St San Francisco CA 94105-1895

LASPADA, CARMELLA, government agency administrator; BS in Psychology and TV Comm., Pa. State U., 1960. Organizer USO tour to S.E. Asia White House Spl. Projects Aid, 1967; founder No Greater Love, 1971—; White House liaison and exec. dir. White House Commn. on the Nat. Moment of Remembrance, 2001—. Initiator Nat. Moment of Remembrance, 2000. Named Washingtonian of the Yr., Unsung Heroine, VFW Women's Aux.; recipient U.S. Spl. Ops. Command medal, Ellis Island Medal of Honor, Dickey Chapelle award, USMC League, Spirit of Enterprise award, U.S. C. of C., Humanitarian award, Rotary Club, Outstanding Alumni award, Pa. State U., Woman of the Yr. award, Christopher Columbus Assn. Office: White House Commn on Remembrance 1750 New York Ave NW Washington DC 20006

LASPINA, PETER JOSEPH, computer resource educator; b. Bay Shore, N.Y., June 28, 1951; s. Peter Celestine and Barbara Elizabeth (Rodee) L.; 1 child, Joseph Peter. BMus with high honors, Performer's Cert. on Piano, N.Y. State Coll., Potsdam, 1973; MS in Music Edn., L.I. U., 1978; MS in Tech. Sys. Mgmt., SUNY, Stony Brook, 1987; postgrad., Nova Southeastern U., 1995-97. Tchr. music E. Meadow (N.Y.) pub. schs., 1974-75, Northport-East Northport Pub. Schs., 1975-86, computer resource tchr., 1986—. Adj. faculty SUNY, Stony Brook, 1991—; writer master trainer N.Y. State Edn. Dept., Albany, 1987-88; cons. ednl. tech., Smithtown, N.Y., 1987—; invited del. U.S./China Joint Conf. on Edn., Beijing, 1992, 95-96, and conf. presenter. Contbr. articles to profl. jours. Mem. Am. Fedn. Tchrs., N.Y. State United Tchrs., Suffolk County Music Educators Assn., Nat. Assn. Sci., Tech. and Soc., N.Y. State Assn. Computers and Techs. (mem. conf. com. 1994), Internat. Soc. for Tech. in Edn., Assn. Ednl. Comm. and Tech., Assn. for

Advancement of Computers in Edn. Presbyterian. Avocations: reading, oenology, home repair, travel. Home: 21 Knolltop Dr Nesconset NY 11767-2221 Office: SUNY Tech And Soc Program Stony Brook NY 11794-0001 E-mail: plaspina@optonline.net.

LASSAR, SCOTT R., lawyer, former prosecutor; b. Evanston, Ill., Apr. 5, 1950; s. Richard Ernest and Jo (Ladenson) L.; m. Elizabeth Levine, May 22, 1977; children: Margaret, Kate. B.A., Oberlin Coll., 1972; J.D., Northwestern U., 1975. Bar: Ill. 1975. With Office U.S. Atty. (No. dist.) Ill., US Dept. Justice, 1975-86, Chgo., ptnr. Keck, Mahin & Cate (formerly Karon, Morrison & Savikas), Chgo., 1986-93; first asst. US atty. (No. dist.) Ill., US Dept. Justice, 1993-97, interim U.S. atty., 1997, U.S. atty., 1997-2001, ptnr., Sidley, Austin, Brown & Wood LLP, Chgo, 2001-; Recipient Bill of Rights in Action award, Constl. Rights Found., 2002. Office: Bank One Plaza 10 South Dearborn St Chicago IL 60603*

LASSEN, BETTY JANE, gifted and talented educator; b. Topeka, Kans., Apr. 19, 1923; d. Harvey Leroy and Anna Elizabeth (Day) Rose; m. Emil Lassen Jr., June 5, 1944 (dec. Sept. 1989); 1 child, Emil III. Instr., guide YMCA-YWCA, Albuquerque, 1975-84, U. N.Mex. Continuing Edn., Albuquerque, 1979—, Ft. Lewis Coll. Continuing Edn., Durango, Colo., 1992-93. Liaison, asst. coord. San Juan Coll. Elder Hostel, Farmington, N.Mex., 1993-94; owner, pres. Outdoor Adventure Tours, Inc., Albuquerque, 1982—; mem. curriculum com., human svcs. tng. coun. gerontology divsn. continuing edn. U. N.Mex., 1979-82; spkr. in field. Designer ski equipment; contbr. articles, poetry to profl. publs. Vol. instr., guide for disabled Easter Seals Soc., Albuquerque, 1983; vol. campground host Nat. Park Svc., Chaco Canyon Ruins, N.Mex., 1990; campaign vol. Dem. Party, Albuquerque, 1976. Recipient Appreciation award Easter Seals Soc., 1983. Mem. Puerto Del Sol Ladies Golf Assn. (pres. 1976-77), N.Mex. Outfitters/Guides, N.Mex. Cross-Country Ski Club (sec. 1973-76), N.Mex. Mountain Club. Avocations: cross country skiing, hiking, bicycling, golf, ballroom dancing. Home: Apt 212 13991 E Marina Dr Aurora CO 80014-3787

LASSEN, JOHN KAI, development company executive; b. Youngstown, Ohio, Mar. 28, 1942; s. Kai Kierulff and Helen Susanne (Elsaesser) L.; m. Marion duPont McConnell, Sept. 26, 1987; children: Christian K., Laura Wick, William duPont, James Tyler. BA, Yale U., 1964; JD, U. Pa., 1967. Bar: Del. 1971, U.S. Dist. Ct. Del. 1972. Ptnr. Morris, Nichols, Arsht & Tunnell, Wilmington, Del., 1977-83, Lassen, Smith Katzenstein & Furlow, Wilmington, Del., 1984-91; pres. Chesapeake Industries, Inc., Wilmington, Del., 1992—2001; vice-chmn., COO Krapfcandoit Co., Wilmington, Del., 1995-2000; pres. Southern Sr. Devel. Svcs., Inc., Wilmington, Del., 2000—02; gen. counsel Pettinaro Enterprises, Wilmington, 2002—. Lt. UNSR, 1967-70. Mem.: SAR, ABA, Nat. Soc. Huguenot Descendants (v.p. Del. chpt.), Del. Bar Assn. (chmn. decedents, estate and trusts 1979—81), Soc. Descendants of War of 1812, Friends of Winterthur, Soc. Mayflower Descs. (dep. gov. 1990—93, capt. 2002—), Soc. Colonial Wars, Yale Club N.Y.C., Lincoln Club, Ocean Reef Club, Vicmead Hunt Club, Wilmington Country Club, Wilmington Club, Rotary. Episcopalian. Home: Crooked Billet PO Box 3712 3510 Kennett Pike Wilmington DE 19807-3019 also: Shore Winds 19 Hall Ave Rehoboth Beach DE 19971-2512 Personal E-mail: kl328@aol.com.

LASSER, GAIL MARIA, psychologist, educator; b. Saddle River, N.J., Feb. 29, 1960; d. Dominick A. and Genevieve M. Sanzo; children: Michael, Jason, Jonathan. B.A., Seton Hall U., 1971; postgrad., Seton HaLL u., 1975—77; tchg. cert., William Paterson Coll., 1973; M.A., Montclair State Coll., 1975. Cert. staff psychologist N.J., 1977; lic. real estate agt. N.J., 1977, notary pub. Pub. rel. rep. European Health Spa, 1970—71; med. asst. Sci. Prevention and Rehab. Assn., 1973; grad. tchg. and rsch. asst. Montclair State Coll., 1973—74; clin. asst. Dr. Brower, 1974; instr. psychology Essex County Coll., 1976—77; clin. psychologist intern Cmty. Mental Health Ctr., Mt. Carmel Guild, Newark, 1976—77; lectr. St. Michaels Med. Ctr.-N.J. Coll. Medicine, 1977—80; instr. psychology Bergen Cmty. Coll., Paramus, NJ, 1977—. Asst. to ct. adminstr. Bergen County Cts., 1977—78; cons. telecom., 1994. Vol. Am. Heart Assn. Mem.: Am. Soc. Phy. Rsch., Am. Psychol. Assn., Psi Chi, Pi Lambda Theta. Home: 234 E Saddle River Rd Saddle River NJ 07458-2614

LASSER, HOWARD GILBERT, chemical engineer, consultant; b. NYC, Nov. 24, 1926; s. Milton and Tessie (Rosenthal) Lasser; m. Barbara Ann Katz, Aug. 24, 1950; children: Cathy, Ellen Lasser-LeVee, Alan. BSChemE, Lehigh U., 1950; postgrad., Columbia U., 1951; DEng, Darmstadt Tech. Inst., Germany, 1956. Registered profl. engr., DC, Va., Calif. Chem. engr. Belvoir Rsch. Engrng. & Devel. Ctr., Ft. Belvoir, Va., 1951-55, 58-72, Naval Sea Sys. Command, Washington, 1955-56, Naval Facilities Engrng. Command, Alexandria, Va., 1972-82, Materials Rsch. Cons., Alexandria, Springfield, Va., 1982—; materials engr. GSA, Washington, 1956-57. Author: Electroplating Facilities, 1991, Chemical Engineering: Electroplating Processes, 1992, Design of Electroplating Facilities, 1992, Lasser's List. The Hamilton Watch Co. American Production, 2004; co-author: Painting of Buildings, 1990, Petroleum Distribution Facilities, 1992; contbr. articles to profl. jours. Fellow: AAAS, Am. Inst. Chemists, Oil and Colour Chemists Assn.; mem.: AIChE, Am. Watch Makers Soc., SSPC Coatings Soc., ASM Internat., NACE Internat., Am. Electroplaters and Surface Finishers Soc., Nat. Watch and Clock Collectors Assn., Sigma Xi, Pi Delta Epsilon, Alpha Chi Sigma, Tau Beta Pi. Achievements include patents for electroplating and metal finishing with medical applications; description of thermodynamic properties of carbon dioxide; development of thermotropic dyes for aluminum oxides; dyes to match laser wavelengths to enhance etching of substrates used in the electronics industry and medicine. Home: 5912 Camberly Ave Springfield VA 22150-2438 Office: Materials Rsch Cons 1121 King St Alexandria VA 22314-2924 Office Phone: 703-683-4288. Personal E-mail: hlasser@cox.net.

LASSER, JOSEPH ROBERT, investment company executive; b. N.Y.C., Sept. 25, 1923; s. Milton and Tessie (Rosenthal) L.; m. Ruth Jean Pollak, May 4, 1925; children: James, Carol Lasser Kornblith, Jean. BS, Lehigh U., 1946; MBA, NYU, 1951. Sr. analyst Lewisohn and Co., N.Y.C., 1946-51; dir. research Walston and Co., N.Y.C., 1951-55, Wertheim and Co., N.Y.C., 1956-67; ptnr. Shufro, Rose, Ehrman, and Stanley Marks, Lasser & Co., N.Y.C., 1967-75; sr. portfolio mgr. C.J. Lawrence, N.Y.C., 1975-76; prin., sr. portfolio mgr. Neuberger & Berman, N.Y.C., 1977—2002. Treas. Bronx House, N.Y., 1978-95; past trusteee United Jewish Appeal/Fedn. Jewish Philanthropies, mem. bd. overseers. 1st lt. USAF, 1943-45. Decorated Air medal with three bronze oak leaf clusters, one silver oak leaf cluster; recipient 1st Lit. award Soc. Paper Money, 1976. Mem. Am. Numismatic Soc. (councillor 1990-93), N.Y. Soc. Security Analysts, Chartered Fin. Analysts Assn., Phi Beta Kappa, Princeton Club (N.Y.C.), Quaker Ridge (Scarsdale N.Y.). Office: 605 3rd Ave 43d Fl New York NY 10158-3698 Home: 22 Glenbrooke Dr White Plains NY 10605-5008 Business E-Mail: jlasser@nb.com.

LASSER, LAWRENCE J., former investment company executive; b. 1942; BA, Antioch Coll.; MBA, Harvard U., 1967. With Putnam Investments, Boston, 1969—2003, v.p., asst. dir. rsch., 1973-75, sr. v.p., dir. rsch. to exec. v.p., chief investment officer, 1975-80, 81-85, CEO, pres., 1985—2003. Bd. govs., exec. com. Investment Co. Inst.; dir. Marsh and McLennan Cos., Inc.; trustee The Putnam Mut. Funds, Vineyard Open Land Found.; pres. Putnam Investment Mgmt.; v.p. The Putnam Funds; chmn. operating, mgmt. and exec. coms. Putnam Investments; bd. govs., exec. com. Investment Co. Inst.; mem. CareGroup Bd. Mgrs. Investment Com., Coun. on Fgn. Rels. Trustee Mus. of Fine Arts, Boston; bd. dirs. United Way of Mass. Bay; trustee, fin. com., exec. com. Beth Israel/Deaconess Med. Ctr., Boston.

LASSETER, JOHN P., film director, computer animator; b. Hollywood, Calif., Jan. 12, 1957; m. Nancy Lasseter; 5 children. BA in Fine Arts in Film, Calif. Inst. Arts. Exec. v.p. creative Pixar Animation Studios, Richmond, Calif. Dir., writer, prodr.: (films) Luxo Jr., 1986 (Silver Berlin Bear award Berlin Internat. Film Festival, 1986, nominated Oscar for Best Short Films, Animated Films, 1986); dir., writer: Red's Dream, 1987, Tin Toy, 1988 (Best Short Films, Animated Films Acad. award 1988), Knick Knack, 1989 (Best Short Film award Seattle Internat. Film Festival 1989), Toy Story, 1995 (Academy award for Spl. Achievement 1995), A Bug's Life, 1998, Toy Story 2, 1999; exec. prodr.: Geri's Game, 1997, For the Birds, 2000, Spirited Away, 2001, Monsters Inc., 2001, Finding Nemo, 2003, Boundin', 2003, Howl's Moving Castle, 2004, The Incredibles, 2004; actor: Computer Illusions, 1998. Recipient Humanitarian award ShoWest Conv., 1997, Outstanding Contribution to Cinematic Imagery award Art Directors Guild, 2004; named one of 50 Most Powerful People in Hollywood, Premiere mag., 2002-05. Office: Pixar Animation Studios 1200 Park Ave Emeryville CA 94608 Office Phone: 510-752-3000.*

LASSETER, KENNETH CARLYLE, pharmacologist; b. Jacksonville, Fla., Aug. 12, 1942; s. James and Retta (Shad) L.; m. Kathy G. Marks, Aug. 6, 1977; children: Kenneth C. III, Susan, Frank L. BS, Stetson U., 1963; MD, U. Fla., 1967. Diplomate Am. Bd. Clin. Pharmacology. Intern, resident in medicine U. Ky. Med. Ctr., 1967-71; asst. prof., assoc. prof. pharmacology and medicine U. Miami (Fla.) Med. Sch., 1971-81, clin. assoc. prof., 1981—. Adj. assoc. prof. pharmacology, Barry U., 1986—; v.p., dir. Clin. Pharmacology Assos., Inc., Miami, 1981-2003; v.p., med. dir. SFBC Internat. Inc., 2003—. Contbr. articles to profl. jours. With USAR, 1971-76. Recipient William B. Peck Sci. Rsch. award Interstate Postgrad. Med. Assn., 1976, Rsch. award Alpha Omega Alpha, 1967. Fellow Am. Coll. Clin. Pharmacology; mem. ACP, Am. Soc. Pharmacology and Exptl. Therapeutics, Am. Soc. Clin. Pharmacology and Therapeutics, Sigma Xi. Republican. Presbyterian. Office: SFBC Internat Inc 11190 Biscayne Blvd Miami FL 33181 Office Phone: 305-895-0304 x2344. Business E-Mail: klasseter@sfbci.com.

LASSETER, ROBERT HAYGOOD, electrical engineering educator, consultant; b. Miami, Fla., Apr. 4, 1938; s. J. Haygood and Elsiemae (Davis) L.; m. Lucy Taylor, Sept. 2, 1979; children: Courtney M., Malahn P., Robert M., Lauren L. BS in Physics, N.C. State U., 1963, MS in Physics, 1967; PhD in Physics, U. Pa., 1971; postgrad., U. Pa., Phila., 1971—80. Cons. engr. GE Co., Phila., 1980—84; asst. prof U. Wis., Madison, 1980—82, assoc. prof., 1982—85, prof., 1985—. Dir. power sys. Engring. Rsch. Ctr.- Wis., 1994—; cons. engr. Siemens AG, Germany, 1985-86. Contbr. articles to profl. jours. Fellow IEEE. Achievements include pioneering work in application of digital methods to the design of high voltage direct current power systems; basic development of analytical methods for design and study of power electronic controllers in power systems; creating a concept of Microgrids as applied to distributed resources in power systems. Office: Univ Wisconsin Electrical & Computer Engineering 1415 Engineering Dr Madison WI 53706-1607

LASSETTER, JAN, artist; b. Knoxville, Tenn., Oct. 27, 1936; d. Roy Lassetter, Jr. and Anita Knotts; m. Michael C. Mead, July 14, 1980. Student, U. Tex., 1954—55, U. Colo., 1955—56, U. Bonn, 1956—57; BFA, Acad. Fine Art, Munich, Germany, 1959. One-woman shows include High Mus. Art, Atlanta, Ga., 1960, Bernanducci Meisel Gallery, N.Y., N.Y., 2001, exhibited in group shows at A.H. Meml. de Young Mus., San Francisco, Calif., 1967, exhibitions include San Francisco (Calif.) Mus. Modern Art, 1980, Santa Barbara (Calif.) Mus., 1985, San Diego (Calif.) Art Mus., 1991, Brock R. Lewin Gallery, N.Y., N.Y., 1993—98, Oakland (Calif.) Art Mus., 2002, Represented in permanent collections Boise (Idaho) Art Mus., El Paso (Tex.) Art Mus., High Mus. Art, Atlanta, Ga., Santa Barbara Art Mus. Recipient Hubbard award, Am. Masters of Realism. Mem.: Charter 100. Republican. Episc. Avocations: skiing, hiking, horseback riding, symphony, ballet. Office: 255 4th St 301 Oakland CA 94607 Home (Summer): Box 4623 Ketchum ID 83340 Office Phone: 510-891-0343, 208-725-2177.

LASSETTER, SCOTT D., lawyer; b. Dallas, Dec. 25, 1958; BA magna cum laude, Tex. Tech U., 1980; JD, U. Tex. Sch. Law, 1983. Bar: Tex. 1983, US Dist. Ct. (So., Ea. and No. Districts Tex.), US Ct. Appeals, 5th Cir., US Supreme Ct. Mng. ptnr. Weil, Gotshal & Manges, LLP, Houston. Lectr. in field. Named "Super Lawyer", Texas Monthly, 2003; named one of Top Forty Lawyers in Am. Under the Age of Forty, Nat. Law Jour., 1995, Top 10 Trial Lawyers in Am., honored in article "Winning", 1996; named to "Go-To Guide", listing of top lawyers in their respective fields, Texas Lawyer, 2002. Mem.: State Bar Tex., Houston Bar Assn., Tex. Bar Found. (bd. certified, personal injury trial law & civil trial law, Tex. bd. legal specialization), ABA, Phi Delta Phi. Office: Weil Gotshal & Manges LLP 700 Louisiana St Ste 1600 Houston TX 77002 Office Phone: 713-546-5101. Office Fax: 713-224-9511. Business E-Mail: scott.lassetter@weil.com.

LASSILA, DAVID H., materials scientist, researcher; b. Renton, Wash., July 21, 1955; s. Jean G. Lassila; m. Rene Marie Wisler, Feb. 29, 1996; children: Elizabeth Marie, Robert Henry. BS in Mech. Engring., Mich. Tech., Houghton, 1977, MS in Engring. Mechanics, 1978; PhD in Metallurgy, U. Ill., Urbana, 1984. Staff Rockwell Internat., Canoga Park, Calif., 1979—81; post doctoral rsch. NASA Ames Rsch. Ctr., Mountain View, Calif., 1984—86; materials tech. leader Lawrence Livermore Nat. Lab., Calif., 1986—. Organizer and author materials rsch. conf. proceedings. Contbr. scientific papers to profl. jours. Recipient Neill Griffiths award, Internat. Symposium on Ballistics, 1998. Mem.: The Minerals, Metals and Materials Soc., Materials Rsch. Soc. (assoc. Corp. Seal 2003), U.S. Windsurfing. Achievements include development of multiscale modeling and experiments. Office: Lawrence Livermore Nat Lab 7000 East Ave L-113 Livermore CA 94551 Office Phone: 925-423-9537. E-mail: lassila1@llnl.gov.

LASSITER, PHILLIP B., insurance company executive; married. Group exec. N. American investment banking and ins. Citicorp; chmn., CEO Ambac Inc., N.Y.C., 1991—2004, pres., 1992—2004, non-exec. chmn. N.Y.C., 2004—. Bd. dirs. HCIA, Inc., Diebold, Inc. Lt. USN. Office: Ambac Inc One State Street Plaza New York NY 10004

LASSMAN, ADRIENNE, community volunteer; b. Chgo., Oct. 18, 1933; d. Irving Morris and Lillian Elizabeth (Root) Berman; m. Joseph Lassman, Aug. 29, 1954; children: Mark Bennett, Mindy Lassman Elkabetz. BS in Journalism, Comm., U. Ill., 1954. Vol. to numerous profl. tng. and devel. ednl. programs. Acting pres. Am. Red Magen David for Israel, Pacific S.W. region, 1987-90, pres., 1990-94, pres. Coun. Am. Jewish Com., L.A., U. Ill. Mem. World Jewish Congress Internat., U. Ill. Found. Jewish. Avocations: travel, bridge. E-mail: jade@socal.rr.com.

LASSONDE, PEIRRE, mining executive; BA, U. Montreal; BSEE, Polytech. Sch. Montreal; MBA, U. Utah, 1973. Registered profl. engr., Assn. Profl. Engrs. Ontario, 1976. Pres. Franco-Nev., 1982—2002; pres., CEO Euro-Nev. Mining Corp., 1985—99; pres., co-CEO Franco-Nev., 1999—2002; pres. Newmont Mining Corp., Denver, 2002—. Office: Newmont Mining Corp 1700 Lincoln St Denver CO 80203

LASSWELL, MARCIA LEE, psychologist, educator; b. Oklahoma City, July 13, 1927; d. Lee and Stella (Blackard) Eck; m. Thomas Lasswell, May 29, 1950 (div. July 1990); children: Marcia Jane, Thomas Ely, Julia Lee. BA, U. Calif., Berkeley, 1949; MA, U. So. Calif., 1952; postgrad., U. Calif., Riverside, U. So. Calif., U. N.C. Individual practice psychotherapy, marriage/family therapy, Claremont, Calif.; asst. prof. Pepperdine Coll., L.A., 1959—60; asst. prof. psychology behavioral sci. dept. Calif. State U., Pomona, 1960—64, assoc. prof., 1965—69, prof., 1970—, chmn. dept., 1964—69; assoc. clin. dir. Human Rels. Ctr. U. So. Calif., 1975—98. Vis. assoc. prof. Scripps Coll., 1968-69, U. So. Calif., 1969-70, Occidental Coll., 1971-72; lectr. various Calif. univs.; mem. staff spl. project alcoholics and narcotics offenders Calif. Prison System, 1970-73; mem. Calif. Accreditation Com. Secondary Schs. and Colls., 1965—1990; mem. commn. accreditation for marriage and family tng. U.S. Dept. Edn., 1981-87. Author: College Teaching of General Psychology, 1967, Love, Marriage and Family, 1973, No-Fault Marriage, 1976, Styles of Loving, 1980, Marriage and Family, 1982, rev. edit., 1987, 91, Equal Time, 1983. Recipient Outstanding Tchrs. award Calif. State U., 1971, Outstanding Contbn. to Marriage and Family Therapy, 1991, Disting. Clin. Mem. award Calif. Assn. Marriage and Family Therapists, 1995, award Outstanding Marriage and Family Therapy Orgn., 1999. Fellow Am. Assn. Marital and Family Therapy (bd. dirs. 1970-72, 87-91, pres. elect 1993-95, pres. 1995-97, past pres. 1997-98); mem. AAAS, Nat. Coun. Family Rels. (exec. com. 1978-80), Am. Acad. Family Therapy, So. Calif. Assn. Marital and Family Therapy (pres. 1972-73), Groves Family Conf. Acad., Groves Family Conf. (sec. 2001-2004), Alpha Kappa Delta, Phi Delta Gamma, Pi Gamma Mu. Home: 800 W 1st St Apt 2908 Los Angeles CA 90012-2444 Office: 250 W First St # 352 Claremont CA 91711 Office Phone: 909-624-4641. Personal E-mail: mlass@aol.com.

LAST, MICHAEL P., lawyer; b. Chgo., July 31, 1946; s. Jules Hilbert and Muriel Esther (Ruekberg) L.; m. Yong-Hee Chyun, Dec. 1970 (div.); m. Jane Antoinette Nooy Bunnell, May 29, 1983. BA magna cum laude, Lawrence U., 1968; JD cum laude, Harvard U., 1971. Bar: Mass. 1971. Ptnr., head real estate, environ. law dept. Warner & Stackpole, Boston, 1972-84; ptnr., head environ. law dept. Gaston & Snow, Boston, 1984-91; ptnr., co-chair environ. law sect. Mintz, Levin, Cohn, Ferris, Glovsky and Popeo P.C., Boston, 1991-99; mng. dir. ML Strategies, Inc., Boston, 1991-99, v.p., 1999; co-counsel Rackemann, Sawyer & Brewster, Boston, 1999—; prin. Nexus Environ. Ptnrs., Boston, 1999—2003; founding mem., prin. Creative Resolutions, LLC, Boston, 2003—. Bd. dirs. Newell Enterprises Inc., 1983-87; co-chair Am. Law Inst./ABA Ann. Course Study Minimizing Liability for Hazardous Waste Mgmt.; lectr. in field. Contbr. articles to profl. jours. Chair wetlands regulation rev. bd. Mass. Dept. Environ. Quality Engring., 1983-85, Town Wellesley Wetlands Protection Com., 1980-82; mem. Town Wellesley Planning Bd., 1983-88; rep. Town Meeting, Wellesley; mem. rev. bd. Mass. Dept. Environ. Protection, 1991-92; mem. bd. environ. mgmt. Mass. Dept. Environ. Mgmt., 1991—2003, chmn., 1994-97, 2000—03; founder, pres. Santa Fe Coun. Excellence, 1991—; founder, pres. Berkshire Inst., Inc.; mem. corp. gifts com. Boston Mus. Fine Arts Capital Fund Dr., 1979; vice chair open space plan implementation com. Town Wellesley, 1978-79; trustee, bd. govs. New Eng. Aquarium, 1995-2002, overseer, 2002—, chmn. David B. Stone award com.; trustee Mass. Eye and Ear Infirmary, 1990-98, Mt. Kearsarge Indian Mus., 1997-2002; trustee, bd. govs., exec. com. Newton-Wellesley Hosp., 1987-94, hon. trustee and overseer, 1994—, chmn. joint trustee staff com., 1992-93; mem. corp. Ptnrs. Healthcare Sys., Inc., 1999—; bd. dirs. Environ. Bus. Coun. New Eng., Inc., 1997—, chmn. Brownfields Com., chmn. ann. retreat, mem. exec. com., 2001-05, vice chmn., 2005—. 1st lt. USAF, 1971-72 Warren Hurst Stevens scholar Lawrence U., 1964. Mem. ABA (standing com. environ. law 1989-91, natural resources sect., corp., banking, bus. law sect., real property, probate, trust law sect.), Boston Bar Assn. (bd. dirs. 1984-87, chair environment com. 1979-81, chair urban affairs sect. 1983-87, co-chair mcpl. planning process com. 1983-87), Greater Boston C. of C. (real estate devel. com. 1979-80, co-chair Boston 2000 project review com. 1982-90, Boston 2000 steering com. 1983-90, co-chair adv. com. Devel. Design Guideline Study Downtown Boston 1983-92), Phi Beta Kappa. Avocations: canoeing, cross country skiing, camping. Office: One Financial Center 29th Fl Boston MA 02111 Office Phone: 617-951-1192. Business E-Mail: mpl@rackemann.com, mlast@lastlaw.com.

LASTELICK, JERRY, lawyer, banker; b. Oct. 17, 1932; s. Joseph and Louise (Gorman) L.; m. Betty Jo Guthrie, Dec. 28, 1959; children— Karen M., J.J. B.B.A. in Acctg., Tex. A&M U., 1953; LL.B., So. Meth. U., 1958. Bar: Tex. 1958, U.S. Supreme Ct. 1962, U.S. Dist. Ct. (no. dist.) Tex. 1959, U.S. Ct. Appeals (5th cir.) 1963, (11th cir.) 1981. Assoc. Daugherty, Bruner & Kelsoe, Dallas, 1958-65; ptnr. Daugherty, Bruner, Lastelick & Anderson, Dallas, 1965-73; sr. ptnr. Lastelick, Anderson & Hilliard, Dallas, 1973—; chmn. bd. 1st Tex. Bank, Dallas, 1977—97. Chmn. bd. Lekemia Soc. N. Central Tex., 1973—2003. Served to 1st lt. U.S. Army, 1953-55. Fellow Tex. Bar Found. (sustaining life); mem. Dallas Bar Found. (trustee 1982—), ABA, State Bar Tex. (bd. dirs. 1984—88, chmn. bd. 1986-87), Tex. Aggie Bar Assn. (pres. 1986), Dallas Bar Assn. (pres. 1983), Dallas Country Club. Democrat. Roman Catholic. Home: 5520 Pebblebrook Dr Dallas TX 75229-5509 Office Phone: 214-360-0338. E-mail: jlastel@attglobal.net.

LASTER, LEONARD, internist, gastroenterologist, academic administrator, educator, writer, biomedical researcher; b. N.Y.C., Aug. 24, 1928; s. Isaac and Mary (Ehrenreich) L.; m. Ruth Ann Leventhal, Dec. 16, 1956; children: Judith Eve, Susan Beth, Stephen Jay. AB, Harvard U., 1949, MD, 1950. Diplomate Nat. Bd. Med. Examiners, Am. Bd. Internal Medicine (gastroenterology). From intern to resident in medicine Mass. Gen. Hosp., Boston, 1950-53; fellow gastroenterology Mass. Meml. Hosp., 1958-59; vis. investigator Pub. Health Rsch. Inst., N.Y.C., 1953-54; commd. lt. USPHS, 1954, advanced through grades to asst. surgeon gen. (rear adm.), 1971; mem. staff Nat. Inst. Arthritis, Metabolic and Digestive Diseases, NIH, Bethesda, Md., 1954-73, chief digestive and hereditary diseases br., 1969-73; from spl. asst. to asst. dir. human resources President's Office Sci. and Tech., 1969-73; exec. dir. Assembly Life Scis., also div. med. scis. NAS-NRC, 1973-74; ret. USPHS, 1973; v.p. acad. affairs and clin. affairs Med. Ctr., also dean Coll. Medicine, prof. medicine Downstate Med. Ctr., SUNY, Bklyn., 1974-78; pres., prof. medicine Oreg. Health Scis. U., Portland, 1978-87; chancellor U. Mass. Med. Ctr., Worcester, 1987-90, chancellor emeritus, 1990—, disting. univ. prof. medicine and health policy, 1990—2002, emeritus, 2002—; adj. scientist Marine Biol. Lab., Woods Hole, Mass., 2002—. Bd. dirs. TEI Biosci., Boston; lab. investigator Marine Biol. Lab., Woods Hole, Mass., 1962—69, chmn. organizer symposia on nat. policy and biomed. scis., 1971—72, libr. reader, 1973—76; chmn. steering com. Falmouth Forum, 1994—2002, mem. coun. visitors, 2003—; cons. in field. Author: Life After Medical School, 32 Doctors Describe How They Shaped Their Medical Careers, 1996; contbr. articles on gastrointestinal disease, inborn errors of metabolism, devel. biology to profl. jours.; contbr. op-ed column and other pieces to Washington Post, essays to Hosp. Practice and MD Mag. columnist Cape Cod Times, 2002—. Active Found. Advanced Edn. Scis., Bethesda, 1965-69, Bedford Stuyvesant Family Health Ctr., Bklyn., 1975-78, Med. Rsch. Found., Oreg., 1979-87, Oreg. Symphony, 1979-85, Oreg. Contemporary Theatre, 1981-83; pres. Burning Tree Elem. Sch. PTA, Bethesda, 1972-73; bd. dirs. Internat. Artists Series, Worcester, 1988-91, Mass. Biotech. Ctrs. for Excellence, Boston, 1988-96, Mass. Biotech. Rsch. Inst., Worcester, 1988-90, Worcester Bus. Devel. Corp., 1988-91; co-chmn. United Way Ctrl. Mass., COMEC Campaign, 1989; mem. exec. com. Worcester Econ. Club, 1988-91; mem. citizen gov. bd. Worcester Fights Back, 1990-95; chmn. corp. liaison com. Marine Biol. Lab., 1991-92; mem. Worcester Com. Fgn. Rels. (affiliated with Coun. Fgn. Rels.), 1992-96. Fellow ACP; mem. Am. Fedn. Clin. Rsch., Am. Gastroenterol. Assn., Am. Soc. Biol. Chemists, Am. Soc. Clin. Investigation (emeritus), Marine Biol. Lab. Corp., Portland C. of C. (dir. 1980-84), Mass. Med. Soc., Cosmos Club, Harvard Club (N.Y.C.), Harvard Club, Harvard Faculty Club, Phi Beta Kappa. Home and Office: 8 Lawrence Farm Rd Woods Hole MA 02543-1416 Personal E-mail: lencolumn@aol.com. *Education is nurturing excellence in others and facilitating its spread as an infectious disease.*

LASTER, RICHARD, biotechnologist, consultant; b. Vienna, Nov. 10, 1923; arrived in U.S., 1940, naturalized, 1944; s. Alan and Caroline (Harband) L.; m. Liselotte (Schneider), Oct. 17, 1948; children: Susan Laster Rubenstein, Thomas. Student, U. Wash., 1941-42; BChE cum laude, Poly. Inst. Bklyn., 1943; postgrad., Stevens Inst. Tech., 1945-47. With Gen. Foods Corp., 1944-82, corp. R & D Hoboken, N.J., 1944-58, ops. mgr. Franklin Baker divsn., 1958-64, ops. mgr. Atlantic gelatin divsn. Woburn, Mass., 1958-64, mgr. R & D Jell-O divsn. White Plains, N.Y., 1967-68, exec. v.p. Maxwell House divsn., 1968-69, pres. Maxwell House divsn., 1969-71, corp. v.p., 1971-73, exec. v.p., 1974-82, also dir. R & D and food-away-from-home, 1975-82. Bd. dirs., DNA Plant Tech. Corp., 1982-94, chmn., 1988-94, CEO, 1982-92, pres., 1982-91; mgmt. cons., 1994—; bd. dirs., Rice Tec; bd. dirs., chmn. Well Gen, Inc. Contbg. articles to profl. pub.; patentee in field. Mem. Sch. Bd., Chappaqua, NY, 1971—74, pres., 1973—74; chmn., bd. dirs., 1st v.p. United Way of Westchester, 1978; chmn. adv. com. Poly. Inst. Westchester, 1977; trustee Poly. Inst. N.Y., 1978—; mem. coll. coun. SUNY Purchase, Purchase Coll. Found., 1986—; mem. corp. NY Bot. Garden; mem. subcom. export adminstrn. Pres.'s Export Coun., 1995; chmn. Westchester Edn.

Coalition, 1992—2001, Westchester Holocaust Edn. Ctr., 1994—, Am. Soc. Plant Physiologists Edn. Found., 1995—2000; mem. New Castle Town Bd., 1996—2001. Recipient Disting. Alumnus award, 1996, Disting. Svc. award-,NCCJ, Poly Inst. N.Y. fellow. Mem. AAAS, AIChE (Food and Bioengring. award 1972), N.Y. Acad. Sci., Am. Chem. Soc., Am. Inst. Chemists, Tau Beta Pi, Phi Lambda Upsilon. Home: 23 Round Hill Rd Chappaqua NY 10514-1622 Office: 103 S Bedford Rd Mount Kisco NY 10549-3440 Office Phone: 914-241-4959. E-mail: rilaster@aol.com.

LASTOWKA, JAMES ANTHONY, former federal agency administrator, lawyer; b. Chester, Pa., Oct. 1, 1951; s. Joseph Edward and Mary A. (O'Malley) L.; m. Sandra L. Pugh, Apr. 28, 1979; children: Conor David, Carey Anna, Austin Tucker. BA in Econs. cum laude, Syracuse U., 1973; JD, Georgetown U., 1976. Bar: Pa. 1976, D.C. 1990, U.S. Ct. Appeals (4th, 5th, 9th, 10th, 11th, D.C. cirs.) 1981. Staff atty. U.S. Occupational Safety and Health Rev. Commn., Washington, 1976-78, asst. gen. counsel, 1979-80; supervisory atty. Fed. Mine Safety and Health Rev. Commn., Washington, 1978-79, dep. gen. counsel, 1980-81, gen. counsel, 1981-84, commr., 1984-90; with Jones, Day, Reavis & Pogue, Washington, 1990-92, McDermott, Will & Emery, Washington, 1992—. Contbr. editor Occupational Hazards Mag. Mem. ABA (mem. labor law sect., com. occupational safety and health law). Office: McDermott Will & Emery 600 13th St NW Fl 12 Washington DC 20005-3096 Office Phone: 202-756-8245. Business E-Mail: jlastowka@mwe.com.

LASUCHIN, MICHAEL, artist, retired art educator; b. Kramatorsk, Russia, July 24, 1923; came to U.S. 1951; s. Sergei F. and Agafia I. (Okolelova) L.; m. Dorothy L. Roschen, Aug. 26, 1988. BFA, Phila. Coll. Art, 1970; MFA, Temple U., 1972. Prof. art The Univ. of the Arts, Phila., 1972-90; ret., 1990. Author/pub.; Interpolated Voids, 1970; one-man shows include Capital Air Ctr. Gallery, Taichung, Taiwan, 1989, U. of the Arts, Phila., 1991; permanent collections include Phila. Mus. Art, Bklyn. Art Mus., Mus. Modern Art, N.Y., Mus. Modern Art, Barcelona, Spain, Libr. Nat., Paris, Berlin Mus. of Art, Russian State Mus., Tretjakow Gallery, Moscow, Pushkin Mus., Moscow, Victoria Albert Mus., London; traveling group exhibit, "A Legacy of Excellence: Artistic Achievements of Older Pennsylvanians," 2004. Mem. Watercolor USA Honor Soc., Nat. Watercolor Soc., Color Print Soc., Soc. Am. Graphic Artists, Phila. Print Club, Boston Printmakers, NAD (academician, 1994-). Avocations: music, books, travel.*

LASYS, JOAN, medical/surgical nurse, educator; b. Siauliai, Lithuania, Sept. 1, 1924; arrived in Can., 1948; came to U.S., 1960; d. Joseph-Apolinarius and Elena (Šlapokaite) Barcevičius; m. Bill Lasys, July 31, 1949. RN degree, Lithuanian Red Cross Sch. Nursing, 1945; student, Ariz. State U., 1981—86, Ea. Ariz. Coll., 1981—86. RN, Can., Nebr.; cert. nursing tchr., Ariz.; C.C., occupl. tchg. cert. Ariz. Staff RN St. Mary's Hosp., Montreal, Canada, 1949—51, Montreal Gen. Hosp., 1951—53, 1959—60; pvt. duty Nurses Registry, Montreal, 1953—56; Can. civil svc. RN R.H.O. Ctr. Dept. Vets. Affairs, Ottawa, 1956—57, Queen Mary Vets. Hosp., Montreal, 1957-58; staff RN St. Joseph's Hosp., Omaha, 1968—69, Meryvale Hosp., Phoenix, 1969—71, Valley View Hosp., Youngtown, Ariz., 1971—72, Boswell Hosp., Sun City, Ariz., 1972—76; RN Kivel Care Ctr., Phoenix, 1986—93, 2000—02. Past v.p. and officer Pine-Strawberry (Ariz.) Health Svcs.; columnist/reporter Payson (Ariz.) Roundup. Pub. (mag.) Small Town U.S.A.; prodr. audio tapes: Time Management, Nursing Communications. Life mem. Pine-Strawberry and Gila County Homemakers, Payson Regional Med. Ctr. Aux.; mem Rep. Presdl. Task Force. Mem.: AAUW, Libr. Congress, Nat. Mus. Women in the Arts, Payson Libr., County Attys. and Sheriffs Assn. (hon.), Kivel Geriatric Ctr. Aux. (life), Arbor Day Found., Nature Conservancy, Cooking Club of Am. (charter). Republican. Roman Catholic. Avocations: cooking, poetry, public speaking, arts and crafts. Home: 506 N William Tell Cir Payson AZ 85541-4050

LASZEWSKI, BOLESLAW TADEUSZ, civic volunteer; b. Gora Ropczycka, Poland, Nov. 22, 1912; s. Jozef and Katarzyna (Toton) L.; m. Sophie Kinel, Sept. 26, 1947 (div. 1968); children: Barbara, Marzena, Dorothy; m. Christine Gaszynski. BSBA, CUNY, 1957; MS, Columbia U., 1956; MA, Jagiellonian U., 1937. Co-founder, hon. pres. Polish Assistance, N.Y.C., 1952—. Co-founder, pres., Polish Combatants Assn., London, 1945-50; v.p. Worldwide Orgn. Poles Abroad, London, 1947-80; mem. Kostiuszko Found., N.Y.C., 1952—; co-founder, pres. Polish Daily News, N.Y.C., 1970—; pres. Polish Am. Army Veterans Assn., 1985—; exec. dir. Polish Inst. Arts & Scis., N.Y.C., 1986-90; v.p., dir. Polish Am. Congress, 1986-88; pres. Polish Fed. Credit Union, Bklyn., 1985-90. Author: From Army to Civilian Life, 1984, Krakow, 1985, East West Russia—USSR—USA—Poland, 1986, Diary of a Soldier, 2000.

LASZEWSKI, RONALD THOMAS, college official; b. Johnson City, N.Y., Sept. 22, 1949; s. Lewis and Mary (Grodecki) L.; m. Donna Suzanne Drews, Aug. 18, 1973; 1 child, Matthew Drews. BA, Colgate U., 1971; MEd, U. Vt., 1975. Asst. dir. fin. aid Vassar Coll., Poughkeepsie, N.Y., 1975-79; dir. fin. aid Bucknell U., Lewisburg, Pa., 1979—2002; asst. v.p. progams, state grant and spl. programs divsn. Pa. Higher Edn. Assistance Agy., 2002—04. Cons. guidance counselor program study com. Pa. Aid Adminstrs. Tng. Program/Pa. Higher Edn. Assistance Agy., Harrisburg, 1986-89, Mem. faculty planning com. Stafford Loan Workshop Series, 1987-90; mem. fin. aid adv. coun. N.Y.C. Urban Corps, 1978-79; faculty, mem. tng. materials com. PAATP Summer Inst., 1990-93; mem. state grant certification com. PHEAA, 1990, mem. state grant adv. com., 1990-93. Mem. Pa. State Democratic Com., Harrisburg, 1988-90, 97-00; mem. exec. com., dir. pub. rels. Union County (Pa.) Dem. Com., 1984-90, chair Union County Dem. com., 1997-00; mem. Union County Econ. Devel. Coun., Lewisburg, Pa., 1989-96, mem. scholarship subcom., 1988-96; founding treas., pres., bd. dirs. Bucknell U. Employees Fed. Credit Union, Lewisburg, 1985-88; mem. nat. coun. Coll. Scholarship Svc., 1998-2001, regional coun. Coll. Bd. Mid. States, 1995-98. Mem. Nat. Assn. Student Fin. Aid Adminstrs. (nat. ethics com. 1977-78, nat. need analysis com. 1995-96, nat. tng. com. 1997-99), Ea. Assn. Student Fin. Aid Adminstrs., Pa. Assn. Student Fin. Aid Adminstrs. (exec. coun. 1989-93, svc. recognition award 1988, pres. 1991-92, govt. rels. com. 2002-04), Adirondack Mountain Club (Glen Falls, N.Y., coun. Elizabethtown, N.J.), N.Y. LWV. Roman Catholic. Avocation: golf. Home: 101 Red Fox Ln Lewisburg PA 17837-9598 Office: Bucknell U Office of Fin Aid Lewisburg PA 17837

LASZYNSKI, ROBERT STEVEN, lawyer; b. Dowagiac, Mich., Aug. 27, 1953; s. Steve and Margaret (Hampel) L.; m. Cheryl Ann Florjancic, Oct. 15, 1977; children: Michael Steven, Jennifer Ann. BS, U. Notre Dame, 1975; JD, Ind. U., 1978. Bar: Ind. 1978, U.S. Dist. Ct. (no. dist.) Ind. 1980. Ptnr. Laszynski & Moore, Lafayette, Ind., 1994—. Bd. dirs, pres. Legal Aid Corp., Lafayette. Bd. dirs. Tippecanoe Arts Fedn., Lafayette, 1985-91; chmn. Lafayette Cath. Elem. Sch. Coun., 1987-89, Lafayette Cath. Sch. Adv. Coun., 1989-92; bd. dirs. Group Homes for Children, Lafayette, 1998-2004, pres. 2003-04. Mem. ABA, Ind. Bar Assn., Tippecanoe County Bar Assn. (sec. 1980-81), Elks. Roman Catholic. Avocation: sports. Home: 3530 Pine Needle Pl West Lafayette IN 47906-8851 Office: Laszynski & Moore PO Box 848 Lafayette IN 47902-0848 Office Phone: 765-423-5626. Business E-Mail: blaszynski@laszynskimoore.com.

LATAIF, LAWRENCE P., lawyer; b. Fall River, Mass., Nov. 1, 1943; s. Louis and Linda Adele Lataif; m. Noha Nader, Dec. 29, 1979; children: Nicole, Lawrence Jr., Christina. BA, Brown U., 1965; JD, Georgetown U., 1968, LLM, 1970. Bar: D.C. 1969, U.S. Ct. Appeals (D.C. cir.) 1969, U.S. Ct. Mil. Appeals 1969, U.S. Supreme Ct. 1973, Va. 1974, U.S. Tax Ct. 1979. Asst. U.S. atty. U.S. Dept. Justice, Washington, 1970-73; pvt. practice Arlington, Va., 1974-75; ptnr. Lataif & Bernsen, Arlington, 1976-77; pvt. practice Fairfax, Va., 1978-85; of counsel Jones Day, Reavis & Pogue, Washington, 1986-88, ptnr., 1989-91, McDermott, Will & Emery, Miami, Fla., 1991-95; prin. Lataif & Assocs, P.A., Ft. Lauderdale, Fla., 1995—. Bd. advisors: Corp. Counsel's Guide to Business-Related Immigration, 1989-95; contbr. articles to Wall St. Jour. and profl. jours. Mem. bd. overseers Children's Hosp., Boston, 1993; bd. dirs. Symphony of the Americas, 1995-96. Recipient Ellis Island medal of honor, 2004; Prettyman fellow Georgetown U. Law Sch., 1968. Mem. Am. Immigration Lawyers Assn. Office: Lataif & Assocs PA 5100 N Federal Hwy Ste 202 Fort Lauderdale FL 33308-3842

LATAIF, LOUIS EDWARD, dean; b. Fall River, Mass., Jan. 24, 1939; s. Louis and Linda Adele (Salwan) L.; m. Najla Ann Koury, June 8, 1963; children: Louis Edward Jr., Nina Walters, Nancy Ruiz, Stephanie P. BS in Bus. Adminstrn., Boston U., 1961, LLD (hon.), 1990; MBA, Harvard U., 1964; DBA (hon.), U. Mass., 1986; LLD Lycoming Coll. (hon.), 1993. Sales and mktg. mgmt. trainee Ford Motor Co., Dearborn, Mich., 1964-66, Calif. mktg. mgr. L.A., 1975-76, dist. sales mgr., regional sales mgr. Chgo., 1976-78, gen. mktg. mgr. Ford divsn. Dearborn, Mich., 1978-81, v.p., gen. mgr. Ford divsn., 1981-84, N.Am. sales ops. v.p., 1984-88, pres. Ford of Europe Brentwood, Eng., 1988-91, v.p. worldwide quality & mktg. Dearborn, Mich., 1991; dean Sch. Mgmt. Boston U., 1991—. Bd. dirs. Sanyo Electric Co. Inc., Interaudi Bank, Group 1 Automotive, 2002-, Magna Entertainment Corp. Mem. editl. bd. European Bus. Jour., London, 1992—. Bd. dirs. Lahey-Hitchcock Clinic, Burlington, Mass., 1991—97, Iacocca Found. Mem. Brae Burn Country Club (Boston). Roman Catholic. Avocations: skiing, piano, golf. Office: Boston U Sch Mgmt 595 Commonwealth Ave Boston MA 02215-1704

LATANÉ, BIBB, social psychologist; b. N.Y.C., July 19, 1937; s. Henry Allen and Felicite Gillman (Bibb) L.; children: Julia Gillman, Claire Augusta, Henry Arbiter. BA, Yale U., 1958; PhD, U. Minn., 1963. Mem. faculty dept. social psychology Columbia U., N.Y.C., 1962-68; prof. psychology, dir. behavioral scis. lab. Ohio State U., Columbus, 1968-82; prof. psychology, dir. Inst. Research Social Sci. U.N.C.-Chapel Hill, 1982-90; prof. psychology Fla. Atlantic U., Boca Raton, 1990—2000. Pres. Social Sci. Confs., Inc.; founder Nags Head Confs., Sea Frolic Conf. Ctr., Ctr. Human Sci. Contbr. articles to profl. jours. Guggenheim fellow, 1974-75; James McKeen Cattell fellow, 1981-82; NSF, Office of Naval Research grantee. Mem. APA (coun. rep. 1971-75), Soc. Personality and Social Psychology (pres. 1976-79, Campbell award 1986), Midwestern Psychol. Assn. (pres. 1981-84), Acad. Mgmt., AAAS (Socio-Psychol. prize 1968, 80), Soc. Exptl. Soc. Psychology (Disting. Scientist award 1998), Am. Sociol. Assn., Animal Behavior Soc. Home: 212 Vance St Chapel Hill NC 27516 E-mail: latane@humanscience.org. *We know so much, yet understand so little about human beings and the social realities they create.*

LATANISION, RONALD MICHAEL, materials science and engineering consultant; b. Richmondale, Pa., July 2, 1942; s. Stephen and Mary (Kopach) Latanision; m. Carolyn Marie Domenig, 1964; children: Ivan, Sara. BS, Pa. State U., 1964; PhD in Metall. Engring., Ohio State U., 1968. Postdoctoral fellow Nat. Bur. Standards, Washington, 1968-69; research scientist Martin Marietta, Balt., 1969-73, acting head materials sci., 1973-74; dir. H.H. Uhlig Corrosion Lab. MIT, Cambridge, 1974—2003, Shell Disting. prof. materials sci. and engring., 1983-88, dir. Materials Processing Ctr., 1984-91; co-founder ALTRAN Materials Engring. Corp., Boston, 1992—; prin., dir. mechanics and materials practice Exponent Inc., 2003—. Mem. tech. adv. bd. Modell Devel. Corp., Framingham, Mass., 1987-94; sci. advisor com. on sci. and tech. U.S. Ho. of Reps., 1982-83; chmn. ad hoc com. Mass. Advanced Materials Ctr., Boston, 1985—; mem. adv. bd. Mass. Office Sci. and Tech.; co-PI, NSF/SSI project PALMS; chmn. MIT Coun. on Primary and Secondary Edn. Editor: Surface Effects in Crystal Plasticity, 1977, Atomistics of Fracture, 1983, Chemistry and Physics of Fracture, 1987, Advances in Mechanics and Physics of Fracture, 1981, 83, 86; contbr. articles to profl. jours. Recipient sr. scientist award Humboldt Found., 1974-75, David Ford McFarland award Pa. State U., 1986, T.P. Hoar award Inst. of Corrosion, U.K., 2001, Henry B. Linford award Electrochem. Soc., 2004; named Henry Krumb lectr. AIME, 1984, Disting. Alumnus, Ohio State U. Coll. Engring., 1991, hon. alumnus MIT, 1992; Centennial fellow Coll. Earth and Mineral Scis., Pa. State U., 1996. Fellow Am. Soc. Metals Internat. (govt. and pub. affairs com. 1984), Nat. Assn. Corrosion Engrs. (A.B. Campbell award 1971, Willis R. Whitney award 1994); mem. New Eng. Sci. Tchrs. (founder, co-chmn.), Nat. Acad. Engring., Am. Acad. Arts and Scis., Nat. Materials Adv. Bd., Masons. Roman Catholic. Office: MIT Materials Sci & Engring 77 Mass Ave Rm 16-206 Cambridge MA 02139-4307 Office Phone: 508-652-8560. Business E-Mail: rlatanision@exponent.com.

LATCH, ISABEL ANN, elementary school educator; m. William W. Latch, June 14, 1980. BS in edn., Bloomsburg State Coll., 1975—79; MS in edn., Bloomsburg U. Gifted support tchr. Pennsbury Sch. Dist., Yardley, Pa., 1980—. Office: William Penn Mid Sch 1524 Derbyshire Rd Yardley PA 19067 Office Phone: 215-428-4280.

LATHAM, AMY MOORE, academic administrator; d. Lawrence and Nannie Lou Moore; m. William Todd Latham, Dec. 12, 1992; children: Will, Ashley. B of Bus. Adminstrn., Delta State U., Miss., 1986. Computer programmer N.W. Miss. CC, Senatobia, Miss., 1986—89, mgr. computer ctr., 1989—96. Dir. of MIS N.W. Miss. CC, Senatobia, Miss., 1996—. Crafts fair chmn. Arkabutla Vol. Fire Dept., Miss., 2003—05. Mem.: COMMON. Baptist. Achievements include development of a pre-registration system for the college. Most of our administrative software is written and maintained in-house, while keeping pace with what other colleges are offering. Avocations: gardening, travel. Office: NW Miss C C 4975 Highway 51 North Senatobia MS 38668 Office Phone: 662-562-3201. E-mail: a_latham@northwestms.edu.

LATHAM, BENJAMIN ERWIN, music educator; b. Belle Fourche, SD, Apr. 7, 1971; s. Erwin and Shirley Latham. BA in Music Edn., Black Hills State U., 1996, BS in Speech and Theater, 1994; M Conducting, Calif. State U., Fresno, 2001. Actor Black Hills Passion Play, Spearfish, SD, 1990—97; prodr., dir. Why Knot Theatre Co., Spearfish, SD, 1992—. Pacificia, Calif., 1992—; dir. music and speech Riverdale (Calif.) H.S., 1997—99; dir. music Corcoran (Calif.) H.S., 1999—2001; carddealer Old Style Saloon No. 10, Deadwood, SD, 2001—02; dir. bands Cabrillo and Vallemar Schs., Pacifica, 2002—. Asst. condr. Fresno Wind Ensemble, Calif. State U., Fresno, 1999—2001. Contbr. articles to Pacific Tribune; composer: (symphonic overture) Civic Overture, 2003. Co-founder, co-dir. Ctrl. Valley United Marching Band, Fresno, 1999—2001; mem., prin. trumpet San Francisco Civic Symphony, 2001—; pres. Civic Symphony Assn., San Francisco, 2003—; mem. Skyline Coll. Concert Band, 2001—; SD Boys State auditor Am. Legion, Aberdeen, SD, 1987. Named Am. Mus. Amb., West Lafayette, Ind., 1988—98. Mem.: Calif. Music Educators Assn., Calif. Band Dirs. Assn. (auditioner 1997—), Lions Club (tail twister 1997—99). Roman Catholic. Home: 1537 Terra Nova Blvd Pacifica CA 94044 Office: Pacifica Sch Dist 375 Reina Del Mar Pacifica CA 94044 Office Phone: 650-738-6660 102. E-mail: lathbe@yahoo.com.

LATHAM, CHRISTOPHER ROBERT, alumni and development director; b. N.Y.C., July 11, 1953; s. Robert Francis and Anne Cardon Latham; m. Cynthia Leah Hunt, Nov. 26, 1977; children: Leah Anne, Robert Hunt, Christopher Charles. BSS, Cornell Coll., Mt. Vernon, Iowa, 1976. Devel. assoc. Holderness Sch., Plymouth, NH, 1976—77, dir. of devel. and alumni rels., 1979—89; mgmt. trainee Princeton Bank & Trust Co., Princeton, NJ, 1977—79; assoc. dir. of maj. gifts Dartmouth Coll., Hanover, NH, 1989—90; dir. of alumni and devel. Tabor Acad., Marion, Mass., 1990—. Mem./pres. CONFR, Concord, NH, 1980—90; lectr. in field. Mem. planning com. N.H. Gov.'s Conf. on Volunteerism, 1989—99, mem. steering com., 1999; vestry mem. St. Gabriel's Episc. Ch., Marion, 1997—99; mem. Sea Change, Inc., Marion, Mass., 1995—97. Mem.: CASE (assoc.; Dist. 1 awards com. 1994—95, nominating com. 1995, Robert Bell Crow Meml. award 1999), NAIS (assoc.), PGGNE (assoc.), AISNE (assoc.; chair devel. com. 1996—2003, bd. dirs. 2005—). Independent. Avocations: ceramics, sailing, jogging, skiing, travel. Home: 94 Olde Knoll Rd Marion MA 02738 Office: Tabor Academy 66 Spring St Marion MA 02738 Office Phone: 508-748-2000 2237. Personal E-mail: crlatham@comcast.net. E-mail: clatham@taboracademy.org.

LATHAM, DENNET WALDRON, architect; b. Kansas City, Mo., May 24, 1950; s. Raymond Waldron and Arline Downs Latham; m. Claire Kamm, June 1, 1974; children: Michelle Arline, Nicole Isabelle. BA in Biology, Princeton U., 1972; M Arch, U. Pa., 1976. Registered architect, Oreg. Intern architect Kaplan & Gaunt Architects, Red Bank, N.J., 1973-77; architect SRG Partnership, P.C., Portland, Oreg., 1977-87; specifications programmer Heery Internat., Atlanta, 1987-92; architect CH2MHILL - Indsl. Design Corp., Portland, 1992—. Mem. AIA, Constrn. Specification Inst. (chpt. pres. 1986-87, 2005-). Avocations: home remodeling, gardening, running, reading. Office: CH2M Hill-IDC 2020 SW 4th Ave Fl 3D Portland OR 97201-4953 E-mail: dennet.latham@idc-ch2m.com.

LATHAM, ERNEST HARGREAVES, JR., historian, educator; b. Lowell, Mass., Aug. 11, 1938; s. Ernest Hargreaves and Anne MacIvor Latham; children: Ernest Hargreaves Latham, III, Charlotte Lucy. BA, Dartmouth Coll., 1960; MA, Roosevlt U., 1966; PhD, U. Bucharest, 1987. Instr. Lowell Technol. Inst., Mass., 1965—66; diplomat US Fgn. Svc., Beirut, 1966—93, Jiddah, 1966—93, Vienna, 1966—93, Nicosia, 1966—93, Berlin, 1966—93, Bucharest, 1966—93, Athens, 1966—93, Washington, 1966—93; spl. asst. to sec. def. Romanian mil. archives Pentagon, Dept. of Defence, 1997—2000; Fulbright prof. U. Babes-Bolyai and Bucharest, Bucharest and Cluj, 2000—00; exec. dir. Fulbright Commn., Bucharest, 2000—00; dir. Ctr. Romanian Studies, Iasi, 2002—. Adj. faculty Fgn. Svc. Inst., Arlington, Va., 1998—. Author: (historical study) A Notable Achievement: the Eleventh Editon of the Encyclopedia Britannica and Romania, (historical study) Watching from the Window: Olivia Manning in Romania, 1939-1940, (historical study) All Thankful: Reports by Neutral Observers of American Prisoners of War in Romania, 1943-1944, (historical study') Prompted to Write: Marcu Beza and World War II, (historical study) Useful Service Rendered: The Romanian Life of Dimitri Demitrius Dimancescu, Efficient nd Rapid: the Lettersof Major Walter Ross of OSS to is Commanding Officer, Lieutrenant Comander Edward Green, During the Evacuation of Allied Airmen from Romania, August 30-September 2, 1944; editor: (memoir) Athene Palace, (folklore) the Mioitsa: An Icon of Romanian Culturei (Am. Romanian Acad. Book award, 2000), (novel) Assignment: Bucharest; co-coordinator (archival study) Structures Involved in the Enforcement of the Armistice Agreement and the Peace Treaty: 1944-1947 (Gen. Radu Rosetti award Excellence Mil. History, 2000). Lic. lay reader Anglican Diocese Gibralter, Bucharest, 1983—90, Athens, 1983—90. Comdr. USCGR, 1961—92. Recipient Knight Comander Order St. George of Carinthia, Grand Bailiff of Austria, 1983, Fgn. Svc. Meritorious Svc. award, USIA, 1989. Fellow: Am. Romanian Acad. Arts and Scis. (sec. 1994—2000); mem.: Am. Hist. Assn., Am. Assn. Advancement Slavic Studies, Diplomatic and Consular Officers Ret., Soc. Romanian Studies, William North Masonic Temple. Independent. Episcopal. Avocation: bibliophile. Home: 942 24th Street NW Washington DC 20037-2201 Office: Foreign Service Institute (NFATC-F4315) 4000 Arlington Blvd Arlington VA 22204 Personal E-mail: ehlathamjr@hotmail.com.

LATHAM, JAMES DAVID, lawyer; b. Lowell, Mass., Apr. 18, 1942; s. Ernest Hargreaves and Anne Crowdis (MacIvor) L.; children: James Benjamin, Timothy David. AB, Dartmouth Coll., 1964; LLB, Boston U., 1967. Bar: Mass. 1967, U.S. Dist. Ct. Mass. 1968. Assoc. Goldman & Curtis, Lowell, 1967-72; ptnr. Goldman, Curtis, Leahey & Latham, Lowell and Boston, 1972-74; assoc. counsel ITT Sheraton Corp., Boston, 1974-78, sr. counsel, 1978-80, asst. gen. counsel, 1982-84, v.p., 1984-92, sr. v.p., sec., gen. counsel, 1992-98; sr. v.p., gen. counsel Hotel Group Starwood Hotels & Resorts Worldwide, Inc., Boston, 1998—. Office: Sheraton 1111 Westchester Ave White Plains NY 10604-3525

LATHAM, JOHN L., lawyer; b. Dallas, Tex., July 12, 1954; BA, Univ. Toledo, 1976; JD, Emory Univ., Atlanta, 1979. Bar: Ga. 1979. Ptnr., securities, litig., capital mkts. group Alston & Bird LLP, Atlanta. Office: Alston & Bird LLP One Atlantic Ctr 1201 W Peachtree St NW Atlanta GA 30309-3424 Office Phone: 404-881-7915. Office Fax: 404-881-7777. Business E-Mail: jlatham@alston.com.

LATHAM, JOHN RONALD, quality assurance professional; s. Jack Will and Mary Nelda Latham; m. Penny Jackson Latham, Sept. 22, 1990; children: Courtney Michele, Charles Dewayne, Dirk Ryan. PhD Applied Mgmt. and Decision Sci., Walden U., 1997. Cert. quality engr., Am. Soc. Quality, 1994. V.p. corp. quality and bus. excellence Dade Behring, Deerfield, Ill., 2000; dir. orgn. assessment Tectura Corp., Seattle, 2000—02; pres., CEO The Latham Group, LLC, Monument, Colo., 2002—04; mng. ptnr. Genitect, LLC, Colo. Springs, Colo., 2004—. Alumni examiner, sr. examiner, examiner Malcolm Baldrige Nat. Quality Award, Gaithersburg, Md., 1996—. Author: Baldrige User's Guide: Organization Diagnosis, Design, and Transformation. Mem.: Am. Soc. Quality (sect. chmn. 1993—94). Avocations: skiing, travel, reading, writing. Office Phone: 719-487-9039. Personal E-mail: john@drjohnlatham.com.

LATHAM, LANCE EMERSON, school disciplinarian; b. Taunton, Mass., Oct. 10, 1963; s. Russell Francis Latham and Virginia Richmond Potter; m. Karen Elizabeth Zolnay, Aug. 20, 1989; children: Hannah Elisabeth, Tristan Roy. BA, Bates Coll., Lewiston, Maine, 1985; MS, Ohio U., 1990. History tchr. Berkshire Sch., Sheffield, Mass., 1990—94, Western Res. Acad., Hudson, Ohio, 1994—97; dean of students/history tchr. Boston U. Acad., Boston, 1997—98; history tchr. Brooks Sch., North Andover, Mass., 1998—2003, dir. of fin. aid, 2003—04, acad. dean, 2004—. Mem.: Am. Hist. Assn. Independent. Avocations: coaching, computers, writing, baseball. Home: 1160 Great Pond Rd North Andover MA 01845 Office: Brooks School 1160 Great Pond Rd North Andover MA 01845 Office Phone: 978-725-6227. E-mail: llatham@brooksschool.org.

LATHAM, PATRICIA HORAN, lawyer; b. Hoboken, N.J., Sept. 5, 1941; d. Patrick John and Rosemary (Moller) Horan; m. Peter Samuel Latham, June 12, 1965; children: John Horan, Kerry Patricia. BA, Swarthmore Coll., 1963; JD, U. Chgo., 1966. Bar: D.C. 1967, U.S. Dist. Ct. D.C. 1967, U.S. Ct. Appeals 1967, U.S. Supreme Ct. 1970, Va. 1989, U.S. Dist. Ct. (ea. dist.) Va. 1989, U.S. Dist. Ct. Md. 1991. Assoc. Fried, Frank, Harris, Shriver & Kampelman, Washington, 1966-69; atty. Office of Gen. Counsel, SEC, Washington, 1969-71; assoc. Martin & Smith, Washington, 1971—, ptnr., 1974-85, Latham & Latham, Washington, 1986—. Lectr. Columbus Sch. Law, Cath. U. Am., Washington, 1978-92; mem. panel of arbitrators N.Y. Stock Exch., 1985—; co-founder, co-dir. Nat. Ctr. Law and Learning Disabilities, 1992—; mem. disability adv. com. GED Testing Svc., 1999—. Co-author: Attention Deficit Disorder and the Law, 1992, Attention Deficit Disorder and the Law, 2d edit., 1997, Learning Disabilities and the Law, 1993, Learning Disabilities and the Law, 2d edit., 2000, Succeeding in the Workplace, 1994, Higher Education Services for Students with Learning Disabilities and Attention Deficit Disorder: A Legal Guide, 1994, Documentation and the Law, 1996, Tales from the Workplace, 1997, Terrorism and the Law: Bringing Terrorists to Justice, 2002; contbg. author: ADD and the College Student, 1993, A Comprehensive Guide to ADD in Adults, 1995, Managing Attention and Learning Disorders in Late Adolescence and Adulthood, 1996, Textbook of Pediatric Neuropsychiatry, 1998, Learning Disabilities and Employment, 1997, ADD in Children and Adults, 1999. Co-founder, trustee Beacon Coll., 1989-93, chmn. bd. trustees, 1990-92; mem. adv. bd. Disability Law Reporter Svc., 1996-2001. Mem.: ABA, Learning Disabilities Assn. Am. (nat. adv. bd. 1996—2000, nat. bd. dirs. 2000—), Nat. Attention Deficit Disorders Assn. (bd. dirs. 1993—98, nat. adv. bd. 1998—), Am. Arbitration Assn. (panel arbitrators and mediators 1982—), Va. Bar Assn., DC Bar Assn., Ft. Myer and Ft. McNair Club. Roman Catholic. Home: The Watergate 2700 Virginia Ave NW # 707 Washington DC 20037 Office: Latham & Latham The Watergate 2700 Virginia Ave NW Washington DC 20037 Office Phone: 202-333-1713. Business E-Mail: lathamlaw@gmal.com.

LATHAM, PATRICIA S., physician; b. Annapolis, Md., Aug. 22, 1946; BS, Simmons Coll., 1968; MD, U. So. Calif., 1972. Intern Yale-New Haven Hosp., 1972-73, resident, 1973-75, fellow in hepatology, 1975-78; resident in anatomic pathology U. Toronto (Can.) Hosp., 1978-80; asst. prof. pathology and medicine U. Md., 1981-88, Nat. Cancer Inst., 1988-90, George Washington U., 1990-92, assoc. prof. pathology and medicine, 1992—. Office: George Wash U 2300 I St NW Washington DC 20037-2336

LATHAM, PETER SAMUEL, lawyer; b. Boston, July 23, 1940; s. Earl Gansen and Margaret (Perrier) L.; m. Patricia Ann Horan, June 12, 1965; children: John Horan, Kerry Patricia. BA with honors, Swarthmore Coll., 1962; LLB, U. Pa., 1965. Bar: D.C. 1966, U.S. Ct. Appeals (D.C. cir.) 1982, U.S. Dist. Ct. Md. 1991. Atty. SEC, Washington, 1965-66; assoc. firm Vom Baur, Coburn, Simmons & Turtle, Washington, 1969-71; mem. firm Wachtel, Ross and Matzkin, Washington, 1971-80; ptnr. Latham & Latham and predecessor firms, Washington, 1980—. Arbitrator Am. Arbitration Assn., 1978-2001. Author: Government Contract Disputes, 1981, 86; co-author: Attention Deficit Disorder and the Law: A Guide for Advocates, 1992, Learning Disabilities and the Law, 1993, Succeeding in the Workplace, 1994, Higher Education Services for Students with Learning Disabilities and Attention Deficit Disorder: A Legal Guide, 1994, Documentation and the Law, 1996, Tales from the Workplace, 1997, Attention Deficit Disorder and the Law, 2d edit., 1997, Learning Disabilities and the Law, 2d edit., 2000, Terrorism and the Law-Bringing Terrorists to Justice, 2002; contbg. author ADD and the College Student, 1993, A Comprehensive Guide to ADD in Adults, 1995, Managing Attention and Learning Disorders in Late Adolescence and Adulthood, 1996, Textbook of Pediatric Neuropsychiatry, 1998, Learning Disabilities and Employment, 1997, ADD in Children and Adults, 1999; producer, dir. The ABC's of ADD, other videos on legal topics. Co-founder, trustee Beacon Coll., 1989-93; co-founder Nat. Ctr. for Law and Learning Disabilities. Lt. USN, 1966-69. Decorated Navy Achievement medal with combat V. Mem.: ABA, D.C. Procurement Reform Taskforce (mem. Alternate Dispute Resolution subcom. 1995—), Nat. Attention Deficit Disorders Assn. (bd. dirs. 1993—97), Ft. Myer and Ft. McNair Club. Republican. Roman Catholic. Avocations: tennis, swimming. Home: The Watergate 2700 Virginia Ave NW # 707 Washington DC 20037 Office: Latham and Latham The Watergate 2700 Virginia Ave NW Washington DC 20037 Office Phone: 202-333-1713. Business E-Mail: plath3@his.com.

LATHAM, TAMARA BERYL, chemist, researcher; b. Brisbane, Australia, July 31, 1944; arrived in U.S., 1946; d. James Samuel and Beryl (Holzheimer) Latham. BS in Chemistry, CUNY, 1979, postgrad., 1979—81. With Novocol Chem. Co., Bklyn., 1980, Sloan Kettering Inst. Cancer Ctr., N.Y.C., 1984; chemist BOC Group, Murray Hill, NJ, 1984—95, Bayer Corp., West Haven, Conn., 1995—99, tchr. sci. on schooner S/V Quinnipiac New Haven, 1997—98; with Grolier/Scholastic, West Haven, 1999—2001; rsch. recruiter 20/20 Rsch., Nashville, 2002—. Forum moderator metric poetry Moontown Cafe Website, 2001; sci. tchr. Schooner s/v Quinnipiack, New Haven, 1997—98. Author: (poetry) Mirror Of My Soul, 1999, The Poet, 2003; contbr. articles to profl. jours. With USN, 1963—66. Recipient Amos Alonzo Stagg award, U.S. Navy, 1965, Editors Challenge award for poetry, Internat. Soc. Authors and Artists, 1996. Mem.: Am. Chem. Soc., Am. Legion, The Workshop Poets. Achievements include patents for cancer anti-emetic. Avocations: singing, reading, gardening, chess.

LATHAM, TOM, congressman; b. Hampton, Iowa, July 14, 1948; s. Willard and Evelyn L.; m. Kathy Swinson, 1975; children: Justin, Jennifer, Jill. Student, Watrburg Coll., Iowa State U. Bank teller, bookkeeper, Brush, Colo., 1970-72; ind. ins. agent Fort Lupton, Colo., 1972-74; mktg. rep. Hartford Ins. Co., Des Moines, 1974-76; with Latham Seed Co., Alexander, Iowa, 1976—, now v.p., co-owner; mem. 104th-108th Congress from 4th Iowa dist. (formerly 5th), 1994—, Ho. Appropriations Com. Sec. Republican Party of Iowa; rep. 5th dist. Republican State Ctrl. com.; co-chair Francklin County Republican Ctrl. com.; whip Iowa del. Republican Nat. Conv., 1992. Past chair Franklin County Extension Coun.; mem. Nazareth Lutheran Ch., past pres.; citizens adv. coun. Iowa State U. Mem. Am. Soybean Assn., Am. Seed Trade Assn., Iowa Farm Bur. Fedn., Iowa Soybean Assn., Iowa Corn Growers Assn., Iowa Seed Assn., Agribusiness Assn. of Iowa. Republican. Lutheran. Office: US House Reps 2447 Rayburn Hob Washington DC 20515-1505*

LATHAM, WELDON HURD, lawyer; b. Bklyn., Jan. 2, 1947; s. Aubrey Geddes and Avril (Hurd) L.; m. Constantia Beecher, Aug. 8, 1948; children: Nicole Marie, Brett Weldon. BA, Howard U., 1968; JD, Georgetown U., 1971; postgrad., George Washington U., 1975-76. Bar: D.C. 1972, U.S. Ct. Appeals (D.C. cir.) 1972, U.S. Ct. Mil. Appeals 1974, U.S. Ct. Claims 1975, U.S. Supreme Ct. 1975, Va. 1981, U.S. Ct. Appeals (fed. cir.) 1988. Mgmt. cons. Checchi & Co., Washington, 1968-71; atty. Covington & Burling, Washington, 1971-73; sr. atty. Fed. Energy Adminstrn., Washington, 1974; asst. gen. counsel Exec. Office Pres. Office Mgmt. and Budget The White House, Washington, 1974-76; atty. Hogan & Hartson, Washington, 1976-79; gen. dep. asst. sec. HUD, Washington, 1979-81; v.p., gen. counsel Sterling Sys., Inc. (subs. PRC.); exec. asst., counsel to chmn., CEO and assoc. gen. counsel Planning Rsch. Corp., McLean, Va., 1981-86; mng. ptnr. Va. office Reed, Smith, Shaw & McClay, McLean, Va., 1986-91; sr. ptnr. Shaw Pittman, Washington, 1992-2000; sr. ptnr., practice area leader corp. diversity counseling Holland & Knight, Washington, 2000—04; sr. ptnr. and chmn. Corp. Diversity Counseling Group Davis Wright Tremaine LLP, 2004—. Chmn. diversity adv. bd. Deloitte & Touche, 2002—; bd. visitors Georgetown U. Law Ctr., 2002—; mem. adv. coun. Coca-Cola Procurement, 2000-03; adj. prof. Howard U. Law Sch., Washington, 1972-82; guest prof. U. Va., Charlottesville, 1976-90; mem. Va. Govs. Bus. and Industry Adv. Com. on Crime Prevention, 1983-85, Va. Govs. Regulatory Reform Adv. Bd., 1982-84; chmn. task force SBA, 1982; legal counsel Md. Mondale for Pres. Campaign, 1984; gen. counsel Nat. Coalition Minority Bus., 1993-03; trustee The Am. Univ., 1999-2002; bd. dirs., chmn. legal com. Metro Washington Airports Authority, 1997-; bd. dirs. Telecomms. Sys., Inc., 1999-; bd. govs. Joint Ctr. Polit. and Econ. Studies, 1998-2004. Columnist Minority Bus. Entrepreneur Mag., 1991-2004, Diversity Jour., 2002--; mem. editl. adv. bd. Washington Bus. Jour., 1985-87. Washington steering com. NAACP Legal Def. Fund, 1975-95, Fairfax County Airports Adv. Com., 1987-88; bd. dirs., gen. counsel Northern Va. Minority Bus. and Profl. Assn., 1985-92; trustee Va. Commonwealth U., Richmond, 1986-90, George Mason U., Fairfax, Va., 1990-94; bd. dirs. Washington Urban League, 1986-90, U. D.C. Found., 1982-87, Washington Coun. Lawyers, 1973, Profl. Svcs. Coun., 1983-88, Minority Bus. Enterprise Legal Def. and Edn. Fund, 1989-91, Wash. Hosp. Ctr. Found., 1996-98; appointee Greater Washington Bd. Trade, Blue Ribbon Task Force on Home Rule, 1985-86, bd. dirs., exec. com., chmn. regional affairs com., corp. sec. Greater Wash. Bd. Trade, 1990-95; adv. bd. First Union Nat. Bank, 1995-99; civilian aide to Sec. of Army, 1995-2000; mem. Small Bus. Adminstrn. Nat. Adv. Coun., 1993-2003, Burger King Corp. Diversity Action Coun., 1996-98, Diversity Best Practices Coun., 2001--, Md. Econ. Devel. Commn., 1996-98, Gov. Bd. Transition Team, 1995, Dem. Nat. Com., 1996, Platform Drafting Com., 1996; prin. coun. for Excellence in Govt., 1989-95; at-large mem. Dem. Nat. Com., 2001--; mayor D.C. Internat. Ins. Adv. Commn., 1994-95; chmn. D.C. Mayors Bus. Adv. Coun., 1994-96; vice-chmn. Dem. Bus. Coun. DNC, 1994-98; co-chmn. UNCF Sportsfest Fundraiser, 1994; hon. vice-chmn. Clinton-Gore Campaign, 1996; mem. corp. adv. coun. Congrl. Black Caucus Found., 1999—; gen. counsels Honors Program Office Sec. Capt. USAF, 1973-74. Recipient SES Effective Mgr. award HUD, 1980, Nat. Assn. for Equal Achievement Opportunity in Higher Edn. award, 1987, A. Philip Randolph award Amtrak, 2001, Ron Brown Legacy award Nat. Black MBA Assn., 2002. Mem. ABA (vice-chmn. subcom. pub. contract law sect. 1988-93), Fed. Bar Assn., Nat. Bar Assn., D.C. C. of C. (gen. counsel 1979), State Va. Bar Assn., Washington Bar Assn.(elected to Hall of Fame, 2001), Bar Assn. D.C., Nat. Contract Mgmt. Assn., Econ. Club Washington. Democrat. Home: 7004 Natelli Woods Ln Bethesda MD 20817-3924 Office: Davis Wright Tremaine LLP 1500 K St NW Ste 450 Washington DC 20005-1272 Office Phone: 202-508-6664. Business E-Mail: weldonlatham@dwt.com.

LATHAN, CORINNA ELISABETH, aerospace engineer; b. Nov. 7, 1967; m. David Kubalak. BA in Biopsychology and Math., Swarthmore Coll., 1988; PhD in Neurosci., MIT, 1994, SM in Aeronautics and Astronautics, 1995. Asst. prof. biomed. engring. Cath. U., Washington, 1995—99, assoc. prof. biomed. engring., 1999—2000; adj. prof. aerospace engring. U. Md., 2002—; founder, pres., CEO AnthroTronix, College Park, Md., 1999—. Mem. editl. bd.: Jour. Human Performance in Extreme Environs., 1998—. Founder Keys to Empowering Youth; spl. projects advisor FIRST, Inc. Named Top Innovator of Yr., Md. Daily Record, 2002, Tech. Pioneer, World Econ. Forum, 2004; named one of Top 100 World Innovators Under the Age of 35, Tech. Review-MIT's Mag. of Innovation, Top 100 Women, Md. Daily Record, 2003; recipient Creating a Future of Opportunity award, Dept. Aeronautics and Astronautics, MIT, 2000, Women in Tech. Leadership award for entrepreneurship, 2002. Mem.: Assn. for Advancement of Med. Instrumentation (mem. human engring. stds. com. 1997—). Office: AnthroTronix Inc 387 Technology Dr Ste 1101 College Park MD 20742

LATHE, ROBERT EDWARD, management and financial consultant; b. Balt., Apr. 8, 1945; s. Warren Calvin Sr. and Margaret Mary (Cavey) L.; m. Hermina Yeghnazarian, Apr. 13, 1967; children: Michelle Gayaneh, Mellina Margaret. MSc in Mgmt., U. Dublin Trinity Coll., 1985. Metrology/field engr. Bendix Field Engring. Corp., Balt., 1967-68; quality assurance supr. space seismology lab. Bendix Aerospace Systems Divsn., Ann Arbor, Mich., 1968-72; programs mgr. Iran Aircraft Industries, Tehran, 1972-76; mgmt. cons. Alexander Proudfoot Co., Chgo., 1977-78; program mgr., field engr. Harris-PRD Electronics Divsn., Syosset, N.Y. & Isfahan, Iran, 1978-80; ops. dir. Airmotive Ireland Ltd., Dublin, 1980-84; project mgr. Handley-Walker Co., Inc., Valencia, Calif., 1986-87; owner, pres. Hyrel Bus. Svcs., Glendale, Calif., 1987-90; fin. planner, investment advisor IDS Fin. Svcs. Inc., Glendale, 1990-94; co-founder, sr. ptnr. Calif. Connection, Glendale, 1994—; co-founder, sec., treas. LaMouche, Inc., Glendale, 1997—. Sgt. USAF, 1963-67, Vietnam. Mem. Am. Legion, Internat. Platform Assn. Avocations: microcomputers, public speaking, golf, swimming, ten-pin bowling. Home: 11014 Mountair Ave Tujunga CA 91042 Office Phone: 818-606-9299. E-mail: relathe@aol.com, ccesthetique@aol.com, Lamoucheinc@aol.com.

LATHI, BHAGAWANDAS PANNALAL, retired electrical engineering educator; b. Bhokar, Maharashtr, India, Dec. 3, 1933; came to U.S., 1956; s. Pannalal Rupchand and Tapi Pannalal (Indani) L.; m. Rajani Damodardas Mundada, July 27, 1962; children: Anjali, Shishir. BEEE, Poona U., 1955; MSEE, U. Ill., 1957; PhD in Elec. Engring., Stanford U., 1961. Rsch. asst. U. Ill., Urbana, 1956-57, Stanford (Calif.) U., 1957-60; rsch. engr. Gen. Electric Co., Syracuse, N.Y., 1960-61; cons. to semicondr. industry India, 1961-62; assoc. prof. elec. engring. Bradley U., Peoria, Ill., 1962-69, U.S. Naval Acad., Annapolis, Md., 1969-72; prof. elec. engring. Campinas (Brazil) State U., 1972-78, Calif. State U., Sacramento, 1979—2001, prof. emeritus, 2002—. Vis. prof. U. Iowa, Owa City, 1979. Author: Signals, Systems and Communication, 1965, Communication Systems, 1968 (transl. into Japanese 1977), Random Signals and Communication Theory, 1968, Teoria Signalow I Ukladow Telekomunikacyjnych, 1970, Sistemy Telekomunikacyjne, 1972, Signals, Systems and Controls, 1974, Sistemas de Comunicacion, 1974, 86, Sistemas de Comunicacao, 1978, Modern Digital and Analog Communication Systems, 1983, 89 (transl. into Japanese 1986, 90, Korean, 2001), Signals and Systems, 1987, Linear Systems and Signals, 1992, 2d rev. edit., 2005, Signal Processing and Linear Systems, 1998; contbr. articles to profl. jours. Fellow IEEE. Office: Calif State U 6000 J St Sacramento CA 95819-2605 Address: 3021 Scenic Height Way Carmichael CA 95608 Personal E-mail: bercamb@yahoo.com.

LATHON, SHERAINE, clergyman; b. Chicago Heights, Feb. 20, 1952; d. Roosevelt Willingham and Norma L. Cobb; m. Willie Lathon, Jr., June 11, 1983; children: Eric, Christopher. AAS, Prairie State Jr. Coll., 1972; BS, Friends Internat. U., 1992, MS, 1994, PhD, 1997. Ordained to ministry, 1999. Collection mgr. Donnelley Directory, Chgo., 1973-87; ch. adminstr. Liberty Temple Full Gospel Ch., Chgo., 1987—, sr. pastor, 1999—. Assoc. prof. Logos Ministerial Tng. Inst., Friends Internat. U. Co-author: Recovery, 2000. Sec.-treas. Bushido-Kan Acad.; pres. Sheraine Lathon Evangelistic Ministries. Mem. NAFE. Office: Liberty Temple Full Gospel Ch 2233 W 79th St Chicago IL 60620-5803 E-mail: slathon1063@aol.com.

LATHROP, IRVIN TUNIS, retired dean; b. Platteville, Wis., Sept. 23, 1927; s. Irvin J. and Marian (Johnson) Lathrop; m. Eleanor M. Kolar, Aug. 18, 1951; 1 child, James I. BS, Stout State Coll., 1950; MS, Iowa State U., 1954, PhD, 1958. Tchr. Ottumwa (Iowa) H.S., 1950-55; mem. faculty Iowa State U., 1957-58, Western Mich. U., 1958-59, Calif. State Coll., 1959-88, prof. indsl. arts, 1966-88, chmn. dept. indsl. edn., 1969-88, assoc. dean extended edn., 1978-88, prof. emeritus, 1988—. Cons. Naval Ordnance Lab., Corona, Calif., 1961—63. Author (with Marshall La Cour): Photo Technology, 1966; author: (with John LIndbeck) General Industry, 1969, with John LIndbeck: rev. edit., 1977; author: Laboratory Manual for Photo Technology, 1973, Photography, 1979, rev. edit., 1992, The Basic Book of Photography, 1979; author: (with Robert Kunst) Photo-Offset, 1979; editl. cons. Am. Tech. Soc.; contbr. articles to profl. jours. Mem. Orange County Grand Jury, 1989—90, Orange County Juvenile Justice Commn., 1991—2002; mem. adv. com. El Camino and Orange Coast Coll. Mem.: Am. Ednl. Rsch. Assn., Internat. Tech. Assn., Nat. Assn. Indsl. and Tech. Tchrs., Am. Vocat. Assn., Am. Coun. Indsl. Arts Tchr. Edn., Nat. Soc. Study Edn., Phi Kappa Phi, Phi Delta Kappa, Psi Chi, Epsilon Pi Tau. Home: PO Box 3430 Laguna Woods CA 92654-3430 Office: 1250 N Bellflower Blvd Long Beach CA 90840-0006 Personal E-mail: ilathrop@sbcglobal.net.

LATHROP, KAYE DON, nuclear scientist, educator; b. Bryan, Ohio, Oct. 8, 1932; s. Arthur Quay and Helen Venita (Hoos) L.; m. Judith Marie Green, June 11, 1957; children: Braxton Landess, Scottfield Michael. BS, U.S. Mil. Acad., 1955; MS, Calif. Inst. Tech., 1959, PhD, 1962. Staff mem. Los Alamos Sci. Lab., 1962-67; group leader methods devel. Gen. Atomic Co., San Diego, 1967-68; mem. staff Los Alamos Sci. Lab., 1968—72, group leader transport theory, 1972—75, asst. divsn. leader theoretical divsn., 1973—75, assoc. div. leader reactor safeguards and reactor safety and tech. div., 1975-77, alt. div. leader energy div., 1977-78, div. leader computer sci. and svcs. div., 1978-79, assoc. dir. for engring. scis., 1979-84; assoc. lab dir., prof. applied rsch. Stanford Linear Accelerator Ctr. Stanford U., 1984-94, prof. emeritus, 1994—. Vis. prof. U. N.Mex., 1964-65, adj. prof., 1966-67; guest lectr. IAEA, 1969; mem. adv. com. reactor physics ERDA, 1973-77; mem. reactor physics vis. com. Argonne Nat. Lab., 1978-83; mem. mgmt. adv. com. y-12 divsn. Union Carbide Corp., 1979-82; mem. engring. nat. adv. com. U. Mich., 1983-92; mem. steering com. Joint MIT-Idaho Nat. Engring. Lab. Rsch. Program, 1985-89; mem. external adv. com. Nuclear Tech. and Engring. divsn. Los Alamos Sci. Lab., 1988-91, 92-93; mem. com. on material control and acctg. for spl. nuclear materials NRC, 1988-89; mem. energy rsch. adv. bd. panel on new prodn. reactor tech. assessment Dept. of Energy, 1988; mem. electric power/energy sys. engring. peer com. NAE, 1992-94, chair, 1994, mem. com. on membership, 1994-97, mem. presdl. nominating com., 1996-97, mem. membership policy com., 1997-99; chair divsn. rev. com. tech. and safety assessment divsn. Los Alamos Nat. Lab., 1994-97, mem. divsn. rev. com. tech. and safety assessment, 1997-99, divsn. rev. com. applied physics divsn., 1997—, mem. weapons program rev. com., 2002-04; mem. burn code rev. panel Dept. Energy, 2000-04; mem. U. Calif. Pres.'s Coun. on Nat. Labs., 1995-99, mem. sci. and tech. panel, 1993-99, mem. nat. sec. panel, 1996-99. Author reports, papers, chpts. to books; mem. editorial adv. bd. Progress in Nuclear Energy, 1983-85 Served to 1st lt. C.E. U.S. Army, 1955-58. Spl. fellow AEC, 1958-61; R.C. Baker Found. fellow, 1961-62; recipient E.O. Lawrence Meml. award ERDA, 1976; Disting. Svc. award Los Alamos Nat. Lab., 1984 Fellow Am. Nuclear Soc. (chmn. math. and computation div. 1970-71, nat. dir. 1973-76, 79-82, treas. 1977-79, Outstanding Performance award 1980); mem. Am. Phys. Soc., Nat. Acad. Engring. Republican. Episcopalian. Home: 190 Cedar Ln E Ridgway CO 81432 E-mail: klathrop@independence.net.

LATHROP, LAWRENCE ERWIN, JR., retired small business owner, retired forester; b. L.A., Dec. 4, 1942; s. Lawrence Erwin and Anna Maxine (Cypert) L.; m. Elaine Dorothy Baudin, May 16, 1964; 1 child, Lawrence Erwin III. AA in Forestry, Lassen Coll., 1968; BA in Pub. Adminstrn., U. San Francisco, 1976. Cert. fire investigator, coll. instr. Forest firefighter Calif. Dept. Forestry and Fire Protection, Santa Clara, 1961, engr. fire apparatus Belmont and Yreka, 1962—64, fire capt. Riverside County, 1964—73, fire prevention officer Clearlake, 1973, state forest ranger I Ione, 1973—82, state forest ranger II Susanville, 1982—93, ret., 1993; cons. pvt. practice Calif., 1993—2000; co-owner Secret Air Aviation Svcs., Janesville, Calif., 1994—2000; owner Larry Lathrop Enterprises, Janesville, 1993—2000. Fire investigation and tng. cons. Nev. Dept. Forestry, Carson City, 1985—2000, U.S. Bur. Land Mgmt., Elko and Winnemuca, Nev., 1985—2000. Author, editor: Tailgate Safety Bull., 1984—91; author: numerous in-svc. tng. programs, including Helicopter Safety, Air Attack, Powerline Inspections, 1978—82. Advisor Demolay, Amador County, Calif., 1976-78; active PTA, Amador County, 1975-82, Lassen County Arson Task Force, 1985-93, State Arson Unit, 1974-93. Master: Masons; mem.: Elks. Republican. Presbyterian. Avocations: hunting, fishing, flying. Home: HC01 Box 86P White Bird ID 83554

LATHROP, MITCHELL LEE, lawyer; b. LA, Dec. 15, 1937; s. Alfred Lee and Barbara (Mitchell) L.; m. Lynn Mara Dalton; children: Christin Lorraine Newlon, Alexander Mitchell BSc, U.S. Naval Acad., 1959; JD, U. So. Calif., 1966. Bar: D.C. 1966, Calif. 1966, U.S. Supreme Ct. 1969, N.Y. 1981; cert. arbitrator Nat. Arbitration Forum, ARIAS-US, Chartered Inst. Arbitrators; cert. civil trial specialist Nat. Bd. Trial Advocacy. Dep. counsel L.A. County, Calif., 1966-68; with Brill, Hunt, DeBuys and Burby, L.A., 1968-71; ptnr. Macdonald, Halsted & Laybourne, L.A. and San Diego, 1971-80; sr. ptnr. Rogers & Wells, N.Y.C., San Diego, 1980-86; sr. ptnr., exec. com. Adams, Duque & Hazeltine, L.A., San Francisco, N.Y.C., San Diego, 1986-94, firm chmn., 1992-94; sr. ptnr. Luce, Forward, Hamilton & Scripps, San Diego and N.Y.C., 1994—2003; ptnr. Duane Morris LLP, NYC, San Diego, 2003—. Presiding referee Calif. Bar Ct., 1984-86, mem. exec. com., 1981-88; lectr. law Calif. Judges Assn., Practicing Law Inst. N.Y., Continuing Edn. of Bar, State Bar Calif., ABA, others. Author: State Hazardous Waste Regulation, 1991, Environmental Insurance Coverage, 1991, Insurance Coverage for Environmental Claims, 1992; mem. editl. bd. Def. Counsel Jour., 1997—, Jour. Ins. Coverage. Western Regional chmn. Met. Opera Nat. Coun., 1971—81, v.p., mem. exec. com., 1971—, now chmn; trustee Honnold Libr. at Claremont Colls., 1972—80; sec. Music Ctr. Opera Assn., 1974—80; v.p. San Diego Opera Assn., 1985—89, pres.-elect, 1993, pres., 1994—96; bd. dirs. Music Ctr. Opera Assn., L.A., 1973—80, San Diego Opera Assn., 1980—2003, Met. Opera Assn., N.Y.C., 1971—; mem. adv. bd. Internat. Dominican Found., Rome. Mem.: ABA, Internat. Assn. Def. Counsel, Judge Advocates Assn. (dir. L.A. chpt. 1974—80, pres. So. Calif. chpt. 1977—78), Am. Bd. Trial Advocates, Assn. So. Calif. Def. Counsel, Am. Intellectual Property Law Assn., Assn. Bus. Trial Lawyers, San Diego County Bar Assn. (chmn. ethics com. 1980—82, bd. dirs. 1982—85, v.p. 1985), DC Bar Assn., Calif. Bar Assn., Fed. Bar Coun., Fed. Bar Assn., NY Bar Assn., S.R. (pres. 1977—79), Calif. Soc., Mensa Internat., Friends Claremont Coll. (dir. 1975—81, pres. 1978—79), Soc. Colonial Wars in Calif. (gov. 1970—72), LA Opera Assocs. (pres. 1970—72), Order St. Lazarus of Jerusalem, Brit. United Svcs. Club (dir. L.A. 1973—75), Univ. Club, Calif. Club (LA), The Naval Club (London), Met. Club (NYC), Phi Delta Phi. Republican. Office: Duane Morris LLP 101 W Broadway 9th Fl San Diego CA 92101-8285 also: 380 Lexington Ave 37th Fl New York NY 10168 Office Phone: 619-744-2200. Business E-Mail: mllathrop@duanemorris.com.

LATHROP, ROBERT W, music educator; s. Ralph and Linda Lathrop; m. Merri-Lynn Lois Roques, Mar. 7, 1999. MusB Edn., Gordon Coll., Wenham, MA, 1993. Music tchr. Triton Regional H.S., Byfield, Mass., 1995—; music dir. Byfield Parish Ch., Georgetown, Mass., 1995. Mem.: Am. Choral Dirs. Assn., Music Educators Nat. Conf.

LATHROP, THOMAS ALBERT, language educator; b. L.A., Apr. 18, 1941; s. Donald C. and Ethel M. (Challacombe) L.; m. Constance Ellen Cook, Aug. 30, 1969; 1 child, Aline. BA, UCLA, 1964, MA, 1965, PhD, 1970. Mem. faculty Romance langs. UCLA, 1964-66, U. Wyo., 1966-68, Transylvania U., 1973-76, Lafayette Coll., 1976-80; prof. Romance langs. U. Del., Newark, 1980—. Founding editor Juan de la Cuesta Hispanic Monographs, 1978—; co-editor The Cabrilho Press, 1974-89; pres. Linguatext, Ltd., 1989—; asst. editor Cervantes Bull. of the Cervantes Soc. Am., 1980-90. Author: The Legend of the Siete Infantes de Lara, 1972; (with F. Jensen) The Syntax of the Old Spanish Subjunctive, 1973, La Vie Saint Eustace, 2000; Espanol--Lengua y cultura de hoy, 1974; The Evolution of Spanish, 1980; De Acuerdo! and Tanto Mejor, 1986; (with E Dias) Portugal, Lingua e Cultura, 1978, 2d edit., 1995, Curso de gramatica historica espanola, 1984, 89, (with E. Dias) Brasil: Lingua e Cultura, 2002, student edit. Don Quijote, 1997, Don Quizote translation, 2005, others; editor: European Classics, 2001-. AID grantee, 1968; Nat. Endowment for Humanities grantee, 1976, 81; Gulbenkian Found. grantee, 1973; Del Amo Found. grantee, 1972. Mem. MLA, Cervantes Soc. Am., Internat. Assn. Hispanists, Am. Coun. on Tchg. of Fgn. Lag., Am. Assn. Tchrs. Spanish and Portuguese. Home: 270 Indian Rd Newark DE 19711-5204 Office: U Del Dept Lang Newark DE 19716 Office Phone: 302-453-8695. Business E-Mail: lathrop@udel.edu.

LATHROPE, DANIEL JOHN, law educator; BSBA, U. Denver, 1973; JD, Northwestern U., 1977; LLM, NYU, 1979. Bar: Ariz. 1977, Calif. 1978. Assoc. Evans, Kitchel & Jenckes, Phoenix, 1977-78; instr. law NYU, 1979-80; assoc. prof. U. Calif. Hastings Coll. Law, San Francisco, 1980-86, prof., 1986—. Assoc. acad. dean U. Calif. Hastings Coll. Law, San Francisco, 1986-87, acting dean, 1987-88, acad. dean, 1988-90, dir. LLM program U.S. legal studies, 2004—; prof., assoc. dean, dir. grad. tax program U. Fla. Coll. Law, Gainesville, 1995-96. Co-author: (with Lind, Schwarz and Rosenberg) Fundamentals of Corporate Taxation, 6th edit., 2005, (with Lind, Schwarz and Rosenberg) Fundamentals of Business Enterprise Taxation, 3d edit., 2005, (with Lind, Schwarz and Rosenberg) Fundamentals of Partnership Taxation, 7th edit., 2005, (with Schwarz) Black Letter on Federal Taxation of Corporations and Partnerships, 5th edit., 2005, (with Freeland, Lind and Stephens) Fundamentals of Federal Income Taxation, 13th edit., 2004, (with McNulty) Federal Income Taxation of Individual in a Nutshell, 7th edit., 2004; author: The Alternative Minimum Tax-Compliance and Planning with Analysis, 1994. Mem. Order of Coif, Beta Gamma Sigma. Office Phone: 415-565-4636.

LATIES, VICTOR GREGORY, psychologist, educator; b. Racine, Wis., Feb. 2, 1926; s. Simon Gregory and Rima (Kapnik) L.; m. Martha Ann Fisher, July 29, 1956; children: Nancy, Andrew, Claire. AB, Tufts U., 1949; PhD, U. Rochester, N.Y., 1954. Ford Found. teaching intern Brown U., 1954-55; instr., asst. prof. dept. pharmacology Johns Hopkins U. Sch. Medicine, 1955-65; assoc. prof. U. Rochester Sch. Medicine and Dentistry, 1965-71, prof., 1971—, dir. toxicology tng. program, 1978-91, 95-96. Mem. preclinical psychopharmacology research rev. com. NIMH, 1967-71; mem. bd. on toxicology and environ. health hazards Nat. Acad. Sci.-NRC, 1977-80, mem. toxicology info. program com., 1981-85; mem. sci. rev. com. for health research EPA, 1981-89. Editor: Jour. Exptl. Analysis of Behavior, 1972-76, exec. editor, 1966-72, 76—; editor: (with B. Weiss) Behavioral Toxicology, 1975, Behavioral Pharmacology, 1976; mem. editorial bd.: Jour. Pharmacology and Exptl. Therapeutics, 1965-71, Psychopharmacology, 1968-78, 81-89, The Behavior Analyst, 1980-82, Experimental and Clinical Psychopharmacology, 1993-99; contbr. articles to profl. jours. Served with USN, 1944-46. Fellow Am. Psychol. Assn. (pres. div. psychopharmacology 1968-69, div. exptl. analysis of behavior 1979-82, bd. sci. affairs 1983-85), Behavioral Pharmacology Soc. (pres. 1966-68), Am. Soc. Pharmacology and Exptl. Therapeutics, Assn. for Behavior Analysis, Soc. Toxicology, Am. Psychol. Soc., Soc. for Exptl. Analysis of Behavior (sec.-treas. 1966—). Home: 55 Dale Rd E Rochester NY 14625-2137 Office: U Rochester Medical Ctr Dept Environ Medicine Box EHSC Rochester NY 14642

LATIF, RAUF, biomedical researcher; PhD. Rsch. instr. MSSM, 2002—04; asst. prof. Mt. Sinai sch. Of medicine, Manhatten, NY, 2004—. Mem.: ATA (assoc.). Achievements include research in Tshr. Office: Mount Sinai sch of Medicine One Gustave L levy Pl Manhatten NY 10029 Office Phone: 212-241-1954. Business E-Mail: rauf.latif@mssm.edu.

LATIFUR RAHAMAN, RASUL BOAKSH, legal association administrator; b. Kushita, Bangladesh, Jan. 1, 1945; arrived in India, Jan. 3, 1945; s. Fazlur Rahman and Rabya Khatun Ruby Rabia Khatun; married; children: Rassel, Boaksel. Diploma, Kushtia Coll., 1963, LLB, 1966; M Commerce, Dhaka U., 1967. Headmaster Talberia High Sch., Kushtia Dist., 1961; head asst. Indsl. Promo Svcs., Dacca, 1966-67; income tax cons. Bangladesh Bar Assn., Segun Bagicha/Dacca, 1967-69; pres. Kushtia Income Tax Bar Assn., 1970-90, Padma Devel., Kushtia, 1980—. Chmn. Bangladesh Coms., Padma, Kushtia, 1971—; chmn. Cen. Capital, Padma; leader of party/chmn., Bangladesh Internat. Moisen Order Internat. Command Party, Padma, 1980—; chmn. Ctrl. Capital of Bangladesh, Padma, 299100; trade consulate Bangladesh Trade, Padma, 1980—; chmn. Bazar com., Padma. Mem. Pub. Libr., Kushtia, 1965-66. Office: The Income Tax Bar Assn B06000 Kushtia Padma Bangladesh

LATIMER, ALLIE B., retired lawyer; b. Coraopolis, Pa. d. Lawnye S. and Bennie Latimer BS, Hampton Inst.; JD, MDiv, DMin, Howard U.; LLM, Cath. U.; postgrad., Am. U., 1960-61. Bar: N.C. bar 1955, D.C. bar 1960. Vol. in projects Am. Friends Service Com., N.J. and, Europe, 1948-49; correctional officer Fed. Reformatory for Women, Alderson, W.Va., 1949-51; personnel clk. NIH, Bethesda, 1953-55; realty officer Mitchell AFB, N.Y., 1955-56; with Office Gen. Counsel, GSA, Washington, 1957-76, chief counsel, after 1966, asst. gen. counsel, 1971-76, gen. counsel, 1977-87; asst. gen. counsel NASA, 1976-77; spl. counsel Gen. Svcs. Adminstrn., Washington, 1987-96. Past chmn. central office com. Fed. Women's Program, GSA; mem. membership and budget com. Health and Welfare Council, 1967-72 Bd. dirs. D.C. Mental Health Assn., pres., 1977-79; bd. dirs. Friendship House, Washington; elder Presbyn. Ch.; mem. com. on office of Gen. Assembly, Presbyn. Ch. USA; pres. Interacial Council, 1964-75; chmn. Presbyn. Econ. Devel. Corp., 1975-81; mem. governing bd. Nat. Council Chs. of Christ in U.S.A.; bd. trustees Johnson C. Smith Theol. Sem. Recipient GSA Sustained Superior Service award, 1959, Meritorious Svc. award, 1964, Commendable Svc. award, 1964, Pub. Svc. award, 1971, Outstanding Performance award, 1971, Presdl. Rank award, 1983, Disting. Svc. award, 1984. Mem. ABA, Nat. Bar Assn. (sec. 1966-74, Hall of Fame award 1999), Fed. Bar Assn., Washington Bar Assn. (Ollie M. Cooper award 1998, Hall of Fame award 2004), NC Bar Assn., Nat. Bar Found. (dir. 1970-71, pres. 1974-75), Hampton Alumni Assn. (pres. Washington chpt. 1970-71), Howard Law Alumni Assn. (v.p. alumni assns. 1962-63), Links (pres. Washington chpt. 1971-74, nat. v.p. 1976-80), Federally Employed Women (co-founder, 1st pres.). Home: 3050 Military Rd NW #520 Washington DC 20015-1364

LATIMER, JAMES HAROLD, musician, conductor, composer, music educator; b. Tulsa, June 27, 1934; s. Major Sylvester and Maria Louise (Wilson) L. MusB, Ind. U., 1956; MusM, Boston U., 1964; postgrad., Harvard U., 1968. Instr., asst. dir. bands Fla. A&M U., Tallahassee, 1957-62; freelance performer Boston, 1963-68; prof. music-percussion U. Wis., Madison, 1968-99; music dir. Wis. Youth Symphony Orchs., Madison, 1972-78. Timpanist Madison Symphony Orch., 1968-99; clinician Ludwig Industries, Chgo., 1971-99; condr. Capitol City Band, Madison, 1981—; marimbist Madison Marimba Quartet, 1982-; Fulbright lectr. Cairo Conservatoire, 1984-85; Commonwealth vis. prof. Radford (Va.) U., 1985-87. Percussionist Boston Pops Orch., 1968-74; contbr. Inquiring About Communities, 1971; composer, arranger various titles for percussion and bands. Mem. ASCAP, Percussive Arts Soc., Am. Fedn. Musicians, Wis. Federated Music Club (hon. life mem.), Rotary (Madison chpt.), Phi Mu Alpha, Kappa Kappa Psi, Phi Beta (hon.). Mem. Soc. Of Friends. Avocations: amateur radio, electronics, woodworking, collecting. E-mail: jhlatime@wisc.edu.

LATIMER, KATHARINE RUTH, lawyer; b. Lafayette, La., Apr. 5, 1961; d. Ewing Craig and Beverly Elise (Dalferes) L. BA magna cum laude, U. Tenn., 1983; JD cum laude, Georgetown U., 1986. Bar: D.C. 1986, US Dist. Ct., Md., DC, US Ct. of Appeals, Third Circuit, Fourth Circuit, Sixth Circuit, Eighth Circuit, Ninth Circuit, Tenth Circuit, Eleventh Circuit. Jud. clk. 19th Jud. Cir. Va., Fairfax, 1986-87; assoc. then ptnr. Spriggs & Hollingsworth, Washington, 1987—. Consulting editor, adv. mem. Expert Evidence Reporter; mem. Toxic Tort Adv. Council. Mem. ABA (litigation sect.), Bar Assn. D.C. Democrat. Roman Catholic. Office: Spriggs & Hollingsworth 1350 I St NW Washington DC 20005-3399 Office Phone: 202-898-5800. Office Fax: 202-682-1639. Business E-Mail: klatimer@spriggs.com.

LATIMER, KENNETH ALAN, lawyer; b. Chgo., Oct. 26, 1943; s. Edward and Mary (Schiller) L.; m. Carole Ross, June 23, 1968; children: Cary, Darren, Wendy. BS, U. Wis., 1966; JD with honors, George Washington U., 1969. Bar: D.C. 1969, Ill. 1970. Atty. U.S. Office of Comptroller, Washington, 1969-70; assoc. Berger, Newmark & Fenchel, Chgo., 1970-74, ptnr., 1975-86, Holleb & Coff, Chgo., 1986-99, Duane, Morris LLP, Chgo., 1999—. Guest speaker Ill. Inst. for Continuing Legal Edn., Chgo., 1975-87; lectr. Banking Law Inst., 1996—. Pres. North Suburban Jewish Cmty. Ctr., Highland Park, Ill., 1985; bd. dirs. Jewish Cmty. Ctrs. Chgo., 1985-95. Mem. ABA Fellows, Ill. Bar Assn. (chmn. sect. coun. on comml. banking and bankruptcy 1990-91), ABA (com. on banking and comml. finance), Chgo. Bar Assn. (com. on fin. instns.), Comml. Fin. Assn. Ednl. Found. (founders coun.), Assn. Comml. Fin. Attys., Am Coll. Comml. Fin Attys.(bd. regents), Standard Club. Avocations: jogging, travel. Office: Duane Morris LLP 227 W Monroe St Ste 3400 Chicago IL 60606-5098 Office Phone: 312-499-6730. E-mail: kalatimer@duanemorris.com.

LATIMER, PAUL JERRY, industrial engineer; b. Springfield, Tenn., July 21, 1943; s. Paul Daniel and Juanita Inez (Richey) L.; m. Sylvia Susan Cole, June 6, 1966; children: Zachary Nathaniel, Matthew Jason. BS in Physics with honors, U. Tenn., 1966, MS in Physics, 1979, PhD in Physics, 1983. Devel. engr. Oak Ridge (Tenn.) Nat. Lab., 1980-81; faculty rsch. assoc. Ohio State U., Columbus, 1981; rsch. asst. U. Tenn., Knoxville, 1981-83; sr. rsch. engr. McDermott Techs. Inc. R&D divsn. Lynchburg Rsch. Ctr., Va., 1983-98; sr. engr. MAST Automation, Inc., Lynchburg, Va., 1998—2001; physicist, scientist Naval Surface Warfare Ctr., Indian Head, Md., 2001—. Contbr. articles to profl. jours.; patentee in field. Co-leader cub pack Lynchburg Area coun. Boy Scouts Am., 1983-84; vol. United Way, 1994; mem. Pacer Club for United Way Support, 1993-98. Mem. ASTM, Am. Soc. Metals, Am. Soc. Non-destructive Testing (cert. Level III untrasonic methods), Am. Welding Soc., Sigma Pi Sigma. Avocations: martial arts, hiking, lapidary, mineral collecting. Home: 376 Juniper Dr Lynchburg VA 24502-5661 Office: Naval Surface Warfare Ctr Bldg 1576-Code 330 PL 101 Strauss Ave Indian Head MD 20640 E-mail: latimerpj@ih.navy.mil.

LATIMER, ROXIE ANN, social services administrator, writer, journalist, publishing executive, television producer; b. Santa Mon Ica, Calif., Feb. 28, 1956; d. Russell Little and Doralee Latimer; married, Jan. 14, 2002; 1 child. Pres., founder Friends Of Russell Latimer, Inc., Whittier, Calif., 1992—; pres. & ceo, exec. prodr, pub. Wim Media & Publ. Group, Whittier, Calif., 1997—. Bd. dirs. Imani Bible Coll., San Diego, 1995—96; chairwoman Nation 2 Nation, L.A., 2000; chairwomen Nation 2 Nation Ohio, Columbus, 2004—. Author: (novel) You Never Know, (poetry) Poetry In Motion Series; editor: (newsletter) I Stand Prison News, Wim Mag. (Women Who Mean Bus. award San Diego Bus. Jour., 1997), (newsletter) Nation 2 Nation News And Reviews; prodr.: (tv show) Ask Lady Diamond, In Da Zone, Dream's World With Ace TV; various paintings and drawings. Grantee, HUD, 1994—96. Mem.: African Womens Writers Guild, AFI (assoc.), Ontario C. of C. Democrat-Npl. Achievements include first to innovative transitional housing program for domestic violence victims In San Diego, 1992-1996. Home and Office: 6521 Ironwood Terr Winterhaven CA 92283 Office Phone: 310-694-1257, 760-562-3911. Personal E-mail: wimmedia1997@aol.com.

LATIMER, ROY TRUETT, museum executive; b. Albany, Tex., Aug. 23, 1928; s. Charles Lee and Zora Neil (Brock) L.; m. Judith Gail Johnson, Nov. 26, 1955 (div. 1975); children: Jeff, Laura, Tiffany; m. Harriet Calvin, Nov. 20, 1976. BA, Hardin-Simmons U., 1951, LLD, 1996. Owner Gen. Ins. Agy., Abilene, Tex., 1951-55; alumni dir. Hardin-Simmons U., Abilene, 1955-62; dir. pub. relations Tex. Assn. of Realtors, Austin, 1962-65; exec. dir. Tex. Hist. Commn., Austin, 1965-81, Tex. Hist. Found., Austin, 1972-81; v.p. pub. relations and mktg. Spaw Glass, Inc., Houston, 1981-85; pres. Houston Mus. Natural Sci., Houston, 1986—2001. Pres. Nat. Conf. State Hist. Preservation Officers, 1974-75; bd. advisors Nat. Trust for Hist. Preservation, Washington, 1981-88; bd. dirs. Houston Conv. and Tourist Bur. Mem. Tex. Ho. Reps., Austin, 1952-62; bd. devel. Hardin-Simmons U., 1974—, pres. 1999—; bd. dirs. Downtown Houston Assn., 1983—, past pres.; bd. dirs. Rice Design Alliance, Houston, 1983-87; chmn. S. Main Ctr. Assn., 1991-93; mem. Pres.' Adv. Coun. on Hist. Preservation, 1974-75. Mem. South Main Ctr. Assn. (bd. dirs. 1988—, pres. 2000—), Giant Screen Theater Assn. (v.p. 1999-2000, pres. 2001-02). Presbyterian. Avocations: running, canoeing, backpacking, travel. Home: 9 Bash Pl Houston TX 77027-5601 Personal E-mail: tlatimer1@houston.rr.com.

LATIMER, STEPHEN MARK, lawyer; b. Bklyn., July 15, 1939; s. Ted and Martha (Goldberg) L.; m. Judith R. Shulman, June 3, 1964 (dec. Mar. 29, 1984); 1 child, Gary. BA, Tufts U., 1961; JD, NYU, 1968. Bar: N.Y. 1968, N.J. 1979, U.S. Dist. Ct. (so. dist.) N.Y. 1970, U.S. Dist. Ct. (ea. dist.) N.Y. 1972, U.S. Dist. Ct. N.J. 1979, U.S. Dist. Ct. (we. dist.) N.Y. 1984, U.S. Dist. Ct. (no. dist.) Tex. 1992, U.S. Ct. Appeals (2d cir.) 1974, U.S. Ct. Appeals (3rd cir.) 1981, U.S. Ct. Appeals (5th cir.) 1986, U.S. Supreme Ct. 1975, U.S. Dist. Ct. (we. dist.) Tex. 2002. Clk. Burke & Parsons, N.Y.C., 1966-67; mng. clk. Otterbourg, Steindler, Houston & Rosen, N.Y.C., 1967-68, assoc., 1968-69, Halpern, Schivitz, Scholer and Steingut, N.Y.C., 1969-71; dir. supervised pre-trial release project N.Y. Lawyers Com. for Civil Rights Under Law, N.Y.C., 1972-73; dir. cmty. devel. and law reform Bronx Legal Svcs., N.Y.C., 1973-79, acting mng. atty., 1974; dir. litigation Camden (N.J.) Regional Legal Svcs., Inc., 1979-81, acting dir., 1981-82; statewide litigation coord. Legal Svcs. of N.J., New Brunswick, 1982-84; sr. litigation atty. Prisoners' Legal Svcs. of N.Y., N.Y.C., 1984-94; asst. dep. pub. defender N.J. Pub. Defender, Newark, 1994-95; ptnr. Loughlin & Latimer, Hackensack, N.J., 1995—. Lectr. Rutgers U. Law Sch., 1975-90. Contbr. articles to profl. jours. Trustee ACLU of N.J., 1982-2001, exec. com. 1984-99, N.J. Assn. Correction, 1986—, Planned Parenthood of Middlesex County, 1981-85. Lt. USN, 1961-66, USNR, 1966-68. Instr. U.S. Marine Acad., Kings Point, N.Y., 1964-66. Mem. N.J. Bar Assn. (vice chmn. individual rights 1998-99, chmn. individual rights, 1999-2001). Home: 120 Floyd Ave Bloomfield NJ 07003-5610 Office: Loughlin & Latimer 131 Main St Hackensack NJ 07601-7140 Office Phone: 201-487-9797. Personal E-mail: slatimer@mindspring.com.

LATIOLAIS, MINNIE FITZGERALD, retired nurse, health facility administrator; b. Dec. 26, 1921; d. Thomas Ambrose and Mildred Surita (Nagle) Fitzgerald; m. Joseph C. Latiolais Jr., July 19, 1947; children: Felisa, Diana, Sylvia, Mary, Amelia, Joseph Clifton III. RN, New Orleans. Asst. night supr. Touro Infirmary, New Orleans, 1943; orthopaedic surg. nurse Ochsner Clinic, New Orleans, 1943-47; asst. DON Ochsner Found. Hosp., 1947; supr. Lafayette (La.) Gen. Hosp., 1960-64; adminstrv. asst., supr. oper. rm. Abbeville (La.) Gen. Hosp., 1964-68; gen. mgr., neurol. surg. nurse J. Robert Rivet, neurol. surgeon, Lafayette, 1968-78; hosp. cons. assoc. B.J. Landry & Assocs.; hosps. cons. Lafayette, 1979-90; DON Acadia St. Landry Hosp., Church Point, 1981-82; supr. supplies, processing and distbn. Univ. Med. Ctr., Lafayette, 1982-90, ret., 1990. Pres. SW La. Rehab. Assn., 1979-80; mem. Mid-La. Health Systems Agy., 1977-82, project rev. chmn., 1978-80; vice chmn. Acadica Regional Clearing House, 1984-86; mem. crafts and practical nurse com. Lafayette Regional Vocat.-Tech. Inst., 1980-84, chmn. 1983-84. Roman Catholic.

LA TORRE, CARISSA DANITZA, counselor; d. Luis Francisco and Elia Danitza La Torre. AA in Spanish, AA in Psychology, Saddleback C.C., Mission Viejo, Calif., 1995, AA in Bus. Adminstrn., 2002; BA in Spanish, BA in Psychology, Calif. State U., Fullerton, 1998, MS in Edn., 2000. Lic. Behavior Modification Case Mgr./Specialist Calif., 1999, cert. Specialist Mild/Moderate/Severe Disabilities Calif., 1999, Multiple Subject Calif., 1999, Single Subject Calif., 1999. Educator Capistrano Unified Sch. Dist., San Juan Capistrano, Calif., 1997—99; bilingual grad. rschr. UCLA/Calif. State U., 1998—2003; office/human resource mgr. GlobalStar Electronics, Inc., Aliso Viejo, Calif., 2002—03; birth mother counselor Adoption Network Law Ctr., Inc., Laguna Beach, Calif., 2003—. Presenter in field of infant devel. Rep. and spkr. MADD, Tustin, Calif., 1996—; youth group ministry leader Mission San Juan Capistrano, 2001—. Recipient Dedication and Svc. in Counseling award, Outreach Concern, Inc., 1997, 1998. Mem.: Coun. Children with Behavioral Disorders (assoc. presenter internat. conf. 2001), Divsn. Early Childhood (assoc. presenter internat. confs. 2000—01), Harley Owners' Group (life), Phi Kappa Phi (life), Zeta Tau Alpha (life; pres. and v.p. 1995—97). Office Phone: 800-455-6055, 800-455-6055. Personal E-mail: xclatorre@collegeclub.com. Business E-Mail: CarissaL@adoptionpro.com, carissal@adoptionnetwork.com.

LATORRE, ROBERT GEORGE, naval architecture and engineering educator; b. Toledo, Jan. 9, 1949; s. Robert James and Madge Violette (Roy) L.; m. Iryna Korol, 2000; 1 child, Marie-Elise. BS in Naval Architecture and Marine Engring. with honors, U. Mich., 1971, MS in Engring., 1972; MSE in Naval Architecture, U. Tokyo, 1975, PhD in Naval Architecture, 1978. Asst. prof. U. Mich., Ann Arbor, 1979—83; assoc. prof. U. New Orleans, 1984—87, prof. naval architecture and marine engring., 1987—, chmn. dept., 1989—95. Assoc. prof. mech. engring., U. Tokyo, 1986-87; rsch. scientist, David Taylor Naval R & D Lab., Bethesda, Md., 1980, 81, Bassin d'Essais des Carenes, Paris, 1983; cons. in field. Contbr. to profl. publs. Mem. ASME, Soc. Naval Architects, Royal Inst. Naval Archtects Gt. Britain, Soc. Naval Architects Japan, Am. Soc. Engring. Edn. (program chmn. ocean engring. divsn. 1989-9O), Japan Club New Orleans. Roman Catholic. Office: U New Orleans 911 Engring Bldg New Orleans LA 70148-0001 Office Phone: 504-280-7180. E-mail: rlatorre@uno.edu.

LATOUR, ROBERT JAMES, animal scientist, educator; b. Holyoke, Mass., Mar. 2, 1972; s. Anne Marie Bourque and Robert Paul Latour. BA in Math., Western New Eng. Coll., Springfield, Mass., 1994; M in Biomath., NC State U., Raleigh, 1996, Ph.D in Biomath., 2000. Tchg. asst. NC State U., Raleigh, NC, 1994—95, rsch. asst., 1996—2000; postdoctoral rsch. assoc. Va. Inst. Marine Sci., Gloucester Point, 2000—01, rsch. asst. prof., 2001—04, asst. prof., 2004—. Contbg. author (book) Elasmobranch Fisheries Management Techniques; contbr. articles to profl. jours. Grantee, Va. Recreational Fishing and Adv. Bd., 2000 - 2001, 2003 - 2005, NOAA, 2001—04, Va. Environ. Endowment, 2001—05, Keith Campbell Found. for the Environment, 2004, EPA, 2005—. Mem.: Estuarine Rsch. Fedn., Am. Fisheries Soc. Avocations: fishing, traveling, hiking, camping, music (drumming). Office: Va Inst Marine Sci 1208 Greate Road Gloucester Point VA 23062 Office Phone: 804-684-7312. E-mail: latour@vims.edu.

LATOURETTE, STEVEN C., congressman; b. Cleve., July 22, 1954; married; 4 children. BA in Hist., U. Mich., 1976; JD, Cleve. State U., 1979. Asst. pub. defender Lake County Pub. Defender's Office, 1980-83; assoc. Cannon, Stern, Aveni & Krivok, Painesville, 1983-86; with Baker, Hackenberg & Collins, Painesville, 1986-88; prosecuting atty. Lake County Prosecutor Office, 1988-93; mem. U.S. Ho. of Reps. from 14th Ohio dist., Washington, 1994—; mem. Com. on Transp. & Infrastructure, econ. devel., pub. bldg. & emergency mgmt. & water resources and environ. U.S. Ho. of Reps., chmn. transit & pipelines, mem. govt. reform and govt. efficiency and fin. mgmt. nat. security, emerging threats, and internat. rels., mem. fin. svcs. com., fin. instn. and consumer credit, vice chair oversight and investigations, mem. U.S. Holocaust Meml. Coun., trans. & infrastructure, 1995—. Republican. Office: US House Reps 2453 Rayburn HOB Washington DC 20515-3519*

LATOURRETTE, JAMES THOMAS, retired electrophysics, electrical engineering and computer science educator; b. Miami, Ariz., Dec. 26, 1931; s. Emery Everest and Carrie D. (Hoffman) LaT.; m. Muriel Ashe, Aug. 28, 1955; children: Mary Beth, John Emery, James Thomas, Joanne. BS, Calif. Inst. Tech., 1953; MA (Gen. Communication Co. fellow), Harvard U., 1954, PhD (NSF fellow), 1958. Rsch. assoc., lectr. physics Harvard U., 1957-59; physicist Gen. Electric Research Lab., Schenectady, 1960-62; sr. supervisory scientist TRG, Inc., Melville, N.Y., 1962-66; sect. head TRG div. Control Data Corp., Melville, 1966-67; prof. electrophysics, elec. engring. and computer sci. Poly. U. (formerly Poly. Inst. Bklyn. and Poly. Inst. N.Y.), Farmingdale, NY, 1967—93, prof. emeritus, 1993. Assoc. dir. Weber Rsch. Inst., Poly. U., 1987-90. Contbr. articles to profl. jours. NSF postdoctoral fellow Physikalisches Institut der U. Bonn, Germany, 1959-60 Mem. IEEE, Sigma Xi, Tau Beta Pi. Home: 2 Candlewood Ct Huntington NY 11743-1827 E-mail: j.latourrette@ieee.org.

LATSON, RICHARD CHARLES, retired audio-visual specialist; b. Nov. 13, 1947; s. Robert Lee and Ruby (Kent) Latson; m. Sherilyn Day (div.). BA in Radio and TV Comm., Tex. Tech U., 1970. Radio-TV broadcaster, 1967-70; TV prodn. specialist Naval Acad., Annapolis, Md., 1974-79; mgr. TV prodn. Walter Reed Army Med. Ctr., Washington, 1979-87; audio visual mgmt. officer Dept. Army, Washington, 1987-90; mgr. audio visual prodn. and distbn. program Dept. Def., Alexandria, Va., 1990—2002. Mem. fed. audio-visual com. Office Mgmt. and Budget, Washington, 1990—96; U.S. judge Internat. Mil. Film Festival, Argentina, 1998, Bracciano, Italy, 2001, Bracciano, 03, U.S. del., Rome, 1998; mgr. DoD Audiovisual Prodn. Awards Program, 1998—2002; judge Clarion Awards-Assn. Women in Comm., 2002, 03. Mem. NATO Mil. Audiovisual Working Group, Joint Svcs. Adv. Group Advanced Distributed Learning, 1995—2002; judge U.S. Army Audiovisual Prodn. Competition, 2000, 2001, 2002, USN Audiovisual Prodn. Competition, 2001. 1st lt. USAF, 1970—74. Decorated Air Force commendation medal; recipient medal for exceptional civilian svc., Office of Sec. of Def. Mem.: NATAS, English-Speaking Union, Brit. & Commonwealth Soc. N.Am. (past pres.), Internat. Imaging Industry Assn. (stds. mgmt. bd. 1992—2002), Am. Nat. Stds. Inst. (image tech. stds. bd. 1990—98, info. sys. stds. bd. 1990—2002). Avocations: old time radio programs, big band music, collecting art. Home: 3364 Gleneagles Dr Apt 1E Silver Spring MD 20906

LATTA, DIANA LENNOX, retired interior designer; b. Lahaina, Maui, Hawaii, Aug. 5, 1936; d. D. Stewart and Jean Marjorie (Anderson) Lennox; m. Arthur McKee Latta, Jan. 26, 1957 (dec.); children: Mary-Stewart, Marion McKee Davidson. Grad., The Bishop's Sch., La Jolla, Calif., 1954; student, U. Wash., 1954—56. Dir. Vero Beach (Fla.) br. of Wellington Hall Ltd., Thomasville, NC, 1970—72; asst. to chief designer Rablen-West Interiors, Vero Beach, 1972—75; design and adminstrv. asst. to pres. Design Studio Archtl. & Interior Design Concepts, Inc., Vero Beach, 1975—82; owner, designer The Designery, Vero Beach, 1983—87; designer's asst. Frank J. Lincoln Interiors, Inc., Vero Beach, Locust Valley, NY, 1987—90; sr. staff designer Chancellor's Inc., Bellingham, Wash., 1992—93; v.p., sec., dir. JADSL Corp., Mill Creek, Wash., 1999—; v.p., sec., bd. dirs. Jadsl Corp. Leading actress (Vero Beach Theatre Guild prodns) The Laughmaker, 1964, Oklahoma, 1966, model Holly Fashion Show, Vero Beach, 1962—69. Mem. Indian River Meml. Hosp. Women's Aux., Vero Beach, 1957—70, chmn. charity ball and gift shop, 1960, v.p., 1962—64; founding mem. Indian River Land Trust, Vero Beach, 1989—90; chmn. Mill Creek for Youth Com., 1994; advisor to steering com. The Malt Shoppe after-sch. program, Mill Creek, 1995—97; mem. coun. Snohomish County Federated Health and Safety Network, 1999—2003; bd. dirs., chmn. hospitality com. Vero Beach Mut. Concert Assn., 1973—76; mem. adv. bd. Indian River 4-H Horsemaster's Club, 1973—76; treas., bd. dirs. McKee Jungle Gardens Preservation Soc., Inc., chmn. fundraising com., pub. rels. com., 1988; bd. dirs. Vero Beach Theatre Guild, 1964; mem. adv. com. Safe and Drug Free Schs. Edmonds (Wash.) Sch. Dist., 1996—2002; mem. key leaders bd. Cmtys. That Care Project Edmonds Sch. Dist., 2001—. Mem.: Internat. Platform Assn., Riomar Bay Yacht Club (chmn. tennis com. 1964—66, club tennis champion 1964, 1966), Kappa Kappa Gamma (mem. adv. bd. U. Wash., Seattle chpt. 1997—2000, founding mem. N. Sound Alumnae Assn. 2002—, founding mem. Indian River Alumnae Club 1968). Republican. Episcopalian. Home: 16018 Village Green Dr # B Mill Creek WA 98012-5874

LATTA, GEORGE HAWORTH, III, neonatal/perinatal nurse practitioner; b. Chattanooga, Sept. 4, 1960; s. George Haworth Jr. and Charlotte (Major) L. BS in Physics, Ga. Inst. Tech., 1982; MD, East Tenn. State U., 1986. Cert. in pediat., neonatology. Intern, resident in pediat. Dartmouth (N.H.) U., 1986-88; resident in pediat. Stanford (Calif.) U., 1988-89; fellow in neonatology Vanderbilt U., Nashville, 1989-90, U. Tenn., Memphis, 1990-92; attending neonatologist Rose Med. Ctr., Denver, 1992-94, Forrest Gen. Hosp., Hattiesburg, Miss., 1994-95, Meth. Hosps., Memphis, 1995-99; neontalogist Intermountain Healthcare, Provo, Utah, 2000—. NIH pulmonary trainee grantee Vanderbilt U., 1989; March of Dimes scholar East Tenn. State U., 1984, Johnny J. Jones scholar, 1981. Fellow Am. Acad. Pediat.; mem. Phi Eta Sigma. Roman Catholic. Avocations: skiing, camping, jazz music, aquariums, scuba diving. Home: 1825 South 2300 East Salt Lake City UT 84108 Office: Utah Valley Regional Med Ctr Intermountain Healthcare 1034 N 500 W Provo UT 84604-3380 Personal E-mail: ghlatta3@comcast.net. Business E-Mail: uvglatta@ihc.com.

LATTA, JEAN CAROLYN, financial analyst, chemist; b. Chgo., Oct. 11, 1943; d. John Oscar and Katherine Helen (Schnitzer) Latta. BS in Chemistry, U. Ill., 1966; MS in Chemistry, Ill. Inst. Tech., 1970; MBA, U. Chgo., 1976. Chemist Gillette Co., Chgo., 1966—67, asst. rsch. chemist, 1969—73; product designer Bunker-Ramo Corp., Chgo., 1973—75; staff exec. George S. May Internat. Co., Park Ridge, Ill., 1977; contr., ind. cons. GBayou City Svc. Co., Houston, 1978; staff acct. Chemtrust Industries, Franklin Park, Ill., 1979; fin. analyst U. Chgo., 1979—84; sr. price/cost analyst Northrop Grumman Corp., Pico Rivera, Calif., 1984—85, pricing coord., engring. cost analyst Hawthorne, Calif., 1989—96; sr. engring. specialist Aerospace Corp., 1997—. Democrat. Roman Catholic. Achievements include Patentee in electronic field. E-mail: jclx@aol.com.

LATTA, RICHARD ALLEN, lawyer; b. Elmhurst, Ill., Sept. 15, 1959; s. James LeRoy and Carol Elaine (Drake) L.; m. Nancy Anne Callan, Aug. 16, 1986. BBA in Acctg., U. Notre Dame, 1981; JD, U. Wis., 1986. Bar: Wis. 1986, Calif. 1987; CPA, Calif. With Arthur Young & Co., Milw., 1981-83; assoc. Pillsbury, Madison & Sutro, San Francisco, 1986-88. Mem. ABA, State Bar Calif.

LATTANZIO, STEPHEN PAUL, astronomy educator; b. Yonkers, N.Y., June 29, 1949; s. Anthony Raymond and Anella Lattanzio; m. Barbara Regina Knisely, Aug. 14, 1976; children: Gregory Paul, Timothy Paul. BA in Astronomy, U. Calif., Berkeley, 1971; MA in Astronomy, UCLA, 1973, postgrad., 1973-75. Planetarium lectr. Griffith Obs., Los Angeles, 1973-75; instr. astronomy El Camino Coll., Torrance, Calif., 1974-75; planetarium lectr. Valley Coll., Los Angeles, 1975; prof. astronomy Orange Coast Coll., Costa Mesa, Calif., 1975—, planetarium dir., 1975—. Mem. adv. commn. Natural History Found. Orange County, Calif., 1988-91; scientific advisor instructional TV series Universe: The Infinite Frontier, 1992—. Contbr. articles to profl. jours. Mem. Astron. Soc. Pacific, The Planetary Soc., Sigma Xi (assoc.), Phi Beta Kappa. Avocation: astronautics. Office: Orange Coast Coll 2701 Fairview Rd Costa Mesa CA 92626-5563 E-mail: slattanzio@cccd.edu.

LATTIMER, GARY LEE, physician; b. Nanticoke, Pa., Dec. 4, 1939; s. Paul Floyd and Gene Elizabeth L.; m. Patricia Sara Weise, June 14, 1958; children: Toni Jo, Gregory Weise. MD, Temple U., 1966; postgrad., Jefferson Med. Coll., 1970-72. Intern Allentown (Pa.) Hosp.; resident Presbyn.-Univ. Hosp., Phila., 1969-70, Jefferson Med. Coll. Hosp., Phila., 1970-71, chief med. resident, 1971-72; chief infectious diseases Allentown-Sacred Heart Hosp. Center, 1972-80; assoc. prof. medicine U. N.D., 1980-81, chief infectious diseases, 1980-81, New Britain (Conn.) Gen. Hosp., 1981—; assoc.

prof. medicine U. Conn., 1981-83; dir. infectious diseases Williamsport Hosp., Divine Providence Hosp., 1983—. Author: Legionnaires' Disease, 1981; contbr. articles to profl. jours. Served with M.C. U.S. Army, 1967-69. Decorated Bronze Star; recipient Disting. Service award Pa. chpt. Am. Legion. Fellow ACP; mem. Am. Soc. Microbiology, AAAS, Nat. Found. Infectious Diseases, Am. Legion. Office: 17 Durban Pl Hilton Head Island SC 29926-2217 Personal E-mail: glattimer@adelphia.net.

LATTIMER, JOHN KINGSLEY, physician, educator; b. Mt. Clemens, Mich., Oct. 14, 1914; s. Eugene and Gladys Soulier (Lenfestey) L.; m. Jamie Elizabeth Hill, Jan. 1948; children: Evan, Jon, Gary. AB, Columbia U., 1935, MD, 1938, ScD, 1943; student, Balliol Coll., Oxford (Eng.) U., 1944, Med. Field Svc. Sch., Paris, 1945. Diplomate Am. Bd. Urology. Surg. intern Meth.-Episcopal Hosp., N.Y.C., 1938-40; urol. resident Squier Urol. Clinic Presbyn. Hosp., N.Y.C., 1940-43, dir. Squier Urol. Clinic, 1955-80, dir. urol. svc., 1955-80, also dir. urology Sch. Nursing. Staff asst., instr. urology Columbia Coll. Physicians and Surgeons, 1940-53, asst. prof. clin. urology, 1953-55, prof. urology, chmn. dept. urology, 1955-80; vis. prof. Med. Coll. S.C., Med. Coll. Va., Mayo Clinic Med. Sch., Rochester, Minn., 1977, Boston U., Tufts U., U. Oreg., Ind. U., UCLA, Leeds Med. Sch. U. Witwatersrand, South Africa; guest lectr. Akron City Hosp., 1977, Reno Surg. Soc., 1977; chief urology Babies Hosp., Vanderbilt Clinic, Frances Delafield Hosp., N.Y.C., 1955; cons. urology VA, N.Y.C., 1947-80, USPHS Hosp., S.I., N.Y.C., Meth. Hosp., Bklyn., Englewood (N.J.), Yonkers (N.Y.) gen. hosps., Harlem, Roosevelt, St. Lukes hosps. (all N.Y.C.); mem. com. surgery in Tb, genito-urinary Tb, VA; med. cons. Time mag.; cons. to com. on therapy Nat. Tb Assn.; mem. expert adv. panel biology human reprodn. WHO; mem. N.Y. Supreme Ct. Med. Arbitration Panel, 1975; Am. Urol. Assn. rep. to NRC-Nat. Acad. Scis.; mem. tng. grants com. NIH, 1968-72; lectr. in field. Contbr. over 350 articles on urology and history to various publs., also chpts. in books; guest author New Eng. Jour. Medicine; rschr., writer, speaker on assassinations of Pres. Lincoln and Kennedy, and Nuremberg Trials. Trustee Presbyn. Hosp., 1974-78; mem. vis. com. Ft. Ticonderoga Mus.; mem. vis. com. sect. arms and armour Met. Mus. Art, 1978, Abraham Lincoln U., Harrogate, Tenn.; chmn. book com. Englewood Hist. Soc., 1984—; mem. Dallas Coun. World Affairs, Phila. Coun. World Affairs; ofcl. historian City of Englewood, N.J. Maj. M.C., AUS, 1943-46; med. officer at Nuremberg Trials, 1945-46. Decorated Croix de Guerre (France and Belgium); recipient Joseph Mather Smith prize for kidney disease rsch. Columbia U., 1943, honor award for meritorious work in field Tb, Am. Acad. Tb Physicians, also prizes for sci. exhibits, gold medal Coll. Physicians and Surgeons Alumni Assn., 1971, Disting. Svc. award, 1993, Hugh Young medal for outstanding work in infectious diseases, 1973, Belfield medal Chgo. Urol. Soc., Burpeau medal N.J. Acad. Medicine, Edward Henderson gold medal Am. Geriat. Soc., 1978, Gt. medal City of Paris, 1979, Normandy Liberation medal Soc. French War Vets., Paris Liberation medal French Govt., medal Nat. Kidney Fedn., 1987, Am. Acad. Pediatric Urology, 1987, Chevalier French Legion Hon., 2004,; named a Knight of French Legion, 2005. Fellow ACS (chmn. adv. com. urology 1962-64, gov. 1966-79, com. on undergrad. tng. 1967-80, chmn. nominating com. 1976-77, com. to study size and composition of bd. govs.), AMA (prize rsch. kidney Tb 1953), Am. Acad. Pediatrics (chmn. com. on pediatric urology, pres. sect. urology 1973-79); mem. AAAS, Am. Assn. Clin. Urologists, Assn. Am. Med. Colls., Clin. Soc. Genito-Urinary Surgeons (pres. 1984), N.Y. Acad. Sci. (trustee), N.Y. Acad. Medicine (chmn. genito-urinary surg. sect. 1956-57, trustee 1978-84, v.p. 1986-87, chmn. bldg. com. 1982-87), Am. Assn. Genito-Urinary Surgeons (pres. 1982), Am. Urol. Assn. (pres. 1975-76, chmn. com. on pediatric urology, pres. N.Y. sect. 1966, exec. com. 1967-80, com. on surgery, rev. and long range planning com., editorial bd. Jour. Urology 1965-68, chmn. com. to gather info. about urology, chmn. coordinating coun. for urology, chmn. nominating com. 1976-77, 1st prize for clin. rsch. 1950, 60, Ramon Guiterez medal 1980, Keyes medal 1996), Am. Thoracic Soc., AAUP, Soc. U. Urologists (pres. 1969), Nat. Inst. Social Scis., St. Nicholas Soc., Assn. Mil. Surgeons Harvey Soc., Nat. Tb Assn., N.Y. State Pediatrics Soc., N.Y. Med. Socs., New York County Med. Soc., Soc. Pediatric Urology (pres. 1961-62), Brit. Assn. Urol. Surgeons (corr.), N.Y. Soc. Surgeons, N.Y. Soc. Professions, Internationale Société d'Urology (v.p. 1967-73, pres.1973-79), Assn. Pediatric Urology (pres. 1961), Spanish Urol. Assn. (hon.), Paleopathology Assn., Charles A. Lindbergh Soc. (ofcl. historian City of Englewood 1990), Dallas Surgical Soc., Japanese Urol. Assn. (hon.), Italian Urol. Assn. (hon.), SAR, Assn. Mil. Historians, Soc. War 1812, Mil. Order Fgn. Wars U.S., Order of Founders and Patriots, Arms and Armour Soc. N.Y., Arms and Armour Soc. Eng., Arms and Armour Soc. Gueurnsey, Soc. Colonial Wars, Englewood Hist. Soc., Manuscript Soc., Revolutionary War Round Table of N.Y., Abraham Lincoln Soc., Lincoln Soc. N.Y., Wis., Ill., Fla., Washington, Civil War Surgeons (hon.), Am. Legion, 82d Airborne Div. Assn., 101st Airborne Div. Assn., Res. Officers Assn., Metropolitan Club, Sigma Xi. Office: Columbia U Med Sch 161 Fort Washington Ave Rm 1156 New York NY 10032-3713

LATTIMORE, RANDY, mathematics professor; b. Macon, Ga., Feb. 11, 1965; s. Robert Lee and Geneva (Clark) L.; m. Sheree Michelle Rivers, Dec. 15, 1990. BS in Math., Savannah State Coll., 1989; MA in Math., Ohio State U., 1992, ABD, 1994. Mem. NCTM, AERA, Benjamin Banneker Assn. Avocations: basketball, reading, television, billiards. Home: 2336 Leeward Ct Hilliard OH 43026-9052

LATTIMORE, STEVEN, classicist, educator; b. Bryn Mawr, Pa., May 25, 1938; s. Richmond and Alice Bockstahler Lattimore; m. Deborah Lee Nourse, July 14, 1976 (div. July 1994); children: Judith, Nicholas, Isabel. BA, Dartmouth Coll., 1960; MA, Princeton U., 1964, PhD, 1968. Instr. Dartmouth Coll., Hanover, NH, 1964, Haverford Coll., Pa., 1965—66; asst. prof. Intercollegiate Ctr. Classical Studies, Rome, 1966—67, U. Calif., L.A., 1967—74, assoc. prof., 1974—98, prof., 1998—. Author: Marine Thiasos in Greek Sculpture, 1976, Isthmia Marble Sculpture 1967-1980, 1996; translator: Thucydides, Peloponnesian War, 1998. Fellow, John Simon Guggenheim Meml. Found., 1975—76. Mem.: German Archaeol. Inst. (elected), Am. Philogical Assn., Archaeol. Inst. Am. Avocations: travel, hiking. Office: UCLA Dept Classics 405 N Hilgard Ave Los Angeles CA 90095 E-mail: lattimor@humnet.ucla.edu.

LATTMAN, LAURENCE HAROLD, retired academic administrator; b. NYC, Nov. 30, 1923; s. Jacob and Yetta (Schwartz) L.; m. Hanna Renate Cohn, Apr. 12, 1946; children— Martin Jacob, Barbara Diane. BSChemE, Coll. City N.Y., 1948; MS in Geology, U. Cin., 1951, PhD, 1953. Instr. U. Mich., 1952-53; asst. head photogeology sect. Gulf Oil Corp., Pitts., 1953-57; asst. prof. to prof. geomorphology Pa. State U., 1957-70; prof., head dept. geology U. Cin., 1970-75; dean Coll. of Mines U. Utah, 1975-83, dean Coll. Engring., 1978-83; pres. N.Mex. Tech., Socorro, 1983-93, pres. emeritus, 1993—. Bd. dirs. Pub. Svc. Co. of N.Mex.; cons. U.S. Army Engrs., Vicksburg, Miss., 1965-69, also major oil cos. Author: (with R.G. Ray) Aerial Photographs in Field Geology, 1965, (with D. Zillman) Energy Law; Contbr. articles to profl. jours. Mem. N.Mex. Environ. Improvement Bd., 1995—. With AUS, 1943-46. Fenneman fellow U. Cin., 1953. Fellow Geol. Soc. Am.; mem. Am. Assn. Petroleum Geologists, Am. Soc. Photogrammetry (Ford Bartlett award 1968), Soc. Econ. Paleontologists and Mineralogists, AIME (Disting. mem. 1981, Mineral Industries Edn., award 1986—), Assn. Western Univs. (chmn. bd. dirs. 1986-87), Sigma Xi. Home: 11509 Penfield Ln NE Albuquerque NM 87111-6526 Personal E-mail: lhlattman@aol.com.

LATTO, LEWIS M., broadcasting company executive; b. Duluth, Minn., Jan. 21, 1940; s. Lewis M. and Ethel S. L.; divorced; children: Aaron, Caroline. BA, U. Minn., 1963. Owner, mgr. Sta. KXTP, Duluth, 1965-94, Sta. WAKX-FM, 1974-94; owner Sta. KRBT-AM, WEVE-FM, Eveleth, Minn., 1978—, Sta. KGPZ-FM, Grand Rapids, Minn., 1995—. Mem. Duluth City Council, 1969-75, pres., 1974. Mem. Nat. Radio Broadcasters Assn. (dir.), Minn. Broadcasters Assn. (pres. 1992-93). Republican. Methodist. Office: Northland Radio Stas 5732 Eagle View Dr Duluth MN 55803-9498 E-mail: lewlatto@aol.com.

LATZA, WILLIAM D., lawyer; b. Neb., May 28, 1955; BS with distinction, Univ. Neb., Lincoln, 1977; grad. fellow, London Sch. Econ. & Polit. Sci.; JD, Georgetown Univ., 1981. Adminstrv. ptnr, insurance practice area Stroock & Stroock & Lavan LLP, NYC. Frequent writer, lectr. in field. Mem.: ABA, Internat. Assn. Insurance Receivers (legal counsel), Insurance Regulatory Examiners Soc., Soc. Fin. Examiners (gen. counsel), NY County Lawyers Assn., Internat. Bar Assn. (sec. on bus. law, com. on insurance), NY State Bar Assn. (insurance, negligence, compensation law sect.), Assn. Bar City NY (com. on insurance law 1998—2001), Omicron Delta Epsilon, Beta Gamma Sigma. Office: Stroock & Stroock & Lavan LLP 180 Maiden Ln New York NY 10038-4982 Office Phone: 212-806-5807. Office Fax: 212-806-6006. Business E-Mail: wlatza@stroock.com.

LAU, CHRISTOPHER SI-LUNG, pharmacologist, biomedical researcher; b. Canton, China, Sept. 1, 1951; s. Man-Wah Lau and Pik-Man Ho. AB, Duke U., 1975; PhD, Duke U., NC, 1982. Sr. scientist Mantech Environ. Scis., Research Triangle Park, NC, 1984—90; pharmacologist U.S. EPA, Research Triangle Park, NC, 1990—; rsch. assoc. Med. Coll. of Pa., Phila., 1982—84. Adj. asst. prof. Duke U. Med. Ctr., Durham, NC, 1984—; adj. prof. NC State U. Sch. of Vet. Medicine, Raleigh, NC, 2004—. Contbr. articles to profl. jours. Mem.: Internat. Soc. for Devel. Neuroscience, Soc. of Toxicology, Teratology Soc., Soceity for Neuroscience. Business E-Mail: lau.christopher@epa.gov.

LAU, DANNY T., mathematics professor, department chairman; b. Hong Kong, Aug. 12, 1959; arrived in U.S., 1978; s. Yim-Nam Lau and Yau-Ngor Ma; m. Christina M. Lau, June 12, 1981; children: Sharon, Charmaine, Joyce. BS, Brigham Young U., 1981; MS, Purdue U., 1983; PhD, Wash. State U., 1990. Assoc. prof., chair Mt. Mercy Coll., Cedar Rapids, 1989—98, Gainesville (Ga.) Coll., 1998—2002, prof., chair, 2003—; assoc. prof., chair Kennesaw (Ga.) State U., 2002—03. Mem.: Math. Assn. Am. Office: Gainesville Coll PO Box 1358 Gainesville GA 30503

LAU, DENYS T., research scientist, educator; b. Hong Kong; BA, Cornell U.; PhD, Johns Hopkins U. Rsch. assoc. Covance Health Economics and Outcomes Rsch., Inc., Washington; program analyst agy. healthcare rsch. and quality U.S. Dept Health & Human Svcs., Gaithersburg, Md.; rsch. fellow U. Mich., Pfizer, Ann Arbor, Mich.; asst. prof. Northwestern U., Chicago, 2004—. Bd. mem. Asian Pacific Islander HIV/AIDS Anti-Stigma Task Force, Chicago, Asian Pacific Islander Health Forum, Washington; co-founder, bd. mem. Asian Pacific Islander Queers United for Action, Washington; bd. mem. Asian Pacific Islander Gay, Lesbian, and Bisexual Task Force, Chicago. Recipient Marilyn Bergner Award in Health Services Rsch., Johns Hopkins U., Jay S. Drotman Meml. Award for Promising Young Pub. Health Profl., APHA, Director's Citation for Outstanding Performance, Agy. for Healthcare Rsch. and Quality; fellow Pub. Health Svc. Pre-Doctoral Tng. Grant, U.S. Dept of Health and Human Services; Pfizer Post-Doctoral fellow, U. of Mich./Pfizer. Mem.: APHA, Gerontol. Soc. Am., Acad. Health, Mortar Bd.

LAU, H. LORRIN, obstetrician, gynecologist; b. Honolulu, Hawaii, Apr. 21, 1932; s. Henry S. and Helen (Lee) L.; m. Maureen Lau; children: David, Marianne, Mike, Mark, Linda. AB cum laude, Harvard U., 1950-54; MD, Johns Hopkins U., 1954-58, MPH, 1970-71. Asst. prof. Sch. Med. Johns Hopkins U. (Balt.), 1964-82; assoc. prof. U. Hawaii, 1982-84; chief ob-gyn. St. Francis West Hosp., Honolulu, 1990-92, Kuakini Hosp., Honolulu, 1994-95. Fellow AMA; mem. ACOG, Internat. Soc. Biology and Medicine. Inventor pregnancy tests, helped introduce alpha-fetoprotein tests into obstetrics in USA, 1971. Home: 1121 Wilder Ave 1700B Honolulu HI 96822 Office: 1010 S King St Honolulu HI 96814-1701 Office Phone: 808-596-0164. Personal E-mail: drhllau@yahoo.com.

LAU, HARRY HUNG-KWAN, acoustical and interior designer, consultant; b. Hong Kong, May 8, 1938; s. Kang Hoi and Yuk Jing (Chan) L.; BArch, Ohio State U., 1965, MArch., 1966; postgrad. in archl. acoustics, MIT, 1967. Acoustical designer Bolt, Beranek & Newman, N.Y.C., 1967-69; archl. designer Marcel Breuer & Asscos., N.Y.C., 1969-70; archl. designer Edward L. Barnes & Assocs., N.Y.C., 1970-74; pres. MKC Design, N.Y.C., 1975-76; pres. Lau & Assocs., N.Y.C., 1977-2004; instr. of design N.Y. Inst. Tech., 1974. Summer grantee Harvard-Cornell Sardis Expdn., 1966. Mem. Acoustical Soc. Am., Nat. Council Interior Design, Am. Soc. Interior Design. Address: 30 E 95th St 7F New York NY 10128-0718

LAU, JOANNA T., information technology executive; BS in Computer Sci. and Applied Math., SUNY, Stony Brook; MS in Computer Engring., Old Dominion U., 1985; MBA in Bus. and Ops., Boston U., 1991; PhD (hon.), Suffolk U., 1999, Bentley Coll., 1998, Bryant Coll., 1997. Software engr. aerospace control systems dept. GE, 1981—83, consumer electronics ops. systems engr., 1983—85, CIM project mgr. aircraft engine bus. group, 1986—89; supr. mfg. engring. Digital Equipment Corp., 1989—90; pres., chmn. bd. LAU Acquisition Corp./LAU Technologies, Littleton, Mass., 1990—. Mem. Army Sci. Bd. Mem. Kennedy Libr. Found., Com. of 200. Named Nat. Turnaround Entrepreneur of the Yr., 1995, 8(a) Small Bus. Person of the Yr. for Mass., 1995; recipient Pinnacle award, Greater Boston C. of C., 1997, Leadership award to Women in Bus., New Eng. Coun., Young Engring. award, GE Aircraft Engine Group. Mem.: Young Pres.'s Orgn., Internat. Women's Forum, Assn. of U.S. Army, Nat. Def. Indsl. Assn.

LAU, LAWRENCE JUEN-YEE, economics professor, consultant; b. Guizhou, China, Dec. 12, 1944; arrived in U.S., 1961, naturalized, 1974; s. Shai-Tat and Chi-Hing (Yu) Liu. BS with great distinction, Stanford U., 1964; MA, U. Calif., Berkeley, 1966, PhD, 1969; D.Social Sci. honoris causa, Hong Kong U. Sci. and Tech. From acting asst. prof. econs. to assoc. prof. Stanford U., Palo Alto, Calif., 1966-76, prof., 1976—, Kwoh-Ting Li prof. econ. devel., 1992—; dir. Stanford Inst. Econ. Policy Rsch., 1997—99; vice chancellor The Chinese U. Hong Kong, 2004—. Co-dir. Asia/Pacific Rsch. Ctr., Stanford U., 1992-96; cons. The World Bank, Wash., 1976-; vice chmn. Bank of Canton of Calif. Bldg. Corp., San Francisco, 1981-85, Complete Computer Co. Far Eat Ltd., Hong Kong, 1981-89; bd. dirs. Taiwan Fund, Inc. Co-author (with D.T. Jamison): Farmer Education and Farm Efficiency, 1982, Models of Development: A Comparative Study of Economic Growth in South Korea and Taiwan, 1986, rev. edit., 1990, Econometrics and the Cost of Capital: Essays in Honor of Dale W. Jorgenson, 2000; co-author: (with C.H. Yoon) North Korea in Transition: Prospects for Economic and Social Reform, 2001; co-author: (with K.C. Fung and J.S. Lee) Direct Investment in China, 2005; contbr. articles to profl. jours. Adv. bd. Self-Help for Elderly, San Francisco, 1982—; bd. dirs. Chiang Ching-Kuo Found. for Internat. Scholarly Exch., 1989—; govs. coun. econ. policy advisors State of Calif., 1993-99; mem. Asian Art Commn., San Francisco, 1998-2001; mem. adv. coun. Innovation and Tech., Hong Kong, 2000-02. John Simon Guggenheim Meml. fellow, 1973, fellow Ctr. for Advanced Study in Behavioral Scis., 1982, Overseas fellow Churchill Coll., Cambridge U., Eng., 1984 Fellow Econometric Soc.; mem. Academia Sinica (academician), Conf. Research in Income and Wealth, Chinese Acad. Social Scis. (hon.), Internat. Eurasian Acad. Scis. (academician). Episcopalian. Office: The Chinese Univ Hong Kong Shatin Hong Kong Hong Kong Office Phone: 852-269-8600. Business E-Mail: lawrencelau@cuhk.edu.hk.

LAU, LUNINDA, director; D in Ednl. Leadership, Nova Southeastern U., 1998. Cert. sch. prin. N.J. State Dept. Edn. Adminstrv. asst. supt. Paramus Pub. Schs., NJ, 2000—02, coord. staff devel. & tech., 2002—. Office: Paramus Public Schs 145 Spring Valley Rd Paramus NJ 07652 Office Phone: 201-261-7800 3045.

LAU, PATRICK HING-LEUNG, radiologist, educator; b. Hong Kong, May 21, 1945; m. Peggy Lau; children: Eric, Chad. BS, St. Louis U., 1970; DO, Midwestern U., 1974. Diplomate Am. Bd. Radiology. Intern Grandview Hosp. Med. Ctr., 1974-75; pvt. practice family medicine, 1975—80; resident Mt. Sinai Med. Ctr., 1981-84; fellow Coll. Medicine U. Ill., 1984-85, radiology instr. Chgo., 1984-85; asst. prof. radiology Phila. Coll. Osteo. Medicine, 1985-86; chief imaging svcs. VA No. Ind. Healthcare Sys., Marion, 1988—; med. dir. radiology tech. program Ivy Tech. State Coll., 2001—. Contbr. articles to profl. jours. Dep. med. examiner, Monroe County, Mich., 1977-80; police surgeon Am. Law Enforcement Officers Assn., 1979-80. Named one of Am.'s Top Physicians, Consumers Rsch. Coun. Am., 2004—05; recipient Abbie Norman Prince award for Outstanding Svc., Mt. Sinai Med. Ctr., 1984, cert. of appreciation, Midwestern U., 1984, 1999, cert. recognition, Am. Osteo. Coll. Radiology, 1985, award of appreciation, SME Boy Scouts Am., 1991, Hands and Heart award VA Affairs, 1995, 2000, Exceptional Svc. award, VFW, 1999, Spl. Contbn. award, Dept. VA, 2004, Cert. of Appreciation, 2004. Mem. Am. Coll. Radiology, Radiol. Soc. N.Am. Office: VA No Ind Healthcare Sys 1700 E 38th St Marion IN 46953-4568

LAU, PAULINE YOUNG, chemist; b. Harbin, China, June 18, 1943; d. Ching-ju and Chuan-erh (Fu) Young; m. Roland Lau, Sept. 16, 1967 (div. 1990); 1 child, Joan Mann. BS in Med. Tech., Nat. Taiwan U., 1964; MS in Chemistry, Wayne State U., Detroit, 1967; PhD in Chemistry, 1984. Med. technologist Detroit Gen. Hosp., 1967-68; adminstrv. asst. in rsch. Purdue U., W. Lafayette, Ind., 1970-72; supr. chemistry dept. Raritan Valley Hosp., Greenbrook, N.J., 1973-75; head chemistry dept. Princeton (N.J.) Med. Ctr., 1975-80; mgr. S.E. region RIA Ctr., Columbia, S.C., 1980-82; rsch. chemist Med. Product dept. DuPont Co., Wilmington, Del., 1984-88; mgr. rsch./devel. Boehringer Mannheim Diagnostics, Indpls., 1988—. Com. mem. Nat. Com. on Clin. Lab. Stds., 1989—. Author: Clinical Chemistry Laboratory Procedures, 1977. Recipient Outstanding Product Devel. award, Boehringer Mannheim Co., 1990. Mem. Chinese Acad. and Profl. Assn. in Mid-Am. (bd. dirs. 1990—), Ind. Assn. Chinese Ams. (pres. 1993), Mt. Jade Assn. (chmn. biomed. div. 1990—), Ctrl. Ind. Clin. Biochemistry Forum (pres. 1993—), Am. Assn. Clin. Chemistry (chpt. treas. 1989-92, divsn. sec. 1992-93), Am. Chem. Soc. (chpt. bd. dirs. 1990-91), Ind. Chinese Profl. Assn. (v.p. 1990-91, pres. 1992-93), N.Am. Chinese Clin. Chemists Assn. (bd. dirs. 1988-91, pres. 1992—). Office: Roche Diagnostic Corp 9115 Hague Rd Indianapolis IN 46256-1025 Home: 4238 Suzanne Dr Palo Alto CA 94306-4335

LAU, STEPHEN C., surgeon; m. Dianne M. Hunt, Apr. 16, 1977; children: Anne Marie, Andrew. MBBS, U. Hong Kong, 1969. Diplomate Am. Bd. of Surgery, 1978, Am. Bd. of Thoracic Surgery, 1985. Resident W.Va. U. Hosp., Mongentown, W.Va., 1971—76; tchg. fellow Royal Alexandra Hosp., Alberta, Canada, 1976—77; attending surgeon Appalachian Regional Hosp., So. Williamson, W.Va., 1977—79; chief of surgery U.S. Pub. Health Svc. Hosp., Boston, 1979—81; attending surgeon St. Elizabeth Hosp., Boston, 1983—89, Fairmont Gen. Hosp., W.Va., 1991—, Davis Meml. Hosp., Elkins, W.Va., 2000—. Office: Stephen C Lau MD Ste 3 909 Gorman Ave Elkins WV 26241 Mailing: PO Box 1633 Elkins WV 26241 Office Phone: 304-637-8700. E-mail: stephenclau@medscape.com.

LAU, VINCENT W., lawyer; BA, Yale U., 1993; MA in higher Edn. Adminstrn., JD, Boston Coll., 1997. Bar: Mass. 1997, Fed. Dist. Ct., MA 1999. Assoc. Fletcher, Tilton & Whipple, P.C., Worcester, Mass., 1998—99, Flynn & Clark, P.C., Cambridge, 1999—. Assoc. editor (conference handbook) Advanced Immigration Solutions for Small Businesses and Entrepreneurs. Mem.: Am. Immigration Lawyers Assn. (co-chmn. New Eng. chpt. young lawyers divsn. com. 2002—03). Office: Flynn & Clark PC 1 Main St Cambridge MA 02142 Office Phone: 617-354-1550. Office Fax: 617-661-2576. Business E-Mail: vlau@flynnclark.com.

LAUB, DORI, psychiatrist; b. Chernovtsy, Romania, June 8, 1937; s. Moshe and Clara (Sattinger) Laub; children: Miri, Avi; m. Johanna Bodenstab. MD, Hebrew U./Hadassah Med. Sch., Jerusalem, Israel, 1961; MA in Clin. Psychology, Bar Ilan U., Ramat Gan, Israel, 1966. Diplomate Am. Bd. Psychiatry and Neurology; cert. in psychoanalysis; lic. Israel, Conn., N.Y., Mass. Intern Rambam Hosp., Haifa, Israel, 1962-63; resident Acre (Israel) Mental Hosp., 1965-66, Boston City Hosp., 1966-67; fellow in psychiatry Austen Riggs Ctr., Inc., Stockbridge, Mass., 1967-69; resident dept. psychiatry Yale U., New Haven, 1969; psychoanalytic tng. We. New Eng. Inst. for Psychoanalysis, 1968-79; psychotherapist, chief group psychotherapy program Conn. Mental Health Ctr., 1970-77; assoc. dir. mental health tng. Connecticut Valley Hosp., 1977-81, dir. residency tng. program, 1981-93, sr. attending physician psychosis study and treatment unit Conn. Mental Health Ctr., 1993-95; attending psychiatrist homeless outreach team Access Project, 1995—2000. Part-time pvt. practice in psychotherapy, 1972—2004, clinician 2004-; from instr. to assoc. clin. prof. dept. psychiatry Yale U., 1969—; co-vis. lectr. Yale Law Sch., 1994; acting dir. Genocide Study Program Yale U., 2000, 2003, dep. dir. trauma studies, 2001—. Co-author: Testimony-Crisis of Witnessing in Literature, Psychoanalysis and History, 1992; contbr. articles to profl. jours. Recipient Sigmund Freud prize, 1962. Fellow Am. Psychiat. Assn.; mem. AMA, Internat. Psychoanalytic Assn., Soc. for Traumatic Stress Studies. Home: 30 Ranch Rd Woodbridge CT 06525-1912 Office: 315 Whitney Ave Ste 2 New Haven CT 06511-3715 also: 267 William St Middletown CT 06457-3212

LAUB, WILLIAM MURRAY, retired utilities executive; b. Ft. Mills, Corregidor, Philippines, July 20, 1924; s. Harold Goodspeed and Marjorie M. (Murray) L.; m. Mary McDonald, July 26, 1947; children: William, Andrew, Mary, David, John. BSBA, U. Calif., Berkeley, 1947, LLB, 1950. Bar: Calif. 1951. Practice law, Los Angeles, 1951-55; with Southwest Gas Corp., Las Vegas, Nev., 1948-88, v.p., gen. counsel, 1958-60, exec. v.p., 1960-64, pres., chief exec. officer, 1964-82, chmn., chief exec. officer, 1982-88. Pres. Boulder Dam Area council Boy Scouts Am., 1967-69, So. Nev. Indsl. Found., 1967-68, So. Nev. Meth. Found., 1967-74; chmn. Nev. Equal Rights Commn., 1966-68; Chmn. Clark County Republican Central Com., 1964-66; nat. committeeman Nev. Rep. Com., 1968-80; trustee Sch. Theology at Claremont, Calif., 1977-2004, emeritus; trustee Inst. Gas Tech., 1983-89; nat. bd. advisors, coll. bus. and pub. adminstrn. The U. Ariz., 1985-89; bd. dirs. Alliance for Acid Rain Control, 1985-89; vice chmn., bd. trustees KNPR Pub. Radio Sta., 1996-2003, emeritus; dir. First Nat. Bank Nev., 1964-88; mem. Defense Orientation Conf. Assn., 1955-. Served to lt. USNR, 1941—45. Mem. ABA, Am. Gas Assn. (bd. dirs., chmn. 1986-87), Pacific Coast Gas Assn. (chmn. 1983), Calif. Bar Assn., Nat. Coal Coun., Def. Orientation Conf. Assn., Jonathan Club, Pauma Valley Country Club, Spanish Trail Golf and Country Club, Las Vegas Country Club. Office: 2810 W Charleston Blvd Ste 53 Las Vegas NV 89102-1906 Office Phone: 702-259-5241.

LAUBACH, ROGER ALVIN, accountant; b. Riegelsville, NJ, July 3, 1922; s. Harry and Daisy (Cyphers) L. Diploma in bus. adminstrn., Churchman Bus. Coll., Easton, Pa., 1941; BS cum laude in Acctg., Rider U., 1949. CPA NY, NJ. Acct. Coopers & Lybrand, CPAs, N.Y.C., 1949-60; asst. to treas. Coca-Cola Bottling Co. N.Y., N.Y.C., 1960-63; mgr. audits and systems Atlantic Rsch. Corp., Alexandria, Va., 1964-65; contr. Ely-Cruikshank Co., Inc., Realtors, N.Y.C., 1965-66, asst. treas., 1966-67, treas., dir., 1967-71; dir. N.Y. Fed. Savs. & Loan Assn., 1970-71; dir. Phila. Acctg. Ctr. Ogden Food Svc. Corp., 1971-72, treas., 1972-77; dir. corp. auditing Ogden Corp., N.Y.C., 1977-79; contr. Burlington County Cmty. Action Program, Burlington, N.J., 1981-84. With U.S. Army, 1942—46, ETO. Decorated Bronze Star, N.J. Disting. Svc. medal, 1998; recipient Cold War cert. recognition, 2000, Burlington County Mil. Svc. medal, 2001, Thank You Am. cert. for participation in liberation of France during World War II, Embassy of France. Mem. AICPA, ARC (vol. bloodmobile 1986—), Inst. Internal Auditors, N.Y. State Soc. CPAs, N.J. Soc. CPAs, Real Estate Bd. N.Y., SAR (registrar, geneal. 1995-2001, War Svc. medal, Liberty medal with 3 bronze oak leaf clusters, cert. of disting. svc.), VFW (life), Am. Legion (life), 100th Inf. Divsn. Assn., Soc. Colonial Wars (life), Laubach Family Assn. (book com. 1989-93), Nat. Trust for Hist. Preservation, Bucks County (Pa.) Hist. Soc., Warren County (N.J.) His. Soc., Delta Sigma Pi (life). Home: 39 Southgate Rd Mount Laurel NJ 08054-2932

LAUBE, LOIS RUTH, librarian; b. St. Peter, Minn., Oct. 23, 1946; d. Richard H. and C. Ruth (Rosel) Laube. BA, Valparaiso U., 1968; postgrad., George Washington U., 1968-69; MLS, Ind. U., 1971. Cert. librarian, Ind. Adminstrv. asst. Am. Hist. Assn., Washington, 1969-70; libr. social scis. div.

Indpls.-Marion County Pub. Libr., 1971-80, section mgr., 1981—2002; mgr. 2d fl. Ctrl. Libr., 2002—. Chmn. profl. relations com. Cen. Ind. Area Library Svcs. Authority, Indpls., 1989. Contbr. articles to profl. jours. Mem. Valparaiso U. Guild, 1980—, Eiteljorg Mus. Am. Indian and Western Art, Indpls., 1989—. Mem. ALA, Ind. Library Fedn., Beta Phi Mu. Avocations: physical fitness, gardening and wildflower crafts, american indian culture. Office: Indpls-Marion County Pub Libr PO Box 211 Indianapolis IN 46206-0211

LAUBE, ROGER GUSTAV, retired banker; b. Chgo., Aug. 11, 1921; s. William C. and Elsie (Drews) L.; m. Irene Mary Chadbourne, Mar. 30, 1946; children: David Roger, Philip Russell, Steven Richard. BA, Roosevelt U., 1942; postgrad., John Marshall Law Sch., 1942, 48-50; LLB, Northwestern U., 1960; postgrad., U. Wash., 1962-64. Cert. fin. cons. With Chgo. Title & Trust Co., Chgo., 1938-42, 48-50, Nat. Bank Alaska, Anchorage, 1950-72, mgr. mortgage dept., 1950-56, v.p., trust officer, mgr. trust dept., 1956-72; v.p., trust officer, mktg. dir., mgr. estate and fin. planning div. Bishop Trust Co., Ltd., Honolulu, 1972-82; instr. estate planning U. Hawaii, Honolulu, 1978-82; exec. v.p. Design Capital Planning Group, Inc., Tucson, 1982-83; pres., sr. trust officer, registered investment adviser Advanced Capital Advisory, Inc. of Ariz., Tucson, 1983-89; registered rep., pres. Advanced Capital Investments, Inc. of Ariz., Prescott, 1983-89; pres., chief exec. officer Advanced Capital Devel., Inc. of Ariz., Prescott, 1983-89; mng. exec. Integrated Resources Equity Corp., Prescott, 1983-89. Pres. Anchorage Estate Planning Coun., 1960-62, Charter mem., 1960-72, Hawaii Estate Planning Coun., 1972-82, v.p., 1979, pres., 1980, bd. dirs., 1981-82; charter mem. Prescott Estate Planning Coun., 1986-90, pres. 1988. Charter mem. Anchorage Community Chorus, 1946, pres., 1950-53, bd. dirs., 1953-72, Alaska Festival of Music, 1960-72; mem. Anchorage camp Gideons Internat., 1947-72, Honolulu camp, 1972-82, mem. Cen. camp, Tucson, 1982-85, Prescott, 1985-90, Port Angeles-Sequim Camp, 1990—; mem. adv. bd. Faith Hosp., Glenallen, Alaska, 1960—, Cen. Alaska Mission of Far Ea. Gospel Crusade, 1960—; sec., treas. Alaska Bapt. Found., 1955-72; bd. dirs. Anchorage Symphony, 1965-72; bd. dirs. Bapt. Found. of Ariz., 1985-90; bd. dirs., mem. investment com. N.W. Bapt. Found., 1991-97; mem. mainland adv. coun. Hawaii Bapt. Acad., Honolulu, 1982—; pres. Sabinovista Townhouse Assn., 1983-85; bd. advisers Salvation Army, Alaska, 1961-72, chmn., Anchorage, 1969-72, bd. advisers, Honolulu, 1972-82, chmn. bd. advisers, 1976-78; asst. staff judge adv. Alaskan Command, 1946-48; exec. com. Alaska Conv., 1959-61, dir. music Chgo., 1938-42, 48-50, Alaska, 1950-72, Hawaii, 1972-82, Tucson, 1982-85, 1st So. Bapt. Ch., Prescott Valley, Ariz., 1985-90; 1st Bapt. of Sequim, Wash., 1990-98; chmn. bd. trustees Hawaii, 1972-81, Prescott Valley, 1986-89, Sequim, Wash., 1991—; worship leader Waikiki Ch., 1979-82. 1st lt., JAGD, U.S. Army, 1942-48. Recipient Others award Salvation Army, 1972 Mem. Am. Inst. Banking (instr. trust div. 1961-72), Am. Bankers Assn. (legis. com., trust div. 1960-72), Nat. Assn. Life Underwriters (nat. com. for Ariz.), Yavapai County-Prescott Life Underwriters Assn. (charter), Anchorage C. of C. (awards com. 1969-71), Internat. Assn. Fin. Planners (treas. Anchorage chpt. 1969-72, exec. com. Honolulu chpt. 1972-82, Ariz. chpt. 1982-90, del. to World Congress Australia and New Zealand 1987), Am. Assn. Handbell Ringers. Baptist. Home: Sunland Country Club 212 Sunset Pl Sequim WA 98382-8515

LAUBE, STEVEN RICHARD, literary agent; b. Anchorage, Alaska, June 6, 1958; s. Roger Gustav and Irene Mary Laube; m. Lisa Kathryn Laube, Aug. 22, 1981; children: Trissina Rose, Geneva Jewel, Fiona Star. BA, Grand Canyon U., 1976—81. Gen. mgr. Berean Christian Stores, Phoenix, 1981—92; editl. dir. non-fiction Bethany Ho. Publishers, Bloomington, Minn., 1992—2003; lit. agt., pres. Steve Laube Agy., Phoenix, 2004—. Author: (book) God's Promises for Your Financial Success. Interim youth dir. Camelback Bible Ch., Paradise Valley, Ariz., 1993—94. Decorated Spl. Recognition award Mt. Hermon Writer's Conf.; recipient Store of the Yr., Christian Booksellers Assn., 1989, Golden Scroll Editor of the Yr., AWSA, 2002, Faculty of the Yr., Fla. Writer's Conf., 2002. Christian. Avocations: reading, basketball. Office: Steve Laube Agency 5501 N 7th Ave #502 Phoenix AZ 85013 Office Phone: 602-336-8910.

LAUCELLO, MICHAEL JAMES, lawyer; b. Utica, N.Y., Aug. 5, 1951; s. Joseph James and Rita Laucello; m. Victoria Pauline Ollino, Aug. 11, 1984; children: Michael J. Jr., Christina G. BA, Union Coll., 1973; JD, SUNY, Buffalo, N.Y., 1978. Bar: N.Y. 1978. Lawyer Kavinoky, Cook, et al., Buffalo, 1978—79, Phillips, Lytle et al., Buffalo, 1979—84; prin. law clk. N.Y. State Unified Ct. Sys., Rome, NY, 1984—89; pvt. practice lawyer Clinton, NY, 1989—. Vol. tchr. English Holy Cross Acad., Oneida Castle, NY, 2005; bd. dirs. Skenandoa Little League, Clinton, 1994—95. Mem.: Oneida County Bar Assn., N.Y. State Bar Assn., Phi Beta Kappa. Roman Catholic. Avocations: reading, swimming, golf, tennis, racquetball. Office: 40 Chenango Ave Clinton NY 13323

LAUCHENGCO, JOSE YUJUICO, JR., lawyer; b. Manila, Philippines, Dec. 6, 1936; came to U.S., 1962; s. José Celis Sr. Lauchengco and Angeles (Yujuico) Sapota; m. Elisabeth Schindler, Feb. 22, 1968; children: Birthe, Martina, Duane, Lance. AB, U. Philippines, Quezon City, 1959; MBA, U. So. Calif., 1964; JD, Loyola U., L.A., 1971. Bar: Calif. 1972, U.S. Dist. Ct. (cen. dist.) Calif. 1972, U.S. Ct. Appeals (9th cir.) 1972, U.S. Supreme Ct. 1975. Banker First Western Bank/United Calif. Bank, L.A., 1964-71; assoc. Demler, Perona, Langer & Bergkvist, Long Beach, Calif., 1972-73; ptnr. Demler, Perona, Langer, Bergkvist, Lauchengco & Manzella, Long Beach, 1973-77; sole practice Long Beach and L.A., 1977-83; ptnr. Lauchengco & Mendoza, L.A., 1983-92; pvt. practice L.A., 1993—. Mem. commn. on jud. procedures County of L.A., 1979; tchr. Confraternity of Christian Doctrine, 1972-79; counsel Philippine Presdl. Commn. on Good Govt., L.A., 1986. Chmn. Filipino-Am. Bi-Partisan Polit. Action Group, L.A., 1978. Recipient Degree of Distinction, Nat. Forensic League, 1955. Mem. Calif. Pub. Defenders Assn., Philippine-Am. Bar Assn. (life), U. Philippines Vanguard Assn. (life), K.C., Beta Sigma. Roman Catholic. Avocations: classical music, opera, romantic paintings and sculpture, camping, shooting. Office: PO Box 767 Los Angeles CA 90078-0767 Office Phone: 323-462-1555.

LAUDA, DONALD PAUL, dean; b. Leigh, Nebr., Aug. 7, 1937; s. Joe and Libbie L.; m. Sheila H. Henderson, Dec. 28, 1966; children: Daren M., Tanya R. BS, Wayne State Coll., 1963, MS, 1964; PhD, Iowa State U., 1966. Assoc. dir. Communications Center U. Hawaii, 1966-67; assoc. prof. indsl. arts St. Cloud (Minn.) State Coll., 1967-69; asst. dean Ind. State U., 1970-73; chmn. tech. edn. W.Va. U., 1973-75; dean Sch. Tech., Eastern Ill. U., Charleston, 1975-83; dean Coll. Health and Human Svcs. Calif. State U., Long Beach, 1983—2002, dean emeritus, 2002—. Cons. traditional Chinese medicine edn. Author: Advancing Technology: Its Impact on Society, 1971, Technology, Change and Society, 1978, 2d edit., 1985; contbr. articles to profl. jours. Pres. Council on Tech. Tchr. Edn.; dir. Charleston 2000 Futures Project, 1978-81. Served with USAR, 1957-59. EPDA research fellow, 1969-70; Eastern Ill. U. faculty research grantee, 1971 Mem. Future Soc. Internat. Tech. Edn. Assn., Coun. Tech. Tchr. Educators (pres., Tchr. of Yr. award 1978), World Future Soc., Internat. Tech. Edn. Assn. (pres. 1990), World Coun. Assn. Tech. Edn., Am. Vocat. Assn., Phi Kappa Phi (pres. 1993), Epsilon Pi Tau (Laureate citation 1982), Long Beach C. of C. (bd. dirs. 1995—), Japan Am. Soc. (adv. bd.). Office: Calif State U Coll Health & Human Svcs Long Beach CA 90840-0001 Personal E-mail: dlauda@aol.com. *Jobs and careers come through a great deal of effort, education, but, most importantly, through the help of others. It is this input that helps one clarify goals, gain new insights, and synthesize information. The process is reciprocal in that one helps others grow. Reflecting on the past always brings to mind people rather than degrees, positions, salaries, etc. When one loses sight of this, he/she is missing the greatest achievement of life.*

LAUDER, AERIN, cosmetics executive; d. Ronald and Jo Carole Lauder; 2 children. Degree, U. Pa. From dir. mktg. Prescriptives to v.p. global adv. Estée Lauder Inc., NYC, 1992—2001, v.p. global adv., 2001—04, sr. v.p. global creative directions, 2004—. Jr. assoc. Mus. Modern Art, NYC; bd. trustees Thirteen WNET, NYC; costume inst. visiting com. Met. Mus. Art, NYC; bd. trustees Animal Med Ctr.; advisory bd. NY Botanical Garden. Office: Estée Lauder Inc Corp HQ 767 Fifth Ave New York NY 10153*

LAUDER, EVELYN H., cosmetics executive; b. Vienna; arrived in U.S., 1940; m. Leonard A. Lauder, 1959; children: William, Gary. BA, Hunter Coll.; hon. degree, Muhlenberg Coll., 1996. Joined as edn. dir. Estée Lauder Cos., N.Y.C., 1959, v.p., sr. corp. v.p., 1989—. Photographer: (book) The Seasons Observed, 1994, An Eye For Beauty, 2002. Founder, chmn. Breast Cancer Rsch. Found., 1993—; mem. bd. overseers Meml. Sloan-Kettering Cancer Ctr.; trustee Ctrl. Pk. Conservancy Inc.; trustee emirata The Trinity Sch., N.Y.C.; bd. dirs. New Yorkers for Parks. Named Disting. Fgn. Born Citizen, Internat. Ctr., 1987; named one of 75 Most Influential Bus. Women, Crain's Newspaper, 1996, Women of Yr., Glamour mag., 1999, Top 200 Collectors, ARTnews Mag., 2004; recipient Spirit Achievement award, Albert Einstein Coll. Medicine, 1991, Mary Waterman award, Breast Cancer Alliance, 1998, Humanitarian award, Coun. Fashion Designers Am., 2001, award for excellence in philanthropy, Soc. Meml. Sloan-Kettering, 2001, Ellis Island Medal of Honor, Nat. Ethnic Coalition Orgns., 2001. Achievements include founder of The Breast Cancer Research Foundation, the largest national organization dedicated solely to breast cancer research; implementing breast cancer awareness programs from Pink Ribbon campaigns to illuminating world landmarks in a pink glow for Breast Cancer Awareness Month. Avocation: Collector of Modern art especially Cubism. Office: Estée Lauder Cos 767 5th Ave New York NY 10153-0023

LAUDER, GEORGE V., marine biologist; AB in biology, Harvard U., 1976, MA in biology, 1978, PhD in biology, 1979. Asst. to assoc. prof. anatomy U. Chgo., 1981—86; assoc. dean grad. studies, Sch. Biol. Scis. U. Calif., Irvine, 1987—96, prof. ecology and evolutionary biology, 1990—99; prof. organismic and evolutionary biology Harvard U., 1999—. Mem. editl. bd. Physiological and Biochemical Zoology, Jour. Morphology, Jour. Exptl. Biology. Contbr. articles to profl. jour. Fellow, Andrew W. Mellon Found., 1981. Fellow: AAAS, Zoological Soc. London, Linnean Soc. London; mem.: Internat. Soc. Neuroethology, Soc. Vertebrate Paleontology, Am. Soc. Zoologists, Soc. Exptl. Biology, Soc. Study Evolution, Soc. Systemic Biology, Soc. Neuroscience, Phi Beta Kappa, Sigma Xi. Office: Harvard U Mus Comparative Zoology 26 Oxford St Cambridge MA 02138 Business E-Mail: glauder@oeb.harvard.edu.

LAUDER, JO CAROLE, art association administrator; m. Ronald S. Lauder, July 1967; children: Aerin, Jane. Mem. bd. dirs. The Ronald S. Lauder Found.; pres. internat. coun. Mus. of Modern Art; mem. bd. trustees Ind. Curators Internat., Mt. Sinai Medical Ctr.; chmn. bd. dirs. Friends of Art & Preservation in Embasies. Named one of Top 200 Collectors, ARTnews Mag, 2004. Avocation: Collector of Old Masters; 19th and 20th century art, especially German. Office: Mus Modern Art 11 W 53rd St New York NY 10019

LAUDER, LEONARD ALAN, cosmetic and fragrance company executive; b. NYC, Mar. 19, 1933; s. Joseph H. and Estée (Mentzer) Lauder; m. Evelyn Hausner Lauder, July 5, 1959; children: William Phillip, Gary Mark. BS, Wharton Sch., U. Pa., 1954. With Estée Lauder Inc., NYC, 1958—, exec. v.p., 1962-72, pres., 1972-82, pres., CEO, from 1982, now chmn., CEO. Vice chmn. bd. CFTA, NYC, 1976—79. Bd dirs. Adv. Commn. on Trade Negotiations, Washington, 1983—87; trustee Aspen Inst. for Humanistic Studies, 1978; bd. govs. Joseph H. Lauder Inst. Mgmt. and Internat. Studies, 1983; chmn. & past pres. Whitney Mus. Art, NYC. Lt. USNR, 1955. Named one of Top 200 Collectors, ARTnews Mag., 2004; recipient (with Evelyn Lauder) Philanthropists of Yr., Greater NY Chapter of Nat. Soc. of Fund Raising Execs., 1993, American Art award, Whitney Mus. of Am. Art, 1996, Am. Spirit award, Nat. Retail Fedn., 1998, Ellis Island Medal of Honor, 2000. Mem.: Chief Execs. Orgn., French-Am. C. of C. in U.S. (coun. fgn. relations). Avocation: collector of modern art, especially Cubism. Office: Estée Lauder Cos Inc 767 5th Ave New York NY 10153-0023 Address: Whitney Mus Am Art 945 Madison Ave New York NY 10021*

LAUDER, RONALD STEPHEN, investor; b. N.Y.C., Feb. 26, 1944; s. Joseph H. and Estee (Josephine) (Mentzer) L.; m. Jo Carole Knopf, July 8, 1967; children: Aerin Rebecca, Jane Alexandra. Degree in French lit., U. Paris, 1964; BS in Internat. Bus., U. Pa., 1965. With Estee Lauder, Inc., Brussels, Paris, N.Y.C., 1965-83; chmn. Estee Lauder Internat., Inc. & Clinique Laboratories Inc.; dep. asst. Sec. of Def., Washington, 1983-85; ambassador to Austria Vienna, 1986-87; chmn., pres. Lauder Investments, Inc.; pvt. investor Ea. and Cen. Europe. Founder, chmn. Cen. European Devel. Corp. Author: Fighting Violent Crime in America, 1985 Mem. N.Y. State Econ. Devel. Bd., 1972-78; fin. chmn. N.Y. State Republican Com., 1979-82; chmn. 500 Club of N.Y. Rep. Com., 1979-83; trustee Mus. Modern Art, N.Y.C., 1975—, chmn. 1995-; pres. Neue Galerie, N.Y.C., 2001-; trustee, Mt. Sinai Med. Ctr., 1981—; Rep. candidate, Conservative nominee for Mayor of N.Y.C., 1989. Recipient Ordre De Merit, France, 1985, Disting. Pub. Svc. medal award Dept. Def., 1986; decorated Great Cross of the Order of Aeronautical Merit with White Ribbon, Spain, 1985; Ronald S. Lauder Drawing Gallery at Mus. Modern Art named in his honor, 1984; Named One of the World's Richest People, Forbes mag., 1999-2002; named one of the Top 200 Collectors, ARTnews mag., 2004 Avocation: Art Collector, Old Masters; 19th and 20th century art, especially German. Office: Estee Lauder Inc 767 5th Ave Ste 4200 New York NY 10153-0023

LAUDER, VALARIE ANNE, editor, educator; b. Detroit, Mar. 01; d. William J. and Murza Valerie (Mann) L. AA, Stephens Coll., Columbia, Mo., 1944; postgrad., Northwestern U. With Chgo. Daily News, 1944-52, columnist, 1946-52; lectr. Sch. Assembly Svc., also Redpath lectr., 1952-55; freelance writer for mags. and newspapers including New York Times, Yankee, Ford Times, Travel & Leisure, Am. Heritage, 1955—; editor-in-chief Scholastic Roto, 1962; editor U. N.C., 1975-80, lectr. Sch. Journalism, 1980—. Gen. sec. World Assn. for Pub. Opinion Rsch., 1988-95; nat. chmn. student writing project Ford Times, 1981-86; pub. rels. dir. Am. Dance Festival Duke U., 1982-83, lectr., instr. continuing edn. program, 1984. Contbg. editor So. Accents mag., 1982-86. Mem. nat. fundraising bd. Kennedy Ctr., 1962-63; bd. dirs. Chapel Hill Mus., Inc., 1996-98. Recipient 1st place award Nat. Fedn. Press Women, 1981, 1st place awards Ill. Women's Press Assn., 1950, 51. Mem. Pub. Rels. Soc. Am. (treas. N.C. chpt. 1982, sec. 1983, v.p. 1984, pres.-elect 1985, pres. 1986, chmn. coun. of past pres., chmn. 25th Ann. event 1987, del. Nat. Assembly 1988-94, S.E. dist. officer, nat. nominating com. 1991, 1st pres.'s award 1993), Women in Comms. (v.p. matrix N.C. Triangle chpt. 1984-85), N.C. Pub. Rels. (mem. Hall of Fame com.), DAR, Soc. Mayflower Desc. (bd. dirs. Ill. Soc. 1946-52), Chapel Hill Hist. Soc. (bd. dirs. 1981-85, 94-2001, chmn. pub. com. 1980-85, pres. 1996-2001), Chapel Hill Preservation Soc. (bd. trustees 1993-96, nominating com. 1994), N.C. Press Club (3d v.p. 1981-83, 2d v.p. 1983-85, pres. 1985, 1st pl. awards 1981, 82, 83, 84), Univ. Women's Club (2nd v.p. 1988), The Carolina Club, The Nat. Press Club. Office: U NC Sch Journalism and Mass Comm CB 3365 Chapel Hill NC 27599-0001 Office Phone: 919-843-8295.

LAUDER, WILLIAM P., cosmetics executive; married; 2 children. Degree, U. Pa.; student, U. Grenoble, France. Assoc. merchandising mgr. N.Y. Divsn./Dallas Store Macy's, 1985—86; from regional mktg. dir. Clinique USA to COO Estée Lauder Inc., N.Y., 1986—2003, COO, 2003—04, CEO, 2004—. Avocations: golf, skiing, tennis, hiking. Office: Estée Lauder Inc Corp HQ 767 Fifth Ave New York NY 10153

LAUDERDALE, VANCE, JR., anesthesiologist; b. N.Y.C., Sept. 11, 1923; MD, Columbia U., 1947. Diplomate Am. Bd. Anesthesiologists. Intern Kings County Hosp., N.Y.C., 1947-49; resident anesthesiology Presbyn. Hosp., N.Y.C., 1949-51; cons. emeritus anesthesiology Columbia-Presbyn. Med. Ctr., N.Y.C., 1985—; spl. lectr. anesthesiology Columbia U., 1985—. Fellow Am. Coll. Anesthesiologists; mem. AMA, Am. Soc. Anesthesiologists, N.Y. County Med. Soc. (mem. peer review com. bd. censors 1975-85).

LAUDONE, ANITA HELENE, lawyer; b. Boston, 1948; m. Colin E. Harley. AB, Conn. Coll., 1970; JD, Columbia U., 1973. Bar: N.Y. 1974. Law clk. to judge Fed. Dist. Ct., N.Y.C., 1973-74; assoc. Davis Polk & Wardwell, N.Y.C., 1974-78, Shearman & Sterling, N.Y.C., 1978-79; with Phelps Dodge Corp., N.Y.C., 1979-85, corp. sec., 1980-85, v.p., corp. sec., 1984-85. Editor: Columbia Law Rev., 1973.

LAUE, BRUCE ANTONIO, financial consultant, writer; b. N.Y.C., July 21, 1953; s. William Rollini and Yolande Violette (Dodelin) Laue; m. Sherry Lynn Locher, May 18, 1996. BA, Fairleigh Dickinson U., 1975. Mng. dir. Geneva Capital Resources, Inc., N.Y.C., 1992—. Chmn. scholarship com. Youth Found., N.Y.C., 1996—2001; mem. French Am. Friendship Found.; mem. adv. bd. Soldier's, Sailor's, Marines' and Airmen's Club, N.Y.C., 1988—; mem. St. George's Soc., N.Y.C., 1989—; steward New Eng. Soc., N.Y.C., 1983—; spl. legate to Principality of Seborga Internat. Federative Alliance of Sovereign Mil. Order of Temple of Jerusalem, 1998. Lt. col. intelligence officer Vets. Corps Arty., 1981—. Recipient Civic Commendation, Coun. City of N.Y., 1989, N.Y. State Hist. Mil. Command commendation, N.Y. Soc. Mil. and Naval Officers, 1998, N.Y. State Mil. Commendation medal, N.Y. State Dept. Mil. and Naval Affairs, 1993, Def. of Liberty medal, 2004. Mem.: Army and Navy Union, Masons, Order of Lafayette (pres.-gen. 1996—), Hospitaller of St. John of Jerusalem (Knight of Grace), Sovereign Order of Orthodox Knights, Old Guard City of N.Y., Nat. Gavel Soc. Roman Catholic. Home and Office: 243 W 70th St New York NY 10023-4318

LAUER, CLINTON DILLMAN, automotive executive; b. Joliet, Ill., Dec. 8, 1926; s. Thomas Ayscough and Francis (Dillman) L.; m. Lea Merrill, Dec. 9, 1950; children: Joanne L. Buckley, John C. BS, U. Ill., 1948; MBA, U. Pa., 1950. Supply mgr. automotive assembly div. Ford Motor Co., Dearborn, Mich., 1971-76, dir. body and assembly purchasing N.Am. automotive ops., 1976-83, exec. dir. N.Am. Automotive Ops. prodn. purchasing, 1983-87, v.p. purchasing and supply, 1987-92; pres. Lauer and Assocs., LLC, Bloomfield Hills, Mich., 1992—. Bd. dirs. Sanderson Industries. Mem. exec. bd. Detroit Area coun. Boy Scouts Am., pres., 1990-92; past bd. dirs. nat. and S.E. Mich. Jr. Achievement, Boys and Girls Club of S.E. Mich. With U.S. Army, 1944-46, 50-52. Mem. Oakland Hills Country Club, Bear Creek Golf Club, S.C. Yacht Club. Republican. Episcopalian. Avocation: golf. Home: 26 Ribaut Dr Hilton Head Island SC 29926-1986

LAUER, ELIOT, lawyer; b. NYC, Aug. 17, 1949; s. George and Doris (Trenk) L.; m. Marilyn Steinberg, June 5, 1977; children: Tamar Rachel, Ilana Jennifer, Michael Jonathan, Samuel Geoffrey. BA, Yeshiva U., 1971; JD cum laude, Fordham U., 1974. Bar: D.C. 1975, N.Y. 1975, U.S. Dist. Ct. (so. and ea. dists.) N.Y. 1975, U.S. Ct. Appeals (2d cir.) 1975, U.S. Supreme Ct. 1984. Assoc. Curtis, Mallet-Prevost, Colt & Mosle, N.Y.C., 1974-82, ptnr., 1982—. Counsel Keren-Or Inc., N.Y.C., 1985—; bd. dirs. Ctr. for Mid. East Peace and Econ. Cooperation, 1991—. Rep. Jewish Coalition, 2002—, Hebrew Acad. Long Beach, NY, 1985—, Young Israel Lawrence, Cedarhurst, NY, 1984—. Mem.: ABA, N.Y. State Bar Assn., Fed. Bar Coun., Assn. of Bar of City of N.Y. Republican. Office: Curtis Mallet-Prevost Colt & Mosle 101 Park Ave Fl 34 New York NY 10178-0061 Office Phone: 212-696-6192. Business E-Mail: elauer@cm-p.com.

LAUER, HARRY CURTIS, retired civil engineer; b. Jersey City, Jan. 23, 1927; s. Harry Carl and Sarah Cecilia Lauer; divorced; children: Harry Curtis, Pamela Elizabeth, Eric Rivard. BSCE, Ind. Inst. Tech., 1950. Rodman Nickel Plate R.R., Ft. Wayne, Ind., 1950-51; with Lederle Labs/Am. Cynamid, Water Supply, Pearl River, N.Y., 1951-52; engr. DuPont/Atomic Energy Plant Constrn., Aiken, S.C., 1952; resident engr. Western Electric/AT&T, Winston-Salem, N.C., 1952-54; plant and project engr. Universal Atlas Cement div. U.S. Steel, various locations, 1955-70; sr. resident mgr. constrn. GE, Columbia, Md. and Research Triangle Park, N.C., 1970-73; project mgr. J. A. Jones Constrn. Co., Charlotte, N.C., 1974-75; project mgr., constrn. mgr. Bendy Engring. Co., Santa Cruz, Calif. and St. Louis, Mo., 1975-85; chief civil engr. Arab Swiss Engring. Co., Cairo, 1983; constrn. and plant engr. Fla. Crushed Stone, Brooksville, 1984—92. Engr., investigator Bahama Cement Co., Freeport, The Bahamas, 1967. Engr., investigator report Silo Failure Investigation (Commendation award 1967). Chief, founder YMCA Indian Guides, Columbia, Md., 1970; deacon Christian Ch., 1963, 68. With USN, 1944-46. Mem. Am. Inst. Plant Engr. (cert., del. to nat. conv. 1987), Ky. Cols., Am. Legion, Elks, Moose, Hernando Beach Yacht Club. Avocations: sailing, construction projects. Home: 27208 Townsend Blvd Brooksville FL 34601-4369 Office: Fla Crushed Stone/CPL Cement Plant Rd Brooksville FL 34601

LAUER, JAMES LOTHAR, physicist, researcher; b. Vienna, Aug. 2, 1920; came to U.S., 1938, naturalized, 1943; s. Max and Friederike (Rapaport) L.; m. Stefanie Dorothea Blank, Sept. 4, 1955; children: Michael, Ruth. AB, Temple U., 1942, MA, 1944; PhD, U. Pa., 1948; postgrad., U. Calif., San Diego, 1964-65. Scientist Sun Oil Co., Marcus Hook, Pa., 1944-52, spectroscopist, 1952-64, sr. scientist, 1965-77; asst. prof. U. Pa., 1952-55; lectr. U. Del., 1952-58; rsch. fellow mech. engring. U. Calif., San Diego, 1964-65; rsch. prof. mech. engring. Rensselaer Poly. Inst., Troy, N.Y., 1978-85, prof. mech. engring., 1985-93, prof. mech. engring. emeritus, 1993—; rsch. sci. Ctr. Magnetic Recording Rsch. U. Calif., San Diego, 1993-95, vis. scholar applied mechanics and engring. sci., 1995—. Sr. faculty summer rsch. fellow NASA-Lewis Rsch. Ctr., 1986-87; vis. prof. Ctr. for Magnetic Rec. Rsch., U. Calif., San Diego, 1991; cons. Digital Equipment Corp., 1992-94, NASA-Lewis Rsch. Ctr., 1993-95. Author: Infrared Fourier Spectroscopy--Chemical Applications, 1978; co-author: Handbook of Raman Spectroscopy, 2001; mem. editl. bd. Tribology Letters, 1995—; contbr. articles to profl. jours.; patentee in field. Active Penn Wynne Civic Assn., 1959—77, Country Knolls Civic Assn., 1978—93. Sun Oil Co. fellow, 1964-65, Air Force Office Sci. Rsch. grantee, 1974-86, NASA Lewis Rsch. Ctr. grantee, 1974-86, Office Naval Rsch. grantee, 1979-82, Army Rsch. Office grantee, 1985-89, NSF grantee, 1987-95, Innovative Rsch. award Soc. Mech. Engrs., 1991, Discovery awards NASA, 1993, 96. Fellow: Inst. Physics (U.K.); mem.: AAAS (life), Optical Soc. Am. (emeritus), Soc. Applied Spectroscopy, Am. Phys. Soc. (emeritus), Am. Chem. Soc. (emeritus), Materials Rsch. Soc., Sigma Chi. Jewish. Home: 7622 Palmilla Dr Apt 78 San Diego CA 92122-4710 Office: U Calif San Diego La Jolla CA 92037 *My advice to those contemplating a career in experimental research is to give much thought to these points: (1) interest, enthusiasm, willingness to work are only basics, (2) a loving and understanding wife is essential, and (3) the knowledge that one can create one's own success at any time is the driving force.*

LAUER, JEANETTE CAROL, dean, history educator, writer; b. St. Louis, July 14, 1935; d. Clinton Jones and Blanche Aldine (Gideon) Pentecost; m. Robert Harold Lauer, July 2, 1954; children: Jon, Julie, Jeffrey. BS, U. Mo., St. Louis, 1970; MA, Washington U., St. Louis, 1973, PhD, 1975. Assoc. prof. history St. Louis C.C., 1974-82, U.S. Internat. U., San Diego, 1982-90, prof., 1990-94, dean Coll. Arts and Scis., 1990-94, rsch. prof., 1997—. Author: Fashion Power, 1981, The Spirit and the Flesh, 1983, Til Death Do Us Part, 1986, Watersheds, 1988, The Quest for Intimacy, 5th edit., 2002, 6th edit. 2006, No Secrets, 1993, The Joy Ride, 1993, For Better of Better, 1995, True Intimacy, 1996, Intimacy on the Run, 1996, How to Build a Happy Marriage, 1996, Sociology: Contours of Society, 1997, Windows on Society, 1999, 7th edit., 2005; Becoming Family: How to Build a Stepfamily that Works, 1999, How to Survive and Thrive in an Empty Nest, 1999, Troubled Times: Readings in Social Problems, 1999, Love Never Ends, 2002, The Play Solution: How to Put the Fun Back into your Relationship, 2002, Social Problems and the Quality of Life, 10th edit., 2005, Marriage and the Family: The Quest for Intimacy, 2005. Woodrow Wilson fellow, 1970, Washington U. fellow, 1971-75. Mem.: Am. Hist. Assn., Orgn. Am. Historians. Democrat. Presbyterian.

LAUER, LEN J., telecommunications industry executive; BS in Managerial Econ., U. Calif., San Diego. With IBM; pres., CEO Bell Atlantic Corp., NJ, 1996—98; pres. consumer svcs. group global mkts. group Sprint Corp., Overland Park, Kans., 1999, pres. global markets group, 2000—03, pres.,

COO, 2003—. Bd. dirs. Children's Mercy Hosp., Maplewood Ptnrs., Nat. Orgn. on Disability, Virgin Mobile USA. Bus. coun. steering com. Nelson-Atkins Mus. Art. Office: Sprint Corp 6200 Sprint Pkwy Overland Park KS 66251

LAUER, MATT, broadcast journalist; b. Dec. 30, 1957; m. Annette Roque Lauer, Oct. 1998; children: Jack Matthew, Romy. BA, U. Ohio. Prodr. WOWK-TV, Huntington, W.Va., 1979—80; program host various locations, 1980—88; substitute host Day's End, ABC-TV, 1989, Esquire Show, King Prodns./Lifetime, 1988—89, 9 Broadcast Plaza, WWOR-TV, N.Y.C., 1989—91; with WNBC, N.Y.C., 1992—96; co-anchor News 4/Live at Five, N.Y.C., 1993—96; news anchor NBC News' Today Show, N.Y.C., 1994—96, co-anchor, 1997—. Office: NBC News "Today" Show 30 Rockefeller Plz Fl 3D New York NY 10112-0002*

LAUER, RONALD MARTIN, pediatric cardiologist, researcher; b. Winnipeg, Man., Can., Feb. 18, 1930; m. Eileen Pearson, Jan. 12, 1959; children: Geoffrey, Judith Lauer. BS, U. Man., 1953, MD, 1954. Diplomate Am. Bd. Pediatrics. Asst. prof. pediatrics U. Pitts., 1960-61; asst. prof. pediatrics U. Kans., 1961-67, assoc. prof. pediatrics, 1967-68; prof. pediatrics, dir. pediatrics cardiology U. Iowa, 1968-95, vice chmn. pediatrics, 1974-82, prof. pediatrics and preventive medicine 1980— . Recipient Sci. Couns. Disting. Achievement award Am. Heart Assn., 1991, award of meritorious achievement, 1998, Eugene Braunwald Mentorship award, 2002, named Disting. Scientist, 2004; Founder's award Am. Acad. Pediatrics, 1997. Office: U Iowa Coll Medicine Divsn Pediat Cardiology 200 Hawkins Dr Iowa City IA 52242-1009 Office Phone: 319-356-2839. Business E-Mail: ronald-lauer@uiowa.edu.

LAUER, WARREN, lawyer; b. Lusk, Wyo., Dec. 3, 1951; BS in Agr., U. Wyo., 1976, JD, 1980. Bar: Wyo. 1981. Pvt. practice, Laramie, Wyo. Bd. dirs. U. Wyo. Coll. Law Alumni Assn., pres., 2002—03; bd. dirs., treas. Laramie Regional Airport. Contbr. articles to profl. jours. Mem. pres. coun. U. Wyo.; mem. state small bus. air quality adv. panel, 1994—97; mem. bd. adjustment Laramie Zoning Bd., 1983—89; mem. Albany County Planning and Zoning Commn., 1998—2000. Mem.: ABA, Wyo. Trial Lawyers Assn., Wyo. State Bar (commr. 1998—2001, sec.-treas. 2002—03, v.p. 2003—04, pres.-elect 2004—), Albany County Bar Assn. (sec., treas. 1995, v.p. 1996, pres. 1997). Office: 208 Garfield St Ste 200 A Laramie WY 82070 Office Phone: 307-742-7288. Office Fax: 307-745-5502.

LAUFER, HANS, developmental biologist, educator; b. Germany, Oct. 18, 1929; s. Sol and Margarete (Freundlich) L.; m. Evelyn Green, Oct. 31, 1953 (dec. May 2001); children: Jessica, Marc, Leonard. BS, CCNY, 1952; MA, Bklyn. Coll., 1953; PhD (James fellow), Cornell U., Ithaca, N.Y., 1954. Research and teaching asst. Cornell U., 1953-57; NRC fellow Carnegie Instn. of Washington, 1957-59; asst. prof. biology Johns Hopkins U., 1959-65; assoc. prof. U. Conn., Storrs, 1965-72, prof., 1972—98, rsch. prof., 1998—. Vis. prof. Karolinska Inst., Stockholm, 1972, Charles U., Prague, 1974, Yale U., 1980, Harvard U., 1987-90, Hebrew U., Jerusalem, 1988, Ben-Gurion U., Beer-Sheva, 1997; Rosenstiel vis. scholar Brandeis U., 1974; participant Nat. Acad. Scis.-Czechoslovak Acad. exchange program, 1974, 77; ad hoc mem. study sect. tropical medicine NIH, 1981, mem., 1982-85; Conklin Meml. fellow Marine Biology Lab., Woods Hole, Mass., 1956, Lalor fellow, 1962, 63, mem. staff, embryology course, 1968-72, mem. corp., 1962, corp. trustee, 1978-82, mem. exec. com., 1979-80; vis. scholar Case Western Res. U., 1962; mem. NSF-NATO Fellowship Rev. Panel, 1974, 76 Contbg. author numerous books; assoc. editor Jour. Exptl. Zoology, 1969-73, 90-93, Archives Insect Physiology and Biochemistry, 1983-95, Invertebrate Reprodn. and Devel., 1984-86, mng. editor, 1991—; contbr. numerous articles to profl. jours. Recipient Rsch. Svc. award NIH, 1989, Marcus Singer medal for rsch., 1986, 95; NATO sr. fellow, 1973, fellow Lady Davis Trust, Hebrew U., 1988; Japan Soc. Promotion of Sci. Fell., 1980; Rosenstiel scholar Brandeis U., 1973; Dozor vis. prof., Ben Gurion U., 1997. Fellow AAAS (chmn. sect. biology 1975), Royal Entomology Soc. London (fgn. fellow); mem. Internat. Soc. Devel. Biology, Internat. Soc. Invertebrate Reprodn. and Devel. (mem. exec. coun. and v.p. 1995—), Rsch. Couns. (nat. bd. on grad. edn. of conf. bd. 1971-75), Am. Soc. Zoology (chmn. divsn. developmental biology 1981-82), Soc. Devel. Biology, Am. Soc. Cell Biology, European Soc. Comparative Endocrinology, Am. Assn. Advancement Aging Rsch., Internat. Soc. Differentiation, Tissue Culture Assn. (coun. 1979-82), World Aquaculture Soc., Conn. Acad. Sci. and Engring. Home: 57 Davis Rd Storrs Mansfield CT 06268-2525 Office: U Conn Dept Molecular & Cell Biology U-3125 91 N Eagleville Rd Storrs Mansfield CT 06269-3125 Office Phone: 860-486-4117. E-mail: laufer@uconn.edu.

LAUFER, LEONARD JUSTIN, management consultant; b. Hartford, Conn., Sept. 30, 1965; s. Hans and Evelyn Alice (Green) L.; m. Terry Gushner; children: Arianna Olivia, Eli Tyler. AB, Harvard U., 1987; MBA, U. Pa., 1992. Assoc. The MAC Group Gemini Cons., N.Y.C., 1992-93; cons. First Manhattan Cons. Group, N.Y.C., 1994; prin. KLH Assocs., White Plains, NY, 1994—. Prin. Argus Info. and Adv. Svcs., LLC, White Plains, NY, 1995—. Mem.: Sunningdale Country Club. Home: 2 Richbell Rd Scarsdale NY 10583-4422 E-mail: llaufer@argusinformation.com.

LAUFER, MARK VLADIMIR, retired engineering educator; b. Kiev, Ukraine, Sept. 30, 1910; arrived in U.S., 1994; s. Vladimir Ieseevich and Ida (Naumovna) Laufer; m. Raisa Lvovna Bespalko, Oct. 21, 1977 (dec.); 1 child, Tatyana; m. Vera Mikhaylovna Vaks, Sept. 25, 1993 (dec. Nov. 2003). Diploma in engring., Kiev Poly. Inst., 1936, M, Tashkent Poly. Inst., Uzbekistan, 1943. Prof. Motion Picture Engr. Inst., Kiev, 1936—41, chief chair, 1944—53; chief engr. Motion Picture Studio, Tashkent, 1942—43; prof. Poly. Inst., Kiev, 1954—78, ret., 2004—. Cons. Acad. Scis. Ukraine, Kiev, 1937—41, Sci. Rsch. Inst., Kiev, 1961—77; pres. Assoc. Magnetic Rec., Kiev, 1937—77. Author: Theory of Magnetic Recording, 1980, Bases on Record Magnetical Carrier, 2004; editor: Questions Radioelectronics, 1962—77. Capt. USSR Air Force, 1941—45. Recipient Hon. medal, Acad. Scis. USSR, 1959, Hon. emblem, Ministry of Comm., 1961. Mem.: N.Y. Acad. Scis. Achievements include 30 inventions. Avocations: swimming, gardening. Home: 174 Ave A Apt 6F New York NY 10009 Office Phone: 212-674-1382.

LAUFER, MILTON RUBÉN, concert pianist, music educator; b. Skokie, Ill., June 28, 1972; s. Guillermo and Carmen Alicia Laufer; m. Valeska Wittek, May 8, 2002. MusB, U. Mich., Ann Arbor, 1995; MusM, Rice U., Houston, 1998, Dr. in Musical Arts, 2003; performer's cert., Gnessin Sch. Music, Moscow, 1990. Phoenix prof. fine arts Peace Coll., Raleigh, NC, 2001—. Artistic dir. Williamson Ctr. for the Performing Arts, Raleigh, NC, 2005—. Editor: (musical composition) La Vega by Isaac Albeniz. Named Man of Yr., Cuban Med. Assn., 1986; recipient Stillman Kelly Award, Nat. Fedn. Music Clubs, 1987, Silver Medal, Stravinsky Internat. Piano Competition, 1988, Young Keyboard Artists Internat. Piano Competition, 1989, Gold Medal, Union League Civic Arts Found., 1990, Nena Wideman Internat. Piano Competition, 1995, Cert. of Merit, Aspira Found. Ill., 2005; Brown Scholar, Rice U., 1999, Fulbright Scholar to Spain, 2000—01. Avocations: cooking, travel. Office Phone: 919-508-2290. Personal E-mail: mlaufer@miltonlaufer.com.

LAUFER, NATHAN, cardiologist; b. Montreal, Mar. 12, 1953; came to U.S., 1981; s. Jack and Pearl (Brachfeld) L.; m. Judy Franceska Egett, Sept. 2, 1986; 1 child, Andrew. DCS, McGill U., 1972, MD, 1977. Diplomate Nat. Bd. Med. Examiners, Am. Bd. Internal Medicine; cert. Profl. Corp. Physicians Que. Intern, resident U. Toronto, Can., 1977-81; fellow cardiology U. Mich., Ann Arbor, 1981-83, faculty dept. cardiology, 1983-84; cardiologist Affiliated Cardiologists, Phoenix, 1984-2001, mng. cardiologist, 1996-2001; med. dir. Heart & Vascular Ctr. Ariz., 2001—; chief cardiovascular svcs. Banner Inteалla Med. Ctr., 2004—. Dir. coronary care Good Samaritan Hosp., Phoenix, 1986—92, dir. interventional cardiology, 1987—; vis. prof. Chigasaki Tokushi-kai Med. Ctr., Kanagawa-ken, Japan, 1988, Leningrad Postgrad. Med. Inst., St. Petersburg, Russia, 1991; bd. dirs. Integrated Cardiovascular Group, Maricopa Med. Ctr., 2002—04. Contbr. articles to profl. jours. Fellow ACP, Am. Coll. Cardiology, Am. Coll. Chest Physicians, Royal Coll. Physicians and Surgeons Can.; mem. AMA, N.Am. Soc. Pacing and Electrophysiology, Soc. Cardiac Angiography and Intervention, Am. Assn. Nuclear Cardiology, Ariz. Med. Assn., Can. Cardiovascular Soc., Maricopa County Med. Assn., Cardiovascular Soc. Ariz. (founder, pres.). Avocations: skiing, tennis, computers, music, films. Home: 9100 N 55th St Paradise Valley AZ 85253-1632 Office: Heart & Vascular Ctr Ariz 1331 N 7th St Ste 375 Phoenix AZ 85006-2712 Office Phone: 602-307-0070.

LAUFER, WILLIAM HERVEY, artist, printmaker; b. Newark, Apr. 2, 1934; s. Edward Basil and Grace (Krudop) L.; m. Guida Miller Jackson, Feb. 14, 1986. Student, Trinity Coll., Hartford, Conn., 1952-53, New Sch. for Social Rsch., N.Y.C., 1971-73; AA, SUNY, Albany, 1973. Commd. ensign USN, 1960, advanced through grades to lt. comdr., 1968, ret., 1973; exhibition artist-printmaker The Woodlands, Tex., 1973—; founder Third Coast Letter Press, 1993—. Vis. lectr. in art Stephen F. Austin State U., Nacogdoches, Tex., 1998. Author, artist: Indochina Suite, 1994, Surrogates, 1995, Four Sea Interludes, 1996, P: An Excursus Into Liminal Space, 1997, Laughing Woman, 1998, Judith & Bluebeard: A Little Something for the Millennium, 1999, Voice: Some Music in the Sanskrit Mode, 1999, Selected Sanskrit Translations from the Bhagavad Gita and RG Veda, 2000; Watching the Worlds Go By, Poetry by Omar S. Pound, 2001; two prose poems, New Tex., Ctr. for Tex. Studies, 2003. Mem. Assn. Difusora obra Grafica Internat. (Barcelona, Spain), Guild Bookworkers.

LAUFF, GEORGE HOWARD, biologist; b. Milan, Mich., Mar. 23, 1927; s. George John and Mary Anna (Klein) L. BS, Mich. State U., 1949, MS, 1951; postgrad., U. Mont., 1951, U. Wash., 1952; PhD, Cornell U., 1953. Fisheries research technician Mich. Dept. Conservation, 1950; teaching asst. Cornell U., 1952-53; instr. U. Mich., 1953-57, asst. prof., 1957-61, asso. prof., 1961-62; research asso. Gt. Lakes Research Inst., U. Mich., 1954-59; dir. U. Ga. Marine Inst., 1960-62; asso. prof. U. Ga., 1960-62; research coord. Sapelo Island Research Found., 1962-64; dir. Kellogg Biol. Sta., 1964-90; prof. dept. fisheries and wildlife and zoology Mich. State U., East Lansing, 1964-91, prof. emeritus, 1991—. Mem. cons. and rev. panels for Smithsonian Inst., Nat. Water Commn., NSF, Nat. Acad. Sci., Am. Inst. Biol. Sci., U.S. AEC, Inst. Ecology, others. Editor: Estuaries, 1967, Experimental Ecological Reserves, 1977. Served with inf. U.S. Army, 1944-46. Office of Naval Research grantee; U.S. Dept. Interior grantee; NSF grantee; others. Fellow AAAS; mem. Am. Inst. Biol. Sci., Am. Soc. Limnology and Oceanography (pres. 1972-73), Ecol. Soc. Am., Freshwater Biology Assn., INTECOL, Societas Internationalis Limnologiae, Orgn. Biol. Field Stas., Sigma Xi, Phi Kappa Phi. Home: PO Box 53185 Kalamazoo MI 49005-3185 Office: 3700 E Gull Lake Dr Hickory Corners MI 49060-9505 Business E-Mail: lauff@msu.edu.

LAUFMAN, HAROLD, surgeon, consultant; b. Milw., Jan. 6, 1912; s. Jacob and Sophia (Peters) L.; m. Marilyn Joselit, 1940 (dec. 1963); children: Dionne Joselit Laufman Weigert, Laurien Laufman Kogut; m. June Friend Moses, 1980 (dec. 1999). BS, U. Chgo., 1932; MD, Rush Med. Coll., 1937; MS in Surgery, Northwestern U., Chgo., 1946, PhD, 1948. Diplomate: Am. Bd. Surgery. Intern Michael Reese Hosp., Chgo., 1936-39; fellow in gen. surgery St. Marks Hosp., London, Northwestern U. Med. Sch., Cook County Hosp., Hines VA Hosp., 1939-46; attending surgeon Michael Reese Hosp., 1940-53; mem. faculty Northwestern U., 1941-65; from clin. asst. to prof., attending surgeon Passavant Meml. Hosp., Chgo., 1953-65; prof. surgery, history of medicine Albert Einstein Coll. Medicine, N.Y.C., 1965-81, prof. emeritus, 1982—; dir. Inst. Surg. Studies, Montefiore Hosp. and Med. Ctr., Bronx, N.Y., 1965-81; pvt. practice gen. and vascular surgery Chgo., 1941-65, N.Y.C., 1965-82; ret. professorial lectr. surgery Mt. Sinai Sch. Medicine, N.Y.C., 1979-83, emeritus, 1983—; attending surgeon Mt. Sinai Hosp., N.Y.C., 1979-83. Cons., lectr. in field; chmn. FDA Classification Panel Gen. and Plastic Surgery Devices, 1975-78; pres. Harold Laufman Assocs., Inc., 1977-2003, sr. ptnr., 1988-2004. Author: (with S.W. Banks) Surgical Exposures of the Extremities, 1953, 2d edit., 1986, (with R.B. Erichson) Hematologic Problems in Surgery, 1970, Hospital Special Care Facilities, 1981, The Veins, 1986; chmn. editorial bd.: Diagnostica, 1974-79; mem. editl. bd. Surgery, Gynecology and Obstetrics, 1974-92, Infection Control, 1980-88, Med. Instrumentation, 1972-83, Med. Rsch. Engring., 1972-79; contbr. articles to sci. publs. Chmn. bd. dirs. N.Y. Chamber Soloists, 1974-80, Chamber Music Conf. and Composers Forum of the East, 1975-91, pres., 1987-90. Maj. AUS, 1942-46. Recipient James IV Traveling Professorship in Surgery, Israel, Vienna and Moscow, 1963, Disting. Alumnus award, Rush Med. Coll., 1993, U. Chgo. Sch. Medicine, 1999. Fellow: ACS, Am. Surg. Assn.; mem.: Surg. Infection Soc. (councillor 1980—84, founding mem.), Soc. Surgery Alimentary Tract (founding mem.), Internat. Cardiovasc. Soc., Soc. Vascular Surgery, N.Y. Surg. Soc., Ctrl. Surg. Assn., Western Surg. Assn., Societe Internationale de Chirurgie, Am. Med. Writers Assn. (pres. 1968—69), Am. Assn. Healthcare Cons., Assn. Advancement Med. Instrumentation (pres. 1974—75, chmn. bd. 1976—77), Harmonie Club (N.Y.C.), Sigma Xi, Alpha Omega Alpha, Zeta Beta Tau. Home and Office: 31 E 72nd St New York NY 10021-4131

LAUGHLIN, CHRISTEL RENATE, translator, consultant; b. Berlin, Dec. 18, 1940; came to U.S., 1966; d. Werner Wilhelm and Rosa Ida (Conrad) Friedrich; m. Phillip Edward Laughlin, July 1, 1966; 1 child, Christina Rosa. Cambridge proficiency diploma, Davies's Sch., London, 1960; French lang. diploma, U. Paris, 1961; Italian lang. diploma, Centri Europei Lingua, Florence, Italy, 1961; BA in Translating, U. Geneva, 1964; accredited travel agt., N.Am. Sch. Travel, Newport, Calif., 1976. Mem. touring svc. Swiss Touring Club, Geneva, 1962-63; hostess, interpreter Intercontinental Hotel, Geneva, 1964, Swiss Nat. Exhbn., Lausanne, 1964; exec. sec. Intercom S.A., Geneva, 1964-65, Soc. Luchard, Paris, 1965-66; outside saleswoman Hunnicutt Travel, Ft. Worth, 1974-76; pres. Simon Stevens Laughlin Travel, Ft. Worth, 1976-81; cons., translator K.T. Lendt & Co., N.Y.C., 1969-96; tax acct. Tarrant Operators, Inc., Ft. Worth, 1996-98. Market rsch. analyst Power Base, Denver, 1997; cons. Schwartzkopf Cosmetics, Duesseldorf, Germany, 1997; traffic cons. ADAC-Automobil Club Germany, Munich, 1997. Pres. Symphony League Ft. Worth, 1972-74; juror host family, interpreter Van Cliburn Internat. Piano Competition, Ft. Worth, 1973-97; host family interpreter XX World Gymnastics Championships, Ft. Worth, 1979, U.S. Gymnastics Internat., Ft. Worth, 1982. Mem. AAUW, Nat. Assn. Market Rsch. Analysts, Bot. Rsch. Inst. Tex. (sponsor), Arts Coun. Ft. Worth, Modern Art Mus. Fort Worth. Avocations: tennis, skiing, classical music, opera, travel. Home: 6212 Indian Creek Dr Fort Worth TX 76107-3526 E-mail: texasmanlaughlin@hotmail.com.

LAUGHLIN, DAVID EUGENE, materials scientist, educator, metallurgist, consultant; b. Phila., July 15, 1947; s. Eugene L. and Myrtle M. (Kramer) L.; m. Diane Rae Seamans, June 13, 1970; children: Jonathan, Elizabeth, Andrew, Daniel BSc, Drexel U., 1969; PhD, MIT, 1973. Asst. prof. materials sci. Carnegie-Mellon U., Pitts., 1974-78, assoc. prof., 1978-82, prof., 1982—, Alcoa prof. phys. metallurgy, 2001—. Rsch. scientist Oxford (Eng.) U., 1985; vis. scientist Alcoa Tech. Ctr., Pa., 1996. Editor: Solid-Solid Phase Transformations, 1982; category editor of copper: Am. Soc. Metals-Nat. Bur. Stds. Phase Diagram Program, 1981-94; assoc. editor: Metall. Trans., 1982-87, editor, 1987—; contbr. more than 350 articles to profl. jours.; holder 8 patents Mem. sch. bd. Trinity Christian Sch., Pitts., 1976-85, 87-95, pres., 1978-83, sec., 1988-91, pres., 1991-94; ruling elder Covenant Presbyn. Ch., Pitts., 1982-96; foster parent Children's Home of Pitts., 1984-90; bd. dirs. Christian Schs. Internat., 1991-98; vestry mem. Ch. of the Ascension, 1998—, clk., 1999—2000, warden, 2001—. Recipient Ladd Tchg. award Carnegie-Mellon U., 1975, B.R. Teare award for excellence in engring. edn., 1999, Outstanding Rsch. award Carnegie-Mellon U.; postdoctoral fellow Nat. Acad. Scis., 1974. Fellow Am. Soc. Metals; mem. Metall. Soc. AIME, Am. Sci. Affiliation, Materials Rsch. Soc., IEEE Magnetics Soc. Avocations: sports, books. Home: 2357 Mcnary Blvd Pittsburgh PA 15235-2779 Office: Carnegie-Mellon U Dept Materials Sci Eng Pittsburgh PA 15213 Office Phone: 412-268-2706. Business E-Mail: Laughlin@cmu.edu.

LAUGHLIN, FELIX B., lawyer; b. New Orleans, Dec. 4, 1942; m. Betty Gayle Laughlin. BS with honors, JD with honors, U. Tenn., 1967; LLM, Georgetown U., 1971. Bar: Tenn. 1967, D.C. 1972, U.S. Ct. Claims 1969, U.S. Tax Ct. 1968, U.S. Dist. Ct. D.C. 1972, U.S. Ct. Appeals (D.C. cir.) 1988, U.S. Ct. Appeals (fed. cir.) 1992, U.S. Supreme Ct. 1970. With interpretation divsn. Office Chief Counsel IRS, 1967-71; assoc. Dewey Ballantine LLP, Washington, 1972-74, ptnr. & chmn. tax dept., 1975—. Dir. Friends of U.S. Nat. Arboretum, Nat. Bonsai Found. (pres.). Fellow ABA (tax sect.); mem. Fed. Bar Assn. (chmn. tax sect. 1989), Met. Club (Washington), George Town Club (Washington), Order of Coif, Sigma Alpha Epsilon, Phi Eta Sigma, Phi Kappa Phi, Phi Delta Phi. Office: Dewey Ballantine LLP 1775 Pennsylvania Ave NW Washington DC 20006-4605 Office Phone: 202-862-1040. Office Fax: 202-862-1093. Business E-Mail: flaughlin@deweyballantine.com.*

LAUGHLIN, GREGORY H. (GREG LAUGHLIN), former congressman; b. Bay City, Tex., Jan. 21, 1942; BA, Tex. A&M U.; LLB, U. Tex. Asst. dist. atty. Harris County, Tex., 1970-74; pvt. practice Tex.; mem. 101st-104th Congresses from 14th Tex. dist., Washington, D.C., 1989-97; of counsel, Legis. Affairs, Public Policy, Energy Policy practices Patton Boggs, LLP, Washington, 1997—. Founder & co-chmn. U.S. / Former Soviet Union Energy Caucus. Col. USAR, active Persian Gulf, Oper. Desert Storm, 1991. Office: Patton Boggs LLP 2550 M St NW Ste 800 Washington DC 20037-1301 Office Phone: 202-457-5662. Office Fax: 202-457-6315. Business E-Mail: glaughlin@pattonboggs.com.*

LAUGHLIN, JAMES HAROLD, JR., lawyer; b. Charleston, W.Va., July 18, 1941; s. James Harold and Pearl Ruby L.; m. Eleanor Blackford Watson, II, Aug. 3, 1968; children: C. Michelle, Jeanette C., Cheryl Adele. BS in Chem. Engring., W.Va. U., 1964; JD, Am. U., 1968. Bar: D.C. 1968, Va. 1969. Atty. Am. Cyanamid Co., Wayne, N.J., 1968-70, Xerox Corp., Rochester, N.Y., 1971-77; ptnr. Benoit, Smith & Laughlin, Arlington, Va., 1977-93, Lane & Mittendorf, LLP, Washington, 1993-97, Shook, Hardy & Bacon, LLP, Washington, 1997-99, Arter & Hadden, LLP, Washington, 2000-01, Swidler Berlin Shereff Friedman, LLP, 2001—05, Holland & Knight, LLP, 2005—. Mem. ABA, Am. Intellectual Property Law Assn. (bd. dirs. 1976-79, treas. 1982-85, councilman 1993-94), Va. State Bar (chmn. PTC sect. 1982-83), Nat. Coun. Patent Law Assns. (Va. del. 1983-2002), Nat. Inventors Hall of Fame Found. (bd. dirs. 1988-93, pres. 1991-92). Office: 2099 Pennsylvania Ave NW Washington DC 20006 Office Phone: 202-828-1866. E-mail: jim.laughlin@jlaughlin.com.

LAUGHLIN, LARRY, communications media executive; b. Taunton, Mass. Grad. Providence Coll. With Taunton Daily Gazette, Mass., AP, Boston, 1976—78, Providence, 1978—82, corr., 1979—82, news editor Richmond, Va., 1982—88, bur. chief No. New England Concord, NH, 1988—. Office: 2 Capital Plz 400 Concord NH 03301-4911

LAUGHLIN, M. PAGE DURKEE, artist; b. Phila., May 7, 1921; m. Henry P. Laughlin, 1941; 5 children. Student, Phila. Coll. Art, Am. U., Hood Coll.; DFA (hon.), Mt. St. Mary's Coll., 2001. Mem. bd. Frederick (Md.) Arts Coun.; mem. arts bd. State of Md.; pres. Montgomery Couunty (Md.) Soc. Aux.; bd. dirs. Frederick County YMCA, pres.; bd. dirs. Frederick Cmty. Concert, United Way Frederick County; past state pres. Daus. Founders Patriots Am. Recipient Alex de Tocqueville award United Way, Pub. Svc. cert. Mental Health Assn., 1995, Pub. Svc. cert. Heartly House, 1995, (with H. P. Laughlin) Benefactor award Frederick County Mental Health Assn., 1996, Good Samaritan of Yr. award Frederick Meml. Hosp., 1999. Mem. Nat. Congress Patriotic Orgns. (charter, Nat. Svc. award 1995), Mensa, D.C. Mayflower Soc. (hon. life), Rotary (sec. inter-city inner wheel 1994-95, founder, 1st pres., Paul Harris fellow 1989). Avocations: genealogy, computers, embroidery, history, reading. Address: Buckingham's Choice 3200 Baker Cir Unit I-035 Adamstown MD 21710-9656 E-mail: page.laughlin@erols.com.

LAUGHLIN, NAOMI MYERS, realtor; b. Oliver, Ill., Mar. 11, 1913; d. Jesse and Mary Grace (Macke) Myers; m. Otis Alton Worthington, July 24, 1936 (dec. Apr. 1948); m. Cyril James Laughlin, Feb. 19, 1955. BA, George Washington U., 1934. Cert. assn. exec. Realtor, Silver Spring, Md., 1943-50, 70—. Recipient 1st A.V. Pisani Lifetime Achievement award, Capital Area Realtors Assn. Mem. AAUW (hon., past pres.), Realtors Land Inst. (hon., pres. 1976-77, ind. land specialist), Montgomery County (Md.) Bd. Realtors (exec. v.p. 1950-70, pres. fed. credit union 1981-84, Lifetime Achievement award, 2003), Manor Country Club (hon.). Democrat. Roman Catholic. Home: 13716 New Hampshire Ave Silver Spring MD 20904-6215

LAUGHLIN, ROBERT B., physics professor; b. Visalia, Calif., Nov. 1, 1950; m. Anita Rhona Perry, Apr. 22, 1979; children: Nathaniel David, Todd William. AB in Math, U. Calif., Berkeley, 1972; PhD in Physics, MIT, 1979. Postdoctoral fellow Bell Tel. Labs., 1979—81. Lawrence Livermore Nat. Lab., 1981—82; research scientist Lawrence Livermore Nat Lab, 1982—; assoc. prof. physics Stanford (Calif.) U., 1985—89, prof. physics, 1989—, Anne T. and Robert M. Bass prof. Sch. Humanities and Scis., 1992—, prof. applied physics, 1993—. Lectr. in field. Author: A Different Universe: Reinventing Physics from the Bottom Down, 2005; contbr. articles to profl. jours. With U.S. Army, 1972—74. Named Eastman Kodak lectr., 1989, Van Vleck lectr., 1994; recipient E.O. Lawrence award for Physics, 1985, Franklin Inst. medal, 1998, Nobel Prize in Physics, 1998; fellow, IBM, 1976—78. Fellow: Am. Phys. Soc. (Oliver E. Buckley prize 1986); mem.: NAS, AAAS (fellow), Aspen Ctr. Physics, Am. Acad. Arts and Scis. (fellow, 1990). Office: Stanford U Dept Physics LAM Rm 342 476 Lomita Mall Stanford CA 94305*

LAUGHLIN, STEVEN L., advertising executive; b. 1948; Copy writer Fuller Biety Connell Agy., Milw., 1968-74, Cramer Krusselt Co., Milw., 1974-75; with Laughlin/Constable Inc., Milw., 1976—, pres., ptnr., creative dir., writer, ptnr. Office: Laughlin/Constable Inc 207 E Michigan St Milwaukee WI 53202-4996

LAUGHLIN, WILLIAM EUGENE, retired electric power industry executive; b. Sheffield, Ala., May 4, 1936; s. Rawlie Wayne and Nina Louise (Campbell) L.; m. Donna Lynn Blackburn, Jan. 3, 1958; children: Kevin McGregor, Christopher Scott, Laura Shannon, Alison Paige. BS, Auburn U., 1961. Registered profl. and electrical engr., Ala., Tenn., Miss. Elec. engr. Dept. Power, Water and Gas, City of Sheffield, 1961-66; chief engr., asst. mgr. Electric Plant Bd., Bowling Green, Ky., 1966-76; systems mgr. Bowling Green Mcpl. Utilities, 1975-77; gen. mgr. Fayetteville (Tenn.) Electric Systems, 1977-81, Talquin Electric Coop. Inc., Quincy, Fla., 1981—2002. Bd. dirs., v.p. Seminole Electric Coop., Inc., Tampa, Fla.; pres. Fla. Rural Electric Coop. Assn., Tallahassee. Pres. Boys Club, Bowling Green, 1972; v.p. Bowling Green C. of C., 1975, Fayetteville C. of C., 1979; dist. chmn. Boy Scouts Am., Bowling Green, 1972, Fayetteville, 1978; pres. Fayetteville United Way, 1980. Mem. Nat. Rural Elec. Coop. Assn. (mem. regional com., nat. water task force 1995), Am. Water Works Assn., Rotary (bd. dirs. 1986-87, pres. Quincy club 1996-97), Fayetteville 1978-79, Paul Harris fellow), Kiwanis (dir. Bowling Green club 1973-74). Democrat. Mem. Ch. of Christ. Home: 2110 Ellicott Dr Tallahassee FL 32308-0818

LAUGHMAN, CHRISTOPHER THEODORE, building services administrator; b. Lakenheath, Eng., May 4, 1969; s. Lyle William and Sharon Ann Laughman; m. Tamara Lynn Buchheit, Oct. 16, 1999; 1 child, Abigail Rose. BS, Ctrl. Mo. State U., 1991; MA with honors, Webster U., St. Louis, 1998. Br. mgr. ABM Janitorial Svcs., St. Louis, 2000—03, Kansas City, Mo., 2003—. Mem.: Internat. Facility Mgmt. Assn. (assoc.), Inst. Real Estate Mgmt. (assoc.), Bldg. Owners and Mgrs. Assn. (assoc.), Toastmasters Internat. (assoc.), Kans. City Club (assoc.), KC (assoc.), Sigma Tau Gamma (life). Roman Catholic. Avocations: golf, wine, cigars. Office: ABM Janitorial Svcs 1927 McGee St Kansas City MO 64108 Home Phone: 816-842-3397; Office Fax: 816-842-3397. Personal E-mail: claughman@abm.com.

LAUGHNER, THOMAS CHRIS, information technology manager; b. McKeesport, Pa., Sept. 7, 1965; s. Frank Thomas and Donna Jean Laughner; m. Lori Ellen DeMien, June 5, 1971; children: Sara Elaine Young, Allison Marie, Michael Ryan, Benjamin Kyle. BS, U. Ariz., 1987; MA, George Wash. U., 1999; PhD, Andrews U., 2004. Acting dir., Kaneb Ctr. tchg. and learning U. Notre Dame, Ind., 2001—03, assoc. dir., ednl. tech. & svcs., 2003—. Various Harris Prairie Ch. of Christ, Granger, Ind., 1999—2004. Mem.: Educause. Office: U Notre Dame 115B DeBartolo Hall Notre Dame IN 46556 Office Phone: 574-631-5545. Personal E-mail: tclaughner@yahoo.com. E-mail: laughner@nd.edu.

LAUGHREY, NANETTE KAY, federal judge; b. Cheyenne, Wyo., Feb. 11, 1946; m. Christopher Sexton Kelly; children: Hugh, Jessica Katherine. BA, UCLA, 1967; JD, U. Mo. Columbia, 1975. Bar: Mo. 1975, U.S. Dist. Ct. (we. dist.) Mo. 1975, U.S. Ct. Appeals (8th cir.) 1976, U.S. Supreme Ct. 1978. Asst. atty. gen. Mo. Atty. Gen.'s Office, Kansas City, 1975-79; assoc. Craig Van Matre, P.C., Columbia, 1980-83; assoc. prof. law U. Mo. Columbia, 1983-87, prof. law, 1987-89, William H. Pittman prof. law, 1989-96; judge U.S. Dist. Ct. (we. dist.) Mo., Kansas City, 1996—. Mcpl. judge City of Columbia, 1979-83; vis. prof. law U. Iowa, 1990; dep. atty. gen. Mo. Atty. Gen.'s Office, 1992-93. Contbr. articles to profl. jours. Bd. dirs. Columbia Housing Authority. Mem.: ABA, Mo. Bar Assn., Am. Law Inst., U. Mo. Alumni Assn., Am. Whitewater Assn., Mo. Whitewater Assn. Office: US Dist Ct 400 E 9th St Ste 7452 Kansas City MO 64106-2670

LAUGHTER, BENNIE M., corporate lawyer; AB with honors, U. N.C., 1973; JD, Georgetown U., 1976. Bar: N.C. 1976, D.C. 1977, Ill. 1979, Ga. 1987. V.p., gen. counsel, corp. sec. Shaw Industries, Dalton, Ga., 1986—. Office: Shaw Industries Inc 616 E Walnut Ave PO Box 2128 Dalton GA 30722-2128

LAULAINEN-SCHEIN, DIANA LYN, history professor, editor; d. Robert Deane and Jean Laulainen; m. Joel Corey Schein, May 27, 1995; children: Ariana Carolyn Schein, Serena Caitlyn Schein, Jordan William Schein, Jared Royse Schein. BA, Washington U., 1989; MA in History, U. Minn., 1997, PhD, 2004. Editor Mosby Pub., St. Louis, 1990—95; tchg. asst. U. Minn., Mpls., 1996—97, instr., 1997—99; faculty assoc. Ariz. State U., Tempe, 2003—. Editor: Pediat. Neurology Jour., 1997—; contbr. articles to profl. jours. Girl scout leader/ svc. team mem. Girl Scouts, Scottsdale, Ariz., 2002—; newsletter editor, webmaster Laguna PTO, Scottsdale, Ariz., 2004—. Scholar, Ednl. Comm. Found., 1985—89, WR Konneker/Washington U., 1986—89; Mellow fellow, Va. Hist. Soc., 2001, Mary McEwen Schimke fellow, Wellesley Coll., 2001—02, Union Pacific Rsch. grantee, U. Minn., Ctr. for Early Modern History, 2001—02, Union Pacific Microfilm grantee, 2001—02, Travel grantee, History Sci. Soc., 2002. Mem.: Omohundro Inst. Early Am. History, N.Am. Conf. on Brit. Studies, Am. Hist. Assn. Presbyterian. Achievements include research in Comparative Counterpoints: Witchcraft Accusations in Early Modern Lancashire and the Chesapeake. Avocations: travel, photography, genealogy.

LAULE, GERHARD HELMUT, chemistry educator, researcher; b. Wilhelmshaven, Germany, June 24, 1949; came to U.S., 1951; s. Helmut Adolph and Rosemarie Luci (Hoffmann) L.; m. Danielle Jeane Guyer, Aug. 17, 1991. BS in Chemistry, U. Ctrl. Ark., 1976; MS in Instrumental Scis., U. Ark., 1986. Lab. supr. Ark. Dept. Health, Little Rock, 1977-81; grad. rsch. asst. U. Ark., Little Rock, 1984-86; grad. tchg. fellow U. Oreg., Eugene, 1986-88; instr. chemistry Seminole (Okla.) State Coll., 1988—, pres. faculty senate, 1992-93. Rsch. assoc. Okla. State U., Stillwater, 1993—; chair math./sci. engring. divsn., Seminole State Coll., 1998-02. With USAF, 1968-72, Vietnam. Mem. Am. Chem. Soc. Avocations: bicycling, sailing, camping. Office: Seminole State Coll 2701 State St Seminole OK 74868-1901 E-mail: laule_g@ssc.cc.ok.us.

LAULICHT, MURRAY JACK, lawyer; b. Bklyn., May 12, 1940; s. Philip and Ernestine (Greenfield) L.; m. Linda Kushner, Apr. 4, 1965; children: Laurie Hasten, Pamela Hirt, Shellie Davis, Abigail Herschmann. BA, Yeshiva U., 1961; LLB summa cum laude, Columbia U., 1964. Bar: N.Y. 1965, N.J. 1968, U.S. Supreme Ct. 1976. Legal staff Warren Commn., Washington, 1964; law clk. Hon. Harold R. Medina U.S. Ct. Appeals, 1964-65; assoc. Kaye, Scholer, Fierman, Hays & Handler, N.Y.C., 1965-68; ptnr. Lowenstein, Sandler, Brochin, Kohl & Fisher, Newark, N.J., 1968-79, Pitney, Hardin, Kipp & Szuch, Florham Park, N.J., 1979—. Mem. N.J. Consumer Affairs Adv. Com., 1991-93; mem. N.J. Commn. on Holocaust Edn., 1991—, chmn. 1992-95; mem. N.J. Commn. on Character Edn., 2002; pres. Jewish Edn. Assn., 1981-84, Jewish Fedn. Metro West, 1996-99, Edah, 2001-02, chmn. Cmty. Rels. Com., 1988-91, chmn. com. on religious pluralism, 1999-2002; exec. comm. Coun. of Jewish Fedn., 1996-99; trustee United Jewish Cmtys., 1999-2003; bd. govs. Jewish Agy. Israel, 2004—. Recipient Julius Cohn Young Leadership award Jewish Fedn. Metrowest, 1976. Mem. ABA, N.J. State Bar Assn. (dist. X ethics com. 1986-89, bd. editors N.J. Law Jour. 1986-93), N.J. Lawyer Mag. (chmn. 1993-95). Democrat. Avocations: jewish studies, communal activities. Home: 59 Cummings Cir West Orange NJ 07052-2268 Office: Pitney Hardin Kipp & Szuch PO Box 1945 200 Campus Dr Florham Park NJ 07932-1007 Office Phone: 973-966-8030. Business E-Mail: mlaulicht@pitneyhardin.com.

LAUMANN, EDWARD OTTO, sociology educator; b. Youngstown, Ohio, Aug. 31, 1938; m. Anne Elizabeth Solomon, June 21, 1980; children: Christopher, Timothy; children by previous marriage: Eric, Lisa. AB summa cum laude, Oberlin Coll., 1960; MA, Harvard U., 1962, PhD, 1964. Asst. prof. sociology U. Mich., Ann Arbor, 1964-69, assoc. prof., 1969-72; prof. sociology U. Chgo., 1973—, George Herbert Mead Disting. Service prof., 1985—, dean divsn. of social scis., 1984—92, provost, 1992—93, chmn. dept., 1981—84, 1997—99, 2002—03. Bd. govs. Argonne Nat. Lab., 1992-93. Author: Prestige and Associations in an Urban Community, 1966, Bonds of Pluralism, 1973, (with Franz U. Pappi) Networks of Collective Action, 1976, (with John P. Heinz) Chicago Lawyers, 1982, (with David Knoke) The Organizational State, 1987, (with John P. Heinz, Robert Nelson and Robert Salisbury) The Hollow Core, 1993, (with John Gagnon, Robert Michael, Stuart Michaels) The Social Organization of Sexuality, 1994, (with Robert Michael, John Gagnon, Gina Kolata) Sex in America, 1994, (with Robert T. Michael) Sex, Love and Health, 2001, (with Stephen Ellison, Jenna Mahay, Anthony Pain, Yoosik Youm), The Sexual Organization of the City, 2004, (with John Heinz, Robert Nelson, Rebecca Sandefur) Urban Lawyers, 2005; editor Am. Jour. Sociology, 1978-84, 95-97. Mem. sociology panel NSF, Washington, 1972-74; commr. CBASSE, NRC, 1986-91; chair bd. trustees NORC, 2001—; trustee U. Chgo. Hosps., 1992-93; mem. Panel on Elder Mistreatment, 2000-02. Fellow AAAS (chmn. sect. K 2001—04), Soc. Sci. Study of Sexuality, Internat. Acad. Sex Rsch.; mem. Sociol. Rsch. Assn., Am. Sociol. Assn., Population Assn. Am. Office: U Chgo 1126 E 59th St Chicago IL 60637 Office Phone: 773-702-8691. E-mail: e-laumann@uchicago.edu.

LAUMONT, PHILIPPE EMILE, communications executive; b. Liege, Belgium, June 17, 1944; came to U.S., 1957; s. Gustave J. and Germaine (Cattet-Thellier de Poncheville) L.; m. Anne Colton Adams, July 19, 1978; children: Anne Sophie, Julia Adams, Laura Philippa. BA, U. Louvain, Belgium, 1964, MA, 1965; MBA, Columbia U., 1978. Film producer CBS Inc., N.Y.C., 1969-78; pres. Laumont Labs Inc., N.Y.C., 1979—, Laumont Photographics, 1993—, Laumont Editions, 1998—. Mem. Coffee House Club, Ausable Club. Office: Laumont Editions 333 W 52nd St New York NY 10019-6238 E-mail: pl@laumont.com.

LAUN, LOUIS FREDERICK, government official; b. Battle Creek, Mich., May 19, 1920; s. Louis Frederick and Roena (Graves) L.; m. Margaret West, Jan. 25, 1947; children: Nancy, Kathryn Webb, Margaret. BA, Yale U., 1942. Asst. advt. mgr. Bates Fabrics, Inc., N.Y.C., 1946-48; asst. to pres., indsl. and public relations Bates Mfg. Co., Lewiston, Maine, 1948-55; advt. dir. Burlington Industries, N.Y.C., 1955-57; gen. merchandising mgr. Celanese Fibers Co., N.Y.C., 1957-60, v.p., dir. mktg., 1960-63, exec. v.p. mktg., 1963-64; pres. Celanese Fibers Mktg. Co. div. Celanese Corp., 1964-71, also v.p. corp., 1964-71; asso. adminstr. ops. SBA, Washington, 1973, dep. adminstr., 1973-77; pres. Am. Paper Inst., N.Y.C., 1977-86; asst. Sec. Commerce for Internat. Econ. Policy Dept. of Commerce, Washington, 1986-89, exec. br. commr., H elsinki Commn. on Security and Cooperation in Europe, 1988-89; cons. Nat. Exec. Svc. Corp, 1989—2001. U.S. pulp and paper rep. food and agrl. orgns. UN; bd. dirs. Overseas Pvt. Investment Corp., Noranda Aluminum, Inc.; exec. br. mem. Commn. on Security and Cooperation in Europe (Helsinki Commn.); vol. cons. Nat. Exec. Svc. Corps, 1989-2001. Bd. dirs. N.Y. Bd. Trade, Better Bus. Bur. N.Y., Alliance to Save Energy, Bus. Adv. Com. on Fed. Reports; bd. dirs., mem. exec. com. The Grace Commn. on Govt. Waste; indsl. asst. to chmn. Opportunities Industrialization Ctrs. Am.; nat. adv. coun. SBA; chmn. Rep. Industry Workshop program; field dir. Com. for Re-election of Pres., 1972; trustee Taft Sch.; mem. exec. com. President's Pvt. Sector Survey on Cost Control; chmn. Kids to Kids Internat., 1999; bd. dirs. New Castle Hist. Soc., 1999-2001, Edwin Gould Svcs. for Families and Children, 1997-2001, United Way of No. Westchester, 1998-2001. Lt. col. USMC, 1942-46. Decorated Bronze Star; recipient Human Rights award Anti-Defamation League, 1968; Achievement award Textile Vets. Assn., 1970; named Young Man of Yr. Lewiston-Auburn C. of C., 1953, Man of Yr. Textile Salesman Assn., 1970, Man of Yr. Fabric Salesmen's Guild, 1971; Gold medal for disting. service SBA, Citation Merit Taft Sch., 1988. Mem. Color Assn. U.S. (sec.), Man-Made Fiber Producers Assn. (chmn. 1967-69), Yale Club (N.Y.C.), Sleepy Hollow Country Club (Scarborough, N.Y.), Met. Club (Washington), Mid-Ocean Club (Bermuda). Home and Office: 25 Spring Ln Chappaqua NY 10514-2607 Personal E-mail: lflcl@aol.com.

LAUNDRA, KENNETH H., sociology educator; b. Hemlock, Mich., May 29, 1967; s. Robert and Ronnie J. Neumann; m. Tamyra Laundra, Aug. 7, 1993. BS in Psychology, Mich. State U., 1990; MA in Sociology, Ctrl. Mich. U., 1995; PhD in Sociology, Utah State U., 1999. Dir. Alpha House, Midland, Mich., Opportunity Ctr., Bay City, Mich.; asst. prof. sociology So. Utah U., Cedar City, Utah. Bd. mem. Obis House, Cedar City. Author: (book) Freeland: Delinquency in Rural America, 2005. Activist So. Utah Wilderness Alliance. Recipient Outstanding Paper award, Utah Acad. Scis., Arts & Letters, 2005. Avocations: skiing, golf, sailing. Office: So Utah U 301 W Center Cedar City UT 84720

LAUPER, CYNDI, musician; b. Queens, N.Y., June 20, 1953; Studied with Katie Agresta, N.Y., 1974. Toured with Doc West's Disco Band Flyer; mem. musical group Blue Angel, N.Y.C., 1980. Featured in German TV music program; rec. artist: (album) She's So Unusual, 1983, A Night To Remember, 1989, Hat Full of Stars, 1993, Twelve Deadly Cyns...and Then Some, 1995, Sisters of Avalon, 1997, Merry Christmas...Have a Nice Life, 1998, Feels Like Christmas, 2001, The Essential Cyndi Lauper, 2003, At Last, 2003; co-writer: (songs) Girls Just Want to Have Fun, She Bop, Money Changes Everything, Time After Time, Goonies R Good Enough, 1985, True Colors, 1986, A Night to Remember, 1989; contbr. A Very Special Christmas, 1992, vol. 2, 1993; star: (videos) Girls Just Want to Have Fun, Time After Time, others; appearance (film) Vibes, 1988, Off and Running, 1991, Life with Mikey, 1993; (TV movie) Mother Goose Rock n' Rhyme, 1990; TV appearances include The Tonight Show, The David Letterman Show, Mad About You (Emmy award, Guest Actress - Comedy Series, 1995); concert tours in Japan, Australia, Hawaii and Eng. Named one of Women of Yr., 1984, Best Female Video Performer, MTV Video Music Awards, 1984, Best Female Performer, Am. Video Awards, 1985; recipient 6 Grammy awards, 1985, 2 Am. Video awards, 1985.

LAUR, WILLIAM EDWARD, retired dermatologist; b. Saginaw, Mich., Nov. 17, 1919; s. Vertner Linton and Ruth Gae (Eyre) L.; m. Mary Elizabeth Kirby, Dec. 31, 1943; children: Eric, Edward, John, J. Michael. BS, Mercer U., Macon, Ga., 1941; MD, U. Mich., 1943; MS in Medicine, Wayne State U., Detroit, 1949. Diplomate Am. Bd. Dermatology. Intern John Sealy Hosp., Galveston, Tex., 1943; resident Wayne State U., 1946-49; pvt. practice Amarillo, Tex., 1949-70; pres. High Plains Dermatology Ctr., P.A., Amarillo, 1975—90; ret., 1990. Cons. VA, USAF, 1952-90; assoc. prof. Tex. Tech. Health Sci. Ctr., Amarillo, 1965-90. Contbr. articles to profl. jours. including Archives of Dermatology, Internat. Jour. Dermatology, Cutis, So. Med. Jour., Jour. Am. Acad. Dermatology, Panhandle Med. Soc. Bull., Urologic and Cutaneous Rev. Dir. Moon Watch, NASA, Amarillo, 1956. Capt. U.S. Army, 1944-46, ETO. Fellow Am. Acad. Dermatology; mem. AMA, Tex. Med. Assn., Noah Worcester Dermatol. Soc., Potter Randall County Med. Soc. (pres. 1964), Alpha Tau Omega. Avocations: cooking, duplicate bridge, computer activities. Home: 1607 S Fannin St Amarillo TX 79102-2412

LAURA, ANTHONY JOSEPH, lawyer; b. Bklyn., July 15, 1961; s. Andrew J. and Edda V. (DePaola) L.; m. Rosemary B. Marino, Sept. 21, 1986; children: Diana, Amanda, Gianna. BA, Yale U., 1983; JD, Fordham U., 1986. Bar: N.J. 1986, U.S. Dist. Ct. N.J. 1986, N.Y. 1987, U.S. Dist. Ct. (so. dist.) N.Y. 1987, U.S. Ct. Appeals (3rd cir.) 1993, U.S. Ct. Appeals (7th cir.) 2003. Assoc. atty. Kelley Drye and Warren, N.Y.C., 1986-87, Morristown, N.J., 1987-89, Parsippany, N.J., 1989-97; ptnr. Reed Smith LLP, Newark, 1997—. Bd. trustee Cmtys. on Cable, Summit, N.J., 1994-97, chair fund distribution com. United Way Summit, New Providence, N.J., 1995-2000, trustee, 1998—. Township committeeman Rep. Com. Union County, Berkeley Hts., N.J., 1994-2000; trustee Runnells Specialized Hosp. Found., 1996-98. Mem. N.J. State Bar Assn. (chair product liability and toxic tort sect. 1999—), The Mory's Assn., Park Ave Club (membership com. 1994-96), Yale Club Ctrl. N.J. Avocation: golf. Office: Reed Smith LLP 1 Riverfront Plz Newark NJ 07102-5470

LAUREANO, MARI, government agency administrator, writer; b. NYC, Nov. 6, 1970; d. Jose Antonio Miranda and Blanca Iris Velez- Miranda; m. Pedro Antonio Laureano, Sept. 16, 1991; children: Laura, Nia. BA, Hunter Coll. CUNY, 1987—91. Immigration officer US Immigration & Naturalization Svc., NYC, 1991—2000; tax examiner US IRS, Holtsville, NY, 2002—04; dist. adjudications officer US Citizenship and Immigration Svc. Dept. Homeland Security, Garden City, NY, 2004—. In-house expert on Nicaraguan adjustment and ctrl. am. relief act US Immigration Svc., N.Y.C., 1998—98. Author: (poetry books) Maelstrom Rising, 2001, By What Light I Shed, 2002, Riverborne, 2003, Into the Quicksilver Mirror, 2004, The Fairytale Journals, 2005. Rudin fellow, The Am. Mus. of Natural History, 1989-1991. Avocations: poetry writing, drawing, spoken word artist. Office: US Citizenship and Immigration Svc Dept Homeland Security 711 Stewart Ave Garden City NY 11530 Personal E-mail: pantha699@aol.com.

LAUREL, DAVID EZEQUIEL, finance educator, academic administrator; b. Great Falls, Minn., Sept. 5, 1952; s. Humberto Reymundo Jr. and Anna Maria Laurel; m. Mary Pat Laurel, Apr. 23, 1977; children: David Anthony, Mallory Patricia. BA in Govt., U. Tex., Brownsville, 1996, MBA, 1998; MA in Profl. Accountancy, Tex. A&M U., Kingsville, 2000, MA in Edn. Self-employed acct., 1972—96; CFO, Tex. Hardware Inc., 1976—81; staff acct. Silva, Cortez, Garza and Garza CPAs, 1981—88; Valley scholar coord. South Tex. Coll., McAllen, 1998—. Program chair acctg. and econ. South Tex. Coll., McAllen, Tex., 2000—02; founder South Tex. Entrepreneurial Program (STEP), 2000, Rising Star summer camp, 2001; spkr. at nat. confs. Contbr. articles to profl. jours. Bd. mem. Boys and Girls Club, Harlingen, Family Crisis Ctr., Candlelight Posada, McAllen, Tex., 2000—04, McAllen Christmas for Kids, 2000—04. Mem.: Lions (treas. 1994—95), Optimists (v.p. 1990—92), Rotary. Home: 1717 Peachtree Ct Harlingen TX 78550 Office: S Tex Coll 3201 W Pecan Mcallen TX 78501 Office Phone: 956-872-2621. Home Fax: 956-872-2620; Office Fax: 956-683-2620. E-mail: dlaurel@southtexascollege.edu.

LAUREN, RALPH, fashion designer; b. Bronx, N.Y., Oct. 14, 1939; s. Frank and Frieda Lifshitz; m. Ricky Low Beer, Dec. 30, 1964; children: Andrew, David, Dylan. Student, CCNY; DFA (hon.), Pratt U., 1988; HDL (hon.), Brandeis U., 1996. Salesperson Brooks Bros., N.Y.C.; asst. buyer Allied Stores, N.Y.C.; rep. Rivetz Necktie Mfrs., N.Y.C.; neckwear designer Polo divsn. Beau Brummel, N.Y.C., 1967-69; founder, chmn. Polo Fashions, Inc. (now Polo Ralph Lauren Corp.), N.Y.C., 1967—; established Polo Men's Wear Co., N.Y.C., 1968—, Ralph Lauren Womenswear, N.Y.C., 1971—, Polo Leathergoods, 1978—, Polo/Ralph Lauren for Boys, 1978—, Polo/Ralph Lauren Luggage, 1982—, Ralph Lauren Home Collection, 1983—; launched fragrances Polo for Men, Lauren for Women, 1979—; opened RL Restaurant, Chgo., 1999. Chmn. Polo Ralph Lauren Corp. (flagship store NYC, 65 other stores in US and 140 stores worldwide); launched fragrances Lauren, Lauren Style, Purple Label, Ralph Lauren Blue, Silver, Polo Blue, Romance for men and women, Polo, Polo Sport, Ralph, Safari for men and woemn, and Glamourous. Served in U.S. Army. Recipient Coty Am. Fashion awards, 1970, 73, 74, 76, 77, 81, 84, also Coty Hall of Fame award for Menswear and Womenswear, Tommy award Am. Printed Fabrics Coun., 1971, Neiman Marcus Disting. Svc. award, 1973, Am. Fashion award, 1975, award Coun. Fashion Designers Am., 1981, CFDA Lifetime Achievement award, 1992, Menswear Designer of Yr. award CFDA, 1996, Womenswear Design of Yr. award CFDA, 1996, Humanitarian Leadership award CFDA, 1998, Humanitarian award Breast Cancer Rsch. Found., 1998, VH1/Vogue Lifetime Achievement award, 2002, Man of Yr. award GQ, 2002. Achievements include established the American Heroes Fund following September 11, 2001; established the Pink Poney Campaign to address the significant lack of access to cancer screening, education, outreach and quality cancer care for people in these communities, 2000; opened the Ralph Lauren Center for Cancer Care and Prevention to provide individuals, many of who are medically underserved, with access to the highest quality cancer screening and treatment services. Office: Polo Ralph Lauren Corp 650 Madison Ave New York NY 10022-1029

LAURENCE, DAN H., writer, editor; b. N.Y.C., Mar. 28, 1920; BA, Hofstra U., 1946; MA, NYU, 1950. Performed in profl. theatre, 1932-41; writer, performer Armed Forces Radio, 1942-45; writer for radio, TV U.S. and Australia, 1946-48; grad. asst. NYU, 1950-52, assoc. prof. English, 1962-67, prof., 1967-70; instr. Hofstra U., 1953-58; editor Readex Microprint Corp., 1959-60; lit. and dramatic adv. Estate of George Bernard Shaw, London, 1973-90. Vis. prof. Ind. U., 1969, U. Tex., 1974-75; vis. fellow Inst. Arts and Humanistic Studies, Pa. State U., 1976; spl. cons. Humanities rsch. Ctr., U. Tex., Austin, 1975-77; Andrew W. Mellon prof. humanities Tulane U., New Orleans, 1981; Montgomery fellow Dartmouth Coll., 1982; disting. vis. prof. humanities Guelph U. (Ont., Can.), 1983, U. B.C. (Can.), 1984; adj. prof. drama Guelph U., 1986-91; literary advisor, mem. acting ensemble of Shaw Festival, Ont., 1982-90, assoc. dir., 1987-2000; co-founder Offstage, Inc., San Antonio, 1972. Author: (with Leon Edel) Henry James: A Bibliography, 3d edit., 1981, Robert Nathan: A Bibliography, 1960, Bernard Shaw: A Bibliography, 1983; playwright: The Black Girl in Search of God, 1977; editor: Uncollected Writing of Bernard Shaw: How to Become a Musical Critic, 1961, Platform and Pulpit, 1961, (with David H. Greene) The Matter with Ireland, 1962, rev. edit., 2001, Selected Non-Dramatic Writings of Shaw, 1965, Collected Letters of Bernard Shaw, 4 vols., 1965-88, Bernard Shaw's Collected Plays with Their Prefaces, 7 vols., 1970-74, (with Daniel J. Leary) Flyleaves, 1977, Shaw's Music, 3 vols., 1981, (with James Rambeau) Agitations, 1985, (with Martin Quinn) Shaw on Dickens, 1985, (with Nicholas Grene) Bernard Shaw, Lady Gregory, and the Abbey, 1993, (with Daniel J. Leary) Shaw: Complete Prefaces, 3 vols. 1993-97, Theatrics, 1995, (with Margot Peters) Unpublished Shaw, 1996, (with Fred D. Crawford) Bibliographical Shaw, 2000. Served with USAAF, 1942-45, PTO. John Simon Guggenheim Meml. fellow, 1960, 61, 72, Pres.'s medal Hofstra U., 1990. Mem. Royal Acad. Dramatic Art (assoc.), Phi Beta Kappa, Phi Alpha Theta, Alpha Psi Omega, Phi Gamma Delta. Home: 101 Arcadia Pl #403 San Antonio TX 78209

LAURENCE, GEOFFREY FRANCIS, artist; b. Paterson, N.J., Dec. 23, 1949; BA, St. Martins, London, 1969—71; MFA, N.Y. Acad., 1993—95. Exhibitions include Arnot Art Mus., Las Vegas Art Mus., one-man shows include Chelsea Arts Club, London, 1990, Bartleys Gallery, Eng., 1990, Kunstsalon Straetz, Freiburg, Germany, 1991, exhibited in group shows at Kline Gallery, Santa Fe, N.Mex., 2003, John Pence Gallery, San Francisco, 2004, 2004, Armory Art Ctr., Fla., 2004, one-man shows include Meisel Art Ctr., Denver, 2005, exhibited in group shows at Klaudia Marr Gallery, Santa Fe, N.Mex., 2005. Recipient Walter Erlebacher, N.Y. Acad., 1995, J. Epstein Travel award, 1995, Robert Rauschenburg award, 2004.

LAURENCE, JEFFREY CONRAD, immunologist, educator; b. N.Y.C., Oct. 21, 1952; s. Harry and Stephanie (Maderic) L.; m. Susan Paley, Mar. 2003; children: Auden, Galen, Luca. BA summa cum laude, Columbia U., 1972; MD, U. Chgo., 1976. Diplomate Am. Bd. Internal Medicine. Rsch. assoc. Inst. for Cancer Rsch., Osaka, Japan, 1974-75; intern, resident, then hematology fellow N.Y.C. Hosp.-Cornell, 1976-82; assoc. physician The Rockefeller U., N.Y.C., 1980-84; asst. prof. Cornell U. Med. Coll., N.Y.C., 1982-87, assoc. prof., 1988-2000, prof., 2001—; dir. Lab. AIDS Rsch. Cornell Med. Coll., N.Y.C., 1986—; attending physician N.Y. Presbyn. Hosp., N.Y.C., 2001—. Sr. dir. Immune Tech., Inc., N.Y.C., 1986-95; sr. scientist Am. Found. AIDS Rsch., N.Y.C. and Beverly Hills, Calif., 1986—. Author: (play) Many Happy Returns, 1982; editor-in-chief The AIDS Reader, 1991—; editor AIDS Targeted Info. Newsletter, 1987-92; assoc. editor AIDS Rsch. and Human Retroviruses, AIDS, 1987-95; editor-in-chief AIDS Patient Care and STDs, 1996—; cons. editor Infections in Medicine, 1987—; patentee in field. Recipient Clinician-Scientist award Am. Heart Assn., 1980-85; William S. Paley Found. fellow, 1982-84; Henry Luce Found. scholar, 1974, Rhodes scholar-elect, 1973. Mem. NIH (mem. study sect.), AMA, Fedn. Am. Soc. Exptl. Biology-Medicine, Am. Soc. Microbiology, Am. Soc. Clin. Investigation, Phi Beta Kappa. Presbyterian. Avocations: collecting ancient med. books and sci. instruments, contemporary art, sports, yoga. Home: 86 Brookside Dr Greenwich CT 06831-5345 Office: NY Presbyn Hosp-Cornell Med Ctr Dept Medicine Lab AIDS Rsch 411 E 69th St New York NY 10021-5608 E-mail: jlaurenc@med.cornell.edu.

LAURENCE, MICHAEL MARSHALL, magazine publisher, writer; b. N.Y.C., May 22, 1940; s. Frank Marshall and Edna Ann (Roeder) L.; m. Patricia Ann McDonald, Mar. 1, 1969; children: Elizabeth Sarah, John Marshall. AB cum laude, Harvard U., 1963. From sr. editor to asst. pub. Playboy mag., Chgo., 1967—77, asst. pub., 1977—82; mng. editor Oui mag., Chgo., 1973-77; editor, pub. Linn's Stamp News, Sidney, Ohio, 1982—2002, also columnist Editor's Choice; sr. v.p., editl. dir. Amos Hobby Pub., Sidney, 2002—. Co-founder, dir. U.S. 1869 Pictorial Rsch. Assocs., 1975-82. Author: Playboy's Investment Guide, 1971; editor: U.S. Mail and Post Office Assistant, 1975; author articles. Recipient G.M. Loeb award for disting. mag. writing U. Conn., 1968; named to Writers Hall of Fame, Am. Philatelic Soc., 1994. Mem. U.S. Philat. Classics Soc. (life, Elliott Perry award 1975, bd. dirs. 1975-81, Disting. Philatelist award 2003), Harvard Club (N.Y.C.), Collectors Club Chgo. (bd. dirs. 1978-82), Collectors Club N.Y.C. Avocations: stamp collecting/philately, gardening. Office: Linn's Stamp News 911 S Vandemark Rd Sidney OH 45365-8974 Business E-Mail: mlaurence@linns.com.

LAURENCE, ROBERT LIONEL, chemical engineering professor; b. West Warwick, RI, July 13, 1936; s. Lionel Gerard and Gertrude Sara (Lefebvre) L.; m. Carol Leah Jolicoeur, Sept. 7, 1959; children: Jonathan, Lisa, Andrew. BSChemE, MIT, 1957; MSChemE, U. R.I., 1960; PhDChemE, Northwestern U., 1966; DSc (honoris causa), Inst. Nat. Poly., Toulouse, France, 1989. Rsch. engr. Gen. Dynamics, Groton, Conn., 1957-59, E. I. du Pont de Nemours, Wilmington, Del., 1960-61, field svc. engr. Beaumont, Tex., 1961-63; asst. prof. chem. engring. Johns Hopkins U., Balt., 1965-68; rsch. engr. Monsanto Co., Springfield, Mass., 1968; assoc. prof. U. Mass., Amherst, 1968-73, head dept. chem. engring., 1982-89, prof., 1973-2001, prof. emeritus, 2001—. Vis. prof. Imperial Coll., London, 1974-75, Coll. de France, Paris, 1982-83, Rijks U. Gent, 1996; invited prof. ENSIGC, Toulouse, France, 1990; vis. rsch.

fellow GE, Schenectady, 1989; cons. UN Devel. Program, Argentina, 1978, 80, Beijing, 1982; mem. Conseil Technologique Groupe Rhone-Poulenc, Paris, 1988-96. Fellow Am. Inst. Chem. Engrs., Am. Inst. Chemists; mem. Am. Chem. Soc., Tau Beta Pi. Roman Catholic. Avocation: rugby. Home: 5 Ashley Terr Waterville ME 04901 Office Phone: 413-545-0470. E-mail: rlaurence@ecs.umass.edu.

LAURENCIN, CATO THOMAS, biomedical engineer, orthopaedic surgeon; b. Phila., Jan. 15; s. Cyril Alexander and Helen Isabella (Moorehead) L. BS in Engring., Princeton U., 1980; PhD, MIT, 1987; MD, Harvard U., Boston, 1987. Diplomate Nat. Bd. Med. Examiners. Instr. biochem. engring. MIT, Cambridge, 1987—92; clin. fellow in orthopaedic surgery Mass. Gen. Hosp.-Harvard Med. Sch., 1988—89; rsch. scientist div. of health sciences & tech. MIT, Cambridge, 1992—97; adjunct prof. biomedical engring. Drexel U., Phila., 1994, rsch. prof. materials engring., 1994, rsch. prof. chemical engring., 1994—98, vice chmn. orthopaedic surgery & Helen I. Moorehead prof. chemical engring., 1998—2002; assoc. prof. orthopaedic surgery Hahnemann U. Sch. Medicine, Phila., 1994—98, clinical assoc. prof. orthopaedic surgery, 1998—2002, rsch. prof. pharmacology & physiology, 2000; prof. biomedical & chemical engring., Lillian T. Pratt disting. prof. & chair orthopaedic surgery U. Va., Charlottesville, Va., 2003—. Asst. dir., clin. coord. Harvard Health Professions Program, 1983-85; Lowell Inst. lectr. Suffolk U., Boston, 1991. Recipient resident rsch. award Am. Orthopaedic Assn., 1991, William Grimes award, Am. Inst. Chemical Engineers, Leadership in Tech. award, New Millennium Found.; named one of Top 100 Black Physicians in Am., Black Enterprise Mag., 2001. Mem. Nat. Med. Assn. (chmn. resident planning com. 1990-91), Nat. Soc. Black Engrs. (mem., chmn. acads. com. 1976-80); fellow Am. Inst. for Med. & Biological Engring.; internat. fellow in Biomaterials Sci. & Engring. Office: Dept Orthopaedic Surgery Univ Va PO Box 800159 Charlottesville VA 22908

LAURENSON, ROBERT MARK, mechanical engineer; b. Pitts., Oct. 25, 1938; s. Robert Mark and Mildred Othelia (Frandsen) L.; m. Alice Ann Scroggins, Aug. 26, 1961; children: Susan Elizabeth Laurenson Matchael, Shari Lynn, Laurenson Lawson. Student, Drury Coll., 1956-58; BS in Mech. Engring., Mo. Sch. Mines, 1961; MS in Mech. Engring., U. Mich., 1962; PhD in Mech. Engring. (NASA tng. grantee), Ga. Inst. Tech., 1968. Registered profl. engr., Mo. Dynamics engr. McDonnell Douglas Corp., St. Louis, 1962-64, sr. dynamics engr., 1968-71, group engr., 1971-74, staff engr., 1974-75, tech. specialist, 1975-78, sr. tech. specialist, 1978-81, sect. chief, 1981-85, prin. tech. specialist, 1985-87, br. chief, 1987-89, prin. mgr. engring., 1989-92; prin. tech. specialist, systems engring. mgr. The Boeing Co., Seabrook, Md., 1992-93, sr. mgr., 1993-95, asst. dir. engring., 1995-97, gen. mgr., 1998-99; ret.; pvt. cons. Crofton, Md., 1999—. Participant 14th Midwestern Mechanics Conf., 1975; lectr. engring. mechanics St. Louis U., part-time 1969-71; adj. assoc. prof. U. Mo.-Rolla Grad. Engring. Ctr., St. Louis, 1980-88; lectr. mech. engring. Johns Hopkins U., 1996-99; participant Symposium on Dynamics and Control of Large Flexible Spacecraft, Blackburg, Va., 1977, In-Space Tech. Experiments Workshop NASA, 1988, Damping, '89 Conf., 1989; mem. panel Am. Astronautical Soc. Symposium on Dynamics and Control of Nonridig Spacecraft, UCLA, 1974; mem. accreditation bd. engr. and tech. Engring. Accredidation Commn., 1998-2003, mem. exec. com., 2000-03, vice chair ops., 2003-04, chair-elect, 2004-05, chair, 2005—, mem. accredidation coun., 2004—, Vol. Participation Project steering com., 2005—; project coord. ASME/NSF Project Grant, 2000-01. Author: How to Write Winning Proposals, 2001; contbr. articles to profl. jour.; reviewer profl. jour.; author tech. papers Jour. Engring. for Industry, 1972, Jour. Spacecraft and Rockets, 1973, AIAA Jour., 1976, 78, 80, 85; numerous papers presented at tech. conf. Vestryman Episcopal Ch., 1972-76, sr. warden, 1976, uscher chmn., 1978-80, Sunday sch. tchr., 1980-84, chmn. every mem. canvas, 1983, mem. steering com., 1983-88, chmn. steering com., 1987-88, mem. search com., 1984-85, mem. exec. com., 1991-92, warden, 1991-92; mem. Commn. on Ministry, Diocese of Mo., 1985-91, chmn., 1989-91; mem. standing com. Diocese of Mo., 1990-92; trustee Corp. of Episcopal Diocese of Mo., 1990-92; mem. seminarian com., 1993-98, 2001-03, chair, 1994-97, engring. mentor Holy Trinity Episcopal Day Sch., chmn. Parish Commn. on Ministry, 1999-2000, chair parish strategic planning com., 2001-03, chair comms. ministry area, 2005—; pres. Crabtown Square Dance Club, 1998-2000. Fellow ASME (structures materials com. aerospace divsn. 1975-84, com. chmn. 1979-81, session organizer, chmn. ann. meeting 1975, participant ann. meeting 1986, 89, mem. exec. com. aerospace divsn. 1980-85, sec.-treas. 1981-82, vice-chmn. 1982-83, chmn. 1983-84, Flag award aerospace divsn. 1990, mem. Guggenheim medal bd. 1989-92, mem. conf. organizing com., session chmn. Structures, Structural Dynamics and Materials Conf., 1977, chmn. tech. program 1978, gen. co-chmn. 1979, gen. chmn. 1981, mem. SDM planning com. 1978-82, chmn. 1981-82, session chmn. 1985, 88, adv. com. 1978-82, participant 1979, 83, 86, 90, mech. engring. evaluator Accreditation Bd. Engring. and Tech. 1985-91, 94-98, organizer symposium on microgravity fluid mechanics 1986, mem. planning com. edn. conf. 1986, editor Advances in Aerospace Structures 1982, Procs. of 1986 Edn. Conf. The Decade Ahead, bd. engring. edn. K thru 12 task force 1992-93, bd. pre-coll. edn. 1992-95, 1st alt. nat. nominating com. 1993-94, bd. on engring. edn. 1998-2003, engring. accreditation com. 1998-2003, exec. com. 1993-2003, sec. 1995-96, vice chair 1996-97, rep. on Am. Assn. Engring. Soc.'s Precoll. Edn. Coun. 1993-95, exec. com. 1993-95, Dedicated Svc. award 1995); mem. AIAA (sr., gen. chmn. dynamics specialist conf. 1981, session chmn. 1987), Edison Electric Inst. (adv. com. power engring. edn. forgivable loan program 1993-94), Sigma Xi, Pi Tau Sigma, Tau Beta Pi, Phi Kappa Phi, Sigma Phi Epsilon. Home: 1104 Jasper Ct Crofton MD 21114-1658

LAURENT, JERRY SUZANNA, information technology executive; b. Oklahoma City, Dec. 28, 1942; d. Harry Austin and M. LaVerne (Barker) Minick; m. Leroy E. Laurent, July 2, 1960; children: Steven, Sandra, David, Debra. AS in Engr. Tech., Okla. State U., 1986. Owner, CEO Technically Write, Mustang, Okla., 1989-95; sr. tech. comm. specialist Applied Intelligence Group, Edmond, Okla., 1995-98, DCA Svcs., Oklahoma City, 1998—2003; owner, CEO Comm. Design Group, 2003—, pres. Oklahoma City, 2003—. Fellow: Soc. Tech. Comm. (assoc.; Superscript editor 1985, v.p. 1985, feature editor 1986, student chpt. pres. 1986, program coord. Okla. chpt. 1992—93, sec. 1993—94, v.p. 1994—95, state pres. 1995—96, state treas. Okla. chpt. 1998—99, dir./sponsor region 5 1999—2002, bylaws com. mgr. 2001—02, Region 5 conf. mgr. 2002, 2nd v.p. 2003—04, 1st v.p. 2004—05, internat. pres. 2005—, Disting. Chpt. Svc. award 1997, Outstanding Achievement award 2001); mem.: Am. Bus. Women's Assn. (area coun. pres. 1987—89, v.p. dist. III 1988—89, sec. 1990—91, conf. gen. chair 1992, chmn. bd. dirs. Help Us Grow Spiritually 1993—95, editor Smoke Signals, Bull. award 1977, Woman of Yr. 1978, Bull. award 1981, 1983, Bus. Assoc. of Yr. 1983—84, Bull. award 1984, 1993, 1995, Woman of Yr. 1996, 1997, Bull. award 1997—99, Nat. Newsletter award 1999, Bull. award 2003—04, named One of Top Ten Bus. Women in Nation 1997). Democrat. Baptist. Avocations: reading, public speaking, motivating people, volunteer activities. Home and Office: Comm Design Group 347 W Forest Dr Mustang OK 73064-3430

LAURENT, LAWRENCE BELL, communications executive, retired journalist; b. Monroe, La., Mar. 09; s. Lewis Emeal and John Ethel (Dawkins) L.; m. Margaret F. Goodwillie, Nov. 1, 1949; children— Richard Sandford, Arthur Halliday, Margaret Funsten, Elizabeth MacLean. Student, U. Colo., 1943—44, U. Va., 1946-49; pvt. study with, Dr. W.Y. Elliott, 1954-56, Dr. Franklin Dunham, 1957-58. With Bluefield (W.Va.) Daily Telegraph, 1949-50, Charlottesville (Va.) Daily Progress, 1950-51; with Washington Post, 1951-82, radio-TV editor, 1953-82, radio-TV editor emeritus, 1982—; cons. Assn. Ind. TV Stas., 1982-85, dir. communication, 1985-86, v.p. communication, 1986-91; congl. cons., 1991—; editor-in-residence Broadcast Pioneers Library, 1985-96; adj. prof. communications Am. U., Washington, 1963-85; chmn. editorial bd. TV Quar., 1963-74, bd. dirs., 1974—. Guest prof. Syracuse U., 1965; vis. prof. U. Detroit, 1967; vis. prof. George Washington U., 1982-95, professorial lectr., 1996—; formerly judge Alfred I. duPont awards, Saturday Rev. Lit. TV awards, Sigma Delt Chi pub. svc. TV awards, Humanitas awards. Editor, author: (with Newton N. Minow) Equal Time, 1964; Contbr. to books, mags. Trustee Human Family Edn. and Cultural Inst.; bd. dirs. Pioneers Edn. Fund, Inc., 1984-94, trustee, 1995-2002. With USNR, 1943-46. Recipient Front Page award Am. Newspaper Guild, 1964, Disting. Tchr. award Am. U., 1978, TV Acad.'s Silver Circle award, 1988, Pres.'s medal George Washington U., 1999; named to Broadcast Pioneers' Hall of Fame, 1984; du Pont Journalism scholar U. Va., 1947-49. Mem. AAUP, NATAS (life), VFW (life), DAV (life), 593rd Joint Assault Signal Co. Assn., USS Belle Grove Historic Assn., Nat. Press Club, White House Corrs. Assn., Washington Post E-Streeters, Am. Legion (life), Thomas Jefferson Soc. Alumni (U. Va.), Sigma Delta Chi, Pi Delta Epsilon, Theta Chi. Episcopalian. Home: Goodwin House Apt 558 4800 Fillmore Ave Alexandria VA 22311

LAURENT, PIERRE-HENRI, history professor; b. Fall River, Mass., May 15, 1933; s. Henri and Harriet (Moriarty) L.; m. Virginia Brayton, 1958; children: Paul-Henri, Bradford Webb, Nicole, Alexa. AB, Colgate U., 1956; AM, Boston U., 1960, PhD, 1964. Instr. polit. economy Boston U., 1961-64; asst. prof. history Sweet Briar Coll., 1964-66; vis. asst. prof. history U. Wis., Madison, 1966-67; asst. prof. history Tulane U., New Orleans, 1967-68, assoc. prof., 1968-70; assoc. prof. history Tufts U., Medford, Mass., 1970—75, prof., 1975—2003, chmn. dept., 1987—89, chmn. Exptl. Coll., 1973-75, adj. prof. diplomatic history/Fletcher Sch. Law and Diplomacy, 1977, 1984, acting dir. internat. rels. program, 1979, dir. internat. relations program, 1984—88, co-dir. internat. relations program France, 1979—80; acad. dir. Tufts European Ctr., 1996; prof. emeritus Tufts U., Medford, Mass., 2003—. Mem. history devel. bd. Ednl. Testing Svc. of Princeton, 1979-82; instr. JFK Inst. Polit., Harvard U., Cambridge, 1989; mem. nat. screening com. Fulbright-Hays program Inst. Internat. Edn., 1988-91; rsch. assoc. Ctr. for Internat. Affairs, Harvard U. Mem. editorial bd. Jour. Social History, 1966-74; sect. editor Am. Hist. Rev., 1967-77; co-editor: The State of the European Union: Deepening and Widening, 1998, NATO and the European Union: Confronting the Challenges of European Security and Enlargement, 1999; contbr. chpts. to books, articles to profl. jours., mags., encys. Mem. Wellesley Hist. Commn., 2003—. With USAF, 1956—58. NATO fellow, 1967, NEH fellow, 1969, Paul-Henri Spaak Found. fellow, 1976-77; Sweet Briar Faculty rsch. grantee, 1965, Tufts Faculty rsch. grantee, 1972, 1994, Inst. European Studies-Exxon Ednl. Fund grantee, 1983; Fulbright Rsch. scholar, 1992-93; Fulbright chair Coll. of Europe, Bruges, 1998. Fellow Inst. des Rels. Internationales, Acad. Assoc. Atlantic Coun.; mem. AAUP (exec. com. Mass. State Conf. 1974-76, pres. Tufts U. chpt. 1982-84, 2000-2002), European Cmty. Studies Assn. (exec. com. 1988-92, 95-99, chmn. 1991-92, vice-chmn. 1997-99). Personal E-mail: ginnypierre@msn.com.

LAURENTS, ARTHUR, playwright; b. N.Y.C., July 14, 1917; s. Irving and Ada (Robbins) L. BA, Cornell U., Ithaca, N.Y., 1937. Radio script writer, 1939-40. Author: (novels) The Way We Were, 1972, The Turning Point, 1977 (screen plays) The Snake Pit, 1948, Rope, 1948, Caught, 1948, Anna Lucasta, 1949, Anastasia, 1956, Bonjour Tristesse, 1958, The Way We Were, 1973, The Turning Point, 1977 (Writer Guild Am. award), (plays) Home of the Brave, 1946, The Bird Cage, 1950, The Time of the Cuckoo, 1952, A Clearing in the Woods, 1956, Invitation to a March, 1960, The Enclave, 1973, Scream, Houston, 1978, Jolson Sings Again, 1995, The Radical Mystique, 1995, My Good Name, 1997, Venecia, 1999, Big Potato, 2000, 2 Lives, 2001, Claudia Lazlo, 2002, Attacks on the Heart, 2003, (mus. plays) West Side Story, 1957, Gypsy, 1959, Do I Hear A Waltz?, 1964, Hallelujah, Baby, 1967 (Tony award), Nick and Nora, 1991; screenwriter, co-producer (film) The Turning Point, 1977 (Golden Glove award, Nat. Bd. Rev. award); co-author, dir.: (dramatic prodns.) My Mother was a Fortune Teller, 1978 (Drama Desk award), The Madwoman of Central Park West, (radio plays in anthologies) Radio Drama in Action, 1945, Best One Act Plays of 1944-45, 1945-46, dir.: (Broadway prodns.) Invitation to a March, 1960, I Can Get It For You Wholesale, 1962, La Cage aux Folles (Tony award for Best Dir. 1984); writer, dir.: (Broadway prodns.) Invitation to the March, 1960, Anyone Can Whistle, 1964, The Enclave, 1973, (one-act play) A Loss of Memory (Best Short Plays of 1983); dir. (London prodn.) Gypsy, 1973, N.Y. revival, 1974 (Drama Desk award), La Cage aux Folles, 1983, Australian prodn. (Best Dir's. award 1985, London prodn. 1986), Birds of Paradise, 1987, Gypsy, revival, 1989, Nick and Nora, 1991, Memoir, Original Story By, 2000. Served with AUS, 1941-45. Recipient Variety Radio award, 1945, Am. Acad. Arts and Letters award; co-recipient Sidney Howard award, 1946. Mem. Dramatists Guild Council, P.E.N., Authors League, Screenwriters Guild, Acad. Motion Picture Arts and Scis., Theatre Hall of Fame. Address: Peter Franklin care William Morris Agency 1325 Avenue Of The Americas New York NY 10019-6026

LAURENZO, VINCENT DENNIS, industrial management company executive; b. Des Moines, May 31, 1939; s. Vincent C. and B.J. (Garver) L.; m. Sherrill S. Mullen, Sept. 10, 1960; children: Lisa, David, Susan, Nancy, James. BBA, U. Notre Dame, 1961; MBA, U. Mich., 1964. With Ford Motor Co., Dearborn, Mich., 1961-66; plant controller Massey Ferguson Inc., 1967-70; with parent co. Massey Ferguson Ltd., Toronto, Ont., Can., 1971-94, dir. fin. Am. div., 1977-78, v.p., comptr. Massey Ferguson Ltd., 1978-80, sr. v.p. planning and adminstrn., 1980-81; pres. Varity Corp. (formerly Massey Ferguson Ltd.), Toronto, 1981-94, vice chmn. bd. Buffalo, 1988-96, vice chmn., pres., 1988-94; ret., 1994; vice chair bd. dirs. Roman Catholic.

LAURI, A. ELIZABETH, artist, art educator; arrived in U.S., 1974; d. Sidney Panting and Maria Ernestina Paz; m. Frank Lauri, May 1, 1979; 1 child from previous marriage, Anelisa. B in Liberal Arts, San Vincente de Paúl, Honduras, 1973; BA in Comml. and Fine Arts, Albert Pels Sch. of Art, N.Y.C., 1978. Asst. art dir. Karoktype, Bklyn., 1978—79; asst. and artist Charles Fazzino, Editions Inc., New Rochelle, 1986—93; tile designer Elon, Inc., Hawthorne, 1995—96; art instr. No. Westchester Ctr. Arts, Mt. Kisco, 1998—, Wooster Arts Ctr., Danbury, Conn., 2001—. Mem. adv. bd. Art-Life Guild, Port Chester, N.Y., 1990—92; mem. grant panel Putnam Arts Coun., Mahopac, 1997—99. Founder and sec. Latin Americans of Putnam County, 2001. Recipient 2d prize, JJenth Art Gallery, Peekskill, N.Y., 1997; grantee, N.Y. State Coun. Arts, 1998. Achievements include teaching "Arte en Español" to low-income children in Westchester and Putnam counties in N.Y., Danbury, Conn. E-mail: lauri@bestweb.net.

LAURIE, CRAIG, real estate company executive; B in Commerce, Queens U. Chartered acct. With Deloitte & Touche, Toronto, Canada; sr. v.p., CFO Brascan Power Corp. Brascan Power, 1997—2003, sr. v.p. fin., 1997—2003; sr. v.p., CFO Brookfield Properties Corp., N.Y.C., 2003—. Office: Brookfield Properties Corp One Liberty Plaza 165 Broadway 6th Fl New York NY 10006

LAURIE, GERALD TENZER, lawyer; b. St. Paul, Jan. 22, 1942; s. Hyman and Leona (Smith) L.; m. Joellyn Kronick, Mar. 12, 1968; children: Ian, Eben, Joshua. BA, U. Minn., 1964, JD, 1967. Bar: Minn. 1967, U.S. Dist. Ct. Minn. 1967, U.S. Ct. Appeals (fed. cir.) 1987. Spl. asst. atty. gen. Minn. Atty. Gen. Office, St. Paul, 1968-70; ptnr. Laurie & Laurie, P.A., Mpls., 2001—. Contbr. articles in field to legal jours. Mem. City of New Hope Indsl. Commn.; chmn. New Hope Liquor Commn. Fellow Am. Coll. Labor and Employment Lawyers; mem. ABA, Assn. Trial Lawyers Am., Minn. Bar Assn. (cert. civil litigation specialist), Minn. Trial Lawyers Assn. (bd. govs. 1983-89), Hennepin County Bar Assn. Avocations: reading, swimming, biking. Office: Laurie & Laurie PA Parkdale Plz Bldg 1660 S Hwy 100 508 East Minneapolis MN 55416-1534 E-mail: Jerry@laurielaurie.com.

LAURIE, HUGH, actor; b. Oxford, Oxfordshire, Eng., June 11, 1959; s. George Ranald and Patricia Mundell; m. Jo Green, June 16, 1989; children: Charlie, Bill, Rebecca. Actor, writer: (TV series) Alfresco, 1983—84; A Bit of Fry and Laurie, 1986—95; actor, dir. Fortysomething, 2003; actor: Blackadder the Third, 1987, Les Girls, 1988, Blackadder Goes Forth, 1989, (voice) Treasure Island, 1993, Tracey Takes On..., 1996, (voice) Preson Pig, 2000, Little Grey Rabbit, 2000, Stuart Little, 2003, House, M.D., 2004—; (TV films) Cambridge Footlights Revue, 1982, The Crystal Cube, 1983, Mrs. Capper's Birthday, 1985, The Laughing Prisoner, 1987, Hysteria 2!, 1989, All or Nothing at All, 1993, The Adventures of Mole, 1995, The Place of Lions, 1997, The Nearly Complete Utter History of Everything, 1999, Life with Judy Garland: Me and My Shadows, 2001, The Young Visitors, 2003; (films) Plenty, 1985, Peter's Friends, 1992, A Pin for the Butterfly, 1994, Sense and Sensibility, 1995, 101 Dalmatians, 1996, The Borrowers, 1997, The Man in the Iron Mask, 1998, Cousin Bette, 1998, Stuart Little, 1999, Blackadder Back and Forth, 1999, Carnivale, 2000, The Piano Tuner, 2001, Stuart Little 2, 2002, Flight of the Phoenix, 2004, The Big Empty, 2005, Valiant, 2005. Office: The Gersh Agy 232 N Canon Dr Beverly Hills CA 90210*

LAURIE, JAMES ANDREW, broadcast executive, consultant, director, television executive producer, journalist; b. Eustis, Fla., June 16, 1947; s. Andrew Louis and Geneva Lavina (Pryor) L. BA in History, Am. U., Washington, 1970; postgrad., George Washington U. Free-lance writer Far Eastern Econ. Review, Washington, 1969, 73-74, Phnom Penh, Cambodia and Saigon, Vietnam, 1970-71; reporter NBC News, Saigon, 1971-73, 75, Tokyo, 1976-78; with ABC News, 1978-99, corr., bur. chief, Hong Kong, 1978-81, opened 1st Am. radio-TV bur. in Peking, 1981, bur. chief, Peking, 1981-82, chief Asia corr., Tokyo, 1983-88, corr., bur. chief Moscow, 1989-91, sr. corr. London, 1991-96, Hong Kong, bur. chief, 1996-99; vice pres. Network News and Current Affairs, Newscorps/Satellite Television, Asia region, 1999—2005; sr. advisor broadcasting U. Hong Kong, 2005—; pres., exec. prodr. Focus Asia Prodns., 2005—; dir. broadcast program U. Hong Kong, 2005—. Writer, narrator: (ABC Closeup documentaries) Japan: Myths behind the Miracle, 1981, The Unruly Dragon: China's Yellow River, 1988, Soviet segment ABC Spl. "Beyond the Cold War", 1989; covered Mikhail Gorbachev in Cuba, East Germany, Rome, Malta, 1989, Tien An Men Crushing of Democrats Movement, 1989, Gorbachev summit in U.S., 1990, Bush-Gorbachev summit, Moscow, 1991, coup d'etat Moscow, 1991, Somalia Famine, 1992, Iraq Crisis, 1993, Bosnia Crises, 1993, Israeli-Palestinian Negotiations, 1993, Russian Crisis October, 1993, South African elections, 1994, U.S. operation in Haiti, 1994, Crisis in Rwanda, 1995, Human Right Coverage China, 1996, Hong Kong Handover, 1997, Reporting from Tibet, 1997, coup d'etat in Cambodia, 1997, Afganistan, 2001; interviewed Pakistan Pres. Musharaf, 2001, Russian Pres. Putin, 2003. Recipient George Foster Peabody Broadcasting award for reporting fall of Saigon, 1976; Columbia-Dupont award for ABC Closeup documentary Cambodia: This Shattered Land, 1981; award for radio news coverage of assassination of Philippine leader Benigno Aquino, Overseas Press Club, 1983; Emmy award, 1987, N.Y. Festivals award. Office: Eliot Hall Journalism Media Studies Ctr U Hong Kong Pokfulam Rd Hong Kong Hong Kong also: U Hong Kong Parkview Tower 3 Ste 2127 Hong Kong Hong Kong Office Phone: 852 2219 4013. Personal E-mail: jlaurie@pacific.net.hk. E-mail: jlaurie@hku.hk.

LAURIE, ROBIN GARRETT, lawyer; b. Mobile, Ala., June 10, 1956; s. George and Margaret Eloise (Garrett) L.; m. Deborah Dockery; children: Elizabeth Anne, Robin Garrett. AA, Marion (Ala.) Mil. Inst., 1976; BS in Bus., U. Ala., Tuscaloosa, 1978; JD, U.Ala., Tuscaloosa, 1988. Bar: Ala. 1988, U.S. Dist. Ct. (no., mid. and so. dists.) Ala. 1988, U.S. Ct. Appeals (11th cir.) 1988. Ptnr. Balch & Bingham LLP, Montgomery, Ala., 1988—. Lead articles editor Ala. Law Rev., 1986-88. Recipient Outstanding Svc. award Ala. Law Rev., 1988. Mem. ABA, Ala. State Bar, Montgomery County Bar Assn., Montgomery Rotary Club, Order of the Coif. Methodist. Avocations: flying small airplanes, fishing, hunting. Office: Balch & Bingham LLP PO Box 78 Montgomery AL 36101-0078 Office Phone: 334-834-6500. Business E-Mail: rlaurie@balch.com.

LAURIN, PIERRE, finance company executive; b. Charlemagne, Que., Can., Aug. 11, 1939; MBA, U. Montreal, 1963; D in Bus. Adminstrn., Harvard U., 1969; PhD (hon.), Concordia U., Montreal, 1983. Dean bus. sch. U. Montreal, 1975-82; v.p. planning and adminstrn. Alcan Co. of Can., 1982-87; vice chmn., pres., Que. Merrill Lynch Can. Inc., Montreal, 1987—99. Exec. in residence, HEC Montréal, 1999. Author mgmt. textbook. Named officer Order Can. Office: HEC Montréal Montreal PQ Canada H3T 2A7 Office Phone: 514-340-7148. Business E-Mail: pierre.laurin@hec.ca.

LAUSE, MICHAEL FRANCIS, lawyer; b. Washington, Mo., Aug. 3, 1948; s. Walter Francis and Junilla Rose (Marquart) L.; m. Ann G. Hellman, Aug. 29, 1981; children: Andrew Edward, Scott Michael. BA, St. Benedict's Coll., 1970; JD, U. Ill., 1973. Bar: Mo. 1973. Ptnr. Thompson Coburn LLP, St. Louis, 1973—. Chmn. corp. dept. Thompson Coburn LLP, St. Louis, 2002-. Gen. counsel Mo. Health and Ednl. Facilities Authority, 1986—, St. Louis Zoo, 1992—. Mem. ABA, Mo. Bar Assn., St. Louis Bar Assn., Nat. Assn. Bond Lawyers, Bellerive Country Club. Roman Catholic. Home: 9822 Old Warson Rd Saint Louis MO 63124-1066 Office: Thompson Coburn LLP One US Bank Plz Saint Louis MO 63101 Office Phone: 314-552-6000. Business E-Mail: mlause@thompsoncoburn.com.

LAUTENBACHER, CONRAD CHARLES, JR., federal agency administrator, retired naval officer; b. Phila., June 26, 1942; s. Conrad Charles and Dorthea Henrietta (Jensen) L.; m. Susan Elizabeth Scheihing, June 20, 1964; children: Elizabeth Lautenbacher Katz, Conrad John. BS, U.S. Naval Acad., 1964; MS, Harvard U., 1965, PhD, 1968. Commd. ensign USN, 1964, advanced through grades to vice adm., 1994, aide to Vice Chief Naval Ops., Chief Naval Ops. Washington, 1974-75, exec. officer USS Benjamin Stoddert Pearl Harbor, Hawaii, 1975-77, program analyst Chief Naval Ops. Washington, 1977-80, comdg. officer USS Hewitt San Diego, 1980-82, dir. program planning Chief Naval Ops. Washington, 1982-86, comdg. officer Naval Sta., Norfolk Va., 1986-88, insp. gen. U.S. Pacific Fleet Hdqrs. Pearl Harbor, 1988-90; comdr. Cruiser-Destroyer Group 5 San Diego, 1990-91; dir. force structure, resources and assessment J-8, Joint Staff, Washington, 1991-94; spl. asst. to asst. sec. navy USN, 1994; commdr. U.S. Third Fleet, 1994-96; dir. office of program appraisal, 1996-97; dep. chief of naval ops. N-8, 1997-2000; ret., 2000; mgmt. cons. Tech., Stategies, and Alliances, Inc., 2000-01; pres., CEO Consortium for Oceanographic Rsch. and Edn., 2001—02; under sec. of commerce, adminstr. NOAA US Dept. Commerce, 2002—. Decorated D.S.M. (4), Legion of Merit with 3 gold stars, Meritorious Svc. medal with 2 gold stars, Navy Commendation medal, Navy Achievement medal. Mem. U.S. Naval Inst. Lutheran. Office: NOAA 1401 Constitution Ave NW Washington DC 20230 Office Phone: 202-482-3436. Business E-Mail: conrad.c.lautenbacher@noaa.gov. *Life is about people and relationships. True happiness begins with sensitivity and responsiveness to the needs of others.*

LAUTENBERG, FRANK R., senator; b. Paterson, N.J., Jan. 23, 1924; s. Samuel and Mollie L.; children: Ellen, Nan, Lisa, Joshua. BS, Columbia U., 1949; DHL, Hebrew Union Coll., Cin. and N.Y.C., 1977; PhD (hon.), Hebrew U., Jerusalem, 1978. Founder Automatic Data Processing, Inc., Clifton, N.J., 1952-55, exec. v.p. adminstrn., 1955-69, pres., 1969-75, chief exec. officer, 1975-82, chmn. bd.; mem. U.S. Senate from N.J., 1982—2001; owner FRL Enterprises, Rochelle Park, NJ, 2001—; U.S. senator from N.J., 2003—. Mem. Commerce Com., Govtl. Affairs Com.; bd. dirs. The Holocaust Mus., Washington, Columbia U., N.Y.C., Cordoza Law Sch. at Yeshiva U., N.Y.C., Rutgers U., N.J.; former disting. vis. prof. Univ. of Medicine & Dentistry, New Brunswick, N.J. Commr. Port Authority N.Y. and N.J., 1978-82, N.J. econ. devel. coun.; trustee Sch. Bus., Columbia U.; nat. pres. Am. Friends Hebrew U., 1973-74; former hon. gen. chmn., pres. Nat. United Jewish Appeal, 1975-77; mem. bd. overseers N.J. Symphony Orch.; founder Lautenberg Cancer Rsch. Ctr., Med. Sch., Hebrew U., Jerusalem, 1971. Served with Armed Forces, 1943-46, ETO; bd. mem. Montclair Art Mus. Recipient Torch of Learning award Am. Friends Hebrew U., 1971, Scopus award, 1975 Mem. Nat. Assn. Data Processing Service Orgns. (pres. 1968-69, dir. from 1974). Democrat. Office: US Senate 324 Hart Senate Office Bldg Washington DC 20510*

LAUTENSCHLAGER, PEGGY A., state attorney general; b. Fond du Lac, Wis., Nov. 22, 1955; d. Milton A. and Patsy R. (Oleson) L.; m. Rajiv M. Kaul, Dec. 29, 1979 (div. Dec. 1986); children: Joshua Lautenschlager Kaul, Ryan Lautenschlager Kaul; m. William P. Rippl, May 26, 1989; 1 child, Rebecca Lautenschlager Rippl. BA, Lake Forest Coll., 1977; JD, U. Wis., 1980. Bar: Wis., U.S. Dist. Ct. (we. dist.). Pvt. practice atty., Oshkosh, Wis., 1981-85; dist. atty. Winnebago County Wis., Oshkosh, 1985-88; rep. Wis. Assembly, Fond du Lac, 1988-92; U.S. atty. U.S. Dept. of Justice, Madison, Wis., 1992—2000; atty. gen. State of Wis., 2003—. Apptd. mem. Govs. Coun. on

Domestic Violence, Madison, State Elections Bd., Madison; bd. dirs. Blandine House, Inc. Active Dem. Nat. Com., Washington, 1992-93; com. Wis., 1989-92. Named Legislator of Yr., Wis. Sch. Counselors, 1992, Legislator of Yr., Wis. Corrections Coalition, 1992. Mem. Wis. Bar Assn., Dane County Bar Assn., Fond du lac County Bar Assn., Phi Beta Kappa. Avocations: gardening, house renovation, sports, cooking. Office: 114 E State Capitol Madison WI 53702

LAUTER, JAMES DONALD, retired stockbroker; b. L.A., Sept. 3, 1931; s. Richard Leo and Helen M. (Stern) L.; m. Neima Zwieli, Feb. 24, 1973; children: Walter James (dec.), Gary. BS, UCLA, 1956. Market rsch. mgr. Germain's Inc., L.A., 1961; sr. v.p. investments, former br. mgr. Dean Witter Reynolds, Inc., Pasadena, Calif., 1961-96, ret., 1996. With Armed Forces, 1954-56. Recipient Sammy award L.A. Sales Execs. Club, 1961. Mem. AARP, UCLA Alumni Assn., UCLA Chancellors Assocs., Pasadena Bond Club (pres. 1995-96), Bruin Athletic Club, Coaches Round Table, UCLA Athletics Life Pass Club. Home: 3717 Marfield Ave Tarzana CA 91356 Personal E-mail: jlauter@flash.net.

LAUTER, M. DAVID, physician; b. Wilmington, Del., Jan. 7, 1951; s. Aaron Mordecai and Anne Marguerite (Scondin) L.; m. Diane Ruel, Oct. 11, 1980; children: Michael, Sara. B in Engring. Scis., Johns Hopkins U., 1973, MA, 1974; MD, Jefferson Med. Coll., 1978. Diplomate Am. Bd. Family Physicians. Resident family practice Ctrl. Maine Med. Ctr., Lewiston, 1978-81; clin. dir. USPHS Indian Hosp., Red Lake, Minn., 1981-84; pvt. practice as family doctor York, Maine, 1984—. With Pub. Health Svc., 1981-84. Office: 12 Hospital Dr York ME 03909-1030 Office Phone: 207-363-3681. Business E-Mail: dlauter@yorkhospital.com.

LAUTERBACH, EDWARD CHARLES, psychiatric educator; b. Chgo., Mar. 21, 1955; s. Edward G. and Virginia C. (Pochelski) L. AB cum laude, Augustana Coll., Rock Island, Ill., 1977; MD, Wake Forest U., 1982. Lic. psychiatrist, Mo., Pa., N.J., N.C., Ga.; diplomate Nat. Bd. Med. Examiners, Am. Bd. Psychiatry and Neurology with qualifications in geriat. psychiatry. Intern Washington U. Sch. Medicine/Barnes Hosp., St. Louis, 1982-83, resident in psychiatry, 1983-86, clin. asst., 1982-86; instr. neurology movement disorder fellow U. Medicine and Dentistry of N.J., New Brunswick, 1986-87; asst. prof. Mercer U. Sch. Medicine, Macon, Ga., 1988-92, chief div. adult and geriatric psychiatry, dept. psychiatry and behavioral scis., 1988-98, coord. grand rounds dept. psychiatry and behavioral scis., 1989-98, assoc. prof., 1992-96, prof., 1996—, prof. internal medicine/neurology, 1996—, prof. radiology, 1996—; pvt. practice Charlotte, NC, 1987-88. Chair free comm. IVth World Congress Biol. Psychiatry, Phila., 1985; mem. neurology staff Lyons VA Hosp., 1986; med. staff privileges in neurology Mercy Hosp., Charlotte, 1987, cons., 1987; privileges in psychiatry Med. Ctr. Ctrl. Ga., 1994—, Coliseum Psychiat. Hosp., 1994—, dir. med. staff continuing edn., 1994-96, Middle Ga. Hosp., 1997-2002; med. dir. geropsychiatry program The Sr. Ctr., Middle Ga. Hosp., 1997-2002. Guest editor Psychiatric Annals, 2002; editor: Psychiatric Management in Neurological Disease, 2000, Psychiatric Management in Neurological Disease, Spanish and Italian edits., 2002; editl. reviewer Neuropsychiatry, Neuropsychology and Behavioral Neurology, Biological Psychiatry, Movement Disorders, assoc. editor Jour. Neuropsychiatry and Clin. Neuroscis., 1999—; contbr. articles to profl. jours. Recipient Med. Dir. of Yr. award S.E. region, Horizon Mental Health Mgmt., Inc., 1999—2001; scholar Rock Sleyster scholar, Wake Forest U., 1981. Fellow: Am. Psychiat. Assn. (course dir. 1990—92, 1994—95, symposium chmn. 1995—97, co-dir. 1998—2001, symposium chmn. 2001, Disting.), Am. Neuropsychiat. Assn. (rsch. com. 1992—, vice-chair 1998—99, chmn. 1999—); mem.: Charlotte Psychiat. Soc., Movement Disorder Soc., Med. Assn. Ga., Mecklenburg County Med. Soc., N.C. Psychiat. Assn., Bibb County Med. Soc., Ga. Psychiat. Physicians Assn. (state com. on contg. med. edn.), Am. Acad. Neurology, AMA.

LAUTERBUR, PAUL C(HRISTIAN), chemistry professor; b. Sidney, Ohio, May 6, 1929; BS, Case Inst. Tech., 1951; PhD, U. Pitts., 1962, DSc (hon.) Honoris Causa, 2004; PhD (hon.), U. Liege, Belgium, 1984; DSc (hon.), Carnegie Mellon U., 1987; DEng (hon.), Copernicus Med. Acad., Cracow, Poland, 1988; DSc (hon.), Wesleyan U., 1989, SUNY, Stony Brook, 1990; DEng (hon.), Rennselaer Poly. Inst., 1991, U. Mons, Hainaut, Belgium, 1996. Rsch. asst. and assoc. Mellon Inst., Pitts., 1951—54, fellow, 1955—63; assoc. prof. chemistry SUNY, Stony Brook, 1963—69, prof. chemistry, 1969—84, rsch. prof. radiology, 1978—85, univ. prof., 1984—85; prof. (4) depts. U. Ill., Urbana, 1985—, Disting. Univ. prof. Coll. Medicine Chgo., 1990—. Mem. sci. couns. Contbr. articles to profl. jours.; mem. editl. bds. Cpl. U.S. Army, 1953—55. Recipient Clin. Rsch. award, Lasker Found., 1984, Nat. Medal of Sci., U.S.A., 1987, Fiuggi Internat. prize, Fondazione Fiuggi, 1987, Roentgen medal, 1987, Gold medal, Radiol. Soc. N.Am., 1987, Nat. Medal of Tech., 1988, Gold medal, Soc. Computed Body Tomography, 1989, The Amsterdam (Alfred Heineken) prize in medicine, 1989, Laufman-Greatbatch award, Assn. for Advancement Med. Instrumentation, 1989, Leadership Tech. award, Nat. Elec. Mfrs. Assn., 1990, Bower award and prize for achievement in sci., Benjamin Franklin Nat. Meml. Commn. of the Franklin Inst., 1990, Internat. Soc. Magnetic Resonance award, 1992, Kyoto prize, Inamori Found., 1994, Nobel prize in physiology or medicine, 2003. Fellow: Am. Inst. Med. and Biol. Engring., Am. Phys. Soc. (Biol. Physics prize 1983), AAAS; mem.: Internat. Soc. Magnetic Resonance in Medicine (Gold medal 1982), IEEE (sr.), Am. Chem. Soc., NAS. Office: Dept Chemistry U Ill 600 S Mathews 51-6 MC-712 Urbana IL 61801 Office Phone: 217-244-0445. Business E-Mail: pcl@uiuc.edu.

LAUTERSTEIN, JOSEPH, cardiologist; b. Vienna, Dec. 1, 1934; came to U.S., 1940; s. Bernard and Hajnalka (Stern) L.; m. Erika Stein, Jan. 24, 1964 (dec. Aug. 1990); children: Deborah Ann Ehret, Brenda Rose Horton; m. Elisabeth Spiegl Lazaroff, Nov. 27, 1994. BA, Syracuse U., 1955; MD, U. Vienna, 1964. Lic. physician, N.Y. Intern, then resident in internal medicine The Bklyn. Cumberland Med. Ctr., 1964-66, 68-69, fellow in cardiology, 1969-70; attending physician, cons. internal medicine and cardiology Hamilton Ave. Hosp., Monticello, N.Y., 1970-78, Catskill Regional Med. Ctr., Harris, NY, 1970—2005, chief cardiology, 1971—2005, chief of staff, 1981—82; mem. courtesy staff dept. internal medicine and cardiology The Bklyn. Hosp. Ctr., 1971-95; clin. asst. dept. internal medicine and cardiology St. Vincent's Hosp. and Med. Ctr. N.Y., 1974-80, asst. attending physician, 1981-86, assoc. attending physician, 1987-94, attending physician, 1995—2005; with Sullivan Internal Medicine Group, P.C., Monticello, 1970—2005; ret. Dir. ICU Catskill Regional Med. Ctr., Harris, 1971—79, dir. CCU, 1978—2005, dir. spl. diagnostics, 1984—2005, pres. med. bd., 1981—82; mem. pacemaker task force Empire State Med. Sci. and Ednl. Found., 1985—89; med. dir. Sullivan County EMT-D Program, 1989—2005; police surgeon Vill. of Monticello, 1974—, Sullivan County, 1972—; med. advisor Monticello Vol. Ambulance Corps, 1970—80, 1989—2004; mem. Sullivan County Emergency Svcs. Coun., 1990, 91; instr. outdoor emergency care, 1991—. Co-contbr. articles to Jour. Cardiovascular Surgery, Annals of Thoracic Surgery, Angiology, Chest. Trustee Catskill Regional Med. Ctr., 1981-82, Catskill Regional Med. Ctr. Found., 1990-2004, hon. trustee, 2004—; mem. Nat. Ski Patrol, 1979—, med. advisor So. N.Y. region, 1989-94, 97—, med. advisor So. Catskill sect., 1994-97; patroller Holiday Mountain Ski Patrol, 1979—. Capt. med. corps USAF, 1966—68. Named Citizen of Yr., SYDA Found. Sullivan County, 1991. Fellow Am. Coll. Cardiology (N.Y. State chpt., del. to N.Y. Med. Soc. Ho. Dels. 1991—, councilor 1991—, com. mem. 1990—), Am. Coll. Chest Physicians (assoc.), Am. Coll. Angiology, Internat. Coll. Angiology, N.Y. Cardiol. Soc. (exec. bd. dirs. 1982—, mem. various coms.), N.Y. Acad. Medicine; mem. AMA, Am. Geriatrics Soc., ACP/Am. Soc. Internal Medicine, Soc. for Critical Care Medicine, N.Y. Acad. Scis., N.Am. Soc. for Pacing and Electrophysiology, Med. Soc. State of N.Y. (cardiology del. to interspecialty com., cardiology del. to ho. of dels.), others. Personal E-mail: joe_lauterstein@yahoo.com.

LAUTTENBACH, CAROL, artist; b. New Haven, Nov. 26, 1934; d. Gustav Fredrick and Wanda M. (Eshner) Stolze; m. Francis John Lauttenbach; children: Daniel M., William J. Grad. with honors in oils, watercolors, Washington Sch. Art, Chgo., 1967. One-woman shows include Greene Art Gallery, Guilford, Conn., Carriage House Gallery Ltd., Guilford, Gallery 53, Meriden, Conn., John Slade Ely House Gallery, New Haven, exhibitions include Mary Lou Fischer Gallery, Guilford, 2005. Recipient First prize, Wallingford Art League, 1967—69, 1972, award, Branford Art League, 1970, Second prize, Wallingford Art League, 1970, Best Conn. Landscape award, Mt. Carmel Art Assn., Inc., Hamden, 1970, Prix de Paris award, Musee Des Raymon Duncan, France, 1972, 1976, 1980, Second prize, Autumn Art Exhbn., Wallingford, 1974, award, Drawing Anthology Internat., Long Beach, NY, 1974, Second New Haven Bank award, Mt. Carmel Art Assn., Inc., Hamden, 1975, Third prize, Old Saybrook Art Exhbn., 1976, Guilford Art League, 1977, award, 1978, Am. Nat. Bank award, Mt. Carmel Art Assn., Inc., Hamden, 1979, Rainbow Cleaners award, 1980, award, Grand Salon Des Surindependants, Paris, 1981, Mt. Carmel Art Assn., Inc., Hamden, 1982, Hilda Levy Meml. award, Brush and Palette Club, New Haven, 1983, Viewers' award, Greene Art Gallery, Shoreline Alliance for Arts, Guilford, 1984, Guilford Savs. Bank award, Guilford Art League, 1985, Best in Show award, Mt. Carmel Art Assn., Inc., Hamden, 1986, Elizabeth Greeley Meml. award, 1987, Jean Cowels award, Shoreline Alliance Arts, 1987, Donald L. Perlroth, Inc. award, Mt. Carmel Art Assn., Inc., Hamden, 1988, Koenig Art Emporium prize, New Haven Brush & Palette Club, 1990, Marc D. Rosenberg Meml. award, Mt. Carmel Art Assn., Inc., Hamden, 1990, Third prize, Nat. League Am. Pen Women, 1992, Merriam Motors award, Arts & Crafts Assn. Meriden, 1995, Stella King Meml. award, 1997, New Haven Savs. Bank award, Mt. Carmel Art Assn., Inc., Hamden, 1998, Jerry's Artarama cert. award, Arts & Crafts Assn. Meriden, 1998, Beazley Realtors award, Mt. Carmel Art Assn., Inc., Hamden, 2000, Harvey Fuller award, Arts & Crafts Assn. Meriden, 2001, Mayor Carl Amento award, Mt. Carmel Art Assn., Inc., Hamden, 2002, Utrech Art Supplies award, Hamden Art League, 2004, Dusa Chipopractic Ctr. award, 2005, Best Theme award, Arts & Crafts Assn., Meriden, 2005, others. Mem.: Arts and Crafts Assn. Meriden (First prize 1976, Best in Show award 1982, Grumbacher Silver medal 1983—84, Hon. mention 1986, 1987, Henry T. and Stella King Meml. award 1990, Jerry's Artarama Cert. award 1990, Gold medal 1993, Grumbacher Gold medal 1993, Merriam Motors award Jubilee 325 Wallingford Theme 1995, Stella King Meml. award 1997, Artist's Alternative award 2004, Best Theme award 2005, Harvey Fuller award 2001), Conn. Classic Arts, Inc. (Third prize 1981, First prize 1982, Third prize 1983, Gabriel D. Luchetti award 1984, 1986, First prize 1987, 1993, Third prize 1994, Rosemary Landino Meml. award 1995, Westport Framing and Art Gallery Award 1997, Second prize in acrylic and oils 1998), Internat. Soc. Artists, Provincetown Art Assn., New Haven Paint and Clay Club (Members' Show award 1978, Hon. mention 1996), Wadsworth Athenium (life), Conn. Acad. Fine Arts (life), Wallingford Hist. Soc. (life). Home: 39 Ridgewood Rd Wallingford CT 06492-2116

LAUTZENHEISER, BARBARA JEAN, insurance company executive; b. LaFeria, Tex., Nov. 15, 1938; d. Fred E. and Verna V. L. BA with high distinction, Nebr. Wesleyan U., 1960. Actuarial trainee Bankers Life Ins. Co. Nebr., Lincoln, 1960-64, programmer and systems analyst, 1964-65, asst. actuary, 1965-69, assoc. actuary, 1969-70, 2d v.p., actuary, 1970-72, v.p., actuary, 1972-80; sr. v.p. Phoenix Mut. Life Ins. Co., Hartford, Conn., 1980-84; pres. Montgomery Ward Life Ins. Co., Montgomery Ward Ins. Co., Forum Ins. Co., Schaumberg, Ill., 1984-85; prin., CEO Lautzenheiser & Assocs., Hartford, 1986—. Spokesperson for ins. industry, witness U.S. Senate and Ho. of Reps. coms., commns. and state legislatures; featured on TV, nat. mags. and newspaper articles; mem. Interim Actuarial Std. Bd., 1986-88, Actuarial Std. Bd., 1989-90; chmn. Com. for Fair Ins. Rates, 1983-86; mem. adv. com. Nat. Assn. Ins. Commrs. Life Disclosure (A) Com. working group, 1993; bd. dirs. LifeUSA Holding Co. Contbr. articles to profl. jours. Mem. Lincoln Electric Sys. Adminstrv. Bd., 1977-79; bd. dirs. Nebr. Wesleyan U., 1977-82, 89-93, Am. Coll., 1987-97. Recipient Young Alumni svc. award Nebr. Wesleyan U., 1971, Corp. Woman award Women Bus. Owners of N.Y., 1983, C.H. Poindexter award for disting. achievement and exceptional svc. to the assn. and ins. industry Nat. Assn. Life Cos., 1989. Fellow: Conf. Cons. Actuaries (dir. 1997—98), Soc. Actuaries (dir. 1975—80, exec. com. 1978—80, chmn. adminstrn. and fin. com. 1981—82, exec. com. 1981—84, dir. 1981—85, pres. 1982—83, assoc. editor The Actuary 1992—93, life nonforfeiture task force 1995—96); mem.: Am. Coun. Life Ins. (risk classification com. 1973—81), Life Office Mgmt. Assn. (corp. fin. planning com. 1974—81, chmn. 1976—78), Nat. Alliance Life Companies (bd. dirs. 1992—95), Soc. of Actuaries Found. (founding trustee 1994—98, trustee emeritus Actuarial Found. 1998—), Am. Acad. Actuaries (dir. 1974—77, chmn. com. on publs. 1980—81, disclosure working group 1994—2001, nonforfeiture working group 1994—, com. on life ins. 1995—98, life practice coun. vice chair 1998, co-chair 1998—99, v.p. life 1999—2001, pres.-elect 2002—03, editl. adv. bd. mem. Contingencies mag. 2002—, pres. 2003—04, immediate past pres. 2004—05, task force revise ASOP no.12 2004—, past pres. 2005—), Greater Hartford C. of C. (nat. policies panel 1980—84), Nebr. Actuaries Club (dir. 1969—70, sec.-treas. 1971—72, dir. 1971—74, pres. 1972—73, chmn. 1973—74, dir. 1992—94). Home: 17 Huntingridge Dr South Glastonbury CT 06073-3614 Office: Lautzenheiser & Assocs City Place II 185 Asylum St Fl 11 Hartford CT 06103-3611 Office Phone: 860-246-0893. Personal E-mail: lautzenheiser@aol.com.

LA VALLEE, ADRIENNE KERNAN, artist, educator; b. Pittsfield, Mass., Feb. 27, 1953; d. Gerard William and Ann Catlin La Vallee. BFA cum laude, U. of Mass., 1975; MFA, Md. Inst. Coll. of Art, Balt., 1977. Visual artist Self Employed, Manchester, NH, 1977—; lectr. St. Anselm Coll., Manchester, NH, 1986—, New Eng. Coll., Henniker, NH, 1980—; asst. dir. Chapel Art Ctr. St. Anselm Coll., 1988—97; edn. coord. N.H. Inst. of Art, Manchester, 1983—95. Bd. dirs. N.H. Citizens' Com. for the Arts, Concord, 2002—; co-founder, bd. dirs. N.H. chpt. Women's Caucus for Art, Concord, 1991—95; bd. dirs. Boston chpt. Caucus for the Arts, 1989—90; reviewer Art New Eng., Boston, 1982—87; mng. editor, co-editor OPTIONS: new hampshire's visual arts quar., Henniker, 1979—85. One person exhibition, Recent paintings at Worcester Polytechnic Institute, 2002, Nature Morte: recent still life paintings and prints, 2001, REMEMBERANCES at Eastern Washington University, Cheney, WA, 2001; author: (published essay) Carlos Barnas, Painter, Citizen of Ecuador, 2000; paintings, Artist's Residency Grant in Wyoming, 1995, painting, 1992, Whiz Bang, 1982 (First Pl. N.H. Art Biennial, 1985), selections, 1985, mono-prints, 1983, installation with poet rodger martin, Our Paradise Lost, 1997. Juror N.H. Congl. Dist. One, Manchester, 1996—96, N.H. Found. for the Blind, Concord, 1985. Mem.: AAUP, Coll. Art Assn. Conservative. Avocation: perennial flower garden design, gardening, travel, haiku. Office: Saint Anselm Coll 100 Saint Anselm Dr Manchester NH 03102 Personal E-mail: atelierdelavie@yahoo.com.

LAVALLEE, DAVID KENNETH, chemistry professor, academic administrator; b. Malone, New York, Oct. 1, 1945; s. Bernard Martin and Eleanor Jane (Magoon) Lavallee; m. Eileen Marie (Gilmartin); children: Jeffrey Michael, Gregory James, Jocelyn Marie. BS, St. Bonaventure U., 1967; MS, U. Ill., Chgo., 1968, PhD, 1971. Asst. prof. Colo. State U., Ft. Collins, Colo., 1972—78; assoc. prof. Hunter Coll., City Univ. of N.Y., N.Y.C., 1978—82; prof. chemistry Hunter Coll., City Univ. of N.Y., N.Y.C., 1983—94; assoc. provost Hunter Coll., City Coll. of N.Y., N.Y.C., 1990—94; provost, v.p. acad. affairs City Coll. of N.Y., N.Y.C., 1994—99, State Univ. of N.Y., New Paltz, NY, 1999—. Edn. adv. bd. Chemtech, Washington, 1978—84. Author: The Chemistry and Biochemistry of N-substituted Porphyrins, 1987; author: (with others) Chemistry, 1978. Mem. NY State Regents Adv. Bd. Accreditation, 2003—. Named USPHS Fellow, Anatomy Dept. U. Ill., Chgo., 1971—72; recipient NATO Rsch. Award, Ecole Normale, Superieure, Paris, 1983—85, Fulbright Rsch. Scholar Award, U. Rene Descartes, Paris, 1985—86, Catalyst Award, Chem. Mfr. Assn., 1986. Mem.: AAAS, Soc. Nuclear Medicine, Am. Chem. Soc. (chair Internat. Chemistry Olympiad 1986—93, soc. com. chem. edn. 1990—96, bd. publs. divsn. chem. edn. 1986—99, chair 1993—97). Democrat. Achievements include patents for N-substituted metalloporphyrins as anti-tumor agents; synthesis of radiolabelled metalloporphyrins via N-substituted precursors. Office: State Univ NY 75 S Manheim Blvd Ste 1 New Paltz NY 12561-2499 Home: 944 Rte 308 Rhinebeck NY 12572-3447 Office Phone: 845-257-3275. E-mail: lavallee@newpaltz.edu.

LAVANI, ROMEEN M., physician; b. Mumbai (Bombay), India, Feb. 25, 1970; s. Mohmed R. and Mumtaz M. Pathan; m. Vaishali R. Mody, June 16, 1998. MBBS, T.N. Med. Coll., Mumbai(Bombay), India, 1993; DCH, L.T.M Med. Coll. and Sion Hosp., Mumbai(Bombay), India, 1995, MD, 1996, U. Ill. at Chgo., Chicago, Ill., 2001, U. Chgo. Hosp., 2004. Lic. Physicians (pediatrics) Ill., 1998, Physicians(pediatrics) Wis., 2003, Ind., 2003. Physician-pediat. residency Sion Hosp., Mumbai, India, 1993—96; physician-pediat. pvt. practice Pvt. practice, Mumbai, India, 1996—98; physician-pediatrics residency U. Ill. at Chgo. Hosp., Chgo., 1998—2001; physician-pediat.c critical care fellowship U. Chgo., Chgo., 2001—04; physician-primary care/critical care St. Anthony Hosp., Chgo., 2004—. Primary care(outpatient) pediatrician, inpatient dir., dir. of residency rotation St.Anthony Hosp., Chicago, Ill., 2004—. Recipient Gold Medal in Pediat., Bombay U., 1996, Sir James Flett Award-second prize, Indian acad. of Pediat., 1997, APA Internat. Health Award, 1997; grantee Travel Grant - APA meeting, Wash., DC, Ambulatory pediat. Assn., 1997, Travel Grant - Am. Heart Assn. Meeting, Orlando, Fla., U. Chgo.-Emergency Resuscitation Ctr., 2003, Travel Grant - Soc. for Pediatric Rsch. Meeting, San Fransisco, Calif., U. Chgo., Emergency Resuscitation Ctr., 2004. Mem.: AHA, AAP, Soc. for Critical Care medicine(SCCM). Achievements include research in Role of Amylase Rich foods in Nutritional rehabilitation of severely malnourished children with diarrhea; Affect of pH/CO2 on global cardiomyocyte ischemia-reperfusion injury. Avocation: cricket. Home: 724 S Oakley # 1 Chicago IL 60612 Office: St Anthony Hosp 2875 West 19th St Chicago IL 60612 Home Fax: 773-521-4587; Office Fax: 773-521-4587. Personal E-mail: yomeen@gmail.com.

LAVE, CHARLES ARTHUR, economics professor; b. Phila., May 18, 1938; s. Israel and Esther Lave; 1 child, Rebecca. BA, Reed Coll., 1960; PhD, Stanford U., 1968. Mem. faculty U. Calif., Irvine, 1966—, prof. econs., chmn. dept. econs., 1978-85, 89-92. Vis. prof., vis. scholar Hampshire Coll., 1972, Stanford U., 1974, MIT, 1982, Harvard U., 1982, U. Calif., Berkeley, 1988, 94. Author: (with James March) An Introduction to Models in the Social Sciences, 1975, Energy and Auto Type Choice, 1981, Urban Transit, 1985, others. Trustee Reed Coll., Portland, Oreg., 1978-82; bd. dirs. Nat. Bur. Econ. Rsch., Cambridge, 1991-97; chmn. bd. Irvine Campus Housing Authority, Inc., 1982-96, asst. to chancellor, 1996-97. With USAF, 1957. Recipient Pyke Johnson award Transp. Rsch. Bd., 1987, Extraordinarius award U. Calif., 1993. Fellow Soc. Applied Anthropology; mem. Am. Econ. Assn., AAAS, Transp. Research Bd. Office: U Calif Dept Econs Irvine CA 92697-5100 E-mail: calave@uci.edu.

LAVE, JUDITH RICE, economics professor; b. Campbellton, May 18, 1939; d. J.H. Melville and G.A. Pauline (Lister) Rice; m. Lester Bernard Lave, June 21, 1965; children: Tamara Rice, Jonathan Melville. BA in Econs., Queen's U., Kingston, Ont., Can., 1957-61; MA in Econs., Harvard U., 1964, PhD, 1967; LLD, Queen's U., 1994. Lectr., asst. prof. econ. Carnegie Mellon U., Pitts., 1966-73, assoc. prof., 1973-78; dir. econ. analysis Office of Sec., Dep. of Asst. Sec. Planning and Evaluation, Washington, 1978-79; dir. office of rsch. Health Care Fin. Adminstrn., Washington, 1980-82; prof. health econ. U. Pitts., 1982—, co-dir. Ctr. for Rsch. on Health Care, 1996—, chair dept. health policy and mgmt., 2003—. Cons. Nat. Study Internal Medicine Manpower, Chgo., 1976, Wash. State Hosp. Assn., 1984, Horty, Springer & Mattern, Pitts., 1984, Hogan and Hartson, Washington, 1989, Ont. Hosp. Assn., Conn. Hosp. Assn., 1991; cons. various agys. U.S. HHS (formerly U.S. HEW), 1971-89; mem. adv. panel Robert Wood Johnson Found., Princeton, N.J., 1983-84, 96—, Leonard Davis Inst., Phila., 1984, U.S. Congress, 1977, 82, 83—; com. mem. Inst. Medicine Coms., Washington, 1975-, Project 2000 Commn. on Future of Podiatry, Washington, 1985-86. Editl. bd. Wiley Series in Health Svcs., 1989-90, Health Svcs. Rsch., 1970-74, Inquiry, 1979-82, AUPHA Press, 1986, Jour. of Health Policy Politics and Law, Health Affairs, 1998—; co-author: Hospital Construction Act - An Evaluation of the Hill Burton Program, 1948-73, 74, Health Status, Medical Care Utilization and Outcome: A Bibliography of Empirical Studies (4 vols.) 1989, Providing Hospital Services, 1989; contbr. numerous articles to profl. jours. Mem. Prospective Payment Assessment Commn., 1993—97, Medicare Payment Adv. Commn., 1997—2000; mem. planning com. ARC, Pitts., 1986—; mem. rev. com. United Way, Pitts., 1988—90; bd. dirs. Craig House, Pitts., 1976—77, Presbyn. Sr. Care, Pitts., Jewish Health Care Found., 2002—. Woodrow Wilson fellow, 1961—62. Disting. fellow Acad. Health (pres. 1977-88, bd. dirs. 1983-93); mem. Found. for Health Svcs. Rsch. (pres. 1988-89, bd. dirs. 1983—), Am. Pub. Health Soc., Am. Econ. Soc. (com. mem.), Inst. Medicine (bd. health svcs. 2005-), Nat. Acad. Social Ins., Robert Wood Johnson Found. (com. on econ. impact of health sys. change 1996—), Internat. Health Eco Assn. Democrat. Home: 1008 Devonshire Rd Pittsburgh PA 15213-2914 Office: U Pitts A649 Pub Health Pittsburgh PA 15213 Office Phone: 412-624-0898. Business E-Mail: lave@pitt.edu.

LAVECCHIA, JAYNEE, state supreme court justice; b. Paterson, NJ, Oct. 9, 1954; m. Michael R. Cole. Grad., Douglass Coll., 1976, Rutgers U., 1979. Bar: N.J. 1980. Pvt. law practice; dep. atty. gen. divsn. of law State of NJ; asst. counsel to Gov. Thomas H. Kean Office of Counsel, dep. chief counsel to Gov. Thomas H. Kean; dir. divsn. of law dept. law anf pub. safety State of NJ, 1984-98; dir., chief admisntrv. law judge Office of Adminstrv. Law, 1989-94; commr. banking and ins. State of NJ, 1998-99; assoc. justice NJ Supreme Ct., Trenton, 2000—. Chair various N.J. Supreme Ct. Coms. Fellow ABA. Office: North Tower 158 Headquarters Pla Morristown NJ 07960

LAVELLE, ARTHUR, anatomy educator; b. Fargo, N.D., Nov. 29, 1921; s. Frank and Lillie (Hanson) LaV.; m. Faith Evelyn Wilson, 1947; 1 dau., Audrey Anne. BS, U. Wash., 1946; MA, Johns Hopkins, 1948; PhD, U. Pa., 1951. USPHS postdoctoral fellow U. Pa., Phila., 1951-52; mem. faculty dept. anatomy U. Ill. Coll. Medicine, Chgo., 1952—, assoc. prof., 1958-65, prof., 1965-87, prof. emeritus, 1987—. Vis. prof. UCLA, 1968-69; cons. Galesburg (Ill.) State Rsch. Hosp., 1965-68; mem. Biol. Stain Commn., 1953-93, trustee, 1978-93, pres., 1981-86, v.p., 1991-92. Mem. editorial bd. Biotechnic and Histochemistry, 1989-93; contbr. articles to profl. jours. USPHS research grantee, 1953-70; Cerebral Palsy Found. grantee, 1964-68; Guggenheim fellow, 1966-69 Mem. Am. Assn. Anatomists, Am. Soc. Cell Biology, Cajal Club, AAAS, Soc. Neurosci., Sigma Xi. E-mail: arthurlavelle@cs.com.

LAVELLE, AVIS, consulting firm executive; b. Chgo., Mar. 5, 1954; d. Adolph Eugene and Mai Evelyn (Hicks) Sampson. BS in Comms. cum laude, U. Ill., 1975. Announcer, pub. affairs dir. Sta. WTAX Radio, Springfield, Ill., 1977-78; news dir., anchor Sta. WLTH Radio, Gary, Ind., 1978-79; reporter, anchor Stas. WJJD/WJEZ, Chgo., 1979-84; chief polit. reporter Sta. WGN-Radio/TV, Chgo., 1984-88; campaign press sec. Richard M. Daley for Mayor, Chgo., 1988-89; mayoral press sec. Officer of the Mayor, Chgo., 1989-92; nat. press sec. Clinton/Gore for Pres., Little Rock, 1992; spl. asst. to chmn. Vernon Jordan Presdl. Transition, Washington, 1992-93; asst. sec. pub. affairs U.S. Dept. Health and Human Svcs., Washington, 1993—95; v.p. comm. Waste Mgmt. Inc., 1995—99; v.p. govt. and pub. affairs U. Chgo. Hosps., 1999—2001; sr. ptnr. bus. devel. The Foster Group, Chgo., 2001—04; pres. A LaVelle Consulting Svcs. LLC, Chgo., 2004—. Mem. Delta Sigma Theta Pub. Svc., Chgo., 1973—; mem. steering com. Black Adoption Taskforce of Ill., Chgo., 1987; v.p. Chgo. Bd. Edn., 1997-2003; bd. dirs. Project Image, Inc., Chgo., 1988-89, Human Resources Devel. Inst., Chgo., 1988; founding mem. bd. dirs. After Sch. Matters Found.; mem. resource com. Met. Planning Coun.; campaign mgr. Mayor Richard M. Daley's Re-election, 1999; commr. Chgo. Cable Commn., 2003—; state dir. Ill. Kerry for Pres. Campaign, 2004. Recipient African Am. Bus. and Profl. Women award Dollars and Sense Mag., 1989, Women at Work award Nat. Commn. Working Women, 1980, First Place Team award AP, 1984; named one of Chicago's 100 Most Influential Women, Crain's Chgo. Bus., 2004. Democrat. Office: A LaVelle Consulting Svcs LLC 25 E Washington St #908 Chicago IL 60602 Office Phone: 312-223-0581.

LAVELLE, BRIAN FRANCIS DAVID, lawyer; b. Cleve., Aug. 16, 1941; s. Gerald John and Mary Josephine (O'Callaghan) L.; m. Sara Hill, Sept. 10, 1966; children: S. Elizabeth, B. Francis D. Jr., Catherine H. BA, U. Va., 1963; JD, Vanderbilt U., 1966; LLM in Taxation, NYU, 1969. Bar: N.C. 1966, Ohio 1968. Assoc. VanWinkle Buck, Wall, Starnes & Davis, Asheville, N.C., 1968-74, ptnr., 1974—. Lectr. continuing edn. N.C. Bar Found., Wake Forest U. Estate Planning Inst., Hartford Tax Inst., Duke U. Estate Planning Inst. Contbr. articles on law to profl. jours. Trustee Carolina Day Sch., 1981-92, sec., 1982-85; bd. dirs. The Salvation Army, 1986—; bd. dirs. Western N.C. Cmty. Found., 1986—, sec., 1987-90; bd. advs. U. N.C. Ann. Tax Inst., 1981—. Capt. JAG USAF, 1966-67. Mem. ABA, Am. Coll. Trust and Estate Counsel (state chmn. 1982-85, regent 1984-90, lectr. continuing edn.), N.C. Bar Assn. (bd. govs. 1979-82, v.p. 1997-2000, councillor tax sect. 1979-83, councillor estate planning law sect. 1982-85, 2002—), N.C. State Bar (splty. exam. com. on estate planning and probate law 1984-90, chmn. 1990-91, cert. 1987), Rotary, Biltmore Forest Country, Royal Brigade of Guards, Asheville Downtown City. Anglican. Home: 45 Brookside Rd Asheville NC 28803-3015 Office: 11 N Market St PO Box 7376 Asheville NC 28802-8506 Office Phone: 828-258-2991. Business E-Mail: blavelle@vwlawfirm.com.

LAVELLE, JOSEPH P., lawyer; b. Scranton, Pa., Sept. 7, 1957; s. Patrick Leo and Anne M. (Antal) L.; m. Kathy A. Mlodzienski, Aug. 14, 1982; children: Remy, Joseph, Taylor. BS in Physics, Wilkes Coll., 1979; JD summa cum laude, U. Pitts., 1982. Bar: D.C. 1982, U.S. Ct. Appeals (Fed. cir.) 1982, U.S. Patent and Trademark Office 1982, U.S. Ct. Appeals (3d, 2d and 6th cir.). Assoc. Howrey & Simon, Washington, 1982-90, ptnr., 1991—. Adj. prof. Georgetown U. Law Ctr., 1995—. Editl. bd. ABA Antitrust Law Developments, III, 1992; contbr. articles to profl. jours.; mng. editor U. Pitts. Law Rev., 1981-82. Mem. ABA, AAAS, Am. Phys. Soc., Order of the Coif. Republican. Office: Howrey Simon Arnold & White Ste 1 1299 Pennsylvania Ave Washington DC 20004-2420 E-mail: lavellej@howrey.com.

LAVENAS, SUZANNE, writer, editor, consultant; b. Buenos Aires, Dec. 17, 1942; arrived in U.S., 1955; d. Carlos Fernando and Mary (Sharp) Lavenas; m. Wesley First, Jan. 9, 1982 (dec. Nov. 2000). Student, Antioch Coll., 1960-64, 65-66. Computer programmer N.Y. Telephone, N.Y.C., 1966-68; prodn. editor, then copy editor Travel Weekly, N.Y.C., 1968-76, chief copy editor, 1976-79; mng. editor Indsl. Chem. News, N.Y.C., 1981-82; editor, writer, cons. N.Y.C., 1986-99; pres. Lavenas & Carson, Montauk, N.Y., 1999—. Author numerous articles. Mem. Overseas Press Club, Soc. Silurians. Republican. Episcopalian. Avocations: reading, cooking, computer hacking, walking, cinema. Home: 236 Edgemere St Montauk NY 11954-5249

LAVENBERG, STEPHEN S., electrical engineer, researcher; b. Mar. 22, 1943; BS in Elec. Engring., Rensselaer Poly. Inst., 1963; MS in Elec. Engring., Calif. Inst. Tech., 1964, PhD in Elec. Engring., 1968. Rsch. staff mem., sr. mgr. IBM Corp. Rsch., Thomas J. Watson Rsch. Ctr., 1970—. Fellow IEEE (Meritorious Svc. award 1984, Koji Kobayashi Computers and Comm. award 1991). Office: IBM Corp Rsch Thomas J Watson Rsch Ctr 30 Saw Mill River Rd Hawthorne NY 10532-1507

LAVENDER, ROBERT EUGENE, state supreme court justice; b. Muskogee, Okla., July 19, 1926; s. Harold James and Vergene Irene (Martin) L.; m. Maxine Knight, Dec. 22, 1945; children— Linda (Mrs. Dean Courter), Robert K., Debra (Mrs. Thomas Merrill), William J. LL.B., U. Tulsa, 1953; grad., Appellate Judges Seminar, 1967, Nat. Coll. State Trial Judges, 1970. Bar: Okla. bar 1953. With Mass. Bonding & Ins. Co., Tulsa, 1951-53, U.S. Fidelity & Guaranty Co., Tulsa, 1953-54; asst. city atty. Tulsa, 1954-55; practice, 1955-60, Claremore, Okla., 1960-65; justice Okla. Supreme Ct., 1965—, chief justice, 1979-80. Guest lectr. Okla. U., Oklahoma City U., Tulsa U. law schs. Republican committeeman, Rogers County, 1961-62. Served with USNR, 1944-46. Recipient Disting. Alumnus award U. Tulsa, 1993. Mem. ABA, Okla. Bar Assn., Rogers County Bar Assn., Am. Judicature Soc., Okla. Jud. Conf., Phi Alpha Delta (hon.) Methodist (adminstrv. bd.). Club: Mason (32 deg.). Home: 2910 Kerry Ln Oklahoma City OK 73120-2507 Office: US Supreme Ct Okla State Capitol Room 208 Oklahoma City OK 73105

LAVENSON, SUSAN BARKER, hotel corporate executive, consultant; b. LA, July 26, 1936; d. Percy Morton and Rosalie Laura (Donner) Barker; m. James H. Lavenson, Apr. 22, 1973 (dec. Sept. 1998); 1 child, Ellen Ruth Stanclift. BA, Stanford U., 1958, MA, 1959; PhD (hon.), Thomas Coll., 1994. Cert. gen. secondary credential tchr., Calif. Tchr. Benjamin Franklin Jr. H.S., San Francisco, 1960; tchr. French dept. Lowell H.S., San Francisco, 1960-61; v.p. Monogram Co., San Francisco, 1961-62, creative dir. N.Y.C., 1973-86; pres. SYR Corp., Santa Barbara, Calif., 1976-89; mng. ptnr. Lavenson Ptnrs., Camden, Maine, 1989—. Mem. commn. on co-edn. Wheaton Coll., Norton, Mass., 1985-87; mem. Relais et Chateaux, Paris, 1978-89; cons. World Bank Recruit Divsn., 1993. Author: Greening of San Ysidro, 1977 (Conf. award 1977). Trustee Camden Pub. Libr., 1989—95, v.p., 1991—93; vice chair bd. trustees Thomas Coll., Waterville, Maine, 1990—2001, trustee emerita, 2001—; trustee Atlantic Ave. Trust, 1989—91; founding pres. Maine chpt. Internat. Women's Forum, 1991—; mem. Coun. of Advisors Coll. of the Atlantic, Bar Harbor, Maine, 1996—2001, Ariz. Women's Forum; chair dean's adv. coun. Ariz. State U., 2002, chair coun. advisors Virginia Piper Creative Writing Ctr., 2004—. Recipient Piper award for entrepreneurial excellence, 2002. Mem. Advice Inc., Camden Yacht Club, Stanford Alumni Assn., Com. of 200 (treas. 1985-86), Women's Entrepreneur Corps, Phi Delta Kappa (Stanford U. chpt., founding mem.). Home and Office: 7841 E Shooting Star Way Scottsdale AZ 85262 Office Phone: 480-575-7722. E-mail: sbl1@cox.net. *Three rules to remember: 1) Never take anything personally. 2) Never lose your sense of humor. 3) Keep your eye on the objective - I also like the Apocryphal words: "I am not made or unmade by things that happen to me, but by my reactions to them.".*

LAVER, RODNEY GEORGE, tennis player; b. Rockhampton, Queensland, Australia, Aug. 9, 1938; ed. pub. schs.; m. Mary Benson, 1966; 1 son. Played on Australian Davis Cup team, 1958-63, 73; Australian champion, 1960, 62, 69; Wimbledon champion, 1961, 62, 68, 69; U.S.A. champion, 1962, 69; French champion, 1962, 69; 1st player to win Grand Slam twice, 1962, 69; French champion, 1962, 69; joined World Championship Tennis, 1970, played for San Diego Friars, 1976, 77, 78. Decorated Order Brit. Empire. Author: How To Play Winning Tennis, 1964; Education of a Tennis Player, 1971.

LAVERDIERE, CLAUDETTE MARIE, nun, head of religious order; BS in Edn., Mary Rogers Coll., Maryknoll, N.Y., 1967; M Theol. Studies, Cath. Theol. Union, Chgo., 1986; licentiate in Sacred Theology, Weston Jesuit Sch. Theology, 2000. Joined Maryknoll Sisters Congregation, 1956. Tchr. Nganza Secondary Sch. for Girls, Mwanza, Tanzania, 1967-71; with devel. dept. Maryknoll Sisters Congregation, 1972-74; tchr. religious edn. dept. secondary schs. Nakuru, Kenya, 1974-76; cathechetical dir. Nakuru Diocese, Kenya, 1976-79; team mem. devel. edn. program Mombasa Diocese, Kenya, 1980-84; registrar, tchr. Theol. Centre Religious, Nairobi, Kenya, 1987-90; pres. Maryknoll Sisters Congregation, 1991-97, student, 1997-2000; tchr. Theological Ctr. Religious, Nairobi, Kenya, 2000-01; tchr. sacred scripture Religious Sisters Inst., Kenya, 2001—03. Home: 18 Poulin St Winslow ME 04901-6958

LAVERS, RICHARD MARSHALL, lawyer; b. Oak Ridge, Tenn., Apr. 15, 1947; s. Willard Douglas and Athena Vashti (Compton) L.; m. Christine Anne Jandl, June 2, 1973; children: Christian Douglas, Ansley McKay, Ti-Patrice, Rickey Elizabeth. BA, U. Mich., 1968; postgrad., Columbia U., 1968-69; JD cum laude, U. Mich., 1972; postdoctoral, U. Wis., 1977-81. Bar: Colo. 1972, U.S. Dist. Ct. (Colo.) 1972, U.S. Ct. Appeals (10th cir.) 1975, Wis. 1978, La. 1983, U.S. Dist. Ct. (mid. dist.) La. 1983, U.S. Ct. Appeals (5th cir.) 1983, N.Y. 1986. Dep. dist. atty. 9th Jud. Dist., Glenwood Springs, Colo., 1972-73; assoc. Martin Dumont, Glenwood Springs, 1972-74, Rovira, Demuth & Eiberger, Denver, 1974-76; assoc. resident counsel Nat. Presto Industries, Eau Claire, Wis., 1976-82; asst. counsel Ethyl Corp., Baton Rouge, 1982-87; ptnr. Mulcahy & Wherry, S.C., Milw., 1987-90, Michael, Best & Friedrich, Milw., 1990-94; gen. counsel RMT, Inc., Madison, Wis., 1994—97; of counsel Whyte Hirschboeck Dudek, S.C., 1994—97; gen. counsel MK Rampage, Inc., 1995—99; exec. v.p., sec., gen. counsel Coachmen Industries, Inc., Elkhart, Ind., 1997—. Gen. counsel Wis. World Trace Ctr., 1987-91; bd. dirs. Nexus Internat., Ltd.; adj. prof. bus. law Cardinal Stritch Coll. Mem. editorial bd. U.S. Trademark Assn., Guide to the Internat. Sale of Goods Conv., Bus. Laws Inc. Counsel U.S. Rep. Steve Gunderson campaign, Eau Claire, Wis., 1980; bd. dirs. Milw. Kickers Soccer Club, Inc., pres., 1992—95. Mem. ABA, N.Y. Bar Assn., Wis. Bar Assn. (bd. dirs. internat. practice sect. 1992—), La. Bar Assn., Eau Claire Jaycees (bd. dirs. 1976-80), Meridian Club (pres. 1981). Republican. Congregationalist. Office: RMT Inc PO Box 8923 Madison WI 53708-8923

LAVERY, DANIEL P., management consultant; b. NYC, June 28, 1932; m. Doris E. Guenther, Oct. 23, 1954; children: Daniel, Brian, Kevin, Michael. BS with honors, Manhattan Coll., 1954; MBA, Rutgers U., 1963. Mem. prodn. mgmt. staff, photo products dept. E.I. DuPont de Nemours & Co., Inc., 1954-65; divsn. mgr. Anken Industries, Williamstown, Mass., 1965-71; gen. mgr. Dymo Industries, N.Y.C., 1971-73; dir. cons. studies Quantum Sci. Corps., N.Y.C., 1973-79; mgr. strategic mktg. ITT, N.Y.C., 1979-80; sr. dir. market rsch. Western Union, 1980-82; v.p. Pactel, Inc., mgmt. cons., N.Y.C., 1982-83; ptnr. Palo Alto Mgmt. Group, Wyckoff, N.J., 1983-98, Matterhorn Group, Wyckoff, N.J., 1998—. Served as capt. USAF, 1955-57. Mem. Inst. Mgmt. Cons. (cert. mgmt. cons.), Am. Arbitration Assn. (panel mem. 1985—). Office: Matterhorn Group 458 Sicomac Ave Wyckoff NJ 07481-1120 Office Phone: 201-891-6162. Business E-Mail: danlavery@matterhorngroup.com.

LAVERY, IAN C., colon and rectal surgeon, medical association administrator; MD, U. Queensland. Residency Cleveland Clinic Found., Cleveland; intern Princess Alexandra Hospital, Australia; residency Repatriation Gen. Hospital, Melbourne, Australia; vice chmn. dept. of colorectal surgery, bd. mem. Cleveland Clinic Found., Cleveland, 1976—. Fellowship Cleveland Clinic Found., Cleveland. Mem.: Am. Bd. of Colon and Rectal Surgery (pres.). Office: Am Bd Colon and Rectal Surgery Ste 600 20600 Eureka Rd Taylor MI 48180 also: Cleveland Clinic 9500 Euclid Ave Cleveland OH 44195

LA VETTE, MAUREEN C., actress, writer; d. William Michael and Mary Elizabeth La Vette. Actor: (films) Hardcase and Fist, 1989, Mind Trap, 1990, Virgin High, 1991, Assault of Party Nerds, 1995, Cyborg II, 1996, Lima: Breaking the Silence, 1998, Johnny Stompanato, 2000, Death Game, 2001, Starfire Mutiny, 2002, Desert Rose, 2002, The Wizard; (TV series) Acting on Intuition, 2003, Mike Hammer, Mama's Family, 9 to 5, Other World, Chevy Chase Show, 1994, Final Justice, America's Most Wanted, Sea Quest (3 episodes), Divorce Law, The Wizard, (TV pilot) This Is America; guest: (TV talk show) Egyptian TV. Sponsor World Vision, Nairobi, 2004—; vol. Smokey Robinson Gospel, L.A., 2004—, Leon Isaac Kennedy Ministries, L.A., 2004—. Named Best Actress-Most Promising Newcomer, Santa Monica Coll., 1979; recipient Jeanie Golden Angel award philanthropic work, So. Calif. Motion Picture Coun., 1988, Bronze Halo award, 1988. Mem.: AFTRA, SAG, Women In Film, Acad. TV Arts and Scis. Roman Catholic. Avocations: ballet, tango, hiking, studying etymology, travel. Office: 9201 Wilshire Blvd #204 Beverly Hills CA 90210

LAVEY, STEWART EVAN, lawyer; b. Newark, July 24, 1945; m. Suzanne Laurence, July 9, 1972. AB, Syracuse U., 1967; JD, Fordham U., 1970. Bar: N.Y. 1971, N.J. 1987, Pa. 1988, D.C. 1988. Assoc. Kelley Drye & Warren, N.Y.C., 1970-71, Emil, Kobrin, Klein & Garbus, N.Y.C., 1971-72, Zimet Haines Moss & Goodkind, N.Y.C., 1972-75; asst. sec., asst. gen. counsel Norlin Corp., N.Y.C., 1975-78, sec., asst. gen. counsel, 1978-85; of counsel Shanley & Fisher, P.C., Morristown, NJ, 1985-87, ptnr., 1987—99; ptnr., bus., fin. dept Drinker Biddle & Reath LLP, Florham Park, NJ, and assoc. head, corp. and securities practice group, 1999—. Adj. assoc. prof. law Fordham U., N.Y.C., 1976-79, adj. prof., 1980-2004, lectr. Fordham U. Continuing Legal Edn., 1991-93. Mem. Fordham Law Rev., 1968-70. Trustee Pingry Sch., Martinsville, N.J., 1996-2000. Recipient Bene Merenti medal Fordham U. Mem. Am. Bar Assn., N.Y. State Bar Assn., Assn. of Bar of City of N.Y., N.J. Bar Assn. (securities law com.), Pa. Bar Assn., D.C. Bar Assn., Pingry Sch. Alumni Assn. (pres. 1996-2000). Office: Drinker Biddle & Reath LLP 500 Campus Dr Florham Park NJ 07932-1047 Office Phone: 973-360-1100. Office Fax: 973-360-9831. Business E-Mail: stewart.lavey@dbr.com.

LAVEY, WARREN G., lawyer; AB MS in Applied Mat., Harvard U., 1975; diploma in Econ., Cambridge U., 1976; JD magna cum laude, Harvard Law Sch., 1979. Spl. asst. to the Chief of the Common Carrier Bur. FCC, 1983, 1984; practice leader for communications Skadden, Arps, Slate, Meagher & Flom, LLP, Chgo. Lectr and panelist at telecommunications seminars; adj. prof. Kellogg Sch. of Mgmt., Northwestern U.; bd. legal advisors Intelsat; mem. Blue Ribbon Panel Ill. Commerce Comm.; mem. steering com. on fgn. telecommunications privatizations and competition US Dept. Commerce; chmn. of conf. on telecommunications mfg. joint ventures, Shanghai; lead spkr. at conf. on global telecom regulatory developments, Tel Aviv. Authorships (to profl. jours.); author: "Can I Do the Deal? Terminated Rules, Bad Rules and Phantom Rules at the FCC", The M&A Lawyer, 2004. Office: Skadden Arps Slate Meagher & Flom LLP 33 W Wacker Dr Chicago IL 60606 Office Phone: 312-407-0830. Office Fax: 312-407-8515. Business E-Mail: wlavey@skadden.com.

LAVEZZI, JOHN CHARLES, retired art history educator, archaeologist; b. Chgo., July 7, 1940; s. Francis M. and Dorothy M. (Kopal) L. AB magna cum laude, Cath. U. Am., 1962; MA, U. Cin., 1965; postgrad., Am. Sch. Classical Studies, Athens, Greece, 1967-70; PhD, U. Chgo., 1973. Sec. of the sch. Am. Sch. Classical Studies at Athens, 1968-70; asst. prof. Sch. Art Bowling Green (Ohio) State U., 1973-80, assoc. prof., 1980—2005, head divsn. art history, 1998—2001, acting head, 2003—04. Sr. assoc. mem. Am. Sch. Classical Studies at Athens, 1972—, rsch. assoc. Corinth Excavations, 1972—. Author: (book chapter) Corinth XX, 2003; contbr. articles to profl. jours. and symposia. Mem. Toledo Mus. Art. Recipient CUA Stratemeier award, 1962, Medici Circle teaching awards, 1986, 94; grantee Am. Philos. Soc., 1973. Mem. Archeol. Inst. Am., Midwest Art History Soc., Soc. for Preservation of Greek Heritage, Nat. Geog. Soc., Smithsonian Instn. Friends, Cyprus Am. Archeol. Rsch. Inst., Cath. Assn. Scientists and Engrs., Blue Key, Phi Beta Kappa (pres. chpt. 1992), Phi Alpha Theta, Delta Epsilon Sigma, Phi Eta Sigma. Roman Catholic. Office Phone: 419-372-2160. E-mail: lavezzi@bgnet.bgsu.edu.

LAVIDGE, ROBERT JAMES, marketing research executive; b. Chgo., Dec. 27, 1921; s. Arthur Wills and Mary Beatrice (James) L.; m. Margaret Mary Zwigard, June 8, 1946; children: Margaret, Kathleen, William, Lynn Elizabeth. AB, DePauw U., 1943; MBA, U. Chgo., 1947. Analyst Pepsodent divsn. Lever Bros., Chgo., 1947-48, new products mktg. rsch. mgr. Pepsodent divsn., 1948-49; asst. dir. mktg. Am. Meat Inst., Chgo., 1950-51; ptnr. Elrick, Lavidge and Co., Chgo., 1951-56; pres. Elrick and Lavidge, Inc., Chgo., 1956-86; pres. emeritus Elrick and Lavidge, Scottsdale, Ariz., 1997—2002; ret. Lectr. mktg. rsch., sales adminstrn. Northwestern U., 1950-80; mem. Nat. Mktg. Adv. Com., 1967-71, also exec. com.; bd. govs. Brand Names Edn. Found., 2000-02. Trustee Village Western Springs, Ill., 1957-61, pres., 1973-77; trustee McCormick Theol. Sem., 1981-90, 92-96; mem. coun. U. Chgo. Grad. Sch. Bus.; dir. Ariz. Faith Counseling Ctr.; mem. coun. Ctr. Svcs. Leadership; dir. Animals Benefit Club Ariz. Mem. Am. Mktg. Assn. (v.p. 1963-64, pres. 1966-67, trustee found. 1992—, chmn. 1992-99), Internat. Rels. Soc. (chmn. 1961-65), DePauw U. Alumni Assn. (pres. 1967-68), Klinger Lake Club (Mich.), Paradise Valley Country Club, Phi Beta Kappa, Beta Gamma Sigma, Sigma Delta Chi. Presbyterian.

LAVIGNE, AVRIL, singer; b. Napanee, Ont., Can. Performer: (albums) Let Go, 2002 (nominee Grammy award Best New Artist, 2002, nominee Grammy award Best Pop Vocal Album, 2002, nominee Grammy award for Song of Year for Complicated, 2002, nominee Grammy award for Best Female Pop Vocal Performance for song Complicated, 2002, nominee Grammy award for Best Female Rock Vocal Performance for song Sk8er Boi, 2002), Under My Skin, 2004. Achievements include signed with L.A. Reid of Arista Records at age 16. Avocations: hockey, basketball, skateboarding. Office: Network Mgmt 1650 W 2nd Ave Vancouver BC Canada V6J 4R3

LAVIGNE, LAWRENCE NEIL, lawyer; b. Newark, June 30, 1957; s. Daniel S. and Alice M. (Melon) L.; m. Benjie Panesh, Oct. 12, 1980; children: Gabriel A., Derek N. BA, Franklin & Marshall Coll., 1979; JD, Seton Hall U., 1982. Bar: N.J. 1982, U.S. Dist. Ct. N.J. 1982, U.S. Ct. Appeals (3d cir.) 1986, U.S. Supreme Ct. 1986, N.Y. 1989. Assoc. Shanley & Fisher, P.C., Newark, 1982-83; ptnr. Hanlon & Lavigne (and predecessor firm), Edison, NJ, 1983—2002; mem. Norris, McLaughlin & Marcus, P.C., 2002—. Instr. Am. Inst. Paralegal Studies, Mahwah, N.J., 1985-88. Mem.: ABA (litigation sect.), Def. Rsch. Inst., Worrall F. Mountain Inn of Ct. (barrister 1991—93), Nat. Assn. Employment Attys., Somerset County Bar Assn., Somerset Bar Assn., Assn. Trial Lawyers Am., N.J. Def. Assn., Trial Attys. N.J., Middlesex County Bar Assn., N.J. Bar Assn. (product liability com.). Republican. Jewish. Avocations: tennis, music, computers, gourmet food and wine. Office Phone: 908-722-0700. Business E-Mail: lnlavigne@nmnlaw.com.

LAVIGNE, ROBERT A., writer; b. Easthampton, Mass., Apr. 10, 1943; s. Donald A. and Janette Lavigne; m. Ann Amelia Grider (div. June 1991). LPN, Pioneer Valley Sch. Nursing, 1970—80; student, Greenfield (Mass.) C.C., 1970. LPN various hosps. and nursing homes; maintenance engr. various casinos, Las Vegas, Nev. Author: Harry, 2002, Escape, 2002, Tamera II, 2002, (screenplays) Deceived, 2000, short stories, novels. With USAF, 1960—64. Avocations: music, sports, fishing, travel, boating. Home: 80 Damon Rd #4106 Northampton MA 01060

LAVIK, BRICKER L., lawyer; b. 1950; BA magna cum laude, Univ. Minn., 1974; JD cum laude, Hamline Univ., 1977. Bar: Minn. 1977. Atty. Legal Aid Soc., Mpls., 1977—86; atty., trial dept. Dorsey & Whitney LLP, Mpls., 1986—93, ptnr., sr. counsel, trial group, dir., pro bono program, 1994—, dir., pro bono dept., 1996—. Adj. prof. Hamline Univ. Sch. Law., 1986—92, 1995, William Mitchell Coll. Law., 1989—92. Lectr. in field. Named a Super Lawyer, Minn. Law & Politics, 2002; recipient Outstanding Svc. award, Minn. Justice Found., 1992, Pro Bono Publico award, Hennepin County Bar Assn., 1994, Disting. Alumni award, Hamline Univ. Law Sch., 2000, Pro Bono Atty. award, Minn. Legal Services Coalition, 2001. Mem.: Minn. State Bar Assn. (construction Law sect. 1998—, gov. coun.), Hennepin County Bar Assn. (co-chair, delivery legal svcs. com. 2001—). Office: Dorsey & Whitney LLP Ste 1500 50 S Sixth St Minneapolis MN 55402-1498 Office Phone: 612-340-5645. Office Fax: 612-340-2868. Business E-Mail: lavik.bricker@dorsey.com.

LAVIN, BERNICE E., cosmetics executive; b. 1925; m. Leonard H. Lavin, Oct. 30, 1947; children: Scott Jay (dec.), Carol Marie, Karen Sue. Student, Northwestern U. Vice chairperson of bd., sec.- treas. Alberto-Culver Co.; dir., v.p., sec.- treas. Alberto-Culver U.S.A., Inc. Sec.-treas., dir. Alberto-Culver Internat., Inc.; sec.-treas. Sally Beauty Co., Inc. Office: Alberto-Culver Co 2525 Armitage Ave Melrose Park IL 60160-1163 E-mail: blavin@alberto.com.

LAVIN, FRANKLIN L., ambassador; b. Canton, Ohio, 1957; married; 3 children. BSc in Fgn. Svc., Georgetown U., 1980, MSc in Chinese Lang. and History, 1985; MA in Internat. Econ./Internat. Rels., Johns Hopkins U., 1990; MBA, U. Pa., 1996. Asst. to dep. dir. personnel The White House, Washington, 1981, asst. dir. Pres. Commn. on Exec. Exch., 1982—83, assoc. dir. Office of Pub. Liaison, 1984—85, dir. Office of Polit. Affairs, 1987—89; dir. pvt. & voluntary programs, Asia Bur. US Agy. for Internat. Devel., 1981—82, spl. asst., asst. adminstr. for African Affairs, 1983—84; dep. exec. sec. for coord NSC, Washington, 1986—87; dep. asst. sec. for East Asia and Pacific US Dept. Commerce, Washington, 1991-93; trade economist, exec. dir. Asia Pacific Policy Ctr., Washington, 1994—96; v.p. emerging markets Citibank; regional mgr. Bank of Am.; US amb. to Singapore US Dept. State, 2001—. Adj. fellow Ctr. Strategic and Internat. Studies; mem. US Com. on Security and Cooperation in the Asia Pacific; mem. Nat. Policy Forum; mem. steering com. Am. Coun. on Germany's Young Leaders' Program. Contbr. chpts. to book, articles to NY Times, Wall St. Jour., Fgn. Affairs, others. Officer USNR. Office: Embassy of the US 27 Napier Rd 258508 Singapore

LAVIN, HOWARD S., lawyer; b. NYC, June 28, 1957; BS in Indsl. and Labor Rels., Cornell Univ., 1979; JD, Emory Univ., Atlanta, 1982. Bar: NY 1983. Adminstrv. ptnr., labor & employment practice area Stroock & Stroock & Lavan LLP, NYC. Frequent lectr. in field. Mem.: NY State Bar Assn., NY C of C. Office: Stroock & Stroock & Lavan LLP 180 Maiden Ln New York NY 10038-4982 Office Phone: 212-806-6046. Office Fax: 212-806-9046. Business E-Mail: hlavin@stroock.com.

LAVIN, LAURENCE MICHAEL, lawyer; b. Upper Darby, Pa., Apr. 27, 1940; s. Michael Joseph and Helen Clair (McGonigle) L. BS, St. Joseph's U., Phila., 1962; JD, Villanova (Pa.) U., 1965. Bar: Pa., S.C. Vol. U.S. Peace Corps, Thika, Kenya, 1966-67; atty. Community Legal Svcs., Phila., 1968-70, exec. dir., 1971-79, Palmetto Legal Svcs., Columbia, S.C., 1981-85; dir. Law Coordination Ctr., Harrisburg, Pa., 1985-88, Nat. Health Law Program, L.A., 1988—; chmn. bd. dirs. L.A. Poverty Dept. Bd. dirs., chmn. civil com. Nat. Legal Aid and Defender, Washington, 1976-78. Founding mem. Pa. Coun. to Abolish Death Penalty, Harrisburg, 1986; bd. dirs. LA Poverty Dept., 1996—, Health Care Access Trust, 2005—. Mem. ABA, Pa. Bar Assn. (chmn. legal svcs. to pub. com. 1985-88). Democrat. Home: 3677 Wellington Rd Los Angeles CA 90016 Office: Nat Health Law Program 2639 S La Cienega Blvd Los Angeles CA 90034-2675 E-mail: lavin@healthlaw.org.

LAVIN, PHILIP TODD, medical educator; b. Rochester, N.Y., Nov. 21, 1946; s. Albert A. and Mary (Rapkin) Lavin; m. Mary Ellen Saunders, Aug. 23, 1970; children: Andrew, Abby. AB, U. Rochester, 1968; PhD, Brown U., 1972. Rsch. asst. prof. Brown U., Providence, 1972-74, SUNY Buffalo, Amherst, 1974-77; asst. prof. sch. pub. health Harvard U., Boston, 1977-83, assoc. prof. surgery, 1983—. Trainee NSF, 1968—72; pres., founder Averion Inc. (formerly Boston Biostatistics, Inc.), 1983—; dir., founder Boston Biostat Rsch. Found., Framingham, 1988—; cons. FDA, 1983—86, spl. govt. employee, 1992—; co-chmn. clinical trial com. Mass. Biotech. Coun. Contbr. articles to scholarly jours. Bd. dirs. William Graves Fund, Boston, 1989—. Grantee, Nat. Cancer Inst., 1976—80, Nat. Heart Lung Blood Inst., 1985—89. Mem.: Regulatory Affairs Profl. Soc., Soc. Clin. Trials, Am. Statis. Assn., Biometric Soc., Phi Beta Kappa. Achievements include support for 32 FDA approvals for drugs, devices and biologics; development of statistical methods for the analysis of serial biomarker data applicable to the detection of biomarker shifts and trends over time; natural history models for cancer, renal faulure and device implants; research in chronic disease models; found a contract research organization and not for profit research foundation. Home: 3 Cahill Park Dr Framingham MA 01702-6105 Office: Averion Inc 4 California Ave Framingham MA 01701 Business E-Mail: plavin@averioninc.com.

LAVIN, STEPHEN MICHAEL, university basketball coach; b. San Francisco, Sept. 4, 1964; s. Cap and Mary Lavin. BS, Chapman U., 1987. Grad. asst. basketball coach, staff mem. Purdue U., 1988-91; staff mem. UCLA, 1991-95, asst. coach, 1995-97, recruiting coord., 1996-97, head coach, 1997—. Dir., founder Lavin Basketball Camps, 1984—; summer camp and coaches clinic spkr., 1989—; cons./advisor Korean Nat. Profl. Team, Samsung Profl. Team, 1992-96. Named Nat. Rookie Coach of Yr. Basketball Times mag., 1997; recipient Internat. Inspiration award Hugh O'Brien Youth Found., 1997. Office: UCLA 325 Westwood Plz Los Angeles CA 90095-8356

LAVIN, SYLVIA, architecture educator; d. Irving and Marilyn (Aronberg) Lavin; m. Greg Lynn; 2 children. BA, Barnard U.; MA, Columbia U., PhD, 1990. Instr. Columbia U., Harvard U., So. Calif. Inst. Arch., U. So. Calif.; joined faculty Sch. Arch. and Urban Planning UCLA, 1992, chair dept. arch. and urban design Sch. Arts and Arch., 1996—. Lectr. in field. Author: Quatremere de Quincy and the Invention of a Modern Language of Architecture, 1992; contbr. articles to profl. jours. Jewish.

LAVIN, TERRENCE J., lawyer; b. May 1954; m. Cynthia Sykes; children: Hillary, Chelsea. Grad. in Journalism, U. Ill.; grad., Chgo.-Kent Coll., 1983. Bd. dirs., claims com., underwriting com. Ill. State Bar Assn. Mut. Ins. Co.; adj. prof. med. malpractice Chgo.-Kent Coll.; lectr. in field. Contbr. articles to profl. jours.; editor: ITLA's Medical Malpractice Trial Notebook, 1990. Mem.: Ill. Trial Lawyers Assn. (bd. mgrs., amicus curiae com., publs. com.), Ill. State Bar Assn. (3d v.p. 2000—, chair task forces on multidisciplinary practice and allocation of judg. scope and correlation, budge and fin., and space and properties coms., pres.-elect 2002—03).

LAVINE, ALAN, columnist, writer; b. Sharon, Pa., Feb. 17, 1948; s. Milton and Doris (Helfman) L.; m. Gail Jeanne Liberman, Dec. 20, 1991. BA, Kent State U., 1970; MA, U. Akron, 1973; MBA, Clark U., 1981. Dir. of rsch. Donoghue Orgn., Holliston, Mass., 1981-83; freelance nat. syndicated fin. columnist North Palm Beach, Fla., 1983—; columnist Dow Jones Market Watch. Presenter papers in field ann. meeting AAAS, 1972, ann. meeting Mass. Psychol. Assn., Wellesley, 1978, ann. meeting APA, 1979, Nat. Symposium on Rsch. in Art, U. Ill., 1980; guest lectr. Cornell U., 1990, 91, 92, 93. Author: Diversify: Investor's Guide to Asset Allocation Strategies, 1990 (alt. selection Fortune Book Club), Your Life Insurance Options, 1993 (endorsed Inst. CFPs), Improving Your Credit and Reducing Your Debt, 1994 (endorsed Inst. CFPs), Getting Started in Mutual Funds, 1994, Diversify Your Way to Wealth, 1994 (alt. selection Fortune Book Club), 50 Ways to Mutual Fund Profits, 1995, The Complete Idiot's Guide to Making Money with Mutual Funds, 1996, Love, Marriage and Money, 1998, Rags To Riches: Motivationing Stories of Ordinary People Who Achieved Extraordinary Wealth, 2000, Short and Simple Guide to Life Insurance, 2000, More Rags to Riches: All New Stories of Ordinary People Who Achieved Extraordinary Wealth, 2002, Short and Simple Guide to Smart Investing, 2002, Rags to Retirement, 2002; contbr. articles to profl. jours. Mem. Nat. Writers Union, Soc. Am. Bus. Editors and Writers, Inc. Office: Alan Lavine Inc PO Box 14697 North Palm Beach FL 33408 Home: PO Box 14697 North Palm Beach FL 33408-0697 Office Phone: 561-630-7112. Personal E-mail: mwliblav@aol.com.

LAVINE, HENRY WOLFE, lawyer; b. Phila., Apr. 21, 1936; s. Samuel Phillips and Sarah Pamela (Leese) Lavine; m. Meta Landreth Doak, Feb. 20, 1960 (div. Feb. 1980); children: Lisa, Lindsay; m. Martha Putnam Cathcart (div. Feb. 1995); children: Samuel Putnam, Gwenn Cathcart; m. Ronda S. McCrea, June 5, 2004. BA, U. Pa., 1957, JD, 1961. Assoc. Squire, Sanders & Dempsey L.L.P., Cleve., 1961-70, ptnr. Washington, 1970-85, mng. ptnr. Washington office, 1985-91, sr. mng. ptnr., 1991—2002, counsellor to the firm, 2003—. Pres. Sawyer & Co. LLC. Mem. The Bretton Woods Com. Mem. Met. Club. Office: Squire Sanders & Dempsey 1201 Pennsylvania Ave NW PO Box 407 Washington DC 20044-0407 Office Phone: 202-626-6689.

LAVINE, STEVEN DAVID, academic administrator; b. Sparta, Wis., June 7, 1947; s. Israel Harry and Harriet Hauda (Rosen) L.; m. Janet M. Sternburg, May 29, 1988. BA, Stanford U., 1969; MA, Harvard U., 1970, PhD, 1976. Asst. prof.-English Lit. U. Mich., Ann Arbor, 1974-81; asst. dir. arts and humanities Rockefeller Found., NYC, 1983-86, assoc. dir. arts and humanities, 1986-88; pres. Calif. Inst. Arts, Valencia, 1988—. Cons. Wexner Found., Columbus, Ohio, 1986-87; selection panelist Input TV Screening Conf., Montreal, Can., and Granada, Spain, 1985-86; faculty chair Salzburg Seminar on Mus., 1989; co-dir. Arts and Govt. Program, The Am. Assembly, 1991; mem. arch. selection jury L.A. Cathedral, 1996, Arch. L.A., 1998-2001; adv. com. The Asia Soc., So. Calif. Ctr., 1998-; co-chair The Arts Coalition for Acad. Progress, L.A. Unified Sch. Dist., 1997-; vis. com. J. Paul Getty Mus., 1990-1997; cons. in field. Editor: The Hopwood Anthology, 1981, Exhibiting Cultures, 1991, Museums and Communities, 1992. Bd. dirs. Sta. KCRW-FM (NPR), Endowments, Inc., Cotsen Family Found., Villa Aurora, Am. Coun. Edn.; trustee Idyllwild Arts Found. Recipient Class of 1923 award, 1979, Faculty Recognition award, 1980 U. Mich.; Charles Dexter traveling fellow Harvard U., 1972, Ford fellow, 1969-74. Jewish. Office: Calif Inst Arts Office Pres 24700 McBean Pkwy Santa Clarita CA 91355-2397 Business E-Mail: slavine@calarts.edu.

LAVINE, THELMA ZENO, philosophy educator; b. Boston; d. Samuel Alexander and Augusta Ann (Pearlman) L.; m. Jerome J. Sachs, Mar. 31, 1944; 1 child, Margaret Vera. AB, Radcliffe Coll., 1936; A.M., Harvard U., 1937, PhD, 1939. Instr. Wells Coll., 1941-43, asst. prof., 1945-46; asst. prof. philosophy Bklyn. Coll., 1946-51; asst. prof. U. Md., 1955-57, assoc. prof., 1957-62, prof., 1962-65; Elton prof. George Washington U., 1965-85, chmn. dept., 1969-77; Clarence J.Robinson Univ. prof. George Mason U., Fairfax, Va., 1985—. Lectr., seminar cons. Inter-Am. Def. Coll., 1975—; exec. bd. Jour. of Speculative Philosophy, 2000—. Author: From Socrates to Sartre, 1980; co-author: introduction to Collected Works of John Dewey, Vol. 16, 1990, contbg. author: Reading Dewey, 1998, contbg. editor: Free Inquiry, 1980—, exec. bd.: Jour. of Speculative Philosophy, 2000—; contbr. articles to profl. jours., chpts. to books; author: (TV course) From Socrates to Sartre: The Philosophic Quest, 1984; co-author: History and Anti-History Philosophy, 1989, contbg. author: Philosophy of Paul Ricoeur, 1995, Rorty and Pragmatism, 1996, contbg. author: Perspectives on Habermas, 2000, contbg. author: Philosophy of Paul Ricoeur, 1995, mem. exec. bd.: Jour. Speculative Philosophy, 2000—; contbr. articles to profl. jours., revs., chpts. to books; series editor Transaction, 2003. Recipient Outstanding Faculty award U. Md., 1965, Outstanding Faculty award George Washington U., 1968, Alumnae Achievement award Radcliffe Coll., 1991; NEH sr. rsch fellow, 1980; Am. Enterprise Inst. Public Policy Research fellow, 1980-81, Va. Found. Humanities fellow, 1990; Herbert W. Schneider award contbns. to Am. Philosophy, 2000. Mem. Am. Philos. Assn. (5th Ann. Romanell lectr. 1991), Soc. Advancement Am. Philosophy (exec. com. 1979-82, pres. 1992-94), Internat. Soc. Sociology Knowledge, Internat. Soc. Polit. Psychology, Metaphys. Soc. Am., Washington Philosophy Club (pres. 1967-68), Washington Sch. Psychiatry, Forum Psychiatry and Humanities (exec. bd.), Cosmos Club, Harvard Club, SOPHIA, Phi Beta Kappa (pres. chpt. 1978-80). Home: 1625 35th St NW Washington DC 20007-2316 Office: George Mason U Robinsons Profs E 207 Fairfax VA 22030 Office Phone: 703-993-2171. E-mail: tzlavine@awol.com.

LAVINGTON, MICHAEL RICHARD, venture capital company executive; b. Purley, Surrey, Eng., Feb. 21, 1943; came to U.S., 1972; s. Richard H. and Patricia (Young) L.; m. June Watford, Aug. 13, 1966; children: Susan, Victoria. BA, Cambridge U., 1964; MA, Columbia U., 1965; PhD, Lancaster U., (Eng.), 1968. Dir. Ralli Australia, 1969-71, Bowater America, N.Y.C., 1971-74; pres. Kay Jewelers Inc., Alexandria, Va., 1974-90, Watford Investment Corp., McLean, Va., 1990-97, Fannie Mae, Washington, 1997—. Chmn. St. Stephen's and St. Agnes Sch., Alexandria, 1981-96; trustee Ch. Schs. in Diocese of Va., 1989-96. Personal E-mail: mlavington@aol.com.

LAVIN-PENNYFEATHER, ROSE, artist; b. Perth Amboy, N.J., Oct. 16, 1952; d. James V.P. and Emma (Kiblosh) Lavin; m. Franco Casentini, Feb. 14, 1974 (div. 1978); 1 child, Franco K. Casentini; m. Stefano Corti, Oct. 24, 1984 (div. 1997); 1 child, Sandro J. Corti; m. Wayne Pennyfeather, May 8, 1999. Student, Georgian Ct., 1970-72, U. Florence (Italy), 1972-73. Saleswoman Correges, Rome, 1977-78; sec. McDonnell-Douglas, Rome, 1978-80, McCann-Erickson, Rome, 1980-82, RAI TV and Radio Corp., N.Y.C., 1983-84; mgr. Benetton, Woodbridge, N.J., 1984-85; sole proprietor Art Studio LC, Woodbridge, 1990-99; art tchr. Perth Amboy Cath. Schs. K-8, 1999—. Artist drawing logo contest, Tarquinia, Italy (Silver medal 1978). Directress St. Peter's Altar Guild, Perth Amboy, 1991-2002. Mem. NOW, Nat. Mus. of Women in the Arts. Democrat. Episcopalian. Avocations: karate (brown belt), swimming, cooking. Home: 677 Parker St Perth Amboy NJ 08861-2913 Office: Perth Amboy Cath Schs 680 Catherine St Perth Amboy NJ 08861-2802

LAVIOLETTE, JOHN WALKER, engineering geologist, civil engineer; b. Crockett, Calif., Mar. 11, 1947; s. John Edwin and Virginia Marguerite LaViolette; m. Alyce Louise Dunn LaViolette (div.); children: John Edwin, Corrine Michelle. BS in Geology, Calif. State U., 1971, MS in Engring., 1980; MS in Civil Engring., U. Calif., Berkeley, 2005. Geologist Fugro, Inc., Long Beach, Calif., 1973—90; project geologist Lindvall Richter & Assocs., L.A., 1980—81; dist. geologist Blackhawk Geologic Hazard Abatement Dist., Danville, 1985—95, Canyon Lakes Geologic Hazard Abatement Dist., Calif., 1986—95; cons. geologist LaViolette and Assocs., Crockett, 1981—98, cons. engr., 2005—; project engr. Ned Clyde Constrn., Concord, 1998—2005. Chmn. preservation subcom. Carquinez Bridge Cmty. Adv. Com. With U.S. Army, 1971—73. Mem.: Soc. Industrial Archaeology, Assn. Engring. Geologists. Home: 1435 Pomona St Crockett CA 94525 Office: LaViolette and Assocs PO Box 158 Crockett CA 94525

LA VISTA, FRANK WILLIAM, author, educator, speaker; b. Bklyn., Nov. 28, 1939; s. Frank William and Constance Edith La Vista; m. Jane Ellen La Vista, 1963 (div. May 1980); 1 child, Kirsten; m. Jacqueline Gable, June 28, 1980. BA in Applied Behavior Sci., Nat. Louis U., 1990; BA in Mgmt., Nat. Coll. of Edn., 1990. With customer svc. United Airlines, N.Y.C., 1960-68, flight ops., 1968-74, faculty mgmt. coll. Chgo., 1974-97; faculty exec. mgmt. program Northwestern U., Evanston, 1985—; pres. La Vista & Assocs. LLC, Scottsdale, Ariz., 1985—. Cons. Wunderlin Co., Louisville, 1998—, E Pluribus Maximus, N.Y., 1999—, Bus. Assoc. Integrity Systems, Phoenix, 2002- Mem.: Nat. Spkrs. Assn. Avocations: jogging, travel, reading, the arts, meditation. Home and Office: 7525 E Gainey Ranch Rd 205 Scottsdale AZ 85258-1610 E-mail: lavistallc@cox.net.

LAVIZZO-MOUREY, RISA JUANITA, medical foundation administrator, academic administrator; b. 1954; MD, Harvard U., 1979; MBA, U. Pa., 1986. Dep. adminstr. Agy. Healthcare Policy and Rsch., U.S. Dept. Health and Human Svcs., 1992—94; Sylvan Eismann prof. of medicine U. Penn, Phila., 1995—2001, dir. Inst. of Aging, 1995—2001, chief, div. geriatric med., assoc. exec. v.p., health policy, 1995—2001; associate chief of staff for geriatrics and extended care Phila. Veterans Admin. Med. Ctr.; sr. v.p., dir., Health Care Group Robert Wood Johnson Found., Princeton, NJ, 2001—02, pres., CEO, 2003—. Mem. Pres.'s Commn. on Consumer Rights and Quality in the Healthcare Industry, 1997-98; mem. advisory com. Task Force on Aging Rsch., Office of Tech. Assessment Panel on Preventive Services for Medicare Beneficiaries, Inst. of Medicine's Panel on Disease and Disability Prevention Among Older Adults, Nat. Com. for Vital and Health Statistics. Mem., IOM, Nat. Acad. Sciences, Amer. Geriatrics Soc., The Assn. of Acad. Minority Physicians, Nat. Med. Assn., Acad. for Health Services Rsch. & Health Policy, Gerontological Soc. Amer. Office: The Robert Wood Johnson Foundation PO Box 2316 College Road East and Route 1 Princeton NJ 08543-2316

LAVOIE, LIONEL A., physician, health science association administrator; b. St. Brieux, Sask., Can., Aug. 24, 1937; s. Athanase T. and Ella Marie (Mevel) L.; m. Mary Tina Luchewski, Oct. 12, 1964; children: Robert, Michelle, Nicole, Andrea. BA, Ottawa U., Ont., Can., 1958, MD, 1964. Intern, then resident Univ. Hosp., Sask.; clin. prof. family medicine U. Sask., 1978—; chief of staff Melfort (Sask.) Union Hosp., 1985-90. Commr. Med. Care Ins. Commn., 1984-88. Chmn. Melfort Dist. Minor Sports, 1978-80, Melfort Pks. and Recreation, 1983-86, Sask. Summer Games 1988, 1986-88. Recipient Ramstead award, Jaycees of Province Sask., 1975, Dedication award, Sask. Parks, Recreation and Culture, 1988, Cmty. Recreation award, Melford C. of C., 1989, Commemorative medal, 125th Anniversary Can. Confedn., 1993, Recognition award, Coll. Medicine, U. Sask., 1999, award of merit, Faculty of Medicine U. Ottawa Alumni Assn., 2001, Rural Long Service award, Soc. Rural Physicians Can., 2002, Queen's Jubilee medal Can., 2002, Award of Merit, Can. Paraplegic Assn., 2005. Fellow Coll. Family Physicians (Can., cert.),; mem. Can. Med. Assn. (sr., bd. dirs. 1978-83, pres. elect 1989-90, pres. 1990-91, life), Sask. Med. Assn. (bd. dirs. 1971-76, v.p. 1974, pres. 1975, life), Can. Acad. Sports Medicine, Am. Geriatric Soc., Coll. Family Physicians Can. (sec. Sask. province 1967-70), Sask. Acad. Sports Medicine (pres. 1986-88, Cert. of Merit 2004), Coun. Med. Assn. (chmn. 1985-89), Sask. Paraplegic Assn. (bd. dirs. 1978—), Can. Cancer Soc. (adv. com. Sask. div. 1986—), Nat. Aerospace Med. Assn., KC (grand knight 1980-81), Rotary (pres. Melfort club 1987-88). Avocations: golf, curling, horticulture. Home: 402 Stovel E Melfort SK Canada S0E 1A0 Office: Can Med Assn 1867 Alta Vista Dr Ottawa ON Canada K1G 0G8 Office Phone: 306-752-2876. E-mail: lionelmarylavoie@hotmail.com.

LAVORATO, LOUIS A., state supreme court justice; s. Charles Lavorato; m. Janis M. Lavorato; children: Cindy, Natalie, Anthony, Dominic. BS in Bus. Adminstrn., Drake U., 1959, JD, 1962. Sole practice, Des Moines, 1962-79; judge Iowa Dist. Ct., Des Moines, 1979-86; justice Iowa Supreme Ct., Des Moines, 1986—2000, chief justice, 2000—. Mem. Iowa Supreme Ct. Administrative Subcom.; former chair Iowa Supreme Ct. Equality in the Courts Task Force Subcom. Recipient Judicial Achievement award, Iowa Assn. of Trial Lawyers, 1985, Merit award, Iowa Judges Assn., 1996. Office: Iowa Supreme Ct St Capitol Bldg Des Moines IA 50319-0001*

LAVORGNA, GREGORY JOSEPH, lawyer; b. Phila., Apr. 30, 1950; s. Emanuel and Mafalda (Gentile) L.; m. Christine J. Scherf, July 15, 1978; children: Stephanie Noelle, Cynthia Faith. BEE, Drexel U., 1972, MEE, 1975; JD cum laude, Temple U., 1981. Bar: Pa. 1981, U.S. Dist. Ct. (ea. dist.) Pa. 1981, U.S. Patent Office 1981, U.S. Ct. Appeals (Fed. cir.) 1982, D.C. 1986, U.S. Supreme Ct. 1988. Electronics engr. RCA Corp., Camden, N.J., 1972-75, Gen. Electric Co., Phila., 1975-79; assoc. Seidel, Gonda, Goldhammer & Abbott, P.C., Phila., 1981-87; ptnr. Seidel, Gonda, Lavorgna & Monaco, P.C., Phila., 1988; ptnr., head, intellectual property practice group Drinker Biddle & Reath LLP, Phila. Editor in chief Drexel U. Tech. Jour., 1971-72; contbr. articles to profl. jours. Trustee 1st Bapt. Ch., Phila., 1978-88, Lower Merion Bapt. Ch., Bryn Mawr, Pa., 1989-92, moderator, 1995—. Mem. ABA, Pa. Bar Assn., Phila. Bar Assn., Am. Intellectual Property Law Assn., Justinian Soc. (sec. 1994—), Am. Law Inst. Office: Drinker Biddle & Reath LLP One Logan Sq 18th & Cherry Sts Philadelphia PA 19103-6996 Office Phone: 215-988-3309. Office Fax: 218-988-2757. Business E-Mail: gregory.lavorgna@dbr.com.

LAVORI, NORA, real estate executive, lawyer; b. S.I., N.Y., Aug. 11, 1950; d. William P. and Mary E. Lavori; div. 1990; children: Liana Sterling, Alexander O. Sterling. BA, Bryn Mawr Coll., 1971; JD, Bklyn. Law Sch., 1976. Bar: N.Y. 1977. Atty., N.Y.C., 1977—; ptnr. Orleans Realty, N.Y.C., 1978—; officer The Culture Ctr., N.Y.C., 1990—. Author: Living Together, Married or Single: Your Legal Rights, 1976. Mem. real estate coun., maj. gifts com. Met. Mus. Art, N.Y.C., 1998—; trustee Bryn Mawr (Pa.) Coll., 1999-2005; vice-chair Columbus Ave. Bus. Improvement Dist., N.Y.C., 2000; bd. advisors Syracuse U., 2005—. Mem. Women's City Club N.Y. (pres. 1995-96; hon. dir.). Home: 100 W 80th St New York NY 10024

LAVRUK, ALEXANDER E., music educator, sales consultant; b. Leninobad, Tajikistan, 1956; s. Eugene E. Lavruk; life ptnr. Pamela Moreland; 1 child, Alexandra Moreland. BA, Coll. Music, Leninobad, 1971—75; MA (hon.), U. Culture, Kuybishev, Russia, 1987—89. Adj. prof. San Bernardino Valley Coll., Calif., 2002—. Sales cons. Piano Music Ctr., Riverside, Calif., 2002—; tchr. music CCS Music, Claremont, Calif., 2003—. Sgt. Soviet Army, 1975—77. Scholar, Glier Music Sch., 1964—71. Mem.: Nat. Assn. Realtors. Republican. Avocations: golf, tennis, reading, cooking, Harley. Home: 14980 Camelia Dr Fontana CA 92337 Office: Piano Music Ctr 3386 Tyler St Riverside CA 92503 Personal E-mail: alavruk@excite.com.

LAW, CLARENE ALTA, small business owner, state legislator; b. Thornton, Idaho, July 22, 1933; d. Clarence Riley and Alta (Simmons) Webb; m. Franklin Kelso Meadows, Dec. 2, 1953 (div.); children: Teresa Lin Meadows, Charisse Meadows Haws, Steven Riley; m. Creed Law, 1973. Student, Idaho State Coll., 1953. Sec., sub. tchr. Grand County Schs., Cedar City, Utah, 1954-57; UPI rep. newspaper agy. Moab, Utah Regional Papers, Salt Lake City and Denver; auditor Wort Hotel, Jackson, Wyo., 1960-62; innkeeper, CEO Elk Country Motels, Inc., Jackson, Wyo., 1962—; rep. Wyo. Ho. of Reps., Cheyenne, 1991—. Bd. dirs. Jackson State Bank, Snow King Resort; mem. bank bd. Wyo. State Ho. Reps., 1991-98, chmn. travel com., 1993-2000, chmn. minerals and econ. devel. com., 2001-04. Chmn. sch. bd. dirs. Teton County Schs., Jackson, 1983-86; bd. dirs. Wyo. Taxpayers Assn., Bus. Coun., 1998—. Named Citizen of Yr. Jackson C. of C., 1976, 99, Bus. Person of Yr. Jackson Hole Realtors, 1987, Wyo. Small Bus. Person SBA, 1977. Mem. Wyo. Lodging and Restaurant Assn. (pres., chmn. bd. dirs. 1988-89, Big Wyo. award 1987), Soroptimists (charter), Bus. Profl. Womens Orgn. (Woman of Yr. 1975, mem. Heritage steering com. 1996—), Gov.'s 15-Mem. Bus. Coun. Republican. Avocations: grandchildren, travel, study, old cars. Address: PO Box 575 Jackson WY 83001-0575 Office: Elk County Motels Inc Box 575 43 W Pearl Jackson WY 83001

LAW, DAVID HILLIS, physician; b. Milw., July 24, 1927; s. David Hillis Law III and Hazel Janice (May) Young; m. Patricia Bicking Thornton, Sept. 14, 1949; children: Linda Clark, Wendy, David, Kimberly Rankin, Cassandra. BA, Cornell U., 1950, MD, 1954. Resident in internal medicine Cornell U. Med. Coll., N.Y.C., 1954-57, fellow in gastroenterology, 1957-59; dir. personnel health services N.Y. Hosp., Cornell Med. Ctr., N.Y.C., 1959-60; asst. prof. medicine, chief gastroenterology Vanderbilt U. Med. Coll., Nashville, 1960-69; prof., vice chmn. dept. medicine U. New Mex. Sch. Med., Albuquerque, 1969-85; chief med. services Vets. Adminstrn. Med. Ctr., Albuquerque, 1969-85; dir. med. services Vets. Adminstrn. Cen. Office, Washington, 1985-86, dep. asst. chief med. dir. for clin. services, 1986-89, asst. chief med. dir. clin. affairs, 1989-91, acting dep. assoc. chief med. dir. for hosp.-based svcs., 1991-95, assoc. dep. chief med. dir. for clin. program, 1993-95, acting chief patient care officer, 1995-96; assoc. chief of staff for edn. Bay Pines (Fla.) Med. Ctr., 1996—2002; prof. internal medicine U. So. Fl., 1998—. Human rsch. com. Los Alamos (N.Mex.) Sci. Lab., 1972-80; sabbatical dept. clin. physiology Karolinska Inst., Stockholm, 1980; officer N.Mex. Nutrition Improvement Program, 1970-75; sub-com. chmn. U.S. Pharmacopeia Commn. on Revision, 1975-80. Editor, Parenteral Nutrition; mem. editorial bd., Am. Jour. Digestive Diseases, 1968-74; rev. numerous med. jours.; contbr. articles to numeous profl. jours. Bd. dirs., officer Albuquerque Friends of Music, 1975-85; active Nat. Digestive Disease Adv. Bd., 1989-95, Interdepartmental Digestive Disease Coordinating Com.; pres. Bay Pines Edn. Found., Inc., 2001, bd. dirs., 2003—. With U.S. Army, 1945-46. Named Tchr. and Attending Physician of Yr. Dept. Medicine House Staff, 1985. Fellow ACP (gov. 1989-96); mem. AMA (lectr.), Western Assn. Physicians, Western Soc. Clin. Rsch., Am. Gastroenterol. Assn., Am. Inst. Nutrition, Alpha Omega Alpha. Republican. Presbyterian. Avocation: hot air ballooning. Office: Vets Adminstrn Med Ctr 11-B Bay Pines FL 33744 Personal E-mail: clawoakhur@aol.com. Business E-Mail: david.law@med.va.gov.

LAW, DAVID JOHN, medical researcher; b. Detroit, Dec. 14, 1945; s. John Harvey and Loretta T. Law; m. Joan Kay Anderson, Apr. 14, 1973 (dec. Nov. 21, 2000); 1 child, John Andrew. BS, U. Mich., 1967; MS, Wayne State U., Detroit, 1973, PhD, 1981. Clin., rsch. microbiologist Children's Hosp. of Mich., Detroit, 1973—77; postdoctoral rsch. scholar U. Mich., Ann Arbor, Mich., 1981—86; rsch. scientist Howard Hughes Med. Inst. at U. Mich., 1986—93; dir., genomic resources core, human genome ctr. U. Mich., 1993—96; rsch. scientist Howard Hughes Med. Inst. at U. Mich., 1996—2002; rsch. investigator U. Mich., Dept. Internal Medicine, 2002—. Mem., bd. of dirs. Joy Southfield Cmty. Devel. Corp., Detroit, 2004—. Contbr. articles to profl. jours. Multicultural collaborator Multicultural Experience in Leadership Devel., Wayne State U., Detroit, 2001—; cmty. outreach and multicultural collaboration First United Meth. Ch. of Northville, Mich., 1989—2005; providing healthcare, housing and econ. devel. Joy Southfield Cmty. Devel. Corp., 2004—05. First lt. Combat Inf. U.S. Army, 1968—70, Republic of Vietnam, U.S. Decorated Bronze Star for Valor, 3 awards US Army, Army Commendation Medal for Valor, 2 Air medals; fellow Nat. Rsch. Svc. award, NIH, 1982—84; grantee Cancer Rsch. grant, 2003—. Mem.: Amer. Gastroent. Assoc, Amer. Assoc. for Advancement of Sci., Phi Kappa Psi (pres. 1966—66, Solon E. Summerfield Scholarship award 1966). Methodist. Achievements include research in First published observation of concerted multiple genetic changes in colon cancer. Avocations: photography, camping, writing, running. Home: 1060 N Center St Northville MI 48167-1183 Office: Univ Mich 1150 W Medical Center Dr Ann Arbor MI 48109-0650 Office Phone: 734-936-6363. Office Fax: 734-763-4686. Personal E-mail: davelaw@umich.edu.

LAW, JANE HINTON, artist, small business owner; b. Dayton, Ohio, Dec. 26, 1928; d. William Guy and Nelle Grant (Royse) Hinton; m. Lillard E. Law, Feb. 5, 1928; children: Melinda Talbot, Laurie Jorgensen, Thomas W. Hinton, Jonathan S. BA, Otterbein Coll., 1947; MA, NYU, 1970. Art supr. Worthington (Ohio) Schs., 1947-51; tchr. Gambler Schs., Mt. Vernon, Ohio, 1954-59; asst. prof. fine arts Union Coll., Elizabeth, N.J., 1969-74; tchr. So. Regional High Sch., Manahawkin, N.J., 1975-78; instr. Ocean County Coll., Toms River, N.J., 1975-76; owner Jane Law Art Studio and Gallery, Surf City, N.J., 1976—. State judge Fed. Art Assn., Westfield, N.J., 1984—; bd. dirs. Internat. Miniature Exhibit, Surf City, Nat. Watercolor Exhibit, Surf City. Editor: Long Beach Island Cookbook, 1981; artist several featured articles in cultural events, Art. Bus. News on show, calendar and cover photos. Remor judge Stafford Twp. Founders Day, MAnahawkin, N.J., 1987, state contest posters Women's History Month, 1990. Recipient Outstanding Community Bus. award Tax Payers Assn., 1988; named one of Outstanding Artists Ocean County Cultural and Heritage Commn., 1989; named Woman of Yr. AAUW, 1990. Mem. AAUW (v.p. 1985—), N.J. Assn. Sch. Adminstrs. (aux. pres. 1972—), Internat. Soc. Marine Painters, N.J. Watercolor Soc. (assoc.), Island Singers (pres. 1984—), Soroptimists (pres. 1983-84), Phila. Watercolor Club. Republican. Episcopalian. Home: 2005 Long Beach Blvd Ship Bottom NJ 08008-5552 Office: Jane Law Art Studio & Gallery 20th St & Long Beach Blvd Surf City NJ 08008

LAW, JOHN HAROLD, biochemistry educator; b. Cleve., Feb. 27, 1931; s. John and Katherine (Frampton) L.; m. Jeannette Ward Belcher, Nov. 9, 2000. BS, Case Inst. Tech., Cleve., 1953; PhD, U. Ill., 1957; D (hon.), U. Sofia, 1995, U. South Bohemia, 2004. Fellow Harvard U., Cambridge, Mass., 1957—59, from instr. to asst. prof. biochemistry, 1960-65; instr. Northwestern U., Evanston, Ill., 1959-60; prof. U. Chgo., 1965-81, U. Ariz., Tucson, 1981-91, Regents prof., 1991—2001, Regents prof. emeritus, 2001—, chmn. dept. biochemistry, 1981-86, dir. biotech. program, 1986-92; dir. Ctr. Insect Sci., 1993-98; assoc. dean coll. agr. U. Ariz., Tucson, 1988-90; prof. entymology U. Ga., 2005—. Gov. bd. Internat. Ctr. Insects, Nairobi, Kenya, 1980-87; mem. bd. trust Gordon Rsch. Conf., 1992-98, chmn., 1996; mem. coun. Am. Soc. Biochem. Molecular Biology, 1993-96. Recipient Gregor Mendel medal Czech Acad. Sci., 1992, J.E. Purkinje medal Czech Acad. Sci., 1994, Alumni Achievement award U. Ill., 2002. Fellow AAAS, ESA (Recognition award 1999); mem. NAS, Am. Soc. Biochem. Molecular Biology, Am. Chem. Soc., Entomol. Soc. Am. Home: 201-8 Hamilton Rd Athens GA 30606-6619 Office: U Ga Dept Entomology Bio Sci 518 Athens GA 30602-2603 Business E-Mail: jhlaw@bugs.ent.uga.edu.

LAW, JOSEPH GILLESPIE, JR., psychologist; b. Mobile, Ala., Feb. 8, 1947; s. Joseph Gillespie and Elma Idonia (Antoine) L.; m. Pamela McFerrin, Dec. 5, 1975; children— Joseph, Jonathan. B.S., Spring Hill Coll., 1969; M.S., U. South Ala., 1976; Ed.D., Auburn U., 1981. Lic. psychologist, Tenn. Psychologist Dept. Mental Health, Eufaula, Ala., 1976-78; sch. psychologist Opelika City Schs., Ala., 1978-80; intern VA Mental Ctr., Tuskegee, Ala., 1980-81; team leader VA Vet. Ctr., Mobile, Ala., 1981—; cons. psychologist Ala. Bd. Polygraph Examiners, 1978— . Contbr. articles to profl. jours.

Served to capt. U.S. Army, 1969-73. Named Employee of Yr., VA Med. Ctr., 1984; recipient Cert. of Recognition, Miss. Coast Assn. Fed. Adminstrs., 1984. Mem. Am. Psychol. Assn., Ala. Psychol. Assn., Am. Mental Health Counselors Assn. Methodist. Avocation: astronomy. Office: Vet Ctr 110 Marine St Mobile AL 36604-3018

LAW, JUDE (DAVID JUDE LAW), actor; b. London, Eng., Dec. 29, 1972; s. Peter and Maggie Law; m. Sadie Frost, Sept. 2, 1977 (div. 2003); children: Rafferty, Iris, Rudy Indiana Otis 1 stepchild, Finlay Munro. Ptnr. production comp. Natural Nylon. Actor: (TV series) The Tailor of Gloucester, 1989, Families, 1990, The Marshal, 1993; (films) Shopping, 1994, The Crane, 1994, I Love You, I Love You Not, 1996, Bent, 1997, Wilde, 1997, Gattaca, 1997, Midnight in the Garden of Good and Evil, 1997, Music from Another Room, 1998, Final Cut, 1998, The Wisdom of Crocodiles, 1998, eXistenZ, 1999, Presence of Mind, 1999, The Talented Mr. Ripley, 1999 (BAFTA award for best supp. actor, 2000, Santa Fe Film Critics Circle award for best supp. actor, 2000), Love, Honour and Obey, 2000, Enemy at the Gates, 2001, Artificial Intelligence: AI, 2001, Road to Perdition, 2002, Cold Mountain, 2003 (Acad. Award nomination for best actor, 2004, Golden Globe nomination for best actor in a drama, 2004), I Heart Huckabees, 2004, Alfie, 2004, Closer, 2004, The Aviator, 2004; actor, prodr. (films) Sky Captain and the World of Tomorrow, 2004; dir.: (TV) Tube Tales (segment "A Bird in the Hand"), 1999; voice Lemony Sniket's A Series of Unfortunate Events, 2004. Named Sexiest Man Alive, People Mag., 2004; named to 50 Most Beautiful List, 2000, 2004. Office: Endeavor Agy 10th Fl 9601 Wilshire Blvd Beverly Hills CA 90212*

LAW, MARCIA ELIZABETH, aide; b. Spokane, Wash., Oct. 9, 1950; d. John Glen and Jean Carolyn (Lines) L.; 1 child, Michael Sean. AA, Spokane C.C., 1973. Notary public. Data entry operator, controller CyCare Sys., Spokane, Wash., 1974-78, tape libr., 1978-79; data entry operator Wash. state Dept. Employment Security, Spokane, 1986-87, Cath. Charities, Spokane, 1987, Cath. Diocese Spokane, 1987-90, Divsn. Vocat. Rehab. Dept. Health & Social Svcs., Seattle, 1990-95, sec. sr., 1994-99, counselor aide, 1999—, regional adv. com.; state internal adv. com. Stakeholders Commn. Avocations: reading, movies, cross stitch, swimming. Home: 3002 S 208th St Apt P3 Seatac WA 98198-5933 Office: 18000 International Blvd Ste 1000 Seattle WA 98188-4251 Fax: 206-439-3753. E-mail: lawm@dshs.wa.gov.

LAW, MARK EDWARD, electrical engineer, educator; b. St. Paul, July 19, 1959; s. Paul Rock and Bernice Edna (Brookshaw) L.; m. Alison Leigh Retz, May 30, 1981; children: Christopher, Heather. BS CprE, Iowa State U., 1981; MSEE, Stanford U., 1982, PhD in Elec. Engring., 1988. Engr. Hewlett Packard, 1982-84; rsch. asst. Stanford (Calif.) U., 1984-87, rsch. assoc., 1988; asst. prof. elec. engring. U. Fla., Gainesville, 1988-93, assoc. prof. elec. engring., 1993-97, prof. elec. engring., 1997—, prof., chair, elec. engring., 2003—. Presenter, spkr. in field; session chmn. various tech. meetings in field. Author: Floods/Floops User's Manual, 1993; contbr. articles to profl. jours., chpts. to books. Recipient Young Faculty Devel. award IBM, 1988, Tech. Excellence award Semicondr. Rsch. Corp., 1993, Outstanding Young Alumnus award Iowa State U., 1994, Profl. Progress award Iowa State U., 1994; Nat. Merit scholar, 1977-81; grantee NSF, 1992—, SRC, 1989—, 93—, IBM, 1991-93; NSF Presdl. fellow, 1992. Fellow IEEE (guest editor publ. 1991, assoc. editor IEEE Transactions on Semicondr. Mfg. 1996-97, editor Jour. on Tech. Computer Aided Design 1996-02, editor Circuits and Devices Mag. 1996-98), Am. Soc. Engring. Edn., Am. Phys. Soc., Electrochem. Soc., Sigma Xi, Phi Beta Pi, Phi Kappa Phi. Avocations: soccer, golf. Office: U Fla 216 Larsen Gainesville FL 32611-6200 Business E-Mail: law@tec.ufl.edu.

LAW, MICHAEL R., lawyer; b. Rochester, N.Y., Nov. 30, 1947; s. George Robert and Elizabeth (Stoddart) L.; m. Cheryl Heller. BS, St. John Fisher Coll., 1969; JD, U. Louisville, 1975. Bar: N.Y. 1976, U.S. Supreme Ct. 1982. Assoc. Wood, P.C., Rochester, N.Y., 1976-77; pvt. practice Rochester, 1977-78; assoc. Sullivan, Peters, et al, Rochester, 1978-80; ptnr., 1980-81, Phillips, Lytle, Hitchcock, Blaine & Huber, Rochester, 1982—. With USAR, 1968—74. Mem.: ABA (alternate dispute resolution com. 1995—, trial law sect., trial techniques com., editor 1986 Trial Techniques), N.Y. State Acad. Trial Lawyers, Genesee Valley Trial Lawyers Assn. (treas. 1992—93, pres.-elect 1993—95, pres. 1995—98), Monroe County Bar Assn. (judiciary com. 1981—88, personal injury com. 1988—, profl. responsibility com. 1996—, bd. dirs. 2003), N.Y. State Trial Lawyers (bd. dirs. 1990—2004), N.Y. State Bar Assn. (trial sec., ins. negligence com.), Am. Bd. Trial Advs. Republican. Roman Catholic. Home: 3373 Elmwood Ave Rochester NY 14610-3425 Office: Phillips Lytle Et Al 1400 1st Federal Plz Rochester NY 14614-1981 Office Phone: 585-238-2000. Business E-Mail: mlaw@phillipslytle.com.

LAW, RANDALL DAVID, history professor; b. Kansas City, Mo., Feb. 25, 1969; s. Elmo Adrian and Patricia Joyce (Hobson) Law; m. Hannah Katherine Wolfson, May 30, 1999. BA in Russian, Amherst Coll., Mass., 1991; MA in Russian and East European Studies, Yale U., New Haven, 1993; PhD in History, Georgetown U., Washington, 2001. Vis. asst. prof. history Northwestern Coll., Orange City, Iowa, 2001—03; asst. prof. history Birmingham-Southern Coll., Birmingham, Ala., 2003—. Scholar, Am. Coun. of Teachers of Russian, 1997—98. Mem.: So. Conf. on Slavic Studies, Am. Assn. Advancement of Slavic Studies, Am. Hist. Assn., Phi Alpha Theta (pres. (Georgetown U. chpt.) 1994—95). Home: 629 46th St S Birmingham AL 35222 Office: Birmingham-Southern Coll Box 549031 900 Arkadelphia Rd Birmingham AL 35254 Office Phone: 205-226-7836. E-mail: rlaw@bsc.edu.

LAW, STEVEN J., federal agency administrator; b. Oakland, Calif. married; 2 children. BA cum laude in Music, U. Calif., Davis, Calif., 1983; JD, Columbia U., 1986. Bar: D.C., N.Y., U.S. Supreme Ct. Dep. sec. U.S. Dept. Labor, Washington, 2004—. Office: US Dept Labor 200 Constitution Ave NW S2018 Washington DC 20210

LAW, STUART A., JR., lawyer; b. Broomall, Pa., 1957; BA, Ind. Univ. of Pa., 1979; JD, Pa. State Univ., 1982. Bar: Pa. 1982, NJ 1989. Law clerk, Hon. John B. Hannum US Dist. Ct. (ea. dist.) Pa.; ptnr., construction litig. Drinker Biddle & Reath LLP, Princeton, NJ, and co-chair, construction law practice group. Nat. panel arbitrators Am. Arbitration Assn. Editor: (newsletter) The Construction Lawyer. Office: Drinker Biddle & Reath LLP Ste 300 105 College Rd E Princeton NJ 08540-6622 Office Phone: 609-716-6548. Office Fax: 609-799-7000. Business E-Mail: stuart.law@dbr.com.

LAW, SYLVIA A., law educator; b. 1942; BA, Antioch Coll., 1964; JD, NYU, 1968. Bar: NY 1968, Pa. 1970. Reginald Heber Smith Cmty. Lawyer Columbia Ctr. Social Welfare Policy & Law, 1968-69; lectr. London Sch. Econ. & Polit. Sci., 1969-70; staff dir. Pa. Health Law Project, 1970-73; asst. prof. NYU Sch. Law, NYC, 1973-76, assoc. prof., 1976-79, prof. law, 1979—94, Elizabeth K. Dollard prof. law, medicine and psychiatry, 1994—, also co-dir. Arthur Garfield Hays Civil Liberties Program. Vis. prof. Harvard U., 1984, CUNY at Queens, 1989; Hon. Phyllis W. Beck prof. law, Beasley Sch. Law Temple U., 2005. Author: Blue Cross: What Went Wrong?, 1973; co-author: (with Steve Polan) Pain and Profit: The Politics of Malpractice, 1978, (with R. Rosenblatt and S. Rosenbaum) Law and the American Health Care System, 1997. Sec. Alan Guttmacher Inst., 1978-90; chmn. Non-Traditional Employment for Women, 1985; bd. mem Ctr. Reproductive Rights, 1993-, Compassion in Dying (now Compassion & Choices), 1996-. MacArthur Fellow, 1983. Fellow Am. Soc. Arts & Sciences; mem. ACLU, SALT (treas. 1974-75, pres. 1988-90; named Lawyer of Yr., 2001), Nat. Lawyer's Guild. Office: NYU Sch Law Vanderbilt Hall Rm 429 49 Washington Sq S New York NY 10012-1099 Office Phone: 212-998-6265. Office Fax: 212-995-4526. E-mail: sylvialaw@aol.com.*

LAW, THOMAS HART, lawyer; b. Austin, Tex., July 6, 1918; s. Robert Adger and Elizabeth (Manigault) L.; m. Terese Tarlton, June 11, 1943 (div. Apr. 1956); m. Jo Ann Nelson, Dec. 17, 1960; children: Thomas Hart Jr., Debra Ann. AB, U. Tex., 1939, JD, 1942. Bar: Tex. 1942, U.S. Supreme Ct. 1950. Assoc. White, Taylor & Chandler, Austin, 1942; assoc. Thompson, Walker, Smith & Shannon, Ft. Worth, 1946-50; ptnr. Tilley, Hyder & Law, Ft. Worth, 1950-67, Stone, Tilley, Parker, Snakard, Law & Brown, Ft. Worth, 1967-71; pres. Law, Snakard, Brown & Gambill, P.C., Ft. Worth, 1971-90; of counsel Law, Snakard & Gambill, P.C., Ft. Worth, 1990—. Gen. counsel Gearhart Industries, Inc., Ft. Worth, 1960-88, Tarrant County Coll. Chmn. Leadership Ft. Worth, 1974-90; bd. regents U. Tex. System, 1975-81, vice chmn., 1979-81. Lt. USNR, 1942-46. Recipient Nat. Humanitarian award Nat. Jewish Hosp./Nat. Asthma Ctr., 1983; named Outstanding Young Man, City of Ft. Worth, 1950, Outstanding Alumnus, Coll. of Humanities, U. Tex., 1977, Outstanding Citizen, City of Ft. Worth, 1984, Bus. Exec. of Yr., City of Ft. Worth, 1987, Blackstone award for contbns. field of law Ft. Worth Bar Assn., 1990, Disting. Alumnus U. Tex., 1992. Fellow Am. Bar Found., Tex. Bar Found., Am. Coll. Probate Counsel, Tarrant County Bar Found. (founding chmn.); mem. Ft. Worth C. of C. (pres. 1972), Mortar Bd., Phi Beta Kappa, Omicron Delta Kappa, Pi Sigma Alpha, Delta Sigma Rho, Phi Eta Sigma, Delta Tau Delta. Clubs: Ft. Worth (bd. govs. 1984-90), Century II (bd. govs. to 1985), River Crest Country, Exchange (pres. 1972), Steeplechase. Lodges: Rotary (local club pres. 1960). Democrat. Presbyterian. Avocation: coin collecting/numismatics. Home: 6741 Brants Ln Fort Worth TX 76116-7201 Office: Law Snakard & Gambill 1600 W 7th St Ste 500 Fort Worth TX 76102-2598 Office Phone: 817-335-7373. Personal E-mail: jnlent@juno.com. Business E-Mail: tlaw@lawsnakard.com.

LAW, THOMAS MELVIN, college president; b. Bristol, Va., Sept. 23, 1925; s. Thomas Keen and Rebecca Ellen (Davis) L; m. Katherine Iris Tillar, Oct. 14, 1954; 1 child, Thomas Fenimore. BS summa cum laude, St. Paul's Coll., 1950, LHD (hon.), 1982; MA, NYU, 1953; EdD, Cornell U., 1962; LHD (hon.), Cuttington U., Liberia, 2001. Dean., prof. St. Paul's Coll., Lawrenceville, Va., 1967-69, pres., trustee, 1989—; v.p. acad. affairs Washington Tech. Inst., 1969-71; pres. Penn Valley Community Coll., Kansas City, Mo., 1971-76, Va. State U., Petersburg, 1976-82; dep. to chancellor spl. programs SUNY, Albany, 1982-86, dep. to chancellor for CC, 1986, assoc. vice chancellor contracts/purchasing, 1986-89, pres., 1989—2001; pres. emeritus St. Paul's Coll. Bd. dirs. Nat. Alumni Assn, Sch. of Human Ecology, Cornell U.; mem. Cornell U. Coun (life). Bd. dirs. Brunswick County C. of C., Lawrenceville, 1990—, Va. C. of C., Brunswick County Indsl. Devel. Authority, 1994-2002, A.L. Philpott Mfg. Extension Partnership1994-2002; life mem. NAACP; mem . commn. black mins. Union Black Episcs., Inc., by-laws com. United Negro Coll. Fund, Inc. Sgt. U.S. Army, 1942-46. Mem. Am. Assn. Higher Edn., Nat. Assn. Ind. Colls. and Univs. (com. campus concerns), Coun. Ind. Colleges in Va. (exec. com., pres.), Assn. Va. Colls. and Univs. (exec com., pres.), Am. Coun. on Edn. (com. leadership), Rotary, Phi Delta Kappa, Alpha Phi Alpha (life), Sigma Pi Phi. Address: 117 Scrimshaw Dr Chester VA 23836-1200

LAWER, BETSY, banker; b. Anchorage, July 27, 1949; d. Daniel H. and Betti Jane Cuddy; m. David A. Lawer, June 9, 1972; 1 child. Vice chair bd., COO 1st Nat. Bank Alaska, 1974—. Emeritus bd. dirs. Providence Health Care Found., 2001; bd. dirs. Commonwealth North. Named one of the Top 25 Most Powerful Alaskans Alaska Jour. Commerce, 1999-2003, one of 25 Women to Watch US Banker, 2003. Mem.: Anchorage Athena Soc. (Athena award 2001).

LAWHEAD, VICTOR BERNARD, education educator; b. Vincennes, Ind., Feb. 26, 1919; s. William Augustus Lawhead and Rilla Belle Wood; m. Doris Jean Barber, July 11, 1953. AB, De Pauw U., 1940; MA, Ohio State U., 1947, PhD, 1950. Hist. tchr. Kokomo (Ind.) Ind. Pub. Schools, 1940—48; prof. of edn. Ball State U., Ind., 1950—84; vis. lectr. Mich. State U., 1952; vis. prof. U. Md., 1957; asst. dean, undergraduate programs Ball State U., 1958—63, dean, undergraduate programs, 1964—84, prof. higher edn., 1984—. Cons. examiner No. Ctrl. Assn. for Colleges and Schools, Chgo., 1962—84; participant/observer United Nations Unesco Offices, Paris, 1967—81; cons., tchg. adv. duties Ball State U., 1984—. Contbr. articles to jours.; co-author: (book) Meanings, Values and Commitment, 1962—66; contbr. author (book) Teachers and Mentors, 1996. Mem., sponsor of programs So. Poverty Law Ctr., 1995—, People for the American Way, 1982—; founding assoc. Minnetrista Ctr. Natural and Cultural Heritage, 1990—. Lt. USN, 1943—46, Pacific Theater, Japan. Recipient Disting. Svc. award, Acad. Affairs Conf. Midwest Univ., 1976; Rector scholar, DePauw U., 1936—40, Univ. fellow, Ohio State U., 1948—50. Mem.: Assn. for Integrative Studies, Assn. for Gen. and Liberal Studies, Kiwanis Club. Avocations: sailing, poetry, fishing. Home: 801 N Briar Rd Muncie IN 47304 Office: Ball State Univ Bracken Libr 304 2000 W Univ Ave Muncie IN 47306 Office Phone: 765-285-8036. Business E-Mail: vblawhead@bsu.edu.

LAWHON, CHARLA, editor; Grad., Drake U. With Apt. Life Mag., Des Moines; dir. editl. svcs. Meredith Design Group, 1990; exec. editor Met. Home, 1992; dep. editor InStyle Mag., N.Y.C., 1994—98, exec. editor, 1998—2002, mng. editor, 2002—. Office: InStyle Mag 1271 Ave of the Ams New York NY 10020

LAWHON, JOHN, III, lawyer, retired county official; b. Denton, Tex., Dec. 14, 1934; s. John E. and Gladys (Barns) L.; m. Tommie Collins, Aug. 27, 1967; 1 son, David Collins. Student, U. N.Tex., 1951-53; BBA, JD, U. Houston, 1958. Bar: Tex. 1958; cert. specialist in estate and probate law, family law; bd. cert. in family law. Asst. dist. and county atty., Denton County, Tex., 1958-61; dist. and county atty., 1961-77; dir. Southridge, Inc., Denton, 1962-72, Lawyers Title Agy. Denton, 1965-74; Legal adviser Denton City-County Day Nursery, 1972-80; tchr. bus. law U. North Tex. (formerly North Tex. State U.), Denton, 1969-71; mem. adv. bd. Tex. Criminal Justice Council, 1973-79; univ. atty. Tex. Woman's U., 1977-83, gen. counsel, 1983—, sec. bd. regents, 1987—. Bd. dirs. Denton County Welfare Coun., 1970-78, Denton Community Coun., 1978-79, 80-82; mem. Denton Forum; chmn. Denton County ARC, 1985-87, Denton County Probation Adv. Bd., 1985-92; mem. City of Denton Land Use Com., 1986-88. Mem. Tex. Bar Assn., Denton Bar Assn. (pres. 1968-69, bd. dirs. 1978-81), Tex. Dist. and County Attys. Assn. (bd. dirs. 1964-66), Denton Jaycees (sec. 1961), Denton C. of C., Tex. Assn. State Univ. Attys. (pres. 1983-84, Denton County crim. justice task force 1992-93, state bar coll. fellow 1995—), K.P., Kiwanis (bd dirs 1981-86, pres 1984-85). Baptist (deacon 1968—). Home: 2810 Carmel St Denton TX 76205-8310 Office: Tex Woman's U Adminstrn Tower Bldg PO Box 44 Denton TX 76202-0044 Office Phone: 940-387-4401.

LAWHON, TOMMIE COLLINS MONTGOMERY, humanities educator; b. Shelby County, Tex., Mar. 15; d. Marland Walker and Lillian (Tinsley) Collins; m. David Baldwin Montgomery, Mar. 31, 1962 (dec. Aug. 1964); m. John Lawhon, Aug. 27, 1967; 1 child, David Collins. BS, Baylor U., 1954; M in Home Mgmt. Edn., M in Home Econs., Tex. Woman's U., 1964, PhD, 1966, M in Child Devel. and Family Studies. Cert. tchr., Tex.; cert. family and consumer scis.; cert. family life educator. Tchr. Victoria (Tex.) Pub. Schs., 1954-55; stewardess, supr. Am. Airlines, Dallas/Ft. Worth, 1955-62; assoc. prof. home econs. Ea. Ky. U., Richmond, 1966-67, U. North Tex., Denton, 1968—, head divsn. child devel. and family studies, 1974—77, program head, 1993-94, mem. faculty senate, 1984-90, chmn. com. on coms., 1987-88, mem. com. status on women, 1984-87, mem. faculty salary student com., 1989-95, chmn., 1989-91, mem. tradition com., 1989-95, recorder, 1989-91. Bd. dirs. U. North Tex., Univ. Union, 1985-88, mem. status of women com., 1984-87, mem. student mentor com., 1990-00, mem. benefits com., 1994-00, vice chair, 1994-95, chair, 1997-98, mem. faculty sen. Faculty Handbook com., 1998-2004, mem. faculty sen. mentor com., 1990-96; presenter in field. Co-author: Children are Artists, 1971, Hidden Hazards for Children and Families, 1982; editor: What to Do with Children, 1974, Field Trips for Children, 1984; contbr. articles to profl. jours. Chmn. United Way North Tex. State U., 1980-81; chmn. crusade Am. Cancer Soc., Denton County, 1982-83; chmn. nominating com. First Bapt. Ch., Denton, 1983-84, 84-85; active Girls Inc. of Met. Dallas; mem. adv. com. Career Action Ctr., 1999, chair, 2000-01; advisor North Tex. Student Coun. on Family Rels., 1994—. Recipient Presdl. award Tex. Coun. on Family Rels., 1979, Fessor Graham award North Tex. State U., 1980, Svc. award Am. Cancer Soc., 1983, Outstanding Home Economists Alumni award Baylor U., 1985; named Hon. Prof. North Tex. State U., 1975, Meritorious award Nat. Coun. on Family Rels. Assn. of Couns., 2004; Disting. Svc. award Outstanding Orgn. Advisor, U. North Tex., 2004. Mem. Tex. Coun. on Family Rels. (pres. 1977-79, chmn. policy advisor com. 1986-88, nominating com. 1986-88, 94-96, chair 1994-96, family life edn. com. 1994-97, Moore-Bowman award 1994), Denton Assn. for Edn. Young Children (pres. 1970-72, 84-85, 85-86, v.p. 1986-87), Tex. Assn. Coll. Tchrs. (nominating com. 1988-89, 89-90, v.p. 1990-92, v.p. U. North Tex. chpt. 1987-88, pres. 1988-89, 89-90), Tex. Home Econs. Assn. (chmn. FLCD nominating com. 1983-84, chmn. child devel. and family rels. sect. 1988-90, sec. rep. bd. 1989-90), Nat. Coun. Family Rels. (com. 1982-83, cert. family life's continuing edn. com. 1996-99, chair elect cert. family life continuing edn. com. 1996, chair 1997-98, cert. family life edn. focus group and regional-state coord., chair 1996-97, coord. of all student asst. annual conf., 2001-02, U. North Tex. Assn. of Couns. Meritorious Svc. award 2004), Nat. Assn. Early Childhood Tchr. Educators (membership com. 1995-97), North Tex. Home Econs. Inter-orgnl. Coun. (adviser 1983-85), Phi Delta Kappa (pres. local chpt. 1991-92), Alpha Iota/Phi Upsilon Omicron (advisor 1970-82, chmn. nat. com. 1984-87, nat. bd. dirs. edn. found. 1990-94, com. pubs. 1991-92, vice chair edn. found. 1992-94), Tri D Club (v.p. Baylor U. chpt. 1953-54), Univ. Grad. Club (pres. Tex. Woman's U. chpt. 1965-66). Democrat. Office: U North Tex Coll Edn Denton TX 76203

LAWI, DAVID STEVEN, utilities executive, merchant banker; b. Baghdad, Iraq, Aug. 3, 1935; came to U.S., 1946, naturalized, 1952; s. Steven David and Marcelle (Masry) L.; m. Anne Shamash, June 9, 1968; children— Nicole, Neil. AA in Sci, N.Y. State Coll., 1955. Registered rep. domestic and fgn. arbitrage Bear, Stearns & Co., N.Y.C., 1956—62; dir. Adobe Brick & Supply, West Palm Beach, Fla., 1962—64; v.p. Molly Corp., Reading, Pa., 1962—64; gen. mgr. United Shoe Machinery Corp., Reading, 1964—65; co-founder, sec., treas., mem. exec. com., dir. Unimax Group Inc. (formerly Riker-Maxson Corp. ASE), N.Y.C., 1966—80; also dir. all subs., v.p., treas. Telepictures Corp. ASE, N.Y.C., 1980—81; chmn. fin. com., sec. Telepictures Corp., N.Y.C., 1980—86; exec. v.p., sec. Helm Capital Group, Inc. (ASE), Greenwich, Conn., 1980—; founder, chmn. exec. com., also bd. dirs. Helm Capital Group, Inc., Greenwich, Conn. Founder, bd. dirs., sec. Teletrak Advanced Tech. Sys., Inc., 1983—, Continuing Care Assocs., 1982—; sec., bd. dirs., founder, chmn. exec. com. Seitel Inc. (NYSE; formerly Seismic Enterprises, Inc.), 1982-84, now bd. dirs.; advisor Lorimar-Telepictures (acquired by Warner Comm., Inc. 1989/NYSE), 1986, now Time-Warner/NYSE, 1990—; founder, bd. dirs., chmn. exec. com. Intersys., Inc. (ASE; formerly Bamberger Polymers, Inc.), Unipix Entertainment, Inc. (EquiFin, Inc., formerly ASE; formerly Majestic Entertainment, Inc.), Cliff Engle Ltd., Unapix Entertainment Inc. Served with AUS, 1968. Home: 120 Polly Park Rd Rye NY 10580 also: 13 Sloans Curve Dr Palm Beach FL 33480

LAWING, JIM L., lawyer; b. Oklahoma City, Feb. 19, 1937; s. Oscar Mitchell and Clara Hattie (Williams) L.; m. Karlin Church, Jar. 24, 1964 (div. Dec. 1979); children: Keith Lawing, Kirsten Spinelli, Chris Lawing; m. Mary Ann, Sept. 2, 1989; children: Jeff Harper, Jennifer Harper, Curry Harper, Gretchen Flatan, Anne Payne, Andy Newlan. BS, Northeastern State U., Okla., 1959; JD, U. Kans., 1965. Bar: Kans. Atty., Wichita, Kans., 1965—. State rep. Kans. House Reps., 1975-76; chmn. Sedgwick County Dem. Party, Kans., 1993-96; lay reader St. Stephen's Episcopal Ch., 1997—. Democrat. Episcopalian. Office: 200 E 1st St N Wichita KS 67202-2111 E-mail: j.lawing@inetmail.att.net.

LAWINGER, JANE M., lawyer; b. Dodgeville, Wis., Feb. 5, 1960; d. William Nicholas and Helena Theresa (Salzmann) L. BS in Criminal Justice, U. Wis., Platteville, 1984; JD, DePaul U., 1991. Ill. 1991, Wis. 1992, U.S. Dist. Ct. (so. dist.) Ill. 1991, U.S. Ct. Appeals (7th cir.) 1991. Pvt. practice, Vandalia, Ill., 1991—; spl. asst. atty. gen. State of Ill., Vandalia, 1994—. Home: PO Box 240 Vandalia IL 62471-2323 Office: PO Box 240 106 S 5th St Vandalia IL 62471-2702 E-mail: lawinger@fgi.net.

LAWLER, BRIDGET ANN, lawyer; b. Marion, Ill., May 27, 1975; d. Raymond and Ellen Marie Lawler; m. Dan Reid, Nov. 24, 2001. BA, St. Louis U., 1997; JD, So. Ill. U., 2000. Bar: Ill. 2000, Ky. 2001. Ptnr. Lawler & Lawler Law Firm, Marion, 2001—. Treas. So. Ill. Workers Compensation Bar, 2000—. Editor: (law jour.) Casenote and Comment, 1999. Mem.: ATLA, Ill. Trial Lawyers Assn., Inns of Ct. Found., Phi Delta Phi. Democrat. Roman Catholic. Avocations: running, reading, volunteering. Office: Lawler & Lawler Law Firm PO Box 1733 Marion IL 62959 Office Phone: 618-967-7682.

LAWLER, JAMES EDWARD, physics professor; b. St. Louis, June 29, 1951; s. James Austin and Dolores Catherine Lawler; m. Katherine Ann Moffatt, July 21, 1973; children: Emily Christine, Katie Marie. BS in Physics summa cum laude, U. Mo., Rolla, 1973; MS in Physics, U. Wis., 1974, PhD in Physics, 1978. Rsch. assoc. Stanford (Calif.) U., 1978-80; asst. prof. U. Wis., Madison, 1980-85, assoc. prof., 1985-89, prof., 1989—, Arthur & Aurelia Schawlow prof., 1999—. Product devel. cons. Nat. Rsch. Group, Inc., Madison, 1977-78; cons. GE, Schenectady, N.Y., 1985-96, Teltech, Inc., 1990—; exec. com. Gaseous Electronics Conf., 1987-89, treas., 1992-94, DAMOP program com., 1993-95. Editor: (with R.S. Stewart) Optogalvanic Spectroscopy, 1991; contbr. articles to profl. jours. Recipient Penning award Internat. Conf. on Phenomena in Ionized Gases, 1995; Schumberger scholar U. Mo., 1971-72; grad. fellow U. Wis. Alumni Rsch. Found., 1973-74, NSF, 1974-76, H.I. Romnes faculty fellow U. Wis., 1987. Fellow Am. Phys. Soc. (Will Allis prize 1992), Optical Soc. Am.; mem. Sigma Xi. Achievements include patent for Echelle Sine Bar for dye laser cavity; development of laser diagnostics for glow discharge plasmas, of methods for measuring accurate atomic transition probabilities and radiative lifetimes. Office: U Wis Dept Physics 1150 University Ave Madison WI 53706-1302 Business E-Mail: jelawler@wisc.edu.

LAWLER, JAMES RONALD, French language educator; b. Melbourne, Australia, Aug. 15, 1929; married, 1954; 2 children. BA, U. Melbourne, 1950, MA, 1952; DUniv., U. Paris, 1954. Lectr. French U. Queensland, Australia, 1955-56; sr. lectr. U. Melbourne, 1957-62; prof., head dept. U. Western Australia, 1963-71; prof., chmn. dept. UCLA, 1971-74; McCulloch prof. Dalhousie U., Halifax, N.S., Can., 1974-79; prof. French U. Chgo., 1979—, Edward Carson Waller Disting. Svc. prof., 1983-97, prof. emeritus, 1998. Vis. prof. Coll. de France, 1985, Tokyo, 1996, 98-99; chmn. vis. com. Romance Langs. and Lits. Harvard U., 1991-94, Soc. Amis U. Paris coun. Author: Form and Meaning in Valery's Le Cimetiere Marin, 1959, Lecture de Valery: Une Etude de Charmes, 1963, The Language of French Symbolism, 1969, The Poet as Analyst, 1974, Rene Char: The Myth and the Poem, 1978, Edgar Poe et les Poetes Francais, 1989, Rimbaud's Theatre of the Self, 1992, Poetry and Moral Dialectic: Baudelaire's Secret Architecture, 1997; co-author: Paul Valery; Poems, 1971, Paul Valery: Leonardo, Poe, Mallarme, 1972, Paul Claudel: Knowing the East, 2004; editor: An Anthology of French Poetry, 1960, Paul Valery: An Anthology, 1977, Paul Valery, 1991; founding editor Essays in French Literature, 1964, Dalhousie French Studies, 1980. Decorated officier Palmes Academiques; recipient Prix Internat. Amities Françaises, Prix du rayonnement de la langue francaise Acad. Francaise, 1999; Brit. Coun. interchange scholar, 1967; Australian Acad. Humanities fellow, 1970, Guggenheim Found. fellow, 1974, NEH fellow, 1985. Mem. MLA (coun. 1978-82), Internat. Assn. French Studies (pres. 1998-2001), Australian Acad. the Humanities. Achievements include rsch. in modern French poetry, poetics, 20th century novel. Office: U Chgo Dept Romance Langs & Lit 1050 E 59th St Chicago IL 60637-1559

LAWLER, JEAN MARIE, lawyer; b. San Francisco, Aug. 7, 1954; d. Jack Wofford and Evelyn Mary (Matkovich) Suggs; m. Timothy Lawler, May 20, 1978; children— Kathleen, Megan, Colleen. A.A., Riverside City Coll., 1974; student San Diego State U., 1974; B.B.A., Loyola Marymount U., Los Angeles, 1976; J.D., Loyola U. Law Sch.-Los Angeles, 1979. Bar: Calif. Supreme Ct. 1979, Oreg. Supreme Ct. 1981. Assoc. law firm David L. Rosner, Los Angeles, 1979-80; instr. Lane Community Coll., Eugene, Oreg., 1981-82; sole practice law, Eugene, 1981-82, and Beaverton, Oreg., 1982-93, ptnr.

Murchison & Cumming, LA, 1993-97, sr. ptnr and chair ins. law and risk mgmt. practice group, 1997-. Editor: Copyright Law, 1979-80; Business Associates Review, 1974; contbr. poetry to Coll. Poetry Rev., 1974, 76. Chmn. legal asst. adv. com. Lane Community Coll., 1981-82. Recipient Riverside County Bar Assn. scholarship, 1977; Loyola U. Jesuit Community scholarship, 1978. Mem. State Bar of Calif., Oreg. State Bar Assn., ABA, Washington County Bar Assn., Fedn. Def. & Corp. Counsel (bd. dir, 1996-, pres. 2004-2005). Democrat. Roman Catholic. Club: Columbia-Edgewater Country. Office: Murchison & Cumming 9th Fl 801 S Grand Ave Los Angeles CA 90017 Office Phone: 213-630-1019. Office Fax: 210-623-6336. Business E-Mail: jlawler@murchison-cumming.com.

LAWLER, JOHN A., publishing executive; BA, Williams Coll.; MBA, Univ. Va. With Dun and Bradstreet, London, 1992—93, head, European mktg. and sales Tokyo, 1994—95, vice-pres. global product devel.; pres. Reed Elsevier New Providence (RENP), which includes Martindale-Hubbell, New Providence, NJ, CEO, 2001—. Office: Martindale-Hubbell 121 Chanlon Ave New Providence NJ 07974*

LAWLER, THOMAS COMERFORD, protective services official; b. Cumberland, Md., Dec. 19, 1920; DHL (hon.), St. Joseph's coll., Standish, Maine, 1974; DDiv (hon.), Notre Dame Pontifical Catechetical Inst., Arlington, Va., 1987. Editor, briefing inspector Freedom of Info. officer CIA, 1951—77, resigned, 1977. Author: (book) various, including Ancient Christian Writers 15, St. Augustine: Sermons for Christmas and Epiphany, 1952; co-author (and co-editor): The Teaching of Christ: A Catholic Catechism for Adults, 1976, 4th edit., 1995; co-editor: The Catholic Catechism (now The Gift of Faith in reprint edit.), 1986, 2001. Recipient Pro Ecclesia et Pontifice award, Pope John Paul II, 2000.

LAWLER, WILLIAM E., III, lawyer; b. Washington, May 21, 1960; BA cum laude, U. Notre Dame, 1982; JD cum laude, Georgetown U., 1985. Bar: Md. 1985, D.C. 1986. Asst. U.S. atty. U.S. Atty.'s Office, DC, 1989—96; ptnr. Vinson & Elkins LLP, Washington. Lectr. FBI Tng. Acad., Quanticio, Va. Contbr. articles to profl. jours. Named Young Lawyer of Yr., D.C., 1992. Mem.: ABA (Ho. of Dels. 1992—93, 2001—03), Bar Assn. D.C. (bd. dirs. 1993—2004, chair Young Lawyers sect. 1994—95, pres.-elect 2000—01, pres. 2001—02). Office: Vinson and Elkins LLP Willard Office Bldg 1455 Pennsylvania Ave NW Washington DC 20004-1008

LAWLESS, MICHAEL RHODES, pediatrics educator; b. Baytown, Tex., Oct. 13, 1942; s. Wallace Ervin and Amy Ruth (Broussard) L.; m. E. Sandra Johnson, Aug. 27, 1967; children: Melanie Lawless York, Stephanie Lawless Setzer. BA in Zoology, U. Tex., 1964, MD, 1968. Diplomate Am. Bd. Pediat. Intern City Memphis Hosp., 1968-69; resident in pediat. U. Tex. Med. Br., Galveston, 1969-71; instr. U. Rochester (N.Y.) Sch. Medicine, 1971-72; staff pediatrician Portsmouth (Va.) Naval Hosp., 1972-74; asst. prof. pediat. Wake Forest U. Sch. Medicine, Winston-Salem, NC, 1974-80, assoc. prof. pediat., 1980-2001, prof. pediat., 2001—, dep. assoc. dean student affairs, 1988-96, chief gen. pediat. and adolescent medicine, 1997—2005. Lt. comdr. USNR, 1972-74. Fellow U. Rochester, 1971-72. Fellow Am. Acad. Pediat. (legis. liaison 1980—); mem. Am. Profl. Soc. on Abuse of Children, N.C. Pediatric Soc. (child adv. 1974—), Coun. Med. Student Edn. in Pediat. (pres. 1998-00), Ambulatory Pediatric Assn., Am. Bd. Pediat. (bd. dirs. 2003—). Avocations: tennis, outdoor activities.

LAWLESS, ROBERT J., food products executive; Distribution mgr. Club House Foods Inc. Canadian subs. McCormick, 1977; from prodn. mgr. to pres. to COO McCormick Can. formerly Club House Foods Inc.; exec. v.p., COO McCormick, Sparks, Md., 1995-96; pres., COO, CEO, 1996—; also bd. dirs. Office: McCormick 18 Loveton Cir Sparks MD 21152

LAWLESS, ROBERT WILLIAM, academic administrator; b. Baytown, Tex., Feb. 13, 1937; s. James Milton and Belva Ambaline (Mode) Lawless; m. Marcella Jane Emmert; children: Christopher, Cheryl, Diana. BS, U. Houston, 1964; PhD, Tex. A&M U., 1968. Instr., asst. prof. Tex. A&M U., College Station, 1967—69; prof., sr. vice chancellor U. Houston, 1969—82; v.p., CFO S.W. Airlines, Dallas, 1982—85, exec. v.p., COO, 1985—89; cons. Tex. Hosp. Assn., 1966—82, banks, savs. and loans, 1970—72, NASA, 1970; pres. Tex. Tech U. and Tex. Tech. U. Health Scis. Ctr., Lubbock, 1989—96, U. Tulsa, Okla., 1996—. Ind. dir. Salomon Bros. Asset Mgmt Co., 1991—2001, Central and SW Corp., 1991—2000, Williams Comms. Group Inc., 2000—02; chmn. Coun. Pub. Univ. Pres. and Chancellors, Tex. Higher Edn. Sys., 1993—95; mem. pres.'s commn. NCAA, 1994—97, mem. exec. com., 1998—2003, chmn., exec. com., 2001—03, bd. dirs. Divsn. 1; bd. dirs. Nat. Assn. Ind. Colls. and Univs., Assn. Presbyn. Coll. and Univs. Contbr. articles to profl jours. Mem formula adv comt Tex State Coordinating Bd, Austin, 1977—89; chmn bd dirs Col Football Asn, 1990—92. Recipient Teaching Excellence Award, Univ Houston, 1972, Disting Alumni Award, 1990, Disting Faculty Award, Col Bus Alumni, 1971, Disting Alumni Award, Lee Col, 1984. Office: Univ of Tulsa 600 S College Ave Tulsa OK 74104-3126 E-mail: robert-lawless@utulsa.edu.

LAWLEY, ALAN, materials engineer, educator; b. Birmingham, Eng., Aug. 29, 1933; s. Archibald and Millicent A. (Olorenshaw) L.; m. Nancy A. Kressler, Mar. 26, 1960; children: Carolyn Ann, Elizabeth Ann, Jennifer Ann. BSc, U. Birmingham, 1955, PhD, 1958. Rsch. assoc. U. Pa., 1958—61; mgr. rsch. labs. Franklin Inst. Labs., 1961—66; A.W. Grosvenor prof. materials engring. Drexel U., Phila., 1993—2003, head dept., 1969—79, 1992—98, prof. emeritus, 2003—. Cons. to govt., industry. Editor-in-chief Internat. Jour. Powder Metallurgy; contbr. chpts. to books, articles to profl. jours. Recipient Disting. Svc. award Metal Powder Industries Fedn., 1991. Fellow APMI Internat., ASM Internat. (life mem., Gold Medal award); mem. NAE, Inst. Metals, Mining and Materials, Minerals, Metals and Materials Soc. (pres. 1982, Educator award 2002), Sigma Xi, Phi Kappa Phi, Tau Beta Pi, Alpha Sigma Mu. Home: 336 Hathaway Ln Wynnewood PA 19096-1925 Office: Drexel Univ Dept Materials Sci Engring Philadelphia PA 19104

LAWLEY, THOMAS JOSEPH, dean, medical educator; b. Buffalo, 1947; m. Christine Lawley, 1969; children: Thomas Jr., John, Megan. Grad., Canisius Coll., 1968; MD, SUNY Sch. Medicine, Buffalo, 1972. Intern SUNY Sch. Medicine, Buffalo, 1973—74; resident Yale U. Affiliated Hosps., 1974—75; sr. investigator dermatology br. Nat. Cancer Inst. NIH; prof. and chair. dept. dermatology Emory U. Sch. Medicine, Atlanta, 1988—96, William Patterson Timmie Prof. Dermatology, 1993—, exec. assoc. dean, 1995—96, dean, 1996—; vice chair Emory U. Sys. Health Care, Atlanta, 1996—; core dir. Emory Skin Disease Rsch. Ctr., Atlanta. Pres. Emory Med. Care Found., Emory Children's Ctr.; adminstrv. coun. Assn. Am. Med. Colls. Mem.: Am. Profs. Dermatology, Soc. Investigative Dermatology, Am. Acad. Dermatology (Marion Sulzberger Award 1995), Assn. Am. Physicians, Am. Soc. Clin. Investigators. Office: Emory U Sch Medicine Woodruff Health Scis Ctr Adminstrv Bldg 1440 Clifton Rd NE Atlanta GA 30322-1053

LAWLIS, PATRICIA KITE, air force officer, computer consultant; b. Greensburg, Pa., May 5, 1945; d. Joseph Powell Jr. and Dorothy Theresa (Allshouse) Kite; m. John Charles Ryan, Feb. 6, 1965 (div. 1973); m. Mark Craig Lawlis, Sept. 17, 1976 (div. 1983); 1 child, Elizabeth Marie. BS in Math., East Carolina U., 1967; MS in Computer Sci., Air Force Inst. Tech., 1982; PhD in Computer Sci., Ariz. State U., 1989. Cert. secondary math. tchr. Employment counselor Pa. State Employment Svc., Washington, 1967-69; math. tchr. Fort Cherry Sch. Dist., McDonald, Pa., 1969-74; commd. 2d lt. USAF, 1974, advanced through grades to lt. col., 1974—94; data base mgr. Air Force Space Command, Colorado Springs, 1974-77; computer sys. analyst USAF in Europe, Birkenfeld, Germany, 1977-80; prof. computer sci. Air Force Inst. Tech., Wright-Patterson AFB, Ohio, 1982-86, 89-94; ret. USAF, 1994; computer cons., pres. C.J. Kemp Systems, Inc., Fairborn, Ohio, 1993—2003; women's dir. Sr. Softball USA, Sacramento, 2002—; pres. 2d Chance Sports, Inc., Phoenix, 2002—; engring. specialist Jacobs Sverdrup, San Antonio, 2003—. Ada cons., Ada Joint Program Office, Washington, 1984-94. State treas. NOW, Pa., 1973-74; active women's adv. coun. Nat. Sr. Softball Summit, Sacramento, 2003—. Recipient Mervin E. Gross award Air Force Inst. Tech., 1982, Prof. Ezra Kotcher award, 1985. Mem. Computer Soc. of IEEE, Assn. Computing Machinery, Tau Beta Pi (v.p. chpt. 1981-82), Upsilon Pi Epsilon. Office: 2nd Chance Sports Inc PO Box 93514 Phoenix AZ 85070-3514 also: Jacobs Sverdrup 1107 Crossbrook San Antonio TX 78253 Office Phone: 210-733-3383. E-mail: lawlis@aol.com.

LAWNER, RON, advertising executive; Exec. v.p., creative dir. Della Femina McNamee, Boston; vice chmn., mng. ptnr., chief creative officer Arnold Comm., Inc., Boston, 1996—. Office: Arnold Comm Inc 101 Huntington Ave Boston MA 02199-7606

LAWNICZAK, JAMES MICHAEL, lawyer; b. Toledo, Sept. 11, 1951; m. Christine Nielsen, Dec. 31, 1979; children: Mara Katharine, Rachel Anne, Amy Elizabeth. BA, U. Mich., 1974, JD, 1977. Bar: Mich. 1977, Ill. 1979, Ohio 1989. Law clk. to the Honorable Robert E. DeMascio U.S. Dist. Ct. (ea. dist.) Mich., Detroit, 1977-79; assoc. Levy and Erens, Chgo., 1979-83; assoc. then ptnr. Mayer, Brown & Platt, Chgo., 1983-88; ptnr. Calfee, Halter & Griswold, LLP, Cleve., 1988—. Contbg. author: Collier on Bankruptcy, 15th rev. edit., 1997—. Mem. Chgo. Bar Assn. (subcom. on bankruptcy 1983-88), Cleve. Bar Assn. (bankruptcy com.). Home: 14039 Fox Hollow Dr Novelty OH 44072-9773 Office: Calfee Halter & Griswold 800 Superior Ave E Ste 1400 Cleveland OH 44114-2601 E-mail: jlawniczak@calfee.com.

LAWRANCE, CHARLES HOLWAY, retired civil and sanitary engineer; b. Augusta, Maine, Dec. 25, 1920; s. Charles William and Lois Lyford (Holway) L.; m. Mary Jane Hungerford, Nov. 22, 1947; children: Kenneth A., Lois R., Robert J. BS in Pub. Health Engring., MIT, 1942; MPH, Yale U., 1952. Registered profl. engr., Calif. Sr. san. engr. Conn. State Dept. Health, Hartford, 1946-53; assoc. san. engr. Calif. Dept. Pub. Health, L.A., 1953-55; chief san. engr. Koebig & Koebig, Inc., Cons. Engrs., L.A., 1955-75; engr., mgr. Santa Barbara County Water Agy., Santa Barbara, Calif., 1975-79; prin. engr. James M. Montgomery Cons. Engrs., Pasadena, Calif., 1979-83; v.p. Lawrance, Fisk & McFarland, Inc., Santa Barbara, 1983-96; cons. engr., retired Santa Barbara, 1996-99. Author: The Death of the Dam, 1972; co-author: Ocean Outfall Design, 1958; contbr. articles to profl. jours. Bd. dirs. Pacific Unitarian Ch., Palos Verdes Peninsula, Calif., 1956-60, chmn. bd. 1st lt. USMCR, 1942-46, PTO. Fellow ASCE (life, Norman medal 1966); mem. Am. Water Works Assn. (life), Am. Acad. Environ. Engrs. (life diplomate), Water Environment Fedn. (life). Republican. Unitarian Universalist. Home and Office: 1340 Kenwood Rd Santa Barbara CA 93109-1224 Personal E-mail: charleslawrance@earthlink.net.

LAWRENCE, ANNETTE, artist; b. N.Y.C., 1965; BFA, U. Hartford, 1986; MFA, Md. Inst., 1990. Mem. artist com. Lawndale Art and Performance Ctr., 1991—95; mem. cmty. arts panel Tex. Commn. on Arts, 1995—96; artist-in-residence Cmty. Artist's Collective, Houston, 1990—91, Housing Authority City of Houston, 1992—93, Glassell Sch. Art, Houston, 1993; guest artist Tex. So. U., Houston, 1992; cons. HSPVA, Houston, 1993—94; affiliate artist U. Houston, 1995; adj. faculty U. Houston-Downtown, 1993—96, U. North Tex., Denton, 1996—. One-woman shows include ArtPace, San Antonio, 1995, Art League of Houston, 1996, Gerald Peters Gallery, Dallas, 1996, one-man shows include, 1998, one-woman shows include Women and Their Work, Austin, 1996, African Am. Mus., Dallas, 1998, exhibited in group shows at Minor Injury Gallery, Bklyn., 1986, Bronx River Art Gallery, N.Y., 1987, Manhattan Cable, N.Y.C., 1988, Meyerhoff Gallery, Balt., 1990, Laguna Gloria Mus. Art, Austin, Tex., 1992, Inman Gallery, Houston, 1993, Tex. Gallery, 1994, Gerald Peters Gallery, Dallas, 1995, 1996, 1997—98, U. Houston, Clearlake, Tex., 1998, numerous others, Represented in permanent collections Dallas Mus. Art, ArtPace, San Antonio, Mus. Fine Arts, exhibited in group shows at Texas Trialogues, 2003, Artists and their Mentors, 2003, Flip, 2003, Dunn and Brown Contemporary, 2004, Perspectives at 25, 2004, For Nothing, 2004, Double Consciousness: Black Conception Art Since 1970, 2005, performances include, Sangoma, 1990, Square One, 1990, Amazon Papers, 1991, Parachute Project, 1995; actor:. Recipient Artist award, Cultural Arts Coun., Houston, 1994, Arch and Anne Giles Kimbrough award, Dallas Mus. Art, 1994; fellow W.E.B. Dubois fellow, W.Va. U., 1987—88, Patricia Robert Harris fellow, Md. Inst., 1988—90, Skowhegan Camille Hanks Cosby fellow, African-Am. Artists, 1996; Art Matters grantee, 1994. Office: care Gerald Peters Gallery 2913 Fairmount St Dallas TX 75201-1455*

LAWRENCE, BRIAN DAVID, wedding professional; b. Bklyn., Feb. 21, 1958; s. Matthew Martin Lawrence and Gloria Blacker Peyser; m. Stacy Fran Lipner, Nov. 23, 1985; children: Eric Harlan, Jordan Allison. BA, Bklyn. Coll. Pres. Bridal Fashions, Inc., Rutherford, N.J., 1983—; v.p. Elite Limosine, West N.Y., N.J., 1987—; pres. Able Mind Cons., Teaneck, N.J., 1990—; v.p. mktg. Encore Studios, Clifton, N.J., 1996—. Seminar spkr., columnist. Author: Wedding Expert's Guide to Sales and Marketing, 1991; developer: (Web site) www.sellthebride.com. Mem. Assn. Bridal Cons. Jewish. Avocations: poetry, tournament paddleball. Home: 268 Griggs Ave Teaneck NJ 07666-3305 Office Phone: 800-526-0497 538. E-mail: marketing@encorstudios.com.

LAWRENCE, BRYAN HUNT, investment company executive; b. N.Y.C., July 26, 1942; s. Bryan and Suzanne (Walbridge) L.; m. Elizabeth D. Lawrence, Sept. 25, 1965; children: Bryan R., E. Corey. BA, Hamilton Coll., 1964; MBA, Columbia U., 1966. Assoc. Dillon, Read & Co. Inc., N.Y.C., 1966-70, v.p., 1971-74, sr. v.p., 1975-81, mng. dir., 1982-97; mem. Yorktown Ptnrs. LLC, N.Y.C., 1997—. Bd. dirs. Vintage Petroleum, Tulsa, D & K Health Care, St. Louis, Transmontaigne Inc., Denver, PetroSantander Inc., Houston, Hallador Petroleum, Denver, Savoy Energy L.P., Traverse City, Mich., Athanor B.V., Geneva, Camden Resources, Dallas, Crosstex Energy, Dallas, ESI Energy Svcs. Inc., Calgary, Ellora Energy Inc., Boulder, Colo., Dernick Resources, Inc. Houston Cinco Natural Resources, Dallas, Peak Energy Resources, Durango, Colo., Approach Resources, Ft. Worth, Compass Energy, Calgary, Nytis Exploration, Denver. Trustee Hamilton Coll., Clinton, N.Y., 1991-94. Republican. Home: 580 Park Ave New York NY 10021-7325 Office: Yorktown Ptnrs LLC 410 Park Ave New York NY 10022-4407

LAWRENCE, CHARLES EDWARD, JR., lawyer, judge; b. Beaumont, Miss., July 29, 1955; s. Charles Edward and Mattie Mae Lawrence; m. Shirley A. Sutton, June 5, 1977; children: Charles E. III (CJ), Chari E. B, U. So. Miss., 1976; JD, Howard U., 1979. Bar: Miss. 1979. Pvt. practice atty., counselor at law, Hattiesburg, Miss., 1979—; mcpl. ct. judge City of Hattiesburg, 1997—. Bd. dirs. BancorpSouth Cmty. Adv. Coun. Contbg. columnist, 1983-85. V.p. Forrest County br. NAACP, Hattiesburg, 1980; councilmember City of Hattiesburg, 1985-97; pres. Hattiesburg City Coun., 1991-97; bd. dirs. Wesley Med. Ctr. Meth. Hosp., Hattiesburg, 1995-97, United Way, Hattiesburg, 1997—. Recipient Svc. award Optimist Internation, 1986, New Medinah Islamic Retreat, 1996. Mem. ATLA, Miss. Bar Assn., Miss. Mcpl. Judge Assn., Magnolia Bar Assn. (so. dist. rep. 1986-87). Baptist. Avocations: camping, reading, bike riding, photography. Home: 606 John St Hattiesburg MS 39401-3948 Office: 606 1/2 John St Hattiesburg MS 39401-3966 Fax: 601-544-9279.

LAWRENCE, CHRISTOPHER RUECKERT, investment banker; b. N.Y.C., May 24, 1953; s. Gerard R. and Nancy Lee (Rueckert) L.; m. Cathy Sogg, Apr. 7, 1979; children: Alexander Edward, Zoe Elizabeth, Charles Joseph. AB, Vassar Coll., 1976; MBA, Harvard U., 1981. With mktg. dept. IBM, N.Y.C., 1976-79; investment banker, mng. dir. to vice chmn. Salomon Bros., Inc. (acquired by Citigroup), N.Y.C., 1981—2000; vice chmn. investment banking, global head telecom group Credit Suisse First Boston, 2000, chief strategic officer, 2003—05; vice chmn. Rothschild, 2005—. Bd. dirs. Playwrights Horizons. Office: Rothschild 1251 Sixth Ave 51st Fl New York NY 10020

LAWRENCE, DAVID, JR., journalist; b. N.Y.C., Mar. 5, 1942; s. David Sr. and Nancy Wemple (Bissell) Lawrence; m. Roberta Phyllis Fleischman, Dec. 21, 1963; children: David III, Jennifer Beth, Amanda Katherine, John Benjamin, Dana Victoria. BS, U. Fla., 1963; postgrad. advanced mgmt. program, Harvard U., 1983; LHD (hon.), Siena Heights Coll., Adrian, Mich., 1985; HHD (hon.), Lawrence Inst. Tech., Detroit, 1986; LHD (hon.), No. Mich. U., 1987; LD (hon.), Barry U., 1991, Fla. Meml. U., 1992, Northwood U., 1993, U. Fla., 1993, Nova Southeastern U., 1997, Colgate U., 1998, Fla. Internat. U., 2005. Reporter, news editor St. Petersburg (Fla.) Times, 1963—67; news editor Style/Washington Post, 1967—69; mng. editor Palm Beach (Fla.) Post, 1969—71, Phila. Daily News, 1971—75; exec. editor Charlotte (N.C.) Observer, 1975—76, editor, 1976—78; exec. editor Detroit Free Press, 1978—85, pub., chmn., 1985—89, The Miami Herald, 1989—99. Univ. scholar for early childhood, devel. and readiness U. Fla. Chair The Children's Trust, Miami-Dade Early Learning. Named Disting. Alumnus, U. Fla., 1982; recipient Nat. Human Rights award, Am. Jewish Com., 1986, First Amendment Freedoms award, Anti-Defamation League, 1988, Ida Wells Nat. award for advancement of minorities, Nat. Assn. Black Journalists and Nat. Conf. of Editl. Writers, 1988, John S. Knight Gold medal, Knight-Ridder, 1988, Silver Medallion award, NCCJ, 1992, Disting. Svc. award, Nat. Assn. Schs. Journalism and Mass Comm., 1992, Scripps Howard First Amendment award, 1993, Lifetime Achievement award, Nat. Assn. Minority Media Execs., 2002, Award of Excellence, Am. Pub. Health Assn., 2002, Lewis Hine award for Children and Youth, 2002. Mem.: Early Childhood Initiative Found. (pres.), Inter-Am. Press Assn. (pres. 1995—96), Am. Soc. Newspaper Editors (pres. 1991—92). Office: 3250 SW 3rd Ave 5th Fl Miami FL 33129 Office Phone: 305-646-7229. Business E-Mail: dlawrence@childreadiness.org.

LAWRENCE, DAVID LONG, radiologist; b. Jamestown, Ky. s. Marshall Marvin Lawrence and Opal Hilden Long; m. Jeanette Wesley, Jan. 30, 1954 (div. 1990); 1 child, Julia L.; m. Sandra B. Hubbard, Feb. 14, 1992; 1 child, David W. AB, Centre Coll., Danville, Ky., 1955; MS, U. Ky., 1958; MD, U. Louisville, 1962. Diplomate Am. Bd. Radiology, Nat. Bd. Med. Examiners. Radiologist, v.p. Springfield (Ohio) Radiology, 1971-96; locum tenens cons. Global Med. Staffing, Salt Lake City, 1995—, Vista Med. Staffing, Salt Lake City, 1997—. Med. staff Mercy Med. Ctr.; chmn. bd. Missionary Health Svc., 1991. Lt. comdr., USNR, 1966-68. Mem. Am. Coll. Radiology, Clark County Med. Soc. (pres. 1983), Ohio State Med. Assn. (alternate del.). Episcopalian. Avocations: fly fishing, cosmology, mind/brain interface, etymology. E-mail: sandavidl@hotmail.com.

LAWRENCE, DAVID MICHAEL, lawyer, educator; b. Portland, Oreg., Dec. 26, 1943; s. Robert A. and Maude (Davis) L.; m. Alice Oviatt, June 18, 1966 AB, Princeton U., 1965; JD, Harvard U., 1968. Asst. prof. Inst. Govt., U. N.C., Chapel Hill, 1968-71, assoc. prof., 1971-76, prof. pub. law and govt., 1976-94; Kenan prof. pub. law and govt. U. N.C., Chapel Hill, 1994—. Counsel N.C. Local Govt. Study Commn., 1972-73, N.C. Open Meetings Study Commn., 1978-79 Author: Local Government Finance in North Carolina, 2d edit., 1991 (award for excellence Rsch. and Publs. Govt. Fin. Officers Assn. U.S. and Can. 1991), numerous other books on local govt. law and fin.; contbr. law articles to profl. jours. Chmn. Durham (N.C.) Hist. Dist. Commn., 1985-89. Recipient Herald prize Princeton U., 1965 Mem. N.C. State Bar, Princeton U. Campus Club, Harvard Club of N.Y. Democrat. Office: University of NC Knapp Bldg Clb # 3330 Chapel Hill NC 27599-0001 Office Phone: 919-966-4214.

LAWRENCE, DEIRDRE ELIZABETH, librarian; b. Lawton, Okla., Mar. 15, 1952; d. Herbert Thomas and Joan Roberta (McDonald) L. BA in Art History, Richmond Coll., 1974; MLS, Pratt Inst., 1979; postgrad., Harvard U., 1981-82. Head cataloging and tech. svcs., coord. rsch. svcs. Mus. Fine Arts, Boston, 1980-83; prin. libr., coord. rsch. svcs. mus. and libr. archives Bklyn. Mus., 1983—. Mem. Rsch Libr. Group, bd. nominating com., 1994, adv. com. Getty Projects, 1996—, N.Y. Met. Reference and Rsch. Libr. Agy, conservation preservation adv. coun., 1988-92, bd. trustees, 1995—; grant reviewer fed. and state agys.; cons. in field; lectr. in field. Author: New York and Hollywood Fashion, 1986, Dressing the Part: Costume Sket, 1989, Modern Art--The Production, 1989, Guide to the Culin Archival Collection, 1996, Formation of an Islamic art library collection in an Am. museum, 1996, Culin: Collector and Documentor of the World He Saw, Fashion and How It Was Influenced by Ethnographic Collections in Museums, Native American Art and Culture: Documentary Resources, Access to Visual Images-Past and Present; contbr. articles to profl. jours.; lectr. at internat. and nat. libr. confs.; curator various collections including Bklyn. Mus., 1989, 96, 97, others. Mem. conservation, preservation adv. coun. N.Y. Met. Reference and Rsch. Libr. Agy., 1988-92, bd. trustees, 1995—. Recipient Samuel H. Kress Travel grant, 1993, 95. Mem. Art Librs. Soc. N.Am. (mem. internat. rels. com. 1996-97, other offices), Spl. Librs. Assn., Native Am. Art Studies Assn., Internat. Fedn. Libr. Assns. Office: Brooklyn Mus 200 Eastern Pkwy Brooklyn NY 11238-6099

LAWRENCE, GERALD, JR., lawyer; b. Phila., Jan. 10, 1968; s. Gerald and Rita Katherine (Duffy) L.; m. Andrea Stewart, Jan. 8, 1994. BSBA, Georgetown U., 1990; JD, Villanova U., 1993. Bar: Pa. 1993, U.S. Dist. Ct. Pa. 1994, U.S. Ct. Appeals (3d cir.) 1994. Atty. Elliott Reihner Siedzikowski & Egan, Blue Bell, Harrisburg, Scranton, Pa. and Woodbury, N.J., 1992-97; counsel Aetna U.S. Healthcare, Inc., Blue Bell, 1997—2000, Aetna, Inc., Hartford, Conn., 2000—, Blue Bell, Pa., 2000—05; ptnr. Lowey Dannenberg, Bemporad & Selinger P.C., West Conshohocken, Pa., 2005—, NYC, 2005—. Counsel Delaware Country Dem. Party, 1996—98; Delaware County counsel Pa. Dem. Party Victory Com., 1996; spl. local counsel Gore 2000 Campaign, 2000; mem. atty. adv. com. Pa. Securities Commn., 2005—. Interviewer Georgetown Alumni Admission Program, 1992—; bd. dirs. James A. Finnegan Found., 1995—; v.p. Georgetown Club Phila., 1996.; treas. Del. County Dem. Party, 1998; mem. Dem. State Com., 1998-02; treas. Southeastern Caucus Pa. Dem. State Com., 1998-02, mem. exec. com., 1999-02; alt. del. Dem. Nat. Conv., 2000; chmn. Radnor Twp. Dem. Com., 1998-02; commr. elections Del County, Pa., 2004—; vice-chmn. Del. County Dem. Party, 2002-04 Named Pa. Super Lawyer, Phila. and Law and Politics Mags., 2005. Mem.: ATLA, ABA (vice chmn. bus. torts com. 1996—2001), Phila. Bar Assn., Pa. Bar Assn. (mem. commn. to rev. and evaluate jud. campaign advt. guidelines 1996, mem. jud. selection and adminstrn. com. 1994—). Home: 407 Saint Davids Rd Wayne PA 19087-5205 Office: Lowey Dannenberg Bemporad & Selinger PC 200 Barr Harbor Dr Ste 400 West Conshohocken PA 19428-2977 also: Lowey Dannenbert Bemporad & Selinger PC One North Lexington Ave White Plains NY 10601 Office Phone: 914-997-0500, 610-941-2760. Business E-Mail: glawrence@ldbs.com.

LAWRENCE, GERALD GRAHAM, management consultant; b. U.K., June 21, 1947; came to U.S., 1962, naturalized, 1967; s. Raymond Joseph and Barbara Virginia Lawrence; 1 child, Ian Andrew; m. Julie Ann Quiram. BA in Math., Northeastern U., 1970, MA in Econs., 1973; MBA, U. Pa., 1975. Optics rsch. technologist Polaroid Corp., Cambridge, Mass., 1968-70; intern Corning Glass Works, Inc., N.Y.C., 1974; asst. brand mgr. Procter and Gamble, Cin., 1975-76; assoc. Theodore Barry & Assocs., N.Y.C., 1976-79; dir. performance improvement systems Stone & Webster Mgmt. Cons., N.Y.C., 1979-84; mgr. utility MAS Deloitte Haskins & Sells, N.Y.C., 1984-86; pres. PMC Mgmt. Cons., Inc., Three Bridges, N.J., 1986—. Advisor Commerce & Econ. Devel. Dept. State of N.J.; speaker in field. Designer: auditor system nuclear power plant constrn; innovator; quality assurance for profl. cons. svcs; contbr. articles to profl. jours. Econs. fellow Northeastern U., 1973, adminstrv. fellow Wharton Sch. U. Pa., 1975. Home: 6 Thistle Ln Flemington NJ 08822-7067 Office: PMC Mgmt Cons PO Box 332 Three Bridges NJ 08887-0332 E-mail: pmc@pmc-management.com.

LAWRENCE, GLENN ROBERT, arbitrator, mediator, lawyer; b. NYC, Nov. 8, 1930; m. Nina M. Scaturro; children: David P., Eric A. JD, Bklyn. Law Sch., 1954; BA, U. Louisville, 1968; MA in Psychology, Cath. U., 1977; PhD, Am. U., 1980. Bar: N.Y. 1955, D.C. 1973, U.S. Supreme Ct. 1976, Va. 1997; cert. family mediator, Va., 2002-04. Atty. N.Y.C. Legal Aid, 1955-57;

ptnr. Lawrence & Lawrence, N.Y.C., 1957-64; agt. N.Y. State, Babylon, N.Y., 1964-66; atty. U.S. Army Engrs., 1966-69; assoc. chief trial atty. U.S. Dept. Navy, Washington, 1969-78; judge adminstrv. law HEW, Camden, N.J., 1978-79, U.S. Dept. Labor, Washington, 1979-93, SEC, Washington, 1993-96; mem. bd. contract appeals U.S. Dept. Labor, Washington, 1981-93; arbitrator Nat. Assn. Securities Dealers, Inc., Washington, 1996—, Superior Ct., Washington, 1996—; mediator Women's Ctr., Vienna, Va., 1996—2001. Adj. prof. law George Mason U., Fairfax, Va., 1980-83, Ctrl. Mich. U., Washington, 1981-95, Nat. Jud. Coll. U. Nev., Reno, 1985-88; lectr. Banares Hindu U., Varanasi, India, 1988, Law Coll., Ernakulum, Cochin, India, 1989, Washington Lee U., Lexington, Va., 1990; mem. adv. com. Georgetown U. State Cts. and Toxic Torts, 1991; advisor Judiciary Leadership Devel. Coun. Inc., 1990-99; v.p. Fed. Bar Found., 1996-99, chair profl. ethics com., 1999-2001, chair sr. lawyers divsn., 1999-2000. Author: Condemnation Law, 1969. Bd. dirs. Democracy Devel. Initiative, Parkinson Found., 2004—. Mem. ABA (chmn. nat. conf. adminstrv. law judges edn. com. 1985-90, chmn. internat. conf. jud. edn. London 1985, pres. fed. adminstrv. law judge conf. 1984-85, chmn. edn. jud. adminstrn. divsn. 1987-91, chmn. confs., chmn. jud. edn. standards program 1991-95, vice chmn. govt. lawyers com. sr. lawyers divsn. 1991-95), Fed Bar Assn. (chmn. adminstrv. judiciary com. 1984-88, continuing edn. bd. 1988-91, chmn. judiciary sect. 1989-91, sect. coord. exec. com. 1992-94, editor Fed. Jurist 1991-96, chair pub. rels. com. 1995-96, chair profl. ethics com. 1996-98), Adminstrv. Trial Lawyers Assn. (pres. 1979-80, chmn. sr. lawyers divsn. 1999—). Office Phone: 703-406-2732. Personal E-mail: nml1@erols.com.

LAWRENCE, J. RODNEY, lawyer; b. 1945; married. BA, Tulane U., 1967; JD, U. Ky., 1972. Inside counsel Long John Silvers, 1975-80, Hydral Co., 1980-83; pvt. practice law, 1983-85; exec. v.p. legal affairs, sec. Pier 1 Imports, Inc. (co. of Internark, Inc.), Ft. Worth, 1985—. Lt. (j.g.) 1967-69. Office: Pier 1 Imports Inc 100 Pier 1 Pl Fort Worth TX 76102 also: 301 Commerce St Ste 600 Fort Worth TX 76102-4106

LAWRENCE, JAMES A., food products executive; m. Mary G. Lawrence; 3 children. BA, Yale U., 1974; MBA with distinction, Harvard U., 1976. With Fidelity Funds, Boston Cons. Group; ptnr. Bain & Co.; co-founder, ptnr. The LEK Partnership, 1983—92; pres., CEO Asia, Africa & Mid. E. bus. units The Pepsi-Cola Co., 1992—96; exec. v.p., CFO Northwest Airlines, St. Paul, 1996—98, General Mills, Inc., Mpls., 1998—. Bd. dirs. Am. Re-Ins. Corp., TransTech., Inc., TWA, U.S. China Bus. Coun., chmn. U.S. South Africa Bus. Devel. Com. Office: Gen Mills 1 General Mills Blvd Minneapolis MN 55426

LAWRENCE, JAMES KAUFMAN LEBENSBURGER, lawyer; b. New Rochelle, NY, Oct. 8, 1940; s. Michael Monet and Edna (Billings) L.; m. George-Ann Adams, Apr. 5, 1969; children: David Michael, Catherine Robin. AB, Ohio State U., 1962, JD, 1965. Bar: Ohio 1965, U.S. Dist. Ct. (so. dist.) Ohio 1971, U.S. Ct. Appeals (6th cir.) 1971, U.S. Ct. Appeals (4th cir.) 1978. Field atty. NLRB, Cin., 1965-70; ptnr. Frost Brown Todd LLC, Cin., 1970—. Adj. prof. econs. dept. and Coll. Law U. Cin., 1975—; adj. prof. Moritz Coll. Law Ohio State U., 1995—; adj. prof. Xavier U., 1995, McGregor Sch., Antioch U., 1993—98; adj. prof. MBA program Otterbein Coll., 2002—; treas. Potter Stewart Inn of Ct., Cin., 1988—90; tchg. fellow Harvard Negotiation Project, 1991; chmn. adv. panel on appointment of magistrate judges U.S. Dist. Ct. for So. Dist. Ohio, 1993—97. Contbr. articles to profl. jours.; editor: (newsletter) Pass the Gavel, 2002—03. Mem. nat. coun. Ohio State U. Coll. Law, 1974—; steering com. Leadership Cin., 1985-89; mem. Seven Hills Neighborhood Houses, Cin., 1973-95, pres., 1992-94; bd. dirs. Beechwood Home, Cin., 1973-85; adv. bd. Emerson Behavioral Health Svcs., 1990-95, chmn., 1995; chmn. Labor Dept., 1978-89, Franciscan Hosp. Devel. Coun., 1995-99, chmn., 1996-97; trustee Ctr. for Resolution of Disputes, Inc., 1988-91, treas., 1990-91; mem. Ohio Gov.'s Ops. Improvement Task Force, 1991. Recipient Outstanding Adj. Faculty award, U. Cin., 1998. Fellow Coll. Labor and Employment Lawyers; mem. ABA, Cin. Bar Assn. (chmn. labor law com. 1979-82, comm. adv. com. 1994-96, alternative dispute resolution com. 1996—), Ohio Bar Assn. (cert. specialist in labor and employment law, vice chmn. labor and employment law sect. 1987-90, chmn. 1990-92, Ohio's Friend of Legal Edn. award 2003), Indsl. Rels. Rsch. Assn. (bd. govs. 1977-80), Alumni Assn. Coll. Law Ohio State U. (pres. 1984-85), Assn. for Conflict Resolution, Cincinnatus Assn. (pres. 1985-86), Collaborative Law Ctr. (steering com. 1996—), Univ. Club; master Potter Stewart Inn of Ct. Avocations: collecting movie posters, Lionel trains. Home: 3300 Columbia Pkwy Cincinnati OH 45226-1044 Office: Frost Brown Todd LLC 2500 PNC Ctr 201 E 5th St Cincinnati OH 45202-4182 Office Phone: 513-651-6822. Business E-Mail: jlawrence@fbtlaw.com.

LAWRENCE, JANICE ELAINE, psychiatric and mental health nurse; b. Brockton, Mass., Jan. 7, 1954; d. George Freemont and Marjorie Elsie Glidden; m. James George Lawrence, Sept. 11, 1971; children: Jennifer Lynn, Jillian Lee, James George, Justin James. AS, Massasoit CC, Brockton, Mass., 1983. RN Mass. Nursing asst. Hallmark nursing Home, East Bridgewater, Mass., 1979—83; evening nursing supr. Blue Hills Nursing Care Ctr., Staughton, Mass., 1983—84; evening charge nurse psychiat. unit, emergency dept. psychiat. evaluator Brockton (Mass.) Hosp., 1984—. Author numerous poems. Active Girl Scouts Am., East Bridgewater, 1978—84, Boy Scouts Am., Bridgewater, 1992—. Baptist. Avocations: writing, horseback riding, music, gardening, dogs. Home: 298 High St Bridgewater MA 02324 Office: Brockton Hosp 680 Centre St Brockton MA 02302 Personal E-mail: jl02324@aol.com.

LAWRENCE, JOHN KIDDER, lawyer; b. Detroit, Nov. 18, 1949; s. Luther Ernest and Mary Anna (Kidder) L.; m. Jeanine Ann DeLay, June 20, 1981. AB, U. Mich., 1971; JD, Harvard U., 1974. Bar: Mich. 1974, U.S. Supreme Ct. 1977, D.C. 1978. Assoc. Dickinson, Wright, McKean & Cudlip, Detroit, 1973-74; staff atty. Office of Judge Adv. Gen., Washington, 1975-78; assoc. Dickinson, Wright, McKean, Cudlip & Moon, Detroit, 1978-81; ptnr. Dickinson, Wright, Moon, VanDusen & Freeman, Detroit, 1981-98, Dickinson Wright PLLC, Detroit, 1998—. Exec. sec. Detroit Com. on Fgn. Rels., 1988—; trustee Ann Arbor (Mich.) Summer Festival, Inc., 1990—; patron Founders Soc. Detroit Inst. Arts, 1979—; dir. Mich. C. of C., 2002—. With USN, 1975-78. Mem. AAAS, ABA, Am. Law Inst., State Bar Mich., D.C. Bar Assn., Am. Judicature Soc., Internat. Bar Assn., Am. Hist. Assn., Mich. C. of C. (bd. dirs. 2002—), Detroit Athletic Club, Econ. Club Detroit, Phi Eta Sigma, Phi Beta Kappa. Democrat. Episcopalian. Office: Dickinson Wright PLLC 500 Woodward Ave Ste 4000 Detroit MI 48226-3416 Office Phone: 313-223-3500.

LAWRENCE, JOHN R., academic administrator; Bachelor's degree, Master's degree, EdS, N.E. Mo. State U.; EdD, U. Mo., Columbia. Supt. Troy (Mo.) R-3 Schs., Mo., 1984—, Schuyler County R-I Pub. Schs., Lancaster, Mo. Mem.: Mo. Assn. Sch. Adminstrs. (pres.), Assn. Sch. Adminstrs. (mem. exec. com. 1999—, pres.-elect 2002, pres. 2003). Office: Lincoln County R-III Sch Dist 951 W College St Troy MO 63379

LAWRENCE, JUDITH M., writer, journalist; b. Rochester, N.Y., Apr. 25, 1944; d. Ralph and Mildred Eaton Lawrence; m. Pat Collins, May 25, 1977; children: Matthew Lillibridge, Lara Lillibridge. BS, U. Rochester, 1976, MS, 1979. Exec. dir. Rochester Ctr. for Ind. Living, 1984—89, Alzheimer's Assn., Rochester, 1989—94; freelance writer Key West, Fla., 1994—; journalist Chautaugua, NY, 2001—. Short story contest judge Key West Women Writers, 2000, 01. Author: Musings, 2001; columnist:, author short stories. Democrat. Unitarian. Avocations: walking, swimming, travel. Home and Office: 2622 Privada Dr The Villages FL 32162

LAWRENCE, LAUREN, author, dreams expert, psychoanalytical theorist, psychoanalyst; b. N.Y.C., June 26, 1950; d. Jack and Elaine (Gaumont) Soefer; m. D. Henry Lawrence, June 24, 1972; 1 child, Graham. MA in Psychology, New Sch. for Social Rsch., 1993. Psychoanalyst, N.Y.C., 1992—. Author: Dream Keys: Unlocking the Power of Your Unconscious Mind, 1999, Dream Keys for Love, 1999, Dream Keys for the Future: Unlocking the Secrets of Your Destiny, 2000, La Llave De Los Suenos, 2001, A Quoi Revent Les Stars, 2002, Private Dreams of Public People, 2002; columnist: N.Y. Daily News, Newport This Week, Swing Mag., George mag., Trader Monthly mag.; contbr. sci. papers and articles to profl. jours. and mags.; performer: (TV series) The Dream Zone, RISE TV, BBC; appeared on numerous TV and radio shows. Friend N.Y. Psychoanalytic Soc. Achievements include founding of a third person analysis, a new method of analysis in clinical practice, which provides the analysand a narrational objectivity; the covert seduction theory, which expounds the dangers of a non-physical parental seduction, the Actualized Dream, a conscious behavioral manifestation of symbolic material-unconscious desires that manifest themselves during consciousness through extreme behavioral acts, the undisclosed visual cliche, as an attribute or assessment drawn from a visual that leads to a cliche, and the externalized dream as a manifestation of a vision. Home and Office: 31 E 72d St New York NY 10021-4146 Office Phone: 212-737-3911. E-mail: LaurenLawrence@aol.com.

LAWRENCE, MARTIN, actor, comedian; b. Frankfurt, Germany, Apr. 16, 1965; s. John and Chlora L.; m. Patricia Southall Jan. 7, 1995 (div. Sept. 17, 1996); 1 child. Actor: (TV series) What's Happening Now, 1985, HBO One Night Stand, 1989, Kid 'N' Play, 1990 (voice only), Russell Simmons' Def Comedy Jam, 1991-93 (host); (films) Do the Right Thing, 1989, House Party, 1990, House Party 2, 1991, Talkin' Dirty after Dark, 1991, Boomerang, 1992, You So Crazy, 1994 (concert film, also exec. prodr.), Bad Boys, 1995, Nothing to Lose, 1997, Life, 1997, Blue Streak, 1999; actor, exec. prodr., writer, dir. A Thin Line Between Love and Hate, 1997; actor, exec. prodr.: Big Momma's House, 2000, What's the Worst That Could Happen, 2001, Black Knight, 2001, National Security, 2003, Bad Boys II, 2003, Rebound, 2005, (TV series) Martin, 1992-97. Office: United Talent Agy 9560 Wilshire Blvd Ste 500 Beverly Hills CA 90212*

LAWRENCE, MARY JOSEPHINE (JOSIE LAWRENCE), artist, retired library official; b. Carbondale, Pa., Mar. 9, 1932; d. Domenick Anthony and Teresa Rose (Zaccone) Gentile; m. John Paul Lawrence, Apr. 25, 1953 (dec. June 1977); children: Mary Josephine, Jane Therese, Susan Michele. BFA, Mass. Coll. Art, 1989; postgrad., Chelsea (Eng.) Sch. Art, 1989, San Pancrazio Art Sch., Tuscany, Italy, 1990, 91, 92; cert. in grad. studies, Guangzhou Acad. Fine Arts, China, 1993; postgrad., Md. Inst. Fine Art, Sorrento, Italy, 1994, Ctrl. Acad. Arts and Design, Beijing, 1997, Skopelos, Greece, 1998, N.Y. Sch. Visual Arts, Barcelona, Spain, 1999, Internat. Sch. Art, Umbria, Italy, 2000. Sales clk. Gorins, 5&10, Jordan Marsh, Boston, 1946-49; clk.-typist, sec. John Hancock Ins. Co., Boston, 1950-53; machine operator, quality control supr. Rust Craft Greeting Cards, Dedham, Mass., 1961-69; restaurant hostess Tony's Villa, Waltham, Mass., 1972-73; mus. sales clk., artist John F. Kennedy Libr., Boston, 1979-87, mgr. mus. store, supr., 1988-2000; freelance artist, 2000—. Tchr.'s asst. San Pancrazio Art Sch., 1992; guest appearance TAKE TWO cable TV, Channel 11, 1996, Walpole Cmty. TV, 2001, WEZE Family 590 Talk Show, 2001. One woman shows include de Havilland Fine Art Gallery, Boston, 1997, Dr. James McDermott Gallery, Boston, 1996, Cranberry Cafe, Boston, 1997; exhibited in group shows at South Shore Arts Ctr., Cohasset, Mass., 1991, North River Arts Soc., Marshfield Hills, Mass., 1994 (Best of Show), de Havilland Fine Art Gallery, Boston, 1997, United South End Open Studios, 1998, Artana Gallery, Framingham, Mass., 2000. Juror Quincy Art Assn., 1996, 98, 2002, 2005, Weymouth Art Assn., 1995, 97, Arts Affair, 1999. Recipient Outstanding Achievement award, Nat. Archives and Rsch. Adminstrn., 1989, 1994, 1996—97, Svc. award, 1990, Blue Ribbon Mems. award, 2003, Best of show award, De Havilland Fine Arts Gallery, 1992, honorium, Weymouth Art Assn., 1995, 1997, Quincy Art Assn. award, 1996, 1998, 2002; grantee Vt. Studio Ctr., 2002, 2004. Mem. de Havilland Fine Art Gallery, South Shore Art Ctr., North River Arts Soc., Nat. Mus. Women in Arts (charter), Milton Art Mus., United S. End Artists, Fuller Mus. Art., South Boston Arts Assn., Portland Mus. Art, Farnsworth Art Mus. Democrat. Roman Catholic. Personal E-mail: josielawrence@comcast.net.

LAWRENCE, MERLOYD LUDINGTON, editor; b. Pasadena, Calif., Aug. 1, 1932; d. Nicholas Saltus and Mary Lloyd (Macy) Ludington; m. Seymour Lawrence, June 21, 1952 (div. 1984); children: Macy, Nicholas; m. John M. Myers, 1985 AB, Radcliffe Coll., 1954, MA, 1957. With Houghton Mifflin Co., 1955-57; free lance translator, 1957-65; editor, treas., v.p. Seymour Lawrence Inc., Boston, 1965-83; pres. Merloyd Lawrence, Inc., Boston, 1983—. Bd. dirs. Island Press. Translator works of Flaubert and Balzac, modern French fiction, German and Swedish children's books. Treas., v.p. Milford House Properties, Ltd., N.S., Can., 1975-80; trustee Milton (Mass.) Acad., 1974-82; mem. com. clin. investigations Beth Israel/Deaconess Hosp.; bd. dirs. Northeast Wilderness Trust, 2002—, Woods Hole Rsch. Ctr., 2004—; bd. dirs. Island Press, 2005—. Mem. Am. Translators Assn., New Eng. Forestry Found. (exec. bd. officer 1989—), Mass. Audubon Soc. (dir. 1974-2001, exec. com. 1992-2001, hon. dir. 2001—), Island Press (bd. dirs. 2005—), Tavern Club, Phi Beta Kappa. Home: 102 Chestnut St Boston MA 02108-1120 Office: 102A Chestnut St Boston MA 02108-1120

LAWRENCE, NINA, publishing executive; married; 2 children. B cum laude, Middlebury Coll., 1982. Media planner Benton & Bowles, Inc., 1983—85; with Mag. Sales Develop. Program Time Inc., 1985—86, with advt. sales dept., 1986—87; advt. sales dir. Diversion mag. Hearst Publishing, 1987—89, pub. Hearst Profl. Magazines, 1989—90; pres. Family Publishing Concepts, 1991—92; advt. dir. Discover mag., 1992—93; pub. Disney Adventures mag., 1993—94; assoc. pub. Mademoiselle mag. Conde Nast Pubs., NYC, 1994-96; pub. Modern Bride mag. Primedia Inc., NYC, 1996-98; pub. Bride's mag. Conde Nast Pubs., NYC, 1999—2005; v.p. & pres. W mag., 2005—. Office: W Mag 7 West 34th St New York NY 10001*

LAWRENCE, PAUL ROGER, retired finance educator; b. Rochelle, Ill., Apr. 26, 1922; s. Howard Cyrus and Clara (Luther) L.; m. Martha G. Stiles, Dec. 14, 1948; children: Anne Talcott, William Stiles. Student, Grand Rapids Jr. Coll., 1939-41; AB, Albion Coll., 1943; MBA, Harvard U., 1947, DCS, 1950. Mem. faculty Harvard U. Bus. Sch., Boston, 1947-91, asst. prof., 1951-56, assoc. prof., 1956-61, prof. organizational behavior, 1961-68, Donham prof. organizational behavior, 1968; retired, 1991. Author (with others): Renewing American Industry, 1983; author: HRM, Trends and Challenges, 1985, Behind the Factory Walls, 1990, Driven, How Human Nature Shapes Our Choices, 2002. Served to lt. USNR, 1943-46. Fellow Acad. Mgmt.; mem. Am. Sociol. Assn. Office: Cumnock Hall Soldiers Field Boston MA 02163 Home: 206 Wintrop Terr Bedford MA 01730 E-mail: plawrence@hbs.edu.

LAWRENCE, RAMON, education educator, consultant; arrived in U.S., 2001; B Computer Sci., U. Manitoba, Winnipeg, Can., 1996; Dr, U. Man., 2001. Asst. prof. U. Iowa, Iowa City, 2001—. Office Phone: 319-335-0561.

LAWRENCE, ROBERT SWAN, physician, educator; b. Phila., Feb. 6, 1938; s. Thomas George and Catherine (Swan) Lawrence; m. Cynthia Starr Cole, July 1, 1960; children: Job Scott, Matthew Swan, Hannah Starr, Jin Sook, Sang Bo. AB magna cum laude, Harvard U., 1960, MD, 1964. Intern, resident in internal medicine Mass. Gen. Hosp., 1964—66; surgeon USPHS, 1966—69; resident in internal medicine Mass. Gen. Hosp., 1969—70; asst. prof., then assoc. prof. medicine, chief divsn. cmty. medicine Med. Sch. U. NC, 1970—74; dir. divsn. primary care Harvard U. Med. Sch., 1974—91, assoc. prof. medicine, 1980—81, Charles S. Davidson assoc. prof. medicine, 1981—91. Chmn. dept. medicine Cambridge (Mass.) Hosp., 1980—91; adj. prof. NYU Sch. of Medicine, 1992—95; prof. health policy and mgmt. Johns Hopkins Bloomberg Sch. Pub. Health, 1995—, assoc. dean for profl. edn., 1995—, Edyth Schoenrich prof. preventive medicine, 2000—; prof. medicine Johns Hopkins Sch. Medicine, 1996—; mem. com. human rights NAS, 1986—97; chmn. bd. health promotion and disease prevention IOM, 1981—86, chmn. com. health and human rights, 1990—94; chmn. U.S. Preventive Svc. Task Force HHS, 1984—89, active mem., 1990—96; fellow Ctr. for Advanced Study in Behavioral Scis., 1988—89; dir. health scis. Rockefeller Found., 1991—95; found. dir. Ctr. for Livable Future, John Hopkins U., 1996—. Editor Am. Jour. Preventive Medicine, 1990—92; contbr. articles to profl. jours., chapters to books. Bd. trustees Columbia U. Tchrs. Coll., 1992—98; bd. dirs. Physicians for Human Rights, 1986—91, 1997—2003, pres., 1999—2003. Recipient Maimonides prize, 1964, John Atkinson Ferrell prize, 1997, Albert Schweitzer Humanitarian prize, 2002. Master: ACP; fellow: Am. Coll. Preventive Medicine (Spl. Recognition award 1988); mem.: APHA, Soc. Tchrs. Preventive Medicine (Spl. Recognition award 1993), Soc. Gen. Internal Medicine (pres. 1978—79, Leadership award 1997), Inst. Medicine NAS, Phi Beta Kappa, Delta Omega. Home: Highfield House 1112 4000 N Charles St Baltimore MD 21218-1760 Office Phone: 410-614-4590. Business E-Mail: rlawrence@jhsph.edu.

LAWRENCE, RUTH, writer, illustrator; b. Bklyn., Aug. 1, 1926; d. Joseph Katz and Sara Rachel Leibick; m. Martin Robert Lawrence, June 4, 1950 (div. June 1975); children: Sandra, Audrey. AA, Nassau C.C., 1968; BA, C.W. Post Coll., 1975. Artist Merrick (N.Y.) Libr., 1973—75; worker U.S. Govt., 1980—95; artist, poet, tchr., lectr., children's book illustrator, 1995—. Cons. Merrick Art Gallery, 1976. Author: My Famous Grandma, 1996, Mostly Limericks for the Millennium, 1998, Columbus, 1999, Barbara Bubbles, 2000. Recipient 1st in oil award, Nassau C.C., Garden City, N.Y., 1975, Best in Show award, 1975. Mem.: Suburban Art League.

LAWRENCE, SALLY CLARK, retired academic administrator; b. San Francisco, Dec. 29, 1930; d. George Dickson and Martha Marie Alice (Smith) Clark; m. Henry Clay Judd Jr., July 1, 1950 (div. Dec. 1972); children: Rebecca, David, Nancy; m. John I. Lawrence, Aug. 12, 1976; stepchildren: Maia, Dylan. Docent Portland Art Mus., Portland, Oreg., 1958-68; gallery owner, dir. Sally Judd Gallery, Portland, Oreg., 1968-75; art ins. appraiser, cons. Portland, Oreg., 1975-81; from interim dir. Mus. Art Sch. to pres. emerita Pacific NW Coll. Art, Portland, Oreg., 1981—2003, pres. emerita, 2003—. Bd. dirs. Contemporary Crafts Gallery, Portland, 1970—73, Portland Arts Alliance, Portland, Oreg., 1987—2003, Assn. Ind. Coll. of Art and Design, 1991—2003, Portland (Oreg.) Contemporary Art, 2005—; pres. Assn. Ind. Coll. of Art and Design, 1995—96, sec., 1996—2001. Fellow: Nat. Assn. Sch. Art and Design (life; bd. dirs. 1984—91, 1994—2002, pres. 1996—99); mem.: Oreg. Ind. Coll. Assn. (bd. dirs. 1981—2003, exec. com. 1989—94, pres. 1992—93, v.p. 2001—03), Pearl Arts Found. (chair bd. dirs. 2000—03). Personal E-mail: sallyl@carrollsweb.com.

LAWRENCE, SANFORD HULL, physician, immunochemist, author; b. Kokomo, Ind., July 10, 1919; s. Walter Scott and Florence Elizabeth (Hull) L. AB, Ind. U., 1941, MD, 1944. Fellow in biochemistry George Washington U., 1941; intern Rochester (N.Y.) Gen. Hosp., 1944-45; resident Halloran Hosp., Staten Island, N.Y., 1946-49; chief med. svce. Ft. Ord Regl. Hosp., 1945-46; dir. biochemistry rsch. lab. San Fernando (Calif.) VA Hosp.; asst. prof. UCLA, 1950—. Cons. internal medicine and cardiology U.S. Govt., Los Angeles County; lectr. Faculte de Medicine, Paris, various colls. Eng., France, Belgium, Sweden, USSR, India, Japan; chief med. svc. Ft. Ord Regional Hosp.; chmn. Titus, Inc., 1982—. Author: Zymogram in Clinical Medicine, 1965, Gyert, 2000, Whitley Heights, 2002; contbr. articles to sci. jours.; author: Threshold of Valhalla, Another Way to Fly, My Last Satyr, and other short stories; traveling editor: Relax Mag. Mem. Whitley Heights Civic Assn., 1952—; pres. Halloran Hosp. Employees Assn., 1947-48. Served to maj. U.S. Army, 1945-46. Recipient Rsch. award TB and Health Assn., 1955-58, Los Angeles County Heart Assn., 1957-59, Pres. award, Queen's Blue Book award, Am. Men of Sci. award; named one of 2000 Men of Achievement, Leaders of Am. Sci., Ky. Col., named Hon. Mayor of West Point, Ky. Mem. AAAS, AMA, N.Y. Acad. Scis., Am. Fedn. Clin. Research, Am. Assn. Clin. Investigation, Am. Assn. Clin. Pathology, Am. Assn. Clin. Chemistry, Los Angeles County Med. Assn. Republican. Methodist. Avocations: bridge, comml. pilot, piano, organist. Home: Whitley Heights 2014 Whitley Ave Los Angeles CA 90068-3235 also: 160 rue St Martin 75003 Paris France

LAWRENCE, TRACEY, country singer, songwriter; b. Atlanta, Tex., Jan. 27, 1968; Started performing in Nashville, 1982; signed with Atlantic Records, Tenn., 1991; currently with Dreamworks, Nashville. Singer: (albums) Sticks & Stones, 1991, Alibis, 1993, I See It Now, 1994, Live and Unplugged, 1995, Time Marches On, 1996, Coast is Clear, 1997, Lessons Learned, 2000, Tracey Lawrence, 2001, Strong, 2004, (singles) Alibis, 1993, Can't Break it to My Heart, 1993, My Second Time, 1993, Any Fool Can See, 1994, If the World Had a Front Porch, 1995, Is That a Tear, 1996, Stars Over Texas, 1996, Better Man Better Off, 1997, While You Sleep, 1998, I'll Never Pass This Way Again, 1998; singer, prodr.: songs "Renegades, Rebels, and Rogues", Maverick (Original Soundtrack), 1994, singer, prodr. with John Anderson: "Hillbilly with a Heartache" Country til' I Die, 1994; singer (with Kenny Chesney and George Jones): (songs) "From Hillbilly Heaven to Honky Tonk Hell", I Will Stand, 1997. Office: Dreamworks Nashville 1516 16th Ave S Nashville TN 37212 Office Phone: 615-463-4600.

LAWRENCE, WALTER, JR., surgeon, educator; b. Chgo., May 31, 1925; s. Walter and Violette May (Matthews) L.; m. Susan Grayson Shryock, June 20, 1947; children: Walter Thomas, Elizabeth, William Amos, Edward Gene. Student, Dartmouth Coll., 1943-44; PhB, U. Chgo., 1944, SB, 1945, MD with honors, 1948. Diplomate Am. Bd. Surgery (examiner 1974-78, sr. mem. 1978—). Intern Johns Hopkins, 1948-49, asst. resident, 1949-51; fellow Meml. Sloan-Kettering Cancer Ctr., 1951-52, 54-56, rsch. fellow, 1956, asst. mem., asst. attending surgeon, 1957-60, assoc. mem., assoc. attending surgeon, 1960-66; practice medicine specializing in surgery NYC, 1956-66, Richmond, Va., 1966—. Instr. surgery Cornell U., 1957-58, asst. profl. clin. surgery, 1958-63, clin. assoc. prof., 1963-66; vis. investigator Queen Victoria Hosp., East Grinstead, Eng., 1964-65; prof. surgery Med. Coll. Va., Richmond, 1966-90, prof. emeritus, 1990--, chmn. divsn. surg. oncology, 1966-90, exec. vice chmn. dept. surgery, 1966-73, acting chmn., 1973-74, Am. Cancer Soc. prof. clin. oncology, 1972-77; dir. Massey Cancer Ctr., 1974-88, dir. emeritus, 1988—; chmn. surgery test com. Nat. Bd. Med. Examiners, 1973-77; med. dir.-at-large Va. divsn. Am. Cancer Soc., 1967—, med. v.p. Am. Cancer Soc., 1975-77, pres., 1977-79, nat. del., 1972-76, mem. nat. coun. for rsch. and clin. investigation, 1974-78, mem. profl. edn. com., 1982-96, bd. dir., 1985-98, vice chmn., chmn. M&S com., 1986-88, chmn. M&S exec. com., 1989-90, pres. elect, 1990-91, nat. pres., 1991-92, past office dir., 1993-99, hon. life mem., 1999—; bd. sci. counsellors Nat. Cancer Inst., 1978-82, chmn. surg. oncology rsch. devel. com.; mem. Nat. Cancer Adv. Bd., 1988-94; governing coun. Internat. Union Against Cancer, 1994-2002. Author: (with J.J. Terz) Cancer Management, 1977, (with J.J. Terz, J.P. Neifeld) Manual of Soft Tissue Surgery, 1983; mem. editl. bd. Va. Med., 1977-93, Jour. Surg. Oncology, 1978—, assoc. editor, 1991—; editl. bd. Jour. Cancer Edn., 1986; asst. editor Cancer, 1962-65, assoc. editor, 1991-2000, mem. editl. bd., 2000--; contbr. articles to med. jour. Served with USNR, 1942-46; Served with US Army, 1952-54. Recipient Cancer Rsch. award Alfred P. Sloan Found., 1964; J. Shelton Horsley award Am. Cancer Soc., 1973; Disting. Svc. award U. Chgo., 1976; Va. Commonwealth U. Univ. Award for Excellence, 1988, Disting. Faculty award Med. Coll. Va. Alumni Assn., 1988, Va. Cultural Laureate award, 1992, OBICI award, 1992, Dean's award for Disting. Svc., 1992; named to Humera Soc. (hon.), 1992, Beckstrand Cancer Found. Cancer Fighter of Yr., 1999, Presdl. medallion Va. Commonwealth U., 2000, Lifetime Sci. Achievement award Sci. Mus. Va., 2002; Distinguished Svc. Award of Richmond Acad. of Medicine, 2003. Fellow ACS (commn. on cancer 1973-85, chmn. 1979-81), NY Acad. Sci., Royal Soc. Medicine, Soc. Black Acad. Surgeons (hon.), So. Suiz Assn.; mem. AAAS, AMA, Am. Assn. Cancer Edn., Am. Assn. Cancer Rsch., Am. Gastroenterol. Assn. (coun. on cancer 1972-76), Am. Surg. Assn., Halsted Soc. (pres. 1975), James Ewing Soc., Soc. Head and Neck Surgeons, Am. Soc. Clin. Oncology, Am. Radium Soc. (exec. coun. 1985-87), Soc. Surgery Alimentary Tract (founder), Soc. Surg. Oncology (exec. com. 1976-77, v.p. 1977-78, pres. 1979-80, chmn. exec. coun. 1980-81, Heritage honoree 2002), Soc. Univ. Surgeons, Surg. Biol. Club III (founding mem.), Transplantation Soc., Collegium Internat. Chirurgiae Digestive, Southeastern Surg. Congress, Pan Am. Med. Assn., Socièté Internationale de Chirurgie, Va. Surg. Soc. (v.p. 1973-74), Richmond Surg. Soc. (pres. 1986-87), Richmond Acad. Medicine (trustee 1986-87, 1st v.p. 1988, Disting. Svc. award 2003), So. Surg. Assn.

(1st v.p. 1999-2000, Hon. fellow, 2004), Argentine Surg. Assn. (hon.), Sigma Xi, Alpha Omega Alpha. Home: 6501 Three Chopt Rd Richmond VA 23226-3118 Office: Med Coll Va Hosps 1200 E Broad St PO Box 980011 Richmond VA 23298-0011 Office Phone: 804-828-9323. Business E-Mail: wlawren1@vcu.edu.

LAWRENCE, WALTER THOMAS, plastic surgeon; b. Balt., Sept. 5, 1950; s. Walter Jr. and Susan (Shryock) L.; m. Marsha Blake, May 30, 1987. BS, Yale U., 1972; MPH, Harvard U., 1976; MD, U. Va., 1976. Diplomate Am. Bd. Surgery, Am. Bd. Plastic Surgery. Intern and resident in gen. surgery U. N.C., Chapel Hill, 1976-78; resident gen. surgery Med. Coll. Va., Richmond, 1978-81; resident plastic surgery U. Chgo., 1981-83; expert NIH, Bethesda, Md., 1983-85; asst. prof. U. N.C., Chapel Hill, 1985-92, assoc. prof., div. chmn., 1992-95; prof., divsn. chmn. U. Mass. Med. Ctr., 1995-99, U. Kans. Med. Ctr., Kansas City, 1999—. Fellow ACS; mem. Am. Assn. Plastic Surgeons, Am. Soc. Plastic and Reconstructive Surgeons, Plastic Surgery Rsch. Coun., Humera Soc., Womack Soc. Avocations: skiing, sailing, tennis. Office: U Kans Med Ctr Sutherland Inst/Pl Surgery 3901 Rainbow Blvd Kansas City KS 66160-0001 Office Phone: 913-588-2000. Business E-Mail: tlawrence@kumc.edu.

LAWRENCE, WENDY B., astronaut; b. Jacksonville, Fla., July 2, 1959; d. William P. Lawrence and Anne Haynes. BS in Ocean Engring., U.S. Naval Acad., 1981; MS in Ocean Engring., MIT and Woods Hole Oceanographic Institution, 1988. Naval aviator USN, 1982; with Helicopter Combat Support Squadron SIX (HC-6); officer in charge of detachment ALFA Helicopter Anti-Submarine Squadron Light THIRTY HSL-30; physics instr., novice women's crew coach U.S. Naval Acad., 1990-92; mission specialist, astronaut NASA, 1992—, flight software verifier Shuttle Avionics Integration Lab., astronaut office asst. tng. officer, ascent/entry flight engr., blue shift orbit pilot on STS-67, 1995, dir. ops. Gagarin Cosmonaut Tng. Ctr. Star City, Russia, with crew on STS-86 on space shuttle Atlantis, 1997, with crew on STS-91 on space shuttle Discovery, 1998, mission specialist 4 (MS-4) for STS-114 (Discovery) Return to Flight mission, 2005. Recipient Defense Superior Svc. medal, Defense Meritorious Svc. medal, NASA Space Flight medal, Navy Commendation medal, Navy Achievement medal, Capt. Winifred Collins award for inspirational leadership Nat. Navy League, 1986. Mem. Assn. Naval Aviation, Women Mil. Aviators, Naval Helicopter Assn., Phi Kappa Phi. Avocations: running, rowing, triathlons. Office: NASA Lyndon B Johnson Space Ctr Houston TX 77058*

LAWRENCE, WILLIAM JOSEPH, JR., retired corporate executive; b. Kalamazoo, Feb. 1, 1918; s. William J. and Borgia M. (Wheeler) L.; m. Doris Luella Fitzgerald, Aug. 19, 1955; children: Aaron Frances, Cleve Moren, Julie Anne, William III. AB, Kalamazoo Coll., 1941. Engaged in personal investments; dir. emeritus Superior Pine Products Co.; dir. LPI. Trustee emeritus Kalamazoo Found.; trustee emeritus Kalamazoo Coll., Borgess Med. Ctr. With AUS, 1942-46. Mem. Kalamazoo C. of C., Kiwanis, Com. of Twenty-Five (Palm Springs, Calif.), O'Donnell Golf Club (Palm Springs), Gull Lake Country Club, Park Club. Roman Catholic. Home: PO Box 37 Richland MI 49083-0037 Office: 136 E Michigan Ave Ste 1000 Kalamazoo MI 49007

LAWRENCE-COX, NANCY NELL, artist, retired executive secretary; b. Columbus, Miss., Mar. 4, 1934; d. James Edward and Elizabeth Caplinger (Land) Lawrence. BFA, U. Ark., Little Rock, 1983, postgrad., 1983-84. Office boy Miss. State Hwy. Dept., Columbus, 1952-53; clk.-typist FBI, Washington, 1953-54; sec.-automation Little Rock AFB, Ark., 1984-2000; ret., 2000. Exhibited sculptures at U. Ark., 1982 (Best of Show 1981-82), Centre International D'Art Contemporain, 1984, photography at Les Editions Arts et Images du Monde, 1990, Who's Who Internat. Art, Lausanne, Switzerland, 1993. Civic vol. Yes We Can Team 314th Supply Squadron Care Team, 1989-94. Recipient Cert. of Recognition, Jacksonville C. of C., 1991, other awards. Home: 13 Phyllis Cir Jacksonville AR 72076-2403

LAWRIE, J. MICHAEL, former software company executive; married; 2 children. BA in History, Ohio U., 1975; MBA in Fin. and Mktg., Drexel U., 1977; grad., Dartmouth Inst.; cert. in fin. planning, U. Pa. Various sales, mktg. and fin. positions IBM, 1977—95, v.p. software Asia Pacific, 1995—97, v.p. industries, 1995—97, gen. mgr. personal software products, head divsn. network computing software, 1997—98, gen. mgr. Europe Mid. E. Africa (EMEA), 1998—2001, sr. v.p., group exec. global sales and distbn., 2001—04; CEO Siebel Systems, Inc., San Mateo, Calif., 2004—05. Me-m.adv. bd. Internet Capital Group; U.S. bd. dirs. NTT DoCoMo. Bd. trustees Ohio U.; bd. dirs. Marymount Sch.

LAWS, KENNETH L., physics professor; b. Pasadena, Calif., May 30, 1935; s. Allen L. and Florence (Windsor) L.; m. Priscilla Watson, June 3, 1965; children: Kevin Allen, Virginia. BS, Calif. Inst. Tech., 1956; MS, U. Pa., 1959; PhD, Bryn Mawr Coll., 1962. Instr. physics Hobart and William Smith Colls., Geneva, N.Y., 1958-59; from asst. prof. to prof. physics Dickinson Coll., Carlisle, Pa., 1962-2000, assoc. dean, dir. summer sch., 1971-77, prof. emeritus, 2000—; adminstrv. dir. summer ballet program Ctrl. Pa. Youth Ballet, Carlisle, 1977-87, pres. bd. dirs., 1988-93. Guest faculty Scientific Aspect of the Art of Dance, U. Washington Med. Sch. and Dance Dept., 1982; bd. reviewers Dance: Current Selected Research, 1985—. Author: The Physics of Dance, 1984; (with Cynthia Harvey) Physics, Dance and the Pas de Deux, 1994, Physics and the Art of Dance, 2002; contbr. articles on dance, physics to profl. jours. Office: Dickinson Coll Dept Physics Carlisle PA 17013 E-mail: laws@dickinson.edu.

LAWS, MAURICE WESLEY, set decorator, museum exhibit designer; b. Ferndale, Mich., Sept. 27, 1925; s. George Winslow Laws and Marion Jane Greenleaf; m. Betty Elaine Stein, June 1955 (div. Sept. 1957). Attended, N.Y. Sch. Interior Design, 1948—50. Set decorator CBS TV, N.Y., 1950—88. Designer mus. exhibits Edward Dean Mus. Decorative Arts, Cherry Valley, Calif., 1995—. Set decorator: (films) A View from the Bridge, 1962. Mem. Palm Springs Desert Mus. Svc. Coun., Calif., 1990—; bd. mem. Friends of Edward Dean Mus., 1996—, Cabots Mus. Commn., Desert Hot Springs, 1998—2001; pres. Cabots Mus. Found., Desert Hot Springs, 2001—. SM2/C USN, 1943—46. Nominee Emmy award six times, Acad. TV Arts & Sci.; recipient 4 Emmy awards. Mem.: Internat. Wedgwood Soc., Wedgwood Soc. So. Calif. Achievements include member of CBS team covering first moon landing of Apollo XI (TV Acad. nomination). Avocations: travel, archaeology. Home: 12075 Highland Ave Desert Hot Springs CA 92240

LAWS, PRISCILLA WATSON, physics professor; b. N.Y.C., Jan. 18, 1940; d. Morris Clemens and Frances (Fetterman) Watson; m. Kenneth Lee Laws, June 3, 1965; children: Kevin Allen, Virginia. BA, Reed Coll., 1961; MA, Bryn Mawr Coll., 1963, PhD, 1966. Asst. prof. physics Dickinson Coll., Carlisle, Pa., 1965-70, assoc. prof., 1970-79, prof. physics, 1979—, chmn. dept. physics and astronomy, 1982-83. Cons. in field. Author: X Rays: More Harm than Good?, 1977, The X-Ray Information Book, 1983, The Workshop Physics Activity Guide, 1997, Real Time Physics Laboratory Guides in Mechanics and Thermodynamics, Explorations in Physics, 2003; contbr. numerous articles to profl. jours.; assoc. editor Am. Jour. Physics, 1989—. Vice-pres. Cumberland Conservancy, 1972-73, pres. 1973; bd. dirs. Pa. Alliance for Returnables, 1974-77; asst. sec., treas. Carlisle Hosp. Authority, 1973-76; pres. bd. Carlisle Day Care Ctr., 1973-74. Fellow NSF, 1963-64, grantee, 1989-95, Commonwealth of Pa., 1985-86, U.S. Dept. Edn. Fund for Improvement of Post-Secondary Edn., 1986-89, 89-93, AEC; recipient Innovation award Merck Found., 1989, Educom NCRIPTAL award for curriculum innovation in sci. labs., 1989, award Sears Roebuck and Co., 1990, Ednl. Software Devel. awards Computers in Physics Jour., 1991, 97, Pioneering Achievement in Edn. award Dana Found., 1993. Mem. Am. Assn. Physics Tchrs. (Disting Svc. citation 1992, Robert A. Milliken award for Outstanding Contbns. to Physics Tchg., 1996), Am. Phys. Soc., Fedn. Am. Scientist, Sigma Xi, Sigma Pi Sigma, Omicron Delta Kappa. Democrat. Home: 10 Douglas Ct Carlisle PA 17013-1714 Office: Dickinson Coll PO Box 1773 Carlisle PA 17013-2896

LAWSON, A. PETER, lawyer; AB, Dartmouth Coll., 1968; JD, Columbia U., 1971. Bar: N.Y. 1971, Ill. 1979. Assoc. Sullivan & Cromwell, 1971-78; sr. counsel Baxter Internat., 1978-79; assoc. gen. attorney Motorola Inc., 1980—84, v.p., gen. attorney, 1985—87, corp. v.p., asst. gen. counsel, 1987—94, sr. v.p., asst. gen. counsel, 1994—96, sr. v.p., sec., gen. counsel, 1996-98, exec. v.p., gen. counsel, sec., 1998—. Mem.: Am. Soc. Corporate Sec., North Shore Gen. Counsel Assn., CLO Roundtable, American Corporate Counsel Assoc., ABA, Association of Gen. Counsel. Office: Motorola Inc 1303 E Algonquin Rd Schaumburg IL 60196-1079*

LAWSON, AMY L., literature and language educator; b. Phila., Pa., Aug. 9, 1961; d. Robert Anthy and Marian Rose Dudek; m. Richard Dreu, Aug. 13, 1983; children: Christopher Dreu, Alexander Dreu. BA, Temple U., 1987. English tchr. Pemberton Twp. HS, Pemberton, NJ, 1987—88, Browns Mills, NJ, 1992, Gloucester City HS, Gloucester, NJ, 1993—. Home: 2 Cross St Sewell NJ 08080 Office: Gloucester City HS Rt 130 and Market St Gloucester City NJ 08030 Office Phone: 856-256-7000. E-mail: alawson@gcsd.k12.nj.us.

LAWSON, BEVERLY ELAINE, nursing administrator; b. St. Louis, Mar. 17, 1946; d. Berrie Sr. and Odessa (Wallace) L. BSN, Dillard U., New Orleans, 1968; MPH, Hunter Coll., 1984, cert. Nurse Practitioner, 1981. RN, N.Y. Family nurse practitioner Dr. Martin Luther King Health Ctr., Bronx, N.Y., 1972-88, co-planner health outreach program in maternal child health, 1988-90, tchr. lamaze, 1990—, co-planner adolescent pregnancy program, 1991—, nutrition educator, nursing rep.; dir. nursing svcs., family nurse practitioner Leake and Watts Svcs., 1988-91, clin. computerliaison; part time family nurse practitioner Planned Parenthood, 1991-99; dir. employee health svcs., family nurse practitioner Leake and Watts, 1991—; clin. preceptor Pace U. Lienhard Sch. Nursing, 1998—; family nurse practitioner Woodfield Correctionsl Facility, Vahalla, N.Y., 1995-2000. Part-time women's health nurse practitioner Planned Parenthood, Yonkers Robert Woods Found. grantee. Mem. Assn. Nurse Practitioners, ANA, N.Y. State Nurse's Assn., N.Y. State Cert. FNP, Delta Sigma Theta. Office: Leake & Watts Svcs Inc 463 Hawthorne Ave Yonkers NY 10705-3441 E-mail: blawson@leakeandwatts.org.

LAWSON, CAROLE JEAN, religious educator, author, poet; b. San Antonio, June 18, 1944; d. Albert Joseph and Pearl Nettie (Garner) Fuller; m. James Ray Lawson, Sept. 7, 1962; children: Regina Anne (Lawson) Kacho, Clinton Ray. Founder Love Makes the World Go Around in Peace, Ft. Worth, 1988—; founder, dir. Healing Thru Love Seminars, Ft. Worth, 1988—; founder Sunshine 'n Rainbows Stress Overcomers, Ft. Worth, 1985-87; founder, head Omni-Vision Pub. and Prodns., Ft. Worth, 1990—93, 2002—. Life mgmt. cons., 2003—. Pub. editor Omni Vision newsletter, 1985-93, 2002-; author: To God Be the Glory, poetry collection, 1988-90, My Rocky Mountain High, 1989, The Reflection of God's Smile, 1991. Sec. Lightly Speaking Forum, Ft. Worth, 1987—89; supporter publicity Campaign for the Earth, 1990—91; founder Omni Vision Ministries, 1993—99, 2002—; dir. Chapel of Light Conf. Ctr., Lake Whitney, 2001—02; founder Universal World Investments, Chi Energy Wholeness Ctr., Lake Whitney, Tex., 2001—02, life mgmt. cons., 2003; Chi technician Fort Worth, 2005. Named Honorary Mayan Centurian. Mem. Internat. Platform Assn. Home and Office: 1112 Edney St Fort Worth TX 76115-4317 Office Phone: 817-924-2920. E-mail: omni_visionministries@yahoo.com. *With the energy shifting at excelerated speed to usher in the new, we must also excelerate our consciousness into the reality of our oneness with God and all creation. We must not live in the past, nor in future daydreams. We must live in the present moment...The Now! If you don't want a part in the play...don't become part of the production! Just watch the performance. If it doesn't serve you don't get involved in it...create your chosen reality with inward harmony and peace. Unconditional love is a must. God is Love!.*

LAWSON, CAROLINA DONADIO, language educator, translator; b. Naples, Italy, Mar. 11, 1920; d. Joseph and Concetta (Bartolomeo) Donadio; m. Allan Leroy Lawson, Sept. 15, 1945; 1 child, John. Laurea in European langs., lit., instns., We. Group Instituto Universitario Orientale, Naples, 1946; PhD in French and Italian, Tulane U., 1971. Lectr. overseas divsn. U. Md., Leghorn, Italy, 1952; tchr. Warren Easton H.S., New Orleans, 1958—61; tchg. asst. Newcomb Coll. Tulane U., New Orleans, 1961—64; instr. Tex. Christian U., Ft. Worth, 1964—65; lectr. Downtown Ctr. U.Chgo., 1967—73; lectr. U. Akron, Ohio, 1975—76; pvt. practice lectr., translator, ind. scholar, freelance writer Moncks Corner, SC, 1985—. Vis. prof. Kent (Ohio) State U., 1977-84; mem., lectr. S.C. Humanities Coun., 1989-93. Author: (textbook) Nuove Letture di Cultura Italiana, 1975; fgn. lang. editl. reviewer Ency. Brit. Chgo., 1971; rev. editor: Italian Culture, 1981-84; contbr. many articles and revs. in lit. criticism, art history, textbooks of fables, fairy tales and biographies to profiles of famous Italians. Recipient cert. of proficiency in Japanese lang. and culture Tokyo Coll., 1958. Mem. MLA, Am. Assn. Tchrs. of Italian, Am. Assn. Italian Studies, Am. Assn. Tchrs. of French, Nat. Italian-Am. Found. Republican. Roman Catholic. Avocations: classical music, painting, sports, world travel.

LAWSON, DARREN PATRICK, academic administrator, educator; s. Garland Ray and Phyllis Tedder Lawson; m. Sarah Jane Goodwin, July 23, 1988; 1 child, Cameron Scott. BA in Rhetoric and Pub. Address, Bob Jones U., 1986, MA in Platform Arts, 1988; PhD in Comm. studies, U. Kans., 1996. Grad. asst. Bob Jones U., Greenville, SC, 1986—88, faculty divsn. of speech comm., 1988—93; grad. tchg. asst. U. Kans., Lawrence, 1993—96; assoc. dean Sch. of Fine Arts, Bob Jones U., Greenville, 1996—97, dean Sch. of Fine Arts, 1997—. Owner Millennium Comm., Inc., Greenville, SC, 1990—. Actor: (classic players) Numerous Shakespearean roles; dir.: (opera association) Andrea Chenier, Elixir of Love, Mefistofele; author: (prisonization) The Prison Journal. Bd. dirs. Met. Arts Coun., Greenville, SC, 2003—04. Recipient award, Am. Legion, 1986, Disting. Tech. Comm. award, S.C. chpt. of Soc. for Tech. Comm., 1993, Best of the Month award, Edn. World, 1997, Knowledge Network Learning Application award, Pacific Bell, 1997, Best of Kans. on the Web award, KeyPlaza, 1999. Mem.: Internat. Comm. Assn., Nat. Comm. Assn. Avocations: drama, opera stage directing, music. Office: Bob Jones Univ 1700 Wade Hampton Blvd Greenville SC 29614 Office Phone: 864-242-5100. Business E-Mail: dplawson@bju.edu.

LAWSON, DIANE SUE, elementary school educator; b. Marion, Ind., Jan. 27, 1948; d. Donald Richard and Reba Maxine (Ulshafer) Jacobs; m. Jay L. Lawson, Oct. 18, 1975; children: Nathan Andrew, Jacob Lawrence. BA, Ind. Wesleyan U., 1970; MS in Edn., Ball State U., 1973. Cert. tchr. K-8 Ind. Tchr. grade 2 Marion Community Schs., 1970-76, 77-79, 81-91, tchr. grade 4, 1976-77, 79-81, 91—. Mem. gov.'s tchr. adv. com., 1985-86. Active Riverview PTO, Girls After Sch. Activity Night, 1973-75, leadership roles in church; pres. Oak Hill Community Youth League, 1988-89. Mem.: Marion Area Reading Assn. (bldg. rep. 1984—87). Office: Riverview Elem Sch 513 W Buckingham Dr Marion IN 46952-2027

LAWSON, EDWARD EARLE, neonatal/perinatal nurse practitioner; b. Winston-Salem, N.C., Aug. 6, 1946; s. Robert Barrett and Elsie Chatterton (Earle) L.; m. Rebecca Newhall Fitts, June 21, 1969; children: Katherine Tabor, Robert Barrett II. BA magna cum laude, Harvard U., 1968; MD, Northwestern U., 1972. Diplomate Am. Bd. Pediat. and Neonatal/Perinatal Medicine. Intern then resident pediat. Children's Hosp., Boston, 1972-75, fellow neonatology, 1975-78; from asst. prof. pediat. to prof. pediat. U. N.C., Chapel Hill, 1978-99, chief divsn. neonatal medicine, 1987-95, interim chmn. dept. pediat., 1993-95; vice chmn., dept. pediat., 1995-99; prof. pediat., vice chair dept. pediat. Johns Hopkins U., Balt., 1999—; chief divsn. neonatology, dept. pediat. Johns Hopkins U. Hosp., Balt., 1999—. Editor-in-chief Jour. Perinatology, 2001—; assoc. editor Jour. of Pediat., 1985-95; contbr. numerous articles to profl. jours. Recipient Sidney Farber Meml. Rsch. award United Cerbral Palsy, 1982, Rsch. Career Devel. award NIH, 1982-87; E.L. Trudeau fellow, 1978-81, Alexander Von Humboldt fellow, 1985-86; NIH grantee, 1979—. Fellow Am. Acad. Pediat.; mem. Am. Lung Assn. (sci. adv. com. 1989-91), Am. Thoracic Soc. (bd. dirs. 1988-90), Am. Pediat. Soc., Perinatal Rsch. Soc. Achievements include research on developmental aspects of respiratory control, particularly physiology and neurobiology. Office: Johns Hopkins Hosp Dept Pediatrics 600 N Wolfe St NH2-133 Baltimore MD 21287-0001 Business E-Mail: elawson@jhmi.edu.

LAWSON, EVE KENNEDY, dancer; b. Washington, Mar. 28, 1964; d. John and Elizabeth Lawson. Student, Sch. Am. Ballet, N.Y.C., 1972-83. Prin. dancer State Ballet Mo., Kansas City, 1983-87; dancer Miami City Ballet, Miami Beach, Fla., 1988-94, coord. edn., 1993-94, ballet mistress, 1994—. Created prin. roles in ballet Voyager (Bolender), 1984, Miniatures (Gamonet), 1990, Tango Tonto (Gamonet), 1991. Office: Miami City Ballet 2200 Liberty Ave Miami Beach FL 33139-1641

LAWSON, FRED RAULSTON, banker; b. Sevierville, Tenn., Mar. 26, 1936; s. Arville Raulston and Ila Mary (Lowe) L.; m. Sharon Sheets, Jan. 1, 1982; children: Terry Lawson Akins, Laura Lawson Rathbone, Kristi Watson Newvine. Student, U. Tenn., 1953—59, La. State U. Sch. Banking of South, 1965—68, Harvard Inst. Fin. Mgmt., 1968; D (hon.), Maryville Coll. From br. mgr. to exec. v.p. Blount Nat. Bank, Maryville, Tenn., 1958-68, pres., 1968-86, also bd. dirs.; pres. Tenn. Nat. Bancshares, Inc., Maryville, 1971-86, Bank of East Tenn., Knoxville, 1986-92; pres., CEO BankFirst, Knoxville, 1993-2001; commr. dept. fin. instns. State of Tenn., 2001—02; chmn. BankEast, 2004—. Mem. Covenant Health Fin./Investment Com., 2000-2001, also bd. dirs. Mem. Blount County Indsl. Devel. bd., 1969—; chancellors assoc. U. Tenn., Knoxville, 1971-78; trustee Carson-Newman Coll., Jefferson City, 1984-94, Harrison-Chilhowee Bapt. Acad., Seymour, Tenn., 1972-85, Pellissippi State Found., 1989-96; adv. bd. U. Tenn. Med. Rsch. Ctr. and Hosp.; bd. regents Mid-South Sch. banking, Memphis, 1982-90; bd. dirs. Thompson Cancer Survival Ctr., Knoxville, 1987-2000, The Downtown Orgn., Tenn. Resource Valley, East Tenn. Hist. Soc., Maryville Coll., 1995—. Recipient Tenn. Indsl. Devel. Vol. award, 1977. Mem. Assn. Bank Holding Cos. (bd. dirs. 1978-82), Tenn. Bankers Assn. (chmn. state legis. com. 1980, banking practice com. 1983, bd. dirs. 1990—, pres. 1994-95). Republican. Baptist. Home: 2101 Cochran Rd Maryville TN 37803 Office: Bank East PO Box 24 607 Market St Knoxville TN 37901 Office Phone: 865-540-5830.

LAWSON, HARRY WILBUR, retired chemist, consultant, writer; b. Chgo., June 22, 1920; s. Harry Wilbur and Maude Lillian (Cleveland) L.; m. Betty Jane Cooper, Mar. 13, 1944; children: Ralph S., Janet Lawson Jenrette, Sally Bailey. BS, U. Ill., 1941; postgrad., U. Cin., 1946-50. Chemist, lab. supr. DuPont, Joliet, Ill., 1941-44; mgr. product devel tech. svc. Procter & Gamble, Cin., 1946-82, founder food svc. rsch. dept., 1947; ret., 1982; chemistry cons., Cin., Florence, Ky., Can., Honduras, 1982—. Hon. mem. faculty Mich. State U., Lansing, 1977; vol. exec. Internat. Exec. Svc., Honduras, 1988; program spkr. Nat. Restaurant Assn., Chgo., 1952-55. Author: Standards for Fats and Oils, 1985, Food Oils and Fats—Technology, Utilization and Nutrition, 1995; contbr. articles to food svc. publs. Mgr. Little League Baseball, Cin., 1954-63; v.p. PTA, Mt. Airy, Ohio, 1957; pres. Aiken H.S. Boosters, Cin., 1966. With USN, 1944-46, PTO. Mem. Am. Chem. Soc., Am. Oil Chemists Soc., Am. Bakers Assn., Am. Assn. Cereal Chemists, Inst. Am. Poultry Industries, Am. Soc. Bakery Engrs. (program chmn.). Republican. Presbyterian. Avocations: travel, reading, walking, volunteering, problem solving. Home and Office: 7152 Cascade Dr Florence KY 41042-2540

LAWSON, H(ERBERT) BLAINE, JR., mathematician, educator; b. Norristown, Pa., Jan. 4, 1942; s. Herbert Blaine and Mary Louise (Corson) L.; m. Carolyn Elaine Pieroni, June 6, 1964 (div. Sept. 1977); children: Christina Corson, Heather Brooke. AB, ScB in Applied Mat. and Russian Lit., Brown U., 1964; MS in Math., Stanford U., 1966, PhD in Math., 1968. Lectr. math. U. Calif., Berkeley, 1968-70, assoc. prof., 1971-74, prof., 1974-80, asst. dean, 1975-77; Disting. prof., chmn. SUNY, Stony Brook, 1978—. Vis. asst. prof. IMPA, Rio de Janeiro, 1970-71; vis. prof. Inst. des Hautes Etudes Scientifiques, Bures-sur-Yvette, France, 1977-78, Ecole Poly., Palaiseau, France, 1983-84; bd. dirs. U.S.-Brazilian Math. Exch., Stony Brook and Rio de Janeiro; trustee Math. Scis. Rsch. Inst., Berkeley; chmn. Nat. Com. Math. NAS, Washington, 1989-91; mem. Inst. Advanced Study, Princeton U., 1973-74; lectr. in minimal submanifolds, 1971. Author: The Theory of Gauge Fields in 4 Dimensions, 1985, Spin Geometry, 1989; editor Jour. Differential Geometry, Topology, The Princeton Mat. Series; contbr. articles to profl. jours. Sloan Found. fellow, 1971, Guggenheim Found. fellow, 1983, Japan Soc. Promotion Sci. fellow, 1985. Mem. Nat. Acad. of Sci., Am. Math. Soc. (coun. 1988-91, v.p. 1997-2000, editor jour., Steele prize 1975), Brazilian Acad. of Scis. Achievements include construction of minimal surfaces in the 3-dimensional sphere, construction of foliations on higher dimensional spheres; characterization of boundaries of analytic varieties; co-creation of Calibrated Geometries; basic results on manifolds of non-positive curvature, on spaces of positive scalar curvature, on stability of Yang-Mills fields, on relations between algebraic cycles and topology, and on structure of Chow Varieties. Home: 29 North Rd Stony Brook NY 11790-1009 Business E-Mail: blaine@math.sunysb.edu.

LAWSON, JANE ELIZABETH, retired bank executive; b. Cornwall, Ont., Can. d. Leonard J. and Margaret Lawson. BA, U. N.B., Can., LLB, 1971. With law dept. Royal Bank Can., Montreal, 1974-78, sr. counsel, 1978-84, v.p., corp. sec., 1988-92, sr. v.p., sec., 1992—, ret., 2005—. Mem.: Am. Soc. Corp. Secs., Inst. Corp. Dirs., Inst. Chartered Secs. and Adminstrs., N.B. Bar Assn., Can. Bar Assn., Royal Can. Yacht Club, Mt. Royal Tennis Club. Office: Royal Bank Plz PO Box 1 Toronto ON Canada M5J 2J15

LAWSON, JENNIFER, broadcast executive; b. Birmingham, Ala., June 8, 1946; d. Willie DeLeon and Velma Theresa (Foster) L.; m. Elbert Sampson, June 1, 1979 (div. Sept. 1980); m. Anthony Gittens, May 29, 1982; children: Kai, Zachary. Student, Tuskegee U., 1963—65; MFA, Columbia U., 1974; LHD (hon.), Teikyo Post U., Hartford, Conn., 1991. Assoc. producer William Greaves Prodns., N.Y.C., 1974-75; asst. prof. film studies Bklyn. Coll., 1975-77; exec. dir. The Film Fund, N.Y.C., 1977-80; TV coord. Program Fund Corp. for Pub. Broadcasting, Washington, 1980-83, assoc. dir. TV Program Fund, 1983-89, dir. TV Program Fund, 1989; exec. v.p. programming PBS, Alexandria, Va., 1989-95; broadcast cons. Md. Pub. TV, 1995—98, exec. cons., 1996—, exec. prodr. Africa, 1998-2001; pres. Magic Box Mediaworks, 1996—; gen. mgr. WHUT-TV32, 2004—. V.p. Internat. Pub. TV, Washington, 1984-88; panelist Fulbright Fellowships, Washington, 1988-90. Author, illustrator: Children of Africa, 1970; illustrator: Our Folktales, 1968, African Folktales: A Calabash of Wisdom, 1973. Coord. Nat. Coun. Negro Women, Washington, 1969. Avocations: painting, reading. Office: 1838 Ontario Pl NW Washington DC 20009-2109 Office Phone: 202-806-3010. Business E-Mail: j_lawson@howard.edu.

LAWSON, JERRY MARSHALL, journalist, educator, genealogist; b. Anderson, Ind., June 18, 1945; s. Ernest Marshall and Dolores May (Gault) L.; m. Marsha Jean Myers, June 20, 1970; children: Eric Marshall, Kurt Marshall. BS, Ball State U., 1972, MA, 1975; MPA, Ind. U., 1993. Furniture designer, builder Lawson Design, Ft. Wayne, Ind., 1982-87; from sports editor to mng. editor New Haven News/New Allen News, 1987-92; product info. writer Navistar Internat., Ft. Wayne, 1992-93; chair writer's bur. Ft. Wayne Bicentennial Exec. Coun., 1993-94; journalist Herald-Press, Huntington, Ind., 1994; freelance writer Ft. Wayne News-Sentinel, 1994-96, Creative Svcs., Ft. Wayne, 1994-99; instr. history and govt. Ivy Tech State Coll., 1994—2000, Indian-U., Purdue U., Ft. Wayne, 2000—01. V.p. Kolor Print, Inc., Ft. Wayne, 1982-83; vis. lectr. Manchester Coll. 2000; personal historian Lifescapes, 1999—. V.p. Preservation Soc., Inc., Ft. Wayne, 1982-83; newsletter editor Leadership Ft. Wayne Alumni Assn., 1993-96, bd. advisors, chair comms. com., Downtown New Haven Task Force, 1991-92. Mem. Assn.

Personal Historians (bd. dirs. 1999-2003, treas. 2000-2003), Writers' Ctr. Ind., Ind. Hist. Soc., Allen County-Ft. Wayne Hist. Soc., Ind. Geneological Soc., Allen County of Ind. Geneological Soc., Ctrl. Ind. Writers Assn., Small Pubs., Arists and Writers Network. Unitarian Universalist. Avocations: reading, photography, wood sculpture, making furniture, music. Home and Office: 2229 Muskoday Pass Fort Wayne IN 46809-1427

LAWSON, JOHN DUVAL, communications educator; b. Richmond, Va. s. John DuVal and Portia Ann Lawson; 1 child, Steven Thomas. BA, St. Andrews Presbyn. Coll., Laurinburg, N.C., 1971; MA, Va. Commonwealth U., Richmond, 1986; PhD, No. Ill. U., DeKalb, 1995. Cmty. organizer Va. Cmty. Devel. Orgn., Petersburg, 1972—74; svc. supr., Cabell Libr. Va. Commonwealth U., Richmond, 1975—80, writing instr., 1984—88; pub. sch. tchr. Henrico County Pub. Schs., Richmond, Va., 1980—84; health comm. rschs. No. Ill. U., DeKalb, 1989—95; comm. prof. St. Andrews Presbyn. Coll., Laurinburg, NC, 1996—98, Robert Morris U., Pitts., 1998—. Mem.: Popular Culture Assn., Pa. Comm. Assn. (pres. 2004—05). Office: Robert Morris Univ 6001 University Blvd Moon Township PA 15108

LAWSON, JOHN JOSEPH, vocational educator, consultant; s. William and Jean Lawson. AAS, Ferris State U., 1976, BE, 1981. Registered social worker Mich., 1990; cert. architectural design Lawrence Inst. Tech., 1974, vocational drafting instr. 1981. Draftsman Penn-Dixie Steel Corp., Grand Rapids, Mich., 1976—78; property mgr. Altman/Allstate Mgmt., Mich., 1979—80; owner Lawson Mgmt. & Constrn., 1980—; life skills instr. Ackco Svcs., Mich., 1985—88; supervising shop foreman Meml. Ctr. Work Reconditioning Svcs., Owosso, Mich., 1988—89; instr. Baker Coll., Owosso, 1989—97; constrn. instr. United Auto Workers, Flint, Mich., 1997—98; drafting tchr. Linden HS, Mich., 2001—; CAD drafting instr. So. Lakes Career Ctr., Flint, 2002—. Cons. Rehab. Svcs., Owosso, 1989—. Mem.: Linden Edn. Assn., Mich. Edn. Assn. Avocation: golf.

LAWSON, JOHN QUINN, architect; b. Tucumcari, N.Mex., Apr. 11, 1940; s. Tom L. and Mable Marie (Hagglund) L.; m. Elizabeth Jo Waddel, June 4, 1961 (div. 1980); children: Bevan Eugene, Cary Augusta; m. Lorna Miriam Katz, Feb. 20, 1981. BA, Rice U., 1961, BSArch, 1962; MFA in Architecture, Princeton U., 1964. Registered architect, Pa., N.J., N.Y. Staff architect Doxiadis Assocs., Phila., 1961, Collins, Uhl, Hoisington, Princeton, N.J., 1963, Frank Schlesinger, Doylestown, Pa., 1964, Kneedler Mirick & Zantzinger, Phila., 1964, Mitchell/Giurgola Architects, Phila., 1965-71, assoc., 1972-73, ptnr., 1974-85, John Lawson Architects, Phila., 1986—. Mem. adj. faculty Grad. Sch. Fine Arts U. Pa., 1972-87, Sch. Arch. Phila. U., 2004-; chmn. archtl. adv. bd. Spring Garden Coll., Phila., 1986-92. Prin. works include United Way hdqrs. bldg., Phila., 1971, Lang Music Bldg. Swarthmore (Pa.) Coll., 1973, Ind. Nat. Hist. Park maintenance bldg., Phila., 1981, Columbia Ave. Sta. improvements, Phila., 1983, all recipients Pa. Soc. Architects awards, Benjamin Franklin Bridge Lighting Competition, Phila., 1986 (1st runner-up), Diamond Park Competition, Phila., 1987 (winner with Chuck Fahlen), Evancich residence, Phila., 1990 (1st prize Best Residential Renovation), Ctr. for Animal Health and Productivity, Sch. Vet. Medicine, U. Pa., 1990, Surg. Edn. Ctr., Hosp. Univ. Pa., 1996, Comparative Orthop. Rsch. Lab., Sch. Vet. Medicine, U. Pa., 1998, The Vistas at Lake Worth Apts., Ft. Worth, 1998, Coll. Hall Interior Renovations South Central Ground Floor, East Wing, U. Pa., 1999-2000, Smart Classroom, Delaware Valley Coll., Doylestown, Pa., 2001, Surg. Seminar Rm., Hosp. of U. Pa., 2003, Kahn Residence, Hillsdale, N.Y., 2004. V.p. Logan Sq. Neighborhood Assn., Phila., 1971-72; mem. Cmty.y Leadership Seminar Alumni, Phila., 1982-85; cons. Friends of Starr Garden, Inc., Phila., 1989; vol. exec., Internat. Exec. Svc. Corps, Cairo, 1998. Lowell M. Palmer fellow Princeton U., 1964, NEA Mid-Career fellow Am. Acad. in Rome, 1980. Fellow AIA (mem. architecture for edn. com. 1976-85, chmn. urban design com. Phila. chpt. 1986-98, Fellows steering com. Phila chpt. 1988—); mem. Pa. Soc. Architects, Soc. Hill Civic Assn., City Pks. Assn. (bd. dirs. 1988-2002), Awbury Arboretum Assn. (bd. dirs. 1989-99), Soc. Hill Towers (coun. 1994-2002). Democrat. Office: John Lawson Architects 812 Chestnut St Apt 2 Philadelphia PA 19107-5115 E-mail: jlawson@johnlawsonarchitects.com.

LAWSON, KAY DONAHUE, music educator; b. Olean, N.Y., May 16, 1954; d. Norman Kay and Louise Lucille (Carter) Donahue; m. Stephen James Lawson, July 1, 1978; children: Erin Louise, Erika Rose. BMus, Crane Sch. Music, 1976; MMus in Edn., Mich. State U., 1983, MMus in Bassoon Performance, 1991. Music tchr. grades 7-8 Pittsfield (Mass.) City Schs., 1976-78; dir. choral music grades 7-12 Schuylerville (N.Y.) Ctrl. Sch., 1978-80; instr. bassoon & oboe Western Carolina U., Cullowhee, N.C., 1983-89; instr. woodwinds Brevard (N.C.) Coll., 1984-89; adj. prof. bassoon and oboe Minot (N.D.) State U., 1991—2002; instr. Marshall U., Huntington, W.Va., 2002—. Bassoonist Asheville (N.C.) Symphony, 1983-89, Brevard Chamber Orch., 1983-89, Audubon Chamber Ensemble, Minot, 1991—, Hungtinton Symphony, 2002—, Kingsbury Woodwing Quintent, 2002—; prin. bassoonist Minot Symphony, 1991—. Mem. Minot Symphony Assn. Bd., 1994-96. Mem. Internat. Double Reed Soc. Avocations: gardening, travel, reading. Home: 5443 Lea Hill Dr Huntington WV 25705

LAWSON, KENNETH L., lawyer; b. Cin., Apr. 19, 1963; m. Marva Lawson; 5 children. BA, Wittenberg U., 1986; JD, U. Cin., 1989. Bar: OH 1989, OH Supreme Ct. 1989. Assoc. Taft, Stettinius & Hollister, 1989—93; mng. ptnr. Kenneth L. Lawson & Assocs., Cin., 1993—. Adj. prof. U. Cin. Bd. dir. Evanston-Walnut Hills Cmty. Health Ctr., 1992, SUMA, 1991, v.p., 1991. Named Nat. Atty. of Yr., WCIN; named one of Am.'s Top Black Lawyers, Black Enterprise Mag., 2003; recipient Wright-Overstreet award, NAACP, 2002, Imagemaker's Pub. Svc. award, US Dist. Ct. (so. dist.), OH, Outstanding and Dedicated Svc. award, Nat. African Am. Leadership Summit, Coalition Concerned Citizens. Mem.: Am. Bar Assn., OH State Bar Assn., Cin. Bar Assn., Black Lawyers Assn. Cin. (v.p., bd. dir.). Office: Kenneth L Lawson & Assocs LPA 808 Elm St Ste 100 Cincinnati OH 45202*

LAWSON, LISA TRACY, nurse, consultant; b. East Meadow, N.Y., Oct. 26, 1966; d. Michael Brent and Lynne Cheryl Kaufman. BS in Nursing, Fla. Atlantic U., Boca Raton, 1988. RN Boca Raton Cmty. Hosp., Fla., 1987—, legal nurse cons., 1993—. Mem.: Am. Assn. Legal Nurse Cons.

LAWSON, RANDALL CLAYTON, II, finance company executive; b. Wabash, Ind., June 20, 1948; s. Randall Clayton and Evelyn Beatrice (Wright) L.; m. Julie Ann Severin, June 30, 1973; children: Randall Clayton III, Erin Elizabeth. BS, Butler U., 1970. CPA, Ind., Ohio. Jr. acct. Price Waterhouse, Indpls., 1970-73, sr. acct. Indpls. and Cin., 1973-76, audit mgr. Cin., 1976-79; unit devel. contr. Ponderosa, Inc., Dayton, Ohio, 1979-81, asst. corp. contr., 1981-82, corp. contr., 1982-84, v.p., corp. contr., 1984-85, sr. v.p., chief acctg. officer, 1985-87, sr. v.p., CFO, 1987; v.p., CFO Tad Tech. Svcs. Corp., Cambridge, Mass., 1988-89; v.p. fin. HydroLogic, Inc., Asheville, N.C., 1993; dir. mgmt. acctg. Rust Indsl. Cleaning Inc., Ashland, Ky., 1994-95; East region contr. Rust Indsl. Svcs., Inc., LaPorte, Tex., 1995, divsn. v.p., contr., 1996-97, v.p., contr., 1997—; group dir. fin. and adminstrn. waste mgmt. indsl. svcs. In Plant Svcs. Group, LaPorte, Tex., 1998—. V.p., CFO Onyx Indsl. Svcs., La Porte, 1999—; adj. prof. Wilmington Coll., 1991; bus. cons., 1987—. Mem. agy. audit com. United Way Greater Cin., 1975; mem. fin. and resource allocation com. United Way Greater Dayton, 1985, mem. com. on agy. fins., 1986-87. Mem. AICPA, Ohio Soc. CPAs, Fin. Execs. Internat., Queen City Assn. Club (bd. dirs. 1978), Dayton Racquet Club, Elks, Phi Kappa Psi. Republican. Presbyterian. Avocations: golf, tennis, reading, antiques, crafts. Home: 2810 Countrylake Dr Cincinnati OH 45233-1735 Office Phone: 713-307-2170. E-mail: jslawson@fuse.net.

LAWSON, ROBERT BERNARD, psychology professor; b. N.Y.C., June 20, 1940; s. Robert Bernard Sr. and Isabella Theresa (McPeake) L.; children: Christina Megan, Steven Robert, Jennifer Erin. BA in Psychology, Monmouth U., 1961; MA in Psychology, U. Del., 1963, PhD in Psychology, 1965. Mem. faculty U. Vt., Burlington, 1966—, asst. prof. psychology, 1966-69, assoc. prof., 1969-74, prof., 1974—, assoc. v.p. acad. affairs, 1978, assoc. v.p. rsch., dean Grad. Coll., 1978-86, dir. gen. exptl. psychology, 1988-90, chmn. dept. pub. adminstrn., 1990-95, acting dir. MPA program, 1998-99, dir. MPA program, 1999—2002, chmn. dept. psychology, 2002—. Presenter, worker in China, Russia, and Italy; cons. Mgmt. Sys., 1986—; vis. scholar Stanford U., 1986-87; pres. Alliance Mgmt. Cons. Group, Burlington, 1987—, N.E. Assn. Grad. Schs., Princeton, N.J., 1983-86; bd. dirs. Grad. Record Exams-ETS, Princeton, 1984-88. Author: (with S.G. Goldstein and R.E. Musty) Principles and Methods of Psychology, 1975, (with W.L. Gulick) Human Stereopsis: A Psychophysical Approach, 1976, (with Zheng Shen) Organizational Psychology: Foundations and Applications, 1998. Mem. bd. govs. Univ. Press New England, 1978-86, bd. dirs., 1979-80. Recipient George V. Kidder Disting. Faculty award U. Vt., 2003; numerous grants NIH, NSF, USDA, numerous awards from Nat. Eye Inst. Mem. AAAS, APA, Psychonomic Soc., Coun. Grad. Schs., N.Y. Acad. Scis., Ea. Psychol. Assn. Avocations: international organizational psychology, leadership, motivation, decision making, organizational culture. Office: U Vt Dept Psychology John Dewey Hl Burlington VT 05405-0001 Business E-Mail: robert.lawson@uvm.edu.

LAWSON, SHERRY LYNN, music educator; b. Morris, Minn., Aug. 9, 1951; d. Roland Henry William and Mable Emma Dorthea Schulz; m. Robert Alan Lawson, July 24, 1971; children: Robert Jr., Heather. BS summa cum laude, St. Cloud U., 1993; lic. cosmetologist, Ritter Beauty Sch., 1970. Hairdresser Sonja's, Morris, Minn., 1970—71, Coif Beauty Salon, Dilworth, Minn., 1971—74; pvt. practice Morris, 1974—77; hairdresser Blue Diamond, Twin Valley, Minn., 1978—82, Mr. Allan's, Mankato, Minn., 1982—86; pvt. practice piano tchr. Bemidji, Minn., 1986—93; music tchr. Milaca (Minn.) Ind. Sch. Dist., 1993—. Organist, choir dir. various churches. Mem.: Minn. Music Educators Assn., Minn. Elem. Music Educators, Phi Kappa Phi. Avocations: gardening, flower arranging, reading, music. Home: 1002 N 3d St Princeton MN 55371 Office: Milaca Ind Sch Dist 500 Hwy 23 W Milaca MN 56353

LAWSON, THOMAS CHENEY, fraud examiner; b. Pasadena, Calif., Sept. 21, 1955; s. William McDonald and Joan Bell (Jaffe) Lawson; m. Susan Sullivan; children: Christopher, Brittany, Courtney, Madison. Student, Calif. State U., Sacramento, 1973-77. Cert. internat. investigator, fraud examiner. Pres. Tomatron Co., Pasadena, 1970-88, Tom's Tune Up & Detail, Pasadena, 1971-88, Tom's Pool Svc., Sacramento, 1975-78, Tomsupply Co., 1975—; mgmt. trainee Permoid Process Co., L.A., 1970-75; prof. automechanics Calif. State U., Sacramento, 1973-75; regional sales cons. Hoover Co., Burlingame, 1974-76; mktg. exec. River City Prodns., Sacramento, 1977-78; territorial rep. Globe div. Burlington House Furniture Co., 1978; So. Calif. territorial rep. Marge Carson Furniture, Inc., 1978-80; pres. Ted L. Gunderson & Assos., Inc., Westwood, Calif., 1980-81; pres., CEO Apscreen, Newport Beach, Calif., 1980—. Founder Creditbase Co., Newport Beach, Calif., 1980-89, Worldata Corp., Newport Beach, 1980-89, Trademark Enforcement Corp., L.A., 1985-86; pres. Carecheck, Inc., Newport Beach, 1990—, CEO Badchex, Inc., Newport Beach, 1992—; expert witness Calif. Superior Ct. Mem. editl. rev. bd. Fraud Mag. Calif. Rehab. scholar, 1974—77. Mem.: Nat. Assn. Profl. Background Screeners (founding mem.), Pub. Record Retrievers Network, Orange County Employment Mgrs. Assn., Forensic Expert Witness Assn., World Investigators Network, Soc. Human Resource Mgmt., World Assn. Detectives, Profls. in Human Resources Assn., Nat. Pub. Records Rsch. Assn., Am. Soc. Indsl. Security (cert., chmn. Orange County chpt. 1990), Coun. Internat. Investigators, Christian Businessmen's Com. Internat., Assn. Cert. Fraud Examiners (life; editl. rev. bd. 1995—). Office: PO Box 1355 Newport Beach CA 92663

LAWSON, THOMAS SEAY, JR., lawyer; b. Montgomery, Ala., Oct. 30, 1935; s. Thomas Seay and Rose Darrington (Gunter) L.; m. Sarah Hunter Clayton, May 27, 1961 (dec. Oct. 2004); children: Rose Gunter, Gladys Robinson, Thomas Seay III. AB, U. Ala., 1957, JD, 1963. Bar: Ala. 1963, U.S. Supreme Ct. 1969. Law clk. to chief judge U.S. Dist. Ct. (no. dist.) Ala., 1963-64; assoc. Steiner, Crum & Baker, Montgomery, 1964-68; ptnr. Capell, Howard, Knabe & Cobbs P.A., Montgomery, 1968-98; asst. dist. atty. 15th jud. cir. of Ala., 1969-70; ptnr. Capell & Howard, P.C., Montgomery, 1999—. Mem. lawyers adv. com. U.S. Ct. Appeals, 5th cir. 1978, 11th cir. 1979-82. Pres. The Lighthouse, 1978-79. Lt. USNR, 1957-60. Fellow Ala. Law Found.; mem. ABA, FBA, Ala. State Bar (pres. young lawyers sect. 1970-71), Montgomery County Bar Assn. (pres. 1980), Am. Judicature Soc., 11th Cir. Hist. Soc. (pres. 1999-2001), Lawyers Adv. Com. U.S. Dist. Ct. (mid. dist.) Ala. (chmn. 2000—), Soc. of Pioneers of Montgomery (pres. 1983), Farrah Law Soc. (pres. 1986-88, Outstanding Alumnus award U. Ala. student chpt. 1989), Montgomery Inn of Ct. (master bencher, bd. dirs. 1989-93, chancellor 1991, pres. 1992-93, emeritus 1994—), Ala. Law Inst. (bd. dirs. 1986—), Ala. Law Sch. Found. (trustee 1985—), Montgomery Country Club. Episcopalian. Home: 1262 Glen Grattan Montgomery AL 36111-1402 Office: Capell & Howard PC PO Box 2069 150 S Perry St Montgomery AL 36102-2069 Office Phone: 334-241-8042, 334-264-9682. Business E-Mail: tsl@chlaw.com.

LAWSON, VICKIE MARIE, education educator; b. Balt., Sept. 19, 1957; d. Willie James and Marjorie (Hughes) Oliver; m. John Juner Lawson, May 18, 1979; children: Alia June, John Courtney. BS, Morgan State U., Balt., 1980, MS, 1987. Cert. Elem. Edn. 2nd asst. mgr. Broadway-Payne, Balt., 1974-78; tchr. Balt. City Pub. Schs., 1979-91, tutor, 1992, futures facilitator, 1992—. Math. tutor, team leader, subcommittee mem., curriculum trainer Balt. City Pub. Schs., 1990-92. Author: Moments With The Almighty One, 1993. Grante Fund for Ednl. Excellence, Balt., 1991-92. Democrat. Baptist. Avocations: reading, watching movies, singing, theater, plays. Home: 6023 Woodcrest Ave Baltimore MD 21209-4008 Office: Balt City Pub Schs 200 W North Ave Baltimore MD 21201-5809

LAWSON, WILLIAM, otolaryngologist, educator; b. N.Y.C., Nov. 23, 1934; s. Alexander and Sophia (Elkind) L.; m. Miriam Patkin, Nov. 7, 1965; 1 child, Vanessa Ann. BA, NYU, 1956, DDS, 1961, MD, 1965. Diplomate Am. Bd. Otolaryngology, Am. Bd. Cosmetic Surgery, Am. Bd. Facial Plastic Surgery. Intern Mt. Sinai Hosp., N.Y.C., 1965-66, rsch. fellow in otolaryngology, 1969-70, resident in otolaryngology, 1970-73; resident in gen. surgery Bronx (N.Y.) VA Hosp., 1966-67, chief otolaryngology, head and neck surgery, 1974—2003, cons., 2003—; prof. Mt. Sinai Sch. Medicine, N.Y.C., 1980—; vice chmn., 1996—. Co-dir. Paranasal Sinus Rsch. Lab.; dir. facial plastic surgery clini Mt. Sinai Hosp., N.Y.C.; cons. Nat. Space Biomed. Rsch. Consortium, cons. in physical anthropology, Am. Mus. Natural History. Author: Paraganglionic Chemoreceptor Systems, 1982, Surgery of the Paranasal Sinuses, 1988, 2nd edit., 1992, External Ear, 1995; contbr. over 200 articles to med. jours., chpts. to books. Capt. Med. Corps. U.S. Army, 1967—69. Fellow ACS, Am. Acad. Facial Plastic and Reconstructive Surgery (svc. awrd), Am. Soc. Head and Neck Surgery, Am. Soc. Maxillofacial Surgeons, Am. Rhinologic Soc., Otologic and Laryngologic Soc., Am. Laryngol. Soc.; mem. Am. Acad. Otolaryngology (svc. award), Am. Bronchoesophagologic Soc. (included in Best Drs. Am., Best Drs. in N.Y.). Avocations: photography, art history, horology. Office: Mt Sinai Med Ctr 1 Gustave L Levy Pl New York NY 10029-6500

LAWSON, WILLIAM BRADFORD, psychiatrist; b. Richmond, Va., Nov. 27, 1945; s. Thomas Henry and Violet Serena (Roane) L.; m. Rosemary Jackson, Aug. 6, 1983; children: Robert, Anthony. BS, Howard U., 1966; MA, U. Va., 1968; PhD, U. N.H., 1971; MD, U. Chgo., 1978. Diplomate Am. Bd. Psychiatry and Neurology. Asst. prof. dept. psychology U. Ill., Urbana, 1971-74; intern, resident Stanford (Calif.) U. Med. ctr., 1979-82; clin. rsch. fellow NIMH, Washington, 1981-84; asst. prof. U. Calif., Irvine, 1984-86, Vanderbilt U. Med. Ctr., Nashville, 1986-91; assoc. prof. U. Ark. Med. Sch., Little Rock, 1991—. Chief chronic mentally ill, psychiat. svc. McClellan VA Med. Ctr., Little Rock; dir. rsch. Met. State Hosp., Norwalk, Calif., 1984-86; cons. Meharry Med. Coll., Nashville, 1988-91; chief med. officer Tenn. Mental Health and Mental Retardation, 1988-91. Contbr. chpts. to books, articles to profl. publs. Bd. dirs. Ctr. Living and Learning, Nashville, 1991. Mem. ACLU (bd. dirs. 1990), NAACP (bd. dirs. 1991), Am. Psychiat. Assn. (rsch. coun., com. on under-represented minorities), Collegium Internat. Neuropsychopharmacologium (pres.-elect), Black Psychiatrists Am. (editor quar.), Omega Psi Phi (Gold medal 1992, 93). Democrat. Baptist.

LAWSON, WILLIAM DAVID, III, retired cotton company executive; b. Jackson, Miss., Oct. 30, 1924; s. William David Jr. and Elizabeth Vaiden (Barksdale) L.; m. Elizabeth Coppridge Smith, June 9, 1948; children: Margaret Monroe, William David IV, Susan Barksdale, Thomas Nelson. Student, Woodberry Forest Sch., 1940-42; BS, Davidson Coll., 1948; MBA, U. Pa., 1949. Trainee T.J. White and Co., Memphis, 1949-52; v.p. W.D. Lawson and Co., Gastonia, N.C., 1952-70, pres., 1971-81, Lawson, Lewis & Peat, Gastonia, 1981-85, Lawson Cotton Co., Gastonia, 1985-95; v.p. Hohenberg Bros. Co. div. Cargill Inc., Memphis, 1988-95; ret., 1995; pres. Lawson-Harris Cotton, Inc., 1997—. Pres. Covenant Village, 1979-81; hon. dir. 1st Union Nat. Bank, Gastonia. Mem. adv. coun. aging Gov., 1998—2000; del. Sr. Tar Heel Legislature, 1998—2004; elder Presbyn. Ch.; pres. Sister Cities Com., Gastonia, 1990—94, Gaston Cmty. Found., 2002—05; bd. advisors Davidson Coll., 1976—80; bd. mgrs. N.Y. Cotton Exch., 1974—80. 1st lt. inf. U.S. Army, WWII. Named Cotton Man of Yr. Cotton Digest, 1969, 76; recipient Duke Kimbrell Lifetime Civic Achievement award, 1999, Harry S. Baker Disting. Svc. award Nat. Cotton Coun., 2002. Mem.: Svc. Corps. Ret. Execs., Gaston County C. of C. (pres. 1972—73), Am. Cotton Exporters Assn. (pres. 1979—80), Cotton Coun. Internat. (pres. 1972—73), Atlantic Cotton Assn. (pres. 1957—58), Am. Cotton Shippers Assn. (pres. 1968—69), Nat. Cotton Coun. (pres. 1975—76, advisor 1976—), Am. Legion, Newcomen Soc., The Point Lake and Golf Club, Gaston Country Club, Bequest Soc. (pres. 1964—65, dist. gov. 1995—96, pres.' rep. 2000, Major Donor award 1999, citation for Meritorious Svc. 2001, Disting. Rotarian award 2004), Rotary Found., Kappa Sigma. Avocations: scuba diving, tennis, golf. Home: 1341 Covenant Dr Gastonia NC 28054-3861 Home Fax: 704-868-3173.

LAWSON-JOHNSTON, PETER, II, investment company executive; BA, Trinity Coll.; MS in Real Estate Devel., Columbia U. Mng. ptnr. Jack Primus Partners LP, Harper Partners; dir. & v.p. Elgerbar Corp. Trustee Solomon R. Guggenheim Found., chmn. investment com.; sr. ptnr. Guggenheim Brothers; dir. Harry Frank Guggenheim Found., chmn. investment com.; dir. emeritus Charles A. & Anne Morrow Lindberg Found. Mailing: c/o Solomon R Guggenheim Found 1071 Fifth Ave New York NY 10128-0173 Fax: 212-423-3650.*

LAWSON-JOHNSTON, PETER ORMAN, foundation executive; b. NYC, Feb. 8, 1927; s. John R. and Barbara (Guggenheim) L.; m. Dorothy Stevenson Hammond, Sept. 30, 1950; children: Wendy, Tania, Peter, Mary. Grad. with honors, U. Va., 1951. Reporter, yachting editor Balt. Sun Papers, 1951-53; exec. dir. Md. Classified Employees Assn., Balt., 1953-54; pub. info. dir. Md. Civil Def. Agy., Pikesville, 1954-56; dir. Zemex Corp., NYC, 1960—, v.p., 1966—72, vice chmn., 1972—75, pres., 1975—76, chmn., 1975—2003, also bd. dirs.; dir. Feldspar Corp., subsidiary of Zemex Corp. (formerly Pacific Tin Consolidated Corp.), 1959—2003, sales mgr., 1956—60, v.p. sales, 1961—66, v.p., 1966—72, chmn., 1972—81. Trustee Solomon R. Guggenheim Found., 1964, v.p. bus. adminstrn., 1965-69, pres., 1969-95, chmn., 1995-98, hon. chmn., 1998—; pres. adv. bd. Peggy Guggenheim Collection; dir. Harry Frank Guggenheim Found., 1968—, chmn., 1971—; ptnr. Guggenheim Bros., 1962-70, sr. ptnr., 1971—; chmn. Anglo Energy, Inc., 1973-86; pres., bd. dirs. Elgerbar Corp.; bd. dirs. Nat. Rev. Inc.; bd. dirs., Jupiter Island Holdings. Author: Growing Up Guggenheim: A Personal History of a Family Enterprise, 2005. Trustee The Lawrenceville Sch., 1977-99, trustee emeritus, 1999—, pres., 1990-97; trustee St. Elmo Found., 1996-2005; mem. adv. bd. U. Va. Art Mus., 1997—, chmn., 1997-2005, chmn. emeritus, 2005-. With AUS, 1945-47 Recipient Gertrude Vanderbilt Whitney award Skowhegan Sch. Painting and Sculpture, 1986, Ellis Island Medal of Honor, Nat. Ethnic Coalition Orgns., 1993, Lawrenceville medal Lawrenceville Sch., 1997. Mem. Pilgrims of U.S., Carolina Plantation Soc., US Srs. Golf Assn., Edgartown Yacht Club, Edgartown Reading Room Club, Century Assn., Links, Bedens Brook Club, Pretty Book Tennis Club, Seminole Golf Club, Jupiter Island Club, Brook Club (NYC), Yeamans Hall Club. Republican. Episcopalian. Office: 25 W 53rd St New York NY 10019-5401 Office Phone: 212-644-4901.

LAWSON-NDU, OVUNDA A., emergency physician, surgeon; b. Elelenwo, Nigeria, 1951; s. Lawson Ngbachi and Esther Adanma (Nwogbe) N.; m. Elsie Nnenne Jenewari, Dec. 13, 1977 (div. Jan. 1980); children: Jennifer Mboma, Sandra Njimole; m. Donna Marie Grimes, June 27, 1986; 1 child, Anuugo Michelle. BS in Chemistry with highest honors, U. Wis., 1977; DO, U. Health Sci., 1980. Diplomate Am. Bd. Emergency Medicine. Intern Metro Health Ctr., Erie, Pa., 1981-82; resident in gen. surgery Howard U. Hosp., Washington; mem. staff Lower Bucks Hosp., Bristol, Pa. Mem. hypertension and diabetes screening program Rivers State, Nigeria, 1992—; vice chmn. dept. emergency medicine Temple U. Hosp., Bristol, Pa., 1997—, asst. dir., 1997-2000, assoc. dir., 2000—. Active Nat. Exch. Club, Amnesty Internat. Fellow Am. Coll. Emergency Physicians, Am. Acad. Emergency Medicine. Address: PO Box 640 Medford NJ 08055-0640

LAWTON, ALEXANDER ROBERT, immunologist, educator; b. Savannah, Ga., Nov. 8, 1938; s. Alexander Robert and Elizabeth (Holdrege) L.; m. Frances Ritchie Crockett, Nov. 25, 1960; children: Julia Beckwith, Alexander Robert IV. BA, Yale U., 1960; MD, Vanderbilt U., 1964. Diplomate Am. Bd. Pediatrics. Resident in pediatrics Vanderbilt U., Nashville, 1964-66; fellow dept. pediatrics U. Ala., Birmingham, 1969-71, from asst. prof. to prof. pediatrics and microbiology, 1971-80; prof. microbiology, Edward C. Stahlman prof. pediatric physiology and cell metabolism Vanderbilt U. Sch. Medicine, Nashville, 1980—. Mem. cancer spl. programs rev. com. Nat. Cancer Inst., 1981-84; mem. allergy, immunology and transplantation rev. com. Nat. Inst. Allergy and Infectious Diseases, 1985-88. Contbr. over 150 articles, book chpts. to profl. publs. Surgeon USPHS, 1966-69. Grantee NIH, March of Dimes Birth Defects Found. Mem. Soc. Pediatric Rsch., Am. Pediatric Soc., Am. Soc. Clin. Investigation, Am. Assn. Immunologists, Am. Assn. Pathologists. Episcopalian. Office: Vanderbilt U Sch Medicine 311 Oxford House Nashville TN 37232-0001

LAWTON, BARBARA, lieutenant governor; b. Wis. m. Cal Lawton; children: Joseph, Amanda Krupp. BA summa cum laude, Lawrence U., 1987; MA, U. Wis., 1991. Lt. gov. State of Wis., Madison, 2003—. Founding mem. Ednl. Resource Found.; founding trustee Cmty. Found.; founding mem. Latinos Unidos; mem. adv. bd. Green Bay Multicultural Ctr., Women's Polit. Voice; mem. bus. planning and resource team Entrepreneurs of Color; bd. mem. Planned Parenthood Advs. Wis., Northeastern Wis. Tech. Coll. Edn. Found. Named Feminist of the Yr., Wis. Chpt. NOW, 1999; recipient Ft. Howard Founds. Humanitarian award. Mem.: AAUW, LWV, Nat. Women's Polit. Caucus. Democrat. Office: Office of Lt Governor Rm 19 E State Capitol Madison WI 53702

LAWTON, DEBORAH SIMMONS, educational association administrator; b. Dover, N.J., Sept. 14, 1950; d. Coryden Jerome Simmons and Marjorie Lynd (Jewell) Weber; children: Catherine Randall, Christopher James. BA, Lebanon Valley Coll., 1972; tchr. cert., Coll. St. Elizabeth, 1974; MLS, Rutgers-The State U., 1994. Cert. ednl. media specialist, profl. libr., supr. Confidential ratings analyst Martindale-Hubbell, Summit, N.J., 1972-74; tchr. St. Rose Sch., East Hanover, N.J., 1975-77, St. Paul Sch., Princeton, N.J., 1977-78; libr. Mary Jacobs Libr., Rocky Hill, N.J., 1988-92, South Brunswick H.S., Monmouth Junction, N.J., 1994—. Reviewer Infolink, 1995—; chair press rev. com. Am. Assn. Univs. Author: Knowledge Quest, Book Report; co-author: Authentic Assessment in South Brunswick, Partnerships at Work in the Library. Chair Montgomery jointure com., Montgomery Twp., N.J., 1985; coach/dir. Montgomery Girls Softball, 1988-91; v.p., exec. bd. Montgomery Twp. PTSA, 1986-90; pres., treas. Lawrenceville (N.J.) Presbyn. Coop. Nursery Sch., 1981-84; ranking chair jrs. N.J. Tennis Dist.; mem. INFOLINK Book Evaluation Criteria Com., KidsConnect, INFOLINK Youth Svcs. Com.; deacon Blawenburg Reformed Ch., elder. Internet grantee N.J. State Libr.,

1994, Instrnl. Coun. grantee South Brunswick Instrnl. Coun., 1995, 96, 97; recipient Pres.'s award N.J. Tennis. Mem. ALA, Am. Assn. Sch. Librs. (assn. Am. univ. presses com. 1996—, legis. com., chair youth svcs. com., intellectual freedom com., bd. tristees), Assn. for Libr. Svc. to Children, Young Adult Libr. Svcs. Assn., Intellectual Freedom Round Table, Ednl. Media Assn. N.J. (legis. chair, intellectual freedom chair), Assn. of Am. Univ. Presses (rev. com.), N.J. Libr. Assn., Beta Phi Mu, Pi Gamma Mu. Avocations: water sports, quilting. Office: South Brunswick HS 750 Ridge Rd Monmouth Junction NJ 08852-0183 Office Phone: 732-329-4044 3256. E-mail: deborah.lawton@sbschools.org.

LAWTON, ERIC, lawyer, artist, photographer; b. N.Y.C., Apr. 9, 1947; s. Leo and Vira L.; m. Gail Schenbaum, July 15, 1989; children: Rebecca Nicole, Alexandra Rose. AB, UCLA, 1969, photographic studies, 1980-81; JD, Loyola U., Los Angeles, 1972. Bar: Calif. 1972, U.S. Dist. Ct. (cen. dist.) Calif. 1974, U.S. Ct. Appeals (9th cir.) 1973, U.S. Supreme Ct. 1976. Assoc. West & Girardi, Los Angeles, 1972-76; pvt. practice Los Angeles, 1976—; of counsel Mahoney, Coppenrath, & Jaffe LLP, 1997—2004. Guest lectr. UCLA Law Sch., 1986; instr. visual arts dept. UCLA Ext.; AV rating Martindale-Hubbell; guest spkr., UCLA Conf. Ctr., 2002, 03, 04. One-man shows include L.A. Children's Mus., 1980-81, Am. Film Inst., 1981, Marc Richards Gallery, L.A., 1986, U. Art Gallery Calif. State U. Northridge, 1987, John Nichols Gallery, Santa Paula, Calif., 1988, Gallery at 817, L.A., 1991, Pacific Asia Mus., Pasadena, Calif., 1993, Bergamot Station Arts Ctr., Santa Monica, 2000, L.A. City Hall, Office of the Mayor, 2001; exhibited in group shows at Stockholm Art Fair, Sweden, 1986, Francine Ellman Gallery, 1986-87, Artists' Soc. Internat. Gallery, San Francisco, 1986-87, Fla. State U. Fine Arts Gallery and Mus., Tallahassee, 1988, Silvermine Gallery, Stamford, Conn., 1988, City Hall of West Hollywood, 1988, Louis Stern Gallery, 2003, 04, 05, Pacific Design Ctr., 2003, Photo LA: The L.A. Internat. Photography Exposition, 2003, TBWA/CHIAT/DAY, 2004; group show P.L.A.N Spring Street Gallery, L.A., 1995, Christie's, Beverly Hills, Calif., 1998, Finegood Gallery, L.A., 1999, Advt. Photographers Am., 2001; spl. film photographer in The Last Day, 1979, Chiva, Getting on in Style, 1980, Child's Play, 1981, others; multi-media prodns. include The Power, 1979, The Tie That Binds, 1981, Large-Screen Visual Montage with performance of L.A. Philharm. Orch. at Hollywood Bowl, 1986, Floating Stone performance, Japan Am. Theater, L.A., 1987, Pacific Asia Mus., 1993, Rejoice Performance at Thousand Oaks Performing Arts Ctr., 1998 (multi-media prodr. and digital visual performance), Wadsworth Theater, L.A., 2003, others; represented in permanent collections including Bibliotheque Nationale, Paris, N.Y. Pub. Libr., Skirball Mus., L.A., L.A. Children's Mus., Credit Suisse/First Boston, L.A.Westwood Nat. Bank, Gibralter Savs., L.A., Mobius Soc., L.A., Western Bank, Internat. Photography Mus., Oklahoma City, Condon & Forsyth, William Morris Agcy.,others; photographer, co-author The Soul of the World, 1993, The Soul Aflame, 2000, A Righteous Soul, 2003; spl. assignment White House photographer, 1983; record album covers include Gyuto Monks, Tibetan Tantric Choir, Jungle Suite, Michael McDonald, A Gathering of Friends, 2001; poster Japanese Boats; contbr. photographs to books, newspapers and mags. including, N.Y. Times Mag., Fortune Mag., Conde Nast Traveler Mag., Comm. Arts. Mag., Am. Photo Mag., Chgo. Tribune, Variety, Gente (Italy), Dukas Femina (Switzerland), The World of Photography (China), Popular Photography, Wraparound Mag., Loyola Lawyer Mag., Pan Am Mag., Travel & Leisure Mag., U.S. News Mag., Time, Newsweek, Nat. Geographic, Harper & Row Books, Harcourt Brace Books, Holt, Rinehart & Winston books, John Wiley & Sons Books, others; world-wide advt. campaign Motorola Iridium, 1998, Citigroup, 2001-02; ann. report Tenn. Valley Authority, 1997; author: (short stories anthologies) Soul Moments, 1997, The Art of Pilgrimage, 1998. Active organizing com., citizens adv. and cultural and fine arts adv. commns. XXIII Olympic Games, Los Angeles, 1983-84; mem Cultural and Fine Arts Adv. Commn, 1983-84; bd. dirs. Adverstising Photographers of Am., L.A., 2004, 05. Recipient award Fla. Nat. '88, Artquest awards, 1987, 88, 1st Prize Sierra Mag. Photo Contest, 1990, Award of Excellence for Photography, Communication Arts Mag., 1994, Cert. of Tribute, City of L.A., 2001; named one of top 40 photographers Internat. Photography Congress, 1988, winner Am. Photo Mag. 3rd Ann. Photography Contest, 1994; Judge's Choice Award, Advertisting Photographers of Am., 2004, Internat. Photography awards, 2004; featured in Alumni Profile, Loyola Lawyer Mag., 2003; quoted in 75th annual Acad. Awards, 2003. Mem. ABA, Consumer Atty. Assn. L.A., Consumer Atty. Assn. Calif., L.A. County Bar Assn., Advt. Photographers Am. (award 2002, 03, 04). Avocations: swimming, music, mountain biking, world traveling, karate (1st degree black belt). Office: Ste 700 233 Wilshire Blvd Santa Monica CA 90401-1207 Office Phone: 310-319-5409. E-mail: elawton@ericlawtonlaw.com.

LAWTON, FLORIAN KENNETH, artist, educator; b. Cleve., June 20, 1921; m. Lois Mari Ondrey, June 19, 1948; children: Kenneth R., David F., Dawn M., Patricia A. Student, Cleve. Sch. Art, 1941-43, Cleve. Inst. Art, 1948-51, John Huntington Polytech. Inst., 1946-50. Instr. Cooper Sch. Art, Cleve., 1976-80, Cleve. Sch. Art, 1980-82. Cons., instr. Orange Art Ctr., Pepper Pike, Ohio, 1978—; cons. in field, juror, 1968—. Exhbns. include Am. Watercolor Soc., N.Y., Cleve. Mus. Art, Butler Mus., Youngstown, Ohio, Canton (Ohio) Mus., Massillon (Ohio) Mus., Nat. Arts Club, N.Y.C., Pitts. Watercolor Soc., Audubon Artists, N.Y.C., Salmagundi Club, N.Y.C., Parkersburg (W.Va.) Art Ctr., Boston Mills Arts Festival, Peninsula, Ohio, Marietta (Ohio) Coll., Nat. Pks. Assn. Exhbn., 1996, 97, 2000, many others; 25 yrs. retrospective exhbn. Amish paintings, Butler Inst. Am. Art, 1989; represented in collections including Am. Soc. Metals, Ctrl. Nat. Bank, Diamond-Shamrock, Diocese Cleve., Kaiser Found., Ohio Conservation Found., Nat. City Bank Ohio, TRW, Standard Oil Co., Huntington Bank, Nat. Mennonite Mus., Lancaster, Pa., Ohio Bell Telephone Co., Day-Glo Corp., Soc. Bank Corp., The White House Collection, Washington, numerous others U.S. and internat., also pvt. collections; featured mags., calendars; Mill Pond Press; cons., artist (documentary) Amish Romance, 1979; official Coast Guard artist; artist Amish Documentary-PBS, 1996. Cons. Aurora (Ohio) Community Libr., 1990—. Cpl. USAF, 1943-46, PTO. Recipient Disting. Alumni award Garfield Hgts. (Ohio) High Sch., 1990, 1st place award Grand Invitational Exhbn., Akron, Ohio, 1996, numerous others. Mem. Ohio Watercolor Soc. (signature, charter, Grand Buckeye award 1983), Am. Watercolor Soc. (signature, Strathmore award 1977), Nat. Watercolor Soc. (signature), Akron Soc. Artists, Assoc. Audubon Artists, Artists Fellowships Inc. (N.Y.), Ky. Watercolor Soc. (signature), Midwest Watercolor Soc., Pa. Watercolor Soc. (signature), Ga. Watercolor Soc., Whiskey Painters Am., Rotary Club Chagrin Valley (Paul Harris fellow 1989). Office: 410-29 Willow Cir Aurora OH 44202-9131 Fax: 330-562-4102.

LAWTON, GREGORY E., sales and marketing executive; BA in Govt., St. Lawrence U. Various pos., to v.p. and gen. mgr. paper divsn. Procter & Gamble Co., 1972—94; pres. NuTone, Inc., Cin., 1994—98; pres., COO CMI, 1998—2000; dir. Comml. Markets Holdco, 2000—; dir., pres., CEO JohnsonDiversey, Inc., Sturtevant, Wis., 2000—. Dir. Johnson Outdoors, Inc. and Gen. Cable Corp.; mem. compensation and audit com. Gen. Cable Corp. Office: JohnsonDiversey World Hdqrs 8310 16th St PO Box 902 Sturtevant WI 53177-0902

LAWTON, KELLY MARIE LEE, secondary school educator, performing arts director; b. Pitts., Sept. 17, 1970; d. Francis Xavier and Helen Louise Lawton. BS in Music Edn., Clarion U. of Pa., 1993; MSEd, Shenandoah U., 2000. Cert. PreK-12 music tchr., adminstr., supr. Va. Dir. performing arts Page County Pub. Schs., Shenandoah, Va., 1996—. Named Tchr. of the Month, Sylvan Learning Ctr. and WHSV-3, 2004; recipient Tchr. Achievement award, McDonald's Ray A. Kroc, 2004, award, Nat. Soc. H.S. Scholars, 2004, Outstanding Educator award, Regional Gov.'s Sch., 2005. Mem.: NEA (assoc.), Music Educators Nat. Conf. (assoc.), Va. Choral Directors Assn. (assoc.), Va. Band and Orch. Dirs. Assn. (assoc.), Va. Music Edn. Assn. (assoc.), Page County Edn. Assn. (assoc.), Women's Nat. Bandmaster's Assn. (life), Tau Beta Sigma (hon.), Beta Sigma Phi (hon.). Office Phone: 540-652-8712.

LAWTON, LORILEE ANN, small business owner, accountant; b. Morrisville, Vt., July 17, 1947; d. Philip Wyman Sr. and Margaret Elaine (Ather) Noyes; m. Lee Henry Lawton, Dec. 6, 1969 (dec. Nov. 2004); children: Deborah Ann, Jeffrey Lee. BBA, U. Vt., 1969. Sr. acct., staff asst. IBM, Essex Junction, Vt., 1969-72; owner, pres., chmn. bd. Red-Hed Supply Inc., Colchester, 1972-2001; owner, pres. Firetech Sprinkler Corp., Colchester, 1992—. Bd. dirs. Mchts. Bank, Burlington, Mchts. Bankshares. Mem. Am. Fire Sprinkler Assn., Nat. Fire Protection Assn., Vt. Subcontractors Assn. Republican. Avocations: reading, gardening. Home: 571 Middle Rd Colchester VT 05446-7310 Office: Firetech Sprinkler Corp 340 Hegeman Ave Colchester VT 05446-3173 Office Phone: 802-655-1800.

LAWTON, NANCY, artist; b. Gilroy, Calif., Feb. 28, 1950; d. Edward Henry and Marilyn Kelly (Boyd) L.; m. Richard Enemark, Aug. 4, 1984; children: Faith Lawton, Forrest Lawton. BA in Fine Art, Calif. State U., San Jose, 1971; MFA, Mass. Coll. Art, 1980. Artist-in-residence Villa Montalvo Ctr. Arts, Los Gatos, Calif., 1971, Noble & Greenough Sch., Dedham, Mass., 1990. One-woman shows include The Bklyn. Mus., 1983, Victoria Munroe Gallery, N.Y.C., 1993, Hirschl & Adler Galleries, N.Y.C., 2002, 05; group shows include San Francisco Mus. Modern Art, 1973, The Bklyn. Mus., 1980, 83, Staempfli Gallery, N.Y.C., 1984, The Ark. Art Ctr. Mus., Little Rock, 1984, 88, 92, 93, Victoria Munroe Gallery, 1985, 87, 88, 92, Butler Inst. Am. Art, Ohio, 1988, Smith Coll. Mus. Art, 1988, NAD, N.Y.C., 1988, Reynolds Gallery, Richmond, 1994, Nancy Solomon Gallery, Atlanta, 1995, Arnot Art Mus., Elmira, N.Y., 2001-03, Hunt Inst. for Bot. Documentation, Carnegie Mellon U., Pitts., 2001-02, Hirsch and Adler Galleries, N.Y.C., 2002-04, John Pence Galleries, San Francisco, 2004, Vose Galleries, Boston, 2004; pub. collections include The Ark. Art Ctr. Mus., Art Inst. Chgo., Bklyn. Mus., Met. Mus. Art, Smithsonian Am. Art Mus., Washington. Scholar Mellon Found., 1982; N.Y. State Creative Artists grantee, 1983, N.Y. State Arts Devel. Fund grantee, 1989. Home and Office: 78 Willett St Albany NY 12210-1001 Office Phone: 518-449-7022. E-mail: nancydraws@aol.com.

LAWTON, PAMELA HARRIS, artist, educator; b. Washington, Jan. 7, 1959; d. Frank Lee and Patricia Anne Harris; m. Eric Christian Lawton, May 31, 1986. BA Studio Art, Sociology, U. Va., Charlottesville, 1981; MFA Printmaking, Howard U., Washington, 1991; EdD, Columbia U., N.Y.C., 2004. Cert. Tchr.art 7-12. Sr. rep. benefits and compensation USA Today, Arlington, Va.; art tchr. Northwestern H.S., Adelphi, Md.; acad. asst. tchr. Columbia U. Coll., N.Y.C.; advisor grads. Bank Str Coll. Edn.; asst. prof. Tyler Sch. Art, Phila. Cons. Phila. Schs.; mem. adv. bd. Heritage H.S. Contbr. chpt. to book Community Connections. Recipient Bernard Hans Hirsch award, Nat. Arts Club, 2002; grantee, Prince George County, Md., 1997; scholar Arthur W Dowd scholarship, Columbia U. N.Y.C., 2002. Democrat. Episcopalian. Home: 12300 Markby Ct Upper Marlboro MD 20774 Office: Temple U Tyler Sch Art 1114 W Rierks St Philadelphia PA 19122 E-mail: lawton@temple.edu.

LAWYER, DAVID JAMES, lawyer; b. Chgo., Mar. 28, 1961; s. Cornelius Bernard and Margaret (Leamy) L.; children: Brandon David, Caitlin Elizabeth, Dylan Thomas. BA in Govt., St. John's U., Collegeville, Minn., 1982; JD, Seattle U., 1986. Bar: Wash., 1986, U.S. Dist. Ct. (we. dist.) Wash., 1986, U.S. Ct. Appeals (9th cir.), 1995. Ptnr. Inslee, Best, Doezie & Ryder, Bellevue, Wash., 1986—. Vol. Vol. Legal Svcs., Seattle, 1991—, Eastside Literacy Coun., 1993—; gen. counsel, pro bono Kids Voting, Wash., Bellevue, 1994—. Mem. Wash. State Bar Assn., King County Bar Assn., Ea. King County Bar Assn. (trustee 1991-95, Oustanding Trustee award, 1994). Roman Catholic. Avocations: baseball, music, theater, coaching youth athletics, writing. Home: 15116 NE 67th Pl Redmond WA 98052-4739 Office: Inslee Best Doezie & Ryder PS PO Box c-90016 777 108th Ave NE Ste 1900 Bellevue WA 98004-5144

LAWYER, STEVEN RANDALL, psychologist, researcher; b. Anderson, Ind., Mar. 14, 1971; s. Steven Howard and Nancy Jo Lawyer; m. Erin Brooke Rasmussen, Apr. 22, 2001; 1 child, Andrew. BA, Western Mich. U., 1995; MSc, Auburn U., 1999, PhD, 2002. Doctorate fellow Med. U. of SC, Nat. Crime Victims Rsch. and Treatment Ctr., 2002—04; adj. prof. Coll. Charleston, SC, 2003; asst. prof. Idaho State U., 2004—. Mem. editl. bd. Jour. of Child and Adolescent Substance Abuse, ad hoc reviewer Jour. of Anxiety Disorders, Jour. Traumatic Stress; contbr. articles. Recipient Rsch. award, Ala. Psychol. Assn., 1998; rsch. grant, Med. U. SC U. Rsch. Com., 2003. Mem.: Am. Psychol. Soc., Soc. for Scientific Study of Sexuality, Assn. for Behaviorial and Cognitive Therapies, Psi Chi. Office: Idaho State U Dept Psychology Campus Box 8112 Pocatello ID 83209-8112 Business E-Mail: lawyster@isu.edu.

LAX, PETER DAVID, mathematician, educator; b. Budapest, Hungary, May 1, 1926; arrived in U.S., 1941, naturalized, 1944; s. Henry and Klara (Kornfeld) Lax; m. Anneli Cahn, 1948; 1 child, John; 1 child, James D. BA, NYU, 1947, PhD, 1949; DSc (hon.), Kent State U., 1976, Brown U., 1993; DHC (hon.), U. Paris, 1979; D. Natural Scis. (hon.), Technische Hochschule Aachen, Germany, 1988; DSc (hon.), Herriot Walt U., 1990; D. (hon.), Leningrad State U., 1991; D. (hon.), U. Md. Baltimore County, 1993; PhD (hon.), Tel Aviv U., 1992, Beijing U., 1993. Asst. prof. NYU, 1949—57, prof., 1957—99; dir. Courant Inst. Math. Scis., 1972—80. Author (with Ralph Phillips): Scattering Theory, 1967; author: Hyperbolic Systems of Conservation Laws and the Mathematical Theory of Shock Waves, 1973, Scattering Theory for Automorphic Functions, 1976; author: (with A. Lax and S.Z. Burstein) Calculus with Applications and Computing, 1976; author: Linear Algebra, 1997, Functional Analysis, 2002. Mem. Pres.'s Com. on Nat. Medal of Sci., 1976; Nat. Sci. Bd., 1980—86. Served with U.S. Army, 1944—46. Recipient Semmelweis medal, Semmelweis Med. Soc., 1975, Nat. medal Sci., 1986, Wolf prize, Israel, 1987, Abel prize, Norway, 2005. Mem.: NAS (applied math. and numerical analysis award 1983), AAAS, Russian Acad. Sci. (fgn. assoc.), Acad. des Scis. (fgn. assoc.), Soc. Indsl. and Applied Math., Am. Philos. Soc., Am. Acad. Arts and Scis., Math. Assn. Am. (bd. govs., Chauvenet prize 1974), Am. Math. Soc. (pres. 1979—80, Norbert Wiener prize 1973, Leroy P. Steele prize 1993), London Math. Soc. (hon.), Moscow Math. Soc. (hon.), Hungarian Acad. Sci. (hon.), Acad. Sinica (hon.). Office: Courant Inst Math Scis 251 Mercer St Rm 910 New York NY 10012-1185 Office Phone: 212-998-3232. Business E-Mail: lax@cims.nyu.edu.

LAX, PHILIP, land developer, space planner; b. Newark, Apr. 22, 1920; s. Nathan and Beckie (Hirschhorn) L; m. Madeline Blondman, June 13, 2004; children from previous marriage: Corinne, Barbara. BS, NYU, 1940, postgrad., 1941-42. With Lax & Co., Newark, 1942-77, v.p., 1950-77; pres. Chathill Mgmt., Inc., 1977—. Cons. World Book of Am. Heritage, 1992. Pres. B'nai Brith Ctr., Rochester, Minn., 1965-70, now hon. pres.; trustee Rutgers U. Hillel; pres. B'nai Brith Rutgers U. Hillel Found. Bldg. Corp., 1969—; chmn. United Jewish Appeal, Maplewood, N.J., 1966, 76; mem. N.J. region exec. bd. Anti-Defamation League, mem. nat. community rels. bd.; mem. Gov.'s Conf. on Edn., N.J., 1966, mem. bd. trustees Soc. Friends of Touro Synagogue, Newport, R.I., 1996; v.p. Touro Synagogue, 2000—; bd. dirs. Hebrew Immigration Soc. (HIAS); hon. chair B'nai B'rith Ctr. for Pub. Policy. 1999; mem. Mayor's Budget Com., Maplewood, 1958-59; co-chmn. N.J. Opera Ball, 1977; trustee B'nai Brith Found., Washington, 1967—(Philip Lax Gallery of B'nai Brith History and Archives named for him in Philip Klutznick Mus., Room named in his honor Stern Sch. Econs., NYU); co-chmn. B'nai Brith Internat. Coun., 1979-84, chmn., 1982-94; voting del. to Jewish Agy., Jerusalem; represented ICBB in UN as NGO, ECOSOC mem. UN, representing coordinated Bd. Jewish Orgns.; attended UNESCO Conf. in Mex., 1982, with Internat. Coun. B'nai Brith and U.S.; trustee, mem. exec. com. N.J. sect. NCCJ, 1981; trustee Henry Monsky Found., Washington, 1968—; trustee Leo N. Levi Hosp., Hot Springs, Ark., 1968-71, B'nai Brith World Jewish Ctr., Jerusalem, 1982, Nat. Arthritis Hosp., 1976—, N.Y. Statue of Liberty Centennial Found., Touro Synagogue, Newport, R.I., 1996—,; hon. trustee Arts Coun. of Suburban Essex, N.J., 1980, Soc. Friends Touro Synagogue, Newport, 1996; mem. Econ. Devel. Commn., Twp. of Maplewood, 1979—; mem. steering com. to Restore Ellis Island, 1977—; nat. pres. Ellis Island Restoration Commn., 1978—, responsible for planning, funding and operating Family History Ctr. on Ellis Island; apptd. to planning team of Statue of Liberty and Ellis Island by Pres. Carter, Dept. of Interior; mem. Statue of Liberty/Ellis Island Centennial Commn., chmn. bd. Com. of Architecture and Restoration of Statue of Liberty-Ellis Island, past chmn.; bd. dirs. Hebrew Immigration Aid Soc. Decorated Cavaliere Ufficiale (Knighted) Order of Merit of the Republic of Italy; recipient Found. award B'nai Brith, 1968, Humanitarian award, 1969, Pres.'s Gold medal, 1975; Pro Mundi Beneficio medal Brazilian Acad. Humanities, 1976; Philip Lax chapel at Rutgers U. Hillel named in his honor; named One of 100 Most Influential New Jersey Jews in the 20th Century, Eminent Wisdom fellow Wisdom Hall of Fame, 2000; honored by N.J. State Senate. Mem. Am. Soc. Interior Designers, Nat. Soc. Interior Designers (trustee 1970-73), Am. Arbitration Assn., Am. Jewish Hist. Com. (v.p.), Am. Jewish Hist. Soc. (trustee 1984), Am. Soc. Israel Philatelists, Masons (32 deg.), Shriners, B'nai Brith (v.p. Supreme Lodge 1968-71, internat. bd. govs. 1971—, mem. exec. com. of internat. coun.), NYU Club (founding mem. 1956), Nat. Press Club. Home: 609 S Orange Ave W South Orange NJ 07079 Office: Chathill Mgmt 40 Main St Chatham NJ 07928-2402

LAXMINARAYANA, DAMA, geneticist, researcher, educator; b. Hyderabad, India, Apr. 20, 1953; came to U.S., 1990; s. Kishtaiah and Sathyamma; m. Dara Jayalakshmi; children: Dama Bhargavi, Dama Sriharsha, Dama Vishnupriya. BSc, Osmania U., Hyderabad, 1974, MSc, 1976, PhD, 1982. Jr. sci. asst. dept. genetics Osmania U., 1977-78, lectr. dept. zoology, 1985-90; jr. rsch. fellow Indian Dept. Atomic Energy, 1978-81, postdoctoral fellow, 1982-83, rsch. assoc., 1983-85; postdoctoral fellow dept. medicine Case Western Res. U. Sch. Medicine, Cleve., 1990-91; rsch. assoc. dept. internal medicine Wake Forest U. Sch. Medicine, Winston-Salem, N.C., 1991-94, rsch. instr., 1994-98, rsch. asst. prof., 1998—. Conf. presenter in field. Contbr. articles to sci. jours., chpts. to books. Mem. AAAS, Am. Assn. Immunologists, Am. Coll. Rheumatology, Environ. Mutagen Soc. India, India Soc. Cell Biology, Soc. Geneticists and Cytologists India, N.Y. Acad. Scis. Home: 444 Lynn Ave Winston Salem NC 27104 Office: Wake Forest U Sch Medicine Dept Internal Medicine Medical Center Blvd Winston Salem NC 27157 Office Phone: 336-716-0616. Business E-mail: dlaxmina@wfubmc.edu.

LAXSON, RUTH KNIGHT, artist; b. Roanoke, Ala, July 16, 1924; d. Edward Wilts and Ruby Melinda (Dunson) Knight; m. C.R. King, Nov. 29, 1942 (div. Aug. 1946); 1 child, Claude Roland King Jr.; m. Robert Earl Laxson, Jan. 31, 1953. Student, Atlanta Coll. Art, 1965-70. Resident fellow Hambridge Ctr., 1995, resident scholarship, 1998. One-women shows include Atlanta Coll. Art, 1991, Pagination Exhibit Press 63 Plus, Atlanta, 1992, Letter Works and Sculpture/Arts Festival of Atlanta, 1995, Bookworks/U. Iowa, 1996,; artist (drawings, paintings) Marcia Wood Gallery, Atlanta, Ga., 1997, 2002; exhibited in group shows Tula Found. Gallery, Atlanta, 1991, San Antonio Art Inst., 1991, City Gallery at Chastain, Atlanta, 1993, Zeitgenossische Handpressendrucke, Hamburg, Germany, 1993, Atlanta Coll. Art, 1994, Banff Ctr., Alta., Can., 1994, Rolling Stone Press, 1996, Art Papers mag., 1996, Am. Fedn. of Arts Internat. Invitational Traveling Exhbn. Artist Books, 1998—, Experimental Narrative, 1999, Unbound-Agnes Scott Col., 2001; represented in permanent collections High Mus., Atlanta, Ga. Coun. Arts, Atlanta, Getty Ctr. Mus., Malibu, Calif., Mus. Modern Art, N.Y.C., N.Y.C. Pub. Libr., Yale U., Stanford U., UCLA, U. Alta., Edmonton, Victoria and Albert Mus., London, Tate Gallery, London, Mus. Contemporary Art of Ga.; author: illustrator: Playfulness Works, 1982, (Ho+Go)2=It, 1986, Measure-Cut-Stitch, 1987, About Change About, 1989, Some Things Are Sacred, 1991, Imaging, 1991, Wheeling, 1992, Measureup, Retell the Tale, 1997, Muse Measures, 2000, A Hundred Years of: LEX FLEX, 2003; contbr. to profl. jours., books Grantee Ga. Coun. for the Arts-Acquisitions, 1989-90, Dekalb Coun. for the Arts, 1986, 2002,NEA, 1980; Installation grantee Arts Festival of Atlanta, 1995. Mem. High Mus. Art (charter), Avocation: gardening. Home: 2298 Drew Valley Rd NE Atlanta GA 30319-3968 Office: Press 63 Plus PO Box 190731 Atlanta GA 31119-0731

LAY, DONALD POMEROY, federal judge; s. Hardy W. and Ruth (Cushing) L.; m. Miriam Elaine Gustafson; children: Stephen Pomeroy(dec.), Catherine Sue, Cynthia Lynn, Elizabeth Ann, Deborah Jean, Susan Elaine. Student, U.S. Naval Acad., 1945—46; BA, U. Iowa, 1948, JD, 1951; LLD (hon.) (hon.), Mitchell Coll. Law, 1985. Bar: Nebr. 1951, Iowa 1951, Wis. 1953. Assoc. Kennedy, Holland, DeLacy & Svoboda, Omaha, 1951—53, Quarles, Spence & Quarles, Milw., 1953—54, Eisenstatt, Lay, Higgins & Miller, 1954—66; judge U.S. Ct. Appeals (8th cir.), 1966—, chief judge, 1980—92, senior judge, 1992—. Faculty mem. on evidence Nat. Coll. Trial Judges, 1964—65, U. Minn. Law Sch., William Mitchell Law Sch.; mem. U.S. Jud. Conf., 1980—92. Mem. editl. bd.: Iowa Law Rev., 1950—51; contbr. articles to legal jours. With USNR, 1944—46. Recipient Hancher-Finkbine medal, U. Iowa, 1980, Disting. Alumni award, 2000. Mem.: ATLA (bd. govs. 1963—65, Jud. Achievement award), ABA, Am. Judicature Soc., Wis. Bar Assn., Iowa Bar Assn., Nebr. Bar Assn., Internat. Acad. Trial Lawyers, Order of Coif, Sigma Chi, Phi Delta Phi, Delta Sigma Rho (Significant Sig award 1986, Herbert Harley award 1988). Presbyterian. Office: US Ct Appeals 8th Cir 316 N Robert St Rm 560 Saint Paul MN 55101-1461

LAY, GREGG R., pharmacist; b. Fremont, Nebr., Aug. 1, 1949; s. Albertus Nies and Rachel Constance Lay; m. Pamela Kay Geu, Sept. 23, 1972 (div. May 1996); children: Cody Michael, Rikki Allison; m. Crystal Lynn Sughroue, May 19, 1997; children: Cari Lee Ferguson, Willie Joe Ferguson. BS in pharm., U. Nebr., 1972; PharmD, U. Kans., 2003. Registered pharmacist State of Nebr. Pharmacy intern Baker's Pharmacy, Lincoln, Nebr., 1970, Mary Lanning Meml. Hosp., Hastings, Nebr., 1971—72, registered pharmacist, 1975—2005, Gibson Pharmacy, Norfolk, Nebr., 1972—75. Clin. asst. prof. pharmacy Creighton U. Sch. Pharmacy, Omaha, 1977—79; cert. pharmacy preceptor Creighton U., 1980—2004, U. Nebr. Med. Ctr., Omaha, 1980—2004; adj. asst. prof. pharmacy Creighton U. Sch. Pharmacy, 1980; clin. instr. U. Nebr. Med. Ctr., 1990. Spkr. YMCA Family Asthma Conf., Hastings, 1998; pharmacist vol. Adams County Vital Signs Health Fair; spkr. Mary Lanning Meml. Hosp. Cardiac/Cardiopulmonary Rehab. Mem.: Am. Soc. Health Sys. Pharmacists, Nebr. Soc. Health Sys. Pharmacists, Am. Soc. Parenteral and Enteral Nutrition. Republican. Presbyterian. Achievements include development of 26 original computer programs to assist physicians and pharmacists with pharmacokinetic dosing and complete dosing calculations for Neonatal ICU and Adult Critical Care Total Parenteral Nutrition. Avocations: fishing, hunting, softball, skiing, travel. Home: 611 N Shore Dr Hastings NE 68901 Office Phone: 402-461-5138. Personal E-mail: grlay1@yahoo.com.

LAY, NORVIE LEE, law educator; b. Cardwell, Ky., Apr. 17, 1940; s. Arlie H. and Opha (Burns) L.; 1 dau., Lea Anne. BS, U. Ky., 1960; JD, U. Louisville, 1963; LL.M. (Cook fellow), U. Mich., 1964, S.JD, 1967. Bar: Ky. 1963. Asst. prof. law U. Louisville, 1964-67, assoc. prof., 1967-70, prof., 1970—; asst. dean U. Louisville (Sch. Law), 1971-73, assoc. dean, 1973-84, acting dean, 1981-82. Vis. prof. Southwestern U. Sch. Law, summer 1983, N.Y. Law Sch., 1983-84, Coll. of Law U. Iowa, summer 1989. Author: Tax and Estate Planning for Community Property and the Migrant Client, 1970; contbr. articles to profl. jours. Trustee St. Joseph's Infirmary, 1974-78, S.W. Jefferson Community Hosp., 1979-80, Suburban Hosp., 1981-84, Humana-Audubon Hosp., 1985-88, U. Louisville Law Sch. Alumni Found., from 1982-85; bd. dirs. Louisville Ballet, from 1982-88, Louisville Theatrical Assn., 1985-88, Louisville Art Gallery, 1984-87, Watertower Art Assn., 1986-89, Chamber Mus. Soc. of Louisville, 1985-88, Louisville Chorus, 1985-88, Ky. Contemporary Theatre, 1984, Ky. Country Day Sch., 1985-88, Ky. Arts Coun., 1991—; mem. Nat. Conf. Commrs. Uniform State Laws. Recipient Scholarship Key Delta Theta Phi, 1963, Outstanding Graduating Sr. award Omicron Delta Kappa, 1963 Fellow Am. Coll. of Trust and Estate Counsel (acad.), Am. Coll. Tax Counsel; mem. ABA, Ky. Bar Assn., Louisville Bar Assn., Am. Judicature Soc. Republican. Baptist. Office: U Louisville Sch Law Belknap Campus Louisville KY 40292-0001 Office Phone: 502-852-6374.

LAY, THORNE, geosciences educator; b. Casper, Wyo., Apr. 20, 1956; s. Johnny Gordon and Virginia Florence (Lee) L. BS, U. Rochester, 1978; MS, Calif. Inst. Tech., 1980. Rsch. assoc. Calif. Inst. Tech., Pasadena, 1983; asst. prof. geosciences U. Mich., Ann Arbor, 1984-88, assoc. prof., 1988-89; prof. U. Calif., Santa Cruz, 1989—, assoc. dean, 2003—05. Cons. Woodward Clyde cons., Pasadena, 1982-84; dir. Inst. Tectonics, 1990-94, chmn. earth sci. dept., 1994-2000; dir. Inst. Geophysics and Planetary Physics, 2002-05, assoc. dean math., 2003-05; chmn bd. dirs., Incorp. Rsch. Instns. Seismology 2005-. Author: Structure and Fate of Subducting Slabs, 1997; co-author: (with T.C. Wallace) Modern Global Seismology, 1995; contbr. numerous articles to profl. jours. NSF fellow, 1978-81, Guttenberg fellow Calif. Inst. Tech., 1978, Lilly fellow Eli Lilly Found., 1984, Sloan fellow, 1985-87, Presidential Young Investigator, 1985-90. Fellow Royal Astron. Soc., Am. Geophys. Union (Macelwane medal 1991), Soc. Exploration Geophysicist, Seismol. Soc. Am., AAAS; mem. Nat. Acad. Sci. (life assoc.). Home: 2114 Harborview Ct Santa Cruz CA 95062-1678

LAYBOURNE, GERALDINE B., broadcast executive; b. Plainfield, NJ, 1947; m. Kit Laybourne; children: Emily, Sam. BA art history, Vassar Coll., 1969; MS elem. ed., U. Pa., 1971. Former high sch. tchr.; joined Nickelodeon as program manager, 1980; created Nick at Nite, 1985; exec. v.p./gen. mgr. Nickelodeon/Nick at Nite, 1986—89, pres., 1989—96; vice chmn. MTV Networks, 1993—96; pres. Disney/ABC Cable Networks, NYC, 1996—98; co-founder and CEO Oxygen Media, NYC, 1998—. Bd. dirs. Insight Comm. Co., The YES Network, Nat. Coun. Families and TV. Bd. dirs. Nat. Coun. Families and TV, Children Affected by AIDS Found., Nat. Ctr. Children's TV, The Nat. Cable TV Assn., Vassar Coll. Named one of 25 Most Influential People in Am., Time mag., 1996; named to, Broadcasting Hall of Fame, 1995, Broadcasting and Cable Hall of Fame, 1995; recipient Idell Kaitz award, Nat. Cable and Telecom. Assn. Vanguard Awards, 1990, Film Muse award, NY Women, 1991, Entrepreneur of Yr. award, U. Mo., Kans. City, 1991, Women in Cable award, 1992, Genii award, Am. Women in Radio and TV, 1992, Govs. award, Nat. Acad. Cable Programming, 1993, Grand Tam award, Cable TV Adminstrn. and Mktg. Com., 1994, Spotlight award, Creative Coalition, 1995, Matrix award for broadcasting, N.Y. Women in Comm., 1996, award for disting. lifetime contbn. to children and TV, Annenberg Pub. Policy Ctr., 1997, Crystal Apple award, Mayor Rudy Giuliani, 2001, award for disting. lifetime contbn. to children and TV, Annenberg Pub. Policy Ctr., Matrix award for broadcasting, N.Y. Women in Comm., Spotlight award, Creative Coalition. Mem.: Nat. Cable TV Assn. (bd. dirs.), Cable Positive (hon. chair), NY Women in Film and TV (adv. bd.). Office: Oxygen Media 75 9th Ave Fl 7 New York NY 10011-7006

LAYBOURNE, STANLEY, computer technology company executive; CPA. With Touche, Ross & Co. (now Deloitte & Touche), 1972—85, audit ptnr., 1983—85; pres., CEO Scottscom Group, 1985—89; exec. v.p. Ovation Broadcasting Co., 1989—90; CFO, treas. Insight Enterprises, Inc., 1991—, sec., 1994—, exec. v.p. Tempe, Ariz., 2002—. Office: Insight Enterprises Inc 1305 W Auto Drive Tempe AZ 85284

LAYCOCK, HAROLD DOUGLAS, law educator, writer; b. Alton, Ill., Apr. 15, 1948; s. Harold Francis and Claudia Anita (Garrette) L.; m. Teresa A. Sullivan, June 14, 1971; children: Joseph Peter, John Patrick. BA, Mich. State U., 1970; JD, U. Chgo., 1973. Bar: Ill. 1973, U.S. Dist. Ct. (no. dist.) Ill. 1973, Tex. 1974, U.S. Dist. Ct. (we. dist.) Tex. 1975, U.S. Ct. Appeals (5th and 11th cirs.) 1975, U.S. Supreme Ct. 1976, U.S. Ct. Appeals (6th cir.) 1987, U.S. Ct. Appeals (8th cir.) 1994, U.S. Ct. Appeals (10th cir.) 1997, U.S. Ct. Appeals (3rd cir.) 2003. Law clk. to judge U.S. Ct. Appeals (7th cir.), Chgo., 1973-74; pvt. practice Austin, Tex., 1974-76; asst. prof. U. Chgo., 1976-80, prof., 1980-81, U. Tex., Austin, 1980—, endowed professorships, 1983-88, assoc. dean for acad. affairs, 1985-86, endowed chair, 1988—, assoc. dean for rsch., 1991—. Vis. prof. U. Mich., 1990; reporter com. on motion practice Ill. Jud. Conf., 1977-78. Author: Modern American Remedies, 1985, 3d edit., 2002, The Death of the Irreparable Injury Rule, 1991; mem. bd. advisors Religious Freedom Reporter, 1990-2001; contbr. articles to profl. jours. Adv. bd. Consumer Svcs. Orgn., Chgo., 1979-80; exec. bd. Ctr. for Ch./State Studies, DePaul U., Chgo., 1982-87; adv. com. on religious liberty Presbyn. Ch. U.S.A., 1983-88, advisor restatement of restitution, 1984-85, 97—; v.p. St. Francis Sch., 1990-92, bd. dirs., 1990—, pres. 1992-2001; bd. adv. J.M. Dawson Inst. Ch./State Studies, Baylor U., 1990—; judicial speech adv. com., Supreme Ct. of Tex., 2002; adv. com. jud. ethics Supreme Ct. Tex., 2004. Fellow AAAS, Internat. Acad. for Freedom of Religion and Belief; mem. AAUP (mem. com. on status of women in acad. profession 1982-85), Am. Law Inst. (mem. coun. 2001—), Chgo. Coun. Lawyers (v.p. 1977-78), Assn. Am. Law Schs. (chmn., sec. on remedies 1983, 94), chmn., sec. on constitutional law, 2000). Home: 8819 Chalk Knoll Dr Austin TX 78735 Office: U Tex Law Sch 727 E Dean Keeton St Austin TX 78705-3224 Business E-Mail: dlaycock@law.utexas.edu.

LAYCOCK, MARY CHAPPELL, gifted and talented education educator, consultant; b. Jefferson City, Mo., Jan. 11, 1915; d. Alvin E. and Ollie (Harris) Chappell; m. James Charles Laycock, June 22, 1937; children: Charles, Ann, Donald E., Jane. AB, Judson Coll., 1937; MA in Math. Edn., U. Tenn., 1961. Math. tchr. various, 1938-41; math. tchr. Kingsport (Tenn.) Jr. High Sch., 1942; math. coord. Oak Ridge (Tenn.) City Schs., 1956-68, high sch. math. tchr., 1945-68; math. specialist Nueva Ctr. for Learning, Hillsborough, Calif., 1968-98; cons. Hayward, Calif., 1990-97. Author many books including Mathematics for Meaning, The Fabric of Mathematics, Algebra in Concrete, Focus on Geometry, Hands On Mathematics for Secondary Teachers, Weaving Your Way from Arithmetic to Mathematics, 1993, The Magician's Castle Fantasy, 1995; developed documentary Don't Bother Me, I'm Learning, 12 videotapes on teaching manipulatives; contbr. articles to profl. jours. Recipient Calif. Educator award, 1989, Elem. Math. Tchr. award Calif. Math. Coun. and State of Calif., 1989, Award of Recognition Calif. Assn. for the Gifted, 1984, Glenn Gilbert Nat. Leadership award for outstanding contbns. to math. edn. Nat. Coun. Suprs. Math., 2003. Mem. NEA, Nat. Coun. Tchrs. Math., Oreg. Math. Coun., Calif. Math. Coun. (life), Fla. Math. Coun., Greater San Diego Math. Coun., San Mateo County Math. Coun., Calif. Assn. for the Gifted. Avocation: geometric art. Home and Office: 20655 Hathaway Ave Hayward CA 94541-3740 Office Phone: 510-782-1300. E-mail: info@activityresources.com.

LAYCRAFT, JAMES HERBERT, retired judge; b. Veteran, Alta., Can., Jan. 5, 1924; s. George Edward and Hattie (Cogswell) L.; m. Helen Elizabeth Bradley, May 1, 1948; children: James B., Anne L. BA, U. Alta., Edmonton, 1950; LLB, U. Alta., 1951; LLD (hon.), U. Calgary, Alta., 1986. Bar: Alta. Barrister Nolan Chambers & Co., Calgary, 1952-75; justice trial div. Supreme Ct. of Alta., Calgary, 1975-79; justice Ct. of Appeal of Alta., Calgary, 1979-85, chief justice of Alta., 1985-91, ret., 1991. Contbr. articles to law jours. Served to lt. Royal Can. Arty., 1941-46, PTO. Named officer, Order of Can., 2002. Mem. United Ch. of Can. Avocations: amateur radio, fishing. E-mail: lacrjh@telus.net.

LAYFIELD, ERIN MARIE, music educator; b. Long Beach, Calif., Sept. 28, 1977; d. P. Bradley and Dawn Marie Logan; m. Benjamin David Layfield, June 19, 1999; 1 child, Morgan Paige. BA, U. Nebr., 1999; MEd, N.D. State U., 2004. Cert. K-12 music tchr. N.C., 2004. Grad. tchg. asst. N.D. State U., Fargo, ND, 2001—04; music tchr. Wake Co. Pub. Schs., Raleigh, NC, 2004—.

LAYFIELD, LESTER JAMES, pathologist, educator; BS magna cum laude, U. Calif., Irvine, 1974; MD, UCLA, 1979. Diplomate in anatomic and clin. pathology, splty. cert. in cytopathology Am. Bd. Pathology; diplomate Nat. Bd. Med. Examiners; lic. physician, Calif., Utah, NC. Intern U. Wash., Seattle, 1979-80; resident UCLA, 1980-83, chief resident, 1983-84, adj. asst. prof. pathology, 1983-84, asst. prof. dept. pathology, 1984-89, assoc. prof., 1989-90; assoc. prof. dept. pathology U. Iowa Hosps. and Clinics, Iowa City, 1990-92, Duke U. Med. Ctr., Durham, N.C., 1992-96, dir. image analysis lab., 1992-97, chief surg. pathology, 1993-97, prof. dept. pathology, 1996-97; prof. dept. pathology, head anatomic pathology, dept. chmn. U. Utah, Salt Lake City, 1997—. Pathologist Childrens Cancer Study Group UCLA, 1984-90, dir. fine needle aspiration svc., 1984-90; co-dir. cytology U. Iowa Hosps. and Clinics, Iowa City, 1990-92; lectr. cytopathology at local, regional and nat. workshops. Contbr. articles to profl. jours., chpts. to books. Am. Cancer Soc. jr. fellow, 1982. Mem. Arthur Purdy Stout Soc., Papanicolaou Soc. Cytopathology, Internat. Acad. Cytology, Internat. Soc. Breast Pathology. Office: Health Scis Ctr Dept Pathology U Utah 50 N Medical Dr Dept U Salt Lake City UT 84132-0001

LAYISH, DANIEL T., internist; BA magna cum laude, Boston U., 1986, MD magna cum laude, 1990. Diplomate Am. Bd. Internal Medicine, Pulmonary Disease and Critical Care Medicine, Nat. Bd. Med. Examiners; ACLS, Advanced Trauma Life Support. Intern/resident, dept. internal medicine Barnes Hosp., St. Louis, 1990-93; pulmonary/critical care/sleep medicine fellow Duke U. Med. Ctr., Durham, N.C., 1994-97; critical care staff, assoc. med. staff Christian Hosp. Northeast, St. Louis, 1993-94; staff, Urgent Care Clinic Carolina Permanente, Raleigh, N.C., 1994-96. Contbr. articles to profl. jours. Recipient Med. Grad. award, Hewlett-Packard Co., 1990, Young Investigator and Alfred Soffer Rsch. awards, Am. Coll. Chest Physicians, 1995. Fellow ACP, Am. Coll. Chest Physicians, Am. Acad. Sleep Medicine; mem. AMA, Am. Thoracic Soc., Alpha Omega Alpha. Home: 1700 King Arthur Cir Maitland FL 32751-5820 Office: Ctrl Fla Pulmonary Group PA 326 N Mills Ave Orlando FL 32803-5734

LAYMAN, DALE PIERRE, medical educator, researcher, writer; b. Niles, Mich., July 3, 1948; s. Pierre Andre and Delphine Lucille (Lenke) L.; m. Kathleen Ann Jackowiak, Aug. 8, 1970; children: Andrew Michael, Alexis Kathryn, Allison Victoria, Amanda Elizabeth. AS in Life Sci., Lake Mich. Coll., 1968; BS in Anthropology and Zoology with distinction, U. Mich., 1971, MS in Physiology, 1974; EdS in Physiology and Health Sci., Ball State U., 1979; PhD in Health and Safety Studies, U. Ill., 1986. Histological technician in neuropathology U. Mich. Med. Sch., Ann Arbor, 1971-72, tchg. fellow in human physiology, 1972-74; instr. in human anatomy, physiology, and histology Lake Superior State U., Sault Ste. Marie, Mich., 1974-75; prof. med. terminology, human anatomy and physiology Joliet (Ill.) Jr. Coll., 1975—. Author: The Terminology of Anatomy and Physiology, 1983, The Medical Language: A Programmed Body-Systems Approach, 1995, Biology Demystified, 2003, Anatomy Demystified, 2004, Physiology Demystified, 2004, Medical Terminology Demystified, 2005; contbr. articles to profl. jours. Founder Robowatch. Mem. Ill. C.C. Faculty Assn. (campus coord.), London Diplomatic Acad. (mem. acad. coun.), European Acad. Informatization (cavalier-knight, prof.), Internat. Assn. Bus. Leaders (life), Phi Kappa Phi, Kappa Delta Pi. Avocations: running, swimming, reading motivational literature. Home: 509 Westridge Ln Joliet IL 60431-4883 Office: Joliet Jr Coll 1215 Houbolt Rd Joliet IL 60431-8938 Business E-Mail: drdlayman@sbcglobal.net.

LAYMAN, DAVID MICHAEL, lawyer; b. Pensacola, Fla., July 28, 1955; s. James Hugh and Winifred (Smith) L. BA with high honors, U. Fla., 1977, JD with honors, 1979. Bar: Fla. 1980. Assoc. Gunster, Yoakley, Criser & Stewart, West Palm Beach, Fla., 1980-83, Wolf, Block, Schorr & Solis-Cohen, West Palm Beach, 1983-87, ptnr., 1987-88; shareholder Shapiro and Bregman P.A., 1988-91, Greenberg, Traurig, Hoffman, Lipoff, Rosen & Quentel, P.A., West Palm Beach, Fla., 1991-93, Prom, Korn & Zehmer, P.A., Jacksonville, Fla., 1993-94, Mahoney Adams & Criser, P.A., Jacksonville, Fla., 1994-96, Greenberg, Traurig, P.A., West Palm Beach, Fla., 1996—. Mem. Attys. Title Ins. Fund. Contbg. editor U. Fla. Law Rev.; contbr. articles to profl. jours. Del. Statewide Rep. Caucus, Orlando, Fla., 1986; mem. Blue Ribbon Zoning Rev. Com., West Palm Beach, 1986; bd. dirs., pres. Palm Beach County Planning Congress, 1984-89; trustee South Fla. Sci. Mus., 1994-96; bd. dirs., sec., v.p. Ronald McDonald House, Jacksonville, 1994-96, Cultural Coun. of Greater Jacksonville; bd. dirs., pres.-elect Children's Pl. at Home Safe Inc., 1996—; mem. vestry, jr. warden Holy Trinity Episcopal Ch., West Palm Beach, 2002-03. Named one of Outstanding Young Men in Am., 1980. Mem. ABA, Fla. Bar Assn. (bd. govs. young lawyers divsn. 1989-91), Palm Beach County Bar Assn. (pres. young lawyers sect. 1987-88), Fla. Blue Key, Palm Beach County Gator Club (pres., bd. dirs.), Omicron Delta Kappa, Sigma Chi, Phi Kappa Phi. Episcopalian. Office: 777 S Flagler Dr Ste 300E West Palm Beach FL 33401-6161 Business E-Mail: laymand@gtlaw.com.

LAYMAN, KIM FLORINDA MARIE, pharmacist, writer; b. New Orleans, Oct. 1, 1959; d. Charles Clifton and Audrey Spann Layman. BS in Biochemistry, Xavier U., 1982, BS in Pharmacy, 1985, PharmD, 2000. Lic. pharmacist La., Ind. Staff pharmacist Ochsner Med. Found., New Orleans, 1985—88; pharmacist Deaconess Hosp., Evansville, Ind., 1989—91; clin. pharmacist West Jefferson Med. Ctr., Marrero, La., 1991—. Author: Poems for Everyday People, 1993, I Got Something to Say, 2002. Storyteller Layman's Pre-sch. Acad., New Orleans, 1982—. Mem.: S.E. La. Soc. Health Sys. Pharmacists, La. Soc. Health Sys. Pharmacists, Am. Soc. Health Sys. Pharmacists, Zeta Phi Beta. Roman Catholic. Avocations: French horn, jazz, yoga, reciting poetry, theater. Home: 2710 Pressburg St New Orleans LA 70122

LAYMAN, LAWRENCE, naval officer; b. Laclede County, Mo., Oct. 28, 1930; s. Archibald A. and Zoe Ellen (Hoke) L.; m. Carmen Elizabeth Meyer, Oct. 5, 1953; children: Linda Carmen, Lawrence, Harry Arthur, John Robert. BS, U.S. Naval Acad., 1952; MS in Internat. Affairs, George Washington U., 1972. Commd. ensign U.S. Navy, 1952, advanced through grades to rear adm., 1979; service to Korea and Vietnam; dep. comdr. Naval Telecommunications Command, 1978-79; dir. command, control and communications systems U.S. European Command, 1979-81; vice dir. Def. Communications Agy., Washington, 1981-83; dir. Naval Communications, Washington, 1983-86; dir. space command and control Office Chief Naval Ops., Washington, 1986-89, ret., 1989. Decorated D.S.M., Def. Superior Svc. medal with oak leaf cluster, Legion of Merit with Gold Star, Bronze Star with combat V, Meritorious Svc. medal. Home: 6800 Fleetwood Rd Unit 323 Mc Lean VA 22101 E-mail: llayman@cox.net.

LAYMON, JOE W., human resources specialist, automotive executive; married; 3 children. BA, Jackson State U.; MA, U. Wis. Various sr. human resouces positions including chief labor negotiator Xerox Corp., 1979—96; dir., v.p. human resources Kodak; with agency for internat. devel. U.S. State Dept.; exec. dir., human resources ops. Ford Motor Co., 2000—01, v.p. corp. human resources, 2001—03, group v.p., corp. human resources and labor affairs, 2003—. Bd. dirs. Am. Soc. Employers, Nat. Action Coun. Minorities in Engring., Douglas A. Fraser Ctr. Workplace Issues, Molex Inc., Nat. Tech. Inst. Deaf Rochester Inst. Tech., U. Wis., Human Resources Policy Assn., Am. Soc. Employers, Volvo Cars. Avocations: golf, cooking. Office: Ford Motor Co 1 American Rd Dearborn MI 48126-2798 Office Phone: 313-322-3000. Office Fax: 313-845-6073.*

LAYNE, JAMES NATHANIEL, vertebrate biologist; b. Chgo., May 16, 1926; s. Leslie Joy and Harriet (Hausmann) L.; m. Lois Virginia Linderoth, Aug. 26, 1950; children: Linda Carrie, Kimberly, Jamie Linderoth, Susan Nell, Rachel Pratt. BA, Cornell U., 1950, PhD, 1954. Grad. teaching asst. Cornell U., Ithaca, N.Y., 1950-54, asst. prof. zoology, 1963-67; asst. prof. zoology So. Ill. U., Carbondale, 1954-55; asst. prof., then assoc. prof. biology U. Fla., 1955-63; asst. curator, then assoc. curator mammals Fla. State Mus., Gainesville, 1955-63, research assoc., 1963-65; dir. research, then exec. dir. Archbold Biol. Sta.; Archbold curator mammals Am. Mus. Natural History, 1967-85; sr. rsch. biologist Archbold Biol. Sta., 1985-94, sr. rsch. biologist emeritus, 1994—. Rsch. assoc. Fla. State Collection of Arthropods, Am. Mus. Natural History; vis. scientist primate ecology sect. Nat. Inst. Neurol. Diseases and Blindness, summers 1961-62; adj. prof. biology U. South fla., 1968-89; adj. prof. biol. scis. Fla. Atlantic U., 1980-84. Contbr. articles and chpt. to profl. jours. and books. Hon. trustee Fla. Defenders of Environment; bd. dirs. Fla. Audubon Soc.; mem. Fla. Nongame Wildlife Adv. Council, Peace River Basin Bd., Fla. Panther Tech. Adv. Council. Served with USAAF, 1944-46. bd., Inst. of Environ. Studies U. of South Fla. Fellow AAAS; mem. Am. Soc. Zoologists, Am. Soc. Mammalogists (pres. 1970-72, hon. mem. 1993, C. Hart Merriam award 1976), Ecol. Soc. Am., Soc. for Study of Evolution, Am. Soc. Naturalists, Wildlife Soc., Wildlife Disease Assn., Nature Conservancy (trustee Fla. chpt.), Fla. Acad. Scis. (pres. 1984-85, medalist 1995), Orgn. Biol. Field Stas. (pres. 1986-87), Phi Beta Kappa, Sigma Xi, Phi Kappa Phi, Phi Sigma. Personal E-mail: jlayne@strato.net.

LAYNE, JONATHAN K., lawyer; b. July 16, 1953; BA in Econ., Coll. of William and Mary, 1975; JD with distinction, Emory Univ., Atlanta, 1979; MBA, Emory Univ., 1979. Bar: Ga. 1979, Calif. 1979. Joined Gibson Dunn & Crutcher LLP, LA, 1979—, now ptnr. and co-chair corp. transactions and securities practice group. Mem. exec. com, Gibson Dunn & Crutcher. Mng. editor Emory Law Jour., 1978—79. Bd. dir. Calif. C. of C.; past chmn. and pres. John Thomas Dye Sch. Mem.: ABA, LA County Bar Assn., State Bar of Calif., Order of Coif. Office: Gibson Dunn & Crutcher 2029 Century Pk E Los Angeles CA 90067-3026 Office Phone: 310-552-8641. Office Fax: 310-552-7053. Business E-Mail: jlayne@gibsondunn.com.

LAYTON, DONALD HARVEY, banker; b. May 9, 1950; s. Irving and Charlotte (Bell) L.; m. Sandra Lynn Lazo, June 1, 1974; children: Todd Samuel, Ross Charles. SB in Econs., SM in Econs., MIT, 1972; MBA, Harvard U., 1974. Rsch. asst. Harvard Bus. Sch., Boston, 1974-75; various positions through sr. mng. dir. Mfrs. Hanover Trust Co., N.Y.C., 1975-91; sr. exec. v.p. Chemical Bank, N.Y.C., 1992—95, vice-chmn., 1995, Chase Manhattan Bank, N.Y.C., 1995-2001, J.P. Morgan Chase & Co., N.Y.C., 2001—04. Mem. vis. com. for econs. MIT, 1999—; bd. dirs. Internat. Exec. Svc. Corps, 2004—, Partnership for the Homeless, 2004—; mem. internat. capital markets adv. coun. Fed. Res. Bank N.Y., 1999—. Gov. Fgn. Policy Assn., 1998—. Baker scholar Harvard U., 1974. Office: JP Morgan Chase & Co 277 Park Ave Fl 42 New York NY 10172 Office Phone: 212-622-9095. Personal E-mail: dhlaytonny@aol.com.

LAYTON, HARRY CHRISTOPHER, art director; b. Safford, Ariz., Nov. 17, 1938; s. Christopher E. and Eurilda (Welker) L.; m. Karol Barbara Kendall, July 11, 1964 (div. Jan. 1989); children: Deborah, Christopher, Joseph, Elisabeth, Faith, Aaron, Gretchen, Benjamin, Justin, Matthew, Peter. LHD, Sussex Coll., Eng., 1969; RE (hon.), PhD (hon.), DRE (hon.), St. Matthew U., Ohio, 1970; DFA (hon.), DSc (hon.), London Inst. Applied Rsch., Ohio, 1972. Cert. clin. hypnotherapist. Pres., mgr. Poems, Art & Myths; pres., CEO Layton Studio Graphic Design, L.A. Lectr. ancient art Serra Cath. H.S., Gardena, Calif., 1963-64, L.A. Dept. Parks and Recreation, summers 1962-64; interior decorator Cities of Hawthorne, Lawndale, Compton, Gardena, and Torrance, Calif., 1960-68. One-man shows Nahas Dept. Stores, 1962, 64; group shows include Gt. Western Savs. & Loan, Lawndale, 1962, Gardena Adult Sch., 1965, Serra Cath. H.S., 1963, Salon de Nations, Paris, 1983; represented in permanent collections Sussex Coll., Culver City-Foshey Masonic Lodge, Gt. Western Savs. & Loan; paintings inlcude The Fairy Princess, 1975, Nocturnal Covenant, 1963, Blindas Name, 1962, Creation, 1962; author numerous poems. Elder LDS Ch., Santa Monica, Calif., 1963—. Mem. Am. Hypnotherapy Assn., Internat. Soc. Artists, Internat. Platform Assn., Am. Security Coun., Soc. for Early Hist. Archaeology, Am. Councilor's Soc. Psychol. Counselors, Salon des Nation Paris Geneva, Ctr. Internat. Art Contemporain, Internat. Soc. Poets (disting.), Internat. Masonic Poetry Soc., Am. Legion, Masons (32d degre), Shriners, KT, Alpha Psi Omega. Republican. Home and Office: Layton Studio Graphic Design Inc 3654 Centinela Ave Apt 10 Los Angeles CA 90066-3147 Office Phone: 310-390-0543. E-mail: LSGD@comcast.net, PoetLayton@hotmail.com.

LAYTON, ROBERT GLENN, radiologist; b. Bklyn., Oct. 14, 1946; s. Irving and Charlotte (Bell) L.; m. Judith Helene Bohrer, May 31, 1969; children: Andrew, Julia. BS, Union Coll., 1968; MD, Boston U., 1972. Diplomate Am. Bd. Radiology. Resident in radiology Boston City Hosp., 1972-75; jr. attending radiologist L.I. Jewish Hosp., Hillside, N.Y., 1975-76; staff radiologist Cedars Med. Ctr., Miami, Fla., 1978-98, chief of radiology, 1999—2003; assoc. med. dir. MedSolutions Inc., Franklin, Tenn., 2004—. Radiologist Highland Park Gen. Hosp., Miami, 1978-84; clin. asst. prof. U. Miami Sch. Med., 1985-87. Pres. Michael-Ann Russell Jewish Cmty. Ctr., Miami, 1980-82; bd. dirs. Jewish Cmty. Ctrs. South Fla., 1982-86; trustee Temple Sinai of North Dade, North Miami Beach, 1982-01, v.p., 1985-92, pres., 1992-94; nat. bd. dirs. Union Am. Hebrew Congregations, trustee, 1999-2004. Served to maj. USAF, 1976-78. Mem. AMA, Am. Coll. Radiology, Colo. Radiol. Soc., Begg Soc., Alpha Omega Alpha. Avocations: contemporary art, skiing, golf. Office Phone: 615-468-4181. Personal E-mail: rglmd1@yahoo.com.

LAYTON, VIRGINIA H., academic administrator; b. Cleve., Feb. 16, 1951; d. Robert E. and Virginia W. Hodgins; m. Dale L. Layton, Sept. 2, 1972; children: Andrew, Chad, Robert. BS, Miami U., Oxford, Ohio, 1991, MBA, 2003. From asst. bursar to assoc. bursar Miami U., Oxford, 1993—2000, bursar, 2000—. Mem.: Ohio Bursars Assn. (pres.-elect 2004—05, bd. dirs. 2002—04), Kiwanis Internat. (bd. dirs. Oxford chpt. 2004—). Avocations: swimming, travel.

LAYTON, WILLIAM GEORGE, retired management consultant, human resources executive, import/export company executive; b. Missouri Valley, Iowa, Sept. 11, 1931; s. George Holbert and Margaret (Wilson) L.; m. Caroline R. Tiffany, June 27, 1953; children: Kathleen Layton Medl, Sara Layton Howe, Thomas William. BA, Coe Coll., 1953; MA, U. Ill., 1955. Indsl. rels. trainee Procter & Gamble Co., Cin., 1955-57, pers. specialist, 1957-62, indsl. rels. mgr. France, 1962-66, pers. mgr. European Tech. Ctr., 1966-69, pers. mgr. internat., 1969-72; v.p. human resources Food Svc. div. Heublein, Inc., Louisville, 1972-77; sr. v.p. human resources Holiday Inns, Inc., Memphis, 1977-83; pres. The Layton Group, St. Petersburg, Fla., 1983—2001; sr. ptnr. Johnson-Layton Co. Mgmt. Cons., L.A. and St. Petersburg, 1985-95; pres. CompCom, Inc., 1994-97; chmn., CEO Appliances Internat., Inc., 1997—2002. Bd. dirs., pres. Jr. Achievement of Memphis, 1981-83; mem. Tenn. Jobs Tng. Coordinating Coun., 1982-88; mem. Pvt. Industry Coun. of Memphis and Shelby County, 1982-88; mem. Pres.'s Coun., Rhodes Coll., Memphis, 1983-90. Served with USAF, 1953-55. Mem.: Coun. Mgmt. Cons. (Sr. Examiner Sterling Quality award Fla. 1994), Inst. Mgmt. Cons. (cert. mgmt. cons.), Am. Mgmt. Assn. (human resources coun. 1981—83), Rotary, Phi Beta Kappa. Republican. Presbyterian. E-mail: wglayton@citcom.net.

LAZAR, ANNA, chemist; b. Budapest, Hungary, Jan. 10, 1931; came to U.S. 1956; d. Lajos and Maria (Grits) Varga; m. Joseph Lazar, Apr. 11, 1955 (div. 1969); 1 child, Julie Anna. Diploma, Eötvös Lorand Sci. U., Budapest, 1955. Chemist Harvard U., Boston, 1957-59, Arthur D. Little, CAmbridge, Mass., 1959-61, Wilkens Instrument and Rsch., Lafayette, Calif., 1961-62, Stanford (Calif.) U., 1962-63, Hercules Inc., Wilmington, Del., 1964-69, Cancer Rsch. Inst., Fox Chase Phila., Pa., 1969-70, Food and Drug Administrn., Phila., 1970--. Roman Catholic. Business E-Mail: alazar@ora.fda.gov.

LAZAR, CHARNA L., retired CIA Officer, private investigator, consultant; BA in Polit. Sci., CCNY, 1968; Cert. in French Lang. & Civilization, U. Paris, 1973; MS in Pub. Adminstrn., George Wash. U., 1979. Lic. pvt. investigator Fla., 2003. Polit. coord. Robert F. Kennedy Presdl. Campaign, Garden City, NY, 1968; clandestine svc. officer US CIA, Washington, 1969—94; pvt. investigator, security cons. Wonder Woman Investigations, Boca Raton, Fla., 2003—; adj. prof. Fla. Atlantic U., 2005—. Regional coord. Safe Cmty. Initiative (Am. Jewish Com. & local police agencies), Boca Raton, Fla., 2003—; adj. prof. Fla. Atlantic U. Grad. Boca Raton Citizens Police Acad., Boca Raton, 1995; mem. fundraising com. Boca Helping Hands, 2003; cert. mem. Cmty. Emergency Response Team, 2003—; v.p. Boca Raton Dog Club, 1999—2001; elected mem. Palm Beach County Dem. Exec. Com., 2000—04; dem. candidate Fla. Ho. Reps., 2001—02; exec. v.p. New Dem. Club Boca-Delray, 2000—02; exec. vice-chair Va. Women's Polit. Caucus, 1979—81; candidate Palm Beach County Commn., 2004; mem. ambassadorial com. Am. Jewish Com., Palm Beach, Fla., 2001—; life mem. Ctrl.

Intelligence Retirees Assn., McLean, Va., 1994; chpt. v.p. Assn. Former Intelligence Officers, 2000. Mem.: Assn. Former Intelligence Officers (life; Palm Beach County chpt. v.p. 2000), Ctrl. Intelligence Retirees Assn. (life; SE Fla. chpt. sec. 1995—2001), Boca Raton Dog Club (v.p. 1999—2001), Boca Raton Martin Luther King Meml. Found. (assoc.; fund-raising com. 1997—2003), Am. Mensa, Weimaraner Club of South Fla. (bd. dirs.). Democrat. Avocations: pure-bred dogs (weimaraners), public speaking (homeland security issues), political activism & consulting. Office: PO Box 272482 Boca Raton FL 33427-2482

LAZAR, HAROLD LEE, cardiothoracic surgeon; AB, Boston U., 1970, MD, 1974. Diplomate Am. Bd. Surgery, Am. Bd. Thoracic Surgery. Resident in gen. surgery U. Mich. Med. Ctr., Ann Arbor, 1974-81; rsch. fellow in cardiac surgery UCLA Med. Ctr., 1977-79; fellow in cardiothoracic surgery Columbia-Presbyn. Med. Ctr., N.Y.C., 1981-83; attending surgeon Univ. Hosp., Boston, 1984—, Boston City Hosp., 1984—, VA Med. Ctr., Boston, 1990—. Asst. dir. thoracic surgery Boston City Hosp., 1990—; chmn. Mass. Consortium Lung Transplantation, Boston, 1992; from asst. prof. to prof. cardiothoracic surgery Med. Sch., Boston (Mass.) U., 1984-98, prof., 1998—. Editor: Current Therapy for Acute Coronary Ischemin, 1993; mem. editl. bd. Jour. Thoracic and Cardiovascular Surgery, 2002-. Fellow ACS, Am. Coll. Cardiology, Mass. Med. Soc.; mem. Am. Coll. Chest Physicians (sec. sect. cardiac surgery 1993—), Am. Assn. Thoracic Surgery, Soc. Thoracic Surgery, Soc. Univ. Surgeons. Office: Boston U Med Ctr 88 E Newton St Boston MA 02118-2308 Office Phone: 617-638-7350. E-mail: harold.lazar@bmc.org.

LAZAR, IRVING, psychologist; b. N.Y.C., Feb. 20, 1926; s. Charles and Sylvia L.; m. Jules M. Marquart, Dec. 24, 1981; children: Kathryn S., James Bradford, Richard Alan. BS, CCNY, 1948; MA, Columbia U., 1950, PhD, 1954. Intern Menninger Clinic, Topeka, 1946—47; instr. clin. psychology U. Rochester, NY, 1948—49; instr. psychology Bard Coll., Amandale-on-Hudson, NY, 1949—50; instr. child devel. U. Ill. Coll. Edn., Urbana, 1950—54; assoc. chief mental health sect. Nev. State Dept. Health, Las Vegas, 1954—60; dir. Peterson-Guedel Family Ctr., Beverly Hills, Calif., 1960—64; exec. dir Neumeyer Found., Beverly Hills, 1963—68; western mgr. Kirschner Assoc., L.A., 1968—70; assoc. dir. Appalachian Regional Commn., Washington, 1969—72; prof. dept. human svc. studies Cornell U., 1972—91, prof. emeritus, 1991—; external faculty Santa Fe Inst., 1994—99; rsch. prof. Peabody Coll. Vanderbilt U., Nashville, 1991—98, resident scholar Kennedy Ctr. Rsch. Human Devel. Peabody Coll., 1991—. Cons. in field. Contbr. articles to profl. jour. Trustee Coalition for Quality Children's Media, Santa Fe, 1994—. Rsch. Fellow Population Inst., East-West Ctr., Honolulu, 1987. Home: 313 Cana Cir Nashville TN 37205 Office Phone: 615-354-1505. Business E-Mail: irving@santafe.edu.

LAZAR, JILL SUE, home healthcare company executive; b. Oak Park, Ill., June 15, 1954; d. Norton David and Carol Ellen (Kaufmann) Freyer; m. Bruce Horwich, Aug. 21, 1976 (div. Sept. 1982); 1 child, Mathew Freyer Horwich; m. Neil Lazar, Nov. 23, 1986. BS in Mktg., No. Ill. U., 1975. Mktg. rsch. assoc. McDonald's Corp., Oak Brook, Ill., 1976-80; renewal coord. Time, Inc., Chgo., 1984-87; product mgr. Macmillan Directory Div., Wilmette, Ill., 1987-92; with DependiCare, Broadview, Ill., 1992—. Mem. provider adv. panels Chad Therapeutics, Aradigm Corp., others. Mem. Chgo. Health Execs. Forum. Avocations: swimming, reading. Office: DependiCare 1815 Gardner Rd Broadview IL 60155-4401

LAZAR, JOHN EDWARD, social services administrator, not-for-profit developer; b. Bklyn., Mar. 24, 1950; s. John and Elizabeth (Titch) Lazar. BA, St. John's U., Bklyn., 1971; postgrad., Bklyn. Coll., 1972-73; MDiv, Sem. of Immaculate Conception, 1980. Ordained Roman Cath. Ch., 1980; cert. tchr. N.Y. English tchr. N.Y.C. Bd. Edn., Bklyn., 1973-79; clergyman Roman Cath. Diocese of Bklyn., 1980-93; pres. POMOC, Inc., N.Y.C., 1981-84; dir. housing Argus Cmty., Inc., Bronx, N.Y., 1993-96; devel. cons. Met. Cmty. Ch., L.A., 1997—; exec. dir. San Fernando Valley Am. Cancer Soc., Sherman Oaks, Calif., 1998—2001; regional v.p. Greater Bay Area Redwood Empire region Am. Cancer Soc., 2001—. Exec. dir. Peregrinatio Ad Petri Sedem-U.S. Office of Pilgrimages, Vatican City, 1985—86. Author: Outpouring the Spirit: Gay and Lesbian Spirituality in the Judeo Christian Tradition, 1996. Commr. City of West Hollywood Lesbian and Gay Adv. Bd., Calif., 1998—2001, co-chair; bd. dirs. City Vol. Corps, N.Y.C., 1990—96; v.p. Polish Am. Congress, N.Y.C., 1989—93; co-prodr. civic celebration Bklyn. Outdoor Mus. Art, 1993; mem. com. Mayor's Planning Com. L.A. Vol. Festival, 1998, 1999; chmn. N.Y.C. Compter.'s Polish Adv. Com., 1982—89, 1994—96; panelist City of West Hollywood Town Hall Election, 2000; co.-chmn. fin. Alice B. Toklas GLBT Dem. Club, 2002—05; co-chmn. PAC Alice B. Toklas GLBT Dem. Club, 2005—; bd. dirs. Stonewall Dem. Club, L.A. Named Hon. Alumnus, Our Lady of the Lake Sem., 1982, Citizen of Yr., Polish Am. World, 1982; recipient Pres.'s award, Stonewall Dem. Club, 1998, Commendation award, N.Y.C. Comptr., 1995. Mem.: Polish Inst. Arts and Scis. in Am., Inc., So. Calif. Assn. Non Profit Housing, Inc., Commonwealth Club (Moderator LGBT Spirituality Panel 2004, chmn. GLBT forums 2005—). Democrat. Avocations: bicycling, reading, prestidigitation, downhill skiing. Home: 2790 19th Ave # 21 San Francisco CA 94132 Office: Am Cancer Soc 1700 Webster St Oakland CA 94612 Office Phone: 415-394-7100. Personal E-mail: JELazer324@aol.com.

LAZAR, JONATHAN KUMIN, computer scientist, educator; b. Columbia, Md., Sept. 24, 1974; s. Martin J. and Libby Kumin Lazar. BBA magna cum laude, Loyola Coll., 1995; MS, PhD, U. Md., Balt., 1999. Asst. prof. computer and info. scis. Towson U., Md., 1999—, assoc. prof., 2004—; affiliate prof. Ctr. Applied Info. Tech., Towson, 1999—. Dir. undergraduate comp. info. sys. Towson U., 2003—, dir. Universal Usability Lab., 2003—. Author: (book) User-Centered Web Development, 2001; mem. editl. rev. bd. Info. Resources Mgmt. Jour., 2001; author, editor: Managing IT/Community Partnerships in the 21st Century, 2002; author: Web Usability: A User Centered Design Approach, 2005; contbr. articles to profl. jours.; assoc. editor: Jour. Informatics Edn. and Rsch., 2003—. Recipient Fr. Daniel J. McGuire Alumni Assn. award, Loyola Coll., 1995, Bronze medal for nat. Latin exam, Am. Classical League, 1990; grantee, Johns Hopkins U./U.S. Ctrs. for Disease Control, 2001—02, Curriculum grantee, Shriver Ctr./Learn and Serve Am., 2000, 2002. Mem.: Info. Resource Mgmt. Assn., Assn. Computing Machinery (chmn. spl. interest group 2001 conf. 2000—01, co-chair 2003 conf. workshops 2002—03, spl. interest group computer human interaction), Green and Grey Soc., Alpha Sigma Nu, Phi Kappa Phi, Beta Gamma Sigma (v.p. 1994—95), Upsilon Pi Epsilon (faculty advisor 2000—01), Omicron Delta Kappa (faculty advisor 1999—2004, Faculty Advisor of Yr. 2000). Office: Towson U Dept COSC 8000 York Rd Towson MD 21252

LAZAR, JULIAN HAMPTON, minister; b. Florence, S.C., Nov. 16, 1927; s. Jamie Tarlton and Mary Alice (Jordan) L.; m. Sara Edna Stoddard, Sept. 2, 1950; children: David Tarlton, John Hampton. BA, Wofford Coll., 1951; BD, Duke U., 1955. Min. Van Wyck United Meth. Ch., 1954-57, St. John's United Meth. Ch., Blacksburg, S.C., 1957-61, Lyman United Meth. Ch., S.C., 1965-72, Epworld United Meth. Ch., Rock Hill, S.C., 1961-65, Union United Meth. Ch., 1972-77, Trinty United Meth. Ch., Sumter, S.C., 1977-81, St. Paul's United Meth. Ch., Orangeburg, S.C., 1981-85, St. Paul United Meth. Ch., Florence, S.C., 1985-93, ret., 1998, min. emeritus. Mem. sr. citizen's bd. Florence County, S.C.; chmn., bd. trustees Meth. Oaks Ret. Ctr., Orangeburg, S.C. Mem. Rotary.

LAZAR, LUDMILA, concert pianist, music educator; b. Celje, Slovenia; married; two children. MusB, Roosevelt U., 1963, MusM, 1964; D of Musical Arts, Northwestern U., 1987. Faculty Roosevelt U., Chgo., 1967—, prof. piano Chgo. Musical Coll., 1988—, prof. emerita, 2003—, chmn. keyboard dept., 1983—2003. Lectr., demonstrator in field. Roosevelt U. rsch. grantee, 1988, 96; recipient Goethe Inst. award, 1987, Outstanding Coll. Tchr. award Roosevelt U., 1981; named to All Star Profs. Team Chgo. Tribune, 1993. Mem. AAUP, Music Tchrs. Nat. Assn. (master tchr. cert. 1991), European Piano Tchrs. Assn., Ill. State Music Tchrs. Assn., Soc. Am. Musicians (pres., v.p.), Coll. Music Soc., Musicians Club of Women (v.p.), Mu Phi Epsilon (pres., v.p.). Office: Roosevelt U 430 S Michigan Ave Chicago IL 60605-1394 Office Phone: 312-341-3779.

LAZAR, MAX SEYMOUR, retired pharmaceutical company executive; b. Bklyn., Dec. 6, 1943; s. Harry and Bessie L.; m. Sherry Dorf, Sept. 5, 1965; children: Lawrence Jay, Lisa Jill. BA in Chemistry, CUNY, 1966. Lab. analyst, supr. Hoffmann-LaRoche Inc., Nutley, NJ, 1966—69; dir. quality control Roche Vitamins & Fine Chems., Belvidere, NJ, 1969—86, dir. tech. svcs., 1986—88, divsnl. dir. quality assurance Nutley, NJ, 1988—89; asst. v.p., dir. corp. quality assurance Hoffmann-LaRoche Inc., Nutley, NJ, 1989—93, v.p. quality assurance, 1993—94, v.p. FDA and drug enforcement adminstrn. (DEA) compliance, 1994—2001; ret., 2001; pres. FDA Regulatory Compliance Cons., Surprise, Ariz., 2001—. Vice-chair pharm. waters expert com. USP, 2000—; U.S. Pharmacopea. Mem. editl. bd. Jour. Current Good Mfg. Practices, 1997—; contbr. articles to profl. jours., including Pharm. Tech. Bd. dirs. Parkette Nat. Gymnastics Tng. Ctr., Allentown, Pa., 1980-2001. Recipient Spl. citation, USA FDA Commr., 2004. Mem. Am. Chem. Soc., Pharm. Rsch. & Mfrs. Assn. (expert work group topic leader for active pharm. ingredients Internat. Conf. on Harmonization Q7A), Am. Soc. Quality. Avocations: amateur radio operator, photography. Home and Office: 15359 W Sierra Vista Dr Surprise AZ 85374 Office Phone: 623-556-0556. E-mail: maxslazar@aol.com.

LAZAR, PAUL ALAN, actor; b. Norwalk, Conn., Mar. 26, 1955; s. Albert Aaron and Carol (Bettman) L.; m. Annie B. Parson, Dec. 5, 1987. Student, Bennington Coll., 1978. Actor, theatre games leader, improvisation tchr. Irondale Ensemble Project, N.Y.C., 1983—. Appeared in (films) Streamers, 1983, Married to the Mob, 1987, Silence of the Lambs, 1989, Twenty Ninth Street, 1990, (tv shows) Gideon Oliver, 1987, Dolan Street, 1988, Miami Vice, 1988, (stage) The False Servant, 2005. Office: Irondale Ensemble Project PO Box 150604 Brooklyn NY 11215-0604*

LAZAR, RANDE HARRIS, otolaryngologist; b. N.Y.C., Feb. 27, 1951; s. Irving and Dorothy (Tartasky) L.; m. Linda Zishuk, Aug. 11, 1974; 1 child, Lauren K. BA, Bklyn. Coll., 1973; MD, U. Autonoma de Guadalajara, Mexico, 1978; postgrad., N.Y. Med. Coll., 1978-79. Diplomate Am. Bd. Otolaryngology-Head and Neck Surgery; lic. physician, N.Y., Ohio, Tenn. Gen. surgery resident Cornell-North Shore Community Hosp., Manhasset, N.Y., 1979-80, Cleve. Clinic Found., 1980-81, otolaryngology-head and neck surgery resident, 1980-84, chief resident dept. otolaryngology & communicative disorder, 1983-84; physician Otolaryngology Cons. Memphis, 1984—. Fellow pathology head and neck dept. otolaryngologic pathology Armed Forces Inst. Pathology, Washington, 1983; pediatric otolaryngology fellow Le Bonheur Children's Med. Ctr., Memphis, 1984-85, dir. pediatric otolaryngology fellowship tng., 1989—, chief surgery, 1989, chief staff East Surgery Ctr.; chmn. dept. otolaryngology head and neck surgery Meth. Health Systems, 1990-91; courtesy staff Bapt. Meml. Hosp., Bapt. Meml. Hosp.-East, Eastwood Med. Ctr., Meth. Hosp., Germantown, Tenn.; chief dept. otolaryngology Les Passees Rehab. Ctr., 1988—. Contbr. articles to profl. jours. Bd. dirs. Bklyn. Tech. Found. Recipient award of honor Am. Acad. Otolaryngology-Head and Neck Surgery, 1991. Fellow Internat. Coll. Surgeons; mem. AMA, Am. Acad. Otolaryngology-Head and Neck Surgery, Am. Acad. Facial Plastic and Reconstructive Surgery, Am. Acad. Otolaryngic Allergy, Centurions Deafness Rsch. Found., Am. Auditory Soc., Nat. Hearing Assn., Soc. Ear, Nose Throat Advances in Children, Am. Soc. Laser Medicine and Surgery, So. Med. Assn., N.Y. Acad. Scis., Tenn. Med. Soc., Tenn. Acad. Otolaryngology-Head and Neck Surgery, Memphis and Shelby County Med. Soc., Memphis/Mid South Soc. Pediatrics Office: Otolaryngology Cons Memphis 791 Estate Pl Memphis TN 38120 E-mail: Lazarent@aol.com.

LAZAR, RAYMOND MICHAEL, lawyer, educator; b. Mpls., July 16, 1939; s. Simon and Hessie (Teplin) L; children: Mark, Deborah. BBA, U. Minn., 1961, JD, 1964. Bar: Minn. 1964, U.S. Dist. Ct. Minn. 1964. Spl. asst. atty. gen. State of Minn., St. Paul, 1964-66; pvt. practice Mpls., 1966-72; ptnr. Lapp, Lazar, Laurie & Smith, Mpls., 1972-86; ptnr., officer Fredrikson & Byron P.A., Mpls., 1986—. Lectr. various continuing edn. programs, 1972—; adj. prof. law U. Minn., Mpls., 1983-99. Fellow Am. Acad. Matrimonial Lawyers; mem. ABA (chair divorce laws and procedures com. family law sect. 1993-94), Minn. Bar Assn., Hennepin County Bar Assn. (chair family law sect. 1978-79). Home: 400 River St Minneapolis MN 55401 Office: Fredrikson & Byron PA 4000 Pillsbury Ctr Minneapolis MN 55402-3314 Office Phone: 612-492-7121. E-mail: rlazar@fredlaw.com.

LAZAR, THEODORE AARON, retired manufacturing executive, lawyer; b. Chgo, Ill, July 16, 1920; s. Philip and Rena (Goodman) L.; m. Betty Jean Papermaster, July 6, 1952; children: Mark D., Paul A., Nancy Paula. JD, John Marshall Law Sch., Chgo., 1951. Bar: Ill. 1951, Wis. 1962, Ohio 1966. Sole practice, Chgo., 1951-62; asst. corp. counsel City of Chgo., 1956-59; atty. NLRB, Chgo., 1962—64, L.A., 1964—65; corp. counsel Lancaster Colony Corp., Columbus, Ohio, 1965-83, v.p. law, 1983-88, ret., 1988. Sgt. Air Corps U.S. Army, 1942—46. Mem. Columbus Bar Assn. Home: 270 Bryant Ave Columbus OH 43085-3009

LAZAR, ZOE L., psychologist; b. N.Y.C., June 27, 1948; d. Ira Gerald and Charlotte (Silverstein) Levy; m. Ira Lazar, Apr. 5, 1970; children: Alexander David, Samantha Chloe, Damien Jacob. BA, Brandeis U., 1969; MEd, Boston U., 1972, EdD, 1974; cert. in psychoanalysis, William Alanson White Inst., N.Y.C., 1984. Lic. psychologist, N.Y. Intern in clin. psychology McLean Hosp./Harvard U. Med. Sch., Belmont, Mass., 1973-74; staff psychologist out-patient clinic Coney Island Hosp., Bklyn., 1974-75; pvt. practice psychology and psychoanalysis Scarsdale, N.Y., 1976—; instr. psychology in psychiatry Cornell U. Med. Coll., NY, 1978—82, clin. asst. prof. psychology in psychiatry, 1982—; profl. assoc. in psychology N.Y. Hosp., 1978-82, asst. attending psychologist, 1982—. Pub. BaBoom Press, 2002. Contbr. articles to profl. jours. Cornell U. fellow, 1975-77. Mem. APA, N.Y. State Psychol. Assn., Westchester Psychol. Assn., William Alanson White Soc. Avocations: theater, dance, hiking, gardening, bicycling. Office Phone: 914-723-4893. Personal E-mail: zoelazer@yahoo.com.

LAZARAN, FRANK, former retail executive; b. 1957; BS, Calif. State U., Long Beach; Master, Calif. State U. Group v.p. sales, advt. and merchandising Ralphs Grocery Co., Compton, Calif.; sr. v.p. sales & merchandising Randalls Food Markets Inc., Houston, 1997—99, pres., 1999—2002; exec. v.p., COO Winn-Dixie Stores, Inc., Jacksonville, Fla., 2002—03, pres., CEO, 2003—04. Mem. bd. dirs. Winn-Dixie Stores, Inc., 2003—04.

LAZARCHICK, JOHN, hematologist, educator; b. Pottsville, Pa., Nov. 1, 1942; s. John and Ann (Peshock) L.; m. Lynda Lazarchick; 1 child, John Jeffery. BA, Lafayette Coll., Easton, Pa., 1964; MD, Jefferson Med. U., 1968. Asst. prof. U. Conn. Health Sci. Ctr., Farmington, Conn., 1977-79; from asst. prof. to prof. Med. U. S.C., Charleston, 1979—. Author: Clinical Hematology and Fundamentals of Hemostasis, 1988; contbr. over 100 articles to profl. jours. Lt. comdr. USN, 1972-75. Rsch. grantee NIH, 1980-83, Ames, Miles Laboratories, 1985-90, Wyeth-Ayerst Corp., 1989-91. Fellow ACP; mem. Assn. Clin. Scientists (chmn. immunohematology, 1988—), Am. Soc. Hematology, Hematopathology Soc. Office: 171 Ashley Ave Charleston SC 29425-0001

LAZARCIK, GREGOR, economist, educator, financial research company executive; b. Horna Streda, Slovakia, Mar. 10, 1923; came to U.S., 1953, naturalized, 1958; s. Gaspar and Maria (Rehak) L.; m. Theresa M. Good, Aug. 14, 1971. BS, State Coll., Slovakia, 1945; MS, Coll. Agr., Brno, Czechoslovakia, 1948; cert., Swiss Inst. Tech., Zurich, 1949; AM, U. Strasbourg, France, 1952; LLM, LLD (fellow), U. Paris, 1953; PhD (fellow), Columbia, 1960. Asst. to mgr. Ctrl. Cutter Dairy, Lucerne, Switzerland, 1948-49; controller dairy products Agrl. Syndicate, Hazebruck, France, 1949-50; with Rsch. Project on Nat. Income Columbia U., N.Y.C., 1956-00, sr. rsch. economist, 1961-70, seminar assoc., 1970—; pres., chmn. bd. L.W. Internat. Financial Rsch., Inc., N.Y.C., 1961-00. Lectr. econs. Hunter Coll., CUNY, 1963-64, Columbia U., 1964-68; prof. econs. SUNY, 1968-85, CUNY, 1984—. Author: Le Commerce en Matiere Agricole Entre l'Europe de l'Ouest et l'Europe deL'Est, 1959; co-author: Czechoslovak National Income and Product, 1947-56, 1962, The Performance of Socialist Agriculture, 1963, Scientific Research and its Relation to Earnings and Stock Prices, 1965, Comparison of Agricultural and Nonagricultural Income, 1937, 48-65, 1968, Defense, Education and Health Expenditures and Their Relation to GNP in Eastern Europe, 1978, Economic Growth in Eastern Europe, 1965-82, 1983, Agricultural Output and Productivity in Eastern Europe and Some Comparisons with the USSR and USA, 1985; contbr. to East European Economics Post-Helsinki, 1977, Pressure for Reform in the East European Economics, Joint Econ. Com., U.S. Congress, 1989, The Development of the Private Sector in East Central Europe, 1993, Overview of Transportation Infrastructure in East Central Europe, 1994, The Status of and Prospects for Agriculture in East Central Europe, 1996, Energy in Eastern Europe: Production, Consumption, and Trade, 1970-1987, 1999. Mem. Am. Econ. Assn., Am. Regional Sci. Assn., Assn. Comparative Economic Studies, Am. Assn. Advancement Slavic Studies. Roman Catholic. Address: 100 La Salle St Apt 17-b New York NY 10027-4730 E-mail: gregorlazarcik@aol.com.

LAZARE, AARON, dean, psychiatrist; b. Newark, Feb. 14, 1936; s. H. Benjamin and Anne (Storfer) L.; m. Louise Cannon; children: Robert, Jacqueline, David, Sam, Sarah, Hien, Thomas, Naomi. AB, Oberlin Coll., 1957; MD, Case Western Reserve U., 1961. Intern in medicine Bronx (N.Y.) Mcpl. Hosp. Ctr., 1961-62; resident in psychiatry Mass. Mental Health Ctr., 1962-65; asst. in psychiatry Mass. Gen. Hosp., Boston, 1967-68; chief day hosp. inpatient unit Yale-New Haven Hosp., 1967-68; assoc. dir. adult outpatient psychiatry Mass. Gen. Hosp., Boston, 1968-70, dir. adult outpatient psychiatry, 1970-75, acting dir. residency tng., 1972, dir. outpatient psychiatry, 1975-82, dep. chief psychiatry, 1976-82, clin. dir. psychiatry, 1978-82; prof., chmn. dept. psychiatry U. Mass. Med. Ctr., Worcester, 1982—90, interim dean, 1989-90, dean, 1990—, chancellor, 1991—. Prof. Harvard U., 1982. Editor: Outpatient Psychiatry, 1979, 1989, 2nd edit.; contbr. articles to profl. jours.; co-author of books in field. Capt. U.S. Army, 1965-67. Named for Disting. Pub. Svc. Commonwealth of Mass., honorable mention U. Mass., 1987, Commonwealth of Mass., U. Mass., Boston, 1988, Brotherhood award NCCJ, 1992, Maimonides award for outstanding commitment as a physician and educator Anti-Defamation League New Eng., 1993, Friend and Leader award Mass. Assn. Mental Health Inc., 2001. Mem. AAAS, AMA, Am. Psychiat. Assn. (Benjamin Rush award 1992), Mass. Psychiat. Soc. Office: U Mass Med Ctr Off Chancellor 55 Lake Ave N Worcester MA 01655-0002

LAZAREFF, JORGE ANTONIO, neurosurgeon, researcher; b. Buenos Aires, Jan. 11, 1953; s. Nicolas and Vera (Budinska) L.; m. Ines Garcia Lloret, May 28, 1982; children: Nicolás, Ana Maria. MD, Nat. Univ. Buenos Aires, 1977. cert. neurosurgeon Edu. Comm. for Foreign Med. Grads., 1980, Mexican Coun. Neurosurgeons, 1991, Medical Bd. of Calif., 1993, Colegio Argentino de Neurocirujanos, 1996. Resident in neurosurgery Hosp. de Niños, Buenos Aires, 1979-83; chief resident in neurosurgery Hosp. Fernandez, Buenos Aires, 1983-84; registrar in neurosurgery Groote Schuur Hosp., Red Cross Meml. Children Hosp., Cape Town, 1984-86; rsch. fellow dept. surgery U. Alberta, Edmonton, Can., 1986-88; head dept. exptl. surgery Hosp. Infantil de Mexico, 1988-91, head dept. neurosurgery, 1991—93; assist. prof. dept. neurosurgery UCLA Med. Ctr., Los Angeles, Calif., 1993—99, dir. pediatric neurosurgery, 1997—, assoc. prof. dept. neurosurgery, 1999—, co. dir., Cerebral Palsy Clinic, co. dir., Pediatric Brain Tumor Prog. Mem. rsch. com. Hosp. Infantil de Mexico, 1991. Inventor biopsy probe for sterotactic brain surgery; separated conjoined twins, 2002; author papers on neurosurgery and neurophistology. Recipient Rsch. award for spasticity Aaron Saenz Found., 1991, Ulrich Batzdorf, M.D. Faculty Teaching award, 2001. Mem. Soc. for Neurosci., 1991, Sociedad Mexicana de Cirugia Neurologica, 1992, Research Soc. of Neurological Surgeons, 1993, Internat. Soc. for Pediatric Neurosurgery, 1993, Academic Senate, UCLA, 1994, Johnson Comprehensive Cancer Ctr. 1994. Roman Catholic. Office: UCLA Med Ctr Divsn Neurosurgery PO Box 957039 Los Angeles CA 90095-7039

LAZARIDIS, MIKE, information technology executive; b. Istanbul, Mar. 14, 1961; married; 2 children. DEng (hon.), U. Waterloo. Founder, pres., co-CEO Rsch. in Motion, 1984—; founder Perimeter Inst., 2000—. Chancellor U. Waterloo, 2003—. Named one of World's 100 Most Influential People, Time Mag., 2005; recipient technical Emmy award, 1994, Oscar award for a film bar-code reader, 1999. Achievements include over 30 patents in field; development of BlackBerry. Office: Rsch in Motion Ltd 295 Phillip St N2L 3W8 Waterloo ON Canada

LAZARIS, PAMELA ADRIANE, community planning and development consultant; b. Dixon, Ill., Oct. 13, 1956; d. Michael Christ and Ellen Euridice (Eftax) L.; m. Eugene Dale Monson, Oct. 17, 1987; children: Anthony Edward, Anna Adriane. BFA in Fine Arts, U. Wis., Milw., 1978; MS in Urban and Regional Planning, U. Wis., 1982; MBA, U. St. Thomas, 1992. Analyst planning Wis. Dept. Natural Resources, Madison, 1979-82; asst. city planner City of Albert Lea, Minn., 1982-83; specialist community devel. City of Winona, Minn., 1983-85; dir. community devel. City of Waseca, Minn., 1985-98; assoc. Real Estate Dynamics, Inc., Madison, Wis., 1998-99; prin. Planning Svc. and Solutions, Lake Mills, Wis., 1999—. Vol. spl. events Farmam-Minn. Agrl. Interpretive Ctr., Waseca, 1985-86; mem. Waseca County Econ. Devel. Commn., 1989-98; com. dir. Waseca Area Found., 1989-98; mem. dist. 2 city coun. City of Lake Mills, Wis., 1999—, city plan commn., 1999—; troop 148 advancement coord. Boy Scouts Am., 2002-. Named one of Oustanding Young Women of Am., 1986. Mem. Am. Inst. Cert. Planners (cert.), Am. Planning Assn. (chpt. bd. dirs. 1986-89), Minn. Planning Assn. (v.p. 1989-90, dist. bd. dirs. 1985-89), Toastmasters (chpt. sgt.-at-arms 1987, ednl. v.p. 1988, 91-98), Lake Mills Area C. of C. Avocations: public speaking, travel, art. Home: PO Box 17 Lake Mills WI 53551-0017 Office: 110 E Madison St Lake Mills WI 53551-1644 Business E-Mail: pal@gdinet.com.

LAZARNICK, SYLVIA, secondary school educator; b. Bklyn., Feb. 6, 1949; d. Emanuel and Karin Lazarnick; m. Timothy Taylor Beaman, June 18, 1973. BA, Bklyn. Coll., 1969; MA, Pa. State U., 1971. Math. tchr. Class. High Sch., Springfield, Mass., 1971-72, Alternative High Sch., Lakewood, N.J., 1972-73, Broadmeadows (Australia) Tech. Sch., 1975-77, Neshaminy-Langhorne (Pa.) High Sch., 1979, Rice Meml. High Sch., Burlington, Vt., 1979-80, Bellows Free Acad., St. Albans, Vt., 1980—2004. Bd. dirs. Franklin County Food Coop., St. Albans; coach Vt. All Stars; coach BFA Math League Team; bd. dirs. Convergence. Mem. Nat. Coun. Tchrs. Math., Assn. Tchrs. Math. in New Eng. (program co-chair fall meeting 1994), Vt. Coun. Tchrs. Math. (pres. 1995-97, finalist Presdl. award for excellence in math. tchg. 1996). Avocations: reading, rock climbing, skiing, hiking, bicycling. Home: 578 Swamp Rd Fairfield VT 05455-9733

LAZAROW, MARTIN SIDNEY, lawyer, accountant; b. Schenectady, N.Y., July 10, 1937; BS, SUNY, Albany, 1968, MS, 1969; LLB, JD, Albany Law Sch., 1966. CPA; Bar: N.Y. 1966, U.S. Dist. Ct. (no. dist.) N.Y. 1966, U.S. Tax Ct. 1967, U.S. Ct. Appeals (2d cir.) 1994. Mem. acctg. faculty Bus. Sch., SUNY, Albany; counsel to Com. on Taxation N.Y. State Senate, Albany; counsel to Zoning Bd. Appeals Town of Clifton, N.Y., town justice; sole practitioner Clifton Park. With U.S. Army, 1956-59, France. Mem. numerous profl. orgns. Office: PO Box 284 Clifton Park NY 12065 also: 313 Ushers Rd Ballston Lake NY 12019 Office Phone: 518-877-9250.

LAZAROW, ROBIN S., lawyer; b. Atlantic City, N.J., Dec. 20, 1958; d. Joseph Aron and Fredlyn (Pogach) Lazarow. BA, U. Pa., 1981; JD, Rutgers U. Sch. Law-Newark, 1988. Bar: N.J. 1989, U.S. Dist. Ct., dist. N.J. 1989, U.S. Tax Ct. 1989, Mass. 2001. Assoc. Brach, Eichler, Rosenberg, Silver, Hammer & Gladstone, PC, Roseland, N.J., 1988—90, Witman,Stadmauer & Michaels, PA, Florham Park, N.J., 1990—98, ptnr., 1998—2000; assoc. Mirick, O'Connel, DeMallie & Lougee, LLP, Worcester, Mass., 2000—. Adj.

prof. The Stillman Sch. of Bus., Seton Hall U., Newark, N.J., 1993—98. Author: (article) IRS, DOL & PBGC Audits of Retirement Plans, 2003; contbg. author: book ERISA: A Comprehensive Guide, 2003, 2004. Mem. personnel com. United Way of Ctrl. Mass., Inc., 2002—; corporator, mem. personnel com. Children's Friend, Worcester, 2003—; mem. advisory bd. Ctr. for Women and Enterprise, Boston, 2004—; bd. dirs. Montachusett Girl Scouts Coun., Worcester, 2004—. Mem.: Worldwide Employee Benefits, Inc. (Mass. Metrowest chpt., pres. 2001—, bd. dirs. nat. bd., Wash.; program chair; ea. region dir.-at-large 1997—2001), IRS Northeast Pension Liasion Group, ABA (mem. section of taxation, employee benefits com. 1989—), Am. Soc. Pension Profls. & Actuaries (assoc.; mem. Dept. Labor subcom. of Govt. Affairs com. 2004—). Office: Mirick O'Connell DeMallie & Lougee LLP 1700 W Park Dr Westborough MA 01581 Office Phone: 508-791-8500. Office Fax: 508-791-8502. Business E-Mail: rslazarow@modl.com.

LAZARUS, ALLAN MATTHEW, retired newspaper editor; b. New Orleans, Nov. 21, 1927; s. Harry Adolph and Edna Mary (Wodiker) L.; m. Martha Elizabeth Ellis, July 26, 1946; children— Kenneth Wayne, Virginia Lynn BA in History, Centenary Coll., 1951. Copy boy The Times, Shreveport, La., 1944-45, reporter, 1945-46, telegraph editor, 1947-58, news editor, 1958-69, mng. editor, 1969-90. Pulitzer Prize Juror, 1978; pres. La.-Miss. AP Assn., 1977-78. Cpl. USAF, 1946—47. Mem.: Soc. Profl. Journalists (pres. Ark.-La.-Tex. chpt. 1971—72), AP Mng. Editors's Assn. (bd. dirs. 1975—80). Roman Catholic. Home: 7713 Tampa Way Shreveport LA 71105-5701

LAZARUS, ARNOLD ALLAN, psychologist, educator; b. Johannesburg, Republic of South Africa, Jan. 27, 1932; came to U.S., 1963; s. Benjamin and Rachel Leah (Mosselson) L.; m. Daphne Ann Kessel, June 10, 1956; children: Linda Sue, Clifford Neil. BA with honors, U. Witwatersrand, Johannesburg, 1956, MA, 1957, PhD, 1960. Diplomate: Am. Bd. Profl. Psychology, Am. Bd. Med. Psychotherapists (fellow), Internat. Acad. Behavioral Medicine, Counseling and Psychotherapy. Pvt. practice clin. psychology, Johannesburg, 1959-63, 64-66; vis. asst. prof. dept. psychology Stanford (Calif.) U., 1963-64; prof. psychology Temple U. Med. Sch., Phila., 1967-70; dir. clin. tng. Yale U., New Haven, 1970-72; disting. prof. Rutgers U., New Brunswick, N.J., 1972-98; pres. Ctr. for Multimodal Psychol. Svcs., Princeton, NJ, 1998—2005; exec. dir. Lazarus Inst., Skillman, NJ, 2005—. Mem. adv. bd. Psychologists for Social Responsibility, 1984—; cons. in field. Author: (18 books including) Behavior Therapy and Beyond, 1971, Multimodal Therapy, 1981, rev. edit., 1989, In the Mind's Eye, 1984, Martial Myths, 1985, Mind Power: Getting What You Want Through Mental Training, 1987, The Essential Arnold Lazarus, 1991, A Dialogue with Arnold Lazarus, 1991, Don't Believe It For A Minute!, 1993, Abnormal Psychology, 1995, Brief But Comprehensive Psychotherapy, 1997, The 60 Second Shrink, 1997, I Can If I Want To, 2000, Marital Myths Revisited, 2001, Dual Relationships and Psychotherapy, 2002; editl. bd.: sci. jours.; contbr. articles to profl. jours. Recipient Disting. Svc. award Am. Bd. Profl. Psychology, Disting. Career Achievement award Am. Bd. Med. Psychotherapists, Outstanding Contbns. to Mental Health award Psychiat. Outpatient Ctrs. of the Americas, 1991, Presdl. award ACA, 2003, NJ Psychol. Assn., 2003. Fellow APA (Disting. Psychologist award divsn. of psychotherapy 1992, 1st Ann. Cummings Psyche award 1996, Disting. Profl. Contbns. award Divsn. Clin. Psychology 1997), Am. Bd. Profl. Psychology (diplomate), Internat. Acad. Eclectic Psychotherapists, Acad. Clin. Psychology, Am. Psychotherapy Assn. (mem. exec. adv. bd. 2001—); mem. Internat. Assn. Marriage and Family Counselors (Disting. Presenter Series award 2000), Am. Acad. Psychotherapy, Assn. for Advancement Psychotherapy, Nat. Acads. Practice in Psychology (disting.), Soc. for Exploration of Psychotherapy Integration, Calif. Psychol. Assn. (Lifetime Achievement award 1999), Assn. Advancement Behavior Therapy (Lifetime Achievement award 1999), Internat. Assn. Marriage and Family Counselors (Disting. Presenter award 2000), Am. Counseling Assn. (presdl. award 2003), N.J. Psychol. Assn. (presdl. award 2003). Home: 56 Herrontown Cir Princeton NJ 08540-2924 E-mail: aalaz@aol.com. *To respect others for their exceptional capacities, but never to deify them, enables one to learn from others instead of envying them and denigrating oneself. This egalitarian view transforms acquisitiveness, power, and aggression into love, intimacy, and productive activity.*

LAZARUS, ARTHUR, JR., lawyer; b. Bklyn., Aug. 30, 1926; s. Arthur and Frieda (Langer) L.; m. Gertrude Chiger, Jan. 8, 1956; children: Andrew Joseph, Edward Peter, Diana Ruth. BA with honors, Columbia U., 1946; JD, Yale U., 1949. Bar: N.Y. 1951, D.C. 1952, U.S. Supreme Ct. 1954. Assoc. Fried, Frank, Harris, Shriver & Jacobson, Washington, 1950-57, ptnr., 1957-91, mng. ptnr. Washington office, 1974-86; of counsel Sonosky, Chambers, Sachse, Endreson & Perry, LLP, Washington, 1994—. Vis. lectr. Yale Law Sch., 1973-81. Trustee Arena Stage, 1987-98, Georgetown Day Sch., 1963-71. Home: 3201 Fessenden St NW Washington DC 20008-2032 Office Phone: 202-682-0240. Business E-Mail: ALazarus@Sonosky.com.

LAZARUS, DAVID, physicist, researcher; b. Buffalo, Sept. 8, 1921; s. Barney B. and Lillian (Markel) L.; m. Betty Jane Ross, Aug. 15, 1943; children: Barbara, William, Mary Ann, Richard. BS, U. Chgo., 1942, MS, 1947, PhD, 1949. Instr. electronics U. Chgo., 1942-43, electronics engr., 1946-49, instr. physics, 1949; research assoc. radio research lab. Harvard, 1943-45; mem. physics faculty U. Ill., Urbana, 1949—, prof., 1959—. Vis. prof. U. Paris, 1968-69, M.I.T., 1978-79, Harvard U., 1978-79; vis. scientist Am. Inst. Physics, N.Y.C., 1962-69; cons. Phys. Sci. Study Com., 1957-59, Hallicrafters Co., Chgo., 1957-69, Gen. Electric Co., Cin., 1960-68, Gen. Atomic, La Jolla, Calif., 1962-63, Lawrence Radiation Lab., 1967-68, Sandia Lab., 1970-72, Addison-Wesley Pub. Co., Reading, Mass., 1964-80; dir. Council on Materials Sci., U.S. Dept. Energy, 1981-85 Author: (with H. de Waard) Modern Electronics, 1966, (with R.I. Hulsizer) The World of Physics, 1972, (with M. Raether) Practical Physics: How Things Work, 1979; also articles. Guggenheim fellow, 1968-69 Fellow AAAS, Am. Phys. Soc. (coun. 1974-78, 80-91, exec. com. 1980-91, editor-in-chief 1980-91, publs. com. 1980-91, exec. com. div. contensed matter physics 1968-70, 74-78, chmn. New Materials prize com. 1976, chmn. Buckley prize com. 1979); mem. Am. Inst. Physics (governing bd. 1981-92, exec. com. 1981-89, publs. policy com. 1981-92). Home (Summer): PO Box 484 Chilmark MA 02535-0484 Home: 502 W Vermont Ave Urbana IL 61801 Personal E-mail: d-lazars@uiuc.edu.

LAZARUS, DAVID, journalist; Crime reporter Daily (Californian) at Berkeley; columnist Japan Times; with San Francisco Chronicle, 1999—. Contbg. writer: Fortune, Wired, Salon.com, Nat. Geographic; author: two books. Recipient Journalist of Yr. award, Consumer Fedn. Calif., 2004, C. Everett Coop award,-2003, Nat. Headliner award, 2002, Calif. Journalism award, Ctr. Calif. Studies Calif. State U., 2002, John Jacobs award, 2001, Journalist of Yr. award, Soc. Profl. Journalists, 2001. Office: San Franccisco Chronicle 901 Mission St San Francisco CA 94103-2988 Office Phone: 415-777-8827. Business E-Mail: dlazarus@sfchronicle.com.

LAZARUS, FRED, IV, academic administrator; b. NYC, Jan. 1, 1942; s. Fred and Irma (Mendelson) L.; m. Jonna Gane, Nov. 27, 1970; children: Anna Mendelson, Fred Lazarus V. BA, Claremont McKenna Coll., 1964; MBA, Harvard U., 1966; PhD (hon.), Osaka U. Arts. Staff assoc. Nat. Council for Equal Bus. Opportunity, Washington, 1969-71; pres. Washington Council for Equal Bus. Opportunity, 1971-74; exec. asst. to chmn. Nat. Endowment for Arts, Washington, 1975-78; pres. Md. Inst. Coll. Art, Balt., 1978—. Vice chmn. Assn. Ind. Colls. Art and Design, 1992-96; trustee Alliance for Ind. Colls. Art, 1978-91, chmn., 1984-86, 89-91; founding chmn. Nat. Coalition for Edn. in Arts, 1988-90; bd. dirs. Midtown Devel. Corp. Trustee St. Paul's Sch., 1988—96, Am. Coun. for Arts, 1980—97, sec., 1991—94; trustee Amns. for the Arts, 1998—, chmn., 1998—2001; trustee Md. Art Place, 1988—96; trustee emeritus Ptnrs. for Livable Places; bd. dirs. Afro-Am. Newspapers, 1990—2003, Balt. Artists Housing Corp.; chmn. Balt. Coun. for Equal Bus. Opportunity, 1978—2002; trustee Md. Ind. Coll. and Univ. Assn., 1978—, vice chmn., 1995—99, chmn., 1999—2003; mem. Thurgood Marshall Meml. Statue Commn., 1996—98; bd. dirs. Greater Balt. Cultural Alliance, 2001—, chmn., 2001—04. Recipient mayor's art award, City of Balt., 1988. Mem. Harvard Club (N.Y.C.) Office: Md Inst Coll Art 1300 W Mount Royal Ave Baltimore MD 21217-4134 Office Phone: 410-669-9200. Business E-Mail: flazarus@mich.edu.

LAZARUS, GERALD SYLVAN, dermatologist, educator, dean; b. NYC, Feb. 16, 1939; s. Joseph W. and Marion (Goldstein) Lazarus; m. Sandra Jacob, Sept. 3, 1961 (dec. 1985); children: Mark, Elyse, Lynne, Laura; m. Audrey Fedyszyn Jakubowski, Apr. 7, 1990. BA, Colby Coll., 1959; MD, George Washington U., 1963. Intern, then resident U. Mich., Ann Arbor, 1963—64, resident in medicine, 1964—65; rsch. asso. NIH, Bethesda, Md., 1965—68; resident in dermatology Harvard U., Cambridge, Mass., 1968—70; rsch. fellow Strangeways Labs., Cambridge, England, 1970—72; assoc. prof. medicine, co-dir. dermatology tng. program Albert Einstein Med. Coll., N.Y.C., 1972—75; J. Lamar Callaway prof. Duke U., Durham, NC, 1977—82, chief dermatology, 1975—82; Milton B. Hartzell prof. U. Pa. Sch. Medicine, Phila., 1982—, chmn. dept. dermatology, 1982—93; dean Sch. Medicine U. Calif., Davis, 1993—97; vis. scholar U. Calif., Inst. Health Policy Rsch., San Francisco, 1997—98; prof. dermatology, biol. chemistry U. Calif. Scholar Inst. for Health Policy, 1998—99; dean, prof. emeritus U. Calif. Davis Sch. Medicine, 1999—; prof. dermatology Johns Hopkins Med. Inst., Balt., 2002—; dir. Johns Hopkins Medicine Wound Healing Ctr. Sr. investigator Arthritis Found., 1972—77; mem. study sect. NIH, 1976—80; prof. dermatology U. Calif., San Francisco; faculty Inst. of Health Policy; advisor to univ. pres. and hosp. dir. advisor Ministry of Health; vis. prof. Peking Union Med. Coll., Beijing, 1999—2002; advisor to pres. Peking Union Med. Coll. Hosp.; co-dir. China Med. Be. Mgmt. Program. Author (with L. Goldsmith): Diagnosis of Skin Disease, 1980; author: (with Herman Beerman) Tradition of Excellance: History of Dermatology at Univ. Pa. Sch. of Medicine; contbr. numerous articles to profl. jours. Bd. trustees George Washington U., DC, 2005. Served with USPHS, 1965—68. Fellow John Simon Guggenheim, U. Geneva, 1986; grantee, NIH. Fellow: ACP, Am. Soc. Clin. Investigation, Assn. Am. Physicians; mem.: Am. Acad. Dermatology (Sultzberger award 1986), Biochem. Soc., Soc. Investigative Dermatology (pres. 1996—97, dir., Disting. Alumnus award George Washington U. 1996), Am. Dermatol. Assn. (Carl Herzog fellow 1970—72). Republican. Jewish. Home: 2010 Bennett Point Rd Queenstown MD 21658 Office: Johns Hopkins Bayview Med Ctr 4940 Eastern Ave Baltimore MD 21224 Office Phone: 410-550-4724. Business E-Mail: lazaruspumc@hotmail.com.

LAZARUS, HAROLD, management educator; b. N.Y.C., Jan. 16, 1927; s. Louis and Anna (Fritz) L.; m. Carol Nunes, June 22, 1952 (dec. Aug. 9, 1987); children: Mark Leander, Eric Lewis. BA in Econs. and Philosophy cum laude, NYU, 1949; MS in Mktg., Columbia U., 1952, PhD in Mgmt., 1963. Asst. prof. mgmt. Hofstra U., Hempstead, N.Y., 1952-63, dean Sch. Bus., 1973-80, also mem. Pres.'s and Provost's Adv. Couns, Mel Weitz Disting. prof. bus., 1980—; prof. mgmt. Grad. Sch. Bus. Adminstrn., NYU, N.Y.C., 1963-73; fellow Internat. Acad. Mgmt., 1989. Research dir. manpower lab. AT&T, N.Y.C., 1970-71; adj. prof. Columbia U. Grad. Sch. Bus. and Tchrs. Coll., N.Y.C., 1969-70; lectr. Harvard U. Grad. Sch. Bus. Adminstrn., Cornell U. Sch. Indsl. and Labor Relations, NBC-TV, UN Office Tech. Cooperation, Advanced Mgmt. Sch. IBM, Fgn. Svc. Inst. U.S. Dept. State, Athens Sch. of Piraeus, Greece, SUNY Stony Brook; mgmt. cons. to govt. agys. and industry; bd. dirs. N.Am. Mgmt. Coun., World Mgmr. Coun.; bd. dirs. Paragon Fin. Corp., MyTurn.com, The Sweet Life, Inc., CompuDawn, Inc., Graham-Field Health Products, Inc., Stage II Apparel Corp., Ideal Toy Corp., Labtron Sci. Corp., Patient Tech., Inc., Diamond Med., Inc., Bristoline, Inc., Ventilator Corp., Medisco, Inc., ExNewt, Inc., M.E. Team, Inc., Graham-Field Temco, Inc., Diplomat Electronics Corp., Aquatherm Corp., Health and Med. Techniques, Inc., Graham Field Distbn., Inc., Graham Field Bandage, Inc., Graham Field Health Care Products Corp., Graham Field European Distbn. Corp., Health Team, Inc., Continental Plastics Corp., Ideal Internat. Ind., Interstate Molding & Hobbing Co., Crown Recreation Inc., Superior Surg. Mfg. Co., Rust Warehousing Corp., Alabe Products Inc., BINY Inc., Superior Surg. Mfg. Co.; mem. planning com. 21st World Mgmt. Coun., 1989; chmn. bd. The Sweet Life, Inc.; lectr. numerous bus. orgns., govt. agys., hosps., univs.; cons. to deans, presidents, chairs and faculty numerous univs. Author: The American Business Dictionary, 1957, (with E. Tomeski) People-Oriented Computer Systems, The Computer in Transition, 1975, rev. edit., 1983,; mem. editorial bd. Acad. Mgmt. Jour., 1969-70; editor: Human Values in Management, 1968; editor: (with others) The Progress of Management: Process and Behavior in a Changing Environment, 2d edit., 1972, 3d edit., 1977; mem. editorial rev. bd. Acad. Mgmt. Rev., 1986-87; mem. editorial adv. bd. The Jour. Mgmt. Devel., 1988—, editor spl. issues, 1993-94; sr. editorial advisor Ency. Mgmt., 1978-2005; contbr. chpts. and intros. to books, articles to bus. jours. With USN, 1945-46 Recipient award for teaching excellence NYU, 1972; recipient award for teaching excellence Hofstra U., 1985; Tchr. of Yr. award Hofstra U., 1987; Met. Life Ins. Co. fellow, 1965; War Service scholar, 1946-49; Columbia U. fellow, 1949-50; Bronfman Found. fellow, 1960-62; Ford Motor Co. fellow, 1964 Fellow Internat. Acad. Mgmt.; mem. Middle Atlantic Assn. Colls. Bus. Adminstrn. (past pres.), Eastern Acad. Mgmt. (past pres.), N.Am. Mgmt. Coun. (past pres.), Soc. for Advancement Mgmt. (past v.p.), Acad. Mgmt. (past dir.), AAUP (past pres. Hofstra U. chpt.), LWV, NOW, Phi Beta Kappa (pres. alumna and alumni of L.I., chmn. 1980-2001), Beta Gamma Sigma, Beta Alpha Psi, Mu Gamma Tau, Omicron Chi Epsilon, Pi Delta Epsilon Home: TH8 20191 E Country Club Dr Aventura FL 33180-3015 Office: Hofstra U Dept Mgmt Weller Hall Hempstead NY 11550 Office Phone: 516-463-5734. Personal E-mail: hallaz@bellsouth.net.

LAZARUS, KENNETH ANTHONY, lawyer; b. Passaic, N.J., Mar. 10, 1942; s. John Joseph and Margaret (Di Cenzo) L.; m. Marylyn Jane Flemming, Aug. 13, 1966; children: Maggi Ann, John, Joseph. BA, U. Dayton, 1964; JD, U. Notre Dame, 1967; LLM in Taxation, George Washington U., 1971. Bar: N.J. 1967, U.S. Tax Ct. 1970, U.S. Ct. Claims 1970, U.S. Supreme Ct. 1971, D.C. 1976. Trial atty. U.S. Dept. Justice, 1967-71; assoc. counsel and chief counsel to Minority Com. on Judiciary, U.S. Senate, 1971-74; assoc. counsel to Pres. U.S., 1974-77; ptnr. Bierbower & Rockefeller, 1977—81, Ward, Lazarus & Grow, Washington, 1981—91; of counsel Dixon & Jessup, Washington, 1991-97, Krooth & Atlman, 1997—. Mem. adv. bd. Sch. Law Dayton U., 1975-85; adj. prof. Sch. Law Georgetown U., 1979—; mem. U.S. Adv. Com. on Trade Negotiations, 1983-87; chmn. Sailors and Mchts. Bank and Trust Co., Vienna, Va., 1987-89. Mem. adv. bd. Houston Jour. Internat. Law, 1983-90; contbr. numerous articles to profl. publs. U.S. reporter to UN, 1975-77; mem. adv. coun. Rep. Nat. Com., 1977-80; mem. Presdl. transition team Office of Pres.-Elect, 1980-81; caucus mgr. George Bush, Rep. Conv., 1988; trustee Internat. Law Inst., pres., 1990-92. Mem.: ABA, Am. Judicature Soc., N.J. Bar Assn., Fed. Bar Assn., Bar Assn. D.C., D.C. Bar Assn., Am. Law Inst. (life). Home: 4501 Connecticut Ave NW Apt 716 Washington DC 20008-3712 Office: Lazarus & Assocs 1850 M St NW Ste 400 Washington DC 20036-5815 Office Phone: 202-457-0380.

LAZARUS, MELL, cartoonist; b. NYC, May 3, 1927; s. Sidney and Frances (Mushkin) L.; m. Eileen Hortense Israel, June 19, 1949; children: Marjorie, Suesan, Catherine; m. Sally Elizabeth Mitchell, May 13, 1995. Cartoonist-writer Miss Peach, 1957—, Momma, 1970—; author anthologies Miss Peach, Miss Peach, Are These Your Children?, Momma, We're Grownups Now!; novels The Boss is Crazy, Too, 1964, The Neighborhood Watch, 1986; plays Everybody into the Lake, Elliman's Fly, Lifetime Eggcreams, 1969-70; juvenile Francine, Your Face Would Stop a Clock, 1975; co-author Miss Peach TV spl. programs Turkey Day Pageant and Annual Heart Throb Ball. Trustee Internat. Mus. Cartoon Art; with USNR, 1945, USAFR, 1951-54. Mem. Nat. Cartoonists Soc. (pres. 1989-93, chmn. membership com. 1965, nat. rep., Humor Strip Cartoonist of Yr. 1973, 79, Reuben award 1981, Silver T-Square award 2000), Writers Guild Am. West, Nat. Press Club, The Century Assn., Am. Mensa, Sigma Delta Chi. Office: Creators Syndicate Inc 5777 W Century Blvd Los Angeles CA 90045-5600 Personal E-mail: kpop3@aol.com.

LAZARUS, PENNY CYD, music educator; b. Pittsburg, Pa., May 11, 1957; d. Norman Nathan and Pearl Ruder Lazarus; m. Joshua Reid Faigen, May 24, 1997; children: Adlai Faigen, Max Faigen. BS, BA, Univ. of Pitts., Pitts., Pa., 1975—79, MA, 1981—84. Cert. soc. sci. in ed. Univ. of Pitts./Pitts., Pa., 1987. Acad. adv. Univ. of Pitts., Pitts., 1984—89; adj. asst. prof. Carnegie Mellon Univ., Pitts., 1991—93; music ed. of piano pvt. studio, Pitts., 1993—2000, Newbury, Mass., 2000—. Lectr. Mid. Atlantic Symposium, 1983, Am. Studies Assoc., 1990. Curator (art exhibitions) Columbus Quincent., 1992. Nature Habitat Dir. Kelly Sch., Newburyport, Mass., 2003. Recipient Nationality Rm. Scholarship for Travel Abroad, Univ. of Pitts., 1982; fellow Andrew Mellon Pre-Doctoral Fellow, 1990—91. Mem.: Music Tchr. Nat. Assoc., Newburyport Choral Society. Democrat. Jewish. Avocations: book club, gourmet, gardening, swimming. Home: 313 Merrimac St Newburyport MA 01950

LAZARUS, ROCHELLE BRAFF (SHELLY LAZARUS), advertising executive; b. NYC, Sept. 1, 1947; d. Lewis L. and Sylvia Ruth (Eisenberg) Braff; m. George M. Lazarus, Mar. 22, 1970; children: Theodore, Samantha, Benjamin. AB, Smith Coll., 1968; MBA, Columbia U., 1970. Product mgr. Clairol, NYC, 1970-71; account exec. Ogilvy & Mather, NYC, 1971-73, account supr., 1973-77, mgmt. supr., 1977-84, sr. v.p., 1981—, account group dir., 1984-87; gen. mgr. Ogilvy & Mather Direct, NYC, 1987-88, mng. dir., 1988-89, pres., 1989-91, Ogilvy & Mather, NYC, 1991-94, pres. N. Am., 1991-94; pres., COO Ogilvy & Mather Worldwide, NYC, 1995-96, CEO, 1996—, chmn., 1997—. Bd. dirs. Merck & Co., Inc., GE, Com. to Encourage Corp., Philanthropy, NY Presbyn. Hosp., Advt. Edn. Found., Am. Mus. Nat. History, World Wildlife Fund; mem. bd. overseers Columbia Bus. Sch. Mem. adv. bd. Judge Inst. Mgmt. Studies Cambridge U., England, Women's Forum, Yale Press Coun. Internat. Activities, Bus. Coun., 4A's Adv. Coun., Deloitte and Touche Coun. Advancement Women, Coun. Fgn. Rels., Advt. Women NY, Com. 200. Recipient YWCA Women Achievers award, 1985, Matrix award, 1995; named Businesswoman of Yr. NYC Partnership and C. of C., 1996, one of 100 Most Powerful Women in World, Forbes Mag., 2005. Mem.: Am. Assn. Advt. Agys. (vice chmn. 1998—99, chmn. 1999—2000, bd. dirs.), Advt. Women N.Y. (coun. fgn. rels., com. to encourage corp. philanthropy, Woman of Yr 1994). Home: 106 E 78th St New York NY 10021-0302 Office: Ogilvy & Mather Worldwide 309 W 49th St New York NY 10019-7316 Office Phone: 212-237-4000.

LAZARUS, STEVEN, technology company exective; b. N.Y.C., May 31, 1931; s. Jesse and Dorothy (Gold) L.; m. Arlene Doris Travin, June 18, 1953; children: Paul M., Scott R., Jeffrey T. AB, Dartmouth Coll., 1952; MBA, Harvard U., 1965. Commd. ensign USN, 1953, advanced through grades to capt., 1973, ret., 1969; asst. maritime adminstr. U.S. Dept. Commerce, Washington, 1969-72, dept. asst. sect. commerce for east-west trade, 1972-74; various positions to group v.p. for health care systems Baxter Travenol Labs. Inc., Chgo., 1974-86; assoc. dean grad. sch. of bus. U. Chgo., 1986—94; founder, mng. dir. Arch Venture Partners, 1986—; chief exec. officer, pres. Arch Devel. Corp., Chgo., 1986—94. Bd. dirs. Amgen Corp., Thousand Oaks, Calif., Primark Corp., McLean, Va, First Consulting Group, R2 Tech., Inc. Trustee Highland Park (Ill.) Hosp., 1985—. Office: Arch Venture Partners 8725 W Higgins Rd Ste 290 Chicago IL 60631*

LAZARUS, STEVEN S., management consultant, marketing consultant; b. Rochester, NY, June 16, 1943; s. Alfred and Ceal H. Lazarus; m. Elissa C. Lazarus, June 19, 1966; children: Michael, Stuart, Jean. BS, Cornell U., 1966; MS, Poly. U. N.Y., 1967; PhD, U. Rochester, 1974. Pres. Mgmt. Systems Analysis Corp., Denver, 1977—; dir. Sci. Application Intern Corp., Englewood, Colo., 1979-84; assoc. prof. Metro State Coll., Denver, 1983-84; sr. v.p. Pal Assocs. Inc., Denver, 1984-85; with strategic planning and mktg. McDonnell Douglas, Denver, 1985-86; mktg. cons. Clin. Reference Systems, Denver, 1986; pres. Mgmt. Sys. Analysis Corp., 1986-89, 95—; assoc. exec. dir. Ctr. Rsch. Ambulatory Health Care Adminstrn., Englewood, 1990-94. Spl. cons. State of Colo., Denver, 1976-81; mktg. cons. IMX, Louisville, 1986-87; speaker Am. Hosp. Assn., Chgo., 1983; asst. sec. Work Group for Elec. Data Interchange, 1995-96, bd. dirs., 1997—, chmn. bd. dirs., 2001-02; trustee WEDI Found., 2003—, sec, 2004-05; pres. Boundary Info. Group, 1995—; founder, bd. dirs. Train for Compliance, Inc., 2003-, vice chmn., 2003—; co-founder Health IT Cert., LLC, 2004—. Co-author: Handbook for HIPAA Security Implementation, 2003, Complete Guide to HIPAA Security Risk Analysis: A Step-by-Step Approach, 2004, Electronic Health Records: Transforming Your Medical Practice, 2005; contbr. chapters to books. NDEA fellow U. Rochester, 1968-71. Fellow Healthcare Info. and Mgmt. Systems Soc.; mem. Med. GroupMgmt. Assn., Optimists (program chmn. Denver club 1976-78). Achievements include patents for med. quality assurance. Home: 7023 E Eastman Ave Denver CO 80224-2845 Office: MSA Corp 4401 S Quebec St Ste 100 Denver CO 80237-2644 Office Phone: 303-488-9911.

LAZEAR, EDWARD PAUL, economist, educator; b. N.Y.C., Aug. 17, 1948; s. Abe and Rose (Karp) L.; m. Victoria Ann Allen, July 2, 1977; 1 child, Julia Ann AB, A.M., UCLA, 1971; PhD, Harvard U., 1974; LLD (hon.), Albertson Coll., 1997. Asst. prof. econs. U. Chgo., 1974-78, assoc. prof. indsl. relations, 1978-81, prof. indsl. relations, 1981-85, Isidore and Gladys Brown prof. urban and labor econs., 1985-92; sr. fellow Hoover Instn. Stanford (Calif.) U., 1985—2002, coord. domestic studies Hoover Instn., 1987-90, prof. econs. and human resource mgmt. Grad. Sch. Bus., 1992-95, Jack Steele Parker prof. econs. and human resource mgmt., 1995—, mem. steering com. Stanford Inst. for Econ. Policy Rsch., 1996—. Econ. advisor to Romania, Czechoslovakia, Russia, Ukraine, Georgia; rsch. assoc. Nat. Bur. Econ. Rsch., Econs. Rsch. Ctr. of Nat. Opinion Rsch. Ctr.; chmn. rsch. adv. bd. World at Work; fellow Inst. Advanced Study, Hebrew U., Jerusalem, 1977-8; lectr. Inst. Advanced Study, Vienna, 1983-84, Nat. Productivity Bd., Singapore, 1982, 85, Adam Smith lctr., Seville, Spain, 2003; vis. prof. Inst. des Etudes Politiques, Paris, 1987; Wicksell lectr., Stockholm, 1993; chmn. Am. Compensation Assoc. Adv. Bd., 1999—; mem. Pres.'s Panel on Tax Reform, 2005. Author: (with R. Michael) Allocation of Income Within the Household, 1988; (with J.P. Gould) Microeconomic Theory, 1989, Personnel Economics, 1995, Personnel Economics for Managers, 1998; editor: Economic Transition in Eastern Europe and Russia, 1995; founding editor Jour. Labor Econs., 1982—; assoc. editor Jour. Econ. Perspectives, 1986-89, German Econ. Rev., 2000—; co-editor; Jour. Labor Abstracts, 1996—; contbr. numerous articles to scholarly jours. Recipient Leo Melamed prize for outstanding scholarship, 1998, prize for outstanding contbns. in labor econs. IZA; NSF grad. fellow, 1971-74, Morris Arnold Cox sr. fellow Hoover Instn., 2002. Fellow Am. Acad. Arts and Scis., Econometric Soc., Soc. Labor Economists (1st v.p. 1995-96, pres. 1997-98), Ctr. Corp. Performance Denmark; mem. Am. Econs. Assn., Inst. Study Labor, Nat. Acad. Scis. (bd. testing and assessment), Bd. Tng. Assessment. Home: 277 Old Spanish Trl Portola Valley CA 94028-8129 Office: Stanford U Grad Sch Bus Stanford CA 94305-5015 Also: Stanford Univ Hoover Inst Stanford CA 94305-6010

LAZERSON, EARL EDWIN, academic administrator emeritus; b. Detroit, Dec. 10, 1930; s. Nathan and Ceil (Stashefsky) L.; m. Ann May Harper, June 11, 1966; children from previous marriage: Joshua, Paul. BS, Wayne State U., Detroit, 1953; postgrad., U. Leiden, Netherlands, 1957-58; MA, U. Mich., 1954, PhD, 1982. Mathematician Inst. Def. Analyses, Princeton, N.J., 1960-62; asst. prof. math. Washington U., St. Louis, 1962-65, 66-69; vis. asso. prof. Brandeis U., 1965-66; mem. faculty So. Ill. U., Edwardsville, 1969—, prof. math., 1973—, chmn. dept. math. studies, 1972-73, dean Sch. Sci. and Tech., 1973-76, univ. v.p., provost, 1977-79, pres., 1980-93; pres. emeritus, 1994—. Chmn. Southwestern Ill. Devel. Authority, City of East St. Louis Fin. Adv. Authority; active Leadership Coun. Southwestern Ill., Gateway Ctr. Met. St. Louis, Inc., St. Louis Symphony Soc.; trustee Jefferson Nat. Expansion Meml. Assn., Ill. Econ. Devel. Bd. Recipient Sr. Teaching Excellence award Standard Oil Found., 1970-71 Mem. Am. Math. Soc., Math. Assn. Am., European Math. Soc., London Math. Soc., Soc. Mathematique France, Fulbright Alumni Assn., Sigma Xi. Home: 122 Forest Grove Dr Glen Carbon IL 62034 E-mail: laze@charter.net.

LAZICH, DANIEL, aerospace engineer; b. Galjipovci, Yugoslavia, Jan. 1, 1941; came to U.S., 1963; s. Stojan and Ljubica Lazic; m. Spomenka Krkljus, Aug. 11, 1968. BS in Engring., U. Ill., 1974; postgrad., U. Tex., Arlington, 1976-78; MA in Internat. Transactions, George Mason U., 1997. Analytical engr. Pratt & Whitney Aircraft, West Hartford, Conn., 1974-75; aircraft structures engr. Gen. Dynamics Corp., Ft. Worth, 1975-78; aerospace engr. Shrike missile Air Systems Commn. USN, Arlington, Va., 1978-81; sr. propulsion engr. Joint Cruise Missiles Project, Dept. Def., Arlington, 1981-85; prin. staff engr., tech. advisor kinetic energy weapons Strategic Def. Commn., Arlington, 1985—. Contbr. articles to profl. jours. Sgt. U.S. Army, 1966-68. Mem. AIAA, Aircraft Owners and Pilots Assn., No. Va. Astronomy Club. Avocations: flying, photography. Home: 12104 Capilla La North Port FL 34287-1302

LAZIO, RICK ANTHONY (ENRICO ANTHONY LAZIO), bank executive, former congressman; b. Amityville, N.Y., Mar. 13, 1958; s. Anthony and Olive E. (Christensen) L. m. Patrica Moriarity, 1990, children: Molly Ann, Kelsey. AB in Polit. Sci., Vassar Coll., 1980; JD, Am. U., 1983. Bar: N.Y. 1984, U.S. Dist. Ct. (ea. and so. dists.) N.Y., 1985. Asst. dist. atty. Suffolk County Rackets Bureau, Hauppauge, N.Y., 1983-88; exec. asst. dist. atty. Suffolk County, N.Y., 1987-88; village atty. Village of Lindenhurst, N.Y., 1988-93; mng. ptnr. Glass, Lazio and Glass, Esqs., Babylon, N.Y., 1988-93; mem. Suffolk County Legislature from 11th Dist., N.Y., 1989-93, 103rd-106th Congresses from 2nd N.Y. dist., Washington, 1993-2001; dep. majority whip 103d-106th Congresses from 2nd N.Y. dist., Washington; asst. majority leader 106th Congress from 2nd N.Y. dist., Washington; pres., CEO Fin. Services Forum, N.Y.C. and Washington, 2001—04; exec. v.p. global govt. relations & pub. policy J.P. Morgan Chase & Co., NYC, 2004—. Mem. commerce com., banking com., subcom. on health and environ., subcom. on fin. and hazardous materials, chmn. subcom. on housing and cmty. opportunity. Republican. Roman Catholic. Avocations: coin collecting/numismatics, guitar. Office: JP Morgan Chase Co 270 Park Ave New York NY 10017-2070

LAZOWSKA, EDWARD DELANO, computer science educator; b. Washington, Aug. 3, 1950; AB, Brown U., 1972; MSc, U. Toronto, Can., 1974, PhD, 1977. Asst. prof. U. Wash., Seattle, 1977-82, assoc. prof., 1982-86, prof. dept. computer sci. & engring., 1986—, chair dept. computer sci. and engring., 1993—2001, Bill and Melinda Gates chair, 2000—. Vis. scholar computer sci. Stanford U., 1984—85; vis. scientist Digital Equipment Corp., 1984—85; vis. scholar computer sci. U. Calif., San Diego, 2001—02; tech. adv. bd. mem. Microsoft Rsch., Voyager Capital, Ignition, Frazier Tech. Ventures, Madrona Venture Group, Impinj; bd. dirs. Washington Software Alliance, Tech. Alliance of Washington, Data I/O Corp., Intrepid Learning Solutions; co-chair Pres.'s Info. Tech. Adv. Com., 2003—05. Fellow: AAAS, IEEE, Am. Acad. Arts and Sci., Assn. Computing Machinery (chmn. spl. interest group on measurement and evaluation 1985—89); mem.: Nat. Acad. Engring. Office: U Wash Dept Computer Sci & Engring PO Box 352350 Seattle WA 98195-2350 Office Phone: 206-543-4755. Business E-Mail: lazowska@cs.washington.edu.

LAZUKA, ROBERT, artist, art educator; BFA in painting, Art Inst. Chgo.; MFA, Ariz. State U. Prof. Sch. Art, Ohio. U., 1984—, interim dir. Represented in permanent collections, Whitney Mus. Art, N.Y., Smithsonian Nat. Mus. Am. Art, Washington, DC, Nelson-Atkins Mus. Art, Kans. City, MO, Clemson U., S.C., Chattahoochee Valley Art Mus., Ga., Baseball Hall Fame Mus. Mem.: Coll. Bd. Advanced Placement Program (mem. 1988—, chief faculty consultant, studio art 1996—2000, devel. com.). Office: Ohio University School of Art 417 Seigfred Hall Athens OH 45701 Office Phone: 740-593-1676. Office Fax: 740-593-0457. E-mail: lazuka@ohiou.edu.*

LAZZARA, BERNADETTE See PETERS, BERNADETTE

LAZZARINI, LORNE, lawyer; b. Thunderbay, Ont., Can., Dec. 29, 1941; came to U.S., 1944; s. Gino and Giselda (Marcuzzi) L.; m. Sheila Robbins, Aug. 22, 1970 (div. July 1983); children: Adrianna, Marcogino. BS in Psychology, U. Calif., Berkeley, 1964; MBA, San Diego State U., 1971; JD, U. San Diego, 1986. Bar: Calif. 1986. Asst. to v.p. U.S. Financial, San Diego, 1971-73; v.p. fin./acct. Keystone Corp., Ontario, Calif., 1973-75; CEO Robbins stores, Hamilton, Mont., 1975-82; pvt. practice San Diego, 1986—. Lt. (j.g.) USN, 1965-68. Avocations: golf, travel, reading. Office: 2454 Heritage Park Row San Diego CA 92110

LAZZARINI, ROBERT, sculptor; b. Parsippany, NJ, 1965; Grad., Parsons Sch. Design, 1985; BFA, Sch. Visual Arts, NYC, 1990. Group exhibitions, Intercourse, Mustard, Brooklyn, 1994, Soup, 10, Brooklyn, 1994, Second Independents Biennial, Galeria El Bohio, NYC, 1994, Self Images, HBO Corp. Gallery, NYC, 1996, Independents Show, Galeria El Bohio, NYC, 1996, Gramercy Internat., Gramercy Hotel, Gina Fiore Salon, NYC, 1996, Genuine Fiction, W-139, Amsterdam, 1997, Gramercy Internat., Gramercy Hotel, Pierogi 2000, NYC, 1997, Current/Undercurrent: Working in Brooklyn, Brooklyn Mus. Art, 1997, NY Drawers, Gasworks Gallery, London, 1997, The CornerHouse, Manchester, 1997, Invitational '98, Stefan Stux Gallery, NYC, 1998, Multiple Sensations, Yerba Buena Ctr. for the Arts, San Francisco, 2000, Haulin' Ass, Post, LA, 2000, Minutiae, Southeastern Ctr. for Contemporary Art, Winston-Salem, NC, 2000, Pierogi Flat Files, Block Artspace, Kansas City, MO, 2001, Bitstreams, Whitney Mus. Art, 2001, Brent Sikkema Gallery, NYC, 2001, Situated Realities: Works from Silicon Elsewhere, Md. Inst. Coll. Art, 2002, On Perspective, Gallery Faurschou, Copenhagen, 2002, The Whitney Biennial, Whitney Mus. Art, 2002, solo exhibitions, Gina Fiore Salon, NYC, 1995, Pierogi 2000, Brooklyn, 1998, 2000, first solo mus. exhibition, robert lazzarini, Va. Mus. Fine Arts, 2003—04 (Award for Best Exhbn. of Digital Art, Internat. Assn. Art Critics/USA, 2005). Visual Arts Grant, NY Found. for Arts, 1985, 1986.*

LAZZARO, ANTHONY DEREK, university administrator; b. Utica, N.Y., Jan. 31, 1921; s. Angelo Michael and Philomena (Vanilla) L.; m. Shirley Margaret Jones, Dec. 20, 1941; 1 child, Nancy. BS in Indsl. and Sys. Engring., U. So. Calif., 1948; LL.D. with honors, Pepperdine U., 1974. Registered profl. engr., Calif. Asst. bus. mgr. U. So. Calif., L.A., 1948-60, asst. bus. mgr., dir. campus devel., 1960-65, asso. bus. mgr., dir. campus devel., 1965-71, asso. v.p. bus. affairs, 1971-72, v.p. bus. affairs, 1972-86, sr. v.p. bus. affairs, 1986-88, univ. v.p., 1988-91, v.p. emeritus, 1991—. Cons. HEW. Editorial cons. College and University Business, 1955-58. Mem. nat. adv. coun. United Student Aid Funds, N.Y.C., 1974-77, chmn., 1976-77; spl. studies cons. div. higher edn. Office Edn. HEW, 1956-59; mem. citizens com. Palos Verdes Bd. Edn., 1955-57; mem. Hoover urban renewal adv. com. Cmty. Redevel. Agy. City of L.A., 1960-88. Lt. USNR, 1941-46, PTO. Recipient Pres.'s Outstanding Svc. award U. Redlands, 2000. Mem. Nat. Assn. Coll. and Univ. Bus. Officers (pres. 1978-79, dir. 1972-80, chmn. goals and programs com. 1978, chmn. large inst. com. 1986-87, Disting. Bus. Officer award 1986), Western Assn. Coll. and Univ. Bus. Officers (pres. 1971-72), Soc. Coll. and Univ. Planning, Blue Key, Golden Key, Phi Kappa Phi, Tau Beta Pi. Clubs: Jonathan (Los Angeles). Home: 4012 Via Larga Vis Palos Verdes Estates CA 90274 Business E-Mail: lazzaro@usc.edu.

LÊ, AN-MY, photographer, educator; BA with honors in Biology and French, Stanford U., 1982, MS in Biology, 1985; MFA in Photography, Yale U., 1993. Rsch. asst. in immunology Blood Ctr., Med. Ch. Stanford (Calif.) U., 1981—86, lectr. photography art dept., 1996—97, lectr. photography continuing studies dept., 1997; tchg. asst. photography dept. Yale U. Sch. Art, New Haven, 1992; lectr. photography Fordham U., NYU, Bard Coll., N.Y.C., 1998; free-lance photographer, 1993—. Staff photographer Compagnons du Devoir, France, 1986—91; vis. asst. prof. Bard Coll., 1999. Author: Dirs. Guild Am., 1993; Exhibited in group shows at Canton (China) Cultural Ctr., 1993, Lowinski Gallery, N.Y., 1994, Houston Ctr. for Photography (traveled to Webster U., St. Louis and Silver Eye Ctr. for Photography, Pitts.), 1994—96, 1997, Mus. Modern Art, N.Y.C., 1997, Fotofest, Houston, 1998, Scott Nicols Gallery, San Francisco, 1999, Represented in permanent collections Mus. Fine Arts, Houston, Mus. Modern Art, N.Y.C., San Francisco, Met. Mus., N.Y.C., Bibliotéque Nationale, Paris. Fellow Photography fellow, N.Y. Found. for Arts, 1996; CameraWorks Inc. grantee, 1995, Guggenheim fellow, 1997.

LE, CHI-DINH, law educator, writer; b. Hatinh, Vietnam, Jan. 2, 1938; arrived in U.S., 1991; s. Hue-Dinh Le and Quang-Kiem Tran; m. Quyen-Tn Huyen, Oct. 6, 1960; children: Chau-Quynh, Ngoc-Tuyet, Bach-Dinh, Chau-Pho, Chau-My, Chau-A. B in Law, Law Sch., Saigon, Vietnam, 1960, M in Pub. Law, 1969, D of Pub. Law, 1971; M in Adminstrn., Nat. Inst. Adminstrn., Saigon, 1969. Chmn. Strategic Estimation Com., Saigon, 1961—62; dir. mgmt. Open Arms U., Saigon, 1970—72; prof. Law Sch., Saigon, 1972—75. Author: Ethnic Minority in South Vietnam, 1971, The Wire-Puller, 1999, (short stories) The Stream of Life, 2003. Mem.: N.Y. Acad. Scis., So. Poverty Law Ctr. Home: 4069 Rue D'Artagnan Stone Mountain GA 30083

LE, SON MINH, philosophy educator; b. Ninh Binh, Vietnam, Jan. 16, 1945; U.S., 1964; s. Chuyen Van Le and Tuyet Thi Dinh; m. Mary Kai Ming Cheung, Apr. 6, 1969 (dec. 1977); children: Trang Minh, Dao Minh, Tri Minh; m. Marilyn Jean Matsumura, Aug. 9, 1980; 1 child, Mai Minh. BA, Fordham U., 1967; MA, Antioch Coll., 1968; PhD, Ohio State U., 1971. Philosophy instr. Franconia (N.H.) Coll., 1968, Antioch Coll., Yellow Springs, Ohio, 1968; rssch. assoc. U. So. Calif. Med. Ctr., L.A., 1974-75; prof. philosophy, dept. chair Mission Coll., Santa Clara, 1975—, weekend coll. and evening adminstr., 1986-95. Founding faculty mem. Mission Coll., 1975, chair, faculty com. to draft original Mission Coll. philosophy, 1976. Author: Behavioral Objectives, 1973, Term Deliveryof Primary Care, 1976, Logic Flip Book: A Modular Approach, 1979, Elements of Critical Thinking and Writing, 2000. Vietnam del. World Youth Forum, 1963. Presdl. scholarship Fordham U., 1964. Mem. Nat. Endowment for the Humanities, State of Calif. Coun. for Pvt. Postsecondary and Vocat. Edn., Am. Philos. Assn. Avocation: reading and reflecting. Office: Philosophy Dept Mission Coll 3000 Mission Coll Blvd Santa Clara CA 95054 Office Phone: 408-855-5269. E-mail: mcphilosopher@yahoo.com.

LE, THUY TRONG, nuclear engineer, educator; b. Vietnam, Jan. 20, 1958; came to US, 1980; s. Thich Trong and Le-Phi Thi (Vuong) V.; m. Nhan Thi Le, Aug. 20, 1985; children: Thuy-Nhu Thi, Thi Trong. BS in Nuclear Engring., U. Calif., 1985, MS in Nuclear Engring., 1987, PhD in Engring., 1990. Nuclear reactor operator, health physicist asst. Nuc. Engring. Dept. U. Calif., Berkeley, 1985-88, grad. student instr. Nuc. Engring. and Physics Dept., 1987-90; rsch. asst. physics divsn. Lawrence Berkeley Nat. Lab., 1988-89; physics instr. Calif. Coll. of Alameda, 1989-90; rsch. engr. sci. computation divsn. applied physics group Westinghouse Savannah River Lab., 1990-93; sr. rschr. high performance computing group Fujitsu Am. Incorporation, Calif., 1993-2000. Cons. engr. Sierra Nuclear Corp., Scotts Valley, Calif., 1989—; adj. prof. U. S.C., Aiken, 1991-93; assoc. prof. San Jose State U., 1996—; cons. Fujitsu America Inc. 2001—. Contbr. numerous articles to profl. jours. Mem. IEEE, Am. Nuclear Soc. (math. and computation divsn.). Achievements include authoring GRIMH3 computer code: multi dimensional reactor analysis code, WINDEX System: detailed energy residence treatment code, research in computer architectures, digital design, networking, numerical methods, parallel computing and algorithms, computational physics and engineering, criticality and radiation shielding, nuclear reactor analysis and design. Address: 44291 Pomace St Fremont CA 94539-6537 Business E-Mail: thuytle@email.sjsu.edu.

LE, TUAN A., architectural engineer, management consultant; BArchE cum laude, Pa. State U., Univ. Park, 1988; post grad. in Mgmt. and Orgnl. Behavior, Wharton Sch. Bus. Mgmt. U.Pa., 1998—2000; post grad. in Sigma Six Leadership and Project Mapping, Eli Broad Sch. Mgmt. Mich. State U., 2001. Project mgr. Toll Bros., Inc., Hopkinton, Mass., 1988—91; dir. prodn. svcs. Realen Homes, Inc., Ambler, Pa., 1991—94; dir. ops. and purchasing Tadian Homes, Troy, Mich., 2000—04; chief exec. advisor Keystone Consulting, Doylestown, Pa., 1994—2000, 2004—. Classical violinist:, jazz violinist: with Chuck Mangione, Maynard Ferguson, Buddy Rich, Lionel Hampton. Address: 17711 Ridgeway Point Pl Tampa FL 33647

LE, VINH TU, language educator, translator; b. Quang-Binh, Vietnam, Apr. 25, 1935; arrived in U.S., 1991; s. Oanh Tu Le and Thuan Thi Lam; m. Phuong Thi Ton, Jan. 29, 1958; children: Thuy K., Hai, Grace K., Vance, Tuong K., Trina, Scott, Thomson. Student, U. Hue, Vietnam, 1961—62, U. Saigon, 1963—65, student, 1972—74. Tchr. English Tang Bat Ho HS, Binh Dinh, Vietnam, 1955—58, Cuong De HS, Binh Dinh, 1958—60; instr. English Armed Forces Lang. Sch., Saigon, Vietnam, 1963—68; asst. course dir. Nat. Def. Coll., Saigon, 1968—70; tchr. English Bode and Chan P. Liem HS, Saigon, 1970—75, GoVap HS, Saigon, 1979—87; tchr. aide St. Anselm Multicultural Ctr., Garden Grove, Calif., 1991—92; ret., 2003. Vice prin. Fgn. Lang. Ctr., Saigon, 1980—87. Translator: The Pride of the Vietnamese, 1992—93, A Vietnamese Girl and An American Soldier, 1997; editor-in-chief Lai Giang Spl. Publ., 1994—2003. Head steering com. AFLS Assn., 1993—98; sec. gen. Quang Binh Assn., 1997—99; pres. Lai Giang Assn., 1994—2003. 1st lt. U.S. Army, 1962—70, Vietnam. Recipient 1st class tng. medal, Joint Gen. Staff, 1966, 1st class Honor Staff medal, 1970. Avocations: reading, watching television. Home: 16537 Mt Michaelis Cir Fountain Valley CA 92708

LEA, LORENZO BATES, lawyer; b. St. Louis, Apr. 12, 1925; s. Lorenzo Bates and Ursula Agnes (Gibson) L.; m. Marcia Gwendolyn Wood, Mar. 21, 1953; children— Victoria, Jennifer, Christopher. BS, MIT, 1946; JD, U. Mich., 1949; grad. Advanced Mgmt. Program, Harvard U., 1964. Bar: Ill. 1950. With Amoco Corp. (formerly Standard Oil Co. Ind.), Chgo., 1949—89, asst. gen. counsel, 1963-71, assoc. gen. counsel, 1971-72, gen. counsel, 1972-78, v.p., gen. counsel, 1978-89. Trustee Village of Glenview, Ill., 1963-64, mem. Zoning Bd., 1961-63; bd. dirs. Chgo. Crime Commn., 1978—, Midwest Coun. for Internat. Econ. Policy, 1973—, Chgo. Bar Found., 1981—, Chgo. Area Found. for Legal Svcs., 1981—; bd. dirs. United Charities of Chgo., 1973—, chmn., 1985—; bd. dirs. Cmty. Found. Collier County, 1997—, Naples Bot. Garden, 2000—. Served with USNR, 1943-46. Mem. ABA, Am. Petroleum Inst., Am. Arbitration Assn. (dir. 1980—), Ill. Bar Assn., Chgo. Bar Assn., Assn. Gen. Counsel (bd. dirs. 1983-89), Order of Coif, Law Club, Econs. Club, Legal, Mid-Am. (Chgo.), Glen View, Wyndemere, Hole-In-The-Wall, Sigma Xi. Republican. Mem. United Ch. of Christ.

LEA, RUSSELL M., writer, historian; b. Mt. Kisco, NY, Nov. 11, 1964; BA, Westchester CC, Valhalla, NY, 1992; BS, Nyack Coll., NY; AAS, Westchester CC; postgrad., Nyack Coll., 2001. Author: W.P. Bicentrivia, 2003, The Long Green Line, 2003. Mem.: US Coast Guard Aux.

LEA, SCOTT CARTER, retired packaging company executive; b. New Orleans, Nov. 14, 1931; s. Leonard G. and Helen (Stoughton) L.; m. Marilyn Ruth Blair, Oct. 25, 1957; children: Scott, Nancy B., Mark S. BA, Amherst Coll., 1954; MBA, U. Pa., 1959. Sales and mktg. positions Riegel Paper, 1959-66, sales mgr. folding carton dept. southeastern div., 1966-67, gen. sales mgr., 1967-69, v.p. folding carton dept., 1969-71; v.p. bd. conversion div. Rexham Corp., Charlotte, N.C., 1971-73, v.p. packaging group, 1973-74, pres., 1974-90; chmn. bd. Rexham Industries, Inc., 1990-92; bd. dirs. Lance Inc., Charlotte, 1994—, chmn. bd. dirs., 1996-99; ret., 1999. Bd. dirs. Speizman Industries, Inc. Trustee Johnson C. Smith U., Charlotte, N.C., 1977-2003, vice chmn. bd. trustees, 1998-2003; bd. dirs. Ctrl. Piedmont C.C. Found., Charlotte. With U.S. Army, 1954-57. Mem.: N.C. Zool. Soc. (bd. dirs. 1996—2002), Charlotte C. of C. (bd. dirs. 1977—78), Wild Dunes Club (Isle of Palms, S.C.), Quail Hollow Country Club, Carmel Country Club. Home: 3704 Stone Ct Charlotte NC 28226-7343 Office: Lance Inc 8600 South Blvd Charlotte NC 28273-6924

LEA, STANLEY E., artist, educator; b. Joplin, Mo., Apr. 5, 1930; s. Everett G. and Edna F. L.; m. Ruth Lowe, Aug. 19, 1951; children: Kristy Ruth, Kraig, Kelly B. B.F.A., Pitts. State U., 1953; M.F.A., U. Ark., 1961. Prof. art Sam Houston State U., Huntsville, 1961-93, Mexican Field Sch., Puebla, Mexico, 1963-65; vis. artist prof. Mus. Fine Arts, Houston, 1968, 69, 70; prof. art study abroad program London, 1977-78. Juror various art exhibits, 1970-81; workshop demonstrator, E. Tex. State U., Commerce, 1977, 10th ann. color print symposium, Tex. Tech. U., Lubbock, 1983, City of Huntsville mural, 1980; one-man shows paintings and/or prints, Valley House Gallery, Dallas, 1963, Inst. Mex. N. Am. de Rels., Mexico City, 1967, Main Place Gallery, Dallas, 1970-71, U. Tex. Med. Ctr., San Antonio, 1970, Moody Gallery, Houston, 1976, Sol Del Rio, San Antonio, 1978, 89, Adelle M. Fine Arts, Dallas, 1978, Dubose Gallery, Houston, 1980, Cultural Activities Ctr., Temple, Tex., 1982, Tex. A&M U., College Station, 1986, Mus. at E. Tex., Lufkin, 1989Cultural Ctr., Bryan, Tex., 1993; numerous group shows, latest being Moody Gallery, Houston, 1975, 77, Pecan Square Gallery, Austin, Tex., 1977, Am. Painters In Paris, 1975-76, Waco Art Center, Waco, Tex., 1977, East Tex. State U., Commerce, 1977, Galveston (Tex.) Art Center, 1978, Twenty Five Nat. Printmaker, Lubbock, Tex., 1978, Beaumont (Tex.) Art Mus., 1978, Art League of Houston, 1978, Gates Gallery, Port Arthur, Tex., 1979, Ars Longa, Houston, 1974, Laguna Gloria Mus., Austin, 1979; represented in permanent collections, Library of Congress, Washington, Smithsonian Mus. Am. Art, Washington, Calif. Palace of Legion of Honor, San Francisco, Brit. Mus., London, Mus. Fine Arts, Houston, USIA, N.Y.C., N.Y. Public Library, N.Y.C., Mpls. Inst. Art, Kalamazoo Inst. Art, Boise (Idaho) Gallery of Art, Madison (Wis.) Art Center, Spiva Art Center, Joplin, Mo., Ft. Worth Art Mus., Convention Ctr., The Woodlands, Tex., Cleve. Mus., Inst. Mexicano Norteamericana de Relationes, Mexico City, also corp. and pvt. collections. (Recipient numerous awards, latest being, Southwest Graphics Invitational award 1971, Dimensions IX Exhbn. award 1974, 68th Nat. Tex. Fine Arts Exhbn. 1979). Sam Houston State U. grantee, 1970, 74, Lakeside (Mich.) Studio grantee 1972, Casa Argentina grantee, Buenos Aires, 1973, Europe, 1982. Home: 3324 Winter Way Huntsville TX 77340-8919 Office Phone: 936-295-2853.

LEAB, DANIEL JOSEPH, history professor; b. Berlin, Aug. 29, 1936; s. Leo and Herta (Marcus) L.; m. Katharine Kyes, Aug. 16, 1964; children: Abigail Elizabeth, Constance Martha, Marcus Rogers. BA, Columbia U., 1957, MA, 1961, PhD, 1969. With Columbia U., N.Y.C., 1966-73, Seton Hall U., 1974—. Co-editor Am. Book Prices Current. Author: A Union of Individuals: The Formation of the American Newspaper Guild, 1970, I Was a Communist for the FBI: the unhappy life and times of Matt Cvetic, 2000; mng. editor: Labor History, 1974—2002, Am. Communist History, 2002—. Bd. of Edn. Region 12 (Washington, Roxbury, Bridgewater), 1997-2002, 2003—; justice of the peace, 2001—. Recipient Commerford award. N.Y. State Labor History Assn., 1997. Fellow Met. Mus. Art; mem. Historians of Am. Communism (gen. sec.), Century Assn., Grolier Club. Home: PO Box 1216 Washington CT 06793-0216 E-mail: danleab@earthlink.net.

LEACH, BERTON JOE, medical educator; b. Tuscola, Ill., Mar. 30, 1932; s. William Howard Leach and Frances Margaret De Haven; m. Barbara English, June 5, 1955; children: Laura Anne, Berton Franklin. AB, Washington U., 1957; MA, U. Mo., 1960, PhD, 1963. Assoc. prof. George Washington U., Washington, 1963—66; scientist adminstr. NSF, Washington, 1966—69; chmn., prof. Ctrl. Meth. Coll., Fayette, Mo., 1969—74; exec. sec. NIH, Bethesda, Md., 1974—76; sr. scientist pvt. industry, Rockville, Md., 1976—89; scientist Omni Rsch., Capital Sys. Group, 1976—89; admissions team leader Shady Grove Adventist Hosp., Rockville, 1988—; adj. prof. neurosci. Georgetown U., Washington, 1989—2003. Vis. scholar Harvard U., Cambridge, Mass., 1969; gen. reader Marine Biol. Lab., Woods Hole, Mass., 1985—87; guest rschr. NIH/Brain Behavior Lab., Poolesville, Md., 1991—92. Author: Structure and Development of Vertebrates, 1973, Vertebrate Biology Courseware, 1979, Human Neuroanatomy, 1999. Program chmn. Rotary Internat., Bethesda, 1975; vol. swimming instr. Rockville Swim Ctr., 2001; pres. Meth. Men's Club, Columbia, Mo., 1960. Decorated Am. Spirit Honor medal U.S. Army; named F. H. Dearing endowed prof., Ctrl. Meth. Coll., Fayette, 1970—74; fellow USPH rsch. fellow, NIH, Bethesda, 1962—63; grantee, NSF, Washington, 1973—74. Mem.: Am. Soc. Mammalogists (life), Sigma Xi. Republican. Methodist. Achievements include first scientist to ovulate polyovular follicles using exogenous hormones. Avocations: gardening, landscaping. Home: 12707 Weiss St Rockville MD 20853 Office: Georgetown Univ Med Ctr Dept Neurosci 3970 Reservoir Rd NW Washington DC 20007

LEACH, CHERI JEAN, elementary and secondary education educator; b. Coldwater, Mich., Oct. 14, 1947; d. Dean T. and Bonnie A. (Byers) Culver; m. Timothy Nathan Leach, Aug. 6, 1971; children: Timothy Thor, Prescott Tarn. BA, Albion Coll., 1969; M, U. Mich., 1991. Cert. tchr., Mich. Sci. tchr. Parma (Mich.) Western Schs., 1969-78; substitute tchr. East Jordan (Mich.) Schs., 1983-84, tchr. presch., summer 1990; tchr. sci. Boyne City (Mich.) Schs., 1984-95. Instr. adult edn. St. Ignace (Mich.) schs., 1983-89, North Ctrl. Mich. Coll., Petoskey, summer 1990; tchr. Coll. for Kids, Petoskey, 1986-94; presenter Charlevoix (Mich.) Emmet-Intermediate Sch., 1987—; founder, CEO Raven Hill Discovery Ctr., East Jordan, 1991—. Contbr. articles to profl. jours. Pres. PTO, East Jordan, 1987. Eleanor Roosevelt fellow, 1991; State of Mich. grantee, 1985, 86. Mem. AAUW, Mich. Sci. Tchrs. Assn., Nat. Sci. Tchr. Assn. (Sheldon Lab Exemplary Facilities award 1991). Avocations: basketry, reading, natural dyes. Home: 4834 Fuller Rd East Jordan MI 49727-9729 Office: Raven Hill Discovery Ctr 4737 Fuller Rd East Jordan MI 49727-9001 Office Phone: 231-536-3369. E-mail: cheri@torchlake.com.

LEACH, DAVE FRANCIS, editor, musician; b. Iowa City, Nov. 12, 1945; s. Joseph Stanley and Thelma Maxine (Strubhar) L.; m. Donna Susan Schoeppner, Dec. 17, 1970 (div. Feb. 1979); children: Arlo Bernard, Cynthia Robin; m. Dorothy Darlene Barnes, Dec. 13, 1986. B Music Edn., Drake U., 1967. Band dir. Melcher (Iowa)/Dallas Schs., 1967-68, Lackland Air Force Band, 1968-70, Coon Rapids (Iowa) Schs., 1970; band instrument repairman Miller Music/Family Music Ctr., Des Moines, 1972—; editor, founder Prayer & Action News, Des Moines, 1989—; producer, host The Uncle Ed Show, 1995—; owner Family Music Ctr., 1999—. Trumpet player Des Moines Mcpl. Band, 1963-78; musician Kingsway, St. Ambrose and St. Augustine Cathedrals, and Simpson United Meth. Ch., 1980-92. Author, composer: (musical comedy) Werld Klas Ejukashun, 1991; author: The Gifts of Governments, 1990, The Prehistoric Angel Diary, 2005 Dem. candidate for state rep., Iowa, 1986, Rep. candidate 1988, 90, 2000, 02; pres., editor Fathers for Equal Rights, Des Moines chpt. 1985-87; mem. Soc. of Mayflower Descendants, 2002—, chaplain, 2005. Avocations: bible study, inventing, construction. Office: 4110 SW 9th Ave Des Moines IA 50315-3643 Office Phone: 515-244-3711. Personal E-mail: leach@saltshaker.us.

LEACH, DONALD PAUL, small business owner; b. Mount Vernon, N.Y., Mar. 17, 1945; s. Alfred Grahame and Anne Marie (Hantz) Leach; m. Nancy Lynne Davis, Jan. 30, 1967; children: Donald Paul, Brian, Deborah. BS, Cedarville Coll., 1968; MBA, U. Dayton, 1974. Acct., mem. corp. staff Top Value Enterprises, Dayton, Ohio, 1969—72; tax analyst, corp. staff Phillips Industries, Inc., Dayton, 1972—73; tax mgr. Danis Industries Corp., Dayton, 1973—76, asst. v.p., 1976—78, v.p., treas. constrn. products group, 1978—82; v.p., treas. Moody Bible Inst., Chgo., 1982—88; v.p., spl. asst. to pres. Moody Consumer Ministries, 1988—89; COO Grabill Corp., Oak Forest, Ill.; owner, pres. Advance Refrigeration Co., Bensenville, Ill., 1990—. Instr. acctg. Sinclair C.C., Dayton, 1974—82. Mem. fin. com. Dayton Christian Schs., 1981—82; treas. Alumni Coun. Cedarville (Ohio) Coll., 1981—83, chmn., 1983—87; pres. Dayton Tax Club, 1977—78; deacon Faith Bapt. Ch., Winfield, Ill., 1984—87; small group leader Cmty. Fellowship Ch., 1996—, elder, 1999—2005; trustee Washington Hts. Bapt. Ch., Dayton, 1981—82, supt., 1977—80. With U.S. Army, 1967—73. Mem.: Christian Ministries Mgmt. Assn., Inst. Internal Auditors, Nat. Assn. Accts. Home: 420 Spring Cress Ln West Chicago IL 60185-1781 Office: Advance Refrigeration Co 1177 Industrial Dr Bensenville IL 60106-1200 Office Phone: 630-766-2000. Personal E-mail: donnandeb@aol.com.

LEACH, HOWARD H., former ambassador, former health care products company executive; b. Salinas, Calif., June 19, 1930; m. Gretchen Cooper, 1977; 5 children. BS, Yale U., 1952; studied at Stanford Grad Sch. of Bus., 1953, studied at Stanford Mgmt. Coll., 1968. Chmn. Sybron Corp., Saddle Brook, NJ, 1995—2000; U.S. amb. to France U.S. Dept. State, 2001—05.

LEACH, JAMES ALBERT SMITH, congressman; b. Davenport, Iowa, Oct. 15, 1942; s. James Albert and Lois (Hill) L.; m. Elisabeth Foxley, Dec. 6, 1975; 1 child, Gallagher BA, Princeton U., 1964; MA, Johns Hopkins U., 1966; postgrad., London Sch. Econs., 1966-68. Mem. staff Congressman Donald Rumsfeld, 1965-66; U.S. fgn. svc. officer, 1968-69, 70-73; spl. asst. to dir. OEO, 1969-70; pres. Flamegas Companies Inc., Bettendorf, Iowa, 1973-76; chmn. bd. Adel Wholesalers, Inc., Bettendorf, 1973-76; mem. 95th-109th Congresses from 2nd Iowa dist. (formerly 1st) Ho. Reps., Washington, 1977—. Chmn. banking and fin. svcs. com. Ho. Reps., chmn. subcom. Asia and Pacific, mem. com. internat. rels., co-chmn. U.S. commn. improving effectiveness of U.N.; trustee Princeton U.; bd. dirs. Century Incidation. Chmn. Iowa Rep. Directions '76 Com. Republican. Episcopalian. Office: 2186 Rayburn Bldg Washington DC 20515-1501*

LEACH, JOHN F., editor, journalist, educator; b. Montrose, Colo., Aug. 6, 1952; s. Darrell Willis and Marian (Hester) L.; m. Deborah C. Ross, Jan. 2, 1982; children: Allison, Jason. BS in Journalism, U. Colo., 1974, MA in Journalism, 1979; MA in Am. Studies, U. Sussex, Brighton, Eng., 1983. News reporter Boulder (Colo.) Daily Camera, 1974-79, The Ariz. Republic, Phoenix, 1979-85, asst. city editor, 1985-93; news editor The Phoenix Gazette, 1993-94; asst. mng. editor Phoenix Gazette, 1994-95, The Ariz. Republic and The Phoenix Gazette, 1995-97; sr. editor The Ariz. Republic, Phoenix, 1997-99, sr. editor for online news, 1999—2002, sr. editor digital media, 2002—; sr. editor for online news azcentral.com, 1999—2002, sr. editor digital media, 2002—. Faculty assoc. Ariz. State U., Tempe, 1990—; pres., dir. Best of the West, Phoenix, 1987—. Bd. Regents scholar U. Colo., 1970-74, Rotary Found. scholar, 1982-83. Mem. Ariz. Press Club (treas. 1984-86, pres. 1986-87), Soc. Profl. Journalists, Online News Assn., Newspaper Assn. Am. New Media Fedn. Office: The Ariz Republic 200 E Van Buren St Phoenix AZ 85004-2238 Personal E-mail: jfleach@hotmail.com. Business E-Mail: jleach@azcentral.com.

LEACH, MAURICE DERBY, JR., librarian, educator; b. Lexington, Ky., June 23, 1923; s. Maurice Derby and Sallie Eleanor (Woods) L.; m. Virginia Stuart Baskett, Mar. 16, 1953; 1 dau., Sarah Stuart. AB, U. Ky., 1945; B.L.S., U. Chgo., 1946. Bibliographer Dept. State, 1947-50; fgn. service officer Dept. State (USIS), vice consul, attache Cairo and Alexandria, Cairo and Beirut, 1950-59; chmn. dept. library sci. U. Ky., 1959-66; regional program officer Ford Found., Beirut, 1967-68; univ. librarian, prof. Washington and Lee U., Lexington, Va., 1968-85, prof., asst. to pres., 1985-88; library adviser Nat. Library, Egypt. Contbr. articles to profl. jours. Served with AUS, 1948-49. Mem. English Speaking Union (pres. Lexington br. 1970-75), Va. Libr. Assn. (pres. 1976), Assn. Preservation of Va. Activities (dir. Lexington br. 1989-91), Rockbridge Hist. Soc., SAR (v.p. 1990-93). Episcopalian. Home: 1 Courtland Cir Lexington VA 24450-1813

LEACH, RALPH F., banker; b. Elgin, Ill., June 24, 1917; s. Harry A. and Edith (Sanders) L.; m. Harriet C. Scheuerman, Nov. 18, 1944; children: C. David, H. Randall, Barbara E. AB, U. Chgo., 1938. Investment analyst Harris Trust & Savs. Bank, Chgo., 1940-48, Valley Nat. Bank, Phoenix, 1948-50; chief govt. finance sect. Fed. Res. Bd., Washington, 1950-53; treas. Guaranty Trust Co., N.Y.C., 1953-59, v.p., 1958-59; v.p., treas. Morgan Guaranty Trust Co., N.Y.C., 1959-62, sr. v.p., treas., 1962-64, exec. v.p., treas., 1964-68, vice chmn. bd. dirs., 1968-71, chmn. exec. com., 1971-77; dir. Merrill Lynch and Co., N.Y.C., 1978—89. Chmn. emeritus Energy Conversion Devices Inc. Bd. trustees The Juilliard Sch., 1963—87, vice chmn., 1968—87. Capt. USMC, 1940—45. Mem.: Coral Ridge Country Club, Phi Kappa Psi. Home: 4211 NE 25th Ave Fort Lauderdale FL 33308-5706 Office Phone: 954-566-8404.

LEACH, RICHARD MAXWELL, JR., (MAX LEACH JR.), corporate professional; b. Chillicothe, Tex., June 14, 1934; s. Richard Maxwell and Lelia Booth (Page) L.; m. Wanda Gail Groves, Feb. 4, 1956; children: Richard Clifton, John Christopher, Sandra Gail, Kathy Lynn. BS in Acctg. magna cum laude, Abilene Christian U., 1955. Registered fin. cons., CLU. Asst. dir. agys. Am. Founders Ins. Co., Austin, Tex., 1960—62; owner A.F. Ins. Planning Assocs., Temple, Tex., 1962—65; v.p. sales Christian Fidelity Life Ins. Co., Waxahachie, Tex., 1966—67; exec. v.p. Acad. Computer Tech., Inc., Dallas, 1968—69; pres., chief exec. officer Insta-Search Internat., Inc., Dallas, 1969—71; prin., chief exec. officer, fin. cons. Leach and Assocs., Albuquerque, 1971—; pres. The Wright Edge, Inc., 1988—90; pres., CEO Action Mktg. Programs, Inc., 1989—92; CEO Vacation Premiums Internat., Inc., 1990—92; pres., CEO ITM Corp., Albuquerque, 1993—98; founder, chmn., CEO Health Maximization Rsch. Studies Inst. Internat., Albuquerque, 1999—. Chmn. bd. United Quest Inc., Albuquerque, Hosanna Inc., Albuquerque; real estate broker; commodity futures broker; exec. dir., bd. dirs. New Heart, Inc., Albuquerque, 1975-85; owner Insta-Copy, Albuquerque, 1973-76, Radio Sta. KYLE-FM, Temple, 1963-64. Editor, author Hosanna newspaper, 1973-74. Gen. dir. Here's Life, New Mexico, Albuquerque, 1976; exec. dir. Christians for Cambodia, Albuquerque, 1979-80. With U.S. Army, 1955-57. Home: 3308 June St NE Albuquerque NM 87111-5029 Office: 10308 Candelaria NE # 345 Albuquerque NM 87112-1505 Office Phone: 505-344-2255. *Personal philosophy: Success is doing what God wants you to do when and where He would have you do it.*

LEACH, ROBERT ELLIS, orthopedist, surgeon, medical educator, department chairman; b. Sanford, Maine, Nov. 25, 1931; s. Ellis and Estella (Tucker) L.; m. Laurine Seber, Aug. 20, 1955; children: Cathy, Brian, Michael, Craig, Karen, Diane. AB, Princeton U., 1953; MD, Columbia U., 1957. Diplomate Am. Bd. Orthopedic Surgery (treas. 1986-93). Resident orthopedic surgery U. Minn., 1957-62; orthopedic surgeon Lahey Clinic, Boston, 1964-68, chmn. dept., 1968-70; prof., chmn. dept. Boston U. Med. Sch., 1970—. Head physician U.S. Olympic Team, 1984; chmn. sports medicine coun. U.S. Olympic Com., 1984-93; vice chmn. sports medicine coun. U.S. Tennis Assn., 1988-2002. Editor-in-chief Am. J. Sports Med.; editor emeritus Am. Jour. Sports Medicine, 2002; contbr. articles to profl. jours. Served to lt. comdr. USNR, 1962-64. Named Sports Medicine Man of Yr., 1988; named to Sports Medicine Hall of Fame, 2003; recipient Rovere Career Tchg. award, 1995, Ernst Jokl Sports Medicine award, 2000; Am., Brit., Can. Orthop. Travelling fellow, 1971. Mem. Am. Acad. Orthopedic Surgeons, Continental Orthopedic Soc. (sec. 1966), Am. Orthopedic Assn. (pres. 1994), Am. Orthopedic Soc. Sports Medicine (pres. 1983), Longwood Cricket Club. Home: 40 Rockport Rd Weston MA 02493-1428 Office: 230 Calvary St Waltham MA 02453-8366 Office Phone: 617-638-5633. Personal E-mail: releachrock@aol.com.

LEACH, ROBIN, producer, writer, television host; b. London, Aug. 29, 1941; came to U.S., 1963; s. Douglas Thomas and Violet Leach. Diploma, Nat. Union Journalists, 1961. Reporter Harrow (Eng.) Observer, 1958-61, Daily Mail, London, 1961-63; mag. pub. GO mag., N.Y.C., 1964-67; show bus. editor The Star, 1970-79; show bus. reporter CNN, 1979-80; reporter Entertainment Tonight, 1980-83; exec. producer Leach Entertainment Enterprises, 1983—. Founder Live From Las Vegas, 2000, Toral Vegas TV, 2005; pres. Total Vegas TV Inc., 2004; host, network spokesman Shop NBC. Author: The Go Rock & Roll Manual, 1966, 2d rev. edit., 1967, Lifestyles of the Rich and Famous, 1983, Healthy Lifestyles, 1995; prodr.: (TV shows) Lifestyles of the Rich and Famous, 1983-96 (Emmy nomination), Runaway with the Rich and Famous, The Rich and Famous Worlds Best, Fame, Fortune & Romance; host: KNBC-TV Year in Review, 1986 (Emmy award), Supermodel of the World, 1986, Home Videos of the Stars, 1991, Nitecap, (ABC-TV) Talking Food and Gourmet Getaways for TVFN, 1993-98, Most Expensive Videos MTV, 1998, 99, 2000, 2002, (ABC network) I'm a Celebrity Get Me Out of Here, (ABC-TV) Life of Luxury, 2003, (AOL) Vegas Super City TV, 2005. Mem. AFTRA, Screen Actors Guild. Avocations: tennis, gourmet cooking. Office: Leach Entertainment Inc 122 East 42d St Ste #1518 New York NY 10168

LEACH, RONALD GEORGE, education educator, librarian; b. Monroe, Mich., Feb. 22, 1938; s. Garnet William and Erma (Erbadine) L.; m. Joy Adeline Moore, Dec. 21, 1956; children— Ronald George, Debra Mabel, Catherine Louise, Shane John. BS in Secondary Edn, Central Mich. U., 1966; MA in L.S. (U.S. Office Edn. fellow 1968-69), U. Mich., 1969; PhD in Higher Edn. Adminstrn, Mich. State U., 1980. Head libr. Ohio State U., Mansfield, 1969-70; asst. dir., then acting dir. libr. Lake Superior State Coll., Sault Ste. Marie, Mich., 1970-76; assoc. dir. librs. Central Mich. U., 1976-80; dean libr. svcs. Ind. State U., Terre Haute, 1980-93, assoc. v.p. info. svcs., dean of librs., 1994-97, prof. higher ednl. adminstrn., 1997—. Prof. edn., mem. accreditation teams North Ctrl. Assn. Author articles in field. Served with N.G., 1955-61. Mem. ALA, INFORMA (steering com. 1990—), Assn. Coll. and Rsch. Librs., Libr. Info. and Tech. Assn., Ind. Libr. Assn., Am. Soc. Info. Sci., Libr. Adminstrn. and Mgmt. Assn. (pres. 1985-86), Online Computer Libr. Ctr. User Council (exec. com. 1986, 88). Office: Ind State U Dept Leadership Admin Found Terre Haute IN 47809-0001

LEACHMAN, CLORIS, actress; b. Des Moines, Apr. 30, 1926; m. George England, April 19, 1953 (div. 1979); 5 children. Attended, Northwestern U. Actress: (films) including Kiss Me Deadly, 1955, Butch Cassidy and the Sundance Kid, 1969, W.U.S.A., 1970, The People Next Door, 1970, Lovers and Other Strangers, 1970, The Steagle, 1971, The Last Picture Show, 1971 (Acad. award for best supporting actress 1971), Charles and the Angel, 1972, Happy Mother's Day...Love, George, 1973, Dillinger, 1973, Daisy Miller, 1974, Young Frankenstein, 1974, Crazy Mama, 1975, High Anxiety, 1977, The Mouse and His Child, 1977 (voice), Foolin' Around, 1979, The North Avenue Irregulars, 1979, The Muppet Movie, 1979, Scavenger Hunt, 1979, Yesterday, 1979, Herbie Goes Bananas, 1980, History of the World, Part 1, 1982, Shadow Play, 1986, My Little Pony, 1986 (voice), Walk Like a Man, 1987, Hansel and Gretel, 1987, Prancer, 1989, Love Hurts, 1990, Texasville, 1990, Walter and Emily, 1991, My Boyfriend's Back, 1993, The Beverly Hillbillies, 1993, A Troll in Central Park, 1994 (voice), Storytime, 1994, Nobody's Girls, 1994, Now and Then, 1995, Music of the Heart, 1999, Hanging Up, 2000, Manna From Heaven, 2002, Alex & Emma, 2003, Bad Santa, 2003, Spanglish, 2004, The Longest Yard, 2005, Sky High, 2005; TV series including Lassie, 1957, Mary Tyler Moore Show, 1970-75, Phyllis, 1975-77, Facts of Life, 1986-88, The Nutt House, 1989, Walter & Emily, 1991, Thanks, 1999; TV movies including Silent Night, Lonely Night, 1969, Suddenly Single, 1971, Haunts of the Very Rich, 1972, Brand New Life, 1973, Dying Room Only, 1973, Crime Club, 1973, Death Sentence, 1974, Thursday's Game, 1974, Hitchhike!, 1974, The Migrants, 1974, A Girl Named Sooner, 1975, Ladies of the Corridor, The New Original Wonder Woman, 1975, Death Scream, 1975, Someone I Touched, 1975, It Happened One Christmas, 1977, Long Journey Back, 1978, Mrs. R.'s Daughter, 1979, Willa, 1979, S.O.S. Titanic, 1979, The Acorn People, 1981, Advice to the Lovelorn, 1981, Miss All-American Beauty, 1982, Dixie: Changing Habits, 1983, The Demon Murder Case, 1983, Ernie Kovacs, Between the Laughter, 1984, Deadly Intentions, 1985, Love is Never Silent, Danielle Steele's Fine Things, 1990, In Broad Daylight, 1991, A Little Piece of Heaven, 1991, Fade to Black, 1993, Without a Kiss Goodbye, 1993, Spies, 1993, Miracle Child, 1993, Double, Double, Toil and Trouble, 1993, Between Love and Honor, 1995, Crazy Love, 2003; (TV miniseries) Backstairs at the White House, 1979, Beach Girls, 2005; theater appearance in Grandma Moses: An American Primitive, Washington, 1990; TV appearances include: Alfred Hitchcok Presents, 1955, 58, 62, Gunsmoke, 1956, 61, Zane Grey Theater, 1956, Rawhide, 1960, The Twilight Zone, 1961, 2003, The Untouchables, 1962, Dr. Kildare, 1965, Perry Mason, 1966, Rhoda, 1974, Wonder Woman, 1975, The Muppet Show, 1977, The Love Boat, 1985, (voice) The Simpsons, 1991, The Nanny, 1994, Touched by an Angel, 1997, 2003, The Norm Show, 2000, Malcolm in the Middle, 2001, 03, 04, Joan of Arcadia, 2004. Recipient 6 Emmy awards; named Miss Chicago in Miss America contest 1946.*

LEACHTENAUER, JON CLARK, optical scientist; b. Kingston, N.Y., Feb. 25, 1936; s. Clark and Ruby Mae L.; m. Christine Catherine Carr, Aug. 24, 1957 (div. 1975); children: Caroline, Jon, Paul; m. Mary Ellen Kevilly, Jan. 14, 1978; 1 child, Amy. AB in Geology, Syracuse U., 1957, MS in Geology, 1959. Rsch. scientist Aero Svc. Corp., Phila., 1961-65; dept. mgr. Photics Rsch., Montgomeryville, Pa., 1965-68; rsch. scientist Boeing Co., Kent, Wash., 1968-78; rsch. mgr. ERIM Internat., Arlington, Va., 1978-99; pres. J/M Leachtenauer Assoc. Inc., 1999—. Author: (with R. Driggers) Surveillance and Reconnaissance Imaging Systems: Modeling and Performance Prediction, 2001; contbr. chpt. to book: Corona Between the Sun and the Earth, 1997, also articles to sci. jours. Pres. PTA, Annandale, Va., 1989-91, treas., 1995-97; divsn. coord. WAGS Soccer Tournament, Springfield, Va., 1993-95. 1st lt. U.S. Army, 1959-61. Mem. Soc. Info. Display, Human Factors Soc., Am. Soc. Photogrammetry and Remote Sensing, Soc. Motion Picture and TV Engrs., Soc. Photog. Inst. Engring., Soc. Imaging Sci. and Tech., Sigma Xi. Avocations: photography, lutherie, model railroading. E-mail: jcleachtr@aol.com.

LEADER, BRUCE ROBERT, secondary school educator; b. Buffalo, Mar. 9, 1967; s. Bennett and Fay (Broder) L. BA in History and Philosophy, SUNY, Binghamton, 1989; MA in History, SUNY, Buffalo, 1991. Programming asst. Sta.-WBFO Radio, NY, 1989-90; supr. computer lab. Williamsville Ctrl. Schs., NY, 1991; tchr. social studies Starpoint Ctrl. Schs., Lockport, NY, 1991—; head of history Anglican Interant. Sch., Jerusalem, 2000—02. Head coach soccer Starpoint Ctrl. Schs., 1992—; tchr. Bridges for Edn., Poland, summer 1995; mem. U.S. Bicycling Tour, summer 1991; English lang. tchr. Yew Wah Lang. Sch., Shanghai, China, summer 1999. Head coach Amherst Soccer Assn., 1989-92. Recipient Nat. Sallie Mae award outstanding first yr. tchr. Democrat. Jewish. Avocations: reading, bicycling, travel, camping. Home: 650 Auburn Ave Buffalo NY 14222-1415 Office: Starpoint Ctrl Schs 4363 Mapleton Rd Lockport NY 14094-9652

LEADER, JOYCE E., ambassador; BA, Denison U, 1964; MA, U. Chgo., 1969; MS, Columbia U Sch of Journalism, 1974. Desk officer U.S. Fgn. Svc., 1982—83, dep. chief of mission, 1983—85; political officer U.S. Embassy, Nigeria, 1985—88, U.S. Fgn Svc., Rwanda, 1991—94; prin. officer U.S. Fgn. Svc., Marseille, 1994—97, counselor Sr. Fgn. Svc., 1997—99, U.S. ambassador to Republic of Guinea, 1999-00; sr. fellow The Fund for Peace, Washington, 2000—01; dir. Office of Assistance to Refugees in Asia & Near E. Bureau for Population, Refugees & Migration, Washington, 2001—03.

LEADER, ROBERT JOHN, lawyer; b. Syracuse, N.Y., Oct. 14, 1933; s. Henry John and Dorothy Alberta (Schad) Leader; m. Nancy Bruce, Sept. 23, 1960 (dec.); children: Henry, William, Catherine, Thomas, Edward. AB, Cornell U., 1956; JD, Syracuse U., 1962. Bar: N.Y. 1963. Assoc. Ferris, Hughes, Dorrance & Groben, Utica, N.Y., 1962-64; ptnr. Cole Leader & Elmer, Gouverneur, N.Y., 1964-66, Case & Leader, Gouverneur, 1966—. Sec. North Country Hosps. Inc., 1972—; atty. Village of Hermon (N.Y.), 1968—, Town of Gouverneur, 1967-94, Town of Pitcairn (N.Y.), 1974—, Town of Edwards, 1974—, Town of Rossie, 1985—, Town of Fowler, 1978—; corp. counsel Village of Gouverneur, 1973—2004; counsel Gouverneur Ctrl. Sch. Dist., 1980—; bd. dirs. Gouverneur Savs. and Loan Trustee Edward John Noble Hosp., Gouverneur, 1972—, Gouverneur Libr., 1973-83, Gouverneur Nursing Home Co., Inc., 1972—, past pres., 1979-81, past chmn. bd. trustees, 1979-81; Republican chmn. Town and Village of Gouverneur, 1969-72; del. N.Y. State Jud. conv., 1981—. Served to capt. USAF, 1956-59. Mem. Rotary (pres. 1988-89). Roman Catholic. Office: 107 E Main St Gouverneur NY 13642-1408 Home: 157 St Croix Ave Cocoa Beach FL 32931 Office Phone: 315-287-2000.

LEADY, VICKIE GONZALES, lawyer; BA, Princeton U., 1988; JD, SMU Dedman Sch. Law, 1991. Bar: Tex. 1991. Assoc. Strasburger & Price, LLP, Dallas, 1991—93; pvt. practice Austin, Tex., 1994—98; exec. asst. to sr. v.p. Schlotzsky's, Inc., Austin, 1998, spl. projects coord., 1999, corp. counsel, 1999—2002, gen. counsel, 2002—05, Schlotzsky's, Ltd., Austin, 2005—. Mem. Travis County Fee Dispute Com., Austin, 1995—97. Dir. D-Art Visual Arts Ctr., Dallas, 1992—93; com. mem. Austin Idea Network, 2001—02. Named Tex. Super Lawyer, Tex. Monthly/Law & Politics Magazines, 2004, Tex. Rising Star Lawyer, 2004. Office: Schlotzsky's Ltd 203 Colorado St Austin TX 78701 Office Phone: 512-236-3752.

LEAF, ALEXANDER, preventive medicine physician, epidemiologist; b. Yokohama, Japan, Apr. 10, 1920; arrived in U.S., 1922, naturalized, 1936; s. Aaron L. and Dora (Hural) Leaf; m. Barbara Louise Kincaid, Oct. 1943; children: Caroline Joan, Rebecca Louise, Tamara Jean. BS, U. Wash., 1940; MD, U. Mich., 1943; MA, Harvard, 1961. Intern Mass. Gen. Hosp., Boston, 1943—44, mem. staff, 1949—, physician-in-chief, 1966—81; resident Mayo Found., Rochester, Minn., 1944—45; rsch. fellow U. Mich., 1947—49; practice internal medicine Boston, 1949—90; faculty Med. Sch., Harvard, 1949—66, Jackson prof. clin. medicine, 1966—81, Ridley Watts prof. preventive medicine, 1980—90, chmn. dept. preventive medicine and clin. epidemiology, 1980—90, Jackson prof. clin. medicine emeritus, 1990—; Disting. physician VA Medical Ctr. Brockton/W. Roxbury Hosps., Boston, 1992—97. Capt. M.C. U.S. Army, 1945—46. Recipient Outstanding Achievement award, U. Minn., 1964; fellow Vis. fellow, Balliol Coll., Eng., 1971—72, Guggenheim, 1971—72. Master: ACP; fellow: Am. Acad. Arts and Scis.; mem.: NAS, Internat. Soc. Nephrology (A.M. Richards award 1997), Assn. Am. Physicians (Kober medal 1995), Biophys. Soc., Am. Physiol. Soc., Am. Soc. Clin. Investigation (past pres.), Inst. Medicine. Home: 5 Sussex Rd Winchester MA 01890-3846 Office: Mass Gen Hosp Bldg 149 13th St Charlestown MA 02129 Office Phone: 617-726-5908. Business E-Mail: aleaf@partners.org.

LEAF, HOWARD WESTLEY, retired military officer; b. Menominee, Mich., Sept. 22, 1923; s. Joseph Conrad and Hilda Eugene (Lavoy) L.; m. Madonna Anne; children: Mary Elizabeth, Timothy M., Barbara Anne, Anne Marie Moore, Thomas M., James D. BS, Colo. Sch. Mines, 1950; MS, St. Louis U., 1955; grad., Command and Staff Coll., 1961, Indsl. Coll. Armed Forces, 1969. Commd. 2d lt. U.S. Air Force, 1951, advanced through grades to lt. gen., 1980, ret., 1985; aviation cadet, 1950-51; jet pilot, 1952-53; test pilot, 1955-60; geophysicist, 1961-64; ops. officer (49th Tactical Fighter Wing), Europe, 1965; squadron comdr. S.E. Asia, 1966; staff officer (Hdqrs. USAF), 1966-68, 69-71; wing comdr. 1st and 366th Tactical Fighter Wings, 1971-74; dep. chief staff for requirements Tactical Air Command, 1974-76; comdr. Air Force Test and Evaluation Ctr., Kirtland AFB, N.Mex., 1976-80; insp. gen. U.S. Air Force, Washington, 1980-83, asst. vice chief of staff, 1983-85; sr. v.p. BDM Internat. Corp., McLean, Va., 1984-91; dir. test and evaluation Hdqrs. USAF The Pentagon, Washington, 1992—. Mem. Air Force Sci. Adv. Bd. Decorated D.S.M., Silver Star with one oak leaf cluster, Legion of Merit, D.F.C.; recipient Eugene M. Zuckert Mgmt. Award, 1978, Disting. Achievement award Colo. Sch. Mines, 1982, Exceptional Svc. award USAF, 1997. Mem. Internat. Test and Evaluation Assn. (sr. adv. bd., Allen R. Mattews Award, 1994). Presbyterian. Home: 16002 Dr Bowen Rd Brandywine MD 20613 Office: Hdqs USAF TE 4E-995 The Pentagon Washington DC 20330-0001 Personal E-mail: leafhq@aol.com.

LEAF, MARTIN NORMAN, lawyer; b. N.Y.C., Feb. 19, 1932; s. Jack and Shirley L.; m. Louise Sarkin, Dec. 29, 1956 d. 1995; children: Marc, Jenifer, Clifton. BA, Washington U., St. Louis, 1952; JD, NYU, 1958. Bar: N.Y., U.S. Dist. Ct. 1958, U.S. Ct. Customs and Patent Appeals 1964, U.S. Ct. Mil. Appeals 1964, U.S. Ct. Claims 1964, U.S. Supreme Ct. 1964. Sr. assoc. Jacob D. Fuchsberg, N.Y.C., 1958-63; sr. ptnr. Leaf, Sternklar & Drogin, N.Y.C., 1963-; ptnr. Morrison Cohen Singer & Weinstein, LLP, 1989-90, counsel, 1999-2003; spl. master N.Y. State Supreme Ct. Arbitrator, Am. Arbitration Assn.; village atty. Hastings-on-Hudson (N.Y.), 1969-82; spl. asst. dist. atty. Westchester Country. Lectr. Far Ea. Law and Bus. Studies, Washington U., Bd. dirs. Buckminster Fuller Inst., Echo Hills Mental Health Clinic, 1973-87, Trailblazers, 1979-, Nat. Black Theatre, 1973-, Am. Arab Affairs Coun., 1983-; mem. internat. adv. bd. World Sikh Centre, 1980-; Hunger Project del. NGO, UN; mem. N.Y. State Conf. Village Ofcls. Served to 1st lt. U.S. Army, 1955-57. Recipient Disting. Svc. award VFW, 1983. Mem. Fed. Bar Coun., ABA, N.Y. State Bar Assn., New York County Lawyers Assn., N.Y. Trial Lawyers Assn., Union Internationale des Avocats. Clubs: Players, St. Anthony (N.Y.C.), N.Y. Athletic, Doubles. Assoc. editor Am. Trial Lawyers Assn. Jour., 1963-73. Home: 71 Pierce Rd East Windsor MA 01270 Office: PO Box 142 Windsor MA 01270-0142 Office Phone: 413-684-3469. E-mail: mleaf@rcn.com.

LEAF, PAUL, film producer, writer; b. N.Y.C., May 2, 1929; s. Manuel and Anna (Dardick) L.; m. Nydia Ellis, Oct. 22, 1955 (div. 1990); children: Jonathan, Alexandra, Ellen; m. Christine Hardy, Dec. 15, 1999. BA in Drama with honors, CCNY, 1952. Pres. Sea Gate Co. Dir., prodr.: 17 Broadway prodns., including The Subject Was Roses, 1964 (Pulitzer prize, 1964), films include: The Anatomy of Cindy Fink, 1967, The Last Mohican, 1967, Bach to Bach, 1968, Sunday Father, 1968, I Never Promised You a Long Run, 1970, The Reason Why, 1970, Nightside, 1972, Desperate Characters, 1972, Hail to the Chief, 1973, Judge Horton and the Scottsboro Boys, 1976 (Peabody award), Sister Aimee, 1977, Every Man a King, 1977, Top Secret, 1979, God, Sex and Apple Pie, 1998, TV prodns. include Sgt. Matlovich vs. the U.S. Air Force, 1978 (Best Feature Austin Film Fesival, Audience Favorite Ariz. Internat. Film Festival, Best Comedy Marco Island Film Festival, Best Dir. Ariz. Film Festival); author: Comrades, 1987, Red, Right, Returning, 1989. Founder, chmn. Santa Monica Arts Commn., Santa Monica Arts Found.; founder, cons., bd. dirs. Santa Monica Coll. Art, Design and Architecture, 1990—; mem. grants panel Nat. Endowment for the Arts, 1993, Nat. Endowment for the Humanities, 1994. With U.S. Army, 1952-54. Decorated Meritorious Service medal; recipient 20 internat. festival and profl. awards, including Venice, 1967, London, 1967, 68, 69, 98-99, N.Y., 1967, 68, 69, Berlin, 1972, Austin, Tucson, N.Y., San Diego film festivals. Mem. Dirs. Guild Am., Writers Guild Am. Home: 2800 Neilson Way Santa Monica CA 90405-4025 Office Phone: 310-392-5276. Personal E-mail: sea.gate@verizon.net.

LEAF, ROBERT STEPHEN, public relations executive; b. N.Y.C., Aug. 9, 1931; s. Nathan and Anne (Feinman) L.; m. Adele Ornstein, June 8, 1958; 1 child, Stuart Nathan. BJ, U. Mo., Columbia, 1952; MA, U. Mo., Columbia, 1954. Account exec. Herbert Kaufman, N.Y.C., 1956-57; various positions Marsteller Orgn., N.Y.C., 1957-65; v.p., gen. mgr. Marsteller Internat., Brussels, 1965-68, v.p. Europe, 1968-70; pres. Burson-Marsteller Internat. and Marsteller Internat., London, 1970-81; chmn. Burson-Marsteller Internat., London, 1985-97, Robert S. Leaf Cons., England, 1997—2005; dir. Burson-Marsteller Europe, Burson-Marsteller S.A., (France). Contbr. articles to profl. jours. Mem. Inst. Pub. Relations Eng., Pub. Relations Consultancy Assn. (London), Fgn. Press Assn., Pub. Relations Soc. Am., Hurlingham Club, Alpha Pi Zeta, Kappa Tau Alpha Clubs: Hurlingham (London). Home: 3 Fursecroft George St London W1H 5LF England Office: Robert S Leaf Cons Ltd 44 Grosvener Hill London W1K 3QL England Office Phone: 0207 491 2926. E-mail: bob_leaf@eu.bm.com.

LEAFBLAD, BRUCE HAROLD, music educator; b. Waukegan, Ill., Oct. 28, 1939; s. Harold Lawrence and Elvera Lilian Leafblad; m. June Darlene McGillivray, Aug. 1, 1964; children: Stewart Bruce, Stefani June Massongill. BA in Music Edn., Bethel U., St. Paul, 1962; BD in Bibl. Studies, Bethel Theol. Sem., St. Paul, 1966; MA in Music Performance/Voice, U. No. Colo., 1967; DMA in Ch. Music, U. So. Calif., 1976. Min. music and worship Lake Ave. Congl. Ch., Pasadena, Calif., 1970—80; prof. ch. music and worship Bethel Coll. and Sem., St. Paul, 1980—83, Southwestern Bapt. Theol. Sem., Ft. Worth, 1983—. Guest lectr, conf. spkr., seminar leader in field, 1970—; ednl. and liturgical cons., 1970—. Contbr. (books) We'll Sing and Shout Hosanna, Experience God in Worship; author: (monograph) Thirty Centuries of Music and Worship. Mem.: Internat. Fedn. for Choral Music, Hymn Soc.

US and Can., Am. Choral Dirs. Assn. (life). Home: 4513 French Lake Dr Fort Worth TX 76133 Office: Southwestern Bapt Theol Sem 2001 W Seminary Dr Fort Worth TX 76122 Personal E-mail: bleafblad@swbts.edu.

LEAHEY, LYNN, editor-in-chief; married; 1 child, Jack. BA in English, Colgate U., 1981. From asst. editor, to mng. ed then editor-in-chief Soap Opera Digest, NYC, 1984—91, editor-in-chief, 1991—; editl. dir. Soap Opera Weekly, NYC, 2001—. Office: Soap Opera Digest 261 Madison Ave Fl 10 New York NY 10016-2303*

LEAHY, ARTHUR STEPHEN, economist, educator; b. N.Y.C., Sept. 4, 1951; s. Arthur Thomas and Agnes (Haslach) Leahy. BA, SUNY, Oneonta, 1973; MA, SUNY, Binghamton, 1977, PhD, 1981. Industry economist FCC, Washington, 1978-88, U.S. Dept. Treasury, Washington, 1991—; economist FAA, Washington, 1988-91. Adj. prof. Strayer U., Washington, 1989—. Contbr. articles to profl. jours. Mem.: So. Econ. Assn., Indsl. Orgn. Soc., Am. Econ. Assn., Omicron Delta Epsilon. Avocation: swimming. Office: 500 N Capitol St NW Washington DC 20221-0003

LEAHY, CHRISTINE A., information technology executive; b. June 1964; Degree, Brown U.; JD, Boston Coll. Former ptnr. Sidley Austin Brown & Wood, Chgo.; v.p. pres., gen. counsel, corp. sec. CDW Computer Ctrs., Vernon Hills, Ill., 2002—. Office: CDW 200 N Milwaukee Ave Vernon Hills IL 60061 Home: 904 Glencoe Dr Glencoe IL 60022-1249

LEAHY, MICHAEL JOSEPH, newspaper editor; b. Chgo., Feb. 24, 1939; s. Joseph Michael and Elizabeth Catherine (Keefe) L.; m. Harriet Smith Friday, Sept. 18, 1971; children: Christine Elizabeth, Thomas Joseph, Christopher Michael. AB, Georgetown U., 1961; MS in Journalism, Columbia U., 1966. From copy boy, news clk., copy editor to editor L.I. Weekly N.Y. Times, N.Y.C., 1961-77, editor Conn. Weekly, 1977-81, travel editor, 1982-86, editor arts and leisure sect., 1986-90, dep. editor The Week in Review, 1990-92, real estate editor, 1992—2004, spl. projects editor, 2004—. Editor: If You're Thinking of Living In All About 115 Great Neighborhoods In & Around New York, (with A.M. Rosenthal, A. Gelb and N. Kerr) The Sophisticated Traveler series. Bd. advisors Georgetown Coll., 1990-96; mem. edn. com. St. David's Sch., 1991-93. 1st lt. U.S. Army, 1961-64. Pulitzer Traveling fellow Columbia U., 1967 Mem. Georgetown Libr. Assocs. (trustee 1981-94, 97—), Columbia Journalism Alumni (pres. 1981-83), Century Assn. Roman Catholic. Office: NY Times Co 229 W 43rd St New York NY 10036-3959

LEAHY, PATRICK JOSEPH, senator; b. Montpelier, Vt., Mar. 31, 1940; s. Howard and Alba (Zambon) L.; m. Marcelle Pomerleau, Aug. 25, 1962; children: Kevin, Alicia, Mark. BA, St. Michael's Coll., Vt., 1961; JD, Georgetown U., 1964. Bar: Vt. 1964, D.C. 1979, U.S. Ct. Appeals (2d cir.) 1966, Vt. Fed. Dist. Ct. 1965, U.S. Supreme Ct. 1968. State's atty., Chittenden County, Vt., 1966-75; U.S. senator from Vt., 1975—; ranking minority mem. com. on the judiciary; mem. com. on agr., nutrition and forestry; mem. appropriations com. Mem. World Hunger bd.; bd. visitors U.S. Mil. Acad. West Point, Gallaudet Coll., Nat. Coll. Deaf, Washington. Recipient 1st Amendment award Soc. Profl. Journalists, John Peter and Anna Catherine Zenger award for outstanding contributions in support of press freedom & the people's right to know, 1999. Mem. Nat. Dist. Attys. Assn. (v.p. 1971-74) Democrat. Office: US Senate 433 Russell Senate Ofc Washington DC 20510-0001*

LEAHY, T. LIAM, business development and technology investor; b. Camp Lejeune, N.C., Apr. 15, 1952; s. Thomas James and Margaret May L.; m. Shannon Kelly Brooks, Apr. 21, 1990. BS, St. Louis U., 1974, MA, 1975. V.p. sales Cablecom Inc., Chgo., 1976-80, Kaye Advt., N.Y.C., 1980-82; group pub. Jour. Graphics Pub., N.Y.C., 1983-85; pres., gen. mgr. Generation Dynamics, N.Y.C., 1985-86; pres., dir. Leahy & Assocs., N.Y.C., 1982—2004, L.A., 1982—2001; v.p. RBAC, Inc., 1999—; pres. Global Area Network, 2001—. Chmn. Global Area Network; bd. dirs. RBAC, Inc. Contbr. articles to profl. jours. Mem. Turnaround Mgmt. Assn., L.A. C. of C. Avocations: jazz, woodwinds, film. Office Phone: 877-810-7295. Business E-Mail: liam@liamleahy.com.

LEAHY, SIR TERRY, food products executive, marketing professional; b. Liverpool, Eng., Feb. 28, 1956; m. Alison Leahy; children: Kate, Tom, David. Attended, St. Edwards Coll.; BSc in mgmt. sci. with honors, UMIST, 1977. Joined Tesco, 1979; comml. dir. fresh foods Tesco PLC, 1986, mktg. dir., 1992—, dep. mng. dir., 1995, CEO, 1997—. Vis. prof. mktg. UMIST, 1984—; co-chancellor Manchester U.; European bus. leader Wall St. Jour., 2005. Dir. Liverpool Vision. Named European Businessman Yr., Fortune mag., 2004, Most Admired Leader in UK, Mgmt. Today, 2004; recipient Alumnus Yr. award, UMIST, 1996, Freedom of the City of Liverpool, 2001, knighthood for svcs. to food retailing, 2002. Avocations: football, theater. Office: Tesco PLC Tesco House Delamare Rd Cheshunt Hertfordshire EN8 9SL England

LEAHY, THOMAS MELVIN, JR., writer; b. Denison, Iowa, Nov. 2, 1923; s. Thomas Melvin and Marie Christiansen Leahy; m. Maudie Lovella Schoolcraft, Oct. 16, 1946; children: Michal Suzanne, Thomas Melvin, Robert Marcus. BA in English and Econs., U. N.Mex., 1960; MA in Journalism and Comm., U. Fla., 1972. Commd. 2d lt. US Army, 1945, advanced through grades to lt. col., ret., 1970; prof. journalism U. Fla., Gainesville, 1973—88; dir. pub. rels. Fla. Sea Grant Coll. Program. Author: Sharron's Song, 2000, Blood Red Sand, 2001, The Steward, 2002. Mem.: Ret. Officers Assn., Gator City Kiwanis (pres. 1993—94), Phi Kappa Phi. Lutheran. Avocation: golf. Home: 10 NW 88 Ter Gainesville FL 32607

LEAHY, WILLIAM PATRICK, academic administrator, historian, educator; b. Omaha, July 16, 1948; s. Edward and Alice (McGinnis) Leahy. Student, Creighton U., 1966—67, Jesuit Coll., 1967—70; BA in Philosophy, St. Louis U., 1972, MA in U.S. History, 1975; MDiv in Theology, Jesuit Sch. Theology, Berkeley, Calif., 1978, STM in Hist. Theology, 1980; PhD in U.S. History, Stanford U., 1986. Ordained to ministry Cath. Ch., 1978. Tchr. Campion Jesuit H.S., Prairie du Chien, Wis., 1973—75; tchg. asst. Stanford U., 1981; instr. history Marquette U., Milw., 1985—86, asst. prof., 1986—91, acting asst. chmn., 1988—90, assoc. prof. history, exec. v.p., 1991—96; pres. Boston Coll., Chestnut Hill, Mass., 1996—. Author: Adapting to America: Catholics, Jesuits and Higher Education in the Twentieth Century, 1991; contbr. articles to profl. jours. Trustee Boston Coll., St. Joseph's U., Phila.; bd. dirs. Weston Jesuit Sch. Theology, Assn. Cath. Colls. and Univs., Nat. ASsn. Ind. Colls. and Univs; mem. pres. com. Bishops and Cath. Coll. and Univs. Mem.: Assn. Jesuit Colls. and Univs. (mem. bd.), History Edn. Soc. Office: Boston Coll Office of the Pres 18 Old Colony Rd Chestnut Hill MA 02467-3934 Office Phone: 617-552-3250. E-mail: leahy@bc.edu.

LEAK, ROBERT EDWARDS, economic development consultant; b. Charlotte, N.C., Sept. 15, 1934; s. James Pickett and Cornelia (Edwards) L.; m. Martha Councill, Aug. 25, 1956; children: Robert E., James Councill. BS, Duke U., 1956; MS, U. Tenn., 1957. With Pan Am. Petroleum Co., Lafayette, La., 1957-59, Allied Securities Corp., Raleigh, NC, 1961-62, Cameron Brown Mortgage Co., Raleigh and Charlotte, 1962-64, N.C. Dept. Natural and Econ. Resources, Raleigh, 1959-61, 64-76, dir. divsn. econ. devel., until 1976; dir. S.C. State Devel. Bd., Columbia, 1976-84; pres. Rsch. Triangle Park Found., NC, 1984-88; prin. Leak-Goforth Co., LLC, Raleigh, 1988—. Mem. U.S. Dept. Commerce Small Bus. Adv. Coun., vice-chmn. Dist. Export Coun.; leader industry organized govt. approved trade and indsl. devel. missions to Can., Europe, S.Am., Australia, Far East. Bd. dirs. Raleigh YMCA, S.C. Tech. and Comprehensive Edn., N.C. Symphony Fedn., Duke Alumni Assn., Carolina Ballet; chmn. bd. dirs. Wake Tech. C.C. Found.; adv. bd. Duke Hosp.; sr. warden vestry Christ Episcopal Ch.; past pres. Internat. Econ. Devel. Coun. Mem. Nat. Assn. State Devel. Agys. (past pres.), Raleigh Rotary Club (bd. dirs., Paul Harris fellow). Episcopalian. Home: 3301 Landor Rd Raleigh NC 27609-7012 Office: 4601 Six Forks Rd Ste 500 Raleigh NC 27609 E-mail: bobbleak@aol.com.

LEAKE, GENEVIEVE ELLEN, chemistry educator; m. David Leake; children: Martha Wolf, Rachel Wolf, Rosemary Wolf. BS in secondary edn., U. Del., Newark, 1975, MInstrn., 2003. Cert. chemistry instrn. Del., 2003. Tchr. chemistry Christiana H.S., Newark, Del., 1993—97, Howard H.S. of Tech., Wilmington, Del., 1997—98, Newark H.S., Del., 1998—99, Christiana H.S., Newark, Del., 1999—2001, Newark H.S., Del., 2001—. Lead H.S. sci. tchr. State of Del., Dover, Del., 2000—. Grantee, MBNA, 2001. Mem.: Nat. Sci. Tchr. Assn., Del. Teachers of Sci. (life), Phi Kappa Phi. Avocations: reading, needlecrafts, sports.

LEAL, J. TERRI, academic facility administrator; b. San Antonio, Apr. 20, 1949; d. Antonio Fernando and Maria Teresa (Narvarte) L.; children from previous marriage: Giovanni DeGerolami, Carla DeGerolami; m. Robert K. Young, Nov. 4, 1990. BA, U. Tex., 1971; MS, Trinity U., 1982; PhD, U. Tex., 1988. Lic. profl. counselor, Tex. Test adminstr., counselor San Antonio Coll., 1972-83; from tchg. asst. to dir. instnl. analysis U. Tex., San Antonio, 1982-95, asst. v.p. assessment, dir. instnl. analysis, 1995—. Owner South Tex. Data Cons., San Antonio, 1994—; CEO Fundamental Orientation for Coll. and U. Survival, 1998—. Author: (personality test) Gender Fair Embedded Figures Test, 1988. Mem. Assn. Instnl. Rsch., Tex. Assn. Instnl. Rsch. Roman Catholic. Avocations: sailing, home repair, writing, reading. Office: U Tex 6900 N Loop 1604 W San Antonio TX 78249-1130

LEAL, JOSEPH ROGERS, chemist; b. New Bedford, Mass., Sept. 14, 1918; s. Joaquim S. and Mary C. (Rogers) L.; m. Mary Desmond, Apr. 25, 1944; children: Joseph E., Michael J., Patricia M., Victoria A. Diploma, U. Mass., Dartmouth, 1940; BS summa cum laude, U. Mass., 1949; PhD, Ind. U., 1953. Asst. chemist CPC Internat., Edgewater, NJ, 1940—42, Revere Copper & Brass Co., New Bedford, 1942-43, 45-46; rsch. chemist Am. Cyanamid Co., Bound Brook, 1952-57, tech. rep. Washington, 1957-63, mgr. contract rels. Stamford, Conn., 1963-67; sr. staff assoc. Celanese Rsch. Co., Summit, N.J., 1967-83; pres. Crescent Cons., Maplewood, N.J., 1983-97, South Hadley, Mass., 1997-2000. Served chem. warfare svc. U.S. Army, 1943—45. Frederick Gardiner Cottrell fellow, 1950, Corn Industries Rsch. fellow, 1951-52. Mem. AAAS, Am. Chem. Soc., SAMPE, Sigma Xi, Sci. Rsch. Soc. Achievements include research in high temperature resistant polymers, nonflammable fibers, high strength high modulus reinforcement materials, fiber reinforced organic, ceramic and metal composites. Home: 30 Lawn St South Hadley MA 01075-1833

LEALE, OLIVIA MASON, small business owner, import marketing executive; b. Boston, May 5, 1944; d. William Mason and Jane Chapin (Prouty) Smith; m. Euan Harvie-Watt, Mar. 11, 1967 (div. Aug. 1979); children: Katrina, Jennifer; m. Douglas Marshall Leale, Aug. 29, 1980. BA, Vassar Coll., 1966. Cert. paralegal, beginning yoga instr. Sec. to dir. Met. Opera Guild, N.Y.C., 1966; sec. to pres. Friesons Printers, London, 1974-75; guide, trainer Autoguide, London, 1977-79; ptnr. Inmark Internat. Mktg. Inc., Seattle, 1980—. Owner and mgr. Argus Ranch Facility for Dogs, Seattle, 2001—. Social case worker Inner London Ednl. Authority, 1975-76. Democrat. Presbyterian. Avocations: reading, making doll house furniture, painting, knitting, dog agility. Home and Office: 1233 Shenandoah Dr E Seattle WA 98112-3727 Office Phone: 253-333-2347. Personal E-mail: oleale@comcast.net.

LEAMAN, DAVID MARTIN, cardiologist, educator; b. Lancaster, Pa., Apr. 24, 1935; s. Benjamin Denlinger and Elise Mae (Martin) L.; m. Doris Jean Heisey; children: Gretchen Jane, Heidi Jean, Erika Ingrid. Student, Franklin & Marshall Coll., 1956-58; BA, Eastern Mennonite Coll., 1960; MD, Temple U., 1964. Intern Mary Hitchcock Hosp., Hanover, N.H., 1964-66; resident U. Vt., Burlington, 1968-71; asst. prof. medicine Pa. State U., Hershey, 1971-77, assoc. prof., 1977-84, prof., 1984—, chief div. of cardiology, 1984-95, asst. dean for student affairs, 1987-91, asst. dean for admissions, 1991-94. Contbr. articles to med. jours. Sch. dir. Lower Dauphin Sch. Dist., Hummelstown, Pa., 1977-83. Served with USPHS, 1966-68. Named Alumnus of Yr. Eastern Mennonite Coll., 1985. Fellow Am. Coll. Cardiology, Am. Coll. Chest Physicians, ACP, Soc. Cardiac Angiology, Am. Heart Assn. (mem. council on clin. cardiology, Service Recognition award 1981, Disting. Service award 1985, bd. dirs. Pa. affiliate 1975—), Alpha Omega Alpha. Republican. Mennonite. Avocations: reading, photography. Office: Pa State Univ Hershey Med Ctr PO Box 850 Hershey PA 17033-0850 Office Phone: 717-531-8407. Business E-Mail: dleaman@psu.edu.

LEAMAN, J. RICHARD, JR., paper company executive; b. Lancaster, Pa., Sept. 22, 1934; s. J. Richard and Margaret B. (Leaman); m. Helen Brown, June 15, 1957; children: Lynda B., J. Richard, III. BA, Dartmouth Coll., 1956, MBA, 1957; PhD (hon.), Widener U., 1988. With Scott Paper Co., Phila., 1960-95, v.p. comml. products, 1975-78, exec. v.p. mktg. and sales, 1978—, pres. Packaged Products div., 1983-86, vice chmn., 1991-94, dir., 1986; pres. Scott Worldwide, 1986-91; pres., CEO, S.D. Warren Co., Boston, 1991-95. Bd. dirs. Church & Dwight Co., Inc., Pep Boys, Elwyn Inc., Stonebridge Fin. Corp. Recipient Disting. Performance in Mgmt. award Widener U. Mem. Conf. Bd.'s Coun. on Global Bus. Mgmt., Dartmouth Club (Phila.). Republican. Episcopalian. Home: 317 Boot Rd Malvern PA 19355-3317 Office: 225 Franklin St Boston MA 02110-2804 E-mail: jrl2assoc@aol.com.

LEAMAN, LEONARD S., JR., science educator; b. N.Y.C., Nov. 30, 1945; s. Leonard S. and Elinore McNamee Leaman. BA, Holy Cross Coll., 1968; MFA, NYU, 1971. Camping and trip leader Camp Winaco, Sebago, Maine, 1970—92; sci. tchr. St. Hilda's and St. Hugh's Sch., N.Y.C., 1976—80, Trinity Sch., N.Y.C., 1980—, dean, 1993—99, 2001—. Writer, dir.: (film) Papa You're Crazy, 1971; writer, dir., photographer: (film) One Year's Spring, 1971; cameraman: (film) Eugene, 1971 (Cine Golden Eagle award 1971). Charles Bluhdorn fellow Trinity Sch., 1983, Earthwatch fellow, 1994. Mem. Assn. Tchrs. in Ind. Schs., Am. Mus. Natural History (assoc.), N.Y. Acad. Scis., Appalachian Mountain Club, Orion Soc., N.Y. Bot. Garden. Roman Catholic. Home: 70 W 95th St New York NY 10025 Office: Trinity Sch 139 W 91st St New York NY 10024 Office Phone: 212-932-6851. E-mail: lennyleaman@netscape.net, winaco@mac.com.

LEAMER, LAURENCE ALLEN, writer; b. Chgo., Oct. 30, 1941; s. Laurence Eugene and Helen Mae (Burkey) L.; m. Eliana Robitschek, Sept. 12, 1968 (div. Sept. 1980); 1 child, Daniela; m. Vesna Obradovic, Dec. 16, 1984. Diploma, U. Besancon, France, 1962; BA, Antioch Coll., 1964; M.Internat. Affairs, U. Oreg., 1968; M.J., Columbia U., 1969. Vol., tchr. Peace Corps, Nepal, 1964-66; assoc. editor Newsweek, NYC, 1969-70; dir. study on underground press 20th Century Fund, NYC, 1970-71. Author: The Paper Revolutionaries, 1972, Playing for Keeps in Washington, 1977 (Notable Book of Yr., NY Times Book Rev. 1977), Assignment, 1981, Ascent: The Spiritual and Physical Quest of Willi Unsoeld, 1982, Make-Believe: The Story of Nancy and Ronald Reagan, 1983, As Time Goes By: The Life of Ingrid Bergman, 1986, King of the Night: The Life of Johnny Carson, 1989 (N.Y. Times Bestseller list), The Kennedy Women: The Saga of an American Family, 1996 (NY Times Bestseller list), Three Chords and the Truth: Hope, Heartbreak, and Changing Fortunes in Nashville, 1997, The Kennedy Men: 1901-1963, 2001 (N.Y. Times Bestseller list), Sons of Camelot: The Fate of an American Dynasty, 2004 (N.Y. Times Bestseller list), Fantastic: The Life of Arnold Schwarzenegger, 2005; contbr. articles to Harper's mag., NY Times mag., New Republic, Playboy, others. Internat. fellow Columbia U., 1968-69; Pulitzer travel fellow, 1969; recipient citation Overseas Press Club, 1973. Address: c/o Author Mail St Martin's Press 175 Fifth Avenue New York NY 10010 Mailing: 2501 M St NW 712 Washington DC 20037-7002

LEAMER, ROBERT ELDON, lawyer, hospital administrator; b. Chgo., Jan. 4, 1950; s. Laurence Eugene and Helen Mae (Burkey) L.; m. Mary Frances Leamer; children: Stephen, Christina. AB, Colgate U., 1972; JD, Albany U., 1976. Bar: N.Y. 1977, U.S. Dist. Ct. (no. dist.) N.Y. 1977. Asst. counsel N.Y. State Assembly, Albany, 1976-79; counsel N.Y. State Assembly Com. on Health, Albany, 1979-86; pvt. practice law Binghamton, N.Y., 1979-88; gen. counsel United Health Svcs., Binghamton, 1988—98; sr. v.p., gen. counsel Met. Jewish Health Sys., Bklyn., 1998—. Adj. prof. New Sch. for Social Rsch., Sch. Mgmt. Binghamton U. Mem. N.Y.-Pa. Health Sys. Agy., 1980-88; bd. dirs. Broome Legal Assistance Corp., 1985-93, Good Shepard Fairview Home, Inc., 1989-96, Broome County Coun. on the Arts, 1988-94, Ctr. for Adolescent Svcs., 1993-98, Partnership 2000. Mem. ABA, N.Y. State Bar Assn., Broome County Bar Assn., Assn. Bar City N.Y., Am. Health Lawyers Assn., Am. Coll. Healthcare Execs. (diplomate). Democrat. Episcopalian. Home: 207 Noe Ave Chatham NJ 07928-1507 Office: MJHS 6323 7th Ave Brooklyn NY 11220-4711 Office Phone: 718-491-7169. E-mail: rleamer@mjhs.org.

LEAMY, NANCY M., professional athletics coach; b. Phila., Dec. 3, 1938; d. John E. and Anna Cecilia Madden; children: Anne Marie-Elizabeth Frances, Charles John, Catherine. BA, Boston Coll.; postgrad., Fairfield U. Dir. Greenwich Skating Sch. Dorothy Hamill Rink, Conn., 1971—; dir. Skating Greenwich Skating Club, Conn., 1971—95; internat., nat., sectional, regional figure skating coach, 1973—; head skating dir. Darien (Conn.) Ice Rink, 1997—2001; coach U.S. internat. team, Milan, 1997; U.S. nat. coach 2001 N. Am. Cup Challenge, 2000—01. Powerskating coach N.Y. Rangers Orgn., 1996—98; coach gold medalist Spl. Olympics, 1996; jr. olympic coach, 1995—2000; dep. governing coun. United States Figure Skating Assn., 2004—. Named to Hall of Fame, New Country Day Sch., Newton, Mass., 2004. Mem.: Profl. Skaters Assn., U.S. Figure Skating Assn., Williams Club. Republican. Roman Catholic. Avocation: horseback riding. Home: 15 Mead Ave Cos Cob CT 06807 Office Phone: 203-622-6634.

LEANDRE, JUAN (JOAN LEANDRE), computer graphics designer, artist; b. Barcelona, May 7, 1968; Organizer OVNI Scanner, Barcelona, 1992—99; author MAP Series Maga Assemble Project, 1994—96; mem. Oigo Rom Project Institut Universitari del Audiovisual, Barcelona, 1996—98. Retroy-ou.org, 1999—, exhibited in group shows at Whitney Biennial, Whitney Mus. Am. Art, 2004. Mailing: c/o Whitney Museum American Art 945 Madison Ave New York NY 10021*

LEANSE, THOMAS J., lawyer; b. L.A., Feb. 21, 1954; BA, U. Calif., San Diego, 1975; JD, U. San Diego, 1978. Bar: Calif. 1978, Ill. 1979, US Supreme Ct. 1982. Asst. state atty. Cook County, Ill., 1979—81; gen. counsel US Ski Assn. and US Ski Team, 1985—94; ptnr. Katten Muchin Rosenman LLP, LA. Mem.: ABA, LA County Bar Assn., Internat. Coun. of Shopping Ctrs., Calif. Bus. Properties Assn., Anti-Defamation League, Cedars-Sinai Med. Ctr. Office: Katten Muchin Rosenman LLP Ste 2600 2029 Century Park E Los Angeles CA 90067 Office Phone: 310-788-4475. Office Fax: 310-712-8426. E-mail: thomas.leanse@kattenlaw.com.

LEAPHART, W. WILLIAM, state supreme court justice; b. Butte, Mont., Dec. 3, 1946; s. Charles William and Cornelia (Murphy) L.; m. Barbara Berg, Dec. 30, 1977; children: Rebecca, Retta, Ada. Student, Whitman Coll., 1965—66; BA, U. Mont., 1969, JD, 1972. Bar: Mont. 1972, U.S. Dist. Ct., U.S. Ct. Appeals (9th cir.) 1975, U.S. Supreme Ct. 1975. Law clk. to Hon. W.D. Murray U.S. Dist. Ct., Butte, 1972—74; ptnr. Leaphart Law Firm, Helena, Mont., 1974—94; justice Mont. Supreme Ct., Helena, 1995—. Office: Mont Supreme Ct Justice Bldg 215 N Sanders St Rm 315 Helena MT 59601-4522 also: PO Box 203001 Helena MT 59620-3001

LEAR, ERWIN, anesthesiologist, educator; b. Bridgeport, Conn., Jan. 1, 1924; s. Samuel Joseph and Ida (Ruth) L.; m. Arlene Joyce Alexander, Feb. 15, 1953; children: Stephanie, Samuel MD, SUNY, 1952. Diplomate Am. Bd. Anesthesiology, Nat. Bd. Med. Examiners. Intern L.I. Coll. Hosp., Bklyn., 1952-53; asst. resident anesthesiology Jewish Hosp., Bklyn., 1953-54, sr. resident, 1955, asst., 1955-56, adj., 1956-58, assoc. anesthesiologist, 1958-64; attending anesthesiologist Bklyn. VA Hosp., 1958-64, cons., 1977—; assoc. vis. anesthesiologist Kings County Hosp. Ctr., Bklyn., 1957-80, staff anesthesiologist, 1980-81; vis. anesthesiologist Queens Gen. Hosp. Ctr., 1955-67; dir. anesthesiology Queens Hosp. Ctr. Jamaica, 1964-67; chmn. dept. anesthesiology Catholic Med. Ctr., Queens and Bklyn., 1968-80; dir. anesthesiology Beth Israel Med. Ctr., N.Y.C., 1981-98; clin. instr. SUNY Coll. Medicine, Bklyn., 1955-58, from clin. asst. prof. to clin. prof., 1958-80, prof., vice-chmn. clin. anesthesiology, 1980-81; prof. anesthesiology Mt. Sinai Sch. Medicine, 1981-94, Albert Einstein Coll. of Medicine, 1994—. Cons. in field. Author: Chemistry Applied Pharmacology of Tranquilizers; contbr. articles to profl. jours. Served with USNR, 1942-45 Fellow: N.Y. Acad. Medicine (sec. sect. anesthesiology 1985—86, chmn. sect. anesthesiology 1986—87), Am. Coll. Anesthesiologists; mem.: AMA, SUNY Coll. Medicine Alumni Assn. (pres. 1983, trustee alumni fund 1980), N.Y. County Med. Soc., N.Y. State Med. Soc. (chmn. sect. anesthesiology 1966—67, sec. sect. 1977—81), N.Y. State Soc. Anesthesiologists (chmn. pub. rels. 1963—73, assoc. editor Bulletin 1963—77, chmn. com. local arrangements 1968—73, dist. dir. 1972—73, bd. dirs. 1972—94, v.p. 1974—75, pres. 1976, chmn. jud. com. 1977—81, editor Sphere 1978—87, Disting. Svc. award 1996), Am. Soc. Anesthesiologists (ho. of dels. 1973—94, dir. 1981—97, chmn. com. on by-laws 1982—83, editor newsletter 1984—98, chmn. adminstrv. affairs com. 1987—94), Alpha Omega Alpha. Address: 1 Harriman Dr Sands Point NY 11050-1246

LEAR, LYN DAVIS, psychologist; m. Norman Lear; children: Benjamin, Brianna, Madeline. BA in Psychology, Calif. State Univ., Sacramento; M in Psychology, Calif. State Univ., Northridge; PhD in Clin. Psychology, Profl. Sch. Psychological Studies, San Diego. Family therapist NY Found. for Manic Depression and Depression; tchr., humanities, psychology, philosophy Brentwood Sch., LA; private practice Beverly Hills; ptnr., co-founder Graham and Statton public rels., San Francisco. Co-founder, bd. dir. Environ. Media Assn., 1989—; assoc. bd. mem. Woodshole Oceanographic Inst.; bd. dir. Rape Treatment Ctr., Women's Polit. Com., Earth Day; founder Retain Our Am. Rights (ROAR), LA, 2003. Grantee Rockefeller Fellow in Humanities, Univ. Mass., Amherst. Office: Environmental Media Assn Ste 210 10780 Santa Monica Blvd Los Angeles CA 90025*

LEAR, M. KATHLEEN, artist, music educator, small business owner; d. Charles Cecil and Margaret Ruth (Burnside) Lear; children: Kamee Lynn, Merry Rose, Jasmine Capri. MusB, Seton Hill U., Greensburg, Pa., 1988; MA in Music Edn., Duquesne U., Pitts., 1991. Music libr. Seton Hill U., Greensburg, Pa., 1983—87, piano tchr., 1987—92; asst. to dir. Sch. Music, Duquesne U., Pitts., 1989—91; piano/voice tchr. Broken Arrow Sch. Fine Arts, Pa., 1992—95; pvt. piano/voice/guitar tchr. Tulsa, 1995—96, Ligonier, Pa., 1997—99; owner Kit's Music, Art, Gifts, Ligonier, Pa., 1999—. Mem.: Music Tchrs. Nat. Assn., Phi Beta Theta. Avocations: art, painting, poetry. Office Phone: 724-516-6892. Personal E-mail: kitsmusic@hotmail.com.

LEAR, NORMAN MILTON, producer, writer, director; b. New Haven, July 27, 1922; s. Herman and Jeanette (Seicol) Lear; m. Lyn Davis; children: Benjamin Davis, Brianna, Madeline; children: Ellen, Kate B. Lear LaPook, Maggie B. Student, Emerson Coll., 1940-42, HHD, 1968. Engaged in pub. relations, 1945-49; founder Act III Comms., 1987—. Comedy writer for TV, 1950—54; dir.(writer): (films, and TV), 1954—59; prodr.: (films) Never Too Late, 1965, Start the Revolution Without Me, 1970; (TV series) Sanford and Son, Maude, 1972, Good Times, 1974, Hot L Baltimore, 1975, All That Glitters, A Year at the Top, 1977, The Baxters, 1979, Sunday Dinner, 1991; exec. prodr.: (films) Fried Green Tomatoes, 1991, Way Past Cool, 2000, Stand By Me, 1986, Princess Bride, 1987; (TV series) The Andy Williams Show, 1962, One Day at a Time, 1975, The Nancy Walker Show, 1976, Heartsounds, 1984, a.k.a. Pablo, 1984, 704 Hauser, 1994, Channel Umptee-3, 1997; prodr.(dir., creator): All in the Family, 1971 (4 Emmy awards 1970-73,

Peabody award, 1977), The Powers That Be, 1992, (screenwriter): (films) Come Blow Your Horn, 1963, Divorce American Style, 1967, The Night They Raided Minsky's, 1968, (dir., screenwriter): Cold Turkey, 1971; screenwriter Scared Stiff, 1953, creator The Jeffersons, 1975, Fernwood 2-Night, 1977. Pres. Am. Civil Liberties Found. So., Calif., 1973—; trustee Mus. Broadcasting; founder Bus. Enterprise Trust; bd. dirs People for the American Way. Served with USAF, 1942—45. Decorated Air medal with 4 oak leaf clusters; named One of Top Ten Motion Picture Producers, Motion Picture Exhibitors, 1963, 1967, 1968, Showman of Yr., Publicists Guild, 1971—77, Assn. Bus. Mgrs., 1972, Broadcaster of Yr., Internat. Radio and TV Soc., 1973, Man of Yr. Hollywood chpt., Nat. Acad. Television Arts and Scis., 1973; named to TV Acad. Hall of Fame, 1984; recipient Humanitarian award, NCCJ, 1976, Mark Twain award, Internat. Platform Assn., 1977, William O. Douglas award Pub. Counsel, 1981, 1st Amendment Lectr. Ford Hall Forum, 1981, Gold medal Internat. Radio and TV Soc., 1981, Disting. Am. award, 1984, Mass Media award, Am. Jewish Com. Inst. of Human Relations, 1986, Internat. award of Yr., Nat. Assn. TV Program Execs., 1987, Nat. Arts Medal, 1992. Mem.: AFTRA, Writers, and Dirs., Caucus Producers, Dirs. Guild Am., Writers Guild Am. (Valentine Davies award 1977). Office: Act III Comm 100 N Crescent Dr, Ste 250 Beverly Hills CA 90210*

LEAR, RICHARD EDWIN, lawyer; b. Keene, N.H., Mar. 10, 1958; s. Robert Charles and Jean (Davis) L.; m. Teresa Jeanne Vasquez, Oct. 17, 1987; children: Charles Edwin II, Courtney Elizabeth, Caroline Elise, Cathleen Erin, Christina Ellen. BA magna cum laude, U. N.H., 1980; JD, Washington & Lee U., 1983. Bar: N.H. 1983, U.S. Ct. Appeals (4th cir.) 1985, U.S. Dist. Ct. D.C. 1986, U.S. Dist. Ct. Md. 1987, U.S. Dist. Ct. (ea. dist.) Va. 1992, U.S. Dist. Ct. (we. dist.) Va. 1992. Law clk. U.S. Bankruptcy Ct. Ea. Dist. Va., Alexandria, 1983-85; assoc. Hazel, Beckhorn & Hanes, Fairfax, Va., 1985-87, Hazel & Thomas, Washington, 1987-91, ptnr., 1991-94, Holland & Knight LLP, Washington, 1994—. Asst. basketball coach, Hayfield Secondary Sch., Fairfax County, Va., 1992-99; youth soccer coach, Lee Mt. Vernon Soccer Assn., 2000—. Mem. Am. Bankruptcy Inst., No. Va. Bankruptcy Bar Assn., Phi Beta Kappa Avocation: coaching youth sports. Office: Holland & Knight LLP 2099 Pennsylvania Ave NW Washington DC 20006-6801 Business E-Mail: richard.lear@hklaw.com.

LEAR, WILLIAM H., lawyer; b. 1939; BA magna cum laude, Yale U., 1961; JD, Duke U., 1965. Bar: Calif. 1966. Sr. v.p., gen. counsel, sec. Fleetwood Enterprises, Inc., Riverside, Calif. Office: Fleetwood Enterprises Inc 3125 Myers St PO Box 7638 Riverside CA 92513-7638

LEARNARD, JAMES MICHAEL, retired finance company executive, secondary school educator; b. Worcester, Mass., June 13, 1947; s. James Felix and Katherine M. (Slater) L.; m. Mary Kathryn Douglas, Mar. 16, 1972 (div. June 1974); 1 child, Sean Patrick; m. Joyce Stanek Hogan, June 10, 1989 (div. Nov. 1991); m. Donna Cecile Courtney, Aug. 12, 1993 (div. Aug. 1995). AA, Fla. Jr. Coll., Jacksonville, 1968; BSBA, Century U., Beverly Hills, Calif., 1987, MBA, 1988; PhD (hon.), Century U., 2001, MA in Edn., 2002; BA, Augusta (Ga.) Coll., 1991. Cert. paralegal, Ga.; cert. nursing asst. Epidemiologist L.A. Dept. Health, 1972-73; credit collector supr. Levy-Wolf, Inc., Jacksonville, 1973-75; correctional officer S.C. Dept. Corrections, Aiken, 1975-76; v.p., office mgr. Nat. Auto Fin. Corp., Aiken, 1976-81; ins. agt. Security Life Ins. Co. of Ga., Augusta, 1981-82, United Ins. Co. of Am., Aiken, 1982-86, Life Ins. Co. of Ga., Atlanta, 1986-87, The Keller Agy., Aiken, 1992-94; collector ARC, Inc., Augusta, Ga., 1994; owner, collector CSRA Recovery Svcs., Inc., Aiken, 1994-99; collection mgr. Service Loan Co., Augusta, 1999—; tchr. Richmond County (Ga.) Bd. Edn. Collector Apex Fin. Co., Inc., Augusta, 1999; telemarketer So. Ind., Augusta, 1999, Hospitality Mktg. Concepts, Inc., Augusta, 1999, DialAm. Mktg., North Augusta, S.C., 1999; nursing asst. Anna Maria Nursing and Rehab. Ctr., North Augusta, 1999. Author: Words of Love, 1985, Thoughts of Love and Inspiration, 1988, Student Protests at Harvard College, 1766-1780, 1986, Catholic Hospitals in the American Healthcare System, 1988, I Praise Your Name, A Collection of Love Poems, 1998, Recipes from the Heart: Cooking for the One You Love, 1999, How Do I Love Thee? A Collection of Love Poems, 2000, Love Lasts Eternal--Love Poems to a Lovely Lady, 2000, The Not So Famous Quotations and Other Writings of James M. Learnard, 20 vols., 2000; composer: Tonight (soul ballad), 1982, (pop rock ballad), 1983, Friends (pop rock ballad), 1983, Do You Remember (soul ballad), 1983, Eastern Morn (hymn), 1983, Christmas Day, 1982, Sunset on Tampa Bay (soul ballad), 1982, 83, My Angel (soul ballad), 1983, What Will She Say? (pop rock ballad), 1983, Easter Morn, 1983; prodr. album: Michael Hicks/Love Songs, 1983. Past chmn. Animal Control Adv. Bd., Aiken. Recipient Golden Poet award World of Poetry, 1986, 87, Silver Poet award, 1988, Recognition by the S.C. House of Reps. for accomplishment as an author, poet and lycricist, 1986, Internat. Peace prize, 2002; commd. admiral S.C. Navy, 1986; recipient Medal of Honor commemorating disting. lifelong achievement Am. Biog. Assn., 1990; Eagle Scout with Bronze Palm, Boy Scouts Am., 1963. Mem. Assn. of MBA Execs., Healthcare Fin. Mgmt. Assn., Fedn. of Am. Health Svcs., Am. Hosp. Assn., Soc. for Hosp. Healthcare and Mktg., K.C. (4th degree). Roman Catholic. Home: 117 Green St Graniteville SC 29829 Office Phone: 706-796-4992. Personal E-mail: jamesmlearnard@aol.com.

LEARNED, VINCENT ROY, electrical engineer, educator; b. San Jose, Calif., Jan. 21, 1917; m. Bernice Evelyn Brown, June 5, 1938; children: Daryl Vincent, Dean Charles, Craig Edwin, Kent Brudeen, Bruce Roy. BSEE, U. Calif., 1938; PhD, Stanford U., 1943. Dir. rsch. and devel. microwave tubes Sperry Rand Corp., 1943-65; prof. elec. and computer engr. San Diego State U., 1968-87, prof. emeritus, 1987—. Fellow Inst. Radio Engrs. Office: 348 Litchfield Ln Houston TX 77024-6042

LEARSY, RAYMOND J., private investor; b. Luxembourg; m. Melva Bucksbaum. Mem. Nat. Coun. on Arts, 1982—88; trustee Whitney Mus. Am. Art. Named one of top 200 collectors, ARTnews Mag., 2004; recipient Gertrude Vanderbilt Whitney Award for outstanding arts patronage & philanthropy (with Melva Bucksbaum), 2004. Mem.: Whitney Mus. Am. Art, Tate Gallery. Avocation: collector of contemporary art. Mailing: 646 Willoughby Way Aspen CO 81611 also: 253 Amenia Union Rd Sharon CT 06069*

LEARY, CAROL ANN, academic administrator; b. Niagara Falls, N.Y., Mar. 29, 1947; d. Angelo Andrew and Mary Josephine (Pullano) Gigliotti; m. Noel Robert Leary, Dec. 30, 1972. BA, Boston U., 1969; MS, SUNY, Albany, 1970; PhD, Am. Univ., 1988. Asst. to v.p. for student affairs, dir. women's programs Siena Coll., Loudonville, N.Y., 1970-72; asst. dir. housing Boston U., 1972-78; dir. residence Simmons Coll., Boston, 1978-84, assoc. dean, 1984-85; assoc. dir. The Washington Campus, Washington, 1985-86; adminstrv. v.p., asst. to pres. Simmons Coll., Boston, 1988-94; pres. Bay Path Coll., Longmeadow, Mass. Bd. dirs. Mass. Mut. Fin. Group. Past pres., bd. govs. Colony Club; past pres. Cooperating Colls. of Greater Springfield; exec. com., chmn. Cmty. Found.; mem. exec. com. Women's Coll. Coalition; past pres. WGBY; bd. dir. United Bank; dir. Frank Stanley Beveridge Found.; bd. mem. Go Fit Found. Mem.: Assn. Ind. Colls. and Univs. Mass. (past chair). Avocations: art, traveling overseas, hiking. Office: Bay Path Coll Office of the President 588 Longmeadow St Longmeadow MA 01106-2212 Office Phone: 413-565-1241. E-mail: cleary@baypath.edu.

LEARY, DANIEL, artist; b. Glens Falls, N.Y., July 20, 1955; s. John Andrew and Maud Houston (Parkhurst) L. BFA, Antioch Coll., 1979; MFA, Syracuse U., 1996. One person exhbns. include Breedlove Gallery, Westark Cmty. Coll., Fort Smith, Ark., 1984, 85, Comart Gallery, Syracuse U., 1985, 87, The Printspace, U. Ark., Fayetteville, 1985, The Fort Smith Art Ctr., 1986, Printworks Gallery, 1991, 99, 2000, Chgo., 1988, 95, The Hyde Collection, Glens Falls, N.Y., 1990, The Blanden Meml. Art Mus., Fort Dodge, Iowa, 1992, The Bobbit Visual Art Ctr., Albion Coll., Mich., 1993, Sharon Campbell Gallery, Greenville, S.C., 1994, We. Mich. State U., Kalamazoo, 1994, Greenville County Fine Arts Ctr., 2002; group exhbns. include East Tenn. State U., Johnson City, 1985, Gallery Sixty-Eight, Belfast, Maine, 1985, The Fort Smith Arts Ctr., 1985, Syracuse U., 1985, The Ark. Arts Ctr. and the Decorative Arts Mus., Little Rock, 1985, The Soc. Am. Graphic Artists, 1986, Westminster Coll., New Wilmington, Pa., 1986, Joe Fawbush Editions, N.Y., 1986, Cazenovia (N.Y.) Coll., 1987, Jan Turner Gallery, L.A., 1987, The Greenville County Mus. Art, 1988, The Mpls. Inst. Arts., 1988, The Munson-Williams-Proctor Inst. Mus. Art, Utica, N.Y., 1989, The Statesville Arts and Scis. Mus., 1989, The Nat. Exhbn. Ctr. Can., Alma, Quebec, 1989, The Pyramid Arts Ctr., Rochester, N.Y., 1989, The Vero Beach Ctr. For the Arts, Fla., 1989, The Jane Voorhees Zimmerli Art Mus., Rutgers U., New Brunswick, N.J., 1990, Bradford Art Galleries and Mus., England, 1990, The Contemporary Arts Ctr., Cin., 1991, Northwest Art Gallery, Ind. U. Northwest, Gary, 1993, Printworks Gallery, Chgo., 1996, 97, Bibliotèque Nat. Québec, Montréal, Can., 1998, 2003, Adirondack C.C., Queensbury, N.Y., 1998, 2003, Parkland Coll., Champaign, Ill., 1998, Wayne State U., Detroit, 1999, S.C.'s Gov's. Sch. Arts and Humanities, Greenville, S.C., 1999, 2000, Jean Albano Gallery, Chgo., 2003; public collections include Adirondack Cmty. Coll., Queensbury, Albion (Mich.) Coll., The Ark. Arts Ctr., The Boston Pub. Library, The Blanden Meml. Art Mus., The Carnegie Mus. Art, Pitts., East Tenn. State U., Greenville (S.C.) County Arts Ctr., Greenville County Mus. Art, The Hyde Collection, Glens Falls, The Library of Congress, Washington, D.C., The Metropolitan Mus. Art., N.Y., The Milw. Art Mus., The Mpls. Inst. Arts, The Munson-Williams-Proctor Inst. Mus. Art, The N.Y. Pub. Library, The Spencer Mus. Art, U. Kans., Syracuse U., The Toledo Mus. Art, U. Ariz. Mus. Art, U. Indpls., The Walker Art Ctr., Mpls., We. Mich. U., The Williams Coll. Mus. Art, Williamstown, Mass., Wright State U., Dayton, Ohio, Yale U. Art Gallery, The Jane Voorhees Zimmerli Art Mus., Rutgers U., New Brunswick, N.J. Visual Artists Fellow NEA, 1989, N.Y. Found. for the Arts fellow, 1988. Home: PO Box 136 Hudson Falls NY 12839-0136 Office Phone: 518-747-1003. Business E-Mail: danielleary@danielleary.com.

LEARY, DAVID EDWARD, psychologist, educator; b. L.A., May 5, 1945; married; 3 children. BA in Philosophy, San Luis Rey Coll., 1968; MA in Psychology, San Jose State Coll., 1971; PhD in History of Sci., U. Chgo., 1977. Instr. psychology Holy Names Coll., Oakland, Calif., 1972-74, U. Calif. Extension Svcs., Berkeley, 1972-74; counseling psychologist Howard Inst., Oakland, 1972-74; instr. psychology San Jose (Calif.) State U. Extension Svcs., 1973-74, San Francisco State U. Extension Svcs., 1973-74, U. Calif. at Santa Cruz Extension Svcs., Monterey, 1973-74, U. Chgo., 1975; asst. prof. history and philosophy of psychology U. N.H., Durham, 1977-81, co-dir. grad. program in history and theory psychology, 1977-89, assoc. prof. psychology and humanities, 1981-87, chmn. dept. psychology, 1986-89, prof. psychology, history and humanities, 1987-89; prof. psychology, dean arts and scis. U. Richmond, Va., 1989—2002, univ. prof., 2002—. Vis. asst. prof. psychology Grad. Theol. Union, Berkeley, 1971-72; fellow Ctr. Advanced Study in Behavioral Scis., Stanford, Calif., 1982-83, co-dir. summer inst. on history of social sci. inquiry, 1986; assoc. prof. humanities Summer Program Cambridge U., Eng., 1984; presenter in field. Editor: A Century of Psychology as Science, 2d rev. edit., 1992 (Assn. Am. Pub. award 1986), An Introduction to the Psychology of Guilt, 1975; editor: Metaphors in the History of Psychology, 1990; author: (with others) Narrative Identities Psychologists Engaged in Self-Construction, 2005, The Anatomy of Impact: What Makes The Great Works of Psychology Great?, 2003, Evolving Perspectives on The History of Psychology, 2002, Encyclopedia of Psychology, 2000, A History of Psychology: Original Sources and Contemporary Research, 2d edit., 1997, The Encyclopedia of Higher Education, 1992, Writing the Social Text: Poetics and Politics in Social Science Discourses, 1992, Annual Review of Psychology, 1991, Metaphors in the History of Psychology, 1990, Reflections on The Principles of Psychology: William James After a Century, 1990, Psychology in Twentieth-Century Thought and Society, 1987, Psychology in its Historical Context, 1985, Thinkers of the 20th Century, 1984, Studies in Eighteenth-Century Culture, 1984, The Problematic Science: Psychology in Nineteenth Century Thought, 1982; contbr. articles to profl. jours. Grantee NEH, 1982-83, 91-94, Social Sci. Rsch. Ctr. Faculty Support, U. N.H., 1988, Coll. Liberal Arts Faculty Rsch. Support, U. N.H., 1987-88, Ctrl. U. Rsch. Fund, U. N.H., 1979, 87, Mellon Found., 1986, NSF, 1980-82, 82-83; rsch. fellow History Psychology Found., 1980, summer fellow NEH, 1979, 2005, U. N.H., 1978, grad. fellow U. Chgo., 1975-77 Fellow Am. Psychol. Soc.; mem. APA (centennial lectr. on history of psychology 1979-80, 91-92, fellow divsn. 24 1988—, fellow divsn. 1 1983—, pres. divsn. 26 1983-84, fellow divsn. 26 1982—, pres. divsn. 24 1994-95), Am. Assn. Higher Edn., Am. Conf. Acad. Deans (bd. dirs. 1994-00, chair 1998-99), Am. Hist. Assn., Assn. Am. Colls. Univs. (grantee 1990-91), Soc. History of Sci. in Am., Cheiron: Internat. Soc. History of Behavioral and Social Scis., Forum History of Human Sci., History of Sci. Soc., Phi Beta Kappa (hon.). Office: Univ Richmond Ryland Hall 302 Richmond VA 23173 Office Phone: 804-289-8302.

LEARY, DENIS, actor, comedian; b. Worcester, Mass., Aug. 18, 1957; s. John and Nora Leary; m. Ann Lembeck, 1989; children: Jack, Devin. BFA, Emerson Coll., 1979. Acting tchr. Emerson Coll. Co-founder Emerson Comedy Workshop, 1976. Actor: (films) Strictly Business, 1991, Loaded Weapon I, 1993, The Sandlot, 1993, Who's the Man?, 1993, Judgment Night, 1993, Demolition Man, 1993, Gunmen, 1994, The Ref, 1994, Operation Dumbo Drop, 1995, The Neon Bible, 1995, Underworld, 1996, Suicide Kings, 1997, The Real Blonde, 1997, The Matchmaker, 1997, Wag the Dog, 1997, Snitch, 1998, Wide Awake, 1998, Small Soldiers, 1998, A Bug's Life (voice), 1998, True Crime, 1999, The Thomas Crown Affair, 1999, Jesus' Son, 1999, Do Not Disturb, 1999, Company Man, 2000, Sand, 2000, Double Whammy, 2001, Lakeboat, 2001, Final, 2001, Bad Boy, 2002, Ice Age (voice), 2002, The Secret Lives of Dentists, 2002; (TV films) Favorite Deadly Sins, 1995, The Second Civil War, 1997, Subway Stories: Tales from the Underground, 1997; (TV series) Crank Yankers (voice), 2002; actor, prodr.: (films) Love Walked In, 1997; actor, writer: (films) Two If by Sea, 1996; (TV series) Remote Control, 1987-90; actor, exec. prodr., writer: (TV series) The Job, 2001-02, Rescue Me, 2004-; (comedy specials) No Cure for Cancer, 1992, Denis Leary: Lock 'N Load, 1997; host: (TV series) Paramount City, 1991; host, co-exec. prodr. (TV series) Comics Come Home, 1999; co-exec. prodr.: (TV series) Contest Searchlight, 2002; exec. prodr.: (TV series) Shorties Watchin' Shorties, 2004; prodr.: (films) Blow, 2001. Founder Leary Firefighter's Found.

LEARY, G. EDWARD, state financial commisioner; m. Betty Chamberlain; 5 children. BS in Polit. Sci., U. Utah, 1971, MBA, 1981. Cert. Internat. Rels. With collections and lending dept. Draper Bank and Trust, 1974-77; examiner Utah Dept. Fin. Instns., Salt Lake City, 1977-82, industry supr., 1982-87, chief examiner, 1987-92, commr., 1992—. Chmn. Bd. Fin. Instns.; mem. Utah Housing Fin. Agy. Bd., Utah Appraiser Registration and Cert. Bd. With USN, 1971-73. Capt. USNR, ret. 1995. Mem. Conf. State Bank Supr. (frmr. chmn.). Office: Utah Dept Fin Instns Box 146800 Salt Lake City UT 84114-6800

LEARY, MARGARET A., law librarian, library director; b. 1942; BA, Cornell U., 1964; MLS, U. Minn., 1966; JD, William Mitchell Coll. Law, St. Paul, 1973. Bar: Minn. 1973, Mich. 1974. Chpt. cataloger U. Minn. Law Libr., 1968—69; cataloger William Mitchell Coll. Law, 1970—72; atty. Legal Aid Soc., Mpls., 1972—73; lectr. U. Mich. Sch. Info. and Libr. Studies, 1974—88; asst. dir. U. Mich. Law Sch. Libr., 1973—81, assoc. dir. Ann Arbor, 1982—84, dir., 1984—. Exec. com. mem. Inst. for Continuing Legal Edn., 2004, Am. Assn. Law Libraries, 1983—86, pres., 1988—89. Contbr. articles to profl. jours. Trustee William Mitchell Coll. of Law, 1993—2002; mem. & vice-chmn., Planning Commn. City of Ann Arbor, Mich., 1994—2004. Named Volunteer of Yr., Habitat for Humanity, Huron Valley, 2002. Achievements include being first woman to head a library at one of the top 5 US law schools. Office: Office of Dir Univ Mich Law Library 801 Monroe Ann Arbor MI 48109-1210 Office Phone: 734-764-4468. Fax: 734-615-0178. Business E-Mail: mleary@umich.edu.

LEARY, ROBIN JANELL, executive secretary, municipal official; b. Hudson, Wis., July 9, 1954; d. Edward James and Marlys Marie (Ensign) L. BA in History, U. Wis., Eau Claire, 1976. From stenographer I to program asst. IV U. Wis., 1977—; sec. 3rd Congl. Dist./Dem. Com. Wis., 1993-95, elected vice chmn., 1999-2001; bd. suprs. Dist. 23, Eau Claire County, 1996—. Chair edn. and agr. com. U. Wis. Extension, 2000—. Mem. Eau Claire County Housing Commn., 2002—, Eau Claire County Groundwater Commn.; mem. steering com. Chippewa Valley Am.'s Promise, 1998—99, chair publicity and mktg. com., 1998—99; mem. appropriations com. United Way of Greater Eau Claire, 1994—96; elected asst. sec. U. Wis.-Eau Claire Found., Inc., 1999—; appointed mem. affirmative action commn. City of Eau Claire, 2004—; chmn. Eau Claire County Dem. Party, 1990—92, 1999—2000, sec., 1986—90, ex-officio mem., 2000—, exec. bd., 1993—95, 2000—, 1st vice chmn., 1996—99, elected mem. exec. bd., 1995—96; mem. credentials com. Wis. Dem. Com., 1990—95, chair com., 1990—92, mem. elections commn., 1990—, alt. platform and resolutions com., 2001—02; del. Dem. Nat. Conv., Atlanta, 1988, N.Y.C., 1992, Chgo., 1996. Recipient Classified Staff Excellence in Svc. award U. Wis.-Eau Clarie, 1995; named Female Dem. Vol. of Yr., Eau Claire County Dem. Party, 1989. Mem. AFL-CIO (Eau Claire area labor coun., treas. 1986-94, trustee 1994-98, 98-99, treas. 1999—, sec. 3d congl. dist. com. on polit. edn. 1993-97, 97—), AAUW, AFSCME Pub. Employees Organized to Promote Legis. Equality (vice chmn. 3d congl. dist. 1992-93, chair com. 1993-95, elected vice-chair 3d congl. dist. P.E.O.P.L.E. 1995-97, coun. 24 family and gender com. 1990-98, 99-2000, tri-coun. state woman's com., coun. 24 contracting out com., exec. bd. liaison, bargaining del. adminstrv. support unit coun. 24 2002--), Internat. Platform Assn., Chippewa Valley-Am.'s Promise (steering Com., chmn. publicity and mktg. com. 1998-99), Wis. State Employees Union (exec. bd. coun. 24 2000-02), Wis. Women's Network. Avocations: reading, bowling. Home: 2104 Providence Ct Eau Claire WI 54703-4103 Office: U Wis 105 Garfield Ave Eau Claire WI 54701-4811 Office Phone: 715-836-5630. Business E-Mail: learyrj@uwec.edu.

LEARY, THOMAS BARRETT, federal agency administrator; b. Orange, NJ, July 15, 1931; s. Daniel and Margaret (Barrett) L.; m. Stephanie Lynn Abbott, Dec. 18, 1954, June 3, 1991; children: Thomas A., David A., Alison Leary Estep. AB, Princeton U., 1952; JD magna cum laude, Harvard U., 1958. Bar: N.Y. 1959, Mich. 1972, D.C. 1983. Assoc. White & Case, N.Y.C., 1958-68, ptnr., 1968-71; atty.-in-charge antitrust Gen. Motors Corp., Detroit, 1971-77, asst. gen. counsel, 1977-82; ptnr. Hogan & Hartson, Washington, 1983-99; commr. FTC, Washington, 1999—. Served to lt. USNR, 1952-55 Mem. ABA (antitrust sect., coun. mem. 1979-83, mem. antitrust adv. bd., BNA antitrust & trade reg. rep., 1981-99). Office: Fed Trade Commn 600 Pennsylvania Ave NW # 520 Washington DC 20580-0002 Business E-Mail: tleary@ftc.gov.

LEARY, WILLIAM JAMES, educational association administrator; b. Boston, Oct. 1, 1935; s. John Gilbert and Josephine Marie (Kelley) L.; m. Joann Linda Parodi, June 25, 1960; children: Lorraine, Lisa, Linda. S.B., Boston Coll.; M.Ed., Boston State Coll.; postgrad. (Fulbright fellow), Sophia U., Tokyo, 1967; cert. advanced study, Harvard U., 1972, Ed.D., 1973, Boston U., 1971. Tchr. pub. schs., Boston, 1960—67; chmn. dept. social studies Dorchester High Sch., Boston, 1967—68; dir. curriculum Boston Dist. Pub. Schs., 1969—72, supt. schs., 1972—75; exec. dir. Met. Planning Project, Newton, Mass., 1975—77; supt. schs. Rockville Centre, NY, 1977—82, North Babylon, NY, 1982—84, Broward County, Ft. Lauderdale, Fla., 1984—88; supt. Gloucester (Mass.) Pub. Schs., 1989—93; assoc. prof. dept. ednl. leadership, dept. chair U. Miss., Oxford, 1993—98, dir. PhD Program; prof. coll. edn. Lynn U., Boca Raton, Fla., 1998—2000. Assoc. prof. dept. continuing studies Bsoton State Coll., 1970-72; assoc. in edn. Harvard U. Grad. Sch. Edn., 1972-75; adj. prof. edn. Boston U., 1973-75, C.W. Post Ctr., L.I. U., 1979-84, Fla. Internat. U., 1984-88, Salem (Mass.) State Coll., 1990-93; prof. Suffolk U., 1977-82; TV commentator Channel 5, Boston, 1975-76; prodr. edn. programs New Eng. Cablevision, 1989-93; keynote spkr. Harvard U. Grad. Sch. Edn., 1976, NYU, 1980; mem. faculty senate U. Miss., 1994-96, chair subcom. on athletics, 1994-95. Edn. columnist Boston Herald, 1975-78, L.I. News, 1982-84, Gloucester Times; edn. commentator New Eng. Cablevision, 1989-93; contbr. articles to profl. jours. Edn. coord. Boston chpt. United Way, 1974, Rockville Centre United Fund, 1979-80, Broward County chpt., 1985-87; trustee Mus. Fin. Arts, Boston, 1972-77; bd. dirs. Boston Youth Symphony, 1972-77, Edn. Devel. Ctr., 1972-77, Broward Com. of 100, Boys Club Broward County, 1985-88; mem. nat. alumni bd. Boston U., 1975—; mem. vis. com. Suffolk U., 1978-80; adv. bd. Harvard N.Y. Alumni Forums, 1980-84; mem. L.I. Regional Planning Bd., 1983-84, Gov.'s Task Force on Alt. Edn., Fla., 1986-88; mem. Atty. Gen.'s edn. adv. com., Mass., 1991-93; lector, Eucharistic min. Ascension Cath. Ch., Boca Raton; bd. dirs., v.p., Mill Pond Homeowners Assn., Boca Raton. Served with 2d armored divsn U.S. Army. Recipient Friend of Youth award Hayden Goodwill Boys' Home, 1973, Ida M. Johnston Outstanding Alumni award Boston U. Sch. Edn., 1976, Man of Yr. award Pope's Hill Assn., 1976, Jenkins Meml. award for ednl. leadership N.Y. State Coun., PTA, 1980, Ednl. Leadership award L.I. chpt. NCCJ, 1980, Broward County Med. Aux., 1984, Lifetime Achievement award Matignon H.S. Alumni, 1995, Civil Rights award NAACP Layfayette County, MS, 1996; selected as mem. Exec. Educator 100, Nat. Sch. Bd. Assn., 1987; named to Matignon H.S. Hall of Fame, 1995. Mem. ASCD (nat. commn. on supervision 1984-85), Am. Assn. Sch. Adminstrs. (del. assembly 1991, 92, 93, resolutions com. 1988-89, 93-94, 94-95, 95-96), Am. Hist. Assn., Horace Mann League, Assn. for Asian Studies, Nat. Coun. Social Studies (nat. urban affairs com. 1977-80), Large City Sch. Supts., Mass. Atty. Gen.'s Adv. Group, Harvard Club N.Y.C., Boston Coll. Alumni Club, Varsity Club, KC, Rotary, Harvard Club of Boston and N.Y., Harvard Club of Palm Beach, Am. Legion, DAV, Comdrs. Club, Phi Delta Kappa. Roman Catholic. Office: Lynn U Grad Sch Edn Boca Raton FL 33431 E-mail: billyjoj@msn.com, bjleary@adelphia.net, gjleary@adenphia.net. *A person's ability for creative and imaginative thinking is limited only by his/her fear to dream.*

LEASE, ROBERT K., lawyer; b. Cleve., 1948; AB magna cum laude, Dartmouth Coll., 1970; JD cum laude, U. Conn., 1976. Bar: Ohio. Ptnr. Baker & Hostetler LLP, Cleve. Mem. Phi Beta Kappa. Office: Baker & Hostetler LLP 3200 Nat City Ctr 1900 E 9th St Ste 3200 Cleveland OH 44114-3485 Office Phone: 216-621-0200. E-mail: rlease@bakerlaw.com.

LEATH, CHERYL LYNN, retired pre-school educator; b. Chgo., Ill., Apr. 10, 1961; d. Wayne Lee Cutliff and Judith Louise Edwards, Sharron Cutliff (Stepmother); m. Thomas Richard Leath, Dec. 6, 1980 (div. Nov. 4, 1987); children: Cristin Lynnette McCoy, Dustin Scott, Allison Rene German. AA in applied sci., Carl Sandburg Coll., 1987—90. Practicum/internship Creative Childhood Ctr., Galesburg, Ill., 1990; preschool tchr./child care provider Children's Sch., Galesburg, Ill., 1991; child care provider Teddy Bear Day Care Ctr., Monmouth, Ill.; preschool tchr./child care provider Cameron Christian Care Ctr., Cameron, Ill., 1994—94; lead early childhood preschool tchr./child care provider Spires Child Care Ctr., Galesburg, Ill., 2003; ret. Painting in acrylics, Back Upon A Time; author: (poetry) A Veteran's Day Poem, Our World's Rainbow (editor's choice award cert., 2004), Pain, A Day Spent With Depression (editor's choice award cert., 2004), From the Heart Poetry, 2005. Mem.: Coalition of Citizens with Disabilities in Ill, Conservative-R. Christian (Faith). Avocations: writing, painting, reading, volunteering. Personal E-mail: cherieskids@yahoo.com.

LEATH, KENNETH THOMAS, plant pathologist, educator, agriculturist, consultant; b. Providence, Apr. 29, 1931; s. Thomas and Elizabeth (Wootten) L.; m. Marie Andreozzi, Aug. 1955; children: Kenneth, Steven, Kevin, Maria Beth. BS, U. R.I., 1959; MS, PhD, U. Minn., 1966. Rsch. plant pathologist U.S. Regional Pasture Rsch. Lab. USDA-ARS, 1966-94; prof. Pa. State U., 1966-94; pvt. agrl. cons. Boalsburg, Pa., 1994—. Advisor numerous state and nat. orgns. Contbr. numerous articles to profl. jours. and chpts. to books. With USN, 1951-55. Recipient state and nat. recognition for contbns. to improvements in grassland agr. Mem. Elks. Achievements include research on root diseases and systemic wilts of forage species.

LEATH, PAUL LARRY, physicist, educator, former university official; b. Moberly, Mo., Jan. 9, 1941; s. James Lewis and Naomia (Burton) L.; m. Rosemary Rippel, June 2, 1962; children: Steven, Kimberly. Grad., Moberly Jr. Coll., 1960; BS, U. Mo., 1961, MS, 1963, PhD, 1966. Rsch. officer Oxford

U., Eng., 1966-67; asst. prof. physics Rutgers U., New Brunswick, 1967-71, assoc. prof., 1971-78, prof., 1978—, assoc. provost for acad. affairs, 1978-87, provost, 1987-92, chair dept. physics and astronomy, 1995—. Sr. vis. fellow Oxford U., 1972-73, 93-94; vis. prof. Mich. State U., 1992-93. Co-author: The Theory and Properties of Randomly Disordered Crystals and Related Physical Systems, 1974. Active Millstone (N.J.) Borough Coun., 1979-84, pres., 1984; bd. dirs. New Brunswick Tomorrow, 1989-92, R&D Coun. N.J., 1980-83; bd. trustees Rutgers Preparatory Sch., 2002-. Mem. Am. Phys. Soc., Inst. Physics, AAAS, N.Y. Acad. Sci., Sigma Xi. Achievements include research in theoretical physics, properties of alloys and disordered materials, percolation processes, breakdown phenomena, and vibrational and electronic properties. Office: Rutgers U Dept Physics and Astro 136 Frelinghuysen Rd Piscataway NJ 08854-8019 Office Phone: 908-445-2521. Business E-Mail: leath@physics.rutgers.edu.

LEATHER, VICTORIA POTTS, college librarian; b. Chattanooga, June 12, 1947; d. James Elmer Potts and Ruby Lea (Bettis) Potts Wilmoth; m. Jack Edward Leather; children: Stephen, Sean. BA cum laude, U. Chattanooga, 1968; MSLS, U. Tenn., 1978. Libr. asst. East New Orleans Regional Libr., 1969-71; libr. Erlanger Nursing Sch., Chattanooga, 1971-75; chief libr. Erlanger Hosp., Chattanooga, 1975-77; dir. Eastgate Br. Libr., Chattanooga, 1977-81; dir. libr. svcs. Chattanooga State Tech. C.C., 1981-95, dean libr. svcs., 1996—. Mem. ALA, Southeastern Libr. Assn., Tenn. Libr. Assn. (past chair legis. com.), Chattanooga Area Libr. Assn. (pres. 1978-79), Tenn. Bd. Regents Media Consortium (chair 1994-95), Phi Delta Kappa. Episcopalian. Avocations: reading, needlecrafts, travel. Office Phone: 615-697-2576. Business E-Mail: vicky.leather@chattanoogastate.edu.

LEATHERBURY, THOMAS SHAWN, lawyer; b. Ft. Worth, Dec. 7, 1955; s. John Raymond and Hester Louise (Hoffecker) L.; m. Patricia Villareal, Nov. 27, 1982; children: Sean, Colin. BA, Yale U., 1976, JD, 1979. Bar: Tex. 1979, U.S. Dist. Ct. (no. dist.) Tex. 1979, U.S. Ct. Appeals (5th cir.) 1982, U.S. Dist. Ct. (we. dist.) Tex. 1984. Law clk. to presiding justice U.S. Dist. Ct. (no. dist.) Tex., Dallas, 1979-80; assoc. Locke, Purnell, Boren, Laney & Neely P.C., Dallas, 1980-86, ptnr., 1987—; ptnr., co-head Appellate Sect. Vinson & Elkins LLP, Dallas. Mem. Tex. Bar Assn., Dallas Bar Assn., Dallas Assn. Young Lawyers. Home: 4430 Woodfin St Dallas TX 75220-6420 Office: Vinson & Elkins LLP Trammell Crow Ctr 2001 Ross Ave, Ste 3700 Dallas TX 75201 Office Phone: 214-220-7792. E-mail: tleatherbury@velaw.com.

LEATHERDALE, DOUGLAS WEST, insurance company executive; b. Morden, Man., Can., Dec. 6, 1936; came to U.S., 1968; s. Walter West and Lena Elizabeth (Gilligan) L.; children: Mary Jo, Christopher BA, United Coll., Winnipeg, Man., 1957. Investment analyst, officer Gt. West Life Assurance Co., Winnipeg, 1957-68; assoc. exec. sec. Bd. Pensions, Luth. Ch., Mpls., 1968-72; exec. v.p., then v.p. St. Paul Investment Mgmt. Co., subs. St. Paul Cos., Inc., 1972-77; v.p.-fin. St. Paul Cos., Inc., 1974-81, sr. v.p.-fin., 1981-82, exec. v.p., 1982-89, also dir., pres., chief oper. officer, 1989-90, chmn.,ceo and pres., 1990—. Bd. dirs. St. Paul Fire and Marine Ins. Co., St. Paul Land Resources, Inc., St. Paul Real Estate of Ill., Inc., John Nuveen & Co. Inc., St. Paul Properties, Inc., St. Paul Oil and Gas Corp., St. Paul Fire & Marine Ins. Co. (U.K.) Ltd., St. Paul Mercury Ins. Co., St. Paul Guardian Ins. Co., St. Paul Surplus Lines Ins. Co., Nat. Ins. Wholesalers, Atwater McMillian, 77 Water St., Inc., Ramsey Ins. Co., St. Paul Risk Services, Inc., St. Paul Plymouth Ctr., Inc. Athena Assurance Co., St. Paul Fin. Group, Inc., Graham Resources, Inc., Carlyle Capital, L.P., United HealthCare Corp. Mem. Twin Cities Soc. Security Analysts, Fin. Execs. Inst. Clubs: Minnesota (St. Paul).

LEATHERMAN, HUGH KENNETH, SR., state legislator, engineering executive; b. Lincoln County, N.C., Apr. 14, 1931; s. John Bingham and Ada Annis (Gantt) L.; m. Jean Helms, Nov. 11, 1978; children: Sheila Dianne, Hugh Kenneth, Karen Ann, Joyce Lynn, Amy Jean, Sarah Ada. BS in Civil Engring., N.C. State U., 1953. Engr. then sec. Florence (S.C.) Concrete Products Inc., 1955-72, pres., 1972-93. Mem. S.C. Senate, 1980—; commr. S.C. Dept. Consumer Affairs. Mem. S.C. State Budget & Control Bd Home: 1817 Pineland Ave Florence SC 29501-5419 Office: 111 Gressette Bldg Columbia SC 29201

LEATHERS, SUSAN LYNN, music educator; d. Richard Dean and Norma Ann (Whitemeyer) Young; m. Ronald Keith Leathers; children: Melissa Miller, Kyle. B. in Music Edn., Mount Union Coll., Alliance, Ohio, 1973; MusM, Ariz. State U., Tempe, 1980. Cert. Music Edn. K-12, Ariz. 1973. Music Educator, K-8 Creighton School District, Phoenix, 1973—85; Group Piano Instructor City of Phoenix, Phoenix, 1989—93; Assistant Program Director Girl Scouts of America, Cactus Pine Council, Phoenix, 1989—90; Private Music Teacher The PLACe Music Academy, Phoenix, 1991—2001; Music, Band and Strings Educator Washington School District, Phoenix, 1990—now. Volunteer Organist Faith United Methodist Church, Phoenix, 1981—95; musician Fiesta Bowl Play It Again Band, Phoenix, 1990—96, Ariz. Winds Concert Band, Glendale, 1990—; substance abuse coord. for Sunburst Sch. Washington Sch. Dist., Phoenix, 1995—99, mem. site coun., 1996—98. Mem.: Music Educators Nat. Conf. Methodist. Avocations: genealogy, needlecrafts, photography. Home: 11437 N 61st Drive Glendale AZ 85304 Office: Sunburst School 14218 N 47th Ave Phoenix AZ 85006 Personal E-mail: leatherssl@aol.com. Business E-Mail: sleathers1@cox.net.

LEAVELL, JULITA ANN, lawyer; JD, U. N.Mex., 1998. Bar: N.Mex. 1998, U.S. Dist. Ct. N.Mex. 2002. Owner and mng. atty. Leavell & Assocs., Albuquerque, 1998—. Commn. appointee Jud. Evaluation Performance Commn., Albuquerque, 2000—. Author: CYFD, Nightmare for Families and Children. Soccer coach AYSO, Albuquerque, 2000—04; bd. dirs., v.p. Summit Park Neighborhood Assn., 2004—; commr. D.R. Task Force, 2004—, Jud. Nominating Com., 2003—; YLD chair Children's Law Sect., 2003—. Fellow UNM Grad. fellow, U. of N.Mex, 1996—98; scholar Phi Alpha Delta Hon. scholar, Phi Alpha Delta Frat., 1987. Mem.: N.Mex. Women's Bar Assn. (bd. dirs. 2000—). Avocations: swimming, bicycling, tennis. Home: 300 Central SW Ste 2500W Albuquerque NM 87102 Office: PO Box 40025 Albuquerque NM 87196-0025 Office Phone: 505-232-2270.

LEAVELLE, TOMMY LEE, mathematics professor; b. Littlefield, Tex., May 18, 1956; s. Carl Eugene and Jo Nell Leavelle; m. Cynthia Ann Hamrick, June 3, 1978; children: Richard Griffith, Robert Galbraith, Stephen Eugene. BS, Wayland Bapt. Coll., Plainview, Tex., 1978; MA, U. N. Tex., 1980, PhD, 1984. Asst. prof. John Brown U., Siloam Springs, Ark., 1984—92; prof. math. Miss. Coll., Clinton, 1992—, London prof., 2002, chair math. and computer sci., 1992—2004. Vis. prof. Nat. U. Def. Tech., Changsha, Hunan, China, 1991; cons. Jackson (Miss.) Pub. Schs., 2002—. Treas. Habitat for Humanity, Clinton, 2002—; tchr. coll. Sunday sch. First Bapt. Ch., Clinton, 2002—. Mem.: Assn. Christians Math. Scis., Nat. Coun. Tchrs. Math., Math. Assn. Am. Avocation: reading. Business E-Mail: leavelle@mc.edu.

LEAVEY, THOMAS EDWARD, international organization administrator; b. Kansas City, Mo., Nov. 10, 1934; BA, Josephinum Coll, 1957; Lic., Cath. Inst., Paris, 1964; MA, Princeton U., 1967, PhD, 1968; cert. in bus. and fin., NYU, U. Tex., U. Va., Duke U., 1969-91. Prof. Tng. and Devel. Inst., Bethesda, Md., 1970-72; dir. Postal Svc. Tng. and Devel. Mgmt. Tng. Ctr., L.A., 1973-75; gen. mgr. employment and placement divsn. USPS Hdqs., 1976-78, 1976-78, dir. postal career exec. svc., 1979; postmaster, sectional ctr. mgr. Charlottesville, Va., 1980; regional dir. human resources cen. region Chgo., 1981; contr. USPS Hdqs., 1982, gen. mgr. internat. mail processing divsn., 1982-87, asst. postmaster gen., sr. dir. internat. postal affairs, 1987-94; dir. gen. internat. bur. Universal Postal Union, Berne, 1995—. Prof. Fairleigh Dickinson U., Teaneck, N.J., George Washington U., Washington, 1968-70. Recipient ASTD award, 1973, Heinrich von Stephan medal German Ministry of Post and Telecomm., 1997, Chevalier de la légion d'honneur, 2004. Office: Universal Postal Union Case postale 3000 Bern 15 Switzerland

LEAVITT, JEFFREY STUART, lawyer; b. Cleve., July 13, 1946; s. Sol and Esther (Dolinsky) L.; m. Ellen Fern Sugerman, Dec. 21, 1968; children: Matthew Adam, Joshua Aaron. AB, Cornell U., 1968; JD, Case Western Res. U., 1973. Bar: Ohio 1973. Assoc. Jones, Day, Reavis & Pogue, Cleve., 1973-80, ptnr., 1981—. Contbr. articles to profl. jours. Trustee Bur. Jewish Edn., Cleve., 1981-93, v.p., 1985-87; trustee Fairmount Temple, Cleve., 1982-2002, v.p., 1985-90, pres., 1990-93; trustee Citizens League Greater Cleve., 1982-89, 92-94, pres., 1987-89; trustee Citizens League Rsch. Inst., Cleve., 1989-98, Great Lakes Region of Union Am. Hebrew Congregations, 1990-93; mem. bd. govs. Case Western Res. Law Sch. Alumni Assn., 1989-92; sec. Kulas Found., 1986-88, 93-99, asst. treas., 1989-92. Named Ohio Super Lawyer, Cin. Mag. and Law and Politics, 2004, 2005. Mem.: ABA (employee benefits coms. 1976—). Jewish. Home: 7935 Sunrise Ln Novelty OH 44072-9404 Office: Jones Day N Point 901 Lakeside Ave E Cleveland OH 44114-1190 Office Phone: 216-586-7188. Business E-Mail: jleavitt@jonesday.com.

LEAVITT, JEROME EDWARD, childhood educator; b. Verona, N.J., Aug. 1, 1916; s. Thomas Edward and Clara Marie (Sonn) L.; m. Florence Elizabeth Wilkins, Aug. 23, 1963. BS, Newark State Coll., 1938; MA, N.Y. U., 1942; Ed.D., Northwestern U., 1952. Tchr. pub. schs., Roslyn Heights, N.Y., 1938-42; instr. Sperry Gyroscope, Bklyn., 1942-45; prin., supr. pub. schs. Los Alamos, N.Mex., 1945-49; prof. edn., exec. asst. to dean Portland (Oreg.) State U., 1952-66; prof. edn. U. Ariz., Tucson, 1966-69; prof. elem. edn., coordinator Child Abuse Project, Calif. State U., Fresno, 1969-81; pres. Jerome Leavitt, Inc., 1981—. Author: Nursery-Kindergarten Edn., 1958, Carpentry for Children, 1959, By Land, By Sea, By Air, 1969, The Beginning Kindergarten Teacher, 1971, America and Its Indians, 1971, The Battered Child, 1974, Herbert Sonn: Yosemite's Birdman, 1975, Child Abuse and Neglect: Research and Innovation, 1983, others; contbr. articles to profl. jours. Mem. ASCD (life), NEA (life), Assn. Childhood Edn. Internat. (life), Soc.Profs. Edn., Calif. Tchrs. Assn., Profs. Curriculum, Phi Delta Kappa, Kappa Delta Pi, Epsilon Pi Tau. Home and Office: Apt 222 7500 Calle Sin Envidia Tucson AZ 85718-7316

LEAVITT, MARY JANICE DEIMEL, special education educator, civic worker; b. Washington, Aug. 21, 1924; d. Henry L. and Ruth (Grady) Deimel; m. Robert Walker Leavitt, Mar. 30, 1945; children: Michael Deimel, Robert Walker, Caroline Ann Leavitt Snyder. BA, Am. U., 1946; postgrad., U. Md., 1963-65, U. Va., 1965-67, 72-73, 78-79, George Washington U., 1966-67. cert. spl. edn. tchr. 1968. Tchr. Rothery Sch., Arlington, Va., 1947; dir. Sunnyside Children's House, Washington, 1949; asst. dir. Coop Sch. for Handicapped Children, Arlington, 1962; dir. Arlington and Springfield, Va., 1963-66; tchr. mentally retarded children Fairfax (Va.) County Pub. Schs., 1966-68; asst. dir. Burgundy Farm Country Day Sch., Alexandria, Va., 1968-69; tchr., substitute tchr. specific learning problem children Accotink Acad., Springfield, Va., 1970-80; substitute tchr. learning disabilities Children's Achievement Ctr., McLean, Va., 1973-82, Psychiat. Inst., Washington and Rockville, Md., 1976-82, Home-Bound and Substitute Program, Fairfax, Va., 1978-84. Asst. info. splst. Ednl. Rsch. Svc., Inc., Rosslyn, Va., 1974-76; docent Sully Plantation, Fairfax County (Va.) Park Authority, 1981-87, 88-94, Children's Learning Ctrs. Vol. Honor Roll, 1987, Walney-Collections Fairfax County (Va.) Park Authority, 1989-97; sec. Widowed PersonsSvc., 1983-85, mem., 1985-90; mem. ednl. subcom. Va. Commn. Children and Youth, 1973-74; den mother Nat. Capital Area Cub Scouts, Boy Scouts Am., 1962; troop and fundraising chmn. Nat. Capitol coun. Girl Scouts U.S.A., 1968-69; capt. amblyopia team No. va. chpt. Delta Gamma Alumnae, 1969; vol. Prevention of Blindness, 1980-95; fund raiser Martha Movement, 1977-78; mem. St. John's Mus. Art, Wilmington, N.C., 1989—, Corcoran Gallery Art, Washington, 1989-90, 94—, Brunswick County Literacy Coun., N.C., 1989—; Sunday sch. tchr. St. Andrews Episcopal Ch., Burke, Va., 1995-99, mem. search com., 1996, libr. project, 1999; mem. World Affairs Coun. Washington DC, 1998—. Recipient award Nat. Assn. Retarded Citizens, 1975, Sully Recognition gift, 1989, Ten Yr. recognition pin Honor Roll, 1990. Mem. AAUW (co-chmn. met area mass media com. DC chpt. 1973-75, v.p. Alexandria br. 1974-76, fellowship co-chmn., historian Springfield-Annandale br. 1979-80, 89-94, 94-95, name grantee ednl. found., 1980, cultural co-chmn. 1983-84), Assn. Part-Time Profls. (co-chmn. Va. local groups, job devel. and membership asst. 1981), Older Women's League, Nat. Mus. Women in the Arts (charter), Libr. Congress Assocs. (nat.), Mil. Dist. Washington Officer's Clubs (McNair, Ft. Myer), Delta Gamma (treas. No. Va. alumnae chpt. 1973-75, pres. 1977-79, found. chmn. 1979-81, Katie Hale award 1989, treas. House Corp. Am. U. Beta Epsilon chpt. 1994-97). Episcopalian. Home: 7129 Rolling Forest Ave Springfield VA 22152-3622 also: 325A Brunswick Ave W Holden Beach NC 28462-1903

LEAVITT, MICHAEL OKERLUND, secretary of health and human services; b. Cedar City, Utah, Feb. 11, 1951; s. Dixie and Anne (Okerlund) L.; m. Jacalyn Smith; children: Michael Smith, Taylor Smith, Anne Marie Smith, Chase Smith, Weston Smith. BA, So. Utah U., 1978. CPCU. Sales rep. Leavitt Group, Cedar City, 1972-74, account exec., 1974-76, mgr. underwriting Salt Lake City, 1976-82, COO, 1982-84, pres., CEO, 1984-92; gov. State of Utah, 1993—2003; adminstr. EPA, Washington, 2003—05; sec. US Dept. Health & Human Services, Washington, 2005—. Bd. dirs. Pacificorp, Portland, Oreg., Utah Power and Light Co., Salt Lake City, Great Western Thrift and Loan, Salt Lake City; vice-chmn. Grand Canyon Visability Transport Commn.; co-chair Western Regional Air Partnership. Chmn. instl. coun. So. UT St. U., Cedar City, 1985-89, chmn, UT St. Bd. Regents, 1989-92, campaign chmn. U.S. Sen. Orrin Hatch, 1982, 88, U.S. Sen. Jake Garn, 1980, 86; cons. campaign Gov. Norman Angerter, 1984; mem. staff Reagan-Bush '84. 2d lt. USNG, 1969-77. Named Disting. Alumni So. Utah State Coll. Sch. Bus., 1986. Mem. CPCU. Republican. Mem. Lds Ch. Avocation: golf. Office: US Dept Health & Human Services Hubert Humphrey Bldg 200 Independence Ave SW Rm 615 F Washington DC 20201*

LEAVITT, THOMAS WHITTLESEY, retired museum director, educator; b. Boston, Jan. 8, 1930; s. Richard C. and Helen M. (Pratt) L.; m. Jane O. Ayer, June 23, 1951 (div. 1969); children: Katherine, Nancy, Hugh; m. Lloyd B. Carter, Sept. 14, 1978 (div. 1985); m. Michele C. McDonald, Apr. 20, 1991; children: Zachary Leavitt, Collin McDonald. AB, Middlebury (Vt.) Coll., 1951; MA, Boston U., 1952; PhD, Harvard, 1958. Asst. to dir. Fogg Mus., Harvard, 1954-56; exec. dir. fine arts com. People to People Program, 1957; dir. Pasadena (Calif.) Art Mus., 1957-63, dir. Santa Barbara (Calif.) Mus. Art, 1963-68; dir. Andrew Dickson White Mus. Art, Cornell U., Ithaca, N.Y., 1968-73, Herbert F. Johnson Mus. Art, 1973-91; univ. prof. history art Cornell U., 1968-91, prof. emeritus, 1991—; interim dir. RISD Mus. Art, 1993-94, Newport Art Mus., 1994-95, The Menil Collection, Houston, 1999-2000. Dir. mus. program Nat. Endowment for Arts, 1971-72, mem. museum panel, 1972-75; vice chmn. Council on Museums and Edn. in Visual Arts, 1972-76; trustee Gallery Assn. N.Y. State, 1972-78; mem. mus. panel N.Y. State Council Arts, 1975-78, 1980-82; chmn. art adv. com. Nat. Air and Space Mus., 1988—. Author exhbn. catalogs, articles. Trustee Am. Fedn. Arts, 1972-91, Newport Art Mus., 1995-2001; bd. dirs. Am. Arts Alliance, 1976-82, Ind. Sector, 1980-84; bd. govs. N.E. Mus. Conf., 1973-76; trustee Williamstown Regional Art Conservation Lab., 1979-91, pres., 1984-87. Mem. Assn. Art Mus. Dirs. (pres. 1977-78, trustee 1978-80), Am. Assn. Museums (council 1976-79, v.p. 1980-82, pres. 1982-85, Disting. Svc. to Museums award 1997). Home: 25 Waterway Rd Saunderstown RI 02874-3906

LEAVY, EDWARD, federal judge; b. 1929; m. Eileen Leavy; children: Thomas, Patrick, Mary Kay, Paul. AB, U. Portland, 1950; LLB, U. Notre Dame, 1953. Dist. judge Lane County, Eugene, Oreg., 1957—61, cir. judge, 1961—76; magistrate U.S. Dist. Ct. Oreg., Portland, 1976—84, judge, 1984—87; cir. judge U.S. Ct. Appeals (9th cir.), 1987—97, sr. judge, 1997—. Mem. Foreign Intelligence Surveillance Ct. of Review, 2002—. Recipient Sid Lezak award, 2003. Office: US Ct Appeals 232 Pioneer Courthouse 555 SW Yamhill St Portland OR 97204-1323*

LEAVY, HERBERT THEODORE, publisher; b. Detroit, July 10, 1927; s. Morris and Thelma (Davidson) L.; m. Patricia J. Moran, June 20, 1953; children: Karen, Kathryn, Jill, Jacqueline. BS in Journalism, Ohio U., 1951. Supervisory editor Fawcett Books, N.Y.C., 1951-60; v.p., editorial dir. Davis Publs., N.Y.C., 1960-69; founder, pres. Internat. Evaluations, Hauppage, N.Y., 1969-70; pub. dir. Countrywide Publs. Inc., N.Y.C., 1970-75; pres. Communications Devel. Co., N.Y.C., 1975-79; editorial dir. Watson-Guptil Publs., N.Y.C., 1979-80; pres. Books from Mags., Inc., Smithtown, N.Y., 1980—, Resumes Unltd., Smithtown, 1984—. Author: 101 Fast Track Resumes, The Pleasure, Executive Handbook, Vegetarian Times Cookbook, McCall's Houseplant and Indoor Landscaping Guide, Working Mother Cookbook, Carpentry, Shoe and Leather Repair at Home, The Complete Book of Beards and Moustaches, Air Conditioning-Repair and Maintenance, Designing and Building Beds, Lofts and Sleeping Areas, Wallcovering, Floor Stripping and Refinishing, Packing and Moving, Recreational Vehicles, Appliance Repair, Plumbing Handbook, Successful Small Farms; numerous others; editor-in-chief: The Ohioan Mag. Ohio U., 1950-51. Acting 1st sgt. USAF, 1946—47. Mem. Sales Exec. Club, Am. Soc. Mag. Editors, Nat. Sporting Goods Assn., Am. Mgmt. Assn., Mag. Advts. Sales Club, Electronics Press Club, U.S. Tennis Ct. and Track Builders Assn., Am. Motorcycle Assn., Am. Horse Council, Authors Guild, Motorcycle Industry Council, Nat. Indoor Tennis Assn., Bus./Profl. Advt. Assn., Sigma Delta Chi.

LEBAN, CELESTE CASDIA, elementary school educator; b. Que., Can., July 24, 1953; d. Carl Vincent and Maria del Carmen (Rodriguez) Casdia; m. Brian John Leban, Oct. 29, 1976; children: Carla Casiopia, Brianne Gem. BE, U. Miami, 1975; MS, Nova Southeastern U., 1998. Cert. elem. tchr., Fla. Tchr. 4th and 6th grades Inter Am. Mil. Acad., Miami, Fla., 1975—76; legal investigator Lloyds of Legals & Property Searchers Inc., Miami, 1977—79; tchr. 1st and 2d grades Shady Acres Sch., North Miami, Fla., 1982—83; med. receptionist Drs. Nichols, Phillips, Elias et al, Miami, 1983—86; tchr. 1st grade Archdiocese of Miami, 1976—77, tchr. 2d, 5th and 6th grades, 1986—89, tchr. 6th grade, 1989—90, Dade County Pub. Schs., Miami, 1990—97, tchr. 4th grade, 1997—, tchr. 4th grade alternative edn., 2002—03. Mem. adv. com., co-writer sch. improvement plan Natural Bridge Elem. Sch., North Miami, 1991—, peer tchr., 1996-97; advisor Future Educators of Am. club Natural Bridge Elem. Sch./Dade County Pub. Schs. and State of Fla., 1993—, grade level chair, 1998-99, 2000-2001, 2005-2006; participant Buddy Reading grant program Dade County Pub. Edn. Fund, 1993-94, chair testing com., 1995-96; co-chair Multicultural com., co-planner Cultural Fair, 1994—; directing tchr. for student tchrs., 1992-93, 95-96, 99-2003, peer tchr. for beginning tchr., 1997-98, 99-2000, 04-05 Avocations: reading, photography, travel, needlecrafts, ceramics. Office Phone: 305-891-8649.

LEBANO, EDOARDO ANTONIO, foreign language educator; b. Palmanova, Italy, Jan. 17, 1934; came to U.S., 1957, naturalized, 1961; s. Nicola and Flora (Puccioni) L.; m. Mary Vangell, 1957; children: Tito Nicola, Mario Antonio. Student, U. Florence, Italy, 1955; MA, Cath. U. Am., 1961, PhD, 1966. Tchr. high sch., Florence, 1955-57; Italian lang. specialist Bur. Programs and Stds., CSC, Washington, 1958; lang. instr. Sch. Langs., Fgn. Svcs. Inst., Dept. State, Washington, 1959-61; lectr. Italian, U. Va., Charlottesville, 1961-66; asst. prof. Italian, U. Wis., Milw., 1966-69, assoc. prof., assoc. chmn. dept. French and Italian, 1969-71; assoc. prof. dept. French and Italian, Ind. U., Bloomington, 1971-83, prof., 1983—2000, prof. emeritus, 2000—. Dir. Sch. Italian, Middlebury Coll., Vt., 1987-95. Author: A Look at Italy, 1976, Buon giorno a tutti, 1983, L'Insegnamento dell'italiano nei colleges e nelle universita del nordamerica, 1983; author introduction and notes to Morgante by Luigi Pulci, 1998; contbr. articles to profl. jours. Decorated cavaliere Ordine al Merito della Repubblica Italiana; recipient Uhrig award U. Wis.-Milw. faculty, 1968. Mem. MLA, AAUP, Am. Assn. Tchrs. Italian (sec.-treas. 1980-84, pres. 1984-87, Disting. Svc. award 1994), Dante Soc. Am., Renaissance Soc. Am., Boccaccio Soc. Am., Nat. Italian Am. Found., Am. Italian Hist. Assn., Am. Assn. Italian Studies, Midwest MLA. Home: 4323 Falcon Dr Bloomington IN 47403-9044 Office: Ind U Ctr for Italian Studies Bloomington IN 47405 Office Phone: 812-855-2508.

LEBARON, RICHARD, ambassador; Polit. officer office European affairs U.S. Dept. of State, Washington, 1989—91, dir. Near East and South Asian affairs, Nat. Security Coun., dir. peace process and regional affairs bur. Near Ea. affairs, pub. affairs advisor Near Ea. bur., 1991—98; minister-counselor polit. and econ. affairs U.S. Embassy, Cairo, 1998—2001, dep. chief of mission Tel Aviv, 2001—04; U.S. amb. to Kuwait US Dept. State, Washington, 2004—. Office: Am Embassy 6200 Kuwait Pl Washington DC 20521*

LEBBIN, CAROLE SUE, artist; b. Washington, Nov. 10, 1948; d. Gary H. and Bernice (Hamburger) L.; m. Phillip Louis Spector, May 11, 1980; children: Adam, David. BFA, Carnegie-Mellon U., 1970; MA, George Washington U., 1972. Lectr. Catholic U., Washington, 1974-75; asst. prof. art No. Va. C.C., Alexandria, 1974-80. Lectr. in field. One-woman shows include Marin-Price Gallery, Bethesda, Md., 2002, 04; represented in permanent collections at High Mus., Atlanta, Corcoran Gallery of Art, Libr. of Congress, Nat. Mus. Am. Art, Dept. State, Washington, State of Md., Portland Mus., Norton Gallery, Mus. Palm Beaches, Fla., Gannett Pub. Co., Dean Witter Reynolds, Reader's Digest, others; exhibitor numerous print exhbns. including Pratt/Silvermine Internat. Print Exhbn., 1985, U. Dallas Nat. Print Invitational, 1988, N.D. Print and Drawing Ann., U. Miss., 1990, 63rd SAGA Nat. Print Exhbn., 1991, Boston Printmakers, 1991 Recipient 1st prize, U. Md., Coll. Park, 1985. Mem. Soc. Am. Graphic Artists (purchase award 1986), Md. Printmakers, Boston Printmakers, So. Graphics Coun., Phila. Print Club, Washington Print Club. Office Phone: 301-442-5696. Business E-Mail: csl@carolesuelebbin.com.

LEBEAU, DICK, professional football coach, retired professional football player; b. Ohio, Sept. 9, 1937; m. Nancy LeBeau; 1 child, Brandon Grant. Attended, Ohio State Univ., 1955—58. Player, cornerback Detroit Lions, 1959—72; asst. coach Green Bay Packers, 1976—79, Phila. Eagles, 1976—79; defensive coord. Cin. Bengals, 1984—91, asst. head coach & defensive coord., 1997—2000, head coach, 2000—02; asst. head coach Buffalo Bills, 2003; asst. coach Pitts. Steelers, 1992—94, defensive coord., 1995—96, 2004—. Office: c/o Pitts Steelers 3400 S Water St Pittsburgh PA 15203-2349*

LEBEAU, MARY DELLE, dancer, educator, writer; b. El Paso, Tex., Oct. 24, 1951; d. George Louis LeBeau, Jr. and Rachel Elaine (McGibboney) LeBeau. BA cum laude in Russian & French, U.Tex., 1974; diploma in Eurythmy, Sch. of Eurythmy, Spring Valley, N.Y., 1982—87; Ma in Russian, SUNY, 1999—2001; PhD ABD, U. So. Calif., 2001—05. Cert. tchr., secondary Edn. in French, Russian, Eng. U. Tex., 1978. Tchr. of English Kashmere Sr. High, Houston, 1980—82; tchr. of eurythmy, Russian, French Hawthorne Valley Sch., Ghent, NY, 1987—93; founding tchr. Acad. of Art of Eurythmy, Moscow, 1993—97; grad. asst. in Russian SUNY, 1999—2001; tchg. asst. U. of So. Calif., 2003—. Rep. Eurythmy Assn. of Am., Garden City, NY, 1991—93; guest artist in eurythmy at confs., NY, 1990—97; guest spkr. on Russia at confs., NY, 1993—97; performer Acad. of the Art of Eurythmy, Moscow, 1993—97. Dir., performer, creator of program (performance: eurythmy, poetry, jazz) And Still I Rise: African Am. poetry & music (N.Y. State Grant, 1993); translator: (transl. of poems) The Russian poet, Ol'ga Sedakova. Recipient Phi Beta Kappa, U. of Tex., 1974; grantee Decentralization Grant, N.Y. State, 1993, Spl. Opportunity Grant, 1992. Mem.: MLA, Am. Coun. of Teachers of Russian, Assn. for Women in Slavic Studies, Am. Assn. of Slavic and East European Languages, Eurythmy Assn. Am. Avocations: gardening, raising exotic finches, collecting Russian folk toys & crafts, observing and reading about nature, weather; reading poetry, birdwatching. Office: U of So Calif SLL 2nd Fl Taper Hall Los Angeles CA 90089 Business E-Mail: mlebeau@usc.edu.

LEBEDEV, ALEXEI NIKOLAEVICH, physicist, researcher; b. Nizhni Tagil, Sverdlovskaya oblast, Russia, Feb. 2, 1949; arrived in U.S., 1994; s. Nikolai Sergeevich Lebedev and Anna Ivanovna Lebedeva; m. Irina Yurevna Bikhovskaya, Sept. 18, 1971; children: Yuliya Mostoufi, Diana Lebedeva. BS in Exptl. Nuc. Physics, Moscow (Russia) Physics Engring. Inst., 1972, PhD in Nuc. Physics, 1989. Rsch. engr., group leader Moscow (Russia) Physics Engring. Inst., 1972—88, sr. staff scientist, 1989—94; vis. rschr. Lawrence Berkeley (calif.) Lab., 1994—97; assoc. Brookhaven Nat. Lab., Upton, NY, 1997—. Contbr. articles to profl. jours. Mem.: Am. Physics Soc. Achievements include patents for 15 patents in nuclear instrumentation; invention of laser system for STAR detector and ALICE detector. Office: Brookhaven National Laboratory Bldg 1006C Upton NY 11973-5000 Office Phone: 631-344-3101. Office Fax: 631-344-3276. Business E-Mail: alebedev@bnl.gov.

LEBEDEV, KONSTANTIN VLADIMIROVICH, oceanographer; s. Vladimir Lvovich Lebedev and Natalia Konstantinovna Lebedeva, Erik Rudolfovich Kolman (Stepfather); m. Marina Sergeevna Lobanova, Oct. 13, 1981 (div. Aug. 9, 1985); 1 child, Julia Lebedeva; m. Alla Pavlovna, Sept. 7, 2001; children: Georgiy, Anna. MS in Aerodynamics and Thermodynamics, Moscow Inst. Physics and Tech., 1978—85; PhD in Phys. Oceanography, P.Shirshov Inst. Oceanology, Moscow, 1995. Sr. rsch. scientist P.Shirshov Inst. Oceanology, Moscow, 1985—98; vis. asst. rschr. Internat. Pacific Rsch. Ctr., SOEST, U. Hawaii, Honolulu, 1998—. Tchr. Moscow Inst. Physics and Tech., 1996—98. Contbr. articles to profl. jours. Grantee, Russian Acad. Scis. Mem.: Am. Geophys. Union. Office: IPRC-SOEST Univ Hawaii 1680 E West Rd Post #401 Honolulu HI 96822 Office Phone: 808-956-9710. Office Fax: 808-956-9425. E-mail: klebedev@soest.hawaii.edu.

LEBEDOFF, DAVID M., lawyer, writer; b. Mpls., Apr. 29, 1938; s. Martin David and Mary Louise (Galanter) Lebedoff; m. Randy Louise Miller, Feb. 7, 1981; children: Caroline, Jonathan, Nicholas. BA magna cum laude, U. Minn., 1960; JD, Harvard U., 1963. Bar: Minn. 1963. Spl. asst. atty. gen. Atty. Gen. of Minn., St. Paul, 1963-65; pvt. practice law Mpls., 1967-81; ptnr. Lindquist & Vennum, Mpls., 1981-91, Briggs & Morgan, Mpls., 1991-95; of counsel Gray, Plant, Mooty, Mooty & Bennett, Mpls., 1995—. Spl. master U.S. Dist. Ct., Mpls., 1974—75. Bd. dirs. Coun. Crime and Justice, 1999—; past bd. dirs. Guthrie Theatre, U. Minn. Found., Blake Sch., Ctr. Am. Experiment; bd. dirs. Mpls. Inst. Art, 1975—, chmn., 1989—91, life trustee, 1997—; bd. regents U. Minn., Mpls., St. Paul, 1977—89, chmn. bd. regents, 1987—89. Recipient Outstanding Achievement award, U. Minn., 1991, Minn. Book award, 1998. Mem.: Minikahda Club, Mpls. Club (former bd. dirs.), Phi Beta Kappa. Home: 1738 Oliver Ave S Minneapolis MN 55405-2222 Office Phone: 612-632-3214.

LEBEDOFF, JONATHAN GALANTER, federal judge; b. Mpls., Apr. 29, 1938; s. Martin David and Mary (Galanter) L.; m. Sarah Sargent Mitchell, June 10, 1979; children: David Shevlin, Ann McNair. BA, U. Minn., 1960, LLB, 1963. Bar: Minn. 1963, U.S. Dist. Ct. Minn. 1964, U.S. Ct. Appeals (8th cir.) 1968. Pvt. practice, Mpls., 1963-71; judge Hennepin County Mcpl. Ct., State Minn., Mpls., 1971-74; dist. ct. judge State of Minn., Mpls., 1974-91; U.S. magistrate judge U.S. Dist. Ct., Mpls., 1991—2002, chief U.S. magistrate judge, 2002—. Mem. Gov.'s Commn. on Crime Prevention, 1971-75; mem. State Bd. Continuing Legal Edn.; mem. Minn. Supreme Ct. Task Force for Gender Fairness in Cts., mem. implementation com. of gender fairness in cts. Jewish. Avocations: reading (biographies, history), family, bridge. Office: 300 S 4th St Minneapolis MN 55415-1320

LEBEDOFF, RANDY MILLER, lawyer; b. Washington, Oct. 16, 1949; m. David Lebedoff; children: Caroline, Jonathan, Nicholas. BA, Smith Coll., 1971; JD magna cum laude, Ind. U., 1975. Assoc. Faegre & Benson, Mpls., 1975-82, ptnr., 1983-86; v.p., gen. counsel Star Tribune, Mpls., 1989—2001; asst. sec. Star Tribune Cowles Media Co., Mpls., 1990—98; pvt. practice Mpls., 2001—02; v.p., gen. counsel Twin Cities Public Television, 2002—. Bd. dirs. Milkweed Editions, 1989-96. Bd. dirs. Minn. Opera, 1986-90, YWCA, 1984-90, Planned Parenthood Minn., 1985-90, Fund for Legal Aid Soc., 1988-96, Abbott-Northwestern Hosp., 1990-94. Mem. Newspaper Assn. Am. (legal affairs com. 1991-2002), Minn. Newspapers Assn. (bd. dirs. 1995-2002, pres. 2002). Home: 1738 Oliver Ave S Minneapolis MN 55405-2222 Office: 172 E Fourth St Saint Paul MN 55101

LEBEDOW, AARON LOUIS, consulting company executive; b. Chgo., Aug. 19, 1935; s. Isidor and Fannie (Perchikoff) L.; m. Madeleine Hellman; children: Ellen, Francine, Sheri, Sherri Michaels, Tracey Michaels. BS in Indsl. Engring, Ill. Inst. Tech., 1957; MBA, U. Mich., 1958. Cert. mgmt. cons. Asst. marketing mgr. Imperial-Eastman, Chgo., 1960-61; mgr. Corplan Assos., Chgo., 1961-66; chmn. bd. Technomic, Inc., Chgo., 1966-87, Technomic Consultants Internat., Deerfield, Ill., 1987-93, Global Devel. Network, Inc., 1993—, Hoganson Venture Group Inc., Hinsdale, IL, 1998-2000, Sheldon Good Auctioneers, 2004—. Bd. dirs. Coun. for Jewish Elderly. Served to 1st lt. USAF, 1958-60. Mem. Am. Mgmt. Assn., Am. Mktg. Assn., Tau Epsilon Phi. Office: Global Devel Network Inc 6540 N Kilbourn Ste A100 Lincolnwood IL 60712-3437 Office Phone: 847-674-7300. E-mail: lebedowa@aol.com.

LEBEL, GREGORY GALEN, director, consultant; b. Portsmouth, N.H., Apr. 12, 1950; s. Emile Henry Jr. and Willetta Jane (Vigue) L. BA, U. N.H., 1972, MPA, 1981; MA, U. Md., 1991, postgrad., 1991—. Chief program ops. to program planner N.H. Dept. of Health and Welfare, Concord, 1974-83; nat. staff Americans with Hart, N.H., 1983-84; campaign mgr. Asbury for Congress, Albuquerque, 1984-85; chief ops. officer Ctr. for a New Democracy, Washington, 1985; spl. asst. U.S. Sen. Gary Hart, Washington, 1985; exec. dir. The Vol. Com., Washington, 1986-87; dir. nat. scheduling Friends of Gary Hart, Denver, 1987; nat. polit. dir. League of Conservation Voters, Washington, 1987; nat. campaign mgr., dep. nat. campaign mgr. Hart for Pres., N.H., 1987-88; rsch. assoc. and adjunct asst. prof. The Grad. Sch. of Polit. Mgmt., 1988-99; asst. dean The Grad. Sch. Polit. Mgmt.; dir. semester in Wash. program George Washington U. Tech. advisor White House Conf. on Aging, Concord, 1981; cons. Global Tomorrow Coalition, Washington, Voter Edn. Project Atlanta, Dem. Congl. Campaign Com., Americans with Hart, N.H. Dept. Health and Human Svcs., The Interfaith Alliance; guest lectr. Williams Coll., U. N.Mex., U. Md., Am. U.; guest scholar John Hopkins U. Ctr. for Study Am. Govt. Co-Author: Sustainable Development: A Guide to Our Common Future, 1989; author: The Advance Manual, 1986. Del. Democratic Nat. Convention, San Francisco, 1984; chair Takoma Park Md. Ethics Comm. Mem. Am. Polit. Sci. Assn., Am. Assn. on Polit. Cons. (ethics com.). Democrat. Episcopalian. Avocations: reading, cooking, sailing. Office: George Washington Semester in Washington 524 Funger Hall 2201 G St NW Washington DC 20052-0001

LEBEL, ROBERT, bishop; b. Trois Pistoles, Que., Can., Aug. 11, 1924; s. Wilfrid and Alexina (Belanger) L. L.Theol., St. Paul U., Ottawa, 1950; D.Theol., Athenee Angelicum, Rome, 1951. Ordained priest Roman Cath. Ch., 1950, consecrated bishop, 1974; tchr. theology Major Sem., Rimouski, Que., 1951-65, rector, 1963-65, Minor Sem., 1965-68; tchr. domatic theology U. Rimouski, 1970-74; aux. bishop St. Jean, Que., 1974-76; bishop Valleyfield, Que., 1976-2000; bishop emeritus, 2000—. Contbr. ch. publs. Mem. Roman Synod on the Christian Family, 1980. Mem. Conf. Can. Cath. Bishops, Soc. Canadienne de Theologie, KC. Roman Catholic. Address: 183 chemin St Louis Beauharnois PQ Canada J6N 2H8 E-mail: robert.lebel@sympatico.ca.

LEBENTHAL, ALEXANDRA, investment firm executive; d. James and Jacqueline Beymer Lebenthal; m. Jeremy Diamond, 1991; children: Benjamin, Charlotte. AB history, Princeton U., 1986. Municipal bond dept. Kidder Peabody & Co., 1986—88; joined sales department Lebenthal & Co., N.Y.C., 1988, bd. dirs., 1992—, v.p., dir. mut. fund dept. N.Y.C., 1993—94, v.p., dir. sales, 1994—95, pres., CEO, 1995—; chmn. Lebenthal Funds Inc., N.Y.C.; bd. dirs. Advest Inc., N.Y.C. Mem. adv. bd. Barbara K. Enterprises. Trustee Nightingale Bamford Sch., Citizen's Budget Commn.; co-founder, bd. dirs. The Women's Exec. Cir.; bd. dirs. United Jewish Appeal Fedn. N.Y. Named one of New York's 100 most influential women, Crain's N.Y. Bus., 1999. Mem.: Bond Market Assn. (bd. dirs. 2004), The Com. of 200, The Young Pres. Orgn. Office: Lebenthal & Co 120 Broadway Fl 12 New York NY 10271-0005

LE BLANC, ALICE ISABELLE, academic administrator; b. New Orleans, Dec. 23, 1949; d. Joseph and Mary Elizabeth (Welsh) Le B.; divorced; 1 child, Matthew. BA in Drama & Comm., U. New Orleans, 1971; MPH, Tulane U., 1996. Sect. editor, feature writer Las Vegas Rev.- Jour., 1972-74; asst. dir. pub. rels. Touro Infirmary, New Orleans, 1980-82; dir. cmty. rels. AMI Riverside Hosp., Corpus Christi, Tex., 1982-84; dir. comm. United Way of the Coastal Bend, Corpus Christi, 1984-86; dir. pub. rels. & devel. Ada Wilson Hosp. Phys. Medicine and Rehab., Corpus Christi, 1986-89; mktg. mgr. nat. sexual trauma program River Oaks Psychiat. Hosp., New Orleans, 1989-90; mktg. cons./physician recruitment contract Eye, Ear, Nose and Throat Hosp., New Orleans, 1990; mgr. prog. svcs./exec. MHA recruitment, dept. health sys. Tulane U. Sch. Pub. Health and Tropical Mediicne, New Orleans, 1990-96; instr., dir. admissions and student affairs Sch. Pub. Health La. State U. Health Scis. Ctr., New Orleans, 1996—. Bd. dirs., bd. exec. com., chmn. standing com. United Way of the Coastal Bend, Corpus Christi, 1986, 87; bd. dirs. Early Childhood Devel. Ctr., Corpus Christi, 1988. Recipient Cert. of Appreciation, Gov. of Nev., 1974, Mayor of New Orleans, 1981, First Pl. award La. Hosp. Assn., 1982, Addy award of Excellence, Corpus Christi Advt. Fedn., 1986, 87, Addy First Place awards, 1988, Cert. of Recognition, United Way of the Coastal Bend, 1986, Cert. of Appreciation, Corpus Christi Jr. League, 1987. Avocations: gardening, carpentry, writing. Office: La State U Med Ctr Health Sci Ctr 1600 Canal St Ste 800 New Orleans LA 70112-2854 Office Phone: 504-599-1299.

LEBLANC, HUGH LINUS, political science professor, consultant; b. Alexandria, La., Oct. 30, 1927; s. Moreland Paul and Carmen Marie (Haydel) LeB.; m. Shirley Jean Smith, Feb. 28, 1953; children: Leslie Ann, Alexander Hugh. BA, La. State U., 1948; MA, U. Tenn., 1950; PhD, U. Chgo., 1958. Asst. prof. George Washington U., Washington, 1955-58, assoc. prof., 1959-63, prof., 1964-90, prof. emeritus dept. polit. sci., 1991—, chmn. dept., 1963-65, 70-76, 82-88; v.p. Area Inc., Arlington, VA, 1961-63. Author: American Political Parties, 1982, (with D. Trudeau Allensworth) The Politics of States and Urban Communities, 1971; contbr. articles to polit. sci. jours. Served to lt. (j.g.) USNR, 1944-45, 52-55. Named Outstanding Prof. Interfraternity Council, George Washington U., 1963 Mem. Amelia Island Plantation Club (Fla.). Personal E-mail: hllssl@aol.com.

LEBLANC, JANET M., addictions and relationship counselor; b. Altamonte Springs, Fla., Oct. 8, 1947; BA, U. Fla., 1969; MA, Rollins Coll., 1989. Lic. mental health counselor, Fla.; cert. addictions profl.; cert. drug counselor level II; cert. master addictions counselor; cert. alcohol and drug counselor; cert. employee assistance profl.; cert. clin. criminal justice specialist. Dir. Mgmt. Consulting Svcs., Altamonte Springs; dir. outpatient adult alcohol and drug treatment program, substance abuse evaluations, and EAP work; substance abuse provider DOT. Mem. Nat. Alcohol and Drug Assn. for Counselors, Employee Assistance Program Assn. (treas. 1996-99, v.p. 2000-04, pres. 2004-05), Mental Health Counselors Ctrl. Fla. (chair cmty. rels. 1999-2002, pres. 2002-04, past pres. 2004, spl. events chair 2005), Fla. Alcohol and Drug Assn. for Counselors. Office: Mgmt Cons Svcs PO Box 450 Altamonte Springs FL 32715-0450 Office Phone: 407-260-8533. E-mail: jmldbamcs@cs.com.

LEBLANC, JEAN EVA, writer, poet, educator; b. Leominster, Mass., Apr. 16, 1961; d. J. Camille and Sydne Grace (Lloyd) LeB. BS in Biology summa cum laude, Fitchburg State Coll., 1986; MA in English, Middlebury Coll., 1993. Adj. instr. English Sussex County C.C., Newton, NJ, 1999—. Contbr. poetry, book revs., and essays to various periodicals, mus. revs. to Classical disCDigest; contbr. natural history articles to Appalachian Trailway News, Gen. Store Mag. Avocations: hiking, visiting museums, reading, art.

LEBLANC, LEONARD JOSEPH, retired electronics company executive; b. Amherst, N.S., Can., Feb. 4, 1941; came to U.S., 1952 naturalized 1959; s. Edgar Marcel and Mary Catherine (Bourgeois) LeB.; m. Janice May Dittrich, Sept. 11, 1965; children: Bryan, Jeffrey, Steven. BS, Coll. of Holy Cross, 1962, MS, 1963, George Washington U., 1966. Fin. analyst to mgr. Philco-Ford Corp., Blue Bell, Pa., 1966-72; asst. corp. controller Centainteed Corp., Valley Forge, Pa., 1972-73; sr. v.p. fin. Data Tech. Corp., Costa Mesa, Calif., 1973-76; v.p., controller Memorex Corp., Santa Clara, Calif., 1976-82; v.p. fin., treas. Saga Corp., Menlo Park, Calif., 1982-87; exec. v.p. fin. and adminstrn. Cadence Design Systems Inc., San Jose, Calif., 1987-92; sr. v.p. fin. and adminstrn., CFO GTech Corp., West Greenwich, R.I., 1993-94; exec. v.p., CFO, COO Infoseek Corp., Santa Clara, Calif., 1996-97; exec. v.p., CFO Vantive Corp., Santa Clara, Calif., 1998-2000, ret., 2000. Bd. dirs. OpLink Comms., Inc., EBest Inc., AXT Inc. Mem. Monte Sereno Archtl. Com., Calif., 1981-93; bd. dirs. Eastfield Children's Ctr., Campbell, Calif., 1984-87. Served to lt.(j.g.) USN, 1963-66. Recipient commendation U.S. Navy Med. Sch., Bethesda, Md., 1966; fellow Coll. of Holy Cross, 1962 Mem. Fin. Execs. Inst. (pres. Santa Clara chpt. 1986-87).

LEBLANC, MARIANNE CAMILLE, lawyer; b. Boston, June 19, 1968; d. Norman Roger and Barbara Ann (Camille) L.; m. John Joseph Cummings III, Sept. 18, 1993. BA with honors, Wellesley Coll., 1990; JD with honors, Boston Coll., 1993. Bar: Mass. 1993, U.S. Dist. Ct. Mass. 1994. Assoc. Sugarman and Sugarman, P.C., Boston, 1993—2000, ptnr., 2000. Co-editor Jour. Mass. Acad. Trial Attys., 1998-2001. Bd. dirs. Support Com. for Battered Women, 1993-98, pres. 1994-96; bd. trustees Ursuline Acad., 2003—. Named one of Lawyers Yr., Mass. Lawyers Weekly, 1999, Top Boston Lawyers, Boston Mag., 2004, Top 100 Mass. Super Lawyers, Law & Politics, 2004, 2005, Top 50 Female Mass. Super Lawyers, 2004, 2005; recipient 40 Under 40 award, Boston Bus. Jour., 2002. Mem. ATLA (new lawyers divsn. gov., 1996-98), New. Eng. Bar Assn. (bd. dirs. 2002—), Mass. Acad. Trial Attorneys (co-editor jour., bd. govs. 1999—, recipient New Lawyers award, 1996), Mass. Bar Assn. (civil litig. sect. coun. 2000-02, ho. dels. 2001-02, chair civil litig. sect. coun. 2001-02), Women's Bar Assn. Mass. (bd. dirs., 1999-, co-chair legis. policy com. 2001-02, ann. gala chair 2003, v.p. 2002-03, pres-elect 2003-04, pres. 2004-05), Women's Bar Found. Mass. (bd. trustees 2001—), New England Bar Assn. (bd. dirs. 2002-), Ursuline Acad. (Bd. trustees 2003-), Children's Law Ctr. Mass. (pro bono atty. program). Democrat. Roman Catholic. Avocations: running, golf. Office: Sugarman and Sugarman PC 1 Beacon St Boston MA 02108-3107 Office Phone: 617-542-1000. Business E-Mail: mleblanc@sugarman.com.

LEBLANC, MATT, actor; b. Newton, Mass., July 25, 1967; m. Melissa McKnight, 2003; 1 child, Marina stepchildren: Tyler, Jacquelyne. Actor (movies) Reform School Girl, 1994, (TV series) TV 101, 1988, Anything to Survive, 1990, Top of the Heap, 1991, Vinnie and Bobby, 1992, Friends, 1994-2004, Joey, 2004- (films) The Killing Box, 1993, Lookin Italian, 1994, Ed, 1996, Lost in Space, 1998, Charlie's Angels: The Movie, 2000, All the Queens Men, 2001, Charlie's Angels: Full Throttle, 2003; TV guest appearances include: Just the Ten of Us, 1989, Monsters, 1988, Married...With Children, 1991, Red Shoe Diaries, 1992-1994.

LEBLANC, ROGER MAURICE, chemistry professor; b. Trois Rivières, Que., Can., Jan. 5, 1942; s. Henri and Rita (Moreau) L.; m. Micheline D. Veillette, June 26, 1965; children: Daniel, Hughes, Marie-Jose, Nancy. BSc, U. Laval, 1964, PhD, 1968. NRC postdoctoral fellow Davy Faraday Rsch. Lab. Royal Inst. Great Britain, London, 1968-70; prof. phys. chemistry U. Que., Trois-Rivières, 1970-93, chmn. dept., 1971-75, dir. Biophysics Rsch. Group, 1978-81, chmn. Photobiophysics Rsch. Ctr., 1981-91; prof., chmn. dept. chemistry U. Miami, Coral Gables, Fla., 1994—. Hon. prof. Jilin U., Changchun, China, 1992. Recipient Barringer award Spectroscopy Soc. Can., 1983, Medaille du Merite Universitaire du Que. a Trois-Rivieres, 1987, Commemorative medal for 125th Anniversary of Confedn. Can., 1993, rsch. award Soc. Cosmetic Chemists Fla. chpt., 1999, Provost's award for scholarly activity, 2002. Fellow Chem. Inst. Can. (Noranda award 1982, John Labatt Ltd. award 1992); mem. Am. Chem. Soc., Assn. Canadienne Francaise pour l'Avancement des Sciences (Prix Vincent 1978), Am. Soc. Photobiology, Biophys. Soc., European Photochem. Assn., Soc. Phys. Chemistry of Serbia (hon.), Royal Sci. Sc. Belgium (corr.). Roman Catholic. Home: 713 Crandon Blvd Apt 203 Key Biscayne FL 33149-2530 Office: U Miami Dept Chemistry Cox Sci Bldg Rm 315 1301 Memorial Dr Coral Gables FL 33124-0431 Office Phone: 305-284-2194. Business E-Mail: rml@miami.edu.

LE BLANC, SUZANNE, museum director; Exec. dir. Lied Discovery Children's Mus., Las Vegas, Nev., 1990—. Office: Lied Discovery Childrens Mus 833 Las Vegas Blvd N Las Vegas NV 89101-2059

LEBLANC, TINA, dancer; b. Erie, Pa. m. Marco Jerkunica, May 1988; children: Marinko James, Sasha Johan. Trained, Carlisle, Pa. Dancer Joffrey II Dancers, NYC, 1982-83, The Joffrey Ballet, NYC, 1984-92; prin. dancer San Francisco Ballet, 1992—. Guest tchr. Ctrl. Pa. Youth Ballet, 1992, 94—. Work includes roles in (with San Francisco Ballet) Con Brio, Bizet Pas de Deux, Swan Lake, Nanna's Lied, Handel--A Celebration, La fille mal gardée, Rubies, Tchaikovsky Pas de Deux, Seeing Stars, The Nutcracker, La Pavane Rouge, Company B, Romeo and Juliet, Sleeping Beauty, The Dance House, Terra Firma, Lambarena, Fly by Night, In the Night, Ballo della Regina, The Lesson, The Tuning Game, Quartette, Etudes, Western Symphony, Maelstrom, Pacific, Criss-Cross, Giselle, Theme and Variations, Gala Performance, The Vertiginous Thrill of Exactitude, Taiko, Sandpaper Ballet, La Bayadere, Night, Serenade, Celts, Stars & Stripes, Tarantella, Symphony in C, Dances at a Gathering, Don Quixote (full length), Square Dance, Apollo, Rush, Paquita, Who Cares, Study in Motion, 7 for Eight, Symphonic Variations, Two Bits, Valses Poeticos, Sea Pictures, Elite Syncopations, Smile with Your Heart, Falling; (with other companies) The Green Table, Les Presages, Le sacre du printemps, Les Noces, Light Rain, Romeo and Juliet, Runaway Train, Empyrean Dances, La Vivandière, L'air D'esprit, Corsaire Pas de deux, Don Quixote pas de deux, Lacrymosa, Confetti, Kettentanz Le Beau Danube, Offenbach in the Underworld, Suite Saint Saens, Forgotten Land, Dream Dances, Postcards, Coppelia, Remembrances, Reflections, Cotillion. Recipient Princess Grace Found. award, 1988, Princess Grace Statuette award, 1995, Isadora Duncan award, 1998-99, 2000-01. Office: San Francisco Ballet Assn 455 Franklin St San Francisco CA 94102-4471 Office Phone: 415-861-5600.

LEBLANG, THEODORE RAYMOND, law educator, lawyer; s. Morton and Leah L.; m. Pamela Kay; children: Danielle Rosalyn, Yale Phillip. BA, Pa. State U., 1970; JD, U. Ill., 1974. Bar: Ill. 1974, U.S. Supreme Ct. 1977. Legal counsel So. Ill. U. Sch. of Medicine, Springfield, 1975-92; prof. med. jurisprudence So. Ill. U. Sch. Law, Carbondale, 1991—; prof., chair dept. med. humanities So. Ill. U. Sch. Medicine, Springfield, 1993—. Adj. prof. Sangamon State U., Springfield, 1984-89; co-annotator AMA Code Med.Ethics with Annotations, 1994—. Co-author: The Law of Medical Practice in Illinois, 1986, 2d edit., 1996; author column Legalities in Am. Druggist mag., 1988-99; editor: Jour. Legal Medicine, 1981-2003, editor emeritus, 2004—; editor: Series in Med. Humanities, So. Ill. U Press, 1993-99, Ill. Bar. Jour., 2000-02; mem. editl. bd. Law, Medicine and Health Care, 1981—, Ill. Bar Jour., 1987—, Jour. Law and Medicine, 1998-2003, Ill. Child Welfare, 2003—; assoc. editor Health Care Lawyer, 1992—; contbg. editor Am. Druggist Mag., 1996—; mem. Textbook Co., Legal Medicine, 6t edit, 2004, Scientific Co., Mem. adv. com. Children Family Stress Cons. Team, Springfield, 1976-99; co-host Children's Miracle Network, 1987-2000; bd. dirs. Mid-Am. Playwrights Theatre, 1990-92; pres. Springfield Jewish Fedn., 1997-99; chair UJA/Fedn. Campaign, 1992-93; chair Endowment Fund Bd., 2001-; mem. finance Com., Jewish Fedn. Metro. Chgo. Pooled Endowment, 2004—. Lt. comdr. ret. JAGC, USNR. Fellow Am. Coll. Legal Medicine (past pres.); mem. ABA (past chair TIPS medicine and law com. 1986-87), Med. Malpractice Nat. Inst. (co-chair 1986-90), Ill. State Bar Assn. (Bd. Govs. award 1995, founding chair, bar publs. bd. 1992-95, past chairperson interprofl. cooperation com. 1985-86, past chair health care sect. coun. 1990-91, past chair CLE com. 1994-95, past chair tellers of election 1998, vice chair spl. com. comm. for next century 1998-2000, rep. assembly 1986-88, interdisciplinary panel life support systems inst. pub. affairs 1986-87), U.S. Agy. Healthcare Rsch. and Policy (mem. task force liability determination 1991), Am. Health Lawyers Assn., Am. Soc. Law, Medicine & Ethics, Am. Acad. Forensic Sci., Ill. Assn. Healthcare Attys., Nat. Bd. Med. Examiners (task force on law and ethics medicine 1980-86, ethics task force 1991—), So. Ill. U. Sch. Law Alumni Assn. (Hon.), World Assn. Med. Law (mem. coun. pres. 2004, Maccabi award Outstanding paper, 1994) Naval Res. Assn. (life). Avocations: alpine skiing, scuba diving, softball. Office: So Ill U Sch Medicine PO Box 19603 913 N Rutledge St Springfield IL 62794-9603

LEBLOND, CHARLES PHILIPPE, anatomy educator, researcher; b. Lille, France, Feb. 5, 1910; s. Oscar and Jeanne (Desmarchelier) L.; m. Gertrude Sternschuss, Oct. 22, 1936 (dec.); children— Philippe L., Paul N., Pierre F., Marie Pascale; m. Odette Lengrand, July 12, 2001 (dec.). L.Sc., U. Lille, 1932, MD, U. Paris, France, 1934, D. Sc., 1945; PhD, U. Montreal, 1942; DSc Acadia (hon.), McGill U., 1982, York U., 1985; DSc (hon.), Sherbrooke Univ., 1988. Asst. histology U. Lille and U. Paris, France, 1934-35; Rockefeller fellow anatomy Yale, 1935-37; charge biology div. Lab. Synthese Atom, Paris, 1937-40; research fellow U. Rochester, N.Y., 1940-41; mem. faculty McGill U., Montreal, Que., Can., 1941—, prof. anatomy, 1948—, chmn. dept., 1957-75. Author: L'Acide Ascorbique dans les Tissues et sa Detection, 1936, Radioautography as a Tool in the Study of Protein Synthesis, 1965; contbr. articles to profl. jours. Decorated companion Nat. Order Can., grand officer Order of Quebec; named to Can. Med. Hall of Fame, 1995; recipient Marie-Victorian Prize, Quebec, 1992, Duncan Graham award, Royal Coll. Physicians and Surgeons of Can., 1986, E-B Wilson Award, 1982, Issac Schour award, 1974; scholar Fogarty scholarship, NIH, 1975. Fellow: Prix. Scientifique du Que., Am. Acad. Arts and Scis., Can. Assn. Anatomists (J.C.B. Grant award 1979), Am. Assn. Anatomy (Centennial award 1979, Henry Grey award 1978), Royal Soc. Can. (McLaughlin Medal 1983), Royal Soc. London. Achievements include research in cell and tissue dynamics. Home: 68 Chesterfield St Montreal PQ Canada H3Y 2M5 E-mail: charles.leblond@staff.mcgill.ca.

LEBLOND, PAUL HENRI, oceanographer, educator; b. Que., Can., Dec. 30, 1938; s. Sylvio and Jeanne (Lacerte) LeB.; m. Josee Michaud (div. 1985); children: Michel, Philippe, Anne. BA, Laval U., Quebec, 1957; BS, McGill U., Montreal, Que., 1961; PhD, U. B.C., Vancouver, Can., 1964; DSc (hon.), Meml. U., Newfoundland, 1992. Prof. depts. oceanography and physics U. B.C., Vancouver, 1965, assoc. dean faculty of sci., 1982-85, head dept. oceanography, 1987-92, dir. program earth and ocean scis., 1992-96, prof. emeritus, 1996—. Chmn. Can. nat. com. World Ocean Circulation Expt., 1987-92; program leader Ocean Prodn. Enhancement Network, Can., 1991-93; pres. Can. Open Frontiers Rsch. Found., 1996-98. Co-author: Waves in the Oceans, 1978, Cadborosaurus, 1995; contbr. articles to profl. jours. Mem. Fisheries Resource Conservation Coun., 1993-98; mem. Pacific Fisheries Resource Conservation Coun., 1998—; chair sci. and industry bd. Inst. Pacific, Ocean Sci. and Tech., 1998-2002; trustee Can. Found. Climate Atmosphere, 2000—. Fellow Royal Soc. Can., Can. Meteorol. and Oceanographic Soc. (Pres.'s prize 1981, Tully medal 1991); mem. Am. Geophys. Union, Galiano Conservancy Assn. (bd. dirs. 1996—2004), Can. Parks & Wilderness Soc. (B.C. chpt. bd. dirs. 2000-05), Galiano Mus. Soc. (pres. 2003—). Avocations: hiking, history, science fiction. Business E-Mail: leblond@gulfislands.com.

LEBLOND, RICHARD KNIGHT, II, banker; b. Cin., Nov. 16, 1920; s. Harold R. and Elizabeth (Conroy) LeB.,; m. Sara Cordial Chapman, Dec. 11, 1948; children— Mary, Richard, E. Chapman, Elizabeth, David, Virginia, William, Thomas, Sara, Joseph BA, Princeton U.; DCS (hon.), St. John's U., Jamaica, N.Y., 1978. Exec. v.p. Chem. Bank, N.Y.C., 1968-73, vice-chmn. bd., 1973-85, sr. advisor, 1985—. Sr. advisor JP Morgan Chase, Bedford Stuyvestant D&S Corp., Bklyn. Pres. Robert T. Jones Jr. Scholarship Fund. 1st lt. U.S. Army, 1943—46, PTO. Mem. N.Y. State Bankers Assn. (pres.

1979-80), Harvard Bus. Sch. Assn. (pres. 1975-76) Republican. Roman Catholic. Office: JP Morgan Chase & Co 11 W 51st St Fl 2 New York NY 10019-6901 Office Phone: 212-307-8710.

LEBLOW, G. HAGNY, artist; b. June 5, 1924; d. Henry Aaron and Mabel Alice (Warn) Hagny; m. Raymond E. Leblow, Mar. 10, 1950; children: Bonnie, Charles, Colin. Grad., h.s., 1942. Formerly sec. with State of Calif., Oakland. Artist, painting country and farm scenes. Republican. Lutheran. Avocations: painting, sewing, reading. Home: 2691 Oakes Dr Hayward CA 94542-1225

LEBMAN, ROBERT RICHARD, social services administrator; b. Amsterdam, N.Y., Sept. 20, 1945; s. Harry and Catherine (Spitzkopf) L. BA cum laude, Harpur Coll., Binghamton, N.Y., 1967; MA, Pa. State U., 1968. With Peace Corps, 1968-72; project dir. AID mission, Afghanistan, 1972-73; cons. Rochester (N.Y.) Sch. Dist., 1973; rsch. assoc. Applied Behavioral Rsch. Assocs., Rochester, 1973-74; from caseworker to clin. dir. Delphi House, Rochester, 1974-78; dir. N.W. Youth Ctr. of Charles Settlement House, Rochester, 1978-80; exec. dir. Livingston County Youth Bur., Rochester, 1981-83, Monroe County Youth Advocacy, Rochester, 1983-86; dir. in-patient svcs. DayBreak Alcoholism Treatment Facility, Rochester, 1986-89; exec. dir. Huther-Doyle Meml. Inst., Rochester, N.Y., 1989—, COO. Author: English Language Teaching in Afghanistan, 1972. Past pres. Helping People with AIDS, Jewish Family Svcs., Region II Consortium on Alcoholism and Substance Abuse Svcs.; mem. profl. adv. HRC, Inc.; mem. behavioral health adv. Excellus Inc.; mem. Monroe County Task Force on Youth and Alcohol, 1976—86, Monroe County Cmty. Svcs. Bd.; mem. 4-H adv. com. Monroe County Coop. Extension, 1978—80; mem. Black Seeds Scholarship Com., 1981—86, Jewish Chm. Dependency Task Force Com. on Youth and Alcohol; mem. budget adv. com. Rochester City Schs., 1983—85; chmn. Regional Youth Workers Tng. Network; mem. harm reduction adv. bd. AIDS Rochester; pres. Recovery Net; treas. Coun. Agy. Execs.; mem. steering com. Rochester Drug Summit; bd. dirs. Finger Lakes Health Sys. Agy., Operation U-Turn, Inc.; vice chair bd. dirs. Rochester Area Task Force on AIDS; bd. dirs. NY State Assn. Alcoholism and Substance Abuse Providers; v.p., bd. dirs. Jewish Family Svcs. NDEA fellow, 1967. Mem.: Arts and Scis. Acad. Rochester (bd. dirs.), Nat. Coun. Crime and Delinquency, Am. Judicature Soc., Acad. Polit. and Social Sci., Am. Polit. Sci. Assn., Acad. Polit. Sci. Democrat. Jewish. Home: 29 Old Winding Ln Fairport NY 14450-1108 Office: 360 East Ave Rochester NY 14604-2612 Office Phone: 585-325-5100. E-mail: rlebman@hutherdoyle.com.

LEBOEUF, SANDRA MENDES, nurse; b. Newark, N.J., Jan. 1, 1974; d. Maria Helena Mendes and Fernando Moises; m. Chad Joseph LeBoeuf, May 21, 2001; 1 child, Dylan Joseph; children: Bailey Mendes Sexton, Gavin Mendes Sexton. Med. specialist, Acad. of Health Sci., Fort Sam Houston, Tex., 1994, practical nurse, 1997, med. lab. specialist, 1999. Lic. Am. Soc. of Phlebotomy Technicians La., 2002, Am. Registry of Med. Asst. U.S.A., 2003. Practical nurse / med. asst. Adult Cardiovasc. Cons., San Antonio, 2004—, Kufoy Med. Clinic, DeRidder, La., 2001—04. Nurse Abrazando Cristo Med. Mission, Nicaragua, 2002—03. Cpl U.S. Army, 1994—2001. Decorated Army Achievement Medal Paul W. Wingo LTC, USA Commdg., Lance S. Maley MAJ, MS, Good Conduct Medal, Affiliation of The US Army Med. Dept. Rgt. Surgeon Gen., Army Svc. Ribbon, Army Overseas Svc. Ribbon. Home: 6712 Meadow Ash Dr Converse TX 78109 Office: Adult Cardiovasc Cons 7434 Louis Pasteur Dr Ste 209 San Antonio TX 78229 Office Phone: 210-949-0304. Personal E-mail: honeybutterfly20@hotmail.com.

LEBOUITZ, MARTIN FREDERICK, diversified financial services company executive, consultant; b. Phila., May 16, 1946; s. William and Sylvia (Magen) L.; m. Helene A. Pepe, Oct. 15, 1977; children: Clarke S., Jacqueline B. BS, U.S. Air Force Acad., Colorado Springs, Colo., 1971, MA, 1972; MA, Fletcher Sch. Law and Diplomacy, Tufts U. Asst. v.p. Bankers Trust Co., N.Y.C., 1976-82; v.p. mgr. of planning Barclays Bank of N. Am., N.Y.C, 1982-85; v.p. corp. devel. Chase Manhattan Bank, N.Y.C., 1985-88; v.p. planning and devel. Paine Webber Group Inc., N.Y.C., 1988-90; prin. DRI/McGraw-Hill, N.Y.C., 1990-91; mng. dir. Fin. Svcs. Cons., N.Y.C., 1991-95; v.p. global payments project exec. and industry issues exec. JP Morgan Chase, N.Y.C., 1995—99; v.p. planning and devel. JP Morgan, Fin. Mkts. Solutions, 1999—; pres. Global Payments Strategies, 2004—. Bd. dirs., chmn. sch. rels. com. N.Y. chpt. Fletcher Sch. Capt. USAF, 1971-76. Mem. Strategic Leadership Forum (dir., chmn. program com. NY chpt.), Assn. for Corp. Growth, Am. Mgmt. Assn., pres., USAF Acad. Assn. of Grad., Tampa Chpt., Harvard Club, Fletcher Sch. Club NY (chmn. sch. rels. com.), Univ. Club, Tampa Club. Office: 2202 West Shore Blvd Ste 200 Tampa FL 33607 E-mail: martin.lebouitz@paymentstrategies.org.

LEBOURGEOIS, CYNTHIA CARRIE, lawyer; b. New Iberia, La., July 23, 1962; d. Paul Arthur (dec.) and Billie (Graham) LeB. BA valedictorian, U. Southwestern La., 1983; JD, Tulane U., 1986. Bar: La. 1986; cert. pilot, real estate agent; family law cert. mediator. Law clk. 15th Jud. Dist. Ct., Lafayette, La., 1986-88; pvt. practice law Lafayette, 1988—; former spl. asst. atty. gen. State of La.; asst. city atty. Lafayette, La.; pros., spl. asst. dist. atty., 1996—. Active Lafayette Vol. Lawyers. Phi Kappa Phi scholar, Tulane Reg. scholar. Mem. ABA, Lafayette Parish Bar Assn., Acadiana Women Bus. Owners Assn., Phi Alpha Delta. Home: 415 Lippi Blvd Lafayette LA 70508-2010 Office: 239 La Rue France Lafayette LA 70508-3103

LEBOUTILLIER, JANET ELA, writer, real estate investment asset manager, minister; b. Marshfield, Mass., May 10, 1936; d. Preston Carleton and Barbara (Higgins) Ela; m. John Walter McNeill, Oct. 10, 1959 (div. 1970); children: Duncan Davis McNeill, Sarah McNeill Treffry; m. Martin LeBoutillier, May 10, 1986 (dec. Feb. 2001). AA, Briarcliff Jr. Coll., 1956; BA in English Lit., U. Colo., 1958; postgrad. Real Estate/Mortgage Banking, NYU, 1973-78; AA, Wagner Leadership Sch., 2004. Lic. N.Y. and Conn. real estate broker; cert. property mgr. Sales, leasing agt. L.B. Kaye Assocs., Ltd., N.Y.C., 1969-74; comml. leasing agt. Kenneth D. Laub & Co., N.Y.C., 1975; dir. leasing, asst. bldg. mgr. Douglas Elliman Gibbons & Ives Co., N.Y.C., 1975-76; adminstr. REIT adv. unit Chase Manhattan Bank, N.A., N.Y.C., 1976-78; asst. dir. real estate investments Mass. Mut. Life Ins. Co., Springfield, Mass., 1978-80; dir. real estate investments Yale U., New Haven, Conn., 1980-81; ind. cons. N.Y.C., 1981-83; sr. analyst, equity mgmt., sales and devel. Aetna Realty Investors, Inc., Hartford, Conn., 1983-84, dir. pub. involvement unit, 1984-86; sr. asset mgr. Cigna Investments, Inc., Hartford, 1986-87; v.p. Wm. M. Hotchkiss Co., New Haven, Conn., 1987-88; pres., prin. LeBoutillier & LeBoutillier, Inc., Lyme, Conn., 1989-93. Author: Mediations on Joy, 1995. Past mem. pastoral care and healing commn., prayer team ministry leader/tng., Grace Episcopal Ch., 1991-2002; co-founder, convener Heart of Compassion chpt. Internat. Order of St. Luke, 1993-2002; prayer minister, equipping tng. Gateway Christian Fellowship, 2002—; apostolic teams, leader to various pastors, ministries, ho. ch. and small groups ARC, 2004— Mem. Soc. Mayflower Descs., Nat. Soc. Colonial Dames (bd. mgrs., sec. 1998-2000). Independent. Avocations: writing, prophetic healing prayer ministry, walking, swimming, sports. Home and Office: 11 Academy Ln Old Lyme CT 06371-2312

LEBOUTILLIER, MEGAN, writer; b. N.Y.C., Apr. 5, 1955; d. Charles and Deirdre Jones (Johnson) LeB. BA, Vt. Coll., 1985; PhD, Union Inst., Cin., 1998. Health educator Planned Parenthood, Missoula, Mont., 1977-80, dir. cmty. edn. Atlanta, 1980-85; pres. Seaglass Publs., Atlanta, 1985-88, pres., writer Pawleys Island, S.C., 1988-88; facilitator The Courage to Teach, Free Union, Va., 1998—; freelance writer, Free Union, 1998—. Vis. author, lectr. Emory U., Atlanta, 1987, 91, Waccamaw Libr., Pawleys Island, 1996, 2000, Coastal Carolina U., Conway, S.C., 1999, 2000; facilitator Leadership Acad., Conway, 1993, 94. Author: Little Miss Perfect, 1990, "No" Is a Complete Sentence, 1995; co-author: Birth Control, The Movie, 1986. Bd. dirs. LWV, Georgetown, S.C., 1989-98, pres., 1993-95; bd. dirs., eductor AIDS Task Force, Georgetown, 1991-96. Avocations: bicycling, hiking, cooking, gardening, weaving. Office: PO Box 325 Free Union VA 22940 E-mail: mimileb@mindspring.com.

LEBOVITZ, HAROLD PAUL (HAL LEBOVITZ), journalist; b. Cleve., Sept. 11, 1916; s. Isaiah and Celia (Levy) L.; m. Margie Glassman, Feb. 20, 1938; children: Neil Ross, Lynn Gail. BA, Case Western Res. U., 1938, MA, 1942. Sci. tchr., coach Euclid (Ohio) High Sch., 1938-46; reporter, baseball writer, columnist Cleve. News, 1946-60; columnist Cleve. Plain Dealer, 1960-84, sports editor, 1964—82; columnist The Sporting News, 1970-92, Gannett Syndicate, 1979-82; dir. Cleve. Jewish News, 1971-89; baseball umpire, 1937-50; football ofcl., 1940-71; basketball ofcl., 1940-60; Cleve. corr. Sporting News, 1950-64. Author: Pitchin' Man, 1948; author: (with Phil R. Gilman) Springboards to Science, 1967; author: The Best of Hal Lebovitz, 2004; contbg. editor: Webster's New World Dictionary, 1983—; syndicated columnist several Ohio newspapers, 1984—; contbr. articles to various periodicals; inventor outdoor playground game Four Sq. Tennis. Mem. recreation com. University Heights, Ohio, 1965-75; bd. dirs. Jewish Community Ctr., Cleve., 1962-63, Alumni Assn. Adelbert Coll. Case-Western Res. U., 1969-83. Named Citizen of Yr. City of University Heights, 1964, Sportsman of Yr. B'rith Emeth Men's Club, 1964, Top Sportswriter Cortron Twelve of Atlantic Fleet, 1961, Sporting News Top Feature Writer, 1963-64; recipient ten best writing awards Cleve. Newspaper Guild, 1948-60, Greater Cleve. Football Coaches Golden Deeds award, 1987, J.G. Taylor Spink award Baseball Hall of Fame, Cooperstown, N.Y., 2000; inducted into Glenville High Sch. Hall of Fame, 1980, JRC-JCC Hall of Fame, 1982, Ohio Baseball Hall of Fame, 1984, Greater Cleve. Softball Hall of Fame, 1989, Sport Media Assn. of Cleve. Hall of Fame, 1990, Cleve. Journalism Hall of Fame, 1991, Euclid (Ohio) Sports Hall of Fame, 1997, Cleve. Sports Stars Hall of Fame, 1998, Glenville C.D. Legends Hall of Fame, 1998, Greater Cleve. Sports Hall of Fame, 1999, Case Western Res. U. Sports Hall of Fame, 2000; recipient Special Tribute award, U. Heights, Ohio, 2000. Mem. Baseball Writers Assn. (pres. 1965-66, bd. dirs. 1966-67), Ohio Sports Editors Assn. (pres. 1965-66), Cleve. Football Ofcls. Assn., Ohio Football Ofcls. Assn., Cleve. Athletic Club (Outstanding Sports Personality award 1984), Cleve. Umpires Assn., Sigma Delta Chi (Disting. Svc. award 1981, Mel Harder Disting. Svc. award 1992). Home: 2380 Edgerton Rd Cleveland OH 44118-3726

LEBOVITZ, STEPHEN D., property manager; With Goldman, Sachs & Co., 1984—86; exec. v.p. devel./acquisitions CBL Properties, exec. v.p. devel., sr. v.p. New Eng. Office, sr. v.p. Cmty. Ctr. Devel., treas., also bd. dirs.; pres., sec. CBL & Assocs. Properties, Inc., Chattanooga, 1999—. Pres. Boston Jewish Family and Children's Svc.; bd. dirs. Children's Hosp. Trust, Boston, Combined Jewish Philanthropic, Boston. Mem.: Internat. Coun. Shopping Ctrs. (trustee, divisional v.p.). Office: CBL & Assocs Properties INc CBL Ctr Ste 500 2030 Hamilton Pl Blvd Chattanooga TN 37421-6000

LEBOW, IRWIN LEON, communications engineering consultant; b. Boston, Apr. 27, 1926; s. Samuel and Ruth (Tobey) L.; m. Grace H. Hackel, July 8, 1951; children: Judith, William, David. SB, MIT, 1948, PhD, 1951. Staff mem. MIT Lincoln Lab., 1951-60, assoc. leader satellite communications surface techniques group, 1960-65, leader, 1965-70, assoc. head communications divsn., 1970-72, assoc. head data systems divsn., 1972-75, mem. steering com., 1970-75; chief scientist, assoc. dir. tech. Def. Communications Agy., Washington, Dept. Def., Washington, 1975-81; v.p. engring. Am. Satellite Co., Rockville, Md., 1981-84; v.p. Systems Research and Applications Corp., Arlington, Va., 1984-87; ind. cons. Washington, 1987—. Adj. prof. U. Md., Univ. Coll., 1998—. Author: (with others) Theory and Design of Digital Machines, 1962, The Digital Connection, 1991, Information Highways and Byways, 1995, Understanding Digital Transmission and Recording, 1997, (with others) Coping with Your Difficult Older Parent, 1999. With USNR, 1944-46. Awarded rank of Meritorious Sr. Exec., 1980; recipient Meritorious Civilian Service medal Dept. Def., 1981. Fellow Am. Phys. Soc., IEEE; mem. AAAS, Sigma Xi. Home and Office: Apt 909 5600 Wisconsin Ave Chevy Chase MD 20815-4411 E-mail: irwinle@cs.net.

LEBOW, MARK DENIS, lawyer; b. Harrisburg, Pa., Apr. 2, 1940; s. Sylvan and Ruth M. (Lebowitz) L.; m. Catherine Maugee, Nov. 22, 1972 (div. 1982); m. Patricia Edith Harris, Jan. 30, 1988; children: Michael, Jeffrey, Alexandra. AB, Yale U., 1961; JD, Harvard U., 1964. Bar: N.Y. 1965, U.S. Ct. Appeals (2d cir.) 1965, U.S. Dist. Ct. (so. and ea. dists.) N.Y. 1966, U.S. Supreme Ct., 1972. Assoc. Coudert Bros., N.Y.C., 1965-71, ptnr., 1972-98; mng. ptnr. Sokolow Carreras LLP, N.Y.C., 1999—. Chmn. N.Y.C. CSC, 1979-92; bd. dirs. Met. Transp. Authority of N.Y. State, 1992—. Chmn. St. Francis Friends of the Poor, Inc., 1991—; trustee St. Bona Venture U., 1997—; pres. Am. Red Magen David for Israel, 2001—. Home: 1067 5th Ave New York NY 10128-0101 Office: Sokolow Carreras LLP 770 Lexington Ave 6th Flr New York NY 10021-8165 Office Phone: 212-935-6000. Personal E-mail: Mark@Lebow.net. Business E-Mail: mlebow@scassocies.net.

LEBOWITZ, ALBERT, lawyer, writer; b. St. Louis, June 18, 1922; s. Jacob and Lena (Zemmel) L.; m. Naomi Gordon, Nov. 26, 1953; children: Joel Aaron, Judith Leah. AB, Washington U., St. Louis, 1945; LL.B., Harvard U., 1948. Bar: Mo. bar 1948. Assoc. Frank E. Morris, St. Louis, 1948-55; partner firm Morris, Schneider & Lebowitz, St. Louis, 1955-58, Crowe, Schneider, Shanahan & Lebowitz, St. Louis, 1958-66; counsel firm Murphy & Roche, St. Louis, 1966-67, Murphy & Schlapprizzi, St. Louis, 1967-81; partner firm Murphy, Schlapprizzi & Lebowitz, 1981-86; editor lit. quar. Perspective, 1961-80; of counsel Donald L. Schlapprizzi, P.C., 1986—, John T. Murphy, Jr., 1986-88. Author: novel Laban's Will, 1966, The Man Who Wouldn't Say No, 1969, A Matter of Days, 1989; also short stories. Served as combat navigator USAAF, 1943-45, ETO. Decorated Air medal with 3 oak leaf clusters. Mem. Mo. Bar Assn., Phi Beta Kappa. Home: 743 Yale Ave Saint Louis MO 63130-3120 Office: 743 Yale Ave Saint Louis MO 63130-3120

LEBOWITZ, CATHARINE KOCH, state legislator; b. Winchester, Mass., June 30, 1915; d. William John and Carolyn Sophia (Kistinger) Koch; m. Murray Lebowitz, Sept. 21, 1971 (dec. Oct. 1978). Student, Northwestern U., 1948-49, Boston Coll., 1949-52; degree (hon.), Ea. Main Tech. Coll., 2003. Sec. ERA, Bangor, Augusta, Maine, 1935-38, WPA, Portland, Maine, 1938-42; pers. officer, exec. sec. USN, Portland, 1942-47; exec. sec. Clark Babbitt, Boston, 1947-48; adminstrv. asst. Moore Bus. Forms, Boston, 1948-52; apt. mgr., wholesale appliance divsn. Coffin-Wimple Inc., 1952-62; clk. U.S. Dist. Ct. Bangor (no. dist.), 1962-79; sec. Portland Credit Bur., 1980-86; mem. Bangor City Coun., 1985-87, Maine State Legislature, 1982-92. Bd. dirs. Eastern Transp., 1989—94; mem. Bus. Adv. Coun., 1991—; active Program Rev. Subcom., 1991—; mem. adv. coun. Ea. Maine Tech. Coll., 1992—; bd. dirs. Rural Health Ctrs. Maine, Inc., 1992—99; chair, adv. bd., Gala decorating com. Maine Ctr. for Arts, U. Maine, 1992—2003. Sec. Symphony Women, Bangor, 1964—84; bd. dirs. Opera House Com., 1978—94; legis. com. United Way of Penobscot Valley, 1988—93, bd. dirs., 1993—99; adv. com. Maine Devel. Found., 1988—90; adv. bd. Aftercare, Cmty. Health & Counseling Svc., 1992; planning bd. St. Joseph Hosp., 1987—92; dir., v.p. St. Joseph Hosp. Aux., 1994—99, Maine Ctr. Arts Adv. Bd., 1994—2002; apptr. by gov. Maine Commn. Cmty. Svc., 1996—2002; mem. Bangor City Hosp. Aux., 1988—99; bd. dirs. Penobscot Theater, 1990; accredited Beauty Pageant judge, 1986—; mem. Eastern Main Commn. Cmty Svc., 1996; del. Rep. Nat. Conv., 1984, 1988. Recipient Civilian Meritorious Svc. award USN, Portland, Maine, 1946, Paul Bunyan award, C. of C., 1997, Cmty. Spirit award Sr. Star recognition Merrill Merchants Bank Bangor, 1999; named Hon. Alumnus Secretarial Sci., Husson Coll., 1980, Ea. Main Tech. Coll. Champion award, 2002. Mem.: Ea. Maine Med. Ctr. Aux., Ret. Fed. Employees (v.p. 1994—, pres. 1996), Newcomb Soc., Penobscot County Reps., Bangor C. of C. (mem. comsumer rels. coun., 1981-90, gov. affairs com. 1996—, coord. 150th ann. prodn. Music Man 1984), Bangor Dist. Nursing Assn. (corp. mem. at large), Credit Women Bangor (sec. 1965—67), Nat. Assn. Ret. Fed. Employees (v.p. bd. dirs. 1993—, sec. 1994), Credit Profls. Bangor Cmty. Theater (treas. 1973—98), Credit Women Internat. (treas. 1975—77), Penobscot County Ext. Svc. (hon.; bd. dirs. 1995—), Main Art N.G. (hon.), Maine N.G. Assn. (hon.), Bangor Hist. Soc. (bd. dirs. 1993—, exec. bd. sec. 1994—99, pres. 1999—2002), U. Maine Maine Masque Theater (judge 1983—90), Mgmt. Club, Bangor City Rep. Club (bd. dirs., treas. 1993—97), Penobscot County Rep. Women's Club (sec. 1979), Zonta Club (pres. Bangor 1962—64, 1980—82, v.p. 1994, adv. bd. Maine migrant health program 2001—, cooperator cmty. health and counseling svcs. 2001—, Outstanding Leader 1991).

LEBOWITZ, JOEL LOUIS, mathematical physicist, educator; b. May 10, 1930; arrived in US, 1946, naturalized, 1951; m. Estelle Mandelbaum, June 21, 1953 (dec. Dec. 1996); m. Ann Keay Beneduce, June 3, 1999. BS, Bklyn. Coll., 1952; MS, Syracuse U., 1955, PhD, 1956; hon. doctorate, Ecole Poly. Federale, Lausanne, Switzerland, 1977, Clark U., 1999. NSF postdoctoral fellow Yale U., New Haven, 1956-57; mem. faculty Stevens Inst. Tech., Hoboken, N.J., 1957-59, Yeshiva U., N.Y.C., 1959-77, prof. physics, 1965-77, acting chmn. Belfer Grad. Sch. Sci., 1964-67, chmn. dept., 1967-76; George William Hill prof math. and physics, dir. Ctr. for Math. Scis., Rutgers U., New Brunswick, N.J., 1977—. Co-editor: Phase Transitions and Critical Phenomena, 1980, editor Jour. Statis. Physics, 1975—, Studies in Statis. Mechanics, 1973—, Com. Math. Physics, 1973—; contbr. articles to profl. jours. Recipient Boltzmann medal Internat. Union Pure and Applied Physics, 1992, Max Planck Rsch. award, 1993, Delmar S. Fahrney medal Franklin Inst., 1995, Henri Poincare prize Internat. Assn. of Math. Physics/Daniel Iagolnitzer Found., 2000, Vito Volterra medal Academia Nazionale dei Lincei, 2001; Guggenheim fellow, 1976-77. Fellow AAAS (Sci. Freedom and Responsibility award 1998), Am. Phys. Soc. (Nicholson medal for humanitarian svc. 2004), N.Y. Acad. Scis. (pres. 1979, A. Cressy Morrison award in natural scis. 1986, Heinz R. Pagels Human Rights of Scientists award 1996); mem. NAS, AAUP, Am. Math. Soc., Phi Beta Kappa, Sigma Xi. Office: Rutgers U Ctr Math Sci Rsch 110 Frelinghuysen Rd Piscataway NJ 08854-8019 Office Phone: 732-445-3117. Business E-Mail: lebowitz@sakharov.rutgers.edu.

LEBOWITZ, MARSHALL, publishing company executive; b. Boston, Mar. 4, 1923; s. Max Nathan and Rissah (Zangwill) L.; m. Charlotte Lily Meyersohn, Aug. 7, 1949; children: Wendy Ann, Marian Kay, Mark Louis. AB, Harvard U., 1942. Statis. analyst U.S. WPB, Washington, 1942-43; periodicals mgr. J.S. Canner & Co., Inc., Needham Heights, Mass., 1946—67, gen. mgr., 1967—96, v.p., 1967—96, Plenum Pub. Corp., 1967—96. Mem. Natick (Mass.) Planning Bd., 1964-69, chmn., 1968-69; mem. Natick Town Meeting, 1954—, chmn. town by-laws revision com., 1965-67; pres. Greater Framingham Mental Health Assn., 1963-64, dir., 1954-63; mem. Greater Framingham Mental Health Area Bd., 1972-78, v.p., 1974-75, pres., 1975-77; mem. Regional Drug Rev. Bd., 1973; chmn. Natick Regional Vocat. Sch. Planning Com., 1974-77; mem. Natick Sch. Com., 1978-81, clk., 1979-81; chmn. legis. impact study commn. Town of Natick, 1980; chmn. town commn. to rev. by-laws and mcpl. charter, 1980-90; mem. trustees adv. coun. Leonard Morse Hosp., 1973-91, vice chmn., 1974-77, mem. mental health adv. com., 1972-91; chmn. Natick Land-Use Com., 1983—; mem. Mcpl. Charter Rev. Com., 1985-88, Framingham-Natick Golden Triangle Planning Com., 1988-93; trustee Morse Inst. Libr., 1989—, pres., 1996—; bd. dirs. Framingham-Natick Cemetery Assn., 1991—; mem. Mcpl. Facilities Planning, 1994-96. With AUS, 1943-46. Named Natick Sr. Man of Yr., 1997; recipient Geshelin Humanitarian award. Jewish (fin. sec. temple 1954-56, treas. 1952-54, vice-chmn. bd. 1958-59). Home: 2 Abbott Rd Natick MA 01760-1913

LEBRA, JOYCE C., retired history educator; b. Mpls. d. Royal N. and Helen A. (Sanborn) Chapman. BA, U. Minn., 1947, MA, 1949; PhD, Harvard/Radcliffe, 1958. Vis. asst. prof. U. Tex., Austin, 1960-61; asst. prof. Rutgers U., Newark, 1961-62; asst. to full prof. U. Colo., Boulder, 1962-91; prof. emerita. Author: Sugar and Smoke, A Novel, 2005, Shaping Hawaii: the Voices of Women, 1999, Durga's Sword, 1995, Women's Voices in Hawaii, 1991, The Rani of Jhansi: A Study in Female Heroism in India, 1986, Okuma Shigenobu Statesman of Meiji Japan, 1981, Japanese Trained Armies in Southeast Asia, 1977, Jungle Alliance, Japan and the Indian National Army, 1971, others; editor: Women and Work in India, 1984, Chinese Women in Southeast Asia, 1977, Women in Changing Japan, 1976, others; contbr. articles to profl. jours. Grantee Fulbright Comms., Japan, 1955-57, India, 1965-66, various grants to Japan, India; recipient fellowships NEH, 1970-71, Japan Found. fellowship, 1981-82, fellowship Indo-U.S. Subcommn. on Edn. and Culture, India, 1983. Home and Office: 566 A Kaleo Pl Kihei HI 96753 Office Phone: 303-246-9963.

LEBRAS, PAUL J., career military officer; b. N.Y.C., Oct. 27, 1949; BA in Edn., Manhattan Coll., 1971; MA in African Area Studies, UCLA, 1979; Grad., Army Command & Gen. Staff Coll., Ft. Leavenworth, 1984; Grad, Air War Coll., Maxwell AFB, 1990. Commd. 2d lt. USAF, 1971, advanced through grades to maj. gen., 2002; target analyst Nakhon Phanom Royal, Thai AFB, Thailand, 1972; operational intelligence officer 8th Tactical Fighter Wing, Ubon Thai Royal AFB, 1972-73; staff officer Hdqrs. Pacific Air Forces, Hickam AFB, Hawaii, 1973-77; air staff tng. program officer Hdqrs. USAF, The Pentagon, Washington, 1977-78, chief Middle East and African br. regional estimates divsn., 1984-87; analyst Def. Intelligence Agy., Washington, 1980-83; dir. White Ho. Situation Rm., Washington, 1987-89; commdr. 12th Tactical Intelligence Squadron, Bergstrom AFB, Tex., 1990-91; dir. intelligence Hdqrs. 4th Air Force, Yokota AB, Japan, 1991-94; dir. of intelligence Hdqrs. Pacific Air Forces, Hickman AFB, 1994-96; dir. intelligence Hdqrs. Air Combat Command, Langley AFB, Va., 1996-97, various assignments, 1997-98; vice comdr. Air Intelligence Agy., Kelly AFB, 1998-99; vice dir. intelligence, Joint Staff (J-2) Def. Intelligence Agy., Washington, 1999—2001; dep. comdr. info. ops. 8th Air Force, Barkdale AFB, La., 2002—; comdr. Air Intelligence Agy. & Joint Info. Ops. Ctr., Lackland AFB, Tex., 2002—. Decorated Def. Superior Svc. medal with two oak leaf clusters, Legion of Merit, Def. Meritorious Svc. medal, Meritorious Svc. medal with four oak leaf clusters, Joint. Svc. Commendation medal, Air Force Commendation medal; Recipient Presdl. Svc. Badge. Office: Air Intelligence Agy 2 Hall Blvd Ste 201 San Antonio TX 78243*

LEBRECHT, THELMA JANE MOSSMAN, retired reporter; b. Indpls., Feb. 21, 1946; d. Elmore Somerville and Lois Thelma (Johnson) Mossman; m. Roger Dublon LeBrecht, May 4, 1968. BS in Journalism, U. Fla., 1968. Pub. affairs reporter WBT and WBTV, Charlotte, N.C., 1967-72; freelance reporter Toronto and N.Y.C., 1972-76; reporter KYW Newsradio, Phila., 1976-80; editor ABC Radio Network, N.Y.C., 1980-81; reporter AP Broadcast, Washington, 1981—2004, ret., 2004. Bd. dirs. Washington Press Club Found., 1995-2004. Mem. Radio and TV Corrs. Assn. in U.S. Capitol (chmn. 1991, AP Oliver S. Gramling Disting. Reporter award 1996).

LEBRUN, GENE N., lawyer; b. Langdon, N.D., July 4, 1939; s. Jules E. and Marie Lebrun; m. Patricia A. Lebrun, Aug. 17, 1963; children: Michael, Kenneth. BA, St. John's U., 1961; JD, U. N.D., 1964. Bar: S.D. 64, 1964. Mem. Lynn, Jackson, Shultz & Lebrun, P.C., Rapid City, S.D., 1964—. Mem. Adv. Commn. on Electronic Commerce, 1999-2000. Mem. Nat. Conf. of Commrs. on Uniform State Laws (pres. 1997-99), SD House Reps., 1971-1974 (speaker 1973-1974). Democrat. Office: Lynn Jackson Shultz & Lebrun PC Ste 400 909 St Joseph St Rapid City SD 57701 Office Phone: 605-342-2592.

LE BRUN, JOHN LEO, education educator, tax specialist; b. Geneva, NY, Aug. 8, 1934; s. Ralph Leo and Mary Elizabeth Le Brun; m. Priscilla S. Costich, Aug. 12, 1961; children: Joseph André, Lisette Johanna. AB, U. Rochester, 1957; MA, Boston Coll., 1963; PhD, Case Western Res. U., 1967. Tech. editor Gen. Dynamics, 1958—61; prof. Kent (Ohio) State U., 1964—2004; camp dir. Boy Scouts Am., Warren, Ohio, 1974—75, 1994, 1996; tax specialist H&R Block, Youngstown, Ohio, 1996—. Health and welfare com. United Way, Youngstown, 1986—92; leader Boy Scouts Am., Warren, 1966—; social justice com. Cath. Conf. Ohio, Columbus, 1994—96; mem. St. Michael Parish Coun., 1984—87, 1999—2002, Youngstown Diocesan Pastoral Coun., 1985—87, 1999—2002. With U.S. Army, 1957—63. Recipient Dist. Merit award, Boy Scouts Am., 1992, Silver Beaver award,

2000, St. George award, Diocese of Youngstown, 1996. Mem.: Orgn. Am. Historians, Peace History Soc., Ohio Hist. Soc., Am. Hist. Soc. Roman Catholic. Avocations: photography, travel. Home: 85 Cardinal Dr Canfield OH 44406

LEBRUN, MARCEL RENÉ, education educator; s. Rene Henri Lebrun and Angela Therese Laramie. B of Edn., U. Man., Winnipeg, 1979, BA, 1982, MEd, 1993; PhD, U. San Jose, 1996. Cert. tchr. Man., spl. edn. Man., spl. edn. dir. Man. Elem. and mid. sch. tchr. Transcona Springfield Sch. Dist., Winnipeg, 1983—2002; clin. dir. MRL Stress and Anxiety Clinic, Winnipeg, 1994—2002; univ. prof. Plymouth (N.H.) State U. Coord. Lakes Region PBIS Ctr. for Effective Behavioral Interventions and Support, Bedford, NH, 2002—; presenter maj. edn. confs. Author: Reflections on Still Waters, 2005, Success in University Manual, 2002; contbr. articles to profl. jours. Mem.: CEC, ASCD, APA, Coun. for Behavioral Disorders, Phi Delta Kappa (exec. bd. dirs. 2004). Democrat. Unitarian Universalist. Avocations: reading, travel, writing, movies, acting. Home: PO Box 1193 Ashland NH 03217 Office: Plymouth State U 17 High St Plymouth NH 03264 Office Phone: 603-535-2288. E-mail: mrlebrun@plymouth.edu.

LECAR, MYRON, astrophysicist, astronomer, educator; b. Bkyln., Apr. 10, 1930; s. Joshua Lecar and Rachel Stoun. SB, MIT, Cambridge, Mass., 1951; MS, Case Inst. Tech., Cleve., 1953; PhD, Yale U., New Haven, Conn., 1963; MS (hon.), Churchill Coll., Cambridge, Eng., 1978. Physicist Goddard Inst. Space Studies, N.Y.C., 1961—65; sr. astrophysicist Harvard-Smithsonian Ctr. Astrophysics, Cambridge, Mass., 1965—. Lectr. astronomy Yale U., New Haven, 1961—65, Harvard U., Cambridge, Mass., 1965—. Contbr. articles to profl. jours. Lt. (j.g.) USN, 1954—58. Democrat. Jewish. Achievements include principal investigator in grant which established first astronomical observatory in Israel. Home: 23 Tobey Rd Belmont MA 02478 Office: Harvard Smithsonian Ctr Astrophysics 60 Garden St Cambridge MA 02138 E-mail: mlecar@cta.harvard.edu.

LE CARRÉ, JOHN (DAVID JOHN MOORE CORNWELL), author; b. Poole, Dorset, Eng., Oct. 19, 1931; s. Ronald Thomas Archibald and Olive (Glassy) Cornwell; m. Alison Ann Sharp, Nov. 27, 1954 (div. dissolved 1972); children: Simon, Stephen, Timothy; m. Valerie Jane Eustace, 1972; 1 son, Nicholas. Student, Bern (Switzerland) U., 1948-49, BA in Modern Langs., 1956; hon. doctorate, U. Exeter, 1990, St. Andrews U., 1996, U. Southampton, U. Bath. Tutor Eton Coll., Berkshire, Eng., 1956-58; mem. Brit. Fgn. Service, 1959-64, 2d sec. embassy Bonn, Germany, 1961-63, consul Hamburg, Germany, 1963-64. Author: Call for the Dead, 1960, A Murder of Quality, 1962, The Spy Who Came in From the Cold, 1963 (Mystery Writers of Am. Novel of Yr., 1963, Brit. Crime Novel of Yr. award 1963, Somerset Maugham award 1963), The Looking-Glass War, 1965, A Small Town in Germany, 1968, The Naive and Sentimental Lover, 1971, Tinker Tailor Soldier Spy, 1973, rev., 1978, The Honourable Schoolboy, 1977 (James Tait Black Meml. prize, Crime Writers Assn. gold dagger), Smiley's People, 1980 (televised 1982), The Little Drummer Girl, 1983, A Perfect Spy, 1986, The Russia House, 1989 (Nikos Kasanzakis prize 1991), The Secret Pilgrim, 1991, The Night Manager, 1993, Our Game, 1995, The Tailor of Panama, 1996 (made into movie 2001), Single & Single, 1999, The Constant Gardener, 2002, Absolute Friends, 2004. Recipient Somerset Maugham award 1964, Edgar Allen Poe award Mystery Writers Am., 1965, Gold dagger Crime Writers Assn., 1978, Black Meml. award, 1978, The Kazamzakis prize, Greece, 1984, Grand Master award Mystery Writers Am., 1986, Malaparte prize, 1987, Diamond Dagger award Crime Writers Assn., 1988; Lincoln Coll., Oxford hon. fellow, 1984.*

LECAT, ROBERT J., retired aeronautical engineer; s. Paul and Suzanne Vigne Lecat; m. Veronica Joan Miller (dec.); children: Nicole, Daphne, Gabrielle(dec.), Paul. BS in aerospace, Cath. U., 1948—49, MS in aerospace, 1953, D in engring. aerospace, 1964. Engr. Wash. Gas Light Co., Washington, 1948—50, McDonnel, St. Louis, 1950—52, Kellex Nitro, Silver Spring, Md., 1953—54, APL/IHLI, Silver Spring, 1954—55; head preliminary design Fairchild Guided Mass, Wyandanch, NY, 1956—57; head aerospace/design specialist Grumman, Bethpage, NY, 1957—90. Cons., 1990—; adj. asst. prof. SUNY, Stony Brook, 1988—93; engr. Pluf Ultra Tech., Stony Brook, 2000—02; project engr. Soc. A/C Restoration, Comack, NY, 1988—2004. Author: Dynamics Reentry Scala, 1963, Goniometric Aerodynamic, 1969; contbr. scientific papers pub. to profl. jour. With French 12th Royal Marine/Militia Brigade, 1976—, Milford, Conn., ensign French Aeronavale, 1944—46. Fellow: Am. Inst. Aero Astro Coun. (assoc.); mem.: Assn. Naval Aviation, Soc. Flight Test Engr. Achievements include patents in field; design of Gruman reentry vehicles; wind tunnel & flight test of a supersonic towed decoy now in prodn; research in exploration of Jovian atmosphere listing a nuc. ramjet flyer. Avocations: model building, aviation, history.

LECAVALIER, VINCENT, professional hockey player; b. Ile Bizard, Que., Can., Apr. 21, 1980; Hockey player Rimouski Oceanic, Tampa Bay (Fla.) Lightning, 1998—. Mem. Team Can., World Cup of Hockey, 2004. Named Tournament MVP, World Cup of Hockey, 2004; named to NHL All-Star Game, 2003. Achievements include mem. Stanley Cup Championship Team, Tampa Bay Lightning, 2004; mem. World Cup Champion Team Can., 2004. Office: Tampa Bay Lightning St Pete Times Forum 401 Channelside Dr Tampa FL 33602

LECCESE, PETER, retired music educator; b. Flushing, N.Y., Oct. 6, 1949; s. James and Jennie Leccese; m. Denise Marie Schlotterbeck, Aug. 5, 1972; children: Amy Buttigieg, Deborah. BS in Edn., Hofstra U., 1972; MA in Music Composition, C.W. Post U., 1977. Vocal music educator Sachem H.S., Lake Ronkonkoma, NY, 1972—75, music educator, 1975—91, jazz band educator, 1984—96; band music educator Merrimac Elem. Sch., 1991—99, band/orch. educator, 1999—; dir. elem. band Grundy Ave. Sch., 1991—, band/orch. educator, 1999—2005, ret., 2005. Disc jockey, 1978—. V.p. Sachem Ctrl. Tchrs. Assn., Lake Ronkonkoma, 2002—05; pres. Sachem Alumni Assn., 1997—. Mem.: S.C. Music Educators Assn., N.Y. State Sch. Music Assn., Sachem Ctr. Sch. Tchrs. Assn. (v.p. 2002—), Music Educators Nat. Conf., Sachem Alumni Assn. (pres. 1997—2001). Avocations: music, disc jockeying. Home: 33 Metzner Rd Lake Ronkonkoma NY 11779-2140 Personal E-mail: lecesse7@optonline.net.

LECHAGO, JUAN, pathologist, educator; b. Barcelona, Aug. 2, 1942; came to U.S., 1973; s. Angel and Dolores (Xicart) L.; m. Lia Virginia Epstein, Feb. 26, 1966 (dec.); children: John Patrick, James Bernard, Sarah Angela; m. Maria Zunilda Nuñez, July 21, 2002; 1 stepchild, Pamela Espino. B of Humanities, Nat. Coll. Monserrat, Cordoba, Argentina, 1959; MD, Nat. U. Cordoba, 1966; PhD in Pathology, Queen's U., Kingston, Ont., Can., 1971. Diplomate Am. Bd. Pathologists. Staff pathologist Harbor UCLA Med. Ctr., Torrance, Calif., 1973-87; asst. prof. pathology UCLA, 1973-79, assoc. prof. pathology, 1979-85, prof. pathology, 1985-87; prof., vice-chmn. dept. pathology U. Tex. So. Med. Sch., Dallas, 1987-90; chief lab. VA Med. Ctr., Dallas, 1987-90; prof. pathology Baylor Coll. Medicine, Houston, 1990—2002, prof. medicine, 1998—2002; head gastrointestinal and endocrine pathology Cedars-Sinai Med. Ctr., LA, 2002—. Dir. morphology Core Ctr. for Study of Inflammatory Bowel Disease, Torrance, 1985-87, Ctr. for Diabetes Rsch., Dallas, 1988-90; dir. surg. pathology svc. The Meth. Hosp., Houston, 1990-2002. Editor: Cellular Basis of Chemical Messengers in the Digestive System, 1981, Endocrine Pathology Update, 1990, Bloodworth's Endocrine Pathology, 3d edit., 1996; contbr. over 120 articles to profl. jours. NIH grantee, 1974-84, 82-86. Mem. U.S. Can. Acad. Pathology (edn. com. 1973—), Gastrointestinal Pathology Soc. (founding mem., pres. 1987-88), L.Am. Pathology Found. (pres. 1994-96), Ctrl. Am. Assn. Pathology (hon.), Argentinian Soc. Pathology (hon.). Achievements include work on ultrastructural and histochemical characterization of the digestive endocrine cells in man and animal species, first immunocytochemical cellular localization of the neuropeptides Bombesin and Ranatensin in animals, first immunolocalization of Granuliberin-like peptide in frog brain, molecular biology of Barrett's esophagus-derived cancer. Office: Cedars-Sinai Med Ctr Dept Pathology 8700 Beverly Blvd Los Angeles CA 90048 Office Phone: 310-423-6604. E-mail: lechagoj@csms.org.

LECHEVALIER, HUBERT ARTHUR, microbiology educator; b. Tours, Indre et Loire, France, May 12, 1926; came to U.S., 1948; s. Jean Gaston and Marie Emilie L.; m. Mary Pfeil, Apr. 10, 1950; children: Marc, Paul. L ès Sci., Laval U., 1947, MS, 1948, DSc (hon.), 1983; PhD, Rutgers U., 1951. Asst. prof. Rutgers U., New Brunswick, N.J., 1951-56, assoc. prof., 1956-66, prof. microbiology, 1966-91, assoc. dir. Waksman Inst., 1980-88; prof. emeritus, 1991—. Vis. scientist Acad. of Scis. USSR, Moscow, 1958-59, Pasteur Inst., Paris, 1961-62 Author: (with others) A Guide to the Actinomycetes and Their Antibiotics, 1953, Neomycin--Its Nature and Practical Application, 1958, Antibiotics of Actinomycetes, 1962, Three Centuries of Microbiology, 1965, Hungarian transl., 1971, The Microbes, 1971, The Development of Applied Microbiology at Rutgers, 1982; co-editor: CRC Critical Reviews in Microbiology (1970-78), CRC Handbook of Microbiology (1970-89); contbr. numerous articles to profl. jours.; 4 patents. Trustee Am. Type Culture Collection, Rockville, Md., 1973-79. Recipient Lindback award 1976, Bergey award 1989; inducted into N.J. Inventors Hall of Fame, 1990. Mem. Soc. Française de Microbiology (hon.), Soc. for Indsl. Microbiology (emeritus); Charles Thom award 1982, Soc. for Actinomycetes Japan (hon.) Home: 131 Goddard-Nisbet Rd Morrisville VT 05661-8041 Personal E-mail: hubartlech@msn.com.

LECHEVALIER, MARY PFEIL, retired microbiologist, educator; b. Cleve., Jan. 27, 1928; d. Alfred Leslie Pfeil and Mary Edith Martin; m. Hubert Arthur Lechevalier, Apr. 7, 1950; children: Marc E.M., Paul R. BA in Physiology-Biochemistry, Mt. Holyoke Coll., 1949; MS in Microbiology, Rutgers U., 1951. Rsch. fellow Rutgers U., New Brunswick, N.J., 1949-51, rsch. assoc. inst. microbiology, 1962-74, from asst. to assoc. rsch. prof., 1974-85, rsch. prof. Waksman inst. microbiology, 1985-91, prof. emerita, 1991—; ind. rschr., 1955-59; microbiologist steroid preparative lab. E.R. Squibb and Sons, New Brunswick, 1960-61; vis. investigator Inst. Biology Czechoslovak Acad. Scis., Svc. de Mycologie Pasteur Inst., Prague, Paris, 1961-62. Cons. in field. Contbr. over 100 chpts. to books and articles to rsch. jours.; mem. adv. com. actinomycetes Bergey's Manual of Determinative Bacteriology, 8th edit.; chair adv. com. muriform actinomycetes Bergey's Manual, 9th edit. Assoc. mem. Bergey's Trust, 1989—92. Recipient Charles Thom award, Soc. Indsl. Microbiology, 1982, Waksman award, Theobald Smith Soc., 1991. Mem. AAAS, Am. Soc. Microbiology (former mem. com. actinomycetales), U.S. Fedn. Culture Collections (exec. com. 1982-85, J. Roger Porter award nominating com. 1983-84, 87-88, chair 1989-90, J. Roger Porter award 1992), N.Am. Mycol. Assn., Soc. for Actinomycetes Japan, Sigma Xi (pres. Rutgers U. chpt. 1977-78). Achievements include patents for immunological adjuvant and process for preparing same, pharmaceutical composition and process, restriction endonuclease Fse I, antibiotic LL-14E605B and O-Methyl LL-14E605B. Home: 131 Goddard-Nisbet Rd Morrisville VT 05661-8041

LECHLEITER, RICHARD A., service industry executive; CPA. V.p., contr. Humana Inc., 1990—93, Galen Health Care, Inc., 1993, Columbia/HCA Healthcare Corp., 1993—95; dir. fin. Vencor, 1995, v.p. fin. corp. contr., 1995—98; v.p., fin. corp. contr., treas. Kindred Healthcare, Louisville, 1998—2002, sr. v.p., CFO, treas., 2002—. Office: Kindred Healthcare 680 S Fourth St Louisville KY 40202

LECHNER, BERNARD JOSEPH, consulting electrical engineer; b. N.Y.C., Jan. 25, 1932; s. Barnard Joseph and Lillian L.; m. Joan Camp Mathewson, Nov. 21, 1953. BSEE, Columbia U., 1957; postgrad., Princeton U., 1957-60. Mem. tech. staff RCA Labs., Princeton, N.J., 1957-62, project leader, 1962-67, group head, 1967-77, lab. dir., 1977-83, staff v.p., 1983-87; cons., Princeton, 1987—. Cons. expert on TV matters including high definition TV and flat-panel displays; bd. dirs. Palisades Inst., N.Y.C.; chmn. adv. commn. Mercer County Coll., Trenton, N.J., 1968-85. Contbr. articles to profl. jours. Reader Recording for the Blind, Princeton, 1967-72. Served to cpl. U.S. Army, 1953-55. Recipient David Sarnoff Gold medal RCA Corp., 1962, Outstanding Contributor award Advanced TV Sys. Com., 2000, TV Engring. Achievement award NAB, 2002. Fellow: IEEE (chpt. chmn. 1964—66, Best Paper award Solid State Cirs. Conf. 1966), Soc. Motion Picture and TV Engrs. (David Sarnoff Gold Medal award 1996, Progress Medal award 2001), Soc. for Info. Display (pres. 1978—80, Frances Rice Darne award 1971, Beatrice Winner award 1983); mem.: Am. Relay Radio League, Princeton Sqs. (pres. 1981-87), Eta Kappa Nu, Tau Beta Pi, Sigma Xi. Episcopalian. Achievements include 10 patents; development of home video tape recorders in the late 1950s; flat-panel matrix displays in the 1960s including pioneering work on active-matrix liquid crystal displays; advanced two-way cable TV systems and pay-TV systems in the early 1970s; electronic tuning systems and CCD comb-filters for TV receivers in the mid-1970s and early 1980s; contributed to the early development of HDTV in the mid-1980s; led the development of many of the standards for HDTV during the 1990s. Avocations: amateur radio, square dancing, stamp collecting/philately, sailing, swimming. Address: 59 Carson Rd Princeton NJ 08540-2207 Office Phone: 609-924-7545. Business E-Mail: tvbernie@ieee.org.

LECHNER, JANE ANN, secondary mathematics educator; b. July 19, 1949; AA, Ottumwa Heights Coll., 1969; BA, William Penn Coll., 1972; MA, N.E. Mo. State U., 1987. Cert. profl. educator. Tchr. aide Ottumwa (Iowa) Community Schs., 1969-71, tchr. substitute, 1972-83; tchr. Indian Hills Community Coll., Ottumwa, 1978, Ottumwa Community Schs., 1983—. Contbg. author: K-8 Mathematics Activity Book Series, 1991. Tchr. ch. Sun. Sch., Ottumwa, 1982—; bd. mem. Ottumwa Cmty. Sch. Credit Union. Recipient Honors Tchr. award NSTA, 1990. Mem. NEA, Iowa State Edn. Assn., Ottumwa Edn. Assn. (past sec. and negotiations chair, v.p.), Nat. Coun. Tchrs. Math., Iowa Coun. Tchrs. Math., Nat. Mid. Sch. Assn., Iowa Assn. Mid. Level Edn., King's Daughters (v.p. 1986—, treas. 1984-86, honor pearl 1990), Alpha Delta Kappa (pres. 2000-02), Delta Kappa Gamma (sec. 2004—), O.E.S. Rose chpt. (treas. 2004—). Avocations: reading, travel, needlecrafts, gardening, aviation. Home: 1213 N Court St Ottumwa IA 52501-1909 Office: Evans Middle Sch 812 Chester Ave Ottumwa IA 52501-4150

LECHNER, JON ROBERT, nursing administrator, educator; b. Detroit, Nov. 5, 1957; s. Monroe Stanley and Helen Cecelia (Schneider) L. Cert. in practical nursing, Oakland C.C., Southfield, Mich., 1983; ADN, Mercy Coll. Detroit, 1991, BSN, 1992; MSA, Ctrl. Mich. U., 1998. Cert. EMT; RN, ANCC, Mich. Coord. emergency med. svcs., paramedic William Beaumont Hosp., Royal Oak, Mich., 1979-84, nurse, 1986—92, asst. nursing mgr., 1992-97, nursing mgr., 1997—2001; pastoral assoc. St. Mary's Parish & Sch., Toledo, 1984-86; adj. clin. instr. Oakland C.C., Waterford, Mich., 1993—; program mgr. Vis. Nurse Assn. of Southeast Mich., Oak Park, 2001—. Cert. BLS instr. Am. Heart Assn., Southfield, 1986—. Vol. Project Health-O-Rama, 1992—, Wellness Networks, Inc., 1992—; voting mem. region I State of Mich. HIV Planning & Prevention Commn., Detroit, 1994-2002. Mem. Am. Assembly Men Nursing, Am. Assn. Neurosci. Nurses, Acad. Med. Surg. Nurses (charter), Assn. Nurses AIDS Care, Sigma Theta Tau. Democrat. Roman Catholic. Avocations: reading, hiking, walking, bicycling, theater. Home: 28450 Universal Dr Warren MI 48092-2441 Office: Visiting Nurse Assn of Southeast Michigan 25900 Greenfield Rd Ste 600 Oak Park MI 48237 Office Phone: 248-967-8377. E-mail: jlechner@vna.org.

LECHOWICZ, LISA MARIE, retired insurance company executive; b. Chgo., Feb. 11, 1954; d. Edmund Lawrence and Gloria Marie (Radtke) L.; m. John F. Hession, Jr. May 26, 1983. BS, MS, Purdue U., 1977. CLU, ChFC; cert. employee benefits specialist, health ins. assoc. Cons. Accenture, Chgo., 1978-79, sr. cons. Omaha, 1979-81; systems analyst Mutual of Omaha, 1981-82, mgr., 1982-87, asst. v.p., mgr., 1987-89, 2nd v.p., dir., 1989-92, v.p., dir., 1992-95, sr. v.p., 1995-96; pres. Health Data Mgmt. Corp., Omaha, 1996—. Part-time instr. Met. C.C., Omaha, 1988-91, adv. bd., 1989-90, Coll. of St. Mary's, 1990-94. Campaign com. various local candidates, Omaha, 1988—; hon. chair A Taste for Independence Easter Seals, 2003. Mem. CLU Soc., WEDI, Omaha Jaycees (bd. dirs. 1988-89, Bronze Key award 1989), Nebr. Choral Arts Soc. (voce chair event 2002, voce silent auction chair 2002-2003). Home: 15611 Burt St Omaha NE 68118-2219 Office: HDM Corp 720 N 129th St Omaha NE 68154-6109 E-mail: ll@hdmcorp.com.

LECHTENBERG, VICTOR L., agricultural studies educator; b. Butte, Nebr., Apr. 14, 1945; m. Grayce Lechtenberg; 4 children. BS, U. Nebr., 1967; PhD in Agronomy, Purdue U., 1971. Prof. agronomy Purdue U., West Lafayette, Ind., 1971—, assoc. dir. Agrl. Experiment Sta., 1982-89, exec. assoc. dean agr., 1989-93, dean agr., 1994—2004, vice provost engagement, 2004—. Contbr. articles to profl. jours., chpts. to books. Scoutmaster Boy Scouts Am., 1983-85. Recipient Nebr. 4-H Dist. Alumni award, 1981. Fellow Am. Soc. Agronomy (Ciba-Geigy award), Crop Sci. Soc. Am. (past pres.); mem. Crop Sci. Soc. Agrnomy, Coun. Agrl. Sci. and Tech. (past pres., bd. dirs.), USDA (past chmn. nat. agrl. rsch., extension, edn. and econs. adv. bd.). Sigma Xi, Alpha Zeta, Gamma Sigma Delta. Roman Catholic. Avocation: woodworking. Office: Purdue Univ Hovde Hall 610 Purdue Mall West Lafayette IN 47907 Office Phone: 765-494-9095. Business E-Mail: vll@purdue.edu.

LECKMAN, JAMES FREDERICK, psychiatry and pediatrics educator; b. Albuquerque, Dec. 3, 1947; s. Frederick Arnold and Alberta Beatrice (Lane) L.; m. Hannah Jean Hone, Dec. 27, 1971; children: Emily Beth, Peter Edwin. BA, Coll. Wooster, 1969; MD, U. N.Mex., 1973; MA (hon.), Yale U., 1990. Diplomate Am. Bd. Psychiatry, Am. Bd. Child Psychiatry. Intern USPHS Marine Hosp., San Francisco, 1973-74; clin. assoc. NIMH, Bethesda, Md., 1974-76; adult and child psychiatric resident Yale U., New Haven, 1976-80, from asst. prof. to assoc. prof., 1980-90, Neison Harris prof. child psychiatry and pediat., 1990—. Mem. psychopathology and clin. biology initial rsch. rev. com. NIMH, 1985-90; Milton M. & Harriet H. Parker lectr. psychiatry and human genetics Ohio State U., 1985; cons. U.S. Army, Heidelberg, 1986, Nat. Adv. Mental Health Coun., 1989-90; chmn. steering com. study of rsch. on child and adolescent mental disorders Inst. Medicine, 1988-89, child psychology and treatment initial rsch. rev. com. NIMH, 1992—; sci. adv. bd. Sophia Found. Med. Rsch., Rotterdam, The Netherlands, 1989-94. Co-author: Tourette's Syndrome and Tic Disorders, 1988, Fragile X Syndrome, 1993; mem. editl. bd. Devel. and Psychopathology, 1988-94. Acta Paedopsychiatrica, 1992—; N. Am. corr. editor Jour. Child Psychology and Psychiatry, 1995—, Neuropsychopharmacol., 1995—; contbr. over 250 articles to profl. jours. Recipient Seymour L. Lustman Rsch. award, 1978, 79; fellow USPHS-AAMC, 1972; William T. Grant Found. Rsch. scholar, 1980-83, Merck Faculty scholar, 1982-91; grantee NIH, 1972-93, 92-95, Nat. Inst. Child Health and Human Devel., 1970-95, Nat. Inst. Neurol. Disease and Stroke, 1980-96, NIMH, 1980-83, 89-93, 92-96. Fellow APA (Blanche Ittelson award 1995, Am. Coll. Neuropsychology, Am.Acad. Child and Adolescent Psychiatry (editl. bd. jour. 1982-88, guest co-editor spl. sect. Tourette's syndrome 1984, sci. program com. 1983-87, Outstanding Mentor 1990,92, 95); mem. ACP (H.P. Laughlin fellow 1981), Tourette Syndrome Assn. (sci. adv. bd. 1991-95), Conn. Coun. Child and Adolescent Psychiatrists (pres. 1991-93), Phi Beta Kappa, Alpha Omega Alpha, Sigma Xi. Home: 125 Spring Glen Ter Hamden CT 06517-1538 Office: Yale U Child Study Ctr 230 S Frontage Rd New Haven CT 06519-1124

LE CLAIR, CHARLES GEORGE, artist, retired dean; b. Columbia, Mo., May 23, 1914; s. Carl Amie and Marie (Fess) LeC.; m. Margaret Foster, May 30, 1945 (dec. Nov. 1991). BS, MS, U. Wis., 1935; posgrad., Acad. Ranson, Paris, 1937, Columbia U., 1940-41. Instr. art U. Ala., 1935-36, asst. prof., head dept., 1937-42; asst. prof. art, head dept. Albion Coll., 1942-43; tchr. painting and design Albright Art Sch., Buffalo, 1943-46; assoc. prof., head dept. Chatham Coll., 1946-52, prof., 1952-60; dean Tyler Sch. Art, Temple U., Phila., 1960-74, dean emeritus, 1981—, prof. painting, 1974-81, chmn. painting and sculpture dept., 1979-81. Founder Tyler Sch. Art, Rome, Italy, 1966. Author: The Art of Watercolor, 1985, rev. edit., 1994, expanded edit., 1999, Color in Contemporary Painting, 1991; contbg. author: Everything You Ever Wanted to Know About Oil Painting, 1994; works exhibited at Pa. Acad. Met. Mus. Art, Carnegie Inst., Whitney Mus., Corcoran Mus., Chgo. Art Inst., Richmond Mus., Butler Mus. Art, Am. Watercolor Soc., Bklyn. Mus.; one-man shows include Carnegie Inst., 1954, Salpeter Gallery, N.Y.C., 1956, 59, 65, Rochester Inst. Tech., 1958, Phila. Art Alliance, 1962, 73, 2000, Franklin and Marshall Coll., 1969, Galleria 89, Rome, 1970, Left Bank Gallery, Wellfleet, 1983, 87, 96, Temple U., 1978, Visual Images, Wellfleet, 1978-80, Gross-McCleaf Gallery, Phila., 1979, 81, 96, 98, 2002, 04, More Gallery Phila., 1983, 87, 89, Villanova U., 1998, Carspecken-Scott Gallery, Wilmington, Del., 1999, Susquehanna Mus. Art, Harrisburg, Pa., 2003. Named Pitts. Artist of Yr., 1957; recipient Pennell medal Pa. Acad. Fine Arts, 1965, Achievement award Am. Artist mag., 1995, Lifetime Achievement award Watercolor Honor Soc., 1997; fellow Fund for Advancement Edn. Ford Found., 1952-53. Achievements include being subject of Elizabeth Leonard's book Painting Flowers, 1986, cover story Watercolor mag., 1999. Home: 2 Franklin Town Blvd Apt 1714 Philadelphia PA 19103

LECLAIR, DONAT R., JR., automotive executive; MBA, U. Mich. Fin. analyst Lorain Assembly Plant Ford Motor Co., contr. N.Am., 2001—03, group v.p. and CFO, 2003—. Office: Ford Motor Co One American Rd Dearborn MI 48126-1899*

LECLAIR, JOHN CLARK, professional hockey player; b. St. Albans, Vt., July 5, 1969; Hockey player Montreal Canadiens, 1987—94, Phila. Flyers, 1995—2005, Pitts. Penguins, 2005—. Named to ECAC All-Star 2d Team, 1990—91, Sporting News All-Star 1st Team, 1994—95, NHL All-Star 1st Team, 1994—95. Office: Pittsburgh Penguins 66 Mario Lemieux Pl Pittsburgh PA 15219 Office Phone: 412-471-4000.*

LECOANET, HELENE FRANCOISE, researcher; b. Managua, Nicaragua, June 17, 1972; BSc in Fluid Mechanics, U. Toulon, 1994; MSc in Oceanography, U. Bretagne, 1995; MSc in Environ. Sci., CERECE-Aûx en Provence, 1997; PhD in Earth Scis., U. Aûx Marseille. Cert. scuba diving and sailing instr. Post-doctral Utrecht U., Netherlands, 2000—01; rsch. assoc. Rice U., Houston, 2001—. Avocations: travel, sailing. Home: 2 E Gaslight Pl The Woodlands TX 77380 Office: Rice U 6100 Main St Houston TX 77005

LECOMPTE, JANET, historian, writer; b. Phila., May 22, 1923; d. Frederic Barr and Dorothy Price Shaw; m. Oliver Philip Lecompte, Oct. 3, 1944 (div. Feb. 1985); Jenny, Ellen, Louisa, Charles, Thomas, Peter. BA, Wellesley (Mass.) Coll., 1944; LLD, Colo. Coll., Colorado Springs, 1979; postgrad., Washington State U., 1988-91, U. N.Mex., 1990. Bd. dirs. Nat. Rev. Hist. Places, Denver, 1968-86, Colo. Hist. Soc., Denver, 1980-86; trustee Colo. Hist. Found., 1973-78; Colo. adv. bd. Nat. Historic Publs. and Records Commn., Denver, 1977-87. Hist. cons. U.S. Army, Fort Carson, Colorado Springs, 1983-85; cons. exhibits Colo. History Mus., Denver, 1977-78; mem. adv. com. Coll. Letters, Arts and Sci., Colo. U., Colorado Springs, 1971-83. Author: Pueblo Hardscrabble Greenhorn, 1978 (4 awards 1980), Rebellion in Rio Arriba, 1985; editor: Emily: Diary of a Hardworked Woman, 1987, French Fur Traders, 1993; bd. editors N.Mex. Hist. Rev., 1982-93; contbr. articles to profl. jours. Founder, pres. bd. Colorado Springs Sch., 1961-76; mem., subcom. chmn. Com. on Ednl. Endeavors, Legis. Coun., Denver, 1961-64. Recipient Best Non-Fiction Book of Yr., Westerners Internat., 1979, Western Writers Am., 1979 award of merit Am. Assn. State and Local History, 1980. Avocations: tennis, bridge, walking dogs, writing letters. Home: 1606 Pine Cone Rd Moscow ID 83843-9317

LE CONGE, MONIQUE ANNE, library director, consultant; b. San Francisco, July 5, 1965; d. Michele Jean Butler; adopted parents: Antoine and Marianne le Conge; m. Jon Benjamin King, June 11, 1988 (div. Nov. 1999); children: Joshua D. King, Marissa R. King, Gregory A. King. BS, U. Calif., Davis, 1987; M of Libr. and Info. Studies, U. Calif., Berkeley, 1988. Libr. Solano County Libr., Fairfield, Calif., 1989-91, children's libr. Vallejo, Calif.,

1991-94; young adult libr. Benicia (Calif.) Pub. Libr., 1994-98, dir., 1998—2004; dir. libr., recreation and arts Richmond (Calif.) Pub. Libr., 2004—. Cons. San Joaquin Valley Libr. Sys., Fresno, Calif., 2001-2002; young adult svcs. cons. North State Coop. Libr. Sys., Willows, Calif., 1997-98; cons. Benicia H.S., 1989. Editor: A Bibliography for Thou Shalt Not Read: Banned and Challenged Books for Children and Young Adults, 1995; contbr. to web site 700 Plus Great Web Sites for Kids, 1995; contbr. Librarian's Index to the Internet (Lii.org), 2001—; contbr. articles to profl. jours. Bd. dirs. Benicia Main St. Program, 1999-2001, Benicia Libr. Found., 2004—, Richmond (Calif.) Pub. Libr. Found., 2004— Mem. ALA, Assn. Children's Librs. of No. Calif. (pres. 1993-94), Bay Area Young Adult Librs., Benicia-Vallejo AAUW (bd. dirs. 2002-2003), Calif. Libr. Assn. (pres. mgmt. svcs. sect. 2003-04, chmn.), Assn. for Libr. Svc. to Children (com. chair), Pub. Libr. Assn. (com. mem.), Young Adult Libr. Svcs. Assn. (com. chair), Libr. Adminstrn. and Mgmt. Assn., BayNet (pres. 2002), Rotary Benicia (bd. dirs. 2000-2002, 2003-04), Rotary. Roman Catholic. Avocations: travel, hiking, museums. Office: Richmond Public Library 325 Civic Center Plz Richmond CA 94804 Office Phone: 510-620-6555. Personal E-mail: josiemo73@hotmail.com. Business E-Mail: monique_leconge@ci.richmond.ca.us.

LECORGNE, LISETTE MARY, family practice nurse practitioner; b. New Orleans, La., Aug. 11, 1955; d. Louis Constant and Nodileen LeCompte LeCorgne. RN, No. Ariz. U., 1978; nurse practitioner, U. of Colo., 1980—82; BS in Health Arts, U. St. Francis, 1982, MS in Healthcare Adminstrn., 2004. NP, Ariz., ANCC, 1983. Med. coord. Hozhoni Found., Flagstaff, Ariz., 1979—83; nurse practitioner U. of Ariz. Campus Health, Tucson, 1983—, coord. urgent care, triage/radiology. Past pres., bd. mem. Flying Samaritans, Tucson, 1996—. Delivery of health care to indigent, Tucson, 1996—2003. Recipient Appreciation award, Associated Students with Disabilities, 1998. Mem.: ANA (assoc.). Episcopal. Avocations: woodworking, travel. Home: 5133 E Adams St Tucson AZ 85713-4105 Office: University of Arizona Campus Health PO Box 210063 Tucson AZ 85721-0063 Office Phone: 520-621-6490. Personal E-mail: lisettelecorgne@hotmail.com. E-mail: lecorgne@health.arizona.edu.

LECOUNTE, LOLA HOUSTON, literature and language professor, educational consultant; d. Simpson and Lillian Edna Houston; widowed; children: Ernest Jerome, Karen Yvette, Mark Houston. BA, U. Md. Eastern Shore, 1956; MA, Trinity U., 1974; EdD, George Washington U., 1982. Tchr. English and French Accomack (Va.) County Pub. Schs., Va., 1957—59; tchr. English and history Fairfax (Va.) County Pub. Schs., 1959—67; tchr. English D.C. Pub. Schs., Washington, 1967—76, supr. English, 1976—81, asst. dir. English, 1981—92; asst. prof. Bowie (Md.) State U., 1996—, chair dept. tchg., 2001—04. Ednl. cons. E & L Consultants, Washington, 1976—88, Scholastic Book Co., N.Y.C., 1991—96, D.C. Pub. Schs., Washington, 1992—97; presenter papers at confs. Co-author: (hist./ednl. kit) Black Women in America Contribute to Our Heritage, 1983, Black Women for Social Change, 1984. Named Disting. Alumnus, Nat. Assn. Equal Opportunity in Higher Edn., 1987; named to Hall of Fame for Disting. Alumni, U. Md. Eastern Shore; recipient Outstanding Svc. award, Alpha Kappa Alpha, 1994, Oustanding Svc. in Edn. award, U. Md. Eastern Shore alumni chpt., 1992; grantee, NSF, 2004—05. Mem.: Nat. Coun. Tchrs. English, Assn. Supervision and Curriculum Devel., Assn. Tchr. Educators. Avocations: reading, poetry, singing, theater. Office: Bowie State U 14000 Jericho Park Rd Bowie MD 20715

LE CROISSETTE, DENNIS HARLOW, writer, consultant; arrived in U.S., 1957; s. Harlow Frederick and Ethel Mabel Le Croissette; m. Jill Campbell McLean, June 9, 1960. BSc in Physics, U. London, 1949, MSc in Physics, 1951, PhD in Atomic Physics, 1957. Physics lectr. U. Southampton, England, 1951—57; asst. prof. elec. engring. U. Kans., Lawrence, 1957—58; assoc. prof. elec. engring. Drexel U., Phila., 1958—62; exec. sci. mgr. Jet Propulsion Lab./Calif. Inst. Tech., Pasadena, Calif., 1962—84; clin. prof. radiology U. So. Calif., L.A., 1976—86; pvt. cons. Carlsbad, Calif., 1986—. Founder biomed. engring. program Drexel U., Phila., 1961; sci. instrument dir. Surveyor Spacecraft Jet Propulsion Lab., Calif. Inst. Tech., Pasadena, 1968; founding mem. cardiology com. Nat. Heart, Lung and Blood Inst., Bethesda, Md., 1975—77; lectr. in field. Author: Transistors, 1963, Condominium Living, 1980, Deadly Voice, 2005; contbr. articles to profl. jours. Recipient Apollo award, NASA, 1972. Achievements include responsible for design and developments of instruments on Surveyor Spacecraft-first soft lander on the moon; project manager first ultrasonic diagnostic lab in an Arab country. E-mail: jand1@mail.com.

LECTKA, THOMAS, education educator; PhD, Cornell U. Prof. Chemistry John Hopkins U., 2002—. Alexander von Humboldt postdoctoral fellow U. of Heidelberg; NIH postdoctoral fellow Harvard U. Recipient Merck Faculty Develop. award, 2002, NSF career award; fellowship, John Simon Guggenheim Meml. Found., 2003, Alfred P. Sloan fellow, Camille Dreyfus Tchr. Scholar, 1999, Duponte ATE grant, grant, Am. Cancer Soc., Eli Lilly Young Faculty grant. Office: John Hopkins U Dept Chemistry Dunning Hall 302 3400 N Charles St Baltimore MD 21218

LECUREUX, LLOYD WILLIAM, scientist; s. Donald and Lavon LeCureux; m. Miriam Patricia Slabaugh, Oct. 11, 1956; children: Marc Christopher, Bethanie Joy, Valerie Annette, Jason Curtis. AS, Delta Coll., 1974; BS, Mich. State U., 1976. Sr. rsch. technician Mich. State U., East Lansing, Mich., 1976—86; rsch. assoc. Mich. Biotechnology Inst., Lansing, Mich., 1986—88; rsch. scientist The Upjohn Co., Kalamazoo, 1988—95, Pharmacia, Kalamazoo, 1995—2002, Pfizer, Kalamazoo, 2002—03; scientist Bristol-Myers Squibb, Lawrenceville, NJ, 2003—. Author: (scientific publication) Protein Expression and Purification, Journal of Cell Science, Atherosclerosis, Journal of Cell Biology, Analytical Biochemistry, Microbiological Technology, Horticulture Science, Plant Physiology, (scientific book) Gaseous Air Pollutants and Plant Metabolism. Office: Bristol-Myers Squibb H4114 Rt 206 Provinceline Rd Lawrenceville NJ 08543 Office Phone: 609-252-7873.

LEDBETTER, CALVIN REVILLE, JR., (CAL LEDBETTER), political science professor, legislator; b. Little Rock; s. Calvin Reville Sr. and Virginia Mae (Campbell) L.; m. Mary Brown Williams, July 26, 1953; children: Grainger, Jeffrey (dec.), Snow. BA, Princeton U., 1951; LLB, U. Ark., 1954; PhD, Northwestern U., 1960. Bar: Ark., 1954. Pvt. practice, Little Rock, 1954; faculty dept. polit. sci. U. Ark., Little Rock, 1960-97, prof., 1960-97, prof. emeritus, 1997—, dean, 1978-88; cons. law enforcement program, advisor pre-law program; mem. Ark. Ho. of Reps., 1967-76; chmn. spl. legis. com., com. on legis. orgn.; vice chmn. legis. com. state agys. and govt. affairs; cons. pub. schs.; mem. Nat. Adv. Com. on Criminal Justice Goals and Standards; mem. adv. com. Nat. Inst. Law Enforcement and Criminal Justice. Dept. head. U. Ark., Little Rock, 1968-78; election night analyst for Ark. congl. and Presdl. elections ABC, 1964-84 Co-author: Politics in Arkansas: The Constitutional Experience, 1972, The Arkansas Plan: A Case Study in Public Policy, 1979, Arkansas Becomes a State, 1985, Carpenter from Conway: George W. Donaghey as Governor of Arkansas 1909-1913, 1993; contbr. articles, book reviews to profl. jours. Mem. Ark. Adv. Coun. on Pub., Elem. and Secondary Edn.; Gov.'s rep. So. Regional Growth Policies Bd.; mem. Ark. Legis. Coun.; del. Ark. Constl. Conv., 1979, v.p., 1979-80; chmn. law enforcement and criminal justice task force Nat. Legis. Conf. Former chmn. coll. and univ. sect. United Fund; del. Dem. Nat. Conv., 1968, 84; mem. exec. com. Ark. Young Dems.; bd. dirs. Health and Welfare Coun. Pulaski County; trustee Philander Smith Coll., chmn. council community advisers; sec. bd. dirs. St. Vincent's Infirmary; bd. dirs. Ark. Humanities Coun., 1989-93, v.p., 1991-93, pres. 1993-94; bd. trustees Ark. Mus. Sci. and History. Served with JAGC AUS, 1955-57. Recipient award for outstanding contbn. to humanities Little Rock Arts and Humanities Commn., 1993; named Educator of Yr., Greater Little Rock Fedn. Women's Clubs, 1968. Mem. ABA, Ark. Bar Assn. (Writing Excellence award 1985-86), Pulaski County Bar Assn., Nat. Conf. State Legislators (exec. com.), Nat. Conf. Acad. Deans (pres. 1987-88), Am. Polit. Sci. Assn., So. Polit. Sci. Assn., Ark. Polit. Sci. Assn. (pres. 1980-81), Ark. Acad. Sci., Am. Acad. Polit. and Social Sci., Ark. Hist. Assn., Ark. Edn. Assn., Pulaski County Hist. Soc. (bd. dirs. 1988-90), Ark. Hist. Commn. (v.p. 1989—, pres. 1990—), Rotary (pres. West Little Rock chpt. 1987-88). Presbyterian. Home: 3416 I St Little Rock AR 72205-4114 Office: Univ Ark Little Rock Polit Sci Dept Little Rock AR 72204

LEDBETTER, DAVID OSCAR, lawyer; b. Santa Rosa, Calif., Mar. 16, 1950; s. Oscar Smith Ledbetter and Nova Nell (Huckaby) Kramer; m. Judith Louise Fischer, Dec. 14, 1976; children: Hannah J., Jordan B. BA, U. Redlands, 1972; JD, Hastings Coll. Law, 1977. Bar: Calif. 1977, Va. 1987. Assoc. Moran, Urich & Evans, San Francisco, 1977-79; trial atty. land and natural resource divsn. U.S. Dept. Justice, Washington, 1979-85; assoc., counsel, ptnr. Hunton & Williams, Richmond, Va., 1985—. Bd. adv. Chem. Waste Litigation Reporter, Washington, 1983—. Co-editor: Outline RCRA/CERCLA Enforcement Issues and Holdings, 2004; contbr. articles to profl. jours. Bd. dirs. John Tyler C.C. Found., Chester, Va., 1992—; ednl. adv. coun. Charles City (Va.) County Vocat., 1990—. Mem. ABA, Va. State Bar Assn., Calif. Bar Assn., Environ. Law Inst., Charles City Ruritan Club. Democrat. Methodist. Avocations: gardening, fishing. Home: 16530 The Glebe Ln Charles City VA 23030-3837 Office: Hunton & Williams 951 E Byrd St Ste 200 Richmond VA 23219-4074 Office Phone: 804-788-8364. Business E-Mail: dledbetter@hunton.com.

LEDBETTER, KENNETH W., federal agency administrator; b. Calif., Sept. 1946; MS in Aerospace Engring., U. Colo., 1969. Mem. Viking Mars landing team NASA, Pasadena, 1976, dep. payload ops mgr. Space Shuttle flight of Space Sextant, 1982, spacecraft ops. mgr. launch and flight of Magellan mission to Venus, 1989—92, Hubble Space Telescope program mgr., 1992—94, flight programs br. chief OSS astrophysics divsn., 1994—95, dir. mission and payload devel. divsn., 1996—2001, dep. assoc. adminstr. for programs Office Space Sci., 2001—04. Co-author: Design of Mission Operations Systems for Scientific Remote Sensing, 1991; contbr. articles to profl. publs. Office: NASA Hdqs Mail SMD 300 E St SW Washington DC 20546

LEDBETTER, KORRIN, reading educator; d. Kirk L. and Ercella Kading; m. Grover Dennis Ledbetter, Sept. 3, 1972; children: Bryan Kirk, Shannon Dee, Bronson Blu. BS in Elem. Edn. (hon.), U. Ariz., 1991; M in Elem. Edn., No. Ariz. U., 1996. Cert. prin. Ariz. State Dept., 1994, in adult edn. Ariz. State Dept., 1994, nat. staff devel. Nat. Staff Devel. Coun., 2004. Elem. tchr. Casa Grande Elem. Sch. Dist., Ariz., 1991—95, K-3 reading tchr., 1996—98, title 1 tchr., 1999—2002, acad. coach, 2002—03, reading first coach, 2003—. Adj. prof. No. Ariz. Coll., Flagstaff, 1996—99, Ctrl. Ariz. Coll., Coolidge, 2004. Mem.: NEA, Ctrl. Reading Coun., Internat. Reading Assn., Nat. Staff Devel. Coun. Home: 2081 N Pebble Beach Dr Casa Grande AZ 85222

LEDBETTER, MICHAEL RAY, lawyer; b. San Bernardino, Calif., June 13, 1956; s. Raymond Leonard and Anna Laura Ledbetter; m. Diane Elizabeth Burger, Jan. 16, 1987 (div. Aug. 1991); 1 child, Lauren Ann; m. Diane Lorraine Errick, June 30, 1993. BA, U. Calif. Irvine, 1978; JD, U. So. Calif., 1981. Bar: Calif. 1981, U.S. Dist. Ct. (ctrl. dist.) Calif. 1982, U.S. Dist. Ct. (ea. dist.) Calif. 1992, U.S. Ct. Appeals (9th cir.) 1990, U.S. Supreme Ct. Assoc. atty. Roger J. Rosen Law Office, L.A., 1981—83; dep. pub. defender Office of Pub. Defender, Santa Barbara, Calif., 1983—90; sr. dep. counsel Office of County Counsel, Santa Barbara, 1990—. Bd. dirs. Calif. Joint Powers Ins. Authority, La Palma, 1992-94, 96-2002. Contbg. editor: California County Counsels Benchbook, 1996, 97, 98. Mem. City Coun., City of Carpinteria, Calif., 1990-94, 96—, mayor, 1991-93, vice-mayor, 2004— Avocations: automobiles, computers, music. Office: Office of County Counsel 105 E Anapamu St Rm 201 Santa Barbara CA 93101-6060 Office Phone: 805-568-2950. E-mail: ldbttr@co.santa-barbara.ca.us, MLdbttr@Netscape.net.

LEDBETTER, PAUL MARK, lawyer, writer; b. San Francisco, Oct. 14, 1947; s. John Paul and Joyce (Mayo) L.; m. Jerald Ann Broyles, Sept. 18, 1971; children: Paul Mark, Sarah Broyles. BA in English, Ouachita Bapt. U., 1970; JD, U. Ark., 1973. Bar: Ark. 1974, Tenn. 1995, U.S. Dist. Ct. (ea. dist.) Ark. 1974, U.S. Ct. Appeals (8th cir.) 1974, U.S. Ct. Appeals (6th cir.) 1991, U.S. Dist. Ct. (mid. dist.) Tenn. 1995. From assoc. to ptnr. Frierson, Walker, Snellgrove & Laser, Jonesboro, Ark., 1974-82; city atty. Monette, Ark., 1979—80; regional def. counsel Sq. D. Co., 1980-82; pres. Mark Ledbetter, P.A., Jonesboro, 1982-86; ptnr. Gerber, Gerber & Agee, Memphis, 1986-89, Taylor, Halliburton, Ledbetter & Caldwell, Memphis, 1989—2002, Taylor, Halliburton & Ledbetter, Memphis, 2003—. Product safety cons., sch. bus safety cons. CNN, 1997—; lectr. dept. mech. engring. U. Memphis, 1997—; lectr. dept. rehab. engring. U. Tenn., 1994—95. Author: The Hearing, 1994, The Thayer Class, 1998, The Wait, 2000. Tutor Memphis Literacy Coun., 2003—; mem. forum commn. City of Jonesboro, 1978—80; co-founder St. Mark's Episcopal Day Sch., Jonesboro, Ark., 1978; mem. vestry St. Mark's Episcopal Ch., 1979. Conservation Found. grantee, 1976; Rotary Internat. grantee, Japan, 1979. Mem. ATLA, Am. Bd. Trial Advs. (assoc.), Tenn. Bar Assn., Ark. Bar Assn. (mem. tort reform com. 1980, ho. of dels. 1979-80), Ark. Trial Lawyers Assn. (chmn. amicus curiae com. 1980-81, gov. 1980—), Tenn. Trial Lawyers Assn., Jonesboro C. of C. (bd. dirs. 1978-80), Human Factors and Ergonomics Soc., Rotary. Office: Taylor Halliburton Ledbetter 254 Court Ave 3d Fl Memphis TN 38103 Office Phone: 901-523-8153. E-mail: mark794@aol.com.

LEDBETTER, STEVEN, musicologist; BA in Music, Pomona Coll.; MA in Musicology, PhD in Musicology, NYU. Mem. faculties NYU and Dartmouth Coll.; lectr. Harvard U., Inst. for Studies in Am. Music, Bklyn. Coll.; musicologist, program annotator Boston Symphony Orch., 1979—98; pres. Steven Ledbetter Program Notes, 1998—. Writer, booklet notes for nearly 200 recordings; conductor, choral ensembles and orchs. Dartmouth Coll. and Providence Coll.; singer Boston Symphony's Tanglewood Festival Chorus. Co-editor: Secular Works of Luca Marenzio; editor: complete operas of Gilbert and Sullivan (both multi-volume edits.), Sennets & Tuckets, 1988; area editor for pre-1918 Am. opera New Grove Dictionary of Opera. Recipient Disting. Print and Media Coverage of Music, ASCAP/Deems Taylor, 1991. Mem.: Nat. Artistic Directorate, Am. Classical Music Hall of Fame, Cin. Office: Steven Ledbetter Program Notes 21 Tennyson St Worcester MA 01610 Business E-Mail: sledbetter@bigplanet.com.

LEDEEN, ROBERT WAGNER, neuroscientist, educator; b. Denver, Aug. 19, 1928; s. Hyman and Olga (Wagner) L.; m. Lydia Rosen Hailparn, July 2, 1982. BS, U. Calif., Berkeley, 1949; PhD, Oreg. State U., 1953. Postdoctoral fellow in chemistry U. Chgo., 1953-54; rsch. assoc. in chemistry Mt. Sinai Hosp., N.Y.C., 1956-59; rsch. fellow Albert Einstein Coll. Medicine, Bronx, NY, 1959, asst. prof., 1963-69, assoc. prof., 1969-75, prof., 1975-91; prof., dir. div. neurochemistry U. Medicine and Dentistry N.J., Newark, 1991—. Contbr. articles to profl. jours.; dep. chief editor Jour. Neurochemistry. Mem. neurol. scis. study sect. NIH; mem. study sect. Nat. Multiple Sclerosis Soc. NIH grantee, 1963—; Nat. Multiple Sclerosis Soc. grantee, 1967-74, 97-2003; recipient Humboldt prize, Javits Neurosci. Investigator award. Mem. Internat. Soc. Neurochemistry, Am. Soc. Neurochemistry, Am. Chem. Soc., Am. Soc. Biol. Chemists, N.Y. Acad. Sci. Jewish. Achievements include discoveries in the biochemistry of brain glycolipids and myelin. Home: 8 Donald Ct Wayne NJ 07470-4608 Office: U Medicine and Dentistry NJ Dept Neuroscis 185 S Orange Ave Newark NJ 07103-2757

LEDER, MIMI, television director, film director, film producer; b. N.Y.C., Jan. 26, 1952; d. Paul and Etyl Leder; m. Gary Werntz, Feb. 6, 1986; 1 child, Hannah. Student, Los Angeles City College, Am. Film Inst. Dir. TV movies A Little Piece of Heaven (also known as Honor Bright), 1991, Woman with a Past, 1992, Rio Shannon, 1992, Marked for Murder, 1992, There Was a Little Boy, 1993, House of Secrets, 1993, The Sandman, 1993, The Innocent, 1994, John Doe, 2002; dir. TV series L.A. Law, 1986, Midnight Caller, 1988, A Year in the Life, 1988, Buck James, 1988, Just in Time, 1988, Crime Story, 1988, ER, 1994- (Emmy award 1995, 96), John Doe, 2002, China Beach (also prodr.), The Beast (also exec. prodr.), 2001; dir. movies, The Peacemaker, 1997, Deep Impact, 1998, Sentimental Journey, 1999, Pay it Forward, 2000; supervising prodr. China Beach, 1988-91 (Emmy nominations for outstanding drama series 1989, 90, and outstanding directing in drama series 1990, 91), Nightingales, 1989 Mem. Dirs. Guild Am. Office: c/o CAA 9830 Wilshire Blvd Beverly Hills CA 90212-1804 also: United Talent Agy 9560 Wilshire Blvd Beverly Hills CA 90212

LEDERBERG, JOSHUA, geneticist, educator; b. Montclair, NJ, May 23, 1925; s. Zwi Hirsch and Esther Lederberg; m. Marguerite S. Kirsch, Apr. 5, 1968; children: David Kirsch, Anne. BA, Columbia U., 1944; PhD, Yale U., 1947. With U. Wis., 1947-58; prof. genetics Sch. Medicine, Stanford (Calif.) U., 1959-78; pres. Rockefeller U., N.Y.C., 1978-90, univ. prof. Sackler Found. scholar, 1990—. Mem. adv. com. WHO, 1971; chmn. adv. bd. Ellison Med. Found., 1997—; mem. bd. sci. advisors Antigenics, N.Y.C., Quark Biotech, Fremont, Calif.; cons. U.S. Def. Sci. Bd., NSF, NIH, NASA. Mem. editl. bd.: The Scientist. Trustee Camille and Henry Dreyfus Found. With USN, 1943—45. Named Sr. Scholar, Stanford U. Ctr. Internat. Security and Arms Control, 1998; recipient Nobel prize in physiology and medicine for rsch. in genetics of bacteria, 1958, U.S. Nat. medal of sci., 1989, Alan Newell award, Assn. Computing Machinery, 1996, John Stearns award, N.Y. Acad. Medicine, 1996, Maxwell Finland award, NCIH, 1997, Morris Collen award, Am. Med. Info. Assn., 1999. Fellow: AAAS, Am. Acad. Arts and Scis., Am. Philos. Soc. (Benjamin Franklin medal 2002); mem.: NAS, N.Y. Acad. Scis. (hon. life gov.), Royal Soc. London (fgn.), Inst. Medicine (David Rall medal), Coun. Fgn. Rels. Office: Rockefeller U Stop 174 1230 York Ave New York NY 10021-6399 Office Phone: 212-327-7809. E-mail: lederberg@mail.rockefeller.edu.

LEDERER, JOHN MARTIN, retired aeronautical engineer; b. Solomon, Kans., May 12, 1930; s. George Martin and Angie Belle (Faubion) L.; m. Joan Elizabeth Patrick, June 15, 1963; children: Jeffrey Mark, Carol Elizabeth. BS in Aero. Engring., Kans. State U., 1953; MSEE, Air Force Inst. Tech., 1955; postgrad., U. N.Mex., 1962-65. Registered profl. aero. engr., Ohio. Project engr. Air Force Spl. Weapons Ctr., Albuquerque, 1955-63, chief project engring. div., 1963-67, chief electromagnetics div., 1967-70; tech. adviser Air Force Weapons Lab., Albuquerque, 1970-73, 76-87, chief nuclear systems surety div., 1988-91; dir. nuclear systems engring. Nuclear Systems Engring. Directorate/USAF Systems Command, Albuquerque, 1991-92; dir. nuclear systems engring. aero. systems ctr. Air Force Materiel Command, Albuquerque, 1992-93; tech. dir. 4900th test group, Albuquerque, 1973-76, ret. Chmn. Dept. of Def. Design Rev. and Acceptance Group, Albuquerque, 1979-91; flying instr. airplanes, instruments. Co-inventor digital distance measuring instrument. Founder One of Ten Young Am. Football League, Albuquerque, 1964. Served to 1st lt. USAF, 1953-58. Recipient Outstanding Performance award Dept. Air Force, Albuquerque, 1965, 66, 68, 73, 74, 79, Sustained Superior Performance award, 1961, 81, 83-86, 88-93, Air Force Disting. Civilian Svc. award, 1993. Mem. NSPE, FAA (cert. flight instr.), Inst. Aerospace Scis. Republican. Episcopalian. Avocations: archery, flying. Home: 3012 El Marta Ct NE Albuquerque NM 87111-5618 E-mail: fishhooks@comcast.net.

LEDERER, KAREN F., lawyer; b. N.Y.C., Sept. 28, 1954; BA, U. Wis., 1975; JD, SUNY, Buffalo, 1978. Bar: N.Y. 1979, U.S. Dist. Ct. (so. and ea. dists.) N.Y. 1979. Atty. N.Y.C. Dept. Consumer Affairs, 1978-80, Weil Gotshal & Manges, N.Y.C., 1980-82, N.Y.C. Corp. Counsel's Office, N.Y.C., 1982-86; ptnr. Parker, Chapin, LLP, N.Y.C., 1986—. Mem. Assn. of Bar of City of N.Y. (consumer affairs com.). Office: Parker Chapin LLP The Chrysler Bldg 405 Lexington Ave New York NY 10174

LEDERER, MARION IRVINE, cultural administrator; b. Brampton, Ont., Can., Feb. 10, 1920; d. Oliver Bateman and Eva Jane (MacMurdo) L.; m. Francis Lederer, July 10, 1941. Student, U. Toronto, 1938, UCLA, 1942-45. Owner Canoga Mission Gallery, Canoga Park, Calif., 1967—, cultural heritage monument, 1974—. V.p. Screen Smart Set women's aux. Motion Picture and TV Fund, 1973, pres., 2002—03; founder sister city program Canoga Park-Taxco, Mex., 1963. Mem. Mayor's Cultural Task Force San Fernando Valley, 1973—, L.A. Cultural Affairs Commn., 1980—85; pres. Women's Aux. of Motionn Pictures, TV Fund. Recipient Pub. Svc. award, mayor, city council, C. of C. Mem. Canoga Park C. of C. (cultural chmn. 1973-75, dir. 1973-75) Presbyterian. Home: PO Box 32 Canoga Park CA 91305-0032 Office: Canoga Mission Gallery 23130 Sherman Way Canoga Park CA 91307-1402 Office Phone: 818-340-2209.

LEDERER, PETER DAVID, lawyer; b. Frankfurt, Germany, May 2, 1930; came to US, 1938; s. Leo and Alice Lederer. BA, U. Chgo., 1949, JD, 1957, M in Comparative Law, 1958. Bar: Ill. 1959, U.S. Supreme Ct. 1966, N.Y. 1967. Law and behavioral sci. rsch. fellow U. Chgo. Law Sch., 1958-59; ptnr. Baker & McKenzie, Zurich, Switzerland, 1960-66, N.Y.C., 1966-94, of counsel, 1994—2002; pres. Japanese Am. Social Svcs., Inc., NYC, 2003—. Chmn. bd. dirs. Coverage Connect, Inc., 1999-2002; mem. adv. bd. TeslaLab LLC, 2002-. Dir. Asian-Am. Legal Def. and Edn. Fund, N.Y.C.; chmn. emeritus bd. dirs. The Midori Found.; pres. bd. trustees The Calhoun Sch., N.Y.C., 1980—83; dir. Asian-Am. Fed. of N.Y.; mem. vis. com. U. Miami Law Sch., Coral Gables, Fla., 1974—, U. Chgo. Law Sch., 1988—91, 2000—; mem. adv. coun. Wildlife Trust, 2000—. With AUS, 1951—53. Fellow Am. Bar Found.; mem. ABA, Assn. of Bar of City of N.Y., Internat. Nuc. Law Assn. Personal E-mail: peterdlederer@verizon.net.

LEDERER, RICHARD HENRY, writer, educator, columnist; b. Phila., May 26, 1938; s. Howard Jules and Leah (Perry) L.; m. Rhoda Anne Spangenberg, Aug. 25, 1962 (div. 1986); m. Simone Johanna van Egeren, Nov. 29, 1991; children: Howard Henry, Anne Labarr, Katherine Lee. BA, Haverford Coll., 1959; student, Harvard U., 1959—60, M of Arts and Tchg., 1962; PhD, U. N.H., 1980. Tchr., coach St. Paul's Sch., Concord, NH, 1962-89. Lectr. in field. Author: Anguished English, 1987, Get Thee to a Punnery, 1988, Crazy English, 1989, The Play of Words, 1990, The Miracle of Language, 1991, More Anguished English, 1993, Building Bridge, 1994, Adventures of a Verbivore, 1994, Literary Trivia, 1994, Nothing Risqué, Nothing Gained, 1995, The Write Way, 1995, Pun and Games, 1996, Fractured English, 1996, The Word Circus, 1998. Sleeping Dogs Don't Lay, 1999, The Bride of Anguished English, 2000, The Circus of Words, 2001, Word Play Crosswords, 2000, A Man of My Words, 2003, The Cunning Linguist, 2003, The Revenge of Anguished English, 2005, Comma Sense, 2005, The Giant Book of Animal Jokes, 2005; weekly columnist Looking at Lang.; contbr. over 3000 articles to mags. and jours.; broadcaster various radio stas.; numerous TV appearances; host A Way With Words KPBS, San Diego. Recipient Chmns. award, Am. Mensa, Ltd., 2000, Toastmasters Internat. Golden Gavel, 2002, Lifetime Achievement award Columbia Scholastic Press Assn., N.Y.C., 1989, Leadership in Comms. award San Diego Toastmasters, Odin award San Diego Writers and Editors, 2004; named Internat. Punster of Yr. Internat. Save the Pun Found., Toronto, 1990, Celebrity in Action, San Diego Found. for Ednl. Achievement, 2002; Paul Harris Rotary fellow. Mem. Am. Mensa, Phi Beta Kappa, Phi Delta Kappa. Avocations: tennis, cards, film. Office: Ste 201 9974 Scripps Ranch Blvd San Diego CA 92131-1825 Office Phone: 858-549-6788. E-mail: richard.lederer@pobox.com. *Whatever you hear about the closing of the American mind and cultural illiteracy, there has never been a more passionate moment in the history of the American love affair with language than right now. I'm exceedingly fortunate to have written books that embrace that passion.*

LEDERER, SUSAN HENDLER, speech/language pathologist, educator; d. Arthur Joel and Gloria Spector Hendler; m. Richard Brian Lederer, July 20, 1986; 1 child, Spencer Michael. BS, N.Y. U., 1979, MA, 1981, PhD, 1996. Lic. speech-lang. pathologist N.Y., cert. tchr. of speech and hearing handicapped N.Y. Speech-lang. pathologist, NY, 1981—; adminstr. SteppingStone Day Sch., Kew Garden Hills, NY, 1984—97; assoc. prof. Adelphi U., Garden City, NY, 1997—, chair depart. comm. sci. and disorders. Author: Pre-Read: An Integrated Emergent Literacy Program. Grantee, N.Y. State Devel.

Disabilities Planning Coun. and Dept. Social Services, 1993—97. Mem.: L.I. Speech-Lang.-Hearing Assn. (univ. counselor 1997—2000), N.Y. State Speech-Lang.-Hearing Assn., Am. Speech-Lang.-Hearing Assn. (cert.). Avocations: yoga, swimming, rollerblading, travel, reading. Office: Adelphi U Hy Weinberg Ctr Cambridge Ave Garden City NY 11530 Office Phone: 516-877-4770. Business E-Mail: lederer@adelphi.edu.

LEDERER, WILLIAM JULIUS, author; b. N.Y.C., Mar. 31, 1912; s. William J. and Paula (Franken) L.; m. Ethel Hackett, Apr. 21, 1940 (div. Jan. 1965); children: Brian, Jonathan, Bruce; m. Corinne Edwards Lewis, July 1965 (div. May 1976). BS, U.S. Naval Acad., 1936; A Nieman fellow, Harvard U., 1950-51. Enlisted USN, 1930, commd. ensign, 1936, advanced through grades to capt., 1952, ret., 1958; Far East corr. Reader's Digest, 1958-63; lectr. colls. and univs., 1949—. Author in residence, Harvard U., 1966-67; Author: All the Ship's at Sea, 1950, The Last Cruise, 1950, Spare Time Article Writing for Money, 1953, Ensign O'Toole and Me, 1957, A Nation of Sheep, 1961, Timothy's Song, 1965, Pink Jade, 1966, (with Eugene Burdick) The Ugly American, 1958, Sarkhan, 1965, Our Own Worst Enemy, 1967, (with Don D. Jackson) The Mirages of Marriage, 1968, (with Joe Pete Wilson) Complete Cross-Country Skiing and Ski Touring, 1970, (with others) Marriage for and Against, Marital Choices, A Happy Book of Happy Stories, I, Giorghos, 1984, Creating a Good Relationship, 1984. Mem. Signet Soc., Authors Guild, Acad. Orthomolecular Psychiatry, European Acad. Preventive Medicine, Internat. Acad. Preventive Medicine, Internat. Coll. Applied Nutrition, Lotos Club, Trap Door Spiders Club, Harvard Faculty Club, Sigma Delta Chi. Home: 1350 Mayflower Ave Melbourne FL 32940-6723 *If one works at being joyful and physically functional, almost everything else seems to come along on its own. Put energy into the "here and now" and do not distract from it by worrying about either the past or the future.*

LEDERIS, KAROLIS PAUL (KARL LEDERIS), pharmacologist, educator, researcher; b. Noreikoniai, Lithuania, Aug. 1, 1920; arrived in Can., 1969; s. Paul Augustus and Franciska (Danisevicius) L.; m. Hildegard Gallistl, Feb. 28, 1952 (dec. Nov. 2000); children: Aldona Franciska, Edmund Paul. Diploma, Tchrs. Coll., Siauliai, Lithuania, 1939; BSc, U. Bristol, U.K., 1958, PhD, 1961, DSc, 1968. From jr. lectr. to reader U. Bristol, 1961-69; prof. pharmacology and therapeutics U. Calgary, Alta., Can., 1969-89, prof. emeritus, 1989—. Vis. prof. univs. in Fed. Republic Germany, Austria, Chile, Argentina, Sri Lanka, Switzerland, Lithuania, France, USA, USSR, 1963-79, U. Bristol, 1979, U. Kyoto, Japan, 1980; career investigator, mem., chair grants com. Med. Rsch. Coun., Ottawa, Ont., Can., 1970-89, coun. mem., exec., 1983-90; mem. internat. com. Centres Excellence Networks, Ottawa, 1988-89. Author, editor: 5 books on hypothalamic hormones; editor in chief Jour. Exptl. and Clin. Pharmacology, 1977-89; contbr. approximately 350 book chpts. and articles to profl. jours.; patentee hormonal peptides. Recipient Upjohn award in pharmacology, 1990, various fellowships and scholarships in U.K., Fed. Republic of Germany, US. Fellow NAS, Royal Soc. Can.; mem. Western Pharmacological Soc. (pres. Brit., Can., U.S. divsns., 1982-83), Kiwanis, Lithuanian Club (London), Men's Can. Club, Cabot Yacht and Cruise Club (Bristol). Avocations: music, sailing, golf. Home: 147 Carthew St Comox BC Canada V9M 1T4 Office: U Calgary Health Scis Centre Calgary AB Canada T2N 4N1 Office Phone: 403-220-6931. Business E-Mail: klederis@shaw.ca.

LEDERLE, FRANK ALLEN, medical educator; b. Chgo., Nov. 16, 1952; s. Frank Allen and Janet Irene (McGanney) Lederle; m. Janet Asselstine, June 4, 1983; children: Lauren, Curt. BA, Pomona Coll., 1974; MD, U. N. Mex., 1979. Cert. Wis., 1980. Asst. to assoc. to prof. of medicine VA Med. Ctr., Mpls., 1982—. Author (prin. investigator) various VA cooperative studies. Grantee numerous grants. Avocations: nordic skiing, racing. Office: U Minn Minn Vet Affairs Med Ctr 3 0 1 Vet Dr Minneapolis MN 55417

LEDERLE, KENNETH JOSEPH, director, secondary school educator; b. St. Louis, Aug. 31, 1979; s. Gary Joseph and Sharon Ann Lederle; m. Jennifer Ann Baumann, Sept. 13, 2003. BA in Music, Truman State U., 2000, MA in Edn., Music, 2001. Music dir. Bishop DuBourg High Sch., St. Louis, 2001—; instr. Nottlemann Music Co., 2001—. Mem.: Bandmaster Mo., Music Educator Nat. Conf. Roman Catholic. Office: Bishop DuBourg High Sch 5850 Eichelberger Saint Louis MO 63109

LEDERMAN, BRUCE RANDOLPH, lawyer; b. N.Y.C., Oct. 12, 1942; s. Morris David and Frances Lederman; m. Ellen Kline, Aug. 4, 1979; children: Eric, Jeffrey, Joshua. Cert., U. London, 1963; BS Econs. cum laude, U. Pa., 1964; LLB cum laude, Harvard U., 1967. Bar: U.S. Dist. Ct. (cen. dist.) Calif. 1967. Law clk. to Hon. Irving Hill U.S. Dist. Ct. Cen. Dist., L.A., 1967-68; sr. ptnr. Latham & Watkins, L.A., 1968—. Avocations: bicycle riding, real estate investments. Office: Latham & Watkins 633 W 5th St Ste 3800 Los Angeles CA 90071-2007

LEDERMAN, EDITH RACHEL, physician, military officer; d. William Albert and Patricia Irene Lederman (Stepmother), Merryl Susan Feldman. AB, Bryn Mawr Coll., Pa., 1989—93; MD, NYU, 1993—97. Cert. Am. Bd. Internal Medicine, 2000, in infectious diseases Am. Bd. Internal Medicine, 2002. Dept. head, clin. medicine U.S. Naval Med. Rsch. Unit No. 2, Jakarta, Indonesia, 2002—. Lt. comdr. USN.

LEDERMAN, GARY, dentist; Grad. rsch. periodontics & oral microbiology, U. Rochester, 1973—77; attended, U. Pa. Sch. Dental Medicine, 1977—81; MS, USAF Regional Med. Ctr. Keesler AFB, 1981—82. Dentist Where Dreams Become Smiles, NY. Mem.: Integrated Dental Study Club, Suffolk County Dental Assn., Nassau County Dental Soc., First Dist. Dental Soc. NY, NYS Dental Assn., ADA, Acad. Gen. Dentistry, Dental Orgn. Conscious Sedation, Am. Acad. Cosmetic Dentistry. Avocations: windsurfing, sailing, reading, theater. Mailing: 100 Centre Ave Bellmore NY 11710 Office Phone: 516-785-0032. Office Fax: 516-785-0066.*

LEDERMAN, IRA SETH, insurance company executive, lawyer; b. N.Y.C., Apr. 25, 1953; m. Carol Susan Jupiter; children: Rachael, Aaron. BA, Queens Coll., NYC, 1975; MPA, NYU, 1977; JD, Hofstra Univ., 1979. Bar: N.Y. 1980. Assoc. Rein Mound and Cotton, N.Y.C., 1979-83; assoc. counsel W.R. Berkley Corp., Greenwich, Conn., 1983-86, v.p., ins. counsel, 1986-89, v.p., asst. gen. counsel, 1989—2001, sr. v.p., gen. counsel, 2001—. Mem. ABA, N.Y. County Lawyers Assn., The Corp. Bar Assn., Am. Soc. Corp. Secs. Office: W R Berkley Corp PO Box 2518 165 Mason St Greenwich CT 06836-2518

LEDERMAN, LAWRENCE, lawyer, writer, educator; b. N.Y.C., Sept. 8, 1935; s. Herman Jack and Lillian (Rosenfeld) Lederman; m. Kitty Hawks; children: Leandra, Evin. BA, Bklyn. Coll., 1957; LLB, NYU, 1966. Bar: NY 1968. Law clk. chief justice Calif. Supreme Ct., 1966—67; assoc. Cravath, Swaine & Moore, NYC, 1968—74; ptnr. Wachtell, Lipton, Rosen & Katz, NYC, 1975—91; ptnr., chmn. corp. practice Milbank, Tweed, Hadley & McCloy, 1991—2004, of counsel, 2005—. Adj. prof. law NYU Law Sch., 1974—, N.Y. Law Sch., 2005—. Author: Tombstones: A Lawyer's Tales from the Takeover Decades, 1992; contbr. articles to profl. jours.; calendar, Trees in Their Seasons at the N.Y. Bot. Garden, 2003, 2005. Chmn. bd. Phoenix House Devel. Corp.; mem. Phoenix House Found.; bd. dirs. The Nat. Mentoring Partnership, Tails in Need. Served with U.S. Army, 1957—59. Mem.: ABA, NY State Bar Assn., Order of Coif. Office: Milbank Tweed Hadley & McCloy 1 Chase Manhattan Plz Fl 47 New York NY 10005-1413 Office Phone: 212-530-5000. Business E-Mail: ledlaw@milbank.com.

LEDERMAN, LEON MAX, physicist, researcher; b. NYC, July 15, 1922; s. Morris and Minna (Rosenberg) Lederman; m. Florence Gordon, Sept. 19, 1945; children: Rena S., Jesse A., Heidi R.; m. Ellen Carr, Sept. 17, 1981. BS, CCNY, 1943, DSc (hon.), 1980; AM, Columbia U., 1948, PhD, 1951; DSc (hon.), No. Ill. U., 1984, U. Chgo., 1985, Ill. Inst. Tech., 1987; 35 additional hon. degrees. Assoc. in physics Columbia U., NYC, 1951, asst. prof., 1952—54, assoc. prof., 1954—58, prof., 1958—89, Eugene Higgins prof. physics, 1972—79; Frank L. Sulzberger prof. physics U. Chgo., 1989—92; dir. Fermi Nat. Accelerator Lab., Batavia, Ill., 1979—89, dir. emeritus, 1989—; Pritzker prof. sci. Ill. Inst. Tech., Chgo., 1992—; resident scholar Ill. Math. and Sci. Acad., 1998—. Dir. Nevis Labs., Irvington, NY, 1962—79; guest scientist Brookhaven Nat. Labs., 1955; cons. Nat. Accelerator Lab., European Orgn. for Nuc. Rsch. (CERN), 1970—; mem. high energy physics adv. panel AEC, 1966—70; mem. adv. com. to divsn. math. and phys. scis. NSF, 1970—72; sci. advisor to gov. State of Ill., 1989—93; chmn. XXIV Internat. Physics Olympiad, 1991—93; co-chair com. on capacity bldg. in sci. Internat. Sci. Unions, 1994—2001; pres. bd. sponsors Bull. Atomic Scientists, 2000—; mem. adv. com. to dean U. Chgo., 2000—; pres.'s coun. The Cooper Union, 2002—. Author: Quarks to the Cosmos, 1989, The God Particle, 1993, Symmetry and the Beautiful Universe, 2005; editor, contbr.: Portraits of Great American Scientists, 2001; editor: Science Education (NATO Sci. series), 2002; contbr. articles over 200 to profl. jours. including. Commr. White House Fellows Program, 1997—2000; Univ. Rsch. Assocs., 1967—71, 1992—; founder sci. edn. program ARISE, 1995; mem. sci. adv. bd. Sec. of Energy, 1991—2001; bd. dirs. Mus. Sci. and Industry, Chgo., 1989—, Weizmann Inst. Sci., Israel, 1988—. Named Hon. Prof., Beijing Normal U., The Lederman Sci. Edn. Ctr. in his name, Fermi Nat. Accelerator Lab., 1997; recipient Nat. medal of Sci., 1965, Townsend Harris medal, CUNY, 1973, Elliot Cresson medal, Franklin Inst., 1976, Wolf prize, 1982, Nobel prize in Physics, 1988, Enrico Fermi prize, 1992, Rosenblith lectr. in Sci. and Tech., NAS, Joseph Priestly award, Dickinson Coll., 1996, Pres.'s medal, CCNY, 1993, Heald prize, Ill. Inst. Tech., 2000, Pupin Med. award, Columbia U., 2000, Faraday award, NSTA, Discover, 2002, Dedication of Science Literacy in the 21st Century, to him and including one of his articles; fellow Guggenheim, 1958—59, Ford Found., European Ctr. for Nuc. Rsch., Geneva, 1958—59, NSF, 1967, Presdl., World Bank, 1996—99; scholar Great Minds program, Ill. Math. Sci. Acad. Fellow: AAAS (pres. 1990—91, chmn. 1991—92, Abelson award 2001), Am. Phys. Soc. (mem. coun., Compton medal 2005); mem.: IEEE, NAS (U.S., Argentina, Finland, Mex., Russia), World Assn. Young Scientists (hon. pres. 2004—), Russian Acad. Scis. (fgn. mem.), Coun. Advancement of Sci. Writing, Italian Phys. Soc. (hon.), Tchrs. Acad. for Math. and Sci. in Chgo. (co-chmn. 1990—2001), Ill. Math. Sci. Acad. (founding vice chmn. 1985—98), Aspen Inst. Physics (pres. 1990—92). Office Phone: 630-907-5911. Business E-Mail: Lederman@fnal.gov. E-mail: lederman@imsa.edu.

LEDERMAN, SUSAN STURC, educational association administrator; b. Bratislava, Slovakia, May 28, 1937; came to U.S., 1948; d. Ludovit and Helen Sturc; m. Peter Bernd Lederman, Aug. 25, 1957; children: Stuart, Ellen. AB in Polit. Sci., U. Mich., 1958; MA in Polit. Sci., Rutgers U., 1970, PhD in Polit. Sci., 1978. Vis. instr. Fairleigh Dickinson U., Madison, N.J., 1973-74, Drew U., Madison, 1975-76; from asst. prof. to assoc. prof. pub. adminstrn. Kean U., Union, N.J., 1977-89, prof., dir. MPA program, 1989-97; exec. dir. Gateway Inst. Regional Devel. Kean U., Union, N.J., 1997-2000; prof. Kean U., Union, N.J., 1990—. Vis. fellow Woodrow Wilson Sch., Princeton (N.J.) U., 1988-89. Co-author: (book) Elections in America—Control and Influence in Democratic Politics, 1980, (monograph) Campaign Watch: A Report on the 1992 Campaign Watch Project, 1993; editor: (book) The SLERP Reforms and Their Impact, 1989; contbr. articles to profl. jours. Mem. nat. gov. bd. Common Cause, Washington, 1994-2000; bd. dirs., sec.-treas. The Jefferson Ctr., Mpls., 1992-2002; dir. Regional Plan Assn., N.Y.C., 1991—; pres. LWV of N.J., 1985-89, program v.p., 1983-85, sec., fiscal policy dir., 1981-83, fiscal policy dir., 1979-81, adminstrn. of justice dir., 1976-79; pres. LWV of U.S., 1990-92, chair edn. fund., 1990-92; mem. bd. trustees exec. com., sec. N.J. Future, 1993—; pub. mem. Supreme Ct. of N.J. Disciplinary Oversight Com., 1994-98, Coun. of Engring. and Sci. Splty. Bds., 1996-2002; mem. Property Tax Commn., 1998; mem. N.J. Legis. Coun. of Acad. Advisors; commr. N.J. State and Local Expenditure Revenue Policy Commn., 1985-88, N.J. Election Law Enforcement Commn., 2000-04; pres. Northeastern Polit. Sci. Assn., 1984-85. Recipient Disting. Svc. award N.J. Polit. Sci. Assn., 1984, Pub. Svc. award ASPA, 1993, Eric Neisser Pub. Svc. award Pub. Interest Law Ctr., 2001; rsch. grantee Fund for N.J., 1981, Florence and John Schumann Found., 1988-89. Mem. Internat. Women's Forum (N.J. Forum bd. dirs. 1998—, bd. trustees 2002-), Phi Kappa Phi, Pi Sigma Alpha, Pi Alpha Alpha. Office: Kean U 1000 Morris Ave Union NJ 07083-7131 Office Phone: 908-737-4311. Business E-Mail: slederma@kean.edu.

LEDET, HENRY JOSEPH, librarian; b. Houston, June 12, 1953; s. Henry Joseph Jr. and Marie (Gaudet) L.; m. Diane Marie Biediger, Nov. 26, 1988; 1 child, Robert Joseph. BS, La. State U., 1976, MLS, 1978. Tchr. English Iberville Parish Schs., Plaquemine, La., 1976-77; asst. dir. Lincoln Lawrence Franklin Regional Libr., Brookhaven, Miss., 1979-81, dir., 1981—. Editor (newsletter) Brookhaven Trust Notes, 1994—; book reviewer Daily Leader Sunday Edition, 1996—. Recipient Pine Hills Culture Program scholar U. So. Miss Ctr. for Oral History and Cultural Heritage, 1996, Leadership in Mgmt. of Info. and Comm. Tech. award Solinet, 1997. Mem. ALA, Miss. Libr. Assn. (treas. 1997-98, pres.-elect 2000, pres. 2001), Brookhaven Trust (pres. 1996), Brookhaven Arts Coun. (sec. 1999). Roman Catholic. Avocations: running, gardening, cooking. Office: Lincoln Lawrence Franklin Regional Libr 100 S Jackson St Brookhaven MS 39601-3347 Fax: 601-833-3381. E-mail: hledet@llf.lib.ms.us.

LEDFORD, BRENDA KAY, writer; b. Young Harris, Ga., Apr. 9, 1952; d. James Ronda and Blanche Willie (Lee) L. BS in Edn., We. Carolina U., Cullowhee, N.C., 1976, MA in Edn., 1979. Cert. tchr. N.C. Clerk, typist FBI, Washington, 1970—71; tchr. Cherokee County Bd. Edn., Murphy, NC, 1976—90; freelance writer Smoky Mountain Sentinel, Hayesville, NC, 1990—2001. Writing instr. John Campbell Folk Sch., Brasstown, NC, 2000; storyteller Clay Revitalization Assn., Hayesville, 1999—2001. Author: poems; editor: Tri-County C.C. newspaper, 1996; contbr. articles Our State mag., 2000. Named winner photo contest, Writers' Jour., 1998; recipient award journalism contest, N.C. Press Assn., 2000. Mem.: DAR, Clay County C. C., Clay County Arts Coun. (bd. dirs. 1999, sec. 1999, poetry contest judge 2000), N.C. Storytelling Guild, N.C. Writer's Network, Order Ea. Star (Clay chpt., Angels Among Us award 1999). Democrat. Baptist. Avocations: travel, piano, drawing, reading, photography.

LEDFORD, FRANK FINLEY, JR., surgeon, military officer; b. Jacksonville, Fla., Apr. 22, 1934; s. Frank F. and Hazel H. (Barrette) L.; m. Marilyn Sue Kain, Aug. 23, 1957; 1 child, Cheryl Lynn. BS, U. Dayton, 1955; MD, U. Cin., 1959; postgrad., Indsl. Coll. Armed Forces, 1976—. Diplomate: Am. Bd. Orthopedic Surgery. Commd. 2d lt. U.S. Army, 1958, advanced through grades to lt. gen., 1988; surgeon, 1958-69; intern Brooke Army Hosp., San Antonio, 1959-60; resident in surgery Womack Army Hosp., 1960-61; resident in orthop. surgery Letterman Gen. Hosp., San Francisco, 1961-64; resident in pediat. orthop. surgery Phoenix Crippled Childrens Hosp., 1964-65; chief orthopedic surgery (Army Hosp.), Landstuhl, W.Ger., 1969-71, dep. commr. Heidelberg, W.Ger., 1971-72; asst. chief surg. cons. Office of Surgeon Gen., Washington, 1972-73, chief grad. med. edn., 1973-76; comdr. U.S. Army Hosp., Fort Riley, Kans., 1977-80, Ft. Benning, Ga., 1980; dir. profl. services Office of Surgeon Gen., U.S. Army, Washington, 1980-82; comdr. Letterman Army Med. Ctr. San Francisco, 1982-85; chief surgeon U.S. Army Europe, 1985-88; The Surgeon Gen. Dept. of the Army, Washington, 1988-92; pres. S.W. Found. for Biomedical Rsch., San Antonio, 1992—; clin. prof. Health Sci. Ctr. U. Tex., San Antonio, 1993—. Clin prof. surgery Uniformed Services U. Health Scis. Contbr. articles to med. jours. Fellow ACS, Am. Acad. Orthopedic Surgeons, Am. Coll. Physician Execs.; mem. AMA, Assn. Mil. Surgeons, Soc. Mil. Orthopedic Surgeons, Argyle Club. Methodist. Address: SW Found For Biomedical Research PO Box 760549 San Antonio TX 78245-0549 E-mail: fledford@sfbr.org.

LEDGER, HEATH, actor; b. Perth, Australia, Apr. 4, 1979; s. Kim and Sally Ledger. Actor: (films) Clowning Around, 1992, Blackrock, 1997, Paws, 1997, 10 Things I Hate About You, 1999, The Patriot, 2000, A Knight's Tale, 2001, Monster's Ball, 2001, Four Feathers, 2002, The Sin Eater, 2002, Ned Kelly, 2002, The Order, 2003, Lords of Dogtown, 2005, The Brothers Grimm, 2005; (TV series) Ship to Shore, 1993, Sweat, 1996, Home and Away, 1997. Mailing: 2222 N Beachwood Dr Apt 408 Los Angeles CA 90068 also: c/o Shanahans Mgmt PO Box 478 Kings Cross NSW 1340 Australia*

LEDGER, WILLIAM JOE, obstetrician, educator; b. Turtle Creek, Pa., 1932; BA, Princeton U., 1954; MD, U. Pa., 1958; MS, Temple U., 1964. Diplomate Am. Bd. Ob-Gyn. Intern Hamot Hosp. Assn., Erie, N.Y., 1958-59; resident Temple U. Hosp., Phila., 1961-64; attending physician Women's Hosp.-Mich. Med. Ctr., 1964-72; assoc. prof. U. Mich., Ann Arbor; prof. U. So. Calif., L.A., 1972-79; Given Found. prof., chmn. ob-gyn. Cornell U. Med. Coll., N.Y.C., 1979—99, chmn. emeritus, 1999—. Served to capt. USMC, 1959-61 Fellow ACS, Am. Coll. Ob-Gyn. Office: NY Presbyn Hosp Weill Med Coll Cornell U 525 E 68th St Ste J-130 New York NY 10021-4870 Office Phone: 212-746-3011. Business E-Mail: wjledger@med.cornell.edu.

LEDGERWOOD, DAVID ROBERT, music educator, department chairman, composer; b. Steubenville, Ohio, Aug. 16, 1953; s. Arthur Robert and Claire Maler Ledgerwood; m. Kim Ellen Wilson, July 12, 1974; children: Naomi, Nathan, Matthew, Joshua, RuthAnn, Joanna, Bethany, Philip. BS in Music Edn., Indiana U. of Pa., 1980; MA in Sacred Music, Pensacola (Fla.) Christian Coll., 1985; MA in Theory and Composition, Indiana U. of Pa., 1986; D (hon.), Maranatha Bapt. Bible Coll., Watertown, Wis., 2004. Tchr. Calvary Christian Sch., Clymer, Pa., 1980—86; prof. music Maranatha Bapt. Bible Coll., 1986—. Arranger: band method/book Heritage Band, 1995, cantatas The Newborn King, 1997, CD Higher Ground, 1998. Staff sgt. USAF, 1973—77. Mem.: Music Educators Nat. Conf., Am. Choral Dirs. Assn. Baptist. Home: 416 S Montgomery Watertown WI 53094 Office: Maranatha Bapt Bible Coll 715 W Main St Watertown WI 53094 Office Phone: 920-206-2356.

LEDIN, PATRICIA ANN, nurse, legal consultant; b. Downey, Calif., May 6, 1959; d. Clyde Burdette and Estelle Angelina (Acceturo) Bornhurst; m. Scott Richard Ledin, Sept. 9, 1989. BSN, U. Ariz., 1981; postgrad., U. Phoenix, 2000. Cert. electronic fetal monitoring, inpatient obstetrics, ACLS, PALS, NRP; RN Ariz., cert. instr. PALS. Labor and delivery nurse Tucson Med. Ctr., 1981-86, childbirth instr., 1983-95, nurse, mother-baby unit, 1995-97, clin. educator obstetrics, 1986—95, CPR instr., 1986—, learning and devel. specialist, 2001—02, clin. nurse specialist, 2001, clin. educator obstetrics, 1997—2001, nurse recruiter, 2002—03, mgr. student placement program, 2004, clin. educator nursing informatics, 2004—. Adj. faculty preceptor U. Ariz., Tucson, 1988—; expert witness for legal cases, 1992—; expert reviewer Lifelines mag., 2002-; faculty, Az. Perinatal Edn. Coalition, 2000—. Contbr. articles to profl. jours. Mem. adv. com. March of Dimes, 1991—95; mentor Nat. Cert. Corp., 2001. Bristol-Meyers fellow, 1994. Mem.: Nat. Nursing Staff Devel. Orgn., Assn. Women's Health, Obstet. and Neonatal Nursing (edn. coord. 1991—98, sec.-treas. 1999—2002, Recognition award for fin. budget submission 2001, 2002, award for outstanding performance in fin. responsibility 2001), Beta mu, Omicron Delta, Sigma Theta Tau (chair nominations 2002—). Avocations: water-skiing, nascar races, boating, travel, aerobics. Office: Tucson Med Ctr 5301 E Grant Rd Tucson AZ 85712-2805

LEDING, ANNE DIXON, artist, educator; b. Fort Smith, Ark., Jan. 29, 1947; d. Charles Victor Dixon and Elizabeth Johanna (Mitchell) Dixon Roderick; m. Larry Joseph Peters (dec), Jan. 6, 1967; m. John Thomas Leding, June 24, 1978; children: Jonathan Brian (Peters) Leding, Caroline Kristen Leding. Student, Memphis State U., Memphis, 1964-66, Westark C.C., Fort Smith, 1976-78. Cert. custom framer; lic. health & life ins., Tex. Art instr. Fort Smith (Ark.) Art Ctr., 1976; pvt. practice art instr. Fort Smith, 1977-78; classical guitar instr. Paul Mendy Guitar Studio, Fort Smith, 1978-79; framing merchandise mgr. MJDesigns, 1983-98; sr. cert. framer, framing supr. Michael Arts and Crafts, 1999—2001; cert. art instr. Robert Garden Sch. Art, 2002; with Worlf Fin. Group, 2004—. Cmty. svc. classical guitar instr. Westmark C.C., 1976. One-woman shows include Ariel Gallery, Fort Smith Art Ctr., Cafe Bliss, La Cima Club; group shows include Del Mar Coll., Ariel Gallery, N.Y.C.; featured in Ency. of Living Artists in Am., 1986-87; listed in N.Y. Art Rev., S.W. Art Rev., 1990-91; critiqued in Artspeak, N.Y., 1990. Mentor Grapevine (Tex.) Mid. Sch. Recipient 1st place Fort Smith Sch. Dist., 1955; letter of recognition Seventeen Mag., 1963; hon. mention Fort Smith Art Ctr. Bicentennial, 1976, Del Mar Coll., 1985, Trinity Arts Competition, 1992, Mid Cities Fine Arts Competition, 1994. Mem. Nat. Mus. Women in the Arts, Nat. Watercolor Soc., Am. Watercolor Soc., Dallas Mus. Art, Kimbel Art Mus., Trinity Arts Guild, Ft. Smith Art Ctr., Toastmasters Internat. (advanced toastmaster bronze competant leader, v.p. pub. rels. local chpt., 1998-99, 99-2000, v.p. edn. 2002-03, pres. 2003-2004), Dallas/Ft. Worth Writer's Workshop. Republican. Anglican. Avocations: photography, music. Home and Office: Anne Leding Illustrations 402 Walden Trl Euless TX 76039-3870 Office Phone: 817-905-6255. E-mail: dibidy@comcast.net.

LEDLEY, ROBERT STEVEN, biophysicist; b. N.Y.C., June 28, 1928; DDS, NYU, 1948; MA in Theoretical Physics, Columbia U., 1949. Rsch. physicist Columbia U. Radiation Labs., Columbia, 1948—50; instr. physics Columbia U., 1949—50; vis. scientist Nat. Bur. Standards, 1951—52; physicist, 1953—54; ops. rsch. analyst Johns Hopkins U., 1954—56; assoc. prof. elec. engring George Washington U., 1957—60; instr. pediat. Johns Hopkins U., Sch. Medicine, 1960—63; prof. elec. engring. George Washington U., 1968—70; prof. physiology, biophysics & radiology Georgetown U., 1970—; pres., rsch. dir. Nat. Biomed. Rsch. Found., 1960—; pres. Digital Info. Sci. Corp., 1970—75. Contbr. articles to profl. jours. and author of several books; editor-in-chief Pattern Recognition, Elsevier Science, Oxford, Eng., Computers in Biology and Medicine, Computerized Medical Imaging and Graphics, Computer Languages. Named to Nat. Inventor Hall of Fame, 1990; recipient Nat. medal of Tech., U.S. Dept. Commerce, 1997, Morris E. Collen, MD award, Am. Coll. of Medical Informatics, 1998, Goldhaber award, Harvard Sch. Dental Medicine, 1998, Cert. of Appreciation, Nat. Inst. Dental Rsch., NIH, 1998, Disting. Alumni NYU, 1999. Mem.: NIH, IEEE, NAS (mem. Inst. Medicine), Pattern Recognition Soc., N.Y. Acad. Scis., Biophys. Soc., Soc. Math. Biophysics. Achievements include invention of CT Scanner. Office: Nat Biomed Rsch Found Georgetown U Med Ctr 3900 Reservoir Rd NW Washington DC 20007 Address: Georgetown U Med Ctr LR-3 Preclinical Science 4000 Reservoir Rd NW Washington DC 20057 Office Phone: 202-687-2121. Office Fax: 202-687-1662. Business E-Mail: ledley@georgetown.edu.*

LEDOGAR, STEPHEN J., retired diplomat; b. N.Y.C., Sept. 14, 1929; m. Marcia Hubert, Sept. 16, 1967; children: Lucy, Charles. BS, Fordham U., 1954, LLB, 1958. Bar: N.Y. 1959. Surety claims atty. Chubb & Son, N.Y.C., 1954-59; with Fgn. Svc., 1959-97, ret., 1997; press spokesman, U.S. del. Vietnam Peace Talks, Paris, 1967-72; with U.S. Mission to NATO, 1973-76; spl. asst. to undersec. of state, 1976-77; dir. Office of NATO Affairs, 1977-80; mem. State Dept. Senior Seminar, 1980-81; dep. chief of mission U.S. Mission to NATO, Brussels, 1981-87; amb., U.S. rep. European Conventional Stability Negotiations and Mutual and Balanced Force Reductions Talks, 1987-89; amb. and head U.S. Del. to Negotiations on Conventional Armed Forces in Europe, 1989; amb. and U.S. rep. Conference on Disarmament, 1989-97; prin. U.S. negotiator of chem. weapons conv., 1993; prin. U.S. negotiator Comprehensive Nuclear Test Ban Treaty, 1996. Lt. USN, 1949-52, USNR, 1954-60 (Naval Aviator). E-mail: hubert.ledogar@verizon.net.

LEDONNE, DEBORAH JANE, secondary school educator; b. Darby, Pa., Mar. 4, 1956; d. Peter Anthony and Camella Jean (Perrone) LeD. Undergrad. credits in Spanish, U. Madrid, 1977; BA in Modern Langs., BS in Edn., Villanova U., 1978; Sorbonne U. Paris, U. Paris, 1979; MA in Modern Langs., Villanova U., 1982. Tchr. French/Spanish Marple Newtown Sch. Dist., Newtown Square, Pa., 1978—. Tutor Phila. area, 1978—; sec. Faculty Adv. Coun., 1990—. Mem. Phila. Mus. Art, Annenberg Ctr. of Phila. Recipient Maria Rosa award for Excellence Am. Inst. Italian Culture, 1978; chosen to attend Nat. Debutante Ball, N.Y.C., 1974, Internat. Debutante Ball, Vienna, 1975; named a Woman of Yr. Am. Biog. Inst., 1993, one of 2,000 Notable Am. Women, 1994. Mem.: NEA, Pa. State Modern Lang. Assn., Alliance

Francaise, Pa. State Edn. Assn., Kappa Delta Pi. Avocations: tennis, swimming, dance, gourmet cooking. Office: Marple Newtown Sch Dist 120 Media Line Rd Newtown Square PA 19073-4614

LEDSINGER, CHARLES A., hotel executive; b. Tenn., 1950; m. Anita Ledsinger; 2 daughters. BS, U. Va.; MBA, Memphis State U. Joined Holiday Inns (divsn. Promus Cos., Inc.), 1978, various fin. mgmt. positions, 1978—83; v.p. fin. and adminstrn. Embassy Suites Hotel (divsn. Promus Cos., Inc.), 1983—86; v.p. project fin. Holiday Inns, 1986—88; treas. Promus, 1988—90, sr. v.p., CFO, 1990, Harrah's Entertainment, Inc., 1995—97; pres., COO The St. Joe Co., 1997—98, Choice Hotels Internat., 1998—. Bd. dirs. Choice Hotels Internat., FelCor Suite Hotels, Inc., Friendly Ice Cream Corp., Perkins Mgmt. Co., Inc., TBC Corp. Mem. Am. Hotel and Motel Assn. (mem., past chmn. real estate fin. adv. counsel). Office: Choice Hotels Internat 10750 Columbia Pike Silver Spring MD 20901-4494

LEDWIDGE, PATRICK JOSEPH, lawyer; b. Detroit, Mar. 17, 1928; s. Patrick Liam and Mary Josephine (Hooley) L.; m. Rosemary Lahey Mervenne, Aug. 3, 1974; stepchildren: Anne Marie, Mary Clare, John, David, Sara Edleman. AB, Coll. Holy Cross, 1949; JD, U. Mich., 1952. Bar: Mich. 1952. Assoc. firm Dickinson, Wright, Moon, Van Dusen & Freeman, Detroit, 1956-63; mem. Dickinson Wright PLLC, Bloomfield Hills, Mich., 1964—. Served to lt. j.g. U.S. Navy, 1952-55. Mem. Mich. Bar Assn., Detroit Bar Assn., Am. Law Inst. Clubs: Detroit Athletic, Detroit Golf. Roman Catholic. Office: Dickinson Wright PLLC 38525 Woodward Ave Ste 2000 Bloomfield Hills MI 48304-5092

LEDWIG, DONALD EUGENE, association executive, consultant, retired broadcast executive, military officer; s. Paul Lawrence and Rose Ledwig; m. Gail Wilcox, Jan. 30, 1965; children: Donald Eugene Jr., David W. BS, Tex. Tech U, 1959; MBA, George Washington U., 1973; disting. grad., Naval War Coll., 1977. Commd. ensign USN, 1959, advanced through grades to capt., 1980; ship's officer U.S. Pacific Fleet, 1959-65, 77-79; mem. staff Adm. H.G. Rickover, Nuclear Propulsion Program, 1966-72; dir. contract policy Naval Materiel Command, Washington, 1979-81; dep. comdr. Naval Electronic Sys. Command, Washington, 1981-84; ret., 1984; v.p., treas. Corp. for Pub. Broadcasting, Washington, 1984-86, pres., CEO, 1987-92; exec. dir. Am. Prodn. and Inventory Control Soc., Falls Church, Va., 1992-95; pres. Am. Logistics Assn., Washington, 1995-96; COO Anchor Health Assn., 1997-98; cons. Assn. Mgmt., 1998—. Chair Alexandria (Va.) Electoral Bd., 2000—. Decorated Legion of Merit; recipient Barrow Meml. award Hastings Coll. Law, 1989, award Nat. Captioning Inst., 1990, Disting. Alumnus award Tex. Tech U., 1992. Mem. Am. Legion, Nat. Press Club, Army-Navy Country Club.

LEDWITH, JOHN FRANCIS, lawyer; b. Phila., Oct. 3, 1938; s. Francis Joseph and Jane Agnes (White) L.; m. Mary Evans, Aug. 28, 1965; children: Deirdre A., John E. AB, U. Pa., 1960, JD, 1963. Bar: Pa. 1965, N.Y. 1984, U.S. Dist. Ct. (ea. dist.) Pa. 1965, U.S. Ct. Appeals (3d cir.) 1965, U.S. Supreme Ct. 1970. Assoc. Joseph R. Thompson, Phila., 1965-71; mem. Schubert, Mallon, Wallheim & deCindis, Phila., 1971-81, LaBrum & Doak, Phila., 1981-95, Marshall, Denchey, Warner, Coleman & Goggins, Phila., 1995—. Author: (with others) Philadelphia CP Trial Manual, 1982. Bd. dirs. Chestnut Hill Cmty. Assn., Pa., 1975-76. With USCG, 1963-71. Mem. ABA, Pa. Bar Assn., Phila. Bar Assn., Def. Rsch. Inst., Fedn. Ins. Corp. Coun., Racquet Club (Phila.), Phila. Cricket Club, Avalon Yacht Club (commodore 1982). Republican. Roman Catholic. Office: Marshall Dennehey Warner Coleman & Goggins 1845 Walnut St Philadelphia PA 19103-4708 Office Phone: 215-575-2604.

LEDYARD, JOHN ODELL, economics professor, consultant; b. Detroit, Apr. 4, 1940; s. William Hendrie and Florence (Odell) L.; m. Bonnie Higginbottom, May 23, 1970; children: Stephen, J. Henry, Meg. BA, Wabash Coll., 1963; PhD, Purdue U., 1967; PhD (hon.), Purdue U./Ind. U., 1993. Asst. prof. Carnegie-Mellon U., Pitts., 1967-70; prof. Northwestern U., Evanston, Ill., 1970-85, Calif. Inst. Tech., Pasadena, 1985—, exec. officer for social sci., 1989-92, chmn. div. humanities and social scis., 1992—2002. Contbr. articles to profl. jours. Fellow Am. Acad. Arts and Scis., Econometric Soc., Pub. Choice Soc. (pres. 1980-82); mem. Econ. Sci. Assn. (exec. com. 1986-88). Office: Calif Inst Tech Dept HHS Pasadena CA 91125-0001

LEDYARD, ROBINS HEARD, lawyer; b. Nashville, Oct. 14, 1939; s. Quitman Robins and Alma Elizabeth (Stevenson) L.; m. Julia Bordeaux Gambill, Dec. 19, 1962; children: Stevenson Gambill, Quitman Robins II, Margaret Dabney. BA, Vanderbilt U., 1965, JD, 1966. Bar: Tenn. 1966, U.S. Supreme Ct. 1975. Atty. Nat. Life & Accident Ins. Co., Nashville, 1966-68, asst. counsel, 1968-69, assoc. counsel, 1969-70, counsel, 1970-72, assoc. gen. counsel, 1972-75, gen. counsel, 1975-80; partner Bass, Berry & Sims, 1980—. Tchr. C.L.U.s, 1967-75 Asst. editor: Vanderbilt Law Rev., 1965-66; contbr. articles to profl. jours. Active United Way, Nashville, 1967—, Heart Fund, 1970-73; vice chmn. United Diocesan Givers, 1975; bd. dirs. St. Thomas Hosp., 1990—. With USMC, 1958-61. Recipient Bennett Douglas Bell Meml. prize, 1966; Marr scholar, 1965-66 Mem. ABA, Am. Coun. Life Ins. (chmn. tax com. 1978-80), Assn. Life Ins. Counsel (chmn. tax com. 1979-80), Tenn. Bar Assn., Nashville Bar Assn., Internat. Assn. Ins. Counsel, Global Leaders for the South, Order of Coif, Phi Delta Phi, Alpha Tau Omega. Clubs: Belle Meade Country, Capitol of Nashville, KC. Democrat. Roman Catholic. Home: 1215 Chickering Rd Nashville TN 37215-4519 Office: Amsouth Ctr Ste 2700 315 Deaderick St Nashville TN 37238-3001

LEE, ADRIAN ISELIN, JR., journalist; b. Miami, Fla, Nov. 6, 1920; s. Adrian Iselin and Adriana Lanier (Owen) L.; m. Marie Lainé Santa Maria, Oct. 14, 1950; children: Adrian Iselin III, Catherine Taney, Thomas Sim, William Owen, Anne Marie, Louisa Carrell. BA, Spring Hill Coll., Mobile, Ala., 1943. With The Bulletin, Phila., 1948—; gen. assignment reporter The Bull., 1960-82, edit. writer, 1967-72, columnist op-ed page, 1972-82; with Phila. Daily News, 1982-88; speech and op-ed writer US Atty. Gen. Edwin Meese III, 1988-89; writer CBS Radio News, 1989-90. Tchr. editorial writing, dept. journalism Temple U. Active Chestnut Hill Community Assn. Lt. (j.g.) USNR, 1943-46, PTO. Decorated Navy Unit Commendation medal. Mem. Nat. Press Club, Pen and Pencil Club, Phila. Press Assn. (prize for coverage John F. Kennedy assassination 1963), Vietnam War, 1966; Sigma Delta Chi (prize for column writing 1978) Republican. Roman Catholic. Home and Office: 20 Haws Ln Flourtown PA 19031-2048

LEE, ALFRED THEODORE, research psychologist; b. Port Washington, Wis., June 25, 1946; s. Alfred and Gladys (Loomis) L. BA cum laude Psychology, San Jose State U., 1972, MA in Exptl. Psychology, 1974; PhD in Exptl. Psychology, U. Calif.-Riverside, 1979. Lic. pvt. pilot. Rsch. scientist U. Dayton (Ohio), 1979-82, NASA-Ames Rsch. Ctr., Moffett Field, Calif., 1983-90; pres. Beta Rsch., Inc., Los Gatos, Calif., 1990—. Lectr. U. Calif., 1978, teaching asst., 1974-78; rsch. cons. U.S. Dept. Justice, 1978-79, VA, 1978; rsch. asst. San Jose State U., 1972-74. Contbr. articles to profl. jours. Sgt. USAF, 1964-68. Regents fellow U. Calif., 1979. Mem.: APA, Human Factors Soc. Avocations: flying, skiing. Office: 18379 Main Blvd Los Gatos CA 95033-8391 E-mail: info@beta-research.com.

LEE, ALVIN A., literary educator, scholar, author; b. Woodville, Ont., Can., Sept. 30, 1930; s. Norman Osborne and Susanna Elizabeth (Found) L.; m. Hope Arnott, Dec. 21, 1957 (dec.); children: Joanna, Monika, Fiona, Alison, Margaret. BA, U. Toronto, Ont., Can., 1953, MA in English, 1958, PhD, 1961; M.Div., Victoria U., Toronto, 1957. Teaching fellow in English U. Toronto, 1957-59; asst. prof. English McMaster U., Hamilton, Ont., 1960-65, assoc. prof., 1966-70, prof., 1970-92, prof. emeritus, 1990—, asst. dean Sch. Grad. Studies, 1968-71, dean Sch. Grad. Studies, 1971-73, acad. v.p., 1974-79, pres., vice-chancellor, 1980-90, pres. emeritus, 1994—; Northrop Frye prof. literary theory U. Toronto, 1992, rsch. assoc. Victoria Coll., 1997—. Mem. Western Ont. coun. Conf. Bd. Can., 1983-90; mem. adv. bd. Medieval and Renaissance History, 1991—. Author: James Reaney, Twayne's World Authors Series, 49, 1968, The Guest-Hall of Eden: Four Essays on the Design of Old English Poetry, 1972, Gold-Hall and Earth-Dragon: 'Beowulf' as Metaphor, 1999; editor: (with Hope Arnott Lee) Wish and Nightmare, 1972, Circle of Stories: One, 1972, Two, 1972, The Garden and the Wilderness, 1973, The Temple and the Ruin, 1973, The Peaceable Kingdom, 1974; (with Robert D. Denham) The Legacy of Northrop Frye, 1994; gen. editor: McMaster Old English Studies and Texts, 1982-92, Collected Works of Northrop Frye, 1995—; editl. bd. English Studies in Canada, 1982-88; contbr. articles to profl. jours. Trustee, mem. exec. com. Chedoke-McMaster Hosps., 1980-90; mem. Community Edn. Coordinating Com., 1981-90; mem. Council Ont. Univs., 1980-90, vice chmn., 1981-83, chmn., 1983-85, mem. exec. com., 1981-87; mem. Health Scis. Liaison Com., 1980-90; dir. Council Ont. Univ. Holdings Ltd., 1981-90; mem. chancellors coun. Victoria U., U. Toronto, 1983—; hon. bd. dirs. Operation Lifeline, Hamilton, 1980-90; hon. Patron Opera Hamilton, 1982-90; vice chmn. bd., mem. exec. com. Royal Bot. Gardens, Hamilton, 1980-90, chmn. provincial and fed. relations com., 1981-90, vice chmn. sci. and ednl. com., 1981-90, mem. nominating com., 1981-90; vice chmn. bus. adv. conf. Regional Municipality of Hamilton-Wentworth, 1983-90; chmn. fund-raising liaison com. McMaster Hosps. Found/McMaster U., 1983-90; hon. patron Edn. Found. of Fedn. Chinese Can. Profls., Ont., 1984-90; mem., vice chair Can. Merit Scholarship Found., 1990-93; bd. dirs. Art Gallery Hamilton, 1991-94; mem. adminstrn. bd. McMaster Mus. Art. Mem. MLA, Mediaeval Acad. Am., Assn. Univs. and Colls. Can. (coun. univ. pres. 1980-90), Hamilton Assn. Advancement Lit., Sci. and Art (hon. pres. 1980-88), Can. Inst. Advanced Rsch., Internat. Assn. Anglo-Saxonists, Corporate-Higher Edn. Forum, McMaster U. Alumni Coun. (hon. pres. 1980-90), McMaster U. Letterman's Assn. (hon.), Hamilton and Dist. C. of C. (dir., mem. program com. 1982-87, Hamilton Gallery of Distinction 1996—). Office: Stormont Box 72, West Flamborough ON L0R 2K0 Canada Office Phone: 905-627-3085. E-mail: alvinlee@mcmaster.ca.

LEE, AMY, singer; b. Riverside, Calif., Dec. 13, 1981; d. John and Sara Lee. Lead singer Evanescence. Musician: (albums) Origin, 2002, Fallen, 2003 (album went Double Platinum, Grammy award best new artist, 2003); musician: (guest vocalist) (songs) "Broken" by Seether; musician: (breakout single) "Bring Me To Life" (Grammy award best hard rock performance, 2003). Office: Wind-Up Records 72 Madison Ave New York NY 10016 Office Phone: 212-895-3100.

LEE, ANDREA JANE, academic administrator, nun; 1 adopted child, Lahens. AA in Italian, Villa Walsh Coll.; BA in music and elem. edn., Northeastern Ill. U.; MEd, PhD in edn. adminstrn., Pa. State U. Instr. tchr. edn. Pa. State U.; dean continuing edn. and cmty. svcs. Marygrove Coll., 1981—84, exec. v.p. and COO, 1984—97, interim pres., 1998; pres. Coll. of St. Catherine, St. Paul, 1999—. Office: Coll of St Catherine 2004 Randolph Ave Saint Paul MN 55105

LEE, ANDREW YANQING, school librarian; b. Beijing, Aug. 13, 1955; arrived in U.S., 1988; s. Pingcun Li and Shantong Kuang; m. Patricia Cong Tang, Aug. 15, 1983; children: Ran, Nathan Bowen. BA in English, Capital Normal U., 1982; MLS, PhD in Anthropology, SUNY, Buffalo, N.Y., 1996. Instr. Capital Normal U., Beijing, 1982—88; reference circuit libr. Upstate Med. U. SUNY, Syracuse, NY, 1997—2000; reference liaison libr. George Mason U., Fairfax, Va., 2000—. Contbr. articles to profl. jours. Mem.: ALA. Office: George Mason Univ Libraries 4400 University Dr Fairfax VA 22030 Office Phone: 703-993-2209.

LEE, ANITA COMBS, writer, speaker, consultant; b. Pt. Arthur, Tex., Apr. 5, 1945; d. Bruce Harrison and Thelma Viola (Turner) Combs; m. Daryl Otis Lee, Aug. 9, 1969; children: Meredith, Adam. BS, Lamar U., 1967; postgrad., Nat. Geog. Summer Inst., 1988; MS, U. North Tex., 1995. Tchr. Hiroshima (Japan) Internat. Sch., 1967-68, Kyoto (Japan) Internat. Sch., 1968-69, Richardson (Tex.) Ind. Sch. Dist., 1969-70, Fairfax County (Va.) Schs., 1970-72; tchr. English Hefei (People's Republic China) Poly. Inst., 1982-83; tchr. world cultures Plano (Tex.) Ind. Sch. Dist., 1987-94, curriculum writer, 1987-94; asst. to headmaster PACE Acad., Atlanta, 1996—2000; asst. dir. children's ministry Roswell (Ga.) United Meth. Ch., 2000—03. Pt. time tchr. dept. continuing edn. Collin County C.C., Plano, 1986; mem. tchr. exch. program, Vilnius, Lithuania, 90; instr. writing Profl. Writers Ctr. Lamear U., 2005; presenter in field. Weekly columnist Plano Star Courier, 1985-87. Avocations: music, watercolor, spinning, international travel. Personal E-mail: alee@altaregos.com.

LEE, BARBARA, congresswoman; b. El Paso, Tex., July 16, 1946; m. Michael Millben (div.); children: Tony, Craig. BA, Mills Coll., 1973; M in Social Welfare, U. Calif. Berkeley, 1976. Chief of staff U.S. Rep. Ron Dellums, 1975—87; rep. Calif. State Assembly, 1990-96; mem. Calif. State Sen., 1996-98, U.S. Congress from 9th Calif. dist., Washington, 1998—; mem. fin. svcs. com., internat. rels. com. Co-chmn. Progressive Caucus; chmn. Congl. Black Caucus Task Force HIV/AIDS; whip Congl. Black Caucus, mem. Minority Bus. Task Force; mem. adv. bd. Alameda Boys Club; bd. dirs. Bay Area Black United Fund; with Black Women Organized Polit. Action; founder Calif. Commn. Status African Am. Male; mem. Calif. Commn. Status Women; mem. bd. Calif. Coastal Conservancy/Dist. Export Coun. Democrat. Office: US Ho Reps 1724 Longworth Ho Office Bldg Washington DC 20515-0509

LEE, BARBARA, political activist, foundation administrator; b. July 1945; d. Sidney and Ruth Fish; m. Thomas Lee, 1968 (div. 1996); children: Zach, Robbie. BA, Simmons Coll., 1967; MSW, Boston U.; degree (hon.), Pine Manor Coll., 2004. Pres., treas., dir. Barbara Lee Family Found., Cambridge, Mass.; vice chair bd. dirs. Inst. Contemporary Art, Boston; pres., treas. Revolutionary Women, Cambridge. Founding chair contemporary arts program Isabella Stewart Gardner Mus., Boston; co-founder The White House Project, 1997. Named one of Top 200 Collectors, ARTnews Mag., 2004, 21 Leaders for the 21st Century, Women's E News, 2005; named to The 100 Women Who Run this Town, Boston Mag., The 100 People Who Run this Town, 2004; recipient Opening Doors award, Women's Inst. for Housing and Econ. Devel., 2003, George Alden Dean Leadership award, Women's Campaign Sch., Yale U., 2003. Democrat. Avocation: Collector of Modern and contemporary art by women. Office: 131 Mt Auburn St, Ste 2 Cambridge MA 02138 Office Phone: 617-234-0355. Office Fax: 617-234-0357.

LEE, BARBARA ANNE, law educator, dean; b. Newton, N.J., Apr. 9, 1949; d. Robert hanna and Keren (Dalrymple) L.; m. James Paul Begin, Aug. 14, 1982; 1 child, Robert James. BA, U. Vt., 1971; MA, Ohio State U., 1972; JD, Georgetown U., 1982; PhD, Ohio State U., 1977. Bar: N.J. 1983, U.S. Dist. Ct. N.J. 1983. Instr. Franklin U., Columbus, Ohio, 1974—75; rsch. asst. Ohio State U., Columbus, 1975—77; policy analyst U.S. Dept. Edn., Washington, 1978—80; dir. data trands Carnegie Found., Washington, 1980—82; asst. prof. Grad. Sch. Edn. Rutgers U., Brunswick, NJ, 1982—84, asst. prof. Sch. Mgmt. and Labor Rels., 1984—88, assoc. prof., 1988—94, prof., 1994—, assoc. provost, 1995—96, dean, 2000—. Mem. Study Group on Excellence in Higher Edn., Nat. Inst. Edn., 1983-84; project dir. Carnegie Corp., N.Y.C., 1982-84. Author: Academics in Court, 1987; co-author: The Law of Higher Education, 3d edit., 1995; contbr. numerous articles to profl. jours. Corse fellow U. Vt., 1971; recipient John F. Kennedy Labor Law award Georgetown U., 1982; grantee Bur. Labor-Mgmt. Rels. and Coop. Programs, 1985-86. Mem. ABA, N.J. Bar Assn. (mem. exec. com. labor and employment law sect. 1987—, women's rights sect.), Am. Ednl. Rsch. Assn., Indsl. Rels. Rsch. Assn., Acad. Mgmt., Assn. Study Higher Edn. (legal counsel 1982-88), Nat. Assn. Coll. and Univ. Attys. (vice chair editl. bd. 1986-89, chair 1995-96, chair publs. com. 1988-91, bd. dirs. 1990-93). Office: Rutgers U Office of Dean Sch Mgmt and Labor Rels 94 Rockafeller Rd Piscataway NJ 08854-8054 Office Phone: 732-445-5993. Business E-Mail: lee@smlr.rutgers.edu.

LEE, BENJAMIN YUEHTUNG, genetic biochemist, nutrition researcher; b. Tianjin, China, July 1, 1930; arrived in U.S., 1986; s. Zhongyao Li and Guizhi Sun; m. Liwei Zhao, Nov. 20, 1985 (div. Oct. 20, 1996); m. Gongfu Bai Lee, Jan. 9, 1998; children: James, John, Hui Lin, Rong Bai. BS, Yenching U. of Am Chs. Union, Beijing, 1952; MD, Peking Union Med. Coll., Beijing, 1957. Intern in internal medicine Beijing Med. Coll. Hosp./Peking Union Med. Coll. Hosp., 1956—57; resident in internal medicine Peking Union Med. Coll. Hosp./Beijing Tiantan Hosp., 1957—58; resident, physician Lake Xingkai State Farm (Concentration Camp) Hosp., Black Dragon River Province, China, 1958—62; physician Beijing Jianguomen Clinic, 1962—85; clin. assoc. prof. Beijing Tropical Medicine Rsch. Inst., 1977—85; rsch. assoc., postdoctoral fellow, instr. pediat. genetics La. State U. Health Scis. Ctr., Shreveport, 1986—. Author: (series) New Nutrition Diseases, 1997; guest editor: Greater Chinese Encyclopedia, 1984—86. Roman Catholic. Achievements include discovery of nutritional diseases; design of nutritional deficiency may be the basic etiology of several surgical diseases. Office: La State U Health Scis Ctr Dept Pediat 1501 Kings Hwy Shreveport LA 71130 Office Phone: 318-675-6339. E-mail: blee1@lsuhsc.edu.

LEE, BLAINE NELSON, psychology educator, writer; b. Olympia, Wash., Apr. 3, 1946; s. Elwyn Earl and Thelma Marie (Woods) Reeder; children: Blaine, Benjamin, Adam, Michal, Joseph, Joshua, Casey, Abraham, Eliza, Gabriel, Celeste, Isaac. BS in Psychology, Brigham Young U., Provo, Utah, 1969, MS in Ednl. Psychology, 1972; PhD in Ednl. Psychology, U. Tex., 1982. Cert. ednl. specialist, secondary edn., ednl. adminstrn. Dir. instrnl. sys. USAF, San Antonio, 1972-75; assoc. prof. USAF Acad., Colorado Springs, Colo., 1975-78; edn. dir. Heritage Sch., Provo, Utah, 1978-81; asst. prof. Utah Valley State Coll., Orem, Utah, 1981-84; pres. Skills for Living, Salem, Utah, 1984-86; v.p. Covey Leadership Ctr., Provo, Utah, 1986-97, Franklin Covey Co., Provo, 1997—. Cons. in field. Author: Affective Objectives, 1972, Personal Change, 1982, Stress Strategist, 1986, Principle Centered Leadership, 1990, Power Principle: Influence with Honor, 1997; contbr. articles to profl. jours. High councilman LDS Ch., mem. gen. bd., 1970-72; pres. Provo PTO. Named one of Outstanding Young Men of Am., U.S. C. of C., 1976, 84. Mem. APA, ASTD, Am. Mgmt. Assn., Nat. Spkrs. Assn., Phi Delta Kappa. Avocations: theater, camping, poetry, soccer. Office: FranklinCovey 2200 W Parkway Blvd Salt Lake City UT 84119-2099 Home: 830 West 830 North Orem UT 84057

LEE, BOK SIN See POWELL GEBHARD, JOY

LEE, BRANT THOMAS, lawyer, educator, federal official; b. San Francisco, Feb. 17, 1962; s. Ford and Patricia (Leong) L.; m. Marie Bernadette Curry, Sept. 20, 1991. BA in Philosophy, U. Calif., Berkeley, 1985; JD, Harvard U., 1990, M in Pub. Policy, 1994. Bar: Calif. 1992. Counsel subcom. on Constitution, U.S. Senate Judiciary Com., Washington, 1990-92; assoc. Breon, O'Donnell, Miller, Brown & Dannis, San Francisco, 1992-96; dep. staff sec., spl. asst. to Pres. (acting) The White House, Washington, 1993; vis. asst. prof. Syracuse (N.Y.) U. Coll. Law, 1996-97; asst. prof. U. Akron (Ohio) Sch. Law, 1997-2001, assoc. prof., 2001—. Commr. San Francisco Ethics Commn., 1995-96. Bd. dirs., Asian Svcs. in Action, Inc., Akron, 1998—; trustee Chinese for Affirmative Action, San Francisco, 1992-96; bd. dirs. Conf. Asian Pacific Am. Leadership, Washington, 1990-92; staff mem. Dukakis for Pres., Boston, 1988. Mem. ABA, Nat. Asian Pacific Am. Bar Assn. Office: U Akron Sch Law Akron OH 44325-0001 Office Phone: 330-972-6616. Business E-Mail: btlee@uakron.edu.

LEE, BRENDA BAKER, real estate company executive; b. Houston, June 9, 1944; d. Leroy Baker and Gloria Betty Nicoletti; m. Arthur Louis Puderbaugh, Feb. 4, 1967 (dec. June 10, 1995); children: Thomas Ance Puderbaugh, Shawn Michael Puderbaugh, Shannon Lee Puderbaugh; m. Edward Brooke Lee Jr., Feb. 12, 1998 (dec. Aug. 20, 2004). Cert. real estate specialist Md., lic. real estate Md., 1988, D.C., 1988. Saleswoman Coldwell Banker, Gaithersburg, Md., 1988—91, Shannon & Luchs, Potomac, Md., 1992—95, Weichert Real Estate, Bethesda, Md., 1996—. Editor: Polit. Comm. Network, 1990. Chmn. casualty com., Washington, 1970; chmn. army cmty. svc., 1974—77; vol. Army Cmty. Svc.; mem. Christ Ch. of Houston. Recipient 7 Achievement awards, Md., 1991. Mem.: DAR, Nat. Assn. Realtors, Nat. Soc. Colonial Dames, Descs. of Signers of the Declaration of Independence, James Town Soc., Princeton Club of NY, Metro Club. Republican. Episcopalian. Avocations: history, politics, antiques. Home and Office: 8806 Connecticut Ave Chevy Chase MD 20815-6737 Office Phone: 301-652-3144.

LEE, BRIAN EDWARD, lawyer; b. Oceanside, NY, Feb. 29, 1952; s. Lewis H. Jr. and Jean Elinor (Andrews) L.; m. Eleanor L. Barker, June 5, 1982; children: Christopher Martin, Alison Ruth, Danielle Andrea. AB, Colgate U., 1974; JD, Valparaiso U., 1976. Bar: N.Y. 1977, U.S. Dist. Ct. (so. and ea. dists.) N.Y. 1978, U.S. Ct. Appeals (2nd cir. 1992). Assoc. Marshall, Bellofatto & Callahan, Lynbrook, N.Y., 1977-80, Morris, Duffy, Ivone & Jensen, N.Y.C., 1980-84; sr. assoc. Ivone, Devine & Jensen, Lake Success, N.Y., 1984-85, ptnr., 1985—. Pres., trustee Trinity Christian Sch. of Montville Inc., N.J., 1985—, also track coach. Mem. ABA, N.Y. State Bar Assn., N.Y. County Lawyers Assn., Christian Legal Soc. Republican. Baptist. Home: 292 Jacksonville Rd Pompton Plains NJ 07444-1511 Office: Ivone Devine & Jensen LLP 2001 Marcus Ave Lake Success NY 11042-1024 Office Phone: 516-326-2400. Personal E-mail: brianelee@verizon.net. Business E-Mail: blee@idjlaw.com.

LEE, BRUCE, editor, writer; b. N.Y.C., Dec. 3, 1930; s. Edward Brooke and Thelma Llewellyn (Lawson) Lee; m. Nancy Faye Hatch, Sept. 28, 1958 (div. Aug. 15, 1980); children: Evalyn Brooke, Bruce Hatch; m. Janetta M. Macpherson of Cluny, Mar. 21, 1981. BA, Rollins Coll., Winter Park, Fla., 1954; MFA, Fordham U., 1959. Reporter Adirondack Daily Enterprise, Saranac Lake, NY, 1952—53, N.Y. Daily News, 1954; assoc. editor Newsweek, N.Y.C., 1954—61; Washington corr. Reader's Digest, Washington, 1961—65, assoc. editor N.Y.C., 1965—66, sr. editor, 1966—72; editor-in-chief Reader's Digest Press, N.Y.C., 1972—78; sr. editor McGraw Hill Gen. Book Divsn., N.Y.C., 1978—82, William Morrow & Co., N.Y.C., 1982—90; author, 1990—. Chmn. bd. Lee Devel. Group, Silver Spring, Md., 1990—95; gen. ptnr. Montgomery Land LLP, Silver Spring, 1981—. Author: (Book) The Boy's Life of John F. Kennedy, 1962, Marching Orders: The Untold Story of World War II, 1995; co-author: Pearl Harbor: Final Judgement, 1992; editor: Bearing The Cross: The Biography of Martin Luther King, Jr., 1997 (Pulitzer prize, 1997). Mem. yachting com. U.S. Olympic Com., 1972—75; pres. U.S. Sailing Assn., 1973—75. SPE5 NY Nat. Guard USAR, 1954—60. Recipient award for advancing knowledge of cryptographic history, Nat. Security Agy., Fort Meade, Md., 1995. Mem.: Royal No. and Clyde Yacht Club, Royal Yacht Squadron, New York Yacht Club, Seawanhaka Corinthian Yacht Club. Home and Office: 115 E 67th St New York NY 10021

LEE, BRYAN, information technology executive; m. Lisa Lee; 4 children. BA in Acctg., U. Miss. With Arthur Andersen & Co., Houston, Sony Pictures Entertainment, Inc., 1987—2000, former exec. v.p. bus. affairs; gen. mgr. bus. devel. home and entertainment group Microsoft, Redmond, Wash., 2000—02, corp. v.p., CFO worldwide mktg. and pub. home and entertainment group, 2002—. Office: Microsoft Corp 1 Microsoft Way Redmond WA 98052-8300

LEE, BYUNG HEE, finance educator; b. Pusan, Republic of Korea, Sept. 9, 1967; s. Sang Woo Lee and Mal Soon Kim. PhD in Strategic Mgmt., Ind. U. Assoc. instr. Ind. U., Bloomington, Ind., 1995—2000, lectr., 2000—01; assoc. prof. Calif. State U., Fullerton, Calif., 2001—04; asst. prof. Hanyang U., Seoul, Republic of Korea, 2005—.

LEE, CARL, statistician, educator; b. Chia-I, Taiwan, June 15, 1954; s. Chin-Fei and Yei-Yin Lee; m. Ye-Fu Kao; children: Marcia, Grace, Michale. PhD, Iowa State U., 1984. Assoc. prof. Ctrl. Mich. U., 1988—92, prof. stats., 1992—, univ. assessment coord., 1999—2001; vis. assoc. prof. Nat. Ctrl. U., Taiwan, 1990—91. Expert statistician Teltech Resource Network Corp., Mpls., 1990—; sr. rsch. fellow Ctr. for Applied Rsch. in Tech., Mt. Pleasant, 2002—; statis. cons. Ctrl. Mich. U. Contbr. articles to profl. jours. Mem.:

Internat. Stats. Inst., Assn. for Advancement of Computing Tech., Biometircs Soc., Internat. Chinese Statis. Assn., Am. Statis. Assn. (pres. 1998—, Outstanding Svc. and Leadership award 2001). Office: PE 206E Dept Math Ctrl Mich U Mount Pleasant MI 48859 E-mail: carl.lee@cmich.edu.

LEE, CARL B., lawyer; b. San Antonio, Tex., Feb. 27, 1947; AB cum laude, Harvard Coll., 1968; JD, Univ. Chgo., 1971. Bar: Tex. 1971. Assoc. Akin Gump Strauss Hauer & Feld LLP, 1974, ptnr. Dallas, 1978—, now ptnr., co-chair firmwide real estate and fin. practice group. Former group leader, Konrad Adenauer Found/Am. Jewish Com. German-Jewish Exchange Program.; past pres. Dallas Chpt. Am. Jewish Com.; trustee and officer Temple Emanu-El; bd. dir. SW Region, Union of Am. Hebrew Congregations; mem. steering com. Hillcrest/Forest Neighborhood Assn. Capt. Quartermaster Corps USAR. Named one of World's Leading Real Estate Attorneys, Euromoney, World's Leading Real Estate Adv., Mondaq's Guide; recipient Excellence in Devel. Highest Honor award for effective citizen planning, No. Ctrl. Tex. sect., Am. Planning Assn. Mem.: ABA (real property sect.), Real Estate Fin. Execs. Assn., Real Estate Coun., Tex. Acad. of Real Estate, Probate and Trust Lawyers, Dallas Bar Assn. (past pres., real property sect., past chair, legal aid and legal svcs. com., past vice chair, lawyer referral com.), State Bar of Tex. (real property sect.), Order of Coif. Office: Akin Gump Strauss Hauer & Feld LLP Ste 4100 1700 Pacific Ave Dallas TX 75201-4675 Office Phone: 214-969-2726. Office Fax: 214-969-4343. Business E-Mail: clee@akingump.com.

LEE, CATHERINE, sculptor, painter; b. Pampa, Tex., Apr. 11, 1950; d. Paul Albert and Alice (Fleming) Porter; m. B. R. Mangham, 1967 (div. 1976); 1 child, Monk Parker; m. Sean Scully, 1977 (div. 2004). BA, San Jose State U., 1975. Asst. prof. sculpture U. Tex., San Antonio, 2000. Artist-in-residence Mpls. Coll. Art and Design, Minn. Inst. Art, 1982; vis. asst. prof. painting U. Tex., San Antonio, 1983, vis. asst. prof. sculpture, 2001; adj. asst. prof. Columbia U., N.Y.C., 1986-87. Group exhbns. include Albright-Knox Mus., Buffalo, 1987, Mus. Art, Carnegie Inst., Pitts., 1988, Am. Acad. & Inst. Arts & Letters, N.Y.C., 1988, Mus. Folkwang, Essen, Germany, 1992, Stadtische Galerie im Lenbachhaus, Munich, 1992, Neue Galerie Der Stadt Linz, Austria, 1992, Cleve. Mus. of Art, 1993, Galleria Nazionale d'Arte Moderna, San Marino, Italy, 1996, The Tate Gallery, 1994, U. R.I. Art Gallery, 1996, Sonoma State U. Art Gallery, 1997, Bemis Ctr. for Contemporary Art, 1998, Städtische Gallery, Lenbachhaus, Munich, 1999, Lafayette Coll. Art Ctr., Easton, Pa., 1999, San Diego State U. Art Gallery, San Diego, 1999, Lyman-Allen Art Mus., New London, Conn., 2000, Grounds for Sculpture, The Johnson Atelier, 2002, S.W. Sch. Arts and Crafts Gallery, 2004, Irish Mus. Modern Art, Dublin, 2005. Creative Artists Pub. Svc. fellow, 1978, NEA grantee, 1989. Office: 106 Spring St New York NY 10012-3814 also: Galerie Karsten Greve Wallrafplatz 3 5000 Koln Germany also: Galerie Lelong 528 W 26th St New York NY 10001 E-mail: catherlee@aol.com.

LEE, CATHERINE A., librarian, educator; b. Jersey City, N.J., Dec. 4, 1961; d. Peter John and Catherine (Powell) Apicella; m. Roger Alan Lee, Sept. 10, 1988. BA in English, U. South Fla., 1988, MLS, 1990; MA in English, Eastern Ky. U., 1993. Crisis counselor Alternative Human Svcs., St. Petersburg, Fla., 1985-90; libr. dir. Greenbrier C.C., Lewisburg, W.Va., 1990-91; pub. svcs. libr. Eastern Ky. U., Richmond, 1991-94; head libr. Pa. State U., DuBois, 1994—. Mem. libr. adv. bd. DuBois Bus. Coll., Pa., 1995—. Contbr. articles to profl. jours., chpts. to books; editor: Nat. Coun. Learning Resources Newsletter, 1996—. Friend DuBois Pub. Libr., 1994—. Recipient Acad. Excellence grants Pa. State DuBois Ednl. Found., 1995, 96; Continuing Edn. scholarship Pa. State Libr., 1994. Mem. AAUW (program chair 1995—, woman of yr. award 1996), ALA, Assn. Coll. & Rsch. Librs., Golden Key Nat. Honor Soc., Phi Kappa Phi (pres. eastern Ky. U. br.), Sigma Tau Delta. Republican. Office: Pa State U DuBois Campus College Pl Du Bois PA 15801

LEE, CECILIA HAE-JIN, artist, writer; b. Seoul, Nov. 14, 1970; came to U.S., 1977; d. Daniel Pal-Woo and Julia Mi-Ja Lee. BA, U. Calif., San Diego, 1992; postgrad., Inst. Allende, San Miguel de Allende, Mex., 1992, Seoul Nat. U., 1994. Writer, artist, poet, photographer, and designer; resident Cottages at Hedgebrook, Langley, Wash., 1999. Pub. art, César Chavéz Meml., U. So. Calif., L.A., 1998, City of L.A. Parks & Recreation Dept., Seattle, Wash., 2002, exhibitions include Rita Dean Gallery, San Diego, 1992, 1993, Installation Gallery, 1992, Loyola Law Sch. Gallery, L.A., 1993, Artspace Gallery, Woodland Hills, Calif., 1993, SITE Gallery, L.A., 1993, Mus. Contemporary Art, San Diego and Centro Cultural de la Raza, San Diego, 1992—94, L.A. Mcpl. Art Gallery, 1996, Gallery 825, L.A., 1997, Barnsdall Art Ctr. Gallery, 1998, Galeria Asociacion de Bancarios del Urugua y, Montevideo, Uruguay, 1998, Cesar Chavez Meml., 1998, Piazza Risorgimento, Sergno, Italy, 1998, Sabina Lee Gallery, 1999, Jr. Arts Gallery, L.A., 1999, Gallery Prince, 1999, Galeria de la Historia de Concepcion, Chile, 1999, UCC Gallery (2nd pl., 2002), Pierce Coll. Gallery, 2002, Hollywood Libr. Gallery, 2002; contbr. Korean Culture Mag., Kabang, Minority Engr., Ency. Sculpture, Ency. Am. Poetry, columns in newspapers L.A. Times, Washington Post, Eating Well, Food & Wine, Northstar Travel Guide, articles to profl. jours. including Asian Pacific Am. Jour.; author (poet): Eating Korean, 2000; author: (and photographer), 2005. Recipient hon. mention Iliad Press, 1995. Mem.: WriteGirl, Women in Photography Internat., Ind. Writers So. Calif., Archive Korean Am. Artists, Soc. Children's Book Writers and Illustrators. Avocations: travel, building furniture, learning languages, cooking. Address: PO Box 36673 Los Angeles CA 90036-0673 Personal E-mail: cecilia@littlececilia.com.

LEE, CHAN-YUN, physicist, process engineer, educator; b. Hwa-Liang, Taiwan, July 19, 1952; came to U.S., 1988; s. Hsiao-Feng and Shu-Yun (Huang) L.; m. Chia-Li Yang, Jan. 13, 1983; children: Yifan E., Ethel Y., Elias Y. BS in Physics, Soochow U., Taipei, Taiwan, 1974; MS, U. So. Calif., 1980; PhD, U. Notre Dame, 1988. Cert. assoc. prof., lectr. Dept. Edn. Asst. prof. physics Tatung Inst. Tech., Taipei, 1982-86, assoc. prof., 1986-88, chmn. physics sect., 1986-88; cons. Tatung Semiconductor Divsn., Taipei, 1985-88; dir. Tatung Natural Sci. Mus., Taipei, 1986-88; lab. instr. U. Notre Dame, Notre Dame, Ind., 1988-94; process engr. Lam Rsch. Co., Fremont, Calif., 1994-96, sr. process engr., 1996-99, mgr. metal etch key accounts, 1998-99; assoc. prof. physics San Jose City Coll., Calif., 1998-99; regional chief process technologist Silicon Valley Group, 1999-2000; West Coast process coord., tech. staff Tokyo Electron Am., Santa Clara, Calif., 2000—. Rsch. asst. U. So. Calif., L.A., 1977-79. Contbr. numerous articles to profl. jours. 2d lt. Chinese Artillery, 1974-76. Recipient Excellent Rschrs. prize Chinese Nat. Sci. Coun., Taipei, 1986-88, Outstanding Acad. Pub. prize Hsieh-Tze Indsl. Revival Com., Taipei, 1987, 88, Sci. & Tech. Pers. Rsch. & Study award Chinese Nat. Sci. Coun., 1989. Mem. Chinese Physics Assn. Achievements include development of model of relativistic corrections to semiconducting properties of selected materials, simulated and calculated the dynamical susceptibility of square lattice antiferromagnets; successfully developed the first large size SAC process in the world on high density plasma TCP etcher with satisfactory yields; designed and developed the single chamber dry clean process with a MW downstream and RF plate chamber for metal via applications; designed and constructed a spectrophotometer to measure the absolute photoabsorption cross section of atomic potassium in VUV region. Home: 471 Via Vera Cruz Fremont CA 94539-5325 Office: Tokyo Electron Am Inc 2953 Bunker Hill Ln Santa Clara CA 95054 Personal E-mail: cylee9334@yahooo.com.

LEE, CHARLES, cytologist; Phd in med. svcs., U. Alberta, 1996. Cert. in clin. cytogenetics Am. Bd. Med. Genetics, 2002. Fellow in clin. cytogenetics Harvard Med. Sch., 1999—2001, asst. prof. pathology; NSERC rsch. fellow, dept. pathology Cambridge U., 1996—98; assoc. cytogeneticist Brigham and Women's Hosp.; asst. dir. Dana Farber/Harvard Cancer Ctr. Cytogenetics Core. Contbr. articles to profl. jour. Office: Brigham and Womens Hosp Dept Pathology 20 Shattuck St Thorn 628 Boston MA 02115

LEE, CHARLES SUNG CHULL, otolaryngologist; b. Korea, Mar. 29, 1963; MD, Washington U., St. Louis, 1989. Cert. in otolaryngology. Intern Loma Linda U., 1989, resident in otolaryngology, 1994; fellow in plastic surgery U. Miami Sch. Medicine, 1996, fellow in microsurgery, 1997; craniofacial surgery fellow Paik-Inje Hosp., Seoul, 1997.

LEE, CHAVA CHERTA, psychotherapist, consultant; arrived in Thailand, 1980, arrived in U.S., 1980; s. Khoua Pao Lee and True Thao; m. Chaeng Moua, Dec. 5, 1963; children: Linda, David L., Elvis, Yen, Tumuakong. AA, Fresno City Coll., 1986, ASc, 1987; BS, MS, Nat. U., 1992; postgrad., Family Therapy Tng. Inst., Milw., 1996—98; PhD, U. Devonshire, 2000. Cert. marriage and family therapist Wis. Psychotherapist Aurora Health Care, Milw., 2001—, Chava Counseling Practice, LLC, Milw., 1996—. Cons. Sebatian Family Psychology Practice, Milw. Mem.: Am. Mental Health Counselor Assn., Am. Assn. Marriage and Family Therapy.

LEE, CHEEGWAN, environmental engineer, consultant; b. Ulleong, Kyungpook, Republic of Korea, Aug. 23, 1967; s. Youngbaik Lee and Youngza Cho; m. Heejeong Son, Dec. 28, 1996; children: Daniel Seunghoon, Samuel Jihoon. PhD, U. Wis., 2002. Post doctoral rschr. NOAA Gt. Lakes Environ. Rsch. Lab U. Mich., Ann Arbor, Mich., 2002—04; rsch. scientist Battelle Meml. Inst., Seattle, 2004—. Contbr. articles to profl. jours. First lt. Korean Air Force Operation Command, 1991—94, Osan, South Korea. Recipient award, NRC, 2002. Achievements include research in sediment transport and hydrodynamic modeling. Avocations: travel, scuba diving, golf. Office: Battelle Memorial Institute 1100 Dexter Ave North Suite 400 Seattle WA 98109 Office Phone: 206-528-3556. Home Fax: 206-528-3556; Office Fax: 206-528-3556. Personal E-mail: cheegwan@hanmail.net. Business E-Mail: leecheeg@battelle.org.

LEE, CHRISTOPHER FRANK CARANDINI, actor, writer, singer; b. London, May 27, 1922; s. Geoffrey Trollope and Estelle Marie (Carandini) L.; m. Birgit Kroencke, Mar. 17, 1961; 1 child, Christina Erika. Scholar, Eton Coll., Wellington Coll. With theatrical and film industry, 1946—; actor: (films) Corridor of Mirrors, 1947, The Curse of Frankenstein, 1956, Dracula, 1958, The Three Musketeers, 1974, The Four Musketeers, 1975, The Man with the Golden Gun, 1974, Airport 77, 1977, Caravans, 1978, Return from Witch Mountain, 1978, Circle of Iron, 1979, The Passage, 1979, The Wicker Man, 1979, 1941, 1980, Bear Island, 1980, The Salamander, 1981, An Eye for an Eye, 1981, Safari 3000, 1982, The Last Unicorn, 1982, The Return of Captain Invincible, 1983, Mio Min Mio, 1987, Roadtrip, 1987, Shaka Zulu, 1987, House of the Long Shadows, 1989, The Return of the Musketeers, 1990, Gremlins II: The New Batch, 1990, Police Academy: Mission to Moscow, 1993, A Feast at Midnight, 1993, Jinnah, 1997, Sleepy Hollow, 1999, The Lord of the Rings: The Fellowship of the Ring, 2001, Star Wars, Episode II, 2002, The Lord of the Rings: The Two Towers, 2002, The Lord of the Rings: The Return of the King, 2003, Crimson Rivers 2, 2004, Star Wars Episode III, 2004, The Corpse Bride (animation), 2004, Charlie and the Chocolate Factory, 2004, Grey Friars Bobby, 2004; (TV miniseries) How the West Was Won, 1978, Goliath Awaits, 1981, The Far Pavillions, 1984, Around the World in Eighty Days, 1989, Ivanhoe, 1997, In The Beginning, 2000; (TV films) Poor Devil, 1973, Once Upon a Spy, 1980, Charles and Diana: A Royal Love Story, 1982, The Disputation, Metier du Seigneur, Treasure Island, 1990, Young Indy, 1992, Death Train, 1992, Moses, 1996, Im Brunnen der Träume, 1996, The Odyssey, 1997, The Many Faces of Christopher Lee, 1997, Gormenghast, 1999; author: Tall Dark and Gruesome, 1977, rev. edit., 1997, Lord of Misrule, 2003, The Great Villains, 1979, Archives of Evil. Served with RAF and Spl. Forces, 1941-46. Decorated Polonia Restituta (Poland); officer Arts, Lettres et Scis. (France); comdr. Order Brit. Empire, Order of St. John of Jerusalem; officier Arts Lettres (France), 2002. Mem. SAG, AFTRA, Brit. Actors Equity, Variety, Clubs Internat. Conservative. Hon. Company Edinburgh Golfers, Bucks's Club (London), Travellers Club (Paris). Mem. Ch. Of Eng. Office Phone: 0044207 631 0400.

LEE, CONRAD S., councilman; b. China; m. Winnie Lee; children: Christopher, Jennifer. BS in Engring., U. Mich., 1962; MBA, U. Wash., 1980. Various positions including engnr., mktg. sls. mgr. and energy analyst Boeing Co., 1962—78; project mgr. City of Seattle Solid Waste Utility, 1979—96; regional administrator US Small Bus. Administration, 2002—. Former pres. Am. Pacific Am. Municipal Officials; mem. Bellevue City Council, 1994—, Econ. Develop. Council of Seattle & King County, King County Solid Waste Adv. Com. Office: SBA Seattle Region 1200 Sixth Ave Park Place Bldg Seattle WA 98101-1128*

LEE, CORINNE ADAMS, retired English teacher; b. Cuba, N.Y., Mar. 18, 1910; d. Duston Emery and Florence Eugenia (Butts) Adams; m. Glenn Max Lee, Oct. 30, 1936 (dec.). BA, Alfred U., 1931. Cert. tchr. N.Y. Tchr. English Lodi (N.Y.) H.S., 1931—36, Ovid (N.Y.) Ctrl. Sch., 1936—67. Author: (light verse) A Little Leeway, 1983, (anecdotes, light verse, quips) A Little More Leeway, 1984, (essays, short stories, poems) Still More Leeway, 1986. Trustee Montour Falls Meml. Libr. Mem.: LWV, Elmira and Area Ret. Tchrs. Assn., Schuyler County Ret. Tchrs. Assn., N.Y. State Ret. Tchrs. Assn., Nat. Ret. Tchrs. Assn., PTA (life). Avocations: reading, travel, writing.

LEE, C.S. (CHUN-SHING LEE), semiconductor company executive; BS in elec. engring., Nat. Cheng-Kung U., 1976; MS in elec. engring., Tex. Tech. U., 1978, MBA, 1981. With Tex. Instruments, 1978—, v.p. worldwide mixed signal products Dallas, 2000—01, sr. v.p. and mgr. high volume analog logic, 2001—; dep. pres. TI Asia, 1996—98; mgr. mixed-signal wireless comm., 1998—2000. Exec. sponsor Tex. Instruments Inc. Chinese Initiative; co-sponsor Tex. Instruments Inc. Annual Juvenile Diabetes Fund-raising Drive. Recipient Asian-Am. Corp. Achievement award, Overseas Chinese Assn., 1997, Disting. Engr. award, Tex. Tech. U., 2004. Office: Tex Instruments Inc 12500 TI Blvd Dallas TX 75243 Office Phone: 972-995-2011. Office Fax: 972-995-4360.

LEE, DAI-KEONG, composer; b. Honolulu; s. Lin Fong and Young Kun (Chang) L.; m. Dorothy Isabelle Moncur, May 16, 1974. Student in pre-medicine, U. Hawaii, 1933-36; scholarship student with Roger Sessions, N.Y.C., 1937-38; fellowship student under Frederick Jacobi, Juilliard Grad. Sch., 1938-41; fellowship student under Aaron Copland, Berkshire Music Ctr., summer 1941; MA under Otto Luening, Columbia U., 1951. Bd. dirs. Am. Music Ctr., N.Y.C., 1960-69. Recorded Prelude, Hula, Symphony No. 1, Polynesian Suite; wrote mus. score for motion picture Letter from Australia, 1945; guest condr., ABC Symphony, Sydney, Australia, 1944-45; composer: orchestral works including Prelude and Hula, 1939, Hawaiian Festival Overture, 1940, Introduction and Allegro for Strings, 1941, Golden Gate Overture for Chamber Orch., 1941, Polynesian Suite, Symphony No. 1, 1941, revised 1947, Symphony No. 2, 1952; chamber works including String Quartet No. 1, 1947, Sonatina for Piano, 1947, Incantation and Dance for Piano and Violin, 1948, Introduction and Allegro for Cello and Piano, 1947; opera Open the Gates, produced by Blackfriars, N.Y.C., 1951; ballet Waltzing Matilda, 1951; mus. score Teahouse of the August Moon, produced by Maurice Evans-George Shaeffer, 1953; Polynesian Suite for Orch., 1958, Violin Concerto, 1947, revised 1955, Mele Olili for Chorus, Solo and Orch., 1960, Canticle of the Pacific, 1968; mus. play Noa-Noa, 1972; Mortal Thoughts of a Buddhist Monk for baritone, chorus and orch., 1976; one-act opera Ballad of Kitty the Barkeep, 1979; mus. plays Jenny Lind, 1981, Gauguin, Maker of Sea and Sky, 1994; Concerto Grosso for string orch., 1952, rev., 1985; contbr. articles to music mags., newspapers. Served with AUS, 1942-45, PTO. Received Albert Metz commn. for violin concerto, 1946; received CBS commn. for Introduction and Allegro for Strings, 1941, Inst. Mus. Art commn. for one-act opera, Poet's Dilemma, 1940; recipient hon. mention Prix de Rome competition Am. Acad. in Rome, 1942; Guggenheim fellow, 1945, 51 Mem. ASCAP, League Composers, Allied MacDowell Club, Dramatists Guild. Achievements include composing orchestral, symphonic, chamber music; 1st orchestral work Valse Pensieroso, performed Honolulu Symphony Orch., 1936; works performed by N.Y. Philharm., Eastman Rochester Philharm., Mpls., San Francisco, Cin., CBS, Nat., Montreal, Manila, N.Y.C. Phila., symphony orchs.; under direction of Kurtz, Monteux, Mitropoulos, Goosens, Barlow, Caston, Dixon, Stokowski, Stoessel, Pelletier, Wallenstein, others. Home: 245 W 104th St New York NY 10025-4249

LEE, DALE W., lawyer; b. Spokane, Wash., Sept. 16, 1948; AB, Brown U., 1970; JD, So. Meth. U., 1974. Bar: Hawaii 1974. Atty. Kobayashi, Sugita & Goda, Honolulu. Mem.: ABA, Am. Judicature Soc., Korean Bar Assn., Hawaii State Bar Assn. (treas. Young Lawyers sect. 1979—80, pres. 2004), Delta Theta Phi. Office: Kobayashi, Sugita & Goda Ste 2600 999 Bishop St Honolulu HI 96813

LEE, DAN M., retired state supreme court chief justice; b. Petal, Miss., Apr. 19, 1926; s. Buford Aaron and Pherbia Ann (Camp) L.; m. Peggy Jo Daniel, Nov. 27, 1947 (dec. 1952); 1 child, Sheron Lee Anderson; m. Mary Alice Gray, Sept. 30, 1956; 1 child, Dan Jr. Attended, U. So. Miss., 1946; LLB, Jackson Sch. Law, 1949; JD, Miss. Coll., 1970. Bar: Miss. 1948. Ptnr. Franklin & Lee, Jackson, Miss, 1948-54, Lee, Moore and Countiss, Jackson, Miss., 1954-71; county judge Hinds County, 1971-77; cir. judge Hinds-Yazoo Counties, 1977-82; assoc. justice Miss. Supreme Ct., Jackson, 1982-87, presiding justice, 1987-95, chief justice, 1995-98; ret., 1998; of counsel Dogan & Wilkinson, PLLC, Jackson, 1999. With U.S. Naval Aviation, 1944-46. Mem. ABA, Hinds County Bar Assn., Miss. State Bar Assn., Aircraft Owners and Pilots Assn., Am. Legion, VFW, Kiwanis Internat. Baptist. Office Phone: 601-351-3200. E-mail: judgeanddr@aol.com.

LEE, DAVID CHANG, physician; b. Seoul, Republic of Korea, Sept. 14, 1940; s. Young C. Lee and Hae W. (Kim) Kim; m. Margaret C. Park, Sept. 10, 1965; children: Edward, Grace, George. MD, Yon-Sei Sch. Med., Seoul, 1965. Diplomate Am. Bd. Otolaryngology. Intern Howard med. Ctr., Washington, 1965-66; resident gen. surgery Roger's Meml. Hosp., Washington, 1966-67; resident otolaryngology St. Louis City Hosp., 1967-70, U. Md. Hosp., Balt., 1970-71; staff physician Ft. Howard (Md.) Vets. Hosp., 1971-73; asst. prof. U. Ill., Chgo., 1973—, Chgo. Osteo. Med. Sch., 1999—. Med. staff St. Francis Hosp., Blude Island, Ill., 1973—, Ingall's Meml. Hosp., Harvey, Ill., 1973—. Contbr. articles to profl. jours. Fellow ACS, Am. Acad. Otolaryncology and Head and Neck Surgery; AMA. Presbyterian. Avocations: tae kwon do (3d degree black belt), golf. Office: 5320 159th St Oak Forest IL 60452-4705

LEE, DAVID HEE-DON, trade association administrator, educator; b. Seoul, Republic of Korea, Mar. 28, 1959; arrived in U.S., 1985; s. Dong Pyo Lee and Boo Nam Han; m. Sun Song Yi, Dec. 18, 1956; children: Grace Eun-Hae, Jonathan Eun-June. BA in Spanish, Hankuk U. of Fgn. Studies, Seoul, 1978—82, MA in Internat. Rels., 1982—84; PhD, Madrid Nat. U., 1984—89; JD, Western State U., Sch. Law, Fullerton, Calif., 1991—92; studied, U. Calif., La Jolla, 1993—95. V.p. for regional devel. and edn. World Trade Ctrs. Assn., N.Y.C., 1997—2002, vice chmn., 2002—. Sr. fellow, coord. Ctr. for U.S.-Mexican Studies, U. Calif. San Diego, La Jolla, 1995—97; disting. fellow Harris Manchester Coll., Oxford (Eng.) U., 1997—2002; pres., CEO World Trade Ctr. U., Palm Springs, Calif., 1998—. Author: Korea-Mexico Cooperation and its Role in the Pcific Economic Community, 1990, The Pacific Economic Cooperation and Strategy for Collective Security, 1997; co-author (with Van Whiting, Jr.): The Triangle and the Star: A New Approach to Comparative Regional Development, 2001. Pres., CEO WTC Corps, Washington, 2000; chmn. bd. dirs. WTC Found., L.A., 2001. Recipient Hon. Citizenship of Mex., Mexican Govt., 1992, Honor Plaque, Nat. Assembly of Republic of Korea, 1998. Mem.: AAUP (assoc.), Am. Polit. Sci. Assn. (assoc.). Republican. Evangelical. Achievements include development of online trade one-stop service in the fields of financing, education and business tourism; World Trade Centers in the disputed countries such as North Korea. Avocation: golf. Office: World Trade Ctrs Assn Ste 1901 60 E 42nd St New York NY 10165 Office Phone: 202-789-1998. Personal E-mail: dlee@wtcu.com. Business E-Mail: dlee@wtca.org.

LEE, DAVID MALLIN, physicist; b. Bklyn., Jan. 18, 1944; s. George Francis Lee and Winifred Rita (Jones) Wyatt; m. Judith Carol Silliman, Aug. 20, 1966; children: David, Timothy, Karen, Jeffrey, Rebecca. BS, Mannhattan Coll., 1966; PhD, U. Va., 1971. Vis. mem. staff Los Alamos (N.Mex) Nat. Lab., 1971-74, mem. staff, 1974-80, 81—; U.S. tech. expert IAEA, Vienna, Austria, 1980-81. Patentee in field. Mem. Am. Phys. Soc., AAAS, Sigma Xi. Democrat. Roman Catholic. Home: 48 Wildflower Way Santa Fe NM 87506-2116 E-mail: dLee@lanl.gov.

LEE, DAVID MORRIS, physics professor; b. Rye, N.Y., Jan. 20, 1931; s. Marvin and Annette (Franks) Lee; m. Dana Thorangkul, Sept. 7, 1960; children: Eric Bertel, James Marvin. AB, Harvard U., 1952; MS, U. Conn., 1955; PhD, Yale U., 1959. Instr. of physics Cornell U., Ithaca, NY, 1959—60, asst. prof. physics, 1960—63, assoc. prof. physics, 1963—69, prof. physics, 1969—99, James Gilbert White disting. prof. phys. scis., 1999—. Vis. scientist Brookhaven Nat. Lab., Upton, NY, 1966—67; vis. prof. U. Fla., Gainesville, 1974—75, Gainesville, 1994, U. Calif., San Diego, 1988, La Jolla, 88; vis. lectr. Peking U., Beijing, 1981; chair mcpl. Joseph Fourier U., Grenoble, France, 1994. Contbr. articles Phys. Rev. Letters, Phys. Rev., Physica and Nature. With U.S. Army, 1952—54. Co-recipient Nobel prize for physics, 1996; recipient Sir Francis Simon Meml. prize, Brit. Inst. Physics, 1976, Wilber Cross medal, Yale U., 1998; fellow John Simon Guggenheim, Guggenheim Found., 1966—67, 1974—75, Japan Soc. Promotion of Scis., 1977. Fellow: AAAS, Am. Acad. Arts and Scis., Brit. Inst. Physics, Am. Phys. Soc. (Oliver Buckley prize 1981); mem.: Russian Acad. Sci. (fgn. mem.), Nat. Acad. Scis. Achievements include co-discovery of superfluid 3He, of the tricritical point of 3He-4He mixtures; co-observation of spin waves in spin polarized hydrogen gas. Office: Cornell U Physics Dept 610 Clark Hall Ithaca NY 14853-2501*

LEE, DAVID STODDART, retired investment company executive; b. Boston, Jan. 12, 1934; s. George Cabot and Kathleen Bowring (Stoddart) L.; m. Lucinda Hopkins, Apr. 29, 1972; children: Alexander Putnam, Madeline Jackson, Alice Ingalls. AB, Harvard U., 1956, MBA, 1960. V.p., dir. Lee Higginson Corp., N.Y.C., 1960-65; mng. dir., Scudder, Stevens and Clark, Boston, 1965-97; ret., 1997. Trustee Cotting Sch., Boston, 1974—, New Eng. Med. Ctr., 1974; bd. dirs. Lakes Region Conservation Trust; bd. dirs., chmn. Rogerson Cmtys., 1978—; corporator Mass. Gen. Hosp., 1975—. Lt. (j.g.) USN, 1956—58. Mem.: Soc. Chartered Fin. Analysts (chartered investment counsellor), Country Club, Somerset Club (Boston), The Boulders, Bald Peak Colony Club. Republican. Episcopalian. Office: 50 Congress St Ste 543 Boston MA 02109-4002 Office Phone: 617-523-0897.

LEE, DEBRA LOUISE, cable television company executive; b. Columbia, SC, Aug. 8, 1954; d. Richard M. and Delma L. Lee; m. Randall Spencer Coleman; children: Quinn Spencer, Ava. B in Polit. Sci., Brown U., 1976; M in Pub. Policy, JD, Harvard U., 1980. Law clk. to Hon. Barrington Parker U.S. Dist. Ct. D.C., 1980—81; atty. Steptoe & Johnson, Washington, 1981—86; v.p., gen. counsel BET (Black Entertainment TV), 1986—92, exec. v.p. legal affairs dept., gen. counsel, 1992—96, corp. sec., pres., pub. pub. divsn., 1992—96; pres., COO BET Holdings, Inc., 1996—2005, CEO, 2005—. Bd. dirs. BET Holdings, Inc., Eastman Kodak Co., Marriott Internat., Wash. Gas & Light Co.; nat. bd. dirs. Nat. Cable & Telecom. Assn., Cable & Telecom. Assn. for Mktg., Alvin Ailey Dance Theater, Nat. Symphony Orch., Telecom. Devel. Fund, Ctr. for Comm., Kennedy Ctr. Community & Friends Bd., Nat. Women's Law Ctr.; trustee emeritus Brown U. Bd. dirs. Kennedy Ctrs. Comty. Bd., Women in Cable, Telecom Devel. Fund, Nat. Symphony Orch. Bd. Named Woman of Yr., Women in Cable and Telecom., 2001; named one of Hundred Heavy Hitters, Cable Fax Mag., 100 Most Powerful Women in Washington, Washingtonian Mag.; recipient Eva A. Mooar award, Brown U., 1976, Nat. Achievement award, Area Chapter of the Nat. Alumnus Assn., 1992, Tower of Power Trumpet award, Turner Broadcasting Sys., 2000, Vanguard award, Nat. Cable & Telecom. Assn., 2003, Quasar award, Nat.

Assn. Minorities in Communication, 2003, Silver Star award, Am. Women in Radio and TV, Par Excellence award, Dollars and $ense Mag., Wonder Woman award, Cablevision Mag. Office: BET Holdings Inc One BET Plaza 1235 W St NE Washington DC 20018-1211*

LEE, DON YOON, publishing executive, academic administrator, writer; b. Seoul, Korea, Apr. 7, 1936; came to U.S., 1957; s. Yoo-ehn and Ch'i-ho (Kim) L. BA, U. Wash., 1963; MA, St. John's U., Jamaica, N.Y., 1967; MS, Georgetown U., 1971; MA, Ind. U., 1975, 90; PhD, World Info. Distributed U., 2003. Founder, pub. Eastern Press, Inc., Bloomington, Ind., 1981—. Author: History of Early Relation Between China and Tibet, 1981, An Introduction to East Asian and Tibetan Linguistics and Culture, 1981, Learning Standard Arabic, 1988, An Annotated Bibliography of Selected Works on China, 1981, Light Literature and Philosophy of East Asia, 1982, An Annotated Bibliography on Inner Asia, 1983, An Annotated Archaeological Bibliography of Selected Works on Norther and Central Asia, 1983, Traditional Chinese Thoughts: The Four Schools, 1990, others. Office: Eastern Press Inc PO Box 881 Bloomington IN 47402-0881 E-mail: dongyoonlee2002@yahoo.com.

LEE, DONALD HAN, surgeon, orthopedist; b. Huntington, W.Va., Oct. 28, 1955; s. Kwan Ho and Kay Hee Lee; m. Dawn Thomas Thomas, May 13, 1989; children: David Thomas, Dana Elizabeth, Diane Louise, Daniel Thomas, Dustin Thomas. BS, Georgetown U., 1977; MD, W.Va. Sch. Medicine, 1982. Diplomate Nat. Bd. Med. Examiners, 1983, Am. Bd. Orthop. Surgeons, 1991. Intern surgery W. Va. U. Sch. Medicine, 1982—83, George Washington U. Sch. Medicine, 1983—84, resident orthop. surgery, 1984—88; Hand fellowship Columbia Presbyn. Med. Ctr., 1988—89; assoc. prof. orthop. surgery U. Ala., Birmingham, 1989—2005; prof. orthop. surgery Vanderbilt U., Nashville, 2005—. Dir. hand fellowship U. Ala., Birmingham, 1993—; bd. examiner Am. Bd. Orthop. Surgery; joint com. surgery of hand Am. Bd. Orthop. Surgeons. Pres. parish coun., 2000—01. Hand fellow, Columbia Presbyn. Med. Ctr., 1988—89, Rsch. grantee, Merck and Co., Biomet, Inc. Mem.: Am. Soc. Reconstructive Microsurgery, Am. Soc. Surgery of Hand, Am. Acad. Orthop. Surgeons, Assn. Bone and Joint Surgeons, Am. Orthop. Assn. Office: Vanderbilt U Dept Orthop Surgery D-4213 MC Nashville TN 37232-2550 Office Phone: 618-322-4683.

LEE, DONALD YOUNG (DON LEE), publishing executive; b. Tokyo, Dec. 11, 1959; s. Victor Young and Jean Ann (Kim) L. BA in English, UCLA, 0982; MFA in Creative Writing, Emerson Coll., 1986. Writing instr. Emerson Coll., Boston, 1985-89; mng. editor Ploughshares, Boston, 1988-92, dir., 1992—. Cons. AGNI, Boston, 1993, Asian Pacific Am. Jour., 1994, New Eng. Rev., 1995, Columbia, 1998, Ga. Rev., 1999, CLMP, 1999, Salamander, 1999, Lannan Found., 2000. Author: Yellow: Stories, 2001, Country of Origin, 2004; contbr. short stories, articles to jours. Recipient Sue Kaufman prize for 1st fiction, 2002; fellow, St. Botolph Club Found., 1990, 1991; Mass. Cultural Coun. Fiction fellow, 1998. Mem.: PEN. Democrat. Office: Ploughshares Emerson Coll 120 Boylston St Boston MA 02116-4624

LEE, DONG HWAN, business administration educator; b. Seoul, Nov. 8, 1952; s. Hee Kwon and Yong Boon (Kim) L.; m. Young Ja Lee, Apr. 16, 1981; 2 children; Hyon Jae and Joan. B of Agr. summa cum laude, Kon-Kuk U., 1977; MBA, Okla. State U., 1984; PhD in Bus., Ind. U., 1989. Cert. internat. trade specialist, Ministry of Commerce and Industry/Seoul; cert. tchr. Ministry of Edn., Seoul. Sr. staff mem. overseas bus. Divsn. Gold Star Telecomm. Co., Inc., Seoul, 1976—80; advisor to comml. counsellor Brit. Embassy in Seoul, 1980—82; lectr. mktg. Sch. of Bus. Ind. U., Bloomington, 1989—90; asst. prof. mktg. SUNY, Albany, 1990—97; assoc. prof. mktg. Manhattan Coll., N.Y.C., 1997—. Mem. editl. rev. bd. Jour. Bus. Rsch., 1997—, Jour. Consumer Satisfaction, Dissatisfaction and Complaining Behavior, 1997—. Elder Stony Point Presbyn. Ch. Recipient Faculty Rsch. awards SUNY, Albany, 1990, 92, 94, 95; Faculty Devel. award, N.Y. State/United U. Profls., 1991, 93, 94; rsch. grantee Manhattan Coll., 1999, 2003; Gabriel Hauge Faculty fellow Manhattan Coll., 1999-2000. Mem. Am. Mktg. Assn. (Outstanding Doctoral Dissertation award 1990), Acad. Mktg. Sci., Assn. Consumer Rsch., Soc. Consumer Psychology, Beta Gamma Sigma. Presbyterian. Home: 9 Old Clave Ct Congers NY 10920-1101 Office: Manhattan College Sch of Business DLS 517 Bronx NY 10471 Office Phone: 718-862-7195. Business E-Mail: dongh.lee@manhattan.edu.

LEE, DONNA A., telecommunications industry executive; b. Norfolk, Va. BS in Math., Mary Washington Coll.; MBA, Ga. State U.; postgrad. in advanced Mgmt., Harvard U. With AT&T, 1988—98; pres. Managed Network Solutions Inc., BellSouth Corp., Atlanta, 1998—2000, chief mktg. officer, 2000—. Bd. dirs. Atlanta Coll. Art, BellSouth Found. Named finalist Woman of Yr. in Tech. award, Women in Tech., 2001; named one of Top 25 Unsung Heroes of the Net, Inter@ctive Week mag., 2000; recipient Ovations award, tele.com mag. and ComNet, 2000. Avocations: tennis, swimming. Office: BellSouth Corp 1155 Peachtree St NE Atlanta GA 30309-3610

LEE, DONNA JEAN, retired hospice and respite nurse; b. Huntington Park, Nov. 12, 1931; d. Louis Frederick and Lena Adelaide (Hinson) Munyon; m. Frank Bernard Lee, July 16, 1949; children: Frank, Robert, John. AA in Nursing, Fullerton (Calif.) Jr. Coll., 1966; extension student, U. Calif., Irvine, 1966-74; student, U. N.Mex., 1982. RN, Calif.; cert. Intraventous Therapy Assn. U.S.A. Staff nurse Orange (Calif.) County Med. Ctr., 1966-71, staff and charge nurse relief ICU, CCU, Burn Unit, ER, Communicable Disease, Neo-Natal Care Unit, 1969-71, charge nurse communicable disease unit, 1969-70; staff and charge nurse ICU, emergency rm., CCU, med./surg. units Anaheim (Calif.) Meml. Hosp., 1971-74; charge and staff nurse, relief Staff Builders, Orange, 1974-82; agy. nurse Nursing Svcs. Internat., 1978-89; asst. DON Chapman Convalescent SNF, Orange, 1982; geriat. and pediat. nurse VNASS, 1985-93; hospice/respite nurse VIA Upjohn Home Healthcare Svcs and VNA Support Svcs. of Orange, 1985-93; ret. Staff relief nurse ICU/CCU various hosps. and labs, including plasmapheresis nurse Med. Lab. of Orange, 1978. Life mem. in honor of spouse Republican. Presdl. Task Force, 1982—, Nat. Rep. Com. Ocean Conservancy, Natl. Park Trust, Wildlife Land Trust, Sierra Club. Mem. AACN, Harvard Med. Sch. Nurses, Am. Lung Assn., Am. Heart Assn., Arthritis Found., Life Extension Found. Baptist. Home: 924 S Hampstead St Anaheim CA 92802-1740

LEE, DOROTHY WONG, secondary art educator; b. L.A., Aug. 17, 1948; d. Leonard G.Y. and Ginger (Hom) Wong; m. Kenny Lee, Nov. 24, 1973; children: Brandon Joel, Brittany Jene. BA cum laude, UCLA, 1971; std. secondary tchg. credential, Calif. State U. L.A., 1973. Secondary art tchr., chmn. dept. art L.A. Unified Sch. Dist., 1973—2005. Buyer, retailer Imperial Dragon Gifts, Inc., Los Angeles, 1978—2002. Recipient Tchg. award Otis Art Inst., L.A., 1992, Bravo award L.A. (County Music Ctr., 1994. Mem. Calif. Art Educator's Assn., United Tchrs. L.A., Art Educators L.A., L.A. County Art Mus. (Bravo award 1994), Mus. Contemporary Art L.A Home: PO Box 29893 Los Angeles CA 90029-0893

LEE, DOUGLAS A., music educator; b. Carmel, Ind., Nov. 3, 1932; s. Ralph Henley and Flossie Ellen (Chandler) Lee; m. Beverly Ruth Haskell, Sept. 2, 1961. MusB with High Distinction, DePauw U., 1954; MusM, U. Mich., 1958, PhD, 1968; postgrad., U. Md., 1985. Instr. Nat. Mus. Camp, Interlochen, Mich., 1959-62, Mt. Union Coll., Alliance, Ohio, 1959-61, chmn. keyboard instrn., 1959-61; asst. prof. Music Wichita (Kans.) State U., 1964-68, assoc. prof., 1968-74, coord. Music History and Lit., 1968-71, coord. grad. studies in Music, 1969-70, chmn. dept. Musicology, 1971-74, prof. Music, 1974-86, administrv. intern, v.p. bus. affairs, 1983, spl. events coord., 1974—85; prof. Musicology Vanderbilt U., Nashville, 1986—, chmn. Music History and Lit., advisor, 1987—98, prof. musicology emeritus, 1998. Radio commentator Sta. KMUW-FM, 1969-76; judge various competitions, Mu Phi Epsilon, 1980, Kans. Music Tchrs. Assn., 1975-83, Baldwin Found. awards, 1979, 80; program annotator Nashville Symphony Orch., 1988-2001; cons. U.S. Dept. Edn. Jacob Javits fellowship program, 1988, 89, United Meth. Publishing Ho., 1988, Mayfield Pub. Co., 1990, Prentice-Hall, Inc., 1993, 97. Author: The Instrumental Works of Christoph Nichelmann: The Thematic Index, 1971, Franz Benda: A Thematic Catalogue of His Works, 1984, Franz Benda: A Musician at Court, 1998, Masterworks of 20th-Century Music, 2002; editor: Christoph Nichelmann: Clavier Concertos in E Major and A Minor, 1977, Six Sonatas for Violin and Bass by Franz Benda, with Embellishments, 1981, The Sonneck Soc. Bull., 1988-90; contbg. editor: Carl Phillip Emanuel Bach: Collected Works, 2003—; contbr. articles to The New Grove Dictionary of Music and Musicians, 1980, The New Grove Dictionary of Music in the United States, 1986, America in the Fifties, 2004; contbr. articles to profl. jours., chpts. to books. With U.S. Army, 1955-57, Japan. Rector Scholar Found., 1950-54; Rackham fellow U. Mich., 1961-63, fellow NEH, 1980, 85, Am. Philos. Soc., 1980, Kans. Arts Coun., 1985, Tenn. Arts Coun., 1988, 89, Packard Humanities Inst., Cambridge, Mass., 2002, 04 Mem. Am. Musicological Soc. (program chmn. Midwest chpt. 1984, South-Ctrl. chpt. 1989, nat. coun. 1986, pres. South-Ctrl. chpt. 1990-91), Music Tchrs. Nat. Assn. (editor 1971-90), Am. Soc. Eighteenth Century Studies, Coll. Music Soc., Sonneck Soc. Am. Music (program coord. 1987-88). Episcopalian. Avocation: photography. Office: 6517 Cornwall Dr Nashville TN 37205-3041 Office Phone: 615-356-8489. Business E-Mail: douglas.lee@vanderbilt.edu.

LEE, EARL WAYNE, library science educator; b. Rockford, Ill., Nov. 8, 1954; s. Earl Ray and Opal (Sharp) L.; m. Kathleen R. DeGrave, Mar. 10, 1978; children: Nathan, Cambria, Erin. BA, Lyon Coll., 1975; MA, U. Ark., Fayetteville, 1978, U. Wis., 1985. Instr. English No. Ill. U., DeKalb, 1979-80; lectr. English U. Wis., Green Bay, 1983-84; info. specialist Dept. of Transp., Madison, Wis., 1985-86; libr. Phillips U., Enid, Okla., 1986-87, Pittsburg (Kans.) State U., 1987—. Author: Drakulya, 1994, Libraries in the Age of Mediocrity, 1998, Drakulya: The Vampire Play, 2001; contbr. articles to profl. jours. Shrenk scholar U. Wis., 1985, McCain scholar Lyon Coll. Mem. ALA, Kans. Libr. Assn. Unitarian Universalist. Office: Axe Bldg Pittsburg State U Pittsburg KS 66762

LEE, EDITH OLIVE MAE, secondary educator; b. Kinston, N.C., Jan. 27, 1929; d. Gaston and Tessie (Jones) L. BS, N.C. Cen. U., Durham, 1951; MA, Columbia U., 1957; postgrad., East Carolina U., Greenville, N.C., 1967, 70-71. Tchr. math., registrar, dormitory supr. Boggs Acad., Keysville, Ga., 1952-67; tchr. math. South Greene High Sch., Snow Hill, N.C., 1967-69, Snow Hill Jr. High Sch., 1969-79, Greene Cen. High Sch., Snow Hill, 1979-87. Mem. Nat. Coun. Tchrs. Math., N.C. Tchrs. Math. (eastern regional v.p. secondary sch. 1975-77), Ret. Govtl. Employee Assn., Nta. Ret. Sch. Pers., N.C. Ret. Sch. Pers., Lenoir-Kinston Ret. Sch. Pers., Am. Assn. Ret. Persons. Democrat. Presbyterian. Avocations: sewing, reading, working crossword puzzles. Home: PO Box 2637 Kinston NC 28502-2637

LEE, ELLA LOUISE, librarian, educator; b. Pitts., Aug. 15, 1929; d. Louis C. and Ida Lily (Ward) Lee; 1 child, Lily I. Lee-Braithwaite. BA in French Lang., History & Culture, San Francisco Coll. for Women, 1971; MA in History, U. San Francisco Jesuit U., 1978; MLS, San Jose State U., 1993. Cert. tchg. K-12 Calif., tchg. 13-14 Calif. Clk. U.S. Fgn. Svc., 1951—61; adult ednl. profl. UN - UNESCO, Paris, 1961—67; tchr. French and history San Francisco Unified Sch., 1972—80; instr. San Francisco C.C., 1994—98; assoc. libr. Richmond Calif. Pub, Libr., 1998—2000, U. San Francisco Jesuit U., 2000—. Home: # 3 415 MacArthur Blvd Oakland CA 94610 Office: U San Francisco 2808 Lakeshore Blvd Oakland CA 94610 E-mail: leee@usfca.edu.

LEE, ERIC MCCAULEY, museum director, art historian; b. Clinton, N.C., Feb. 23, 1966; s. Harry McCauley and Mary Thompson Lee; m. Rima Canaan, June 12, 1994; children: Edward Marshall, Graham William. BA, Yale U., 1988, MA, 1991, PhD, 1997. Rsch. asst. U.S. Senate Select Com. on Intelligence, Washington, 1989—90; acting asst. curator paintings Yale Ctr. for Brit. Art, New Haven, 1995—96; acting dir. Fred Jones Jr. Mus. Art, U. Okla., Norman, 1997—98, Wylodean and Bill Saxon dir., 1998—. Co-author: (book) The Fred Jones Jr. Museum of Art at the University of Oklahoma: Selected Works; author: (exhibition catalogue) Translations: Turner and Printmaking. A. Bartlett Giamatti fellow, Yale U., 1990—91, Theodore Rousseau fellow, Met. Mus. of Art, N.Y., 1994. Mem.: Coll. Art Assn., Accreditation Vis. Com., Am. Assn. Mus. Home: 1105 Riviera Dr Norman OK 73072 Office: Fred Jones Jr Mus Art Univ Okla 555 Elm Ave Norman OK 73019-3003 Office Phone: 405-325-0843.

LEE, ERNEST J., SR., lawyer; b. Ft. Bragg, N.C., June 21, 1956; s. Major Lee, Sr. and Lucille L. Lee; 1 child, Ernest L. Lee, Jr. BA in Mass Comm., U. Mo., St. Louis, 1996; JD, U. Mo., Kansas City, 1999. Bar: Calif. 2001, U.S. Dist. Ct. (so. dist.) Calif. 2001, U.S. Dist. Ct. (central dist.) Calif. 2003. Mgr., owner Queensway Dry Cleaning Co., St. Louis, 1981—88; owner, operator Ernest Lee Bail Surety Co., St. Louis, 1988—90; pres., CEO, chmn. LEECORP Corp., Inc., St. Louis, 1990—98; pvt. practice San Diego, 2001—. Founder, chmn., 1st pres. Liberty Coalition, San Diego, L.A., 2002—. Avocations: horseback riding, dogs, jogging, golf, tennis, reading.

LEE, ERNEST WILLIAM, II, lawyer; b. Sweetwater, Tenn., Feb. 26, 1960; s. Ernest William and Ruth Ellen (Burris) Lee. BA in Psychology, Mercer U., 1982; diploma, U. London, King's Coll., 1985; JD, Samford U., 1989; diploma, Generative Learning Inst., Atlanta, 2001. Bar: U.S. Superior Ct. Ga. 1989, U.S. Supreme Ct. 1990, U.S. Ct. Appeals 1990, U.S. Dist. Ct. (no. dist.) Ga. 1990, cert.: Ga. Office Dispute Resolution (mediator) 1996. Acctg. clk., parts mgr. Lee Bros., Inc., Conley, Ga., 1982—83, v.p., 1985—88; atty. Law Offices of Ernest W. Lee, Atlanta, 1989—90; law clk. JD Lee and Assocs., Knoxville, 1989; atty. Desiderio and Lee, PC, Atlanta, 1990—91; interim dir. Ga. Minority Supplier Devel. Coun., Atlanta, 1992—93, v.p., staff atty., 1993—94, interim dir., 1994; staff atty., regional sales rep. West's Legal Directory, Atlanta, 1994—96; risk mgr. Life Sources, Inc., Lilburn, Ga., 1996—98; sr. staff devel. tng. coord. Dept. Revenue State of Ga., Atlanta, 1999—2000, computer tech. instr., mobile PC lab oper. Dept. Tech. and Adult Edn., 2000—01, legis. policy analyst, spl. projects dir. Dept. Human Resources, Divsn. Pub. Health, 2001—03; legal counsel Savannah (Ga.) Coll. Art and Design, 2003—. Author: Introduction to Tobacco Use Prevention (Atlanta Bronze Flame award Internat. Assn. Bus. Communicators, 2003). Mem. tng. and devel. com. Ga. Equality, Atlanta, 1997—2003; chair St. Bart's Arts, Atlanta, 2003. Mem.: ABA, Nat. Assn. Univ. and Coll. Attys. (membership com. 2004—05), First City Club (assoc.; membership com. 2004—05). Democrat. Episcopalian. Avocations: travel, dogs, reading, antiques, fountain pens. Office: Savannah Coll Art and Design 618 Drayton St Savannah GA 31401 Office Phone: 912-525-5549. E-mail: elee@scad.edu.

LEE, E(UGENE) STANLEY, engineering educator; b. Hopeh, China, Sept. 7, 1930; s. Ing Yah and Lindy (Hsieng) L.; m. Mayanne Lee, Dec. 21, 1957 (dec. June 1980); children: Linda J., Margaret H.; m. Yuan Lee, Mar. 8, 1983; children— Lynn Hua Lee, Jin Hua Lee, Ming Hua Lee. BS, Chung Cheng Inst. Tech., Taiwan, Republic of China, 1953; MS, N.C. State U., 1957; PhDChemE, Princeton U., 1962. Rsch. engr. Phillips Petroleum Co., Bartlesville, Okla., 1960-66; asst. prof. chem. engring. Kans. State U., Manhattan, 1966-67, assoc. prof. indsl. engring., 1967-69, prof. indsl. engring., 1969—; prof. chem. and elec. engring. U. So. Calif., 1972-76. Hon. prof. Chinese Acad. Sci., 1987—; chaired prof. Yuan-ze Inst. Tech., Taiwan, Republic of China, 1993—; cons. govt. and industry. Author: Quasilinearization and Invariant Imbedding, 1968, Coal Conversion Technnology, 1979, Operations Research, 1981, Fuzzy and Evidence Reasoning, 1996, Fuzzy and Multi-level Decision Making, 2000; editor: Energy Sci. and Tech., 1975; assoc. editor: Jour. Math. Analysis and Applications, 1974—, Computers and Mathematics with Applications, 1974, editl. bd.: Jour. Engring. Chemistry and Metallurgy, 1989—, Jour. of Nonlinear Differential Equations, 1992—, Jour. Chinese Fuzzy Sys. Assn., 1995—, Fuzzy Optimization and Decision Making, 2000—, Internat. Jour. Modeling and Optimization, 2001—, Math. Scis. Rsch. Hot-line, An Internat. Jour. Rapid Publ., 2001—, author over 300 papers in profl. jours. Grantee Dept. Def., 1967-72, Office Water Resources, 1968-75, EPA, 1969-71, NSF, 1971—, USDA, 1978-90, Dept. Energy, 1979-84, USAF, 1984-88. Mem. Soc. Indsl. and Applied Math., Ops. Rsch. Soc. Am., N. Am. Fuzzy Info. Processing Soc., Internat. Neural Network Soc., Sigma Xi, Tau Beta Pi, Phi Kappa Phi. Office: Kans State U Dept Indsl Engring Manhattan KS 66506 Business E-Mail: eslee@ksu.edu. *Nothing can replace hard work and persistence.*

LEE, EUNICE, music educator; b. Yong San, Seoul, Republic of Korea, Mar. 16, 1967; d. Jung In and Byung Joo Lee; m. Steve Rhee, July 5, 2000. DMA, San Francisco Conservatory of Music, 1991; MusB (hon.), U. So. Calif., 1998, MusM, 2000; grad., Am. Coll. Musicians, Calif., 2005. Accompanist San Jose Korean Bapt., San Jose, 1985—92; keyboard collaborator various univs., LA, San Francisco, NY, Aspen, Ohio, 1987—2000; accompanist Foothill Coll., Palo Alto, Calif., 1988—89; dir. San Jose Piano Studio, Santa Clara, Calif., 1991—95; condr. Ch. of Love, San Jose, Calif., 1993—94; faculty De Anza Coll., Cupertino, Calif., 1993—94; tchg. asst. U. So. Calif., L.A., 1995—2000, Aspen Summer Music Festival, Colo., 1998—98; accompanist Santa Monica First Christian Ch., Santa Monica, Calif., 1999—2002; pvt. piano tchr. Bakersfield, Calif., 2004—. Adjudicator Nat. Guild Piano Audition, Am. Christian Sch. Instn. Piano Festival, 2004—05. Music dir., organist, LA, 1994—2002. Recipient Grand prize, Concerto Competitions, 1989, Leo Poldofsky award, 1996—99, Keyboard Ensemble, 1996-2000; scholar, San Francisco Conservatory of Music, 1986—91, U. of So. Calif., 1995—2000. Mem.: Nat. Guild Piano Tchrs. (assoc.), Music Tchrs. Assn. Calif. (assoc.; second v.p. 2004—). Mem. Citizens Party. Avocations: breeder, cooking, interior decorating. Office: Music Tchrs Assn Calif 10818 Whitburn St Bakersfield CA 93312 Office Phone: 661-205-9300. Home Fax: 661-654-0398. Personal E-mail: e.rhee04@sbcglobal.net.

LEE, FRANCES HELEN, editor; b. NYC, Jan. 6, 1936; d. Murray and Rose (Rothman) Lee. BA, Queens Coll., 1957; MA, NYU, 1962. Editl. asst. Christian Herald Family Bookshelf, N.Y.C., 1957-62; with Gordon and Breach Sci. Pubs., Inc., N.Y.C., 1964-66, Am. Electric Power Svc. Corp. AEP Operating Ideas, N.Y.C., 1966-69, Indsl. Water Engring. Mag., N.Y.C., 1969-71; directory editor photographic divsn. United Bus. Publs., N.Y.C., 1971-80; editor Am. Druggist Blue Book Hearst Books/Bus. Publs. Group, 1980-81; spl. projects coord. motor manuals Hearst Book Divsn., 1981-82; editor New Price Report, 1982-84, Am. Druggist Blue Book, 1982-88; freelance editor, cons., 1988—. Supr. Bronx divsn. N.Y. State Civil Defense, 1953-59; mem. com. on N.Y.C. charter revision, Citizens Union, 1975, com. on city mgmt., 1977-92, bd. dirs., co-chmn. com. on N.Y.C. cultural concerns, 1979-97, chmn., 1997-98; vol. N.Y.C. Opera, 1988—, info. project mgr., 2001—. Recipient cert. of honor NYU Alumni Fedn., 1985, Meritorious Svc. award, 1986. Mem. N.Y. Bus. Press Editors (bd. dirs. 1988-90, sec. 1990-91), Women's Equity Action League (chmn. rsch. com.), NYU Alumnae Club (dir. 1976-78, rec. sec. 1978-80, v.p. 1980-82, pres. 1982-84, rep. to bd. dirs. fedn. 1984-86), NYU Alumni Fedn. (dir.-at-large 1986—), Villa-Lobos Music Soc. (sec. 1989-91, treas. 1992-95), NYU Club (bd. govs. 1987-89). Home: 170 2nd Ave New York NY 10003-5754 Personal E-mail: franceslee397@hotmail.com.

LEE, FRED C., electrical engineering educator; b. China, 1946; naturalized Am. citizen; BS, Nat. Cheng Kung U., Taiwan, 1968; MSA, Duke U., 1972, PhD, 1974. Tchg. asst. Duke U., Durham, N.C., 1970-72; rsch. asst. Spacecraft Sys. Rsch. Lab., 1972-74; mem. tech. staff TRW Systems, 1974-77; from asst. prof. to prof. Va. Poly. Inst. and State U., Blacksburg, 1977-83, James S. Tucker prof., 1986-94, Lewis A. Hester engring. chair, 1994-99, univ. disting. prof., 1999—, dir. Va. Power Electronics Ctr., 1985-98; bd. dirs. Zytec, 1986-97; dir. NSFERC Ctr. for Power Electronics Sys., 1998—. Bd. dirs. Artesyn Techs., 1997—2004, Delta Electronics, 2003-, Delta Environ. and Ednl. Found., 2002-; mem. adv. bd. Power Integrations Inc., 1988-94; chmn., CEO Va. Power Techs., Inc., 1994—, Primarion Inc., 2004-. Recipient, PCIM award for Outstanding Power Electronics Edn., 1990, Arthur Fury award for Outstanding Powere Electronics Innovation, 1998, IEEE Millennium medal, 2000. Fellow IEEE William E. Newell Power Electronics award 1989, IEEE Power Electronics Soc. (chmn. meeting com., mem. advt. com., mem. fellow evaluation com., chmn. power electronics specialists conf. 1987, v.p. 1988, pres. 1993-94), IEEE Engrs. Indsl. Applications Soc., Brit. Inst. Engrs. Office: NSFERC Ctr for Power Electronics Sys 655 Whitemore Blacksburg VA 24061-0111 E-mail: fclee@art.edu.

LEE, FREDERICK DREXEL, lawyer; b. Savannah, Ga., Sept. 27, 1937; d. Frederick Charles and Geneva (Futch) Drexel; m. Julian Ralson Lee, June 7, 1959; children: Dawn, Courtney. BS in Edn., U. Ga., 1959, MEd, 1960; JD summa cum laude, Woodrow Wilson Coll. Law, Atlanta, 1978. Bar: Ga. 1979. Pvt. practice, Atlanta, 1978-92, Ellabell, Ga., 1992—. Editor Ga. Profl. Engr., 1982-86. Pres. Pembroke (Ga.) Garden Club, 1996-99. Recipient Chief Justice Robert Benham's Supreme Ct. of Ga. award for cmty. svc., 1998. Mem. Phi Beta Kappa, Phi Kappa Phi, Kappa Delta Pi. Methodist. Avocations: gardening, reading, bible study, exercise. Home: 505 Bill Futch Rd Ellabell GA 31308-4600 Personal E-mail: FAD485@aol.com.

LEE, GARY, lawyer; b. Feb. 1955; BA, JD, U. N.D. Bar: N.D. 1980. With Olson Burns Lee, P.C., Minot, ND. Mem.: State Bar Assn. N.D. (pres. 2002). Address: PO Box 1180 Minot ND 58702

LEE, GEORGE TERRY, JR., lawyer; b. Dallas, Oct. 28, 1935; s. George Terry and Isabel (Breckenridge) T.; m. Natalie Blythe Henderson, Aug. 17, 1957; children: George Terry III, Blythe, Rebecca, Hamilton. BA, Yale U., 1957; LLB, Stanford U., 1960. Assoc. Goldberg, Fonville, et al, Dallas, 1960-65; gen. counsel George A. Fuller Co. and OKC Corp., Dallas, 1965-73; ptnr. Akin, Gump, Strauss, Hauer & Feld, L.L.P., Dallas, 1973—. Trustee Found. for Arts, Dallas, 1963—, St. Mark's Sch. of Tex., Dallas, 1966-72; bd. dirs. Dallas Mus. Fine Arts; pres. Brit.-Am. Commerce Assn., Dallas, 1986. Fellow (life) Tex. Bar Found.; mem. ABA, University Club (N.Y.C.), Brook Hollow Golf Club (Dallas), Koon Kreek Klub (Athens, Tex.), Crescent Club (Dallas). Home: 3101 Greenbrier Dr Dallas TX 75225-4603 Office: Akin Gump Strauss Hauer & Feld LLP 1700 Pacific Ave Ste 4100 Dallas TX 75201-4675

LEE, GLENN RICHARD, medical association administrator, educator; b. Ogden, Utah, May 18, 1932; s. Glenn Edwin and Thelma (Jensen) L.; m. Pamela Marjorie Ridd, July 18, 1969; children— Jennifer, Cynthia. BS, U. Utah, 1953, MD, 1956. Intern Boston City Hosp.-Harvard U., 1956-57, resident, 1957-58; clin. asso. Nat. Cancer Inst., NIH, 1958-60; postdoctoral fellow U. Utah, 1960-63; instr. U. Utah Coll. Medicine, 1963-64, asst. prof. internal medicine, 1964-68, assoc. prof., 1968-73, prof., 1973-96, assoc. dean for acad. affairs, 1973-76, dean, 1978-83, prof. emeritus, 1996—; chief of staff Salt Lake VA Med. Ctr., 1985-95. Author: (with others) Clinical Hematology, 10th edit, 1998; Contbr. (with others) numerous articles to profl. jours.; editorial bd.: (with others) Am. Jour. Hematology, 1976-79. Served with USPHS, 1958-60. Markle Found. scholar, 1965-70; Nat. Inst. Arthritis, Metabolic and Digestive Disease grantee, 1977-82. Mem. A.C.P., Am. Soc. Hematology, Am. Soc. Clin. Investigation, Western Assn. Physicians, Am. Inst. Nutrition. Mem. Lds Ch. Home and Office: 194 Harvest Run Idaho Falls ID 83404 Personal E-mail: grichardl@cableone.net.

LEE, GORDON KENNETH, physician assistant; b. Harlingen, Tex., Jan. 2, 1959; s Ralph Gordon and Enedelia Lee; m. Barbara Jo Lee, Aug. 10, 1985; children: Joseph Randolf, Mark Kenneth. B in Physician Asst. Studies, U. Tex., Galveston, 1985; M in Physician Asst. Studies, U. Nebr., 1997. Physician asst. McGregor Med. Assn., Houston, 1985-87, Tex. Dept. Corrections, Rosharon, Tex., 1987, USAF Regional Hosp., Sheppard AFB, Tex., 1987-89, 432d Med. Group, Misawa AB, Japan, 1989-91, Wright-Patterson AFB, Ohio, 1992-93, Parkview Regional Hosp., Mexia, Tex., 1993-97; pres. Paladin Healthcare Assocs., P.C., Wortham, Tex., 1997—. Bd. dirs., pres. Eagle Crest Therapeutic Ctr., Inc., 1998-99; bd. dirs. Freestone County Soccer Assn, 1997—; vice chmn. exec. com. Ctr. for Rural Health Initiative, Austin, Tex., 1998-2001. Capt. USAF, 1987-93. Fellow Am. Acad. Physician

Assts., Tex. Acad. Physician Assts. (bd. dirs. 1998). Avocations: scuba, motorcycling, parachuting. Home: RR 3 Box 486 Mexia TX 76667-9301 Office: Paladin Healthcare Assocs PC 618 S 3rd St Wortham TX 76693-9722 E-mail: glee@mexia.com.

LEE, GREG W., food company executive; With Wal-Mart Stores, Inc., Swift & Co., Tyson Foods, Inc., 1980—, exec. v.p. sales, marketing, research and development and quality assurance, 1995—99, pres. food svc. group Springdale, Ark., 1999—2001, CO-COO, group pres., 2001—03, international pres., chief admin. officer, 2003—. Office: Tyson Foods Inc 2210 W Oaklawn Dr Springdale AR 72762-6999

LEE, GREGORY A., human resources specialist; BS in mktg., So. Ill. U. V.p. human resources PepsiCo, 1983—92; sr. v.p. human resources St. Paul Companies, 1992—98, Whirpool, 1998—2000, Sears, Roebuck and Co., 2001—. Bd. dirs. Boys and Girls Club of Chgo. Mem.: Human Resources Policy Assn. (bd. dirs.). Avocations: photography, woodworking, golf, history. Office: Sears Roebuck and Co 3333 Beverly Rd Hoffman Estates IL 60179 Office Phone: 847-286-2500. Office Fax: 847-286-7829.*

LEE, GREGORY PRICE, neuropsychology educator; b. Orange, N.J., July 3, 1952; s. John Landon and Olga (Squeo) Lee. BA in Psychology, U. No. Colo., 1975; MA in Clin. Psychology, Lone Mountain Coll., 1975; PhD in Clin. Psychology, Fla. Inst. Tech., 1980. Diplomate Am. Bd. Clin. Neuropsychology, Am. Bd. Profl. Psychology; lic. psychologist, Ga. Predoctoral intern Harlem Valley Psychiat. Ctr., White Plains, NY, 1977—79; instr. dept. psychology Coll. V.I., St. Thomas, 1981—82; rsch. assoc. Tex. Rsch. Inst. Mental Sci., Tex. Med. Ctr., Houston, 1983—84; postdoctoral fellow dept. psychology, sect. neuropsychology U. Houston, Baylor Coll. Medicine, 1983—84; postdoctoral fellow dept. neurology U. Wis. Med. Sch., Milw., 1984—86; dir. neuropsychology svc. neurosurgery and psychiatry Med. Coll. Ga., Augusta, 1986—2002, med. student ednl. enrichment program, 1987—2003, asst. prof. dept. neurology, 1986—2001, prof., 2001—. Dir. adult neuropsychology svc., reviewer work samples Am. Bd. Clin. Neuropsychology, 1989—; cons. editor Jour. of the Internat. Neuropsychol. Soc., 1994-97, Archives of Clin. Neuropsychology, 2002—; chair Med. Student Promotions Com. Med. Coll. Ga., 1989-2001, Med. Student Admissions Com., 1998-2001, course dir. Ga., Applied Pathophysiology, 2002—05, clin. rsch. I and II, 2001—05, Neuroscience, 2001-05, Brain & Behavior, 2003-05. Co-author: Amobarbital Effects and Lateralized Brain Function: The Wada Test; contbr. numerous articles to profl. jours.; contbr. chpts. to books. Mem. med. adv. com. Alzheimer's Disease and Related Disorders Assn., 1986-97; bd. dirs. Red Devil, Inc., 1985-92. Grantee, Med. Coll. of Ga. Found./Smith Kline Glaxo grantee, 2003—, Med. Coll. of Ga. Rsch. Inst. grantee, 2002—04, NIH/NINDS, 2003—, Berlex Labs. grantee, 2002—03. Fellow APA (divsn.40, membership program com. 2000—, chair awards com., 2000—), Nat. Acad. Neuropsychology (chair publs. com., mem.a investment com. 2001-04, program com. 2000-05); mem. Internat. Neuropsychol. Soc. (com. for dictionary neuropsychology 1987-98, editor neuroanatomy and neuropsychiatry sect. dictionary neuropsychology), Am. Acad. Neurology, Am. Epilepsy Soc., Sigma Xi. Office: Med Coll Ga Dept Neurology (BA-3278) 1120 15th St Augusta GA 30912-3275 Office Phone: 706-721-3851. E-mail: glee@mcg.edu.

LEE, H. HELEN, music educator; arrived in U.S., 1969; d. Chin Din Lee and Yeh Yin Lin; m. Mingyee Richard Lee, Dec. 12, 1969; children: Felix, Eileen. BA in Vocal Performance, Chinese Culture U., 1969; MusM in Vocal Performance, U. Nev., 1976. Resident solo artist BCC Network, Taipei, Taiwan, 1967—69; grad. tchg. asst. music Brigham Young U., Provo, Utah, 1969—71; voice instr. U. Nev., Reno, 1980—. Music adviser Sierra Nev. Chorale, Reno, 1979—, Melodia Sinica Choir, Northridge, Calif., 1993—97; music dir. Sierra Youth Choir, Reno, 1997—2000. Solo album, Favorite Folk Songs, 1968, Famous Arts Songs, 1969, solo performances, Lincoln Ctr., N.Y.C., 1983, Carnegie Hall, 1993, 1997; musician: (solo TV performance) skating music for Olympic Gold Medalist Figure Skater, Katarina Witt, 1996, concert tour to Japan. Named Nat. Winner Singing, Nat. Dept. Edn., Taipei, Taiwan, 1965, Dist. Winner, Met. Opera Co., Reno, 1976, Disting. Alumna, Chinese Culture U. Alumni, San Francisco, 1993. Mem.: Am. Univ. Profs. Assn., N.Am. Taiwanese Women's Assn. (music adviser 1997—), Internat. Honor Soc. for Internat. Scholars (chpt. pres. 1998—2001), Sigma Alpha Iota (patroness 1995—). Office: Univ Nev Music Dept 1664 N Virginia St MS226 Reno NV 89557 Office Phone: 775-784-6145.

LEE, HAMILTON H., education educator; b. Zhouxian, Shandong, China, Oct. 10, 1921; s. Beiyuen and Huaiying Lee; m. Jean Chang, Aug. 14, 1945; children: Wei, Clarence, Karen, Kate. BA, Nat. Beijing Normal U., 1948; MA, U. Minn., 1958; EdD, Wayne State U., 1964. Rsch. assoc. Wayne State U., Detroit, 1958-64; asst. prof. Moorhead (Minn.) State U., 1964-65; assoc. prof. U. Wis., LaCrosse, 1965-66; prof. edn. East Stroudsburg (Pa.) U., 1966—, now prof. emeritus. Vis. prof. Seton Hall U., summer 1964; vis. scholar Harvard U., summer 1965, 66; vis. fellow Princeton U., 1976-78; hon. mem. adv. coun. Internat. Biog. Ctr., Cambridge, Eng., 1995. Author: Readings in Instructional Technology, 1970, (chapbook I) Reflection, 1989, (chapbook II) Revelation, 1991; contbg. editor Edn. Tomorrow, 1972-74; contbr. articles and poetry to profl. jours. and anthologies. Recipient numerous poetry contest awards; fellow World Lit. Acad. Mem. World Future Soc. (profl.), Acad. Am. Poets, Poetry Soc. Am., Pa. Poetry Soc., Internat. Soc. Poets (life, adv. panel), Am. Biol. Inst. (rsch. bd.), Phi Delta Kappa. Home: 2694-4 Lenox Rd Atlanta GA 30324 Address: PO Box 980 Los Altos CA 94023-0980 also: 30 Hacienda Dr Woodside CA 94062-2420

LEE, HARLAN Y.M., small business owner, retired government agency administrator; b. Honolulu, July 3, 1945; s. Henry K.H. and Hattie Pang Lee, Nellie Chock Goo Lee (Stepmother); m. Mary Jane Williams, Oct. 29, 1977. BA, Stanford U., 1967; MA, U. Hawaii, 1978. Cert. mtg. profl. Conv. Industry Coun., 2002. Fgn. svc. officer U.S. Dept. State, Washington, 1968—95, ret., 1995; prin., owner Harlan Lee & Assocs. LLC, Falls Church, Va., 1996—. Bd. sec., chmn. supr. com. State Dept. Fed. Credit Union, Alexandria, Va., 1994—99. Office: Harlan Lee & Associates LLC 7700 Leesburg Pike Falls Church VA 22043 Office Phone: 703-442-7727.

LEE, HARRISON HON, librarian, consultant; b. Stockton, Calif., Sept. 20, 1943; s. Hon Bo and Lulu Joyce Lee; m. Estelle Toby Wlosko, May 11, 1980. AA, Stockton Coll., 1967; BA, Stanislaus State Coll., Turlock, Calif., 1969; MA, Sonoma State U., Cotati, Calif., 1973; MLS, Simmons Coll., 1978. Lectr. Ecole d'Humanite, Reuti, Switzerland, 1973-75; libr. M. Rosenblatt & Son, Inc., N.Y.C., 1978-89; libr. cons. SELF, Stockton, 1989—. Mem.: Soc. Naval Archs. and Marine Engrs., Spl. Libr. Assn. Unitarian Universalist. Personal E-mail: josun@msn.com.

LEE, HARRY ANTONIUS, allergist, immunologist; b. West Java, Indonesia, June 27, 1954; arrived in US, 1973, naturalized, 1991; s. Djoe Eng and Jan Nio (Tjan) L.; m. Johanna Francisca Setiawan, Nov. 23, 1977; children: Edwin Christopher, Vanessa Theresa. BS in Biology, magna cum laude, Fairmont State Coll., 1977; MD, St. George's U., 1982. Cert. allergy & immunology, pediat. Resident in pediat. Marshall U. Sch. Medicine, Huntington, W.Va., 1983-86; fellow in allergy and immunology U. South Fla./All Children's Hosp., St. Petersburg, 1989-91; chief Air U. Regional Hosp.-Maxwell AFB, Montgomery, Ala., 1991-93; with Bapt. Med. Ctr., Montgomery, 1994—, Jackson Hosp., Montgomery, 1994—. Contbr. articles to profl. jours. Maj. USAF, 1986—93. Decorated USAF Commendation medal; recipient Schering Travel award, Schering-Plough Pharm., 1990. Fellow Am. Acad. Pediats., Am. Acad. Allergy, Asthma, and Immunology, Am. Coll. Allergy, Asthma, and Immunology; mem. Ala. Soc. Allergy & Immunology (treas. 2004-05), Joint Coun. Allergy, Asthma, and Immunology, Med. Assn. State Ala., Soc. Air Force Physicians. Republican. Roman Catholic. Avocations: travel, golf, swimming, reading, computers. Office: Allergy Asthma & Immunology Montgomery 1420 Narrow Ln Pky Montgomery AL 36111-2654 Fax: 334-284-4256. Office Phone: 334-284-4196. Business E-Mail: dochlee@knology.net.

LEE, HELIE, writer; b. Seoul, S. Korea, Aug. 29, 1964; arrived in US, 1970; BS in Polit. Sci., UCLA, 1986. Mem. Asian Am. Writers Workshop. Writer (TV series) In Living Color, Saved By The Bell, Martin Lawrence Show; author: (novels) Still Life With Rice, 1996, In The Absence of Sun, 2002, (articles) Mademoiselle, Essence, KoreAm Journal. Office: c/o Harmony Books 1745 Broadway New York NY 10019*

LEE, HENRY C., forensic scientist; b. China, Nov. 22, 1938; came to U.S., 1965; s. An-Fu and Ho-Ming Lee; m. Margaret Song, 1962; children: Sherry, Stanley. Degree in Police Sci., Ctrl. Police Coll., Taiwan, Republic of China, 1960; BS in Forensic Sci., John Jay Coll. Criminal Justice, NYC, 1972; MS in Sci., NYU, 1974, PhD in Biochemistry, 1975; DSc (hon.), U. New Haven, West Haven, Conn., 1990; LHD (hon.), St. Joseph's Coll., West Hartford, Conn., 1996; LLD (hon.), Roger Williams U., RI, 1997; LHD (hon.), U. Bridgeport, Conn., 1999; DSc (hon.), Am. Internat. Coll., Springfield, Mass., 2002; attended several special tng. courses offered by the FBI Acad., ATF, post grad. schs., post med. schs. and profl. orgns. cert. Am. Bd. Criminalists, 1992. From police lt. to capt. Taipei Police Hdqs., Taiwan, 1960—63; newspaper reporter, editor; rsch. tech., biochemistry dept. NYU Med. Ctr., 1968—74, rsch. scientist, biochemistry dept., 1974—75; asst. prof. criminal justice U. New Haven, West Haven, Conn., 1975—77, assoc. prof. forensic sci., 1977—78, prof. forensic sci., program chmn., 1978, dir. forensic sci. lab., 1975—79, dir., Ctr. of Applied Rsch., 1977—80, disting. prof., 2000—; dir., founder HCL Inst. Forensic Sci., 1996; chief criminologist Conn. State Police Forensic Lab., Meriden, 1980—2000, lab. dir., 1980—2000; commr., Conn. State Police Dept. Pub. Safety, 1998—2000, chief emeritus, divsn. scientific svcs., 2000—. DNA analysis expert in cases including Helle Crafts, William Kennedy Smith, O.J. Simpson, among others; assisted prosecutors across the country and the world with difficult forensic investigations including mass grave identification in Bosnia and Herzegovina, Branch Davidian (Waco, Tex.) cult; cons. in cases including reivestigation of Sacco-Vanzetti affair, JonBenet Ramsey murder, John F. Kennedy assassination, and Vincent Foster's death; served as expert witness, testified and investigated several criminal and civil cases; cons. to NJ Burlington County Forensic Sci. Lab., Conn. State Pub. Defender's Office, Tech. Adv. Svcs. for Attys., Pa., PRC Pub. Mgmt. Svcs., Vir. U. Ala., John Jay Coll. of Criminal Justice, NYC, U. SC, Elmira Coll., NYC, Nat. Inst. Justice, Maine State Police, Del. Dept. Justice, Allegheny County Dept. Lab., Pa., Rothman Arch. Inc., Mass., County of Prince William, Va., Pub. Defender's Office, Sullivan County, NY, NJ, Del., Dist. Atty's office, Cambridge, Mass., Anchorage, State Atty's Office, Va. Beach, Miami, Taiwan Nat. Police Criminal Investigation Bur., Bur. Investigation, Ministry of Justice, Taiwan, Dept. Pub. Safety, State Miss., Jackson, Miss., Crown Atty's office, Ottawa, Can., and Hawaii Police Dept., Hilo, Hawaii and others; guest lectr. several prominent univs. and acads.; instr. Nat. Coll. Dist. Atty's., 1986, Mcpl. Police Tng. Acad., Meriden, Conn., 1980, Conn. State Police Acad., 1980; vis. prof., Bilingual Edn., Seton Hall U., 1976, Sch. Law, People's U., Peking, China, 1985; adj. prof., Forensic Sci. Program, Inst. Chemical Analysis, Northeastern U., Mass., 1977-79, forensic sci. program, sch. criminal justice, Northeastern U., 1983, dept. adminstrn. justice, Western Conn. State U., 1984, biology dept., biology program, grad. program, Bridgeport U., Conn., forensic sci. program, John Jay Coll. Criminal Justice, CUNY, 1987, U. Conn. Sch. Law, 1992 & 2000, dept. sociology, Ctrl. Conn. State U., 1993, Tze An Med. Sch., China, 1998, Quinnipiac U. Law Sch., Hamden, Conn., 1998-; vis. faculty, biochemistry detp., Yale U., New Haven, Conn., 1978; Disting. prof., criminology, Ctrl. Conn. U., 2000, rsch. prof., U. Conn., 2000; prof., Pub. Safety U. & Criminal Police Coll., People's Republic of China; instructed/conducted several courses, workshops, and seminars. Author and co-author of more than 30 books and monographs on forensic sci.; contbr. more than 300 articles to profl. jours.; editor fot the following jours.: Hwa-Lian Daily News, Forensic Serology News, Jour. of Forensic Sci., Crime Lab. Digest, Advances in Forensic Scis., Jour. Forensic Identification, Great Crime Cases, Forensic Sci. Review, Crime Lab. Digest, FBI, Am. Jour. Forensic Pathology, Ency. Forensic Scis.; featured in Trace Evidence: The Case Files of Dr. Henry Lee, Court TV, 2005. Docent scholarship fund U. New Haven, Conn. Dept. Pub. Safety; mem., Forensic Serology Cert. Com. Nat. Inst. Justice/Acad. Forensic Sci, 1978, Conn. State Rape Com., Dept. Health/ Dept. Public Safety, 1980, Forensic Scis. Svcs. Comt, Conn. Justice Com., 1981, Nat. Steering Com. Arson Evidence, ATF/NBS, 1982, Ad Hoc Com. on the Reliability of Genetic Marker Typing in Blood and Body Fluid Stains, AAFS, 1984; chmn., Forensic Science Operation and Program Com., FBI/ ASCLD, 1985, Capitol Region Investigative Support Team, 1991; accreditation inspector, Am. Crime Lab. Accreditation, 1983; assoc. referee. forensic sci., Assn. Official Analytical Chemists, 1981; Chief Del., Chinese-Am. Police Conf., Taipei, Taiwan, 1986; bd. dir., University of New Haven, 1987; com. mem., Nat. Orgn. Against Liquor in Candy for Children, 1987, Conn. State Rape Com., 1987; Oral Boards, Mass. State Police, Framingham, MA, 1997. Recipient Disting. Svc. award. for distinguished svc. in criminal investigation., Taipei Police Hdqs., 1962, Commendation award, Greenburgh Police Dept. for assistance in solving homicide case, 1976, Alumni Achievement award, John Jay College of Criminal Justice for achievement, contribution and svcs. in forensic science, 1979, 1990, Disting. Mgr. Award, Gov. Connecticut, 1982, State Conn. General Assembly Citation received in recognition of disting.managerial svcs., 1982, Recognition Citation, Conn. State General Assembly for distinguished svc. to the State of Connecticut in solving difficult crimes, 1983, Special award, Conn. Divsn. Criminal Justice in recognition of the svc. to the criminal justice system, 1984, Lewis Memorial Lecture award, St. Joseph's College Chemistry Club, 1984, Special award. Connecticut Law Foundation for innovation and dedication to the advancement of professionalism in law enforcement, 1984, Recognition award, The People's University of China in recognition of outstanding svc. to forensic science and training, 1985, Lecture award, Am. Chemical Soc., Hartford State Technical Coll., 1986, Disting. Svc. award, Acad. of Forensic Scis. for outstanding contribution to criminalistics and forensic science, 1986, Commendation award, Criminal Investigation Bur., Taiwan Nat. Police for outstanding contribution in criminal investigation and training, Police medal, The Ministry of Interior, Republic of China, distinguished svcs. in police work, 1986, Alumni award, The Central Police Coll., Taiwan, Republic of China for outstanding achievements and svcs. to the community, 1989, J. Donero award, Internat. Assn. for Identification, 1989, Svc. Award, Am. Bd. Criminalistics, 1990, Svc. award, ATF, 1990, Svc. award, Taiwan Criminal Investigation Bur., 1991, Disting. Svc. award, Police Commr. Assn. Conn., Inc., Norwalk, 1992, Appreciation award, NH State Police, Concord, 1993, Svc. award, Drug Enforcement Agency, 1995, VIDOCQ Medal of Honor, VIDOCQ Soc., Phila., 1996, Alfred C. Fones award, Conn. State Dental Assn.,1996, NESCAN award, New England Coll. Sexual Assault Network, Storrs, CT, 1996, State Ethics award, presented by State Ethics Comm., Hartford,1996; named Hon. Deputy Sheriff. Middlesex County Sheriff's Assn., Hon. Deputy Sheriff. Bergen County Sheriff's Office, NJ, Hon. Captain. Maine State Police, Maine, Hon. Lt. Colonel, State Ga., Hon. Tex. Lawman, State Tex. Fellow Am. Acad. Forensic Sci., Disting. Fellow, 1990, chmn. nomination com., 1983, 1984, chmn., Ad Hoc Com. on DNA Typing, 1989, 1990, 1991), Northeastern Assn. Forensic Scientists (reg. dir., 1977-80, chmn., Ethics Com., 1978, 1980), Forensic Sci. Soc., England, Am. Acad. Criminal Justice, Northeastern Criminal Justice Educator's Assn., Internat. Assn. Identification (Cert. Latent Fingerprint Examiner, com. chmn. 1985, disting. mem., 1988, mem., lab. safety com., 1985, mem. Scholarship Com., 1985, publication com., 1986, advisor, crime scene cert. com., 1987, chmn., forensic lab. analysis com., 1988), NY Acad. Sci., AAAS, Am. Soc. for Testing and Materials, Am. Soc. of Crime Laboratory (dir., bd. dir., chmn., edn. and tng. com., 1980, 1982, 1986, 1990), Internat. Assn. Forensic Sci., Assn. Official Analytical Chemists, (Referee 1980), Conn. Chromatography Coun., Fingerprint Society, England (Fellow, 1984), Internat. Assn. Bloodpattern Analysis (reg. v.p., 1987), Puerto Rico Forensic Scis. Assn. (hon. mem.), Fla. Homicide Investigators Assn. (hon. mem.), Conn. Arson Investigator Assn. (hon. mem.), Internat. Homicide Detective's Assn, (Advisor, 1990), Internat. Assn. Bloodstain Analysts (v.p., 1990). Avocations: cooking, gardening, chinese calligraphy, fossils. Office: Dept Pub Safety 278 Colony St Meriden CT 06451 Address: U New Haven Forensic Science Program 300 Orange Ave West Haven CT 06516 also: Forensic Rsch and Tng Ctr 82 Limewood Ave Branford CT 06405 Office Phone: 203-639-6400, 203-932-6119, 203-488-1475. Office Fax: 203-639-6485.*

LEE, HI YOUNG, physician, acupuncturist; b. Seoul, Republic of Korea, Oct. 18, 1941; arrived in U.S., 1965, naturalized, 1976; s. Jung S. and Hwa J. (Kim) Lee; m. Sun M. Lee, June 4, 1965; children: Sandra, Grace, David. MD, Yon Sei U., Seoul, 1965. Diplomate Am. Bd. Family Practice. Intern Grasslands Hosp., Valhalla, NY, 1965-66; resident VA Hosp., Dayton, Ohio, 1966-70; mem. staff Eastern State Hosp., Medical Lake, Wash., 1970-74; practice family medicine, acupuncturist Empire Med. Office, Spokane, Wash., 1974—. Active staff St. Lukes Meml. Hosp., Spokane, 1974—; courtesy staff Deaconess Med. Ctr., Spokane, 1974—, Sacred Heart Med. Ctr., Spokane, 1974—; sr. disability analyst, diplomate Am. Bd. Disability Analysts, 2000. Author: Von Recklinghousen's Disease, 1970; columnist: Rainier Forum Korea Post Weekly News, 1996—. Trustee St. Georges Prep Sch., Wash., 1986—; elder First Presbyn. Ch., Spokane, 1975. Fellow: Am. Acad. Family Practice; mem.: Christian Med. Soc., Ctr. Chinese Medicine, Nat. Acupuncture Rsch. Soc., Spokane County Med. Soc. Home: 2006 W Liberty Ave Spokane WA 99205-2570 Office: Empire Med Office 17 E Empire Ave Spokane WA 99207-1707 Personal E-mail: drhileemd@yahoo.com.

LEE, HOWARD D., academic administrator; B Indsl. Edn., M Indsl. Edn., U. Wis., Stout; PhD Edn., U. Minn., 1981. Grad. program dir. master's program vocat. and tech. edn. U. Wis., exec. dir. Stout Solutions Menomonie, 2002—. Office: U Wis Stout Solutions 140 Vocat Rehab Bldg Menomonie WI 54751-0790

LEE, HOWARD DOUGLAS, academic administrator; b. Louisville, Ky., Mar. 15, 1943; s. Howard W. and Margaret (Davidson) L.; m. Margaret Easley, Nov. 20, 1965; children: Gregory Davidson, Elizabeth Anna. BA in English, U. Richmond, 1964; ThM, Southeastern Seminary, Wake Forest, N.C., 1968; PhD in Religion, U. Iowa, Iowa City, 1971. Prof. religion, devel. dir. Va. Intermont Coll., Bristol, 1971-73; dir. univ. relations Wake Forest (N.C.) U., 1973-78; v.p. devel. Stetson U., DeLand, Fla., 1978-80, v.p. planning and devel., 1980-83, exec. v.p., 1984-86, pres.-elect, 1986-87, pres., 1987—. Contbr. articles to profl. jours. Founding dir. Atlantic Ctr. for Arts, New Smyrna Beach, Fla., 1978—; chmn. DeLand C. of C., 1994; chair Volusia Vision Com., 1994-96. Mem. So. Assn. Colls. and Schs. (exec. coun. 1993-94), Rotary, Deland Country Club, Omicron Delta Kappa. Avocations: running, golf, wood carving, woodworking/antiques, reading. Office: Stetson U Campus Box 8258 421 N Woodland Blvd Deland FL 32720-3761

LEE, HOWARD N., educational association administrator; b. Lithonia, Ga., July 28, 1934; m. Lillian Lee; 3 children. BA, Ft. Valley State Coll., 1959; MSW, U. N.C., 1966. Mem. faculty U. N.C., Chapel Hill; mem. N.C. Senate, Raleigh, 1990—94, 1997—2003; chmn. N.C. State Bd. of Edn., Raleigh, 2003—. Chmn. appropriations on edn. and higher edn. com., edn. and higher edn. com., mem. appropriations/base budget com., fin. com., inf. tech. com., judiciary II com., vice chmn. commerce com., transp. com. Mayor, Chapel Hill, NC, 1969—75; sec. N.C. Dept. Environment and Natural Resources, 1977—81. With U.S. Army, 1959—61, with USAR, 1961—63. Democrat. also: 109 Glenview Pl Chapel Hill NC 27514-1948 Office: NC State Bd of Edn 301 N Wilmington St 6302 Mail Svc Ctr Raleigh NC 27699-6302 also: Dobbs Bldg Raleigh NC 27699-6302 Personal E-mail: hlee@nc.rr.com.

LEE, HWA-WEI, librarian, educator, consultant; b. Guangdong, China, Dec. 7, 1933; came to U.S., 1957, naturalized, 1962; s. Luther Kan-Chun and Mary Hsiao-Huei (Wang) L.; m. Mary F. Kratochvil, Mar. 14, 1959; children: Shirley, James, Pamela, Edward, Charles, Robert. BEd, Nat. Taiwan Normal U., 1954; MEd, U. Pitts., 1959, PhD, 1964; MLS, Carnegie Mellon U., 1961. Asst. libr. U. Pitts. Librs., 1959-62; head tech. svcs. Duquesne U. Libr., Pitts., 1962-65; head libr. U. Pa., Edinboro, 1965-68; dir. libr. and info. ctr. Asian Inst. Tech., Bangkok, 1968-75; assoc. dir. librs., prof. libr. adminstrn. Colo. State U., Fort Collins, 1975-78; dean librs., prof. Ohio U., Athens, 1978-99, dean emeritus, librs., 1999—; disting. vis. scholar OCLC, 2000—02; chief Asian divsn. Libr. of Congress, 2003—. Fulbright sr. specialist, 2001; cons. FAO, UNESCO, U.S. AID, World Bank, Internat. Devel. Rsch. Ctr., Asia Found., OCLC; del.-at-large White House Conf. Libr. and Info. Svcs., 1991. Author: Librarianship in World Perspectives, 1991, Fundraising for the 1990s: The Challenge Ahead, 1992, Modern Library Management, 1996, Knowledge Management: Theory and Practice, 2002; exec. editor Jour. Ednl. Media and Libr. Sci., 1982—; mem. editl. bd. Internat. Comm. in Libr. Automation, 1975-76, Jour. Libr. and Info. Sci., 1975-78, Libr. Acquisition: Practice and Theory, 1976-83; adv. bd. Jour. Info., Comm. and Libr. Sci., 1994—; contbr. articles to profl. jours. Recipient Disting. Svc. award Libr. Assn. of China (Taiwan), 1989; new bldg. on Ohio U. campus named in his honor: Hwa-wei Lee Libr. Annex, and 1st flr. of the main libr.: Hwa-wei Lee Ctr. for Internat. Collections, 1999. Mem. ALA (councilor 1988-92, 93-97, John Ames Humphry/Forest Press award 1991), Acad. Libr. Assn. Ohio, Am. Soc. Info. Sci., Asian-Pacific Am. Librs. Assn. (Disting. Svc. award 1991), Internat. Fedn. Libr. Assns. and Instns. (standing com. univ. librs. and other gen. rsch. librs. 1989-93), Assn. Coll. and Rsch. Librs. Chinese-Am. Librs. Assn. (Disting. Svc. award 1983), Internat. Assn. Orientalist Librs., Ohio Libr. Coun. (bd. dirs. 1991-92, Libr. of the Yr. 1987, Hall of Fame Libr. 1999), Online Computer Libr. Ctr. (users coun. 1987-91), Ohio Chinese Acad. and Profl. Assn. (founding pres. 1988-90). Home: 2800 Clarendon Blvd W608 Arlington VA 22201 Office: Libr of Congress Asian Divsn Washington DC 20540 Office Phone: 202-707-5919. Business E-Mail: hlee@loc.gov.

LEE, IARA, filmmaker; Co-founder, acting pres. Calpirinha Prodns., N.Y.C. Filmmaker: Prufrock, 1991; Neighbors, 1992 (Best of Festival, Dysfunctional Family Film Festival Chgo., 1993, Jury prize Rochester Internat. Film Festival, 1993, Silver award Houston Internat. Film Festival, 1993, Bronze award Festival Der Nationen-Ebensee, Germany, 1993); An Autumn Wind, 1993; Synthetic Pleasures, Modulations--cinema for the ear, 1998; participant numerous festival screenings including:, 1992, 1992; Karlsruhe Film Festival, 1992; Hawaii Internat. Film Festival, 1992; Film Front Film Festival, 1992; Ind. Feature Film Market, 1992, 1993; Mill Valley Film Festival, 1993; Internat. Film Festival Dhaka, 1993; Worldfest Houston, 1993; New Orleans Film and Video Festival, 1993; St. Petersburg Internat. Film Festival, 1994; Social Outcast Film and Video Festival, 1994; others. Office: C/O The Presidio 39 Mesa St Ste 300 San Francisco CA 94129-1019

LEE, IN-YOUNG, lawyer; b. In-Cheon, Kyonggi-do, Korea, Dec. 5, 1952; came to U.S. 1978; s. In-Seok and Hyun-Bo (Rim) L.; m. Young-Lae Hong, July 1, 1978; children: Casey K., Brian K. LLB, Seoul Nat. U., Korea, 1975; LLM, Harvard U., 1980; JD, UCLA, 1983. Bar: Ill. 1983, N.Y. 1987, D.C. 1989, U.S. Ct. Internat. Trade. Assoc. Baker & McKenzie, Chgo., 1983—86, Marks & Murase, N.Y.C., 1986—87, Baker & McKenzie, N.Y.C., 1987—91; ptnr. Marks & Murase, N.Y.C., 1991—96, McDermott, Will & Emery, N.Y.C., 1996—. Gen. counsel Korean C. of C. and Industry in USA, Inc., 1993—, Assn. Korean Fin. Instns. Am., Inc. Articles editor Pacific Basin Law Jour. Presbyterian. Avocations: fishing, golf. Office: McDermott Will & Emery 50 Rockefeller Plz Fl 11 New York NY 10020-1600 E-mail: ilee@mwe.com.

LEE, J. PATRICK, academic administrator; b. Leitchfield, Ky., Nov. 30, 1942; s. Herman G. and Josephine (Pearl) L.; m. Louise Sipple, June 8, 1972. BA, Brescia Coll., 1963; postgrad., U. Paris, 1966-67; PhD, Fordham U., 1971. Asst. prof. French Brescia Coll., Owensboro, Ky., Univ. of Ga., Athens, Ga.; v. p. acad. affairs Belmont N.C. Abbey Coll.; provost Barry Univ., Miami, Fla. Researcher 18th Century French lit., Voltaire works. Woodrow Wilson fellow, 1963, Danforth fellow, 1963-67, Fulbright fellow, 1966-67. Mem. AAUP (exec. bd.), SEASECS (exec. bd., past pres.), Delta Epsilon Sigma (nat. sec./treas.), Phi Beta Kappa. Home: 1341 NE 103rd St Miami FL 33138-2623

LEE, JACK (JIM SANDERS BEASLEY), broadcast executive; b. Buffalo Valley, Tenn., Apr. 14, 1936; s. Jesse McDonald and Nelle Viola (Sanders) Beasley; m. Barbara Sue Looper, Sept. 1, 1961; children: Laura Ann, Elizabeth Jane, Sarah Kathleen. Student, Wayne State U., 1955-57; BA, Albion Coll., 1959. Announcer Sta. WHUB-AM, Cookeville, Tenn., 1956; news dir., program dir. Sta. WALM-AM, Albion, Mich., 1957-59; radio-TV personality WKZO-Radio-TV, Kalamazoo, 1960-62; prodn. dir. Stas. WKMH-WKNR, Detroit, 1962-63; gen. mgr. Sta. WAUK-AM-FM, Waukesha, Wis., 1963-65; asst. program mgr. Sta. WOKY, Milw., 1965-70; program mgr. Sta. WTMJ-WKTI, Milw., 1970-76; gen. mgr. Sta. WEMP-WMYX, Milw., 1976-88; pres. Jack Lee Enterprises Ltd., Milw., 1977—; pres., CEO, Milw. Area Radio Stas., 1989—. Instr. dept. mass comm. U. Wis.-Milw., 1972-81. With U.S. Army, 1959, 61-62; maj. CAP, 1964-01, ret. Decorated Army Commendation medal; cert. radio mktg. cons., Broadcasters Hall of Fame, 1999; Milw. Air awards Lifetime Achievement, 2003 Mem. AFTRA, Actors Equity, Omicron Delta Kappa, Alpha Epsilon Rho. Home and Office: W277 W N Chicory Ln # 2793 Pewaukee WI 53072 Office Phone: 262-691-3707. E-mail: jbeasley@wi.rr.com. *It is a constant struggle to balance my greatest gift—the ability to express myself—with my biggest failing—the inability to keep my mouth shut.*

LEE, JAEJIN, computer scientist; b. Gyeongju, South Korea, Aug. 13, 1967; s. Young-Hee Lee and Young-Hee Sohn; m. Yookyung Chung, Mar. 14, 1975; 1 child, Sungho. PhD, U. Ill. Urbana-Champaign, 1999. Asst. prof. Mich. State U., Lansing, 2000—02; assoc. prof. Seoul Nat. U., Republic of Korea, 2002—. Vis. lectr. U. Ill. at Urbana-Champaign, 1999. Cpl. Korean Army, 1991—92, Korea. Recipient Best Paper Award, 5th Workshop on Multi-threaded Execution, Architecture and Compilation, 2001; IBM Coop. Fellowship, IBM, 1997-1999. Mem.: IEEE, Assn. Computing Machinery, Korea Informaiton Sci. Soc. (life). Office: Seoul National Univ Sch Computer Sci & Engring Seoul 151-744 Republic of Korea Office Phone: +82-2-880-1863. Personal E-mail: jlee@cse.snu.ac.kr.

LEE, JAMES A., health facility finance executive; b. Red Level, Ala., Dec. 19, 1939; s. H. Alton Lee; m. Charlotte Phillips, Dec. 19, 1963 (div. July 1971); children: Phillip, Michele, Jenifer; m. Melanie Cooper, Dec. 14, 1973; children: Christopher, Amanda. BBA in Acctg., Jacksonville State U., 1964; MS in Hosp. and Health Adminstrn., U. Ala., 1980. CPA, Ala. Sr. acct. Macke, Eldredge, McIntosh, Birmingham, Ala., 1964-67, Touche, Ross, Bailey & Smart, Birmingham, 1967-68; bus. functions mgr. Druid City Hosp., Tuscaloosa, Ala., 1968-71; sr. assoc. adminstr., fin. Univ. Ala. Hosp., Birmingham, 1971-94; CFO Montgomery Cardiovasc. Assocs., PC, 1994—. Asst. prof. health services adminstrn. Univ. Ala. Birmingham, 1980—; asst. prof. Dept. Pub. Health, Univ. Ala. Birmingham, 1984—. Mem. AICPA, Health Care Fin. Mgmt. Assn., Ala. Soc. CPAs. Republican. Baptist. Home: 109 Pemberton Pl Pelham AL 35124-2817 E-mail: jleecpa@aol.com.

LEE, JAMES ALAN, writer, editor; b. Windber, Pa., Oct. 4, 1958; s. Robert Lohman Lee and Catherine Alene Machtley. Student, Univ. Pitts., Johnstown, Pa., 1976—78. Contbr. articles over 1,700 pub. to profl. jour. Mem.: So. Alleghenies Writers Guild (pres. 1987—93, sec./treas. 1993—), Penn Writers Inc. Democrat. Avocations: gardening, hiking, reading. Home and Office: 801-26th St Windber PA 15963

LEE, JAMES EDWARD, JR., educational consultant; b. Pitts., Mar. 9, 1939; s. Willard and Gladys Hilda (Jenkins) L.; children: Stephen Michael, Monica Michelle, Brian Patrick, Priscilla Demone. BS, Wayne State U., 1962, EdS, 1969; MA, U. Mich., 1964; postgrad., Mich. State U., Wayne State U., U. Minn., U. Colo., 1964—65, Ctrl. Mich. U. Cert. tchr., adminstr., Mich. Tchr. Miller, Durfee and Michael Jr. High Schs., Detroit, 1962—67; team leader Nat. Tchr. Corps, Detroit, 1967—69; dept. head Noble Jr. High Sch., Detroit, 1969—74; asst. prin. MacKenzie High Sch., Detroit, 1974—80, Drew Mid. Sch., Detroit, 1980, prin., 1980—97. Chandler Park Acad., Detroit, 1997—98; ops. supr. Detroit Mfg. Partnership, 1999—2000; exec. dir. Detroit Pub. Schs., 2000—01; prin. Rivers Mid. Sch., Charleston, SC, 2001—02, ednl. cons., 2002—; prin. mentor, coach Detroit Pub. Schools, 2004—. Instr. Wayne State U., Detroit, 1967-69, edn. cons., 1970-71; instr. Wayne C.C., 1967-81; prin. adult evening sch., 1974-80, summer gifted program, Detroit, 1986-92; profl. stds. commn. for sch. adminstrs. Mich. Dept. Edn., 1992-96, adminstrv. waiver com., 1992-94; mem. sch. improvement team Wayne County Regional Ednl. Svc. Agy., 1996-97. Contbg. author: The Development of Micro Teaching as an Evaluative Instrument in Teacher Training, 1969, (manual) The Principalship, 1990. Co-chair ednl. audit com. Oak Park (Mich.) Sch., 1988-90; bd. dirs. Scott Community Ctr., Detroit, 1988-97; adv. bd. Adrian/Scott Program To Inspire Readiness for Ednl. Success, Detroit, 1990-97; adv. coun. Christ Child House, Detroit, 1990-92. With USMC, 1956-58. Recipient Prins. and Educators award Booker T. Washington Bus. Assn., Detroit, 1986, 90, Citation for Outstanding Leadership Detroit Bd. Edn., 1986; named finalist Boss of Yr., Detroit chpt. Am. Bus. Women's Assn., 1987. Mem. Nat. Assn. Secondary Sch. Prins., Nat. Mid. Sch. Assn., Mich. Assn. Supervision and Curriculum Devel., Mich. Assn. Secondary Sch. Prins. (exec. bd. 1986-88, Outstanding Mid. Level Prin. of Yr. 1991), Mich. Assn. Mid. Sch. Educators (bd. dirs. 1988-91). Avocation: tennis. Home: 16500 North Park Dr Apt 1117 Southfield MI 48075 Office Phone: 248-443-7169.

LEE, JAMES WADE, humanities educator, writer, actor; b. Lansing, Mich., Mar. 13, 1945; s. James Lester Lee and Thelma Evelyn (Marrison) Lee Parks; m. Erin Gail Taylor (div.); 1 child, Robert Clifford. AA, L.A. City Coll., 1971; BA, Calif. State U., L.A., 1978, MA, 1979; PhD, U. Utah, 1984; LLB, Blackstone Sch. Law, Chgo., 1971. Actor, scriptwriter, L.A., 1968-80; performer, copywriter Salt Lake City, 1980-88; dean acad. affairs Salt Lake City Coll., 1985-87; actor, scriptwriter Las Vegas, Nev., 1988-96; mng. editor Am. Lit. Svc., Las Vegas and Clovis, N.Mex., 1990—; instr. Clovis (N.Mex.) C.C., 1997—. Part-time lectr. U. Nev., Las Vegas, 1988-89; adj. prof. Nat. U., Las Vegas, 1988-90; adj. asst. prof. Embry-Riddle Aero. U., Clovis, 1996—; founder Sho'Biz Job Finder, L.A., 1973. Author various stage plays, 1971-84, including Will Someone Please Tell me What's Going On Here?, 1974; author: (ednl. video) How to Study, 1988. Mem. MLA, SAG (under profl. name Lee James), Masquer's Club (Hollywood). Avocations: drawing, painting, music, cooking, developing new talented writers, innovation in higher education.

LEE, JANET MENTORE, psychologist, educator; b. NYC, July 21, 1972; d. Percy Edward and Celina Mentore (Stepmother); m. Ryan Todd Lee, Aug. 5, 2000; 1 child, Jordyn Olivia. BA, Ithaca Coll., 1994; MS in Edn., Fordham U., 1997, PhD, 1999. Lic. psychologist Conn., 2001, N.Y., 2001, cert. sch. psychologist Conn., 2000, N.Y., 1999. Psychologist Westport (Conn.) Pub. Schs., 2000—. Psychologist Hawthorne (N.Y.) Union Free Sch. Dist., 1999—2000; adj. asst. prof. Fordham U., N.Y.C., 2000—03, Fairfield (Conn.) U., 2002—03; panelist Conn. State Advanced Learning Disability Seminar, 2002—03; presenter in field. Advisory editor: The School Psychologist-APA; contbr. articles to profl. jours. Bd. mem. Cmty. Free Dems., N.Y.C., 1997—99. Grad. Assistantship, Fordham U., 1995—99, Internat. Congress on Obesity scholar, Pfizer Pharmaceuticals, 1998. Mem.: NASP, APA (Hon. Mention Outstanding Dissertation award Divsn. 16 2000), Conn. Assn. Sch. Psychologists, Conn. Psychol. Assn., N.Y. Assn. Sch. Psychologists (Ted Bernstein Outstanding Student award 1999), N.Y. State Psychol. Assn. (future psychologists sect. chair 1997—99, Conv. scholar 1998, Spl. Citation award 1999). Democrat. Achievements include co-investigator baseline levels of obesity and weight gain among patients taking antipsychotic medications. Home: 55 Kelley Green New Canaan CT 06840 Office: Westport Public Schs/Long Lots Elem 13 Hyde Ln Westport CT 06880 Office Phone: 203-341-1933. Personal E-mail: jmentore@yahoo.com. E-mail: jmlee@westport.k12.ct.us.

LEE, JANIE C., curator; b. Shreveport, La., Apr. 22, 1937; d. Birch Lee and Joanna (Glassell) Wood; m. David B. Warren, Jan. 2, 1980. Student, Nat. Cathedral Sch., 1951-55; BA, Sarah Lawrence Coll., 1959. Asst. to Cheryl Crawford, Actors Studi o, N.Y.C., 1962-63; co-prodr. Off Broadway Theatre Co., N.Y.C., 1963-65; owner, pres. Janie C. Lee Gallery, Dallas, 1967-74, Houston, 1973-96, Janie C. Lee Master Drawings, N.Y.C., 1983-96; curator of drawings Whitney Mus. Am. Art, 1997—2004. Mem. art appraisal panel IRS, Washington, 1987-94; trustee Menil Found., Inc., 2000—. Prodr. ann. catalogue on 20th Century drawings, 1979-93. Mem. Alumnae Bd. Sarah Lawrence Coll. (1972-74); pres. Nancy Graves Found., 1996—. Mem. Art Dealers Assn. Am. (bd. dirs. 1980-88, 92-94, v.p. 1984-88). Office: 3711 San Felipe # 4E Houston TX 77027 Office Phone: 713-355-5300. E-mail: janieclee@aol.com.

LEE, JEN-SHIH, biomedical engineering educator; b. Kwangtong, China, Aug. 22, 1940; parents Y. and Yao-Ze (Lai) L.; m. Lian-Pin Ma Lee, June 11, 1966; children: Lionel, Grace, Albert. BS, Nat. Taiwan U., 1961; MS, Calif. Inst. Tech., 1963, PhD, 1966. Advance rsch. fellow San Diego Heart Assn., U. Calif., San Diego, 1966-69; asst. prof. dept. Biomedical Engring. U. Va., Charlottesville, 1969-74, assoc. prof., 1974-83, prof., 1983—, chmn. dept. Biomedical Engring., 1988—. Editor: Microvascular Mechanics, 1988; assoc. editor Jour. Biomech. Engring., 1987-93; contbr. articles to Jour. Applied Physiology, Jour. Biomech. Engring., others. Recipient Rsch. Career Devel. award NIH, 1974-80. Fellow ASME, Am. Inst. Med. and Biol. Engring., Am. Physiol. Soc.; mem. IEEE, Microcirculatory Soc., Biomed. Engring. Soc. (bd. dirs. 1991-93, pres. 1994-95), Coun. of Socs. Am. Inst. Med. and Biol. Engring. (bd. dirs. 1995-97, chair 1995-97). Office: U Va Health Sci Ctr Dept Biomed Engring PO Box 337 Charlottesville VA 22902-0337 Home: PO Box 5777 Charlottesville VA 22905-5777

LEE, JEROME G., lawyer; b. Chgo., Feb. 23, 1924; m. Margo B. Lee, Dec. 23, 1947; children: James A., Kenneth M. BSChemE, U. Wis., 1947; JD, NYU, 1950. Bar: N.Y. 1950, U.S. Supreme Ct. 1964. Assoc. Jeffery, Kimball, Eggleston, N.Y.C., 1950-52, Morgan, Finnegan, Durham & Pine, N.Y.C., 1952-59; ptnr. Morgan, Finnegan, Pine, Foley & Lee, N.Y.C., 1959-86; sr. ptnr. Morgan & Finnegan, N.Y.C., 1986-95, of counsel, 1995—. Lectr. in field. Author (with J. Gould): Intellectual Property Counseling and Litigation, 1988; author: USPTO Proposals to Change Rule 56 and the Related Rules Regarding a Patent Applicant's Duty of Candour, Patent World, 1992; contbr. articles to legal jours. Fellow: Am. Bar Found.; mem.: ABA (mem. coun. intellectual property law sect., chmn. com. fed. practice and procedure, chmn. com. Ct. Appeals Fed. Cir., chmn. com. ethics and profl. responsibility, mem. stds. com., mem. fed. cir. adv. com. 1992—97), ATLA, others, N.Y. Patent, Trademark and Copyright Law Assn. (bd. dirs. 1975—80, pres. 1981), N.Y. County Bar Assn., Assn. Bar City of N.Y., N.Y. Bar Assn., Found. Creative Am. (bd. dirs.), Internat. Fedn. Indsl. Property Attys., Am. Judicature Soc., Am. Intellectual Property Law Assn. (bd. dirs. 1984—90, pres. 1991). Office: Morgan and Finnegan 3 World Financial Ctr New York NY 10281-2101 Home: 3328 Sabal Cove Ln Longboat Key FL 34228 Office Phone: 212-415-8700.

LEE, JHEMON HOM, physician; b. Redwood City, Calif., July 1, 1970; s. Billy Tom and Yuen Han Lee. BA in Engring. summa cum laude, Harvard U., 1990; MD cum laude, U. Md., 1994. Diplomate Nat. Bd. Med. Examiners. Residency in diagnostic radiology U. Chicago, 1994—98; fellowship in abdominal imaging Brigham and Women's Hospital/ Harvard Med. Hosp., Boston, 1998—99; vice chair, radiology dept. Los Alamitos Med. Ctr., Los Alamitos, Calif.; radiologist, ptnr. MemRAD Med. Group, Long Beach, Calif. Bd. dir. Radiologic Practice Mgmt., Inc. Editor-in-chief UMAB news, 1993; news editor East Wind, 1987-90; contbr. articles to profl. jours. Mem. steering com. United Asian Am. Orgns., Chgo., 1996-98; mem. Leadership Ctr. for Asian Ams., Chgo., 1997-98. Mem. Radiol. Soc. N.Am., Nat. Assn. Asian Am. Professionals (nat. pres., 1998-2000, exec. v.p., 2002-04; Lifetime Achievement award, 2002), Chgo. Radiol. Soc., Asian Pacific Am. Med. Students Assn. (pres. adv. bd.), Asian Profl. Exchange (chair, Healthcare Spl. Interest Group, dir. profl. devel., 2000-01), Orgn. Chinese Ams. (pres. orange county chap.), Phi Beta Kappa, Alpha Omega Alpha. Avocations: computers, asian american culture, writing, film, television. Office: MemRAD Med Group 100 Oceangate 1000 Long Beach CA 90802 also: Los Alamitos Med Ctr 3751 Katella Ave Los Alamitos CA 90720

LEE, JOE R., food service executive; b. 1940; married. Store mgr. Red Lobster Inns, Lakeland, Fla., 1967-69, supr., dir. ops., 1969-72, v.p. ops., 1972-75, pres., CEO, 1976-79; pres. Gen. Mills Restaurant, Inc., 1979-91; with Gen. Mills, Inc., Mpls., 1970-95, v.p., 1976-80, exec. v.p., 1980-91, exec. v.p. fin., 1991-92, CFO, 1992, vice-chmn., 1992-95; chmn. Darden Restaurants, Inc., Orlando, Fla., 1995—, CEO, 1995—2004. Bd. dirs. Tupperware Worldwide Econ. Devel. Commn. Mem. Nat. Restaurant Assn. (former pres.). Office: Darden Restaurants Inc 5900 Lake Ellenor Dr Orlando FL 32809-4634

LEE, JOHN JIN, lawyer; b. Chgo., Oct. 20, 1948; s. Jim Soon and Fay Yown (Young) L.; m. Jamie Pearl Eng, Apr. 30, 1983. BA magna cum laude, Rice U., 1971; JD, MBA, Stanford U., 1975. Bar: Calif. 1976. Assoc. atty. Manatt Phelps & Rothenberg, L.A., 1976-77; asst. counsel Wells Fargo Bank N.A., San Francisco, 1977-79, counsel, 1979-80, v.p., sr. counsel, 1980, v.p., mng. sr. counsel, 1981-98, v.p., asst. gen. counsel, 1998—2001; gen. counsel, sec. Westlake Global Mgmt., San Mateo, Calif., 2002—. Mem. governing com. Conf. on Consumer Fin. Law, 1989-93. Bd. dirs. Asian Bus. League San Franciscon, 1980—, gen. counsel, 1980—81, chmn., 2004—. Fellow Am. Coll. Consumer Fin. Svcs. Lawyers, Inc. (bd. regents 1995-96); mem. ABA (chmn. subcom. housing fin., com. consumer fin. svcs., bus. law sect. 1983-90, vice chmn. subcom. securities products, consumer fin. svcs., bus. law sect. 1995-96, chmn. subcom. elec. banking, com. consumer fin. svcs., bus. law sect. 1996-2000, co-chmn. joint subcom. elec. fin. svcs., bus. law sect. 1997-2000, co-chmn. directory com. minority in-house counsel group 1995-98), Consumer Bankers Assn. (lawyers com.), Soc. Physics Students, Stanford Asian-Pacific Am. Alumni/ae Club (bd. dirs. 1989-93, v.p. 1989-91). Democrat. Baptist. Office: PO Box 1304 San Carlos CA 94070-7304 Office Phone: 650-579-1010 157. Business E-Mail: johnjinlee@stanfordalumni.org.

LEE, JOHN MARSHALL, mathematics professor; b. Phila., Sept. 2, 1950; s. Warren W. and Virginia (Hull) L.; m. Pm Weizenbaum, May 26, 1984; children: Nathan Lee Weizenbaum, Jeremy Lee Weizenbaum. AB, Princeton U., 1972; student, Tufts U., 1977-78; PhD, MIT, 1982. Systems programmer Tex. Instruments, Princeton, N.J., 1972-74; Geophys. Fluid Dynamics Lab., GFDL/NOAA, Princeton, 1974-75; tchr. math. and physics Wooster Sch., Danbury, Conn., 1975-77; programmer and cons. info. processing svcs. MIT, Cambridge, Mass., 1978-82; asst. prof. math. Harvard U., Cambridge, 1982-87, U. Wash., Seattle, 1987-89, assoc. prof. math., 1989-96, prof. math., 1996—. Sr. tutor Harvard U., Cambridge, 1984-87. Author: Riemannian Manifolds: An Introduction to Curvature, 1997, Introduction to Topological Manifolds, 2000, Introduction to Smooth Manifolds, 2002; contbr. articles to profl. jours. Rsch. fellow NSF, 1982. Mem. Am. Math. Soc. (Centennial fellow 1989). Avocations: hiking, wine tasting, music. Office: Univ Wash Math Dept PO Box 354350 Seattle WA 98195-4350 Office Phone: 206-543-1735. E-mail: lee@math.washington.edu.

LEE, JONATHAN OWEN, financial services company executive, lawyer; b. Boston, Mar. 12, 1951; s. Herbert C. and Mildred (Schiff) L.; m. Barbara Ruth Cole, Mar. 24, 1984; children: Suzanna Cole, Alexander Philip. AB in Architecture, U. Calif., Berkeley, 1973; JD, Boston Coll., 1976. Bar: Mass. 1976. Staff atty. SEC, N.Y.C., 1976-79; pres. Lee Capital Holdings, LLC, Boston, 1979—. Chmn. bd. dirs. Globe Metall., Inc., Cleve., 1986—, HSC Hospitality, Inc., Dallas, 1995—, Heritage Brands, LLC, Wilton, Conn., 1997, Hafslund Metall.As, Sarpsborg, Norway, 1998, Fesil Asa, Oslo, Norway, 1998; bd. dirs. So. Energy Homes, Inc., Adison, Ala., 1st Security Svcs., Inc., Boston, Mass., P.A.R. Assocs., Inc., Boston, Citizens Capital, Inc., Boston. Bd. dirs. Combined Jewish Philanthropies, Boston, 1987—, The Park Sch., Brookline, Mass, 1998—, Wang Ctr. Performing Arts, Boston, 1998—, Project Hope, Dorchester, Mass., 1999; mem. bd. overseers Mus. Fine Arts, Boston. Mem. Young Presidents Orgn., Explorers Club.

LEE, JONG HYUK, accountant; b. Hamheung, Korea, May 6, 1941; s. Jung Bo and Wol Sun Lee; m. Esther Kim, Jan. 24, 1970. BA, Sonoma State U., Rohnert Park, Calif., 1971; MBA in Taxation, Golden Gate U., 1976; postgrad., Argosy U., 2004—. CPA, Calif. Cost acct., internal auditor Foremost-McKesson Co., San Francisco, 1971-74; sr. acct. Clark, Wong, Foulkes & Barbieri, CPAs, Oakland, Calif., 1974-77; pres. J.H. Lee Accts. Corp., Oakland, 1977-97, J. Lee Assocs., Oakland, 1997—. Instr. Armstrong Coll., Berkeley, Calif., 1977-78; lectr. acctg., dir. Sch. Bus., U.S. Korea Bus. Inst., San Francisco State U., cross cultural seminars info. tech. industry major U.S. cities, France, Mex.; mem. adv. bd. Ctr. for Korean Studies, Insts. East Asian Studies, U. Calif., Berkeley; bd. dirs. United Labor Bank, Oakland. Columnist tax and bus. column Korea Times, 1980. Commr. Calif. OEO, 1982—86; regional chmn. Adv. Coun. on Peaceful Unification Policy, Republic of Korea; commr. Asian Art Mus., San Francisco, 1988—91, Oakland Cmty. and Econ. Devel., 1997; bd. dirs., dir. East Bay Asian Local Devel. Corp.; pres. Oakland Masonic Ctr., Communities United Com., Korean Am. Dem. Network, Dem. Nat. Fin. Coun.; chmn. caucus Calif.-Nev. Ann. Conf. United Meth. Ch., 1977; bd. dirs. Korean Residents Assn., 1974, Multi-Svc. Ctr. for Koreans, 1979, BBB, 1984—87. Cpl. Korean Marine Corp, 1961—64, 1st lt. Calif. Mil. Res. Named March 5, 2004 Jong H. Lee Day, Mayor of Oakland. Mem. AICPA, Nat. Assn. Asian Am. CPAs (bd. dirs.), Am. Acctg. Assn., Nat. Assn. Accts., Internat. Found. Employee Benefit Plans, Calif. Soc. CPAs, Oakland C of C., Korean Am. C. of C. (pres. Pacific North Coast), Rotary. Home: 180 Firestone Dr Walnut Creek CA 94598-3645 Office: 369 13th St Oakland CA 94612-2636 Office Phone: 510-836-7400. Business E-Mail: jlee@jhleecpa.com.

LEE, JONG Y., medical scientist, educator; b. Seoul, Korea; MD, PhD in Pathology, U. Minn., 1987. Postdoctoral fellowship U. Minn., Mpls., 1987—92, educator, 1992—; pres. LGen Medtech, Ltd., Mpls., 1996—. Pres. Korean Scientists and Engrs. Assoc., Mpls., 1993—94; com. Bus. Cooperation, Dept. of Commerce, U.S. Govt., Washington, 1996—99. Author: (pioneering achievements/researcher) Brain microsurgery methodology: the central nervous system and hypertension (Am. Heart Association's Internat. Fellowship Award, 1990); contbr. articles to profl. jours. Recipient Scholastic achievement, Phi Kappa Phi, 1986, Outstanding Leadership Achievement Nat. award, Korean Scientist and Engrs. Assoc., 1994, Outstanding Leadership Achievement award, Govt. of State of Minn., 1994, Coun. of Asian Pacific Minnesotans, 1994, Most Outstanding Manuscript Award of Yr., Assn. for Advancement of Med. Instrumentation, 1998, Young Investigator's award mentorship honor, 1998. Mem.: Am. Heart Assn., Amerian Soc. of Hypertension, Twin Cities Catholoc Chorale, U. of Minn. Pres. Club (life), Phi Kappa Phi (life Academic excellence GPA 4.0/4.0 1986). Roman Catholic. Achievements include patents for Expression vector using human gene to purify pure protein and its antobody; R&D and trials on invention of products; patents pending for Differential diagnostic Test kits for clinical use; Invention product for Hypertension; research in brain microsurgery, methodology, hypertension, the central nervous system, salt generic hypertension and chronobiological hypertension. Avocations: music, gardening, reading, travel, camping.

LEE, JOSEPH, musician, educator; b. Bogor, Indonesia, June 6, 1941; arrived in U.S., 1968; s. Njan Fie and Kiun Fong; m. Lois Lee, July 6, 1973; 1 child, Jason. Artist diploma, Jakarta (Indonesia) Nat. Conservatory of Music, 1965; performance cert., U. Oreg., 1972; artist diploma, Bklyn. Conservatory of Music, 1982. Performer Ret. Execs. and Profls. Roslyn, NY, 1989—. Named ARTS award, Nat. Found. for Advancement in Arts, 1987. Fellow: Music Tchrs. Nat. Assn.; mem.: Piano Guild. Home: 8544 Homelawn Jamaica NY 11432

LEE, JOSEPH WILLIAM, sales executive; b. Florence, S.C., Sept. 19, 1943; s. Warner Lou and Rosalee (Hyman) L.; m. Rita Martin, Sept. 8, 1962; children: Mark Stephen, Allison Lynette. Grad. high sch., Florence. Clk. Atlantic Coast Line R.R., Florence, 1962-69; sales rep. Durham (N.C.) & So. Rwy., 1969-74; dist. sales mgr. Westmoreland Coal Sales Co., Charlotte, N.C., 1974-82, v.p. purchasing Phila., 1982-85, v.p. purchasing distbn., 1985-88, v.p. purchasing and northern sales, 1988-91, sr. v.p., 1991, pres., 1991-95; v.p. sales TECO Coal Corp., 1995. Mem., trustee So. Coals Conf., Inc., 1989—92. Mem. N.C. Coal Inst., Charlotte C. of C. Republican. Personal E-mail: jlee17@carolina.rr.com.

LEE, JUHNYOUNG, electronics engineer, researcher; s. G. B. and H. S. Lee; m. Hye Soon Kim, June 1, 1991; children: Rachel Nahye, Sophie Jeehye. PhD, U. of Va., 1994. Sr. rschr. Lexis-Nexis, Dayton, Ohio, 1996—97; rsch. staff mem. IBM T. J. Watson Rsch. Ctr., Hawthorne, NY, 1997—. Contbr. articles to profl. jours. 2d lt. Korean Army, 1987—88. Fellow, U. of Va., 1990. Mem.: IEEE. Achievements include patents for 30 patent aiplications in software/E-Commerce.

LEE, JUNG-KOO, economist, educator; b. Kwangju, Korea, June 12, 1939; s. Hae Dong Lee and Hyung Ok Choi; m. Soon Ja Ha, Jan. 30, 1969; children: Sungji, Sungmi, Sunghwa, Sangjin. BA in Econs., Chonnam Nat. U., 1962, MA in Econs., 1966, PhD in Econs., 1979. Instr. Chonnam Nat. U., Kwangju, 1966-70, asst. prof., 1970-77, assoc. prof., 1977-83, prof. econs., Coll. Bus. Adminstrn., dir. the Ctr. for Regional Devel., 1983—. Vis. prof. IGS, Stockholm U., Sweden, 1979-80; acting mem. Labor Rels. com. Chonnam Province, 1981—; mem. adv. com. Korea Land Devel. Corp., 1985—. Rsch. fellow SIET Inst. Hyderabad, India. Mem.: Korean Econ. Assn. (v.p. 2000—01, 2004—05). Office: Chonnam Nat U 300 Yong Bong Dong Buk ku Kwangju 500-808 Republic of Korea

LEE, JUNGOK PAIK, music educator; b. TaeGoo, KyungBook, Korea (South), Mar. 30, 1969; d. Tae-Young and Duk-Joo Shin Paik; m. Sang Ki Lee, July 26, 1994. MusM, Northwestern U., 1996. Studio tchr. North Pk. U., Chgo., 1996—; piano faculty Creator Arts Ctr., Winnetka, Ill., 2000—; staff accompanist Lake Forest Coll., Ill., 2002—. Musician: (performance) Korean Artist Association, Chosun Daily News Award. Music dir. Trinity Presbyn. Ch., Vernon Hills, Ill., 1991—. Recipient Grand prize, Korean Artist Assn., 1983; scholar, Chosun Daily News, 1993. Home: 47 Monterey Dr Vernon Hills IL 60061 Personal E-mail: slee000@aol.com.

LEE, KANGOH, economics educator; b. Seoul, Korea, Apr. 4, 1955; s. Kise and Hyangran (Kim) L.; m. Jungnyeon Lee, May 30, 1984; children: Ann, Jay. BA in Econs., Seoul Nat. U., 1979; PhD in Econs., U. Ill., 1990. Sect. chief Economic Planning Bd., Seoul, 1979-84; lectr. U. Ill., Champaign, 1988-90; prof. econs. Towson U., Md., 1990—. Contbr. articles to profl. jours. NSF grantee, 1999—. Mem. Am. Econ. Assn. Avocations: hiking, travel. Office: Economics Dept Towson U 8000 York Rd Towson MD 21252-0001 E-mail: klee@towson.edu.

LEE, KATHLEEN MARY, administration and nursing executive; b. Phila., Apr. 12, 1948; d. Daniel Joseph and Mary Ann (Daly) Glackin; m. Gary Douglas MacClay, May 2, 1970 (div. 1980); 1 child, Jeffrey Daniel; m. Glenn Patrick Lee, Feb. 14, 1981. RN diploma, Phila. Gen. Hosp., 1969; BS, St. Joseph Coll., 1985; M Health Svcs. Adminstrn., St. Josephs Coll., 1990; PhD in Health Svcs., Walden U., 1992. RN, Ga., R.I., Pa., Miss.; cert. nursing adminstr. Head nurse, nursery Jeanes Hosp., Phila., 1969-78; adminstrv. supr. Roger Williams Hosp., Providence, 1981-83; head nurse, nursery svcs. King Fahad Hosp., Rivadh, Saudi Arabia, 1983-85; charge nurse psychiatric N.E. Ga. Med. Ctr., Gainesville, 1986-87; v.p. patient svcs. St. Joseph's Hosp., Dahlonega, Ga., 1987-95, Coffee Regional Med. Ctr., Douglas, Ga., 1996-98; assoc. adminstr. Nursing and Profl. Svcs., Ocean Springs, Miss., 1998—. Founder, UNITE, Parent Support Group, Phila., 1976; co-founder, Neonatal Soc. San Antonio, 1979. Capt. USAF, 1978-81. Fellow: Am. Coll. Healthcare Execs.; mem.: ANA, Ga. Nurses Assn. (Ga. Nurses Make a Difference award 1991, dist. honoree 1992), Am. Orgn. Nurse Execs., Miss. Nurses Assn. (Dist. Specialty Nurse of Year award 2000), Sigma Theta Tau (Excellence in Nursing Adminstrn. award Zeta Gamma chpt. 2005). Democrat. Roman

Catholic. Home: 1509 Amberjack Dr Gautier MS 39553-7133 Office: Nursing and Profl Svcs 3109 Bienville Blvd Ocean Springs MS 39564-4361 Office Phone: 228-818-1193. Business E-Mail: k_lee@srhsealth.com.

LEE, KENNETH STUART, neurosurgeon, educator; b. Raleigh, N.C., July 23, 1955; s. Kenneth Lloyd and Myrtie Lee (Turner) L.; m. Cynthia Jane Anderson, May 23, 1981; children: Robert Alexander, Evan Anderson. BA, Wake Forest U., 1977; MD, East Carolina U., 1981. Diplomate Nat. Bd. Med. Examiners, Am. Bd. Neurol. Surgeons; med. lic. N.C., Ariz. Intern, then resident in neurosurgery Wake Forest U. Med. Ctr., Winston-Salem, N.C., 1981-88; fellow Barrow Neurol. Inst., Phoenix, 1988-89; clin. asst. prof. neurosurgery East Carolina U., Greenville, NC, 1989-93, clin. assoc. prof. neurosurgery, 1994—2001, clin. prof. neurosurgery, 2001—, adj. assoc. prof. health edn., 1997—. Assoc. editor Current Surgery, 1990—; contbr. 30 articles to profl. jours. and 5 chpts. to books. Mem. Ethicon Neurosurgical Adv. Panel, 1989-95. Bucy fellow, 1988. Fellow ACS, Am. Heart Assn. (stroke coun.); mem. AMA, N.C. Med. Soc., Am. Assn. Neurol. Surgeons, Am. Soc. Stereotactic and Functional Neurosurgery, So. Med. Assn., Congress Neurol Surgeons, N.C. Neurosurg. Soc. (sec.-treas. 1991-93, pres. 1994-95), So. Neurosurg. Soc., Alpha Omega Alpha. Republican. Baptist. Achievements include research on the efficacy of certain surgical procedures, particularly carotid endarterectomy, in the prevention of strokes. Home: 792 Lexington Dr Greenville NC 27834 Office: Ea Carolina Neurosurg 2325 Stantonsburg Rd Greenville NC 27834-7534 Office Phone: 252-752-5156.

LEE, KEUN SOK, business educator, consultant; b. Pusan, Korea, May 12, 1954; came to the U.S., 1981; s. Namho and Okki (Ryo) L.; m. Youn Bin Lee, Apr. 15, 1980; children: Grace, Danny. BA, Hankuk U. of Fgn. Studies, Seoul, 1979; MBA, U. No. Iowa, 1983; DBA, U. Ky., 1987; postgrad., Columbia U. Rsch. cons. U. No. Iowa, Cedar Falls, 1982-83; rsch. asst. U. Ky., Lexington, 1983-84, tchg. asst., 1984-85; instr. Hofstra U., Hempstead, NY, 1986-87, asst. prof., 1987-93, assoc. prof., 1998—. Author numerous publs. in mktg. jours. and confs. Recipient best article award Mu Kappa Tau, 1989, Acad. Mktg. Sci., 1991. Mem. Acad. Mktg. Svc. (Best Paper award 1991), Am. Mktg. Assn. (assoc.). Avocation: tae kwon do (2d degree black belt). Home: 1503 John St Fort Lee NJ 07024-2560 Office: Hofstra U 141 Weller Hall Hempstead NY 11550 Office Phone: 516-463-5332.

LEE, KUO-HSIUNG, medicinal chemistry professor; b. Kaohsiung, Taiwan, Jan. 4, 1940; came to U.S., 1965; s. Ching-Tsung Lee and Chin-Yeh Yang; m. Lan-Huei Chen; children: Thomas Tung-Ying, Catherine Tung-Ling. BS, Kaohsiung Med. Coll., Taiwan, 1961; MS, Kyoto U., Japan, 1965; PhD, U. Minn., 1968. Postdoctoral scholar dept. chemistry UCLA, 1968-70; asst. prof. Sch. Pharmacy, U. N.C., Chapel Hill, 1970-74, assoc. prof., 1974-77, prof. medicinal chemistry, 1977-91, dir. natural products lab., 1983—, Kenan prof. medicinal chemistry, 1992—, chair divsn. med. chem. and natural products, 1998-99. Adj. prof. Kaohsiung Med. Coll., 1977—; mem. devel. therapeutics contract rev. com. Nat. Cancer Inst., NIH, 1984-88, Bio-organic and natural products chemistry study sect., 1990-94, mem. reviewers res., 1994-98; external assessor, res grants coun., Hong Kong, 1994—; cons. natural products program divsn. life scis. NSC, Taiwan, 1986-87, Food and Drug Bur., Dept. Health, Exec. Yuan of Republic of China, Taiwan, 1986-92, Genelabs, Inc., Redwood City, Calif., 1988—2000, Nat. Rsch. Inst., Chinese Medicine, Taiwan, 1989—, Sphinx Pharms. Corp., Durham, N.C., 1990-94; sci. advisor Nat. Lab. Foods and Drugs, Dept. Health, Exec. Yuan of Republic of China, Taiwan, 1990—; mem. sci. adv. bd. Pharmagenesis, 1992—2003; mem. acad. adv. com. planning sect. Nat. Health Rsch. Inst., Dept. Health, 1992-95, mem. recruitment and adv. com., 1996—2000, mem. sci. rev. and sci. coun. com. pharm. and biotech. sect., 1996—; mem. internat. adv. com. Biotech. Rsch. Inst., Hong Kong U. Sci. and Tech., 1997—; mem. strategic adv. panel Hong Kong Jockey Club Inst. Chinese Medicine, 2002—; mem. adv. com. Inst. of Botany, Academia Sinica, Taiwan, 2001—, Genomic Rsch. Ctr., Academia Sinica, 2004—, Inst. of Zoology, Academia Sinica, 2004—, Nat. Sci. Coun.'s Nat. Sci. and Tech. Program in Pharmacy and Tech., Taiwan, 2002—; chair sci. adv. bd. Plantaceutica, Inc., Research Triangle Park, N.C., 2001-04; chair com. for promotion of Chinese herbal medicine industry and tech. Ministry of Econ. Affairs, Taiwan, 2000–; hon. advisor Chinese Medicinal Material Rsch. Ctr., Chinese U. of Hong Kong, 1999—, hon. prof. Inst. Med. Plant Devel., Chinese Acad. Med. Scis., 1999. Mem. editl. adv. bd. Abstracts of Chinese Medicines, 1986-, Oriental Healing Arts Internat. Bull., 1987-, Bot. Bull. Academia Sinica, 1988-, The Chinese Pharm. Jour., 1988-, Jour. Pharm. Sci., 1990-92, Jour. Chinese Medicine, 1990-, Internat. Jour. Oriental Medicine, 1989-, Kaohsiung Jour. Med. Sci., 1992-, Internat. Jour. Pharmacognosy, 1991-, Jour. Nat. Prod., 1994-, Jour. Asian Nat. Prod. Rsch., 1998-, Jour. Med. Chem., 1999-2003, Jour. Biomed. Sci.; contbr. more than 550 articles to profl. jours. Grantee NIH, Am. Cancer Soc., U.S. Army, 1971—; recipient Soine Meml. award U. Minn., 1990, Achievement award Genelabs, 1993, Lifu Acad. award Chinese Medicine, 1994, T.M. Tu Sci. award, 1995, Merit award Nat. Health Rsch. Insts., 1996, Editor's award Japan Oil Chem. Soc., 1997; named Hon. Prof., Shanghai Inst. Materia Medica, 1996-; recipient Outstanding Achievement award U. Minn., 1999, Achievement award Taiwanese-Am. Found. Sci. and Engring., 2003, Kitasato Microbial Chemistry medal, Japan, 2005. Fellow AAAS, Am. Assn. Pharm. Scientists, Acad. Pharm. Sci.; mem. Am. Chem. Soc., Chem. Soc., Am. Soc. Pharmacognosy, Am. Assn. Pharm. Sci., Am. Assn. Coll. Pharm., Phytochemistry Soc. N.Am., Soc. Syn. Organic Chemistry, Am. Assn. Cancer Rsch., Academia Sinica (academician). Achievements include over 40 patents on synthesis of anti-cancer drugs, anti-fungal agts., anti-AIDS compounds, discovery of more than 2,000 novel plant anti-tumor agts. and synthetic analogs; elucidation of structure-activity relationships, mechanisms of action of bioactive products, herbal medicine including Chinese herbal medicine. Office: U NC Sch Pharmacy Chapel Hill NC 27599-7360 Office Phone: 919-962-0066. Business E-Mail: khlee@unc.edu.

LEE, KYO RAK, radiology educator; b. Seoul, Korea, Aug. 3, 1933; s. Ke Chong and Ok Hi (Um) L.; came to U.S., 1964, naturalized, 1976; MD, Seoul Nat. U., 1959; m. Ke Sook Oh, July 22, 1964; children: Andrew, John. Intern, Franklin Sq. Hosp., Balt., 1964-65; resident U. Mo. Med. Center, Columbia, Mo., 1965-68; instr. dept. radiology U. Mo., Columbia, 1968-69, asst. prof., 1969-71; asst. prof. dept. radiology U. Kans., Kansas City, 1971-76, assoc. prof., 1976-81, prof., 1981—. Served with Republic of Korea Army, 1950-52. Diplomate Am. Bd. Radiology (cert. added qualification in pediat. radiology). Recipient Richard H. Marshak award Am. Coll. Gastroenterology, 1975. Fellow Am. Coll. Radiology; mem. Radiol. Soc. N.Am., Am. Roentgen Ray Soc., Assn. Univ. Radiologists, Kans. Radiol. Soc., Greater Kansas City Radiol. Soc., Wyandotte County Med. Soc., Korean Radiol. Soc. N.Am., Soc., Soc. Pediat. Radiology. Contbr. articles to med. jours. E-mail: klee@kumc.edu. Home: 9800 Glenwood St Shawnee Mission KS 66212-1536 Office: U Kans 39th St and Rainbow Blvd Kansas City KS 66103 Office Phone: 913-588-6832.

LEE, KYUNG SUN, music educator; b. Masan, Korea, Jan. 11, 1965; arrived in U.S., 1988; d. Han-Pil Lee and Suk-Sun Choi; m. Brian John Suits, Mar. 20, 1994; 1 child, Amy Lee Suits. BS, Seoul Nat. U., 1988; MS, Peabody Conservatory, 1990; profl. studies program, Juilliard Sch., 1993—95. Asst. prof. Oberlin Conservatory, Oberlin, Ohio, 2001—. Home: 356 W Lorain St B Oberlin OH 44074 Office: Oberlin College Oberlin OH 44074

LEE, LANSING BURROWS, JR., lawyer; b. Augusta, Ga., Dec. 27, 1919; s. Lansing Burrows and Bertha (Barrett) Lee; m. Natalie Krug, July 4, 1943; children: Melinda Lee Clark, Lansing Burrows III, Bothwell Graves, M. B. Richard Hancock. BS, U. Va., 1939; postgrad., U. Ga. Sch. Law, 1939-40; JD, Harvard U., 1947. Bar: Ga. 1947. Pvt. practice, Augusta, Ga., 1947—; corp. officer Ga.-Carolina Warehouse & Compress Co., Augusta, 1957-89, pres., CEO; co-owner Ga.-Carolina Warehouse. Chmn. bd. trustees James Brice White Found., 1962—; sr. councillor Atlantic Coun. U.S.; sr. warden Episcopal Ch., chancellor, lay min. Capt. USAAF, 1942—46. Fellow: Am. Coll. Trust and Estate Counsel; mem.: Med. Coll. Ga. Found. (bd. dirs.), U.S. Supreme Ct. Hist. Soc., State Bar Ga. (former chmn. fiduciary law sect.), Augusta Bar Assn. (pres. 1966—67), Ga. Bar Found., U. Va. Thomas Jefferson Soc. Alumni, Harvard U. Law Sch. Assn. Ga. (pres. 1966—67), Pres.'s Club Med. Coll. Ga., Harvard Club Atlanta, Augusta Country Club, Internat. Order St. Luke the Physician, Soc. Colonial Wars Ga. Office: Wachovia Bldg 699 Broad St Ste 1001 Augusta GA 30901-1461 Office Phone: 706-722-7503. Personal E-mail: lawlee@worldnet.att.net.

LEE, LAURIE NEILSON, lawyer; b. Portland, Oreg., Jan. 22, 1947; d. Duncan Reese and Lilian (Schwichtenberg) Neilson; m. Douglas Caldwell, Sept. 13, 1968 (div. Aug. 1987); children: Jessica, Ashley; m. Alan M. Lee, Jan. 1, 1988; stepchildren: Erin Lee, Sam Lee. BA, U. Oreg., 1969; JD, Lewis & Clark Coll., 1980. Bar: Oreg. 1980, U.S. Dist. Ct. Oreg. 1980. Assoc. Urbigkeit, Hinson & Abele, Oregon City, Oreg., 1980-85, Gleason, Scarborough, McNeese, O'Brien & Barnes, P.C., Portland, Oreg., 1985-88; ptnr. Bullivant, Houser, Bailey, Pendergrass & Hoffman, Portland, 1989-94, Foster Pepper & Shefelman, Portland, 1994-98, Miller Nash LLP, Portland, 1998—. Spkr. legal seminars Oreg. State Bar, 1984-86, 88, 90, 92-95, 97-98, Oreg. Law Inst., 1989, Oreg. Soc. CPAs, 1986-90, 92, 95, Nat. Bus. Inst., 1990, Portland Tax Forum, 1991. Contbr. articles to profl. jours.; contbg. author: Administering Trusts in Oregon, 1994. Mem. N.W. Planned Giving Roundtable, 1992—; past chair, past sec., com. mem. exec. com. estate planning and adminstrn. sect. Oreg. State Bar, Lake Oswego, 1982-88; bd. trustees Nat. Multiple Sclerosis Soc., Oregon chpt., 2000—. Fellow Am. Coll. Trust and Estate Coun.; mem. ABA, Oreg. Women Lawyers (charter), Estate Planning Coun. Portland Inc. (bd. dirs. 1992—), Oreg. State Bar, Multnomah County Bar Assn. E-mail: leel@millernash.com.

LEE, LEA, education educator; b. Seoul, Republic of Korea, Sept. 11, 1965; arrived in U.S., 1988; d. Jowon Lee and Myoung Jang. MS, Chgo. State U., 1990; PhD, U. Minn., 1993. Rsch. asst. Chgo. State U., 1988—90, U. Minn., Mpls., 1991—93; asst. prof. Murray State U., Ky., 1994—98, Old Dominion U., Norfolk, Va., 1998—2004, assoc. prof., 2004—. Cons. Dumfried Elem. Sch., Va., 2001—02. Contbr. chapters to books. Grantee, Va. Edn. Tech. Alliance, 1998—99; scholar, U. Minn., 1990. Mem.: World Orgn. Early Childhood Edn., Assn. Childhood Edn. Internat., Intenrat. Reading Assn. Office: Old Dominion U 145 Edn Bldg Norfolk VA 23529

LEE, LEONA LIPARI, writer; b. Patterson, La., Mar. 4, 1941; d. Michael and Lucy Listi Lipari; m. Michael Sr. Vinson Lee, June 20, 1964; children: Michael Vinson Jr., Allison Lee Neal. BA in Psychology, MA in English, U. New Orleans, 1978. RN Miss. Author: (nonfiction book) How To Survive Menopause Without Going Crazy, (novels) Taxing Tallula, The Sisters: Lost in Brooklyn, The Sisters: Found in San Antonio, (story) Vital Chatter in Chicken Soup for the Sisters Soul. Avocation: reading. Personal E-mail: lee3731@bellsouth.net.

LEE, LESLIE WARREN, marketing executive, educator; b. Mpls., Nov. 21, 1949; s. Adolph Orlando and Eunice Celia (Akerson) L.; m. Kathleen Karen Frie, June 2, 1973; children: Megan Christine, Maren Elisabeth, Matthew Warren. BA in History magna cum laude, Augsburg Coll., Mpls., 1971. CLU, ChFC. Dir. YMCA, Mpls., 1971-73; dist. sales mgr. Chrysler Mtr. Corp., Marshfield, Wis., 1973-75; agt. Northwestern Mut. Life, Marshfield, 1975-81; mgr. advanced underwriting The Rural Co., Madison, Wis., 1981-83; advanced life mktg. specialist Am. Family Ins., Madison, 1983-95; nat. sales dir., v.p. mktg. Flexsystem, Madison, 1995-98; specialist Farmers Ins. Group Life, 1999—; trainer Farmers Fin. Svc., 1999—. Instr. dept. bus. U. Wis., Madison, 1981-82, instr. dept. econs., Stevens Point, 1978-81; lectr., cons. in field. Mem. Nat. Assn. Ins. & Fin. Advisors, Madison Assn. Ins. and Fin. Adv., Nat. Spkrs. Assn., Wis. Profl. Spkrs. Assn., Soc. Fin. Svc. Profls. Republican. Lutheran. Avocation: stamp collecting/philately. Office: Motivation and Tng for Arena Life PO Box 620305 7522 E Hampstead Ct Middleton WI 53562-3609 Office Phone: 608-831-4857. E-mail: leslee@itis.com.

LEE, LEWIS SWIFT, lawyer; b. Dallas, Nov. 19, 1933; s. Lenoir Valentine and Margaret Louise (Clendon) L.; m. Frances Ann Childress, Mar. 16, 1956; children; Frances Ann Lee Webb, Lewis S. Jr., George Childress, Lenoir Valentine Lee II. AB, U. South, 1955; postgrad., Washington & Lee U., 1954-55; MA, Emory U., 1956, LLB (replaced by JD), 1960. Bar: Fla. 1960. Trainee Citizens & So. Nat. Bank, Atlanta, 1956, 58-59; assoc. Adair, Ulmer, Murchison, Kent & Ashby, Jacksonville, Fla., 1960-63; shareholder Ulmer, Murchison, Ashby & Ball, Jacksonville, 1963-95; of counsel LeBoeuf, Lamb, Greene & MacRae, LLP, Jacksonville, 1996-99, Martin, Ade, Birchfield & Mickler, PA, Jacksonville, 2000, McGuire Woods LLP, Jacksonville, 2001—05. Gen. counsel Fla. Rock Industries, Inc., Jacksonville, 1972-2004, Patriot Transp. Holdings, Inc., Jacksonville, 1989-2004; dir. Fla. Sch. Book Depository, Jacksonville, 1990—. 1st lt. AUS, 1956-58. Mem. ABA, Jacksonville Bar Assn., Ponte Vedra Inn & Club, Timuquana Country Club, Fla. Yacht Club, The River Club, Haile Plantation Golf & Country Club (Gainesville). Republican. Epsicopalian. Avocations: hiking, skiing, swimming, hunting, travel. Home: 3733 Ortega Blvd Jacksonville FL 32210-4347 Office: McGuire Woods LLP 50 N Laura St Ste 3300 Jacksonville FL 32202

LEE, LILLIAN VANESSA, microbiologist; b. N.Y.C., June 1, 1951; d. Wenceslao and Ada (Otero) Cancel; m. Thomas Christopher Lee, June 11, 1972; children: Tovan, John-Peter, Phillip-Michael. BS in Biology, St. Johns U., 1972; MS in Microbiology, Wagner Coll., 1974. Cert. registered biologist Nat. Registry Microbiologists, specialist in microbiology Nat. Registry Microbiologists, Am. Soc. Clin. Pathologists. Grad. lab. asst. in microbiology Wagner Coll., S.I., NY, 1972—74; clin. microbiology technobiologist Queens Hosp. Ctr., Jamaica, NY, 1974—81, supr. clin. microbiology, 1981—84; sect. head microbiology Nyack Hosp., NY, 1984—93, acting lab. mgr., 1992—93; mgr. microbiology Beth Israel Med. Ctr., N.Y.C., 1994—97, Cabrini Med. Ctr., N.Y.C., 1997—98, Columbia Presbyn. Med. Ctr., N.Y.C., 1998—2002; chief gen. and spl. microbiology lab., chief microbiology biothreat response lab. N.Y.C. Dept. Health and Mental Hygiene, 2002—, chief molecular testing lab, acting chief mycbacteriology and parasitology lab. Mem. Mayor's Task Force on Biol. Warfare, 1997-2003; mem. adv. com. to Asst. Commr. on Bioterrorism and Emerging Pathogens, 2004-. Mem.: Clin. Lab. Mgmt. Assn. (program com. 1996—97), N.Y.C. Soc. Infectious Diseases, Med. Mycology Soc. N.Y., Am. Acad. Microbiology, Am. Soc. Microbiology (N.Y.C. br. coun. 1992—, chair program com. 1993—96, co-chair program com. 1997—2001, pres. N.Y.C. br. 1999—2001), Am. Soc. Clin. Pathologists. Home: 530 E 23rd St Apt MF New York NY 10010-5046 Office: NYC DOHMH Pub Health Labs 455 First Ave New York NY 10016 Office Phone: 212-447-6970. Personal E-mail: lvlee5@yahoo.com. Business E-Mail: llee2@health.nyc.gov.

LEE, LORIN L., obstetrician, gynecologist; b. Seattle, 1942; MD, U. Wash., 1968. Intern William Beaumont Gen. Hosp., El Paso, Tex., 1968-69; resident Tripler Gen. Hosp., Honolulu, 1970-73; ob-gyn. St. Francis Hosp., Indpls. Mem. ACOG, AMA. Office Phone: 317-865-6252.

LEE, LORRIN L., internet marketing entrepreneur, architect, writer; b. Honolulu, July 22, 1941; s. Bernard Chong and Betty (Lum) L.; m. Nina Fedoroscko, June 10, 1981. BArch, U. Mich., 1970; MBA, PhD in Psychology, Columbia Pacific U., 1981. Registered arch., Skidmore, Owings & Merrill Archs., Hawaii, 1967, NBBJ Archs., 1974. Arch. Clifford Young AIA, Honolulu, 1971-72, Aotani & Oka AIA, Honolulu, 1972—73, Geoffrey Fairfax FAIA, Honolulu, 1974-76; seminar leader Lorrin Lee Program, Honolulu, 1976-81; star grand master coord. Enhance Corp., 1981-83; 5-diamond supr. Herbalife Internat., L.A., 1983—, mem. Global Expansion Team, 1993—; presdl. dir. Uni-Vite Internat., San Diego, 1989-92; agt. Internat. Pen Friends, 1995—; mgr. Cyber Media Sales, 1996-2000; dealer Cajun Country Candies, 2000—; distributor Tahitian Noni Internat., 2002—; agt. FriendFinder, 2001—. Author: Here is Genius, 1980. Editor Honolulu Chinese Jaycees, Honolulu, 1972, v.p., 1983; active Makiki Cmty. Ctr., Honolulu, 1974. 1st lt. U.S. Army, 1967-70, Okinawa, 2nd Logistical Command. Recipient Braun-Knect-Heimann award, 1959, 1st Prize in Design Kidjel Cali-Pro Internat., 1975, Kitchen Design award Sub-Zero Contest, 1994; named Honolulu Chinese Jaycee of Yr., Honolulu Chinese Jaycees, 1973. Mem. Nature Conservancy, Sierra Club. Avocations: international travel, hiking, desktop publishing, photography, reading. Office: 500 University Ave #2415 Honolulu HI 96826 Office Phone: 808-949-5000. Personal E-mail: lorrin@lorrinlee.com.

LEE, LOW KEE, electronics engineer, consultant; b. Feb. 12, 1916; s. Hing Wing and Yan Hai (Louie) L.; m. Alice Jing, Nov. 29, 1953; children: Elliott James, Elizabeth Joanne. BS, U. Calif., Berkeley, 1937, MS, 1939; PhD, Calif. Western U., 1977. Group leader Aerophysics Lab., L.A., 1946—50; lab. mgr. Stanford Rsch. Inst., Menlo Park, Calif., 1950—55; asst. to dir. Gen. Mills, Mpls., 1955—57; dept. mgr. product engring. TRW, Redondo Beach, Calif., 1957—62, asst. dir. product assurance, 1962—78; ret., 1978. Cons. Omni Corp., Rancho Santa Fe, 1983—, Control Data Inc., City of Industry, Calif. Co-author: Design and Construction of Electronic Equipment, 1961; contbr. to books, encys. Fellow: IEEE; mem.: Chinese Am. Inst. Engrs. and Scientists (pres. San Francisco 1945—46, trustee 1979—81, 1989—91, Meritorious award 1985), Masons. Home: 33 Linda Ave 1301 Oakland CA 94611 Office Phone: 510-985-0452.

LEE, MARGARET BURKE, college president, language educator; b. San Diego, Dec. 28, 1943; d. Peter John and Margaret Mary (Brown) Burke; m. Donald Harry Lee, June 30, 1973 (dec. June 2002); children: Katherine Louise, Kristopher Donald. BA summa cum laude, Regis Coll., 1966; MA with honors, U. Chgo., 1970, PhD, 1978; IEM Cert., Harvard U., 1992, Seminar for New Pres., 1996. Asst. to humanities MIT, Cambridge, 1969; instr. Dover-Sherborn H.S., Dover, 1973-75, Alpena (Mich.) C.C., 1975-80, dean liberal arts, 1980-82; dean instrn. Kalamazoo Valley C.C., 1982-85; v.p. Oakton C.C., Des Plaines, Ill., 1985-95, pres., 1995—. Cons. evaluator North Ctrl. Assn., Chgo., 1982—, commr.-at-large, 1988-92, commn. on inst. of higher edn. bd. dirs., 1992—, vice chair, 1996-98, chair, 1998-2001, now v.p.; vice chair Am. Coun. on Internat. Intercultural Edn., 2000—, chair, 2002-05; cons., field faculty Vt. Coll., Montpelier, 1982-85; mem. admissions com. Ill. Math and Sci. Acad., 1988—; bd. govs. North Cook Ednl. Svc. Ctr., 1988—2004, bd. dirs., 1989—, vice chair, 1990-91, chair, 1992-94; bd. dirs. Academic Search Cons. Svcs., 2001—. Mem. Bd. Edn. Dist. 39, Wilmette, Ill., 1990-92, Des Plaines Sister Cities, 1995—; bd. dirs. Ill. C.C. Atty.'s Assn., 1994—; mem. Career Edn. Planning Dist., Kalamazoo, 1982, Kalamazoo Forum/Kalamazoo Network, 1982, Needs Assessment Task Force, 1984. Ford Found. fellow, 1969—73, Woodrow Wilson Found. fellow, 1975, fed. grantee, 1978—84. Mem. Am. Assn. of C.C.'s (bd. dirs.), Am. Assn. Cmty. and Jr. Colls., Mich. Assn. C.C. Instrnl. Adminstrs. (pres. 1983-85), Mich. Occupl. Deans Adminstrs. Coun. (exec. bd. 1983-85), Mich. Women's Studies Assn. (hons. selection com. 1984), North Ctrl. Assn. Acad. Deans (pres. 1988-90), Kalamazoo Consortium Higher Edn. (pres.'s coun. coord. com. 1982-85), Kalamazoo C. of C. (vocat. edn. subcom. indsl. coun. 1982), North Ctrl. Assn. Acad. Deans (v.p., pres. 1985-87), Des Plaines C. of C. (mem. bd. dirs. 1995—). Democrat. Lutheran. Avocations: quilt collecting, reading, listening to classical music, sports spectating, theatre-going. Home: 2247 Lake Ave Wilmette IL 60091-1410 Office: Oakton CC 1600 E Golf Rd Des Plaines IL 60016-1234 Business E-Mail: plee@oakton.edu.

LEE, MARGARET NORMA, artist; b. Kansas City, Mo., July 7, 1928; d. James W. and Margaret W. (Farin) Lee; PhB, U. Chgo., 1948; MA, Art Inst. Chgo., 1952. Lectr., U. Kansas City, 1957-61; cons. Kansas City Bd. Edn., Kansas City, Mo., 1968-86; guest lectr. U.Mo.-Columbia, 1983, 85, 87, 89, 91, 93-95, 97; one-woman shows Univ. Women's Club, Kansas City, 1966, Friends of Art, Kansas City, 1969, Fine Arts Gallery U. Mo. at Columbia, 1972, All Souls Unitarian Ch. Kansas City, Mo., 1978; two-Woman show Rockhurst Coll., Kansas City, Mo., 1981 exhibited in group shows U. Kans., Lawrence, 1958, Chgo. Art Inst., 1963, Nelson Art Gallery, Kansas City, Mo., 1968, 74, Mo. Art Show, 1976, Fine Arts Gallery, Davenport, Iowa, 1977; represented in permanent collections Amarillo (Tex.) Art Center, Kansas City (Mo.) Pub. Library, Park Coll., Parkville, Mo. Mem. Coll. Art Assn. Roman Catholic. Contbr. art to profl. jours.; author booklet. Home: 4109 Holmes St Kansas City MO 64110-1127

LEE, MARILYN MODARELLI, lawyer, retired library director; b. Jersey City, Dec. 8, 1934; d. Alfred E. and Florence Olga (Koment) Modarelli; m. Alfred McClung Lee III, June 8, 1957 (div. July 1985); children: Leslie Lee Ekstrand, Alfred McClung IV, Andrew Modarelli. BA, Swarthmore (Pa.) Coll., 1956; JD, Western New Eng. Sch. of Law, 1985. Bar: Mass. 1986. Claims rep., supr. region II Social Security Adminstrn., Jersey City, 1956—59; law libr. County of Franklin, Greenfield, Mass., 1972—78; head law libr. Mass. Trial Ct., Greenfield, 1978—2001. Mem. Franklin County Futures Lab Project (Mass. Cts.), 1994—. Vice chmn. Greenfield Planning Bd., 1987—95; mem. bldg. com. Greenfield Sch., 1995—2003, clerk, 2002—03; active Greenfield Bd. Registrar of Voters, 2003—, Jennie L. Bascomb Fund, 2004—; mem. Franklin Regional Planning Bd., 1988—98; moderator All Souls Unitarian Ch., 1996—2000, asst. treas., 1997—98, treas., 1998—2001; exec. bd. Franklin Regional Planning Bd., 1992—95; mem. western regional bd. Mass. Soc. for Prevention of Cruelty to Children, 2002—; chmn. Franklin County (Mass.) Tech., Turners Falls, 1974—76; bldg. com. chair Franklin County (Tech) Sch., Turners Falls, 1974—76; clk. Franklin County (Mass.) Tech., Turners Falls, 1976—81; mem. Greenfield C.C. Found., 1990—, Franklin Regional Transp. Com., 1992—; mem. alumni coun. Swarthmore Coll., 1994—97. Mem. Franklin County Bar Assn. (chmn. lawyer referral com. 1992-94, 97-99, vice-chmn. 1994-97, chmn. libr. com. 1992—), Law Librs. of New Eng. (treas. 1993-97), Am. Assn. Law Librs. (mem. state ct. and county law librs. sect. 1972—, bylaws com. 1996-99, chair bylaws com. 1997-98), Greenfield Charter (commn. clk. 1979-83), Western Mass. Libr. Club (bd. clk. 2003—). Avocations: swimming, gardening.

LEE, MARK RICHARD, lawyer, educator; b. St. Louis, Jan. 23, 1949; s. Bernard and Leatrice Lee; m. Elaine D. Edelman, June 7, 1980; 3 children. BA, Yale U., 1967; JD, U. Tex., 1971. Bar: Tex. 1974, U.S. Ct. Appeals (2d, 4th, and 7th cirs.) 1975, U.S. Ct. Appeals(D.C. cir.) 1976. Asst. atty. gen. State of Tex., Austin, 1974-75; atty. antitrust div. U.S. Dept. of Justice, Washington, 1975-76; instr. law U. Miami, 1976-77; prof. law So. Ill. U., Carbondale, 1977—. Vis. lectr. U. Warwick, Coventry, Eng., 1984; vis. prof. law U. San Diego, 1990-91, 93, 95, 97, 2001-02, Cath. U. of Brussels, 1992, Washington U., 1997, U. Colo., 1998, Georgetown U., 1999, 2000, Am. U., 1999, 2000, U. Salerno, Italy, 2004, U. Macerata, 2004, U. Naples, Italy, 2004, Gonzaga U., Spokane, Wash., 2004, 05; mem. Ill. Blue Ribbon Telecomm. Commn., 1990-91; arbitrator Nat. Assn. Securities Dealers, Am. Arbitration Assn., NY Stock Exch. Author: Antitrust Law and Local Government, 1985, Organizing Corporate and Other Business Enterprises, 6th edit.(with Gross), 2000; contbr articles to profl. jours. Mem. Gov.'s Task Force on Utility Regulation Reform, Springfield, 1982-84. Rsch. scholar Max Planck Inst. for Fgn. and Internat. Pvt. Law, Hamburg, Germany, 1986; Fulbright awardee U. Erlangen-Nuremberg, 1992; recipient (with Edelman)Belgian Nat. Fund for Sci. Rsch. award, 1992. Mem. ABA, Order of the Coif, Phi Kappa Phi. Avocations: volleyball, tennis, bridge. Home: 350 Union Grove Rd Carbondale IL 62903-7685 Office: So Ill U Sch Law Carbondale IL 62901

LEE, MARTHA, artist, writer; b. Chehalis, Wash., Aug. 23, 1946; d. William Robert and Phyllis Ann (Herzog) L.; m. Peter Reynolds Lockwood, Jan. 25, 1974 (div. 1982). BA in English Lit., U. Wash., 1968; student, Factory of Visual Art, 1980-82. Reporter Seattle Post-Intelligencer, 1970; personnel counselor Theresa Snow Employment, 1971-72; receptionist Northwest Kidney Ctr., 1972-73; proprietress The Reliquary, 1974-77; travel agt. Cathay Express, 1977-79; artist, 1980—. Painter various oil paintings; exhibited in numerous one-woman shows; numerous group shows including most recently: Columbia River Artists Gallery, Chinook, Washington, Blackwood Beach Cottages, Ocean Pk., Washington; author: To The Beach and Other Poems, 1998. Avocations: horseback riding, beachcombing, reading, music. Home: PO Box 1157 Ocean Park WA 98640-1157 Office Phone: 360-665-4579. E-mail: arowhead@pacifier.com.

LEE, MICHAEL, leasing company executive, real estate company executive; b. Chgo., Nov. 26, 1953; s. Joseph A. and Mildred M. Kathrein; m. Victoria Lee; children: Jane Emily, Joseph Andrew, Theodore Michael, Elizabeth Grace, Fay Golda. BS in Acctg., U. Nebr., 1978; M in Mgmt., Northwestern U., 1985. CPA, Ill.; lic. real estate broker, pilot. Tax mgr. Touche Ross & Co., Chgo., 1978-84; corp. contr., v.p. Lettuce Entertain You Enterprises, Chgo., 1984-86; pres., CEO Kathrein Leasing Co., Chgo., 1983—; also bd. dirs.; pres., chief exec. officer Empire Real Estate Investment Co., Chgo., 1986—. Bd. dirs., speaker Nat. Speakers Bur., N.Y.C., 1985-94; cons. Fla. Investor, Inc., Cocoa, 1986—. Author: (how-to book) Real Estate Comparative Analysis, 1986. Bd. dirs. Revenue Crusade of Mercy, United Way, Chgo., 1980. Mem. AICPA, Cert. Mgmt. Accts. Assn. (cert.), Cert. Internal Auditors Assn. (cert.), Nat. Assn. Realtors, Young Pres.'s Orgn., Northwestern U. Alumni Assn., Mensa. Avocations: aviation, lecturing. Home: 7601 N Eastlake Ter Chicago IL 60626-1421

LEE, MORDECAI, political scientist, educator; b. Milw., Aug. 27, 1948; s. Jack Harold and Bernice (Kamesar) L.; 1 child, Ethan. BA, U. Wis., 1970; MPA, Syracuse U., 1972, PhD, 1975. Guest scholar Brookings Instn., Washington, 1972-74; legis. asst. to Congressman Henry Reuss Washington, 1975; asst. prof. polit. sci. U. Wis.-Whitewater and Parkside, 1976; mem. Wis. Ho. Reps., 1977-82, Wis. Senate, 1982-89; exec. dir. Milw. Jewish Coun. Cmty. Rels., 1990-97; asst. prof. govt. U. Wis.-Milw., 1997—2002, assoc. prof., 2002—. Author: The First Presidential Communications Agency: FDR's Office of Government Reports, 2005. Grantee, Franklin and Eleanor Roosevelt Inst., 2002, Hoover Presdl. Libr. Assn., 2003, IBM Ctr. for Bus. of Govt., 2003. Mem.: ASPA (co-chair program com. 64th conf. 2003, exec. com. sect. pub. adminstrn. edn. 1998—2003), Assn. for Rsch. on Nonprofit Orgns. and Voluntary Action (vice-chair sect. tchg. 2001—03). Business E-Mail: mordecai@uwm.edu.

LEE, NANCY RANCK, management consultant; b. Yonkers, N.Y., Oct. 31, 1932; d. William Edward and Marion Edna Ranck; children: John Gregory, Paul Edward. BS, Cornell U., 1953; postgrad., Boston U., 1974-75. Social worker Tompkins County, Ithaca, N.Y., 1953-54; pers. adminstr. GE Advanced Electronics Ctr., Ithaca, 1954-55; fashion publicist Macy's, N.Y.C., 1956-59; mgr. advt. and pub. rels. Josiah Wedgwood & Co., N.Y.C., 1959-65; dir. comms. Gregory Fosella Assocs., Boston, 1969-71; dir. mktg. Kuras & Co., Boston, 1971-73; internat. sales mgr. Laser Focus Mag., Boston, 1973-75; pres. Lee Assocs., Boston, 1975-82; exec. v.p. Infotech, Boston, 1982-92; pres. Requisite Orgn. Assoc., Sarasota, Fla., 1992—. Lectr. Simmons Coll. Author: Targeting the Top: Everything a Woman Needs to Know to Succeed in Business, 1980. Mem. Cornell Cb. Ivy League Club, Phi Kappa Phi. Avocation: skiing. Home: 1590 1st St Sarasota FL 34236

LEE, PALI JAE (POLLY JAE STEAD LEE), retired librarian, writer; b. Nov. 26, 1925; d. Jonathan Everett Wheeler and Ona Katherine (Grunder) Stead; m. Richard H.W. Lee, Apr. 7, 1945 (div. 1978); children: Catherine Lani Honcoop, Karin Elizabeth Robinson, Ona G., Laurie Brett, Robin Louise Halbert; m. John K. Willis, 1979 (dec. 1994). Student, U. Hawaii, 1944-46, Mich. State, 1961-64. Cataloguer and processor U.S. Army Air Force, 1945-46; with U.S. Weather Bur. Film Library, New Orleans, 1948-50, FBI, Wright-Patterson AFB, Dayton, Ohio, 1952, Ohio Wholesale Winedealers, Columbus, Ohio, 1956-58, Coll. Engring., Ohio State U., Columbus, 1959; writer tech. manual Annie Whittenmeyer Home, Davenport, Iowa, 1960; with Grand Rapids (Mich.) Pub. Library, 1961-62; dir. Waterford (Mich.) Twp. Libraries, 1962-64; acquisition librarian Pontiac (Mich.) Pub. Libraries, 1965-71, dir. East Side br., 1971-73; rsch. asst. dept. anthropology Bishop Mus., Honolulu, 1975-83; pub. Night Rainbow Pub., Honolulu, 1984—. Author: HIstory of Wine Growing in America, 1952, House Parenting at its Best, 1960, Mary Dyer, Child of Light, 1973, Giant: Pictorial History of the Human Colossus, 1973, History of Change: Kaneohe Bay Area, 1976, English edit., 1983, Na Po Makole-Tales of the Night Rainbow, 1981, rev. edit., 1988, Mo'olelo O Na Pohukaina, 1983, Ka Ipu Kukui, 1994, Ho'opono, 1999, Remembrance: The History of a Family, 2003; contbr. articles to profl. jours. Chmn. Oakland County br. Multiple Sclerosis Soc., 1972-73, co-chmn. Pontiac com. of Mich. area bd., 1972-73; sec. Ohana o Kokua, 1979-83, Paia-Willis Ohana, 1982-91, Ohana Kame'ekua, 1988-91; bd. dirs. Detroit Multiple Sclerosis Soc., 1971; mem. Mich. area bd. Am. Friends Svc. com., 1961-69; mem. consumer adv. bd. Libr. for Blind and Physically Handicapped, Honolulu, 1997—, bd. dirs. 1999—; pres. consumer 55 plus Hawaii Ctr. for Ind. Living, 1990-94, pres., 1995-96; pres. Honolulu chpt. Nat. Fedn. of Blind, 1991-93, 1st v.p. #93 state affiliate, 1991-93, editor Na Na Maka Aloha newsletter, 1990-94 Recipient Mother of the Yr. award Quad City Bus. Men, 1960, Bowl of Light award Cmty. Hawaii, 1989. Mem. Soc. Friends, Talking Book Readers Club (1st v.p. Hawaii chpt. 1994-95, pres., 1996, corr. sec. 2000-05), Nahnmenalima Club (chmn. youth outreach com.), Peace and Social Concerns Soc. Friends (corr. dinajor, peace sub com.) Office: PO Box 10706 Honolulu HI 96816-0706 Personal E-mail: palijae@juno.com.

LEE, PATRICIA, lawyer, diplomat; b. Honolulu; Cert., U. Paris, 1964; BA, U. Hawaii, 1965; MA, Columbia U., 1966; PhD, Northwestern U., 1973; JD, U. Hawaii, 1979. Ptnr. Goodsill Anderson Quinn & Stifel, Honolulu, 1979—; hon. consul of France, 1997—. Chairperson bd. regents U. Hawaii, 2000—; mem. bd. regents Hon. Consulate, France. Office: France Hon Consulate 1099 Alakea St 1800 Alii Pl Honolulu HI 96813 Office Phone: 808-547-5600. E-mail: plee@goodsill.com.

LEE, PATRICIA ANN, secondary school educator; b. Lynn, Mass., Nov. 21, 1944; d. Patrick Joseph and Irma Helen (Howard) Lee. BS cum laude, Salem State Coll., 1966, MA in Teaching History, 1970. Tchr. Sisson Elem. Sch., Lynn, Mass., 1966, Hood Elem. Sch., Lynn, 1967, Breed Jr. High Sch., Lynn, 1967-74, Classical High Sch., Lynn, 1974—. Sec., voting mem. Lynn Hist. Commn., 1989—; active Friends of Lynn Woods, 1992—, Friends of Lynn Pub. Libr., 1992—. Horace Mann grantee State of Mass., 1986, 87. Mem.: Classical H.S. Coun., Lynn Hist. Soc., Phi Alpha Theta, Delta Tau Kappa. Democrat. Roman Catholic. Avocations: reading, hooking rugs, gardening, writing historical book. Home: 205 Edgemere Rd Lynn MA 01904-2087 Office: Lynn Classical High 235 O'Callaghan Way Lynn MA 01905

LEE, PATRICK A., physics educator; b. Hong Kong, Sept. 8, 1946; m. Jeanne M. Tran, June 7, 1969; children: Eric, Brian. BS, MIT, 1966, PhD, 1970. Gibbs instr. Yale U., New Haven, 1970-72; asst. prof. U. Wash., Seattle, 1973-74; mem. tech. staff Bell Labs., Murray Hill, N.J., 1974-82; prof. physics MIT, Cambridge, 1982—. Fellow Am. Phys. Soc. (Oliver Buckley prize 1991); mem. NAS, Am. Acad. Arts and Scis. Office: MIT 77 Massachusetts Ave Cambridge MA 02139-4307

LEE, PAUL, broadcast executive; b. London, July 8, 1960; m. Deirdre Lee, Aug. 19, 1987; 2 children. MA in modern lang., Oxford U. Prodn. mgr. Rede Globo, Rio de Janeiro, 1983; gen. trainee BBC, 1984, reporter, 1985—90, documentary prodr., drama dir., 1990—93, exec. prodr., 1994—97, channel editor BBC Prime, 1997—98, gen. mgr. BBC Am., 1998—99, COO BBC Am., 1999—2002, CEO BBC Am., 2002—04; pres. ABC Family, 2004—. Office: ABC Family 500 S Buena Vista St Burbank CA 91521

LEE, PAUL LAWRENCE, lawyer; b. NYC, Mar. 7, 1946; AB, Georgetown U., 1969; JD, U. Mich., 1972. Bar: N.Y. 1974. Editor-in-chief Mich. Law Rev., 1971-72; law clk. to Hon. Walter R. Mansfield US Ct. Appeals (2d cir.), 1973-74; spl. asst. to gen. counsel US Treasury Dept., 1977-78, exec. asst. to dep. sec., 1978-79; dep. supt. and counsel NY State Banking Dept., 1980-81; ptnr. Shearman & Sterling, NYC, 1982-94; exec. v.p., gen. counsel Republic N.Y. Corp., NYC, 1994-2000; sr. exec. v.p., gen. counsel HSBC USA Inc., NYC, 2000—04; ptnr., head Banking Practice, mem. Fin. Insts. Group Debevoise & Plimpton LLP, NYC, 2004—. Office: Debevoise & Plimpton LLP 919 Third Ave New York NY 10022 Office Phone: 212-909-6955. Office Fax: 212-521-7955. Business E-Mail: plee@debevoise.com.

LEE, PAUL W., lawyer; BS in Elec. Engring. and Computer Sci., Columbia U., 1972; JD cum laude, Cornell U., 1976. Ptnr., bus. law dept. Goodwin Procter LLP, Boston, chair corp. dept., assoc. compensation and legal pers. supervision com. Apptd. mem. Govs. Asian Am. Commn. Editor: Cornell Internat. Law Jour. Mem.: ABA (minority members-at-large 2000—03, bd. govs., former mem. commn. on opportunities for minorities in the profession), Asian Am. Lawyers Assn. Mass. (founder, first pres.), Nat. Asian Pacific Am. Bar Assn. (pres. 1995—96). Office: Goodwin Procter LLP Exchange Place 53 State St Boston MA 02109*

LEE, PAUL YUE-YAN, surgeon; b. Hong Kong, Aug. 30, 1938; arrived in U.S., 1959; MD, U. Oreg., 1967. Intern Wayne County Gen. Hosp., Eloise, Mich., 1967-68; resident Kern Gen. Hosp., Bakersfield, Calif., 1968-72; with Bellflower Kaiser-Permanente Med. Ctr., Calif., 1972—. Mem.: ACS. Office: Kaiser Permanente Med Ctr 9400 Rosecrans Ave Bellflower CA 90706-2217 Office Phone: 562-461-4622. Personal E-mail: mabalee@aol.com. Business E-Mail: pauly.lee@kp.org.

LEE, PETER ALLEN, pediatrician, educator; b. Watertown, N.Y., Feb. 28, 1939; s. Chester Hildreth and Doris Eleanor (Rathbun) L.; m. Karin Christine Landin, Aug. 25, 1962; children: Kristen Ann, Daniel Landin. BA magna cum laude, Houghton Coll., 1961; MS, U. Mich., 1962, PhD, 1965, MD, 1969. Diplomate Am. Bd. Pediatrics. Resident U. Mich. Med. Ctr., Ann Arbor, 1969-71; fellow in pediatric endocrinology Johns Hopkins U. Sch. Medicine, Balt., 1971-73, assoc. prof. pediatrics, 1975-81; prof. pediatrics U. Pitts. Sch. Medicine, Pitts., 1981—. Cons. TAP Pharms., North Chicago, Ill., 1988—. Editor (book) Congenital Adrenal Hyperplasia, 1977; assoc. editor (book) Pediatric and Adolescent Gynecology, 1994; co-editor (book) The Neurobiology of Puberty, 1995; contbr. chpts. to books; contbr. 140 articles to profl. jours. and 40 chpts. to textbooks. Chmn. bd. dirs. Saltworks Theater Co., Pitts., 1986-87; bd. dirs. Pitts. Pastoral Inst., 1993—, Human Growth Found., 1993—; med. advisor Turner Syndrome Soc., Pitts., 1992—. Lt. comdr. USN, 1973-75. U. Mich. Cancer Rsch. Inst. fellow, 1963-64, Med. Scientist fellow, 1965-69, Ford Found. Rsch. fellow, 1968-69, Rockefeller Found. scholar, 1988, Nat. Inst. Child Human Devel. grantee, 1992—. Mem. Am. Fedn. Clin. Rsch., Am. Pediatric Soc., Lawson Wilkins Pediatric Endocrinology Soc. (program chair 1987-88, dir. 1994—), Soc. for Pediatric Rsch., The Endocrine Soc., N.Am. Soc for Pediatric and Adolescent Gynecology (sec. 1993—), Sigma Xi. Presbyterian. Avocations: travel, gardening, history. Office: Children's Hosp Pitts 3705 5th Ave Pittsburgh PA 15213-2524

LEE, PETER JAMES, bishop; b. Greenville, Miss., May 11, 1938; s. Erling Norman and Marion (O'Brien) L.; m. Kristina Knapp, Aug. 28, 1965; children: Stewart, Peter James Jr. AB, Washington and Lee U., 1960; LittD, U. of the South, 1999; MDiv, Va. Theol. Sem., 1967; postgrad, Duke U. Law Sch., 1963-64; DD (hon.), Va. Theol. Sem., 1984, St. Paul's Coll., Lawrenceville, Va., 1985, U. of the South, 1993; LittD, Washington and Lee U., 1997. Ordained priest Episc. Ch., 1968, bishop, 1984. Newspaper reporter, editor, Pensacola, Fla., Richmond, Memphis, 1960-63; deacon St. John's Cathedral, Jacksonville, Fla., 1967-68; asst. min. St. John's Ch. LaFayette Sq., Washington, 1968-71; rector Chapel of the Cross, Chapel Hill, N.C., 1971-84; bishop coadjutor Episcopal Diocese of Va., Richmond, 1984-85, bishop, 1985—. Pres. trustees of the funds Diocese of Va., 1985—; dir. Presiding Bishop's Fund for World Relief, 1986-93. Rector bd. trustees Episcopal H.S., Alexandria, Va., 1985—; chmn. Meml. Trustees, Richmond; trustee Wash. Nat. Cathedral, Ch. Pension Fund, 1999—, Berkeley Div. Sch. at Yale, 1999-2002. Recipient duPont Fund Lifetime Achievement award, 1997. Mem. Phi Beta Kappa, Omicron Delta Kappa. Episcopalian. Office: Diocese Va 110 W Franklin St Richmond VA 23220-5010 Office Phone: 804-643-8451. E-mail: pjlee@thediocese.net.

LEE, RANDY JAY, music educator, musician; b. Staples, Minn., Nov. 28, 1960; s. Gordon Ellsworth and Doris Marie (Farber) Lee; m. Mary Frances Claveau, Aug. 7, 1982; children: Robert, Jerome, Nathan, Peter. B of Music Edn., U. Minn., Duluth, 1982; MS in Edn., U. Wis., Superior, 1990. Cert. tchr. Minn. Dir. choral and instrumental music McGregor Schs., Minn., 1982—87; dir. bands mid. sch. Hermantown Schs., 1987—. Adj. faculty U. Minn., Duluth, 1995—2000; artistic dir. Big Time Jazz Orch., 1990—; guest condr., clinician various honor bands and sch. bands, 1995—, Wis., 1995—, Des Moines, 1995—; presenter in field. Composer: (big band jazz CD) Sometimes Down, 1999. Organizer, coord. concerts, performer various charity orgn. benefits, Duluth, 1990—. Grantee, Arrowhead Regional Arts Coun., Duluth, 1995, 1997, 1998, 2005. Mem.: Quality Tchr. Network for Arts, Minn. Band Dirs. Assn., Internat. Assn. Jazz Educators, Minn. Music Educators Assn., Am. Sch. Band Dirs. Assn. (chair 1992—). Roman Catholic. Avocations: exercise, camping. Office: Hermantown Mid Sch 4289 Ugstad Rd Hermantown MN 55811

LEE, RAPHAEL CARL, plastic surgeon, biomedical engineer; b. Sumter, SC, Oct. 29, 1949; s. Leonard Powell and Jean Maurice (Langston) L.; m. Kathleen Kelley, Feb. 11, 1983; children: Rachel, Catherine. BS, U. SC, 1971, ScD (hon.), 1999; MS, Drexel U., 1975; MD, Temple U., 1975; ScD, MIT, 1979. Diplomate Am. Bd. Plastic Surgeons, Am. Bd. Surgery. Chief resident gen. surgery U. Chgo. Hosps., 1980-81; chief resident plastic surgery Mass. Gen. Hosp., 1982-83; assoc. in surgery Brigham and Women's Hosp., 1984-89; assoc. surgeon The Children's Hosp., 1985-89; dir. Elec. Trauma Rsch. Program, 1991—; med. dir. U. Chgo. Burn Unit, 1991-97. Asst. prof. surgery Harvard Med. Sch., 1984—89; VanTassel asst. prof. elec. and bioengring. MIT, 1983—89; asst. prof. bioengring. and surgery Harvard MIT, Divsn. Health Scis. and Tech., 1983—89; prof. surgery, medicine, anatomy and bioengring. U. Chgo., 1992—; chmn. bd. dirs. Avocet Polymers Techs., Inc., 1996—; exec. com. Biomed. Engring. Inst., Ill. Inst. Tech.; chmn. bd. dirs. Maroon Biotech., Inc. Author: Electrical Injury, Multidisciplinary Approach, 1994, Occupational Electrical Injury, 1999; editor: Electrical Trauma, Pathophysiology, 1992; assoc. editor Bioelectromagnetics, 1993—; contbr. more than 200 articles to profl. jours. Recipient Alumni Achievement award Class of 1975 Temple Med. Sch., 1995, Searle Scholar award The Searle Found., 1985-88, Disting. Engring. Sch. Alumnus award U. SC, 1998, award for advancing safety and health Am. Electric Power Assn.; named Ams. 100 Brightest Young Scientists Sci. Digest, 1984; MacArthur Prize fellow John D. and Catherine T. MacArthur Found., 1981-86. Fellow ACS (Schering scholar in Surgery 1978), Am. Inst. Med. and Biol. Engring.; mem. IEEE, AAAS, Am. Burn Assn. (Lindberg award), Am. Phys. Soc., Am. Soc. for Cell Biology, Am. Assn. Plastic Surgeons (James Barrett Brown award 1988), Biophys. Soc., Nat. Med. Assn. (plastic surgery sect. chmn. 1989-91), Soc. for Phys. Regulation in Biology and Medicine (pres. 1995), Soc. Univ. Surgeons, Surg. Biology Club III, Tau Beta Pi, Alpha Omega Alpha, Sigma Xi. Achievements include 12 patents. Office: U Chgo Hosps Pritzker Sch Medicine-Surgery MC6035 5841 S Maryland Ave Chicago IL 60637-1463 Office Phone: 773-702-6302. E-mail: rlee@uchicago.edu.

LEE, RAYMOND WILLIAM, III, institutional stockbroker; b. Atlanta, Feb. 20, 1960; s. William Jr. and Marianne (Hollingsworth) Lee; m. Suzanne Bobbelle Smith, July 7, 1984; children: Virginia Stuart, Catherine Coleman. Student, Furman U., 1978; BBA, U. Ga., 1982; MBA, Ga. State U., 1984. Lic. broker series 7, 63, 4, 24, 27, 55. Sales rep. Harris/Lanier, Atlanta, 1984, maj. account rep., 1985-86; asst. v.p. Donaldson and Co., Inc., Atlanta, 1986, v.p., CFO, 1987-94; pres., founder, bd. dirs. Paragon Fin. Group, Inc., Atlanta, 1994—, Tradewinds Fin. Group, Inc., Atlanta, 2004—; pres., founder Paragon Property Ptnrs. LLC, 2003—. Holy Innocents Episcopal Ch.; mem. Holy Innocents Epis. Ch., 2003; bd. dir. Prevent Blindness Ga., 2001—, Ga. Coop. Svc. Blind, 2001—, Sandy Springs Cmty. Found., 2002—, Bonanza Five, Inc., 2000—03. Named one of Outstanding Young Men Am., 1985. Mem.: World Entreprenuers Orgn., Securities Industry Assn. (mem. instnl. com. 2002—04), Young Entreprenuers Orgn. (bd. dirs., pres. 2000), Cherokee Town and Country Club, Delta Tau Delta (bd. dirs., v.p. 1992—94, Karnea chmn. 1994, bd. dirs., v.p. 1998—2000). Republican. Home: 5290 Cross Roads Manor Atlanta GA 30327 Office: Tradewinds Fin Group Ste 100 1355 Terrell Mill Rd Bldg 1476 Marietta GA 30067 Business E-Mail: rwl@pfgi.com.

LEE, RICHARD DIEBOLD, lawyer, educator; b. Fargo, ND, July 31, 1935; s. Sidney Jay and Charlotte Hannah (Thompson) L.; m. Patricia Ann Taylor, June 17, 1957; children: Elizabeth Carol, Deborah Susan, David Stuart. BA with distinction, Stanford U., 1957; JD, Yale U., 1960. Bar: Calif. 1961, U.S. Dist. Ct. (no. dist.) Calif. 1961, U.S. Ct. Appeals (9th cir.) 1961. Dep. atty. gen. Office of Atty. Gen., Sacramento, 1960-62; assoc. McDonough, Holland, Schwartz, Allen & Wahrhaftig, Sacramento, 1962-66, ptnr., 1966-69; asst. dean U. Calif. Sch. Law, Davis, 1969-73, assoc. dean, 1973-76; assoc. prof. law Temple U. Sch. Law, Phila., 1976-77, vis. prof., 1975-76, prof., 1977-89; dir. profl. devel. Baker & McKenzie, Chgo., NYC, 1981-83; dir. Am. Law Inst.-ABA In-House (formerly Am. Inst. for Law Tng.), Phila., 1985—89, mem. adv. bd., 1989—; dir. profl. devel. Morrison & Foerster, San Francisco, 1989—93; dir. Continuing Edn. of the Bar, Berkeley, Calif., 1993—97; v.p. JusLaw.com, 2000—01, LawyersTV Continue Learning Networks L.L.C., 2002. Mem. Grad. and Profl. Fin. Aid Coun., Princeton, NJ, 1974-80; trustee Law Sch. Admission Coun., Washington, 1976-78; mem. internat. adv. com. Internat. Juridical Orgn., Rome, 1977-88; mem. bd. advisors Lawyer Hiring and Tng. Report, Chgo., 1983-95. Author: (coursebook) Materials on International Efforts to Control the Environment, 1977, 78, 79, 80, 84, 85, 87; co-editor: Orientation in the U.S. Legal System annual coursebook, 1982-92; contbr. articles to profl. jours. Trustee Grad. Theol. Union, Berkeley, 1991—2000, vice chair, 1994—99; mem. bd. of coun. Episc. Cmty. Svcs., Phila., 1984—88; trustee Grace Cathedral, San Francisco, 1989—2004, chair bd. trustees, 1992—95; trustee Coll. of Preachers, Washington Nat. Cathedral, 1999—2004, mem. cathedral coll. bd., 2004—; adv. bd. Ch. Div. Sch. of the Pacific, 2000—; bd. dirs. Lung Assn. of Sacramento-Emigrant Trails, 1962—69, pres., 1966—68; bd. dirs. Sacramento County Legal Aid Soc., 1968—74, pres., 1971—72; chmn. bd. overseers Phila. Theol. Inst., 1984—88, bd. overseers, 1979—80, 1984—88; mem. bd. visitors John Marshall Law Sch., Chgo., 1989—93; bd. dirs. Earplay, 2004—; chair, bd. dirs. The Ghiberti Found., 2002—04. Mem. ABA (chmn. various coms., spl. cons. on continuing legal edn. MacCrate Task Force on Law Schs. and the Profession: Narrowing the Gap, 1991-93, standing com. on specialization 1998-2001, standing com. paralegals 2003—), State Bar Calif. (chair standing com. on minimum continuing legal edn. 1990-92, com. mem. 1990-93), Bar Assn. San Francisco (legal ethics com., conf. of delegates 1987—), Profl. Devel. Consortium (co-founder, chair 1990-93), Am. Law Inst., Yale Club (N.Y.C., San Francisco). Democrat. Episcopalian. Home and Office: 2001 Sacramento St Ste 4 San Francisco CA 94109-3342 Personal E-mail: RichardDLee@earthlink.net.

LEE, RICHARD FRANCIS JAMES, evangelical clergyman, media consultant, lawyer; b. Yakima, Wash., Sept. 13, 1967; s. Richard Francis and Dorothy Aldean (Blackwell). Diploma, Berean Coll., Springfield, Mo., 1989; BA, U. Wash., Seattle, 1990; JD, Gonzaga Sch. Law, 1997; MDiv, Fuller Theol. Seminary, 2001. Bar: Wash. 2002; ordained Assemblies of God, So. Calif. dist., 1999. Lic. clergyman N.W. dist. Assemblies of God, Seattle, 1989. Author: Tell Me the Story, 1982, The Crimson Detective Motion Picture, 1996. Named Most Likely to be President, Franklin High Sch., Seattle, 1986. Pentecostal. Avocations: collector, writer, itinerant speaker, filmmaker. Office: 2604 E Boone Ave Spokane WA 99202-3718 Office Phone: 509-536-0986. Business E-Mail: info@richardlee.ministries.org. E-mail: lsrc@comcast.net.

LEE, RICHARD KENNETH, software company executive; b. Birmingham, Eng., Dec. 10, 1942; came to U.S., 1964; s. Kenneth Jesse Lee and Eleanor Margaret (Bellsham) Dean; m. Melinda Elena Noback, Aug. 20, 1966; children: Sonja Eleanor, Alyssa Claire. BSc with upper 2d class honours, No. Poly. U. London, 1964; MS in Inorganic Chemistry, Northwestern U., 1965; PhD in Inorganic Chemistry, U. London, 1968. Various corp. rsch. positions UOP Inc., Des Plaines, Ill., 1965-74, mgr. catalyst R & D automotive products divsn., 1974-77; v.p., gen. mgr. portable battery div. Gould Inc., St. Paul, 1977-82; v.p., gen. mgr. Elgar Corp., an Onan/McGraw Edison Co., San Diego, 1982-85; v.p. R & D, Pharmaseal div. Baxter Healthcare Corp., Valencia, Calif., 1985-88; v.p. strategic bus. ops. Manville Sales Corp., Denver, 1988-92; pres., chief exec. officer Rocklite Inc., Denver, 1992-99; prin. LeeVarage Internat., Castle Rock, 1993-00; chmn., pres., CEO Value Innovations, Inc., Denver, 1999—; mng. dir. Edgeguard Internat. Ltd., Castle Rock, 2002—03. Adj. prof. masters tech. program U. Coll., U. Denver, 1993-95; bd. dirs. Q.E.D., Denver; mem. adv. bd. Kodiak, Denver, 1998-99. Author: (videotape) U.S. Competitiveness—A Crisis?, 1992; patentee for vehicle emission control system. Chmn. Summit 91, Denver, 1991, mem. organizing com. Summit 92, Pacoima, Calif., 1992; bd. dirs. Indsl. Rsch. Inst., Inc., Washington, 1991-92, chmn. emeritus, 2003-04. Recipient IR-100 award, Indsl. R & D, 1978; Fulbright travel scholar, 1964—65. Mem. Rocky Mountain World Trade Ctr. (vice chmn. 1992-94, exec. com. 1992-94, bd. dirs. 1990-95). Office Phone: 303-688-4143. Business E-Mail: dick_lee@valueinnovations.net. *The quality of life for U.S. citizens in the early 21st Century will be primarily determined by the results of U.S. industry and government efforts to improve our ability to commercialize technology successfully.*

LEE, RICHARD VAILLE, internist, educator; b. Islip, N.Y., May 26, 1937; s. Louis Emerson and Erma Natalie (Little) L.; m. Susan Bradley, June 25, 1961; children: Matthew, Benjamin. BS, Yale U., 1960, MD cum laude, 1964. Diplomate Am. Bd. Internal Medicine, Am. Bd. Family Practice. Intern Grace-New Haven Hosp., 1964-65, asst. resident in internal medicine, 1965-66, 69-70; fellow in inflammatory disease Yale U., New Haven, 1970-71, asst. prof. medicine, 1971-74, assoc. prof. clin. medicine, 1974-76; practice medicine specializing in internal medicine New Haven, 1969-76, Buffalo, 1976—; family practice Poplar, Mont., 1966-68, Chester, Mont., 1968-69; prof. medicine SUNY, Buffalo, 1976—, prof. pediat., 1985—, adj. prof. anthropology, 1989—, prof. obstetrics, 1992—, chief divsn. gen. internal medicine, 1979-82, chief divsn. maternal and adolescent medicine, 1982—, chief divsn. geog. medicine, 1991—; dir. primary care ctr. Yale-New Haven Hosp., 1975-76, dir. med. clinics, 1971-75; chief med. svc. Buffalo VA Hosp., 1976-79; head dept. medicine Children's Hosp. Buffalo, 1979-96; fellow WHO Collaborating Ctr. for Health in Housing, 1985—, chief med. officer, 1995—. Cons. internal medicine N.Y. Zool. Soc., 1973—; cons. physician Buffalo Zool. Soc., 1980—2001; aviation med. examiner, 1980—2001; med. dir. Ecology and Environment, Inc., Lancaster, NY; mem. N.Y. State Bd. for Medicine, 1995—2002; mem. com. Nat. Bd. Med. Examiners, 1999—; mem. N.Y. State Office for Profl. Med. Conduct, 2001—. Author: Outside Rounds, 2005; editor: When I Was a Boy in China, 2003; sr. editor: Current Obstetric Medicine, 1989—95; corr. editor Jour. Obstetrics and Gynecology, London, 1989—; mem. editl. bd.: Internat. Jour. Environ. Health, 1994—; cons. editor Am. Jour. Medicine, 1976—86; contbr. chapters to books on obstetrics and toxicology, articles to profl. jours. Served with USPHS, 1966-68. Fellow: ACP (sr. editor Med. Care of the Pregnant Patient 2000, Laureate award 2002), Royal Soc. Asian Affairs, Royal Geog. Soc., Explorers Club N.Y.C.; mem.: AMA, Am. Coll. Occupl. and Environ. Medicine, Internat. Soc. of Travel Medicine, Soc. Obstetric Medicine (pres. 1991—93), Infectious Disease Soc. Am., Am. Soc. Tropical Medicine and Hygiene, Gen. Internal Medicine, Am. Fedn. Clin. Rsch. Soc., N.Y. Acad. Sci., Yale China Assn. (trustee 1992—2001, sec. 1995—2001), Nat. Bd. Med. Examiners, Am. Soc. History of Medicine, Royal Soc. Medicine, Great Lakes Interurban Clin. Club, Alpha Omega Alpha. Achievements include editing and reprinting, with introduction and photographs, his grandfather's book When I Was a Boy In China, 2003. Home: 7664 East Quaker Rd Orchard Park NY 14127-2015

LEE, ROBERT, engineer; b. Seoul, Republic of Korea, Jan. 18, 1963; arrived in U.S., 1973; s. Il Sang and Soon Keun Lee; m. Susan E. Lee, Jan. 18, 1969; children: Jennifer Melissa, Johnathan Robert, James. BS, Boston U., 1985. Sr. rsch. scientist Sci. Applications Internat. Corp., Fort Washington, Pa., 1985—94, Combustion Rsch. and Flow Tech., Inc., Dublin, Pa., 1995—2001; sr. aerodynamic engr. SAGE Sys. Techs., King of Prussia, Pa., 2001—03, Mil. Sys. Tech., LLC, 2003—. Mem.: AIAA. Home: 2545 Marshall Dr Quakertown PA 18951 Office: Military Sys Tech LLC 408 E Fourth St Ste 204 Bridgeport PA 19405 Office Phone: 610-272-5050. Business E-Mail: robert@milsystech.com.

LEE, ROBERT E., lawyer; b. Nashville, Oct. 4, 1963; s. Sherwood C. and Vada Ann Lee; children: Frances Margaret Ann, Robert E. Jr. BBA, Francis Marion U., Florence, S.C., 1987; JD, U. S.C., 1990. Bar: S.C. 1991, U.S. Dist. Ct. S.C. 1991, U.S. Ct. Appeals (4th cir.) 1991, cert.: S.C. Supreme Ct. (lead counsel in capital litigation), lic.: (arbitrator). Assoc. McIntosh & Lee, Florence, SC, 1990—2000; mng. shareholder Aiken, Bridges, Nunn, Elliott & Tyler, P.A., Florence, 2000—. Mem. ho. of dels. S.C. Bar, 1998. Chmn. bd. trustees Francis Marion U., Florence, 1999—2003; bd. mgrs. S.C. Hist. Soc., 2002—. Recipient Pres.'s award, Nat. Assn. Criminal Def. Lawyers, 1996. Mem.: Am. Kennel Club (mem. test rules adv. com. 1999—). Office: Aiken Bridges Nunn Elliott & Tyler PA Ste 409 181 E Evans St Florence SC 29506

LEE, ROBERT J. Y., marketing professional; b. Xixia, Henan, China, Dec. 28, 1929; arrived in U.S., 1975; s. Guo Jun Lee and Shih Yang; m. Shirley Pei-Chi, May 15, 1965; children: Alice P.C., Bowen. MA, U. Manila, 1973. Asst. fgn. svc. Ministry Fgn. Affairs, Taipei, Taiwan, 1966—69; consul Chinese Embassy, Manila, Philippines, 1969—75; v.p. OTC Inc., Columbus, Ohio, 1975—. Avocations: classical music, opera, gardening. Office: OTC Inc 40 Clairedan Dr Powell OH 43065 Home: 2065 Strathshire Hall Ln Powell OH 43065

LEE, RONALD DEMOS, demographer, economist, educator; b. Sept. 5, 1941; s. Otis Hamilton and Dorothy (Demetracopoulou) Lee; m. Melissa Lee Nelken, July 6, 1968; children: Sophia, Isabel, Rebecca. BA, Reed Coll., 1963; MA, U. Calif., Berkeley, 1967; PhD, Harvard U., 1971; D (hon.), Lund U., Sweden, 2004. Postdoctoral fellow Nat. Demographic Inst., Paris, 1970-71; asst. prof. to prof. U. Mich., Ann Arbor, 1971-79; prof. demography and econs. U. Calif., Berkeley, 1979—. Dir. Berkeley Ctr. Econs. and Demography Aging; chair com. population NAS, 1993—97; cons. in field. Author, editor: Population Patterns in the Past, 1977, Econometric Studies of Topics in Demographic History, 1978, Population, Food, and Rural Development, 1988, Economics of Changing Age Distributions in Developed Countries, 1988, others; editor: Population Change in Asia: Transition, Development and Aging, 2000, Demographic Change and Fiscal Policy, 2000, United States Fertility: New Patters, New Theories, 1996; contbr. articles to profl. jours. Vol. Peace Corps, Ethiopia, 1963—65. Recipient Mindel C. Sheps award, Population Assn. Am. and U. N.C. Sch. Pub. Health, 1984, MERIT award, Nat. Inst. Aging, 1994—2003, Taeuber award, Population Assn. Am. and Princeton U., 1999; fellow, Social Sci. Rsch. Coun., 1970—71; NIH fellow, 1965—67, NSF fellow, 1968—69, NIH grantee, 1973—, Guggenheim fellow, 1984—85. Fellow: Brit. Acad. (corr.); mem.: AAAS, NAS, Internat. Union Sci. Study Population, Am. Acad. Arts and Scis., Am. Econ. Assn., Population Assn. Am. (pres. 1987). Democrat. Home: 2933 Russell St Berkeley CA 94705-2333 Office: U Calif Dept Demography 2232 Piedmont Ave Berkeley CA 94720-2120 Office Phone: 510-642-4535. E-mail: rlee@demog.berkeley.edu.

LEE, RONALD DEREK, lawyer; b. Seattle, Aug. 10, 1959; s. Frank B. and Mary Lee. AB, Princeton (N.J.) U., 1980; M of Philosophy, Oxford U., 1982; JD, Yale U., 1985. Bar: N.Y. 1986, D.C. 1987, Calif. 1991. Law clk. to Judge Abner J. Mikva U.S. Ct. Appeals (D.C. cir.), Washington, 1985-86; law clk. to Justice John Paul Stevens U.S. Supreme Ct., Washington, 1986-87; assoc. Arnold & Porter, Washington, 1987-91, L.A., 1991-92, ptnr., 1993-94; gen. counsel Nat. Security Agy., 1994—98; chief of staff CIA, 1996; assoc. dep. atty. gen. U.S. Dept. Justice, Washington, 1998—2000; ptnr., Nat. Security Law & Policy Practice group Arnold & Porter LLP, Washington, 2001—. Rhodes scholarship Rhodes Trust, 1980. Mem. Phi Beta Kappa. Avocations: tennis, table tennis. Office: Arnold & Porter LLP 555 Twelfth St NW Washington DC 20004-1206 Office Phone: 202-942-5380. Office Fax: 202-942-5999. Business E-Mail: ronald.lee@aporter.com.

LEE, SALLY A., editor-in-chief; m. Rob Niosi. Grad., Durham U., Eng.; MA, Clark U., Mass. Tchr. writing and lit. Clark U.; reporter Worcester (Mass.) Telegram; mng. editor Worcester (Mass.) Monthly; spl. features editor Woman's World mag., NYC; articles editor Woman's Day mag., NYC; sr. editor Redbook mag., NYC; editor-in-chief YM, NYC, 1994—96, Fitness Mag., NYC, 1996—98, Parents Mag., NYC, 1998—; editl. dir. YM mag., NYC, 2004. Corr. E! Entertainment Network. Author: The Best Advice I Ever Got, 2001. Bd. dirs. Room to Grow, Women for Women Internat. Mem.: Parenting Network. Office: Parents Mag 375 Lexington Ave Fl 10 New York NY 10017-5514 Office Phone: 212-499-2050, 212-449-2083.*

LEE, SANDRA ANN, investment company executive; b. Houston, Nov. 28, 1942; d. Herman and Lillian (Bily) Sporn; m. Kenneth Phillip Veit, June 2, 1962 (div. June 1989). BA, U. Tex., 1963; MS, Am. U., Washington, 1971; MBA, U. Conn., 1979. CFA. Programmer GE, Bethesda, Md., 1963-64; assoc. mem. tech. staff Rsch. Analysis Corp., McLean, Va., 1964-66; mem. tech. staff MITRE Corp., McLean, 1966-72; systems mgr. Travelers Ins. Cos., Hartford, Conn., 1972-74; data base adminstr. Mass. Mut. Life Ins. Co., Springfield, Mass., 1974-75; investment mgr. cons. West Hartford, Conn., 1975-79, 87-92; trust officer Conn. Nat. Bank, Hartford, 1979-87; sr. v.p. investments The T.O. Richardson Co., Farmington, Conn., 1992—95; prin. Sandra A. Lee Investment Cons., West Hartford, Conn., 1995—. Mem. Hartford Soc. Fin. Analysts (pres., bd. mem. 1982-89). Republican. Congregationalist. Avocations: hiking, biking, reading, running.

LEE, SANG-HEE, communications engineer; b. Joomoonjin, Gangwondo, Republic of Korea, Apr. 28, 1971; s. Hee-sung Lee and Jung-ja Kim; m. Hyun-ju Lee, May 5, 1972. BS magna cum laude, Korea Advanced Inst. of Sci. and Tech., Daejon, 1993, MS, 1995, PhD, 2000. Sr. engr. ImpressTek, Inc., Daejon, Republic of Korea, 2000—02; prin. engr. Thin Multimedia, Inc., Palo Alto, Calif., 2002—. Cons. ImpressTek, Inc., Daejon, Republic of Korea, 1999—99, Havin, Inc., Daejon, Republic of Korea, 2000—01, Shellcomm, Inc., Daejon, Republic of Korea, 2001—02. Contbr. over 40 articles to profl. jours. Recipient award of the Min. of Comm., Korea Nat. Personal Programming Contest., Korea Govt., 1986; scholarship, Korea Advanced Inst. of Sci. and Tech., 1989-1993, Samsung Electronics, 1993, Hyundai Electronics. (currently Hynix Semiconductor), 1996-2000, Travel grant, Japan Internat. Sci. and Tech. Exch. Ctr., 1996. Mem.: IEEE (assoc.). Achievements include patents for two core US(US6215905) and Korean(KR303685) patents of the MPEG-4 video (Simple Profile), which is the world-famous technology for mobile phones, internet video, and digital cameras; first to Developed mobile video codecs for the world-first wireless multimedia service in 6 countries (US, Korea, Israel, Taiwan, Italy, India). Office: Thin Multimedia Inc 1731 Embarcadero Rd Ste 220 Palo Alto CA 94303 Office Phone: 650-856-2700. Personal E-mail: neoshlee1@hotmail.com.

LEE, SARENA JANEEN, public health service officer; b. Chicago, Ill., Feb. 4, 1976; d. Alfred B. Lee Sr. and Felicia J. Riley. BA in profl. and Tech. Writing, Chgo. State U., 1994—2001; MA in Writing Theory and Pedaogogy, DePaul U., Chgo., Ill., 2002—04. Buyer Provident Hosp. Cook County, Chgo., 1993—; disaster preparedness/readiness journeyman USAF Res., Grissom ARB, Ind., 2002—. Sr. airman Res. USAF, 2002, Grissom ARB, Ind. E-mail: sarenajlee@yahoo.com.

LEE, SE-HEE, electrical engineer, researcher; b. Yechon, Kyungbuk, Korea, Aug. 3, 1971; s. Sang-Seop Lee and Sun-Deok Kim; m. In-Sook Heo, June 19, 1975; 1 child, Eun-Jae. PhD, Sungkyunkwan U., 2002. Part-time lectr. Daelim Coll., Anyang, Republic of Korea, 1998—99; vis. lectr. ANSOFT Korea Corp., Seoul, 1999—2000; sr. rschr. Sungkyunkwan U., Suwon, Republic of Korea, 2002—, part-time lectr., 2003; post-doctoral fellow MIT, Cambridge, 2003—04, post-doctoral assoc., 2004—. Contbr. articles to profl. jours. Post-doctoral Fellowship, Korea Sci. and Engring. Found., 2003—04. Mem.: Korea Inst. Elec. Engrs. Office: Massachusetts Institute of Technology 155 Massachusetts Ave BldgN10 Cambridge MA 02139 Office Phone: 617-253-5019. Personal E-mail: shlees@mit.edu.

LEE, SEHEE, energy scientist; b. Ulsan, Republic of Korea, Mar. 03; s. Boonsun Kim; m. Huwon Lee, July 11; children: Justin, Michelle. PhD, Seoul Nat. U., 1997. Sr. scientist Nat. Renewable Energy Lab, Golden, Colo., 1997—. Mem.: Electrochem. Soc. Office: Nat Renewable Energy Lab 1617 Cole Blvd Golden CO 80401 Home: 8814 W Center Ave Lakewood CO 80226 Office Fax: 303-384-6432. Personal E-mail: seheelee87@hanmail.net. Business E-Mail: se_hee_lee@nrel.gov.

LEE, SEONG-JAE, research scientist; b. Kwangyang, Chunnam, South Korea, Apr. 30, 1963; s. Yong-Dae Lee and Il-Lim Suh; m. Sung-Hye Yoon; children: Sharon, Amy. BS, Yonsei U., Seoul, 1986, MS, 1988; PhD, Iowa State U., 1998. Rsch. asst. Iowa State U., Ames, 1993—98, rsch. assoc., 1998—2003, rsch. scientist Ctr. for Nondestructive Evaluation, 2004—. Contbr. articles to profl. jours. Mem.: Sigma Xi. Home: Apt 4 240 Raphael Ames IA 50014 Office: Iowa State U Ames Lab 258H Metals Devel Bldg Ames IA 50011 Office Phone: 515-294-9066. Business E-Mail: sjlee@ameslab.gov.

LEE, SHARON GAIL, lawyer; b. Madisonville, Tenn., Dec. 8, 1953; d. Charles James and Judith Ann (Burris) L.; children: Sarah, Laura Elizabeth. BS, JD, U. Tenn. Bar: Tenn. 1978. Assoc. J.D. Lee & Assocs., Madisonville, 1978-80; ptnr. Lee & Alliman Law Offices, Madisonville, 1980—90; sole practice Madisonville, 1990—. Atty. Town of Madisonville, 1982-88, County of Monroe, 1990—, City of Vonne, 1998—; judge City of Madisonville, 2002—. Mem. ABA, Tenn. Trial Lawyer Assn., Am. Trial Lawyers Assn. Democrat. Episc. Home: 495 Dyer Rd Madisonville TN 37354 Office: PO Box 425 Madisonville TN 37354-0425

LEE, SHAU KEE, real estate developer; married; 5 children. With Henderson Land Devel., Hong Kong; chmn. Hong Kong & China Gas; chmn., mng. dir. Henderson Land Group, 1976—, Henderson Investment Ltd.; chmn. Henderson Cyber Ltd.; vice chmn. Sun Hung Kai Properties. Avocation: golf. Office: 23d Fl 363 Java Rd Northpoint Hong Kong Hong Kong

LEE, SHEPARD, automobile dealership owner; b. Lewiston, Maine, Nov. 13, 1926; s. Joseph and Ethel (Richelson) Lifshitz; m. Nancy Margolis (div.); children: Jonathan, Catherine, Adam, Beth; m. Candice Thornton, Feb. 24, 1995. AB magna cum laude, Bowdoin Coll., 1947. Owner Lee Auto Malls, Westbrook, Auburn, Topsham, Augusta, Saco, Norway and Windham, Maine, 1947—. Spkr. Nat. Can. Auto Dealers Assn.; cons. French Bank, Credit Gen. Indsl.; lectr. in China on free enterprise Brandeis U.; bd. dirs. Fin. Authority of Maine. Former mem. New Eng. adv. coun. Fed. Res. Bank, Boston; former bd. dirs. Cumberland Club, Portland, Maine, ACLU; bd. dirs. George J. Mitchell Scholarship Rsch. Inst.; former mem. adv. bd. U. Maine Inst. Family Owned Bus.; mem. bd. govs. U. Maine Law Sch., Edmund S. Muskie Sch. Pub. Affairs, adv. bd. Sch. Bus. Recipient Dealer of Distinction award AIADA Sports Illustrated, 1985, Robert R. Masterson award Westbrook C. of C., 2003, Access to Justice award, 2004, Roger Baldwin award ACLU; named one of eight Outstanding Dealers in Country, Time Mag., 1992. Mem. ACLU (bd. dirs., Roger Baldwin award), Nat. Auto Dealers Assn. (mem. project 2000 Commn.), Phi Beta Kappa. Democrat. Office: Lee Auto Malls 200 Main St Westbrook ME 04092 Business E-Mail: slee@leeautomall.com.

LEE, SHUISHIH SAGE, pathologist; b. Soo-chow, Kiang su, China, Jan. 5, 1948; came to U.S., 1972, naturalized, 1979; m. Chung Seng Lee; children: Yvonne Claire, Michael Chung. MD, Nat. Taiwan U., 1972; PhD, U. Rochester, 1976. Resident in pathology Strong Meml. Hosp., Rochester, N.Y., 1976-78, Northwestern Meml. Hosp., Chgo., 1978-79; dir. cytology and electron microscopy Parkview Meml. Hosp., Ft. Wayne, Ind., 1979—. Clin. prof. Ind. U. Med. Sch. Contbr. articles to profl. jours. Fellow: Am. Soc. Clin. Pathologists, Coll. Am. Pathologists; mem.: AMA, Internat. Assn. Chinese Pathologists (pres. 1999—2001), Ft. Wayne Acad. Physicians and Surgeons (pres. 1990), Ft. Wayne Med. Soc. (pres. 2001—02, chairperson of bd. 2002—), Electron Microscopy Soc. Am., Internat. Acad. Cytology, Internat. Acad. Pathology, Am. Soc. Cytology, Am. Assn. Pathologists, N.Y. Acad. Scis., Ind. Assn. Pathologists, N.E. Ind. Pathologists Assn. (sec. 1984), Ind. Med. Assn. Home: 5728 The Prophets Pass Fort Wayne IN 46845-9659 Office: Parkview Meml Hosp 2200 Randallia Dr Fort Wayne IN 46805-4699

LEE, SIDNEY PHILLIP, chemical engineer, state senator; b. Pa., Apr. 20, 1926; s. Samuel L. and Mollie (Heller) L. B.Sc., U. Pa., 1939; McMullin fellow, Cornell U., 1939-40, then M.Ch.E. Chem. engr. Atlantic Richfield Co., 1938-42; sr. chem. engr., 1942-45; pres. Dallas Labs., 1945—, Asso. Labs., Dallas, 1945—, West Indies Investment Co., 1957—; chmn. exec. com. West Indies Bank & Trust Co. Dir., mem. exec. com. Am. Ship Bldg. Co.; prin. West Indies Investment Co., St. Croix, 1956— Writer of Lee Lets Loose column for local Carribean newspapers. Mem. V.I. Senate, 1976—, now v.p.; chmn. com. govt., chmn. com. on fin. ops. V.I. Govt. Dem. nat. committeeman for V.I., 1969—; mem. V.I. Bd. Edn., 1969-76; mem. Gov.'s Blue Ribbon Commn. for Econ. Devel., 1995—; commr. V.I. Port Authority, 1997—. Fellow Am. Inst. Chemists; mem. AIChE (sr.), AIME (sr.), AARP (chmn. legis. com. 1984—), St. Croix C. of C. (v.p. 1995), Rotary (pres. 1971-73), Lions (pres. 1960), Tau Beta Pi, Sigma Tau. Home and Office: 135 E 54th St Apt 11C New York NY 10022-4511 Office: PO Box 130 St Croix VI 00821-0130 *In retrospect, elation from supposed triumphs or defeats is blurred in memory; and of greater importance is the quality of one's life or how one played the game.*

LEE, SIN HANG, pathologist, educator; b. Hong Kong, Nov. 17, 1932; came to U.S., 1963, naturalized, 1976; s. Yat Sun and Siu Tsing (Wong) L.; m. Kee Hung Hau, Dec. 31, 1958; children: Emil, Karen. MD, Wuhan Med. Coll., China, 1956. Diplomate Am. Bd. Pathology. Intern South Balt. Gen. Hosp., 1963-64; resident N.Y. Hosp., 1964-66; bacteriologist Sichuan Med. Coll., Chengdu, China, 1956-61; demonstrator in pathology U. Hong Kong, 1961-63; instr. pathology Cornell-N.Y. Hosp., 1966-67; fellow in pathology Meml. Hosp. for Cancer, N.Y.C., 1967-68; asst. prof. McGill U., Montreal, 1968-71; assoc. prof. Yale U., New Haven, 1971-73, assoc. clin. prof., 1973—2003; attending pathologist Hosp. St. Raphael, New Haven, 1973—2003, Milford (Conn.) Hosp., 2004—. Guest prof. Wuhan Med. Coll. (China), 1984—. Contbr. articles in field to profl. jours.; patentee in field. Mem. AAAS, Royal Coll. Physicians and Surgeons of Can., Internat. Acad. Pathology. Office: Milford Hosp 300 Seaside Ave Milford CT 06460-4603 also: Milford Hosp 300 Seaside Ave Milford CT 06460 Office Phone: 203-385-3836. E-mail: drleestea@teaforhealth.com.

LEE, SOH YEONG, music educator; b. Seoul, Rep. of Korea, Mar. 21, 1966; arrived in US, 1993; d. Sang Jin Yoo and Kyung Suk Baik; m. Jae Hwan Lee, Aug. 21, 1993. MusB in piano performance, Han Yang U., Rep. of Korea, 1991; MusM in piano performance, Han Yang U., 1993; MusM in piano pedagogy, West Chester U., 1999; MusD in piano performance, Rutgers U., 2005. Piano adj. faculty Valley Forge Christian Coll., Phoenixville, Pa., 2000—01; group piano class instr. Del. County C. C., Media, Pa., 2002—03; piano faculty Cmty. Music Sch., Trappe, Pa., 1998—; piano adj. faculty Ursinus Coll., Collegeville, Pa., 2004—. Ch. pianist Pughtown Bapt. Ch., Pughtown, Pa., 2003—, Soh Mang Ch., Ambler, Pa., 1995—2001, Lower Providence Bapt. Ch., Eagleville, Pa., 2001—02. Contbr. articles various recital papers. Mem.: Coll. Music Soc., Pi Kappa Lamda. Avocations: walking, swimming. Office Phone: 484-680-1665. Personal E-mail: ssoppong@yahoo.com.

LEE, SPIKE (SHELTON JACKSON LEE), filmmaker; b. Atlanta, Mar. 20, 1957; s. William and Jacqueline (Shelton) L.; m. Tonya Lewis; 1 child: Satchel Lewis Lee. BA, Morehouse Coll., 1979; MA, NYU, 1982. Pres. Spike/DDB. Dir. (films) Last Hustle in Brooklyn, 1977, The Answer, 1980, Sarah, 1981, Boyz n the Hood, 1991, Come Rain or Come Shine, 2001, (TV series) Sucker Free City, 2004, (TV films) Freak, 1998, (documentary) A Huey P. Newton Story, 2001; actor, dir., prodr. writer (films) Summer of Sam, 1999; actor, dir., prodr., writer (films) School Daze, 1988, Do the Right Thing, 1989, Mo' Better Blues, 1990, Jungle Fever, 1991, Malcolm X, 1992, Crooklyn, 1994, Clockers, 1995; dir., prodr., writer (films) He Got Game, 1998, Bamboozled, 2000, She Hate Me, 2004; dir., prodr., writer, editor Joe's Bed-Stuy Barbershop: We Cut Heads, 1983 (student dir. award Acad. Motion Pictures Arts and Scis.); actor, dir., prodr., writer, editor (films) She's Gotta Have It, 1986 (New Generation award L.A. Film Critics, Prix de Jeunesse, Cannes Film Festival 1986); prodr. (films) The Best Man, 1999, Love and Basketball, 2000; exec. prodr. (films) Drop Squad, 1994, New Jersey Drive, 1995, Tales from the Hood, 1995, Home Invaders, 2001 (TV films) Good Fences, 2003; dir., exec. prodr. (documentary) Get on the Bus, 1996, (TV films) Sucker Free City, 2004; actor, dir., prodr Girl 6, 1996; dir., prodr. (documentary) 4 Little Girls, 1997, The Original Kings of Comedy, 2000, (documentary) Jim Brown All American, 2002, 25th Hour, 2002; actor, co-exec. prodr., prodr. 3 A.M., 2001; author: Spike Lee's Gotta Have It: Inside Guerilla Filmmaking, 1987, Uplift the Race: The Construction of School Daze,1988, Do the Right Thing: A Spike Lee Joint, 1989, Mo' Better Blues, 1990, By Any Means Necessary: The Trials and Tribulations of the Making of "Malcolm X", 1992. Trustee Morehouse Coll., 1992—. Office: 40 Acres & a Mule 124 Dekalb Ave Ste 2 Brooklyn NY 11217-1200*

LEE, STAN (STANLEY MARTIN LIEBER), cartoon publisher, writer; b. NYC, Dec. 28, 1922; s. Jack and Celia (Solomon) Lieber; m. Joan Clayton Boocock, Dec. 5, 1947; 2 children, Joan C., Jan (dec.). Hon. degree, Bowling Green State U. Copy writer, then asst. editor, editor Timely Comics, NYC, 1939—42; editor, creative dir. Atlas Comics (formerly Timely Comics), 1945—61; with Marvel Comics, 1961—72, pub., editl. dir., 1972—78; creative dir. Marvel Prodns., 1978—89, chmn. Marvel comics; partnered with DC Comics, 2000—. Founder, Stan Lee Media. Creator, former writer and editor Fantastic Four, Incredible Hulk, Amazing Spiderman, numerous others; author: Origins of Marvel Comics, 1974, Son of Origins, 1975, Bring On The Bad Guys, 1976, Mighty Marvel Strength & Fitness Book, 1976, Mighty Marvel Superheroes Fun Book, 1976, The Marvel Comics Illustrated Version of Star Wars, 1977, The Amazing Spiderman Vol. No. 3, 1977, The Superhero Women, 1977, The Mighty World of Marvel Pin-up Book, 1978, The Mighty Marvel Superhero Fun Book Vol. No. 3, 1978, The Silver Surfer, How to Draw Comics the Marvel Way, 1978, Marvel's Greatest Superhero Battles, 1978, Incredible Hulk, 1978, Marvelous Mazes to Drive You Mad, 1978, Fantastic Four, 1979, Doctor Strange, 1979, Complete Adventures of Spider-Man, 1979, Captain America, 1979, The Best of the Worst, 1979, Marvel Word Games, 1979, Omnibus Fun Book, 1979, Dunn's Conundrum, 1985, The Best of Spider-Man, 1986, Marvel Team-Up Thrillers, 1987, The Amazing Spiderman, No. 2, 1980, Hulk Cartoons, 1980, Marvel Masterworks Vol. 2: Fantastics Four, 1987, X-Men, 1987, Marvel Masterworks, Vol. 1: Amazing Spider-Man, 1987, Masterworks, Vol. 6: Fantastic Four, 1988, Silver Surfer: Judgement Day, 1988, Silver Surfer: Parable, 1988, Spider-Man, 1988, Avengers, 1988, The God Project, 1990, Silver Surfer: The Enslavers, 1990, Marvel Masterworks, Vol. 13: Fantastic Four, 1990, Best of Marvel Comics, 1991, Night Cat, 1991, Marvel Masterworks, Vol. 17: Daredevil, 1991, Marvel Masterworks, Vol. 18: Thor, 1991, Spider-Man Wedding, 1991, Spider-Man Masterworks, 1992, Uncanny X-Men Masterworks, 1993, Marvels Greatest Super Battles, 1994, The Ultimate Spiderman, 1994, The Very Best of Spiderman, 1994, The Incredible Hulk: A Man-Brute Berserk, 1995, others; creator (TV series), Iron Man, 1966, Hulk, 1966, Spider-Man, 1994-98, The Fantastic Four, 1994, The Incredible Hulk, 1996-97, Avengers, 1999-2000, Spider-Man: The New Animated Series, 2003, Striperella, 2003; cameos in several movie adaptations of comic book characters including X-Men, 2000, Spider-Man, 2002, Daredevil, 2003, Hulk, 2003, Spider-Man 2, 2004, Fantastic Four, 2005; guest appearences include (voice) The Incredible Hulk, 1997, (voice) Spider-Man, 1998, 2003, Turn Ben Stein On, 2001, To Tell the Truth, 2001, (voice) The Simpsons, 2002, Mad TV, 2003, 2004, and several talk shows. With Signal Corps U.S. Army, 1942—45. Recipient Alley Award, 1963-68; Comic Art Award, Soc. for Comic Art Rsch. & Preservation, 1968; Eureka Award, Il Targa 1970; Publisher of the Year, Periodical & Book Assn. of America, 1978; ann. award Popular Culture Assn., 1974 Mem. (founder), Acad. Comic Book Arts (award 1973), Nat. Acad. TV Arts and Scis., Nat. Cartoonists Soc., AFTRA. Clubs: Friars (N.Y.C.). Office: Marvel Comics Group Wilshire Blvd Ste 1400 Los Angeles CA 90024 also: Marvel Entertainment Group Inc Fl 9 10 E 40th St New York NY 10016-0201 Mailing: Attn: Ross Fineman William Morris Agency 151 ElCamino Dr Beverly Hills CA 90212 Address: Attn: Gill Champion POW! Entertainment 9440 Santa Monica Blvd Ste 620 Beverly Hills CA 90210*

LEE, STANLEY TAK, dentist; b. Chungshan, Canton, China, Mar. 1, 1946; s. Man Hoy and Bo Yuk (Lau) Lee; m. Rita Sook Chin, July 3, 1976; children: Winnie Sita, Jennie Wanda. AS, City Coll. San Francisco, 1971; BS, U. Calif., Berkeley, 1973; DDS, Loma Linda U., 1977. Diplomate Misch Implant Inst. Gen. practice dentistry, San Jose, Calif., 1978—. Fellow: Internat. Congress Oral Implantologists, Am. Congress Oral Implantology, Am. Soc. Ossteo (assoc.); mem.: ADA, Am. Endodontic Soc., Santa Clara County Dental Soc. (dental care com. 1983—84), Calif. Dental Assn., Chinese Cultural Assn., Chungshan Benevolence Assn., Beta Gamma Sigma, Alpha Gamma Sigma. Home and Office: Lee Dental Ctr Suite #101 1095 Branham Ln San Jose CA 95131 Office: 1628 Hostetter Rd # J San Jose CA 95131 also: 1698 S Wolfe Rd # 108 San Jose CA 95131 Office Phone: 408-978-8888. Personal E-mail: leestanley88@yahoo.com.

LEE, STEPHEN SUBERS, investment advisor; b. Allentown, Pa., June 13, 1967; s. John Newbold and Mary S. Lee; m. Deborah E. Ernst, May 14, 1994; children: Savannah, Amanda. BS, Lehigh U., 1994. V.p. Mercer Capital Mgmt., Inc., Phila., 1992—93; mng. dir. Logan Capital Mgmt., Inc., Phila., 1994—. Office: Logan Capital Mgmt Inc 1650 Market St Ste 5200 Philadelphia PA 19103 Home: 108 Booth Ln Haverford PA 19041 Office Fax: 215-851-9444. Business E-Mail: sslee@logancapital.com.

LEE, STEPHEN W., lawyer; b. New Castle, Ind., Oct. 25, 1949; s. Delmer W. Lee and Loma F. (Thurston) McCall; m. Pamela A. Summers, Aug. 2, 1969; children: Erin E., Stephanie M. BS, Ball State U., 1971; JD summa cum laude, Ind. U., 1977. Bar: Ind. 1977, U.S. Dist. Ct. (so. dist.) Ind. 1977, U.S. Ct. Appeals (7th cir.) 1977, U.S. Supreme Ct. 1982. Officer, lt.(j.g.) USNR, Phila., 1971-74; law clk. U.S. Dist. Ct. (no. dist.) Ind., Ft. Wayne, 1977-78; assoc. Barnes, Hickam, Pantzer & Boyd, Indpls., 1978-82, Barnes & Thornburg, Indpls., 1982-83, ptnr., 1984—. Dir. The Julian Ctr., Indpls., 1999—; mem. Ind. U. Sch. of Law Bd. of Visitors, 1999—. Editor-in-chief: Indiana Law Jour., 1976-77. Dir. Ind. Repertory Theatre, Indpls., 1986-91; exec. coun. Ind. U. Alumni Assn., Bloomington, 1989; dir. Ind. U. Sch. of Law Alumni Assn., Bloomington, 1984-90, pres., 1991-92; mem. Ball State U. Coll. Bus. Alumni Bd., 1991-2000, Ball State U. Entrepreneurship Adv. Bd., 1994-2002. Mem. Ind. State Bar Assn., Indpls. Bar Assn. (chmn. bus. sect. 1985), Highland Golf & Country Club. Republican. Avocation: golf. Office: Barnes & Thornburg 11 S Meridian St Indianapolis IN 46204-3535 Office Phone: 317-231-7200. Business E-Mail: slee@btlaw.com.

LEE, STEVEN XAVIER, museum director, communication and environmental designer; b. Balt., Dec. 25; s. Francis Xavier Lee and Dolores Carroll Lucas. BFA, Howard U., 1974; MS, Pratt Inst., 1977. News reporter WHUR Radio, Washington, 1972—74; exhbn. designer Manasse Assocs., N.Y.C., 1975—77, Warren Displays, N.Y.C., 1976—77; art dir. The Continental Group, N.Y.C., 1978—80; art and animation dir. Le Centre Bossuet, Paris, 1980—81; lectr./assoc. prof. U. Md., Baltimore County/College Park, 1982—87; asst. curator Office of the Mayor, Balt., 1988—91; dir. The Heritage Mus., Balt., 1991—, Benjamin Banneker Hist. Pk. and Mus., Oella, Md., 1997—. Dir. The Found. for Minority Film, Balt., 1984—90; art and culture com. chmn. Balt. Cable Access Corp., 1984—94; instr. Md. Inst. Coll. Art, Balt., 1985—86; adj. assoc. prof. U. Balt., 1988—90; bd. mem. Friends of the Gwynns Falls/Leakin Pk., Balt., 1989—, Consortium African Am. Museums Md., Annapolis, 2002—. Co-author: Understanding & Exploring Community-Based Approaches to Ecosystem Management in the U.S.; prodr., author: exhibition Remember Maryland - A History of Free African American and Native Americans in the Making of Early Maryland (Md. Humanities Coun. award, 1995), hist. exhbn. Remember Maryland, prodr., interviewer:

public radio program Living Voices/Voces Vivas; commentator, historian (pub. TV prodn.) American Almanacs - A Living History; book (non-fiction), Windsor Hills - A Century of History 1895 to 1995, digital painting, Embers - Tribute to Haile Gerima (Sigraph Art Show award, 1986), exhbn., Design (Design Excellence award, 1979), History of Trade Shows (First Pl. in Hist. Exhbn., 1977). Task force appointee Mayor's Task Force for the Gwynns Falls Freenway, Balt., 1993—96; com. mem. Md. Stream ReLeaf Coordinating Com., Annapolis, 1998—2002; steering com. mem. Revitalizing Balt., 1995—2000; monument com. chmn. Balt. Cultural Alliance, 1999—2005; dir. Gwynns Falls Conservancy, Balt., 1993—2005. Named Living Maker of History, Gov. Paris Glendening & Iota Phi Lambda; recipient Stream Action award, Md. Save Our Streams, 1995, Hose Resolution - In Recognition of Exceptional Achievement in the Devel. Diverse Cultural Arts, Md. Ho. Dels., 1997, CityArts award, Mayor's Adv. Com. on Art and Culture, 1998. Mem.: Internat. Coun. Museums, Am. Assn. Mus. Achievements include design of modular pneumatic exhibition structures; development of The Heritage Museum - first organization for the combined development of African, African American, Carribean, Latin American and Native American cultures; The Gwynns Falls Conservancy - minority organization for environmental education and conservation. Home: Hamlet Court 4509 Prospect Circle Baltimore MD 21216 Office: Banneker Historical Park & Museum 300 Oella Ave Baltimore MD 21228 Office Phone: 410-887-1081. Office Fax: 410-203-2747. Personal E-mail: sxlee@co.ba.md.us.

LEE, SUN, surgeon; b. Korea, June 2, 1920; 6 children. MD, Seoul Nat. (Kyung Sung Med. Sch.), Seoul, Korea, 1945, Cook County Grad. Sch. of Medicine, Chgo., Calif., 1950. Intern Wheeling Gen. Hosp., W.Va., 1951; gen. residency Ohio Valley Gen. Hosp., Wheeling, 1952; gen. surg. residency Pitts., 1955; fellow asst. prof. surgery Univ. Pitts., 1955—64; assoc. immunopathology Scripps Clinic, La Jolla, Calif., 1967; dir. San Diego Microsurg. Inst., San Diego, 2003—; vol. clin. prof. surgery U. Calif. San Diego Med. Sch., 2003—05. Mem.: Transplanation, Internat. Soc. For Experimental Microsurgery (founder), Worlds Microsurgical Soc. (hon.). Achievements include research in began to explore rat blood vessel surgery under Prof. Bernard Fisher in 1957; development of rat organ transplants except heart, intestine. Studying tech-immunological, pathophysiological investigation using rodents; the use of rodents in the organ transplant rsch., we were able to replace use of domestic animals thus reducing pub. sentiments and rsch. expenditures; research in consecutive organ transplant study. Older vital organs are transplanted into young, when these rats get old, removed the same organ, and transplant into a young rat; Rats life span is around 24 months, we were able to extend pancreas to survive to 52 months, by this technique, one can observe endocrine glands implanted into the spleen can be observed much lolnger; the benign turmors at usual rats life term showed malignant at a prolonged period, we are predicting human vital organs can be recycable in the future to fight the organ shortage problem.

LEE, SUNG HO, psychiatrist; b. Seoul, June 28, 1934; s. Suk K. Lee and Chung Won Kim; m. Myung H. Lee, Nov. 17, 1959; children: Benjamin, May. Student, Yonsei U., 1953-55, MD, 1959; MSc, Ohio State U., 1967; postgrad. med. cert., UCLA, 1968. Diplomate Am. Bd. Psychiatry and Neurology, Korean Bd. of Psychiatry and Neurology. Psychiat. resident Brentwood Psychiat. Hosp., VAMC, L.A., 1967-68, Ohio State U. Hosp., Columbus, 1965-67; neurology resident Cin. Gen. Hosp., 1964-65; psychiat. resident Yonsei U. Hosp., Seoul, 1960-62, staff psychiatrist, 1968-69; chief psychiatrist Ewha U. Hosp., Seoul, 1969-70; clin. dir. unit B Broughton State Hosp., Morganton, N.C., 1970-71; chief psychiatrist VA Med. Ctr., Dayton, Ohio, 1971-79; staff psychiatrist Eastway Cmty. Mental Health Ctr., Dayton, 1975-95; med. dir. South Cmty. Inc., Centerville, Ohio, 1990-95; pvt. practice Dayton, 1975-95; chief psychiatrist Kyung Hee Pundang CHA Gen. Hosp., Seoul, 1995-96; staff psychiatrist Accord Behavioral Healthcare, Dayton, 1996—2004; staff psychiatrist, dep. med. dir. Eastway Corp., Dayton, 1996—2004. Cons. psychiatrist South Cmty Inc., Centerville, 1980-90, Dayton Mental Health Ctr., 1975-95, Eastway Cmty. Mental Health Ctr., 1975-79; assoc. clin. prof. Wright State U., Dayton, 1979—, asst. clin. prof., 1975-79; prof. Kyung Hee U., 1975-76; asst. clin. prof. Ohio State U., Columbus, 1971-75; asst. prof. Ewha U. Coll. of Medicine, 1969-70; instr. Yonsei U. Coll. of Medicine, 1968-69, 1961-64. Home: 7706 Normandy Ln Dayton OH 45459-4118 Office: Eastway Behavioral Health 600 Wayne Ave Dayton OH 45410-1122

LEE, SUNGHO H., education educator, consultant, academic administrator; b. Kyonggi-do, Rep. of Korea, Nov. 3, 1946; s. Kiwon and Imae (Song) L.; m. Hwadong Kim, Feb. 17, 1973; children: Haichung, Haiseok. BA, Yonsei U., Seoul, Rep. of Korea, 1970, MA, 1975; student, Ruhr U., Bochum, Germany, 1976-77; EdD, George Washington U., 1980. Instr. Yonsei U., 1975-76, asst. prof., 1981-85, assoc. prof., 1986-90, prof., 1991—, dean Coll. Edn., 1998-2000, dean Grad. Sch., 2000—02, v.p., 2002—04. Asst. min. Ministry of Edn., Rep. of Korea, 1993; dir. univ. evaluation Korean Coun. for Univ. Edn., Korea, 1983-90; mem. Presdl. Commn. 21st Century, 1989-93. Author: Shaking Parents and Straying Children, 1997 (award Chosun Daily Newspaper Co. 1997); co-author: Scientific Development and Higher Education, 1989 (award NSF 1986), Academic Profession in the World, 1995, Teaching Methods in Schools, 1999; contbr. chpts. to books. Cons. New Cmty. Devel. Movement Assn., Korea, 1996-99; mem. Nat. Commn. UNESCO, Korea, 1993-95; bd. trustees Nat. Inst. Curriculum Devel., 1998-99; mem. nat. adv. com. for edn. policy, Korea, 1996-99; mem. standing com. Presdl. Com. for Rebuilding Korea, 1998-2000; mem. adv. com. Korean Air Force, 2001—; chmn. Nat. Edn. Policy Adv. Com., 2001-2003. Sgt. US I Corps., 1970-73. Decorated U.S. Army Commendation medal, Order of Svc. Merit Pres. of Korea; recipient award, Nat. Carnegie Found., 1992; grantee, Nat. Assn. Trade and Tech. Schs., 1980, Ford Found., 2001. Mem. Korean Soc. for Study Edn. (bd. trustees 1981-83, 86-90, 98-2000), Korean Higher Edn. Assn. (bd. trustees 1994—). Evangelical. Avocation: golf. Office: Yonsei U Dept Edn Shinchon-dong 134 Sodaemoon-ku Seoul 120-749 Republic of Korea Office Phone: 82-2-2123-3176. Business E-Mail: leesh@yonsei.ac.kr.

LEE, SUNG-WOO, medical physicist; s. Chang Koo Lee and Kyu Soon Kim; m. Yeon Ju Yoon, July 9, 1972; children: Isaiah Doo-Hyoung, Michelle Da-Eun. BS, Hanyang U., Seoul, 1993, MS, 1995, Tex. A&M U., 1999, PhD, 2003. Grad. rsch. asst. Tex. A&M U., College Station, 1997—2003; post doctoral fellow Henry Ford Hosp., Detroit, 2003—04. Mem.: Health Physics Soc., Am. Nuc. Soc., Am. Assn. Physicists in Medicine. Achievements include research in clinical assessment and characterization of a dual tube kV x-ray localization system in the radiotherapy treatment room; dosimetric characterization of an intensity modulated X-ray brachytherachy system; dose calculation of 142Pr microspheres as a potential treatment for arteriovenous malformations and 142Pr beta sources in water; image-guided procedures for intensity-modulated spinal radiosurgery and novel needle-based miniature x-ray generating system; dose backscatter factors for selected beta sources as a function of source, calcified plaque, and contrast agent using Monte Carlo calculations; image-guided intensity-modulated x-ray brachytherapy system; parallel Monte-Carlo electron and photon transport simulation code (PM-CEPT code). Avocations: swimming, travel. Office: Berkshire Med Ctr Dept Radiol Oncology 725 North St Pittsfield MA 01201

LEE, SUSAN C., state legislator, lawyer; b. San Antonio, Tex., May 14, 1954; BA in Polit. Sci., U. Md., Coll. Park, 1976; JD, U. San Francisco Sch. of Law, 1982. Bar: DC 1983, Calif. 1983. Law clerk to Judge Richard Figone San Francisco Superior Ct., 1981—82; exec. dir. Nat. Dem. Council of Asian and Pacific Am., 1983—86; atty. Alexander, Bearden, Hairston, & Marks, LLP, 1993—97; of counsel Pena & Assoc., 1997—2001; legislative asst. to pres. Montgomery County Council, 2000—01; of counsel Gebhardt & Assoc., 2001—; mem. Md. Ho. of Delegates, 2002—, mem. judiciary com., 2002—, deputy majority whip, 2003—. Atty. US Commn. on Civil Rights, 1983—86, US Patent and Trademark Office, 1988—93; mem. US Patent and Trademark Public Adv. Com., Dept. of Commerce, 2000—01; co-founder Asian Pacific Am. Inst. for Congressional Studies, bd. dirs., 1995—2001. Mem.: Asian Pacific Am. Bar Assn. of Greater Wash. (pres. 1985), Nat. Asian Pacific Am. Bar Assn. Office: Md Ho of Delegates Lowe Ho Office Bldg Rm 221C 84 College Ave Annapolis MD 21401-1991*

LEE, SUSAN M., librarian; b. Great Falls, Mont., Feb. 10, 1960; d. Walter T. and Alma A. (Gardner) L. BA with honors, U. Mont., 1982; MLS, U. Ariz., 1984. Readers' svcs. libr. Coll. of Great Falls Library; info. svcs. libr. U. Great Falls, Mont. Mem. Mont. Library Assn., Beta Phi Mu. E-mail: slee@ugf.edu.

LEE, THEODORE BO, real estate developer; b. Stockton, Calif., Dec. 28, 1932; s. Wong Bo and Daisy (Lum) L.; m. Doris Shoong, June 14, 1969; children: Gregory T.H., Ernest T.H. BA, Harvard Coll., 1954; JD, U. Calif., Berkeley, 1959, MBA, 1966. Bar: Hawaii 1962, Calif. 1960. Jr. lectr. U. Singapore, 1960—61; legal assoc. Fong, Miho, etal, Honolulu, 1961—62; assoc. dir. East West Ctr., Honolulu, 1962—64; real estate atty. Urban Cons., San Francisco, 1964—82; chmn. Urban Group, San Francisco, 1971—. Dir. Ind. Nev. Casino Operators, Las Vegas, Nihonmachi Cmty. Devel. Corp., San Francisco. Author: Laws of the Commonwealth (Singapore), 1961. Pres. St. Pauls Parents Assn., Concord, N.H., 1980-88; trustee, vice chair Berkeley Found., 1984-97. Recipient internat. legal fellowship U. Calif., Berkeley, 1959, Wheeler Oak award Berkeley Found., 1985. Mem. Harvard Alumni Assn. (trustee, dir. 1982-85, overseer 1994-2000, alumni award), Boalt Hall Alumni Assn. (pres.). Avocation: foreign travel. Office: Urban Land Nev 3271 S Highland Dr Ste 704 Las Vegas NV 89109-1051 Office Phone: 702-369-9595.

LEE, THERESA K., chemicals executive; b. Gary, W.Va., Nov. 21, 1952; BS in Polit. Sci. and History, East Tenn. State U., 1974; JD, U. Tenn., 1977; postgrad., Harvard U., 1999. Staff atty. Legal Svcs. Upper East Tenn., 1977—79; sr. law clk. to Judge H. Emory Widener, Jr. U.S. Ct. Appeals (4th cir.), 1979—87; atty. Eastman Chem., 1987—91, asst. to pres., 1991—92, asst. sec., sr. counsel Tex. Eastman divsn., 1992—93, asst. sec., asst. gen. counsel legal dept. health safety and environ. group, 1993—95, asst. sec., asst. gen. counsel legal dept., corp. group, 1995—97, v.p., sec., assoc. gen. counsel, 1997—2000, sec. Memphis, 1997—, chief legal officer, 2000—, sr. v.p., 2002—. Recipient Outstanding Alumna award, East Tenn. State U. Nat. Alumni Assn., 2002. Mem.: ABA (gen. counsel com.), Soc. Corp. Secs. & Governance Profls., Kingsport Bar Assn., Tenn. Bar Assn. (ho. of dels.), Am. Corp. Counsel Assn. (bd. dirs.). Address: Eastman Chem PO Box 1975 Kingsport TN 37662-5075 Office: Eastman Chem PO Box 511 100 N Eastman Rd Kingsport TN 37662-5075

LEE, THOMAS ALEXANDER, accountant, educator; b. Edinburgh, Scotland, May 18, 1941; s. Thomas Henderson and Dorothy Jane (Norman) L.; m. Ann Margaret Brown, Sept. 14, 1963; children: Sarah Ann, Richard Thomas. Chartered acct., Inst. Chartered Accts.Scotland, Edinburgh, 1964; tax acct., Inst. Tax, Glasgow, Scotland, 1965; MS, U. Strathclyde, Glasgow, Scotland, 1969, DLitt, 1984. Audit asst., Edinburgh, 1959-64, Glasgow, 1964-66; lectr. U. Strathclyde, 1966-69, U. Edinburgh, 1969-73, prof., 1976-90, U. Liverpool, Eng., 1973-76; dir. rsch. Inst. Chartered Accts. Scotland, 1983-84; prof. U. Ala., 1990—2001, dir. PhD program, 1991—2001, emeritus prof., 2001—; hon. prof. U. Newcastle, 2003—. Vis. prof. U. Md., 1986, U. Utah, 1987-88, U. Edinburgh, 1991-94, Deakin U., 1994—, U. Newcastle; hon. prof. U. Dundee, Scotland, 1995—. Editor: Internat. Jour. Auditing; mem. editl. bd. various jours., 1971—. Acad. Acctg. Historians, pres., 1999, past pres., 2000. Recipient Burnum award U. Ala., 1997. Mem. Inst. Chartered Accts. Scotland (coun. 1989-90), Inst. Taxation, Brit. Acctg. Assn. (Lifetime Achievement award 2004, Hall of Fame 2005). Presbyterian. Avocations: church, road running, cricket history. Office: Dept Accountancy U Dundee Nethergate Dundee DD1 4HN Scotland Home: 5 Alderston Gardens Haddington EH41 3RY England Office Phone: 011 44 1382 344000. E-mail: leeatom@aol.com.

LEE, THOMAS F., art association administrator; Sec. Federation of Musicians, Local 161-710, Wash., DC; v.p. Am. Fedn. Musicians, 1995—99, sec., treas., 1999—2001, pres., 2001—. Mem. exec. com. Am. Fedn. Musicians. Office: Am Fedn Musicians 1501 Broadway Ste 600 New York NY 10036 Office Phone: 212-869-1330. Office Fax: 212-764-6134. E-mail: presoffice@afm.org.

LEE, THOMAS H., investor; m. Ann Tenenbaum; children: Stephen Zachary, Robert Schiff. B, Harvard U., 1965. With First Nat. Bank Boston, 1966—74, mgr. high tech. leading group, 1968—74, v.p., 1973—74; chmn. T.H. Lee Mezzanine; chmn. & CEO THLee Putnam Ventures; founder, chmn., CEO Thomas H. Lee Ptnrs., Boston, 1974—. Nat. adv. bd. JP Morgan; dir. Metris Companies Inc., Miller Import Corp., Wyndham Internat. Inc., Snapple Beverage Corp., Gen. Nutrition Companies, Playtex Products Inc., Vail Resorts Inc., 1993—, Safelite Glass Corp., Vertis Holdings Inc., First Security Svcs. Corp. Established Henry Rosovsky Fund, Faculty of Arts and Scis., Harvard U., 1984; trustee Intrepid Mus., Lincoln Ctr. for Rockefeller U., NYU Med. Ctr., Mus. Modern Art, NYC; v.p. bd. Whitney Mus. Am. Art. Named one of Top 200 Collectors, ARTnews Mag., 2004. Avocation: Collector of Modern and contemporary art; Egyptian art. Office: Thomas H Lee Ptnrs LP 100 Federal St, 35th Fl Boston MA 02110-1802 Office Phone: 617-227-1050. Office Fax: 617-227-3514.*

LEE, THOMAS HENRY, internist, cardiologist, healthcare executive; b. Schenectady, NY, Dec. 2, 1953; Grad., Harvard Coll., 1975; MD, Cornell U., 1979; MSc, Harvard U., 1987. Bd. cert. internal medicine 1982, bd. cert. cardiovasc. disease. Intern Harvard Med. Sch., Boston, 1980—82; resident Brigham and Women's Hosp., Boston, 1982—84, cardiology fellow, 1984—85, internist, cardiologist; assoc. prof. dept. health policy and mgmt. Harvard Med. Sch., Boston; chief med. officer Partners Cmty. Healthcare, Inc., network pres., 2004—, CEO, 2004—. Bd. dirs. Mass. Quality Partnership, Bridges to Excellence; dir. Partners Signature Initiatives. Assoc. editor: The New England Journal of Medicine, editor-in-chief: The Harvard Heart Letter, author numerous scholarly articles. Office: Partners Cmty Health Care Inc Prudential Twr Ste 1150 800 Boylston St Boston MA 02199 also: Brigham Internal Medicine Assoc 75 Francis St Boston MA 02115

LEE, TIMOTHY EARL, international agency executive, paralegal; b. Seattle, May 23, 1947; s. Charles Augusta and Esther Letty (Young) L.; m. Marcia Lea Wulff, July 6, 1968 (div. May 1976); children: Vincent Dean, Dante' Claude; 1 stepson, Kevin Paul McCorkle; m. Jayne Elizabeth Ashley, Apr. 28, 1984 (div. Apr. 1995). Cert., Ivy Tech., 1981, Am. Inst. Paralegal Studies, 1988. Mgr. Gen. Fin. Corp., Evanston, Ill., 1970-74, FBT Capital Corp., South Bend, Ind., 1974-76; owner Lee's Internat. Investigative Rsch. Agy., Ft. Wayne, Ind., 1978—. Mem. Heritage Foun., Citizens Against Govt. Waste; spl. adv. Allen Superior Ct. With U.S. Army, 1966-68, Vietnam. Recipient Cert. of Appreciation, DAV, 1968. Mem. VFW, Ind. Assn. Pvt. Detectives (v.p. N.E. region Ind. 1984—), Ind. Sheriff's Assn., Ft. Wayne Allen County Security Assn., Coun. for Inter-Am. Security, Nat. Security Ctr., Nat. Def. Inst., 27th Field Artillery Assn. (v.p., founding father), Am. Legion, Vietnam Vets, Internat. Platform Assn., Concord Coalition. Address: PO Box 15028 Fort Wayne IN 46885-5028 Office Phone: 260-437-7167. E-mail: Liira@gte.net.

LEE, TOM STEWART, judge; b. 1941; m. Norma Ruth Robbins; children: Elizabeth Robbins Maron, Tom Stewart Jr. BA summa cum laude, Miss. Coll., 1963; JD cum laude, U. Miss., 1965. Ptnr. Lee & Lee, Forest, Miss., 1965-84; pros. atty. Scott County, Miss., 1968-71; judge Scott County Youth Ct., Forest, 1979-82, U.S. Dist. Ct. (so. dist.) Miss., Jackson, 1984-96, chief judge, 1996—2003. Asst. editor: Miss. Law Jour. Pres. Forest Pub. Sch. Bd., Scott County Heart Assn.; bd. trustees Miss. Coll. Named one of Outstanding Young Men Am. Fellow: Found. of Fed. Bar Assn. (life); mem.: 5th Cir. Jud. Coun. (CACM com. Jud. Conf., Disting. Svc. award), Fed. Judges Assn., Fed. Bar Assn., Hinds County Bar Assn., Scott County Bar Assn., Miss. Bar Assn., Ole Miss. Alumni Assn. (pres.), Am. Legion. Office: US Dist Ct 245 E Capitol St Ste 110 Jackson MS 39201-2414 Office Phone: 601-965-4963. Business E-Mail: tom_lee@mssd.uscourts.gov.

LEE, TSUNG-DAO, physicist, researcher; b. Shanghai, Nov. 24, 1926; arrived in U.S., 1946; s. Tsing-Kong L. and Ming-Chang (Chang); m. Jeannette Chin, June 3, 1950; children: James, Stephen. Student, Nat. Chekiang U., Kweichow, China, 1943-44, Nat. S.W. Assoc. U., Kunming, China, 1945-46; PhD, U. Chgo., 1950; DSc (hon.), Princeton U., 1958; LLD (hon.), Chinese U., Hong Kong, 1969; DSc (hon.), CCNY, 1978. Rsch. assoc. in astronomy U. Chgo., 1950; rsch. assoc. Yerkes Astron. Obs., Lake Geneva, Wis., 1950; rsch. assoc., lectr. physics U. Calif., Berkeley, 1950—51; mem. Inst. Advanced Study, Princeton U., NJ, 1951—53, prof. physics, 1960—63; asst. prof. Columbia U., N.Y.C., 1953—55, assoc. prof., 1955—56, prof., 1956—60, adj. prof., 1960—62, Enrico Fermi prof. physics, 1963—, univ. prof., 1984—. Loeb lectr. Harvard U., Cambridge, Mass., 1957, Cambridge, 64. Editor: Weak Interactions and High Energy Nutrino Physics, 1966, Particle Physics and Introduction to Field Theory, 1981; contbr. articles to profl. jours. Decorated grande ufficiale Order of Merit (Italy); recipient Albert Einstein Sci. award Yeshiva U., 1957, (with Chen Ning Yang) Nobel prize in physics, 1957, Ettore Majorana-Erice-Sci. for Peace prize, 1990. Mem. NAS, Acad. Sinica, Am. Acad. Arts and Scis., Am. Philos. Soc., Acad. Nazionale dei Lincei, Acad. Sci. China. Achievements include investigation of the so-called parity laws that have led to important discoveries regarding the elementary particles. Office: Columbia U Dept Physics 829 Pupin Hall 120th St New York NY 10027*

LEE, UNJOO H., library director; b. Seoul, May 30, 1959; d. Chul Soo Han and Byung Sun Kim; children: Euno, Sono. MLS, M in Info. Scis., Sch. Libr. and Info. Sci., San Jose State U., 1995. Children's libr. A.C. Bilbrew Libr., County LA Pub. Libr., 1995—97, Hacienda Heights Libr., County LA Pub. Libr., 1998—99; cataloging libr. County LA Pub. Libr., Downey; cmty. libr. mgr. Alondra Libr., County LA Pub. Libr., Norwalk, 2000—. Sunday sch. tchr. Na Sung Ch., La Habra Heights, Calif., 2002—05. Calif. Minority scholar, Calif. State Libr., 1993-1995, scholar, Korean Am. Libr.'s Assn., 1993. Mem.: Korean Am. Libr. and Info. Profls. Assn. (sec. 1997—99), Norwalk Woman's Club. Office: Alondra Libr County LA Pub Lib 11949 Alondra Blvd Norwalk CA 90650 Office Phone: 562-868-7771. Office Fax: 562-863-8620. Personal E-mail: unjoohlee@yahoo.com. E-mail: unjool@gw.colapl.org.

LEE, V. PAUL, entertainment software company executive; B in Commerce, U. BC. Prin. Distinctive Software, Inc.; with Elec. Arts, Redwood City, Calif., 1991—, gen. mgr. Canada, COO, CFO sports, v.p. fin. and adminstrn., sr. v.p., COO Redwood City, Calif., 1998—2002, exec. v.p., COO, 2002—05, pres. worldwide studios, 2005—. Office: Elec Arts 209 Redwood Shores Pky Redwood City CA 94065 Office Phone: 650-628-1500.*

LEE, VERNON ROY, minister; b. Jackson, Miss., Feb. 1, 1952; s. Samuel Rayford and Evie Mae (Abel) L.; m. Rhonda Sue Parker, Nov. 6, 1970; 1 child, Shannon Grant. Pastor Mt. Moriah Bapt. Ch., Junction City, Ark., 1971-72, Pleasant Grove Bapt. Ch., El Dorado, Ark., 1972-74, Pilgrims Rest Bapt. Ch., Spearsville, La., 1974-76, Bethany Bapt. Ch., Bastrop, La., 1976-78, 1st Bapt. Ch., Taylor, Ark., 1978-83, Farmington Bapt. Ch., Corinth, Miss., 1983-86, Wyatt Bapt. Ch., El Dorado, 1986—. Trustee Southeastern Bapt. Coll., Laurel, Miss., 1983-86, Ctrl. Bapt. Coll., Conway, Ark., 1992-96, 99—, asst. chmn. bd. trustees, 1993-95, 2001—03, chmn., 1995-96, 2004-; vol. Boy's Clubs, El Dorado, 1986-91, YMCA, Corinth, 1983-86. Mem. Bapt. Missionary Assn. Am. (v.p. 1986-88, 2000-02, pres. 1990-92, clk. missionary com. 1989-91, asst. ch. adv. com. 1992-95, v.p. pastors and laymen's conf. 1996-98, pres. pastors and laymen's conf. 1998-2000, chmn. adv. com. 2000—, asst. chmn. missionary com. 2002—), Miss. Bapt. Assn. (pres. 1984-86), Bapt. Missionary Assn. Ark. (v.p. 2000-02, pres. 2002—, asst. chmn. missionary com. 2002—). Avocations: golf, fishing, basketball, softball. Home: 625 Royal Oak El Dorado AR 71730 Office: Wyatt Bapt Ch 4621 W Hillsboro El Dorado AR 71730-6768

LEE, VIRGINIA FERN, community volunteer; b. Mar. 14, 1921; BA, Coll. of St. Scholastica, 1943; postgrad., Stanford U., 1970. Dir. med. info. Hosp. Dept. Universitario for Rockefeller Found., Cali, Colombia, 1956-58, VA Med. Ctr., Palo Alto, Calif., 1962-82; chief coord. VA Registrar Svc. Workshop, Boulder, 1965. Bd. dirs., v.p., sec., chmn. fin. com. Palo Alto Aux. to Packard Children's Hosp., 1987—93; bd. dirs., sec. Children's Health Coun. Aux., Palo Alto, 1997—99, nominating chmn., 2002—03. Mem. Am. Health Info. Mgmt. Assn. (hon.), Calif. Health Info. Mgmt. Assn. (hon., pres., treas. 1968-70), Ctrl. Calif. Health Info. Mgmt. Assn., (v.p., then pres. 1965-68), Minn. Health Info. Mgmt. Assn. (pres., chmn. pub. rels. com. 1953-59). Avocations: collecting teddy bears, public speaking. Address: 433 Guinda St Palo Alto CA 94301-2110

LEE, W. BRUCE, management consultant; b. Sacramento, Calif., Jan. 23, 1953; s. Wade Bruce and Marguerite (Stogner) L.; m. Nell Jeanette Alford, Aug. 13, 1977; children: Jessica, Amanda. BA in Adminstrn., U. Calif., Davis, 1971-75; MPA in Adminstrn., MA in Internat. Affairs, Calif. State U., 1977. Cert. in bus. and industry mgmt., mktg. and distbn., govt., pub. adminstrn. Adminstr./cons. State of Calif., Sacramento, 1973-76; mng. dir. Horizon Rsch. and Managerial Cons., Sacramento, 1978-87; exec. dir. Calif. Bus. League, Sacramento, 1987-90, Calif. Refuse Removal Coun., Sacramento, 1990-94; pres. Horizon Mgmt. and Assn. Svcs., Roseville, Calif., 1995—. Commentator internat. affairs KXPR Pub. Radio, Sacramento, 1977-78; newspaper columnist Sacramento Union, 1990-94. Author: Beyond Accounting, 1985; contbr. articles to profl. jours. Mayor, City of Loomis, Calif., 1991-96; chmn. Placer County Flood Control Dist., Auburn, Calif., 1993-96; treas. Sierra Econ. Devel. Dist., Auburn, 1994; founder South Placer Cmty. Prayer Breakfast, Rocklin, 1993—; mem. Local Agy. Formation Commn., Auburn, 1991-92; mem. Placer County Water Agy., Auburn, 1996—; co-chmn. fin. com. Billy Graham Crusade, Sacramento, 1995-96. Recipient Calif. Senate Rules Com. Resolution of Commendation, Calif. Assembly Resolution of Commendation. Mem. Calif. Soc. Assn. Execs., Am. Soc. Assn. Execs., Sacramento Jaycees (state dir. 1978, Outstanding Lt. Gov. 1971), Calif. Jaycees (Presdl. Award of Merit, mem. legis. coun. 1977). Avocations: photography, travel, cross country skiing, flying, scuba. Home: 5629 Montclair Cir Rocklin CA 95677-3374

LEE, WAYNE J., lawyer; b. New Orleans, Jan. 26, 1950; BA, Tulane U., 1971, JD, 1974. Bar: La. 1974. Atty. Stone Pigman Walther Wittmann LLC, New Orleans, 1974—. Mem. La. Indigent Defender Bd.; chair Civil Justice Reform Act Adv. Group, Fed. Dist. Ct. for Ea. Dist. La.; appointed La. Bd. of Regents for Higher Edn., 1989—94; bd. dirs. Attys.' Liability Assurance Soc., Ltd.; spkr. in field. Adv. bd. editors Tulane Law Review; contbr. La. Appellate Procedure Handbook. Fellow: Am. Coll. Trial Lawyers; mem.: ABA (sect. on litigation and antitrust), Tulane U. Inn of Ct., Fifth Cir. Bar Assn., New Orleans Bar Assn., La. State Bar Assn. (bd. govs. 1993—96, Ho. of Dels. 1997—2002, pres.-elect 2002—03, Pres.'s award 1993, 1998), Def. Rsch. Inst., Nat. Bar Assn., Louis A. Martinet Soc., Order of Coif. Office: Stone Pigman Walther Wittmann 546 Carondelet St New Orleans LA 70130-3588

LEE, WHITNEY FIELDING, literary agent; b. Bryn Mawr, Pa., Jan. 22, 1977; s. Robert Greenwood and Ann (Fielding) Lee. BA, Northwestern U., Evanston, Ill., 1999. Asst. Nicholas Ellison, Inc., N.Y.C., 1999—2000; dir. fgn. rights Carlisle & Co., N.Y.C., 2000—03; pres. The Fielding Agy., Beverly Hills, Calif., 2003—. Mem.: Bayhead Yacht. Office: The Fielding Agy LLC 269 S Beverly Dr Ste # 341 Beverly Hills CA 90212 Office Phone: 310-276-7517. E-mail: wlee@fieldingagency.com.

LEE, WILLIAM CHARLES, judge; b. Ft. Wayne, Ind., Feb. 2, 1938; s. Russell and Catherine (Zwick) L.; m. Judith Anne Bash, Sept. 19, 1959; children: Catherine L., Mark R., Richard R. AB, Yale U., 1959; JD, U. Chgo.,

1962; LLD (hon.), Huntington Coll., 1999. Bar: Ind. 1962. Ptnr. Parry, Krueckeberg & Lee, Ft. Wayne, 1963-69, chief dep., 1966-69; U.S. atty. No. Dist. Ind., Ft. Wayne, 1970-73; ptnr. Hunt, Suedhoff, Borror, Eilbacher & Lee, Ft. Wayne, 1973-81; U.S. dist. judge U.S. Dist. Ct. (no. dist.) Ind., Ft. Wayne, 1981—. Instr. Nat. Inst. Trial Advocacy; lectr. in field. Co-author: Business and Commercial Litigation in Federal Courts, 1998; author: Volume I Federal Jury Practice and Instructions, 1999; contbr. to numerous publs. in field. Co-chmn. Fort Wayne Fine Arts Operating Fund Drive, 1978; past bd. dirs., v.p., pres. Fort Wayne Philharm. Orch.; past bd. dirs., v.p. Hospice of Fort Wayne, inc.; past bd. dirs. Fort Wayne Fine Arts Found., Fort Wayne Civic Theatre, Neighbors, Inc., Embassy Theatre Found.; past bd. dirs., pres. Legal Aid of fort Wayne, Inc.; past mem. chm. coun., v.p. Trinity English Lutheran Ch. Coun.; past trustee, pres. Fort Wayne Cmty. Schs., 1978-81, pres., 1980-81; trustee Fort Wayne Mus. Art, 1984-90; past bd. dirs., pres. Fort Wayne-Allen County Hist. Soc. Griffin Scholar, 1955-59; chmn. Fort Wayne Cmty. Schs. Scholarship Com.; bd. dirs. Arts United of Greater Fort Wayne, Fort Wayne Ballet. Weymouth Kirkland scholar, 1959-62; named Ind. Trial Judge of Yr., 1988. Fellow Am. Coll. Trial Lawyers, Ind. Bar Found.; mem. ABA, Allen County Bar Assn., Ind. State Bar Assn., Fed. Bar Assn., Seventh Cir. Bar Assn., Benjamin Harrison Am. Inn of Ct., North Side High Alumni Assn. (bd. dris., pres.), Fort Wayne Rotary Club (bd. dirs.), Phi Delta Phi (past bd. dirs., 1st pres.). Republican. Lutheran. Office: US Dist Ct 2145 Fed Bldg 1300 S Harrison St Fort Wayne IN 46802-3495

LEE, WILLIAM F., lawyer; b. 1950; BA magna cum laude, Harvard U., 1972; MBA with distinction, JD magna cum laude, Cornell U., 1976. Bar: Mass. 1977, U.S. Supreme Ct. Assoc. counsel to Lawrence E. Walsh Ind. Counsel in Iran-Contra Investigation, 1987—89; joined Hale & Dorr LLP, Boston, 1976, mng. ptnr., 2000—04; co-mng. ptnr. Wilmer, Cutler, Pickering, Hale & Dorr LLP, Boston, 2004—. Visiting prof. Harvard U. Law Sch.; appointed by chief judge Ct. Appeals Fed. Cir. to Ct. Adv. Com., 2000; Ct. Adv. Com. U.S. Dist. Ct. Mass., Com to Evaluate Adminstrn. Criminal Justice Act, Merit Selection Panel Magistrate Judges; Intellectual Property Adv. Com. U.S. Dist. Ct. Del.; spl. Judicial Nominating Com. Mass. Supreme Judicial Ct. Named one of top ten super lawyers in Mass., Boston Mag., 2004, top Boston lawyers, 2002, 100 most influential lawyers in Am., Nat. Law Jour., 2000. Fellow: Am. Coll. Trial Lawyers; mem.: Cornell Law Sch. (visiting com.), Harvard U. (bd. overseers 2002), Tenacre Country Day Sch. (chmn. bd. trustees), Order Coif. Office: Wilmer Cutler Pickering Hale & Dorr LLP 60 State St Boston MA 02109 Office Phone: 617-526-6556. Office Fax: 617-526-5000. Business E-Mail: william.lee@wilmerhale.com.

LEE, WILLIAM FRANKLIN, III, composer, musician; b. Galveston, Tex., Feb. 20, 1929; s. William Franklin Jr. and Anna Lena (Keis) L.; children: William Franklin IV, Robert Terry, Patricia Lynn, Peggy Ann. MusB, N. Tex. State U., 1949, MS, 1950; MusM, PhD, U. Tex., 1956. Prof. music St. Mary's U., San Antonio, 1952-55; asst. to dean fine arts U. Tex., 1955-56; chmn. dept. music Sam Houston State Coll., 1956-64; dean Sch. Music U. Miami (Fla.), 1964-82, provost, exec. v.p., 1982-86, disting. prof., composer in residence, 1986-88; dir. arts Fla. Internat. U., Miami, 1988-90; dean coll. fine arts and humanities U. Tex., San Antonio, 1990-94; exec. dir. Internat. Assn. Jazz Educators, 1994-98, ret., 1998. Performances with Houston, Dallas symphony orchs., performances with Gene Krupa and Artie Shaw, guest clinician, condr., composer, 1952—; composer, author, arranger more than 100 published works.; author: Music Theory Dictionary, 1962; also articles, music publs.; biographer, discographer of Stan Kenton, 1981, Maynard Ferguson, 1997, Bill Evans, 2000, America's Big Bands, 2002, Taylor Made (biography., discogaphy of Billy Taylor), 2003; editor, co-founder: Southwestern Brass Jour., 1958, Belwin New Dictionary of Music and Musicians, 1988. Mem. AAUP, ASCAP (recipient ann. awards 1968— including Deems Taylor awards 1981, 85), Nat. Assn. Am. Composers and Condrs., Music Educators Nat. Conf., Am. Fedn. Musicians, Music Tchrs. Nat. Assn., Pi Kappa Lambda, Kappa Kappa Psi, Phi Mu Alpha.

LEE, WILLIAM JOHN, petroleum engineering educator, consultant; b. Lubbock, Tex., Jan. 16, 1936; s. William Preston and Bonnie Lee (Cook) L.; m. Phyllis Ann Bass, June 10, 1961; children: Anne Preston, Mary Denise. B in Chem. Engring., Ga. Inst. Tech., 1959, MSChemE, 1961, PhD in Chem. Engring., 1963, NAE, 1993; Disting. Engring. Alumni, Ga. Tech. Acad., 1994. Registered profl. engr., Tex. Sr. rsch. specialist Exxon Prodn. Rsch. Co., Houston, 1962-68; assoc. prof. petroleum engring. Miss. State U., Starkville, 1968-71; tech. advisor Exxon Co., Houston, 1971-77; prof. petroleum engring. Tex. A&M U., College Station, 1977—, holder Noble chair in petroleum engring., 1985-93, Peterson chair in petroleum engring., 1993—. Dir. Crisman Inst. for Petroleum Reservoir Mgmt. at Tex. A&M U., 1987-93; exec. v.p. S.A. Holditch & Assocs., Inc., College Station, 1979-99. Author: Well Testing, 1982, Gas Reservoir Engineering, 1996, Pressure Transient Testing, 2003. Recipient award of excellence Halliburton Edn. Found., 1982, Meritorious Engring. Tchg. award Tenneco, Inc., 1982, 2000, Disting. Tchg. award Assn. Former Students Tex. A&M U., 1983, Continuing Edn. award, 2001; Tex. Engring. Experiment Sta. fellow, 1987-88, sr. fellow, 1990; named to Dream Team, Tex. Soc. Profl. Engrs., 2001. Mem. Soc. Petroleum Engrs. (hon., disting., chmn. edn. and accreditation com. 1985-86, disting. lectr. 1980, Disting. Faculty Achievement award 1982, Reservoir Engring. award 1986, Regional Svc. award 1987, Disting. Svc. award, 1992, Carll award 1995, dir. 1996-99, disting. lectr. 2005—, Lucas medal 2003, DeGolyer Disting. Svc. medal 2004), Am. Inst. Mining Metal. and Petroleum Engrs. (hon.). Presbyterian. Avocation: travel. Home: 9310 Lake Forest Ct S College Station TX 77845-8758 Office: Tex A&M U Dept Petroleum Engring 3116 TAMU College Station TX 77843-3116 Personal E-mail: johnlee@tca.net. Business E-Mail: lee@spindletop.tamu.edu.

LEE, WILLIAM JOHNSON, lawyer; b. Jan. 13, 1924; s. William J. and Ara (Anderson) L. Student, Akron U., 1941-43, Denison U., 1943-44, Harvard U., 1944-45; JD, Ohio State U., 1948. Bar: Ohio 1948, Fla. 1962, U.S. Dist. Ct. (no. dist.) Ohio 1960, U.S. Dist. Ct. (so. dist.) Fla. 1965, U.S. Dist. Ct. (so. dist.) Ohio 1970. Research asst. Ohio State U. Law Sch., 1948-49; asst. dir. Ohio Dept. Liquor Control, chief purchases, 1956-57, atty. examiner, 1951-53, asst. state permit chief, 1953-55, state permit chief, 1955-56; asst. counsel, staff Hupp Corp., 1957-58; spl. counsel City Attys. Office, Ft. Lauderdale, Fla., 1963-65; asst. atty. gen. Office Atty. Gen. State of Ohio, 1966-70; administr. State Med. Bd. Ohio, Columbus, 1970-85. Mem. Federated State Bd.'s Nat. Commn. for Evaluation of Fgn. Med. Schs., 1981-83; mem. Flex 1/Flex 2 Transitional Task Force, 1983-84; pvt. practice law, Ft. Lauderdale, 1965-66; acting municipal judge, Ravenna, Ohio, 1960; instr. Coll. Bus. Adminstrn., Kent State U., 1961-62. chmn. legal aid com. Portage County, Ohio, 1960. Mem. editl. bd. Ohio State Law Jour., 1947—48; contbr. articles to profl. jours. Mem. pastoral relations com. Epworth United Meth. Ch., 1976; troop awards chmn. Boy Scouts Am., 1965; mem. ch. bd. Melrose Park (Fla.) Meth. Ch., 1966. Served with USAAF, 1943-46. Mem. ATLA, Exptl. Aviation Assn. S.W. Fla., Franklin County Trial Lawyers Assn., Am. Legion, Fla. Bar Assn., Columbus Bar Assn., Akron Bar Assn., Broward County Bar Assn., Ohio State Bar Assn., Delta Theta Phi, Phi Kappa Tau, Pi Kappa Delta. Home: Apple Valley 704 Country Club Dr Howard OH 43028-9530

LEE, WILLIAM MARSHALL, lawyer; b. NYC, Feb. 23, 1922; s. Marshall McLean and Marguerite (Letts) L.; m. Lois Kathryn Plain, Oct. 10, 1942; children: Marsha (Mrs. Stephen Derynck), William Marshall Jr., Victoria C. (Mrs. Larry Nelson). Student, U. Wis., 1939-40; BS, Aero. U., Chgo., 1942; postgrad., UCLA, 1946-48, Loyola U. Law Sch., L.A., 1948-49; JD, Loyola U., Chgo., 1952. Bar: Ill. 1952, U.S. Supreme Ct., 1972. Thermodynamicist Northrop Aircraft Co., Hawthorne, Calif., 1947-49; patent agt. Hill, Sherman, Meroni, Gross & Simpson, Chgo., 1949-51, Borg-Warner Corp., Chgo., 1951-53; ptnr. Hume, Clement, Hume & Lee, Chgo., 1953-72; pvt. practice Chgo., 1973-74; ptnr. Lee and Smith (and predecessors), Chgo., 1974-89, Lee, Mann, Smith, McWilliams, Sweeney & Ohlson, Chgo., 1989—2002; ind. expert intellectual property Barrington, Ill., 1999—. Cons. Power Packaging, Inc., 1982-2002. Speaker and contbr. articles on legal topics. Pres. Glenview (Ill.) Citizens Sch. Com., 1953-57; v.p. Glenbrook High Sch. Bd., 1957-63. Lt. USNR, 1942-46, CBI. Recipient Pub. Svc. award Glenbrook High Sch. Bd., 1963 Mem. ABA (chmn. sect. intellectual property law 1986-87, sect. fin. officer 1976-77, sect. sec. 1977-80, sect. governing coun. 1980-84, 87-88), Ill. Bar Assn., Chgo. Bar Assn., 7th Fed. Cir. Bar Assn., Am. Intellectual Property Law Assn., Intellectual Property Law Assn. Chgo., Licensing Execs. Soc. (pres. 1981-82, treas. 1977-80, trustee 1974-77, 80-81, 82-83, internat. del. 1980—), Phi Delta Theta, Phi Alpha Delta. Republican. Office: 84 Otis Rd Barrington IL 60010-5128

LEE, WINNIE SITA, dentist; b. Loma Linda, Calif., Mar. 20, 1978; d. Stanley Tak and Rita Sook Lee. BA in Applied Scis., U. of Pacific, Calif., 2003; DDS, U. Pacific Sch. Dentistry, Calif., 2001. Dental Lic. Calif., 2001. Pre-clin. instr. U. Pacific Sch. Dentistry, San Francisco, 2002—04; dentist pvt. practice, Sunnyvale, 2003—. Presenter in field. Recipient Athena award, San Jose Alumni Panhellenic, Calif., 1996. Fellow: Internat. Congress Oral Implantologists, Am. Acad. Implant Dentistry (assoc.); mem.: Acad. Gen. Dentistry, Santa Clara Dental Soc., Alpha Lambda Delta. Avocations: running, exercise. Office Phone: 408-830-0888.

LEE, WON JAY, radiologist; b. Seoul, Korea, Feb. 2, 1938; arrived in U.S., 1965; s. Kang Sei and Choon Ja (Park) L.; m. Moon Jung, Feb. 24, 1968; children: Julie, Lisa, Jennifer. MD, Yonsei U., Seoul, 1962. Diplomate Am. Bd. Radiology, Am. Bd. Nuclear Medicine. Intern Wyckoff Heights Hosp., Bklyn., 1965-66; resident in radiology N.Y. U. Med. Ctr., N.Y.C., 1966-69; fellow, asst. radiologist L.I. Jewish Med. Ctr., New Hyde Park, 1969-71, staff radiologist, 1975-82, chief uroradiology, 1983—2001, hon. staff, 2001—; assoc. radiologist Binghamton Gen. Hosp., 1971-75. Asst. prof. SUNY, Stony Brook, 1975-86, assoc. prof. radiology, 1987-89; prof. radiology Albert Einstein Coll. Medicine, 1989-2002, prof. emeritus radiology, 2002-; clin. prof. diagnostic radiology Yonsei U. Coll. Medicine, Seoul, 1996—; cons. in field. Asst. editor: Jour. Endourology, 1987-96; assoc. editor: Jour. Korean-Am. Med. Assn., 1995-98, editor-in-chief, 1999-2000; contbr. chpts. to books and articles to profl. jours. First lt. Republic of Korea Army M.C., 1962-65. Recipient Sci. Paper award Soc. Uroradiology, 1994, Clin. award Can. Assoc. Radiologists, 1979, Disting. Svc. award Yonsei U. Col. Med. Alumni Assn., 1998. Fellow Am. Coll. Radiology, Soc. Interventional Radiology (emeritus), Soc. Uroradiology (emeritus); mem. Am. Roentgen Ray Soc. (Merit award 1983), Radiol. Soc. N.Am., Korean-Am. Med. Assn. (chmn. sci. and edn. divsn. 1996), Korean Radiol. Soc. N.Am., Severance Alumni Assn. Am. (pres. 1997). Democrat. Presbyn. Avocations: gardening, golf, travel. Office: Lee Radiol Cons 6306 Adirondack Ct Gainesville VA 20155 Office Phone: 703-743-1382. Personal E-mail: wjaylee@yahoo.com.

LEE, WON-CHAN, psychometrician; arrived in US, 1992; PhD, U. of Iowa, 1998. Grad. rsch. asst. U. of Iowa, Iowa City, 1995—98; rsch. staff Iowa Testing Programs, Iowa City, 1998—99; rsch. assoc. ACT, Inc., Iowa City, 1999—2004; rsch. scientist U. Iowa, 2004—. Contbr. articles to profl. rsch. jours. Recipient T. Anne Cleary Psychol. Rsch. award, U. of Iowa, 1998, Brenda H. Loyd Outstanding Dissertation award, Nat. Coun. on Measurement in Edn. Mem.: Psychometric Soc., Nat. Coun. on Measurement in Edn., Am. Ednl. Rsch. Assn. Office Phone: 319-335-5546.

LEE, YEU-TSU MARGARET, surgeon, educator; b. Xian, Shensi, China, Mar. 18, 1936; m. Thomas V. Lee, Dec. 29, 1962 (div. 1987); 1 child, Maxwell M. AB in Microbiology, U. S.D., 1957; MD, Harvard U., 1961. Diplomate Am. Bd. Surgery. Assoc. prof. surgery Med. Sch., U. So. Calif., L.A., 1973-83; commd. lt. col. U.S. Army Med. Corps, 1983, advanced through grades to col., 1989; chief surg. oncology Tripler Army Med. Ctr., Honolulu, 1983-98; ret. U.S. Army, 1999; assoc. clin. prof. surgery Med. Sch., U. Hawaii, Honolulu, 1984-92, clin. prof. surgery, 1992—. Author: Malignant Lymphoma, 1974; author chpts to books; contbr. articles to profl. jours. Pres. Orgn. Chinese-Am. Women, L.A., 1981, Hawaii chpt., 1988; active U.S.-China Friendship Assn., 1991—. Decorated Nat. Def. Svc. medal, Army Commendation medal, Army Meritorious Svc. medal, Army Humanitarian Svc. medal; recipient Chinese-Am. Engrs. and Scis. Assn., 1987; named Sci. Woman Warrior, Asian-Pacific Womens Network, 1983. Mem. ACS, Soc. Surg. Oncology, Assn. Women Surgeons. Avocations: classical music, movies, hiking, ballroom dancing. Address: PO Box 29726 Honolulu HI 96820 E-mail: ytm_lee@hotmail.com.

LEE, YOON MO, state official; arrived in US, 1970; m. Hwa Kim; 2 children. BS in Agricultural Sci., Seoul Nat. U.; MDiv in Christian Social Ethics, Seoul Methodist Theological Seminary; ThM, Asbury Theological Seminary; MA in Sociology, PhD in Sociology, Loyola U. Former reporter, mng. editor & chief editor Korea Times, Chicago; former CEO Korean Am. TV of Chicago; chief rsch., planning and develop., fed. grant project dir. & webmaster Ill. Dept. of Human Rights, 2000—. Lead rsch. adv. Asian Am. Inst. of Chicago. Author: Seventy Years' History of the First Korean United Methodist Church of Chicago, 1995. Office: Ill Dept of Human Rights James R Thompson Ctr 100 W Randolph St Ste 10-100 Chicago IL 60601*

LEE, YUAN TSEH, chemistry professor; b. Hsinchu, Taiwan, China, Nov. 19, 1936; arrived in U.S., 1962, naturalized, 1974; s. Tsefan and Pei (Tasi) Lee; m. Bernice Wu, June 28, 1963; children: Ted, Sidney, Charlotte. BS, Nat. Taiwan U., 1959; MS, Nat. Tsinghua U., Taiwan, 1961; PhD, U. Calif., Berkeley, 1965; PhD (hon.), U. of Waterloo, 1986. From asst. prof. to prof. chemistry U. Chgo., 1968—74; prof. emeritus U. Calif., Berkeley, 1974—, former prin. investigator Lawrence Berkeley Lab., 1974—97, Miller Professorship, 1981—82; pres. Academia Sinica, Taiwan, 1994—. Hon. prof. Chinese Acad. Sci., 1980, Fudan U., Shanghai, 1980; Sherman Fairchild Disting. Scholar Calif. Inst. Tech., 1983; hon. prof. Chinese U. Sci. & Tech., Hofei, Anhuei, 1986. Contbr. articles to profl. jours. on chem. physics. Recipient Nobel Prize in chemistry, 1986, Ernest O. Lawrence award, Dept. Energy, 1981, Nat. Medal of Sci., 1986, 1990, Peter Debye award for phys. chemistry, 1986, Harrison Howe award, 1983, Sherman Fairchild Disting. Scholar, Calif. Inst. Tech., 1983; fellow, Alfred P. Sloan, 1969—71, John Simon Guggenheim Found., 1976—77, Amer. Acad. of Arts and Sciences, 1975; scholar Tchr. scholar, Camille and Henry Dreyfus Found., 1971—74. Fellow: Am. Phys. Soc.; mem.: Academia Sinica, 1980, Am. Chem. Soc., Am. Acad. Arts and Scis., AAAS, NAS. Office: Acad Sinica Pres Office 128 Academia Rd Sec 2 Nankang Taipei 11529 Taiwan

LEE, YUNG-KEUN, physicist, researcher; b. Seoul, Korea, Sept. 26, 1929; came to U.S., 1953, naturalized, 1968; s. Kwang-Soo and Young-Sook (Hur) L.; m. Ock-Kyung Pai, Oct. 25, 1958; children: Ann, Arnold, Sara, Sylvia, Clara. BA, Johns Hopkins, 1956; MS, U. Chgo., 1957; PhD, Columbia, 1961. Research scientist Columbia U., N.Y.C., 1961-64; prof. physics Johns Hopkins U., Balt., 1964—2004, prof. emeritus physics, 2004—. Vis. mem. staff Los Alamos Sci. Lab., 1971; vis. researcher Institut Scis. Nucléaires, Grenoble, France, 1975; cons. Idaho Nat. Engring. Lab., 1988-91; mem. Brahms collaboration Brookhaven Nat. Lab., 1996—. Contbr. articles to profl. jours. Mem.: Johns Hopkins Club. Democrat. Methodist. Home: 1318 Denby Rd Baltimore MD 21286-1627 Office: Johns Hopkins U 34th and Charles Sts Baltimore MD 21218 Office Phone: 410-516-7355. E-mail: yklee@jhu.edu.

LEEB, CHARLES SAMUEL, clinical psychologist; b. July 18, 1945; s. Sidney Herbert and Dorothy Barbara (Fishstrom) Leeb; m. Storme Lynn Gilkey, Apr. 28, 1984; children: Morgan Evan, Spencer Douglas. BA in Psychology, U. Calif., Davis, 1967; MS in Counseling and Guidance, San Diego State U., 1970; PhD in Edn. and Psychology, Claremont Grad., 1973. Assoc. So. Regional Dir. Mental Retardation Ctr., Las Vegas, Nev., 1978—79; pvt. practice Las Vegas, 1978—79; dir. biofeedback and athletics Menninger Found., Topeka, 1979—82, dir. children's divsn. biofeedback and psychophysiology ctr., 1979—82; pvt. practice Claremont, Calif., 1982—. Dir. psychol. svcs. Horizon Hosp., 1986—88; dir. adolescent chem. dependence and children's program Charter Oak Hosp., Covina, Calif., 1989—91; founder, CEO Rsch. and Treatment Inst., Claremont, Calif., 1991—2002; co-founder, dir. Live Oak Canyon Sch., 1992—; lectr. in field. Contbr. articles to profl. jours. Mem.: APA, Calif. State Psychol. Assn. Office: 1420 N Claremont Blvd #102-A Claremont CA 91711-3358 Office Phone: 909-624-4864. Business E-Mail: ChuckL@liveoaknps.org.

LEEBENS, PATRICIA KAY, psychiatrist; b. Austin, Minn., Aug. 21, 1951; d. William Moore and Jean Elizabeth (Stubbee) Leebens. BA in English and Psychology, Grinnell Coll., 1973; MAT in English Edn., Brown U., 1974; MA in Psychology, U. No. Colo., 1978; MD, U. Colo., 1986; postgrad., Yale U., 1986—94. Diplomate Am. Bd. Psychiatry and Neurology. English tchr., guidance counselor Charles M. Russell Jr. H.S., Colorado Springs, 1974—77, 1978—79, 1981—82; resident psychiatry Yale U. Sch. Medicine, New Haven, 1986—90, fellow child psychiatry, 1990—94; unit chief dept. children and families Riverview Hosp., Middletown, Conn., 1994—2000; dir. psychiatry Dept. Children and Families, State Conn., Hartford, 2001—. Warden Trinity Episcopal Ch. on the Green, New Haven, 1997—2001; bd. dirs. Elm City Girls Choir, New Haven, 1995—99. Democrat. Avocations: reading, gardening, travel, movies. Office: State Conn Dept Children and Families Dir Psychiatry 505 Hudson St Hartford CT 06106 Office Phone: 860-560-5020.

LEEBRON, DAVID WAYNE, academic administrator, law educator; b. Phila., Feb. 12, 1955; m. Y. Ping Sun; children: Daniel, Merissa. BA, Harvard U., 1976, JD, 1979. Bar: Hawaii 1980, Pa. 1981, NY 1982. Law clk. to Judge Shirley Hufstedler US Ct. Appeals Ninth Cir., LA, 1979—80; adj. prof. UCLA Sch. Law, Los Angeles, Calif., 1980; assoc. Cleary, Gottlieb, Steen & Hamilton, NYC, 1981—83; prof., dir. Internat. Legal Studies Program NYU Sch. Law, NYC, 1983—89; prof. Columbia U. Sch. Law, NYC, 1989—2004, dean, Lucy G Moses Prof. of Law, 1996—2004; pres. Rice University, Houston, 2004—, prof. polit. sci., 2004—. Vis. fellow Max Planck Inst. Fgn. and Internat. Pvt. Law, Hamburg, Germany, 1988; Jean Monnet vis. prof. law, Bielefeld, Germany, 1992—93; mem. editl. bd. Found. Press; bd. dirs. IMAX Corp. Co-editor: Human Rights, 1999. Pres. Columbia Cmty. Services. Mem.: Coun. Fgn. Rels., Assn. of the Bar of the City of NY, Am. Soc. of Internat. Law, Am. Law Inst., Am. Law Deans Assn., ABA, Am. Assn. of Law Schools. Office: Rice U Office of Pres 6100 Main St Houston TX 77005 E-mail: president@rice.edu.*

LEECH, CHARLES RUSSELL, JR., lawyer; b. Coshocton, Ohio, July 29, 1930; s. Charles Russell and Edna (Henry) L.; m. Patricia Ann Tubaugh, June 20, 1953; children— Charles Russell III, Timothy David (dec.), Wendy Ann. AB cum laude, Kenyon Coll., 1952; JD, Ohio State U., 1955; MA, U. Toledo, 1969. Bar: Ohio 1955. Assoc. Fuller & Henry Ltd. and predecessors, Toledo, 1957-64, ptnr., 1964-97, counsel, 1997-99. Mng. editor: Ohio State Law Jour, 1955. Mem. exec. com. alumni council Kenyon Coll., 1967-72, trustee coll., 1974-80. Served with USNR, 1955-57. Fellow Ohio State Bar Found.; mem. ABA, Ohio Bar Assn., Kenyon Coll. Alumni Assn. Maumee Valley (past pres.), Beta Theta Pi, Phi Delta Phi. Republican. Home: 20285 Zion Rd Gambier OH 43022-9643

LEECH, FREDERICK C., lawyer; b. Pitts., Aug. 21, 1954; BA with high honors, U. Mich., 1976; JD, Northeastern U., Boston, 1980. Bar: Pa. 1980. Joined Reed Smith LLP, Pitts., 1980, now ptnr., practice group leader investment mgmt. group, 2002—. Hearing officer Pa. Disciplinary Bd. Mem.: Allegheny County Bar Assn., Pa. Bar Assn. Office: Reed Smith LLP 435 Sixth Ave Pittsburgh PA 15219 Office Phone: 412-288-4178. Office Fax: 412-288-3063. Business E-Mail: fleech@reedsmith.com.

LEECH, JAMES WILLIAM, investment company executive; b. St. Boniface, Man., Can., June 12, 1947; s. George Clarence and Mary Elizabeth (Gibson) L.; m. Deborah Barrett; children: Jennifer Hilton Cumming, Joanna Marjorie Thiessen, James Andrew Douglas. BS in Math. and Physics with hons., Royal Mil. Coll. Can., 1964; MBA, Queen's U., Can., 1973. Exec. asst. to pres. Commerce Capital Corp., Ltd., Montreal, Que., Can., 1973-74, v.p., 1974-75; exec. v.p. Commerce Capital Trust Co., Calgary, Alta., Can., 1976-78; sr. v.p. Eaton/Bay Fin. Services Ltd., Toronto, Ont., Can., 1979; pres., bd. dirs. Unicorp Canada Corp., Toronto, 1979-88; pres., CEO, bd. dirs. Union Energy, Inc., Toronto, 1985-93, Disys Corp., Toronto, 1993-96; vice-chmn., bd. dirs. Kasten Chase Applied Rsch. Ltd., Mississauga, Ont., 1996-99; pres., CEO, bd. dirs. InfoCast Corp., Toronto, 1999-2001; sr. v.p. Tchrs. Pvt. Capital, Ont. Tchrs. Pension Plan, Toronto, 2001—. Bd. dirs. Harris Steel Group, Inc., Chemtrade Logistics Income Fund, Yellow Pages Group, Maple Leaf Sports & Entertainment, WorldSpan Techs. Vice-chmn. adv. coun. sch. bus. Queens U., 1979-83, chmn. 1998-2001, mem. gen. coun., 1978-97, mem. investment com. bd. trustees, 1980-97, trustee, 1984-96, mem. fund coun., 1988-97; bd. dirs., chmn., pres., mem. exec. com. Can. Stage Co., 1989-94; v.p., bd. dirs. Toronto Arts Coun., 1994-2000; trustee Toronto Gen. and Western Hosp. Found., 1996—; bd. govs. Stratford Festival of Can., 2002—; bd. dirs. Right to Play, 2002—. D.I. McLeod scholar, 1971-73; Seagram rsch. fellow, 1983, Samuel Bronfman Found. fellow, 1973, Transp. Devel. Agy. fellow, 1972, Gold Medalist, Canadian Securities Course, 1974. Mem. World Pres. Orgn., The Nat. Club, Muskoka Lakes Golf and Country Club, Canadian Club Toronto (bd. dirs. 2004—). United Ch. Can. Home: 51 Mathersfield Dr Toronto ON Canada M4W 3W4 E-mail: jim_leech@otpp.com.

LEECH, MARLA RENÉE, media specialist, educator; b. San Diego, Calif., Apr. 6, 1961; d. Thomas Franklin Leech and Margaret Vernon Blaisdel-Johnson. BA in Psychology, U. Calif., Davis, Calif., 1983; cert. in Film, U. Calif., Santa Cruz, Calif., 1987; MA in Broadcasting, U. Calif., San Francisco, Calif., 1993; B in Tchg., New Coll., 1996. Prof. broadcasting City Coll., San Francisco, 1996—. Self employed video prodr., editor, San Francisco, 1993—; prof. media Laney Coll., Oakland, Calif., 2003—; instr. online Nat. Acad. TV Arts and Scis., San Francisco, 1999; prodn. mgr. Mission Movie, San Francisco, 2003; bd. dirs. Women in Film and TV, 2004. Prodr.: (films) Breakin' The Glass, 1999, It's A Boy! Journeys From Female to Male, 2000; editor: (films) Love Makes a Family, 1993, 2004, Strings Attached, 1998, Radical Harmonies, 2002 (Best Documentary award Frameline Fest, 2002). Outdoor educator Environ. Travel Companions, San Francisco, 1999—; vol. Film Arts Found., San Francisco, 1993—95. Named Woman of Vision, Coll. San Mateo, 1999; grantee Sheldon Fay grant, Nat. Acad. TV Arts and Scis., 1993. Democrat. Avocations: drums, kayaking, guitar, politics, meeting people. Home: PO Box 460542 San Francisco CA 94146

LEECH, NOYES ELWOOD, lawyer, educator; b. Ambler, Pa., Aug. 1, 1921; m. Louise Ann Gallagher, Apr. 19, 1954; children: Katharine, Gwyneth. AB, U. Pa., 1943, JD, 1948. Bar: Pa. 1949. Assoc. Dechert, Price & Rhoads (and predecessors), Phila., 1948-49, 51-53; mem. faculty law sch. U. Pa., Phila., 1949-57, prof., 1957-78, Ferdinand Wakeman Hubbell prof. law, 1978-85, William A. Schnader prof. law, 1985-86, prof. emeritus, 1986—. Co-author: The International Legal System, 3d edit., 1988; gen. editor: Jour. Comparative Bus. and Capital Market Law, 1978-86. Mem. Order of Coif, Phi Beta Kappa. Home: 6300 Greene St 505 Philadelphia PA 19144-2510

LEEDER, ELLEN LISMORE, literature and language professor, literary critic; b. Vedado, Havana, Cuba, July 8, 1931; came to U.S., 1959; d. Thomas and Josefina (Jorge) Lismore; m. Robert Henry Leeder, Dec. 20, 1957 (dec. 1994); 1 child, Thomas Henry. D of Pedagogy, U. Havana, Cuba, 1955; MA, U. Miami, 1966, PhD, 1973. Lang. tchr. St. George's Sch., Havana, 1952-59; from part-time instr. to full prof. Spanish Barry U., Miami Shores, Fla., 1960—75, prof. Spanish, 1975—, chmn. dept. for lang., 1975-76, coord. fgn. lang., 1976—89; dir. Spanish immersion program, 1986-88. Part-time prof. Miami-Dade C.C., 1974-75; vis. prof. U. Madrid, 1982; prof. Forspro Program Studies Abroad, 1989, 90; cons. HEH, 1981-83; judge Asociación Críticos y Comentaristas del Arte, Miami, 1985—; judge Silver Knight Awards, 1979-83; oral examiner juror Dade County Pub. Schs., Miami, 1986-87. Author: El Desarraigo en Las Novelas de Angel María de Lera, 1978, Justo Sierra y el Mar, 1979, Dimensión Existencial en la Narrativa de Lera, 1992; co-editor: El arte narrativo de Hilda Perera, 1996. Bd. dirs. Vis.

Nurse Assn., 1978-80. Mem. MLA, South Atlantic MLA, Am. Coun. Tchg. Fgn. Langs., Am. Assn. Tchrs. Spanish and Portuguese (pres. 1978-84, v.p. 1984-87, pres. Southeastern Fla. chpt.), Fla. Fgn. Assn., Círculo de Cultura Panamericano, Assn. Internat. Hispanistas, Assn. Cubana de Mujeres Universitarias (pres.), Cuban Women Club, Phi Alpha Theta, Kappa Delta Pi, Sigma Delta Xi, Alpha Mu Gamma, Coral Gables Country Club. Avocations: tennis, piano, singing, coin collecting/numismatics. Home: 830 SW 101st Ave Miami FL 33174-2836 Office: Barry Univ 11300 NE 2nd Ave Miami FL 33161-6695 E-mail: eleeder@mail.barry.edu.

LEEDOM, JOHN NESBETT, manufacturing executive, state legislator; b. Dallas, July 27, 1921; BSEE, Rice U., 1943. Engr. Naval Rsch. Lab., Washington, 1943-45; asst. sales mgr. Sprague Products Co., North Adams, Mass., 1945-50; founder, CEO Wholesales Electronic Supply Inc., Dallas, 1950—. Pres. Levco, Inc., 1973—; mem. Tex. Senate, 1980-96. Author: The Group and You, 1994, Whose Water, 2002, Words of God, 2004. Chmn. Dallas County Rep. Com., 1962-66, mem. state exec. com., 1966-68; mem. Dallas City Coun., 1975-80. Served to lt. (j.g.) USNR, 1943-45. Mem.: Nat. Assn. Wholesale Distbrs. (pres. 1972—73), Nat. Electronic Distbrs. Assn. (pres. 1971—72), Weather Modification Assn. (chmn. legis. com. 2001—), Mil. Order World Wars, Navy League, Tau Beta Pi. Office: 2809 Ross Ave Dallas TX 75201-2519 Office Phone: 214-969-2400 ext. 200.

LEEDS, BARRY HOWARD, literature and language professor; b. NYC, Dec. 6, 1940; s. Andrew Samuel and Paula (Stark) Leeds; m. Robin Leigh Flowers, Apr. 20, 1968 (div. Dec. 2000); children: Brett Ashley, Leslie Lion(dec.). BA, Columbia U., 1962, MA, 1963; PhD, Ohio U., 1967. Lectr. CUNY, 1963-64; instr. U. Tex., El Paso, 1964-65; asst. prof. Cen. Conn. State U., New Britain, 1968-71, assoc. prof., 1971-76, prof., 1976-91; disting. prof., 1991—. Cons. Am. lit. Choice mag., Middletown, Conn., 1968—; vis. faculty Yale U., 1984-85. Author: The Structured Vision of Norman Mailer, 1969, Ken Kesey, 1981, The Enduring Vision of Norman Mailer, 2002; editor: Conn. Rev., 1989-92, mem. editl. bd., 1986-95; contbg. editor D.C. Heath Anthology Am. Lit., 1986—; contbr. articles to profl. jours. incl. Saturday Rev., Modern Fiction Studies, Jour. Modern Lit. Alumni interviewer Columbia Coll., N.Y.C., 1982-95. Conn. State U. grantee, 1986—; recipient Disting. Svc. award Cen. Conn. State U., 1982. Mem.: Norman Mailer Soc. (v.p. 2002—), Conn. Acad. Arts and Scis. Avocations: scuba diving, weightlifting, ballroom dancing, competition target shooting. Home: 200 Blakeslee St Apt 121 Bristol CT 06010-8800 Office: Cen Conn State U Dept English 1615 Stanley St New Britain CT 06053-2439 E-mail: bhleeds01@snet.net.

LEEDS, CHARLES ALAN, publishing executive; b. Mpls., Aug. 20, 1951; s. Charles Phillips and Irene (Pollard) L.; m. Karen Sue Biggs, Aug. 2, 1986; children: Charles Austin, Tyler Dixon. BA, Drake U., 1973, MPA, 1978. Mktg. coord. Register and Tribune Syndicate Inc., Des Moines, Iowa, 1973-79; sales mgr. Washington Post Writers Group, Washington, 1979-89; pres. and editorial dir. L.A. Times Washington Post News Svc., Washington, 1989—. Asst. professorial lectr. George Washington U., Washington, 1986, 88. Mem. nat. adv. bd. Sch. Journalism and Mass Comm. Drake U., 1996—2001, chmn. Bus. Basics, 1999—2003. Recipient Best in Bus. award Am. Journalism Rev., 1995. Mem. Internat. Press Inst. (assoc.), Soc. Profl. Journalists, Sigma Delta Chi, Kappa Tau Alpha. Presbyterian. Avocations: jogging, tennis, golf. Home: 4714 17th St N Arlington VA 22207-2031 Office: LA Times-Washington Post News Svc 1150 15th St NW Washington DC 20071-0001

LEEDS, DOUGLAS BRECKER, advertising executive, theater producer; b. NYC, Mar. 15, 1947; s. Richard Henry and Nancy Ann (Brecker) L.; m. Christine (Anki) Castler, Jan. 14, 1980; 1 child, Victoria Brecker. BS, Babson Coll., 1970. V.p., dir. Auto Data Systems, Inc., Natick, Mass., 1970-72; dir. leasing Beacon Cos., Inc., Boston, 1972-77; account exec. Thomson-Leeds Co., Inc. divsn. The WPP Group, N.Y.C., 1977-84, exec. v.p., 1985-88, pres., 1988-97, chmn., CEO, 1989—2002. Chmn. ednl. rels. com. Point of Purchase Advt. Inst., 1986—, elected bd. dirs., 1989, vice chmn., 1994—; bd. dirs. Checker Board Found.; pres. The Tori Group, Inc., 2002—. Co-prodr.: (Broadway musical) Streetheat, 1985; assoc. prodr.: (Broadway play) Sleight of Hand, 1986; patentee in field. Chmn., founder Lobby Gallery Assocs. Whitney Mus. Am. Art, N.Y.C., 1983-90; trustee Guild Hall of East Hampton (Mus. and Theatre), 1990-92, John Drew Theatre; chmn. men's com. Boys Club N.Y., 1989; bd. dirs. chmn. Friends Henry Street Settlement House, N.Y.C., 1977-80; trustee Whitney Mus. Am. Art, 1992-99, co-chmn. membership com., 1993—, Worcester Acad., 1982-85; also trustee emeritus; trustee Babson Coll., 1979-86, also co-chmn. devel. and pub. affairs com.; mem. dream team Meml. Sloan-Kettering Cancer Ctr.; bd. dirs. Am. Theatre Wing, 1991—, vice chmn., treas., sec. bd. dirs., pres., 2003—, mem. adminstrn. com. Tony Awards; mem. coun. Frick Collection, 2000—. Mem. Babson Coll. Alumni Assn. (bd. dirs., v.p. 1975-79), Union Club, Doubles Club, Royal Tennis Court Club (Middlesex, Eng.).

LEEDS, NORMA STERNE, chemistry educator; b. N.Y.C. d. Harry Archer and Teenie Sterne; m. Morton W. Leeds, Feb. 4, 1945; 1 child, Valerie Ann. PhD, Rutgers U., 1950. Rsch. assoc. Sloan Kettering Inst. Cancer Rsch., N.Y.C., 1950-55; supr. Gen. Aniline & Film, Linden, N.J., 1955-58; asst. prof. Fairleigh Dickinson U., Florham Park, N.J., 1959-62; assoc. prof. Caldwell (N.J.) Coll. for Women, 1962-64; from assoc. prof. to prof. chemistry Kean Univ., Union, N.J., 1964-91, chair dept. chemistry, 1970-72, prof. emeritus, 1991—. Contbr. articles to profl.jours.; editor: Opera at Florham Assn., 1992—97. Cottrell grantee Rutgers U., 1946-48; Univ. Rsch. Coun. fellow Rutgers U., 1946-48. Mem. Fortnightly Club (chair membership 1993-95), Sigma Xi. Unitarian Universalist. Home: 6 Sunningdale Ct Maplewood NJ 07040-2420 E-mail: normaleeds@yahoo.com.

LEEDS, NORMAN E., medical educator, radiologist; b. Jersey City, N.J., June 9, 1928; m. Bette G. Leeds, June 12, 1953; children: Frederick G., Patrice G. BA, Yale Coll., 1948; MD, NY Med. Coll., 1953. Diplomate in radiology and in neuroradiology Am. Bd. Radiology. Asst. prof. radiology U So. Calif. Sch. Medicine, L.A., 1961—63; asst. prof. U. Pa. Grad. Sch. and Grad. Hosp., Phila., 1962—64, U. Pa. Children's Hosp., 1964—69, Albert Einstein Hosp. Temple U., 1964—69; assoc. prof. Albert Einstein Coll. Medicine, Montefiore Hosp., Bronx, 1969—74, prof., 1974—85, Mt. Sinai Sch. of Medicine, N.Y.C., 1985—90; chair dept. radiology Beth Israel Hosp., N.Y.C.; prof., Kennedy chair U. Tex. M.D. Anderson Cancer Ctr., Houston, 1991—2003; clin. prof. Mt. Sinai Sch. Medicine, Mt. Sinai Hosp., 2003—. With USPHS, 1955—57. Fellow: Am. Heart Assn., Am. Coll. Radiology; mem.: Am. Soc. Neuroradiology (pres. 1973, Gold medal 2003). Home: 50 Sutton Pl S Apt 5E New York NY 10022 E-mail: norman.leeds@msnyuhealth.org.

LEEDS, RICHARD, computer marketing executive; Chmn., CEO Systemax Inc. (formerly Global DirectMail), Port Washington, NY. Office: Systemax 11 Harbor Park Dr Port Washington NY 11050-4656*

LEEDS, ROBERT X., writer; b. Detroit, Feb. 24, 1927; s. Harry Leeds and Beatrice Burnett; m. Peggy Baran, July 4, 1948; children: Leslie A. Kemper, Marc B., Gail Arlyne. BA, Wayne State U., 1956, MBA, 1960. Dir. methods engring. GM, Detroit, 1954—71; pres. Am. Pet Motels, Chgo., 1972—99; creative editor Epic Pub. Co., Las Vegas, 1988—. Cons. Associated Mgmt. Engrs., Chgo., 1970—72. Author: Christmas Tails, 1999, Love is A 4 Legged Word, 2001; editor: Doctor Leeds' Selection of Popular Epic Recreations, 1999. Mem.: Rotary. Avocation: flying.

LEEDS, SUSANNE, special education educator, writer; d. Joel and Hilda (Reiss) Leibowitz. BA, Queens Coll. of CUNY, 1972; MA, NYU, 1978. Cert. spl. edn. tchr. N.Y., 1978. Spl. edn. tchr. N.Y.C. Bd. Edn., 1972—82; tchr. Palm Beach County Sch. Bd., Boca Raton, Fla., 1994—. Author: (poem) Illumination (In Honor of Ethiopian Jews), 1999, At The U.S. Holocaust Meml. Mus., 2002, Gone (In Memory of Victims of 9/11), 2001; contbr. numerous poems publ. in jours. and mags.; singer: (performed with Barry Harris Jazz Ensemble) Beacon Theater, N.Y.C., 1984. Recipient 3rd prize Vi Bagliore Mem. award, Nat. League Am. Pen Women, 2000, 1st prize, 11th Ann. Sylvia Wolens Jewish Heritage Writing Competition, 2002, finalist, 15th Ann. Robert Penn Warren Poetry awards, 2002, 1st prize Grandmother Earth Nat. Writing awards (Haiku category), 2002, Wall of Tolerance honoree, Civil Rights Meml. Ctr., 2005. Mem.: Nat. Fedn. State Poetry Socs., Fla. State Poetry Assn., Nat. League of Am. Pen Women. Avocations: music, singing, opera, piano. Home: 6507 Royal Manor Cir Delray Beach FL 33484-2411 Personal E-mail: susanneleeds@yahoo.com.

LEEF, JAMES LEWIS, biology professor, immunology research executive, immunologist, director; b. San Francisco, Mar. 6, 1937; married, 1964; 4 children. BA, U. Calif., San Francisco, 1967; PhD in Biology, U. Tenn., 1974. Sr. investigator cryobiology, head Malaria Rsch. dept. Biomed. Rsch. Inst., Rockville, Md., 1976-82, exec. dir., 1982—. Cons. Sci. and Indsl. Rsch. and Devel. Co., 1967-69; guest scientist Navy Med. Rsch. Inst., 1976—. U. Ill. fellow, 1973-76. Mem. AAAS, Soc. Cryobiology, Tissue Culture Assn., Am. Assn. Tissue Banks, N.Y. Acad. Sci. Achievements include research in malariology; mechanisms of freezing injury; study of various developmental stages of malaria and schistosomiasis parasites as antigens in developing a malaria and schistosomiasis vaccine and preservation of these forms at low temperatures. Office: Biomed Rsch Inst 12111 Parklawn Dr Rockville MD 20852-1709

LEEFE, JAMES MORRISON, architect; b. N.Y.C., Aug. 28, 1921; s. Charles Clement and Suzanne (Bernhardt) L.; m. Miriam Danziger, Oct. 31, 1949; 1 dau., Molly Elizabeth. Cert., U.S. Mcht. Marine Acad., 1943; B.Arch., Columbia U., 1950. Practice architecture, San Francisco, 1955-60; chief architect power and indsl. div. Bechtel Inc., San Francisco, 1960-64, prin. urban designer, 1974-80; chief architect San Francisco Power div. Bechtel Power Corp., 1980-89; v.p., asst. sec. Bechtel Assos. (P.C.), N.Y., 1978-89, v.p., 1978-89; pvt. cons. architect Sausalito, Calif., 1989—; ptnr. Leefe & Ehrankrantz Architects, San Francisco, 1964-68; v.p. Bldg. Systems Devel. Inc., San Francisco and Washington, 1965-70; also dir.; dir. architecture Giffels Assos. Inc., Detroit, 1971-74. Lectr. in architecture Columbia U., 1951-52, U. Calif., Berkeley, 1954-60; mem. faculty U. for Pres's., Young Pres's. Orgn., 1967; adj. prof. U. Detroit, 1971-72; mem. adv. bd. Nat. Clearing House for Criminal Justice Planning and Architecture, 1974-76 Works include Mus. West of Am. Craftsmen's Council, San Francisco, 1964 (Archtl. Record award for interior design 1971), Wells Hydrocombine Dam and Power Generating Facility, Columbia River, Wash., 1965, Boundary Dam, Pend Orielle River, Wash., 1965 (Am. Public Power Assn. honor award 1975), Detroit Automobile Inter-Ins. Exchange Corp. Hdqrs, Dearborn, Mich., 1972 (Detroit chpt. AIA honor award 1975), PPG Industries Research Center, Allison Park, Pa., 1973 (Detroit chpt. AIA honor award 1975, Am. Inst. Steel Constrn. Archtl. award of excellence 1975, Mich. Soc. Architects honor award 1976), Gen. Electric Research Center, Twinsburg, Ohio, 1973 (Detroit chpt. AIA honor award 1977), Appliance Buyers Credit Corp. Hdqrs. Office, Benton Harbor, Mich., 1974 (Engring. Soc. Detroit Design award 1976), Standard Tng. Bldg. Commonwealth Edison, 1989-90, Strybing Arboretum, San Francisco, 1990; contbr. articles to profl. jours.; originator various techniques for analysis of human factors in the working environment. Chmn. bd. Mus. West of Am. Crafts Coun., San Francisco, 1966-68; vice chmn. Franklin (Mich.) Hist. Dist. Commn., 1973-74; trustee So. Marin Land Trust. With U.S. Mcht. Marine, 1942-46. Recipient Hirsh Meml. prize Columbia U., 1950, 1st prize (with Miriam Leefe) Dow Chem. Co. Competition for Interior Design, 1960 Fellow AIA; hon. mem. Internat. Union Architects Working Group Habitat, trustee, So. Marin Land Trust. Home and Office: James Leefe FAIA Architect 131 Spencer Ave Sausalito CA 94965-2022 *I think of architecture as a celebration of life, of the buildings we make for ourselves as stepping stones on the path of history. This forces me to be an optimist, always searching to find a manifestation of the joy of being in my work.*

LEEK, JAY WILBUR, management consultant; b. Albany, Ind., Apr. 24, 1928; s. Cecil and Hazel (Lindley) Leek; m. Laurayne M. DelaHunt, Sept. 22, 2001; children from previous marriage: Roderick Jay, Stacy LeAnn, Scott Lee, Timothy Lane, Debra Jan, Marilynn Sue, James Jay. BS in Indsl. Engring., Pacific Western, 1969, MS in Mgmt., 1976, D in Bus. Adminstrn., 1980. Registered profl. engr., Calif. Mgr. Nutone, Inc., Cin., 1951-53, Bulova Watch Co., N.Y.C., 1953-59, Martin Marietta Corp., Orlando, Fla., 1959-75; v.p. Northrop Corp., L.A., 1975-80; pres., COO Philip Crosby Assocs., Winter Park, Fla., 1980-87, also bd. dirs.; mgmt. cons., Ft. Myers, 1987-91; pres., CEO Carchi-Resources, Inc., Ocala, Fla. Bd. dirs. So. Bank, Longwood, Fla., Electro-World, Orlando. Author: Workmanship Standards, 1974; co-author: (with others) AMA Management Handbook, 1986, Quality Management Handbook, 1986. Trustee Orlando Sports Inc., 1985-87, Fla. State Univ. Found., Tallahassee, 1986-96; bd. dirs. Fla. Citrus Sports Assn., Orlando, 1984-90. With USN, 1944-46. Recipient Academician award Internat. Acad. for Quality, Grobenzell, Fed. Republic Germany, 1985; named to Wall of Fame, Am. Mgmt. Assn., 1979. Fellow: Am. Soc. Quality Control (pres. 1980—81); mem.: Sapphire Lakes Country Club, Sawgrass Country Club, Ponte Vedra Beach Country Club, Shriners, Masons. Republican. Home: 951 Spinnakers Reach Dr Ponte Vedra Beach FL 32082 E-mail: bearj824@aol.com.

LEEKLEY, JOHN ROBERT, lawyer; b. Phila., Aug. 27, 1943; s. Thomas Briggs and Dorothy (O'Hora) L.; m. Karen Kristin Myers, Aug. 28, 1965 (dec. Mar. 1997); children: John Thomas, Michael Dennis; m. Gerry Lee Gildner, June 5, 1999. BA, Boston Coll., 1965; LLB, Columbia U., 1968. Bar: N.Y. 1968, Mich. 1976. Assoc. Curtis, Mallet-Prevost, Colt & Mosle, N.Y.C., 1968-69, Davis Polk & Wardwell, N.Y.C., 1969-76; asst. corp. counsel Masco Corp., Taylor, Mich., 1976-77, corp. counsel, 1977-79, v.p., corp. counsel, 1979-88, v.p., gen. counsel, 1988-96, sr. v.p., gen. counsel, 1996—. Bd. visitors Columbia U. Law Sch., N.Y.C., 1994-96; mem. Freedom Twp. Bd. Tax Appeals, 1984-85. Mem. ABA (com. long range issues affecting bus. practice 1976-96), Mich. State Bar Assn. Democrat. Roman Catholic. Avocations: percheron horse breeding, hunting, fishing, outdoor activities. Office: Masco Corp 21001 Van Born Rd Taylor MI 48180-1300

LEEMAN, SUSAN EPSTEIN, neuroscientist, educator; b. Chgo., May 9, 1930; d. Samuel and Dora (Gubernikoff) Epstein; m. Cavin Leeman (div.); children: Eve, Raphael, Jennifer. BA, Goucher Coll., 1951; MA, Radcliffe Coll., 1954, PhD, 1958; DS (hon.), SUNY, Utica, 1992; hon. degree, Goucher Coll., 1993. Instr. Harvard Med. Sch., Boston, 1958-59; postdoctoral fellow Brandeis U., Waltham, Mass., 1959-62, 62-66; rsch. assoc., adj. ast. prof., asst. rsch. prof. Brandieis U., Waltham, Mass., 1966-68, 68-71; asst. prof. Harvard Med. Sch., 1972-73, assoc. prof., 1973-80; prof. U. Mass. Med. Ctr., Worcester, 1980-92, dir. interdept. neurosci. program, 1984-92; prof. dept. pharmacology Boston U. Sch. Medicine, 1992—. Burroughs Wellcome vis. prof. U.Ky., 1992. Fogarty scholar NAS, 1994; recipient Women in Sci. award N.Y. Acad., 1995. Mem. NAS (197th Lilly lectr. 1994, Fred Conrad Koch award 1994, Women in Sci. award 1995), Am. Acad. Arts and Scis. (Isadore Rosenberg lectr. 1999). Office: Boston U Sch Medicine Dept Pharmacology 715 Albany St # R-616 Boston MA 02118-2526 Office Phone: 617-638-4364. E-mail: sleeman@bu.edu.

LEEMANS, WIM PIETER, physicist; b. Gent, Belgium, June 7, 1963; BS in Elec. Engring., Free U. Brussels, 1985; MS in Elec. Engring., UCLA, 1987, PhD in Elec. Engring., 1991. Teaching asst. UCLA, 1986-87, rsch. asst., 1987-91; staff scientist Lawrence Berkeley Lab., Berkeley, Calif., 1991—. Group leader exptl. beam physics group, 1994—; chair ICFA panel on advanced and novel accelerators; presenter numerous seminars. Contbr. articles to profl. jours. Recipient Simon Ramo awd., Am. Physical Soc., 1992; grad. scholar IEEE Nuclear and Plasma Soc., 1987. Fellow Belgian Am. Ednl. Found., Francqui Found.; mem. IEEE (Nuclear and Plasma scis. soc. grad. scholar 1987), Soc. Photo-Optical Instrument Engrs., Am. Phys. Soc., Royal Flemish Engrs. Soc. Achievements include research in high intensity laser-plasma interaction, interaction of relativistic electrons with lasers and plasmas, novel radiation sources, advanced accelerator concepts, non-linear dynamics of free electron lasers. Office: Lawrence Berkeley Lab Divsn Accelerator Fusion Rsch 1 Cyclotron Rd Ms 71 259 Berkeley CA 94720-0001

LEEMPUTTE, PETER G., manufacturing executive; BS in chem. engring., Wash. U.; MBA, U. Chgo. Grad. Sch. of Bus. Product devel. engr. Proctor & Gamble Co.; fin. Armco Inc., FMC Corp., BP Amoco; v.p., ptnr. Mercer Mgmt. Cons., 0196—1998; Exec. v.p., CFO, admin. officer Chgo. Title Corp., 1998—2000; v.p., contr. Brunswick, Lake Forest, Ill., 2000—03, sr. v.p., CFO, 2003—. Office: Brunswick 1 N Field Ct Lake Forest IL 60045-4811

LEENEY, ROBERT JOSEPH, newspaper editor; b. New Haven, May 10, 1916; s. Patrick Joseph and Mary Alice (Ross) L.; m. Anne King Coyne, June 28, 1941; children: Robert Joseph, David Coyne, Anne Patricia. Student pub. and pvt. schs.; L.H.D. (hon.), U. New Haven, 1983, Albertus Magnus Coll., 1985. Reporter, book page editor, drama critic New Haven Register, 1940-47, editorial writer, 1947-55; editor editorial page New Haven Jour.-Courier, New Haven Register, 1956-61, exec. editor, 1961-72, editor, 1972-81, editor emeritus, 1981, v.p., dir., 1970—. V.p., sec. Register Pub. Co.; dir. Conn. Savs. Bank.; examiner adminstrv. reports, editor Ofcl. Digest State Reports, Conn., 1951-52 Author: New Haven in the 20th Century, 2000; columnist. Conn. pub. info. chmn. Am. Cancer Soc.; v.p. Arts Council Greater New Haven; mem. Conn. Edn. Council, Edn. Commn. of States, Conn. Commn. on Freedom of Info., 1981-86; bd. dirs. St. Raphael's Hosp. Found., Long Wharf Theatre, New Haven, 1990; trustee Albertus Magnus Coll., 1984, Conn. Found. Open Govt. Served with USAAF, World War II. Named to New Eng. Journalism Hall of Fame, 1977; recipient Seal of the City award for disting. cmty. svc., 1994; named Hon. Capt. 2d Co. Gov.'s Footguard 1775. Mem. SAR (hon. mem., Humphreys br. 2005), Nat. Conf. Editl. Writers, Am. Soc. Newspaper Editors, New Eng. Soc. Newspaper Editors (pres. 1961), New Eng. AP News Execs. Assn. (pres. 1977), Conn. Editl. Assn., Conn. Cir. AP (pres.), New Haven C. of C. (v.p., dir., Disting. Svc. award), Outer Circle, NH Colony Hist. Soc., Kiwanis, Woodbridge Club, Mory's Club, Quinnipiak Club, Sigma Delta Chi (pres. Conn. chpt. 1963-69). Home: R 69 424 Carrington Rd Bethany CT 06524-3160 Office: New Haven Register 40 Sargent Dr New Haven CT 06511-5939 E-mail: rjleeney@snet.net.

LEEPER, KATHLEEN MARIE, elementary school educator; b. L.A., Dec. 5, 1962; d. Carl L. and Mary E. (Parker)_L. BA, Calif. Poly. Inst., 1985, MEd, 1988. Cert. adminstrn. 2001. Tchr. New Lexington Sch., El Monte, Calif., 1985—2001; asst. prin. Frank M. Wright Elem. Sch., El Monte, Calif., 2001—. Mem. leadership team New Lexington Sch.; tchr. transition English, 1990-2001; grant writer El Monte City Sch. Dist., 1990-2001. Sunday sch. tchr. El Monte 1st Presbyn. Ch., 1980-2001, elder; mem. Village Presbyn. Ch., 2005-. Mem. Delta Kappa Gamma. Avocations: travel, reading, swimming, walking, spanish.

LEEPER, RAMON JOE, physicist; b. Princeton, Mo., Apr. 1, 1948; s. Joe Edd and Jeanne (Gaul) Leeper; m. Sumiko Yasuda, Dec. 21, 1976; 1 child, Joe Eric. BS, MIT, 1970; PhD, Iowa State U., 1975. Rsch. assoc. Ames (Iowa) Lab. U.S. Dept. Energy, 1975-76; mem. tech. staff Sandia Nat. Labs., Albuquerque, 1976-86, dept. mgr. diagnostics and target physics dept., 1986—. Guest scientist Argonne Nat. Lab., Ill., 1971—76; invited lectr. NATO Advanced Study Inst., Italy, 1983, Internat. Sch. Plasma Physics, Italy, 2001. Contbr. articles to profl. jours. Recipient Outstanding Tchg. award, Iowa State U., 1973; fellow NDEA, 1971—73. Mem.: IEEE (session chmn. 1984), Am. Phys. Soc. (chmn. high temperature plasma diagnostics conf. 1992), Sigma Xi. Republican. Achievements include patents in field. Home: 6905 Rosewood Rd NE Albuquerque NM 87111-1021 Office: Diagnostics & Target Physics Dept 1677 Sandia Nat Labs Albuquerque NM 87185 E-mail: rjleepe@sandia.gov.

LEEPSON, MARC, freelance/self-employed writer; b. Newark, June 20, 1945; s. Arthur and Selma Ruth (Levin) L.; m. Janna Lee Murphy, Aug. 29, 1970; children: Devin Patrick Murphy, Cara Rose. BA, George Washington U., 1967, MA, 1971. Staff writer Congl. Quar., Washington, 1976-86; freelance writer, 1986—. Author: Executive Fitness, 1982, The Alive and Well Stress Book, 1984, Saving Monticello, 2001, Flag: An American Biography, 2005; contbg. author: What Should We Tell Our Children About Vietnam?, 1989, Vietnam War Films, 1994; editor: Webster's New World Dictionary of the Vietnam War, 1998. Cons. Vietnam Vets. of Am., 1987—, arts editor, columnist newspaper, 1986—; pres. adv. bd. Middleburg (Va.) Libr. Bd., 1995—; bd. dirs. YMCA of Loudon County, Leesburg, Va., 1996—. With U.S. Army, 1967-69. Mem. Nat. Book Critics Cir., Washington Ind. Writers. Home and Office: PO Box 1889 Middleburg VA 20118-1889 Mailing: c/o Joseph Brendan Vallely Flaming Star Literary Enterprises 320 Riverside Dr New York NY 10025 E-mail: Marc527psc@aol.com.*

LEER, STEVEN F., mining executive; Pres., CEO Arch Coal Inc., St. Louis, 1992—. Bd. dir. Western Business Roundtable, Norfolk Southern Corp. Office: Arch Mineral Corp City Place One Saint Louis MO 63141*

LEES, ALFRED WILLIAM, writer, former magazine editor; b. Kansas City, Kans., June 12, 1926; s. Alfred Whitaker and Blanche (Pontius) L. BA, Stanford U., 1950. Editor and writer Home Craftsman, N.Y.C., 1953—59, Family Handyman, 1960, Popular Sci., N.Y.C, 1960—62, sr. editor and writer, 1967—71; editor and writer Popular Mechanics, 1962—66; home care columnist Cosmopolitan, 1965—67; group editor reader activities Popular Sci., 1972—88; dir. and judge nat. ann. design competition Am. Plywood Assn., Tacoma, 1976—86. Pres. Nat. Assn. Home and Workshop Writers, 1990—92. *Upon retiring from his 35-year career as a how-to writer-editor, Lees tackled a book unlike the six he'd already published: an anthology of autobiographies by committed male couples across America. It took four years to find a publisher-not because the accounts were sensational, but because they were not. Even publishers with "gay lists" had scant interest in solid-citizen couples, preferring to present from-another-planet stereotypes, fey celebrities or wry comics. When Haworth Press bought the manuscript, the 28 authors persisted in telling their tales without compromise, resulting in a book that pioneered the marriage equality movement.* Author: Leisure Homes, 1980, 67 Prizewinning Plywood Projects, 1984; co-author: Wood Finishing and Painting, 1955, DIY Projects for Your Own Backyard, 1978, 2d edit., 1984, What's Wrong with My Car?, 1990, Decks and Sunspaces, 1991, Longtime Companions, 1999, Year of the B's: An Illustrated Chronicle of '04, 2005. With USAAF, 1944—45. Mem. Delaware Valley Arts Alliance, Dutch Treat Club, Traveler's Century Club (122 countries visited). Avocations: world travel, photography. Home: 140 Nassau St Apt 9B New York NY 10038-1548

LEES, FRANCIS, economics professor; b. Bklyn., Jan. 19, 1931; s. Roy A. and Mary (Ozustowicz) L.; m. Kathryn V. Murphy, June 6, 1959; children: Veronica Ann, Francis, Daniel, Jeannette Marie. BA, Bklyn. Coll., 1952; MA, St. Louis U., 1953; PhD, NYU, 1961. Instr. Fordham U., N.Y.C., 1956-60; asst. prof. St. Johns U., Jamaica, NY, 1960-61; fin. analyst Dominick & Dominick, N.Y.C., 1961-62; assoc. prof. St. John's U., 1962-68, prof., 1968—. Cons. Conf. Bd., 1979-86, U.S. Govt., 1985 fin. analyst, Internat. Report, 1982-84, CIA, 1985-86; prof. global fin. St. John's U., 1999—. Author: Capital Controls and the US Balance of Payments, 1968, International Banking and Finance, 1974, International Financial Markets, 1975, Foreign Banking and Investment in the United States, 1976, Economic and Political Development of the Sudan, 1977, International Lending, Risk, and the Euromarkets, 1979, Foreign Multinational Investment in the U.S., 1986, Banking and Financial Deepening in Brazil, 1990, Global Finance, 1995, 98, Foreign Participation in China's Banking and Securities Markets, 1996, China Superpower, 1997, The Euro, Capital Markets and Dollarization, 2002, Russia Inc., 2005; founder, co-editor Jour. Emerging Markets, 1996—; contbr. articles to profl. jours. Served with AUS, 1953-56. Am. Bankers Assn. Summer Rsch. fellow, 1969; Fulbright rsch. scholar, 1987-88. Home: 14 Hunting Hill Rd Woodbury NY 11797-1404 Office: St Johns U Grand Central And Utopia Pkwy Jamaica NY 11439-0001 Office Phone: 718-990-7305.

LEES, MARJORIE BERMAN, biochemist, neuroscientist; b. N.Y.C., Mar. 17, 1923; d. Isadore I. and Ruth (Rogalsky) Berman; m. Sidney Lees, Sept. 17, 1946; children: David E., Andrew, Eliot. BA, Hunter Coll., 1943; MS, U. Chgo., 1945; PhD, Harvard U./Radcliffe Coll., 1951. Assoc. biochemist, asst. biochemist McLean Hosp., Belmont, Mass., 1953-62; rsch. assoc. Dartmouth Med. Sch., Hanover, 1962-66; assoc. biochemist McLean Hosp., Belmont, 1966-76; prin. and sr. rsch. assoc. Harvard Med. Sch., Boston, 1966-85; biomed. scientist E.K. Shriver Ctr., Waltham, Mass., 1976-98; prof. biochemistry (neurology) Harvard Med. Sch., Boston, 1985-94, prof. emerita, 1994—; biochemist Mass. Gen. Hosp., Boston, 1976-98; assoc. dir. biochemistry E.K. Shriver Ctr., Waltham, 1982-90, dir. biochemistry, 1990-93, assoc. dir. mental retardation rsch. ctr., 1994-97, sr. biomed. sci., 1998—; prof. emerita U. Mass. Med. Sch., 1999—. Mem. adv. com. biomed. and behavioral rsch. NASA/NIH, 1993—; mem. sci. adv. com. Nat. Multiple Sclerosis Soc., 1988-93. Chief editor Jour. of Neurochemistry, 1986-90; author (with others) books; contbr. articles to profl. jours. Mem. adv. coun. Nat. Inst. Neurological Disorders, Bethesda, Md., 1979-82; chmn. Radcliffe Grad. Soc., Cambridge, Mass., 1978-80. Predoctoral fellow USPHS, 1947-50, postdoctoral fellow Am. Cancer Soc., 1951-53; Javits Neurosci. grantee NIH, 1983-90, 91-97, prin. grantee NIH, 1962-98; named to Hunter Coll. Hall of Fame, 1982. Mem. Am. Soc. Biochemistry and Molecular Biology, Internat. Soc. Neurochemistry, Am. Soc. Neurochemistry (treas. 1975-81, pres. 1983-85), Soc. for Neurosci., Am. Assn. Neuropathology (assoc.), Phi Beta Kappa. Office: Shriver Ctr U Mass Med Sch Neurobiology Program 200 Trapelo Rd Waltham MA 02452-6332 Office Phone: 781-642-0129. Business E-Mail: marjorie.lees@umassmed.edu.

LEESON, JOSEPH FRANCIS, JR., lawyer; b. Allentown, Pa., Apr. 15, 1955; s. Joseph Francis and Mary Louise (Kennedy) L. BA cum laude, De Sales U., 1977; JD, Cath. U. Am., 1980. Bar: Pa. 1980, U.S. Supreme Ct. 1986. Ptnr. Leeson, Leeson & Leeson, Bethlehem, Pa., 1980—. Co-author: Home Rule Charter for Northampton County, Pennsylvania, 1976. Chmn. bd. dirs. Lehigh Valley Cmty. Found., 1989-91; chmn. bd. govs. Lehigh-Northampton Airport Authority/Lehigh Valley Internat. Airport, 1995-98. Named Bethlehem Outstanding Young Man award, 1988. Mem. Northampton County Bar Assn., Pa. Bar Assn., Fed. Bar Assn. Roman Catholic. Home: 2721 Briarwood Pl Bethlehem PA 18017-3801 Office: Leeson Leeson & Leeson 70 E Broad St Bethlehem PA 18016-1426

LEESON, LEWIS JOSEPH, pharmacist, researcher; b. Paterson, N.J., Apr. 26, 1927; s. Alfred Elias and Rose (Sandow) L.; m. Barbara Rothstein, Dec. 20, 1953; children: Suzanne, Erica, Alex. BS in Pharmacy, Rutgers U., Newark, 1950, MS in Pharm. Chemistry, 1954; PhD in Pharm. Chemistry, U. Mich., 1957. Registered pharmacist, N.J., N.Y., Mich. Pharmacist Mack Drug Co., Paterson, N.J., 1950-52, Fried's Drugs, Paterson, 1952-54; lab. asst. Rutgers U. Coll. Pharmacy, Newark, 1952-54, U. Mich., Ann Arbor, 1954-57; rsch. pharmacist, project leader Lederle Labs., Pearl River, NY, 1957—67; dir. product R & D, Union Carbide Co., Greenburgh, N.Y., 1967-69; asst. dir. product R & D, Geigy Pharm., Suffern, N.Y., 1969-71; dir., sr. dir., sr. rsch. fellow Ciba-Geigy Pharm., Summit, N.J., 1971-84; disting. rsch. fellow Ciba-Geigy Corp., Summit, 1984-93, ret., 1993; pres. LJL Assocs. Inc, Pharm. R&D Cons., Montville, N.J., 1993—. Dean Louis W. Busse lectr. U. Wis., 1993; mem. exec. com. USP, 1990—95, mem. expert adv. com., 2000—; mem. exec. com. N.J. DURC, 1984—89; founder, chief sci. officer Cogent Pharm., 1997—. Editor: Dissolution Technology, 1971; contbr. over 40 articles to profl. jours; patentee in field. Recipient Disting. Alumnus award U. Mich., 1990. Fellow Acad. Pharm. Sci., Am. Assn. Pharm. Scientists; mem. Am. Pharm. Assn., Sigma Xi, Rho Chi, Phi Lambda Upsilon. Jewish. Achievements include 14 patents in field. Home and Office: LJL Assocs Inc 134 Ridge Dr Montville NJ 07045-9473 Office Phone: 973-265-4637. Personal E-mail: blll@optonline.net.

LEESTMA, ROBERT, retired federal agency administrator, educational association administrator; b. Detroit, Oct. 15, 1927; s. Richard and Jeanne (Nivarre) L.; m. Margaret Elizabeth Bell, Aug. 13, 1955 (dec. 1982). AB, U. Mich., 1949, AM, 1951, PhD, 1956. Rsch. teaching asst., cmty. adult edn. program U. Mich., Ann Arbor, 1949-50; tchr. English and social studies Ann Arbor pub. schs., 1950-51; asst. dir. Audio-Visual Edn. Ctr., lectr. sch. edn. U. Mich., 1951-55, assoc. prof., dir. Peace Corps tng. program, 1961-64; ICA edn. and mass. comm. advisor Govt. of Vietnam, 1955-58; edn. adviser Govt. of Thailand, 1958-61; dep. chief edn. div. Bur. Africa, AID, 1964-65; dir. Office Multilateral Policy and Programs, Multilateral Policy Planning Staff, Bur. Ednl. and Cultural Affairs, Dept. State, 1965-67; asst. to asst. sec. edn. for internat. edn. HEW, 1967-68; dir. Inst. Internat. Studies, assoc. commr. internat. edn. U.S. Office Edn., 1968-74, assoc. commr. instl. devel. and internat. edn., 1974-79; dep. dir. planning and implementation Office Edn. for Overseas Dependents, U.S. Dept. Edn., 1980-82; assoc. dir. dissemination and improvement of practice Nat. Inst. Edn., 1982-83, assoc. dir. field initiated and internal studies, 1984-85; dir. U.S. study edn. in Japan, Office Ednl. Rsch. and Improvement Dept. Edn., 1986-89; v.p. internat. programs Am. Assn. State Colls. and Univs., Washington, 1989-91; dir. spl. studies staff U.S. Dept. Edn. Office Ednl. Rsch. and Improvement, 1991-94; also sr. policy advisor Edn. Rsch. and Devel. Bur. AID, 1992-94; interim dir. Nat. Libr. Edn., 1994; edn. cons., 1995—. Mem., chmn. and/or adviser U.S. dels. internat. confs.; U.S. rep., chmn. edn. com. OECD; U.S. rep. governing coun. Internat. Bur. Edn., UNESCO; mem. Indo-U.S. Subcommn. on Edn. and Culture, U.S.-Egyptian Joint Working Group on Edn. and Culture, U.S.-Japan Culcon Edn. Com., U.S. Nat. Commn. for UNESCO; alt. mem. U.S.-Japan Friendship Commn., also Am. panel Joint Culcon Com.; mem. adv. com. Hanna Collection, Hoover Instn., Com. on Edn. and Successor Generation of Atlantic Coun. U.S.; bd. dirs. Pericles Inst., Abraham A. Low Inst. Author, co-author and/or editor books, chpts. and articles in profl. jours., including Japanese Education Today, 1987, Japanese Educational Productivity, 1992. With AUS, 1946-47. Payne scholar U. Mich., 1951-52, Hinsdale scholar, 1953-54. Mem. Comparative and Internat. Edn. Soc., Assn. Asian Studies, Phi Delta Kappa. Home: 2712 George Mason Pl Alexandria VA 22305-1620

LEET, MILDRED ROBBINS, social welfare administrator, consultant; b. NYC, Aug. 9, 1922; d. Samuel Milton and Isabella (Zeitz) Elowsky; m. Louis J. Robbins, Feb. 23, 1941 (dec. 1970); children: Jane, Aileen; m. Glen Leet, Aug. 9, 1974 (dec. 1998). BA, NYU, 1942; LHD (hon.), Coll. Human Svcs., 1988; LLD honoris causa, Marymount Coll., Tarrytown, N.Y., 1991; HHD, Lynn U., 1993; D Humanitarian Svc. (hon.), Norwich U., 1994; DHL, Conn. Coll., 1996; DHL (hon.), Wilson Coll., 2003. Pres. women's div. United Cerebral Palsy, N.Y.C., 1951-52, bd. dirs., 1953-55; rep. Nat. Coun. Women U.S. at UN, 1957-64, 1st v.p., 1959-64, pres., 1964-68, hon. pres., 1968-70; sec., v.p. conf. group U.S. Nat. Orgns. at UN, 1961-64, 76-78, vice chmn., sec., 1962-64, mem. exec. com., 1961-65, chmn. hospitality info. svc., 1960-66; vice chmn. exec. com. NGO's UN Office Public Info., 1976-78, chmn. ann. conf., 1977; chmn. com. on water, desertification, habitat and environment Conf. NGO's with consultative status with UN/ECOSOC, 1976-77; mem. exec. com. Internat. Coun. Women, 1960-73, v.p., 1970-73; chmn. program planning com., women's com. OEO, 1967-72; chmn. com. on natural disasters N.Am. Com. on Environment, 1973-77; N.Y. State chmn. UN Day, 1975; ptnr. Leet & Leet (cons. women in devel.), 1979—98. Co-founder Trickle Up Program, 1979—, pres., 1991—2000, chair, 2001—; mem. task force on Africa UN, 1995—. Contbr. articles to profl. jours.; editor UN Calendar & Digest, 1959-64, Measure of Mankind, 1963; editorial bd.: Peace & Change. Co-chmn. Vols. for Stevenson, N.Y.C., 1956; vice chmn. task force Nat. Dem. Com., 1969-72; commr. N.Y. State Commn. on Powers Local Govt., 1970-73; chmn. Coll. for Human Svcs. Audrey Cohen Coll., 1985-2000; former mem. bd. dirs. Am. Arbitration Assn., New Directions, Inst. for Mediation and Conflict Resolution, Spirit of Stockholm; bd. dirs. Hotline Internat.; v.p. Save the Children Fedn., 1986-93 rep. Internat. Peace Acad. at UN, 1974-77, Internat. Soc. Cmty. Devel., 1977-98, del. at large 1st Nat. Women's Conf., Houston, 1977; chmn. task force on internat. interdependence N.Y. State Women's Meeting, 1977; mem. Task Force on Poverty, 1977; chmn. Task Force on Women, Sci. and Tech. for Devel., 1978; U.S. del. UN Status of Women Commn., 1978, UN Conf. Sci. and Tech. for Devel., 1979, Brazzaville Centennial Celebration, 1980; mem. global adv. bd. Internat. Expn. Rural Devel., 1981—; mem. Coun. Internat. Fellows U. Bridgeport, 1982-88; trustee overseas edn. fund LWV, 1983-91; v.p. U.S. Com. UN Devel. Fund for Women, 1983-94, trustee, 1998-2000; mem. Nat. Consultative Com. Planning for Nairobi, 1984-85; co-chmn. women in devel. com. Interaction, 1985-91; mem. com. of cooperation Interam. Commn. of Women, 1986; bd. dirs. Internat. Devel. Conf., 1991-2001; mem. UN task force informal sector devel. Africa, 1995—. Recipient Crystal award Coll. Human Svcs., 1983, Ann. award Inst. Mediation and Conflict Resloution, 1985, Woman of Conscience award Nat. Coun. Women, 1996, Temple award Inst. Noetic Scis., 1987, Presdl. End Hunger award, 1987, Giraffe award Giraffe Project, 1987, Woman of the World award Eng.'s Women Aid, 1989, Mildred Robbins Leet award Interaction, 1995; co-recipient Rose award World Media Inst., 1987, Human Rights award UN Devel. Fund for Women, 1987, Leadership award U.S. Peace Corps, Woman of Vision award N.Y.C. NOW, 1990, Matrix award Women in Comm., Inc., Spirit of Enterprise award Rolex Industries, 1990, Ann. Bush's Ann. Points of Light award, 1992, Internat. Humanity award ARC Overseas Assn., 1992, Excellence award U.S. Com. for UNIFEM, 1992, Champion of Enterprise award Avon, 1994, Achievement award NYU-Washington Sq. Coll. Alumni. Assn., 1995, Lizette H. Sarnoff Vol. Svc. award Yeshiva U., 1996, Disting. Svc. award N.Y. African Studies Assn., 1996, Disting. Svc. award 50th Anniversary United Cerebral Palsy, 1997, Eleanor Schnurr award UN Assn./USA, Women of Distinction honoree Birmingham So. Coll., Spirit award Nat. Assn. Women Bus. Owners, 1998, Nat. Caring Inst. award, 2001, Nat. Women's Hall of Fame, 2003, Met. Coll. NY Leadership award, 2004, Philippine Kalayan award, 2004, Global Summit of Women Internat. Hall of Fame award, 2005. Mem. AAAS, Women's Forum, Coun. on Fgn. Rels., Cosmopolitan Club, Princeton Club. Home and Office: 54 Riverside Dr New York NY 10024-6509 E-mail: millieleet@aol.com.

LEET, RICHARD HALE, oil industry executive; b. Maryville, Mo., Oct. 11, 1926; s. Theron Hale and Helen Eloise (Rutledge) L.; m. Phyllis Jean Combs, June 14, 1949; children: Richard Hale II, Alan Combs, Dana Ellen. BS in Chemistry, N.W. Mo. State Coll., 1948; PhD in Phys. Chemistry, Ohio State U., 1952. Rsch. chemist Standard Oil Co., Whiting, Ind., 1953-64; dir. long-range and capital planning, mktg. dept. Am. Oil Co., Chgo., 1964-68, mgr. ops. planning, mfg. dept., 1968-70, regional v.p. Atlanta, 1970-71, v.p. supply Chgo., 1971-74; v.p. planning and adminstrn. Amoco Chems. Corp., Chgo., 1974-75, v.p. mktg., 1975-77, exec. v.p., 1977-78, pres., 1978-83; dir. Amoco Corp., Chgo., 1983-91, vice chmn., 1991-92; chmn. bd. OSCN. Bd. dirs. emeritus Gt. Lakes Chem., Vulcan Materials Corp., ITW, Landauer, Inc. Former chmn. bd. mgrs. Met. YMCA, Chgo.; former pres. Boy Scouts Am.; former chmn. bd. Am. Indsl. Health Coun.; former bd. visitors Emory U., 1970-71; hon. v.p. found. bd. Ohio State U; trustee Brenau U. With USNR, 1944-46. Mem. Am. Chem. Soc., Soc. Chem. Industry (exec. com.), Am. Petroleum Inst. (bd. dirs.), Société Industrielle de Chemie, Chem. Mfrs. Assn. (dir.), Phi Sigma Epsilon, Gamma Alpha. Office: Lighthouse Acres 3631 Lantern Dr Gainesville GA 30504-5420

LEETCH, BRIAN JOSEPH, professional hockey player; b. Corpus Christi, Tex., Mar. 3, 1968; Student, Boston Coll. Player N.Y. Rangers, 1988—2004, Toronto Maple Leafs, 2004—05, Boston Bruins, 2005—. Mem. Team U.S.A., Olympic games, 1988, 98, 2002, Team U.S.A., Canada Cup, 1991, Team U.S.A., World Cup of Hockey, 1996, 2004; player NHL All-Star game, 1990—92, 1994, 1996—98, 2001—02. Named to NHL All-Rookie team, 1989, NHL First All-Star team, 1992, 1997; recipient Calder Memorial Trophy, 1989, James Norris Memorial Trophy, 1992, 1997, Conn Smythe Trophy, 1994. Achievements include mem. Stanley Cup Champion New York Rangers, 1994; mem. World Cup Champion Team U.S.A., 1996. Office: c/o Boston Bruins 1 TD BankNorth Garden Boston MA 02114

LEETE, WILLIAM WHITE, artist; b. Portsmouth, Ohio, June 12, 1929; s. Bernard Emerson and Lois Trowbridge (Denison) L.; m. Doris Louise Knight, Sept. 19, 1952; children: Amy MacDonald, Robin Schodt. BA, Yale U., 1951, BFA, 1955, MFA, 1957. Mem. faculty dept. art U. R.I., Kingston, 1957-95, prof. emeritus, 1995, acting dept. chmn., 1968, 69-70, 76. Represented in permanent collections, De Cordova Mus., Lincoln, Mass., Cleve. Mus., Worcester Mus., Fleet Bank, also various pvt. collections. Served with USMC, 1951—53. Mem.: Coll. Art Assn. Home: 202 Silver Lake Ave Wakefield RI 02879-4231 Personal E-mail: wleete@aol.com.

LEEVES, JANE, actress; b. Essex, England, Apr. 18, 1961; m. Marshall Coben, 1996; 2 children. Actress (TV series) The Benny Hill Show, 1983-84, Double Trouble, 1984, Throb, 1986-88, Murphy Brown, 1989-1993, Just Deserts, 1992, Frasier 1993-2004 (Emmy award nom. sup. actress, 1998, SAG award outstanding performance ensemble, 2000); (TV movies) Red Dwarf, 1992, Pandora's Clock, 1996, Just Deserts, 1999; (films) The Hunger, 1983, To Live and Die in L.A., 1985, Miracle on 34th Street, 1994, The Meaning of Life, 1983, Mr. Write, 1994, James and the Giant Peach (voice), 1996, Don't Go Breaking My Heart, 1999, Music of the Heart, 1999, Adventures of Tom Thumb and Thumbelina (voice), 2002, The Event, 2003; (TV guest appearances) Murder, She Wrote, 1987, It's a Living, 1989, Hooperman, 1989, Mr. Belvedere, 1989, My Two Dads, 1990, Who's the Boss?, 1990, Blossom, 1991, Seinfeld, 1992-93, 98, Caroline in the City, 1995, Hercules (voice), 1998, The Simpsons, 2003; (Broadway show) Cabaret, 2002. Avocations: reading, cooking, sports, dance. Office: Talent Group Inc 5670 Wilshire Blvd #820 Los Angeles CA 90036-5602

LEEVY, CARROLL MOTON, medical educator, hepatology researcher; b. Columbia, S.C., Oct. 13, 1920; s. Isaac S. and Mary (Kirkl) L.; m. Ruth S. Barboza, Feb. 4, 1956; children: Carroll Barboza, Maria Secora. AB, Fisk U., 1941; MD, U. Mich., 1944; ScD (hon.), N.J. Inst. Tech., 1973, U. Nebr., 1989; HHD (hon.), Fisk U., 1981. Intern Jersey City Med. Ctr., 1944-45, resident, 1945-48, dir. clin. investigation, 1947-57; fellow Banting-Best Inst., U. Toronto, Ont., Can., 1953; research assoc. Harvard U. Med. Sch., Cambridge, Mass., 1959; assoc. prof. U. Medicine and Dentistry of N.J., 1960-64, prof., 1964, Disting. prof., 1990—; chief of medicine EOVA Hosp., 1966—77; physician in chief Univ. Hosp., 1975-91; dir. Liver Ctr. U. Medicine and Dentistry N.J., 1983-85; dir. div. hepatology and nutrition N.J. Med. Sch., 1959-75, acting chmn. dept. medicine, 1966-68, chief of medicine, 1968-71, chmn. dept. medicine, 1975-91; disting. prof. medicine Univ. Hosp., physician in chief, 1975-91; acting chmn. Sammy Davis Jr. Nat. Liver Inst., 1984-86, pres., sci. dir., 1989—, dir., 1991—, N.J. Med. Sch. Liver Ctr., 1991—. Chief medicine VA Hosp., East Orange, N.J., 1966-71; cons. NIH, 1965-, FDA, 1970-80, VA, 1971-, Alcohol and Nutrition Found., 1970-80, Am. Liver Found., 1979-84; cons. Health Care Fin. Adminstrn., 1990-, mem. adv. com. on liver transplantation, 1991-; mem. Nat. Commn. on Digestive Disease, 1975-78; mem. expert com. on chronic liver disease WHO, 1978; mem. nat. adv. com. digestive disease HHS, 1989-93; chmn. monitoring com. VA Coop. Study on Alcoholic Hepatitis, 1989-94, VA Rsch. Study on Colchicine Alcoholic Cirrhosis, 1994-; med. dir. Univ. Hosp. Liver Transplant Program, 1989-; disting. prof. U. Medicine and Dentistry N.J., 1991-; chmn. Newark Hepatitis C Study Group, 2000-; mem. N.J. State Commn. on Viral Hepatitis C, 2002-; med. dir. Medicare Liver Transplant Program, 1991-. Author: Practical Diagnosis and Treatment of Liver Disease, 1957, Evaluation of Liver Function in Clinical Practice, 1965, 2d edit., 1974, Liver Regeneration in Man, 1973, The Liver and Its Diseases, 1973, Diseases of the Liver and Biliary Tract, 1977, Guidelines for Detection of Drug and Chemical-Induced Hepatotoxicity, 1979, Alcohol and the Digestive Tract, 1981, Standardization of Nomenclature, Diagnostic Criteria and Prognosis for Diseases of the Liver and Biliary Tract, 1994; contbr. numerous articles to med., sci. jours.; patentee in field. Bd. dirs. U. Cape Town, South Africa Fund, 1984-2001; active Pilgrim Congl. Ch. Comdr. USNR, 1954-59. E.V. Gabriel scholar, 1938, Kellog Med. scholar, 1942; recipient Modern Med. award, 1972, Edward Ill award, 1973, United Negro Coll. Fund award, 1980, Key to City of Newark, 1981, Key to City of Columbia, S.C., 1987, Key to City of Secaucus, N.J., 1981, 50th N.J. Achievement award U. Medicine and Dentistry N.J., 1995, Honor and Commendation for viral hepatitis rsch. N.J. State Senate and Gen. Assembly, 1999, Disting. Achievement award U. Mich. Med. Ctr. Alumni Soc., 1999; 40th Anniversary Faculty Honoree, U. Medicine and Dentistry N.J., 1995; comdr. chief pulmonary disease USN Disease Sect., developer liver ctr., 1954-56; chmn. organizing com. for establishing med. sch. in NJ. Mem. AAAS, ACP (publs. com. 1969-74, master), AMA (vice-chmn., chmn. program com. sect. on gastroenterology 1971-74), NAACP, Am. Assn. for Study Liver Diseases (pres. 1967-68, chmn. steering com. 1968-74, Disting. Svc. award 1991), Internat. Assn. for Study Liver (pres. 1970-74, chmn. criteria com. 1972—), Am. Gastroenterol. Assn. (edn. and tng. com. 1967-71), Assn. Profs. Medicine (Robert Williams Disting. Chmn. award 1991), Assn. Am. Physicians, Soc. Exptl. Biology and Medicine, Am. Soc. Clin. Nutrition, Am. Inst. Nutrition, Nat. Med. Assn. (award 1987, Centenial award 1995), Am. Fedn. Clin. Rsch., Assn. Acad. Minority Physicians (pres. 1986-88, chmn. bd. trustees 1988—, Disting. Achievement award 1995), Internat. Com. on Informatics in Hepatology (chmn. 1986—), Internal Hepatology Informatics Group (chmn. 1984-01, UNOS cert. transplant hepatologist med. dir. 1989—), N.J. Acad. Medicine, N.J. Liver Study Group (chmn. 1996—), Detection Counseling on Treatment Hepatitus Cir. Inner City Residents (chmn., 1986-2001, chmn. exec. com. 1986-2003), N.J. Commn. on Hepatitis, 2002—, Phi Beta Kappa, Alpha Omega Alpha, Sigma Pi Phi. Home: 35 Robert Dr Short Hills NJ 07078-1525 Office: UMDNJ Med School 100 Bergen St Newark NJ 07103-2484 E-mail: Leevyc.m.@umdng.edu. *My goal has been to help improve quality of life of all people, the disadvantaged and advantaged. Efforts have been made through medical education and research to decrease the incidence and untoward effects of disease, as well as improve communication and the social environment.*

LEFAUVE, LINDA MARIE, college administrator; b. Buffalo, Apr. 9, 1955; d. Richard F. and Teresa LeFauve; m. Robert A. Moss, Sept. 17, 1977 (div. Mar. 1993); m. Craig Bove, Aug. 7, 1995. BA, Wells Coll., 1977; MA, SUNY, Geneseo, 1980, SUNY, Buffalo, 1996. Program evaluator N.Y. State Psychiat. Ctr. at Helmuth, N.Y., 1980; assoc. instnl. rsch. SUNY, Buffalo, 1986-96; dir. instnl. rsch. Middlebury (Vt.) Coll., 1996-98; dir. planning and instnl. rsch. Davidson (N.C.) Coll., 1998—. Cons. higher edn. orgns. and mktg. firms on qualitative rsch. tech. Mem. So. Assn. for Instnl. Rsch., Assn. Instnl. Rsch. (policy and analysis com.), Higher Edn. Data Sharing Consortium. Avocations: marathon running, triathlons, british literature. Office: Davidson Coll Davidson NY 28036 E-mail: lilefauve@davidson.edu.

LEFCO, KATHY NAN, law librarian; b. Bethesda, Md., Feb. 24, 1949; d. Ted Lefco and Dorothy Rose (Fox) Harris; m. Stephen Gary Katz, Sept. 2, 1973 (div. May 1984); m. John Alfred Price, Nov. 24, 1984 (dec. Jan. 1989); m. Richard Louis Edmonds, Apr. 12, 2002. BA, U. Wis., 1971; MLS, U. Wis., Milw., 1975. Rsch. asst. Ctr. Auto Safety, Washington, 1971-73; asst. to dir. Ctr. Consumer Affairs, Milw., 1973-74; legis. libr. Morgan, Lewis & Bockius, Washington, 1976-78; dir. library Mulcahy & Wherry, Milw., 1978; paralegal Land of Lincoln Legal Assistance, Springfield, Ill., 1979-80; reference and interlibrary loan libr. So. Ill. U. Sch. Medicine, Springfield, 1980; reader svcs. libr. Wis. State Law Library, Madison, 1981-83; ref. libr. Mudge Rose Guthrie Alexander & Ferdon, N.Y.C., 1983-85; sr. legal info. specialist Cravath, Swaine & Moore, N.Y.C., 1985-86; asst. libr. Kaye, Scholer, Fierman, Hays & Handler, N.Y.C., 1986-89; head libr. Parker Chapin Flattau & Klimpl, N.Y.C., 1989-94; dir. libr. svcs. Winston & Strawn LLP, Chgo., 1994—. Author: (with others) Mobile Homes: The Low-Cost Housing Hoax, 1973. Mem. Chgo. Assn. Law Librs., Am. Assn. Law Librs. Democrat. Jewish. Avocations: biking, backgammon, politics. Home: 543 Oakdale Ave Glencoe IL 60022 Office: Winston & Strawn LLP 35 W Wacker Dr Ste 4200 Chicago IL 60601-1695 Office Phone: 312-558-5813. E-mail: klefco@winston.com.

LEFCOURT, GERALD B., lawyer; b. N.Y.C., June 1, 1942; s. Albert Lefcourt and Ethel (Saltzman) L.; children: Jeffrey Michael, Karen Elizabeth. BS, NYU, 1964; JD, Bklyn. Law Sch., 1967. Bar: N.Y. 1967, U.S. Dist. Ct. (ea. and so. dists.) N.Y., U.S. Ct. Appeals (2nd and D.C. cirs.), U.S. Supreme Ct. Staff atty. Legal Aid Soc., N.Y.C., 1967-68; legislative dir. Nat. Emergency Civil Liberties Com., N.Y.C., 1968-69; sole practice N.Y.C., 1971—. Adj. prof. law Hofstra U., 1978; adv. bd. dirs. Law Sch. NYU, 1985—. Author various legal publs. Mem. ABA (ho. of dels., lawyers coalition for criminal justice), ACLU, NACDL (past pres., Robert C. Heeney Meml. award 1993), Nat. Coll. Criminal Def. Attys., N.Y. State Bar Assn. (Outstanding Practitioner award 1985, 93), N.Y. Criminal Bar Assn. (past pres.), founder, mem. N.Y. State Assn. Criminal Defense Lawyers (Thurgood Marshall Lifetime Achievement award 1997). Office: 148 E 78th St New York NY 10021-0406 Office Phone: 212-737-0400. E-mail: lefcourt@aol.com.

LEFEBER, NATHAN JOHN, music educator; b. Elgin, Ill., Sept. 18, 1979; s. John Edward and Carol Jeane LeFeber; m. Julie Andrea Stenberg, Dec. 30, 2000. B of Music Edn., U. Nebr., 2002. Tchr. mid. sch. band Mt. Homb Pub. Schs., Wis., 2003; instr. grades 6-12 instrumental music Lincoln Christian Sch., Nebr., 2003—. Composer: (albums) Fallen-Seven, 2003. Mem.: Nebr. State Bandmasters Assn., Nebr. Music Educators Assn. Republican. Mem. Covenant Ch. Office: Lincoln Christian Sch 5801 S 8th St Lincoln NE 68516

LEFEBVRE, VLADIMIR A., psychologist, researcher; b. Leningrad, USSR; came to U.S., 1974; s. Alexander Voinov and Olga Lefevr; m. Victorina Dubovskaya, Apr. 26, 1959; 1 child, Andrei; 1 adopted child, Dung Le. MS in Math., Lomonosov State U., Moscow, 1968, PhD in Psychology, 1971; D honoris causa, Internat. Info. Acad., 2000. Engr., lab. technician Rsch. Inst. of Ministry of Def., Moscow, 1961-64; rsch. scientist, head sci. team Automatic Equipment Inst., Moscow, 1965-69; rsch. scientist Cen. Math. Econs. Inst. Acad. of Scis., Moscow, 1969-73; lectr. in psychology Lomonosov State U., 1972-73; researcher dept. psychology U. Calif., L.A., 1974-75, lectr. Russian program Humanities Sch. Irvine, 1975-77, researcher Sch. of Social Scis., 1977—. Cons. Scis. Application Internat., Inc., 1981—, RAND Corp., 1985-88. Author: Conflicting Structures, 1967, enlarged edit., 1973, The Structure of Awareness: Toward a Symbolic Language of Human Reflexion, 1977, Algebra of Conscience, 1982, enlarged edit., 2001, The Structure of Human Reflexion: The Reflexional Psychology of Vladimir Lefebvre, 1990, A Psychological Theory of Bipolarity and Reflexivity, 1992, The Cosmic Subject, 1997; mem. editl. bd. Jour. of Social and Biol. Structures, 1985-89. Sgt. Soviet Army, 1955-58. Recipient gold medal Moldova br. Internat. Info. Acad., 2000. Mem. AAAS, Am. Psychol. Soc., Soc. for Math. Psychology, Internat. Soc. for Sys. Studies, Russian Acad. Natural Scis. (fgn. mem.), N.Y. Acad. Scis., U. Calif. Univ. Club. Office: U Calif Sch Social Sciences Irvine CA 92697 E-mail: valefebv@uci.edu.

LEFER, ALLAN MARK, physiologist; b. NYC, Feb. 1, 1936; s. I. Judah and Lillian G. Lefer; m. Mary E. Indoe, Aug. 23, 1959; children: Debra Lynn, David Joseph, Barry Lee and Leslie Ann (twins). BA, Adelphi Coll., 1957, Western Res. U., 1959; PhD, U. Ill., 1962. Instr. physiology, USPHS-NIH fellow Western Res. U., 1962-64; asst. prof. physiology U. Va., 1964-69, assoc. prof., 1969-71, prof., 1972-74; vis. prof. Hadassah Med. Sch., Jerusalem, 1971-72; prof., chmn. dept. physiology Jefferson Med. Coll., Thomas Jefferson U., Phila., 1974—2001, prof. emeritus, 2001—; dir. Ischemia-Shock Rsch. Inst., 1980-95. Cons. Merck & Co., Upjohn Co., Genentech Inc., Syntex, Inc., Ciba-Geigy, NIH, Nitromed, IBEX Technologies, Bristol-Myers Squibb, Cytel Corp., Wellcome Found.; vis. prof. 1985-86, Pfizer vis. prof. cardiovasc. medicine, 1995; Nat. Bd. of Med. Examiners, Step 1, 1993-95; vis. prof. U. Calif., San Diego, 1995-96. Author: Pathophysiology and Therapeutics of Myocardial Ischemia, 1977, Prostaglandins in Cardiovascular and Renal Function, 1979, Cellular and Molecular Aspects of Shock and Trauma, 1983; Leukotrienes in Cardiovascular and Pulmonary Function, 1985; mng. editor: Eicosanoids, 1988-93; cons. editor Circulatory Shock, 1973-80; field editor Jour. of Pharmacology and Exptl. Therapeutics Cardiovasc., 1994-2000; mem. editl. bd. Critical Care Medicine, Shock Am. Jour. Physiology, Endothelium, Cardiovasc. Pathology, Drug News and Perspectives; contbr. to World Book Ency. Sci. Yearbook, 1979, Cardiovasc. Drug Reviews, Circulation Rsch. Drugs Today; contbr. over 600 articles to profl. jours. Chmn. United Jewish Appeal of Charlottesville, Va., 1973-74; coach basketball and baseball Huntingdon Valley Athletic Assn., 1975-78. Recipient Pres. and Visitor's prize in rsch. U. Va., 1970, Disting. Alumnus award U. Ill., 1996, Disting. Svc. award Coll. Grad. Studies, Thomas

Jefferson U., 1999; NSF fellow U. Ill., 1960-62. Fellow Am. Coll. Cardiology; mem. AAAS, Am. Physiol. Soc. (Carl J. Wiggers award 2003), Am. Soc. Pharmacology and Exptl. Therapeutics, Internat. Heart Rsch. Soc., Am. Heart Assn. (established investigator 1968-73, fellow circulation coun., nat. grant rev. com. 1993-95), Pa. Heart Assn. (rsch. com.), Shock Soc. (hon. life, chmn. membership com., pres. 1983-84, chmn. devel. com. 1985-89, chmn. internat. rels. com. 1993), Internat. Fed. Shock Socs. (coun. 1994-2002, pres. 4th internat. shock congress 1996-99), Soc. Exptl. Biology and Medicine, Soc. Leukocyte Biology, Israel Soc. Physiology and Pharmacology, Phila. Physiol. Soc. (pres. 1978-79), Sierra Club, B'nai B'rith (Charlottesville chpt., v.p. 1967-68, chmn. Va. Hillel 1970-71), Sigma Xi. Democrat. Home: 57 Oyster Reef Dr Hilton Head Island SC 29926 E-mail: allefer@aol.com.

LEFEVER, BRYCE EDWIN, psychologist; b. Washington, Sept. 13, 1957; s. Ernest Warren and Margaret Briggs Lefever; m. Shyla Rae Welch; 1 child, Paris Ann. BA in Psychology and English, Bucknell U., 1980; MA in Psychology, U. Ill., Chgo., 1986, PhD in Clin. Psychology, 1989. Bd. cert. clin. psychology Am. Bd. Profl. Psychology. Psychologist Navy Survival Sch., San Diego, 1990—93; head outpatient psychology Naval Hosp., Portsmouth, Va., 1993—96, head mental health Sigonella, Italy, 1996—98; command psychologist Naval Spl. Warfare, Dam Neck, Va., 1998—2003; head Substance Abuse Rehab. Program, Norfolk, Va., 2003—. Assoc. prof. Old Dominion U., Norfolk, Va., 2003—. Capt. USN, 1987—. Decorated Def. Meritorious Svc. medal USN, Meritorious Svc. medal. Mem.: APA, Internat. Critical Incident Stress Found. Presbyterian. Avocations: tennis, scuba diving.

LEFEVER, GRETCHEN B., clinical psychologist, educator; b. New Hartford, N.Y., Mar. 30, 1960; d. Merritt Wesley and Carol (Perry) Bremer; m. Bryce E. LeFever, June 29, 1985; 1 child, Paris Ann. BA in Psychology, Boston U., 1982; PhD in Clin. and Devel. Psychology, U. Ill., 1987; postgrad., Georgetown U., 1988. Lic. clin. psychologist, Va. Clin. psychologist in pediats. Naval Hosp., San Diego, 1990-93; assoc. prof. pediat. and psychiatry Ea. Va. Med. Sch., Norfolk, 1994—. Adj. assoc. prof. psychology Coll. of William & Mary, Williamsburg, Va., 1999—; head, behavioral sci. sect. Ctr. for Pediat. Rsch., Norfolk, 1997—; dir. psychol. assessment Children's Hosp. of the King's Daus., Norfolk, 1995—. Contbr. articles to profl. jours. including Am. Jour. Pub. Health, Family and Cmty. Health, Jour. Pharmacology, Biochemistry and Behavior. Chair cmty. coalition Sch. Health Initiative for Edn., SHINE, South Eastern Va., 1996—. Grantee NIMH; recipient scholarship Rotary. Mem. APA, APHA, Soc. Developmental and Behavioral Sci., Phi Beta Kappa. Republican. Presbyterian. Avocations: long-distance running, social development and behavioral pediatrics. Home: 3309 Glen Eden Quay Virginia Beach VA 23452-6240 Office: Ctr for Pediat Rsch 855 W Brambleton Ave Norfolk VA 23510-1005

LEFEVRE, DAVID E., lawyer, professional sports team executive; b. Cleve., Oct. 25, 1944; s. Fay A. and Amy (Eaton) LeF. BA, Yale U., 1966; JD, U. Mich., 1971. Bar: N.Y., U.S. Dist. Ct. (so. and ea. dists.) N.Y. Assoc. Reid & Priest, N.Y.C., 1971-78, ptnr., 1979-92; owner Houston Astros Baseball Club, 1979-84, Cleve. Indians Baseball Club, 1984-86; dir. Tampa Bay Lightning, NHL. Bd. dirs. TDC (USA), Inc., NHL Pension Soc.; chmn. bd. dirs. Chertsey Corp.; bd. govs. NHL, 1992—; bd. dirs. Fla. Sports Found., 1996—. Bd. dirs. Tampa Downtown Partnership; vol. Peace Corps, Uruguay, 1966-68. Recipient Spl. award Tampa Sports Club.; named Hon. Alumnus, Cleve. State U., 1985. Mem. ABA, Sports Lawyers Assn., Canyon Club (pres. Armonk, N.Y. 1986—), Alexis de Tocqueville Soc., Univ. Club of Tampa. Address: 303 E 57th St New York NY 10022-2947

LEFEVRE, DONALD KEITH, electrical engineer; b. Casper, Wyo., Feb. 12, 1956; s. Lorin Durward and Margery Phyllis (Green) L.; m. Susan Lesley Nichols, May 31, 1975; children: Justin, Michelle, Mark, Kristen, Gregory, Sean, Brendan, Eric. BS in Physics, Elec. Engring., S.D. Sch. Mines and Technology, 1978; MS in Elec. Engring., U. Utah, 1985. Sr. engr. Sperry Def. Systems, Salt Lake City, 1978-84; chief engr. Anderson Scientific, Rapid City, S.D., 1984-86; asst. prof. elec. engring. S.D. Sch. Mines and Technology, Rapid City, 1986-90; pres. Wesha Technologies, Inc., Rapid City, 1987; pres., founder Cynetics Corp., Rapid City, 1988—, Wireless Control Sys., Inc., 1990-94, dir., 1990—. Leader of team for world's first multiple-channel compressed digital video broadcast sys.; founder, pres. African TV Investors, LLC; bd. dirs. Tepco. Mem. bd. advisors Black Hills Bus. Innovation Ctr., Rapid City, 1986-90; founding mem. Black Hills Entrepreneur Network, 1988, dir., 1991-95; chmn. Ptnrs. in Entrepreneurship Com. Rapid City, 1993-95; mem. audit com. S.D. Sch. Mines and Tech. Found. Recipient Nat. Merit scholar; named Outstanding Recent Grad. in Elec. Engring. award S.D Sch. Mines and Tech., 1989. Mem. IEEE, Soc. Photo-Optical Instrumentation Engrs., Planetary Soc., Soc. Physics Students (chpt. pres. 1977), Eta Kappa Nu, Tau Beta Pi, Sigma Pi Sigma, Pi Mu Epsilon. Lodges: KC. Republican. Roman Catholic. Achievements include patents in field. Home: 4911 S Canyon Rd Rapid City SD 57702-1876 Office: Cynetics Corp PO Box 2422 Rapid City SD 57709-2422

LEFEVRE, PERRY DEYO, minister, theologian, educator; b. Kingston, N.Y., July 12, 1921; s. Johannes and Faye (McFerran) LeF.; m. Carol Baumann, Sept. 14, 1946; children: Susan Faye, Judith Ann, Peter Gerret. AB, Harvard U., 1943; BD, Chgo. Theol. Sem., 1946, DD, 1992; PhD, U. Chgo., 1951. Ordained to ministry Congl. Ch. (now United Ch. of Christ), 1946. Instr. religion Franklin and Marshall Coll., 1948-49; asst., then assoc. prof. religion Knox Coll., 1949-53, Fed. Theol. Sem., U. Chgo., 1953-61; prof. constructive theology Chgo. Theol. Sem., 1961-92, dean of faculty, 1961-81, acting dean, 1990-91. Author: The Prayers of Kierkegaard, 1956, The Christian Teacher, 1958, Introduction to Religious Existentialism, 1963, Understandings of Man, 1966, Philosophical Resources for Christian Thought, 1968, Conflict in a Voluntary Association, 1975, Understandings of Prayer, 1981, Aging and the Human Spirit, 1981, Radical Prayer, 1982; editor: Paul Tillich: The Meaning of Health, 1984, Spiritual Nurture and Congregational Development, 1984, Daniel Day Williams Essays in Process Theology, 1985, Pastoral Care and Liberation Praxis, 1986, Bernard Meland Essays in Constructive Theology, 1988, Creative Ministries in Contemporary Christianity, 1991, Modern Theologies of Prayer, 1995, Challenge and Response, 1999. Mem. Phi Beta Kappa. Address: 1314 Foulkeways Gwynedd PA 19436-1033

LEFEVRE, THOMAS VERNON, retired utilities executive; b. Dallas, Dec. 5, 1918; s. Eugene H. and Callie E. (Powell) L.; m. Lillian Herndon Bourne, Oct. 12, 1946; children: Eugene B., Nicholas R., Sharon A., Margot P. BA, U. Fla., 1939, LLB, 1942; LLM, Harvard U., 1946. Bar: Fla. 1945, N.Y. 1947, D.C. 1951, Pa. 1955, U.S. Supreme Ct. 1953. Atty. IRS and various firms, N.Y.C., Washington, and Phila., 1946-55; ptnr. Morgan, Lewis & Bockius, Phila., 1956-79; pres., chief exec. officer UGI Corp., Valley Forge, Pa., 1979-85, chmn., 1983-89. Chmn. G.P. Hospitality, Inc., 1981—; mem. Commr.'s Adv. Group IRS, 1976-77. Bd. dirs. Zool. Soc. Phila., 1982-91, WHYY Inc., 1982-96; chmn. U. Arts, 1986-89; trustee Franklin Inst., 1980-89, Fox Chase Cancer Ctr., 1979-88. With USMC, 1942-46. Fellow ABA (vice chmn. govt. rels. sect. of taxation 1976-79), Am. Bar Found.; mem. Pa. Bar Assn., Merion Cricket Club, Merion Golf Club, Sankaty Head Golf Club, Nantucket Yacht Club. Episcopalian. Office: 5 Radnor Corp Ctr Wayne PA 19087-4526 Office Phone: 610-964-8131.

LEFF, ALAN RICHARD, medical educator, researcher; b. May 23, 1945; s. Maurice D. and Grace Ruth (Schwartz) Leff; m. Donna Rae Rosene, Feb. 14, 1975; children: Marni, Karen, Alison. AB cum laude, Oberlin Coll., 1967; MD, U. Rochester, 1971. Diplomate Am. Bd. Internal Medicine, Am. Bd. Pulmonary Disease. Intern U. Mich. Hosp., Ann Arbor, 1971—72, resident, 1974—76; fellow U. Calif., San Francisco, 1976—77, postdoctoral fellow, 1977—79; asst. prof. medicine U. Chgo., 1979—85, assoc. prof. medicine and clin. pharm., 1985—89, prof. medicine, anesthesia, critical care and clin. pharm., 1989—, prof. cell physiology, 1992—, prof. pediats., neurobiology, physiology, 1999—, dir. pulmonary medicine svc., 1984—87, dir. Pulmonary Function Lab., 1979—87, chief sect. pulmonary and critical care medicine, 1987—2000, sr. dir. R&D biol. scis., 2000—02. Dir. NIAID Asthma and Allergic Disease Coop. Rsch. Ctr., Chgo., 1993—97; co-chair asthma sect. NIAID Task Force on Immunology, 1996—98; advisor San Francisco Dept. Pub. Health, 1977—79, Chgo Dept. Health, 1979—89; dir. Ctr. of Excellence in Asthma Glaxo Smith Kline, 2000—. Editor: Am. Jour. Respiratory Critical Care Medicine, 1994—99, Procs. Am. Thoracic Soc., 2004—; contbr. articles to profl. jours. Bd. dirs. Chgo. Lung Assn., 1984—93. With USPHS, 1972—74. Recipient Citation of Merit, Chgo. Lung Assn., 1974, Am. Lung Assn., 1998; fellow, Leopold Schepp Found., 1967—69. Fellow: Am. Coll. Chest Physicians; mem.: Am. Assn. Immunologists, Ctrl. Soc. for Clin. Investigation, Am. Thoracic Soc. (Spl. Citation 1999), Assn. Am. Physicians, Am. Physiol. Soc., Am. Soc. Clin. Investigation, Am. Fedn. Clin. Rsch. (councilor 1983—86), Sigma Xi. Avocation: music. Home: 5730 S Kimbark Ave Chicago IL 60637-1615 Office: U Chgo Pritzker Sch Medicine Div Biological Scis MC 6076 5841 S Maryland Ave Chicago IL 60637-1463 Office Phone: 773-702-1859. Business E-Mail: aleff@medicine.bsd.uchicago.edu.

LEFF, DANIEL V., venture capitalist; b. 1969; BS in Chemistry, U. Calif., Berkeley; MBA, Anderson Venture Fellow, PhD in Phys. Chemistry, UCLA. With Redpoint Ventures, L.A.; sr. process engr. Fab Capital Equipment Devel. Group Intel Corp., sr. strategic mktg. engr. Desktop Products Group, mgr. Strategic Investments Intel Capital; sr. assoc. Sevin Rosen Funds, Dallas, 2001—04; exec. v.p., mng. dir. Harris & Harris Group, L.A., 2004—. Mem. adv. bd. bus. NanoBusiness Alliance; mem. adv. bd. Calif. NanoSystems Inst. (CNSI). Contbr. several articles to profl. sci. jours. Achievements include role in funding Luxtera, Sana Security (aka: Company 51), Nanomix, D2Audio, InnovaLight, and airBand Communications, Sevin Rosen Funds, Dallas; two patents in the field of Nanotechnology; founded a nanotechnology company to develop and commercialize next-generation products based on metal and semiconductor nanomaterials. Office: Harris & Harris Group Inc 1150 Santa Monica Blvd Ste 1200 Los Angeles CA 90025 also: Harris & Harris Group Inc 111 W 57th St Ste 1100 New York NY 10019

LEFF, DEAN, music educator; s. Nathan and Shirley Leff; m. Rebecca Lyden, July 8, 1979; children: Benjamin, Jamie. MusB in Edn., MusM in Edn., U. Ill., 1972; MusM in Music Performance, U. Wis., 1973. Tchg. asst. Sch. Music U. Wis., Madison, Wis., 1972—73; dir. band Morrison (Ill.) Jr. H.S., 1974—75, Howard Jr. H.S., Wilmette, Ill., 1975—76, Eastview Jr. H.S., Bartlett, Ill., 1977—82, Elgin (Ill.) H.S., 1983—. Condr. No. Ill. U. Wind Ensemble. Nominee Golden Apple award, Golden Apple Found.; recipient Outstanding Tchg. award, U. Chgo. Mem.: Ill. Edn. Assn., Ill. Music Educators Assn.

LEFF, DEBORAH, government executive; b. Washington, Oct. 25, 1951; d. Sam and Melitta Leff. AB, Princeton (NJ) U., 1973; JD, U. Chgo., 1977. Trial atty. Civil Rights divsn. U.S. Dept. Justice, Washington, 1977-79; dir. office of pub. affairs Fed. Trade Commn., Washington, 1980-81; sr. producer Nightline-ABC News, Washington and London, 1983-89, World News Tonight-ABC News, N.Y.C., 1990-91; pres. The Joyce Found., Chgo., 1992-99, also bd. dirs.; pres., CEO Am.'s Second Harvest, Chgo., 1999-2001; dir. John F. Kennedy Presdl. Libr., Boston, 2001—. Bd. dirs. Sound Portraits; chmn. Midwest Rhodes Scholars Selection Com., Chgo., 1992. Office: John F Kennedy Presdl Libr Columbia Point Boston MA 02125

LEFF, ILENE J(AFNEL), management consultant, cosmetics executive, federal official; b. N.Y.C., Mar. 29; d. Abraham and Rose (Levy) L. BA cum laude, U. Pa., 1964; MA with honors, Columbia U., 1969. Statis. and computer analyst McKinsey & Co., N.Y.C., 1969-70, rsch. cons., 1971-74; mgmt. cons. N.Y.C. and Europe, 1974-78; dir. exec. resources Revlon, Inc., N.Y.C., 1978-81, dir. human resources, 1981-83, dir. pers., 1983-86; cons. APM Inc., 1986-88; mgmt. cons. The Estee Lauder Cos., 1988-92; dep. asst. sec. for mgmt. HUD, Washington, 1993-94; pres. Leff Mgmt. Cons., N.Y.C., 1995-97; mng. dir. Eisner LLP, N.Y.C., 1997-2000; pres. Leff Mgmt., 2000—. Rsch. asst. U. Pa., Phila., 1964-65; employment counselor State of N.J., Newark, 1965-66; tchr., Newark, 1966-69; lectr. Grad. Program in Pub. Policy, New Sch. for Social Rsch., Wharton Sch., Duke U.; chmn. com. on employment and unemployment, mem. exec. com. Bus. Rsch. Adv. Coun., U.S. Bur. Labor Stats., 1980; sr. del. econ. rels. and trade Sino-U.S. Conf., 1986; mem. nat. adv. bd. First Book. Contbr. issues papers and program recommendations to candidates for U.S. Pres., U.S. Senate and Congress, N.Y. State gov., mayor N.Y.C. Mem. ops. coun. Jr. Achievement Greater N.Y., 1975-78; cons. Com. for Econ. Devel., N.Y. Hosp., Regional Plan Assn., Am. Cancer Soc.; mem. adv. bd. First Book; vol. for dep. mayor for ops. N.Y.C., 1977-78. Mem. N.Y. Human Resource Planners (treas. 1984), Fin. Women's Assn. N.Y. (exec. bd. 1977-78, 83-84), Fashion Group (treas. 1989). Office Phone: 212-674-1140. Personal E-mail: ileneleff@aol.com.

LEFF, JOSEPH NORMAN, yarn manufacturing company executive; b. N.Y.C., Dec. 17, 1923; s. Phillip and Lillian (Wiesen) L.; m. Joyce Hochberg, June 12, 1954 (div. 1958); 1 child, Julie; m. Juanita Hughey, Dec. 17, 1967; 1 child, Valerie. BS, Columbia U., 1944, AB, 1946. Treas. Nat. Spinning Co. Inc., N.Y.C., 1949-63, pres., CEO, 1963-83, chmn., CEO, 1983-97, chmn. bd. dirs. Mem. bd. visitors Columbia Coll., N.Y.C., 1987-92; trustee Park Ave. Synagogue, N.Y.C., 1987-95; bd. dirs., pres. 92d St. YM/YWHA, N.Y.C., 1994-97, chmn., 1997—; bd. dirs. Inst. Textile Tech., Va., 1982-97; mem. Purchase Coll. Found., 1999—. With U.S. Army, 1944-45. Mem. Harmonie Club (pres. 1974-75) (N.Y.C.), Quaker Ridge Golf Club (Scarsdale, N.Y.), Boca Rio Country Club (Boca Raton, Fla.), Regency Whist Club. Jewish.

LEFFEK, KENNETH THOMAS, retired chemist, educator; b. Nottingham, Eng., Oct. 15, 1934; emigrated to Can., 1959, naturalized, 1966; s. Thomas and Ivy Louise (Pye) L.; m. Janet Marilyn Wallace, Sept. 26, 1958; children: Katharine, Geoffrey. BS, Univ. Coll., London, 1956, PhD, 1959. Asst. prof. chemistry Dalhousie U., Halifax, N.S., 1961-67, assoc. prof., 1967-72, prof., 1972-94, dean grad. studies, 1972-90, prof. chemistry, 1990-94, ret., 1994. Chmn. Atlantic Provinces Interuniv. Com. on Scis., 1975-77. Author: Sir Christopher Ingold, a Biography; contbr. articles on phys.-organic chemistry to profl. jours. Leverhulme fellow U. Kent (Eng.), 1967-68 Fellow Chem. Inst. Can., Royal Soc. Arts (London; chmn. Atlantic Can. chpt. 1987-91); mem. Chem. Soc. London, Chem. Inst. Can. (nat. dir. tech. and sci. affairs 1980-83, nat. v.p. 1985-86, pres. 1986-87) Home: 980 Kentwood Ter Victoria BC Canada V8Y 1A6 E-mail: kleffek@vanisle.net.

LEFFELL, DAVID JOEL, dermatologist, surgeon, health facility administrator, educator, writer; b. Montreal, Feb. 28, 1956; came to U.S., 1973; s. Allen Bernard and Freda (Deckelbaum) L. BS, Yale U., 1977; MD, McGill U., Montreal, 1981. Diplomate Am. Bd. Dermatology, Am. Bd. Internal Medicine. Resident in internal medicine Meml. Sloan-Kettering Cancer Ctr., N.Y.C., 1981-84; instr. medicine Cornell U. Sch. Medicine, N.Y.C., 1983-84; resident in dermatology Yale U. Sch. Medicine, New Haven, 1984-86; lectr., fellow dermatologic surgery U. Mich., Ann Arbor, 1987-88; chief Mohs micrographic surgery and laser surgery Yale U. Sch. Medicine, New Haven, 1988—, dir. Yale skin cancer detection program, 1988—, med. dir. faculty practice plan, 1996-98, prof. dermatology, plastic surgery and otolaryngology, 1998—, assoc. dean clin. affairs, 1999-2000; dir. Yale Med. Group, New Haven, 1999—; sr. assoc. dean clin. affairs Yale U. Sch. Medicine, New Haven, 2001—05, dep. dean clin. affairs, 2005—. Sci. advisor Nat. Hereditary Hemorrhagic Telangiectasia Found., New Haven, 1991—; bd. dirs. Am. Coll. Mohs Micrographic Surgery and Cutaneous Oncology. Author: Manual of Skin Surgery, 1996, Total Skin: The Definitive Guide to Whole Skin Care for Life, 2000; contbg. editor Jour. Dermatologic Surgery and Oncology, 1992-97; assoc. editor Med. and Surg. Dermatology; mem. editl. bd. Archives of Dermatology, Jour. Aesthetic Dermatology and Cosmetic Surgery, 1999—; assoc. editor Skin and Aging, 1996-98; editor: Faculty of 1000; inventor laser fluorescence device to measure photoaging; patent: PTC skin cancer gene, 2003. Bd. dirs., Conn. Pub. TV, 2001-2004. Recipient Frederic Mohs award Skin Cancer Found., 1988, 91. Mem. Conn. Dermatology Soc. (pres.). Home: 460 St Ronan St New Haven CT 06511-2251 Office: Yale Sch Medicine PO Box 208059 New Haven CT 06520-8059 Office Phone: 203-785-7999.

LEFFERTS, GEORGE, television producer; b. Paterson, N.J. BA in English, U. Mich., 1942. Exec. prodr., writer, dir. NBC, 1947-57; pres. George Lefferts Assocs., 1968—; exec. prodr. ABC, 1966-67, Time-Life Films, 1980-81; tchr. John Hopkins U., Balt., 1989-90, Rutgers U., 1992—; prodr., writer, dir. Network for Continuing Med. Edn., 1990—95. Program cons. ABC, 1981. Exhibited sculpture, Sculpture Gallery, N.Y.C., 1960; producer: series Report from America, U.S. Dept. State, Tactic, Am. Cancer Soc., others; (Recipient Nat. Media award 1961, Fame award 1962, Fgn. Press award 1963, Golden Globe award 1967, Plaudit award Producers Guild 1968, 69, Cine Golden Eagle award 1974, Peabody award 1970, 75, 1st prize San Francisco Film Festival 1970; nominee Humanitas Prize 1988); author: plays Nantucket Legend, 1960, The Boat, 1968, Hey Everybody, 1969; columnist N.Y. Observer, Litchfield County Times, 1984-87 (1st place New England Journalism award, 1984, 85); also author mag. articles, works on piano method, syndicated columns, others; prodns. include Biographies in Sound (Peabody award 1956), NBC Theatre, (Ohio State award 1955), Kraft Theatre, Armstrong Circle Theatre, Studio One, Lights Out, Frank Sinatra Show; spl. program Pain, 1971, Bravo Picasso!, 1972, What Price Health; program NBC Investigative Reports, 1972 (Albert Lasker award), CBS, Ben Franklin Series (Peabody award 1975, Emmy award 1975), Ryan's Hope, 1977 (Emmy award 1977), Purex Specials, 1966 (Emmy award 1966), The People vs. Jean Harris, 1981; exec. prodr., writer, dir., NBC, Spls. for Women (2 Emmy awards 1965); series (Emmy award 1962), 1961 (Golden Globe award 1961); exec. prodr.: series Breaking Point, 1962-64 (Prodrs. Guild Plaudit award 1963), CBS, Smithsonian Spls., 1974-75, ABC, Wide World of Entertainment, 1973-74, Bing Crosby Prodns., 1962-64; exec. prodr.: Wolper Prodns., 1974-75, Time/Life Films, 1978-79; original films produced include: The Living End, 1959, The Stake, 1960, The Teenager, 1965, The Harness, 1972, The Night They Took Miss Beautiful, 1977, Bud & Lou, 1978, Mean Dog Blues, 1979, The Search for Alexander the Great, 1981, Dressed to Kill, 1980; prodr.: series Hallmark Hall of Fame, 1969-70, Never Say Goodbye, 1987 (Emmy award 1988, Humanitas award nomination 1988), TV play Teacher, Teacher, 1974 (Emmy award 1974). With AUS, 1942-45. William Rose scholar Drew U., 1940. Mem. NATAS, Am. Acad. Motion Picture Arts and Scis., Christopher Morley Knothole Assn. Clubs: South Bay Cruising (Babylon, (N.Y.).

LEFFERTS, GILLET, JR., architect; b. N.Y.C., May 6, 1923; s. Gillet and Helen Willets (Lambert) L.; m. Lucia Beverly Hollerith, Apr. 21, 1951; children: Helena Gillet (dec.), Robert Beverly, John Willets, Sarah Fox, David Hollerith. AB, Williams Coll., 1947; MFA, Princeton, 1950. Apprentice Moore & Hutchins, N.Y.C., 1947-48, 50-55, assoc., 1955-66, ptnr., 1967-72, Hutchins, Evans & Lefferts, N.Y.C., 1972-89; mem. The Hall Partnership, Archs., LLP, N.Y.C., 1990—. Instr. Mechanics Inst., N.Y.C., 1955-58. Prin. works include SUNY-Binghamton, Buffalo, master plan Coll. Agr., Malaya, St. Johnland Nursing Home, L.I., N.Y., Clark Gymnasium, Cooperstown, N.Y., Nat. Baseball Hall of Fame and Mus. Expansion, Cooperstown, Scholes Libr. Coll. Ceramics, Alfred U., Ice Arena, Broome CC, Binghamton. Mem. zoning bd. appeals Town of Darien, Conn., 1961-69, mem. planning and zoning commn., 1969-77, chmn., 1973-77, mem. bd. selectmen, 1983-89; bd. dirs. Darien Hist. Soc., 1978-83, pres., 1982-83; trustee Darien Pub. Libr., 1991-97; bd. dirs. Darien Nature Ctr., 1997-2004, pres., chmn. 1999-2001. With USAAF, 1943-46. Decorated Air medal with oak leaf cluster. Fellow AIA; mem. Fairfield County Alumni Assn. Williams Coll. (v.p. 1965-67), Nat. Inst. Archtl. Edn. (chmn. bd. trustees 1963-65, treas. 1970-73), Soc. Alumni Williams Coll. (exec. com. 2004—), Williams Club N.Y.C., Delta Psi. Episcopalian. Office: 42 E 21st St New York NY 10010-7216 Office Phone: 212-777-2090. Business E-Mail: glefferts@hallarchitect.com.

LEFFERTS, WILLIAM GEOFFREY, internist, educator; b. Towanda, Pa, Mar. 24, 1943; s. William LeRoy and Beatrice (Smith) L.; m. Susan Lynn Hiles, Oct. 31, 1970. BA, Hamilton Coll., 1965; MD, Hahnemann Med. Coll., 1969. Intern Hahnemann Hosp., 1969-70; resident in internal medicine Cleve. Clinic Hosp., 1970-73, chief med. resident, 1972-73; asst. prof. internal medicine Hahnemann Med. Coll., 1973-77; assoc. prof. Med. Coll. Pa., 1978-82, dir. primary care unit, 1978-82, dir. div. gen. internal medicine, 1979-82; staff physician Cleve. Clinic Found., 1982—. Fellow ACP. Office: 9500 Euclid Ave Cleveland OH 44195-0001

LEFFLER, CAROLE ELIZABETH, mental health nurse, women's health nurse; b. Sidney, Ohio, Feb. 18, 1942; d. August B. and Delores K. Aselage; children: Veronica, Christopher. ADN, Sinclair C.C., Dayton, Ohio, 1975. Cert. psychiat. nurse supr. Nurse Grandview Hosp, Dayton, 1961—76; substitute sch. nurse Fairborn City Schs., Ohio, 1981—82; dir. nursing Fairborn Nursing Home, 1983; supr. psychiat. nurse Twin Valley Behavioral Health Ctr., 1984—. Mem. exec. bd. 1199; chmn. disaster mental health com. ARC Ohio. Vol., instr., disaster health nurse ARC, chmn. State of Ohio disaster mental health com.; officer, leader, camp nurse for Girl Scouts, Boy Scouts; Ch. Parish Coun. Recipient Fleur de Lis award Girl and Boy Scouts, Svc. award ARC, Fairborn Mayor's Cert. of Merit for Civic Pride, State of Ohio Govs. award Innovation Ohio, Ohio State Gov.'s award for assistance in N.Y.C. disaster, 2001. Mem. ANA, Ohio Nurses Assn. Home: 1711 Port Jefferson Rd Sidney OH 45365-1939

LEFFLER, JEAN RIISE, religious organization administrator; b. N.Y.C., Mar. 5, 1949; d. Morris Mike and Muriel Rita Riise; m. David Lawrence Leffler, Oct. 17, 1946; children: Catherine, Virginia. AA in Comml. Art, Palm Beach C.C., 1968; BS in Bus. magna cum laude, Ctrl. Baptist Coll., 2002; BA in Theology, St. Gregory's U., 2003. Sr. citizen meal site supr. West Ctrl Ind. Econ. Devel. Dist., Terre Haute, Ind., 1983—86; sr. citizen ctr. dir. Shelby Sr. Svcs., Shelbyville, 1986—93; tech. writer Leisure Arts, Little Rock, 1993—95; activity dir. St. Andrews Pl., Conway, Ark., 1995—97; asst. cmty. dir. Outlook Pointe Assisted Living, Maumelle, Ark., 1997—98; social svc., mktg. dir. Faulkner Nursing & Rehab. Ctr., Conway, Ark., 1998—2000; dir. religious edn. St. Joseph Cath. Ch., Conway, Ark., 2000—. Profl. workshop leader, facilitator, Ark., 1998—2004. Author (designer): (nat. publs.) Crafts, Crafting Traditions, Etc., 1978—99, (booklet) Leisure Arts Publications, 1995, newspaper articles. Leadership at county and state level 4-H, Ind., 1988—93; com. chair Ptnrs. for Pinnacle, Little Rock, 1993—99; sec. Union Pacific Employees Club #54, Little Rock, 1998—2000; adv. coun. Hospice Home Care, Conway, Ark., 2002—; profl. workshop leader Diocese of Little Rock, 2002—. Republican. Roman Catholic. Avocations: historical reenactment 1840s, gardening, writing. Home: 33 Bernard Dr Conway AR 72032 Office: St Joseph Cath Ch 1115 College Ave Conway AR 72032 Office Phone: 501-513-6812.

LEFFLER, MARVIN, foundation administrator, writer; s. Saul Leffler and Bertha Cohen; m. Charlotte K. Frank, Dec. 23, 1989; m. Shirley Schleicher, Sept. 3, 1944 (dec. Sept. 15, 1988); children: Bruce, Nancy. BS, NYU, 1942, MBA, 1951. Pres. Continous Sales Corp., L.I., NY, 1945—92, Flexible Fabricators, Inc., Port Jervis, NY, 1954—90, Town Hall Found., N.Y., 1978—. Pres. Nat. Coun. Sales Orgn., N.Y., 1960—85, P.J. Co., Port Jervis, 1954—. Author: How To Become A Successful Sales Rep, 1951, How To Increase Your Sales Volume, 1954. Mem. policy com. for disciplinary com. first appellate divsn. Ct. of Appeals, 2004—; mem. midtown com. Mayor, N.Y., 1980—. Sgt. U.S. Army, 1942—46. Named Disting. Alumnus award, NYU, 2005; recipient Presdl. citation, 1990. Mem.: NYU Alumni Assn. (exec. com., pres. 1984—2000), Am. Arbitration Assn. (panelist 1970—), Fenway Golf Club (dir., sec. 2000—03). Avocations: golf, travel, writing. Office: Town Hall 123 West 43rd St New York NY 10036 Business E-Mail: Leffler@the-townhall-nyc.org.

LEFFLER, MELVYN P., history professor; b. NYC, May 31, 1945; s. Louis and Mollie (Fuchs) L.; m. Phyllis Koran, Sept. 1, 1968; children: Sarah Ann, Elliot. BS, Cornell U., 1966; PhD, Ohio State U., 1972. Asst. prof. Vanderbilt U., Nashville, 1972-77, assoc. prof., 1977-86; Coun. Fgn. Rels. internat. affairs fellow Dept. Def., Washington, 1979-80; prof. U. Va., Charlottesville, 1986-94, Edward R. Stettinius prof. history, 1994—, chmn. hist. dept., 1990-95, Edward R. Stettinius prof. history dept., 1995-97, dean Coll. and Grad. Sch. Arts and Scis., 1997-2001. Harmsworth prof. Am. history Oxford

(Eng.) U., 2002-03; Henry Kissinger chair Libr. Congress, 2005. Author: The Elusive Quest, 1979, A Preponderance of Power, 1992 (Bancroft, Ferrell & Hoover prizes 1993), The Specter of Communism, 1994; contbr. articles to profl. jours. Fellow Woodrow Wilson Internat. Ctr., 1979, 2001-02, Am. Coun. Learned Socs., 1984, Nobel Peace Inst., 1994, 98, U.S. Inst. Peace, 2004-2005. Mem. Am. Hist. Assn., Orgn. Am. Hists., Soc. Hists. Am. Fgn. Rels. (v.p. 1993, pres. 1994, Bernath Article prize 1984). Jewish. Home: 1612 Concord Dr Charlottesville VA 22901-3135 Office: U Va Dept History PO Box 400180 Charlottesville VA 22904-0180

LEFGREN, JULIE P., business development manager; b. Ft. Worth, Jan. 26, 1968; d. James I. and Loretta J. Lefgren. BA in Comparative Lit., Brigham Young U., 1994; MA in Chinese Lang. and Lits., U. Oreg., 1998. Web tech. lead Lionbridge, Framingham, Mass., 1999—2001; bus. devel. mgr. Globalmart, Logan, Utah, 2001. Cons., web designer Regis Coll., 2001; small bus. owner, entrepreneur Sister's Remodeling, 2002. Ch. leader Church of Jesus Christ of Latter Day Saints, Boston, 1998—2001. Fellow grad. tchg. fellow, U. Oreg., 1995—98. Mem. Lds Ch.

LEFKOVITS, ALBERT MEYER, dermatologist; b. N.Y.C., June 30, 1937; s. Aaron Melchoir and Muriel (Mark) L.; A.B., Cornell U., 1958; M.D. (Lederle research fellow), N.Y. Med. Coll., 1962; m. Cheryl Beth Kornberg, Apr. 25, 1971; children— Ari Nathan, Lauren Blair. Intern, Newark Beth Israel Hosp., 1962-63; resident in dermatology Kings County Hosp. Center, SUNY, Downstate Med. Center, Bklyn., 1963-65; chief resident dermatology Mt. Sinai Hosp., N.Y.C., 1965-66, research fellow in dermatology, 1966-67, asst. attending physician, 1966—; practice medicine specializing in dermatology, N.Y.C., 1966—; asst. attending physician Beekman-Downtown Hosp., N.Y.C., 1968-75; instr. dermatology Mt. Sinai Sch. Medicine, 1966-68, clin. asso. dermatology, 1968-73, asst. prof., 1974, acad. council, 1973-78, 1886—; instr. dermatology N.Y. Med. Coll., 1966-69. Alumni fund-raising chmn. Horace Mann Sch., 1976-78; treas. Mt. Sinai Alumni, 1988-90, sec., 1991-93, v.p., 1993-95, pres. 1995-97. Served to maj. M.C., AUS, 1969-71. Recipient Fredrick Wise Dermatology award N.Y. Acad. Medicine, 1965, Torch of Liberty award Anti-Defamation League, 1987, Maimonides award Keren Or Found. for Handicapped Blind Children, 1994; mem. med. adv. bd. Skin Cancer Found. Mem. Harvey Soc., Soc. Investigative Dermatology, Dermatology Found., Soc. Tropical Dermatology, Am. Acad. Dermatology (task force on therapeutics and FDA liaison com., comm. coun., physicians practice com.), Am. Acad. Dermatology (comm. coun., physicians practice com.), AMA, Internat. Soc. Human and Animal Mycology, Mycology Soc. Ams., N.Y. Acad. Sci., Am. Physicians Fedn. (trustee, exec. com.), Jewish Chautaugua Soc. (life), Dermatology Soc. Greater N.Y. (pres., chmn. physicians advocacy com.), N.Y. State Med. Soc., Cornell Alumni Assn. N.Y. (bd. govs. 1974-76) Med. Adv. Bd. Skin Cancer Found., 1986—. Jewish (dir. congregation Emanu-El men's club). Clubs: Harmonie, Town, Cornell (N.Y.C.), Friar's, Lawrence Yacht (fleet surgeon 1982-83, sec. 1984, treas. 1985, commodore 1987). Address: 1040 Park Ave New York NY 10028-1032

LEFKOW, JOAN HUMPHREY, federal judge; b. Kans., Jan. 9, 1944; d. Otis L. and Donna Grace (Glenn) Humphrey; m. Michael F. Lefkow (dec. 2005), June 21, 1975; children: Maria Aithne, Helena Claiborne, Laura Bethany, Margaret Frances. AB, Wheaton Coll., 1965; JD, Northwestern U., 1971. Bar: Ill. 1971, U.S. Dist. Ct. (no. dist.) Ill. 1972, U.S. Ct. Appeals (7th cir.) 1972, U.S. Ct. Appeals (5th cir.) 1980. Law clerk to Hon. Thomas E. Fairchild U.S. Ct. Appeals (7th cir.), 1971-72; atty. Legal Assistance Found. Chgo., 1972-75; adminstrv. law judge Ill. Fair Employment Practices Commn., 1975-77, chief adminstrv. law judge, 1977-79; instr. sch. law U. Miami, Fla., 1980-81; exec. dir. Cook County Legal Assistance Found., 1981-82; magistrate judge U.S. Dist. Ct. (no. dist.) Ill., 1982-96; judge U.S. Bankruptcy Ct. (no. dist.) Ill., 1996—. Editor Northwestern U. Law Rev. Active PTA. Mem. Chgo. Bar Assn. (legal aid com. 1982, Alliance for Women 1992—), Chgo. Coun. Lawyers (gov. bd. 1975-77), 7th Cir. Bar Assn. Episcopalian. Office: Everett McKinley Dirksen Bldg 219 S Dearborn St Ste 662 Chicago IL 60604-1702

LEFKOWITZ, DAVID S., lawyer; b. NYC, Nov. 3, 1960; BS, Northwestern U., 1982; JD cum laude, Georgetown U., 1986. Bar: NY 1987. Ptnr. Weil, Gotshal & Manges, NYC, co-head capital markets group. Named a Leading Capital Markets Lawyer, Chambers USA, 2005; named an Am. Lawyer Dealmaker of Yr., 2004; named one of 40 Under 40 for Rising Stars in Law, Nat. Law Jour. Office: Weil Gotshal & Manges 767 Fifth Ave New York NY 10153 Office Phone: 212-310-8000. Office Fax: 212-310-8007. Business E-Mail: david.lefkowitz@weil.com.

LEFKOWITZ, HOWARD N., lawyer; b. Utica, N.Y., Oct. 28, 1936; s. Samuel I. and Sarah Lefkowitz; m. Martha Yelon, June 16, 1958; children: Sarah, David. BA, Cornell U., 1958; LLB, Columbia U., 1963. Bar: N.Y. 1963. Ptnr. Proskauer Rose LLP, N.Y.C., 1963—. Co-author: New York LLC and LLP Forms and Practice Manual, Data Trace, rev. edit. 2003; co-author: Transactional Lawyers Deskbook: Advising Business Entities West, 2001; editor Columbia Law Rev., 1963; contbg. editor Encyclopedia of Private and Venture Capital. Lt. (j.g.) USN, 1958-61. Kent scholar, Columbia U. Law Sch. Mem.: N.Y. Pvt. Investment Funds Forum (chmn. 2004), N.Y. County Lawyers Assn. (chmn. com. on comm. entertainment and arts-related law 1983—86), Assn. Bar City of N.Y. (chmn. com. on corp. law 1990—93, com. on corp. law 1997—2000), ABA (mem. partnership and uninc. bus. orgns. 1993—). Office: Proskauer Rose LLP 1585 Broadway Fl 23 New York NY 10036-8299

LEFKOWITZ, IVAN MARTIN, lawyer; b. Winston-Salem, N.C., Jan. 4, 1952; s. Ernest W. and Matilda C. (Center) L.; m. Fern Deutsch, Apr. 14, 1972; children: Aaron M., Shira B. BBA, U. Cen. Fla., 1973; JD, U. Miami, 1979, LLM Estate Planning, 1980. Bar: Fla. 1979, U.S. Dist. Ct. (mid. dist.) 1980, U.S. Tax. Ct. 1980; CPA, Fla. Sr. acct. Alexander Grant & Co. CPA, Orlando, Fla., 1974-76; assoc. Gray, Harris & Robinson P.A., Orlando, 1980-82; pvt. practice, Orlando, 1982-88; ptnr. Lefkowitz & Miner, P.A., Orlando, 1988-93; sr. ptnr. Lefkowitz & Bloom, P.A., Orlando, 1993—. Adj. prof. Am. Coll., Denver, 1984-90, Mgmt. Inst., U. Cen. Fla., Orlando, 1988—; sec., dir. Employee Benefits Coun. Fla., 1987-89, pres., 1990. Mem. dean's exec. coun. U. Ctrl. Fla. Coll. of Bus., 2000—; mem. governing bd. Princeton Hosp., Orlando, 1997—98; mem. Ctrl. Fla. Estate Planning Coun.; treas. Holocaust Meml. Resource and Edn. Ctr. Ctrl. Fla., 2000—01; mem. U. Ctrl. Fla. Found. Orlando, 1981—96, 2001—; U. Ctrl. Fla. Found. Orlando, 1981—96; bd. dirs., pres. Nat. Kidney Found. Ctrl. Fla., Orlando and Tampa, 1984—91. Recipient Induction to Coll. of Bus. Adminstrn. Hall of Fame, U. Ctrl. Fla., 2001. Democrat. Office: 430 N Mills Ave Orlando FL 32803-5746 Office Phone: 407-425-1974. Business E-Mail: firm@orlandolaw.org, lefkowitz@orlandolaw.org.

LEFKOWITZ, JAY, diplomat; b. NYC, 1962; married; 3 children. AB, Columbia U., 1984, JD, 1987. Law firm assoc., 1987—91; assoc. Kirkland & Ellis LLP, Washington, 1993—2001, ptnr., 2003—05; dep. exec. sec. of domestic policy, dir. cabinet affairs The White House, 1991—93, gen. counsel Office of Mgmt. & Budget, 2001—02, dep. asst. to pres., dir. domestic policy coun., 2002—05; U.S. spl. envoy on human rights to N. Korea US Dept. State, 2005—. Pub. mem. U.S. delegation to UN Human Rights Commn., Geneva, 1990. Office: The White House 1600 Pennsylvania Ave Washington DC 20500*

LEFKOWITZ, JOEL M., psychologist, educator; b. N.Y.C., Oct. 17, 1940; s. Frank Morris and Charlotte (Van Dam) L.; m. Merle Ellen Goldner, Sept. 12, 1965 (div. May 1982); children: Jared, Melanie; m. Setha M. Low, June 26, 1994. BBA, CCNY, 1961; MS, Case Western Res. U., Cleve., 1963, PhD, 1965. Lic. psychologist, N.Y.; diplomate Am. Bd. Profl. Psychology. Asst. prof. to prof. psychology Baruch Coll. CUNY, N.Y.C., 1965—. Ind. cons., N.Y.C., 1965—; nat. bd. mem. Am. Bd. Profl. Psychology, 1995—. Author: Ethics and Values in Industrial-Organizational Psychology, 2003; contbr. articles to profl. jours. Fellow: APA, Soc. Indsl. Orgn. Psychology. Avocations: tennis, photography. Office: Baruch Coll Box B8-215 1 Bernard Baruch Way New York NY 10010 Office Phone: 646-312-3789. E-mail: Joel_Lefkowitz@Baruch.CUNY.edu.

LEFKOWITZ, ROBERT JOSEPH, physician, educator; b. N.Y.C., Apr. 15, 1943; s. Max and Rose (Levine) Lefkowitz; m. Lynn Tilley, May 26, 1991. BA, Columbia U., 1962, MD, 1966. Diplomate Am. Bd. Internal Medicine. Assoc. prof medicine Duke U., Durham, NC, 1973—77, prof. medicine, 1977—, James B. Duke prof. medicine, 1982—, prof. biochemistry, 1985—. Investigator Howard Hughes Med. Inst., Durham, 1976—; vis. prof. NYU, 1996. Author: Receptor Binding Studies in Adrenergic Pharmacology, 1978, Receptor Regulation, 1981, Principles of Biochemistry, 1983. Named Am. Heart Assn. established investigator, 1973—76; recipient Basic Rsch. prize, 1990, Young Scientist award, Passano Found., 1978, George Thorn award, Howard Hughes Med. Inst., 1979, Oppenheimer award, 1982, Gordon Wilson medal, Am. Clin. and Climatol. Assn., 1982, Lita Annenberg Hazen award, 1983, Outstanding Rsch. award, Internat. Soc. for Health Rsch., 1985, H.B. van Dyke award, Coll. Physicians and Surgeons Columbia U., 1986, Steven C. Beering award, Ind. U. Sch. Medicine, 1986, N.C. award in sci., 1987, Internat. award, Gairdner Found., 1988, Novo Nordsk Biotech. award, 1990, Biomed. Rsch. award, Assn. Am. Med. Colls., 1990, City of Medecin award, N.C., 1991, Alumnus award for disting. achievement in cardiovasc. rsch., Columbia U. Coll. of Physicians and Surgeons, 1992, The Giovani Lorenzini prize for basic biomed. rsch., 1992, Joseph Mather Smith prize, Columbia U. Coll. Physicians and Surgeons, 1993, The Endocrine Soc. Gerald D. Aurbach Lectr. award, Inst. of Medicine NAS, 1995, J. David Gladstone Insts. Disting. Lecture award, 1996, Bio/Tech. Winter Symposia Feodor Lynen award, Ciba award, Hypertension Rsch. award, 1996, Glorney-Raisbeck award in cardiology, N.Y. Acad. Medicine, 1997, Novartis/Drew award in biomed. rsch., 2000, F.E. Shideman-Sterling award, U. Minn., 2001, Louis and Artur Lucian award for rsch. in circulatory disease, 2001, Peter Harris Disting. Scientist award, Internat. Soc. for Heart Rsch., 2001, 15th Ann. Pasarow Cardiovasc. Rsch. award, The Robert J. and Claire Pasarow Found., 2002, Medal of Merit, Internat. Acad. Cardiovasc. Scis., 2003, IPSEN Endocrinology prize, Found. IPSEN, Paris, 2003, Found. Lefoulon-Delalande Grand Prize for Sci. award, Inst. France, 2003, Founding Disting. Scientist award, Am. Heart Assn., 2003, Herbert Tabor Lecture award, Am. Soc. Biol. Chemistry and Molecular Biology, 2004;, Internat. Acad. Cardiovasc. Scis., 2002. Mem.: NAS (Jessie Stevenson Kovalenko medal 2001), Am. Heart Assn. Basic Rsch. Soc., Am. Acad. Arts and Scis., Am. Fedn. Clin. Rsch. (sec.-treas. 1980—83, mem. nat. coun. 1978—83), Endocrine Soc. (Fred Conrad Koch award 2001), Am. Soc. Pharmacology and Exptl. Therapeutics (John J. Abel award 1978, Goodman and Gilman award 1986), Assn. Am. Physicians (treas. 1989—94, Francis Gilman Blake award 2001), Am. Soc. Clin. Investigation (counselor 1982—85, pres.-elect 1986—87, pres. 1987—88), Am. Soc. Biol. Chemists, Japanese Biochem. Soc. (hon.). Office: Duke Univ Med Ctr PO Box 3821 Durham NC 27710-0001

LEFLER, SHERRY LYNETTE, elementary school educator; d. Charles William and Mary Jones Ridge; m. David Donald Lefler, July 28, 1973; children: Jamie Lynn Irvin, Jacob Alan. BS in Edn., SW Tex. State U., 1972; M in Elem. Edn., Prairie View A&M U., Tex., 1977. Kindergarten endorsement SW Tex. State U. Educator Needville (Tex.) Consol. Ind. Sch. Dist., 1973—82, Lamar Consol. Ind. Sch. Dist., Rosenberg, Tex., 1982—. Trainer NJ. Writing Project in Tex., Rosenberg, 1999—; mem. Districtwide Student Improvement Coun. Lamar Consol. Ind. Sch. Dist., Rosenberg, 2002—. Named Tchr. of Yr., Travis Elem. Sch., 1992. Mem.: West Houston Area Coun. Tchrs. English (pres. 2004—), Tex. State Tchrs. Assn. (rec. sec. 1973—74), Tex. Classroom Tchrs. Assn. (assoc.), Delta Kappa Gamma (rec. sec. 1993—95). Home: 1500 Band Rd Rosenberg TX 77471 Office: Lamar Consolidated Independent School Di 3911 Avenue I Rosenberg TX 77471

LEFLER, WADE HAMPTON, JR., ophthalmologist; b. Statesville, NC, Feb. 27, 1937; s. Wade Hampton and Eunice Trudye (Chilcoat) L.; m. Katherine Webb Davis, Apr. 1, 1961; children: Elizabeth Ashley Wilson, Rosemary Kirsten, Ririe. AB, U. N.C., 1959; MD, Bowman Gray Sch. Medicine, 1963. Diplomate Am. Bd. Ophthalmology. Intern N.Y. Hosp./Cornell Med. Ctr., 1963-64; resident in ophthalmology Duke U. Med. Ctr., Durham, N.C., 1966-69; practice medicine specializing in ophthalmology, Hickory, N.C., 1969—; ptnr. Graystone Eye, Ear, Nose and Throat Ctr., Hickory, 1974—; clin. assoc. prof. ophthalmology Duke Med. Ctr., 1969—. Mem. staff Catawba Meml. Hosp., Hickory, Frye Regional Med. Ctr., Hickory, Western Carolina Center, Morganton, N.C., Duke Eye Center, Durham, N.C., Oteen VA Hosp., Asheville, N.C. Trustee Catawba Meml. Hosp., 1990-94. Served to capt. M.C., U.S. Army, 1964-66. Duke U. Med. Ctr. grantee, 1968-70. Mem. AMA, N.C. Med. Soc., Catawba County Med. Soc., Med. Alumni Assn. Bowman Gray Sch. Medicine (pres. 1993, Disting. Svc. award 1995), Lake Hickory Country Club, Phi Beta Kappa, Alpha Omega Alpha. Presbyterian. Home: 1260 6th St NW Hickory NC 28601-2408 Office: PO Box 2588 Hickory NC 28603-2588 E-mail: khlefler@charter.net.

LEFRAK, EDWARD ARTHUR, cardiovascular and thoracic surgeon; b. Newark, Apr. 21, 1943; s. Bernard David and Lillian (Hollander) L.; m. Trudy Glaser, Aug. 8, 1973; children: Lisa, Allison, Shayna, Ashley, Mikaela. BA cum laude, SUNY, Buffalo, 1965; MD, Ind. U., 1969. Diplomate Am. Bd. Surgery, Am. Bd. Thoracic Surgery. Intern in gen. surgery Baylor Coll. Medicine Affiliated Hosps., Houston, 1969-70, resident in gen. surgery, 1970-75; resident cardiopulmonary surgery U. Oreg. Med. Sch., 1975-77; chief cardiac surgery Inova Heart Ctr. at Fairfax Hosp., Falls Church, Va., 1977—, dir. cardiac surgery rsch.; pres. Cardiovascular and Thoracic Surgery Assocs., P.C., Annandale, Va.; med. dir. cardiac surgery Inova Heart and Vascular Inst., Falls Church, Va.; clin. assoc. profl. surgery Uniformed Svcs. U. Health Scis., Bethesda, Md.; asst. clin. prof. surgery Georgetown U. Sch. Medicine, Washington; active staff Cardio-Thoracic Surgery Svc. Nat. Naval Med. Ctr., Bethesda; prof. surgery Va. Commonwealth U. Sch. Medicine. Asst. prof. surgery U. Oreg. Med. Sch., 1977; mem. courtesy staff Alexandria (Va.) Hosp.; active staff Arlington (Va.) Hosp., Alexandria (Va.) Hosp.; cons. Clin. Ctr. NIH, Bethesda; mem. med. adv. com. Washington Regional Transplant Consortium; dir. heart and lung transplantation Va. Heart Ctr. Fairfax, 1986-96; mem. critical care com. Fairfax Hosp., 1978-93; jour. cons. Chest, Cancer Chemotherapy Reports, Ann. Thor. Surg. Author: Cardiac Valve Prostheses, 1979; prodr. films in field; contbr. articles to profl. publs. Fellow ACS, Am. Coll. Cardiology, Am. Coll. Chest Physicians, Internat. Coll. Surgeons; mem. AMA, Am. Heart Assn. (bd. dirs. No. Va. chpt. 1978), Albert Starr Surg. Soc., Fairfax County Med. Soc., Med. Soc. Va., Met. Washington Soc. Thoracic and Cardiovascular Surgeons, Michael E. DeBakey Internat. Cardiovascular Soc., Soc. Thoracic Surgeons, Internat. Soc. for Heart and Lung Transplantation, So. thoracic Surg. Assn., Washington Area Transplant Soc., Am. Assn. Thoracic Surgery, Colegio Interamericano de Médicos y Cirujanos. Address: 3301 Woodburn Rd Annandale VA 22003-1229 Office Phone: 703-280-5858. Business E-Mail: edward.lefrak@inova.com.

LEFTON, IRA S., lawyer; b. Pitts., June 23, 1952; BA in English cum laude, Yale U., 1974; JD with honors, U. NC, 1978. Bar: Pa. 1978. Joined Reed Smith LLP, 1978, now ptnr., chair firmwide pro bono com. Phila. Sec. bd. dirs. Citizens for the Arts in PA. Rotary Internat. Found. Grad. Fellow, 1974—75. Mem.: Allegheny County Bar Assn. (co-founder & past pres. arts and law com.), Pa. Bar Assn. Office: Reed Smith LLP 2500 One Liberty Pl 1650 Market St Philadelphia PA 19103 Office Phone: 215-851-8236. Office Fax: 215-851-1420. Business E-Mail: ilefton@reedsmith.com.

LEFTWICH, BYRON ANTRON, professional football player; b. Jan. 14, 1980; Quarterback Jacksonville Jaguars, Fla., 2003—. Finalist Offensive Player of Yr award, Walter Camp Nat.; recipient Vern Smith Leadership award, Mid-Am. Conf., Offensive Player of Yr. award. Office: Jacksonville Jaguars 1 Alltel Stadium Pl Jacksonville FL 32202

LEGATES, JOHN CREWS BOULTON, information scientist; b. Boston, Nov. 19, 1940; s. Eber Thomson and Sybil Rowe (Crews) LeGates; m. Nancy Elizabeth Boulton, Apr. 28, 1993. BA in Math., Harvard U., 1962. Edn. svcs. mgr. Bolt Beranek & Newman, Cambridge, Mass., 1966-67; v.p. Washington Engring. Svcs., Cambridge, 1967-69; v.p., co-founder Cambridge Info. Systems, 1968-69; v.p., founder Computer Adv. Svc. to Edn., Wayland, Mass., 1966-72; exec. dir. Educom Interuniversity Communications Coun., Boston, 1969-72; founder, mng. dir. Program on Info. Resources Policy Harvard U., 1973—, founder, pres. Ctr. Info. Policy Rsch., 1978—. Mem. Arpanet NWG, core Arpanet/Internet design team, 1970-72; U.S. del. First World Conf. on Computer Comms., Amsterdam, 1970; cons. in field; pioneer ednl. computing. Photo exhbn., Boston Mus. Fine Arts; contbr. articles to profl. jours. Bd. dirs. Nat. Telecommunications Conf., Washington, 1979. Kent fellow, 1964. Mem. NAS/NRC (panelist), IEEE, NSF, Soc. for Values in Higher Edn., Nashoba Valley Hunt Club (pres. 1974-80). Unitarian Universalist. Achievements include pioneering educational computers, building world's first hospital integrated information system at Mass. Gen. Hosp. Corp. Bds. Avocations: sailing, fox-hunting, mountain climbing, classical music. Home: PO Box 6331 Lincoln MA 01773-6331 Office Phone: 617-495-4114.

LEGATO, MARIANNE, internist, medical educator; b. N.J., Aug. 17, 1935; MD, NYU, 1962. Bd. cert. internal medicine. Intern Columbia U. Coll. Physicians and Surgeons, N.Y.C., 1962—63, resident internal medicine, 1963—64, Presbyn. Hosp., N.Y.C., 1964—65, fellow cardiology, 1965—68, assoc. attending physician, 1993—; sr. attending physician St. Luke's/Roosevelt Hosp., N.Y.C., 1980—; founder, dir. Partnership for Gender Specific Medicine Columbia U., N.Y.C., 1997—; prof. clin. medicine Columbia U. Coll. Physicians and Surgeons, 1998—. Charter mem. adv. bd. Office Rsch. on Women's Health, NIH. Author: The Female Heart: The Truth About Women and Heart Disease, 1992; author: (with Carol Colman) What Women Need to Know: From Headaches to Heart Disease and Everything in Between, 1997; author: Eve's Rib: The New Science of Gender-Specific Medicine and How It Can Save Your Life, 2002, Why Men Never Remeber and Women Never Forget, 2005; editor: The Principles of Gender Specific Medicine, 2004; founder, editor: Gender Medicine, mem. editl. bd.: Cardiovasc. Risk Factors, Prevention Mag. Named Am. Health Hero, Am. Health for Women, 1997, Heroine of Women's Health, Ladies Home Jour., 2000; named one of 300 Am. Women Changing the Face of Medicine, Nat. Libr. Medicine, 2004; named to 1,000 Women for the Nineties, Mirabella Mag., 1994; recipient Howard W. Blakeslee award, Am. Heart Assn., 1992, Leadership in Action award, Women's Action Alliance, 1994, Woman in Sci. award, Am. Med. Women's Assn., 2002, Heart of Gold award, L.I. Heart Coun., J. Murray Steele award, Sr. Investigator award, Am. Heart Assn., N.Y. Affiliate, Rsch. Career Devel. award, NIH; Martha Lyon Slater fellow. Home and Office: Partnership for Gender-Specific Medicine 962 Park Ave New York NY 10028-0313 Office Phone: 212-737-5663. Business E-Mail: mjl2@columbia.edu.

LEGENDRE, LOUIS, oceanographer, educator, research scientist; b. Montreal, Que., Can., Feb. 16, 1945; s. Vianney and Marguerite (Venne) Legendre. BA, U. Montreal, 1964, BSc, 1967; PhD, Dalhousie U., Halifax, 1971; Doctorat honoris causa, U. Liege, 1997. Postdoctoral fellow U. Paris VI, Villefranche-sur-Mer, France, 1971-73; rsch. assoc. U. Laval, Quebec City, Canada, 1973, asst. prof., 1974-77, assoc. prof., 1977-81, prof., 1981-2000, emeritus prof., 2001—; rsch. prof. CNRS, France, 2000—; dir. Villefranche-sur-Mer Oceanography Lab., 2001—; dep. sci. dir. European Network Excellence EUR-OCEANS, 2004—. V.p. Groupe Interuniversitaire de Recherches Océanographiques du Que., 1989—2000; group chmn. Natural Scis. and Engring. Rsch. Coun. Can., Ottawa, 1989—92. Author (with P. Legendre): (book) Numerical Ecology, 1983, 1998; author: Scientific Research and Discovery: Process, Consequences and Practice, 2004; contbr. articles to profl. jours. V.p. Model Environ., Liege, Belgium, 1993—; mem. standing adv. group Nua Pear Applications Imstrumental Atomic Enbergy Agumey, 2005—. Decorated Knight of Malta; recipient Léo-Pariseau award, Assn. Canadienne-Française pour l'Avancement des Scis., 1985, Michel-Jurdant award, 1986, Que. Sci. prize, Pure and Applied Scis., 1997, Excellence in Ecology prize, Internat. Ecology Inst., 2001; fellow Killam Rsch., Can. Coun., 1996—98. Fellow: Internat. Ecology Inst., Royal Soc. Can.; mem.: European Geosci. Union, Am. Geophys. Union, Am. Soc. Limnology and Oceanography (G. Evelyn Hutchinson award 2002). Office: LOV BP 28 06234 Villefranche-sur-Mer Cedex France Office Phone: 33 4 9376 3836. Business E-Mail: legendre@obs.vlfr.fr.

LEGER, PHILIPPE, legal administrator; b. 1938; Mem. judiciary Min. of Justice, 1966-70; head of and subsequently tech. advisor Pvt. office of Min. for Living Stds., 1976; tech. advisor Pvt. Office of Garde des Sceaux, 1976-78; dep. dir. criminal affairs and reprieves Min. Justice, 1978-83; sr. mem. Ct. of Appeal, Paris, 1983-86; dep. dir. Pvt. Office of Garde des Sceaux, Min. for Justice, 1986; pres. Regional Ct. Bobigny, 1986-93; head pvt. office Ministre d'État, the Garde des Sceaux, Min. for Justice, 1993-94; advocate gen. Ct. Appeal, Paris, 1993-94; assoc. prof. René Descartes U., Paris, 1988-93; advocate gen. Ct. Justice, Luxembourg, 1994—. Office: European Ct of Justice Blvd Konrad Adenauer L-2925 Kirchberg Luxembourg

LEGER, WALTER JOHN, JR., lawyer; b. New Orleans, Nov. 11, 1951; s. Walter John Sr. and Mildred Veronica (Brown) L.; m. Catherine Ann Buras, Aug. 4, 1973; children: Walter John III, Rhett Michael, Elizabeth Catherine. BA, La. State U., 1973; JD, Tulane U., 1976. Bar: La. 1976, U.S. Dist. Ct. (ea. dist.) La. 1976, U.S. Dist. Ct. (ea. dist.) La. 1976, U.S. Dist. Ct. (we. dist.) La. 1978, U.S. Ct. Appeals (5th and 11th cirs.) 1981, U.S. Supreme Ct. 1981, U.S. Dist. Ct. (mid. dist.) La. 1989. Assoc. Phelps, Dunbar, Marks, Claverie & Smith, New Orleans, 1976-78; ptnr. George & George, New Orleans, 1978-79; sr. ptnr. Leger & Mestayer, New Orleans, 1979—; pres. CBL Barge Co., 1979—. Lectr. law Tulane U. 1983-85, U. New Orleans, Para-Legal Inst., 1987-88; adv. bd. dirs. First Nat. Bank of St. Bernard, Chalmette, La.; bd. dirs. Bergeron Marine Svc., Inc., New Orleans, Ryan Marine, Inc., Pearlington, Miss. Chmn. March of Dimes, Met. New Orleans and Southeastern La., 1980-84; adv. com. bd. commrs. Port of New Orleans, 1986-88; bd. dirs. St. Bernard Community Coll. Found., Chalmette, La., 1986-92; bd. dirs., vice chmn. Nunez Community Coll., Chalmette, 1992—; adv. counsel St. Bernard Parish Home Rule Charter Commn., 1988, econ. devel. commn., 1989—, pers. bd., 1990—, chmn. Appointments Rev. Bd; Disting. fellow Govt. Leadership Inst., U. New Orleans. Named one of People to Watch in 1982 New Orleans Mag., 1982. Mem. ABA, Fed. Bar Assn., Assn. Trial Lawyers Am., La. Trial Lawyers Assn. (pres.'s adv. council 1982-88, bd. govs. 1988—, exec. com. 1991—), Miss. Trial Lawyers Assn., Maritime Law Assn., Southeastern Admiralty Law Inst., La. State U. Fedn. (pres.-elect St. Bernard chpt. 1986-87), St. Bernard Council C. of C. (chmn. 1986, 92—), New Orleans/River Region C. of C. (bd. dirs. 1986—, vice-chmn. bd. dirs. 1987-88), Omicron Delta Kappa. Democrat. Roman Catholic. Avocations: jogging, sailing, tennis. Home: 20 Carolyn Ct Arabi LA 70032-1955 Office: Leger & Mestayer 600 Carondelet St New Orleans LA 70130-3511

LEGESSE, SOLOMON, technology executive; s. Feleke and Sewnete Legesse; m. Jemanesh Legesse; children: Eric M., Matthew J. BS, Calif. State U., L.A., 1981. Network engr. ATT Paradyne, Largo, Fla., 1980—84; sr. network engr. Western Airlines (Delta), L.A., 1984—87; dir. info. tech. EMJ Co., Brea, Calif., 1987—. Recipient Process Innovation award, AIIM, 1998, Top 100 Co. for Innovative Info. Tech., InfoWorld, 1999, recognition for Cost-Effective Comm. on IP Tech., Cisco Sys., 2002. Achievements include design of document imaging process. E-mail: slegesse@emjemtals.com.

LEGETT, BENJAMIN J., III, choral director, composer; b. San Diego, Apr. 28, 1952; s. Benjamin J. and June Drumm Legett; m. Robin Stavely, Dec. 23, 1977; children: Stavely Michael, Joshua Chapman. MusB, Rhodes Coll., Memphis, 1974; MusM, U. Memphis, 1978. Founder and dir. The Germantown (Tenn.) Chorale, 1976—80; music dir. Colonial Pk. United Meth. Ch., Memphis, 1985—90; music dir. and tchr. Hutchison Sch., Memphis, 1986—97; founder and music dir. The Wolf River Singers, Memphis,

1993—2005; music dir. Our Lady of Perpetual Help Ch., Germantown, 1996—. Composer and arranger, 1974—; condr. All-West Tenn. Honor Choir, Memphis, 1978, Memphis All-City H.S. Honor Choir, 1979; founder of the honor choir Tenn. Assn. of Ind. Schools, 1988; instr. Liturgical Ministries Inst., Memphis, 2001—. Composer: (choral anthem) We Walk By Faith; music dir. (musicals) Cardigans (Memphis Theater Award for Excellence in Music Direction, 1995), Company, Man of La Mancha, Kiss Me Kate, Germantown Cmty. Theater, condr. Annie Get Your Gun, Theatre Memphis. Mem.: Am. Choral Directors Assn., Omicron Delta Kappa, Pi Kappa Lambda. Avocations: boat building, fly fishing. Office: Our Lady of Perpetual Help 8151 Poplar Ave Germantown TN 38138 Office Phone: 901-754-1204 130.

LEGG, BENSON EVERETT, federal judge; b. Balt., June 8, 1947; s. William Mercer Legg and Beverly Mason; m. Kyle Prechtl Legg; children: Jennifer, Charles, Matthew. BA in English Literature, magna cum laude, Princeton U., 1970; JD, U. Va., 1973. Bar: Md. 1973. Summer assoc. Venable, Baetjer & Howard, 1971, Goodwin, Procter & Hoar, Boston, 1972; law clk. to Hon. Frank A. Kaufman, Balt., 1973-74; assoc. Venable, Baetjer & Howard, Balt., 1975-81, ptnr., 1982-91; judge U.S. Dist. Ct., Dist. Md., Balt., 1991—2003, chief judge, 2003—. Faculty mem. Md. Inst. for Continuing Profl. Edn. of Lawyers; instr., Trial Advocacy Inst. U. Va. Editl. bd. Va. Law Review, 1971—73. Adv. bd. Nat. Aquarium, Balt., 1987—; trustee, mem. exec. com., mem. fin. com. Balt. Zool. Soc., 1990—. Mem.: Order of Coif. Office: US Dist Ct 101 W Lombard St Ste 3D Baltimore MD 21201-2605 Office Phone: 410-962-0723.*

LEGG, HAROLYN LEE, librarian; b. Crawley, W.Va., Aug. 17, 1955; d. Harold Lee and Emma Irene (Miller) L. BS in Edn., Bowling Green State U., 1976, MEd, 1980, postgrad., 1990-91. Cert.tchr., K-12 ednl. media, Ohio. Dist. libr. Liberty-Benton High Sch., Findlay, Ohio, 1977—. Contbr. articles to profl. jours.; book reviewer The Book Report, 1982—. Recipient Cable in Classroom award Continental Cablevision, 1992. Mem. Ohio Ednl. Libr. Media Assn. (co-chmn. intellectual freedom dept. 1988-91, chmn. 1992-93, Social Issues Resource Series Intellectual Freedom award 1987), Hancock County Librs. Assn. (chmn. 1985—), Phi Delta Kappa. Democrat. Methodist. Avocations: reading, music, sports. Office: Liberty-Benton High Sch 9190 CR 9 Findlay OH 45840-9303 Home: 107 Warrington Ave Findlay OH 45840-6328 Office Phone: 419-424-5351. Business E-Mail: hlegg@lb.noacsc.org.

LEGG, J. IVAN, academic administrator; Exec. v.p., provost No. Ill. U., DeKalb. Office: No Ill U Office Of Provost Dekalb IL 60115-2886 Office Phone: 815-753-0493. Business E-Mail: ilegg@ntu.edu.

LEGG, TIMOTHY JAMES, nursing educator; BS, Wilkes U., Pa., 1993—96; MS, SUNY, 1996—2000; PhD, Touro U. Internat., Cypress, Cal., 2000—04. Cert. in Long Term Care Adminstrn., Marywood U., Scranton, Pa., 1999, Gerontol. Nurse Practitioner, ANCC, DC, 2000, Fellow, Am. Coll. of Health Care Administrators, Va., 2003. Don Mountain Rest Nursing Home, Scranton, Pa., 1993—97; dir. of staff edn. Taylor Nursing & Rehab. Ctr., Pa., 1997—2000; gerontol. nurse practitioner VA Med. Ctr., Wilkes Barre, 2000—02; faculty Wilkes Univ., 2003—; regional dir. of staff devel. Beverly Healthcare, 2003—. Mem. Pa. State Nurses Assn., Harrisburg, 2000, Sigma Theta Tau, Indpls., Ind., 1995; pres. Sigma Phi Omega- Alpha Sigma Chpt., Scranton, 2000. Mem.: Am. Coll. of Health Care Executives, Gerontol. Soc. of Am., Nat. Gerontol. Nurses Assn. Home: 141 Country Club Estates Thornhurst PA 18424 Office: Beverly Healthcare 101 E Mountain Blvd Wilkes Barre PA 18702 Personal E-mail: timrn@ptd.net.

LEGG, WILLIAM JEFFERSON, lawyer; b. Enid, Okla., Aug. 20, 1925; s. Garl Paul and Mabel (Gensman) L.; m. Eva Imogene Hill, Dec. 16, 1950; children: Melissa Lou, Eva Diane, Janet Sue. Grad., Enid Bus. Coll., 1943; student, Pittsburg State U., 1944; BBA, U. Tex., Austin, 1946; JD, U. Tulsa, 1954. Bar: Okla. 1954, U.S. Supreme Ct., U.S. Ct. Appeals (10th cir.), U.S. Dist. Ct. (we. dist.) Okla. With aviation sales Phillips Petroleum Co., 1946-48; atty. Marathon Oil Co., 1954-61; pvt. practice Oklahoma City, 1962—; with Andrews Davis Legg Bixler Milsten & Price, Inc. and predecessor firms, Oklahoma City, 1962—2002, pres., 83-86, also dir., 1973-77, 80-81, 83-86, 90, sec., 1975-80, 82-83, 90; sr. counsel, 1991—2002. Adj. prof. law Oklahoma City U., 1975-80; lectr. Okla. U. Law Sch., 1986; dir., v.p. Woods Petroleum Corp. subs., Turkey, Australia, Brunei, 1967-82; dir., gen. counsel NJR Energy Corp., Wall, NJ, 1986-91; rsch. fellow The Ctr. for Am. and Internat. Law (formerly Southwestern Legal Found.), Dallas, 1989—, CLE adv. bd., 1998—; lectr. in field. Contbr. articles to profl. jours. Legal com. Okla. Gov.'s Energy Adv. Coun., 1973, Okla. Blue Ribbon Com. on Natural Gas Well Allowables, 1983; dir. Skillpath, Inc., Kansas City, Mo., 1994—98; ordained Cmty. of Christ (formerly Reorganized Ch. of Jesus Christ of Latter Day Saints), 1964, dist. pres., 1975—80, br. pres., 1986—91, evangelist, 1993—; trustee Am. Inst. Discussion, 1962—88, chmn., 1969—72; trustee Restoration Trails Found., 1975, Jenkins Found. Rsch., sec., 1975—81; exec. com., chmn. bus. affairs com. Graceland U., Lamoni, Iowa, 1988—98, trustee, 1986—2000, investment com., 1998—2000, trustee emeritus, 2000—; trustee Met. Lib. Endowment Trust, 1986—99, treas., 1988—99, chmn. investment com. With USN, 1943—46, lt. (j.g.) USNR, 1946—66. Mem. ABA, Okla. Bar Assn. (past com. chmn.), Oklahoma County Bar Assn. (past com. chmn.), Internat. Bar Assn., Internat. Assn. Energy Econs., Econ. Club Okla., Men's Dinner Club, Petroleum Club. Home: 3017 Brush Creek Rd Oklahoma City OK 73120-1855

LEGGE, CHARLES ALEXANDER, federal judge; b. San Francisco, Aug. 24, 1930; s. Roy Alexander and Wilda (Rampton) L.; m. Janice Meredith Sleeper, June 27, 1952; children: Jeffrey, Nancy, Laura. AB with distinction, Stanford U., 1952, JD, 1954. Bar: Calif. 1955. Assoc. Bronson, Bronson & McKinnin, San Francisco, 1956-64, ptnr., 1964-84, chmn., 1978-84; U.S. Dist. Ct. judge U.S. Dist. Ct. (no. dist.) Calif., San Francisco, 1984—. Served with U.S. Army, 1954-56. Fellow Am. Coll. Trial Lawyers; mem. Calif. Bar Assn. (past chmn. adminstrn. justice com.). Clubs: Bohemian, World Trade (San Francisco); Orinda (Calif.) Country. Republican.

LEGGE KEMP, DIANE, architect, landscape architect; b. Englewood, N.J., Dec. 4, 1949; d. Richard Claude and Patricia (Roney) L.; m. Kevin A. Kemp; children: Alloy Hudson, McClelland Beebe, Logan Roney. BArch, Stanford U., 1972; MArch, Princeton U., 1975. Registered arch., Ill., Wis., Minn., Ind., landscape arch., Ill. Architect Northrop, Kaelber & Kopf, Rochester, NY, 1971—73, Michael Graves, Architect, Princeton, NJ, 1973—75, The Ehrenkrantz Group, NYC, 1975-77; ptnr. Skidmore Owings & Merrill, Chgo., 1977-89; pres. Diane Legge Kemp Architecture and Landscape Consulting, Riverside, Ill., 1993—, DLK Architecture, 1993—. Chair Princeton U. adv. bd. Sch. Architecture, 1991—; dir. Newhouse Archtl. Found., Chgo., 1991—. Designer, architect: Boston Globe Satellite Printing Plant, 1984, Mfrs. Hanover Plaza, Wilmington, 1987, Herman Miller Showroom, Chgo., 1988, Arlington Internat. Racecourse, 1989, Phila. Newspapers Espansion and Retrofit, 1989, Navy Pier R constrn., 1990, McCormick Place Retrofit and Expansion, 1991, L.A. Times Master Plan, 1992, CRSS capital project mgmt. Chgo. Park Dist., 1993, Chgo. Hist. Blvds. Restoration, 1993, Roosevelt Rd. Reconstruction, Chgo., 1993, Field, Shedd, Adler Mus. Campus, Goodman Theater, Chgo., 1995, Job Corps Tng. Campus, 1995, Chgo. area Circulator Urban Design, 1995, Cook County Hosp., 1996, Ft. Sherman Base, 1997, Girl Scouts Svc. Ctr., 1997, Michigan Ave. Renovation, 1997. Mem. bd. govs. Sch. of Art Inst., Chgo., 1991—; dir., past pres. Soc. for Contemporary Art, Chgo., 1991—. Named one of 100 Most Influential Women in Chgo., Crain's, 1996; recipient Urban Design award, Progressive Architecture, 1984, Nat. Designer award, 1986, 40 under 40 award, N.Y. Archtl. League, 1986, Waterfront Honor award, World Trade Ctr., 1988, Excellence award, Inst. & Mcpl. Parking Congress, Northwestern U., 1993, Chicagoan of Yr., Chgo. Tribune, 1996, Woman of Achievement award, Ill. Crossroads Coun. Girl Scouts Am., 1997, Disting. Built award, AIA Chgo. Chpt., Disting. Unbuilt award, Richard H. Driehaus Statewide Ill. Preservation award, Project of Yr., Ill. Engring. Coun. Fellow: AIA (Disting. Bldg. award 1983, Interiors award 1988, Nat. Urban Design award 1996); mem.: NCARB, The Chgo. Network, Am. Soc. Landscape Architects, Urban Land. Inst., The Econ. Club Chgo. Avocations: piano, flute, skiing, sailing, gardens. Office: DLK CINC Design 410 S Michigan Ave Chicago IL 60605-1308 Office Phone: 312-322-0911 ext. 102. Business E-Mail: dleggekemp@dlkinc.com.

LEGGETT, ANTHONY J., physics professor, researcher; b. London, 1938; Student, Balliol Coll., Oxford, Eng.; degree in physics, PhD in Theoretical Physics, Merton Coll., Oxford. Mem. faculty U. Sussex (UK), 1967-71, reader, 1971-78, prof., 1978-83; John D. and Catherine T. Macarthur prof. U. Ill., Urbana-Champaign, 1983—. Rschr. Urbana, Ill., Kyoto, Japan; lectr. in field. Author: The Problems of Physics, 1987, Quantum Tunnelling in Condensed Media, 1992; contbr. articles to profl. jours. Recipient Maxwell Medal and Prize, Inst. Physics, UK, 1975, Simon Meml. prize, 1981, Fritz London Meml. award, 1981, Paul Dirac Medal and prize, Inst. Physics, UK, 1992, John Bardeen prize, 1994, Wolf Prize, 2003, Nobel prize in physics, 2003. Fellow: American Physical Soc., Inst. Physics, UK (hon.), Royal Soc., UK; mem.: Russian Acad. of Sciences, Nat. Acad. of Sciences (assoc.), Am. Acad. Arts & Sciences, Am. Philol. Soc. Achievements include research in condensed matter physics, high-temperature superconductivity, foundations of quantum mechanics. Office: U Ill 1110 W Green St Urbana IL 61801-9013 E-mail: aleggett@uiuc.edu.

LEGGETT, GLORIA JEAN, minister; b. Buffalo, June 6, 1941; d. Richard Howard and Mary Alice (Jumper) Pope; m. Arthur William Leggett, June 17, 1961; children: Wendy Irene, Pamela Jean. MusB, Va. Commonwealth U., 1986; MDiv, Wesley Theol. Sem., 1991. Ordained to ministry Christian Ch., 1991. Choir dir. St. Mark's United Meth. Ch., Richmond, Va., 1974-80; vol. hosp. chaplain Johnston-Willis Hosp., Richmond, Va., 1991—; interim minister Westville Christian Ch., Mathews, Va., 1992-93, Crewe (Va.) Christian Ch.; vol. police chaplain Chesterfield County (Va.) Police Dept., 1995—; pastor Westside Christian Ch., Richmond, Va., 1997—, Ind. Christian Ch., Ashland, Va., 1998—; interim Unity Christ Ch. of Bon Air, 1999; min. Colonial Christian Ch., Colonial Heights, Va., 1991—2005. Tchr. music, Richmond, 1972—; supply preacher, keynote spkr. Main Line Denomination Chs., Va., 1990—. Counselor rape crisis YWCA, Richmond, 1992; bd. dirs. Va. Wildlife Fedn., 1986—92. Recipient Achievement award, Dale Carnegie Course, 1979. Mem.: NOW, AAUW, Phi Kappa Phi. Avocations: travel, crossword puzzles, music, camping, pets. Home and Office: 9216 Groomfield Rd Richmond VA 23236-3402 E-mail: revgjleggett@aol.com.

LEGGETT, JAMES DANIEL, bishop; b. Williamston, N.C., Oct. 21, 1939; s. James S. and Hazel Louise (Wynn) L.; m. Clara Faye Watts, June 25, 1961; children: James Jr., Joseph Talmadge, Cynthia Faye, John David. BA, Pembroke State U.; ThB, Holmes Coll. of the Bible, hon. doctorate, 1988. Ordained to ministry Pentecostal Holiness Ch., 1960. Pastor Swan Quarter Pentecostal Holiness Ch., 1962-64, Pinetown Pentecostal Holiness Ch., 1962-64, Mt. Olive Pentecostal Holiness Ch., Pembroke, 1964-70, Culbreth Meml. Pentecostal Holiness Ch., Falcon, 1970-86; supr. N.C. Conf. Pentecostal Holiness Ch., 1986-89; asst. gen. supt. Internat. Pentecostal Holiness Ch., Bethany, Okla., 1989-93, vice chmn., 1993-97. Exec. dir. Evangelism USA, 1989-97; pres. Extension Loan Fund, 1989-97; gen. supt. (bishop) Internat. Pentecostal Holiness Ch., 1997—; co-chmn. exec. com. Pentecostal/Charismatic Chs. N.A.; bd. dirs. Nat. Assn. Evangs.; mem. adv. com. Pentecostal World Fellowship; mem. adv. coun. Internat. Charismatic Consultation; mem. Mission Am.; former mem. Evang. Curriculum Commn., writer Sunday Sch. lit., instr. extension classes Holmes Coll. of Bible, Emmanuel Coll. Sec. bd. trustees Holmes Coll. of the Bible, past bd. dirs. Mem. Pentecostal Holiness Ch. Office: Pentecostal Holiness Ch 7300 NW 39th Expy Bethany OK 73008-2340

LEGGETT, JAMES EVERETT, JR., infectious diseases physician, educator; s. James Everett and Hattie Leggett; m. Alba Carla Orsi, June 15, 1976; children: Matteo, Giulia. MD, U. Ky., 1980. Cert. Am. Bd. Internal Medicine (cert. in infectious diseases and internal medicine). Clin. instr. U. Wis., Madison, 1986—89; asst. dir. med. edn. Providence Portland (Oreg.) Med. Ctr., 1989—; assoc. prof. divsn. infectious diseases, dept. internal medicine Oreg. Health and Sci. U., Portland, 1994—. Mem. anti-infective drug adv. bd. FDA, Rockville, Md., 1999—2004. Fellow: ACP, Infectious Diseases Soc. Am. Office: Infection Consultants Llp Ste 540 5050 NE Hoyt St Portland OR 97213 Office Phone: 503-215-6600.

LEGGETT, ROBERTA JEAN (BOBBI LEGGETT), retired social services administrator; b. Kankakee, Ill., Nov. 30, 1926; d. Clyde H. and Sybil D. (Billings) Karns; m. George T. Leggett, Aug. 25, 1956. Sec. Cardov div. Chemetron Corp., Chgo., 1951-60; sec., asst. mgr. Ravisloe Country Club, Homewood, Ill., 1961-65; sec. Nationwide Paper Co., Chgo., 1966-68; exec. dir. Am. Bd. Oral and Maxillofacial Surgery, Chgo., 1969-87. Mem. Chgo. Soc. Assn. Execs., Conf. Med. Soc. Execs. of Greater Chgo., Profl. Secs. Internat. Methodist.

LEGGETT, WILLIAM C., biology professor, academic administrator; b. Orangeville, Ont., Can., June 25, 1939; s. Frank William and Edna Irene (Wheeler) L.; m. Claire Holman, May 9, 1964; children: David, John. BA, Waterloo U. Coll., 1962; MSc, U. Waterloo, 1965, DSc, 1992; PhD, McGill U., 1969, DSc, 2001; LLD, Wilfred Laurier U., 1994, Queen's U., 2005; DSc, Laval U., 1996. From rsch. scientist to rsch. assoc. Essex (Conn.) Marine Lab., 1965-73; asst. prof. McGill U., Montreal, Que., Can., 1970-72, assoc. prof., 1972-79, prof., 1979—2004, chmn. dept. biology, 1981-85, dean of sci., 1986-91, acad. v.p., 1991-94; prin., vice chancellor Queen's U., Kingston, Canada, 1994—2004, prin. emeritus, prof. emeritus, 2004—; chmn. bd. Huntsman Marine Lab., 1980-89; pres. Groupe Interuniversitaire de Recherche Oceanographique du Que., 1986-91. Chmn. grant selection com. for population biology Natural Scis. and Engring. Rsch. Coun. Can., 1980-81, chmn. grant selection com. for oceans, 1986-87; exec. com. Coun. Ontario Univs., 1996-2004, vice-chair, 2002-04; mem. com. internationalization Assn. Univ. Colls. Can., 2001-04; bd. dirs. Office for Partnerships for Advanced Skills, 2000-04; chair Ont. Commn. on Interuniv. Athletes, 2002-04; sec. Connecticut River Ecol. Study Found., 2004—. Mem. editl. bd.: Can. Jour. Fisheries and Aquatic Sciences, 1980-85, Le Naturaliste Canadien, 1980-91, Can. Jour. Zoology, 1982-86; contbr. articles in field. Chair svc. learning adv. com. McConnell Found., 2004—. Recipient Dwight D. Webster award Am. Fisheries Soc., 1989, Award for Excellence for Fisheries Edn., 1990, Fry medal Can. Soc. Zoologists, 1990, Outstanding Biologist award Can. Coun. Biol. Chmn., 1993, Disting. Svc. award Queen's U., 2004, John Orr award Queen's U., 2003; grantee in field. Fellow Rawson Acad., Royal Soc. Can., Order of Can.; mem. Am. Fisheries Soc. (pres. North-East divsn. 1977-78, EO Sette award 1996, Excellence award 1997, Stirling medal 2004), Can. Com. for Fishery Rsch., Can. Soc. Zoologists, Am. Soc. Limnology and Oceanography, Am. Soc. Naturalists. Office: Queen's U Dept Biology Kingston ON Canada K7L 3N6 Office Phone: 613-533-6534. Business E-Mail: wleggett@post.queensu.ca.

LEGINS, SARAH OTIS, information scientist, librarian; b. White Plains, N.Y., Oct. 10, 1971; d. Christopher and Pamela Wimpress Mitchell; m. Keith Legins, Nov. 7, 1998. AB in Art History, Bowdoin Coll., 1993; MS in Libr. and Info. sci. and MS in Art and Archtl. History, Pratt Inst., Bklyn., 2002. Rschr. Art Resource, Inc., N.Y.C., 1993—95; mgr. Christie's images Christie's, Inc., N.Y.C., 1995—96; account exec. SuperStock, Inc., N.Y.C., 1995—96; libr. asst. Skidmore, Owings & Merrill, LLP, N.Y.C., 2001—02; visual resources/ref. libr. Clemson U., SC, 2002—04; prin. Edifiche, LLC, Easley, SC, 2004—. Recipient Pratt Cir. award for acad. excellence, Pratt Inst., 2002. Mem.: ALA, AIA, Assn. of Ind. Info. Profls. Episcopalian. Avocations: running, travel, sewing. Home: 306 Glazner St Easley SC 29640 Office: Edifiche LLC 1027 S Pendleton St Easley SC 29642 Office Phone: 864-320-3035. Personal E-mail: slegins@juno.com. Business E-Mail: sarah@edifiche.com.

LEGLER, APRIL ARINGTON, librarian, educator; b. Gary, Ind., Apr. 20, 1946; d. James Berry Arington and Charlotte Bushong Arington Canine; m. Theodore Rex Legler II, Aug. 26, 1967; children: Melinda, Sara, Tad. AB in Comparative Lit., Ind. U., 1968, MLS, 1971. Various capacities in pub. and acad. librs., 1961-70; head librarian Math., Physics and Astronomy Libr. Ind. U. Librs., Bloomington, 1970-71; instr. Big Bend C.C., Berlin, 1986-88, Midlands Tech. Coll., Columbia, S.C., 1988-91, U. Md., Heidelberg, Germany, 1992, Schiller Internat. U., Heidelberg, 1991-92, head libr., 1992-95; career counselor Ind. U. Kelley Sch. of Bus., 1997-99; course mgr. I.U. Kelley Sch. of Bus., 1999-2000, career edn. assoc., 2000—03, lectr. undergrad. programs, 2003—. Author monograph. Life mem. Girl Scouts U.S., 1979—, instr. adult leader devel., 1983-85, bd. dirs. Congaree coun., Columbia, 1989-91, bd. dirs. North Atlantic, Europe, 1992-95; adult mem. Boy Scouts Am., 1973-99, instr. adult leader devel., 1973-92; instr. outdoor living skills Am. Camping Assn., 1985-87; vol. ARC. Recipient Silver Beaver award Boy Scouts Am., 1987, Congaree award Girl Scouts U.S., 1991. Mem. German-Am. Women's Club (v.p. 1992-93), Am. Found. for Visual Awareness (Ind. state trustee 1996-98, Ind. state sec. 1998-2000), Ind. U. Alumni Assn. (life), Ind. U. Women's Club (2nd v.p. 1999-00, program chair 2000-2001), Beta Phi Mu, Psi Iota Xi (treas. 1999—). Avocations: needlecrafts, gourmet cooking. Office: Kelly Sch Bus Ind U 1309 E 10th St Bloomington IN 47405-1701 Home: 4630 Chatham Dr Bloomington IN 47404-1319

LEGLER, CHRISTINE KAY, music educator; d. Doyle Gene and Sandra Kay Whitton; m. Mark R. Legler, May 19, 1984; children: Victoria, Noah, Elijah. BA in music, St. Joseph's Coll., 2002. Church pianist/organist various churches, Ind., 1976—; music tchr. Tippecanoe Piano Tchr. Assn., Remington, Ind., 1979—; elem. music tchr. Tri-County Sch. Corp., Remington and Wolcott, Ind., 1998—. Music dir. Remington Town Theatre, 1988—91; choir dir. Remington First Christian Ch., Ind., 1991—99, Tri-County Bible Ch., Rensseleer, Ind., 2003—04. Recipient Earl Poindexter award, Tri-Kappa Sorority, 1990. Mem.: Tippecanoe Ind. Music Tchr. Assn., Ind. State Tchr. Assn., Am. Coll. Musicians, Ind. Music Educators Assn. Protestant. Avocations: travel, reading. Office: Tri County Primary Sch 300 W Michigan St Remington IN 47977 Office Phone: 219-261-2214. E-mail: leglerc@trico.k12.in.us.

LEGLER, MITCHELL WOOTEN, lawyer; b. Alexandria, Va., June 3, 1942; s. John Clarke and Doris (Wooten) L.; m. Harriette Dodson; children: John Clarke, Dorothy Trumbull, Harriette Holland. BA in Polit. Sci. with honors, U. N.C., 1964; JD, U. Va., 1967. Bar: Va. 1967, Fla. 1967. Pres. Commander, Legler, Werber, Dawes, Sadler & Howell, Jacksonville, Fla., 1976-91; dir., gen. counsel Stein Mart, Inc., 1991—; ptnr. Foley & Lardner, Jacksonville, 1991—95; pres. Mitchell W. Legler, P.A., 1995—2001, Kirschner & Legler, P.A., 2001—. Chmn. Fla. Bar Consumer Protection Law Com. Editorial bd. Va. Law Rev., 1966-67. Mem. Va. Bar Assn., Fla. Bar Assn. (lectr. continuing legal edn.), Order of Coif, Phi Beta Kappa, Phi Eta Sigma, Delta Upsilon, Delta Theta Phi. Office: 300A Wharfside Way Jacksonville FL 32207-8153 E-mail: MWLegler@leglerlaw.com.

LEGO, PAUL EDWARD, retired manufacturing executive; b. Centre County, Pa., May 16, 1930; s. Paul Irvin and Sarah Elizabeth (Montgomery) L.; m. Ann Sepety, July 7, 1956; children: Paul Gregory, Debra Ann, Douglas Edward, Michael John. BS in Elec. Engring, U. Pitts., 1956, MS, 1958. With Westinghouse Electric Corp., 1956-93, gen. mgr. Westinghouse semiconductor div. Pitts., 1970-74, gen. mgr. electronic tube div. Elmira, NY, 1974-75, bus. unit gen. mgr. electronic components divs. Pitts., 1975-77, v.p., gen. mgr. lamp divs. Bloomfield, NJ, 1977-80, exec. v.p. electronics and control group Pitts., 1980-83, exec. v.p. control equipment, 1983-85, sr. exec. v.p. corp. resources, 1985-87, pres., COO, 1988-90, chmn., CEO, 1990-93, also bd. dirs.; ret., 1993; pres. Intelligent Enterprises, Pitts., 1993—; chmn. bd. Commonwealth Industries, Inc., Louisville, 1995—2004. Bd. dirs. Lincoln Electric Co., Aleris Internat. Trustee U. Pitts.; mem. bd. visitors U. Pitts. Sch. Engring. With U.S. Army, 1948-52. Recipient Westinghouse Order of Merit 1975, Disting. Alumni award U. Pitts. Sch. Engring., 1986, Bicentennial Medallion of Distinction award U. Pitts., 1987, Legacy Laurette award U. Pitts., 2000. Mem. Am. Soc. Corp. Execs., Valley Brook Country Club, Duquesne Club, The Club Pelican Bay (Naples, Fla.), Laurel Valley Golf Club, Rolling Rock Club (Ligonier, Pa.), Golf Club of Everglades (Naples). Republican. Roman Catholic. Office: Exec Assocs One PPG Pl Ste 2970 Pittsburgh PA 15241 Office Phone: 412-263-3344. E-mail: plego10@aol.com. *I believe that every individual should take ownership of his or her job and have the authority and responsibility to make continuous improvements in the processes by which the objectives of that job are accomplished.*

LEGRADY, GEORGE, photographer, educator; Assoc. prof. San Francisco State U. Vis. assoc. prof. dept. design, prof. electronic media Merz Akademie, Stuttgart, Germany. Interactive installations, Kunst und AustellungHalle der Bundes Republik, Bonn, 1997—98, Haus der Kunst, Munich, 1997, Kunstforum, Berlin, 1997, Nat. Gallery Can. and Can. Mus. Contemporary Photography, 1997—98, Palais des beaux-arts, Brussels, 1997, Nat. Gallery Prague, 1997, Inst. Contemporary Art Phila., 1997, Kunstmus, Dusseldorf, 1998, PSI, N.Y., 1998, Henry Art Gallery, Seattle, 1998; photographer (CD-ROM) Artintact 3, 1996, Actualizing the Virtual, 1996, George Legrady: From Analogue to Digital, 1998. Recipient New Voices, New Visions prize, The Voyager Co., 1994, Computer Integrated Media award, Can. Coun., 1996, 1997; fellow Visual fellow, Nat. Endowment Arts, 1995. Office: Postmasters Gallery Dept Art 459 W 19th St New York NY 10011-3803

LEGRAND, CHRIS, lab administrator; BS in Math. Scis., Clemson U.; MS in Info. Mgmt. and Info. Sys., George Washington U. Various bus. and tech. positions BDM Internat., Inc.; dir., info. tech. and scientific data mgmt. divsn. Constella Health Scis., 1998; COO, health scis. Constella Group, pres., health scis., 2004—. Chair, clin. info. techs. and sys. com. Drug Info. Assn., 2002. Named one of N.C.'s Top 40 Under 40, The Bus. Jour. of Raleigh-Durham, 2001, the Top 100 Bus. Impact Leaders in the Rsch. Triangle, Bus. Leader Mag., 2002. Office: Constella Group Inc 2605 Meridian Pkwy Durham NC 27713

LEGRAND, MICHEL JEAN, composer; b. Paris, Feb. 24, 1932; came to U.S., 1955; s. Raymond and Marcelle Legrand; children: Hervé, Benjamin, Eugénie, Dominique. Diploma, Conservatoire Nationale Superieur de Musique, Paris, 1951. Composer, condr., pianist, 1965—. Composer: (score, song, adaptation) I Will Wait for You, 1965 (3 Acad. award nominations), Windmills of Your Mind, 1968 (Acad. award 1968), film scores include Summer of 42, 1970 (Acad. award 1970), Brian's Song, 1971, Lady Sings the Blues, 1972, The Three Muscateers, 1973, Ode to Billy Joe, 1975, The Other Side of Midnight, 1977, Atlantic City, 1980, The Mountain Men, 1980, Never Say Never Again, 1983, Yentl, 1984 (Acad. award 1984), The Pickle, 1993, Ready to Wear, 1994, Madeline, 1998, also over 100 albums; arranger (album) I Love Paris, 1954; contbr. jazz pianist with numerous orchs. including Pitts. Symphony, Minn. Orch., Buffalo Philharm.; collaborated with various artists including Barbra Streisand, Sarah Vaughan, Jack Jones, Lena Horne, Dame Kiri Te Kanawa, Ray Charles, Miles Davis, Neil Diamond, Johnny Mathis, Jessye Norman; dir. (film) 5 Days in June, 1989. Mem. Dramatists Guild, Songwriters Guild of Am., Am. Fedn. Musicians, AFTRA, ASCAP, Acad. Motion Picture Arts and Scis. (Oscar award 1967, 70, 83). Avocations: boating, airplane pilot, tennis, horseback riding. Office: care Jim DiGiovanni PO Box 2040 New York NY 10101-2040 E-mail: jjosie157@aol.com.

LEGRAND, ROBIN LEA, music educator; b. Hayward, Calif., Aug. 13, 1953; d. Gene E. and Carolyn Rose Haney; m. Stephen Ross LeGrand, May 24, 1975; children: Katherine Elizabeth, Charles Ross. MusB, Ea. Ill U., Charleston, 1978. Cert. tchr. Ill. Tchr. vocal music k-12 County Unified Sch. Dist. #20, Lawrenceville, Ill., 1979—. Pt. time faculty Frontier CC, Fairfield, Ill., 2001—; bd. mem. Lawrence County Arts Coun., Lawrenceville, 2001—, dir. plays and musicals, 2001—; freelance pianist and accompanist. Mem.: Ill. Edn. Assn., Am. Choral Dir. Assn., Ill. Music Educators Assn. (dist. V sr.

choral co-chair 1994—). Avocations: gourmet cooking, choral music arrangement, piano. Home: 1205 Elm St Bridgeport IL 62417 Office: Lawrenceville HS 503 8th St Lawrenceville IL 62439 Office Phone: 618-943-3389. E-mail: legrandr@yahoo.com.

LEGRO, PATRICE, museum director; b. Dec. 1953; m. Alan Legro. BA in Art History, Old Dominion U., 1977; MA in internat. transaction, George Mason U., 1996. Program officer Office Internat. Affairs Nat. Acad., Wash., DC, 1987—93, mgr. Nat. Sci. Edn. Standards Project, co-study dir. Tchg. About Evolution and Nature of Sci., 1998, dir. Divsn. Comm. and Special Projects Ctr. Sci., Math., and Engring. Edn., 1998, dir. Philanthropy Svcs., 1998—2002; dir. Marian Koshland Sci. Mus. Nat. Acad. Scis., Wash., DC, 2002—. Office: Marian Koshland Sci Mus Nat Acad 500 Fifth St NW Washington DC 20001 Office Phone: 202-334-2728.

LEGRO, STANLEY WAYNE, environmental lawyer; b. Muskogee, Okla., July 3, 1936; s. Wayne Leo and Monta Catherine (Cottingham) L.; m. Marcia Louise West, Aug. 17, 1963 (div. Aug. 1986); children: Susan Louise, Stanley Wayne Jr. BS in Engring. with distinction first in class, U.S. Naval Acad., 1959; JD cum laude, Harvard U., 1966. Bar: Calif. 1967, DC 1977, US Supreme Ct. 1971. Pvt. practice, San Diego, 1967—75, 1977—82; asst. adminstr. U.S. EPA, Washington, 1975—77; nat. sec., bd. dirs. Harvard U. Alumni Assn., 1977—80; pvt. practice Washington, 1983—; of counsel Piper Rudnick, Washington, 2002—05; chairman Pacific Action Resources, Rancho Santa Fe, Calif., 2005—. Adj. prof. U. San Diego Law Sch., 1968-75; adj. fellow Ctr. for Strategic and Internat. Studies, Washington, 1989-93. Author (movie and tchg. material): A Model Criminal Trial, 1975 (Golden Gavel award ABA); mem. editl. bd. Harvard Environ. Law. Rev., 1977—88. Appt. by Pres. mem. Nat. Adv. Com. on Oceans and Atmosphere, Washington, 1985-89; mem. San Diego Planning Commn., 1971-73; bd. vis. U. San Diego Law Sch., 1974-83, 2001—; mem. Select Com. to Rev. Calif. Postseconary Edn., 1971-73; bd. overseers U. Calif., San Diego, 1980-84. Officer USMC, 1959-63. Recipient Cert. of Appreciation City of San Diego, 1973; named San Diego's Outstanding Young Man, San Diego Jaycees, 1971. Mem.: Environ. Law Inst. Coun., U.S. Naval Acad. Pres.'s Cir., U. Calif. San Diego Med. Sch. Assocs. (pres. 1972—74), U. Calif. San Diego Chancellor's Assocs., Harvard Faculty Club, Rancho Santa Fe Golf Club, Harvard Club of N.Y.C. Republican. Methodist. Avocations: golf, running, reading, music. Office: PO Box G Rancho Santa Fe CA 92067-0479 Office Phone: 858-756-6638. E-mail: Par4u@earthlink.net.

LEGUEY-FEILLEUX, JEAN-ROBERT, political scientist, educator; b. Marseilles, France, Mar. 28, 1928; came to U.S., Aug. 1949; s. E. Feilleux and Jeanne (Leguey) Feilleux Levassort; m. Virginia Louise Hartwell, Sept. 19, 1953; children— Michele, Monique, Suzanne, Christiane. M.A., Ecole Superieure de Commerce, France, 1949; Diplome Superieur d'Etudes Coloniales, U. d'Aix-Marseille, France, 1949; M.A., U. Fla., 1951; Ph.D., Georgetown U., 1965. Lectr. Sch. Foreign Service Georgetown U., Washington, 1957-66; dir. research Inst. World Polit. Georgetown U., 1960-66; asst. prof. St. Louis U., 1966-70, assoc. prof., 1970—, chmn. polit. sci. dept., 1983-96; vis. scholar Harvard Law Sch., Cambridge, Mass., 1974-75; chmn. Fulbright Commn. for France Inst. Internat. Edn., N.Y.C., 1974-76; vis. researcher UN, N.Y.C., 1981; mem. academic delegation, Jordan, 1988, Israel, 1990, Syria, Bahrain, Kuwait, 1991, Kuwait, Syria, 1992, Syria, 1993—, Yemen, 1995, Morocco, Tunisia, Spain, 1996, Tunisia, 1997, Yemen, 1998. Author (with others): Law of Limited International Conflict, 1965. Contbr. chpt. to books Implications of Disarmament, 1977, Democracy in a High-technology Society, 1988, The External Environment, 1991, Proceedings of First Gobal Village Conference, 1992, Great Events from History II: Human Rights, 1992, Science and Politics of Food, 1995. Contbr. articles to profl. jours. Author testimony Pres.'s Commn. on 25th Anniversary of UN, 1970. Recipient Medaille d'Or Institut Comml., France, 1949, Fulbright award U.S. State Dept., 1950, Cert. Disting. Service Inst. Internat. Edn., 1976; named Outstanding Educator Nutshell Mag., 1982; Malone fellow in Jordan, 1988. Mem. UN Assn. (mem. nat. coun. chpt. and div. pres. 1972-73, steering com. 1973-75), Am. Biog. Inst. (named to Hall of Fame, 1986), Internat. Human Rights Task Force (chmn. 1975-81), Character Research Assn. (pres. 1980-83, 89-90), Acad. Coun. on UN System, Am. Coun. for UN Univ., Georgetown U. Gold Key Soc., Alpha Sigma Nu, Phi Alpha Theta, Pi Sigma Alpha, Delta Phi Epsilon, Pi Delta Phi. Roman Catholic. Home: 6139 Kingsbury Ave Saint Louis MO 63112-1101 Office: Saint Louis U Dept Polit Sci 221 N Grand Blvd Saint Louis MO 63103-2006

LEGUILLON, ROLANDE LUCIENNE, French educator; b. Etréchy, Essonne, France, Mar. 4, 1924; came to U.S., 1946; d. Marcel Charles and Fernande Léone (Mansion) Pipereau; m. Harry Sylvain Leguillon, Aug. 24, 1946; children: Philippe, Catherine Leguillon Conrad, Michael. BA, U. St. Thomas, Houston, 1962; MA, U. Houston, 1966; PhD, Rice U., 1970. Tchr. Lamar High Sch., Houston Ind. Sch. Dist., 1962-66; instr. Tex. So. U., Houston, 1966-68; prof. French U. St. Thomas, 1968—, chmn. dept., 1970—, dir. French Program, 1980—, chmn. modern lang. dept., 1981-90. Lectr. various univs. in SW U.S., 1974—. Contbr. articles to profl. jours. Spkr. various Alliances Françaises, S.W. U.S., 1970—, pres., Houston, 1981-82, 96—, bd. dirs., 1988—. Decorated chevalier Palmes Acadèmiques (France), decorated officier Palmes Acadèmiques, 1995; recipient Coll. Tchr. of Yr. award Tex. Fgn. Lang. Assn., 1993-94. Mem. Am. Assn. Tchrs. French (regional rep. 1974-80), Fedn. French Alliance in U.S. (bd. dirs. 1987-2002, dir. scholarships Houston chpt. 1987—, oral examiner baccalaureate 1982-93), Houston Assn. Tchrs. French Lang. (pres. 1975-76), Houston French Alliance (bd. dirs. 1970—, pres. 1982-83, 1994—), Pi Delta Phi (nat. v.p. 1981-91, pres.-elect 1991, nat. pres. 1992-1998, reader advanced program in French 1987-94, spkr. at meetings 1981—). Avocations: movies, theater, travel. Office: U St Thomas 3800 Montrose Blvd Houston TX 77006-4626 Business E-Mail: rolandel@stthom.edu.

LE GUIN, URSULA KROEBER, writer; b. Berkeley, Calif., Oct. 21, 1929; d. Alfred Louis and Theodora (Kracaw) Kroeber; m. Charles A. Le Guin, Dec. 22, 1953; children: Elisabeth, Caroline, Theodore. BA, Radcliffe Coll., 1951; MA, Columbia, 1952; 9 hon. degrees. Vis. lectr. or writer in residence numerous workshops and univs., U.S. and abroad. Author: Rocannon's World, 1966, Planet of Exile, 1966, City of Illusion, 1967, A Wizard of Earthsea, 1968, The Left Hand of Darkness, 1969, The Tombs of Atuan, 1970, The Lathe of Heaven, 1971, The Farthest Shore, 1972, The Dispossessed, 1974, The Wind's Twelve Quarters, 1975, A Very Long Way from Anywhere Else, 1976, Orsinian Tales, 1976, The Word For World is Forest, 1976, The Language of the Night, 1989, rev. edit., 1992, Leese Webster, 1979, Malafrena, 1979, The Beginning Place, 1980, Hard Words, 1981, The Compass Rose, 1982, The Eye of the Heron, 1983, Cobbler's Rune, 1983, King Dog, 1985, Always Coming Home, 1985, Buffalo Gals, 1987, Wild Oats and Fireweed, 1988, A Visit from Dr. Katz, 1988, Catwings, 1988, Solomon Leviathan, 1988, Fire and Stone, 1989, Catwings Return, 1989, Dancing at the Edge of the World, 1989, revised edit., 1992, Tehanu, 1990, Searoad, 1991, Fish Soup, 1992, A Ride on the Red Mare's Back, 1992, Blue Moon Over Thurman Street, 1994, Wonderful Alexander and the Catwings, 1994, Going Out With Peacocks, 1994, A Fisherman of the Inland Sea, 1994, Four Ways to Forgiveness, 1995, Unlocking the Air, 1996, (with Diana Bellessi) The Twins, The Dream, 1997, Lao Tzu: Tao Te Ching: A Book About the Way and the Power of the Way, 1997, Steering the Craft, 1998, Jane on Her Own, 1999, Sixty Odd, 1999, The Telling, 2000, The Other Wind, 2001, Tales From Earthsea, 2001, The Birthday of the World, 2002, Tom Mouse, 2002, Kalpa Imperial, 2003, Selected Poems of Gabriela Mistral, 2003, Changing Planes, 2003, The Wave in the Mind, 2004, Gifts, 2004, also numerous short stories, poems, criticism, screenplays. Recipient Jupiter award 1975, 76, Lewis Caroll Shelf award 1979, Internat. Fantasy award 1988, Howard D. Vursell award Am. Acad. Arts and Letters, 1991, Pushcart prize, 1991, Boston Globe-Hornbook award for excellence in juvenile fiction, 1968, Newbery Honor medal, 1972, Nebula award (novel) 1969, 75, 90, (story) 1996, Hugo award (novel) 1969, 75, (story) 1974, 88, Gandalf award, 1979, Kafka award, 1986, Nat. Book award, 1972, H.L. Davis award Oreg. Inst. Literary Arts, 1992, Hubbub annual poetry award, 1995, Asimov's Reader's award, 1995, 2003, James Tiptree Jr. award, 1995, 97, Retrospective award, 1996, Theodore Sturgeon award (story), 1995, Locus Readers award (novel), 1973, (story) 1984, 95, 2002, 03, (collection) 1996, (novel and story) 2001, 02, Prix Lectures-Jeunesse award, 1987, Bumbershoot Arts award, Seattle, 1998, Lifetime Achievement award Robert Kirsch/L.A. Times, 2000, Lifetime Achievement award Pacific NW Booksellers Assn., 2001, Endeavor award, 2001, 2003, Willamette Writers Lifetime Achievement award, 2002, PEN/Malamud award for short fiction, 2002, World Fantasy award, 2002, Grandmaster SWFA, 2003, Margaret A. Edwards Award for lifetime contbn. in writing for young adults, 2004; Arbuthnot lectr. ALA, 2004. Mem. NARAL, Amnesty Internet. USA, Environ. Def. Fund, Nat. Resources Def. CTEE, Planned Parenthood Fedn. of Amer., Oreg. Nature Conservancy, Sci. Fiction Research Assn., Sci. Fiction Writers Assn. (Grand Master 2003), Authors League, PEN, Writers Guild West, Phi Beta Kappa. Office: care Virginia Kidd Lit Agy PO Box 278 Milford PA 18337-0278 also: c/o William Contandi 244 Madison Ave #E1 New York NY 10016-4702

LEGUIZAMÖ, JOHN, actor, comedian; b. Bogota, Columbia, July 22, 1964; s. Alberto and Luz Leguizamo; m. Yelba Osorio, Sept. 1994 (div. Nov. 1996); m. Justine Mauer, July 5, 2003; children: Allegra Sky, Ryder Lee. Studied, Sylvia Leigh's Showcase Theater, NY, Lee Strasberg Inst., HB Studio; studied Theater, NYU. Movies include Mixed Blood, 1985, The Burning Question, 1988, Casualties of War, 1989, Street Hunter, 1990, Gentille alouette, 1990, Revenge, 1990, Die Hard 2, 1990, Poison, 1991, Hangin' with the Homeboys, 1991, Out for Justice, 1991, Regarding Henry, 1991, Time Expired, 1992, Whispers in the Dark, 1992, Night Owl, 1993, Super Mario Bros., 1993, Carlito's Way, 1993, A Pyromaniac's Love Story, 1995, To Wong Foo, Thanks for Everything, Julie Newmar, 1995, Executive Decision, 1996, The Fan, 1996, Romeo & Juliet, 1996, The Pest, 1996 (also co-prodr.), A Brother's Kiss, 1997, Spawn, 1997, Frogs for Snakes, 1998, Body Count, 1998, Doctor Doolittle (voice), 1998, Joe the King, 1999 (also exec. prodr.), Summer of Sam, 1999, Titan A.E. (voice), 2000, Moulin Rouge!, 2001, What's the Worst That Could Happen?, 2001, King of the Jungle, 2001, Empire, 2002 (also co-prodr.), Zigzag, 2002, Ice Age (voice), 2002, Spun, 2002, Sueño, 2004, Crónicas, 2004, The Alibi, 2005, Assault on Precinct 13, 2005, The Honeymooners, 2005, Land of the Dead, 2005; (video) Rayman 3: Hoodlum Havoc (voice), 2003; (TV films) Words in Your Face, 1991, N.Y.P.D. Mounted, 1991, Arabian Nights, 2000, Point of Origin, 2002, Undefeated, 2003, (also exec. prodr., dir., writer); (TV series) House of Buggin, 1995 (also writer, prodr.), The Brothers Garcia (voice), 2000, ER, 2005-; (music video for Madonna) Borderline, 1984, Madonna: The Immaculate Collection, 1990; co-exec. prodr. Piñero, 2001; exec. prodr. Nuyorican Dream, 1999; writer (one person show) Freak: A Semi-Demi-Quasi-Autobiographical Comedy, 1997 (Tony award nomination), John Leguizamo LIVE, Sexaholix...A Love Story, 2001 (also prodr.); writer (TV film) Mambo Mouth, 1991, Spic-O-Rama, 1993; guest appearances include Miami Vice, 1986, 1987, 1989 and several talk shows. Recipient OBIE award for Mambo Mouth, 1991, Tony award for play Freak, 1998, Entertainer of Yr. ALMA, 2002 Office: William Morris Agy 151 S El Camino Dr Beverly Hills CA 90212-2775*

LEGUM, JEFFREY ALFRED, holding company executive; b. Balt., Dec. 16, 1941; s. Leslie and Naomi (Hendler) L.; m. Harriet Cohn, Nov. 10, 1968; children: Laurie Hope, Michael Neil. BS in Econs., Wharton Sch. U. Pa., 1963; grad., Chevrolet Sch. Merchandising and Mgmt., 1966. With Park Circle Motor Co. DBA Pk. Cir. Investments, Balt., 1963—, exec. v.p., 1966—67, pres., 1977—, CEO, 1982—; pres. and dir. Legum Chevrolet-Nissan, 1977—89; ltd. ptnr. Pkwy. Indsl. Ctr., Dorsey, Md., 1965-91, Circle Ltd. Partnership, Glen Burnie, Md., 1991—99; v.p., dir. P.C. Parts Co., 1967—, pres., 1995—, One Forty Corp., Westminster, Md., 1972—97; pres. and CEO Westminster Motor Co., 1973—. Dir., exec. com. United Consol. Industries, 1970-73; dist. chmn. Chevrolet Dealers Coun., 1975-77; chmn. Washington zone, 1982-83. *The Park Circle Motor Company, DBA Park Circle Investments, is a holding company with interests in large locally based corporation, i.e., Legg Mason Inc., Mercantile Bankshares, Black & Decker, McCormick & Company, St. Paul Travelers (USF&G) and T. Rowe Price. In addition, Park Circle owned auto dealerships from 1921 until 1997.* Chmn. transp. divsn. Assoc. Jewish Charities, Balt., 1966—69; mem. investment com. Balt. Hebrew Congregation, 1980—99, bd. elecors, 1990—93; bd. dirs. Assoc. Placement Bur. (Jewish Vocat. Svc.), Balt., 1964—76, v.p., 1972—76; mem. adv. bd. The Competitive Edge, Albuquerque, 1977—81; mem. Md. Svc. Acad. Rev. Bd., 1975—77, Bus. Adv. Bd. to Atty. Gen., 1985—87; trustee Balt. Mus. Art, 1992—, fine arts accessions com., 1992—, chaired legal panel, 1996—99, investment com., 1992—, chair, 1996—98, chair fine arts accessions com., 2001—04, mem. exec. com., 1993; fin. com. Mus. Fine Arts, 1995—, contr., 1994—96, sec., treas., 1996—2001, sec., 2001—04; pres.'s com. U. Toronto, 1983—99, The Park Sch., Balt., 1979—94; chmn. investment com. The Park Sch. Balt., 1980—96, mem. exec. com., chmn. fin. com. and treas., 1981—91; treas. The Legum Found., 1967—; trustee, mem. fin. com. Johns Hopkins Med. Insts., 1997—; mem. inst. rev. bd. for human subjects rsch. Johns Hopkins Bayview Med. Ctr., 1992—98; mem. steering com. Govt. House Trust, 1996—2002; v.p. Preakness Celebration, Inc., 1988—89; sponsor endowment for Jeffrey and Harriet Legum professorship in acute neurol. medicine Johns Hopkins U.; adv. coun. Wilmer Eye Inst., The Johns Hopkins Hosp., 1991—. Recipient award of honor, Assn. Jewish Charities of Balt., 1967, 1968, Cadillac Master Dealer award, 1980—88, 1991, Cadillac Pinnacle of Excellence award, 1986, Young Pres.'s Orgn. Cert. Appreciation, 1984, Nissan Nat. Merit Master award, annually, 1979—89, Sales Giant award, Automotive News, 1987, Minute of Gratitude, The Park Sch. Bd. Trustees, 1994. Mem. Young Pres. Orgn. (pres.'s forum 1977-92), World Pres.' Orgn., Benjamin Franklin Assocs., Johns Hopkins Assocs., Md. Hist. Soc. (exec. com. Library of Md. History 1981-90), Suburban Club (Balt. County), U. Pa., Center Club. Home: 10 Stone Hollow Ct Baltimore MD 21208-1860 Office: 1829 Reisterstown Rd Baltimore MD 21208-6320

LEGVOLD, ROBERT, political science professor; b. Mpls., Feb. 26, 1940; s. Oscar and Hazel Legvold; m. Gloria Dee Welch, Mar. 17, 1940; children: Nancy Diane Rubbico, Nathan Cameron. BA, U. S.D., 1962, LLD (hon.); MA, Tufts U., 1962—67, MA in Law and Diplomacy, 1964, PhD, 1967. From asst. to assoc. prof. Tufts U., Medford, Mass., 1967—77; sr. fellow Coun. on Fgn. Rels., N.Y.C., 1979—84; from assoc. prof. to prof. Columbia U., N.Y.C., 1984—. Author: (book) Soviet Policy in West Africa; editor: Thinking Strategically: The Major Powers, Kazakhstan, and the Central Asian Nexus, Swords and Sustenance: The Economics of National Security in Belarus and Ukraine, Statehood and Security: Georgia After the Rose Revolution. Mem. and com. chair Tufts U. Bd. of Trustees, Medford, Mass., 1991—2001; mem. Carnegie Endowment for Internat. Peace, Washington, 1993—2005; mem. and com. chair Watson Inst., Brown U., Providence, 1998—2005; mem. Davis Ctr., Harvard U., Cambridge, Mass., 2000—05. Named one of 500 Most Influential People in U.S. in Field of Fgn. Policy, World Affairs Couns. of Am., 2004; recipient Disting. Svc. to Profession award, Tufts U., 1991. Mem.: AAAS, Internat. Inst. of Strategic Studies, Coun. on Fgn. Rels. Avocations: tennis, gardening, carpentry. Home: 11 Fenwick Rd Winchester MA 01890 Office: Columbia Univ New York NY 10027 Office Phone: 212-854-5426. Office Fax: 212-666-3481. Business E-Mail: rhl1@columbia.edu.

LEHANE, DENNIS, writer; b. Dorchester, Mass., Aug. 4, 1965; Author: A Drink Before the War, 1994, Darkness Take My Hand, 1996, Sacred, 1997, Gone, Baby, Gone, 1998, Prayers for Rain, 1999, Mystic River, 2001 (Anthony award, Barry award, Mass. Book award), Shutter Island, 2003. Office: c/o Ann Rittenberg Ste 708 1201 Broadway New York NY 10001

LEHISTE, ILSE, retired language educator; b. Tallinn, Estonia, Jan. 31, 1922; came to U.S., 1949, naturalized, 1956; d. Aleksander and Julie M. (Sikka) L. Dr.Phil., U. Hamburg (Ger.), 1948; PhD, U. Mich., 1959; D.Univ. (hon.), U. Essex (Eng.), 1977; Dr. Phil. (hon.), U. Lund (Sweden), 1982, U. Tartu, Estonia, 1989; LHD (hon.), Ohio State U., 1999. Lectr. U. Hamburg, 1948-49; assoc. prof. modern langs. Kans. Wesleyan U., 1950-51, Detroit Inst. Tech., 1951-56; rsch. assoc. U. Mich., 1957-63; faculty Ohio State U., Columbus, 1963-87, prof. linguistics, 1965-87, prof. emeritus, 1987—, chmn. dept., 1965-71, 85-87. Dir. Linguistic Inst. Ohio State U., 1970; vis. prof. U. Cologne, Germany, 1965, UCLA, 1966, U. Vienna, 1974, U. Tokyo, 1980, U. Graz, 2004. Author 18 books, including The Temporal Structure of Estonian Runic Songs (with Jaan Ross), 2001; contbr. articles to profl. jours., book revs. Recipient medal for sci. achievement, Internat. Speech Comm. Assn., 2002; fellow Ctr. for Advanced Study in Behavioral Scis., 1975—76; grantee Am. Coun. Learned Socs., 1971; Guggenheim fellow, 1969, 1975. Fellow: AAAS, Acoustical Soc. Am., Am. Acad. Arts and Scis.; mem.: MLA, Internat. Speech Comm. Assn., Finnish Acad. Scis. (fgn.), Societas Linguistica Europaea, Internat. Soc. Phonetic Scis., Linguistic Soc. Am. (exec. com. 1971—73, pres. 1980). Home: 985 Kennington Ave Columbus OH 43220-4018 E-mail: ilsele@ling.ohio-state.edu.

LEHMAN, ARNOLD LESTER, museum official, art historian; b. N.Y.C., July 18, 1944; s. Sidney and Henrietta F. L.; m. Pamela Gimbel, June 21, 1969; children— Nicholas Richard, Zachary Gimbel. BA, Johns Hopkins, 1965, MA, 1966, Yale U., 1968, PhD, 1973. Chester Dale fellow Met. Mus. Art, N.Y.C., 1969-70; lectr. art history Cooper Union and Hunter Coll., 1969-72; dir. Urban Improvements Program, N.Y.C., 1970-72, Parks Council of N.Y.C., 1972-74, Met. Mus. and Art Centers, Miami, Fla., 1974-79, Balt. Mus. Art, 1979-97, Bklyn. Mus. Art, 1997—. Adj. prof. dept. art history Johns Hopkins U., 1986-97; dir. or trustee several corps. and non-profit orgns. Author: The Architecture of Worlds Fairs 1900-1939, 1972, The New York Skyscraper: A History of its Development 1870-1939, 1974, various mus. catalogues; editor: Oskar Schlemmer, 1986; exhibitions include. Mem. Bklyn. Arts Coun.; trustee Am. Fedn. Arts, NY, several non-profit orgns.; mem. exec. planning com. The Bard Grad Ctr. for Studies in the Decorative Arts. Mem.: Assn. Art Mus. Dirs. (trustee 1987—93, pres. 1990—91). Office: Bklyn Mus Art 200 Eastern Pkwy Brooklyn NY 11238-6052

LEHMAN, DONALD RICHARD, physicist, educator, academic administrator; b. York, Pa., Dec. 13, 1940; s. Frederick Hinkle and Wilhelmina Emma (Ruesskamp) Lehman; m. Elyse Joan Brauch, Aug. 24, 1962. BA in Physics, Rutgers U., 1962; PhD in Theoretical Physics, George Washington U., 1970. NAS NRC postdoctoral rsch. assoc. Nat. Bur. Stds., Gaithersburg, Md., 1970-72; from asst. to assoc. prof. physics George Washington U., Washington, 1972-82, prof., 1982—2002, George Gamow prof. theoretical physics, 2003—, dep. chair physics, 1986-87, chair physics, 1987-93, dir. ctr. nuclear studies, 1990-93, assoc. v.p. rsch. and grad. studies, 1993-96, v.p. acad. affairs, 1996—2002, exec. v.p. acad. affairs, 2003—. Guest worker Nat. Bur. Stds., Gaithersburg, 1972—89, program analyst, 1974; vis. staff mem., collaborator Los Alamos (N.Mex.) Nat. Lab., 1973—2001; spkr. internat. confs. Contbr. articles to profl. jours. Grantee, Rsch. Corp., N.Y., 1974—76, Dept. Energy, Germantown, Md., 1979—98, NATO, Belgium, 1987—91. Fellow: Am. Phys. Soc.; mem.: Southeastern Univs. Rsch. Assn. (trustee 1993—, chair bd. trustees 2002—03, mem. exec. com. 1996—). Achievements include elucidation of the physics of the 3 body structure of 6Li; unraveling of the physics underlying the role of exact three body continuum states in the photodisintegration of 3He. Office: George Washington U Academic Affairs 2121 I St NW Washington DC 20037-2353 Office Phone: 202-994-6510.

LEHMAN, EDWARD WILLIAM, social studies educator, researcher; b. Regensburg, Germany, Feb. 7, 1936; arrived in US, 1939; s. William and Kate (Hoffman) Lehman; m. Ethna V O'Flannery, May 26, 1962; 1 child, Robert. BS, Fordham U., 1956, MA, 1959; PhD, Columbia U., 1966. Lectr. Fordham U., 1958-59; vis. research sociologist dept. psychiatry Montefiore Hosp., Bronx, N.Y., 1959-61; lectr. Sch. Nursing, Columbia U., N.Y.C., 1964-67; research sociologist Cornell U. Med. Coll., N.Y.C., 1961-67; asst. prof., then assoc. prof. sociology NYU, 1967-78; prof., 1978—; chmn. dept., 1978-84, 93-96. Assoc dir Ctr Policy Research, New York, NY, 1976—85, sr research assoc, 1969—89; mem minority adv comt NY State Dept Mental Hygiene, 1981—90. Author: (book) Coordinating Health Care: Explorations in Interorganizational Relations, 1975, Political Society: A Macrosociology of Politics, 1977, The Viable Polity, 1992; editor (with others): A Sociological Reader in Complex Organizations, 1980, Autonomy and Order: A Communitarian Anthology, 2000. Served to capt U.S. Army, 1957. Mem.: Soc. for Advancement of SocioEcons., Am. Polit. Sci. Assn., Am. Sociol. Assn. Democrat. Roman Catholic. Home: Apt 8B 1 Washington Square Village New York NY 10012-1632 Office Phone: 212-998-8379. Business E-Mail: ewl1@nyu.edu.

LEHMAN, ELYSE BRAUCH, psychologist, educator; b. Apr. 5, 1942; BA with honors, Rutgers U., 1962; MA, George Washington U., 1967, PhD, 1970. Rsc. assoc. psychology George Washington U., 1970-72; cons. clin. investigations svc. devel. metabol. neurol. br. Nat. Inst. Neurol. Diseases and Stroke, 1972-75; from asst. prof. to assoc. prof. psychology George Mason U., Fairfax, Va., 1976-97, prof., 1997—. Adj. asst. prof. George Washington U., 1972—76. Vis. scholar, U. N.C., Chapel Hill, 1993. Office: George Mason U Dept Psychology (MSN-3F5) Fairfax VA 22030-4444 Office Phone: 703-993-1352. Business E-Mail: elehman@gmu.edu.

LEHMAN, I(SRAEL) ROBERT, biochemist, educator; b. Tauroggen, Lithuania, Oct. 5, 1924; arrived in U.S., 1927; s. Herman Bernard Lehman and Anne Kahn; m. Sandra Lee, July 5, 1959; children: Ellen, Deborah, Samuel. BA, Johns Hopkins U., 1950, PhD, 1954; MD (hon.), U. Gothenberg, Sweden, 1987; DSc, U. Paris, 1992. Asst. prof. Stanford (Calif.) U., 1959-62, assoc. prof., 1962-67, prof. biochemistry, 1967—, chmn. dept. biochemistry, 1974—79. Mem. sci. adv. bd. U.S. Biochem., Cleve., 1984-98, RPI Pharms., Boulder, Colo., 1991-96, Genetrol, Oakland, Calif., 1998-2003; cons. Abbott Labs, Chgo., 1990-94. Author: Principles of Biochemistry, 7th edit., 1984. Sgt. U.S. Army, 1943-46, ETO. Recipient Merck award Am. Soc. Biochemistry and Molecular Biology, 1994. Fellow: Am. Acad. Arts and Scis.; mem.: Am. Soc. Biochemistry and Molecular Biology (pres. 1995), Nat. Acad. Scis. Democrat. Jewish. Office: Sch of Medicine Stanford U Stanford CA 94305

LEHMAN, J. LEE, writer, consultant, astrologer; b. Wakefield, Nebr., Sept. 9, 1953; d. Alan D. and Katheryn E. (Kennedy) L. BS, U. Wis., Green Bay, 1972; MS, Rutgers U., 1974, PhD, 1979. Post doctoral Pub. Health Rsch. Inst., N.Y.C., 1978-81; pvt. practice N.Y.C., San Francisco, 1981—. Cons. Nat. Council Geocosmic Rsch., Mass., 1986-98, United Astrological Congress, Calif., 1990—. Author: The Ultimate Asteroid Book, 1988, Essential Dignities, 1989, The Book of Rulerships, 1992, Classical Astrology for Modern Living, 1996, Martial ARt of Honory Astrology, 2002; mem. editl. bd. Culture & Cosmos, Bristol, England, 1996—. Recipient Marc Edmund Jones award Marc Edmund Jones Trust, 1995. Mem. Internat. Soc. Astrological Rsch., Astrological Assn. Great Britain, Fedn. Australian Astrologers. Office: Lehman Associates PO Box 501107 Malabar FL 32950-1107

LEHMAN, JEFFREY ALAN, music educator; b. Freeport, Ill., Dec. 30, 1956; s. Merlyn Robert and Eleanor Jane Lehman; m. Martha Ann Gastel, July 19, 1986; children: Kara Jane, Kelsey Jean, Katie Marie. B in Music Edn., Morningside Coll., 1978; MA in Music Edn., U. Iowa, 1985. Cert. K-12 tchr. Ill. Choir dir. Shenandoah H.S., 1979—81; dir. choral music Freeport (Ill.) H.S., 1981—. Home: 1113 S Stewart Ave Freeport IL 61032 Office: Freeport High Sch 701 W Moseley St Freeport IL 61032

LEHMAN, JEFFREY SEAN, former academic administrator; b. Bronxville, NY, Aug. 1, 1956; s. Leonard and Imogene (McAuliffe) L.; m. Kathy Okun; children: Rebecca Colleen, Jacob Keegan, Benjamin Emil. AB, Cornell U., 1977; M of Pub. Policy, U. M of Pub. Policy, JD, U. Mich., 1981. Bar: DC 1983, US Ct. Appeals (fed. cir.) 1984, US Ct. Appeals (D.C. cir.) 1987, US Supreme Ct. 1987. Law clk. to chief judge US Ct. Appeals (1st cir.), Portland, Maine, 1981-82; law clk. to assoc. justice US Supreme Ct., Washington, 1982-83; assoc. Caplin & Drysdale, Chartered, Washington, 1983-87; asst. prof. U. Mich. Law Sch., Ann Arbor, 1987-92, prof., 1992-93, prof. law and pub. policy, 1993—2003, dean, 1994—2003; pres. Cornell U., Ithaca, NY, 2003—05; sr. scholar Woodrow Wilson Internat. Ctr. for Scholars, Washington, 2005—. Vis. prof. Yale U., 1993, U. Paris II, 1994. Co-author: Corporate Income Taxation, 1994; editor-in-chief: Mich. Law Rev., 1979-80. Trustee Skadden Fellowship Found., 1995-. Mem. Am. Law Inst., Order of Coif.

LEHMAN, JOAN ALICE, real estate executive; b. Jamaica Queens, N.Y., May 8, 1938; d. Hans Newman and Margot (Deutsch) Senen; m. Eugene Lehman, June 17, 1956 (div. Mar. 1990); children: Joel, Peter, Alan, Ira, Helen Ann, Helen Beth, Robert, Jacqueline, John, Steven, Robin, Elizabeth, Jody, Lisa, David, Andy, Jeremy, Jay. AA, Nassau C.C., East Meadow, N.Y., 1971; BS, Nova U., 1982. Lic. real estate broker, Fla. Owner Joan Lehman Real Estate Mgmt. Co., Old Bethpage, N.Y., 1961-82; tchr. Broward County Schs., Ft. Lauderdale, Fla., 1982-86; owner Joan Lehman Real Estate, Pompano Beach, Fla., 1986—; pres. Jo Al 1 Inc., Pompano Beach. Mem. Sunset Sch. Adv. Bd., Ft. Lauderdale, 1994-96; pres. The Pointe Condo Assn., 2001—; bd. dirs. Property Owners Ctrl. Lauderhill, Fla., 1996; den mother Boy Scouts Am., Old Bethpage, N.Y.; leader Girl Scouts U.S., Old Bethpage. Avocations: bowling, travel, theater.

LEHMAN, JOHN F., JR., manufacturing executive; b. Phila., Sept. 14, 1942; s. John F. and Constance (Cruice) L.; m. Barbara Wieland, 1975; children: John F., Alexandra, Grace. BS in Internat. Rels., St. Joseph's Coll., 1964; BA in Law with honors, MA in Internat. Law and Diplomacy, Cambridge U., 1967; PhD in Internat. Rels., U. Pa., 1974. Sr. staff mem. Nat. Security Council, 1969-74; dep. dir. U.S. Arms Control and Disarmament Agy., 1975-77; pres. Abingdon Corp., 1977-81; sec. USN US Dept. Def., Washington, 1981-87; mng. dir. Paine Webber, 1988-91; chmn. J.F. Lehman & Co., N.Y.C., 1991—, OAOT Corp., 2001—. Bd. dirs. Ball Corp., ISO, Inc.; commr. The Nat. Commn. on Terrorist Attacks Upon the U.S. (The 9-11 Commn.), 2002—04. Author: Command of the Seas, 1989, Making War: The 200-Year Old Battle Between Over the President and Congress Over How America Goes to War, 1992, On Seas of Glory: Heroic Men, Great Ships and Epic Battles of the Great American Navy, 2001. Capt. USNR, 1968—93.

LEHMAN, LARRY L., retired state supreme court justice; Judge Wyo. County Ct., 1985-88, Wyo. Dist. Ct. (2nd dist.), 1988-94; chief justice Wyo. Supreme Ct., Cheyenne, 1998—2002, justice, 1994—2005.

LEHMAN, LAWRENCE HERBERT, consulting engineering executive; b. N.Y.C., Apr. 30, 1929; s. Samuel and Shirley (Freiberg) L.; m. Susan E. Green, June 29, 1957; children: Scott Jeffrey, Christopher Adam. BCE, NYU, 1949; MBA, Iona Coll., 1978. Registered profl. engr., N.Y., N.J., Ky., Ill., Mass., Conn., Ind., Pa., Md., Fla. Project engr. Andrews & Clark (Cons. Engrs.), N.Y.C., 1951-57; project mgr. Barstow, Mulligan & Vollmer (Cons. Engrs.), N.Y.C., 1957-59; chief engr., ptnr. Vollmer Assos. (Cons. Engrs.), N.Y.C., 1959-67; chief exec. officer, dir. Berger, Lehman Assos. (P.C.), Rye, N.Y., 1967—. Recipient Third award U.S. Steel Corp., 1966, Bridge award Pre-stressed Concrete Inst., 1975, Honor award Nat. ACEC, 1995, nat. awards USDOT, 2000, Am. Cons. Engrs. Coun., 2000, others. Fellow ASCE (life); mem. NSPE, Am. Cons. Engrs. Coun., Soc. Am. Mil. Engrs., Transp. Rsch. Bd., Am. Ry. Engring. Assn., Internat. Assn. Bridge and Structural Engrs., Inst. Transp. Engrs., Am. Arbitration Assn. (nat. panel arbitrators), N.Y. Assn. Cons. Engrs. (Engring. Excellence awards 1975, 79, 90, 95), Conn. Engrs. in Pvt. Practice, West County Profl. Engrs. Soc. (Engr. of Yr. award 1991), The Moles. Home: 10 Chester Dr Rye NY 10580-2204 Office: 411 Theodore Fremd Ave Rye NY 10580-1410 Office Phone: 914-967-5800. E-mail: blalehman@aol.com.

LEHMAN, LEONARD, retired lawyer, consultant; b. Bklyn., July 5, 1927; s. Samuel and Marcy (Dolgenas) Lehman; m. Imogene McAuliffe, June 11, 1954; children: Jeffrey, Toby, Amy, Zachary. BA, Cornell U., 1949; JD, Yale U., 1952. Bar: N.Y. 1953, U.S. Supreme Ct. 1969, D.C. 1979, U.S. Ct. Internat. Trade 1981, U.S. Ct. Appeals (fed. cir.) 1982. Atty.-advisor U.S. Tax Ct., Washington, 1952—55; practice N.Y.C., 1955—63; sr. counsel Office Tax Legis. Counsel, U.S. Dept. Treasury, Washington, 1963—65; asst. to chief counsel U.S. Customs Svc., 1965—67, dep. chief counsel, 1968—71, asst. commr., 1971—79; ptnr. Barnes, Richardson and Colburn, N.Y.C., Washington and Chgo., 1979—89, counsel, 1989—95; mem. industry functional adv. com. on customs/trade policy U.S. Dept. Commerce, 1989—95. Contbr. articles to profl. jours. Recipient Meritorious Svc. award, U.S. Dept. Treasury, 1971, Exceptional Svc. award, 1979, U.S. Customs Honor award, 1977. Mem.: ABA (standing com. on customs law 1974—80, chmn. 1980, customs and tariff com., adminstrv. law sect. 1971—88, vice chmn. 1981—83, chmn. 1984—88), Phi Kappa Phi, Phi Beta Kappa. Home and Office: 18 Rich Branch Ct North Potomac MD 20878-2461

LEHMAN, MARK E., lawyer; b. Bklyn., Mar. 14, 1951; s. Edward Berton and Aileen Sally (Tarrow) L.; m. Diane Carol Goller, Aug. 15, 1976; children: David, Abigail. BA, Columbia Coll., 1973; JD, NYU, 1976. Bar: N.Y. 1977, U.S. Dist. Ct. (so. dist.) N.Y. 1977. Litigation atty. Merrill Lynch, Pierce, Fenner & Smith, Inc., N.Y.C., 1976-79; gen. coun. Bear Stearns & Co. Inc., N.Y.C., 1986—2004, spl. advisor to c.e.o., 2004—. Arbitrator Am. Stock Exchange, Nat. Assn. Securities Dealers. Mem. Securities Industry Assn., Future Industry Assn. Office: 245 Park Ave New York NY 10167-0002

LEHMANN, CORINNE E., medical educator; d. Terry W. and Hannah Lehmann; 1 child, Miro Calderas. BS in Chemistry, Ohio State U., 1988; MS in Chemistry, Yale U., 1989; MD, U. Cin., 1993, MEd, 2005. Intern, resident internal medicine, pediat. U. Cin., 1993—97; physician West Suburban Hosp., Oak Park, Ill., 1998—2000; asst. prof. dept. internal medicine, pediat. U. Cin., 2000—04; dir. resident edn. divsn. adolescent medicine Cin. Children's Hosp., 2002—. Mem. admissions com. U. Cin., Coll. Medicine, 2003—04; fellow adolescent medicine Cin. Children's Hosp. Med. Ctr., 2000—02. Grantee, U. Cin., 2003, 2004. Fellow: Am. Acad. Pediat.; mem.: Ohio Med. Pediat. Assn., Am. Coll. Physicians, Soc. Adolescent Medicine (sec., treas. 2004). Avocations: tennis, music, art. Office: Cin Childrens Hosp Med Ctr Divsn Adolescent Medicine 3333 Burnet Ave ML 4000 Cincinnati OH 45229 also: U Pediat Internal Medicine Assoc 234 Goodman Ave ML 665X Cincinnati OH 45219 Office Phone: 513-636-6859. E-mail: corinne.lehmann@uc.edu.

LEHMANN, DORIS ELIZABETH, retired elementary school educator; b. Ramsey, NJ, Aug. 17, 1933; d. Alfred Harrison and Anna Elizabeth (Gerhold) Rockefeller; m. Victor S. Lehmann, June 25, 1955; children: Joanne E. Cathy Lynn, Victor A., Kristie Sue. BS in Edn. magna cum laude, Wagner Coll., 1955; student in edn., Columbia U., summers 1988-91, Jersey City State, 1990—, William Paterson, 1971. Elem. tchr. Sch. St. Sch., Ramsey, 1955-56; bedside instr. N. Bergen County schs., NJ, 1966-71; elem. tchr. Edith A. Bogert Sch., Upper Saddle River, NJ, 1971-2000; ret., 2000. Author numerous poems; author: (with others) Curriculum for Values Education in New Jersey, 1991. Indian cons. Bergen County Mus. Art Sci., Paramus, NJ, 1983—. Recipient Fellowship Life award Luth. Layman's Movement, 1955. Fellow Upper Saddle River Edn. Assn. (social sec. 1972-73, v.p. 1974-75, 84-85, liaison to USR hist. soc. 1986—) NJ Edn. Assn., NJ North Edn. Assn., VFW Aux. (historian, sr. v.p. 2000-05), Alpha Omicron Pi (life, treas. 1954, v.p. 1955). Republican. Lutheran. Personal E-mail: vlcco@aol.com.

LEHMANN, (A) SPENCER, retired chemist, retired chemical engineer; b. L.A., Sept. 23, 1916; s. Aldo Mayer and Elsie Thompson Lehmann; m. Rosalie Belle Lowther, Dec. 28, 1943; children: Lawrence Spencer, Bruce Aldo. AB, Stanford U., 1938; PhD, Brown U., 1941. Registered profl. chem. engr. Rsch. chemist, engr. Naval Rsch. Lab, Washington, 1941—42, Tenn. Eastman Co., Oak Ridge, Tenn., 1942—46; rsch. chemist, gen. mgr. Shell Oil, Houston, 1946—76. Dir. Fallbrook Pub. Utility Dist., 1983—96; exec. bd., dir. Joint Powers Ins. Authority, Sacramento, 1986—96. Chair-water supply and distbn. Houston C. of C., 1972—75; dir. Houston/Galveston Subsidence Dist, 1973—76; bd. dirs., pres. San Diego Blood Bank Found., San Diego, 1986—98. Recipient Cert. Of Appreciation, Am. Petroleum Inst., 1967. Mem.: Am. Chem. Soc., Rotary Club of Fallbrook, Sigma Xi, Phi Beta Kappa.

LEHMANN, WILLIAM K., pilot; b. Washington, Nov. 11, 1960; s. W. Kemp and Katherine K. Lehmann; m. Cynthia Renee Hershberger. BS in Cartography, U. Md., College Park, 1994. Cert. airline transport pilot FAA. Firefighter, emergency vehicle driver Balt. Fire Dept., 1982—90, fire lt., 1990—91; contract tng. mgr. Comair Aviation Acad., Sanford, Fla., 1996—98; pilot Continental Express, Houston, 1998—2000; asst. chief pilot ExpressJet Airlines, Newark, 2000—. Vol. firefighter, fire officer Berwyn Heights (Md.) Vol. Fire Dept., 1992—96. Recipient Exemplary Performance award, Balt. Fire Dept., 1991. Mem.: AIAA (chair subcom. air traffic mgmt. program com. 2001—05). Avocations: running/fitness, golf, travel, photography. Home: 1040 Johnston Dr Bethlehem PA 18017 Office: ExpressJet Airlines Terminal C Newark Liberty Internat Airport Newark NJ 07114 Office Phone: 973-681-0053. Personal E-mail: cfihammer@aol.com. E-mail: blehma@coair.com.

LEHMANN, WILLIAM LEONARDO, electrical engineer, educator; b. Milw., Dec. 17, 1924; s. William Christian and Johanna Alma (Schrumpf) L.; m. Barbara Taylor, June 29, 1948; children: Johanna, William, Katherine, Wendy, Christianne. AB, Haverford (Pa.) Coll., 1944; MS, Syracuse (N.Y.) U., 1948, PhD, 1953. Registered profl. engr., Ohio. Prof. physics acting dean Air Force Inst. Tech., 1951-66; lectr. Ohio State U., 1957-60; dep. for labs. Office Asst. Sec. Air Force Research and Devel., 1966-74; dir. Air Force Office Sci. Research, 1974-78, Air Force Weapons Lab., Kirtland AFB, N.Mex., 1978-81; chief scientist Combat Devel. Experimentation Ctr. U.S. Army Sci. Support Lab, Ft. Ord, Calif., 1982-85; sr. sci. analyst N.Mex. Engring. Research Inst., 1985-93; prof. elec. engring. U. N.Mex., Albuquerque, 1988-93; sr. assoc. Ctr. for Occupational R & D, 1993—. Vis. prof. U. N.Mex., 1981-82, also adv. bd. Coll. Engring.; Past mem. Gov. N.Mex. Tech. Excellence Com.; mem. USAF Scientific Adv. Bd., 1985-92. Patentee solar orientation device. Mem. Beaver Creek (Ohio) Sch. Dist. Bd., 1965-66; trustee Lovelace Med. Found. Served with AUS, 1944-45. Recipient Air Force Exceptional Civilian Service medal with three oak leaf cluster, 1981, Ohio Engr.'s award, 1966, award Ohio Soc. Profl. Engrs., 1965 Fellow AAAS; mem. Air Force Assn. (citation honor 1978), Am. Soc. Engring. Edn., AIAA, Am. Def. Preparedness Assn., Sigma Xi, Sigma Pi Sigma, Tau Beta Pi. Lodges: Rotary. Republican. Episcopalian. Home: 700 Island Retreat Rd Port Aransas TX 78373-6012 Office: Port Aransas High Sch PO Box 1297 Port Aransas TX 78373-1297 Office Phone: 361-749-7136. E-mail: bblehmann@aol.com.

LEHMANN-HAUPT, CHRISTOPHER CHARLES HERBERT, book reviewer; b. Edinburgh, Scotland, June 14, 1934; came to U.S., 1934; s. Hellmut Otto Emil and Letitia Jane H. (Grierson) Lehmann-H.; m. Natalie Robins, Oct. 3, 1965; children: Rachel Louise, Noah Christopher. BA, Swarthmore Coll., 1956; M.F.A., Yale U., 1959. Editor A.S. Barnes & Co., Inc., N.Y.C., 1961-62, Holt, Rinehart & Winston, 1962-63; sr. editor Dial Press, 1963-65; mem. staff N.Y. Times Book Review, 1965-69; sr. daily book reviewer N.Y. Times, 1969-95, daily book reviewer, 1995-2000, chief obituary writer, 2000—. Asst. prof. lit. CUNY, 1973-75 Author: Me and Di Maggio, 1986, A Crooked Man, 1995, The Mad Cook of Pymatuning, 2005. Mem.: Century. Office: New York Times 229 W 43rd St New York NY 10036-3959 Office Phone: 212-556-1706. Business E-Mail: clhaupt@nytimes.com.

LEHMBECK, JOHN PIERCE, journalist, writer; b. Pinehurst, Ga., Nov. 26, 1936; s. John Wesley Sullivan and Jewell Ellen Powell, Norman Gene Lehmbeck (Stepfather); m. Karen Barbara Armel, June 18, 1998; m. Nancy Jane Voss, June 12, 1959 (div. Nov. 26, 1980); children: Cynthia Lynne, John Pierce Jr., Michael Sean. BS in Journalism, Fla. State U., 1958. Newsman The AP, 1955—76, chief bur. Albany, NY, 1968—72, N.Y.C., 1972—76; account exec. Hill & Knowlton Inc., N.Y.C., 1976—77; bus. svcs. ombudsman N.Y. State Dept. Commerce, Albany, 1977—79, dir. state info., 1980; editor Fin. News & Daily Record, Jacksonville, Fla., 1980—84; mng. editor Clay TODAY, Orange Park, 1986—88; reporter, columnist St. Augustine Record, 1994—98; pres. Media Lehmbeck, Jacksonville, 1998—2002, O'Sullivan Gold, 2002—. Bd. mem. Journalism Adv. Bd., St. Bonaventure U., Olean, NY, 1968—72; supervising dir. NYC Election Svc., 1972—76. Author: (novels) Sullivan Road, 2004. Served with US Army N.G., 1959—76. Recipient Gold Key Scholastic and Leadership Soc., Fla. State U., 1958, Outstanding Contbn. Journalism, for creation of Empire Audio, NY State Broadcasters Assn., 1971—72, Outstanding Contributions Journalism, Morrisville State U., 1972, Outstanding Contributions Broadcast Journalism, NY State AP Broadcasters Assn., 1972; Grantland Rice Meml. scholar, Fla. State U., 1958. Independent. Avocations: post-graduate study, special education, reading, writing, sports. Home and Office: O'Sulllivan Gold 8767 Como Lake Dr Jacksonville FL 32256 Office Phone: 904-620-8643. Personal E-mail: plehmbeck@hotmail.com.

LEHMBERG, ROBERT HENRY, research physicist; b. Phila., Dec. 4, 1937; s. Henry and Marguerite Elenore (Schock) L.; m. Norma Geder, Dec. 29, 1966; 1 child, Karl Robert. BSc, Pa. State U., 1959; MSc, U. Ariz., 1961; PhD, Brandeis U., 1968. Rsch. physicist Naval Air Devel. Ctr., Warminster, Pa., 1966-72, Naval Rsch. Lab., Washington, 1972—. Chmn. program com. Conf. on Lasers and Electro-Optics, Washington, 1991. Contbr. articles to profl. jours.; patentee in field. Recipient E.O. Hulbert Ann. Sci. award Naval Rsch. Lab., 1997. Fellow Am. Phys. Soc. (Excellence in Plasma Physics Rsch. award 1993); mem. IEEE, Sigma Xi. Achievements include development of optical beam smoothing techniques for laser fusion, optical design of the Naval Research Laboratory's Nike laser facility, and research in nonlinear optics, excimer laser physics and laser-plasma interaction physics. Office: Naval Rsch Lab Plasma Divsn 4555 Overlook Ave SW Washington DC 20375-0001 E-mail: lehmberg@this.nrl.navy.mil.

LEHMBERG, STANFORD EUGENE, historian, educator; b. McPherson, Kans., Sept. 23, 1931; s. Willard Eugene and Helen (Stanford) L.; m. Phyllis Barton, July 23, 1962; 1 son, Derek Grantham. BA, U. Kans., 1953, MA, 1954; PhD, Cambridge (Eng.) U., 1956, DLitt, 1990. Mem. faculty U. Tex., Austin, 1956-69; mem. faculty U. Minn., 1969-98, prof. history, 1967-98, chmn. dept., 1979-85. Author: Sir Thomas Elyot, Tudor Humanist, 1960, Sir Walter Mildmay and Tudor Government, 1966, The Reformation Parliament, 1970, The Later Parliaments of Henry VIII, 1977, The Reformation of Cathedrals, 1988, The People of the British Isles to 1688, 1991, 2d edit., 2001, Cathedrals Under Siege, 1996, (with Ann M. Pflaum) The University of Minnesota, 1945-2000, 2001, Holy Faith of Santa Fe, 2004, English Cathedrals: A History, 2005; also articles, revs. Fulbright scholar, 1954—56, Guggenheim fellow, 1965—66, 1985—86. Fellow Royal Hist. Soc., Soc. of Antiquaries; mem. Am. Hist. Assn., Midwest Conf. Brit. Studies (pres. 1982-84), Renaissance Soc. Am., Am. Soc. Reformation Research. Episcopalian. Home: 1005 Calle Largo Santa Fe NM 87501-1068 Personal E-mail: lehmberg@earthlink.net.

LEHMKUHL, LYNN, publishing executive; m. David Lehmkuhl; 1 child, Mia. Various sales and mktg. positions Newsweek; pub. Disney Adventures mag., 1990—93; v.p., pub. Nickelodeon mag. Nickelodeon Online, 1993—96; v.p., group pub. Kids Mag. Divsn. The Walt Disney Co., 1996—98; pres., Youth Pub. Peterson's Pub., 1998—2002; pres. Teen Magazine, LA, 1998—2002; v.p. corp. sponsorship Sesame Workshop, NYC, 2002; pub., v.p. Ladies Home Jour., 2002—04; pub. Yoga Jour., NY, 2004—. Yoga practitioner and a certified yoga teacher. Office: Yoga Journal 2054 University Ave Berkeley CA 94704 Office Phone: 510-841-9200. Office Fax: 510-644-3101. E-mail: lynn.lehmkuhl@meredith.com.

LEHN, JEAN-MARIE PIERRE, chemistry professor; b. Rosheim, Bas-Rhin, France, Sept. 30, 1939; s. Pierre and Marie (Salomon) Lehn; m. Sylvie Lederer, 1965; 2 children. Grad., U. Strasbourg, France, 1960, PhD, 1963; PhD (hon.), U. Jerusalem, 1984, U. Autonoma, Madrid, 1985, U. Göttingen, 1987, U. Brussels, 1987, U. Herakliou, Greece, 1989, U. Bologna, 1989, Charles U., Prague, 1990, U. Twente, 1991, U. Sheffield, 1991, U. Athens, 1992, U. Polytech. Athens, 1992, Poly. U. Bucharest, 1994, Ill. Wesleyan U., 1995, U. Montreal, 1995, Bielefeld U., 1998, USTC, Hefei, 1998, Southeast U., Nanjing, 1998, Weizmann Inst., Rehovoth, 1998; DSc (hon.), U. Brussels, 1999, U. Nagoya, 2000, U. Sherbrooke, 2000, U. Trieste, 2001, Jiao Tong U., Shanghai, 2003, Nanjing U., 2003, KTH, 2003, U. St. Andrews, 2004. Various positions Nat. Ctr. Sci. Rsch., France, 1960—66; postdoctoral rsch. assoc. Harvard U., Cambridge, Mass., 1963—64; asst. prof. U. Strasbourg, France, 1966—69; assoc. prof. U. Louis Pasteur of Strasbourg, 1970, prof. of chemistry, 1970—79; prof. Coll. France, Paris, 1979—. Vis. prof. chemistry Harvard U., 1972—74, E.T.H., Zurich, Switzerland, Cambridge (Eng.) U., 1984, Barcelona (Spain) U., 1985, Fankfurt (Germany) U., 1985—86; Heinrich-Hertz Gast prof. Karlsruhe U., 1989; Woodward vis. prof. Harvard U., Cambridge, Mass., 1997; Newton-Abraham vis. prof. Oxford U., 1999—2000. Contbr. articles to sci. publs. Decorated commandeur Légion d'Honneur, officer Order Nat. du Mérite, Ordre pour le Mérite for Scis. and Arts, Austrian Cross of Honor for Sci. and Art, First Class; recipient Bronze, Silver and Gold medals, Ctr. Nat. Sci. Rsch. (CNRS), Pontifical Acad. Sci., 1981, Swiss Chem. Soc., 1982, von Humboldt prize, 1983, Nobel prize for chemistry, 1987, Karl-Ziegler prize, 1989, Bonner Chemiepreis, 1993, Ettore Majorana-Erice-Sci. for Peace prize, 1994, Gold medal, Soc. Acad. Arts, Scis., Lettres, 1995, Davy medal, Royal Soc., 1997, Lavoisier medal, SFC, 1997, A.R. Day award, 1998, others. Mem.: Chinese Acad. Scis., Acad. Bibliotheca Alexandrinae (pres.), Slovenian Acad. Arts and Scis., Hungarian Acad. Scis., Russian Acad. Scis., Royal Irish Acad., Acad. Scis. Torino, Pontifical Acad. Scis., Third World Acad. Scis., The Czech Learned Soc., Korean Acad. Sci. and Tech., Royal Soc., Acad. Roumaine, Inst. Grand Ducal (Luxembourg), Acad. Scis. Ukraine, Acad. Arts and Scis. P.R., Royal Acad. Scis., Letters and Fine Arts (Belgium), Polish Acad. Scis., Indian Acad. Scis., Yugoslav Acad. Arts and Scis. Zagreb, Acad. Wissenschaften, Acad. Wissenschaften Literatur-Mainz, Acad. Europaea, Am. Philos. Soc. (Phila., fgn. mem.), Royal Netherlands Acad., Acad. Nazionale dei Lincei, Deutsche Acad. der Naturforscher Leopoldina, Inst. de France, AAAS (fgn.) (hon.), NAS (fgn.) (assoc.). Home: 6 rue des Pontonniers 67000 Strasbourg France Office: Coll France 11 pl Marcelin Berthelot 75005 Paris France also: ISIS U Louis Pasteur 8 allee Gaspard Monge 67000 Strasbourg France

LEHNER-QUAM, ALISON LYNN, library administrator; b. Oak Harbor, Wash., Apr. 25, 1960; d. Paul Elias and Johanna Marie (Vinson) Q.; m. Matthias Karl-Eugen Lehner, Oct. 3, 1997; 1 child, Peter Elias Bernhard Lehner. BA, U. Wash., 1983; cert. tech. theater, Yale U., 1985; MS in Libr. Sci., Columbia U., 1991. Freelance costumer various prodns., N.Y.C., 1984-90; cataloging asst. Fashion Inst. of Tech., N.Y.C., 1986-91; intern Bank St. Sch., N.Y.C., 1991; asst. dir. Columbia Children's Lit. Inst., N.Y.C., 1990; libr. dir. Lincoln Ctr. Inst., N.Y.C., 1991—. Project dir. Arts Edn. Reference Window on the Work, 1992—. Pub. mgr.: (periodical) The Institute View, 1996—, website mgr. www.lcinstitute.org, 2000—; resource round-up editor Teaching Artist Jour., 2002-2003. Vol. mgr. Lincoln Ctr. Inst., N.Y.C., 1995-2001. Recipient Dirs.' Emeriti award Lincoln Ctr. for Performing Arts, 1997; scholar Sch. Libr. Svcs., Columbia U., 1989, 90. Mem. ALA, N.Y. Arts in Edn. Roundtable (steering com. 1995-98), Theater Libr. Assn., Beta Phi Mu (bd. dirs. Theta chpt. 1997-2004, v.p. 1994-96). Avocations: reading, the arts. E-mail: alquam@lincolncenter.org.

LEHOCZKY, JOHN PAUL, statistics educator; b. Columbus, Ohio, June 29, 1943; s. Paul Nicholas and Thelma Marie (Heisterkamp) L.; m. Mary Louise Zimmerman, Sept. 10, 1966; children: Jennifer Lynne, Jessica Augusta. BA, Oberlin Coll., 1965; MS, Stanford U., 1967, PhD, 1969. Asst. prof. stats. Carnegie Mellon U., Pitts., 1969-73, assoc. prof., 1973-81, prof., 1981-96, head dept., 1984-95, Thomas Lord prof. stats., 1997—, dean humanities & social scis., 2000—; assoc. editor IEEE Transactions on Computers, 1995-98. Cons. in field. Dept. editor Mgmt. Sci., 1981-86; assoc. editor Jour. Real-Time Systems, 1989—; contbr. over 100 rsch. papers in various diciplines. Fellow INFORMS, Am. Statis. Assn. (statistician of yr. Pitts. chpt. 1987), Inst. Math. Stats.; mem. IEEE, AAAS, Assn. for Computing Machinery, Internat. Statis. Inst., Informs. Office: Carnegie Mellon Univ Dept Stats Pittsburgh PA 15213 Business E-Mail: jpl@stat.cmu.edu.

LEHR, DENNIS JAMES, lawyer; b. N.Y.C., Feb. 7, 1932; s. Irwin Allen and Teeny (Scofield) L.; m. Enid J. Auerbach, June 10, 1956; children—Austin Windsor, Bryant Paul, Amy Lynn BA, NYU, 1954, LLM, 1961; LLB, Yale U., 1957. Bar: N.Y. 1959, D.C. 1967. Atty. Allstate Ins. Co., N.Y.C., 1958-59; atty. Regional Office SEC, N.Y.C., 1959-61; assoc. Borden and Ball, N.Y.C., 1961-63; atty. Office Spl Counsel Investment Co. Act Matters SEC, Washington, 1963-64; assoc. chief counsel Office Comptroller Currency U.S. Treasury Dept., Washington, 1964-67; assoc. Hogan & Hartson, Washington, 1967-69, ptnr., 1969-94, of counsel, 1994—. Bd. advs. So. Meth. U. Grad. Sch. Banking; adj. prof. Georgetown Law Sch., 1964-68; legal adv. com. Nat. Ctr. on Fin. Svcs., U. Calif.; lectr. Practicing Law Inst.; adv. coun. Banking Law Inst.; pub. mem. Adminstrv. Conf. of the U.S. Bd. contbrs. Fin. Services Law Report. Contbr. articles to profl. jours. Mem. ABA (coun. mem. sect. bus. law, former chmn. com. on Long Range Issues Affecting Bus. Law Practice, former chmn., com. on devels. in investment svcs, chmn. standing com. on Gavel Awards.). Office: Hogan and Hartson 555 13th St NW Ste 800E Washington DC 20004-1161 Office Phone: 202-637-6560.

LEHR, JEFFREY MARVIN, immunologist, allergist; b. N.Y.C., Apr. 29, 1942; s. Arthur and Stella (Smellow) L.; m. Suzanne Kozak, June 10, 1946; children: Elisa, Alexandra, Vanessa, Ryan. BS, City Coll., Bklyn., 1963; MD, NYU, 1967. Intern, resident Beth Israel Hosp., N.Y.C., 1967-69; resident in allergy/immunology, internal medicine Roosevelt Hosp., N.Y.C., 1969-72; chief of allergy/immunology USAF, Wright Patterson AFB, Ohio, 1972-74; allergist, immunologist Monterey, Calif., 1974—. Chmn. Monterey Bay Ari Pollution Hearing Bd., 1982-95; v.p. Lyceum of Monterey, 1977-83. Fellow Am. Acad. Allergy/Immunology, Am. Coll. Allergy/Immunology, Am. Assn. Cert. Allergists; mem. Am. Lung Assn. (v.p. 1989-91), Monterey County Med. Soc. (pres. 1988-89). Avocations: tennis, jogging, golf, hiking, backpacking. Office: 798 Cass St Monterey CA 93940-2918 Office Phone: 831-649-4044. E-mail: jlehrmd@sbcglobal.net.

LEHR, MICHAEL L., lawyer; b. NYC, Mar. 8, 1948; s. Hanns and Friederike (Gross) L.; children: Jackson M., Samuel G., Genevieve E. BA, U. Pa., 1969; JD, Harvard U., 1973. Bar: Pa. 1973, U.S. Dist. Ct. (ea. dist.) Pa. 1973, U.S. Ct. Appeals (3d cir.) 1975, D.C. 1976, U.S. Ct. Appeals (D.C. cir.) 1977, U.S. Tax Ct. 1984. Assoc. Ballard Spahr Andrews & Ingersoll, Phila., 1973-74, 79-82; asst. spl. prosecutor Watergate Spl. Prosecution Office, Washington, 1974-76; asst. U.S. atty. U.S. Atty.'s Office, Washington, 1976-79; ptnr. Ballard Spahr Andrews & Ingersoll, 1982—; now mng. shareholder, co-chair nat. public fin. practice Greenberg Traurig, LLP, Phila. Dir. Pub. Interest Law Ctr. of Phila., 1992—. Office: Greenberg Traurig LLP Two Commerce Sq Ste 2700 2001 Market St Philadelphia PA 19103 Office Phone: 215-988-7800. Office Fax: 215-988-7801. Business E-Mail: lehrm@gtlaw.com.

LEHR, MIRA TAGER, artist; b. Bklyn., Sept. 22, 1936; d. Charles Tager and Pearl Goodstein; m. David Lehr, 1956 (dec. 1996); children: Alison Fryd, John, Elizabeth Matthews, Paul. Degree in art history, Vassar Coll., 1956. Artist Elaine Baker Gallery, Boca Raton, Fla., 2003, Flomenhaft Gallery, N.Y.C., NY, 2005. Co-founder, mem. Continuum Gallery, Miami, 1960—97. Numerous painting exhbns. Trustee Miami Dade County Art in Pub. Pl. Trust, 1993—98; chairperson Art in Pub. Places Com., Miami Beach, Fla., 1991—96. Recipient 1st Prize works on paper. nat. exhbn., U. Tex., 1986, Grumbacher award, Nat. Assn. Women Artists, 1993, Vasari Project, Miami Dade Pub. Libr., 2002. Home: 5215 Pinetree Dr Miami Beach FL 33140 Personal E-mail: mira@miralehr.com.

LEHRER, JAMES CHARLES, reporter, journalist; b. Wichita, Kans., May 19, 1934; s. Harry Frederick and Lois Catherine (Chapman) Lehrer; m. Kate Staples, June 4, 1960; children: Jamie, Lucy, Amanda. AA, Victoria Coll., 1954; BJ, U. Mo., 1956. Reporter Dallas Morning News, 1959—61; reporter, columnist, city editor Dallas Times Herald, 1961—70; exec. prodr., corr. Sta. KERA-TV, Dallas, 1970—72; pub. affairs coord. PBS, Washington, 1972—73; corr. NPACT-WETA-TV, Washington, 1973—; exec. editor, anchor The NewsHour with Jim Lehrer, 1995—; instr. creative writing Dallas Coll., So. Meth. U., 1967—68. Author: (novels) Viva Max, 1966, We Were Dreamers, Kick the Can, 1988, Crown Oklahoma, 1980, The Sooner Spy, 1990, Lost and Found, 1991, Short List, 1992, A Bus of My Own, 1992, Blue Hearts, 1993, Fine Lines, 1994, The Last Debate, 1995, White Widow, 1997, Purple Dots, 1998, The Special Prisoner, 2000, No Certain Rest, 2002, Flying Crows, 2004, The Franklin Affair, 2005, (plays) Chili Queen, 1986, Church Key Charlie Blue, 1987, The Will and Bart Show, 1992. With USMC, 1956—59. Named to Acad. TV Arts and Scis. Hall of Fame, 1999; recipient Columbia-Dupont award, George Polk award, Peabody award, Emmy award, Nat. Humanities medal, 1999. Fellow: Soc. Am. Historians; mem.: Coun. on Fgn. Rels., Tex. Inst. Letters, Dramatists Guild, Authors Guild, Am. Acad. Arts and Scis. Office: Sta WETA-TV 3620 27th St S Arlington VA 22206-2302

LEHRER, KENNETH EUGENE, real estate company executive, educator; b. N.Y.C., Apr. 17, 1946; s. Charles Carlton and Evelyn Estelle (Rosenfeld) L.; m. M. Newman, 1981 (div. 1988); m. Geraldine Trudy Fishman, Mar. 18, 1994. BS, NYU, 1967, MBA, 1969, MA, 1972, D in Pub. Adminstrn., 1980. Registered investment advisor; cert. real estate appraiser; lic. real estate broker. Asst. treas. Banker's Trust Co., N.Y.C., 1970-73; dir. devel. Coventry Devel. Corp., N.Y.C., 1974-77; asst. v.p. Affiliated Capital Corp., Houston, 1977-80; dir. fin. Allison/Walker Interests, Houston, 1980-82; mng. dir. Lehrer Fin. and Econ. Adv. Svcs., Houston, 1982—. Prof. real estate fin. U. Houston Grad. Sch. Bus. Adminstrn., 1984-2002; adj. prof. econ. and fin. U. Phoenix (Houston div.) 2003—; dir., CFO Aztec Oil & Gas, Houston, 2005-; chmn., bd. dirs. Acadia Savings and Loan Assn., Crowley, La., French Market Homestead Savs. Assn., Metairie, La., Twin City Savs. Bank, West Monroe, La., 1st Savs. La., LaPlace, 1988-89, Integrated Resource Techs., Inc., 1992-95. Pres. Cornerstone Mcpl. Utilities Dist. 1978-85; bd. dirs. Ft. Bend County Mcpl. Utility Dist #106, 1987-98, Houston Caliber Fin. Group chmn. 1994-96; Tex. Rep. Assn., Rep. Senatorial Inner Cir. (life, Medal of Freedom 1994). Mem. Am. Horse Show Assn. (life), Nat. Steeplechase and Hunt Assn. (life), U.S. Tennis Assn. (life), Am. Real Estate and Urban Econs. Assn., Am. Real Estate Soc., Nat. Assn. Bus. Economists, NYU Money Marketeers, Nat. Forensic Ctr., Nat. Assn. Corp. Dirs., Am. Acad. Econ. and Fin. Experts, Internat. Coll. Real Estate Cons. Profls., Internat. Assn. Corp. Real Estate Execs., Nat. Assn. Forensic Economists, Am. Arbitration Assn., Houston Bus. Economists, Western Econ. Assn., Fin. Club N.Y.C., Real Estate Educators Assn., Am. Econ. Assn., N. Am. Econs. and Fin. Assn., So. Econ. Assn., NYU Alumni Fedn. (bd. dirs. 1974-77), Houston C. of C. (mem. govtl. rels. com.), Princeton Club (N.Y.), St. James's Club (London), Capitol Hill Club (Washington), Royal Oaks Country Club (Houston). Episcopalian. Home: 5555 Del Monte Dr Unit 802 Houston TX 77056-4117 Office: Lehrer Fin & Econ Adv Svcs 1775 Saint James Pl Ste 110 Houston TX 77056-3403 Office Phone: 713-972-7912. Business E-Mail: drken@lehecoserv.com.

LEHRER, LEONARD, artist, educator; b. Phila., Mar. 23, 1935; s. Abraham and Bessie Lehrer; m. Marilyn Bigard, May 29, 1977; 1 child, Anna-Katrina Picard (dec.); stepchildren: Tracy Peel, Janna Peel Paulson, John Peel, Jamye Peel. BFA, Phila. Coll. Art, 1956; MFA, U. Pa., 1960. Faculty Phila. Coll. Art, 1956-70, co-dir. found. program, 1965-70; prof. art U. N.Mex., 1970-74, chmn. dept., 1970-73; prof. U. Tex., San Antonio, 1974-77, dir. divsn. art and design, 1974-75; prof., dir. Sch. Art, Ariz. State U., Tempe, 1977-90; dir. Visual Art Rsch. Studios, 1984-91; prof. art NYU, 1991-99, chair dept. art and art professions, 1991-96, prof. emeritus, 1999; dean Sch. Fine and Performing Arts Columbia Coll., Chgo., 2001. Cur. Large Scale Am. Prints in Art Multiple, Dusseldorf, Germany, 1992. One-man shows include Utah Mus. Fine Arts, Salt Lake City, 1973, 1982, Marian Locks Gallery, Phila., 1974, 1977, 1984, McNay Art Mus., San Antonio, 1975, Galerie Kühl, Hannover, Germany, 1976, 1979, 1982, 1991, Bomann Mus., Celle, Germany, 1980, Marilyn Butler Fine Art, Scottsdale, Ariz., 1980, Assoc. Am. Artists, Phila., 1984, Am. Cultural Affairs Ctr., Madrid, 1984, MyungSook Lee, NY, 1997, Crecloo Art Gallery, Phila., N.Y., 2004, others, exhibited in group shows at Ljubljana Internat. Print Biennial, 1981, Graphic Arts Biennial of Ams., Cali, Colombia, 1981, Brit. Internat. Print Biennial, Bradfrod, Eng., 1982, Internat. Printmaking Invitational, San Bernardino, Calif., 1983, XXXV Art Fair, Munich, 1992, XXIV Art Fair, Hannover, 1993, 2000 (XX Yrs. Heitland prizes, Kunstalle, Darmstadt, Germany, 2000), Contemporary Korean and Am. Art, Seoul, 1999, Miami Art Basel, 2002, Represented in permanent collections Met. Mus. Art, N.Y.C., Mus. Modern Art, Phila. Mus. Art, Nat. Gallery Art, Fed. Res. Bd., Corcoran Gallery, Libr. Congress, Albright-Knox Art Mus., Buffalo, Sprengel Mus. Art, Hannover, Bibliotheque Nationale, Paris, France; author: (introductory essay) The Art of the Book; works featured in the Art of Leonard Lehrer, 1986; contbr. articles. Bd. trustees Internat. Print Ctr. N.Y., Inc.; chair Arts Acad. Adv. Com., The College Bd., 1995-2004; bd. dirs. Apex Art Curator Program, N.Y. Recipient 1st prize Miami Internat. Print Biennial, 1980, Western States Art Found. Printmaking Fellowship award, 1979, Heitland Found. prize, Celle, 1980, Gold Medal award Ariz. chpt. Nat. Soc. Arts and Letters, 1981; Acad. Specialist grant USIA to Colombia, 1997; Fulbright scholar, 2001—, Fulbright Sr. Scholar AIA grantee, 2003. Business E-Mail: llehrer@colum.edu.

LEHRER, STANLEY, magazine publisher, editorial director, museum exhibitor; b. Bklyn., Mar. 18, 1929; s. Martin and Rose L.; m. Laurel Francine Zang, June 8, 1952; children: Merrill Clark, Randee Hope. BS in Journalism, NYU, 1950; postgrad. in Edn., San Antonio Coll., 1952. Editor and pub. Crossroads mag., Valley Stream, NY, 1949-50; youth svc. editor Open Road mag., N.Y.C., 1950—51; mng. editor School & Society, N.Y.C., 1953-68, v.p., 1956-68; pub. School & Society Books, N.Y.C., 1963-86; pres., pub. School & Society mag., N.Y.C., 1968-72; founder, pres., pub. Intellect mag., N.Y.C., 1972-78, editl. dir., 1974-78; founder, pres., pub., editl. dir. USA Today, Valley Stream, 1978—99, Newsview newsletter, 1979—99, Your Health newsletter, 1980-99; pres., pub., editl. dir. The World of Sci. newsletter, 1980-99. Cons. Child Care Publs., N.Y.C., 1955; guest spkr. Midwestern Writers' Conf., Chgo., 1950, Writers and Artists Group Nat. Music Camp, Interlochen, Mich., 1950, World of the Little Mag., Sta. WNYC-AM, N.Y.C., 1977, Titanic Symposium Mariners' Mus., Newport News, Va., 1998, Titanic Revealed, Nat. Geog. Ch., 2004; auction insider Fine Living Network, Time-Warner Ch., 2005; prodr., commentator Report on Edn. radio program Sta. WBAI-FM, N.Y.C., 1960—61; internat./nat. mus. exhibitor. Author: John Dewey: Master Educator, 1959, Countdown on Segregated Education, 1960, Religion, Government, and Education, 1961, A Century of Higher Education: Classical Citadel to Collegiate Colossus, 1962, Automation, Education, and Human Values, 1966, Conflict and Change on the Campus: The Response to Student Hyperactivism, 1970, Leaders, Teachers, and Learners in Academe: Partners in the Educational Process, 1970, Education and the Many Faces of the Disadvantaged: Cultural and Historical Perspectives, 1972, Titanic: Fortune & Fate, 1998; contbr. articles to nat. mags., newspapers, and profl. jours.; exhibited Stanley Lehrer maritime collection on transatlantic ships, N.Y. Yacht Club, 1983, on Cunard Line's 150th Anniversary, Forbes Mag. Galleries, N.Y.C., 1989—90, on French Line's Normandie, French Embassy, N.Y.C., 1992, Bass Mus. Art, Miami, 1993, on Ships of State: The Great Transatlantic Liners, PaineWebber Art Gallery, N.Y.C., 1994—95, on the Wreck of the Titanic, Nat. Maritime Mus., London, 1994—95, on S.O.S. Safety on Ships: Learning from New York's Maritime Tragedies, Water St. Gallery, Seamen's Ch. Inst., NYC, 1996, on Titanic: Fortune & Fate, Mariners' Mus., Newport News, Va., 1998, on Titanic: The Artifact Exhibition at World Trade Center, Boston, 1998, on Titanic: The Exhibition, Union Depot, St. Paul, 1998—99, on Blue Ribband: Quest for Speed Across the Atlantic, U.S. Courthouse, N.Y.C., 1999, on Titanic: The Experience, Tropicana, Atlantic City, N.J., 1999, on Titanic, Better Living Ctr., Toronto, Ont., Can., 1999—2000, on Titanic: The Artifact Exhibit, Fair Park, Dallas, 2000, on Titanic: The Exhibn., Mus. Sci. and Industry, Chgo., 2000, on Titanic, Mus. Ctr., Cin., 2000, Tropicana, Atlantic City, NJ, 2000, Opryland Hotel, Nashville, 2001, Kans. City Mus., Union Station, 2001, on Dazzle & Drab: Ocean Liners at War, Water Street Gallery, Seamen's Ch. Inst., N.Y.C., 2001—02, on Destination Hoboken: The Great Ocean Liners of Hamburg-American & North German Lloyd, Hoboken (N.J.) Hist. Mus., 2002, on Titanic: The Exhibition, Orlando, Fla., 2002—04, on Titanic: Made in Belfast (No. Ireland) City Hall, 2004, on Titanic:Branson, Mo., 2005—, life jackets for Broadway musical Titanic (based on Stanley Lehrer Titanic Collection), Lunt-Fontanne Theatre, N.Y.C, 1997, An Evening with "Mr. Titanic", Stanley Lehrer, Melville Gallery, South Street Seaport Mus., 2004, collector photographs and artifacts featured in books and videos including On Board The Titanic, 1996, Lost Liners, 1997, Titanic: Legacy of the World's Greatest Ocean Liner, 1997, Titanic: Fortune & Fate, 1998, Nat. Geog. Soc. booklet on Titanic, 1998, Eyewitness: Titanic, 1999, Molly Brown: Unraveling the Myth, 1999, The Lost Ships of Robert Ballard, 2005, Titanica (video), 1998, Steamboats: On the Hudson (video), 2004. V.p. Garden City Park (N.Y.) Civic Assn., 1961-63; treas. Citizens' Com. Edn., Garden City Park, 1962; mem. nat. jr. book awards com. Boys' Clubs Am., 1954; mem. nat. hon. com. for Richard H. Heindel Meml. Fund, Pa. State U., 1979-80. With Signal Corps, U.S. Army, 1951-53. Recipient non-fiction awards Midwestern Writers Conf., Chgo., 1948, 1950. Mem. New Hyde Park (N.Y.) C. of C. (dir. 1961-62), Titanic Hist. Soc., S.S. Hist. Soc. Am., Titanic Internat., Soc. Advancement of Edn. (treas. 1953-99, trustee 1963-99, pres. 1968-99), Ocean Liner Mus. (1983-2002), N.Y.C., Psi Chi Omega. Home: 82 Shelbourne Ln New Hyde Park NY 11040-1044

LEHRER, STEVEN, health products executive; Degrees in chem. engring. and econs., U. Md.; MBA, Harvard U. Former tech. brand mgr. Procter and Gamble Co., Inc.; former engagement mgr. McKinsey & Co., Inc.; former co-leader strategic bus. team, developer Integrated Protein Techs. Monsanto Group; chief bus. officer DNA Scis., Inc., Fremont, Calif., 2000—01, chmn., CEO, acting pres., COO, 2001—. Office: DNA Scis Inc PO Box 787 Fremont CA 94537-0787

LEHRMAN, EMILY ROSENSTEIN, retired librarian; b. Samara, USSR, Mar. 1, 1923; arrived in USA, 1935; d. Joseph L. Rosenstein and Sima B. (Glashow) Yaffe; m. Nathaniel S. Lehrman, June 18, 1944; children: Leonard, Paul, Betty. BS, Simmons Coll., Boston, 1945; MA, Columbia U., 1947; MLS, Long Island U., Brookville, NY, 1967. Asst. to editor American Review of Soviet Medicine, NYC, 1946-48; instr. of Russian Columbia U., 1948; instr. Russian Adelphi U., Garden City, 1962-66; librarian Hofstra U., Hempstead, 1969-73, SUNY, Farmingdale, 1974, Kingsboro Psychiatric Ctr., Bklyn., 1975-78; staff editor Macmillan Pub. Co., NYC, 1980; libr., assoc. prof. C.W. Post Campus, Long Is. U., Brookville, 1980—2001; ret., 2001. Translator Folktales of the Amur, 1980, Novella, appeared in Mass. Rev., "A Week Like Any Other Week", 1974. Mem.: Acad. and Spl. Library Div., Nassau County Library Assn., Beta Phi Mu. Avocations: travel, language study. Home: 10 Nob Hl Gate Roslyn NY 11576-2533

LEHRMAN, MARGARET MCBRIDE, broadcast executive, television producer; b. Spokane, Wash., Sept. 25, 1944; d. John P. and Ruth A. McBride; m. Michael L. Lehrman, June 27, 1970. BA, U. Oreg., 1966; MS, Columbia U., 1970. Staff Peace Corps, Washington, 1966-69; with The Morning News Co., Washington, 1970-72; radio and newspaper reporter Albright Comms., Washington, 1973-74; tv assignment editor ABC News, Washington, 1974; press asst. Senator Robert P. Griffin, Washington, 1975-79; rschr. Today Show, NBC News, Washington, 1979, assoc. prodr., 1979—83, Washington prodr., 1983-89, dep. bur. chief, 1989-95, sr. Washington prodr. spl. coverage and events, 1995—. Trustee U. Oreg. Found., 1990-2000. Recipient Edwin M. Hood award for diplomatic reporting (China), adv. bd. Internat. Women's Media Found., Women's Fgn. Policy Group, World Affairs Coun. Office: NBC News 4001 Nebraska Ave NW Washington DC 20016-2733 Business E-Mail: margaret.lehrman@nbc.com.

LEHTIHALME, LARRY K. (LAURI LEHTIHALME), financial planner; b. Montreal, Que., Can., Feb. 26, 1937; came to U.S., 1964; s. Lauri Johann and Selma Maire (Piispanen) L.; m. Elizabeth Speed Smith, Sept. 9, 1961; children: Tina Beth, Shauna Lyn. Student, Sir George Williams U., Montreal, 1960-64, Mission Coll., San Fernando, Calif., 1978-80, Pierce Coll., Woodland Hills, Calif., 1990-92. Lic. in variable annuity, life and disability ins., Calif.; lic. securities series 7 SEC, series 63. Acct., customer svc. cons. No. Electric, Montreal, 1957—64; salesman Remington Rand Systems, Wilmington, Del., 1964—67; account exec., comm. cons. Pacific Tel. & Telegraph Co., L.A., 1968—84; tech. customer support specialist AT&T, L.A., 1984—85; fin. adv., registered rep. Ameriprise Fin. Svc., Inc., L.A., 1987—. Mem. L.A. World Affairs Coun., 1998—. Mem. ctrl. com. Calif. 39th Assembly Dist. Rep. Com., 1976-81, City of L.A., 12th dist. adv. com., Calif.; pres. North Hills Jaycees, 1969-70; sec.-treas. Com. Ind. Valley City and County Govt., 1978-82; subchmn. allocations United Way, Van Nuys, Calif., 1990; fundraiser North Valley YMCA, 1986-98; formerly active numerous comty. and polit. orgns. in San Fernando Valley. Named Jaycee of Yr., Newark (Del.) Jaycees, 1966, Granada Hills Jaycees, 1971; recipient cert. of merit U.S. Ho. of Reps., 1973, award of merit, City of L.A., 1970, cert. appreciation, 1980, 84, tribute, 2003, State of Calif., 20th senate dist., 1983, Comty. Spirit award, 1990. Mem. L.A. Olympic Organizing Com. Alumni Assn., Jr. Chamber Internat. (life, senator 1973), U.S. Jaycees (life, Jaycee of Yr. 1965, Outstanding Local Jaycee 1965-66, Presdl. award Honor 1967, Jaycee of Month 1966-67, asst. gen. chmn. 1970-71, state dir. N. Hollywood chpt. 1970-71, Cert. Merit 1971, state gen. chmn., 1971-72, 72-73, Outstanding State Chmn. Calif. dist. 22 1973-74), Granada Hills C. of C. (bd. dirs. 1976-83, Man of Yr. award 1973), Granada Hills Jr. C. of C. Episcopalian. Avocation: community service. Home: 11408 Haskell Ave Granada Hills CA 91344-3959 Office: Am Express Fin Advisors 17050 Chatsworth St Ste 235 Granada Hills CA 91344-5898 Office Phone: 818-360-0390. Personal E-mail: llehti@aol.com.

LEHTO, GAIL S., education educator, musician; d. Gerald William and Alice Lehto. BA in Applied Clarinet, U. Wisconsin, 1991; MusM in Clarinet Performance, Ohio State U., 1994, DMA in Clarinet Performance, 2002. Second clarinet Kenosha (Wis.) Symphony Orch., 1990—92; prin. clarinet Westerville (Ohio) Symphony, 1994—; assoc. musician Columbus (Ohio) Symphony Orch., 1994—; clarinet instr. Ohio Wesleyan U., Delaware, 1997; asst. prof. clarinet Capital U. Conservatory Music, Columbus, 1999—. Substitute second clarinet Roanoke (Va.) Symphony Orch., 2002; substitute prin., second clarinet Richmond (Va.) Symphony Orch., 2003; second clarinet Wintergreen Summer Festival Orch., 2003. Scholar, U. Wis., 1987—91; Grad. fellow, Ohio State U., 1992—93, Mary Hubbell Osburn Grad. fellow, 1996. Mem.: Coll. Music Soc., Internat. Clarinet Assn. Office: Capital Univ Conservatory Music 2199 E Main St Columbus OH 43209 Business E-Mail: glehto@capital.edu.

LEI, HUI, computer scientist; b. Wuhan, Hubei, China, Oct. 14, 1966; s. Zichao Lei and Shuzheng Yao; m. Huiwei Wu, July 6, 1995; children: Ethan children: Jason Hui. BS, Zhongshan U., Guangzhou, China, 1987; MS, NYU, 1989; MPhil, Columbia U., 1995, PhD, 1997. Sr. software engr. Syncsort Inc., Woodcliff Lake, NJ, 1990—93; rsch. staff mem. IBM T. J. Watson Rsch. Ctr., Yorktown Heights, NY, 1998—. Chair Mobile Computing Profl. Interests Cmty., IBM Rsch., 2002—; program co-chair Second ACM Internat. Workshop on Mobile Commerce, 2002; conf. chmn. internat. conf. on mobile data mgmt. IEEE, 2004, program co-chair, internat. conf. on e-bus. engring., 05. Guest editor: jour. spl. issue IEEE Pervasive Computing, IEEE Wireless Comm., ACM/Baltzer Mobile Networks and Applications; arch. comml. software; contbr. articles to profl. jours. Achievements include patents for the system and method for performing joins and self-joins in a database system; the system and method for disconnected database access by heterogeneous clients; patents pending for the method and apparatus for content prefetching and preparation; the method and apparatus for providing a flexible and scalable context service; the method and apparatus for providing extensible scalable transcoding of multimedia content; the system and method for sorting embedded content in Web pages; system and method for enabling disconnected Web access; the method and apparatus for fusing context data; the system and method for web services QoS observation and dynamic selection; the method and system for context-aware unified communication; the system and method for pervasive enablement of buisness processes; the apparatus and method of semantic-based publish-subscribe systems. Avocations: music, travel, volleyball. Home: 15 Clarendon Pl Scarsdale NY 10583 Office: IBM T J Watson Rsch Ctr Route 134 Yorktown Heights NY 10598 Office Phone: 914-945-3624. E-mail: hlei@us.ibm.com.

LEIBACHER, LISE HELENE, French language and literature educator; b. Flers, Orne, France, Jan. 29, 1952; came to U.S., 1976; d. Georges and Jane (Guillaume) Ouvrard; m. John W. Leibacher, Dec. 21, 1976. Degree in English, U. Lille III, 1975; MA in French, San Jose State U., 1977; PhD in French, Stanford U., 1982. Asst. prof. French U. Ariz., Tucson, 1985-91, assoc. prof. French, 1991—, interim dept. head, 1991-92. Mem. adv. bd. Syracuse (N.Y.) U. Press, 1988—; reviewer, panelist NEH, Washington, 1992-94. Author: Libertinage et Utopies, 1989; editor: (collected essays) Pascal Corneille Desert, 1984, Utopian Studies IV, 1991, Esprit Créateur, Winte,r 1994; mem. editl. bd. Utopian Studies, 1988—. Mem. MLA, Am. Assn. Tchrs. French, Am. Soc. for Eighteenth Century Studies, N.Am. Soc. for 17th Century French Lit., N.Am. Soc. for Utopian Studies, Popular Culture Assn. Office: U Ariz Dept French Modern Langs 549 Tucson AZ 85721-0001

LEIBEL, STEVEN ARNOLD, radiologist; MD, U. Calif., San Francisco, 1972. Bd. cert. radiation oncology, bd. cert. therapeutic radiology. Intern U. Calif., San Francisco, 1972—73, resident radiation oncology, 1973—76, assoc. prof. radiation oncology, 1982—88; vice chmn., clin. dir. dept. radiation oncology Meml. Sloan-Kettering Cancer Ctr., N.Y.C., 1988—98; chmn. radiation oncology Meml. Sloan Kettering Cancer Ctr., N.Y.C., 1998—. Office: Stanford Cancer Ctr 875 Blake Wilbur Dr Mc 5827 Stanford CA 94305-5827

LEIBER, GERSON AUGUST, artist; b. Bklyn., Nov. 12, 1921; s. William and Rebecca (Margulis) L.; m. Judith Maria Peto, Feb. 5, 1946. Student art, Art Students League, N.Y., 1947-52, Bklyn. Mus. Art Sch., 1952-53; DFA (hon.), Bar Ilan U., Israel, 1993. Instr. Newark Sch. Fine and Indsl. Arts; v.p. Judith Leiber, Inc., N.Y.C., 1963—. One-man shows Oakland (Calif.) Mus., 1960, N.Y.C., 1961, 62, 63, 64, 68, 69, 72, 76, 85, 95, 96, 98, 99, Fine Arts Mus. L.I. (N.Y.), 1991, Steinbaum-Kraus Gallery, 1998, Denise Bibro Gallery, East Hampton, 2001, 2003, Guild Hall Mus., 2003; exhibited in numerous nat. and internat. group shows, prints and paintings represented in pvt. and permanent collections. With US Army, 1942-47. Recipient numerous prizes including Bklyn. Mus. Purchase awards, 1953-66, 2d prize of $1,000, Assoc. Am. Artists Nat. Print Exhbn., 1959, Soc. Washington Printmakers prize, 1962, purchase award Hunterdon County Art Center 6th nat. print exhbn., 1962, Audubon medals of Honor for Graphics, 1963, 65, Sonia Watter award Am. Color Print Soc., 1968, 1000 Purchase award Assn. Am. Artists, 1968, John Taylor Arms Meml. prize NAD, 1971; Tiffany fellow, 1957, 60 Mem. NAD (assoc., 1978-91, academician, 1991-), Soc. Am. Graphic Artists (past pres.), Art Students League N.Y. Studio: 27 E 31st St New York NY 10016-6810 Office Phone: 212-481-3436.

LEIBERT, BURTON M., lawyer; b. Brooklyn, NY, Sept. 6, 1945; AB, Franklin & Marshall Coll., 1966; JD, Georgetown U., 1969, LLM, 1973. Bar: Va. 1969, DC 1970, NY 1981. Asst. dir. Div. Investment Mgmt. SEC; counsel ERISA Regulation and Fiduciary Responsibility US Dept. Labor; ptnr. Corp. and Fin. Svcs. Dept. Willkie Farr & Gallagher LLP, NYC. Mem.: ABA, Assn. Bar of City NY. Office: Willkie Farr & Gallagher LLP 787 Seventh Ave New York NY 10019 Office Phone: 212-728-8238. Office Fax: 212-728-9238. E-mail: bleibert@willkie.com.

LEIBHOLZ, STEPHEN WOLFGANG, physicist, information technology executive, entrepreneur; b. Jan. 28, 1932; s. Ernest S. and Louise (Stern) L.; m. Ann Esther Greenberg, May 29, 1958; children: Judith, Robert, Daniel. BA in Physics, NYU, 1952. Prin. engr. Repub. Fairchild Co., Farmingdale, N.Y., 1957-60; mgr. sys. design and analysis Auerbach Corp., Phila., 1960-67; founder, chmn. Analytics, Inc., Willow Grove, Pa., 1967-91; advisor, cons. scientist U.S. govt. agys., Washington, 1970—; founder, COO Gentor Inc., 1996—; cofounder, vice chmn., CEO, VizorNet, Inc., 2002—; cofounder, CEO, EntroLabs LLC, 2004—. Founder, CEO Chesapeake TechLabs Inc., 1986—, ACS, Inc., 1987-90. Author and editor 7 books; contbr. articles to profl. publs. Bd. dirs. Jenkintown Music Sch., 1970-74; advisor Kansas City Camerata Chamber Orch. Cons. U. of Arts, Pa. Conv. Ctr.; mem. adv. bd. Inst. for Adv. Psychology; trustee Cheltenham Ctr. for Arts. Fellow Fgn. Policy Rsch. Inst. (sr.); mem. AAAS, IEEE (sr.), Mil. Ops. Rsch. Soc. (past bd. dirs.), NY Composers Cir. (chair), Cosmos Club (Washington). Office: 2333 Huntingdon Pike Huntingdon Valley PA 19006-6109 Office Phone: 215-938-7800. E-mail: swe@techlabs.com.

LEIBLEIN, MICHAEL, finance educator; b. East Northport, N.Y., Apr. 1965; s. Carl and Frances Leiblein. PhD, Purdue U., West Lafayette, Ind., 1995. Account exec. Johnson Controls, N.Y.C., 1987—90; cons. Accenture, Hartford, Conn., 1990—91; asst. prof. U. of S.C., Columbia, SC, 1995—98; assoc. prof. Fisher Coll.; Ohio State U., Columbus, 1998—. Cons. in field. Contbr. articles to profl. jours. Office: Ohio State University 2100 Neil Ave Columbus OH 43220 Office Phone: 614-292-0071.

LEIBLER, KENNETH ROBERT, finance company executive; b. N.Y.C., Feb. 21, 1949; s. Max and Martha (Dales) L.; m. Marcia Kate Reiss, July 15, 1973; children: Jessica Hope, Andrew Ethan. BA magna cum laude, Syracuse U., 1971; postgrad., U. Pa., 1972. Mgr. options Lehman Bros., 1972-75; v.p. options Am. Stock Exchange, N.Y.C., 1975-79, sr. v.p. adminstrn. and fin., 1979-81, exec. v.p. adminstrn. and fin., 1981-85, sr. exec. v.p., 1985-86, pres., 1986-90, Liberty Fin. Cos., Boston, 1990—2001; chmn. Boston Stock Exchange, 2001—03, Boston Options Exchange, 2004—. Instr. N.Y. Inst. Fin.; bd. dirs. ISO New Eng., Ruder Finn Group, Optimun Funds. Contbg. author: Handbook of Financial Markets: Securities, Options Futures, 1981. Mem. Securities Industry Assn., Phi Beta Kappa, Phi Kappa Phi.

LEIBOLD, ARTHUR WILLIAM, JR., lawyer; b. Ottawa, Ill., June 13, 1931; s. Arthur William and Helen (Cull) L.; m. Nora Collins, Nov. 30, 1957; children: Arthur William III, Alison Aubry, Peter Collins. AB, Haverford Coll., 1953; JD, U. Pa., 1956. Bar: Pa. 1957. With Dechert, Price & Rhoads, Phila., 1956—69, ptnr., 1965—69, Washington, 1972—97. Gen. counsel Fed. Home Loan Bank Bd. and Fed. Savs. & Loan Ins. Corp., Washington, 1969-72, Fed. Home Loan Mortgage Corp., 1970-72; lectr. English St. Joseph's Coll., Phila., 1957-59 Contbr. articles to profl. publs. Mem. Pres. Kennedy's Lawyers Com. Civil Rights, 1963, Adminstrv. Conf. U.S., 1969-72; bd. dirs. Marymount Coll. Va., 1974-75; Mem. Phila. Com. 70, 1965-74, Fellowship Commn. Mem. ABA (mem. ho. dels. 1967-69, 79-88, treas. 1979-83, mem. fin. com., mem. bd. govs. 1977-83), Fed. Bar Assn. (mem. nat. coun. 1971-80), D.C. Bar Assn., Phila. Bar Assn., Am. Bar Found. (treas. 1979-83), Am. Bar Ret. Assn. (dir. 1978-83), Am. Bar Endowment (bd. dirs. 1984-97, pres. 1995-97), Am. Bar Ins. (bd. dirs. 1999—), Phila. Country Club (Gladwyne, Pa.), Chester River Yacht and Country Club (Chestertown, Md.), Skating Club Phila., Order of Coif, Phi Beta Kappa. Republican. Roman Catholic. Office: Dechert 1775 Eye St NW Ste 1100 Washington DC 20006-2424 Home: 170 Satin Leaf Dr Jupiter FL 33458 Office Phone: 202-261-3301. Personal E-mail: leibold1@aol.com. Business E-Mail: aleibold@dechert.com.

LEIBOLD, GARY ALAN, school system administrator; b. Barberton, Ohio, Mar. 16, 1949; s. Raymond Fredrick and Mildred Carol Leibold; m. Cynthia Kay Wagner; 1 child, Heather S. Witter. BSc in edn., Bowling Green State U., 1967—70; MA in tchg., U. of Louisville, 1987—89; EdD, U. of Cin., 1998—2000. Dir. of small schools, amelia h.s. West Clermont Local Sch. Dist., Cin., 2002—; prin. Warren County Ednl. Svc. Ctr. Virtual Sch., Lebanon, Ohio, 2000—02; tech. services coord. Regional Profl. Devel. Ctr., Cin., 2000—02; dir. Warren-Butler Consortium Interactive Video Distance Learning, Lebanon, Ohio, 2000—02. Cons. Regional Com. of Practice, Cin., 2000—02, Regional Tech. Com., Cin., 2000—02; advisor CERTI at the U. of Cin., 2000—02. Pres. Cin. Youth Symphony Orch., 1991—92. U. Rsch. scholarship, U. of Cin., 1993—2000, U. scholarship, U. of Louisville,

1987—89. Mem.: NEA, AFCA, ASCD, OASSA, NASSP. Avocations: sailing, golf, photography, birdwatching. Office: Amelia High School 1351 Clough Pike Batavia OH 45103 Office Phone: 513-947-7421. Personal E-mail: gleibold@cinci.rr.com. E-mail: leibold_g@westcler.org.

LEIBOVICH, SIDNEY, engineering educator; b. Memphis, Apr. 2, 1939; s. Harry and Rebecca (Palant) L.; m. Gail Barbara Colin, Nov. 24, 1962; children: Bradley Colin, Adam Keith. BS, Calif. Inst. Tech., Pasadena, 1961; PhD in Theoretical and Applied Mechanics, Cornell U., 1965. NATO postdoctoral fellow U. Coll., London, 1965-66; asst. prof. thermal engring. Cornell U., Ithaca, NY, 1966-70, assoc. prof. thermal engring., 1970-78, prof. mech. and aerospace engring., 1978-89, Samuel B. Eckert prof. mech. and aerospace engring., 1989—, S.C. Thomas Sze dir. Sibley Sch. Mech. and Aerospace Engring, 1998—2005. Chmn. U.S. Nat. Com. for Theoretical and Applied Mechanics, 1990—92. Editor: Nonlinear Waves, 1974; assoc. editor: Jour. Fluid Mechanics, 1982-93; co-editor: Acta Mechanica, 1986-92; mem. editl. bd. Ann. Revs. of Fluid Mechanics, 1989-93; gen. editor Cambridge U. Press Monographs on Mechanics, 1994-04. Disting. lectr. Naval Ocean Rsch. Devel. Activity, 1983. Recipient MacPherson prize Calif. Inst. Tech., 1961. Fellow ASME (chmn. applied mechanics div. 1987-88), Am. Phys. Soc. (chmn. div. fluid dynamics 1987-88), Am. Acad. Arts and Scis.; mem. Nat. Acad. Engring. Office: Cornell U Upson Hall 246 Ithaca NY 14853 Office Phone: 607-255-3477. E-mail: SL23@cornell.edu.

LEIBOVITZ, ANNIE, photographer; b. Waterbury, Conn., Oct. 2, 1949; BFA, San Francisco Art Inst., 1971. Photographer Rolling Stone, 1970-83, chief photographer, 1973-83; photographer Conde Nast Vanity Fair, Vogue, 1980—; proprietor Annie Leibovitz Studio, N.Y.C. Works exhibited in various galleries and mus. including the National Portrait Gallery, Washington DC, 1991, The Corcoran Gallery, 1999; author: Photographs: Annie Leibovitz 1970-1990, 1992, Olympic Portraits: Annie Leibovitz, 1996, Annie Leibovitz: Women,(with essay by Susan Sontag) 1999, American Music, 2003; creator offcl. portfolio for 26th Olympic Games, Atlanta, 1995. Recipient Photographer of Yr. award Am. Soc. Mag. Photographers, 1984, Innovation in Photography award Am. Soc. Mag. Photographers, 1987, Clio award, 1987, Campaign of Decade award Advt. Age mag., 1987, Infinity award for applied photography Internat. Ctr. for Photography, 1990; named one of Top 10 Living Artists, ARTnews mag., 1999. Achievements include first woman and second photographer to have a solo exhibit at The National Portrait Gallery. Office: Annie Leibovitz Studio 547 W 26th St New York NY 10001-5503 also: Art & Commerce Care Jim Moffat 755 Washington St New York NY 10014-1746 E-mail: als@leibovitzstudio.com.

LEIBOW, RONALD LOUIS, lawyer; b. Santa Monica, Calif., Oct. 4, 1939; s. Norman and Jessica (Kellner) L.; m. Linda Bengelsdorf, June 11, 1961 (div. Dec. 1974); children: Jocelyn Elise, Jeffrey David, Joshua Aaron; m. Jacqueline Blatt, Apr. 6, 1986. AB, Calif. State U., Northridge, 1962; JD, UCLA, 1965. Bar: Calif. 1966, U.S. Dist. Ct. (cen. dist.) Calif. 1966, U.S. Dist. Ct. (no., so. and ea. dists.) Calif. 1971. Spl. asst. city atty. City of Burbank, Calif., 1966-67; from assoc. to ptnr. Meyers, Stevens & Walters, L.A., 1967-71; ptnr. Karpf, Leibow & Warner, Beverly Hills, Calif., 1971-74, Volk, Newman Gralla & Karp, L.A., L.A., 1979-81, Spector & Leibow, L.A., 1982-84, Stroock & Stroock & Lavan, L.A., 1984-94, Kaye Scholer LLP, L.A., 1994—, mng. ptnr., 1996-97. Lectr. law UCLA, 1968-69, Practicing Law Inst., 2001-; asst. prof. Calif. State U., Northridge, 1969-71. Contbr. articles to profl. jours. Pres. Jewish Cmty. Ctr., Greater L.A., 1983-86; vice chair Jewish Cmty. Ctr. Assn. N.Am., N.Y.C., 1988—; vice chair Jewish Fedn. Greater L.A., 1988—, chair planning and allocations com., 1998-01; internat. bd., exec. com. Starlight Starbright Children's Found., 1997-05, co-chair exec. com., 2005-; treas. Modern and Contemporary Arts Coun., LA County Mus. Art, 2003-. Mem. ABA (bus. bankruptcy com.), Phi Alpha Delta. Avocations: writing, tennis, skiing, travel. Office: Kaye Scholer LLP 1999 Avenue Of The Stars Fl 17 Los Angeles CA 90067-6022 Office Phone: 310-788-1220. Business E-Mail: rleibow@kayescholer.com.

LEIBOWITT, SOL DAVID, lawyer; b. Bklyn., Feb. 18, 1912; s. Morris and Bella (Small) Leibowitt; m. Ethel Leibowitt, June 18, 1950 (dec. Aug. 1985); m. Babs Lee, Dec. 28, 1986 (dec. June 2000). BA, Lehigh U., 1933; JD, Harvard U., 1936. Bar: N.Y. 1937, Conn. 1970. Pvt. practice, N.Y.C., 1937-84, Stamford, Conn., 1970-78, Milford, Conn., 1978-79; gen. counsel New Haven Clock and Watch Co., 1955-59, pres., 1958-59, Diagnon Corp., 1981-83, vice chmn., 1983-86. Chmn. Card Tech. Corp., 1983-85; Phi Beta Kappa 1977-79. Author: (folk poetry) Wit and Whimsy. Pres. Ethel and David Leibowitt Found.; dir. Am. Com. for Weizmann Inst. Sci.; mediator family law Supreme Ct. State Fla. 15th Jud. Ct., 1990—; arbitrator Am. Arbitration Assn., Fla.; chmn. Israel Cancer Assn. USA; dir. Am. Assocs., Ben-Gurion U., 1999. Recipient Human Rels. award Anti-Defamation League, 1969, Ethel Leibowitt Fund Johns Hopkins U. Sch. Medcine Meml. award Anti-Defamation League, 1971, Tikvah award Israel Cancer Assn., 1995. Mem.: ABA, Am. Soc. for Technion U. (bd. dirs., v.p., Conn. pres., life trustee), Anti-Defamation League (commr.), NY State Bar Assn., Assn. Bar N.Y.C., Harvard Club (N.Y.C.), Lotos Club.

LEIBOWITZ, HAL J., lawyer; s. Allan E. and Frances A. Leibowitz; m. Jill M. Leibowitz. BA, Brandeis U., Waltham, Mass., 1982; JD, Suffolk U. Law Sch., Boston, Mass., 1985. Bar: Mass. 1985. Ptnr. Wilmer Cutler Pickering Hale Dorr LLP, Boston, 1985—. Dir. Mass. Telecom. Coun., 1984. Recipient Mass. Super Lawyer, Representation Pub. Companies, 2004. Mem.: MBA, BBA, ABA. Office: Wilmer Cutler Pickering Hale Dorr LLP 60 State St Boston MA 02109 Office Phone: 617-526-6461.

LEIBOWITZ, HERBERT AKIBA, literature and language professor, writer; b. Staten Island, N.Y., Apr. 26, 1935; s. Morris and Rose (Rabinowitz) L.; m. Susan Yankowitz, May 3, 1978; 1 son, Gabriel. BA, Bklyn. Coll., 1956; MA, Brown U., 1958; PhD, Columbia U., 1966. Asst. prof. English Columbia U., 1967-70; asst. prof. humanities Richmond Coll., Staten Island, N.Y., 1971-73, assoc. prof., 1973-76; assoc. prof. English Coll. S.I., 1976-81; prof. English Coll. Staten Island, CUNY and Grad. Ctr., CUNY, 1981—; prof. English emeritus, 1991—. Fannie Hurst vis. prof. Washington U., St. Louis, 1995; Fulbright prof. U. Barcelona, 1999, U. Autonoma, 1999. Author: Hart Crane: An Introduction to the Poetry, 1968, Fabricating Lives, 1989; editor: Selected Music Criticism of Paul Rosenfeld, 1970, Parnassus: Poetry in Review, 1972, Parnassus: Twenty Years of Poetry in Review, 1994, Asphodel, That Greeny Flower and Other William Carlos Williams Love Poems, 1994. Recipient Fels award for edil. distinction Coordinating Coun. Lit. Mags., 1975, Elizabeth Kray award Poets House, 2002; postdoctoral fellow U. Ill. Ctr. Advanced Study, 1968-69, Chamberlain fellow Columbia U., 1970, fellow N.Y. Inst. Humanities, 1987—, Mellon Seminar fellow NYU, 1988, Guggenheim fellow, 1991-92. Fellow N.Y. Pub. Libr. Ctr. Scholars and Writers; mem. PEN (Nora Magid award for disting. editing of lit. mag. 1995), Nat. Book Critics Circle (bd. dirs. 1988-94, pres. 1992-94). Jewish. Home: 205 W 89th St New York NY 10024-1828 Office: Poetry Rev Found 205 W 89th St Apt 8F New York NY 10024-1835 E-mail: Parnew@aol.com.

LEIBOWITZ, JACK RICHARD, physicist, educator; b. Bridgeport, Conn., July 21, 1929; BA, MS, NYU; PhD in Physics, Brown U., 1962. Rsch. physicist MIT Lincoln Lab., 1956—61, Westinghouse Rsch. Labs., Pitts., 1961—64; asst. prof. U. Md., College Park, 1964—69; assoc. prof. physics Cath. U. Am., Washington, 1969—73, prof. physics, 1974—95, prof. physics emeritus, 1995—, assoc. dean for grad. studies, 1988—93, chmn. art dept., 1982—86, acad. senate. Sci. cons. govt. agys. Contbr. numerous rsch. articles to sci. jours. and books. Fellow: Washington Acad. Scis., Am. Phys. Soc.; mem.: Sigma Xi. Achievements include research in condensed matter physics; superconductivity, electron-phonon interaction, band structure. Address: PO Box 31761 Santa Fe NM 87594-1761 Personal E-mail: jrleib@earthlink.net.

LEIBOWITZ, JONATHAN STEWART See **STEWART, JON**

LEIBOWITZ, MARK ALAN, lawyer; b. N.Y.C., Jan. 22, 1950; s. Philip and Muriel Shirley Leibowitz; m. Ann, Nov. 30, 2002; children: Joan, Jonathan. BA, Syracuse U., 1972; JD, U. Miami, 1975. Bar: Fla. 1975, U.S. Dist. Ct. (so. dist.) Fla. 1976, Colo. 1994. Lawyer Wolfson & Diamond, Miami Beach, Fla., 1976-82, Wolpe & Leibowitz, Miami, Fla., 1982—2002, Wolpe, Leibowitz, Alvarez & Fernadez LLP, 2002—. Recipient Voted Best Lawyers in South Fla., South Fla, Legal Guide. Mem.: Dade County Trial Lawyers Am. Bar Assn., Dade County Bar Assn., Fla. Bar Assn. (bd. cert. civil trial lawyer). Avocations: skiing, hiking, golf. Office: Wolpe Leibowitz Alvarez & Fernandez LLP 44 W Flagler Penthouse Miami FL 33130-4400 Office Phone: 305-372-0060. Business E-Mail: mleibowitz@wlaf-law.com.

LEIBOWITZ, MARVIN, lawyer; b. Phila., Jan. 24, 1950; s. Aaron and Ethel (Kashoff) L.; m. Faye Rebecca Liepack, Nov. 12, 1983; children: Cheryl Renée, Ellen Paulette. BA, Temple U., 1971, postgrad., 1971-72; JD, Widener U., 1976. Bar: Pa. 1977, N.J. 1977, U.S. Dist. Ct. N.J. 1977, U.S. Dist. Ct. (we. dist.) Pa. 1980. Atty.-advisor SSA, Pitts., 1977-95, sr. atty., 1995—2001; quality assurance reviewer Office of Program and Integrity Revs., 1997; pvt. practice Pitts., 1979—. Active Phila. Dem. Com., 1973—77. Pa. State Scholar Pa. Higher Edn. Assistance Agy., Harrisburg, 1967-71; recipient U.S. Dept. Health and Human Svcs. Assoc. Commr.'s citation, 1994. Mem. Nat. Treasury Employees Union (regional steward 1982-99, regional v.p. 1999-2001), Pa. Bar Assn., Allegheny County Bar Assn. Democrat. Jewish. Home: 6501 Landview Rd Pittsburgh PA 15217-3000 Office Phone: 412-391-1191. Personal E-mail: marvleibo@yahoo.com.

LEIBRECHT, MURL EDWIN, preventive medicine physician, consultant, retired military officer; b. Spokane, Wash., June 21, 1945; s. Frank John and Minnie Louise Leibrecht; m. Karen Rae Kappel, Aug. 12, 1967. BA, Whitman Coll., Walla Walla, Wash., 1967; MD, U. Utah Coll. Medicine, Salt Lake City, 1971; MPH, Harvard U., Boston, 1986. Diplomate Nat. Bd. Med. Examiners, 1972, preventive/aerospace medicine Am. Bd. Preventive Medicine, 1988. Chief physician aeromedical svcs. McChord AFB Clinic, Tacoma, 1977—80; clinic dir. and embassy med. advisor USAF Clinic, Oslo, 1980—85; command chief physician aerospace medicine SAC, Omaha, 1987—90; program dir. residency in aerospace medicine USAF Sch. Aerospace Medicine, San Antonio, 1990—93; chief physician/command surgeon USAF Space Command, Colorado Springs, 1993—96; clinic dir. Bad Aibling Sta. Clinic, Germany, 1996—2004; consulting physician Landstuhl Regional Med. Ctr. Med. advisor US Embassy, Oslo, 1980—85; asst. prof. Uniformed Svcs. U. Health Sciences, Bethesda, Md., 1990—96; chmn. dept. aerospace medicine USAF Sch. of Aerospace Medicine, San Antonio, 1992; med. mem.astronaut selection bd. USAF Astronaut Selection Bd., Washington, 1993—96; mem. and med. advisor USAF Space Shuttle Support Team, Patrick Air Force Base, Fla. Editor: (report) Integrating Women into High Altitude Reconaissance Aircraft Flight Operations; contbr. scientific papers. Working mem. Habitat for Humanity, San Antonio, 1990—. Col. USAF, 1972—96. Decorated Legion of Merit USAF; recipient First prize, Student AMA Sci. Rsch. Competition, 1971. Fellow: Am. Coll. of Preventive Medicine (life), Aerospace Med. Assn. (life); mem.: Soc. of Air Force Flight Surgeons (pres. 1995—96), Nat. Wildlife Fedn. (life), Nat. Audubon Soc. (life), Order of Waiilatpu (life), Tau Kappa Epsilon (life). Independent. Avocations: travel, photography, skiing, creative writing, scuba diving. Home: En Bout Tournus 71700 France Office: Landstuhl Regional Med Ctr CMR 402 Box 1147 APO AE 09098 Office Phone: 01149 637186 8048. E-mail: murl.leibrecht@lnd.amedd.army.mil.

LEIBY, JOHN SEVERN, historian, educator; s. Austin Nelson and Judith Winifred Leiby. BA, Ariz. State U., 1977, MA, 1979; PhD, No. Ariz. U., 1983. Prof. history Navajo C.C., Tsaile, Ariz., 1993—96; adj. instr. history Paradise Valley C.C., Phoenix, 1998—. Editor: (hist.) Memoria sobre el Nuevo Reino de Granada, 1803; author: Colonial Bureaucrats and the Mexican Economy, The Royal Indian Hospital of Mexico City, 1553-1680, The Historian, 1992, San Hipólito's Treatment of the Mentally Ill in Mexico City, 1589-1650, (hist. entries) Dictionary of the Vietnam War. Rsch. Fellowhip, Ariz. Ctr. for Medieval & Renaissance Studies, 1982—83. Mem.: Am. Hist. Assn. Office: Paradise Valley Cmty Coll 18401 North 32d St Phoenix AZ 85032 Business E-Mail: john.leiby@pvmail.maricopa.edu.

LEICHTLING, MICHAEL ALFRED, lawyer; b. N.Y.C., Mar. 30, 1943; s. Stanley Arthur and Roslyn Priscilla (Fuhr) L.; m. Arlene Dorf, July 30, 1966; children: Julie Karen Nacos, Nina Anastasia, Noah James. BA, SUNY, Binghamton, 1963; JD, Northwestern U., 1966; postgrad., Columbia U., 1968. Bar: N.Y. 1969, U.S. Ct. Appeals (2d cir.) 1969. Assoc. Aranow Brodsky Bohlinger Einhorn & Dann, N.Y.C., 1966, Parker Chapin & Flattau, N.Y.C., 1969-77; ptnr. Parker Chapin Flattau & Klimpl, LLP, N.Y.C., 1977-2001, Jenkens & Gilchrist Parker Chapin LLP, N.Y.C., 2001—05, Troutman Sanders LLP, N.Y.C., 2005—, mem. exec. com. Bd. dirs. H. Warshow & Sons Inc., N.Y.C. Editor Northwestern U. Law Rev., 1965-66, Equipment Leasing Jour., 1986—; co-editor Commercial Finance Guide, 1997—, Commercial Loan Documentation Guide, 1997—. Bd. dirs., exec. com. Friends of Israel Disabled Vets., N.Y.C., 1986—; bd. trustees, vice chmn., exec. com. Equipment Leasing and Fin. Found., Arlington, Va., 1998—. With U.S. Army, 1966-68; Vietnam. Decorated Bronze Star; Regents scholar, 1963, Newman scholar, 1963-66. Mem. N.Y. State Bar Assn. (corp. law sect.), N.Y. County Lawyers Assn. (banking law com., secured lending com.), Equipment Leasing Assn. Am. (bd. dirs. 2001-2004, exec. com. 2004, industry future coun.), Ea. Assn. Equipment Lessors (gen. counsel 1986—) Avocations: reading, painting, swimming, golf. Home: 148 Quinn Rd Briarcliff Manor NY 10510-2133 Office: 405 Lexington Ave New York NY 10174-0002 Office Phone: 212-704-6257. Business E-Mail: michael.leichtling@troutmansanders.com.

LEICHTMAN, MARIA LUISA, mental health services professional; b. Philippines; B, Assumption Coll.; D of Clin. Psychology, U. Kans. With Irving Schwartz Inst. Children, Phila. Psychiat. Ctr., until 1979, Menninger, Topeka, 1979—, dir. child & adolscent residential treatment program, 1999—. Fulbright scholar.

LEIDEN, JEFFREY MARC M., pharmaceutical executive, molecular biologist, cardiologist; b. Chgo., Oct. 12, 1955; s. Irving and Rosemary (Rebelsky) L.; m. Lisa Leyland, June 23, 1982; children: Benjamin Bradford, Alexander Dow. BA in Biol. Sci. with honors, U. Chgo., 1975, MD with honors, 1979, PhD, 1981. Diplomate Am. Bd. Internal Medicine, Am. Bd. Cardiovascular Diseases; lic. cardiologist, Mass., Ill. Intern Brigham and Women's Hosp. Harvard Med. Sch., Boston, 1981, resident in internal medicine, 1982-84, cardiology fellow, 1984-87; clin. fellow Dana-Farber Cancer Inst. Harvard Med. Sch., Boston, 1984-87; from asst. to assoc. investigator Howard Hughes Med. Inst., Ann Arbor, 1987-92; from asst. to assoc. prof. internal medicine div. cardiology U. Mich. Sch. Medicine, Ann Arbor, 1986-92, asst. prof. dept. microbiology, immunology, 1987-92, assoc. chief div. cardiology, dir. Cardiovascular Rsch. Ctr., 1990-92; prof. pathology U. Chgo., 1992—, Rowson prof. medicine, chief sect. cardiology, 1992—; Blout prof. biol. scis. Harvard Sch. Pub. Health, 1999—2000, Bloat prof. biol. scis., 1999—2000; prof. medicine Harvard Med. Sch., 1999—2000; bd. dir. Abbott, Abbott Park, Ill., 1999—, chief sci. officer, 2000—, exec. v.p., 2000—01; pres., COO global pharms., 2001—. Pres. Am. Soc. Clin. Investigation, 1998. Chmn. molecular biology session Am. Heart Assn. Nat. Meeting, 1992, Katz Prize selection com., 1992-93. Recipient John Van Prohaska award, 1981, Ctrl. Soc. for Clin. Rsch. Presdl. award, 1991. Mem.: Assn. Prof. Cardiology, Basic. Sci. Coun., Am. Heart Assn., Am. Fedn. Clin. Rsch., Inst. Medicine of Nat. Acad. Scis., Am. Acad. Arts and Scis., Am. Soc. Clinical Investigation, Alpha Omega Alpha, Phi Beta Kappa. Achievements include research in transcriptional regulation of T-cell development, regulation of cardiovascular development, and gene therapy approaches in cardiac and skeletal muscle. Office: Abbott Labs Dept 0392 Bldg AP6D-2 100 Abbott Park Rd Abbott Park IL 60064-6020

LEIDHEISER, HENRY, JR., retired chemistry educator, consultant; b. Union City, N.J., Apr. 18, 1920; s. Henry and Margaret Marie (Steinel) L.; m. Virginia Townsend, Feb. 21, 1944; children: Margaret Frances, Henry III. BS in Chemistry, U. Va., 1941, MS in Phys. Chemistry, 1943, PhD in Phys. Chemistry, 1946. Research associate U. Va., Charlottesville, 1946-49; research chemist, dir. Va. Inst. for Sci. Research, Richmond, 1949-68; prof. chemistry Lehigh U., Bethlehem, Pa., 1968-90, prof. emeritus, 1990—. Cons. space science NASA, 1972-84; cons. numerous indsl. orgns. Author or editor of 8 books; 275 publs. in tech. lit.; 7 patents on crystal growth and metal surface treatment. NATO fellow to Cambridge U., England, 1969; recipient J. Shelton Horsley Rsch. award Va. Acad. Sci., 1948, Oak Ridge Inst. Nuclear Studies Rsch. award, 1949, Westinghouse Signal and Brake Award of Inst. Metal Finishing, 1954, Silver medal Am. Electroplaters' Soc., 1978, Arch T. Colwell award Soc. Automotive Engrs., 1979, Humboldt Sr. Scientist award, 1985, Tambour award 11th Congress Metal Finishing, 1984, Silver medal South African Corrosion Inst., 1986, Libsch Rsch. award Lehigh U., 1987, Mattiello Rsch. award Fedn. Soc. Coatings Tech., 1990 Fellow AAAS; mem. Am. Chem. Soc., Electrochem. Soc. (Young Author's award 1948, Rsch. award 1986, 91), Nat. Assn. Corrosion Engrs. (Whitney award 1983), Rotary. Republican. Presbyterian. Avocations: bridge, golf, collecting ceramics. Home: 822 Carnoustie Dr Venice FL 34293-4343 E-mail: hleid@worldnet.att.net.

LEIDIG, MARGOT HELENE, retired elementary and secondary education educator; b. Fresno, Calif., May 31, 1945; d. Euvelle R. and Anita S. Enderlin; m. Leigh Arthur Leidig, June 11, 1972; children: Bonnie Chrisman, Kimberly Minnick. BA, Chico State U., 1967, MA, 1970. 3/5 faculty appt. phys. sci. dept. Chico (Calif.) State Coll., 1967-68; tchr. math., sci. Oak Grove Intermediate Sch. Mt. Diablo Unified Sch. Dist., Concord, Calif., 1968-73; tchr. resource maths. John Still Jr. High Sch. Sacramento City Unified Sch. Dist., 1973-80, tchr., maths. Kit Carson Middle Sch. Sacramento, 1980-86, tchr. maths. John F. Kennedy High Sch., 1986-96; tchr. maths., sci. Capital City Schs., 1996—; ret., 2002. Presenter No. Calif. Maths. Conf., Asilomar; chair No. Calif. Math Project U. Calif., Davis, 1985. Author: 5 math books. Mem. AAUW, Calif. Math Coun., Order of Ea. Star (# 150, 25 Yr. Pin), Daus. of the Nile, Phi Delta Kappa. Avocations: golf, gardening, travel, reading, bridge.

LEIER, CARL VICTOR, internist, cardiologist; b. Bismarck, N.D., Oct. 20, 1944; married; 3 children. Grad., Creighton U., MD cum laude, 1969. Diplomate Am. Bd. Internal Medicine, Cardiovascular Medicine, Critical Care Medicine, Geriatric Medicine, Electrocardiography, Nat. Bd. Med. Examiners; lic. med., surgical Nebr., med. Ohio. Intern Ohio State U. Coll. Medicine, Columbus, 1969-70, med. resident (instr.) dept. medicine, 1971-73, chief resident (instr.), 1973-74, fellowship divsn. cardiology, 1974-76; pathology resident dept. pathology St. Vincent Hosp., Worcester, Mass., 1970-71; trainee NIH Tng. Grant, 1974-75; asst. prof. medicine cardiology dept., Ohio State U. Coll. Medicine, Columbus, 1976-80, asst. prof. pharmacology, 1976-80, assoc. prof., 1980-84, faculty mem. grad. sch., 1980—, dir. rsch. divsn. cardiology, 1980-83, James W. Overstreet prof. of medicine, 1983—, prof. of medicine divsn. cardiology, 1984—, prof. pharmacology, dept. pharmacology, 1984—, dir. divsn. cardiology, 1986-98. Mem. rsch. com. ctrl. Ohio chpt. Am. Heart Assn., 1977-84, bd. trustees, 1979-88, exec. rsch. com., 1979-84, vice chmn. rsch. com., 1980-82, chmn. rsch. peer rev. com., 1982-84, v.p., 1984-86, pres. elect, 1986-88; numerous other coms.; cons. cardiorenal adv. bd. Smith-Kline Labs., 1982-85, com. on cardiovascular rsch. and devel., 1982-85., AMA on Drugs and Tech., 1985—, FDA Cardiorenal adv. com. 1986-92; mem. chmn. Annual Sci. Sessions of the Am. Coll. of Cardiolog, 1996-97; vis. prof., lectr. and presenter at numerous sci. confs., insts. in U.S. and internationally. Editor: (book) Cardiotonic Drugs, 1986, 2d rev. edit., 1991; co-author: (with H. Boudoulas) CardioRenal Disorders and Diseases, 1986, 2d edit., 1992 (with J. Vincent) Critical Care Medicine: Recent Advances in Cardiovascular Medicine, 1990; contbr. more than 40 chpts. to other medical books and almost 200 articles to peer reviewed jours. including: Circulation, Brit. Heart Jour., Jour. Clin. Investigation, Jour. Am. Coll. Cardiology, Am. Jour. Cardiology, Chest, Am. Jour. Medicine, Am. Heart Jour., Annals of Internal Medicine and others; editor in chief Congestive Heart Failure: Index and Revs., 1988-94; mem. editorial bds. of ten medical jours. concerned with heart diseases, the review bds. of others including New Eng. Jour. Medicine, Internat. Jour. Cardiology, Jour. of Lab. and Clin. Medicine. Recipient Upjohn award, 1969, Lange Scholar award, 1969, Golden Apple Student Tchg. award, 1973, 75, Young Investigator award Ctrl. Ohio Heart Chpt., Am. Heart Assn., 1976-78, Rsch. Recognition award, 1978. Fellow Am. Heart Assn., Am. Coll. Cardiology, Am. Coll. Physicians, Coun. on Geriatric Cardiology; mem. AAAS, Am. Fedn. for Clin. Rsch., Ctrl. Soc. for Clin. Rsch., Am. Soc. Clin. Investigation, Assn. Univ. Cardiologists, Assn. Profs. of Cardiology. Office: Ohio State U Med Ctr Divsn Cardiology 473 W 12th Ave Columbus OH 43210-1250

LEIFER, EDGAR, physician, retired medical educator; b. N.Y.C., Aug. 20, 1918; s. Moses and Rose (Greenfield) Leifer; m. Violet S. Beerman, June 17, 1945; 1 child, Dana. BS, CCNY, 1937; PhD, Columbia U., 1941, MD, 1946. Diplomate Am. Bd. Internal Medicine. Rsch. chemist Corning (N.Y.) Glass Works, 1941—43; radiobiologist Los Alamos (N.Mex.) Sci. Lab., 1947—48; chief Isotope Lab. Walter Reed Med. Ctr., Washington, 1948—49; resident physician Presbyn. Hosp., N.Y.C., 1949—51, attending physician, 1951—, dir. med. affairs, 1977—83. Prof. clin. medicine Columbia Presbyn. Med. Ctr., N.Y.C., 1951—2000, prof. emeritus, 2000—03; ret., 2003. Contbr. articles to profl. jours. Capt. U.S. Army, 1947—49. Office: Presbyn Hosp 161 Ft Washington Ave New York NY 10032

LEIGH, CHERI J., engineering consulting executive; BS Civil Eng., Southern Methodist U.; MS Eng. Mgmt., Kansas U. Positions with GM, Norfolk & Western Railway; founder and principle partner Leigh & O'Kane LLC, 1983—. Volunteer Reach to Recovery. Fellow: Soc. Women Engineers (Entrepreneur award 2003); mem.: Missouri Soc. Profl. Engineers. Achievements include being the first woman engineer to be appointed to the Missouri Board for Architects, Professional Engineers, and Land Surveyors. Office: Leigh & O'Kane LLC 9201 Ward Pkwy Kansas City MO 64114-3339

LEIGH, GLORIA LORRAINE, retired religious studies educator; b. Columbus, Ohio, May 6, 1939; d. William Franklin and Catherine Aileen Leigh; 1 child, Anthonia McDaniel. AA, Monterey Peninsula Coll., 1961; cert. in black cath. studies, Xavier U., 1990; MA in Religion, Athenaeum Of Ohio, 1996. Dir. religious edn. Resurrection Cath. Ch., Dayton, Ohio, 1988—96, Mary, Help of Christians Cath. Ch., Fairborn, Ohio, 1996—2001; coord. christian initiation for adults St. Martin De Porres Cath. Ch., Lincoln Heights, Ohio, 2001—. Adv. Tribunal Archdiocese Cinn., 1990; catechetical leader Archdiocese Cinn., 1996, Fedn. Christian Ministries, 2000; cons. St. Anthony Messenger Press, Cinn., 1997—; coord. Nguzo Saba, Cinn., 2002—; adj. faculty mem. Athenaeum of Ohio, 2003. President Greater Dayton Christian Coun., 1992—94; bd. dirs. Greater Dayton Christian Connection, 1998—2002; pres. Interfaith Ministers for Reconciliation, 2001; rep. Southwest Priority Bd., Dayton, 1988—91; steering com. Dayton Dialogue on Race Rels., Dayton, 1998—2002. Named to, Peace Bridge Hall of Fame, Dayton, 2003; grantee, Epiphany Found., 1994; scholar, Benjamin E. Mays, 1992, Gabrielle Bouscaren, 1994—96. Mem.: Dayton Area Religious Edn. Assn. (co-chair 1999—2001), Fedn. Christian Ministries, Delta Sigma Theta (life; chaplain 1999—2001). Roman Catholic. Avocations: travel, reading, weaving, yoga, gardening. Home: 148 N Ardmore Avenue Dayton OH 45417 Home Fax: 937-268-0521. Personal E-mail: GloriaLeigh300@CS.com.

LEIGH, HOYLE, psychiatrist, educator, writer; b. Seoul, Korea, Mar. 25, 1942; came to U.S., 1965; m. Vincenta Masciandaro, Sept. 16, 1967; 1 child, Alexander Hoyle. MA, Yale U., 1982; MD, Yonsei U., Seoul, 1965. Diplomate Am. Bd. Psychiatry and Neurology. Asst. prof. Yale U., New Haven, 1971-75, assoc. prof., 1975-80, prof., 1980-89, lectr. in psychiatry, 1989—. Dir. Behavioral Medicine Clinic, Yale U., 1980-89; dir. psychiat. cons. svc. Yale-New Haven Hosp., 1971-89; chief psychiatry VA Med Ctr., Fresno, Calif., 1989—; prof., vice chmn. dept. psychiatry U. Calif., San

Francisco, 1989—, head dept. psychiatry, 1989—; cons. Am. Jour. Psychiatry, Archives Internal Medicine, Psychosomatic Medicine. Author: The Patient, 1980, 2d edit., 1985, 3d edit., 1992; editor: Psychiatry in the Practice of Medicine, 1983, Consultation-Liaison Psychiatry: 1990's & Beyond, 1994, Biopsychosocial Approaches in Primary Care: State of the Art and Challenges for the 21st Century, 1997. Fellow ACP, Internat. Coll. Psychosomatic Medicine (v.p.), Am. Acad. Psychosomatic Medicine; mem. AMA, AAUP, World Psychiat. Assn. Avocations: reading, music, skiing. Office: U Calif Dept Psychiat 2615 E Clinton Ave Fresno CA 93703-2223

LEIGH, JENNIFER JASON (JENNIFER LEIGH MORROW), actress; b. L.A., Feb. 5, 1962; d. Barbara Turner and Vic Morrow. Student, Lee Strasberg Inst. Appearances include (films) Eyes of a Stranger, 1980, Fast Times at Ridgemont High, 1982, Wrong is Right, 1982, Easy Money, 1983, Grandview U.S.A., 1984, Flesh + Blood, 1985, The Hitcher, 1986, The Men's Club, 1986, Sister, Sister, 1987, Under Cover, 1987, Heart of Midnight, 1988, The Big Picture, 1989, Last Exit to Brooklyn, 1989, Miami Blues, 1990, Crooked Hearts, 1991, Backdraft, 1991, Rush, 1992, Single White Female, 1992, Short Cuts, 1993, The Hudsucker Proxy, 1994, Mrs. Parker and the Vicious Circle, 1994, Dolores Claiborne, 1994, Kansas City, 1996, Bastard Out of Carolina, 1996, A Thousand Acres, 1997, Washington Square, 1997, eXistenZ, 1998, The King is Alive, 2000, Skipped Parts, 2000, Beautiful View, 2000, The Quickie, 2001, Hey Arnold! The Movie, (voice) 2002 Road to Perdition, 2002, In the Cut, 2003, The Machinist, 2004; (TV movies) Angel City, 1980, The Killing of Randy Webster, 1981, The Best Little Girl in the World, 1981, The First Time, 1982, Girls of the White Orchid, 1983, Buried Alive, 1990, The Love Letter, 1998, Crossed Over, 2002 (mini series) Thanks of a Grateful Nation, 1998; prodr., actress Georgia, 1995; writer, dir., prodr., actor The Anniversary Party, 2001; TV guest appearances include The Waltons, 1972, Tracey Takes On..., 1996, King of the Hill, 1997; (TV series) Hercules (voice), 1998. Office: ICM c/o Tracey Jacobs 8942 Wilshire Blvd Beverly Hills CA 90211-1934 also: care Elaine Rich 2400 Whitman Pl Los Angeles CA 90068-2464

LEIGH, MIKE, film director; b. Salford, England, Feb. 20, 1943; s. A.A. and P.P. (Cousin) Leigh; m. Alison Steadman, 1973 (div. 2001); 2 children. Student, Royal Acad. Dramatic Art, London, Camberwell Sch. Arts and Crafts, Cen. Sch. Art and Design, London Film Sch. Writer, dir.: (plays) The Box Play, 1965, My Parents Have Gone to Carlisle, The Last Crusade of the Five Little Nuns, 1966, Nenaa, 1967, Individual Fruit Pies, Down Here and Up There, Big Basil, 1968, Epilogue, Glum Victoria and the Lad with Specs, 1969, Bleak Moments, 1970, A Rancid Pong, 1971, Wholesome Glory, The Jaws of Death, Dick Whittington and His Cat, 1973, Babies Grow Old, The Silent Majority, 1974, Abigail's Party, 1977, Ecstasy, 1979, Goose-Pimples, 1981 (Critics' Choice Best Comedy award London Evening Std. 1981, Critics' Choice Best Comedy award Drama London 1981), Smelling A Rat, 1988, Greek Tragedy, 1989, It's a Great Big Shame!, 1993, (feature films) Bleak Moments, 1971 (Golden Leopard award Locarno Film Festival 1972, Golden Hugo award Chgo. Film Festival 1972), High Hopes, 1988 (Internat. Critic's prize Venice Film Festival 1988, Best Film Coup de Coeur Geneva 1989, Peter Sellers Best Comedy Film award London Evening Std. 1990), Life is Sweet, 1990, Naked, 1993 (Best Dir. award Cannes Internat. Film Festival 1993), Secrets and Lies, 1996 (Palme d'Or Cannes 1996), Career Girls, 1997, Topsy-Turvy, 1999, All or Nothing, 2002, Vera Drake, 2004, (TV films) A Mug's Game, Hard Labour, 1972, The Permissive Society, The Birth of the 2001 F.A. Cup Final Goalie, Old Chums, Probation, A Light Snack, Afternoon, 1975, Nuts in May, 1976, Knock for Knock, 1976, The Kiss of Death, 1977, Abigail's Party, 1977, Who's Who, 1978, Grown Ups, 1980, Home Sweet Home, 1981, Meantime, 1983, Four Days in July, 1984, The Short and Curlies, 1987, A Sense of History, 1992, (radio play) Too Much of a Good Thing, 1979. Address: Peters Fraser & Dunlop Drury House 34-43 Russell London WC2B 3HA England*

LEIGH, RICHARD E., JR., lawyer; b. 1959; m. Desiree Blackwell; 1 child, Trey. BA, Brown U., 1981; MA, John Hopkins U.; JD, Columbia U., 1986. Bar: 1987. Ptnr. Foster Pepper & Shefelman, Seattle, 1989—97; v.p., gen. counsel Seattle Seahawks NFL, Seattle, 1997; v.p., gen. counsel Vulcan Inc., Seattle; exec. v.p., gen. counsel, corp. sec. Cell Therapeutics, Inc., Seattle, 2004—. With Gr. Seattle C. of C., Kingdome Renovation Task Force, Seattle Seahawks Charitable Found. Office: Cell Therapeutics Inc 501 Elliot Ave W Ste 400 Seattle WA 98119 Office Phone: 206-282-7100. Office Fax: 206-284-6206.*

LEIGH, STEPHEN, industrial designer; b. N.Y.C., May 21, 1931; s. Herman Lerner and Rhea (Drinkhouse) L.; children: Harvey Alan, Madeleine Beth; m. Wendy Horton, June 6, 1999. BFA, Cooper Union, 1951. Interior designer Robert Gruen Assocs., N.Y.C., 1951-55; designer, project dir. Michael Saphier Assocs., N.Y.C., 1955-59; pres. Stephen Leigh & Assocs. Inc., N.Y.C., 1959—. Interior designers, cons. specializing in comml. usage, United Jewish Appeal, 1963, U.S. Pavilion, Venezuelan Pavilion, N.Y. World's Fair, 1964-65, Random House, 1969, Mitsubishi Internat. Corp., 1980, Rapid Am. Corp., 1982, Bowery Savs. Bank, 1986; lectr. NYU. Columnist Real Estate Weekly, 1963-65, The Office Mag., 1985—; one-man shows of sculpture at Cartier and East River Savings Bank; recent prin. works include Union Chelsea Nat. Bank, Faberge, Fino Restaurant, Il Menestrello Restaurant, Schenley, redesign of landmark facade at 111 8th Ave., 1989; sculpted permanent team trophy for Eisenhower Golf Tournament. Recipient AIA design award for Venezuelan Pavilion N.Y. World's Fair, 1964-65, Excellence award The Archtl. Woodwork Inst., 1988. Mem. Am. Soc. of Interior Designers (N.Y. chpt.), Charge des Missions of the Confrerie de la Chaine des Rotisseurs (Bronze Star of Excellence), Brotherhood of the Knights of the Vine Avocations: sculpture, painting, cooking, travel, collecting americana and american flags. Office: 157 E 57th St New York NY 10022-2104

LEIGH, VINCENTA M., health administrator; b. N.Y.C., June 27, 1947; d. Emanuel and Ines Masciandara; m. Hoyle Leigh, Sept. 16, 1967; 1 child, Alexander. BA, Lehman Coll., 1968; MSN, Yale U., 1973. Psychiat. clinician Jacobi Hosp., Bronx, N.Y., 1971; pediatric nurse Conn. Mental Health Ctr., New Haven, 1971-73; instr. in psychiat. nursing Yale U., New Haven, 1973-77; asst. dir. mental health nursing edn. Conn. Valley Hosp., Middletown, 1980-81; nurse coord. Inst. of Living, Hartford, Conn., 1981-85, asst. dir. nursing, 1985-89; asst. clin. profl. psychiatry U. Calif., San Francisco, 1989—; coord. Intensive outpatient program Kaiser Permanent, Fresno, Calif., 1996—. Contbr. articles to profl. jours. Mem. ANA, Am. Psychosomatic Soc., Internat. Coll. Psychosomatic Medicine, Am. Orthopedic Assn., Jr. League. Avocations: piano, reading, trombone, skiing.

LEIGHTON, ALBERT CHESTER, history educator; b. Chester, N.H., Sept. 6, 1919; s. Arthur Edmund and Sarah Elizabeth (Edwards) L.; m. Estella Ruth Dietel, Jan. 17, 1958; children: Cedric Edmund George. AB, U. Calif., Berkeley, 1960, MA, 1961, PhD, 1964. Enlisted U.S. Army, 1937, commd. 2d lt., 1946, advanced through grades to capt., 1953, ret., 1957; ops. officer, Germany, 1947-50, staff officer Hdqrs., Washington, 1950-53, 55-57, ops. officer, Korea, Japan, Taiwan, 1954-55; assoc. prof. history SUNY-Oswego, 1964-69, prof., 1969-85, prof. emeritus, 1985—; adj. prof., lectr. U. Tex. at San Antonio, 1987—; Fulbright Rsch. prof. U. Munich, 1978-79; faculty exchange scholar SUNY, 1981-85; coord. internat. rsch. in hist. cryptanalysis, 1969—; speaker Internat. Congress, St. Petersburg formerly Leningrad, 1970, Moscow, 1971, Tokyo, 1974, Edinburgh, 1977. Author: Transport and Communication in Early Medieval Europe, 1972; contbr. Ency. Americana; contbr. articles to profl. jours. Rsch. fellow Ctr. Medieval and Renaissance Studies UCLA, 1984, Medieval Insts. fellow Duke U., 1976, SUNY Binghamton fellow, 1985. Mem. Am. Hist. Assn., Medieval Acad. Am., Am. Cryptogram Assn., Beale Cypher Soc., Ancient and Honorable Arty. Co. Mass., New Eng. Hist. and Genealogical Soc., Ret. Officers Assn. Home: 8406 Burwell San Antonio TX 78254-2538

LEIGHTON, CAROLYN, foundation administrator; b. Providence, R.I. BS in Human Devel., Pacific Oaks Coll. Founder Leighton Corp., 1978—82, Legal Talent Directory, 1982—; chmn. Core Competency Database Project Stanford (Conn.) U., 1982—84; founder Criterion Rsch., Sherman Oaks, Calif., 1984—89, Women in Tech. Internat., Sherman Oaks, 1989—. Office: Women in Tech Internat 13351 0 Riverside Dr 441 Sherman Oaks CA 91423

LEIGHTON, CHARLES MILTON, retired specialty consumer products executive; b. Portland, Maine, June 4, 1935; s. Wilbur F. and Elizabeth (Loveland) L.; children: Julia Loveland, Anne Throop; m. Roxanne Brooks McCormick, May 23, 1992. AB, Bowdoin Coll., 1957, LLD (hon.), 1989; MBA, Harvard U., 1960. Product lines mgr. Mine Safety Appliances Co., Pitts., 1960-64; instr. Harvard Bus. Sch., 1964-65; group v.p. Bangor Punta Corp., Boston, 1965-69; chmn., CEO CML Group, Inc., Acton, Mass., 1969-97; pvt. investor, cons. mergers and acquisitions Bolton, Mass., 1997—. Exec. dir. U.S. Sailing, 2005—; bd. dirs. Met. Life Ins. Co., N.Y.; trustee Lahey Clinic; chmn. Lahey Clinic Pension Fund. Past pres. Alumni Coun. Harvard Bus. Sch., Cambridge, Mass.; past pres. trustees Concord (Mass.) Acad. Mem. N.Y. Yacht Club (commodore 1993-94, chmn. trustees Am.'s Cup 2000 Challenge), Chatham (Mass.) Yacht Club (vice commodore 1957), Harvard of N.Y.C., Harvard Faculty Club, Tarratine Club, Carnegie Abby Golf Club. Republican. Episcopalian. Home: 330 Gray Craig Rd Middletown RI 02842 Office Phone: 401-683-0800. Personal E-mail: whitecap20@aol.com. Business E-Mail: cleighton@ussailing.org.

LEIGHTON, FRANCES SPATZ, writer, journalist; b. Geauga County, Ohio; m. Kendall King Hoyt, Feb. 1, 1984 (dec. Aug. 2001). Student, Ohio State U. Washington corr. Am. Weekly, Internat. News Svc.; corr. and Washington editor This Week Mag.; Washington corr. Met. Group Sunday Mags.; contbg. editor Family Weekly; freelance journalist Metro Sunday Group, Washington. Lectr. summer confs. Dellbrook-Shenandoah Coll., Georgetown U., Washington. Author over 30 books on hist. figures, celebrities, Hollywood, psychiatry, the White House and Capitol Hill, 1957—; (with Louise Pfister) I Married a Psychiatrist, 1961, (with Francois Rysovy) A Treasury of White House Cooking, 1968, (with Frank S. Caprio) How to Avoid a Nervous Breakdown, 1969, (with Mary B. Gallagher) My Life with Jacqueline Kennedy, 1969, (with Traphes Bryant) Dog Days at the White House, 1975, (with William Fishbait Miller) Fishbait— the Memoirs of the Congressional Doorkeeper, 1977, (with Lillian Rogers Parks) My 30 Years Backstairs at the White House (made into TV mini-series), 1979, (with Hugh Carter) Cousin Beedie, Cousin Hot--, My Life with the Carter Family of Plains, Georgia, 1978, (with Jerry Cammarata) The Fun Book of Fatherhood-or How the Animal Kingdom is Helping to Raise the Wild Kids at Our House, 1978, (with Natalie Golos) Coping with Your Allergies, 1979, (with Ken Hoyt) Drunk Before Noon— The Behind the Scenes Story of the Washington Press Corps, 1979, (with Louis Hurst) The Sweetest Little Club in the World, The Memoirs of the Senate Restaurateur, 1980, (with John M. Szostak) In the Footsteps of Pope John Paul II, 1980, (with Lillian Rogers Parks) The Roosevelts, a Family in Turmoil, 1981, (with June Allyson) June Allyson, 1982, (with Beverly Slater) Stranger in My Bed, 1985 (made into TV movie, 1987), The Search for the Real Nancy Reagan, 1987, (with Oscar Collier) How To Write and Sell Your First Nonfiction Book, 1990, How to Write and Sell Your First Novel, 1986, rev. edit., 1998, (with Stephen M. Bauer) At Ease at the White House, 1991; contbg. author: Katherine Graham's Washington, 2002; contbr. numerous feature stories on polit., social and govtl. personalities to various publs. Bd. dirs. Nat. Found., 1963-. Recipient Edgar award, 1961. Mem. AAUW, Senate Periodical Corr. Assn., White House Corr. Assn., Am. News Women's Club, The Writers Club, Nat. Press Club, Writers League of Washington (pres.), Washington League Am. Pen Women (pres.), Washington Ind. Writers, Smithsonian Assocs., Nat. Trust Hist. Preservation, Lake Barcroft Women's Club, Delta Phi Delta, Sigma Delta Chi. Unitarian Universalist. Office: Lake Barcroft 6336 Lakeview Dr Falls Church VA 22041-1331 Office Phone: 703-256-9664.

LEIGHTON, GEORGE NEVES, retired judge; b. New Bedford, Mass., Oct. 22, 1912; s. Antonio N. and Anna Sylvia (Garcia) Leitao; m. Virginia Berry Quivers, June 21, 1942; children: Virginia Anne, Barbara Elaine. AB, Howard U., 1940; LLB, Harvard U., 1946; LLD, Elmhurst Coll., 1964; LLD., John Marshall Law Sch., 1973; LLD, U. Mass., 1975, New Eng. U. Sch. Law, 1978, R.I. Coll., 1992, So. New Eng. Sch. Law, 2000; LLD (hon.), Loyola U., Chgo., 1989. Bar: Mass. 1946, Ill. 1947, U.S. Supreme Ct. 1958. Ptnr. Moore, Ming & Leighton, Chgo., 1951-59, McCoy, Ming & Leighton, Chgo., 1959-64; judge Cook County Circuit Ct., Chgo., 1964-69, Ill. Appellate Ct. (1st dist.), 1969-76; U.S. dist. judge U.S. Dist. Ct. (no. dist.) Ill., 1976-86, sr. dist. judge, 1986-87; ret.; of counsel Earl L. Neal & Assocs., 1987—. Adj. prof. John Marshall Law Sch., Chgo., 1965—; commr., mem. character and fitness com. for 1st Appellate Dist., Supreme Ct. Ill., 1955-63, chmn. character and fitness com., 1961-62; joint com. for revision Ill. Criminal Code, 1959-63; chmn. Ill. adv. com. U.S. Commn. on Civil Rights, 1964; mem. pub. rev. bd. UAW, AFL-CIO, 1961-70; Asst. atty. gen. State of Ill., 1950-51; pres. 3d Ward Regular Democratic Orgn., Cook County, Ill., 1951-53; v.p. 21st Ward, 1964; spl. counsel to chmn. bd. Chgo. Transit Authority, 1988. Contbr. articles to legal jours. Bd. dirs. United Ch. Bd. for Homeland Ministries, United Ch. of Christ, Grant Hosp., Chgo.; trustee U. Notre Dame, 1979-83, trustee emeritus, 1983—; bd. overseers Harvard Coll., 1983-89. Capt., inf. AUS, 1942-45. Decorated Bronze Star; recipient Civil Liberties award Ill. div. ACLU, 1961, U.S. Supreme Ct. Justice John Paul Stevens award, 2000, Father Agustus Tolton awardCath. Archdioceses Chgo., 2000; named Chicagoan of Year in Law and Judiciary Jr. Assn. Commerce and Industry, 1964, Laureate, Acad. Ill. Lawyers, 2000. Fellow ABA (chmn. coun. 1976, mem. coun. sect. legal edn. and admissions to bar), Am. Coll. Trial Lawyers; mem. NAACP (chmn. legal redress com. Chgo. br.), John Howard Assn. (bd. dirs.), Chgo. Bar Assn., Ill. Bar Assn. (joint com. for revision jud. article 1959-62, sr. counselor 1996), Nat. Harvard Law Sch. Assn. (mem. coun.), Howard U. Chgo. Alumni Club (chmn. bd. dirs.), Phi Beta Kappa. Office: Neal Murdock & Leroy Ste 2300 203 N LaSalle St Chicago IL 60601-1213 Office Phone: 312-641-7144. Business E-Mail: gleighton@nealmurdock.com, gleighton@nealleroy.com.

LEIGHTON, JACK RICHARD, small business owner, former educator; b. Boise, Idaho, May 10, 1918; s. Ralph Waldo and Lucia Marie (Strub) L.; m. Helen Louise Wirtenberger, July 24, 1942; 1 child, James Carl. Student, U. Wash., 1938—39; BS, U. Oreg., 1941, MS, 1942, PhD, 1954; postgrad., U. Iowa, 1950. Dir. phys. edn. and athletics Montpelier (Idaho) H.S., 1941-42; exec. asst. phys. medicine rehab. svc. Vancouver (Wash.) VA Hosp., 1946-50; assoc. prof. phys. edn. Pa. State U., State College, 1952-53; assoc. prof. Ea. Wash. U., Cheney, 1953-56, prof., 1956-81, dir. divsn. health, phys. edn., recreation and athletics, 1953-81; pres. Leighton Flexometer Co. Inc., Spokane, Wash., 1985—. Mem. com. on secondary sch. health and phys. edn. Idaho Dept. Edn., Boise, 1942; cons. state adv. com. on sch. activity and phys. edn. Wash. Dept. Pub. Instrn., Olympia, 1954-55, mem. com. on phys. edn. curriculum guide, 1957-58. Author: Physical Education for Boys, 1942, Objective Physical Education, 1946, Progressive Weight Training, 1961, Fitness, Body Development & Sports Conditioning Through Weight Training, 1983; assoc. editor Rsch. Quar. AAHPERD, 1960-63, Jour. Health, Phys. Edn. and Recreation, 1967-68; editor Jour. Assn. for Phys. and Mental Rehab., 1963-67; mem. editl. bd. Am. Corrective Therapy Jour., 1972-79; contbr. articles to profl. jours., chpts. to books; patentee instrument to measure range of joint motion. Mem. Ea. Wash. U. Retirees Bd., 1996-99; mem. Spokane County Cmty. Svcs. Devel. Disabilities Adv. Bd., 2000—. With AUS, 1942-46. Fellow Am. Coll. Sports Medicine; mem. AAHPERD (necrology com. 1955-58, chmn. fitness sect. 1960-61, mem. rsch. coun., com. to study purpose and propose revisions of structure and procedures gen. divsn. 1960-61; mem. N.W. dist. honor awards com. 1955-57, 76-79, chmn. 1976-77, mem. constn. com. 1957-60, chmn. rsch. sect. 1957-58, v.p. phys. edn. 1957-58, chmn. fitness sect. 1963-64, pres. 1971-72), Wash. Assn. Health, Phys. Edn. and Recreation (phys. fitness steering com. 1955-57, constn. com. 1957-58, chmn. tchr. tng. sect. 1956-57, phys. fitness steering com. 1957-59, v.p. ea. dist. 1957-58, pres. 1959-60), Spokane United Sch. Groups (Ea. Wash. U. rep. 1957-60), Spokane Area C. of C. (small bus. coun. 1993—2003), Phi Delta Kappa, Phi Epsilon Kappa. Home and Office: 3118 E Chaser Ln Spokane WA 99223-7267 Office Phone: 509-448-0392.

LEIGHTON, JAMES H., law educator, department chairman; b. N.Y.C., Mar. 28, 1947; s. Martin and Rosalyn A. (Brown) Leighton. BA in Polit. Sci. cum laude, SUNY, Binghamton, 1969, M in Polit. Sci., 1971; JD, Hofstra U., 1985. Bar: Fla. 1987. Prof., dept. chair legal assisting and pvt. investigations dept. City Coll., Ft. Lauderdale, Fla., 1995—. Committeeman East Norwich (N.Y.) Dems., 1973—78; staff McGovern for Pres. 1972, Binghamton, 1971—72; faculty advisor chair Ambassadors Svc. and Honors Soc., Ft. Lauderdale, 1997—2000. Tchg. fellow, SUNY Binghamton, 1969—71. Mem.: Fla. Bar Assn. (licentiate). Democrat. Avocations: travel, reading, baseball. Office: City Coll 1401 W Cypress Creek Rd Fort Lauderdale FL 33309 Personal E-mail: jleighton@citycollege.edu.

LEIGHTON, LAWRENCE WARD, investment banker; b. NYC, July 1, 1934; s. Sidney and Florence (Ward) Leighton; m. Mariana Stroock, June 21, 1959; children: Sandra L. Galvin, Michelle S. BSE, Princeton U., 1956; MBA, Harvard U., 1962. V.p. Kuhn Loeb & Co., N.Y.C., 1962-69, Clark, Dodge & Co., Inc., 1970-74; dir. Norton-Simon, Inc., 1974-78; ltd. ptnr. Bear, Stearns & Co., 1978-82; mng. dir. Chase Investment Bank, 1983-88; pres., CEO Union d'Etudes et d'Investissements Mcht. Bank of Credit Agricole, 1989-93; vice-chmn. 2I, Inc., 1993-94; mng. dir. LM Capital Corp., 1994-96, Bentley Assocs., LP, N.Y.C., 1997—. Chmn. Princeton Schs. Com. N.Y., 1965—85. Mem. exec. com. alumni coun. Lawrenceville Sch., 1999—2002; mem. nat. fin. com. Pete DuPont for Pres., 1986—88; mem. exec. com. alumni coun. Princeton (N.J.) U., 1975—80, vice-chmn. nat. schs. com., 1980—; chmn. Harvard Bus. Sch. Fund. N.Y., 1964—65; trustee Waterford Inst., 1985—. Lt. (j.g.) USN, 1957—60. Mem.: Mid Ocean Club (Bermuda), Coral Beach and Tennis Club (Bermuda), Princeton Club N.Y. (mem. scholarship com. 1970—, bd. govs. 1989—96), Stanwich Club (Greenwich, Conn.). Avocations: flying, golf, photography. Home: 1088 Park Ave New York NY 10128-1132 Office: Bentley Assocs Rm 2201 101 Park Ave New York NY 10178-2101 Office Phone: 212-763-0374. Business E-Mail: lwleighton@bentleylp.com.

LEIGHTON, RICHARD FREDERICK, retired dean; BA, Western Md. Coll., 1951; MD, U. Md., 1955; ScD (hon.), Med. Coll. Ohio, Toledo, 2000. Diplomate Am. Bd. Internal Medicine (Specialty Cardiovascular Disease). Intern U. Hosp., Balt., 1955—56; flight surgeon USN, 1956—58; resident Ohio State U. Hosp., 1959—61, resident, cardiology fellow, 1961—64; from asst. prof. to assoc. prof. medicine Coll. Medicine Ohio State U., 1965—74, dir. coronary care unit, 1968—69, dir. cardiac catheterization labs., 1970—74; prof. medicine, chief cardiology Med. Coll. Ohio, 1974—90, acting chmn. dept. medicine, 1988, vice chmn., 1988—90, v.p. acad. affairs, dean Sch. Medicine, 1990—95, sr. v.p. acad. affairs, dean Sch. Medicine, 1995—96, emeritus, ret., 1997; prof. medicine Mercer U. Med. Sch., 1998—; chmn. instnl. rev. bd. Meml. Health U. Med. Ctr., 1998—. Editl. bd. La Lettre du Cardiologue, 1985—; contbr. numerous articles to profl. jours. Fellow ACP, Am. Coll. Cardiology (gov. Ohio chpt. 1985-88), Am. Heart Assn (coun. circulation, epidemiology, clinical cardiology, coun. rep. Ohio 1977-80), Royal Soc. Medicine; mem. Ctrl. Soc. Clin. Rsch., U. Md. Med. Alumni Assn. (Honor award, Gold Key 2005), Societe Francaise Cardiologie (corr.), Alpha Omega Alpha. Office: Meml Health U Med Ctr Dept Internal Med Edn PO Box 23089 Savannah GA 31403-3089 Business E-Mail: leighril@memorialhealth.com. E-mail: rflfsl@bellsouth.net.

LEIGHTON, ROBERT JOSEPH, lawyer; b. Austin, Minn., July 7, 1965; s. Robert Joseph Sr. and JoAnn (Mulvihill) L. BA, U. Minn., 1988; JD, U. Calif., Berkeley, 1991. Minn. state rep. Dist. 27B, 1995—2002; atty. Nolan, MacGregor, Thompson & Leighton, St. Paul, 2002—. Presdl. and Waller scholar U. Minn., 1988. Mem. Minn. Bar Assn., Minn. Trial Lawyers Assn., Phi Beta Kappa. Home: 4243 Wexford Way Eagan MN 55122 Office: Nolan MacGregor Thompson & Leighton Lawson Commons Ste 710 380 St Peter St Saint Paul MN 55102 Office Phone: 651-227-6661. Business E-Mail: rleighton@nmtlaw.com.

LEIGHTON, TODD EDWARD, band director; b. Lewiston, Maine, Jan. 19, 1971; s. Lawrence Jon and Carol Susan Leighton; m. Rebecca Marie Leighton, Feb. 29, 1996; children: Todd Michael, Kailyn. AA, Polk CC, Winter Haven, Fla., 1993; BA in Music Edn., U. Central Fla., Orlando, 1999. Profl. musician Walt Disney World Co., Lake Buena Vista, Fla.; band dir. Gotha Mid. Sch., Fla., 1999—2000, Lake Howell HS, Winter Park, Fla., 2000—. Percussion clinician Lake Howell HS, Buchholz HS, Winter Park. Guest conductor Tangerine Bowl, 2003. Nominee Disney Tchr. Hand award, 2004; named Tchr. of Week, Orlando Sentinel, 2004; recipient Principal's award, Lake Howell HS, 2004. Mem.: Fla. Music Educators Assn., Percussive Arts Soc., Fla. Bandmasters Assn. Office: Lake Howell HS 4200 Dike Rd Winter Park FL 32792 Business E-Mail: todd_leighton@scps.k12.fl.us.

LEIGHTON, WILLIAM D., plastic and reconstructive surgeon; b. Battle Creek, Mich., Sept. 27, 1952; m. Judith Peltier, July 2, 1976; children: Joshua, Jason. BA, U. Colo., 1974; MD, U. Ill., 1978. Diplomate Am. Bd. Plastic Surgery. Intern Phoenix Integrated Surg. Residency, 1978, gen. surgery resident, 1979-83, resident in plastic surgery, 1983-85; micro-surgery fellow So. Ill. U., 1985; chief plastic surgery Good Samaritan Hosp., Phoenix, 1988-93, Phoenix Children's Hosp., 1989-92, Maricopa Med. Ctr., 1987-91, Scottsalde (Ariz.) Meml. North, 1994—. Mem. Ariz. Soc. Plastic and Reconstructive Surgeons (pres.), Am. Soc. Plastic Surgeons, Am. Soc. Aesthetic Plastic Surgery. Office: 10210 N 92d St # 200 Scottsdale AZ 85258

LEIJONHUFVUD, AXEL STIG BENGT, economics professor; b. Stockholm, Sept. 6, 1933; came to U.S., 1960; s. Erik Gabriel and Helene Adelheid (Neovius) L.; m. Marta Elisabeth Ising, June 10, 1955 (div. 1977); m. Earlene Joyce Craver, June 18, 1977; children— Carl Axel, Gabriella Helene, Christina Elisabeth Fil. kand., U. Lund, Sweden, 1960; MA, U. Pitts., Pa., 1961; PhD, Northwestern U., 1967; Fil. Dr. (hon.), U. Lund, Sweden, 1983; Dr. (hon.), U. Nice, Sophia-Antipolis, France, 1995. Acting asst. prof. econs. UCLA, 1964-67, assoc. prof. econs., 1967-71, prof. econs., 1971—, chair dept. econs., 1980-83, 90-92; dir. Ctr. for Computable Econs., 1992-97; prof. monetary theory and policy U. Trento, Italy, 1995—. Co-dir. summer workshops Siena Internat. Sch. Econ. Rsch., 1987-91; dir. program in econ. dynamics U. Trento, 2000—; participant profl. confs.; cons., lectr., vis. prof. econs. various colls. and univs.; cons. Republic of Tatarstan, 1994. Author: On Keynesian Economics and the Economics of Keynes: A Study in Monetary Theory, 1968, Keynes and the Classics: Two Lectures, 1969, Information and Coordination: Essays in Macroeconomic Theory, 1981; co-author (with D. Heymann): High Inflation, 1995, Macroeconomic Instability and Coordination, Selected Essays, 2000; editor: Monetary Theory as a Basis for Monetary Policy, 2001, Monetary Theory and Policy Experience, 2001, Informazione, coordinamento e instabilità macroeconomica: a cura di Elisabella de Antonz, 2004. Econ. expert com. of pres. Kazakhstan, 1991-92. Brookings Instn. fellow, 1963-64; Marshall lectr. Cambridge U., Eng., 1974; Overseas fellow Churchill Coll., Cambridge, 1974; Inst. Advanced Study fellow, 1983-84 Mem. Am. Econ. Assn., Western Econ. Assn., History of Econs. Soc. Business E-Mail: axel@ucla.edu.

LEIKEN, EARL MURRAY, lawyer; b. Cleve., Jan. 19, 1942; s. Manny and Betty G. L.; m. Ellen Kay Miner, Mar. 26, 1970; children: Jonathan, Brian. BA magna cum laude, Harvard U., 1964, JD cum laude, 1967. Asst. dean, assoc. prof. law Case Western Res. U., Cleve., 1967-71; ptnr. Hahn, Loeser, Freedheim, Dean & Wellman, Cleve., 1971-86, Baker & Hostetler, Cleve., 1986—. Adj. faculty, lectr. law Case Western Res. U., 1971-86. Pres. Shaker Heights (Ohio) Bd. Edn., 1986-88, Jewish Community Ctr., Cleve., 1988-91, Shaker Heights Family Ctr., 1994-97; mem. Shaker Heights City Coun., 2000—. Named one of Greater Cleve.'s 10 Outstanding Young Leaders, Cleve. Jaycees, 1972; recipient Kane award Cleve. Jewish Community Fedn.,

1982. Mem. ABA, Greater Cleve. Bar Assn. (chmn. labor law sect. 1978). Home: 20815 Colby Rd Cleveland OH 44122-1903 Office: Baker & Hostetler 3200 Nat City Ctr 1900 E 9th St Ste 3200 Cleveland OH 44114-3475

LEIKIN, JERROLD BLAIR, emergency room physician, toxicologist; b. Chgo., Aug. 28, 1954; s. Mitchell and Evelyn (Ucitel) L.; m. Robin Ellen Goldman, June 6, 1982; children: Scott Michael, Eryn Nicole. BS, U. Iowa, 1976; MD, Chgo. Med. Sch., 1980. Diplomate Am. Bd. Internal Medicine, Am. Bd. Emergency Medicine, Am. Bd. Med. Toxicology, Am Bd. Quality Assurance and Utilization Rev. Physicians. Resident Evanston (Ill.) Hosp., 1980-82, Northwestern Meml. Hosp., Chgo., 1982-84; fellow Cook County Hosp., Chgo., 1984-87; chief med. emergency svcs. U. Ill. Hosp., Chgo., 1984-88; assoc. dir. Rush Emergency Svcs. Rush Presbyn. St. Luke Med. Ctr., Chgo., 1988—2001, med. dir. Rush Poison Control Ctr., 1989-98; dir. med. toxicology Evanston Northwestern Healthcare-OMEGA, Glenview, Ill., 2001—; prof. medicine Rush Med. Coll., Feinberg Sch. Medicine, Northwestern U. Cons. Underwriter Labs., Northbrook, Ill., 1991—; reviewer Jour. Clin. Toxicology, Omaha, 1990—. Co-author: Poisoning and Toxicology Compendium; contbr. articles to profl. jours. Fellow ACP, Am. Coll. Emergency Physicians; mem. AMA, Am. Acad. Clin. Toxicology. Achievements include research on immunotoxicity, immunotherapy and management of drug overdose and carbon monoxide evaluation. Office: Evanston Northwestern Healthcare-OMEGA 2150 Pfingston Rd Ste 3000 Glenview IL 60025

LEIMKUHLER, GERARD JOSEPH, diversified financial services company executive; b. Phila., June 13, 1948; s. Gerard Joseph and Dorothy Joan (Gaffney) L.; m. Karen Roberta Hall, Oct. 13, 1973; 1 child, Courtney Hall. BBA, Temple U., 1970. Mem. Phila. Stock Exch., 1971-75; sr. v.p., exec. v.p., vice chmn. Oxford First Corp., Phila., 1975—95; sr. v.p., sec. Oxford Communities, Inc., Oxford Fin. Cos. Inc., Phila., 1975—95; pres. Gen. Acquisitions Corp., Phila., 1977-95; chmn., pres., chief officer Eagle Capital Corp. and Eagle Capital Mortgage, Ltd., 1997—99; mng. dir. Berwyn Capital Group, 1995—2001. Vice chmn., chmn. restructure com. Medshares, Inc., Memphis, 1999—2003; pres., CEO Wescott Strategic Mgmt. LLC, Phila., 2001—. Vice-chmn. Newtown Twp. Planning Commn., Delaware County, Pa., 1976-98; chmn. investment adv. bd. Newtown Twp. Investment, 1987-99. With U.S. Army, 1970-71. Mem. Internat. Found. Timesharing (former chmn. investment com.) 1990, Turnaround Mgmt. Assn. Phila. (founding bd. dirs., treas.), Urban Land Inst., Am. Resort Devel. Assn., HFCA, Rep. Congl. Com., Federalist Soc., Mensa, Union League Phila., Aronimink Golf Club. Republican. Roman Catholic. Office: One Liberty Place Ste 4200 Philadelphia PA 19103

LEINART, MATT, college football player; b. Santa Ana, Califorina, May 11, 1983; s. Bob and Linda. Student, soc. major, U. So. Calif., 2001—. Quarterback USC Trojans, 2001—. Named Pac-10 Offensive Player of the Yr., 2003, Rose Bowl MVP, 2003; named to All-American first team, 2003, All-Pac-10 first team; recipient Heisman Trophy, 2004. Achievements include quarterback, co-nat. champions USC Trojan's, 2004, nat. champions, 2005; set Orange Bowl record with 5 touchdown passes, 2005. Mailing: USC Football 3501 Watt Way HER 203 A Los Angeles CA 90089*

LEINBACH, PHILIP EATON, retired librarian; b. Winston-Salem, N.C., Sept. 17, 1935; s. Gray Newton and Martha Elizabeth (Eaton) L.; m. Nancy Lee Yocom, July 27, 1957; children— Jonathan Eaton, David Timothy AB, Duke U., 1956; MA in History, Ind. U., 1963, M.L.S., 1964. Adminstrv. asst. Harvard U. Library, Cambridge, Mass., 1964-66; asst. librarian for acquisitions Harvard U., Cambridge, 1966-67, specialist in book selection, 1967-71, asst. univ. librarian, 1972-82; univ. librarian Tulane U., New Orleans, 1982-99; ret. Acting chief libr. Harvard U. Div. Sch., Cambridge, 1978-79; dep. libr. Queen Mary Coll., London, 1970-71. Author: Handbook for Librarians, 1977, Personnel Administration in an Automated Environment, 1990. Served with USNR, 1957-61 Fellow Ind. U., 1963-64; UCLA Grad. Sch. Library and Info. Sci., 1982; NDEA modern lang. fellow, 1962-63 Mem. ALA (council 1984-88), La. Library Assn., Omicron Delta Kappa, Beta Phi Mu, Pi Sigma Alpha Home: 122 Solterra Way Durham NC 27705-7314

LEINBACH, TRACY A., transportation executive; BBA in Acctg., Coll. William and Mary; MBA, U. N.C. CPA. From asst. controller Ryder Integrated Logistics to exec. v.p., CFO Ryder System. Inc., Miami, 1988—2002, exec. v.p., 2002—, CFO, 2002—. Office: Ryder System 3600 Northwest 82nd Ave Miami FL 33166

LEINENWEBER, HARRY D., federal judge; b. Joliet, Ill., June 3, 1937; s. Harry Dean and Emily (Lennon) L.; m. Lynn Morley Martin, Jan. 7, 1987; 5 children; 2 stepchildren. AB cum laude, U. Notre Dame, 1959; JD, U. Chgo., 1962. Bar: Ill. 1962, U.S. Dist. Ct. (no. dist.) Ill. 1967. Assoc. Dunn, Stefanich, McGarry & Kennedy, Joliet, Ill., 1962-65, ptnr., 1965-79; city atty. City of Joliet, 1963-67; spl. counsel Village of Park Forest, Ill., 1967-74; spl. prosecutor County of Will, Ill., 1968-70; spl. counsel Village of Bolingbrook, Ill., 1975-77, Will County Forest Preserve, 1977; mem. Ill. Ho. of Reps., Springfield, 1973-83, chmn. judiciary I com., 1981-83; ptnr. Dunn, Leinenweber & Dunn, Joliet, 1979-86; fed. judge U.S. Dist. Ct. (no. dist.) Ill., Chgo., 1986—. Bd. dirs. Will County Bar Assn., 1984-86, State Jud. Adv. Coun., 1973-85, sec. 1975-76; tchr. legis. process seminar U. Ill., Chgo., 1988-2001; coord. U. Ill. Disting. Lecture Series, 2002--; mem. U. Ill. Inst. Govt. and Pub. Affairs Nat. Adv. Com., 1998-2001. Bd. dirs. Will County Legal Assistance Found., 1982-86, Good Shepard Manor, 1981—, Am. Cancer Soc., 1981-85, Joliet (Ill.) Montessori Sch., 1966-74; del. Rep. Nat. Conv., 1980; precinct committeeman, 1966-86; mem. nat. adv. com. U. Ill. Inst. Govt. and Pub. Affairs, 1998-2001. Recipient Environ. Legislator Golden award. Mem. Will County Bar Assn. (mem. jud. adv. coun., 1973-85, sec. 1975-76, bd. dirs. 1984-86), Nat. Conf. Commrs. on Uniform State Laws (exec. com. 1991-93, elected life mem. 1996), The Law Club of Chgo. (bd. dirs. 1996-98). Roman Catholic. Office: US Dist Ct 219 S Dearborn St Ste 1946 Chicago IL 60604-1801 Office Phone: 312-435-7612. E-mail: harry_leinenweber@ilnd.uscourts.gov.

LEINIEKS, VALDIS, classicist, educator; b. Liepaja, Latvia, Apr. 15, 1932; came to U.S., 1949, naturalized, 1954; s. Arvid Ansis and Valia Leontine (Brunaus) L. BA, Cornell U., 1955, MA, 1956; PhD, Princeton U., 1962. Instr. classics Cornell Coll., Mount Vernon, Iowa, 1959-62, asst. prof. classics, 1962-64; assoc. prof. classics Ohio State U., 1964-66, U. Nebr., Lincoln, 1966-71, prof. classics, 1971—2005, chmn. dept. classics, 1967-95, chmn. program comparative lit., 1970-86, interim chmn. dept. modern langs., 1982-83, prof. emeritus, 2005—. Author: Morphosyntax of the Homeric Greek Verb, 1964, The Structure of Latin, 1975, Index Nepotianus, 1976, The Plays of Sophokles, 1982, The City of Dionysos, 1996; contbr. articles to profl. jours. Mem. AAUP, Am. Philol. Assn Home: 2505 A St Lincoln NE 68502-1841 Office: U Nebr Dept Classics Lincoln NE 68588-0337

LEININGER, MADELEINE MONICA, nursing educator, consultant, anthropologist, editor, writer, theorist; b. Sutton, Nebr., July 13, 1925; d. George M. S. and D. Irene (Sheedy) L. BS in Biology, Scholastic Coll., 1950, LHD, 1976; MS in Nursing, Cath. U. Am., 1953; PhD in Anthropology, U. Wash., 1965; DSc (hon.), U. Indpls., 1990; PhDN (hon.), 1990, U. Kuopio, Finland, 1991. RN; cert. transcultural nurse FAAN/Am. Acad. Nursing. Instr., mem. staff, head nurse med.-surg. unit, supr. psychiat. unit St. Joseph's Hosp., Omaha, 1950-54; assoc. prof. nursing, dir. grad. program in psychiat. nursing U. Cin. Coll. Nursing, 1954-60; research fellow Nat. League Nursing, Papua New Guinea, 1960—62, 1978, 1992, 1994; research assoc. U. Wash. Dept. Anthropology, Seattle, 1964-65; prof. nursing and anthropology, dir. nursescientist PhD program U. Colo., Boulder and Denver, 1966-69; dean sch. nursing, prof. nursing, lectr. anthropology U. Wash., Seattle, 1969-74; dean coll. nursing, prof. nursing and anthropology U. Utah, Salt Lake City, 1974-80; Anise J. Sorell prof. nursing Troy (Ala.) State U., 1981; prof. nursing, adj. prof. anthropology, dir. Ctr. for Health Research, dir. transcultural nursing offerings Wayne State U., Detroit, 1981-95, prof. emeritus, 1995—; prof. Coll. Nursing U. Nebr. Med. Ctr., 1997—2001; ret., 2001—. Adj. prof. anthropology U. Utah, 1974-81; adj. prof. nursing U. Nebr., 1997—; disting. vis. prof. over 200 univs., U.S. and overseas, 1970—; docent Boys and Girls Town of Am., Omaha Father Flanaghan Ctr., 1996; cons. and lectr. in field. Author: 30 books including Nursing and Anthropology: Two Worlds to Blend, 1970, Contemporary Issues in Mental Health Nursing, 1973, Caring: An Essential Human Need, 1981, Reference Sources for Transcultural Health and Nursing, 1984, Basic Psychiatric Concepts in Nursing, 1960, Care: The Essence of Nursing and Health, 1984, Qualitative Research Methods in Nursing, 1985, Care: Discovery and Clinical-Community Uses, 1988, Ethical and Moral Dimensions of Caring, 1990, Culture Care, Diversity and Universality: A Theory of Nursing, 1991, 2002, 2d edit. 2003, 3d edit., 2004, Care: The Compassionate Healer, 1991, Caring Imperative for Nursing Education, 1991, Transcultural Nursing, 3d edit., 2005, (with M. McFarland) Transcultural Nursing Concepts, Theories, Research and Practice, 3d edit., 2004; editor, founder Jour. Transcultural Nursing, 1988-2000 (AJN award 2003); contbr. over 400 articles to profl. jours., chpts. to books; prodr. Leininger Nursing Autobiography, 2005. Recipient Outstanding Alumni award Cath. U. Am., 1969, Hon. award Am. Assn. Colls. Nursing, 1976, 96, Nurse of Yr. award Dist. 1 Utah Nurses Assn., 1976, Lit. award Utah Nurses Assn., 1978, Trotter Disting. Pub. Lectr. award U. Tex., 1985, Disting. Faculty Tchg. Recognition award Wayne State U., 1985, Outstanding Faculty Rsch. scholar award Wayne State U. and Gerontology Inst., 1985, Gershenson Rsch. award Wayne State U., 1985, Pace Inst. Rsch. award, 1992, Hewlett Packard Rsch. award, 1992, award for Acad. Excellence AAUW-Detroit, 1986, Disting. award Bd. Govs., 1987, Pres. Excellence in Tchg. award, 1988, Women of Sci. award U. Calif., Fullerton, 1990, Outstanding U. Grad. Mentor award Wayne State U., 1995, 97, Nightingale Rsch. award Oakland U., 1995, Outstanding Nursing Leader Russell Sage Coll, Sigma Theta Tau Intl. Disting. scholar award Russell Sage Coll., 1995, Nobel prize nominee, 1999, Can. Outstanding Rsch. award Can. Nurses Assn., 2003, Deans award Wayne State U. Coll. Nursing, 2005, Outstanding Public Nursing Svc. award, Wayne State U., 2005; Womens Hall of Fame, 2004, Leininger Learning and Transcultural Nursing Collection libr. and reading sects. at Madonna U., Livonia, Mich. named in her honor, 1996; Leininger Archival Room at Trinity Coll., Moline, Ill. named in her honor, 2002; Mary Boynton Disting. lectr., 1998; Disting. vis. scholar Jimmy Crockett Lectr. Series, Disting. Vis. scholar U. Nebr., 1999, U. (Fresno) Calif. State U., 2005; named Disting. scholar U. Wis., 2001-02, Disting lectr. Arab Am. Internat. Conf., 2005, several other colls. and universities, 2004-05; Worldwide Transcultural Nursing Ctr. named in her honor, 2001; Dist. honoree Worldwide Transcultural Nursing Soc., 2003; Nominee Women's Hall of Fame, 2003; nominee Nobel Peace prize, 2000. Fellow ANA, Am. Anthrop. Soc. for Applied Anthropology (exec. com. 1980-84, nominee Nobel Perce award), Am. Acad. Nursing (Living Legend award 1998), Royal Coll. Nursing Australia (First Internat. Achievement award 2000, First Qualitative Achievement award 2003); mem. Am. Assn. Humanities, Am. Applied Anthropol. Soc., Royal Coll. Nursing Australia, Mich. Nurses Assn. (Bertha Culp Human Rights award 1994), Ctrl. States Anthropology, Amnesty Internat., Transcultural Nursing Soc. (founder, bd. dirs., pres. 1974-80), Cultural Cmty. Group Assn. (ethics, humanities heritage study group), Australian Nat. Rsch. Care Confs. (leader human care rsch.), Internat. Assn. Human Caring (founder, pres., bd. dirs.), Nordic Caring Soc. Sweden (hon.), Sigma Xi, Pi Gamma Mu, Sigma Theta Tau (Lectr. of Yr. 1987—, Disting. Spkr. at conf. 1995-2005), Delta Kappa Gamma, Alpha Tau Delta. Office: 11211 Woolworth Plz Omaha NE 68144-1875

LEIPER, ROBERT DUNCAN, local government official; b. Houston, July 22, 1953; s. William Harper Leiper and Frances Ann (Wright) Freeman; m. Glynna Dell Wilson, May 18, 1985; children: Kelsey Allison, Chad Wilson. AAS in Fire Protection, San Jacinto Coll., 1983; BA in Pub. Mgmt., U. Houston, 1988; MS in Pub. Adminstrn., Grand Canyon U., Phoenix, 2003. Master fire fighter, Tex.; cert. fire protection specialist. Lt. Spring Br. Fire Dept., Houston, 1973-75; asst. svc. mgr. Archer Motor Sales, Houston, 1975-77; fire fighter Baytown (Tex.) Fire & Rescue, 1977-80, driver, 1980-83, lt., 1983-88, capt., 1988-92, fire chief, 1992—2002; asst. city mgr. City of Baytown, 2002—04, deputy city mgr., 2004—. Instr. Tex. A & M U., College Station, 1988-92, Lamar U., Beaumont, Tex., 1990-92. Chmn. bd. Baycoast Med. Ctr., Baytown, Tex., 1994-95. Named Exec. Fire Officer, Nat. Fire Acad.; recipient Fire Fighter of Yr. award VFW, 1987, 90. Mem. Nat. Fire Protection Assn., Tex. Fire Chief's Assn. (dir.), Hispanic C. of C., Baytown C. of C., Kiwanis Club (pres. 1994, Rookie of Yr. award 1989). Avocations: wood working, camping, photography. Office: City of Baytown PO Box 424 Baytown TX 77522-0424 E-mail: bob.leiper@baytown.org.

LEIPOLD, CRAIG L., professional sports team executive; m. Helen; children: Chris, Kyle, Conner, Curtis, Bradford. Grad., Hendrix Coll. With Kimberly-Clark Corp., Neenah, Wis.; founder Ameritel Corp.; owner Rainfair Corp., 1987; owner, gov. Nashville Predators Hockey Team, 1998—; chmn. Gaylord Entertainment, Nashville. Bd. dirs. Rainfair Corp. Named Sports Person of the Year, 1999, Father of the Year, Nashville Father's Day Coun., 1999, Nashvillian of the Year, Easter Seals, 1999; named to Seton Society, St. Thomas Health Services, 2004. Office: c/o Nashville Predators 501 Broadway Nashville TN 37203-3932*

LEIPOLD, JAMES G., lawyer; BA magna cum laude, Brown U.; JD magna cum laude, Temple U. Law Sch. Dir. admissions Temple U. Law Sch.; sr. mgmt. team Law Sch. Admissions Council, asst. dir. Admissions, Edn. and Pre-law Programs, dir. Electronic Services Support and asst. dir. Edn. and Pre-law; exec. dir. Nat. Assn. for Law Placement, 2004—. Office: Nat Assn for Law Placement 1025 Connecticut Ave Ste 1110 Washington DC 20003-5413 Office Phone: 202-835-5413. Office Fax: 202-835-1112. Business E-Mail: jleipold@nalp.org.

LEIPZIG, ARTHUR, photographer, retired educator; b. Bklyn., Oct. 25, 1918; s. Julius M. and Esther Pearl (Rubin) L.; m. Mildred Levin, Mar. 21, 1942; children: Joel Myron, Judith Anne. Student, Photo League, 1942-43, Paul Strand Photo Workshop, 1946. Staff photographer PM newspaper, N.Y.C., 1942-46, Internat. News Photos, N.Y.C., 1946; freelance photographer, Sea Cliff, N.Y., 1946-68; prof. art, dir. photography C.W. Post Sch. of Arts, L.I. U., Greenvale, N.Y., 1968-90, prof. emeritus, 1990—. Contbr. photographs to Fortune, Look, Parade, Life, Natural History, Sunday Times, also indsl. mags.; guest editor Infinity Mag., N.Y.C., 1970, mem. editorial bd., 1973-75; interview and photographs included Life Documentary Photo Book, N.Y.C., 1972, 83; exhibited works Mus. Modern Art, 1946-51, 55-58, Met. Mus. Art, 1961, 62, Nassau Mus. Art, 1975, Queens Mus. Art, 1982, Transco Gallery, Houston, 1985, Daniel Wolf Gallery, N.Y.C., Houston Foto Fest, 1986, Photo Find Gallery, Woodstock, Coll. Art Gallery, New Paltz, N.Y., Smithsonian Mus., Washington, 1987, Mus. of the City of N.Y., Children's Games, 1988, Photofind Gallery, N.Y.C., 1990, ICP, Bklyn., 1992; one-man shows include Midtown Y Gallery, 1978, Henry St. Settlement, Arts for Living Ctr., 1986, Frumkin Adams Gallery, N.Y.C., 1990, 92, Photofind Gallery, 1990, Howard Greenberg Gallery, 1991, 98, Salena Gallery, Bklyn., 1992, Port Washington Libr., 1994, Mus. of the City of N.Y., 1995, 96, Albin O. Kuhn Gallery, Balt., Md., Milw. Inst. Art & Design, 1998, Firehouse Gallery, Nassau C.C., 2001; Arthur Leipzig: A Tribute to Influence; group shows include Balt. Mus. Art, 1998, Whitney Mus. Am. Art, 1999, Am. Embassy, Copenhagen Art in Embassies, 1999, The Jewish Mus., The Changing Face of Family, 1999, N.Y.: Capital of Photography, The Jewish Mus., 2002; represented in permanent collections Mus. Modern Art, Bklyn. Mus., Eastman House, Nat. Gallery Art, Nassau Mus. Art, Houston Mus. Fine Arts, Midtown Y Gallery, Visual Studies Workshop, Pablo Casals Mus., Internat. Ctr. Photography, Nat. Mus. Am. Art, Washington, Consol. Freightways, San Francisco, Bank of Am. Art Program, San Francisco, Bibliotheque Nationale, Paris, The Jewish Mus., N.Y.C., Mus. Folkwang, Essen, Germany, Nat. Portrait Gallery, Washington, The Gilman Paper Co., Queens Coll., N.Y., Madison Art Ctr., Wis., Univ. Tex., Dallas, Dreyfus, N.Y.C., Soho Grand Hotel, Columbus Mus. Art, Nassau C.C., Kresge Mus. Art, East Lansing, Mich., Milbank Meml. Fund, Santa Barbara Mus. Art; retrospective exhbn. Hillwood Gallery, Brookville, N.Y., 1989, Musée De La Civilisation, Quebec City, 1990, Balt. Mus. Art, Reader's Digest Corporate Art Gallery; featured on World of Photography, Sta. WABC-TV; pub. Classic Photographs from the Brooklyn Museum Collection, 1987, Sarah's Daughters, 1988, Master Photographs Photography in Fine Arts Exhbt. Internat. Ctr. Photography, 1988, 92, The Nat. Portrait Gallery, 1992, High Mus., Atlanta, 1992, Growing up in N.Y., 1995; photographer: Shari Lewis Puppet Book, Sara's Daughter, 1987, Growing Up in N.Y., 1995, Arthur Leipzig On Assignment, 2005 Adv. bd. Midtown Y Gallery, 1983; bd. dirs. Nassau Mus. Fine Art, 1973-75. Recipient Nat. Urban League award, 1962, ORT award, 1976, Nassau County Office Cultural Devel. award, 1982, Award for Scholarly Achievement, L.I. U. Trustees, 1983, 89, David Newton Excellence in Tchg. award, 1989, Lucie award Internat. Photography Awards, 2004 Mem. Am. Soc. Mag. Photographers (bd. govs., trustee 1960-65, treas. 1965). *My photogrpahy is very personal, my focus the human condition, exploring people, their humanity and inhumanity. I am not a cerebral photographer. My Images come as intuitive responses and they deal with my feelings about life. Through my work I have learned about myself and the world.*

LEIPZIG, MELVIN, art educator; b. Bklyn., N.Y., May 23, 1935; s. Irving and Anne Leipzig; m. Mary Jo Michelessi, Sept. 14, 1968; children: Francesca Leipzig Picone, Joshua Michael. 3-yr. cert., The Cooper Union, 1956; BFA, Yale U., 1958; MFA, Pratt Inst., 1972. Instr. Columbia U., N.Y.C., 1968—70, Queens (N.Y.) Coll., 1968—73; prof. Mercer County C.C., Trenton, NJ, 1968—. Bd. dirs. Trenton Artists Workshop Assn., 1979—, Assn. Art Edn. N.J., 1986—, N.J. Sch. for Arts, 2001—. Recipient grant for painting, NEA, 1995, award, Louis Comfort Tiffany, 1959, grant to Paris, Fulbright Found., 1958; grantee, N.J. State Coun. on Arts, 1982, 1986, 1992, 2002. Office: Mercer County C C 1200 Old Trenton Rd Trenton NJ 08690 Office Phone: 609-586-4800 3353.

LEISEY, DONALD EUGENE, wholesale distribution executive; b. Pa., Sept. 23, 1937; s. Alvin L. and E. Marie L.; m. Patricia M. Leisey; children: Kristen, Kendra. BS in Edn., West Chester (Pa.) U., 1959; MA in Adminstrn., Villanova U., 1962; cert. in bus. adminstrn., U. So. Calif., 1970, EdD in Adminstrn., 1973. Cert. gen. adminstrv., gen. secondary, gen. elem., Calif. Tchr., Coatesville, Pa., 1959-62; prin. Downingtown, Pa., 1962-64, Dept. Def. Dependent Schs., Japan, 1964-67; asst. supt. Lennox Schs., Inglewood, Calif., 1967-71; dir. adminstrv. svcs. San Rafael (Calif.) City Sch. Dist., 1971-73, supt. schs., 1973-79; instr. Dominican Coll., 1973-79; v.p., regional mgr. Am. Learning Corp., Huntington Beach, Calif., 1979-80; v.p., treas. Kittredge Sch. Corp., San Francisco, 1980-83; instr. Calif. State U., Hayward, 1981; chmn., CEO Merryhill Schs., Inc., Sacramento, 1981-89; pres., chmn. bd., CEO The Report Card, Citrus Heights, Calif., 1990—; co-dir. Internat. Acad. Ednl. Entrepreneurship, 2000—. Apptd. bd. councilors U. So. Calif., Rossier Sch. Edn., 1999; trustee Fund West Chester U., 2000. Co-author: The Educational Entrepreneur: Making a Difference, 2000. Apptd. to Gov.'s Child Care Task Force, Calif., 1984, Gov.'s Child Devel. Program Adv. Com., Calif., 1985—. Recipient Disting. Alumnus award West Chester U., 1983, Disting. Svc. award L.A. County Sheriff, 1969, Hon. Svc. award PTA, 1970. Home and Office: 23 Peacock Dr San Rafael CA 94901-8301 Office: 6366 Tupelo Dr Citrus Heights CA 95621-1700 Office Phone: 415-459-6019. Personal E-mail: delaplus@aol.com.

LEISH, KENNETH WILLIAM, retired publishing company executive; b. Cambridge, Mass., Dec. 31, 1936; s. Frank and Lillian (Kargir) L.; m. Barbara Lynn Ackerman, Nov. 27, 1966; children: Matthew, Emily, Adam. AB magna cum laude, Harvard U., 1958; MS in Journalism, Columbia U., 1959. Interviewer Oral History Office, Columbia, 1960; free lance drama reviewer Variety, 1961-66; editor Am. Heritage Pub. Co., Inc., N.Y.C., 1961-69, v.p., gen. mgr. book div., 1971-77; editor-in-chief Am. Heritage Press, 1970-71; mgr. large-format paperbacks Bantam Books Inc., N.Y.C., 1977-81; editor-in-chief Grolier Inc. Project Editorial Group, 1981-87; v.p., dir. product devel. Grolier Internat., Inc., Danbury, Conn., 1988-91; v.p. new product devel. Grolier Inc., Danbury, Conn., 1992-95; v.p., mng. editor Grolier Ednl., Danbury, Conn., 1996—2003. Author: The White House, 1972, A History of the Cinema, 1974. Served with U.S Army, 1959-60. Home: PO Box 1681 White Plains NY 10602-1681 E-mail: leishbk@aol.com.

LEISNER, ANTHONY BAKER, publishing company executive; b. Evanston, Ill., Sept. 13, 1941; s. A. Paul and Ruth (Solms) L.; children: Justina, William, Sarah; m. Patricia Anne Leisner, 1996. BS, Northwestern U., 1964, MBA, 1983; PhD, Walden U., 2005. Salesman Pitney Bowes Co., 1976-77; with Quality Books Inc., Lake Bluff, Ill., 1968—, v.p., 1972—, gen. mgr., 1979—91. Adj. faculty Lake Forest (Ill.) Sch. Mgmt., 1983—92, Kellogg Grad. Sch. Mgmt. Northwestern U., Evanston, Ill.; assoc. prof. internat. mktg. Schiller Internat. U., Dunedin, Fla., 1995—,faculty, Walden U. 2005-; head global strategic planning, spl. asst., CEO Dawson Group, Folkestone, Eng. pres. Watersedge Properties Inc., Tarpon Springs, Fla.; ptnr. Wikle Properties Mgmt., Palm Harbor, Fla.; bd. dirs. Highland Properties, Inc., Palm Harbor; mem. Pinellas Workforce Bd., Pinellas County, Fla. Author: Official Guide to Country Dance Steps, 1980; contbr. articles to jours. Pres. bd. dirs. Lake Villa Pub. Libr., 1972-78; bd. dirs. No. Ill. Libr. Sys., 1973-78, St. Petersburg (Fla.) Coll. Found.; chmn. Leepa-Rattner Mus., Libertarian Party Lake County (Ill.), 1980-81, 2002, Econ. Devel. Tarpon Springs, Fla.; probation officer Lake County CAP, 1981. Mem.: ALA (councilor, del. pub. com. White House conf. on librs. and info. svcs.), World Future Soc., Am. Mktg. Assn., Acad. Mgmt., Ill. Libr. Assn. (Gerald L. Campbell award 1980), Tarpon Springs C. of C. (chmn. econ. devel.), World Isshin Ryu Karate Assn., Tarpon Springs Yacht Club. Home and Office: 1350 Riverside Ave Tarpon Springs FL 34689-6614

LEIST, SUSAN MONDSCHEIN, communications educator, consultant; d. George Wright Richardson and Beatrice Elaine Dickerson; m. Charles Howard Leist, May 25, 1996; children: Susan Cecilia George, Thomas Richardson George, Franz William Mondschein. BS, W.Va. U., 1964, MA, 1967; EdD, U. Va., 1990. Asst. prof. Lehigh Carbon C.C., Allentown, Pa., 1968—73; instr. Buckingham H.S., Buckingham, Va., 1980—88; prof. SUNY Buffalo., 1991—2003. Author: (textbook) Grammatical Literacy, 1991, A Guidebook for using writing to Teach, 2005, Writing to Teach: Writing to Learn for Higher Education, 2005. Pers. com. chair Just Buffalo Lit. Soc., 2000—03. Recipient Innovative Excellence Tchg., Learning, and Tech., Tenth Internat. Conf. Tchg., Learning, and Tech., 1999, Pres.'s award for Excellence in Tchg., SUNY, 2001. Mem.: Nat. Coun. Tchrs. English. Democrat. Methodist. Avocations: travel, dance, reading, swimming. Office: SUNY Coll 1300 Elmwood Ave Buffalo NY 14222 Office Phone: 716-878-5401.

LEISTYNA, PEPI, linguistics educator; b. Oneida, N.Y. s. Joseph A. Leistyna and Rita R. Geoffrion; m. Susan Kubik, 1999. BA in Journalism, U. Mass., 1986, BA in French, 1987; MEd, Harvard U., 1992, EdD, 1998. Lang. instr. Berlitz, Boston, 1988—89; lang. literacy instr. Brockline (Mass.) Adult and Comty. Edn., 1989—2001; lang. instr. English Lang. Ctr., Boston, 1989—94; vis. instr. Salem (Mass.) State Coll., 1993; vis. lectr., asst. prof. U. Mass., Boston, 1995—2004, assoc. prof. applied linguistics grad. studies, 2004—. Rsch. fellow Edn. Policy Rsch. Inst., Phoenix, 2001—; assoc. editor Jour. English Linguistics, N.Y.C., 1999—; v.p. curriculum devel. ACME: Action Coalition for Media Edn., 2004—; bd. dirs. Radical Tchr. Author: Presence of Mind: Education and the Politics of Deception, 1999, Defining and Designing Multiculturalism, 2002; editor: Breaking Free: The Transformative Power of Critical Pedagogy, 1996, Corpus Analysis: Language, Structure and Language Use, 2003, Cultural Studies: From Theory to Action, 2005; contbr. articles to profl. jours.; mem. editl. bd.: Jour. for Critical Edn. Policy Studies, Simile: Studies in Media and Informatics Literacy, Taboo: The Jour. of Culture and Edn. Mem. civil liberties task force ACLU, Boston, 2001—; co-founder, mem. Human Rights Working Group, Boston, 2001—; mem. Working Class Studies Assn., SUNY, Stony Brook, NY, 2004—, Ctr. for Constnl. Rights, N.Y.C., 2004. Recipient Dr. Stephen G. and Wanda W. Jones scholarship, Harvard Grad. Sch. Edn., 1997, Roy E. Larson Rsch. fellowship, 1992; scholar, Nat. Conf. for Comty. and Justice, 2001. Mem.: Global Exch., Amnesty Internat., Bill of Rights Def. Com. Avocations: photography, painting, guitar, fishing, travel. Home: 111 Hatherly Rd Scituate MA 02066 Office: U Mass Applied Linguistics Grad Studies 100 Morrissey Blvd Brighton MA 02135 Office Phone: 617-287-6737.

LEISURE, PETER KEETON, federal judge; b. N.Y.C., Mar. 21, 1929; s. George S. and Lucille E. (Pelouze) L.; m. Kathleen Blair; Feb. 27, 1960; children: Lucille K. (dec.), Mary Blair, Kathleen K. BA, Yale U., 1952; LL.B., U. Va., 1958. Bar: N.Y. 1959, U.S. Supreme Ct. 1966, D.C. 1979, U.S. Dist. Ct. Conn. 1981. Assoc. Breed, Abbott & Morgan, 1958-61; asst. U.S. atty. So. Dist. N.Y., 1962-66; partner firm Curtis, Mallet-Prevost, Colt & Mosle, 1967-78; ptnr. Whitman & Ransom, NYC, 1978-84; judge U.S. Dist. Ct. (So. Dist.), NYC, 1984—, sr. judge, 1997—. Bd. dirs. Retarded Infants Svcs., 1968-78, pres., 1971-75; bd. dirs. Community Coun. of Greater N.Y., 1972-79, Youth Consultation Svcs., 1971-78; trustee Ch. Club of N.Y., 1973-81, 87-90; mem. jud. ethics com. Jud. Conf., 1990-93, fin disclosure com. 1st lt. USAR, 1953-55. Recipient Ellis Island medal of honor, 2000. Fellow: Am. Coll. Trial Lawyers, Am. Bar Found.; mem.: ABA, Fed. Bar Coun. (trustee, v.p. 1973—78), D.C. Bar Assn., Am. Judges Assn., Fed. Judges Assn., Am. Law Inst., Nat. Lawyers Club (hon.). Office: US Dist Ct 1910 US Courthouse 500 Pearl St New York NY 10007-1316 Office Phone: 212-805-0226.

LEITCH, MARTHA TERRY, retired secondary school educator; b. Lexington, Ky., June 20, 1949; d. Ned and Mary Loretta L. AB in Secondary Edn., U. Ky., 1971, MS in Secondary Vocat. Edn., 1978. Cert. tchr., Ky. Bus. tchr. Notre Dame Acad., Covington, Ky., 1971-74; exec. sec. Phillips Industries, Inc., Nicholasville, Ky., 1974-75; bus. tchr. Jessamine County Jr. HS, Nicholasville, 1975-76, Jessamine County Sr. HS, Nicholasville, 1976—2002, ret., 2002. Mem. Ky. Bus. Edn. Adv. Coun., Frankfort, 1991-93. Sec. bd. dirs. Jessamine County Hospice, Inc., Nicholasville, Ky., 1987-90; comm. chairperson Jessamine County Heart Assn., Nicholasville, 1990-91; dir. choir St. Luke Cath. Ch., Nicholasville, Ky., 1980—, sec., 2002— Mem. Jessamine County Edn. Assn. (v.p. 1985-86, pres. 1986-87, treas. 1989-90, pres. elect 1992-93, pres. 1993-94), Delta Kappa Gamma (2d v.p. 1988-90, pres. 1990-92, parliamentarian 1992-94). Roman Catholic. Avocations: reading, singing, piano.

LEITER, AL (ALOIS TERRY LEITER), professional baseball player; b. Toms River, N.J., Oct. 23, 1965; Pitcher N.Y. Yankees, 1984—89, Toronto Blue Jays, 1989—95, Fla. Marlins, Miami, 1995—97, 2004—, N.Y. Mets, 1998—2004. Founder Leiters Landing charitable orgn.; donated $100,000 to build youth league baseball field Berkeley Twp., NJ. Named Lefthanded Pitcher Nat. League All-Star Team, The Sporting News, 1996. Achievements include mem. of World Series Champion Florida Marlins, 1997. Office: Florida Marlins 2269 Dan Marino Blvd Hollywood FL 33028

LEITER, AMANDA C., lawyer; BS, M Engring., Stanford Univ.; MS Oceanography, Univ. Wash.; JD, Harvard Univ., 2000. Law clk. to Hon. John Paul Stevens U.S. Supreme Ct., Washington, 2003—04; atty. Natural Resources Def. Council, Washington, 2004—. Editor (mng.): Environmental Law Rev. Grantee Beagle Harvard Law Sch. Fellowship, 2004. Office: Natural Resources Defense Council Suite 400 1200 New York Ave NW Washington DC 20005 Office Phone: 202-289-2398.

LEITER, EDWARD HENRY, cell biologist, researcher; b. Columbus, Ga., Apr. 17, 1942; m. Susan Shaw, Sept. 5, 1964. BS, Princeton U., 1964; MS, PhD in Cell Biology, Emory U., 1968. Fellow U. Tex., Austin, 1968-71; asst. prof. in Genetics of Diabetes and Inflammatory Bowel Disease CUNY, Bkyn., 1971-74; assoc. staff scientist Jackson Lab., Bar Harbor, Maine, 1974-75, staff scientist, 1975-90, sr. staff scientist, 1990—. Recipient rsch. award, Juvenile Diabetes Found., 1994. Achievements include research in include research in genetics and immunology of diabetes. Office: Jackson Lab 600 Main St Bar Harbor ME 04609-1500 Office Phone: 207-288-6370.

LEITER, JOHN M., lawyer; b. Marietta, Ga., July 14, 1951; s. Hans David and Lilo (Shwarzschild) L.; m. Mary Clayton, May 8, 1976; children: Jonathan, Elizabeth, Kristin. BA, Emory U., 1973; JD, U. S.C., 1978. Bar: S.C. 1978, Ga. 1978, U.S. Dist. Ct. S.C. 1978, U.S. Dist. Ct. (no. dist.) Ga. 1978, U.S. Ct. Appeals (4th and 5th cirs.), U.S. Supreme Ct. Assoc. Harmon, Smith & Bridges, Atlanta, 1978-82, Lawn & Leiter, Myrtle Beach, S.C., 1982-87; ptnr. Leiter & Tall, Myrtle Beach, 1988-92; pvt. practice Myrtle Beach, 1992-94; prin. Leiter and Snook, P.A., 1994—2005, Law Offices of John M. Leiter, 2005—. Intern World Peace Through Law Conf., Manila, 1977. Bd. dirs. Myrtle Beach Housing Authority, 1987—. David Means scholar, 1977. Mem. ABA, S.C. State Bar Assn., Ga. State Bar Assn., Horry County Bar Assn. (pres. 1995). Office: PO Box 7516 Myrtle Beach SC 29572-0013 Office Phone: 843-449-1451. E-mail: mblaw@sccoast.net.

LEITER, RICHARD ALLEN, law librarian, educator; b. Sacramento, Mar. 21, 1952; s. Lionel and Lois Rose Leiter; m. Wendy Ellin Werges, Dec. 30, 1978; children: Emily Grace, Madeline Rose, Anna Joy, Rebecca Hope. BA in Anthropology and Religious Studies with honors, U. Calif., Santa Cruz, 1976; JD, Southwestern U., 1981; M of Libr. and Info. Sci., U. Tex., 1986. Libr. asst. Irell & Manella, L.A., 1977-78; libr. Hopkins, Mitchell & Carley, San Jose, Calif., 1982-84; head of reference Law Sch., U. Tex., Austin, 1984-86; pub. svcs. libr. Law Sch., U. Nebr., Lincoln, 1986-88; head libr. Littler, Mendelson, Fastiff & Tichy, San Francisco, 1988-91; dir. law libr., assoc. prof. law Regent U. Sch. Law, Virginia Beach, Va., 1991-94; assoc. prof. law Howard U. Sch. Law, A.M. Daniels Law Libr., Washington, 1994-98, dir. law libr., 1994—2000; assoc. dean, prof. Howard U., Washington, 1998-2000; dir. Schmid Law Libr., prof. law U. Nebr., Lincoln, 2000—. Mem. Westlaw Acad. Adv. Bd., 1990-93; sec. bd. dirs. StoneBridge Sch., 1993-94; mem. adv. bd. Oceana Publs., Inc., 1994-98. Editor: (book sect.) Yellow Pads to Computers, 1986, 91; author: (bibliography) New Frontiers of Forensic & Demonstrative Evidence, 1985; editor: Automatome, 1987-89, The Spirit of Law Librarianship, 1991, 3d edit., 2005, National Survey of State Laws, 1993, 5th edit., 2005; (with A. White) Concordance of Federal Legislation, 1999; editor Southwestern U. Law Review; contbr. articles to profl. jours. Mem. adv. com. StoneBridge Ednl. Found. Mem. ABA, Am. Assn. Law Librs. (so. chpt., automation and sci. devel. spl. interest sect. 1986—, chair 1989-90, indexing of periodical lit. adv. com. 1990-91, 2001-04, chair 1990-91, mem. spl. com. to promote development of resources for legal info. cmty. 1994-96, recruitment com. 1995-97, chair rsch. com. 1998-99, mem. law libr. jour. adv. com. 2004—, chair 2005), San Francisco Pvt. Law Librs. (steering com. 1989), Mid Am. Law Sch. Libr. Consortium, Scribes. Avocations: bicycling, reading, running. Home: 1301 N 37th St Lincoln NE 68503-2015 Office: U Nebr Schmid Law Libr Coll Law Lincoln NE 68583-0902 Business E-Mail: rleiter@unl.edu.

LEITER, ROBERT ALLEN, journalist, editor, writer; b. Phila., Apr. 21, 1949; s. Samuel Simon and Beverly (Agins) L.; m. Barbara Ann Field, May 6, 1973; children: Lauren, James, Rebecca. BA in English and Creative Writing with honors, U. Iowa, 1970. Freelance writer short stories, book revs., feature articles The Nation, The New Republic, Redbook, Am. Scholar, N.Y. Times, Partisan Rev., The Forward, others, 1973—; mng. editor, book columnist Inside mag., Phila., 1983-87; gen. reporter, book editor Jewish Exponent, Phila., 1987-98. Co-editor Friday, lit. supplement newspaper Jewish Exponent, Phila., 1983-87, mgn. editor Jewish Exponent 100th Anniversary edit., 1987, editor Extra Extra, weekly mag. sect., 1987-94; news editor Jewish Exponent, 1994-95, lit. supplement editor, 1995-98, interim editor-in-chief, 1998-99, lit. editor, 1999—; editor-in-chief, Inside Mag., 2000—; contbr. editor Am. Poetry Rev., Phila., 1987—; instr. writing, Am. lit., theater Cheltenham (Pa.) Adult Sch., 1983-87; instr. Jewish Am. lit., Jews in politics Daroff Campus Adult Studies, Pa., 1984, 99-2001; mem. selection com. Ann. Chaim Potok Lit. Award. Author: (with others) Jewish Profiles, 1992. Asst. to vice chmn. U.S. Commn. on Civil Rights, Washington, 1987-88. Recipient Smolar award for excellence in N.Am. Jewish journalism for article series, 1989, Simon Rockower award, 1990, (2), 1993, 1996, 1998, 2000, Keystone Press award, 1994, 2003, Soc. Profl. Journalists award, 1996, 2001. Mem. Phi Beta Kappa. Jewish. Avocations: collecting books, antique furniture and paintings. Home: 1002 Prospect Ave Elkins Park PA 19027-3058 Office: Phila Jewish Exponent 2100 Arch St Philadelphia PA 19103-1300 Office Phone: 215-832-0726. E-mail: bleiter@jewishexponent.com.

LEITH, CECIL ELDON, JR., retired physicist; b. Boston, Jan. 31, 1923; s. Cecil Eldon and Elizabeth (Benedict) L.; m. Mary Louise Henry, July 18, 1942; children: Ann, John, Paul. AB, U. Calif. at, Berkeley, 1943, PhD, 1957. Exptl. physicist Lawrence Radiation Lab., Berkeley, 1946-52, theoretical physicist Livermore, Calif., 1952-68; sr. scientist Nat. Center for Atmospheric Research, Boulder, Colo., 1968-83, div. dir., 1977-81; physicist Lawrence Livermore Nat. Lab. (Calif.), 1983-90. Symons Meml. lectr. Royal Meteorol. Soc., London, 1978; chmn. com. on atmospheric scis. NRC, 1978-80, sci. program evaluation com. Univ. Corp. for Atmospheric Rsch., 1991-96; mem. joint sci. com. world climate research program World Meteorol. Organ. and Internat. Council Sci. Unions, 1976-83; mem. program adv. com. Office Advanced Sci. Computing, NSF, 1984-85. Served with AUS, 1944-46. Fellow Am. Phys. Soc., Am. Meteorol. Soc. (Meisinger award 1967, Rossby research medal 1982) Home: 627 Carla St Livermore CA 94550-2316 Office: Lawrence Livermore Nat Lab PO Box 808 Livermore CA 94551-0808 Office Phone: 925-423-1612.

LEITH, EMMETT NORMAN, electrical engineer, educator; b. Detroit, Mar. 12, 1927; s. Albert Donald and Dorothy Marie (Emmett) Leith; m. Lois June Neswold, Feb. 17, 1956; children: Kim Ellen, Pam Elizabeth. BS, Wayne State U., 1950, MS, 1952, PhD, 1978; DSc (hon.), U. Aberdeen, Scotland, 1996. Mem. rsch. staff U. Mich., 1952—, prof. elec. engring., 1968—. Cons. several indsl. corps. Contbr. articles to profl. jours. With USNR, 1945—46. Named Man of Yr., Indsl. Rsch. mag., 1966; recipient Gordon Meml. award, SPIE, 1965, citation, Am. Soc. Mag. Photographers, 1966, Achievement award, U.S. Camera and Travel mag., 1967, Excellence of Paper award, Soc. Motion Picture and TV Engrs., 1967, Daedalion award, 1968, Stuart Ballantine medal, Franklin Inst., 1969, Alumni award, Wayne State U., 1974, cited by Nobel Prize Commn. for contbns. to holography, 1971, Holley medal, ASME, 1976, Nat. medal of Sci., 1979, Russel lecture award, U. Mich., 1981, Denins Gabor medal, Soc. Photo-Instrumentation Engrs., 1983, Gold medal, 1990, Mich. Trailblazer award, 1986. Fellow: IEEE (Liebmann award 1967, Inventor of Yr. award 1976), Optical Soc. Am. (Wood medal 1975, Herbert Ives medal 1985), The Royal Photographic Soc. of Great Britain (hon.), Engring. Soc. Detroit (hon.); mem.: NAE, Sigma Pi Sigma, Sigma Xi. Achievements include patents in field; first demonstrating (with colleague) capability of holography to form high-quality 3-dimensional image. Home: 51325 Murray Hill Dr Canton MI 48187-1030 Office: Univ Mich Inst Sci and Tech PO Box 618 Ann Arbor MI 48106-0618 Business E-Mail: leith@umich.edu.

LEITMANN, GEORGE, mechanical engineer, educator; b. Vienna, May 24, 1925; arrived in U.S., 1940, naturalized, 1944; s. Josef and Stella (Fischer) Leitmann; m. Nancy Lloyd, Jan. 28, 1955; children: Josef Lloyd, Elaine Michèle. BS, Columbia U., 1949, MA, 1950; PhD, U. Calif., Berkeley, 1956; D Engring. honoris causa, Tech. U. Vienna, 1988; D honoris causa, U. Paris, 1989, Tech. U. Darmstadt, 1990. Physicist, head aeroballistics sect. U.S. Naval Ordnance Sta., China Lake, 1950-57; mem. faculty U. Calif., Berkeley, 1957—, prof. engring. sci., 1963—, first acad. ombudsman, 1968—70, prof. grad. sch., 1995—, assoc. dean acad. affairs, 1981-90, assoc. dean rsch., 1990-94, acting dean, 1988, chair faculty, 1994-98, assoc. dean internat. rels., 2003—. Cons. to aerospace industry and govt.; lectr. in field. Author: (book) An Introduction to Optimal Control, 1966, Quantitative and Qualitative Games, 1969, The Calculus of Variations and Optimal Control, 1981; editor: (jour.) Math Analysis Applications, 1985—2002; assoc. editor Optimizing Theory Applications; contbr. 300 articles to profl. jours.; assoc. editor, mem. editl. bd. (to 11 jour.); translator: The Mantle of Dreams. Mem. adv. com. ARTSHIP Found.; master knight Order of Knights of Vine; mem. Acad. Italiana della Cucina. With AUS, 1944—46, ETO, combat engrs., special agent CIC. Decorated Croix de Guerre France, Fourragere Belgium, Comdr.'s Cross, Order of Merit Germany, commendatore Order of Merit Italy; named Miller Rsch. prof., 1966; recipient Pendray Aerospace Lit. award, AIAA, 1979, Mechanics and Control of Flight award, 1984, Von Humboldt U.S. Sr. Scientist award, Von Humboldt Found., 1980, Levy medal, Franklin Inst., 1981, Berkeley citation, U. Calif.-Berkeley, 1991, von Humboldt medal, von Humboldt Found., 1991, Rufus Oldenburger medal, ASME, 1995, Distng. Engring. Alumni award, 2002, Disting. Emeritus of Yr., 2004, 1st recipient Isaacs award, Internat. Soc. Dynamic Games, 2004, Werner Heisenberg medal, von Humboldt Found., 2005; Berkeley fellow, 2002. Mem.: NAE, World Innovation Found., Georgian Acad. Sci., A. V. Humboldt Assn. Am. (pres. 1994—97), Bavarian Acad. Sci., Georgian Acad. Engring., Russian Acad. Natural Sci., Argentine Nat. Acad. Engring., Internat. Acad. Astronautics, Acad. Sci. Bologna. Avocations: art, swimming, oenology, international relations. Office: U Calif Coll Engring Berkeley CA 94720-0001 Office Phone: 510-642-3984. Business E-Mail: gleit@coe.berkeley.edu.

LEITNER, ALFRED, retired mathematical physicist, educator, educational film producer; b. Vienna, Nov. 3, 1921; came to U.S., 1938, naturalized, 1944; s. Philipp and Lona (Machlup) L.; m. Marzia O'Neil, Nov. 24, 1948; children: Kathleen, Deborah Jones, David. BA, U. Buffalo, 1944; MS, Yale U., 1945, PhD, 1948. Research assoc. Courant Inst. Math. Scis., N.Y. U., 1947-51; from asst. prof. to prof. physics Mich. State U., 1951-67; prof. physics Rensselaer Poly. Inst., 1967-88, prof. emeritus, 1988—; research assoc. Harvard U., 1965-66; ret., 1988. Cons. Harvard project physics, 1966-68; vis. prof. U.S. Mil. Acad., West Point, 1983-85. Author papers on theory spl. functions, boundary value problems, antennas, history of sci., teaching.; Films Liquid Helium, 1963, Superconductivity, 1966, Project Physics, 1965-68; Dispersion, 1973, Fraunhofer (2 films), 1974, A Story of Research, 1981; (videotapes) Our Favorite Physics Demonstrations, 1987. Guggenheim fellow, 1958-59; Deutscher Akademischer Austauschdienst fellow, 1977 Fellow Am. Phys. Soc.; mem. Phi Beta Kappa, Sigma Xi. Home: 1201 8th Ter N Naples FL 34102-5411 Personal E-mail: ltnr@aol.com.

LEITNER, PAUL REVERE, lawyer; b. Winnsboro, SC, Nov. 11, 1928; s. W. Walker and Irene (Lewis) L.; m. Jeannette C. Card, Mar. 16, 1985; children by previous marriage: David, Douglas, Gregory, Reid, Cheryl. AB, Duke U., 1950; LLB, McKenzie Coll., 1954. Bar: Tenn. 1954; cert. civil trial specialist Nat. Bd. Trial Advocacy and Tenn. Commn. on CLE and Specialization. Pvt. practice law, Chattanooga, 1954; assoc. Leitner, Williams, Dooley & Napolitan and predecessor firms, 1952-57; ptnr. Leitner, Williams, Dooley & Napolitan and predecessor firms, 1957—. Tenn. chmn. Def. Rsch. Inst., 1978-89. Bd. dirs. Family Service Agy., 1957-63, Chattanooga Symphony and Opera Assn., 1986-89, sec., 1987-89, Prison and Prevention Ministries, 1992—, chmn. 1996-99; mem. Chattanooga-Hamilton County Community Action Bd.; mem. Juvenile Ct. Commn., Hamilton County, 1955-61, chmn., 1958-59; chmn. Citizens Com. for Better Schs.; mem. Met. Govt. Charter Commn. Served with U.S. Army, 1946-47. Named Young Man of Yr. Chattanooga Area, 1957. Fellow Am. Coll. Trial Lawyers, Tenn. Bar. Found, Chattanooga Bar Found. (founding); mem. ABA, Tenn. Bar Assn., Jaycees (Chattanooga, pres. 1956-57), Chatanooga Bar Assn., Fed. Bar Assn., Fed. Def. Corp. Counsel, Internat. Assn. Def. Coun., Trial Attys. Am., Tenn. Def. Lawyers Assn. (pres. 1975-76), Am. Bd. Trial Advs. (advocate), U.S. Sixth Cir. Jud. Conf. (life), Am. Inns of Ct. Methodist. Home: 3926 Windward Ln Soddy Daisy TN 37379 Business E-Mail: paul.leitner@leitnerfirm.com.

LEITZEL, GALEN EUGENE, music educator, director, musician, conductor; b. Winfield, Penn., Nov. 30, 1953; s. Robert Eugene and Fay Inic; m. Jennifer Clare Summers, July 12, 2004; stepchildren: Daniel Summers, Ryan Summers; children: Adam, Patrick. BS in Music Edn., Mansfield State Coll., 1975; MusM, Ithaca Coll., 1982; MusD, Shenandoah U., 2005. Music instr. Penn., 1982, cert. in music supervision 1997. Band dir. Loyalsock Twp Sch. Dist., Williamsport, Pa., 1975—86, Hanover Pub. Sch. Dist., Pa., 1986—2002; woodwind instr. Lycoming Coll., Williamsport, Pa., 1982—86; music supervisor Conestoga Valley Sch. Dist., Lancaster, Pa., 2002—. Adjudicator Nat. Judges Assn., Mechanicsburg, Pa., 1988—. V.p., pres. Lycoming County Band Dir. Assn., 1981—82; officer, mem. Hanover Baseball Parents Assn., Pa., 1994—96; music dir., conductor Lyric Band of Hanover, Inc., Pa., 2001—; officer, mem. United Methodist First Ch., 1998—99. Mem.: Assn. Supervision and Curriculum Develop., Am. Fedn. Musicians, Music Educators Nat. Conf. Democrat. Methodist. Avocations: reading, chess, sports, bicycling, music. Home: 2531 Eldorado Dr York PA 17402 Office: Conestoga Valley Sch Dist 2110 Horseshoe Rd Lancaster PA 17601 Office Phone: 717-397-5231. Personal E-mail: galen_leitzel@cusd.k12.pa.us.

LEITZEL, JOAN RUTH, retired university president emerita; BA in Math., Hanover Coll., 1958; MA in Math., Brown U., 1961; PhD in Math., Ind. U., 1965. Instr. math. Oberlin (Ohio) Coll., 1961-62; asst. prof. math. Ohio State U., Columbus, 1965-70, assoc. prof., 1970-84, prof., 1984-92, vice-chmn. dept., 1973-79, acting chmn., 1978, assoc. provost, 1985-90; prof. dept. math. and stats. U. Nebr., Lincoln, 1992-96, sr. vice chancellor for acad. affairs, 1992-96, interim chancellor, 1995-96; pres. U. N.H., Durham, 1996—2002, pres. emerita, 2002—. Adv. com. Griffith Ins. Found., 1979-82; cons. Ohio Dept. Edn., 1980-83; participant Am. Coun. on Edn., 1980, 82; cons. Nat. Commn. on Excellence in Edn., U.S. Dept. Edn., 1982; univ. math. edn. del. to China, 1983; dir. divsn. materials devel., rsch. and info. sci. edn. NSF, 1990-92; presenter in field, 1980—; bd. dirs. Am. Assn. Higher Edn., chmn.-elect, 1996-97, chmn., 1997-98; mem. interpretive reports adv. bd. Nat. ssessment Ednl. Progress, 1995-98; trustee Consortium on Math. and Its Applications, 1994-95; mem. exec. coun. com. on acad. affairs Nat. Assn. State Univs. and Land-Grant Colls., 1994-96, bd. dirs., 1997-99, chmn. com. on faculty, 1994-96; coord. coun. for edn. NRC, 1993-95, mem. bd. on math. scis. edn., 1985-87, math. scis. edn. bd., chmn. 2000-2005. Bd. dirs. United Way Lincoln, 1995-96, 1st Plymouth Ch., 1996, Lincoln Partnership for Econ. Devel., 1996, N.H. Charitable Found., 1998-02, Durham Cmty. Ch., 1996-02. Recipient Disting. Alumni award Hanover Coll., 1986, dir.'s award for mgmt. excellence NSF, 1991; Disting. Tchg. award Ohio State U., 1982, Disting. Svc. award Ohio State U., 2002, Pettee medal U. N.H., 2002; grantee NSF, 1976-798, 84-88, Battelle Found., 1981-83, SOHIO, 1983-85. Mem. AAAS (edn. com. 1981-84), Am. Math. Soc. (com. on excellence in scholarship 1993-95), Assn. for Women in Math., Math. Assn. Am. (nominating com. 1978-79, com. on tchr. tng. and accreditation Ohio sect. 1976-79, nat. com. on undergrad programs 1982-85, chmn. joint task force on curriculum for grades 11-13 with Nat. Coun. Tchrs. Math. 1986-88), Nat. Coun. Tchrs. Math., Mortar Bd., Sigma Xi, Phi Kappa Phi. E-mail: joan.leitzel@unh.edu.

LEITZELL, TERRY LEE, lawyer; b. Williamsport, Pa., Apr. 15, 1942; s. Ernest Richard and Inez Mae (Taylor) L.; m. Lucy Acker Emmerich, June 18, 1966; children: Thomas Addison, Charles Taylor, Robert Davies. AB, Cornell U., 1964; JD, U. Pa., 1967. Bar: D.C. bar 1967. Consular officer Dept. State, Bombay, India, 1968-70, atty.-adv. for oceans affairs Washington, 1970-77, chief U.S. negotiator UN law of sea negotiations Geneva, also N.Y.C., 1974-77; asst. adminstr. for fisheries and dir. Nat. Marine Fisheries Service, NOAA, Dept. Commerce, Washington, 1978-81; practice law Washington, 1981-92, Seattle, 1992—; gen. counsel Icicle Seafoods, Seattle. Mem.: Wash. Bar Assn. Democrat. Home: 3150 W Laurelhurst Dr NE Seattle WA 98105-5346 Office: Icicle Seafoods 4019 21st Ave W Ste 300 Seattle WA 98199-1299 Office Phone: 206-281-5372. Business E-Mail: terryl@icicleseafoods.com.

LEIVE, CINDI, editor-in-chief; m. Howard Bernstein; 1 child, Lucy. BA in English Literature, Swarthmore Coll., 1988. With The Paris Rev, The Saturday Rev.; editl. asst., then dep. editor Glamour Mag., 1988—99; editor-in-chief Self Mag., 1999—2001, Glamour Mag., 2001—. Named one of Top 40 Under 40 Executives in NY, Crain's NY Bus., 2002. Mailing: Glamour Mag 4 Times Square 17th Floor New York NY 10036*

LEKAS, MARY DESPINA, retired otolaryngologist; b. Worcester, Mass., May 13, 1928; d. Spyridon Peter and Merciny S. (Manoliou) Lekas; m. Harold William Picozzi (dec.). Student, Boston U.; BA, Clark U., 1949, DSc, ScD, Clark U., 1997; MD, Athens (Greece) U., 1957; MA, Brown U., 1986. Diplomate Am. Bd. Otolaryngology. Sci. instr. Hahnemann Hosp. Sch. Nursing; rotating intern Meml. Hosp., Worcester, 1957-58; resident in otolaryngology R.I. Hosp., Providence, 1958-62; resident in otolaryngology and otorhinolaryngology U. Pa. Grad. Sch. Medicine, 1960; surgeon in chief, dept. otolaryngology R.I. Hosp., 1984-96, surgeon-in-chief emerita; pvt. practice Providence, 1962—. Chmn. dept. otolaryngology Brown U., Providnce, 1984, clin. prof. emerita surgery divsn. otolaryngology, head and neck; cons. Cleft Palate Clin. and Craniofacial of R.I. Hosp., 1964—. VA Hosp., Providence, 1967—, St. Joseph Hosp., Providence, 1983—, Miriam Hosp., Providence, 1984—; lectr. profl. orgns.; mem. Project Hope in Columbia, Ceylon/Sri Lanka, SS Hope Hosp. Ship, People-to-People, Inc., Washington, 1968-69. Mem. editl. bd. Am. Jour. Rhinology, 1987—; contbr. articles to profl. jours. Mem. alumni coun. Clark U.; pres. Providence Med. Assn., 1987-88. Named R.I. Woman Physician of Yr., 1992; recipient Disting. Svc. award, Providence Med. Assn., 1996, Emeriti award, Brown U., 1999, Outstanding Svc. award, Brown Med. Alumni Assn., 1999, cert. of recognition, People-to-People, Inc.; fellow Jonas Clark fellow. Fellow ACS, Soc. Univ. Otolaryngologists-Head and Neck Surgeons, Triological Soc. (ea. sect. sec., Presdl. Citation 1993), Am. Acad. Otolaryngology-Head and Neck Surgeons (gov. R.I. chpt. bd. of govs. 1985-), Am. Acad. Facial Plastic and Reconstructive Surgeons, Am. Acad. Broncho-Escophalogy (treas., v.p. 1990); mem. AMA, Assn. Acad. Dept. Otolaryngology-Head and Neck Surgery, Deafness Rsch. Found., Am. Cleft Palate Assn., Am. Med. Women's Assn. (R.I. Woman Physician of Yr. 1992), Am. Broncho-Esophagological Assn. (hon.), New Eng. Otolaryng. Soc. (pres. 1987-88, Cert. of Recognition 1980-81), Centurion Club. Greek Orthodox. Avocations: bicycling, swimming, church choir. Home: 129 Terrace Ave Riverside RI 02915-4726 Home Fax: 401-433-0941.

LEKBERG, BARBARA, sculptor; BFA, MA, Univ. Iowa; DFA (hon.), Simpson Coll. Instr. Univ. of the Arts, Phila., Nat. Acad. Sch. of Fine Arts, NYC. Exhibitions include Sculpture Ctr., NYC, Marmara Manhattan, NYC, Mt. Holyoke Coll, Glass Art Gallery, Toronto, Pa. Acad. Fine Arts, Whitney Mus. Am. Art, Mus. Modern Art; represented in collections of NAD, Whitney Mus. Am. Art, George Washington Univ., Des Moines Art Ctr., General Electric Corp., Birmingham Mus. Art, New Sch. Univ., NY, Bayfield Clark Collection, Berauda, Michener Mus., Pa., Brookgreen Gardens, SC, . Grantee 2 Guggenheim Fellowships, Inst. Arts & Letters, Richard Florsheim Art Fund. Mem.: Century Assn., NAD (academician, Saltus Gold medal 1990), Nat. Sculpture Soc. (sec., Gold medal 1991, Fellow). Studio: Apt 2A 195 Stanton St New York NY 10002 Office Phone: 212-996-1908.

LEKUS, DIANA ROSE, librarian; b. Washington, Feb. 5, 1948; d. Max and Eleanor (Kruger) L. Student, Hofstra U., 1965-66; BA, Emerson Coll., 1969; MLS, U. Pitts., 1970. Asst. dept. head. search dept. Temple U., Phila., 1970-71; cataloging supr. weekly record sect. R.R. Bowker, N.Y.C., 1972-75; cataloger, asst. prof. U. Ill., Champaign-Urbana, Ill., 1975-78; customer svc. rep. Res. Fund, N.Y.C., 1979-81; list libr. Kleid Co., N.Y.C., 1981-94; subject classifier Reed Pub. Co., New Providence, N.J., 1995-99; with Am. Lung Assn., N.Y.C., 1997; libr. Queens Borough Pub. Libr., Jamaica, N.Y., 1999—. Sr. editor Am. Book Pub. Record, 1974; book reviewer Libr. Jour., 1979. Devel. asst. Pearl Theatre Co., 1995-96. Mem. ALA, Nat. Hist. Preservation and Trust, N.Y. Sheet Music Soc., Hadassah (life). Democrat. Avocations: travel, theater, reading. Home: 28-05 37th St Astoria NY 11103-4350 E-mail: dlekus@aol.com, dlekus@queenslibrary.org.

LELAND, CHRISTOPHER TOWNE, writer, language educator; b. Tulsa, Oct. 17, 1951; s. Benjamin Towne L. and Julia Elizabeth Sanford; m. Osvaldo R. Sabino, June 13, 1979. BA, Pomona Coll., 1973; MA, U. Calif., San Diego, 1980, PhD, 1982. Briggs Copeland asst. prof. Harvard U., Cambridge, Mass., 1983-88; faculty mem. Bennington (Vt.) Coll., 1988-90; prof. English Wayne State U., Detroit, 1990—. Author: Mean Time, 1982, The Last Happy Men: The Generation of 1922, Fiction, and the Argentine Reality, 1986, Mrs. Randall, 1987, The Book of Marvels, 1990, The Professor of Aesthetics, 1994, Letting Loose, 1996, The Art of Compelling Fiction, 1998, The Creative Writers Style Guide, 2002. Fulbright grantee, 1979, 89, 96. Office: Wayne State U Dept English 5057 Woodward Ste 9408 Detroit MI 48201

LELAND, DAVID D., timber company executive; b. Austin, Minn., July 26, 1935; s. P.C. and Leona (Christensen) L.; m. Maralee Brown (div.); children: D. Mark, Todd D., Reid H.; m. Leslie S. Gibbs, Aug. 21, 1987. BS in Forestry, U. Wash., 1958. Various positions Simpson Timber Co., Shelton, Wash., 1959-71, v.p. Calif. ops., 1971-76; sr. v.p. S.W. Forest Industries, Phoenix, 1976-77, exec. v.p. bldg. products, 1977-83; pres., chief exec. officer Plum Creek Timber Co., Seattle, 1983-93, chmn., pres., CEO, 1993—, chmn., 1994—. Bd. dirs. Plum Creek Mgmt. Co., Seattle. Mem. Nat. Forest Products Assn. (bd. dirs., chmn., 1st vice chmn., 2d vice chmn., treas. 1989-92), Am. Plywood Assn. (trustee 1986-93), Am. Forest & Paper Assn. (bd. dirs. 1993), World Forestry Ctr. (bd. dirs. 1988—), Rainier Club, Seattle Yacht Club, Seattle Golf Club. Office: Plum Creek Timber Co LP 999 3rd Ave Ste 2300 Seattle WA 98104-4096

LELAND, JOY HANSON, retired anthropologist, researcher; b. Glendale, Calif., July 29, 1927; d. David Emmett and Florence (Sockerson) Hanson; m. David A. Riegert, Nov. 14, 1993. BA in English Lit., Pomona Coll., Claremont, Calif., 1949; MBA, Stanford U., 1960; MA in Anthropology, U. Nev., 1972; PhD in Anthropology, U. Calif., Irvine, 1975. With Desert Research Inst., U. Nev., 1961—, asst. research prof., 1975-77, assoc. research prof., 1977-79, rsch. prof., 1979-89, rsch. prof. emerita, 1990—. Author: monograph Firewater Myths, Frederick West Lander-A Biographical Sketch; contbg. author: Smithsonian Handbook of North American Indians; also articles, book chpts. Trustee Robert and Joy Leland Charitable Trust, 1992—. NIMH grantee, 1972-73; Nat. Inst. Alcohol Abuse and Alcoholism grantee, 1974-75, 79-81 Mem. Am. Anthrop. Assn., Southwestern Anthrop. Assn., Soc. Applied Anthropology, Soc. Med. Anthropology, Gt. Basin Anthrop. Conf., Phi Kappa Phi. Address: 6126 Carriage House Way Reno NV 89509-7326

LELAND, MARC ERNEST, trust company executive, consultant, lawyer; b. San Francisco, Apr. 20, 1938; s. Herbert and Sarah Betty (Robinson) L.; m. Elisabeth Gustava De Rothschild, July 7, 1970 (div. Sept. 1980); children: Natasha Hanna, Olivia Mitzi; m. Jacqueline de Botton, 1989. AB in Govt., Harvard U., 1959; MA in Law, St. John's Coll.-Oxford U., Eng., 1961; JD, U. Calif.-Berkeley, 1963. Ford Found. fellow Inst. Comparative Law-U., Paris, 1963-64; assoc. Cerf Robinson & Leland, San Francisco, 1964-68, ptnr., 1972-76; faculty fellow Harvard U. Law Sch., Boston, 1968-70; gen. counsel Peace Corps, Washington, 1970-71, ACTION, Washington, 1971-72; ACDA rep. Force Reduction Talks, Vienna, Austria, 1976-78; resident ptnr. Proskauer Rose Goetz & Mendelsohn, London, 1978-81; asst. sec. internat. affairs Dept. Treasury, Washington, 1981-84; pres. Marc E. Leland & Assocs., Washington, 1984—. Republican. Jewish. Office: 1001 19th St N Ste 1700 Arlington VA 22209-1725

LELAND, NITA ELLEN SHANNON, artist, writer; b. Dayton, Ohio, June 24, 1933; d. Carl E. Shannon and Martha J. Spicer; m. Robert G. Leland, July 2, 1955; children: Kurt, Carl, Wes, Kathleen. BA (hons.), Otterbein Coll., 1955. Prin., owner Nita Leland Studio, Dayton, Ohio, 1972—; pub. Moonflower Books, 2000—. Workshop instr. in field. Author: Exploring Color, 1985, The Creative Artist, 1990, Exploring Color revised edition, 1998, Exploring Coloring Book, 2000; co-author: Creative Collage Techniques, 1994; video Basic Color Mixing, 1996, All About Painting, 1998; contbr. articles to profl. jours.; patentee in field. Vol. Building Bridges Juvenile Ct., Dayton, 1987-91, Otterbein Retirement Cmty., Lebanon, Ohio, 1975-97. Mem. Nat. Art Materials Trade Assn., Soc. Layerists in MultiMedia, The Authors Guild, Western Ohio Watercolor Soc. Office: Nita Leland Studio 1210 Brittany Hills Dr Dayton OH 45459-1418 Personal E-mail: nita@nitaleland.com.

LELAND, RICHARD G(UY), lawyer; b. Oceanside, NY, Jan. 25, 1949; s. Arnold Joseph and Eunice (Himlyn) L.; m. Jane E. Schwartz; children: Jennifer Schultz, David Jarett. BS, Cornell U., 1971; JD with distinction, Hofstra U., 1974. Bar: N.Y. 1975, U.S. CT. Appeals (2nd cir.) 1975, U.S. Dist. Ct. (so., ea., no. and we. dists.) N.Y. 1976, U.S. Supreme Ct. 1979. Assoc. Winer, Neuburger & Sive, N.Y.C., 1974-76; law sec. to Justice Douglas F. Young Supreme Ct. N.Y. Nassau County, Mineola, 1976-79; assoc. Ruskin, Schlissel, Moscou & Evans, P.C., Mineola, 1979-82, ptnr., 1982-89, Rosenman & Colin LLP, N.Y.C., 1989—2002, Kramer Levin Naftalis & Frankel LLP, N.Y.C., 2002—. Spl. prof. Hofstra U., Hempstead, N.Y., 1991—; mem. Real Estate Bd. of N.Y., Inc.; chair Commn. on Environ. Law. Contbr. articles to profl. jours. Mem.: Assn. Bar City N.Y., N.Y. State Bar Assn. (task force downtown redevelopment, land use and energy com. 2002), Hofstra Law Sch. Alumni Assn. (pres. 1995—99). Office: Kramer Levin Naftalis & Frankel LLP 1177 Avenue of the Americas New York NY 10036 Office Phone: 212-715-8087. Business E-Mail: rleland@kramerlevin.com.

LELAND, TIMOTHY, retired newspaper executive; b. Boston, Sept. 24, 1937; s. Oliver Stevens and Frances Chamberlain (Ayres) L.; m. Natasha Bourso, Sept. 26, 1964 (div. 1981); children: Chris Bourso, London Chamberlain; m. Julie S. Hatfield, Nov. 23, 1984. AB cum laude, Harvard U., 1960; MS with honors, Columbia Sch. Journalism, 1961. Med. editor Boston Herald, 1963-64; sci. editor Boston Globe, 1965-66, State House bur. chief, 1966-67, asst. city editor, 1968-69, investigative reporter, 1970-71, asst. mng. editor, 1972, mng. editor (Sunday), 1976-81, mng. editor (daily), 1981-82, asst. to pub., 1984-97, asst. to chmn., 1997-98, v.p., 1990-98. Bd. dirs. Boys and Girls Clubs of Boston. Recipient Am. Polit. Sci. award, 1968; Pulitzer Prize for investigative reporting, 1972; Sigma Delta Chi award for civic service (reporting), 1972; award for pub. service A.P. Mng. Editors, 1974; Sevellon Brown award, 1974; U.S.-South African Leader Exchange Program traveling grantee, 1969; Internat. fellow Columbia, 1961. Mem. Harvard Club. Office: Boston Globe 3 School St Boston MA 02108

LELAS, SNJEZANA, pharmacologist, researcher; b. Zagreb, Croatia, Apr. 29, 1971; d. Srdan and Jasmina Lelas. BA, U. Oxford, 1989—92, DPhil, 1993—96. Postdoctoral fellow La. State U. Med. Ctr., New Orleans, 1996—98, Harvard Med. Sch., Southborough, Mass., 1999—2001; sr. rsch. investigator Bristol-Myers Squibb, Wallingford, Conn., 2001—. Contbr. articles to profl. jours. Scholar, U. Oxford, 1991. Mem.: Am. Soc. for Pharmacology and Exptl. Therapeutics, Behavioral Pharmacology Soc., Soc. for Neuroscience. Avocations: travel, writing, sports, theater. Home: 3B Oak Hill Dr Clinton CT 06413 Office: Bristol-Myers Squibb 5 Research Pkwy Wallingford CT 06492 Office Phone: 203-677-7441. Office Fax: 203-677-7569. Business E-Mail: snjezana.lelas@bms.com.

LELE, AMOL SHASHIKANT, obstetrician, gynecologist; b. Chhindnara, India, May 23, 1944; came to U.S., 1970; d. Gajanan S. and Sarala S. (Manjrekar) Karande; m. Shashikant Lele, Feb. 28, 1970; children: Kedar, Rajal. MBBS, Bombay U., 1967, MD, 1970; D Ob-Gyn., Coll. Physicians, Bombay, 1969. Diplomate Am. Bd. Ob-Gyn. Clinician ob-gyn. clinic St. Luke's Hosp., Cleve., 1974; instr. SUNY, Buffalo, 1974-76, asst. prof., 1978-84, clin. assoc. prof., 1984—; fellow Children's Hosp., Buffalo, 1976-78, dir. women's svcs., 1976—, dir. outreach program, 1991-97; dir. prenatal care Erie County Med. Ctr., Buffalo, 1979-97; clin. chief ob-gyn. CHOB Kaleida Health Sys., 1999—. Mem. health com. Planned Parenthood, Buffalo, 1992-97; mem. infant mortality task force Health Systems Agy., Buffalo, 1994—. Avocations: reading, theater, light music. Home: 75 Nottingham Ter Buffalo NY 14216-3620 Office: 11 Summer St Buffalo NY 14209-2256

LELEU, JONATHAN PAUL, lawyer; b. Chgo., Feb. 10, 1974; s. Henri Ignatious and Inalynn Marie Leleu; m. Jacquelyn Sue Dietz, Nov. 3, 2001. BA, Loyola U., Chicago, 1996; JD, Coll. of Law DePaul U., Chgo., 1999. Bar: Nev. 2000, Ill. 2000. Atty. Zenoff & Zenoff, Chartered, Chgo., 1999—2001, Rawlings Olson Cannon Gormley & Desruisseaux, Las Vegas, Nev., 2001—03, Kummer Kaempfer Bonner & Renshaw, Las Vegas, 2003—. Legis. intern U.S. Senator Carol Moseley Braun, Chgo., 1995—96. Mem.: ABA (assoc.), Clark County Bar Assn. (assoc.), Nev. Am. Inn of Ct. (assoc.), Pi Alpha Delta (life). Roman Catholic. Avocations: baseball, hockey, culinary arts, travel. Office: Kummer Kaempfer Bonner & Renshaw 7th Fl 3800 Howard Hughes Pkwy Las Vegas NV 89109 Office Phone: 702-792-7000. Office Fax: 702-796-7181. E-mail: jleleu@kkbr.com.

LELYVELD, GAIL ANNICK, actress; b. Boston, May 22, 1948; d. Edward I. and Beatrice Elizabeth (Hewitt) L. BA in Polit. Sci., Boston U., 1970; MA in Polit. Sci., Goddard Coll., 1974; studies with Paul Barry, Peter Donat, Ray Reinhardt, Darrell Lauer, others. Actress, 1970—; tech. staff USA Prodns. and Midseason, Hempstead, N.Y., 1986-87, prodn. stage mgr., 1987—. Tech. staff Gray Wig, Hempstead, 1986, 87; cons. Talking With prodn. M.A., C.W. Post. Appeared in numerous films including Frances, Halloween III, Children On Their Birthdays, Project 1917, Rocky II, Happy Endings, Seeds of Innocence, Bonfire of the Vanities, The Music of the Heart, The Bird's Eye View, Insomnia, Monster Math, The Lesson, I'm Not Rappaport, City Hall, The House of the Venus Flytrap (ind. film), Believe for Hofstra University (film), Baby Buyer (NYU short film); (TV): Archie Bunker's Place, Mister Clown Says, White Noise, The Gentle Creature, (ABC Afterschool Spl.) Summer Stories: The Mall, Mathnet, Bill Cosby Murder Mystery, Cosby: You're OK, I'm Hilton, Upright Citizen Brigade; actor: Alice in Wonderland, Not So Grimm Fairytale Players; actress (Littletop Theater Co.) Toby Tyler, Marmalade Gumdrops, Bohemian Lights, King Lear - Tenant, Doctor & Knight Plainedge Playhouse, The Hostage, USA Prodns., The Cherry Orchard, Broadhollow Theater Bay Way Art Ctr., The House of Blue Leaves, The Lady of Larkspur Lotion, Broadhollow Theatre Bay Way Arts Ctr., Sarah Good and the Voice of Martha Corey, BDR Repertory Co., The Worst Play in the World, Women's Theatrical Collective, The Man Who Came to Dinner, U.S.A. Prodns., Holocaust Survivor-Columbia U.; Singer: Gospel Oedipus at Colonus evangelist, townsperson, choir, Musicum Collegium Hofstra U., Pala Opera Assn., St. Patrick's Cathedral Choir, Temple Emanuel New Hyde Park Choir; singer and leader Christmas Carols Garden City Group Christmas Party, Garden City Group Chorus Holiday Songs and Soloist; soloist piano recital, solo singer Ecumenical Thanksgiving Svc.; one-person performance, Dona Gracia Nasi, Memoirs of Glüchel of Hameln, Temple Emanuel of New Hyde Park, Karen Finley Workshop Performance Arts, Actors Bootcamp, Purple Rose Theatre Co.; theater tech. involvement includes stage mgr., sound asst. Wings; sound asst. Danton's Death; asst. stage mgr. props, fx, dresser Accomplice; cons. on reading The Sisters Rosenweig. Reader Yom Kippur svcs. Temple Emanuel, San Francisco. Mem. AFTRA Jewish. Avocations: reading, knitting, walking. Home: 4 Grafton St Greenlawn NY 11740 Personal E-mail: berrydoor863@yahoo.com. Business E-Mail: gail_lelyveld@gardencitygroup.com.

LELYVELD, JOSEPH SALEM, editor, writer, writer, news correspondent; b. Cin., Apr. 5, 1937; s. Arthur Joseph and Toby (Bookholtz) L.; m. Carolyn Fox, June 14, 1959 (dec. May, 2004); children: Amy, Nita. BA summa cum laude, Harvard U., 1958, MA, 1959; MS in Journalism, Columbia U., 1960. Reporter, editor N.Y. Times, 1963—2001, fgn. corr., Johannesburg, New Delhi, Hong Kong, London, 1965-86, columnist mag., staff writer, 1977, 84-85, fgn. editor, 1987-89, mng. editor, 1990-94, exec. editor, 1994—2001, interim exec. editor, 2003. Author: Move Your Shadow, 1985 (Pulitzer prize, L.A. Times Book prize, Sidney Hillman award, all 1986), Omaha Blues: A Memory Loop, 2005. Recipient George Polk Meml. award, 1972, 84; Guggenheim fellow, 1984. Mem. Coun. Fgn. Rels., The Century Assn. Business E-Mail: lelyveld@nytimes.com.

LEMAIRE, JACQUES, professional hockey coach; b. Lasalle, Que., Can., Sept. 7, 1945; Player Montreal Canadiens, 1967-79, head coach, 1983-85; head coach, player Sierre Hockey Club, Switzerland, 1979-81; asst. coach SUNY Coll., Plattsburgh, 1981-82; coach Longueuil Chevaliers, maj. jr. league, Que., 1982-83; dir. of hockey pers. Montreal Canadiens, 1985-87, asst. to mng. dir., 1987-93; head coach N.J. Devils, 1993-98; cons. to gen. mgr. Montreal Canadiens, 1998-00; head coach Minnesota Wild, Saint Paul, 2000—. Mem. Stanley Cup Championship teams, 1968, 69, 71, 73, 76-79; coach 1995. Named NHL Coach of Yr., Sporting News, 1993, 94; inducted into Hockey Hall of Fame, 1984

LEMAISTRE, CHARLES AUBREY, retired internist, epidemiologist, educator; b. Lockhart, Ala., Feb. 10, 1924; s. John Wesley and Edith (McLeod) LeM.; m. Joyce Trapp, June 3, 1952 (dec. Dec. 2003), Andreae Preyer Behlen, Jan. 29, 2005; children: Charles Frederick, William Sidney, Joyce Anne, Helen Jean; m. Andreae Preyer Behlen, Jan. 29, 2005. BA, U. Ala., 1943, LLD (hon.), 1971; MD, Cornell U., 1947; LLD (hon.), Austin Coll., 1970; DSc (hon.), U. Dallas, 1978, Southwestern U., 1981; D honoris causa, U. Guadalajara (Mex.), 1989. Intern, then resident in medicine N.Y. Hosp., 1947-49; rsch. fellow infectious diseases Cornell U. Med. Coll., 1949-51, mem. faculty, 1951-54, asst. prof. medicine, 1953-54; mem. faculty Emory U. Sch. Medicine, 1954-59, prof. preventive medicine, chmn. dept., 1957-59; prof. medicine U. Tex. Southwestern Med. Sch., 1959-78, assoc. dean, 1965-66; vice chancellor health affairs U. Tex. Sys., Austin, 1966-68, exec. vice chancellor, 1968-69, dep. chancellor, 1969-70, chancellor, 1971-78, prof. medicine, 1978-96; pres., internist, prof. medicine U. Tex. M.D. Anderson Cancer Ctr., 1978-96; ret., 1996. Cons. epidemiology Communicable Disease Ctr., USPHS, 1953-69; cons. medicine VA, 1954-59; area med. cons. VA (Atlanta area), 1958-59; vis. staff physician Grady Meml. Hosp., Atlanta, 1954-59, Emory U. Hosp., 1954-59; sr. attending staff mem. Parkland Meml. Hosp., Dallas, 1959-66; med. dir. chest divsn. Woodlawn Hosp., Dallas, 1959-65; mem. Surgeon Gen.'s Adv. Com. Smoking and Health, 1963-64, AMA-Edn. Rsch. Found. com. rsch. tobacco and health, 1964-66; chmn. Gov. Tex. Com. Tb Eradication, 1963-64; cons. internal medicine Baylor U. Med. Ctr., Dallas, 1962-66, St. Paul Hosp., Dallas, 1966; cons. divsn. hosp. and med. facilities USPHS, 1966; mem. N.Y.C. Task Force on Tb, 1967; cons. Bur. Physician, HEW, 1967-70; mem. grad. med. edn. nat. adv. com. Health Resources Adminstrn., 1977-80; mem. Tex. Legislature Dept. Health, Edn. and Welfare, 1967, Tex. Legislature Com. on Organ Transplantation, 1968, Carnegie Commn. on Non-Traditional Study, 1971-73; mem. bd. commrs. Nat. Commn. on Accrediting, 1973-76; mem. joint task force on continuing competence in pharmacy Am. Pharm. Assn.-Am. Assn. Coll. in Pharmacy, 1973-74; mem. exec. com. Legis. Task Force on Cancer in Tex., 1984-86; adv. bd. 6th World Conf. on Smoking and Health. Contbr. articles to med. jours.; contbg. author: A Textbook of Medicine, 10 and 11th edits, 1963, Pharmacology in Medicine, 1958; translating author: The Tubercle Bacillus, 1955; mem. editl. bd. Am. Rev. Respiratory Diseases, 1955-58. Mem. President's Commn. White House Fellows, 1971; chmn. subcom. on diversity and pluralism Nat. Coun. on Ednl. Rsch., 1973-75; bd. dirs. Assn. Tex. Colls. and Univs., 1974-75; mem. devel. coun. United Negro Coll. Fund, 1974-78; mem. nat. adv. coun. Inst. for Svcs. to Edn., 1974-78; mem. exec. com. Assn. Am. Univs., 1975-77; mem. Project HOPE com. on Health Policy, 1977; chmn. steering com. Presbyn. Physicians for Fgn. Missions, 1960-62; mem. Ministers Cons. Clinic, Dallas, 1960-62; trustee Austin Coll., 1979-83, Stillman Coll., 1978-84; bd. dirs. Ga. Tb Assn., 1955-59; bd. dirs. Damon Runyon-Walter Winchell Cancer Fund, 1976-85, chmn. exec. com., v.p., 1978, pres., 1979-83; trustee Biol. Humanics Found., Dallas, 1973-82; chmn. health manpower com. Assn. Am. Univs., 1975-78; sec. Coun. So. Univs., Inc., 1976-78, pres., 1977-78; hon. life trustee Menninger Found.; host com. Houston Econ. Summit, 1990. Recipient Cornell Univ. Alumni of Distinction award, 1978, Disting. Alumnus award U. Alabama Sch. Medicine, 1982, Pres.' award Am. Lung Assn., 1987, Gibson D. Lewis award for Excellence in Cancer Control Tex. Cancer Coun., 1988, award of Honor Am. Soc. Hosp. Pharmacists, 1988, Svc. to Mankind award Leukemia Soc. Am. Tex. Gulf Coast chpt., 1991, People of Vision award Tex. Soc. to Prevent Blindness, 1991, Outstanding Tex. Leader award 7th Ann. John Ben Sheppard Pub. Leadership Forum, 1991; Inst. Religion's Caring Spirit Tribute, 1993, AMA Disting. Svc. award, 1995, Ala. Acad. of Honor, 1998, Disting. Svc. award NASA, 1998, Charles A. LeMaiste Clinic Bldg. U. Tex. M.D. Anderson Cancer Ctr., Houston, 1997; named Houstonian of Yr., Houston Sch. for Deaf Children, 1987, Lamar award Assn. Tex. Colls. and Univs., 2000; named to Ala. Healthcare Hall of Fame, 1999. Mem. AMA, (Disting. Svc. award 1995), NASA, NIH (chair joint adv. com. behavioral rsch. 1992), Am. Thoracic Soc. (past v.p.), So. Thoracic Soc. (past pres.), Nat. TB Assn., Tex. Med. Assn., Ga. Med. Assn., Soc. Assn. Oncology (bd. dirs.), Am. Cancer Soc. (Tex. bd. dirs. 1977-89, med. and sci. com. 1974, chmn. study com. on tobacco and cancer 1976, pub. edn. com. 1976-87, chmn., mem. various nat. coms., v.p., pres. 1986, med. dir.-at-large 1977-89, Ted C. Mars award 1998, medal of Honor 1998), Houston C. of C. (dir. 1979-89), Philos. Soc. Tex. (pres. 1980-81), Greater Houston Partnership (bd. dirs. 1989-96), Alpha Omega Alpha. Presbyterian. Home: 7 Bristol Grn San Antonio TX 78209-1846 E-mail: charles_lemaistre@hotmail.com.

LEMAN, EUGENE D., meat industry executive; b. Peoria, Ill., Dec. 1, 1942; s. Vernon L. and Viola L. (Beer) L.; m. Carolyn Leman, June 14, 1964; children— Jill C., Jennifer A. BS, U. Ill., 1964. Dir. various depts. Wilson Foods, Oklahoma City, 1964-78, v.p. fresh and processed pork, 1978-80, v.p. fresh meat group, 1980-81; group v.p. IBP, Inc., Dakota City, Nebr., 1981-86, exec. v.p., 1986—95, CEO, exec. v.p., 1986—95, pres. Allied Group, 1996—98; pres. IBP Fresh Meats, Dakota City, Nebr., 1998, CEO, 2000, sr. group v.p., 2001, Tyson Fresh Meats, Dakota City, Nebr., 2003. Bd. dirs. Wells Fargo Bank, Dakota Valley Bus. Coun.; bd. trustees BSA Mid-Am. Coun. Bd. mem. United Way of Siouxland, 2003—05, campaign chmn., 2004—05; bd. trustees Siouxland Cmty. Found. Mem. Am. Meat Inst. (chmn. pork com. 1980-81), Nat. Pork Producers Council (packer rep. Pork Value Task Force 1981-82, 88, pork export com. 1985) Clubs: Sioux City Country (Iowa), Dakota Dunes Country Club. Republican. Office: Tyson Fresh Meats Ste 820 800 Stevens Port Dr Dakota Dunes SD 57049-5005 E-mail: gene.leman@tyson.com.

LEMAN, LOREN DWIGHT, lieutenant governor, civil engineer; b. Pomona, Calif., Dec. 2, 1950; s. Nick and Marian (Broady) L.; m. Carolyn Rae Bratvold, June 17, 1978; children: Joseph, Rachel, Nicole. BSCE, Oreg. State U., 1972; MS in Civil, Environ. Engring., Stanford U., 1973; studied Arctic engring., U. Alaska, Anchorage. Registered profl. engr., Alaska. Project mgr. CH2M Hill, San Francisco, 1973, Reston, Va., 1973-74, Ketchikan, Alaska, 1974-75, Anchorage, 1975-87; owner Loren Leman, P.E., Anchorage, 1987—; mem. Alaska Ho. of Reps., 1989-93, Alaska Senate, Dist. G, Juneau, 1993—2003; lt. gov State of Alaska, 2003—. Mem. Anchorage Hazardous Materials Commn., Local Emergency Planning Com., 1989-93. Contbr. articles to profl. jours. Mem. Breakthrough Com., Anchorage, 1978; del. to conv. Rep. Party of Alaska, 1976-90; basketball coach Grace Christian Sch., Anchorage, 1985-88; commr. Pacific States Marine Fisheries Commn.; past chmn. Pacific Fisheries Legis. Task Force. Mem. ASCE, Alaska Water Mgmt. Assn., Am. Legis. Exch. Coun., Water Environment Fedn., Toastmasters (pres.). Republican. Avocations: reading, fishing, biking, music, basketball. Home: 2699 Nathaniel Ct Anchorage AK 99517-1016 Office: 550 W 7th Ave, Ste 1700 Anchorage AK 99501*

LEMANN, THOMAS BERTHELOT, lawyer; b. New Orleans, Jan. 3, 1926; s. Monte M. and Nettie E. (Hyman) L.; m. Barbara M. London, Apr. 14, 1951 (dec. 1999); children: Nicholas B., Nancy E.; m. Sheila Bosworth Bell, June 1, 2000. AB summa cum laude, Harvard U., 1949, LLB, 1952; MCL, Tulane U., 1953. Bar: La. 1953. Assoc. Monroe & Lemann, New Orleans, 1953-58, ptnr., 1958-98; of counsel Liskow & Lewis, New Orleans, 1998—. Bd. dirs. B. Lemann & Bro., Mermentau Mineral and Land Co., Avrico Inc.; adv. bd. dirs. Riviana Foods. Contbr. articles to profl. publs. Mem. coun. La. State Law Inst., sec. trust adv. com.; chmn. Mayor's Cultural Resources Com., 1970-75; pres. Arts Coun. Greater New Orleans, 1975-80, bd. dirs.; mem. vis. com. art museums Harvard U., 1974-80; trustee Metairie Park Country Day Sch., 1956-71, pres., 1967-70, New Orleans Philharm. Symphony Soc., 1956-78, Flint-Goodridge Hosp., 1960-70, La. Civil Svc. League, pres., 1974-76, New Orleans Mus. Art, 1986-92; bd. dirs. Zemurray Found., Hever Found., Parkside Found., Azby Fund, Azby Art Fund, Greater New Orleans Found., 1996-2005, Arts Coun. New Orleans, Musica da Camera. Served with AUS, 1944-46, PTO. Mem. ABA, La. Bar Assn. (bd. govs. 1977-78), New Orleans Bar Assn., Assn. Bar City N.Y., Am. Law Inst., Soc. Bartolus, New Orleans Country Club, Wyvern Club (New Orleans), Phi Beta Kappa. Jewish. Home: 6020 Garfield St New Orleans LA 70118-6039 Office: Liskow & Lewis 701 Poydras St Ste 5000 New Orleans LA 70139-5099 Office Phone: 504-581-7979. E-mail: tblemann@liskow.com.

LEMANSKE, ROBERT F., JR., allergist, immunologist; b. Milw., 1948; MD, U. Wis., 1975. Diplomate Am. Bd. Pediats., Am. Bd. Allergy and Immunology. Intern U. Wis. Hosp., Madison, 1975-76, resident in pediats., 1976-78, prof. pediats. medicine, divsn. head pediat. allergy, immunology & rheumatology. Fellow: Am. Acad. Allergy and Immunology, Am. Acad. Pediat. Office: Clin Sci Ctr Rm K4/916 600 Highland Ave Madison WI 53792-0001 Office Phone: 608-265-2206.

LEMANSKI, LARRY FREDRICK, medical educator, academic administrator; b. Madison, Wis., June 5, 1943; s. Fredrick Everett and Marjery Ulila (Hill) L.; m. Sharon Lee Wulf, Aug. 6, 1966; children: Scott Fredrick, Jennifer Lee. *Married Sharon Lee Wulf in 1966. Sharon taught third grade from 1966-1971 before pursuing a career as a research support specialist in an academic environment. Son, Scott F. Lemanski, B.A. 1997, Colgate University, J.D., 2001, St. Mary's University, San Antonio, TX. Daughter, Jennifer L. Lemanski, B.A., 2000, Colgate University, M.A. with honors, 2002, Univeristy of Florida and is now pursuing a Ph. D. degree in Mass Communication at the Univeristy of Florida, Gainseville. Scott was heavily involved in the Boy Scouts of America where he earned the 3 palm Eagle Scout rank. Jennifer was a member of the National Honor Society in high school.* BS, U. Wis., Platteville, 1966; MS, Ariz. State U., 1968, PhD, 1971. Asst. prof. U. Calif., San Francisco, 1975-77; assoc. prof. U. Wis., Madison, 1977-79, prof., 1979-83; prof., chmn. dept. anatomy and cell biology SUNY, Syracuse, 1983-97, cell & molecular biology doctoral tng. program & consortium, 1987-97; rsch. prof. biology Syracuse U., 1988-97; assoc. v.p. for rsch. Tex. A&M. U., College Station, 1997—2001; v.p. rsch. and grad. studies, prof. biomed. sci., biology, chemistry, dean grad. programs, pres., chmn. Bd. Rsch. Found. Fla. Atlantic U., 2001—. Mem. ad hoc rev. panel NIH, mem. cardiovasc. study sect., 1993—97, chmn. special study sect.; bd. dirs. Fla. Rsch. Consortium; gov. apptd. bd. dirs.' position Ctr. Human and Machine Cognition, 2004—; mem. NIH review panel Roadmap Rsch. Programs, 2004—05; bd dirs. Fla. Space Rsch. Inst., 2004—; spkr. in field. *Over 25 years as an educator, research scientist, and university administrator, Dr. Larry F. Lemanski continues his research interests in medical embryology of the heart. As a Basic Science Department Chairman in a major medical school in New York, he excelled as an administrator and researcher. His department's overall research funding increased over 800 percent during the last ten years (1987-1997) and was awarded the "Outstanding Basic Science Teaching Award" for medical students (1988-97). He continues to be a national and international leader in research while involved in university administration as the Vice President for Research and Graduate Studies and President of the Research Corporation at Florida Atlantic University.* Bd. dirs. Oak Ridge Assoc. Univs., 1999-02, 2004—, Fla. Rsch. Consortium, Ctr. Human Machine Cooperation (gov.'s appointee 2004-); adult leader for Boy Scouts Am., mem. nat. staff Boy Scout Jamboree 1989, coun. tng. chmn., 1992-94. Officer USAR, 1965-69. Recipient Pres'. award Rsch. SUNY HSC, 1987, Disting. Alumnus award U. Wis., 1990, Profl. Excellence award N.Y. State/United Univ. Professions, 1990, 95, Pres.'s award for affirmative action, 1995, Outstanding Rschr. award SUNY Coll. of Medicine, 1997; NIH fellow, 1968-71, 71-73, Muscular Dystrophy fellow, 1973-75; grantee NIH, 1975—. Mem. AAAS, Am. Heart Assn. (Wis. affiliate rsch. com. 1982-83, peer review panel, Louis N. Katz Rsch. prize 1978, Outstanding Rsch. award 1982, Established Investigator award 1976-81, symposium chair Internat. Soc. Heart Rsch. Conf., Brisbane, Australia, 2004, Fla.-Puerto Rican rsch. com. 2004-), Electron Microscopy Soc. Am., Tex. Soc. for Biomed. Rsch. (bd. dirs. 1999-2001), Am. Assn. Anatomy, Cell Biology, and Neurobiology (chairperson nat. coun. 1997—), Am. Assn. Anatomists, Am. Soc. Cell Biology (congrl. liaison com. 1993—), Soc. Devel. Biology, Am. Assn. Anatomy Chmn., N.Y. Acad. Scis., Masons (3d degree master), Sigma Xi, Beta Beta Beta, Phi Beta Delta. Methodist. Avocations: gardening, fishing, boating, camping, music. Home: 6762 Camille St Boynton Beach FL 33437 Fax: 561-297-2141. Office Phone: 591-267-0267. Business E-Mail: lemanski@fau.edu.

LE MASTER, DENNIS CLYDE, forester, educator, economist, department chairman; b. Startup, Wash., Apr. 22, 1939; s. Franklin Clyde and Delores Ilene (Schwartz) Le M.; m. Kathleen Ruth Dennis, Apr. 4, 1961; children: Paul, Matthew. BA, Wash. State U., 1961, MA, 1970, PhD, 1974. Asst. prof. dept. forestry and range mgmt. Wash. State U., Pullman, 1972-74, assoc. prof., 1978-80, prof., chair dept., 1980-88; prof., head dept. forestry and natural resources Purdue U., West Lafayette, Ind., 1998—2004; dir. resource policy Soc. Am. Foresters, Bethesda, Md., 1974-76; staff counsel subcom. on forests Ho. of Reps., Washington, 1977-78. Cons. USDA Forest Svc., Washington, 1978, Com. on Agr., Ho. of Reps., 1979-80, Forest History Soc., Durham, N.C., 1979-83, The Conservation Found., 1989-90, Office Tech. Assessment, Washington, 1989-91, Consultative Group on Biol. Diversity, 1991. Author: Decade of Change, 1984; co-editor 8 books; contbr. articles to profl. jours. Bd. dirs. Pinchot Inst. for Conservation, treas., 1996-97, vice-chair, 1998-99, chair, 2000-01. Sr. fellow, Pinchot Inst. for Conservation. Fellow Soc. Am. Foresters (chair house of soc. dels. 1982, coun. 1988); mem. AAAS, Inland Empire Soc. Am. Foresters (chair 1980-81, Forester of Yr. award 1982), Inst. Forest Biotech., Internat. Union Forest Rsch. Orgns., Omicron Delta Epsilon, Beta Gamma Sigma, Epsilon Sigma Phi, Xi Sigma Pi. Democrat. Episcopalian. Avocation: fishing. Home: 626 40th Pl Everett WA 98201 Office: Purdue U Dept Forestry and Natural Resources West Lafayette IN 47907 Personal E-mail: dclmstr@comcast.net.

LEMASTER, SUSAN M., marketing executive, writer; b. Cody, Wyo., May 9, 1953; d. Floyd Morris and Virginia Kristena (Renner) LeM. AA, Casper Coll., 1977; BA, U. Wyo., Casper, 1979. Reporter, night editor Casper Star Tribune, 1972-76; copy editor, editor In Wyo. mag., Casper, 1979; info. dir. Wyo. Rural Electric Assn., Casper, 1980-81; story editor Wyo. Horizons mag., Casper, 1981-82; asst., instr. English lab. Casper Coll., 1982-84; mktg. mgr. Chen & Assocs., Inc., 1984-87; mktg. cons., 1987-90; dir. mktg. KaWES and Assocs., Inc., 1990-91, pub. rels. and mktg. cons., 1992-95; comm. mgr. Arthur Andersen, L.A., 1995-97, assoc. dir. sales and mktg., 1997-99, mktg. dir., 1999-2000, Pacific Region Bus. Consulting, 2000—01, mktg. mgr. healthcare, 2001—02; mktg. dir. PacifiCare Dental & Vision, Santa Ana, Calif., 2002—03; west unit mktg. leader Mercer HR Consulting, L.A., 2003—04, U.S. mktg. strategist, 2004—. Freelance writer and editor, 1982—; night sch. instr. Casper Coll., 1983-84, summer sch. instr., 1984. Editor Casper Jour., 1983-84. Recipient 1st Place News Story award Wyo. Press Assn., 1973, 1st Place Editing award Wyo. Press Women, 1980. Mem. L.A. Press Club, Phi Theta Kappa, Phi Kappa Phi, Alpha Mu Gamma. Democrat. Home: 1059 E Cypress Ave Burbank CA 91501-1309 Office: Mercer HR Consulting 777 S Figueroa St Los Angeles CA 90017 Office Phone: 213-346-2522. Business E-Mail: susan.lemaster@mercer.com.

LEMASURIER, WESLEY ERNEST, geology educator, researcher; b. Washington, May 3, 1934; s. E. Howard and V. May (Van Arnum) LeM.; m. C. Heather Nelson, Sept. 21, 1963; children: Michelle, Susanne, John. *Great-grandfather, Philippe A. LeMasurier, was a piano maker from St. Helier, Jersey. He moved to England in 1952, then to Ontario, Canada, then to St. Vincent, Minnesota. Great-grandfather, Dr. John W. Van Arnum, was Surgeon General in the Spanish American War, from April until August, 1898. Great-uncle, Elihu S. Riley, wrote "History of Annapolis".* Student, St. Andrews U., Fifeshire, Scotland, 1954-55; BS, Union Coll., Schenectady, N.Y., 1956; MS, U. Colo., 1962; PhD, Stanford U., 1965. Geologist U.S. Geol. Survey, Denver, also Menlo Park, Calif., 1956-63; asst. prof. geology Cornell U., Ithaca, N.Y., 1964-68; from assoc. prof. to prof. geology U. Colo., Denver, 1968—2003, prof. geology, 2004—; fellow, sr. rsch. scientist Inst. Arctic-Alpine Rsch., Boulder, 2003—. Dir. Guilin Coll. (China)-U. Colo. Denver Scholarly Exch. Program, 1986—. Editor, author: Volcanoes of the Antarctic Plate and Southern Oceans, 1990. Pvt. U.S. Army, 1960. Recipient Antarctic Svc. medal, 1971; NSF grantee, 1968-85; Mt. LeMasurier named in his honor, 1971; exch. scholar St. Andrews U., 1954-55. Fellow Geol. Soc. Am.; mem. Am. Geophys. Union, Internat. Assn. Volcanology. Presbyterian. Home: 1333 Mariposa Ave Boulder CO 80302-7841 Office: Inst Arctic-Alpine Rsch U Colo Boulder CO 80309-0450 Office Phone: 303-735-8170. E-mail: wesley.lemasurier@colorado.edu.

LEMAY, CURTIS EMERSON, former United States Air Force Chief of Staff; b. Columbus, Ohio, Nov. 15, 1906; m. Helen Maitland, 1934; 1 child, Patricia. BCE, Ohio State U., 1932, DSc (hon.); LLD (hon.), John Carroll U., Kenyon Coll., U. So. Calif., U. Akron, Bradley U., C.W. Post Coll.; DSc (hon.), Tufts U., U. W.Va.; ED (hon.), Case Inst. Tech. Flying cadet AC, U.S. Army, 1928, commd. 2d lt., 1930; advanced through grades maj. gen. USAAF, 1943; temp. gen. USAF, 1951; chief staff AUS Stategic Air Forces, 1945; dep. chief Air Staff for R & D, Washington, 1945; comdg. gen. USAF in Europe, 1947; vice chief staff Hdqrs. USAF, Washington, 1957-61, chief staff, 1961-65; chmn. bd. Networks Electronic Corp., after 1965. Author: (with MacKinlay Kantor) Mission with LeMay, 1965. Trustee Nat. Geog. Soc. Decorated D.S.C., D.S.M. with 3 oak leaf clusters, Air medal with 3 clusters, DFC. with 2 clusters; comdr. Legion of Honor (France), MacKay Trophy; comdr. Order Ouissam Alaouite Chefifien (Morroco), Medal for Humane Action, Crois de Guerre with palm (Belgium), Silver Star medal, Order of So. Cross (Brazil), D.F.C. (Eng.), Order of Patriotic war (USSR), Order Svc. Merit 1st class (Korea), Most Exalted Order of White Elephant 1st class (Thailand), Cross of Phoenix (Greece); recipient Robert J. Collier Trophy. Mem. Masons (33d degree), Sigma Tau, Tau Beta Pi, Theta Tau. Home: Moreno Valley, Calif. Died Oct. 1, 1990; buried USAF Acad., Colo.

LEMAY, HARRY ADRIAN, artist, educator; b. Lewiston, Pa., Dec. 19, 1929; s. Joseph Adrian LeMay and Edna May Price; m. Yves Lindsay, July 24, 1954 (dec. Dec. 28, 1974); children: Nina(dec.), Peter(dec.); m. Nancy Potenzano, Jan. 24, 1986. BS with honors, U.S. Mcht. Marine Acad., 1952; diploma, Cooper Union, N.Y.C., 1958; diploma in vocat. edn., CUNY, 1976. Cert. tchr. N.Y.C., LA. Art dir. Mann Assoc., N.Y.C., 1960—63; designer, art dir. Rapid Art, N.Y.C., 1963—65; mgr. art & prodn. RCA Victor Record Club, 1965—67; v.p. creative Capitol Record Club, 1967—69; tchr. HS Art & Design, N.Y.C., 1972—91; pres. LeMay Co., NY, 1975—. Judge Suburban Art League, JP Morgan Estate, NY, 1965. Exhibited in group shows, N.Y.C., LA, 1955—2005, one-man shows include, Saratoga Springs, 1970, LA, 1970—2004, N.Y.C., 1980—91; pub.: Keynotes Mag., 1967—69; guest (TV series) You're Part of Art, 1971—72; lighting design, tech. dir.: Folklorico Philipino Dance Performances, 1973, 1974; designer, pub.: Day of the Wounded Eagle (Daisy Alden), 1990. U.S. rep. Donatello Awards, Italy, 1962—63. Lt. (j.g.) USN, 1953—55. Mem.: Art Students League (life), Acad. Magical Arts, Inc., Am. Philatelic Soc. Avocations: stamp collecting/philately, collecting movie posters, collecting books. Home: 357 S Curson Ave #6B Los Angeles CA 90036 Personal E-mail: halemay@comcast.net.

LEMAY, J.A. LEO, American literature educator; b. Bristow, Va., Jan. 17, 1935; s. Joseph Albert and Valencia Lee (Winslow) L.; m. Muriel Ann Clarke, Aug. 11, 1965; children: John Clarke, Lee Clarke, Kate Clarke. AB, U. Md., 1957, AM, 1962; PhD, U. Pa., 1964. From instr. to asst. prof. English George Washington U., Washington, 1963-65; asst. prof. English UCLA, 1965-70, assoc. prof., 1970-75, prof. English, 1975-77; H.F. du Pont Winterthur prof. English U. Del., Newark, 1977—. Author: Men of Letters in Colonial Maryland, 1972, The Canon of Benjamin Franklin New Attributions, 1986, The American Dream of Captain John Smith, 1991, Did Pocahontas Save Captain John Smith?, 1992, Finding Colonial Americans: Essays Honoring J.A. Leo Lemay, 2001; (internet book) A Documentary History of Benjamin Franklin, 1997—; editor Robert Bolling Woos Anne Miller, 1990. Adv. com. Ctr. Editions of Am. Authors, 1974-76; mem. Inst. Early Am. History and Culture, 1978-81, Cosmos Club, 1984—. With U.S. Army, 1957-59. Fellow Inst. Advanced Study, U. Del., 1980-81, 98-99, Guggenheim Found., 1974-75. Mem. MLA (Hon. Scholar award 1999), Am. Humor Studies Assn. (pres. 1981), Am. Antiquarian Soc., Soc. for Study of So. Lit. Office: Univ Del Memorial Hall Newark DE 19716-2595 Home: 55 Sunset Rd Newark DE 19711-5237 Office Phone: 302-831-8011. Business E-Mail: lemay@udel.edu.

LEMAY, JACQUES, lawyer; b. Quebec City, Can., July 10, 1940; s. Gerard and Jacqueline (LaChance) LeMay. BA, Que. Sem., 1959; LL.L., Laval U., 1962; postgrad., U. Toronto, 1964; D.E.S., 1965. Bar: Que. 1963. Practice in, Quebec City, 1964—; mem. firm Prevost, Gagne, Flynn, Chouinard & Jacques, 1964-67; ptnr. Flynn, Rivard, Jacques, Cimon, Lessard & LeMay, 1968-86, Flynn, Rivard, 1986—2003, Desjardins, Ducharme, Quebec, 2003—. Legal adv. Soc. des Ajusteurs d'Assurance, 1969. Mem.: Soc. des Etudes Juridiques (pres. 1969), Cercle de la Garnison (Que.). Home: 265 ch duBout de l'Ile Sainte-Petronille PQ Canada G0A 4CO Office: 900 Place d'Youville Bureau 6W Quebec City PQ Canada G1K 3P7 Office Phone: 418-640-4450. Business E-Mail: jacques.lemay@ddsm.ca.

LEMBARK, CONNIE WERTHEIMER, art consultant; b. Omaha, Mar. 8, 1934; d. Sam Wertheimer and Elinor (Livingston) Wertheimer-Dombrowsky; m. Daniel Lembark, July 10, 1955; 1 child, Steven. Student, U. Ariz. Docent UCLA, 1964-71; owner, art cons. Connie W. Lembark, Nashville, 1992—2000, L.A.; owner, founding ptnr. Art Posters Ltd., L.A., 1971-82; art cons., 1983—. Lectr. L.A. County Mus. Art, 1994; founder Mus. Contemporary Art L.A. Author: The Prints of Sam Francis, 1992, The Life of Frank Stella, 2005; organizer (one-man shows) Tenn. State Mus. Recipient Herb Alpert honoree, Lincoln Ctr., N.Y., 2001. E-mail: clembark@earthlink.net.

LEMBERG, LOUIS, cardiologist, educator; b. Chgo., Dec. 27, 1916; s. Morris and Frances Lemberg; m. Dorothy Feinstein, 1940 (dec. 1969); children: Gerald, Laura Bott, Paula Saltzman; m. Miriam Mayer, Jan. 29, 1971. BS, U. Ill., Chgo., 1938; MD, U. Ill., 1940. Intern Mt. Sinai Hosp., Chgo., 1940-41, resident, 1945-48, asst. prof. med., 1955-58, assoc. prof. med., 1958-70; prof. clin. cardiology U. Miami (Fla.) Sch. Medicine, 1970—, dir. coronary care unit, 1965-75. Chief cardiology Mercy Hosp., 1974-79; chief staff Nat. Children's Cardiac Hosp., 1959-66; cons. cardiology VA Hosp., Miami, 1953-64; dir. cardiology Dade County Hosp., 1953-64, dir. Heart Sta. and Electrocardiography, U. Miami Jackson Meml. Med. Ctr., 1952-75, program dir. Courses in Coronary Care for Practicing Physician, 1970-2003, Courses in Coronary Care for Nurses, 1970-90; Master Approach to Cardiovascular Problems, 1972-82, Cardiology Update for Intensive Care Nurses, Am. Coll. Cardiology, 1978-92, Cardiology Update, 1987-2002. Author: Vectorcardiography, 1969, 2d edit., 1975, Electrophysiology of Pacing and Cardioversion, 1969; editor-in-chief Current Concepts in Cardiovascular Disorders, 1984-86; contbr. to med. publs. Served to maj. AUS, 1941-55, ETO. Recipient U. St. Torres (Philippines) Luis Guerrero hon. lectr. award, 1977, Recognition award U. Miami Sch. Medicine, Lifetime Achievement award Jackson Meml. Med. Ctr. U. Miami, 1997, Key to City of Miami Beach, Fla., Nurses Pioneering Spirit award Am. Assn. Critical Care, 2000, Physicians Recognition awards AMA. Fellow ACP, Am. Coll. Cardiology (editl. bd. jour.); mem. Heart Assn. Greater Miami (pres.), Fla. Heart Assn. (pres.), Am. Heart Assn. (fellow coun. clin. cardiology). Democrat. Jewish. Achievements include pioneer in development Demand Pacemaker, 1964, a chair in cardiology established at the U. Miami Sch. of Medicine entitled The Louis Lemberg Professor of Cardiology, 1990. Home: 720 NE 69th St Apt 18 South Miami FL 33138-5738 Office: U Miami Sch Medicine Divsn Cardiology PO Box 016960 Miami FL 33101 Office Phone: 305-243-3515.

LEMBERGER, LOUIS, pharmacologist; b. Monticello, N.Y., May 8, 1937; s. Max and Ida (Siegel) L.; m. Myrna Sue Diamond, 1959; children: Harriet Felice Schor, Margo Beth. BS magna cum laude, Bklyn. Coll. Pharmacy, L.I. U., 1960; PhD in Pharmacology, Albert Einstein Coll. Medicine, 1964, MD, 1968; Doctorate (hon.), L.I. U., 1994. Pharmacy intern VA Regional Office, Newark, summer 1960; postdoctoral fellow Albert Einstein Coll. Medicine, 1964-68; intern in medicine Met. Hosp. Center, N.Y. Med. Coll., N.Y.C., 1968-69; rsch. assoc. NIH, Bethesda, Md., 1969-71; clin. pharmacologist Lilly Lab. for Clin. Rsch., Eli Lilly & Co., Indpls., 1971-75, chief clin. pharmacology, 1975-78, dir. clin. pharmacology, 1978-89, clin. rsch. fellow, 1982-93; asst. prof. pharmacology Ind. U., 1972-73, asst. prof. medicine, 1972-73, assoc. prof. pharmacology, 1973-77, assoc. prof. medicine, 1973-77, prof. pharmacology, 1977—, prof. medicine, prof. psychiatry, 1977—, mem. grad. faculty, 1975—; adj. prof. clin. pharmacology Ohio State U., 1975-86; physician Wishard Meml. Hosp., 1976-98. Cons. U.S. Nat. Commn. on Marijuana and Drug Abuse, 1971-73, Can. Commn. Inquiry into Non-Med. Use of Drugs, 1971-73; mem. Pharm. Mfrs. Assn. Commn. on Medicines for Drug Dependence and Abuse, 1990-93, Ind. Optometric Legend Drug Adv. Com., 1991-96; guest lectr. various univs., 1968—; lectr. U. Minn., 1993—; mem. adv. com. Faseb Life Scis. Rsch. Office, 1993-96. Author: (with A. Rubin) Physiologic Disposition of Drugs of Abuse, 1976; contbr. numerous articles on biochemistry and pharmacology to sci. jours.; editorial bd.; Excerpta Medica, 1972-96, Clin. Pharmacology and Therapeutics, 1976-96, Communications in Psychopharmacology, 1975-91, Pharmacology, Internat. Jour. Exptl. and Clin. Pharmacology, 1978-94, Drug and Alcohol Abuse Rsch., 1979-86, Drug Devel. Rsch., 1980-87, Trends in Pharmcol. Scis., 1980-85. Post adviser Crossroads of Am. coun. Boy Scouts Am., 1972-77; commdr. Jewish War Vet. Post 114, 2005—. Lt. cmdr. USPHS, 1969-71 Recipient Disting. Alumnus award, Albert Einstein Coll. Medicine, 1989, L.I. U., 1990, Pres. award, 1998, Cornerstone award for Oustanding Lifetime Achievement in Health Scis., Am. Drugstore Mus., 2000. Fellow ACP, AAAS, Am. Coll. Neuropsychopharmacology (chmn. credentials com. 1993), Am. Coll. Clin. Pharmacology; mem. Am. Soc. Pharmacology and Exptl. Therapeutics (com. div. clin. pharmacology 1972-78, chmn. com. 1978-83, coun. 1980-83, chmn. long-range planning com. 1984-86, pres. 1987-88, ASPET award in Therapeutics, 1985, Harry Gold award for rsch. and teaching excellence in clin. pharmacology 1993), Am. Soc. Clin. Pharmacology and Therapeutics (chmn. sect. neuropsychopharmacology 1973-80, chmn. fin. com. 1976-83, 89-92, v.p. 1981-82, pres. 1983-84, dir. 1975-81, 84-87, Rawls-Palmer award 1986, Henry Elliot Disting. Svc. award 1992, Oscar B. Hunter award for outstanding achievement in exptl. therapeutics 2003), Am. Soc. Clin. Investigation, Collegium Internat. Neuro-Psychopharmacologicum, Am. Fedn. Clin. Rsch. Ctrl. Soc. Clin. Rsch., Soc. Neurosci., Sigma Xi, Alpha Omega Alpha, Rho Chi. Jewish. Achievements include being first person to administer and study the actions in humans of the antidepressant drug Prozac (fluoxetine), Permax (pergolide) the drug used to treat Parkinson's disease, and the cannabinoid drug Cesamet (nabilone) utilized for the treatment of nausea and vomiting secondary to cancer chemotherapy and Zyprexa (Olanzepine) the drug utilized in schizophrenia and Strattera (atomoxetine) the drug utilized in attention deficit hyperactivity disorder; responsible for directing and spearheading the clinical development of Prozac, Permax and Cesamet through clinical trials, regulatory approval and eventually into the marketplace. Home: 3315 Walnut Creek Dr N Carmel IN 46032-9038 Office: Ind Univ Sch Medicine Dept Pharmacology and Medicine Indianapolis IN 46202

LEMEIN, GREGG D., lawyer; b. Chgo., Feb. 2, 1950; BS with high honors, U. Ill., 1972; MM with distinction, JD magna cum laude, Northwestern U., 1976. Bar: Ill. 1976, U.S. Claims Ct. 1978, U.S. Tax Ct. 1979. Ptnr. Baker & McKenzie, Chgo. Office: Baker & McKenzie 1 Prudential Plz 130 E Randolph St Ste 3700 Chicago IL 60601-6342

LEMENS, WILLIAM VERNON, JR., banker, finance company executive, lawyer; b. Austin, Tex., Oct. 26, 1935; s. William Vernon and Lylia (Engberg) L.; m. Jean Lemens, May 31, 1959; children: William Vernon III, Shandra Christine. BA, U. Tex., 1958, LLB, JD, U. Tex., 1962. Bar: Tex. 1962; lic. real estate broker, Tex. Pvt. practice, Austin, 1962—; pres. Standard Fin. Co., Austin, 1963-67, First State Loan, Austin, 1967—; chief exec. officer Southwest Computer Svcs., Inc., Austin, 1965—. Pres., chief instr., mgmt. cons. Decision Dynamics, Inc., Austin, 1965-75; exec. v.p., atty. Northwest Savs. Assn., Austin, 1975-78; chmn. bd. First State Bank, Jarrell, Tex., 1975-87; pres., chief exec. officer First Am. Fin. Co., Ft. Worth, 1982—, Eagle Bank, Jarrell, 1987—. Author: Elements of Objective Orientation, 1971, SSAM-The Power of Perfect Decisions, 1972, Successful Financial Institution Operation, 1978, National Standard Financial Company Operations, 1981. Pres. Ballet Austin, 1967, Southwest Regional Ballet Assn., 1968; deacon Univ. Bapt. Ch., Austin, 1979—. Mem. State Bar Tex., Austin Bd. Realtors, Tex. Fin. Inst. (bd. dirs. 1975—), Tex. Consumer Fin. Asns. (bd. dirs. 1995—). Office: 1509 Guadalupe St Ste 200 Austin TX 78701-1608 Office Phone: 512-476-2608. E-mail: vlemens@aol.com.

LEMER, ANDREW CHARLES, engineer, economist; b. Maxwell Field, Ala., Dec. 25, 1944; s. Samuel Theodore and Carol (Oppenheimer) L.; m. Patricia Spear, Aug. 1967 (div. Dec. 1981); m. Janet Felsten, Aug. 1992; children: Elizabeth Catherine, Daniel Evan, Rebekah Simone. SB, MIT, 1967, SM, 1968, PhD, 1971. Assoc. Alan M. Voorhees & Assoc., Inc., McLean, Va., 1971-76; sr. assoc. PRC Planning & Econs., Inc., McLean, 1976-80; chief planner PRC (Nigeria) Ltd., Lagos, 1980-82; divsn. v.p. PRC Engring., Inc., McLean, 1982-85; pres. Matrix Group, LLC, Balt., 1985—; dir. bldg. rsch. bd. Nat. Acad. Scis., Balt., 1988—93. Cons. Fed. Rail Adminstrn., Washington, 1975, FAA, Washington, 1986—, World Bank, Washington, 1980—, Abell Found., Balt., 1993—, Transp. Rsch. Bd., Washington, 1993—; vis. prof. civil engring. Purdue U., West Lafayette, Ind., 1995-96; adj. faculty Johns Hopkins U., Balt., 1994—. Prin. author: In Our Own Back Yard: Principles for Improving the Nation's Infrastructure, 1993, Toward Infrastructure Improvement: A Research Agenda, 1994, Solving the Innovation Puzzle: Challenges Facing the U.S. Design and Construction Industry, 1996, Getting the Most Out of Your Infrastructure Assets, 2002; editl. adv. bd. Jour. Infrastructure Sys., Constrn. Bus. Rev., Constrn. Mgmt. and Econs., Pub. Works Mgmt. and Policy. Loeb fellow Harvard U., 1992-93. Mem. ASCE, The Am. Soc. Macroengring. (bd. dirs. 1997—, pres. 2000—), Royal Inst. Chartered Surveyors, Cosmos Club (Washington), 14 W. Hamilton St. Club (Balt.), Lambda Alpha Internat (pres. Balt. chpt. 2002—). Office: 4701 Keswick Rd Baltimore MD 21210-2322

LEMESIS, GUNTIS VICTOR, human resources specialist; b. Jekabpils, Latvia, May 17, 1943; came to U.S., 1950; s. Alberts and Alma Lemesis; m. Mara Kalva, Aug. 2, 1979 (div. 1988); m. Susan Durden, Aug. 26, 1989. BA, Wesleyan U., 1966. Compensation specialist Honeywell, Inc., Phoenix, 1978—79, human resources planning specialist, 1979—80, mgr. benefits planning Mpls., 1980—82; dir. compensation & benefits United Airlines, Elk Grove Village, Ill., 1982—86; dir. compensation & mgmt. resources Contel Corp., Atlanta, 1986—91; v.p. compensation GTE Corp., Stamford, Conn., 1991—93; dir. compensation & human resources planning Sci.-Atlanta, Inc., Norcross, Ga., 1993—2000; pres. Lemesis & Assocs., Inc., 2000—. Instr. World at Work, Scottsdale, Ariz., 1985—; mem. exec. adv. panel Acad. Mgmt., Boston, 1997-2001. Co-author: Determining Compensation Costs, 1992, Compensation Guide, 1993, Academy of Management Executive, 2003; mem. editl. bd. Executive Compensation Reports, 1999—2002. Mem. employee benefits com. U.S. C. of C., Washington, 1981-86. Recipient 1st pl. Pub. Utilities Advt. Assn., 1972, 1st pl. Ariz. Assn. Bus. Communicators, 1974. Mem.: World at Work. Republican. Methodist. Avocations: music, wine collecting, amateur photography, chess.

LEMIEUX, CLAUDE, former professional hockey player, professional sports team executive; b. Buckingham, Que., July 16, 1965; Right wing Montreal Canadiens, 1983—90, N.J. Devils, 1990—95, 1999—2000, Colo. Avalanche, 1995—99, Phoenix Coyotes, 2000—03; pres. Phoenix Roadrunners, 2005—. Mem. Stanley Cup Championship Team, 1986, 95, 96. Named to Que. Major Jr. League All-Star 2nd Team, 1983; recipient Guy Lafleur Trophy, 1985, Conn Smythe Trophy MVP in Playoffs, 1995. Office: Phoenix Roadrunners Am W Arena 201 E Jefferson St Phoenix AZ 85004*

LEMIEUX, LINDA DAILEY, museum director; b. Cleve., Sept. 6, 1953; d. Leslie Leo LeMieux Jr. and Mildred Edna (Dailey) Tutt. BA, Beloit Coll., 1975; MA, U. Mich., 1979; A cert., Mus. Mgmt. Program, Boulder, Colo., 1987. Asst. curator Old Salem, Inc., Winston-Salem, NC, 1979-82; curator Clarke House, Chgo., 1982-84, Western Mus. Mining and Industry, Colorado Springs, Colo., 1985-86, dir., 1987—. Author: Prairie Avenue Guidebook, 1985; editor: The Golden Years--Mines in the Cripple Creek District, 1987; contbr. articles to mags. and newspapers. Fellow Hist. Deerfield, Mass., 1974—. Rsch. grantee Early Am. Industries Assn., 1978. Mem. Am. Assn. Mus., Am. Assn. State and Local History, Colo.-Wyo. Mus. Assn., Colo. Mining Assn., Mountain Plains Assn. Mus., Women in Mining, Colo. Mont. Wyo. State Conf. Edn. Com. NAACP. Mem. First Congl. Ch. Home: 1337 Hermosa Way Colorado Springs CO 80906-3050 Office: Western Mus Mining & Industry 1025 N Gate Rd Colorado Springs CO 80921-3018 E-mail: director@wmmi.org, lindalemieux1@aol.com.

LEMIEUX, MARIO, professional hockey player, professional sports team executive; b. Montreal, P.Q., Can., Oct. 5, 1965; m. Natalie Asselin, June 26, 1993; children: Lauren, Stephanie, Austin, Alexa. Player Pitts. Penguins, 1984—97, 2000—, owner, chmn., CEO, 1998—. Mem. Team Can., Olympic Games, Salt Lake City, 2002, Team Can., World Cup of Hockey, 2004. Named Player of the Yr., Can. Hockey League, 1983—84, MVP, NHL All-Star game, 1985, 1988, 1990; named to NHL All-Star game, 1986—89, 1990, 1992—93, 1996—97, 2001; recipient Calder Memorial Trophy, 1985, Hart Meml. trophy for most valuable player, 1988, 1993, 1996, Conn Smythe Trophy, 1991—92, Art Ross Meml. trophy, 1988—89, 1992—93, 1996—97, Michel Briere trophy, 1983—84, Jean Beliveau trophy, 1983—84, Michael Bossy trophy, 1983—84, Guy LaFleur trophy, 1983—84, Bill Masterson Meml. trophy, 1993. Achievements include only player in NHL history to score a goal 5 different ways in a single game, 1988; mem. Stanley Cup Champion Pittsburgh Penguins, 1991-92; inducted to Hockey Hall of Fame without manditory 3 year waiting period, 1997; mem. Gold medal Can. Hockey Team, Salt Lake City Olympic games, 2002; mem. World Cup Champion Team Can., 2004. Office: Pitts Penguins Mellon Arena 66 Mario Lemieux Drive Pittsburgh PA 15219

LE MIN, THOMAS FRANCIS, law enforcement official, educator; s. Joseph D. and Rita R. Le Min; m. Charupin Charoenthep. BA in Polit. sci., Widener U., Chester, Pa., 1983—87; MS in Criminal Justice, U. Ala., Tuscaloosa, 1996—98. Cert. Assessor Commn. on Accreditation for Law Enforcement Agencies, 1995, Master Police Instructor Del. Coun. on Police Tng., 1995, Nationally Credentialed Law Enforcement Officer Nat. Law Enforcement Credentialing Bd., 1997. Asst. prof., mil. sci. U. Del., Newark, 1994—2003; traffic divsn. comdr. Newark Police Dept., Del., 2000—; adj. prof., criminal justice Wilmington Coll., New Castle, Del., 2000—. Contbr. articles to profl. jours. Decorated Parachutist Badge U.S. Army Inf. Ctr. and Sch., Army Achievement Medal U.S. Army; recipient Police Officer of Yr., Newark Lion's Club, 1993, Police Officer of Yr. Award, VFW, Post 475, 1994. Mem.: European Assn. for Forensic Entomology. Office: Newark Police Dept 220 Elkton Rd Newark DE 19711 Office Phone: 302-366-7111. E-mail: tlemin@msn.com, tlemin@newarkpd.state.de.us.

LEMIRE, RONALD JOHN, pediatrician, educator; b. Portland, Apr. 20, 1933; s. Lucile Frances Morelock; m. Kathy H. Brazeau, Aug. 1, 1993; children: Gregory, Suzy McNabb, Jennifer, Anne Kondra, Alisa Brooks, Brian Brazeau, Leisa Houlahan. MD, U. Wash., 1962. Prof. pediatrics U. Wash. Sch. Medicine, Seattle, 1977—; dir. impatient svcs. Children's Hosp. & Regional MEd. Ctr., 1978—. Author: Normal and Abnormal Development of the Human Nervous System, 1975, Anencephaly, 1978, Mental Retardation and Congenital Malformations of the Cedntral Nervous System, 1981, Holoprosencephaly: An Overview and Atlas of Cases, 1990, Catalog of Teratogenic Agents, 11th edit., 2004; mem. editl. bd.: Jour. Child Neurology, 1985—91, Pediatric Neurosci., 1985—91, Pediatric Neurosurgery, 1992—2002. With USN, 1951—55. Mem.: AAUP, Soc. Pediatric Rsch., Teratology Soc. Avocations: flying, fishing. Home: 10037 NE 127th Pl Kirkland WA 98034 Office: Childrens Hosp and Regional Med Ctr 4800 Sand Point Way NE Seattle WA 98105 Office Phone: 206-987-2025. Business E-Mail: ron.lemire@seattlechildrens.org.

LEMKE, ALAN JAMES, environmental specialist; b. Appleton, Wis., May 22, 1945; s. Edwin R. and Ethel Mae (Noe) L.; m. Joyce Eileen Kruse, May 24, 1975; 1 child, David Edwin. BS in chemistry, Coll. Idaho, 1968. Rsch. chemist Am. Med. Ctr., Denver, 1972-74; chemist U.S. Geol. Survey, Denver,

1975-77; chemist II Occupl. Health Lab., Portland, Oreg., 1977-80, State Hygienic Labs., Des Moines, 1980-82; indsl. hygienist Iowa Divsn. Labor, Des Moines, 1982-88; environ. specialist Iowa Dept. Natural Resources, Spencer, 1988—. Small bus. owner Al's Stamps and Collectables. Author: The Noe Family's Involvement in the Civil War: A History of Wisconsin's 19th Volunteer Infantry Regiment, 1994. Republican. Evangelical. Avocations: camping, hiking, fishing, history, reading. Home: 1110 15th Ave W Spencer IA 51301-2943 Office: Iowa Dept Natural Resources 1900 N Grand Ave Spencer IA 51301-2200

LEMKE, HERMAN ERNEST FREDERICK, JR., retired elementary school educator, consultant; b. Argo, Ill., July 13, 1919; s. Herman and Augusta Victoria (Statt) L.; m. Geneva Octavene Davidson, Sept, 5, 1942 (dec.); children: Patricia, Herman E.F. III, Gloria, John, Elizabeth. BA, George Peabody Coll., 1949, MA, 1952. Cert. social sci. tchr., Tenn., elem. tchr., Calif. Tchr. Cadd Parish Sch., Shreveport, La., 1950-55, Pacific Sch. Dist., Sacramento, 1956-58, Sacramento (Calif.) Sch. Dist., 1958-89; part-time tchr. Sacramento (Calif.) County Sch., 1974-84, ret., 2002. Substitute tchr., 1989—. Co-author: Natural History Guide, 1963, (field guide) Outdoor World of Sacramento Region, 1975; contbr. articles to profl. jours. Asst. dist. Commn. Boys Scouts Am., Shreveport, 1954, cubmaster, 1954; leader 4-H Club, Shreveport, 1950-54; elder Faith Luth. Ch., Fair Oaks, Calif., 1981-88. Recipient Scouter award, Boy Scouts Am., Shreveport, 1954, Honorary Svc. award Am. Winn Sch. PTA, 1982, Calif. Life Diploma Elem. Schs., 1961. Mem. Calif. Congress Parents Tchrs. Inc. (life). Democrat. Avocations: backpacking, coin collecting/numismatics, stamp collecting/philately, antiques, fishing. Home: 7720 Magnolia Ave Fair Oaks CA 95628-7316 E-mail: herman.lemke@worldnet.att.net.

LEMKE, JAMES UNDERWOOD, physicist; b. Grand Rapids, Mich., Dec. 26, 1929; s. Andrew Bertram and Frances (Underwood) L.; m. Ann Stickley, Aug. 1, 1953; children: Catherine, Susan, Michael. BS in Physics, Ill. Inst. Tech., 1959; MS in Physics, Northwestern U., 1960; PhD in Physics, U. Calif., Santa Barbara, 1966. From assoc. to tech. v.p. Armour Rsch. Found., Chgo., 1957-60; dir. Bell & Howell Rsch. Labs., Pasadena, Calif., 1960-68; pres. Spin Physics, Inc. subs. Eastman Kodak, San Diego, 1968-82; fellow rsch. labs. Eastman Kodak, Rochester, N.Y., 1982-86; pres. Rec. Physics, Inc., San Diego, 1986—; founder, dir. Visqus Corp., 1989. Adj. prof. U. Calif. at San Diego, LaJolla, 1982—. Contbr. numerous sci. and tech. articles to phys. jours.; patentee in field. Bd. dirs. San Diego Aero-Space Mus., 1982—. Recipient Revelle medal U. Calif. San Diego. Mem. NAE, AAAS, Am. Phys. Soc., Magnetic Soc. (IEEE (Reynold Johnson medal 1995). Democrat. Avocation: airplane pilot. E-mail: james@lemke.com.

LEMKE, JUDITH A., lawyer; b. New Rochelle, N.Y., Sept. 28, 1952; d. Thomas Francis and Sara Jane (Blish) Fanelli; m. W. Frederick Lemke, Apr. 1, 1980; 1 child, Morgan Frederick. Student, Manhattanville Coll., Purchase, N.Y., 1970-72; BA, Case Western Res. U., Cleve., 1974, MA, 1975, JD, 1978. Sr. cert. pub. acct. Price Waterhouse, Cleve., 1978-81; assoc. Benesch Friedlander Coplan & Aronoff, Cleve., 1981-85; adjunct faculty Cleve. Marshall Coll. Law, 1982-86; ptnr. Benesch Friedlander Coplan & Aronoff, Cleve., 1986-94; prin. Kahn Kleinman Yanowitz & Arnson Co., Cleve., 1994-95; tax mgr. N.Am./L.Am. tax planning and compliance Chiquita Brands Internat., Cin., 1995-97, tax mgr. Europe, Colombia, Panama, 1998—, asst. v.p. taxation, 1998-99; v.p. tax Pepsi Bottling Group, Somers, N.Y., 1999—. Adj. faculty Case Western Res. U. Sch. of Law, 1993-95. Recipient Elijah Watt Sells award for highest distinction AICPA, N.Y.C. 1979. Mem. ABA, Ohio State Bar Assn., Internat. Fiscal Assn., Case Western Res. U. Undergrad. Alumni Assn. (exec. com. 1987-95, trustee 1987-95, chmn. spl. events com. 1989-90, pres. 1990-92, v.p. 1993-94). Avocations: wilderness canoe camping, guitar. Home: 39 Brundige Dr Goldens Bridge NY 10526-1413 Office: Pepsi Bottling Group 1 Pepsi Way Somers NY 10589-2204 Office Phone: 914-767-6772.

LEMKIN, JEFFREY W., lawyer; b. June 1945; m. Donna K. Lemkin. AB, Bowdoin Coll., 1966; JD cum laude, Boston U., 1972. Ptnr., mem. firm exec. mgmt. com., chmn. firm fin. com. McDermott Will & Emery LLP. Lectr. Am. Hosp. Assn., Am. Health Lawyers Assn., Calif. Soc. Healthcare Attys., Healthcare Fin. Mgmt. Assn. Mem.: Calif. Soc. Healthcare Attys. (former pres.), Am. Health Lawyers Assn. Office: McDermott Will & Emery LLP 2049 Century Pk E Los Angeles CA 90067-3208 Home: 3655 Sweetwater Mesa Rd Malibu CA 90265-4924 Office Fax: 310-277-4730, 310-551-9309. Business E-Mail: jlemkin@mwe.com.

LEMLE, ROBERT SPENCER, lawyer; b. N.Y.C., Mar. 6, 1953; s. Leo Karl and Gertrude (Bander) L.; m. Roni Sue Kohen, Sept. 5, 1976; children: Zachary, Joanna. AB, Oberlin Coll., 1975; JD, NYU, 1978. Bar: N.Y. 1979. Assoc. Cravath, Swaine & Moore, N.Y.C., 1978—82; assoc. gen. counsel Cablevision Sys. Corp., Bethpage, NY, 1982—84, v.p., gen. counsel, 1984—86, sr. v.p., gen. counsel, sec., 1986—94, bd. dirs., 1988—2003, exec. v.p., gen. counsel, sec., 1994—2001, vice chmn., gen. counsel, sec., 2001—02, vice chmn., sec., 2002—03; vice chmn. Madison Sq. Garden, N.Y.C., 1999—2002. Bd. editors Cable TV and New Media Law and Fin., N.Y.C., 1983-99. Trustee L.I. Children's Mus., 1990—, pres., 1996—; trustee Oberlin Coll., 1996—, vice-chair, 2001-05, chair, 2005—. Mem. ABA, N.Y. State Bar Assn. Avocation: real estate. Office: Ste 400 50 Charles Lindbergh Blvd Uniondale NY 11553 Office Phone: 516-390-4775. E-mail: rlemle@optonline.net.

LEMLEY, MARK ALAN, law educator; b. St. Louis, Nov. 20, 1966; s. Alan Norman Lemley and Linda Leigh (Allen) Huheey; m. Rose Anne Hagan, Mar. 11, 1995. AB in Economics & Polit. Sci., Stanford U., 1988; JD, U. Calif., Berkeley, 1991. Bar: Calif. 1991, US Ct. Appeals 9th Cir. 1991, US Ct. Appeals 7th Cir. 1996, US Ct. Appeals Fed. Cir. 1997, US Ct. Appeals 2nd Cir. Law clk. to Judge Dorothy W. Nelson US Ct. of Appeals 9th Cir., Pasadena, Calif., 1991-92; atty. Brown & Bain, Palo Alto, Calif., 1992-93, Fish & Richardson P.C., Menlo Park, Calif., 1993—94, of counsel Austin, Tex., 1995—2001, Keker & Van Nest, San Francisco, 2001—; asst. prof. U. Tex. Sch. Law, Austin, 1994-98, prof., 1998—99, Marrs McLean prof. law, 1999—2000; prof. law Boalt Hall Sch. Law, U. Calif., Berkeley, 2000—04, co-dir. Berkeley Ctr. for Law & Tech., 2000—04, Elizabeth Josslyn Boalt Chair in Law, 2003—04; William H. Neukom prof. law Stanford Law Sch., 2004—, dir. Program in Law, Sci. & Tech., 2004—. Vis. prof. Boalt Hall Sch. Law, U. Calif., Berkeley, 1998, Stanford Law Sch., 2003; bd. editors Am. Intellectual Property Law Assn. Quarterly Jour., 1994-2000; mem. No. Dist. Calif. Working Com. on Model Patent Jury Instruction, 2000-, Calif. Blue Ribbon Task Force on Nanotechnology, 2004-. Co-author: Antitrust, 1996, 2004, Intellectual Property in the New Technological Age, 1997, 2000, 03, Software and Internet Law, 2000,03, IP and Antitrust, 2001. Adv. bd. Electronic Frontier Found., 2004-. Named Young Alumnus of Yr., Boalt Hall Sch. Law, 2002. Mem. Am. Intellectual Property Law Assn., Am. Law and Economics Assn., U. Coop. Soc. (bd. dirs. 1995-99), Assn. of Am. Law Schools (chair law and computers sect. 1997). Avocations: cooking, hiking, skiing. Office: Stanford Law Sch Crown Quadrangle 559 Nathan Abbott Way Stanford CA 94305 Office Phone: 650-723-4605. Office Fax: 650-725-0253. E-mail: mlemley@law.stanford.edu.

LEMLICH, ROBERT, chemical engineer, educator; b. Bklyn., Aug. 22, 1926; s. Marcus S. and Mary L.; m. Elizabeth Ann Murphy, Jan. 31, 1976. B Chem. Engring. summa cum laude, NYU, 1948; M Chem. Engring., Poly. Inst. Bklyn., 1951; PhD, U. Cin., 1954. Registered profl. engr., N.Y., Ohio. Rsch. chem. engr. Allied Chem. & Dye Corp., 1948-49; mem. faculty U. Cin., 1952—, prof. chem. engring., 1962-85, prof. emeritus, 1985—; fellow U. Cin. Grad. Sch., 1971—, chmn. fellows, 1976-78. Fulbright lectr., Israel, 1958-59, Argentina, 1966, USSR, 1991, rschr., cons. in field. Rsch. Corp. grantee, 1954-55, NSF grantee, 1956-59, 73, 77-81, 85-88, NIH grantee, 1959-69, P & G grantee, 1976-77. Editor: Adsorptive Bubble Separation Techniques, 1972; editor, originator: Jour. Chem. Engring. Edn, 1962-65. Served in USN, 1944-46. Recipient Sigma Xi award disting. rsch. U. Cin., 1969 Fellow AAAS, AIChE (named Chem. Engr. of Yr. Ohio Valley sect. 1979); mem. Am. Chem. Soc., Am. Soc. Engring. Edn., Sigma Xi, Tau Beta Pi, Phi Lambda Upsilon. Home: 346 Bonnie Leslie Ave Bellevue KY 41073-1718

LEMLY, THOMAS ADGER, lawyer; b. Dayton, Ohio, Jan. 31, 1943; s. Thomas Moore and Elizabeth (Adger) L.; m. Kathleen Brame, Nov. 24, 1984; children: Elizabeth Hayden, Joanna Marsden, Isabelle Stafford, Kate Brame. BA, Duke U., 1970; JD with honors, U. N.C., 1973. Bar: Wash. 1973, U.S. Dist. Ct. (we. dist.) Wash. 1973, U.S. Ct. Appeals (9th cir.) 1975, U.S. Supreme Ct. 1980. Assoc. Davis Wright Tremaine, Seattle, 1973-79, ptnr., 1979—. Contbg. editor Employment Discrimination Law, 1984-87, 94—; editor Wash., Oreg., Alaska and Calif. Employment Law Deskbooks, 1987—. Chmn. Pacific Coast Labor Conf., Seattle, 1983; trustee Plymouth Congregational Ch., 1980-84, Seattle Opera Assn., 1991—. Fellow Am. Coll. Trial Lawyers; mem. ABA (labor employment law sect. 1975—, subcom. chmn. 1984-90, govt. liaison com. 1982-94), Seattle-King County Bar Assn. (chmn. labor sect.), Assn. Wash. Bus. (sec.-treas. 2002-03, trustee 1992—, vice chair 2003-2004, bd. chair 2004-2005, chmn. human resources coun. 1993-2002, chmn. employment law task force 1987-93), U. N.C. Bar Found. (bd. dirs. 1973-76), Seattle Duke Alumni Assn. (pres. 1979-84), Order of Coif, Wash. Athletic Club (Seattle), Rotary. Republican. Presbyterian. Home: 1614 7th Ave W Seattle WA 98119-2919 Office: Davis Wright Tremaine 2600 Century Sq 1501 4th Ave Seattle WA 98101-1688 Office Phone: 206-628-7716. E-mail: tomlemly@dwt.com.

LEMMER, ROBERT E., geologist, consultant; b. Little Rock, Nov. 3, 1954; s. Carmelita F. and Robert Lopez; m. April A. Brewer, May 20, 1994; 1 child, Caleb M. Brewer. BS in Geology, Memphis State U., 1987, MS in Geology, 1990. Registered Profl. Geologist Calif., 2001, cert. Engring Geologist Calif., 2002, Hydrogeologist Calif., 2003, registered Profl. Geologist Ark., 1995. Geologist supr. Ark. Dept. Environ. Quality, Little Rock, 1994—98; geology instr. U. of Ark., 1997—2001; project cons. ECI, Tustin, Calif., 2001—. Pres. South Coast Geol. Soc., Irvine, Calif., 2005—; presenter in field. Contbr. articles to profl. jours. Nat. Earthquake Hazard Reduction Program rsch. grant, US Geol. Soc., 2000. Mem.: South Coast Geol. Soc. (pres. 2004—05), Assn. of Engring. Geologists, Am. Geophys. Union, Seismol. Soc. of Am., Geol. Soc. of Am. Avocations: travel, sports, bicycling. Personal E-mail: geolemmer@hotmail.com.

LEMMER, WILLIAM C., lawyer; BA, Mich. State U., 1966; JD, U. Va., 1971. Assoc. Bigham, Englar, Jones & Houston, NY, 1971—76; staff atty. Overseas Pvt. Investment Co., 1976—79; various sr. mgmt. positions Sunoco, Inc., 1979—88; chief counsel Oryx Energy Co., 1988—94, v.p., gen. counsel, corp. sec., 1994—99; v.p., gen. counsel, sec. Cooper Cameron Corp., Houston, 1999—. Office: Cooper Cameron Corp 1333 W Loop South Ste 1700 Houston TX 77027-9109 Office Phone: 713-513-3336. Office Fax: 713-513-3355.

LEMMO, PETER S., writer, educational consultant; b. N.Y.C., June 6, 1949; s. Angelo "Charles" and Lillian K. Lemmo; m. Janice M. Braff, Oct. 25, 1975; 1 child, David. BA, CCNY, N.Y.C., 1970, MA, 1972. Cert. tchr. social studies 7-12 N.Y., N.J., tchr. English N.Y. Tchr. Jr. High Schs., Bronx, NY, 1970—73; tchr. and mentor Harry S. Truman H.S., 1973—76; tchr. and coord. Evander Childs H.S., 1977—2004; writer and cons., 2004—. Co-author: Human Heritage: A World History 5 edits., 1989—; editor: A Place Called Whippany, 1998—; contbr. A Handbook for the Teaching of Social Studies. County committeeman Dem. Party, Parsippany, 1985—98; trustee Citizens for Controlled Devel., Inc., Morristown, 1990—98; Dem. candidate Borough Coun., Mountain Lakes, 2000, 2005; bd. dir. Morris County Art Assn., Inc., Morristown, NJ, 2004—. Mem.: ASCD, Nat. Coun. Social Studies, Natural Resources Def. Coun., Morris Land Conservancy, Nature Conservancy, Sierra Club. Avocations: photography, travel, hiking. Home: 5 Pickwick Ln Mountain Lakes NJ 07046 Office: PSL Assoc PO Box 557 Whippany NJ 07981-0557

LEMNIOS, ANDREW ZACHERY, aerospace engineer, educator, researcher; b. Newburyport, Mass., Nov. 23, 1931; s. Zaharias Vasilios and Evangelia (Malamoglou) L.; m. Aspasia Soula Hanos, Sept. 26, 1954; children: Karen Eve, Keith Harold. SB, MIT, 1953, SM, 1954; PhD, U. Conn., 1967; grad. advanced mgmt. program, Harvard U., 1983; grad mgmt. program, Rensselaer Poly. Inst., 1970. Rsch. engr. United Techs. Rsch., East Hartford, Conn., 1954-60; sr. analytical engr. Kaman Aerospace Corp., Bloomfield, Conn., 1961-63, chief fluid mechanics, 1963-68, chief rsch. engr., 1969-76, dir. rsch. and tech., 1976-89, asst. v.p. rsch. and tech. programs, 1989-93; mem. rotorcraft adv. com. Rensselaer Poly. Inst., Troy, N.Y., 1985-92, clin. prof., dir. Rotorcraft Tech. Ctr., 1993—99; v.p., dean Rensselaer at Hartford, Conn., 1999—2002, adj. prof., 2002—03. Adj. prof. Western New Eng. Coll., Springfield, Mass., 1956-76, U. Mass., Amherst, 1976-78, U. Hartford, Conn., 1997-99; mem. aeronautics adv. com. NASA, Washington, 1979-84; mem. rotorcraft adv. com. U. Md., College Park, 1985-92, Ga. Inst. Tech., Atlanta, 1985-92. Patentee controllable twist rotor, rotor trim tab. Fellow AIAA (assoc.), Am. Helicopter Soc. (hon.). Republican. Greek Orthodox. Avocations: carpentry, gardening, music, reading. Home: 144 Primrose Dr Longmeadow MA 01106-2534 E-mail: andrewlemnios@comcast.net.

LEMOINE, FRANK EUGENE, lawyer, judge; b. Montgomery, La., Oct. 17, 1953; s. Frank Lucian LeMoine and Frances Pauline (Jones) LeMoine Birchfield; m. Geraldine Guidry, Oct. 1, 1971; children: Frank Lucian II, Stephanie Antoinette, Monique Angele. BS summa cum laude, U. Southwestern La., 1983; JD cum laude, So. U., 1986. Bar: La. 1986, U.S. Dist. Ct. (we. dist.) La. 1987, U.S. Ct. Appeals (5th cir.) 1990. Oilfield constrn. worker, La., 1972-77; pvt. practice Abbeville, La., 1986—; mcpl. judge, 2003—. Mem. ABA, La. State Bar Assn., Vermilion Parish Bar Assn., Am. Inns of Ct., Phi Eta Sigma, Phi Kappa Phi, Kappa Delta Pi, Phi Alpha Delta. Democrat. Roman Catholic. Avocations: woodworking, hunting, fishing, knife collecting. Office: 511 N Cushing Ave PO Box 121 Kaplan LA 70548 also: 116 S State St PO Box 1199 Abbeville LA 70511-1199 Office Phone: 337-893-4382, 337-643-6611. Business E-Mail: frank@lemoinelaw.com, kaplancitycourt@kaplantel.net.

LEMOLE, GERALD MICHAEL, surgeon; b. S.I., NY, Dec. 17, 1936; s. Joseph Michael and Mary (Boylan) L.; m. Emily Jane Asplundh, Dec. 8, 1962; children: Lisa Jane, Laura Leigh, Emily Anne, Gerald Michael Samantha Mary, Christopher Robin. BS in Biology, Villanova U., 1958; MD, Temple U., 1962. Diplomate Am. Bd. Surgery, Am. Bd. Thoracic Surgery. Intern S.I. Hosp., 1962-63; resident Temple U., Phila., 1963-67, Baylor Affiliated Hosps., Houston, 1967-69; practice medicine specializing in throacic surgery Phila., 1969—, Browns Mills, N.J., 1972-84. Chief sect. cardiac and thoracic surgery Temple U. Hosp., Phila., 1970-77; prof. surgery Temple U. Health Scis. Ctr., 1975-77; chmn. dept. surgery Deborah Heart and Lung Ctr., Phila., 1972-84; chief sect. cardiovascular surgery Med. Ctr. Del.; vis. prof. cardiac surgery U. Dublin, Ireland, 1974, u. Istanbul, Turkey, 1982, Mil. Med. Coll., Ankara, Turkey, 1985, Beijing Heart Inst., 1991; clin. prof. surgery U. Pa., 1979, Rutgers Med. Sch., Thomas Jefferson U., 1999—; rschr. in field. Contbr. numerous articles on cradiovascular surgery and disease to med. jours. Recipient Disting Alumnus award Villanova U., 1987. Fellow ACS, Coll. Cardiology, Am. Coll. Chest Physicians (cardiovascular com. 1974—); mem. AMA, Am. Assn. Thoracic Surgery, Am. Fedn. Clin. Rsch., Pan Am. Thoracic Soc., Am. Heart Assn. (cardiovascular coun. 1973—, pres. Del. chpt. 1991, chmn. bd. dirs. 1992), Pa. Med. Soc., Pa. Assn. Thoracic Surgery (program chaor 1975—), Pa. Assn. Thoracic Surgeons, Phila. County Med. Soc., Phila. Acad. Surgery, Phila. Acad. Cardioloby (pres. 1976-79, chmn. exec. com. 1976—), Phila. Coll. Physicians, Internat. Cardiovascular Soc., Assn. Acad. Surgeons, Soc. Casvular Surgery, Denton A. Cooley Cardiovascular Surg. Soc. Home: 404 Tomlinson Rd Huntingdon Valley PA 19006-4818 Office: Med Ctr Del 4745 Ogletown Stanton Rd # 20 Newark DE 19713-2067 Personal E-mail: gmlmd17@aol.com.

LEMON, LESLIE GENE, retired diversified financial services company executive, lawyer; b. Davenport, Iowa, June 14, 1940; BS, U. Ill., 1962, LLB, 1964. Bar: Ill. 1964, Ariz. 1972. Asst. gen. counsel Am. Farm Bur. Fedn., Chgo., 1964-69; sr. atty. Armour and Co., Chgo., 1969-71; with Viad Corp (formerly The Dial Corp and Greyhound Corp.), Phoenix, 1971-99; gen. counsel The Dial Corp (formerly Greyhound Corp.), Phoenix, 1977-96, v.p., 1979-99; ret., 1999; chmn. State of Ariz. Citizens Clean Elections Commn., 1999—2003. Vestryman All Saints Episcopal Ch., Phoenix, 1975-81; trustee Phoenix Art Mus., 1985-98; bd. dirs. Phoenix Children's Hosp., 1985-98; bd. visitors U. Calif. Med. Sch., Davis, 1983—. Mem. ABA, Nat. Conf. Uniform Law Commrs., Assn. Gen. Counsel, Maricopa County Bar Assn., State Bar Ariz., Phoenix C. of C. (bd. dirs. 1989-95), Am. Arbitration Assn. (bd. dirs. 1996-2004). Home: 1136 W Butler Dr Phoenix AZ 85021-4428 E-mail: l.lemon@azbar.org.

LEMON, LESLIE ROY, radar meteorologist; b. Greenville, S.C., Jan. 19, 1947; s. Carlson Howard and Diora Elizabeth (Hyre) L.; m Betty Louise Vest, June 15, 1968; children: Kirsten M., Allison M., Jonathan M. BS, postgrad., Okla. U., 1970. Phys. sci. aide Nat. Severe Storms Lab., Norman, Okla., 1968-70, rsch. meteorologist, 1975-76; mem. NOAA Commn. Corps, 1970—75; meteorologist, forecaster Nat. Severe Storms Forecast Ctr., Kansas City, Mo., 1976, rsch. meteorologist techniques devel. unit, 1976-81; mgr. Nexrad ops. compatibility assurance Sperry Corp., Great Neck, NY, 1981-89; NEXRAD rsch. meteorologist, program control mgr. Unisys Corp., Great Neck, NY, 1989-95; chief meteorologist, mgr. advanced weather sys., rsch. ops. Loral Def. Sys. East, 1995-96; chief meteorologist, mgr. advaned weather sys. Lockheed Martin Tactical Def. Sys., 1996-97; chief meteorologist, weather and ATC programs Lockheed Martin Ocean, Radar & Sensor Sys., Syracuse, N.Y., 1997-99; radar and severe storms meteorologist, cons., 1999—2001; rsch. meteorologist Basic Commerce and Industry, Inc., Moorestown, NJ, 2001—. Cons. USAF, Scott AFB, Ill., Tech. Svc. Corp., Corp., Silver Spring, Md., 1984, 91, TV Sta. tng. weather radar use and interpretation, 1990—, domestic and internat. weather radar interpretation, 1996—. Designer/creator nat. severe thunderstorm radar warning technique The Lemon Technique; co-discoverer Doppler Weather Radar Tornadic Vortex Signature; contbr. chpt. to textbook, articles to profl. jours. Mem. sch. bd. Blue Ridge Christian Sch., Kansas City, 1984; mem. ch. bd. Blue Ridge Bible Ch., Kansas City, 1977-81. Lt. (s.g.) NOAA, 1970-75; bd. trustees Calvary Bible Coll., 2004—. Fellow U. Okla., 1997—, Am. Meteorol. Soc. Fellow Am. Meteorol. Soc. (Outstanding Contbn. to the Advance of Applied Meteorology award 1997), Nat. Weather Assn. (pres. local chpt. 1989, councillor 1998, v.p. 1999, pres. 2001), Sigma Tau. Republican. Achievements include discovered and documented the first recorded tornado in Romanian history in 2003. Avocations: cosmology, walking, public speaking, reading. Home: 16416 S Cogan Dr Independence MO 64055-2257 Office Phone: 816-373-3533. Personal E-mail: lrlemon@comcast.net.

LEMON, WILLIAM JACOB, lawyer; b. Covington, Va., Oct. 25, 1932; s. James Gordon and Elizabeth (Wilson) L.; m. Barbara Inez Boyle, Aug. 17, 1957; children: Sarah E. Lemon Ludwig, William Tucker, Stephen Weldon. BA, Washington & Lee U., 1957, JD, 1959. Bar: Va. 1959. Assoc. Martin, Martin & Hopkins, Roanoke, Va., 1959-61; ptnr. Martin, Hopkins & Lemon, Roanoke, 1962—. Trustee Washington and Lee U., Lexington, Va., 1988-97, North Cross Sch., Roanoke, 1995—; pres. Specific Reading and Learning Difficulties Assn. Shedd Early Learning Ctr., 1985-86, George C. Marshall Found., Lexington, Va., 1997-2004. With U.S. Army, 1952-54. Mem. Va. Bar Assn., Roanoke Bar Assn. (pres. 1982-83), Va. State Bar, Shenandoah Club. Presbyterian. Avocations: farming, hunting, travel. Office: Martin Hopkins Lemon Wachovia Tower 10 S Jefferson St Ste 1000 Roanoke VA 24011-1314 also: PO Box 13366 Roanoke VA 24033-3366

LEMONE, MARGARET ANNE, atmospheric scientist; b. Columbia, Mo., Feb. 21, 1946; d. David Vandenberg and Margaret Ann (Meyer) LeMone; m. Peter Augustus Gilman; children: Patrick Cyrus, Sarah Margaret. BA in Math., U. Mo., 1967; PhD in Atmospheric Scis., U. Wash., 1972. Postdoctoral fellow Nat. Ctr. for Atmospheric Rsch., Boulder, Colo., 1972-73, scientist, 1973-92, sr. scientist, 1992—; chief scientist Globe, 2003—. Mem. bd. on atmospheric sci. and climate NRC, 1993-97, 2001-04; mem. sci. adv. com. U.S. Weather Rsch. Program, 1997-99. Contbr. articles to profl. jours.; contbg. author: D.C. Heath Earth Science, 1983-93; editor Jour. Atmospheric Scis., 1991-95. Woodrow Wilson fellow, NSF fellow, NDEA fellow, 1967. Fellow AAAS, Am. Meteorol. Soc. (councillor, mem. exec. com. 1992-96, Editor's award, Charles Anderson award); mem. Am. Geophys. Union, Nat. Acad. Engring. Achievements include research in dynamics of linear convection (roll vortices) in daytime atmospheric boundary layer and its relationship to clouds; demonstrating that bands of deep convection (like squall lines) can increase the vertical shear of horizontal wind (contrary to conventional wisdom at that time); developing technique to estimate small fluctuations in air pressure from aircraft flying over land, used to estimate pressure field around clouds and storms. Home: 2048 Balsam Dr Boulder CO 80304-3618 Office: Nat Ctr Atmospheric Rsch PO Box 3000 Boulder CO 80307-3000 Business E-Mail: lemone@ucar.edu.

LEMONS, DONALD W., state supreme court justice; b. Feb. 22, 1949; BA, U. Va., JD, 1976. Bar: Va. 1976. Former asst. dean U. Va. Law Sch.; judge Richmond Circuit Ct., 1995—2000; justice va. Supreme Ct., 2000—. Mem. Commn. on Family Violence Prevention. Mem.: ABA, Va. Bar Assn., Am. Inns of Ct. (trustee). Office: Supreme Ct Bldg 100 N Ninth St, 5th Floor Richmond VA 23219 also: PO Box 1315 Richmond VA 23218-1315

LE MONS, KATHLEEN ANN, securities company executive, branch manager, investment officer, portfolio manager; b. Trenton, NJ, Apr. 6, 1952; d. Albert Martin and Veronica Grace (Kerr) LeM.; m. Walter Everett Faircloth, Apr. 15, 1978 (div. Dec. 1988); m. Jeffery West Benedict, June 29, 1991. Student, Rollins Coll., 1970-71, Fla. State U., 1971-76; BSBA magna cum laude, Christopher Newport U., 1995; MBA in Fin., Coll. William and Mary, 1998; postgrad., U. Pa., 2005—. Registered rep. NASD/NYSE; registered investment advisor; cert. portfolio mgr.; accredited asset mgmt. specialist. Sci. rsch. assoc. NASA, Hampton, Va., 1973-76; fin. cons. Merrill Lynch Pierce Fenner Smith, Hampton, 1985-88; investment officer, portfolio mgr. Wheat First Butcher Singer (now Wachovia Securities), Newport News, Va., 1988—; sr. v.p. Wachovia Securities (formerly First Union Securities), investment officer, br. mgr. Life mem. Capital Dist. Found., 1992; mem. exec. panel fund distbn. Va. Peninsula United Way, 1996-97; Hampton Rds. chair March of Dimes Walk Am., 1996-98; bd. dirs. Greater Hampton Rds. March of Dimes Found., 1997—. George F. Hixson fellow Kiwanis Internat., 1996. Mem. Am. Mktg. Assn., Va. Peninsula C. of C. (transp. task force 1993-97, govtl. affairs task force 1993-99), Rotary, Oyster Point Kiwanis (charter, pres. 1991-92, 98-99), Coll. of William and Mary Part-Time MBA Assn. (charter, curriculum com. chair 1995-97, v.p. 1996-97, bd. dir.), Christopher Newport U. Pres.' Coun., Christopher Newport Univ. Alumni Soc. (bd. dirs., v.p. bd. dirs. 1998—), Mensa, James River Country Club (9-hole golf group), Smithfield Women's Club, Smithfield Rotary Club, Kiwanis Internat. (life), Alpha Chi. Republican. Avocations: golf, snowskiing. Home: 20454 Gatling Pointe Pkwy S Smithfield VA 23430-5756 also: 20454 Gatling Pointe Pkwy S Smithfield VA 23430-5756 Office: Wheat First Butcher Singer 11817 Canon Blvd Newport News VA 23606-2569

LEMONS, L. JAY, academic administrator; b. Chadron, Nebr., Aug. 30, 1959; s. Larry Dean and LaVana Lee (Smith) L.; m. Marsha Louise Schone Lemons, May 27, 1984; children: Olivia Jaye, Magdalene Marie, Thomas Potter, Meredith. BS in phys. edn. and health edn., BA in philosophy, Nebr. Wesleyan U., 1983; MEd in ednl. psychology and coll. student devel., U. Nebr., 1985; PhD in higher edn. adminstrn., U. Va., 1991. Cert. phys. edn. tchr., health edn. tchr. Hall dir. office residence life Nebr. Wesleyan U., Lincoln, 1982-84; grad. asst. to dir. admissions office admissions and advising U. Nebr., Lincoln, 1984-85; asst. area coord. dept. student affairs Tex. A&M U., College Station, 1985-86, area coord. dept. student affairs, 1986-88; grad. asst. to dean Curry Sch. Edn. U. Va., Charlottesville, 1988-89, intern Curry Sch. Edn. Found., 1989, intern office of pres., 1989-90, asst. to pres.,

1990—92; chancellor U. Va. Coll. at Wise, 1992—2001; pres. Susquehanna U., 2001—. Contbr. articles to profl. jours. Recipient Outstanding Young Men of Am. award, 1986, Gov.'s fellowship, 1988-90, Annette Gibbs Rsch. and Publ. award, 1990. Mem. Am. Assn. Counseling and Devel., Am. Coll. Personnel Assn. (presenter nat. conf. 1986), Nat. Assn. Student Personnel Adminstrs. (participant new profl.'s inst. region III 1987, local arrangements com. mem. fall conf. 1988, registration chair Tex. state conf. 1988, program coord. state conf. 1989, 90, presenter region IV west conf. 1986, nat. conf. 1988, region III chief student affairs officers workshop 1988, ann. conf. 1991, Outstanding New Profl. award region III 1987), Assn. Study Higher Edn., So. Assn. Coll. Student Affairs (registration chair devel. theories workshop 1988, presenter ann. conf. 1987), Blue Key Nat. Honor Soc., Kappa Delta Pi (Outstanding Edn. Student award 1983). Office: Susquehanna U 514 Univ Ave Selinsgrove PA 17870-1025

LEMOS, ARTHUR, retired music educator; b. Mt. Vernon, NY, Feb. 1, 1932; s. Antonio Tavares de Lemos and Silvina de Almeida Santos. BS, NYU, 1953; MA, Montclair State U., N.J., 1956. Cert. Music Tchr. N.J. Edn. Dept., 1953, N.Y. State Edn. Dept., 1956, Elem. Sch. Prin. N.Y. State Edn. Dept., 1956. Music tchr. Paterson Pub. Schs., NJ, 1953—56, New Hyde Pk. Pub. Schs., NY, 1956—67, Brentwood Pub. Schs., NY, 1967—68, Scarsdale Pub. Schs., NY, 1968—69, Lakeland Pub. Schs., Shrub Oak, NY, 1969—92; sub. pianist, organist 1st Presbyn. Ch., 1983—. Tuba player Mt. Vernon Symphony, NY, 1949—50, Mt. Vernon Mcpl. Band, Mt. Vernon, NY, 1950—65, Herricks Cmty. Band, NY, 1956—67, Lynbrook Symphony, NY, 1957—58; conductor New Hyde Park Adult Edn. Band, 1965—66; tuba player Mamaroneck Cmty. Band, NY, 2001—, Westchester Seasonal Pops Band, Larchmont, NY, 2001—02, Pleasantville Fire Dept. Band, 2001, Merry Tuba Christmas Band, Rockefeller Ctr., N.Y.C., 2001, Bronxville Pops Concert Band, NY, 2002—; pres. New Hyde Pk. Rd. Sch. Tchrs. Assn., NY, 1960—63; nominating com. mem. Sole Supervisory Dist. Tchrs. Assn., Floral Park, NY, 1961—66; del. N.Y. State Tchrs. Assn., Albany, NY, 1961—66, resolutions com. mem., NY, 1962—65, activities com. mem., Albany, NY, 1966—66, activities com. chmn., NY, 1966—66; del. N.Y. State Tchrs. Retirement Sys., Albany, NY, 1962—66; salary com. mem. New Hyde Pk. Tchrs. Assn., New Hyde Park, NY, 1964—66, treas., 1964—67, Sole Supervisory Dist. Tchrs. Assn., Floral Park, NY, 1965—66, v.p., 1966—67. Author: A Speck of Dust, 2001; musician (musical composition): (paso doble for concert band) El Hillside, 1960, El Pancho, 1961, El Torero, 2003, El Vencedor, 2004, (march for concert band) The Mount Vernon Band March, 1960, (composition) The Hartley Park March, 1960, (vocal or piano solo) O Destino, 1974, A Tristeza, 2003, Solitude, 2003, Saudades de Portugal, 2004, (vocal solo) A Bright White Star, 1960, The United States of America, 2001; corr. Portuguese Heritage Jour., 1991—93, Mundo Portugues, 1994—95. Mem. citizens adv. com. City of Mt. Vernon, NY, 1985—88, mem. city centennial com., 1992; deacon First Presbyn. Ch., Mt. Vernon, NY, 1975—77, Mount Vernon, NY, 1980—82, 1988—89, elder Mt. Vernon, NY, 1983—85, 1990—92, 1997—2001, worship and music com. chmn., 1984—85, mem. centennial com., 1987—87, mem. centennial plus ten, com., 1997—97, missions com. mem., 1993—94, nominating com. mem., 1997—98. Decorated Medal of the Order of Merit Govt. of Portugal; recipient Honored vol. svc., 1994. Mem.: Berkeley Coll. (Arthur Lemos Scholarship award 1994), NEA (life; del. 1965—66, 1967), Am. Found. for Charities of Portugal (assoc.; mem. bd. dirs. 1984—88), Westchester County Stamp Club (assoc.; sec. 1984—85), Portuguese Civic Assn. of N.Y. (life; sec. 1978—95, Elected Hon. mem. 1984), Portuguese Civic Assn. of N.Y. (life; sec. 1978—95, Elected Man of Yr. 1986), Portuguese Am. Club (life; sec. 1976—94, hon. 1983, Elected Meritorious mem. 1992). Conservative. Presbyterian. Avocations: travel, photography, computer, movies, current events. Home: 130 Elm Ave Mount Vernon NY 10550-2362 Personal E-mail: arthur13@netzero.net.

LEMOS, MARGARET H., lawyer; BA, Brown Univ.; JD, N.Y.U., 2001. Law clk. U.S. Solicitor Gen., Washington, 2001, 2003, U.S. Ct. Appeals (1st cir.), Portland, Maine, 2002—03; law clerk to Hon. John Paul Stevens U.S. Supreme Ct., Washington, 2003—04; vis. faculty N.Y.U. Law Sch., New York, 2004—. Editor (sr. notes): N.Y.U. Law Rev. Bristow fellow, 2002, Furman fellow, 2004. Office: NYU Law School 40 Washington Sq So New York NY 10012

LEMOV, MICHAEL R., lawyer; b. NYC, Jan. 21, 1935; BA in Polit. Sci., magna cum laude, Colgate U., 1956; LLB, Harvard U., 1959. Bar: NY 1960, DC 1971, Md. 1995. Gen. counsel Nat. Commn. on Product Safety; spl. counsel consumer protection subcom. US Ho. of Reps., 1972—75, chief counsel interstate and fgn. commerce subcom. on oversight and investigation, 1975—77; ptnr. Leighton Lemov Jacobs & Buckley, Washington; named exec. dir. Food Rsch. and Action Ctr., Washington, 1984; ptnr. Winston & Strawn, Washington; dep. gen. counsel Office Compliance US Congress; of counsel Sonnenschein Nath & Rosenthal LLP, Washington, 2004—. Author: Consumer Product Safety Commn. Regulatory Manual, 1981. Bd. dirs. John E. Moss Found. Office: Sonnenschein Nath & Rosenthal LLP Ste 600, E Tower 1301 K St NW Washington DC 20005 Office Phone: 202-408-6445. Office Fax: 202-408-6399. Business E-Mail: mlemov@sonnenschein.com.

LEMPERT, PHILIP, advertising executive, writer, news correspondent; b. East Orange, NJ, Apr. 17, 1953; s. Sol and Lillian E. L.; m. Laura Gray; 1 son. BS in Mktg., Drexel U., 1974; degree in Package Design, Pratt Inst., 1978. With Lempert Co., Belleville, N.J., 1974-89; pres. Consumer Insight, Inc., 1990—; sr. v.p., sr. ptnr. AGE Wave Inc., 1991-93; pres., CEO Supermarketguru.com. Founder, CEO Supermarket Alliance, 1993—; adj. prof. Fairleigh Dickinson U., Seton Hall U. Pub., editor newsletter The Lempert Report; editor Factus, Figures and the Future e-Newsletter; lectr. in field. Author: Phil Lempert's Supermarket Shopping and Value Guide, 1996, Top Ten Trends for Baby Boomers for Business, 1997, Being the Shopper: Understanding Consumer Choices for the Second Millenium, 2002; columnist Chgo. Tribune, 1993-98, Knight-Ridder/Tribune Syndicate, LA Times, 2000-02, Progressive Grocer mag., 2003—; editor (newsletter) Facts, Figures and the Future; food editor, corr. Today Show, KNBC-TV, BBC Radio 5; talk show host WOR Radio Network; news corr. Discovery Health Network. Chmn. Tribune Food Task Force, 1996-98; bd. dirs. Powerhouse Theatre, 2001—, Partnership for Food Safety, 2002; adv. bd. Partnership for Food Safety. Mem. Am. Assn. Advt. Agys. (bd. govs. 1986-88, legis. liason 1988-90, legis. coord. 1987-90), Nat. Food Brokers Assn. (chmn. food svcs. com.). Office: Consumer Insight Inc 3015 Main St Ste 320 Santa Monica CA 90405-6401 E-mail: Plempert@lempertreport.com.

LEMPERT, RICHARD OWEN, lawyer, educator; b. Hartford, Conn., June 2, 1942; s. Philip Leonard and Mary (Steinberg) L.; m. Cynthia Ruth Willey, Sept. 10, 1967 (div.); 1 child, Leah Rose; m. Lisa Ann Kahn, May 26, 2002. AB, Oberlin Coll., 1964; JD, U. Mich., 1968, PhD in Sociology, 1971. Bar: Mich. 1978. Asst. prof. law U. Mich., Ann Arbor, 1968-72, assoc. prof., 1972-74, prof. law, 1974—, prof. sociology, 1985—, Francis A. Allen collegiate prof. law, 1990—2001, acting chair dept. sociology, 1993-94, chair dept. sociology, 1995-98, dir. life scis., values and society program, 2000—04, Eric Stein Disting. Univ. prof. law and sociology, 2001—; dir. divsn. social and econ. scis. NSF, 2002—. Mason Ladd disting. vis. prof. U. Iowa Law Sch., 1981; vis. fellow Centre for Socio-Legal Rsch., Wolfson Coll., Oxford (Eng.) U., 1982; mem. adv. panel for law and social sci. div. NSF, 1976-79, mem. exec. com. adv. com. for social sci., 1979; mem. com. law enforcement and adminstrn. of justice NRC, vice chmn., 1984-87, chmn., 1987-89; mem. adv. panel NSF program on Human Dimensions of Global Change, 1989, 92-94; mem. com. on DNA technology in forensic sci. NRC, 1989-92, com. on drug testing in workplace, 1991-93; vis. scholar Russell Sage Found., 1998-99; vis. scholar Russell Sage Found., 1998-99. Author: (with Stepehn Saltzburg) A Modern Approach to Evidence, 1977, 2d edit., 1983, 3d edit. (with Sam Gross and James Liebman), 2000; (with Joseph Sanders) An Invitation to Law and Social Science, 1986, Under the Influence, 1993; editor: (with Jacques Normand and Charles O'Brien) Under the Influence? Drugs and the American Work Force, 1994; editorial bd. Law and Soc. Rev., 1972-77, 89-92, 98—, editor, 1982-85; mem. editl. bd. Evaluation Rev., 1979-82, Violence and Victims, 1985—, Jour. Law and Human Behavior, 1980-82; contbr. articles to profl. jours. Fellow Ctr. for Advanced Study in Behavioral Scis., 1994-95; vis. scholar Russell Sage Found., 1998-99. Fellow Am. Acad. Arts and Scis.; mem. Am. Sociol. Assn. (chair sect. sociology of law 1995-96), Law and Society Assn. (trustee 1977-80, 90-93, exec. com. 1979-80, 82-87), Order of Coif, Phi Beta Kappa, Phi Kappa Phi. Office: U Mich Law Sch 412 Hutchins Hall 625 S State St Ann Arbor MI 48109-1215 Personal E-mail: rol25@hotmail.com. E-mail: rlempert@umich.edu.

LEMY, MARIE EDITH, psychologist, educator; d. Josette Jean-Louis and Andre Louis. MPH, Hunter Coll., NY; PhD, Seton-Hall U., NJ. Lic. Psychologist N.Y. Psychologist So. Westchester BOCES, Rye, NY; asst. prof. CUNY, NY. Cons. Nassau BOCES, Seacliff, NY. Translator legal documents. Mem.: APA (assoc.). Independent. Roman Catholic. Avocations: travel, reading. Mailing: 59 New Drop Ln Hopewell Junction NY 12533 Personal E-mail: m-lemy@msn.com.

LENARD, GEORGE DEAN, lawyer; b. Joliet, Ill., Aug. 26, 1957; s. Louis George and Jennie (Helopoulos) L.; m. Nancy Ilene Sundquist, Nov. 11, 1989. BS, Ill. State U., 1979; JD, Thomas Cooley Law Sch., 1984. Bar: Ill. 1984, U.S. Dist. Ct. (no. dist.) Ill. 1984, U.S. Ct. Appeals (6th cir.) 1998, U.S. Supreme Ct. 1990, Mich. 1998, Ariz. 1999, Calif. 2001, Fla. 2003. Asst. states atty. Will County States Attys. Office, Joliet, 1984-88; pvt. practice law Joliet, 1988—. Mem. ABA (mem. Ill. capital litigation trial bar, lead counsel), ATLA, Nat. Assn. Criminal Def. Lawyers, State Bar Ariz., State Bar Mich., State Bar Calif., State Bar Fla., Phi Alpha Delta (Isaac P. Christiancy chpt.). Avocation: golf. Office: 81 N Chicago St Ste 206 Joliet IL 60432-4383

LENART, CRISTIAN PAUL, mathematician, educator; b. Cluj-Napoca, Romania, May 29, 1965; arrived in U.S., 1996; s. Arpad and Ileana Romana Lenart; m. Camelia Ileana Voiculescu, Aug. 10, 2000; children: Cristina Celia Inceu, Alison Flavia Inceu, Andrew Christian. PhD in Computer Sci., Babes-Bolyai U., 1992; cert. of Advanced Study in Math., Cambridge U., Eng., 1993; PhD in Math., U. Manchester, Eng., 1996. Instr. applied math. MIT, Cambridge, 1996—98; vis. scientist Max Planck Inst. Math., Bonn, Germany, 1998—99; assoc. prof. SUNY, Albany, 1999—. Contbr. articles to profl. jours. Recipient First prize Romanian Nat. Math. Competition, Ministry of Edn., 1979, 1980, 1983, Magdalene Coll. prize in Math., Cambridge, Eng., 1993; grantee Nat. Sci. Found., 2004—; scholar, Cambridge Overseas Trust and Soros Found., 1992—93, Rsch., U. of Manchester, Eng., 1993—96. Mem.: Am. Math. Soc. Orthodox. Achievements include research at the interface of algebraic combinatorics, representation theory, algebraic geometry, and algebraic topology; research in clustering algorithms. Avocations: literature, classical music, travel, skiing. Office Phone: 518-442-4635. E-mail: lenart@albany.edu.

LENCZ, TODD, psychologist, researcher; BA magna cum laude, Yale U., 1989; PhD in Clin. Psychology, U. So. Calif., 1995. Lic. psychologist N.Y., 1997. Intern in psychology Bellevue Hosp., NYC, 1994—95; postdoc. fellow clin. neurosci. Hillside Hosp., Glen Oaks, NY, 1995—97, asst. psychologist, 1997—98, rsch. psychologist, 1998—; assoc. dir. Recognition and Prevention Program, Lake Success, NY, 1998—; asst. prof. psychiatry Albert Einstein Coll. Medicine, Bronx, NY, 1999—. Recipient Young Investigator's award, Internat. Congress of Schizophrenia Rsch., 1993, Meml. Travel Award, Am. Coll. of Neuropsychopharmacology, 2003; grantee Mentored Rsch. Scientist Devel. award, NIMH, 2003—, Young Investigator's award, Nat. Alliance Rsch. in Schizophrenia and Depression, 2001-2003. Mem.: APA, Internat. Prodromal Rsch. Network, Internat. Early Psychosis Assn., Orgn. Human Brain Mapping, Soc. Rsch.Psychopathology. Office: RAP Program 444 Lakeville Rd Ste 303 Lake Success NY 11042 Office Phone: 516-470-6951. E-mail: lencz@lij.edu.

LENDSEY, JACQUELYN L., foundation administrator; BS, Adelphi U.; MEd, Howard U. With pub. sch. sys., Prince George County, Md.; v.p. corp. and cmty. devel. Greater S.E. Healthcare; v.p. pub. policy Planned Parenthood Fedn. Am., N.Y.C., 1998—2001; pres., CEO Women in Cmty. Svc., Alexandria, Va., 2001—. Bd. dirs. Nat. Assembly Health and Human Svcs. Orgns., Reproductive Health Tech. Project. Mem.: Leadership Washington. Office: 1900 Beauregard St Ste 103 Alexandria VA 22311

LENEAVE, CORTNEY SCOTT, lawyer; b. Lavonia, Mich., May 25, 1961; s. C. Wayne and A. Anita (Johnson) L.; m. Kristen E. Hill, Aug. 15, 1987; children: Sarah, Sam, Kathryn. BA in Pol. Sci., U. Minn., 1983; JD, William Mitchell Law Sch., 1987. Bar: Minn. 1987, U.S. Dist. Ct. Minn. 1988. Law clk. Hennepin County Dist. Ct., Mpls., 1987-88; assoc. Meagher & Geer, Mpls., 1988-95; ptnr. Hunegs, Stone, LeNeave, Kvas & Thornton, Mpls., 1995—. Arbitrator Am. Arbitration Assn., Mpls., 1994—; designated legal counsel United Transp. Union. Hockey/soccer coach Wayzata Youth Hockey/Plymouth Soccer Assn., 1994—. Mem. ABA, ATLA, Minn. Bar Assn., Minn. Trial Lawyers Assn. Avocations: golf, hockey. Office: Hunegs Stone LeNeave Kvas & Thornton PA 1650 Internat Ctr 900 2d Ave S Minneapolis MN 55402 E-mail: CLeNeave@hunegslaw.com.

LENEHAN, JAMES T., pharmaceutical executive; married; 3 children. BA in econs., U. Akron, 1971; MBA in mktg., Northwestern U. With golf divsn. Wilson Sporting Goods; mktg. positions, McNeil Consumer Products Co. Johnson & Johnson, 1976—90; pres., 1990—94; group chmn. Johnson & Johnson, 1993—94, worldwide chmn. consumer pharms. and professional group, 1994—99, mem. exec. com., 1994—2004, worldwide chmn. med. devices and diagnostic group, 1999—2004, vice chmn., 2001—04, pres., 2002—04. Office: Johnson and Johnson 1 Johnson and Johnson Plza New Brunswick NJ 08933

LENEY, GEORGE WILLARD, retired consulting engineer; b. Nov. 13, 1927; s. Bert and Iva Irene (Skoog) L.; m. Arax G. Tefankjian, June 25, 1955 (dec. Aug. 1983); children: Sara Ann, Janet Ellen, John Alan, Ruth Alison. BS, U. Mich., 1950, MS, 1952, MA, 1955. Tchg. fellow U. Mich., 1951—53, 1953—55; geophysicist Gulf Oil Co., Harmarville, Pa., 1955—56; chief geophysicist Hanna Mining Co., Cleve., 1956—64; staff geophysicist Shell Oil Co., Houston, 1964—66; chief geologist H.K. Porter Co., Inc., Pitts., 1966—76; cons., 1976—77, 1981—86; regional geologist U.S. Dept. Energy, 1977—81; adminstr. air pollution Allegheny County Health Dept., Pa., 1986—97; ret., 1997. Organizer minerals exploration programs for asbestos, iron ore, base metals, gold, oil and gas, and uranium in the US, Can., Brazil and Cameroon; v.p. Pacific Asbestos Corp., 1970—75. With USN, 1946—48. Recipient Robert Peele Meml. award AIME, 1965 for pioneering work in geophysical exploration of iron ore. Mem. Soc. Econ. Geologists, Am. Inst. Mining Engrs., Soc. Exploration Geophysicists, Geologic Soc. Am., Pa. Acad. Sci., Air and Waste Mgmt. Assn. Achievements include rsch. in mineral exploration and mining geophysics, emissions inventory and ozone planning; discovery of Pilot Knob iron ore body in Missouri; on canoe reconnaissance in Labrador and the Northwest Territories in Can. Address: 5335 Tomfran Dr Pittsburgh PA 15236-2477

LENFANT, CLAUDE JEAN-MARIE, physician; b. Paris, Oct. 12, 1928; arrived in U.S., 1960, naturalized, 1965; s. Robert and Jeanine (Leclerc) Lenfant; children: Philipe, Bernard, Martine Lenfant Wayman, Brigitte Lenfant Martin, Christine. BS, U. Rennes, France, 1948; MD, U. Paris, 1956; DSc (hon.), SUNY, 1988. Asst. prof. physiology U. Lille, France, 1959—60; from clin. instr. to prof. medicine physiology and biophysics U. Wash. Med. Sch., 1961—72; assoc. dir. lung programs Nat. Heart, Lung and Blood Inst. NIH, Bethesda, Md., 1970—72, dir. divsn. lung diseases, 1972—80; dir. Fogarty Internat. Ctr. NIH, 1980—82, assoc. dir. internat. rsch., 1980—82; dir. Nat. Heart, Lung and Blood Inst., 1982—2003, disting. scientist emeritus, 2003—; pres. World Hypertension League, 2003. Mem. editl. bd.: Undersea Biomed. Rsch., 1973—75, Respiration Physiology, 1971—78, Am. Jour. Physiology and Jour. Applied Physiology, 1970—76, Am. Rev. Respiratory Disease, 1973—79, Jour. Applied Physiology, 1976—82, Am. Jour. Medicine, 1979—82; editor: Lung Biology in Health and Disease. Recipient Nathan Davis award, AMA, 1998, Gold Heart award, Am. Heart Assn., 2002. Fellow: Royal Soc. Medicine, Royal Coll. Physicians; mem.: French Nat. Acad. Medicine, USSR Acad. Med. Scis., Inst. Medicine of NAS, Undersea Med. Soc., N.Y. Acad. Scis., Am. Physiol. Soc., French Physiol. Soc., Am. Soc. Clin. Investigation, Assn. Am. Physicians, Alpha Omega Alpha. Home: PO Box 83027 Gaithersburg MD 20883-3027 E-mail: lenfantc@prodigy.net.

LENFEST, HAROLD FITZ GERALD, former cable television executive, lawyer; b. Jacksonville, Fla., May 29, 1930; s. Harold Churchill and Herrena (FitzGerald) L.; m. Marguerite Brooks, July 9, 1955; children: Diane, H. Chase, Brook. AB, Washington and Lee U., 1953; LLB, Columbia U., 1958; DHL (hon.), Ursinus Coll., 2002, Temple U., 2003, Washington and Lee U., 2004. Bar: N.Y. 1959. Assoc. Davis Polk & Wardwell, N.Y.C., 1958-65; assoc. counsel Triangle Publs., Phila., 1965-70, mng. dir. comm. divsn. N.Y.C., 1970-74; editorial dir., pub. Seventeen mag., N.Y.C., 1970-74; pres. Suburban Cable TV Co.; pres., CEO Lenfest Comm., Inc., 1974-2000. Bd. dirs. TCI West, Inc., Seattle, Liberty Media Corp., Cable Advt. Bur., Vidéopole, France, Australis Media Ltd., Australia, Voice FX, Inc.; chmn. Video JukeBox, Inc.; CEO Cable AdNet, Inc., 1981—92, StarNet, Inc., 1989—, TelVue, Inc., 1990—, CAM Sys., 1995—. Trustee Walter Kaitz Found., Oakland, Calif., 1986—88; trustee, nat. campaign chmn. Washington and Lee U., 1990—98, hon. chair campaign, 2000—04; mem. bd. regents Mercersburg Acad., 1989—97, pres., 1994—97; trustee Columbia U., 2000—; mem. James Madison Coun. Libr. of Congress, 1989—; trustee, exec. com. Chesapeake Bay Found., 1995—; bd. trustees Phila. Mus. Art, 1993—; bd. dir. Smithsonian, 2003—04; bd. dirs., v.p. Columbia U. Sch. Law, N.Y.C., 1960—65, 1974—78, mem. bd. visitors, 1992—; chair Phila. Mus. Art, 2001—; bd. dirs. C-SPAN, 1995—2000. Capt. USNR, 1953—76, active duty USNR, 1953—56, active duty USNR, 1962. Named Man of Yr., Phila. Area Easter Seal Soc., 1992, Citizen of Yr., PenJerDel Coun., 2004, Individual Philanthropist of Yr., Assn. Fundraising Profls., Pjila. Chpt., 2004; recipient Disting. Achievement award, Columbia U. Sch. Law, 1997, Individual Leadership award, Phila. Arts and Bus. Coun., 2002, Patron of Yr. award, Gov. of Pa., 2002, Russell H. Conwell award, Temple U., 2003, Vision for Phila. award, Phila. Hospitality, Inc., 2003, Americanism award, Antidefamation League, 2004, Woodrow Wilson award for pub. svc., Internat. Ctr. Scholars of Smithsonian Instn., 2005, Internat. Outstanding Philanthrophist award, Assn. Fundraising Profls., 2005, Robert P. Casey medal for commitment to ind. higher edn., Assn. Ind. Colls. and Univs. Pa., 2005; fellow, Phila. Coll. Physicans, 2005. Mem. Pa. Cable TV Assn. (bd. dirs., officer 1976-79), Mayflower Soc., Am. Philos. Soc., Soc. Colonial Wars, Order of the Coif. Office: The Lenfest Group 300 Barr Harbor Dr Ste 460 West Conshohocken PA 19428 Business E-Mail: gerry@lenfestgroup.com.

LENG, QIBIN, immunologist, virologist; b. Songtao, China, July 10, 1970; m. Lin Jiao, Oct. 8, 1998. BSc in Biology, Beijing Normal U., 1994; MSc in Pharmacology and Virology, Peking Union Med. Coll., Beijing, 1997; student, Hebrew U., Jerusalem, 1997—2002. Rsch. asst. Chinese Acad. Sci., 1994; immunologist, virologist Weizmann Inst. Sci., 2003, Ctr. for Cancer Rsch., MIT, Cambridge, Mass., 2003—. Contbr. articles to profl. jours. Achievements include research in immunopathogenesis of chronic infectious diseases and development of the concept of immure fuzzy recognition model and of heterologous vaccination. Home: 58 Holmes St Apt 21 Quincy MA 02171-2452 E-mail: qibin_leng@yahoo.com.

LENG, YONGSHENG, research scientist; b. Tianjin City, China, Feb. 12, 1962; arrived in U.S., 1999; s. Yinpu Leng and Guizhen Shi; m. Guiping Yang, Aug. 15, 1989; 1 child, Ziwie. B Engring. (hon.), North China U. Tech., Beijing, 1984; MSc, Tsinghua U., Beijing, 1987, PhD, 1999. Tchg. assoc. North China U. Tech., Beijing, 1987—89, lectr., 1990—95, assoc. prof., 1995—99; rsch. assoc. Kans. State U., Manhattan, 1999, U. Wash., Seattle, 1999—2001; sr. rsch. assoc. U. Tenn., Knoxville, 2001—02, Vanderbilt U., Nashville, 2002—. Contbr. articles to profl. jours. Recipient Young Investigator award, NSF of China, 1997—98. Mem.: ASME, AIChE (mem. internat. tribology conf. 1998). Achievements include development of hybrid molecular simulations in atomic force microscopy; research in contact mechanics, adhesion mechanics, nanoindentation, self-assembled monolayers molecular simulation, molecular electronics simulation, nanotribology of liquid ultrathin films.

LENGAUER, MARY IRENE, elementary school educator; b. Mercer, Pa., Nov. 24, 1942; d. Sylvester Everton McKean and Forresteene Jane Fletcher; m. Gary Neil Lengauer, June 5, 1965; 1 child, Carrie Jane Lengauer Gault. BS in Elem. Edn., Clarion U., Pa., 1964. 2nd grade tchr. Brockway Sch. Dist., Pa., 1964—65; 4th grade tchr. Lakeview Sch. Dist., Oakview Elem., Stoneboro, Pa., 1965—2005, mem. curriculum coun., basketball cheerleading advisor, 1985—91. Coun. mem. Sandy Lake Boro. Republican. Presbyterian. Avocations: golf, travel. Home: Box 184 15 Cathie Dr Sandy Lake PA 16145

LENGEMANN, FREDERICK WILLIAM, retired physiology educator; b. N.Y.C., Apr. 8, 1925; s. Peter and Dorathea Johanna (Wolter) L.; m. J. Joan Doremus, Dec. 23, 1950; children: Frederick William Jr., David Munson. Student, N.Y. State Sch. Agr., Farmingdale, 1942—43; BS with distinction, Cornell U., 1950, M in Nutrition Sci., 1951; PhD, U. Wis., 1954. Rsch. assoc. U. Tenn.-AEC Agrl. Rsch. Program, Oak Ridge, 1954-55; asst. prof. dept. chemistry U. Tenn. Med. Sch., Memphis, 1955-59; prof. dept. physiology N.Y. State Coll. Vet. Medicine, Cornell U., 1959-88, prof. physiology emeritus, 1988—; biochemist divsn. biology and medicine AEC, 1962-63. Cons. FAO-IAEA, Vienna, Austria, 1966-67, 76-77, Fed. Radiation Coun., 1964-65, NRC, 1970-73, Nat. Com. on Radiation Protection, 1970-73, 79, 82; IAEA expert U. Nacional Agraria, Peru, 1978; lectr., dir. tng. courses. Contbr. articles to profl. jours. Mem. planning bd. Town of Dryden, N.Y., 1963-68; treas. Rome (Pa.) Presbyn. Ch. Served with USNR, 1943-46. Decorated Air medal with 2 stars. Fellow AAAS; mem. Coun. Agrl. Sci. and Tech., Am. Dairy Sci. Assn., Am. Nutrition Soc., Fed. Am. Socs. for Exptl. Biology, Nat., N.Y. State Christmas Tree Growers Assns., Sigma Xi, Phi Kappa Phi. Home: RR3 Box 3000J Rome PA 18837 Office: Cornell U NY State Coll Vet Medicine Dept Physiology Ithaca NY 14853

LENGER, JOHN RICHARD, journalism educator; b. Washington, Mo., Jan. 26, 1964; s. Juan Rafael Joseph and Bev (stepmother) Lenger and Joan and Craig (stepfather) Hart; m. Maria Cristina Caballero, Aug. 5, 2000; 1 child, Juan Rafael Lenger BJ, BA in Polit. Sci., U. Mo., 1986; MEd, Harvard U., 2002. Editor The LaBelle (Mo.) Star, 1986, Suburban Newspapers Greater St. Louis, 1986-90; Sunday editor The Post-Star, Glens Falls, NY, 1990-92; copy editor Gazette Newspapers, Schenectady, NY, 1992-93; freelance editor, writer Foxboro, Mass., 1993-94; asst. editor Harvard U. Gazette, Cambridge, Mass., 1994-95, editor-in-chief, 1995-98; publs. dir. Harvard U. Office News & Pub. Affairs, Cambridge, 1998—; instr. journalism Harvard U., Cambridge, 1997—. Bd. dirs. New England Press Assn. Co-author: (chpt.) The Writer's Handbook, 2001, Living Ethics: Developing Values in Mass Communication, 1996; editor: The Harvard Guide, 2000, 2002; contbr. articles to profl. jours. Mentor Graham & Parks Alternative Pub. Sch., Cambridge, 1995—2002; bd. dirs. New England Press Assn., 2005—. Recipient James E. Conway Excellence in Tchg. Writing award, Harvard U., 2005. Mem. Soc. Profl. Journalists, New Eng. Press Assn. (vol. coord. 1999—, bd. dirs. 2005). Office: Harvard U News & Pub Affairs 1060 Holyoke Ctr Cambridge MA 02138 E-mail: john_lenger@harvard.edu.

L'ENGLE, MADELEINE (MRS. HUGH FRANKLIN), writer; b. N.Y.C., Nov. 29, 1918; d. Charles Wadsworth and Madeleine (Barnett) Camp; m. Hugh Franklin, Jan. 26, 1946 (dec., 1986); children: Josephine Franklin Jones, Maria Franklin Rooney, Bion. AB, Smith Coll., 1941; postgrad., New Sch., 1941-42, Columbia U., 1960-61; holder 19 hon. degrees. Tchr. St. Hilda's and St. Hugh's Sch., 1960—; mem. faculty U. Ind., 1965-66, 71; writer-in-residence Ohio State U., 1970, U. Rochester, 1972, Wheaton Coll., 1976—, Cathedral St. John the Divine, N.Y.C., 1965—. Author: The Small Rain, 1945, Ilsa, 1946, Camilla Dickinson, 1951, A Winter's Love, 1957, And Both Were Young, 1949, Meet the Austins, 1960, A Wrinkle in Time, 1962, The Moon by Night, 1963, The 24 Days Before Christmas, 1964, The Arm of the Starfish, 1965, The Love Letters, 1966, The Journey with Jonah, 1968, The Young Unicorns, 1968, Dance in the Desert, 1969, Lines Scribbled on an Envelope, 1969, The Other Side of the Sun, 1971, A Circle of Quiet, 1972, A Wind in the Door, 1973, The Summer of the Great-Grandmother, 1974, Dragons in the Waters, 1976, The Irrational Season, 1977, A Swiftly Tilting Planet, 1978, The Weather of the Heart, 1978, Ladder of Angels, 1980, A Ring of Endless Light, 1980, Walking on Water, 1980, A Severed Wasp, 1982, And It Was Good, 1983, A House Like a Lotus, 1984, Trailing Clouds of Glory, 1985, A Stone for a Pillow, 1986, Many Waters, 1986, Two-Part Invention, 1988, A Cry Like a Bell, 1987, Sole Into Egypt, 1989, From This Day Forward, 1988, An Acceptable Time, 1989, The Glorious Impossible, 1990, Certain Women, 1992, The Rock That Is Higher: Story As Truth, 1993, Anytime Prayers, 1994, Troubling a Star, 1994, Penguins and Golden Calves, 1996, A Live Coal in the Sea, 1996, Glimpses of Grace, 1996, Wintersong, 1996, Mothers and Daughters, 1997, Friends for the Journey, 1997, Bright Evening Star: Mystery of the Incarnation, 1997, The Other Dog, 2001, Madeleine L'Engle Herself: Reflections on a Writing Life (with Carole Chase), 2001 Pres. Crosswicks Found. Recipient Newbery medal, 1963, Sequoyah award, 1965, runner-up Hans Christian Andersen Internat. award, 1964, Lewis Carroll Shelf award, 1965, Austrian State Lit. award, 1969, Bishop's Cross, 1970, U. South Miss. medal, 1978, Regina medal, 1985, Alan award Nat. Coun. Tchrs. English, 1986, Kerlan award, 1990, Margaret Edwards award, 1998; collection of papers at Wheaton Coll. Mem. Authors Guild (mem. council), Authors League (mem. council), Writers Guild Am. Episcopalian. Office: Cathedral Libr St John the Divine 1047 Amsterdam Ave New York NY 10025-1747 also: care Random House Children's Media 1540 Broadway New York NY 10036-4039 *Over the years I've worked out a philosophy of failure which I find extraordinarily liberating. If I'm not free to fail, I'm not free to take risks, and everything in life that's worth doing involves a willingness to take a risk and involves the risk of failure. Each time I start a new book I am risking failure. Although I have had over 60 books published, there are at least 6 full unpublished books which have failed, but which have been necessary for the book which then gets published. The same thing is true in all human relationships. Unless I'm willing to open myself up to risk and to being hurt, then I'm closing myself off to love and friendship.**

LENGYEL, ALFONZ, art educator, archeology educator, museology educator; b. Godollo, Hungary, Oct. 21, 1921; arrived in U.S., 1957; s. Aurel and Margit (Furedy) L.; m. Hongying Liu. Terminal degree in law and polit. sci., Miskolc Law Acad., Budapest, 1944; MA, San Jose State Coll., 1959; PhD, U. Paris, 1964; LLD (hon.), London Inst. Applied Rsch., 1973. Asst. prof. San Jose State Coll., Calif., 1961-63; faculty U. Md. European Div., Paris and Heidelberg, Germany, 1963-68; intern museology Ecole du Louvre, Paris, 1965-66; prof. Wayne State U., Detroit, 1968-72, No. Ky. U., Highland Heights, 1972-77; dean, prof. Inst. Mediterranean Art and Archaeology, Cin., 1977-82; coord. art history Rosemont Coll., Pa., 1982-86; rsch. prof. art history, dir. Goebel's Print Collection, 1986-88; pres. Fudan Mus. Found., China, 1988—. Adj. curator Detroit Inst. Arts, 1968-72; cons. Paris Am. Acad., 1963—; dir. UPAO, Washington, 1983—; adv. prof. Fudan U., Shanghai, People's Republic of China; cons. prof. Xian Jiaotong U., Xian, People's Republic of China, founder Sino-Am. Summer Field Sch. Archaeology; mem. governing bd. Mus. Asian Art, Sarasota, Fla. Author: Pub. Rels. for Mus., 1992, Archaeology for Museologists, 1993, Chinese Chronological History, 1993, Field Work in Archaeology, 2001, Chinese Chronological History, 2001; co-author: The Archaeology of Roman Pannonia, 1983; contbr. numerous articles to profl. jours. Bd. dirs. Hungarian-Am. Fedn., Cleve., 1983-91, exec. v.p., Ft. Lauderdale, Fla., 1951—; mem. Rep. Presdl. Task Force, Washington, 1982—; mem. adv. bd. U.S. Dept. Interior Nat. Pk. Svc., 1987-91; bd. dirs. Mus. Asian Art, Sarasota, Fla., 2001—. Rockefeller Found. grantee U. Vienna, 1957; Govt. of France grantee U. Paris, 1962-63; S.H. Kress Found. lectureship Denison U. (Ohio), 1967-68; Smithsonian Instn. grantee, 1968; NEH grantee, 1971, 76. Fellow Internat. Acad. Sci. and Lettres, Arpad Acad. (pres. 1982—), Szechenyi Acad., Am. Assn. Swiss, German, Austrian Profs.; mem. Internat. Coun. Mus., Renaissance Soc. Am., Coll. Art Assn. Am., Archaeol. Inst. Am., Nat. Fedn. Hungarian-Ams., Soc. Architectural Historians, N.Y. Acad. Scis., Hungarian Acad. Scis., Mich. Acad. Scis. and Letters, Register of Profl. Archaeologists, Christopher Giest Hist. Soc., Detroit Classical Assn., Mich. Acad. Arts and Scis., Am. Assn. Mus. Republican. Roman Catholic. Home: 4206 73d Terrace E Sarasota FL 34243 Office: Sino-Am Field Sch Archaeology Fudan Mus Found Sarasota FL 34243 Personal E-mail: fmfsafsa@juno.com.

LENGYEL, ISTVAN, chemist, educator; b. Kaposvar, Hungary, July 12, 1931; came to the U.S., 1958; s. István and Margit (Palásthy) L. Diploma in chemistry, Eötvös Lóránd U., Budapest, 1955; PhD in Organic Chemistry, MIT, 1964. Rsch. chemist G. Richter Pharm. Works, Inc., Budapest, 1953-55; chemist State Geophys. Inst., Budapest, 1955-56; rsch. chemist Biochemie GmbH, Kundl, Austria, 1957-58; rsch. asst. Johns Hopkins Med. Sch., Balt., 1958-59; predoctoral fellow MIT, Cambridge, 1959-63, postdoctoral fellow, 1964; NIH postdoctoral fellow Techn. U., Munich, 1964-65; rsch. assoc. MIT, Cambridge, 1965-67; prof. chemistry St. John's U., Jamaica, N.Y., 1967-98, chmn. dept. chemistry, 1985-91, prof. emeritus, 1999—. Vis. scholar U.S. Nat. Acad. Sci. and Hungarian Acad. Sci., 1973. Sr. Award Recipient, Alexander von Humboldt Found., 1973-74. Avocations: swimming, travel. Home: 84-01 169th St Jamaica NY 11439-0001 Office: Saint Johns U 8000 Utopia Pkwy Jamaica NY 11432-1335 Office Phone: 718-990-6291. Office Fax: 718-990-1876.

LENHART, CYNTHIA RAE, conservation organization executive; b. Cheverly, Md., Nov. 3, 1957; d. Donald Edward and Vesta Jean Lenhart. BS in Environ. Studies, Coll. William & Mary, 1979; MS in Environ. Sci., SUNY, Syracuse, 1983. Asst. to pres. Environ. Policy Inst., Washington, 1979-81; wildlife policy analyst Nat. Audubon Soc., Washington, 1984-90; exec. dir. Hawk Mountain Sanctuary, Kempton, Pa., 1990—2004; prin., owner Salamander, Saluda, NC, 2004—. Bd. dirs. Am. Bird Conservancy, Washington, Pa. Environ. Coun., Phila. Contbr. chpts. to Audubon Wildlife Report, 1985, 87, 88, 89. Chair Everglades Coalition, Washington, 1986-88.

LENHART, LORRAINE MARGARET, county official; b. Schuylkill County, Pa., Nov. 18, 1944; d. Thomas Edward and Margaret Elizabeth (Klinger) Kimmel; m. William Charles Reber II, May 10, 1964 (div. 1968); 1 child, William Charles II; m. Kenneth Edward Lenhart, June 30, 1972; children: Vickie Elaine Lenhart Marino, Sonya Lynn Lenhart Yost. Grad. H.S., Mifflinburg, Pa., 1962; Cert. sect. I, II, III, Pa. Land Title Inst., 1988; instrn. course cert., Pa. State Mcpl. Ofcl. Instrn., 1992; Newly Elected Officials Tng. I, II Cert., Commonwealth of Pa., 1994, Mcpl. Fin. Elected Officials, 1995; genealogy cert., Williamsport Area C.C.; estate planning course cert., Pa. State Co-op Ext. Various positions; deputy register and recorder Union County Pa., Lewisburg, 1978-95, register of wills, recorder of deeds, 1996—. Mem. Preservation Mifflinburg Inc.; former dir. Am. Cancer Soc., Susquehanna Valley, Lewisburg, Pa.; past coun. mem. Postal Customer Adv. Coun., Mifflinburg; past mem. Union County Hist. Soc., Lewisburg, Bald Eagle State Forest Roundtable, Mifflinburg, OUE, Allenwood, Pa.; vol. Union County Emergency Svcs., Lewisburg; past dir. Ctrl. Susquehanna unit Am. Cancer Soc., Union County Found., Lewisburg, 1997—2003; former councillor and v.p. Mifflinburg Borough Coun.; cert. Leadership Susquehanna Valley; past treas. Mifflinburg Hist. Soc.; past dir. Buffalo Creek Watershed Alliance; mem. Union County Con. of Rep. Women, Pa. Coun. Rep. Women; committeeperson Union County Rep. Com., East Ward, Mifflinburg; past bd. dirs. Mifflinburg Hist. Soc. Mem.: Register of Wills and Clk. of Orphan's Ct. Assn. Pa., Pa. Recorder of Deeds Assn., Internat. Assn. Clks., Recorders, Election Ofcls. and Treas., Mifflinburg Buggy Mus., Kiwanis Club of Buffalo Valley A.M. of Lewisburg (1st v.p. 2004—05, past sec.). Republican. Lutheran. Avocations: reading, needlecrafts, gardening. Office: Union County Court House 103 S 2d St Lewisburg PA 17837-1996 Office Phone: 570-524-8761. E-mail: llenhart@unionco.org.

LENHART, SUZANNE, mathematician, education educator; Prof. math. U. Tenn., Knoxville. Rschr. Oak Ridge Nat. Lab. Mem.: Assn. for Women in Math. (pres. 2001—03). Office: Univ Tenn Math Dept 317 C Ayres Hall Knoxville TN 37996

LENHOFF, HOWARD MAER, biological sciences educator, academic administrator; b. North Adams, Mass., Jan. 27, 1929; s. Charles and G. Sarah Lenhoff; m. Sylvia Grossman, June 20, 1954; children: Gloria, Bernard. BA, Coe Coll., 1950, D.Sc. (hon.), 1976; PhD, Johns Hopkins U., 1955. USPHS fellow Loomis Lab., Greenwich, Conn., 1954-56; vis. lectr. Howard U., Washington, 1957-58; rsch. assoc. George Washington U., Washington, 1957-58; postdoctoral fellow Carnegie Instn., Washington, 1958; investigator Howard Hughes Med. Inst., Miami, 1958-63; prof. biology, dir. Lab. for Quantitative Biology U. Miami, Coral Gables, 1963-69; prof. biol. scis. U. Calif., Irvine, 1969—96, prof. polit. sci., 1986, assoc. dean biol. scis., 1969-71, dean grad. div., 1971-73, faculty asst. to vice chancellor of student affairs, 1986-88, 90-96, chair faculty senate, 1988-90, prof. emeritus, rsch. prof., 1993—; adj. prof. psychology U. Mass., Amherst, 2001—03. Adj. prof. biology U. Miss., Oxford, 2001—; vis. scientist, Louis Lipsky fellow Weizmann Inst. Sci., Rehovot, Israel, 1968-69; vis. prof. chem. engring., Rothschild fellow Israel Inst. Tech., 1973-74; vis. prof. Hebrew U., Jerusalem, spring 1970, fall 1971, 77-78; Hubert Humphrey Inst. fellow Ben Gurion U., Beersheva, Israel, 1981; sr. rsch. fellow Jesus Coll., U. Oxford, 1988; dir. Nelson Rsch. & Devel. Co., Irvine, 1971-73; bd. dirs. BioProbe Internat., Inc., Tustin, Calif., 1983-89, chmn. bd., 1983-86. Editor/author: Biology of Hydra, 1961, Hydra, 1969, Experimental Coelenterate Biology, 1972, Coelenterate Biology— Review and Perspectives, 1974, Hydra: Research Methods, 1983, Enzyme Immunoassay, 1985, From Trembley's Polyps to New Directions in Research on Hydra, 1985, Hydra and the Birth of Experimental Biology, 1986, Biology of Nematocysts, Conception to Birth, 1988; mem. editorial bd. Jour. Solid Phase Biochemistry, 1976-80. Vice chmn. So. Calif. div. Am. Assn. Profs. for Peace in Middle East, 1972-80; bd. dirs. Am. Assn. for Ethiopian Jews, 1974-93, pres., 1978-82; bd. govs. Israel Bonds Orange County, Calif., 1974-80, Dade County Heart Assn., Miami, 1958-61, So. Calif. Technion Soc., 1976; pres. Hillel Coun. of Orange County, 1976-78; nat. chmn. faculty div. State of Israel Bonds, 1976; mem. sci. adv. bd. Am. Friends of Weizman Inst. Sci., 1980-84; bd. dirs. Hi Hopes Identity Discovery Found., Anaheim, Calif., 1982-87, pres. bd. govs., 1983-85, William Syndrome Found., trustee, 1992, 99—, pres., bd. dirs., 1993-95, exec. v.p., 1995-99; v.p. edn. Williams Syndrome Assn., 1994, bd. dirs., 1993-94, mem. adv. bd., 2001—; founder, mem. adv. bd., founder Berkshire Hills Music Acad., 2000—; founder, mem. adv. bd. Guardian Angel Initiative, 2004—. 1st lt. USAF, 1956-58. Recipient Career Development award USPHS, 1965-69; Disting. fellow Iowa Acad. Sci., 1986. Fellow AAAS; mem. Soc. Physics and Natural History of Swiss Acad. Scis. Geneva (hon.), Am. Chem. Soc., Am. Biophys. Soc., Am. Soc. Zoologists, History of Sci. Soc., Am. Soc. Cell Biologists, Am. Soc. Biol. Chemists, Biophysics Soc., Soc. Gen. Physiologists, Soc. Growth and Devel. Home: 304 Dogwood Dr Oxford MS 38655-9670 Office: U Calif Sch Biol Scis Irvine CA 92697-2300 Office Phone: 949-824-7259. Business E-Mail: hlenhoff@uci.edu.

LENINGTON, SARAH, statistician, researcher; d. Thales and Theo Lenington; m. Arthur Ruppin, Oct. 14, 1990. PhD, U. of Chgo., Ill., 1977. Assoc. prof. Inst. Animal Behavior Rutgers U., Newark, 1979—95; dir. clin. develop. Mirabel Med., Austin, Tex., 2000—. Lectr. in field. Contbr. over 45 articles to profl. jours. Grantee, several grants from NIH, NSF and the Harry Frank Guggenheim Found., 1980—93. Avocation: travel.

LENK, EDWARD C. (TOBY), Internet company executive; Grad. summa cum laude, Bowdoin Coll.; MBA, Harvard U. Stragegy cons. LäEäK Partnership; corp. v.p. strategic planning group Walt Disney Corp.; founder eToys, Inc., Santa Monica, Calif., 1996—, pres., CEO, uncle of the bd. Office: eToys Direct Inc Ste 1800 1099 18th St Denver CO 80202*

LENKE, JOANNE MARIE, publishing executive; b. Chgo., Aug. 27, 1938; d. August Julian and Dorothy Anna (Gold) L. BS, Purdue U., 1960; MS, Syracuse U., 1964, PhD, 1968. Tchr. pub. schs., Evanston, Ill., 1960-63; editor Test Dept. Harcourt, Brace & World, Inc., N.Y.C., 1967-70; rsch. psychologist Harcourt Brace Jovanovich, Inc., N.Y.C., 1970-73, exec. editor, 1973-75; asst. dir. ednl. measurment divsn. The Psychol. Corp., N.Y.C., 1975-83, dir. ednl. measurement and psychometrics Cleve., 1983-85, San Antonio, 1986, v.p. dir. measurement divsn., 1986-88, sr. v.p., 1988-91, exec. v.p., 1991-97, pres., 1997-99; cons., 1999—2002; assoc. v.p. Ednl. Testing Svc., 2002—. Field reader U.S. Office Edn., 1972. Adv. editor Jour. Ednl. Measurement, 1974-78. NSF grantee, 1963-64. Mem. APA, Nat. Coun. Measurement in Edn., Am. Ednl. Rsch. Assn. Home: 2534 Winding VW San Antonio TX 78258-7257 Personal E-mail: jlenke@usa.net.

LENKOSKI, LEO DOUGLAS, psychiatrist, educator; b. Northampton, Mass., May 13, 1925; s. Leo L. and Mary Agnes (Lee) L.; m. Jeannette Teare, July 12, 1952; children— Jan Ellen, Mark Teare, Lisa Marie, Joanne Lee. AB, Harvard, 1948, spl. student, 1948-49; MD, Western Res. U., 1953; grad., Cleve. Psychoanalytic Inst., 1964. Intern Univ. Hosps., Cleve., 1953-54, resident in psychiatry, 1956-57, dir. psychiatry, 1970-86, chief of staff, 1982-90; dir. profl. services Horizon Ctr. Hosp., 1980; asst. resident in psychiatry Yale U., New Haven, 1954-56; teaching fellow Case Western Res. U., Cleve., 1957-60, from instr. to prof. psychiatry, 1960-93; prof. emeritus, 1993—; assoc. dean Sch. Medicine Case Western Res. U., Cleve., 1982-93, dir. Substance Abuse Ctr., 1990-93. Cons. Cleve. Ctr. on Alcoholism, DePaul Maternity and Infant Home, St. Ann's Hosp., Def. Dept., Cleve. VA Hosp., Psychiat. Edn. br. NIMH; mem. Cuyahoga County Mental Health and Retardation Bd., 1967-73, 94-2002, 2004—, Health Planning and Devel. Commn., 1967-73, Ohio Mental Health and Retardation Commn., 1976-78; mental health advisor Jewish Family Svcs. Assocs., 2003—. Contbr. articles to profl. jours. Bd. dirs. Hough-Norwood Health Ctr., Hitchcock Ctr., Hopewell Inn, Woodruff Found, 2001—. 1st lt. USAAF, 1943-46. Decorated D.F.C., Air medal with oak leaf cluster.; Career Tchr. grantee NIMH, 1958-60 Fellow Am. Psychiat. Assn. (life), Am. Coll. Psychiatrists, Am. Coll. Psychoanalysts (pres. 1988-89); mem. AMA, AAAS, Ohio Psychiat. Assn. (pres. 1974—), Am. Psychoanalytic Assn., Assn. Am. Med. Colls., Cleve. Acad. Medicine (bd. dirs. 1987-90), Ohio Med. Assn., Pasteur Club, Am. Assn. Chairmen Depts. Psychiatry (pres. 1978-79), Alpha Omega Alpha. Home: 1 Bratenahl Pl Apt 1010 Cleveland OH 44108-1155 Office: 11000 Euclid Ave Cleveland OH 44106-1714

LENMAN, BRUCE PHILIP, historian, educator; b. Aberdeen, Scotland, Apr. 9, 1938; s. Jacob Philip and May (Wishart) L. MA in History with 1st class honors, Aberdeen U., 1960; MLitt, U. Cambridge, 1965, LittD, 1986. Asst. prof. U. Victoria, Canada, 1963; lectr. Queen's Coll., Dundee, Scotland, 1963—67, U. Dundee, 1967—72, U. St. Andrews, Scotland, 1972—78, sr. lectr., 1978—83, reader, 1983—92, prof. modern history, 1992—2003, emeritus, 2003—. James Pinckney Harrison prof. history Coll. William and Mary, Williamsburg, Va., 1988-89; Bird prof. history Emory U., Atlanta, 1998; mem. humanities com. Coun. for Nat. Acad. Awards, London, 1985-87. Author: From Esk to Tweed, 1975, Economic History of Modern Scotland, 1977 (Scottish Arts Coun. award 1977), The Jacobite Risings 1689-1746, 1980 (Scottish Arts Coun. award 1980), Scotland 1746-1832, 1981, The Jacobite Clans of the Great Glen, 1984, The Jacobite Cause, 1986, The Eclipse of Parliament, 1992, England's Colonial Wars, 2000, Britain's Colonial Wars, 2001; co-author: (with John S. Gibson) The Jacobite Threat, 1990; editor: Chambers Dictionary of World History, 1993, 3d edit., 2005. Brit. Acad.-Newberry Library fellow, 1982, John Carter Brown Library fellow, 1984, Mellon fellow Va. Hist. Soc., 1990, Mayers fellow Huntington Libr., 1996, Folger Libr. fellow, 1997, Hill fellow, 2004. Fellow Royal Hist. Soc., Royal Soc. Edinburgh; mem. 18th Century Scottish StudiesSoc., Soc. for History of Discoveries, Hakluyt Soc., Royal Commonwealth Club (London). Avocations: golf, hill walking, swimming, scottish country dancing, badminton. Office: Apt 4 55 Victoria Pl Stirling FK8 2QT Scotland Office Phone: 0044 01334 462923. Business E-Mail: bl@st-andrews.ac.uk.

LENN, MARJORIE PEACE, educational association administrator, consultant; b. Bowling Green, Ohio, Jan. 17, 1946; d. Frederick Elwynn and Nelvia P. Peace; m. D. Jeffrey Lenn; 1 child, Rebecca. BA, Transylvania Coll., 1968; M in Arts and Religion, Yale U., 1970; MEd, U. Mass., 1973, EdD, 1978. Dir. student svcs. U. Mass., Amherst, 1970-79, dir. residential life, 1979-82; dir. profl. svcs. Coun. on Postsecondary Accreditation, Washington, 1982-89, v.p., 1989-92; exec. dir. Ctr. for Quality Assurance in Internat. Edn., Washington, 1992—, Global Alliance for Transnat. Edn., Washington, 1996—2000. Cons. govts. China, India, Indonesia, South Africa, Mex., Belize, Argentina, Chile, Mauritius, Romania, Hungary and others in higher edn. reform, 1991—; spl. adviser on trade in edn. svcs. U.S. Govt., 2000—. Author: International Developments in Assuring Quality in Higher Education, 1994, Ambassadors of U.S. Higher Education: Quality Credit Bearing Programs Abroad, 1997, Globalization of the Professions and the Quality Imperative, 1997, Multinational Discourse on Professional Accreditation, Certification, and Licensure: Bridges for the Globalizing Professions, 1998, The Foundations of Globalization of Higher Education and the Professions, 1999, The Globalization of the Professions in the United States and Canada: A Survey and Analysis, 2000, Higher Education and Training in the Global Marketplace: Exporting Issues and the Trade Agreements, 2002; author: (with others) Ethics in Higher Education, 1990; editor: New England Consultation Network, 1978, Site Visitors in the Accreditation Process: A Guide to Issues and Practical Concerns, 1988, International Education and Accreditation: Uncharted Waters, 1990, Conflicts of Interest in the Accreditation Process, 1991, Distance Learning and Accreditation, 1991, Diversity, Accessibility, and Quality: An Introduction to Education in the United States for Educators for Other Countries, 1995; editor, contbr. Globalization of Higher Education and the Professions: The Mobility of Students, Scholars, and Professionals, 1993, Globalization of Education and the Professions: The Case of North America, 1994, (series) Studying in the United States, 1994; contbr. articles to profl. jours. Bd. dirs. Regents Coll., 1996-98, Hong Kong Coun. Acad. Accreditation, 1989-92; v.p. adminstrv. Women's Nat. Dem. Club, Washington, 1990-91; elder Old Presbyn. Meeting House, Alexandria, Va., 1983—. Recipient Outstanding Alumni award Transylvania U., 1998, Outstanding Contbn. to Global Higher Edn. award Assn. Christian Colls. and Univs., Internat. Ecumenical Forum, 1998. Fellow Soc. for Values in Higher Edn. (bd. dirs. 1994-95); mem. Women Adminstrs. in Higher Edn. (bd. dirs. 1984-90), Internat. Network Quality Assurance Agys. in Higher Edn. (bd. dirs. 1994—), Sigma Kappa (Colby award for outstanding svc. 2000). Democrat. Presbyterian. Avocations: choral music, travel. Office: Ctr for Quality Assurance in Int Edn Nat Ctr for Higher Edn 1 Dupont Cir NW Ste 515 Washington DC 20036-1135 E-mail: cqaie@aacrao.org.

LENN, STEPHEN ANDREW, investment banker; b. Ft. Lauderdale, Fla., Jan. 6, 1946; s. Joseph A. and Ruth (Kreis) L.; 1 child, Daniel Lenn. BA, Tufts U., 1967; JD, Columbia U., 1970. Assoc. Kronish, Lieb, Shainswit, Weiner & Hellman, N.Y.C., 1970-72, Shereff, Friedman, Hoffman & Goodman, N.Y.C., 1972-75; exec. v.p., gen. counsel Union Commerce Bank, Union Commerce Corp., Cleve., 1975-83; ptnr., mng. ptnr. Porter, Wright, Morris & Arthur, Cleve., 1983-88; ptnr. Baker & Hostetler, Cleve., 1988-97; CEO Capital Strategies Inc., Cleve., 1997—. Trustee Gt. Lakes Sci. Ctr.; corp. bd. mem. Ohio Motorists Assn.; bd. dirs. Cuyahoga County Pub. Libr. Found. Mem.: ABA. Office: Capital Strategies Inc 1801 E 9th St 1350 Cleveland OH 44114

LENNARZ, WILLIAM JOSEPH, research biologist, educator; b. N.Y.C., Sept. 28, 1934; s. William and Louise (Richter) L.; m. Roberta S. Lozensky, June 16, 1956 (div. June 1973); children: William, Matthew, David; m. Sheila Jackson, July 13, 1973. BS, Pa. State U., 1956; PhD, U. Ill., 1959; research fellow, Harvard, 1959-62. Mem. faculty Johns Hopkins Sch. Medicine, 1962-83, assoc. prof. biochemistry, 1966-70, prof., 1971-83; R.A. Welch prof. and chmn. dept. biochemistry and molecular biology U. Tex. Cancer Ctr., M.D. Anderson Hosp., Houston, 1983-89; disting. prof., chmn. dept. biochemistry and cell biology SUNY, Stony Brook, 1989—; dir. Inst. for Cell and Devel. Biology, Stony Brook, 1990—. Cons. NIH, Seminars in Cell and Developmental Biology and Degradation; sec. adv. bd. Ceptor Corp. Co-editor in chief: Encyclopedia of Biological Chemistry, 2005, mem. editl. bd.: Biochem. Biophys. Rsch. Commn. Clayton Found. scholar, 1962-64; grantee NIH, 1963-2005, Lederle, 1965-67; recipient Disting. Young Scientist award Md., 1967. Mem. NAS, Am. Chem. Soc., Am. Soc. Biol. Chemists and Molecular Biologists (pres. 1989-90, coun. 2002—), Am. Soc. Cell Biology (pub. affairs com.), Assn. Med. Grad. Sch. Dept. Biochemistry (pres. 1993), Internat. Union Biochemistry and Molecular Biology (exec. com.), Worcester Found. (mem. scientific adv. bd.), Soc. Glycobiology (pres. 1993, Karl Meyer award 2004), Sigma Xi, Phi Kappa Phi, Alpha Chi Sigma. achievements include rsch. in biosynthesis and degradation of glycoproteins and of fertilization. Home: 43 Erland Rd Stony Brook NY 11790-1124 Office: SUNY at Stony Brook 450 Life Sci Stony Brook NY 11790 Office Phone: 631-632-8560. Business E-Mail: wlennarz@notes.cc.sunysb.edu.

LENNON, JOSEPH LUKE, retired academic administrator, priest; b. Providence, Sept. 21, 1919; s. John Joseph and Marjorie (McCabe) L. AB, Providence Coll., 1940; STB, Immaculate Conception Coll., 1946; MA, U. Notre Dame, 1950, PhD, 1953; LLD, Bradford Durfee Coll. Tech., 1963; LittD (hon.), U. Southeastern Mass., 1975; DHL (hon.), Roger Williams Coll., 1980. Ordained priest Roman Cath. Ch., 1947; instr. U. Notre Dame, 1948-50; mem. edn. dept. Providence Coll., 1950-51, 53-56, asst. dean men, 1953, dean of men, 1954-56, dean of coll., 1956-68, v.p. community affairs, 1968-88, ret., 1988. Dir. Tchrs. Guild of Thomistic Inst., 1953-56, Pennywise Shop; bd. trustees So. New Eng. Sch. of Law, 1994—. Author: The Role of Experience in the Acquisition of Scientific Knowledge, 1952, The Dean Speaks, 1958, College is for Knowledge, 1959; rev. as 30 Ways to Get Ahead at College, 1964. Mem. adv. council Citizens Ednl. Freedom; adv. bd. Perceptional Edn. and Research Center; co-chmn. Easter Seals, 1968; arbitrator R.I. Bd. Labor; adv. com. Mental Retardation, R.I.; chmn. Nat. Library Week, 1962; mem. R.I. Adv. Com. Vocational Edn.; ann. lectr. Psychology and Everyday Life, WJAR-TV, 1960-75; mem. Gov. R.I. Com. to Study R.I. State Inst. at, Howard; chmn. speaker's bur. United Fund Campaign, 1971; coordinator Civil Rights Affirmative Action Program, 1970-78; mem. Com. Future Jurisprudence in, R.I; com. clergy renewal Diocese Providence; mem. Com. for CROP-Community Hunger Appeal of Ch. World Service, 1974-75; mem. subcom. on family law Gov.'s Commn. on Jurisprudence of Future; mem. membership com. Cancer Control Bd., R.I., 1977; mem. Gov.'s Commn. on Consumer's Council, 1977, Gov.'s Leadership Conf. on Citizen Participation.; bd. dirs. Blue Cross and Blue Shield, Progress for Providence, R.I. Legal Services, Fed. Hill House, Pawtucket YMCA, The Samaritans, Handgun Alert, Vols. in R.I. Schs., Meeting St. Sch., Big Sisters, Big Bros. Assn. R.I., R.I. Easter Seal, Blackstone Valley Surgicare, R.I. Heart Assn.; chmn. 1975 Heart Fund campaign; trustee R.I. chpt. Leukemia Soc. Am.; adv. bd. Parents Without Partners; bd. govs. John E. Fogarty Found., Irish Scholarship Found.; bd. dirs., trustee Big Sisters Assn., R.I.; bd. dirs. Diabetes Assn.; adv. bd. St. Joseph's Merged Hosps.; mem. corp. R.I. Hosp.; trustee Emma Pendleton Bradley Hosp., 1984—, Southern New Eng. Sch. Law, 1994—; chmn. Laborer's Internat. Union North Am. Scholarship Program, 1995—; mem. adv. council Quirk Inst.; mem. Spl. Legis. Commn. Created on Catastrophic Health Ins., 1979-82, Gov.'s Screening Com. for the Judiciary, 1980-89; mem. Save the Bay, 1986-88; bd. dirs. John Burke Scholarship Found., 1973— Scholarship Funds of the Laborers' International Union of North America. Recipient Seal of Approval R.I. Automobile Dealers Assn., 1978; Father Lenon O.P. Park established in his honor, City of Providence, 1998; inducted into R.I. Heritage Hall of Fame, 1999. Mem. Nat. Cath. Edn. Assn., Am. Cath. Sociol. Soc., Nat. Soc. Study Edn., Am. Philosophers Edn. Assn., New Eng. Ednl. Assn., New Eng. Guidance and Personnel Assn., Greater Providence Epilepsy Assn., Nat. Soc. Study Edn., Am. Arbitration Assn., Alpha Epsilon Delta, Delta Epsilon Sigma (pres. 1966-69)

LENNOX, DONALD D(UANE), automotive and housing components company executive; b. Pitts., Dec. 3, 1918; s. Edward George and Sarah B. (Knight) L.; m. Jane Armstrong, June 11, 1949; children: Donald D., J. Gordon. BS with honors, U. Pitts., 1947. CPA, Pa. With Ford Motor Co.,

1950-69, Xerox Corp., 1969-80, corp. v.p. and sr. v.p. info. tech. group Rochester, N.Y., 1969-73, group v.p. and pres. info. tech. group, 1973-75, group v.p., pres. info. systems group, 1975-80, sr. v.p., sr. staff officer Stamford, Conn., 1973-74; sr. v.p. ops. staff Navistar Internat. Corp., Chgo., 1980-81, exec. v.p., 1981-82, pres., chief operating officer, 1982, chmn., chief exec. officer, 1983-87, also bd. dirs.; chmn., chief exec. officer Schlegel Corp., Rochester, N.Y., 1987-89; chmn. Internat. Imaging Materials, Inc., Amherst, N.Y., 1990-97; ret., 1997. Bd. dirs. Prudential-Securities Mut. Funds, Gleason Corp. Served with AC USN, 1942-45. Decorated D.F.C. with 2 gold stars, Air medal with 4 gold stars. Mem. Rochester Area C. of C. (pres. 1979), Country Club of Rochester, Genesee Valley Econ. Club, Chgo. Club, Order of Artus, Beta Gamma Sigma. Republican. *What modest success I have enjoyed is the result of hard work and dedication to the success of the organization public or private. Rarely is one's contribution to the success of the organization not recognized or rewarded.*

LENNOX, HEATHER, lawyer; b. Cleve., Sept. 22, 1967; d. Rand Tru and Leilani Marie L.; m. Douglas Robert Krause, Sept. 17, 1994. BA summa cum laude, John Carroll U., 1989; JD cum laude, Georgetown U., 1992. Bar: Ohio 1992, U.S. Dist. Ct. (no. dist.) Ohio 1993. Ptnr. Jones Day, Cleve., 1992—. Contbr. articles to law jours. Mem. Am. Bankruptcy Inst., Cleve. Bar Assn. Office: Jones Day North Point 901 Lakeside Ave E Cleveland OH 44114-1190 Office Phone: 216-586-3939. Business E-Mail: hlennox@jonesday.com.

LENNOX, PAMELA CHATTERTON, academic administrator; b. L.A. BA, MA, Calif. State U., Long Beach; EdD, UCLA. Adj. prof., coll. profl. studies U. San Francisco, 1986—91; dir. coop. edn. Calif. State U., Stanislaus, 1987—91; exec. dir. Higher Edn. Consortium of Ctrl. Calif., 1991; dir., profl. experience and career planning Long Island U., 1992—95, assoc. provost, 1995—. Mem., bd. dirs. Girl Scouts of Nassau County, 1999—2004; membership com. chair Coop. Edn. Assn., 1989—90; mem., conf. planner Stanislaus County Literacy Network, 1989—91; bd. mem., vol Brookville Park Found., 1999—2002, bd. v.p., vol., 2002—; higher edn. grants field reader U.S. Dept. Edn., 1991—. Recipient Vol. Merit Award, Jr. League of Long Island, 1999, 90 Women for 90 Years Award, Girl Scouts of Nassau County, 2002, "Thanks" Badge, 2004, Mentor Award, Nassau County Edn. Leadership Ctr., 2003. Office: CW Post Campus Long Island Univ 720 Northern Blvd Greenvale NY 11548 Office Phone: 516-299-2824.

LENNOX, WILLIAM J., JR., academic administrator, career military officer; BS, U.S. Mil. Acad., 1971; MLitt, Princeton U., DLitt, 1979; student, Command & Gen. Staff Coll., Ft. Leavenworth, Kans., 1985—86. Commd. 2d lt. US Army, 1971, advanced through grades to lt. gen., 2001, forward observer later exec. officer, C battery, later Fire Support Officer, 1st bn., 29th field arty., 4th infantry (mechanized) Ft. Carson, Colo., 1972—74, aide de camp to the asst. divsn. comdr. for support, 4th infantry divsn. (mechanized), 1974—75; instr., later asst. prof. english US Mil. Acad., West Point, NY, 1979—82; S-3 (ops.) later exec. officer, 2nd bn., 41st field arty., 3rd infantry divsn. (mechanized) US Army, Germany, 1982—85, comdr. B battery, 2nd bn., 20th field arty., 4th infantry divsn. (mechanized) Ft. Carson, Colo., 1975—76, comdr. 5th bn. 29th field arty., 4th infantry divsn. (mechanized), 1988—90, spl. asst. to sec. Washington, 1991—92, comdr., divsn. arty. 24th Infantry divsn. Ft. Stewart, Ga., 1992—94, exec. officer for dep. chief of staff ops. and plans Washington, 1994—95; dep. commdg. gen. US Army Field Arty. Ctr., Ft. Sill, Okla., 1995—97, asst. comdt., 1995—97; chief of staff III Corps, Ft. Hood, Tex., 1997—98; asst. chief of staff, C-3/J-3, UN Command/Combined Forces Command US Forces Korea, commdg. gen., 8th Army US Army, Republic of Korea, 1998—99; chief legis. liaison, Office Sec. Army The Pentagon, Washington, 1999—2001; supt. US Mil. Acad., West Point, NY, 2001—. Decorated Legion of Merit with 4 oak leaf clusters, Def. Disting. Svc. medal, Disting. Svc. medal, Meritorious Svc. medal with oak leaf cluster, Army Commendation medal with two oak leaf clusters, Army Achievement medal, Korean Order of Mil. Merit, Inheon medal, . Office: US Mil Acad West Point NY 10996*

LENNY, RICHARD HERBERT, food products executive, marketing professional; b. Atlanta, Jan. 5, 1952; s. Julian I. and Helen (Prozan) L.; m. Roxanne Hager, Jan. 1985. BBA in Mktg. magna cum laude, Ga. State U., 1974; MBA in Mktg. with distinction, Northwestern U., 1977. Research assoc. Atlanta Newspapers, Inc., 1974-76; market analyst Kraft, Inc., Chgo., 1977-78, asst. mktg. mgr., 1978-80, brand mgr. Glenview, Ill., 1980-82, group brand mgr., 1982-84, v.p. mktg. Celestial Seasonings Boulder, Colo., 1985-87, corp. v.p. sales and mktg. promotion Glenview, 1987—97; pres., CEO Hershey Foods Corp., 2001—, chmn., 2002—. Bd. dirs. Kraft Employee Credit Union, Glenview, Fortune 44 Co., Boulder. Recipient Disting. Scholar award Northwestern U., 1977, Advt. Age Mag. award 1986, Rising Young Advt. Clients award, 1986. Mem. Northwestern Alumni Assn. (fund raising chmn. 1984, adminstrv. bd. mgmt. alumni 1985—), Am. Mktg. Assn. Office: Hershey Foods Corp 100 Crystal A Dr Hershey PA 17033

LENO, JAY (JAMES DOUGLAS MUIR LENO), television personality, comedian, writer; b. New Rochelle, N.Y., Apr. 28, 1950; s. Angelo and Cathryn Leno; m. Mavis Nicholson Nov. 30, 1980. Grad., Emerson Coll., 1972. Worked as Rolls-Royce auto mechanic and deliveryman. Stand-up comedian playing Carneigie Hall, Caesar's Palace, others; numerous appearances on Late Night with David Letterman; exclusive guest host The Tonight Show, NBC-TV, 1987-92, host, prodr., writer, 1992— (Emmy award, 1995); host, prodr. Showtime Spl. Jay Leno and the American Dream, 1986, Saturday Night Live, 1986, Jay Leno's Family Comedy Hour (Writers Guild Am. nomination), 1987, Our Planet Tonight; film appearances include: The Silver Bears, Fun with Dick and Jane, 1977, American Hot Wax, 1978, Americathon, 1979, Collision Course, 1989, Dave, 1993, Wayne's World 2, Major League 2, The Flintstones, 1994, The Birdcage, 1996, (voice) What's up Hideous Sun Demon?, We're Back! A Dinosaur's Story, 1993, The Flinstones, 1994, (voice) Robots, 2005; (TV series) (voice) The Fairly Odd Parents, 2001; prodr. (TV films) Roadside Attractions, 2002; writer: (TV series) Good Times, 1974-79; author: Leading with my Chin, 1996, If Roast Beef Could Fly, 2004. Avocation: antique motorcycles and automobiles.*

LENO, SAM R., corporate financial executive; BS in Acctg., N. Ill. U.; MBA, Roosevelt U. CFO, exec. v.p. Corp. Express Inc., Broomfield, Colo., 1995-1999; CFO, sr. v.p. Arrow Electronics, Inc., Melville, NY, 1999—2001; sr. v.p. Zimmer Holdings, Inc., 2001—03, exec. v.p. corp. fin. operations, 2003—, CFO, 2003—. Office: Zimmer Holdings PO Box 708 Warsaw IN 46581-0708

LENOBEL, JEFFREY A., lawyer; b. Bklyn., 1951; BA, Gettysburg Coll., 1973; JD cum laude, Cumberland Sch. Law, 1978. Bar: NY 1979. Assoc. Demov & Morris, 1978—84, ptnr., 1985—87, Mudge Rose Guthri Alexander & Ferdon, 1987—90, Baker & McKenzie, 1990—94, Orrick Herrington & Sutcliffe LLP, 1994—97; chmn., real estate dept. Schulte Roth & Zabel LLP, NYC, ptnr. Adv. bd. Chgo. Title Ins. Co., 1994—, Stewart Title Ins. Co., 2001—, First Am. Ins. Co., 2002—04. Assoc. editor Cumberland Law Rev., 1976—77, exec. editor, 1977—78; contbr. articles to profl. jour.; spkr. in field. Exec. com. UJA-Fedn. Real Estate Lawyers Div., Fund to Cure Asthma, Nat. Jewish Med. Rsch. Ctr.; commr. Village of Scarsdale Cable TV Commn., 1994—2001, chmn., 1998—2000; mem. Internat. Coun. Shopping Ctrs. Recipient Burton Award legal achievement, 2003. Mem.: Am. Coll. Real Estate Lawyers, Comml. Mortgage Securities Assn., Mortgage Bankers Assn., ABA (securitized mortgage lending 1998—2002, chmn., pension fund investments com. 2002—), NY State Bar Assn. (cooperatives & condominiums com. 1986—), Assn. Bar City NY (housing & urban devol. com. 1986—89, 1991—94), Phi Alpha Delta. Office: Schulte Roth & Zabel LLP 919 Third Ave New York NY 10022 Office Phone: 212-756-2444. Office Fax: 212-593-5955. Business E-Mail: jeffrey.lenobel@srz.com.

LENOIR, GLORIA CISNEROS, secondary school educator, consultant; b. Monterrey, Nuevo Leon, Mex., Aug. 18, 1951; came to U.S., 1956, naturalized; d. Juan Antonio and Maria Gloria (Flores) Cisneros; m. Walter Frank Lenoir, June 6, 1975; children: Lucy Gloria, Katherine Judith, Walter Frank IV. Student, Inst. Am. Univs., 1971-72; BA in French Art, Austin Coll., 1973, MA in French Art, 1974; MBA in Fin., U. Tex., 1979, postgrad. in Ednl. Policy and Planning, 2001—03. Region XIII behavior coach cert. 2005. French tchr. Sherman (Tex.) H.S., 1973-74; French/Spanish tchr, dept. chmn. Lyndon Baines Johnson H.S., Austin, 1974-77; legis. aide Tex. State Capitol, Austin, Tex., 1977-81; stock broker Merrill Lynch, Austin, 1981-83, Schneider, Bernet and Hickman, Austin, 1983-84; bus. mgr. Holleman Photographic Labs., Inc., Austin, 1984-87, 88-90; account exec., stock broker Eppler, Guerin & Turner, 1987-88; ind. distbr. Austin, 1990-93; owner, cons. Profl. Cons. Svcs., Austin, 1991—2001; adj. faculty Spanish for internat. trade St. Edwards U., 1991-99; bilingual interviewer The Gallup Orgn., 1997-98; Spanish tchr., club sponsor Hyde Park Bapt. Schs., 1997-99; tchr. computer applications Travis H.S. Comm. Acad., 1999-2000, 9th grade coord., 2000—01; tchr. langs. Travis HS, 2001—. Group counselor, organizer Inst. Fgn. Studies, U. Strasbourg, France, 1976; mktg. intern IBM, Austin, 1978; mktg. cons. Creative Ednl. Enterprises, Austin, 1980-81; hon. speaker Mex.-Am. U. Tex., Austin, 1984; coord. small bus. workshops, 1985; group sponsor, advisor Travel Selections, 1997-2003, Explorica, Inc., 2003—; mem. campus adv. coun. Travis H.S., 1999-2002; Southwest area rep. Travel Selections from Campbell, Calif., 2000—03; spkr. in fields of bus, fin., edn. and travel, 1974— Photographs pub. in Women in Space, 1979, Review, 1988; exhibited in group shows, Tex. and US, 1979, 88-89, 99, 2005 Neighborhood capt. Am. Cancer Soc., Austin, 1982-86, 90, Am. Heart Assn., 1989; active bds. various PTA orgns., chmn., 1989—, chmn. numerous coms., 19986-96; active Advantage Austin, 1988; mem. Bryker Woods Elem. PTA Bd., 1990-92, pres., 1990-91, mem. Austin City coun. PTA Bd., 1991-96, Kealing Jr. H.S. PTA Bd., 1992-94, chair 50th anniversary celebration com., 1990, hospitality chmn., 1st grade coord., Austin, 1986, legis. com. Tex. State, 1990-92; vol. liaison leads program Austin Coll., 1983-2000; peer panelist Maj. Art Insts., Austin; elder Ctrl. Presbyn. Ch., 1988-90, 2000-02, mem. ch. choir, 1975-78, 2003-04, mem. adminstrn., fin., membership, staff coms., 1988—, tchr. H.S. Sunday sch., 2002-03, mission com., 2003-04; Megaskills leader Austin Ind. Sch. Dist., 1991-96; bd. dirs. Magnet Parents Coalition, 1995-98; cultural arts chair Dist. 13 PTA Bd., 1996-97; participant NASA Urban and Rural Cmty. Enrichment Program, 2002; mem. smaller learning cmtys. com. Travis H.S., Austin, Tex., 2002-04, mem. partnership for behavioral success com., 2003—. Recipient Night on the Town award IBM, 1978. Mem.: NEA, Edn. Assn., Tex. Fgn. Lang. Assn., Am. Assn. French Tchrs. Democrat. Home and Office: 1801 Lavaca St Apt 11E Austin TX 78701-1331 Personal E-mail: mrs_lenoir@hotmail.com.

LE NOIR, MICHAEL A., allergist; b. Tex., Feb. 22, 1942; married, 4 children. MD, U Tex, 1967. Allergist Childrens Hosp., Oakland, Calif., Summit Med. Ctr., Oakland, Calif.; assoc. clinical prof. pediatrics U. Calif., San Francisco; COO & med. dir. Bay Area MultiCultural Clinical Rsch. & Ed. Ctr., San Francisco; chief of allergy services San Francisco General Hospital, San Francisco. Named one of Top 100 Black Physicians in Am., Black Enterprise Mag., 2001. Fellow: Am. Acad. of Pediatrics; mem.: Nat. Med. Assn. (chair allergy & asthma initiative). Office: 401 29th St Ste 201 Oakland CA 94609-3581

LENOX, ADRIANE, actress; b. Memphis, Sept. 11, 1965; m. Zane Mark; 1 child, Crystal Joy. Performer: (Broadway plays) Ain't Misbehavin', 1978—82, Dreamgirls, 1981—85, How To Succeed in Business Without Really Trying, 1995—96, The Gershwins' Fascinating Rhythm, 1999, Kiss Me, Kate, 1999—2001, Caroline, or Change, 2004, Doubt, 2005— (Outer Critics Circle award nomination for Outstanding Featured Actress in a Play, 2005, Drama Desk award for Outstanding Featured Actress in a Play, 2005, Tony award for Best Performance by a Featured Actress in a Play, 2005), Buddy Holly Story, (off-broadway plays) Spunk, 1981, The American Play, 1994, Merrily We Roll Along, 1994, Identical Twins from Baltimore, 1995, The Venus, 1995, Broken Sleep: Three Plays, 1997, Dinah Was, 1998 (Obie award for Performance, 1998, Audelco award), The Broadway Musicals of 1943, 2001, Miss Evers Boys, 2002, Crowns, 2002, Our Town, 2002, Cavedweller, 2003, Caroline, or Change, 2004, Beehive, 1986, On the Town, 1989 (Helen Hayes award for Outstanding Lead Actress in a Musical), The Color Purple, 2004, Doubt, 2004 (Lucille Lortel award for Outstanding Featured Actress, 2005); actress (TV series) Third Watch, 2000, 2004, Law and Order, 1999, Law and Order: Special Victims Unit, 2001, 2003, (films) Forever, Lulu, 1987, On the One, 2004, (TV films) Double Platinum, 1999. Mem.: Actors Equity Assn. Address: c/o Walter Kerr Theatre 219 West 48th St New York NY 10036*

LENT, JOHN ANTHONY, journalist, educator; b. East Millsboro, Pa., Sept. 8, 1936; s. John and Rose (Marano) L.; children: Laura, Andrea, John, Lisa, Shahnon. BS, Ohio U., 1958, MS, 1960; PhD, U. Iowa, 1972; cert., Press Inst. of India, Sophia U., Tokyo, U. Oslo, Guadalajara, Mex., Summer Sch. Dir. pub. rels., instr. English W.Va. Tech., Montgomery, 1960-62, asst. prof., 1965-66; Newhouse rsch. asst. and asst. to dir. comm. rsch. Syracuse (NY) U., 1962-64; lectr. De La Salle Coll., Manila, 1964-65; asst. prof. journalism U. Wis., Eau Claire, 1966-67; asst. prof. journalism, head tchrs.' journalism sequence Marshall U., Huntington, W.Va., 1967-69. Vis. assoc. prof. U. Wyo., Laramie, 1969—70; asst. editor Internat. Comm. Bull., Iowa City, 1970—72; coord. mass comm. U. Sains Malaysia, Penang, 1972—74; assoc. prof. comm. Temple U., Phila., 1974—76, prof. comm. journalism, 1976—95, prof. comm. broadcasting, telecom. and mass media, 1995—, Benedum vis. disting. prof., 1987; Rogers disting. prof. U. Western Ont., Canada, 2000; guest prof. Shanghai U., 2002—, China Comm. U., 2004—. Author: Asian Newspapers Reluctant Revolution, 1971, Asian Mass Communications: A Comprehensive Bibliography, 1975, 2d edit., 1978, Third World Mass Media and Their Search for Modernity, 1977, Broadcasting in Asia and Pacific, 1978, Topics in Third World Mass Media, 1979, Caribbean Mass Communications: A Comprehensive Bibliography, 1981, Asian Newspapers: Contemporary Trends and Problems, 1982, Videocassettes in the Third World, 1989, Asian Film Industry, 1990, Caribbean Popular Culture, 1990, Caribbean Mass Communications, 1990, Transnational Communications, 1991, Women and Mass Communications: An International Annotated Bibliography, 1991, Bibliographic Guide to Caribbean Mass Communications, 1992, Bibliography of Cuban Mass Communications, 1992, Cartoonometer, 1994, Animation, Caricature, and Gag and Political Cartoons in the U.S. and Canada: An International Bibliography, 1994, Comic Art of Europe: An International, Comprehensive Bibliography, 1994, Comic Books and Comic Strips in the United States: An International Bibliography, 1994, Asian Popular Culture, 1995, A Different Road Taken, 1995, Comic Art in Africa, Asia, Australia and Latin America: A Comprehensive, International Bibliography, 1996, Global Productions, 1998, Themes and Issues in Asian Cartooning, 1999, Pulp Demons, 1999, Women and Mass Communications in the 1990's, 1999, Illustrating Asia, 2001, Animation in Asia and the Pacific, 2001, Cartooning in Africa, 2005, Comic Art in Africa, Asia, and Latin America Through 2000: An Internat. Bibliography, 2004, Comic Art of Europe Through 2000: An Internat. Bibliography, 2 vols., 2003, Cartooning in Latin America, 2005, Centennial Reflections on Cinematic China, 2005, Comic Art of the United States Through 2000: Animation and Cartoons, 2005, others; founding editor: Berita, 1975—2002, Internat. Jour. Comic Art, 1998—, founding mng. editor: WittyWorld, 1987—; editor: Westview Press Internat. Comm. series, 1992—95, Asian Cinema, 1994—, Hampton Books Popular Culture series, Hampton Books Comic Art series. Anchor Hocking scholar, 1954-58, U. Oslo scholar, 1962, Fulbright scholar, Philippines, 1964-65; recipient Benedum award, 1968, Broadcast Preceptor award (2), 1979, Paul Eberman Outstanding Rsch. award, 1988, Ray and Pat Browne Nat. Book award, 1995, Temple U. Exceptional award, 1995, John A. Lent Travel award ICAF, 2003; decorated Chapel of Four Chaplains' Legion of Honor. Mem. Malaysia/Singapore/Brunei Studies Group (founding chmn. 1975-82), Caribbean Studies Assn., Assn. Asian Studies, Internat. Assn. Mass Comm. Rsch. (visual and comic art organizer, chair 1984—), Asian Cinema Studies Soc. (chmn. 1994—), Popular Culture Assn. (founding chmn. Asian popular culture group 1996—), Sigma Delta Chi, Sigma Tau Delta, Kappa Tau Alpha, Phi Alpha Theta. Home: 669 Ferne Blvd Drexel Hill PA 19026-3110 Office: Temple Univ Broadcasting/Telecom Dept Philadelphia PA 19122 Business E-Mail: jlent@temple.edu. *I have cherished the principles of hard work over long hours, accuracy, comprehensiveness, and honesty in my intellectual and scholarly endeavors. I have considered it important to set and meet goals, to share my work with others, to remain untainted by organizations or individuals who, I feel, are not working for the good of humankind. I also cherish, and protect and use, my right to speak out on those issues which I feel are offensive to the public; the result has been that my writings have incurred the wrath of government ministers in at least two countries.*

LENT, NORMAN FREDERICK, JR., former congressman; b. Oceanside, N.Y., Mar. 23, 1931; s. Norman Frederick and Ellen (Bain) L.; m. Barbara Ann Morris, Aug. 4, 1979; children from previous marriage: Norman Frederick III, Barbara Anne, Thomas Benjamin (dec.). BA, Hofstra U., 1952; JD, Cornell U., 1957; LLD (hon.), Kyung Hee U., Seoul, Republic of Korea, 1975, Molloy Coll., 1985, Hofstra Coll., 1988. Bar: N.Y. 1957, Fla. 1976. Assoc. police judge, East Rockaway, N.Y., 1958-60; confidential law sec. to N.Y. State Supreme Ct., 1960-62; mem. N.Y. State Senate, 1963-70, chmn. joint legislative com. public health, 1966-70; mem. 92nd Congress 5th Dist. N.Y., 1971-73; mem. 93rd-102d Congresses 4th Dist. N.Y., 1973-93; vice chmn. Energy and Commerce com. 100th-102nd Congresses U.S. Ho. Reps., 1986-93, vice chmn. Mcht. Marine subcom., 1987-93; cons. Lent Scrivner & Roth, Washington, 1993—. Lt. (j.g.) USNR, 1952—54. Recipient George Estabrook Disting. Service award Hofstra U., 1967, Israeli Prime Minister's medal, 1977, Disting. Achievement medal N.Y.C. Holland Soc., 1987, Tree of Life award Jewish Nat. Fund, 1987, Anatoly Sharansky Freedom award L.I. Com. for Soviet Jewry, 1983. Republican. Office: Lent Scrivner & Roth 1420 New York Ave NW Washington DC 20005-2302 Personal E-mail: nlent@lentdc.com.

LENTINI, ERNEST JOHN, physician; b. Brookling, Mass., July 22, 1953; BS in Biology; DO, U. New Eng., 1983. Pres. SUNY, L.I., Stoney Brook, 1983-87; pvt. practice Eagle Lake, Maine, 1987-90; physician Braintree (Mass.) Family Physician Inc., 1990—. Mem. exec. com., chmn. family practice S. Shore Hosp., Weymouth, Mass., 1994-98; mem. credentials com. Blue Cross Blue Shield Mass., Boston, 1995-2001. Fellow Am. Acad. Family Physicians (commn. on continuing med. edn. 2000-04); mem. Mass. Acad. Family Physicians (chmn. edn. com. 1995—, pres. 2004—), Mass. Osteo. Assn., Mass. Med. Soc. Avocations: poetry, consciousness research, wine tasting. Office: Braintree Family Physician Inc 382 Grove St Braintree MA 02184-7324 Office Phone: 781-848-1555.

LENTINI, FRANCINE, physical education educator; b. Brooklyn, Dec. 6, 1950; d. Jack and Ida Cutinella Morales; m. Joseph Lentini (div. 1983); 1 child, Christopher; m. John Andreacchio (dec. Sept. 11, 2001). BA, Hunter Coll., 1972; MS in physical edn., Brooklyn Coll. Tchr. sci., health, phys. edn. St. Mary Elem. Sch., Brooklyn, 1972—73; tchr. health, phys. edn. and gymnastics coach Bishop Kearney HS, 1973—74; tchr. health, phys. edn. Wingate HS, 1974—76, Erasmus Hall HS, 1973—96; A.P. coord. health, phys. edn. EHC: HS for Humanities, 1996—. Author: (book) Heart and Soul - A Poetic Journey Since 9/11, 2003. Recipient N.Y.C. Recognition Award, 1989, N.Y.C. Zone Excellence in PE Award, 1989. Mem.: The Acad. Am. Poets. Democrat. Roman Catholic. Avocations: writing, poetry, reading, country line dancing. Home: 2233 W 5th St Brooklyn NY 11223 Office: Erasmus Hall HS Campus Humanities & Performing Arts 911 Flatbush Ave Brooklyn NY 11226

LENTINI, JOHN J., fire investigator, chemist; b. Boston; s. Joseph Raymond and Joan Woods Lentini; m. Judith Kaye Lentini, Aug. 4; children: Julia, Jerald. BA in Natural Scis., New Coll., Sarasota, Fla., 1973. Cert. Internat. Assn. Arson Investigators, Nat. Assn. Fire Investigators. Crime lab scientist Ga. Bur. Investigation, Atlanta, 1974—77; scientist, fire investigator Metall. Engrs. of Atlanta, 1977; mgr. fire investigations Applied Tech. Svcs., Inc., Marietta, Ga., 1978—. Expert witness in field; peer reviewer U.S. Dept. Justice, Nat. Inst. Justice-Office Sci. and Tech.; chair forensic sci. com. Internat. Assn. Arson Investigators; mem. planning panel U.S. Dept. Justice, Nat. Inst. Justice Tech. Working Group on Fire Investigations; presenter in field. Contbr. articles to profl. jours.; mem. editl. bd. Jour. Forensic Scis., 2003—. Recipient Silver Beaver award, Boy Scouts Am., 2003. Fellow: Am. Acad. Forensic Scis. (chair criminalistics sect. nominating com. 1999—), Am. Bd. Criminalistics (bd. dirs. 1993—, chair proficiency adminstrn. com. 1993—99); mem.: ASTM (chmn. com. E30 on forensic scis. 1999—, past chair subcom. E30.01 on criminalistics, Forensic Sci. award 1996, award of merit 2001), Am. Chem. Soc., Metro Atlanta Fire Investigators Assn., Ga. Fire Investigators Assn., Nat. Assn. Fire Investigators, Nat. Fire Protection Assn. (tech. com. 921 on fire investigations 1996—, tech. working group on fire and explosion investigations). Avocations: astronomy, camping. Office: Applied Tech Svcs Inc 440 Atlanta Indsl Dr Marietta GA 30066

LENTINI, JOSEPH CHARLES, retired government agency management analyst; b. Washington, Oct. 2, 1943; s. Joseph and Pearl (Crosman) L.; m. Colleen Gail Sargent, Dec. 5, 1983; children: Randolph, Lois, Steven, Suzanne, Richard. AA cum laude, Prince Georges C.C., Largo, Md., 1977; BS cum laude, U. Md., 1982; MS in Pub. Adminstrn., Am. U., 1991; CIO cert., Info. Resources Mgmt. Coll., 1997. Owner, operator N.Am. Van Lines, Ft. Wayne, Ind., 1974-79; materiel bus. adminstr. E-Systems, Inc., Falls Church, Va., 1979-81; adminstrv. mgr. MA/COM, Inc., Rockville, Md., 1981-83; computer specialist VA, Washington, 1983-89; web master, mgmt. analyst, IRM expert EPA, Washington, 1989—2005. Mem. adv. com. Nat. Multiple Sclerosis Soc., Washington, 1993-95. Served with USN, 1961-69. Decorated Purple Heart, Presdl. Unit citation, 1967. Mem. ASPA, DAV, Assn. Fed. Info. Resources Mgrs., Armed Forces Comm. and Electronics Assn., Am. Legion, Fleet Res. Democrat. Avocations: biking, camping, reading, Judo, music. Home: 6502 Pleasant Ridge Rd Sparta TN 38583 E-mail: lentini.joseph@gmail.com.

LENTON, ROBERTO LEONARDO, environmental services administrator; b. Buenos Aires, Feb. 28, 1947; s. Leonard Gersham and Katie (McCulloch) L.; m. Julia Anne Frend, June 11, 1971; children: Alexandra, James, Christopher, Jessica. Civil Engr., U. Buenos Aires, 1971; SM in Civil Engring., MIT, 1973, PhD in Water Resources Systems, 1974. Planning asst. Ministry Pub. Works, Buenos Aires, 1970-71; vis. rsch. engr. MIT, Cambridge, 1971-72, rsch. asst., 1972-74, asst. prof., 1974-77; project specialist Ford Found., New Delhi, 1977-80, program officer, 1980-83, N.Y.C., 1983-86; dep. dir. gen. Internat. Irrigation Mgmt. Inst., Kandy, Sri Lanka, 1986-87, dir. gen. Colombo, Sri Lanka, 1987-94; dir. sustainable energy and environ. divsn. UN Devel. Programme, N.Y.C., 1995-2000; sr. advisor for internat. affairs and devel. Internat. Rsch. Inst. for Climate Prediction, Columbia U., N.Y.C., 2001—. Co-author: Applied Water Resources Systems Planning, 1979. Bd. dirs., treas. Am. Embassy Sch., New Delhi, 1981-83; bd. dirs. Overseas Children's Sch., Colombo, 1989-93; trustee Iwokrama Internat. Ctr. for Rain Forest Conservation and Devel., Georgetown, Guyana, 1998—2001. Mem. ASCE, Am. Geophys. Union, Centro Argentino Ingenieros. Avocations: windsurfing, tennis, running. Home: 48 Rye Rd Rye NY 10580-2231 Office: IRI Lamont-Doherty Earth Observatory Columbia U Lamont Hall Palisades NY 10964-8000 Office Phone: 845-680-4414. Business E-Mail: rlenton@iri.ldeo.columbia.edu.

LENTS, DON GLAUDE, lawyer; b. Kansas City, Mo., Nov. 4, 1949; s. Donald Victor and Helen Maxine (Draper) L.; m. Peggy Lynn Iglauer, Aug. 27, 1972; children: Stacie Lee, Kelsey Lynn. BA magna cum laude, Harvard U., 1971, JD magna cum laude, 1974. Bar: Mo. 1974, U.S. Dist. Ct. (ea. dist.) Mo. 1975, U.S. Ct. Appeals (8th cir.) 1975. Jr. ptnr. Bryan Cave LLP, St. Louis, 1974-81, ptnr., 1982, 84—, London, 1982-84, mem. exec. com. St. Louis, 1988—, mgr. internat. dept., 1984-88, mgr. corp. and bus. dept., 1988-95, chair corp. and bus. dept., 1995-96, head transactions group, 1996—. Instr. law Washington U., 1979-80. Co-author: Missouri Corporate Law and Practice, 1989, 91 and ann. supplements. Bd. dirs. Leadership St. Louis, Inc., 1978-81, 86-91, pres., 1989-91; bd. dirs. Coro Found., St. Louis, Inc., 1986-91, gen. counsel, sec., 1988-90; vol. St. Louis Lawyers and Accts. for Arts, 1988-93, v.p., 1990-92, pres., 1992-93; bd. dirs. Brit. Am. Project,

1989-94, pres., 1993-94; bd. dirs., exec. com. Confluence St. Louis, 1995-96; bd. dirs., exec. com. Focus St. Louis, 1996—. Sheldon fellow Harvard U., 1974-75. Mem. ABA, Mo. Bar Assn. (coun. corp. and bus. law sect. 1987-93, vice chmn. 1988-92), Met. St. Louis Bar Assn. (sec. bus. law sect. 1980-81), Harvard Alumni Assn. (regional dir. 1993-96), Hasty Pudding Club, Harvard Club (exec. com. St. Louis Club 1978-82, v.p. 1987-92, pres. 1992-93). Office: Bryan Cave One Metropolitan Sq 211 S Broadway Saint Louis MO 63102-1705 Office Phone: 314-259-2119. Office Fax: 312-552-8119. E-mail: dglents@bryancave.com.

LENTS, PEGGY IGLAUER, marketing professional; b. St. Louis, Apr. 14, 1950; d. Hank S. and Elizabeth Ruth (Metzger) Iglauer; m. Don G. Lents, Aug. 27, 1972; children: Stacie Lee, Kelsey Lynn. BA magna cum laude, Tufts U., 1971; MPA, Harvard U., 1974. Legis. aide Congressman Symington, Washington, 1971; adminstrv. mgr. May Co., London, 1974; buyer Famous Barr subs. May Co., St. Louis, 1976-78; gen. mdse. mgr. Roman Co., St. Louis, 1978-80, mktg. dir., 1981-82, v.p., 1982; mktg. cons., 1983-86; ptnr. Andrew & Lents, St. Louis, 1987-89; pres. Lents & Assocs., St. Louis, 1990—. Cons. Human Resources Adminstrn., NYC; cons. in field. Chmn. nat. leadership program NCD, 1974; bd. dirs. Springboard to Learning, 1987—, Mo. Bot. Garden, 1988—92, Ctr. Contemporary Arts, 1989—, Jewish Family and Children's Svcs., 1998—2005; v.p. planning and devel. NCJW, 1986—90, adv. bd., 2000—, Metro Link Arts Transit; counsel Direct Mktg. Assn., 2001—; chmn. adv. bd. Alzheimer's Assn., 1993—; dir. comm. Mo. Botanical Garden, 2002—; v.p. Jewish Family and Children's Svcs., 2004—05; dir. comm. Mo. Botanical Garden, 2004—; v.p. St. Louis Forum, 2004—; chancellor's com. arts U. Mo., St. Louis, 1999—2004; devel. bd. univ. fellow Tufts U., 1971. Named one of Top 25 Most Influential Women, St. Louis Bus. Jour., 2003; grantee, Harvard U., 1974; Tchg. fellow, Tufts U., 1971—72. Mem.: Directory Group (U.K.), Women in Bus., Direct Mktg. Assn. (sr. cons. 2000—), Am. Mgmt. Assn., Jewish Hosp. Sch. Nursing Alumni Assn. (life), Westwood Country Club, Pioneers. Address: 1750 S Brentwood Blvd Ste 552 Saint Louis MO 63144-1302 Office Phone: 314-968-3060. Business E-Mail: plents@lentsandassoc.com.

LENTZ, EDWARD ALLEN, consultant, retired health administrator; b. Superior, Wis., May 30, 1926; s. Otto Albert and Martha Mary Ann (Gruhel) L.; m. Margaret Ann Denier, May 30, 1952; 1 child, Elizabeth Ann Clark. BS, U. Cin., 1951; MHA, Wayne State U., Detroit, 1957. Asst. dir. Pub. Health Fedn., Cin., 1954-57; dir. health planning United Cmty. Coun., Columbus, Ohio, 1957-62; asst. dir. Columbus Hosp. Fedn., 1962-65; assoc. exec. dir. Ohio Hosp. Assn., Columbus, 1965-69; exec. dir. Health Planning Assn. of Ohio River Valley, Cin., 1969-70; asst. prof. grad. program in health svcs. adminstrn. Coll. of Medicine, Ohio State U., Columbus, 1970-72, adj. assoc. prof. preventive medicine, 1957—; dep. dir. med. care adminstrn. Ohio Dept. Health, Columbus, 1972-75; pres., CEO Med. Advances Inst., Columbus, 1975-79; v.p. corp. devel. Mt. Carmel Health System, Columbus, 1979-95, cons., 1995-97. Cons. cmty. health planning USPHS; bd. dirs. Scioto Valley Health Sys. Agy. Contbr. articles to profl. jours. Mem., chair Ohio Dept. Jobs and Family Svcs./Ohio Med. Care Adv. Com., Columbus, 1975—; bd. dirs., vice chair Netcare Corp., Columbus, 1989—. Served with USN, 1944-46; 1st lt. U.S. Army, 1951-53, Korea. Recipient Spl. Citation for hosp. planning and mktg. in Ohio and Delbert L. Pugh Conf., Ohio State U. Coll. Medicine and Ohio Hosp. Assn., 1991. Fellow Am. Pub. Health Assn. (bd. dirs., vice chmn. bd. trustees 1979-83); mem. Ohio Pub. Health Assn. (pres. 1969-70), Am. Assn. Areawide Planning Agencies (pres. 1969-70), Ohio Hosp. Assn. Soc. for Hosp. Planning and Mktg. (pres. 1987-88), Columbus Rotary (com. chair). Presbyterian. Avocations: fishing, photography, tennis. Home: 585 Keyes Ln Worthington OH 43085-3503

LENTZ, EDWIN LAMAR, art historian; b. Houston, Mar. 31, 1951; s. Edwin Lonzo and Gerald Dwain (Flack) L. BA, U. Tex., 1973, MA, 1991. Spl. asst. to Harry H. Ransom Harry Ransom Humanities Rsch. Ctr., U. Tex., Austin, 1971-73, curator Coral Maud Oneal Rm., 1975—; mus. registrar Lyndon Baines Johnson Libr. and Mus., Austin, 1974-75; asst. to registrar Mus. Fine Arts, Houston, 1975-76; dir. libr. and mus. collections Festival-Inst. at Round Top, Tex., 1976—. Author (catalog): Cora Maud Oneal Room, 1979, 85; contbr. articles to profl. jours. Ransom Ctr. rsch. grantee, 1985, 86, 88; Victorian Soc. Am. scholar, 1992. Mem. Coll. Art Assn. (mem. mus. com. 1993-99), Am. Friends of Attingham, Victorian Soc. Am., Phi Kappa Phi. Avocations: rare books, theater. Office: Festival-Inst at Round Top PO Box 89 Round Top TX 78954-0089 E-mail: lamarl@festivalhill.org.

LENTZ, JOSEPH EDWARD, music educator, protective services official; s. Joseph Warren and Franed Lentz; m. Shelley Lynn Lentz, Sept. 5, 1992. A, Ferris State U., 1998, BA in Criminal Justice, 1988; B in Music Edn., Mich. State U., 2003. Cert. tchr. Mich. Police officer Jackson (Mich.) Police Dept., 1989—97, Napolean (Mich.) Twp. Police Dept., 1998—2001, Spring Arbor (Mich.) Police Dept., 1999—2004. Tchr. Napolean Cmty. Schs., 1999—2004. Composer: A Police Officer's Life, 2002. Mem.: Fraternal Order of Police (treas., v.p. 1989—), Am. Choral Dir. Assn., Music Educator's Nat. Conf., Twp. and Village Officer's Assn., Gold Key Nat. honor Soc. Republican. Roman Catholic. Office: Ackerson Lake Cmty Ctr Napoleon Sch 4126 Brooklyn Rd Jackson MI 49201

LENTZ, THOMAS W., museum director, curator; m. Mary Pfeifer Lentz. BA, Claremont Men's Coll.; MA in Near Eastern studies, U. Calif., Berkeley; MA in Islamic art, Harvard U., PhD in fine arts, 1985. Curator Asian art RISD; from asst. curator to curator and head Dept. Ancient and Islamic Art LA County Mus. Art; asst. dir. rsch. and collections Freer and Sackler Galleries Smithsonian Inst., Washington, DC, 1992, dep. dir. to dir. internat. art mus. div.; Elizabeth and John Moors Cabot Dir. Harvard U. Art Mus., Cambridge, Mass., 2003—. Curator Timur and the Princely Vision: Persian Art and Culture in the 15th Century, LA Co. Mus. Art. Office: Harvard U Art Mus 32 Quincy St Cambridge MA 02138 Office Phone: 617-459-9400.*

LENWELL, JOHN D., music educator; b. Panama City, Fla., Oct. 9, 1967; s. Douglas D and Sue Larrison Lenwell; m. Lovella M Lenwell, Jan. 27, 1990; children: Todd D, Susan E, Andrew D. BSc, Indiana State U., 1991. Music tchr. Watseka Unit 9 Schools, Watseka, Ill., 1991—93; orchestra/music tchr. Herscher Unit 2 Schools, Ill., 1993—98; vocal music tchr. Franklin County Schools, Brookville, Ind., 1999; orch. tchr. Newport News Pub. Schools, 1999—. Edn. chmn. York River Symphony Orch., Newport News, Va., 2003; jr. regional orch. chmn. Va Bd. of Orch. Directors Assn., 2004, sr. regional orch. chmn., 00. Mem.: Nat. Edn. Assn., Music Educators Nat. Conf., Masonic Lodge. Republican. United Meth. Office: Dozie Mid Sch 432 Industrial Park Dr Newport News VA 23608 Home: 203 Vista Dr Newport News VA 23608 Personal E-mail: jlenwell@aol.com.

LENZ, DEBRA LYNN, auditor; b. Watertown, Wis., June 8, 1973; d. Ron Floyd and Sandy Jean Lenz. BS in Acctg., Marquette U., Milw., 1996, MBA, 2003. CPA Wis., cert. Internal Auditor. Sr. auditor Deloitte & Touche LLP, Milw., 1996-99; sr. fin. analyst Rockwell Automation, Milw., 1999-2000, Harley-Davidson, Milw., 2000—. Mem. AICPA, Bus. Profl. Women, Wis. Inst. CPAs, Alpha Sigma Nu, Beta Gamma Sigma. Home: 8472 Northview Dr Pleasant Prairie WI 53158 Office: Harley-Davidson 3700 W Juneau Ave Milwaukee WI 53208 Office Phone: 414-343-8764. Business E-Mail: debra.lenz@harley-davidson.com.

LENZ, EDWARD ARNOLD, trade association administrator, lawyer; b. White Plains, N.Y., Sept. 28, 1942; s. Fritz and Hildegarde (Bunzel) L.; m. Anna Maria Bartusiak, Mar. 21, 1987; children: Scott, Eric. BA, Bucknell U., 1964; JD, Boston Coll., 1967; LLM, NYU, 1968. Bar: N.Y. 1968, D.C. 1973, Mich. 1982. Trial atty. U.S. Dept. Justice, Washington, 1970-72; assoc. gen. counsel litigation U.S. Cost of Living Coun., Exec. Office of the Pres., Washington, 1973; assoc. Miller & Chevalier, Washington, 1973-80; counsel Health Ins. Assn. Am., Washington, 1980-82; v.p., asst. gen. counsel Kelly Svcs. Inc., Troy, Mich., 1982-89; chmn. legis. com. Am. Staffing Assn., Alexandria, Va., 1985-89, sr. v.p., gen. counsel, 1989-93, sr. v.p. legal and govt. affairs, 1993-99, sr. v.p. pub. affairs, gen. counsel, 1999—. Author: Co-employment--Employer Liability Issues in Third-Party Staffing Arrangements, 1994, 5th edit., 2003. Capt. U.S. Army, 1968-70, Vietnam. Decorated Bronze Star. Fellow Coll. Labor and Employment Lawyers; mem. ABA, N.Y. Bar Assn., D.C. Bar Assn., Pi Sigma Alpha, Sigma Alpha Epsilon. Home: 818 S Lee St Alexandria VA 22314-4334 Office: Am Staffing Assn 277 S Washington St Ste 200 Alexandria VA 22314-3675 Office Phone: 703-253-2020.

LENZ, HENRY PAUL, management consultant; b. NYC, Nov. 24, 1925; s. Ernest and Margaret (Schick) L.; m. Norma M. Kull, Jan. 25, 1958; children: Susan, Scott, Theresa. AB, U. N.C., 1946; MBA, Coll. Ins., 1974. Underwriter U.S. Casualty Co., N.Y.C., 1948-55; underwriting mgr. Mass. Bonding & Ins. Co., N.Y.C., 1955-60; with Home Ins. Co., N.Y.C., 1960-85, sr. v.p., 1972-75, exec. v.p., dir., 1975-85; chmn. bd. Lenz Enterprises Ltd., Chatham, NJ, 1985—. Former pres., dir. Home Indemnity Co.; pres., dir. Home Ins. Co. Ind., Home Ins. Co. Ill., City Ins. Co., Home Group Risk Mgmt.; chmn. bd. Home Reins. Co., Scott Wetzel Services Inc.; chmn., pres. Cityvest Reins. Ltd., City Ins. Co. (U.K.) Ltd.; trustee Am. Inst. Property and Liability Underwriters, Ins. Inst. Am. Served with USNR, 1944-47, 52-53. Decorated Army Commendation medal. Mem. Soc. CPCU's, Phi Beta Kappa, Sigma Nu. Office Phone: 973-377-2949.

LENZ, JACQUELYN L, literature and language educator; b. Pitts., Oct. 27, 1945; s. Virgil Philip and Dorothy Elizabeth Moccia; children: Matthew, Joseph. BS in Edn., Ctrl. Mo. State U., 1967; M of English Edn., U. Mo., 1970. Tchr. English Independence Pub. Schs., Mo., 1967—71, St. Peter and Paul Cath. Sch., Boonville, 1971—73, Columbia Pub. Schs., 1973—75, Blue Springs Pub. Schs., 1977—84, Katy Ind. Schs., Tex., 1985—89, Blue Valley Sch. Dist., Overland Park, Kans., 1989—. Home: 605 W 131st Terr Kansas City MO 64145

LENZEN, GLENN HOWARD, JR., lawyer; b. 1947; B in Welding Engr./MSc, Ohio State U., 1970; JD, Loyola U., Chgo., 1979; MBA, St. Mary's Coll. of Calif., 1990. Bar: Ill. 1979, CA 1981. Asst. gen. counsel, chief patent counsel Raytheon Co., Waltham, Mass., 1995—2000, v.p. intellectual property and licensing, 2000—04, ptnr., 2004. Office: Lathrop & Gage LC Ste 300 4845 Pearl East Cir Boulder CO 80301 Office Phone: 720-931-3017. Business E-Mail: glenzen@lathropgage.com.

LENZER, IRMINGARD ISOLDE, psychology professor; b. 1938; arrived in Can., 1979; d. Johann and Maria (Pfaffinger) L.; children: Alexander Lemond, Anna Lemond. BA in Psychology, UCLA, 1964; PhD of Psychology, Ind. U., 1969. Diplomate Am. Bd. Forensic Examiners. Asst. prof. psychology St. Mary's U., Halifax, Canada, 1969—73, assoc. prof., 1973—81, prof., 1981—2004; ret., 2004. Cons., Halifax, 2004—. Mem. Internat. Neuropsychol. Soc., Can. Psychol. Assn. Home: 1232 Edward St Halifax NS B3H 3H4 Canada

LEO, JACQUELINE M., editor-in-chief; Feature writer AP; sr. editor Modern Bride; co-founder Child, N.Y.C., 1986, editor-in-chief, 1987-88, Family Circle, N.Y.C., 1988-94; editl. dir. women's mags. group N.Y. Times Co., N.Y.C., 1994, dir. mag. and media devel., 1994-95; editl. dir. Good Morning America ABC-TV News, N.Y.C., 1995—97; editl. dir. Consumer Reports, 1997-99; v.p., editl. dir. Interactive Media/Meredith Corp., 1999—2001; editor-in-chief Reader's Digest, Pleasantville, NY, 2000—. Author: New Woman's Guide To Getting Married. Recipient Matrix award Women in Comm., 1993. Mem. Am. Soc. Mag. Editors (bd. dirs., pres.), N.Y. Acad. Scis. (bd. govs.). Office: Office of Editor-in-Chief Reader's Digest Reader's Digest Rd Pleasantville NY 10570 Fax: 914-244-5900. Office Phone: 914-238-1000, 914-244-5567. Office Fax: 914-238-4559. E-mail: jacqueline_leo@rd.com.*

LEO, JOHN P., columnist; b. Hoboken, N.J., June 16, 1935; s. Maurice M. and Maria M. (Trincellita) L.; m. Stephanie Wolf, Dec. 30, 1967 (div.); children: Kristin, Karen; m. Jacqueline Jasous, Jan. 21, 1978; 1 child, Alexandra. BA, U. Toronto, 1957; LittD (hon.), Marietta Coll., 1996. Reporter Bergen Record, Hackensack, N.J., 1957-60; editor Cath. Messenger, Davenport, Iowa, 1960-63; assoc. editor Commonweal mag., N.Y.C., 1963-67; reporter The New York Times, N.Y.C., 1967-69; dep. adminstr. N.Y.C. Dept. Environ. Protection, 1970-73; press columnist Village Voice, N.Y.C., 1973-74; assoc. editor, sr. writer Time mag., N.Y.C., 1974-88; columnist U.S. News & World Report, N.Y.C., 1988—. Author: How the Russians Invented Baseball, 1989, Two Steps Ahead of the Thought Police, 1994. Mem. ch.-state com. ACLU, 1964-66; bd. advisors Columbia Journalism Rev., 1994—. Office: US News & World Report 1290 6th Ave Ste 600 New York NY 10104-0101*

LEO, LEONARD A., legal association administrator, lawyer; b. 1965; m. Sally Leo; children: Margaret, Anthony, Elizabeth, Thaddeus. AB, Cornell U., 1987, JD, 1989. Cons. various legis. and litigation projects; exec. v.p. Federalist Soc. Law and Pub. Policy Studies, Washington; mem. U.S. govt. delegation to UN Commn. on Human Rights. Co-chmn. Rep. Nat. Com. Cath. Outreach; Cath. strategist Bush-Cheney campaign, 2004. Contbr. articles to profl. jours.; co-editor: Presidential Leadership: Rating the Best and Worst in the White House, 2004. Bd. dirs. Nat. Cath. Prayer Breakfast, Youth Leadership Found., Men's Leadership Found., Cath. Action Network. Office: The Federalist Soc 1015 18th St NW Ste 425 Washington DC 20036 Office Phone: 202-822-8138.*

LEO, PETER ANDREW, newspaper columnist, writing educator; b. Aug. 3, 1943; s. Maurice Matthew and Mary (Trincellita) L.; m. Sylvia Weed, July 26, 1970; children: Steven, Jane. AB, U. Toronto, 1966; MA, NYU, 1967. Tchr. H.S. Peace Corps, Nairobi, Kenya, 1968-69; reporter AP, N.Y.C., 1970, Greenboro (N.C.) Record, 1971-72, Wilmington (Del.) News Jour., 1973-78; reporter, asst. city editor, columnist, assoc. editor Pitts. Post-Gazette, 1978—. Instr. U. Pitts., 1999—. Recipient Headliners award Atlantic City Press Club, 1972, Golden Quill award Pitts. Press Club, 1980, 95, Keystone award Pa. Newspaper Pubs. and Editors Assn., 1984. Home: 5266 Beelermont Pl Pittsburgh PA 15217-1010 Office: PG Pub Co 34 Blvd Of The Allies Pittsburgh PA 15222-1200

LEOGRANDE, WILLIAM MARK, political science professor, writer; b. Utica, N.Y., July 1, 1949; s. John James and Patricia Ann (Ryan) LeoG; m. Martha J. Langelan AB, Syracuse U., 1971, MA, 1973, PhD, 1976. Asst. prof. Hamilton Coll., Clinton, NY, 1976-78; dir. polit. sci. Am. U., Washington, 1980-82, asst. prof. polit. sci., 1978-83, assoc. prof., 1984-89, prof., 1989—, chair dept. govt., 1992-96, dean Sch. Pub. Affairs, 1997-99, 2002—. Mem. profl. staff U.S. Senate, 1982-83, cons., 1984-85 Author: Cuba's Policy in Africa, 1980; editor: (with Morris Blachman) Confronting Revolution; Security Through Diplomacy in Central America, 1986, (with Louis Goodman) Political Parties and Democracy in Central America, Our Own Backyard: The United States in Central America, 1998; dir. Latin Am. Rsch. Rev., 1982-86, World Policy Jour., 1983-93. Dir. svc. com. Unitarian-Universalist Ch., Boston, 1983-86; mem. staff Michael Dukakis Presdl. Campaign, 1988. Council Fgn. Relation Internat. Affairs fellow, 1982-83, Pew Faculty fellow, 1994-95. Mem. Coun. Fgn. Rels., Am. Polit. Sci. Assn., Latin Am. Studies Assn. (exec. council 1984-87) Democrat. Home: 7215 Chestnut St Bethesda MD 20815-4051 Office: Am U Sch Pub Affairs Ward Cir Washington DC 20016 Business E-Mail: wleogra@american.edu.

LEON, ARTHUR SOL, research cardiologist, exercise physiologist; b. Bklyn., Apr. 26, 1931; s. Alex and Anne (Schrek) L.; m. Gloria Rakita, Dec. 23, 1956; children: Denise, Harmon, Michelle. BS in Chemistry with high honors, U. Fla., 1952; MS in Biochemistry, U. Wis., 1954, MD, 1957. Intern Henry Ford Hosp., Detroit, 1957-58; fellow in internal medicine Lahey Clinic, Boston, 1958-60; fellow in cardiology Jackson Meml. Hosp.-U. Miami (Fla.) Med. Sch., 1960-61; dir. clin. pharmacology research unit Hoffmann-La Roche Inc.-Newark Beth Israel Med. Ctr., 1969-73; from instr. to assoc. prof. medicine Coll. Medicine and Dentistry N.J., Newark, 1967-73; from assoc. prof. to prof. div. epidemiology U. Minn., Mpls., 1973—, H.L. Taylor prof. exercise sci. and health enhancement, dir. lab. physiol. hygiene and exercise sci., div. kinesiology, Coll. Edn., 1991—, dir. applied physiology and nutrition, 1973-91. Mem. med. eval. team Gemini and Apollo projects NASA, 1964-67. Editor Procs. of the NIH Consensus Conf. on Phys. Activity and Cardiovasc. Health, 1997; assoc. editor Surgeon Gen.'s Report on Health Benefits of Exercise, 1996; contbr. numerous articles to profl. publs. Trustee Vinland Nat. Sports Health Ctr. for Disabled, 1978—; mem. gov.'s coun. physical fitness sports, 1979-90. Served as officer M.C. U.S. Army, 1961-67, 90-91, col. Res. 1978-92, ret. Recipient Anderson award AAHPER, 1981, Presdl. award for exercise sci. rsch. Internat. Olympic Com., 1999; Am. Heart Assn. fellow, 1960-61 Fellow Am. Coll. Cardiology, Am. Coll. Chest Physicians, Am. Coll. Clin. Pharmacology, N.Y. Acad. Scis., Am. Coll. Sports Medicine (trustee 1976-78, 82-83, v.p. 1977-79, pres. Northland chpt. 1975-76, Citation award 1995), Am. Assn. Cardiovasc. and Pulmonary Rehab. (trustee 1989-90), Am. Acad. Kinesiology and Phys. Edn.; mem. Am. Physiol. Soc., Am. Soc. Pharmacology and Exptl. Therapeutics, Am. Inst. Nutrition, Am. Heart Assn. (v.p. Hennepin County divsn. 1980-81, pres. 1982-83), Am. Coll. Nutrition, Am. Fedn. Clin. Rsch., Minn. Lung Assn. (trustee 1978-81), Phi Beta Kappa, Phi Kappa Phi. Jewish. Home: 5628 Glen Ave Minnetonka MN 55345-6610 Office: U Minn Sch Kinesiology & Leisure Studies 202 Cooke Hall Minneapolis MN 55455-0136 Office Phone: 612-624-8271. Business E-Mail: leonx002@umn.edu.

LEON, BRUNO, architect, architecture educator; b. Van Houten, N.Mex., Feb. 18, 1924; s. Giovanni and Rosina (Cunico) L.; m. Louise Dal-Bo, Sept. 4, 1948 (dec. 1974); m. Bonnie Bertram, Sept. 12, 1976; children: Mark Jon, John Anthony, Lisa Rose. Student, Wayne State U., 1942, U. Detroit, 1945-48, LHD (hon.), 1984; BArch, N.C. State U., 1953. Registered architect, Mich., N.C., Mass., N.Y., N.Mex., Fla. Head design staff Fuller Research Found., Raleigh, N.C., 1954-55; archtl. designer I.M. Pei & Assos., N.Y.C., 1955-56; instr. Mass. Inst. Tech., 1956-59; designer Catalano & Belluschi (architects), Cambridge, Mass., 1958-59; asst. prof. U. Ill., Urbana, 1959-61; dean Sch. Architecture, U. Detroit, 1961-93, dean emeritus, 1993; pvt. practice architecture, 1956—. With USAAF, 1942-45. Fellow AIA (dir. Detroit 1963-64); mem. Alpha Sigma Nu (hon.), Phi Kappa Phi. Home: 9 Redondo Ct Santa Fe NM 87508-8308 Office Phone: 505-466-1583. E-mail: volterra@newmexico.com. *I believe the integral quality of the human spirit to be the ability to dream rather than to rationalize.*

LEON, EDWARD, investor; b. Benton, Ill., May 2, 1925; s. John and Mary (Letukas) L.; m. Mary Ellen Cooper, Aug. 29, 1953; children: Ellen, Edward, Carol. BS in Chemistry, U. Ill., 1949; MS in Chemistry, U. Mich., 1950, PhD in Chemistry, 1956. Rsch. supr. Occidental Petroleum, Grand Island, NY, 1954—68; rsch. mgr. Borg-Warner Chems., Parkersburg, W.Va., 1968—77, dir. ctrl. rsch. lab. Des Plaines, Ill., 1977—88; owner, pres. Cooper-Leon Fin. Svcs., Inc., Barrington, Ill., 1988—92. Contbr. articles to profl. jours.; holder 12 U.S. patents, numerous fgn. patents. With U.S. Army, 1944-46, ETO. Decorated Purple Heart. Mem. Am. Chem. Soc. (chmn. Mid-Ohio Valley sect. 1972, nat. counselor 1973-75), Internat. Assn. for Fin. Planning (bd. dirs. Greater O'Hare chpt. 1990). Avocations: foreign languages, music, painting. Office: 1280 Village DR Apt 113 Arlington Heights IL 60004-4692

LEON, KAREN RENÉE, elementary school educator; b. Sept. 3, 1963; BS in Elem. Edn., Fla. A&M U., Tallahassee, 1988, MEd, 1998. 3d grade tchr. Leon County Sch. Dist., Tallahassee, 1988, 2d grade tchr., 1988—. Mem. NEA, Internat. Reading Assn., Leon County Tchrs. Union, Pi Lambda Theta, Alpha Delta Kappa. Office: 2465 Atlas Rd Tallahassee FL 32303-3703 E-mail: kleon@nettally.com.

LEON, RICHARD J., federal judge; b. South Natick, Mass., Dec. 3, 1949; s. Silvano B. and Rita (O'Rorke) L.; m. M-Christine Costa; Nicholas Cavanagh. AB, Holy Cross Coll., 1971; JD cum laude, Suffolk Law Sch., 1974; LLM, Harvard U., 1981. Bar: R.I. 1975, U.S. Ct. Appeals (2d cir.) 1977, U.S. Dist. Ct. R.I. 1976, U.S. Supreme Ct. 1984, D.C. 1991, U.S. Dist. Ct. D.C. 1991, U.S. Ct. Appeals (D.C. cir.) 1991. Law clk. to justices Superior Ct. Mass., 1974-75, to justice R.I. Supreme Ct., 1975-76; spl. asst. U.S. atty. U.S. Attys. Office (so. dist.) N.Y., 1977-78; asst. prof. law St. John's U. Law Sch., 1979-83; adj. prof. law Georgetown U. Law Ctr., 1997—; sr. trial atty., criminal sect., tax div. U.S. Dept. Justice, Washington, 1983-87, dep. asst. U.S. atty. gen. environment and natural resources divsn., 1988-89; ptnr. Baker & Hostetler, Washington, 1989-99,Vorys, Sater, Seymour and Pease, Washington, 1999-2002; judge U.S. Dist. Ct., 2002—; dep. chief minority counsel House Select "Iran-Contra" Com., 1987; active Jud. Conf. D.C. cir., 1991—, mem. Pres.'s Commn. on White House Fellowships, 1990-93; chief minority counsel House Fgn. Affairs Com. 'October Surprise' Task Force, 1992; spl. counsel House banking com. "Whitewater investigation", 1994; spl. counsel House ethics reform task force, 1997; mem. Jud. Rev. Commn. on Fgn. Asset Control, 2000-01. Author: (chpt.) Environmental Crime, Lawyers' Desk Book on White Collar Crime, 1991; contbr. articles to legal jours. Trustee Suffolk U., 1990-98. Mem. ABA, Order of Barristers, R.I. Bar Assn., Fed. Bar Coun., Suffolk Law Sch. Assn. Met. N.Y. (past pres.), Suffolk Law Sch. Assn. Met. Washington (past pres.), Chevy Chase Club. Republican. Roman Catholic. Office: US Courthouse 333 Constitution Ave NW Washington DC 20001

LEON, ROBERT LEONARD, psychiatrist, educator; b. Denver, Jan. 18, 1925; s. Louis and Rae (Brown) L.; m. Willena Lee, Sept. 14, 1947; children: Alexis Kay, Mark Robert, Jeffrey Clayton, Stacy Lee. MD, U. Colo., 1948. Diplomate Am. Bd. Psychiatry and Neurology. Intern U. Mich. Hosp., Ann Arbor, 1948-49; resident in psychiatry U. Colo. Med. Ctr., Denver, 1949-52, child psychiatry fellow, 1951-52, Bur. Mental Hygiene, New Haven, Conn. Dept. Health/Student Health Svc., Yale U., 1952-53; asst. dir., acting dir. child psychiatry Greater Kansas City Mental Health Found., 1953-54; instr. psychiatry U. Kans. Sch. Medicine, Kansas City, 1956-57; asst. prof. psychiatry U. Tex. Health Sci. Ctr. at Dallas, Southwestern Med. Sch., 1957-61, assoc. prof., 1961-65, prof., 1965-67; prof., chmn. dept. psychiatry Sch. Medicine U. Tex. Health Sci. Ctr., San Antonio, 1967-95, interim chmn., 1995-96; Ashbel Smith prof. U. Tex. Health Sci. Ctr., San Antonio, 1990—2003, prof. emeritus, 2003—. Chief psychiatry U. Health Sys., Bexar County, San Antonio, 1967-96; mem. Am. Assn. Chmn. Depts. Psychiatry, 1967-96, pres., 1982-83; cons. psychiatry Audie Murphy Vet.'s Hosp., 1973—; cons. Mental Health Orgn., region IV, HEW, 1957-73; mem. Psychiat. Tng. Rev. NIMH, Rockville, Md., 1970-74; hon. cons. World Health Orgn., Geneva, 1996. Author: Psychiatric Interviewing: A Primer, 1982, 2d edit., 1989; contbr. articles to profl. jours. Sr. surgeon USPHS, 1954-57. Fellow ACP (pres. 1987-88), Am. Psychiat. Assn. (life), Am. Orthopsychiat. Assn. (life), Am. Acad. Child and Adolescent Psychiatry (life), Am. Assn. Social Psychiatry (pres. 1990-92); mem. Benjamin Rush Soc., World Assn. for Social Psychiatry. Avocation: photography. Home: 6866 Stonykirk St San Antonio TX 78240-2743 Office: U Tex Health Sci Ctr 7703 Floyd Curl Dr MS 7792 San Antonio TX 78229-3900 Office Phone: 210-567-5408. Business E-Mail: leon@uthscsa.edu.

LEON, TANIA JUSTINA, composer, music director, pianist; b. Havana, Cuba, May 14, 1943; came to U.S., 1967; d. Oscar and Dora (Ferran) L. BA in Piano and Theory, Peyrellade Conservatory Music, Havana, 1963; MA in Music Edn., Nat. Conservatory Music, Havana, 1965; BA in Acctg., U. Havana, 1965; BS Music Edn., BS in Music Edn., NYU, 1973, MA in Composition, 1975; PhD (hon.), Colgate U., 1999. Prof. Bklyn. Coll. Conservatory of Music, 1985—2000, Tow disting. prof., 2000—. Vis. prof. Yale U., New Haven, 1993; vis. lectr. Harvard U., Cambridge, Mass., 1994; resident composer Lincoln Ctr. Inst., 1985, teaching artist, 1982-88; composer in residence Nat. Black Music Festival, 1990, Cabrillo Music Festival, 1990, Yaddo, 1991, Ravinia Festival, 1991, Cleve. Inst., 1992, Bellagio Ctr., Italy, 1992, Cornish Coll., Seattle, 1993, Billings Symphony, 1993, Carnegie Mellon U., Pitts., 1993, Harvard Coll., Cambridge, Mass., 1993, Voices of Change, Dallas, 1993; panelist N.Y. State Council on the Arts, 1980, 81, 86, NEA composing program, 1980-82, recording program, 1985-87; mem. adv. bd. Bklyn. Coll. Conservatory, 1982-84, Meet the Composer, 1983—,

Children TV Workshop; artistic dir. Composers Forum Inc., N.Y.C., 1987—; assoc. prof. composition Bklyn. Coll., 1987—; bd. dirs. Am. Music Ctr., N.Y. Found. for Arts; with Cin. Symphony Orch., 1991—, Revson Composer fellow N.Y. Philharmonic, 1993—; U.S. rep. U.S.-Mex. Fund for Culture, 1994. Piano soloist, Cuba, 1964-67; piano soloist, N.Y. Coll. of Music Orch., N.Y.C., 1967, NYU Orch., N.Y.C., 1969, Buffalo Symphony Orch., 1973; staff pianist, condr., Dance Theatre of Harlem, N.Y.C., 1968—, assoc. condr., 1983—, music dir., 1968-79; founder, Dance Theatre of Harlem Orch., 1975; concert series Meet the Performer, 1977; music dir. concert series Dance in Am. Spl., Sta. WNET-TV; guest condr. concert series, Genova (Italy) Symphony Orch., 1972, Juilliard Orch., Festival Two Worlds, Spoleto, Italy, Symphony New World, 1974, Royal Ballet Orch., 1974, 76, BBC Orch., 1974, 76, Halle Orch., 1974, Buffalo Philharm. Orch., 1975, Concert Orch. of L.I., 1979, Sadler's Wells Orch., 1979, London Universal Symphony, 1979, Composer's Forum, 1979, Lincoln Ctr. Outdoor Festival, 1980, Bklyn. Coll. Symphony, 1981, J. F. Kennedy Ctr. Opera House Orch., 1981, 82, Radio City Music Hall, 1982, Spoleto Festival, Charleston, 1983, Orch. of Our Time, N.Y., N.Y. Grand Opera, Colonne Orch., Paris, Mich. Opera, Human Comedy, Royale Theatre, Broadway, Pasadena Orch., P.R. Symphony, Met. Opera Orch., Phoenix Symphony, Columbus Symphony Orch., Fund. Latinoamericana Musica Contemporanea P.R., Am. Women Condr./Composer Symposium, Eugene, Oreg., New Music Am., Houston, New Music in Am., 1989 and Concert in the Pk., 1990 both with Bklyn. Philharm., Cabrillo Festival, 1990, Nat. Black Arts Festival, Atlanta, 1990, La Crosse Symphony, Wis., 1991, Dance Theater of Harlem, 1991, 92, 93, 25th Anniversary Season-94, Celebrate Bklyn. Festival, 1991, Bklyn. Philharm., 1991, New World Symphony, Miami, Fla., 1991, 94, Cosmopolitan Symphony Orch., N.Y.C., 1991, Beethovenhalle Symphony Orch., Bonn, Germany, 1992, Opera Orch. of Johannesburg, 1992, Nat. Symphony Orch., Johannesburg, 1992, Louisville Symphony, 1992, RIAS Orch., Berlin, 1992, Billings Symphony, 1993, Dance Theater of Harlem, 1993, 94, Carnegie Mellon Orch., 1993, Alvin Ailey 35th Anniversary Season, 1993, Am. Composers Orch. Chamber Ensemble, 1994, Munich Biennale, 1994, others; royal command performer concert series, London Palladium, 1974, 76, Concert Orch. L.I., 1976, concert pianist, Sta. WNYC-FM, 1968-70; conductor coord.: concert series Music by Black Composers Series, Bklyn. Philharmonia, 1978-79; music dir., condr., Bklyn. Philharm. Community Concert Series, 1977—; mus. dir., condr. The Wiz, Broadway Theatre, 1978; music dir. Death, Destruction and Detroit, 1979, Alvin Ailey Am. Dance Theatre, 1983—, Whitney Mus. Contemporary Music Concert Series, 1986, 87; mus. dir., composer: Maggie Magalita, J.F. Kennedy Ctr. Performing Arts, 1980, The Golden Windows, 1982; apptd. music dir. concert series, Intar Theatre, N.Y.C.; condr., mus. dir. concert series Godspell, NYU, 1978, Carmencita, 1978; composer (ballet music) Haiku, 1974, (piano concerto) Tones, 1970, Sailor's Boat, (score for musical) Dougla, 1974, (African ballet) La Ramera de la Cueva, 1974, (score for musical) Namiac Poems, 1974, (for voice, chorus and orch.) Spiritual Suite, 1975, (2 sopranos, chorus and mixed ensemble with narrator), Concerto Criollo, 1976, (concerto for piano, 8 timpanies and orch.) Pet's Suite, 1979, (for flute and piano) I Got Ovah, 1980, (for soprano, piano and percussion, based on poems by Carolyn M. Rodgers) Concerto Criollo, 1980, Four Pieces for Cello, 1981, De-Orishas, 1982, Ascend, Fanfare for Brass and Percussion, 1983, (for solo piano) Momentum, 1984, Bata, 1985, Permutation Seven, 1985, A La Par, 1986, Ritual, 1987, Pueblo Mulato, 1987, Heart of Ours, a piece, 1988, Parajota Delaté, 1988, Kabiosile, 1988, Latin File, 1988, Indigena for instrumental ensemble, 1991, Solisti Chamber Orch N.Y., 1991, Carabali for orch., 1992, Crossings for brass ensemble, 1992, Arenas d'un Tempo for clarinet, cello and piano, 1992, Son Sonora for flute and guitar, 1993, Scourge of Hyacinths: chamber opera, 1994, Para Viola y Orquesta for viola and orch., 1994, Sin Normas Ajenas for chamber orch., 1994, Sol de Doce for men's vocal ensemble Chanticleer with poetry by Pedro Mir, Singing Sepia song cycle in collaboration with poet Rita Dove for chamber ensemble continuum, orchestra Para Viola y Orquesta, Hechizos, 1995, multimedia work Drummin, 1997, opera Scourge of Hyacinthe, 1999; records on CRI, WesternWind, Albany Records, Newport Classics, Leonarda Records, Mode labels. Bd. dirs. Am. Composers Orch. Recipient Young Composers prize Nat. Council Arts, Havana, 1966, Alvin Johnson award Am. Council Emigres in the Profession, 1971, Cintas award in composition, 1974-75, 78-79, Achievement award Nat. Council Women of U.S., 1980, Byrd Hoffman Found. award, 1981, Key to City of Detroit, 1982, Queens Council on Arts award, 1983, Meet The Composer awards, 1978-94, Manhattan Arts award, 1985, Dean Dixon Achievement award, 1985, N.Y. State Coun. on Arts award, 1988, Mayor's citation, City of N.Y., 1989, Celebrate Bklyn. Achievement award, 1990, award in music Am. Acad. and Inst. of Arts and Letters, 1991, N.Y. State Govs. Lifetime Achievement award, 1999; Nat. Endowment for Arts fellow, 1975. Mem. ASCAP (Composers award 1978-94, Morton Gould award), French Soc. Composers, Am. Acad. Poets (bd. dirs.), Am. Composers Orch. (bd. dirs.), Am. Fedn. Musicians, Ctr. New Music, Am. Music Ctr. (bd. dirs. 1985—), Internat. Artists Alliance, Am. Women Composers, AFL-CIO.

LEONARD, SISTER ANNE C., school system administrator; b. N.Y.C., Dec. 22, 1936; d. Patrick A. and Mary T. (McAlpin) L. BS in Edn. and Social Sci., Fordham U., 1962, MA, 1965; CAGS, Boston U., 1972; postgrad., Hunter Coll., U. San Francisco, U. Northern Ill., Notre Dame U. Cert. tchr. K-12, adminstr. N.Y. Tchr., asst. prin., prin. Notre Dame Acad., Staten Island, N.Y., 1957-68; prin. Maternity B.V.M. Sch., Bourbonnais, Ill., 1968-69, St. Jude the Apostle Sch., South Holland, Ill., 1969-78; dir. Cath. Elem. Schs. Archdiocese of Chgo., 1978-83, dir. ednl. svcs., mem. Cardinal Bernadin's cabinet, 1983-90, exec. officer commn. ednl. svcs., 1983-90; supt. schs., dir. edn. Archdiocese of Okla. City, 1990-96; U.S. province leader Congregation of Notre Dame, Ridgefield, Conn., 1996—. Chair edn. divisn. Cath. Conf. Ill., 1988-90; del. gen. chpt. Congregation Notre Dame, mem. provincial coun.; mem. edn. com. U.S. Cath. Conf. Bishops, Washington, 1985-88; mem. Nat. Cath. Bishops' Millennium Com.; speaker in field; lectr., presenter workshops; mem. Fortune 500 panel edn. and bus.; devel. mission statement, just principles compensation, new models compensation for prins., 1987-91; initiated, organized Dirs. Edn. Wis., Ill., Ind., Ohio, Mich.; attended symposia in field; mem. com. prep. Office of Cath. Edn. Conciliation Process; exec. officer local sch. bds.; initiated individually guided edn. program St. Jude Sch. Cons. textbooks William H. Sadlier, Inc.; contbr. articles to profl. jours. Trustee DePaul U., 1986—; trustee Midwestern U., 1999—, bd. dirs., vice chair acad. affairs com.; bd. dirs. Jr. Achievement, Chgo., 1984-90, Oklahoma City, 1991-96; mem. NCCJ, 1992-96, Gov. Ill. adv. com. on non-pub. schs., Springfield, 1978-82, planning com. Big Shoulders Project, officer Leadership Conf. of Women Religious (Region I), 1997—; active Congregation of Notre Dame Mem. ASCD, Nat. Cath. Ednl. Assn. (pres. chief adminstrs. Cath. edn. 1991-94, v.p. 1989-91, vice chair bd. 1991-94, task force 1990-91, centennial com. 1997—, supervision, pers., curriculum, Educator of Yr. award 1990), Archdiocesan Prins. Assn. (pres. 1973-78), Nat. Religious Retirement Bd. (grant com.), Chgo. Coun. Fgn. Rels., Phi Delta Kappa (Educator of Yr. 1984). Avocations: reading, swimming, travel. Home and Office: 5809 E Circle Dr Chicago IL 60631 Office Phone: 203-438-5282. Personal E-mail: anneleonardcard@juno.com, provsec@juno.com.

LEONARD, DAVID MORSE, lawyer; b. Akron, Ohio, Dec. 4, 1949; s. Frank O. and Barbara J. Leonard. BS in Chem. Engring., Purdue U., 1972; JD, Emory U., 1975. Bar: Ga. 1975, N.Y. 2005, U.S. Ct. Appeals (4th, 5th and 11th cirs.), U.S. Dist. Ct. (no., mid. and so. dists.) Ga., U.S. Dist. Ct. (so. dist.) Ala., U.S. Dist. Ct. (we. dist.) La.; registered atty. U.S. Patent and Trademark Office. Assoc. Montet & Smith, Atlanta, 1975-79, Hurt, Richardson, Garner, Todd & Cadenhead, Atlanta, 1979-83, ptnr., 1983-85; of counsel Lord, Bissell & Brook, Atlanta, 1985-87, ptnr., 1987—. Mem. panel of arbitrators Am. Arbitration Assn., 1995—, arbitrator, mediator. Mem. ABA (litigation sect., intellectual property sect., tort and ins. practice sect.), Profl. Liability Underwriting Soc., Atlanta Lawyers Club, Atlanta C. of C., Am. Arbitration Assn. (panel of arbitrators). Office: Lord Bissell & Brook Ste 1900 1170 Peachtree St NE Atlanta GA 30309-7675 Office Phone: 404-870-4676.

LEONARD, DOROTHY, business educator; b. Elsah, Ill., Mar. 18, 1942; d. Edwin Stanley and Gladys Eugenia (Lee) L.; m. Walter C. Swap; children: Gavin B. Barton, Michelle A. Barton. BA, Principia Coll., 1963; MA, U. Va., 1968; PhD, Stanford U., 1979. Peace corp vol., Bangkok, Thailand, 1965-67; journalist freelance, Bangkok, 1968-70, Jakarta, Indonesia, 1970-75; research analyst S.R.I. Internat., Menlo Park, Calif., 1979-80; asst. prof. Sloan Sch. Mgmt. MIT, Cambridge, Mass., 1980-83, Harvard Grad. Sch. Bus., Boston, 1983-89, assoc. prof., 1989-92, chaired prof., 1993—. Bd. dirs. Am. Mgmt. Systems; cons. in field. Author: Wellsprings of Knowledge, 1995, 98, (with W. Swap) When Sparks Fly, 1999, (with W. Swap) Deep Smarts, 2005; sr. editor Orgn. Sci.; contbr. numerous articles to profl. jours. Com. mem. Nat. Research Council, Washington, 1981-83; panel mem. Nat. Research Council, 1982. Recipient Kaiser Found. Grant, 1982, Whitaker Health Sciences Fund, 1981. Mem. Technology Innovation Div. Acad. Mgmt. Office: Harvard Bus Sch Soldiers Fld Boston MA 02163-1317 Home: 3815 W Tohono View Pl Tucson AZ 85745

LEONARD, EDWIN DEANE, lawyer; b. Oakland, Calif., Apr. 22, 1929; s. Edwin Stanley and Gladys Eugenia (Lee) L.; m. Judith Swatland, July 10, 1954; children: Garrick Hillman, Susanna Leonard Hill, Rebecca Leonard McCauley, Ethan York. BA, The Principia, 1950; LLB, Harvard U., 1953; LLM, George Washington U., 1956. Bar: D.C. 1953, Ill. 1953, N.Y. 1957. Assoc. Davis Polk Wardwell Sunderland & Kiendl, N.Y.C., 1956-61; ptnr. Davis Polk & Wardwell, N.Y.C., 1961-97, sr. counsel, 1998—. Trustee the Brearley Sch., N.Y.C., 1980-90; pres. Millbrook Equestrian Ctr., 1983-98. Served to 1st lt. JAGC, 1953-56. Mem. ABA, N.Y. Bar Assn., N.Y. County Bar Assn., Assn. of Bar of City of N.Y. (chmn. various coms.). Home: 157 Conklin Hill Rd Stanfordville NY 12581-5639 Office: Davis Polk & Wardwell 450 Lexington Ave New York NY 10017-3982 Personal E-mail: deaneleonard@worldnet.att.net.

LEONARD, ELIZABETH ADNEY, social worker; b. Lebanon, Ind., Apr. 27, 1917; d. Frank Brown and Ethel Fern (Coons) Adney; m. Alan J. Leonard, Aug. 4, 1949; children: Arthur Alan, Jean Elizabeth. BA, Ind. U., 1939, MSW, 1947; postgrad., Columbia U., N.Y.C., 1948. Lic. clin. social worker, Calif. With Psychiat. Clinic for Youth, Long Beach, Calif., 1958-74, chief social worker, 1974-82, ret., 1982. Mem. AAUW, NASW, Am. Orthopsychiat. Assn., Zeta Tau Alpha. Home: 2339 Avenida Sevilla Apt A Laguna Woods CA 92637-0836

LEONARD, ELMORE JOHN, writer, scriptwriter; b. New Orleans, Oct. 11, 1925; s. Elmore John and Flora Amelia (Rivé) L.; m. Beverly Claire Cline, Aug. 30, 1949 (div. 1977); children: Jane, Peter, Christopher, William, Katherine; m. Joan Leanne Lancaster, Sept. 15, 1979 (dec. 1993); m. Christine Kent, Aug. 19, 1993. PhB, U. Detroit, 1950. Author over 30 novels including Hombre, 1961, Swag, 1976, Unknown Man No. 89, 1977, City Primeval, 1980, Split Images, 1982, Cat Chaser, 1982, La Brava, 1983, Stick, 1983, Glitz, 1985, Bandits, 1987, Touch, 1987, Freaky Deaky, 1988, Killshot, 1989, Get Shorty, 1990, Maximum Bob, 1991, Rum Punch, 1992, Pronto, 1993, Riding the Rap, 1995, Out of Sight, 1996 (Edgar Allan Poe award 1999), Tishomingo Blues, 2002, Mr. Paradise, 2004, The Hot Kid, 2005 (Publishers Weekly Hardcover Bestseller list, 2005); author of screenplays including The Moonshine War, 1970, Joe Kidd, 1972, Mr. Majestyk, 1974, (with Joseph Stinson) Stick, 1985, (with John Steppling) 52 Pick-Up, 1986, (with Fred Walton) The Rosary Murders, 1987, (with Jim Borrelli and Alan Sharp) Cat Chaser, 1990, Jackie Brown, 1997, Cuba Libre, 1998, Be Cool, 1999; cons. (ABC TV) Karen Sisco, 2003—. With USN, 1943-46. Recipient Mystery Writers of Am. Grand Master award, 1992. Mem. Writers Guild of Am., Authors Guild, Mystery Writers of Am., Western Writers of Am. Roman Catholic. Address: care Michael Siegel 11532 Thurston Cir Los Angeles CA 90049-2427

LEONARD, FLORENCE IRENE, retired educator; b. Trenton, Apr. 12, 1934; d. Esau and Alverine (Arnold) Courtney; B.A., Trenton State Coll., 1968, M.Ed., 1979, supr./prin. cert., m. Henry L. Leonard, Feb. 21, 1953 (dec.); children: Guy Anthony, Carl Henry, Celeste Alverine, Troy Courtney. Librarian asst. dept. edn. N.J. State Library, 1960-64; tchr. Harrison Elem. Sch., Trenton, 1968-93, supr., 1981-93, asst. prin. Trenton (N.J.) Hedgepeth/Williams Mid. Sch., Trenton, N.J., 1993-96, disciplinarian, 1997-2000, ret., 2000; active Holy Temple Chs. of God in Christ, Phila. Mem. NEA, N.J. Edn. Assn., Trenton Edn. Assn., Mercer County Edn. Assn. Author: The Xerox Intermediate Dictionary, 1973; designer mural girls' dormitory for Chs. of God in Christ, Monrovia, Liberia, 1959. Home: 9 James Cubberly Ct Trenton NJ 08610-2722 Office: Harrison Sch Genesee St Trenton NJ 08611-1908 also: Trenton Bd Edn N Clinton Ave Trenton NJ 08609

LEONARD, GEORGE EDMUND, real estate agent, finance company executive, consultant; b. Phoenix, Nov. 20, 1940; s. George Edmund and Marion Elizabeth (Fink) L.; m. Gloria Jean Henry, Mar. 26, 1965 (div. Feb. 1981); children: Tracy Lynn McKinney, Amy Theresa Blanchard, Kristin Jean Steel; m. Mary C. Short, Sept. 22, 1990. Student, Ariz. State U., 1958-60; BS, U.S. Naval Acad., 1964; postgrad., Pa. State U., 1969-70; MBA, U. Chgo., 1973. Commd. ensign USN, 1964, advanced through grades to lt. comdr., 1975; v.p. 1st Nat. Bank Chgo., 1970-75; exec. v.p., chief banking, CFO, chief lending officer Mera Bank, Phoenix, 1975-90, also bd. dirs., 1982-90; pres., CEO Ctrl. Savs., San Diego, 1985-87; chmn., CEO AmBank Holding Co. of Colo., Scottsdale, Ariz., 1990-91, Consumer Guarantee Corp., Phoenix, 1996; pres., CEO Diversified Mgmt. Svcs., Inc., Phoenix, 1991-96, GEL Mgmt. Inc., Phoenix, 1991—; v.p. CFO Western Pacific Airlines, Colorado Springs, 1996-98, bd. dirs., 1996-98; exec. v.p., CFO, treas., sec., dir. fin. Radi Sys. Microware Sys. Corp., Des Moines, 1998—2002, COO, bd. dirs., 2000—01; sr. v.p., chief credit officer Harris Bank N.A., Scottsdale, Ariz., 2002—. Active Phoenix Thunderbirds, 1979—; bd. dirs. Maricopa C.C.s Found., treas., 2nd v.p., 1991-93, 1st v.p., 1993-94, pres., 1994-95, past pres., 1995-96, Camelback Charitable Trust, 1991-92, The Samaritan Found., 1993-96, chmn. fin. com., 1994-96, vice chmn., 1996; bd. dirs. Westminster Village, Inc., 2003—, sec., 2004—; bd. trustees Desert Bot. Gardens, 2004—; mem. City Scottsdale Housing Bd., 2005-. Mem. Phoenix Met. C. of C. (bd. dirs. 1975-82), Inst. Fin. Edn. (bd. dirs. 1980-87, nat. chmn. 1985-86), Ariz. State U. Coll. of Bus. Deans Coun. of 100, Paradise Valley Country Club (bd. dirs. 1991-98, treas. 1992-95, pres. 1995-97), White Mountain Country Club, Kiwanis. Republican. Roman Catholic. Office: Harris Bank NA 6720 N Scottsdale Rd Ste 111 Scottsdale AZ 85253 Home: 11113 E North Ln Scottsdale AZ 85259-4853 Office Phone: 480-951-4616. Personal E-mail: geljr@aol.com.

LEONARD, HERMAN BEUKEMA (DUTCH LEONARD), public finance and management and leadership educator; b. Carlisle Barracks, Pa., Dec. 26, 1952; s. Charles Frederick and Margery Alden (Beukema) L.; m. Kathryn Anne Angell, Oct. 9, 1983; children: Whitney Angell, Dana Angell. AB summa cum laude, Harvard U., 1974, AM, 1976, PhD, 1979. Asst. prof. pub. policy John F. Kennedy Sch. Govt., Harvard U., Cambridge, Mass., 1979-83, assoc. prof., 1983-86, George F. Baker, Jr. prof. pub. mgmt., 1986—, acad. dean for curriculum and instrn., 1992—96, acad. dean for teaching programs, 1996—2000; prof. bus. adminstrn. Harvard Bus. Sch., Harvard U., Cambridge, Mass., 2004—. Bd. dirs., Harvard Pilgrim Health Care, 2000—; mem. Gov.'s Coun. Econ. Policy, Alaska, 1980-82; chmn. Gov.'s Task Force on Coll. Opportunity, Mass., 1987-88; bd. dirs. Mass. Health and Ednl. Facilities Authority, 1988-99; mem. adv. bd. N.Y.C. Debt Mgmt., 1990-94; mem. Mass Performance Enchancement Commn., 1997-98. Co-author: Discrimination in Rural Housing, 1976, The Federal Budget and the States, 1993-99; author: Checks Unbalanced: The Quiet Side of Public Spending, 1986, By Choice or By Chance? Tracking the Values in Massachusetts Public Spending, 1992; contbr. numerous articles on pub. fin. and mgmt. to jours. in field. Bd. dirs. Hitachi Found., 2004—. Recipient grad. fellowship NSF, 1974; jr. fellow Soc. Fellows, Harvard U., 1976-79; Presdl. scholar, 1970. Mem. Phi Beta Kappa. Office: Harvard U John F Kennedy Sch Govt 79 JFK St Cambridge MA 02138-5801 Business E-Mail: dutch_leonard@harvard.edu.

LEONARD, J. WAYNE, energy company executive; BA in Acctg., Ball State U., 1973; MBA, Ind. U., 1987. CPA, Ind. Various positions PSI Energy, sr. v.p., CFO, 1989-94; group v.p., CFO, Cinergy, 1994-96, pres. energy commodities strategic bus. unit, 1996-98; pres. Cinergy Capital and Trading, 1996-98; pres., COO domestic bus. units, in-charge for internat. ops. Entergy Corp., New Orleans, 1998, CEO, 1999—. Leader BusinessLINC, Mississippi River Delta bus.-to-bus. mentoring. Mem. AICPA. Office: Entergy Corp 639 Loyola Ave New Orleans LA 70113-3125

LEONARD, JAMES JOSEPH, physician, educator; b. Schenectady, June 17, 1924; s. James Joseph and Helena (Flood) L.; m. Helen Louise Mitchell, Oct. 24, 1953; children: James Joseph, W. Jeffrey, Paul Mitchell, Kathleen Marie. MD, Georgetown U., 1950. Intern medicine Georgetown U. Hosp., 1950-51, jr. asst. resident, 1951-52, fellow cardiology, 1953-54; asst. resident medicine Boston City Hosp., 1952-53; resident pulmonary diseases D.C. Gen. Hosp., 1954-55, med. officer, 1955-56; instr. medicine Georgetown U. Med. Sch., 1955-56, Duke Med. Center, 1956-57; asst. prof. medicine, dir. div. cardiology Georgetown U. service D.C. Gen. Hosp., 1957-59; asst. prof. medicine U. Tex. Med. Br., Galveston, 1959-62; asso. prof. medicine Ohio State U. Med. Sch., 1962-63; dir. div. cardiology U. Pitts. Med. Sch., 1963-70, asso. prof. medicine, 1963-67, prof. medicine, 1967-77, acting chmn. dept., 1970, chmn. dept., 1971-77; prof., chmn. dept. medicine Uniformed Services U. of Health Scis., 1977—. Master ACP; mem. So. Soc. Clin. Investigation, Am. Clin. and Climatol. Assn., Central Soc. Clin. Research, Assn. Am. Physicians, Assn. Profs. Medicine, Assn. U. Cardiologists. Home: 4901 Connecticut Ave NW Washington DC 20008 Office: 4301 Jones Bridge Rd Washington DC 20008-2022 Office Phone: 202-977-3401.

LEONARD, JAMES KEVIN, mechanical engineer; b. Bklyn., Oct. 7, 1950; s. James Joseph and Virginia Isabel (Curtin) L. Student, Marquette U., 1969—73; AAS, NYC C.C., 1975; postgrad., Fordham U., 1976. V.p. Lencon, Bklyn., 1978, 1986—; technician Bd. of Higher Edn., Bklyn., 1979-81; safety engr. Dept. Housing, Preservation & Devel., Bklyn., 1982-83; asst. rschr. Bklyn. Hist. Soc., 1985. Author: (plays) Pictures, 1979, Siblings, 1985. Mem. Alpha Delta Gamma. Republican. Roman Catholic. Avocations: literature, tennis, swimming. Home: 2101 Bedford Ave Apt 6H Brooklyn NY 11226

LEONARD, JOHN FRANCIS, psychiatrist; b. LA, May 11, 1931; s. Albert and Jean Taylor Leonard; m. Barbara Jean Ferris, June 15, 1957; children: Deborah Ann, Elaine Marie, Meredith Lynn, Cara Lee. BA, UCLA, 1953, MD, 1957. Diplomate Am. Bd. Psychiatry and Neurology, Child and Adolescent Psychiatry. Gen. rotating intern U.S. VA Gen. Med. and Surg. Hosp.; resident in psychiatry UCLA/U.S. VA Neuropsychiat. Hosp., Brentwood, Calif.; pvt. practice L.A., 1963—; from clin. asst. prof. psychiatry to clin. assoc. prof. U. Calif., LA, 1978—2005, clin. prof., 2005—. Med. dir. Culver City (Calif.) Clinic, 1965-71, Westwood Hosp. Cmty. Psychiat. Ctrs., Inc., L.A., 1971-74; clin. dir. child/adolescent psychiatry Harbor/UCLA Med. Ctr., Torrance, Calif., 1990—. Capt. USAF, 1961-63. Mem. Phi Beta Kappa. Avocations: high sierra pack trips, fishing, skiing, trekking. Office: 14229 W Sunset Blvd Pacific Palisades CA 90272-3916 E-mail: leonardj@ucla.edu.

LEONARD, JOHN HARRY, advertising executive; b. N.Y.C., June 28, 1922; s. Frederick H. and Florence (Kiechlin) L.; m. Marjorie Jane Haslun, Oct. 19, 1946; children— John Kiechlin, Janet Ann. BS, N.Y. U., 1942, MBA, 1951. Advt. mgr. Autographic Register Co., 1946-47; promotion mgr. Macfadden Pub. Co., 1947-50; successively copywriter, account exec., v.p. and account supr. Batten, Barton, Durstine & Osborn, 1950-64; with DDB Needham Worldwide (formerly Doyle Dane Bernbach, Inc.), N.Y.C., 1964-87, group sr. v.p., 1972-87. Lectr. Grad. Sch. Bus., N.Y. U., 1959-61 Bd. dirs., past exec. com. Am. Bible Soc.; past chmn. bd. dirs. Wartburg Home, Mt. Vernon, N.Y.; trustee NYU, 1978-84. With USAF, 1943—46. Recipient Alumni Meritorious Service award N.Y. U., 1969 Mem. NYU Grad. Sch. Bus. Alumni Assn. (pres.), NYU Commerce Alumni Assn. (pres. 1979-80), Alpha Delta Sigma. Home: 310A Heritage Vlg Southbury CT 06488-1752 E-mail: johnleonard@charter.net.

LEONARD, JOHN MILTON, elementary school educator; b. Texarkana, Ark., Aug. 12, 1952; s. David Warren and Bernadine Leonard; m. Debra Ruth Newton, Oct. 17, 1980; 1 child, Jeffrey John. AA, Jefferson Coll., 1972; BS in Edn., S.E. Mo. State U., 1974; MA in Tchg., Webster U., 1983. Cert. tchr. elem. edn. Mo. Dept. Edn., 1974, tchr. reading Mo. Dept. Edn., 1983. Tchr. Sacred Heart Sch., Festus, Mo., 1974—76; instr., coach tennis Jefferson Coll., Hillsboro, Mo., 1976—78; tchr. Festus (Mo.) R-6 Sch. Dist., 1978; instr. tennis, desk clk. Concord Tennis Club, St. Louis, 1979—80; tchr. reading Blue Hills Homes Corp., St. Louis, 1980—2003, Nonpublic Ednl. Svcs., Inc., St. Louis, 2003—. Coach tennis Nat. Youth Sports Program Forest Pk. C.C., St. Louis, 1985—2000; coach basketball and baseball St. David Ch., Arnold, Mo., 1999—. Chmn. choir, musician St. David Ch., Arnold, Mo., 1982—2005. Named Coach of Yr., Forest Pk. C.C. NYSP, 1982, 1983. Mem.: Internat. Reading Assn. (assoc.). Avocation: tennis. Home: 2137 Thrush Arnold MO 63010 Office: Nonpublic Educational Services Inc 3700 Hampton Saint Louis MO 63109 Personal E-mail: adjleonard3_1@juno.com.

LEONARD, JOSEPH HOWARD, association organization executive; b. Cambridge, Md., Oct. 20, 1952; s. Joseph Francis and Catherine (Hill) L.; m. Jacquelyn Lee McCall, June 7, 1975 (div. Dec. 1981); m. Margaret Ann Shenton, June 26, 1982 (div. Dec. 2004); children: Stephanie Kristina, Jacquelyn Margaret. BA in Psychology, Salisbury State U., 1976; MA in Rehab. Counseling, Gallaudet U., 1979; postgrad., Washington Coll., 1984, Wasington Coll., 1988, U. Md., 1986—87, San Diego State U., 1996, Johns Hopkins U., 1998. Cert. profl. counselor, Md. Instr., program coord. Dorchester Devel. Unit, Inc., Cambridge, 1976—77; rehab. counselor Tex. Rehab. Commn., Austin, 1979; instr. Am. Sign Lang., develop. disabilities Chesapeake Coll., Wye Mills, Md., 1979—90; case mgr., coord. spl. programs Dorchester County Health Dept., Cambridge, 1979—90; ind. interpreter Am. Sign Lang. Md., 1979—; exec. dir. Deaf Ind. Living Assn., Inc., Salisbury, Md., 1990—2005; adj.faculty, interpreter tng. program Catonsville C.C., Md., 1995—2000; state coord. Deaf Svcs. divsn. Rehab. Svcs., Balt., 2005—. V.p. bd. dirs. Deaf Ind. Living Assn., Inc., Md., 1984-90; trustee Md. Sch. for the Deaf, 1985-2002, pres., 1996-97; mem. adv. bd. Devel. Disabilities program Chesapeake Coll., 1986-90; mem. Gov.'s Commn. on the Hearing Impaired, Md., 1984-90; surveyor Applied Rsch. and Evaluation U., U. Md., 1988-89; mem. mental health adv. com. for deaf and hearing impaired, Md., 1986—; mem. adv. coun. Office for the Deaf and Hard of Hearing, Md., 2001—, chair 2003—. Contbr. articles to profl. jours. Asst. scoutmaster Boy Scouts Am., Cambridge, 1973-78; v.p. bd. dirs. Dorchester County Family YWCA, 1985; pres. bd. dirs. Dorchester Assn. for Devel. Disabled, 1979-88; bd. dirs. Ea. Shore Ctr. Ind. Living, 1998-2005, v.p., 2003-04, Md. Assn. of Deaf, 1982-86; pres. Trappe Little League Baseball and Softball Assn., 2000-02. With USN, 1970-73, with USCGR, 1975-86. Recipient Founder's award Gallaudet U., 1993, Disting. Svc. award Md. Assn. of the Deaf, 1995. Mem. Am. Deafness and Rehab. Assn., Md. Rehab. Assn., Nat. Assn. Deaf, Registry of Interpreters for the Deaf (bd. dirs. Potomac chpt. 1996-2000), Chi Sigma Iota, Psi Chi, Rho Sigma Chi. Roman Catholic. Avocations: photography, boating, canoeing, sailing, scuba diving. Home: 32655 Meadowlark Ln Easton MD 21601 Office: Divsn Rehab Svcs Workforce and Tech Ctr 2301 Argonne Dr Baltimore MD 21218 E-mail: JHLDILA@aol.com.

LEONARD, JUDITH PRICE, educational advisor; b. Milw., July 10, 1941; d. Ralph H. and Sylvia (Shames) Price; m. Richard Black Leonard Jr., Dec. 15, 1962 (dec. Dec. 1978); m. Norman Crasilneck, Aug. 31, 1991. BS in Math., Antioch U., 1963; MS in Math., St. Louis U., 1970. Tchr. math. Ferguson Florissant (Mo.) Schs., 1963—94, coord., 1971—73; mentor, co-dir., faculty advisor Engelmann Math. & Sci. Inst., U. Mo., St. Louis, 1988—96; supr. student tchrs. U. Mo., St. Louis, 1995—96; coord. Regional Inst. Sci. Edn., St. Louis, 1996—2000; evaluator and cons. math. programs St. Louis Pub. Schs., 1994—2005; faculty advisor NSF Young Scholars, U. Mo., St. Louis, 1997, NSF Students & Tchrs. as Rsch. Scientists, U. Mo., St. Louis, 1998—99. Co-dir. Post Dispatch and Monsanto Greater St. Louis Sci. Fair, 1998—99; adv. bd. Greater St. Louis Sci. Fair, 1997—2005, Intel

Internat. Sci. and Edn. Fair, 1996—99, adults in charge, 1997—99, fair dir., 1999, mem. leadership coun., 2005; chair Discovery Young Scientist Challenge, St. Louis, 1999—2005; sec. exec. bd. Math. Educators Greater St. Louis, 2001—05; mem. Math. Sci. Network of Greater St. Louis, 1995—2005; math. cons. U. Mo., St. Louis, 2002—03; presenter, judge, chmn. judges for math. computer sci., physics and engring. Jr. Sci., Engring. and Humanities Symposium, 1995—2001, 2003—05; mem. leadership coun. Greater St. Louis Sci. Fair, 2005. Author: Word Problems, Basic Skills Instructional Fair, 1996; author, editor: (brochure) Teacher Linking Collaborative, 1997, 2002; editor 3 Math. Books, 2002, 5th and 6th Pre Algebra, 2002. Hon. Engelmann scholar Engelmann Math. and Sci. Inst., St. Louis, 1993, NSF Young scholar U. Mo., St. Louis, 1997; recipient Math. Edn. award Math. Educators Greater St. Louis, 1994, NSF STARS award U. Mo., St. Louis, 2000. Mem. NEA, Nat. Coun. Tchrs. Math., Mo. Coun. Tchrs. Math. (life), Ferguson Florissant NEA (life). Avocations: tennis, biking, walking. Home: 22 Bellerive Acres Saint Louis MO 63121-4321 Personal E-mail: judy@judyleonard.net.

LEONARD, KURT JOHN, retired plant pathologist, director; b. Holstein, Iowa, Dec. 6, 1939; s. Elvin Elsworth and Irene Marie (Helkenn) L.; m. Maren Jane Simonsen, May 28, 1961; children: Maria Catherine, Mary Alice, Benjamin Andrew. BS, Iowa State U., 1962; PhD, Cornell U., 1968. Plant pathologist Agrl. Rsch. Svc. USDA, Raleigh, N.C., 1968-88, dir. Cereal Disease Lab. U. Minn. St. Paul, 1988—2001. Author: (with others) Annual Review of Phytopathology, 1980; co-editor: Plant Disease Epidemiology, vol. 1, 1986, vol. 2, 1989, Fusarium Head Blight of Wheat and Barley, 2003; editor-in-chief: Phytopathology, 1981-84, Am. Phytopathol. Soc. Press, 1994-97; contbr. over 120 articles to profl. jours., chpts. to books. Fellow Am. Phytopathol. Soc. (coun. 1981-84, 94-97); mem. Am. Mycol. Soc., Internat. Soc. Plant Pathology (councilor 1982-93), Brit. Soc. Plant Pathology, Phi Kappa Phi, Sigma Xi, Gamma Sigma Delta. Achievements include description of new species and genera of plant pathogenic fungi; research on spread of disease through crop mixtures, on relationships between virulence and fitness in plant pathogenic fungi. Office: U Minn Dept Plant Pathology Saint Paul MN 55108

LEONARD, LAURA L. L., lawyer; b. 1956; AB, U. Calif., Davis, 1978; JD, Loyola U., Chgo., 1983. Bar: Ill. 1983. With Sidley & Austin, Chgo., 1983—, ptnr., 1991—. Lectr. on environ. aspects of bus. trans., including Northwestern U. Kellogg Grad. Sch. Mgmt.; mem. adv. bd. BNA's Environ. Due Digigence Guide. Office: Sidley & Austin Bank One Plz 10 S Dearborn St Chicago IL 60603 Fax: 323-853-7620. E-mail: lleonard@sidley.com.

LEONARD, MARKUS DAYLE, software systems engineer; b. Florence, Ariz., Apr. 12, 1964; s. Harold Lee and Lynda Mae L.; m. Shauna Morgan, Nov. 7, 1998. BS, Ariz. State U., 1987. Programmer analyst Motorola Semiconductor Products Sector, Phoenix, 1988-90, info. sys. engring. analyst Tempe, Ariz., 1990-92; sr. engr. computer integrated mfg. SEMATECH, Austin, Tex., 1992-94, Motorola, Tempe, 1994-96; tech. cons. Transarc, Pitts., 1996-98; mgr. Andersen Consulting, Overland Pk., Kans., 1998-2000; software engr. Sprint, Overland Pk., 2000—; dir. Reflections of Life Images, Inc., Olathe, Kans. Cons. Goldman Sachs, N.Y.C., 1997, Circadence, Boulder, Colo., 2000, SBC Comm., St. Louis, 2000, mem. working com. establishment of internat. software engring. standards; spkr. in field. Contbg. author, editor reports in profl. jours. Campaign fin. mgr. Kathryn Bailey for Ariz. State Legislature, 1996. Mem.: IEEE. Republican. Assembly of God. Avocations: photography, golf. Office: Sprint PCS 6000 Sprint Pky Overland Park KS 66210 Office Phone: 913-390-4888.

LEONARD, MICHAEL A., retired automotive executive; b. Cadillac, Mich., Aug. 3, 1937; s. Hugel A. and Mildred (Johnson) L.; m. Frances Erickson, June 18, 1960; children: Kristin, Anne. MA, Alma Coll., 1959; MBA, Wayne State U., 1964; MS, MIT, 1971. Exec. Chrysler Corp., Highland Park, Mich., 1959—75; group v.p. Bendix Corp., Southfield, Mich., 1975—83; v.p., group exec. Allied Signal Automotive, Bloomfield Hills, Mich., 1983—91; pres. Harman, Inc., Southfield, 1991—94; mng. ptnr. Exec. Resources Inc., Bloomfield Hills, 1994—2002. Bd. dirs. Kalyani Brake Co., Pune, India, Bendix France, Paris, Bendix Italy, and fgn. subs. Trustee Alma (Mich.) Coll.; chmn. Presbyn. Villages of Mich. Sloan fellow, MIT. Mem. Soc. Automotive Engrs., Delta Sigma Phi (pres. 1958-59). Presbyterian. Avocations: swimming, golf, boating. Home: 37215 S Summit Crest Ct Tucson AZ 85739-1438

LEONARD, MICHAEL STEVEN, industrial engineering educator; b. Salisbury, N.C., Feb. 2, 1947; s. Charles Thomas and Dorothy Francis (Loflin) L.; m. Mary Elizabeth Stewart, June 21, 1969; children: Dorothy Elizabeth, Amanda Brooke, Gabrielle Francis. B in Engring., U. Fla., 1970, M in Engring., 1972, PhD, 1973. Registered profl. engr., Mo., S.C. Asst. prof. health systems rsch. ctr. Georgia Tech, Atlanta, 1973-75; asst. prof. indsl. engring. U. Mo., Columbia, 1975-79, assoc. prof. indsl. engring., 1979-82, prof. indsl. engring., 1982-90, dept. chmn. indsl. engring., 1985-90; chmn. dept. indsl. engring. Clemson (S.C.) U., 1990—95, 2001—03; sr. assoc. dean Mercer U., Sch. Engring., Ga., 2004—. Bd. dirs. Accreditation Bd. Engring. and Tech., Balt., 1999—. Editor Jour. Soc. for Health Systems, 1989-91; contbr. articles to profl. jours. Evaluation adv. com. Am. Blood Commn., Washington, 1977-80; bd. dirs. Am. Cancer Soc. Boone County Mo. unit, Columbia, 1978-90. Mem. Soc. Health Systems (bd. dirs. 1989-94, pres. elect 1991-92, pres. 1992-93), Inst. Indsl. Engrs. (nat. dir. career guidance 1987-95, v.p. acad. affairs 1997), Mo. Soc. Profl. Engrs. (cen. chpt. treas. 1988-89, v.p. 1989-90). Office: Mercer Univ Sch Engring Macon GA 31207-0001 Office Phone: 478-301-2520. E-mail: leonard_ms@mercer.edu.

LEONARD, MONA FREEMAN, communications educator; d. Jack Robinson and Ruth Olivia Freeman; m. Jeffrey Allen Leonard, Oct. 27, 1989; 1 child, Jared Alexander. BA, Howard U., Washington, 1986, MA, 1989; postgrad., U. Ky., Lexington, 1994—97. Adj. prof. U. Louisville, 1991—2002; assoc. prof. Jefferson C.C., Louisville, 1993—2005, prof., 2005—, chmn., 2005—. Author (chpt.): Our Voices: Essays in Culture, Ethnicity and Communication, 2004. Mem.: Nat. Comm. Assn. Office: Jefferson CC 109 E Broadway Louisville KY 40202 Business E-Mail: mona.leonard@kctcs.edu.

LEONARD, NAOMI EHRICH, aerospace engineer, engineering educator; BSE, Princeton U., NJ, 1985; MS, U. Md., College Park, 1991, PhD, 1994. Engr. elec. power ind.; asst. prof., mech. and aerospace engring. Princeton U., 1994—99, assoc. prof., 1999—2003, prof., 2003—. Author: of numerous sci. jour. articles, including Journal of Dynamical Control Systems, Physica D, and Automatica. Named a MacArthur Fellow, 2004. Office: Dept Mech and Aerospace Engring Engring Quad Princeton Univ Princeton NJ 08544

LEONARD, R. MICHAEL, lawyer; b. Atlanta, Feb. 27, 1953; s. Charles C. and Catherine (Martin) L.; m. Margaret Ellen Mead, June 29, 1985 (div. 1993); 1 child, Sarah Marie; m. Michelle Merritt, May 27, 2001, 1 child, Eleanor Iris. AB, U. N.C., 1975, JD with honors, 1978. Bar: Ala. 1978, N.C. 1987. Assoc. Cabaniss, Johnston, Gardner, Dumas & O'Neal, Birmingham, Ala., 1978-85, ptnr., 1985-86; assoc. Womble Carlyle Sandridge & Rice, Winston-Salem, N.C., 1986-88, ptnr., 1988—. Author: Trail and Naturalist's Guide to Oak Mountain State Park, Alabama, 1982. Bd. dirs. Ala. Conservancy, Birmingham, 1981-85, Ruffner Mountain Nature Ctr., Birmingham, 1982-86, pres. 1985-86, Nature Sci. Ctr., Winston-Salem, N.C., 1987-91, Piedmont Land Conservancy, Greensboro, N.C., 1989-91; bd. dirs. Ala. Trails Assn., Birmingham, 1985—, founder, pres., 1985-87; trustee N.C. Nat. Heritage Found., Raleigh, 1989-92; gov.'s appointee bd. trustees N.C. Natural Heritage Trust Fund, 1994—, Ala. scenic Byways Program Adv. Coun., 2000-02; nat. adv. coun. Trust for Pub. Land, San Francisco, 1991—; mem. adv. coun. N.C. Yr. of the Mtns., 1995-96; mem. Nat. Coun. Conservation Fund, Arlington, Va., 1997—; pres. Bethania (N.C.) Hist. Property Owners Assn., Inc., 1996—; founding chmn. Ga. Pinhoti Trail Assn., Rome, 1996—; bd. dirs. Bethania Historical Assn., 1996—, Coalition for the Blue Ridge Pkwy, Asheville, N.C., 1997-2000, Bethabara Hist. Park, Winston-Salem, 2001—, Conservation Fund, 2004—; adv. coun. Blue Ridge Pkwy. Found., Winston-Salem, 1998—, High Country Conservancy, Boone, N.C., 1999-2003; bd. visitors Warren Wilson Coll., Black Mtn., N.C., 1999—, U. N.C., Chapel Hill, 1999—. Recipient Chevron Conservation award, San Francisco, 1998, Leon E. Rice Cmty. Svc. award, Winston-Salem, 1998, E-Town E-chievement award, Boulder, Colo., 1997, Pres.'s Conservationist of Yr. award Conservation Fund, Arlington, 1996, Oak Leaf award Nature Conservancy, Washington, 1991, Sol Feinstone Environ. award Coll. Environ. Sci. & Forestry, SUNY, Rochester, 1991, Chpt. Svc. award N.C. Chpt. Sierra Club, 1990, Malcolm Stewart Conservationist of Yr. award Ala. Conservancy, Birmingham, 1983, N.C. Wildlife Fedn. Environ. Essay award, 1970. Mem. Ala. Bar Assn., N.C. Bar Assn., Forsyth County Bar Assn., Winston-Salem Rotary Club, Carolina Club, Order of Coif, Phi Beta Kappa, Phi Eta Sigma. Democrat. Avocations: writing, hiking, mountain climbing, camping, turkey hunting. Office: Womble Carlyle Sandridge & Rice One West Fourth St Winston Salem NC 27101-4019

LEONARD, RICHARD DAVIS, minister; b. Detroit, Mich., Sept. 24, 1927; s. Richard Hovey and Frances Jane (Davis) Leonard; m. Barbara Louise Manzella, May 26, 1951 (div. 1968); children: Suzanne, Elizabeth; m. Anna Mary Barr, Apr. 4, 1970; stepchildren: Helen Louise Mason, Kenneth Mason, Martha Mason. BA, Yale Coll., 1949; MDiv, Union Theol. Sem., 1952. Min. Bethany Congl. Ch., East Rockaway, 1955—59; alum. affairs and devel. officer Walden Sch., N.Y.C., 1968—71; min. edn. Cmty. Ch. N.Y., N.Y.C., 1959—68; alum. affairs and devel. officer Horace Mann Sch., Bronx, 1971—75; min. Flatbush Unitarian Ch., Bklyn., 1968—78; alumn. affairs and devel. officer Columbia Grammar and Prep. Sch., N.Y.C., 1975—83; min. emeritus Unitarian Ch. All Souls, N.Y.C., 1979—. Author: (book) Call to Selma, 18 Days of Witness, 2002, Ports of Call, Journeys in Ministry, 2004. Violinist Riverside Orch., N.Y.C., 1972—97. Mem.: Liberal Religious Educators Assn., Nat. Soc. Fund Raising Execs., Yale Band Alumni (pres.), Assn. Yale Alumni. Independent. Unitarian Universalist. Avocations: music, chess instruction, lecturing on Rubik's cube, travel. Home: 142 West End Ave New York NY 10023 Office: All Souls Ch 1157 Lexington Ave New York NY 10021 E-mail: revdickleonard@hotmail.com.

LEONARD, RICHARD HART, journalist, educator; b. NYC, May 23, 1921; s. Richard Barstow and Stella Burnham (Hart) L.; m. Barbara Klausner, July 11, 1948; children: Laurie, Lisa. BA, U. Wis., 1947. Reporter Milw. Jour., 1947, picture editor, 1948, with Madison (Wis.) bur., 1949-50, state desk, 1951-52, state editor, 1953-62, mng. editor, 1962-66; editor, v.p. Milw. Jour. Co., 1967-85; ret., 1986; editor-in-residence East-West Ctr., Honolulu, 1987. Sr. fellow East-West Ctr., 1988-89; mem. Pulitzer Prize Bd., 1976-86; Nieman prof. journalism Marquette U., 1989-99, emeritus, 1999—. With AUS, 1942-46. Recipient Carr Van Anda award, Ohio U., 1972, Disting. Svc. award, East-West Ctr., U. Wis. Mem. Am. Soc. Newspaper Editors, Internat. Press Inst. (chmn. 1984-86), Milw. Press Club (pres. 1965, elected Hall of Fame), Sigma Delta Chi (nat. pres. 1976), Phi Kappa Phi. Presbyterian. Home: 330 E Beaumont Ave Milwaukee WI 53217-4867 Office Phone: 414-963-0598. E-mail: bkleonard@mixcom.com.

LEONARD, ROBERT HAIGH, theater educator, stage director; b. Williamstown, Mass., Aug. 20, 1942; s. Richard Lewis and Ruth Marsden Leonard; m. Deborah Ann McClintock, Sept. 5, 1983; children: Seth H, Tanya Cox, Brook Pyhtila. BA, Wesleyan U., 1965; grad studies in theatre, Catholic U. of Am., 1965—67. Stage mgr. Wash. Theatre Club, DC, 1968—70; founding artistic dir. The Road Co., Johnson City, Tenn., 1972—98; prof. theatre arts Va. Tech., 1989—. Founding bd. mem. Alternate ROOTS, Atlanta, 1976—; co-dir. Cmty. Arts Network, 1998—; founding bd. mem. Network of Ensemble Theatres, NYC, 2000—; bd. mem. Theater Commn. Group, NYC, 2002—. Co-chair Liberal Arts and Human Sciences Diversity Com., 2003—; chair Arts and Sciences Cultural Diversity Com., 1996—2000. Avocations: gardening, sailing, walking, theater. Home: 113 Southampton Ct Blacksburg VA 24060 Office: Va Tech Dept Theatre Arts Performing Arts Bldg 203 Blacksburg VA 24061 Office Phone: 540-231-9299. Business E-Mail: robert.leonard@vt.edu.

LEONARD, ROBERT SEAN, actor; b. Westwood, NJ, Feb. 28, 1969; s. Robert Howard and Joyce (Peterson) L. Stage debut in Oliver; stage appearences include Coming of Age in Soho, Sally's Gone, She's Left Her Name, 1985, The Beach House, Brighton Beach Memoirs, 1986, Breaking the Code, 1987, When She Danced, Biloxi Blues (tour), Romeo and Juliet, The Speed of Darkness, Our Town, Candida, Arcadia, The Invention of Love (Tony award for Best Featured Actor 2001), Long Days Journey into Night; film appearences include The Manhattan Project, 1986, My Best Friend Is A Vampire, 1988, Dead Poets Society, 1989, Mr. & Mrs. Bridge, 1990, Married to It, 1993, Swing Kids, 1993, Much Ado About Nothing, 1993, The Age of Innocence, 1993, Safe Passage, 1994, Killer: A Journal of Murder, 1996, Standoff, 1998, The Last Days of Disco, 1998, Ground Control, 1998, Tape, 2001, Driven, 2001, Chelsea Walls, 2001, The I Inside, 2003; TV movies include My Two Loves, 1986, Bluffing It, 1987, The Boys Next Door, 1996, In the Glooming, 1997, A Glimpse of Hell, 2001, A Painted House, 2003; TV series Corsairs, 2002-, House M.D., 2004-. Office: William Morris Agency 151 S El Camino Dr Beverly Hills CA 90212-2775*

LEONARD, SEAN TIMOTHY, psychologist, researcher; b. Columbus, Ohio, Jan. 1, 1972; s. John Timothy and Mary Dillon Leonard, Leo Winkelman and Janice Smith. BA with honors, Miami U., Oxford, 1993; MS, Nova Southeastern U., Fort Lauderdale, Fla., 1995, PhD, 2001. Lic. clin.psychologist Fla., 2002. Disting. undergraduate tchg. fellow Miami U., Oxford, Ohio, 1992—93; rsch. cons. Family Life Inst. HIV Prevention Project, Lauderdale Lakes, Fla., 1994—95; rsch. coord. Nova Southeastern U., Fort Lauderdale, 1995—98; treatment dir. REACH Sexual Offender Treatment Program, Davie, 1997—99; lead psychologist unit 27 Fla. State Hosp., Chattahoochee, 2000—02; rsch. specialist Broward County Pub. Schs., Fort Lauderdale, 2002—; pvt. practice rsch. and forensic clin. psychologist Fort Lauderdale, Fla., 2002—. Lead rschr., sexual decision making project Miami U., Oxford, Ohio, 1991—96; lead rschr. MMPI project Nova Southeastern U., Fort Lauderdale, Fla., 1995—98, adj. prof., 2003—; treatment dir. REACH Sexual Offender Treatment Program, Davie, 1997—99, rsch. dir., 1999—2000; ind. cons. in field, 2002—. Contbr. articles to profl. jours. Grantee, Albers Found., 2001; scholar Leader scholarship, Miami U., 1993; Crannell Rsch. grantee, 1991, 1992, 1993. Achievements include development of sexual offender treatment program inpatient and outpatient settings; adult mental retardation and psychosis inpatient treatment program; sexual behavior management and self-regulation inpatient treatment program; constrn. and devel. Broward County Benchmark Assessment Test (BAT); research in profiling and predicting future criminal behaviors among known sexual offenders; impact of sexual reasoning on high risk behaviors, relationship satisfaction, other psychological/behavioral factors over time; positive psychology interventions for enhancement of satisfaction in intimate relationships. Office: Fla Psychology Ste 307 915 Middle River Dr Fort Lauderdale FL 33304 Office Phone: 954-566-2166. Office Fax: 954-566-1186. E-mail: drsleonard@floridapsychology.us.

LEONARD, SUGAR RAY (RAY CHARLES LEONARD), retired professional boxer; b. Wilmington, N.C., May 17, 1956; s. Cicero and Getha L.; m. Juanita Wilkinson, Jan. 19, 1980 (div. 1990); children: Ray Charles, Jr., Jarrell Giulio. Profl. boxer, 1977-82, 84, 1987-91, 1997; pres. SRL Mgmt., Inc. With Franklin Sports Industries, Inc. Commentator boxing broadcasts; exercise video: Boxout with Sugar Ray Leonard, 1993. Recipient Gold medal Olympic Games, 1976; winner World Boxing Coun. Welterweight Championship, 1979, World Boxing Assn. Championship Jr. Middleweight div., 1981, World Boxing Coun. Championship and World Boxing Assn. Welterweight Championship, 1981, World Boxing Coun. Middleweight Championship, 1987, World Boxing Coun. Light Heavyweight and Super Middleweight Championship, 1988.

LEONARD, THOMAS, lawyer; b. Phila., Sept. 5, 1946; s. Thomas Aloysius and Mary Teresa (Kelly) Leonard; m. Kathleen Mary Duffy; children: Sarah, Mary Kate, Tom. BS, Drexel U., 1968; JD, Temple U., 1971. Bar: Pa., U.S. Supreme Ct., U.S. Ct. Appeals (3d cir.), U.S. Dist. Ct. (ea., mid., we. dists.) Pa., U.S. Dist. Ct. (so. dist.) N.J., U.S. Dist. Ct. Utah, U.S. Dist. Ct. (so. dist.) N.Y. Assoc. Dilworth, Paxson, Kalish & Kauffman, Phila., 1972-76, ptnr., 1976—79, 1983—91, sr. ptnr., mem. exec. com., 1979—83; controller City of Phila., 1991—; chmn. litigation dept., sr. ptnr., permanent mem. mgmt. com. Obermayer, Rebmann, Maxwell and Hippel, Phila., 1991—. Bd. dirs. Fed. Nat. Mortgage Assn., Independence Blue Cross, World Affair Coun. Phila., Cora Social Svcs., Pa. Bus. Bank, U.S. Facilities, Hahnemann Hosp.; chmn. Permalith Plastics. Mem. editl. bd. Amran's Pa. Practice, 1972; contbr. articles to profl. jours. Vice chmn. Phila. Gas Commn., 1979—83; register wills City of Phila., 1976—79; mem. disciplinary bd. Supreme Ct., Pa., 1991—95, vice chmn., 1995—96, chmn., 1996—, Delaware Valley Real Estate Investment Fund, 1999—; mem. coun. Phila. Orch., 1981—86; mem. Dem. Nat. Com., Washington, 1976—83, mem. fin. com., 1988, vice chair fin., 1993—, Pa. fin. chair, 1993—, bd. dirs.; del. Dem. Nat. Conv., 1976, 1980, 1992, 1996; chmn. Pa. fin. com. Clinton for Pres., 1992, 1996; co-chair Rendell for Mayor, 1991, 1995; bd. dirs. Acad. Scis., Phila., 1981—85; pres. Pa. chpt. Irish Am. Partnership. Capt. U.S. Army, 1971—77. Recipient Man of the Yr. award, Emerald Soc., 1979, Korean-Am. Friendship Soc., 1982, Carmel Humanitarian award, Haifa U., 1981, Merit award, Chapel of Four Chaplains, 1983. Mem.: ABA, Phila. Bar Assn. (bd. govs. 1979—82), Pa. Bar Assn., Sierra Club (past pres.), Racquet Club, Union League. Roman Catholic. Office: Obermayer Rebmann Maxwell and Hippel 1617 John F Kennedy Blvd Fl 19 Philadelphia PA 19103-1821 Office Phone: 215-665-3220. Business E-Mail: thomas.leonard@obermayer.com.

LEONARD, THOMAS, dean, librarian; BA (hon.), Univ. Mich., 1966; PhD, Univ. Calif., 1973. Libr. Univ. Calif., Berkeley. Spkr., cons. in field. Author: Above the Battle: War-Making in America from Appomattox to Versailles, 1978, The Power of the Press: The Birth of American Political Reporting, 1986, News for All: America's Coming of Age with the Press, 1995; contbr. numerous articles to profl. jours. Office: U Calif Berkeley Libr 245 Doe Libr MC 6000 Berkeley CA 94720-6000 Office Phone: 510-642-3773. Business E-Mail: tleonard@library.berkeley.edu.

LEONARD, THOMAS MICHAEL, university program director, educator; b. Elizabeth, N.J., Nov. 8, 1937; s. Edward Carroll and Amelia Teckla (Chap) L.; m. Yvonne Ann-Marie Clements, Aug. 13, 1960; children: Thomas Jr., Robert, Randall, Edward, David, Stacy. BS, Mt. St. Mary's Coll., Emmitsburg, Md., 1959; MA, Georgetown U., 1963; PhD, The Am. U., Washington, 1968. Sales exec. Weston Instruments, Newark, 1959-60; tchr. social studies Balt. County Bd. Edn., Towson, Md., 1960-62; instr. to assoc. prof. history St. Joseph Coll., Emmitsburg, 1962-73; assoc. prof. to prof., dir. internat. studies U. North Fla., Jacksonville, 1973—. Bd. dirs. N.E. Fla. Export Trading Co.; vis. prof. Inst. Advanced Studies, Guadalajara, Mex., 1978, Mt. St. Mary's Coll., Emmitsburg, 1979-84, U. San Diego, Guadalajara, 1992, U. Warsaw, Poland, 2002, Beijing Internat. Studies, 2003; Fulbright lectr. Inst. Juan XXIII, Bahía Blanca, Argentina, 1984; adj. instr. U. Fla., 1980—; cons. U.S. Dept. Edn., 1996-97. Author: Day By Day: The Forties, 1977, United States and Central America, 1944-49: Perceptions of Political Dynamics, 1984, Central America and United States Policies: Guide to Issues and Sources, 1985; author: (with others) Day By Day: The Seventies, 1988; author: Central America and the United States: The Search for Stability, 1991, Panama and the United States: Guide to Issues and Sources, 1993, Guide to Archival Material in the United States on Central America, 1994, The United States and Latin America, 1850-1903: Establishing a Relationship, 1998, Castro and the Cuban Revolution, 1999, James K. Polk: Clear and Unquestionable Destiny, 2001, Fidel Castro: A Biography, 2004, Encyclopedia of U.S.- Cuban Relations, 2004; contbr. chapters to books, articles to profl. jours. Grantee Fla. Endowment for the Humanities, 1976, Coun. for Internat. Exchange of Scholars, 1981, Fulbright Scholar, 1984, Coun. for Internat. Exchange of Scholars, 1985, Agy. for Internat. Devel., 1987, Breezewood Found., 1988, Fulbright Scholar, 1990, Franklin D. Roosevelt Presdl. Libr., 1991, US Dept. Edn., 1992, U. North Fla., 1993, US Dept. Edn., 1994, Andrew W. Mellon Found., 1994, Fulbright Scholar, 1997, US Dept. Edn., 1998, U.S. Dept. Edn., 1998—2003, John F. Kennedy Libr., 2000, Lyndon Baines Johnson Found., 2001, US Dept. Edn., 2001. Avocations: travel, reading, sports. Home: 1104 Pond View Ct Jacksonville FL 32259-2950 Office: U North Fla St John's Bluff Rd Jacksonville FL 32224 Office Phone: 904-620-1873. E-mail: tleonard@unf.edu.

LEONARD, TIMOTHY DWIGHT, judge; b. Beaver, Okla., Jan. 22, 1940; s. Dwight and Mary Evelyn Leonard; m. Nancy Louise Laughlin, July 15, 1967; children: Kirstin Dione, Ryan Timothy, Tyler Dwight. BA, U. Okla., 1962, JD, 1965; student, Mil. Naval Justice Sch., 1966. Bar: Okla. 1965, U.S. Dist. Ct. (no. and we. dists.) Okla. 1969, U.S. Ct. Appeals (10th cir.) 1969, U.S. Supreme Ct. 1970. Asst. atty. gen. State of Okla., 1968-70; mem. Okla. Senate, 1979-88; ptnr. Blankenship, Herrold, Russell et al, Oklahoma City, 1970-71, Trippet, Leonard & Kee, Beaver, 1971-88; of counsel Huckaby, Fleming et al, Oklahoma City, 1988-89; U.S. atty. Western Dist. Okla., 1988-92; judge U.S. Dist. Ct. (we. dist.) Okla., 1992—. Guest lectr. Oklahoma City U., 1988—89; mem. U.S. Atty. Gen.'s Adv. Com., 1990—92, chmn. office mgmt. and budget subcom., 1990—92, jud. conf. com. on fin. disclosure, 1998—, jud. coun. of 10th cir., 1999—2001, 10th cir. adv. coun., 2002—; adj. prof. Okla. U. Sch. Law, 2000—. Co-author: 4 Days, 40 Hours, 1970. Rep. Party candidate for lt. gov. of Okla.; minority leader Okla. State Senate, 1985-86; White House mil. aide, Washington, 1966-67; ex officio mem. Okla. State Fair Bd., Oklahoma City, 1987-90; mem. Gov.'s Coun. on Sports and Phys. Edn., Oklahoma City, 1987-89; mem. Donna Nigh Found., Edmond, Okla., 1987-9. Lt. USN, 1965-68. Named Outstanding Legislator, Okla. Sch. Bd. Assn., 1988. Fellow ABA; mem. Okla. Bar Assn., Okla. County Bar, Phi Alpha Delta, Beta Theta Pi. Republican. Presbyterian. Avocations: golf, basketball, running, reading. Office: US Courthouse 200 NW 4th St Ste 5012 Oklahoma City OK 73102-3031

LEONARD, VENELDA HALL, writer; b. Tifton, Ga., Jan. 7, 1914; d. Alonza Clayton and Bessie Lee (Shiver) Hall; m. James W. Leonard, June 14, 1931; children: James W. Leonard, Jr., Doris Delle Carr, Joan Le Mai Kyser. AA, Gulf Coast C.C., Panama City, Fla., 1964; BS, Fla. State U., 1965, MS, 1966. Instr. English, journalism Mosley H.S., Panama City, Fla., 1969-78; instr. remedial English Gulf Coast C.C., Panama City, 1979. Author: Sourwood, 1995. Mem. Phi Theta Kappa. Home: 2302 Country Club Dr Lynn Haven FL 32444-1994

LEONARD, WALTER RAYMOND, retired biology professor; b. Scott County, Va., July 5, 1923; s. Homer Stanley and Minnie Eunice (Neal) L.; m. Alice Ann McCaskill, Sept. 1, 1951; children— Leslie Ann, Walter Raymond. BA, Tusculum Coll., Greeneville, Tenn., 1946; MA, Vanderbilt U., 1947, PhD, 1949. Mem. faculty Wofford Coll., Spartanburg, S.C., 1949-93, John M. Reeves prof. biology, 1954-87, William R. Kenan Jr. prof. biology, 1987-93, William R. Kenan Jr. prof. emeritus, 1993—. Instl. rev. bd. mem. Spartanburg Regional Med. Ctr., 1994-98; faculty athletic rep. NCAA. Served with USAAF, 1942—43. Named to Sports Hall of Fame, Tusculum Coll., 1983; Walter Raymond Leonard scholarship created Wofford Coll., 1973; W. Ray Leonard award established Beta Beta Beta, 1993; W. Ray Leonard Retirement Fund established Former Students Wofford Coll., 1993, disting. citizen award Wofford Coll. Nat. Alumni Assn., 1999. Mem. AAAS, S.C. Acad. Sci., Scabbard and Blade (hon.), Lamda Chi Alpha (named to Hall of Fame 1996), Letterman's Club (hon.). Methodist. Achievements include rsch. on cell metabolism. Home: 110 Pinetree Cir Spartanburg SC 29307-2938 Office: Wofford Coll N Church St Spartanburg SC 29301 E-mail: wrleonard11@msn.com.

LEONARD, WILLIAM, food services company executive; BA, NYU. Pres., global food & support services Aramark Corp., Phila., 1993—96, pres., COO, 1997—2003, pres., CEO, 2004—. Office: Aramark Corp Aramark Tower 1101 Market St Ste 45 Philadelphia PA 19107-2988

LEONARD, WILLIAM NORRIS, economist, educator; b. Pitts., Dec. 13, 1912; s. Burt Hayes and Mabel Etta (Norris) L.; m. Elizabeth Flora Waugh, Aug. 24, 1939 (dec. Nov. 2004); children: Virginia Leonard Ewing, John Waugh. AB, U. Va., 1936; AM, U. Tex., 1938; PhD, Columbia U., 1945. Oil field worker Devonian Oil Co., Tulsa, 1930—32; instr., then asst. prof. econs. U. Conn., 1939—42; indsl. analyst, transp. officer WPB, 1942—45; asst. coord. planning Trans-World Airlines, Kansas City, Mo., 1945—46; assoc. prof., chmn. dept. econs. Rutgers U., 1946—49; prof. econs., head dept. econs. and commerce Pa. State Coll., 1949—53; chmn. dept. econs. and divsn. social sci. Hofstra U., Hempstead, NY, 1953—59, asst. pres., 1965—66; Fulbright prof. Haiti, 1974; prof., chmn. dept. econs. H. Lehman Coll., CCNY, 1974—78; ret., 1978; Disting. lectr. econs. U. South Fla., Tampa, 1978—79; vis. prof. U. Tampa, 1980—84. Cons. FTC, 1968, Senate Antitrust and Monopoly Subcom., 1969-74; pres. Fed. R.R. Progress, 1953-56. Author: Business Size, Market Power and Public Policy, 1969; contbr. articles to profl. jours Planning commr. Nassau County, 1962, chmn., 1963-65; mem. Hillsborough Area Regional Transit, 1979-90; bd. dirs. The Population Inst., 1997-. Mem. Am. Econ. Assn., Ea. Econ. Assn. (pres. 1984-85), UNA/USA (pres. Tampa Bay chpt. 2003), Rotary (gov. dist. 6950, 1986-87), Raven Soc., Phi Beta Kappa. Home: 1010 American Eagle Blvd Apt 408 Sun City Center FL 33573-7019

LEONARDI, LISA DIANA, secondary school educator; b. Bklyn, NY; d. Salvatore John and Constance Elizabeth Leonardi. M in music edn., Syracuse U., 1984; B in music edn., SUNY at Postdam, 1979. Cert. music tchr. and elem. tchr. K-12. Orch. tchr. Vernon-Sherill Sch., 1980—83; jr. high orch. tchr. William Floyd Sch., Mastic Beach, NY, 1984—86; mid. sch. orch. tchr. Shoreham Wading River, NY, 1990—2001; orch. tchr. Huntington H.S., NY, 2001—.

LEONARDS, KENNETH STANLEY, medical educator, researcher; b. Detroit, July 19, 1950; s. Stanley M. and Emily (Lukasik) L.; m. Royce Marie Hazard, June 2, 1980; 1 child, Amelia Royce. BA, Kalamazoo Coll., 1972; MS, Mich. State U., 1975, PhD, 1980. Assoc., postdoctoral fellow SUNY Med. Sch., Buffalo, 1980-82; NIH postdoctoral trainee U. Va. Med. Sch., Charlottesville, 1982-83, Am. Heart Assn. postdoctoral fellow, 1983-84; asst. prof. UCLA Med. Sch., 1984-90; msr. rsch. scientist Ciba Pharm. (now Novartis Pharm. Corp.), Cambridge, Mass., 1990-99; scientific data officer rsch. Novartis Pharm. Corp., Summit, N.J., 1999—. Mem. editorial bd. Molecular and Cellular Biochemistry, 1987-90; contbr. articles to profl. jours. Recipient New Investigator award NIH, 1985-88; fellow Dept. Energy, 1975-80; grantee NSF, 1971-72, Am. Heart Assn., 1986-89. Mem. Am. Chem. Soc., Am. Physiol. Soc., Biophys. Soc., Protein Soc. Avocations: hiking, fly fishing, chess, classical music. Office: Novartis Institutes for BioMedical Rsch Inc 400 Technology Square Rm 146 Cambridge MA 02139

LEONE, DEANNA JOSEPHINE, director; b. Reading, Pa., Sept. 10, 1977; d. Robert Charles Leone Sr. and Regina Joanna Leone. BA, Juanita Coll., Huntingdon, Pa., 1999; MEd, U. Mass., Amherst, 2001. Therapeutic support staff Skills of Ctrl. Pa., Huntingdon, Pa., 1997—99; residence dir. Juanita Coll., Huntingdon, Pa., 1998—99; asst. residence dir. U. Mass., Amherst, 1999—2001; residence dir. So. New Hampshire Univ., Manchester, 2001—03; assoc. mgr. for student life Boston U. Tanglewood Inst., Lennox, Mass., 2000—03; resident dir. Art Inst. of Seatt;e, 2003—. Named to Nat. Honor Soc., Muhlenburg H.S., Reading, Pa., 1995, Soc. for Acad. Achievement, 1994, 1995, Comm. Honor Soc., Juanita Coll., Huntingdon, Pa., 1999. Mem.: Am. Coll. Pers. Assn., Nat. Assn. for Student Affairs Profls. Democrat. Roman Catholic. Avocations: hiking, backpacking, marathon running, reading, skiing.

LEONE, JOSEPH M., finance company executive; BBA, CUNY; student in Mgmt., Harvard U. From mem. staff to sr. v.p., controller Mfrs. Hanover Corp., 1982—87, sr. v.p., controller, 1987—91; exec. v.p. Sales and Fin. Unit CIT Group, Livingston, NJ, 1991—95, exec. v.p., CFO, 1995—. Vice chmn. Children's Specialized Hosp. Found., Mountainside, NJ; bd. trustees Ramapo Coll. Found. Mem.: AICPA, Fin. Execs. Inst., N.Y. Soc. CPAs. Office: CIT Group 1 CIT Drive Livingston NJ 07039

LEONE, WILLIAM CHARLES, retired manufacturing executive; b. Pitts., May 3, 1924; s. Joseph and Fortuna (Sammarco) L.; m. Sara Jane Hollenback, Aug. 26, 1950; children: William Charles, David M., Patricia Ann, Mary Jane. BS, Carnegie Inst. Tech., 1944, MS, 1948, DSc, 1952. Asst. prof. engring. Carnegie Inst. Tech., Pitts., 1946-53; mgr. Indsl. Sys. divsn. Hughes Aircraft, L.A., 1953-59; v.p., gen. mgr., dir. Rheem Califone, L.A., 1960, Rheem Electronics, L.A., 1960-68; group v.p. Rheem Mfg. Co., 1968-71, exec. v.p. N.Y.C., 1971-72, pres., 1972-76, also dir.; pres. City Investing Co. Internat., Inc., 1972-76; pres., dir. Farah Mfg. Co., El Paso, Tex., 1976-77; bus. cons., 1977-79; acting vice chmn. McCulloch Oil Corp. (MCO), L.A., 1979-80, also bd. dirs.; pres., dir. MAXXAM Inc. (formerly MCO Holdings, Inc.), 1980-90; vice chmn. MAXXAM Inc., 1990-92. Chmn., CEO, dir. Pacific Lumber Co., 1986-90, Horizon Corp., 1984-89. Author: Production Automation and Numerical Control; contbr. articles to tech. jours.; patentee in field. Trustee Carnegie Mellon U., 1986-92. Lt. (j.g.) USN, 1944—46. Mem. ASME, IEEE, Am. Inst. Aerospace and Aeronautics, Sigma Xi, Tau Beta Pi, Pi Tau Sigma, Theta Tau, Pi Mu Epsilon. Home: 2209 Chelsea Rd Palos Verdes Peninsula CA 90274-2603 Personal E-mail: wcle@aol.com.

LEONE, WILLIAM J., prosecutor, lawyer; b. Trinidad, Colo., Oct. 16, 1956; s. John Valentine and Virginia Claire (Sexauer) L.; m. Cheryl Leone, 1978; children: Amanda, Victoria, Nicholas, Theresa. BA in Polit. Sci., Colo. State U., 1978; JD, U. Colo., 1981. Bar: Colo. Assoc. Sparks Dix Enoch Suthers, Colorado Springs, Colo., 1985-86; assoc., officer, dir. Ireland, Stapleton, Pryor, Denver, 1982-84; ptnr. Cooley Godward Castro, Denver, 1994—2001; first asst. US atty. dist. Colo. US Dept. Justice, Denver, 2001—, acting US atty., 2005—. Author: Immunity to a Direct Action: Is It a Defense, 1978. Active Colo. and Adams County Rep. Orgn., 1978—; bd. dirs. Cath. Cmty. Svcs., Colorado Springs, 1985; pres. Brandy Chase East Homeowner's Assn., Aurora, Colo., 1981-84. Mem. ABA, Colo. Bar Assn., Denver Bar Assn., El Paso County Bar Assn., Order of Coif, Denver Athletic Club, Phi Beta Kappa. Avocations: basketball, golf. Office: US Atty 1225 17th St Ste 700 17th St Plz Denver CO 80202*

LEONETT, ANTHONY ARTHUR, banker; b. Summit, N.J., Jan. 4, 1929; s. Joseph J. and Margaret (DiGuglielmo) L.; m. Ann Marino, Oct. 6, 1974; 1 son by previous marriage, Anthony Arthur. BS, Seton Hall U., 1950; cert., Am. Inst. Banking, 1956; postgrad., U. Wis., 1962. Mgr. First Nat. Bank & Trust Co., Summit, 1950-56; sr. v.p., auditor Nat. State Bank, Elizabeth, N.J., 1956-91; ret., 1991. Instr. principles of auditing and bank ops. Am. Inst. Banking; mem. faculty N.J. Data Processing Sch., Princeton, Bank Adminstrn. Sch. of U. Wis. Bd. dirs. N.J. affiliate Am. Heart Assn. With U.S. Army, 1951-53. Recipient Irving Grabiel award for outstanding leadership in banking, 1979 Mem. Am. Inst. Banking (dir. chpt.), Bank Adminstrn. Inst. (N.J. state dir. 1977-79, pres. N.J. chpt., dist. dir. 1979-81) Clubs: K.C., Minisink (Chatham). Republican. Roman Catholic. Home: 102 N Hillside Ave Chatham NJ 07928-2825

LEONETTI, MICHAEL EDWARD, financial planner; b. Oak Park, Ill., Aug. 23, 1955; s. Michael Louis and Dolores Mary (DiOrio) L. BA, St. Marys Coll., 1977. Cert. fin. planner, fund specialist; registered investment advisor. Sales rep. Metropolitan Life, Des Plaines and Rosemont, Ill., 1977-80; fin. planner Money Masters Inc., Buffalo Grove, Ill., 1980-82, Leonetti & Assocs., Buffalo Grove, 1982—. Instr. fin. planning Harper Coll., 1982-84. Author: Retire Worry Free: Financial Strategies for Tomorrow's Independence; adv. bd. Practical Fin. Planning; contbr. articles to profl. jours. Named one of Best Fin. Planners in U.S., Money Mag., 1987, One of Top Balanced Style Money Managers in U.S., 1992. Mem. Nat. Assn. Personal Fin. Advisors (pres. 1986-87), United Shareholders Assn., Internat. Assn. Fin. Planning (bd. dirs.), Inst. Cert. Fin. Planners (bd. dirs. 1986—), Registry Fin. Planning Practitioners, Investment Rsch. Inst. (cert. fund specialist), St. Mary Coll. Weight Lifting Club (pres., founder 1973-77). Republican. Roman Catholic. Avocations: golf, weight training, bodybuilding. Home: 4468 Kettering Dr Long Grove IL 60047 Office: Leonetti & Assocs 1130 W Lake Cook Rd Ste 300 Buffalo Grove IL 60089-1976

LEONG, ALBIN B., allergist, educator, pediatric pulmonologist; b. Astoria, Oreg, 1950; MD, U. Calif., San Diego, 1977. Resident Children's Hosp. of L.A., 1977-79; resident in pediat. U. Calif., San Diego, 1979-80, fellow in pediat. pulmonology, immunology and allergy, 1980-82; clin. asst. prof. U. Calif. Med. Sch., Davis; pediat. pulmonologist and allergist Sacramento Kaiser Found. Hosp. Office: Sacramento Kaiser Found Hosp Pediatric Pulmonology & Allergy 2025 Morse Ave Sacramento CA 95825-2115 Office Phone: 916-973-7342. Business E-Mail: albin.leong@kp.org.

LEONG, JONATHAN R., insurance company executive; BA, San Francisco State U. Pres. JLA Cos. Former consultant San Francisco Public Transp. Commn., Bay Area Rapid Transit Dist.; mem. Caltrans Small Bus. Adv. Council; delegate White House Conference on Small Bus., 1986, 95; commr. President's Adv. Commn. on Asian Am. and Pacific Islanders, 2000—02. Founding mem. Dem. Leadership Council, San Francisco, Asian Pacific Dem. Caucus, Nat. Council of Asian Am. Bus. Assn.; bd. dirs. Chinese Performing Arts Found.; former pres. Asian Am. Theater Co.; bd. mem. Calif. Small Bus. Admn.; founder, pres. Asian Am. Donor Program, 1989—. Recipient Excellence 2000 award, US Pan Asian Am. Chamber of Commerce. Office: JLA Cos 7700 Edgewater Dr Oakland CA 94621*

LEONG, STEPHANIE MEI, financial planner; b. Stockton, Calif., July 21, 1947; d. Edward G. and Ly H. (Ng) L.; m. Truman D. Wong, Aug. 24, 1969 (div. Mar. 1995); 1 child, Alexandra G.; m. Raymond Tom, June 17, 1995. BA, Mills Coll., 1970. Software cons. ComputerLand, San Francisco, 1983-86; trainer acctg. software Data Integrity, San Francisco, 1986-88; fin. cons. Shearson Lehman Bros., San Francisco, Larkspur, Calif., 1988-92, FN Investment Ctr., San Francisco, 1992-95; registered prin. Assoc. Securities Corp., Santa Rosa, Calif., 1995-99, Investment Architects, Inc., 1999—. Vol. Donaldina Cameron House, San Francisco, 1962-83; mem. fin. com. Santa Rosa Symphony Assn., 1996-2003, bd. dirs., 1998-2004; bd. dirs. Jr. League Napa-Sonoma, 1996-1997, San Francisco Opera Guild, 1998—; docent coun. Asian Art Mus., San Francisco, 2000—, bd. dirs., 2003—; alumnae admissions rep. Mills Coll., 2000-2003. Named to Golden Scale Coun., Putnam Investments, Boston, 1993. Mem. Internat. Assn. Fin. Planning, Kiwanis (bd. dirs. Santa Rosa, suburban chmn. interclub 1996-98, Outstanding Achievement award 1998). Presbyterian. Avocations: sailing, art, classical music, dance, travel. Office: Investment Architects Inc 2513 Saddleback Ct Santa Rosa CA 95401-0805 Office Phone: 707-526-2666. E-mail: stephanieleong@yahoo.com.

LEONHARD, MATTHEW BRENT, prosecutor; s. George Ludwig and Rubye Hannah Leonhard; m. Carolyn E. Eyestone, Aug. 10, 1997. BA in philosophy, West. Wash. U.; JD, U. of Wash., Seattle, 1997. Bar: Wash. 1997. Lead pub. defender Confederated Tribes of the Colville Reservation, Nespelem, Wash., 1997—99; chief prosecutor White Mountain Apache Tribe, Whiteriver, Ariz., 1999—2002; spl. asst. u.s. atty. US Atty Office, Phoenix, 2000—02; dep. pros. atty. City of Walla Walla, Walla Walla, Wash., 2002—, asst. city atty., 2004—. Recipient Outstanding Grad. in Philosophy, Western Wash. U., 1993. Mem.: ABA. Democrat. Office Phone: 509-522-2843. Personal E-mail: mbleonhard@hotmail.com.

LEONHARDT, CLIFTON ANDREW, lawyer, public information officer; b. New Orleans, Dec. 27, 1947; s. Robert Crawford and Mary Gay (Labrot) L.; m. Mary Alice Leonhardt, Dec. 18, 1988 (div. Jan. 2004); children: Theodore Lawrence, Christine Alexandra. AB with honors, Cornell U., 1969; JD cum laude, Harvard U., 1972; postgrad., Balliol Coll., Oxford (Eng.) U., 1972-73. Assoc. Robinson & Cole, Hartford, Conn., 1973-74; legis. counsel Com. on Govt. Ops., U.S. Senate, Washington, 1974-75; dep. sec. State of Conn., Hartford, Conn., 1975-78, state senator, 1979—83; dir. Atlantic Wood Industries, Savannah, Ga., 1978-85; assoc. Wiggin & Dana, New Haven, 1984-89; chairperson Dept. Pub. Utility Control, State of Conn., 1991-93; prin. de Fontenay, Savin & Kiss, Greenwich, Conn., 1994-95; chief counsel Freedom of Info. Commn., State of Conn., 1996—. Law lectr. U. Conn., Hartford, 1983—85. Contbr. articles to profl. jours. Del. Dem. Nat. Conv., San Francisco, 1984; bd. dirs. Conn.Correctional Ombudsman, Hartford, 1994—; corporator Renbrook Sch., West Hartford, 2000—05. Mem. N.Y. Yacht Club, Hartford Tennis Club, Phi Beta Kappa. Democrat. Episcopalian. Avocations: tennis, reading. Home: 46 Mountain Spring Rd Farmington CT 06032 Office: Freedom of Info Commn 18-20 Trinity St Hartford CT 06106 Office Phone: 860-566-3234 ext. 311. Business E-Mail: clifton.leonhardt@po.state.ct.us.

LEONHARDT, FREDERICK WAYNE, lawyer; b. Daytona Beach, Fla., Oct. 26, 1949; s. Frederick Walter and Gaetane Laura Leonhardt; m. Victoria Ann Cook, Dec. 27, 1975; children: Ashley Victoria, Frederick Whitaker. BA, U. Fla., 1971, JD, 1974. Bar: Fla. 1974, N.C. 1984, D.C. 1985; cert. real estate lawyer, Fla. Gen. cousnel Fla. Ho. of Reps., 1974-75; ptnr. Cobb, Cole and Bell, Daytona Beach, 1975-79; pres. Leonhardt & Upchurch, 1979-87; ptnr. Holland & Knight, Orlando, Fla., 1987-93, Gray Robinson, Orlando, Fla., 1993—. Chmn. bd. dirs. Orlando/Orange County Compact, 1989-90, Orlando/Orange County Civic Facilities Authority, 1998-2000; founder Leadership Daytona Beach; grad. Leadership Fla., mem. bd. regents, 1995—, chmn. state program, 1997-98, chair-elect 1999, chair, 2000-2001; active Leadership Ctrl. Fla., Leadership Orlando; past chmn. Ctrl. Fla. Sports Commn., bd. dirs., 1992-98; bd. dirs. Enterprise Fla.; mem. Orange County Civic Facilities Authority, 1998-2001; bd. dirs. Orlando/Orange County Conv. and Visitors Bur.; founder VCARD; past gen. campaign mgr. Volusia County United Way; bd. dirs. Celebration Health Found., Ctr. for Drug Free Living, Prevent Blindness Fla.; mem. Gov.'s Growth Mgmt. Study Commn.; exec. com. Floridians for Better Transp., 2000—; treas. U. Ctrl. Fla. Found., 2000—; bd. dirs. Econ. Devel. Commn. Mid-Fla., 2001—, Enterprise Fla.; mem. adv. bd. Ronald McDonald House. Mem.: ABA (chmn. state and local govt. law sect. 1997—98, editor sect. newsletter 1991—94), Fla. C. of C. (bd. dirs. 1984—90, 1993—, chair 2004), Daytona Beach Area C. of C. (pres. 1985), Greater Orlando C. of C. (chmn. 1991—92), Orange and Volusia Counties Bar Assn., Delta Chi, Phi Alpha Delta. Office: Gray Robinson PA PO Box 3068 301 E Pine St Ste 1400 Orlando FL 32801-2731 Business E-Mail: fleonhardt@gray-robinson.com.

LEONHARDT, THOMAS WILBURN, librarian, library director; b. Wilmington, N.C., Feb. 7, 1943; s. Thomas Beauregard and Rachel Virginia (Callicutt) L.; m. Margaret Ann Pullen, Sept. 19, 1966; children: Hilary, Thomas, Rebecca, Benjamin. AA, Pasadena (Calif.) City Coll., 1968; AB, U. Calif., Berkeley, 1970, MLS, 1973. Head gift and exch. div. Stanford (Calif.) U. Librs., 1973-76; head acquisition dept. Boise (Idaho) State U. Libr., 1976-79, Duke U. Librs., Durham, N.C., 1980-82; asst. univ. libr. U. Oreg., Eugene, 1982-87; dean librs. U. of the Pacific, Stockton, Calif., 1987-92; dir. tech. svcs. U. Okla. Librs., Norman, 1992-97; libr. dir. Oreg. Inst. Tech., Klamath Falls, 1997—2001; founding libr. Internat. U., Bremen, Germany, 2001; cons., 2002—; dir. Scarborough-Phillips Libr./St. Edward's Univ., Austin, Tex., 2002—. Editor RTSD Newsletter, Chgo., 1986-89, Info. Tech. & Librs., Chgo., 1990-95. Editor Advances in Collection Development and Resource Management, JAI Press, 1994-97, Internat. Leads, 2004-05; publisher, editor Callicutt Family Chronicle; contbr. articles to profl. jours. Bd. dirs. No. Regional Libr. Facility, Richmond, Calif., 1988-92, Feather River Inst. for Libr. Acquisitions, Blairsden, Calif.; del. Online Computer Libr. Ctr. AMIGOS Bibliog. Coun., Inc., 1996-97; chair Orbis Coun., 1999-2001; mem. Klamath Symphony, 1997-2001; chair Am. Libr. Assn. Com. on Accreditation, 2005—. Mem. ALA (chair com. on accreditation 2005—), Assn. Coll. Rsch. Librs., Libr. and Info. Tech. Assn. (pres. 1997-98), Assn. for Libr. Collections and Tech. Svcs., Ctrl. Assn. Librs. (bd. dirs. Stockton chpt. 1987-92). Democrat. Avocations: trumpet, guitar. Office Phone: 512-448-8470. Personal E-mail: twleonhardt@earthlink.net. Business E-Mail: thomasl@admin.stedwards.edu.

LEONI, TEA (ELIZABETH TEA PANTALEONI), actress; b. NYC, Feb. 25, 1966; m. Neil Tardio, Feb. 1992 (div. Oct. 1995); m. David Duchovny, May 6, 1997; Madeline West Duchovny, Kyd Miller Duchovny. Attended, Sarah Lawrence Coll. Actor (TV series): Santa Barbara, 1989, Flying Blind, 1992-93, The Naked Truth, 1995-98; (TV movies) The Counterfeit Contessa, 1994; (films) Switch, 1991, A League of Their Own, 1992, Wyatt Earp, 1994, Bad Boys, 1995, Flirting with Disaster, 1996, Deep Impact, 1998, There's No Fish Food in Heaven, 1998, The Family Man, 2000, Jurassic Park 3, 2001, Hollywood Ending, 2002, People I Know, 2002, House of D, 2004, Spanglish, 2004. Recipient Saturn Award, best actress for "The Family Man", 2001.*

LEON-PORTILLA, MIGUEL, historian, educator; b. Mexico City, Mex., Feb. 22, 1926; s. Miguel and Luisa (Portilla) L.; m. Ascension Hernandez Treviño, May 2, 1965; 1 child, Marisa. BA, Loyola U., L.A., 1948, MA, 1951; PhD, Nat. U. Mex., 1956; PhD (hon.), So. Meth. U., 1980; DHL (hon.), U. Tel Aviv, 1987, So. Calif. U., 1989, Toulouse U., France, 1990, Colima U., San Andres, 1994, U. La Paz, Bolivia, 1994, Brown U., 1996; PhD (hon.), U. Carolina, Prague, 2000, Calif. State U., San Diego, 2002, U. Iberoamericana, Mexico City, 2002, Cath. U., Peru, 2003. Sec. Interam. Indian Inst., Mexico City, 1955-58, asst. dir., 1958-60, dir., 1960-66; prof. faculty philosophy Nat. U. Mex., 1957—, dir. Inst. Hist. Rsch., 1966-76; researcher emeritus Inst. Hist. Rsch. Nat. Univ. Mexico, Mexico City. Sec.-gen. Internat. Congress Americanists, Mexico City, 1962; disting. lectr. Am. Anthrop. Assn., 1974. Author: La Filosofia Nahuatl estudiada en sus fuentes, 10th edit., 2001, Vision de las Vencidos, 18th edit., 2001, Broken Spears-Aztec Account of Conquest of Mexico, 10th edit., 1994, Aztec Thought and Culture, 1964, 20th edit., 2003, Le Crepuscule des Azteques, 1965, Trece Poetas del Mundo Azteca, 1967, Pre-Columbian Literatures of Mexico, 1969, Testimonios Sudcalifornianos, 1970, Religion de los Nicaraos, 1972, Time and Reality in the Thought of the Maya, 1972, The Voyages of Francisco de Ortega to California, 1932-36, 1972, Historia Natural y Cronica de la Antiqua California, 1973, Il Rovescio della Conquista, Testimoniaze Asteche Maya e Inca, 1974, Anthropology and the Endangered Cultures, 1976, New Light on the Sources of Torquemada's Monarchia Indiana, 1979, Native Mesoamerican Spirituality, 1980, Toltecayotl, Aspectos de la Cultura Nahuatl, 1980, The Natural History of Baja California, 1980, The Testaments of Culhuacan, 1984, La Pensèe Azteque, 1985, Time and Reality in the Thought of the Maya, 1988; editor: Monarquia Indiana (Father Juan de Torquenada), 1975, Hamnotzejim Jazon, 1976, Culturas en peligro, 1976, Indian Place Names in Baja California, 1977, Los manifiestos en nahuatl de Emilian Zapata, 1978, Native Mesoamerican Spirituality, Ancient Myths, Discourses, Stories, Doctrines, Hymns, Poems from the Aztec, Yucatec, Quichè-Maya, and Other Sacred Traditions, 1980, The Natural History of Baja California, 1980, Place Names in Nahuatl: Their Morphology, 1981, Fifteen Poets of the Aztec World, 1992, Aztec Image of Self and the Others, 1994, Tonantzin Guadalupe, 2000, El Retorno de Quetzalcoatl, 2002; (with Earl Shorris) In the Language of Kings, 2002, The Ancient Books of the New World, 2003, Antigua y Nueva Palara, 2004. Bd. regents Nat. U. Mex., 1976-86; amb. of Mex. to UNESCO, 1987-92, permanent del., Paris, 1987-92. Decorated Order of Great Cross, Alfonso X the Wise (Spain), Palmes Academiques (France), Great Cross Civil Merit, Spain, 2003; recipient Elias Sourasky prize in Humanistic Rsch. Mex. Sec. Edn., 1966; recipient Serra award of the Ams., 1978, Nat. prize in Social Scis. Govt. of Mex., 1981, Gamio award, 1983, Raphael Heliodoro Valle prize in History, 1984, Nat. U. Mex. prize, 1994, Alfonso Reyes Internat. prize, Mex., 2000, Menédez Pelayo Internat. prize, Santander, 2001, B. de las Casas prize, 2001, Thamatine prize, 2005; Guggenheim fellow, 1969; Fulbright fellow, 1975. Mem. NAS (fgn.), Mex. Acad. History (pres. 1996), Royal Spanish Acad. Lang., Smithsonian Coun., Am. Hist. Assn. (hon.), Sociètè des Americanistes de PAris, Inst. Different Civilizations, Sociedad Mexicana de Antropologia, Am. Anthrop. Assn., El Colegio Nacional Mex., Royal Acad. Letters of Extremadura, Nat. Acad. of Sci., Wash., DC. Home: Coyoacán 103 Alberto Zamora 04000 Mexico City Mexico Office: Ciudad U Inst de Investig Históricas 04510 Mexico City Mexico Fax: (52) 56 65 00 70. Office Phone: 52 55 5665 4417. Business E-Mail: portilla@servidor.unam.mx.

LEONSIS, TED, media executive, professional sports team executive; b. Bklyn., Jan. 8, 1956; BA magna cum laude, Georgetown U., 1976; postgrad., Suffolk U. Law Sch., 1980. Copywriter, advt. mgr. Wang Labs., Inc., 1976-78, corp. publicity/pub. rels. dir., 1978-81; dir. mktg. comm. Harris Corp., Melbourne, Fla., 1981-83; founder, CEO Redgate Pub. Co., Vero Beach, Fla., 1983—, also dir.; founder, CEO Redgate Comm. Corp., 1986-94; pres. Am. Online Svcs. Co., Vienna, Va., 1994-96, vice chmn., pres. AOL audience bus., 2002—; pres., CEO AOL Studios, Vienna, 1996—; majority owner Washington Capitals; founder Lincoln Holdings; minority shareholder Washington Wizards. Founder Collegiate Entrepreneurs Fund; dir. Preview Travel Inc., Thrive, Interzine, The Hub, Digital City, Planet Out, Tribune Interactive, Best Buddies, Georgetown U. Internat. TV & Radio Soc., Brevard Venture Fund. Chmn. Author: Software Master for the IBM Pc, Mastering the IBM Assistant Series, Software Master for PFS, Blue Magic; pub. The Macintosh Buyer's Guide, Apple II Rev., The Apple IIGS Buyer's Guide, COMPAQ, FYI, The Harris Mag. ofr INfo. Mgmt.; contbr. articles to profl. jours. Chmn. United Fund campaign, Wang Labs. Inc., 1980; bd. dirs. Big Bros. Brevard County, 1981, Brevard Art Ctr. and Mus., Brevard Coun. of Arts, 1981, Juvenile Employment Project, Lowell, Mass., Merrimack Regional Theatre. Named one of entrepreneurs of yr. Chivas Regal, 1989, one of 200 global leaders of tomorrow World Econ. Forum, 1993; recipient Andrew Heiskell Community Service Award. Mem. Pub. Rels. Soc. Am. (cert.), Publicity Club Boston, Bus. Profl. Advt. Adminstrs., Am. Mktg. Assn. Office: AOL Studios 490 Sea Oak Dr Vero Beach FL 32963-3245 also: c/o Washington Capitals 401 9th St NW Ste 750 Washington DC 20004-2132*

LEOPOLD, A. CARL, plant physiologist; BA, U. Wis., 1941; MA, Harvard U., 1947, PhD, 1948; DSc (hon.), Purdue U., 1997. Prof. horticulture Purdue U., West Lafayette, Ind., 1949-74; sr. policy analyst NSF, 1974-75; dean Grad. Coll. U. Nebr., 1975-77; W. C. Crooker Disting. scientist Boyce Thompson Inst., 1977-90, scientist emeritus, 1990—. Am. Soc. of Plant Physiol. (Charles Reid Barnes Life Membership award 1994). Office: Cornell U Boyce Thompson Inst Ithaca NY 14853 E-mail: acl9@cornell.edu.

LEOPOLD, LUNA BERGERE, geology educator; b. Albuquerque, Oct. 8, 1915; BS, U. Wis., 1936, DSc (hon.), 1985; MS, UCLA, 1944; PhD, Harvard, 1950; D Geography (hon.), U. Ottawa, 1969; DSc (hon.), Iowa Wesleyan Coll., 1971, St. Andrews U., 1981, U. Murcia, Spain, 1988. With Soil Conservation Service, 1938-41, U.S. Engrs. Office, 1941-42, U.S. Bur. Reclamation, 1946; head meteorologist Pineapple Research Inst. of Hawaii, 1946-49; hydraulic engr. U.S. Geol. Survey, 1950-71, chief hydrologist, 1957-66, sr. research hydrologist, 1966-71; prof. geology U. Calif. at Berkeley, 1973—. Author (with Thomas Maddock, Jr.): The Flood Control Controversy, 1954; author: Fluvial Processes in Geomorphology, 1964, Water, 1974; author: (with Thomas Dunne) Water in Environmental Planning, 1978; author: A View of the River, 1994, Water, Rivers and Creeks, 1997, also tech. papers. Capt. air weather svc. USAF, 1942—46. Recipient Disting. Svc. award, Dept. of Interior, 1958, Veth medal, Royal Netherlands Geog. Soc., 1963, Cullum Geog. medal, Am. Geog. Soc., 1968, Rockefeller Pub. Svc. award, 1971, Busk medal, Royal Geog. Soc., 1983, Berkeley citation, U. Calif., David Linton award, Brit. Geomorphol. Rsch. Group, 1986, Linsley award, Am. Inst. Hydrology, 1989, Caulfield medal, Am. Water Resources Assn., 1991, Nat. Medal Sci., NSF, 1991, Palladium medal, Nat. Audubon Soc., 1994, Joan Hodges Queneau Palladium medal, Am. Assn. Engring. Socs., 1994. Mem.: Am. Philos. Soc., Am. Acad. ARts and Scis., Am. Geol. Inst. (Ian Campbell medal), Am. Geophys. Union (Robert E. Horton medal 1993), Geol. Soc. Am. (pres. 1972, Kirk Bryan award 1958, Disting. Career award geomorphological group 1991, Penrose medal 1994), ASCE (Julian Hinds award), NAS (Warren prize), Cosmos Club (Washington), Phi Kappa Phi, Sigma Xi, Chi Epsilon, Tau Beta Pi. Office: U Calif Dept Geology Berkeley CA 94720-0001 Home: 400 Vermont Ave Berkeley CA 94707

LEOPOLD, MARK F., lawyer; b. 1950; s. Paul F. and Corinne (S.) L.; m. Jacqueline Rood, June 9, 1974; children: Jonathan, David. BA, Am. U., Washington, 1972; JD, Loyola U., 1975. Bar: Ill. 1975, U.S. Dist. Ct. (no. dist.) Ill. 1975, Fla. 1976, U.S. Ct. Appeals (7th cir.) 1976, U.S. Ct. Appeals (8th cir.) 1979, U.S. Supreme Ct., 2003. Assoc. McConnell & Campbell, Chgo., 1975-79; atty. U.S. Gypsum Co., Chgo., 1979-82, sr. litigation atty., 1982-84, USG Corp., Chgo., 1985-87, corp. counsel, 1987, sr. corp. counsel, 1987-89; asst. gen. counsel G.D. Searle & Co., 1989-93, Household Internat., Inc., Prospect Heights, Ill., 1993—2004; dep. gen. coun. HSBC Fin. Corp., Prospect Heights, Ill., 2004—; asst. gen. counsel HSBC N.Am. Holdings Inc., 2004—. Mem. adv. bd. Roosevelt U. Legal Asst. Program, 1994-2000; legal writing instr. Loyola U. Sch. Law, Chgo., 1978-79. Pres., bd. dirs. Internat. Policyholders Assn., 1992-93; del. candidate Rep. Nat. Conv., 1996; mem. Lake County Study Commn. II, Waukegan, Ill., 1989-90; commr. Lake County, Waukegan, 1982-84, Forest Preserve, Libertyville, Ill., 1982-84, Pub. Bldg. Commn., Waukegan, 1980-82; chmn. Deerfield Twp. Rep. Cen. Com., Highland Park, Ill., 1984-86, officer, 1981-89; vice chmn. Lake County Rep. Cen. Com., Waukegan, 1982-84; bd. dirs. Am. Jewish Com., Chgo., 1988-91; bd. dirs. A Safe Place, Lake County, Ill., 2001—, treas., 2004—, chmn. fin. com., 2004—; chmn. amicus sub-com. Civil Justice Reform, bus. round table, 2002-05 Recipient Disting. Svc. award Jaycees, Highland Park, 1983. Mem. ABA, (antitrust com. 1976—, litigation com. 1980—, torts and ins. practice com. 1989—), Pi Sigma Alpha, Omicron Delta Kappa. Republican. Office: HSBC-NAm 2700 Sanders Rd Prospect Heights IL 60070-2701

LEPAGE, CLIFFORD BENNETT, JR., lawyer; b. Reading, Pa., May 17, 1944; s. Clifford B. and Minnie H. (Himmelreich) LeP.; m. Elleen M. McCullough, Mar. 6, 1970; children: Clifford III, Alexander P. AB, Brown U., 1966; JD, U. Pa., 1969. Bar: Pa. 1969, U.S. Dist. Ct. (ea. dist.) Pa., 1970. Ptnr. Austin, Boland, et al, Reading, Pa., 1969—. Bd. mem. Family Guidance, Reading. Mem. Pagoda Pacers Running Club. Unitarian Universalist. Avocations: running distance races, college basketball, bridge, travel. Home: 10 Phoebe Dr Wyomissing PA 19610-2857 Office: Austin Boland et al PO Box 8521 Reading PA 19603-8521 Office Phone: 610-374-8211.

LEPAGE, ROBERT, actor, playwright; b. Quebec City, Canada, 1957; Cert. in acting, Conservatoire d'Art Dramatique, Quebec, 1978; studied with Alain Knapp, Paris, 1978; PhD in Arts (hon.), Univ. Laval, Que., 2019; PhD in Lit. (hon.), McGill U., Montreal, 1997, U. Toronto, 1997; PhD in Law (hon.), Concordia U., Monteal, 2019. Actor Ligue Nationale d'Improvisation, 1984—88; artistic co-dir., actor Théâtre Repère, 1986—89; founder, pres. Robert Lepage Inc., 1988; artistic dir. French theatre Nat. Arts Ctr., Ottawa, 1989—93; founder, pres., artistic dir. Ex Machina, Que., 1994—, In Extremis Images, Inc., Montreal, 1995; founder La Caserne Dalhousie, 1997; v.p. Ex Aqueo Films Inc., 2004. Dir. Nat. Theatre Sch. Can., Montreal, 1990—91; gen. commr. Le Printemps du Québec en France, 1999; cons. New Millennium Dome Experience, 1999. Dir., set designer Et Drömspel, 1994, dir., actor (adapted French version) Elseneur, 1995, writer, dir., actor (one-man shows) Needles and Opium, 1991, La face cachée de la Lune, 2000, (films) Far Side of the Moon, 2003, (plays) Le projet Andersen, 2005; dir.: Los Cincos soles, 1991, Macbeth, 1992, (French version) La Tempête, 1992, A Midsummer Night's Dream, 1992, Alanienouidet, 1992, Le cycle de Shakespeare: Macbeth, Coriolan et La tempête, 1992, National Capitale Nationale, 1993, (Japanese version) Macbeth and La Tempête, 1993, Shakespeare's Rapid Eye Movement, 1993, Noises, Sounds and Sweet Airs, 1994, Le songe d'une nuit d'été, 1995, (Japanese version) The Polygraph, 1996, (adapted English version) Elsinore, 1997, (Swedish version) La Celestina, 1998, (Spanish version), 2004, Kindertotenlieder, 1998, La tempête, 1998, Jeanssans-mom, 1999, Zulu Time, 1999, (original French version) La Casa Azul, 2001; co-writer, dir. La géométrie des miracles, 1998, The Seven Streams of the River Ôta, 1994, (Spanish and Italian versions) The Polygraph, 2000, La trilogie des dragons, 2003, co-writer, dir., actor Les plaques tectoniques, 1991, numerous other plays; actor: (TV series) Court-circuit, 1984, Les grands Esprits, 1987; (films) Jesus de Montreal, 1988, Montreal vu par..., 1991, Ding et Dong, le film, 1992, Stardom, 2000; player Ligue Nationale d'Improvisation, 1984; dir.: Le groupe Sanguin, prise I, 1986, Le groupe Sanguin, prise II, 1987, (ads) Loto-Quebec, 1988, Syndicat de la Fonction Publique du Quebec, 1988, (video) Diane Dufrene's L'Enfant lumière, 1999; (films) Possible Worlds, 2000; (Operas) Bluebeards Castle, 1992, Erwartung, 1992, Die Dreigroschenoper, 2002, The Busker's Opera, 2004, 1984, 2005, Peter Gabriel's Secret World Tour, 1993, Peter Gabriel's Growing Up Tour, 2002; stage dir. La damnation de Faust, 1999, creator, dir. KÀ, 2004, co-writer, actor (films) Suspect No. 1, 1989, scriptwriter, dir. (screenplays) The Confessional, 1995, The Polygraph, 1996, Nô, 1997. Nominee Oscar for Best Fgn. Lang. Feature Film, 2004; recipient Pierre Curzi trophy, Ligue Nationale d'Improvisation, 1985, Profil du Public award, 1986, O'Keefe trophy, 1987, People's Choice award, La Presse Newspaper, Montreal, 1985, Best Directing award, Fondation de Théâtre du Trident, 1986, Conseil de la culture de Quebec award, Vinci, 1986, Best dir., best prodn., best sound realization awards, Que. Theatre Critics Assn., 1986, Best Show of Yr. award, 1987, Nat. Bank award, 1992, Best Show of Yr. award, Le Cercle des critiques de la Capitale, 1987, Grand prize, Festival de Théâtre des Amériques, 1987, Coup de Pouce award, 1987, Dora Mavor Moore award, Toronto Theatre Alliance, 1988, Dora Maver Moore award, 1990, Gascon-Roux award, 1988, 1989, 2003, Knight of the Order of Arts and Lit., Le Ministère de la Culture, 1990, Floyd S. Chalmers award, 1991, 1995, award, Nat. Arts Ctr., 1994, Genie award for best motion picture, 1995, Officer of Order of Can., Gov. Gen. Can., 1995, Best Screenplay award, SARDEC, 1996, Internat. Critics award, Istanbul Internat. Film Festival, 1997, City TV award, Toronto Internat. Film Festival, 1998, Best Can. Film award, Sudbury's Internat. Film Festival, 1999, Spl. Jury award, La Semana de Cine exptl. de Madrid, 2001, Chevalier of Legion of Hon., French Embassy, 2002, Queen's Golden Jubilee medal, Dept. Can. Heritage, 2002, Prix Denise-Pelletier, 2003, Hans Christian Andersen prize, 2004, Bayard d'Or, 19th Namur Internat. French-Speaking Film Festival, 2004, Audience prize, Festival of Theatre Spotkania, 2004, Cooper Wing award, Phoenix Film Festival, 2005, numerous others. Fax: 418-692-5400. Business E-Mail: rli@exmachina.qc.ca.

LEPELEY, MARIA-TERESA, educational association administrator; d. Enrique Lepeley and Manola Gonzalez; m. Eduardo Bancalari, Mar. 4, 1967 (div. Nov. 31, 1988); children: Eduardo Enrique Bancalari Jr., Claudia Andrea Bancalari. B in Edn. and English, U. Santiago, Chile, 1966; MS in Edn., U. Miami, Coral Gables, 1981, MA in Econs., 1987. Cert. quality examiner Nat. Inst. Stds. and Tech. Rsch. asst. dept. econs. U. Miami, Coral Gables, 1984—87; prof., dir. econs. divsn. dept. econs. U. Chile, Santiago, 1995—99; pres. Inst. Entrepreneurial Edn., Santiago, 1998—99; dir. Internat. Inst. U. Conn., Hartford, 2000—03; pres., founder Global Inst. for Quality Edn., Orlando, 2003—. Examiner Malcolm Baldrige Nat. Quality Award, Washington, 2002—. Author: Quality Management in Education. A Model for Assessment. Recipient grad. assistantship, U. Miami, 1984—86; Ann. Conf. fellow, Coleman Found., 2002—03. Master: Miami Bus. Economists Assn. (pres. 1990—91); fellow: Chile-U.S. C. of C. (dir. 1990—94); mem.: U.S. Small Bus. and Entrepreneurial Assn., Acad. Mgmt. (corr.; reviewer), Am. Assn. for Quality. Republican. Roman Catholic. Avocations: arts, travel, swimming, reading, dancing. Office Phone: 569-355-1757. E-mail: mtlepeley@globalqualityeducation.org.

LEPKE, CHARMA DAVIES, musician, educator; b. Delavan, Wis., Oct. 1, 1919; d. Ithel B. and Florence Mary (Jones) Davies; m. John Richard Lepke, Dec. 22, 1949 (div. July 1974). BA, Wellesley Coll., 1941, MA, 1942; MMusic, Am. Conservatory of Music, Chgo., 1946. Piano tchr., organist Fairfax Hall Jr. Coll., Waynesboro, Va., 1942-44; piano tchr. U. Nebr., Lincoln, 1946-50; ch. organist Trinity Methodist, Unitarian, Lincoln, 1946-50; missionary Am. Bd. Congl. Ch., Durban, Johannesburg, South Africa, 1950-56; ch. organist, choir dir. Congl. United Ch. of Christ, Oconomowoc/Sheboygan, Wis., 1957-70; organist Coloma, Mich., 1970-73; ch. organist Brick Bapt. Ch., Walworth, Wis., 1974, United Meth. Ch., Delavan, 1974-77, Congl. United Ch. of Christ, Delavan, 1977—; with Walworth County Arts Coun. Music editor revised Zulu hymnal Amagama Okuhlabalela, South Africa, 1951-56; composer preludes for organ, piano pieces, song and anthem. Recipient 1st prize for song Wis. Fedn. Music Clubs, 1960, others. Mem. Am. Guild of Organists, Music Tchrs. Nat. Assn., Wis. Alliance for Composers, Delavan Musical Arts Soc. (founder, pres.), Phi Beta Kappa. Congregationalist. Home: 223 W Geneva St Delavan WI 53115-1626

LEPKOWSKI, WIL (WILBERT CHARLES LEPKOWSKI), journalist; b. Salem, Mass., Sept. 3, 1934; s. Charles J. and Alice (Bartnicki) L.; m. Jane Littlefield, Oct. 28, 1961 (div. May 1975); children: David E., Rebecca A., Thomas M.C.; m. Helene Kay Hollander, Feb. 4, 1984; 1 child, Katherine Angela. BS in Chemistry, U. Mass., 1956; MS in Biochemistry, Ohio State U., 1961. Asst. chemist Doeskin Products Inc., Easthampton, Mass., 1956; asst. editor Chem. Abstracts Svcs., Columbus, Ohio, 1956—58; reporter UP Internat., Columbus, 1960, Providence Jour.-Bull., Westerly, RI, 1961; sci. writer Johns Hopkins Med. Instn., Balt., 1961—63, Newhouse Newspapers, Washington, 1963—65; head bur. S.E. Chem. & Engring. News, Washington, 1965—69, sr. corr., 1977—99, contbg. editor, 1999—2003; sci. corr. Bus. Week, Washington, 1969—75; free-lance writer, cons., 1975—77. Adj. prof. sci. and tech. studies Va. Poly. and State U., 2002—; journalist in residence Columbia U. Ctr. for Sci., Policy and Outcomes, 1999—2003. Contbr. articles to jours. in field. Sloan/Rockefeller fellow Advanced Sci. Writing Prgram, Columbia U. Grad. Sch. Journalism, 1959-60. Fellow AAAS; mem. Nat. Press Club, Nat. Assn. Sci. Writers, Am. Sci. Affiliation, Latin Am. Parents Assn., Mended Hearts. Roman Catholic. Avocations: natural history, geography, poetry, spiritual reading. E-mail: willep@comcast.net. *Tell the truth.*

L'EPLATTENIER, NORA SWEENY HICKEY, nursing educator; b. N.Y.C., Mar. 16, 1945; 1 child, Brendan Sweeny Hickey. Diploma, Bellevue Mills Sch. Nursing, 1965; BS in Health Sci. summa cum laude, Bklyn. Coll., 1978; MS in Psychiat.-Mental Health Nursing, Adelphi U., 1982, PhD, 1988. RN N.Y., cert. clin. specialist in adult psychiat. mental health, in group psychotherapy, lic. nurse practitioner in psychiatry, N.Y., Reiki therapist, cert. advanced practice holistic nurse, RN N.J. Dir. psychiat. staff devel. Bellevue Hosp. Ctr., N.Y.C., 1980-82; group psychotherapist Jewish Inst. Geriatric Care, New Hyde Park, NY, 1983; staff psychotherapist New Hope Guild, N.Y.C., 1984; prof. L.I. U. Bklyn., N.Y.C., 1986—; nurse rschr. Englewood (N.J.) Hosp. and Med. Ctr., 1994-97; pvt. practice NY, 1982—2000; psychiat. nurse practitioner Alternatives Counseling Project, Riverhead, NY, 2000—04. Maj. USAR, 1977—2003. Am. Legion scholar, 1962, Isabel McIsaac scholar, 1983. Mem.: Soc. Rogerian Scholars, Nurse Practitioner Assn. N.Y. State, Sigma Theta Tau. Personal E-mail: nhickey@lui.edu.

LEPLEY, RICK ALLEN, consumer products company executive; b. Lewistown, Pa., Apr. 16, 1950; s. Robert Kenneth and Eva Louise L.; m. Deborah Gail Ohmer, Sept. 8, 1982; children: Robert O., Lauren A. BA in Polit. Sci., Lycoming Coll., 1972. Field sales mgr. Chrysler Corp., Detroit, 1977-78, asst. zone mgr., 1978-79, regional sales mgr. Los Angeles, 1979-80; gen. sales mgr. Mid-Atlantic Toyota, Glen Burnie, Md., 1980-81, corp. mktg. mgr., 1981-82; dir. eastern ops. Mitsubishi Motor Sales Am., Inc., Bridgeport, N.J., 1982-87, gen. sales mgr. Fountain Valley, Calif., 1987-88, v.p. to sr. v.p., sales and marketing Cypress, Calif.; former pres. Retail Investment Concepts, Inc., Fla.; pres. Office Depot- Japan, 2001—. Mem. Am. Internat. Automotive Dealers Assn., S. Jersey C. of C. Republican. Avocations: golf, history, baseball.

LEPORE, DAWN GOULD, Internet company executive; BA, Smith Coll. With Cin. Bell, Informatics, San Francisco, Charles Schwab Corp., San Francisco, 1983—2004, exec. v.p., chief info. officer, 1993—99, vice chmn. tech., operations and admin., 1999—2004; CEO drugstore.com inc., 2004—. Bd. dirs. Wal-Mart Stores, Inc., 2001—, eBay. Bd. dirs. Catalyst; trustee Smith Coll. Named one of Bay Area's Most Powerful Corp. Women, San Francisco Chronicle, Top 100 Women in Computing, Open Computing mag., Ten Hottest CIOs, Future Banker mag., 1999, 50 Most Powerful Women in Am. Bus., Fortune mag., 2000, 2001, 2002; recipient Aiming High Conf., NOW, 2003. Office: 13920 SE Eastgate Way Ste 300 Bellevue WA 98005 Office Phone: 425-372-3200. Office Fax: 425-372-3800.

LEPORE, FREDERICK EVERETT, neurologist, educator; b. N.Y.C., Nov. 23, 1949; s. Michael Joseph and Ardean Clough (Everett) L.; m. Adlynn McKeel Gordon, Sept. 9, 1978; children: Adlynn Everett, Meredith Ardean. AB, Princeton U., 1971; MD, U. Rochester, 1975. Diplomate Am. Bd. Psychiatry and Neurology. Intern in internal medicine U. Mich., Ann Arbor, 1975-76; resident in neurology U. Va., Charlottesville, 1976-79; fellow in neuro-ophthalmology Bascom Palmer Eye Inst.-U. Miami, Fla., 1979-80; asst. prof. neurology U. Med. & Dentistry N.J./Rutgers Med. Sch., Piscataway, 1980-86; assoc. prof. neurology U. Med. and Dentistry/Robert Wood Johnson Med. Sch., Piscataway, 1986-94, prof. neurology, 1994—, prof. ophthalmology, 1998—; acting chmn. dept. neurology U. Med. and Dentistry Robert Wood Johnson Med. Sch., Piscataway, 1995—97. Attending physician Robert Wood Johnson Univ. Hosp., New Brunswick, N.J., 1980—; chief neurology svcs., 1994-98; cons. VA Hosp., East Orange, N.J., 1982—. Guest editor (jour.) Seminars in Neurology, 1986; designer Optic Nerve Test Card, 1985. Fellow Am. Acad. Neurology; mem. AAUP (pres. coun. chpts. 2004—), Am. Neurol. Assn., Assn. for Rsch. in Nervous and Mental Disease, Queen Square Alumnus Assn. Presbyterian. Avocations: photography, running. Office: Robert Wood Johnson Med Sch Dept Neurology 97 Paterson St New Brunswick NJ 08901-1928 Office Phone: 732-235-7731. Business E-Mail: leporefe@umdnj.edu.

LEPORE, JILL, history professor, writer; BA in English, Tufts Univ., 1987; MA in Am. Culture, Univ. Mich., Ann Arbor, 1990; MPhil in Am. Studies, Yale Univ., 1993, PhD in Am. Studies, 1995. Asst. prof., history dept. Univ. Calif., San Diego, 1995—96, Boston Univ., 1996—2001, assoc. prof., history dept., 2001—03; prof., history dept. Harvard Univ., 2003—, and chair, history and lit. program, 2005—. Bd. dir. Boston History Collaborative, 1999—2000. Author: Encounters in the New World, 2000, The Name of War: King Philip's War and the Origins of American Identity, 1998 (Bancroft Prize, Ralph Waldo Emerson Prize, Berkshire Prize, New England Hist. Assn. Book Prize), A is for American, 2002 (Kahn award), New York Burning: Liberty, Slavery and Conspiracy in Eighteenth-Century Manhattan, 2005; co-founder, co-editor Common-place, 1999—2004, adv. bd. (TV series) History of America, American Experience, WGBH-TV, 2003, cons. TimeLab 2000, Smash Prodn./The History Channel, 1998—99, The Murder of Dr. Parkman, Spy Pond Prodn., 1999, writer Out of Time, Partners in Time Prodn., 1993—94, American Families: A History of Change, Paradise Prodn/SCETV, 1994—95, editl. bd. Penguin History of Am. Life, 2003—. Named a Disting. Lectr., Orgn. Am. Historians, 2002—05; grantee Gilder Lehrman Inst. Am. History fellowship, 2002, Nat. Endowment for Humanities fellowship, 2003—04. Mem.: Cambridge Hist. Soc., Soc. Am. Historians, Am. Antiquarian Soc. Office: History Dept Harvard Univ 209 Robinson Hall Cambridge MA 02138 Office Phone: 617-496-5083. Office Fax: 617-496-3425. Business E-Mail: jlepore@fas.harvard.edu.

LEPORE, RALPH THOMAS, III, lawyer; b. Framingham, Mass., Oct. 11, 1954; s. Ralph Thomas Jr. and Barbara (Ablondi) L.; m. Marianne Moruzzi, June 20, 1986; children: Cristina Marie, Timothy James. BA in Polit. Sci., U. Mass., 1976; JD, Boston Coll., 1979; LLD (hon.), Framingham State Coll., 2002. Bar: Mass. 1979, US Dist. Ct. Mass. 1980, US Ct. Appeals (1st, 5th and fed. cirs.), pro hac vice admissions RI, NJ, Md., Maine, Pa., Ala., Conn., Vt. Fla., Tex., Calif., NY. Assoc. Sheridan, Garrahan & Lander, Framingham, 1979-81, Warner & Stackpole, Boston, 1981-86, ptnr., 1987—98, Holland & Knight LLP, Boston, 1998—, mem. dir. com. Mem. Mass. Jud. Nominating Coun., 1991-97, vice chmn., 1994-. Co-editor: Massachusetts Liability Insurance Manual, 2000, 2004. Trustee Framingham State Coll., 1991-2001, chmn., 1995-1997, 1999-2001. bd. advisors found. bd. 1992-; bd. advisors Christa McAuliffe Ctr. 1998-; served fundraising activities Jimmy Fund 1988-, S. Middlesex Legal Svcs.1999-; mem. Framingham Town Mtg. 1986-91. Mem. ABA, Mass. Bar Assn., Boston Bar Assn., Justinian Law Soc., Def. Rsch. Inst., Framingham Country Club (mem. bd. dirs. 1995-97, v.p. 1998-99, pres. 2000-2001. Democrat. Roman Catholic. Avocation: golf. Home: 7 Gaslight Ln Framingham MA 01702-5539 Office: Holland & Knight LLP 10 St James Ave 11th Fl Boston MA 02116 Office Phone: 617-523-2700. Business E-Mail: ralph.lepore@hklaw.com.

LEPPARD, RAYMOND JOHN, conductor, musician; b. London, Aug. 11, 1927; arrived in U.S., 1976; s. Albert Victor and Bertha May (Beck) Leppard. MA, U. Cambridge, Eng., 1955; DLitt (hon.), U. Bath, Eng., 1973; PhD (hon.), U. Indpls., 1991, Purdue U., 1992, Butler U., 1994, Wabash Coll., 1995; MusD (hon.), Ind. U., 2001. Fellow Trinity Coll., Cambridge; lectr. music U. Cambridge, 1958—68; music dir. English Chamber Orch., London, 1959—77; prin. condr. BBC Philharm., Manchester, England, 1972—80; condr. symphony orchs. in Am. and Europe, Met. Opera, N.Y.C., Santa Fe Opera, N.Mex., San Francisco Opera, Calif., Covent Garden, Glyndebourne, Paris Opera, Paris; prin. guest condr. St. Louis Symphony Orch., St. Louis, 1984—90; music dir. Indpls. Symphony Orch., 1987—2001, condr. laureate, 2001—. Music dir. European tours, 1993, 97. Rec. artist, composer numerous film scores; author: Authenticity in Music, 1989, Raymond Leppard on Music/An Anthology of Critical and Personal Writings, 1993. Decorated Commendatore Della Republica Italiana, comdr. Order Brit. Empire; recipient Gov.'s Arts Award, 1997. Office: care Michal Schmidt 59 E 54th St Ste 83 New York NY 10022 also: Indianapolis Symphony Orch 45 Monument Circle Indianapolis IN 46204-2919

LEPPER, MARK ROGER, psychologist, educator; b. Washington, Dec. 5, 1944; s. Mark H. and Joyce M. (Sullivan) L.; m. Jeanne E. Wallace, Dec. 22, 1966; 1 child, Geoffrey William. BA, Stanford (Calif.) U., 1966; PhD, Yale U., 1970. Asst. prof. psychology Stanford U., 1971-76, assoc. prof., 1976-82, prof., 1982—, chmn., 1990—94, 2000—04. Fellow Ctr. Advanced Study in Behavioral Scis., 1979-80; chmn. mental health behavioral scis. rsch. rev. com. NIMH, 1982-84, mem. basic sociocultural rsch. rev. com., 1980-82. Co-editor: The Hidden Costs of Reward, 1978; cons. editor Jour. Personality and Social Psychology, 1977-85, Child Devel., 1977-86, Social Cognition, 1981-84, Jour. Ednl. Computing Rsch., 1983—, Media Psychology, 1999—; contbr. articles to profl. jours. Recipient Cattell Found. award, 1999; Woodrow Wilson fellow, 1966-67, NSF fellow, 1966-69, Sterling fellow, 1969-70, Mellon fellow, 1975; grantee NSF, 1978-82, 86-88, NIMH, 1978-86, 88—, Nat. Inst. Child Health and Human Devel., 1975-88, 90-98, U.S. Office Edn., 1972-73. Fellow APA, AAAS, Am. Psychol. Soc., Soc. Personality and Social Psychology, Soc. Psychol. Study Social Issues, Am. Acad. Arts and Scis.; mem. Am. Ednl. Rsch. Assn., Soc. Exptl. Social Psychology, Soc. Rsch. in Child Devel. Home: 1544 Dana Ave Palo Alto CA 94303-2813 Office: Stanford U Dept Psychology Jordan Hall Bldg 420 Stanford CA 94305-2130

LEPPERT, CYNTHIA L., lawyer; b. Balt., Nov. 26, 1956; d. Peter and Mary R. Leppert; m. Douglas J. Stanley, Sept. 30, 2001. BA with honors, Johns Hopkins U., 1978; JD, UCLA, 1982. Bar: Md. 1982. Assoc. Semmes, Bowen & Semmes, Balt., 1982—83; staff atty. FTC, Washington, 1983—86; from assoc. to ptnr. Frank, Bernstein, Conaway & Goldman, Balt., 1986—92; prin. Neuberger, Quinn, Gielen, Rubin & Gibber, P.A., Balt., 1992—. Mem., peer rev. panel Atty. Grievance Com., Md., 1998—; mem. faculty professionalism course Md. State Bar Assn., 2002—. Comments editor UCLA Law Rev., 1981—82. Mktg. and comm. com. Jr. Achievement Ctrl. Md., Inc., Balt., 2005—; mem. policy com. Alzheimer's Assn. Ctrl. Md., 2000—01; commr. Md. Commn. for Women, Annapolis, 2002—; bd. dirs. Wakefield Improvement Assn., Timonium, Md., 2003—, v.p., 2005—. Regents' fellow in econs., UCLA, 1978—79. Fellow: Md. Bar Found.; mem.: ABA, Bar Assn. Balt. City (chair continuing legal edn. com. 2005—, exec. com. 2005), Balt. Women's Bar (exec. com. 1996—2001, sec. 1998—99, pres. 1999—2000), Bankruptcy Bar Assn. Md., Md. State Bar Assn., Women's Bar Assn. Md. (bd. dirs. 2000—05, treas. 2004—05, v.p. 2005—05, chair jud. selections com. 2000—04, Pres.'s award 2004). Office: Neuberger Quinn Gielen Rubin & Gibber One South St 27th Fl Baltimore MD 21202

LEPPERT, PHYLLIS CAROLYN, obstetrician, gynecologist; b. Phila., July 7, 1938; d. Walter Jennings and Alice (Brubach) Leppert. BS, Columbia U., 1961, MS, 1964, PhD, 1986; MD, Duke U., 1973; DSc (hon.), DePauw U., 2000. Diplomate Nat. Bd. Med. Examiners, Am. Bd. Ob-Gyn. Clin. scholar Duke U., Durham, NC, 1973-74, resident in pediatrics Med. Ctr., 1974-76; resident in ob-gyn. Med. Sch. Yale U., New Haven, 1976-79; assoc. in ob-gyn. Columbia U., N.Y.C., 1979-81, asst. prof. ob-gyn., 1981-88; chmn. dept. ob-gyn. Rochester (N.Y.) Gen. Hosp., 1989-95; from assoc. prof. to prof. Sch. Medicine and Dentistry U. Rochester, 1989-95; prof. SUNY, Buffalo, 1996-98, chmn. ob-gyn., 1996-98; chief reproductive scis. br. Nat. Inst. Child Health and Human Devel./NIH, Bethesda, Md., 1999—, sr. staff scientist reproductive endocrinology unit reproductive biology and medicine br., 1999—2004. Vis. prof. Tokyo Coll. Pharmacy, 1989, St. Louis U., 1999—; mem. adv. com. women's health initiative program NIH, 1993—97, mem. ad hoc study sect., mem. Buffalo Vanguard Ctr. Women's Initiative, 1996—98; mem. N.Y. State Coun. Grad. Med. Edn., 1994—99, Bd. Profl. Med. Conduct, NY, 1990—99; founder Internat. Confs. Extra Cellular Matrix Reproductive Tract; program dir. We. N.Y. Perinatal Database, 1997—98; adj. prof. Uniform Svcs. U., Bethesda, 2000—. Co-editor: (book) The Extracellular Matrix of the Reproductive Tract, 1992; sr. editor: book Primary Care for Women, 1996, 2d edit., 2004; contbr. articles to profl. jours. Mem. adv. com. Office Tech., U.S. Congress, 1984; mem. Monroe County Bd. Health, 1992—96, St. Albans Ch., Washington; mem. vestry Christ Ch. Riverdale, Bronx, NY, 1984—86; bd. dirs. Maternity Ctr. Assn., N.Y.C., 1988—96, Preferred Care, Rochester, 1990—94, Riverdale Mental Health Assn., 1986—89, St. Luke/Roosevelt Hosp., N.Y.C., 1986—88. Fellow: ACOG (past mem. com. underserved, mem. com. acad. rsch. fellowship, past mem. gynecol. practice com., mem. obstetrics practice com., mem. genetics com.), Am. Coll. Nurse Midwives; mem.: AAAS, Am. Soc. Reproductive Medicine, Soc. Study Reproduction, Am. Soc. Profs. Ob-gyn. (region I rep. to coun. grad. med. edn. ob-gyn. 1999), Soc. Gynecol. Investigation (mem. coun. 2003—), N.Y. Obstet. Soc., Soc. Exptl. Biology and Medicine, Coun. Resident Edn. Ob-gyn. (rep. retion I 1999—, mem. residency rev. com. ob-gyn.), Am. Gynecol. Obstet. Soc., Alpha Omega Alpha. Avocations: gardening, reading, singing, music, Scottish Country Dancing. Office: NIH 6100 Executive Blvd Bethesda MD 20892-0001 Business E-Mail: leppert@mail.nih.gov.

LEPPIK, ILO E., neurologist, educator; b. Tartu, Estonia, Aug. 18, 1942; arrived in U.S., 1950; s. Elmar Emil and Lilly (Hanson) L.; m. Margaret Ann White, June 18, 1967; children: Peter, David, Karina. BS, Haverford (Pa.) Coll., 1964; MD, U. Pa., 1968. Diplomate Am. Bd. Neurology and Psychiatry, Am. Bd. Clin. Neurophysiology. Rsch. fellow Montreal Neurol. Inst., McGill U., Canada, 1974-76; asst. prof. neurology U. Minn., Mpls., 1976-80, assoc. prof. neurology, 1980-87, prof. neurology, 1987-89, clin. prof. neurology, 1989—, clin. assoc. prof. pharmacy, 1986-89, clin. prof. pharmacy, 1987—2004, prof. pharmacy, 2004—; dir. rsch. MINCEP Epilepsy Care, Mpls., 1990—. Author: Contemporary Diagnosis and Management of the Patient with Epilepsy, 1993, 5th edit., 2000, 2d printing, 2002; founding editor Jour. Epilepsy Rsch., 1987—; contbr. articles to profl. jours. Bd. dirs. Am. Bd. Clin. Neurophysiology, 1992-94; prin. investigator NIH program epilepsy in elderly, 1997-; mem. ctrl. com. Rep. Party Minn. Maj. USAF, 1969-71. Fellow Am. Acad. Neurology; mem. Am. Epilepsy Soc. (pres. 1992-94, treas. 1983-86), Ctrl. Soc. Neurol. Rsch. (pres. 1991-92), Assn. Neurologists of Minn. (pres. 1983-89), Epilepsy Found. Am. (chmn., profl. adv. bd. 1989-91, bd. dirs. 1982-92). Unitarian Universalist. Achievements include development of new drugs for treatment of epilepsy. Avocation: cross country skiing. Office: 7-115 Weaver Deusford Hall Univ Mn Coll Pharmacy 308 Harvard St SE Minneapolis MN 55455 Business E-Mail: leppi001@umn.edu.

LEPPIK, MARGARET WHITE, municipal official; b. Newark, June 5, 1943; d. John Underhill and Laura (Schaefer) White; m. Ilo Elmar Leppik, June 18, 1967; children: Peter, David, Karina. BA, Smith Coll., 1965. Rsch. asst. Wistar Inst., U. Pa., Phila., 1967-68, U. Wis., Madison, 1968-69; mem.

Minn. Ho. Reps., St. Paul, 1991—2003, chair higher edn. fin. com.; mem. Met. Coun., 2003—. Active Golden Valley (Minn.) Planning Commn., 1982—90, Golden Valley Bd. Zoning Appeals, 1985—87; commr. Midwest Higher Edn. Commn., 1999—2003; bd. dirs. Minn. Partnership Action Against Tobacco, 1998—2003. Named Citizen of Distinction, Hennepin County Human Svcs. Planning Bd., 1992, Legislator of Yr., U. Minn. Alumni Assn., 1995, 1998—2001, Minn. State U. Student Assn., 1999; recipient Presdl. medallion, North Hennepin CC, 2003. Mem.: LWV (v.p., dir. 1984—90), Hubert H. Humphrey Inst. (adv. coun. 2003—), Nature Conservancy (bd. trustees 2003—), Minn. Opera Assn. (pres. 1986—88), Optimists, Rotary. Republican. Avocations: gardening, bicycling, canoeing. Home: 7500 Western Ave Golden Valley MN 55427-4849 Personal E-mail: peggy@leppik.net.

LEPPMAN, ELIZABETH JANE, geographer, educator; b. Chgo., Dec. 6, 1943; d. Ulrich Leppman and Ruth Louise (Armstrong) Leppman; m. Gary Robert Hovinen, June 28, 1974 (div. July 9, 1995); children: Karen Louise Hovinen, Bradford Gary Hovinen. BA, Middlebury Coll., 1966; MA, York U., 1976; PhD, U. Ga., 1997. Cartographer Rand McNally & Co., Chgo., 1966—67, asst. editor geography, 1967—70; editor J.M. Dent Ltd., Toronto, Canada, 1970—71, Gage Pub., Toronto, 1971—74; instr. Millersville U., Pa., 1984—91; English instr. Northeastern U., Shenyang, China, 1993—95; instr. U. Ga., Athens, 1997; vis. asst. prof., geography Miami U., Oxford, Ohio, 1997—98; assoc. prof. geography St. Cloud State U., Minn., 1998—2005. Freelance map and book editor, 1975—. Author: Teaching Map and Globe Skills: A Handbook; co-author Pennsylvania Dutch Country: A Pictorial History; author: The Quakers of Yonge Street, (workbook) Map Activities, Changing Rice Bowl: Economic Development and Diet in China; co-author: Student Atlas of World Politics, 6th edit.; contbr. chapters to books Sharing Our World, articles to profl. jours. Fact-finding team Academics Against War in Iraq, Atlanta, 2003—03; vol. Dem. Farmer Labor Party, Saint Cloud, 2002—04; lay reader Episcopal Ch., 1978—; vestry mem. St. John's Episcopal Ch., Saint Cloud, 1999—. Fellow, Sasakawa Found., 1999; scholar Athena Award, AAUW, 1993. Mem.: Nat. Coun. Geog. Edn. (editor Jour. Geography 2001—04), Assn. Am. Geographers (sec.-treas. cultural geography specialty group 2004—, editor Geographies Religions and Belief Sys. 2004—), St. Cloud Stamp Club (pres. 2000—03), Gamma Theta Upsilon, Phi Kappa Phi. Avocations: photography, sewing. Personal E-mail: ejleppman@alltel.net.

LEPRE, JERRY, risk management consultant, media consultant; BA in Journalism, Loyola Coll., 1977, MA in Comm., 1985. CCFC Faith Fin. Ministries, 2002. Trainer, risk mgr. Citizens Consulting, Inc., New Orleans, 2004—; trainer, spkr., cons. Jerry LePre Productions, Destrehan, La., 1996—; compliance officer Maxicare, New Orleans; asst. v.p. mktg. Advantage Health, New Orleans; dir. Ochsner Health Plan, Metairie, La. Dir. Faith Fin. Ministries, Inc., Destrehan, La., 1991—, Christian Fin. Network, Inc., Destrehan, Inst. of Principle-Based Selling, Inc., New Orleans. Author: Don't Steal My Popcorn- 12 Secrets for Ultimate Success and Extreme Happiness, File Gumbo for the Soul, God's Money-Back Guarantee- The Seven Steps to Financial Security, Silver Security/Financial Tips for Senior Adults. Forums moderator St. John the Bapt. Parish, LaPlace, La., 2003—04. Recipient Superior Rating, La. Fedn. Music Clubs, 1965—75, Key to City, City of New Orleans, 1967.

LEPS, THOMAS MACMASTER, civil engineer, consultant; b. Keyser, W.Va., Dec. 3, 1914; s. Thomas Davis and Grace (King) L.; m. Catherine Mary Sacksteder, June 22, 1940; 1 son, Timothy. BA, Stanford U., 1936; MS, MIT, 1939. Jr. and asst. civil engr. Calif. Divsn. Hwys., U.S. C.E. & Bur. of Reclamation, 1936-41; chief civil engr. So. Calif. Edison Co., L.A., 1946-61; chief engr. Shannon & Wilson Co., Seattle, 1961-63; cons. civil engr. U.S. and abroad, Dinuba, Calif., 1963—. Mem. over 90 bds. of cons. on hydro, steam and nuclear power projects. Contbr. articles to profl. jours., chpts. to engring books. Served to comdr. USNR, 1943-46, 46-60. Recipient certificate of Appreciation Calif. Dept. Water Resources, 1971 Mem. NAE (life mem., nominations com. for officers 1981), ASCE (life mem., cert. of appreciation 1961), U.S. Com. on Large Dams (life mem. vice-chmn. exec. com. 1980-81), Phi Beta Kappa, Tau Beta Pi. Presbyterian. Address: PO Box 217 Dinuba CA 93618-0217 Office Phone: 559-595-9001.

LE QUÉRÉ, JEAN FRANÇOIS MARIE, scientific instrumentation researcher; b. Pabu, France, Apr. 7, 1933; s. Yves Marie and Yvonne Marie Rose (Ollivier) Le Q.; m. Jacqueline Marie Le Colas, Mar. 26, 1964; children: Anne Marie, Isabelle Marie, Jean-Yves Marie, Blandine Marie. Upper tech. diploma, Nat. Conservatory Arts-Trade, Paris, 1965, engr. physicist grad., 1968; DEng, U. Pierre and Marie Curie, Paris, 1983. Electrician Regie Renault, Paris, 1950-61; lab. technician, Paris, 1961-65; lab. upper rsch. technician, 1965-68; engr. physicist U. Paris 6, 1968-72, engr. rschr., 1972-96; mem. faculty U. Paris 7, 1972-94, engr. rschr., 1972—. Contbr. articles to profl. jours. With French Army, 1953. Mem. Assn. Tchg. (pres. 1996). Home: 22 rue Pierre Brossolette 93160 Noisy-le-Grand France E-mail: jean_lequere@laposte.net.

LE QUESNE, PHILIP WILLIAM, chemistry educator, researcher; b. Auckland, New Zealand, Jan. 6, 1939; came to U.S., 1967; s. Ernest W. B. and Bettie A. (Colwill) Le Q.; m. Mary E. Kinloch, 1965 (dec. 1988); children: Elizabeth Ruth, Martin James. BS, U. Auckland, 1960, MS, 1961, PhD, 1964, D.Sc. (hon.), 1979. Asst. prof. U. Mich., Ann Arbor, 1967-72; assoc. prof. Northeastern U., Boston, 1973-78, prof., 1978—, chmn. dept. chemistry, 1979-87, vice provost for rsch. and grad. edn., 1991-93. Assoc. dir. Barnett Inst. for Chem. analysis and Materials Sci., 1993-97. Mem. editl. bd. Bioactive Natural Products, 2004—; contbr. articles on chemistry to profl. jours. Sr. warden Ch. of the Advent, Boston, 1990-96. Home: 17 Stafford Rd Newton Center MA 02459-1818 Office: Northeastern U Chemistry Dept 360 Huntington Ave Boston MA 02115-5000 Office Phone: 617-373-2858. E-mail: p.lequesne@neu.edu.

LEQUIRE, ALAN RUSSELL, sculptor, educator; b. Nashville, Dec. 16, 1955; s. Virgil Shields and Louise Fairfax (Lasseter) LeQ.; m. Andrée Lejeune Akers, Oct. 14, 1990. BS, Vanderbilt U., 1978; MFA, U. N.C., Greensboro, 1981. Mem. faculty Watkins Inst., Nashville, 1987—. Prin. works include Athena Parthenos, 1990, Musica, 2003, bronze portraits and statues. Founding mem. Nashville Visual Artists Alliance, 1991. Recipient Tenn. Art League Young Artist award Tenn. Art League, 1988, Gov.'s Citation, State of Tenn., 1988. Mem. Nashville Artist Guild (exhibitor bi-annual group shows), Coll. Art Assn. Office: LeQuire Gallery 4304 Charlotte Ave Ste C Nashville TN 37209

LERAAEN, ALLEN KEITH, financial executive; b. Mason City, Iowa, Dec. 4, 1951; s. Myron O. and Clarice A. (Handeland) L.; m. Mary Elena Partheymuller, Apr. 14, 1978. BBA in Data Processing and Acctg., No. Ariz. U., 1975. CFA. Data processing supr. Stephenson & Co., Denver, 1978-81, contr., 1981-85, arbitrageur, trader, 1985-88, v.p., 1985-90, exec. v.p., portfolio mgr., 1990—. V.p., sec. bd. dirs. Circle Corp., Denver, 1985—; v.p. StarTek, Inc., Denver, 1997—. Mem. Assn. Investment Mgmt. and Rsch., Denver Soc. Security Analysts. Avocation: flying. Home: 5692 S Robb St Littleton CO 80127-1942 Office: 100 Garfield St Fl 4 Denver CO 80206-5597 E-mail: al@great.net.

LERACH, WILLIAM S., lawyer; b. Pitts., Mar. 14, 1946; BA, U. Pitts., 1967, JD magna cum laude, 1970. Bar: Pa. 1970, Calif. 1976. Ptnr. Milberg, Weiss, Bershad, Hynes & Lerach LLP, San Diego. Presenter numerous seminars, confs. Contbr. articles to profl. jours. Mem. ABA, Assn. Trial Lawyers Am., Pa. Bar Assn., State Bar Calif., Calif. Trial Lawyers Assn., San Diego Bar Assn., San Diego County Trial Lawyers Assn., Order of Coif. Office: Milberg Weiss Bershad Hynes & Lerach LLP 401 B St Ste 1700 San Diego CA 92101-4297 E-mail: wsl@mwbhl.com.

LEREW, LLOYD EUGENE, consultant; b. Carlisle, Pa., Sept. 27, 1949; s. Lloyd Miller and Kathryn Maxine (Karns) L.; m. Jane E. Myers, Aug. 18, 1994; 1 child, Ryan Kyle. BS, Mich. State U., 1971, MS, 1972, PhD, 1978. Engring. trainee USDA, Soil Conservation Svc., Harrisburg, Pa., 1968-69; undergrad. rsch. assoc. dept. agrl. engring. Mich. State U., East Lansing, 1970, grad. asst., 1971-73, 75-76, instr., 1977-78, asst. prof., 1979-80; gen. mgr., bus. mgr. Lerew's Farm Market, Inc., Dillsburg, Pa., 1974-80, v.p., 1981-86, pres., 1986—; cons. Dillsburg, 1990—. Chmn. York County Solid Waste and Refuse Authority, York, Pa., 1983-89, vice-chmn., 1990-91; mem. No. York County Sch. Dist. Vocat. Agrl. Adv. Bd., Dillsburg, Pa., 1985-87. Author: Primer for the Michigan State University CDC 6500, 1973; contbr. articles to profl. jours. Mem. Am. Soc. Agrl. Engrs., Alpha Epsilon. Republican. Avocations: computers, antique toys, nature, gardening. Home: 2130 Old York Rd Dillsburg PA 17019-8911 E-mail: lelerew@earthlink.net.

LERITZ, LAWRENCE R., choreographer, singer, actor, dancer, producer; b. Alton, Ill., Sept. 26, 1952; s. Leonard Henry and Marcella Rose (Fravle) L. Student, Harkness Ballet Sch., 1973-74, Sch. Am. Ballet, 1975-76. Debut: State Fair, St. Louis Muny Opera, 1969, appeared in Can Can, 1983; TV appearances include Capitol, 1982, All My Children, 1981-85, Home Sweet, Homeless; Rodney Dangerfield: It's Lonely at the Top, HBO, 1992, various comms.; guest expert on various talk shows including Rolonda, Charles Perez, Maury Povich, Show Biz Today, Am. Muscle Mag., Rosie O'Donnell Show; film debut: Stardust Memories, 1979; appeared in Easy Money, 1982, Stag, 1997; star Leritz and His Girls, 1983-85; Broadway appearances include: Fiddler on the Roof, 1981, Fonteyn and Nureyev on Broadway, 1975; prodr., choreographer Boobs!, N.Y.C., N.Y., 2000, Boobs! The Musical, off Broadway, 2003-04; appeared Met. Opera telecast of Manon Lescaut, 1980; choreographer feature film musical The Last Dragon, 1984; choreographer, co-star home video Treehouse Trolls Birthday Day, 1993; dancer with Harkness Ballet, Paris Opera, Hamburg Ballet, Chgo. Ballet, world wide guest star; dir., choreographer own co. Dance Celebration which represented U.S. at Internat. Choreographic Competitions, Paris, 1979; dir. mus. numbers for Shields and Yarnell; creator mus. indsls. for Lily of France, Bausch & Lomb, Christian Dior; pres. Leritz Prodns., Ltd., N.Y.C. and L.A., 1983—; star exercise cruise on Queen Elizabeth II, 1995; rec. artist: It Takes Two to Tango, 1984, Crank It Up, 1989, Bright Light, 1992; song lyricist, composer; East coast prodr. Day of Compassion, 1995-97; choreographer, guest dancer Placido Domingo's L.A. Music Ctr. Opera, 1987. Writer Muscular Devel. mag., Ironman mag., Men's Fitness mag., Muscle & Fitness mag.; creator, star of video Total Stretch! with Lawrence Leritz, 1992. Full scholar Sch. Am. Ballet, Harkness Ballet Sch.; Lawrence R. Leritz Day declared; recipient Key to City, Wood River, Ill., 1983, Alton, Ill., 1987; appeared on cover Dance Pages mag., fall 1987, spring 1989 Time Mag.'s Local Hero, 1996. Mem. AFTRA, ASCAP (Pop Music awards for songwriting 1985—), SAG (film nominating com. 1996), Actors Equity Assn., Am. Guild Musical Artists (bd. govs. 1979-92, 94—, prodn. supr./choreographer 50th Ann. Gala 1986, Life Membership award for disting. svc. 1991). Office: 250 W 19th St Apt 10M New York NY 10011-4054 E-mail: lleritz@aol.com.

LERMA, EDGAR VILLANEUVA, nephrologist; b. Manila, Jan. 27, 1969; arrived in U.S., 1995; s. Jesus Sr. Lerma and Norma Cuenca Villanueva. BS in Biology, U. Santo Tomas, Manila, 1987, MD, 1991. Diplomate Am. Bd. Internal Medicine, 2000, Am. Bd. Med. Specialties, 2001, Am. Bd. Nephrology, 2002, cert. clin. specialist in hypertension Am. Soc. Hypertension, diplomate Nephrology Ambd. Internal Med., 2002. Resident in internal medicine Mercy Hosp. and Med. Ctr./U. Ill. Chgo. Med. Ctr., 1995—98, chief resident, 1997—98; fellow in nephrology and hypertension Northwestern Meml. Hosp./Northwestern U. Med. Sch., Chgo., 1998—2000; staff physician Altru Health Sys./Altru Hosp., Grand Forks, ND, 2000—; clin. asst. prof. U. N.D., Grand Forks, 2000—. Mem. manuscript rev. bd.: Hosp. Physician Med. Jour., 2000—, peer reviewer: Archives Internal Medicine, 2003—, Jour. Gen. Internal Medicine, 2003—, Am. Jour. Kidney Disease, 2003—, Kidney Internat., 2003—, Nephrology Med. Jour., 2003—, Jour. Am. Soc. Nephrology, 2003—, Physicians Info. Ednl. Resource, 2003—. Fellow: ACP (chmn. N.D. chpt. 2001—, sentinel reader); mem.: AMA, ACP Jour. Club (sentinel reader, commentator/rater), Am. Soc. Diagnostic and Interventional Nephrology, N.D. Med. Assn. (mem. commn. med. edn. 2001—, commn. med. ethics 2003—), Am. Heart Assn. (mem. coun. blood pressure rsch./kidney disease 2000—), Am. Soc. Hypertension, Nat. Kidney Found., Am. Soc. Nephrology, U. Santo Tomas Med. Alumni Assn. Home: 3543 S Wisconsin Ave Berwyn IL 60402 Office: Altru Health Sys 1000 S Columbia Rd Grand Forks ND 58206 Personal E-mail: edgarvlermamd@pol.net.

LERMAN, TERRY ALLEN, lawyer; b. Pitts., July 11, 1946; s. Robert Marvin and Celia (Berger) L.; m. Beverly Dee Lipscher, Mar. 25, 1972 (div. 1977); m. Cynthia Schulhof, Mar. 1994. BS, U. Pitts., 1968; JD, Duquesne U., 1971. Bar: Pa. 1971. Atty. Urban Redevel. Authority, Pitts., 1972-74; counsel, v.p. Babb Investments, Inc., Pitts., 1974-76; atty., counsel Security Pacific, Inc., Seattle, 1976-77; pres., counsel First Capital Corp., Pitts., 1977—. Bd. dirs. Nat. Multi-Housing Coun., Washington; mem. Real Estate Tax Inst., Washington, 1988—, Securities-Syndication Inst., Chgo., 1983-85; co-chmn. Colition for Low and Moderate Income Housing., Washington, 1984-86. Bd. dirs. Forward Shady Housing Corp., Pitts., 1987—, Riverview Ctr. for Sr. Citizens, 1989—, S.W. Community Loan Fund, Pitts., 1990—, Jewish Assn. on Aging, 1997; trustee Tree of Life Endowment Fund, Pitts., 1987—. Recipient Law Week award Bur. Nat. Affairs, 1971. Mem. ABA, Pa. Bar Assn., Allegheny County Bar Assn., Westmoreland Club, Downtown Club. Democrat. Avocations: tennis, golf. Office: First Capital Corp 1350 Old Freeport Rd Pittsburgh PA 15238-3122

LERMOND, CHARLES AFTON, artist, educator; b. Brunswick, Maine, Aug. 1, 1927; s. Earle and Mabel Elizabeth (Rogers) L.; m. Martha Evelyn (Leeman, Sept. 19, 1948; children: Kent, Nancy. BA, Bowdoin Coll., 1949; MS in Analytical Chemistry, MIT, 1953. Owner, artist The Loom Shed, Oberlin, Ohio, 1981—. Lectr., workshop leader, instr. in block-switching, drafting, rug weaving, special overshot techniques, exploration of Theo Moorman techniques. Exhibited in group shows at Mannings Handweaving, 1978-85, Ohio State Fair, 1985, Convergence 1986, 92, 93, Toronto, Can., 1986, Gund Gallery, Columbus, Ohio, 1989; two-man show at Loomworks, Columbus, 1988; contbr. articles to profl. jours. Past pres., founder Firelands Weavers Guild, Oberlin. Recipient Ind. Artist's fellowship in traditional crafts Ohio Arts Coun., 1988. Mem. Firelands Assn. for Visual Arts (founding trustee, sec.). Address: 13 S Main St 2nd flr Oberlin OH 44074-1602 Office Phone: 440-774-3500. Business E-Mail: loomshed@oberlin.net.

LERNER, ABRAM, museum director, artist; b. N.Y.C., Apr. 11, 1913; s. Hyman and Sarah (Becker) L.; m. Pauline Hanenberg, Oct. 7, 1940; 1 child, Aline. BA, NYU, 1935; student, Ednl. Alliance, Art Students League, Bklyn. Mus.; pvt. studies, Florence, Italy. Asso. dir. A.C.A. Gallery and Artist's Gallery, N.Y.C., 1945-57; curator Joseph H. Hirshhorn Collection, N.Y.C., 1957-66; dir. Hirshhorn Mus. and Sculpture Garden, Washington, 1967-85; founding dir. emeritus, ret. Hirshhorn Mus. and Sculpture Garden, Smithsonian Instn., Washington, 1985. Adv. bd. Archives Am. Art, 1970— Author: Hirshhorn Museum and Sculpture Garden - Inaugural Book, 1974, Gregory Gillespie, 1977; contbr. to mags., mus. catalogues.; one man show, Davis Gallery, N.Y.C., 1958, group shows include, A.C.A. Gallery, Peridot Gallery, Bklyn.-Mus., Pa. Acad., Davis Gallery; represented in pvt. collections. Decorated comdr. Order Oranje-Nassau (Netherlands); chevalier Order Arts and Letters (France). Home: 98 Lewis St Southampton NY 11968-5006

LERNER, ALAN CHARLES, financial market economist, educator; b. Bklyn., July 24, 1944; s. Isidore and Florence (Leschinski) L.; m. Bonnie Marilyn Taub, Jan. 28, 1967 (div. Apr. 1980); children: Lisa, Jennifer; m. Linda Joy Hunter, Feb. 1, 1981 (dec. Sept. 1982); 1 child, Kali; m. Wendy Watson, Aug. 20, 1985. BA, Bklyn. Coll., 1966; MBA, NYU, 1968. Instr. econs. NYU, 1969-72; economist Salomon Bros., N.Y.C., 1972-74; economist, sr. v.p. Banker Trust Co., N.Y.C., 1974—93; pres. Lerner Cons., 1993—. Adj. prof. econs. and fin. NYU, 1974— Author: weekly market letter Prospects for the Credit Markets, 1976—93. NDEA fellow, 1967-69 Mem. Am. Fin. Assn., Money Marketeers (v.p. 1981—, past pres.). Jewish.

LERNER, ALEXANDER ROBERT, insurance company executive; b. Chgo., June 26, 1946; s. Peter Lerner and Lillian Orlinsky Joseph; m. Marianne Ryan, Apr. 21, 1979; 1 child, Lindsey Anne. BS, No. Ill. U., 1970. Adminstrv. asst. Gov. of Ill., 1970-72; adminstrv. asst. spkr. Ill. Ho. of Reps., Springfield, 1973-74; asst. dir. pub. affairs divsn. AMA, Chgo., 1974-75; dir. Ill. State Med. Soc., Chgo., 1975-78; pres. Govtl. Affairs, Inc., Chgo., 1978—81; CEO ISMIE Mut. Ins. Co., Chgo., 1981—. Mem. adv. com. to dir. Ctrs. Disease Control and Prevention, 2001—04, NIH. Bd. dirs. Lincoln Park Zoo; chmn. Ill. Sports Facilities Authority, 1992—2004. Fellow: Inst. Medicine Chgo.; mem.: Assn. Forum Chgo., Chgo. Soc. Assn. Execs., Am. Soc. Assn. Execs., Am. Assn. Med. Soc. Execs., Conway Farms Golf Club, Execs. Club of Chgo., Michigan Shores Club, Chgo. Yacht Club, Union League Club. Avocations: nautical antiques, presidential history, travel, golf. Office: Ill State Med Soc 20 N Michigan Ave Chicago IL 60602-4811 Office Phone: 312-580-2412.

LERNER, BARBARA, writer, researcher; b. Chgo., Mar. 31, 1935; d. Jacob Israel and Mary (Turen) Lerner. BA with honors, U. Ill., 1956; MA, U. Chgo., 1961, PhD, 1965, JD, 1977. Bar: Ill. 1977. Intern U. Chgo. Hosp. and Clinic, 1962-63; instr. Coll. Medicine U. Ill., 1963-64; clin. psychologist Ill. Mental Health Ctr., Chgo., 1965-68; assoc. prof. Ohio U., Athens, 1968-70; pvt. practice clin. psychologist Chgo., 1970-78; assoc. prof. Roosevelt U., Chgo., 1972-74; study dir. Nat. Acad. Scis., Washington, 1977-78; pres. Lerner Assocs., Princeton, NJ, 1981-96. Vis. scholar Ednl. Testing Svc., Princeton, 1978—79, sr. rsch. scientist, 1980—81; expert witness fed. cts. Debra P. vs. Turlington, Tampa, Fla., Marshall vs. Ga., 1983; vis. prof. U. Tex., Austin, 1989. Author: Therapy in the Ghetto, 1972, Minimum Competence, Maximum Choice, 1980; assoc. editor: U. Chgo. Law Rev., 1975—77, columnist: Phila. Inquirer, 1992—93; contbr. articles to profl. jours., newspapers and mags. Mem. U.S. Commn. Civil Rights, NJ, 1985—87; Pres. nominee U.S. Dept. of Edn., Washington, 1986. Recipient Cert. of Appreciation award for outstanding svc., U.S. Dept. of Edn., 1985. Mem.: Sigma Xi, Phi Beta Kappa. Avocation: gardening. Office: 5050 S East End Ave Chicago IL 60615-5901 E-mail: xlerner@ameritech.net.

LERNER, BETH M., non-profit consultant; b. Phila., Dec. 9, 1972; d. Craig and Zena Lerner; life ptnr. Kartik Krishnaiyer. BA, Temple U., 1995. Cmty. svc. coord. SE Fla. chpt. Alzheimer's Assn., Palm Beach, 2001—02; resource devel. dir. United Way of Palm Beach County, Boynton Beach, Fla., 2002—04; polit. cons. JKRB Inc., Coral Springs, Fla., 2003—04; legis. asst. State Rep. Mary Brandenburg, Palm Beach, Fla., 2004—05; non-profit cons. Am. Cancer Soc., 2005—. Exec. com., Jewish cmty. rels. coun. Jewish Fedn. South Palm Beach County, Boca Raton, 2004; pub. affairs com. Planned Parenthood of Palm Beaches and Treasure Coast, West Palm Beach, 2004; team devel. chair Am. Cancer Soc., West Palm Beach, 2004; pres. Palm Beach County Young Democrats, Boynton Beach, Fla., 2003—05, Lake Worth (Fla.) Dem. Club, 2005; precinct capt. Palm Beach County Dem. Party, Lantana, Fla., 2002—; bd. dirs. Children's Case Mgmt. Orgn., Inc., West Palm Beach, 2005—. Recipient Svc. Award, Fla. Young Democrats, 2003. Mem.: NOW, AAUW, Nat. Assn. Notaries, LWV. Democrat. Jewish. Avocations: travel, politics, history. Personal E-mail: bethrenrel@aol.com.

LERNER, ERIC M., lawyer; b. Bklyn., July 18, 1957; BA cum laude, SUNY, Binghamton, 1979; JD, U. Chgo., 1982. Bar: NY 1983. Ptnr. Katten Muchin Zavis Rosenman, NYC. Mem.: ABA (mem. Bus. Law Sect.), Pi Sigma Alpha, Phi Beta Kappa. Office: Katten Muchin Zavis Rosenman 575 Madison Ave New York NY 10022 Office Phone: 212-840-7157. Office Fax: 212-940-8776. E-mail: eric.lerner@kmzr.com.

LERNER, GERDA, historian, educator, author; b. Vienna, Apr. 30, 1920; came to U.S., 1939, naturalized, 1943; d. Robert and Ilona (Neumann) Kronstein; m. Carl Lerner, Oct. 6, 1941 (dec.); children: Stephanie, Daniel. BA, New Sch. Social Research, 1963; MA (faculty scholar), Columbia U., 1965, PhD, 1966. Lectr. New Sch. Social Research, N.Y.C., 1963-65; asst. prof. L.I. U., 1965-67, assoc. prof., 1967-68; mem. faculty Sarah Lawrence Coll., Bronxville, N.Y., 1968-80. Dir. Master's Program in Women's History, 1972-80; ednl. dir. Summer Inst. in Women's History, 1976, 79; scholar-in-residence Rockefeller Found. Conf. Center, Bellagio, Italy, 1975, 91; Robinson-Edwards prof. history U. Wis., Madison, 1980—, prof. emeritus, 1991—; sr. disting. rsch. prof. Wis. Alumni Rsch. Found., 1984-91; co-dir. Fund Improvement Post-Secondary Edn. grant for Promoting Black Women's History, 1980-83 Author: screenplay Black Like Me, 1964; novel No Farewell, 1955, The Grimke Sisters from South Carolina: Rebels Against Slavery, 1967; The Woman in American History, 1971, Black Women in White America: A Documentary History, 1972, The Female Experience: Documents in American History, 1976, A Death of One's Own, 1978, The Majority Finds its Past: Placing Women in History, 1979, Teaching Women's History, 1981, The Creation of Patriarchy, 1986, The Creation of Feminist Consciousness, 1993, Why History Matters, 1997, The Feminist Thought of Sarah Grimke, 1998. Rsch. fellow AAUW, 1968-69, Social Sci. Research Council research fellow, 1970-71, Rockefeller Found. fellow, 1975, 77, 91; Rockefeller Found. grantee, 1972-76, NEH grantee, 1976, Ford Found. grantee, 1978-79, Lilly Found. grantee, 1979, FIPSE grantee, 1980-83, Knapp grantee, 1982-88, Anonymous Fund and Knapp Found. grantee, 1990-93; Recipient Guggenheim award, 1980-81, Ednl. Found. Achievement award AAUW, 1986, Berkshire Conf. Women Historians Spl. Book award, 1980, Lucretia Mott award, 1988, Kathe Leichter prize/Austrian state prize for women's history and history of labor movement, 1995, Austrian Cross of Honor for sci. and art, 1996. Fellow Wis. Acad. Scis., Arts, and Letters; mem. Am. Acad. Arts., Am. Hist. Assn. (Scholarly Distinction award 1992), Orgn. Am. Historians (pres. 1981-82), AAUP, Authors League, Am. Studies Assn., PEN. Home: 6005 Hammersley Rd Madison WI 53711-3113

LERNER, HARRY JONAS, publishing company executive; b. Mpls., Mar. 5, 1932; s. Morris and Lena (Liederschneider) L.; m. Sharon Ruth Goldman, June 25, 1961 (dec. 1982); children: Adam Morris, Mia Carol, Daniel Aryeh, Leah Anne; m. Sandra Karon Davis, Aug. 24, 1996. Student, U. Mich., 1952, Hebrew U., Jerusalem, 1953-54; BA, U. Minn., 1957. Founder Lerner Publs. Co., Mpls., 1959, chief exec. officer, 1959—; founder Muscle Bound Bindery, Inc., 1967, chief exec. officer, 1967—; founder Carolrhoda Books, Inc., 1969; gen. mgr. Interface Graphics Inc., 1969—, CEO, 1993—. Bd. visitors U. Minn. Press; del. White House Conf. on Libr. and Info. Svcs., 1979; chmn. North Loop Bus. Assn., Mpls., 1972-79, Minn. Book Pubs. Roundtable, 1974; bd. overseers Hill Monastic Manuscript Libr., St. John's U., Collegeville, Minn., 1986-89; bd. dirs., libr. dir. Jewish Community Ctr. Pres. Twin City chpt. Am. Jewish Com., 1980-85; bd. dirs. Fgn. Policy Assn. Minn., 1970-71, bd. dirs. Children's Book Coun., N.Y.C., 1991-94, Minn. Libr. Assn. Found., 1997; bd. advisors Books for Africa, 1996. Recipient Brotherhood award, NCCJ, 1961, Kay Sexton award, 2002, numerous graphic arts awards, Minn. Innovative Communicator award, Minn. State U., 2004. Mem. Mpls. Inst. Art, Walker Art Ctr., St. Paul-Mpls. Com. on Fgn. Affairs, Jewish Hist. Soc. Upper Midwest, Ampersand Club, Daybreakers Breakfast Club (Mpls.). Home: 2215 Willow Ln N Minneapolis MN 55416-3862 Office: Lerner Pub Group 241 1st Ave N Minneapolis MN 55401-1676 Business E-Mail: hjl@lernerbooks.com.

LERNER, HERBERT J., tax consultant; b. Newark, Aug. 19, 1938; s. Morris David Lerner and Evelyn L. (Shapiro) Kaplan; m. Dianne Joan Prag, Aug. 23, 1959; children— Joy Ellen, Mark Allen BS, Rutgers U., 1959; LL.B., Georgetown U., 1963. Bar: D.C. 1964; C.P.A., D.C. With Ernst & Young, Washington, 1963-96, ptnr., 1970-83, 83-89, vice chmn. tax Washington, 1990—, nat. dir. tax policy and standards; ret. Mem. IRS Commrs. Adv. Group, 1982-83, 96-98; treas., trustee Am. Tax Policy Inst., 1990-97. Author: (with others) Federal Income Taxation of Corporations Filing Consolidated Returns, 4 vols., 1975, with ann. supplement thru 1997; contbr., editor pvt. letter rulings column Jour. Taxation. Mem. AICPA (exec. com. tax divsn. 1979-82, 85-89, past chmn., bd. dirs. 1990-94, co-chmn. nat. conf. lawyers and CPAs), ABA, George Town Club (bd. govs.). E-mail: Herblerner@aol.com.

LERNER, JONATHAN J., lawyer; b. Bklyn., 1948; BA, SUNY, Binghamton, 1970; JD magna cum laude, St. John's U., Jamaica, N.Y., 1973. Bar: NY 1974. Ptnr., corp., securities and commercial litigation Skadden, Arps, Slate, Meagher & Flom, LLP, NYC. Lectr. bus. judgement rule and fed. practice and procedure Practising Law Inst. and bar associations confs.; lectr. at law Columbia U. Sch. of Law, 1989—92; mem. Dept. Disciplinary Com., Appellate Divsn., First Jud. Dept., 1983—90, 1993, hearing panel chmn., 1984—90, 1992—; adj. prof. Bklyn. Law Sch., 2000—. Published numerous articles on the liability of corp. dirs., corp. takeovers, litigation strategy and legal ethics. Mem.: Assn. of the Bar City NY (mem. com. on profl. and jud. ethics 1981—84, mem. com. on the fed. courts 1989—92, chmn. 1999—2002). Office: Skadden Arps Slate Meagher & Flom LLP 4 Times Sq New York NY 10036 Office Phone: 212-735-2550. Office Fax: 917-777-2550. Business E-Mail: jlerner@skadden.com.

LERNER, JOSHUA, finance educator; b. Chgo., May 26, 1960; s. Ralph Lerner, Carol Lerner; m. Wendy Wood. BA, Yale U., 1982. Jacob H. Schiff prof. investment banking Harvard Bus. Sch., Boston, 1991—. Organizer innovation policy and the economy group, entrepreneurship working group Nat. Bur. Econ. Rsch., Boston, 1999—2005. Author: The Venture Capital Cycle, 1999, Venture Capital and Private Equity, 2000, 3d edit., 2004, The Money of Invention, 2001, Innovation and Its Discontents, 2004. Office: Harvard Bus Sch Rock Ctr Rock Ctr Rm 214 Boston MA 02163 Office Phone: 617-495-6065. Business E-Mail: jlerner@hbs.edu.

LERNER, LAURENCE M., college administrator; b. N.Y.C., Aug. 21, 1939; s. Meyer Philip and Rose (Goss) L.; m. Susan Goodstein, sept. 8, 1963; children: Elisabeth, Marc. BA, NYU, 1961; MA, U. Wis., 1963, PhD, 1970. Asst. adminstr. history U. Wis., Madison, 1964-66; instr. Hofstra U., Hempstead, N.Y., 1967-68; sr. assoc. Drummond Assocs., Inc., N.Y.C., 1968-71; lectr. Am. history Barnard Coll., N.Y.C., 1971; asst. editor Bus. Internat., Inc., N.Y.C., 1972-73, asst. editor mgmt. practices, 1972-73; dir. rsch. United Jewish Appeal, N.Y.C., 1973-79; dir. devel. Am. Jewish Congress, N.Y.C., 1979-80; exec. v.p. Alumni Fedn. of NYU, Inc., N.Y.C., 1980-89; sr. v.p., spl. asst. to the pres. Manhattan Coll., Riverdale, 2000—, v.p. coll. advancement, 1989-95, sr. v.p. capital campaign, 1996—2000. Bd. dirs. Hamilton-Madison House, N.Y.C., 1985-91, U.S. Com./Sports for Israel, N.Y.C., 1979-81; mem. historian's com. Am. Mus. Immigration, N.Y.C., 1982—; bd. advisors Coun. of Mcpl. Performance, N.Y.C., 1977-84; bd. trustees Horace Mann-Barnard Sch., Riverdale, 1979-82. Mem. NYU Alumni Assn. (bd. dirs. 1996—), Alumni Fedn. NYU (bd. dirs. 1982-96), NYU Club (ex-officio bd. govs. 1983-89), Univ. Club of Washington, Princeton club of N.Y., Univ. Glee Club of N.Y.C. Democrat. Jewish. Avocation: singing. Office: Manhattan College Lavelle Hall Manhattan Coll Pkwy Bronx NY 10471 E-mail: llerner@manhattan.edu.

LERNER, MARTIN, museum curator; b. N.Y.C., Nov. 14, 1936; s. Joseph and Rose (Kolberg) L.; m. Roberta M. Rubenstein, Feb. 26, 1968; children: Benjamin Louis, Seth Laurence, Jocelyn Ann. BA, Bklyn. Coll., 1959; postgrad., Inst. Fine Arts, NYU, 1961-65. Asst. prof. U. Calif., Santa Barbara, 1965-66; asst. curator Oriental art Cleve. Mus. Art, 1966-72; asst. prof. Case Western Res. U., 1968-72; vice chmn. charge Far Eastern art Met. Mus. Art, N.Y.C., 1972-75, curator Indian and S.E. Asian art, 1978—2004, curatorial advisor for South and S.E. Asian art, 2004—. Adj. prof. Columbia U., 2004; cons. in field; internat. lectr. Author: Bronze Sculptures from Asia, 1975, Blue and White: Early Japanese Export Ware, 1978, The Flame and the Lotus, 1984, (with W. Felten) Cambodian and Thai Sculpture: From the 6th to the 14th Century, 1989, Entdeckungen: Skulpturen der Khmer und Thai, 1989, (with S. Kossak), The Lotus Transcendent, 1991, Ancient Khmer Sculpture, 1994; contbr. articles to profl. jours. Served with U.S. Army, 1959-61. Mem.: East India; Devonshire (London). Home: Giglio Ct Croton On Hudson NY 10520 Office: Met Mus Art 82nd & Fifth Ave New York NY 10028 Personal E-mail: mlerneraaa@aol.com.

LERNER, MARTIN A., infectious disease physician; b. St. Louis, Mo. s. Bernard and Sarah Lerner; m. Lueva Dixon Lerner, July 2, 1989; children: Joshua Dodek, Joel Seth, Dara Elizabeth. BA, Wash. U., 1946—50, MD, 1950—54. Attending physician Beaumont Hosp., Royal Oak, Mich.; dir. divsn. of infection diseases Wayne State U., 1963—82; chief, dept. of medicine Hutzel Hosp., 1970—82; gov. Mich. Am. Coll. of Physicians, 1990—94. Asst. surgeon U.S. Pub. Health Svc., 1955—57. Recipient Achievement award, Wash. U., Sch. of Medicine, 1994. Master: Am. Coll. Physicians. Jewish. Achievements include patents for. Home: 590 Wallace Birmingham MI 48009 Office Phone: 248-540-9866. Business E-Mail: lerner@cdlmed.com.

LERNER, RANDOLPH D., finance company executive; s. Alfred and Norma Lerner. Grad., Columbia U., 1984, grad., 1987. Bar: N.Y., D.C. With Bear Stearns; ptnr. Securities Advisors, L.P., 1991; dir. MBNA Corp., 1993—, vice chmn., 2002, chmn., 2002—; owner, chmn. Cleve. Browns, 2002—. Chmn. bd. trustees N.Y. Acad. Art; trustee Hosp. for Spl. Surgery, N.Y.C. Mem.: D.C. Bar Assn., N.Y. State Bar Assn. Office: MBNA 1100 N King St Wilmington DE 19884-0131*

LERNER, RICHARD E., lawyer; b. Queens, NY, May 19, 1961; BA, SUNY, Albany, 1985; JD, St. John's U., 1989. Bar: Conn. 1989, NY 1989, US Dist. Ct. Ea. Dist. NY, US Dist. Ct. So. Dist. NY, US Ct. Appeals 2nd Cir., US Ct. Appeals DC Cir. Ptnr. Wilson, Elser, Moskowitz, Edelman & Dicker LLP, NYC. Mem.: Queens County Bar Assn., Assn. of the Bar of the City of NY, NY State Bar Assn. Office: Wilson Elser Moskowitz Edelman & Dicker LLP 23rd Fl 150 E 42nd St New York NY 10017-5639 Office Phone: 212-490-3000 ext. 2414. Office Fax: 212-490-3038. Business E-Mail: lernerr@wemed.com.

LERNER, SANDRA, artist. One-woman shows: Mercer Gallery, N.Y.C., 1969, Nassau County Mus. Fine Arts, Roslyn, N.Y., 1976, Soho Ctr. Visual Artists, N.Y.C., 1977, Betty Parsons Gallery, N.Y.C., 1982, Kampo Mus., Kyoto, Japan, 1983, 84, Gallery Don, Fukuoka, Japan, 1984, Tokyo Mus. Art, 1984, 86, 87, 89, Kampo Mus., Kyoto, 1984, 93, June Kelly Gallery, N.Y.C., 1992, 92, 96, 99-2000, June Kelly Gallery, NYC, 2004, Washington Assn. Gallery, Conn., 2005; group shows include: NAD, 1966, 72, 73, Hechscher Mus., N.Y.C., 1963, 68, 69, 74, Guild Hall Mus., Easthampton, N.Y., 1974, N.Y. Carlsberg Blyptotek Mus., Copenhagen, 1980, N.Y.C. Cultural Ctr., 1983, Mus. Stony Broook, NY, 1996, Zimmerli Mus., NEw Brunswick, N.J., 1999, Jeollabuk-do, Republic Korea, 2003, Art in Embassies Program, Bangladesh, Washington, 2004; represented in permanent collections: Aldrich Mus. Contemporary Art, Kampo Mus., Fukuoka, Japan, Zimmerli Mus., Rutgers U., Heckster Mus., Huntington, NY. ICA lectr., Japan, 1981; stage designer LAND Dance Performance, 1991, slide image for ECHO, 1995. Recipient Purchase award Nassau Community Coll., 1970, 74, Anne Eisner Putnam prize Nat. Assn. Women Artists, 1973, Benjamin Altman prize NAD, 1972; grantee ICA, 1981. Mailing: Ten E 18th St 6th Fl New York NY 10003 Office Phone: 212-929-2721. E-mail: sandralerner@aol.com.

LERNER, STEPHEN ALEXANDER, microbiologist, physician, educator; b. Chgo., Oct. 4, 1938; s. David G. and Florence (Trace) L.; m. June 6, 1963 (div. 1990); children: Deborah, Daniel, Susan; m. Aug. 18, 1991; children: Helena, Thomas. AB magna cum laude, Harvard U., 1959, MD magna cum laude, 1963. Intern, then resident Peter Bent Brigham Hosp., 1963-65; rsch. assoc. NIH, 1965-68; postdoctoral fellow Stanford (Calif.) U., 1968-71; asst. prof. then assoc. prof. U. Chgo., 1971-86; prof. medicine and infectious diseases Wayne State U., Detroit, 1986—, assoc. dean faculty affairs, 2002—. Convenor Soviet-Am. Symposium Antibiotics and Chemotherapy, Moscow, 1988; mem. merit rev. subcom. on infectious disease VA, 1998-2001; co-chair exec. coun. Mich. Antibiotic Resistance Reduction Coalition, 1999—. Editor: Aminoglycoside Ototoxicity, 1981; mem. editl. bd. Antimicrobial Agts. and Chemotherapy, 1981—, European Jour. Clin. Microbiology and Infectious Diseases, 1992-2005, Antibiotic Resistance Updates, 1997—; contbr. articles to profl. jours. With USPHS, 1965-67. Recipient Borden Rsch. award, 1963. Fellow Infectious Disease Soc. Am., Am. Acad. Microbiology (com. on awards 1993-96); mem. Am. Soc. Microbiology (chmn. antimicrobial chemotherapy 1987-88, divsn. group rep. 1990-92, councillor 1990-92, chmn. confs. com. 1993-96, internat.com. 1993—, chmn. 1996-2003), Inter-Am. Soc. for Chemotherapy (pres. 1986-88, bd. dirs., chmn. 1988-93), Internat. Union Microbiol. Socs. (U.S. nat. com. 2001—, chmn. 2005—), Internat. Soc. Chemotherapy (exec. com. 1987-93), Phi Beta Kappa, Sigma Xi, Alpha Omega Alpha. Democrat. Jewish. Avocations: travel photography, russian language, collecting antique maps. Office: Harper Hosp Div Infectious Diseases 3990 John R St Detroit MI 48201-2097 Business E-Mail: slerner@med.wayne.edu.

LERNER, VLADIMIR SEMION, computer scientist, educator; b. Odessa, Ukraine, Sept. 12, 1931; arrived in U.S., 1990; s. Semion N. and Manya G. (Grosman) L.; m. Sanna K. Gleyzer, Sept. 28, 1954; children: Alex, Tatyana, Olga. BSEE, Odessa Poly. Inst., 1954; MEE, Inst. Problem's Controls, Moscow, 1959; PhD in Elec. Engring., Moscow Power Inst., 1961; D Sci. in Systems Analysis, Leningrad State U., 1974. Prof. elec. engring. Kishinev (Moldova) State U., 1962-64; prof. elec. engring. and control systems Kishinev Poly. Inst., 1964-79; sr. scientist in applied math. Acad. Sci., Kishinev, 1964-79; dir. math. modeling and computer sci. lab. Rsch. Inst., Odessa, 1979-89; sr. lectr. UCLA, 1991-93, rschr., 1993—; chmn. computer sci. dept. West Coast U., L.A., 1993-97, Nat. U., L.A., 1997-99. Mem. adv. bds. Acad. Sci., Kishinev, 1964—79, Poly. Inst. Kishinev, 1964—79; vis. prof. Leningrad State U., 1971—73; cons., mem. adv. bd. Poly. Inst. Odessa, 1979—89. Author: Physical Approach to Control Systems, 1969, Superimposing Processes in Control Problems, 1973, Dynamic Models in Decision Making, 1974, Special Course in Optimal and Self Control Systems, 1977, Lectures in Mathematical Modelling and Optimization, 1995, Mathematical Foundations of Informational Macrodynamics, 1996, Lectures in Informational Macrodynamics, 1996, Information Systems Analysis and Modelling: An Informational Microdynamics Approach, 1999, Variation Principle in Informational Macrodynamics, 2003, Introduction to Information Systems Theory, 2004. Recipient Silver medal for rsch. achievements, Moscow, 1961, outstanding achievements in edn., Kishinev, 1975. Achievements include development of new scientific discipline Informational Macrodynamics. Avocations: bicycling, travel. E-mail: vslerner@yahoo.com.

LERNER, WARREN, historian, educator; b. Boston, July 16, 1929; s. Max and Rebecca (Rudnick) L.; m. Francine Sandra Pickow, Aug. 16, 1959; children: Suzanne Rachel Knuiman, Amy Florence Coyle, Daniel Joseph. BS, Boston U., 1952; MA and cert. of Russian, Inst. Columbia U., 1954, PhD, 1961. Asst. prof. history Roosevelt U., 1959-61; asst. prof. Duke U., 1961-65, assoc. prof., 1965-72, prof., 1972—2002, chmn. dept., 1985-90, prof. emeritus, 2002—. Cons. NEH, 1974—80. Author: Karl Radek: The Last Internationalist, 1970, A History of Socialism and Communism in Modern Times, 1982, rev. edit., 1993; editor: The Development of Soviet Foreign Policy, 1973, (with Clifford M. Foust) The Soviet World in Flux, 1967; contbr. articles to profl. jours.; mem. editl. bd. Studies in Comparative Communism, 1973-91. Served with U.S. Army, 1954-56. Am. Philos. Soc. fellow, 1972, 82; NEH, 1974-75; Am. Council Learned Socs.-Social Svc. Rsch. Coun. fgn. area fellow. Mem. Conf. Slavic and East European History (exec. council 1978-80, pres. 1986-87), Am. Assn. Advancement Slavic Studies, Am. Hist. Assn., So. Conf. Slavic Studies (Outstanding Svc. award, 2003) Jewish. Office: Duke U Dept History PO Box 90719 Durham NC 27708-0719 Office Phone: 919-684-5078. Business E-Mail: wlerner@duke.edu.

LERNER, WAYNE M., health care executive; b. Chicago, Ill. BS, U. Ill.; MHA, U. Mich., DPH, 1988. Adminstrv. positions Rush Presbyterian St. Luke's Med. Ctr., Chicago; v.p. Lash Group, Bannockburn, Ill., 1996; pres. Jewish Hosp., St. Louis, 1991—96; developer. exec. v.p. BLC Health System, 1993—96; pres., CEO Rehab. Inst. Chgo., 1997—. Chmn. Am. Hosp. Assn. Com. of Commissioners; mem. exec. com., bd. of commissioners Joint Commn. on Accreditation of Healthcare Orgn. Fellow Am. Coll. of Healthcare Executives. Office: Rehab Inst Chgo 345 E Superior St Chicago IL 60611-2654 Office Phone: 312-908-2720.

LERNER, WILLIAM C., lawyer; b. Phila., July 17, 1933; m. Billie Campbell, Aug. 15, 1957; children: Bonnie, Edwina. BA, Cornell U., 1955; LLB, NYU, 1960. Bar: NY 1961, Pa. 1992. Counsel SEC, 1960—65; asst. v.p. Am. Stock Exch., 1965—68; sr. v.p., sec. Carter, Berlind & Weill, Inc., NYC, 1968—71; pvt. practice Buffalo, 1971—85; counsel Snow, Becker & Krauss, PC, NYC, 1990—95; pvt. practice Pitts., 1991—. V.p., gen. counsel The Geneva Cos., Irvine, Calif., 1986—89, Hon. Devel. Co., Laguna Hills, Calif., 1990—91; pub. arbitrator NASD, 1995—. Bd. dirs. Rent-Way, Inc., MTM Techs., Inc., The Cortland Trust; chmn. Erie County Pub. Utilities Task Force, 1974—75; mem. Art Coll. Coun. Cornell U., 1977—85; mem. NY Gov.'s Hazardous Waste Facilities Task Force, 1983—85. 1st. lt. Q.M.C. U.S. Army, 1955—57. Mem.: ABA, NY State Bar Assn., Phi Alpha Delta. Office: 423 E Beau St Washington PA 15301-3605 also: 5905 La Rosa Ln Apollo Beach FL 33572-2908 Office Phone: 724-225-7177.

LERNER-LAM, EVA I-HWA, transportation executive; b. N.Y.C., Dec. 27, 1954; d. Sau-Wing and Jean (Lu) Lam; m. Arthur Lawrence Lerner-Lam, Sept. 4, 1977; children: Timothy Chi-Wen, Matthew Ta-Wen, Katherine I-Wen. AB, Princeton U., 1976; MS, MIT, 1978. Asst. planner County of San Diego, San Diego, 1977-78; dir. transp. planning group PRC Toups/Voorhies, La Jolla, Calif., 1978-79; assoc. planner Orange County Transit Dist., Garden Grove, Calif., 1979-80, San Diego Met. Transit Devel. Bd., 1980, sr. planner, 1981, dir. planning and ops., 1982-84; gen. mgr. Regency Motors, Montclair, N.J., 1984-85; asst. v.p., dir. planning and adminstrn. The Dah Chong Hong Trading Corp., N.Y.C., 1985-88; prin., cons. The Palisades Cons. Group Inc., Tenafly, N.J., 1988—; transport sys. advisor Economist Confs. Group, 1994—; co-founder ChinaTransport.net, 2000—. Mem. coun. on Fgn. Rels., 1996—, bd. adv. ENO Transp. Found., 1997—; chair Transit Cooperative Rsch. Program Transit-IDEA, Transp. Rsch. Bd., 1998—; bd. dirs. Transit Stds. Consortium, Inc. Founder, coord. Asian-Am. Admissions Vols. Group, Princeton, N.J., 1985—; chmn. bd. dirs. Si-Yo Music Soc. Found., N.Y.C., 1988—; bd. dirs. Princeton U., 1984-88, founder, bus. mgr. and condr. Princeton U. Jazz Ensemble, 1973-76; mem. Coun. on Fgn. REls., 1996—; bd. advisors Eno Transp. Found., 1997—. Outstanding student fellow State Farm Cos., Princeton, 1974; recipient Outstanding Achievement award Tribute to Women in Industry, San Diego, 1983; named Auto Dealer of Yr., N.J. Living Mag., 1985. Mem. NSF (transp. rsch. bd.), ASCE (vice chmn. planning com. urban transp. divsn. 1987-91, vice chairperson exec. com. 1991-92, chmn. exec. com. 1992-93, Frank M. Masters Transp. Engring. award 1998), Am. Planning Assn., Inst. Transp. Engrs. (best paper award 61st ann. meeting 1991, Innovative Intermodal Solutions for Urban Transp. award 1993, Ivor S. Wisepart Engr. award 1995), IVHS Am. (founding mem.), Asian Alumni of Princeton (mem. exec. com. Beijing 2000—, Outstanding Achievement award 1988), Campus Club (bd. dirs. 1984-94), San Diego Princeton Club (pres. 1983-84). Avocations: piano, swimming, running, bicycling, hiking. E-mail: elernerlam@palisadesgroup.com.

LE ROUX, PETER DAVID, neurosurgeon; b. Durban, Republic of South Africa, May 14, 1960; came to U.S., 1985; s. Petrus Andries Jacobs and Sally Ann LeRoux; m. Eleanor Merle LeRoux, Nov. 6, 1993; children: Peter Donlon, James Patrick, Margot Katherine. MB ChB, U. Cape Town, Republic South Africa, 1983, MD, 1995. Diplomate Am. Bd. Neurological Surgery. Resident in neurosurgery U. Wash., Seattle, 1985-93; fellow neurosci. Ecole Normale Superieure, Paris, 1993-94; asst. prof. neurosurgery NYU, 1994-2000, assoc. prof. neurosurgery, 2001; assoc. prof., vice chmn. dept. neurosurgery U. Pa., Phila., 2001—. Coord. NYU Neurosurgery Residency Program, 1998-2000, acad. coord. dept. neurosurgery, U. Pa., 2001—. Editor: Current Management of Cerebral Aneurysms, 1998, 2004—; ad hoc reviewer Jour. of Neurosurgery, Neurosurgery, Jour. of Neurology, Neurosurgery and Psychiatry, Surg. Neurology Jour. Neurosci., Brain Rsch.; contbr. articles to profl. jours. Named Young Neurosurgeon World Fedn. of Neurosurg. Socs., 1993; faculty rsch. fellowship ACS, 1996, Charles Elsberg Neurosurgery fellowship N.Y. Acad. of Medicine, 1993, Whitehead fellowship NYU, 1999; recipient Clin. Investigator Devel. award NIH, 1997. Fellow ACS, Am. Heart Assn. (Stroke fellowship); mem. Am. Assn. of Neurologic Surgeons, Am. Congress of Neurologic Surgeons, Soc. for Neurosci., AANS/CNS (joint sect. on cerebrovascular surgery), Neurotrauma Soc., Neurocritical Care Soc. Office: U Pa Dept Neurosurgery 330 S 9th St Philadelphia PA 19107 E-mail: lerouxp@uphs.upenn.edu.

LEROY, CLAUDE, physics professor, researcher; b. Charleroi, Hainaut, Belgium, Sept. 30, 1947; s. Bernard and Renée (Jacobeus) L. Mathématique Spéciale, Faculté St. Louis, Brussels, 1967; Lic. en Sci., U. Louvain, Belgium, 1971, D in Scis., 1976. Rsch. assoc. McGill U., Montréal, 1977-80; attaché de rsch U. Montréal, 1978-80; rsch. assoc. Northwestern U., Evanston, Ill., 1980-81; chercheur du fonds du devel. scis. U. Louvain, 1981-83; rsch. scientist Inst. Particle Physics, Montréal, 1983-90; assoc. prof. physics McGill U., 1983-90; titular prof. physics U. Montréal, 1990—, dir. nuclear physics lab., 1991-94, 2000—. Vis. rsch. fellow U. Southampton, Eng., 1976-77; sci. assoc. Ctr. European Rsch. Nuclear physics, Geneva, Switzerland, 1980—, dept. energy U. Florence; hon. prof. Nat. U. Peru, 1994—; mem. bd. mgmt. Inst. for Exptl. and Applied Physics, Prague, TRIUMF Can.'s Nat. Lab. for Particle and Nuc. Physics. Contbr. over 400 articles to profl. jours. Recipient prize for Achievements in Physics, Sci. Coun. Joint Inst. Nuclear Rsch., Moscow, 2000; Killam Rsch. fellow, The Can. Coun., 1993—95. Fellow Royal Soc. Can. (Rutherford prize for physics, 1988, mem. Acad. Scis.); mem. Inst. Particle Physics Can., Can. Assn. Physicists. Roman Catholic. Avocations: hieroglyphics, history, fishing. Home: 335 Hauterive Laval PQ Canada H7G 4L5 Office: U Montréal Nuclear Physics Lab CP 6128 succursale Centre-ville Montreal PQ Canada H3C 3J7 Office Phone: 514-343-6722. Business E-Mail: leroy@lps.umontreal.ca. E-mail: claude.leroy@cern.ch.

LEROY, DAVID HENRY, lawyer; b. Seattle, Aug. 16, 1947; s. Harold David and Lela Fay (Palmer) L.; 2 children. BS, U. Idaho, 1969, JD, 1971; LLM, NYU, 1972; JD (hon.), Lincoln Coll., 1993. Bar: Idaho 1971, N.Y. 1973, U.S. Supreme Ct. 1976. Law clk. Idaho 4th Dist. Ct., Boise, 1969; legal asst. Boise Cascade Corp., 1970; assoc. firm Rothblatt, Rothblatt, Seijas & Peskin, N.Y.C., 1971-73; dep. prosecutor Ada County Prosecutor's Office, Boise, 1973-74, pros. atty., 1974-78; atty. gen. State of Idaho, Boise, 1978-82, lt. gov., 1983-87; ptnr. Runft, Leroy Coffin & Matthews, 1983-88, Leroy Law Offices, 1988—. Candidate for Gov. of Idaho, 1986, U.S. Congress, 1994; U.S. nuc. waste negotiator, 1990-93; U.S. Presdl. elector, 1992; chmn. com. on improving practices for regulatory and mng. low-activity radioactive waste NAS, 2002--; lectr., cons. in field. Mem. State Task Force on Child Abuse, 1975; mem. Ada County Coun. on Alcoholism, 1976; del. Rep. Nat. Conv., 1976, 80, 84, 2004; chmn. Nat. Rep. Lt. Gov.'s Caucus, 1983-86; bd. dirs. United Fund, 1975-81; del. Am. Coun. Young Polit. Leaders, USSR, 1979, Am. Coun. for Free Asia, Taiwan, 1980, U.S./Taiwan Investment Forum, 1983; del. leader Friendship Force Tour USSR, 1984; legal counsel Young Reps., 1974-81; candidate for Gov. Idaho, 1986; presdl. elector, 1992; candidate U.S. Ho. Reps. 1st Dist., Idaho, 1994. Mem. Nat. Dist. Attys. Assn., Idaho Prosecutors Assn., Am. Trial Lawyers Assn., Idaho Trial Lawyers Assn., Nat. Assn. Attys. Gen. (chmn. energy subcom., exec. com., del to China 1981), Western Attys. Gen. Assn. (vice chmn. 1980-83, chmn. 1981), Nat. Lt. Govs. Assn. (exec. bd. 1983), Idaho Bar Assn., Ada County Lincoln Day Assn. (pres. 2000), Found. for Idaho History (pres. 2001-05), NAS (chmn. com. on improving practices for regulating and mng. low activity radioactive waste 2002-), Idaho State Repub. Conv. (vice chmn. 2004), Sigma Alpha Epsilon. Presbyterian. Office: The Leroy Offices PO Box 193 Boise ID 83701-0193 Office Phone: 208-342-0000.

LEROY, G. PALMER, art dealer; b. N.Y.C., July 15, 1929; s. John Minturn and Georgiana Kip (Palmer) LeR.; m. Kyra Hawkins, June 18, 1955; children: Kyra, Nina, Pamela. BA, Harvard U., 1951. With N.Y. Times, 1951-52, Frank Best & Co., N.Y.C., 1952-53, Kenyon & Eckhardt, Inc., N.Y.C., 1953-55, Inmont Corp., U.S. and Europe, 1955-83; v.p. sales Inmont Internat., Inc., N.Y.C., 1974-83; ptnr. Clinton R. Howell, Inc. Antiques, Pound Ridge, N.Y., 1984-85; mng. dir. Met. Opera Guild, Inc., N.Y.C., 1985-94; pub. Opera News, N.Y.C., 1985-94; dealer 19th and 20th Century Am. Art Palmer LeRoy Fine Art, Nantucket, Mass., 1994—. Mem. industry sector adv. com. chem. industry U.S. Commerce Dept., 1976-83. Pres. Friends of John Jay Homestead, Inc., Katonah, N.Y., 1977-95, chmn., 1995-98, chmn. emeritus, 1998—; bd. dirs. The Bedford Assn., 1972-85, pres., 1975-80, bd. dirs. emeritus, 1986-97; bd. dirs. Wildlife Preservation Trust Internat., Inc., Phila., 1983-94, pres., 1990-93, emeritus coun., 1994—; bd. dirs. N.Y. br. English Speaking Union, 1993-98, chmn., 1994-97; sr. warden St. Matthew's Ch., Bedford, 1985-89.*

LEROY, MISS JOY, model, apparel designer; b. Riverdale, Ill., Sept. 8, 1927; d. Gerald and Dorothea (Wingebach) Reasor. BS, Purdue U., 1949. Model, sales rep. Jacques, Lafayette, Ind., 1950; book dept. sales rep. Loebs, 1951-52; window trimmer Marshall Field's and Co., Evanston, Ill., 1952-53; sales and display rep. Emerald Ho., 1954-55. Model, narrator, designer J. L. Hudson Co., GM Corp., Coca Cola Co., Hoover Vacuum Co., Jam Handy Orgn., Rambler and Kelvinator divsn. Am. Motors Corp., Speedway Petroleum Corp., Ford Motor Co., auto, tractor & implement divsn., Sykes Co., Detroit, 1956—61; tour guide, model, freelance writer Christian Sci. Publ. Soc. and Monitor; spl. events coord. Prudential Ins. Co.; model Copley 7, Boston, 1962—70; dep. dir., vice consul Internat. Biog. Inst. Author: Puzz-its, 1986—2002. Founding angel Asolo Theatre, Sarasota, 1960; mem. Ft. Lauderdale Internat. Film Festival, 1990, Mus. of Art, 1978, Fla. Conservation Assn., Rep. Senatorial Com. Inner Cir., 1990, Rep. Nat. Hall of Honor, 1992, Congl. Com., 1990, Nat. Trust for Hist. Preservation, 1986, Fla. Trust for Hist. Preservation, 1987; one of founding friends 1000 Friends of Fla., 1991; sec. gen. World Cultural Conv.-Noble Prize and Internat. Peace Prize; life mem. Rep. Presdl. Task Force, 1993; mem. Grand Club Rep. Party Fla., 1996. Named Woman of Yr., 2004, Internat. Visual Artist of Yr., 2004; named to Internat. Hall Fame, 2004; recipient Rep. Presdl. Legion Honor medal, 1993, Rep. medal of Freedom and Wall of Honor, 1994, Disting. 20th Century Rep. Leader, 1994, 1998, Founder's Wall award, 1995, Hallmark medal of honor, Rep. Presdl. Roundtable, 2000—05, Internat. Order of Merit, Am. Order of Excellence, 2000, Order of Internat. Ambs., 2000, World Laureate of Eng., 1999, Rep. Senatorial Millennium medal of freedom, Congl. medal of excellence, 2002, Am. medal of honor, 2003, DaVinci Diamond award, 2004, Statesman award, Amb. Grand Eminence, 2004, Lifetime Achievement award, World Congress of Arts, Sci. and Comm. Mem.: Am. Rivers, Stratford Shakespearean Festival of Can., USS Constn. Mus. (charter mem. 1993), Am. Queen Inaugural Soc., Libr. of Congress (nat. mem.), Wilderness Soc., Heritage Found., The Crystal Soc., Nat. Parks and Conservation Assn., Internat. Honour Soc. (charter mem.), Ellis Island Found. (charter), Cousteau Soc., Heralds of Nature Soc., Purdue U. Alumni Assn. (pres.'s coun.), Paddlewheel Steamboatin' Soc. Am., Nat. Corvette Owners Assn., Soc. Honorary Mariners, INTRAV-Pinnacle-Elite Explorer Club, Internat. Gov.'s Club (continental gov.), Maupin Travelers Club, Captain's Cir., Ducks Unltd., Skald Club, Seabourn Club, Cunard World Club, Magic Kingdom Entertainment Club, Order Internat. Fellowship (charter mem., Internat. Woman of Yr. 1996—99, Woman of Yr. 1998—99, 2001—03, Internat. Visual Artist of the Yr. 2004), Zeta Tau Alpha. Avocations: travel, art, education, design, photography. Home: 2100 S Ocean Ln Apt 2104 Fort Lauderdale FL 33316-3827

LE ROY, ROBERT POWELL, retired minister, educator, writer; b. Ellensburg, Wash., Oct. 5, 1923; s. Bernard Rayme Jr. and Sibyl Powell Le Roy; m. Marion Knutson, July 30, 1946 (div. Jan. 1960); children: Marcie Jane Le Roy Root, Sibyl Marie Le Roy Ward; m. Shirley June Passmore, May 25, 1962; children: Kenny, Margaret, Beth, Roberta. BA in Edn., Pacific Luth. U., Tacoma, 1950; MS in Edn., Chadron (Nebr.) Tchrs. Coll., 1965; postgrad.,

U. Mo., Independence, 1972—73. Ordained min. Presbyn. Ch., 1950. Educator, Bapt. pastor Riverside Bible Ch., Puyallup, Wash., 1948-52; founder, editor Alarming Cry Newspaper, Pasadena, Calif., 1953—; editor Western Voice Newspaper, Englewood, Colo., 1955-57; tchr. Colo. State Reform Sch., Golden, 1958-60; co-founder Minutemen, Independence, 1962-80; Bapt. evangelist, 1957—90; founder Christian Sons of Liberty, Liberty, Mo., 1970—. Lectr. in field of scis. Author: Scientific Approach to Creation, 1965, All About UFOs, 1973, From My Foxhole to Tokyo (World War II History of 11th Airborne Division 1943-46), 1990, The Bible and UFOs, 1997, LeRoy Family History, 50 Years for God & Country, 1987. Founder, pastor All-Am. Bible Bapt. Ch., Langley, 1980-00; chaplain, historian Am. Legion, Clinton, Wash., 1993-99; co-founder Wash. State Populist Party, Seattle, 1984—; candidate Gov., Wash., 1984—. With U.S. Army, 1943-46. Recipient Bronze Star, 2 Purple Hearts; WWII Vet.'s fellow Christian Sons of Liberty. Mem. VFW (life, post 7348). Avocations: gardening, farming. Home: 3339 S Le Roy Cir Clinton WA 98236 Office: PO Box 48 Langley WA 98260-0048

LEROY, SPENCER, III, lawyer; b. Oak Park, Ill., Apr. 13, 1946; s. Spencer and Priscilla LeRoy; m. Barbara LeRoy. AB with high honors, U. Mich., 1968, JD, 1974. Bar: Ill. 1974, US Dist. Ct. No. Dist. Ill. 1974. Assoc. Lord, Bissell & Brook, 1974—82, ptnr., 1982—92; sr. v.p., sec., gen. counsel Old Republic Internat. Corp., Chgo., 1992—. Sgt. U.S. Army, 1970—73. Mem.: Ill. State Bar Assn., ABA, Phi Beta Kappa. Office: Old Republic International Corp 19th Fl 307 N Michigan Ave Chicago IL 60601

LESAGE, GENE, gastroenterologist, educator; b. Kansas City, Mo., Feb. 19, 1958; s. Robert and Roberta LeSage; m. Jannette Johnson, Apr. 14, 1984; children: Jonathan, Renee, Christopher. MD, U. Mo. Kansas City, 1977. Diplomate Gastroenterology Am. Bd. of Internal Medicine, 1984. Chief hepatology Scott and White Clinic, Temole, Tex., 1984—2001; chief gastroenterology U. Tex. Houston, 2001—. Home: 4026 Colony Oaks Dr Sugar Land TX 77479 Office: Univ Tex 6431 Fannin St Houston TX 77030 Office Phone: 713-500-6671. Personal E-mail: gene_lesage@yahoo.com.

LESAR, DAVID J., oil industry executive; BS, MBA, U. of WI. Ptnr. in charge of energy mfg. and retail practices Arthur Andersen & Co., Dallas; exec. v.p. fin. and adminstrn. Halliburton Energy Svcs. bus. segment, 1993-95; exec. v.p., CFO Halliburton Co., 1995—96; Pres., CEO Brown and Root, Inc., 1996—97; pres., COO Halliburton Co., 1997—2000, chmn., pres., CEO, 2000—. Bd. dirs. Lyondell Chemical Co., Mirant Co., 2000—; Mem. Am. Petroleum Inst., Upstream Com. Office: Halliburton Co 5 Houston Ctr 1401 McKinney Ste 2400 Houston TX 77020*

LESAVOY, MALCOLM A., plastic surgeon, educator; b. Allentown, Pa., June 27, 1942; BA, U. NC, 1964; MD, Chgo. Med. Sch., 1969. Diplomate Am. Bd. Plastic Surgery 1977. Resident gen. surgery U. Chgo., 1969—74; resident plastic and reconstructive surgery U. Miami, 1974—76; chief plastic surgery Harbor-UCLA Med. Ctr., Torrance, 1976—99; plastic surgeon Encino Outpatient Surgery Ctr., Calif. Clin. prof. plastic and reconstructive surgery UCLA Sch. Medicine, LA, 1976—; nat. pres. Millard Plastic Surgery Soc., 1987—89; Frank Hawkins Kenan vis. prof. dept. surgery Duke U., Durham, NC, 2003; Kazanjian vis. prof. divsn. plastic and reconstructive surgery Harvard U., Boston, 2003; presenter in field; symposium chair in field. Author: Reconstruction of the Head and Neck, 1981, Hand Surgery Review, 1981, 2d edit., 1985, over 25 book chpts., over 70 articles to profl. jours. in field. Nat. pres. Reconstructive Surgeons Vol. Program, 1990—92. With USAR, 1969—76. Named a Disting. Alumnus, Chgo. Med. Sch., 1983; recipient Excellence in Clin. Tchg. award, UCLA Sch. Medicine, 1978, 1992, 1993. Mem.: ACS, World Soc. Reconstructive Microsurgery, Plastic Surgery Rsch. Coun., Plastic Surgery Ednl. Found. (bd. dirs. 1984—93, pres. 1991—92), Internat. Coll. Surgeons, Am. Soc. Plastic Surgeons (bd. dirs. 1990—94, chmn. bd. trustees 1995—96), Am. Soc. Maxillofacial Surgeons, Am. Assn. Plastic Surgery (named Clinician of Yr. 2002). Office: 16311 Ventura Blvd Ste 550 Encino CA 91436 Office Phone: 818-986-8270. Business E-Mail: mlesavoy@surgicalrenaissance.com.

LESCH, ANN MOSELY, political scientist, educator; b. Washington, Feb. 1, 1944; d. Philip Edward and Ruth (Bissell) Mosely. BA, Swarthmore Coll., 1966; PhD, Columbia U., 1973. Rsch. assoc. Fgn. Policy Rsch. Inst., Phila., 1972-74; assoc. Middle East rep. Am. Friends Svc. Com., Jerusalem, 1974-77; Middle East program officer Ford Found., N.Y.C., 1977-80, program officer Cairo, 1980-84; assoc. Univs. Field Staff Internat., 1984-87; prof. Villanova U., 1987—2004, assoc. dir. ctr. Arab and Islamic studies, 1992-95; dean humanities & social scis. Am. U. Cairo, 2004—. Author: The Politics of Palestinian Nationalism, 1973, Arab Politics in Palestine, 1979, Political perceptions of the Palestinians on the West Bank and Gaza, 1980, (with Mark Tessler) Israel, Egypt and the Palestinians, 1989, Transition to Palestinian Self-Government, 1992, (with D. Tschirgi) Origins and Development of the Arab-Israeli Conflict, 1998, The Sudan: Contested National Identities, 1998, (with Steven Wondu) Battle for Peace in Sudan, 2000, (with Osman Fadl) Coping with Torture: Images from Sudan, 2004; contbr. articles to profl. jours. Co-chair Middle East Program Com., Am. Friends Svc. Com., 1989—94; mem. Quaker UN Com., 1979—80; U.S. adv. com. Interns for Peace, 1978—82; bd. dirs. Am. Near East Refugee Aid, 1980—86, Middle East Report, 1989—93, Human Rights Watch/Middle East, 1989—. Fellow Catherwood Found., 1965; NDFL, 1967-71; Am. Rsch. Ctr. grant Egypt, 1988, U.S. Inst. of Peace Rsch. grants, 1990-91, 97, 2002-03, Wilson Ctr. Guest scholar Smithsonian, 1990, Rockefeller Fdn. Bellagio Ctr., 1996, Fulbright scholar, Cairo, 1999-2000, Beirut, 2003. Mem.: Palestinian Am. Rsch. Ctr. (co-chair 1998—2001, U.S. dir. 2001—04), Coun. on Fgn. Rels., Sudan Studies Assn. (sec. 1993—96, pres. 1998—2000), Am. Polit. Sci. Assn., Mid. East Inst., Mid. East Studies Assn. (bd. dirs. 1988—91, pres. 1993—96, bull. editor 1997—99). Unitarian Universalist. Office: American Univ HVSS Dean 113 Qasr al-Aini Cairo Egypt

LESCH, MICHAEL OSCAR, lawyer; b. Berlin, May 28, 1938; came to U.S., 1940, naturalized, 1946; s. Adolf F. and Maria E. Leschnitzer; m. Judith Willis, Aug. 31, 1965; children: Sara, Benjamin. AB, Columbia U., 1958; LLB, Harvard U., 1961. Bar: N.Y. 1961, U.S. Dist. Ct. (so. dist.) N.Y. 1963, U.S. Dist. Ct (ea. dist.) N.Y. 1965, U.S. Ct. Appeals (2d cir.) 1968, U.S. Supreme Ct. 1975, U.S. Ct. Appeals (3d cir.) 1979, U.S. Ct. Appeals (7th cir.) 1979, U.S. Ct. Appeals (9th cir.) 2001. Assoc. Shea & Gould and predecessors, N.Y.C., 1961-69, ptnr., 1970-94, LeBoeuf, Lamb, Greene & MacRae, N.Y.C., 1994—. Dir. Apple Bank for Savs., N.Y.C., 2001—. Contbr. articles to profl. jours. Mem. ABA, N.Y. State Bar Assn., Assn. Bar City N.Y., Fed. Bar Coun., Am. Arbitration Assn. (panel of arbitrators). Office: LeBoeuf Lamb Greene & MacRae 125 W 55th St New York NY 10019-5369 Business E-Mail: michael.lesch@llgm.com.

LESCHLY, JAN, retired consumer products company executive; m. Lotte Leschly; 4 children. BS in Pharmacy, Copenhagen Coll. Pharmacy; BSBA, Copenhagen Sch. Econs. & Bus. V.p. comml. devel. Squibb Corp.; exec. v.p., pres. pharm. divsn. Novo Nordisk; CEO SmithKline Beecham, Phila., 1994—2000; ret., 2000—. Chmn. Brit. Pharma Group. Mem. dean's adv. coun. Emory Bus. Sch. Mem. Pharm. Rsch. and Mfrs. Am. (bd. dirs.), Pharm. Rsch. and Mfrs. Found., Nat. Found. for Infectious Diseases (trustee).

LESCROART, JOHN THOMAS, writer, composer, singer; b. Houston, Jan. 14, 1948; s. Maurice Eugene and Loretta Therese (Gregory) L.; m. Leslee Ann Miller, 1976 (div. 1978); m. Lisa Sawyer, Sept. 2, 1984; children: Justine Rose Lescroart, John Jack Sawyer Lescroart. BA in English Lit. with honors, U. Calif., Berkeley, 1970. Author: Sunburn, 1981 (Joseph Henry Jackson award, 1978), Son of Holmes, 1986, Rasputin's Revenge, 1987, Dead Irish, 1989, The Vig, 1990, Hard Evidence, 1993, The 13th Juror, 1994, A Certain Justice, 1995, Guilt, 1997, The Mercy Rule, 1998, Nothing But The Truth, 2001, The Hearing, 2001, The Oath, 2002, The First Law, 2003, The Second Chair, 2004, The Motive, 2005; composer (album) Date Night, 2003; composer and singer As The Crow Flies, 2003. Bd. trustees U. Calif., Davis. Named N.Y. Times Best Seller list for 13th Juror, 1995, Guilt, 1998, The Mercy Rule, 1999, Nothing But the Truth, 2001, The Hearing, 2002, The Oath, 2002, The First Law, 2003, The Second Chair, 2004. Mem. El Macero Country Club, Wine & Food Soc. Sacramento/San Joaquin. Avocations: fishing, baseball, food and wine. E-mail: jles@calweb.com.

LESH, PHILIP CHAPMAN, musician, composer; b. Berkley, Calif., Mar. 15, 1940; s. Frank Hamilton and Barbara Jewel (Chapman) L.; m. Jill Winifred Johnson, Sep. 12, 1984; children: Graham Hamilton, Brian James. Student, Coll. San Mateo, 1958-61, Mills Coll., 1962. Co-founder, bass and vocals group Grateful Dead, 1965—. Albums include American Beauty, Grateful Dead, 1967, Anthem of the Sun, Aoxomoxoa, 1969, Live Dead, 1970, Workingman's Dead, 1970, The Grateful Dead, 1971, Bear's Choice: History of the Grateful Dead, Vol. 1, 1973, Skeletons From the Closet, 1974, What A Long Strange Trip It's Been: The Best of the Grateful Dead, 1977, Wake Of the Flood, 1973, From Mars Hotel, 1974, Blues for Allah, 1975, Steal Your Face, 1976, Terrapin Station, 1977, Shakedown Street, 1978, Built to Last, 1989, Dead Set, Europe, 1972, Reckoning, 1986, Go To Heaven, In the Dark, 1987, Without a Net, 1990, One From the Vault, Two From the Vault, and others; songwriter (with Robert Hunter) Box of Rain, 1970, (with Robert M. Petersen) New Potato Caboose, 1967, Unbroken Chain, 1974, Pride of Cucamonga, 1974; composer Foci for 4 orchs., 1963; author: Searching for the Sound: My Life With the Grateful Dead, 2005 (NY Times Bestseller list, 2005). Inducted into Rock and Roll Hall of Fame, 1994. Office: care Grateful Dead Prodns PO Box 1073 San Rafael CA 94915-1073 also: Arista Records 6 W 57th St New York NY 10019-3901*

LE SHANA, DAVID CHARLES, retired academic administrator; b. Lucknow, India, Nov. 15, 1932; came to U.S., 1949; naturalized, 1958; s. Newman John and Gwendolyn Beatrice (White) Le S.; m. Rebecca Ann Swander, June 8, 1951; children: Deborah Lynn, James David, Catherine Ann, Christine Joy. AB, Taylor U., Upland, Ind., 1953; AM in Edn, Ball State U., 1959; PhD, U. So. Calif., 1967; LHD (hon.), George Fox Coll., 1982; EdD (hon.), Taylor U., 1996; DD (hon.), Western Evang. Sem., 1996. Ordained to ministry Friends Ch., 1953; pastor Ypsilanti (Mich.) Friends Ch., 1953-54; dir. pub. relations, chaplain Taylor U., 1954-61; pastor 1st Friends Ch., Long Beach, Calif., 1961-67; mem. staff George Fox Coll., Newberg, Oreg., from 1967, acting pres., 1967—68, exec. v.p., 1968—69, pres., 1969-82, pres. emeritus, 1996—; pres. Seattle Pacific U., 1982-91, pres. emeritus, 1991—; pres. Western Evang. Sem., Portland, Oreg., 1992-96, pres. emeritus, 1996—. Min. Pacific N.W. Conf. of Free Meth. Ch.; bd. dirs. Coun. Ind. Colls., 1971-80, chmn., 1976-78; chmn. commn. higher edn. Nat. Assn. Evangelicals, 1973-75; chmn. Oreg. Ind. Colls. Assn., 1971-72, 81-82; mem. So. Calif. Radio and TV Commn., 1963-67; bd. dirs. Christian Coll. Consortium, chmn., 1984-86; mem. fact-finding group to Bangladesh, 1972; mem. adv. bd. Oriental Missionary Soc.Internat.; bd. advs. Latin Am. Mission, 1984-2002, Friends Ctr., Azusa Pacific U., 1986—; mem. capital campaign com. Taylor U., 1995-2000; bd. dirs. N.W. Christian Cmty. Found., 1999—, Westlake Home Owners Assn., KWI Found., 1984-2000. Author: Quakers in California, 1969; Rec.: album Songs of Discipleship, 1965. Bd. dirs. Oreg. Ind. Coll. Found., 1969-82, 92-96, George Fox Coll. Found., 1971-82, Herbert Hoover Found., Oreg., 1975-82, Ind. Colls. of Wash., 1982-91, Wash. Friends of Higher Edn., 1982-91, Latin Am. Mission, 2002—, Significant Living, 2002—; bd. assocs. Pacific Sci. Ctr., 1989-92; mem. Wash. Gives Leadership Coun., 1989-92, mem. edn. commn. States Task Force on State Policy and Ind. Higher Edn., 1986-89; trustee CRISTA Ministries, 1982-88, 90-96, bd. dirs., 1982—; chmn. bd. Christian Coll. Coalition, 1991; trustee Azusa Pacific U., 2003—. Recipient Alumni Service award Taylor U., 1961, Chamber of Achievement award, 1978; Tchr. of Yr. award Ball State U., 1978 Mem. Nat. Assn. Evangs. (bd. dirs. 1980-99, chmn. theology com. 1992-94).

LESHER, ROBERT OVERTON, lawyer; b. Phoenix, Apr. 6, 1921; s. Charles Zaner and Alice Marguerite (Heckman) L.; children: Stephen Harrison, Janet Kay. BA, U. Ariz., 1942, LLB, 1949. Bar: Ariz. 1949, Ill. 1949. Atty. Atcheson, Topeka & Santa Fe Ry., 1949-54; pvt. practice, Tucson, 1954—. Adj. prof. Law Sch., U. Ariz., 1954-84; mem. Supreme Ct. Ariz., 1960. With AUS, 1942-46, 50-52. Fellow Am. Coll. Trial Lawyers; mem. Am. Law Inst., Am. Bd. Trial Advs. (diplomate), Internat. Assn. Ins. Counsel, Tucson Country Club. Home: 659 N Richey Blvd Tucson AZ 85716-5040

LESHER, WILLIAM RICHARD, retired academic administrator; b. Carlisle, Pa., Nov. 14, 1924; s. David Luther and Carrie LaVerne (Adams) L.; m. Veda E. Van Etten, June 16, 1946; children— Eileen Fern, Martha Zoe Lesher Keough Th.B., Atlantic Union Coll., South Lancaster, Mass., 1946; MA, Andrews U., 1964; PhD, NYU, 1970. Ordained to ministry Seventh-day Adventist Ch., 1951. Pastor No. New Eng. Conf. Seventh-day Adventists, 1946-56; pastor, mission dir. Delta sect. Nile Union Seventh-day Adventists, Alexandria, Egypt, 1957-58; prin. Nile Union Acad., Cairo, Egypt, 1959-61; sec. Middle East Div. Seventh-day Adventists Beirut, Lebanon, 1962-64; assoc. prof. religion, dir. summer sch., asst. to pres. Atlantic Union Coll., 1964-71; assoc. dir. Sabbath sch. dept. Gen. Conf. Seventh-day Adventists, Washington, 1971-79; dir. Bibl. Research Inst., Gen. Conf. Seventh-day Adventists, Washington, 1979-84; gen. v.p. Gen. Conf. Seventh-day Adventists, Washington, 1981-84; pres. Andrews U., Berrien Springs, Mich., 1984-94; ret., 1994. Author: Tips for Teachers, 1979; editor adult Sabbath Sch. lessons, 1971-79, studies in sanctuary and atonement, 1980-81; contbr. articles to religious jours. Recipient Founders Day award NYU, 1970 Home: 4703 Greenfield Dr Berrien Springs MI 49103-9566 Business E-Mail: lesher@andrews.edu.

LESH-LAURIE, GEORGIA ELIZABETH, academic administrator, biology professor, medical researcher; b. Cleve., July 28, 1938; d. Howard Frees and Josephine Elizabeth (Taylor) Lesh; m. William Francis Laurie, Aug. 16, 1969. BS, Marietta Coll., 1960; MS, U. Wis., 1961; PhD, Case Western Reserve U., 1966. Asst. prof. SUNY, Albany, 1966-69; asst., then assoc. prof. Case Western Reserve U., 1969-77, asst. dean, 1973-76; interim dir. Cleve. State U., Ohio, 1980, prof., chairperson, 1977-81, dean grad. studies, 1981-86, dean arts and scis., 1986-91, interim provost, v.p. academic and student affairs, 1989-90; vice chancellor acad. and student affairs U. Colo., Denver, 1991-95, interim chancellor, 1995-97, chancellor, 1997—2003, chancellor emerita, 2003—. Cons. in field; reviewer numerous granting agencies, profl. jours., 1968—; advanced placement exam. Edn. Testing Service, Princeton, N.J., 1982-83. Contbr. sci. articles to profl. pubs. Trustee Marietta Coll., Ohio, 1980-84, 85-95; mem. city/univ. interchange com., Cleve., 1983-91; chmn. commn. on women Am. Coun. Edn., 2002-2003; bd. mem. Girl Scouts Mile High Coun., Found. for Edn. Excellence, Rocky Mountain Inst. for Internat. Edn., Arapahoe C.C. Fellow NSF, NIH; grantee NIH, Am. Cancer Soc., Am. Heart Assn., Research Corp., 1968—; recipient Wright fellowship Bermuda Biol. Station; named among AAUW Women of Distinction; named to Girl Scouts Women's Leadership Cir. Fellow AAAS; mem. Am. Soc. Zoologists, Soc. Devel. Biology, Am. Soc. Cell Biology, Phi Beta Kappa. Home: 5677 S Park Pl Unit 311B Greenwood Village CO 80111 E-mail: georgia.lesh-laurie@cudenver.edu.

LESHNER, ALAN IRVIN, science administrator; b. Lewisburg, Pa., Feb. 11, 1944; s. Saul S. and Martha (Schmidt) L.; m. Agnes Farkas, May 18, 1969; children: Sarah, Michael. AB, Franklin and Marshall Coll., 1965; MS, Rutgers U., 1967, PhD, 1969. Asst. prof. psychology Bucknell U., 1969-73, assoc. prof., 1973-78, prof., 1978-82; program assoc. divsn. behavioral and neural scis. NSF, Washington, 1979-80, dep. dir. divsn. behavioral and neural scis., 1983-85, dir. divsn. precoll. materials devel. and rsch., 1984-85, exec. officer biol., behavioral and social scis., 1985-87; project mgr. Office Dir., 1980-82; dep. exec. dir. Commn. on Precoll. Edn., Nat. Sci. Bd., 1982-83; dep. dir. NIMH, 1988-90, acting dir., 1990-92; dir. Nat. Inst. Drug Abuse NIH, Wash., DC, 1994—2001; CEO AAAS, Wash., DC, 2001—. Vis. scientist U. Wis., 1976-77, lectr. Weizmann Inst. Sci., Rehovoth, Israel, 1977-78; Am.-Hungarian Acads. Sci. exchange scientist Postgrad Med. Sch., Budapest, 1974; bd. dirs. Nat. Sci. Bd. Author: An Introduction to Behavioral Endocrinology, 1978; exec. publisher Jour. Sci., 2001-; contbr. chpts. to books, numerous articles on roles of hormones in behavior, sci. and tech. policy, higher edn. to profl. publs. Fulbright scholar Weizman Inst. Sci.; recipient Nat. Rsch. Svc. award, 1976, Pres. Merit Exec. Rank award, 1990, Pres. Dist. Exec. Rank award, 1996. Fellow AAAS, APA, Am. Psychological Soc., N.Y. Acad. Scis., Internat. Soc. Rsch. on Aggression; mem. I.O.M., Phi Beta Kappa. Democrat. Jewish. Office: AAAS 1200 New York Ave NW Washington DC 20005 Office Fax: 202-371-9526.

LESHY, JOHN DAVID, lawyer, educator, solicitor; b. Winchester, Ohio, Oct. 7, 1944; s. John and Dolores (King) L.; m. Helen M. Sandalls, Dec. 15, 1973 (div. 2005); 1 child, David Alexander. AB cum laude, Harvard U., 1966, JD magna cum laude, 1969. Trial atty. Civil Rights Divsn. Dept. Justice, Washington, 1969-72; atty. Natural Resources Def. Coun., Palo Alto, Calif., 1972-77; assoc. solicitor energy and resources Dept. Interior, Washington, 1977-80; prof. law Ariz. State U., Tempe, 1980—2002; spl. counsel to chair Natural Resources Com. U.S. Ho. Reps., Washington, 1992-93; solicitor (gen. counsel) Dept. Interior, 1993-2001. Cons. Calif. State Land Commn., N.Mex. Atty. Gen., Western Govs. Assn., Congl. Rsch. Svc., Ford Found., Hewlett Found., Pew Charitable Trusts, Wyss Found.; mem. com. Onshore Oil & Gas Leasing, NAS Nat. Rsch. Coun., 1989-90; vis. prof. Sch. Law U. San Diego, 1990; disting. vis. prof. law U. Calif. Hastings Coll. Law, 2001-02, Harry D. Sunderland disting. prof. real property, 2002-2005; vis. prof. Harvard Law Sch., 2004. Author: The Mining Law: A Study in Perpetual Motion, 1987, The Arizona State Constitution, 1993; co-author Federal Public Land and Resources Law, 5th edit., 2002, Legal Control of Water Resources, 3rd edit., 2000; contbr. articles, book chpts. to profl. jours., environ. jours. Bd. dirs. Ariz. Ctr. Law in Pub. Interest, 1981—86, Grand Canyon Trust, 1987—92, 2002—, Natural Heritage Inst., 2002—, Ariz. Raft Adventures, 1982—92, 2002—; mem. Gov.'s Task Force Recreation on Fed. Lands, 1985—86, Gov.'s Task Force Environ. Impact Assessment, 1990, City of Phoenix Environ. Quality Commn., 1987—90; pres. Wyss Found., 2002—. Robinson Cox vis. fellow U. Western Australia Law Sch., Perth, 1985, rsch. fellow U. Southampton, Eng., 1986; Ford Found. grantee, Resources for the Future grantee. Democrat. Avocations: piano, hiking, whitewater rafting, photography. Office: Calif Hastings Coll Law 200 McAllister St San Francisco CA 94102-4978 Business E-Mail: leshyj@uchastings.edu.

LESIAK, KAREN ANN, librarian; b. Meriden, Conn., June 1, 1953; AA, Mt. Ida Coll., Newton, Mass., 1974; BLS, So. Conn. State U., 1979, MLS, 1990. Asst. libr. sch. of music libr. Yale U., New Haven, 1979-86; asst. libr. Harcourt Wood Meml. Libr., Derby, Conn., 1986-89, dir., 1989—2003; libr. dir. Archbiship O'Brien Libr. St. Thomas Seminary, Bloomfield, Conn., 2003—. Coord., facilitator writer's group Harcourt Wood Meml. Libr. Violinist with contemporary choir St. Stanislaus Ch., Meriden, Conn. Avocations: music, art, poetry.

LESICK, JOHN RICHARD, retired lawyer, consultant; b. Homestead, Pa., June 11, 1917; s. Michael Joseph Lesick and Mary Teresa Gavalek; m. Mary Eleanor Gillespie, May 29, 1942; children: John Richard II, Lawrence Thomas. BA, Ohio Wesleyan U., 1941; grad., U.S. Naval Sch., Port Hueneme, Calif., 1946; LLB, U. Cin., 1948. Bar: Ohio 1949. Lawyer, Cin., 1949—; ins. salesman W.E. Lord Co., Cin., 1952—56; assoc. C.L. Scroggins Assocs., Cin., 1957—62; pres. Profl. Mgmt. Assn. Inc., Cin., 1963—90; ret., 1990. Contbr. articles to profl. jours. Co-founder Village of Forest Park; vol., chmn. bd. Forest Park Hist. Soc.; mem. Forest Park Hall of Fame Commn.; pres. pro-tem City of Forest Park, Ohio, coun. mem. Maj. USMC, 1941—46, PTO. Republican. Avocations: writing, sports, public speaking. Home: 509 Curly Maple Sq Cincinnati OH 45246-4170

LESK, ANN BERGER, lawyer; b. N.Y.C., Feb. 7, 1947; d. Alexander and Eleanor A. (Dickinson) Berger; m. Michael E. Lesk, June 30, 1968. AB cum laude, Radcliffe Coll., 1968; JD with high honors, Rutgers U., 1977. Bar: N.Y. 1979. Law clk. to justice N.J. Supreme Ct., Mountain, 1977-78; assoc. Fried, Frank, Harris, Shriver & Jacobson, N.Y.C., 1978-84, ptnr., 1984—. Editor-in-chief Rutgers Law Rev., 1976—77. Mem.: ABA, Assn. of the Bar of City of N.Y. (com. estate and gift taxation 1997—2000, com. trusts, estates and surrogates cts. 1992-95, 2000—03, com. estate and gift taxation 2004—), N.Y. State Bar Assn. (mem. ho. of dels. 2003—), New York County Lawyers Assn. (co-chair com. trusts and estates legislation and govtl. affairs 1995—98, co-chair com. trusts and estates sect. 1998—2001, bd. dirs. 2001—04, sec. 2004—). Office: Fried Frank Harris Shriver & Jacobson LLP 1 New York Plz Fl 22 New York NY 10004-1980 Office Phone: 212-859-8113. Business E-Mail: ann.lesk@friedfrank.com.

LESKE, M. CRISTINA, medical educator, medical researcher; MD with highest honors, U. Chile, 1964; MPH, Harvard U., 1966; DSc (hon.), U. West Indies, 2004. Resident preventive medicine Harvard Sch. Pub. Health, Boston, 1966; resident pub. health Mass. Dept. Pub. Health, Boston, 1966—67, asst. dir. divsn. local health svcs., 1967—68; resident preventive medicine U. Rochester, NY, 1974, asst. prof. preventive medicine, 1975; asst. clin. prof. epidemiology and biostats. SUNY Coll. Optometry, N.Y.C., 1976—77, assoc. clin. prof., 1977—79; asst. prof. preventive medicine SUNY Sch. Medicine, Stony Brook, 1979—82, assoc. prof., 1982—89, prof. preventive medicine and ophthalmology, 1989—97, disting. svc. prof., 1997—, disting. prof., 2001—, head divsn. epidemiology, 1986—2002, chair dept. preventive medicine, 1991—2002; med. staff Univ. Hosp., Stony Brook, 1981—. Nat. adv. eye coun. NIH, 1987—91. Contbr. over 300 articles to profl. jours. Named Woman of the Yr. in Health, Three Village Times, N.Y., 1996, Outstanding Woman of Yr. in Sci., Town of Brookhaven, N.Y., 1998, Local Legend, Am. Med. Women Assn.; recipient Bicentennial medal, U. Cath. Chile, 1988, Disting. Achievement award in rsch., N.Y. Optometric Assn., 2000, Alumni Merit award, Harvard Sch. Pub. Health, 2004; Pub. Health fellow, Orgn. Am. States, 1965—67. Fellow: Am. Coll. Epidemiology, Am. Coll. Preventive Medicine; mem.: Inst. of Medicine of NAS. Achievements include research in in breast cancer; epidemiology of eye diseases, especially open-angle glaucoma and cataract. Office: 086L3 Health Sciences Ctr Stony Brook NY 11794-8036

LESKES, ANDREA, educational association administrator, educator; b. Washington, Sept. 9, 1943; d. Theodore and Florence Mildred L.; m. Tommy Olof Elder, June 27, 1981; 1 child, Ambjörn Olaf. BA magna cum laude in Zoology, Vassar Coll., 1964; PhD in Life Scis., Rockefeller U., 1969; MA in French, U. Mass., 1986. Asst. dean faculty of arts and scis. Dartmouth Coll., Hanover, NH, 1986—90; assoc. dean humanities, arts and social scis. Brandeis U., Waltham, Mass., 1990—91; vice provost undergrad. edn. Northeastern U., Boston, 1991—96; v.p. acad. affairs, dean faculty, prof. comparative lit. Am. U. Paris, 1996—99, interim pres., 1997—98; v.p. edn. and quality initiatives, dir. Greater Expectations initiative, dir. Inst. gen. edn. Assn. Am. Colls. and Univs., Washington, 1999—. Adj. asst. prof. comparative lit. Dartmouth Coll., 1989-90; adj. assoc. prof. French Brandeis U., 1990-91; adj. assoc. prof. modern langs. Northeastern U., 1991-96; cons. New England Resource Ctr. Higher Edn., Boston, 1994-96, New Eng. Assn. Schs. and Colls., 1995-99, many colls. and univs., NSF, 1990—. Translator: Leonora: The Buried Story of Guadeloupe, 1995, Tribaliks, 1987; editor: Grants for Graduate Students 1986-88, 1986, Greater Expectations: A New Vision for Learning as a Nation Goes to College, 2002. Trustee Am. U. Bulgaria, 2003—. Mem. Internat. Sch. Theory in the Humanities (faculty assoc.), Assn. U. Adminstrs. (exemplary model adminstrv. leadership award 1996), Phi Beta Kappa, Sigma Xi. Office: Assn Am Colls and Univs 1818 R St NW Washington DC 20009 E-mail: leskes@aacu.org.

LESKO, DIANE, museum director, curator; BA, Harpur Coll., 1971; MA in Art History, SUNY, Binghamton, 1975, PhD in Art History, 1982. Part-time instr. Sch. Gen. Studies SUNY, Binghamton, 1974-75, acting curator Univ. Art Gallery, 1975-76; vis. lectr. art history Hartwick Coll., Oneonta, N.Y., 1976-77; asst. prof. art history, co-dir. Coll. Art Gallery Lycoming Coll., Williamsport, Pa., 1978-85; curator of collections Mus. of Fine Arts, St. Petersburg, Fla., 1985-89, sr. curator collections and exhbns., 1989-93, asst. dir./sr. curator; exec. dir. Telfair Mus. Art, Savannah, Ga. Lectr. in field; on-site evaluator Fla. Maj. Cultural Instn. Program. Author: Gari Melchers: A Retrospective Exhibition, 1990, Jon Corbino: An Heroic Vision (mus.

catalogues); author: (book) James Ensor, The Creative Years, 1985; contbr. articles and essays to profl. jours.; editor: Catalogue of the Collection of the Museum of Fine Arts, 1993, Gari Melchers: A Retrospective Exhibition, 1990, Album Amicorum Kenneth C. Lindsay, 1989, Jon Corbino: An Heroic Vision, 1987, Binghamton Collects, 1974; editor Pharos, 1984-85, 86-87. Harpur Coll. Found. scholar, 1968-71; SUNY-Binghamton grad. fellow in art history, 1971-73, doctoral fellow in art history, 1978-79; Lycoming Coll. Doctoral Dissertation grantee, 1981, faculty profl. devel. grantee, summer 1982; recipient AAM Excellence in Peer Review Service Award, 2004, Visionary Award, Savannah Area Tourism and Leadership Coun., 2004. Mem. NOW, Women's Caucus for Art, Coll. Art Assn., Am. Assn. Mus. (reviewer), Phi Beta Kappa. Office: Telfair Mus Art PO Box 10081 Savannah GA 31401*

LESKO, HARRY JOSEPH, transportation executive; b. Cleve., Dec. 6, 1920; s. Theodore Prokop and Bertha Barbara (Trojack) L.; m. Evelyn Martha Culley, Feb. 3, 1945; children— Harry Richard, Larry J., Garry E., Mark J., John M., Joseph. BBA, Cleve. State U., 1956. Schedule analyst Cleve. Ry. System, 1938-40; pres., dir. Greyhound Lines, Inc., Phoenix, 1940—; pres. Atlantic Greyhound Lines of Va., Inc.; v.p. Gelco Bus Leasing Co., 1979—; pres. Trailways Lines Inc., Dallas, 1979—. Pres., dir. The Trailways Corp., Trailways, Inc.; dir. Trailways Lines Inc. (25 subs.), Southeastern Stages, Inc., Atlanta, N.Mex. Transp. Co., Roswell, KG Lines, Tulsa, Okla. Transp. Co., Lubbock, Tex., Jefferson Lines Inc., Mpls., Kerrville Bus. Co., Tex., Continental Lines, Amarillo, Tex., Service Coach Co., Jacksonville, Fla., Gen. Fire and Casualty Co. Served to capt. USMC, 1942-46. Mem. Am. Bus. Assn. (dir.) Roman Catholic.

LESKO, LEONARD HENRY, historian, educator, writer; b. Chgo., Aug. 14, 1938; s. Matthew Edward and Josephine Bernice (Jaszczak) L.; m. Barbara Jadwiga Switalski, Dec. 29, 1966. BA, Loyola U., Chgo., 1961, MA, 1964; PhD, U. Chgo., 1969; MA ad eundem, Brown U., 1983. Tchr. Quigley Prep. Sem. South, Chgo., 1961-64; Egyptologist, epigrapher, epigraphic survey Oriental Inst., U. Chgo., Luxor, Egypt, 1964-65; acting instr. U. Calif. at Berkeley, 1966-67, acting asst. prof., 1967-68, asst. prof., 1968-72, assoc. prof., 1972-77, prof. Egyptology, 1977-82, dir. Ctr. Nr. Eastern Studies, 1973-75, chmn. dept., 1975-77, 79-81, chmn. grad. program in ancient history and Mediterranean archaeology, 1978-79, chmn. humanities council, 1980-81, dir. Seila project, 1981; C.E. Wilbour prof. Egyptology, chmn. dept. Brown U., 1982—2005, prof. emeritus, 2005—. Author: The Ancient Egyptian Book of Two Ways, 1972, Glossary of the Late Ramesside Letters, 1975, King Tut's Wine Cellar, 1977, Index of the Spells on Egyptian Middle Kingdom Coffins and Related Documents, 1979; co-author: Religion in Ancient Egypt, 1991, Pharoah's Workers: The Villagers of Deir el-Medina, 1994; editor: A Dictionary of Late Egyptian, vol. I, 1982, vol. II, 1984, vol. III, 1987, vol. IV, 1989, vol. V, 1990, 2d edit., Vol. I, 2002, Vol. II, 2004, Egyptological Studies in Honor of Richard A. Parker, 1986, Exodus: The Egyptian Evidence, 1997, Ancient Egyptian and Mediterranean Studies in Memory of William A Ward, 1998; co-editor: Joseph Lindon Smith: Paintings from Egypt, 1998; contbr. articles to profl. publs. and encys. Active Friends of Libr., Brown U.; assoc. John Carter Brown Libr. Recipient award computer oriented rsch. in humanities Am. Coun. Learned Socs., 1973; NEH fellow, 1970-71, grantee, 1975-79, co-dir. Summer Inst., 1995; FIAT faculty fellow U. Torino, 1990; grantee R.I. Com. for the Humanities, 1998. Mem.: Soc. Francaise d' Egyptologie, Found. Egyptologique Reine Elizabeth, Egypt Exploration Soc., Archaeol. Inst. Am. (pres. San Francisco chpt. 1976—78, pres. Narragansett chpt. 1994—95), Am. Oriental Soc., Am. Rsch. Ctr. in Egypt (gov. 1973—75), Maserati Club Internat., Chevalier de Ordre Mondial des Gourmets Dègustateurs, John Russell Bartlett Soc. (pres. 1997—98), R.I. Acad. of Wine, Chevalier de Confrèrie de la Chaine des Rotisseurs (vice chargè de presse 1999), U.S. Lighthouse Soc., Ferrari Club Am., Lighthouse Preservation Soc., The Club of Odd Vols. (Boston), Univ. Club (Providence), Explorers' Club (N.Y.). Office: Brown U Dept Egyptology PO Box 1899 Providence RI 02912-1899 E-mail: Leonard_Lesko@Brown.edu.

LESKO, NEWLAND A., paper company executive; b. 1945; BA, Colby Coll., 1965. Staff Internat. Paper Co., Stamford, 1967, staff v.p., dir. quality mgmt., 1990, v.p., coated papers, 1990—92, v.p., gen. mgr., specialty indsl. papers, 1992, sr. v.p., indsl. packaging, chmn., leadership coun., exec. v.p., 2003—. Office: Internat Paper Co 400 Atlantic St Stamford CT 06921

LESKO, RONALD MICHAEL, osteopathic physician; b. Homestead, Pa., Mar. 25, 1948; s. Andrew Paul and Elizabeth Ann (Tarasovic) L.; m. Helena Alexandra Shalayeva, July 29, 1990. BS, U. Pitts., 1970; DO, Coll. Osteo. Medicine & Surgery, Des Moines, 1973; MPH, Loma Linda U., 1985. Diplomate Am. Osteo. Bd. Family Physicians, Am. Osteo. Bd. Preventive Medicine (bd. dirs., chmn. pub. health rep., chmn. bd. exam. com. 1991-97). Family physician pvt. practice, Port Richey, Fla., 1974-80; flight surgeon USN, NAS Chase Field Beeville, Tex., 1981-83; resident gen. preventive medicine Loma Linda (Calif.) U. Med. Ctr., 1983-85; pvt. practice family and preventive medicine, pvt. practice, Del Mar, Calif., 1988—; flight surgeon, capt. USNR, NAS Miramar, San Diego, 1988-95, ret. Loma Linda, Calif., 1996; attending physician ambulatory care svc. J.L. Pettis Meml. VA Hosp., Loma Linda, Calif., 1986-88; staff physician Scripps Meml. Hosp., La Jolla, Calif., 1990—. Lectr., 1985—; cons. Jour. Am. Osteo. Assn., Chgo., 1987, phys. rediness div. USN, Washington, 1988; med. advisor blue ribbon adv. com. Nutrition Screening Initiative, Washington, 1991. Contbr. articles to med. jours.; rschr. in nutrition and metabolism in human physiology. Med. adviser March of Dimes Suncoast chpt., New Port Richey, 1977-79; bd. dirs. Fla. Gulf Health Systems Agy., Region IV, 1977-79, Price-Pottenger Nutrition Found., San Diego, 1988—. Fellow Am. Osteo. Coll. Occupational and Preventive Medicine (trustee 1989-91, chmn. pub. health divisional com. 1989-91), Am. Coll. Preventive Medicine; mem. APHA, Am. Osteo. Assn., San Diego Osteo. Med. Assn., Osteo. Physicians and Surgeons Calif., Am. Coll. Family Physicians-Osteo., U.S. Naval Flight Surgeons. Avocations: scuba diving, photography, marksmanship, art, music. Office: 13983 Mango Dr Ste 103 Del Mar CA 92014-3146

LESLIE, ALFRED, painter, filmmaker; b. Bronx, N.Y., Oct. 29, 1927; Attended, N.Y.U., 1947—49. Vis. artist Amherst Coll., Youngstown State Univ.; vis. prof. painting Boston Univ. Exhibitions include Mus. Fine Arts, Boston, Hirshhorn Mus., Washington, Mus. Contemporary Art, Chgo., Butler Inst. Am. Art, 1984, Newport Harbor Art Mus., 1985, Boca Raton Mus. Art, 1989, St. Louis Art Mus., 1991, Joseloff Gallery, Univ. Hartford, 1991, Oil & Steel Gallery, N.Y., 1992, Manny Silverman Gallery, L.A., 1995; represented in collections of Met. Mus. Art, NYC, Stedelijk Mus., Amsterdam, Kunstmuseum, Basel, Moderna Museet, Stockholm; films include Pull My Daisy, 1959, The Last Clean Shirt, 1963, The Cedar Bar, 2002; author of 100 Views Along the Road, 1988; founding editor, The Hasty Papers, 1959. Recipient lifetime achievement award, Chgo. Underground Film Festival; grantee Guttman Found. for Avant-Garde Film, 1962. Mem.: NAD (academician 1994—). Business E-Mail: aleslie@nyc.rr.com.*

LESLIE, DONALD S., information technology manager; Bachelor's Degree, Dickinson Coll.; MBA, U. Pa. Industry and govt. bus. mgr. 3M Libr. Sys. Mem. Nat. Mus. and Libr. Svcs. Bd., Washington, 2004—. Mem.: ALA (com. on legislation), Minn. Libr. assn., Assn. Coll. and Rsch. Librs., Internat. Fedn. Libr. Assn. (vendor coun.), Am. Assn. Sch. Librs. Alliance (participant @ your libr. task force). Achievements include instrumental in the establishment of the ALA Vendor Alliance; instrumental in the formation of the 3M/AASL Salute to Schools Grant Program. Mailing: Inst Mus and Libr Svcs 1100 Pennsylvania Ave NW Washington DC 20506

LESLIE, DOUGLAS L., law educator; b. Des Moines, Iowa, 1942; BA, U. Iowa, 1964; JD, U. Mich., 1968. Bar: Ohio 1968, DC 1970, Mass. 1970. Appellate branch atty. Office Gen. Counsel NLRB, 1969; pvt. practice Washington, 1970-73; assoc. prof. Ariz. State U. Coll. Law, 1973-75, prof., 1976-78, U. Va. Sch. Law, Charlottesville, 1978-85, Charles O. Gregory prof. law, 1985—. Vis. prof. U. Mich., fall 1976, U. Va., 1977, Stanford U., fall 1982. Author: Cases and Materials on Labor Law: Process and Policy, 1979, 1985, 1992, Labor Law in a Nutshell, 1979, 1986, 1992, 2000; co-author (with Robert E. Scott): Contract Law and Theory, 1988, 1993; editor: The Railway Labor Act, 1995. Guggenheim fellow, 1982-83. Mem. ABA (sec. labor and employment sect. 1987-88). Office: U Va Sch Law 580 Massie Rd Charlottesville VA 22903-1789 Office Phone: 434-924-3853. E-mail: dll2k@virginia.edu.*

LESLIE, GREGG P., lawyer; b. 1963; BA, JD, Georgetown U. Bar: DC 1990. Staff atty. Reporter Com. for Freedom of the Press, legal defense dir. Office: Reporters Com for Freedom of Press 1101 Wilson Blvd Ste 1100 Arlington VA 22209

LESLIE, HENRY ARTHUR, lawyer, retired bank executive; b. Troy, Ala., Oct. 15, 1921; s. James B. and Alice (Minchener) L.; m. Anita Doyle, Apr. 5, 1943; children: Anita Lucinda Leslie Bagby, Henry Arthur Jr. BS, U. Ala., 1942, JD, 1948; JSD, Yale U., 1959; grad., Rutgers U., 1964. Bar: Ala. 1948. Asst. prof. bus. law U. Ala., 1948-50, 52-54; prof., asst. dean U. Ala. Sch. Law, 1954-59; v.p. trust officer Birmingham Trust Nat. Bank, Ala., 1959-64; sr. v.p., trust officer Union Bank & Trust Co., Montgomery, Ala., 1964-73, sr. v.p., sr. loan officer, 1973-76, exec. v.p., 1976-78, pres. CEO, 1978-91, also bd. dirs.; ret., 1991; pvt. practice Montgomery, Ala., 1991—. Mem. Ala. Oil and Gas Bd., 1984-85. Pres. Downtown Unltd., 1983-84; mem. Ala. Bd. Bar Examiners, 1973-78, bd. dirs. YMCA, 1992—; mem., vice-chmn. Ala. Jud. Campaign Oversight Com., 1999-2001; mem. Bus. Com. for Arts, 2003—, Com. for Cmty. Found., 2003. With U.S. Army, WWII, with USAR, retired as ltd. col. JAGC Res., 1970. Decorated Bronze Star. Mem. ABA, Ala. Bar Assn., Montgomery Bar Assn. (Liberty Bell award 1989), Ala. Ind. Bankers (chmn. 1983-84), Ala. Bankers Assn. (trust div. pres. 1963-65), Ind. Bankers Assn. Am. (dir. 1983-90), Ala. World Affairs Coun. (past pres.), Farrah Order Jurisprudence (pres. 1973), Order of Coif Alumni, Montgomery C. of C. (dir. 1983-84, pres. 1987-88), Maxwell Officers Club, Montgomery Country Club, Kiwanis, Delta Sigma Pi, Phi Delta Phi, Omicron Delta Kappa, Pi Kappa Phi. Episcopalian (past sr. warden). Home: 3332 Boxwood Dr Montgomery AL 36111-1702 Office Phone: 334-269-2740.

LESLIE, JACQUES ROBERT, JR., journalist; b. L.A., Mar. 12, 1947; s. Jacques Robert and Aleen (Wetstein) L.; m. Leslie Wernick, June 21, 1980; 1 child, Sarah Alexandra. BA, Yale U., 1968. Tchr. New Asia Coll., Chinese U., Hong Kong, 1968-70; free-lance journalist Washington, 1970-71; fgn. corr. L.A. Times, Saigon, 1972-73, Phnom Penh, 1973, Washington, 1974, chief New Delhi (India) bur., 1974-75, Madrid, 1975-76, chief Hong Kong bur., 1976-77; freelance journalist, 1977—; contbg. writer Wired Mag., 1993—2002. Author: The Mark: A War Correspondent's Memoir of Vietnam and Cambodia, Deep Water: The Struggle Over Dams, Displaced People and the Environment, 2005. Recipient Best Fgn. Corr. award Sigma Delta Chi, 1973, citation for reporting Overseas Press Club, 1973, J. Anthony Lukas Book-in-Progress award, 2002; Individual Artist grantee Marin Arts Coun., 1999, 2003; grantee, William and Flora Hewlett Found., 2001, Fred Gellert Family Found., 2001. Home: 124 Reed St Mill Valley CA 94941-3448 Office Phone: 415-380-1875. Personal E-mail: jacques@well.com.

LESLIE, JOHN WEBSTER, JR., (JACK LESLIE), communications company executive; b. Milw., July 20, 1954; s. John and Joanne Marie (Chamberlain) L.; m. Laura Elizabeth Bafford, June 7, 1986; children: Finn Elizabeth, John Webster III. BS in Fgn. Service, Georgetown U., 1976. Legis. asst. Senator Edward Kennedy, Washington, 1976-80; campaign dir. northeast region Kennedy for Pres., Washington, 1980-81; polit. dir. Senator Edward Kennedy for U.S. Senate, Washington, 1981-82; exec. dir. Fund for Dem. Majority, Washington, 1982-83; pres. Sawyer/Miller Group, N.Y.C., 1983-93; ptnr. Robinson Lerer Sawyer Miller, N.Y.C., 1993-96; pres. BSMG Worldwide, N.Y.C., 1997; chmn. Weber Shandwick, N.Y.C. Bd. dirs. Internat. Policy Research, Inc., N.Y.C., Creative Media, Inc., N.Y.C. Contbr. articles to profl. jours.; speaker in field. Bd. dirs. Nat. Student Edn. Fund, Washington, 1977-79, USA for UNHCR, 1997—. Fellow Circumnavigators Found., Am. Assn. Polit. Cons, Coun. on Fgn. Rels, bd. of the Found. for Accountability. Roman Catholic.

LESLIE, JOHN WILLIAM, public relations and advertising executive; b. Indpls., Nov. 22, 1923; s. John Edward and Catherine (Harris) L.; m. Joan Williams, Dec. 26, 1970; 1 dau. by previous marriage, Catherine Alexandra. Student, U.S. Naval Acad., 1943-44, George Washington U., 1949, Indsl. Coll. Armed Forces, 1956. Dep. excise adminstr., Ind., 1946-47; pvt. pub. relations bus., 1947-49; dir. pub. relations Ind. Democratic State Central Com., 1948-49, Ind. Dept. Vets. Affairs, 1949; press officer Dept. Labor, 1949-51, acting asst. dir. info., 1951-52, asst. dir., 1952-56, dep. dir., 1956-59, dir., 1959-81; sr. assoc. Kamber Group, Washington, 1981-84, counselor, 1984-88, exec. v.p., COO, 1988-96, vice chmn., sec., 1997-98, pub. rels. cons., 1998—, also bd. dirs. Mem., dir. pub. D.C. Com. Employment Physically Handicapped, 1952-53; charter mem. U.S. Sr. Exec. Svc., 1979—. Author numerous articles in field. Advt. cons. Pres.'s Com. on Youth Employment, 1964-80; U.S. del Internat. Graphic Design Coun., Japan, 1973; trustee Washington chpt. Leukemia Soc. Am., 1976-82; chmn. Pub. Printers Adv. Com. on Printing and Publs, 1977-79. Served with USN and USNR, 1941-46. Recipient commendation President's Com. Employment Physically Handicapped, 1954; Disting. Service award Dept. Labor, 1962; citation outstanding service Navy Dept., 1964; Presdl. citation, 1966; Merit award Internat. Labor Press Assn., 1969; Disting. Career Service award Dept. Labor, 1973; Communications award Ga. chpt. Pub. Relations Soc. Am., 1972; Sec. Labor's Recognition award, 1974; Communicator of Yr. award Nat. Assn. Govt. Communicators, 1981 Mem. Am. Assn. Polit. Cons., Am. League Lobbyists, Nat. Press Club, English Speaking Union, Univ. Club (Winter Park, Fla.), Stag Club of Winter Park. Episcopalian. Home and Office: Sweetwater Country Club 2433 Orchard Dr Apopka FL 32712-2562 E-mail: TwoLeslies@aol.com.

LESLIE, LISA DESHAUN, professional basketball player; b. Gardena, Calif., July 7, 1972; Grad., U. So. Calif., 1994. Basketball player USA Women's Nat. Team, 1996, L.A. Sparks WNBA, 1997—. Mem. gold medal winning 1994 Goodwill Games Team, US Women's Basketball Team, Athens Olympics, 2004; color commentary USC Basketball Games; guest corr. NBA Inside Stuff. Named 1993 USA Basketball Female Athlete of Yr.; recipient gold medal Atlanta Olympics, 1996, Sydney Olympics 2000; named MVP 1st WNBA All-Star Game, 1999; named MVP of season, WNBA Championship & All-Star Game, 2001, MVP WNBA Championship and All-Star Game, 2002, WNBA Defensive Player of the Yr., 2004; named 2003 Sportswoman of the Year for a team sport, Women's Sports Foundation; named to All-WNBA First Team, 1997, 2000, 01, 02. Office: Los Angeles Sparks 555 N Nash St El Segundo CA 90245

LESLIE, MARY LANE, lawyer; b. Lubbock, Tex., Aug. 12, 1949; d. James Ray and Margaret T. (Matthews) Chapman; m. John Morgan Broaddus III, June 28, 1980 (div.); m. Douglas David Leslie, Feb. 22, 1990. BA, Tex. Tech. Univ., 1971, JD, 1979; postgrad., William & Mary, Exeter, Eng., 1977. Atty. Ederer, Holmes, Neill & Broaddus, El Paso, Tex., 1979-83; landman-oil & gas El Paso Exploration Co., El Paso, 1984-85; atty. Edmunds Real Estate, El Paso, 1985-86; sr. counsel El Paso Elec., El Paso, 1986-88; atty. El Paso, 1988-96; mediator Taos, N.Mex., 1985—; exec. dir. Taos Talking Pictures Festival, 1996-98; county atty. Taos County, N.Mex., 2000—01; pvt. practice real estate, probate, and mediation Taos, N.Mex., 2001—. Bd. dirs. YWCA of El Paso, 1980-96, Homeless Coalition, El Paso, 1995-97; mem. vestry St. James Episc. Ch., 2002—; bd. dirs. Taos Land Trust, 2003— Mem. Tex. State Bar, New Mex. State Bar. Avocations: skiing, hiking, reading, cooking, horses. Office: 110 Cruz Alta Ste E Taos NM 87571 Mailing: PO Box 1568 Taos NM 87571-1568 Office Phone: 505-737-9762. Business E-Mail: leslielaw@zianet.com.

LESLIE, MAUREEN HEELAN, university director; b. Bronx, N.Y. d. James Joseph, Sr. and Evelyn (McDonald) H.; m. Bruce Allan Leslie; children: James Christopher, Michael Patrick. BA in Bus. Mgmt. cum laude, Molloy Coll., 1997. Adminstrv. asst., A placement dir., counselor Berkeley Coll., N.Y.C., 1965—71; entrepreneur The Silk Floral Gallery, Huntington, 1984-86; gen. orgn. treas. South Huntington Sch. Dist., 1984-98; devel. assoc. Molloy Coll., Rockville Ctr., 1998-99, dir. alumni rels., 1999—2002; exec. dir. L.I. (N.Y.) Ctr. Bus. and Profl. Woemn, 2003—04; asst. dir. off-campus programs Adelphi U., Garden City, NY, 2004—. Mem. industry adv. bd. South Huntington Sch. Dist., 1998—, Mt. Sinai (N.Y.) Sch. Dist., 1999—; bd. dirs. L.I. (N.Y.) Ctr. Bus. and Profl. Women V.p. St. Hugh of Lincoln Sch. Bd., Huntington Sta., N.Y., 1983; mem. LIA/Long Isalnd Works Coalition, Melville, N.Y., 1998—. Mem. AAUW (mem. com. industries initiatives 2005—), Exec. Women's Golf Assn., Long Island Women's Agenda, Long Island Ctr. Bus. and Profl. Women, L.I. Regional C. of C. to Bus. Partnership (mem. industry adv. bd. 2001—), Young Profls. C. of C. (mem. industry adv. bd. 1998—, edn. and tng. com. 2005—), Soc. Human Resource Profls., Delta Epsilon Sigma, Delta Epsilon Pi, Lambda Pi Eta, Phi Delta Kappa Roman Catholic. Avocations: tennis, golf, swimming, dance, reading.

LESLIE, SEAVER, artist; b. Boston, Aug. 22, 1946; s. John Frederick and Joan (Warland) L.; m. Anne Cleland Rogers; children: Genevieve, Marion, Frances. BFA, RISD, 1969, MEd, 1970. Instr. painting RISD, Providence, 1971-81, 97-2000, Parsons sch. Design, N.Y.C., 1980-82, Wellesley (Mass.) Coll., 1983-84; artist-in-residence U Calif., San Diego, 1984-85,1987-88. Exhibited in shows at Hirschl & Adler Gallery, N.Y.C., 1981, Tatistcheff Gallery, N.Y.C., 1982, DeCordova Mus., Lincoln, Mass., 1989, Maine Coast Artists, Rockport, 1993, 2000, Portland (Maine) Mus. Art, 1993, 2000; author: 12 Points: Putting the Case for Customary Measure, 1979, Why America Should Not Go Metric, 1993. Founder Ams. for Customary Weight and Measure, N.Y.C., The Morris Farm Trust; co-founder Maine Trans. Coalition, Wicasset. Studio: PO Box 248 Old Stone Farm Wiscasset ME 04578

LESLIE, SEYMOUR MARVIN, communications executive, director; b. N.Y.C., Dec. 16, 1922; s. Harry and Fay (Goldstein) L.; m. Barbara Miller, Mar. 30, 1947; children: Ellen, Jane, Carol. EE, Syracuse U., 1945; grad., Advanced Mgmt. Program, Harvard U., 1971; DHL, Hofstra U., 1974; Mus D, 5 Towns Coll. Music and Pa., 2005. Sales mgr. Voco, Inc., N.Y.C., 1946-52; founder, chmn. Pickwick Internat., Inc., Woodbury, NY, 1953, chmn. bd., pres., 1953-77; chmn. Leslie Group, Inc., 1977—; pres. CBS Video Enterprises div. CBS, Inc., N.Y.C., 1980-82; chmn., CEO MGM/UA Home Entertainment Group, Inc., 1982-87; co-chmn. Leslie/Linton Entertainment Corp., 1993—. Vice chair Songwriters Hall of Fame; vis. disting. prof. Syracuse U. Sch. Music, 1984. Active Boy Scouts Am., 1947-50; mem. corp. adv. coun. Syracuse U.; mem. coun. Hofstra U.; bd. govs. Anti Defamation League, 1960—; v.p., dir. T.J. Martell Found.; pres. Friars Found.; vice chmn., bd. dirs. Songwriter's Hall of Fame. Sgt. U.S. Army, 1942-46, PTO. Recipient Presdl. award Nat. Assn. Record Merchandisers, 1976, Disting. Svc. award, 1977, Outstanding Arendts Alumnus award Syracuse U., 1978; named Man of Yr. Time Mag., 1987; named to Video Hall of Fame, 1987. Mem. ASCAP, N.Y. Coun. for Humanities (dir.), Record Industry Assn. Am. (profl. group), B'nai B'rith, Friars Club, Harvard Club, Harvard Bus. Club. Office: Leslie Group Inc Ste 1103 1350 Avenue Of The Americas New York NY 10019-4651 E-mail: Cyleslie01@aol.com.

LESLIE, WILLIAM BRUCE, history professor; b. Orange, N.J., July 21, 1944; s. William and Annette (Riedell) L.; stepmother, Dorothy Kaul; children: William Andrew, Sarah Acton. BA, Princeton U., 1966; PhD, Johns Hopkins U., 1971. Asst. prof. history SUNY, Brockport, 1970—79, assoc. prof., 1979—96, prof., 1996—; vis. prof. Jordanhill Coll., Scotland, 1972, dir. grad. studies in history, 1984—90, 1997—99. Vis. scholar U. Cambridge, 2003, 05; co-dir. SUNY Social Sci. Program, London, 1978-79, 82-83, 89; cons. ETS, AP Exams., Fulbright, Scandinavian Selection. Author: Gentlemen and Scholars, 1993, 2d edit., 2005; mem. editl. bd. History of Higher Edn. Ann., 1991—; contbr. articles and revs. to profl jours. Fulbright scholar, Denmark, 1996-97. Mem.: Hist. of Edn. Soc., Am. Hist. Assn., Orgn. Am. Historians, U. Cambridge, Wolfson Coll., Princeton Club N.Y. Democrat. Avocations: camping, travel, gardening. Office: SUNY History Dept Brockport NY 14420-2956 Office Phone: 585-395-5691. E-mail: bleslie@frontiernet.net.

LESNICK, HOWARD, legal educator; b. NYC, Apr. 22, 1931; s. George L. and Sadie (Rovner) Lesnick; m. Carolyn M. Schodt, May 1, 1976; children: Alice, Caleb, Abigail. AB, NYU, 1952; AM, Columbia U., 1953, LLB, 1958. Bar: NY 1958, Pa. 1968. Law clk. to justice John M. Harlan U.S. Supreme Ct., 1959—60; prof. law U. Pa., Phila., 1960—80, Jefferson B. Fordham prof. law, 1988—; disting. prof. CUNY Law Sch. at Queens Coll., 1982—88. Impartial umpire AFL-CIO Internal Disputes Plan; dir. Ctr. for Law and Human Values. Author: Becoming a Lawyer: A Humanistic Perspective on Legal Education and Professionalism, 1981; contbr. articles to law jours. Served as pfc. U.S. Army, 1953—55. Mem.: Am. Law Inst. Office: U Pa Law Sch 3400 Chestnut St Philadelphia PA 19104-6204 Office Phone: 215-898-7495. Office Fax: 215-573-2025. E-mail: hlesnick@law.upenn.edu.*

LESNICK, IRVING ISAAC, lawyer; b. Bronx, Dec. 23, 1932; s. George L. and Sadie (Rovner) L.; m. Sheila H. Chorney, June 5, 1954; children: Charles Schorr, Grace. BA, Columbia U., 1954; LLB, Yale U., 1959. Bar: N.Y. 1960, Fla. 1982, U.S. Dist. Ct. (so. and ea. dists.) N.Y. 1961, U.S. Dist. Ct. (so. and middle dists.) Fla. 1983. Assoc. Poletti, Friedin, Prashker & Harnett, N.Y.C., 1959-60, Koeppel, Sommer, Lesnick & Martone, P.C. and predecessor firms, Mineola, N.Y., 1961, ptnr., 1962-81; pvt. practice Garden City, N.Y. and Boca Raton, Fla., 1981-86; ptnr. Dryer & Traub, New York, 1986-88; v.p. Harnett, Lesnick & Ripps, P.A., Boca Raton, 1988—. Spl. prof. Hofstra U. Co-author: The Law of Life and Health Insurance, 1988; contbr. articles to profl. publs. With U.S. Army, 1954-56. Mem. ABA, N.Y. State Bar Assn., Fla. Bar Assn., Assn. of Bar of City of N.Y., Yale Club. Democrat. Jewish. Office: Harnett Lesnick & Ripps PA 150 E Palmetto Park Rd Ste 500 Boca Raton FL 33432-4834 E-mail: ilesnick@harnettlesnick.com.

LESONSKY, RIEVA, editor-in-chief; b. NYC, June 20, 1952; d. Gerald and Muriel (Cash) L. BJ, U. Mo., 1974. Rschr. Doubleday & Co., N.Y.C., 1975-78, Entrepreneur Mag., L.A., 1978-80, rsch. dir., 1983-84, mng. editor, 1985-86, exec. editor, 1986-87, editor Irvine, Calif., 1987-90; sr. v.p., editor dir. Entrepreneur Media, Inc., Irvine, 1990—; rsch. dir. LFP Inc., L.A., 1980-82; editor-in-chief Entrepreneur Mag., Irvine. Spkr., lectr. in field. Author: Start Your Own Business, 1998, 3d edit., 2004, Young Millionaires, 1998, Get Smart!, 1999, 303 Marketing Tips, 1999, Ultimate Guide to Franchises, 2004; editor: Complete Guide to Owning a Home-based Business, 1990, 168 More Businesses Anyone Can Start, 1991, 111 Businesses You Can Start for Under $10,000, 1991; contbr. articles to mags. Mem. adv. bd. disting. counselors Women's Leadership Exch.; nat. adv. coun. SBA, 1994—2000; bd. dirs. Students in Free Enterprise, Jr. Achievement, Orange County. Named Dist. Media Adv. of Yr., SBA, 1993, Dist. Women in Bus. Adv., SBA, 1995; Bus. Luminaries award. Mem. Women's Network for Entrepreneurial Tng. (bd. dirs., advisor, nat. steering com.). Avocations: books, magazines, baseball. Office: Entrepreneur Media Inc 2445 Mccabe Way Irvine CA 92614-6244 Business E-Mail: rieva@entrepreneur.com.

LESOURD, FRANCIS ANCIL, lawyer; b. Seattle, June 22, 1908; s. Charles Lawson and Edna Blanche (Ball) LeS.; m. Elizabeth Burgess Roberts, Feb. 18, 1935 (dec. 1979); children: Peter Charles, Christopher Roberts. LLB, U. Wash., 1932. Bar: Wash. 1932. Assoc. Chadwick, Chadwick & Mills, Seattle, 1932-33; atty. PWA, Washington, 1933-34; spl. asst. to atty. gen. tax. divsn. Dept. Justice, Washington, 1934-37; assoc. William Stanley, Washington, 1937-38; pvt. practice law Seattle; also regional atty. lands divsn. Dept. Justice, 1938-40; ptnr. LeSourd & Patten and predecessors, Seattle, 1941-86, of counsel, 1986—. Lectr. taxation and constl. law U. Wash., Washington Coll. Law; sec., dir. TBC Inc., Bryant Corp., Seattle. Former Wash. State rep., nat. adv. bd. Coun. Pub. Lands; mem. Seattle Mcpl. Civil Svc. Commn., 1945-50; commr. Housing Authority Seattle, 1939-41; ednl. dir. Wash. Dem.

Ctrl. Com., 1954; mem. Wash. Dem. Fin. Com., 1955-56. Mem. ABA, Wash. Bar Assn., Seattle Bar Assn., Seattle Opera Assn. (past pres.), Order of Coif, Phi Beta Kappa. Clubs: Corinthian Yacht (Seattle). Home: 3143 W Laurelhurst Dr NE Seattle WA 98105-5342

LESOURD, NANCY SUSAN OLIVER, lawyer, writer; b. Atlanta, Aug. 22, 1953; d. Carl Samuel and Jane (Meadows) Oliver; m. Jeffrey Alan LeSourd, Oct. 18, 1986; children: Jeffrey Luke, Catherine Victoria. BA in Polit. Sci., Agnes Scott Coll., 1975; MA in History, Edn., Tufts U., 1977; JD, Georgetown U., 1984. Bar: Pa. 1985, D.C. 1986, Va. 1992, Fed. Cir. Ct. Appeals., 1988, U.S. Claims Ct., 1988, U.S. Supreme Ct. Instr. Newton H.S., Mass., 1976—78, Stony Brook Sch., NY, 1978—81; assoc. Gammon and Grange, Washington, 1984—88; shareholder Gammon and Grange, P.C., 1988—; mgr. Marshall-LeSourd L.L.C., 1996—. Legal commentator (radio shows) UPI News, Washington, 1985-91, Focus on the Family (Washington corr.), Colorado Springs, Colo., 1987-94; legal columnist Christian Mgmt. Rev., Downers Grove, Ill., 1987-90; spkr. in field. Author: No Longer The Hero, 1992, Liberty Letters: Underground Railroad, 2003, Liberty Letters: The Story of Pocahontas, 2003, Liberty Letters: Civil War Spies, 2004, Liberty Letters: Pearl Harbor, 2004, Christy: Christmastime in Cutter Gap, 2003; editor: Georgetown Law Jour., 1982-84; contbr. articles to profl. jours.; cons., prodr. three TV movies based on Christy, 2000—. Founder, vice-chmn. bd. trustees Ambleside Sch., 1998—2001; Bd. dirs. Arlington County Equal Employment Opportunity Commn., 1985. William Robertson Coe fellow SUNY, Stony Brook, 1978. Mem. D.C. Bar Assn., Va. Bar Assn., Christian Legal Society (bd. dirs. 1990-93). Republican. Office: Gammon and Grange PC 8280 Greensboro Dr Fl 7 Mc Lean VA 22102-3807 Home: PO Box C Lincoln VA 20160 Office Phone: 703-761-5000. Business E-Mail: nol@gg-law.com.

LESS, ANTHONY ALBERT, retired naval officer; b. Salem, Ohio, Aug. 31, 1937; s. Joseph Anthony and Mildred Gertrude (Bair) L.; m. Leanne Carol Kuhl, Mar. 3, 1962; children: Robyn, Pamela, Theresa, Christina. BS in Chemistry, Heidelberg Coll., 1959. Designated naval aviator. Commd. ensign USN, 1960, advanced through grades to vice adm., 1991, ret., 1994; comdg. officer USS Wichita (AOR-1), 1979-81, USS Ranger (CV-61), 1982-83; chief of staff Comdr. 7th Fleet, Yokosuka, Japan, 1983-84; dir. Polit. Mil Br. JCS, Washington, 1985-87; comdr. Carrier Group One, Pacific, 1987-88, Mid. East Force, Manama, Bahrain, 1988-89; dir. Plans and Policy Navy Staff, Washington, 1989-91; comdr. Naval Air Force Atlantic Fleet, Norfolk, Va., 1991-94; pres. Assn. Naval Aviation, Washington, 1995. Cons. Kaman Aerospace, Bloomfield, Conn., 1994-2003; v.p. govt. programs Kaman Aerospace, Arlington, Va.; sr. v.p. navy programs Burdeshaw Assocs., Ltd., Bethesda, Md., 2003—. Mem. Assn. Naval Aviation (pres. 1994), Soc. Naval Engrs. Roman Catholic. Avocations: racquetball, farming, reading. Office: Burdeshaw Assocs Ltd 4701 Sangamore Rd Bethesda MD 20816-2500 Office Phone: 301-229-5800. Business E-Mail: tonyless@burdeshaw.com.

LESSARD, MICHEL M., finance company executive; b. Quebec City, Can., Aug. 31, 1939; s. Maurice and Jacqueline (Lacasse) Lessard; children: Eric, Christine. BA, Laval U., Que., Can., 1958, B in Commerce, 1961, M in Commerce, 1962; MBA, Harvard U., 1967. With Can. Ingersoll Rand, Allied Chem. Can., DomGlass Ltd., Montreal, Canada; with Credit Foncier, Montreal, 1970-86, asst. gen. mgr., treas., 1978-79, sr. asst. gen. mgr., 1979-80, exec. v.p., 1980-81, pres., dir., mem. exec. com., 1981-86, pres., CEO, 1984-86; pres. Sogexfi Inc., 1986—; pres., CEO Immobiliere Natgen Inc., 1993-95; gen. mgr. Hippodrome De Montreal Inc., 1997-99; pres. Domaine de L'isle au oyes Inc., 2000—. Bd. dirs. Fonds de Solidarite, FTQ Groupe Redressement, 2004, Hydro-Mobile Inc., 2005, Denmarco Inc. Fellow: Trust Cos. Inst.; mem.: Club de Golf de la Vallee du Richelieu, Winchester Club. Home: 11 O'Reilly Apt 1503 Verdun PQ Canada H3E 1T6 E-mail: mlessard@sogexfi.ca.

LESSARD, STEFAN, musician; b. June 4, 1974; s. Ron and Janaki Lessard; 1 child, Diego. Mem., bassist Dave Matthews Band, 1991—. Musician: (albums) (with Dave Matthews Band) Remember Two Things, 1993, Crash, 1996, Live at Red Rocks 8.15.95, 1997, Before These Crowded Streets, 1998, Everyday, 2001, Busted Stuff, 2002, Central Park Concert, 2003, Gorge, 2004, (others) Best of Columbia Records Radio Hour, Vol. 2, Various Artists, 1996, Live on Letterman: Music from the Late Show, Various Artists, 1997, Scream 2 Original Soundtrack, 1997, Devon, Devon Sproule, 2000, Deep End, Vol. 1, Gov't Mule, 2001, Long Sleeve Story, Devon Sproule, 2001, Beauty of the Rain, Dar Williams, 2003. Recipient with Dave Matthews Band, Grammy award for Best Rock Performance by a Duo or Group with Vocal for So Much to Say, 1996, Chmns. award, NAACP Image Awards, 2004. Office: RCA Records 1540 Broadway New York NY 10036

LESSENCO, GILBERT BARRY, lawyer; b. Balt., June 19, 1929; s. Jacob David and Sarah (Bank) L.; m. Elaine Beitler, Sept. 3, 1952; children: Susan Donna, Amy Gail, Robert Howard. BS, Johns Hopkins U.; JD, Harvard U. Bar: D.C. 1953, Md. 1955. Atty. Wilner and Bergson, Washington, 1955; ptnr. Wilner & Scheiner, Washington, 1960—90; 1990ptnr. Semmes, Bowen & Semmes, Washington, 1990—95, mng. ptnr., 1992—95; of counsel Thompson & Hine, Washington, 1995—. Prof. bus. law and mktg. law Johns Hopkins U. Sch. Profl. Studies in Bus. and Edn., 1997—. Chmn. Internat. Visitors Svc. Coun., 1962; bd. dirs. Mental Health Assn. Montgomery County, 1996, pres., 1981—82; mem. Johns Hopkins U. Com. for Washington, 1996; trustee Meridian Ho. Found.; commr. Washington Suburban San. Commn., 1987—93, chmn., 1989—90; co-chmn., fundraiser St. Luke's Ho., 1989; mem., treas. Dem. Ctrl. Com., Montgomery County, Md., 1970—74; bd. dirs. Jewish Social Svc. Agy. Greater Washington, 1978—, pres., 1984—86. Lt. USAF, 1953—55. Named Outstanding Young Lawyer of Yr., D.C. Jr. Bar, 1965, St. Luke's Ho. Cmty. Leadership award, 2002. Mem. Phi Sigma Delta (v.p.). Home: 10731 Gloxinia Dr Rockville MD 20852-3442 Office: Thompson Hine 1920 N St NW Washington DC 20036-1601 Office Phone: 202-973-2724. Business E-Mail: gil.lessenco@thompsonhine.com.

LESSER, HENRY, lawyer; b. London, Feb. 28, 1947; came to U.S., 1976; s. Bernard Martin and Valerie Joan (Leslie) L.; m. Jane Michaels, June 29, 1969. BA with honors, Cambridge (Eng.) U., 1968, MA with honors, 1972; LLM, Harvard U., 1973. Bar: Eng. 1969, N.Y. 1977, U.S. Dist. Ct. (so. and ea. dists.) N.Y. 1977, Calif. 1984, U.S. Dist. Ct. (cen. dist.) Calif. 1984. Pvt. practice, London, 1969-71; assoc. Spear & Hill, N.Y.C. and London, 1974-75, Webster & Sheffield, N.Y.C. and London, 1976-77, Wachtell, Lipton, Rosen & Katz, N.Y.C., 1977-80, ptnr., 1980-83, Gibson, Dunn & Cutcher, L.A., 1983-87, Fried, Frank, Harris, Shriver & Jacobson, L.A., 1987-91, Irell & Manella, LLC, L.A., 1991-97, Heller, Ehrman, White & McAuliffe, Palo Alto, Calif., 1997-2000, Gray, Cary, Ware & Friedenrich, Ea. Palo Alto, 2000—04; ptnr., co-chmn. Private Equity practice group DLA Piper Rudnick Gray Cary, Ea. Palo Alto, Calif., 2005—. Lectr. law Oxford (Eng.) U., 1968-69, Cambridge U., 1970-71, UCLA, 1989. Editor-in-chief emeritus (bi-monthly) Corporate Governance Adviser; contbr. articles to profl. publs. Chmn. bd. Schola Cantorum, Mountain View, Calif.; bd. mem. Redwood Symphony Orch. Harkness fellow Commonwealth Fund, N.Y., 1971; named one of No. Calif. Top 100 Super Lawyers, San Francisco mag., 2004. Mem. ABA, Internat. Bar Assn., Calif. Bar Assn. (chmn. corps. com. 1990-91, vice chmn. bus. law sect. exec. com. 1993-94), Am. Law Inst., Assn. Bar City N.Y. Avocations: running, golf. Office: DLA Piper Rudnick Gray Cary 2000 University Ave East Palo Alto CA 94303 Office Phone: 650-833-2425. Office Fax: 650-833-2001. Business E-Mail: henry.lesser@dlapiper.com.*

LESSER, JOAN L., lawyer; b. L.A. BA, Brandeis U., 1969; JD, U. So. Calif., 1973. Bar: Calif. 1973, U.S. Dist. Ct. (cen. dist.) Calif. 1974. Assoc. Irell and Manella LLP, L.A., 1973-80, ptnr., 1980—2005, v.p. fin., 2005—. Mem. planning com. Ann. Real Property Inst., Continuing Edn. Bar, Berkeley, 1990-96; spkr. profl. confs. Trustee Windward Sch., 1994-00, bd. dirs., v.p. devel. UCLA Design for Sharing, 2005—, v.p. fin. devel Mem. Orgn. Women Execs. (past pres., bd. dirs.), Order of Coif., In2Books.org (bd. dirs.). Office: Irell & Manella LLP 1800 Avenue Of The Stars Los Angeles CA 90067-4276 Office Phone: 310-203-7577. Business E-Mail: jlesser@irell.com.

LESSER, LAURENCE, musician, educator; b. Los Angeles, Oct. 28, 1938; s. Moses Aaron and Rosalyne Anne (Asner) L.; m. Masuko Ushioda, Dec. 23, 1971; children— Erika, Adam AB, Harvard U., 1961; student of Gaspar Cassadó, Germany, 1961-62; student of Gregor Piatigorsky, 1963-66. Mem. faculty U. So. Calif., Los Angeles, 1963-70, Peabody Inst., Balt., 1970-74, New Eng. Conservatory Music, Boston, 1974—, pres., 1983-96, pres. emeritus, 1997—. Former vis. prof. Eastman Sch. Music, Rochester, NY; vis. prof. Toho Gakuen Sch. Music, Tokyo, 1973—95; performed with New Japan Philharm., Boston Symphony, London Philharm., L.A. Philharm. and Marlboro, Spoleto, Casals, Santa Fe and Banff festivals; rec. artist. Trustee emeritus WGBH Ednl. Found.; mem. adv. coun. Chamber Music Am. Recipient prize Tchaikovsky Competition, Moscow, 1966; Fulbright scholar, 1961-62; Ford Found. grantee, 1972. Mem. Am. Acad. Arts and Scis., Harvard Mus. Assn., Phi Beta Kappa, Pi Kappa Lambda, Sigma Alpha Iota. Jewish. Home: 26 Walker St Cambridge MA 02138-2404 Office: New Eng Conservatory Music 290 Huntington Ave Boston MA 02115-5018 Personal E-mail: ldlesser@comcast.net.

LESSER, RICHARD G., retired apparel executive; Pres. The Marmaxx Group; exec. v.p. The TJX Cos. Inc., Framingham, Mass., 1999, also bd. dirs., ret. Office: The TJX Cos Inc 770 Cochituate Rd Framingham MA 01701-4672

LESSER, WENDY, editor, writer, consultant; b. Santa Monica, Calif., Mar. 20, 1952; d. Murray Leon Lesser and Millicent Dillon; m. Richard Rizzo, Jan. 18, 1985; 1 child, Nicholas 1 stepchild, Dov Antonio. BA, Harvard U., 1973; MA, Cambridge (Eng.) U., 1975; PhD, U. Calif., Berkeley, 1982. Founding ptnr. Lesser & Ogden Assocs., Berkeley, 1977-81; founding editor Threepenny Rev., Berkeley, 1980—. Bellagio resident Rockefeller Found., Italy, 1984. Author: The Life Below the Ground, 1987, His Other Half, 1991, Pictures at an Execution, 1994, A Director Calls, 1997, The Amateur, 1999, Nothing Remains the Same, 2002; editor: Hiding in Plain Sight, 1993, The Genius of Language, 2004. Fellow, NEH, 1983, Guggenheim Found., 1988, NEH, 1992, ACLS, 1996, Open Soc. Inst., 1998, Columbia U., 2000—01, Am. Acad. Berlin, 2003, Remarque Inst., 2004, Callman Ctr. for Scholars and Writers. Democrat. Office: The Threepenny Rev PO Box 9131 Berkeley CA 94709-0131

LESSER, WILLIAM HENRI, marketing educator; b. N.Y.C., Dec. 19, 1946; s. Arthur and Ethel (Boissevain) L.; m. Susan Elizabeth Bailey, Dec. 27, 1975; children: Andrew, Jordan. BA in Geography, U. Wash., 1968; MS in Resource Econs., U. R.I., 1974; PhD in Agrl. Econ., U. Wis., 1978. From asst. to assoc. prof. mktg. Cornell U., Ithaca, NY, 1978—91, prof., 1991—, dir. undergrad. program, 1998—99, dept. chmn., 2003—. With Internat. Acad. Environ., Geneva, 1993-94, FAO vis. scientist, 2002; grad. field rep. Dept. Agrl. Econs., Ithaca, 1985-88; dir. Cornell Western Socs. Program, 1991-93; cons. World Bank, Washington, US/AID, Winrock Internat., Morrilton, Ark. Editor: Animal Patents: The Legal Economic and Social Issues, 1990; author: Equitable Patent Protection in the Developing World, 1991, Marketing Livestock and Meat, 1993, Sustainable Use of Genetic Resources under the Convention on Biological Diversity, 1998. Zone capt. Dem. com. Town of Ithaca, 1985-90, mem. planning bd., 1987-93, councilman, 1999—. Nat. fellow, Kellogg Found., 1988—91. Mem. Am. Agrl. Econ. Assn., Patent and Trademark Office Soc. Avocations: gardening, painting, antique cars. Home: 406 Coddington Rd Ithaca NY 14850-6012 Office: Cornell U Dept Applied Econs & Mgmt 154 Warren Hall Ithaca NY 14853-7801 Office Phone: 607-255-4576. Business E-Mail: whl1@cornell.edu.

LESSEY, SAMUEL KENRIC, JR., foundation administrator; b. Newark, Oct. 9, 1923; s. Samuel Kenric and Ruth (Turner) Lessey. BS, U.S. Mil. Acad., 1945; student, Vanderbilt U., 1945; LLB, Harvard U., 1951; postgrad., George Washington U., 1951—52, U. Md., 1951—53; MBA, Harvard U., 1956; postgrad., Air War Coll., 1974—75. Bar: N.Y., U.S. Dist. Ct. D.C., U.S. Ct. Claims, U.S. Tax Ct., U.S. Ct. Mil. Appeals, U.S. Ct. Appeals (D.C. cir.), U.S. Supreme Ct. Commd. USAF, 1945, advanced through grades to brig. gen., active duty, 1942-54, 76-78; with USAFR, 1954-83; v.p., bd. dirs. Nat. Aviation Corp. Investment Trust, 1957-68; v.p. Shearson Hammill and Co., Inc., 1968-74; moblzn. asst. to dir. Fed. Emergency Mgmt. Agy., 1979-82; insp. gen. U.S. Synthetic Fuels Corp., 1982-86; dir. Selective Svc. System, 1987-91. Civilian aide to Sec. of Army, 1992; bd. visitors U.S. Mil. Acad., West Point, NY, 2003—. Bd. dirs. Nat. Stroke Assn., 1991—, chmn. bd., 1994—2000, chmn. emeritus, 2001—. Decorated Legion of Merit with Oak Leaf Cluster, Army Outstanding Civil Svc. award, Selective Svc. Disting. Svc. medal, WWII Victory medal, Occupation medal, Nat. Def. Svc. medal, Am. Campaign medal, UN Svc. medal, Air Force Outstanding Unit award; Korean Svc. medal. Mem. AIAA, IEEE, Aerospace Analysts Soc. (past pres.), Am. Fighter Pilots Assn., Air Force Assn. (past v.p. Iron Gate chpt.), Am. Astronautical Soc., Am. Def. Preparedness Assn., Am. Helicopter Soc., Assn. U.S. Army (N.H. pres.), Aviation Space Writers Assn., Elec. and Electronic Analysts Group, Assn. Investment Mgmt. and Rsch., N.Y. Soc. Security Analysts, Mil. Order of World Wars, Res. Officers Assn., Air Force Pub. Affairs Alumni Assn., Am. Assoc. Royal Acad. Arts, Def. Orientation Conf. Assn. (past dir.), Wings Club (past bd. dirs.), Ctr. for Mil. Readiness (adv. bd.), Nat. Aviation Club, N.Y. Athletic Club, Lincoln's Inn Soc., Capitol Hill Club, Army & Navy Club. Avocations: skiing, tennis, swimming, traditional jazz, antiques. Home: Brimstone Corner PO Box 57 Hancock NH 03449-0057 Office: Nat Stroke Assn 9707 E Easter Ln Englewood CO 80112-3754

LESSICK, MIRA LEE, nursing educator; b. Hazleton, Pa., Jan. 25, 1949; d. Jack H. and Shirley E. (Frumkin) Lessick. Diploma in Nursing, Albany (N.Y.) Med. Ctr., 1969; BSN, Boston U., 1972; MS, U. Colo., 1973; PhD, U. Tex., 1986. Staff nurse Boston City Hosp. and Mass. Gen. Hosp., 1969-72; instr. to asst. prof. nursing, genetics clinician U. Rochester, NY, 1973-79; asst. prof. nursing, practitioner Rush U. Coll. Nursing, Chgo., 1986-91, assoc. prof. nursing, 1992—2001, project dir. genetic health nursing program, 1993—2001; assoc. prof. U. Toledo, 2001—. Mem. human genome rsch. initial rev. group, ethical, legal, and social implications subcom. Nat. Human Genome Rsch. Inst., NIH, 1996-99; peer reviewer Bur. Health Professions, HHS, 2001-02; spl. enphasis peer rev. panel Nat. Inst. Nursing Rsch., 2004. Mem. editl. adv. bd. AWHONN Lifelines, 1999—, Manuscript Rev. Panel, Rsch. in Nursing and Health Jour.; genetics column editor Medsurg Nursing: The Jour. of Adult Health, 2001-2005; contbr. articles to profl. jours. and textbooks. Recipient Bd. of Govs. award, Excellence in Pediatric Nursing award Albany Med. Ctr., 1969, Outstanding Nurse Recognition award March of Dimes Birth Defects Found., 1991, Recognition award for Individual Contbn. to Maternal-Child Health Nat. Perinatal Assn., 1993, Founders Award in Edn., Internat. Soc. Nurses in Genetics, 1997, Urologic Nursing Jour. Literary Writers award, 2004. Mem. AAAS, ANA, APHA, Internat. Soc. Nurses in Genetics (chair rsch. com. 1993-2002, co-chair rsch. com. 2003—, mem. Genetic Nursing Credentialing Commn., 2001-2004, mem. web site editl. bd., 2001—, hon. mention Genetic Nursing Writer's award, 2002), Assn. Women's Health, Obstetric, and Neonatal Nurses, Am. Soc. Human Genetics, Chgo. Nurses Assn. (legis. com. 1990-91), N.Y. Acad. Scis., Midwest Nursing Rsch. Soc., Sigma Theta Tau (Luther Christman award for excellence in published writing 1993, Luther Christmas award Excellence Pub. Writing, 1998), Phi Kappa Phi. Achievements include development of a genetic health area of concentration within a graduate level nursing program. Office: U Toledo Coll Health and Human Svcs Bancroft Campus Toledo OH 43606-3390 E-mail: mira.lessick@utoledo.edu.

LESSIG, L. LAWRENCE, III, lawyer, law educator, writer; b. Rapid City, SD, June 3, 1961; m. Bettina Neuefeind, 1999; 1 child, Willem Dakota Neuefeind. BA in economics, BS in mgmt., U. Pa., 1983; MA with honors in philosophy, Trinity Coll., 1986; JD, Yale U., 1989. Law clk. to Hon. Richard Posner US Ct. Appeals 7th cir., 1989—90; law clk. to Hon. Antonin Scalia US Supreme Ct., 1990—91; asst. prof. law U. Chgo., 1991—95, prof. law, 1995—97, co-dir. Ctr. for the Study of Constitutionalism in Ea. Europe; prof. law Harvard U., Cambridge, 1997—2000, Jack N. and Lillian R. Berkman Prof. Entrepreneurial Legal Studies, 1998; prof. law Stanford U., 2000—, exec. dir. Ctr. for Internet and Soc., 2000—, Wilson Faculty Scholar, 2002, John A. Wilson Disting. Faculty Scholar, 2003—. Vis. prof. law Yale U., 1995, Harvard U., 1997; bd. mem. RedHat Ctr. for Pub. Domain, 2000—01; bd. dirs. Electronic Frontier Found., San Francisco, Pub. Knowledge, Washington; mem. Penn Nat. Commn. Soc., Culture and Cmty. U. Pa., Phila.; moderator Constl. Law Discussion Group Lexis Counsel Connect, 1994—95; editl. adv. bd. Lexis-Nexis Electronic Authors Press, 1995—97; monthly columnist The Industry Standard, 1998—2001, Wired Mag., 2003—; bimonthly columnist Red Herring, 2002—03; columnist CIO Insight, 2002—03; lectr. in field. Author: Code, and Other Laws of Cyberspace, 1999, The Future of Ideas: The Fate of the Commons in a Connected World, 2001 (Editor's Choice Award for Best Non-Tech. Book, Linux Jour., 2002), Free Culture: How Big Media Uses Technology and the Law to Lock Down Creativity, 2004. Chmn. bd. dirs. Creative Commons, Stanford, 2001—; bd. dirs. Pub. Libr. Sci., San Francisco, 2003—. Named one of Top 25 eBiz Leaders, BusinessWeek, 2000, 2001, 100 Most Influential Lawyers, Nat. Law Jour., 2000, Top 50 Innovators, Sci. Am., 2002; recipient Annual Award, Internat. Tech. Network, 2001, World Tech. Award for Law, 2001, Awarrd for the Advancement of Free Software, Free Software Found., 2003; fellow Program on Ethics and the Professions, Harvard U., 1996—97, Wissenschaftskolleg zu Berlin, Germany, 1999—2000. Fellow: World. Acad. Art and Sci. Office: Stanford Law Sch Crown Quadrangle 559 Nathan Abbott Way Stanford CA 94305-8610*

LESSIN, ANDREW RICHARD, accounting executive; b. Bklyn., Nov. 13, 1942; s. Andrew and Ruth L. m. Phyllis Elaine Pinto, June 27, 1970. BBA, Hofstra U., Hempstead, N.Y., 1965. CPA, N.Y., Tex. Auditor Coopers & Lybrand, CPAs, N.Y.C., 1967-77; mgr. acctg. and fin. standards Internat. Paper Co., N.Y.C., 1977-80, mgr. acctg. and fin. reporting, 1980-83, dir. corp. acctg., policies and controls, 1983-86, sector contr., chief fin. officer Timberlands div. Dallas, 1986-88, staff v.p. tax Purchase, 1988-90, corp. contr., chief acctg. officer, 1990—95, v.p. controller, 1995—2000, v.p. finance, 2000—02, sr. v.p. internal audit, 2002—. Bd. dirs. Carter Holt Harvey Ltd. With AUS, 1965-67. Mem. AICPA, N.Y. State Soc. CPAs. Office: International Paper Co 400 Atlantic St Stamford CT 06921

LESSIN, LAWRENCE STEPHEN, hematologist, oncologist, educator; b. Washington, Oct. 14, 1937; s. Maurice and Anna (Brodsky) L.; m. Judith Ann Lustok, Dec. 23, 1961; children: Jennifer Lynn, Jonathan Lustok, Martine Rose. Student, U. Mich., 1955-58; MD, U. Chgo., 1962. Diplomate Am. Bd. Internal Medicine (assoc. mem. 1976-82). Intern, resident in internal medicine, chief resident, fellow in hematology Hosp. U. Pa., 1962-67; spl. fellow Nat. Heart Inst., Inst. for Cell Pathology, Paris, 1967-68; asst. prof. medicine Duke U., 1968-70; assoc. prof. medicine and pathology George Washington U., 1970-74, prof. medicine and pathology, dir. div. hematology and oncology, 1974—; dir. George Washington U. Cancer Ctr., Washington, 1991-93; med. dir. Washington Cancer Inst. Washington Hosp. Ctr., 1993—. Vis. physician medicine br. Nat. Cancer Inst., 1971-74; cons. hematology Washington VA Hosp., 1971—; cons. ARC Blood Bank, 1972—, Nat. Naval Med. Ctr., Bethesda, Md., 1974—, NHLBI, 1974, Walter Reed Army Med. Ctr., 1978—; mem. NASA Biomed. Rev. Panel, 1981-88; chmn. div. blood diseases and resources adv. com. Nat. Heart, Blood and Lung Inst., NIH, 1985-86, mem. inst. sci. rev. com., 1997-99; mem. data safety monotoring bd. NHLBI, NIH, 2000—; chmn., program dir. Assn. Hematology-Oncology, 1983-87; vol. spl. emphasis panel Comprehensive Sickle Cell SCOR Applications, 1997-99; mem. FDA panel on spongiform encephalopaties, cons. panel on oncology drugs, ODAC; mem. internat. adv. bd. King Hussein Cancer Ctr., Amman, Jordan, 2003—; mem. sci. adv. bd. Capital Tech. Info. Svcs., 2004—; bd. dirs. Internat. Spirit of Life Found., Rockville, Md., 2002—, Ceylinco Health, Colombo, Sri Lanka, 1999—. Editorial reviewer: Annals of Internal Medicine, 1969—, Nouvelle Revue de Hematologie, 1970—, Blood, Jour. Hematology, 1971—, Archives of Internal Medicine, 1972—, Nature, 1973, Jour. Clin. Investigation, 1973—, New Eng. Jour. Medicine; mem. editorial Blood Cells, 1979—, Hematologic Pathology, 1985—; contbr. articles to profl. jours., chpts. to books. Served to capt. M.C. USAR, 1963-69. Named Intern of Year U. Pa. Hosp., 1963; nominee for Golden Apple award, 1975; Nat. Heart Inst. spl. fellow Paris, 1967-68 Master ACP (chair Hematology Med. Knowledge Self-Assessment program 1992-); fellow Internat. Soc. Hematology; mem. Am. Soc. Hematology, Am. Fedn. Clin. Rsch., Am. Soc. Clin. Oncology (pub. info. com. 1999-2003, oncology manpower task force 2003-), Am. Blood Commn., Am. Soc. Internal Medicine, D.C. Med. Soc., Internat. Blood Cells Club, Am. Soc. Clin. Oncology (mem. oncology manpower coms., 2004-), Sigma Xi, Alpha Omega Alpha. Clubs: Cosmos (Washington). Office: Washington Cancer Inst 110 Irving St NW Washington DC 20010-2976 Business E-Mail: Lawrence.Lessin@Medstar.net.

LESSING, BRIAN REID, actuary; b. Miami, Fla., Feb. 2, 1954; s. Kenneth Oliver Ralph and Margaret (Takash) L. AB magna cum laude, Princeton (NJ) U., 1976; MS, NYU, 1979. Cert. FSA, Soc. Actuaries, 1989, CLU, Am. Coll., 1992. Tech. asst. Mut. of NY, 1980-84; from actuarial asst. to v.p. AXA Equitable Life Ins. Co., N.Y.C., 1984—98, v.p., 1998—. Adj. instr. NY Inst. Tech., 1979, Pace U., NYC, 1979, 80; adj. asst. prof. The Coll. of Ins., NYC, 1989-91; rsch. asst. NYU, 1976-80. Mem. ch. coun. exec. com. Cmty. Ch. of NY, 1984-87, fin. com., 1989-99. Fellow Soc. of Actuaries; mem. Soc. Fin. Svc. Profls., Am. Acad. Actuaries, Phi Beta Kappa. Unitarian Universalist. Office: AXA Equitable Life Ins Co 14th Fl Location 14 093 1290 Avenue Of The Americas New York NY 10104-0101

LESSING, DORIS (DORIS MAY), writer; b. Kermanshah, Persia, Oct. 22, 1919; d. Alfred Cook Tayler and Emily Maude McVeagh; m. Frank Charles Wisdom, 1939 (div. 1943); m. Gottfried Anton Nicholas Lessing, 1945 (div. 1949); children: John W. (dec.), Jean W., Peter L. Educated in, So. Rhodesia; DLitt (hon.), Princeton U., 1989, Durham U., 1990; D Fellow in Lit., Sch., Eng. Am. Studies, U. East Anglia, 1991; DLitt (hon.), Warwick U., 1994; LittD (hon.), Bard Coll., 1994, Harvard U., 1995, Open Univ., 1999, Univ. London, 1999. Author: (novels) The Grass is Singing, 1950, Five Short Novels, 1953, Retreat to Innocence, 1959, The Golden Notebook, 1962 (Prix Medicis award, 1976), Children of Violence, 5 vols., 1964—69, Briefing For a Descent Into Hell, 1971, The Summer Before the Dark, 1973, The Memoirs of a Survivor, 1975, Shikasta, 1979, Marriages Between Zones Three, Four and Five, 1980, The Sirian Experiments, 1981, The Making of the Representative for Planet 8, 1982, Documents Relating to the Sentimental Agents in the Volyen Empire, 1983, The Good Terrorist, 1985 (W.H. Smith Lit. award, 1986, Palermo prize, 1987, Premio Internazionale Monello, 1987), The Libretto of the Making of the Representative for Planet 8, 1988, The Fifth Child, 1988, Playing the Game, 1995, Love, Again, 1996, Mara and Dann, 1999, Ben, In The World, 2000, The Old Age of El Magnifico, 2001, The Sweetest Dream, 2001, Love Child, 2003, The Grandmothers, 2003, The Story of General Dann and Mara's Daughter Griot and the Snow Day, 2005, (nonfiction) In Pursuit of the English, 1961, Particularly Cats, 1967, Going Home, 1968, Prisons We Choose to Live Inside, 1987, The Wind Blows Away Our Words...and Other Documents Relating to the Afghan Resistance, 1987, Particularly Cats and More Cats...And Rufus, 1991, African Laughter: Four Visits to Zimbabwe, 1992, Under My Skin: Volume One of My Autobiography, to 1949, 1994, Walking in the Shade: Volume Two of My Autobiography, 1949-62, 1994, On Cats, 2002, (essays) Time Bites, 2004; author: (under pseudonym Jane Somers) Diary of a Good Neighbour, 1983, and If the Old Could..., 1984; author: (short stories) This Was the Old Chief's Country, 1952, The Habit of Loving, 1957, A Man and Two Women, 1963, African Stories, 1965, The Temptation of Jack Orkney and Other Stories, 1978, The Story of a Non-Marrying Man, 1972, Collected African Stories, 1978, The Sun Between Their Feet, 1981, London Observed: Stories and Sketches (U.K.)/The Real Thing (U.S.), 1992, (collections) To Room 19, vols. 1 and 2, 1978, The Doris Lessing Reader, 1990, (plays) Each in His Own Wilderness, 1958, Play with a Tiger, 1973, The Singing Door, 1973, (essays) A Small Personal Voice, 1974, (poetry) Fourteen Poems, 1959, (Operas) (music by Philip Glass) The Making of the Representative for Planet 8, 1988; contbr. columns in newspapers. Recipient Somerset Maugham award Soc. of Authors, 1954, Austrian State prize for European Lit., 1981, Shakespeare prize, Hamburg, 1982, Grinzane Cavour award, Italy, 1989, David Cohen prize, 2001, Golden PEN award for Lifetime Distingushed Services, 2002;

named Woman of Yr. Norway, 1995, awarded Premi Internatl. Catalunya, 1999, Principe de Asturias, Spain, 2001. Fellow MLA (hon.); mem. Nat. Inst. Arts and Letters., Am. Acad. Arts & Letters (assoc. mem. 1974), Inst. Cultural Rsch. (Companion of Honor 2000). Office: care Jonathan Clowes Ltd 10 Iron Bridge House London NW1 8BD England

LESSNAU, KLAUS DIETER, pulmonologist, director, medical educator; b. Nuremberg, Bavaria, Germany, Jan. 22, 1955; s. Lothar and Magda Lessnau; m. Cynthia DeLuise, July 26, 1995; 1 child, Mikaela Zoe. MD, Friedrich Alexander U., Erlangen, West Germany, 1985; grad., Friedrich-Alexander U. Diplomate Germany, 1985. Resident Cabrin Med. Ctr., Bklyn., 1988—91; mem. staff Lenox Hill Hosp. NYU Med. Ctr., N.Y., 2001—, med. dir. Pulmonary Physiology Lab., 2001—. Contbr. articles to profl. jours. Named Best Tchg. Physician, Med. Residents Bklyn Hosp. Ctr., 2001; fellow, Cabrini Med. Ctr., 1991—93, Mt. Sinai Med. Ctr., 1993—94, SUNY, Bklyn., 1994—95. Mem.: Am. Coll. Chest Physicians. Achievements include patents for pulmonary artery catheter. Home: 300 East 93rd 18B New York NY 10128 Office: Lenox Hill Hospital 100 East 77th Street New York NY 10021 Office Phone: 212-434-2000. Personal E-mail: klessnau@pol.net.

LESSON, DAVID, photojournalist; m. Kim Ritzenthaler; 3 children. With Abilene Reporter News, 1977—82, The Times-Picayune/The States-Item, New Orleans, 1982—84; sr. staff photographer Dallas Morning News, 1984—. Recipient Robert F. Kennedy Journalism award, 1986, Pulitzer Prize for breaking news photography, 2004. Office: Dallas Morning New 508 Young St PO Box 655237 Dallas TX 75265-5237

LESTAGE, DANIEL BARFIELD, retired military officer, physician; b. Jennings, La., July 7, 1939; s. Henry Oscar Jr. and Juliet Xavier (Barfield) L.; m. Helen Newcomer, Mar. 9, 1963; children: Juliet Lestage Hirsch, Diane Lestage Davis, Daniel B. Jr. Grad., La. State U., 1959, MD, 1963; grad., Naval Sch. Aviation, 1964; MPH, Tulane U., 1969; diploma, Indsl. Coll. Armed Forces, 1978. Diplomate Am. Bd. Preventive Medicine, 1971, Am. Bd. Family Practice, 1978. Commd. ensign USN, 1960, advanced through grades to rear adm., 1986; rotating intern Charity Hosp., New Orleans, 1963-64; resident in family practice Lafayette (La.) Charity Hosp., 1964; student flight surgeon Naval Sch. Aviation Medicine, Pensacola, Fla., 1964; staff flight surgeon/med. officer Carrier Air Wing 16 USS Oriskany, NAS Lemoore, Calif., 1965-67; sr. med. officer Naval Med. Clinic, NAS New Orleans, 1967-68; resident in aerospace medicine Naval Aerospace Med. Inst., Pensacola, 1969-71; sr. med. officer USS John F. Kennedy, Norfolk, Va., 1971-73, Br. Clinic, Jacksonville NAS, 1973-77; chief preventive medicine dept. Naval Regional Med. Ctrs., Jacksonville, 1973-77; spl. asst. to surgeon gen. Navy Bur. Medicine and Surgery Dept. Navy, Washington, 1978-81; head operational medicine br., aeromed. advisor Office of Chief Naval Ops., Washington, 1978-81; dir. clin. svcs., dir. med. edn., exec. officer Naval Regional Med. Ctr., Portsmouth, Va., 1981-83; comdg. officer Naval Hosp., Millington, Tenn., 1983-84; comdr. U.S. Naval Med. Command, London, 1984-86; fleet med. officer U.S. Naval Forces Europe, 1984-86; fleet surgeon U.S. Atlantic Fleet, Norfolk, 1986-88; command surgeon U.S. Atlantic Command/U.S. Atlantic Command/Supreme Allied Comdr., Norfolk, 1986-89; asst. dir. naval medicine Office of Chief Naval Ops., 1989; insp. gen. Navy Bur. of Medicine and Surgery, 1989-90; comdr. Naval Med. Ctr., Portsmouth, 1990-92; from corp. med. dir. to v.p. healthcare svc. Blue Cross/Blue Shield of Fla., Jacksonville, 1992—. Asst. dean Ea. Va. Med. Sch., Norfolk, 1981-83, assoc. dean, 1990-92; trustee Am. Bd. Preventive Medicine, 1988-94; bd. dirs. Health Options, Inc. Bd. dirs. Blood Bank, Jacksonville, 1973-77, Cath. Family Svcs., Portsmouth, 1981-83, Fraser-Millington Mental Health Ctr., Memphis, 1983-84, Fla. Assn. HMOs, 1999-2001, USO N.E. Fla., 1999—, We Care Jacksonville, 1999—, Fla. Assn. Health Plans, 2002—, Health Planning Coun. N.E. Fla., Inc., 2003—, Fla. Patient Safety Corp., 2004—; mem. Gov.'s Diabetes Adv. Coun., 1998-2000, Fla. Commn. Mental Health and Substance Abuse, 1999-2000, Gov.'s Strategic Panel on Tobacco, 2002, Gov.'s Destination Fla. Commn. Decorated Legion of Merit with four oak leaf clusters, Meritorious Svc. medal, Air medal with oak leaf cluster, Navy Commendation medal; recipient Physician's Recognition award AMA, 1972, 75, 78, 81, 85, 88, 91, 94, 97, 2000, 03, 06 Fellow ACP, Am. Coll. Preventive Medicine, Am. Acad. Family Physicians, Aerospace Med. Assn. (pres. 1988-89, chair fellows group 1997—); mem. AMA (del. 1993—), Fla. Acad. Family Physicians (bd. dirs. 1995-2001, found. bd. dirs. 2001—, found. pres. 2005—), Fla. Soc. for Preventive Medicine (pres. 1995-96), Fla. Med. Assn. (del. 1995—), VFW, DAV, Am. Legion, Disabled Am. Vets., Internat. Acad. Aviation and Space Medicine (bd. dirs. 2000-04, chancellor 2003-), Assn. Mil. Surgeons U.S., Soc. Med. Cons. to Armed Forces, Rotary, Elks. Roman Catholic. Avocations: travel, cooking. Home: 1782 Long Slough Walk Orange Park FL 32003-7033 Office: Blue Cross/Blue Shield Fla 4800 Deerwood Campus Pkwy DC3-3 Jacksonville FL 32246-8273 Office Phone: 905-905-5829. Business E-Mail: daniel.lestage@bcbsfl.com.

LESTELLE, TERRENCE J., lawyer; b. New Orleans, May 31, 1949; s. August Jr. and June Rose (Pays) L.; m. Andrea Sucherman, Sept. 21, 1975; children: Evan Pays, Nicole Jessica. BA, Tulane U., 1971; JD, Loyola U., 1974; LLM, U. London, 1976. Bar: La. 1974, U.S. Dist. Ct. (ea. dist.) La. 1974, U.S. Ct. Appeals (5th cir.) 1975, U.S. Dist. ct. (we. dist.) La. 1977, U.S. Dist. Ct. (mid. dist.) La. 1979, U.S. Ct. Appeals (11th cir.) 1981, U.S. Supreme Ct. 1983, Miss. 1990, Colo. 1990, U.S. Dist. Ct. (so. and no. dist.) Miss. 1990. Law clk. to Hon. James A. Comiskey U.S. Dist. Ct. (ea. dist.) La., New Orleans, 1974-75; law clk. to Hon. Frank Summers La. Supreme Ct., New Orleans, 1975; assoc. Deutsch, Kerrigan & Stiles, New Orleans, 1975, Lemle, Kelleher, Kohlmeyer, Dennery, Hunley, Moss & Frilot, New Orleans, 1976-78, Law Firm of Amato & Creely, Gretna, La., 1978-81; prin. Law Office of Terrence J. Lestelle, New Orleans, 1981-84; ptnr. Lestelle & Lestelle, New Orleans, 1984—. E-mail: lestelle@lestellelaw.com.

LESTER, ALICIA LOUISE, financial analyst; b. Niagara Falls, NY, Aug. 28, 1955; d. Belmira Hinto Harris and James Lester; children: Deláno Thompson, Michael, Jr. Thompson. BS in Commerce, Niagara U., 1977. Underwriting cert. Robert Morris Assn., 1997. Mktg., acctg. analyst Carborundum Abrasives Co., Niagara Falls, NY, 1978—87; pvt. practice contractor Buffalo, 1990—96; comml. fin. analyst Fleet Boston Financial - Corp. Banking, Buffalo, 1996—2000; fin. analyst Motorola Inc., Elma, NY, 2000—02; fin. analyst II, banking officer M & T Bank, Buffalo, 2002—05; sr. fin. analyst, asst. v.p. fin. ops. HSBC, Bank NA, Buffalo, 2005—. Owner Thunder Solutions Programming and Mktg., Buffalo, 1997—. Bd. dirs. Buffalo Prenatal-Perinatal Network, 2005—; chair Clark Acad. Performing Arts, 1990—. Mem.: Inst. Mgmt. Accts., Harriet Tubman 300, Inc., Fin. Women Internat. (comm. chair 1997—99), The Links, Inc. (Niagara Falls chp., co-chair tech. 1997—2002, chair arts facet 1997—2002, fin. sec. 2003—). Personal E-mail: A.Lester@Verizon.net.

LESTER, ANDREW WILLIAM, lawyer; b. Mpls., Feb. 17, 1956; s. Richard G. and Marion Louise (Kurtz) L.; m. Barbara Regina Schmitt, Nov. 22, 1978; 1 child, Susan Erika. Student, Ludwig-Maximilians Univ., Munich, 1975-76; BA, Duke U., 1977; MS in Fgn. Service, JD, Georgetown U., 1981. Bar: Okla. 1981, D.C. 1985, Tex. 1990, U.S. Supreme Ct. 1992, Colo. 1995. Cons. Dresser Industries, Inc., Washington, 1979-81; assoc. Conner & Winters, Tulsa, 1981-82; asst. atty. City of Enid, Okla., 1982-84; ptnr. various law firms Enid, Oklahoma City, 1984-96; ptnr. Lester, Loving & Davies P.C., Edmond, 1996—. Adj. prof. Okla. City Univ. Sch. of Law; lectr. in field; U.S. magistrate judge Western Dist. Okla., 1988-96; constl. law specialist Ctrl. and East European Law Initiative, ABA, Ukraine, Belarus and Moldova, 1993; adj. scholar Okla. Coun. Pub. Affairs. Author: Constitutional Law and Democracy, 1994; contbr. book revs. and articles to profl. jours. Intern Office of Senator Bob Dole, Washington, 1977-78; mem. transition team EEOC Office Pres.-Elect Reagan, Washington, 1980-81; chmn. law enforcement and corrections transition team, mem. budget and fin. transition team Office of Gov.-Elect Brad Henry, 2002-03; chmn. Enid Police Civil Service Commn., 1985-87; bd. dirs. Enid Habitat for Humanity, 1986-88, Booker T. Washington Cmty. Ctr., Enid, 1987-90, St. Mary's Episcopal Sch. of Edmond, 1999-2001; bd. dirs. U. Ctrl. Okla. Found., 2005—; mem. bd. advisors Oklahoma City Command Salvation Army, 2002—; mem. Martin Luther King, Jr. Holiday Commn. of Enid, 1988-91; deacon First Bapt. Ch. of Oklahoma City. Fellow Okla. Bar Found.; mem. Okla. Bar Assn., Colo. Bar Assn., Okla. Assn. Mcpl. Attys. (bd. dirs. 1987-91, 94-98, 00-, gen. counsel 1987-88, pres. 1988-90), Okla. County Bar Assn., Def. Rsch. Inst. (govt. liability com.), Federalist Soc. (vice chmn. civil rights practice group 1996—, pres. Ctrl. Okla. chpt. 1996-99), Hist. Soc. of Tenth Jud. Cir. (bd. dirs. 2005-). Republican. Avocations: german language, cartography. Office: Lester Loving & Davis PC 1701 S Kelly Ave Edmond OK 73013-3623 Office Phone: 405-844-9900. Business E-Mail: alester@lldlaw.com.

LESTER, BARNETT BENJAMIN, retired foreign affairs officer; b. Toronto, Can., Aug. 7, 1912; came to U.S., 1917; s. Louis and Lena (Rubenstein) L.; m. Rita Constance Hatcher, May 31, 1943 (dec.); m. Claudette Yvonne Gionet, Apr. 19, 1970. Student, Cleve. Coll., Western Res. U., 1933; AB (Miller Scholar), Oberlin Coll., 1934, postgrad., 1934-35, Fletcher Sch. Law and Diplomacy, 1935-36; student, Fgn. Service Inst., 1952, 56. Mem. staff, corr. Cleve. Plain Dealer and Cleve. News, 1928-33; feature writer Boston Sunday Post, 1935-38; mng. editor, later editor Exclusive Features Syndicate, Boston, 1936-38; asso. editor The Writer mag., Boston, 1936-38; info. officer Dept. Justice, 1938-41; asst. dir. feature div. Office Inter-Am. Affairs, 1941-45; info. publicist Dept. State, 1945; pub. relations exec. Al Paul Lefton Co., Inc., Phila., 1945-46; info. specialist, chief motion pictures, acting chief audio-visual sect. USPHS, Office Surgeon Gen., 1947-48; info. specialist Fed. Security Agy., 1948-49; chief editorial and prodn. sect. Nat. Heart Inst. (info. specialist, sci. reports br. NIH), 1949-52; pub. info. chief NIH, 1950; review officer Dept. State, 1952-61, supervisory publs. editor, 1961-63, editor-writer, 1963-73, pub. info. officer, 1973-85; assoc. editor Newsletter, 1977-81, State Mag., 1981-86, sr. editor, 1986-89, on contract, 1989; pub. affairs specialist, 1985-89. Fgn. svc. res. officer, 1965-73, assigned to policy and pub. info. affairs program, 1962-67; assigned to policy and pub. info affairs program Newsletter and Info. Office, Office Dir. Gen. Fgn. Svc., 1967-81, Office Pub. Affairs and State Mag., Office Dir. Gen. Fgn. Svc., 1981-89, Career counselor Oberlin Coll., 1940—, pub. affairs officer Inter-Am. Air Pilot Program, sponsored by War Dept. and Office of Inter-Am. Affairs, 1942-44; rep. Office Surg. Gen., USPHS, on Interdepartmental com. med. tng. aids, 1947-48; invited participant U.S. Commr. Edn. Conf. Audio-Visual Aids to Edn., 1948; mem. info. staff Pres.'s Midcentury White House Conf. on Children and Youth, 1950; mem. spl. survey audio-visual tchg. and tng. aids Nat. Heart Inst., USPHS and Assn. Am. Med. Colls., 1951; invited participant symposium The White House: The First 200 Yrs., White House Hist. Assn., 1992; invited participant, symposium Two Hundred Years at the White House: Actors and Observers, White House Hist. Assn., 2000; invited participant, symposium The West Wing-Workshop of Democracy, White House Hist. Assn., 2002. Author: (with others) The Writer's Handbook, 1936. Recipient War Service award Coord. Inter-Am. Affairs, 1945, Meritorious Honor Group award Dept. State, 1967, 40 Year Service award, 1979, Spl. Achievement award, 1979, Superior Honor award, 1983, Superior Honor Group award, 1984; Loy W. Henderson—Joseph C. Satterthwaite award for pub. service, 1987; Bicentennial award Am. Revolution Bicentennial Adminstrn., 1977; award for excellence Soc. Tech. Communications, 1982; award for achievement Soc. Tech. Communication, 1985; 50 Yr. Pin, Fletcher Sch. Law and Diplomacy, 1986; 50 Yr. Svc. award, bronze plaque for 51 yrs. U.S. Govt. Svc., 1989; John Jacob Rogers award for outstanding career achievement, Dept. State, 1989; cert. commendation Dept. State, 1989. Mem. Am. Fgn. Svc. Assn., Am. Polit. Sci. Assn., Acad. Polit. Sci., Diplomatic and Consular Officers Ret., Fed. Editors Assn. (Blue Pencil award 1975), Nat. Assn. Govt. Communicators (Blue Pencil Publs. award 1983), Marquis Libr. Assn. (adv. mem.), U.S. Diplomatic Courier Assn. (hon., Silver Diplomatic Courier medal and cert. appreciation 1990), Nat. Press Found. (charter), Nat. Trust for Hist. Preservation, White House Hist. Assn. (charter), U.S. Capitol Hist. Soc., Assn. for Diplomatic Studies and Tng., Fgn. Affairs Retirees of No. Va., Internat. Club (charter, honored as founding mem.), Nat. Press Club, Silver Owls Club, Am. Fgn. Svc., Diplomatic and Consular Officers Ret. Achievements include having two suggestions adopted by U.S. Postal Service resulted in issuing Treaty of Paris stamp and Great Seal of U.S. embossed stamped envelope. Home: 2507 N Lincoln St Arlington VA 22207-5023

LESTER, CHARLES TURNER, JR., lawyer; b. Plainfield, NJ, Jan. 31, 1942; s. Charles Turner and Marlyn Elizabeth (Tate) L.; m. Nancy Hudmon Simmons, Aug. 19, 1967; children: Susan Hopson, Mary Elizabeth. BA, Emory U., 1964, JD, 1967. Bar: Ga. 1966, U.S. Dist. Ct. (no. dist.) Ga. 1967, D.C. 1970, U.S. Ct. Appeals (5th cir.) 1967, U.S. Ct. Appeals (11th cir.) 1982, U.S. Ct. Appeals (10th cir.) 1984, U.S. Supreme Ct. 2001. Assoc. Sutherland, Asbill & Brennan, Atlanta, 1970-77, ptnr., 1977—. Mem. Leadership Atlanta, 1980-81; pres. Atlanta Legal Aid Soc., 1979-80. Lt. JAGC, USNR, 1967-70. Fellow Am. Bar Found; mem. ABA, State Bar of Ga. (pres. young lawyers sect. 1977-78, bd. govs. 1977-78, 80-93, chmn. formal adv. opinion bd. 1987-90, exec. com. 1977-78, 1987-93, pres. 1991-92), Atlanta Bar Assn., Am. Judicature Soc., Lawyers Club Atlanta (treas. 1982-83, exec. com. 1982-90, 2d v.p. 1986-87, 1st v.p. 1987-88, pres. 1988-89), D.C. Bar Assn., Ga. C. of C. (bd. dirs. 1994-2000), Lawyers Com. for Civil Rights Law (bd. dirs., vice-chmn. S.E. region, co-chair 1999-2001). Democrat. Methodist. Home: 1955 Musket Ct Stone Mountain GA 30087-1703 Office: Sutherland Asbill & Brennan LLP 999 Peachtree St NE Ste 2300 Atlanta GA 30309-3996 Office Phone: 404-853-8116. Business E-Mail: charles.lester@sablaw.com.

LESTER, HELEN DOUGHTY, writer; b. Evanston, Ill., June 12, 1936; d. William Howard and Elizabeth Sargent Doughty; m. Robin Lester, Aug. 26, 1967; children: Robin Debevoise, James Robinson. BA, Wheelock Coll., Boston, 1959. Cert. elem. tchr. State of Mass. Elem. tchr. Lexington (Mass.) Pub. Schs., 1959—62; children's book author Houghton, Mifflin Co., Boston, 1981—; elem. tchr. San Francisco, 1987—89, Francis W. Parker Sch., Chgo., 1962—69, 1991—95. Author: (children's books) Tacky the Penguin, 1988, Fluffy the Porcupine, 1986, Princess Penelope's Parrot, 1996, Three Cheers for Tacky, 1994, The Wizard, the Fairy and the Magic Children, 1983, It Wasn't My Fault, 1984, Hooray for Wodney Wat (Winner of state Children's Choice awards in Calif., Colo., Del., Ga., Ind., Ky., Md., Mo., Nebr., Nev., N.C., N.D., S.C., Tenn. Utah, Va., Wash., Wyo., 1990), Me First, 1992, Listen Buddy, 1995, A True Story, 1997, Tacky in Trouble, Score One for the Sloths, 2004, Tacky and the Emperor, 2001, Tacklocks and the Three Bears, 2002, Something Might Happen, 2003, Hurty Feelings, 2004, Tacky and the Winter Games, 2005 (Smithsonian Notable Book, 1997, Parenting Mag. Reading Magic award, 1997, 1999, Sch. Libr. Jour. Best Books of 1997, Sch. Libr. Jour. Best Books of 1999, others). Vol. dir., arts and crafts Bedford (N.Y.) Correctional Instn. for Women, 1998—2005. Named Adm. in the Nebr. Navy, Gov. of the State of Nebr., 1994. Mem.: Soc. of Children's Book Authors and Illustrators. Avocations: travel, hiking. Home: PO Box 63 Pawling NY 12564

LESTER, JULIUS B., author; b. St. Louis, Jan. 27, 1939; s. W.D. and Julia (Smith) L.; m. Milan Sabatini; children: Jody Simone, Malcolm Coltrane, Elena Milad, David Julius, Lian Sifuentes. BA, Fisk U., 1960. Prof. Judaic studies U. Mass., Amherst, 1971—2003, prof. emeritus, 2004—. Profl. musician and singer, recording for Vanguard Records, folklorist and writer, dir., Newport Folk Festival, 1966-68; author: (with Pete Seeger) The 12-String Guitar as Played by Leadbelly, 1965, Look Out, Whitey, Black Power's Gon' Get Your Mama, 1968, To Be a Slave, 1968 (Newberry Honor book 1968), Black Folktales, 1969, Revolutionary Notes, 1969, Search for the New Land, 1970, The Knee-High Man and Other Tales, 1972, Long Journey Home: Stories from Black History, 1972, Two Love Stories, 1972, Who I Am, 1974, All Is Well, 1976, This Strange New Feeling, 1982, Do Lord Remember Me, 1985, The Tales of Uncle Remus: The Adventures of Brer Rabbit, 1987, The Tales of Uncle Remus, The Further Adventures of Brer Rabbit, 1988, Lovesong: Becoming a Jew, 1988, How Many Spots Does A Leopard Have?, 1989, Further Tales of Uncle Remus, 1990, Falling Pieces of the Broken Sky, 1990, Last Tales of Uncle Remus, 1994, And All Our Wounds Forgiven, 1994, The Man Who Knew Too Much, 1994, John Henry, 1994 (Boston Globe-Horn Book award 1995), Othello: A Novel, 1995, Sam and the Tigers, 1996, From Slave Ship to Freedom Road, 1998, Black Cowboy, Wild Horses, 1998, What A Truly Cool World, 1999, When the Beginning Began, 1999, Pharaoh's Daughter, 2000, Albidaro and the Mischievous Dream, 2000, The Blues Singers: Ten Who Shook the World, 2001, Ackamarackus: Julius Lester's Sumptuosly Silly Fantastically Funny Fables, 2001, When Dad Killed Mom, 2001, Why Heaven is Far Away, 2002, Shining, 2003, Let's Talk About Race, 2004, On Writing for Children and Other People, 2004, The Autobiography of God, 2004, Day of Tears, 2005, The Old African, 2005; editor: Seventh Son: The Thoughts and Writings of W.E.B. DuBois, vol. 1 and 2, 1971; assoc. editor: Sing Out, 1964-69; contbg. editor: Broadside of New York, 1964-70. Office: 306 Old Springfield Rd Belchertown MA 01007 Personal E-mail: jbles@charter.net. *The older I become, the greater the mystery of my life. I think I see my life as journey into mystery, in awe and fear, with joy and apprehension. Whatever my accomplishments, my life is more than and other than, and finally, best expressed by the silence of winter snow, prairie skies, or a feathered serpent. To be as true and eloquent as a drop of water hanging from a twig— that is my ideal.*

LESTER, JUNE, library and information scientist, educator; b. Sandersville, Ga., Aug. 25, 1942; d. Charles DuBose and Frances Irene (Cheney) L.; 1 child, Anna Elisabeth Engle. BA, Emory U., 1963, M in Librarianship, 1971; D in Libr. Sci., Columbia U., 1987, cert. in advanced librarianship, 1982. Asst. prof., cataloger U. Tenn. Libr., Knoxville, 1971-73; libr. divsn. libr. and info. mgmt. Emory U., Atlanta, 1973-81, asst. prof. div. libr. and info. mgmt., 1976-80, assoc. prof., 1980-87; accreditation officer Am. Libr. Assn., 1987-91; assoc. dean, assoc. prof. Sch. Libr. and Info. Scis. U. North Tex., Denton, 1991—93; prof. U. Okla., Norman, 1993—, dir. Sch. Libr and Info. Studies, 1993—2000. UCLA sr. fellow, 1987. Mem. ALA (coun. mem. 1987), Assn. for Libr. and Info. Sci. Edn. (bd. dirs. 1985-87, 94-97, pres. 1995-96), Am. Soc. Info. Sci. and Tech. (treas., 2004—, bd. mem., 2004—), Okla. Libr. Assn., Phi Beta Kappa, Beta Phi Mu. Unitarian Universalist. Home: 2006 Trailview Ct Norman OK 73072-6654 Office: U Okla Sch Libr and Info Studies 401 W Brooks St Norman OK 73019-6030 Office Phone: 405-325-3921. E-mail: jlester@ou.edu.

LESTER, MARK CHARLES, neurosurgeon; b. Pitts., Sept. 23, 1952; AB, Cornell U., 1973; MD, U. Pitts., 1977; MBA, U. Pa., 2002. Diplomate Am. Bd. Neurol. Surgery. Intern gen. surgery U. Health Ctr. Hosps., Pitts., 1977—78, resident in neurological surgery, 1978—83; neurosurgeon Allentown, Pa., 1983—; chief, Divsn. Neurol. Surgery Lehigh Valley Hosp., Allentown, 1992—2001, co-med. dir. trauma/neuro ICU, 1998—2001, vice-chmn. for opers., dept. surgery, 1999—, med. dir. oper. rm., 1999—; clin. assoc. prof. Pa. State Coll. of Medicine, Hershey, Pa., 1995—; head sect. neurotrauma Lehigh Valley Hosp., Allentown, 1991-95. Adj. clin. asst. prof. Hahnemann U., Phila., 1988— Fellow: ACS; mem.: AAAS, Am. Assn. Neurolog. Surgeons. Office: Neurosurg Assocs Lehigh Valley Physician Group Ste 1100 1210 S Cedar Crest Blvd Allentown PA 18103

LESTER, PAMELA ROBIN, lawyer; b. NYC, Aug. 5, 1958; d. Howard M. and Patricia B. Lester; married; 1 child. Student, Princeton U., 1978-79; BA cum laude, Amherst Coll., 1980; JD, Fordham U., 1983. Bar: NY 1984, DC 1985. With Advantage Internat., Inc., Washington, 1984-89, gen. counsel, 1987-89; assoc. Akin, Gump, Strauss, Hauer & Feld, Washington, 1989-90; sr. v.p. bus. affairs and gen. counsel Time Warner Sports, NYC, 1991-99; COO HBO Properties, 1998—2000; pres. Lester Sports and Entertainment, Inc., 2001—. Adj. lectr. sports law Am. U. Law Sch., 1989-91; adj. faculty sports law Fordham U. Law Sch., 1992-96; bd. advisors Ctr. for Protection of Athletes Rights, 1994-97; head girls varsity lacrosse coach and vol. asst. field hockey coach Montgomery HS, NJ, 2001-04. Contbr. chpt. to: The Law of Professional and Amateur Sports, 1989, 95. Recipient Profl. Sports Lawyer of Yr., Fordham Law Sch., 2004. Mem. ABA (program and sports divsn. chair forum entertainment and sports industries' governing com. 1992-96, chair elect 1996, chair 1997-99, immediate past chair 1999-2001, governing com. standing com. on forum-coms. 1994), Assn. Bar City NY (sports law com. 1991-95, 2004—), Sports Lawyers Assn. (bd. dirs., pres.-elect 2000-01, pres. 2001-03), NY State Bar Assn., Women's Sports Found. (mem. bd. adv. 1991-99), Va. Commonwealth U. Sportscenter (adv. bd. 1999-2000), US Field Hockey (mktg. com. mem.) Office: Lester Sports and Entertainment, Inc PO Box 481 Hopewell NJ 08525 Business E-Mail: pam.lester@lestersports.com.

LESTER, RICHARD GARRISON, radiologist, educator; b. NYC, Oct. 24, 1925; s. L. I. and Pauline (Smolan) L.; m. Marion Louise Kurtz, Jan. 17, 1949; children: Elizabeth P., Andrew W. AB, Princeton U., 1946; MD, Columbia U., 1948. Intern N.Y.C. Hosp., 1948-49; asst. resident radiology Stanford Hosp., 1950-51, 53-54; from instr. to asso. prof. radiology U. Minn., 1954-61; prof. radiology, chmn. dept. Med. Coll. Va., 1961-65, Duke Sch. Medicine, 1965-76; prof. radiology U. Tex. Med. Sch., Houston, 1976-84, chmn. dept., 1977-81; interim pres. Meharry Med. Coll., Nashville, 1981-82; dean Eastern Va. Med. Sch., Norfolk, 1984-89, prof. radiology, 1984-93, chmn. dept., 1989-91; prof. emeritus, 1993—; v.p. acad. affairs Med. Coll. of Hampton Roads, formerly Eastern Va. Med. Authority, Norfolk, 1984-89. Trustee Meharry Med. Coll., 1975— Author: (with others) Congenital Heart Disease, 1965, Exposure of the Pregnant Patient to Diagnostic Radiations, 1985, 2d edit., 1997; also numerous articles. Deacon Freemason St. Bapt. Ch. Capt. USAF, 1951-53. Fellow Am. Coll. Radiology, Am. Coll. Chest Physicians; mem. Assn. Univ. Radiologists, Am. Roentgen Ray Soc., Soc. Pediatric Radiology, Radiol. Soc. N.Am. (dir. 1976—, chmn. bd. 1981, pres. 1983). Home: 1362 De Bree Ave Norfolk VA 23517-2131 Office: Ea Va Med Sch PO Box 1980 Norfolk VA 23501-1980 Office Phone: 757-446-6037. Personal E-mail: rglester@aol.com.

LESTER, ROBIN DALE, education educator, writer, former headmaster; b. Holdrege, Nebr., Mar. 1, 1939; s. Earl L. and Evelyn Grace (Robinson) L.; m. Helen Sargent Doughty, Aug. 26, 1967; children: Robin Debevoise, James Robinson. Student, St. Andrews U., Scotland, 1960—61; BA, Pepperdine U., 1962, MA, 1963; MAT, U. Chgo., 1966, PhD, 1971. Resident head, dean students office U. Chgo., 1964-72, Ferdinand Schevill fellow dept. history, 1966-68; asst. prof. history Columbia Coll., Chgo., 1966-70, chmn. social scis. dept., 1970-72; chmn. history dept. Collegiate Sch., N.Y.C., 1972-75; headmaster Trinity Sch., N.Y.C., 1975-86, San Francisco U. Sch., 1986-88, Latin Sch. of Chgo., 1989-92; tchr. Francis W. Parker Sch., Chgo., 1994-97. Adj. prof. Columbia Coll., Chgo., 1992-95; interim head Blake Sch., Mpls., 1997-98. Author: Dictionary of American Biography, 1978, Stagg's University, 1995, Wuzzy Takes Off, 1995, Roy Foy, 1996, Going to School and Awww!, 1997; contbg. author: Problems in American Sports History, 1997; contbr. to N.Y. Times, Jour. Am. History, Chgo. Tribune, Jour. Sports History, History Edn. Quar., U. Chgo. mag. Mem. Manhattan Borough Dem. Com., N.Y.C., 1977-86; commr. Commn. on Ednl. Issues, 1980-84; mem. edn. com. Chgo. Hist. Soc., 1991-95; mem. Chgo.-Prague Sister Cities Com., 1991-97; trustee, treas. St. Andrews U. Am. Found., 1985—; precinct capt. Dem. Party, Chgo., 1964. Lauder fellow Aspen Inst., 1985. Mem. Am. Hist. Assn., Am. Studies Assn., N.Am. Soc. Sport Historians (Book of the Yr. award 1995), Orgn. Am. Historians, Headmaster's Assn., University Club (N.Y.C.), Quadrangle Club (Chgo.). Episcopalian. E-mail: rl1709@hotmail.com.

LESTER, SUSAN E., bank executive; CFO U.S. Bancorp, Mpls., to 2000; exec. v.p., CFO HomeSide Lending. Bd. dirs. VisionShare, Inc., First Community Bancorp, Rancho Sante Fe, Calif., Derma, Inc., Edinda, Minn.; strategic advisor thedatabank, Inc. Trustee Coll. Saint Benedict. Mem.: Hazeltine Nat. Golf Club (bd. govs.).

LESTER, VIRGINIA LAUDANO, academic administrator; b. Phila., Jan. 5, 1931; d. Edmund Francis and Emily Beatrice (Downes) Laudano; children: Pamela Lester Golde, Valerie Lester. BA, Pa. State U., 1952; MEd, Temple U., 1955; PhD, Union Grad. Sch., 1972; JD, Stanford U. Law Sch., 1988. Tchr. pub. schs., Abington, Pa., 1952-55, Greenfield Center, N.Y., 1956; instr. edn. dept. Skidmore Coll., Saratoga Springs, N.Y., 1962-64, dir. ednl. research, 1967-72, asst. to the pres., 1968-72; asst. dir. Capitol Dist. Regional Supplementary Edn. Ctr., Albany, NY, 1966-67; assoc. dean, asst. prof. state-wide programs Empire State Coll., State U. N.Y., Saratoga Springs, 1973-75, sr. assoc. dean, assoc. prof., 1975-76, acting dean state-wide programs, 1976; pres., prof. interdisciplinary studies Mary Baldwin Coll.,

Staunton, Va., 1976-85, cons. to bd. trustees, 1985-88; assoc. Hunton & Williams, Richmond, Va., 1988-90; interim pres. Friends World Coll., Huntington, N.Y., 1990-91; dir. presdl. search consultation svc. Assn. of Governing Bds. of Univs. and Colls., 1991-94; of counsel spl. projects office of exec. dir. Am. Assn. Retired Persons, 1994—2001. Mem. cons. core faculty Union Grad. Sch., Union for Experimenting Colls. and Univs., Cin., 1975—82; vis. faculty fellow Harvard U. Grad. Sch. Edn., 1976; bd. dirs. So. Bankshares, So. Bank, Coun. Advancement of Small Colls., 1977—81, Am. Council Edn., 1983-85; adj. faculty mem. Grad. Sch. George Washington U., 1996, 2002—; cons. Nat. Exec. Svc. Corp., 1991—; state legis. lobbyist AARP, 2004—. Mem. com. on criminal sexual assault Va. State Crime Commn., 1976; v.p. Costume Collection, Inc., 1971-73; v.p. Warren, Washington, Saratoga Counties Planned Parenthood, 1972-74, bd. dirs., 1970-74; mem. Saratoga Springs Housing Bd. Appeals, 1966-76, Commn. on Future of Va., 1982-84; bd. dirs. Nat. Urban League, 1979-86; pres. commn. NCAA, 1984-85. Mem. Am. Acad. Polit. and Social Scis., Va. Found. Ind. Colls. (trustee, exec. com.), Va. Council Ind. Colls., Am. Council on Edn. (commn. on women in higher edn. 1977-80, bd. dirs. 1981-85), Nat. Assn. Ind. Colls. and Univs. (dir.), Assn. Va. Colls. (sec.-treas. 1978-79, pres. 1980-81, dir.), Assn. Ch. Related Colls. and Univs. of South (pres. 1983), Pi Lambda Theta, Pi Gamma Mu, Chimes. Mem. Soc. Of Friends. E-mail: vlester55@msn.com.

LESTER, W. HOWARD, retail executive; Chmn. Williams-Sonoma Inc., San Francisco, 1986—. Chmn. bd. dir. Harold's Stores, Inc.; exec. coun. UCSF; mem. adv. bd. Retail Mgmt. Inst. Santa Clara Univ. Mem.: Internat. Assoc. Shopping Centers (assoc.). Office: Williams-Sonoma Inc 3250 Van Ness Ave San Francisco CA 94109

LESTER, WILLIAM ALEXANDER, JR., chemist, educator; b. Chgo., Apr. 24, 1937; s. William Alexander and Elizabeth Frances (Clark) L.; m. Rochelle Diane Reed, Dec. 27, 1959; children: William Alexander III, Allison Kimberleigh. BS, U. Chgo., 1958, MS, 1959; postgrad., Washington U., St. Louis, 1959-60; PhD, Cath. U. Am., 1964. Phys. chemist Nat. Bur. Stds., Washington, 1961-64; asst. dir. Theoretical Chemistry Inst./U. Wis., Madison, 1965-68; rsch. staff IBM Rsch. Lab., San Jose, Calif., 1968-75, mgr., 1976-78; tech. planning staff IBM T.J. Watson Rsch. Ctr., Yorktown Heights, N.Y., 1975-76; dir. Nat. Resource for Computation in Chemistry, Lawrence Berkeley (Calif.) Lab., 1978-81, also assoc. dir., staff sr. scientist, 1978-81, faculty sr. scientist, 1981—; prof. chemistry U. Calif., Berkeley, 1981—, assoc. dean Coll. Chemistry, 1991-95. Lectr. chemistry U. Wis., 1966-68; cons. NSF, 1976-77, mem. chem. divsn. adv. panel, 1981-83, adv. com. Office Advanced Sci. Computing program, 1985-87, chmn., 1987, sr. fellow for sci. and engring., asst. to dir. for human resource devel., 1995-96; mem. U.S. nat. com. Internat. Union Pure and Applied Chemistry, 1976-79; mem. com. on recommendations for U.S. Army Basic Sci. Rsch. NRC, 1984-87, mem. steering com., 1987-88; chemistry rsch. evaluation panel AF Office Sci. Rsch., 1974-78; chmn. Gordon Conf. Atomic and Molecular Interactions, 1978; mem. NRC panel on chem. physics Nat. Bur. Stds., 1980-83; mem. com. to survey chem. scis. NRC, 1982-84, Fed. Networking Coun. Adv. Com., 1991-95; mem. blue ribbon panel on high performance computing NSF, 1993; mem. com. on high performance computing and comm.: status of a major initiative NRC, 1994-95, mem. com. on math. challenges from theoretical computational chemistry, NRC, 1994-95; mem. tech. assessment bd. Army Rsch. Lab., NRC, 1996-99; coun. mem. Gordon Rsch. Conf., 1997-2000, selection and scheduling com., 2000—; mem. adv. bd. Model Instns. Excellence Spelman Coll., 1997—; mem. external vis. com. Nat. Partnership Advanced Computational Infrastructure, 1999-2002; mem. pres. com. Nat. Medal Sci., 2000-02; mem. dept. energy adv. com. on advanced sci. computing, 2000—; mem. bd. on chem. scis. and tech. NRC, 2004—. Editor: Procs. of Conf. on Potential Energy Surfaces in Chemistry, 1971, Recent Advances in Quantum Monte Carlo Methods, 1997; co-editor (with J. Govaerts and M.N. Houkonnou): Contemporary Problems in Mathematical Physics, 2000; co-editor: (with S.M. Rothstein and S. Tanaka) Recent Advances in Quantum Monte Carlo Methods, Part II, 2002; co-author (with Brian L. Hammond and Peter J. Reynolds): Monte Carlo Methods in Ab Initio Quantum Chemistry, 1994; mem. editl. bd. Jour. Phys. Chemistry, 1979—81, Jour. Computational Chemistry, 1980—87, Computer Physics Comm., 1981—86, mem. adv. bd. Sci. Yr., 1989—93, Comms. on Analysis, Geometry and Physics, 1997—. Recipient Alumni award in sci. Cath. U. Am., 1983; named to U. Chgo. Athletic Hall of Fame, 2004. Fellow AAAS (com. on nominations 1988-91, nat. bd. dirs. 1993-97), Calif. Acad. Scis., Am. Phys. Soc. (chmn. div. chem. physics 1986); mem. Am. Chem. Soc. (sec.-treas. Wis. sect. 1967-68, chmn. div. phys. chemistry 1979, treas. div. computers in chemistry 1974-77), Nat. Orgn. Black Chemists and Chem. Engrs. (Percy L. Julian award 1979, Outstanding Tchr. award 1986, exec. bd. 1984-87). Home: 4433 Briar Cliff Rd Oakland CA 94605-4624 Office: U Calif Dept Chemistry Berkeley CA 94720-1460 Office Phone: 510-643-9590. E-mail: walester@lbl.gov. *Perseverance is the watchword-the will to hold on.*

LESTON, PATRICK JOHN, judge; b. Maywood, Ill., May 2, 1948; s. John R. and Lorraine (McQueen) L.; m. Kristine Brzezinski; children: Alison, Adam. BS in Communications, U. Ill., 1970; JD cum laude, Northwestern U., Chgo., 1973. Bar: Ill. 1973, U.S. Dist. Ct. (no. dist.) Ill. 1973, U.S. Ct. Appeals (7th cir.) 1973. Ptnr. Jacobs & Leston, Villa Park, Ill., 1973-79; atty. Patrick J. Leston Ltd., Glen Ellyn, Ill., 1979-89; ptnr. Keck, Mahin & Cate, Oakbrook Terrace, Ill., 1989-95; judge 18th Cir. Ct., DuPage County, Ill., 1995—. Presenter at profl. confs. Editor Ill. State Bar Assn./Young Lawyers Divsn. Jour., 1983-85. Class rep. Northwestern U. Law Sch. Fund, 1982-88; organizer DuPage County (Ill.) Law Explorers. Fellow ABA (Ill. del. to ABA/Young Lawyers divsn. assembly 1982-85), Ill. Bar Assn. (chmn. fellows 1991-92, bd. govs. 1990-97, chmn. young lawyers divsn. 1985, chmn. agenda com. 1986, del. to 18th jud. cir. assembly 1982-88), Ill. Judges Assn. (bd. dirs. 1997-2004, chmn. benefits and pension com. 1999—, chmn. govt. affairs 2004—), Ill. Bar Found. (charter), Am. Bar Found.; mem. DuPage County Bar Assn. (bd. dirs. 1979-84, pres. 1987, chmn. judiciary com. 1988, gen. counsel 1989), Lions, Chi Psi. Avocations: volleyball, skiing, scuba diving, travel, golf. Office: 18th Jud Cir Ct 505 N County Farm Rd Wheaton IL 60187-3907 Office Phone: 630-407-8858. Business E-Mail: patrick.leston@dupageco.org.

LESZINSKE, WILLIAM O., investment company executive; Chief investment officer Texas Commerce Investment Mgmt. Co.; sr. ptnr. and and equity portfolio mgr. Harris Investment Mgmt. Inc., Harris Bankcorp., Inc., Chgo., 1995, pres., chief investment officer, 1966—. Office: Harris Bankcorp Inc 190 S Lasalle St Chicago IL 60603-3410

LETAI, JOHN LECZA, retired corporate financial executive; b. Kisleta, Hungary, Aug. 28, 1926; arrived in U.S., 1957; children: Stephen, Tony. LLD, U. Budapest, 1951; MS, U. Mich., 1962. Exec. dir. Health and Welfare Coun., Trenton, NJ, 1969—71, Comprehensive Health Planning Coun., Southeastern Pa., 1971; sr. exec. v.p. Hosp. & Highter Edn. Authority, Phila., 1972—93; ret., 1993. 1st lt. judge, atty., sec. Revolutionary com. Atty. Gen. Office, Hungary, 1956. Recipient Pa. Gov. citation for outstanding work as exec. dir. Hosp. & Health Planning Coun., 1970, Phila. Bowl award, City of Phila., 1993, City of Phila. citation for outstanding svc., 1993, Commemorative award for disting. svc. to City of Phila., 1993. Republican. Avocation: chess. Home: 1236 Princeton Ln West Chester PA 19380

LETCHER, NAOMI JEWELL, quality engineer, educator, counselor; b. Belle Point, W. Va., Dec. 29, 1924; d. Andrew Glen and Ollie Pearl (Meadows) Presley; m. Frank Philip Johnson, Oct. 5, 1945 (div. Dec. 1953); m. Paul Arthur Letcher, Mar. 6, 1954; children: Frank, Edwin, Richard, David. AA, El Camino Jr. Coll., 1964; BA, Calif. State U., 1971. Inspector N. Am. Aviation, Downey, Calif., 1964-71; substitute tchr. ABC Unified sch. Dist., Artesia, Calif., 1971-72; recurrence control rep. Rockwell Internat., Downey, Calif., 1972-80, quality engr., 1981-86; counselor Forest Lawn Cemeteries, Cerritos, Calif., 1980-81; tech. analyst Northrop, Pico Rivera, Calif., 1986-89; ret. Gov. divsn. D-2 area T.M. Internat., Downey, Calif., 1978-79. Author: History of the Letcher Family, 1995. Docent Temecula (Calif.) Valley Mus., 1994—. Mem. AAUW, Nat. Mgmt. Assn., NOW, Srs. Golden Yrs. Club, Alpha Gamma Sigma. Democrat. Baptist. Avocations: genealogy, needlecrafts, stamp collecting/philately, dance, bowling. E-mail: OMIE8@aol.com.

LETCHER, WILLIAM, dentist; BA in math., Wash. U., St. Louis, 1971, DMD, 1975; grad., The Pankey Inst., Fla., Misch Implant Inst., U. Pitts. Pvt. practice dentist, Tulsa, Okla. Fellow: Acad. Gen. Dentistry. Achievements include patents for crown fabrication. Office: 5522 S Lewis Ave Tulsa OK 74105 Office Phone: 918-743-4496. Office Fax: 918-743-4436.*

LETHBRIDGE, FRANCIS DONALD, retired architect; b. Hackensack, N.J., Oct. 5, 1920; s. Berry B. and Florence A. (Lapham) L.; m. Mary Jane Christopher, June 21, 1947; children: Catherine B. (Mrs. Robert A. Grove), Mary P. (Mrs. Christopher G. Cromwell), Christopher B., Margaret F. (Mrs. Arsim Cejku). Student, Stevens Inst. Tech., 1937-40, Yale Sch. Architecture, 1945-46. Ptnr. archtl. firm Keyes, Smith, Satterlee & Lethbridge, Washington, 1951-55, Keyes, Lethbridge & Condon, Washington, 1956-75, Francis D. Lethbridge & Assocs., Washington, 1975-90. Mem. fgn. bldgs. archtl. rev. panel U.S. State Dept., 1977-80; mem. archtl. adv. panel Fed. Res. Bd., 1979-83; mem. Potomac Planning Task Force, 1965-67; bd. advisers Nat. Trust for Hist. Preservation, 1969-71; mem. Joint Com. Landmarks Nat. Capital, 1964-79, chmn., 1964-73 Co-author: Guide to the Architecture of Washington, D.C; prin. works include Pine Spring Community, Fairfax County, Va., 1951-54, Potomac Overlook, 1955-58, U.S. Chancery, Lima, Peru, 1957, Forest Industries Bldg., Washington, 1961, Carderock Springs Community, Montgomery County, Md., 1963-65, Unitarian Ch, River Road, Md., 1964, master plan Arlington Nat. Cemetery, 1966-68, Ft. Lincoln New Town, 1968, Visitors Ctr., Arlington Nat. Cemetery, 1988. Trustee Nantucket Atheneum; advisor Nantucket Hist. Assn. Officer, pilot USNR, 1942-45. Decorated D.F.C., Air medal; recipient Design Merit award AIA, 1955, 66, 1st honor award, 1966, Potomac Valley Chpt. archtl. award, 1956, 58, 60, 62, 64, 66, 68, 70, 72, 74, 76, joint award of honor AIA-Nat. Assn. Home Builders, 1960; award in architecture Washington Bd. Trade, 1953, 55, 61, 63, 65, 67, 69, 71, 73; Renchard prize for historic preservation, 1983 Fellow AIA (pres. Washington Met. chpt. 1964, v.p. 1969-70, pres. AIA found. 1971-73); mem. Cosmos Club (Washington). Home and Office: 48 Orange St Nantucket MA 02554-3937

LETICHE, JOHN MARION, economist, educator; b. Uman, Kiev, Russia, Nov. 11, 1918; came to U.S., 1941, naturalized, 1949; s. Leon and Mary (Grossman) L.; m. Emily Kuyper, Nov. 17, 1945; 1 son, Hugo K. BA, McGill U., 1940, MA, 1941; PhD in Econs, U. Chgo., 1951. Rockefeller fellow Council Fgn. Relations, N.Y.C., 1945-46; Smith-Mundt vis. prof. U. Aarhus and U. Copenhagen, Denmark, 1951-52; spl. tech. econ. adv. UN ECA, Africa, 1961-62; prof. U. Calif. at Berkeley, 1960—. Cons. AID, U.S. Depts. State, Labor, HUD and Treasury, 1962—; emissary to Japan and Korea, Dept. State, 1971; cons. Econ. Coun. Can., 1972—, World Bank, 1981—, Bank of Eng., London, Bundesbank, Frankfurt, Germany; lectr. Stockholm, Paris, Uppsala, Hamburg, Kiel, Oxford (Eng.), 1973—, Vancouver, Toronto, Montreal, Zagreb, 1983, Frankfurt, Bonn, Moscow and Nakhodka Acad. Scis. USSR, 1986, Hong Kong, Shanghai, Wuhan, Beijing, London, Bonn, Frankfurt, De Hague, 1987, Bundesbank, 1992-93, 99, China, Beijing, Shanghai, 1988, 90, 94, New Delhi, Addis Ababa, Kuala Lumpur and Seoul, 1996, 99, U.S. War Coll., Quintico, Va., 1997, Acad. Scis., Taipei, 1989, Moscow, 2001, joint session Calif. legis., 1975; ext. examiner adv. degrees U. Hong Kong, U. Calcutta, India. Author: Reciprocal Trade Agreements in the World Economy, 1948, in Japanese, 1951, System or Theory of the Trade of the World, 2d edit., 1957, Balance of Payments and Economic Growth, 2d edit., 1976, A History of Russian Economic Thought, 2d edit., 1977, The Key Problems of Economic Reconstruction and Development in Nigeria, 1970, Dependent Monetary Systems and Economic Development, 1974, Lessons of the Oil Crisis, 1977, Gains from Trade, 1979, Controlling Inflation, Recession, Federal Deficits and the Balance of Payments, 1980, The New Inflation and Its Urban Impact, 1980, Monetary Systems of Africa in the 1980s, 1981, International Economic Policies and Their Theoretical Foundations, 1982, 2d edit., 1992; Russian Statecraft: An Analysis and Translation of Iuril Krizhanich's Politika, 1985, Economics of the Pacific Rim, 1989; editor Royer Lectures, 1980-90, Toward a Market Economy in China, 1992, China's Emerging Monetary and Financial Markets, 1995, India's Economic Reforms, 1996, Causes of the Financial and Economic Crisis in Southeast Asia, 1998, Lessons from the Euro Zone for the East Asian Economies, 2000, Writ of Certiorara, Supreme Court of the U.S., 2004; contbr. articles to profl. jours. Supervisory bd. Sch. Econs., St. Petersburg, Russia, 1994—. Recipient certificate merit Ency. Brit., certificate merit Inst. World Affairs, certificate merit Internat. Legal Center, U. Mich., U.S. Office Personnel Mgmt. Sr. Fed. Govt. Execs. and Mgrs., U. Calif.-Berkeley, Adam Smith medal U. Verona, 1977, Medal, Ioffe Inst. Physics and Tech., 1998, Laureate Living Sci. award NBC Cambridge, Eng., 2004; Guggenheim fellow, 1956-57. Mem. Am. Econ. Assn. (nominating com. 1968-69), Econometric Soc., Royal Econ. Soc., U.S.-Asian Econ. Com. (bd. dirs. 1983—), African Studies Assn., Am. Soc. Internat. Law (bd. 1969-72). Home: 968 Grizzly Peak Blvd Berkeley CA 94708-1549 Office Phone: 510-642-8407. Business E-Mail: letiche@econ.berkeley.edu.

LETONA-HOLLOWAY, MARIA E., music educator; b. San Salvador, El Salvador, Feb. 23, 1962; d. Mauricio Andres Letona and Clelia Moreno Solorzano; m. Thomas E. Holloway, Aug. 20, 1998; children: Christina Maria Holloway, Thomas Andres Holloway. M in Piano performance (hon.), New Eng. Conservatory Music, 1993; B in Piano performance, New Eng. Conservatory, 1991; D of Musical Arts, U. Miami, 2003. Music prof. Barry U., Miami Shores, Fla., 1998—; music dir. Miami's Children Theater, 2003. Music dir. Bethune Sch. of Performing Arts, Ft. Lauderdale, Fla., 2002—02, Miami City Theater, Miami, Fla., 2002—02; piano accompanist U. Miami, Coral Gables, Fla., 1997—. Musician (classical pianist): (concert performance) Barry University; classical pianist (live performance) El Salvador Television, (piano recital) Miami SubTropics Music Festival, (piano soloist) Miami Youth Symphony, (concert performance) Lake Charles Symphony Orquestra (First Prize, 1979), (live radio broadcast) Performance and Interview, (invited to play as the guest of honor) Rene Touzet Concert, (piano recital) First Ibero-American Music Festival, (piano soloist) University Of Miami Concerto Competition (First Prize, 1997), (television performance), (piano soloist) New Orleans Philharmonic Auditions (First Prize, 1980), El Salvador National Symphony Orquestra, (piano recital) Recital Series in Italy. Recipient Hon. Citizen, The city of New Orleans, 1978. Mem.: AAUP. Office: Barry University Dept Fine Arts 11300 NE 2nd Ave Miami FL 33161 Personal E-mail: maria@tritonestudios.com.

LETOURNEAU, JEAN-PAUL, professional society administrator; b. St.-Hyacinthe, Que., Can., May 4, 1930; s. Eugene and Annette (Deslandes) L.; m. Claire Paquin, Sept. 26, 1956. Counsellor in Indsl. Relations, U. Montreal, Que., 1953; cert. c. of c. adminstrn., U. Syracuse, 1962; cert. advanced mgmt. U.S. C. of C, 1965. Mcpl. sec. Mont St.-Hilaire, Que., 1950-53; personnel mgr. Dupuis Freres (mail order house), 1953; editor Jeune Commerce, weekly tabloid Fedn. Que. Jr. C's. of C., 1953. Sec. gen. Montreal Jr. C. of C., 1953-56; asst. gen. mgr. Province Que. C. of C., Montreal, 1956-59, gen. mgr., 1959-71, exec. v.p., 1971-90. Author: Quebec, The Price of Independence, 1969, Report on Corporate Social Responsibilities, 1982. Mem. C. of C. Execs. Can. (pres. 1982-83, mem. coun. excellence 1986), Corp. Counsellors in Indsl Rels. of Que., Am. C. of C. Execs. (bd. dirs. 1982-83), Can. Exec. Svc. Orgns. (bd. dirs. 1991-95, vice chair 1993-95), Office Persons Handicapped of Que. (bd. dirs. 1992-98, exec. com. 1994-98). Roman Catholic. Office: 165 Cote Ste-Catherine #202 Outremont PQ Canada H2V 2A7 *Liberty is priceless; but liberty imposes responsibility, and if one is not responsible he will lose his liberty.*

LETSINGER, ROBERT LEWIS, chemistry professor; Student, Ind. U., 1939-41; BS in Chemistry, Mass. Inst. Tech., 1943, PhD in Organic Chemistry, 1945; DSc (hon.), Acadia U., Can., 1993. Research assoc. MIT, 1945-46; research chemist Tenn. Eastman Corp., 1946; faculty Northwestern U., 1946—, prof. chemistry, 1959—, chmn. dept., 1972-75, joint prof. biochemistry and molecular biology, 1974—92, Clare Hamilton Hall prof. chemistry, 1986—91, Clare Hamilton Hall prof. emeritus chemistry, 1991—; co-founder Nanosphere Inc., 2000—; adj. prof. Ind. U., 2002—. Med. and organic chemistry fellowship panel NIH, 1966-69, mem. physiol. chemistry review group, 1984, bio-organic and natural products chemistry study sect., 1985, chmn. spl. proposal rev. com., 1992; medicinal chem. A study sect., 1971-75; bd. on chem. scis. and tech. NRC, 1987-90, chmn. site visit NRC rsch. assocs., Frank J. Seiler rsch. lab, 1990; mem. steering com. Inst. Medicine Workshop; mem. AIDS project concept rev. panel, 1987; mem. program rev. divsn. biochem. and biophysics, FDA; mem. spl. rev. com. human genome program, 1992; mem. spl. emphasis panel for nat. coop. drug discovery groups for treatment of HIV infection. Recipient Rosenstiel medallion, 1985, MIH merit award, 1988, Arthur C. Cope scholar award, 1993, B.F. Goodrich Collegiate Inventors award, 1997; fellow Guggenheim Fellow, 1956, JSPS fellow, Japan, 1978. Fellow Am. Acad. Arts and Scis., Nat. Acad. Scis., Am. Assn. Arts and Scis.; mem. Am. Chem. Soc. (bd. editors 1969-72, bioconjugate chemistry 1992—), Sigma Xi, Phi Lambda Upsilon (hon. mem.). Methodist. Achievements include introduction of rapid chemical methods for synthesis of DNA segments, including solid phase synthesis and application of phosphite intermediates; development of base for efficient automated synthesis of gene fragments that has facilitated rapid development of molecular biology. Avocations: golf, hiking. Home: 1034 Sassafras Cir Bloomington IN 47408

LETSON, RUTH STAFFORD, librarian; b. Oak Ridge, Tenn., Oct. 21, 1944; d. Claude E. and Lillie (White) Stafford; m. G. Paul Letson, June 13, 1970; children: Stacey Rene, Danielle Michelle, Todd Shane. BS, East Tenn State U., 1966; MLS, George Peabody Coll., 1972. Tchr. Holston High Sch., Blountville, Tenn., 1966-67; tech. svcs. libr. Joint Univ. Librs., Nashville, 1968-77; serials libr. Tenn. State U., Nashville, 1977; libr. II Tenn. Dept. Transp., 1978—. Treas. LaVergne (Tenn.) H.S. Band Boosters, 1992-93. Mem. Tenn. Libr. Assn. (treas. 1991-92). Avocations: bridge, sewing. Office: Tenn Dept Transp Libr JK Polk Bldg Ste 300 Nashville TN 37243 Office Phone: 615-741-2330.

LETTEN, JAMES B., prosecutor; b. New Orleans; married; 2 children. Degree, U. New Orleans, 1976; JD, Tulane Law Sch., 1979. With New Orleans Dist. Attys. Office, 1979—82; with Organized Crime and Racketeering Strike Force US Dept. Justice, La., 1982—94, 1st asst. US atty. New Orleans, 1994—2005, interim US atty. ea. dist. LA, 2000—05, US atty., 2005—. Advanced through ranks to comdr. USNR, 1986—. Office: Hale Boggs Fed Bldg Rm 210 501 Magazine St New Orleans LA 70130

LETTERIE, KATHLEEN, broadcast executive; Head, talent WB Network, 1994—97, sr. v.p. talent and casting Burbank, Calif., 1997—2001, exec. v.p. talent and casting, 2001—. Office: WB TV Network 4000 Warner Blvd Bldg 34R Burbank CA 91522-0001

LETTERMAN, DAVID, television personality, producer, comedian, writer; b. Indpls., Apr. 12, 1947; s. Joseph and Dorothy L.; m. Michelle Cook, 1969 (div. 1977); 1 child. Grad., Ball State U., 1969. Weatherman and TV announcer, 1970—74; radio talk show host, 1974—75. Co-owner Rahal Letterman Racing. Performer The Comedy Store, Los Angeles, 1975; appearances on TV include (variety series) Mary, 1978, frequent guest host The Tonight Show; host (morning comedy/variety program) David Letterman Show, NBC, 1980 (2 Daytime Emmy awards), Late Night with David Letterman, NBC, 1982-1993, (5 Emmy awards) The Late Show with David Letterman, CBS, 1993— (also writer, exec. prodr.) (Emmy award for Outstanding Variety, Music or Comedy Program, 1994, 1998, 1999, 2000, 2001 and 2002); host, Emmy Awards, 1991, Academy Awards, 1995; writer for TV including Bob Hope Special, Good Times, Paul Lynde Comedy Hour, John Denver Special; author: (with others) The Late Night with David Letterman Book of Top Ten Lists, 1990, An Altogether New Book of Top Ten Lists, 1991; film appearances include: Cabin Boy, 1994; prodr. Worldwide Pants Inc.(TV series) The Bonnie Hunt Show, 1995-96, The Late Late Show With Tom Synder, 1995-99, The High Life, 1996, Everybody Loves Raymond, 1996-2005, Late Late Show with Craig Kilburn, 1999-2005, Welcome to New York, 2000-01, Ed, 2000-04, Late Late Show with Craig Ferguson, 2005-. Avocations: baseball, basketball, auto racing, running. Office: Late Show with David Letterman Ed Sullivan Theater 1697 Broadway New York NY 10019-5904*

LETTIERI, RICHARD J(OSEPH), lawyer; b. Chelsea, Mass., May 29, 1947; s. Rosario and Genevieve Helen (Sokoloski) L. AB in History, Villanova U., 1969; JD, Boston Coll., 1974. Bar: Mass. 1975, U.S. Dist. Ct. Mass. 1975, U.S. Ct. Appeals (1st cir.) 1979, U.S. Ct. Appeals (D.C. cir.) 1985. Pvt. practice, Boston, 1975-77; staff atty. Mass. Port Authority, Boston, 1977-81, chief legal counsel, 1981-86; assoc. Ropes & Gray, Boston, 1987-90, ptnr., 1990—. Mem. Boston Bar Assn., Justinian Law Soc. Office: Ropes & Gray 1 International Pl Fl 4 Boston MA 02110-2624 E-mail: rlettieri@ropesgray.com.

LETTON, ALVA HAMBLIN, surgeon, educator; b. Tampa, Fla., May 23, 1916; s. James Hervey and Minerva (Hamblin) L.; m. Roberta Rogers, Oct. 7, 1938; children: Robert Hamblin (dec.), Alice Roberta Zachodski. Student, U. Tampa, 1933-35, U. Fla., 1935-37; MD, Emory U., 1941. Diplomate Am. Bd. Surgery. Intern Ga. Baptist Hosp., Atlanta, 1941-42, resident, 1942-43; pvt. practice medicine specializing gen. surgery (oncology) Atlanta, 1946—; chief staff, attending surgeon Ga. Bapt. Hosp., 1965-73; sr. mem. Letton and Mason Surgery, Atlanta, 1980-95; dir. breast cancer demonstration project Bapt. Med. Ctr., 1972-78, chmn. exec. com. oncology dept.; clin. prof. surgery Med. Coll. Ga.; A. Hamblin Letton chair surg. oncology Ga. Bapt. Med. Ctr., 1990—95; founder Atlanta Cancer Ctr. Vis. prof. Egypt Cancer Inst., 1985, Med. and Dental Sch. N.J., 1986, Coll. Medicine U. Ill., Peoria, 1990; cons. Cobb. Gen. Grady Meml., Scottish Rite hosps.; chmn. cancer task force a. Regional Med. Program, 1966—71; mem. Ga. Sci. and Tech. Com., 1969—70; active Am. Cancer Soc., 1947—, nat. chmn. pub. edn., 1965—68, nat. chmn. svc. com., 1968—69, nat. chmn. med. and sci. com., 1969—70, v.p., nat. pres. elect, 1970—71, nat. pres., 1971—72, hon. bd. dirs. life, 1979—; pres. Atlanta Med. Ctr., 1965—90, Atlanta Health Evaluation Ctr., 1973—82; mem. Gov.'s Sci. Adv. Coun., 1972—75, U.S. nat. com. NAS, 1976—79; Roswell Park Meml. lectr., 1983; A. Hamblin Letton ann. lectr. Southeastern Surg. Congress, 1985—; bd. judges Criss Award; mem. Ethicon Gen. Surg. Adv. Panel, 1975—85; mem. cancer control adv. com. Nat. Cancer Inst., 1975—79; chmn. first cancer postgrad. course USA/USSR/ Union Internat. Contre Cancer, Leningrad, Former Soviet Union, 1999; mem. profl. edn. com. Union Internat. Contre Cancer, 1966—78; cons., Budapest, Hungary, 1986; cons. to exec. sec., Budapest, 72; cons. to forming Russian Cancer Soc., 1991—93; vis. prof. Pacific N.W. Cancer Found., 1998; mem. adv. bd. Ga. U. Sys., 1999—. Mem. editorial bd. Internat. Advances in Surg. Oncology, Jour. Cancer Prevention and Detection, 1985—; chmn. editorial bd. Oncology Times, 1979-90; guest editor Seminars in Surg. Oncology; contbr. articles to profl. jours., films. Deacon Bapt. ch. With M.C. USNR, 1943-46. Recipient Presdl. citation, 1944, Aven Citizenship award Fulton County Med. Soc., 1960, Honor Alumnus award Emory U., 1973, Hardman award Med. Assn. Ga., 1973, highest award John Muir Med. Film Festival, 1978; Disting. Svc. award Am. Cancer Soc., 1980, Nat. divsn. award, 1986, Vaughn award Ga. divsn., 1987, Atlanta Cmty. Svc. award, 2000, Pioneering Spirit award Ga. Cancer Coalition, 2003. Fellow: ACS, Southeastern Surg. Congress (hon.; sec.-dir 1960—86, Disting. Svc. award 1982); mem.: Letton Cancer Found. (pres. 1999), Soc. Internat. de Chirugie, Am. Thyroid Assn., Soc. Nuclear Medicine, So. Surg. Assn., Soc. Surg. Oncology, Univ. Yacht Club (Flowery Branch, Ga.), Capital City Club (Atlanta). Baptist. Home: 3747 Peachtree Rd NE Apt 1508 Atlanta GA 30319-1374

LETTOW, CHARLES FREDERICK, federal judge; b. Iowa Falls, Iowa, 1941; s. Carl Frederick and Catherine L.; m. Sue Lettow, 1963; children: Renee, Carl II, John, Paul. BS in Chem. Engring., Iowa State U., 1962; LLB, Stanford U., 1968; MA, Brown U., 2001. Bar: Calif. 1969, Iowa 1969, D.C.

1972, Md. 1991. Law clk. to Hon. Ben C. Duniway U.S. Ct. Appeals (9th cir.), San Francisco, 1968-69; law clk. to Hon. Warren E. Burger U.S. Supreme Ct., Washington, 1969-70; counsel Council on Environ. Quality, Washington, 1970-73; assoc. Cleary, Gottlieb, Steen & Hamilton, Washington, 1973-76, ptnr., 1976—2003; judge US Ct. Fed. Claims, Washington, 2003—. Contbr. articles to profl. jours. Trustee Potomac Sch., McLean, Va., 1983-90, chmn. bd. trustees, 1985-88. 1st lt. U.S. Army, 1963-65. Mem. ABA, Am. Law Inst., D.C. Bar, Iowa Bar Assn., Order of Coif. Clubs: University. Office: US Ct Fed Claims 717 Madison Pl NW Washington DC 20005 Business E-Mail: charles_lettow@ao.uscourts.gov.

LETTOW, LUCILLE JANE, school librarian, education educator; b. Eldora, Iowa, Mar. 8, 1942; d. Emily Barnhart and Harold W. C. Ziesman; m. Gary J. Lettow, July 25, 1964; 1 child, Karl Josef. BA, U. No. Iowa, 1964; MLS, U. Mo., 1969; M in English, U. No. Iowa, 1984. Iowa Permanent Profl.Tchg. Cert. 1973, Mo. Permanent Profl. Tchg. Cert. 1970. Jr. high tchr. Yale-Jamaica-Bagley Cmty. Schs., Iowa, 1964—66; sch. libr. media specialist Cedar Falls Cmty. Schools, Iowa, 1969—79; youth collection libr. and prof. U. No. Iowa, Cedar Falls, 1980—. Co-director, uni children's lit. workshops U. of No. Iowa, 1986—. Co-author: (profl. book) Picture Books to Enhance the Curriculum; contbr. articles to profl. jours. Recipient IEMA/SIRS Intellectual Freedom award, Iowa Ednl. Media Assn., 1990, Lamplighter award, 2000. Mem.: Assn. for Childhood Ednl. Internat., Internat. Reading Assn., ALA, Iowa Ednl. Media Assn. (pres. 1994—95, Presdl. Citation 1995). Office: Rod Library University of Northern Iowa 1227 West 27th St Cedar Falls IA 50613 Office Phone: 319-273-6167. E-mail: lucille.lettow@uni.edu.

LETTS, TRACY, actor, playwright; b. Tulsa; s. Dennis and Billie Letts. Ensemble mem. Steppenwolf Theatre Co., Chgo. Playwright (plays) Bug, 1996, Killer Joe, 1996 (Fringe First award, Edinburgh's Fringe Festival), Man From Nebraska, 2003 (One of Top 10 Plays of 2003, Time mag.); actor: (plays) Who's Afraid of Virginia Woolf?, Picasso at the Lapin Agile, Three Days of Rain, The Dazzle, The Glass Menagerie, Glengarry Glen Ross, Homebody/Kabul, The Dresser, Orson's Shadow, 2004, The Pain & the Itch, 2005; dir.: Great Men of Science, 21 & 22; actor: (films) Paramedics, 1987, Straight Talk, 1992, US Marshals, 1998, Chicago Cab, 1998, Guinevere, 1999, (TV appearances) Home Improvement, 1995, Seinfeld, 1997, The Drew Carey Show, 1998, Profiler, 2000, The District, 2001. Finalist Pulitzer Prize for Drama, 2004; named one of Best of 2003, Time mag. Office: Steppenwolf Theatre Co 1650 N Halsted St Chicago IL 60614*

LETWIN, LEON, law educator; b. Milw., Dec. 29, 1929; s. Lazar and Bessie (Rosenthal) L.; m. Alita Zurav, July 11, 1952; children— Michael, Daniel, David Ph.B., U. Chgo., 1950; LL.B., U. Wis., 1952; LL.M., Harvard U., 1964. Bar: Wis. 1952, Calif. 1969. Teaching fellow Harvard Law Sch., Boston, 1963-64; faculty Law Sch. UCLA, 1964—, prof., 1968-92, prof. emeritus, 1993—. Coord. Native-Am. Grave Protection and Repatriation Act, UCLA, 1998—2002. Contbr. articles to profl. jours. Active ACLU. Mem. Lawyers Guild, State Bar Calif. Home: 2226 Manning Ave Los Angeles CA 90064-2002 Office: UCLA Law Sch 405 Hilgard Ave Los Angeles CA 90095-9000

LETZIG, BETTY JEAN, financial consultant; b. Feb. 18, 1926; d. Robert H. and Alina Violet (Mayes) L. BA, Scarritt Coll., 1950, MA, 1968. Ednl. staff The Meth. Ch. Ark., Okla., Tex., 1953-60; with Internat. Deaconess Exch. Program, London, 1961-62; staff exec. nat. divsn. United Meth. Ch., N.Y.C., 1962-95, cons. current and deferred giving, 1995—. Coord. Mission Pers. Support Svcs., 1984-88; exec. sec. Deaconess Program Office, 1989-95. Contbr. articles to profl. jours. Bd. dirs. Global Health Action, Atlanta, 1974-88, Vellore Christian Med. Coll., N.Y.C., 1984-94; mem. U.S. com. Internat. Coun. Social Welfare, Washington, 1983-89; active Nat. Interfaith Coalition on Aging, Athens, Ga. and Washington, 1972—, pres., 1981-85. Mem.: LWV, AAUW, Older Women's League, Nat. Coun. Social Welfare, Nat. Voluntary Orgns. Ind. Living for Aging, Nat. Coun. Aging. Avocations: travel, beachcombing, photography, needlecrafts. Home: 266 Merrimon Ave Asheville NC 28801 Office: St Paul's United Meth Ch 223 Hillside St Asheville NC 28801

LEUBBERT, TERRY LYNNE, elementary school educator; b. Kans. City, Mo., Aug. 5, 1963; d. Esten E. and Beverly Lea Gray; m. David Luebbert, Oct. 26, 1989; 1 child, Kelsey Lynne Luebbert. B in edn., William Woods U., 1999; M in edn., Lesley U., 2002. Art tchr. Williamsburg Elem., Williamsburg, Mo., 1999—2000, New Bloomfield R III, New Bloomfield, Mo., 2000—. Author: (poem) Nature's Gentle Kiss, 2003, The Best Poems and Poets, 2003. Cath. Avocations: painting, photography, horse shows. Home: 1113 Ashton Cir W Fulton MO 65251 Office: New Bloomfield Elem 307 Redwood New Bloomfield MO 65063 Office Phone: 573-491-3352. E-mail: tlbbrt@sbcglobal.net.

LEUBERT, ALFRED OTTO PAUL, management consultant; b. N.Y.C., Dec. 7, 1922; s. Paul T. and Josephine (Haaga) L.; m. Celestine Capka, July 22, 1944 (div. 1977); children: Eloise Ann Cronin, Susan Beth; m. Hope Sherman Drapkin, June 4, 1978 (div. 1982). Student, Dartmouth Coll., 1943; BS, Fordham U., 1946; MBA, NYU, 1950. Account mgr. J.K. Lasser & Co., N.Y.C., 1948-52; controller Vision, Inc., N.Y.C., 1952-53, Old Town Corp., 1953-54, sec., controller, 1954-56, sec.-treas., 1956-57, v.p., treas., 1957-58; dir. subsidiaries Old Town Corp. (Old Town Ribbon & Carbon Co., Inc.), Mass. and Calif., 1955-58; v.p., controller Willcox & Gibbs, Inc., N.Y.C., 1958-59, v.p., treas., 1959-65, pres., dir., CEO, 1966-76; founder, pub., pres. Leubert's Compendium of Bus. (Fin. and Econ. Barometers), 1978-82; pres. Alfred O.P. Leubert Ltd., 1981-82, chmn. CEO, 1993—; chmn., CEO Solidyne, Inc., 1982; chmn. bd., pres., CEO, dir. Chyron Corp., 1983-91; dir. K & E Real Estate Ltd., China, 1994-96; chmn. bd. CEO Leubert & Co. (H.K.) Ltd., 1994-98; dir. Laser-Pacific Media Corp., 1995-96; chmn. bd., CEO, bd. dirs. Chyron Group (U.K.) Ltd., 1985-89; dir., vice chrmn. Advanced Definition Systems, Inc., 1996-97; chmn. bd., CEO, bd. dirs. CMX Corp., 1983-91; strategic advisor PlasmaNet, Inc., 1999—, Tru-You.Com, Inc., 2000—01, Dir. Media, Inc., 2000—01, Planet Playier, Inc., 2001—. CEO, dir. CGS Units, Inc., 1988-90, chmn. bd., 1989-90; bd. dirs. Digital Svcs. Corp.; vice chmn. bd. dirs. CMX Laser Sys., Inc., 1988-93; instr. accountancy Pace Coll., 1955-57. Bd. dirs. United Fund of Manhasset, 1963-69, pres., 1964-65; bd. dirs. Actor's Studio, 1972-76; adv. bd. St. Anthony's Guidance Clinic, 1967-69. Served to capt. USMCR, 1943-46. Decorated Bronze Star; recipient Humanitarian award Hebrew Acad., N.Y.C., 1971 Mem. AICPA, N.Y. State Soc. CPAs, Fordham U. Alumni Assn., N.Y. Athletic Club. Roman Catholic. Home and Office: 1 Lincoln Plz New York NY 10023-7129 Office Phone: 212-595-4900.

LEUBSDORF, CARL PHILIPP, publishing executive; b. NYC, Mar. 17, 1938; s. Karl and Bertha (Boschwitz) Leubsdorf; m. Carolyn Cleveland Stockmeyer, Mar. 26, 1963 (div. 1978); children: Carl Philipp Jr., Loma Stockmeyer, E. William Stockmeyer Jr., C. Cleveland Stockmeyer, Claire C. Goodwin; m. Susan Page, May 23, 1982; children: Benjamin Page, William Page. BA in Govt., Cornell U., 1959; MS in Journalism, Columbia U., 1960. Staff writer AP, New Orleans, 1960—63, Washington, 1963—75; corr. Balt. Sun, Washington, 1976—81; Washington bur. chief Dallas Morning News, Washington, 1981—. Recipient Columbia Journalism Sch. Alumni award, 1999. Mem.: Nat. Press Club (Washington), White Ho. Corrs. Assn. (pres. 1995—96), Gridiron Club (sec. 2004—05), Phi Beta Kappa. Office: Dallas Morning News 1325 G St NW Ste 250 Washington DC 20005-3115 Personal E-mail: cleubsdorf@dallasnews.com.

LEUCHOVIUS, DEBORAH, advocate, special education services professional, consultant; b. Litchfield, Minn., Dec. 22, 1954; d. David Robert Leslie and Corinne Ardell Shiell; m. James Raphael Poole, Aug. 18, 1979; 1 child, Frederick Winston Leuchovius Poole. BA, Hamline U., 1978; MA, Rutgers U., 1981. Americans with Disabilities Act specialist PACER Ctr., Inc., Mpls, tech. assistance specialist Mpls., 1994—96, project dir. TATRA project, 1996—, nat. coord., transition tech. assistance programs, 2001—. Cons. Change Agy., St. Paul, 1990—. Editor: (newsletter) Point of Departure, (book) The Americans with Disabilities Act: A Guide for People with Disabilities, Their Families and Advocates. Advisor to nat. leadership team Assn. Sci. and Tech. Ctrs., Mus. and Access; mem. Spina Bifida Assn. Minn., 1994—, sec., 2000; advisor VSA Arts Minn., Mpls., 1995—99; advisor to access com. Walker Art Ctr.; bd. dirs. ADA Minn., St. Paul, 1992—95; founding mem. Minn. Ind. Scholars Forum, 1981—89. Mem.: Nat. Rehab. Assn., Coun. Exceptional Children (parent rep. divsn. career devel. 1997—99). Office: PACER Ctr 8161 Normandale Blvd Minneapolis MN 55437 Office Phone: 952-838-9000. Business E-Mail: tatra@pacer.org.

LEUCHTMAN, STEPHEN NATHAN, lawyer; b. Detroit, Oct. 14, 1945; s. Alexis C. and Frances J. (Boucher) L.; m. Jacque Ward, Nov. 29, 1991; children: Stephen, John II, Lucinda. BA, U. Mich., 1967, JD, 1970. Bar: Mich. 1970, Calif. 1993, U.S. Dist. Ct. (ea. and so. dists.) Mich. 1970, U.S. Ct. Appeals (6th cir.) 1982. Assoc. Eggenberger, Eggenberger, McKinney & Weber, Detroit, 1970-75, Tyler & Canham, Detroit, 1975-80; ptnr. Sommers, Schwartz, Silver & Schwartz, Southfield, 1980-97; founding ptnr. Trowbridge Law Firm, P.C., Detroit, 1997-2001; atty. Stephen N. Leuchtman, P.C., Detroit, 2001—; of counsel Ravid & Assocs., 2005—. Contbr. articles to profl. jours. Mem. ABA, ATLA, Am. Bd. Trial Advocates, Million Dollar Advocates Forum, Consumer Attys. of Calif., Mich. Bar Assn., Calif. Bar Assn. Democrat. Achievements include Alll-Big-Ten, Track, 1965, 1966. Avocations: writing, golf, travel. Office: 23855 Northwestern Hwy Southfield MI 48075 Office Phone: 248-948-9696 143. Personal E-mail: leuchlaw@attglobal.net.

LEUCK, MARK JOSEPH, lawyer; b. Kenosha, Wis., Mar. 8, 1953; s. Donald and Jeanette Leuck; m. Rosanne M. Stella, Aug. 3, 1974; children: Vanessa, Matthew. BA, U. Wis., Kenosha, 1974; JD, Harvard U., 1977. Bar: Wis. 1977. Assoc. Heide, Hartley, Tom, Wilk & Guttormsen, Kenosha, 1977-83; ptnr. Schoone, Leuck, Kelley, Pitts & Knurr, S.C., Racine, Wis., 1983—. Mem. Urban League, Racine, 1992-94; trustee St. Joseph H.S., Kenosha, 1999-2001. Mem. ABA, ATLA, State Bar Wis., Wis. Acad. Trial Lawyers. Home: 3615 13th St Kenosha WI 53144 Office: 6800 Washington Ave Racine WI 53406-3928

LEULIETTE, CONNIE JANE, secondary school educator; b. Buckhannon, W.Va., Mar. 07; d. Audie Nelson and Sadie Laura (Gregory) Ware; m. Charles Benjamin Leuliette, Jr., Sept. 5, 1964; 1 child, Eric Wesley. BS, W.Va. U., 1963, MA, 1965. Tchr. grades 1-4 Point Mountain Elem. Sch., Webster Springs, W.Va., 1959-60; tchr. gen. sci. Webster Springs (W.Va.) High Sch., 1963-64; tchr. 2d grade Norwood Elem. Sch., Clarksburg, W.Va., 1965-66, tchr. 6th grade, 1966-67; circulation clk., librarian Clarksburg-Harrison Pub. Library, 1981-83, reference librarian, 1983-89; tchr. sci. South Harrison High Sch., Lost Creek, W.Va., 1989-90, Roosevelt-Wilson Middle Sch., Nutter Fort, W.Va., 1990-96, Washington Irving Mid. Sch., Clarksburg, W.Va., 1996—2003. Pres. Nutter Fort PTA, 1978-79; elder Presbyn. Ch. NSF grantee, 1964-65. Mem. NEA, AAUW (sec. W.Va. divsn. 1981-83, conv. chmn. 1978-80, treas. 1992-96, br. pres. 1983-85, chair W.Va. Ednl. Found. 2000-02), W.Va. Sci. Tchrs. Assn., W.Va. Assn. Parliamentarians (unit sec. 1986-90, treas. 1991-94, 1999-2001), W.Va. Fedn. Woman's Club (chmn. edn. dept. 1982-86, continuing edn. divsn. 1990-92, cmty. improvement program 1992-94, dist. edn. dept. 1990-92, dist. treas. 1994-98, dist. 2d v.p. 1998-2000, dist. 1st v.p. 2000-02, dist. pres. elect 2002-04, North Ctrl. dist. pres. 2004—), Woman's Club Nutter Fort (pres. 1990-92), Alpha Delta Kappa (W.Va. chpt. v.p. 1992-94, chpt. pres. 1994-96, state historian 2000-02, state treas. 2002—). Democrat. Presbyterian. Avocations: reading, crosswords, walking, photography, stamp collecting/philately. Home: 107 Arbutus Dr Clarksburg WV 26301-4301

LEULIETTE, TIMOTHY D., automotive executive; married; 4 children. BSME, MBA, U. Mich. Founding ptnr., sr. mng. dir. Heartland Indsl. Ptnrs.; with Ford Motor Co.; exec. dir. product planning Am. Motors; chmn. Metaldyne, Plymouth, Mich., pres., CEO. Pres., COO Penske Corp.; pres., CEO ITT Automotive Inc.; sr. v.p. ITT Industries, Inc.; pres., CEO Siemens Automotive L.P.; from group dir. to group v.p. AlliedSignal Automotive, v.p. Bendix Electronics Group; corp. v.p. Siemens AG, mem. mng. bd.; chmn. bd. Detroit (Mich.) Br. The Fed. Res. Bank Chgo. Mem. Citizen's Rsch. Coun. Mich.; mem. citizens adv. com. U. Mich., Dearborn, Mich. Named World Trader of Yr., Detroit (Mich.) Regional C. of C. Mem.: Engring. Soc. Detroit, Soc. Automotive Engrs., Detroit (Mich.) Econ. Club (bd. dir.). Office: Metaldyne 47603 Halyard Dr Plymouth MI 48170

LEUNG, BETTY BRIGID, nursing administrator; b. Shanghai, Oct. 28, 1949; arrived in U.S., 1972; d. Chek Sang and Si Iun (Vong) Leung. Diploma, St. James Sch. Nursing, 1974; BSN, Hunter-Bellevue Sch. Nursing, 1985; MSN, CUNY, 1989. Nurse ICU St. James Mercy Hosp., Hornell, N.Y., 1974-80; sr. staff ICU NYU Med. Ctr., N.Y.C., 1980-81, nurse clinician, 1981-85, asst. clin. coord., 1985-88, clin. coord., 1988-91, nursing supr., 1991-97, organ transplant coord., 1997-98; clin. coord. White Plains (N.Y.) Hosp. Ctr., 1998-2001, nurse mgr., 2001—. Recipient Women's Bd. award, 1974, Therese Cornell Meehan Nursing Rsch. award, 1990; scholar Nursing, St. James Sch., 1972—74. Mem.: AACN, Am. Orgn. Nurse Execs., Nat. Assn. Orthop. Nursing. Roman Catholic. Avocations: photography, travel, collecting coins and stamps. Office: White Plains Hosp Ctr Davis Ave at E Post Rd White Plains NY 10601 Business E-Mail: bleung@wphospital.org.

LEUNG, FRANKIE FOOK-LUN, barrister; b. Guangzhou, China, 1949; (div.); 1 child. BA in Psychology with honors, Hong Kong U., 1972; MS in Psychology, Birmingham (Eng.) U., 1974; BA, MA in Jurisprudence, Oxford (Eng.) U., 1976; JD, Coll. of Law, London, 1977. Bar: Calif. 1987. Barrister Eng. and Hong Kong, 1977—. Lectr. Chinese law for businessmen Hong Kong U., 1984-85, 85-86; vis. scholar Harvard U. Law Sch., 1983; barrister, solicitor Supreme Ct. of Victoria, Australia, 1983—, Calif. Bar, 1987—; cons. prof. Chinese Law Diploma Program, U. East Asia, 1986-87; adj. prof. Loyola Law Sch., L.A., 1988-2000, Pepperdine U. Law Sch., 1989-90; lectr. Stanford U. Law Sch., 1995-96, U. So. Calif. Law Sch., 1998-2003. Author books on Chinese and Hong Kong law, Asian politics, Asian trade and bus. mgmt.; contbr. numerous articles to profl. jours., and 6 books. Bd. advisors Hong Kong Archives Hoover Instn.-Stanford U., 1988—; adv., Ctrl. Policy Unit, Hong Kong govt., 1997-99, dir. YMCA, Pasadena, Calif., 1997-99. Mem. Am. Arbitration Assn. (bd. dirs.), Calif. State Bar (mem. exec. coun. internat. sect. 1989-92, Wiley W. Manuel award 1993), Hong Kong Bar Assn., European Assn. for Chinese Law (mem. exec. coun. 1986—, country corr. 1985—), Am. C. of C. (chmn. subcom. on Chinese intellectual property law 1985-86), Am. Soc. Internat. Law (judge moot ct. 1984-2005). Office: 444 S Flower St Ste 3010 Los Angeles CA 90071-2901 Office Phone: 213-228-8922. Personal E-mail: frankieleunglaw@aol.com.

LEUNG, KA-CHEONG, education educator; B in Engring. in Computer Sci., Hong Kong U. Sci. and Tech., 1994; MSc in Elec. Engring. and Computer Networks, U. So. Calif., 1997, PhD, 2000. Rsch. asst. U. Hong Kong, 1998—2000; sr. rsch. engr. Nokia Rsch. Ctr., Irving, Tex., 2001—02; asst. prof. Tex. Tech U., 2002—05. Ind. cons. Tex. Internat. Edn. Consortium, 2004. Contbr. articles to profl. jours. Mem.: IEEE. Office Phone: 852 2859 7093. Personal E-mail: kcleung@ieee.org.

LEUPOLD, HERBERT AUGUST, physicist; b. Bklyn., Jan. 6, 1931; s. August John and Josefa (Thalmyer) L. BS in Physics, CUNY-Queens Coll., 1953; AM in Physics, Columbia U., 1958, PhD in Physics, 1964. Instr. physics CUNY-Queens Coll., Flushing, 1957; fellow Lawrence Livermore Lab., Livermore, Calif., 1964-67; instr. physics Monmouth Coll., West Long Branch, N.J., 1967-70, 84-85; instr. chemistry Trenton (N.J.) State Coll., 1984-85; rsch. physicist U.S. Army Rsch. Lab., Ft. Monmouth, N.J., 1967-97, U.S. Army Rsch. Lab. at U.S. Mil. Acad., West Point, N.Y., 1997—. Sr. technologist U.S. Army, 1995. Co-author: Rare Earth-Iron Permanent Magnetics, 1996; contbr. over 100 articles to profl. jours.; over 100 patents in fields of magnetics and electronics. With U.S. Army, 1953-55. Fellow IEEE (mem. assoc. editors of IEEE transactions), Army Rsch. Lab.; mem. Magnetics Soc. of IEEE (mem. adminstrv. com. 1991-93, mem. various conf. organizing coms.), Am. Phys. Soc., Sigma Xi. Roman Catholic.

LEUPP, EDYTHE PETERSON, retired education educator; b. Mpls., Nov. 27, 1921; d. Reynold H. and Lillian (Aldridge) Peterson; m. Thomas A. Leupp, Jan. 29, 1944 (dec.); children: DeEtte(dec.), Patrice, Stacia, Roderick, Braden. BS, U. Oreg., 1947, MS, 1951, EdD, 1972. Tchr. various pub. schs., Idaho, 1941-45, Portland, Oreg., 1945-55; dir. tchr. edn. N.W. Nazarene Coll., Nampa, Idaho, 1955-61; sch. adminstr. Portland Pub. Schs., 1963-84; dir. tchr. edn. George Fox Coll., Newberg, Oreg., 1984-87; ret., 1987. Vis. prof. So. Nazarene U., Bethany, Okla., 1988—95, Asia Pacific Nazarene Theol. Sem., 1996, prof., 2000; adj. prof. Warner Pacific Coll., Portland, 1996—97; pres. Portland Assn. Pub. Sch. Adminstrs., 1973—75; dir.-at-large Nat. Coun. Adminstrv. Women Edn., Washington, 1973—76; state chmn. Oreg. Sch. Prins. Spl. Project, 1978—79; chair Confdn. Oreg. Sch. Adminstrs. Ann. Conf.; rschr. 40 tchr. edn. programs in colls. and univs.; designer tchr. edn. program George Fox Coll. Author: tchr. edn. materials. Pres. Nampa PTA, 1958, Idaho State Aux. Mcpl. League, 1957. Named Honored Tchr. of Okla., 1993; recipient Golden Gift award, 1982; fellow, Charles Kettering Found., 1978, 1980, 1987, 1991, 1992, 1993, 1994; scholar Hazel Fishwood, 1970. Mem.: Am. Assn. Colls. Tchr. Edn., Pi Lambda Theta, Phi Delta Kappa, Delta Kappa Gamma (pres. Alpha Rho State 1986—88). Republican. Nazarene. Avocations: travel, crafts, photography. Home: 8100 SW 2nd Ave Portland OR 97219-4602

LEUSCH, MARK STEVEN, microbiologist; b. Cleve., June 8, 1961; s. Thomas Arthur and Elaine Margaret (Torma) L.; m. Cindy June Campos, Feb. 4, 1989; children: Steven Alexander, Kristen Denise, Monica Renée. BA, U. Ariz., 1984, PhD, 1990. Postdoctoral assoc. Monsanto Co., St. Louis, 1990-92; sr. scientist healthcare divsn. Procter and Gamble Co., Cin., 1992—2001; assoc. dir. U.S. regulatory affairs Procter & Gamble Pharmaceuticals, Inc., 2001—. Devel. team Crest Gum Care, 1995, Clean Mint Scope, 1994, Crest Multicare, 1996-97, Crest Extra Whitening, 1997, Crest Multicare with Extra Whitening, 1997-98; tech. support for advt. claims Scope, 1994. Contbr. articles to profl. jours. including Infection and Immunity, Pros. NAS, Biochem. and Biophys. Rsch. Commn., Gene., Jour. Clin. Dentistry, Abstracts to Jour. Dental Rsch. Roman Catholic. Achievements include patents for method of producing recombinant eukaryotic viruses in bacteria; anti-caries oral care compositions and their methods of use. Office: Health Care Rsch Ctr PO Box 8006 Mason OH 45040-8006 Office Phone: 513-622-2620. E-mail: leusch.ms@pg.com.

LEUTHOLD, RAYMOND MARTIN, agricultural economics professor; b. Billings, Mont., Oct. 13, 1940; s. John Henry and Grace Irene L.; m. Jane Hornaday, Aug. 20, 1966; children— Kevin, Gregory. Student, Colo. U., 1958-59; BS, Mont. State U., 1962; MS, U. Wis., 1966, PhD, 1968. Faculty U. Ill., Urbana-Champaign, 1967—, now prof. emeritus dept. agrl. econs., T.A. Hieronymus disting. prof. Vis. scholar Stanford U., 1974, Chgo. Mercantile Exch., 1990, 91. Co-author: The Theory and Practice of Futures Markets, 1989; editor: Commodity Markets and Futures Prices, 1979; co-editor: Livestock Futures Research Symposium, 1980. Served with U.S. Army, 1962—64. Fulbright research scholar Institute de Gestion Internationale Agro-Alimentaire, Cergy, France, 1981 Mem. Am. Econ. Assn., Am. Agrl. Econs. Assn. (Disting. Policy award 1980, Outstanding Instr. award 1986, 88, 90, 92, College Funk award 1993). Office: 305 Mumford Hall 1301 W Gregory Dr Urbana IL 61801-9015

LEUTY, GERALD JOHNSTON, osteopathic physician, surgeon; b. Knoxville, Iowa, July 23, 1919; s. John William and Mable Reichard (Johnston) L.; m. Martha L. Weymouth, Jan. 24, 1940 (div. 1957); children: Maxine Joanne, Robert James, Gerald Johnston Jr., Karl Joseph; m. Norma Jean Hindman, Dec. 30, 1969; children: Barbara Jayne, Patrick Jack. AB, Kemper Mil. Sch., Boonville, Mo., 1939; postgrad., Drake U., Des Moines, 1944-45; DO, Des Moines Coll. Osteopathy, 1949; embalmer, Coll. Mortuary Sci., St. Louis, 1941. Mortician/embalmer Cauldwell-McJihon Funeral Home, Des Moines, 1939-40; aero. engr. Boeing Aircraft Co., Wichita, Kans., 1941-42; osteopathic physician and surgeon Knoxville (Iowa) Ostepathic Clinic, 1949-56; dir. Leuty Osteopathic Clinic, Earlham, Iowa, 1957-77; osteopathic physician and surgeon in pvt. practice Santa Rosa, Calif., 1977—; prof. clin. med. Western U. Health Svcs., Pomona, Calif., 1985—. Mem. Iowa's Gov. Blue Med. Adv. Bd., 1972-77. With U.S. Army, 1942-46. Named Physician of the Yr., 6th Dist. Iowa Ostepathic Soc., 1975, Disting. Leadership award, Am. Biog. Inst., 1988, others. Fellow Internat. Co. Angiologists; mem. Am. Ostepathic Assn. (ho. of dels., life mem. 1989), Iowa Osteopathic Soc. (pres. 6th dist. 1974), Soc. Osteopathic Physicians, No. Calif. Osteopathic Med. Soc. (pres. 1981), Osteopathic Physicians and Surgeons of Calif. (pres. 1982), Am. Acad. Osteopathy (chmn. component socs. com. 1988, pres. Calif. divsn. 1987, pres. No. Calif. divsn. 1989, 91-93, 95), North Coast Osteopathic Med. Assn. (pres. 1992), Am. Med. Soc. Vienna (life mem.), Am. Legion (6th dist. comdr. 1974-75), Lions (pres. 1946). Republican. Presbyterian. Avocations: photography, travel. Home: 5835 La Cuesta Dr Santa Rosa CA 95409-3914

LEUTZE, JAMES RICHARD, former academic administrator; b. Charleston, S.C., Dec. 24, 1935; w. Willard Parker and Magdalene Mae (Seith) L.; m. Kathleen Shirley Erskine, Feb. 13, 1960; children: Magdalene Leigh, Jay, James Parker; m. Margaret Gates, June 7, 1997. BA, U. Md., 1957; MA, U. Miami, 1959; PhD, Duke U., 1968. Legis. asst. U.S. Senator Hubert Humphrey, Washington, 1963-64; prof. history U. N.C., Chapel Hill, 1968-87, chmn. curriculum peace, war, and def., 1979-87, Bowman and Gordon Gray prof., 1982, Dowd prof. Peace and War, 1986; TV host-producer N.C. Ctr. for Pub. TV, Chapel Hill, 1984—; pres. Hampden-Sydney (Va.) Coll., 1987-90; chancellor U. N.C., Wilmington, 1990—2003, chancellor emeritus, 2003—. Author: Bargaining for Supremacy: Anglo-American Naval Collaboration, 1937-41, 1977 (Bernath prize 1978), A Different Kind of Victory: The Biography of Admiral Thomas C. Hart, 1981 (John Lyman Book award 1981); editor: London Journal Gen. Raymond E. Lee, 1972, The Role of the Military in a Democracy, 1974; contbr. articles to profl. jours. Mem. N.C. Progress Bd.; chair Rural Internet Access. Served to capt. USAF, 1960-63. Recipient Standard Oil award for teaching U. N.C., 1971, Tanner award for teaching, 1978, Order of Golden Fleece award, 1983, J.W. Pate award for creating environ. awareness, 1995. Mem. Orgn. Am. Historians, Royal U.S. Inst. (London), Am. Hist. Assn., Univ. Club (N.Y.), N.C. Nature Conservancy, Bald Head Island Conservancy, George C. Marshall Found., Phi Beta Kappa. Democrat. Episcopalian. Avocations: sportsman, hunting, fishing. Office: U NCW 601 S College Rd Wilmington NC 28403-5931 E-mail: leutzej@uncw.edu.

LEV, AVI MEIR, lawyer; b. L.A., Mar. 28, 1956; BA, U. Calif., L.A., 1977; JD, U. Oreg., 1980; LLM in Taxation, Boston (Mass.) U., 2002. Bar: Oreg. 1980, Mass. 1998. With Sullivan & Worcester LLP, Boston, 1980—. Office: Sullivan & Worcester LLP One Post Office Sq Boston MA 02109 Office Phone: 617-338-2800.

LEVACK, BRIAN PAUL, history professor; b. N.Y.C., N.Y., Apr. 6, 1943; s. Arthur Paul and Helen Gertrude Levack; m. Nancy Buecker Levack, Dec. 17, 1966; children: Christopher Paul, Brian Andrew. BA, Fordham Coll., 1965; PhD, Yale U., 1970. Asst. prof. U. of Tex., Austin, 1970—74, assoc. prof., 1974—87, prof., 1987—94, John Green Regents prof., 1994—. Scholar in residence Wash. and Lee U. Sch. of Law, Lexington, Va., 1994. Author: (book) The Civil Lawyers in England, 1603-1641: A Political Study, 1973, The Formation of the British State: England, Scotland and the Union, 1603-1707, 1987, The Witch-Hunt in Early Modern Europe, 1987; editor, 1995, The Witchcraft Sourcebook, 2004; author: (textbook) The West: Encounters and Transformations, 2004; editor: (book) The Jacobean Union: Six Tracts of 1604, 1985; author: Witchcraft and Magic in Europe: The Eighteenth and Nineteenth Centuries, 1999. Fellow, John Simon Guggenheim Meml. Found., 1975—76. Mem.: North Am. Conf. on Brit. Studies (exec. sec. 1999—2002). Democrat. Avocations: running, carpentry, scuba diving.

Home: 2209 Greenlee Dr Austin TX 78703 Office: U Tex Dept History 1 University Station B7000 Austin TX 78712 Office Phone: 512-475-7204. Business E-Mail: levack@mail.utexas.edu.

LEVACK, EDNA BEVAN, music educator, choir director; b. Cheyenne, Wyo., Sept. 21, 1922; d. Christopher Henry Droegemueller and Charlotte Adelheit Mueller; m. Elmer Wayne Bevan, Nov. 4, 1944 (div. Dec. 1988); children: David Wayne, Ronn Merrill, Paul Bevan (dec.), Philip Neal; m. John B. Humphries, Feb. 18, 1989 (dec. Aug. 2003); m. Norman T. Levack, June 18, 2004 BS, U. Minn., 1943. Nat. and state cert. piano tchr. Freelance writer, Seattle, 1955—; piano tchr., 1955—; organist Luth. Ch., Seattle, 1950—80, choir dir., 1965—80; dir. bell choir John Knox Presbyn. Ch., Seattle, 1989—2002, Glendale Luth. Ch., Seattle, 1989—, Southminster Presbyn. Ch., Seattle, 2002—. Handbelll choir dir. Lutheran and Presbyn. chs., Seattle; conductor adult and children choirs Lutheran Chs., 1980—95. Author: Christian Finger Plays and Games, 1955. Mem.: Wash. State Music Tchrs. Assn. (past treas., past pres. South King County chpt.). Avocation: square and folk dancing. Home: 830 SW Shoremont Ave Normandy Park WA 98166-3646 E-mail: ehumphr812@aol.com.

LEVADA, WILLIAM JOSEPH, archbishop; b. Long Beach, Calif., June 15, 1936; s. Joseph and Lorraine (Nunez) Levada. BA, St. John's Coll., Camarillo, Calif., 1958; STL, Gregorian U., Rome, 1962, STD, 1971. Ordained priest in St. Peter's Basilica, Rome 1961; assoc. pastor Archdiocese of LA, 1962—67; prof. theology St. John's Sem., Camarillo, Calif., 1970—76; exec. dir. Calif. Cath. Conf. of Bishops, Sacramento, 1982—84; ordained bishop, 1983; Titular Bishop of Capri & Aux. Bishop of LA, 1983—86; episcopal vicar Santa Barbara County, 1984—86; chancellor & moderator of the curia Archdiocese of LA, 1986; Archbishop of Portland Oreg., 1986—95; Coadjutor Archbishop of San Francisco, 1995; Archbishop of San Francisco, 1995—; apostolic adminstr. Diocese of Santa Rosa, Calif., 1999—2000. Mem. editl. com. Commn. for the Catechism of the Cath. Ch., 1986—93; ofcl. Congregation for the Doctrine of the Faith, 1976—82, mem., 2000—, prefect, 2005—; co-chair Anglican-Roman Cath. dialogue in the US, 2000. Mem.: Canon Law Soc. Am., Cath. Theol. Soc. Am., US Cath. Conf. Bishops (chmn. com. on doctrine 2003—). Office: Roman Cath Archdiocese of San Francisco One Peter Yorke Way San Francisco CA 94109 Office Phone: 415-614-5500.*

LEVAI, PIERRE ALEXANDRE, art gallery executive; b. Paris, Mar. 6, 1937; came to U.S., 1967; s. Paul Victor and Jeanne (Illa) L.; m. Rosemary Hare, Aug. 22, 1969; children: Paula, Max. Degree in bus. and polit. sci., Inst. d'Etudes Politiques, 1959. With Marlborough Gallery, London, 1964-67, pres., dir. N.Y.C., 1967—. Decorated chevalier dans l'ordre des Arts et des Lettres. Mem. Chelsea Arts Club (London). Roman Catholic. Office: Marlborough Gallery 40 W 57th St Fl 2 New York NY 10019-4069

LEVAL, PIERRE NELSON, federal judge; b. NYC, Sept. 4, 1936; s. Fernand and Beatrice (Reiter) L. BA cum laude, Harvard U., 1959, JD magna cum laude, 1963. Bar: N.Y. 1964, U.S. Ct. Appeals 2d Circuit 1964, U.S. Dist. Ct. So. Dist. N.Y 1966. Law clk. to Hon. Henry J. Friendly, U.S. Ct. Appeals, 1963—64; asst. U.S. atty. So. Dist. N.Y., 1964—68, chief appellate atty., 1967—68; assoc. firm Cleary, Gottlieb, Steen & Hamilton, N.Y.C., 1969—74; ptnr. firm, 1973—75; 1st asst. dist. atty. Office of Dist. Atty., N.Y. County, 1975—76, chief asst. dist. atty., 1976—77; U.S. dist. judge So. Dist. N.Y., N.Y.C., 1977—93; judge U.S. Ct. of Appeals (2d cir.), N.Y.C., 1993—2002; sr judge, 2002—. Adj. faculty NYU Sch. of Law. Contbr. articles to profl. jours. With U.S. Army, 1959. Recipient Learned Hand Medal, Fed. Bar Council, 1997; grantee Fowler Harper Mem. Fellowship, Yale Law Sch., 1992; Melville Nimmer Lectureship, UCLA Law Sch., 1997, Intellectual Property Keynote Lecturship, U. Conn Sch. of Law, 2001. Mem.: N.Y. County Lawyers Assn., Assn. Bar City N.Y., Am. Law Inst. (coun.). Office: US Courthouse 40 Foley Sq New York NY 10007-1502*

LEVALLIANT, DEBBIE, information technology executive; BS in Bus. Admin., Acadia Univ. Stockbroker; pres., CEO Amirix Systems, Halifax, Canada, 1990—. Exec. com. NovaKnowledge; mem. Halifax Chamber Commerce. Mem.: Soc. Mgmt. Accts. Nova Scotia (mem. bd. dir.), CMA Soc. (adjudication panel for CMA candidates case presentation). Achievements include leading devel. global lic. program, AMIRIX; negotiating company transition from non-profit to for-profit status. Office: Amirix Systems 77 Chain Lake Dr Halifax NS B35 1E1 Canada

LEVAN, MARTIN DOUGLAS, chemical engineering professor; b. Chattanooga, Aug. 30, 1949; s. Martin Douglas and Charlotte Irene (McAmis) LeV.; m. Barbara Lynn Verkins, Sept. 24, 1977; children: Theodore Douglas, Gregory William. BSChemE, U. Va., 1971; PhD in Chem. Engring., U. Calif., Berkeley, 1976. Sr. research engr. Amoco Prodn. Co., Tulsa, 1976-78; asst. prof. chem. engring. U. Va., Charlottesville, 1978-83, assoc. prof., 1983—89, prof., 1989—96; Centennial prof. and chair chem. engring. Vanderbilt U., Nashville, 1997—2003, J. Lawrence Wilson prof. engring., 2004—. Cons. Amoco Prodn. Co., Tulsa, 1984—, Amoco Chems. Co., Chgo., 1986—; vis. prof. Perpignan U., France, 1994. Contbg. author: Perry's Chemical Engineer's Handbook, 1984; contbr. more than 120 articles to profl. jours. and proceedings. Cub scout officer Boy Scouts Am., Charlottesville, 1986—; coach boys and girls soccer, Charlottesville, 1987—. Fulbright sr. scholar Coun. for Internat. Exchange of Scholars, U. Porto, Portugal, 1985-86, CNRS-LIMSI, Orsay, France, 1993-94; grantee NSF, Petroleum Research Fund of Am. Chem. Soc., others. Mem. Am. Inst Chem. Engrs. (chmn. com. on absorption and ion exchange 1985-87, chmn. symposia 1981—), Am. Chem. Soc., Alpha Chi Sigma, Phi Eta Sigma, Tau Beta Pi, Sigma Xi. Avocations: golf, art. Office: Vanderbilt U Dept Chem Engring Nashville TN 37235 Business E-Mail: m.douglas.levan@vanderbilt.edu.

LEVANDER, ANDREW JOSHUA, lawyer; b. NYC, Aug. 15, 1953; s. Seymour S. and Ellenore B. L.; m. Carol A. Loewenson, Sept. 18, 1983; children: Samuel, Benjamin. BA summa cum laude, Tufts U., 1973; JD, Columbia U., 1977. Bar: NY 1978, DC 1978, U.S. Supreme Ct., U.S. Ct. Appeals (2d, 3d, 4th, 5th, 7th and 10th DC cirs.), U.S. Dist. Ct. (so. and ea. dists.) N.Y. Law clk. Judge Wilfred Feinberg, U.S. Ct. Appeals, N.Y.C, 1977-78; asst. Solicitor Gen.'s Office, US Dept. Justice, Washington, 1978-81; asst. U.S. atty. US Attys. Office, NYC, 1981-85; ptnr. Shereff, Friedman, Hoffman & Goodman, NYC, 1985-98; assoc. ind. counsel Washington, 1987; ptnr. Swidler Berlin Shereff Friedman LLP, Washington, 1998—2004, Dechert, LLP, NYC, 2005—. Bd. dirs. Swidler, Berlin, Shereff Friedman, exec. com., 1998-2004 Co-author: The Prosecution and Prevention of Computer and High Technology Crime, 1986, Settling Commercial Litigation, 1999; contbr. articles to profl. jours. Chmn. scholar com. Westside Youth Soccer League, N.Y.C., 1996-2003. Mem. ABA (White Collar Com. 1997-99, lectr. white collar convention 2002), Bar Assn. City of N.Y. (securities regulation com. 1997-99). Avocations: tennis, travel, coaching. Office: Dechert LLP 30 Rockefeller Plz New York NY 10112-2200 Office Phone: 212-698-3683. Office Fax: 212-698-3599. Business E-Mail: andrew.levander@dechert.com.*

LEVANDOWSKI, BARBARA SUE, education educator; b. Mar. 16, 1948; d. Earl F. and Ann (Klee) L. BA in Edn. and Spanish, North Park Coll., 1970; MS in Elem. Edn., No. Ill. U., 1975, degree in curriculum and supervision/, 1977, EdD, 1979. cert. elem. tchr.; cert. secondary tchr.; cert. in administrv. with supt. endorsement; cert. sr. reviewer, Ill. Tchr. Round Lake (Ill.) Sch. Dist., 1970-75, Schaumburg (Ill.) Sch. Dist., 1975-87, asst. prin., 1977-87; prin., staff devel. dir. Dist. 200 Northwood Elem. Sch., Woodstock, Ill., 1987-94, dir. curriculum and instrn., 1994—2002; developer, dir. Woodstock Mentor-Instrn. for Tchrs., 1998—2002; assoc. prof. Sch. Edn., North Park U., Chgo., 2003—. Curriculum cons. Spring Grove (Ill.) Sch. Dist., 1980-81; instr. various courses, Schaumburg, 1984-86; dir. Einstein Sch. Writing Project, 1986-87; dir. Dist. 200 Thinking Thinking Skills, 1988—; co-instr. Dist. 200 Tchg. Thinking Skills Across the Curriculum, 1992—, dir. curriculum and instrn.; chair north ctrl. assn. visitation team Huntley Sch. Dist, 1989; co-developer 4 yr. tchr. mentor program, 1994—. Mem. editorial bd. Ill. Sch. R & D Jour., 1981—; contbr. articles to profl. jours. Chair Computer/Tech. Strategic Action Team, Woodstock, 1988-89. Recipient numerous awards for excellence in teaching, Those Who Excel award State of Ill., 1979; fed. grantee. Mem. NAESP, NAFE, ASCD (insvc. presenter 1984—, presenter state and nat. conv. 1989—), Am. Biog. Rsch. Assn. (bd. dirs. 1985—, publs. com. 1983), Nat. Staff Devel. Coun., Nat. Coun. of States for Insvc., Ill. Staff Devel. Coun., Ill. Assn. for Supervision and Curriculum Devel. (chair rsch. com. 1982), Ill. Computer Educators, Inst. Ednl. Rsch. (editorial bd. advisors, co-chair effective teaching characteristics observation 1990—, Omega award), Ill. Prin. Assn. Phi Delta Kappa, Delta Kappa Gamma. Home: 426 Normandie Ln Round Lake IL 60073-3711 Office: North Park Univ 3225 W Foster Ave Chicago IL 60625 Office Phone: 773-244-5789. E-mail: blevandowski@northpark.edu.

LEVANDOWSKI, JACK, sales executive; BSBA in Mktg., Calif. State U., Northridge, 1987; M in Aero. Sci. Mgmt., Embry-Riddle Aeo. U., 2000. Regional sales mgr. Latin Am. Pemco World Air Svcs., Denver, 1995—98; sr. sales and mktg. mgr. CresSoft, Inc., Denver, 1998—2000; sr. sales cons. aviation PSDI, Denver, 2000; dir. sales Idmon Corp., Denver, 2000—01, Pan Am Internat. Flight Acad., Denver, 2002—. Home: 2902 Culebra Peak Dr Loveland CO 80538

LEVANT, BRIAN, film director; b. Highland Park, Ill., Aug. 6, 1952; m. Alison Logan. Grad., U. N.Mex. Dir. (TV series) Married...With Children, 1987-97; dir. (films) Problem Child 2, 1991, Beethoven, 1992, The Flintstones, 1994, Jingle All the Way, 1996, Flintstones in Viva Rock Vegas, 2000, It's a Dog's Life, 2001, Snow Dogs, 2002, Are We There Yet?, 2005; writer (TV series) Happy Days, 1974-84, Mork & Mindy, 1978-82; prodr. (TV series) The Bad News Bears, 1979-80, Still The Beaver, 1985-89; writer, exec. prodr. (TV films) Poonchinski, 1990, The Adventures of Captain Zoom in Outer Space, 1995. also: United Talent Agy 9560 Wilshire Blvd Fl 5 Beverly Hills CA 90212-2401

LEVAR, ALAN JEDDY, lawyer; b. Orlando, Fla., July 31, 1970; s. Callis Jeddy and Karma (Huntsman) LeV.; m. Erika Dahl Bisbee, Mar. 10, 1995; 1 child, Christopher Alan. BA, Brigham Young U., 1993; JD, U. Ark., 1996. Bar: Ark. 1996. Owner, mgr. LeVar Laminating, Springdale, Ark., 1994-96; ptnr. Medlock & LeVar, Arkadelphia, Ark., 1996-2000; pvt. practice Arkadelphia, 2000—; pub. defender 9th Jud. Dist. East, Ark. Pub. Defender Commn., Arkadelphia, 1996-98, mng. pub. defender, 1998—. Bd. dirs. Arkadelphia Housing Authority, 1998—; pres. Arkadelphia br. LDS Ch., 1998—. Mem. Clark County Bar Assn. (pres. 1999-00). Democrat. Mem. Lds Ch. Avocation: reading. Home: 108 Apple Blossom Dr Arkadelphia AR 71923-7904 Office: 423 Crittenden St Arkadelphia AR 71923-6139 Fax: 870-246-9234. E-mail: alevar@ezclick.net.

LEV-ARI, HANOCH, electrical engineering educator; b. Klodzko, Poland, Mar. 18, 1949; s. Moshe and Leah (Neiman) Lipschitz; m. Aviva Avraham, Oct. 28, 1971; 1 child, Edan. BScEE summa cum laude, Technion, Haifa, Israel, 1971, MScEE, 1978; PhDEE, Stanford (Calif.) U., 1984. Tech. officer Israeli Def. Forces, 1971-76; rsch. engr. Systems Control, Inc., Palo Alto, Calif., 1980-82, Integrated Systems, Inc., Palo Alto, 1982-84; adj. rsch. prof. Naval Postgrad. Sch., Monterey, Calif., 1984-85; rsch. assoc. Stanford U., 1984-86, sr. rsch. assoc., 1986-90; cons. Saxpy Computer corp., Sunnyvale, 1987-88; assoc. prof. Northeastern U., Boston, 1990—, dir. Comms. and Digital Signal Processing Rsch. Ctr., 1994-96. Assoc. editor Circuits, Systems and Signal Processing, 1989-92, Integration, the VLSI Jour., 1992—; reviewer Procs. of IEEE, IEEE Transactions on Info. Theory, IEEE Transactions on Cirs. and Systems, IEEE Transactions on Acoustics, Speech and Signal Processing, IEEE, Transactions on Automatic Control, IEEE Transactions on Comm., Circuits, Systems and Signal Processing, The Inst. of Math. and Its Applications, others; contbr. numerous articles to profl. jours. Capt. Signal Corps, Israeli Army, 1971-76. Avocations: reading, guitar, singing, stamp collecting/philately. Home: 83 Mandalay Rd Newton MA 02459-1318

LEVASHOV, NICOLAI, writer, researcher; b. Kislovodsk, Stavropolskiy krai, Russia, Feb. 8, 1961; s. Victor and Valentina Levashov; m. Svetlana de Rohan-Levashov, Dec. 1, 1991. MS in Theoretical Physics, Khar'kov U., 1984; MS in Bioenergetics, Ukraine Ministry Health, 1991. Master of Psychotronics Internat. Ctr. of Phenomen, 1991. Sr. rsch. assoc. Ctr. for Functional Rsch., Sausalito, Calif., 1996—. Author: (book) The Final Appeal to Mankind, Spirit and Mind. Vol.1, Anisotropic Universe, Spirit and Mind. Vol. 2. Achievements include first to Anisotropic Universe; Origin of the life; Origin of the memory; Origin of the consiousness; Law Of The Evolution. Home: 122 Wawona St San Francisco CA 94127 Office: Chateau Du Temple Touraine L'ile Bouchard 37220 France Office Phone: (332) 4795-2469. Home Fax: 415-731-8843; Office Fax: (332) 4795-2321. Personal E-mail: nlevashov@comcast.net.

LEVASSEUR, GUY J., lawyer; b. Amityville, NY, Sept. 3, 1965; BA, Dowling Coll., 1987; JD, Thomas E. Cooley Law Sch., 1991. Bar: Mich. 1992, NY 1993, Conn. 1993, US Dist. Ct. Ea. Dist. NY, US Dist. Ct. So. Dist. NY, US Ct. Appeals 2nd Cir., US Supreme Ct. Legal clk. Legal Aid of Ctrl. Mich., 1990—91; ptnr. Wilson, Elser, Moskowitz, Edelman & Dicker LLP, White Plains, NYC. Mem.: ABA (torts, ins. & compensation sect., litig. sect.), Ins. Brokers Assn. NY, NY Self Insurers Assn., Transp. Lawyers Assn., NY State Bar Assn. (torts, ins. & compensation sect.), Delta Theta Phi. Office: Wilson Elser Moskowitz Edelman & Dicker LLP 3 Gannett Dr White Plains NY 10604 Office Phone: 914-323-7000. Office Fax: 914-323-7001. Business E-Mail: levasseurg@wemed.com.

LEVASSEUR, LEE ALLAN, artist; b. Hartford, Conn., Apr. 8, 1950; s. Euclid Roland and Beatrice Marie (Daigle) LeVasseur; m. Evelyn M. Tucker, June 30, 1973 (div. Mar. 1986); 1 child, Robert Aaron. BS in Art Edn., So. Conn. State U., 1973. Cert. art tchr. K-12. Artist Organic Surrealism, Branford, Conn., 1989—, prodr., dir., 1991; custom picture framer APN Gallery, Branford, Conn., 1990-92, Off the Wall Gallery, Madison, Conn., 1992-93; archival picture framer Northlight Gallery, Branford, 1995—; fine arts restoration Brandon Gallery, Madison, Conn., 1995—2004. Lectr. Rotary, Guilford, Conn., 1990; co-prodr., dir. Am. 500 Quintcentennial, Buenos Aires, New Haven, Boston, NYC, 1992. Exhibitions include Festival of Arts and Ideas, New Haven, 1999, Brandon Gallery, Madison, Conn., 2001—04. Recipient cert. Excellence Artitudes, Internat. Art Competition, NYC, 1989, Blue ribbon, Branford Festival, 1991, prize E, SoHo Internat. Art Competition, 1992, 1st pl. mixed media, Cheshire Art League, 2000. Mem.: Art Coun. New Haven, Shoreline Alliance Artists, Branford C. of C. Democrat. Roman Catholic. Avocations: hiking, herbalism, camping, gardening, environmental conservator. Office: Organic Surrealism and Out of Context Photos 525 E Main St Trlr 40 Branford CT 06405-2930 E-mail: leelevasseur@aol.com.

LEVAUX, HUGH PIERRE, pharmaceutical executive, consultant; b. Lubumbashi, Congo, Jan. 23, 1965; s. Rene Alfonse Levaux and Mireille Marie-Rose Lambrechts; m. Kimberly Levaux; children: Lena children: Eric, Roger. MA in Internat. Rels., U. Libre de Bruxelles, Brussels, Belgium, 1989; MA in Internat. Econ. & Internat. Rels., Johns Hopkins U., 1991; PhD in Policy Analysis, RAND U., 1999. Coord. sales promotions Matsushita Electric Co., Osaka, Japan, 1991—94; analyst The RAND Corp., Santa Monica, Calif., 1994—99; from v.p. health economics to sr. v.p. Quintiles Inc. d/b/a Lewin-TAG, San Francisco, 1999—2001; sr. v.p. Quintiles Inc d/b/a Quintiles Late Phase, 2001—02; from exec. v.p. bus. devel.strategic planning to CEO Poinpoint Solutions d/b/a Ninaza, San Mateo, Calif., 2003—. Dir. BelCM, Brussels, 1988. Author: The Cutting Edge-A Half Century of US Fighter R&D, 1998. Fellow Rsch. fellowship, NATO, Brussels, Belgium, 1988. Mem.: Drug Info. Assn., Coun. on Fgn. Rels. Avocations: running, languages, travel.

LEVE, ALAN DONALD, electronics executive; b. Los Angeles, Dec. 15, 1927; s. Milton Lewis and Etta L.; m. Annette Einhorn, Sept. 3, 1962; children— Laura Michelle, Elise Deanne. BS, UCLA, 1951. CPA, Calif. Staff acct., mgr. Joseph S. Herbert & Co. (C.P.A.s), Los Angeles, 1951-57, ptnr., 1957-63; CEO, sec., treas. Mica Corp., Culver City, Calif., 1963-82, also bd. dirs., 1963-82, chmn. bd., chief exec. officer, 1982-83; v.p., bd. dirs. Micaply Internat. Inc., 1968-1982; v.p. Micaply AG, Switzerland, 1972-83, also bd. dirs., chief exec. officer, also bd. dirs., 1982-83; v.p., bd. dirs. Micaply Internat., Ltd., U.K., 1971-82; chmn. bd., mng. dir., chief exec. officer Micaply Internat. Ltd., U.K., 1982-83; v.p., bd. dirs. Titan Chem. Corp., Edgecraft Corp., Culver Hydro-Press, Inc., L.A., 1963-75; chmn. bd., pres., chief exec. officer Ohmega Techs., Inc., Culver City, Calif., 1983—, Ohmega Electronics, Inc., Culver City, 1986—. Served with USAAF, 1946-47. Home: 16430 Dorado Dr Encino CA 91436-4118 Office: 4031 Elenda St Culver City CA 90232-3723

LEVEE, BARBARA POE, artist; b. N.Y.C., Mar. 4, 1922; d. Bernard Joseph and Rebecca Greenberg Reis; m. James W. Poe, 1943 (dec. 1968); children: Adam Poe, Lorna Poe(dec.); m. Michael Levee, 1984 (dec. 1988). Student, Temple U., 1940—42. Exhibitions include Surrealist Show, 1942, Art of this Century, N.Y.C., 1943, U. Calif., Santa Barbara, 1966, one-woman shows include Wakefield Gallery, 1943, PVI Gallery, N.Y.C., 1963, Rex Evans Gallery, L.A., 1970, 1972, 2 person show, J. Brown Studio Gallery, 1976, exhibitions include Glazer Gallery, La Jolla, Calif., 1974, one-woman shows include Art Space, L.A., 1978, exhibitions include Swope Gallery, 1983, 1984, Sharon Truex Fine Arts, 2000, 2001. Bd. dirs. UCLA Art Coun., Plaza de la Raza, Lincoln Park; villa coun. Getty Mus. East L.A., Malibu. Home: 2110 Mandeville Canyon Rd Los Angeles CA 90049

LEVEEN, ROBERT FREDERICK, radiologist; b. Jersey City, July 24, 1946; s. Harry Henry and Jeanette Lois (Rubricius) LeV.; m. Sandra Sue Hickstein, May 28, 1974; children: Emily, Rob. BA, Grinnell Coll., Iowa, 1968; MD, U. Nebr., Omaha, 1974. Diplomate Am. Bd. Radiology. Intern dept. surgery U. Wash., 1974-75; resident in radiology Coll. Medicine U. Nebr., 1975-78; asst. prof. radiology U. Nebr. Med. Ctr., Omaha, 1978-80; from asst. prof. radiology to assoc. prof. U. Pa., Phila., 1980-90; rsch. assoc. VA Med. Ctr., Phila., 1980-83, clin. investigator, 1985-90; coord. angiography rsch. Dept. Radiology U. Pa., 1985-90; assoc. prof. radiology U. Nebr. Med. Ctr., 1991-99; chief radiology svc. VA Med. Ctr., Omaha, 1991-99; assoc. prof. U. Fla., Gainesville, 1999—. Recipient Career Devel. award, VA, 1985; Stauffer award, Assn. U. Radiologists, 1986. Fellow Am. Coll. Radiology; mem. Soc. Cardiovasc. and Interventional Radiology, Radiologic Soc. N.Am., Assn. U. Radiologists, Nebr. Radiol. Soc. (pres. 1998-99), Fla. Radiol. Soc. Presbyterian. Office: U Fla Coll Medicine Dept Radiology PO Box 100374 Gainesville FL 32610-0374 E-mail: leveer@radiology.ufl.edu.

LEVEILLE, GILBERT ANTONIO, food products executive; b. Fall River, Mass., June 3, 1934; s. Isidore and Rose (Caron) L.; divorced; children: Michael, Kathleen, Edward; m. Carol A. Phillips, Aug. 7, 1981. B in Vocat. Agr., U. Mass, 1956; MS, Rutgers U., 1958, PhD in Nutrition and Biochemistry, 1960. Prof. nutritional biochemistry U. Ill., Urbana, 1965-71; chmn. dept. food sci. and human nutrition Mich. State U., East Lansing, 1971-80; dir. nutrition and health sci. Gen. Foods Corp., Tarrytown, NY, 1980-86; v.p. for rsch. and tech. svcs. Nabisco Inc., East Hanover, NJ, 1986-96; pres. Leveille Assocs., Denville, NJ, 1996-99, 2004—; v.p. worldwide, sci. and regulatory affairs McNeil Consumer Healthcare, Fort Washington, Pa., 1999—2001; v.p. tech. food sys. design, dir. food tech. devel. ctr. Cargill, Inc., 2002—04. Author: The Set Point Diet, 1985 (N.Y. Times nonfiction bestseller); also over 300 articles to profl. jours. Served to 1st lt. U.S. Army, 1960-62. Recipient rsch. award Poultry Sci. Assn., 1965, Disting. Faculty award Mich. State U., 1980, Chancellor's Medal, U. Mass., 2000. Mem. AAAS, Am. Chem. Soc., Am. Soc. Nutritional Sci. (pres. 1988-89, Mead Johnson rsch. award 1971, Elvehjem award 2002), Am. Soc. for Clin. Nutrition, Inst. Food Technologists (pres. 1983-84, fellow 1983, Carl Fellers award 1992, Indsl. Scientist award 2004). Personal E-mail: leveilleg@optonline.net.

LEVEL, LEON JULES, computer company executive; b. Detroit, Dec. 30, 1940; s. Leon and Madeline G. (Mayea) L.; m. Constance Kramer, June 25, 1966; children— Andrea, Aileen BBA, U. Mich., 1962, MBA, 1963. CPA, Mich. Asst. accountant Deloitte Haskins & Sells, Detroit, 1963-66, sr. accountant, 1966-69, prin., 1969-71; asst. corp. controller Bendix Corp., Southfield, Mich., 1971-81; v.p. fin. planning Burroughs Corp., Detroit, 1981-82, v.p., treas., 1982-86, Unisys Corp., Blue Bell, Pa., 1986-89; v.p., chief fin. officer Computer Scis. Corp., El Segundo, Calif., 1989—. Mem. adv. bd. U. Mich., Ann Arbor, 1984-90, Providence Hosp., Southfield, Mich., 1984-86, Western FM Global Ins.; bd. dir. UTi Worldwid, Inc. Trustee Walnut St. Theatre, Phila., 1988-89, Autry Nat. Ctr., 2000. Mem. Fin. Execs. Inst. (sec. Detroit chpt. 1983-85, v.p. 1985-86, pres. 1986-87, bd. dirs. 2001), Am. Inst. C.P.A.s, Mich. Assn. C.P.A.s, Inst. Mgmt. Accts. Office: Computer Scis Corp 2100 E Grand Ave El Segundo CA 90245-5024

LEVELL, EDWARD, JR., retired airport terminal executive, aviation consultant; b. Jacksonville, Ala., Apr. 2, 1931; m. Rosa M. (Casellas) L, Aug. 3, 1951 (dec.); children: Edward III (dec.), Ruben C., Kenneth W., Randy C., Raymond C. (dec.), Cheryl D. Levell Rivera, Michael K. BS, Tuskegee Inst., 1953; MA in Urban Sociology, U. No. Colo., 1972; M in Mgmt., Indsl. Coll./Air War Coll., 1974. Commd. 2d lt. USAF, 1953, advanced through grades to col., 1978, various flight tng., air ops. and command positions, 1953-69; comdr. cadet group, then dep. commandant cadet wing USAF Acad., 1969-73; dep. comdr., wing comdr., vice comdr. 1st spl. ops. wing USAF, 1973-77, wing comdr. 58th tactical air command tng. wing, 1977-78, col., vice comdr., comdr. 20th air divsn., 1978-83, ret., 1983; dep. commr. aviation City of Chgo. Dept. Aviation, 1983-89; dep. dir. aviation, fin. and adminstrn. City of New Orleans Dept. Aviation, 1989-90, dep. dir. aviation, ops. and maintenance, 1990-92, dir. aviation, 1992—99; ret., 2000. Bd. dirs. Tourist & Conv. Commn., New Orleans; trustee Dryades YMCA, New Orleans; mem. transp. com. World Trade Ctr. Decorated Legion of Merit, D.F.C. (2), Meritorious Svc. Medal (2), Air Medal (8), Air Force Commendation Medal; recipient Disting. Svc. award Jacksonville, Ala., 1974, State of Fla. Commn. Human Rels. award for spl. recognition, 1977, Air Force Assn. Spl. Citation of Merit, 1977, Disting. Svc. award City of Chgo. Dept. Aviation, 1986, 87, 88; inducted in Tuskegee Univ. Hall of Fame, 1991. Mem. Airport Ops. Coun. Internat. (task force chmn. ann. conf. New Orleans 1991), Am. Assn. Airport Execs., Gulf Coast Internat. Hispanic C. of C. Home: 13881 Cinch Ln Gainesville VA 20155

LEVEN, ANN RUTH, museum director; b. Canton, Ohio, Nov. 1, 1940; d. Joseph J. and Bessie (Scharff) L. AB, Brown U., 1962; cert. with distinction in Bus. Adminstrn., Harvard-Radcliffe U.s, 1963; MBA, Harvard U., 1964. Product mgr. household products div. Colgate-Palmolive, N.Y.C., 1964-66; account exec. Grey Advt., 1966-67; fin. asst. Met. Mus. Art, 1967-69, asst. treas., 1970-72, treas., 1972-79; v.p., sr. corp. planning officer Chase Manhattan Bank, 1979-83; pres. ARL Assoc., NY, 1983—; treas. Smithsonian Instn., Washington, 1984-90; dep. treas. Nat. Gallery Art, 1990-94, treas. and CFO, 1994-99. Adj. asst. prof. Grad. Sch. Bus. Columbia U., N.Y.C., 1975—77, adj. assoc. prof., 1977—79, adj. prof., 1980—93; exec.-in-residence Amos Tuck Sch. Dartmouth Coll., Hanover, NH, 1976, 84; bd. dir. Del. Group Family of Funds, Systemax; bd. gov. Investment Co. Inst., 1997—2004. Artist (awarded prizes for painting and graphic arts); contbr. articles to profl. jours. Exec. bd. new leadership divsn. Fedn. Jewish Philanthropies, 1968-70; coun. mem. N.Y. Pub. Libr., exec. com., 1976-79; mus. adv. panel N.Y. State Coun. Arts, 1977-79; bd. dirs. Camp Rainbow, 1970-84, v.p., 1976-78, treas., 1982-84; bd. overseers Amos Tuck Sch., 1978-84, chmn. ednl. affairs com., 1979-84; trustee Brown U., 1976—, fin. and budget com., student life com., devel. com., adv. and exec. coms., bd. dirs. Ctr. Fgn. Policy Devel.; bd. dirs. Am. Arts Alliance, 1990-92, Twyla Tharp Dance Found., 1982-87, Reading Is Fundamental, 1987-91, adv. coun., 1991-94, Carngie Corp.; trustee Carnegie Corp. N.Y., 1981-1987, Artists'Choice Mus., 1979-87; vis. com. Harvard U. Bus. Sch., 1979-84; bd.

overseers Hood Mus.-Hopkins Ctr. Dartmouth Coll., 1984-91, chmn., 1988-91; trustee ARC Endowment Fund, 1985-90, N.Y. Sch. Interior Design, 1996—, Andy Warhol Found., 1999—; staff Presdl. Task Force on Arts and Humanities, 1981. Recipient Young Leadership award Council Jewish Fedns. and Welfare Funds, 1968; named N.Y. State's Outstanding Young Woman, 1976. Mem. Harvard Bus. Sch. Alumni Assn. (exec. coun. 1976-79, v.p. 1978-79), Women's Fin. Assn., Women's Forum, Econ. Club of N.Y., Cosmopolitan Club, Harvard Bus. Sch. Club, Radcliffe Club, Brown Club, Art Table, Century Assn. Home: 785 Park Ave New York NY 10021-3552

LEVEN, CHARLES LOUIS, economics professor; b. Chgo., May 2, 1928; s. Elie H. and Ruth (Reinach) R.; m. Judith Danoff, 1950 (div. 1970); m. Dorothy Wish, 1970 (div. 1999); children: Ronald L., Robert M., Carol E., Philip W., Alice S. Student, Ill. Inst. Tech., 1945-46, U. Ill., 1947; BS, Northwestern U., 1950, MA, 1957, PhD, 1958. Economist Fed. Res. Bank of Chgo., 1950-56; asst. prof. Iowa State U., 1957-59, U. Pa., 1960—62; assoc. prof. U. Pitts., 1962-65; chmn. dept. econs. Washington U., St. Louis, 1975-80, prof. econs., 1965-91, 2005—, prof. emeritus, 1991—; dir. Inst. Urban and Regional Studies, 1965-85. Disting. prof. U. Mo., St. Louis, 1991—2001; cons. EEC, Ill. Auditor Gen., Polish Ministry of Planning and Constrn., St. Louis Sch. Bd., Ukrainian Ctr. for Markets and Entrepreneurship, Northeast-Midwest Found.; mem. internat. adv. bd., com. spatial econ. and regional planning Polish Acad. Scis. Author: Theory and Method of Income and Product Accounts for Metropolitan Areas, 1963, Development Benefits of Water Resource Investment, 1969, An Analytical Framework for Regional Development Policy, 1970, Neighborhood Change, 1976, The Mature Metropolis, 1978. Served with USNR, 1945-46. Ford Found. fellow, 1956, Weiner Sch. Real Estate Fin. and Urban Econs. fellow, 2005; recipient Disting. Alumni award Sullivan HS, Chgo., 2002; grantee Social Sci. Rsch. Coun., 1960, Com. Urban Econ., 1965, NSF, 1968, 73, Merc. Bancorp., 1976, HUD, 1978, NIH, 1985, 2001 Mem.: Am. Econ. Assn., Regional Sci. Assn. (pres. 1964—65, Walter Isard award for disting. scholarship 1995), Western Regional Sci. Assn. (pres. 1974—75, Disting. Fellow 1999), So. Regional Sci. Assn. (Disting. Fellow 1991). Home: 151 Marigold Ln Milford PA 18337-7322 Office: Washington U Box 1208 1 Brookings Dr Saint Louis MO 63130-4899 E-mail: leven@ptd.net. *Achievement is satisfying, but especially so when one can win without others losing. At the same time, it appears unnecessary to be a failure to prove one's sincerity.*

LEVEN, LINDA, application developer, writer, actress, model, artist; b. Pa. d. Albert L. BA in Maths., NYU, N.Y.C., MA in Maths. Edn., 1967. Cert. Bpt-Spt IBM, 1969. Application and sys. software developer IBM Corp., N.Y.C., 1969—92; application software designer and developer Safe Horizon, N.Y.C., 1993—2004. Designer software various instns. Mem. various objectivist orgns., N.Y.C. Avocations: acting, modeling, writing, graphic art. Personal E-mail: actress666@att.net.

LEVEN, STEPHEN H., human resources professional; BS, Cornell U.; MBA, So. Meth. U. Adminstr. Tex. Instruments, Dallas, 1973-80, employee rels. profl., 1980-82, mgr. human resources, 1982-92, sr. v.p. human resources semiconductor group, 1992-98, sr. v.p. and mgr. worldwide human resources, 1998—. Office: Texas Instruments Inc 12500 TI Blvd Dallas TX 75243 E-mail: s-leven@ti.com.

LEVENDUSKY, PHILIP GEORGE, psychologist, academic administrator, educator; b. Lowell, Mass., Oct. 21, 1946; s. Harry George and Phyllis Mary (Cowgill) Levendusky; m. Cynthia Ann Becton; children: Jason Philip, Anya Prentiss, Katya Sprague. BA magna cum laude, U. Mass, 1968; MS, Wash. State U., 1971, PhD, 1973. Diplomate Am. Bd. Profl. Psychology. Asst. to dir. Human Rels. Ctr., Wash. State U., Pullman, 1971-73; asst. psychologist McLean Hosp., Belmont, Mass., 1974-82, assoc. psychologist, 1982-92, psychologist, 1992—, dir. cognitive behavior therapy unit, 1974-94, dir. ambulatory care, 1991-95, asst. gen. dir., 1993-95, v.p. network devel., 1995—, dir. dept. psychology, dir. clin. tng., 1996—; instr. psychiatry Harvard Med. Sch., Boston, 1974-88, asst. prof., 1988-97, assoc. prof., 1997—; dir. Levendusky and Assocs., Arlington, Mass., 1980—. Cons. VA Hosp., Boston, 1977—85, Boston Cardiovasc. Health, 1983—85, Mass. Dept. Mental Health, 1987—, Mass. Dept. Mental Retardation, 1997—; bd. dirs. Bain & Co., Employee Consultation, Boston, 1987—, Parthenon Group Mem. Assistance Program; mem. Mass. Bd. Psychology, 1988—93. Contbr. articles to profl. jours., mags., newspapers, chapters to books; guest numerous TV and Radio programs, Boston. Mem. Sch. Bd., Manchester, Mass., 1999—2002; bd. dirs. Feeding Ourselves, 1980, Anorexia Bulimia Care, 1991—93. Mem.: APA, New Eng. Soc. Behavior Analysis and Therapy (bd. dirs. 1991), Assn. Advancement Behaviour Therapy, Blue Hill Country Club, Phi Beta Kappa. Republican. Roman Catholic. Avocations: skiing, jogging. Office: McLean Hosp 115 Mill St Belmont MA 02478-1048 E-mail: levendp@mclean.harvard.edu.

LEVENFELD, MILTON ARTHUR, lawyer; b. Chgo., Mar. 18, 1927; s. Mitchell A. and Florence B. (Berman) L.; m. Iona R. Wishner, Dec. 18, 1949; children— Barry, David, Judith Ph.B., U. Chgo., 1947, JD, 1950. Bar: Ill. 1950. Ptnr. Altman, Levenfeld & Kanter, Chgo., 1961-64, Levenfeld and Kanter, Chgo., 1964-80, Levenfeld, Eisenberg, Janger & Glassberg, Chgo., 1980-99; of counsel Levenfeld Pearlstein, Chgo., 1999—. Former dir. Bank of Chgo., Garfield Ridge Trust & Savs. Bank; lectr. in fed. taxation Contbr. articles to profl. jours. Bd. dirs. Spertus Coll. Judaica, Jewish Fedn. Chgo., 1975-84, Am. Israel C. of C., 1st nat. v.p.; chmn. legacies and endowments com., 1982-84; co-gen. chmn. Chgo. Jewish United Fund, 1977, vice chmn. campaign, 1979; gov. mem. Orchestral Assn. Chgo. Symphony Orch.; vis. com. U. Chgo. Law Sch., 1989-91; pres. Am. Israel C. of C. of Met. Chgo., 1993-95, 96-98. With USNR, 1944-45. Recipient Keter Shem Tov award Jewish Nat. Fund, 1978 Mem. ABA, Ill. Bar Assn., Chgo. Bar Assn., Am.-Israel C. of C. (past pres.). Home: 866 Stonegate Dr Highland Park IL 60035-5145 Office: 2 N LaSalle St Chicago IL 60602 Office Phone: 312-476-7531. Business E-Mail: mlevenfeld@lplegal.com.

LEVENS, DORSEY (HERBERT LEVENS), professional football player; b. Syracuse, N.Y., May 21, 1970; Student, U. Notre Dame, Ga. Poly. U. Running back Green Bay (Wis.) Packers, 1994—2001, Phila. Eagles, 2002—, New York Giants, 2003—04; co-owner Premier K-9 Inc.; owner World Gym, Atlanta. Named to Pro-Bowl, 1997. Achievements include mem. of Super Bowl XXXI Championship Team, 1996.

LEVENSON, ALAN IRA, psychiatrist, physician, educator; b. Boston, July 25, 1935; s. Jacob Maurice and Frances Ethel (Biller) Levenson; m. Myra Beatrice Katzen, June 12, 1960 (div. 1993); children: Jonathan, Nancy; m. Linda Ann Nadell, Jan. 30, 1994. AB, Harvard U., 1957, MD, 1961, MPH, 1965. Diplomate Am. Bd. Psychiatry and Neurology. Intern U. Hosp., Ann Arbor, Mich., 1961-62; resident in psychiatry Mass. Mental Health Ctr., Boston, 1962-65; staff psychiatrist NIMH, Chevy Chase, Md., 1965-66, dir. divsn. mental health svc. programs, 1967-69; prof. psychiatry U. Ariz. Coll. Medicine, Tucson, 1969-2000, prof. emeritus, 2000—, head dept. psychiatry, 1969-89; CEO Palo Verde Mental Health Svcs., Tucson, 1971-91, chief med. officer, med. dir., 1991-93; chmn. bd. dirs., CEO Psychiatrists' Purchasing Group, 1991—; chmn. bd. dirs. Psychiatrists' Risk Retention Group, 1991-2000. Author: (book) The Community Mental Health Center: Strategies and Programs, 1972; contbr. papers and articles to profl. jours. Bd. dirs. Tucson Urban League, 1971—78, Pima Coun. Aging, 1976—83. With USPHS, 1965—69. Fellow: Am. Coll. Mental Health Adminstrn. (v.p. 1980—82, pres. 1982—83), Am. Coll. Psychiatrists (regent 1980—83, v.p. 1983—85, pres.-elect 1985—86, pres. 1986—87), Am. Psychiat. Assn. (treas. 1986—90); mem.: Group Advancement Psychiatry, Harvard Alumni Assn. (bd. dirs. 1988—91). Office: 75 N Calle Resplendor Tucson AZ 85716-4937

LEVENSON, JACOB CLAVNER, language educator; b. Boston, Oct. 1, 1922; s. Joseph Mayer and Frances (Hahn) L.; m. Charlotte Elizabeth Getz, June 6, 1946; children: Anne L. Brown, Jill L. Eisenberg, Paul G. AB, Harvard U., 1943, PhD, 1951. Tutor in history and lit. Harvard, 1946-50, vis. lectr. English and gen. edn., 1951-52; instr. English U. Conn., 1950-54; asst. prof. to prof. English U. Minn., 1954-67; Edgar Allan Poe prof. English U. Va., Charlottesville, 1967-99, chmn. dept., 1971-74, prof. emeritus Charlottesville, 1999—; faculty Salzburg (Austria) Seminar in Am. Studies, 1947, 49. Mem. Com. of Cons., Notable Am. Women, 1607-1950, 63-72. Author: The Mind and Art of Henry Adams, 1957, Hist. and Critical Introductions The Works of Stephen Crane, II-V, VII, 1969-76; editor: Stephen Crane: Prose and Poetry, 1984, Mark Twain Life on the Mississippi, 1967, Discussions of Hamlet, 1960, The Letters of Henry Adams I-III, 1982, IV-VI, 1988; mem. editorial bd.; Am. Quar., 1964-70, Va. Quar. Rev., 1968-99, New Literary History, 1969-2000, Am. Lit., 1988-91; contbr. articles to profl. jours. Served with AUS, 1943-45. Decorated Bronze Star; Guggenheim fellow, 1958-59; Am. Council Learned Socs. fellow, 1961-62; Am. Philos. Soc. Penrose grantee, 1956; recipient E. Harris Harbison award for disting. teaching Danforth Found., 1966 Fellow: U. Va. Soc. (hon.); mem.: MLA, Am. Studies Assn., Signet Soc., Phi Beta Kappa. Home: 1581 Belvedere Dr Charlottesville VA 22901-1862

LEVENSON, LAURIE L., law educator; b. Inglewood, Calif., Dec. 7, 1956; d. Daniel and Irene (Moses) L.; m. Douglas E. Mirell, Sept. 3, 1984; children: Solomon, Hava. AB, Stanford U., 1977; JD, UCLA, 1980. Bar: Calif. 1981, U.S. Dist. Ct. (cen. dist.) Calif. 1981, U.S. Ct. Appeals (9th cir.) 1981. Law clk. to Hon. James Hunter III US Ct. Appeals (3rd cir.), L.A., 1980-81; asst. U.S. atty., criminal sect. U.S. Dept. of Justice, 1981-89; adj. prof. Southwestern U., 1982—89; prof. law Loyola U., 1989—, assoc. dean, acad. affairs, 1996—99. Mem. Calif. Bar Assn. (sec., treas. exec. com. criminal law sect. 1988—), LA County Bar Assn., 1994-. Democrat. Jewish. Office: Loyola Law Sch 919 Albany St Los Angeles CA 90015-1211 E-mail: laurie.levenson@lls.edu.

LEVENSON, MARC DAVID, optics and lasers specialist, editor; b. Phila., May 28, 1945; s. Donald William and Ethyl Jean Levenson; m. Naomi Francis Matsuda, Oct. 24, 1971. SB, MIT, 1967; MS, Stanford U., 1968, PhD, 1971. Rsch. fellow Harvard U., Cambridge, Mass., 1971-74; asst. prof. physics U. So. Calif., L.A., 1974-77, assoc. prof., 1977-79; mem. rsch. staff IBM Rsch. div., San Jose, Calif., 1979-93, head mgr. OSC, 1987, mgr. quantum metrology, 1990; v.p. Focused Rsch., Inc., Sunnyvale, Calif., 1993-95; propr., cons. Marc D. Levenson Optics, Saratoga, 1993—. Vis. fellow Joint Inst. for Lab. Astrophysics, U. Colo., Boulder, 1995-96; vis. prof. Rice U., Houston, 1996. Author: Introduction to Nonlinear Laser Spectroscopy, 1988; editor: Lasers, Spectroscopy, New Ideas, 1987, Resonances, 1991; contbg. editor Solid State Tech. mag., 1993—; editor-in-chief Microlithography World Mag., 1995—; contbr. articles to profl. jours. Alfred Sloan rsch. fellow, 1975. Fellow IEEE, Optical Soc. Am. (Adolph Lomb medal 1976), Am. Phys. Soc., Bay Area Chrome Users Soc./Soc. Photog. and Instrumentation Engrs. (award 1991); mem. Nat. Acad. Engring. Avocations: gardening, reading. Office Phone: 650-941-3438 x26. Business E-Mail: marcl@pennwell.com.

LEVENSON, ROBERT MONTIE, retired physician; b. Yakima, Wash., Jan. 10, 1921; s. Montie T. and Ellen (Sharkey) L.; m. Marie E. Hofmeister, Sept. 21, 1947; children: Robert Jr., Albert D., David A., Nancy, Linda, Mary. MD, U. Louisville, 1946. Diplomate Am. Bd. Internal Medicine, 1955. Intern King County Hosp., Seattle, 1946-47; pvt. practice in internal medicine Seattle, 1954-88; resident Providence Hosp., Seattle, 1949-51, U. Calif. Hosp., San Francisco, 1951-52. Clin. prof. U. Wash. Med. Sch., Seattle, 1974—. Trustee Swedish Hosp. Med. Ctr., Seattle, 1985-88, King County Med. Blue Shield, Seattle, 1985—, J.L. Locke Trust, Seattle, 1974—. Fellow Am. Coll. Cardiology, Am. Coll. Physicians, Council Clin. Cardiology; mem. Am. Heart Assn. (award of merit 1982). Home: 3406 72nd Pl SE Mercer Island WA 98040-3342

LEVENSON, STANLEY RICHARD, public relations and advertising executive; b. Cin., Dec. 28, 1933; s. Irven Philip and Dorothy (Aftel) L.; m. Barbara Lind, July 23, 1962; children: Laura, Amy. BA, U. Mich., 1956; postgrad., Am. U. S.W. sales and promotion mgr. DOT Records, Hollywood, Calif., 1959-62; S.W. sales and mktg. rep. Pickwick Internat. Co., 1963-65; pres., chmn. bd. Stan Levenson Assos., Dallas, 1966-76; exec. v.p., gen. mgr. public relations div. S.W., Bozell & Jacobs, Dallas, 1976-81; pres., CEO Levenson & Levenson, Dallas, 1981-83; CEO Levenson Pub. Rels., 1984—; dir. Fidelity Nat. Bank, Dallas. Adj. prof. in pub. relations mgmt. So. Meth. U., 1987-88, mem. adv. bd. Pub. Rels. sequence studies. Group leader comm. task force Dallas Police Dept.; assoc. mem. Dallas Assembly; bd. dirs. Dallas Arboretum, Vis. Nurses Assn., Family Place, Dallas Coun. World Affairs, Dallas Urban League, 2001, Dallas Trees and Parks Found., Thanksgiving Found.; mem. adv. bd. Crystal Charity Ball; co-chmn. Dallas Mayor's Task Force on Mktg.; mem. exec. com., bd. dirs. Ctrl. Downtown Assn., Dallas, 1993-94; mem. Dallas Citizens Coun., 1997—; arts adminstrn. and corp. comm. adv. bd. So. Meth. U., 2000—; trustee TACA, 1980, bd. dirs., 2000; trustee Dallas Alliance, 1988; mem. exec. com. Ctrl. Dallas Assn.; state com. chmn. March of Dimes, 2002. With U.S. Army, 1956-58. Mem. Pub. Rels. Soc. Am. (accredited, North Tex. Teich award), Soc. Profl. Journalists, Am. Heart Assn. (bd. dir., com. chmn. 2002—), Greater Dallas Chamber (mktg. and comm. adv. coun. 2000—). Home: 4545 Mill Run Rd Dallas TX 75244-6432 Office: 717 N Harwood 20th Fl Dallas TX 75201-7484 Office Phone: 214-932-6076. Business E-Mail: s.levenson@levensonbrinkerpr.com.

LEVENTHAL, BENNETT LEE, psychiatry and pediatrics educator, administrator; b. Chgo., July 6, 1949; s. Howard Leonard and Florence Ruth (Albert) L.; m. Celia G. Goodman, June 11, 1972; children: Matthew G., Andrew G., Julia G. Student, Emory U., 1967-68, La. State U., 1968-70, BS, 1972, postgrad., 1970-74, MD, 1974. Diplomate Am. Bd. Psychiatry and Neurology in Psychiatry, Am. Bd. Psychiatry and Neurology, Child Psychiatry; lic. physician N.C., La., Ill., Va. Undergrad. rsch. assoc. Lab. Prof. William A. Pryor dept. chemistry La. State U., 1968-70; house officer I Charity Hosp. at New Orleans, 1974; resident in psychiatry Duke U. Med. Ctr., Durham, NC, 1974-78, chief fellow divsn. dept. psychiatry, 1976-77, chief resident dept. psychiatry, 1977-78, clin. assoc. dept. psychiatry, 1978-80; staff psychiatrist, head psychiatry dept. Joel T. Boone Clinic, Virginia Beach, Va., 1978-80; staff psychiatrist, faculty mem. dept. psychiatry Naval Regional Med. Ctr., Portsmouth, Va., 1978-80; asst. prof. psychiatry and pediats. U. Chgo., 1978-85, dir. Child Psychiatry Clinic, 1978-85, dir. Child and Adolescent Psychiatry Fellowship tng. program, 1979-88, Irving B. Harris prof. child and adolescent psychiatry, 1998—, dir. Sonia Shankman Orthogenic Sch., 2002—05, emeritus, 2005—; prof. psychiatry, dir. Ctr. Child Mental Health U. Ill., Chgo., 2005—. Psychiat. cons. Caledonia State Prision/Halifax Mental Health Ctr., Tillery, N.C., 1976-77, Fed. Correctional Inst., Butner, N.C., 1977-78; cons. Norfolk Cmty. Mental health Ctr., 1978-80; adj. prof. psychology, biopsychology, and devel. psychology U. Chgo., 1990, adj. assoc. prof. dept. psychology and com. on biopsychology, 1987-90; meed. dir. Child Life and Family Edn. program Wyler Children's Hosp. of U. Chgo., 1983-95; dir. child and adolescent programs Chgo. Lakeshore Hosp., 1986-2000; Pfizer vis. prof. dept. psychiatry U. P.R., 1992; examiner Am. Bd. Psychiatry and Neurology in Gen. Psychiatry and Child Psychiatry, 1982—; mem. steering com. Harris Ctr. for Devel. Studies, U. Chgo., 1983—; mem. com. on evaluation of GAPS project AMA, 1993-97; treas. Chgo. Consortium for Psychiat. Rsch., 1994; pres. Ill. Coun. Child and Adolescent Psychiatry, 1992-94; vis. scholar Hunter Inst. Mental Health and U. New Castle, NSW, Australia, 1995; mem. Gov.'s Panel on Health Svcs., 1993-94; prof. psychiatry & pediats. U. Chgo., 1990—, chmn. dept. psychiatry, 1991-98, Irving B. Harris prof. child & adolescent psychiatry, 1998—; presenter in field. Mem. editl. bd. Univ. Chgo. Better Health Letter, 1994-96; cons. editor: Jour. Emo tional and Behavioral Disorders, 1992-96; reviewer: Archives of Gen. Psychiatry, 1983—, Biol. Psychiatry, 1983—, Am. Jour. Psychiatry, 1983—, Jour. AMA, 1983—, Jour. Am. Acad. Child and Adolescent Psychiatry, 1983—, Sci., 1983—; book rev. editor Jour. Neuropsychiatry and Clin. Neuroscis., 1989-92, mem. editl. bd., 1989-92; contbr. articles to profl. jours. Lt. comdr. MC USNR, 1978—80. Recipient Crystal Plate award Little Friends, 1994, Individual Achievement award Autism Soc. Am., 1991, Merit award Duke U. Psychiat. Resident's Assn., 1976, Bick award La. Psychiat. Assn., 1974; Andrew W. Mellon Found. faculty fellow U. Chgo., 1983-84; John Dewey lectr. U. Chgo., 1982. Fellow Am. Acad. Child and Adolescent Psychiatry (Outstanding Mentor 1988, dep. chmn. program com. 1979—, chmn. arrangements com. 1979—, new rsch. subcom. for ann. meeting 1986—, mem. work group on rsch. 1989—), Am. Psychiat. Assn. (Falk fellow, mem. Ittleson Award Bd. 1994-97, mem. Am. Psychiat. Assn./Wisniewski Young Psychiatrists Rsch. Award Panel 1994—), Am. Acad. Pediats., Am. Orthopsychiat. Assn.; mem. AAAS, Am. Coll. Psychiatrists, Brain Rsch. Inst., Ill. Coun. Child and Adolescent Psychiatry, Ill. Psychiat. Soc., Soc. for Rsch. in Child Devel., Soc. of Profs. of Child and Adolescent Psychiatry, Soc. Biol. Psychiatry, Nat. Bd. Med. Examiners, Mental Health Assn. Ill. (profl. adv. bd. 1991—), Sigma Xi. Office: Inst for Juvenile Rsch Dept Psychiatry (M/C 747) U Ill at Chgo 1747 W Roosevelt Rd Rm 155 Chicago IL 60608 Office Phone: 312-355-3026. E-mail: bll@uic.edu.

LEVENTHAL, CARL M., neurologist, consultant, retired government agency administrator; b. N.Y.C., July 28, 1933; s. Isidor and Anna (Semmel) L.; m. Brigid Penelope Gray, 1962 (dec. 1994); children: George Leon, Sarah Elizabeth Roark, Dinah Susan, James Gray. AB cum laude, Harvard Coll., 1954; MD, U. Rochester (N.Y.), 1959. Diplomate: Am. Bd. Psychiatry and Neurology. Fellow in anatomy U. Rochester, 1956—57; intern, then asst. resident in medicine Johns Hopkins Hosp., 1959-61; asst. resident, then resident in neurology Mass. Gen. Hosp., Boston, 1961-64; commd. officer USPHS, 1963-96, asst. surgeon gen., 1979-83; asso. neuropathologist Nat. Inst. Neurol. Diseases and Blindness, 1964-66; neurologist Nat. Cancer Inst., 1966-68; asst. to dep. dir. sci., 1968-73; acting dep. dir. sci. NIH, 1973-74; dep. dir. bur. drugs FDA, Rockville, Md., 1974-77; dep. dir. Nat. Inst. Arthritis, Diabetes and Digestive and Kidney Diseases, 1977-81; div. dir. Nat. Inst. Neurol. Disorders and Stroke, 1981-96; sr. policy analyst for life scis. Office of Sci. and Tech. Policy, Exec. Office of Pres., 1983. Asst. clin. prof. neurology Georgetown U. Med. Sch., 1966-76 Recipient Commendation medal USPHS, 1970, Meritorious Svc. medal, 1974, 77, 91, Outstanding Svc. medal, 1988, dir's. award NIH, 1992, Disting. Svc. medal, 1997. Fellow Am. Acad. Neurology; mem. Am. Assn. Neuropathologists, Am. Neurol. Assn., Soc. for Exptl. Neuropathology, Am. Soc. for Exptl. Neurotherapeutics, Internat. Tremor Found. (dir.), Alpha Omega Alpha. Home: 10924 Brewer House Rd Rockville MD 20852-3422

LEVENTHAL, ELAINE A., internist; MD, U. Wis., 1974; PhD, Yale U., 1966. Diplomate Am. Bd. Internal Medicine. Resident in gynecolory U. Hosps., Madison, Wis., 1974—77; resident in internal medicine Mt. Sinai Med. Ctr., Milw., 1977—79; fellow in geriat. Williams S. Middleton Vets. Meml., Madison, 1979—81; physician divsn. gen. internal medicine Robert Wood Johnson U. Med. Group, New Brunswick, NJ, 1988—. Office: Robert Wood Johnson U Med Group Clinical Acad Bldg 125 Paterson St Ste 5100A New Brunswick NJ 08901-1977 Office Phone: 732-235-6577. Business E-Mail: eleventh@umdnj.edu.

LEVENTHAL, ELLEN IRIS, portfolio manager; b. N.Y.C. d. Harry and Laura (Schapira) L. BA, Barnard Coll., N.Y.C., 1971; MA, Columbia U., 1973; MBA, NYU, 1978; student, Harvard U., 1968. Registered rep. NASD. Sr. investment analyst Comptrollers Office, City of N.Y., 1978-79; asst. investment officer Chem. Bank, N.Y.C., 1980-81; v.p., portfolio mgr. E.F. Hutton, N.Y.C., 1981-87, Shearson Lehman Bros., N.Y.C., 1987-89, Ellaure Corp., N.Y.C., 1989—. Portfolio mgr. Delta Capital Mgmt., 1993—. Mem. Investment Tech. Assn., N.Y. Soc. Security Analysts, NYU Bus. Forum, NYU Fin. Club, Money Marketeers of NYU, Princeton Club of N.Y., Barnard Coll. Club of N.Y., City Club of N.Y., Women's City Club of N.Y., Kappa Delta Pi. Avocations: golf, piano, ballet, tennis.

LEVENTHAL, HOWARD, health psychology educator, researcher; b. Bklyn., Dec. 7, 1931; s. Elias and Mildred (Turetsky) L.; m. Elaine A. Silverman, June 6, 1954; children: Edith A. Leventhal Burns, Sharon G. Student, CCNY, 1948-50; BS, CUNY, 1952; MA, U. N.C., 1954, PhD, 1956. Asst. prof. psychology Yale U., New Haven, 1958-64, assoc. prof., 1964-67; prof. depts. psychology and sociology U. Wis., Madison, 1967-88, dir. social and personality grad. program, 1967-77, acting dir. Inst. on Aging, 1986-87, chmn. dept. psychology, 1987-88; bd. govs. prof. dept. psychology Rutgers U., New Brunswick, N.J., 1988—, Inst. for Health, Health Care Policy and Aging, New Brunswick, N.J., 1988—; chmn. div. on health, assoc. dir. for program devel. Inst. Rutgers U., New Brunswick, N.J., 1988-97. Vis. lectr. Justus Liebig U., Giessen, Germany, summer 1981, U. Tilberg, The Netherlands, summers 1989-90, Rijks U., Leiden, The Netherlands, summer 1992; mem. adv. com. on cancer control Fox Chase Cancer Ctr., Phila., 1980—, mem. sci. adv. com., Phila., 1987—, mem. behavioral medicine study sect. NIH, 1986-90, chmn. 1990-91, mem. nat. reviewer res., 1991—, mem. sci. adv. bd. USAF Project Heart; reviewer Behavioral Medicine, Health Psychology, Psychol. Bull., Psychol. Rev., numerous others. Assoc. editor Health Psychology, 1982-87, mem. editl. bd., 1992; adv. editor Contemporary Psychology, 1987-91; mem. editl. bd. jour. Personality and Social Psychology, 1969-70, cons. editor, 1989; mem. editl. bd. Jour. Applied Social Psychology, 1981—, Motivation and Emotion, Psychosomatic Medicine, 1991—; former mem. editl. bd. Jour. Personality, Jour. Exptl. Social Psychology, Social Psychology; mem. editl. adv. bd. Cognition and Emotion; others; contbr. over 250 articles to psychol. and med. jours. Lt. USPHS, 1956-58. Recipient Disting. Alumnus award U. N.C. at Chapel Hill Carolina Psychology Alumni Assn., 1984, merit award Nat. Inst. on Aging, 1990, Bd. Trustees award for excellence in rsch. Rutgers U., 1992; grantee nat. Heart, Lung and Blood Inst. 1979-83, Nat. Inst. Aging, 1982-90, 93—, Nat. Cancer Inst., 1983-86, Nat. Inst. on Drug Abuse, 1984-87. Fellow AAAS, APA (fellow divsns. 1, 8, 38, pres.-elect divsn. 38 1995, pres. 1995—, Sr. Investigator award 1987), Am. Psychol. Soc., Acad. Behavioral Medicine Rsch. (adv. bd. 1988-91); mem. Inst. Medicine NAS, Am. Psychosomatic Soc., Soc. Exptl. Social Psychologists, Internat. Soc. Rsch. in Emotion, Sigma Xi. Office: Rutgers U Inst for Health 30 College Ave New Brunswick NJ 08901-1283*

LEVENTHAL, LAWRENCE JAY, rheumatologist, educator; b. N.Y.C., June 5, 1958; s. Samuel and Anne Leventhal; m. Linda Currao, May 15, 1988; 2 children. BA in Biology magna cum laude, Brandeis U., 1980; MD, Hahnemann U., 1984. Resident in internal medicine Albert Einstein Med. Ctr., Phila., 1984-87; fellow in rheumatology U. Pa., Phila., 1987—90, clin. assoc. in medicine, 1989—91, clin. asst. prof. medicine, 1989—97; clin. asst. prof. Med. Coll. Pa., Phila., 1990—; assoc. prof. medicine Hahnemann U., 1997. Dir. arthritis rsch. edn. Presbyn. Hosp., Phila., 1990—93; assoc. chief rheumatology Grad. Hosp., Phila., 1993—98, chief rheumatology, 1998—, vice chair dept. medicine, 2001—03, chair of medicine, 2003—. Author: Primer of Rheumatic Disease, 1994; editor: Jour. Clin. Rheumatology; contbr. articles to profl. jours. Named one of Best Drs. in Am., Ctr. for the Study Svcs., 1996—2001. Fellow ACP, Am. Coll. Rheumatology, Phila. Coll. Physicians; mem. AMA (physicians recognition award 1987—), Am. Soc. Internal Medicine, Phila. Rheumatism Soc. (pres. 1996), Arthritis Found. (exec. bd.). Office: Grad Hosp 1800 Lombard St Philadelphia PA 19146-1497 Personal E-mail: ljlmd@yahoo.com.

LEVENTHAL, MARVIN, physicist; b. N.Y.C., Dec. 4, 1937; s. Jerome and Helen (Treppel) L.; m. Alice Judith Smilowitz, Apr. 16, 1961; children: Liza, Tama. BS in Physics, CCNY, 1958; PhD in Physics, Brown U., 1964. Postdoctoral fellow Yale U., New Haven, Conn., 1964-66, asst. prof., 1966-68; mem. tech. staff AT&T Bell Labs., Murray Hill, N.J., 1968-91; NRC sr. rsch. assoc. NASA/Goddard Space Flight Ctr., Greenbelt, Md., 1992—; prof., chmn. dept. astronomy U. Md., College Park, 1993—. Contbr. numerous articles to profl. jours. Owens-Ill. fellow, 1962-64. Fellow Am. Phys. Soc.; mem. Am. Astron. Soc. (exec. com. high energy astrophysics div. 1984-86), Sigma Xi. Avocations: tennis, movies, hiking, theater. Home: 7207 Maple Ave Chevy Chase MD 20815-5109 Office: U of Maryland/Dept Astronomy Rm 1207 Computer & Space Sci Bldg College Park MD 20742-2421

LEVENTHAL, NATHAN, performing company executive, lawyer, municipal official; b. N.Y.C., Feb. 19, 1943; s. Harry Leventhal and Fay L. (Bronstein) Levethal; m. Gretchen Dykstra, Feb. 12, 1993. BA in Pub. Affairs, Queens Coll., 1963; JD cum laude, Columbia U., 1966. Bar: N.Y. 1967. Commr. Rent and Housing Maintenance, N.Y.C., 1972-73; chief counsel U.S. Senate Subcom. Adminstrv. Practice and Procedure, Washington, 1973-74; assoc. and ptnr. Poletti, Freidin, Prashker, Feldman & Gartner, N.Y.C., 1974-78; commr. Housing Preservation and Devel., N.Y.C., 1978-79; dep. mayor ops. City of N.Y., 1979-84; pres. Lincoln Ctr. for Performing Arts, 1984—2000; dir. Dreyfus Mutual Funds, 1987—; chmn. N.Y.C. Mayor's Com. on Appointments, 2002—. Lectr. govt. housing policy New Sch. Social Rsch, N.Y.C, 1979; lectr. health care and pub. policy Columbia Law Sch., N.Y.C, 1974. Editor (Editor-in-chief): Columbia Law Rev., 1965—66. Bd. visitors City Univ. Law Sch., N.Y.C, 1983—, Columbia Law Sch., 1989—, The New Sch., N.Y.C, 1992—; chmn. Citizens Union, 1994—; active Coun. on Jud. Adminstrn. Bar Assn., N.Y.C., 1983—90; dir. Nat. Youth Svc. Corp. for N.Y.C., 1983—85; commr. N.Y.C. Charter Revision Commn., 1986—89, N.Y. State Commn. on Constl. Revision, 1993—95; dir. Queen's Coll. Found., 1988—; chair David M. Dinkins Mayoral Transition Com., NY, 1989—90, Michael Bloombergs Mayoral Transition Com., NY, 2001—02. Recipient Disting. Svc. award, Citizens Housing and Planning Coun., N.Y.C, 1984, Am. Soc. Pub. Adminstrn. Outstanding Pub. Adminstr. award, 1982, Columbia Univ. Medal for Excellence, 1985, Austrian Grand Decoration of Honor, 1992, Theodore L. Kesselman award, San Arts Edn., 1998; Harlan Fiske Stone scholar, Columbia Law Sch., 1963—65, Jerome Michael scholar, 1965—66.*

LEVENTHAL, RUTH, retired parasitology educator, university official; b. Phila., May 23, 1940; d. Harry Louis Mongin and Bertha (Rosenberg) Mongin Blai; children: Sheryl Anne, David Alan. BS, U. Pa., 1961, PhD, 1973, MBA, 1981; HHD (hon.), Thomas Jefferson U., 1995; student, Pa. Acad. Fine Arts, 2000—03. Cert. med. technologist, clin. lab. scientist. Trainee NSF, 1971, USPHS, 1969-70, 73; asst. prof. med. tech. U. Pa., Phila., 1974-77, acting dean, 1977-81; dean Hunter Coll., CUNY, 1981-84; provost, dean, prof. biology Capital Coll., Pa. State U., Middletown, 1984-95; prof. biology Pa. State U. Hershey Med. Ctr., 1996—2002; ret., 2002. Site visitor Mid. State Assn. Colls. and Secondary Schs., Phila., 1983—98. Author (with Creadle): Medical Parasitology: A Self Instructional Text, 1979; author: 5th edit., 2002. Chmn. founds. Tri-County United Way, South Central Pa., 1996, 97; mem. health found. bd. Harrisburg Hosp., Pa., 1984-92; pres. bd. dirs. Open Stage Harrisburg, 1996-97, bd. dirs. 1996-2000; bd. dirs. Tri-County Planned Parenthood, 1984-87, Harrisburg Acad., Wormleysburg, Pa., 1984-88, Metro Arts of Harrisburg, 1984-87, Tech. Coun. Ctrl. Pa., 1996-99; founding chmn. Coun. Pub. Edn., 1984-99. Recipient Alice Paul award Women's Faculty Club, U. Pa., 1981; Recognition award NE Deans of Schs. of Allied Health, 1984, Athena award Capital Region C. of C., 1992, John Baum Humanitarian award Am. Cancer Soc., 1992, Lifetime Achievement award Family and Children's Svcs., 1996, Coll. and Cmty. Svc. award Harrisburg Area C.C., 1993; named Disting. Dau. Pa. by Gov. of Pa., 1995. Avocations: painting, sculpture.

LEVER, ALVIN, health science association administrator; b. St. Louis, Jan. 27, 1939; s. Jack I. and Sabina (Vogel) L.; m. Norine Sue Schwedt, Jan. 27, 1963; children: Daniel Jay, Michael Leonard. BS in Archtl. Scis., Washington U., St. Louis, 1961, BArch, 1963; MA in Applied Psychology, U. Santa Monica, 1992. Registered architect, Mo., Ill. Project designer Sir Basil Spence, Architects, Edinburgh, Scotland, 1963-65; sr. project designer Hellmuth, Obata & Kassabaum, St. Louis, 1965-68, v.p., project mgr., 1968-72; v.p. facility devel. Michael Reese Med. Ctr., Chgo., 1972-74; v.p., gen. mgr. Apelco Internat., Ltd., Northbrook, Ill., 1974-90; dir. membership and fin. Am. Coll. Chest Physicians, Northbrook, 1990-92, exec. dir., 1992-95, exec. v.p., CEO, 1995—. Pub. jour. Chest. Pub. Chest. Bd. dirs. Chest Found., 1997; v.p. Congregation B'nai Tikvah, 1987-91, pres., 1993-95. Mem. Profl. Conv. Mgmt. Assn., Am. Soc. Med. Soc. Execs., Am. Soc. Assn. Execs., Chgo. Soc. Assn. Execs., Chgo. Assn. Healthcare Execs., Alliance for Continuing Med. Edn., Mission Hills Country Club. Avocations: scuba diving, bicycling, travel, golf. Office: Am Coll Chest Physicians 3300 Dundee Rd Northbrook IL 60062-2303 Office Phone: 847-498-8300. E-mail: alever@chestnet.org.

LEVER, JACK Q., JR., lawyer; b. Washington, July 8, 1948; BSME emphasis electrical engring., Clemson U., 1970; JD, Catholic U., 1974. Bar: Md. 1974, U.S. Ct. Customs and Patent Appeals 1975-82, D.C. 1978, U.S. Ct. Appeals (fed. and D.C. cirs.) 1982, U.S. Dist. Ct. D.C. 1990, U.S. Dist. Ct. Md. 1990, U.S. Ct. Appeals (8th cir.) 1990; registered to practice U.S. Patent and Trademark Office. Patent examiner U.S. Patent and Trademark Office, 1970-76; patent atty. Dept. Energy, 1976-81, dep. gen. counsel patents, 1980-82; atty. Willian, Brinks, Olds, Gilson & Lione PC, Washington, 1982; ptnr., chmn. firm intellectual property dept. McDermott Will & Emery LLP, Washington. Spl. counsel and rep. office tech. assessment, U.S. Congress, 1981. Editor: U.S. Intellectual Property Legislative Review: An Annual Review (Clark Boardman); contbr. articles to profl. jours. Mem. ABA (mem. sect. patent trademark and copyright law, litigation, corp banking and bus. law, antitrust), Am. Intellectual Property Law Assn., Inter-Am. Bar Assn., D.C. Bar, Bar Assn. D.C., Md. State Bar Assn., Internat. Trade Commn. Trial Lawyers Assn. Office: McDermott Will & Emery LLP 600 13th St NW 12th Fl Washington DC 20005-3096 Office Phone: 202-756-8365. Office Fax: 202-756-8087. Business E-Mail: jlever@mwe.com.

LEVER, O. WILLIAM, JR., chemist; b. Greenville, S.C., Sept. 11, 1944; s. Oscar William and Dorothy (Smith) L.; m. Andrea Maria Lance, July 31, 1993; 1 child, O. William III. BS, MS, U. S.C., 1969; PhD, MIT, 1974; MBA, U. Rochester, 2001. Sr. medicinal chemist Burroughs Wellcome Co., Research Triangle Park, N.C., 1974-84; group leader drug discovery Ortho Pharm. Corp., Raritan, N.J., 1984-88; dir. rsch. Bausch & Lomb, Rochester, NY, 1988-95, dir. clin. affairs, 1995-96, dir. global bus. devel., 1996-98, dir. global bus. devel. and solution programs, 1999—2000, v.p. chem. and pharm. devel., 2000—05, v.p. global sci. affairs, 2005—. Mem. Commn. on MIT Edn., 1970. Contbr. 35 articles to profl. jours.; reviewer for profl. jours. Mem. AAAS, AAPS, Am. Chem. Soc., Assn. for Rsch. in Vision and Ophthalmology, Contact Lens Assn. Ophthalmologists, Indsl. Rsch. Inst., N.Y. Acad. Sci., Soc. Biomaterials, Sigma Xi. Democrat. Methodist. Achievements include 8 U.S. patents and numerous foreign patents for antiallergic, cardiovascular, ophthalmics; research in analgesics, antiinflammatories, allergy, cardiovascular; development of OTC health care products, surgical products, ophthalmic pharmaceuticals, vision care. Home: 208 Royal View Pittsford NY 14534 Office: Bausch & Lomb 1400 Goodman St N Rochester NY 14609-3596

LEVERE, RICHARD DAVID, internist, educator; b. Bklyn., Dec. 13, 1931; s. Samuel and Mae (Fain) L.; m. Diane L. Gonchar, Jan. 15, 1978; children: Elyssa C., Corinne G., Scott M. Student, NYU, 1949-52; MD, SUNY, N.Y.C., 1956. Intern Bellevue Hosp., N.Y.C., 1956-57, resident, 1957-58, Kings County Hosp., 1960-61; asst. prof. medicine SUNY Downstate Med. Center, 1965-69, assoc. prof., 1969-73, prof., 1973-77, vice-chmn. dept. medicine, 1975-77, chief hematology/oncology div., 1970-77; asst. prof. Rockefeller U., 1964-65; prof., chmn. dept. medicine N.Y. Med. Coll., 1977-93, vice dean, 1991-93; med. dir. Westchester County Med. Ctr., 1991-92; v.p. med. affairs St. Agnes Hosp., 1991-93; sr. v.p. Bklyn. Hosp. Ctr., 1994-98; assoc. dean NYU Sch. Medicine, 1994-99, prof. medicine, 1994-2000, adj. prof., 2000—; v.p. med. affairs Westchester Med. Ctr.-St. Agnes Hosp. Mgmt. Corp., 2002—03. Adj. prof. Rockefeller U., 1973—98, 2002—, vis. prof., 1998—2000; pres. Cantigny Rsch. Found., 1986—; dep. dir. Lang Rsch. Ctr., N.Y. Hosp., Queens, 1999—2001; clin. prof. medicine Weill Cornell Sch. Medicine, N.Y.C., 2001—02, NY Med. Coll., 2002—; exec. dir. Resurgens Charitable Fedn., 2005—; bd. dirs. The Wellness Cmty., Atlanta. Contbr. articles to profl. jours. Trustee Our Lady of Mercy Med. Ctr., 1993—96; exec. dir. Resurgens Charitable Found., 2005—; bd. dirs. Leukemia Soc. Am., 1970—85, Am. Heart Assn., 1978—94, Wellness Cmty., Atlanta, 2004—. NIH grantee, 1971-76, 65-86. Master ACP (gov. N.Y. State 1990-94, pres. N.Y. State chpt. 1992-93, Physician Recognition award 1986); fellow N.Y. Acad. Medicine; mem. Harvey Soc., Am. Soc. Clin. Investigation, Soc. Study of Blood (pres. 1973-74), Soc. Devel. Biology, Am. Soc. Pharm. Exptl. Therapeutics (William Dock Teaching award, Tinsley Harrison Rsch. award), Den Tiroler Adler-Ordern of Austria, Alpha Omega Alpha. Home: 514 Reston Mill Ln SE Marietta GA 30067 Office Phone: 404-459-3785. Personal E-mail: drdoc1313@aol.com.

LEVERETT, ALLEN L., energy executive; BS summa cum laude in elec. engring., Vanderbilt U.; MS in elec. engring., Stanford U.; MBA in fin., Auburn U. Various positions in transmission planning, integrated resource planning, startegic planning, wholesale mktg. and fin.; v.p., treas. Southern Co. Svcs.; exec. v.p., CFO Ga. Power Co.; CFO Wis. Energy Corp., Milw., 2003—. Mem.: Ga. Coun. Econ. Edn. (dir.), Energy Ins. Mutual (dir.), Piedmont Pk. Conservancy (resource devel. dir.), Agnes Scott Coll. (trustee), Decatur-DeKalb YMCA (dir.). Office: Wis Energy Corp PO Box 2949 Milwaukee WI 53201

LEVERICH, DENNIS, protective services official, educator; b. Twin Falls, Idaho, July 11, 1955; s. Thomas Lewis and Viola May Leverich; children: Brenda King, Joseph, Gregory, Christopher, Jeramine, Rachel. Certificate, Crowder Coll., Neesho, Mo., 1974; AGS, Ctrl.Tex. Coll., Kalvertex, 1981; student, Kaplan U., Davenport, Ohio, 2004. Enlisted U.S. Army, Clarksville, Tenn., 1976; rose through ranks to Master Sgt. 101st Airborne; retired, 1992; correctional officer Clellenberg Correctional Ctr., Wash., 1993—96, Cedar Crook Correctional Ctr., 1996—2000; list sgt. Stafford Creek Correctional Ctr., Aberdeen, Wash., 2000—, list lt. (acting), 2004. Field tng. officer Dept. Corrections, Aberdeen, Wash., 2000; fire arms instructor Section Law Enforcement, 1995. Master sgt. Washington State Nat. Guard 21st Inf. F.A., 1993—2002. Mem.: Correctional Peace Officers Foundation, Western Correctional Assn., Am. Legion. Home: 1406 N Simpson St #3 Montesano WA 98563 Office: Dept Corrections 191 Constantine Way Aberdeen WA 98520 Office Phone: 360-537-1947. E-mail: ariesdenis@yahoo.com.

LEVERING, ARTHUR CHESTER, composer; b. Balt., Mar. 6, 1953; BA, Colby Coll., 1976; MusM in Performance, Yale U., 1979; MusM in Composition, Boston (Mass.) U., 1988. Composer: (compositions) Roulade (for flute, harp, string trio), 1991 (Lee Ettelson Composer's award, 1992), School of Velocity (for piano), 1992, Twenty Ways Upon the Bells (for 7 players), 1994 (Heckscher Found. Composition prize, 1997), Cloches II (for 8 players), 1997, Catena (for piano and chamber orchestra), 2000. Fellow, Aspen Music Festival, 1987, June in Buffalo Festival, 1988, 1989, Yale at Norfolk Chamber Music Festival, 1990, MacDowell Colony, 1990—96, Bowdoin Summer Music Festival, 1991, Yaddo, 1993, NEA, 1994, Guggenheim Found., 2002; grantee, Barlow Found., 1996; Rome Prize fellow, Am. Acad. Rome, 1996—97.

LEVERING, KATHRYN H., lawyer; b. Providence, Apr. 6, 1950; BA, Wheaton Coll., 1972; MA, Byrn Mawr Coll., 1973; JD, U. Pa., 1976. Bar: Pa. 1976. Joined Drinker, Biddle & Reath, Phila., 1976, sr. ptnr., labor, employment practice group, mng. ptnr., mem. mgmt. com., and chair, litig. dept., 2002—. Mem.: ABA (mem., labor, employment sect.), Phi Beta Kappa. Office: Drinker Biddle & Reath One Logan Sq 18th & Cherry Sts Philadelphia PA 19103-6996 Office Phone: 215-988-2919. Office Fax: 215-988-2757. Business E-Mail: kate.levering@dbr.com.

LEVERT, FRANCIS EDWARD, nuclear engineer, researcher; b. Tuscuoosa, Ala., Mar. 28, 1940; s. John Clemins and Bessie Leona (Williams) LeV.; m. Faye Burnett, June 5, 1965; children: Francis Edward, Gerald Clemins, Lisa Ann. BSME, Tuskegee Inst., 1964; MS in Nuclear Engring., U. Mich., 1966; PhD in Nuclear Engring., Pa. State U., 1971. Registered profl. engr, Tenn. Assoc. prof., head mech. engring. dept. Tuskegee (Ala.) Inst., 1972-73; nuclear engr. Commonwealth Edison, Chgo., 1973-74, Argonne (Ill.) Nat. Lab., 1974-79; sr. scientist Tech. for Energy Corp., Knoxville, Tenn., 1979-85; v.p. K.E.M.P. Corp., Knoxville, 1985—2002; co-founder, v.p. Spira Footwear, Inc., 2002—. Author: (book) Literature Review and Commercial Source Evaluation of AM.-261 (AEC-ORO-4333), 1973, (book) A Guide to Patent Applications, (Van Nostrand Reinhold 1993); contbr. over 65 articles to tech. publs. AEC fellow, 1964-66, Def. Nat. Edn. Act fellow, 1968-70, Am. Soc. Engring. Edn. Ford Found. fellow, 1973-74. Mem. Am. Soc. Mech. Engrs. (exec. com. Plant Main div. 1989—). Achievements include 26 patents for Heat Flux Monitor, Slag Depositor Monitor, Level Gages, Solid State Neutron Sensor, Directional Sensitive Self-power Gamma Detectors, self-power hair curlers, upwardly deployed venetian blinds, spring cushioned shoe. Home: 1909 Matthew Ln Knoxville TN 37923-1340 Office: KEMP Corp Knoxville TN 37917 Office Phone: 615-525-3372. E-mail: kempcorp@comcast.net.

LEVESON, IRVING FREDERICK, economist; b. NYC, June 28, 1939; s. Hyman Wolf and Minnie L.; m. Barbara Diane Wurtzelman, Jan. 28, 1961; children: Stephen Martin, Scott Owen. BA (NY State Regents scholar), CCNY, 1960, MBA, 1963; PhD, Columbia U., 1968. Rsch. analyst, rsch. asst. Nat. Bur. Econ. Rsch., 1963-67; rsch. economist NYC Health Svcs. Adminstrn., 1967-68; economist RAND Corp., 1968-69; dir. rsch. Office Comprehensive Planning, NYC, Planning Commn., 1969-71; asst. adminstr. health systems planning NYC Health Services Adminstrn., 1971-74; sr. profl. staff, dir. econ. studies Hudson Inst., N.Y.C., 1974-84; sr. v.p., dir. rsch. Hudson Strategy Group, NYC, 1984-90; pres. Leveson Cons., Jackson, NJ, 1990—, ForecastCenter.com, LLC, Jackson, NJ, 1999—. Adj. sr. fellow Hudson Inst.; lectr., cons. in field. Author: The Future of the Financial Services Industry, 1982, American Challenges, 1991; editor: Quantitative Explorations in Drug Abuse Policy, 1980; co-editor: Western Economies in Transition, 1980, Analysis of Urban Health Problems, 1976. Mem. Am. Econ. Assn., Nat. Assn. Bus. Econs Jewish. Home and Office: 10 Inverness Ln Jackson NJ 08527-4047

LEVESON, NANCY G., aeronautical engineer; PhD, UCLA, 1980. Prof. computer sci. U. Calif., Irvine; Boeing prof. computer sci. and engring. U. Wash., 1993; prof. aeronautics and astronautics MIT, Cambridge. Author: Safeware: System Safety and Computers, 1995; contbr. articles to profl. jours.; past editor-in-chief IEEE Transactions on Software Engring. Recipient Info. Sys. award AIAA, 1995. Fellow ACM (mem. com. on computers and pub. policy, Allen Newell award 1999); mem. IEEE, NAE, Internat. Coun. on Sys. Engring. (past bd. dirs.), Computing Rsch. Assn., NRC (commn. on engring. and tech. sys., liaison to aeronautics and space engring. bd.), NASA Langley Adv. Subcom. on Air Frame Sys. Rsch. Achievements include research in software safety, which is concerned with the problems of building software for real-time systems where failures can result in loss of life or property. Office: Dept Aeronautics and Astronautics Rm 33-406 MIT 77 Mass Ave Cambridge MA 02139 E-mail: leveson@mit.edu.

LEVESQUE, RENE JULES ALBERT, retired physicist; b. St. Alexis, Que., Can., Oct. 30, 1926; s. Albert and Elmina Louisa (Veuilleux) L.; m. Alice Farnsworth, Apr. 6, 1956 (div.); children: Marc, Michel, Andre; m. Michèle Robert, Feb., 1992. B.Sc., Sir George Williams U., 1952; PhD, Northwestern U., 1957. Research assoc. U. Md., 1957-59; asst. prof. U. Montreal, 1959-64, assoc. prof., 1964-67, prof., 1967-87, dir. nuclear physics lab., 1965-69, chmn. dept. physics, 1968-73, vice dean arts and scis., 1973-75, dean, 1975-78, v.p. research, 1978-85, v.p. research and planning, 1985-87, prof. emeritus, 1987; mem. Atomic Energy Control Bd., Ottawa, Can., 1985-87, pres., 1987-93; ret., 1993. Mem. adv. com. ING project Atomic Energy of Can. Ltd., 1966-69; mem. adv. bd. physics NRC Can., 1972-74, pres. nuclear physics grant selection, 1973; mem. adv. bd. on TRIUMF, 1979-87; v.p. Commn. Higher Studies Que. Ministry Edn., 1976-77, Natural Scis. and Engring. Research Council Can., 1981-87; v.p. bd. dirs. Can.-France-Hawaii Telescope Corp., 1979-80, pres., 1980-81; pres. permanent research com. Conf. Rectors and Prins. Que. Univs., 1979-80; pres. Mouvement Laïc de Langue française, 1961. Decorated officer Order of Can.; recipient Queen Elizabeth Golden and Silver Jubilee medals. Mem. Can. Assn. Physicists (pres. 1976-77), U. Montreal Faculty Assn. (pres. 1971), Fedn. Que. Faculty Assn. (pres. 1971-72), Interciencia Assn. (v.p. bd. dirs. 1979-80), Assn. Scis., Engring. and Tech. Comty. Can. (v.p. 1979-80, pres. 1980-81). Home: 190 Willowdale PH 1 Outremont PQ Canada H3T 1G2 E-mail: levesqur2@sympatico.ca.

LEVETOWN, ROBERT ALEXANDER, lawyer; b. Bklyn., July 20, 1935; s. Alfred A. and Corinne L. (Cohen) L.; m. Roberta S. Slobodkin, Oct. 18, 1959. Student, U. Munich, Fed. Republic Germany, 1954-55; AB, Princeton U., 1956; LLB, Harvard U., 1959. Bar: D.C. 1960, N.Y. 1982, Va. 1984, Pa. 1985. Assoc. Pierson, Ball & Dowd, Washington, 1960-62; asst. U.S. atty. Washington, 1962-63; atty. Chesapeake & Potomac Telephone Cos., Washington, 1963-66, gen. atty., 1966-68, gen. solicitor, 1968-73, v.p., gen. counsel, 1975-83; exec. v.p., gen. counsel Bell Atlantic, 1983-91, vice chmn., 1991-92, also bd. dirs., 1989-92. Chmn. H.R. com., 1995-99; bd. dirs. Telecom NZ. Mem. ABA (vice chmn. comm. com., pub. utility law sect. 1986-93), Washington Met. Corp. Counsels' Assn. (bd. dirs. 1981-83), Nat. Legal Ctr. (legal adv. coun. 1986-92). Republican. Jewish. Address: PMB 606 10645 N Tatum Blvd #200 Phoenix AZ 85028-3053

LEVEY, GERALD SAUL, dean, internist, educator; b. Jersey City, N.J., Jan. 9, 1937; s. Jacob and Gertrude (Kantoff) Levey; m. Barbara Ann Cohen, June 4, 1961; children: John, Robin. AB, Cornell U., 1957; MD, N.J. Coll. Medicine, 1961. Diplomate Am. Bd. Internal Medicine. Med. intern Jersey City Med. Ctr., 1961—62, asst. med. resident, 1962—63; postdoctoral fellow dept. biol. chemistry Harvard U. Med. Sch., 1963—65; med. resident Mass. Gen. Hosp., Boston, 1965—66; clin. assoc. clin. endocrinology br. Nat. Inst. Arthritis and Metabolic Diseases NIH, Bethesda, Md., 1966—68, clin. assoc. Nat. Heart and Lung Inst., 1968—69, sr. investigator Nat. heart and Lung Inst., 1969—70; assoc. prof. medicine U. Miami Sch. Medicine, Fla., 1970—73, prof. medicine, 1973—79; prof., chmn. dept. medicine U. Pitts. Sch. Medicine, 1979—91; physician-in-chief Presbyn.-Univ. Hosp., Pitts., 1979—91; sr. v.p. for med. and sci. affairs Merck and Co., Inc., Whitehouse Sta., NJ, 1991—94; prof., dept. medicine UCLA, dean, David Geffen Sch. of Medicine, 1994—, vice chancellor med. scis., 1994—. Harold Jeghers lectr. N.J. Coll. Medicine, 1977; Marian Blankenhorn lectr. Cin. Soc. Internal Medicine, 1982—; co-prin. investigator Nat. Study of Internal Medicine Manpower, 1984—. Mem. editl. bd.: Endocrinology, 1972—76, Am. Jour. Physiology, 1972—76, Jour. Applied Physiology, 1972—76, Annals of Internal Medicine, 1981—84, cons. editor: Hosp. Medicine, 1981—91; contbr. articles to profl. jours. Mem. United Jewish Fedn. Pitts. Leadership Devel., 1981—82; bd. dirs. Jewish Family and Children's Svcs., 1982—83, Am. Jewish Com., Miami, 1975—79. Grantee, NIH, 1971—91, Fla. Heart Assn., 1971—74. Fellow: ACP; mem.: AMA, Assn. Am. Physicians, Soc. Gen. Internal Medicine, So. Soc. Clin. Investigation, Assn. Profs. Medicine (chmn. ad hoc com. for use of animals in rsch. 1982—85, chmn. task force on internal medicine manpower 1983—90, nat. pres. 1990—91), Endocrine Soc., Am. Soc. Clin. Investigation, Am. Fedn. Clin. Rsch. (councillor so. sect. 1973—76, pres. so. sect. 1977—78), Am. Thyroid Assn. (mem. membership com. 1977—80), Alpha Omega Alpha. Office: UCLA Deans Office Sch Medicine 10833 Le Conte Ave Los Angeles CA 90095-3075

LEVEY, ROBERT FRANK, columnist, not-for-profit fundraiser; b. N.Y.C., June 2, 1945; s. Stanley Victor and Sylvia Rose (Frank) L.; m. Jane Ellen Freundel, May 17, 1980; children: Emily Susanna, Alexander Freundel. BA, U. Chgo., 1966. Reporter Albuquerque Tribune, 1966-67; reporter, editor Washington Post, 1967-81, columnist, 1981—2004; sr. v.p. for devel. Washington Hosp. Ctr. Found., 2004—. Vis lectr. Duke U., Durham, N.C., 1979—; adviser journalism Cath. U. Am., Washington, 1979-81. Co-author: Washington Album, 2000; talk show host Sta. WRC, 1981—83, Sta. WBAL, 1988—92, Sta. WJLA-TV, 1984—86, Sta. WETA-FM, 1985—90, Sta. WTOP, 1997—2001, Newschannel 8, 2000—02. Woodrow Wilson fellow. Mem. Reporters Com. for Freedom of the Press, Newspaper Guild (chmn. Washington Post unit 1972-75), AFTRA, U. Chgo. Alumni Assn. (bd. govs. 1992-2000, pres. 1998-2000), Sigma Delta Chi. Jewish. Office: Washington Post 110 Irving St NW Washington DC 20010 Office Phone: 202-877-7983. Personal E-mail: bob.levey@comcast.net. Business E-Mail: bob.levey@medstar.net.

LEVEY, STUART A., federal agency administrator; b. 1963; Grad. summa cum laude, Harvard Coll., 1986; grad. magna cum laude, Harvard U., 1989. Bar: 1990. Law clerk U.S. Ct. Appeals (DC cir.), 1989—90; pvt. practice Miller, Cassidy, Larroca & Lewin LLP (now Baker Botts LLP), 1990—2001; with US Dept. Justice, Washington, 2001—04, assoc. dep. atty. gen., chief of staff to dep. atty. gen., prin. assoc. dep. atty. gen.; under sec. terrorism & fin. crimes US Dept. Treasury, Washington, 2004—, head Office Terrorism and Fin. Intelligence, 2004—, head Office Intelligence & Analysis. Office: US Dept Treasury 1500 Pennsylvania Ave Washington DC 20220*

LEVI, DAVID F., federal judge; b. 1951; BA, Harvard U., MA, 1973; JD, Stanford U. Bar: Calif. 1983. U.S. atty. ea. dist. State of Calif., Sacramento, 1986-90; judge US Dist. Ct. (ea. dist.) Calif., Sacramento, 1990—, chief judge, 2003—. Chmn. task force on race, religious and ethnic fairness U.S. Ct. Appeals (9th cir.), 1994-97, mem. jury com., 1993-95. Adv. com. on Civil Rules, 1994—2003, chair, 2000—2003; chair Standing com.on Rules Practice and Procedure, 2003-; vis. com. U. Chgo. Law Sch., 1995-98. Mem. Am. Law Inst. (mem. coun. 2004—), Milton L. Schwartz Inn of Ct. (pres. 1992-95). Office: US Dist Ct Rom 14-230 501 "I" St Sacramento CA 95814-7300*

LEVI, HERBERT WALTER, biologist, educator; b. Frankfurt, Germany, Jan. 3, 1921; came to U.S., 1938, naturalized, 1945; s. Ludwig and Irma (Hochschild) L.; m. Lorna Rose, June 13, 1949; 1 child, Frances. Student, Art Students League, N.Y.C., 1938-39; BS, U. Conn., 1946; MS, U. Wis., 1947, PhD, 1949; MA (hon.), Harvard U., 1970. Instr., then asst. prof. to asso. prof. zoology, extension div. U. Wis., 1949-56; asst. curator arachnology Mus. Comparative Zoology Harvard U., 1956-57, assoc. curator, 1957-66, curator, 1966-91, prof. biology, 1970-91, Agassiz prof. zoology, 1972-91, prof. emeritus, 1991—. Sec. Rocky Mountain Biol. Lab., 1959-65; vis. prof. Hebrew U., Jerusalem, 1975; bd. govs. Nature Conservancy, 1956-62; taxonomic cons. Smithsonian project, 1979; cons. Syntax, Cambridge, Mass., 1986. Author: (with L.R. Levi) Spiders and Their Kin, 1968, 69, Aranas y especies afines, 1971; also numerous articles; translator, editor: Invertebrate Zoology (Kaestner), 3 vols.; bd. reviewers Pacific Insects, 1980-85; bd. editors Psyche, 1957-92, Zoomorphology, 1980-85, Sci. Bull. de Mus., Paris, 1980—, (internat.) Annales Zoologici Warszawa Poland, 1993—, Memorias do Instituto Butantan, São Paulo, Brazil, 1994—. Fellow AAAS; mem. Am. Soc. Zoologists, Soc. Study Evolution, Soc. Systematic Zoology (councillor 1967-69), Am. Micros. Soc. (bd. reviewers 1973-94), Am. Arachnol. Soc. (hon. mem., bd. editors 1974—, dir. 1975-83, pres. 1979-81), Am. Ecol. Soc., Am. Inst. Biological Scis., Wildlife Soc., Am. Ornithol. Union, Assn. Systematics Collections (council nat. systematic collections and resources 1975), British Arachnological Soc., Cambridge Entomology Club, Internat. Soc. Arachnology (v.p. 1965-68, pres. 1980-83, hon. mem. 1995—), Japanese Arachnological Soc. (hon.), Soc. Systematic Biologists, Spider Club So. Africa (hon.), Wilson Ornithological Soc., Wilderness Soc. Home: 45 Wheeler St Pepperell MA 01463-1025 Office: Harvard U Mus Comparative Zoology Cambridge MA 02138-2902 Office Phone: 617-495-2447.

LEVI, JAMES HARRY, real estate executive, investment banker; b. Boston, Oct. 28, 1939; s. Robert Emmett and Doris (Cohen) L.; m. Constance Jo Adler, Dec. 30, 1967; children: James H. II, Andrew R., Deanne D., Constance Jo. AB, Harvard U., 1961, MBA, 1964. Past pres. Value Properties Inc., N.Y.C.; now pres. Levi Co., Larchmont, N.Y. Chmn. bd. dirs. New Millenium Energies, Inc., St. Louis; pres. Gt. Train Store co., Dallas, others; prof. Bus. Sch. Columbia U., N.Y.C.; past pres. Oppenheimer Properties, Inc., N.Y.C.; exec. v.p., mem. exec. com. Oppenheimer & Co., Inc.; pres., chmn. bd. dirs. numerous affiliated cos. Mem. Bus. Sch. coun. Tulane U., N.Y.; mem. bd. govs. Hebrew Union Coll./Jewish Inst. Religion; mem. bd. overseers Sch. Architecture, Ill. Inst. Tech.; mem. exec. bd. Westchester Putnam coun. Boy Scouts Am.; mem. traffic commn. Village of Larchmont,

N.Y.; mem. joint planning commn. Villages of Larchmont and Mamaroneck; trustee Larchmont Hist. Soc. Ensign USN, 1961-62. Named Man of Yr., St. Louis Rabbinical Coll., 1986. Mem. Real Estate Securities and Syndication Inst. (former gov.), Nat. Assn. Realtors, Nat. Assn. Rev. Appraisers (cert.), Soc. for Indsl. Archeology, Soc. Archtl. Historians, Nat. Assn. Security Dealers (registered prin.), Sheldrake Yacht Club (past treas.). Avocations: boating and sailing, collecting antiques, travel, opera, kinetic sculpture. Home: 85 Larchmont Ave Larchmont NY 10538-3748 Office: Levi Co 85 Larchmont Ave Larchmont NY 10538-3748 Office Phone: 917-834-5500. Business E-Mail: jameshlevi@cs.com.

LEVI, JOHN G., lawyer; b. Chgo., Oct. 9, 1948; s. Edward H. and Kate (Sulzberger) L.; m. Jill Felsenthal, Oct. 7, 1979; children: Benjamin E., Daniel F., Sarah K.H. BA with honors, U. Rochester, 1969; JD, Harvard U., 1972, LLM, 1973. Bar: Ill. 1973, US Dist. Ct. (no. dist.) Ill. 1973, US Ct. of Appeals (7th cir.) 1973, US Supreme Ct. 1977. Ptnr. Sidley Austin Brown & Wood LLP, Chgo. Chmn. bd. Francis W. Parker Sch., Chgo.; bd. dirs. Chgo. Child Care Soc.; U. Chgo. Brain Rsch. Found., Jane Addams Juvenile Ct. Found., Ctr. for Wrongful Convictions, Chgo. Inst. for Psychoanalysis, High Jump. Mem. ABA, Ill. Bar Assn., Chgo. Bar Assn., Lawyers Club Chgo. Office: Sidley Austin Brown & Wood LLP Bank One Plz 10 S Dearborn St Chicago IL 60603

LEVI, JOSEF ALAN, artist; b. New York, Feb. 17, 1938; s. Jacob and Evelyn D. (Speizer) L. BA, U. Conn., 1959; postgrad., Columbia U., 1960. Artist in residence Appalachian State U., N.C., 1969, vis. prof. art, Pa. State U., 1976 One-man shows of paintings include Stable include N.Y.C., 1966, 67, 68, 69, 70, Arts Club of Chgo., 1967, J.B. Speed Art Mus., Louisville, Ky., 1968, Appalachian State U., Boone, N.C., 1969, Lambert Gallery, Los Angeles, 1971, Gertrude Kasle Gallery, Detroit, 1971, Jacobs Ladder Gallery, Washington, 1972, Images Gallery, Toledo, Ohio, 1972, A.M. Sachs Gallery, N.Y.C., 1975, 76, 78, O.K. Harris Gallery, N.Y.C., 1983, 85, 87, 90, 92, 94, 96, 99, Adams-Middleton Gallery, Dallas, 1986, Harmon Meek Gallery, Naples, Fla., 1996, 2001; numerous group shows, 1965—, latest being, Balt. Mus. Art, 1975, Mus. Art, R.I. Sch. Design, 1976, Art Mus., U. N.C., Greensboro, 1977, Russell Sage Coll., Troy, N.Y., 1977, Washington U., St. Louis, 1977, Whitney Mus., N.Y.C., 1978-79, Meml. Art Gallery, U. Rochester, N.Y., 1979, Aldrich Mus. Contemporary Art, Ridgefield, Conn., 1980, Western Assn. Art Museums, 1981, Worcester (Mass.) Art Mus., 1981, Palace Theatre of Arts Gallery, Stamford, Conn., 1984, Randolph Macon Coll., Ashland, Va., 1985, Robert I. Kidd Galleries, Birmingham, Mich., 1985, Elaine Benson Gallery, Bridgehampton, N.Y., 1985; others; represented in numerous permanent collections including, Aldrich Mus. Contemporary Art, Albright-Knox Gallery, Buffalo, N.Y., Mus. Modern Art, N.Y.C., Krannert Art Mus., U. Ill., Urbana, Va. Mus. Fine Arts, Richmond, AT&T, N.Y.C., Corcoran Gallery, Washington, U. Md., College City, Chrysler Corp., Detroit., Spellman Coll., Atlanta, Exxon Corp., N.Y.C., Minolta Corp., N.Y.C., Des Moines Art Ctr., Newark Mus., Dartmouth Coll., Hanover, N.H., Storm King Art Ctr., Mountainville, N.Y., U. Notre Dame Art Gallery, South Bend, Ind., J. B. Speed Art Mus., Louisville, Bank of N.Y., N.Y.C., Lewis and Clark Coll., Portland, Oreg., Technimetrics Inc., N.Y.C., Best Products Corp., Ashland, Va., Southland Corp., Dallas, TRW Corp., Cleve., Bklyn. Mus. Art, Worcester (Mass.) Art. Mus., Nat. Gallery of Art, Washington, Albion (Mich.) Coll., Prudential Ins. Co. Am., Newark. Served to 1st. lt. Adj. Gen. Corps U.S. Army, 1959-60. Mem. N.Y. Artist Equity Assn. Office Phone: 212-799-8777.

LEVIE, HOWARD S. (HOWARD SIDNEY LEVIE), lawyer, educator; b. Wolverine, Mich., Dec. 19, 1907; s. J. Walter and Mina (Goldfarb) L.; m. S. Blanche Krim, July 24, 1934 AB, Cornell U., 1928, JD, 1930; LL.M., George Washington U., 1957. Bar: N.Y. 1931, Mo. 1965, U.S. Dist. Ct. (ea. dist.) N.Y. 1934, U.S. Dist. Ct. (so. dist.) N.Y. 1935, U.S. Supreme Ct. 1947, U.S. Ct. Appeals (D.C. cir.) 1949, U.S. Ct. Mil. Appeals 1953. Assoc. Weit & Goldman, N.Y.C., 1931-42; with JAGC, U.S. Army, 1942, advanced through grades to col., 1954; staff officer UN Command Armistice Del., Korea, 1951-52; chief internat. affairs div. Office of JAG, 1954-58; legal adviser U.S. European Command, Paris, 1959-61; ret. 1963; prof. law St. Louis U., 1963-77, prof. emeritus, 1977—; prof. U.S. Naval War Coll., Newport, R.I., 1971-72, Charles H. Stockton prof. internat. law, 1971-72; instr. internat. law Salve Regina Coll., Newport, R.I., 1984-88. Adj. prof. Naval War Coll., 1991—. Author: Prisoners of War in International Armed Conflict (Internat. Soc. for Mil. Law and the Law of War Ciardi prize 1982), 1979, Documents on Prisoners of War, 1980, Protection of War Victims, 4 vols., 1979-81, The Status of Gibraltar, 1983, The Code of International Armed Conflict, 1986, The Law of Non-International Armed Conflict, 1987, The Law of War and Neutrality: A Selected English-Language Bibliography, 1988, Mine Warfare at Sea, 1992, Terrorism in War: The Law of War Crimes, 1993; editor vols. 7-12: Terrorism: Documents of International and Local Control, 1997, Levie on the Law of War, 1998. Decorated Legion of Merit, Bronze Star; grantee Ctr. for Advanced Rsch., Naval War Coll., 1980-82, U.S. Inst. Peace, 1991; Howard S. Levie Mil. Chair of Operational Law established by U.S. Naval War Coll., 1994; recipient Outstanding Civilian Svc. medal Dept. of the Army, 1995; named Disting. Mem. of Judge Advocate Gen.'s Corps Regiment, 1995, The Col. Howard S. Levie Libr., established at the Army Judge Advocate's School is named in his honor. Mem. ABA, Am. Soc. Internat. Law (exec. coun. 1969-70), Internat. Law Assn., Ret. Army Judge Advs. Assn., Internat. Soc. for Mil. Law and Law of War, Phi Beta Kappa. Home and Office: 125 Quaker Hill Ln Apt 316 Portsmouth RI 02871-4075 E-mail: hlevie41@aol.com.

LEVIE, JOSEPH HENRY, lawyer, banker; b. N.Y.C. s. Mortimer Joseph and Pearl (Seelig) L.; m. Hallie Ratzkin, Jan. 26, 1963; children: Matthew Benjamin, Jessica Ruth. AB, Columbia U., 1949, LLB, 1951. Bar: N.Y. 1952, U.S. Supreme Ct. 1954. Assoc. Laporte & Meyers, N.Y.C., 1955-59; asst. gen. counsel Loew Theatres Inc., N.Y.C., 1959-63; from assoc. to ptnr. Rathheim, Hoffman, Kassel & Levie, N.Y.C., 1964-81; ptnr. Rogers & Wells, N.Y.C., 1982-94, ret., 1994, sr. counsel, 1995—. Arbitrator N.Y. Stock Exch., NASD; former dir. Chinese Am. Bank N.Y. Contbr. articles to profl. jours. With JAGC, U.S. Army, 1952-55. Fellow: Am. Coll. Comml. Fin. Attys. Home: 131 Riverside Dr New York NY 10024-3713 Personal E-mail: leviej@verizon.com.

LEVIE, MARK ROBERT, lawyer; b. Chgo., Sept. 2, 1951; s. Harold M. and Muriel L.; m. Gail M., Aug. 19, 1973; children: Melissa, Allison, David. BA in rhetoric & composition, U. Ill., 1973; JD magna cum laude, Harvard U., 1976. Bar: Calif. 1978, U.S. Dist. Ct. (no. dist.) Calif. 1978. Clk. to Hon. James R. Browning, chief judge U.S. Ct. Appeals (9th cir.), San Francisco, 1976-77; assoc. Orrick, Herrington & Sutcliffe, San Francisco, 1977-82, ptnr., 1983—, mem. exec. com., mng. dir. corp. practices. Mem. ABA (corp. banking & bus. law sect., com. devel. bus. fin., sub-com. on securitization of assets, fin. task force), State Bar of Calif., San Francisco Bar Assn., San Francisco Lawyers Com. for Civil Rights (treasurer 1995-1998). Avocations: golf, reading. Office: Orrick Herrington & Sutcliffe LLP 405 Howard St San Francisco CA 94105 Office Phone: 415-773-5955. Office Fax: 415-773-5759. Business E-Mail: mlevie@orrick.com.

LEVIEN, DAVID HAROLD, surgeon; b. N.Y.C., Aug. 4, 1948; s. Maurice Berryl and Gloria Anita (Siff) L.; m. Merril Ann Lirette, Aug. 6, 1977; children— Michael, William, Rachel. BA, Johns Hopkins U., 1970; MD, Georgetown U., 1974. Diplomate Am. Bd. Surgery, Am. Bd. Med. Examiners. Resident Mt. Sinai Hosp., N.Y.C., 1974-76; coordinated surg. resident U. Mass., 1976-79; surg. edn. coordinator New Rochelle Hosp., N.Y., 1980-88; instr. surgery N.Y. Med. Coll., Valhalla, 1980-83, asst. prof. surgery, 1983-90, clin. assoc. prof., 1990-91; cons. in surgery Castle Point VA Hosp., 1980-90; clin. assoc. prof. surgery Med. Coll. Pa./Hahnemann U., 1991—, clin. prof. surgery Jefferson Med. Coll., 1996—; dir. surgery Episcopal Hosp.; chmn. surgery St. Vincent's Med. Ctr., Bridgeport, Conn., 2000-03; prof. clin. surgery NY Med. Coll., 2001-03; surgeon Houlton (Maine) Regional Hosp., 2003—. Author textbook on surgery; contbr. articles to profl. jours. Mem. alumni admissions com. Johns Hopkins U., Balt., 1984-90. Fellow ACS, Am. Soc. Colon and Rectal Surgeons; mem. AMA, Soc. Critical Care Medicine, Assn. Acad. Surgery, Pa. Soc. Colon and Rectal Surgery (pres. 1997-98), Acad. Surgery Phila. (sec. 1998—). Home: 82 Military St Houlton ME 04730-2014 Office Phone: 207-532-7936. Business E-Mail: dlevien@houltonregional.org.

LEVIEN, ROGER ELI, strategy and innovation consultant; b. Bklyn., Apr. 16, 1935; s. Abraham Mark and Rosalind (Horowitz) L.; m. Carla Johanna Sherow, Oct. 9, 1960; children: Royce Adam, Alisa Tova. BS, Swarthmore Coll., 1956, MS, 1958; PhD, Harvard U., 1962. Mem. rsch. staff RAND Corp., Santa Monica, Calif., 1960-67, head sys. scis. dept., 1968-71, dir. Washington domestic program Washington, 1971-74; program leader Internat. Inst. Applied Sys. Analysis, Laxenburg, Austria, 1974-75, gen. dir., 1975-81; dir. strategic sys. analysis Xerox Corp., Stamford, Conn., 1981-85, corp. v.p. strategy office, 1985-92, corp. v.p. strategy and innovation, 1992-97. Adj. prof. UCLA, 1970-81; mem. adv. bd. Carnegie-Bosch Inst., Pitts., 1995-2002, Poly. U., Bklyn., 1995-97; chmn. com. on internet addressing and the domain name sys. NRC, 2000-05. Author: The Emerging Technology, 1972, Research and Development Management, 1975, Taking Technology to Market, 1997, Repent-Signparts in Cyberspace, 2005; contbr. chpts. to books. Bd. dirs. Nat. Corp. Theatre Fund, N.Y.C., 1985-2003, Conn. Grand Opera and Orch., Stamford, 1994—. Recipient Ehrenkreuz First Class in Arts and Sci. award Austrian Govt., 1982. Mem. Mfrs. Alliance Coun. on Strategy (chmn. 1990-91), Coun. Planning Execs. (conf. bd.), Coun. on Mgmt. of Innovation and Tech. (chmn. conf. bd. 1996-97), Phi Beta Kappa, Sigma Xi, Tau Beta Pi. Avocations: skiing, photography, collecting north american indian art, musical theater. Office: Strategy and Innovation Cons 2 River Ln Westport CT 06880-1925 E-mail: rlevien@aol.com.

LE VIET, STEPHANE, financial consultant; b. Paris, France (incl. Monaco), July 12, 1979; s. Dominique and Sabine Le Viet. BS, Ecole Polytechnique, Paris, 1999—2002; MS in applied math., Harvard U., 2002—03. Cons. McKinsey & Co., NYC, 2004—; pvt. equity analyst Eurazeo - Lazard Group, Paris, 2002; internat. rels. analyst French Ministry of Defence, Paris, 1999—2000. Founder, chmn. 6Nema Group (Ind. Media Co.), Paris, 2000—04. Fin. com. Zamani Found., Cambridge, Mass., 2004—05. Officer (french lt.) Min. of Def., 1999—2000, Paris. Decorated Bronze medal for excellence in svc. French Army; recipient Entrepreneurship Winner, ANVAR (French Agy. for Innovation), 2002. Mem.: Harvard Club of NYC. Office Phone: 212-446-7907. Office Fax: 212-891-4676. E-mail: stephane_le_viet@mckinsey.com.

LEVI-MONTALCINI, RITA, neurobiologist, researcher; b. Turin, Italy, Apr. 22, 1909; came to U.S., 1947; naturalized, 1956; d. Adamo Levi and Adele Montalcini. MD, U. Turin, 1936. Asst. in neurology Inst. Anatomy, Neurology Clinic, Turin Sch. Medicine, 1936—37; researcher Neurol. Inst. Brussels, 1939; with Allied Health Svc., Italy, 1944—45; resident, assoc. zoologist Washington U., 1947—51, assoc. prof., 1951—58, prof., 1958—81, prof. emeritus St. Louis, 1977; dir. neurobiology rsch. program CNR (Nat. Rsch. Coun.), Rome, 1961—69, dir. cellular biology lab., 1969—79, guest prof. cellular biology lab., 1979—89; pres. Inst. della Enciclopedia Italiana Treccani, 1993—98. Pres. Ency. Italiana, 1993, Italian Nat. Commn. of United World Colls., 1993. Author: In Praise of Imperfection: My Life and Work, 1988. Named Sen. for Life, Italian Parliament, 2001; recipient Albert Lasker Med. Rsch. award, 1986, Nobel prize in physiology or medicine for work on chemical growth factors which control growth and development in humans and animals, 1986, Lewis S. Rosenstiel award, U.S. Nat. Medal of Sci. Mem. AAAS, Soc. Devel. Biology, Am. Assn. Anatomists, Tissue Culture Assn., NAS, Pontifical Acad., Nat. Acad. dei Lincei, Harvey Soc., Am. NAS, Belgian Royal Acad. Medicine, NAS of Italy, European Acad. Scis., Arts and Letters, Acad. Arts and Scis. of Florence. Office: European Brain Rsch Inst EBRI Via del Fosso di Fiorano 64 65 00143 Rome Italy

LEVIN, A. LEO, law educator, retired government official; b. N.Y.C., Jan. 9, 1919; s. Issaachar and Minerva Hilda (Shapiro) L.; m. Doris Feder, Dec. 28, 1947; children— Allan, Jay Michael BA, Yeshiva Coll., 1939; JD, U. Pa., 1942; LLD (hon.), Yeshiva U., 1960, NY Law Sch., 1980, Quinnipiac Coll., 1995; PhD (hon.), Bar-Ilan U., Israel, 1990. Bar: N.Y. 1947, U.S. Supreme Ct. 1982. Instr., then asst. prof. law U. Iowa, 1947-49; law faculty U. Pa., Phila., 1949-69, 70-89, Meltzer prof. law, 1987-89, Meltzer prof. emeritus, 1989—, vice provost, 1965-68; v.p. for acad. affairs Yeshiva U., N.Y.C., 1969-70; dir. Fed. Jud. Ctr., Washington, 1977-87. Chmn. Pa. State Legis. Reapportionment Commn., 1971-73; founding dir. Nat. Inst. Trial Advocacy, 1971-73; conf. coord. Nat. Conf. on Causes of Popular Dissatisfaction with Adminstrn. of Justice (Pound Conf.); chmn. bd. cert. Circuit Execs., 1977-87; mem. adv. bd. Nat. Inst. Corrections, 1977-87. Author: (with Woolley) Dispatch and Delay: A Field Study of Judicial Administration in Pennsylvania, 1961; (with Cramer) Problems on Trial Advocacy, 1968; editor: (with Schuchman and Yablon) Cases on Civil Procedure, 1992, Supplement, 1997. Hon. trustee Bar Ilan U., Ramat Gan, Israel, 1967—; hon. pres. (former pres.) Jewish Publ. Soc. Am. Served to 1st lt. USAF, 1942-46, ETO Recipient Mordecai Ben David award Yeshiva U., 1967, Disting. Svc. award U. Pa. Law Sch. Alumni, 1974, Bernard Revel award Yeshiva Coll., 1963, Justice award Am. Judicature Soc., 1995; White lectr. La. U., 1970, Jeffords lectr., N.Y. Law Sch., 1980, Murrah Lectr. U. Pa. Law Sch., 1989. Fellow Am. Acad. Arts and Scis.; mem. Am. Law Inst., Am. Judicature Soc. (pres. 1987-89), Order of Coif (nat. pres. 1967-70) Jewish. Office: U Pa Law Sch 3400 Chestnut St Philadelphia PA 19104-6204

LEVIN, ALAN M., television journalist; b. Bklyn., Feb. 28, 1926; s. Herman and Shirley (Levinstein) L.; m. Hannah Alexander, Oct. 30, 1948; children: Marc, Nicole, Danielle, Juliet. BA, Wesleyan U., Middletown, Conn., 1946. Reporter, columnist Plainfield (N.J.) Courier News, 1957-60; statehouse corr. AP, Trenton, N.J., 1960-61; writer N.Y. Post, 1961-63; press sec. Sen. Harrison Williams, Washington, 1963-64; news producer, writer WABC-TV, N.Y.C., 1965-67; owner Levin Mediaworks Inc., producers documentaries for comml. and pub. TV, N.Y.C.; sr. prodr. Blowback Prodns. Documentary film maker, NET, N.Y.C., 1968-69, documentary film maker, pub. affairs, news writer, dir., producer, WNET-TV, N.Y.C., 1969-82 Served with AUS, 1944-46. Recipient numerous awards including George Polk Meml. award, Dupont Columbia award, Emmy awards. Home: 88 Claremont Ave Maplewood NJ 07040-2024 Office: Levin Prodns 601 W 26th St Fl 17 New York NY 10001-1101 E-mail: avanti11@comcast.net.

LEVIN, ALAN SCOTT, pathologist, allergist, immunologist, lawyer; b. Chgo., Jan. 12, 1938; s. John Bernhard and Betty Ruth (Margulis) L.; m. Vera S. Byers, June 15, 1971. BS in Chemistry, U. Ill., Champaign-Urbana, 1960; MS in Biochemistry, U. Ill., Chgo., 1963, MD, 1964; JD, Golden Gate U., 1995. Diplomate Am. Bd. Allergy and Immunology, Am. Bd. Pathology; bar: Calif. 1995, Tex. 1996, Nev. 1999, U.S. Patent Office 2002. Intern Children's Hosp. Med. Ctr., Boston, 1964-65; postdoctoral fellow Harvard U., Boston, 1965-66; adj. instr. pediatrics U. Calif., San Francisco, 1971-72, asst. prof. immunology dept. dermatology, 1972-78, adj. assoc. prof., 1978-88; dir. lab. immunology U. Calif. & Kaiser Found. Rsch. Inst. Joint Program Project, San Francisco, 1971-74; attending physician dept. medicine Mt. Zion/U. Calif. San Francisco Hosps., 1971—; dir. div. immunology Western Labs., Oakland, Calif., 1974-77; med. dir. MML/Solano Labs. Div. Chemed-W.R. Grace, Inc., Berkeley, Calif., 1977-79; med. dir. Levin Clin. Labs., Inc., San Francisco, 1979-81; pvt. practice San Francisco, 1981—. Contbr. articles to profl. jours., chpts. to books. Lt. USN, 1966-69, Vietnam. Decorated Silver Star medal, Bronze Star medal with Combat V, 4 Air medals; Harvard Med. Sch. traineeship grantee, 1964, USPHS hematology tng. grantee U. Calif., San Francisco Med. Ctr., 1969-71; recipient Faculty Rsch. award Am. Cancer Soc., 1970-74. Fellow Coll. Am. Pathologists, Am. Coll. Emergency Physicians, Am. Soc. Clin. Pathologists; mem. AMA, Am. Acad. Allergy and Immunology, Am. Coll. Allergy and Immunology, Am. Assn. Clin. Chemists, Am. Acad. Environ. Medicine, Calif. Med. Assn., San Francisco Med. Soc. Jewish. Office Phone: 775-831-5603. E-mail: flitequack@aol.com.

LEVIN, ALLEN JOSEPH, lawyer; b. Lewistown, Pa., Jan. 17, 1948; s. Norman Lewis and Dorothy Sanford (Herbster) L.; m. Mary Gwendolyn McAdoo, Aug. 14, 1974. Cert., Ecole d'art Americaines, Fontainebleau, France, 1968; BA, Dickinson Coll., 1969; JD, Dickinson Sch. Law, 1974. Bar: Pa. 1974, US Supreme Ct., US Ct. Appeals (3d cir.), US Dist. Ct. (Mid. Dist. Pa.). Assoc. Brugler & Levin Law Offices, Lewistown, 1974-80, ptnr., 1980-2000, Levin Law Offices, Lewistown, 2000—. Counsel Mifflin County Ind. Devel. Corp., Lewistown, 1978—, Mifflin County Ind. Devel. Authority, Lewistown, 1980—; solicitor Midd-West Sch. Dist.; pres. Pa. Sch. Bd. Solicitors Assn., 1989; v.p., assoc. gen. counsel Pocono Mountain R.R., Scranton, Pa., 1994-96; pres. Lewistown Ctrl. R.R. Co., Mt Union Connecting R.R. Co. Pres. Greater Lewistown Corp., 1983-95, v.p., 1995-99. Recipient Outstanding Svc. to Edn. award Pa. Sch. Bd. Assn., 1989. Mem. Pa. Bar Assn., Mifflin County Bar Assn. (pres. 1992-93), Juniata Valley C. of C. (pres. 1983-85), Rotary Club Lewistown, Elks (# 663). Jewish. Avocations: fishing, reading. Home: 9 N Grand St Lewistown PA 17044-2040 Office: Levin Law Offices 27 West 3d St Lewistown PA 17044-0231

LEVIN, ARNOLD MURRAY, social worker, psychotherapist, educator; b. Bklyn., Dec. 26, 1924; s. William and Pauline Levin; m. Elaine M. Zimmerman, Dec. 19, 1946 (dec. Aug. 1971); children: Michael, Nancy Jo Noteman, Amy Louise. BA, U. Mass., 1948; MA, U. Chgo., 1950, PhD, 1975; Cert., Chgo. Inst. Psychoanalysis, 1955. ACSW, LCSW, BCD. Case worker Jewish Family Svcs., Chgo., 1950-53; group therapist Portal House Clinic Alcoholism, Chgo., 1952-55; exec. dir. Family Svc., Mental Health Ctr. So. Cook County, Park Forest, Ill., 1953-60; pvt. practice in social work Chgo., 1960—. Founder, pres. Inst. Clin. Social Work, Chgo., 1979—; bd. dirs. Jewish Childrens Bur., Chgo., 1987—; founder, pres., Ill. Soc. Clin. Social Workers, Chgo., 1971-76; mem. 90 for the 90's, Ill. Author: Private Practice of Psychotherapy, 1983. Sgt. U.S. Army, 1943-46. NIMH grantee, 1971; recipient Gov.'s award, Chgo., 1975, Alumnus of Yr. award U. Chgo., 1976. Mem. Nat. Registry of Health Care Providers in Clin. Social Wk. (bd. dirs. 1985-88), Nat. Fedn. Socs. for Clin. Social Work (founder 1971-75), Am. Acad. of Practice (diplomate, disting. practitioner). Avocations: acting, theater, biking. Home: 333 N Michigan Ave Chicago IL 60601-7543 Personal E-mail: arnielev@aol.com.

LEVIN, BARRY STEVEN, lawyer; b. St. Louis, Dec. 16, 1954; AB, Washington U., St. Louis, 1976; JD, Northwestern U., 1979. Bar: Calif. 1979. Atty. Heller Ehrman White & McAuliffe, LLP, San Francisco, 1979—, chmn. ins. coverage practice group, 1995—97, chmn. litigation dept., 1997—99, shareholder, chmn., 1999—2005. Lectr. in ins. coverage and law firm mgmt. Named one of Leading Ins. Coverage Attorneys in Calif., Chambers & Partners America's Leading Bus. Lawyers, 2003, 2004; recipient Atty. of Yr. award, Calif., 2003. Mem. ABA, Order of Coif, Bar Assn. San Francisco, Phi Beta Kappa. Office: Heller Ehrman White & McAuliffe 333 Bush St San Francisco CA 94104-2806 Office Phone: 415-772-6646. Fax: 415-772-6268. E-mail: blevin@hewm.com.

LEVIN, BERNARD, physician; b. Johannesburg, Apr. 1, 1942; came to U.S., 1966, naturalized, 1972; m. Ronelle DuBrow; children: Adam, Katherine. MB, BCh, U. Witwatersrand, 1964. Resident Presbyn. St. Lukes Hosp, Chgo., 1966-68; rsch. fellow U. Chgo., 1968-71, NIH fellow, 1971-72, instr. medicine, 1971-73, asst. prof. medicine, 1973-78, assoc. prof., 1979-84; prof. medicine, chmn. dept. gastro. oncology and digestive U. Tex. Med. Ctr./M.D. Anderson Hosp., Houston, 1984-94, Robert R. Herring prof., 1986-91, Ellen F. Knisely chair, 1991-94, v.p. for cancer prevention, 1994—, Betty Marcus chair, 1994—. Mem. large bowel cancer working group Nat. Cancer Inst., 1984-85; cons. spl. study sect. Nat. Cancer Inst., 1976-84, chair nat. adv. com. on colorectal cancer, 1990—; chair Nat. Colorectal Cancer Roundtable, 1998—. Mem. editl. bd. Jour. Nat. Cancer Inst., Cancer Epidemiology, Biomarkers, Prevention; contbr. articles to profl. jours. Grantee USPHS, 1976-80, Melamid Found. grantee U. Chgo., 1978-83, NCI grantee, 1980-84, 1994; recipient award for sci. excellence in medicine Am. Italian Cancer Found., 2001, Janssen-Cilag Masters in Gastroenterology award, 2005 Fellow ACP, Am. Coll. Nutrition; mem. AAAS, Am. Assn. Cancer Rsch., Am. Gastroenterol. Assn., Am. Soc. Gastrointestinal Endoscopy, Am. Pancreatic Assn., Am. Soc. Preventive Oncology, Am. Soc. Clin. Oncology (chmn. cancer prevention com. 2002-04, award 2004), Am. Cancer Soc. (chair nat. adv. com. on colorectal cancer, award 2004), Sigma Xi. Jewish. Office: UT M D Anderson Cancer Ctr 1155 Pressler St Unit 1370 Houston TX 77030-4009

LEVIN, BRUCE R., biology professor; b. NYC, June 7, 1940; BS in Zoology, Univ. Mich., 1963, MS in Genetics, 1964, PhD in Genetics, 1967. Instr., zoology Univ. Mich., 1967; asst. prof. biol. sci. Brown Univ., 1967—71; assoc. prof., zoology Univ. Mass., 1971—80, prof., dept. zoology, 1980—92; prof., dept. biology Emory Univ., Atlanta, 1992—. Vis. prof. Fla. Internat. Univ., 1997. Contbr. articles to profl. journals. Recipient Career Devel. award, NIH, 1975—80. Fellow: Am. Acad. Arts & Sci.; mem.: Am. Soc. of Naturalists (v.p. 1988), Soc. for Study of Evolution (v.p. 1985), Sigma Xi. Office: Rollins 1109 Dept Biol Emory Univ 1510 Clifton Rd NE Atlanta GA 30322 Office Phone: 404-727-2826. Business E-Mail: blevin@emory.edu.*

LEVIN, BURTON, diplomat; b. N.Y.C., Sept. 28, 1930; s. Benjamin and Ida (Geller) L.; m. Lily Lee, Jan. 4, 1960; children: Clifton, Alicia. BA, CUNY, 1952; M Internat. Affairs, Columbia U., 1954; postgrad., Harvard U., 1964; LLD (hon.), Carleton Coll., 1993. Commd. fgn. service officer Dept. State, 1954; counselor/econ. officer Am. Embassy, Taipei, Taiwan, 1954-56, polit. officer, 1969-74; intelligence research specialist Dept. State, Washington, 1956-58, dir. Republic China affairs, 1974-77; polit. officer Am. Embassy, Jakarta, Indonesia, 1959-63, Am. Consulate Gen. Hong Kong, 1965-69, dep. chief mission, 1977-78, consul gen., 1981-86; dep. chief mission Am. Embassy, Bangkok, Thailand, 1978-81; amb. to Burma, 1987-90; dir. Asia Soc. Hong Kong Ctr., 1990-95. Vis. prof. Carleton Coll., 1995; vis. fellow Stanford U., 1974; vis. lectr. Harvard U., 1986, Carleton Coll., 1994; bd. dirs. Mansfield Found.; mem. coun., chmn. emeritus Hopkins-Nanjing U. Ctr. for Chinese and Am. Studies Johns Hopkins U. Mem. Am. Fgn. Service Assn. Clubs: Am., Hong Kong Country. Home: 314 2nd St E Northfield MN 55057-2204 Office Phone: 507-645-0086. Personal E-mail: brtnlevin@aol.com.

LEVIN, CARL, senator; b. Detroit, June 28, 1934; m. Barbara Halpern, 1961; children: Kate, Laura, Erica. BA, Swarthmore Coll., 1956; JD, Harvard U., 1959. Ptnr. Grossman, Hyman & Grossman, Detroit, 1959-64; asst. atty. gen., gen. counsel Mich. CRC, 1964-67; chief appellate defender City of Detroit, 1968-69, mem. coun., 1970-73, pres. coun., 1974-77; ptnr. Schlussel, Lifton, Simon, Rands & Kaufman, 1971—73, Jaffe, Snider, Raitt, Garratt & Heuer, 1978—79; U.S. senator from Mich., 1979—. Past instr. Wayne State U., U. Detroit; chmn. Armed Svcs. Com., Govtl. Affairs Com., Com. on Small Bus., Senate Dem. Steering & Coordination Com., Senate Select Com. on Intelligence. Mem. Mich. Bar Assn., D.C. Bar. Democrat. Office: US Senate 269 Russell Senate Ofc Bldg Washington DC 20510-2202 E-mail: senator@levin.senate.gov.*

LEVIN, CHARLES EDWARD, lawyer; b. Chgo., Oct. 6, 1946; m. Barbara Serwer, Dec. 28, 1975. BA with high honor, DePaul U., 1968; JD cum laude, Northwestern U., Chgo., 1971. Bar: Ill. 1971. Asst. instr. legal writing and rsch. Northwestern U. Law Sch., 1970-71; assoc. D'Ancona & Pflaum, Chgo., 1971-76, ptnr., 1977-90, Jenner & Block, Chgo., 1990-2000, McDermott, Will & Emery, Chgo., 2000—. Governing bd. Comml. Fin. Assn. Edn. Found., 1990-2000; asst. instr. legal writing, rsch. Northwestern U., 1970-71. Mem. bd. editors Northwestern U. Law Rev., 1970-71. Aux. bd. Chgo. Architecture Found., 1989-99; founders leadership coun. C omml. Fin. Assn. Edn. Found., NY. Mem. ABA (bus. sect. 1992—), Chgo. Bar Assn. (vice chmn. architecture and law com. 1974-75, vice chmn. divsn. D, mem. exec. com. fed. tax com. 1983-84, comml. fin. and trans. com. 1990—, Article 9 drafting subcom.), East Bank Club Chgo., Met. Club. Avocations: acquisition fine arts, support arts organizations, jogging. Office: McDermott Will & Emery LLP 227 W Monroe St Ste 4400 Chicago IL 60606-5016

LEVIN, CHARLES LEONARD, state supreme court justice; b. Detroit, Apr. 28, 1926; s. Theodore and Rhoda (Katzin) L.; children: Arthur, Amy, Fredrick. BA, U. Mich., 1946, LL.B., 1947; LL.D. (hon.), Detroit Coll. of Law, 1980. Bar: Mich. 1947, N.Y. 1949, U.S. Supreme Ct. 1953, D.C. 1954. Pvt. practice law, N.Y.C., 1948-50, Detroit, 1950-66; ptnr. Levin, Levin, Garvett & Dill, Detroit, 1951-66; judge Mich. Ct. Appeals, Detroit, 1966-73; assoc. justice Mich. Supreme Ct., 1973-96. Mem. Mich. Law Revision Commn., 1966 Trustee Marygrove Coll., 1971-77, chmn., 1971-74; mem. vis. coms. to Law Schs., U. Mich., U. Chgo., 1977-80, Wayne State U. Mem. Am. Law Inst. Office: Mich Supreme Ct 500 Woodward Ave Fl 20 Detroit MI 48226-5498

LEVIN, EDWARD JESSE, lawyer; b. Balt., Oct. 31, 1951; s. Cyril and Virginia Lee (Kremer) Levin; m. Cheri Wyron, Feb. 18, 1973; children: Paul Clifford, Benjamin Lawrence. BA, Johns Hopkins U., 1973; JD, U. Va., 1976. Bar: Md. 1976, U.S. Supreme Ct. 1980. Assoc. Piper & Marbury, Balt., 1976-84; ptnr. DLA Piper Rudnick Gray Cary US LLP (formerly Piper & Marbury LLP), Balt., 1984—. Co-author: Maryland Real Estate Leasing Forms and Practice, 1988. 1st v.p. Balt. Bd. Jewish Edn., 1987—89, pres., 1989—91; trustee Hebrew U., Balt., 1999—2000. Fellow: Am. Coll. Real Estate Lawyers (chmn. atty.'s opinions com. 1992—99); mem.: Balt. City Bar Assn. (co-chmn. spl. joint com. lawyers' opinions comml. transactions 1989—90), Md. State Bar Assn. (chmn. sect. real property, planning and zoning 1988—90, co-chmn. spl. joint com. lawyers' opinions comml. transactions 1989—90). Democrat. Jewish. Office: DLA Piper Rudnick Gray Cary US LLP 6225 Smith Ave Baltimore MD 21209 Office Phone: 410-580-4700. Business E-Mail: edward.levin@dlapiper.com.

LEVIN, EDWARD M., lawyer; b. Chgo., Oct. 16, 1934; s. Edward M. and Anne Meriam (Fantl) L.; children from previous marriage: Daniel Andrew, John Davis; m. Margot Aronson, Apr. 4, 1993. BS, U. Ill., 1955; LLB, Harvard U., 1958. Bar: Ill. 1958, U.S. Supreme Ct. 1968. Mem. firm Ancel, Stonesifer, Glink & Levin and predecessors, Chgo., 1958, 61-68; draftsman Ill. Legis. Reference Bur., Springfield, 1961; spl. asst. to regional adminstr. HUD, Chgo., 1968-71, asst. regional adminstr. community planning and mgmt., 1971-72; asst. dir. Ill. Dept. Local Govt. Affairs, Chgo., 1973-77; of counsel Holleb, Gerstein & Glass, Ltd., Chgo., 1977-79; chief counsel Econ. Devel. Adminstrn., U.S. Dept. Commerce, Washington, 1979—85, 1997—2001; sr. fellow Nat. Gov's. Assn., 1985-86; sr. counsel U.S. Dept. Commerce, Washington, 1987-96. Lectr. U. Ill., 1972—73, adj. assoc. prof. urban scis., 1973—79; lectr. Loyola U., 1976—79, No. Va. Law Sch., 1988; instr. Mgmt. Concepts, Inc., Vienna, 2001—. Assoc. editor Assistance Mgmt. Jour., 1990-95; contbr. articles to profl. jours. Mem. Ill. Nature Preserves Com., 1963-68, Northea. Ill. Planning Commn., 1974-77, Ill.-Ind. Bi-State Commn., 1974-77; bd. dirs. Cook County Legal Assistance Found., 1978-79, D.C. Appleseed Ctr., 1994—; bd. dirs. Ill. divsn. ACLU, 1965-68, 77-79, v.p., 1977-78; chmn. ABA fed. assistance com., 1995-96. With AUS, 1958-60. Recipient Lincoln award Ill. Bar Assn., 1977, Gold medal U.S. Dept. Commerce, 2000, Corrigan award Econ. Devel. Adminstrn., 2000. Mem. FBA (chmn. fed. grants com. 1991-95), Nat. Grants Mgmt. Assn. (bd. dirs. 1988-92, Pres.'s award 1994), Appleseed Found. (bd. dirs. 1994—, mem. exec. com. 1994-2002). Home: 3201 Porter St NW Washington DC 20008-3212 Personal E-mail: elevin111@erols.com.

LEVIN, EDWARD ROSS, lawyer; b. Norfolk, Va., Mar. 18, 1943; s. Charles P. and Estelle N. (Nagle) Levin; m. Susan Israel, Mar. 3, 1945; children: Matthew D., Emily R. BA, Brown U., 1965; LLB, U. Va., 1968. Bar: Va. 1968, DC 1969, U.S. Supreme Ct. 1973. Law clk. to chief judge U.S. Dist. Ct. (ea. dist.) Va., 1968—69; assoc. Danzansky, Dickey, Tydings, Quint & Gordon, Washington, 1969—75, ptnr., 1975—81, Finley Kimble Wagner Heine Underberg Manley & Casey, Washington, 1981—. Mem. minimum wage counsel Greater Washington Bd. Trade, 1972—82, mem. regulatory affairs com., 1980—84. Mem.: ABA (mem. labor sect. EEO com. 1968—82), Anti-Defamation League (mem. regional bd. 1980—84, chmn. law com. 1982—84), Va. Bar Assn., Brown Univ. Club (pres. Washington chpt. 1973, dir. Alumni Assn. 1975). Office: Finley Kimble Wagner et al 1120 Connecticut Ave 10th Fl Washington DC 20036

LEVIN, ERIC MATHEW, secondary school educator; b. Oakland, Calif., Jan. 8, 1959; s. Ben and Barbara Ann Levin; m. Michele Ann Levin, June 20, 1991; 1 child, Kyle David. PhD, U. of Oreg., 1996. Cert. tchr. Calif. Dept. of Edn., 2000. Tchr. Marion County Ednl. Programs, Salem, Oreg., 1987—89; instr. Pacific U., Forest Grove, Oreg., 1989—90; asst. prof. Dickinson State U., ND, 1995—97; instr. Coll. of the Sequoias, Visalia, Calif., 1998—2000; tchr. Hanford Joint Union H.S., Hanford, Calif., 2000—. Dir.: (theatre) The Madwoman of Chaillot, The Odd Couple, More Fun than Bowling, Huey, A Moon For the Misbegotten; scenographer (educational theatre) Various Productions. Tchr. Congregation Rodef Sholem, San Rafael, Calif., 1979—82, Congregation B'nai David, Visalia, Calif., 2003—04. Recipient Intercultural Playwright award, Portland Theatre Assn., 1993; fellow Tchg. fellow, U. of Oreg., 1992—95, Western Oreg. State Coll., 1987; grantee Grad. Rsch. grantee, U. of Oreg., 1995. Mem.: Eugene O'Neill Soc., Am. Theatre and Drama Soc., Ednl. Theatre Assn. Avocations: bowling, nintendo, theater. Office: Hanford High School 120 N Grangeville Blvd Hanford CA 93230 Office Phone: 559-583-5941 3146. Personal E-mail: patcheslevin@sbcglobal.net. E-mail: elevin@huhsd.k12.ca.us.

LEVIN, EVANNE LYNN, lawyer, educator; b. LA, Nov. 6, 1949; d. Marshall Levin and Rose (Tolchin) Levin Albert; m. Jeffrey Neal Oliver, 1992 (div. 1996); m. Al Gerisch Jr., Sept. 2005. BA in Polit. Sci. cum laude, UCLA, 1971; JD, Loyola Law Sch., L.A., 1974. Bar: Calif. 1995; lic. real estate broker Calif. Assoc. Ervin, Cohen & Jessup, Beverly Hills, Calif., 1977-78, Mason & Sloane, LA, 1978-82; atty. Orion Pictures Corp., LA, 1982-84; sr. dir. TV prodn. legal affairs Twentieth Century Fox Film Corp., Beverly Hills, 1986-89; of counsel Weinberg, Zipser, Arbiter & Heller, L.A., 1990; v.p., gen. counsel Zodiac Entertainment, Studio City, Calif., 1991-95; prin., owner Law Offices Evanne L. Levin, LA, 1995—; instr. entertainment law UCLA, 1999—; prin. Levin Realty, 2004—. Instr. personal mgmt. pub. and music career courses Learning Network, 1985—86; instr., asst. atty. UCLA, Learning Network, Entertainment Law Tng. Program, 1999—; devel. and fund-raising cons. Acad. for Jewish Religion, Calif., 2004—. Contbr. articles to profl. jours.; columnist: LA Women in Music Newsletter, 1986—88. Bd. dirs. Hollywood Women's Coalition, 1985—86, bd. dirs. arts festival, 1985; mem. exec. bd. Wellness Guild; mem. Planned Giving Round Table So. Calif.; mem. exec. com., bd. dirs. Weingart Ctr. Assn. Ptnrs., 2001—04; maj. gifts officer Woodbury U., 2002—04; v.p. event chair City Live!, 2003. Mem.: Calif. Copyright Conf., LA Women Music (bd. dirs. 1986—88, mem. adv. com.), Women Entertainment Law, Beverly Hills Bar Assn. (former bd. govs., barristers bd. govs., founding mem./co-chair com. arts, mem. entertainment law com., del. to state bar and ABA convs.), Los Angeles County Bar Assn. (vols. in parole, exec. bd. intellectual property sect.), Assn. Profl. Fundraisers, Coun. Advancement Support Edn. Avocations: scuba diving, collecting kaleidoscipes, travel. Office: 14937 Rhinestone Dr 1st Fl Sherman Oaks CA 91403 Personal E-mail: ellesq@adelphia.net. E-mail: ellesq@yahoo.com.

LEVIN, FRANCES R., psychiatrist, educator; b. Newton, Mass., Nov. 29, 1959; m. Howard Robert Levin; children: Allison Paula, Tamara Stephanie, Charles Jacob. BS magna cum laude, Brown U., 1981; MD, Cornell U., 1985. Diplomate Am. Bd. Psychiatry and Neurology. Q.J. Kennedy assoc. prof. clin. psychiatry Columbia U.; assoc. attending psychiatry N.Y. Presbyn. Hosp.; resident in psychiatry N.Y. Hosp., Payne Whitney Clinic, N.Y.C., 1985—89, asst. unit chief, 1988—89; rsch. and addiction psychiatry fellow Nat. Inst. on Drug Abuse, U. Md., Balt., 1989—90; asst prof. dept. psychiatry U. Md. Med. Ctr., 1990—92; asst. prof. clin. psychiatry dept. psychiatry Columbia U. Coll. Physicians and Surgeons, 1992—99, assoc. pro. clin. psychiatry dept. psychiatry, 1999—; asst. attending psychiatrist N.Y. Presbyn. Hosp., 1992—99, assc. attending psychiatrist, 1999—. Mem. numerous panels and coms.; presenter in field. Reviewer: numerous profl. jours., mem. editl. bd.: Am. Jour. on Addictions, 2000; contbr. over 70 articles to profl. jours. Recipient Connie Guion scholarship, 1983, AMA-ERF Rock Sleyster Meml. scholarship, 1985; numerous rsch. grants. Fellow: N.Y. Acad. Medicine, Am. Psychiat. Assn.; mem.: AMA, Group for Advancement of Psychiatry, Coll. on Problems of Drug Dependence, Am. Soc. Addiction Medicine (N.E. region subcom. 1991), Assn. for Med. Edn. and Rsch. in Substance Abuse, Md. Psychiat. Soc. (com. on addiction 1989), Am. Acad. Addiction Psychiatrists (chair area dirs. 2001, bd. dirs. 2001), Sigma Xi, Phi Beta Kappa. Office: NYSPI Columbia Univ 1051 Riverside Unit 66 New York NY 10032

LEVIN, FRANK S., physicist, researcher; b. NYC, Apr. 14, 1933; s. James J. and Celia (Aronovitch) L.; m. Madeline Carol McMurrough, Apr. 1973; 4 children. BA, Johns Hopkins U., 1955; PhD, U. Md., 1961. Rsch. assoc. Rice U., Houston, 1961-63, Brookhaven Nat. Lab., Upton, N.Y., 1963-66, U.K. Atomic Energy Authority, Harwell, Eng., 1965-67; mem. faculty Brown U., Providence, 1967—, prof. physics, 1977-98, emeritus prof., 1998—. Co-organizer 9th Internat. Conf. on Few-Body Problems, 1980. Author: An Introduction to Quantum Theory, 2002; co-editor (series): Finite Systems and Multiparticle Dynamics. Recipient Sr. U.S. Scientist award Alexander von Humboldt Stiftung, 1979. Fellow Am. Phys. Soc. (founder, 1st chmn. topical group on few body systems and multiparticle dynamics) Office: Brown U Physics Dept PO Box 1843 Providence RI 02912-1843 Business E-Mail: levin@physics.brown.edu.

LEVIN, FREDRIC GERSON, lawyer; b. Pensacola, Fla., Mar. 29, 1937; s. Abraham I. and Rose (Lefkowitz) L.; m. Marilyn Kapner, June 14, 1959; children: Marci Levin Goodman, Debra Levin Dreyer, Martin, Kimberly Levin Brielmayer. BSBA, U. Fla., 1958, JD, 1961. Bar: Fla. 1961, U.S. Dist. Ct. (no. dist.) Fla., U.S. Ct. Appeals (5th cir.). Assoc. Levin, Papantonio, Thomas, Mitchell, Echsner & Proctor, P.A., Pensacola, 1961—. Counsel Fla. Senate, 1981-82. Author: Effective Opening Statements, 1983; contbr. articles to profl. jours. Fellow Acad. Fla. Trial Lawyers (dir. 1977-84), mem. Inner Circle of Advocates, Ala. Trial Lawyers Assn., Tex. Trial Lawyers Assn., Pa. Trial Lawyers Assn. Democrat. Jewish. Home: 533 Deer Point Dr Gulf Breeze FL 32561-4543 Office: Levin Papantonio Thomas Mitchell Echsner & Proctor PA 316 S Baylen St Pensacola FL 32501-5900 Office Phone: 850-435-7123. Business E-Mail: flevin@levinlaw.com.

LEVIN, GAIL, writer, educator, photographer; d. Barron and Shirley Levin. BA, Simmons Coll., 1969, D (hon.), 1996; MA, Tufts U., 1970; PhD, Rutgers U., 1976. Instr. New Sch. for Social Rsch., N.Y.C., 1973—75, Baruch Coll., CUNY, 1974; asst. prof. art history Conn. Coll., New London, 1975—76; vis. prof. art history Grad. Ctr. CUNY, 1979—80; curator Whitney Mus. Am. Art, N.Y.C., 1976—84; vis. prof. Nesbit Coll. Design, Drexel U., 1985—86; asst. prof. art Baruch Coll. CUNY, 1986—87, assoc. prof. art, 1988—89, prof., 1990—. Will and Ariel Durant prof. humanities St. Peter's Coll., Jersey City, 1987—88; chair excellence U. Tenn., Chattanooga, 1995—96. Prodr., host Art at Issue, Manhattan Cable TV, 1985—86; author: Synchromism and American Color Abstraction, 1910-25, 1978, Edward Hopper: The Complete Prints, 1979, Edward Hopper as Illustrator, 1979, Edward Hopper: The Art and the Artist, 1980, Edward Hopper, 1984, Twentieth Century American Painting The Thyssen-Bornemisza Collection, 1987, Edward Hopper: An Intimate Biography, 1995, Edward Hopper: A Catalogue Raisonné, 1995; editor: The Poetry of Solitude: A Tribute to Edward Hopper, 1995, Silent Places: A Tribute to Edward Hopper, 2000; co-author: Abstract Expressionism: The Formative Years, 1978, Aaron Copland's America: A Cultural Perspective, 2000; author, photographer Hoppers Places, 1985, Marsden Hartley in Bavaria, 1989, film Edward Hopper, 1981; contbr. articles to profl. jours. and exhibition catalogues; one-woman shows include Kingston Artists Group, Gallery Rondout, 1984, Kennedy Galleries, Inc., N.Y.C., 1985, Jane Voorhees Zimmerli Art Mus., 1985, Meml. Art Gallery, U. Rochester, 1985, Fay Gold Gallery, Atlanta, Barridoff Gallery, Portland, 1986, Cedar Rapids Art Mus., 1986, Hopper House Art Ctr., Nyack, NY, 1986, Hilton Head Art League, SC, 1986, U. Iowa Art Mus., 1987, St. Peter's Coll. Art Gallery, Jersey City, 1987, Pa. Acad. of Fine Arts, 1987, Ariz. State U., Tempe, 1988, Emerson Gallery, Hamilton Coll., Clinton, NY, 1989, Milw. Art Mus., 1990, Bowdain Coll. Art Mus., 1990, Cress Gallery U. Tenn., Chattanooga, 1995, Trustman Art Gallery Simmons Coll., Boston, 1995, Provincetown (Mass.) Monument Mus., 1996, exhibited in group shows at Catskill Ctr. for Photography in Woodstock, N.Y., 1985, A.I.R. Gallery, N.Y.C., 1985, 1986, 1987, 2002, The 9th Precinct Gallery, 1986, Baruch Coll. Art Gallery, 1987. Recipient Alumnae Achievement award, Simmons Coll., 1986, The Hadassah Internat. Rsch. Inst. on Jewish Women at Brandeis U. Rsch. award, 2001—02, Rsch. award, Schlesinger Libr. Harvard U., 2005—; grantee, Rockefeller Found., 1993, Smithsonian Inst., 1993; rsch. grantee, NEH, 1984, 1989, 1992, 1993—95, Am. Coun. Learned Socs., 1988, fellowship for univ. profs., NEH, 1998—99. Mem.: Coll. Art Assn., Pen Freedom to Write, Internat. Assn. Art Critics. Address: CUNY Baruch Coll B7-235 1 Bernard Baruch Way New York NY 10010-5518 Office Phone: 646-312-4062.

LEVIN, GEOFFREY ARTHUR, botanist; b. Los Alamos, N.Mex., Dec. 7, 1955; s. Jules Samuel and Jane Walden (Settle) L.; children: Tobias, Madeline; m. Lori E. Davis, 2001. BA, Pomona Coll., 1977; MS, U. Calif., Davis, 1980, PhD, 1984. Asst. prof. Ripon (Wis.) Coll., 1982-84; curator, chmn. botany dept. San Diego Natural History Mus., 1984-93; lectr. U. San Diego, 1984-90; asst. profl. scientist Ill. Natural History Survey, Champaign, 1994-96, assoc. profl. scientist to profl. scientist, dir. Ctr. for Biodiversity, 1996—. Adj. asst. prof. dept. plant biology U. Ill., 1995—; rsch. assoc. Mo. Bot. Garden, 1994—. Contbr. articles to jours. in field. Bd. dirs. Fond du Lac Audubon Soc., 1983-84, San Diego Audubon Soc., 1986-87; pres. Summit Unitarian Universalist Fellowship, El Cajon, Calif., 1989-91; treas. Unitarian Universalist Ch., Urbana, Ill., 1996-98, moderator, 1998-2000. Recipient Jesse M. Greenman award. Mo. Bot. Garden, 1987; NSF grad. fellow, 1977-81. Mem. Am. Inst. Biol. Scis., Am. Soc. Plant Taxonomists, Bot. Soc. Am., Soc. Systematic Biologists, Calif. Bot. Soc. (bd. editors 1992-95), Phi Beta Kappa, Sigma Xi. Democrat. Office: Ill Natural History Survey Ctr for Biodiversity 607 E Peabody Dr Champaign IL 61820-6970 Business E-Mail: glevin@inhs.uiuc.edu.

LEVIN, GEORGE MARTIN, association and organization administrator, aeronautical engineer; b. Atlantic City, Oct. 21, 1940; m. Patricia Anne Sever; children: Courtney Anne Avnaim, Suzanne Michelle Griffin. BS, U. of MD, 1962, MS, 1967; diploma, Inst. Von Karman de Dynamique Des Fluides. Dir. Aero. and Space Engring. Bd. Nat. Acad. Scis., Washington, 1997—; engr. Goddard Space Flight Ctr. NASA, 1962—71, mgr. devel. Hubble Space Telescope, 1972—81, mgr. devel.secondary payloads Space Shuttle and Delta II, 1981—97, program mgr. orbital debris, 1990—97. Mem.: Internat. Acad. of Astronautics. Office: Nat Academies 500 5th St NW Washington DC 20001 Office Phone: 202-334-2858. Business E-Mail: glevin@nas.edu.

LEVIN, GERALD M., former media and entertainment company executive; b. Phila., May 6, 1939; m. Barbara J. Riley. BA, Haverford Coll., 1960; LLB, U. Pa., 1963; LLD (hon.), Tex. Coll., 1985; LLD (hon.), Middlebury Coll., 1994; LHD (hon.), U. Denver, 1995. Assoc. Simpson, Thacher & Bartlett, N.Y.C., 1963-67; gen. mgr., chief operating officer Devel. and Resources Corp., N.Y.C., 1967-71; rep. Internat. Basic Economy Corp., Tehran, Iran, 1971-72; v.p. programming Home Box Office, N.Y.C., 1972-73, pres., chief exec. officer, 1973-76, chmn., chief exec. officer, 1976-79; group v.p. video Time Inc., N.Y.C., 1979-84, exec. v.p., 1984-88, vice chmn., dir., 1988-90, Time Warner Inc., N.Y.C., 1990—93, chief oper. officer, 1991-92, pres., co-chief exec. officer to chmn. and CEO, 1992—2000; CEO, chmn. AOL Time Warner, Inc., N.Y.C., 2000—02. Trustee emeritus Hampshire Coll.; bd. dirs. N.Y. Stock Exch., Inc. Bd. dirs., treas. N.Y. Philharm., Ctr. for Comm., A Living Meml. to the Holocaust—Mus. of Jewish Heritage. Mem.: The Trilateral Commn., Coun. on Fgn. Rels., Nat. Cable TV Ctr. and Mus., The Aspen Inst., N.Y. City Partnership, Phi Beta Kappa.

LEVIN, GILBERT VICTOR, health facility administrator; b. Balt., Apr. 23, 1924; s. Henry I. and Lillian R. (Richman) L.; m. Karen Bloomquist, Oct. 25, 1953; children: Ron L., Henry L., Carol Y. BE, Johns Hopkins U., 1947, MS, 1948, PhD, 1963. Registered profl. engr., D.C., Md. With Md. State Dept. Health, 1948-50, Calif. Dept. Health, 1950-51, D.C. Dept. Pub. Health, 1951-55; v.p. Resources Research, Inc., Washington, 1955-63; dir. life systems div. Hazleton Labs., Inc., Reston, Va., 1963-67; CEO, chmn. bd. Spherix Inc. (formerly Biospherics, Inc.), Beltsville, Md., 1967—2003, exec. officer for sci., chmn. bd., 2003—. Contbr. 120 articles to profl. jours.; mem. editorial bd. BioScience, 1960-63; over 100 patents in field. Trustee John Hopkins U., 1982-85. Merchant Marine USCG, 1944-46. Recipient Pub. Svc. medal NASA, 1977; Whiting medal Johns Hopkins U., 1987, Disting. Alumnus award, 1995. Fellow Am. Pub. Health Assn.; mem. ASCE, AAAS (Newcomb Cleveland prize 1977), Am. Water Works Assn., Water Pollution Control Fedn., Am. Soc. Microbiology, N.Y. Acad. Scis. Clubs: Cosmos. Achievements include being NASA experimenter Mariner 9 mission, 1971; Viking Mission Labeled Release Life Detection experiment producing evidence of extant microbial life in Martian soil, 1976; mem. team Mars oxidant expt. for Russian Mars lander, 1996; inventor PhoStrip process for wastewater nutrient removal, microbial radiorespirometry, nonfattening sweeteners, use of D-tagatose as antihyperglycemic agent and in diabetes treatment; applications of chiral chemistry to foods and environmental products; application of firefly bioluminescent assay for adenosine triphosphate to biomass determination and to microbial enumeration. Office: BioSphorix Divsn Spherix Inc 304A Harry S Truman Pkwy Annapolis MD 21401 Business E-Mail: glevin@spherix.com. *Man's ability to accumulate information through learning and to pass it on to his descendents frees his generations from endless repetition. He may hope to understand the universe and his place in it.*

LEVIN, GOLAN, artist, composer, engineer; BS in Art and Design, MIT, 1994, MS in Media Arts and Scis., 2000. Mem. rsch. staff Interval Rsch. Corp., 1994—98; undergraduate rsch. asst. MIT Media Lab., 1990—94, rsch. asst., 1998—2000; cons. Design Machine, NY, 2000—02; adj. prof. Columbia U., 2000; vis. artist and lectr. Cooper Union Sch. Art, 2001—02; adj. faculty Parsons Sch. Design, 2001—03; asst. prof., electronic time-based media, dept. art, sch. art Carnegie Mellon U., 2004—. Invited lectr. in field; interface design cons. Boston Digital Corp., Woburn, Mass., 1993—94; cons. Design Machine, NYC, 2000—02. Composer numerous interactive and multimedia compositions, performances, recordings and other works.; artist with Paul Debevec Rouen Revisited, 1996, artist with Gregory Shakar and Scott Gibbons Scribble, 2000, artist with Gregory Shakar, Scott Gibbons, Yasmin Sohrawardy Dialtones: A Telesymphony, 2001—02, artist with Jonathan Feinberg and Cassidy Curtis Alphabet Synthesis Machine, 2001, artist with Jonathan Feinberg, S. Wynecoop, M. Wattenberg The Secret Lives of Numbers, 2002, artist with Zachary Lieberman RE:MARK, 2002, The Hidden Worlds of Noise and Voice, 2002, The Manual Input Sessions, 2004, artist with Zachary Lieberman, Jooap Blonk, Joan La Barbara Messa di Voce, 2003; exhibitions include Mus. of Innovation, San Jose, Calif., 1999, NY Digital Salon Exhbn., NYC, 2000, MoMA Contemporary Art Ctr., 2001, Am. Mus. of the Moving Image, 2002, Microwave Internat. Media Art Festival, Hong Kong, 2003, Whitney Biennial, Whitney Mus. Am. Art, 2004, Neuberger Mus. of Art at SUNY, Purchase, NY, 2005, and several others, Represented in permanent collections Am. Mus. of the Moving Image, Rouen Revisited, NYC, Ars Electronica Mus. of the Future, Linz: AVES, Australian Ctr. for the Moving Image, Sydney:AVES, Computer Fine Arts Collections: Blobby (Tiles), Zeum.org, San Francisco: Meshy, Whitney Mus. of Am. Arts:Axis, Ars Electronica Mus. of the Future, Linz: Hidden Worlds, Am. Mus. of the Moving Images, Floccus, NYC. Named New Artist Under 30, Print Mag., 2002; named one of Top 100 Young Innovators Under 35, MIT Tech. Review, 2004; recipient Bronze Medal, ID Mag. Interaction Design Award, 2002, Award Distinction, Net Art, Prix Ars Electronica, 2004. Achievements include co-holder three US patents; winner ASCI Digital2000 Competition, 2000; winner Comm. Arts Interactive Design Annual 6, 2000; finalist, Adobe Pub. Art Commn. Competition, 2003. Office: Carnegie Mellon U Sch Art CFA 300 5000 Forbes Ave Pittsburgh PA 15213-3890 Office Phone: 917-520-7456. Office Fax: 412-268-7817. Business E-Mail: golan@flong.com.*

LEVIN, HENRY MORDECHAI, economist, educator; b. N.Y.C., Dec. 7, 1938. B.S. cum laude, NYU, 1960; M.A., Rutgers U., 1962, Ph.D., 1966. assoc. research scientist, Grad. Sch. Pub. Adminstrn., NYU, 1965-66; research assoc. social econs. Econ. Studies div. Brookings Inst., Washington, 1966-68; asst. prof. edn. and econs. Stanford U., Calif., 1968-69, assoc. prof. econs., 1969-75, prof. econs. and edn., 1975—, David Jacks Prof. of Higher Edn. and Econs., 1992—, William Heard Kilpatrick prof. econ. and edn., Tchrs. Coll., Columbia U.; fellow Ctr. for Advanced Studies in Behavioral Scis., 1976-77, dir. Inst. Research on Ednl. Fin. and Governance, 1978-84; Fulbright prof. U. Barcelona, 1989; vis. scholar Russell Sage Found., 1996-97. Office: Tchrs Coll Columbia U Box 181 525 W 120th St New York NY 10022 E-mail: hl361@columbia.edu.

LEVIN, HERBERT, retired diplomat, foundation administrator; b. NYC, Jan. 14, 1931; s. Sol and Kate (Gottlieb) L.; m. Cornelia Rose, Feb. 21, 1954; children: Martha, Jonathan C. BA, Harvard U., 1952; MA, Fletcher Sch. Law Diplomacy, 1956. Internat. economist Dept. of State, 1956-58, staff mem. policy planning coun., 1983-85, dep. dir. Japanese affairs, 1971-74, spl. asst. Office of Sr. Rep. for Strategic Tech. Policy, 1988-90, exec. asst. to amb.-at-large and spl. asst. to sec. of state for non-proliferation and nuc. energy affairs, 1990-91; Chinese lang. and area tng. Taichung, Taiwan, 1959-61; econ. officer Am. Consulate Gen., Hong Kong, 1961-64; polit. officer Am. Embassy, Taipei, 1964-67, Tokyo, 1967-70, dep. chief mission Dar-es-Salaam, 1975-77, Colombo, 1977-79, New Delhi, 1979-81; asst. nat. intelligence officer East Asia East and South Asia Nat. Intelligence Coun., 1981-83; staff mem. East Asia NSC, 1970-71; staff dir. subcom. Asian and Pacific Affairs Ho. of Reps., 1985; diplomat-in-residence, dir. studies Asia Found., San Francisco, 1986-88; spl. advisor to UN under-sec. gen. Ji Chaozhu NYC, 1991-94; exec. dir. Am.-China Soc., NYC, 1994-99. Adviser U.S. Del. to 14th Gen. Assembly of UN, 1985. With U.S. Army, 1953-55, Far East Command; U.S. Fgn. Svc. 1956-91. Fellow Ctr. Internat. Affairs, Harvard U., 1974-75. Fellow: Atlantic Coun. (assoc. sr. mem.), Am.-China Forum; mem.: UN Assn. NY, Fairbank Ctr. East Asian Rsch. Harvard U. (assoc. in rsch.), Assn. Asian Studies (life), Am. Fgn. Svc. Assn. (life), Diplomatic & Consular Officers Ret. (life), Coun. Fgn. Rels., Asia Soc., Cosmos Club, Harvard Club NY, Lake Mansfield Trout Club (life), Hong Kong Cricket Club (life), Sri Lanka Hill Club (life), Dar-es-Salaam Yacht Club (life). Home: 650 Park Ave Apt 4A New York NY 10021-6115 Office Phone: 212-861-8758.

LEVIN, IRA, writer, playwright; b. NYC, Aug. 27, 1929; s. Charles and Beatrice (Schlansky) L.; m. Gabrielle Aronsohn, Aug. 20, 1960 (div. 1968); children: Adam, Jared, Nicholas; m. Phyllis Finkel, Aug. 26, 1979 (div. 1982). Student, Drake U., Des Moines, 1946-48; AB, N.Y. U., 1950. Freelance writer, 1950—; author: A Kiss Before Dying, 1953, Rosemary's Baby, 1967, This Perfect Day, 1970, The Stepford Wives, 1972, The Boys from Brazil, 1976, Sliver, 1991, Son of Rosemary, 1997; playwright: No Time for Sergeants, 1955, Interlock, 1958, Critic's Choice, 1962, General Seeger, 1962, Drat! the Cat, 1965, Dr. Cook's Garden, 1967, Veronica's Room, 1973, Deathtrap, 1978, Break a Leg, 1979, Cantorial, 1989, Sliver, 1991, Son of Rosemary: The Sequel to Rosemary's Baby, 1997. Served with U.S. Army, 1953-55. Recipient Edgar Allan Poe award, 1953, 80, Bram Stoker award, 1997, Grand Master award, Mystery Writers of Am., 2003. Mem. Dramatists Guild (council mem. 1980—). Office: c/o Harold Ober Assocs 425 Madison Ave New York NY 10017-1110

LEVIN, JACK, physician, educator, biomedical investigator; b. Newark, Oct. 11, 1932; s. Joseph and Anna (Greengold) L.; m. Francine Corthesy, Apr. 13, 1975. BA magna cum laude, Yale U., 1953, MD cum laude, 1957. Diplomate: Am. Bd. Internal Medicine. Intern in medicine Grace-New Haven Hosp., 1957-58, asst. resident in medicine, 1960-62; chief resident in medicine Yale-New Haven Med. Ctr., 1964-65; clin. assoc. Nat. Cancer Inst., Bethesda, Md., 1958-60; fellow in hematology Johns Hopkins U. Sch. Medicine and Hosp., Balt., 1962-64, mem. faculty, 1965-82, prof. medicine, 1978-82; prof. lab. medicine, prof. medicine U. Calif. Sch. Medicine, San Francisco, 1982—; dir. hematology lab. and blood bank San Francisco VA

Med. Ctr., Calif., 1982-93, dir. flow cytometry facility, 1987-90; dir. Anticoagulation Clinic, San Francisco VA Med. Ctr., San Francisco, 1996—. Cons. in field. Author: (with P.D. Zieve) Disorders of Hemostasis, 1976; editor: (with E. Cohen and F.B. Bang) Biomedical Applications of the Horseshoe Crab (Limulidae), 1979, (with S.W. Watson and T.J. Novitsky) Endotoxins and Their Detection with the Limulus Amebocyte Lysate Test, 1982, Detection of Bacterial Endotoxins with The Limulus Amebocyte Lysate Test, 1987, (with others) Bacterial Endotoxins. Structure, Biomedical Significance, and Detection with the Limulus Amebocyte Lysate Test, 1985, Megakaryocyte Develop. and Function, 1986, Bacterial Endotoxins. Pathophysiological Effects, Clinical Significance, and Pharmacological Control, 1988, Molecular Biology and Differentiation of Megakaryocytes, 1990, Bacterial Endotoxins: Cytokine Mediators and New Therapies for Sepsis, 1991, Bacterial Endotoxin: Recognition and Effector Mechanisms, 1993, Bacterial Endotoxins: Basic Sci. to Anti-Sepsis Strategies, 1994, Bacterial Endotoxins: Lipopolysaccharides from Genes to Therapy, 1995; mem. editorial bd. Blood, Jour. Endotoxin Rsch.; contbr. numerous articles to profl. jour; editor-in-chief, Jour. Endotoxin Rsch., 1998-2004; developer (with F.B. Bang) Limulus test for bacterial endotoxins. Mem. Yale Alumni Sch. Com. for Md., 1967-82, for San Francisco, 1986-1997; mem. sci. adv. bd. Nat. Aquarium, Balt., 1978-82; mem. corp. Marine Biol. Lab., 1965—; trustee Marine Biol. Lab., 1988-93; mem. panel ind. assessors for rsch. project grants awards Nat. Health and Med. Rsch. Coun. Australia, 1982—. Served with USPHS, 1958-60. Markle scholar, 1968-73; recipient USPHS Rsch. Career Devel. award, 1970-75; Royal Soc. Medicine fellow Oxford (Eng.) U., 1972; Josiah Macy Jr. Found. faculty scholar, 1978-79; fellow, Found. for Med. Rsch., Paris, France, 1998; Fonds Nat. de la Rechorche Scientifique (FNRS) fellowship, Liege (Belg.), 2003; Frederik B. Bang award for rsch. in bacterial endotoxins, 1986. Fellow ACP; mem. Am. Soc. Hematology, Am. Soc. Clin. Investigation, Internat. Soc. Hematology, Internat. Soc. Explt. Hematology, Am. Soc. Investigative Pathology, Am. Fedn. Clin. Rsch., Soc. Exptl. Biology and Medicine, Internat. Endotoxin Soc., So. Soc. Clin. Investigation, Western Assn. Physicians, Soc. Invertebrate Pathology, Soc. Analytical Cytology, Cell Kinetics Soc., Internat. Soc. Artificial Cells, Blood Substitutes and Immobilization Biotech., Calif. Acad. Medicine, Phi Beta Kappa, Sigma Xi. Clubs: 14 W Hamilton St, Tudor and Stuart; Yale (San Francisco). Office Phone: 415-750-6913. Business E-Mail: levinj@medicine.ucsf.edu.

LEVIN, JACK S., lawyer; b. Chgo., May 1, 1936; s. Frank J. and Judy G. (Skerball) L.; m. Sandra Sternberg, Aug. 24, 1958; children: Lisa, Laura, Leslie, Linda. BS summa cum laude, Northwestern U., 1958; LL.B. summa cum laude, Harvard U., 1961. Bar: Ill. 1961; C.P.A. (gold medalist), Ill., 1958. Law clk. to chief judge U.S. Ct. of Appeals 2d Circuit, N.Y.C., 1961-62; asst. for tax matters to Solicitor Gen. of U.S., Washington, 1965-67; assoc. law firm Kirkland & Ellis, Chgo., 1962-65, ptnr., 1967—. Frequent lectr. legal aspects of pvt. equity and venture capital transactions, mergers, acquistions, buyouts, workouts, fed. income tax matters; vis. com. Harvard Law Sch., 1987-93, lectr., 1997—; lectr. Law Sch. U. Chgo., 1988—. Author book on structuring venture capital, pvt. equity and entrepreneurial transactions; co-author multi-volume treatise on mergers, acquisitions and buyouts; case editor Harvard Law Rev., 1959-61; contbr. numerous articles to legal jours. and chpts. to law books. Parliamentarian Winnetka (Ill.) Town Meetings, 1974-83, 89, 93-96; chmn. nat. fundraising drives Harvard Law Sch., 1985-86, 90-91, 95-96, 2001, 03-05, chmn. lawyer's divsn. Jewish United Fund Chgo., 1993-95. Recipient Learned Hand award, Am. Jewish Com., 2000, Fellows award, Ill. Venture Capital Assn., 2002. Mem. ABA (chmn. subcom. 1968-79), Fed. Bar Assn., Chgo. Bar Assn. (tax sect. exec. com. 1985—2000), Am. Jewish Com., Midwest (bd. dirs., exec. com. 2003-, nat. bd. govs. 2005-), Am. Coll. Tax Consel, Mid-Am. Club (bd. dirs. 1985-88), Birchwood Club (Highland Park, Ill.) (pres. 1980-82). Home: 985 Sheridan Rd Winnetka IL 60093-1558 Office: Kirkland & Ellis 200 E Randolph St 57th Fl Chicago IL 60601-6608 Office Phone: 312-861-2004. Business E-Mail: jlevin@kirkland.com.

LEVIN, JANNA, physicist, educator; BS in Astronomy and Physics, Barnard Coll., 1988; PhD in Theoretical Physics, MIT, 1993. Postdoctoral fellow Canadian Inst. for Theoretical Astrophysics, 1993—95; postdoctoral fellow, Ctr. for Particle-Astrophysics U. Calif Berkeley, 1995—98; advanced fellow, Dept. of Applied Mathematics and Theoretical Physics (DAMTP) Cambridge U., 1999—2003; Nat. Endowment for Sci. Technol. and Arts (NESTA) fellow, Astophysics Dept. Oxford U., 2003; asst. prof. Barnard Coll., 2004—. NESTA Dream Time Fellow, Scientist-in-Residence Ruskin School of Drawing and Fine Art, Oxford, 2003. Author: How the Universe Got Its Spots: Diary of a Finite Time in a Finite Space, 2002. Recipient Kilby award, 2003. Achievements include first official scientist in residence at the Ruskin School of Drawing and Fine Art at Oxford U. Office: Barnard Altschul 505 Dept Physics & Astronomy 3009 Broadway New York NY 10027

LEVIN, JONATHAN A., language educator; b. St. Louis, Nov. 10, 1960; s. Milton and Rona Levin; m. Erica Wilens, Oct. 23, 2004. AB, U. Mich., 1983; MA, UCLA, 1985; PhD, Rutgers U., 1992. From asst. prof. to assoc. prof. Columbia U., NYC, 1991—2001; assoc. prof. Fordham U., Bronx, NY, 2001—, chmn. English dept., 2004—. Author: The Poetics of Transition, 1997 (Choice Outstanding Title award); editor: Walt Whitman, 1997, Walden and Civil Disobedience, 2003; mem. editl. bd.: Ravitan: A Quarterly Rev., 1991—2003. Fellow, NEH, 1997—98. Mem.: MLA, Am. Studies Assn., Assn. for the Study of Lit. and Environ. Avocations: guitar, squash, tennis.

LEVIN, JOSHUA ZEV, computer scientist, consultant, transportation engineer; b. Cambridge, Mass., Feb. 5, 1949; s. Betty Louise Zimmermann; m. Susan Evelyn Goldsmith, 1982 (div. 2003); children: Barry Naphtali, David Reuven. PhD, Rensselaer Poly. Inst., 1980; MSEE, NYU, 1974; BA, CUNY, Flushing, 1971. Chief computer scientist Epoch Engring., Lower Gwynedd, Pa., 1988—94; cons. in field. Mem. MetaNexus Inst., Phila., 2002—03, Beth Sholom Congregation, Elkins Park, Pa., 2000—03. Mem.: IEEE, Soc. Indsl. Applied Math., Assn. Computing Machinery, Phi Beta Kappa. Democrat. Jewish. Achievements include development of software pricing engine; theatre anti-submarine warfare war gaming program; algorithm for tracing intersection curves of quadric surfaces; design of a maglev vehicle. Mailing: 106 Mansfield Blvd S Cherry Hill NJ 08034-3613 Office Phone: 866-538-4227. Personal E-mail: josh-levin@ieee.org.

LEVIN, KENNETH MITCHELL, economist, accountant; BA, UCLA, 1985; MA, U. Mass-Amherst, 1996; PhD, U. Mass.-Amherst, 2004. CPA 1989. Sr. acct. Broman & Greig, CPAs, Santa Monica, Calif., 1987—89; vis. lectr. Drew U., Madison, N.J., 2001—03. Chair Conf. Outreach Assn. Economic and Social Analysis, South Bend, Ind., 1998—2001. Author: (doctoral dissertation) Enterprise Hybrids and Alternative Growth Dynamics (Polit. Economy Rsch. Inst. fellowship, 1999). Mem.: Assn. Economic and Social Analysis.

LEVIN, KIM, writer, curator; b. NY, NY, June 29, 1945; d. Aaron Arthur and Jean Lien Levin; m. John A Pateman (div. 1987). AB, Vassar Coll.; MA, Columbia U.; postgrad., NYU Inst. Fine Arts. Contbr. The Village Voice, 1983—. Adv. to Kwang Ju Biennial, Republic of Korea, 1995; guest curator at mus. exhibitions Korea, Japan, Poland, Norway, Sweden, Germany, U.S., 1988—; curator of the nordic biennial Borealis 8, Arken Mus. of Modern Art, 1996—97; commnr. Busan Biennale, 2002. Author: (book) Beyond Modernism, 1989; contbr. articles. Recipient Artworld award for Disting. Newspaper Criticism, 1986; fellow, U. S.C. Annenberg/Getty Arts Journalism Program, 2004; SECA fellowship for criticism, San Francisco Mus. of Modern Art, 1993. Mem.: Internat. Assn. of Art Critics (U.S. sect. pres. 1990—92, internat. pres. 1996—2002, pres. emerita). Office: The Village Voice 36 Cooper Square New York NY 10003 Office Phone: 212-475-3333. Office Fax: 212-475-8944.

LEVIN, LAWRENCE DANIEL, lawyer; b. Chgo., May 10, 1959; s. Sandra Morrison, June 22, 1986; children: Phillip David, Laura Michelle. BS in Accountancy, U. Ill., 1981, JD, 1985. Bar: Ill. 1985, U.S. Dist. Ct. (no. dist.) Ill. 1985. Ptnr. Katten Muchin Rosenman LLP, Chgo., 1985—. Mem. ABA, Chgo. Bar Assn. (chmn. securities law com. 1996-97). Office: Katten Muchin Rosenman LLP 525 W Monroe St Ste 1900 Chicago IL 60661-3693

LEVIN, LAWRENCE SCOTT, plastic surgeon; b. Phila., Apr. 1, 1955; MD, Temple U., Phila., 1982. Resident, gen. surgery Duke U. Med. Ctr., 1982—84, resident, orthopedic surgery, 1984—88, resident, plastic and reconstructive surgery, 1984—91, hand surgery fellow, 1989, chief, divsn. of plastic and reconstructive surgery, 1991—, assoc. prof., orthopedics and plastic surgery, 1991—; hand and microsurgery fellow Christine Kleinert Inst., Louisville, 1988. Office: Duke Univ Med Ctr 134 Baker House Durham NC 27710-0001

LEVIN, MARK REED, legal foundation administrator, lawyer; b. Phila., Sept. 21, 1957; s. Jack Eugene and Norma (Rubin) Levin; m. Kendall Edwards, Aug. 24, 1985. BA magna cum laude, Temple U., 1977, JD, 1980. Asst. counsel Tex. Instruments, Inc., Dallas, 1980-81; adminstrv. asst. Action Agy., Washington, 1981-82; dep. asst. sec. US Dept. Edn., Washington, 1982-84; assoc. dir. for Presdl. personnel The White House, Washington, 1984-85; assoc. dep. atty. gen. US Dept. Justice, Washington; dir. legal policy Landmark Legal Found., Leesburg, Va., pres. Legal analyst MSNBC. Author: Men in Black: How the Supreme Court is Destroying America, 2005. Mem. Cheltenham Twp. Sch. Bd., Pa., 1977-80 Mem.: Pa. Bar Assn., Phi Beta Kappa. Republican. Jewish. Office: Landmark Legal Found 19415 Deerfield Ave Ste 312 Leesburg VA 20176 Office Phone: 703-554-6100. Office Fax: 703-554-6119.

LEVIN, MARTIN P., publishing executive, lawyer; b. Phila., Dec. 20, 1918; s. Harry and Sarah (Chaimovitz) L.; m. Marcia Obrasky, Apr. 2, 1939; children: Jeremy, Wendy, Hugh Lauter. BS, Temple U., postgrad. (personnel Council fellow), 1950; JD, N.Y. Law Sch., 1983. Adminstrv. officer U.S. War Dept., 1940-44, VA, 1945-50; sr. v.p. Grosset & Dunlap, Inc., N.Y.C., 1950-66; pres. book pub. div. Times Mirror Co., N.Y.C., 1966-83; cons. Times Mirror; counsel Cowan, Liebowitz and Latman, PC, 1984—; with Van Tulleken Co., NYC, 2003—04. Adj. prof. N.Y. Law Sch., 1986—; resident fellow pub. course Stanford U., 1977—; cons. Ford Found., India, 1957-58; mem. Pres.'s Working Com. on Books and Publs. Abroad; mem. exec. com. Ctr. for the Book, Libr. of Congress; trustee Harvard U. Press; mem. Assn. Am. Pubs. delegation to USSR, 1976, to People Republic of China, 1979; former chmn. Franklin Book Programs. Author: Be Your Own Literary Agent, ed edit., 2002; contbr. articles to profl. jours. Trustee William Alanson White Inst.; chmn. Assn. Am. Book Pubs., 1982. With AUS, 1944-45. Recipient Pub. of Yr. award ADL, 1980, Friend of Jerusalem award, 1985, Curtis Benjamin award for Lifetime Achievement in Publ., 1999, Erich Fromm award for disting. svc. William Alanson White Inst., 2003. Mem. Assn. Am. Pubs. (chmn., dir. exec. com.), Pubs. Lunch Club (past pres.), Friars Club, Dutch Treat Club. Home: 221 Kirby Ln Rye NY 10580-4321 also: 9150 Blind Pass Rd Sarasota FL 34242-2978 Office: Cowan Liebowitz and Latman PC 1133 Avenue of the Americas New York NY 10036 Office Phone: 212-790-9219. E-mail: mlevin7276@aol.com, mpl@cll.com.

LEVIN, MARVIN EDGAR, physician; b. Terre Haute, Ind., Aug. 11, 1924; s. Benjamin A. and Bertha Levin; m. Barbara Yvonne Symes; 3 children. BA, Washington U., St. Louis, 1947, MD, 1951. Diplomate Am. Bd. Internal Medicine. Intern Barnes Hosp., St. Louis, 1951-52, asst. resident in internal medicine, 1952-53; Nat. Polio Found. fellow in metabolism and endocrinology Sch. Medicine, Washington U., St. Louis, 1953-55; adj. prof. medicine Washington U. Sch. Medicine, St. Louis, 1980—98. Vis. prof. endocrinology and diabetes People's Republic of China, 1982, Jakarta, Indonesia, Cairo, 92, Taipei, 94, Malvern, England, 96; med. dir. Harry and Flora D. Freund Meml. Found.; adj. prof. medicine Endocrine, Diabetes and Metabolism Clinic Washington U., St. Louis, 2000—. Contbr.: Levin and O'Neal's The Diabetic Foot, 6th edit., 2001; contbr. articles to profl. jours., book chpts. Recipient Disting. Alumni award, Washington U., 1989, Arts and Scis. Disting. award, 1998. Fellow ACP, Soc. Vascular Medicine and Biology; mem. AMA, Am. Diabetes Assn. (nat. bd. dirs. 1984-86, chmn. publ. com. 1986-87, bd. dirs. Mo. chpt. 1987-93, editor in chief Clin. Diabetes 1988-93, co-editor Diabetes Spectrum 1988-93, Outstanding Clinician award 1979, Outstanding Physician Educator award 1991), Am. Dietetic Assn. (hon., Marvin E. Levin, MD Scholarship Program for rsch. in diabetic lower extremity disease named in his honor), St. Louis Clin. Diabetes Assn. (pres. 1965-66), Am. Thyroid Assn., Endocrine Soc., St. Louis Soc. Internal Medicine, St. Louis Internist Club (pres. 1972), Sigma Xi, Alpha Omega Alpha. Avocations: golf, collecting belle epoque french prints. Office: 732 Fairfield Lake Dr Town And Country MO 63017-5928 Office Phone: 314-469-6918. Personal E-mail: blevin0001@aol.com.

LEVIN, MARVIN EUGENE, lawyer; b. Antigo, Wis., June 20, 1924; s. Jacob and Lillian (Goldberg) L.; m. Ruth Ganzfried, June 10, 1948; children: Randal Mark, Gregary. BS, U. So. Calif., 1948, JD, 1951. Bar: Calif. 1952. Pvt. practice, L.A., Santa Monica, Calif., 1952-68; sr. ptnr. Levin & Freedman, Santa Monica, 1968-97, of counsel, 1997—2003; arbitrator and mediator Santa Monica, Calif., 2004—. Lectr. in field. Bd. dirs., founding mem. NCCJ, Santa Monica, 1959—, chmn., 1965, So. Calif. regional bd., 1984-92; regional bd. Anti-Defamation League, 1958—, exec. com., 1960-81, 87-2003; pres. Santa Monica Family YMCA, 1985-86, bd. dirs., 1987—, chmn. endowment com., 1990-2004; bd. dirs. U. Synagogue, West L.A., Calif., 1970-74. Capt. USAAF, 1943-46. Decorated Air medal with oak leaf cluster; recipient Brotherhood award Santa Monica Bay Area chpt. NCCJ, 1968. Fellow Am. Coll. Trust and Estate Counsel; mem. ABA (sect. dispute resolution real property, probate and trust law), State Bar Calif. Assn. (sect. real property, probate, trust law), L.A. County Bar Assn., Santa Monica Bay Dist. Bar Assn. (trustee 1971-74, pres. 1973-74, chmn. sect. real property law 1982-84), Am. Arbitration Assn. (panel of arbitrators 1968-90), Rotary Internat. Found. (chmn. world cmty. svc. Santa Monica chpt. 1985-98, chmn, 2001—). Office: 2530 Wilshire Blvd Ste 200 Santa Monica CA 90403 Office Phone: 310-828-6688. Business E-Mail: mandrlevin@verizon.net.

LEVIN, MICHAEL JOSEPH, lawyer; b. Detroit, Feb. 1, 1943; s. Bayre and Lydia Ruth (Kahn) L.; m. Adah Hanson, Aug. 3, 1974; children: Andrew, Stephen. BA, Johns Hopkins U., 1964; JD, U. Mich., 1967. Bar: Mich. 1968, N.Y. 1973. Assoc. Milbank, Tweed, Hadley & McCloy, N.Y.C., 1971-86; ptnr. Boyle, Vogeler & Haimes, N.Y.C., 1986-93, Sutherland, Asbill & Brennan, N.Y.C. and Washington D.C., 1993-97; of counsel Menaker & Herrmann LLP, N.Y.C., 1997-2000, Barger & Wolen LLP, N.Y.C., 2000—. Served to lt. col. USMCR, 1963-90. Mem. Mich. Bar Assn., N.Y. State Bar Assn., Assn. of Bar of City of N.Y. Office: Barger & Wolen LLP 10 East 40th St New York NY 10016 Office Phone: 212-557-2800.

LEVIN, MICHAEL STUART, steel company executive; b. N.Y.C., Aug. 2, 1950; s. Morton Sheldon and Ruth Jean (Leff) Levin; m. Laurence Diane Daisy deBardon deSegonzac, Dec. 13, 1984; children: Alex-Rene-Philippe, Max-André Simon, Sebastien Pierre. BA (hon.), U. Wis., 1972; MBA, Harvard U., 1974. Asst. trader Titan Indsl. Corp., N.Y.C., 1974—75, trader, 1975—76, export mgr., 1976—78, v.p., 1978—80, sr. v.p., 1980—82, pres., 1982—98, chmn., 1988—; CEO, chmn., founder e-STEEL, N.Y.C., 1999—. Bd. dirs. Mus. Modern Art, N.Y.C. Mem.: Coun. of Fgn. Rels., Explorers Club, Mashomack Fish and Game Preserve, River Club, Millbrook Golf and Tennis Club, N.Y. Yacht Club. Avocations: polo, sailing, skiing, shooting. E-mail: mlevin@titansteel.com.

LEVIN, MIKE DOUGLAS, performing arts educator; b. Long Beach, Calif., Feb. 9, 1971; s. Lawrence Alan and Karen Bennett Levin; m. Janet Lynn Taylor, July 25, 1973; children: Aria Quinn, Iris Mikaela. BS, Edinboro U. of Pa. Teaching Ariz., 1997. Lang./theatre arts instr. Flagstaff Arts and Leadership Acad., Flagstaff, Ariz., 1997—. Co. mem. Canyon Moon Theatre. Mem.: Nat. Coun. of the Teachers of English (assoc.). Republican. Christian. Avocations: guitar, writing. Home: PO Box 1769 Flagstaff AZ 86002 Office: Flagstaff Arts and Leadership Academy 3100 North Fort Valley Rd #41 Flagstaff AZ 86001 Personal E-mail: mlevin@apscc.org.

LEVIN, MORTON D(AVID), artist, printmaker, educator; b. N.Y.C., Oct. 7, 1923; s. Louis and Martha (Berusch) L. BS in Art Edn, CCNY, 1948; student in painting, Andre LHote, Paris, 1950; in sculpture, Ossip Zadkine, 1950; etching and engraving, Federico Castellon, N.Y.C., 1948, Stanley W. Hayter, Paris, 1951; student in lithography, Pratt Graphic Art Center, N.Y.C., 1966. Founder, dir., instr. printmaking, painting Morton Levin Graphics Workshop, San Francisco, 1972-91. One-man shows include Galerie Breteau, Paris, 1952, Winston Gallery, San Francisco, 1972, 80, 83, 85-97, 98-2003, 2005; exhibited in group shows at Seattle Art Mus., 1946-49, Libr. of Congress, Washington, 1946, 49, Pa. Acad. Fine Arts, 1948, Mus. Modern Art, Paris, 1951, Pallazzo del Academia, Genoa, Italy, 1951; represented in permanent collections at N.Y. Pub. Libr., Libr. of Congress, History of Medicine Divsn. Nat. Libr. Medicine; work featured in Jour. Erotic Arts, Yellow Silk #34, 1990. Served with inf. U.S. Army, 1943-45. Recipient Bryan Meml. prize Villager Travel Exhbn., N.Y.C., 1964, prize Washington Sq. Art Exhbn., 1964 Office Phone: 415-392-8824. Personal E-mail: mlevin@mortonlevin.com. *My goal has been to define our world and the primal forces of desire, love, procreation, death, and rebirth. To this end, I have created a universe in my art inhabited by the natural and fantastic. Humans, birds, and beasts, male and female, interact and strive on an elemental level. In a romantic expressionistic style, I have attempted to illuminate the human condition.*

LEVIN, MURRAY NEWMAN, retired surgeon; b. Burlington, Vt., Jan. 14, 1918; s. Charles and Sophie (Newman) L.; m. Patricia Etta de Young, June 6, 1948; children: Susan Ella Fisher, Carol Betsy Levin Adelman. BS, U. Vt., 1939, MD, 1943. Diplomate Am. Bd. Surgery, Nat. Bd. Med. Examiners. Intern New Rochelle (N.Y.) Hosp., 1943-44; resident in surgery Mt. Sinai Hosp., N.Y.C., 1947-48; ward surgeon Vet. Adminstrn. Hosp., Hampton, Va., 1948-50, Manchester, N.H., 1950-56, asst. chief surg. svc., 1956-58, chief surg. svc., 1958-62, acting chief surg. svc. Dayton, Ohio, 1963, chief surg. svc. Rutland, Mass., 1963-65; active staff mem. Holden (Mass.) Dist. Hosp., 1965-81, chief of staff, 1976-77, chief of surgery, 1976-77, emergency rm. physician, 1977-78; physician, indsl. medicine Indsl. Med. Ctr., Lawrence, 1978-81. Courtesy staff Hahnemann Hosp., Worcester, 1965-72; cons. in surgery Rutland Heights State Hosp., 1963-65; asst. clin. prof. surgery Boston U. Sch. of Medicine, Boston, 1959-61. Contbr. articles to profl. jours. Trustee Nesmith Libr., Windham, N.H., 1983-93, 99-2003, bldg. com., 1995-97, fundraising com., 1995-98; vol. Golden Brook Sch., Windham, 1981-2001, Elliot Hosp., Manchester, 1990-97. Capt. Med. Corps, U.S. Army, 1944-46. Recipient Carl Heidenblad award Friends of Libr., 1993, You've Made the Difference award N.H. Sch. Adminstrv. Unit #28, 1995, N.H. Vol. Tchr. award N.H. Ptnrs. in Edn., Pub. Svc. Co. of N.H. and N.H. Dept. of Edn., 1999, N.H. Libr. Trustee of Yr. award N.H. Libr. Trustee Assn., 2002. Fellow ACS; mem. AMA, N.H. Med. Soc., Mass. Med. Soc., Rockingham County Med. Soc. Jewish. Avocations: stamp collecting/philately, golf. Home: 2 Rolling Ridge Rd Windham NH 03087-2120 E-mail: murraylevin@msn.com.

LEVIN, MURRAY SIMON, lawyer; b. Phila., Feb. 8, 1943; s. Sidney Michael and Eva (Goldstein) L.; m. Jalond Marie Robinson, June 9, 1968; children: Adrianne Lesley, Alexandra Amber-Rose. BA, Haverford Coll., 1964; MA, LLB, Harvard U., 1968; cert., Hague Internat. Acad. Law, 1967. Bar: Pa. 1968, U.S. Dist. Ct. (ea. dist.) Pa. 1970, U.S. Ct. Appeals (3d cir.) 1970, U.S. Supreme Ct. 1979. Instr. English Harvard U., 1965-68; law clk. to U.S. Dist. Ct. Judge, 1968-70; instr. govt. Haverford Coll., 1970-71; litigation ptnr. Pepper, Hamilton LLP, Phila., 1970—, mem. firm exec. com., 1993-95. Mem. mng. bd. dirs. Atlas Pipeline Ptnrs.; overseas lectr., U.K., Sweden, Germany, Senegal, Kenya, Cameroon, Morocco, Israel, Vietnam, Italy, Portugal, Spain, 1988—; law seminar speaker. Weekly commentator radio Sta. WCAU Dick Clayton Show, TV program Morningside, 1973-76; weekly host, interviewer Sta. WHYY, 1974-79; TV commentator O.J. Simpson trial, 1995; contbr. articles to profl. jours. Chmn. Phila. Coun. Experiment in Internat. Living, 1968—70; mem. Phila. Urban Coalition Housing Task Force, 1968—80; chmn. coll. divsn. Allied Jewish Appeal, 1968—70; pres. Ctrl. Phila. Reform Dems., 1973—74; candidate for Dem. Party nomination for U.S. Senate from Pa., 2000; chair Dem. Party Lower Merion/Narberth, 2003—; del. Dem. Nat. Conv., 2004; mem. exec. com. Pa. Dem. Party State Com., 2002; bd. dirs. Grad. Hosp. Phila., 1976—96, mem. patient safety com., 2002—; bd. dirs. Friends Ctrl. Sch., 1988—96, divsn. Fgn. Policy Rsch. Com. Mid. East Coun., 1992—94; mem. mng. bd. dirs. Atlas Pipeline Ptnrs. L.P., 2003—05, Mid. East Forum, 1994—; bd. dirs. French Internat. Sch. Phila., 2002—, Jewish Family and Children's Svc. Greater Phila., 2003—, Resource Capital Corp., 2005—. Root-Tilden fellow, 1964. Mem. ABA, Pa. Bar Assn. (ho. of dels.), Phila. Bar Assn. (young lawyers exec. bd. 1973, bd. govs. 1985-88, zone del. 1988—, chmn. profl. guidance com. 1989-92, co-chmn. internat. human rights com. 1990-91), Phila. Trial Lawyers Assn., Assn. Internat. des Jeunes Avocats Brussels (bd. dirs. 1981-85, 1st Am. pres. 1985-88), Union Internationale des Avocats Paris (advisor to pres., mem. exec. com. 1993—, pres. Am. chpt. 1995-97, congress pres. 1997, pres. tort law commn. 2003—), Am. Law Inst., Am. Judicature Soc., Phi Beta Kappa. Office: Pepper Hamilton LLP 3000 2 Logan Sq 18th & Arch Sts Philadelphia PA 19103-2799 Office Phone: 215-981-4335. Business E-Mail: levinm@pepperlaw.com.

LEVIN, OSCAR, lawyer; b. Havana, Cuba, July 14, 1954; came to the U.S., 1960; s. Samuel and Sara (Wolson) L.; m. Andrea Joy Peltz, Nov. 21, 1982; children: Brooke Ashley, Garrett Ian, Haylee Paige. AA, Miami Dade C.C., 1973; BA, U. Fla., 1975, JD, 1978. Bar: Fla. 1978, U.S. Dist. Ct. (so. dist.) Fla. 1979, U.S. Ct. Appeals (5th and 11th cir.) 1981. Pub. defender, Miami, Fla., 1981-82; assoc., local ptnr. Barst & Mukamal, Miami, 1982-90; local ptnr., of counsel Baker & McKenzie, Miami, 1990-92; shareholder, nat. co-chair immigration law practice group Greenberg Traurig, P.A., Miami, 1992—. Lectr. in field. Mem. Am. Immigration Lawyers Assn. (bd. dirs. South Fla. chpt.), Internat. Bar Assn., Fla. Bar Assn., Phi Beta Kappa. Democrat. Jewish. Office: Greenberg Traurig PA 1221 Brickell Ave Fl 23 Miami FL 33131-3224 Office Phone: 305-579-0880. Office Fax: 305-579-0717. E-mail: levin@gtlaw.com.

LEVIN, PETER S.W., lawyer; b. 1952; BA, Yale U., 1974; JD, NYU, 1981. Bar: N.Y. 1982. Assoc. Davis, Polk & Wardwell, N.Y.C., 1981—89, Paris, 1984—86, ptnr. N.Y.C., 1989—, coord. credit practice group. Office: Davis Polk & Wardwell 450 Lexington Ave New York NY 10017 Office Phone: 212-450-4630. Office Fax: 212-450-3630. Business E-Mail: peter.levin@dpw.com.

LEVIN, PHILLIS, education educator, writer; Prof. English, poet in residence Hofstra U., Hempstead, NY, 2001—. Fellow The MacDowell Colony, Yaddo, The Liguria Study Ctr. for the Arts and Humanities, Bogliasco, Italy. Author: (books of poetry) Temples and Fields (Poetry Soc. of Am. Norma Farber First Book award), The Afterimage, Mercury, 2001; editor: (anthology) The Penguin Book of the Sonnet, 2001, John Simon Guggenheim Meml. Found. fellow, 2003, Amy Lowell Poetry Travelling scholarship, Fulbright fellowship, Slovenia, grant, Ingram Merrill Found., 1995. Office: Rm 200 Hofstra Hall 101 Hofstra U Hempstead NY 11549-1010

LEVIN, RICHARD LOUIS, retired language educator; b. Buffalo, Aug. 31, 1922; s. Bernard and Meta (Block) Levin; m. Muriel Abrams, June 22, 1952; children: David, Daniel. BA, U. Chgo., 1943, MA, 1947, PhD, 1957. Mem. faculty U. Chgo., 1949-57, asst. prof. English, 1953-57; prof. English, SUNY, Stony Brook, 1957—, acting chmn. English dept., 1960-63, 65-66, ret., 1994. Mem. adv. bd. World Ctr. Shakespeare Studies; mem. acad. adv. coun. Shakespeare Globe Ctr.; Fulbright lectr., 1984—85. Editor: Tragedy: Plays, Theory and Criticism, 1960, The Question of Socrates, 1961, Tragedy Alternate, 1965, Michaelmas Term (Thomas Middleton), 1966, The Multiple Plot in English Renaissance Drama, 1971, New Readings vs. Old Plays: Recent Trends in the Reinterpretation of English Renaissance Drama, 1979, Looking for an Argument: Critical Encounters with the New Approaches to the Criticism of Shakespeare and His Contemporaries, 2003. Served to lt. (j.g.) USNR, 1943—46, ETO. Recipient Explicator award, 1971; fellow, Am. Coun. Learned Socs., 1963—64; Rsch. fellow, SUNY, 1961, 1965—68, 1971, 1973, Faculty Exch. scholar, NEH Sr. fellow, 1974, Guggenheim fellow, 1978—79, Nat. Humanities Ctr. fellow, 1987—88. Mem.: MLA (mem. adv. com. publs., mem. del. assembly), Medieval and Renaissance Drama Soc. (mem. coun.), Shakespeare Assn. Am. (trustee), Internat. Shakespeare Assn., Columbia U. Shakespeare Seminar, Joseph Crabtree Found. Democrat. Jewish. Home: 26 Sparks St Melville NY 11747-1727 Office: SUNY English Dept Stony Brook NY 11794-5350 Personal E-mail: rlevin@ms.cc.sunysb.edu.

LEVIN, RICK (RICHARD CHARLES LEVIN), academic administrator, economist; b. San Francisco, Apr. 7, 1947; s. D. Derek and Phylys M. (Goldstein) Levin; m. Jane Ellen Aries, June 24, 1968; children: Jon, Daniel, Sarah, Rebecca. BA, Stanford U., 1968; LittB, Oxford U., Eng., 1971; PhD, Yale U., 1974; LLD (hon.), Princeton U., 1993, Harvard U., 1994; D in Civil Law (hon.), Oxford U., 1998; Doctorate (hon.), Peking U., 2003. With Yale U., New Haven, 1974—, pres., 1993—, chmn. econs. dept., 1987—92, Frederick William Beinecke prof. econs., 1992—, dean Grad. Sch., 1992—93. Rsch. assoc. Nat. Bur. Econ. Rsch., Cambridge, Mass., 1985—90; program dir. Internat. Inst. Applied Sys. Analysis, Vienna, 1990—92; trustee Tanner Lectures on Human Values; bd. dirs. Lucent Techs.; cons. numerous law and bus. firms. Trustee Hopkins Sch., New Haven, 1988—95, Yale-New Haven Hosp., 1993—, Univs. Rsch. Assn., 1994—99; bd. dirs. Yale-New Haven Health Svcs. Corp., Inc., 1993—; mem. bd. sci., tech. and econ. policy Nat. Rsch. Coun.; mem. The William and Flora Hewlett Found.; mem. presdl. commn. U.S. Postal Svc., 2003; mem. Commn. on the Intelligence Capabilities of the U.S. Regarding Weapons of Mass Destruction, 2004. Fellow, Merton Coll. Oxford U., 1996. Fellow: Am. Acad. Arts and Scis.; mem.: Satmetrix, Econometric Soc., Am. Econ. Assn. Democrat. Jewish. Office: Yale U Office of Pres 105 Wall St New Haven CT 06511-6608 also: Yale University Office of Public Affairs 265 Church Street, Suite 901 New Haven CT 06511 Office Phone: 203-432-2550. Business E-Mail: richard.levin@yale.edu.*

LEVIN, ROBERT J., finance company executive; BA in Econs. with high honors, U. N.C.; MBA, U. Chgo. With Fannie Mae, Washington, 1981—, various positions including sr. v.p. mktg. and mortgage-backed securities and sr. v.p. corp. fin., exec. v.p. mktg., 1990—98, exec. v.p. housing and cmty. devel., 1998—, interim CFO, 2004—. Trustee Morehouse Coll. Exec. Program Club fellow, U. Chgo. Mem.: Phi Beta Kappa. Office: Fannie Mae 3900 Wisconsin Ave NW Washington DC 20016-2892*

LEVIN, ROBERT JOSEPH, food products executive; b. Everett, Mass., Mar. 19, 1928; s. Edward A. and Rose E. L.; m. Carrol Silverman, June 21, 1948; children: Richard J., Cathy Levin Shuman. BA cum laude, U. Wis., 1948. From dir. store ops. and purchasing to pres., treas. C.B. Perkins Tobacco Co., Boston, 1948-73; from dir. store ops. and purchasing to pres., treas. C.B. Perkins Tobacco Co. (co. merged with Stop & Shop), Boston, 1970; v.p., then pres. Medi Mart div. Stop & Shop, 1971-75; group v.p. Stop & Shop Cos., Inc., Boston, 1975-79, sr. v.p., 1979-82, vice. chmn., 1982—, also dir. Bd. dirs. S.A.Y. Industries, Sterling Inc.; chmn. bd. S.A.Y. Packaging, 1988—. Bd. dirs. U. Wis. Found. Mem. Nat. Mass Retailing Inst. (dir.) Jewish. Home: 4762 Exeter Estate Ln Lake Worth FL 33467-8105 Office: 1776 Heritage Dr Quincy MA 02171-2119 also: PO Box 369 Boston MA 02101-0369

LEVIN, ROGER MICHAEL, lawyer; b. N.Y.C., Oct. 20, 1942; s. Harold F. and Blanche M. (Tarr) L. BA in Polit. Sci., U. Chgo., 1964; MA with distinction in polit. sci., U. Calif.-Berkeley, 1966; JD, NYU, 1969. Bar: N.Y. 1970, D.C. 1982, U.S. Dist. Ct. (so. and ea. dists.) N.Y., 1971, U.S. Ct. Appeals (2d cir.) 1971, U.S. Ct. Appeals (D.C. cir.) 1979, U.S. Customs Ct. 1974, U.S. Tax Ct. 1981, U.S. Ct. Customs and Patent Appeals 1974, U.S. Supreme Ct. 1974. Personal asst. to U.S. rep. Dept. State, Quang Nam Province, South Vietnam, 1966; asst. to dir. Nr. East/South Asia Bur. Office Internat. Security Affairs, Office Sec. of Def., Washington, 1967. Rsch. editor NYU Jour. Internat. Law and Politics. Fulbright scholar U. Sri Lanka, 1964-65; Woodrow Wilson fellow U. Calif.-Berkeley, 1966; named Best Oralist, Jessup Internat., Law Moot Ct. Regional Competition, NYU, 1969. Office: 15 E 90th St New York NY 10125-0001 Office Phone: 212-987-8000. E-mail: rmlevin@hotmail.com.

LEVIN, RONALD MARK, law educator; b. St. Louis, May 11, 1950; s. Marvin S. and Lois (Cohn) L.; m. Anne Carol Goldberg, July 29, 1989. BA magna cum laude, Yale U., 1972; JD, U. Chgo., 1975. Bar: Mo. 1975, D.C. 1977. Law clk. to Hon. John C. Godbold U.S. Ct. Appeals, 5th cir., 1975-76; assoc. Sutherland, Asbill & Brennan, Washington, 1976-79; asst. prof. law Washington U., St. Louis, 1979-80, assoc. prof. law, 1980-85, prof. law, 1985-2000, assoc. dean, 1990-93, Henry Hitchcock prof. law, 2000—. Cons. Adminstrv. Conf. U.S., 1979-81, 93-95. Co-author: Administrative Law and Process, 4th edit., 1997, State and Federal Administrative Law, 2d edit., 1998. Chair senate coun. Washington U., 1988-90. Mem.: ABA (chair sect. adminstrv. law and regulatory practice 2000—01), Assn. Am. Law Sch. (chair sect. adminstrv. law 1993, chair sect. legis. 1995). Home: 7352 Kingsbury Blvd Saint Louis MO 63130-4142 Office: PO Box 1120 Saint Louis MO 63188-1120

LEVIN, RONALD MITCHELL, geriatrician; b. Phila., July 29, 1958; s. Herbert A. and Marlene (Axelrod) L.; m. Carol Lynn Most, June 17, 1979; children: Jay Samuel, Marc Andrew, Eric Brian. BA cum laude, LaSalle U., 1980; MD with hons. in Pediats., distinction in medicine, Hahnemann U., 1984. Diplomate Am. Bd. Internal Medicine, Nat. Bd. Med. Examiners; cert. of advanced qualifications in geriatric medicine, Am. Bd. Internal Medicine, 1994, 2004. Intern, resident internal medicine Bryn Mawr Hosp., Phila., 1984-87; physician Lawndale Family Practice, Phila., 1987-88; pvt. practice, Phila., 1988—95, 2001—03; clin. instr. medicine Hahnemann MCP Sch. Medicine, 1993—2003, Allegheny U. Health Scis., 1993—2003; internist Abington Meml. Hosp., 1995-2001; med. dir. U.S. Homecare, Phila., 1991-94; staff physician Salisbury Va. Med. Ctr., 2003—. Interviewer med. sch. admissions com. Hahnemann Med. Coll. Pa. Sch. Medicine, 1995-97. Fellow ACP; mem. AMA (Physician's Recognition award 1991, 94, 97, 2000, 03), Am. Geriatric Soc. Office: W G (Bill) Hefner VA Med Ctr 1601 Brenner Ave Salisbury NC 28144-1623 Home: 4838 Noras Path Rd Charlotte NC 28226-3463 Office Phone: 704-638-9000. E-mail: rmlmdfacp@aol.com.

LEVIN, SANDER M., congressman, lawyer; b. Detroit, Sept. 6, 1931; s. Saul R. and Bess (Levinson) L.; m. Victoria Schlafer, 1957 BA, U. Chgo., 1952; MA, Columbia U., 1954; LLB, Harvard U., 1957. Atty. priv. practice, 1957—64; supr. Oakland County Bd. Suprs., Mich., 1961-64; mem. Mich. Senate, 1965-70; atty. priv. practice, 1971—77; fellow Kennedy Sch. Govt., Inst. Politics, Harvard U., Cambridge, Mass., 1975; asst. adminstr. Agency for Internat. Develop., Washington, 1977-81; mem. U.S. Congresses from 12th (formerly 17th) Mich dist., 1983—; mem. ways and means com. Adj. prof. law Wayne State U., Detroit, 1971—74. Chmn. Mich. Dem. Com., 1968-69; Dem. Candidate for Gov., 1970, 74. Democrat. Office: US Ho of Reps 2300 Rayburn Ho Office Bldg Washington DC 20515-0001*

LEVIN, SIMON, lawyer; b. Newark, Aug. 4, 1942; m. Barbara Leslie Lasky; children: David, Jennifer Menken, Yale, Michael, Jacob. BS cum laude, Lehigh U., 1964; JD, NYU, 1967, LLM in Taxation, 1974. Bar: N.J. 1967, U.S. Tax Ct. 1971, U.S. Ct. Claims 1972, N.Y. 1980. Assoc. Stanley & Fisher, Newark, 1970, Hannoch Weisman, Newark, 1970-73; ptnr. Robinson, Wayne, Levin, Riccio & La Sala, Newark, 1973-88; mem., chmn. tax dept. Sills Cummis Radin Tischman Epstein & Gross, Newark, 1988—. Civillian aide to Sec. Army for N.J., 1992-95; mem. N.J. Dept. Treasury Transition Team for Gov. Christine Todd Whitman, 1993-94; mem. Treas. Adv. Group N.J. Dept. of Treasury, 1995—; lectr., panelist numerous orgns. Co-author: Taxation Investors in Securities and Commodities, 1983, 2d edit., 1984, supplement, 1986, Estate Planning and Administration in New Jersey, 1987; contbr. articles to profl. jours. Trustee, mem. exec. com. Jewish Comty. Found., MetroWest, Whippany, N.J., pres., 1979-83; trustee, mem. exec. com. Israel Bond Campaign MetroWest, Livingston, N.J., chmn., 1988-89; trustee Monmouth Healthcare Ctr. Found., 1997—, N.J. Vietnam Vets. Meml. and Edn. Ctr. Found., Holmdel, 1994—. Capt. U.S. Army, 1968-69, Vietnam. Recipient Cohn Leadership award Jewish Fedn. MetroWest, 1982, Endowment Achievement award Coun. Jewish Fedns., 1986, N.J. Meritorious Svc. medal, 1995. Fellow Am. Coll. Tax Counsel; mem. ABA, N.J. Bar Assn. (chmn. commodities sect. 1982-86), Essex County Bar Assn. (chmn. sect. taxation 1974-76), Monmouth County Bar Assn., Phi Delta Phi. Avocations: tennis, skiing, politics, opera, community service. Office: Sills Cummis Radin Tischman Epstein & Gross 1 Riverfront Plz Fl 10 Newark NJ 07102-5401

LEVIN, SIMON ASHER, mathematician, ecologist, educator; b. Balt., Apr. 22, 1941; s. Theodore S. and Clara G. L.; m. Carole Lotte Leiffer, Aug. 4, 1964; children: Jacob, Rachel. BA in Math., Johns Hopkins U., 1961; PhD in Math. (NSF fellow), U. Md., 1964; DSc (hon.), Ea. Mich. U., 1990. Teaching asst. U. Md., 1961-62, research assoc., 1964, visitor, 1968; NSF fellow U. Calif., Berkeley, 1964-65; asst. prof. math. Cornell U., 1965-70, assoc. prof. applied math., ecology, theoretical and applied math., 1971-77, Charles A. Alexander prof. biol. scis., 1977—92, adj. prof., 1992—, chmn. sect. ecology and systematics div. biol. scis., 1974-79, dir. Ecosystems Rsch. Ctr., 1980-87, dir. Ctr. for Environ. Rsch., 1987-90; George Moffett prof. biology Princeton U., 1992—, associated faculty applied math., 1992—, dir., Princeton Environ. Inst., 1993-98, dir., Del. Ctr. for Biocomplexity, 2001—. Vis. scholar U. Wash., 1973-74, Inst. for Advanced Study, 1999; vis. scientist Weizmann Inst., Rehovot, Israel, 1977, 80; hon. prof. U. B.C., 1979-80; Lansdowne lectr. U. Victoria, 1981; disting. vis. scientist SUNY, Stony Brook, 1984; vis. fellow All Souls Coll., U. Oxford, 1988; vis. scientist, Woods Hole Oceanographic Instn., Geophysical Fluid Dynamics Summer Prog., 1994; Ostrom lectr. Wash. State U., Pullman, 1994; lectr. Third Annual Stanislaw Ulam Meml., Santa Fe Inst., 1996; The Per Brinck Lecture, U. Lund, Sweden, 1999, Chesley Lecture, Carleton Coll., 2002; co-chmn. Gordon Conf. on Theoretical Biology, 1970, chmn. Gordon Conf. on Theoretical Biology and Biomath., 1971; chmn. Am. Math. Soc./ Soc. Indsl. and Applied Maths. Com. on Maths. in Life Scis., 1973-79; mem. core panel on math. in biol. scis., program com. Internat. Congress Mathematicians, 1977-78; co-convenor Biomath. Conf., Oberwolfach, West Germany, 1978; co-dir. Internat. Ctr. for Theoretical Physics Autumn Course on Math. Ecology, Trieste, Italy, 1988, 92, 96, 2000; mem. adv. com. divsn. environ. scis. Oak Ridge Nat. Lab., 1978-81; vice chmn. math. Com. Concerned Scientists, N.Y.C., 1979—; mem. sci. panel Hudson River Found., 1982-86, chmn., 1985-86, bd. dirs., 1986-96; mem. Commn. on Life Scis., NRC, 1983-89, mem. com. ecosys. mgmt. of sustainable marine fisheries ocean studies bd., 1995-98; mem. Health and Environ. Rsch. Adv. Com. Dept. of Energy, 1986-90; prin. lectr. Conf. Bd. on Math. Scis. course on math. ecology, 1985; mem. oversight rev. bd. U.S. Nat. Acid Precipitation Assessment Program; spkr. commencement address Ea. Mich. U., 1990; sci. bd. Santa Fe Inst., 1991—, Inst. Med. Bio Math., Bene Ataroth, Israel, 1999—; bd. dirs. Beijer Inst., 1994-99, chmn. 1997-99; The H. John Heinz III Ctr. for Sci., Econs. and the Environment, 1994-99; tech. adv. bd. Brit. Petroleum, 2001—. Author: Fragile Dominion: Complexity and the Commons, 1999; editor: Lectures on Mathematics in Life Sciences, vols. 7-12, 1974-79, Ecosystem Analysis and Prediction, 1974, (with R.H. Whittaker) Niche: Theory and Application, 1975, Studies in Mathematical Biology, 2, vols., 1978, New Perspectives in Ecotoxicology, 1983, Mathematical Population Biology, 1984, Mathematical Ecology, 1984, Math Ecology: An Introduction, 1986, (with others) Mathematical Ecology, 1988, Ecotoxicology: Problems and Approaches, 1989, Perspectives in Theoretical Ecology, 1989, (with T. Hallam and L. Gross) Applied Mathematical Ecology, 1989, (with T. Powell and J.H. Steele) Patch Dynamics, 1993, Frontiers in Mathematical Biology, 1994, (with Abe and Higashi) Biodiversity: An Ecological Perspective, 1997 (with A. Okuba) Diffusion and Ecological Problems,2d edit.2001, (with P. Kareiva) The Importance of Species, 2003; editor-in-chief Ecological Applications, 1988-95, Ency. of Biodiversity, 1997-2000; Mathematical and Computational Biology Book Series, 1997-2000; editor: Ecology and Ecol. Monographs, 1975-77, Princeton Series in Theoretical and Computational Biology, 2000; editor Jour. Math. Biology, 1976-79, mng. editor, 1979-95; mng. editor Biomath., 1976-95, Lecture Notes in Biomath., 1973-95; mng. editor Princeton U. Press, Monographs in Population Biology, 1992—; assoc. editor Theoretical Population Biology, 1976-84; mem. editl. bd. Evolution Theory, 1976—, Ecol. Issues, 1995—, Conservation Ecology, 1995—, Discrete Applied Math., 1978-87, Internat. Jour. Math. and computer Modelling, 1979—, SIAM Rev., 1997—, Santa Fe Inst., 1998—, Philosophical Transactions of the Royal Soc., Series B, 1998—, Jour. Biomath., 1999, Procs. Nat. Acad. of Scis., 2000—; mem. editl. bd. Princeton U. Press, Complexity series, 1992—; mem. adv. bd. Jour. Theoretical Biology, 1977—, Ecological Rsch., 1996—, Ecosystems, 1996—; also various other editl. positions. Bd. dirs. N.J. chpt. Nature Conservancy, 1995-97. Recipient Robert MacArthur award, Ecol. Soc. Am., 1988, Disting. Statis. Ecologist award, Internat. Assn. Ecology, 1994, Okubo award, Japanese Assn. for Math. Biology/Soc. for Math. Biology, 2001, A.H. Heineken prize for Environ. Scis., Royal Netherlands Acad. Arts and Scis., 2004, Kyoto prize (Basic Scis.), Inamori Found., 2005; fellow, Guggenheim, 1979—80, Japanese Soc. for Promotion of Sci., 1983—84. Fellow AAAS (bd. dirs. 1994-98), Am. Acad. Arts and Scis.; mem. Ecol. Soc. Am. (chmn. Mercer awards subcom. 1976, mem. coun. 1975-77, ad hoc com. to evaluate ecol. consequences of nuclear war 1982-83, pres. 1990-91, MacArthur award 1988, Disting. Svc. citation 1998, chmn. MacArthur award com. 1999-2000), Soc. and Indsl. and Applied Math. (mem. coun. 1977-79, coun. exec. com. 1978-79, coun. rep. to bd. trustees 1978-79, chmn. human rights com. 1980-83, mng. editor Jour. Applied Math. 1975-79), Am. Inst. Biol. Scis., Am. Soc. Naturalists, Soc. Math. Biology (pres. 1987-89), Soc. for Conservation Biology, Brit. Ecol. Soc., Soc. Study Evolution, Japaneses Soc. Theoretical Biology (Okuba Lifetime Achievement award), U.S. Com. for Israel Environ., Sigma Xi. Jewish. Home: 11 Beechtree Ln Princeton NJ 08540-7428 Office: Princeton U Dept Ecology & Evolutionary Biology Eno Hall Princeton NJ 08544-1003*

LEVIN, VICTOR A., neurologist, oncologist, educator; b. Milw. MD, U. Wis., 1966. Diplomate Am. Bd. Psychiatry and Neurology. Intern medicine Washington U., St. Louis City Hosp., 1966—67; staff assoc. Lab. Chem. Pharmacology Nat. Cancer Inst., Bethesda, Md., 1967—69; resident neurology Mass. Gen. Hosp., Boston, 1969—72, NINDS spl. fellow dept. neurology, 1971—72; faculty Schs. Medicine and Pharmacy U. Calif., San Francisco, prof. dept. neurosurgery, pharm. chemistry and pharmacology, 1981, chief neuro-oncology svc. Brain Tumor Rsch. Ctr., 1977; prof. dept. neuro-oncology U. Tex. M.D. Anderson Cancer Ctr., Houston, 1988—, chair dept. neuro-oncology, 1988—99, dir. Brain Tumor Ctr., 1993—99. Cofounder Asilomar Conf. for Brain Tumor Rsch. and Therapy, 1975; exec. devel. program Rice U., Houston, 1990—91. Contbr. chapters to books, over 350 articles to profl. jours. Recipient medal med. faculty, Tokyo U., 1982, award in neuro-oncology, Farber Found., 1988, Heath Meml. award for cancer care, 1997. Mem.: Soc. for Neuro-Oncology (founding pres. 1995—97, Gold medal 2003), Nat. Brain Tumor Found., Am. Soc. Clin. Oncology, Am. Soc. Advancement Sci., Am. Brain Tumor Assn., Am. Assn. Neurol. Surgeons (joint sect. on tumors), Am. Assn. for Cancer Rsch., Am. Acad. Neurology. Achievements include research in defining pharmacokinetics of anticancer drugs; new anticancer agents to selectively inhibit protein tyrosine kinase pathways critical to tumor growth; development of drug and radiation combination therapies for brain tumors. Office: Victor A Levin MD Neuro Oncology Unit 431 UT MD Anderson Cancer Ctr PO Box 301402 Houston TX 77230-1402 Office Phone: 713-792-8297.

LEVIN, WARREN MAYER, family practice physician; b. Phila., Aug. 20, 1932; s. Israel and Clara Deborah (Cherim) L.; m. Marsha Ann Beinstein, Dec. 24, 1955 (div. 1975); children: Beth Ann, Julie Ruth; m. Frances Susan Teitler, Mar. 20, 1982; 1 child, Erika Alexandra. BS, Ursinus Coll., 1952; MD, Jefferson Med. Coll., 1956. Diplomate Am. Bd. Family Practice, Am. Bd. Bariatric Medicine, Am. Bd. Environ. Medicine, Am. Bd. Chelation Therapy, Internat. Bd. Advanced Longevity Medicine; cert. homeopath. Intern U.S. Naval Hosp., Newport, R.I., 1956-57; pvt. practice S.I., N.Y., 1959-74; founder, med. dir. Heights Holistic Health Ctr., Bklyn., 1974-79, World Health Med. Group, N.Y.C., 1979-94; physician Physicians for Complementary Medicine, N.Y.C., 1994-97, Comprehensive Med. Svcs., N.Y.C., 1998—2000, Americas Med. Ctr., Ridgefield, Conn., 1998—2000, Integrative Med. of Conn., 2001—. Mem. bd. examiners Internat. Bd. Advanced Longevity Medicine, 1998—; founder & med. dir. Integrative Medicine of Conn., 2001—. Contbr. to books Nutrition in Pregnancy, 1981, to books Challenging Orthodoxy, 1991, to books Alternative Medicine, 1994, to books The Cholesterol Hoax, 1998, to books Whole Body Dentistry, 1999. Bd. govs. Internat. Coll. Applied Nutrition, 1974-76; chmn. med. adv. bd. Survive Until a Cure, advisory coun.-Chemical Awareness Rsch. Educ. & Solutions; prin. investigator-A Study on Use of Human Growth Hormone. Lt. M.C., USNR ret. Recipient Disting. Pioneer in Alternative Medicine award Found. for Advancement of Innovative Medicine Fund, 1995, Presdl. Commendation, Am. Coll. for Advancement in Medicine, 1995. Fellow: Am. Acad. Family Pactice, Am. Coll Nutrition, Am. Acad. Environ. Medicine; mem.: Am. Soc. Bariatric Medicine (v.p. 1980—82), Am. Coll. Advancement Medicine (treas.). Avocations: ice skating, sailing, swimming. Home: 11659 E Bloomfield Dr Scottsdale AZ 85259 Office: 13832 N 32nd St #126 Phoenix AZ 85032 Office Phone: 480-323-6649. E-mail: drwmlevin@aol.com.

LEVINE, ALAN, lawyer; b. Middletown, N.Y., Jan. 17, 1948; s. Jacques and Florence (Tananbaum) L.; m. ALison Newman; children: Emily Jane, Malcolm Andrew. BS in Econs., U. Pa., 1970; JD, NYU, 1973. Bar: N.Y. 1974, U.S. Dist. Ct. (so. dist.) N.Y. 1974, U.S. Dist. Ct. (ea. dist.) N.Y. 1980, U.S. Tax Ct. 1980, U.S. Ct. Appeals (2d cir.) 1975, U.S. Supreme Ct. 2000. Law clk. U.S. Dist. Ct. (so. dist.) N.Y., N.Y.C., 1973-75; asst. U.S. atty. U.S. Attys. Office, so. dist. N.Y., Dept. Justice, N.Y.C., 1975-80; assoc. Kronish, Lieb, Weiner & Hellman, N.Y.C., 1980-82, mem., 1982—, mng. ptnr., 1998—. Bd. dirs. Legal Aid Soc., NYC, mem. exec. com., 2003—, treas., 2005—; chmn. lawyers divsn. United Jewish Appeal Fedn. NY, 2004—; mem. NY Commn. Pub. Authority Reform, NY, 2005—. Chmn. bd. dirs. Park Ave. Synagogue, N.Y.C., 1993-98; bd. dirs. Jewish Theol. Sem., 1998, MYF Legal Svcs. Inc., 1990-93; law chmn. N.Y. County Rep. Com., 1991-93. Recipient Atty. Gen. Dirs. award U.S. Dept. Justice, 1980, Torch of Learning award Am. Friends Hebrew U., 1995, Human Rels. award Anit-Defamation League, 2001. Fellow Am. Bar Found., Am. Coll. Trial Lawyers; mem. ABA (ho. of dels. 1983-84, chmn. spl. com. for youth edn. for citizenship, 1988-91, vice chmn. white collar crime com. 1996—), N.Y. State Bar Assn. (chmn. com. on citizenship edn. 1979-84, ho. of dels. 1982-84, award of achievement 1984), Sunningdale Country Club (bd. trustees 1988-90 Scarsdale, N.Y.), Mask and Wig Club (Phila.). Republican. Jewish. Home: 755 Park Ave New York NY 10021 Office: Kronish Lieb Weiner & Hellman 1114 Avenue Of The Americas New York NY 10036-7703 Office Phone: 212-479-6260. Business E-Mail: alevine@knonishlieb.com.

LEVINE, ARTHUR ELLIOTT, academic administrator, educator; b. NYC, June 16, 1948; s. Meyer and Katherine (Kalman) L.; m. Linda Christine Fentiman, Aug. 18, 1974; children: Jamie Sloan Fentiman, Rachel Elizabeth Fentiman. BA in Biology, Brandeis U., 1970; PhD, SUNY-Buffalo, 1976; PhD (hon.), St. Thomas Aquinas Coll., 2001; LHD (hon.), U. Puget Sound, 1981, William Jewell Coll., 1995, U. NH, 1995; DHL (hon.), U. New Eng, Biddeford, Maine, 1983, Unity Coll., Maine, 1984, Bradford Coll., 1989, Capitol U., 1991, Taitung Nat. Tchrs. Coll., Taiwan, 1991, Albright Coll., 1993, U. NH, 1995, William Jewell Coll., 1995, Mt. Union Coll., 1995, Niagara U., 1996, LaGuardia CC, 1998, Wilmington Coll., 1998; LittD (hon.), Greensboro Coll., 1988, Jewish Theol. Seminary, 1996, others. Sr. fellow Carnegie Council on Policy Studies in Higher Edn., Berkeley, Calif., 1975-80, Carnegie Found., Washington, 1980-82; pres. Bradford Coll., Mass., 1982-89; chmn. Inst. for Edn. Mgmt. Harvard U., Cambridge, Mass., 1989-94; pres., prof. edn. Tchrs. Coll., Columbia U., N.Y.C., 1994—. Cons. to numerous colls., univs., U.S. Co-author: Reform of Undergraduate Education, 1973 (Am. Coun. on Edn. Book of Yr. award 1974), Quest for Common Learning, 1982, Opportunity in Adversity, 1985, Shaping Higher Education's Future, 1989, Higher Learning in America, 1993, Beating the Odds, 1996, When Hope and Fear Collide, 1998; author: Handbook on Undergraduate Curriculum, 1978, Why Innovation Fails, 1980, When Dreams and Heroes Died, 1980. Recipient Edn. Press Assn. Am. award, 1981, 89, 90, 94; book named Book of Yr., Am. Coun. on Edn., 1974; Spencer fellow, 1979. Office: Tchrs Coll Columbia U 525 W 120th St New York NY 10027-6625

LEVINE, ARTHUR SAMUEL, pediatric hematologist, dean, educator, oncologist, researcher; b. Cleve., Nov. 1, 1936; s. David Alvin and Sarah Ethel (Rubinstein) L.; m. Ruth Eleanor Rubin, Oct. 14, 1959; children: Amy Elizabeth, Raleigh Hannah, Jennifer Leah. AB, Columbia U., 1958; MD, Chgo. Med. Sch., 1964. Diplomate Am. Bd. Pediatrics, Am. Bd. Pediatric Hematology-Oncology. Intern in pediatrics U. Minn., Mpls., 1964-65, resident in pediatrics, 1965-66, USPHS fellow in hematology and genetics, 1966-67; capt. USPHS, 1967-92, rear adm., asst. surgeon gen., 1992-98; clin. assoc. div. cancer treatment Nat. Cancer Inst., Bethesda, Md., 1967-69, sr. staff fellow, 1969-70, sr. investigator, 1970-73, head sect. infectious disease, pediatric oncology br., 1973-75, chief pediatric oncology br., 1975-82; sci. dir. Nat. Inst. Child Health and Human Devel., Bethesda, 1982-98; sr. vice chancellor for health scis., dean Sch. Medicine, U. Pitts., 1998—, prof. medicine and molecular genetics and biochemistry, 1998—. Clin. prof. medicine and pediatrics Georgetown U., Washington, 1975-98; clin. prof. pediatrics Uniformed Svcs. U. Health Scis., Bethesda, 1983-98; vis. prof. Cold Harbor Spring Lab., N.Y., 1973, Benares Hindu U., India, 1975, U. Minn., 1974, Hebrew U., Israel, 1981, U. Bologna, 1989, Northwestern U., 1992, Moscow State U., 1996; Karon meml. lectr. U. So. Calif., 1983; Seham lectr. U. Minn., 1983; Harris lectr. Va. Commonwealth U., 1995; Markey lectr. Wash. U., 1996; Green lectr. European Molecular Biology Lab. Heidelberg, 1997; Walter Rubin meml. lectr. Drexel U., 2003; John Conley lectr. in med. ethics Am. Acad. Otolaryngology, 2003; vis. dean U. Mich., 2003. Author: Cancer in the Young, 1982; editor-in-chief The New Biologist, 1989-92; contbr. articles to profl. jours. Recipient Disting. Alumnus award Chgo. Med. Sch., 1972, NIH Dir.'s award, 1984, Meritorious Svc. award USPHS, 1987, Disting. Svc. award, 1991, Surgeon Gen.'s Exemplary Svc. award, 1993. Mem. AAAS, Am. Soc. Clin. Investigation, Soc. Pediatric Research, Am. Assn. Cancer Research, Am. Soc. Hematology, Am. Soc. Clin. Oncology, Am. Fedn. Clin. Research, Am. Soc. Microbiology, Am. Soc. Pediatric Hematology/Oncology, Alpha Omega Alpha. Office: U Pittsburgh 3550 Terrace St Pittsburgh PA 15261-0001 Office Phone: 412-648-8975. Business E-Mail: alevine@hs.pitt.edu.

LEVINE, AUDREY PEARLSTEIN, foundation administrator; b. N.Y.C., July 6, 1934; d. Irving and Flora Malkin Pearlstein; m. Arthur Levine, Mar. 15, 1958; children: Michael S., Charles T., Andrew S. Student, Hofstra U., 1952, student, 1957. Sec., treas. Pearlstein Found., 1976—; gen. ptnr. Adams County Realty LLP, McSherrystown, Pa., 2003—. Specialist trade shows Stone Care Internat. Inc., Owings Mills, Md., 1991—; adminstr., gen. ptnr. Pearlstein Partnership, Palm Beach, Fla., 1998—; gen. ptnr. Audrey Realty, Pikesville, Md., 2003, Pikesville, 04, Pikesville, 05. V.p. PTA Ft. Garrison Sch., Pikesville, Md., 1968—69; chmn. Hadassah Ho. & Garden Tour, Balt., Palm Beach, 1969, 1970, 1999, Booster Club Pikesville H.S., Pikesville, 1970, 1971, 1975—76, 1980—82; v.p. PTA Pikesville Sr. H.S., Pikesville, 1970, 1976, 1980—82; v.p. parents-student bd. Am. U., Washington, 1978—79, 1984—86; chmn. Save Ft. Garrison, Pikesville, 1965—66, 2001; mem. com. Senator Henry Jackson Save Soviet Jews, Washington, 1972—73; v.p. Jewish Nat. Fund Women, Balt., 1973—75; pres. Balt. (Md.) Suburban Hadassah, 1963—64; bd. dirs. Women's Aux. Sinai Hosp., Balt., 1985—88, Nat. Coun. Johns Hopkins, Balt., 1990—92, Pikesville Recreation Coun., Pikesville, 1968—71; chmn. Rededication of Fort Garrison, Pikesville, Md. Mem.: Nat. Mus. Women in the Arts (charter). Republican. Jewish. Avocations: sculpting, painting, flower arranging, boating, tennis. Home (Winter): Bldg 1 Apt 2A 2500 S Ocean Blvd Palm Beach FL 33480 Home (Summer): 3421 Garrison Farms Rd Pikesville MD 21208

LEVINE, BENJAMIN, lawyer; b. May 22, 1931; s. George and Frances (Levovsky) L.; m. Arleen Ella Rosenblatt, Jan. 14, 1962; children: Joshua, Sarah. BA, U. Conn., 1953; JD, Rutgers U., 1963. Bar: N.Mex. 1964, N.Y. 1965, N.J. 1967, U.S. Supreme Ct. 1980; cert. trial atty., 1986; diplomate Nat. Bd. Trial Advocacy, 1989. Law clk. N.Mex. Sup. Ct., 1963-64; spl. asst. N.J. Commr. Conservation and Econ. Devel., 1965-67; dep. atty. gen. State of N.J., 1967-70; pvt. practice Newark and N.Y.C., 1970—. Adj. prof. law Ramapo Coll., Mahwah, N.J., 1978-80; arbitrator U.S. Dist. Ct. N.J., 1989. Author: Medical Malpractice; Zoning Guide for Local Officals; contbr. articles to profl. jours. Pres. Environ. Action Inst. N.J., 1977-80; chmn. North Plainfield (N.J.) Environ. Commn., 1974-76; trustee South Branch Watershed Assn., 1976-80, Rabbinical Coll. Am., 1994—. Lt. (j.g.) USN, 1956-60. Mem.: ATLA, Million Dollar Advocates Forum, NY County Lawyers Assn. (chmn. state legis. com. 1976—80, mem. com. on constn., com. on civil cts. 1980—82), Am. Arbitration Assn. (nat. panel arbitrators 1973—), NJ Bar Assn. (bd. dirs. med.mal.com, cert. trial lawyers sect.). Office: 1 Gateway Ctr Ste 2500 Newark NJ 07102-5315 Office Phone: 973-639-1315. E-mail: levine@ix.netcom.com.

LEVINE, DANIEL, historian, educator; b. N.Y.C., Dec. 31, 1934; s. Morris Simeon and Margaret (Hirsch) L.; m. Susan Rose, July 29, 1954; children—Timothy, Karen. BA in History, Antioch Coll., 1956; PhD in History (Woodrow Wilson fellow, Social Sci Research Council fellow), Northwestern U., 1961. Asst. prof. history Earlham Coll., 1960-63; asst. prof. Bowdoin Coll., Brunswick, Maine, 1963-66, assoc. prof., 1966-72, prof., 1972—, Thomas Bracket Reed prof. history and polit. sci., 1974—. Fulbright sr. lectr., Munich, 1979-80; vis. prof. U. Copenhagen, 1991. Author: Varieties of Reform Thought, 1964, Jane Addams and the Liberal Tradition, 1971, Poverty and Society, 1988, Bayard Rustin and the Civil Rights Movement, 2000; contbr. articles to profl. jours.; editl. bd.: Explorations in Entrepreneurial History, 1962-70. Bd. dirs. Maine Civil Liberties Union, 1988-94. Fulbright lectr. Denmark, 1969-70; mem. jury Ralph Waldo Emerson prize Phi Beta Kappa, 1973-74; Guggenheim fellow, 1972-73. Mem. Am. Hist. Assn., Orgn. Am. Historians, AAUP, Social Welfare History Group (v.p. 1975-76), Arbeitskreis: Geschichte Sozialer Sicherung un Sozialer Disziplinierung. Democrat. Home: 785 Mere Point Rd Brunswick ME 04011 Office: Bowdoin Coll History Dept Brunswick ME 04011 Office Phone: 207-725-3293. Business E-Mail: dlevine@bowdoin.edu.

LEVINE, DANIEL BLANK, classical studies educator; b. Cin., July 22, 1953; s. Joseph and Elizabeth (Blank) L.; m. Judith Robinson, Aug. 14, 1984; children: Sarah Ruth, Amy Elizabeth. Student, Am. Sch. Classical Studies, Athens, 1974, student, 1978—79; BA in Greek and Latin magna cum laude, U. Minn., 1975; PhD in Classics, U. Cin., 1980. Seymour fellow Am. Sch. Classical Studies, 1978-79; asst. prof. U. Ark., 1980-84, assoc. prof., 1984-98, prof., 1998—. Dir. Summer Session Am. Sch. Classical Studies, Athens, 1987, 95; dir. study tour in Greece Vergilian Soc., 1990, Greece Univ. Ark., 2000, 01, 03, 05; referee Classical Jour., 1984-88, Helios, 1984-88, Cornell U. Press, 1988-89, 91—, Classical Outlook, 1988-89; panelist NEH, Washington, 1986; co-dir., instr. gifted and talented H.S. students summer program State of Ark. Dept. Edn. Grant, 1988; mem. mng. com. Am. Sch. Classical Studies Athens, 1991—. Contbr. articles to profl. jours. Grantee NEH 1981, 82, 83, 84, 92; recipient Outstanding Tchr. award Mortar Bd. Sr. Honor Soc., U. Ark., 1991, Master Tchr. award Fulbright Coll., 1995. Mem. Am. Philological Assn. (Excellence in Teaching Classics award 1992), Am. Classical League, Classical Assn. Mid. West and South (Ovatio 1996, v.p. com. promotion Latin in Ark. 1980-86, 91-95, chmn. regional rep. com. for promotion Latin, Outstanding State V.P. for 1982-83), U. Ark. Teaching Acad., Golden Key, Phi Beta Kappa. Home: 904 Park Ave Fayetteville AR 72701-2027 Office: U Ark Dept Fgn Langs 425 Kimpel Hall Fayetteville AR 72701 Business E-Mail: dlevine@uark.edu.

LEVINE, DAVID, artist; b. Bklyn., Dec. 20, 1926; s. Harry L.; children: Matthew, Eve. B.F.A., BS in Edn, Temple U., 1949; postgrad., Hans Hoffman Sch. Paintings, 1950. One-man shows Forum Gallery, N.Y.C., 1966—, Ga. Mus. Art, 1968, Calif. Palace Legion of Honor, 1968-69, 71-72, 83, Wesleyan U., 1970, Bklyn. Mus., 1971, Princeton U., 1972, Galerie Yves Lambert, Paris, 1972, Yale U., 1973, Hirshhorn Mus. and Sculpture Garden, Washington, 1976, Galerie Claude Bernard, 1979, Phillips Gallery, 1980, Pierpont Morgan Library, 1981, Santa Fe East Gallery, 1983, Ash Molean Mus., Meredith Long, Houston, 1984; represented by Forum Gallery; author: The Man From M.A.L.I.C.E., 1966, Pens and Needles, 1969, No Known Survivors, 1970, The Arts of David Levine, 1978, Aesop's Fables. Served with U.S. Army, 1945-46. Recipient Tiffany award, 1955, Isaac N. Maynard prize, 1958, Julius Halligarten prize, 1960, Thomas B. Clark prize, 1962, George Polk award, 1965, Childe Hassam Purchase prize 1972, Benjamin Altman prize, 1973, Gold medal for Graphic Work, Am. Acad. Inst. Arts and Letters, 1992, Thomas Nast award, 1995; Guggenheim fellow, 1967. Mem. AAAL, Century Assn. Address: care Forum Gallery 745 5th Ave New York NY 10151-0099

LEVINE, EDWARD A., surgeon, educator; b. Chgo., May 2, 1959; s. Franklin and Joan L.; m. Joan, 1981. BS magna cum laude, No. Ill. U., 1981; MD, Chgo. Med. Sch., 1985. Resident in surgery Michael Reese Hosp., Chgo., 1985-90; fellow in oncology U. Ill., Chgo., 1990-92; asst. prof. surgery La. State U., New Orleans, 1992-97, assoc. prof. surgery, 1997-98, chief surg. oncology, 1994-98; assoc. prof., chief surg. oncology Bowman Gray Sch. Medicine Wake Forest U., Winston Salem, NC, prof. surgery, chief surg. onc. Winston Salem, NC, 2002—. Contbr. articles to profl. jours., chpts. to books. Office: Wake Forest U Sect Surg Oncology Medicial Center Blvd Winston Salem NC 27157-0001

LEVINE, ELAINE PRADO, psychologist, music educator, artist; b. Inglewood, Calif., Feb. 16, 1962; d. John Franklin, Jr. and Carolyn Mae (Cable) Walter; m. Paul David Prado, Mar. 2, 1985 (div. 1994); children: Paul David Prado, Lauren Mae Prado; m. Leonard Ralph Levine, Jan. 8, 2000 (dec. May 2001). BA in Music Composition and Theory, Flute, Univ. Calif. at Los Angeles, 1986; MA in Edn. counseling, Calif. State U., 1999. Tchr. multiple subjects Torrance (Calif.) Unified Sch. Dist., 1994-96, tchr. music, dir. band and choir, 1996-99, counselor, 1999-00; sch. psychologist Hemet (Calif.) Unified Sch. Dist., 2000—02, Palm Springs (Calif.) Unified Sch. Dist., 2002—04; music tchr., dir. band & choir Temecula Valley Unified Sch. Dist., 2003—. Part-time asst. prof. Calif. State U., Dominguez Hills, 1999—2000; prodr., dir., pub. Prado Prodn. and Publ., Hemet, 2000—. Author: He Always Goes First!, 1998; prodr., dir. (CD) Dreams of the Jaguar, 1999. Sec., faculty rep. Jefferson Sch. Site Coun., Torrance, 1998—99. Mem.: SAG, Wiseburn Faculty Assn. (scholar 1985), So. Calif. Vocal Assn., Calif. Tchrs. Assn., Calif. Assn. Sch. Psychologists, Nat. Assn. Sch. Psychologists, UCLA Alumni Assn., Phi Kappa Phi. Avocations: tennis, skiing, swimming, travel, gardening. Home and Office: Prado Prodn and Pub 26208 Avenida Hortensia Hemet CA 92544-6548 Personal E-mail: musesmaker@aol.com.

LEVINE, ELLEN R., editor-in-chief; b. NYC, Feb. 19, 1943; d. Eugene Jack and Jean (Zuckman) Jacobson; m. Richard U. Levine, Dec. 21, 1964; children: Daniel, Peter. Student, Wellesley Coll. Reporter The Record, Hackensack, NJ, 1964—70; editor Cosmopolitan mag., NYC, 1976—82; editor-in-chief Cosmopolitan Living mag., NYC, 1980—81, Woman's Day mag., NYC, 1982—91, Redbook mag., NYC, 1991—94, Good Housekeeping, NYC, 1994—; editorial cons. O, The Oprah Mag., 2000—. Commr. U.S. Atty. Gen.'s Commn. on Pornography, 1985—86; bd. dirs. Finlay Enterprises, Inc., Lifetime TV; bd. adv. NY Women in Comm. Author: Planning Your Wedding, Waiting for Baby, Rooms That Grow With Your Child; mem. editl. bd. O mag.; contbr. articles to profl. jours. Bd. dirs. Lifetime TV, Christopher Reeve Paralysis Found., NY Restoration Project. Named to Writers Hall of Fame, 1981, Acad. Women Achievers, YWCA, 1982; recipient Outstanding Profl. Achievement award, N.J. Fedn. Women's Clubs, 1984, Matrix award, N.Y. Women in Comm., Inc., 1989, Am. Health Found., 1996, 2d Century award, Columbia U. Sch. Nursing, 1997, Nat. Mag. award for personal svc., 1999. Mem.: Am. Soc. Mag. Editors (named to Hall of Fame). Achievements include being first woman named editor-in-chief of Good Housekeeping. Office: Good Housekeeping 250 W 55th St New York NY 10019*

LEVINE, FELICE, educational association administrator; AB in Psychology, AM in Sociology and Psychology, PhD in Psychology, U. Chgo. Sr. rsch. social scientist Am. Bar Found., 1974—79; program dir. NSF, 1979—91; exec. officer Am. Sociol. Assn., Washington, 1991—2002; exec. dir. Am. Ednl. Rsch. Assn., Washington, 2002—. Mem. nat. human rsch. protections adv. com. U.S. Dept. Health and Human Svcs., co-chair social and behavioral sci. working group; exec. com. Consortium of Social Sci. Assns., chair, 1997—2000; mem. adv. com. Decennial Census; bd. mem. Nat. Humanities Alliance; mem. adv. com. Nat. Consortium of Violence Rsch. Fellow: AAAS, Am. Psychol. Soc. Office: Am Ednl Rsch Assn 1230 Seventeenth St NW Washington DC 20036

LEVINE, FRAN, elementary school educator; b. Bklyn. d. Milton B. and Roma J. Levine. BA, Bklyn. Coll., 1977, MS, 1982. Cert. reading. Tchr. Yeshiva Rambam, Bklyn., 1978—82, PS 219, Bklyn., 1984—. Item writer, field scorer, test creator social studies NYSED, Albany. Contbr. columns in newspapers, articles to magazines. Facilitator Penny Harvest Roundtable, PS 219, 2005. Mem.: Nat. Council Social Studies, Nat. Council Tchrs. English, Internat. Reading Assn. Avocations: travel, photography.

LEVINE, GAIL CARSON, writer; b. N.Y.C., Sept. 17, 1947; d. David and Sylvia Carson; m. David Matthew Levine, Sept. 2, 1967. BA, CCNY, 1969. Employment interviewer NY State Dept. of Labor, NYC, 1970—82; adminstrv. asst. NY State Dept. of Commerce, NYC, 1982—86; welfare adminstr. NY State Dept. of Social Services, NYC, 1986—96. Author: (children's books) Ella Enchanted, 1997 (Newbery Honor Book, 1998), Dave at Night, 1999, The Fairy's Mistake, 1999, The Princess Test, 1999, Princess Sonora and the Long Sleep, 1999, The Wish, 2000, Cinderellis and the Glass Hill, 2000, The Two Princesses of Bamarre, 2001, For Biddle's Sake, 2002, The Fairy's Return, 2002, (children's picture book) Betsy Who Cried Wolf, 2002. Mem.: Soc. Children's Book Writers and Illustrators, PEN, Author's Guild. Office: HarperCollins Children's Books 1350 Ave of Americas New York NY 10019

LEVINE, GEORGE LEWIS, literature and language professor, literary critic; b. N.Y.C., Aug. 27, 1931; s. Harris Julius and Dorothy Sara (Podolsky) L.; m. Margaret Bloom, Aug. 19, 1956; children: David Michael, Rachel Susan. BA, NYU, 1952; MA, U. Minn., 1953, PhD, 1959. Instr. Ind. U., Bloomington, 1959-62, asst. prof., 1962-65, assoc. prof., 1965-68; prof. English Rutgers U., New Brunswick, N.J., 1968—, chmn. dept., 1979-83, Kenneth Burke prof., 1985—. Vis. prof. U. Calif.-Berkeley, 1968, Stanford U., Calif., 1974-75; vis. rsch. fellow Girton Coll., Cambridge U., Eng., 1983; Avalon prof. lit. Northwestern U., 1998; dir. Ctr. for Critical Analysis of Contemp. Culture. Author: Boundaries of Fiction, 1968, The Endurance of Frankenstein, 1975, The Realistic Imagination, 1981, One Culture, 1987, Darwin and the Novelists, 1988, Lifebirds, 1995, Dying to Know, 2002; author, editor: The Art of Victorian Prose, 1968, Mindful Pleasures, 1975, Constructions of the Self, 1992, Realism and Representation, 1993, Aesthetics and Ideology, The Politics of Research, 1994, Cambridge Companion to George Eliot; editor Victorian Studies, 1959-68. With U.S. Army, 1953—55. Guggenheim Found. fellow, 1971-72; NEH fellow, 1978-79; Rockefeller Found. fellow, 1983; Rockefeller Found. Bellagio fellow, 1996, Bogliasco Found. fellow, 1999, 2004. Mem. MLA, AAUP Democrat. Jewish. Home: 108 Wesley Ave Atlantic Highlands NJ 07716 Office: Rutgers U Ctr Critical Analysis Cont Culture New Brunswick NJ 08903

LEVINE, GEORGE RICHARD, language educator; b. Boston, Aug. 5, 1929; s. Jacob U. and Rose Lillian (Margolis) L.; m. Joan Adler, June 8, 1958 (div. 1977); children— David, Michael; m. Linda Rashman, Apr. 17, 1977. BA, Tufts Coll., Medford, Mass., 1951; MA, Columbia, 1952, PhD, 1961. Lectr. English Columbia, 1956-58; instr. Northwestern U., 1959-63; mem. faculty SUNY, Buffalo, 1963—2001, prof. emeritus, 2001—; prof. English State U. N.Y., 1970—, dean faculty arts and letters, 1975-81. Author: Henry Fielding and The Dry Mock, 1967; editor: Harp on the Shore: Thoreau and the Sea, 1985, Jonathan Swift: A Modest Proposal and Other Satires, 1995; contbr. articles to profl. jours. Chmn. bd. dirs. Youth Orch. Found., Buffalo, 1974-75; trustee Buffalo Chamber Music Soc., Arts Devel. Svcs.; bd. dirs. Buffalo Philharm. Orch., 1992-97; pres. Arts in Edn. Inst. Western N.Y. With AUS, 1952-54. Univ. fellow Columbia U., 1958-59, Faculty Research fellow SUNY, 1966-67; Fulbright lectr. W. Ger., 1969-70; recipient Chancellor's award excellence in teaching SUNY, Buffalo, 1973-74. Mem. MLA, Am. Soc. 18th Century Studies, Internat. Assn. Univ. Profs. English, Adirondack Mountain Club. Jewish. Home: 66 Woodbury Dr Snyder NY 14226 Business E-Mail: grlevine@buffalo.edu.

LEVINE, HAROLD, lawyer; b. Newark, Apr. 30, 1931; s. Rubin and Gussie (Lifshitz) L.; children: Brenda Sue, Linda Ellen Levine Gersen, Louise Abby, Jill Anne Levine Lipari, Charles A., Cristina Gussie, Harold Rubin II; m. Cristina Cervera, Aug. 29, 1980. BS in Engring., Purdue U., 1954; JD with distinction, George Washington U., 1958. Bar: D.C. 1958, Va. 1958, Mass. 1960, Tex. 1972, U.S. Patent Office 1958. Naval arch., marine engr. U.S. Navy Dept., 1954-55; patent examiner U.S. Patent Office, 1955-58; with Tex. Instruments, Inc., Attleboro, Mass., 1959-77, asst. sec. Dallas, 1969-72, asst. v.p. and gen. patent counsel, 1972-77; ptnr. Sigalos & Levine, Dallas, 1977-93; prin. Levine & Majorie LLP, Dallas, 1994-2000, Levine & Starr LLP, 2001—. Chmn. bd. Vanguard Security, Inc., Houston, 1977—; chmn. Tex. Am. Realty, Dallas, 1977—; lectr. assns., socs.; del. Geneva and Lausanne (Switzerland) Intergovtl. Conf. on Revision, Paris Pat. Conv., 1975-76. Editor George Washington U. Law Rev., 1956-57; mem. adv. bd. editors Bur. Nat. Affairs, Pat., Trdmk. and Copyright Jour.; contbr. chpt. to book and articles to profl. jours. Mem. U.S. State Dept. Adv. Panel on Internat. Tech. Transfer, 1977. Mem. ABA (chmn. com. 407 taxation pats. and trdmks. 1971-72), Am. Patent Law Assn., Dallas Bar Assn., Assn. Corp. Pat. Csl. (sec.-treas. 1971-73), Dallas-Ft. Worth Patent Law Assn., Pacific Indsl. Property Assn. (pres. 1975-77), Electronic Industries Assn. (pres. pat. com. 1972), NAM, Southwestern Legal Inst. on Patent Law (planning com. 1971-74), U.S. C. of C., Dallas C. of C., Kiwanis, Alpha Epsilon Pi, Phi Alpha Delta. Republican. Jewish. Office: Levine & Starr LLP Bank Am Pl Tower 101 E Park Blvd Ste 755 Plano TX 75074

LEVINE, HENRY DAVID, lawyer; b. NYC, June 7, 1951; s. Harold Abraham and Joan Sarah (Price) L.; m. Barbara Wolgel, Aug. 28, 1976; children: David, Rachel, Daniel. AB, Yale U., 1972; JD, M in Pub. Policy, Harvard U., 1976. Bar: N.Y. 1977, D.C. 1978, U.S. Supreme Ct. 1980. Assoc. Wilmer, Cutler & Pickering, Washington, 1976-80, Morrison & Foerster, Washington, 1981-83, ptnr., 1983-92, Levine, Blaszak, Block & Boothby LLP, Washington, 1993—. Cons. to GSA on FTS2001, 1994—; chmn. bd. TechCaliber, LLC, 1999—; mem. exec. bd. NY Telecon Reliability Adv. Coun., 2005—. Bd. dirs. Washington Hebrew Congregation, 1996—, 1st v.p., 2004—; bd. dirs. Appleseed Found., 2001—; exec. bd. mem. NY Telecomm. Reliability Adv. Coun., 2005—, mem., 2005—. Named one of the twenty-five most powerful people in networking Network World, 1996. Mem. ABA, Fed. Communication Bar Assn., Forum Com. on Comm. Law. Home: 5208 Edgemoor Ln Bethesda MD 20814-2342 Office: Levine Blaszak Block & Boothby 2001 L St NW Ste 900 Washington DC 20036-4940 Office Phone: 202-857-2550. E-mail: hlevine@lb3law.com.

LEVINE, HERBERT, lawyer; b. June 5, 1924; s. Barnet and Mollie (Morris) L.; m. Pearl H. Kahn, Mar. 30, 1946; children: Barbara, Susan, Deborah, Steven. BBA, JD, U. Wis., 1950. Bar: Wis. 1950, U.S. Dist. Ct. (ea. dist.) Wis. 1950. Pvt. practice, Milw., 1950-66; assoc. Bernstein, Wessel & Lewis, Milw., 1967-75; shareholder Stupar, Schuster & Cooper S.C., Milw., 1976-2000; sole practitioner Milw., 2000—. Instr. Am. Inst. Banking, Milw., 1964-88; lectr. Marquette U., 1968-79, Milw. Bd. Realtors, 1961. Pres. Bayside PTA, Wis., 1965-66; active Indian Guides, Bayside, Wis., 1972-73. Sgt. USAAF, 1943-46. Mem. Wis. Bar Assn., Milw. Bar Assn. Home: 9055 N King Rd Milwaukee WI 53217-1848 Office: 633 W Wisconsin Ave Milwaukee WI 53203-1918 Office Phone: 414-271-8833. E-mail: ssc@ssclaw.com.

LEVINE, HOWARD ARNOLD, judge; b. Mar. 4, 1932; m. Barbara Joan Segall, July 25, 1954; children: Neil Louis, Ruth Ellen, James Robert. BA, Yale U., 1953, LLB, 1956; LLD (hon.), Union U., 1994. Bar: N.Y. 1956. Asst. in instrn., research assoc. in criminal law Yale Law Sch., 1956-57; assoc. firm Hughes, Hubbard, Blair, Reed, N.Y.C., 1957-59; practiced in Schenectady, 1959-70; asst. dist. atty. Schenectady County, N.Y., 1961-66, dist. atty., 1967-70; judge Schenectady County Family Ct., 1971-80; acting judge Schenectady County Ct., 1971-80; adminstrv. judge family cts. N.Y. State 4th Jud. Dist., 1974-80; assoc. justice appellate div. 3d dept. N.Y. State Supreme Ct., 1982-93; assoc. judge N.Y. Ct. of Appeals, 1993—2003; Robert H. Jackson disting. prof. law Albany Law Sch., Union U., 2003—; sr. counsel Whiteman, Osterman & Hanna, Albany, NY, 2003—. Vis. lectr. Albany Law Sch., 1972-81; mem. N.Y. Gov.'s Panel on Juvenile Violence, N.Y. State Temp. Commn. on Child Welfare, N.Y. State Temp. Commn. on Recodification of Family Ct. Act, N.Y. State Juvenile Justice Adv. Bd., 1974-80; mem. ind. rev. bd. N.Y. State Div. for Youth, 1974-80; mem. rules and adv. com. on family ct. N.Y. State Jud. Conf., 1974-80 Contbr. articles to law revs. Bd. dirs. Schnecatady County Child Guildance Ctr., Carver Community Ctr., Freedom Forum of Schnectady. Mem. ABA, Am. Law Inst., N.Y. State Bar Assn. (chmn. spl. com. juvenile justice), Assn. Family Ct. Judges State N.Y. (pres. 1979-80) Home: 2701 Rosendale Rd Niskayuna NY 12309-1300 Office: Whiteunau Osterman & Hanna Commerce Plaza Albany NY 12210 Office Phone: 518-487-7684.

LEVINE, HOWARD R., retail executive; b. 1959; With merchandising dept. Family Dollar Stores, Matthews, N.C., 1981-87, v.p., gen. merchandise mgr. softlines, 1996, sr. v.p. merchandising and advt., 1996-97, pres., COO, 1997-98, CEO, 1998—. Office: Family Dollar Stores PO Box 1017 Charlotte NC 28201-1017*

LEVINE, IRVING R., commentator, dean, writer, educator; b. Pawtucket, R.I. s. Joseph and Emma (Raskin) L.; m. Nancy Cartmell Jones, July 12, 1957; children— Jeffrey Claybourne Bond, Daniel Rome, Jennifer Jones. BS, Brown U., 1944, LHD (hon.), 1969; MS, Columbia, 1947; LHD (hon.), Bryant Coll., 1974; D.Journalism (hon.), Roger Williams Coll., 1985; LLD (hon.), U. R.I., 1988; LHD (hon.), Lynn U., 1992; LLD (hon.), Northeastern U., 1993; D in Journalism (hon.), R.I. Coll., 1996. Writer obits. Providence Jour., 1940-43; fgn. news editor Internat. News Service, 1947-48; chief Vienna (Austria) bur., 1948-50; with NBC, 1950-95, war corr. in Korea, 1950-52; radio anchor World News Roundup, N.Y.C., 1953-54; chief corr. NBC, Moscow, 1955-59, Rome, 1959-71, London, 1967-68, chief econs. corr. Washington, 1971-95; dean Coll. Internat. Comms., Lynn U., Boca Raton, Fla., 1995—; ret. Commentator Consumer News and Bus. Channel Cable TV affiliate svc. NBC TV News, 1990-96; commentator Pub. Broadcasting Sys. TV, Nightly Bus. Report, 1997—; spl. writer London Times, 1955-59; covered assignments in Can., China, Czechoslovakia, Bulgaria, Poland, Japan, Vietnam, Formosa, Thailand, Eng., France, Germany, Switzerland, Algeria, Congo, Israel, Turkey, Tunisia, Greece, Yugoslavia, Union of South Africa, Denmark, Sweden, Ireland; press group with pres. Ford, Carter, Reagan, Bush, Clinton; attended G-7 Econ. Summits, 1975-95; world affairs lectr. Holland Am. Cruise Line. 1995-97, Cunard Cruise Line, 1998-2001, Radisson Seven Seas Cruise Line, 2000-04, Celebrity Cruise Lines, 2004—; lectr. univs., bus. groups, cruise ships; writer Internet World Traveler Column, 1997-99; moderator Bus. Update TV Program, Fla. TV programs, 1998-99; nat. spokesperson First Penn-Pacific Life Ins. Co., 1997-99; anchor Bus. Trends TV program, 2000. Author: Main Street, USSR, 1959, Travel Guide to Russia, 1960, Main Street, Italy, 1963, The New Worker in Soviet Russia, 1973; contbr. articles to nat. mags.; guest on numerous TV shows including Murphy Brown, 1989, David Letterman Show, 1990, Jay Leno Show, 1990. 2d lt. Signal Corps, U.S. Army, 1943-46, Philippines, Japan. Recipient award for best radio-TV reporting from abroad Overseas Press Club, 1956, award for outstanding radio network broadcasting Nat. Headliners Club, 1957, 50th Anniversary award Columbia Sch. Journalism, 1963, Emmy citation 1966, Martin R. Gainsbrugh award for best econ. reporting, 1978, William Rogers award Brown U., 1988, Silver Circle award Nat. Acad. TV Arts and Scis., 1990; named one of 10 Outstanding Young Men, U.S. Jaycees, 1956; named to R.I. Hall of Fame, 1972, Pawtucket Hall of Fame, 1986, Nat. Broadcasters Hall of Fame Lifetime Achievement award, 1995, TJFR and Master Card award as one of 100 top bus. news luminaries, 2000; named Among 100 Most accomplished Grads. 20th Century Brown Alumni mag., 2000; honoree Loyola Coll.'s Beta Gamma Sigma, 1994, Mem. Coun. on Fgn. Rels. (fellowship 1952-53), Cosmos, Phi Beta Kappa, Beta Gamma Sigma. Office: Lynn U 3601 N Military Trail Boca Raton FL 33431-5598

LEVINE, JACK, artist; b. Boston, Jan. 3, 1915; s. Samuel Mayer and Mary (Grinker) L.; widowed; 1 child, Susanna Levine Fisher. AFD, Colby Coll., Waterville, Maine, 1956. One-man shows include Downtown Gallery, N.Y.C., 1938, Artists, 1942, Mus. Modern Art, N.Y.C., 1943; exhibited in group shows at Jeu de Paume, Paris, 1938, Carnegie Internat. exhbns., 1938-40, Artists for Victory, Met. Mus., N.Y.C., 1942, retrospective at Jewish Mus., N.Y.C., 1978-79, Bklyn. Mus., 1999; represented in permanent collections Mus. Modern Art, Met. Mus. Art, N.Y.C., William Hayes Foggs Mus., Harvard U., Addison Gallery, Andover, Mass., Mus. Vatican, D.C. Moore Gallery, N.Y. With AUS, 1942-45. Mem. Am. Acad. Arts and Letters (pres., chancellor), Inst. Arts and Letters (pres. 1993), Nat. Acad. Design, Century Club.

LEVINE, JACK ANTON, lawyer; b. Monticello, N.Y., Dec. 23, 1946; s. Milton and Sara (Sacks) L.; m. Eileen A. Garsh, Sept. 7, 1974; children: Matthew Aaron, Dara Esther. BS with honors, SUNY, Binghamton, 1968; JD with honors, U. Fla., 1975, LLM in Taxation, 1976. Bar: Fla. 1975, U.S. Ct. Appeals (11th cir.) 1981, U.S. Tax Ct., 1982. Tax atty. legis. and regulations divsn. Office chief counsel IRS, Washington, 1977-81; assoc. Holland & Knight, Tampa, Fla., 1981-83, ptnr., 1984—. Lectr. in field. Contbr. articles to profl. jours. Mem. ABA, Fla. Bar Assn. (sect. taxation exec. coun. 1984-2003, chmn. partnership com. 1985-88, chmn. taxation regulated pub. utilities com. 1988-92, co-chmn. corps. and tax-exempt orgns. com. 1992-2001, bd. cert. in tax law 1984—). Democrat. Jewish. Avocations: golf, reading, travel. Home: 10905 Carrollwood Dr Tampa FL 33618-3903 Office: Holland & Knight Ste 4100 100 N Tampa St Tampa FL 33602-3644 Office Phone: 813-227-6531. E-mail: jack.levine@hklaw.com.

LEVINE, JAMES, conductor, performing company executive, pianist; b. Cin., June 23, 1943; s. Lawrence M. and Helen (Goldstein) Levine. Theory and interpretation student with Walter Levin, piano student with Rosina Lhevinne and Rudolf Serkin, conducting student with Jean Morel, Fausto Cleva and Max Rudolf; student, Juilliard Sch. Music, 1961—64; degree (hon.), U. Cin., New Eng. Conservatory, Northwestern U., SUNY, Potsdam, The Juilliard Sch. Debut as pianist Cin. Symphony Orch., 1953; debut as condr. Aspen (Colo.) Music Festival, 1961; assist. condr. Cleve. Orch., 1964—70; condr. The Met. Opera, N.Y.C., NY, 1971—73, prin. condr., 1973—75, music dir., 1976—85, 2004—, artistic dir., 1986—2004; chief condr. Munich Philharm., 1999—2004; music dir. UBS Verbier Festival Orch., 2000—04, Boston Symphony Orch., Boston, 2004—, Ravinia Festival, Highland Park, Ill., 1973—93, Cin. May Festival, 1974—78; guest condr. Vienna Philharm. Orch., Berlin Philharm. Orch., Chgo. Symphony Orch., Phila. Orch., Boston Symphony Orch., NY Philharm. Orch., Dresden Staatskapelle, Philharmonia Orch., Israel Philharm. Orch., Bayreuth Festival, Salzburg Festival. Guest lectr. Sarah Lawrence Coll., Harvard U., Yale U. Recipient Smetana medal, 1987, Nat. Medal of Arts, 1997, Kennedy Ctr. Honors, 2002, 8 Grammy awards. Office: The Met Opera Lincoln Ctr New York NY 10023

LEVINE, JEROME, psychiatrist, educator; b. N.Y.C., July 10, 1934; s. Abraham and Sadie (Glowatz) L.; children: Ross W., Lynn R., Andrew R. BA, U. Buffalo, 1954, MD, 1958. Intern, then psychiat. resident E.J. Meyer Meml.

Hosp., Buffalo, 1958-61; sr. psychiat. resident St. Elizabeth's Hosp., Washington, 1961-62; staff psychiatrist USPHS Hosp., Lexington, Ky., 1962-64; research psychiatrist, asst. chief psychopharmacology research br. NIMH, 1964-67, chief of br., 1967-81, chief pharmacologic and somatic treatments research br., 1981-84; research prof. psychiatry U. Md. Sch. Medicine, Balt., 1985-94; dep. dir. Nathan Kline Inst. for Psychiat. Rsch., Orangeburg, N.Y., 1994—; rsch. prof. psychiatry NYU, 1994—. Instr. psychiatry Johns Hopkins Med. Sch., 1964-72; vis. prof. U. Pisa, Italy, 1977 Author books and papers on psychopharmacology, clin. trial methodology, somatic treatment assessment for psychiat. disorders. Mem. Soc. Clin. Trials, Am. Psychiat. Assn. (Hofheimer Research prize 1970), Am. Coll. Neuropsychopharmacology, Collegium Internationale Neuropsychopharmacologicum, Am. Soc. Clin. Pharmacology and Therapeutics. Home: 15 Stony Hollow Chappaqua NY 10514-2014 Office: Nathan Kline Inst Bldg 35 140 Old Orangeburg Rd Ste 35 Orangeburg NY 10962-1159 Office Phone: 845-398-5503. E-mail: levine@nki.rfmh.org.

LEVINE, JEROME "JERRY" LESTER, lawyer; b. LA, July 20, 1940; m. Maryanne Shields, Sept. 13, 1966; children: Aron Michael, Sara Michelle. BA, U. So. Calif. San Francisco State U., 1962; JD, U. Calif. Hastings Law Coll., 1965. Bar: Calif. 1966, U.S. Dist. Ct. (Ctrl. Dist. Calif.) 1966, U.S. Ct. Appeals (9th Cir.) 1985, U.S. Supreme Ct. 1986, U.S. Dist. Ct. (Ea. Dist. Calif.) 1988, U.S. Ct. Appeals (Fed. Cir.) 1989. Dir. operational svcs., assoc. dir. Western Ctr. on Law and Poverty, L.A., 1968-72; assoc. Swerdlow, Glikbarg & Shimer, Beverly Hills, Calif., 1972-77; ptnr. Lans Feinberg & Cohen, L.A., 1977-79, Albala & Levine, L.A., 1980-83, Neiman, Billet, Albala & Levine, LA, 1983-90, Levine & Assocs., LA, 1991-2000, Holland & Knight LLP, LA, 2000—, mem. dir. com. Lectr. U. So. Calif. Law Ctr. 1970, Loyola U. Sch. Law 1971; corp. counsel Nat. Indian Gaming Assn.(NIGA)(chmn. task force on IGRA regulations, mem. NIGA-Nat. Congress American Indians Tribal-State negotiating team (NCAI)), Calif. Nations Indian Gaming Assn. (CNIGA), Wash. Indian Gaming Assn.(WIGA); mem. bd. dir. Law and Legis. Com. 1988-92, co-chmn. 1992-95; spkr. in field. Contbr. articles to profl. jours.; regular contbr. Indian Gaming Mag., 1990—97, Internat. Gaming and Wagering Mag., oversees editing and publication Indian Gaming Handbook. Mem. ABA (sects. on corp., banking and bus. law, litig., patent, trademark and copyright law, mem. forum com. on the entertainment and sports industries 1979), Beverly Hill Bar Assn. (mem. corp. and commercial law com. 1977-, entertainment law com. 1977-), LA County Bar Assn. (mem. antitrust sect.), Fed. Bar Assn. (indian law sect.), State Bar Calif., Internat. Assn. Gaming Lawyers, Internat. Masters Gaming Law Assn. Office: Holland & Knight LLP 633 W 5th St 21st Fl Los Angeles CA 90071 Office Phone: 213-896-2565. E-mail: jllevine@hklaw.com.

LE VINE, JEROME EDWARD, retired ophthalmologist; b. Pitts., Mar. 23, 1923; s. Harry Robert and Marian Dorothy (Finesilver) L.; m. Marilyn Tobey Hiedovitz, Apr. 14, 1957; children: Loren Robert, Beau Jay, Janice Lynn. BS, U. Pitts., 1944; MD, Hahnemann Med. Sch., Phila., 1949; postgrad. in ophthalmology, U. Pa., 1951-52. Diplomate Am. Bd. Disability Cons., Am. Bd. Quality Assurance & Utilization Rev. Intern St. Francis Hosp., Pitts., 1949-50; resident in ophthalmology Jefferson U. Med. Sch. Hosp., Phila., 1952-54; ophthalmologist Leech Farm VA Hosp., Pitts., 1955-59; chief eye dept. Stanocola Clinic, Baton Rouge, 1959-64; sole practice medicine specializing in ophthalmology Baton Rouge, 1959-86; ret., 1986. Cons. La. State U., East La. State Hosp. Infirmary, Villa Feliciana Geriatric Hosp., disability dept. Social Security Adminstn., div. blind La. State Pub. Welfare dept.; mem. staff Our Lady of the Lake Hosp., Baton Rouge Gen. Hosp., Women's Hosp.; instr. spl. edn. U. Southeastern La., 1971. Mem. Am. Bd. Quality Assurance and Utilization Rev., 1990. With MC, AUS, 1942-44. Fellow Am. Geriatric Soc., Royal Soc. Health; mem. AMA, La. State Med. Soc., East Baton Rouge Parish Med. Soc., 6th Dist. Med. Soc., New Orleans Acad. Ophthalmology, So. Med. Assn., La. Med. Soc., Baton Rouge Parish Med. Soc., Pi Lambda Phi, Phi Delta Epsilon. Democrat. Jewish. Office: PO Box 66787 Baton Rouge LA 70896-6787 Office Fax: 225-924-6801.

LEVINE, JONATHAN CHARLES, urban planner, educator; b. Berkeley, Calif., May 26, 1958; s. Hillel Benjamin and Rose A. Levine; m. Noga Morag; 1 child, Adam Shira. PhD, U. Calif., Berkeley, 1986—90. Assoc. prof., coord. of doctoral studies Taubman Coll. Arch. and Urban Planning, U. Mich., Ann Arbor, 1997—2004, chair, assoc. prof., 2004—. Author: (book) Zoned Out: Regulation, Markets, and Choice in Transportation and Land Use. Office: Urban and Regional Planning Program Univ Mich 2000 Bonisteel Blvd Ann Arbor MI 48109-2069 Office Phone: 734-763-0039.

LEVINE, JOSHUA H., medical products executive; BA in Comm., U. Ariz. Various exec. level sales and mktg. positions to v.p., gen. mgr., Home Health Care Divsn. Kinetic Concepts, Inc., San Antonio, 1989—96; v.p., sales and aesthetic products Mentor Corp., Santa Barbara, Calif., 1996—98, v.p., sales and mktg., aesthetic products, 1998—2000, v.p., domestic sales and mktg., aesthetic products, 2000—01, head of global aesthetic sales and mktg., 2001—02, sr. v.p., global sales and mktg., 2002—03, pres., COO, 2003—04, pres., CEO, 2004—, also bd. dir.; chief develop. officer The Plastic Surgery Co., 2000. Office: Mentor Corp 201 Mentor Dr Santa Barbara CA 93111*

LEVINE, JUDY KENDALL, real estate broker, interior designer, writer; d. Allen Harvern Emerman and Serena Roth; m. Ira Bradley Levine, Jan. 10, 1975; children: Jonathan Alexander, Ross Stewart. BA, Finch Coll., 1972. Sales broker Gumley Haft Kleier, N.Y.C., 1997—; interior designer Kendall Assocs., Inc, N.Y.C., 1980—; v.p. Douglas Elliman, N.Y.C., 2003—. Poetry studies N.Y. Pub. Libr., N.Y.C., 2000—02; advisor emergency housing for victims of Sept.11th, N.Y.C., 2001. Author: (poetry) A Childs' Prayer, 2001. Pediatric dir. donor affairs N.Y. Presbyn. Hosp., N.Y. Weil Cornell Med. Ctr., N.Y.C., 1989—93. Mem.: Soc. Libr., Real Estate Bd. of N.Y., Soc. of Journalists & Authors. Avocations: cultural activities, charitable affilations, crafts, golf. Home: 23 East 74th St New York NY 10021 Office: Douglas Elliman 575 Madison Ave New York NY 10022

LEVINE, LAURENCE HARVEY, lawyer; b. Cleve., Aug. 23, 1946; s. Theodore and Celia (Chaikin) Levine; m. Mary M. Conway, May 13, 1978; children: Abigail, Adam, Sarah. BA cum laude, Case Western Res. U., 1968; JD, Northwestern U., 1971. Bar: Ill. 1971, U.S. Dist. Ct. (no. dist.) Ill. 1972, U.S. Ct. Appeals (6th, 7th, 10th, 11th and D.C. cirs.), U.S. Ct. Claims 1997, U.S. Ct. Appeals (fed. cir.) 2000. Law clk. to presiding judge U.S. Ct. Appeals (6th cir.), Detroit, 1971-72; assoc. Kirkland & Ellis, Chgo., 1972-76; ptnr. Latham & Watkins, Chgo., 1976—. Bd. editors Northwestern Law Rev., 1968-71. Mem. ABA, Chgo. Bar Assn., Mid-Am. Club. Office: Latham & Watkins Sears Tower Ste 5800 Chicago IL 60606-6306 E-mail: laurence.levine@lw.com.

LEVINE, LOUIS D., museum director, archaeologist; b. NYC, June 4, 1940; s. Moe Wolf and Jeanne (Greenwald) L.; m. Dorothy Abrams, Dec. 30, 1962 (div. 1991); children: Sarra L., Samuel E.; m. Pat Molholt, May 25, 1997. Student, Brandeis U., 1960; BA with honors, U. Pa., 1962, PhD with distinction, 1969. Instr. of Hebrew U. Pa., Phila., 1966-69; asst. curator Royal Ont. Mus., Toronto, Can., 1969-75, assoc. curator, 1975-80, curator, 1981, assoc. dir., 1987-90; asst. commr., dir. N.Y. State Mus., Albany, 1990-98; dir. collections & exhbns. Mus. Jewish Heritage, N.Y.C., 1998—. Vis. sr. lectr. Hebrew U., Jerusalem, 1975-76; vis. prof. U. Copenhagen, 1985; asst. prof. U. Toronto, 1969-74, assoc. prof. U. Toronto, 1974-81, prof., 1981-90; dir. Seh Gabi Expdn., western Iran, 1971-73, dir. Mahidasht Project, western Iran, 1975-79. Author: The Neo-Assyrian Zagros, 1974; editor: Scream the Truth at the World, 2001, Lives Remembered, 2002; contbr. articles to profl. jours. NDEA fellow U. Pa., 1962-65, Fulbright fellow, 1965, W.F. Albright fellow, Am. Schs. of Oriental Rsch., 1966, fellow Inst. for Advanced Studies, Hebrew U. Mem. Brit. Inst. of Persian Studies, Brit. Sch. of Archaeology in Iraq, Am. Assn. Mus., Am. Oriental Soc. Jewish. Office: Mus Jewish Heritage 36 Battery Pl New York NY 10280 Office Phone: 646-437-4249. E-mail: llevine@mjhnyc.org.

LEVINE, MACY IRVING, physician; b. Johnstown, Pa., May 19, 1920; s. Elliott B. and Ida (Leuin) L.; m. Evelyn B. Levine, June 28, 1948 (dec. July 1996); children: Alan, Amy, Paul, Robert. BS, U. Pitts., 1940, MD, 1943. Diplomate Am. Bd. Internal Medicine, Am. Bd. Internal Medicine and Allergy. Intern U. Pitts. Med. Ctr., 1944; resident in allergy VA Hosp., Aspinwall, Pa., 1947-48, resident in medicine, 1948-49; fellow in medicine Lahey Clinic, Boston, 1950-51; USPHS postdoctoral fellow in medicine Peter Bent Brigham Hosp.-Harvard Med. Sch., Boston, 1951-52; pvt. practice Pitts., 1952—. Clin. prof. medicine U. Pitts. Sch. Medicine. Editor: Monograph on Insect Allergy, 4th edit., 2003; editor Bull. of the Allegheny County Med. Soc., 1975-86, Pitt Medicine Med. Alumni Assn., U. Pitts., 1987-99; contbr. more than 70 articles to profl. jours. Bd. dirs. Self Help Group Network, 1989-95, B'nai Israel Congregation, Pitts., 1965-71, Hebrew Free Loan Assn. Pitts., 1980—. Capt. U.S. Army, 1944-46, PTO. Recipient Disting. Svc. award Am. Acad. Allergy and Immunology, 1987, Frederick M. Jacob, M.D. Physician Merit award for Outstanding Svc. Allegheny County Med. Soc., 1988. Fellow Am. Acad. Allergy, Asthma and Immunology (v.p. 1982-83, Outstanding Vol. Clin. Faculty award 1996), Pa. Allergy Assn. (pres. 1970-71, Spl. Recognition award 1989), fellow, ACP; mem. Pitts. Allergy Soc. (pres. 1959-61), U. Pitts. Med. Alumni Assn. (pres. 1976-77), U. Pitts. Alumni Assn. (pres. 1984-85). Avocations: tennis, bridge. Home: 220 N Dithridge St Apt 400 Pittsburgh PA 15213-1421 Office Phone: 412-621-2393.

LEVINE, MADELINE GELTMAN, literature and language educator, translator; b. N.Y.C., Feb. 23, 1942; d. Herman and Nettie (Kritman) Geltman; m. Steven I. Levine; children: Elaine, Daniel. BA, Brandeis U., 1962; MA, Harvard U., 1964, PhD, 1971. Asst. prof. Grad Sch. CUNY, N.Y.C., 1971-74; assoc. prof. U. N.C., Chapel Hill, 1974-80, prof., 1980-94, Kenan prof. Slavic lits., 1994—, chmn. dept. Slavic langs., 1979-87, 94-99. Chmn. joint com. on Ea. Europe, Am. Coun. Learned Socs.-Social Sci. Rsch. Coun., 1989-92; chmn. bd. govs. U. N.C. Press, 1999-2005. Translator: A Memoir of the Warsaw Uprising (Miron Bialoszewski), 1977, 2d edit. 1991, The Poetry of Osip Mandelstam: God's Grateful Guest (Ryszard Przybylski), 1987, Beginning With My Streets: Essays and Recollections (Czeslaw Milosz), 1992, A Year of the Hunter (Czeslaw Milosz), 1994, Bread for the Departed (Bogdan Wojdowski), 1997, Lost Landscapes: In Search of Isaac Bashevis Singer and the Jews of Poland (Agata Tuszynska), 1998, Milosz's ABCs (Czeslaw Milosz), 2001, The Woman from Hamburg and Other True Stories, (Hanna Krall), 2005; translator with Francine Prose: A Scrap of Time and Other Stories (Ida Fink), 1986, 2d edit., 1995; author: Contemporary Polish Poetry, 1925-75, 1981; co-editor (with Bogdana Carpenter): To Begin Where I Am: Selected Essays (Czeslaw Milosz), 2001. NEH fellow, 1984, 2000; recipient (with Francine Prose) award for lit. translation PEN-America, 1988. Mem. Am. Assn. for Advancement of Slavic Studies, Polish Inst. of Arts and Scis. Am., Am. Assn. Tchrs. of Slavic and East European Langs., Am. Literary Translators Assn., Pen-Am. Home: 5001 Whitehorse Rd Hillsborough NC 27278-9399 Office: U NC CB # 3165 425 Dey Hall Chapel Hill NC 27599-3165 Office Phone: 919-962-7553. Business E-Mail: mgl@unc.edu.

LEVINE, MARK DAVID, science administrator, director; b. Cleve., May 26, 1944; s. Hyman and Rebecca (Spector) Levine; m. Irma Herrera, June 1990. AB summa cum laude, Princeton U., 1966; PhD, U. Calif., Berkeley, 1975. Staff scientist Ford Found. Energy Policy Project, Washington, 1972-73; sr. energy policy analyst SRI Internat., Menlo Park, Calif., 1974-78; staff scientist Lawrence Berkeley Lab., Berkeley, 1978-84, dept. program leader, 1984-86, leader energy analysis program, 1986-96, dir. environ. energy techs. divsn., 1996—. Cons. Ford Found., TEM, Inc., Pacific Gas & Electric Co., QED Rsch., Inc., Energy Found. Contbr. articles to profl. jours. Lead author Intergovernmental Panel Climate Change; bd. dirs. Am. Coun. Energy Efficient Econ., Ctr. Clean Air Policy, Ctr. Resource Solutions, chair; bd. dirs. Calif. Clean Energy Fund, Beijing Energy Efficient Ctr., Shanghai Pacific Energy Ctr. Woodrow Wilson fellow, 1966, Fulbright scholar, 1966. Fellow: Calif. Coun. Sci. and Tech.; mem.: Consortium Electricity Reliability (vice-chair). Jewish. Home: 5701 Barrett Ave El Cerrito CA 94530-1408 Office: Lawrence Berkeley Lab Bldg 90 Room 3125 Berkeley CA 94720 Business E-Mail: mdlevine@lbl.gov.

LEVINE, MARTIN, printmaker, art educator; b. N.Y.C., N.Y., 1945; MFA Calif. Coll. Arts & Crafts, 1972. Assoc. prof. SUNY, Stony Brook. Represented in collections of Art Inst. Chgo., Boston Mus. Art, Brooklyn Mus. Art, Calif. Palace of Legion of Honor, Libr. Congress, Milw. Art Ctr., Montclair Mus. Art, Mus. Fine Arts Boston, N.Y. Hist. Soc., N.Y. Public Libr., S.F. Mus. Modern Art, Victoria & Albert Mus., Zimmerli Mus. Grantee Nat. Endowment for the Arts. Mem.: Audubon Artists, Boston Printmakers, Soc. Am. Graphic Artists (past pres.), NAD (academician). Office: Staller Center for the Arts State University of New York Stony Brook NY 11794-5400 Office Phone: 631-632-7250. Business E-Mail: mlevine@notes.cc.sunysb.edu.

LEVINE, MELDON EDISES, lawyer, retired congressman; b. LA, June 7, 1943; s. Sid B. and Shirley B. (Blum) L.; children: Adam Paul, Jacob Caplan, Cara Emily. AB, U. Calif., Berkeley, 1964; MPA, Princeton U., 1966; JD, Harvard U., 1969. Bar: Calif. 1970, D.C. 1972. Assoc. Wyman, Bautzer, Rothman & Kuchel, 1969-71; legis. asst. U.S. Senate, Washington, 1971-73; ptnr. Levine Krom & Unger, Beverly Hills, Calif., 1973-77; mem. Calif. Assembly, Sacramento, 1977-82, 98th-102d Congresses from 27th Calif. dist., Washington, 1983-93; ptnr. Gibson, Dunn & Crutcher, L.A., 1993—. Author: The Private Sector and the Common Market, 1968; contbr. articles to various publs. Mem. governing bd. U.S.-Israel Sci. and Tech. Commn., U.S. Holocaust Meml. Mus.; mem. amateur baseball team Hollywood Stars, 1971—. Mem.: LA Bar Assn., Calif. Bar Assn. Office: Gibson Dunn & Crutcher 2029 Century Park E Ste 4000 Los Angeles CA 90067-3032 Office Phone: 310-557-8098. E-mail: mlevine@gibsondunn.com.

LEVINE, MELVIN CHARLES, lawyer; b. Bklyn., Nov. 12, 1930; s. Barnet and Jennie (Iser) Levine. BCS, NYU, 1952; LLB, Harvard U., 1955. Bar: N.Y. 1956, U.S. Supreme Ct. 1964. Assoc. Kriger & Haber, Bklyn., 1956-58, Black, Varian & Simon, N.Y.C., 1958; pvt. practice N.Y.C., 1959—. Devel. multiple dwelling housing; dir. Am. ORT, mem. nat. campaign com.; trustee Bramson ORT Coll.; del. World ORT Gen. Assembly; mem. housing ct. adv. coun. N.Y. State Unified Ct. Sys.; mem. ind. Dem. jud. screening panel N.Y.C. civil ct. judges; mem. Character and Fitness Com. Trustee Jewish Ctr. Hamptons. Recipient Cmty. Achievement award, N.Y. ORT Scholarship Fund. Mem.: Assn. Bar City of N.Y. (adj. mem. jud. com.), N.Y. County Lawyers Assn. (dir., mem. civil ct. com., mem. housing ct. com., mem. uniform housing ct. rules com., liaison Assn. Bar City N.Y. selection housing, civil, criminal judges, mem. com. jud., mem. task force tort reform, co-chair civil ct. practice sect., Civil Ct. Practice Sect. Disting. Svc. award). Democrat. Jewish. Home: 146 Waverly Pl New York NY 10014-3848 Office: 271 Madison Ave Ste 1404 New York NY 10016-1001

LEVINE, MICHAEL, public relations executive, writer, television personality; b. NYC, Apr. 17, 1954; s. Arthur and Virginia (Gaylor) L. Student, Rutgers U., 1978. Owner, operator TV News Mag., Los Angeles, 1977-83; owner Levine/Schnieder Pub. Rels., now Levine Comms. Office, Los Angeles, 1982—. Gov.'s adv. bd. State Calif., Sacramento, 1980-82; pres., owner Aurora Pub., LA, 1986—; moderator Thought Forum; lectr. in field; founder, moderator LA Media Roundtable; media expert KFWB Radio; radio host Access LA, Spiritual Seeker, Inside/Out Author: The Address Book: How to Reach Anyone Who's Anyone, 1984, The New Address Book, 1986, The Corporate Address Book, 1987, The Music Address Book, 1989, Environmental Address Book, 1991, Kid's Address Book, 1991, Guerrilla P.R., Lessons at Halfway Point, 1995, Take It From Me, Selling Goodness, 1998, The Princess & The Package, 1998, Guerrilla PR Wired, A Branded World, 2003, The 7 Life Lessons of Noah's Ark, 2004; editor (newsletter): For Consideration. Mem. Ronald Reagan Pres.'s Libr.; founder The Actor's Conf., Aurora Charity, 1987; bd. dirs. Felice Found., Micah Ctr.; adv. bd. Dare America; founder, moderator L.A. Media Roundtable; moderator U. Judaism Thought Forum. Mem. TV Acad. Arts and Scis., Entertainment Industries Coun., Musician's Assistance Program, West Hollywood C. of C. (bd. dirs. 1980-82). Jewish. Office: 1180 S Beverly Dr Los Angeles CA 90035 E-mail: mlevine@lcoonline.com.

LEVINE, NAOMI BRONHEIM, academic administrator; b. N.Y.C., Apr. 15, 1923; d. Nathan and Malvina (Mermelstein) Bronheim; m. Leonard Levine, Apr. 11, 1948; 1 child, Joan. BA, Hunter Coll., 1944; LLB, Columbia, 1946, JD, 1970. Bar: N.Y. 1946. With Scaadrett, Tuttle & Chalaire, N.Y.C., 1946-48, Charles Gottleib, N.Y.C., 1948-50, Am. Jewish Congress, 1950-78, exec. dir., 1972-78; v.p. to sr. v.p. external affairs NYU, N.Y.C., 1978—2002, spl. advisor to pres., 2002—; chmn., dir. Heyman Ctr. for Philanthropy and Fund Raising, 2002—. Asst. prof. law and police sci. John Jay Coll., N.Y.C., 1969—73, L.I. U., 1965—69. Author: (book) Schools in Crisis, 1969, The Jewish Poor-an American Awakening, 1974, Politics, Religion and Love, 1990; mem. editl. bd. Columbia Law Rev., 1945—46; author: For Her Days Not Her Nights. Chmn. N.Y.U. Bronfman Ctr., N.Y.U. Ctr. for Israeli Studies; com. on character and fitness N.Y. Supreme Ct.; co-chair Taub Ctr. for Israel Studies, NYU; bd. dirs. N.Y. Ctr. Philanthropy and Fund Raising. Named to Hunter Coll. Hall of Fame, 1972. Office: NYU 29 Washington Square West New York NY 10011 Office Phone: 212-998-2380, 212-998-2384.

LEVINE, NORMAN M., academic administrator; b. Chgo., 1943; BS Engring., Ill. Inst. Tech., 1964; MBA, Marquette U., 1969. Sr. v.p., CFO DeVry Inc., Oakbrook Terrace, 2001—. Mem. Fin. Execs. Internat. Office: DeVry Inc Ste 1000 One Tower Ln Oakbrook Terrace IL 60181 Office Phone: 630-574-1906. Business E-Mail: nlevine@devry.com.

LEVINE, PAMELA GAIL, business owner; b. Alameda, Calif., Nov. 20, 1942; d. Carl B. and Lucille N. (Lua) Leverenz; m. George David Barth (div. 1974); children, Claudia Anne, Shanette Michelle; m. Leonard Stuart Levine; children: Leslie, Julie, Susan, Stuart Carl. BA in Archtl. Design/Fine Arts, U. Calif., Berkeley, 1965. Designer Trude of Calif., San Francisco, 1965-66; tchr. TWA, Kansas City, Mo., 1966-69; ptnr., owner, archtl. designer Leverenz of N.Y., 1970—; owner, designer Ressco, Katonah, N.Y., 1974—. Cons. archtl. design and real estate devel.; founder, owner Sintec-Internat. Bus. Opportunities, 1989—; founder, co-owner TheArtsMarket.com, I-The Arts Market. Designer of Sets/Costumes, Chappaqua Drama Group, 1973—. Devel. com. Mount Holyoke Coll., S. Hadley, Mass., 1987—; co-founder Looking Glass Players, Mt. Kisco, N.Y., 1985—; active Jr. League, Caramoor, Katonah Mus. Mem. No. Westchester Ctr. for the Arts (exec. com., v.p. bd. dirs., bd. dirs. devel. com., co-chmn. bldg. com.), Chappaqua Drama Group (bd. dirs.). Republican. Avocations: painter, costume design, set design, doll design, artist. Home: RR 6 Katonah NY 10536-9806 Office: Real Estate Support Svcs PO Box 574 Katonah NY 10536-0574

LEVINE, PAUL MICHAEL, paper company executive, consultant; b. Bklyn., Apr. 15, 1934; s. Isaac Bert and Jessie Sue (Palevsky) L.; m. Lois Jaffin, June 11, 1954 (div.); children: Daniella Sarah, Julie Ann, Carl Joseph; m. 2d Noelle Tenedou, July 14, 1974; children: Simone Allana, Alexander Owen. AB in Econs., Harvard Coll., 1954; A.M. in Internat. Econs., Fletcher Sch. Internat. Law and Diplomacy, 1955. Sales mgr. U.S. Industries, Stamford, Conn., 1956-61; chief exec. officer subs. cos. Parsons and Whittemore-Black Clawson, N.Y.C., 1962-69; dep. adminstr. City of N.Y., 1970-72; v.p. S&S Corrugated Paper Machinery Co., Bklyn., 1973-76, Continental Group, Stamford, Conn., 1977-83; chmn. New Lehigh Corrugated Products, Farmingdale, N.Y., United Container Corp., Phila. Lectr., fellow Yale U., U. Conn., Fordham U., 1979-90; Neeltran Inc., New Milford, Conn., Shulz Electric Corp., New Haven, Conn., Gulf Copper Mfg. Co., Port Arthur, Tex., Gas Tech Engring., Tulsa, Okla. Author: Proceedings 6th World Forestry Congress, 1966; editor: Study of Peoria County Model Program, 1970, Practical Exporting, 1962, The Role of Venture Capital in Europe and the World Trustee Hartman Regional Theatre, Stamford, 1981-82; bd. dirs. Ridgefield Orch., 1978-83, Bklyn. Arts and Culture Assn., 1973-92. Mem. /Turnaround Mgmt. Assn., Explorers Club. Democrat. Jewish. Office: Paul M Levine & Assocs 466 Ridgebury Rd Ridgefield CT 06877-1228 E-mail: levassoc@aol.com. *Creativity, innovation and laughter are the glories of the world.*

LEVINE, PHILIP, classics educator; b. Lawrence, Mass., Sept. 8, 1922; s. Samuel and Jennie (Derdak) L.; m. Dinnie Moseson, June 19, 1955; children— Jared Elliott, Harlan Alcon. AB, Harvard, 1946, A.M., 1948, PhD, 1952; DHL (hon.), U. Judaism, 1986. Instr., asst. prof. classics Harvard, 1952-59; assoc. prof. classical langs. U. Tex. at Austin, 1959-61; assoc prof., prof. classics UCLA, 1961-91, prof. emeritus, 1991—, dean div. humanities, 1965-83; Biggs resident lectr. Washington U., 1993. Info. officer Coun. U. Calif. Emeriti Assn. Author: Lo Scriptorium Vercellese da S. Eusueblo ad Attone, 1958, St. Augustine, City of God, Books 12-15, 1966; editor: Latin lt. sect. Twayne World Author Series, 1964—; adv. editor, U. Calif. Publs. in Classical Studies, 1963-72; assoc. editor, contbr. to U. Calif. Studies in Classical Antiquity, 1967-75, sr. co-editor, 1975-78; mem. editorial bd. Classical Antiquity, 1986-93. Mem. rev. com., sr. fellowship program Nat. Endowment for Humanities, 1966-70; bd. govs. U. Judaism, 1968-90, coun. visitors, 1990-94, acad. adv. coun., 1994—. With AUS, 1943-46. Sheldon fellow Italy; Guggenheim fellow; Fulbright Research grantee; recipient Bromberg Humanities award; decorated Cavaliere dell' Ordine al Merito della Repubblica Italiana. Mem. Am. Philol. Assn. (dir. 1968-70), Mediaeval Acad. Am. (exec. council 1969-72), Renaissance Soc., Am. Philol. Assn., Pacific Coast (chmn. gen. lit. 1964-65), Phi Beta Kappa. Home: 224 S Almont Dr Beverly Hills CA 90211-2507 Office: U Calif Dept Classics Los Angeles CA 90095-0001 Office Phone: 310-825-4171. Business E-Mail: levine@ucla.edu.

LEVINE, PHILLIP PAUL, application developer, poet, actor; b. Bklyn., Feb. 27, 1956; s. Paul Philip and Betty Lee Levine; m. Meredith Auerbach, Mar. 21, 2004; 1 child, Piper Jaden. BS Math., SUNY Binghamton, 1978. Asst. v.p. Johnson & Higgins, New York, NY, 1983—87, v.p. - mgr. micro products divsn./risk mgmt. svcs., 1987—89; application programmer/computer cons. Saugerties, NY, 1989—; poetry editor Chronogram Mag. Luminary Pub., Kingston, NY, 2003—; pres. Woodstock Poetry Soc., NY, 2003—. Tech. dir. Tech. Coordination Com. FUSE, New York, 1985—97. Actor: (performance (co-lead: austin) True West; author: (poetry chapbook) 13 Poems As Of; actor: (performance (co-lead: moon) The Real Inspector Hound, (performance (lead: charlie baker) The Foreigner, (performance (co-lead: don) The Universal Language, (performance (co-lead: antipholus of syr) The Comedy of Errors; actor/director (performance (he) Savage/Love; dir.: (performance) How To Roast a Pepper; actor: (performance (principal: edgar) King Lear; performance poet (performance) 2000 National Poetry Slam - Woodstock Team. Coord. Performing Arts of Woodstock, NY, 1999—2005; host - weekly open mic poetry Colony Cafe, Woodstock, 2001—05. Scholar Regents Scholarship, N.Y. State, 1973—78. Mem.: U.S. Chess Fedn. (life Postal Chess Master 1995). Independent. Home: 235 Manorville Rd Saugerties NY 12477 Personal E-mail: pprod@mindspring.com.

LEVINE, RAPHAEL DAVID, chemistry professor; b. Alexandria, Egypt, Mar. 29, 1938; brought to U.S., 1939; s. Chaim S. and Sofia (Greenberg) L.; m. Gillah T. Ephraty, June 13, 1962; 1 child, Ornah T. MSc, Hebrew U., Jerusalem, 1959; PhD, Nottingham (Eng.) U., 1964; DPhil, Oxford (Eng.) U., 1966; PhD honoris causa, U. Liege, Belgium, 1991, Tech. U., Munich, Germany, 1996. Vis. asst. prof. U. Wis., 1966-68; prof. theoretical chemistry Hebrew U., Jerusalem, 1969—, chmn. research ctr. molecular dynamics, 1981—, Max Born prof. natural philosophy, 1985—; faculty Dept. Chemistry and Biochemistry UCLA, L.A. Battelle prof. chemistry and math. Ohio State U., Columbus, 1970-74; Brittingham vis. prof. U. Wis., 1973; adj. prof. U. Tex., Austin, 1974-80, MIT, 1980-88, UCLA, 1989—; Arthur D. Little lectr. MIT, 1978; Miller rsch. prof. U. Calif., Berkeley, 1989, A.D. White prof. at large Cornell U., 1989-95. Author: Quantum Mechanics of Molecular Rate Processes, 1969, Molecular Reaction Dynamics, 1974, 2005, Lasers and Chemical Change, 1981, Molecular Reaction Dynamics and Chemical

Reactivity, 1986, Algebraic Theory of Molecules, 1995, Molecular Reaction Dynamics, 2005; mem. editorial bds. several well known scientific jours.; contbr. articles to profl. jours. With U.S. Army, 1960—62. Co-recipient Chemistry prize, Wolf Found., 1988; named Ramsay Meml. fellow, 1964—66, Alfred P. Sloan fellow, 1970—72; recipient Ann. award, Internat. Acad. Quantum Molecular Sci., 1968, Landau prize, 1972, Israel prize in exact scis., 1974, Weizman prize, 1979, Rothschild prize, 1992, Max Planck prize for internat. cooperation, 1996, EMET prize, 2002, MOLEC award, 2004. Fellow Am. Phys. Soc.; mem. Israel Chem. Soc., Israel Acad. Scis., Max Planck Soc. (fgn. mem.), Academia Europaea (fgn.), Am. Acad. Arts and Scis. (fgn. hon. mem.), Am. Philos. Soc. (fgn.), Royal Danish Acad. Scis. and Letters (fgn.), Natl. Acad. of Sci., US, (fgn.). Office: UCLA Dept Chemistry & Biochemistry 607 Charles E Young E Dr Los Angeles CA 90095-1569 also: Hebrew U Jerusalem Fritz Haber Rsch Ctr Molecular Dynamics Jerusalem 91904 Israel Office Phone: 310-206-0476. Business E-Mail: rafi@fh.huji.ac.il.

LEVINE, REBECCA-SUE, lawyer; b. N.Y.C., July 1, 1946; d. Isaac and Jeanette (Katz) Kurash; m. Paul Edward Levine, Dec. 22, 1968 (dec. Aug. 1976). BS in Journalism, Ohio U., 1967; JD, Bklyn. Law Sch., 1982. Bar: N.Y. 1983. Sr. editor Women's Wear Daily, N.Y.C., 1972-75; editor-in-chief Men's Wear Mag., N.Y.C., 1975-78; editor Booke and Co., N.Y.C., 1983-85; sole practice, N.Y.C., 1985—; adj. instr. journalism Fashion Inst. Tech., N.Y.C., 1972-87. Pres. Quality-Ruskin Tenants Fedn., Forest Hills, N.Y., 1974, 75; fundraiser Mental Health Assn. Greater N.Y., 1976-90; vol. Humane Soc. N.Y., 1978-79; mem. Older Women's League, N.Y.C., 1985-90; v.p. 27 Victoria Owners Coop., N.Y.C., 1985-86; active Bronx Zoo, Mus. Natural History. Mem. ABA, N.Y. State Bar Assn., Bklyn. Bar Assn., Bklyn. Women's Bar Assn., Women in Communications, Networks Unlimited, Mortar Bd., Chimes. Avocations: photography, travel, wildlife study. Home and Office: 200 E 27th St New York NY 10016-9202

LEVINE, RICHARD A., statistics educator; b. Queens, NY, Sept. 1, 1969; s. Samuel J. and Rhoda L. Levine; life ptnr. Juanjuan Fan. BS, SUNY at Binghamton, 1991; MS, Cornell U., 1994, PhD, 1996. Assoc. prof. San Diego State U., San Diego, 2002; asst. prof. U. of Calif., Davis, 1996—2002. Fellow Grad. rsch., Dept. of Def., Office of Naval Rsch., 1987-1991; grantee Rsch. awards, NSF, 1999-2005. Mem.: Phi Beta Kappa. Achievements include research in Markov chain Monte Carlo methods; Bayesian models. Office: San Diego State Univ Dept of Math 5500 Campanile Rd San Diego CA 92128 Office Fax: 619-594-6746. Personal E-mail: ralevine@sciences.sdsu.edu.

LEVINE, RICHARD E., lawyer; b. Flushing, N.Y., Aug. 6, 1950; s. Sol and Betty Levine; m. Lori A. Balter, Oct. 28, 1979; 1 child, Jamie Balter. BS in Mech. Engring., Bucknell U., 1972; JD, U. Md., 1975; LL.M. in Taxation, Georgetown U., 1978. Bar: Md. 1975, U.S. Tax Ct. 1979, D.C. 1980, U.S. Supreme Ct. 1983, U.S. Ct. Appeals (4th cir.) 1984. Assoc. Miles & Stockbridge, Balt., 1978-83, prin., 1983—2001; ptnr. DLA Piper Rudnick Gray Cary LLP, Balt., 2002—. Adj. prof. U. Md. Law Sch., Balt., 1988. Contbr. articles to profl. jours. Bd. dirs. Har Sinai West Sr. Citizens Housing, Balt., 1983—92; trustee McDonogh Sch., 2002—. Fellow Am. Coll. Tax Counsel; mem. ABA (tax sect., chair partnerships 1990-92), Md. State Bar Assn. (tax sect. coun. 1983-86), The Center Club (house com. 1990—, bd. govs. 1996—). Avocations: golf, music. Office: DLA Piper Rudnick Gray Cary LLP 6225 Smith Ave Baltimore MD 21209-3600

LEVINE, RICHARD JAMES, publishing executive; b. N.Y.C., Jan. 24, 1942; s. Irving Joseph and Dorothy Joyce (Thome) L.; m. Neil Ann Stuckey, June 1, 1963; children: Jonathan Donald, Russell Neilan. BS, Cornell U., 1962; MS with high honors, Columbia U., 1963. Gen. assignment reporter Wall St. Jour., Washington, 1966—67, labor corr., 1967—70, mil. writer, 1970—75, chief econ. writer, outlook columnist, 1976—80; editl. dir., data base pub. Dow Jones & Co., Princeton, NJ, 1980—87, v.p. info. svcs. group, 1987—89, v.p. and editl. dir. info. svcs. group, mem. mgmt. com., 1989—92, v.p., mng. editor info svcs. segment, mem. mgmt. com. N.Y.C., 1992—95; v.p. fin. info. svcs. group, mng. editor Dow Jones News Svcs., Dow Jones & Co., N.Y.C., 1995—97; v.p., mng. editor Dow Jones Newswires, Dow Jones & Co., Jersey City, 1997—2001, v.p., exec. editor Jersey City and Princeton, NJ, 2001—. Dep. chmn. VWD GmbH, 1996-2004; pres. Dow Jones Newspaper Fund, Econ. Rsch. Co. Inc., Dow Jones AER Co. Inc. Author: (with others) The Wall Street Journal Views America Tomorrow, 1977. Trustee Opera Festival N.J., 1998-2003, McCarter Theatre Ctr., Princeton, N.J., Princeton (N.J.) Symphony Orch. 1st lt. U.S. Army, 1964-66. Pulitzer fellow, 1963—64. Mem. Cornell U. Coun., Cornell U. Tower Club, Soc. Profl. Journalists, Cornell Club (N.Y.C.), Princeton Indoor Tennis Ctr. Home: 108 Parkside Dr Princeton NJ 08540-4815 Office: Harborside Fin Ctr 800 Plaza Two Jersey City NJ 07311-1199

LEVINE, ROBERT A., cardiologist; b. N.Y.C., Jan. 29, 1953; s. Jules and Shirley (Krupnick) L. AB summa cum laude, Harvard Coll., 1974; MD, Harvard Med. Sch., 1978. Diplomate Am. Bd. Internal Medicine. Intern, resident in medicine Beth Israel Hosp., Boston, 1978-81; fellow in cardiology Mt. Sinai Hosp., N.Y.C., 1981-83; clinical & rsch. fellow Mass. Gen. Hosp., Boston, 1983-85; instr. in medicine Harvard Med. Sch., Boston, 1985-87, from asst. prof. to assoc. prof. medicine, 1987-2000, prof., 2000—. Staff physician cardiac unit Mass. Gen. Hosp., Boston, 1985—, dir. cardiac ultrasound labs., 1995—; sci. session abstract chmn. Am. Soc. Echocardiography, 1993-95, program chmn., 1996-98, bd. dirs.; adj. prof. bioengring. Ga. Inst. Tech., Atlanta, 1995—. Editl. bd. Jour. Am. Coll. Cardiology, 1991-95, 99-2001, Circulation, 1996—2002, Jour. Amer. Soc. Ech., 1998-2002. Recipient awards NIH, 1985, 87, 95, 98, 2001, 02, 03, 04, Israel Heart Soc., 1999, Doris Duke Charitable Found. Innovations Med. Rsch. award, 2000; clinician-scientist, established investigator Am. Heart Assn., 1986, 91, Atna Found. Quality Care Rsch. Fund, 2001, Richard Popp award for mentoring Am. Soc. Echocardiography, 2002, Henry N. Neufeld award U.S.-Israel Binational Sci. Found., 2002. Office: Mass Gen Hosp Cardiac Ultrasound YOCC5068 Boston MA 02114 E-mail: rlevine@partners.org.

LEVINE, ROBERT ARTHUR, economist, educator, policy writer; b. Bklyn., July 7, 1930; s. Isaac Bert and Jessie Sue (Palevsky) L.; m. Esther Carol Knudsen, Mar. 2, 1953; children: David Knudsen, Peter Kemmerer, Joseph Karl. BA, Harvard U., 1950, MA, 1951; PhD, Yale U., 1957. Economist Rand Corp., 1957-61, sr. economist, 1962-65, 69-73, 87—, sr. economist emeritus, cons., 1994-98, 98—; research assoc. Harvard U. Center Internat. Affairs, 1961-62; asst. dir. for research, plans, programs and evaluation OEO, Washington, 1966-69; pres. N.Y.C.-Rand Inst., 1973-75; dep. dir. Congl. Budget Office, Washington, 1975-79; v.p. System Devel. Corp., Santa Monica, Calif., 1979-85; pres. Canyon Analysts, 1985—. Sr. fellow Nat. Security Studies Program, UCLA, 1964-65; vis. prof. public policy Stanford U. Grad. Sch. Bus., 1972; adj. prof. econs. Pepperdine U. Sch. Bus. and Mgmt., 1984 Author: The Arms Debate, 1963, The Poor Ye Need Not Have With You, 1971, Public Planning: Failure and Redirection, 1972, Evaluation Research and Practice, 1981, Still the Arms Debate, 1990, Turmoil and Transition in the Atlantic Alliance, 1991. With USN, 1951—54. Ford Found. grantee, 1969, 1985, German Marshall Fund grantee, 1979, Carnegie Corp. grantee, 1986. Clubs: Beverly Glen Democratic. Home and Office: 10321 Chrysanthemum Ln Los Angeles CA 90077-2812 E-mail: ral@rand.org.

LEVINE, ROBERT JAY, lawyer; b. Hackensack, NJ, Aug. 7, 1950; s. Nathan R. and Naomi (Bendel) Levine; m. Joan Beth Mirviss, Aug. 10, 1975. AB, Brown U., 1972; JD, U. Pa., 1975. Bar: N.Y. 1976, U.S. Dist. Ct. (so. and ea. dists.) N.Y. 1976. Assoc. Davis Polk & Wardwell, N.Y.C., 1975-82, ptnr., 1983—2002, sr. counsel, 2003—. Pres., bd. dirs. Sylvan Winds, Inc. Trustee NY Youth Symphony, Inc. Mem.: ABA, Internat. Bar Assn., Assn. Bar City of N.Y., N.Y. State Bar Assn., Brown Club N.Y.C., Phi Beta Kappa. Democrat. Jewish. Avocations: golf, travel, cooking, film. Home: 115 Central Park W New York NY 10023-4153 Office: Davis Polk and Wardwell 450 Lexington Ave New York NY 10017-3982 Office Phone: 212-450-4000.

LEVINE, ROBERT JEFFREY, lawyer; b. Miami Beach, Fla., Nov. 27, 1956; s. I. Stanely and Elaine (Martz) L. BSBA magna cum laude, U. Fla., 1978; JD, George Washington U., 1981. Bar: Fla. 1981, U.S. Dist. Ct. (so. dist.) Fla. 1981, U.S. Ct. Appeals (5th and 11th cirs.) 1981, U.S. Supreme Ct. 1986; cert. civil mediator, Fla. Supreme Ct.; lic. sea capt. USCG. Assoc. Barron, Lehman & Cardenas, Miami, 1981-82; ptnr. Haves & Levine, Miami, 1982-83; pvt. practice law Miami, 1983-85; ptnr. Toland & Levine, Miami, 1985-90, Levine & Geiger, P.A., Miami, 1990-94, Levine & Ptnrs., P.A., Miami, 1994—2002. Mem.: ATLA, Acad. Fla. Trial Lawyers, Fla. Bar Assn. Avocations: diving, fishing, skiing, golf, tennis. Office: Levine & Ptnrs PA 1110 Brickell Ave 7th Fl Miami FL 33131-3132 E-mail: RJL@levinelawfirm.com.

LEVINE, ROBERT JOHN, internist, educator; b. N.Y.C., Dec. 29, 1934; s. Benjamin Bernard and Ruth Florence (Schwartz) L.; m. Jeralea Fooshee Hesse, Nov. 28, 1987; children from previous marriage: John Graham, Elizabeth Hurt Braun; stepchildren: Stephen B. Hesse, Katherine F. Hesse. Student, Duke U., 1951—54; MD with distinction, George Washington U., 1958. Diplomate Am. Bd. Internal Medicine. Med. house officer Peter Bent Brigham Hosp., Boston, 1958-59, asst. resident in medicine, 1959-60; clin. assoc. Nat. Heart Inst., Bethesda, Md., 1960-62, investigator, 1963-64; chief med. resident VA Hosp., West Haven, Conn., 1962-63; mem. faculty depts. medicine and pharmacology Yale U., New Haven, 1964-73, chief sect. clin. pharmacology, 1966-74, prof. medicine, lectr. pharmacology, 1973—, co-chair exec. com. interdisciplinary program bioethics, 1999—; mem. med. staff Yale-New Haven Med. Ctr., 1964-68, attending physician, 1968—, co-dir. Ctr. Interdisciplinary Rsch. on AIDS, Law, Policy and Ethics Core, 1997—2000, dir., 2000—. Mem. Conn. Adv. Com. on Foods and Drugs, 1967-82, sec. 1969-71, chmn., 1971-73; mem. adv. com. AIDS program U.S. HHS, 1989-95; cons. Nat. Commn. Protection of Human Subjects of Biomed. and Behavioral Rsch., 1974-78; bd. dirs. Medicine in the Pub. Interest, Inc., 1976-2002, sec., 1983-2002; mem. ethics subcom. of dir.'s adv. com. Ctrs. for Disease Control and Prevention, 1997-2001, 05—; HIV prevention scis. working group NIH: Office of AIDS Rsch., 1998-2002; mem. adv. com. Nat. Human Rsch. Protections, 2000-02. Author: Ethics and Regulation of Clinical Research, 1981, 2d edit., 1986; editor Clin. Rsch., 1971-76, IRB: Rev. Human Subjects Rsch., 1978-2000, chairperson editl. bd., 2000—; contbr. numerous articles to profl. jours. Mem. Conn. Humanities Coun., 1983-89, chmn. 1988-89, Coun. Internat. Orgn. Med. Scis., co-chmn. steering com. revision internat. ethical guidelines for biomed. rsch. involving human subjects, 1991-93, chmn., 1998-02; chair working group for revision of Declaration of Helsinki, World Med. Assn., 1998-99. Multiple rsch. grantee. Fellow ACP, The Hastings Ctr., AAAS (coun. del. 1987-91); mem. Am. Soc. Clin. Investigation, Am. Soc. Clin. Pharmacology and Therapeutics (bd. dirs. 1981-85), Am. Fedn. Clin. Rsch. (nat. coun. 1967-76, exec. com. 1971-76), Am. Soc. Pharmacology and Exptl. Therapeutics (exec. com. 1974-77), Am. Soc. Law, Medicine and Ethics (bd. dirs. 1986-96, pres. 1989-90, 94-95), Pan Am. Health Orgn. (internat. bioethics adv. bd. 2000-03), Pub. Responsibility in Medicine and Rsch. (bd. dirs. 1984—), Soc. for Bioethics Consultation (bd. dirs. 1988-94), Nat. Inst. Mental Health (human subjects rsch. coun. working group 1999—), Sigma Xi, Alpha Omega Alpha. Office: Yale Univ Interdisciplinary Bioethics Project PO Bxo 208300 New Haven CT 06520-8300 Office Phone: 203-432-8807. E-mail: levinerj@att.net.

LEVINE, ROBERT SIDNEY, chemical engineer, consultant; b. Des Moines, June 4, 1921; s. George Julius and Betty (Dennen) L.; m. Sharon Lorraine White; children: George, Gail, Tamara, Michelle, James. BS in Chem. Engring, Iowa State U., 1943; S.M. (Std. Oil Co. Ohio fellow 1947-48), M.I.T., 1946, Sc.D., 1949. With Rocketdyne div. Rockwell Internat. Co., 1948-66; assoc. research dir. NASA, 1966-74; chief liquid rocket tech. Nat. Bur. Stds., Washington, 1974-97; chief fire dynamics Nat. Bur. Stds. (now Nat. Inst. Stds. and Tech.), Washington, 1975-97. Mem. faculty UCLA, 1962-64, George Washington U., 1977; pres. Combustion Inst., 1974-78; chmn. Am. and Soviet Com. on Fire Rsch. in Housing, 1977-82. Author papers in field; mem. Washington editl. rev. bd. NIST, 1976-97. Named Engr. of Year Los Angeles sect. Am. Inst. Chem. Engrs., 1961 Mem. Am. Chem. Soc., AIAA, Nat. Fire Prevention Assn. Home: 19017 Threshing Pl Gaithersburg MD 20886-3143 Office Phone: 301-926-8868. Personal E-mail: rslevine@erols.com.

LEVINE, RONALD JAY, lawyer; b. Bklyn., June 23, 1953; s. Louis Leon and Marilyn Priscilla (Markovich) L.; m. Cindy Beth Israel, Nov. 18, 1979; children: Merisa, Alisha. BA summa cum laude, Princeton U., 1974; JD cum laude, Harvard U., 1977. Bar: N.Y. 1978, U.S. Dist. Ct. (so. and ea. dists.) N.Y. 1978, D.C. 1980, N.J. 1987, U.S. Supreme Ct. 1982, U.S. Ct. Apeals (2d cir.) 1983, N.J. 1987, U.S. Dist. Ct. N.J. 1987, U.S. Dist. Ct. (we. dist.) N.Y. 1991, U.S. Ct. Appeals (3d cir.) 1991, Pa. 1995. Assoc. Phillips, Nizer, Benjamin, Krim & Ballon, N.Y.C., 1977-80, Debevoise & Plimpton, N.Y.C., 1980-84, Herrick, Feinstein, N.Y.C., 1984-85, ptnr., 1985—. Gen. counsel Greater N.Y. Safety Council, N.Y.C., 1979-81; arbitrator Small Claims Ct. of Civil Ct. of City of N.Y., 1983-85; chmn. fee arbitration com. Mercer County, N.J. Mem. Site Plan Rev. Adv. Bd., West Windsor, N.J., 1986, planning bd., 1987. Mem. ABA (litigation sect.), N.Y. State Bar Assn. (chmn. com. on legal edn. and bar admission 1982-92, com. on profl. discipline 1989-90), N.J. State Bar Assn. (product liability com. 1991—, profl. responsibility com. 1992-96), Assn. of Bar of City of N.Y. (coun. jud. adminstrn. 1994-95, com. on profl. responsibility 1980-83, com. on legal assistance 1983-86, product liability com. 1987-91, trustee career devel. awards 1989-90), Phi Beta Kappa. Home: 6 Arnold Dr Princeton Junction NJ 08550-1521 Office: Herrick Feinstein 2 Park Ave Fl 20 New York NY 10016-9302

LEVINE, SOLOMON BERNARD, business and economics educator; b. Boston, Aug. 10, 1920; s. Isaac William and Sybil (Mannis) l.; m. Elizabeth Jane Billett, Dec. 24, 1943; children: Janet Ruth Levine Thal, Michael Alan, Samuel Billett, Elliott Mannis. AB magna cum laude, Harvard Coll., 1942; cert. Japanese Lang., U. Colo., 1944; MBA with honors, Sch. Bus. Adminstrn., Harvard U., 1947; postgrad., MIT, 1947-49, PhD in Indsl. Econs., 1951. Teaching asst. dept. econs. and social sci. MIT, 1947-49; faculty U. Ill., 1949-69, prof. labor and indsl. relations and Asian studies, 1964-69; prof. bus. and econs. U. Wis.-Madison, 1969-89, prof. emeritus, 1989—, mem. East Asian Studies Program, chmn., 1968-77, co-chmn., 1982-88, dir. Nat. Resource Ctr. for East Asian Studies, 1985-87, participating faculty mem. Indsl. Relations Research Inst. Fulbright prof. Keio U., Tokyo, 1959; vis. prof. dept. econs. Pa. State U., 1960; vis. prof. labor relations dept. econs. MIT, 1962-63; vis. prof. econs. U. Singapore, 1968; vis. lectr. and rsch. scholar various univs., Indonesia, 1973, Australia, 1973, N.Z., 1973, vis. scholar univs., Japan, 1978, Australia, 1978, N.Z., 1978, Singapore, 1978, South Korea, 1978; vis. prof., sr. scholar Monash U., Australia and Japan, 1981-82, vis. rsch. scholar Macquarie U., Australia, 1985; vis. prof. Internat. U. Japan, 1984, Nanzan U., Nagoya, Japan, 1989-91, U. Hawaii, Manoa, 1991; vis. fellow Swinburne Inst. Tech., Australia, 1992; vis. scholar Japan Ctr. for Mich. U., Japan, 1994. labor arbitrator. Author: Industrial Relations in Postwar Japan, 1958, Japanese transl., 1959, (with Hishashi Kawada) Human Resources in Japanese Industrial Development, 1980; co-editor, co-author: chpts. and preface Workers and Employers in Japan: The Japanese Employment Relations System, 1973, (with Koji Taira) Japan's External Economic Relations: Japanese Perspectives, 1991; contbr. to sect. Ency. Americana; chpts. to books, articles to profl. jours. Treas. Stevenson for Pres. Campaign, Champaign-Urbana, Ill., 1952; active Cmty. Integration Coun., 1965-69 Sheldon traveling fellow Harvard U., Mex., 1942; Social Sci. Rsch. Coun. tng. fellow, 1948-49; Fulbright rsch. scholar and Ford Found. rsch. fellow Hitotsubashi U., Tokyo, 1953-54; Social Sci. rsch. Coun. fellow Carnegie Inst. Tech., 1957; life fellow Found. Keio U., 1961; Fulbright-Hays faculty rsch. scholar Japan, 1968, 73, 78, Singapore, 1968, 78, Australia, 1978; Fulbright-Hays faculty scholar N.Z., 1978, Japan Found. scholar, 1978; hon. Fulbright sr. scholar Australia, 1981. Mem. Indsl. Rels. Rsch. Assn., Assn. for Asian Studies, Midwest Conf. of Asian Affairs (pres. 1961), Japan Soc., Internat. House of Japan, Internat. Indls. Rels. Assn., Japan Illini Club (hon. life), Wis. Alumni Assn. Japan (pres. 1990), Phi Beta Kappa, Beta Gamma Sigma. Home: 333 W Main St Apt 501 Madison WI 53703-2779

LEVINE, STANLEY WALTER, chemical company executive; b. Boston, Dec. 13, 1929; s. Bernard T. and Sonia (Spector) L.; m. Tochia Levine; children: Robert, Douglas, Elizabeth. BS in Journalism, Butler U., 1952; postgrad., Boston Coll., 1967; grad., FBI Citizens Acad. Nat. mktg. dir. Bates Mfg. Co., N.Y.C., 1965-68; mgmt. cons. Frederick Chusid Co., N.Y.C., 1971-76, Fashioncade, N.Y.C., 1968-71; pres., CEO Internat. Coating & Chem. Co. Inc., Fairfield, Conn., 1976—. Contbr. articles to Nat. Chem. Weekly, Harpers. Mem. Nat. Republican Congl. Com., Rep. Com. Fairfield County (Conn.); bd. dirs. Butler U., So. Poverty Law Ctr., Ariz. and Nat. regional rep., Ariz. Humane Soc., Phoenix Meml. Hosp.; trustee Butler Univ.; bd. mem. Audubon Soc., Arthritis Found., Home Base for Homeless Kids, Anti-Defamation League, St. Joseph Hosp.-Barrow Neurological, Boys Scouts of Am., Ariz. Animal Welfare League; capt. posse edivsn., spl. dep. Sheriff's Dept. Maricopa County; pres. Am. Jewish Com.; mem. Phoenix Environ. Quality Commn. Served to capt. USAF, 1952-55. Decorated Korean Honor medal, Disting. Svc. to Cmty. award Salvation Army. Mem. Am. Mgmt. Assn., Chem. Week Contbrs., Pres.'s Club N.Y., Nat. Chem. Club, N.Y. Acad. Scis., Internat. Platform Assn., Harmonie Club, Paradise Valley Country Club, Plaza Club (bd. dirs.), Rolls Royce Club (chmn. pres. S.W. region), Coddington Landing Assn. (bd. dirs.), Camelback Estates I (bd. dirs.), Gainey Ranch Country Club (bd. dirs.), Alexis de Tocqueville Soc., Sigma Delta Chi, Sigma Alpha Mu, Alpha Phi Omega. also: PO Box 6345 Scottsdale AZ 85261-6345 Office Phone: 480-948-8089. E-mail: stantoch@aol.com.

LEVINE, STEPHEN M., psychologist, educator; b. N.Y.C., Feb. 22, 1945; s. Abraham and Nettie Levine; m. Michelle Mahler; children: Aaron, Sharon, David. AB, Hunter Coll., CUNY, 1967; MSE, CUNY, 1970; PhD, Hofstra U., 1972. Cert. school psychologist N.Y., N.J., Md., psychologist Md. School psychologist Nanuet (N.Y.) Pub. Schs., 1970—72; asst. prof. Salisbury State Coll., Md., 1972—73; assoc. dir. sch. psychol. program U. Md., College Park, 1973—79; asst. prof. Kean Coll., Union, NJ, 1979—81; dir. spl. svcs. Carteret (N.J.) Schs., 1981—86, Colts Neck Twp. Schs., NJ, 1994—2000; prof. psychology Georgian Ct. U., Lakewood, NJ, 1985—. Cons. U.S. Dept. Edn.; rep. Nat. Assn. of Pupil Pers. Orgns. Reviewer: Book Research Methods and Statistics, 2002. Com. mem. Howell Twp. Bd. Edn. Mem.: Am. Psychol. Assn. (exec. officer divsn. sch. psychologists 1973—76), Ea. Psychol. Assn., Nat. Assn. Sch. Psychologists. Home: 24 Poplar St Howell NJ 07731 Office: Georgian Ct Univ 900 Lakewood Ave Lakewood NJ 08701 E-mail: levine@georgian.edu.

LEVINE, STEVEN JON, lawyer; b. N.Y.C., Sept. 27, 1942; s. Irving I. and Freda S. Levine; m. Linda Jane Silberman, Apr. 23, 1967; 1 child, Lawrence Alan. BS, Syracuse U., 1964; JD, St. John's U., 1966; MA, CCNY, 1973; LLM, NYU, 1978. Bar: NY 1967. Assoc. Augustin J. San Filippo & Steven Jon Levine, PC, predecessor, N.Y.C., 1968-78; mem. Vittoria & Forsythe and predecessor, N.Y.C., 1978-93, Levine & Zelman, 1993—. Arbitrator N.Y. County Civil Ct. Panel, 1980-93; asst. csl. N.Y. State Senate Judiciary Com., 1977. Author: of legal column Tomorrow newspapers, 1991-2000; co-author: Divorce Q & A: Answers to Questions about Divorce, Equitable Distribution, Maintenance, Custody and Child Support; host weekly radio law program Sta. WVOX, 1990-91; creator, narrator: (audio cassette program) Coping with Separation and Divorce. Committeeman, Bronx County, 1970-76; bd. dirs. Jewish Conciliation Bd. Am., 1973-93. Mem. ABA, N.Y. State Bar Assn., Westchester County Bar Assn., Assn. Bar City N.Y. (sect. vice chmn. matrimonial com. 1977-80), Am. Arbitration Assn. (no-fault, comml. panels 1975-88). Office: 50 Main St Ph White Plains NY 10606-1901 also: Levine & Zelman 630 5th Ave New York NY 10111-0100 also: Levine & Zelman 1940 Commerce St PO Box 427 Yorktown Heights NY 10598 Office Phone: 914-946-6641.

LEVINE, STEVEN NEIL, endocrinologist; b. NYC, June 10, 1946; s. Milton and Miriam (Gerofsky) L.; m. Laurie Rita Winkler, July 27, 1969; children: Amy, Karen, Jonathan. BA in Gen. Sci. with distinction, U. Rochester, 1968; MD, NYU, 1971. Diplomate Am. Bd. Internal Medicine 1979, cert. Endocrinoogy & Metabolism 1974. Intern N.C. Meml. Hosp., Chapel Hill, 1971-72, resident in medicine, 1972-74; fellow in endocrinology U. N.C. Sch. Medicine, Chapel Hill, 1976-79, clin. instr. medicine, 1976-79; asst. prof. medicine La. State U. Health Scis. Ctr., Shreveport, 1979-84; assoc. prof. medicine, chief sect. endocrinology La. State U. Med. Ctr., Shreveport, 1984-91, prof. medicine, chief sect. endocrinology, 1991—. Instr. dept. medicine N.C. Meml. Hosp., Chapel Hill, 1976-79; staff physician La. State U. Health Sci. Ctr., 1979, Shreveport VA, 1979; courtesy staff Schumpert Med. Ctr., Shreveport, 1980, Highland Hosp., Shreveport, 1981. Reviewer Archives of Internal Medicine, 1981—, Jour. Clin. Endocrinology and Metabolism, 1985—, Obstetrics and Gynecology, 1985—, Clin. Toxicology, 1985—, Biochem. Pharmacology, 1991—; contbr. numerous articles to profl. jours.; also abstracts. Recipient 1st ann. Outstanding Attending award House Staff of Dept. Internal Medicine, La. State U. Med. Ctr., 1990, 2000, 04; Outstanding Clin. Sci. Instr. award, 1994, 2000, 01, 02, 03, Allen A. Copping Excellence in Tchg. award, 2005; grantee Am. Heart Assn.-La. Inc., 1981-82, 83-84, 84-85, 85-88, 89-91, NIH, 1976-79, 81-82, 82-83, Edward P. Stiles Trust Fund, 1979-80, 82-83, 85-87, La. State Bd. Regents, 1984-85, VA Rsch. Adv. Group, 1987-89, Am. Diabetes Assn, 1988-89. Fellow ACP; mem. Shreveport Med. Soc., La. State Med. Soc., Am. Fedn. Clin. Rsch., Am. Diabetes assn. (N.W. La. chpt. bd. dirs. 1980-83, pres. 1983-84), Endocrine Soc. (program dirs. com. 1988—), Alpha Omega Alpha. Office: La State U Health Sci Ctr PO Box 33932 1501 Kings Hwy Shreveport LA 71103-4228 Office Phone: 318-675-5960. Business E-Mail: slevin@lsuhsc.edu.

LEVINE, STEVEN RICHARD, neurology educator, medical facility administrator; b. Bay Shore, N.Y., June 29, 1955; s. Harry Arnold and Elaine Judith (Fink) L.; m. Joanne Miriam Traurig; children: Aaron Marc, David Benjamin, Aliza Rachael. BS, U. Mich., 1977; MD, Med. Coll. Wis., 1981. Resident in neurology U. Mich. Med. Ctr., Ann Arbor, 1982-85; fellow in cerebrovascular disease Henry Ford Hosp., Detroit, 1985-87, staff neurologist, dir. clin. stroke svc., 1987-98; prof. neurology, dir. stroke program Wayne State U. Sch. Medicine, Detroit, 1998—. Mem. edit. Bd. Stroke, Henry Ford Hosp. jour., 1990—. Rsch. fellow Am. Heart Assn., 1986-87; recipient Harold G. Wolff Lectr. award Am. Assn. Study of Headache; grantee NIH-NINDS, 1990-01. Fellow Am. Acad. Neurology, Stroke Coun. Am. Heart Assn. (chmn. Mich. unit 1991-93), Am. Neurol. Assn.; mem. Phi Beta Kappa. Jewish. Achievements include research in cerebrovascular and neurological diseases associated with antiphospholipid antibodies, cerebrovascular complications in use of crack form of akla1oidal cocaine, MRI and stroke, t-PA for stroke, telemedicine for stroke "telestroke". Office: WSU Sch Medicine WSU Sch Med/U Health Ctr 4201 Saint Antoine St 8 Fl Detroit MI 48201-2153

LEVINE, STEVEN Z, humanities educator, department chairman; Leslie Clark prof. of Humanities Byrn Mawr Coll., 1975—; dir., ctr. for visual culture Bryn Mawr Coll. Author: (book) Monet, Narcissus, and Self-Reflection: The Modernist Myth of the Self, 1994, several essays on art history. Fellowship, John Simon Guggenheim Meml. Found., 2003. Office: Bryn Mawr Coll 101 N Merion Ave Bryn Mawr PA 19010

LEVINE, SUMNER NORTON, industrial engineer, educator, editor, writer, financial consultant; b. Boston, Sept. 5, 1923; s. Frank and Lillian (Gold) L.; m. Caroline Gassner, Nov. 27, 1952; 1 dau., Joanne. BS, Brown U., 1946; PhD, U. Wis., 1949; postgrad., M.I.T., 1956. Instr. U. Chgo., 1949-50; sr. research fellow Columbia, 1950-54; dir. research labs. VA, East Orange, N.J., 1954-56; adv. scientist comml. atom power div. Westinghouse Electric Co., Pitts., 1956; dir. chemistry Metallurgy and Materials Labs.; also staff adv. engr. Gen. Engring. Labs., Am. Machine & Foundry Co., Greenwich, Conn., 1956-58; sect. head, materials and advanced electronic devices RCA, 1958-61; chmn. materials scis. dept., prof. engring., also prof., dir. grad. program in indsl. adminstrn. SUNY, Stony Brook, 1961-91; dir. urban research, vis. prof. CUNY Grad. Center, 1967-68; Danforth vis. lectr., 1968-69; vis. prof. Yale Sch. Orgn. and Mgmt., 1976; prof. fin. Coll. Urban and Policy Scis., SUNY, Stony Brook, 1978—. Cons. to industry; bd. dirs. Norteck Assocs.; editl.

adviser Ocean Engring. Author textbooks, profl. articles; editor: Financial Analysts Handbook, 1975, 2d edit., 1987, Investment Manager's Handbook, Dow Jones-Irwin Bus.and Investment Almanac, 1976—, Acquisition Manual, 1990, Turnaround and Bankruptcy Investing, 1991, Handbook of Global Investing, 1992, Internat. Bus. and Investment Almanac, 1992—; editor-in-chief Jour. Biomed. Materials Rsch., 1966-78, Jour. Socio-Econ. Planning Scis., 1966, Advances in Biomed. Engring. and Med. Physics, 1966. Recipient award for disting. contbn. to biomed. materials rsch., 1973. Mem. IEEE, World Conf. Planning Scis., Am. Chem. Soc., Am. Soc. Metals, Electrochem. Soc., Ops. Research Soc. Am., Inst. Mgmt. Scis., Fgn. Policy Assn., N.Y. Acad. Scis. (chmn. conf. materials in biomed. engring. 1966, chmn. colloquia socioecon. planning 1966-68), Soc. for Biomaterials (dir. 1974-76), N.Y. Soc. Security Analysts (chmn. edn. and seminar com., Vols. award 1984), Mus. Modern Art, Met. Mus. of Art, Princeton Club N.Y., Brown U. Club, Sigma Xi. Office: 29 Brandywine Dr Setauket NY 11733-0883

LEVINE, SUZIN NANCY LEAH, religious organization administrator; b. L.A., Mar. 5, 1952; d. Ciprano C. Ortega and Wanda Laurie Murphy; m. Ronald Stuart Levine, Oct. 23, 1972; children: Jason, Elizabeth, Justin, Joshua. Grad., Willow Glen H.S., San Jose, Calif., 1969. Dir. I Care Ministry, Visalia, Calif., 1995—; tchr. Cath. Apostles of Christ, Visalia, 1999—. Author: Don't Cry Anymore, 1995, This is How I Pray, 2000, God Awaits Us, 2003; pub. Chaplet of Reconciliation, Cath. Apostle of Christ Handbook, originator Spiritual Care Packets. Home and Office: I Care Ministry PO Box 7164 Visalia CA 93290 E-mail: jle1172801@hotmail.com.

LEVINE, THOMAS JEFFREY PELLO, lawyer; b. Santa Monica, Calif., Mar. 6, 1952; s. Allan Lester and Shirley Elaine (Pello) Levine; children: Marissa, Matthew, Molly. Student, U. Denver, 1970-71, Calif. State U., Northridge, 1971-73, Uppsala U., Sweden; BA, Calif. State U., Sacramento, 1974; JD, Southwestern U., 1977; postgrad., Yale U., 1999. Bar: Calif. 1977, U.S. Dist. Ct. (ctrl. dist.) Calif. 1978. Ptnr. Levine & Levine, L.A., 1977-83; staff atty. Fed. Deposit Ins. Corp., Newport Beach, Calif., 1983-85; v.p., assoc. counsel Imperial Bank, Inglewood, Calif., 1985-88; v.p., counsel Community Bank, Pasadena, Calif., 1988; gen. counsel, sr. v.p., sec. Calif. Commerce Bank, Banamex USA Bancorp, L.A., 1988-2001; gen. counsel, sr. v.p. Banamex-Citibank, 2001; spl. counsel Office Gen. Counsel L.A. Unified Sch. Dist., 2002—04; sr. v.p., gen. counsel Center Bank, L.A., 2005—. Sec., bd. dirs. Carroll Ave. Restoration Found., L.A., 1979—87; bd. dirs. Angelino Heights Hist. Preservation Assn., L.A., 1985—95, Wilshire C. of C., L.A., 1982. Mem.: Los Angeles County Bar Assn., Calif. Bankers Assn. (mem. legal affairs com. 1990—), Braemar Country Club (bd. govs. 1979—83). Jewish. Office: Center Bank 3435 Wilshire Blvd # 700 Los Angeles CA 90010 Office Phone: 213-251-2227. E-mail: thomasl@centerbank.com.

LE VINE, VICTOR THEODORE, retired political science professor; b. Berlin, Dec. 6, 1928; came to U.S., 1938; s. Maurice and Hildegard (Hirschberg) LeV.; m. Nathalie Jeanne Christian, July 19, 1958; children: Theodore, Nicole. BA, UCLA, 1950, MA, 1958, PhD, 1961. Research assoc. UCLA, 1958-60; prof., head dept. polit. sci. U. Ghana, Legon, 1969-71; Fulbright prof. U. Yaounde, Cameroon, 1981-82; prof. polit. sci. Washington U., St. Louis, 1961—2003, prof. emeritus, 2003—. Cons. U.S. Dept. State, Dept. Def., 1971—; lectr. USIA, 1981—; mem. U.S. Nat. Commn. UNESCO, 1964; dir. Office Internat. Studies, Washington U., 1975-76; vis. lectr. Fudan U., U. Nanjing (China), 1987, Ibn Saud and King Abdulazziz Univs., Saudi Arabia, 1990; mem. Carter Ctr. Internat. monitoring team to Ghana nat. elections, 1992; vis. prof. Hebrew U., Jerusalem, 1978, U. Tex., Austin, 1980, Sabanci U., Turkey, 2003, Athens U., Greece, 2003. Author: Cameroons: Mandate to Independence, 1964, 70, Cameroon Federal Republic, 1971, Political Corruption: Ghana, 1975, (with Timothy Luke) Arab-African Connection, 1979; (with Heidenheimer and Johnston) Political Corruption: A Handbook, 1990; Conceptualizing Ethnicity and Ethnic Conflict: A Controversy Revisited, 1997 Parapolitics: Mapping The Terrain of Informal Politics, 2002, Politics in Francophone Africa, 2004. Mem., dir. UN Assn., St. Louis, 1964-74; mem. Coun. on World Affairs, 1969-2000; pres. Ctr. for Internat. Understanding, 1988-2000. With U.S. Army, 1951-54. Ford. Found. fellow Cameroon, 1960-61; Hoover Instn. fellow, 1974; Lester Martin fellow Truman Instn., Jerusalem, 1978; Fulbright lectr. U.S. Fulbright Commn., Yaounde, Cameroon, 1981-82, Greece and Turkey, 2003. Mem. Am. Polit. Sci. Assn., African Studies Assn., Mideast Studies Assn., Midwest Polit. Sci. Assn., Mo. Polit. Sci. Assn. Office: Washington U Dept Polit Sci Saint Louis MO 63130 Business E-Mail: vlevine@wustl.edu.

LEVINE, WILLIAM MICHAEL, lawyer; b. Rockville Ctr., NY, May 21, 1952; s. Leonard and Regina (Bloom) L.; m. E. Chouteau Levine, Feb. 29, 2004; children: Katie M., Diana R. BA, Northwestern U., Evanston, Ill., 1974; JD, Suffolk U., 1978. Bar: Mass. 1978, U.S. Dist. Ct. Mass. 1978, U.S. Ct. Appeals (1st cir.) 1981; U.S. Tax Ct. 1982. Asst. regional counsel Dept. Pub. Welfare, Boston, 1978-80; dep. regional counsel Dept. Social Svcs., Boston, 1980-81; assoc. Atwood & Wright, Boston, 1981-83, Peabody & Arnold, Boston, 1983-85, Bowser & Lee (now Lee & Levine LLP), Boston, 1985-87, ptnr., 1987-88, Lee & Levine (formerly Lee, Levine & Bowser), Boston, 1988—. Contbg. author: Massachusetts Family Law Manual, 1986-88; contbr. articles to profl. jours. Named one of top Boston lawyers, Boston Mag., 2004. Fellow Internat. Acad. Matrimonial Lawyers, Am. Acad. Matrimonial Lawyers (bd. mgrs. 1988-91, chpt. pres., pres.-elect, v.p., treas. 1997-2005); mem. Mass. Bar Assn. (family law sect. coun. 1987-88), Boston Bar Assn. (chmn. family law sect. 1988-91). Office: Lee & Levine LLP 222 Berkeley St Ste 1400 Boston MA 02116-3750 Office Phone: 617-266-6262. Office Fax: 617-266-8250.

LEVINE, WILLIAM SILVER, electrical engineer, educator; b. Bklyn., Nov. 19, 1941; s. Louis Nathan and Gertrude (Silver) Levine; m. Shirley Johannesen, Feb. 14, 1963; children: Bruce Jonathan, Eleanor Joan. BEE, MIT, 1962, MEE, 1965, PhD in Elec. Engring., 1969. Project engr. Data Tech. Inc., Cambridge, Mass., 1962—64; grad. asst. MIT, Cambridge, 1964—69; asst. prof. U. Md., College Park, 1969—73, assoc. prof., 1973—81, prof., 1981—. Cons. IBM Fed. Sys. divsn., Gaithersburg, Md., 1972—75, Computational Engring. Inc., Laurel, Md., 1980—90. Co-author: Using MATLAB to Analyze and Design Control Systems, 1992, 2d edit., 1995; editor: The Control Handbook, 1996, Control Engineering Series, 1996—; contbr. articles to profl. jours. Rsch. grantee, 1969—. Fellow: IEEE, IEEE Control Sys. Soc. (pres. 1990, disting. mem. 1990); mem.: Soc. Indsl. and Applied Math., Am. Automatic Control Coun. (v.p. 2002—03, pres. 2004—). Office: U Md Dept Elect & Computer Engring College Park MD 20742-0001 Business E-Mail: wsl@eng.umd.edu.

LEVINGER, JEFFREY S., lawyer; b. Yankton, S.D., Feb. 13, 1957; s. Joseph Charles and Leta (Weiner) Levinger; m. Terry Kaufman, Sept. 6, 1987; children: Jacob D., Samuel J. AB, Dartmouth Coll., 1979; JD, U. Va., 1982. Bar: Tex. 1982, U.S. Dist. Ct. No. Tex., U.S. Dist. Ct. So. Tex., U.S. Dist. Ct. Ea. Tex., U.S. Dist. Ct. West. Tex., U.S. Supreme Ct. 1989, U.S. Ct. Appeals (5th cir.), U.S. Ct. Appeals (6th cir.), U.S. Ct. Appeals (10th cir.), U.S. Ct. Appeals (11th cir.), bd. cert. in civil appellate law: Tex. Bd. Legal Specialization. Law clk. Hon. Patrick E. Higginbothom (5th cir.), Dallas, 1982—83; assoc. Carrington, Coleman, Sloman & Blumenthal, LLP, 1983—89, ptnr., 1990—. Former chmn. Civil Appellate Law Advisory Com. Tex. Bd. Legal Specialization, Austin, 1998—2005; mem. State Bar Tex. Commn. on Pattern Jury Changes, Austin, 2002—. Co-author: (book) Fifth Circuit Trial Practice Guide, 1998. Exec. bd. mem. Anti-Defamation League, 2004—; supporter U.S. Holocaust Mus., Wash., 1995—. Named Texas Super Lawyer, Tex. Monthly, 2003, 2004, 2005; named one of Best Lawyers in Dallas, D Mag., 2001, 2003, 2005. Master: William "Mac" Taylor Am. Inn of Ct.; fellow: Tex. Bar Found.; mem.: Am. Law Inst., Order of the Coif, Phi Beta Kappa. Jewish. Avocations: tennis, running, hiking, reading, bicycling. Office: Carrington Coleman Sloman & Blumenthal 200 Crescent Ct Ste 1500 Dallas TX 75201 Office Phone: 214-855-3036. Office Fax: 214-855-1333. Business E-Mail: jlevinger@ccsb.com.

LEVINGER, JOSEPH SOLOMON, physicist, researcher; b. N.Y.C., Nov. 14, 1921; s. Lee J. and Elma (Ehrlich) Levinger; m. Gloria Edwards, Aug. 14, 1943 (dec. Jan. 20, 1987); children: Sam, Laurie, Louis, Joe; m. Hedi McKinley, Sept. 4, 1998. BS, U. Chgo., 1941, MS, 1944; PhD, Cornell U., 1948. Physicist Metall. Lab., U. Chgo., 1942-44, Franklin Inst., Phila., 1945; instr. Cornell U., 1948-51, vis. prof., 1961-64; from asst. prof. to prof. La. State U., 1951-61; prof. physics Rensselaer Poly. Inst., 1964-92, prof. emeritus, 1992—; Fulbright fellow, asso. prof. U. Paris— Sud, 1972-73. Author: Nuclear Photo-Disintegration, 1961, Secrets of the Nucleus, 1967, The Two and Three Body Problem, 1974. Guggenheim fellow, 1957—58. Fellow: Am. Phys. Soc. Home: PO Box 411 Altamont NY 12009-0411 Office: Rensselaer Poly Inst Dept Physics Troy NY 12180 Personal E-mail: levinj@rpi.edu.

LEVINGS, THERESA LAWRENCE, lawyer; b. Kansas City, Mo., Oct. 24, 1952; d. William Youngs and Dorothy (Neer) Frick; m. Darryl Wayne Levings, May 25, 1974; children: Leslie Page, Kerry Dillon. BJ, U. Mo., 1973; JD, U. Mo., Kansas City, 1979. Bar: Mo. 1979, U.S. Dist. Ct. (we. dist.) Mo. 1979, U.S. Ct. Appeals (8th cir.) 1982, U.S. Ct. Appeals (10th cir.) 1986, U.S. Dist. Ct. (ea. dist.) Mo. 1989, U.S. Dist. Ct. Kans. 1995. Copy editor Kansas City Star, 1975-78; law clk. to judge Mo. Supreme Ct., Jefferson City, 1979-80; from assoc. to ptnr. Morrison & Hecker, Kansas City, 1980-94; founding ptnr. Badger & Levings, L.C., Kansas City, 1994—2004. Mem. fed. practice com. U.S. Dist. Ct. (we. dist.), 1990-95; mem. fed. adv. com. U.S. Ct. Appeals (8th cir.), 1994-97. Mem. Mo. Bar (bd. govs. 1990—03, pres. 2001-02, young lawyers coun. 1982-89, chair 1988-89, Pres. award 1989, Outstanding Svc. award young lawyers coun. 1985, 86), Assn. Women Lawyers Greater Kansas City (pres. 1986-87, Woman of Yr. 1993), Kansas City Met. Bar Assn. (chair civil practice and procedure com. 1988-89, chair fed. practice com. 1990-91, Inns of Court (master 1996-2000, 2002—). Office: Badger & Levings LC 1101 Walnut St Kansas City MO 64106-2134 Office Phone: 816-421-2828. Business E-Mail: tlevings@badgerlevings.com.

LEVINGSTON, ERNEST LEE, engineering company executive; b. Pineville, La., Nov. 7, 1921; s. Vernon Lee and Adele (Miller) L.; m. Kathleen Bernice Bordelon, June 23, 1944; children: David Lewis, Jeanne Evelyn, James Lee. BME, La. State U., 1960. Registered profl. engr., La., Tex., Miss., Ark., Tenn., Pa., Md., Del., N.J., D.C., Okla., Colo. Gen. forman T. Miller & Sons, Lake Charles, La., 1939-42; sr. engr., sect. head Cities Svc. Refining Corp., Lake Charles, 1946-57; group leader Bovay Engrs., Baton Rouge, 1957-59; chief engr. Augenstein Constrn. Co., Lake Charles, 1959-60; pres. Levingston Engrs., Inc., Lake Charles, 1961-85; gen. mgr. SW La. Austin Indsl., 1985-88; pres. Levingston Engrs., Lake Charles, 1989-96, chmn. bd., 1996-2000, pres., chmn. bd., 2000—. Mem. Lake Charles Planning and Zoning Commn., 1965-70; adv. bd. Sowela Tech. Inst., 1969—; mem. Regional Export Expansion Coun., 1969-70, chmn. code com., 1966—; mem. La. Bd. Commerce and Industry, 1978—; bd. dirs. Lake Charles Meml. Hosp.; bd. dirs., regional chmn. La. Chem. Industry Alliance, 1990—. With USNR, 1942-46. Named Jaycee Boss of Yr., 1972. Mem. La. Engring. Soc. (pres. 1967-68, state bd. dirs. 1967-68, 90-91), Nat. Inst. Cert. Engring. Technologists (past trustee, mem. exam. com.), La. Assn. Bus. and Industry, Lake Area Industries/McNeese Engring., Lake Charles C. of C. (dir. 1969-73). Baptist (deacon 1955—). Office: PO Box 1865 Lake Charles LA 70602-1865 Office Fax: 337-474-3789.

LEVINS, ILYSSA, public relations executive; b. New Hyde Park, N.Y., Dec. 3, 1958; d. Jack and Marlene (Newman) L. BA, NYU, 1980. Asst. account exec. Gross, Townsend, Frank, Hoffman, Inc., N.Y.C., 1982, account exec., 1983, sr. account exec., 1984, account supr., 1985, group account supr., 1986, v.p., dir. pub. rels., 1987-88, sr. v.p., dir. pub. rels., 1988-90, pres. pub. rels. divsn., 1990-94, mng. dir., 1994-96; vice-chmn., pres. pub. rels. Grey Healthcare Group (formerly Gross, Townsend et al, Inc.), 1996—; chmn., chief creative officer GCI Health, N.Y.C., 1998—. Mem. Pub. Rels. Soc. Am., Am. Soc. for Hosp. Mktg. and Pub. Rels., Women in Communications, Pharm. Advt. Coun., Food and Drug Law Inst., Am. Med. Writer's Assn., Am. Soc. for Health Care Mktg. and Pub. Rels. Jewish. Avocations: poetry, biking, swimming. Office: GCI Health Care 825 Third Ave New York NY 10022

LEVINS, JOHN RAYMOND, investment advisor, educator, management consultant; b. Jersey City, Aug. 4, 1944; s. Raymond Thomas and Catherine (Kelly) L. BS in Acctg., U. N.H., 1973; MBA, U. N.H., Plymouth, 1976. Registered investment advisor; cert. mgmt. cons., enrolled to practice IRS; cert. licensing instr., real estate and multiple lines ins. broker, comml. arbitration panelist; accredited tax advisor; cert. mediator; registered securities prin. Office Supervisory Jurisdiction. Mgmt. risk analyst Express Treaty Mgmt. Corp., N.Y.C., 1962-67; asst. risk mgr. Bigelow-Sanford, Inc., N.Y.C., 1967-71; cons., broker BYSE, Inc., Laconia, N.Y., 1971-74; asst. prof. Nathaniel Hawthorne Coll., Antrim, N.H., 1975-82, Keene (N.H.) State Coll., 1982—; prin. Levins & Assocs., Concord, N.H., 1986—; investment advisor Reality Techs., Internat. Fin., Concord, 1991—; prin. Levins & Assocs. Dir. Small Bus. Inst. Keene State Coll., 1982-86; exec. seminar leader Strategic Mgmt. Group, Inc., 1986—, Boston U., 1976-99; mem. bd. advisors Am. Biog. Inst.; pvt. practice real estate, ins. cons., Concord, 1981; panelist securities arbitration Nat. Assn. Security Dealers, Am. Stock Exch., N.Y. Stock Exch., Gen. Securities Prin.; consumer affair mediator Dept. Justice, Office of Atty. Gen., NH, NASA Svc. Bureau-Compliance; mortgage banker; comml. financing broker; mem. SEC, spkr., seminar leader in field; fin. faculty grad. programs Boston U., 1996 fin. and investment provider Dun & Bradstreet, 1997; exepert witness investments and securities WestLaw.com, FindLaw.com, Martindale and Hubbelle; compliance NASD Svc. Bureau; sr. v.p. Investment Source Captial Group, Inc. Author: Finance and Accounting, 1979 (Excellence award 1980), Financial Analysis, 1981 (Excellence award 1980), Managing Cash Flow, 1988 (Excellence award 1988), Finance and Management, 1989. Incorporator Spaulding Youth Ctr., Tilton, N.H., 1990; colleague Found. for Acctg. Edn., assoc., profl. standing, 1988; mem. Nat. Consortium Edn. and Tng., Madison, Wis., 1989. With USN, 1969-71, S.E. Asia. Named Outstanding Support Leader U.S. Small Bus. Adminstrn., Concord, 1985, Oustanding Svc. Leader Community Leaders Am., N.H., 1990, One of Outstanding Young Men Am. U.S. Jaycees Bd. Adv.'s, 1983. Mem. AICPA (mem. Profl. Devel. Inst., sponsor trainer 1988-89), Found. Acctg. Acctg., Investment Co. Inst. (assoc., nat. standing 1987), Inst. Mgmt. Cons. (assoc., nat. standing 1985, cert. profl. cons. to mgmt.), Nat. Soc. Pub. Accts. (del., profl. standing 1985), Nat. Soc. Non-Profit Orgns. (svc. provider 1989, colleague), Accreditation Coun. for Accountancy (fed. taxation accreditation 1987, colleague). Avocations: boating, teaching, community service, athletics. Office Phone: 603-629-0056. Personal E-mail: Levinsjohnr@comcast.net.

LEVINSOHN, GARY, producer; b. 1959; Prodr., prin. Mutual Film Co. (with Mark Gordon), L.A., 1996—. Exec. prodr. films including: Blue Ice, 1992, The Real McCoy, 1993, Twelve Monkeys, 1995, Angus, 1995, The Relic, 1997, The Jackal, 1997, (TV) The Ripper, 1997, Black Dog, 1998, A Simple Plan, 1998, Virus, 1999, All the Rage, 1999, Isn't She Great? 2000, Timeline, 2003; prodr. Hard Rain, 1998, Paulie, 1998, Saving Private Ryan, 1998, Primary Colors, 1998, Man on the Moon, 1999, The Patriot, 2000, The Core, 2003.

LEVINSON, ARNOLD IRVING, allergist, immunologist; b. Balt., 1944; MD, U. Md. Sch. Medicine, 1969. Diplomate Am. Bd. Internal Medicine, Am. Bd. Allergy and Immunology. Intern Balt. City Hosps., 1969-70, resident internal medicine, 1970-71; prof. medicine and neurology U. Pa., Phila., 1987—. Fellow, U. Pa., Phila., 1971—72, U. Calif., San Francisco, 1972—73. Fellow Am. Acad. Allergy, Asthma and Immunology, Am. Assn. Immunologists, Am. Fedn. for Clin. Rsch., Am. Soc. for Clin. Investigation; mem. Clin. Immunology Soc. Office: U Pa Hospital 3400 Spruce St Philadelphia PA 19104-4206

LEVINSON, BARRY L., film director; b. Balt., Apr. 6, 1942; Ed., Am. U., Washington; D of fine arts (hon.), Am. U., 1999. Film writer, actor: Silent Movie, 1976, High Anxiety, 1978; writer: ...And Justice for All, 1979, Inside Moves, 1980, Best Friends, 1982, Unfaithfully Yours, 1984; dir.: The Natural, 1984, Young Sherlock Holmes, 1985, Good Morning Vietnam, 1987, Rain Man, 1988 (Academy award 1989, Dirs. Guild Am. award 1989); screenwriter, dir.: Diner, 1982, Tin Men, 1987, Avalon, 1990 (Writers Guild Am. award 1990); co-prodr., dir. Bugsy, 1991, Disclosure, 1994, Wag the Dog, 1997, Sphere, 1998, An Everlasting Piece, 2000, Bandits, 2001, Envy, 2004; co-writer, dir., prodr. Toys, 1992; prodr. Donnie Brasco, 1997, An Everlasting Piece, 2000, Bandits, 2001, Possession, 2002; exec. prodr. Analyze That, 2002, Deliver Us from Eva, 2002; writer, dir., prodr. Jimmy Hollywood, 1994 (also actor), Sleepers, 1996, Liberty Heights, 1999; actor: Quiz Show, 1994; dir., exec. prodr. (TV) Homicide: Life on the Street, 1993 (Emmy award, Outstanding Individual Achievement in Directing in a Drama Series, 1993, Peabody award 1993, Humanitas award, 1999); exec. prodr. (TV) Oz, 1997, American Tragedy, 2000, Shot in the Heart, 2001, Baseball Wives, 2002, Strip Search, 2004; dir, and prodr. (TV), The Beat, 2000, The Jury, 2004. Recipient ACE Golden Eddie Filmmaker of Yr. award, 2002. Mem. Dirs. Guild Am., Writers Guild Am. Address: c/o Baltimore Pictures 4000 Warner Blvd Bldg 133 Burbank CA 91522-0208

LEVINSON, DANIEL RONALD, federal agency administrator, lawyer; b. Bklyn., Mar. 24, 1949; s. Gerald Sam and Risha Rose (Waxer) L.; m. Luna Frances Lambert, Sept. 13, 1980; children: Luna Claire, Hannah Louise. AB, U. So. Calif., 1971; JD, Georgetown U., 1974; LLM, George Washington U., 1977. Bar: N.Y. 1975, Calif. 1976, D.C. 1976, U.S. Supreme Ct. 1978; cert. fraud examiner. Law clk. appellate divsn. N.Y. Supreme Ct., Bklyn., 1974-76; assoc. McGuiness & Williams, Washington, 1977-81, ptnr., 1982-83; dep. gen. counsel U.S. Office Personnel Mgmt., Washington, 1983-85; gen. counsel U.S. Consumer Product Safety Commn., Washington, 1985-86; chmn. U.S. Merit Sys. Protection Bd., Washington, 1986-93; of counsel Shaw Bransford & O'Rourke, Washington, 1993-94; chief of staff U.S. Rep. from Ga. Bob Barr, Washington, 1995-98; prin. Law Offices of Daniel R. Levinson, Washington, 1998—2000; insp. gen. General Svc. Admin., Washington, 2001—05; acting insp. gen. U.S. Dept. HHS, Washington, 2004—05, insp. gen., 2005—. Adj. lectr. Am. U., Washington, 1981-82, Cath. U. Am., Washington, 1982. Editor-in-chief Jour. Pub. Inquiry, 2002—; notes and comments editor Am. Criminal Law Rev., 1973-74; contbr. articles to profl. jours. Bd. dirs. Washington Hebrew Congregation, 1993-96; prin. Coun. for Excellence in Govt., 1993-94. Mem. Adminstrv. Conf. U.S. (govt. mem. 1984-93), Phi Beta Kappa. Office: US Dept HHS 330 Independence Ave SW Rm 5250 Washington DC 20201

LEVINSON, DARYL J., law educator; b. 1968; BA, Harvard U., 1990; MA in Modern Studies, JD, U. Va., 1995. Asst. prof. U. Va. Sch. Law, 1996—97, assoc. prof., 1997—2001, prof. law & Harrison Found. rsch. prof., 2001—02; prof. law NYU Sch. Law, 2002—, Bonnie and Richard Reiss prof. constl. law. Vis. assoc. prof. U. Chgo., 2000, NYU Sch. Law, 2001. Office: NYU Sch Law Vanderbilt Hall Rm 503 40 Washington Sq S New York NY 10012-1099 Office Phone: 212-998-6237. E-mail: daryl.levinson@nyu.edu.

LEVINSON, HARRY, psychologist, educator; b. Port Jervis, N.Y., Jan. 16, 1922; s. David and Gussie (Nudell) L.; m. Roberta Freiman, Jan. 11, 1946 (div. June 1972); children— Marc Richard, Kathy, Anne, Brian Thomas; m. Miriam Lewis, Nov. 23, 1990. BS, Emporia (Kans.) State U., 1943, MS, 1946; PhD, U. Kans., 1952; DHL (hon.), Mass. Sch. Profl. Psychology, 2004. Coordinator profl. edn. Topeka State Hosp., 1950-53, psychologist, 1954-55; dir. div. indsl. mental health Menninger Found., Topeka, 1955-68; visiting prof. MIT, 1961-62, U. Kans. Bus. Sch., 1967, Texas A&M U., 1976; Thomas Henry Carroll-Ford Found. distinguished vis. prof. Harvard Grad. Sch. Bus., Boston, 1968-72; adj. prof. Coll. Bus. Administrn., Boston U., 1972-74; lectr. Harvard Med. Sch., 1972-85; adj. prof. Pace U., 1972-83; clin. prof. psychology Harvard Med. Sch., 1985-92, emeritus prof., 1992—; head sect. orgnl. mental health Mass. Mental Health Ctr., 1983-92; pres. The Levinson Inst., 1968-91, chmn. bd., 1991—. Mem. Am. Bd. Profl. Psychology, 1972-80, chmn., 1978-80; Ford Found. prof. Mathur Inst., Jaipur India, 1974; conducted internat. course on social psychiatry Finnish Govt. Inst., 1979. Author: Emotional Health In the World of Work, 1964, Executive Stress, 1970, The Exceptional Executive (McKinsey Found. and Acad. Mgmt. awards), 1968 (James A. Hamilton Hosp. Adminstrs. Book award), Organizational Diagnosis, 1971, The Great Jackass Fallacy, 1973, Psychological Man, 1976, Casebook for Psychological Man; (with S. Rosenthal) CEO: Corporate Leadership in Action (Am. Coll. Health Care Adminstrs. Book award 1986), 1984, Ready, Fire, Aim, 1986, Designing and Managing Your Career, 1989, Career Mastery, 1992, Organizational Assessment, 2002. Chmn. Kans. adv. com. U.S. Civil Rights Commn., 1962-68; chmn. Topeka Human Relations Commn., 1967-68. Served with F.A. AUS, 1944-46. Recipient Perry Rohrer Cons. Psychology Practice award, 1984, Career award Mass. Psychol. Assn., 1985, Disting. Svc. award Soc. Consulting Psychology, 2004, First award Soc. Psychologists in Mgmt.; Eminent scholar in bus. Fla. Atlantic U., 1995. Fellow APA (award for disting. profl. contbn. to knowledge 1992, Gold medal for life achievement in the application of psychology 2000), Am. Psychol. Found. Address: 4889 Pineview Cir Delray Beach FL 33445-4318 E-mail: handmlevinson@earthlink.net.

LEVINSON, HERBERT SHERMAN, civil and transportation engineer; b. Chgo., Sept. 25, 1924; s. Israel and Tillie (Gash) Levinson; m. Sally Farver, July 3, 1977. BSCE, Ill. Inst. Tech., 1949; cert. in hwy. traffic, Yale U., 1952. Jr. traffic engr. Chgo. Park Dist., 1949-51; from assoc. to sr. v.p. Wilbur Smith & Assocs., New Haven, 1952-80; prin. Herbert S. Levinson Transp. Cons., New Haven, 1980—; prof. civil engring. U. Conn., Storrs, 1980-86; prof. transp. Poly. Inst. of N.Y., N.Y.C., 1986-88. UTRC mentor CCNY, 1999—; vis. lectr. Yale U., New Haven, 1961—80. Author: Future Highways and Urban Growth, 1961; author: (with D. Votaw) Elementary Sampling for Traffic Engineers, 1961; author: Transportation and Parking for Tomorrow's Cities, 1966; author: (with R. Weant) Urban Transportation Perspectives and Prospects, 1983, Parking, 1990; contbr. numerous articles to profl. jours. Cpl. USAF, 1943—46. Recipient Presdl. Design award, Nat. Endowment for Arts, 1988, Leadership award, XIII Pan-Am. Conf. Traffic and Transp. Engring., 2004. Fellow: ASCE (Benjamin Wright award 1993, Wilbur S. Smith award 1997, Frank Turner lectr. 2003), Inst. Transp. Engrs. (hon., Transp. Engr. of Yr. 1976, Tech. Coun. award 1982, Theodore M. Matson award 1997); mem.: NAE (nat. assoc.), Conn. Acad. Sci. and Engring. (Disting. Svc. award 2003), Am. Planning Assn., Transp. Rsch. Bd. (Roy W. Crum award 1997). Office Phone: 203-389-2092. E-mail: hslevinson@aol.com.

LEVINSON, JOHN MILTON, obstetrician, gynecologist; b. Atlantic City, Aug. 17, 1927; m. Elizabeth Carl Bell; children: Patricia Anne, John Carl, Mark Jay. BA, Lafayette Coll., Easton, Pa., 1949; MD, Thomas Jefferson U., 1953. Diplomate Am. Bd. Ob-Gyn. Intern Atlantic City Hosp., 1953-54; Am. Cancer Soc. clin. fellow Jefferson Med. Coll. Hosp., Phila., 1954-55; resident in ob-gyn. Del. Hosp., Wilmington, 1955-57; pvt. practice ob-gyn. Wilmington, 1957-85; prof. dept. ob-gyn. Jefferson Med. Coll., Thomas Jefferson U., Phila., hon. clin. prof., 1990—; sr. attending physician emeritus Med. Ctr. Del., Wilmington, 1986—; attending chief dept. ob-gyn. St. Francis Hosp., Wilmington, chief emeritus, 1986-92. Founder, pres. Aid for Internat. Medicine, Inc., 1966—; med. dir., chief surgeon Quark Expeditions, 1991-95; cons. Riverside Hosp., 1972-86, Wilmington Pa. Blue Shield, 1982—: cons. gynecology U.S. VA, 1974-85; founding mem., treas., bd. dirs. Physicians Health Svcs., Del., Ltd., 1985-87; vis. prof., cons., ship's surgeons, practicing physician various orgns. in Africa, Antarctica, Arctic regions, Ctrl. Am., Europe, S.E. Asia, S.W. Asia, 1963—; lectr. in field; internat. med. cons. to Sen. Edward M. Kennedy, 1967—; chmn. Antarctic expdns. study group to advise NSF, 1992-93; co-chmn. Com. for Safety in Arctic and Antarctic Frontier Expeditions, 1992-93. Author: Shorebirds: The Birds, the Hunters, the Decoys, 1991, Safe Passage Questioned: Medical Care and Safety for the Polar Tourist, 1998, Advanced First Aid Afloat, 2000; assoc. prodr. 3 films on explorer Ernest Shackleton; contbr. articles to profl. jours., chpts. to books. Bd. dirs. Del. com. Project H.O.P.E., 1965-75, ARC, 1968-70, Charles A. Lindbergh Fund, Inc., 1985-90; trustee Blue Cross/ Blue Shield Del., Inc., 1968-86, Brandywine Coll., 1972-77; bd. dirs. Nat. Assn. Blue Shield Plans, 1971-77; mem adv. com. Trinity Alcohol and Drug Program, 1978-85; mem.

Del. Gov.'s Commn. on Health Care Cost Mgmt., 1985-87; bd. dirs. founding mem. World Affairs Coun. Wilmington Inc, v.p., 1981-86; pres. Rockland Mills Cmty. Assn., 1992-94; mem. bd. advisors World Sportsmen Ctr., Orlando, 1997—, With USN, 1945-47; col. M.C., USAFR, 1984-87. Recipient Brandywine award Brandywine Coll., 1968, cert. of appreciation for med. svcs. Ministry of Health, Republic of Vietnam, 1963-66, commendation Pres. of U.S., 1971, The Eisenhower award People to People Internat., 1986, Commemorative medal Charles A. Lindbergh Fund, 1987, Phila. Explorers award 1987, Citation for Outstanding Contbn. to People of Del., Med. Soc. Del., 1992. Fellow Am. Coll. Ob.-Gyn., Royal Geog. Soc. London; mem. AMA, Am. Assn. Gyn. Laporoscopists (founding, bd. dirs.), Del. Obstetric Soc. (pres. 1980-82), Phila. Obstetric Soc., Med. Soc. Del. (Citation of Merit award 1992), New Castle County Med. Soc., Soc. Ob-Gyn. Vietnam (hon.), Ducks Unltd. (sponsor, mem. Del. com. 1980-92), Explorers Club (fellow 1966—, chmn. Phila. chpt. 1983-85, bd. dirs. 1981-88, pres. N.Y.C. 1985-87), Univ. and Whist Club Wilmington (life, bd. govs. 1961-64), Rotary (bd. dirs. local club 1991-93), Theta Chi (pres. 1945) Phi Beta Pi (pres. 1952), Kappa Beta Phi (pres. 1952). Avocations: hunting, polar history, sailing, carving bird decoys. Home: 55 Millstone Ln Rockland DE 19732 Office Phone: 302-655-8290.

LEVINSON, JOSEPH E., retired internist, rheumatologist, educator; b. Cin., Apr. 7, 1920; s. Samuel W. and Rebecca (Lewin) L.; m. Mimi Freiberg, Mar. 21, 1945 (dec. Apr. 1992); children: Steven Henry, Henry Samuel, Richard Peter (dec.); m. Carol Weihl, Oct. 10, 1993 (dec. Mar. 1999); m. Sophia Ralson, Nov. 10, 2001. Student, Columbia U., 1937-40; BA, Stanford U., 1941; MD, U. Cin., 1944. Clin. and rsch. fellow in medicine Harvard U./Mass. Gen. Hosp., Boston, 1950-52; instr. medicine U. Cin., 1953-61, assoc. prof. medicine, 1961-73, prof. medicine and pediatrics, 1973-85, dir. divsn. pediatric rheumatology, 1975-86, assoc. dir. Multipurpose Arthritis Ctr., 1978-82, prof. emeritus medicine and pediatrics, 1985—. Dir. arthritis tchg. svc. Cin. Gen. Hosp., 1960-64. Contbr. chapters to books, articles to profl. jours. Bd. dirs. Seven Hills Sch., Cin., 1993-2001, Cancer Family Care, Cin., Anthem Found. of Ohio, 1999-2004, Friends of the Spl. Treatment Ctr.; bd. dirs. Planned Parenthood S.W. Ohio Region, 2000— Master Am. Coll. Rheumatology (master). Avocations: tennis, horse and mule wilderness pack trips, travel. Office: Children's Hosp Med Ctr 3333 Burnet Ave Cincinnati OH 45229-3026 Home: Apt 802 2121 Alpine Pl Cincinnati OH 45206-3697 Fax: 513-221-7091. Office Phone: 513-636-8854. Personal E-mail: jelevinson@fuse.net.

LEVINSON, KATHY, former investment company executive, philanthropist; 2 children. BA in Econs., Stanford U., 1977. With Charles Schwab, 1981-94, sr. v.p. credit svc., 1989-94; cons. E*TRADE Securities, Inc., E*TRADE Group, Palo Alto, Calif., 1995, pres., COO, 1996—2000, corp. sr. v.p., 1996—2000, dir., 1996—2000, corp. exec. v.p. ops., 1996; pres., COO E*Trade Group, 1999—2000. Founder Mishkan HaLev. Recipient Davidson/Valenti award, Gay & Lesbian Alliance Against Defamation, 2000.

LEVINSON, KENNETH S., lawyer, corporate financial executive; b. Mineola, NY, Oct. 27, 1947; s. Max Leonard and Eva (Klamen) L.; m. Laura R. Levinson, Sept. 14, 1969 (div. 1981); 1 child, Barbara Ann Schmidt; m. Jerelyn E. Jarmacz, Feb. 6, 1982; children: Alexander T., Brianna F., Joshua K. BA in Polit. Sci. with distinction, U. Wis., 1969; JD with honors, George Washington U., 1975; LLM in Taxation, Georgetown U., 1978. Bar: D.C. 1975, Va. 1975, U.S. Ct. Claims 1976, U.S. Dist. Ct. (D.C. dist.) 1976, U.S. Tax Ct. 1976, U.S. Ct. Appeals (D.C. cir.) 1976, U.S. Supreme Ct. 1979. Atty., advisor Office Chief Counsel Interpretative div. IRS, Washington, 1975-78, reviewer, asst. br. chief Office Chief Counsel, 1978-79; sr. tax atty. Pepper, Hamilton & Scheetz, Washington, 1979-81; v.p., mng. tax dir. Marriott Corp., Bethesda, Md., 1981-85, v.p. internat. project fin., 1985-90; from v.p. tax to v.p. tax, risk mgmt. & ins. Northwest Airlines, Inc., Eagan, Minn., 1990—96, v.p. tax, risk mgmt. and ins., 1996—2001; mng. dir. KPMG, 2002—. Adj. prof. Georgetown U. Law Ctr., Washington, 1978-86; asst. sec., v.p. various Marriott Corp. subs., Bethesda, 1981-90; v.p. Wings Holdings, Inc./N.W. Airlines Corp., 1990-2001; v.p. tax N.W. Airlines, Inc., 1990-2001, v.p. various subs.; cons. Chechhi Group, Beverly Hills, Calif., 1989-90; bd. dirs. City Harbour Hotel, Ltd., London. Contbr. articles to profl. jours. Bd. dirs. Minn. Taxpayers Assn., Mpls. Lt. USN, 1969-72. Mem.: ABA (subcom. chair 1978—84), Minn. Taxpayers Assn. (bd. dirs. 1998—, exec. com. 1998—, pres. 2004—), Nat. Taxpayers Assn. (bd. dirs. 1999—2002, nominating com. 2003—), Internat. Air Transport Assn. (chair taxation com. 1991—92, chmn. ins. com. 1994, chair internat. risk mgrs. forum 1995, chmn. ins. com. 1997—99, chair internat. risk mgrs. forum 1998—2001, vice chmn. 1999, chair taxation com. 1999—2000, conf. chair 2001, chmn. air 2002), Air Transport Assn., Washington Tax Group, Tax Execs. Inst. (bd. dirs. Minn. chpt. 1999—2003), Va. State Bar, D.C. Bar. Avocations: golf, art appreciation/collection, boating, equestrian show jumping, skiing.

LEVINSON, LAWRENCE EDWARD, lawyer; b. N.Y.C., Aug. 25, 1930; s. Samuel Keever and Sara Lee (Tarvin) L.; m. Margaret Anne Bishop, Aug. 20, 1989; children: Elizabeth, Suzanne, Lucia. BA magna cum laude, Syracuse U., 1952; LLB, Harvard U., 1955. Bar: N.Y. 1957, D.C. 2002; U.S. Supreme Ct. 1958. Atty. Office Sec. Air Force, Washington, 1957-63; spl. assignments Office Sec. Def., Washington, 1963-65; dep. counsel to Pres. U.S., Washington, 1965-69; sr. v.p. Paramount Communications, Inc., N.Y.C., 1969-94; sr. Washington counsel VIACOM Internat., 1994-95; ptnr. Verner, Liipfert, Bernhard, McPherson and Hand, Washington, 1995—2002, DLA Piper Rudnick, Washington, 2002—04, DLA Piper Rudnick Gray Cary, Washington, 2005—. Mem. Nat. Council on Health Planning and Devel., Washington, 1978-84; host pub. affairs TV program Capital Notebook, 1991-95. Mem. bd. visitors Syracuse U. Coll. Arts and Scis., 1981—; mem. bd. dir. Assn. Am. Publishers. Served with Judge Adv. div. U.S. Army, 1955-57. Mem. N.Y. State Bar Assn., Assn. Am. Pubs. (bd. dirs. 1989-95), Army-Navy Country Club (Washington), Phi Beta Kappa. Home: 5715 Little Falls Rd Arlington VA 22207-1554 Office: 1200 Nineteenth St NW Washington DC 20036-2412 Office Phone: 202-861-6463. Office Fax: 202-689-8568. Business E-Mail: lawrence.levinson@dla.piper.com.

LEVINSON, MARINA, information technology executive; arrived in US, 1980; BS in computer sci., Leningrad Inst. Precision Mechanics and Optics. Various positions with TRW, San Jose, Calif., Tandem Computers (now part of HewlettPackard), SpectralPhysics; sr. dir. global integration 3Com Corp., Mass.; v.p., CIO PalmOne Inc., Milpitas, Calif., 1999—. Named one of Premier 100 IT Leaders, Computerworld mag., 2004. Office: PalmOne Inc 400 N McCarthy Blvd Milpitas CA 95035 Office Phone: 408-503-7000.

LEVINSON, NANETTE SEGAL, international relations educator, academic administrator; b. Boston, Nov. 8, 1946; d. Oscar and Rose (Menicks) Segal; m. Peter Joseph Levinson, Mar. 30, 1968; children: Sharman Risa, Justin David. AB cum laude, Harvard U., 1968, EdM, 1969, EdD, 1979. Asst. prof. Am. U., Washington, 1980-86, dir. advanced tech. mgmt. program, 1983-88, assoc. prof., 1986—, assoc. dean sch. internat. svc., 1988—2004, sr. assoc. dean, 2004—; visiting prof. Inst. Etudes Politiques, Paris, 2001. Cons. David Taylor Naval Ship Rsch. and Devel. Ctr., 1984-86, Xerox Corp., Leesburg, Va., 1986-91; chair bd. dirs. Nat. Conf. on Advancement of Rsch., 1992-93, bd. dirs., 1996-2000; bd. dirs. Women's Rsch. Policy Group, 1997-2000, mem. adv. cou., 2000-2003; bd. dirs. Transatlantic Info. Exch. Svcs., sec.-gen., 1997-99; vis. scholar Ritsumeikan U., Kyoto, Japan, 1993; bd. dirs. Internat. Adv. Bd. Transatlantic Internet Seminars, 2000—; vis. prof. Fondation Nationale des Sciences Politiques/Inst. d'Etudes Politiques de Paris, 2001. Contbr. numerous articles to profl. jours. Bd. dirs. Joint Bd. on Sci. and Engring. Edn., Washington, 1982-85; co-chair The Rsch. Project on Women Leaders in Internat. Affairs, 1995-99. Mem. Internat. Studies Assn., Am. Polit. Sci. Assn. Office: Am U Office of Dean 4400 Massachusetts Ave NW Washington DC 20016-8071 E-mail: nlevins@american.edu.

LEVINSON, PETER JOSEPH, retired lawyer; b. Washington, June 11, 1943; AB in History cum laude, Brandeis U., Waltham, Mass., 1965; JD, Harvard U., 1968. Summer supr. Harvard Legal Aid Bur., Cambridge, Mass., 1968; rsch. asst. Harvard Law Sch., 1968-69; tchg. fellow Osgoode Hall Law Sch. York (Can.) U., 1969-70, rsch. assoc., 1969-70, asst. prof., 1970-71; dep. atty. gen. State of Hawaii, 1971-75; vis. fellow Harvard U., 1976-77; ptnr. Levinson and Levinson, Honolulu, 1977-79; spl. asst. to dir. office program support Legal Svcs. Corp., Washington, 1979; cons. Select Commn. on Immigration and Refugee Policy, Washington, 1980-81; minority counsel subcom. on immigration, refugees and internat. law com. on judiciary U.S. Ho. of Reps., Washington, 1981-85, minority counsel subcom. monopolies and comml. law, 1985-89, minority counsel subcom. econ. and comml. law, 1989-95, counsel com. on judiciary, 1995-2001, ret., 2001. Mem.: ABA.

LEVINSON, ROBERT ALAN, textiles executive; b. Balt., July 26, 1925; s. Louis and Frieda Levinson; m. Patricia S. Schulte, Apr. 23, 1954; children: Margot, Andrew, John. AB, MBA, Dartmouth Coll., 1946; postgrad., London Sch. Econs., 1946-47. With Burlington Industries, N.Y.C., 1949-51; v.p., dir. Bangor Punta, Inc., N.Y.C., 1964-68; chmn. bd. Duplan Corp., N.Y.C., 1968-79. Bd. dirs. World Policy Inst., Nat. Dance Inst.; trustee Bklyn. Mus., chmn., 1972—84; bd. dirs., mem. exec. com. Nat. Commn. U.S.-China Rels.; vice-chmn. Nat. Acad. Mus., Harlem Sch. Arts, chmn. With USNR, 1943—45, with USNR, 1952—54. Home: 1035 5th Ave New York NY 10028-0135 Office: 1065 Avenue of the Americas Fl 28 New York NY 10018

LEVINSON, STEVEN HENRY, state supreme court justice; b. Cin., June 8, 1946; BA with distinction, Stanford U., 1968; JD, U. Mich., 1971. Bar: Hawaii 1972, U.S. Dist. Ct. Hawaii 1972, U.S. Ct. Appeals (9th cir.) 1972. Law clk. to Hon. Bernard H. Levinson Hawaii Supreme Ct., 1971-72; pvt. practice Honolulu, 1972-89; judge Hawaii Cir. Ct. (1st cir.), 1989-92; assoc. justice Hawaii Supreme Ct., Honolulu, 1992—. Staff mem. U. Mich. Jour. Law Reform, 1970-71. Active Temple Emanu-El. Mem. ABA (jud. divsn. 1989—), Hawaii State Bar Assn. (dir. young lawyers divsn. 1975-76, dir. 1982-84), Am. Judges Assn., Am. Judicature Soc. Jewish. Office: Supreme Ct Hawaii Aliiolani Hale 417 S King St Honolulu HI 96813-2912 Office Phone: 808-539-4735. Business E-Mail: steven.h.levinson@courts.state.hi.us.

LEVINSON, WARREN MITCHELL, broadcast journalist; b. Bklyn., Feb. 23, 1953; s. Abraham and Roslyn Anne (Bell) L.; m. Debra Lynn Galant, Sept. 1, 1985; children: Margot, Noah. BA, Duke U., 1975. Reporter Sta. WCHL Radio, Chapel Hill, N.C., 1974-77; news dir. Sta. WBLG/WKQQ Radio, Lexington, Ky., 1977-78; newswriter AP, N.Y.C., 1979-82; corr. AP Radio, N.Y.C., 1982—. Co-host (radio talk program) Newsweek on Air, 1985-2005. Recipient Silver medal for News Mag. Internat. Radio T.V. Soc., 1989, Crystal award of Excellence, Nat. Communicator Awards, 2000. Avocations: bicycling, poetry. Office: Associated Press 450 W 33rd St New York NY 10001 Business E-Mail: wlevinson@ap.org.

LEVINSTEIN, MARK STEVEN, lawyer, educator; b. Pitts., June 17, 1958; s. Hyman Joseph and Myrna Carol (Cohen) L.; m. Teresa K. Wellman, Aug. 31, 1991; children: Brian Philip, Kimberly Jael, Carly Ann. BA with honors, U. Va., 1979; JD, Harvard U., 1982. Bar: D.C. 1983, N.J. 1983, Md. 1983, U.S. Dist. Ct. N.J. 1983, Va. 1985, U.S. Dist. Ct. (ea. dist.) Va. 1985, U.S. Dist. Ct. D.C. 1985, U.S. Dist. Ct. Md. 1986, U.S. Ct. Appeals (4th cir., D.C. cir.) 1986, U.S. Ct. Appeals (9th cir.) 1989, U.S. Supreme Ct. 1990. Law clk. to presiding justice U.S. Dist. Ct. Mass., Boston, 1982-83; assoc. Williams & Connolly, Washington, 1983-90, ptnr., 1991—. Adj. prof. law Cath. U., Washington, 1985-92, George Washington U., Washington, 1991-94, Georgetown U., Washington, 1992-1999; chmn. Laws Jour.-Seminars Press Sports Law Program, 1996-2000. Co-author: Sports and the Law: Cases and Materials, 1997; contbr. articles to profl. jours. Echols scholar. Mem. ABA, Md. Bar Assn., Va. Bar Assn., D.C. Bar Assn., Assn. Trial Lawyers Am., Sports Lawyer Assn., Raven Soc., Phi Beta Kappa, Omicron Delta Kappa. Home: 8609 Meadow Edge Ter Fairfax Station VA 22039-3349 Office: Williams & Connolly LLP 725 12th St NW Washington DC 20005-5901 Office Phone: 202-434-5012. E-mail: mlevinstein@wc.com.

LEVIS, DONALD JAMES, psychologist, educator; b. Cleve., Sept. 19, 1936; s. William and Antoinette (Stejskal) L.; children: Brian, Katie. PhD, Emory U., 1964. Postdoctoral fellow clin. psychology Lafayette Clinic, Detroit, 1964-65; asst. prof. psychology U. Iowa, Iowa City, 1966-70, assoc. prof., dir. research and tng. clinic, 1970-72; prof. SUNY-Binghamton, 1972—. Author: Learning Approaches to Therapeutic Behavior Modification, 1970, Implosive Therapy, 1973; cons. editor: Jour. Abnormal Psychology, 1974-80, Jour. Exptl. Psychology, 1976-77, Behavior Moedifications, 1977-81, Behavior Therapy, 1974-76, Clin. Behavior Therapy Rev., 1978—; contbr. articles to profl. jours. Served to capt. AUSR, 1958-66. Fellow Behavior and Therapy Research Soc. (charter, clin.), Am. Psychol. Assn.; mem. Assn. Advancement Behavior Therapy (publ. bd. 1979-82), AAAS, Psychonomic Soc., N.Y. State Psychol. Assn., Sigma Xi Home: 48 Riverside Dr Binghamton NY 13905-4402 Office: SUNY at Binghamton Dept Psychology Binghamton NY 13901 Office Phone: 607-772-9710.

LEVIT, HÉLOÏSE B. (GINGER LEVIT), art historian, art dealer, art consultant, journalist; b. Phila., Apr. 2, 1937; d. Elmer and Claire Frances (Schwartz) Bertman; m. Jay Joseph Levit, July 14, 1962; children: Richard Bertman, Robert Edward, Darcy Francine Honker. BA in French Literature, U. Pa., 1959; MA in French Literature, U. Richmond, 1975; MA Art History, Va. Commonwealth U., Richmond, 1998; Cert., Alliance Française, Paris, 1991, Chambre de Commerce et d'Industrie de Paris, 1991, La Sorbonne, Paris, 1994, Istituto Lorenzo di Medici Firenze, Italy, 1996, Ecole du Louvre, 1998. Arts broadcaster, Richmond, Va., 1976-82; dir. Fine Arts Am., Inc., Richmond, 1982-84; tchr. Henrico County Pub. Schs., Richmond, 1984-88; dir. devel. Sta. WVST-FM Va. State U., Petersburg, 1987-88; mgr., dir. devel. Richmond Philharm. Orch., 1988-99; fine arts and media cons. Art-I-Facts, Richmond, 1988—; cons., 1997-98. Author: Moments, Monuments & Monarchs, 1986 (Star award, 1986); arts writer: Richmond Rev., 1989—90, Mid Atlantic Antiques mag., Mid-Atlantic Antiques News, Washington Jewish Week, Tidewater Women Richmond Jewish News; anchor, prodr. (syndicated radio series) Va. Arts Report, 1978—83, Va. Women, 1984. V.p. Va. Mus. Collector's Cir., Richmond, 1986-91, mem. steering com.; pres. Richmond Area Dem. Women's Club, 1992-93; mem. Va. Mus. Coun., Richmond; rec. sec. Richmond Symphony Orch. League, 1998-2000, dir. pub. rels., 2000—, guest condr., 2000. Mem. Va. Press Women (2d pl. award 2001, 02, 03), U. Pa. Alumni Club (v.p. 1980-90, Ben Franklin award 1990), Am. Symphony Orch. League, L'Accueil Francais, Alliance Francaise, La Table Francaise (chmn. 1996—), World Affairs Coun. Avocations: antiques, art collecting, classical music, foreign travel. Home and Office: Art-I-Facts 419 Dellbrooks Pl Richmond VA 23238-5559 Business E-Mail: ginger@vcw.org.

LEVIT, JAY J(OSEPH), lawyer; b. Phila., Feb. 20, 1934; s. Albert and Mary Levit; m. Heloise Bertman, July 14, 1962; children: Richard Bertman, Robert Edward, Darcy Francine. AB, Case Western Res. U., 1955; JD, U. Richmond, 1958; LLM, Harvard U., 1959. Bar: Va. 1958, US Ct. Appeals (DC cir.) 1961, US Ct. Appeals (4th cir.) 1967, US Ct. Appeals (11th cir.) 1989, US Supreme Ct. 1961. Trial atty. U.S. Dept. Justice, Washington, 1960-64; sr. atty. Gen. Dynamics Corp., Rochester, N.Y., 1965-67; ptnr. Stallard & Levit, Richmond, Va., 1968-77, Levit & Mann, Richmond, 1978—. Instr. U. Mich. Law Sch., Ann Arbor, 1964—65; adj. assoc. prof. U. Richmond Law Sch., 1974—77; adj. lectr. Va. Commonwealth U., Richmond, 1970—85; lectr. in field. Contbg. editor The Developing Labor Law, 4th edit., Bur. Nat. Affairs, 1974—, guest columnist on labor and employment Va. Lawyers Weekly. Recipient ABA and Bur. Nat. Affairs Books cert. of appreciation for significant contbns. to advancement of the law, 1999—2005. Mem.: ABA (labor com.), Fed. Bar Assn. (labor and employment com.), Va. Bar Assn. (labor and employment com., Chair's award for extraordinary contbns. to labor and employment law sect. 1999). Avocations: art collecting, jogging, swimming, travel. Home: 419 Dellbrooks Pl Richmond VA 23238-5559 Office: Levit & Mann Ste 100 1301 N Hamilton St Richmond VA 23230-3959 Office Phone: 804-355-7766. Personal E-mail: levmanhal@mindspring.com.

LEVIT, MAX, wholesale distribution executive, food service executive; s. Joe and Dora Levit. V.p., 1958-1993; pres. Grocers Supply Co., Houston, 1993—. Recipient Torch of Liberty award, Anti-Defamation League, 2001. Office: Grocers Supply Co 3131 E Holcombe Blvd Houston TX 77021

LEVIT, WILLIAM HAROLD, JR., lawyer; b. San Francisco, Feb. 8, 1938; s. William Harold and Barbara Janis Kaiser L.; m. Mary Elizabeth Webster, Feb. 13, 1971; children: Alison Jones Baumler, Alexandra Bradley Kovacevich, Laura Elizabeth Fletcher, Amalia Elizabeth Webster Todryk, William Harold, III. BA magna cum laude, Yale U., 1960; MA Internat. Rels., U. Calif., Berkeley, 1962; LLB, Harvard U., 1967. Bar: N.Y. 1968, Calif. 1974, Wis. 1979. Fgn. service officer Dept. State, 1962-64; assoc. Davis Polk & Wardwell, NYC, 1967—73; assoc. ptnr. Hughes Hubbard & Reed, N.Y.C., L.A., 1973-79; sec. and gen. counsel Rexnord Inc., Milw., 1979-83; ptnr., chair internat. practice group, loss prevention ptnr., former dir and chair litigation prsctice group Godfrey & Kahn, Milw., 1983—. Substitute arbitrator Iran-U.S. Claims Tribunal, The Hague, 1984-88; lectr. Practicing Law Inst., ABA, 7th Cir. Bar Assn., Nat. Assn. Corp. Dirs., Calif. Continuing Edn. of Bar, State Bar of Wis.; trustee State of Wis. Investment Bd., 2003—. Contbr. to: Mergers and the Private Antitrust Suit: The Private Enforcement of Section 7 of the Clayton Act, 1977. Chmn. Bd. Ad Oversight Supreme Ct. Wis. Office Lawyer Regulation, 2000—; bd. dirs. Wis. Humane Soc., 1980—90, pres., 1986—88; bd. dirs. Vis. Nurse Corp., Milw., 1980—90, chmn., 1985—87; bd. dirs. Vis. Nurse Found., 1986—95, chmn., 1986—91; bd. dirs. Aurora Health Care Inc., 1988—93, Aurora Health Care Ventures, 1993—2004, chair, 1998—2000, 2002—03; trustee Columbia Coll. Nursing, 1992—, chair, 2002—04; trustee Mt. Mary Coll., 2002—04; dir. adv. bd. Med. Coll. Wis. Cardiovasc. Ctr., 1994—, chmn., 1999—2002; rep. Assn. Yale Alumni, 1976—79, 1981—84, 1990—93; pres. Yale Club So. Calif., 1977—79; neutral advisor panel and franchise and ins. panels CPR Inst. Inst. for Conflict & Resolution. Ford Found. fellow, U. Pa., 1960—61, NDEA fellow, U. Calif., Berkeley, 1961—62. Fellow: Wis. Law Found., Am. Bar Found.; mem.: ABA, Am. Arbitration Assn. (comml., internat., large complex case, and mediation panels), Inst. Jud. Adminstrn., Am. Soc. Internat. Law, N.Am. Coun. London Ct. of Internat. Arbitration, N.Y. Stock Exch. (panel arbitrators 1988—), Chartered Inst. Arbitrators (London), Nat. Assn. Security Dealers (panel arbitrators 1988—), Am. Br. Internat. Law Assn., Bar Assn. 7th Cir. (pres. 2002—03), State Bar Wis. (dir. internat. bus. transactions sect. 1985—92, dist. 2 Wis. Supreme Ct. bd. attys. profl. responsbility com. 1985—94, chmn. 1993—94), L.A. County Bar Assn. (ethics com. 1976—79), State Bar Calif. (com. on continuing edn. of bar 1977—79), Assn. Bar City N.Y., Am. Soc. Corp. Secs. (dir. 1981—92, pres. Wis. chpt. 1982—83), Am. Law Inst., Town Club, Milw. Athletic Club, Phi Beta Kappa. Office: 780 N Water St Ste 1200 Milwaukee WI 53202-3512 Office Phone: 414-273-3500. Business E-Mail: wlevit@gklaw.com.

LEVITAN, DAVID M(AURICE), lawyer, educator; b. Tver, Lithuania, Dec. 25, 1915; (parents Am. citizens); m. Judith Morley; children: Barbara Lane Levitan, Stuart Dean Levitan. BS, Northwestern U., 1936, MA, 1937; PhD, U. Chgo., 1940; JD, Columbia U., 1948. Bar: N.Y. 1948, U.S. Dist. Ct. (so. dist.) N.Y. 1948, U.S. Supreme Ct. 1953. Various U.S. Govt. adminstrv. and advisory positions with Nat. Youth Adminstrn., Office Price Adminstrn., War Prodn. Bd., Fgn. Econ. Adminstrn. Supreme Hdqrs. Allied Expeditionary Force, and Cen. European div. Dept. State, 1940-46; cons., sec. joint-com. of 5th and 6th coms., 2d Gen. Assembly, dir. com. of experts for establishing adminstrv. tribunal UN, 1946-47; cons. pub. affairs dept., producer series of pub. affairs programs on TV and radio ABC, 1946-53; pvt. practice N.Y.C., 1948-66; counsel Hahn & Hessen, N.Y.C., 1966-68, ptnr., 1968-86, counsel, 1986-96; instr. U. Chgo., 1938-41; adj. prof. public law Columbia U., 1946-65; adj. prof. John Jay Coll. Criminal Justice, CUNY, 1966-75; adj. prof. polit. sci. Post Coll., 1964-66; adj. prof. law Cardozo Sch. Law, 1978-82; pvt. practice, N.Y.C., 1996—. Asst. to Ill. state adminstr. Nat. Youth Adminstrn., chief budget sect., Washington, 1940-41; mgmt. analyst Office of Price Adminstrn., 1941; spl. asst. to chmn. War Prodn. Bd., 1942-43; chief property control divsn. Fgn. Econ. Adminstrn., Washington, 1944-45; with U.S. Group of Control Coun. for Germany at SHAEF, London, 1944; advisor Ctrl. European divsn. U.S. Dept. State, 1945; cons. UN, 1946-47, Sect. Joint Com. 5th and 6th Coms., 1946-47, 2d session of 1st Gen. Assembly, 1946-47; dir. Com. of Experts on Establishment of Adminstrn. Tribunal, 1946-47; cons. pub. affairs dept. ABC, 1946-53. Contbr. articles to legal jours. Mem. Nassau County (N.Y.) Welfare Bd., 1965-69; chmn. Planning Bd., Village of Roslyn Harbor, N.Y., 1965-66; chmn. Bd. of Zoning Appeals, Village Roslyn Harbor, 1967-86. Recipient Demobilization award Social Sci. Rsch. Coun., 1946-48. Fellow Am. Coll. Trust and Estate Counsel; mem. ABA, Am. Polit. Sci. Assn., Am. Soc. Internat. Law, Am. Law Inst., Assn. Bar City N.Y. Office: Ste 704 455 North End Ave New York NY 10282

LEVITAN, KENNETH MARK, psychiatrist; b. Chgo., Dec. 4, 1946; s. Leonard and Esther (Newman) L.; m. Marla Barnow, Aug. 4, 1974; children: Samuel, Emily, Aaron. BS, U. Ill., 1969; MD, U. Ill., Chgo., 1973; postgrad., Chgo. Inst. Psychoanalysis, 1979—. Resident in psychiatry Michael Reese Hosp., Chgo., 1973-76; practice psychiatry Chgo., 1976—. Asst. clin. prof. Rush Med. Sch. Mem. Am. Psychiatric Assn., Ill. Psychiatric Soc., Am. Psychoanalytic Soc. (assoc.), Chgo. Psychoanalytic Soc., Chgo. Soc. Adolescent Psychiatry, Am. Soc. Adolescent Psychiatry. Office: 180 N Michigan Ave Ste 1010 Chicago IL 60601-7454 Office Phone: 312-236-0766.

LEVITAN, LAURENCE, lawyer, retired state senator; b. Oct. 22, 1933; s. Maurice and Nathlie (Rosenthal) L.; m. Barbara E. Levin, 1957; children: Jennifer, Michelle, Lisa. BS, Washington and Lee U., 1955; JD, George Washington U., 1958. Bar: Md. 1964. With Levitan, Cramer & Weinstein, 1959-72, Levitan Ezrin, West & Kenxton, 1973-85, Beckett Cromwell & Goldman, 1990-92; of counsel Baker & Hostetler, 1992-95; ptnr. Rifkin, Livingston, Levitan and Silver, LLC, Annapolis, Md., 1995—. Mem. Md. Ho. of Dels., 1971-74; mem. Md. Senate, 1975-94, chmn. budget and taxation com., policy com., spending affordability com, mem. joint com. on mgmt. pub. funds, legis. com. on budget and audit, gov.'s commn. to rev. state taxes and taxes structure, joint legis. com. on tax refrm, govtl. commn. to revise annotated code of Md., joint subcom. on program open space, chmn. drunk and drugged driving task force, chmn. joint com. on ins. tax reform; mem. Montgomery County Exec.'s Commn. for Higher Edn. in High Tech.; past mem. Gov.'s Commn. to Study Unification of Cir. Ct., Gov.'s Commn. to Study Condominium Laws, Gov.'s Commn. Law Enforcement and Adminstrn. Justice, Gov.'s Subcom. on Revenue Structure of Task Force to Study State-Local Rels.; mem. Gov.'s Commn. to Study Feasability of Biennial Budget, Gov.'s Task Force on Real Property Closing Costs, Task Force to Study Md. Tax Ct., Gov.'s Commn. Sch. Funding, Joint Task Force on Md.'s Procurement Law; apptd. co-chmn. transition team on budget rev. Gov. Glendening; chmn. Gov.'s Jud. Compensation Commn., 1998—; mem. Commn. on Md.'s Fiscal Structure, 2002-03. Mem. ABA, D.C. Bar Assn., Md. Bar Assn., Nat. Conf. State Legislatures (mem. subcom. on fed. budget and taxation com., fiscal affairs govt. oversight com.), So. Legis. Conf. (chmn. fiscal affairs and govt. ops. steering com. 1992-93), Am. Legis. Exch. Coun. (tax task force). Democrat. Jewish. Office: 225 Duke Of Gloucester St Annapolis MD 21401-2506 also: 11426 Georgetowne Dr Potomac MD 20854-3722 Office Phone: 301-922-8774. E-mail: checkoffLL@aol.com.

LEVITAS, ANDREW STEPHEN, child psychiatrist, educator; b. Bklyn., Feb. 17, 1948; s. Louis and Laura (Perlman) L.; m. Phyllis Malin, Apr. 19, 1970; children: Joshua, Matthew. BS, Union Coll., 1968; MD, Albert Einstein Coll. Medicine, 1972. Diplomate Am. Bd. Psychiatry and Neurology. Intern Montefiore Hosp. and Med. Ctr., Bronx, 0971—1973; resident in psychiatry Downstate-Kings County Hosp. Ctr., Bklyn., 1973—75; fellow in child psychiatry U. Colo. Health Scis. Ctr., Denver, 1975—77, asst. clin. prof., 1982—86; staff psychiatrist Denver Children's Hosp., 1977—79; pvt. practice Denver, 1979—86; asst. prof. U. Nebr. Med. Ctr., Omaha, 1986—88, U. Medicine and Dentistry N.J. Sch. Osteo. Medicine, Cherry Hill, 1988—96, assoc. prof. psychiatry, 1996—; med. dir. divsn. prevention and treatment of devel. disorders Sch. Osteo. Medicine, Cherry Hill, 1992—. Cons. psychiatrist T.I.M. House, Devel. Pathways, Aurora, Colo., 1982-86; mem. sci. adv.

bd. Fragile-X Soc. Assoc. editor: Mental Health Aspects of Developmental Disabilities, 1997—; contbr. numerous articles to profl. jours. Mem. MLA, Am. Psychiat. Assn., Am. Acad. Child and Adolescent Psychiatry. Office: U Medicine and Dentistry NJ Sch Oste Medicine Dept Psy 101 Laurel Rd Stratford NJ 08084-1352

LEVITAS, MIRIAM C. STRICKMAN, documentary filmmaker; b. Aug. 3, 1936; d. Morris and Bella (Barsky) Cherrin; m. Bernard Strickman, June 3, 1956 (dec. Jan. 1975); children: Andrew, Brian, Craig, Deron; m. Theodore Clinton Levitas, Apr. 25, 1976; children: Steven, Leslie, Anthony. Student, Temple U., 1953-56; studied interior design, LaSalle U., Chgo., 1968; cert. in gerontology/cmty. svc., Ga. State U., 1988. Intergenerational Connections Contact State of Ga., 1989—. V.p. programming interior design Nat. Home Fashions League, Atlanta, 1974—75, Ga. Bd. Realtors, 1971—; founding adminstr. Stanley H. Kaplan Ednl. Ctr., Atlanta, 1974—84; owner, pres. Levitas Svcs. Inc. (Internat. Destinations), Atlanta, 1984—85; owner, v.p. Nat. Travel Svcs. and Internat. Destinations, Atlanta, 1984—85; realtor Philip White Properties Inc./Sotheby's Internat. Realty, 1985—91, Coldwell Banker Previews, 1991—; intergenerational programs and events cons.; interior designer for loft living. *Ms. Levitas has secured funding for and produced/co-produced television programming for cable, and produced Rap the Gap for intergenerational workshop for Gerontology Conferences. She wrote "A Casual Presence," an intergenerational program, to be implemented into public schools to enhance the family unit and specifically address violence, truancy, and delinquency. She reorganized leadership structure in volunteer organizations and developed new avenues for increasing membership and participation in a multigenerational setting. She has designed and published two publications and developed the distribution and marketing plan for both. She is a producer, writer and orchestrator for local amateur productions.* Prodr.(host cmty. svc. videos TV cable broadcast):, 1988—91. Pres. Ahavath Achim Sisterhood, Atlanta, 1977—79, 1996—98; bd. dirs. Jewish Family Svcs., 1993—96; bd. dirs. Atlanta chpt. Nat. Osteoporosis Found., 1990—91, Outings in the Park, 1989—91; chmn., coord. Tea at the Ritz Scottish Rite Children's Med. Ctr., 1987—90; chmn. women's divsn. Israel Bond, Atlanta, 1987, 1988, 1989, mem. aux.; chmn., coord. Who's Bringing in the Great Chefs Scottish Rige Children's Med. Ctr., 1990, 1991, 1992; mem. Atlanta Symphony, High Mus. Art, Nat. Mus. of Women in Arts, William Bremen Jewish Heritage Mus., Alliance Theater Atlanta, Atlanta Hist. Ctr.-Atlanta Hist. Soc., Alliance No. Dist. Dental Soc.; charter mem. U.S. Holocaust Mus.; bd. dirs. Jewish Ednl. Loan Fund; nat. bd. advisors Brevard Mus. Ctr., 1993—. Named Woman of Achievement, Atlanta Jewish Fedn., 1993; scholar, Phila. Bd. Edn. Music, 1952. Mem.: NAFE, Nat. Assn. Realtors, Image Film and Video Ctr., Am. Women in Radio and TV, Women in Film (Atlanta chpt.), Internat. Furnishings and Design Assn., Spl. Children of the South (chmn. 1991—93), Atlanta Bd. Realtors, Ga. Gerontology Soc., Scots (life), B'nai Brith (life), Nat. Coun. Jewish Women (life), Hadassah (life), Brandeis Nat. Women (life), Ga. Dental Assn. Aux., Children's Med. Ctr. Aux. Office Phone: 404-431-9846. Personal E-mail: mslprod1@biltmorecomm.com.

LEVITCH, JOSEPH See **LEWIS, JERRY**

LEVITE, LAURENCE A., publishing executive; b. Buffalo, Apr. 26, 1940; s. Samuel and Estelle (Tishman) L.; m. Sharon Cohen, Aug. 15, 1965; children: Adam, Joshua. Student, U. Pa., 1958-60; grad., Am. Acad. Dramatic Arts, 1962; student, U. Buffalo Law Sch., 1965. Gen. mgr. McLendon Broadcasting, WYSL and WPHD Radio, Buffalo, 1970-74; exec. v.p., gen. mgr. Queen City Radio Corp., WEBR Radio, Buffalo, 1974-77; founder, pres., CEO Algonquin Broadcasting Corp., Buffalo, 1977-94; chmn. bd. dirs., pres. Algonquin Comm., Inc., Buffalo, 1995—; chmn., pub. David Lawrence Pubs., Inc., Williamsville, N.Y., 1998—. Bd. govs. Jewish Fedn. Buffalo, 1982—; chmn. media divsn. United Way campaign, 1985; mem. adv. bd. Jr. League, 1981, Medaille Coll., 1980, Jewish Ctr. of Buffalo, 1979-82, Episcopal Charities, 1981-83; bd. dirs. Bryant and Stratton Coll., 1998—, Shea's Buffalo Theatre, 1998—. Mem. Profl. Communicators of Western N.Y. (pres.), Buffalo Radio Assocs. Group (pres. 1972), N.Y. Broadcasters, N.Y. State Broadcasters Assn. (bd. dirs. 1983—, chmn. 1987), Nat. Assn. Broadcasters, Radio Advt. Bur., Buffalo Exec. Assn., Buffalo Club. Jewish. also: David Laurence Publs Inc 6215 Sheridan Dr Williamsville NY 14221 Office Phone: 716-634-0820 x 2220.

LEVITEN, RIVA SHAMRAY, artist; b. L.A., Oct. 26, 1928; d. Peter Leo and Edythe (Smith) Shamray; m. Paul Leviten, Oct. 15, 1950 (dec. Oct. 19, 1988); children: Priscilla Leviten Warner, Marcia Leviten, Peter Leviten. BS in Apparel Design, UCLA, 1950; postgrad., Cal Arts, L.A., 1949-50, Exptl. Etching Studio, Boston, 1980-90. 1st v.p. R.I. chpt. Nat. Mus. Women in the Arts, 1997-99. Visual Rev. Bd. Newport Rev., 1997-98, R.I. Women Speak, Nat. Mus. Women in the Arts, Crone elderwoman, 1997, Monotype Printmaking and Painting Travel Show, 1998—; represented in collections at R.I. Sch. Design Mus., Danforth Mus., Slater Mus., El Paso Mus., Midwest Mus. Am. Art, Mass. Coll. Art, R.I. Coll., Tougaloo Coll., U. Ark., Marist Coll., Muscatine Art Ctr., Laura Musser Mus. Dickenson State U., Art in Embassies U.S. Dept. State, Saginaw Art Mus.; exhibited Russia, Australia, Mex., Can. Founding mem. Gallery of Social and Polit. Justice, Boston, 1996—. Recipient Herbert Cross prize South County Art Assn., Kingston, R.I., 1979. Founding mem. Showcase for Collage; elected artist mem. Mystic Art Assn.; mem. Providence Art Club, Monotype Guild of New Eng., Providence Art Club (Providence Art Club award 1998, J. Bannigan Sullivan award 1995, Bradford Swan award 1987), Nat. Assn. Women Artists (Martha Reed award 1994). Avocations: urban gardening, interior design, poetry, innkeeping, public speaking at art symposiums. Home and Office: 425 Benefit St Providence RI 02903-2933

LEVITIN, LEV BEROVICH, research scientist, educator; b. Moscow, Sept. 25, 1935; came to U.S., 1981; s. Ber L. and Tzetzilia (Gushansky) L.; m. Yulia Shmukler, 1959 (div. 1970); 1 child, Boris. MSc, Moscow U., 1960; PhD, Acad. Scis. USSR, 1969. Sr. rsch. scientist Inst. Info. Transmission Problems/USSR Acad. Scis., 1961-73; sr. lectr. Tel-Aviv U., 1974-80; vis. prof. Bielefeld U., W.Ger., 1980-81, Syracuse (N.Y.) U., 1981-82; prof. engring. Boston U., 1982-86, disting. prof. engring. sci., 1986—. Vis. scientist Heinrich-Hertz Inst., Berlin, 1980, Inst. for Optoelektronik, Oberpfaffenhofen, W.Ger., 1981; cons. Vishay Israel, Ltd., Tel-Aviv, 1979, SEL Forschungszentrum, Stuttgart, Germany, 1987, Humboldt U., Berlin, 1997—. Editor: Principles of Cybernetics (in Russian), 1967; contbr. articles to profl. jours. Fellow IEEE, Internat. Acad. of Informatics; mem. AAUP, AAAS, Am. Math. Soc., Assn. Computing Machinery, Soc. Indsl. and Applied Math., N.Y. Acad. Scis., Am. Soc. for Engring. Edn., Math. Assn. Am., Memento, Resistance Internat., Amnesty Internat. Office: Boston U Coll Engring 8 Saint Marys St Boston MA 02215-2421 Office Phone: 617-353-4607. Business E-Mail: levitin@bu.edu.

LEVITON, ALAN EDWARD, curator; b. N.Y.C., Jan. 11, 1930; s. David and Charlotte (Weber) L.; m. Gladys Ann Robertson, June 30, 1952; children: David A., Charlotte A. Student, NYU, 1948; AB, Stanford U., 1949, MA, 1953, PhD, 1960; postgrad., U. Nebr., 1954, Columbia U., 1948; student, U. Nebr., 1954. Asst. curator herpetology Calif. Acad. Scis., San Francisco, 1957—60, assoc. curator, 1960—61, chmn., curator, 1962—82, 1989—92, 2001—, curator, 1983—88, 1993—2000, chmn. computer svcs., 1983—92, editor sci. publs., 1994—; assoc. curator zool. collections Stanford U., 1962—63, lectr. biol. sci., 1963—70; professorial lectr. Golden Gate U., 1953—63; adj. prof. biol. sci. San Francisco State U., 1967—2000, rsch. prof., 2000—. Author: North American Amphibians, 1970, Reptiles of the Middle East, 1992, T.H. Hittel's California Academy of Sciences, 1997; contbr. articles to profl. jours. Grantee Am. Philos. Soc., 1960, NSF, 1960-61, 77-79, 80, 83-89, 91-93, 2002—, Belvedere Sci. Fund, 1958-59, 62; recipient Fellows' medal Calif. Acad. Scis., 1999. Fellow AAAS (coun. 1976-97, com. coun. affairs 1983-85, sec.-treas. Pacific divsn. 1975-79, exec. dir. 1980-98, 2000-2001, pres.-elect 1998, pres. 1999-2000, counselor 2001—), Calif. Acad. Scis., Geol. Soc. Am. (vice-chmn. history geology divsn. 1989-90, chmn. 1990-91); mem. Am. Soc. Ichthyologists and Herpetologists (mem. bd. govs. 1960-84), Soc. Systematic Zoology (sec.-treas. Pacific sect. 1970-72), Forum Historians of Sci. Am. (coord. com. 1986-88, sec.-treas. 1988-90), Herpetologists League (pres. 1961-62), History of Sci. Soc. Home: 571 Kingsley Ave Palo Alto CA 94301-3225 Office: Calif Acad Scis 875 Howard St San Francisco CA 94103

LEVITSKY, MELVYN, former ambassador; b. Sioux City, Iowa, Mar. 19, 1938; s. David and Mollie (Schwartz) L.; m. Joan Daskovsky, Aug. 12, 1962; children: Adam, Ross Josh. BA, U. Mich., 1960; MA, U. Iowa, 1963. Polit. officer U.S. Embassy, Moscow, 1972-75; officer-in-charge Soviet-U.S. bilateral relations Dept. State, Washington, 1975-78, dep. dir. UN polit. affairs, 1978-80, dir. UN polit. affairs, 1980-82, dep. asst. sec. for human rights and humanitarian affairs, 1982-83; dep. dir. Voice of Am., Washington, 1983-84; U.S. amb. to Bulgaria, 1984-87; exec. sec., spl. asst. to sec. Dept. State, Washington, 1987-89, asst. sec. state internat. narcotics matters, 1989-94, U.S. amb. to Brazil Brasilia, 1994—; prof. Internat. Relations & Pub. Adminstrn. Maxwell School of Citizenship & Pub. Affairs, Syracuse U., Syracuse, NY; Disting. Fellow of Moynihan Inst. of Global Affairs Syracuse U., Syracuse, NY; professorial lectr. Johns Hopkins U. Sch. Advanced Internat. Studies, Washington, 2001—. Bd. dirs. Drug Free Am. Found. Recipient Meritorious Honor award Dept. State, 1968, Superior Honor award Dept. State, 1975, 82, Presdl. Meritorious Svc. awards, 1986-91. Mem. Am. Fgn. Svc. Assn., Am. Acad. Diplomacy, Washington Inst. Fgn. Affairs. Office: Maxwell School of Citizenship & Pub Affairs Syracuse U 351 Eggers Hall Syracuse NY 13244-0001 E-mail: mlevitsk@maxwell.syr.edu.*

LEVITT, ARTHUR, JR., investment company executive; b. Bklyn., Feb. 3, 1931; s. Arthur and Dorothy (Wolff) L.; m. Marylin Blauner, June 12, 1955; children: Arthur III, Lauri. BA, Williams Coll., 1952, LLD (hon.), 1980, Pace U., 1980, Hamilton Coll., 1981, L.I. U., 1984, Hofstra U., 1985; LLD (hon.), Columbia U., 1999. Asst. promotion dir. Time, Inc., N.Y.C., 1954-59; exec. v.p., dir. Oppenheimer Industries, Inc., Kansas City, Mo., 1959-62; with Shearson Hayden Stone Inc. (now Citigroup), N.Y.C., 1962-78, pres., 1969-78; chmn., CEO, Am. Stock Exch., N.Y.C., 1978-89; chmn. Levitt Media Co., N.Y.C., 1989-93, N.Y.C. Econ. Devel. Corp., 1989—93, SEC, Washington, 1993—2001; sr. adv. The Carlyle Group, NYC, 2001—; spl. advisor Am. Internat. Group Inc., NYC, 2005—. Chmn. President's Pvt. Sector Survey on Cost Control, 1982-84, President's Task Force on Pvt. Sector Initiatives, 1981-82, White House Small Bus. Conf. Commn., 1978-80; mem. N.Y. State Coun. on Arts, 1969—; chmn. bd. dirs. Spl. Adv. Task Force on Future Devel. West Side Manhattan, President's Base Closure and Realignment Commn.; former trustee Williams Coll.; bd. dirs. Bloomberg LLP, Rand Corp. With USAF, 1952—54, maj. res. Recipient Medal of Excellence Bd. Regents State of N.Y. Mem. Am. Bus. Conf. (chmn. 1980-89), Phi Beta Kappa. Office: The Carlyle Group 520 Madison Ave New York NY 10022 Business E-Mail: arthur.levitt@carlyle.com.

LEVITT, GEORGE, retired chemist; b. Newburg, N.Y., Feb. 19, 1925; m. Julie Zeto; children: Barbara Klein, Jeffrey, David, Gregory. BS, Duquesne U., 1950, MS, 1952; PhD, Mich. State U., 1957. Rsch. chemist Exptl. Sta. E.I. du Pont de Nemours & Co., Inc., 1956—63, rsch. chemist Stine Lab., 1963—66, rsch. chemist Exptl. Sta., 1966—68, sr. rsch. chemist, 1968—80, rsch. assoc., 1981—86. Instr. Del. Tech. and C.C., 1975—80. Pres. Ronald McDonald House of Del, 1986—87, bd. dirs., 1986—94. Recipient Internat. pesticide rsch. award, Swiss Soc. Chem. Industries, 1982, award, Chesapeake chpt. Nat. Agrl. Mktg. Assn., 1987, disting. alumni award, Duquesne U. Coll. Arts and Sci., 1988, Nat. Medal of Tech., 1993, Disting. Inventor award, Intellectual Property Owners Am., 1983. Mem.: AAAS, Internat. Union Pure & Applied Chemistry, Am. Chem. Soc. (Creative Invention award 1989, Kenneth Spencer award 1991, internat. award for rsch. in agrochems. 1998, Hero of Chem. award 1999), Sigma Xi. Achievements include research in organic syntheses, herbicides, fungicides, medicinals, pesticides; synthesis of heterocyclic compounds; characterization and identification of novel organic compounds for biological evaluation; defined and optimized chemical structure-biological activity relationships and sulfonylurea herbicides. Home: 82 Via del Corso Palm Beach Gardens FL 33418-3773 Personal E-mail: gleanr@msn.com.

LEVITT, GERALD STEVEN, engineering executive; b. Bronx, NY, Mar. 21, 1944; s. Charles and Beatrice (Janet) L.; m. Natalie Lillian Hoppen; children: Mark, Roy. B in Mgmt. Engring., Rensselaer Poly. Inst., 1965; MBA, DePaul U., 1972. Registered profl. engr., Ill. Tech. rep. Worthington Air Conditioning Co., Ampere, N.J., 1965-67; indsl. sales engr. Peoples Gas Light & Coke Co., Chgo., 1967-71; planning specialist Peoples Gas Co., Chgo., 1971-72; v.p. Stone & Webster Mgmt. Cons., Inc., N.Y.C., 1972-82; exec. v.p., chief staff officer South Jersey Gas Co., Folsom, N.J., 1982-98; v.p., CFO South Jersey Industries, Inc., Folsom, N.J., 1987-98; sr. v.p., treas., CFO Greenhorne & O'Mara, Inc., Greenbelt, Md., 1998—. Past bd. dirs. Camden County coun. Boy Scouts Am., West Collingswood, N.J., Rowan Coll. Found. Mem. Greater Atlantic City C. of C. (past bd. dirs.), N.J. State C. of C. (past bd. dirs.), Greenhorne O'Mara, Inc. (bd. dirs.). Office: Greenhorne & O'Mara Inc 9001 Edmonston Rd Greenbelt MD 20770-1083 Office Phone: 301-982-2800. Business E-Mail: glevitt@g-and-o.com.

LEVITT, HARRY, speech and hearing scientist; b. Johannesburg, May 19, 1937; came to U.S., 1964; s. Boris and Thelma (Kagan) L.; m. Eleanor Claire Sosnow, June 15, 1969 (dec. Sept. 2000); 1 child, David Avrum. BSc, U. Witwatersrand, Johannesburg, 1958; PhD, Imperial Coll. Sci. and Tech., London, 1964. Tech. staff mem. AT&T Bell Labs., Murray Hill, N.J., 1964-69; assoc. prof., prof., disting. prof. CUNY, 1969-2000. Cons. AT&T Bell Labs., 1980-99, BBN, 1970—, Audimax, 1970—, various univs.; reviewer NIH, NSF, Office Edn., VA, 1970—. Beit fellow, 1960-63; fellow Acoustical Soc. Am., 1970, Am. Speech and Hearing Assn., 1980; recipient Nat. Winner for Computing to Aid the Handicapped Johns Hopkins, 1981, N.Y.C. Mayor's award for contbns. to sci. and tech., 1999, Lifetime Achievement award Am. Auditory Soc., 2001. Achievements include introducing computer assisted adaptive testing to the field of audiology; developed first digital hearing aid. Office: CUNY Grad Sch 365 5th Ave New York NY 10016-4334 Home: PO Box 610 Bodega Bay CA 94923-0610 E-mail: harrylevitt@earthlink.net.

LEVITT, JAREN, real estate company officer; b. N.Y.C., Mar. 19, 1946; s. Seymour and Harriet (Finorsky) L.; children: Jaden, Janna; m. Theresa Julyun Kim, Oct. 16, 1995. BS in Psychology and Biology, Syracuse U., 1965; MS in Clin. Psychology, U. Tex., 1967; PhD in Clin. Psychology, UCLA, 1974. Spl. asst Mayor's Office, N.Y.C., 1968-71, Pres. U.S., Washington, 1971; pres. Med. Cons. Internat., Woodland Hills, Calif., 1973-78; mktg. dir. vacation planning Playboy Internat., McAffe, N.J., 1978-80; regional mktg. dir. Gen. Devel. Co., Miami, Fla., 1981-88, asst. v.p., 1988, v.p. Cen. Region and Far East Norridge, Ill., 1988-90, pres. Am. Real Estate Devel. Corp. Fla.; pres. Global Acquisition and Devel. Corp., 1990-95, Stone Trend Internat., Inc., Sarasota, 1995—, owner, RoadWarriorTrading.com. Cons. substance abuse projects to bus. and fgn. govts., 1968-78. Contbr. articles to profl. jours. Mem. Heritage Found. Republican. Jewish. Avocations: scuba, skiing, sky-diving, tennis, flying. Office: 6244 Clark Center Ave Bldg 3 Sarasota FL 34238-2752 E-mail: thinkpad@msn.com, stonetrend@aol.com, jaren@roadwarriortrading.com.

LEVITT, JERRY DAVID, medical educator; b. Phila., Apr. 11, 1941; s. Abraham and Nettie (Dash) L.; m. Julie Meranze, June 2, 1967; children: Rachel, Daniel, Gabriel. BA, U. Pa., 1962, MD, 1966. Diplomate Am. Bd. Anesthesiology, Pain Mgmt.; lic. physician, Pa., Maine. Intern Mt. Sinai Hosp., N.Y.C., 1966—67; resident in anesthesia U. Pa. Hosp., Phila., 1967—69, rsch. fellow, 1971—72; instr. anesthesia U. Pa., Phila., 1972—73, asst. prof. anesthesia, 1973—82; assoc. prof. anesthesiology Med. Coll. Pa. Hahnemann Sch. Medicine, Phila., 1982—2002, Drexel U. Coll. of Medicine, Phila., 2002—. Author: (with others) Basic Pharmacology in Medicine, 1990; contbr. articles to profl. jours. With USPHS, 1969-71. Avocations: photography, sailing, music, motorcycles. Office: Hahnemann Univ Hosp Broad & Vine Sts Philadelphia PA 19102 Office Phone: 215-762-3544.

LEVITT, JESSE, retired foreign language educator; b. N.Y.C., June 15, 1919; s. Louis and Mollie (Goldstein) L.; m. Selma Kojan, May 9, 1958; children: Vera Louise, Lorraine Elizabeth Levitt Katz. BA magna cum laude, CCNY, 1938; MA in French, Columbia U., 1940, PhD in Romance Philology, 1963. Translator, news wire editor U.S. Fgn. Broadcast Info. Svc., Washington, 1941-54; tchr. high sch. Balt., 1955-56; tchr. jr. high sch. Greenlawn, N.Y., 1956-57; tchr. French, Spanish, Latin Rye Neck High Sch., Mamaroneck, N.Y., 1957-59; asst. prof. Wash. State U., Pullman, 1960-65; prof. fgn. langs. U. Bridgeport, Conn., 1965-89; ret., 1989. Tchr. French history, lit. and current world history in sr. learning program, Bridgeport, Conn., 1999—; spkr. annual conf. The Names Inst., The Am. Soc. Geolinguistics, Baruch Coll., N.Y.C. Author: The Grammaire des Grammaires of Girault Divivier, A Study of 19th Century French, 1968; co-editor: Geolinguistic Perspectives, 1987, Justice: Interdisciplinary and Global Perspectives, 1988, Language in Contemporary Soc., 1993, Constructed Languages and Language Construction, 1996, Language and Communication in the New Century, 1998; contbr. articles in linguistics, onomastics and French lit. to scholarly publs. Mem. MLA, Soc. Internat. de dialectologie et geolinguistique, Am. Soc. Geolinguistics (editor 1973-98, sec., editor internat. conf. 1992), Am. Name Soc., Simon Wiesenthal Ctr., Handgun Control Inc., Phi Beta Kappa. Democrat. Home: 485 Brooklawn Ave Fairfield CT 06825-1805

LEVITT, ROBERT E., gastroenterologist; b. Phila., Oct. 22, 1948; s. Martin E. and Miriam G. (Elson) L.; m. Linda Levitt, Mar. 13, 1976; children: Adam, Ashley. BA summa cum laude, Temple U., 1970, MD, 1974. Diplomate Am. Bd. Internal Medicine, Am. Bd. Gastroenterology. Chief hepatology and gastrointestinal rsch. Presbyn. U. of Pa. Med. Ctr., Phila., 1979-88, staff gastroenterologist, 1979—, assoc. dir. Inst. Gastroenterology, 1981-89; chief svc. gastroenterology Bryn Mawr (Pa.) Hosp., 1985—, chief gastrointestinal sect. dept. medicine, 1988—, dir. endoscopy ste., 1988—; asst. prof. medicine U. Pa. Sch. Medicine, 1979—; dir. endoscopy suite Bryn Mawr Hosp., 1988—. Clin. assoc. prof. medicine, Jefferson Med. Coll., Thomas Jefferson U., Phila. Contbr. articles to med. jours., chpts. to med. books; mem. editorial adv. bd. Post-Grad. Medicine. Fellow ACP; mem. AMA (Physicians Recognition award 1978, others), Am. Gastroenterol. Assn., Am. Coll. Gastroenterology, Am. Soc. for Gastrointestinal Endoscopy, Pa. Soc. Gastroenterology, Med. Club Phila., Phi Eta Sigma, Alpha Omega Alpha. Office: 933 E Haverford Rd Bryn Mawr PA 19010-3819

LEVITT, SEYMOUR HERBERT, radiologist, educator; b. Chgo., July 18, 1928; s. Nathan E. Levitt and Margaret (Chizever) D.; m. Phillis Jeanne Martin, Oct. 31, 1952 (div. Oct. 1981); children: Mary Jeanne, Jennifer Gaye, Scott Hayden; m. Solveig I. Ostberg, Feb. 6, 1983. BA, U. Colo., 1950, MD, 1954, DSc (hon.), 1997. Diplomate Am. Bd. Radiology. Intern Phila. Gen. Hosp., 1954-55; resident in radiology U. Calif. at San Francisco Med. Center, 1957-61; instr. radiation therapy U. Mich., Ann Arbor, 1961-62, U. Rochester, N.Y., 1962-63; asso. prof. radiology U. Okla., Oklahoma City, 1963-66; prof. radiology, chmn. div. radiotherapy Med. Coll. Va., Richmond, 1966-70; prof., head dept. therapeutic radiology U. Minn., Mpls., 1970—99. Cons. in field. Exec. bd. Am. Joint Com. for End Result Reporting and Cancer Staging; com. radiation oncology studies Nat. Cancer Inst.; trustee Am. Bd. Radiology, 1977-89; chmn. bd. dirs. Found. for Rsch. and Edn.; fgn. adj. prof. Karolinska Inst., Stockholm, 2002. Bd. dirs., mem. exec. com. Am. Cancer Soc., 1990-95. With M.C., AUS, 1955-57. Recipient Disting. Svc. award U. Colo., 1988. Fellow: Royal Coll Radiology (hon.), Am. Coll. Radiology (bd. chancellors, Gold medal 1995); mem.: Am. Soc. Therapeutic Radiologists (exec. bd. 1974—78, pres. 1978—79, chmn. bd. 1979—80, Gold medal 1991), Am. Soc. Clin. Oncology, Soc. Nuclear Medicine, Internat. Soc. Radiation Oncology (pres. 1981—85), Soc. Chmn. Acad. Radiation Oncology Programs (pres. 1974—76), German Soc. Radiology (hon.), European Cong. Radiology (hon.), German Soc. Radiation Oncology (hon.), Am. Roentgen Ray Soc., Am. Cancer Soc. (pres. Minn. divsn. 1979—80, nat. bd., exec. com.), Am. Assn. Cancer Rsch., Radiol. Soc. N.Am. (bd. dirs. 1991—2000, chmn. bd. dirs. 1997—98, pres.-elect 1998, pres. 1999—, Gold medal 2004), Am. Radium Soc. (sec. 1981—83, pres. 1983—84, Janeway medal 1989), Alpha Omega Alpha, Sigma Xi, Phi Beta Kappa. Office: U Minn Med Sch PO MMC 436 Minneapolis MN 55455

LEVITT, STEVEN D., economics professor; BA in Econ. summa cum laude, Harvard Univ., 1989; PhD in Econ., MIT, 1994. Mgmt. cons. Corporate Decisions, Inc., 1989—91; Jr. Fellow Harvard Soc. of Fellows, 1994—97; Rsch. Fellow Am. Bar Found., 1997—; asst. prof., econ. Univ. Chgo., 1997—98, assoc. prof., 1998—99, prof., 1999—2002, Alvin H. Baum prof., 2002—. Assoc. editor Quarterly Jour. Econ., 1998—99; editor: Jour. Polit. Economy, 1999—; co-author (with Stephen J. Dubner): Freakonomics: A Rogue Economist Explores the Hidden Side of Everything, 2005 (NY Times Bestseller list, Publishers Weekly Bestseller list). Co-recipient Duncan Black Prize, Public Choice, 2000; recipient Nat. Sci. Found. CAREER award, 1999, Nat. Sci. Found. Presdl. Early Career award for scientists and engrs., 2000, John Bates Clark Medal for best Am. economist under 40; grantee Faculty Rsch. Fellow, Nat. Bur. Econ. Rsch., 1994—, John M. Olin Rsch. Fellow in law and econ., Harvard Law Sch., 1995—97, Nat. Fellow, Harvard Univ. Program in Inequality and Social Policy, 1998—, Alfred P. Sloan Rsch. Fellowship, 1999. Fellow: Ctr. for Adv. Study Behavioral Sci., Stanford, Calif., Am. Acad. Arts and Sci.; mem.: Phi Beta Kappa. Office: Dept Econ Univ Chgo 1126 E 59th St Chicago IL 60637 Business E-Mail: slevitt@midway.uchicago.edu.*

LEVITTE, JEAN-DAVID, ambassador; b. Moissac, France, June 14, 1946; married; 2 children. Grad., Inst. Polit. Scis. With Secs. Fgn. Affairs (the East), 1970—71; vice consul Hong Kong, 1971; 3d sec. Peking, 1972—74; dir. econ. affairs Min. Fgn. AFfairs, 1974—75; sec. gen., 1975—81; permanent mission France UN, 1981—84; sub-mgr. West AFrice Min. Fgn. Affairs, 1984—86; dir. asst. Cabinet Fgn. Min., 1986—88; ambassador France UN, Geneva, 1988—90; dir. Asia and Oceania Min. Fgn. Affairs, 1990—93, gen. mgr. cultural rels., scientific and tech., 1993—95; diplomatic advisor Pres. Sherpa, 1995—2000; ambassador France UN, N.Y.C., 2000—; ambassdor to the U.S. France, 2003—. Office: French Embassy 4101 Reservoir Rd NW Washington DC 20007

LEVITZ, PAUL ELLIOT, publishing executive; b. Bklyn., Oct. 21, 1956; s. Alfred Lazarus and Hannah (Brenner) L.; m. Jeanette Francine Cusimano, Nov. 2, 1980; children: Nicole, Philip, Garret. Student, N.Y. U., 1973-76. Editor, pub. The Comic Reader, Bklyn., 1971-73; writer, asst. editor Nat. Periodical Publs., Inc., N.Y.C., 1973-76; editor, editorial coordinator, writer DC Comics, N.Y.C., 1976-80, mgr. bus. affairs, 1980-82, v.p. ops., 1982-84, exec. v.p., 1984-89, exec. v.p., pub., 1989—2002, MAD mag., 1993—2002; pres. & publ. DC Comics & MAD mag., 2002—. Jewish. Home: 23 Stony Hollow Rd Chappaqua NY 10514-2014 Office: DC Comics 1700 Broadway New York NY 10019-5905 E-mail: paul.levitz@dccomics.com.

LEVITZKY, MICHAEL GORDON, physiology educator, researcher; b. Elizabeth, NJ, Jan. 3, 1947; s. Edward and Shirley (Worfman) L.; m. Ellen Marie De Roxtro, June 27, 1969 (div. Dec. 18, 1984); m. Elizabeth Gouaux, Mar. 13, 1985; children: Edward Benjamin, Sarah Elizabeth. BA, U. Pa., 1969; PhD, Albany Med. Coll., 1975. Physiology instr. Albany (N.Y.) Med. Coll., 1974-75; asst. prof. physiology La. State U. Health Scis. Ctr., New Orleans, 1975-80, assoc. prof. physiology, 1980-85, prof. physiology, 1985—, prof. anesthesiology, 1991—. Adj. prof. pediats. Tulane U. Sch. Medicine, New Orleans, 1990—, adj. prof. physiology, 1991—; dir. basic sci. curriculum La. State U. Med. Sch., 1998—. Author: Pulmonary Physiology, 6th edit., 2003; co-author: Cardiopulmonary Physiology in Anesthesiology, 1997, Introduction to Respiratory Care, 1990. Grantee NIH, 1976-78, 78-86. Mem. Am. Physiol. Soc. (edn. com. 1988-91, Arthur C. Guyton Tchr. of Yr. 1998), Am. Thoracic Soc., Coun. Sci. Editors, N.Y. Acad. Scis., Soc. for Exptl. Biology and Medicine, Sigma Xi. Office: La State U Health Scis Ctr Dept Physiology Box P7-3 1901 Perdido St New Orleans LA 70112-1393 Office Phone: 504-568-6184. Business E-Mail: mlevit@lsuhsc.edu.

LEVMORE, SAUL, dean, law educator; b. 1953; BA, Columbia Coll., 1973, PhD, 1978; JD, Yale U., 1980; LLD (hon.), Ill. Inst. Tech. Chgo.-Kent Law Sch., 1995. Bar: Va. 1983. Dean Jonathan Edwards Coll. Yale U., 1979-80; asst. prof. U. Va., Charlottesville, 1980-84; prof. U. Va., Charlottesville, 1984—98, Brokaw prof. of law; William B. Graham prof. law U. Chgo. Law Sch., 1998—, dean, 2001—. Lectr. econs. Yale U., 1976-80, vis. prof., 1986-87; vis. prof. Harvard U., 1990-91, U. Chgo., 1993. Office: U Chgo Law Sch 1111E 60th St Chicago IL 60637 Office Phone: 773-702-9590. Office Fax: 773-702-0730. Business E-Mail: s-levmore@uchicago.edu.*

LEVOUNIS, PETROS, psychiatrist; b. Piraeus, Greece, Apr. 16, 1962; s. Panagiotis Levounis and Eugenia Varangis-Levounis; life ptnr. Klaus Hassel. BS in Chemistry and Biology, MS in Biology, Stanford U., 1986, MA in Sociology, 1989; MD, Med. Coll. Pa., 1994. Cert. in psychiatry Am. Bd. Psychiatry and Neurology, 1999, in addiction psychiatry Am. Bd. Psychiatry and Neurology, 2000, in addiction medicine Am. Soc. Addiction Medicine, 2002, in psychiatric adminstrn. and mgmt. Am. Psychiat. Assn., 2003. Intern in internal medicine Columbia U. and N.Y. State Psychiat. Inst., N.Y.C., 1994—95, resident in psychiatry, 1995—98; fellow in addiction psychiatry NYU and Bellevue Hosp., N.Y.C., 1998—2000, dir. of the dual diagnosis tng. unit, assoc. dir. of the divsn. on alcoholism and drug abuse, 2000—02; dir. Addiction Inst. of N.Y., chief of divsn. of addiction psychiatry St. Luke's and Roosevelt Hosps., N.Y.C., 2002—. Asst. prof., clin. psychiatry Columbia U. Coll. Physicians and Surgeons, N.Y.C., 2002—; adj. clin. assoc. prof., nursing NYU, N.Y.C., 2002—; adj. asst. prof., psychiatry NYU Sch. Medicine, N.Y.C., 2002—; chief, alcohol and substance abuse sect. Mental Illness Prevention Ctr., N.Y.C., 2003—. Mem. The Jonathan Lax Scholarships for Gay Men, Phila., 1994—2004. Recipient Outstanding Resident Award, NIMH, 1996, U.S. Spkr. and Specialist Award, U.S. Dept. State, 2004; Profl. in Residency Scholarship, Betty Ford Ctr., 1994. Mem.: Assn. Gay and Lesbian Psychiatrists (chair, com. on residents and fellows 1997—99), Am. Soc. Addiction Medicine (chair, med. edn. com. & co-chair, pub. policy com. 1999—2004, chmn. com. on addiction treatment), Am. Psychiat. Assn. (assembly rep., examiner 2002, Nancy CA Roeske Award, APA/CMHS Fellowship 1998—2002), Assn. for Med. Edn. and Rsch. in Substance Abuse, Assn. for Academic Psychiatry (jr. faculty devel. award), Am. Coll. Psychiatrists (Laughlin Fellowship 1998), Am. Assn. Psychiat. Adminstrs., Am. Assn. Dirs. Psychiat. Residency Tng., Internat. Soc. Addiction Medicine, Hellenic Am. Psychiat. Assn., Am. Acad. Addiction Psychiatry, Athens Coll. Alumni Assn., Phi Beta Kappa. Achievements include designing and developing the Addiction Bellevue Courses: The ABCs of Addiction Medicine. Avocations: classical music, skiing, theater, movies. Home: 328 W 17th St #5W New York NY 10011 Office: The Addiction Inst NY 1000 Tenth Ave New York NY 10019 Office Phone: 212-523-6876. Office Fax: 212-523-8057. E-mail: plevounis@addictioninstituteny.org.

LEVOVITZ, PESACH ZECHARIAH, rabbi; b. Poland, Sept. 15, 1922; came to U.S., 1923; s. Reuben and Leah Zlate (Kustanowitz) L.; m. Bluma D. Feder, Feb. 5, 1945 (dec. 1970); children: Sivya, Yaakov; m. Eleanore Herman Klugmann, 1972 (dec. Nov. 1980); children: Maurice, Danny, Renee, Jackie; m. Frayde Twersky Perlow, Dec. 18, 1989; stepchildren: Yitzchok, Faige, Joseph. BA, Yeshivah U., 1942. Rabbi Mesivtha Tifereth Jerusalem Rabbinical Sem., 1943, Congregation Sons of Israel, Lakewood, N.J., 1944—; founder, 1945; since dean Bezalel Day Sch.; Pres. Rabbinical Council Am., 1966-68, chmn. commn. on internat. affairs, 1972; asso. chmn. Soviet Jewry commn., 1980. Mem. exec. com. Synagogue Coun. Am., 1953—; standing com. Conf. European Rabbis and Asso. Rabbis, 1964—; steering com. World Conf. Ashkenazi and Sephardi Synagogues; Co chmn. rabbinic cabinet Bonds for Israel, 1972; chaplain Lakewood Police Dept., 1950—; vis. chaplain Naval Air Sta., Lakehurst, N.J., 1945—; nat. chmn. ann. conv. Rabbinical Coun. Am., 1971, chmn. internat. conf., 1966; v.p. Religious Zionists Am., 1974; nat. chmn. Vaad Haroshi Religious Zionists Am., 1975; pres. Beth Din of Am., 1986; rsch. prof. U. Tenn. Mem. adv. bd. Lakewood Housing Council, Nat. Cmty. Rels. Adv. Coun., United Jewish Appeal; chmn. bd. Sons of Israel Sr. Citizens Housing Inc., 1980; mem. N.J. Drug Utilization Coun.; chmn. adv. coun. on protection kosher legislation to Atty. Gen., State of N.J.; mem. exec. Ocean County Jewish Fedn., 1988, chmn. Jewish Family and Children Svc., 1997; co-chmn. Blue Ribbon Panel Lakewood Twp., 1992—; apptd. Jewish chaplain Vis. Nurses Assn. Ctrl. N.J. Hospice Program, 2000. Recipient Revel Meml. award in religion and religious edn. Yeshivah Coll. Alumni Assn., 1967; award for outstanding rabbinic leadership Union of Orthodox Jewish Congregations Am., 1969; Nat. Assn. Hebrew Day Schs., 1980; chief Rabbi Issas Halevi Herzog Torah Fellowship award Religious Zionists Am., 1972; chmn. nat. conv., 1974; named Rabbi of Yr., Israel Bond Orgn., 1991. Mem. Conf. Presidents Nat. Jewish Orgns., Am. Conf. Soviet Jewry, Vis. Nurses Assn. (spiritual counselor 2000). Home: 403 6th St Lakewood NJ 08701-2705 Office: Congregation Sons of Israel Madison Ave Lakewood NJ 08701

LEVOX, GARY (GARY WAYNE VERNON JR.), country/rock singer; b. July 10, 1970; m. Tara Levox; children: Brittany Kay, Brooklyn Leigh. Performer Printers Alley, Nashville; founder, singer Rascal Flatts, 2000—, engr.: (albums) Gospel, 1998; singer Rascal Flatts, 2000, Melt, 2002, Feels Like Today, 2004 (Group/Duo Video of Yr., Country Music Television Music awards, 2005); performer: (songs) "Walk the Llama Llama", Emperor's Last Groove (Original Soundtrack), 2000. Recipient Vocal Group Yr., Country Music Assn., 2002, 2004, Song Yr. for "I'm Movin On", Acad. Country Music Awards, 2002, Top Vocal Group, 2003, 2005. Avocations: hunting, fishing.

LEVOY, MYRON, author; b. NYC, Jan. 30, 1930; s. Bernard and Elsie Levoy; m. Beatrice Fleischer, Jan. 27, 1952; children: David, Deborah. BS in Chem. Engring., CCNY, 1952; MS in Chem. Engring., Purdue U., 1953. Engr. Pratt & Whitney Aircraft Co., East Hartford, Conn., 1953-56; project engr. Reaction Motors Inc., Rockaway, N.J., 1956-67; engr. specialist Polytech. Design, Livingston, N.J., 1973-81; writer, 1955—. Author: A Necktie in Greenwich Village, 1968, Penny Tunes and Princesses, 1972, The Witch of Fourth Street and Other Stories, 1972 (Book World Honor Book, 1972, Children's Book Showcase award, 1973), Alan and Naomi, 1977 (Boston Globe-Horn Book award, Honor Book, 1978, Jane Addams Honor Book award, 1978, Nat. Book award finalist, 1980, Silver Pencil award The Netherlands, 1981, Austrian State prize for children's lit, 1981, German State prize for young adult lit., 1982, Buxtenhuder Bulle award Fed. Republic Germany, 1982), A Shadow Like a Leopard, 1981 (ALA Best Book for Young Adults, 1981), Three Friends, 1984, The Hanukkah of Great-Uncle Otto, 1984, Pictures of Adam, 1986 (ALA Best Book for young adults, 1986, Internat. Reading Assn. young adult choice, 1986), The Magic Hat of Mortimer Wintergreen, 1988 (Jr. Lit. Guild selection, 1988), Kelly 'N' Me, 1992, Eine Liebe in Schwarz-weiss, 1999, poetry and plays. Mem. PEN, The Authors Guild, The Dramatists Guild. Jewish. Avocations: tennis, cross country skiing, swimming, museums, films. Office: Writers House Inc 21 W 26th St New York NY 10010

LEVY, ADAM B., lawyer; b. Bklyn. BA, SUNY, Albany, 1989; JD, Hofstra U., 1992. Bar: N.Y., U.S. Dist. Ct. (so. and ea. dists.) N.Y. Asst. dist. atty. Suffolk County Atty.'s Office, Riverhead, NY, 1992—96; ptnr. Maher & Broyman, LLP, Carmel, NY, 1996—98, Levy, Santoro & Santoro, Carmel, 1998—. Mem.: Putman County Bar Assn. (pres. 2000—02). Office: Levy Santoro and Santoro 105 Gleneida Ave Carmel NY 10512 Business E-Mail: ablevy@rcn.com.

LEVY, ALBERT, family physician; b. Stanleyville, Congo, Nov. 8, 1948; came to U.S., 1977; s. Moise and Eugenie J. (Menache) L.; children: Antonia G., Eric M.; m: Linda Vartannes. MD, Fed. U. Brazil, Rio de Janeiro, 1973, MS in Field Medicine, 1976. Diplomate Am. Bd. Family Physicians, Am. Bd. Family Practice, Am. Bd. Geriatric Medicine. Chief family medicine sect. Our Lady of Mercy Hosp., Bronx, NY, 1989-96; pvt. practice family medicine Manhattan Family Practice, NYC, 1990—; physician Montefiore Med. Ctr., Bronx, 1994—; asst. clin. prof. dept. family medicine Albert Einstein Coll. Medicine, Bronx, 1994—; asst. prof. NY Med. Coll., Valhalla, 1994—; asst. prof. medicine Mt. Sinai Sch. Medicine, 1999—. With Beth Israel Med. Ctr., 1986, St. Luke's/Roosevelt Med. Ctr., 1986, Lenox Hill Hosp., 1995, Mt. Sinai Med. Ctr., 1999. Fellow Am. Acad. Family Physicians, Royal Soc. Medicine, (Eng.), NY Acad. Medicine; mem. AMA, Am. Geriatric Soc., World Orgn. Nat. Colls./Acads. Family Physicians, NY Acad. Scis., Med. Soc. State of NY, NY County Acad. Family Physicians (v.p. 1992), Soc. Tchrs. Family Medicine. Jewish. Avocations: tennis, opera, travel, wind surfing. Home: 311 Wilton Rd Westport CT 06880-1426 also: 25 Sutton Pl S New York NY 10022-2441 Office: Manhattan Family Practice 911 Park Ave New York NY 10021-0337 Office Phone: 212-288-7193. E-mail: alevymd@earthlink.net.

LEVY, ARNOLD S(TUART), real estate company executive; b. Chgo., Mar. 15, 1941; s. Roy and Esther (Scheff) L.; m. Eva Cichosz, Aug. 8, 1976; children: Adam, Rachel, Deborah. BS, U. Wis., 1963; MPA, Roosevelt U., 1970. Dir. Neighborhood Youth Corps, Chgo., 1966-68; v.p. Social Planning Assn., Chgo., 1968-70; planning dir. Office of Mayor, Chgo., 1970-74; dep. dir. Mayor's Office Manpower, Chgo., 1974-75; sr. v.p. Urban Investment & Devel. Co., Chgo., 1975-93; pres., CEO Stone-Levy, LLC, Chgo., 1994—. Mem. S-L Hospitality Group, LLC, 1995—; pres. JMB/Urban Hotels, Hotel and Resort Devel. Group, JMB/Urban Devel. Co., 1985-93; bd. dirs. Hostmark Mgmt. Group, Inc.; mem. Urban Land Inst. Pres. Ark, Chgo., 1970-72, Parental Stress Svcs., Chgo., 1978-79; past lectr. DePaul U., Roosevelt U., Loyola U.; v.p. Inst. Urban Life, Chgo., 1983—. Co-editor: The Professionals' Guide to Commercial Property Development, 1988. Bd. dirs. Mus. Broadcast Comms., Am. Shalom; pres. Ill. Humane Soc.; steering com. Radio Hall of Fame; chmn. Spertus Inst. Jewish Studies, Glencoe Plan Commn.; bd. dirs. Inst. for Computers in Jewish Life. Mem.: Hospitality Asset Mgrs. Assn., Twin Orchard Club, Glen Club. Home: 535 Park Ave Glencoe IL 60022-1501 Office: Stone-Levy LLC 630 Dundee Rd Ste 220 Northbrook IL 60062-2750 E-mail: alevy@stonelevy.com.

LEVY, COLEMAN B., lawyer; b. New Haven, Conn., May 9, 1939; s. Samuel and Esther Levy; m. Judith S. Siegal; children: Perry (deceased), Dean, Matthew and Evan. BA, U. Conn., 1961, MA in Psychology, 1962, JD, 1966. Bar: Conn. 1966, U.S. Dist. Ct. Conn. 1966, N.Y. 1967, U.S. Dist. Ct. (so. dist.) N.Y. 1967, U.S. Supreme Ct. 1976. Ptnr. Levy & Droney, P.C., Farmington, Conn., 1971—. Office: Levy & Droney PC 74 Batterson Park Rd Farmington CT 06032-2565 Fax: 860-676-3200. E-mail: clevy@ldlaw.com.

LEVY, DAVID, retired lawyer, insurance company executive, consultant; b. Bridgeport, Conn., Aug. 3, 1932; s. Aaron and Rachel (Goldman) L. BS in Econs., U. Pa., 1954; JD, Yale U., 1957. CPA Conn.; bar: Conn. 1958, U.S. Supreme Ct. 1963, D.C. 1964, Mass. 1965, N.Y. 1971, Pa. 1972. Acct. Arthur Andersen & Co., N.Y.C., 1957-59; sole practice Bridgeport, 1959-60; specialist tax law IRS, Washington, 1960-64; counsel State Mut. Life Ins. Co., Worcester, Mass., 1964-70; assoc. gen. counsel taxation Penn Mut. Life Ins. Co., Phila., 1971-81; sole practice Washington, 1982-87; v.p., tax counsel Pacific Life Ins. Co., Newport Beach, Calif., 1987-2001; ret., 2001. Author: (with others) Life Insurance Company Tax Series, Bureau National Affairs Tax Management Income Tax, 1970-71. Mem. adv. bd. Tax Mgmt., Washington, 1975-90, Hartford Inst. on Ins. Taxation, 1990-97; bd. dirs. Citizens Plan E Orgn., Worcester, 1966-70. With AUS, 1957. Mem. ABA (vice-chmn. employee benefits com. 1980-86, ins. cos. com. 1984-86, torts and ins. practice sect., subcom. chair ins. cos. com. tax sect. 1994—), Assn. Life Ins. Counsel, AICPA, Beta Alpha Psi. Jewish.

LEVY, DAVID ALFRED, immunologist, educator; b. Washington, Aug. 27, 1930; s. Stanley A. and Blanche B. (Berman) L.; m. Anne Levy-Badoux; children: Jill, William, Stanley. BS, U. Md., 1952, MD, 1954. Diplomate Am. Bd. Internal Medicine, Am. Bd. Allergy and Immunology. Intern, resident in medicine U. Hosp., Balt., 1954-59; physician VA Hosp., Balt., 1961-62; fellow dept. microbiology Sch. Medicine Johns Hopkins U., 1962-66, asst. prof. radiol. sci. Sch. Hygiene and Pub. Health, 1966-68, assoc. prof., 1968-71, prof. radiol. sci. and epidemiology, 1972-73, prof. biochemistry, 1973-82, with joint appointments in epidemiology and medicine, 1973-82, in pathobiology, 1980-82, prof. immunology and infectious diseases, 1982-86. Mem. FDA Panel on Rev. of Allergenic Extracts, 1975-83; mem. allergy and immunology rev. com. Nat. Inst. Allergy and Infectious Diseases, 1975-77; adj. dir. Centre d'Immunologie et de Biologie, Pierre Fabre, S.A., 1985-90; cons. to pharm. industry, 1990—. Mem. editl. bd. Clin. Immunology and Immunopathology, 1971-76, Revue Francaise d'Allergologie et Immunologie Clinique; assoc. editor Clin. Revs. in Allergy and Immunology; contbr. articles to med. jours. and books. Clin. rsch. Centre d'Allergie, Hopital Tenon, Paris, 1991—. With U.S. Army, 1959-61. Fellow: Am. Acad. Allergy and Immunology; mem.: Franco-Am. Allergy Assn., French Soc. Allergology, Am. Assn. Immunologists, Internat. Union Immunol. Socs. (vice chmn. allergen standardization subcom. 1980—83), Sigma Xi. Home and Office: 11 Quai St Michel 75005 Paris France E-mail: dalevy2@wanadoo.fr.

LEVY, DAVID CORCOS, museum director; b. NYC, Apr. 10, 1938; s. Edgar Wolf and Lucille (Corcos) L.; m. Janet Meyer, June 7, 1959 (div.); children: Jessica Anne, Thomas William; m. Carole L. Feld, May 19, 1992; 1 child, Alexander Wolf. BA, Columbia U., 1960; MA, NYU, 1969, PhD, 1979; DFA (hon.), New Sch. for Social Rsch., 1989, Cedar Crest Coll., 1998. Asst. dir. admissions Parson Sch. Design, NYC, 1961-62, dir. admissions, 1962-67, v.p., 1967-70, dean, chief adminstrv. officer, 1970-79, exec. dean, chief adminstrv. officer, 1979-89; chancellor New Sch. for Social Rsch., NYC, 1989-90; pres., dir. The Corcoran Gallery of Art, Washington, D.C., 1991—. Photographer of works exhibited in Guggenheim Mus., Mus. Modern Art, State Mus., Dortmund, Germany; art dir. jours., books, posters; contbr. articles to jours. and newspapers. Decorated Chevalier des Arts et des Lettres (France). Office: Corcoran Gallery of Art 500 17th St NW Washington DC 20006-4804 Office Phone: 202-639-1736.*

LEVY, DAVID HENRY, lawyer; b. Chgo., Apr. 16, 1951; s. Louis J. and Carolyn A. (Abraham) L. m B in Gen. Studies, Ohio U., 1973; JD, Ill. Inst. Tech/Kent Coll. Law, Chgo., 1976. Bar: Ill. 1976, U.S. Dist. Ct. (no. dist.) Ill. 1976, U.S. Ct. Appeals (7th cir.) 1976. Assoc., Law Offices of John Hirsch, Chgo., 1976-78; assoc. firm Feiwell, Galper Lasky & Berger Ltd., Chgo., 1978-82, ptnr., 1982-87, Kalcheim, Schatz & Berger, Chgo., 1976—, mng. ptnr., 1996—. Faculty Ill. Inst. Continuing Legal Edn., 1986—; lectr. Young Single Parents Orgn.; guest lectr. Loyola U. Law Sch., Chgo., 1986; commentator WCIU-TV, Chgo.; spkr. in field. Chmn. fundraising com. Lincoln Ctrl. Assn., Chgo., 1982-84, bd. dirs., 1983-86, v.p., 1987, pres., 1988; mem. caucus Village of Northfield, Ill., 1988-92, chmn. platform com., 1992; chmn. Avoca Sch. Dist. 37 Caucus, 2002—. Mem. ABA (family law sect.), Ill. State Bar Assn. (chmn. Family Law Sect., 1995-97, vice chmn. family law sect. 1994-96, sec. 1993-94; Supreme Ct. rules com. 1996—, chmn., 2001-2003; atty. children/GAL task force 1997; unauthorized practice of law task force 2002—, moderator cable TV programming 1995—), Am. Acad. Matrimonial Lawyers (pres. Ill. chpt. 1993-94, bd. dirs. 1988-2001, nat. bd. govs. 1996-98, nat. treas. 2003-04, mem. exec. bd. 2003—, chmn. econs. of law practice com., admissions procedures and chmn. site selection coms.), Lincoln Park Conservation Assn. Office: Kalcheim Schatz & Berger 161 N Clark St Ste 2800 Chicago IL 60601-3245 Office Phone: 312-782-3456. E-mail: dlevy@ks6familylaw.com.

LEVY, DAVID LAWRENCE, retired lawyer, legal association administrator; b. N.Y.C., Nov. 7, 1936; s. Arthur Morgan and Shirley (Lanz) L.; 1 child from previous marriage, Justin; m. Virginia Carey, May, 1974 (div. 1980); m. Ellen Dublin, Dec., 1984; 1 child, Diana. BA, U. Fla., 1958, JD, 1961. Bar: D.C. 1968, U.S. Supreme Ct. 1983. Lawyer U.S. Copyright Office, Libr. Congress, Washington, 1962-69, 77-97, ret., 1997; co-founder, CEO Children's Rights Coun., Washington, 1985—. Author: Potomac Conspiracy, 1976; editor: The Best Parent Is Both Parents, 1993; editor-in-chief student newspaper, U. Fla., 1957-58 (recipient awards). Chmn. Students for Kennedy for Pres., 1959, 60. Recipient Civic award Prince George's County (Md.) Civic Fedn., 1989, Disting. Svc. to Children award Parents Without Ptnrs. Internat., 1996, Lifelong Achievement award for untiring efforts on behalf of children U.S. Fed. Child Support Office, 2000, Svc. to Children award N.J. Coun. for Children's Rights, 2000. Mem.: U.S. Supreme Ct. Bar, D.C. Bar Assn., Supervised Visitation Network (bd. dirs.), Stepfamily Assn. Am. (psat bd. dirs.), Masons, Elks. Jewish. Office: Children's Rights Coun 6200 Editors Park Drive Ste 103 Hyattsville MD 20782 E-mail: davidlevy1@juno.com.

LEVY, DEBORAH, security company executive; b. Chgo. d. Sam and Ruth Gadlin; m. Barry W. Levy (dec.); children: Scott B., Todd B. Student, So. Ill. U. Exec. v.p., sec., officer, dir. Levy Security Corp., Chgo., until 1994, chair, CEO, 1994—. Mem. Women Bus. Enterprise Initiative (Mem. of Yr. award 1997), Nat. Assn. Women Bus. Owners, Am. Soc. Indsl. Security. Achievements include being listed in Working Woman 500 Magazine. Office: Levy Security Corp Ste 1200 8750 W Bryn Mawr Ave Chicago IL 60631-3560 Office Phone: 773-867-9204. Business E-Mail: dlevy@levysecurity.com.

LEVY, DENA CHRISTINE, television producer, director; b. Woodland Hills, Calif., Sept. 28, 1965; d. Stanley Gerald and Deanna Marie (Coury) L.; children: Lonna Weber, Dena Levy. BA in Journalism, U. So. Calif., 1986. Profl. tennis player Women's Tennis Assn., USTA, 1986-88; prodr., dir. Two-D Prodns., Hollywood, Calif., 1989—. Recipient Best Documercial award Nat. Infomercial Mktg. Assn., 1994. Avocations: tennis, golf, skiing, softball. Office: 4714 Park Olivo Calabasas CA 91302-1733 Fax: 818 222 0589.

LEVY, EDWARD CHARLES, JR., manufacturing executive; b. Detroit, Nov. 14, 1931; s. Edward Charles and Pauline (Birndorf) Levy; 2 children. SB, MIT, 1952. From staff to exec. v.p. Edw. C. Levy Co., Detroit, 1952-70, pres., 1970—. Bd. dirs. Julie and Ed Levy Jr.Found., Karmanos Cancer Inst., Detroit, Round Table of Christians and Jews, Mackinac Ctr. for Pub. Policy; trustee Children's Hosp. of Mich., Citizens Rsch. Coun. Mich., Washington Inst. for Near East Policy; officer Am. Israel Pub. Affairs Com. Mem. ASTM, Am. Concrete Inst., Engring. Soc. Detroit, Detroit Athletic Club, Renaissance Club, Franklin Hills Country Club. Jewish. Office: Edw C Levy Co Inc 8800 Dix St Detroit MI 48209-1096

LEVY, ELAINE ANN, music educator; b. Fall River, Mass., Mar. 20, 1927; d. Max and Sarah Brodsky Ritter; m. Jack Kirstein Levy, Aug. 18, 1951 (dec. Nov. 1981); children: Steven Mark, Richard Allan. Diploma in Theory & Music, N.Eng. Conservatory Music, 1942; student, Boston U., 1945; AA, Cin. Coll. Music, 1948; MusB, Calif. State U., Fullerton, 1972. Cert. music tchr. Calif., 1990, Music Tchrs. Nat. Assn., 1990. Music tchr. Indep. Music Tchrs. Assn., La Palma, Calif., 1940—. Music aide Thomas M. Erwin Sch., La Puente, Calif., 1958—65; pres. Musical Arts Orange County, La Palma, 1978—80; adv. bd. Music Tchrs. Assn. Calif., Long Beach, Calif., 1988—97. Composer music for Music Tchrs. Assn. Calif. Regional chairperson So. Calif. Jr. Bach Festival, L.A. and Orange County, 1963—; active Dem. Party, La Puente, 1964. Mem.: AAUW, Mu Phi Epsilon. Avocations: social dancing, bowling, swimming, walking. Home: 7811 Norann Circle La Palma CA 90623-1648

LEVY, ELLEN KAPLAN, artist, educator; b. N.Y.C. d. Max Victor and Mae Klein Kaplan; m. David E. Levy. BA in Zoology, Mt. Holyoke Coll.; MFA, Mus. Sch. Fine Arts, Boston. Artist Chapel Art Ctr., Hamburg, Germany, 1990-98, Associated Am. Artists, N.Y.C., 1995—; disting. vis. fellow in arts and scis. Skidmore Coll., Saratoga Springs, N.Y., 1999—; instr. Bklyn. Coll., Sch. Visual Arts. Pres. Ctr. for Photography, Woodstock, N.Y., 1995—. Works commd. by NASA, 1985. Pub. arts commn. State of N.J., Transit Authority. Mem Coll. Art Assn. (guest editor art jour. issue 1995-96, pres. 2004—). Studio: 40 E 19th St Apt 3R New York NY 10003-1303

LEVY, EUGENE, actor, director, screenwriter; b. Hamilton, Ont., Can., Dec. 17, 1946; m. Deborah Divine, 1977; 2 children. Appearences include (films) Cannibal Girls, 1972, Running, 1979, Nothing Personal, 1980, Heavy Metal, 1981, Strange Brew, 1983, Going Berserk, 1983, National Lampoon's Vacation, 1983, Splash, 1984, Armed and Dangerous, 1986, The Canadian Conspiracy, 1986, Club Paradise, 1986, Speed Zone, 1989, Father of the Bride, 1991, Once Upon A Crime, 1992, Stay Tuned, 1992, I Love Trouble, 1994, Father of the Bride, Part II, 1995, Waiting for Guffman, 1996, Multiplicity, 1996, Waiting for Guffman (also wrote), 1996, Dogmatic, 1996, Creature Crunch (voice only), 1996, Almost Heroes, 1998, Richie Rich's Christmas Wish, 1998, Akbar's Adventure Tours, 1998, The Secret Life of Girls, 1999, American Pie, 1999, Best in Shown (also wrote), 2000, The Ladies Man, 2000, Silver Man, 2000, Down to Earth, 2001, American Pie 2, 2001, Serendipity, 2001, Repli-Kate, 2002, Like Mike, 2002, Bringing Down the House, 2003, A Mighty Wind (also wrote), 2003, Dumb and Dumberer: When Harry Met Lloyd, 2003, American Wedding, 2003, New York Minute, 2004, The Man, 2005; actor: (TV) Second City TV, 1977-81, Lovebirds, 1979, From Cleveland, 1980, George Burn's Comedy Week, 1985, SCTV Network, 1981-83, The Last Polka, 1985, Dave Thomas: The Incredible Time Travels of Henry Osgood, 1986, Billy Crystal-Don't Get Me Started, 1986, Bride of Boogedy, 1987, Ray Bradbury Theatre, 1988, Autobiographies: The Enigma of Bobby Bittman, 1988, Hiller and Diller, 1997, Hercules (voice only), 1998, D.O.A., 1999, The Sports Pages, 2001, Club Land, 2001, Committed (TV series), 2001, The Kid, 2001, Greg the Bunny (TV series), 2002; dir.: (TV) Second City's 50th Anniversary Special, 1988, Once Upon a Crime..., 1992, Partners in Love, 1992, Sodbusters, 1994. Office: United Talent Agy 9560 Wilshire Blvd Ste #500 Beverly Hills CA 90212*

LEVY, EUGENE PFEIFER, architectural firm executive, architect; b. Little Rock, Dec. 14, 1936; s. Emmanuel Gabe and Elizabeth (Pfeifer) L.; m. Candy Sue Hood, Sept. 21, 2004; children: Edwin Cromwell, Andrew Stewart, Charles Pfeifer. B.Arch., U. Va., 1959. Registered architect, Ark., Calif., Ga., Tex. Apprentice Erhart, Eichenbaum, Rauch & Blass, Little Rock, 1959-60; arch., pres. Cromwell, Truemper, Levy, Thompson & Woodsmall, Inc., Little Rock, 1962-85, chmn., CEO, 1985—2002; v.p. State Bd. Archs., 1998—; chmn. emeritus Cromwell Archs. Engrs., 2002—. Bd. dirs. Little Rock Boys' Club, 1973—, Temple B'nai Israel, Little Rock, 1975-78; chmn. Ctrl. Ark. chpt. ARC, 1989; mem. Fifty for Future. Capt. U.S. Army, 1960-62. Recipient numerous awards including: U.S. Corps. of Engrs. 1985 Design award for Resident Office and Visitors Ctr., Greers Ferry Lake, Ark., USAG 1985 First Honor award for commissary, Camp Foster, Okinawa, Japan, AIA 1980 Design award for Master Plan and First Phase Design for Multi Agy. Office Bldg., State of Ark. Capitol Ground, Little Rock, AIA Honorable Mention award for Systematics, Inc., Corp. Hdqrs., 1982, AIA Design award for Winthrop Rockefeller Meml. Gallery Ark. Arts Ctr., Little Rock, 1982, Little Rock Riverfront Belvedere, AIA Design award, 1987, AIA Design award for Itzkowitz residence, Little Rock, 1991. Fellow AIA (Design award Commissary USAF, UAMS Stephens Spine and Neurosci. Inst. 2004); mem. Greater Little Rock C. of C. (com. 1983-84). Office: Cromwell Archs Engrs Cromwell Bldg 101 S Spring St Little Rock AR 72201-2413 Home: 1911a W 2d Little Rock AR 72205

LEVY, EZRA CESAR, aerospace scientist, real estate agent; b. Habana, Cuba, Sept. 22, 1924; s. Mayer D and Rachel Levy; m. Margot Webb, 2000; children from previous marriage: Daniel M, Diana M Levy Friedman, Linda R Levy Brenden. MS, UCLA, 1951. Sect. head Douglas Aircraft Co., Santa Monica, Calif., 1951—54; dept. head Lockheed Aircraft Co., Van Nuys, Calif., 1954—56, Librascope, Glendale, Calif., 1956—57, Radioplane, Van Nuys, 1957—58; asst. dept. mgr. Space Tech. Labs., Redondo Beach, Calif., 1958—60; asst. divsn. dir. TRW, Redondo Beach, Calif., 1960—74; now real estate broker, owner Jaunty Real Estate, Valencia, Calif., 1984—. Rschr. ECG analysis Heart Rsch. Found, 1953—68; spec traffic consult South Bay Cities, 1960—65; tchr. Real Estate. Author: (book) Laplace Transform Tables, 1958, Selling Your Property?, 1995, Sample Contractual (Real Estate) Terms, 1996, A Glossary of Real Estate Terms, 1998, A Glossary of Real Estate Terms, 2d ed, 2000, Masonry in Los Angeles Silver Trowel Lodge, 2001; contbr. articles to profl jours. With U.S. Army, 1944—46. Mem.: Temple City C. of C. (bd. dirs. 1992—97, pres. 2000—01), Eastern Star (past patron), Masons (past master and sec.). Democrat. Jewish. Avocations: art, music, philately. Home and Office: 24688-A Brighton Dr Valencia CA 91355 Office Phone: 818-259-3549. E-mail: levymasonman@aol.com.

LEVY, GAD, atmospheric scientist, educator, statistician; b. Tel Aviv, Nov. 22, 1954; came to U.S., 1981; s. Rudi and Zipora Loewy; m. Felice S. Tiu, July 8, 1990; children: Tal Adam, Kai Tiu. BSc, Hebrew U., 1980; MS, Colo. State U., 1982; PhD, U. Wash., 1987. Rsch. asst. Hebrew U., Jerusalem, 1979-80, Colo. State U., Ft. Collins, 1981-82; rsch. asst./assoc. U. Wash., Seattle, 1982-88, sr. rsch. scientist, 1993—2000; rsch. assoc. Oreg. State U., Corvallis, 1988-89, asst. prof., 1989-96, assoc. prof., 1996—. Co-chair flux modeling group TOGA-COARE Internat. Data Workshop, Toulouse, France, 1994; mem. radarsat sci. adv. team NASA, Washington, 1995—, mem. atmospheres panel, Mission to Planet Earth, 1989-94; cons. applied stats. Boeing Co., Seattle, 2001-2002; sr. scientist NorthWest Rsch. Assocs., Bellevue, Wash., 2002—; faculty U. Phoenix, 2002—, exec. sec. and sci. organizing com. Pan Oceanic Remote Sensing Conf. Assn., 2004-; spkr. in field. Editor: Remote Sensing of the Pacific Ocean By Satellites, 1998; contbr. articles to profl. jours. Coord. edn. task force Amnesty Internat., 1984-94; charter mem. Com. for Israeli Palestinian Peace, Seattle, 1983-86; bd. dirs. Found. for Internat. Understanding Through Students, Seattle, 1987. Recipient Elizabeth Gould award for Internat. Understanding, Found. for Internat. Understanding Through Students, 1987, Pres. Fund for Innovative Rsch., Calif. Inst. Tech., 1990. Mem. Am. Meteorological Soc. (Travel award 1989), Am. Geophys. Union (Travel award 1991). Achievements include innovative research on the marine atmosphere boundary layer and the use of satellite based observations to develop and test hypotheses about the dynamics of the marine atmosphere, maritime atmospheric fronts, and equatorial climate dynamics of the atmosphere.

LEVY, GERHARD, pharmacologist; b. Wollin, Germany, Feb. 12, 1928; came to U.S., 1948, naturalized, 1953. s. Gotthold and Eliesabeth (Luebeck) L.; m. Rosalyn Mincer, June 8, 1958; children: David, Marc, Sharon. BS, U. Calif. at San Francisco, 1955, Pharm.D., 1958; Dr. honoris causa, Uppsala (Sweden) U., 1975, Phila. Coll. Pharmacy and Sci., 1979, L.I. U., 1981, U. Ill., 1986, Hoshi U., Japan, 1996, Ohio State U., 1998, U. Minn., 2001. Asst. prof. pharmacy U. Buffalo, 1958-60; assoc. prof. pharmacy State U. N.Y. at Buffalo, 1960-64, prof. biopharmaceutics, 1964-72, distinguished prof. pharmaceutics, 1972-75, chmn. dept. pharmaceutics, 1966-70, univ. disting. prof. emeritus, 1995. Vis. prof. Hebrew U., Jerusalem; cons. WHO, 1966, Bur. Drugs Adv. Panel System, FDA, 1971-74; mem. com. on problems of drug safety NRC, 1971-75; mem. pharmacol.-toxicol. com. NIH, 1971-75 Mem. editorial bd. Jour. Pharm. Sci, 1970-75, Clin. Pharmacology and Therapeutics, 1969-2002, Internat. Jour. Clin. Pharmacology, 1968-78, Drug Metabolism and Disposition, 1973-78, Jour. Pharmacokin Biopharm, 1972-97, Internat. Jour. Pharm., 1977-95, Jour. Pharmacobi-Dynamics, 1979-93, Pharm. Res., 1983-95; contbr. articles to profl. jours. Served with AUS, 1950-51. Recipient Ebert prize, 1969, Am. Pharm. Assn. Research Achievement award, 1969, McKeen Cattell award Am. Coll. Clin. Pharmacology, 1978, Host-Madsen medal Internat. Pharm. Fedn., 1978, Oscar B. Hunter award in exptl. therapeutics Am. Soc. Clin. Pharmacology and Therapeutics, 1982, Volwiler Research Achievement award Am. Assn. Colls. Pharmacy, 1982, Scheele award Swedish Acad. Pharmaceutical Scis., 1992, 1st Lifetime Achievement in the Pharm. Scis. award Internat. Pharm. Assn., 1994; named Alumnus of Year U. Calif. Sch. Pharmacy Alumni Assn., 1970 Fellow Am. Pharm. Assn., Acad. Pharm. Scis. (Takeru Higuchi Research prize 1983), AAAS; mem. Inst. Medicine of Nat. Acad. Scis., Am. Assn. Pharm. Scientists (Dale E. Wurster Rsch. award 1992), Am. Soc. Exptl. Pharmacology and Therapeutics. Home: 4832 Peregrine Point Cir W Sarasota FL 34231-2335 Office Phone: 941-925-3655. Personal E-mail: glevypkpd@aol.com.

LEVY, H. RICHARD, biochemistry educator; b. Leipzig, Germany, Oct. 22, 1929; came to U.S., 1946; s. Berthold and Charlotte Agnes Hedwig (Frank) L.; m. Betty Louise Samuels, June 12, 1960; 1 child, Karen. BSc in Chemistry, Rutgers U., 1950; PhD in Biochemistry, U. Chgo., 1956. Instr. Ben May Lab. for Cancer Rsch., U. Chgo., 1959-61, asst. prof., 1961-63; asst. prof. dept. bacteriology and botany Syracuse (N.Y.) U., 1963-66, assoc. prof. dept. bacteriology and botany, 1966-70, assoc. prof. dept. biology, 1970-71, prof. of biochemistry, 1971-2000, chmn. dept. biology, 1993-99, prof. emeritus, 2000—. Contbr. articles and revs. to profl. publs. Grantee NIH, NSF, 1963-99. Mem. AAAS, AAUP, Am. Chem. Soc., Am. Soc. for Biochemistry and Molecular Biology, Protein Soc. Home: 604 Scott Ave Syracuse NY 13224-2132 Personal E-mail: rlevy1@twcny.rr.com. Business E-Mail: hrlevy@syr.edu.

LEVY, HAROLD DAVID, psycholinguist; b. Rochester, N.Y., Aug. 25, 1938; s. Barnet Lewis and Ada Sylvia (Zimmerman) L.; m. Jan Patricia Schwartz, Mar. 3, 1959 (div. 1961); 1 child; m. Natalie Miller, Nov. 27, 1969 (div. 1982); 1 child; m. Judy Weiner, Sept. 9, 1987. BS in Gen. Studies, U. Rochester, 1969, MA in Edn., 1971. Permanent cert. to teach French, grades 7-12. Sociotherapist Convalescent Hosp. for Children, Rochester, 1971-72; tutor spl. edn. City Sch. Dist., Rochester, 1973-83; editor, ednl. dir. Operaton Friendship, Rochester, 1983-88; pvt. tutor home and social agencies Rochester, 1982-91; vol. and activities asst. therapist Genesee Hosp., Rochester, 1983-93. Dramatics instr. Hochstein Music Sch., Rochester, 1972; lang. tchr. Harley Sch. and Talmudical Inst. Upstate N.Y., 1974-75. Author: Forced Categories: A Taxonomy for Languages, 1971, Languages: Their Common Elements, 1990, Language Learning by Slices, 1990, Linguistics: The Binary System, 1990, Psycholinguistic Interpretation of Names as Language Field Universals, 1995, Lexical Transformations: The Brain's Code, 1996, The Psycholinguistic Development of Terminal Information Systems, 1997; contbr. articles to sci. jours. Avocations: jazz piano, mental health education, nutrition. Home: 111 East Ave Apt 719 Rochester NY 14604-2542

LEVY, IRA HOWARD, marketing professional, real estate developer; b. NYC, Dec. 28, 1937; s. Samuel B. and Ada Levy. Student, UCLA, 1956-58. Sr. v.p. corp. creative mktg. Esteé Lauder Cos., 1961-91; co-owner Sta. WKZE-AM-FM, Conn.; co-founder Conifer Ptnrs., Salisbury, Conn. Former chmn. Contemporary Arts Coun., Mus. Modern Art, N.Y.C.; bd. dirs. emeritus Pilobolus Dance Co., Cunningham Dance Co.; mem. advisory coun. Coll. of Atlantic, Maine; mem. exec. com. bd. trustees Sharon Hosp., Conn.; mem. coun. design excellence Coll. Arch., Ariz. State U. Fellow: Royal Soc. Arts. Avocations: sailing, cross country skiing. Home: Deer Run Salisbury CT 06068 Office: Conifer Ptnrs 308 Main St Lakeville CT 06039 Home (Summer): PO Box 6 East Blue Hill ME 04629 Office Phone: 860-435-8282. Personal E-mail: conifer2@sbcglobal.net.

LEVY, JAY A., medical educator; b. Wilmington, Del., Nov. 21, 1938; BA, Wesleyan U., 1960; MD, Columbia U., 1965; DS (hon.), Wesleyan U., 1996. Intern in medicine Hosp. U. Pa., Phila., 1965—66, 1st yr. resident in medicine, 1966—67; staff assoc. Nat. Cancer Inst. NIH, Bethesda, Md., 1967—70; collaborator N.Y. Blood Ctr., N.Y.C., 1970; 2d yr. resident in medicine San Francisco Sch. Medicine U. Calif., 1970—71, asst. clin. prof. and rsch. assoc. Cancer Rsch. Inst. and Sch. Medicine, 1972—77, assoc. prof. in residence and rsch. assoc. dept. medicine Cancer Rsch. Inst., 1978—82, prof. in residence and rsch. assoc. dept. medicine Cancer Rsch. Inst., 1985—96, prof. dept. medicine div. hematology/oncology Cancer Rsch. Inst., Sch. Medicine, 1996—. Vis. scientist and NATO fellow INSERM, Paris, 1971—72; vis. scientist and Eleanor Roosevelt fellow dept. chem. immunology Weizmann Inst. Sci., Rehovot, Israel, 1978—79, vis. scientist and ICRETT fellow, 1982; disting. lectr. in field; mem. sci. adv. bd. Agence Nationale de Recherches sur le Sida, Govt. France, 1999—; mem. Mayor Willie Brown's AIDS Sci. Adv. Coun., 1997—; mem. sci. adv. com. Brown U./Tufts U. Ctr. AIDS Rsch., 1997—; mem. internat. sci. adv. bd. Rhone-Poulenc-Rorer, 1997; mem. exec. bd. Am. com. Weizmann Inst. Sci., 1987—; mem. sci. adv. bd. HIV vaccine design and devel. team NIH, 2001; mem. internat. adv. com. Internat. Conf. on AIDS, 1986—96; mem. cell and devel. biology study sect. Am. Cancer Soc., 1983—87. Editor: AIDS, 1988—2000; editor in chief:, 2000—, mem. numerous editl. bds.:. Mem. adv. bd. Internat. Alliance for Haiti, 1989—; mem. adv. com. United Religious Initiative Found., 2000—; bd. trustees Wesleyan U., 1988—91. Fellow, USPHS, 1962; Rsch. fellow, U. Paris, 1961, Lederle Med. fellow, Karolinska Inst., Stockholm, 1963, La. State U. Med. fellow, Makerere Univ. Coll., Kampala, Uganda, 1964. Fellow: Am. Acad. Arts & Sciences, Infectious Diseases Soc. Am.; mem.: AAAS, People to People Ethiopian/Am. AIDS Assn. (bd. dirs. 1999—), HIV Med. Assn. Infectious Diseases Soc. Am., We. Soc. Clin. Rsch., We. Assn. Physicians, Internat. AIDS Soc. (mem. adv. bd. 1993—96), Assn. IUCC Fellows, Assn. Am. Physicians, Am. Soc. Virology, Am. Soc. Tropical Medicine and Hygiene, Am. Soc. Microbiology (Abbott award in clinical and diagnostic immunology 2004), Am. Soc. Clin. Investigation, Am. Assn. Cancer Rsch. (mem. long-range planning com. 1987—90, bd. dirs. 1988—91, chair local com. ann. meeting 1989, mem. spl. confs. com. 1989—92, mem. long-range planning com. 1990—93, mem. minority issues com. 1990—93, chair by-laws com. 1992—93, rep. physicians for human rights 1992—, mem. legis. com. 1992—, chair fin. com. 1993—96, mem. local com. ann. meeting 1994, mem. program com. ann. meeting 1996, mem. minority issues com. 1996—2000, mem. program com. ann. meeting 1997, Spl. Recognition award for outstanding leadership as chair fin. com. 1997), Am. Assn. Immunologists, Am. Found. AIDS Rsch. (chair sci. policy com. 1994—, mem. exec. com. 1994—, mem. opportunity fund com. 1998—, mem. sci. adv. bd. 1986—), Internat. Union Against Cancer. Office: U Calif San Francisco Sch Medicine Dept Medicine Lab Tumor and AIDS Virus R Box 1270 S 1280 San Francisco CA 94143 Business E-Mail: jalevy@itsa.ucsf.edu.*

LEVY, JEROME, dermatologist, retired military officer; b. Bklyn., Aug. 17, 1926; s. Alexander and Pauline (Wollkof) L.; m. Leona Elsie Eligator, June 6, 1948; children: Andrew B., Eric J., Peter C., David J. Student, Wesleyan U., 1944—45, postgrad., 1952—54; BA, Yale U., 1947; MD, Albany Med. Coll., 1958. Diplomate Am. Bd. Dermatology. Commd. ensign USN, M.C., 1957, advanced through grades to capt., 1972; intern U.S. Naval Hosp., Newport, RI, 1958—59; resident Phila. (Pa.) Naval Hosp., 1960—62, U. Pa. Grad. Sch. Medicine, Phila., 1962—63, chief dept. dermatology Memphis, 1963—67, Yokosuka, Japan, 1967—70, Long Beach, Calif., 1974—75; head outpatient dermatology clinic San Diego Naval Hosp., 1970—72; sr. med. officer Keflavik, Iceland, 1972—74; ret., 1975; med. dir. dermatology Westwood Pharm. Co., Buffalo, 1975—82; acting chief dermatology dept. Buffalo Gen. Hosp., 1981—82; practice medicine specializing in dermatology Coronado, Calif., 1982—90. Cons. Erie County Health Dept., 1979-82; clin. assoc. prof. SUNY, Buffalo Med. Sch., 1980-82. Contbr. articles to med. jours. and popular mags. Decorated Navy Commendation medal, Joint Svc. Commendation medal; Knight's Cross of the Order of Falcon (Iceland). Fellow ACP, Am. Acad. Dermatology; mem. AMA, So. Med. Assn., Assn. Mil. Surgeons, U.S. Navy League, City Club San Diego, Univ. Club San Diego, Yale Club N.Y.C., Alpha Omega Alpha. Democrat. Jewish. Home: 3352 Lucinda St San Diego CA 92106-2932 Personal E-mail: zitzapper@aya.yale.edu.

LEVY, JON D., state supreme court justice; Grad., Syracuse U., West Va. U. Coll. of Law. Law clerk U.S. Dist. Ct., Charleston, W.Va., court monitor; chief judge Dist. Ct., deputy chief judge; judge Dist. Ten; assoc. justice Maine Supreme Ct., 2002—. Chmn. Maine Family Law Adv. Commn., 1996—2000; ct. liaison Adv. Com. on Professional Responsibility, CASA Adv. Bd., Com. on Jud. Responsibility & Disability; chair Jud. Resource Team. Author: (book) Maine Family Law, 1988. Office: Maine Supreme Ct 142 Federal St PO Box 368 Portland ME 04112-0368*

LEVY, JOSEPH, lawyer; b. N.Y.C., June 9, 1928; s. Morris Joseph and Dora (Cohen) L.; m. Gertrud C. Roeder, Jan. 20, 1967; children— Diana N., Susan R. BBA cum laude, CCNY, 1950; JD cum laude, NYU, 1954. Bar: N.Y. 1955, D.C. 1968. Assoc. Parker, Chapin and Flattau, N.Y.C., 1954-62; ptnr. firm Rivkin, Sherman & Levy (and predecessors), N.Y.C., 1962-84, Schnader, Harrison, Segal & Lewis, 1984-93; v.p., sec., dir. Trecom Bus. Sys., Inc., Edison, N.J., 1993-97. Sec., dir. Horizons Comms. Corp., 1970-78, Quad Typographers, Inc., 1965-79; sec. Savin Bus. Machines Corp., 1959-84, On-Line Systems, Inc., 1968-78, Lambda Tech., Inc., 1970-78, Programming Methods, Inc., 1969-72, Kreisler Mfg. Cor., 1969-72, Peck & Peck, 1970-73, v.p., sec., dir. Trecom Bus. Systems, Inc., 1985-97, Business Edge Solutions, Inc., Edison, N.J., 1999—. Served to capt. AUS, 1951—53. Home: 254 University Way Paramus NJ 07652-5516

LEVY, JOSEPH BRUNO, foundation administrator, educator; b. Milan, Nov. 8, 1930; arrived in Argentina, 1957; s. Moise Joseph and Alice Levy; m. Suzanne Eskenazi, June 12, 1956 (div. 1965); children: Andrew David, Alexandra Alice. BSc, Manchester (Eng.) U., 1950, 51, 52; MS, U. Mass., 1954; MA, Princeton (N.J.) U., 1956, PhD, 1957; fellow, Textile Inst., Manchester, 1958. Chartered textile technologist. Dir. Du Pont Argentina, Buenos Aires, 1957-75, 81-87; gen. dir. Du Pont Italiana, Milan, 1976-78; group dir. Du Pont Mex., Mexico City, 1979-80; pres. Internat. Human Ecology Found., Buenos Aires, 1990—. Contbr. articles to profl. jours. Mem. N.Y. Acad. Sci., Sci. and Med. Network, Soc. for Sci. Exploration, Sigma Xi. Jewish. Avocations: trout fishing, golf, travel, physics, cooking. Home: Libertador 356 (1001) Buenos Aires Argentina Office: Triar SA Cordoba 950 (1054) Buenos Aires Argentina

LEVY, KENNETH, music educator; b. N.Y.C., Feb. 26, 1927; s. Meyer and Sylvia Levy; m. Clara Brooks Emmons, Jan. 25, 1956; children: Robert Brooks, Helen Gardner. AB, Queens Coll., 1947; MFA, Princeton U., 1949, PhD, 1956; Doctorate (hon.), U. Athens, 2004. Instr. music Princeton (N.J.) U., 1952-54; from asst. prof. to Fredrick R. Mann. prof. Brandeis U., Waltham, Mass., 1954-66; prof. music Princeton U., 1966—, chmn. dept. music., 1967-70, 88, Scheide prof. music history, 1988-95. Author: Music: A Listener's Introduction, 1983, Gregorian Chant and the Carolingians, 1998; assoc. editor: Anthologie de la Chanson Parisienne au Seizieme Siecle, 1953; Festschrift: The Study of Medieval Chant: In Honor of Kenneth Levy (edited by P. Jeffery), 2001; mem. editl. bd. Monumenta Musicae Byzantinae, 1968—, Grove's Dictionary, 6th edit, Early Music History, 1980—; contbr. articles to profl. jours. With USNR, 1945-46. Recipient Fulbright award Italy, 1962-63, Howard T. Behrman award for disting. achievements in humanities, 1983, Deems Taylor award ASCAP, 1989, Pres.'s Disting. Teaching award Princeton U., 1995; Guggenheim fellow, 1955-56, Am. Coun. Learned Socs. fellow, 1970-71, sr. fellow Dumbarton Oaks, Harvard U., 1992-96; vis. fellow Cambridge U., 1995. Fellow Medieval Acad. Am.; mem. Am. Philos. Soc., Am. Musicological Soc. (hon.). Office: Princeton U Dept Music Woolworth Ctr Mus Studies Princeton NJ 08544-0001

LEVY, KENNETH, computer company executive; BS engring., MS engring. Former CEO KLA Tencor, San Jose, Calif., chmn., 1999—; with start up team Computervision Corp.; founder KLA Instruments Corp., 1976; chmn. bd. dir. KLA-Tencor. Dir. emeritus Semiconductor Equipment Materials Inst. Recipient numerous awards. Office: KLA-TENCOR CORP One Technology Dr Milpitas CA 95035*

LEVY, KENNETH JAY, psychology educator, academic administrator; b. Dallas, Sept. 18, 1946; s. Reuben and Ruth (Okon) L.; children: Ryan S., Scott D. BA, U. Tex., 1968, MA, 1969; PhD, Purdue, 1972. Asst. prof. psychology SUNY, Buffalo, 1972-75, assoc. prof., 1976-78, prof., 1979—, chmn. dept. psychology, 1976-78, dean social scis., 1978-82, various adminstrv. positions, 1985—, assoc. provost, 1987—. Contbr. numerous articles to profl. jours.; editorial cons. Psychometrika. Home: 39 Shire Dr S East Amherst NY 14051-1816 Office: SUNY at Buffalo Capen Hall Buffalo NY 14260

LEVY, LEAH GARRIGAN, federal official; b. Miami, Fla., Apr. 29, 1947; d. Thomas Leo and Mary (Flaherty) Garrigan; m. Roger N. Levy, May 2, 1977; children: Philip, Aaron. BA in Polit. Sci., George Mason U., 1998, postgrad., 2001—. Mem. legis. staff U.S. Ho. Reps., 1973-75; mem. scheduling staff U.S. Senate, 1975-77, mem. administrv. scheduling staff, 1977-81; staff asst. pub. liaison The White House, 1982-84; spl. asst. U.S Dept. Transport, Washington, 1984-89, U.S. Dept. Housing, Washington, 1989—; scheduling asst. Empower Am., Washington, 1993-94; scheduler majority leader Dick Armey U.S. Ho. of Reps., Washington, 1995-2001; dir. scheduling and advance Sec. of Labor, Washington, 2001—02, spl. asst. Office of the Sec., 2002—03; dir. scheduling U.S. Senator Elizabeth Dole, Washington, 2003—; v.p. devel. Empower Am., Washington, 2003—05; dir. scheduling and advance US Dept. Labor, Washington, 2005—, dir. operations, 2005—. Contbr. to Rep. Nat. Com., Washington. Contbr. Rep. Nat. Conv. Va. Rep. Party, Washington; del. Va. State GOP Conv., Richmond, 1994. Mem. Alpha Chi. Roman Catholic. Avocations: tennis, golf, reading. Office: Empower Am Washington DC 20006 Office Phone: 202-693-6001. Personal E-mail: thelevys@aol.com. Business E-Mail: levy.leah@dol.gov.

LEVY, LEONARD WILLIAMS, history professor, writer; b. Toronto, Ont., Can., Apr. 9, 1923; s. Albert and Rae (Williams) L.; m. Elyse Gitlow, Oct. 21, 1944; children: Wendy Ellen, Leslie Anne. BS, Columbia U., 1947, MA, 1948, PhD (Univ. fellow), 1951; LHD, Brandeis U., 1987; DHL (hon.), Claremont Grad. Sch., 1991, Ripon Coll., 1996. Research asst. Columbia U., 1950-51; instr., asst. prof., assoc. prof., prof. Brandeis U., Waltham, Mass., 1951-70, first incumbent Earl Warren chair constl. history, 1957-70, dean Grad. Sch. Arts and Scis., 1958-63, dean faculty arts and scis., 1963-66; Andrew W. Mellon prof. humanities, history, chmn. grad. faculty history Claremont (Calif.) Grad. Sch., 1970-90, prof. emeritus, 1990—; Disting. scholar in residence So. Oreg. State Coll., 1990—. Reiser lectr. U. Chgo. Law Sch., 1964; Gaspar Bacon lectr. Boston U., 1972; Elliott lectr. U. So. Calif. Law Sch., 1972; Hugo Black lectr. U. Ala., 1976; Bicentennial lectr., City of St. Louis, 1976; disting. lectr. U. Cin., 1978, U. Idaho, 1991. Author: The Law of the Commonwealth and Chief Justice Shaw, 1957, Legacy of Suppression; Freedom of Speech and Press in Early American History, 1960, Jefferson and Civil Liberties; The Darker Side, 1963, Origins of the Fifth Amendment, 1968 (Pulitzer Prize in history 1969), Judgments: Essays on American Constitutional History, 1972, Against The Law: The Nixon Court and Criminal Justice, 1974, Treason Against God: History of the Offense of Blasphemy, 1981, Emergence of a Free Press, 1985, Constitutional Opinions, 1986, The Establishment Clause, 1986, Original Intent and the Framers' Constitution, 1988, Blasphemy: Verbal Offense Against the Sacred, 1993, Seasoned Judgments, 1994, A License to Steal: The Forfeiture of Property, 1996, Origins of the Bill of Rights, 1999, The Palladium of Justice, 1999, Ranters Run Amok, 1999, The Bill of Rights, 2004, The Fourth Amendment, 2004, Facets of Freedom, 2004, A Bookish Life, 2003; editor: Major Crises in American History, 1962, The American Political Process, 1963, The Presidency, 1964, The Congress, 1964, The Judiciary, 1964, Parties and Pressure Groups, 1964, Freedom of the Press from Zenger to Jefferson, 1966, American Constitutional Law, 1966, Judicial Review and the Supreme Court, 1967, Freedom and Reform, 1967, Essays on The Making of the Constitution, 1969, rev. edit. 1987, The Fourteenth Amendment and the Bill of Rights, 1970, The Supreme Court Under Earl Warren, 1972, Jim Crow in Boston, 1974, Essays on the Early Republic, 1974, Blasphemy in Massachusetts, 1974, The Framing and Ratification of the Constitution, 1987, The American Founding, 1988, American Constitutional History, 1989; co-editor: Ency. Am. Presidency, 4 vols., 1993; gen. editor: Am. Heritage Series, 60 vols., Harper Documentary History of Western Civilization, 40 vols.; editor-in-chief Ency. Am. Constn., 4 vols., 1986, supplement, 1991; gen. editor: Bicentennial History of the American Revolution; adv. bd.: Revs. in Am. History, John Marshall Papers, Salmon P. Chase Papers; contbr. articles to profl. jours. Mem. nat. bd. Commn. on Law and Social Action, Am. Jewish Congress; mem. U.S. Bicentennial Commn. Am. Revolution, 1966-68; mem. exec. council Inst. for Early Am. History and Culture; mem. nat. adv. council ACLU, Pulitzer prize juror, chmn. biog. jury, 1974, history jury, 1976. With AUS, 1943-46. Recipient Sigma Delta Chi prize for journalism history, 1961, 86; Frank Luther Mott prize Kappa Tau Alpha, 1961; Pulitzer prize for history, 1969; Commonwealth Club prize for non-fiction, 1975; Oboler Meml. Prize of Am. Library Assn. for Intellectual Freedom, 1986; Cert. Merit ABA, 1986; Henry L. Mencken award Free Press Assn., 1986; Dartmouth Medal Am. Library Assn., 1987, 95; Guggenheim fellow, 1957-58; Center For Study Liberty in Am. fellow Harvard, 1961-62; Am. Bar Found. sr. merit fellow, 1973-74; Am. Coun. Learned Socs. fellow, 1973; NEH sr. fellow, 1974. Mem. Am. Hist. Assn. (Littleton-Griswold com. legal history), Orgn. Am. Historians, Am. Soc. Legal History (dir.), Am. Antiquarian Soc., Soc. Am. Historians, Inst. Early Am. History and Culture (exec. coun.), Mass. Hist. Soc., Kappa Delta Pi. Democrat. Home: 1025 Timberline Ter Ashland OR 97520-3436 Office Phone: 541-552-9488.

LEVY, LESLIE ANN, application developer; b. N.Y.C., Dec. 25, 1941; d. Paul and Ruth Candace (Tachna) Bauman; m. Marc Gersan Gerard Levy, Oct. 1962 (div.); children: Benjamin Gerard, Remy Marcel Gerard. BA summa cum laude in philosophy and history, Smith Coll., 1962; MBA, Harvard U., Boston, 1976, DBA, 1980. Cert. French Fashion Acad., 1964. Tchg. asst. in philosophy UCLA, 1962-63; pres. Commonwealth Collaborative, Inc., Cambridge and Sarasota, Fla., 1976—99; sr. rsch. assoc. Harvard Sch. Bus. Adminstrn., Boston, 1979-81; asst. prof. mgmt. policy, industry analysis Case Western Res. U., Cleve., 1981-84; pres., CEO Acad. for Corp. Governance, Fordham U. Grad. Sch. Bus., 1990-91; pres., dir., treas., sec. Directors, Data, Inc., 1999—; pres., sec. Life Choices and Death Wishes, 2000—. Sr. advisor, pres., dir. Inst. Rsch. on Bd. Dirs., 1998-; with Honeywell Info. Sys., Boston, 1971-75; former cons. and lectr. in field. Author: Director Motivation: Incentives and Disincentives to Board Service, 1996, Separate Chairmen of the Board: Their Roles, Legal Liabilities, and Compensation; editor, co-author: Boards of Directors Part II; columnist: Directors and Boards, 1996-97; contbr. aricles to profl. jours. Mem. Boston and Tampa Bay Com. on Fgn. Rels. Acad. Corp. Governance rsch. fellow; Fulbright scholar. Mem. Am. Soc. Corp. Secs., Nat. Assn. Corp. Dirs., Acad. Mgmt. (article reviewer), Nat. Investor Rels. Inst., Inst. of Dirs., Federalist Soc., Women in Pensions, So. Fin. Assn., Harvard Club of Sarasota, Am. Jewish Com., Am. Jewish Congress, Nat. Coun. Jewish Women. Avocations: hiking, art history, construction, whitewater canoeing. E-mail: dirsdata@drleslielevy.com, irbd@drleslielevy.com.

LEVY, LOUIS EDWARD, retired accounting firm executive; b. Cleve., Nov. 16, 1932; s. Jerome and Bessie (Goldberg) L.; m. Sandra Harris, Mar. 4, 1956; children: Jerold, Richard, Lawrence. BBA, Case Western Res. U., 1956. CPA, N.Y. Agt. IRS, Cleve., 1956; ptnr., vice chmn. KPMG Peat Marwick, N.Y.C., 1958-90. Bd. dirs. ISI Mut. Funds; former mem. emerging issues task force Fin. Acctg. Standards Bd.; former adj. prof. Columbia U. Grad. Sch. Bus. Trustee, chmn. Nat. Multiple Sclerosis Soc., N.Y.C., 1978-2000; trustee New Coll. Fla. Found., sarasota, 2003—. Recipient Braden award Weatherhead Sch. Mgmt. Case Western Res. U., 1984, Community Svc. award Brandeis U., 1980; fellow Brandeis U., Boston, 1981—. Mem. AICPA (former chmn. quality control inquiry com.), Maplewood Country Club (N.J.), Longboat Key Country Club. Republican. Jewish. Avocations: tennis, boating, golf. E-mail: loulevy@msn.com.

LEVY, MARK, art educator; b. NYC, June 24, 1947; s. Sidney and Mitzi Levy; m. Jamie Bronson Levy, June 20, 1987. BA, Clark U., 1968; MA, Ind. U., 1970, PhD, 1977. Asst. prof. Kenyon Coll., Gambier, Ohio, 1974—79, U. Nevada, Reno, 1980—81; asst. to full prof. Calif. State U., Hayward, Calif., 1981—, dept. chair, 1983—89. Vis. critic & prof. San Francisco Art Inst., 1982—88; vis. prof. JFK U., Orida, Calif., 1995—; lectr. in field; cataloguer exhbns. Author: The Modern Artist as Shaman, 1993; contbr. articles to profl. jours.; exhibitions include U. Art Gallery, 2000, 2002, catalogue texts and book intros., Nevada Art Mus., 1981, Triton Art Mus., 1981, Last Gasp Press, 1982, Foster-Goldstrom Fine Arts, 1983, Calif. State U., 1983, 1986, 80 Langton Street Arts Catalogue, 1985, Monterey Peninsula Mus. Art, 1991, U. Art Gallery, 2000. Mem. Alameda County Art Commn., Oakland, Calif., 1985; advisor Fox Restoration Project, Oakland, 2004. Grantee Fellowship for Japan Studies, 1977, Fellowship for Study of Chinese Painting, NEH, 1978, Fulbright-Hays Fellowship to study tribal art in Malaysia, 1990, Fellowship for rsch. in Morocco & Spain, RISCA, 1995; Fulbright-Mays grant, US Govt. Mem.: Internat. Assn. Art Critics (exec. bd. 1990), Media Alliance, Coll. Art Assn., Found. Shamanic Studies, Internat. Assn. Art Critics. Avocations: meditation, drawing, swimming, tai chi.

LEVY, MARK HIRSCH, internist, researcher, medical educator; b. Birmingham, Ala., Nov. 13, 1964; s. Irving Hirsch and Marcie Seligman L.; m. Susan May Levy, Apr. 26, 1992; 1 child, Robert. BS in Chemistry, U. Mich., 1986; MD, 1990. Diplomate Am. Bd. Internal Medicine; cert. advanced cardiac life support, 2003. Intern U. Cin. Hosp., 1990—92; resident Jewish Hosp. Cin., 1992—93; med. dir. Manor Care Rehab. Ctr., Highland Park, Ill., 1997—; asst. prof. medicine Rush Presbyn. St. Lukes Med. Ctr., Chgo., 1998—. Profl. spkr. in field. Contbr. articles to profl. jours. Mem. AMA, ACP, CMS, AMDA, ASC. Office: Rush North Shore Med Ctr 9700 Kenton # 302 Skokie IL 60076

LEVY, MARK IRVING, lawyer; b. Chgo., June 28, 1949; s. Kenneth Warren and Arleen (Langhaus) L.; m. Judith Jarrell Levy, Sept. 8, 1979; children: Elizabeth Sara, Mitchell Bennett. BA summa cum laude with exceptional dist., Yale U., 1971, JD, 1975. Bar: D.C. 1976, U.S. Dist. Ct. D.C. 1977, U.S. Supreme Ct. 1980, Ill. 1986, U.S. Ct. Appeals (D.C. cir.) 1990, U.S. Ct. Appeals (6th, 7th and 8th cirs.) 1990, U.S. Tax Ct. 1990, U.S. Ct. Appeals (9th cir.) 1993, U.S. Ct. Appeals (2d, 4th and 10th cirs.) 1994, U.S. Ct. Appeals (3d, 5th, 11th and Fed. cirs.) 1996, U.S. Ct. Appeals (1st cir.) 2000. Law clk. Judge Gerhard A. Gesell, Washington, 1975-76; assoc. Covington & Burling, Washington, 1976-79, 81-83; asst. to solicitor gen. U.S. Dept. Justice, Washington, 1979-81, 83-86; ptnr. Mayer, Brown & Platt, Chgo., 1987-93; dep. asst. atty. gen. (Appellate) Civil Divsn. U.S. Dept. Justice, Washington, 1993-95; ptnr. Howrey & Simon, Washington, 1995—2003; of counsel Kilpatrick Stockton LLP, 2004—. Adj. faculty, appellate sem. U. Va. Sch. Law, 1999-2000, 2001-2002, 2004-2005; mem. adv. com. on procedures U.S. Dist. Ct. (D.C. cir.), adv. com. fed. rules of appellate procedure Exec. editor Yale Law Jour., 1974-75; contbr. columns to jours. Recipient Israel H. Peres prize Yale Law Sch., 1975. Fellow Am. Acad. Appellate Lawyers; mem. Lawyers Club of Chgo., Yale Law Sch. Alumni Assn. (former treas., exec. com. mem. 1987-90), Edward Coke Appellate Am. Inn of Ct. (master), Phi Beta Kappa (fellow). Home: 7609 Winterberry Pl Bethesda MD 20817-4847 Office: Kilpatrick Stockton LLP 607 14th St NW Ste 900 Washington DC 20005-2018 Office Phone: 202-824-1437. Business E-Mail: mlevy@kilpatrickstockton.com.

LEVY, MARK RAY, lawyer; b. Denver, Mar. 2, 1946; s. Richard C. and Hilde (Lindauer) L.; m. Patricia Loeb, June 13, 1971; children: Betsy, Robert. BA, U. Colo., 1968, JD, 1972. Bar: Colo. 1972, U.S. Dist. Ct. Colo. 1972. Assoc. Holland & Hart LLP, Denver, 1972-78, ptnr., 1978—. Adj. prof. the lawyering process U. Denver Law Sch., 1990-93; mem. spl. adv. com. Colo. Securities Bd., 1996-97. Author: (with others) Colorado Corporations Manual, 1987, Colorado Corporation Law and Practice, 1990. Trustee Congregation Emanuel, Denver, 1984-90, mem. legal com., 1989—; chmn. Denver Alumni Phonathon U. Colo. Law Sch., 1989-90, mem. alumni bd., 1992-96, chmn. alumni bd., 1994-95; trustee Nat. Repertory Orch., 1995-96. Mem. ABA, Colo. Bar Assn. (Blue Sky Law task force 1980-81, co-chmn. Colo. securities law rev. com. 1988-91, Article 8 of UCC com. 1995-96, chmn. ann. conv. com. 1999-2000, mem. annual conv. com. 1998-2002, mem. planning com. annual bus. law inst. 2000), Denver Bar Assn. Office: Holland & Hart LLP 555 17th St Ste 3200 Denver CO 80202-3950 E-mail: mlevy@hollandhart.com.

LEVY, MATTHEW DEGEN, investment company executive, consumer products company executive, management consultant; b. N.Y.C., Dec. 5, 1958; s. Herbert Monte and Marilyn (Wohl) L.; m. Laura Ann Goldin, Aug. 20, 1989; children: Ely Samuel, Philip Benjamin. BA magna cum laude and spl. honors, Tufts U., 1980; MBA, Yale U., 1983. Rsch. assoc. State St. Cons., Boston, 1980-81; cons. to vice chmn. Yankelovich, Skelly & White, Inc., Stamford, Conn., 1982; staff fin. analyst IBM Corp., White Plains, N.Y., 1983-86; co-founder, COO White, Skelly, Yankelovich Cons. Group, Inc., Greenwich, Conn., 1986-93; area dir. and mng. cons. Renaissance Strategy Group, N.Y.C., 1993-95; dir. bus. planning and devel. Sara Lee Corp., N.Y.C., 1995-97; v.p. global ops. Salomon Bros. Inc., N.Y.C., 1997; v.p. tech. and ops. Salomon Smith Barney Inc., N.Y.C., 1997-98; v.p. info. tech. Goldman Sachs, N.Y.C., 1999—. Cons. Yale Sch. Mgmt. Alumni Assn., 1989; bus. mgr., anchorman WMFO Radio, Medford, Mass., 1977-80; co-instr. course on decision-making Tufts U., 1977. Contbr. articles to mags. Bd. dirs. DOROT, N.Y.C., 1986-97, pres. bd., 1991-94; mem. allocations com. United Way of Greenwich, 1984-86; bd. dirs. Am. Jewish World Svc., N.Y.C., 1997—. Home: 160 Riverside Dr Apt 8C New York NY 10024-2111 Office: Goldman Sachs 180 Maiden Ln 13th Fl New York NY 10038-4958 E-mail: mdlnyc@aol.com.

LEVY, MICHAEL, electronic manufacturing company executive; b. Gainesville, Fla., Dec. 19, 1946; s. Leon and Geneva (Shore) Levy; m. Jo-Lynn Nelson, July 3, 1986; children: Susan Elizabeth, Amanda Christine. BSEE, Ga. Inst. Tech., 1969. Design engr. Harris Corp., Melbourne, Fla., 1969—73; mgr. engring. Racal-Milgo, Inc., Miami, Fla., 1973—78; chmn., CEO Lexicon Corp., Ft. Lauderdale, Fla., 1978—93, Scope Inc. subs. Lexicon, Reston, Va., 1985—93; pres., CEO SportsLine USA (now CBS.SportsLine.com Inc.), Ft. Lauderdale, 1994—. Bd. dirs. Sports-Tech Internat. Inc. subs. Lexicon, Ft. Lauderdale, Cosmo Comm. Corp., Miami. Named Named hon. Ky. Col.; named one of 100 Most Powerful People in Sports (3 times), Sporting News. Mem.: Mem. Am. Electronics Assn. Republican. Achievements include patents for electronic dictionary, five others. Office: SportsLine 2200 W Cypress Creek Rd Fort Lauderdale FL 33309-1825*

LEVY, MICHAEL B., business educator; b. Balt., July 12, 1947; m. Bonny B. Wolf; 1 child. BA, Brown U., 1969; PhD, Rutgers U., 1979. Tchr. social studies, coach Loyola High Sch., Balt., 1969—72; teaching asst. Rutgers U., New Brunswick, NJ, 1973—76, instr., 1978; asst. prof. Tex. A&M Univ., College Sta., 1978-84, assoc. prof. polit. sci., 1984-85; economist joint econ. com. U.S. Congress, Washington, 1985-87; adminstrv. asst. to Sen. Lloyd Bentsen U.S. Senate, Washington, 1987-93; asst. sec. legis. affairs U.S. Dept. Treasury, Washington, 1993-95; adj. instr. Georgetown U., Washington, 1986-93, disting. prof., 1995—; sr. advisor to U.S. Treas. Sec. Robert Rubin U.S. Dept Treas., Washington, 1995. Legis. cons. Brownstein, Hyatt & Farber, Denver and Washington, 1995—. Editor: Political Thought in America, 1981, 87, (with Philip Abbot) The Liberal Future in America: Essays in Renewal, 1985, (with Edward Portis) Handbook of Political Theory and Policy Sciences, 1989; contbr. articles to profl. jours. Bevier fellow Rutgers U., 1979; R.J. Reynolds fellow for So. High Sch. Tchrs. Office: Georgetown U Sch Bus 411 Ol North Washington DC 20057-0001 Business E-Mail: levymb@msb.edu.

LEVY, MICHAEL LEE, neurosurgeon; b. San Diego, Calif., Sept. 20, 1960; s. Lee Issaac and Sharline Sheridan (Day) Levy; m. Karen Marie Lorman, Jan. 7, 1989; children: Danielle Montana, Dillon Michael. BA, U. Calif. San Diego, 1981; MD, U. Calif. San Francisco, 1986, PhD, 2001. Resident U. So. Calif. Sch. Medicine, L.A., 1986-93; resident supr. U. So. Calif., L.A., 1992, fellow in pediatric neurol. surgery dept. neurol. surgery, 1993; dir. surg. epilepsy team, dir. neurotrauma Children's Hosp. L.A., 1993—2002; prof., head divsn. pediat. neurosurgery Children's Hosp. San Diego, 2002—; assoc. dir. residency tng. program U. Calif. Sch. Medicine, San Diego, 2003—. Cons. in field. Editor: Neurosurgery News, 2000—02; contbr. numerous articles to profl. jours. Recipient Rudolph Taussig scholarship, U. Calif. San Francisco, 1982—84, CHOMP scholarship, 1983—86, Tucker scholarship, 1984—86, numerous awards in field. Mem.: L.A. Acad. Medicine, Los Angeles County Med. Assn., Calif. House Officer Med. Soc., Calif. Med. Assn., Am. Assn. Neurol. Surgeons, Congress of Neurol. Surgeons (exec. com. 1996—2002, editor newsletter 1996—99), Alpha Omega Alpha. Achievements include development of an endoscopic system for the treatment of hydrocephalus, heads-up virtual displays for microneurosurgery, three dimensional anatomic image reconstruction and stereolithography; specialization in pediat. vascular and midline tumor surgery. Avocations: surfing, diving. Home: 7401 Luna De Oro Rancho Santa Fe CA 92067 Office Phone: 858-966-8574. Business E-Mail: mlevy@chsd.org.

LEVY, NELSON LOUIS, immunologist, educator, surgeon; b. Somerville, NJ, June 19, 1941; s. Myron L. and Sylvia (Cohen) L.; m. Joanne Barnett, Dec. 21, 1963 (div. 1972); children: Scott, Erik, Jonathan; m. Louisa Douglas Stiles, Dec. 21, 1974; children: Michael, Andrew, David. BA/BS summa cum laude, Yale U., 1963; MD, Columbia U., 1967; PhD, Duke U., 1972. Diplomate Am. Bd. Allergy and Immunology. Intern U. Colo. Med. Ctr., Denver, 1967-68; resident Duke U. Med. Ctr., Durham, N.C., 1970-73; rsch. assoc. NIH, Bethesda, Md., 1968-70; asst. prof. immunology Duke U. Med. Ctr., Durham, 1972-75, assoc. prof. immunology and neurology, 1975-80, prof., 1980-81; dir. biol. rsch. Abbott Labs., Abbott Park, Ill., 1981, v.p. rsch., 1981-84; pres. Fujisawa Pharm., Deerfield, Ill., 1992-93; CEO Ill. Tech. Devel. Corp., 1993-95, The Core Techs Corp., Lake Forest, Ill., 1984—92, chmn. bd. dirs., CEO, 1995—. Chmn. bd. dirs. Horizon Quest Inc., Laguna Hills, Calif., 1996—97, ColesCraft Corp., 1997—, IMM UVA Corp., New Orleans, 1997—, Targeted Pharmaceuticals LLC, Lake Forest, Ill.; bd. dirs. ChemBridge Corp., San Diego, Targeted Genetics Corp., Seattle, Biona PTY Ltd., Laguna Beach, Cary Pharm. Co., Bethesda, Md., ChemBridge Rsch. Labs., LLC, San Diego, zuChem, Inc., Chgo.; chmn. sci. adv. bd. Neoprobe Corp., First Horizon Pharms., Inc.; mem. sci. adv. bd. Ligand Pharms. Inc.; cons. Alcide Corp., 1991—, Ameritech, 1993—, U.S. Dept. Treasury, FTC, 1999—; others. Contbr. chapters to books, articles to profl. jours. Mem. Gov.'s Task Force on Econ. Devel., 1993-98; mem. corp. adv. bd. Family Svc. of South Lake County, 1991—; commr. Lake County, Ill., 1998--. Surgeon USPHS, 1968-70. Grantee Am. Cancer Soc., 1970-75, NIH, 1971-81. Nat. Multiple Sclerosis Soc., 1974-81, Ill. Dept. Commerce and Cmty. Affairs, 1993—. Mem. Am. Assn. Immunologists, Am. Assn. Cancer Rsch., Licensing Execs. Soc., Rotary, Phi Beta Kappa, Sigma Xi, Alpha Omega Alpha, Phi Gamma Delta. Avocations: triathlons, biking, rhythm 'n blues. Office: 1391 Concord Rd Lake Forest IL 60045-1506

LEVY, NORMAN B., psychiatrist, educator; b. NYC, 1931; s. Barnett Theodore and Lena (Gulnick) L.; m. Lya Weiss (dec.); children: Karen, Susan, Joanne; m. Carol Lois Spiegel, 1 son, Robert Barnett. BA cum laude, NYU, 1952; MD, SUNY. Diplomate Am. Bd. Psychiatry and Neurology (examiner). Intern Maimonides Med. Center, Bklyn.; resident physician in medicine U. Pitts.-Presbyn. Hosp.; resident in psychiatry Kings County Hosp. Center, Bklyn.; instr. psychiatry SUNY Downstate Med. Ctr. Coll. Medicine, Bklyn., asst. prof., assoc. prof.; prof. State U. N.Y. Downstate Med. Center Coll. Medicine, 1980-95; presiding officer faculty SUNY Downstate Med. Ctr. Coll. Medicine, assoc. dir. med-psychiat. liaison service, 1965-80; prof. psychiatry, medicine, surgery and coordinator psychiat. liaison services N.Y. Med. Coll., 1980-95; clin. prof. psychiatry, adj. prof. of medicine Health Science Ctr. SUNY, Bklyn., 1996—; dir. psychiatry Kingsboro (Bklyn.) Psychiat. Ctr., 2000—. Dir. liaison svcs. psychiatry divsn. Westchester County Med. Ctr., 1980-95, mem. exec. com. med. staff, 1981-85, 89-92, N.Y. Med. Coll., 1980-95; clin. prof. psychiatry, adj. prof. medicine health sci. ctr. SUNY, Bklyn., 1996—; dir., consultation-liaison and emergency psychiatry Coney Island Hosp., Bklyn., 1996-2000; vis. prof. psychiatry and medicine So. Ill. U. Sch. Medicine; vis. prof. psychiatry John A. Burns Sch. Medicine, U. Hawaii, 1981; coord. 1st Internat. Conf. Psychol. Factors in Hemodialysis and Transplantation, 1978, 2d-9th Internat. Confs. on Psychonephrology; cons. NIMH; chief med. svcs. USAF Hosp., Ashiya, Japan; clin. prof. psychiatry, adj. prof. medicine SUNY Health Sci. Ctr., Bklyn., 1996. Author: (with others), editor: Living or Dying: Adaptation to Hemodialysis, 1974, Psychonephrology I: Psychological Factors in Hemodialysis and Transplantation, 1981, Men in Transition: Theory and Therapy, 1982, Psychonephrology II: Psychological Problems in Kidney Failure and their Treatment, 1983; contbr. articles to jours., chpts. to textbooks in field.; assoc. editor: Gen. Hosp. Psychiatry, 1978-82, sect. editor, 1982-2005; sect. editor: Internat. Jour. Psychiatry in Medicine, 1977-78; mem. editl. bd., book rev. editor Jour. Dialysis and Transplantation, 1979-97, Facta Universitatis, 1997—; mem. editl. bd. Resident and Staff Physician, 1981-91, Internat. Jour. Artificial Internal. Organs, 1983-93, Geriatric Nephrology and Urology, 1990—, Kidney: A Current Survey of World Literature, 1990—, Dialysis and Transplantation, 1979—. Served to capt. M.C. USAF. Recipient William A. Console Master Tchr. award, SUNY, Bklyn., 1991. Fellow ACP, Am. Coll. Psychiatrists, Am. Psychiat. Assn. (pres. Kings County dist. br. 1981-82), Acad. Psychosomatic Medicine (Thomas P. Hackett award 1993); mem. AAAS, Am. Psychosomatic Soc. (coun. 1994-97), N.Y. Acad. Scis., Psychonephrology Found. (pres. 1978—), Internat. Soc. Nephrology, Am. Soc. Nephrology, Soc. Liaison Psychiatry (bd. dirs. 1979-80, sec. 1980-81, pres.-elect 1991-92, pres. 1992-94, bd. dirs. 1995-98, award 1998), Serbian Acad. Medicine, Phi Beta Kappa, Sigma Xi. Home: 169 Westminster Rd Brooklyn NY 11218-3445 Office: Kingsboro Psychiat Hosp 681 Clarkson Ave Brooklyn NY 11203 Office Phone: 718-693-6280. E-mail: nephropsyc@aol.com.

LEVY, PAUL FINANQUE, health facility administrator; b. Oceanside, NY; BS in Economics, BS in Urban Studies, M in City Planning, MIT. Adj. prof. urban studies and planning MIT, Cambridge, Mass.; exec. dir. Mass. Water Resources Authority, Cambridge; exec. dean adminstrn. and strategic Harvard Med. Sch., Boston, 1998—2000; pres., CEO Beth Israel Deaconess Med. Ctr., Boston, 2000—. Chmn. Mass. Dept. Pub. Utilities; dir. Ark. Dept. Energy; bd. dirs. Harvard Clin. Rsch. Inst., Water Solutions Group, LLC, Silent Spring Inst., Providence Energy Group; cons. in field. Co-author: Negotiating Environmental Agreements, 1999. Achievements include responsibility for the Boston Harbor clean-up, one of the largest pollution control projects in the world; operation of a water transmission system for 46 communities; administering an aggressive demand management program that descreased water consumption by 15% over a 3-year period. Avocation: soccer. Office: Beth Israel Deaconess Med Ctr 330 Brookline Ave Boston MA 02215

LEVY, PETER A., lawyer; b. Apr. 17, 1949; BA, Univ. Ill., Urbana-Champaign, 1971; JD, Univ. Chgo., 1974. Bar: Ill. 1974. Ptnr., co-chmn. Lodging & Timeshare practice group DLA Piper Rudnick Gray Cary, Chgo. Lectr. Practicing Law Inst., Georgetown Univ. Law Ctr. Co-author: Ill. Real Estate Forms. Mem.: ABA, Ill. State Bar Assn., Chgo. Bar Assn., Phi Beta Kappa. Office: DLA Piper Rudnick Gray Cary 203 N LaSalle St Chicago IL 60601-1293 Office Phone: 312-368-4068. Office Fax: 312-630-5342. Business E-Mail: peter.levy@dlapiper.com.

LEVY, RALPH, engineering executive, consultant; b. London, Apr. 12, 1932; came to U.S., 1967, naturalized, 1978; s. Alfred and Esther L.; m. Barbara Dent, Dec. 12, 1959; children: Sharon E., Mark S. BA, Cambridge U., 1953, MA, 1957; PhD, Queen Mary Coll. U. London, 1966. Mem. sci. staff GEC, Stanmore, Middlesex, Eng., 1953-59; mem. sci. staff Mullard Research Labs., Redhill, Eng., 1959-64; lectr. dept. elec. and electronic engring. U. Leeds, 1964-67; v.p. research Microwave Devel. Labs., Inc., Natick, Mass., 1967-84; v.p. engring. KW Engring., San Diego, 1984-88; v.p. research Remec Inc., San Diego, 1988-89; R. Levy Assocs., 1989—. Author: (with J.O. Scanlan) Circuit Theory, 1970, 2d vol., 1973; contbr. articles in field; patentee in field. Fellow IEEE (editor Transactions on Microwave Theory and Techniques 1986-88, Career award IEEE Microwave Theory and Techniques Soc. 1997); mem. Inst. Elec. Engrs. (London). Office: 1897 Caminito Velasco La Jolla CA 92037-5725 Office Phone: 858-459-2286. E-mail: r.levy@ieee.org.

LEVY, RALPH JACOB, JR., retired theater educator; b. Northampton, Mass., Dec. 1, 1927; s. Ralph Jacob and Dorothy Levy. BA in Speech and Dramatic Art, State U. Iowa, 1951; MA in theater, Case Western Res. U., 1952. Cert. tchr. Mass. Fin. clk. US Army, Fort Dix, NJ, 1946—48; speech and theater educator Duquesne U., Pitts., 1952—54; pres. and mgr. Harry Daniel's Inc., Northampton, Mass., 1956—76; speech and theater educator Northampton H.S., 1976—87; adminstr. aide Commonwealth of Mass., Boston, 1989—2002. Author: (column) Hampshire Mag., (books) The Career of Milton Aborn: 50 Years of Musical Theatre, Biography of Morris J. Raphall. Chmn. Downtown Merchants Assn., Northampton, 1956—76; co-founder, dir. Dollars for Scholars, Northampton, 1975—; program chair, host Radio Sta. WHMP, Northampton, 1959—2000; bd. dirs., campaign chair Hampshire Cmty. United Way, Northampton, 1956—76; ex-officio mem. bd. dirs. C. of C., Northampton, Mass., 1956—76; founder, chmn. bd. dirs. Cmty. Multi-Svc. Agy. Inc., 1971—89; ednl. coord., dir. Northampton Honor Ct., 1982—89; bd. dirs., actor, dir. Circle Players, Northampton, 1954—76; actor, dir. Malone Summer Theatre, NY, 1952—56; senator Jr. Chamber Internat. Cpl. T-5 US Army, 1946—48, New Jersey. Named Northampton's Outstanding Young Man, 1960, Citizen of Yr., Northampton C. of C., 1973, Jaycee of Yr., Mass. Jaycees, 1961; recipient Disting. Svc. award, Hampshire Cmty. United Way, 1960, Awards for Svc., Northampton Cmty. Ct., 1983—85, Northampton Cmty. Arts award, 1985, Helping Hands for Youth award, Cmty. Multi-Svc. Agy., Inc., 1988, Spl. Svc. award, Citizens Scholarship Found. of Am., 1989, New England Dollars for Scholars, 1993—94. Mem.: Northampton Cable TV (bd. mem., sec. 1980—2000), WGBY-TV Channel 57 (Pub. TV Sta.) (mem. bd. of Tribunes 1973—78), Phi Beta Kappa. Democrat. Jewish. Avocations: walking, acting, reading, research. Home: 19 Hancock St 1st Fl Rear Northampton MA 01060

LEVY, RICHARD C., television production executive, author, producer, inventor; b. Wilkes-Barre, Pa., Jan. 7, 1947; s. Sidney Z. and Bettie (Abrahamson) L.; m. Sheryl G. Slate; 1 child, Bettie. Student, U. Madrid, 1965; diploma, U. Paris, 1966; BA in Communications, Emerson Coll., 1968. Asst. to pres. Paramount Internat. Pictures, N.Y.C., 1968; dir. Cen. Am. advt., publicity Paramount Films of Panama, Panama City, 1968-69; dir. fgn. advt., publicity Avco Embassy Pictures, Inc., N.Y.C., 1970-71; pres. Ricsher Prodns. Ltd., N.Y.C., 1971-82; dep. dir. USIA TV and Film Service/Worldnet, Washington, 1982-85; pres. Richard C. Levy Assocs., Washington, 1986—. Author: Wife Beating: The Silent Crisis, 1976, How to Use the Freedom of Information Act, 1978, Plane Talk: The Consumer's Air Travel Guide, 1980, Secrets of Selling Inventions, 1984, Desperately Seeking: Romance in the Want Ads, 1986, Inventing and Patenting Sourcebook: How to Sell and Protect Your Ideas, 1989, Inside Santa's Workshop, 1990, Inventor's Desktop Companion, 1990, 2d edit., 1995, From Workshop to Toy Store, 1992, The Complete Idiot's Guide to Cashing in on Your Inventions, 2002, The Toy and Game Inventor's Handbook, 2003; producer: (documentaries) Hal David: Expressing a Feeling, We the People, (UN Presentation video) KAL-007; co-producer more than 35 TV documentaries; contbr. articles to profl. jours.; inventor Adverteasing, 1988, Noteability, 1990, Screen Challenge, 1991, Adverteasing II, 1992, Oops and Downs, 1992, Blirds, 1992, Wayne's World: VCR board game, 1992; producer (video) Speed Force, 1996, Family Reunion, 2002, Route 66: The Great American Road Trip Game, 2002, Men Are From Mars, Women Are From Venus: The Game, 1998, 2003. Bd. dirs. Intellectual Property Owners, Inc. Recipient Best Game award Inventors Clubs of Am., 1989, Innovation award SBA D.C., 1987, Irma S. Mann award Emerson Coll., 2000. Mem. NATAS. Republican. Avocations: scuba diving, hiking, painting. Office: PO Box 34828 Bethesda MD 20827-0828

LEVY, ROBERT A., academic administrator; BA, Ohio Wesleyan U.; MA in English, Temple U. Asst. to v.p. acad. affairs U. Tenn., Knoxville, 1973—85, assoc. v.p., 1985—2004, v.p. acad. affairs, 2004—. Office: Univ Tenn 810 Andy Holt Tower 1331 Circle Pk Knoxville TN 37996

LEVY, ROBERT EDWARD, management consultant; b. Cin., May 23, 1939; s. Aaron F. and Elizabeth W. (Hirsch) L.; m. Candace Ann Wolfe, June 20, 1970; children: Brian D., Jessica A. BChemE, Cornell U., 1962; PhDChemE, U. Calif. at Berkeley, 1967. Various positions, including mgr. synthetic fuels devel., rsch. and engring. Exxon Co., Florham Park, N.J., 1967-80, 84-86; mgr. tech. dept. Lago Oil & Transport Co., Esso Interam. divsn. Exxon Co., Aruba, Netherlands Antilles, 1980-84; v.p., dir. tech. devel. M.W. Kellogg Co., Houston, 1987-93; v.p. govt. and regulatory affairs Energy Biosystems Corp., The Woodlands, Tex., 1993-97; mgmt. cons. Houston, 1997-99; sr. v.p. Allan F. Dow & Assocs., Houston, 1998-99, UniPure Corp., Houston, 2000—04, dir., 2001—04; pres., CEO AstroVelos, LLC, Houston, 2005—. Cons. in field. Patentee in field. Indsl. mem. Com. for Prevention of Shoreline Pollution by Oil, Aruba, 1982—84; founder Industry Profls. for Clean Air, Houston, 2004. Mem. AIChE, Indsl. Rsch. Inst. (bd. editors 1992-95, pre-coll. edn. com. 1995-2000, chmn., 1996-97), Sigma Xi (pres. Kellogg chpt. 1991-92). Avocations: tennis, jogging, sailing. Personal E-mail: boblevy@houston.rr.com. E-mail: bob@astrovelos.com.

LEVY, ROBERT MORRIS, judge; BA, Harvard Coll., 1971; JD, NYU, 1975. Bar: N.Y., U.S. Dist. Ct. (so. and ea. dists.) N.Y., U.S. Ct. Appeals (D.C. and 2d cirs.), U.S. Supreme Ct. Staff atty. juvenile rights divsn. Legal Aid Soc., N.Y.C., 1976-77; staff atty. mental health law project N.Y. Civil Liberties Union, N.Y.C., 1977-80, dir. mental health law project, 1980-85, sr. staff atty., 1985-93; gen. counsel N.Y. Lawyers for the Pub. Interest, N.Y.C., 1993-94; U.S. magistrate judge Ea. Dist. N.Y., Bklyn., 1995—, overseer ct.'s mediation and arbitrator programs, 2000—; cons. ADR design program Fed.Jud. Ctr., 2003—. Advisor criminal prosecution, Thailand, 2002; advisor on jud. reform in the Republic of Georgia, Ctrl. and East European Law Initiative ABA, 1998; adj. prof. Bklyn. Law Sch., 1989—, NYU Law Sch., 1991—, Columbia U. Law Sch., 1993—. Author: (with V. Rosenthal) Rights of Nursing Home Residents in New York, 1984, (with L. Rubenstein) Rights of People with Mental Disabilities, 1996. Bd. dirs. NYU Pub. Interest Law Found., N.Y.C., 1980-82; mem. Gov.'s Task Force on Advocacy, N.Y., 1988-91; mem. adv. bd. Protection and Advocacy Svcs. for the Mentally Ill, N.Y.C., 1991-93; vol. factfinding missions Human Rights Watch, No. Ireland and Romania, 1990, 91, 92, 93. Mem. Fed. Bar Coun. (2nd cir. cts. com. 1998—, com. on pub. svc. 2001—), Assn. Bar of the City of N.Y. (sect. ethics and profl. responsibilities 2002-), com. on internat. human rights 1995-98). Office: 225 Cadman Plz E # 621 Brooklyn NY 11201-1818 Fax: 718-260-2647.*

LEVY, ROBERT S., lawyer; b. N.Y.C., May 27, 1932; s. Harry Victor and Betty Ruth L.; m. Lorna Iris Klein, June 30, 1957; children— Jill Arden, Kenneth Arlan. B.S. cum laude, N.Y.U., 1954, LL.B. cum laude, 1955. Bar: N.Y. 1956, U.S. Dist. Ct. (so. and ea. dists.) N.Y. 1962, U.S. Supreme Ct. 1967, U.S. Ct. Appeals (2d cir.) 1973. Assoc., Nordlinger, Reigelman, Benetar & Charney, N.Y.C., 1955-59; sr. assoc. Reich, Spitzer & Feldman, N.Y.C., 1959-64; pvt. practice, N.Y.C., 1964-88; ptnr. Levy, Stopol & Camelo, LLP, Uniondale, NY; gen. counsel Audiovox Corp., Hauppauge, NY; mem. nat. panel arbitrators Am. Arbitration Assn., N.Y.C., 1961— . Author: Guide to Franchise Investigation and Contract Negotiation, 1967; Woman's Guide to Franchises, 1967; Directory of State and Federal Funds for Business, 1968. Mem. N.Y. State Bar Assn., Phi Beta Kappa.Tam O'Shanter (Brookville, N.Y.). Office: Levy Stopol & Camelo LLP 1425 EAB Plaza Uniondale NY 11556-1425 Office Phone: 516-802-7008.

LEVY, ROCHELLE FELDMAN, artist; b. N.Y.C., Aug. 4, 1937; d. Harry and Eva (Krause) Feldman. m. Robert Paley Levy, June 4, 1955; children: Kathryn Tracey, Wendy Paige, Robert Paley, Angela Brooke, Michael Tyler. Student, Barnard Coll., 1954—55, U. Pa., 1955—56; BFA, Moore Coll. Art, 1979, HHD (hon.), 1998. Mgmt. cons. Woodlyn Sch., Rosemont, Pa., 1983—2003; sr. ptnr. DRT Interiors, Phila., 1983—2003; ptnr. Phila. Phillies, 1981—94. One-woman shows include Watson Gallery Wheaton Coll. Norton, Mass., 1977, U. Pa., 1977, Med. Coll. Pa. Phila., 1982, Aquaduct Race Track, 1982, Phila. Art Alliance, 1983, Paley Gallery, Moore Coll. Art and Design, 1984, 2003, Art Alliance, 1994, Frost & Reed Gallery, Saratoga, NY, 2000-05, Frost & Reed Ltd, N.Y.C., 2004. Pres. League of Children's Hosp. Phila., 1969-70; bd. overseers Ctr. for Judaic Studies U. Pa., 1993-96; bd. mgrs. Moore Coll. Art and Design, 1970—, chmn. exec. com., 1982-99, trustees 1979-99, chmn. emerita bd. trustees, 1999-2004. Recipient G. Allen Smith Prize Woodmere Art Gallery, Chestnut Hill, Pa., 1979, Disting. Alumni award Moore Coll. Art, 2005, Woman honoree Samuel Paley Day Care Ctr., Phila., 1990, Jefferson Bank Declaration award, 1991, Nat. Philanthropy honoree Nat. Soc. Fund Raising Execs. Greater Phila. chpt., 1994, Hon. Alumni award Moore Coll. Art, 2005. Mem. Pa. Acad. Fine Arts (selections and acquisitions com. 1970—, bd. mgrs. 1975—, chmn. exec. com. 1982—, trustee 1990—), Artist's Equity, Phila. Art Alliance, Phila. Mus. Art (assoc.), Phila. Print Club. Office: 200 W Montgomery Ave Ardmore PA 19003

LEVY, RONALD, medical educator, researcher; b. Carmel, Calif. BS, Harvard U., 1963; MD, Stanford U., 1968. Cert. Internal Medicine, 1973, Med. Oncology, 1979, lic. Commonwealth Mass., 1970, State Calif. Med. License, 1975. Intern, internal medicine Mass. Gen. Hosp., Boston, 1968-69, residency, internal medicine, 1969-70; clin. assoc., immunology branch Nat. Cancer Inst., 1970—72; Helen Hay Whitney Found. fellow in dept. chem. immunology Weizmann Inst. Sci., Rehovot, Israel, 1973-75; fellow, dept. medicine, divsn. oncology Stanford U. Sch. Medicine, 1972—73, mem. faculty, 1975—, asst. prof. medicine, divsn. oncology, 1975—81, assoc. prof. dept. medicine-oncology, 1981—87, prof. medicine, divsn. oncology, 1987—, Robert K. Summy and Helen K. Summy prof., 1987—; Frank and Else Schilling Am. Cancer Soc. Clin. Rsch. prof., 1987—; chief divsn. oncology Stanford U. Sch. Medicine, Calif., 1993—. Investigator Howard Hughes Med. Inst., 1977—82; chmn., bd. scientific counselors, divsn. cancer treatment NIH, 1989—93; mem. scientific advisory bd. Fred Hutchinson Cancer Rsch. Ctr., 1994—, Coley Pharm. Group, 2001, XTL Therapeutics, Rehovoth, Israel, Therion Inc., Cambridge, Mass., Xeyte Therapeutics, Seattle, Agensys, Santa Monica, Calif., Pointilliste, Mountain View, Calif., Cell Genesis, Foster City, Calif., Five Prime, South San Francisco, Calif.; Woodward vis. prof. Meml. Sloan Kettering Cancer Ctr., NY, 1994; Morton Mason lecture U. Tex. Southwestern, 1995; vis. prof. U. Minn. Cancer Ctr., 1996, U. Nebr. Cancer Ctr., 1999; lectr. in field. Contbr. articles to profl. jours.; Author, co-author of several books and publs. Mem. Dorothy P. Landon Am. Assn. for Cancer Rsch. Translational Cancer Rsch. com., 2001; bd. dir. Damon Runyon Cancer Rsch. Fund, 2002—; mem., Conflict of Interest Com. Stanford U. Sch. Medicine, 2001—; mem. Am. Assn. Med. Sch. Task Force on Fin. Conflicts of Interest in Clin. Rsch., 2001, GM Cancer Rsch. Found. Awards Assembly, 1992—96, 2001—. Recipient Armand Hammer award for Cancer Rsch., 1982, Ciba-Geigy/Drew award in Biomedical Rsch., 1983, Dr. Josef Steiner prize for Cancer Rsch., 1989, Karnofsky award, Am. Soc. Clin. Oncology, 1999, Charles F. Kettering award, GM Cancer Rsch. Found., 1999, Centeon award, 6th Internat. Conf. on Bispecific Antibodies, 1999, C. Chester Stock award, Meml. Sloan-Kettering Cancer Ctr., 2000, Medal of Honor, Am. Cancer Soc., 2000, Key to the Cure award, Cure for Lymphoma Found., 2000, Evelyn Hoffman Meml. award, Lymphoma Rsch. Found. Am., 2001, Jeffrey A. Gottlieb Meml. award, M.D. Anderson Cancer Ctr, 2003, Discovery Health Channel Med. Honors, 2004. Mem. ACP, Am. Soc. Clin. Oncology, Am. Cancer Soc. (chmn. immunology study sect., 1988-92, mem., rsch. coun., 2003-), Am. Soc. Clin. Investigation, Assn. Am. Physicians, Am. Assn. for Cancer Rsch. (chmn., Joseph H. Burchinal award com., 2002, Joseph H. Burchenal Clin. Cancer Rsch. award, 1997), Am. Assn. Immunology (program com. and block chmn. for tumor immunology, 1992-96), Am. Fed. for Clin. Rsch., Am. Soc. Hematology, Western Soc. Medicine, Acad. of Cancer Immunology. Achievements include first to the development of idiotype-based therapeutic vaccines for the treatment of non-Hodgkin's B-cell lymphoma. Office: Levy Lab Divsn Oncology 269 Campus Dr CCSR 1126 Stanford CA 94305-5151 Address: Stanford Sch Medicine 300 Pasteur Dr M207 Stanford CA 94305 Office Phone: 650-725-6452. Office Fax: 650-725-1420. E-mail: levy@stanford.edu.*

LEVY, S. WILLIAM, dermatologist, educator; b. San Francisco, Sept. 28, 1920; s. Joseph and Dora (Taylor) L.; m. Elisabeth Rellstab, Mar. 17, 1974; children: David Lewis, Ann Louise. BS, U. Calif., San Francisco, 1943, MD, 1949. Practice medicine specializing in dermatology, San Francisco; research dermatologist Biomechanics Lab., U. Calif., San Francisco; mem. staff Children's Hosp. of the Calif.-Pacific Med. Ctr., Mt. Zion Hosp. and Med. Center. Cons. to Letterman Army Hosp.; central med. adv. Calif. Blue Shield, San Francisco; clin. prof. dermatology U. Calif.; cons. in field. Author: Skin Problems of the Amputee, 1983; co-author: The Skin in Diabetes, 1986, Dermatology, 3rd edit., 1992, Dermatology in General Medicine, 5th edit., 1998, Atlas of Limb Prosthetics, 2d edit., 1992, 3d edit., 2004, Cutis, 1995, Biomechanics, 1999, In Motion-Amputee Coalition of America, 2000; lectr. on skin problems of amputees, skin problems of diabetics, landmines and effects on soc., 2001-03. Served with USN, 1943-46. Recipient Lehn and Fink Gold Medal award. Fellow Am. Acad. Dermatology (life, Gold medal); mem. San Francisco Dermatol. Soc. (pres.), Pacific Dermatologic Assn. (v.p.), AMA, Calif. Med. Assn. (sci. council 1977-84), San Francisco Med. Soc. Office: 136 S Eliseo Dr #210 Greenbrae CA 94904 Office Phone: 415-461-8620.

LEVY, SHAWN ANTHONY, writer; b. NYC, Oct. 22, 1961; s. Jerome Sanford and Agnes Madeline (Shand) L.; m. Mary Elizabeth Bartholemy, Dec. 30, 1985; children: Vincent Bartholemy Levy, Anthony Augustine Levy. BA, U. Pa., 1982; MFA, U. Calif., Irvine, 1985, MA, 1989. Assoc. editor Box Office Mag., LA, 1989-90; sr. editor Am. Film Mag., LA, 1990; film critic Portland Oregonian. Author: (books) King of Comedy: The Life and Art of Jerry Lewis, 1997, Rat Pack Confidential: Frank, Dean, Sammy, Peter, Joey and the Last Great Show Biz Party, 1998, Ready, Steady, Go! The Smashing Rise and Giddy Fall of Swinging London, 2003, The Last Playboy: The High Life of Porfirio Rubirosa, 2005. Office: Author Mail InkWell Mgmt 26th fl 521 Fifth Ave New York NY 10175*

LEVY, STANLEY HERBERT, lawyer; b. Phila., Apr. 11, 1922; s. Max and Rose (Cohen) L.; m. Gloria Kamber, Dec. 20, 1953; children: Steven M., Peter B. BA, Cornell U., 1943; LL.B., Harvard U., 1968, JD, 1968. Bar: N.Y. 1949, U.S. Dist. Ct. (ea. and so. dists.) N.Y., U.S. Treasury 1949, U.S. Supreme Ct. 1961. Practiced in N.Y.C., 1949—. Mem. Republican Town Com., Scarsdale, 1963-65, Temple Emanu-el, Westchester, N.Y. Served to 1st lt. F.A., AUS, 1943-47. Mem. Assn. Bar City N.Y., Confrérie des Chevaliers du Tastevin (officier commandeur), Commanderie de Bordeaux (comdr.), Harvard Club, Yale Club, Century Country Club (Purchase, N.Y.), Mashomack Fish and Game Preserve (Pine Plains, N.Y.). Home: 3 Richbell Rd Scarsdale NY 10583-4421 Office: 551 Fifth Ave New York NY 10176-0003 Office Phone: 212-672-1500 ext. 206. Business E-Mail: stanley@kamberllc.com.

LEVY, STEPHEN RAYMOND, retired data processing executive; b. Everett, Mass., May 4, 1940; s. Robert George and Lillian (Berfield) L.; m. Sandra Helen Rosen, Aug. 26, 1961; children: Phillip, Susan. BBA, U. Mass., 1961, LLD (hon.), 2001. Chmn. emeritus Bolt Beranek and Newman Inc., Cambridge, Mass., CEO, 1976—94; gen. ptnr. Levy Venture Ptnrs. LP; ret. Chmn. bd. dirs. Kaon Interactive Corp. Bd. dirs. Pharos LLC. Decorated Army Commendation medal. Mem. Am. Electronics Assn. (chmn. 1986), Mass. High Tech. Coun. (chmn. 1987-89), Mass. Network Comms. Coun. (chmn. 1996), Common Angels (chmn. 2004). Home: 300 Boylston St Apt 1204 Boston MA 02116-3940 Office: Levy Venture Ptnrs LP 20 Pk Plz Ste 436 Boston MA 02116-2322

LEVY, STUART B., molecular biologist, educator, science administrator, researcher; b. Wilmington, Del., Nov. 21, 1938; m. Cecile Pastel, 1983; 3 children. AB, Williams Coll., 1960; MD, U. Pa., 1965; Degree in Biology (hon.), Wesleyan U., 1998; Degree in Sci. (hon.), Des Moines U., 2001. Intern, med. resident Mt. Sinai Hosp., N.Y.C., 1965-67, rsch. fellow dept. cellular biology, 1966-67; from asst. prof. to assoc. prof. Tufts U., Boston, 1971-80, prof. medicine molecular biology & microbiology Med. Sch., 1980—; dir. Ctr. Adaptation Genetics & Drug Resistance, 1992—. Rsch. fellow dept. microbiology U. Milan, Italy, 1962, Keio U., Tokyo, 1964; publiker nutrition fellow Kenyatta Nat. Hosp., Nairobi, 1964; staff assoc. NIH, Italy, 1967-70, Pasteur Inst., Paris, 1976; fellow hematology New Eng. Med. Ctr., Boston, 1970-71; collaborator East African Viral Inst., Entebbe, Uganda, 1971; staff physician NE Med. Ctr. Hosp., Boston, 1976—; staff scientist Cancer Rsch. Ctr. Med. Sch. Tufts U., 1976—; sci. adv. Biomed. Rsch. Ctr. U. Nat. Pedro Henriquez Urena, Santa Domingo, Dominican Republic, 1977-83; cons. FDA, Washington, 1978-80, 85-87; adv. Fate of the Earth, Inc., 1981—; pres. Alliance for the Prudent Use of Antibiotics, 1981—, Boston Blood Club, 1984; overseas vis. Bd. Postgrad. Med. Edn. Royal Melbourne Hosp., Australia, 1983-84; gen. chmn. Int. Task Forces on Use of Antibiotics Worldwide Fogarty Int. Ctr. NIH, 1983-86; mem. subcom. Gram-Negative Facultatively Anaerobic Rods Am. Soc. Metals, 1985-88; subcom. health & antibiotic resistance EPA, 1988—; lectr. Am. Soc. Microbiology Found., 1989-90, Australian Soc. Microbiology, 1990—; mem. sci. evaluation com. Pasteur Inst., Paris, 1990; dir. Ctr. for adaptation genetics and Drug Resistance, Tufts U. Sch. Medicine. Mem. Am. Assn. Cancer Rsch., Am. Soc. Biochem. & Molecular Biology, Am. Soc. Clin. Investigation, Am. Soc. Hematology, Infectious Disease Soc. of Am., Am. Soc. Microbiology (collection com. on genetic & molecular microbiology 1986, mem. com. environ. microbiology 1989—, pres. 1998—, Hoechst-Roussel award 1995), Am Soc. Microbiology. Achievements include research in resistance to antibiotics and anticancer drugs. Office: Tufts U Sch Medicine Molecular Biology & Microbiology Dept 136 Harrison Ave Boston MA 02111-1817

LEVY, VALERY, publisher; b. Khartoum, Sudan, Feb. 16, 1946; came to U.S., 1959; d. Robert and Victorine (Malka) Braunstein; m. Joseph Levy, Aug. 24, 1968; children: Nomi, Berti. BA in Polit. Sci., Fairleigh Dickinson U., 1976, MA in Internat. Studies, 1978. Eng. tchr. Am. Inst. Cultural Affairs, Barcelona, 1965-66; Montessori tchr. Ft. Lee (N.J.) Community Ctr., 1974-81; project coord. Friends of Hebrew U., N.Y.C., 1981-83; devel. cons. Ft. Lee, 1983-85; editor, sr. editor Holt, Rinehart & Winston, N.Y.C., 1986-88; sr. editor, exec. editor Simon & Schuster Edn. Co., Morristown, Englewood, N.J., 1988-90; pres. Wonder Well Publishers, Ft. Lee, 1990-98; v.p., mng. editor Sch. divsn. McGraw-Hill, 1999—2001; assoc. pub. Macmillan-McGraw Hill, 2003—. Author: Alphabet Connections, 1990; editor: Room Of Mirrors, 1991.

LEVY, WENDY, psychologist; b. Sao Paulo, Brazil, Sept. 21, 1956; d. Merwin Ronald and Edith (Pressburger) L.; m. Leo Massarani, Sept. 4, 1993; children: Julian, Marcel. BA, Coll. William and Mary, 1978; MA, MEd, Columbia U., 1985; D of Psychology, Yeshiva U., 1995. Lic. psychologist, Conn. Dual diagnosis therapist Gracie Square Hosp., N.Y.C., 1991-94; psychologist Karen Horney Clinic, N.Y.C., 1992-94; intern Yale Sch. Medicine, New Haven, 1994-95; coord. domestic violence program Hill Health Ctr., New Haven, 1995-96; clin. instr., clin. supr. Yale Sch. Medicine, 1997—; pvt. practice Westport, Conn., 1998—. Mem. APA, Conn. Psychol. Assn. Avocations: choral singing, biking, hiking. Office: 31 Imperial Ave Westport CT 06880-4303 Office Phone: 203-221-8377. E-mail: wlevyma@hotmail.com.

LEVYN, THOMAS STANLEY, lawyer, former mayor; b. L.A., Apr. 2, 1949; s. Stanley Miles and Toni (March) L.; children: Adam, Stacy. BS in Bus., U. So. Calif., L.A., 1971, JD, 1974. Mng. ptnr. Agapay, Levyn & Halling, L.A., 1974—2004; mem. city council City of Beverly Hills, 1992—2003, vice mayor, 1995—96, 1998—99, mayor, 1996—97, 1999—2000, 2003—04; ptnr. Christensen, Miller, Fink, Jacobs, Glaser, Weil & Shapiro, L.A., 2004—. Judge trial advocacy program U. So. Calif. Law Ctr., 1982—83; landlord tenant settlement officer & judge pro tempore LA mcpl. ct., 1984—86. Bd. govs. Cedars Sinai Med. Ctr., L.A., 1986—, Beverly Hills Pub. Access Corp., 1989-92; bd. trustees, Temple Isaiah, 1991-92. Jewish. Avocations: golf, reading, listening well. Office: Chritensen Miller Fink Jacobs Glaser Weil & Shapiro LLP 10250 Constellation Blvd 19th Fl Los Angeles CA 90067 Office Phone: 310-282-6214. E-mail: tlevyn@chrismill.com.

LEW, JACOB, public administration educator; b. N.Y.C., Aug. 29, 1955; married; 2 children. AB, Harvard U., 1978; JD, Georgetown U., 1983. Bar: D.C., Mass. Legis. aide, Washington, 1973—75; prin. domestic policy advisor Spkr. Thomas P. O'Neill Jr. Ho. of Reps., 1979—87, asst. dir., then exec. dir. Dem. steering and policy com.; pvt. practice law, 1987—91; spl. asst. to pres. Office Mgmt. and Budget, Washington, 1993—94, exec. assoc. dir., assoc. dir. legis. affairs, 1995, dep. dir., 1995—98, dir., 1998—2001; vis. prof. Georgetown U. Pub. Policy Inst., 2001; exec. v.p. and prof. pub. admin. N.Y.U., 2001—. Exec. dir. Ctr. Mid. East Rsch. Dep. dir. office program analysis City of Boston Office Mgmt. and Budget, 1978; issues dir. Dem. Nat. Com. Campaign '88. Office: NYU Office of Exec VP 70 Washington Sq S Rm 1219 New York NY 10012*

LEW, LESLIE, artist; b. N.Y.C., Jan. 3, 1953; BFA, The Sch. of the Art Inst. of Chgo., 1981, postgrad., 1981—82. One-woman shows include Sensory Evolution Gallery, N.Y.C., 1985—86, Bernice Steinbaum Gallery, 1987, Margulies Taplin Gallery, Bay Harbor Island, Fla., 1990, OK Harris Gallery, N.Y.C., 1992, Vered Gallery, East Hampton, N.Y., 1992, Margulies Taplin Gallery, Miami, 1995, Light Gallery, L.A., 1996, Chappaqua Libr. Gallery, Chappaqua, NY, 2001, Hamilton Galleries, Santa Monica, Calif., 2003, Cilia Hirsch Gallery, Chappaqua, NY, 2003, exhibited in group shows at numerous, including Westchester Arts Coun., White Plains, N.Y., 2001, "Comic Release!"/Traveling Mus. Exhbn., Pitts., Pa., 2003—04, Represented in permanent collections various, including Bellevue Hosp., N.Y., Bank of Sicily, N.Y., Elektra Asylum Records, N.Y., Mayo Clinic, Minn., MCA Records, N.Y.; contbr. book The Best of Acrylic Painting, 1996, book The Best of Oil Painting, 1996. Grantee Pollack Krasner grant, N.Y., 1991, Rauchenberg grant, 1991. Studio: 628 Chappaqua Rd Briarcliff Manor NY 10510

LEW, ROGER ALAN, manufacturing executive; b. N.Y.C., Mar. 16, 1941; s. Louis Arthur and Estelle Bebe (Marcus) L.; m. Marilyn Drourr, May 29, 1962; children— William, Jeffrey, Richard. BS in Fin, NYU, 1963. With Franklin Nat. Bank, N.Y.C., 1963-66; sr. v.p. Security Nat. Bank, N.Y.C., 1966-75; v.p. NVF Co., N.Y.C., 1975-78, sr. v.p., 1978-81, treas., 1979-81; pres., dir. Wormuth Bros. Foundry, Inc., Athens, NY, 1981—2003, Richmond Builders LLC, Sag Harbor, NY, 2004—. Pres., bd. dirs. Mirage Fin., Inc., 1985-2003, transmission Gear Sales, Inc., 1985-2003; former sr. v.p., treas. Sharon Steel Corp., Pa. Engring. Corp., DWG Co., Southeastern Pub. Svc. Co.; former sr. v.p., treas., bd. dirs. Wilson Bros.; former mem. small bus. and agr. adv. coun. to N.Y. Fed. Res. Bank. Trustee, former exec. v.p. Universal Housing & Devel. Co.; former v.p. Security Mgmt. Corp. Served with U.S. Army, 1959-60. Mem. Am. Iron and Steel Inst. Clubs: Sag Harbor (N.Y.) Yacht. E-mail: mirage700@aol.com.

LEW, SALVADOR, radio station executive; b. Camajuani, Las Villas, Cuba, Mar. 6, 1929; s. Berko and Clara (Lewinowicz) Lew; 1 child, Esther Maria. JD magna cum laude, U. Havana, 1952. Editor Sch. Mural Newspaper, Camajuani, Cuba, 1941-43; pres. youth sect., nat. sect. Cuban People's Party, 1948-53; Lat. Am. cons. Waltes, Moore & Costanzo, Miami, 1961-72; news dir. Sta. WMIE and Sta. WQBA, Miami, 1961-70; gen. mgr., news dir. Sta. WRHC, Miami, 1973-89; host talk show, 1989—2001. Pres. adv. bd. Cuba Broadcasting, 1992—2001; dir. Office of Cuba Broadcasting, Radio & TV Marti, appointed by President Geroge W. Bush; sr. cons. Everet Clay Assocs., 1989—2001. Trustee, dir. United Way, 1985—. Recipient Lincoln Marti award, Sec. HEW, 1964, FBI award for cmty. svcs., 1983, cmty. svc. awards, various orgns. Mem.: Cuban Lawyers Assn., Exile. Jewish. Home: 2863 SW 23rd St Miami FL 33145-3309

LEW, SUSIE Q., nephrologist; b. N.Y.C., Oct. 28, 1954; married. BS Chemistry, Bklyn. Coll., 1976; MD, SUNY Downstate, Bklyn., 1979. Diplomate Am. Bd. Nephrology. Intership Medicine Brookdale, 1980, residency, 1982; fellowship nephrology Mt. Siani, N.Y., 1985; physician George Washington U., Washington, 1985—, prof. of medicine, 1999—. Contbr. articles on kidney disease and dialysis to profl. jours. Achievements include research in renal disease and dialysis. Office: George Washington U 2150 Pennsylvania Ave NW 4-425 Washington DC 20037 Office Phone: 202-741-2283.

LEWANDO, ALFRED GERARD, JR., oceanographer; b. Boston, Apr. 17, 1945; s. Alfred Gerard and Marie Helen (Coughlin) L.; m. Carol Ann Kologe, Nov. 8, 1969; children: Jennifer Ann, Christina Marie. BS in Earth Sci., State Coll. Boston, 1967; MBA, U. So. Miss., 1986, MS in Polit. Sci., 1989, MS in Pub. Rels., 1990, MEd in Adult Edn., 1991; grad., USAF Air War Coll., 2001. Lic. real estate broker and notary pub., Miss. Staff oceanographer Naval Oceanographic Office, Washington, 1967-76, head fleet support br., 1976-80, dir. tactical analysis div. Bay St. Louis, Miss., 1980-86, dir. oceanographic programs div., 1986-88; dep. asst. chief of staff for ops. Naval Oceanography Command, Stennis Space Ctr., Miss., 1988-94; asst. chief staff for command mgmt. and inspector gen. Naval Meteorology and Oceanography Command, Stennis Space Center, 1994-98; dir. ocean surveys dept. Naval Oceanographic Office, Stennis Space Ctr., 1998—; mem. policy bd. Ctr. of Higher Learning, Stennis Space Ctr., Miss., 1990—; sr. exec. fellow John F. Kennedy Sch. Govt. Harvard U., 1996; founder, pres. Navy Cares!, 1997—, HSA Gulf Coast, 1998—. Mem. adv. com. Cape Fear Jr. Coll., Wilmington, N.C., 1974—, Miss. State U. Rsch. Ctr., 1988—; mem. steering com. Summer Indsl. fellowships for Gulf Coast Tchrs., 1990—; mem. organizing com. 44th Internat. Sci. and Engring. Fair, 1993. Contbr. articles to profl. publs. Commr. City of Long Beach (Miss.) Port Authority, 1986—88; bd. dirs. United Way of South Miss., 1999—, 2000—. Sr. Exec. fellow Harvard U., 1996. Mem. Miss. Acad. Scis., Gamma Theta Upsilon. Home: 553 Mockingbird Dr Long Beach MS 39560-3134 Office: Naval Oceanographic Office Bay Saint Louis MS 39529 E-mail: aglewando@aol.com.

LEWANDOSKI, ROBERT HENRY, editor, publisher; b. N.Y.C., Jan. 21, 1951; BA, Pace U., N.Y.C., 1972. Editor, pub. The Former Presidents Quar., RHL Enterprises, Fullerton, Calif., 1993—; freelance author Model Ship Builder, Cedarburg, Wis., 1981-92. Avocations: model ship building, autograph collecting. Office: RHL Enterprises PO Box 6443 Fullerton CA 92834-6443

LEWANDOWSKI, ANDREW ANTHONY, utilities executive, consultant; b. Kiel, Germany, Nov. 29, 1946; arrived in US, 1949; s. Kazimierz and Emily (Lewandowski) L.; m. Mary Ann Zuza; 1 child, Adam Christopher. Student, Rutgers U., 1964-66; BS in Mech. Engring., N.J. Inst. Tech., 1969; postgrad., Pa. State U., 1969-70; MS in Mech. Engring., N.J. Inst. Tech., 1973. Registered profl. engr., N.J.; cert. profl. planner, N.J. NSF trainee N.J. Inst. Tech., 1970-72; Engr. I DeLeuw, Cather & Co., Newark, 1970; from gas utilities engr. to chief specifications DeLeuw, Cather & Co. of NY, Inc., NYC, 1972—75; from supv. engr. to mgr. planning, budgets Elizabethtown Gas Co., Iselin, NJ, 1976—86, internal cons., computer mgmt. Elizabeth, N.J., 1986-87, internal cons. ops., engring. Iselin, N.J., 1987-89, from internal cons. engring., budgets to sr. planning engr. Union, NJ, 1989—98, sr. planning engr. Stewartsville, 2004; sys. adminstr. NUI/Utility Bus. Svcs., Union, NJ, 1998-99, mgr. applications, 2000—04; sr. engr. AGLR/Elizabethtown Gas Co., Union, 2004—. Editor Jaycee newsletter, 1979-80, local Rep. newsletter, 1986; monthly contbr. Film Score Monthly, 1993-97. Den leader, asst. cubmaster Cub Scouts Boy Scouts Am., sec. troop com., merit badge counselor; active various local govt. religious, polit. and charitable orgns. Recipient Dir. of Yr. award South Plainfield Jaycees, 1972, Disting. Svc. award, 1975, Outstanding Young Man of Yr. award N.J. Jaycees, 1975, South Plainfield Jaycees, 1976, den leader award Boy Scouts Am. 1994; inducted into South Plainfield H.S. Hall of Fame, 1997. Mem. NSPE, ASME, KC, South Plainfield Polish Nat. Home, The Film Music Soc. Republican. Roman Catholic. Home: 1910 Murray Ave South Plainfield NJ 07080-4713 Office: AGLR/Elizabethtown Gas Co 520 Green Ln Union NJ 07083 Personal E-mail: el_cid@att.net.

LEWANDOWSKI, E. DOUGLAS, medical educator; b. 1957; BA, U. Chgo., 1979; MS, U. Ill., 1982; PhD, U. Tex., Dallas. Asst. prof. medicine Baylor Coll. Medicine, Houston, 1986—91; asst. prof. radiology Harvard Med. Sch. and Mass. Gen. Hosp., Boston, 1991—96, assoc. prof. oradiology, 1996—2000; prof. Coll. of Medicine U. Ill., Chgo., 2000—. Dir. Program in Integrative Cardiac Metabolism, Chgo., 2000—. Recipient Young Investigator award, Soc. for Magnetic Resonance in Medicine, 1990, MERIT Award, Nat. Heart Lung and Blood Inst., 2003; grantee, Nat. Heart Lung and Blood Inst./NIH, 1993—, 1996—, 1999—; Argonne Nat. Lab. scholar, U. Chgo., 1975—79. Fellow: Am. Heart Assn.; mem.: AAAS, Internat. Soc. Heart Rsch. (coun. mem. 2003—), Internat. Soc. Magnetic Resonance in Medicine (study group chmn. 1996—97). Achievements include research in Carbon-13 isotope kinetics and nuclear magnetic resonance (NMR) evaluations of heart disease. Office: U Ill Chgo Coll Medicine Dept Physiology MC901 Chicago IL 60612

LEWCOCK, RONALD BENTLEY, architect, educator; b. Brisbane, Australia, Sept. 27, 1929; s. Harry Kingsley and Ena (Orrock) L.; m. Barbara Sansoni, Aug. 8, 1981. Student, U. Queensland, 1947-49; BArch, Cape Town U., South Africa, 1951; PhD, U. Cape Town, South Africa, 1961; MA, Cambridge U., Eng., 1970; DArch (hon.), Natal U., South Africa, 1999. Pvt. practice architecture, 1951—; Whitehead research fellow Clare Hall, Cambridge U., Eng., 1970-72, ofcl. fellow, 1976-84; research officer Middle East Centre, Cambridge U., Cambridge, 1973-80; Aga Khan prof. architecture for Islamic culture, dir. program in architecture for Islamic socs. MIT, Cambridge, 1984-91; chmn. Aga Khan program for Islamic architecture MIT and Harvard U., 1985-87; prof. architecture Ga. Inst. Tech., Atlanta, 1991—. Cons. UNESCO, 1978-98, Habitat, World Bank, British Coun., Am. Rsch. Ctrl., Egypt, 1978-83; lectr. U. Natal, 1952-57, sr. lectr., 1958-69; lectr., examiner Cambridge U., 1973-85; unit leader design in developing world Archtl. Assn., London, 1977-81; lectr. Archtl. Assocs. Sch., London, 1971-82; vis. prof. grad. sch. architecture Ga. Inst. Tech., 1979-84, Harvard, 1984, Louvain U., 1984; vis. Aga Khan prof., MIT, 1991-93, UQT, Australia, 1996. Author: Early 19th Century Architecture in South Africa, 1963, Traditional Architecture in Kuwait and the Northern Gulf, 1978, 2d edit. 81, Wadi Hadramawt and the Walled City of Shibam, 1986, The Old World City of San'a', 1986, The Architecture of an Island—Sri Lanka, 1998; editor: (with R.B. Serjeant) San'a' an Arabian Islamic City, 1983; contbr. articles to profl. jours., Architecture in the Islamic World, 1976, New Grove Dictionary of Music and Musicians, 1980, 97. Mem. coun. Inst. History and Archaeology East Africa, London, 1976-86, Middle East Centre, Cambridge, Eng., 1981-88, British Sch. Archaeology in Jerusalem, London, 1981-98; tech. coord. Internat. Campaign for the Conservation of Sana'a in Yemen Arab Rep. and Shibam and Wadi Hadramaut in Peoples Dem. Rep. of Yemen, 1978-93, UNESCO/UNDP Campaign for Conservation of Monuments and Cities in Uzbekistan, 1994-97; steering com. mem. Aga Khan award, 1990-93, Aga Khan Trust for Culture, Geneva, 1993—. Eliza Howard vis. fellowship Columbia U., 1963. Mem. Royal Inst. Brit. Archs. (assoc.). Office: Georgia Inst of Technology 225 North Ave NW Atlanta GA 30332-0002 also: 13 Norwich St Cambridge CB2 1ND England

LEWELLEN, WILBUR GARRETT, management educator, consultant; b. Charleroi, Pa., Jan. 21, 1938; s. Anthony Garrett and Cozie Harriett (Watson) L.; m. Jean Carolyn Vanderlip, Dec. 8, 1962 (div. 1982); children— Stephen G., Jocelyn A., Jonathan W., Robyn E.; m. Eloise Evelyn Vincent, Mar. 5, 1983 BS, Pa. State U., University Park, 1959; MS, MIT, Cambridge, 1961, PhD, 1967; LhD (hon.), Budapest U. of Econ. Scis., 1996. Asst. prof. mgmt. Purdue U., West Lafayette, Ind., 1964-68, assoc. prof. mgmt., 1968-72, prof., 1972-83, Loeb prof. mgmt., 1983-88, Krannert disting. prof. mgmt., 1988—, dir. exec. edn. programs West Lafayette, Ind., 1985—. Cons. Bank Am., San Francisco, 1975—90, Ind. Bell Tel. Co., Indpls., 1976—90, Am. Water Works Co., Wilmington, Del., 1978—94, Indpls. Power and Light Co., 1993—99, NiSource, Inc., 2000—; bd. dirs. Indsl. Dielectrics, Inc. Author: Executive Compensation in Large Industrial Corporations, 1968, Ownership Income of Management, 1971, The Cost of Capital, 1981, Financial Management: An Introduction to Principles and Practice, 2000. Recipient Salgo-Noren award as Outstanding Tchr. in Grad. Profl. Programs, Salgo-Noren Found., 1973, 77, 79, 84. Mem. AAUP, Fin. Mgmt. Assn. (v.p. 1973-74), Am. Fin. Assn., Western Fin. Assn., Lafayette Country Club. Methodist. Office: Purdue Univ Grad Sch Mgmt West Lafayette IN 47907 Office Phone: 765-494-4493.

LEWENSTEIN, BRUCE VOSS, science historian; b. Palo Alto, Calif., Sept. 18, 1957; s. Harry and Marion (Marcus) L.; m. Claudia Voss, May 29, 1983; children: Joel, Gabriel, Ari. AB, U. Chgo., 1980; MA, U. Pa., 1985, PhD, 1987. Chief researcher U.S. News Books, Washington, 1980-82; advt. copywriter SS&W, McLean, Va., 1982-83; editorial coord. History of Sci. Soc., Phila., 1983-85; pub. edn. officer Ctr. for History of Chemistry, Phila., 1985-87; asst. prof. dept. communication, dept. sci. & tech. studies Cornell U., Ithaca, N.Y., 1987-93, assoc. prof., 1993—. Cons. in field. Editor: Public

Understanding of Sci., 1998-2003, When Science Meets the Public, 1992; contbr. numerous articles to profl. jours. Recipient Disting. Tech. Communication award Soc. for Tech. Communication, 1986. Fellow AAAS; mem. Assn. for Edn. in Journalism and Mass Communication, Forum for History of Sci. in Am., History of Sci. Soc., Nat. Assn. Sci. Writers, Soc. for Social Studies of Sci. Office: Cornell Univ 321 Kennedy Hall Ithaca NY 14853-4203

LEWENT, JUDY CAROL, pharmaceutical executive; b. Jan. 13, 1949; BA, Goucher Coll., 1970; MS in Mgmt., MIT, 1972. With corp. fin. dept. E.F. Hutton & Co., Inc., 1972—74; asst. v.p. for strategic planning Bankers Trust Co., 1974—75; sr. fin. analyst corp. planning Norton Simon, 1975—76; divsn. contr. Pfizer, Inc., 1976—80; dir. acquisitions and capital analysis Merck & Co., Inc., Whitehouse Station, NJ, 1980—83, asst. contr., 1983—85, exec. dir. fin. evaluation and analysis, 1985—87, v.p., treas., 1987—90, v.p. fin., CFO, 1990—92, sr. v.p., CFO, 1993—2001, exec. v.p., CFO, 2001—02, exec. v.p., CFO, pres., human health Asia, 2003—. Bd. dirs. Dell Inc., Motorola Inc., Nat. Bur. Econ. Rsch.; life mem. MIT Corp.; trustee Rockefeller Family Trust. Mem. exec. com. Penn Medicine. Mem.: Am. Acad. Arts and Scis. Office: Merck & Co Inc PO Box 100 One Merck Dr Whitehouse Station NJ 08889-0100

LEWIN, BETSY R., illustrator; b. Pa., May 12, 1937; m. Ted B. Lewin. Grad., Pratt Inst. Illustrator: Itchy, Itchy Chicken Pox, 1992, Ho, Ho, Ho: The Complete Book of Christmas Words, 1993, Somebody Catch My Homework, 1993, Mattie's Little Possum Pet, 1993, Yo, Hungry Wolf, 1995, The Classroom Pet, 1995, My Tooth is About to Fall Out, 1995, A Thousand Cousins, 1996, Recess Mess, 1996, No Such Thing, 1997 (SLJ Honor Book, 1997, Bulletin for Ctr. on Childrens Books Blue Ribbon, Nebr. Golden Sower award), Snake Alley Band, 1998, Araminta's Paint Box, 1998, The Class Trip, 1999, Aunt Minnie McGrannahan, 1999, Click, Clack, Moo: Cows That Type, 2000 (N.Y.. Times best-seller, Soc. Illustrators Original Art, 2000, Caldecott Honor, 2003), Purrfectly Purrfect, 2000, Promises, 2000, Is It Far To Zanzibar?, 2000 (Parents Choice Gold award, 2000), Dumpy La Rue, 2001 (10 Best Illustrated Books N.Y. Times, 2001), A Houseful of Christmas, 2001, Giggle, Giggle, Quack, 2002, Aunty Minnie and the Twister, 2002, Two Eggs Please, 2003, Duck for President, 2004, author, illustrator: Booby Hatch, 1995, Walk a Green Path, 1995, What's the Matter Habibi?, 1997, Animal Snackers, 2004, co-author with Ted Lewin and illustrator: Gorilla Walk, 1999 (Smithsonian Notable Books, 1999, NSTA CB Outstanding Sci. Trade Book, 2000, N.Y. Pub. Libr. Children's Books, 1999), Elephant Quest, 2000 (NSTA CBC Outstanding Sci. Trade Book, 2001, John Burroughs award for outstanding nature book for young readers); exhibitions include Bklyn. Pub. Libr., N.Y., 2004, Children's Mus. Manhattan, 2004. Avocation: travel. Office: c/o Simon & Schuster Childrens Pub 1230 Ave of the Americas New York NY 10020

LEWIN, KLAUS JONATHAN, pathologist, educator; b. Jerusalem, Aug. 10, 1936; came to U.S., 1968; s. Bruno and Charlotte (Nawratzki L.; m. Patricia Coutts Milne, Sept. 25, 1964; children: David, Nicola, Bruno. Attended, King's Coll. U. London, 1954-55; MB, BS, Westminster Med. Sch. London, Eng., 1959; MD, U. London, 1966. Diplomate Am. Bd. Pathology, Royal Coll. Pathologists (London), lic. Calif. Casualty officer Westminster Med. Hosp., 1960; resident Westminster Hosp. Med. Sch., London, 1960-68; pediatric house physician Westminster Hosp. Med. Sch., Westminster Children's Hosp., 1961; house physician St. James Hosp., Balham, London, 1961; asst. prof. pathology Stanford (Calif.) U., 1979-86; assoc. prof. pathology UCLA, L.A., 1977-80, vice chmn. dept. pathology, 1970-86; attending physician Dept. Medicine Gastroenterology divsn. UCLA-Wadsworth VA Hosp., 1978—; prof. pathology UCLA Med. Sch., 1980—2002, prof. dept. medicine divsn. gastroenterology, 1986—2002; dir. divsn. surg. pathology UCLA Ctr. Health Scis., 1986-95, mem. diagnostic surg. pathology svc., dir. divsn. liver, pancreas and gastrointestinal pathology, 1996—2002. Resident pathologist clinical chemistry, bacteriology, hematology, blood transfusion, serology, Westminster Hosp. Med. Sch., 1961-62, registrar dept. morbid anatomy, 1962-64, rotating sr. registrar morbid anatomy, Royal Devon, Exeter Hosp., 1964-68; vis. asst. prof. pathology, Stanford U. Med. Sch., 1968-70; vice chmn. pathology UCLA, L.A., 1979-86; pres. L.A. Soc. Pathologists Inc., 1985-86; mem. curriculum com. U. Calif. Riverside, 1977-84; cons. Wadsworth VA Hosp., L.A., carcinoma of esophagus intervention study, Polyp Prevention study, Nat. Cancer Inst., Cancer Preservation Studies br., Bethesda, Md.; chief gastrointestinal liver/pancreas sect. surg. pathology; rschr. structure, function, pathologic disorders of gastrointestinal tract and liver; vis. prof. U. Leeds, Eng., Porto Alegre, Brazil, Nat. Cancer Inst., Washington, 1999. Co-author (Riddel R., Weinstein W.): Gastrointestinal Pathology and Its Clinical Implications, 1992; co-author: (Henry Appelman) Atlas of Tumor Pathology: Tumors of the Esophagus and Stomach, 1997; editl. bd. Human Pathology, 1986—, Am. Jour. Surg. Pathology, 1990—, reviewer Gastroenterology and Archives of Pathology; contbr. 170 papers, 80 abstracts, 26 book chpts., 250 invited lectures. Recipient Chesterfield medal Inst. Dermatology, London, 1966; named Arris and Gale lectr. Royal Coll. Surgeons, London, 1968; Welcome Trust Rsch. grantee, 1968; fellow Found. Promotion Cancer Rsch., Tokyo, 1992. Fellow Royal Coll. Pathologists (Eng.); mem. Pathological Soc. Great Britain, Am. Gastroenterology Soc., Gastrointestinal Pathology Soc. (founder, pres. 1985-86, exec. com., edn. com. 1990-99), U.S. Acad. Pathology, Can. Acad. Pathology, Assn. Clin. Pathologists, Pathological and Bacteriological Soc. Great Britain, Internat. Acad. Pathology, L.A. Pathology Soc. (bd. dirs.), Calif. Soc. Pathology (edn. com. 1983—), So. Calif. Soc. Gastrointestinal Endoscopy, Arthur Purdy Stout Soc., Gastrointestinal Pathology Soc. (pres., by-laws com., chmn. edn. com., exec. com.). Avocations: travel, geographic pathology, hiking, swimming. Home: 333 Las Casas Ave Pacific Palisades CA 90272-3307 Office: UCLA Sch Medicine Dept Pathology 10833 Le Conte Ave Los Angeles CA 90095-3075

LEWIN, NANCY S., actress; d. Derek Jonathan Lewin and Harriet Ria Lihs. BA in Humanities, U. Calif., Berkeley, 1988, MA in History, 1989; voice cert., John Ford Sch. Voice, 1992. Musician various bands, San Francisco, 1986—94; cons. Fore-1, San Francisco, 1992—2002; actress, model Wilhelmina Scouting Network, Houston, 2003. Contbr. poetry to anthologies; composer: (songs) Music Folios I and II, 2000; musician, performer: benefits Amnesty Internat., 2000, musician, performer: S.E. Texans Organized for Peace. Mem. ACLU, Beaumont, 2003—. Mem.: Inst. Noetic Sci., Nat. Mus. Women in Arts, The Art Studio, Inc., Beaumont Art League. Achievements include discovery of answer to Einstein's theory of relativity; invention of Synopses. Avocations: exhibiting art, poetry, bicycling, metaphysics. Office: Starseed Rear Apt 612 Elgie St Beaumont TX 77705 E-mail: nlewin@gt.rr.com.

LEWIN, PETER ANDREW, electrical engineer, educator; b. Oct. 27, 1945; BSc and MSc, U. Denmark, 1969, PhD, 1979. Project leader Bruel & Kjaer Naerum, Copenhagen, Denmark, 1969-78; project mgr. Danish Inst. Biomed. Engring., Copenhagen, 1978-80; rsch. fellow U. Denmark, 1980-83; prof. dept. elec. and computer engr. Drexel U., 1983—, Richard B. Beard disting. prof. Fellow IEEE (mem. tech. com. IEEE Ultrasonics Symposium 1985, mem. stds. subcom. on ultrasonics, sensors, session chmn. IEEE Ultrasonics Symposia, session chmn./organizer, Lithotripsy, Engring. in Medicine and Biology conf. 1990, co-chmn. med. ultrasound track EMBS conf. 1990, co-chmn. indsl. exhibits com. EMBS conf. 1990, co-editor IEEE Med. Ultrasound Parameter Measurement Guide 1984-88, reviewer IEEE Transactions, co-editor spl. issue IEEE Transactions on Ultrasonics, Frequency and Frequency Control 1988), Acoustical Soc. Am., Am. Inst. Ultrasound in Medicine. Office: Drexel U Dept Electrical & Computer Eng Philadelphia PA 19104

LEWIN, RALPH ARNOLD, biologist; b. London, Apr. 30, 1921; came to U.S., 1947; s. Maurice and Ethel Lewin; m. Joyce Mary Chismore, June, 1950 (div. 1965); m. Cheng Lanna, June 3, 1969. BA, Cambridge U., Eng., 1942, MA, 1946; PhD, Yale U., 1950; ScD, Cambridge U., Eng., 1973. Instr. Yale U., New Haven, Conn., 1951-52; sci. officer Nat. Rsch. Coun., Halifax, N.S., Can., 1952-55; ind. investigator NIH, Woods Hole, Mass., 1956-59; from assoc. prof. to prof. U. Calif., La Jolla, 1960—. Editor: Physiology and Biochemistry of Algae, 1962, Genetics of Algae, 1976, Biology of Algae, 1979, Biology of Women, 1981, Origins of Plastids, 1993, Internacia Vortaro de Mikroba Genetiko, 1994; co-editor: Prochloron, a microbial enigma, 1989; transl. Winnie-La-Pu (Esperanto), 1972, La Dektri Horlogoj, 1993, Merde, 1999, Abacus & Swallows, 2000, Poems on Politics, Pollution and Religion, 2003, Blue Green, 2003. Served with British Army, 1943-46. Mem. Phycological Soc. Am. (pres. 1970-71, Darbaker prize 1963). Avocations: Esperanto, recorders, badminton. Office: U Calif San Diego Scripps Instn Oceanography 9500 Gilman Dr La Jolla CA 92093-0202 Business E-Mail: rlewin@ucsd.edu.

LEWIN, ROBERT, lawyer; b. NYC, July 11, 1952; BA with honors, Johns Hopkins Univ., 1974; JD, NYU, 1977. Bar: NY 1978. Ptnr., insurance/reinsurance litig. Stroock & Stroock & Lavan LLP, NYC, chmn., pro bono com. Arbitrator Reinsurance Assn. Am. Mem.: ABA, Assn. Internationale de Droit des Assurances, Assn. Bar City NY, NY Lawyers for Pub. Interest (bd. dir.). Office: Stroock & Stroock & Lavan LLP 180 Maiden Ln New York NY 10038-4982 Office Phone: 212-806-5643. Office Fax: 212-806-6006. Business E-Mail: rlewin@stroock.com.

LEWIN, STANTON MORRIS, advertising executive; b. Chgo., Feb. 27, 1959; s. Philip M. and Judith (Langert) L.; m. Terri L. Sugarman, Nov. 12, 1988; children: Alexa, Matthew. BS in Advt., U. Ill., 1981. Account exec. The Schram Co., Chgo., 1982-83; sr. account exec. Jacobs & Clevenger, Chgo., 1984; account supr. Bozell, Jacobs, Kenyon and Eckhardt, Chgo., 1985-87; v.p. Stone & Adler, Chgo., 1988-91; chmn. LKH&S, Chgo., 1992—. Avocations: astronomy, science, golf, computers, reading. Home: 1239 Hohlfelder Rd Glencoe IL 60022-1020 Office: LKH&S 360 N Michigan Ave Chicago IL 60601-3806

LEWINS, STEVEN, financial analyst, investment company executive, legislative staff member, retired military officer; b. N.Y.C., Jan. 22, 1943; s. Bruno and Kaethe (Czhoeck) L.; m. Rayna Lee Kornreich, July 4, 1968 (div. 1991); children: Shani Nicole, Scott Asher. BA, Queens Coll., CUNY, 1964, MA in Diplomatic-Econ. History, 1966; postgrad. in pub. adminstrn., NY-SCSC, SUNY, 1967; MBA, CUNY, 1972; postgrad. in info. tech., U. Va., 1979. Park ranger, historian Nat. Park Svc., Statue of Liberty, N.Y.C., 1964-66; traffic asst. AT&T, White Plains, N.Y., 1966; adminstrv. intern N.Y. State, Albany, 1966-67; asst. to commr. N.Y. State Narcotics Addiction Control Commn., N.Y.C., 1967—69; security analyst Value Line Investment Survey, N.Y.C., 1969-71, assoc. rsch. dir., 1971-74, rsch. dir., directing editor, 1975-80; creator Value Line Fin. Database, N.Y.C., 1974; v.p. Arnold Bernhard & Co., N.Y.C., 1975-80, dir., 1976-80, mem. exec. com., 1977-80; ptnr. Ray-Lux Products, N.Y.C., 1978-80; pres. RayLux Assocs., N.Y.C., 1980-81, dir., 1980-86. Founder RayLux Fin. Svc., 1980 (1st SEC-registered electronic investment adv. svc., dissolved 1986); v.p. unit head investment divsn. Citibank N.A., 1981-86, v.p. Citicorp Investment Mgmt., Inc., 1986-88; v.p. transp. and aerospace investment mgmt; chancellor Capital Mgmt., 1988-92; mng. dir., rsch. dir., head of equity First Capital Advisers/F.C. Fin. Svcs., N.Y.C., 1992-93; v.p. Investment Rsch. Gruntal & Co., Inc., 1994-2000; adv. corp. disclosure com. SEC, 1977-78, ICC, 1982-92, Dept. Transp., 1982-2000, interval funds investment cons., 1997-2000, Dept. Justice, 1982-92, 95-96, 2003, Dept. State, 1986-92, Surface Transp. Bd. Legal Panel, 1996-97; advisor surface transport. bd., 1965-2000, Fed. Res. Bd., 1996-2000, 2003, dept. treasury, 2003, infrastructure com. U.S. Ho. of Reps., 1997-2000, Summit Bank, 1998-2000; spkr. security analysis, econs., transp., aerospace, def., corp. disclosure, deregulation, air traffic control, terrorism and airline safety, fin. data svcs., U.S. megatrends, USSR Glastnost and Perestroika, C.I.S. resurgent economy. Author: Fashoda Crisis of 1898, 1966, Knowing Your Common Stocks, 1979, The Social Overhaul of the USSR, 1986, Economic Reform in the U.S.S.R., 1990, USA: 21st Century World Transportation Crossroads, 1994, U.S. Needs World-Class Transportation System, 1994, Transports as Economic Indicators, 1995, The New Union Pacific, 1996, Transportation Trends into the 21st Century, 1996, The Global Terrorist Threat, 1996, The Boeing Company: Firing on All Cylinders, 1997, U.S. Transportation "Consolidations" and "Surprise," 1997, Secular Trends in Global Transportation, 1997; co-author: (with Parkanskii) US-USSR Summit Agenda, 1995, (with Bogdanov and Bobrakov) US-USSR Anti-International Terrorist Protocol, 1989, Rights of Terrorists, 1990, (with Semenov) US-USSR Sub-Orbital Space Cooperation, 1990; editor: Megatrends, 1980, Witch Doctor of Wall Street, 1990; creator Global Transportation and Orbital Space Transport Investment Trust, Gruntal & Co., L.L.C., 1998-2000. Participant U.S.-USSR Emigration/Jackson Vanek, 1984-91, U.S.-USSR Pan Am.-Aeroflot Aviation Agreement, 1985, USSR Student Exch., 1985-86, U.S.-USSR Anti-Internat. Terrorism, 1985-91, U.S.-USSR Rights of Terrorists, 1985, U.S.-USSR Trans-Siberian-CSX Corp. Initiative, 1989, TRW, Inc-Energia N.P.O. Look Down Satellite Agreement, 1989-90, U.S.-USSR Sub-Orbital Space Coop. Agreement, 1989-90, U.S.-USSR Def. Conv. Projects, 1990-93, Reagan-Gorbachev Summit Preparations, 1986, 87, 88, Bush-Gorbachev Summit Preparations, 1990, U.S.-USSR AMR Corp.-Aeroflot Bilateral Discussion, 1989, U.S.-USSR Spl. Mission/Secure Info. Negotiation, 1983-92, U.S.-Japan airline bilateral negotiation, 1996, CSX Corp./CIS indsl. negotiation, 1996-97; sponsor U.S.-USSR Pace U., rsch. exch., 1990; Citicorp liaison USSR mission to UN, 1982-88, Inst. U.S. and Can., Acad. Scis. USSR, 1985-88, econs. dept. Acad. Scis. USSR, 1988; liaison Chancellor Capital Mgmt., USSR, 1988-92; overseas fact-finding visits include Saudi Arabia, Egypt, Jordan, Israel, 1979, Peoples Republic of China, Japan, Hong Kong, 1981, USSR, 1985, 86, 89, 90, Georgia SSR, 1985, 90, Uzbekistan SSR, 1986, Baykhal, Irkutsk, Olha, Siberia, 1989, Kazakhstan SSR, Republic of Georgia, Baykonour-Soyuz Launch Ctr., 1990, Bangkok, Thailand, 1988, Rio de Janeiro, Brazil, 1990, Athens, Greece, 1998, Constantinople, Turkey, 1998; mem. Croton-on-Hudson Narcotics Guidance Coun., 1972-75, Cortland Indsl. Com., 1975-77; dist. leader Dem. Party, 1979-83; founding mem. Challenger Found., 1987, Nat. Space Mus., Dalles, Tex., 1998. Acting col. Secure Information Negotiation, USAF, Mil. Airlift Command, Baikonour, Kazakhstan, 1990, brigadier, 1999—. Recipient Commendation citations for Gulf War, 1992, Reagan-Gorbachev Summit preparartions and diplomatic achivements, 1990, USSR Supreme Soviet Red Bannerr election for 50th birthday anniversary award in svc. to USSR for peace, 1990. Fellow Fin. Analyst Fedn.; mem. N.Y. Soc. Security Analysts (sr. security analyst, membership com., computer applications symposium, airline splinter group, motor carrier splinter group, aerospace splinter group), Bus. Economists Coun., Washington Transp. Roundtable, Assn. Computer Users, Internat. Platform Assn., N.Y. Assn. Bus. Economists, Nat. Assn. Bus. Economists, Nat. Planetary Soc., Nat. Space Soc., Nat. Air and Space Mus., Nat. Air and Space Soc. (founding mem. 1998), Tau Delta Phi (pres. 1963, 64, Undergrad. of Yr. 1963, Spl. Student Senate Recognition 1964, Coll. Distinction medal French 1964). Democrat. Home: 66 Grand St Croton On Hudson NY 10520-2519 E-mail: sniwelist@aol.com.

LEWIS, ALAN JAMES, pharmaceutical executive, pharmacologist; b. Newport Gwent, UK; BSc, Southampton U., Hampshire, 1967; PhD in Pharmacology, U. Wales, Cardiff, 1970. Postdoctoral fellow biomedical sci. U. Guelph, Ont., Can., 1970-72; rsch. assoc. lung rsch. ctr. Yale U., 1972-73; sr. pharmacologist Organon Labs., Ltd., Lanarkshire, Scotland, 1973-79; rsch. mgr. immunoinflammation Am. home products Wyeth-Ayerst Rsch., Princeton, N.J., 1979-82, assoc. dir. exptl. therapeutics, 1982-85, dir., 1985-87, asst. v.p., 1987-89, v.p. rsch., 1989-93; pres. Signal Pharms. Inc., San Diego, 1994-96, pres., CEO, 1996-2000; pres. signal rsch. divsn. Celgene Corp., 2000—. Editor allergy sect. Agents & Internat. Archives Pharmacodynamics Therapy; reviewer Jour. Pharmacology Exptl. Therapy, Biochemical Pharmacology, Can. Jour. Physiol. Pharmacology, European Jour. Pharmacology, Jour. Pharm. Sci. Mem. Am. Soc. Pharmacological and Exptl. Therapeutics, Am. Rheumatism Assn., Mid-Atlantic Pharmacology Soc. (v.p. 1991-93, pres. 1993-94), Pulmonary Rsch. Assn., Inflammation Rsch. Assn. (pres. 1986-88), Pharm. Mfrs. Assn., Internat. Assn. Inflammation Socs. (pres. 1990-95), Bio Bd. Achievements include research in mechanisms and treatment of inflammatory diseases including arthritis and asthma cardiovascular diseases, metabolic disorders, central nervous system diseases, osteoporosis and viral diseases. Office: Celgene Signal Research 4550 Towne Centre Ct San Diego CA 92121-1900 E-mail: alewis@signalpharm.com.

LEWIS, ALAN LAIRD, academic administrator; m. Barbara George Lewis; children: Evan George, Keith Durland. BS in optometry, Mass. Coll. of Optometry, 1965, OD, 1970; MSc, PhD, Ohio State U., 1971. Prof. SUNY, New York, NY, 1972—91; dean Mich. Coll. Optometry, Big Rapids, Mich., 1991—99; pres. New England Coll. Optometry, Boston, 1999—. Pres. Assn. Sch. Coll. Optometry, 1998—99, US Nat. Com., 1996—99, Illuminating Engring. Soc., 2005—. Capt. USN, 1965—95. Fellow, Am. Acad. Optometry, 1972, Illuminating Engring. Soc., 1991. Office Phone: 617-266-2030. Office Fax: 617-424-9202.

LEWIS, ALBERT B., lawyer; b. N.Y.C., Oct. 16, 1925; children: David, Eric, Jonathan; m. Leila Stein, Oct. 6, 1987. BA, Bklyn. Coll., 1948; LLB, St. John's U., 1954. Bar: N.Y. 1954, U.S. Dist. Ct. (so. and ea. dists.) N.Y.; CPA, N.Y. Sec. to Hon. James S. Brown N.Y. Supreme Ct, Kings County, N.Y., 1962-67; mem. N.Y. State Senate, Albany, 1967-78; supt. N.Y. Ins. Dept., N.Y.C., 1978-83; ptnr. Bower & Gardner, N.Y.C., 1983—. Author: Danger: Insurance Fraud in Progress, 1987, Gotcha, Swindles, Frauds, Ripoffs. With U.S. Army, 1944-46. Home: 1025 5th Ave New York NY 10028-0134 Office: D'Amato & Lynch 70 Pine St New York NY 10270

LEWIS, AMY BETH, newswriter, reporter, writer, photographer; b. Silver Creek, N.Y., Dec. 12, 1964; d. Jon Michael Lewis and Elizabeth Jean Chodacki-Berns, Mary Lewis (Stepmother) and Charles Johnson (Stepfather); life ptnr. Michael Ohl. Degree in Comm. and Media Arts, Erie C.C. South, 2000. Supr. sheltered workshop Suburban Adult Services, Inc., Sardina, NY, 1996—98; sec., receptionist William Shoemaker Associates, Inc., Hamburg, 1996—98. Reading tutor Erie C.C., Boston, 1999—2001; writer-reporter, freelance photographer Dunkirk Observer, 2000—03. Author of poems. Orgnl. mem. Bus. and Profl. Women, Silver Creek, NY, 2001—02. Recipient Outstanding News Writing, Irving-Chautauqua County C. of C., 2002. Avocations: horseback riding, gardening, creative writing, travel, movies. Office: Dunkirk Observer 10 East Second St Dunkirk NY 14048-1602

LEWIS, ANDRÉ LEON, artistic director; b. Hull, Que., Can., Jan. 16, 1955; s. Raymond Lincoln and Theresa Lewis. Student, Classical Ballet Studio, Ottawa, Royal Winnipeg (Man.) Ballet Sch., 1975; studies with David Moroni, Arnold Spohr, Rudi van Dantzig, Jiri Kylian, Peter Wright, Hans van Manen, and Alicia Markova, among others. Mem. corps de ballet Royal Winnipeg (Man.) Ballet, 1979-82, soloist, artistic coord., 1984-89, interim artistic dir., 1989-90, assoc. artistic dir., 1990-96, artistic dir., 1996—. Staged Danzig's Romeo and Juliet, Teatro Comunale, Florence, Italy, Greek Nat. Opera, Athens. Dancer soloist (ballets) Song of a Wayfarer, Fall River Legend, Nuages, Lento A Tempo E Appassionatto, Nutcracker, Four Last Songs, Romeo and Juliet, The Ecstasy of Rita Joe, (TV films) Belong, Romeo and Juliet, The Big Top, Firebird, (ballets) performed at many events including the opening Gala in Jackson Miss., Le Don Des Etoiles, Montreal, spl. gala honoring Queen Beatrix of Holland and at a Gala performance in Tchaikovsky Hall, Moscow, appeared as a guest artist throughout, N.Am., the Orient and USSR. Avocation: listening to opera. Office: Can Royal Winnipeg Ballet 380 Graham Ave Winnipeg MB Canada R3C 4K2 Office Phone: 204-956-0183. E-mail: ballet@rwb.org.

LEWIS, ANDREA ELEN, editor; b. Detroit, June 4, 1957; d. Frank Joe and Mae (Shaw) L. BS, Ea. Mich. U., 1982. Arts and entertainment editor Plexus: West Coast Women's Press, Oakland, Calif., 1984-88; rsch. editor Mother Jones mag., San Francisco, 1990-92; editl. asst. Harper Collins Pubs., San Francisco, 1992-94; sr. editor Third Force mag., Oakland, 1992—; assoc. editor Pacific News Svc., San Francisco, 1996—2000; writer NBCi.com, San Francisco, 1997—. Mem. adv. bd. Nat. Radio Project, 1996—. Contbg. writer: The Black Women's Health Book, 1990, Beyond Identity Politics, 1996; contbg. artist (CD rec. project) Bob Ostertag's Fear No Love, 1995; commentator (radio broadcasting) Pacifica Radio, 1995, 96, 97; co-host/prodr. The Morning Show KPFA Radio, Berkeley, Calif., 2000-. Chorus mem. San Francisco Symphony Chorus, 1987—, sect. leader, alto, 1991, 92, 93, 95, 99, mem. artistic adv. com., 1995, 96, 98, 99; mem. planning com., panelist, spkr. Media and Democracy Congress, San Francisco, 1996; fellow Vallecitos Mountain Refuge, N.Mex., 1998. Recipient Merit award Local Music Series, 2001, Nat. Fedn. Comty. Broadcasters Golden Reel awards, 2001. Mem. NARAS (Grammy awards for best choral recording 1992, 95). Avocations: massage therapist, musician, golfer, outdoor activities. Office: KPFA Radio 1929 Martin Luther King Jr Way Berkeley CA 94704

LEWIS, ANN FRANK, former government official; b. Jersey City, Dec. 19, 1937; d. Samuel and Elsie (Golush) Frank; m. Myron Sponder, 1989; children from previous marriage: Patricia Fay, Beth Ellen Susan Jane. Student, Radcllfe Coll., 1954-55. Asst. to mayor City of Boston, 1968-75; dep. campaign mgr. Bayh for Pres., 1975-76; adminstrv. asst. to Congressman Stan Lundine, U.S. Ho. of Reps., Washington, 1976-81, adminstrv. asst. to Congresswoman Barbara Mikulski, 1978-81; polit. dir. Dem. Nat. Com., Washington, 1981-85; nat. dir. Ams. for Dem. Action, Washington, 1985-87; nat. affairs columnist MS mag., 1988-92; analyst Monitor Radio and Sta. WHDH-TV, 1992; v.p. for pub. policy Planned Parenthood Fedn. Am.; pres. Politics, Inc.; co-chmn. Back to Bus. Com., 1994; dep. campaign mgr. Clinton-Gore, 1996; dep. dir. comm. and strategic planning The White House, Washington, 1997, counselor to Pres., dir. comm. and strategic planning, 1997-2000. Inst. Politics of Kennedy Sch. Govt. fellow Harvard U., 1989. Office: Office of the President Rm GLF, West Wing White House Washington DC 20500

LEWIS, ANNE DAVISON, social worker; b. Clarksville, Tenn., Apr. 15, 1928; d. John Alexander and Anne Victoria (Greene) Davison; m. William Phelpa Lewis, Sept. 22, 1956 (dec.); children: Elizabeth Anne, John. BA, Randolph Macon Woman's Coll., 1946—50; MA, Marywood U., 1970—73. Social worker Scranton Sch. Dist., Pa., 1971—90, elem. tchr., 1990—93. Spkr. Meth. Women's Conf., Tenn., 1969; participant Inst. for Advanced Pastoral Studies, Bloomfield, Mich., 1964. Bd. mem. Abington Bapt. Assn., Scranton, 1970, Girl Scouts, 1968—69, YWCA, 1959. Republican. Bapt. Avocations: gardening, classical music, reading, cooking, tennis. Home: 414 Carnation Dr Clarks Summit PA 18411

LEWIS, ANNE MCCUTCHEON, architect; b. New Orleans, Oct. 15, 1943; d. John Tinney and Susan (Dart) McCutcheon; m. Ronald Burton Lewis, Oct. 2, 1971; children: Matthew, Oliver. BA magna cum laude, Radcliffe Coll., 1965; MArch, Harvard U., 1970. Registered architect, D.C., Md., Va., Pa. Architect Skidmore, Owings & Merrill, Washington, 1969—72, Keyes, Lethbridge & Condon, Washington, 1972—75; ptnr. McCartney Lewis Architects, Washington, 1981—98; prin. Anne McCutcheon Lewis AIA, Washington, 1976—81, 1999—. Mem. Harvard U. Grad. Sch. Design Alumni Coun., Cambridge, Mass., 1979-82; bd. dirs. Friends Non-Profit Housing, Washington, 1981-98, Washington Humane Soc., 1990—, D.C. Hist. Preservation Rev. Bd., 2003—. Fellow: AIA (dir.-at-large Washington chpt. 1982—84, Design awards 1979, 1983, 1989, 1990, 1991, 1992, 1993, 1996, 1998, 2000, 2001). Office: Anne McCutcheon Lewis FAIA 3400 Reservoir Rd NW Washington DC 20007-2328

LEWIS, ANTHONY, columnist, educator; b. NYC, Mar. 27, 1927; s. Kassel and Sylvia (Surut) L.; m. Linda Rannells, July 8, 1951 (div.); children: Eliza, David, Mia; m. Margaret H. Marshall, Sept. 23, 1984 AB, Harvard U., 1948. Deskman Sunday dept. NY Times, 1948-52, reporter Washington bur., 1955-64, chief London bur., 1965-72, editl. columnist (column Abroad at Home), 1969—2001; staff Dem. Nat. Com., 1952; reporter Washington Daily News, 1952-55. Lectr. on law Harvard U., 1974-89; James Madison vis. prof. Columbia U., 1983—. Author: Gideon's Trumpet, 1964 (Mystery Writers Am. Award for best factual crime book of yr.), Portrait of a Decade: The Second American Revolution, 1964, Make No Law: The Sullivan Case and the First Amendment, 1991; contbr. articles to profl. jours. Recipient Heywood Broun Award, 1955, Pulitzer Prize for Nat. Reporting, 1955, 63, Presdl. Citizens' Medal, 2001; Nieman Fellow, Harvard U., 1956-57. Mem.: Am. Acad. Arts and Scis., Am. Philos. Soc., Tavern Club. Office Phone: 617-354-2229. Personal E-mail: tlewis@galaxy.net.

LEWIS, ARTHUR DEE, aerospace transportation executive; b. Greenville, Tex., Sept. 13, 1918; s. Carl Hamilton and Maxie (Curtis) L.; m. Hildegard Bair, Dec. 7, 1946; children: Gregory Scott, Kimberly Kealani. Student, U. Tex., 1935-41, Advanced Mgmt. Program, Harvard, 1952; Sc.D., Clarkson Coll. Tech. With Am. Airlines, 1941-55, beginning as cargo research analyst, successively supr. spl. projects, mgr. econ. analysis br., dir. econ. planning div., 1941-54, asst. v.p. planning, 1954-55; exec. v.p. Hawaiian Airlines, 1955, pres., dir., chief exec. officer, 1955-64; sr. v.p., gen. mgr., dir. Eastern Air Lines, 1964-67, pres., chief operating officer, dir., 1967-69; gen. partner F. S. Smithers & Co., 1969—; chmn., pres., chief exec. officer F. Smithers & Co., 1969-73. Chmn., chief exec. officer U.S. Ry. Assn., 1974-77; pres., dir., chief exec. officer Am. Bus Assn., 1977-82; chmn., chief exec. officer U.S. Africa Airways, 1990-94, bd. dirs., chmn. emeritus, cons.; chmn. bd. Airline Media Assocs., Inc.; organizer Consol. Ry. Corp., Conrail; organizer Nat. Ry. Passenger Corp., Amtrak; dir. Riegel Paper Corp., Rexham Corp., Bankers Security Life Ins. Soc., Bank of Commerce, Iroquois Brands Ltd., C. Brewer & Co., Bishop Trust Co., Internat. Bank; chmn. Mid Pacific Airlines, Honolulu; cons. airline moblzn., transp. div. Nat. Security Resources Bd., Korean War; cons. Def. Air Transp. Adminstrn., 1951-55, Dept. Transp., 1969. Bd. regents U. Hawaii; bd. govs. Pacific and Asian Affairs Council, Iolani Sch. Boys; bd. dirs. Hawaii Visitors Bur.; trustee, chmn. emeritus Clarkson Coll. Tech. Mem. Am. Mgmt. Assn. (dir., mem. exec. com.), Honolulu C. of C. (dir. 1958-59), Young Pres. Orgn., World Bus. Coun. (pres., dir. 1973-74), Conquistadores del Cielo (dir.), Burning Tree Club (Bethesda, Md.), Soc. of Sr. Aerospace Execs., Inc. (pres., dir. 1995-97).

LEWIS, AYLWIN B., retail executive, former food service executive; BS in Bus. Mgmt. & English Lit, MBA, Houston U. Sr. v.p., mktg. & ops. devel KFC, PepsiCo, Inc., 1995—96; sr. v.p., ops. Pizza Hut, Inc., 1996—97, COO, 1997—99; exec. v.p., ops. & new bus. devel YUM! Brands, Inc., 2000, COO, 2000—03, pres., chief multibranding & operating officer, 2003—04; pres., CEO Kmart Holding Corp., Troy, Mich., 2004—. Bd. dirs. Halliburton Co., 2001—05, The Walt Disney Co., 2004—. Office: Kmart Holding Corp 3100 W Big Beaver Rd Troy MI 48084*

LEWIS, BENJAMIN PERSHING, JR., pharmacist, retired public health officer; b. Danville, Ky., June 2, 1942; s. Benjamin Pershing Lewis and Juanita Elizabeth Applewhite; m. Patricia Glover, 1968; children: Laura, Jason. BS in Pharmacy, Auburn U., 1966, MS in Pharmacy, 1972; PhD of Health Svcs. Mgmt., Century U., 1989; postgrad., Johns Hopkins U., 1993. Registered pharmacist Ky., Ala. Instr. Auburn U. Sch. Pharmacy, Ala., 1972—73, now affiliate asst. prof.; commd. lt. comdr. USPHS, 1976, advanced through grades to capt., 1985; pharmacy officer Bur. Drugs FDA, Rockville, Md., 1976—82, health scientist adminstr. orphan products devel., 1982—87, AIDS coord., 1987—89, spl. asst. to assoc. dir. Ctr. Biologics Evaluation-Rsch. Bethesda, Md., 1989—92, dir. regulatory ops. divsn. of transfusion and emerging transmitted diseases Ctr. Biologics Evaluation and Rsch. Rockville, 1993—2002; with Brand Inst., Inc., Rockville, 2002—03; v.p. regulatory affairs Prestwick Pharm., Inc., Washington, 2003—. Adj. prof. San Diego State U., 1998. Co-author: Veterinary Drug Index, 1982; editor: FDA Role in AIDS, 1988, The International Ramifications of Drug Development, 1988, Report of the Criticism Task Force on Career Development, 1989; co-editor: Poliovirus Attenuation: Molecular Mechanisms and Practical Aspects, 1993, Combined Vaccines and Simultaneous Administration, 1995; contbr. articles to profl. jours. Officer U.S. Army, 1972-76. Recipient letter of appreciation Sec. Md. Dept. Econ. and Employment Devel., 1991, Secs. award for disting. svc. Dept. Health and Human Svcs., 2001, PHS Meritorious Svc. medal FDA, 2002. Mem. COA of USPHS, Regulatory Affairs Profl. Soc. (Cert. Appreciation 1993), Drug Info. Assn., Am. Pharm. Assn., Am. Acad. Pharm. Rsch. and Sci., Drug Info. Assn., FDA Alumni Assn., Sigma Xi. Methodist. Achievements include assignment by FDA to San Diego State U. to create one of the first Master of Science degrees in Regulatory Affairs in the U.S., 1998. Office: 1825 K St NW Ste 1475 Washington DC 20006 Office Phone: 202-296-1400. Business E-Mail: benl@prestwickpharma.com.

LEWIS, BERNARD, retired social studies educator; b. London, May 31, 1916; s. H. Lewis; m. Ruth Helene Oppenhejm, 1947 (div. 1974); 2 children. BA, PhD, U. London; postgrad., Univs. of London and Paris; doctorate (hon.), Hebrew U., Jerusalem, 1974, Tel Aviv U., 1979, SUNY, Binghamton, 1987, U. Pa., 1987, Hebrew Union Coll., 1987, Yeshiva U., 1991, Haifa U., 1991, Bar-Ilan U., 1992, Brandeis U., 1993, Ben-Gurion U., 1996, Ankara U., 1996, New Sch. U., NY, 2002, Princeton U., 2002, Northwestern U., Evanston, Ill., 2003, U. Judaism, LA, 2004. Asst. lectr. in Islamic history Sch. Oriental Studies U. London, 1938, prof. history Near and Mid. East, Sch. Oriental and African Studies (formerly named Sch. Oriental Studies), 1949-74; Cleveland E. Dodge prof. near ea. studies Princeton (NJ) U., 1974-86, prof. emeritus, 1986—, hon. Ataturk prof., 1992-93; A.D. White prof. at large Cornell U., 1984-90; dir. Annenberg Rsch. Inst., Phila., 1986-90. Vis. prof. history UCLA, 1955-56, Columbia U., 1960, Ind. U., 1963; vis. prof. College de France, 1980, Ecole des Hautes Etudes, Paris, 1983-86; Class of 1932 lectr. Princeton U., 1964; vis. mem. Inst. for Advanced Study, Princeton, N.J., 1969, long-term mem., 1974-86; Gottesman lectr. Yeshiva U., 1974; Jefferson lectr. NEH, 1990; Tanner lectr. Oxford U., 1990; Weizmann lectr. in Humanities, 1991; Henry M. Jackson meml. lectr., 1992; Siemens Stiftung lectr., Munich, 1993; Merle-Curti lectr., Madison, Wis., 1993; lectr. N.Y. Pub. Libr., 1993. Author: The Origins of Ismailism, 1940, Turkey Today, 1940, British Contributions to Arabic Studies, 1941, Handbook of Diplomatic and Political Arabic, 1947, The Arabs in History, 1950, new edit., 1993, Notes and Documents from the Turkish Archives, 1952, The Emergence of Modern Turkey, 1961, 3rd edit. 2002, (transl. from Ibn Gabirol) The Kingly Crown, 1961, rev. edit. 2003, Istanbul and the Civilization of the Ottoman Empire, 1963, The Middle East and the West, 1964, The Assassins, 1967, Race and Color in Islam, 1971, Islam in History, 1973, new edit., 1993, Islam from the Prophet Muhammad to the Capture of Constantinople, 2 vols., 1974, History Remembered, Recovered, Invented, 1975, Studies in Classical and Ottoman Islam, 7th-16th centuries, 1976, The Muslim Discovery of Europe, 1982, The Jews of Islam, 1984, Semites and Anti-Semites, 1986, rev. edit., 1997, The Political Language of Islam, 1988, Race and Slavery in Islam, 1990, Islam and the West, 1993, The Shaping of the Modern Middle East, 1994, Cultures in Conflict: Christians, Muslims and Jews in the Age of Discovery, 1995, The Middle East: A Brief History of the Last 2000 Years, 1996, The Future of the Middle East, 1997, The Multiple Identities of the Middle East, 1999, A Middle East Mosaic: Fragments of life, letters and history, 2000, Music of a Distant Drum, 2001, What Went Wrong? Western Impact and Middle Eastern Response, 2002, The Crisis of Islam: Holy War and Unholy Terror, 2003, From Babel to Dragomans: Interpreting the Middle East, 2004; (with Amnon Cohen) Population and Revenue in the Towns of Palestine in the Sixteenth Century, 1978; author, editor: Land of Enchanters, 1948, 3d edit. (with Stanley Burstein) 2001, The World of Islam: Faith, People, Culture, 1976; author, co-editor: Historians of the Middle East, 1962, Ency. of Islam, 1956-87; editor: (with others) The Cambridge History of Islam, vols. 1-11, 1971; co-editor: Muslims in Europe, 1992, Religionsgespräche im Mittelalter, 1992; also articles. Served with Royal Armoured Corps and Intelligence Corps, Brit. Army, 1940-41; with dept. Fgn. Office, 1941-45. Recipient Cert. of Merit for svcs. to Turkish culture, Turkish Govt., 1973, Harvey prize, 1978, Ataturk Peace prize, 1998; Univ. Coll. of London fellow, 1976; hon. fellow U. London. 1986. Fellow Brit. Acad., Royal Hist. Soc., Turkish Hist. Soc. (hon.), Sch. of Oriental and African Studies (hon.); mem. Am. Acad. Arts and Scis., Am. Philos. Soc., Am. Hist. Assn., Soc. Asiatique (hon.), Inst. d'Egypte (Cairo, assoc.), Inst. de France (corr.), Turkish Acad. Scis. (hon.). Office: Near East Studies Dept Princeton Univ Princeton NJ 08544-0001

LEWIS, BETTE LOUISE, school principal; b. Chandler, Ariz. m. Gladstone S. Lewis (dec. 1987); 1 child, Clinton H. BA, Marymount Coll., 1964; MA, U. Md., 1970. Cert. tchr., adminstr., supr., Md. Tchr. Palos Verdes (Calif.) Peninsula Unified Sch. Dist., 1963-65, Prince George's County Pub. Schs., Upper Marlboro, Md., 1965-69, vice-prin., 1969-72, prin., 1972—. Recipient Washington Post Dist. Ednl. Leadership Award, Prince George's County C. of C. Outstanding Adminstr. Award, Prince George's County Public Schools Outstanding Adminstr. Award, Sigma Sigma Sigma Alumna Achievement Award. Fellow Inst. Devel. Ednl. Activities (asst. dir. 1990); mem. ASCD, Am. Assn. Sch. Adminstrs., Nat. Assn. Secondary Sch. Adminstrs., Nat. Middle Sch. Assn., Md. Middle Sch. Assn., Md. Assn. Secondary Sch. Adminstrs., Rotary Internat., Sigma Sigma Sigma. Roman Catholic. Avocations: classical music, ballroom dancing, tennis, gardening, antiques. Office: Martin Luther King Jr Mid Sch 4545 Ammendale Rd Beltsville MD 20705-1113

LEWIS, BRIAN KREGLOW, retired physiologist, computer scientist; b. Durban, Rep. South Africa, Sept. 2, 1932; s. Arthur Armington and Isabel (Kreglow) L.; m. Mary Helen Kidwell, July 14, 1953; children: Brian E., James A., Charles A., Carol J., Robert E., Sharon H. BS secondary sci. edn., Ohio State U., 1950—54; PhD med. physiology, Tufts U., 1966—71. Biology tchr. Lincoln-Sudbury (Mass.) Regional High Sch., 1965-66; rsch. assoc. May Inst. for Med. Rsch., Cin., 1971-75; from asst. to assoc. prof. health sci. Grand Valley State U., Allendale, Mich., 1975-81; assoc. prof. Ponce Sch. Medicine, PR, 1981—84, prof. chmn. physiology, 1987—91; prin. Lewis Assocs., Sarasota, Fla., 1984—2003, ret., 2004. Adj. asst. prof. physiology Cin. Coll. Medicine, 1972-75; assoc.; instr. Macintosh computer for beginners Sarasota County Tech. Inst., 1995-97. Editor: Search of Far Horizons; developer business and ednl. software, editor Search of Far Horizons, 2004; contbr. articles to profl. jours. Cubmaster, scoutmaster Boy Scouts Am., 1963-78; mem. Choral Polifonica, Ponce, PR, 1982-84, ch. choir, St. Andrew Ch., Sarasota, 1984—, mem. fin. com., 1991-98, treas., 1999-2001, chmn. 2004-, chmn. fin. com. 2005—; bd. dirs. Sarasota chpt. Soc. Preservation and Encouragement Barbershop Quartet Singing in Am., 1994, sec., 1995-99; active Village Voices, Greenhills, Ohio, 1972-75; active Meadows Chorus, 1996—; mem. Manatee chpt. SPEBSQSA, 2002-, treas., 2005— Lt. supply corps USN, 1954—62. NIH fellow, 1965-71. Mem. Endocrine Soc., Soc. for Study Reproduction, Soc. for Study Fertility, Sarasota PC Users Group (spreadsheet SIG leader 1993-94, software reviewer 1992—, moderator TechForum 1996-2003, editor TechTalk, 1995—), Sigma Xi. Personal E-mail: bwsail@yahoo.com.

LEWIS, BROCK, investment company executive; b. New Bedford, Mass., July 16, 1930; s. Frank Edward and Mary (Brock) L.; m. Susan Wahl, Sept. 4, 1954 (div.); children: Juliana D., Christopher B., Josiah E., Victoria D. BA, Dartmouth Coll., 1952; LLB, Boston U., 1955; postgrad., NYU, 1959-61. Asst. v.p. Fidelity Union Trust Co., Newark, 1955-64; v.p., trust officer County Nat. Bank, Poughkeepsie, N.Y., 1964-67, Capital Nat. Bank, Houston, 1967-69; v.p. Lionel D. Edie & Co., Houston, 1969-72, Dominick Mgmt. Co., N.Y.C., 1972-75, Marine Midland Bank, N.Y.C., 1975-80; 1st v.p. Lehman Mgmt. Co., N.Y.C., 1980-82; owner, pres. Brock Lewis Assocs. Ltd., Lawrenceville, N.J., 1982—; pres. Living Daylight, Inc., Yardley, Pa., 2004—. Cons. State of N.J. Adminstrn. Office of Cts., Trenton, 1993—; dir. Inst. Social and Econ. Policy Middle East, Cambridge, Mass., 1993-99. Pres. Greater Trenton Symphony, 1993-2001, pres. emeritus, 2001—; dir. Steinway Soc., Princeton, 1990-2000; trustee emeritus Tabor Acad., Marion, Mass.; mem. Republican Presdl. Roundtable, 2000—. Mem. Nat. Assn. Bus. Economists, Tabor Acad. Alumni Assn. (chmn. 1995-98, trustee 1995-98), Dartmouth Rowing Club.

LEWIS, CALVIN FRED, architect, educator; b. Chgo., Mar. 27, 1946; s. Howard George and Fern Teresa (Voelsch) L.; m. L. Diane Johnson, Aug. 24, 1968; children: Nathan, Miller, Cooper, Wilson. BArch, Iowa State U., 1969. Architect Charles Herbert and Assocs., Des Moines, 1970-86; prin. Herbert Lewis Kruse Blunck Architecture, Des Moines, 1987—2003; prof. Iowa State U., 2000—, chmn. Dept. Arch., 2000—. Peer reviewer Gen. Svcs. Adminstrn. Design Excellence Program, 2003; lectr., awards juror. More tha 50 projects published in profl. jours. Recipient Best in Design award Time mag.; named one of Top Young Architects in Country, Met. Home mag.; firm named Nat. AIA Firm of Yr., 2001. Fellow AIA (over 70 Design awards 1972—, 3 Nat. Honor awards 1997, 2002), Internat Design award Bus. Week/Archtl. Record 1998, Internat. Design mag. awards 1998-99, Nat. Design award AIA-AISC 1999). Avocations: sports, photography. Office: Dept Arch 156A Coll of Design Ames IA 50011 Office Phone: 515-294-2665. Business E-Mail: calewis@iastate.edu.

LEWIS, CARL (FREDERICK CARLTON LEWIS), Olympic track and field athlete; b. Birmingham, Ala., May 1, 1961; s. William McKinley Lewis, Jr. and Evelyn (Lawler) Lewis. Student, U. Houston. Mem. U.S. Olympic Team, 1980, 1984, 1988, 1992, 1996. Musician: (albums) Break it Up, 1986. Founder Carl Lewis Found. Recipient James E. Sullivan award best amateur athlete, 1981, Jesse Owens award, 1982, Athlete of Yr. award Assoc. Press Sports, 1983; named World Athlete of the Decade Track & Field News, 1980-89, Olympic Athlete of the Century, 2000, U.S. Athlete of the Yr., 1981, 82, 83, 84, 87, 88, 91, World Athlete of the Yr., 1982, 83, 84, named to U.S. Olympic Hall of Fame, 1985. winner 1 Bronze medal Pan Am. Games, 1979, 2 Gold medals, 1981, 1 Gold medal World Cup, 1981, 3 Gold medals, 100m, long jump, 400m relay, World Championships, 1983, 1987, 9 Olympic Gold medals, Long Jump 1984, 1988, 1992, 1996, 100m, 1984, 1988, 200m, 1980, 4x100m relay, 1984, 1992, Silver medal, 200m, 1988; world record holder in 4x100m relay, 1981, 83, 84, 91, 92, in 4x200m relay, 1989, 100 meter dash, 1991; Am. record holder in 4x100 relay, 1981, 83, 84, 90, 91, in 200 meter dash, 1983, 100 meter dash, 1987, 88, 91, 4x200m relay, 1989; world and Am. indoor record holder in long jump, 1981, 82, 84, in 60 yd. dash, 1983, holds current world record of 37.40 seconds in the 4x100m relay, 1992-.

LEWIS, CHANCE WAYNE, education educator, researcher; s. Brenda Clem Davis and Lloyd Odgen Lewis; m. Mechael Brown Brown, June 17, 2000; 1 child, Myra Nicole. PhD, Colo. State U., 1998—2001. Tchr. East Baton Rouge Parish Schools, 1994—98; dept. head-computer info. systems dept. Front Range C.C., Fort Collins, Colo., 1998—2001; prof. Colo. State U., 2001—. Rsch. assoc. R&D Ctr. for the Advancement of Student Learning, Fort Collins, Colo., 2001—. Exec. dir. Abyssinian Christian Ch., Fort Collins, Colo., 2001. Recipient Tenure-Track Faculty Tchg. Excellence, Colo. State U., 2004. Fellow: Bros. of the Acad. Inst. (assoc.; leadership team and regional dir. 2004); mem.: Am. Edn. Rsch. Assn. Office: Colo State Univ Room 223-Sch of Edn Fort Collins CO 80523 Office Phone: 970-491-1807. Personal E-mail: chance.lewis@colostate.edu.

LEWIS, CHARLES A., foundation administrator; b. Orange, N.J., Oct. 23, 1942; s. F. Donald and Edna H. L.; m. Gretchen Smith, July 1967 (div.); m. Penny Bender Sebring, June 9, 1984. BA, Amherst Coll., 1964; MBA, U. Pa., 1966; LHD (hon.), Amherst Coll., 2003. Asst. to pres. Computer Tech., Inc., Skokie, Ill., 1969-70; 1st v.p. White, Weld, & Co., 1970-78; vice chmn. investment banking Merrill Lynch & Co., Chgo., 1978—2004. Mem. adv. com. Database of Black Performers of Instrumental Concert Music, 1999—. Life trustee Amherst Coll., Folger Shakespear Libr., 1989—; life trustee, vice chair Chgo. Symphony Orch., 1989—; life dir. Juvenile Diabetes Rsch. Found. Ill.; vis. com. divsn. social scis. U. Chgo.; trustee Ravinia Festival, 1995—98; leadership coun. Chgo. Pub. Edn. Fund, 2000—; governing bd. North Kenwood/Oakland Charter Sch., 2000—03; co-chair The Amherst Coll. Campaign, 1993—2001; mem. policy bd. Ctr. Urban Sch. Improvement U. Chgo., 2003—; bd. dirs. Juvenile Diabetes Rsch. Found. Internat., 1994—95. Named to, Shaker H.S. Sports Hall of Fame, 2003; recipient Cmty. Ptnr. award, People's Music Sch., 2002. Mem. Chgo. Club, Glen View Club. Office: Coach House Capital and Lewis-Sebring Family Found 2735 Sheridan Rd Evanston IL 60201 Office Phone: 847-864-9615. E-mail: calewis@lewissebringff.org.

LEWIS, CHARLES JEREMY (JERRY LEWIS), congressman; b. Spokane, Wash., Oct. 21, 1934; BA, UCLA, 1956. Former life ins. underwriter; field rep. for former U.S. Rep. Jerry Pettis; mem. Calif. State Assembly, 1968-78; vice chmn. rules com., chmn. subcom. on air quality; mem. U.S. Congress from 41st (formerly 35th) Calif. dist., 1979—; mem. appropriations com.; chmn., 2005—. Former chmn. VA-HUD subcom., mem. defense subcom., select com. on intelligence, chmn. subcom. on human intelligence; co-chair Calif. Congl. Delegation, 1996-2001. Republican. Presbyterian. Office: US Ho Reps 2112 Rayburn Ho Office Bldg Washington DC 20515

LEWIS, CHARLES JOSEPH, journalist; b. Bozeman, Mont., July 10, 1940; s. Vern Edward James and Mary (Brooke) L.; m. Sarah Withers (div. 2002); children: Peter, Patrick, Barbara. BS in Humanities with Honors, Loyola U., Chgo., 1962; JD, Columbia U., 1965. Bar: Ill. 1965. Atty. McDermott, Will & Emery, Chgo., 1965-67; reporter City News Bur., Chgo., 1967-68; reporter, editor Chgo. Sun-Times, 1968-73; with AP, 1974-89, reporter, editor, Washington, 1974-78, reporter, editor, L.A., 1978-80, personnel mgr., N.Y.C., 1981-83, bur. chief, Hartford, Conn., 1980-81, bur. chief, Washington, 1984-89; bur. chief Hearst Newspapers, Washington, 1989—. Bd. dirs. Nat. Press Found., Washington, 1985-2003, treas., 1987-88, vice chmn., 1988-90, chmn., 1990-92; dir. Reporters Com. for Freedom of the Press, 1993-98, SDX Found. Washington, 1996—; mem. adv. bd. Paul Miller Washington Reporting Fellowships, 1999—. Lance cpl. USMCR, 1963-67. Mem. Am. Soc. Newspaper Editors, Gridiron Club, Sigma Delta Chi (v.p. Washington chpt. 1988-89). Office: Hearst Newspapers 1850 K St NW Ste 1000 Washington DC 20006

LEWIS, CHARLES LEONARD, psychologist; b. Wellsville, Ohio, Jan. 6, 1926; s. Cleo L. and Charlotte (Hahn) L.; m. Charlotte J. Wynn, Sept. 8, 1948 (dec. Mar. 1987); children: Stephen C., Janet J., Judith A.; m. Jane E. McCormick, Oct. 1, 1988. BS in Edn. with honors, Ohio U., 1949; MA, U. Minn., 1953, PhD, 1955. Asst. dean of men Ohio U., 1948-50; assoc. dir. activities U. Minn., 1950-55; dean student affairs, assoc. prof. psychology U. N.D., 1955-62; exec. dean, assoc. prof. ednl. psychology U. Tenn., 1962-67; v.p. student affairs Pa. State U., 1967-72; exec. dir. Am. Personnel and Guidance Assn., Washington, 1972-74, exec. v.p., 1974-83, exec. v.p. emeritus, 1984—; pres. Charles L. Lewis & Assocs., Annandale, Va., 1983-85, Chuck Lewis et al, Lancaster, Pa., 1985—. Guest prof. U. Md., 1973; mem. Nat. Adv. Com. for Devel. Guidance Components-Career Edn., 1972-76. Founding editor Jour. Coll. Students Pers., 1958-64; mem. editl. bd. Pers. and Guidance Jour., 1954-57. Mem. Pres.'s Com. for Handicapped, 1972-80; bd. dirs. Ctr. Cmty. Hosps., Bellefonte, Pa. With U.S. Army, 1944-47. Named Outstanding Alumnus, Coll. Edn. Ohio U., 1988; recipient George Hill Disting. Alumni award, Ohio U., 1981. Mem.: AAUP, APA, Willow Valley Computer Sig. (pres. 1999—2001), Ohio U. Alumni Soc. and Friends Coll. Edn. (coun. 1985—92, bd. dirs. 1986—92), Coun. Advancement of Stds. (bd. dirs.), Am. Assn. Univ. Adminstrs. (dir. 1973), Am. Pers. and Guidance Assn. (dir. 1967—70), Nat. Assn. Woman Deans and Counselors, Nat. Assn. Student Pers. Adminstrs., Am. Coll. Pers. Assn. (pres. 1968—69, honoree Diamond Anniversary 1999, Lifetime Achievement award 2001), Am. Assn. Higher Edn., Psi Chi, Chi Sigma Iota (founding dir. 1984—90), Beta Theta Pi, Kappa Delta Pi. Episcopalian.

LEWIS, CHARLES RAYMOND, II, traffic engineer, consultant; b. Charleston, W.Va., May 29, 1947; s. Charles Raymond and Jane Ann (Veazey) L.; m. Constance Maria Gratop, Aug. 29, 1970; 1 child, Brian Anthony. BSCE, Ohio U., 1970; MEng in Civil Engring., Pa. State U., 1971. Registered profl. engr., W.Va., profl. surveyor, W.Va.; lic. master electrician, W.Va. Asst. planning and rsch. engr. W.Va. Dept. Hwys., Charleston, 1970-73; planning and rsch. engr. Dept. Transp. Traffic Engr. Divsn. W.Va. Divsn. Hwys., Charleston, 1973—2004; ADA compliance officer Dept. of Transp., W.Va., 2002—, staff engr. traffic rsch. and spl. projects traffic engring. divsn. W.Va. divsn. hwys., 2004—; value engring coord. Dept. of Transp., 1994—. Com. mem. Transp. Rsch. Bd., Washington, 1983—, com. chmn., 1984-90; project and synthesis panel mem. Nat. Coop. Hwy. Rsch. Program, Washington, 1991—; adj. instr. Marshall U., 2003—. Asst. scoutmaster Boy Scouts Am., Charleston, 1991—; co-clerk Charleston Friends Meeting, 2001—. Fellow Automotive Safety Found.; recipient Silver Beaver award Boy Scouts Am., 1998, Lifetime Achievement award W.Va. Operation Lifesaver, 2001. Mem. Inst. Transp. Engrs., Am. Railway Engring. and Maintenance of Way Assn. Avocations: photography, geology, amateur astronomy. Office: Traffic Engring Divsn WVa Dept Transp 1900 Kanawha Blvd E Charleston WV 25305-0009 E-mail: rlewis@dot.state.wv.us.

LEWIS, CHERIE SUE, lawyer, writer, language educator; b. Cleve., Feb. 6, 1951; d. Samuel D. and Evelyne P. L., 1 child, Danielle Anne Lewis. BA, U. Mich., 1973; MS, Boston U., 1975; PhD, U. Minn., 1986; JD, Southwestern U., L.A., 1996. Cert. ESL tchr., Calif. Prof. Pa. State U., State College, 1988—89, Nat. Chengchi U., Taipei, Taiwan, 1989—91, Syracuse U., 1992—93, Nat. U., L.A., 1993—; atty.-advisor U.S. Social Security Adminstrn., L.A., 1998—. Cons. Pacific Rim Inst., L.A., 1992-95, participant Fulbright Program, Cairo, Egypt, 1993 Author: (book chpt.) Disability Rights, International, 1994, ednl. brochures, 1994; mng. editor Southwestern U. Jour. Law and Trade, 1995-96. Mem. AAUP, ABA. Avocations: music, skiing, international travel. Office: 12121 Wilshire Blvd Ste 400 Los Angeles CA 90025 Office Phone: 310-966-4802. Personal E-mail: Cherie0206@hotmail.com.

LEWIS, CHERYL M., foundation executive; b. Tiffin, Ohio, Nov. 2, 1962; d. Jack R. and Madeline R. Staib; m. Murphy J. Lewis, May 5, 2000. AB in English, Heidelberg Coll., 1985, MEd, 1990. Cert. fundraising exec. English tchr. Clearcreek Schs., Springboro, Ohio, 1985-86; alumni dir. Heidelberg Coll., Tiffin, 1986-93; ann. fund dir. Youngstown (Ohio) State U., 1993-99; dir. devel. Shepherd's Found., Youngstown, 1999—. Bd. dirs. Thrivent Fin. for Luths., 2003—. Vol. New Start treatment Ctr., Warren, Ohio, 1995. Mem. Assn. Fundraising Profls. (pres. Youngstown 2001—02), Assn. Lutheran Devel. Execs., No. Ohio Planned Giving Coun., Rotary. Office: Shepherd's Found 6000 Mahoning Ave Ste 410 Youngstown OH 44515 E-mail: clewis@shepherdofthevalley.com.

LEWIS, CHRIS A., manufacturing executive; b. Apr. 22, 1931; BA, Wittenberg U. CPA. With KPMG Peat Warwick; US contr. Peek PLC, 1989—95; treas. Jabil Circuits, 1995—96, CFO, 1996—2004, v.p. global bus. units, 2004—. Recipient CFO Excellence award for planning and performance mgmt., CFO Mag., 2001. Office: Jabil Cir 10560 9th St N Saint Petersburg FL 33716

LEWIS, CYNTHIA LYNN, literature educator, writer; b. Middletown, Ohio, Oct. 11, 1951; d. Richard Lynn and Gwendolyn Conn Lewis; 1 child, Henry. BA, Ohio State U., 1974; MA, Harvard U., 1975, PhD, 1980. Prof. English Davidson (N.C.) Coll., 1980—. Author: Particular Saints: Shakespeare's Four Antonios, 1997; contbr. articles to profl. jours. Recipient Tchr. of Yr. Silver medal, Coun. Advancement and Support Edn., 1987. Office: Davidson College English Dept PO Box 6982 Davidson NC 28035-6982 Office Phone: 704-894-2257.

LEWIS, DAN ALBERT, education educator; b. Chgo., Feb. 14, 1946; s. Milton and Diane (Sabath) L.; m. Stephanie Riger, Jan. 3, 1982; children: Matthew, Jake. BA cum laude, Stanford U., 1968; PhD, U. Calif., Santa Cruz, 1980. Rsch. assoc. Arthur Bolton Assocs., Sacramento, 1969-70; survey contr. Sci. Analysis Corp., San Francisco, 1971; dir. Stanford Workshops on Polit. and Social Issues Stanford (Calif.) U., 1971-74; projects adminstr. Ctr. Urban Affairs and Policy Rsch., Northwestern U., Evanston, Ill., 1975-80, asst. prof. edn., 1980-86, assoc. prof. edn., 1986-90, assoc. dir., chair grad. program human devel./social policy, 1987-90, prof. edn., 1990—. Vis. scholar Sch. Edn., Stanford U., 1990-91; mem. task force on restructuring mental health svcs. Chgo. Dept. Health, 1982; mem. human rights authority Ill. Guardianship and Advocacy Commn., 1980-82; adv. mem. com. on planning and inter-agy. coordination Commn. Mental Health and Devel. Disabilities, 1979;

interim adv. com. on mental health City of Chgo., 1978; adv. mem. Gov.'s Commn. to Revise Mental Health Code Ill., 1975-77;dir. Univ. Consortium on Welfare Reform, 1999-2003; presenter at profl. confs.; presenter workshops. Editor: Reactions to Crime, 1981; co-author: Fear of Crime: Incivility and the Production of a Social Problem, 1986, The Social Construction of Reform: Crime Prevention and Community Organizations, 1988, The Worlds of the Mentally Ill, 1991, The State Mental Patient in Urban Life, 1994, Race and Educational Reform, 1995; contbr. articles, book revs. to profl. publs. Bd. dirs. Designs for Change, Ill. Mental Health Assn.; rsch. adv. com. Chgo. Urban League, Chgo. Panel Pub. Sch. Finances, 1989-91; needs assessment tech. com. United Way Chgo., 1989-90; ednl. coun. Francis W. Parker Sch., Chgo., 1988-90; task force on restructuring mental health svcs. Chgo. Dept. Health, 1982; com. on mentally disabled Ill. State Bar Assn., 1983-89; dir. U. Consortium on Welfare Reform, 1999-2002; rsch. policy com. Ill. Dept. Mental Health, 1978; bd. dirs. Mental Health Assn. Greater Chgo., 1977-84, v.p. pub. policy, 1979-83 Recipient Excellence in Tchg. award Northwestern U. Alumni Assn., 1998; named to Faculty Honor Roll Associated Student Govt., 2001-04. Office: Northwestern Univ 2040 Sheridan Rd Evanston IL 60208-0855 Business E-Mail: dlewis@northwestern.edu.

LEWIS, DANIEL MARTIN, lawyer; b. N.Y.C., Feb. 3, 1944; s. David W. and Muriel (Osafs) L.; m. Claudia Vera Dean, Oct. 2, 1971; children: Matthew, Ethan, Jennifer. BA, Yale U., 1966, LLB, 1969. Bar: D.C., U.S. Ct. Appeals (9th, 5th and 4th cirs.). Legis. asst. U.S. senator Joseph D. Tydings, Md., 1969-70; chief legis. asst. U.S. senator Edmund S. Muskee, Maine, 1971-72; assoc. Arnold & Porter, Washington, 1973-79, ptnr., Antitrust and Trade Regulation Practice Group, 1979—. Office: Arnold & Porter 555 12th St NW Washington DC 20004-1206 Office Phone: 202-942-5661. Office Fax: 202-942-5999. Business E-Mail: daniel.lewis@aporter.com.

LEWIS, DAVID BAKER, lawyer; b. Detroit, June 9, 1944; BA, Oakland U., 1965; MBA, U. Chgo., 1967; JD, U. Mich. Law Sch., 1970. Bar: Mich. 1970. Law clk. to Honorable Theodore Levin, US Dist. Ct., Ea. Dist. Mich., 1970—71; pres. Lewis, Clay & Munday, Detroit, 1972—82, chmn. corp. svcs. practice group, 1982—, founder, shareholder; assoc. prof. law, law and social change Detroit Coll. Law, 1973—78. Mem., sec. State of Mich. Atty. Discipline Bd., 1978—83; mem. steering com. Bond Attys. Workshop, 1979, 89; mem. exec. com. Met. Ctr. High Tech., 1983—89, bd. dirs., 1983—89; mem. exec. com. HGH Health Sys., 1984—88, bd. trustees, 1984—88, Inst. Am. Bus., 1984—, mem. exec. com., 1984—; mem. Met. Affairs Corp., 1985—91, vice-chmn., 1989—91, bd. dirs., 1989—91, Booker T. Washington Bus. Assn., 1989—91, Consolidated Rail Corp. (Conrail), 1989—, mem. audit com., 1989—, mem. fin. com., 1989—; mem. audit com. LG&E Energy Corp., 1992—, mem. devel. com., 1992—, bd. dirs., 1992—, TRW, Inc., 1995—, mem. compensation com., 1995—, mem. retirement funding com., 1995—; mem. audit and legal com. Comerica Bank, Mich., 1995—, mem. trust and investment com., 1995—, bd. dirs., 1995—; life mem. Sixth Circuit Judicial Conf. Mem. Greater Detroit Area Hosp. Coun., Inc., 1977—79, 1983—87, Detroit Inst. Arts Dir. Search Com., 1983—85, Greater Detroit and Windsor Japan-Am. Soc., 1989; bd. trustees Harper-Grace Hosp., 1979—88, mem. exec. com., 1979—88; bd. trustees Oakland U., 1970—81, vice chmn. bd. trustees, 1976—78, chmn. bd. trustees, 1978—80, trustee emeritus bd. trustees; pres. Franklin-Wright Settlement, Inc., 1975—76; v.p. Mich. Assn. Governing Bds. Colls. and Univs., 1977—79; chmn. com. vis. U. Mich. Law Sch.; bd. trustees Ctr. Creative Studies, 1983—95, Grosse Pointe Acad., 1984—87, 1993—94; bd. dirs. Detroit Symphony, 1983—, Detroit. Zoological Soc., 1983—89, Musical Hall Ctr. Performing Arts, 1983—94, Founders Soc., Detroit Inst. Arts, 1984—89, Greater Detroit Interfaith Round Table, Nat. Conf. Christian and Jews, Inc., 1990—, Detroit Club, 1989—95, sec., 1989—95. Named one of Am. Top Black Lawyers, Black Enterprise Mag., 2003. Mem.: Nat. Assn. Securities Profl., Inc. (sec. 1985—87, chair-elect 1987, chair 1988, exec. com.), Nat. Assn. Bond Lawyers (bd. dirs. 1993—95). Office: Lewis & Munday 1300 First Nat Bldg 660 Woodward Ave Detroit MI 48226-3531 Office Phone: 313-961-2550 ext. 4110. Business E-Mail: dlewis@lewismunday.com.

LEWIS, DAVID CARLETON, medical educator, academic administrator; b. Hartford, Conn., May 19, 1935; s. Theodore and Lillian (Levin) L.; m. Eleanor Grace Levinson, Aug. 23, 1959; children: Deborah, Steven. AB magna cum laude, Brown U., 1957; MD, Harvard U., 1961. Intern Beth Israel Hosp., Boston, 1961-62, jr. resident, 1962-63, chief med. resident, 1966-67, dir. emergency unit and med. outpatient dept., 1969-71; sr. resident U. Hosps. Cleve., 1963-64, Parkland Meml. Hosp., Dallas, 1964-66; fellow U. Tex. Southwestern Med. Hosp., Dallas, 1964-66; Sloan Found. fellow Harvard Med. Sch., Boston, 1971-72; med. dir. Washingtonian Ctr. for Addictions, Boston, 1972-77; dir. div. alcohol and substance abuse Roger Williams Gen. Hosp., Providence, 1976-82; dir. program in alcoholism and drug abuse Brown U., Providence, 1976-82, prof. medicine and community health, 1982—, Donald G. Millar prof. alcohol and addiction studies, 1987—, chmn. dept. community health, 1981-86, dir. Ctr. Alcohol and Addiction Studies, 1982-2000. Nat. adv. coun. Nat. Alcohol Inst., Rockville, Md., 1981-85, cons. to dir., 1985-93; sci. adv. bd. Children of Alcoholics Found., 1985-95; cons. WHO, 1986-2000, cocaine global adv. com., 1992-95; chair Physician Consortium on Substance Abuse Edn., 1989—99; mem. Carnegie Substance Abuse Adv. com., 1989-92; scholar-in-residence Nat. Inst. Med., 1991-92; adv. panel to U.S. Pharmacopoeia, 1995—99; mem. Drug Strategies Nat. Adv. Panel, 1994—2000, dir. WHO Collaborating Ctr. at Brown U., 1995-2000; nat. adv. com. Robert Wood Johnson Found. Fighting Back program, 1996—2002; bd. dirs. Nat. Coun. Alchoholism and Drug Dependence, 1995-, dep. chair 2002-04, chair, 2004—; bd. dirs. Drug Policy Alliance. Author: The Drug Experience: Data for Decision Making, 1970; editor: Providing Care for Children of Alcoholics, 1986; editor Brown U. Digest of Addiction Theory and Application, 1986—2001; exec. editor Substance Abuse jour., 1984—; contbr. numerous articles to profl. jours. Med. dir. Beacon Hill Free Clinic, Boston, 1968—71; chmn. Mayor's Coun. on Drug Abuse, Boston, 1972—80; project dir. Physician Leadership on Nat. Drug Policy, 1997—. Grantee Nat. Alcohol and Drug Insts., 1986—, Robert Wood Johnson Found., 1996—, John D. and Catherine T. MacArthur Found., 1997—99, Open Study Inst., 1997—99; Edward John Noble fellow Harvard U. Med. Sch., 1957-91; receipient Assn. Med. Edn. and Rsch. in Substance Abuse award for Excellence in Medical Edn., 1986, Norman E Zinberg Meml. Lectr. award Harvard Med. Sch., 1996, AMA award, 1997, Excellence in Med. Edn. AMA-ERF, 1997. Fellow: ACP; mem.: NAS, Assn. for Edn. and Rsch. in Substance Abuse (bd. dirs. 1985—), Brown Med. Alumni Assn. (pres. 1974—76), Assn. Med. Edn. and Rsch. in Substance Abuse (pres. 1983—88, Excellence in Medicine award 1986), Inst. Medicine Study on Treatment Alcohol Problems, Am. Acad. on Physician and Patient (bd. dirs. 1998—2001), Am. Soc. Addiction Medicine (bd. dirs. 1995—, 1994—, sec. 2003—, John P. McGovern award 2004), Sigma Xi, Phi Beta Kappa. Avocations: choral singing, sailing, photography. Office: Brown Univ Ctr Alcohol & Addiction Studies Box G Providence RI 02912 E-mail: David_Lewis@brown.edu.

LEWIS, DAVID JOHN, lawyer; b. Zanesville, Ohio, Feb. 4, 1948; s. David Griff and Barbara Ann (Hoy) L.; m. Susan G. Smith; 1 child, Ann Elizabeth. BS in Fin., U. Ill., 1970, JD, 1973. Bar: Ill. 1973, D.C. 1974. Law clk. to Judge Philip W. Tone U.S. Dist. Ct. For North Dist. Ill., Chgo., 1973-74; assoc. Sidley Austin Brown & Wood, LLP, Washington, 1974-80, ptnr., 1980—. Comml. arbitrator Am. Arbitration Assn.; mem. Washington panel CPR Inst. Dispute Resolution. Mem. ABA. Office: Sidley Austin Brown & Wood LLP 1501 K St NW Washington DC 20005 Office Phone: 202-736-8183. E-mail: dlewis@sidley.com.

LEWIS, DAVID LANIER, business history educator; b. Bethalto, Ill., Apr. 5, 1927; s. Donald F. and Edith (Jinkinson) L.; m. Florence Yuri Tanaka, Apr. 5, 1953; children: Kim, Leilani, Sumi, Lance. BS, U. Ill., 1948; MS, Boston U., 1955; MA, U. Mich., 1956, PhD, 1959; postgrad. (Fulbright scholar), London Sch. Econs., 1956-57. Reporter Edwardsville (Ill.) Intelligencer, 1948; bur. chief, state editor Alton (Ill.) Telegraph, 1948-50; editor employee publs. St. Louis Lincoln-Mercury Plant, 1950-51; press relations rep. Borden Co., N.Y.C., 1952, Ford Motor Co., Dearborn, Mich., 1952-55; pub. relations exec. Gen. Motors Corp., Detroit, 1959-65; asso. prof. bus. history U. Mich., Ann Arbor, 1965-68, prof., 1968—. Author: The Public Image of Henry Ford: An American Folk Hero and His Company, 1976, The Automobile and American Culture, 1983, Ford, 1903 to 1984, 1984, Ford Country, 1987, Ford Chronicle: A Pictorial History From 1893, 1992, The Car and The Camera, 1996, Ford Country II, 1999, 100 Years of Ford: A Centennial Celebration of the Ford Motor Company, 2003; assoc. editor, columnist: Cars & Parts; guest editor: Mich. Quar. Rev, 1980-81. Trustee Nat. Automotive History Collection, Detroit. Served with USNR, 1945-46. Mem. Mich. Hist. Soc., Soc. Automotive Historians (past pres.), Am. Hist. Assn., Bus. Hist. Conf. Home: 2588 Hawthorn Rd Ann Arbor MI 48104-4032 Office: U Mich Ross Bus School Ann Arbor MI 48109-1234 E-mail: lewisdl@umich.edu.

LEWIS, DAVID P., music educator; b. Ravenna, Ohio, Apr. 4, 1958; s. David E. and Joan L. Lewis; m. Belinda L. Breitenbach, Jan. 6, 1996; 1 child, Jordan. BS in Music Edn., Ind. U., Pa., 1981, MA in Music Edn., 1994; postgrad., Shenandoah U. Permanent cert. Pa. Music dir. Bishop Carroll H.S., Ebensburg, Pa., 1984—89, Williamsburg (Pa.) H.S., 1989—. Lectr. music woodwinds Junsota Coll., Huntingdon, Pa., 2002—. Mem.: Nat. Band Assn., Pa. Music Educators Assn., Music Educators Nat. Conf. Avocations: model railroading, composing and arranging music, bicycling. Office: Williamsburg High Sch PO Box 45 Williamsburg PA 16693

LEWIS, DEBORAH ALICE, tax company executive, writer; b. Griffin, Ga., Mar. 26, 1947; d. Durward and Imogene Hinds L. AA, Miss. Gulf Coast Jr. Coll., Gulfport, 1973; student, William Carey Coll., 1973; BA in English cum laude, U. So. Miss., 1978. Vets. counselor Miss. Gulf Coast Jr. Coll., Gulfport, 1973-76; spl. agt. Dept of Def., 1976-84; instr., adj. faculty Phillips Coll., Gulfport, 1979-81; mgr. H&R Block Inc., Jacksonville, 1984—, tax edn. specialist Anniston, Ala., 1986—; owner Village Tax Team, 2004—. Author: Duty, 1992, (poetry) Dan River Anthology, 1988; regional editor Feminist Lit., 1984. With USMC, 1965—68, with USMCR, 1968—75. Recipient Outstanding Young Women of Am. award, 1980. Mem. Nat. Tax Preparers Assn., Women Marines Assn., League for Animal Welfare (life mem.), Lambda Iota Tau, Nat. Assn. Tax Profls. Avocation: historian. Office: The Village Tax Team 100 Church St North Jacksonville AL 36265 Fax: 256-435-4189. E-mail: dlewis2233@aol.com.

LEWIS, DELANO EUGENE, ambassador, retired broadcast executive; b. Arkansas City, Kans., Nov. 12, 1938; s. Raymond Ernest and Enna (Wordlow) L.; m. Gayle Carolyn Jones; children: Delano Jr., Brian, Geoffrey, Phillip. BA, U. Kansas, 1960; JD, Washburn U., 1963; LHD (hon.), Marymount U., 1988; D of Humane Letters, Bowie State U., 1992; D of Pub. Svc., George Washington U., 1991; DHL (hon.), Barry U., 1994, Kent State U., 1995, Lafayette Coll., 1996; LLD (hon.), Nova Southeastern U., 1997; DFA (hon.), So. Ill. U., 1997. Staff atty. U.S. Dept. of Justice, Washington, 1963-65, EEOC, Washington, 1965-66; assoc. dir., country dir. U.S. Peace Corps, Nigeria, Uganda, 1966-69; legis. asst. Sen. Edward Brooke Mass., Washington, 1969-71; adminstrv. asst. Congressman Walter Fauntroy, Washington, 1971-73; mgr. pub. affairs Chesapeake & Potomac Telephone Co., Washington, 1973-76, asst. v.p., 1976-83, v.p., 1983-88, pres., 1988-93; pres., CEO Nat. Public Radio, Washington, 1994-98; amb. to South Africa Dept. of State, Pretoria, South Africa, 1999-2001. Bd. dirs. Eastman Kodak, Africare, Colgate-Palmolive, Herman T's Smokehouse BBQ Rest. Pres. Greater Washington Bd. Trade, 1988; chmn. Mayor's Transition Com., 1978, D.C. Youth Employment Adv. Coun., 1992; co-chair D.C. Vocational Edn. and Career Opportunities Com., 1991, NPR Found.; emeritus bd. dirs. Washington Performing Arts Soc., 1990—; bd. dirs. Lincoln Theatre, Found. Schs., The Menninger Found., 1996. Named Washingtonian of Yr. Washingtonian mag., 1978, Man of Yr., Greater Washington bd. trustees, 1992; recipient Pres. medal Cath. U., Washington, 1978, Tree of Life award NCCJ, 1989, Social Responsibility award George Washington U. Sch. Bus., 1990, Spl. award Women of Washington, Disting. Alumni Citation U. Kans.; Disting. Leadership award Amnesty Internat., 1997, US Media Spotlight award, 1997. Mem. Kans. Bar Assn., D.C. Bar Assn., Georgetown Club. Democrat. Roman Catholic. Avocation: tennis. Address: PO Box 1389 Mesilla NM 88046 E-mail: delanolewis@zianet.com.

LEWIS, DEXTER GERMAINE, small business owner; b. Albany, Ga., Dec. 28, 1972; s. Joe P. and Minnie Mae (Johnson) Lewis; m. Vickie Ann Christan (div. June 2003); children: Dexter Jr., Reginald, Gregory. AS in Bus. Mgmt., Honolulu CC, 1995. Profl. boxing license Ga. State Boxing Commn. Clk. U.S. Army, Honolulu, 1993—97; CEO Lewis Enterprise Inc., Albany, Ga., 1997—. V.p. Tip Top Nail Inc., Albany, Ga., 2000—. Founder Minorities Against the Injustice of the System, Albany, Ga., 2005. E-4 U.S. Army, 1993—97. Democrat. Baptist. Avocations: horseback riding, fishing, camping. Home: 2004 Jones Ave Albany GA 31707 Office: Minorities Against the Injustice 2004 Jones Ave Albany GA 31707

LEWIS, DONALD EMERSON, banker; b. Orange, N.J., Apr. 3, 1950; s. Donald Emerson Lewis and Marie (Gannon) Slaght; m. Suzanne Kimm, Oct. 12, 1974; children: Andrew Gannon, Meredith Marie, Carolyn Ann. AB, Villanova U., 1972; MBA, Boston Coll., 1974. V.p. Citibank N.A., N.Y.C., 1974-85, Boston Safe Deposit & Trust Co., N.Y.C., 1985-87; sr. v.p. United Jersey Banks, Princeton, NJ, 1987-91; v.p. Fleet Bank, N.A., Bridgewater, NJ, 1991-2000; ptnr. Wachovia Wealth Mgmt. Group, Summit, NJ, 2000—. Mem.: Canoe Brook Country. Republican. Roman Catholic. Avocations: golf, platform tennis. Office: Wachovia Bank NA 190 River Rd Summit NJ 07901-1412 Office Phone: 908-598-3705. E-mail: donald.lewis@wachovia.com.

LEWIS, DONALD SYKES, JR., artist; b. Norfolk, Va., Dec. 13, 1947; s. Donald Sykes and Beverly Porter Lewis; m. Elizabeth Caldwell McCauley, Jan. 15, 1993; children: Davidson, Byron, Peyton. BA in Fine Arts, Randolph-Macon Coll., 1970; MA in History of Art, U. Va., 1973. V.p. Auslew Gallery Inc., Norfolk, Va., 1974—86; instr. Old Dominion U., Norfolk, Va., 1975—76, Hermitage Mus., Norfolk, Va., 1978—79; pres. Auslew Gallery Inc., Norfolk, Va., 1987—93; dir., sec., treas. Granby & Main Corp., Norfolk, Va., 2004—. One-man shows include Auslew Gallery, Norfolk, Va., 1982, Art Works, 1994, Hermitage Found. Mus., 1996, Warm Springs (Va.) Gallery, 2000, exhibited in group shows at Randolph-Macon Coll., Ashland, Va., 1985, exhibitions include Springville (Utah) Mus. Art, 1981, Gallery Mayo, Richmond, Va., 1983—95, 20th Century Gallery, Williamsburg, Va., 1985, Peninsula Fine Arts Ctr., Newport News, Va., 1997, Salmagundi Club, N.Y.C., 2002, Pleiades Gallery, 2002, Am. Artist and Profl. League, 2003, Salmagundi Club, 2003; author: (exhbn. catalog) Brandywind Mus., 1992; contbr. articles to profl. jours. Chmn. fundraising com. Chrysler Mus., Norfolk, Va., 1982—84; v.p. alumni bd. Randolph-Macon Acad., Front Royal, Va., 1983—87; advisor Va. Opera Assn., Norfolk, 1988. Home: 708 Cavalier Dr Virginia Beach VA 23451

LEWIS, DOUGLAS, retired art historian; b. Centreville, Miss., Apr. 30, 1938; s. Charles Douglas and Beatrice Fenwick (Stewart) L. BA in History; BA in History of Art, Yale U., 1960, MA, 1963, PhD, 1967; BA in Fine Arts, Clare Coll., Cambridge (Eng.) U., 1962, MA, 1966. Asst. in instrn. Yale U., 1962-64; asst. prof. art Bryn Mawr Coll., 1967-68; vis. lectr. U. Calif., Berkeley, spring 1970, fall 1979; adj. prof. Johns Hopkins U., 1973-77; curator sculpture and decorative arts Nat. Gallery Art, Washington, 1968—2004. Professorial lectr. Georgetown U., 1980-93; adj. prof. U. Md., 1988-91, 93-2003; mem. art adv. coms. U. Va. Art Mus., Mt. Holyoke Coll. Art Mus., Lawrenceville Sch.; chmn. nat. citizens stamp adv. com. U.S. Postal Svc.; adv. coun. Humanities West, San Francisco, 1991-98; adv. bd. Centro Palladiano, Vicenza, Italy, Audubon and Rosedown (La.) State Hist. Sites, Natchez Lit. and Cinema Celebration. Author: The Late Baroque Churches of Venice, 1979, The Drawings of Andrea Palladio, 1981, rev. and enlarged edit., 2000, intro. to Renaissance Master Bronzes, 1986. Mem. Am. fellowship com. Belgian-Am. Ednl. Found., 1971—. Recipient Copley medal Nat. Portrait Gallery, 1981; Chester Dale fellow; David E. Finley fellow Nat. Gallery Art, 1964-67; Rome Prize fellow Am. Acad. Rome, 1964-66, Bruce Curatorial fellow Nat. Gallery Art, 1997-98. Mem. Assn. for Art History (mem. adv. bd.), Coll. Art Assn. Am., Soc. Archtl. Historians, Nat. Trust Historic Preservation, Manuscript Soc. Clubs: Yale (N.Y.C.); Falcons (Cambridge U.). Episcopalian.

LEWIS, EARL, academic administrator; b. Va. m. Susan Whitlock. BA in History and Psychology magna cum laude, Concordia Coll., Moorhead, Minn., 1978; MA in Am. History, U. Minn., 1981, PhD in History, 1984. Various positions U. Calif., Berkeley, 1984—89; mem. faculty U. Mich., 1989—2004, dir. Ctr. for Afroamerican and African Studies, 1990—93, interim dean Rackham Grad. Sch., 1997—98, dean, vice provost Rackham Grad. Sch., 1998—2004; provost Emory U., Atlanta, 2004—. Chair bd. dirs. Coun. Grad. Schs., 2002. Author: In Their Own Interests: Race, Class and Power in Twentieth-Century Norfolk, 1993; co-author: Love on Trial: An American Scandal in Black and White, 2001, Defending Diversity, 2004; contbr. articles to publs.; co-author: The African American Urban Experience, 2004. Recipient Disting. Achievement award, U. Minn., 2001. Office: Office of Provost Emory Univ Atlanta GA 30322

LEWIS, E(ARL) B(RADLEY), artist, illustrator; b. Phila., Dec. 16, 1956; Student, Temple Univ. Sch. Art League; BFA in Graphic Design & Illustration and Art Edn., Temple Univ., 1979, MFA. Art tchr., freelance artist; now adj.assoc. prof. Univ. of the Arts, Phila. Illustrator: (children's books) Fire on the Mountain, 1994, Down the Road, 1995, Magid Fasts for Ramadan, 1996, Creativity, 1997, The Bat Boy and His Violin, 1998, I Love My Hair!, 1998, The Jazz of Our Street, 1998, Dirt on Their Skirts, 2000, Bippity Bop Barbershop, 2002, Talkin' About Bessie, 2002 (Coretta Scott King award, 2003), Coming On Home Soon, 2004, others. Mem.: Soc. Illustrators, NYC. Office: Illustration Univ of the Arts 320 S Broad St Philadelphia PA 19102 E-mail: eblewis@eticomm.net.*

LEWIS, EDWARD CLARK, lawyer; b. Lamesa, Tex., June 14, 1966; m. Suzanne Lewis. BSChemE, Tex. A&M U., 1988; JD, U. Tex., 1992. Bar: Tex. 1993, U.S. Dist. Ct. (so. dist.) Tex. 1996, U.S. Ct. Appeals (5th cir.) 1997. Ptnr. Fulbright & Jaworski LLP, Houston, 1993—. Author: Texas Environmental Law Handbook, 5th edit., 2000; contbr. articles to profl. jours. Mem. ABA (natural resources, energy and environ. law sect.), Tex. State Bar (environ. law sect.), Houston Bar Assn. (environ. law sect., dir.). Office: Fulbright & Jaworski LLP 1301 Mckinney St Ste 5100 Houston TX 77010-3031 E-mail: elewis@fulbright.com.

LEWIS, EDWIN AUGUSTUS STEVENS, physics educator; b. Balt., Mar. 4, 1940; s. H. H. Walker and Eleanor (Nelson) L.; m. Mary Ann Glasgo, Jan. 27, 1968; children: Catherine, Walker. AB, Princeton U., 1961; Diploma in Edn., Makerere U. Coll., Uganda, 1962; PhD in Physics, U. Ill., 1969. Asst. prof. physics Union Coll., Schenectady, N.Y., 1970-77; tchr. The Key Sch., Annapolis, Md., 1977-80, Gilman Sch., Balt., 1980—. Tchr. Greyhills Acad. High Sch., Tuba City, Ariz., 1996-97. Contbr. articles to profl. jours. Mem. vestry Meml. Episc. Ch., Balt., 1981-83, 90-92; mem., chmn. bd. dirs. Samaritan Cmty., Balt., 1993—. Mem. Am. Assn. Physics Tchrs., Md. Assn. Sci. Tchrs. Democrat. Home: 8 Over Ridge Ct Apt 4032 Baltimore MD 21210-1129 Office: Gilman Sch 5407 Roland Ave Baltimore MD 21210-1989

LEWIS, EDWIN REYNOLDS, biomedical engineering educator; b. LA, July 14, 1934; s. Edwin McMurtry and Sally Newman (Reynolds) L.; m. Elizabeth Louise McLean, June 11, 1960; children: Edwin McLean, Sarah Elizabeth. AB in Biol. Sci., Stanford U., 1956, MSEE, 1957, Engr., 1959, PhD in Elec. Engring., 1962. With research staff Librascope div. Gen. Precision Inc., Glendale, Calif., 1961-67; mem. faculty dept. elec. engring. and computer sci. U. Calif., Berkeley, 1967—, dir. bioengring. tng. program, 1969-77, prof. elec. engring. and computer sci., 1971-94, prof. grad. sch., 1994-99, prof. emeritus, 1999—, assoc. dean grad. div., 1977-82, assoc. dean interdisciplinary studies coll. engring., 1988-96. Chair joint program bioengring. U. Calif., Berkeley and San Francisco, 1988-91. Author: Network Models in Population Biology, 1977, (with others) Neural Modeling, 1977, The Vertebrate Inner Ear, 1985, Introduction to Bioengineering, 1996; contbr. articles to profl. jours. Grantee NSF, NASA, 1984, 87, Office Naval Rsch., 1990-93, NIH, 1975-2001; Neurosci. Rsch. Program fellow, 1966, 69; recipient Disting. Tchg. citation U. Calif., 1972, Berkeley citation, 1997; Jacob Javits Neurosci. investigator NIH, 1984-91. Fellow IEEE, Acoustical Soc. Am.; mem. AAAS, Assn. Rsch. in Otolaryngology, Soc. Neurosci., Toastmasters (area lt. gov. 1966-67), Sigma Xi. Office: U Calif Dept Elec Engring & Computer Scis Berkeley CA 94720-1770 Business E-Mail: lewis@eecs.berkeley.edu.

LEWIS, ELEANOR ROBERTS, lawyer; b. Detroit, Jan. 5, 1944; m. Roger Kutnow Lewis, June 24, 1967; 1 child, Kevin Michael. BA, Wellesley Coll., 1965; MA, Harvard U., 1966; JD, Georgetown U., 1974. Bar: DC 1975. Atty. HUD, Washington, 1974-76, asst. gen. counsel, 1979-82; atty. Brownstein Zeidman & Schomer, Washington, 1976-79; chief counsel internat. commerce U.S. Dept. Commerce, Washington, 1982—. Author, editor (with others): book Street Law, 1975; contbr. chapters to books, articles to legal and fin. jours. Bd. dirs. Dana Pl. Condominium, Washington. Mem.: ABA (U.S. govt. liaison to internat. sect.), Sr. Execs. Assn. (bd. dirs. local chpt.), DC Bar Assn. Home: 5034 1/2 Dana Pl NW Washington DC 20016-3441 Office: US Dept Commerce 14th & Constitution Ave NW Washington DC 20230-0001

LEWIS, ELIZABETH R., director; d. Edward Warren and Grace Stevens Rice; m. Gary F. Lewis, June 30, 1973; children: Karen Elizabeth, Kelly Ann. BA, U. Vt., 1973, MEd, 1983, cert. of advanced study, 2005. Cert. tchr. Vt., lic. reading specialist Vt. Reading tchr. Addison NW Supervisory Union, Vergennes, Vt., 1990—97, literacy coord., 2001—, co-dir. curriculum, 2004—; reading recovery tchr. leader Addison Rutland Consortium, Middlebury, Vt., 1997—2001. Adj. faculty U. Vt., Burlington, 1998—2001. Del. Congregational Ch. of Vergennes, 2005—. Named Outstanding Tchr., U. Vt., 1997. Mem.: Vt. Coun. on Reading, Internat. Reading Assn., Delta Kappa Gamma. Congregationalist. Avocations: gardening, winemaking, sewing. Office: Addison NW Supervisory Union 48 Green St Vergennes VT 05491

LEWIS, EMANUEL RAYMOND, historian; b. Oakland, Calif., Nov. 30, 1928; s. Jacob A. and Rose Lewis; m. Joan R. Wilson, Feb. 7, 1954; 1 son, Joseph J.; m. Eleanor M. Gamarsh, Aug. 24, 1967. BA, U. Calif., Berkeley, 1951, MA, 1953; PhD, U. Oreg., 1962. Asst. prof. psychology We. Oreg. U., 1961-62, Oreg. State U., 1962-67; project mgr. System Devel. Corp., Falls Church, Va., 1968-69; vis. postdoctoral research asso. in Am. history Smithsonian Instn., Washington, 1969-70; chief historian, dir. research Contract Archeology, Alexandria, Va., 1971-73; librarian U.S. Ho. of Reps., Washington, 1973-95, libr. emeritus, 1995—. Author: Seacoast Fortifications of the United States, 1970, 2d edit. 1979, 3d edit. 1993; editor: The Educational Information Center, 1969. Served with M.I. U.S. Army, 1954-56. NIMH research fellow, 1960

LEWIS, ERIC JOSEPH, dermatologist; b. Santa Rosa, Calif., Apr. 29, 1964; s. Albert Abraham and Ilse Paula Lewis; m. Sarah Jean Schulz, Dec. 29, 1984; children: Marena Elaine, Janile Olivia, Kristen Adele. BS in Chemistry, SD Sch. Mines and Tech., 1986; PhD in Chemistry, U. Calif., Davis, 1990, MD, 1994. Diplomate Am. Bd. Dermatology. Intern Hennepin County Med. Ctr., Mpls., 1994—95; resident in dermatology U. Minn., Mpls., 1995—98; dermatologist Affiliated Cmty. Med. Ctrs., Willmar, Minn., 1998—2000, Stevens Cmty. Med. Ctr., Morris, Minn., 2000—. Clin. asst. prof. dermatology U. Minn., Mpls., 1998—2003; resident adv. bd. Cutis, Cutaneous Medicine for the Practitioner, Chatham, NJ, 1998; co-chief resident Dept. Dermatology, U. Minn., Mpls., 1997—98. Contbr. articles to profl. jours. Recipient Outstanding Grad. award, SD Sch. Mines and Tech., 1997. Fellow: Am. Acad. Dermatology; mem.: AMA, Minn. Dermatol. Soc., Am. Soc. for Mohs Surgery (assoc.), Honor Med. Soc., Alpha Omega Alpha. Roman Catholic. Avocations: running, reading, sailing. Office: Stevens Cmty Med Ctr 400 E 1st St Morris MN 56267 Office Phone: 320-589-1313.

LEWIS, FLOYD WALLACE, former electric utility executive; b. Lincoln County, Miss., Sept. 23, 1925; s. Thomas Cassidy and Lizzie (Lofton) L.; m. Jimmie Etoile Slawson, Dec. 27, 1949; children: Floyd Wallace, Gail, Julie, Ann, Carol, Michael Paul. BBA, Tulane U., 1945, LL.B., 1949. Bar: La. 1949. With New Orleans Pub. Service Inc., 1949-62, v.p., chief fin. officer, 1960-62; v.p. Ark. Power & Light Co., Little Rock, 1962-63, sr. v.p., 1963-67; exec. v.p., dir. La. Power & Light Co., New Orleans, 1967-68, pres., 1968-70, chief exec. officer, 1968-71, chmn. bd., 1970-72; pres. Middle South Utilities, Inc., 1970-79, 80-85, chmn. bd., 1979-85, also dir., chief exec. officer, 1972-85. Pres., dir. Middle South Services, Inc., New Orleans, 1970-75, chmn., 1975-85, chief exec. officer, 1972-79; pres., dir. Middle South Energy, Inc., 1974-85; chmn. bd. System Fuels, Inc., 1972-85; dir. New Orleans br. Fed. Res. Bank, 1974-75, chmn., 1975; past dir. Fed. Res. Bank of Atlanta, Breeder Reactor Corp., New Orleans Pub. Service Inc., Ark. Power and Light Co., La. Power & Light Co., Miss. Power and Light Co., U.S. Chamber Commerce; mem. adv. com. Elec. Cos. Advt. Program, 1969-72, chmn., 1970-71; mem. electric utility adv. com. to Fed. Energy Adminstrn., 1975-76; chmn. Edison Electric Inst., 1976-77, mem. exec. com., 1974-78; mem. exec. com. Assn. Edison Illuminating Cos., 1973-80; dir. Electric Power Research Inst., 1977-82, chmn., 1979-81; dir. Am. Nuclear Energy Council, 1982-86; pres. Provident Housing Corp., 1999-2001. Mem. exec. bd. New Orleans area council Boy Scouts Am., 1967-80, v.p., 1970-74, pres., 1975-76, mem. regional exec. com., 1968-80; v.p. Com. for a Better La., 1975-76, sr. v.p., 1976-77, pres., 1977-78; bd. dirs. La. World Expn. Inc., 1976-89, chmn., 1980-81, 83-89, pres., 1981-83; chmn. Utility Nuclear Power Oversight Com., 1979-81; vice chmn. campaign United Fund, New Orleans, 1970, chmn., 1971; bd. dirs. New Orleans Symphony Soc., 1974-75, Atomic Indsl. Forum, 1982-86, vice chmn., 1985-86; bd. dirs. Pub. Affairs Research Council of La.; pres. New Orleans Bapt. Sem. Found., 1973-76, 91-92; trustee La. Coll., 1984-90; New Orleans Baptist Theol. Sem., 1954-62, 1968-78, v.p., 1970-78; bd. adminstrs. Tulane U., 1973-88, bd. visitors, 1968-71; bd. govs. Med. Center, 1969-73, vice chmn., 1969-71; chmn. alumni adv. council Grad. Sch. Bus., 1970-73; bd. dirs. U.S. Com. Energy Awareness, 1982-85, vice-chmn., 1983-84, chmn., 1985; v.p. Internat. House, 1970; trustee Com. Econ. Devel., 1972-87; mem. bd. Ochsner Med. Found., 1976-96, mem. exec. com., 1977-96; 1st chmn. Parents Council, Furman U.; mem. Parents Council, Wake Forest U., 1980-81; trustee La. Bapt. Found., 1995-2000, chmn. 1996; chmn. Kaken-Am. Found., 1999-2005. Served to ensign USNR, 1945-46. Recipient Silver Beaver, Silver Antelope Boy Scouts Am.; Oliver Townsend medal Atomic Indsl. Forum; Outstanding Alumni award Grad. Sch. Bus., 1970; Disting. Alumnus award Tulane U., 1983 Mem. Order of Coif, Beta Gamma Sigma, Omicron Delta Kappa, Beta Theta Pi, Phi Delta Phi. Baptist (deacon).

LEWIS, FRANK RUSSELL, JR., surgeon; b. Willards, Md., Feb. 23, 1941; m. Janet Christensen, 1996. AB in Physics, Princeton U., 1961; MD, U. Md., 1965; postgrad. in med. physics, U. Calif., Berkeley, 1970. Surg. dir. M/SICU San Francisco Gen. Hosp., 1973-80, dir. emergency dept., 1980-83, chief of staff, 1983-85, asst. chief of surgery, 1981-86, chief of surgery, 1986-92; prof. surgery Case We. Res. U., Cleve., 1994—2002; chmn. dept. surgery Henry Ford Hosp., Detroit, 1992—2002; exec. dir. Am. Bd. Surgery, 2002—. Fellow: ACS (gov. 1988—93, 1st v.p. 1995—96); mem.: So. Surg. Assn., Shock Soc. (coun. 1978—, pres.), We. Surg. Soc., Ctrl. Surg. Soc., Am. Assn. for Surgery of Trauma (pres. 1999—2002), Am. Surg. Assn. Office: Am Bd Surgery 1617 JFK Blvd Ste 860 Philadelphia PA 19130 Office Phone: 215-568-4000. E-mail: flewis@absurgery.org.

LEWIS, GENE EVANS, retired medical equipment company executive; b. Terrell, Tex., May 17, 1928; s. John Evans and Helen Elizabeth (Patterson) L.; m. Sonya Dolishny, Jan. 21, 1950; children: Robert, Melissa. BSEE, Tex. A&M U., 1949. Sales, mktg. and engring. mgr. GE, Schenectady, Dallas, Pittsfield, Holyoke, Lynn, 1950-68, gen. mgr. various bus. Milw., 1970-77; group product mgr. Picker X-Ray, Cleve., 1968-70; pres. sci. instruments div. Am. Optical Corp., Southbridge, Mass., 1977-78, pres. internat. div., 1978-79, pres., 1979—84, Baker Instruments Corp., Allentown, Pa., 1985—88; bd. mem. Novecon Technologies, 1994—99. CEO Sterling Semicondr., Inc., 1996-2001. With Signal Corps U.S. Army, 1949. Mem. Calibogue Club, Sea Pines Country Club. Home: 25 Spartina Cres Hilton Head Island SC 29928-2925 Personal E-mail: gelsl@aol.com.

LEWIS, GEORGE RALPH, consumer goods company executive; b. Burgess, Va., Mar. 7, 1941; s. Spencer Harcum and Edith Pauline (Toulson) L.; m. Lillian Charlotte Glenn, Oct. 11, 1963; children: Tonya, Tracey. BS, Hampton U., 1963; MBA, Iona Coll., 1968. Product analyst Gen. Foods Corp., White Plains, N.Y., 1963-66; fin. analyst W.R. Grace, N.Y.C., 1966-67; corp. analyst Philip Morris Inc., N.Y.C., 1967-69, sr. planning analyst, 1969-70, mgr. fin. rels., 1970-72, mgr. fin. svcs., 1972-73, asst. treas., 1973-75; v.p. fin. and planning, treas. Philip Morris Indsl., Milw., 1975-82; v.p., treas. Philip Morris Cos., Inc., N.Y.C., 1984—; v.p. fin. The Seven Up Co., St. Louis, 1982-84. Bd. dirs. Ctrl. Fidelity Bank, Richmond, Va., Kemper Nat. Ins. Cos., Ceridian Corp.; nat. adv. com. Profl. Golfers' Assn. Am. Trustee Hampton (Va.) U.; bd. dirs. Nat. Urban League, N.Y.C. Recipient Arthur A. Loftus Achievement award in Fin., Iona Coll., 1981, Outstanding Twenty Yr. Alumnus award Hampton U., 1983. Mem. Nat. Corp. Treas. Assn., Nat. Bankers Assn. (corp. adv. bd.), Omega Psi Phi, Sigma Pi Phi.

LEWIS, GERALD DAVID, music educator; b. Elkhart, Ind., Dec. 14, 1922; s. Russell Kinkaid and Ruth Elnora (Horein) L.; m. Marjorie Louise Lewis, June 17, 1951; children— Julia, Scott, Jacqueline. B.S., Juilliard Sch. Music, N.Y.C., 1950; M.M., U. So. Calif., 1954. Violinist, St. Louis Symphony and Sinfoniette, 1950-53, L.A. Philharm., 1953-57; tchr. South Bend (Ind.) Community Schs., 1960-70; concertmaster South Bend Symphony, 1960-70; assoc. prof. orch. dir., violin theory Gustavus Adolphus Coll., St. Peter, Minn., 1970-88, prof. emeritus, 1988—; tchr. New Eng. Music Camp, Oakland, Maine, summers 1978-86; 1st violin Res. String Quartet, West S. Bend, Ind., 1964-70, past sec. Minn. String Task Force. Served with U.S. Army, 1943-46. Decorated Bronze Star. Mem. Am. Fedn. Musicians, Music Educators Nat. Conf., Am. String Tchrs. Assn. (gold merit award Ind. chpt. 1964). Home: 2223 Knolls Dr Santa Rosa CA 95405-8343

LEWIS, GERALD JORGENSEN, judge; b. Perth Amboy, N.J., Sept. 9, 1933; s. Norman Francis and Blanche M. (Jorgensen) L.; m. Laura Susan McDonald, Dec. 15, 1973; children by previous marriage: Michael, Marc. AB magna cum laude, Tufts Coll., 1954; JD, Harvard U., 1957. Bar: D.C. 1957, N.J. 1961, Calif. 1962, U.S. Supreme Ct. 1968. Atty. Gen. Atomic, La Jolla, Calif., 1961-63; ptnr. Haskins, Lewis, Nugent & Newnham, San Diego, 1963-77; judge Mcpl. Ct., El Cajon, Calif., 1977-79, Superior Ct., San Diego, 1979-84; assoc. justice Calif. Ct. of Appeal, San Diego, 1984-87; dir. Fisher Scientific Group, Inc., 1987-98, Bolsa Chica Corp., 1991-93, Gen. Chem. Group, Inc., 1996—; of counsel Lathan & Watkins, 1987-97; dir. Invesco Mut. Funds, Denver, 2000—03, AIM Mutual Funds, Houston, 2003—. Adj. prof. evidence Western State U. Sch. Law, San Diego, 1977-85, exec. bd., 1977-89; dir. Invesco Mutual Funds, 2000—03, AIM Mutual Funds, 2003-; faculty San Diego Inn of Ct., 1979—, Am. Inn of Ct., 1984— . Cons. editor: California Civil Jury Instructions, 1984. City atty. Del Mar, Calif., 1963-74, Coronado, Calif., 1972-77; counsel Comprehensive Planning Orgn., San Diego, 1972-73; trustee San Diego Mus. Art, 1986-89; bd. dirs. Air Pollution Control Dist., San Diego County, 1972-76. Served to lt. comdr. USNR, 1957-61. Named Trial Judge of Yr., San Diego Trial Lawyers Assn., 1984; recipient Heritage award, Am. Ireland Fund, 2004. Mem. Am. Judicature Soc., Soc. Inns of Ct. in Calif., Confrerie des Chevaliers du Tastevin, Order of St. Hubert (knight comdr.), Friendly Sons of St. Patrick (Irishman of Yr. 2000), The Irisn 50 Aztec Big 50, Bohemian Club, La Jolla Country Club (dir. 1980-83), Prophets, The K Club (County Kildare), Pauma Valley Country Club. Republican. Episcopalian. Home: PO Box 325 Pauma Valley CA 92061 also: 600 W Broadway Ste 1800 San Diego CA 92101-8197 Office Phone: 619-238-2843.

LEWIS, GOLDA, artist; studied painting with Hans Hofmann, Jack Tworkov, Vaclav Vytlacil, studied sculpture with Robert Laurent, studied papermaking with Douglas Howell. Lectr. numerous workshops and seminars on art. One-woman shows include Balin-Traube Gallery, N.Y., 1963, Drawing Shop Gallery, N.Y., 1963, XXth Century West Galleries, N.Y., 1967, Benedicta Arts Ctr. Gallery, Coll. St. Benedict, St. Joseph, Minn., 1967, 74, Court Gallery, Copenhagen, 1970, Alonzo Gallery, N.Y., 1971, Peter M. David Gallery, Mpls., 1974, Gallery K, Washington, 1979, Mus. Art, RISD, Providence, 1981, Centro Cultural Costarricense Norteamericano, San Jose, Costa Rica, 1983, Galeria Enrique Echandi, Museo De Arte Costarricense, San Jose, 1984, Galerie Faust, Geneva, 1986, Discerning Images Gallery, Montclair, N.J., 1987, Gallery of Inter-Am. Devel. Bank, Washington, 1988; group exhbns. include Mus. Modern Art, N.Y.C., 1963-64, 76, XXth Century West Galleries, N.Y., 1966, John Michael Kohler Gallery, Sheboygan, Wis., 1967, Phoenix Gallery, N.Y., 1969, Weatherspoon Gallery, Greensboro, N.C., 1969, 74, Bergen County Mus., N.J., 1971, Hudson River Mus., Yonkers, N.Y., 1971, Landmark Gallery, N.Y., 1972, 76, N.Y. Cultural Ctr. Mus., N.Y., 1973, Alonzo Gallery, N.Y., 1974, John Nelson Bergstrom Mus., Appleton, Wis., 1975, Buecker and Harpsichord, N.Y., 1976, Art Guild, N.Y., 1976, Nat. Collection of Fine Arts, Smithsonian, Washington, 1977-78, Visual Images Art Gallery, Wellfleet, Mass., 1977, The Gallery of Peters Valley, Layton, N.J., 1978, San Francisco Mus. Art, 1978, Wildcliff Mus., New Rochelle, N.Y., 1978, Peter M. David Gallery, Mpls., 1979, The Gallery of Clayworks, 1980, Am. Cultural Ctr., Tel Aviv, 1981, 84, Visual Art Ctr., Beersheva, Israel, 1981, Gallery Momoyo, Tokyo, 1981, Getler/Pall Gallery, N.Y., 1981, Am. Craft Mus., N.Y., 1982-84, Fine Arts Mus. L.I., Hempstead, N.Y., 1982-83, C.D.S. Gallery, N.Y., 1983, Craftsman Gallery, Scarsdale, N.Y., Gallery Beni, Kyoto, Japan, 1983, Arts Coun. Gt. Britain, 1983-84, Byer Mus. Art, Evanston, Ill., 1983, Kouros Gallery, N.Y., 1984, Montpelier Cultural Arts Ctr., Laurell, Md., 1984, Municipality of Netanya, Israel, 1985, Kenkelba Gallery, N.Y., 1985, Gallery de Isla, U. Guam, 1985, Royal Libr. of the Hague, The Netherlands, 1986, Arad (Israel) Mus., 1986, Leopold-Hoesch Mus., Duren, Germany, 1986, N.J. Ctr. for Visual Arts, Summit, N.J., 1988, Nat. Sch. Art, Brussels, 1989, Koninklijke Bibliotheek, Royal Libr., The Netherlands, 1989, Aaron Gallery, Washington, 1989, Petit Format De Papier, Cul-Des-Sarts, Couvin, Belgium, 1989, Nysted (Denmark) Kunstforening, 1989, Anita Shapolsky Gallery, N.Y., 1991, 92, 94, Museo Banco Central, San Jose, Costa Rica, 1993, numerous others. Studio: 31 Union Sq W Apt 9C New York NY 10003-3204

LEWIS, GOLDY SARAH, real estate developer, real estate company executive; b. West Selkirk, Man., Can., June 15, 1921; d. David and Rose (Dwor) Kimmel; m. Ralph Milton Lewis, June 12, 1941; children: Richard Alan, Robert Edward, Roger Gordon, Randall Wayne. BS, UCLA, 1943; postgrad., U. So. Calif., 1944-45. Pvt. practice acctg., L.A., 1945-57; law office mgr., 1953-55; dir., exec. v.p. Lewis Homes, Upland, Calif., 1955—, Lewis Construction Co. Inc., Upland, 1959—, Lewis Bldg. Co., Inc., Las Vegas, 1960—, Republic Sales Co., Inc., 1956—, Kimmel Enterprises, Inc., 1959—; mng. partner Lewis Homes of Calif., 1973—; mng. ptnr. Lewis Homes of Nev., 1972—, Western Properties, 1972—, Foothill Investment Co., 1971—, Republic Mgmt. Co., 1978—. Contbr. articles to mags., jours. Mem. Dean's Coun. UCLA Grad. Sch. Architecture and Urban Planning; mem. UCLA Found., Chancellor's Assocs.; endowed Ralph and Goldy Lewis Ctr. for Regional Policy at UCLA, 1989, Ralph and Goldy Lewis Hall of Planning and Devel. at U. S.C., 1989, others. Co-recipient Builder of Yr. award, Profl. Builder Mag., 1988, Housing Person of Yr. award, Nat. Housing Conf., 1990, Entrepreneur of Yr. award, Inland Empire, 1990; named Ralph and Goldy Lewis Sports Ctr. in their honor, City of Rancho Cucamonga, 1988, also several other parks and sports fields including Lewis Park in Claremont; named one of Women of Yr., Calif. 25th Senate Dist., 1989, (with husband Ralph M. Lewis) Disting. CEO, Calif. State U., San Bernadino, 1991, Mgmt. Leaders of the Yr., Univ. Calif., Riverside, 1993; recipient 1st award of distinction, Am. Builder mag., 1963, Homer Briggs Svc. to Youth award, West End YMCA, 1990, Spirit of Life award, City of Hope, 1993, Builder of Century award, Bldg. Industry Assn., Baldy View chpt., 1999. Mem. Nat. Assn. Home Builders, Bldg. Industry Assn. So. Calif. (Builder of Yr. award Baldy View chpt. 1988), Internat. Coun. Shopping Ctrs., Urban Land Inst. Office: Lewis Homes PO Box 670 Upland CA 91785-0670

LEWIS, GORDON GILMER, golf course architect; b. Shawnee, Okla., Sept. 7, 1950; s. Ted Eugene and Janet Garvin (Panner) Lewis; m. Karen Louise McKenzie, June 2, 1973 (div. Dec. 1981); children: Melanie Marie Lewis-Lehr, Katie McKenzie Lewis-Lehr; m. Susette Mamie London, June 11, 1988; children: London Marshall, Sarah June Victoria. B in Landscape Architecture, Kans. State U., 1974. Registered landscape arch., Ala., Kans., Fla. Golf course architect David Gill, St. Charles, Ill., 1974-75; golf course arch. Charles M. Graves Orgn., Atlanta, 1975-78, Gordon G. Lewis, Naples, Fla., 1978—. Prin. works include Meadowbrook Links, Rapid City, S.D. (Top 50 Pub. Courses in U.S.), Hulman Links at Los Creek, Terre Haute, Ind. (Top 50 Pub. Courses in U.S.), Lagoon Pk., Montgomery, Ala. (Top 75 Pub. Courses in U.S.), The Forest, Ft. Myers, Fla., The Vines, Estero, Fla. (One of Top New Courses Golf Digest, 1986), Worthington, Bonita Springs, Fla., Tsai-Hsing, Taipei, Taiwan, others. Republican. Presbyterian. Avocation: golf. Home: 5980 Golden Oaks Ln Naples FL 34119

LEWIS, GORDON RICHARD, lawyer; b. Rockford, Ill., June 12, 1949; s. H. Walter and Elizanne (Hanitz) L. BS in Environ. Sci., Mich. State U., 1971; JD, U. Mich., 1974. Assoc. atty. Warner Norcross & Judd LLP, Grand Rapids, Mich., 1974-79, ptnr., 1979—. Dir. Bay Plastics Machinery Corp., Bay City, Mich., 1997—; dir., sec. Scheer Bay Co., Bay City, 1998—. Dir. Little Manistee Watershed Conservation Coun., Irons, Mich., 1996—. Named to Best Lawyers in Am., Woodward-White, 1994—. Mem. Indian Club (dir., sec. 1986—), Kent Country Club. Avocations: fly fishing, golf, hunting. Office: Warner Norcross & Judd LLP 111 Lyon St NW Grand Rapids MI 49503-2406 E-mail: glewis@wnj.com.

LEWIS, GUY A., prosecutor; b. Chattanooga, Tennessee; m. Loyda Lewis; 1 child, Rose Marie. BS, U. Tennessee, 1983; Juris Doctor, U. Memphis Sch. of Law, 1986. Law clerk Hon. Thomas E. Scott, U.S. Dist. Ct., Fla., Hon. William Cowen, U.S. Ct. Appeals, Federal Circuit, Washington; prosecutor State's Atty.'s Office, 1988—, first asst.; U.S. atty. so. dist. U.S. Dept. Justice, 2000—02; dir. Exec. Off. for U.S. Atty., 2002—. Co-counsel trial U.S. vs. Gen. Manuel Noreiga, Matthew Block Prosecution; deputy chief Narcotics Section. Office: EOUSA 950 Pennsylvania Ave NW Rm 2616 Washington DC 20530*

LEWIS, HANNA BALLIN, German educator; b. Berlin, Aug. 20, 1931; came to U.S., 1938; d. Jack Hellmut and Ilse Julie (Blumenthal) Ballin; m. Bernard Melvin Lewis, June 11, 1950; children: Ellen Rose, Anne Carol, Paul Ballin, Kay Elizabeth. Student, U. Pa., 1949-50; BA, Rice U., 1952, MA, 1961, PhD, 1964. Tchr. Cleveland (Tex.) Independent Sch. Dist., 1953-55; teaching asst. Rice U., Houston, 1959-62, instr., 1962-65; tech. translator Fluor Corp., Houston, 1965-67; asst. prof. Stephen F. Austin State U., Nacogdoches, Tex., 1967-69, assoc. prof., 1969-74, Sam Houston State U., Huntsville, Tex., 1974-80, prof., 1980—, program coord., 1988—. Contbr. articles to profl. publs. Grantee Fulbright Found., 1978, NEH, 1980, 87, 89. Mem. MLA, South Cen. Modern Lang. Assn., Am. Assn. Tchrs. German, Am. Literary Translators Assn., German-Texan Heritage Soc. (book editor 1982—). Avocations: cinema, bridge, reading, travel, music. Home: 165 Circle Dr Cleveland TX 77327-5113 Office: Sam Houston State U Fgn Langs Dept Huntsville TX 77341

LEWIS, HENRY RAFALSKY, manufacturing executive; b. Yonkers, N.Y., Nov. 19, 1925; s. Jasper R. and Freda (Rafalsky) L.; m. Barbara Connolly, June 15, 1957; children: Peter, Susan, Abigail. AB, Harvard U., 1949, MA, 1951, PhD, 1957. Group head Ops. Evaluation Group, Washington, 1955-57; staff electronic rsch. lab. RCA, Princeton, N.J., 1957-66, dir., 1966-70; v.p. R & D Itek Corp., Lexington, Mass., 1970-74; pres. Optel Corp., Princeton, N.J., 1974; sr. v.p. Dennison Mfg. Co., Waltham, Mass., 1974-85, vice-chmn., 1986-91, also bd. dirs.; CEO Celadon Scis. Inc., Boston, 1996-98. Bd. dirs. Dyax Corp., Cambridge, Pericor, Boston, 1998-. Contbr. articles to profl. jours. Chmn. investment com. Powers (Mass.) Music Sch., 1978-90; mem. Harvard Grad. Soc. Coun., 1992-95. With U.S. Army, 1944-46. Mem. IEEE, Am. Phys. Soc., Harvard Club, Phi Beta Kappa, Sigma Xi. Home: 975 Memorial Dr # 805 Cambridge MA 02138 Office Phone: 617-576-1498. Personal E-mail: hhrrlewis@aol.com.

LEWIS, HOMER DICK, retired nuclear engineer; b. Covington, Ky., Oct. 4, 1926; s. Homer Dewey and Viola Mabel Lewis; m. Marjorie Louise Hacker; children: Homer Daniel, Holly J., Laurel Marion Williams, Heather Eileen Wheat. BS Metallurgical Engring., U. Cin., 1952; MS Nuclear Engring., U. N.Mex., 1964, MSc Materials Sci., 1971. Lic. profl. engr., N.Mex., 1957. Staff mem. Los Alamos Sci. Lab., N.Mex., 1952—57; lead engr. Boeing Airplane Co., Seattle, 1957—58; staff mem. Los Alamos Sci. Lab./Los Alamos Nat. Lab., 1958—86; lab. assoc./staff mem. Los Alamos Nat. Lab., 1986—94. Sect. leader - enriched uranium casting sect. Los Alamos Sci. Lab., 1953—57; lead engr. - manufacturing/welding rsch. Boeing Airplane Co., 1957—58; prin. investigator/experimenter - measurement of high temperature phys., chem., properties of lmfbr fuels and fuel/clad interactions Los Alamos Sci. Lab., 1975—79; rep. Nat. Task Group for Fast Breeder Reactor Fuels Properties US Dept. of Energy, Los Alamos Nat. Lab., 1977—80; sect. leader nonferrous and enriched uranium melting/casting tech. sect. Los Alamos Nat. Lab., 1981—86. Contbr. articles to profl. jours. Instr./assoc. dir. Los Alamos Ski Sch. at Pajarito Mtn., 1967—71. With USNR, 1944—49, capt. USAF Res., 1952—68. Mem.: Am. Soc. Metals (life), Los Alamos Ski Club (pres. 1962—63), NRA (life), Rocky Mountain Ski Instructors Ass./ Profl. Ski Instructors of Am., Emeritus mem., Sangre deCristo # 16 Knights Templar (comdr. 1970—71), Los Alamos York Rite, Col. Clay Lodge 159 Free and Accepted Masons (life), Phi Kappa Phi (life). Achievements include patents for powder metallurgy. Home: 3201 Wellington Pl Farmington NM 87402 E-mail: marjlulew@obci.net.

LEWIS, HUNTER, investment advisor, consultant, writer; b. Dayton, Ohio, Oct. 13, 1947; s. Welbourne Walker and Emily (Spivey) L.; m. Elizabeth Sidamon-Eristoff, July 3, 1993. AB magna cum laude, Harvard U., 1969. Asst. to office of pres. Boston Co., 1970, v.p., 1972-73; prs. Boston Co. Fin. Strategies, Inc., 1971-72; co-founder Cambridge Assocs., Inc., Boston, 1973—. Author: The Real World War, 1982, A Question of Values, 1990, other books; contbr. articles to N.Y. Times, Atlantic Monthly, Washington Post, others mags. and newspapers; author monographs on specialized fin. subjects. Former mem. pension fin. com. World Bank; former dir. Worldwide Fund Nature; chmn., dir. Nat. Environ. Trust; former trustee, chmn. fin. com. Groton Sch.; former chmn. adv. bd. Dumbarton Oakes affil. of Harvard U.; former trustee Thomas Jefferson Found., Monticello, Va.; former chmn., bd. dirs. Worldwatch Inst.; former treas., dir. World Wildlife Fund; former trustee Pierpont Morgan Libr., N.Y.C., Rockefeller Bros. Fund; pres. emeritus, trustee Am. Sch. Classical Studies at Athens; chmn. bd. Inst. Edn. Foster Children. Served with USMC, 1969—70. Mem. Univ. Club (N.Y.C.), Knickerbocker Club (N.Y.C.), Met. Club (Washington). Office: 4100 N Fairfax Dr Ste 1300 Arlington VA 22201

LEWIS, JACK (CECIL PAUL LEWIS), publishing executive, editor; b. North English, Iowa, Nov. 13, 1924; s. Cecil Howell and Winifred (Warner) L.; children: Dana Claudia, Brandon Paul, Scott Jay, Suzanne Marie. BA, State U. Iowa, 1949. Publicist savs. bonds U.S. Treasury Dept., Des Moines, 1948-49; reporter Santa Ana (Calif.) Register, 1949-50; motion picture writer Monogram Pictures, 1950; reporter Daily Pilot, Costa Mesa, Calif., 1956-57; editor Challenge Pub., North Hollywood, Calif., 1957-60; pres. Gallant/Charger Publs. Inc, Capistrano Beach, Calif., 1960-98; editor, pub. Gun World, 1960-97. Author: (autobiography) White Horse, Black Hat, 2002, 14 novels, 30 other books, 11 TV shows, 8 motion pictures; editor 27 books; contbr. articles to mags. Served to lt. col. USMCR, 1942-46, 50-56, 58, 70. Decorated Bronze Star, Air medal (4), Meritorious Service medal, Navy Commendation medal. Mem. Writers Guild Am., U.S. Marine Corps Combat Corrs. Assn. (pres. 1970-71, 73-74, 80-81, chmn. bd. 1972-78), Sigma Nu, Sigma Delta Chi. Republican. Home: RR 2 Box 4784 Pahoa HI 96778-9779 E-mail: wandcres@hilo.net.

LEWIS, JAMES EARL, investor; b. Chgo., Aug. 1, 1939; s. J. Earl and Elsie L. (Danneberg) Lewis; m. Patricia Ann Martin, Jan. 19, 1980. BA, DePauw U., 1961; MBA, U. Chgo., 1966. Analyst Harris Trust & Savs. Bank, Chgo., 1966-68; v.p. Paine, Webber, Jackson & Curtis, Boston, 1968-70; mgr. corp. loan component Gen. Electric Credit Corp., Stamford, Conn., 1971-77; v.p. Rauscher Pierce Refsnes Inc., Dallas, 1978-82; sr. v.p., mgr. corp. fin. dept. First Okla. Bancorp. Inc., Dallas and Oklahoma City, 1982-84; v.p., mgr. corp. fin. group PNC Mcht. Banking Co., Phila., 1984-87; v.p., dir. corp. fin. Ferris & Co., Inc., Washington, 1987-88; v.p. Washington Sq. Capital Markets Inc., Bala Cynwyd, Pa., 1988-90; pres., founder Mid. Atlantic Capital, Wayne, Pa., 1990-94; founder, pres. PFI Fin. LLC, 1993—. Bd. dirs. PFI Fin. LLC, chmn. bd. dirs., 2002—04. With U.S. Army, 1962—64. Mem.: Internat. Factoring Assn. Office: 3650 Winding Way Newtown Square PA 19073 Home: 200 Garden Pl Radnor PA 19087 Personal E-mail: jelewis.home@verizon.net. Business E-Mail: jim@pfifinancial.com.

LEWIS, JAMES LEE, JR., actuary; b. Toungoo, Burma, June 11, 1930; s. James Lee and Lilly (Ryden) L.; m. Tamra Dell Johns, June 30, 1954; children: James Lee III, David Alexander, Stephen John, Susan Kim, Michael Ryden. BA, U. Mich., 1952, MA, 1956. Actuary Lincoln Nat. Life Ins. Co., Ft. Wayne, Ind., 1956-74; sr. v.p. Mutual Security Life Ins. Co., Ft. Wayne, 1974-83; v.p., actuary Montlife Corp., Itaska, Ill., 1983-84; v.p., sr. actuary Covenant Life Ins. Co., Phila., 1984-94; actuary provident Mut. Life Ins. Co., Phila., 1994-96; ret., 1996. Pres. Associated Chs., Ft. Wayne., 1982; chmn. Project Commitment, Ft. Wayne, 1969. With U.S. Army, 1952-54. Fellow: Soc. of Actuaries (com. chmn. 1988—91); mem.: Am. Acad. Actuaries (charter). Baptist. Avocations: racquetball, barbershop singing.

LEWIS, JAMES (JIM) M., lawyer; b. Richmond, Va., Feb. 21, 1946; BA, U. Va., 1968, JD, 1974. Bar: Va. 1974, U.S. Ct. Appeals (4th Cir.), 1975, U.S. Supreme Ct., 1983; cert. specialist, bus. bankruptcy law, Am. Bankruptcy Bd. of Certification. Joined Boothe, Prichard and Dudley (merged with McGuire, Woods, LLP), Va.; ptnr. McGuire, Woods, LLP, Va.; exec. ptnr. Holland & Knight LLP, McLean, Va., 2000—. Gen. counsel 1998 World Congress on Info. Tech., 1996—99, Va. Chamber Orchestra; mem., gen. counsel World Info. Tech. and Svcs. Alliance, 1998—, Internat. Trade Assn. No. Va., 1995—; former mem., panel of bankruptcy trustees U.S. Bankruptcy Ct. (Ea. Dist. Va.), 1983—90; served Internat. Adv. Com., 2000 World Congress on Info. Tech., Taiwan, 2000; mem. steering com. Global Internet Summit, George Mason U., 2000. Exec. bd. advisors to the Nat. Ctr. for Tech. George Mason U. Sch. Law. Lt. USNR, 1968—71. Mem.: Info. Tech. Assn. Am. (mem. legal roundtable, "Yr. 2000 Challenge"), Omicron Delta Kappa. Office: Holland & Knight LLP 1600 Tysons Blvd Ste 700 Mc Lean VA 22102 Office Phone: 703-720-8638. Business E-Mail: james.lewis@hklaw.com.

LEWIS, JEFFREY E., dean, law educator; BA, Duke U., 1966, JD, 1969. Asst. prof. law U. Akron Sch. Law, 1970—72, U. Fla. Coll. Law, 1972—75, assoc. prof., 1975—77, prof., 1977—99, prof. emeritus, 1999—, assoc. dean, 1982—88, dean, 1988—96, dean emeritus, 1996—; dean. prof. law Saint Louis U. Sch. Law, 1999—. Vis. prof. law Escuela Libre de Derecho, 1996, Johann Wolfgang Goethe U., 1997, U. Ala., 1999. Contbr. articles to law jours. Fellow: ABA; mem.: Omicron Delta Kappa, Phi Kappa Phi. Office: St Louis U Sch Law 3700 Linden Blvd Saint Louis MO 63108 E-mail: lewisje@slu.edu.

LEWIS, JERRY (JOSEPH LEVITCH), comedian; b. Newark, Mar. 16, 1926; s. Danny and Rae Levitch; m. Patti Palmer, 1944 (div., 1982); children: Gary, Ron, Scott, Chris, Anthony, Joseph; m. Sandra Pitnick, 1983; 1 child, Danielle Sara. Edn., Irvington (N.J.) High Sch.; DHL (hon.), Mercy Coll., 1987. Prof. cinema U. So. Calif.; pres. JAS Prodns., Inc., PJ. Prodns., Inc. Began as entertainer with record routine at Catskill (N.Y.) hotel; formed comedy team with Dean Martin, 1946-56, The Martin and Lewis Show, 1949-53, performed at Copa, 1948, 1950, Las Vegas Performances, 1952; performer with Sammy Davis Jr., Playboy Afterdark, 1969; performed as a single, 1956—, The Diamond Jubilee of the Royal Variety Performance, The Palladium, London, 1966 (for Her Majesty Queen Elizabeth The Queen Mother), 1966, (Her Majesty The Queen Elizabeth II), 1969, Olympia, 1976; formed Jerry Lewis Prodns. Inc., prod., dir., writer, star, 1956; films include: How to Smuggle a Hernia Across the Border, 1949 (also dir., writer), My Friend Irma, 1949, My Friend Irma Goes West, 1950, At War with the Army, 1950, That's My Boy, 1950, Sailor Beware, 1951, The Stooge, 1952, Jumping Jacks, 1952, Road to Bali, 1952, The Stooge, 1953, Scared Stiff, 1953, The Caddy, 1953, Money From Home, 1954, Three Ring Circus, 1954, Living it Up, 1954, You're Never Too Young, 1955, Artists and Models, 1955, Pardners, 1956, Hollywood or Bust, 1956, The Delicate Delinquent, 1957(also prodr.), The Sad Sack, 1957, The Geisha Boy, 1958 (also prodr.), Rock-a-bye Baby, 1958 (also prodr.), The Jazz Singer, 1959, Don't Give Up the Ship, 1959, Li'l Abner, 1959, It's a Mad, Mad, Mad, Mad World, 1959, Visit to a Small Planet, 1960, The Bellboy, 1960 (also writer, dir., prodr., co-author), Cinderfella, 1960 (also prodr.), The Ladies Man, 1961(also dir., prodr., co-author), It's Only Money, 1962, The Errand Boy, 1962 (also dir., composer, co-author), The Nutty Professor, 1963(also dir., co-author), Who's Minding The Store, 1963, The Patsy, 1964 (also dir., co-author), The Disorderly Orderly, 1964, Ben Casey, 1964 (also dir., one episode), The Family Jewels, 1965 (also dir., prodr., co-author), Boeing-Boeing, 1965, Three On A Couch (also dir., prodr.), 1966, Way ... Way ... Out, 1966, The Big Mouth, 1967 (also dir., prodr., co-author), Don't Raise the Bridge, Lower the River, 1968, Hook, Line and Sinker, 1969 (also prodr.), One More Time, 1969 (also dir.), Which Way To the Front?, 1970 (also dir., prodr.), The Day the Clown Cried, 1972 (also dir., co-author), Hardly Working, 1981 (also dir., co-author), King of Comedy, 1983, Smorgasbord, 1983 (also dir., co-author), Cracking Up, 1983 (also dir., writer), Slapstick of Another Kind, 1984, To Catch A Cop, 1984, How Did You Get In?, 1985, Fight for Life, 1987, Cookie, 1989, Boy, 1990 (also writer, dir.), Arrowtooth Waltz, 1991, Arizona Dream, 1991, Mr. Saturday Night, 1992, Funny Bones, 1994, Miss Cast Away, 2004; appeared on Broadway in Damn Yankees, 1995, on nat. tour, 1995-1997, internat. tour., 1997; (TV series) Wiseguy, 1988-89; dir. (TV Series) The Bold Ones: The New Doctors, 1969, Good Grief, 1991, Super Force, 1993; writer, exec. prodr. (films) Nutty Professor, 1996, Nutty Professor II: The Klumps, 2000; writer (TV Series) The Jerry Lewis Show, 1963; author: The Total Film-Maker, 1971, Jerry Lewis in Person, 1982; guest appearances include: Toast of the Town, 1948, 1960-62, 1961, What's My Line?, 1954, 1956, 1960-62, 1966, This is Your Life, 1956, Rowan & Martin's Laugh-In, 1968, Saturday Night Live, 1983, Mad About You, 1993, (voice) The Simpsons, 2003, and several famous talk shows 1970-; principal TV appearances include master of ceremonies ann. Labor Day Muscular Dystrophy Telethon, 1966—. Comdr. Order of Arts & Letters, France, 1984; nat. chmn. Muscular Dystrophy Assn. Recipient most promising male star in TV award Motion Picture Daily's 2nd Ann. TV poll, 1950, (as team with Dean Martin), one of TV's 10 money making stars award Motion Picture Herald - Fame poll, 1951, 53-54, 57, The Number One Top Money Actors, Independent Film Jour., 1953, best comedy team award Motion Picture Daily's 16th annual radio poll, 1951-53, Top Men in the Movies, Look Mag., 1953, Nobel Peace Prize nomination, 1978, French Legion of Honor, 1984, Lifetime Achievement award, Am. Comedy Awards, 1998, Governors award, Creative Arts Prime-time Emmy Awards, 2005; Honored by the Eleanor Roosevelt Inst. for Cancer Rsch. Mem. Screen Producers Guild, Screen Dirs. Guild, Screen Writers Guild. Office: Jerry Lewis Films Inc 3180 W Sahara Ave # 16C Las Vegas NV 89102-6003 also: William Morris Agy Inc 151 S El Camino Dr Beverly Hills CA 90212-2704

LEWIS, JERRY LEE, country-rock singer, musician; b. Ferriday, La., Sept. 29, 1935; s. Elmo and Mary Ethel L.; m. Kerrie Lee; children: Phoebe, Jerry Lee Jr. Student, Waxahachie (Tex.) Bible Inst. Rock and roll performer, recs. on Sun Records label, Whole Lotta Shakin' Goin' On, 1957, Great Balls of Fire, Mercury/Phonogram, 1963-78, Elektra Records, 1978-81; shifted to country and rock repertoire: recs. include Golden Hits, Odd Man In, Country Class, Roll Over Beethoven, High Heel Sneakers, Jerry Lee Lewis, Southern Roots, Good Rockin' Tonight, Taste of Country, Sunday After Church, Rural Route #1, Drinkin Wine Spo Dee O Dee, Golden Cream of Country, Monsters, Old Tyme Country Music, Rockin with From the Vaults of Sun; appeared in films American Hot Wax, Disc Jockey Jamboree, High School Confidential; albums include Sold Gold, 1986, The Killer Rocks On, 1987, Rocket, 1988, 1992, Killer: The Mercury Years Vol. One, Vol. Two, Vol. Three, 1989, Great Balls of Fire, 1989, Whole Lotta Shakin' Goin' On, 1992, Rockin' My Life Away, 1992, Heartbreak, 1992, All Killer, No Filler: The Anthology, 1993, Young Blood, 1995, Back to Back, 1996, By Invitation Only, 2000. Named to Rock and Roll Hall of Fame, 1986; recipient Lifetime Achievement Grammy Award, 2005. Office: Warner Bros Records 75 Rockefeller Plz New York NY 10019-6908

LEWIS, JERRY M., psychiatrist, educator; b. Utica, N.Y., Aug. 18, 1924; s. Jerry M. and Margaret (Miller) L.; m. Patsy Ruth Price, Sept. 24, 1949; children: Jerry M., Cynthia Lewis-Reynolds, Nancy Minns, Tom. MD, Southwestern Med. Sch., Dallas, 1951. Diplomate Am. Bd. Psychiatry and Neurology. Staff psychiatrist Timberlawn Psychiat. Hosp., Dallas, 1957-63, chief women's svc., 1963-66, chief adolescent svcs., 1966-70, dir. profl. edn., 1970-79, psychiatrist-in-chief, 1979-88, dir. rsch., 1988-93. Dir. rsch. and tng. Timberlawn Psychiat. Rsch. Found., Dallas, 1967-88, sr. rsch. psychiatrist, 1988—; clin. prof. psychiatry, family practice and cmty. medicine Southwestern Med. Sch.; cons. in psychiatry Baylor U. Med. Ctr., Dallas. Author: No Single Thread, 1976, How's Your Family, 1978, To Be a Therapist, 1979, The Long Struggle, 1983, Swimming Upstream: Teaching Psychotherapy in a Biological Era, 1991, The Monkey-Rope, 1995, Marriage as a Search for Healing: Theory, Assessment & Therapy, 1997, (with John Gossett, Ph.D.) Disarming the Past: How an Intimate Relationship Can Heal Old Wounds, 1999. Served with USN, 1943-45. Fellow Am. Coll. Psychiatrists (pres. 1985), Am. Psychiat. Assn., So. Psychiat. Assn. (pres. 1979); mem. Group for Advancement of Psychiatry (pres. 1987), Benjamin Rush Soc. (pres. 1994-95), AMA, Tex. Med. Assn. Office: PO Box 270789 Dallas TX 75227-0789 Office Phone: 214-275-4001.

LEWIS, JOHN BRUCE, lawyer; b. Poplar Bluff, Mo., Aug. 12, 1947; s. Evan Bruce and Hilda Kathryn (Kassebaum) L.; m. Diane F. Grossman, July 23, 1977; children: Samantha Brooking, Ashley Denning. BA, U. Mo., 1969, JD, 1972; LLM in Labor and Employment Law, Columbia U., 1978; diploma, Nat. Inst. Trial Advocacy, 1982. Bar: Mo. 1972, U.S. Ct. Appeals (8th cir.) 1973, U.S. Dist. Ct. (ea. dist.) Mo. 1974, U.S. Dist. Ct. (no. dist.) Ohio 1979, Ohio 1980, U.S. Ct. Appeals (6th cir.) 1982, U.S. Dist. Ct. (ea. dist.) Mich. 1983, U.S. Ct. Appeals (3d cir.) 1987, U.S. Supreme Ct. 1987, U.S. Dist. Ct. (no. dist.) Calif. 1987, U.S. Ct. Appeals (7th cir.) 1990, U.S. Dist. Ct. (so. dist.) Ohio 2003. Assoc. Millar, Schaefer & Ebling, St. Louis, 1972-77, Squire, Sanders & Dempsey, Cleve., 1979-85; ptnr. Arter & Hadden, Cleve., 1985-2001, Baker & Hostetler, Cleve., 2001—. Lectr. in field. Author: Employment Practices Self-Assessment Guide, 2d edit., 2000; contbr. articles to legal jours. Mem. Cleve. Council on World Affairs. Fellow: Coll. Labor and Employment Lawyers; mem. ABA (sec. labor and employment law, com. EEO law, comm. law forum), Ohio State Bar Assn. (sec. labor and employment law), Cleve. Bar Assn. (sec. labor law), St. Louis Met. Bar Assn., Am. Law Inst., Selden Soc., Ohio C. of C. (employment law com.), William K. Thomas Inn of Ct. (master bencher). Office: Baker & Hostetler LLP 3200 Nat City Ctr 1900 E 9th St Cleveland OH 44114-3485 Office Phone: 216-861-7496. Business E-Mail: jlewis@bakerlaw.com.

LEWIS, JOHN CHRISTOPHER, allergist; b. Boston, Oct. 15, 1950; MD, Loyola U., Maywood, 1982. Asst. prof. medicine Mayo Clinic Coll. Medicine (formerly Mayo Med. Sch.), Scottsdale, Ariz. Office: Mayo Clinic Scottsdale 13400 E Shea Blvd Scottsdale AZ 85259-5499 Office Phone: 480-301-8227.

LEWIS, JOHN FRANCIS, lawyer; b. Oberlin, Ohio, Oct. 25, 1932; s. Ben W. and Gertrude D. Lewis; m. Catharine Monroe, June 15, 1957; children: Ben M., Ian A., Catharine G., William H. BA, Amherst Coll., 1955; JD, U. Mich., 1958. Bar: Ohio 1958, U.S. Dist. Ct. (no dist.) Ohio 1959, U.S. Supreme Ct. 1972. Assoc. firm Squire, Sanders & Dempsey, Cleve., 1959—67; ptnr. Squire, Sanders & Dempsey LLP, 1967—2002, mng. ptnr. Cleve. office to sr. coun., 1985—2002, sr. coun., 2002—. Co-author: Baldwin's Ohio School Law, 1980-91, Ohio Collective Bargaining Law, 1983. Hon. trustee Found. for Sch. Bus. Mgmt., Leadership Cleve., 1977-78; trustee Playhouse Sq. Found., chmn., 1980-85; chair Cleve. Initiative for Edn., 1988-95; chmn. Cleanland Cleve., 1992-95; trustee Ohio Found. Ind. Colls., Case Western Res. U., chmn., 1995-2001; trustee, chmn. Ohio Aerospace Coun., 2001-03; trustee Ohio Aerospace Inst., Univ. Circle, Inc., Inst. for Unlimited Love Recipient Malcolm Daisley Labor-Mgmt. Rels. award, 1991, Tree of Life award Jewish Nat. Fund, 1993, NCCJ award, 1995, Franklin D. Roosevelt March of Dimes award, 1999, Case Western Reserve U. Presidl. medal, 2001. Mem. Cleve. Bar Assn., Ohio Bar Assn., Nat. Sch. Bd. Assn., Edn. Law Assn. (past pres.), Ohio Assn. Sch. Bus. Ofcls. (hon. life, Marion McGehey Edn. Law award 1998), Fifty Club of Cleve., Ohio Council Sch. Bd. Attys. (founding chair), Edn. Law Inst. Episcopalian. Home: 2 Bratenahl Pl Ste 7ef Bratenahl OH 44108-1183 Office: Squire Sanders & Dempsey 4900 Key Tower 127 Public Sq Ste 4900 Cleveland OH 44114-1304 Office Phone: 216-479-8553. Business E-Mail: Jlewis@ssd.com. E-mail: capeoceans@aol.com.

LEWIS, JOHN HARDY, JR., lawyer; b. East Orange, N.J., Oct. 31, 1936; s. John Hardy and Sarah (Ripley) L.; m. Mary Ann Spurgeon, June 25, 1960; children: Peter, David, Mark. AB magna cum laude, Princeton U., 1958; JD cum laude, Harvard U., 1961. Bar: Pa. 1962. Assoc. Morgan, Lewis & Bockius, Phila., 1965-69, ptnr., 1969-99, Montgomery McCracken Walker & Rhoads, LLP, Phila., 1999—. Trustee Blair Acad., Blairstown, N.J. Served to maj. USAF, 1962-65. Fellow Am. Coll. Trial Lawyers. Home: 1000 Green Valley Rd Bryn Mawr PA 19010-1912 Office: Montgomery McCracken Et Al 123 S Broad St Philadelphia PA 19109-1029 Office Phone: 215-772-7596.

LEWIS, JOHN MILTON, cable television company executive; b. Slocomb, Ala., Mar. 29, 1931; s. Phil Truman and Vermell Beatrice (Avery) L.; m. Mary Lee Robledo, June 9, 1951; children: Janet Lee, Lee Michael. Grad. high sch., Panama City, Fla. With Gulf Power Co., Panama City, Fla., 1949-56; self-employed Vehicle Svc. Co., Panama City, 1956-58; dir. Burnup & Sims of Fla., Inc., W. Palm Beach, 1958-70; pres., bd. dirs. Wometco Cable Corp., Miami, Fla., 1970-94; pres., CEO SP1 Holding, Inc., Richardson, Tex., 1988-89; bd. dirs., CEO Spectradyne, Inc., Richardson, 1988-89; pres. Key Capital Group, Inc., Miami, 1995—, St. Joe Comms., Inc., Port St. Joe, Fla., 1996—2000. Bd. dirs. Allied Waste Mgmt., Phoenix; pres. St. Joe Telephone Co., Inc., Port St. Joe, Fla.; cons. in field. Recipient Tower Club award So. TV Assn. Mem. Cable TV Pioneers, Masons. Office: Key Capital Group Inc PO Box 561009 9500 S Dadeland Blvd Ste 603 Miami FL 33156-2848

LEWIS, JOHN PRIOR, economist, educator; b. Albany, NY, Mar. 18, 1921; s. Leon Ray and Grace (Prior) L.; m. June Estelle Ryan, July 12, 1946; children— Betsy Prior, Sally Eastman, Amanda Barnum. Student, St. Andrews U., Scotland, 1939-40; AB, Union Coll., Schenectady, 1941; M.Pub. Adminstrn., Harvard, 1943, PhD in Polit. Economy and Govt, 1950; D.C.L., Union Coll., 1970. Instr., asst. prof. econs. and govt. Union Coll., Schenectady, 1946-50; mem. staff, asst. to chmn. Council Econ. Advisers, Exec. Office of Pres., Washington, 1950-53; cons. UN Korean Reconstrn. Agy., Pusan, Korea, 1953; assoc. prof. Ind. U., 1953-56, prof. bus. econs. and pub. policy, 1956-64, disting. service prof. bus. econs. and pub. policy, 1964, chmn. dept., 1961-63; mem. Council Econ. Advisers, Exec. Office of Pres., Washington, 1963-64; minister-dir. USAID mission to India, 1964-69; dean Woodrow Wilson Sch. Pub. Affairs, 1969-74; prof. econs. and internat. affairs Princeton (N.J.) U., 1969-91, prof. emeritus, 1991—; on leave as chmn. devel. assistance com. OECD, Paris, 1979-81, as DAC chmn. ann. OECD vols. on devel. cooperation, 1979-81; sr. advisor Overseas Devel. Coun., 1981—99. Sr. staff mem. in India Brookings Instn., Washington, 1959-60; mem. UN Com. on Devel. Planning, 1970-83, rapporteur, 1972-78 Author: Business Conditions Analysis, 1959, 2d edit., (with R.C. Turner), 1967, Quiet Crisis in India: Economic Development and American Policy, 1962, (with Ishan Kapur) The World Bank, Multilateral Aid, and the 1970's, 1973, (with V. Kallab) U.S. Foreign Policy and the Third World, 1983, Development Strategies Reconsidered, 1986, Strengthening the Poor, 1988, India's Political Economy, 1995, (with Devesh Kapur and Richard Webb) The World Bank: Its First Half Century, 1997, The Goliath Problem: The Wages of Hegemony, 2004. Served to lt. USNR, 1943-46, PTO. Home: 12 Valencia Ct Skillman NJ 08558-2354 Office: Princeton U Woodrow Wilson Sch Princeton NJ 08544-0001

LEWIS, JOHN R., congressman; b. Troy, Ala., Feb. 21, 1940; m. Lillian Miles, 1968; 1 child, John-Miles. BA, Am. Bapt. Theol. Sem., Nashville, 1961, Fisk U., 1963. Mem. City Coun., Atlanta, 1983—86, U.S. Congress from 5th Ga. dist., Washington, 1987—, former chief dep. majority whip; community affairs dir. Nat. Consumer Coop. Bank, 1980—82. Civil rights leader; mem. Martin Luther King Ctr. for Social Change, African Am. Inst., Robert F. Kennedy Meml. Recipient Allies for Justice award, Nat. Lesbian and Gay Law Assn., 2004. Democrat. Baptist. Office: US Ho of Reps 343 Cannon 40 B Washington DC 20515-1005 Office Fax: 202-225-0351.

LEWIS, JOHN WILSON, political science professor; b. King County, Wash., Nov. 16, 1930; s. Albert Lloyd and Clara (Lewis) Seeman; m. Jacquelyn Clark, June 19, 1954; children: Cynthia, Stephen, Amy. Student, Deep Springs Coll., 1947-49; AB with highest honors, UCLA, 1953, MA, 1958, PhD, 1962; hon. degree, Morningside Coll., 1969, Lawrence U., 1986, Russian Acad. Sci., 1996. Asst. prof. govt. Cornell U., 1961-64, assoc. prof., 1964-68, asst. prof. govt., 1961-64; prof. polit. sci. Stanford U., 1968-97, William Haas prof. Chinese politics, 1972-97, William Haas prof. emeritus, 1997—, co-dir. arms control and disarmament program, 1971-83, co-dir. NE Asia U.S. Forum on Internat. Policy, 1980-90, co-dir. Ctr. for Internat. Security and Arms Control, 1983-91, sr. fellow, 1991—; dir. Project on Peace and Cooperation in the Asian-Pacific Region, 1990—; coord. Five-Nation Project on Asian Regional Security and Econ. Cooperation, 2001—; chmn. Internat. Strategic Inst., 1983-89; chmn. joint com. on contemporary China Social Sci. Rsch. Coun.-Am. Coun. Learned Socs., 1976-79; mng. dir. Generation Ventures, 1994-99. Former vice chmn. Nat. Com. on U.S.-China Rels.; cons. Senate Select Com. on Intelligence, 1977-81, Los Alamos Nat. Lab., 1987-92, Lawrence Livermore Nat. Lab., 1982-2002, Dept. of Def., 1994-96; mem. Def. Policy Bd., 1994-96; chmn. com. advanced study in China Com. Scholarly Comm. with People's Republic of China, 1979-82; com. on internat. security and arms control Nat. Acad. Scis., 1980-83; organizer first univ. discussion arms control and internat. security matters Chinese People's Inst. Fgn. Affairs, 1978, first academic exch. agreement Dem. People's Repb. of Korea, 1988; negotiator first univ. tng. and exch. agreement People's Rep. of China, 1978; coord. Five-Nation Project on Asian Regional Security and Econ. Devel., 2002-05; co-chmn. Nat. Com. North Korea, 2004. Author: Leadership in Communist China, 1963, Major Doctrines of Communist China, 1964, Policy Networks and the Chinese Policy Process, 1986; co-author: The United States in Vietnam, 1967, Modernization by Design, 1969, China Builds the Bomb, 1988, Uncertain Partners: Stalin, Mao, and the Korean War, 1993, China's Strategic Seapower: The Politics of Force Modernization in the Nuclear Era, 1994; editor: The City in Communist China, 1971, Party Leadership and Revolutionary Power in China, 1970, Peasant Rebellion and Communist Revolution in Asia, 1974; contbr.: Congress and Arms Control, 1978, China's Quest for Independence, 1979, others; mem. editl. bd. Chinese Law and Govt., China Quarterly. Served with USN, 1954-57. Recipient Helios award, 2001. Home: 541 San Juan St Stanford CA 94305-8432 Office: Stanford U Encina Hall Stanford CA 94305-6105 Office Phone: 650-723-9627. Business E-Mail: jwlewis@stanford.edu.

LEWIS, JONATHAN JOSEPH, surgical oncologist, molecular biologist, educator; b. Johannesburg, May 23, 1958; s. Myer Philip and Maisie (Bagg) Lewis; m. Nanci Lynn Vicedomini, May 20, 1990. MB BCH, Witwatersrand U., Johannesburg, 1982; PhD, Yale U., 1990. Registrar in surgery Witwatersrand U. Sch. Medicine, Johannesburg, 1982-87; postdoctoral assoc. Yale U. Sch. Medicine, New Haven, 1987-90, chief resident, surgery, 1990-92; fellow dept. surgery Meml. Sloan-Kettering Cancer Ctr., N.Y.C., 1992-94, attending surgeon, 1994—, asst. mem., 1994-99, assoc. mem., 1999—; chmn., CEO, pres. Ziopharm, N.Y.C., 2004—. Asst. prof. surgery Cornell U. Med. Coll., 1994—99, assoc. prof., 1999—; chief med. officer Antigenics Inc., N.Y.C., 2000—03. Contbr. articles to profl. jours. Recipient Abelheim medal, Med. Coun., 1982, Trubshaw medal, Coll. Surgeons, Johannesburg, 1984; Winston fellow, Sloan-Kettering Inst., 1994—95. Fellow: ACS, Royal Coll. Surgeons; mem.: N.Y. Acad. Scis., Soc. Surg. Oncology, Assn. Acad. Surgeons, Am. Soc. Clin. Oncology (Young Investigator award 1994), Am. Assn. Cancer Rsch., Am. Soc. Cell Biology. Jewish. Achievements include research in oncogenes; growth factors; signal transduction; immunotherapy; gene therapy. Office: Ziopharm 300 George St New Haven CT 06511 Office Phone: 203-848-3400. Business E-Mail: jlewis@ziopharm.com.

LEWIS, JONE JOHNSON, clergy member; b. May 15, 1951; married, Sept. 1999. BA in Mgmt., Mundelein Coll., 1981; MDiv, Meadville/Lombard Theol. Sch., 1991. Ordained minister Unitarian Universalist Ch., 1991. Various tng. and edn. mgmt. positions, 1980-90; Unitarian Universalist min. Berrien U. U. Fellowship, St. Joseph, Mich., 1991-93; ethical culture leader Chgo. Ethical Humanist Soc., 1991-96, No. Va. Ethical Soc., Vienna, Va., 1997—. Cyberminister Unitarian Universalist Ch. of Larger Fellowship, 2003—04.

LEWIS, JOSEPH BRADY (JAY LEWIS), lawyer; b. Shreveport, La., Nov. 27, 1946; s. Joseph Peter and Gwendolyn (Pate) L. Student, U. So. Miss., 1964-67; BS summa cum laude, Troy State U., 1982; JD magna cum laude, Jones Sch. Law, Montgomery, Ala., 1991. Bar: Ala. 1992. News reporter Sta. WDAM-TV, Hattiesburg, Miss., 1968-69, Sta. KTVT-TV, Ft. Worth, 1969-70, Sta. WFAA-TV, Dallas, 1970-72; news anchor Sta. KTOK/Okla. News Network, Oklahoma City, 1972-74; editl. dir. Sta. WSFA-TV, Montgomery, Ala., 1974-77; pres. Ala. Info. Network, Montgomery, 1977-80, Amendment One, Inc., Montgomery, 1980-82; owner Lewis Comm., Montgomery, 1977-92; comm. dir. Augat Inc., 1983-92; prin., owner Law Offices of Jay Lewis, LLC, Montgomery, 1992—. Cons. Gen. TV Network, Montgomery, 1980-83; v.p., dir. Am. Community TV Assn., Montgomery, 1980-82. Contbr. articles to jours. and newspapers. Pres. Community Counseling and Guidance Ctr., Oklahoma City, 1973; trustee Ft. Toulouse Found., Montgomery. Named Communicator of Yr., Ala. Wildlife Fedn., 1977. Mem. Ala. Bar Assn., Ala. Criminal Def. Lawyers Assn., Ala. Trial Lawyers Assn., Montgomery County Trial Lawyers Assn., Montgomery County Bar Assn., Soc. Profl. Journalists (pres. chpt. 1974, 75, 78, Nat. Disting. Svc. award 1974, 78), Mensa, Citizens Against Fgn. Control of Am. (pres.), Alpha Epsilon Rho, Sigma Delta Kappa. Roman Catholic. Avocations: flying, sailing, tennis, golf, scuba diving. Office: 847 S McDonough St Montgomery AL 36104 Office Phone: 334-263-7733. Business E-Mail: J-Lewis@JayLewisLaw.com.

LEWIS, JUDITH SUSANNA, artist; b. Ithaca, Ohio, Apr. 16, 1940; d. Kenneth William and Mildred Pauline Coates; m. Harry Robert Lewis, Aug. 18, 1967; children: Lucianna Doré, Brishen Marie. BS, Miss. State Coll. for Women, 1962; MS, Ind. U., 1966. Cert. tchr., Miss., Ind. Elem. tchr. Seymour (Ind.) Cmty. Schs., 1963-74. Muralist pub. schs. and bldgs. One-woman shows include Shaker Seed Box Co. Gallery, Mariemont, Ohio, 1991, exhibited in group shows at Madison (Ind.) Fine Arts Gallery, 1997, exhibitions include So. Ind. Ctr. Arts, Seymour, 1997, 2002 (Best of Show, 1st place), 2005 (Best of Show, Merit award), Columbia Club, Indpls., 1999, Hilbert Ctr. Theatre, 2000, Hoosier Salon, New Harmony, Ind., 2003, 2005 (Merit award, Purchase award), Hoosier Salon-Broad Ripple, Indpls., 2003, Ind. Heritage Arts, 2004 (Merit award), 2005 (Merit award), Represented in permanent collections The Honeywell Found., Inc., Wabash, Ind.; artist (permanent collections) Lilly Found., Indpls. Recipient 1st pl. award, Madison Art Club Exhibit, Ind., 1999, Best of Show and 1st pl. award, 2002, 1st pl. and Best of Show awards, Brown County Art Gallery Patrons Show, Nashville, Ind., 1998, 1999. Mem.: Oil Painters of Am., Brown County Art Assn., Southside Art League (Merit award 2000), Ind. Heritage of the Arts (Merit award 1999), Plein Air Painters, Hoosier Salon (Merit award and Purchase award 2000, Best Traditional Oil Painting award 2001, Best Oil Painting award, Purchase award 2002), So. Ind. Ctr. for the Arts. Avocations: travel, writing, photography, plays and musicals. Home: 602 N Walnut St Seymour IN 47274-1539

LEWIS, JULIETTE, actress; b. San Fernando Valley, Calif., June 21, 1975; d. Geoffrey L. and Glenis Batley; m. Stephen Berra, 1999. TV appearances include The Wonder Years, 1987, The Facts of Life, 1988, Dharma & Greg, 2001; TV Movies include Homefires, 1987, I Married Dora, 1988, Too Young To Die, 1989, A Family For Joe, 1990, My Louisiana Sky (Emmy nominee), Hysterical Blindness, 2002, Chasing Freedom, 2004; films include My Stepmother is an Alien, 1988, Runnin' Kind, 1989, Meet the Hollowheads, 1989, National Lampoons Christmas Vacation, 1989, Cape Fear, 1991 (Academy Award and Golden Globe nomination best supporting actress 1991), Crooked Hearts, 1991, Husbands and Wives, 1992, Kalifornia, 1993, That Night, 1993, What's Eating Gilbert Grape, 1993, Romeo is Bleeding, 1994, Natural Born Killers, 1994, Mixed Nuts, 1994, Strange Days, 1995, The Basketball Diaries, 1995, Audition, 1996, From Dusk Till Dawn, 1996, The Evening Star, 1996, Full Tilt Boogie, 1997, Somegirl, 1998, The 4th Floor, 1999, The Other Sister, 1999, Way of the Gun, 2000, Room to Rent, 2000, Picture Claire, 2001, Gaudi Afternoon, 2001, Armitage: Dual Matrix, 2001, Enough, 2002, Old School, 2003, Cold Creek Manor, 2003, Blueberry, 2004, Starsky & Hutch, 2004; singer, Juliette Lewis and the Licks. Office: William Morris Agy care Norman Brokaw 151 S El Camino Dr Beverly Hills CA 90212-2775 also: care Michelle Bega Rogers & Cowan PR 1888 Century Pk E Ste 500 Los Angeles CA 90006

LEWIS, KENNETH D., bank executive; b. Meridian, Miss., Apr. 9, 1947; BA, Ga. State U., 1969. Pres. NCNB Nat. Bank Fla., 1986-88, NCNB Tex., Dallas, N.C., 1988-90, Gen. Bank NationsBank, Atlanta, 1991-93, NationsBank Corp., Charlotte, NC, 1993-99; pres., COO Bank Am. Corp. (formerly NationsBank Corp.), Charlotte, NC, 1999—2001; chmn., pres., CEO Bank Am. Corp. (merged with FleetBoston), Charlotte, NC, 2001—04; pres., CEO, chmn. Bank Am. Corp., Charlotte, NC, 2004—. Bd. dir. Health Mgmt. Assocs., Inc. Naples, Fla., 1991-2004, Lowe's Companies, Inc., 2000-2004, Fin. Svcs. Roundtable. Past chmn. bd. United Way Cen. Carolinas Inc., Charlotte; dir. Homeownership Edn. and Counseling Inst.; chmn. bd. trustees Nat. Urban League; chmn. Arts and Sci. Coun., campaign dr., Charlotte, 1998; bd. dirs. Presbyn. Hosp. Found., Charlotte. Named Banker of the Year, Am. Banker, 2002, Top CEO, US Banker, 2002. Office: Bank Am Corp Ctr 100 N Tryon St Fl 58 Charlotte NC 28255-0001 Office Phone: 704-386-5666. Office Fax: 704-386-4578.*

LEWIS, KIM, microbiologist; b. N.Y.C., Feb. 3, 1953; s. Tom John Lewis and Fainna Solasko; m. Tanya Genina, May 20, 1976; children: Alexandra, Maria. BS, Moscow U., 1976, PhD, 1980, D of Biology, 1984. Rschr. Moscow U., 1976-79, sr. rschr., 1979-84; rsch. assoc. U. Wis., Madison, 1987-88; asst. prof. MIT, Cambridge, Mass., 1988-94; assoc. prof. U. Md., Balt., 1994-97, Tufts U., Medford, Mass., 1997-2001; prof. biology Northeastern U., Boston, 2001—. Contbr. numerous papers to profl. jours. Rsch. grantee NSF, 1992, 94, 2001, ACS, 1992, NIH, 1996, 99, 2000, 2001,2004 Dept. Energy, 1997, 2004. Mem.: Am. Chem. Soc., Soc. Indsl. Microbiology, Am. Soc. Microbiology. Avocations: reading, art, music. Office: Northeastern Univ Mugar 405 360 Huntington Ave Boston MA 02115 E-mail: k.lewis@neu.edu.

LEWIS, LARRY, communications educator, film producer; b. Cleve., Sept. 14, 1948; s. Richard and Mary Ann Wynn. MA in Radio, TV and Film, Bowling Green State U., 1979; degree in electronic communication, Omega

Sch. Communication, Chgo., 1983; PhD in Mass Communication, Bowling Green State U., 1989. Lic. FCC 1st class. Asst. prof. comm. Albion (Mich.) Coll., 1989-90, Defiance (Ohio) Coll., 1990-92; assoc. prof. comm. Del. State U., Dover, 1992—. Advisor WOSU Radio, Del. State U., 1997-98, advisor Cable Channel 6, 1997—, faculty senator, 1996-98, mem. alumni bd. trustees, 1998—. Author: (book of poetry) Maria's Reprise, 1998. Literacy instr. Kent County Adult Literacy program, Dover, 1995—; teenage intervention vol. 1st State Cmty. Action, Georgetown, Del., 1996—; mentor Upward Bound program, Dover, 1999—; mem. alumni bd. Bowling Green State U. Mem. Nat. Coun. English Tchrs., Soc. Profl. Journalists. Avocations: coins, writing folk songs, acoustic guitar. Office: Del State U Dept Mass Comm 1200 N Dupont Hwy Dover DE 19901-2202 E-mail: apple4jack@aol.com.

LEWIS, LARRY LISLE, human resources specialist company executive; b. 1945; With Homefinders Inc., Jackson, Miss., 1970-90; pres. People Lease Inc., Jackson, Miss., 1984—. With U.S. Army, 1968-70. Office: People Lease 689 Town Center Blvd #A Ridgeland MS 39157

LEWIS, LEONARD J., lawyer; b. Rexburg, Idaho, Jan. 10, 1923; s. Jack and Hannah (Beesley) L.; m. Lois Ann Cannon, Sept. 3, 1947; children—Leslie Ann, L. John, James C., Janet. B.S., U. Utah, 1947; J.D., Stanford U., 1950. Bar: Utah 1950. With firm Van Cott, Bagley, Cornwall & McCarthy, Salt Lake City, 1950—, sr. atty. Temple St. Investment Co. Past trustee U. Utah; past chmn. Utah State Bldg. Bd.; past chmn. bd. visitors Stanford Law Sch., 2003—. Served with U.S. Army, 1941-43. Mem. ABA, Assn. Trial Lawyers Am., Salt Lake County Bar Assn., Internat. Bar Assn., Utah Bar Assn. (past chmn. ct. adminstrv. com., 1974-75), Alta Club, Salt Lake Country Club, Beta Theta Pi. Home: 10 W 1st St # 703 Salt Lake City UT 84108 Office: Jones Walto Holbrook & McDonough 1500 Wells Fargo Plz Salt Lake City UT 84101

LEWIS, LESLIE JOY, music company executive, artist; b. Glendale, Calif., May 28, 1968; d. Thomas Reynolds and Linda Lewis. Dir. arts & repertoire RCA Records/BMG, 1991—94; co-founder Grammy Recordings Record Label Nat. Acad. Recording Arts & Scis., 1994—95; dir./product mgr. artists & repertoire PolyGram Soundtracks, 1995—98; v.p. artists & repertoire A&M Records (now Interscope/Geffen/A&M), 1998—99; v.p. motion picture music Miramax Film Corp., 1999—2000; dir. of prodrs. and engrs. wing Nat. Acad. Recording Arts & Scis., 2000—05. Cons. Musicians Inst., 1997, Grammy Concert Series, 1998, Interscope Records, 1998. Prodr.: albums Grammy nom. CD's, 1995, 1996, Grammy Nominees CD, 2001, 2002, 2003, 2004, 2005, Latin Grammy Nominees CD, 2001, 2002, 2003, 2004; prodr. (albums) James Bond 18: Tomorrow Never Dies, 1999 (Golden Globe nomination, 1999), Sheryl Crow: The Globe Sessions, 1999 (2 Grammy awards, 1999); assoc. prodr./coord.: albums The Songs of West Side Story, 1994—95, contbr.: over 80 films and soundtracks including The Titanic, Truth About Cats & Dogs, Tomorrow Never Dies, Mr. Holland's Opus, Romeo & Juliet, Slingblade, Grosse Pointe Blank, projects including Life Soundtrack, City High, Sheryl Crow, including Scream III, Scary Movie, Boys & Girls. Office Phone: 310-271-1003. Business E-Mail: lesliel@leslielewisconsulting.com.

LEWIS, LINDA DONELLE, neurologist, educator; b. Columbus, Ohio, Nov. 27, 1939; d. Donald Peter and Ann Elizabeth (Karn) L.; m. Gary Gambuti, Oct. 6, 1979. BS, Bethany Coll., 1961, DSc (hon.), 1981; MD, W.Va. U., 1985. Intern U. Wis., Madison, 1965-66; resident in medicine St. Luke's Hosp., N.Y.C., 1966-68; resident in neurology Case Western Res. U., Cleve., 1968-69; sr. resident in neurology Columbia Presbyn. Med. Ctr., N.Y.C., 1969-70, chief resident, 1970-71; pvt. practice, N.Y.C., 1971—. Prof. neurology Coll. Physicians and Surgeons, Columbia U., N.Y.C., from 1971, clin. prof., student affairs, 1979-2005; cons. in field; mem. N.Y. State Bd. for Profl. Med. Conduct, 1979—. Contbr. articles to med. jours. Trustee Bethany Coll., 1987—, A.P. Gold Found. Mem. AMA, AAAS, Am. Acad. Neurology, Am. Assn. Med. Colls., N.Y. State Med. Soc., New York County Med. Soc. Home: 320 Central Park W New York NY 10025-7659 Office: 710 W 168th St New York NY 10032-2603

LEWIS, LINDA SUE, retired elementary school educator; b. San Francisco, Sept. 16, 1947; d. Harry John and Virginia Ruth (Benbow) Walter; m. Danny Morton Lewis, June 28, 1969; children: Mark, Geoffrey. BA in Polit. Sci., U. Calif., 1969; MS in Edn. Curriculum, So. Ill. U., 1998. Cert. elem. edn. tchr. Tchr. Effingham Cmty. Unit 40, Edgewood, Ill., 1971—2005, mem. adminstrv. bd., 1999—2001, 2004—05; ret., 2005. Mem. missions com. Effingham Cmty. Unit 40, 2001—03. Assessor Summit Twp., Effingham County, 1986-93; chair Effingham County Edm. Women, 1985; bd. dirs. Effingham Child Devel. Ctr., 1975-78; bd. dirs., adminstrv. bd. Centenary United Meth. Ch., Effingham, 1989-92, 2004—, trustee, 1992-95, adminstrv. bd. 1999-2001, 04—, missions com., 2001-03 Mem. AAUW (bd. dirs. Ill. state 1981-87, treas. 1990-92, pres.-elect 1992, pres. 1993-95, mgr. e-mail network 1998—), Ill. Edn. Assn. (membership chair region 7 1985-86, membership com. region 7 1982-86), Effingham Classroom Tchrs. Assn. (sec. 1974-76, regional coun. del. 1990-92, exec. com. 2002-05) Democrat. United Methodist. Avocations: reading, counted cross-stitch. Home: 9337 E Nees Ave Effingham IL 62401-7629

LEWIS, LISA, psychologist, administrator; B of Psychology and Biology, Pa. State U.; M of Clin. Psychology, Conn. Coll.; D of Clin. Psychology, Miami U., Oxford, Ohio. Intern Fla. Med. Sch.; dir. clin. psychology Menninger, Topeka. Presenter in field. Contbr. articles to profl. jours. Recipient David Rappaport Excellence in Teaching award; postdoctoral fellow Menninger. Address: Menningers PO Box 809045 Houston TX 77280

LEWIS, LOIDA NICOLAS, food products holding company executive; b. The Philippines, Dec. 23, 1942; m. Reginald Lewis, 1969 (dec. 1993). BA, St. Theresa's Coll., 1963; LLB, U. Philippines, 1967. Immigration atty., N.Y.C.; with Immigration and Naturalization Svc.; chmn., CEO TLC Beatrice Internat., N.Y.C., 1994—. Chmn. Nat. Federation of Filipino Americans Assoc. Author: How the Filipino Veteran of World War II Can Become a U.S. Citizen (According to the Immigration Act of 1990), 1991, How to Get a Green Card According to the Immigration Act of 1990, 1992, How to Get a Green Card: Legal Ways to Stay in the U.S.A., 1993. Office: TLC Beatrice Internat 115 E 57th St Ste 1430 New York NY 10022-2110

LEWIS, LYNN C., language educator, writer; b. Nashville; d. Edward Clayton Jr. and Audrey Eubanks Lewis. MA in English, Tenn. State U., 1979; MBA, Columbia U., 1983; PhD in English, U. Mo., Columbia, 1999. Advt. salesperson Newspaper Printing Corp., Nashville, 1974-75; supr., staff specialist South Ctrl. Bell Tel. Co., Memphis and Birmingham, Ala., 1976-81; mktg./brand asst. Procter & Gamble Co., Cin., 1983-85; divsn. mgr., dir. job tng. Tenn. Valley Ctr., Memphis, 1985-88; instr. English U. Memphis, 1988-93; grad. rsch. asst. Ctr. for Studies in Oral Tradition U. Mo., Columbia, 1993-96; asst. prof. English Tenn. State U., Nashville, 1996—2002, assoc. prof. English, 2002—. Editor, manuscript proofreader U. Mo. Press, Columbia, 1995—; editl. asst. Ctr. for Studies in Oral Tradition, Columbia, 1994-96. Contbg. author: (preface) Not All Okies are White, 2000, (chpt.) Teaching Oral Traditions, 1998; contbr. poetry to jour. Mem. adv. bd. Beale St. Repertory Theater, Memphis, 1989-92. Recipient Leadership award Johnson & Johnson Cos., N.Y.C. and Milltown, N.J., 1981-83, Creative Writing award Memphis Arts Coun., 1988-90. Mem.: So. Conf. on African Am. Studies, Coll. Lang Assn., Nat. Coun. Tchrs. English, Am. Soc. Authors, Composers and Pubs., Black Expressive Culture Studies Assn. (assoc.). Office: 3500 John A Merritt Blvd Nashville TN 37209-1500 E-mail: llewis@Tnstate.edu.

LEWIS, MARGARET MARY, marketing professional; b. Bridgeport, Conn., Sept. 27, 1959; d. Raymond Phillip and Catherine Helen (Gayda) Palovchak; m. William A. Lewis Jr., Oct. 4, 1980. BS summa cum laude, Sacred Heart U., 1986; postgrad., U. Bridgeport; AS, Katherine Gibbs Sch., 1980. Program mgr. sales svc. group Newspaper Coop. Couponing, Inc., Westport, Conn., 1985-87; sales adminstr. Supermarket Communication Sys., Inc., Norwalk, 1987—88, mgr. mktg. support, 1988—89; asst. project mgr. sales promotion Mktg. Corp. Am., Westport, 1989—91, account exec., 1991—92; mgr. program svcs. Ryan Partnership, 1992—93, sr. program mgr., 1993—95, mng. dir., 1995—96; account dir. Creative Alliance, 1996—97; promotion mktg. cons. CSC Weston Group, Wilton, 1997—98; account dir. TLP Inc., 1998—2000, group account dir., 2000—01; sr. dir. Source Mktg., Westport, 2001—02; mng. dir. Ryan Partnership, Wilton, 2002—04, v.p., 2004—. Democrat. Roman Catholic. Home: 16 Nickel Pl Monroe CT 06468-3010 Office: Ryan Partnership 50 Danbury Rd Wilton CT 06897-4411 E-mail: mlewis@ryanpartnership.com.

LEWIS, MARJORIE EHRICH, lawyer; b. Nov. 21, 1954; BA magna cum laude, Tufts U., Mass., 1976; JD, NYU, 1979. Bar: Calif. 1979. Law clk. to Hon. Warren J. Ferguson U.S. Ct. Appeals (9th cir.), 1979-80; joined Gibson, Dunn & Crutcher, 1981—, ptnr. bus. litig. LA, 1988—, now ptnr.-in-charge, LA and Century City offices. Mem. exec. com. Gibson Dunn & Crutcher, 1996—2000, mem. mgmt. com., 1999—2000. Mem. NYU Law Rev., 1977—78. Office: Gibson Dunn & Crutcher 333 S Grand Ave Ste 4400 Los Angeles CA 90071-3197 Office Phone: 213-229-7462. Office Fax: 213-229-6462. Business E-Mail: mlewis@gibsondunn.com.

LEWIS, MARK, lawyer; b. Blanket, Tex., Feb. 11, 1949; s. Clayton M. and Jean R. Lewis; m. Nancy Stock (div.); children: Clayton Michael, Megan Ann(dec.); m. Linda K. Crawford, Aug. 12, 1983; children: Amy Katherine, Andrew Franklin. BA with honors, Ea. Tex. State U., 1971; JD, SMU Law Sch., 1980. Cert.: Tex. (mediator) 1983, Tex. (family law) 1997, lic.: Tex. 1980. Atty., asst. city atty. City of Dallas Atty's Office, Dallas, 1980—81; atty., ptnr. Adams and Lewis, Dallas, 1981—82; atty., assoc. Law Offices Hayden and Cooper, Dallas, 1982—83; atty. shareholder Brown, Lewis and Nagler, Dallas, 1983—92; atty., assoc. Law Office of Curtis Loveliss, Denton, Tex., 1992—97; atty. owner Law Office of Mark Lewis, Denton, Tex., 1997—. Chmn. Denton County Bar Assn. Fellow: Tex. Bar Foun.; mem.: St. Bar of Tex. Law Office Mgmt. Com., State Bar of Tex., Denton County Bar Assn., Tex. Acad. of Family Law Specialists, Collaborations Law Inst. of Tex., Coll. St. Bart. Presbyn. Office: Law Office of Mark Lewis 509 S Carroll Blvd Denton TX 76201 E-mail: mark@dentonmedicator.com.

LEWIS, MARK EARLDON, city manager; b. Boston, June 27, 1951; s. Frederick Cole Lewis and Barbara (Forsyth) Corrigan; m. Kate Lewis; children: Anna Kristine, Benjamin Mark. BA, Washington State U., 1975; BS, We. State U., 1993, JD, 1995. Bar: Calif. 1996. Adminstrv. asst. City and Borough of Juneau, Alaska, 1975-77; city mgr. City of Valdez, Valdez, 1978-82; commr. State of Alaska Dept. Cmty. and Regional Affairs, Juneau, 1982-83; dep. city mgr. City of South San Francisco, Calif., 1984-87, city mgr., 1987-88, City of Monterey Park, Calif., 1988-91, City of Colton, Calif., 1991-93, City of Union City, Calif., 1995-2001, City of Stockton, Calif., 2001—. Mem.: Calif. City Mgrs. Assn. (mem. exec. com. 1996—98), State Bar Calif. Avocation: sailing. Home: 3901 Pine Lake Cir Stockton CA 95219 Office: 425 N El Dorado St Stockton CA 95202 Personal E-mail: marklewis0627@aol.com.

LEWIS, MARK J., civilian military employee, aerospace engineer; BS in earth and planetary sci., BS in aeronautics and astronautics, MIT, 1984, MS in aeronautics and astronautics, 1985, DSc, 1988. Asst. to assoc. prof. aerospace engring. A. James Clark Sch. Engring., U. Md., College Park, 1988—99, prof. and assoc. chair aerospace engring., 1999—2004; dir. Space Vehicle Tech. Inst., College Park, 2002—04; chief scientist USAF, Washington, 2004—. Author: more than 220 tech. publ. Recipient Henry Webb Salisbury award, MIT, 1984, E. Robert Kent Tchg. award, 1989, A. James Clark Svc. award, 1992, Meritorious Civilian Svc. award, 2004; Office of Naval Rsch. Fellow, 1984. Fellow: AIAA (Nat. Capital Section Young Scientist/Engr. Yr. 1994, Abe Zarem award mentor 1998), Nat. Inst. Aerospace; mem.: ASME. Office: Air Force Pentagon Communcaitons Agency Washington DC 20001

LEWIS, MARK K., lawyer; b. Bellmore, N.Y., Aug. 8, 1965; BS magna cum laude, Univ. Md., 1987; JD magna cum laude, Georgetown Univ., 1990. Bar: Md. 1990, D.C. 1991. Ptnr., mem. exec. com. & dep. chmn. global projects dept. Baker Botts LLP, Washington. Mem.: Assn. Internat. Petroleum Negotiators, Energy Bar Assn. Office: Baker Botts LLP The Warner 1299 Pennsylvania St NW Washington DC 20004-2400 Office Phone: 202-639-7732. Office Fax: 202-639-7890. Business E-Mail: mark.lewis@bakerbotts.com.

LEWIS, MARTIN EDWARD, transportation executive; b. Chgo., Dec. 27, 1958; s. Martin Luther and Anna Adlene (Gaines) L. BA, Johns Hopkins U., 1981; postgrad., Rush Med. Coll., 1983-85. Chmn. bd., chief exec. officer Internat. Financier Inc., Chgo., 1987—; co. rep. Assn. S.E. Asia Nations Secretariat Gen., Jakarta, Indonesia, 1995—. Co. rep. OPEC, Vienna, 1988—, Supreme Coun. States of Cooperation Coun., Summit Confs. Countries of Cooperation Coun. for Arab States of Gulf, Secretariat Gen., Riyadh, Saudi Arabia, 1989—; corp. amb. plenipotentiary GM Overseas Ops., N.Y.C., 1977, Adam Opel, Russelsheim, Fed. Republic Germany, 1977. Mem. Asia Soc., Japan Soc. Republican. Avocations: golf, tennis, yachting, scuba diving. Personal E-mail: ifiworld1@yahoo.com. E-mail: info@ifiworld.com.

LEWIS, MARTIN R., paper company executive, consultant; b. Feb. 14, 1929; s. William and Ida (Goldman) L.; m. Renee Raines, Aug. 13, 1950 (div.); children: Jeffrey, Wendy, Lisa; m. Diane Carol Brandt, July 4, 1975. BA, NYU, 1949, LLB, 1951; LLM, U. Mich., 1952. CEO Williamhouse-Regency, Inc., N.Y.C., 1955-95; vice-chmn. DIMAC Corp., N.Y.C., 1998-99; owner Martin Lewis Assocs., N.Y.C., 1999—. Cons. in field. Mem. Envelope Mfg. Assn., Paper Club N.Y., N.Y. Jewish. Office Phone: 212-253-6474. Business E-Mail: marty@mlewis.com.

LEWIS, MARY JANE, retired elementary school educator; b. Hot Springs, SD, Dec. 11, 1939; d. LeRoy Allen and Mary Jane (Casey) Y.; m. Robert Melroy Lewis; children: Patrick, Christopher, Timothy, Eric. BS, U. Wyo., 1962, MA in Curriculum and Instrn., 1979. Cert. elem. tchr., reading specialist (kindergarten through twelfth grades). Elem. tchr. 2nd and 3rd grade, Medicine Bow, Wyo., 1962-63; elem. tchr. 3rd and 4th grade Shirley Basin, Wyo., 1964—66; jr. high reading, study skills tchr. Laramie, Wyo., 1967—98; reading dept. head, 1967—98; ret., 2003. Adj. prof. undergrad. studies U. Wyo. Coll. Edn., 1998—2003, student tchr. cons.; presenter, spkr. in field. Sect. vice-chair Albany County Reps., Laramie, 1990-92, sect., 1986-90; mem. Albany County United Way; v.p. Little League Baseball; cub scout leader; chpt. vol. Red Cross Mothers, March of Dimes. State Innovative grant State Dept. Wyo., 1989. Mem. IRA Snowy Range Internat. Reading Assn. (pres.), NRA Nat. Reading Assn., U. Wyo. Alumni Assn. (life), Phi Delta Kappa, Alpha Delta Kappa (chaplain, v.p., co-pres.), Delta Kappa Gamma (sect. v.p.), Alpha Kappa PEO(guard). Episcopalian. Avocations: reading, golf, bridge. Home: 203 Arrowhead Rd Torrington WY 82240

LEWIS, MARY JANE, film producer, film director, scriptwriter; b. Kansas City, Mo., July 22, 1950; d. J.W. Jr. and Hilda (Miller) L. BA, Stephens Coll., Columbia, Mo., 1971; MA, NYU, 1984, PhD, 1996. Office mgr. Crazy Shirts, Inc., Honolulu, 1974-79; creator Exotic Exports, Honolulu, 1979-80; asst. buyer Bloomingdale's, N.Y.C., 1980-82; office mgr., media dir. Andiamo, Inc., N.Y.C., 1982-85; freelance stylist Condé Nast, Inc., N.Y.C., 1985-86; tchg. fellow NYU, 1988-90, adj. prof., 1990-92. Adj. faculty Fashion Inst. Tech., N.Y.C., 1983; lectr. U. Hawaii, creator adult edn. programs and credit classes, 1986—97; lectr. NYU Sch. Cont. Edn., 1991—94; freelance video stylist, asst. prodr. State of Hawaii, Honolulu, 1994—2003; TV prodr. Office of the Mayor, City and County of Honolulu, 1998; video prodr. Olelo Cmty. TV, Honolulu. Author: Careers in Fashion Manual, 1992, (screenplays) The Last Rose of Summer, 1992, (TV movie scripts) The Mustard Seed, 1992 (Maui Writers Conf. Screenwriting Competition award, 1998); prodr., dir., writer, narrator (video) Learning Through Community Service, 1998 (Communicator award, 1998, Videographer award, 1999); prodr.: (live TV show) City Lights, Honolulu City Lights, 1998; prodr., dir., writer (documentary) Sarah Josepha Hale and The Godey Girls, 2000—. Mem. Friends of the Richards Free Libr., Newport, NH; sponsor Women Make Movies. Mem. AAUW, The Fashion Group Internat., Inc., NYU Alumni Assn., Nat. Trust for Historic Preservation, Nat. Women's History Project, Kappa Alpha Theta Alumni (pres. pledge class 1968), Elks Club. Avocations: psychic tarot readings, harpsicord, sailing, gardening, cats. Home: 91 513 B Hapalua St Ewa Beach HI 96706 Office Phone: 808-689-4225. E-mail: godeygirls@yahoo.com.

LEWIS, MARY MAY SMITH, retired family practice nurse practitioner; b. Curtis, Okla., May 18, 1919; d. James Thomas and Maggie May (Patten) Smith; m. Leo Burch Lewis, July 11, 1993; m. Leslie Wilson Enis, Nov. 8, 1965 (dec. Oct. 11, 1991); 1 child, Mary Corliss Enis. RN, Okla. City Gen. Hosp. Sch. Nursing, 1945. RN, Okla., 1945—50, 1993—, 1950—54, 1958—92, 1948. Author poetry. Second lt. U.S. Army, 1945—46, South Pacific. Mem.: VFW Ladies Aux. (life), Am. Legion (life). Republican. Christian. Avocations: genealogy, gardening, flower arranging, cooking, research. Mailing: PO Box 932 Perkins OK 74059

LEWIS, MELVIN, psychiatrist, pediatrician, psychotherapist; b. London, May 18, 1926; came to U.S., 1956; s. Abraham George and Kitty (Merrick) L.; m. Dorothy S. Otnow, May 30, 1963; children: Gillian Io, Eric Anthony. M.B., BS, Guy's Hosp. Med. Sch., London, 1950; D.C.H., 1954; MA (hon.), Yale U., 1972. Diplomate Am. Bd. Psychiatry and Neurology, Am. Bd. Child Psychiatry; cert. in psychoanalysis, child and adolescent psychoanalysis. Intern Lambeth Hosp., 1950, Fulham Hosp., 1951 (both Eng); resident in pediatrics Yale U. Sch. Medicine, 1956-57, resident in psychiatry and child psychiatry, 1957-61; from instr. child psychiatry to sr. rsch. sci., prof. child psychiatry and pediats. Yale U. Child Study Ctr., New Haven, 1961—2002, prof. emeritus, sr. rsch. sci., 2002—. Author: Clinical Aspects of Child and Adolescent Development, 1971, 3d edit. (with Fred Volkmar), 1991; editor: Jour. Am. Acad. Child & Adolescent Psychiatry, 1975-87, Child and Adolescent Psychiatry, A Comprehensive Textbook, 2002, 3d edit., 1996; cons. editor: Child and Adolescent Psychiatric Clinics of North America, 1991—. Served with M.C. Royal Army, 1951-53. Fellow: Royal Coll. Psychiatrists, Am. Psychiat. Assn. (disting. life fellow), Am. Acad. Child and Adolescent Psychiatry; mem.: Am. Psychoanalytic Assn., Western New Eng. Psychoanalytic Inst. and Soc., Am. Pediat. Soc. Home: 10 St Ronan Ter New Haven CT 06511 Office: Yale U Child Study Ctr 230 S Frontage Rd New Haven CT 06520-7900 E-mail: melvin.lewis@yale.edu.

LEWIS, MELVIN MATTHEW, music educator; b. Chgo., Ill., Jan. 14, 1971; s. Melvin and Paula Marie Lewis; m. Tunya Marie Leonard, Sept. 19, 1998; children: Tyrone Malcolm Cleveland, Trichelle Margaret Wiley, Christian Emmanuel. BA in Music Edn., Bethune-Cookman Coll., Daytona Beach, Fla., 1994; MusM Edn., Fla. State U., Tallahassee, Fla., 1996. Instr. woodwinds/asst. dir. bands Bethune-Cookman Coll., Daytona Beach, Fla., 1997—2005. Mem.: Fla. Music Educators Assn., Phi Mu Alpha (hon.), Kappa Kappa Psi (hon.). Home: 1649 Stocking St Daytona Beach FL 32117 Office: Bethune-Cookman Coll 647 Dr Mary McLeod Bethune Blvd Daytona Beach FL 32114 Office Phone: 386-481-2747. Office Fax: 386-481-2777. Business E-Mail: lewism@cookman.edu.

LEWIS, MICHAEL ROBERT, medical researcher, educator; b. Madison, Wis., Sept. 29, 1962; s. Robert Glenn and Sue Ann Lewis; m. Varyanna Chryzhtjanok Ruthengael, Sept. 28, 1991. PhD, City of Hope Grad. Sch. of Biol. Scis., Duarte, Calif., 1994—97. NIH post doc. fellow Wash. U., St. Louis, 1997—2000; asst. prof. U. of Mo. Columbia, 2000—. Study sect. reviewer NIH, Bethesda, Md., 2002—; ad hoc reviewer Bioconjugate Chemistry Internat. Jour. Pharmaceutics, Jour. Nuclear Medicine; mem. bd. dirs. Radiopharmaceutical Scis. Coun. Grantee, Dept. Health and Human Svcs. Nat. Cancer Inst., 2003—, Dept. of Def., 2001—, 2002—, Dept. of Vet. Affairs, 2005—. Mem.: AAAS, Soc. of Radiopharmaceutical Chemistry and Biology, Soc. of Nuc. Medicine (bd. dirs.), Am. Chem. Soc., Alpha Chi Sigma. Office: U MO Columbia 379 E Campus Dr Columbia MO 65211 Business E-Mail: lewismic@missouri.edu.

LEWIS, NORMAN G., academic administrator, researcher, consultant; b. Irvine, Ayrshire, Scotland, Sept. 16, 1949; came to U.S., 1985; s. William F. and Agnes H. O. L.; m. Christine I. (div. Oct. 1994); children: Fiona, Kathryn; m. Laurence Beatrice Davin, July 1997; 1 child, Sebastien. BSc in Chemistry with honors, U. Strathclyde, Scotland, 1973; PhD in Chemistry 1st class, U. B.C., 1977. NRC postdoctoral fellow U. Cambridge, Eng., 1978-80; rsch. assoc. chemistry dept. Nat. Rsch. Coun., Can., 1980; asst. scientist fundamental rsch. divsn. Pulp and Paper Rsch. Inst. Can., Montreal, 1980-82, group leader chemistry and biochemistry of woody plants, grad. rsch. chemistry divsn., 1982-85; assoc. prof. wood sci. and biochemistry Va. Poly. Inst. and State U., Blacksburg, 1985-90; dir. Inst. Biol. Chemistry, Wash. State U., Pullman, 1990—; Eisig-Tode disting. prof. Wash. State U., Pullman. Cons. NASA, DOE, USDA, NIH, NSF, Am. Inst. Biol. Sci., other industries, 1985—; mem. sci. adv. bd. Ctr. for Marine Sci., U. NC, 2004—, Nat. Ctr. for Natural Products Rsch., U. Miss., Oxford, 2003—, Donald Danforth Plant Sci. Ctr., St. Louis, 2002—. Mem. editl. bd. Holzforschung, 1986, TAPPI, 1986, 89, Jour. Wood Chemistry and Tech., 1987, Polyphenols Actualities, 1992—; mem. editl. bd. Wood Sci. and Tech., 2001—, The Ams., Asia regional editor Phytochemistry, 1992—; exec. editor Advances in Plant Biochemistry and Molecular Biology, 2004—; monitoring editor Plant Physiology, 2005—; author or co-author more than 180 publs., books, articles to profl. jours. Hon. mem. Russian Assn. Space and Mankind. Recipient ICI Merit awards Imperial Chem. Industries, 1968-69, 69-70, 70-71, 71-72, ICI scholar, 1971-73, Chemistry awards Kilmarnock Coll., 1969-70, 70-71; NATO/SRC scholar U. B.C., 1974-77; named Local Hero, Prestwick Acad., Ayrshire, Scotland. Mem. TAPPI, Am. Chem. Soc. (at-large cellulose divsn., organizer symposia, programme subcom. cellulose, paper and textile divsn. 1987-90, editl. bd.), Am. Soc. Plant Biologists, Am. Soc. Gravitational and Space Biology (pres. 1998-99), Phytochem. Soc. N.A. (phytochem. bank com. 1989—), Chem. Inst. Can. (treas. Montreal divsn. 1982-84, Am. Inst. Chemists and Chem. Inst. Can. Montreal conf. 1982-84), Can. Pulp and Paper Assn., Societe de Groupe Polyphenole, Gordon Rsch. Conf. (vice-chmn. renewable resources com. 1993). Presbyterian. Achievements include numerous patents in field; consultant on a project on bioprospecting in Brazil (funded by FAPESP), which has goals of bioassay-guided fractionation, as well as studying biosynthetic pathways and ecological interactions. Home: 1710 NE Upper Dr Pullman WA 99163-4624 Office: Washington State U Inst Biol Chemistry Clark Hall Pullman WA 99164-6340 Fax: 509-335-8206. E-mail: lewisn@wsu.edu.

LEWIS, ORME, JR., real estate company executive, land use adviser; b. Phoenix, Apr. 26, 1935; s. Orme and Barbara (Smith) L.; m. Elizabeth Bruening, Oct. 17, 1964; children: Joseph Orme, Elizabeth Blaise Hazelblood. BS, U. Ariz., 1958. Assoc. Coldwell Banker, Phoenix, 1959-64; v.p. Braggiotti Constrn., Phoenix, 1964-65; pvt. practice investment brokerage Phoenix, 1966-69; dep. asst. sec. Dept. Interior, Washington, 1969-73; dir. devel. Ariz. Biltmore Estates, 1973—76; exec. World Resources Co., Phoenix and McLean, Va., 1978-91; mng. mem. Applewhite Laflin & Lewis, Phoenix, 1979-96; gen. ptnr. Equity Interests, Phoenix, 1982—; mng. dir. Select Investments, Phoenix, 1996—. Co-chmn. U.S. Adv. Com. on Mining and Mineral Rsch., Washington, 1982-94; mem. U.S. Emergency Minerals Adminstrn., 1987-01, Gov.'s Regulatory Rev. Coun., 1992-95, State Plant Site Transmission Line Com., Phoenix, 1974-85; co-chmn. Disease Control Rsch. Commn., 1995-2002; adv. bd. U.S. Minerals Mgmt. Bd., 2002—. Mem. Ariz. Senate, 1966-70 (chmn. Phoenix Children's Hosp., 1981—; mem. bds. Boyce Thompson Arboretum, 1999—); mem. governing bd. Polycystic Kidney Rsch. Found., Kansas City, Mo., 1983—, Ariz. Cmty. Found., 1986-91, Ariz. Parks and Conservation Coun., 1985-96, Ariz. State U. Found., Tempe, 1981—, Ariz. Hist. Found., 1984—, Desert Bot. Garden, 1987-89, Men's Art Coun., 1962-. Recipient Dept. Interior Conservation Svc. award, 1996; inductee Wisdom Hall of Fame, 1997. Mem. Ariz. C. of C. (dir. 1990-96), Met. Club (Washington), Ariz. Valley Field Riding and Polo Club,

Paradise Valley Country Club (Scottsdale), Rotary. Republican. Home: 4325 E Palo Verde Dr Phoenix AZ 85018-1127 Office: Select Investments LLC 5070 N 40th St Ste 140 Phoenix AZ 85018-2193 Office Phone: 602-952-8800. Personal E-mail: adviser_az@msn.com.

LEWIS, PATSY JOANNE, religious studies educator, writer; b. Alexandria, La., Jan. 27, 1943; d. William Neilson Eznack and Faye M. Dryden; m. C. S. Lewis, Sept. 15, 1961; children: Arita J. Johnson, Charlene A., Carson A., Jennifer J. Everett, Jason N. Grad. h.s., Alexandria. Cert. tchr. religion La. Sec. to sr. acct. Continental Lines, Alexandria, 1962—64; tchr. Christian curriculum Christian Sch., Alexandria, 1982—84. Tchr. United Pentecostal Ch. Internat., Alexandria, 1980—96. Author: (novels) The Morning of the White Stone, The Sins of Boggy Creek, (poetry) Immortality, Dawn (Anthology Publ., 2004), (song) The Fellowship of His Suffering. Writer, counselor United Pentecostal Ch., Alexandria, 2000—04. Recipient Songwriter award, Paramount Records, 2002. Mem.: Internat. Soc. of Poets (corr.). Home: 49 Ashton Rd Boyce LA 71409 Personal E-mail: patsylws@aol.com.

LEWIS, PAUL, architecture educator; BA, Wesleyan U., 1988; MArch, Princeton U., 1992. Instr. Ohio State U., Barnard Coll., Columbia Coll., Parsons Sch. Design, Cooper Union; assoc. Diller & Scofidio, 1993—97; co-founder Lewis.Tsurumaki.Lewis, N.Y.C., 1993—; dir. grad. studies Princeton (N.J.) U. Sch. Arch. Fellow: Am. Acad. in Rome (Mercedes T. Bass Rome prize in arch. 1998). Office: Lewis Tsurumaki Lewis 147 Essex St New York NY 10002 also: Sch Arch Princeton Univ Princeton NJ 08544-5264

LEWIS, PERRY JOSHUA, investment banker; b. San Antonio, Feb. 11, 1938; s. Perry Joshua and Zelime L. L.; m. Memrie Taylor Mosier, May 12, 1962 (div. 1994); children— Perry Joshua, IV, Memrie Fraser; m. Basha Szymanska, May 15, 1997. BA, Princeton U., 1959. Registered rep. Lee Higginson Corp., N.Y.C., 1960-63; comml. project mgr. Parsons & Whittemore, Inc., N.Y.C., 1964-67; sr. v.p., mgr. corp. fin. div. Smith Barney, Harris Upham & Co. Inc., N.Y.C., 1967-79; pres. MacKay-Lewis Inc., N.Y.C., 1980-81; ptnr. Morgan Lewis Githens & Ahn, Conn., 1982—2004; sr. mng. dir. Heartland Indsl. Ptnrs., Greenwich, Conn., 2000—01; adv. dir. CRT Capital Group LLC, Stamford, Conn., 2001—. Bd. dirs. Clear Channel Comm., Inc., San Antonio, Superior Essex Inc., Atlanta. With U.S. Army, 1959-60, 61-62. Mem.: Knickerbocker of N.Y. Office: CRT Capital Group 262 Harbor Dr Stamford CT 06902 Business E-Mail: pjlewis@crtllc.com.

LEWIS, PETER BENJAMIN, insurance company executive; b. Cleve., Nov. 11, 1933; s. Joseph M. and Helen (Rosenfeld) Lewis; children: Ivy, Jonathan, Adam. AB, Princeton U., 1955. Underwriting trainee Progressive Ins. Cos., 1955; exec. trainee Progressive Casualty Ins. Co., pres., CEO, 1965-94, The Progressive Corp., Ohio, 1965-2000, chmn. bd., 2000—. Named one of Top 200 Collectors, ARTnews Mag., 2004. Avocation: Collector of Contemporary art including Am. conceptualism. Office: Progressive Corp 6300 Wilson Mills Rd Cleveland OH 44143-2109

LEWIS, PHILIP, educational association administrator, consultant; b. Chgo., Oct. 23, 1913; s. Solomon and Fannie (Margolis) L.; m. Geraldine Gisela Lawenda, Sept. 1, 1947; 1 child, Linda Susan. BS, DePaul U., Chgo., 1937, MA, 1939; EdD, Columbia Tchrs. Coll., 1951. Chmn. dept. edn. Chgo. Tchrs. Coll.; also asst. prin., tchr. South Shore High Sch., Chgo., 1940-51; prin. Herman Felsenthal Elementary Sch., Chgo., 1955-57; dir. Bur. Instructional Materials, Chgo. Pub. Schs., 1957-63, Bur. Research Devel. and Spl. Projects, 1963-67; pres. Instructional Dynamics Inc., Chgo., 1967-89, ret., 1989; ednl. and tech. cons., 1991—. Nat. cons. TV and instructional techniques, 1955—; ednl. cons. to accrediting bur. Health Edn. Schs., 1971-89; chmn. adv. com. U.S. Office Edn., Title VII, 1964-67 Author: Educational Television Guidebook for Electronics Industries Association, 1961, also numerous articles.; mem. editorial bd. Nation's Schs. and Colls; multimedia tech. editor: Tech. Horizons in Edn; cons.: Jour. Ednl. Tech. and Communications; producer ednl., multimedia, tng. and mental health and human devel. materials. Served to lt. comdr. USNR, 1942—45. Mem. Soc. Programmed and Automated Learning (pres. 1960-65), NEA (v.p. dept. audiovisual instrn., chmn. commn. on tech. standards dept. audiovisual instrn. 1965-85), Nat. Assn. Ednl. Broadcasters, Am. Legion, Council for Ednl. Facilities Planners (editorial adv. bd. 1972-80) Ill. C. of C. (edn. com. 1970-77), Chgo. Assn. Commerce and Industry (chmn. edn. com. 1970-80), Nat. Audio-Visual Assn. (profl. devel. bd. 1969-76, chmn), Chgo. Press Club, Masons, Shriners, Rotary, Phi Delta Kappa.

LEWIS, R. FRED, state supreme court justice; b. Beckley, W.Va., Dec. 14, 1947; m. Judith Lewis, 1969; children: Elle, Lindsay. Grad. cum laude, Fla. So. Coll., 1969; JD cum laude, U. Miami, 1972; grad., U.S. Army A.G. Sch.; PhD in Public Service (hon.), Fla. So. Coll., 2000; LLD (hon.), St. Thomas U., 2002. Pvt. practice, Miami; justice Fla. Supreme Ct., 1998—. Mem. Fla. Commn. on Legal Needs of Children; active in Justice Teaching Inst.; liaison Fla. Bd. of Bar Examiners, Judicial Management Council; mem. Fla. Supreme Ct. Com. on Rules of Civil Procedure, Fla. Supreme Ct. Com. on Standard Civil Jury Instructions, Fla. Supreme Ct. Code & Rules of Evidence Com. Contbr. pubs. Continuing Edn. Legal Program. Bd. dirs. Miami Children's Hosp.; inventory atty. The Fla. Bar. Recipient Friends of Justice award ABOTA, 1999; Jud. Pub. Trust and Confidence award FLREA, 2001; Citizen Yr. award, Fla., 2001; Everyday Hero award for outstanding contbn. to cmty. svc. in Fla.; Justice R. Fred Lewis award U. Ctrl. Fla., 2002, Great Am. Law in Edn. award, 2005; NCAA postgrad. grantee, 1969; Guardian of the Constitution Citizenship award for Law-Related Edn., others. Mem. Omicron Delta Kappa, Psi Chi, Sigma Alpha Epsilon. Address: Fla Supreme Ct 500 S Duval St Tallahassee FL 32399-6556 Office Phone: 850-488-0007. E-mail: supremecourt@mail.flcourts.org.

LEWIS, RAY, professional football player; b. May 15, 1975; children: Ray Anthony Lewis, Jr., Rayshad, Dymond Deseree. Degree in arts and scis. Profl. football player Balt. Ravens, 1996—. Vol. charitable orgns. Named NFL Defensive Player of the Yr., 2000, 2003, Super Bowl XXV MVP, 2000; named to NFL Pro-Bowl, 1998—2000, 2003—04. Achievements include became the 2nd player in NFL history to win both NFL Defensive MVP and Super Bowl MVP; mem. Super Bowl XXXV Champion Balt. Ravens, 2000; led NFL in tackles (210), 1997. Avocations: fishing, camping, swimming, basketball. Office: Balt Ravens Ravens Stadium 1101 Russell St Baltimore MD 21230 E-mail: inquiries@baltimoreravens.com.*

LEWIS, REGINALD DEMETRICE PAGAN, education educator; s. Gennell P Lewis. BS, Mercer U., 1995—97; MBA, Troy State U., 1999—2000; PhD, Walden U., 2003—. Certified Internet Webmaster Ga., 2001. Cons. Crown 1 Comm., Union City, Ga., 1995—; dir. of edn. A Rare View, Inc., Atlanta, 2000—. Bd. mem. Miss Fulton County Scholarship Pageant, Atlanta, 2001. Mem.: Nat. Assn. of Black Accountants (assoc.), Nat. Black MBA Assn. (assoc.), Phi Mu Alpha Sinfonia Frat., Inc. (assoc.), Alpha Phi Alpha Frat., Inc. (assoc.). Home: 3335 Estate Lake Drive Fairburn GA 30213 Office: Crown 1 Communications 1605 Summerglen Drive Union City GA 30291 Office Phone: 707-560-0313. Personal E-mail: reggielewis3@aol.com.

LEWIS, RICHARD, actor, comedian; b. Bklyn., June 29, 1948; s. Bill and Blanche L. Student, Ohio State U., 1970. Head copywriter N.J. advt. agency, 1970-71. Appearances include Greenwich Village club, The Improv, The Tonight Show. Co-writer: (TV special) Diary of a Young Comic; actor (TV series) Harry, 1987, King of the Building, 1987, Anything But Love, 1990-92, Daddy Dearest, 1993, over 40 appearances on Late Night With David Letterman, 1982; appeared in (cable special) I'm In Pain, 1985, I'm Exhausted, 1988 (ACE award nomination 1988), All-Star Toast to the Improv, 1988, I'm Doomed, 1990; films include The Wrong Guys, 1988, That's Adequate, 1989, Once Upon a Crime, 1992, Robin Hood: Men in Tights, 1993, Wagons East, 1994, Leaving Las Vegas, 1995, Drunks, 1995, Hugo Pool, 1997; A Weekend in the Country, 1996 (TV Movie).

LEWIS, RICHARD LAURENCE, academic administrator, computer graphics designer; b. Queens, N.Y., Oct. 9, 1955; s. Henry Louis and Joan Ann Lewis; m. Susan Roberta Ingalls, Aug. 2, 1981; 1 child, Robert Andrew. BFA in Visual Arts, SUNY, 1977; MFA in Painting, U. Mich., 1983. From asst. prof. to assoc. prof. art Marist Coll., Poughkeepsie, NY, 1984—2004, prof. art, 2004—, studio art coord., 1989-95, chair dept. art & art history, 1995-97, 2001—, dean acad. programs, asst. acad. v.p., 1997-2000, chair faculty, 2002—04. Mem. steering com. Joint Study with IBM, 1992—2001. Author (with Susan I. Lewis): The Power of Art, 1995; author: (with James Luciana) Digital Media: An Introduction, 2005. Mem.: Am. Assn. Mus., Coll. Art Assn. Office: Art and Art History Marist Coll 3399 North Rd Poughkeepsie NY 12601-1326

LEWIS, RICHARD PHELPS, cardiologist, educator; b. Portland, Oreg., Oct. 26, 1936; s. Howard Phelps and Wava Irene (Brown) L.; m. Penny A. Brown, Oct. 12, 1982; children: Richard Phelps, Heather Brown. BA, Yale U., 1957; MD, U. Oreg., 1961. Intern Peter Bent Brigham Hosp., Boston, 1961-62, resident, 1962-63; Howard Irwin fellow in cardiology U. Oreg., Portland, 1963-65; sr. resident Stanford U., 1965-66, instr. dept. medicine, 1968-69; asst. chief cardiology Madigan Gen. Hosp., Tacoma, 1966-68; asst. prof. medicine div. cardiology Ohio State U., 1969-71, assoc. prof., 1971-75, prof., 1975-2000, dir. Divsn. Cardiology, 1972-86, dir., 1972-86, assoc. chmn. for hosp. and clin. affairs, 1980-86, prof. emeritus, 2000—. Mem. cardiovascular sect. Am. Bd. Internal Medicine, 1981-87, critical care medicine, 1988-92. Contbr. articles to profl. jours. Served with M.C. U.S. Army, 1966-68, col. res. Decorated Army Commendation medal Master Am. Coll. Cardiology (Ohio gov. 1988-91, chmn. bd. govs. 1990-91, trustee 1991-2000, editor self assessment program ACCSAP, 1991-96, 2000—, v.p. 1994-95, pres.-elect 1995-96, pres. 1996-97); fellow ACP (gov. Ohio chpt. 1976-80, chmn. MKSAP cardiovascular sect. 1989-82, master tchr. 1998), Am. Heart Assn. (coun. on clin. cardiology), Am. Clin. and Climatological Assn.; mem. Am. Fedn. Clin. Rsch., Ctrl. Soc. Clin. Rsch., Laennec Soc., Am. Heart Assn., Assn. U. Cardiologists, Alpha Omega Alpha. Republican. Episcopalian. Home: 5088 Stratford Ave Powell OH 43065-8771 Office: 473 W 12th Ave Columbus OH 43210-1240

LEWIS, RITA HOFFMAN, plastic products manufacturing company executive; b. Phila., Aug. 6, 1947; d. Robert John and Helen Anna (Dugan) Hoffman; 1 child, Stephanie Blake. Student, Jefferson Med. Coll. Sch. Nursing, 1965—67, Gloucester County Coll., 1993—. Gen. mgr. Sheets & Co., Inc. (now Flower World, Inc.), Woodbury, NJ, 1968—72; dir., exec. v.p., treas. Hoffman Precision Plastics, Inc., Blackwood, 1973—. Ptnr. Timber Assocs. Author: The Part of Me I Never Really Meant to Share, 1979, In Retrospect: Caught Between Running and Loving; editor: SPOTLIGHTER; columnist: Innovative Singles Mag., 1989—. Commr. N.J. Expressway Authority, 1990—, sec., 1990—91, treas., 1991—, chmn. pers., 1991—; apptd. mem. N.J. Senate Forum on Budget and Revenue Alternatives, 1991; guest spkr. various civic groups, 1974; active Coun. for Citizens of Glen Oaks, NJ, 1979—, Cloucester Twp. Econ. Devel. Com., 1981—, Cloucester Twp. Day Scholar Com., 1984—; adv. coun. Gloucester Twp. Econ. Adv. Coun., 1985—; chair Gloucester Twp. Day Scholar Found., 1985—96; bd. dirs. Diane Hull Dance Co. Recipient Winning Eagle award, 1982, Mayor's award for Womens' Achievement, 1987, Outstanding Cmty. Svc. award Mayor, Coun. and Com., 1987, Don L. Stackhouse Achievement award, 1996. Mem.: NAFE, Soc. Plastic Engrs., Blackwood Businessmen's Assn., Sales Assn. Chem. Industry, Stratford-Lindenwold Rotary (sargent-at-arms 2003, sec. 2004, dist. RYLA com. 2004, pres. 2005—, membership chair, dist. RYLA com. 2005). Roman Catholic.

LEWIS, ROBERT DAVID, ophthalmologist, educator; b. Thomasville, Ga., Aug. 27, 1948; s. Ralph N. and E. Margaret (Klaus) L.; m. Cathleen Ann Polster, May 26, 1996. BS, St. Louis Coll. Pharmacy, 1971; MD, St. Louis U., 1975. Diplomate Am. Bd. Ophthalmology; registered pharmacist. Intern, Cardinal Glennon Hosp. Children, St. Louis, 1975-76; resident St. Louis U., 1976-79; dir. pediatric ophthalmology St. Louis U., 1980-82, 85, asst. prof., 1980-88, assoc. prof., 1988-97, clin. prof. ophthalmology, 1998; pres. St. Louis Ophthalmological Soc., 1991-92; dir. pediatric ophthalmology Cardinal Glennon Hosp. for Children, St. Louis, 1980-82, 85; adv. bd. Delta Gamma Found. for Visually Handicapped Children. Recipient St. Louis U. Award for Teaching, 1982. Fellow ACS; mem. AMA, Mo. Med. Assn., St. Louis Med. Soc., Am. Acad. Ophthalmology, Contact Lens Assn. Ophthalmology, Internat. Assn. Ocular Surgeons, Am. Intraocular Implant Soc., St. Louis Ophthalmol. Soc. (pres. 1991-92), Am. Bd. Club. (pres. 1991-92). Office: 12700 Southfork Rd Ste 205 Saint Louis MO 63128-3201 Office Phone: 314-842-0582.

LEWIS, ROBERT EDWIN, JR., pathology and immunology educator, researcher; b. Meridian, Miss., Mar. 11, 1947; s. Robert Edwin and Cecille (Ryan) Lewis. BA in Biology and Chemistry, U. Miss., 1969, MS in Microbiology, 1973, PhD in Pathology, 1976; specialty tng., Barnes Hosp., U. Miami Med. Ctr., U. Tenn. Ctr. for Health Scis., City of Memphis Hosps., St. Jude Children's Research Hosp. Instr. pathology, anesthesiology U. Miss. Med. Ctr., Jackson, 1976-77, asst. prof. pathology, 1977-84, asst. prof. anesthesiology, 1977-85, asst. dir. clin. immnuopathology lab., 1978-81, assoc. dir. tissue typing lab., 1980-84, dir. paternity testing lab., 1981—, assoc. dir. clin. immunopathology lab., 1981-84, asst. prof. nurse anesthesiology, 1981-85, assoc. prof. pathology, 1984-91, prof., 1991—, dir. clin. immunology, tissue typing lab., 1984—, mem. grad. council, 1981—, prof., 1991—. Co-author: Illus. Dictionary of Immunology, 1995, 2003, Atlas of Immunology, 1999, 2d edit., 2004, Immunology Guidebook, 2004, Historical Atlas of Immunology, 2005; editor (with J.M. Cruse): Concepts in Immunopathology, Vols. 1-8, 1985—91; editor: The Yr. in Immunology-1984-85, 1985, The Yr. in Immunology-1986-8, 1987, The Yr. in Immunology-1988, 1989, The Yr. in Immunology-1989-90, 1990, Progress in Exptl. Tumor Rsch. Vol. 32, 1987, Contributions to Microbiology and Immunology, Vol. 8, 1986, Vol. 9, 1987, Vol. 10, 1989, Vol. 11, 1989, The Yr. in Immunopathology, 1987, Complement Profiles, Vol. 1, 1992, Historical Atlas of Immunology, 2004; sr. editor Immunologic Research, 1981, Pathology and Immunopathology Rsch., 1982—90, Pathobiology, 1990—98, Pathology, 1990—98, Transgenics, 1993, Exptl. and Molecular Pathology, 1999, series editor Concepts in Immunopathology, The Yr. in Immunology, Contributions to Microbiology and Immunology, vol. editor Progress in Exptl. Tumor Rsch, immunology editor Dorland's Illus. Med. Dictionary, 26th and 27th edits., dep. editor-in-chief Pathobiology, 1990—98; contbr. chpts. to books. Am. Cancer Soc. grantee, NIH grantee, Wilson Found. grantee, 1990-2002. Fellow Royal Soc. Health, Royal Soc. Medicine; mem. AAAS, Am. Assn. Pathologists, Am. Assn. Immunologists, Clin. Immunology Soc., Can. Soc. Immunology, Reticuloendothelial Soc., Am. Soc. Microbiology, Am. Soc. Histocompatibility and Immunogenetics (chmn. publs. com. 2000-03, bd. dirs. 2004—), Exptl. Biology and Medicine, N.Y. Acad. Scis., Miss. Acad. Scis., Sigma Xi. Office: U Miss Med Ctr Pathology Dept Dept Pathology 2500 N State St Jackson MS 39216-4500 Office Phone: 601-984-1562. Business E-Mail: rlewis@pathology.umsmed.edu.

LEWIS, ROBERT ENZER, editor, educator; b. Windber, Pa., Aug. 12, 1934; s. Robert Enzer and Katharine Torrence (Blair) L.; m. Julie Fatt Cureton, May 14, 1977; children: Perrin Lewis Rubin, Torrence Evans Lewis; stepchildren: Sarah Cureton Kaufman, James S. Cureton. BA, Princeton U., 1959; MA, U. Pa., 1962, PhD, 1964. Tchr. English Mercersburg (Pa.) Acad., 1959-60; teaching fellow U. Pa., Phila., 1961-63; lectr. Ind. U., Bloomington, 1963-64, asst. prof., 1964-68, assoc. prof., 1968-75, prof. English, 1975-82, U. Mich., Ann Arbor, 1982—2003, prof. emeritus, 2004—. Author: (with A. McIntosh) Descriptive Guide to the Manuscripts of the Prick of Conscience, 1982, (with others) Index of Printed Middle English Prose, 1985; editor: De Miseria Condicionis Humane (Lotario dei Segni), 1978; co-editor: Middle English Dictionary, 1982-83, editor-in-chief: vols. 8, 9, 10, 11, 12, 13, 1984-2001; gen. editor: Chaucer Libr., 1970—, chmn. editl. com., 1978-89, 97—. Bd. regents Mercersburg Acad., 1975-87. U.S. Army, 1954-56. Recipient Sir Israel Gollancz Meml. prize for English studies Brit. Acad., 2003; vis. rsch. fellow Inst. Advanced Studies in the Humanities, U. Edinburgh, 1973-74; Am. Coun. Learned Socs. fellow, 1979-80. Fellow: Dictionary Soc. N.Am. (mem. nominating com. 2005—); mem.: New Chaucer Soc., Medieval Acad. Am. (mem. publs. com. 1987—92). Episcopalian. Office: U Mich Dept English 3187 Angell Hall Ann Arbor MI 48109-1003 Business E-Mail: relewis@umich.edu.

LEWIS, ROBERT JOHN CORNELIUS KOONS, retired library director; b. Feb. 15, 1938; s. Frank Ashby and Dorothy Elaine (Koons) L.; m. Martha Marie Popejoy, Dec. 22, 1957 (div. 1964); 1 child, Stephen Ashley; m. Helena Barbara Vaughn Schumacker, Sept. 11, 1968 (div. 1976); children: Matthew, Randolph; m. Marguerita S. Kris, July 28, 1985 (dec. Feb. 2001). BA in History of Religion, George Washington U., 1961, MA in Secondary Edn., 1966; MSLS, Cath. U. Am., 1974. Intelligence analyst CIA, Washington, 1958-62; tech. libr. supr. Bell Aerospace, Tucson, 1968-70; info. officer Ambionics Inc., Washington, 1970-73; law libr. Patton, Boggs & Blow, Washington, 1973-75; rschr. George Washington U., Washington, 1976-78; libr. dir. Benjamin Franklin U., Washington, 1979—2003; ret. Oriental art cons. Silverman Galleries, Alexandria, Va., 1978—; libr. dir. Cushman, Darby & Cushman, 1988-90, Nat. Geneal. Soc., 1990-93; libr. Met. Club, 1994—. Author, compiler: Brief History of the Rose Mount Branch of the Surles (Searles) Lewis Family of Virginia, 1976, collected poems: Quatrains based on the Love Poems of the 6th Dalai Lama and other poems, 1979, Lewis Patriarchs of Early Va. and Md., 1989, rev. edit., 1991, rev. 3d. edit., 1998, Welsh Family Coats of Arms, 1995. With U.S. Army, 1963-65. Awarded title of Gyalwa Karma Lozang Dondrup, by Kalu Rinpoche of Darjeeling, 1977; hon. grantee of arms Coll. of Arms, London, 1998. Mem. ALA (pres. com. 1982), Assn. Former Intelligence Officers, Spl. Librs. Assn., Nat. Geneal. Soc. (councilor 1990-93), Soc. Geneal. of London, Jamestowne Soc., The Augustan Soc., Mahikari of Am. Club, Subud Club, Theosophical Soc. Club, Sigma Phi Epsilon. Episcopalian. Home: 18612 Sage Way Germantown MD 20874-2041 Office Phone: 301-972-9211. E-mail: robertjcklewis@aol.com.

LEWIS, ROBERT KAY, JR., fundraising executive; b. Danville, Ky., Aug. 10, 1935; s. Robert K. and Mona (Hyden) L.; m. Wendy Gardiner, June 18, 1960; children: Mary Elizabeth, Mona Hyden, Robert K. III. BA, Ctr. Coll., Danville, 1957; MS, George Washington U., 1972. Advanced through ranks to lt. U.S. Navy, 1958-63; alumni/annual giving dir. Ctr. Coll., 1963-67; served to capt. U.S. Navy, 1967-81; alumni/pub. affairs dir. Ctr. Coll., 1981-83; pub. affairs dir. Va. Tech., Blacksburg, 1983-87; sr. v.p. Host Comm., Lexington, 1987-89; pres. Ky. C. of C., Frankfort, 1990; chmn., CEO Global Advancement, Lexington, Ky., 1991—. Trustee Severn Sch., Severna Park, Md., 1979-83; bd. visitors McCallie Sch., Chattanooga, 1983-86; bd. dirs. Ky. Advocates for Higher Edn., Lexington, 1990—. Mem. Assn. Fund Raising Profls. (bd. dirs. Bluegrass chpt. 1991-2003), Henry Clay Found. (bd. dirs. Lexington, 1994—), Nat. Press Club, Coun. Advancement and Support of Edn. (bd. dirs. Ky. chpt. 1991-98), Assn. of Philanthropic Counsel (nat. bd. dirs., exec. com. 2000—), Lexington Rotary Endowment (bd. dirs. 1995-2001). Presbyterian. Home: Forest Hill Farm 2667 Lexington Rd Danville KY 40422 Office: Global Advancement 333 W Vine St Ste 300 Lexington KY 40507-1626 Office Phone: 859-231-8575. E-mail: Bob@global-advt.com.

LEWIS, ROBERT LAWRENCE, lawyer, educator; b. N.Y.C., Sept. 25, 1919; s. Isador and Sadie (Holzinger) L.; m. Frieda Friedman, Nov. 24, 1940 (dec. 1961); children— Brian S., Paul E., David N.; m. Joanne Marcia Waxman, June 16, 1963; children— Pavia S., Eraclea S. AB, Hamilton Coll., 1940; LL.B., Case Western Res. U., 1948. With firm Ulmer & Berne, Cleve., 1948-64, ptnr., 1956-64; ret., 1964. Prof. law, dir. grad. div. Cleve.-Marshall Law Sch. (now Cleve. State U.), 1948-53; bd. dirs. Banner Industries, Inc., Cleve.; scholar-in-residence, prof. classics Cuayhoga C.C.; adj. prof. non-profit governance Case Western Res. U., Cleve. Author: Five Angry Women, 1990, Agatharcus, 1993. Cons., evaluator North Central Assn. Colls. and Schs., Middle States Assn. Mem. Cleve. Area Arts Council, 1971-73; pres. Fairmount Center for Creative and Performing Arts, 1973-75; trustee, chmn. bd. Cuyahoga Community Coll.; trustee Cuyahoga Community Coll. Found., Playhouse Sq. Found., Cleve., Cleve. Commn. Higher Edn., Lake Erie Coll., Council for Interinstnl. Leadership, Pace Assn., New Orgn. for Visual Arts; bd. dirs. Assn. Governing Bds. Univs. and Colls.; bd. advisers Cleve. Ballet; trustee, v.p. New Cleve. Opera Co. Served to 1st lt., arty. and ordnance corps AUS, 1942-46, NATOUSA. Decorated Legion of Merit, Purple Heart Mem. Exec. Order Ohio Commodore, Phi Beta Kappa. Home: Cleveland, Ohio. *There is neither a standard nor a uniform set of qualities which best fits one to be a member of society, and anyone who contends to the contrary, may be equated with the infamous and mythical Procrustes. I for one prefer the preservation of individuality. No one of us should be fitted to the bed of Procrustes. I prefer that we shall all survive; and each of us shall then be the richer for the survival of the other.* Died Aug. 3, 2005.

LEWIS, RODERIC W., electronics executive, lawyer; b. Nyssa, Oreg., May 17, 1955; BA in Economics & Asian studies, Brigham Young U., 1980; JD, Columbia U., 1983. Bar: Utah 1983. Assoc. LeBoeuf, Lamb, Leiby & MacRae, N.Y.C., 1983-89, Rogers, MacKay, Price & Anderson, 1989-91; asst. gen. counsel Micron Tech., 1991-95; v.p., legal and corp. sec. Micron Electronics, 1995-96; v.p. legal affairs, gen. counsel, corp. sec. Micron Techs., Inc., Boise, 1996—. Vice-chmn. Utah Bus. Corp. Act Revision Com. Mem. ABA, Idaho State Bar, Utah State Bar (chmn. bus. law sect. 1988-89). Office: Micron Technology Inc PO Box 6 8000 S Federal Way Boise ID 83716-9632 E-mail: rodlewis@micron.com.

LEWIS, ROGER KUTNOW, architect, educator, author; b. Houston, Jan. 9, 1941; s. Nathan D. and Betty K. Lewis; m. Eleanor Draper Roberts, June 24, 1967; 1 child, Kevin Michael. BArch, MIT, 1964, MArch, 1967. Registered architect, D.C., Va., Md. Vol. architect Peace Corps, Nabeul, Tunisia, 1964-66; designer Wilkes & Faulkner, Washington, 1967-68; ptnr. Chavarria/Lewis Assocs., Washington, 1968-71; prin. Roger K. Lewis AIA & Assocs., Washington, 1971-80; pres. Pecla Corp., Washington, 1971-81; ptnr. Chesapeake Design Group, Balt., 1980-81; prin. Roger K. Lewis FAIA, Architect & Planner, Washington, 1981—. Prof. U. Md. Sch. Arch., 1968—; mem. D.C. Com. on Design Arts, Washington, 1988-92; design advisor City of Alexandria, Va.; nat. peer profl. Gen. Svcs. Adminstrn. Pub. Bldg. Svc. Design Excellence Program. Author: Architect? A Candid Guide to the Profession, 1985, revised edit., 1998, Shaping the City, 1987; co-author Growth Management Handbook, 1989; author articles in jours.and periodicals, chpts. in books, encys.; columnist The Washington Post, 1984—. Trustee Nat. Children's Mus. Recipient Fed. Design Achievement award Nat. Endowment for the Arts, Washington, 1988, numerous awards Am. Planning Assn., AAUW, 1985—. Fellow AIA (numerous design awards 1973—); mem. Faberge Arts Found. (bd. advs.), Cosmos Club. Home: 5034 1/2 Dana Pl NW Washington DC 20016-3441 Office: Univ Md Sch Arch Planning and Preservation College Park MD 20742-0001 Office Phone: 301-405-6289. Personal E-mail: rogershome@aol.com.

LEWIS, ROGER TIMOTHY, mathematics professor, researcher; AB, U. Tenn., 1964, PhD, 1972; MS, Fla. Inst. Tech., 1968. Mathematician Ballistics Rsch. Labs., Aberdeen Proving Grounds, Md., 1964-66, RCA Svc. Corp., Patrick AFB, Fla., 1966-67; engr. Radiation, Inc., Melbourne, Fla., 1967-68; asst. prof. Slippery Rock (Pa.) State Coll., 1972-75, U. Ala., Birmingham, 1975-77, assoc. prof., 1977-81, prof., 1981—, chair dept. math., 1984—87, 1997—2001. Asst. prof. dir. for math. NSF Exptl. Program to Stimulate Competitive Rsch., Ala., 1986-98; Fulbright prof. U. Oslo, 1995; project dir. NSF-DMS, 2001-03. Referee various jours. including London Math. Soc., Jour. D'Analyse Mathématique, Procs. of the Royal Soc. Edinburgh, Dynamics of Continuous, Discrete and Impulsive Sys., Jour. Math. Analysis and Applications, others; contbr. articles to profl. jours. Recipient U.S.-Norway Fulbright Found. Lectr./Rsch. award, 1995; grantee NSF-MCS, 1980-82, 1982-84, 83, NSF-DMS, 1985-87, 87-89, 94, NSF EPSCoR, 1986-91, 95-98, NATO-Collaborative Rsch. grantee, 1992-94. Office: Univ Ala Dept Math Birmingham AL 35294-0001

LEWIS, RON, congressman; b. Greenup County, Ky., Sept. 14, 1946; m. Kayi Gambill, 1966; children: Ronald Brent, Allison Faye. Student, Morehead State U.; BA in History and Polit. Sci., U. Ky., 1969; MA in Higher Edn., Morehead State U., 1981; student, USN Officer Candidate Sch. Ordained to ministry Bapt. Ch. With Ky. Hwy. Dept., Ea. State Hosp.; with sales various cos.; tchr. Watterson Coll., 1980-85; pastor White Mills Bapt. Ch.; owner small bus. Elizabethtown, Ky.; mem. 103rd-108th Congresses from 2d Ky. Dist., 1994—, mem. ways & means com., subcoms., mem. govt. reform com. Past pres. Hardin and Larue County Jail Ministry. Named Guardian of Srs.' Rights, Tax Fairness Srs.; League Pvt. Property Rights, Coun. Citizens Against Govt. Waste, Nat. Fed. Ind. Bus. Mem. Severns Valley Ministerial Assn., Elizabethtown C. of C. Republican. Office: US Ho of Reps 2418 Rayburn Ho Office Bldg Washington DC 20515-1702*

LEWIS, RONALD JAMES, director, music educator; b. Chula Vista, Calif., July 19, 1964; s. Crawford Howard and Marilyn Sands Lewis; m. Gina Lynn Dunegan, July 4, 1984; children: Saxon James, Kelci Lynn. BA, Northeastern State U., Tahlequah, Okla., 1987. Dir. bands Salina Pub. Schs., Salina, Okla., 1987—89, Muldrow Pub. Schs., Muldrow, Okla., 1989—94, McAlester Pub. Schs., McAlester, Okla., 1994—98; h.s. band dir./music supr. Bartlesville Pub. Schs., Bartlesville, Okla., 1998—; dir. bands Okla. Wesleyan U., Bartlesville, Okla., 2003—. Condr. Bartlesville Town Band, Bartlesville, Okla., 2004—05; performing artist/musician Bartlesville Symphony Orch., Bartlesville, Okla., 1998—2005; guest condr./clinician Various Honor Bands, Okla., 1989—2005. Recipient Tchr. of the Yr., Muldrow Pub. Schs., 1993-94. Mem.: Okla. Bandmasters Assn. (pres. elect 2003—04), Okla. Music Adjudicators Assn., Music Educators Nat. Conf., Okla. Music Educators Assn., Okla. Bandmaster's Assn. (pres. 2004—05). Avocation: golf. Home: 1625 Macklyn Ln Bartlesville OK 74006 Office: Bartlesville HS 1700 Hillcrest Dr Bartlesville OK 74003 Office Phone: 918-336-3311. Home Fax: 918-335-3102; Office Fax: 918-337-6226. Personal E-mail: lewbruin@yahoo.com. Business E-Mail: lewisrj@bartlesville.k12.ok.us.

LEWIS, RUSSELL T., publishing executive; BA, SUNY, Stony Brook; JD, Bklyn. Law Sch. Atty. Cahill, Gordon and Reindel, 1973—77; staff atty. The N.Y. Times Co., 1977; circulation sales dir. The N.Y. Times newspaper, N.Y.C., NY, 1981, asst. dir. consumer mktg., 1982, v.p., circulation, 1983, sr. v.p., circulation, 1984—88, sr. v.p., prodn., 1988—92, exec v.p., dep. gen. mgr., 1992—93, pres., gen. mgr., 1993—96; pres. The N.Y. Times Co., N.Y.C., 1996—, CEO, 1997—. Bd. dirs. NY Times Co., 1997—, Dex Media. Office: NY Times 229 W 43rd St New York NY 10036-3959*

LEWIS, RYAN CARL, music educator, youth director; b. Charleston, SC, Mar. 14, 1977; s. Robert Clearance and Karla Lange Lewis; m. Marie Louise Griscom, June 24, 2000. MusB Edn., Furman U., 1999; MusM in Percussion Performance, Fla. State U., 2001, Grad. assistantship in percussion Fla. State U., Tallahassee, 1999—2001, Caribbean steel drum ensemble dir., 2001—04; music tchr. George W. Munroe Elem. Sch., Quincy, Fla., 2001—03; youth dir. St. Paul's United Meth. Ch., Tallahassee, 2003—05; grad. assitanceship in percussion Univ. S.C., 2005—. Musician: performance at Carnegie Hall with Zheng artist Haiqiong Deng, 2004. Recipient Tchr. of the Yr. award, George W. Munroe Elem. Sch., 2002. Methodist. Achievements include research in measuring tonal characteristics of various snare drum batter heads. Avocations: music, reading, cooking, racquetball. Office Phone: 850-385-5146. Personal E-mail: rclewis7@earthlink.net.

LEWIS, SALLY ANN, music educator; b. Tulsa, Okla., Apr. 22, 1955; d. Richard Clarence and Dorothy Marie Bearden; m. Thomas Robert Lewis, Dec. 21, 2000. BA, Okla. State U., Stillwater, 1982. Elementary Education Okla. State Bd. of Edn., 2002. Teen counselor More Than Music Inc. Suzuki Inst., Kingston, Canada, 1995—2001; internat. master class clinician Talpaz Piano Studio, Herzliya, Israel, 1996—2004; teen counselor Internat. Music Festivals of Ams., Cleve., 2000—. Continuing edn. Suzuki instr. Northeastern Okla. State U. Ctr. Lifelong Edn., Tahlequah, Okla., 1994—. Mem.: Suzuki Assn. of Ams. (licentiate). Avocations: long-distance bicycling, hiking, fly fishing, jogging, gardening. Office Phone: 918-456-0131.

LEWIS, SAMELLA SANDERS, artist, educator; b. New Orleans, Feb. 27, 1924; d. Samuel and Rachel (Taylor) Sanders; m. Paul Gad Lewis, Dec. 22, 1948; children: Alan Stephen, Claude Anthony. Student, Dillard U., 1941-43; BS, Hampton Inst., 1945; MA, Ohio State U., 1947, PhD, 1951; postgrad., U. So. Calif., 1964-66; LHD (hon.), Chapman Coll., 1976, U. Cin., 1993; DHL (hon.), Hampton U., 1990, U. Cin., 1993. Asst. prof. Hampton (Va.) Inst., 1945-47; asso. prof. art Morgan State Coll., 1950-52; chmn. dept. art, prof. Fla. A&M U., 1953-58; prof. SUNY, Plattsburgh, 1958-67; coordinator edn. Los Angeles County Mus. Art, 1968-69; prof. Asian, African, Afro-Am. Art History Scripps Coll., Claremont, Calif., 1970-84, prof. emerita, 1984—. Author: Art, African American Textbook, 1978, The Art of Elizabeth Catlett, 1984, African American Art for Young People, 1991, African American Art and Artists Textbook, 1993; producer five films on Black Am. artists; founder Mus. African Am. Art, L.A., 1976; founder, dir., The Gallery, L.A., 1969-79, Asanti Gallery, Pomona, Calif., 1980; art editor Internat. Rev. African Am. Art, 1976—; one woman shows include Clark Mus., Claremont, Calif., 1979, Univ. Union Gallery, 1980, Delta Art Ctr., Winston-Salem, N.C., 1989, Bennett Coll., Greensboro, N.C., 1994; group shows include, Huntsville (Ala.) Mus., 1979, Smithsonian Instn. travelling exhbn., 1980-81, Vorpal Gallery, San Francisoc, 1989, Hampton (Va.) U. Mus., 1990, Am. Fedn. Arts, 1993—, Bomani Gallery, San Francisco, 1994; curator Masters Exhbn., Salvador, Bahia, Brazil, 1988, curator Two Sculptures Two Eras-Richmond Barthe and Richard Hunt, travel to mus., 1992—; solo: James E. Kemp Gallery, Dallas, Tex., 1995, Nat. Conf. Artists Gallery, Detroit, 1995; represented in permanent collections, Balt. Mus. Art, Oakland Mus. Art, High Mus., Atlanta, Palm Spring Mus., Va. Mus. Art; editor and curator: (catalog) Caribbean Visions: Contemporary Painting and Sculpture, 1995. Recipient Faculty Recognition award Scripps Coll., 1984, Disting. Alumni award Ohio State U., 1986, Honor award for outstanding achievement in visual arts Women's Caucus for Art, 1989, Legends in Our Time award Essence Mag., 1990, James Van Der Lee Lifetime Svc. to Arts award Brandywine Workshop, Phila., 1992, Lifetime Achievement award Brandywine Workshop, 1992, UNICEF award for visual arts, 1995; Fulbright fellow, 1962, NDEA postdoctoral fellow, 1964-66; Ford Found. grantee, 1965, 81. Mem. Assn. Asian Studies, Nat. Conf. Artists, So. Calif. Art History Assn., Coll. Art Assn. Am. (bd. dirs. 1990—). Home: 1237 Masselin Ave Los Angeles CA 90019-2544 E-mail: samellalewis@yahoo.com.

LEWIS, SAMUEL WINFIELD, retired federal agency administrator, retired diplomat; b. Houston, Oct. 1, 1930; s. Samuel Winfield and Sue Roselle (Hurley) L.; m. Sallie Kate Smoot, June 20, 1953; children: Pamela Gracelle, Richard Winfield. BA magna cum laude, Yale U., 1952; MA, Johns Hopkins U., 1954; PhD (hon.), Tel Aviv U., 1985, Hebrew U. Jerusalem, 1985, Weizman Inst. Sci., 1985; DHL (hon.), Hebrew Union Coll., 1986, Balt. Hebrew U., 1988; LLD (hon.), Salem-Teikyo U., 1991. Exec. asst. Am. Trucking Assn., Washington., 1953-54; fgn. svc. officer Dept. State, Washington, 1954-85; consular officer Naples, Italy, 1954-55; consul Florence, Italy, 1955-59; officer-in-charge Italian affairs Washington, 1959-61; spl. asst. to undersec. state, 1961; spl. asst. to spl. rep. of pres., 1961-63; dep. asst. dir. US AID Mission to Brazil, Rio de Janeiro, 1964-65; exec. officer embassy, Rio de Janeiro, 1965-67; dep. dir. Office Brazil Affairs, Washington, 1967-68; sr. staff mem. for Latin Am. Affairs Nat. Security Council, White House, Washington, 1968-69; spl. asst. for policy planning Bur. Inter-Am. Affairs, Washington, 1969; spl. asst. to dir. gen. Fgn. Svc., 1970-71; dep. chief mission and counselor embassy Kabul, Afghanistan, 1971-74; dep. dir. policy planning staff Dept. State, 1974-75, asst. sec. state for internat. orgn., 1975-77; U.S. ambassador to Israel, 1977-85; lectr., diplomat-in-residence Johns Hopkins Fgn. Policy Inst., Washington, 1985-86; pres. U.S. Inst. of Peace, Washington, 1987-93; dir. policy planning staff U.S. Dept. State, Washington, 1993-94, cons., 1994-95. Sr. internat. fellow The Dayan Ctr., Tel Aviv U., 1986-87; chmn. bd. overseers Harry S. Truman Rsch. Inst. for Advancement of Peace, Hebrew U., 1986-91; guest scholar The Brookings Inst., Washington, 1987; mem. bd. advisors Washington Inst. Near East Policy, 1986-93, 98—, counselor, 1995-98; adv. com. Search for Common Ground in the Mid. East, Washington, 1994—; vis. prof. Hamilton Coll., spring 1995, fall 1997, adj. prof. Sch. Fgn. Svc., Georgetown U., 1996; sr. advisor Israel Policy Forum, 1998—; lectr. in field. Author: Making Peace Among Arabs and Israelis, 1991; contbg. author: The Middle East: Ten Years After Camp David, 1988, Soviet-American Competition in the Middle East, 1988, Israel: The Peres Era, 1987, The United States States and Israel: Evolution of an Unwritten Alliance, 1999; contbr. articles to profl. jours., also N.Y. Times, Washington Post. Bd. dirs. Inst. for Study Diplomacy, Georgetown U., 1994—; vice chmn. Ctr. Preventive Action, Coun. Fgn. Rels., 1994-97. Recipient William A. Jump award for outstanding service in pub. adminstrn., 1967, Meritorious Honor award Dept. State, 1967, Meritorious Honor award AID, 1967, Pres.' Mgmt. Improvement cert., 1971, Distinguished Honor award Dept. State, 1977, 85, Disting. Alumnus award Johns Hopkins U., 1980, Wilbur J. Carr award Dept. State, 1985; vis. fellow Princeton U., 1963-64. Mem. Am. Acad. Diplomacy (bd. dirs. 1995-, vice chmn. bd. dirs. 1995-99), Am. Fgn. Svc. Assn., U.S. Interreligious Com. for Peace in the Middle East, UN Assn., Middle East Inst., Assn. Diplomatic Studies and Tng. (bd. dirs. 1995-2005), Inst. World Affairs (bd. dirs. 1996-2005), Ptnrs. for Dem. Change (bd. dirs. 2004-), Cousteau Soc., Sierra Club, Phi Beta Kappa. Episcopalian. Office Phone: 703-448-1997. Personal E-mail: sixtymeter@aol.com.

LEWIS, SANDRA COMBS, research psychologist, writer; b. Troup County, Ga., Oct. 8, 1939; d. Robert Milton and Imogene (Richardson) Combs; children: Virginia Susan Lewis, Charles James III. AB, Wesleyan Coll., 1961; MEd, Mercer U., 1972, Ga. State U., 1976; PhD, U. Ga., 1980. Personnel asst. Sears Roebuck & Co., Atlanta, 1961—62; rsch. asst. bd. regents U. Sys. Ga., 1962—63; asst. psychol. svcs. Bibb County Bd. Edn., Macon, 1972—73; instr. Macon Jr. Coll., 1973, 1982, Wesleyan Coll., 1973—75, 1981; psychometrist Middle Ga. Psychoednl. Ctr., 1975—76; instr. Mercer U., 1980—82. Presenter at profl. confs. Co-author: Christian Love and Problems of Living, 1992, God and Positive Christianity, 1998, Psychology for Life, 2000, A Revolutionary View of Education and Teaching for the Third Millennium, 2002; assoc. editor Truth Seekers Newsletter, 1998—. Pres. Macon Wesleyan Alumnae Club, 1973-74; bd. dirs. Family Counseling Ctr., Macon, 1975-76; ruling elder, clk. of session Northminster Presbyn. Ch., Macon, 1988-90, 94-96, vice moderator Presbyn. Women, 1989-90, 2002, moderator Presbyn. Women, 1990-91, 2003; v.p. Fore(In)Sight Found., 1991—. Mem.: APA (life), Mid. Ga. Psychol. Assn., Ga. Psychol. Assn. (life). Avocations: gardening, photography. Home and Office: 4976 Oxford Rd Macon GA 31210-3059 Office Phone: 478-474-3869. Business E-Mail: foreignsight@excite.com.

LEWIS, SHARON KAY, artist, craftsman; b. Aug. 25, 1962; AS, Cin. Tech. Coll., 1991. Data entry operator IRS, Cin., 1989-91; data input operator Def. Fin. and Acctg. Ctr., Columbus, Ohio, 1992-96; freelance fine artist, craftsman, Columbus, 1993—. One-woman shows include water colors Columbus State C.C., 1997, one-woman shows include handpainted silk scarves Studios on High Gallery, Columbus, 2000, exhibitions include Bexley Summer Fest Show, 2002, Represented in permanent collections. Home: 3840 Lamarque Ct Columbus OH 43232-4954 E-mail: sharonartiste43232@peoplepc.com.

LEWIS, SHELDON NOAH, technology consultant; b. Chgo., July 1, 1934; s. Jacob Joseph and Evelyn (Mendelsohn) Iglowitz; m. Suzanne Joyce Goldberg, June 17, 1957; children: Sara Lynn, Matthew David, Rachel Ann. BA with honors, MS (Univ. fellow), Northwestern U., 1956; PhD (Eastman Kodak fellow), UCLA, 1959; postgrad. (NSF fellow), U. Basel, Switzerland, 1959-60; postgrad. cert. in research mgmt, Indsl. Research Inst., Harvard U., 1973. With Rohm & Haas Co., 1960-78, head lab., 1963-68, research supr., 1968-73, dir. splty. chem. research, 1973-74; gen. mgr. DCL Lab. AG subs., Zurich, Switzerland, 1974-75; dir. European Labs. Valbonne, France, 1975-76; corp. dir. research and devel. worldwide for polymers, resins and monomers Spring House, Pa., 1976-78; with The Clorox Co., Oakland, Calif., 1978-91, v.p. R&D, 1978, group v.p., 1978-84, exec. v.p., 1984-91, also bd. dirs.; pres. SNL Inc., Lafayette, Calif., 1991—. Mem. indsl. panel on sci. and tech. NSF. Referee: Jour. Organic Chemistry; patentee in field; contbr. articles to profl. publs. Mem. Calif. Inst. Adv. Bd., World Affairs Council, UCLA Chemistry Adv. Council, Bay Area Sci. Fair Adv. Bd., Mills Coll. Adv. Council for Sci. and Math. Recipient cert. in patent law Phila. Patent Law Assn., 1962, Roon award for coatings research Fedn. Socs. Coatings Tech., 1966, cert. of service Wayne State U. Polymer Conf. Series, 1967, cert. in mgmt. by objectives Am. Mgmt. Research, Inc., 1972 Mem. Soap and Detergent Assn. (bd. dirs.), Chem. Ind. Inst. of Toxicology (bd. dirs.), Indsl. Rsch. Inst., Am. Chem. Soc. (chmn. Phila. polymer sect. 1970-71), Soc. Chem. Industry London, Sigma Xi. Jewish. Office: SNL Inc 3711 Rose Ct Lafayette CA 94549-3030

LEWIS, SHIRLEY, artist; b. Bklyn., Oct. 13, 1921; d. Nathan Shapiro and Jennie (Zimmerman) Schwartz; m. Alfred E. Lewis, Aug. 16, 1953 (dec. Mar. 1968); children: Leora, Sanford, Roland, Elena; m. Hananiah Harari, Sept. 1, 1979. Art therapist, New Sch. for Social Rsch., 1968; BFA, Manhattanville Coll., 1972; MA, cert. art tchr., NYU, 1976. Cert. art therapist. Tchr. fine arts Our Lady of Sorrows Sch., White Plains, N.Y., 1972-74, Blythedale Children's Hosp., Valhalla, N.Y., 1972—. Counselor art therapy Albert Einstein Med. Ctr., Bronx, N.Y., 1978, Wiltwyck, Ossining, 1980. One-man shows include Manhattanville Coll., Purchase, N.Y., 1972, Town Hall, Greenburgh, N.Y., 1975, Hudson River Gallery, Ossining, N.Y., 1989; exhibited in group shows at Cork Gallery Lincoln Ctr., N.Y.C., 1989, Rotunda Gallery, Bklyn., 1991, Nat. Acad. Design, N.Y.C., 1992, Putnam Arts Coun., Mahopac, N.Y., 1993, Susan Teller Gallery, N.Y.C., 1992, North Westchester Ctr. Arts, 1996, Krasdale Galery, White Plains, N.Y., 1997. Recipient First prize Beaux Arts Westchester, 1990. Mem. Art Students League (life), Garrison Art Ctr., Artists Equity, Audubon Artists (nat. juried ann. exhbns. 1991-96). Home: 34 Prospect Pl Croton On Hudson NY 10520-1942

LEWIS, SHIRLEY JEANE, retired psychologist; b. Phoenix, Aug. 23; d. Herman and Leavy (Hutchinson) Smith; m. Edgar Anthony Lewis (div.); children: Edgar Anthony (dec.), Roshaun, Lucy Ann Jonathan. AA, Phoenix C.C., 1957; BA, Ariz. State U., 1960; MS, San Diego State U., 1975, MA, 1985, Azusa Pacific U., 1982; PhD, U. So. Calif., 1983. Cert. tchr. Calif. Recreation leader Phoenix Parks and Recreation Dept., 1957-62; columnist Ariz. Tribune, Phoenix, 1958-59; tchr. phys. edn. San Diego Unified Schs., 1962—; adult educator San Diego C.C., 1973—; assoc. prin. El Camino H.S., Oceanside, Calif., 1997—98; head counselor Gomper Secondary Sch. San Diego (Calif.) Unified Schs., 1998—2003, ret. Gomper Secondary Sch., 2003. Instr. psychology, health, Black studies, 1977—, counselor, 1981—; cmty. counselor S.E. Counseling and Cons. Svcs. and Narcotics Prevention and Edn. Sys., Inc., San Diego, 1973-77; counselor educator, counselor edn. dept. San Diego State U., 1974-77; marriage, family, child counselor Counseling and Cons. Ctr., San Diego, 1977—; inservice educator San Diego Unified and San Diego County Sch. Dists., 1973-77; Fulbright Exch. counselor, London, 1994-96; instr. San Diego (Calif.) C.C., 1977-94, counselor, 1981-94; lectr. in field. Contbr. articles to profl. jours. Girl Scout phys. fitness cons., Phoenix, 1960-62; vol. cmty. tutor for high sch. students, San Diego, 1963; sponsor Tennis Club for Youth, San Diego, 1964-65; troop leader Girl Scouts U.S., Lemon Grove, Calif., 1972-74; vol. counselor USN Alcohol Rehab. Ctr., San Diego, 1978; mem. sch. coun.'s adv. bd. San Diego State U. Named Woman of Yr., Phoenix, 1957, One of Outstanding Women of San Diego, 1980; recipient Phys. Fitness Sch. award and Demonstration Sch. award Pres.'s Coun. on Phys. Fitness, Taft Jr. H.S., 1975, Excel award Corp. Excellence Edn., 1989; Delta Sigma Theta scholar, 1957-60; Alan Korrick scholar, 1956. Mem. NEA, Calif. Tchrs. Assn., San Diego Tchrs. Assn., Assn. Marriage and Family Counselors, Am. Personnel and Guidance Assn., Calif. Assn. Health, Phys. Edn. and Recreation (v.p. health), Am. Alliance of Health, Phys. Edn. and Recreation, Assn. Black Psychologists (corr. sec. 1993), Assn. African-Am. Educators, Delta Sigma Theta (Delta of Yr. 1987). Democrat. Baptist. Home: 1226 Armacost Rd San Diego CA 92114-3307 Office: Gompers Secondary Sch 1005 47th St San Diego CA 92102-3699 Personal E-mail: slewis@mail.sandi.net. *Personal philosophy: High self-esteem, responsibility, self-discipline and striving to achieve personal goals are necessary for a healthful lifestyle regardless of one's personal, historical circumstances. The initial access to such characteristics, in reality, may only be in one's invention of fantasy.*

LEWIS, STEPHEN E., lawyer; b. Rock Hill, SC, 1966; BS with honors, Univ. NC, 1988, JD with high honors, 1991. CPA NC, 1988; bar: Ga. 1991. Assoc. Troutman Sanders LLP, Atlanta, 1991—98, ptnr., corp. and securities group leader, 1999—, hiring ptnr., 2002. Mem. NC Law Rev., 1989—90. Named a Super Lawyer, Atlanta Mag., 2004, Legal Elite in corp. law, Ga. Trend Mag., 2004. Mem.: Beta Alpha Psi, Phi Beta Kappa, Order of Coif. Office: Troutman Sanders LLP One Union Sq Ste 5200 600 Peachtree St Atlanta GA 30308-2216 Office Phone: 404-885-3448. Office Fax: 404-962-6616. Business E-Mail: stephen.lewis@troutmansanders.com.

LEWIS, STEPHEN RICHMOND, JR., economist, educator; b. Englewood, NJ, Feb. 11, 1939; s. Stephen Richmond and Esther (Magan) Lewis; m. Judith Frost, 1996; children from previous marriage: Virginia, Deborah, Mark. BA, Williams Coll., 1960, LLD, 1987; MA, Stanford U., 1962, PhD, 1963; LHD, Doshisha U., 1993, Macalester Coll., 2002; LLD, Carleton Coll., 2002. Instr. Stanford U., 1962—63; research advisor Pakistan Inst. Devel. Econs., Karachi, 1963—65; asst. prof. econs. Harvard U., 1965—66, Williams Coll., 1966—68, assoc. prof., 1968—73, prof., 1973—76, Herbert H. Lehman prof., 1976—87, provost of coll., 1968—71, 1973—77, spl. asst. to pres., 1979—80, dir. Williams-Botswana Project, 1982—88, chmn. dept. econs., 1984—86; vis. sr. research fellow Inst. Devel. Studies, Nairobi, Kenya, 1971—73; econ. cons. to Ministry of Finance and Devel. Planning, Govt. of Botswana, 1975—; vis. fellow Inst. Devel. Studies, Sussex, England, 1986—87; pres., prof. econs. Carleton Coll., Northfield, Minn., 1987—2002, pres. emeritus, 2002—. Trustee Carnegie Endowment for Internat. Peace, 1988—, Minn. Humanities Commn., 2004—; bd. dirs. Am. Express Funds, XDX Innovative Refrigeration, Inc., Xenomosis, LLC, Valmont Industries, Inc.; cons. in field. Author (with others): Relative Price Changes and Industrialization in Pakistan, 1969; author: Economic Policy and Industrial Growth in Pakistan, 1969, Pakistan: Industrialization and Trade Policy, 1970, Williams in the Eighties, 1980, Taxation for Development, 1983, South Africa: Has Time Run Out?, 1986, Policy Choice and Development Performance in Botswana, 1989, The Economics of Apartheid, 1989; mem. editl. bd.: Jour. Econ. Lit., 1985—87; contbr. chapters to books, articles to profl. jours. Mem. chmn.'s coun. No. Star coun. Boy Scouts Am., 1989—. Decorated Presdl. Order of Meritorious Svc. Botswana; recipient Disting. Eagle Scout award, 1993; fellow, Danforth Found., 1960—63, dissertation, Ford Found., 1962—63. Mem.: Am. Econ. Assn., Nat. Tax Assn., Coun. on Fgn. Rels., Phi Beta Kappa. Office: Ste 440 222 S Ninth St Minneapolis MN 55402

LEWIS, SYLVIA DAVIDSON, foundation executive; b. Akron, Ohio, Apr. 28, 1927; d. Harry I. and Helen E. (Stein) Davidson; m. Allen D. Lewis, Oct. 12, 1947; children: Pamela Lewis Kanfer, Randy, Daniel, Cynthia Lewis Lagdameo. Student, U. Mich., 1945—47, U. Akron, 1961—62. Editor Akron Jewish News, 1948-50; tchr. Revere Rd. Congregation, Akron, 1964-70; office mgr. Acme Lumber & Fence Co., Akron, 1970-85; nat. pres. NA'AMAT USA (Movement of Working Women & Vols.), N.Y.C., 1993-97. Pres. Planned Parenthood Summit Portage and Medina Counties, 1999-2001; founding mem. Govt. Affairs Com., Columbus, Ohio, 1981—, exec. com., 1988-89; v.p. Akron Jewish Cmty. Fedn., 1988-94, pres. women's divsn., 1987-90; elect mem. Akron Jewish Cmty. Bd., 1999—; nat. v.p. Na'amat USA, 2004—. Named Woman of Distinction, YWCA Summit County, 2001; named one of No. Ohio's Top Women Profls., No. Ohio Live mag., 1997; named to Ohio Women's Hall of Fame, 1995; recipient Golden Rule award, J.C. Penney, 1994, Vol. of Yr. award, Lippman Cmty. Day Sch., 1992, Commendation of Honor award, Ohio Gen. Assembly, 1993, Women of Achievement award, YWCA of Summit County, 1999. Democrat. Jewish. Avocations: reading, writing, travel, grandchildren. Home: 4389 Everett Rd Richfield OH 44286 Personal E-mail: syllewis1@aol.com.

LEWIS, THOMAS HOWARD, psychiatrist, educator; b. Red Lodge, Mont., July 28, 1919; s. William Michel and Charlotte Amanda (Johnson) L.; m. Ruth Danielson, May 5, 1944; children: William Richard, Daniel John, Thomas Morgan, Linda Ruth, David Gryffdd. BS, U. Wash., 1941; MD, Duke U., 1946. Commd. lt. USN, 1946, advanced through grades to capt., 1962, resident U.S. Naval Hosp. Bethesda, Md., 1951-53; resident NIMH, 1960; dir. resident tng. in psychiatry Nat. Naval Med. Ctr. USN, 1963-68, chief neurology and psychiatry, 1969-73, ret., 1973; prof. psychiatry Georgetown U., Washington, 1975—. Author: Forgotten Battles Along the Yellowstone, 1985, The Medicine Men, 1990; contbr. over 270 articles on medicine, anthropology, biology, ethnology and anatomy to profl. jours.; assoc. editor Am. Indian Quar., 1975—. Fellow ACP, Am. Psychiat. Assn.; mem. AMA, AAAS, Wash. Psychoanalytic Soc., Wash. Psychiat. Soc., N.Y. Acad. Sci., Sigma Xi, Phi Sigma. Clubs: Cosmos, St. David's Soc. (Washington). Democrat. Home and Office: PO Box 162 Boyd MT 59013-0162

LEWIS, VICTOR WAYNE, I, minister; b. Pasedena, Calif., Dec. 9, 1963; s. Charles Edward and Dorothy Lee Lewis; m. Dana Williete Lewis, Apr. 23, 1993; children: DaVida, DaMonique, Dy'lan-Victoria, Victor II. BA, Washington U, 1985—89; AA, A.L. Hardy Theological Sem., Seattle, Wash., 1988—90; MA, Golden Gate Seminary, 1992—96. Pastor Morning Star Bapt. Ch., Pasadena, Calif., 1994—97, Praise Tabernacle Ch., Pasadena, 1997—2001, organizer San Bernadino, Calif., 2003—; ch. facilitator New Revelation Ch., Pasadena, 2003—; case mgr. D'Veal Family Youth Svc., Pasadena, 2003—. Pub. liason Bapt. Ministers Conf., L.A., 1993—98; pres. Inter-Denominational Ministerial Alliance, Pasadena, 1999—2003; founder Praise Tabernacle Ch., Pasadena; founded New Life Rehab. Ctr., Rising Star Christian Acad. Author: Praise Tabernacle Ch. Mem. Handbook, Tithing Principles, 1997, The Nuts and Bolts of Streets Evangelism, Family Matters, A Guide To A Wholesome Home, 1998, Narrow Escape: The Anthony Lewis Story, 2001, (plays) Claira's Song, Unstrung Pearls: Devotional Readings For Daily and Practical Living. II v.p. NAACP, Pasadena, 1995—97; pres. of tolerance City of Pasadena (Calif.), 1997—2000; arbitrator Coalition For Non-Violence, Pasadena, 2000—03; designer Prison Relief Program, Juvenile Detention Alternative Program, Teenage Mothers Residential Support Program, Feed The Nations Program, Youth Alternative Activities, Organized L.A. County's First City Wide Park Revival, Substance Rehabilitation Residential Program. Recipient Humanitarian of the Yr., Pasadena Jour., 1992, Young Man of the Yr. Award, Mekenzie Boys Club, 1994, Journalism Award, New Authors Soc., 2002. Mem.: NAACP, Ctrl. Dist. Assn. (Moderator), Jesus Joy Jubilee (Nat. Evangilist 2003—), Congress of Christian Edn. (pres. 1997—2000). Democrat. Christian. Avocations: writing, singing, grant writing, bowling, movies. Office: Praise Tabernacle Ch 2075 E Highland Ave Ste G San Bernardino CA 92404 also: VW Lewis Ministries 1965 E Coulston St #6 Loma Linda CA 92354 Home: 796 E Merrett Pasadena CA 91104

LEWIS, W. WALKER, strategic and financial advisory company executive; b. Middletown, Ohio, Sept. 15, 1944; s. W. Walker Jr. and Emily S. (Spivy) L.; m. Ellen Anschuetz, Mar. 30, 1970; children: Walker, Alexandra (Sasha), Morgan. AB, Harvard U., 1967. Mgr. Boston Cons. Group, 1970-72; chmn. Strategic Planning Assocs., Washington, 1972-92; pres. Avon Products, N.Y.C., 1992-94; mng. dir. Kidder Peabody, N.Y.C., 1994-96; sr. advisor Dillon Read & Co., N.Y.C., 1997—; chmn. Devon Value Advisers, N.Y.C., 1997—. Mem. Coun. on Fgn. Rels., Washington Inst. Fgn. Affairs. Office: Devon Value Advisers 399 Park Ave Fl 38 New York NY 10022-4616 Business E-Mail: wlewis@devonvalue.com.

LEWIS, WALTER DAVID, historian, educator; b. Towanda, Pa., June 24, 1931; s. Gordon Cleon and Eleanor Esther (Tobias) L.; m. Carolyn Wyatt Brown, June 12, 1954 (div. 1980); children: Daniel Kent, Virginia Lorraine, Nancy Ellyn; m. Patricia L. Freeman, Apr. 26, 1986. BA cum laude, Pa. State U., 1952, MA, 1954; PhD, Cornell U., 1961. Instr. pub. speaking Hamilton Coll., Clinton, N.Y., 1954-57; fellowship coordinator Eleutherian Mills-Hagley Found., Wilmington, Del.; also lectr. history U. Del., 1959-65; assoc.

prof. history SUNY, Buffalo, 1965-71, prof., 1971; Hudson prof. history and engrng. Auburn (Ala.) U., 1971-95, disting. Univ. prof., 1994—. Dir. univ. project tech., human values and so. future, 1974-79; sr. fellow in Am. civilization Cornell U., 1958-59; vis. prof. history U. Tex.-Dallas, summer 1982, 83, 84; pres., dir. conf. on history of civil and comml. aviation (ICCA 92), Swiss Transport Mus., Lucerne, Switzerland, 1992; Charles A. Lindbergh prof. of aerospace history Nat. Air and Space Mus., 1993-94. Exec. co-prodr. (documentary film): About Us: A Deep South Portrait, 1977; author: From Newgate to Dannemora: The Rise of the Penitentiary in New York, 1965, Iron and Steel in America, 1976, Sloss Furnaces and The Rise of the Birmingham District: An Industrial Epic, 1994, Eddie Rickenbacker: An American Hero in the Twentieth Century, 2005; co-author: Delta: The History of an Airline, 1979, Hopewell Furnace, 1983, The Airway to Everywhere: A History of All American Aviation, 1937-53, 1988; contbg. author: The Professions in America, 1965, Technology in Western Civilization, 1967, The Development of an American Culture, 1969, Notable American Women, 1971, Great Engineers and Pioneers in Technology, 1981, Technology in America, 2d edit., 1990, Science-Technology Relationships, 1993, Eli Whitney's Cotton Gin, 1793-1993, 1994, Bring History Alive, 1996, Econsidering A Century of Flight, 2003; editor: Fighting the Flying Circus, 1997, Airline Executives and Federal Regulation: Case Studies in American Enterprise from the Airmail Era to the Dawn of the Jet Age, 2000, The Americanization of Edward Bok, 2000; co-editor: Economic Change in the Civil War Era, 1965, The Southern Mystique: Technology and Human Values in Changing Region, 1977; gen. editor Procs. of the Internat. Conf. on the History of Civil and Commercial Aviation, 1995; contbr. articles to profl. jours. Grantee NEH, 1973-79, 80—, Delta Airlines Found. 1973-79, Eleutherian Mills Hist. Libr., 1970-73, 80; postdoctoral fellow Nat. Humanities Inst., U. Chgo., 1978-79, Mellon fellow Va. Hist. Soc., 1988, 89, 92; recipient Leonardo da Vinci medal, (Soc. for the Hist. of Tech., 1993). Mem. Soc. History Tech., Hist. Soc., Internat. Congress for History of Tech., Phi Beta Kappa. Episcopalian. Home: 210 Lee Dr Auburn AL 36832-6722 E-mail: wdavidandpat@bellsouth.net, lewiswd@mindspring.com.

LEWIS, WILBUR H., educational management consultant; b. Belmont, Ohio, Sept. 16, 1930; s. Charles W. and Lily B. (Dunfee) L.; m. Jean E. Lewis, Aug. 23, 1958; children— David, Deretta, Denise, Dawn, Darrin. Student, Miami U., Oxford, Ohio, 1948-51; BSBA, Ohio State U., 1953; M.Ed., Ohio U., 1961, PhD, 1964. Tchr. pub. schs., Scioto County, Ohio, 1957; tchr., adminstr. public schs. Belmont County, Ohio, 1958-60; grad. asst. Ohio U., 1960-61; prin. high sch., adminstrv. asst. to supt. public schs. Athens, Ohio, 1961-64; asst. prof., adviser to Govt. of Nigeria, 1964-66; asst. supt. pub. schs. Athens, Ohio, 1966-67; prin. high sch. public schs. Wilmington, Ohio, 1967-68; with Parma (Ohio) City Schs., 1968-77, asst. to supt., 1968-70, asst. supt., 1970-72, assoc. supt., 1972-75, supt., 1975-77, Tucson Unified Sch. Dist., 1977-79; cons. ednl. mgmt. Tucson, 1979—. Vice chmn. nat. adv. coun. Edn. Disadvantaged Children, 1972-80; supt. Ariz. State Schs. for Deaf and Blind, 1994-98; semi-ret. edn. cons., 2002. Planning divsn. United Way, Tucson, 1978-80; bd. dirs. Jr. Achievement, 1978-80. 1st lt. QMC, U.S. Army, 1954-56. Recipient numerous civic awards for community service; Kettering Found. fellow, 1970 Mem. Am. Assn. Sch. Adminstrs., Buckeye Assn. Sch. Adminstrs., Masons, Shriners, Rotary Internat. (v.p. Tucson 1987—, past pres., dist. gov.'s rep. group study exch. dist. 9120 Nigeria, dist. 5500, chmn. group study exch. dist. 5490 1991-93), Phi Delta Kappa, Lambda Chi Alpha, Sigma Phi Epsilon. Achievements include rsch. in orgnl. devel., adminstrv. behavior patterns, tchr. job satisfaction, student achievement. Home: 10481 E Barbara Pl Tucson AZ 85748 Personal E-mail: wlewis_5@msn.com. *To achieve one must aspire. To aspire one must dream. But if dreams and aspirations are to become achievements one must persevere. The perseverance necessary to turn dreams and aspirations into achievements has always been made easier for me knowing that children and youth were the benefactors of my efforts.*

LEWIS, WILLIAM D., writer, educator; b. Sarepta, La., Nov. 2, 1943; s. Lonnie D. and Lenora Lewis; children: Sharon, Debra, Holly, Michael. BS in Polit. Sci. and Journalism, U. Colo., 1991; postgrad., So. U. Cert. tchr. La. Educator Orleans Parish Sch. Dist., Houston Ind. Sch. Dist., So. U., Shreveport. Author: (book) Serious Players Only, 1997, Imagine: Losing Everything Your Mind, 2000, The Call to a Purposeful Life, 2002. Dist. fin. chmn. Dem. Party, Denver, 1980. Served with U.S. Army, 1975. Mem.: Am. Fedn. Tchrs. Democrat. Avocations: chess, publishing. Home: PO Box 78272 Shreveport LA 71137 E-mail: hard-life@earthlink.net.

LEWIS, WILLIAM HEADLEY, JR., manufacturing executive; b. Washington, Sept. 29, 1934; s. William Headley and Lois Maude (Bradshaw) L.; m. Carol Elizabet Cheek, Apr. 22, 1967 (dec. Jan. 17, 2005); children: Teresa Lynne, Bret Cameron, Charles William, Kevin Marcus BS in Metall. Engrng., Va. Poly. Inst., 1956; postgrad. Grad. Sch. Bus. Adminstrn., Emory U., 1978. Registered profl. engr., Calif. Various positions Lockheed Corp., Marietta, Ga., 1956-87, mgr. engring. tech. services, 1979-83, dir. engring. Getex divsn., 1983-86; mgr. Inspection Systems divsn. Lockheed Air Terminal, Inc., 1986-87; CEO Measurement Sys. Inc., Atlanta, 1987—. Chmn. Lockheed Corp. Task Force on NDE, 1980-86; mem. Com. to Study Role of Advanced Tech. in Improving Reliability and Maintainability of Future Weapon Systems, Office of Sec. of Def., 1984-85; co-founder Applied Tech. Svcs., Inc., 1967—; pres., CEO Applied Tech. Fin. Corp., Atlanta, 1983-86; mng. ptnr. Tech. Fin. Co., LLC; lectr. grad. studies and continuing edn. Union Coll., Schenectady, N.Y., 1977-82. Editor: Prevention of Structural Failures: The Role of Fracture Mechanics, Failure Analysis, and NDT, 1978; patentee detection apparatus for structural failure in aircraft. Served to 1st lt. USAF, 1957-60. Fellow: Am. Soc. for Nondestructive Testing (nat. dir. 1976—78, chmn. nat. tech. coun. 1977—78, chmn. aerospace com. 1972—74, nat. nominating com. 1982—85); mem.: NAS (mem. com. on compressive fracture 1981—83), AIAA, Am. Soc. for Metals, Brotherhood of the Knights of the Vine, Country Club Sapphire Valley, St . Ives Country Club. Home: 3127 St Ives C Club Pky Duluth GA 30097-2038 E-mail: bill@whlewis.com.

LEWIS, WILLIAM HENRY, JR., lawyer; b. Durham, N.C., Nov. 12, 1942; s. William Henry Sr. and Phyllis Lucille (Phillips) L.; m. Jo Ann Whitsett, Apr. 17, 1965 (div. Sept. 1982); 1 child, Kimberly N.; m. Peyton Cockrill Davis, Nov. 28, 1987. Student, N.C. State U., 1960-63; AB in Polit. Sci., U. N.C., 1965, JD with honors, 1969. Bar: Calif., D.C., U.S. Dist. Ct. (cen. dist.) Calif., U.S. Ct. Appeals (D.C. cir., 2nd and 5th cirs.), U.S. Supreme Ct. Assoc. Latham & Watkins, Los Angeles, 1969-74; exec. officer Calif. Air Resources Bd., Los Angeles and Sacramento, Calif., 1975-78; dir. Nat. Com. on Air Quality, Washington, 1978-81; counsel Wilmer, Cutler & Pickering, Washington, 1981-84; ptnr. Morgan, Lewis & Bockius LLP, Washington, 1984—2004, mgr. nat. environ. practice, 1999—2000, sr. counsel, 2004—. Spl. advisor on environ. policy State of Calif., L.A. and Sacramento, 1975; lectr. Law Sch. U. Va., 1993-97. Bd. dirs. For Love of Children, Inc., Washington, 1985-95, pres., 1987-91; bd. dirs. Advs. for Families, Washington, 1985-87, Hillandale Homeowners Assn., Washington, 1986-87, Thurgood Marshall Ctr. Trust, Washington, 1989-95; mem. EPA Clean Air Act Adv. Com., 1994—; chmn. bd. dirs., co-founder The Montpelier Found., 1998—. Mem. ABA. Home: 3900 Georgetown Ct NW Washington DC 20007-2127 also: 18454 Monteith Farm Rd Gordonsville VA 22942-7560 Office: Morgan Lewis and Bockius LLP 1111 Pennsylvania Ave NW Washington DC 20004 Office Phone: 202-739-5145. Business E-Mail: wlewis@morganlewis.com.

LEWIS, WILLIAM WALKER, management consultant; b. Roanoke, Va., Mar. 29, 1942; s. William Walker and Nancy Katherine (Phipps) L.; m. Jutta Maria Schwarzkopf, Dec. 27, 1966; children: Christopher William, Monica Gisela. BS in Physics with honors, Va. Poly. Inst. and State U., 1963; PhD in Theoretical Physics, Oxford U., 1966. Mem. staff Office of Asst. Sec. for Systems Analysis, Dept. Def., Washington, 1966-69; assoc. provost for resource planning, lectr. public and internat. affairs Princeton U., 1969-71; dir. office of analytical studies U. Calif., Berkeley, 1971-73; sr. ops. officer World Bank, 1973-77; prin. dep. asst. sec. for program analysis and evaluation Dept. Def., Washington, 1977-79; asst. sec. policy and evaluation Dept. Energy, Washington, 1979-81; pres. Dist. Heat and Power, Inc., Washington, 1981-82; ptnr. McKinsey & Co., Inc., Washington, 1982—; dir. McKinsey Global Inst., Washington, 1990—. Trustee, chmn. bd. dirs. Holy Cross Hosp.; trustee Ctr. for Econ. Rsch. and Grad. Edn. Charles U.; trustee Nat. Bur. Econ. Rsch., Com. for Econ. Devel. Rhodes scholar, 1963-66 Office: 600 14th St NW Washington DC 20005-2008 E-mail: bill_lewis@mckinsey.com.

LEWISON, EDWARD FREDERICK, surgeon; b. Chgo., Feb. 11, 1913; s. Maurice and Julia (Trockey) Lewison; m. Elizabeth Oppenheim, July 24, 1938 (dec. 1947); 1 child, John Edward; m. Betty Fleischmann, Mar. 21, 1948; children: Edward M., Robert S., Richard J. BS, U. Chgo., 1932; MD, Johns Hopkins U., 1936. Lic. MD Ill., Md., Fla., diplomate Am. Bd. Surgery. Chief, Breast Clin. Johns Hopkins Hosp., Balt., 1948-72; asst. prof. surgery Johns Hopkins U. Sch. Med., Balt., 1954-69, assoc. prof. surgery, 1969-80, assoc. prof. surgery, emeritus, 1980—. Vice-chmn. breast cancer com. WHO, Geneva, 1968—70; chmn. nat. conf. breast cancer Am. Cancer Soc., Washington, 1969, Swiss Cancer League, Lucerne, 1976; mem. H.S. Nat. Commn. Nat. Rsch. Coun., Washington, 1983—87; mem. adv. bd. Annie Casey Found., 1996—2001. Author: Breast Cancer and Its Diagnosis and Treatment, 1955; editor: Breast Cancer, 1977, Conference on Spontaneous Regression of Cancer, 1974; co-author: Diagnosis and Treatment of Breast Cancer, 1981. Bd. dirs. United Way Md., Balt., 1986—94. Lt. col. M.C. U.S. Army, 1946. Named Disting. Citizen, Gov. State Md., 1980, Humanitarian of the Yr., Wyman Guild, 1990, oncology libr. in his honor, Johns Hopkins Hosp., 1980; recipient Cert. of Merit award, European Theater Ops., 1945, Heritage award, Johns Hopkins U. and Sch. Medicine, 2003. Fellow: ACS, AMA, Royal Soc. Medicine; mem.: Am. Bd. Surgery (diplomat 1946), Am. Cancer Soc. (life Vol. Leadership award 1984, Premier award 1995), N.Y. Acad. Scis. Achievements include invention of of rayable gauze for surgery. Home: 4100 N Charles St Baltimore MD 21218-1028

LEWIS RIFFLE, MURIEL ANN, retired secondary school educator; b. Yonkers, NY, Sept. 29, 1936; d. Paul S. and Anne M. (Koyce) Monahan; children: Amy, Scott, Brian, Michael. BS, Coll. Misericordia, 1958; MS, Purdue U., 1977; EdD, Ind. U., 1996. Lic. tchr. Ind. Tchr. Bergenfield (N.J.) H.S., 1958-62; owner, operator Strawberry Barn, Campbellsburg, Ind., 1969-72; tchr. West Washington H.S., Campbellsburg, 1972-97; ret. Bd. dirs. Life Spring, Salem, Ind., 1991-93, Washington County Substance Abuse coun., 1993-99, Washington County Cmty. Found., 1996-99, Project RESPECT, Salem, 1996-99; mem. parish coun. St. Patrick's Ch., Salem, 1990-93; coun. St. Agnes Ch., Nashville, Ind., 2004—. Mem. Am. Assn. Family and Consumer Scis., Ind. Assn. Family and Consumer Scis. (v.p. 1990-93, other offices), Ind. State Tchrs. Assn., West Washington Edn. Assn., U. Notre Dame Alumni Assn.(ct. appt. special adv., 2000—). Roman Catholic. Avocations: travel, reading, interior design, flower arranging, music, water sports.

LEWIS-WHITE, LINDA BETH, elementary school educator; b. Fresno, Calif., June 30, 1950; d. Lloyd Ernest and Anne Grace (Barkman) Lewis; m. Francis Everett White, Feb. 15, 1975; children: Anna Justine, Christopher Andrew Arthur. BA in Home Econs., Calif. State U., Sacramento, 1972, MA in Social Scis., 1973; postgrad., Tex. Women's U., 1976-79; PhD in Reading, East Tex. State U., 1994. Cert. bilingual and elem. edn. tchr., Tex. Tchr. bilingual Arlington Sch. Dist., 1977-96; prof. reading Eastern Mich. U., 1996—. Adj. prof. reading Tex. Women's U., Denton, 1989, adj. prof. ESL East Tex. State U., 1993; mem. tchr. trainer cadre, Dallas Ind. Sch. Dist., 1985-92; freelance cons., 1987—; presenter TESOL Internat. Conf., San Antonio, 1989. Cons., writer (book) Ciencias-Silver Burdett, 1988. Troop leader Girl Scouts U.S., Dallas, 1980-82. Mem. Nat. Reading Conf., Nat. Writing Project, Internat. Reading Assn., Tchrs. of English to Spkrs. of Other Langs. (nominating com. 1990-91), TEXTESOL V (chair elem. edn. com. 1989-91), Tex. Assn. Bilingual Edn., Phi Delta Kappa, Phi Mu. Mem. Christian Ch. Avocations: sewing, knitting, quilting, reading, gourmet cooking. Office: Eastern Mich U 313A Porter Bldg Ypsilanti MI 48197-2210 Business E-Mail: llewiswh@emich.edu.

LEWIT, EUGENE MYRON, foundation executive, educator, researcher; b. N.Y.C., Aug. 20, 1946; s. Solomon and Violet (Stoneberg) L.; m. Judith Lynn Kennis, Aug. 27, 1967; children: Samantha T., Mathew L. Student, Harvard U., 1963-66; BA, CCNY, 1968; PhD, CUNY, 1977. Rsch. asst. Harvard U., Cambridge, Mass., 1964-66; from rsch. asst. to rsch. analyst Nat. Bur. Econ. Rsch., Inc., N.Y.C., 1969-77, vis. scholar, rsch. assoc., 1978—; instr. Mt. Sinai Sch. Medicine, N.Y.C., 1972-77; assoc. prof. U. Med. and Dentistry of N.J., Newark, 1986-91; dir. rsch. and grants-econs. Ctr. for Future of Children, David and Lucile Packard Found., Los Altos, Calif., 1991—98, sr. program mgr., children, families and cmtys. program, 1998—. Cons. assoc. prof. Stanford (Calif.) U. Sch. Medicine, 1991—; cons. Nat. Cancer Inst., Bethesda, Md., 1984-89, World Bank, Washington, 1986-87, WHO, Geneva, 1984-89, Office on Smoking and Health, Rockville, Md., 1987-88. Contbr. articles to profl. jours. Herbert H. Lehman fellow, 1968-72; Nat. Ctr. for Health Svcs. Rsch. grantee, 1979-81, Nat. Inst. on Drug Abuse grantee, 1984-86, N.J. Dept. Health grantee, 1987-88, Nat. Cancer Inst. grantee, 1989-96. Mem. APHA, Am. Econ. Assn., Health Econs. Rsch. Orgn., Western Econ. Assn. Home: 2448 Emerson St Palo Alto CA 94301-4220 Office: Children Families and Cmtys Program David & Lucile Packard Fdn 300 2nd St Los Altos CA 94022-3694

LEWITT, MILES MARTIN, computer engineering company executive; b. N.Y.C., July 14, 1952; s. George Herman and Barbara (Lin) L.; m. Susan Beth Orenstein, June 24, 1973; children: Melissa, Hannah. BS summa cum laude, CCNY Engring., 1973; MS, Ariz. State U., 1976. Software engr. Honeywell, Phoenix, 1973-78; architect iRMX line ops. systems, x86 line microprocessors Intel Corp., Santa Clara, Calif., 1978; engring. mgr. Intel, Hillsboro, Oreg., 1978-80, 1981-89, corp. strategic staff, 1981-82, engring. mgr. Israel, 1980-81; v.p. engring. Cadre Techs., Inc., Beaverton, Oreg., 1989-91; v.p. rsch. and devel. ADP, Portland, Oreg., 1991—2001; v.p. tech. group Intuit, San Diego, 2001—. Instr. Maricopa Tech. Coll., Phoenix, 1974-75; spkr., keynote spkr. at confs. Contbr. articles to profl. jours. Bd. dirs. Portland Computer Tng. Inst., 1995—98; mem. adv. bd. Daid Intensive Sys. Ctr., Portland State U., Oreg. Grad. Inst Recipient Engring. Alumni award CCNY, 1973, Eliza Ford Prize CCNY, 1973, Advanced Engring. Program award, Honeywell, 1976, Product of Yr. award Electronic Products Mag., 1980. Mem. IEEE (sr.), IEEE Computer Soc. (voting mem.), Assn. Computing Machinery (voting mem.), Am. Electronics Assn. (exec. com. Oreg. Coun.). Democrat. Avocations: photography, travel, walking. E-mail: miles_lewitt@intuit.com.

LEWITT, SOL, artist; b. Hartford, Conn., 1928; BFA, Syracuse U., 1949. Instr. Mus. Modern Art Sch., 1964-67, Cooper Union, 1967, Sch. Visual Arts, N.Y.C., 1969-70, NYU, 1970. Contbr. articles on sculpture, drawing, conceptual art to jours., mags.; one-man shows include, Visual Arts Mus., N.Y.C., 1976, San Francisco Mus. Art, 1975, Wadsworth Atheneum, Hartford, Conn., 1981, Musee d'Art Contemporain, Bordeaux, France, 1983, retrospective travelling exhbn., Mus. Modern Art, N.Y.C., 1990-95, Mus. Contemporary Art, Montreal, Krannert Mus., Champaign, Ill., Mus. Contemporary Art, Chgo., La Jolla (Calif.) Mus., 1978-79, Stedelijk Mus., Amsterdam, 1984, Stedelijk Van Abbe Mus., Eindhoven, 1984, Musee d'Art Moderne de la ville de Paris, 1987, Tate Gallery, 1986, Walker Art Ctr., Mpls., 1988, Kunstlalle Bern, Switzerland, 1989, Touko Mus., 1990, Porticus, Frankfort, Fed. Republic Germany, 1990, Drawings 1958-92 Haags Gemeentemus., The Hague and tour, Structures 1962-93 Mus. Modern Art, Oxford and tour, 25 Years of Wall Drawings 1968-93 Addison Gallery, Phillips Acad., Andover, Mass., Prints 1970-95 Mus. Modern Art, N.Y.C., San Francisco Mus. of Art, 2000, retrospective exhbn. Mus. Contemporary Art, Chgo., Whitney Mus. Am. Art, N.Y.C.; group exhbns. include Sculpture Ann, Whitney Mus. Am. Art, N.Y.C., 1967, Minimal Art, The Hague, 1968, Documenta, Kassel, W. Ger., 1968, 72, 77, 82, Prospect, 1968, Dusseldorf, 1968, Stadtische Kuntshalle, Dusseldorf, 1969, La Jolla Mus. Contemp. Art, 1970, Tokyo Biennale, 1970, Guggenheim Internat., N.Y.C., 1971, Whitney Biennial, Whitney Mus. Am. Art, N.Y.C., 1979, Hayward Gallery, London, 1980, Internat. Sculpture exhbn., Basel, Switzerland, 1980, Westkunst, Cologne, Fed. Republic Germany, 1981, Musee Nat. d'Art Moderne, Paris, 1981, Art Inst. Chgo., 1982, Mus. Modern Art, N.Y.C., 1983, Mus. Contemporary Art, Los Angeles, 1986, Whitney Biennial, 1987, Skulptur Projekt, Münster, Fed. Republic Germany, 1987, Venice (Italy) Biennale, 1988, Zeitlos, Hamburg, Fed. Republic Germany; represented in permanent collections, Stedelijk Mus., Albright-Knox Art Gallery, Buffalo, Art Gallery Ont., Toronto, Los Angeles County Mus. Art, Los Angeles, Mus. Modern Art, N.Y.C., Tate Gallery, London, Centre Georges Pompidou, Paris, Whitney Mus. Am. Art, N.Y.C., Met. Mus. Art, N.Y.C., Art Inst. Chgo., Mus. Contemporary Art, Chgo.; work also in German, Swiss, Australian, Dutch, Belgian and Am. mus. Office: c/o Susanna Singer 50 Riverside Dr New York NY 10024-6555 E-mail: susanna50@aol.com.

LEWITTES, DON JORDAN, clinical psychologist; b. Bklyn., Jan. 21, 1950; s. Morton H. and Laura C. L.; m. Andrea D. Jordon, June 15, 1978; 1 child, Jason D. BA, NYU, 1971; PhD, SUNY, Albany, 1976. Diplomate Am. Bd. Med. Psychotherapists, Am. Bd. Forensic Examiners, Am. Bd. Forensic Medicine, Am. Bd. Psychol. Specialities. Instr. dept. psychiatry Albany Med. Coll., 1976-78; clin. affiliate, prof. of psychology St. John's U., 1983-85; sr. psychologist Schenectady Shared Svcs., Ellis Hosp., 1976-77; dir. adminstrv. and clin. inpatient svcs. South Richmond-South Beach Psychiat. Ctr., S.I., N.Y., 1977-81; chief psychologist South Nassau Cmty. Hosp., Oceanside, N.Y., 1982-87; cons. Nassau Coalition on Child Abuse and Neglect, Hempstead, N.Y., 1989-98. Psychol. cons. Gracie Sq. Hosp., N.Y.C., 1989-91; expert cons. N.Y.C. Office Legal Affairs/ACS, 1991—. Kings County and Bronx County Dist. Atty's. Office, 1994—; adjunct faculty Grad. Sch. Social Svc. Fordham U., 1995-96; intern dept. psychiatry Rutgers Med. Sch., Piscataway, N.J., 1974-75. Contbr. articles to profl. jours. Mem. Am. Psychol. Soc., Am. Profl. Soc. on the Abuse of Children. Office: Ste 150 30 Hempstead Ave Rockville Centre NY 11570-4033 Office Phone: 516-763-1631.

LEWRIS, BASIL J., lawyer; b. Manhattan, N.Y., Feb. 26, 1949; BChE cum laude, CUNY, 1972; JD with high honors, George Washington U., 1977, LLM in Patent and Trade Regulation Law, 1980. Bar: Va. 1977, US Ct. Fed. Claims 1978, DC 1979, US Supreme Ct. 1981, US Ct. Appeals (Fed. Cir.) 1982, registered: US Patent & Trademark Office. Law clerk to assoc. judge Donald E. Lane US Ct. Customs and Patent Appeals, 1977-79; lectr. Patent Resources Group, Inc., 1982-91; ptnr. Finnegan, Henderson, Farabow, Garrett & Dunner LLP, Washington, mem. exec. com. Co-author (with Matthew Bender): Patent Law Perspectives, 1984—88. Named one of best lawyers in intellectual property law, Best Lawyers in Am., 2005—06. Mem.: Order of Coif, Va. State Bar Assn., Fed. Cir. Bar Assn., DC Bar, Assn. Trial Lawyers Am., ABA, Am. Intellectual Property Law Assn., Omega Chi Epsilon, Tau Beta Pi, Delta Theta Phi. Office: Finnegan Henderson Farabow Garrett & Dunner LLP 901 New York Ave NW Washington DC 20001-3315 Office Phone: 202-408-4000. Office Fax: 202-408-4400. Business E-Mail: bill.lewris@finnegan.com.

LEWTER, HELEN CLARK, retired elementary school educator; b. Millis, Mass., Jan. 14, 1936; d. Waldimar Kenville and Ida Mills (Currier) Clark; m. Alvin Council Lewter, June 18, 1966; children: Lois Ida, David Paul, Jonathan Clark. BA, U. Mass., 1958; MS, Old Dominion U., 1978. Tchr. Juniper Hill Sch., Framingham, Mass., 1960—63, Aragona Elem. Sch., Virginia Beach, Va., 1963—65, Park Elem., Chesapeake, Va., 1965—67; edn. specialist Riverview Sch., Portsmouth, Va., 1977—78; reading tchr. Truitt Jr. H.S., Chesapeake, 1979—83; reading resource tchr. Southeastern Elem., Chesapeake, 1983—86; tchr. Deep Creek Elem. Sch., Chesapeake, 1986—99, ret., 1999. Pers. task force, textbook adoption com. Chesapeake Pub. Schs., Va., 1984—85, employee handbook com., Va., 1986—87, K-6 writing curriculum com., Va., 1988—89. Active PTA, 1979—99; mem. mayor's adv. coun. City of Chesapeake, Va., 1988—89; tchr., workshop leader, dir., mem. various coms. Fairview Heights Bapt. Ch., Deep Creek Bapt. Ch., Va. So. Bapt. Retreats, 1968—; mem. summer missionary Va. So. Bapts., 1993. Mem.: NEA, Va. Reading Assn., Internat. Reading Assn., Chesapeake Reading Assn. (v.p., pres., honor and merit coun., chmn. various coms.), Chesapeake Edn. Assn., Va. Edn. Assn., Phi Kappa Phi, Kappa Delta Pi, Delta Kappa Gamma (legis. chmn.). Republican. Avocations: church related activities, reading. Home: 745 Mandarin Ln Chesapeake VA 23323

LEWY, HELEN CROSBY, artist, writer, translator, painter; d. Hewitt Crosby and Helen Louise Pratt; m. Hans Lewy (dec.); 1 child, Michael Robert. Studies with Edward Shenton, Swarthmore Coll., 1936—39; AB in Cinematography, U. So. Calif., 1947; studies with Fred Reichman, San Francisco, 1967—69; student, Nat. Art Sch. Analyst strategic svcs. OSS, Wash., N.Y.; polit. cons. Allied Election Mission to Greece; editor Portfolio, Phila., 1937—40; editor polit. intelligence Office Strategic Svcs., London, 1942—44, Naples, Italy, 1944—45; translator German Stories, N.Y.C., 1953—54, Christian Morgenstern Poems, N.Y.C., 1955—60. Exhibited in group shows at U. Calif. Ext., San Francisco, 1969, Richmond Art Ctr., 1972, Brickwall Gallery, Berkeley, 1972, Vacaville Art League Open Competition, 1973 (Blue Ribbon, 1973), ACCI Gallery, Berkeley, 1973, Crown Zellerbach Gallery, San Francisco, 1973, 1st winter ann. art co-op, 1974, Camelia Capital Art Exhbn., Sacramento, 1974; artist (invitational show) Hayward Area Art Festival, 1974; one-woman shows include Mezzanine Gallery, Bank of Calif., Berkeley, 1971, Athena Gallery, Oakland, 1974, Retrospective, Galerie de la cité, Lausanne, Switzerland, 1996, Represented in permanent collections, Italy, Israel, Germany, Switzerland, US (Oreg., Calif., NY); featured in (Italian mag. piece written by Adriano Sofri) Panorama, 2003; contbr. articles to profl publs. Mem.: Berkeley Art Co-op, Oakland Art Assn., Marin Soc. Artists, Artists Equity Assn., San Francisco Women Artists. Avocations: languages, art, dogs. Personal E-mail: hclewy@speakeasy.net.

LEWY, JOHN EDWIN, pediatric nephrologist; b. Chgo., Apr. 22, 1935; s. Stanley B. and Lucille (Mayer) L.; m. Rosalind Portnoy, June 9, 1963; children— Karen, Steven. BA, U. Mich., 1956; MD, Tulane U., 1960. Diplomate Am. Bd. Pediat. (oral examiner 1985-89, oral exam com. 1987-89, certifying exam. com. on clin. problems 1989-92, com. on rsch. and rev. 1992-98), Am. Bd. Pediatric Nephrology. Intern Michael Reese Hosp. Med. Center, Northwestern U., 1960-61, resident in pediatrics, 1961-62, Michael Reese Hosp. Med. Center, 1963-64, chief resident, 1964, pediatric nephrology fellow, 1965, dir. sect. pediatric nephrology, 1967-70; fellow dept. pediatrics Cornell U. Med. Coll., N.Y.C., 1966, research fellow physiology, 1966-67, asst. prof. pediatrics, 1970-71, assoc. prof., 1971-75, prof., 1975-78, dir. div. pediatric nephrology, 1970-78; Reily prof., chmn. dept. pediat. Tulane U. Sch. Medicine, New Orleans, 1978—; physician-in-chief Tulane Hosp. for Children, New Orleans, 1993—. Pediatrician La. Handicapped Children's Program; mem. exec. com., sci. adv. com. La. End Stage Renal Disease Coun.; mem. life options adv. bd. Rehab. Digest for Nephrologists, 1999—; mem. sci. adv. bd. Nat. Kidney Found., 1979—86, mem. health and sci. affairs com., 1989—95, mem. pub. policy com., 1990—96, chmn. pub. policy com., 1994—96, bd. dirs., 1994—96, mem. task force on early intervention and prevention, 1996—; mem. clin. sci. coun. Tulane U., chmn., 1980—90, 1995—, mem. exec. com. of clin. sci. coun., 1978—, mem. faculty senate, 1987—90; mem. task force on cmty. health care Tulane Sch. Pub. Health and Tropical Medicine, 1993—; bd. dirs. Kidney Found. La., 1984—, mem. med. adv. bd., 1981—, mem. sci. adv. bd., 1982—, rep., regional dir., 2000—, task force early intervention and prevention, 1996—. Contbr. over 200 articles and abstracts to profl. jours. Mem. profl. adv. com. Nat. Found. March of Dimes; sci. adv. com. U.S. Renal Data System, HHS, 1990—93; mem. com. on future of pediat. nephrology NIDDK, 1991—; spl. com. on ctrs. of excellence in kidney and urology diseases HHS Nat. Kidney and Urology Diseases Adv. Bd., 1994—96. Served with M.C. USAF, 1962—63. Named Intern of Year, Michael Reese Hosp. Med. Ctr., 1961; recipient award, La. Pediatric Soc., 1960, Ronald McDonald Children's Charities Gift of Love award, 1996, Disting. Svc. award, Nat. Kidney Found., 1996, Julio Figueroa Gift of Life award, Nat. Kidney Found. La., 1999, Disting. Svc. award, Tulane U. Med. Alumni Assn., 1999. Mem.: AAAS, APHA, Nat. Assn. Children's Hosps. (liason from comm. on Federal Gov. Affairs 2002), So. Soc. Pediatric Rsch. (Founder's award 2003), Greater New Orleans Pediatric Soc., Orleans Parish Med. Soc. (pub. health com. 1981—, media resource panel 1999—, Award for excellence in rsch. 2003), Am. Soc. Artificial Internal Organs, Assn. Med. Sch. Pediatric Dept. Chairmen, La. State Med. Soc., Internat. Pediatric Nephrology Assn. (asst. sec. gen. 1977—78), Internat. Pediatric Chairs Assn., N.Y. Acad. Scis., Midwest Soc. Pediatric Research, Internat. Soc. Nephrology, Am. Soc. Nephrology, Am. Soc. Pediatric Nephrology (sec.-treas. 1974—80, pres. 1980—81, pub. policy com. 1991—94, 1996—2000, Founder's award 2000), Am. Pediatric Soc. (co-chair work group on pub. policy), Soc. Pediatric Rsch., Am. Acad. Pediat. (liaison from AMSPDC 1992—95, coun. fed. govt. affairs 1992—, task force on access 1999—, coun. on coms. 2002—, rsch./edn./orgn. action group 2002—, chmn. 2002, Henry L. Barnett award 1999), Am. Soc. Transplant Physics, Inst. Medicine (end stage renal disease com. 1989—91), Salt and Water Club, Alpha Omega Alpha (faculty advisor 1987—92). Home: 700 S Peters St New Orleans LA 70130-1663 Office: Tulane U Sch Medicine 1430 Tulane Ave New Orleans LA 70112-2699

LEWY, ROBERT MAX, physician; b. N.Y.C., Oct. 18, 1945; s. Martin and Ellen (Newmark) L.; m. Barbara, Oct. 4, 1987; children: Jennifer, Sarah. AB, U. Rochester, 1967; MD, U. Medicine and Dentistry N.J., Newark, 1971; MPH, Columbia U., 1977. Diplomate Nat. Bd. Med. Examiners, Am. Bd. Family Practice. Intern Dartmouth Affiliated Hosps., Hanover, N.H., 1971-72; resident Maine-Dartmouth Family Practice Program, Augusta, 1974-75; clin. scholar Columbia U., N.Y.C., 1975-77; dir. employee health svcs. Presbyn. Hosp., Columbia-Presbyn. Med. Ctr., N.Y.C., 1977-88, dir. office physician affairs, 1988-91, sr. v.p. med. affairs, 1991-98; assoc. prof. medicine Columbia U., N.Y.C., 1991—, sr. assoc. dean health affairs, 1998—. Author: Preventive Primary Medicine, 1981, Employees at Risk, 1991; contbr. articles to profl. jours. With USPHS, 1972-74. Fellow Am. Occupational Med. Assn. (sec. chmn. 1984-88), Am. Coll. Preventive Medicine; mem. Am. Pub. Health Assn., N.Y. Occupational Med. Assn. (bd. dirs. 1985—). Home: 864 Bradley Pky Blauvelt NY 10913-1127 Office: Columbia U Box 100 630 W 168th St New York NY 10032-3795 E-mail: rl10@columbia.edu.

LEWYN, ANN SALFELD, retired English as a second language educator; b. N.Y.C., Dec. 1, 1935; d. Henry and Betty (Ahrens) Salfeld; m. Thomas Mark Lewyn, July 15, 1955; children: Alfred Thomas, Mark Henry. BA, Hunter Coll., 1967, MA, 1982. Mem. faculty UN Hospitality Extension Lang. Program, N.Y.C., 1974-86; adj. instr. ESL NYU, 1986-90, adj. asst. prof., 1990-95, adj. assoc. prof., 1995-2000, adj. prof., 2001—02; ret., 2003—. Editor-in-chief (Newsletter) UN Hospitality Com., 1967-86. Mem. exec. bd. Small Press Ctr., N.Y.C., 1990-98; mem. adv. coun. Hospitality Com. for UN Dels. Inc., 1991-98; bd. dirs. Hunter Coll. Scholarship and Welfare Fund, N.Y.C., 1992—, sec., 1998-2000, 3d v.p., 2000-2001, 2d v.p., 2001—. Mem. Teachers of English as Second Lang. (author in Aug. 1990 newsletter), N.Y. State Tchrs. of English as Second Lang., Pi Sigma Alpha, Kappa Delta Pi. Avocations: travel, tennis, needlepoint, photography, golf. Home: 911 Park Ave New York NY 10021-0337

LEWYN, THOMAS MARK, lawyer; b. N.Y.C., July 2, 1930; s. Oswald and Agnes (Maas) L.; m. Ann Salfeld, July 15, 1955; children— Alfred Thomas, Mark Henry. BA, Stanford, 1952, postgrad., 1952-54; LL.B., Columbia, 1955. Bar: N.Y. 1957. Assoc. Simpson, Thacher & Bartlett, N.Y.C., 1957-64, ptnr., 1965-75, sr. ptnr., 1976-90, of counsel, 1991—95. Bd. dirs. Metro-Goldwyn-Mayer, Inc. Contbr. articles to profl. jours. Served to 1st lt., F.A. AUS, 1955-57. Mem. ABA, Assn. of Bar of City of N.Y., N.Y. State Bar Assn. Home: 911 Park Ave New York NY 10021-0337 Office: Simpson Thacher & Bartlett 425 Lexington Ave Fl 15 New York NY 10017-3954 Office Phone: 212-455-2820.

LEY, RONALD, psychologist, educator; b. Buffalo, Oct. 19, 1929; s. August Andreas and Marie (Jerge) L.; m. Carmen De Brito, Jan. 16, 1965; 1 child, Jessica Elizabeth. BA, U. Buffalo, 1951; PhD, Syracuse U., 1963. Rsch. dir. Madison Area Project, Syracuse, 1962—63; asst. prof. psychology No. Ill. U., DeKalb, 1963—64; asst. prof. grad. faculty New Sch. U., N.Y.C., 1964—66; prof. psychology and stats. SUNY Albany, 1966—99, rsch. prof., 1999—. Cons. Nat. Inst. for Occupational Safety and Health; vis. prof. psychology U. P.R., 1969, cardiac dept., Charing Cross Hosp., London, 1988. Author: A Whisper of Espionage, 1990, Rumores de Espionaje: Wolfgang Köhler y los Monos en Tenerife, 1995; co-editor: Behavioral and Psychological Approaches to Breathing Disorders, 1994; mem. editl. bd. Jour. Behavior Therapy and Exptl. Psychiatry, 1983—, Applied Psychophysiology and Biofeedback, 1997—, Behavior Modification, Jour. Anxiety Disorders, guest editor Biofeedback and Self-Regulation, 1994; guest editor: Behavior Modification, 2001; guest editor Behavior Modification, 2003; contbr. articles to profl. jours. and encys. Bd. dirs. Father's Assn. of the Albany Acad. for Girls, 1981-84. Rsch. fellow SUNY, 1967-68, 70, 74, 76, 78, 91, Rsch. grantee, 1967-72, 74-76, 78, 87-88, 91-92, 96-97, Nat. Inst. Occupl. Safety and Health grantee, 1982-83, 87-88, others. Fellow Am. Psychol. Soc., Behavior Therapy and Rsch. Soc.; mem. APA, Am. Statis. Assn., Assn. Advancement Behavior Therapy, Assn. Applied Psychophysiology and Biofeedback (chmn. sect. applied respiratory psychophysiology 1998-99), Author's Guild, Author's League Am., Ea. Psychol. Assn., Internat. Soc. Advancement Respiratory Psychophysiology (co-founder, pres. 1994-96), Psychol. Assn. Northeastern N.Y. (sec. 1967-68, pres. 1983-84, Disting. Psychologist award 1996), Soc. Psychophysiol. Rsch., Psychonomic Soc., Sigma Xi. Home: 22 Marion Ave Albany NY 12203-1823 Office: Univ at Albany SUNY 233 ED Bldg 1400 Washington Ave Albany NY 12222-1000 Office Phone: 518-442-5055.

LEYDEN, MICHAEL JOSEPH, II, (LEI JIE MING), communications executive, academic administrator, finance educator, writer; b. Feb. 26, 1950; m. Michele Vespier, 1972 (div. 1987); children: Sophia Dion, Søren Nicholas; m. Ivy Zhong Yu Xu, Nov. 1991; 1 child, Sophia Qian Yu. AA in Econs., Wenatchee Valley Coll., 1970; student, Charlotte Amailie, St. Thomas U. V.I., 1970—71; BA in Philosophy and Psychology, Ctrl. Wash. U., 1972; MA in Philosophy, Wash. State U., 1974; various mktg. diplomas, U. Hawaii, 1975-89; DBA, Newport U., Utah and Beijing, 1997. Corp. mgr., tng. dir. Colwell Bankers-Davenport Inc., Wenatchee, Wash., 1977—81; v.p. sales and mktg. John's Real Estate and Securities Corp., Bellevue, Wash., 1981—82; pres., founder Aero-Brokers Inc., Aero-Brokers Internat. Securities Co., ABI Comm. Group Svcs. Co., Aero-Brokers Internat. Real Estate Corp., Honolulu, Hawaii, Long Beach, Calif., Wenatchee, Wash., 1983—86; gen. mgr. Tadashi & Sons Ltd., Truk Islands, 1987; CEO, adminstrv. and fin. mgr. Zorro's Pizza and Italian Restaurants, Honolulu, 1988; gen mgr., tile and marble import wholesaler Coast Enterprises Hawaii Inc., Honolulu, 1990; exec. v.p., gen. mgr. Eternity (Tianjin) Internat. Trade Devel. Co., Ltd., Honolulu, 1992—93; prof. Sch. Internat. Bus. Nankai U., Tianjin, China, 1994; prof. dept. internat. politics Sch. Internat. Rels. Beijing U., China, 1995; prof. dept. econ. and mgmt. Qinghua (Tsinghua) U., Beijing, 1996; internat. bus. affairs dir. Michael Trading and Cons. Co. Ltd., Beijing City, 1997; prof. dept. econ. and mgmt. Shanghai U., China, 1998; dean, adminstrn. and devel. Coll. Marshall Islands, Majuro, 1998; project dir. employment, tng. coord. not for profit orgn. Honolulu Cmty. Action Program, Inc., Honolulu, 1999—2000; prof. grad. sch. mgmt. Tianjin Polytechnic U., 2002; acting dean Coll. Bus. Adminstrn. Kazakhstan Inst. Mgmt. Econs. Strategic Policy, Almaty, Kazakhstan, 2004; dean Coll. Continuing Edn. Kazakhstan Inst. Mgmt., Econs. Strategic Policy, Almaty, 2004. Spl. asst. to commr. edn. and rsch., statistician No. Marianas Islands Pub. Sch. Sys., 1991; program mgr. ed. and trng. Workforce Investment Act, Samoan Svc. Providers Assn., Honolulu, 2001—; dep. vice gen. mgr. Beijing and Prosperity Advt. Co., Ltd., Tianjin, 2003; prof., v.p. acad. affairs Tianjin Pacific Profl. Coll., 2004-05. Author: (poems) Man Atop Banana Leaves, 1970, The Poet: Peu á Peu pp 120-1, The Sacred Human Body, Intruders, Volcano Island Colours, 1976, Recruitment Strategies: A Model for Executive Decision-Making, 1980, Writing a Business Plan for the Five-Minute Reader, 1999, Guidelines for Entrepreneurs on How to Prepare an International Business Plan, 1992, China Treaty Port - Tientsin: Mystery Unraveled "Basic Rsch. Opens yor Philatelic Eye, pp 151-170, 1997; The Collectors Club, "Philatelist" vol. 76 No. 3; China (Tianjin) Postal and Cultural History 1887-1947, 2002, The CIA Story 1785-2004 Narrative and pictorial rev. of The Chinese in America, 2005; contbr. articles and revs. in field. Recipient Pres.'s medal for leadership, 1970, Sophia Newspaper Editors award, 1973, Honolulu Mayor's award bus. honour, 1975, INDEPEX, 1997, Internat. Philatelic Exbn., New Dehli, 1997, Bronze medal in Philatelic Lit., CCNY Jour., Large Silver medal Bangkok Internat. Philatelic Exhibit philatelic lit., 2003, Tianjin Mcpl. Archive Hon. Achievement award to First Foreigner, Dir. Sun, Silver medal, Chgo. PEX, 2003, Silver medal, Postal History Lit. Book APS Stamp Show, Columbus, OH, 2003, Large Silver medal, No. 1 of 56 Philatelic entries, ACPF Nat. Expn. Chong Qing City. Mem. Am. Mgmt. Assn. (mem. pres. club 1980, 87, 92), N.Ctrl. Wash. Oriental Rug Soc. (editor Oriental Textile newsletter 1977-80), Shanghai Am. C. of C. Edn.-Pub. Com. (chmn. 1997-99), All China Philatelic Fed. Beijing Assn., Tianjin Philatelic Assn., Royal Philatelic Soc. London, Am. Philatelic Soc., China Stamp Soc., NC Wash. Writers Guild, Executive Club of Honolulu (sec. 1987), Collectors Club (NY), Lions, Rotary, Inernat. Honolulu Downtown Club, SESCAL, So. Calif. Philatelic Soc., COLOPEX. Roman Catholic. Home: PO Box 22124 Honolulu HI 96823-2124 Address: OuYa Hua Yuan/European-Asian Garden Tower Door 4 Ste 1205 Penthouse Binshui Rd Hexi Dist Tianjin 300060 China Office Phone: 86-22-8835-3948. Office Fax: 86-22-8835-3948. E-mail: michaelleyden@yahoo.com.

LEYDENS, JON A., director; PhD, Colo. State U. Instr. of English, Wall St. Inst. of Langs., Bologna, Italy, 1989—92; writing ctr. dir. Colo. State U., Fort Collins, 1994—97; writing program adminstr. Colo. Sch. of Mines, Golden, 1997—. Mem.: Nat. Coun. of Tchrs. of English, Phi Beta Kappa. Office: Colo School of Mines 1500 Ilinois St Golden CO 80401-1887 Office Phone: 303-273-3180.

LEYDORF, FREDERICK LEROY, lawyer; b. Toledo, Ohio, June 13, 1930; s. Loftin Herman and Dorothy DeRoyal (Cramer) L.; m. Mary MacKenzie Malcolm, Mar. 28, 1953; children: Robert Malcolm, William Frederick, Katherine Ann, Thomas Richard, Deborah Mary. Student, U. Toledo, 1948-49; BBA, U. Mich., 1953; JD, UCLA, 1958. Bar: Calif. 1959, U.S. Supreme Ct. 1970. Assoc. Hammack & Pugh, L.A., 1959-61; ptnr. Willis, Butler, Scheifly, Leydorf & Grant, L.A., 1961-81, Pepper, Hamilton & Scheetz, L.A., 1981-83, Hufstedler & Kaus, L.A., 1983-95. Lectr., cons. Calif. Continuing Edn. of Bar, 1965-92; mem. planning com. Probate and Trust Conf., U. So. Calif., 1984-92. Contbg. author: California Non-Profit Corporations, 1969; contbr. articles to profl. jours. Chmn. pub. adminstr.-pub. guardian adv. commn. Los Angeles County Bd. Suprs., 1972-73; v.p. J.W. and Ida M. Jameson Found., 1995—, bd. dirs., 1967—; bd. dirs. Western Ctr. on Law and Poverty, Inc., 1980-82, L.A. Heart Inst., 1988-90; mem. legal com. Music Ctr. Found., 1980-95; mem. lawyers adv. coun. Constl. Rights Found., 1982-85; mem. devel. adv. bd. U. Mich. Sch. Bus. Adminstrn., 1984-90; mem. adv. bd. UCLA-CEB Estate Planning Inst., 1979-92; Lt. USNR, 1953-55. Mem. Libbey H.S. Hall of Fame (Toledo), 1999. Mem. L.A. County Bar Assn. (bd. trustees 1973-75), State Bar Calif. (chmn. conf. dels. 1977, Alumnus of Yr. award, conf. of dels. 1983, mem. exec. com. estate planning, trust and probate law sect. 1979-80), L.A. County Bar Found. (pres. 1977-79, bd. dirs. 1975-87), Internat. Acad. Estate and Trust Law (v.p. N.Am. 1978-82), Life Ins. and Trust Coun. L.A. (pres. 1983-84), UCLA Law Alumni Assn. (pres. 1982), L.A. World Affairs Coun. (mem. internat. cir.), Chancery Club (pres. 1991-92), Jonathan Club, Laguna Woods Golf Club, Sunrise Country Club (Rancho Mirage, Calif.), Phi Delta Phi, Phi Delta Theta. Republican. Lutheran. Home: 75 Majorca Dr Rancho Mirage CA 92270-3826

LEYHANE, FRANCIS JOHN, III, lawyer; b. Chgo., Mar. 29, 1957; s. Francis J. and Mary Elizabeth (Crowley) L.; m. Diana M. Urizarri, May 8, 1982; children: Katherine, Francis J. IV, Joseph, Brigid Rose, James Matthew. BA, Loyola U., Chgo., 1977, JD, 1980. Bar: Ill. 1980, U.S. Dist. Ct. (no. dist.) Ill. 1980, U.S. Ct. Appeals (7th cir.) 1986. Assoc. Condon, Cook & Roche, Chgo., 1980-87; ptnr. Condon & Cook, Chgo., 1988-98, Boyle & Leyhane, Ltd., Chgo., 1998—2003, Leyhane & Assocs. Ltd., 2003—. Contbr. articles to profl. jours. Mem. Sch. bd. Immaculate Conception Parish, Chgo., 1993-96. Fellow Ill. Bar Found.; mem. Appellate Lawyers Assn. Ill., Ill. State Bar Assn. (mem. assembly 1987-90), Chgo. Bar Assn., Blue Key. Office: Leyhane and Assocs Ltd 11 E Adams Ste 1600 Chicago IL 60603 Office Phone: 312-922-2996. Business E-Mail: leyhane329@aol.com.

LEZHAN, ERLENE, artist; d. Stephen Walter Etherton and Florence Ida (Galbraith) L.; 5 children. Piano tchr., Greeley, Colo., 1981-85; art tchr. for handicapped children, 1981-86. Author: Sinners of the Surf, 1992, (manuscript) A New Day, 1981; exhibited at U. No. Colo., 1976. Recipient Cert. and Flag Union Pacific R.R., 1976. Mem. Nat. Soc. Lit. and the Arts. Home: 1240 28th Ave Apt 1C Greeley CO 80634-5442

L'HEUREUX, RICHARD ALLEN, academic administrator, consultant; b. International Falls, Minn., Mar. 6, 1953; s. John Joseph and Agnes Frances L'heureux; m. Meeta Goel; children: Autumn Paige, Brea Elizabeth, Samuel Husing, Kyle Praveen Singhal, Maia Natalya Goel-L'heureux. BS in Polit. Sci., U. Minn., 1975; MS in Acquisition Mgmt., Air Force Inst. Tech., 1988; PhD in Bus. Adminstrn., Fla. State U., 1994. Commd. 2d lt. USAF, 1980, advanced through grades to lt. col., with San Antonio, 1978—99; exec. v.p. New West Strategies, Helena, Mont., 1999—; provost Mountain State U., Beckley, Minn., 2000—. Contbr. articles to profl. jours. Vol. Spl. Olympics, 1980—99, Habitat for Humanity, Beckley, W.Va., 2000—04; com. mem. Beckley (W.Va.) C. of C., 2003—04; tchr. St. Francis de Sales, Beckley. Recipient Ezra Kotcher award for Curriculum Devel., Air U., 1998. Mem.: Nat. Contract Mgmt. Assn. (cert. profl. contract mgr. 1990). Roman Catholic. Avocations: skiing, golf, canoeing, camping, Native American art. Home: 220 N Alaska Butte MT 59701 Office: Synesis 7 Butte MT 59701

LHUILLIER, MONIQUE (DIANE MONIQUE LHUILLIER), apparel designer; b. Philippines; m. Tom Bugbee. Grad., Fashion Inst. of Design and Merchandising, Los Angeles. Founder, designer Monique Lhuillier & Co., Los Angeles, 1996—; opened Monique Lhuillier Boutique, Beverly Hills, 2001—. Designs featured in numerous magazines including W, In Style, Modern Bride, Elle. Recipient Glamorous Bridal Designer award, 2001, Avant Garde Bridal Designer award, Wedding Dresses Mag., 2002. Mem.: Council of Fashion Designers of Am. Office: Monique Lhuillier & Co 1201 S Grand Ave 3rd Fl Los Angeles CA 90015*

LI, BAOZHEN, electronics engineer, researcher; s. X. Li and Y. Liu; m. Ning Lai, May 2, 1983; 1 child, Kevin. PhD, U. Notre Dame, 1990. Devel. engr. Westinghouse Tech. Ctr., Pitts., 1993—96, IBM Microelectronics, Essex Junction, Vt., 1996—. Achievements include patents for novel process and macro designs for seminconductor ICs; Solid Oxide Fuel Cell development; novel chemical sensor development; research in Seminconductor Reliability Model development. Office: IBM Systems and Tech Group 1000 River St Essex Junction VT 05452 Office Fax: 802-769-4287. Personal E-mail: li5188us@yahoo.com.

LI, BO, semiconductor manufacturing engineer; m. Sherry Li, Aug. 15, 1986; children: Bryan, Catherine. PhD, Ga. Inst. Tech., 1999. Sr. arch. and developer GuangSha Electronic Co., Beijing, 1994—95; rschr. So. Ill. U., Carbondale, 1995—96, Ga. Inst. Tech., Atlanta, 1997—99; sr. staff engr. Intel Corp., Hillsboro, Oreg., 1999—. Author: Semiconductor Manufacturing Handbook; contbr. articles to profl. jours. Recipient Outstanding award for flexible fixture design in automobile mfg., Ford Co., 1999, Tech. and Mfg. Quality award, Intel Corp., 2002, Mfg. Excellence award, 2004. Mem.: IEEE, ASME, Assn. Computing Machinery, Soc. Mfg. Engrs. Achievements include patents pending for proactive staging of semiconductor materials to improve factory throughput; semiconductor material storage management to optimize throughput and minimize stocker overflow; design of automated material handling system execution control framework in 300mm manufacturing; research in unattended and continuous semiconductor manufacturing process system modeling and design; development of semiconductor manufacturing equipment maintanance planning and scheduling. Avocations: travel, reading, piano, hiking, dance. Office Phone: 503-613-9961.

LI, CATHERINE, literature educator, writer; b. Shenyang, China, Sept. 10, 1946; d. Min Chiu and Pei Chia Li; m. Herbert H. Chen (dec.); 1 child, Christine Hsiao-Ching. BA, NYU, 1969; MA, UCLA, 1972; PhD, UCLA, LA, 1987. Tchr. lit., English as second lang. U. Calif., San Diego, 1989—93, Irvine, Calif., 1982—86, Calif. State U., Long Beach, Calif., State U. Fullerton, Calif. State U., LA, Occidental Coll. Contbr. articles to profl. jours. Avocation: travel. E-mail: clichen@cox.net.

LI, CHIEN-PIN, political scientist, educator; PhD, U. Iowa, 1988. Assoc. rsch. fellow Academia Sinica, Taipei, Taiwan, 1988—90; asst. prof. U. Wis., Stevens Point, 1990—94; assoc. prof. Kennesaw State U., Kennesaw, Ga., 1994—2000; prof. Kennesaw (Ga.) State U., 2000—, chair dept. polit. sci. and internat. affairs, 2002—. Vis. prof. Nanjing (China) Normal U., 1998; rsch. assoc. China Rsch. Ctr., Atlanta, 1999—. Contbr. articles to profl. jours. Fellow Sr. fellow, Atlantic Coun. US, 1990, Pacific Cultural Found., 1995—96. Mem.: Chinese-Am. Acad. PA Southeastern US, Assn. Third World Studies, Ga. Polit. Sci. Assn., Internat. Studies Assn. Office: Kennesaw State Univ 1000 Chastain Rd # 2302 Kennesaw GA 30144-5591 E-mail: cli@kennesaw.edu.

LI, CHING-CHUNG, electrical engineering educator; b. Changshu, Kiangsu, China, Mar. 30, 1932; arrived in U.S., 1954, naturalized, 1972; s. Lung-Han and Lien-Tseng (Hwa) L.; m. Hanna Wu, June 10, 1961; children: William Wei-Lin, Vincent Wei-Tsin. BSEE, Nat. Taiwan U., 1954; MSEE, Northwestern U., 1956, PhD, 1961. Jr. engr. analytical dept. Westinghouse Electric Corp., East Pittsburgh, Pa., 1957; inst. fellow Northwestern U., Evanston, Ill., 1957-59; asst. prof. elec. engring. U. Pitts., 1959-62, assoc. prof., 1962-67; vis. assoc. prof. elec. engring. U. Calif.-Berkeley, 1964; vis. prin. scientist Alza Corp., Palo Alto, Calif., 1970; faculty rsch. participant Pitts. Energy Tech. Ctr., Dept. Energy, 1982, 83, 85, 88, 89; prof. elec. engring. U. Pitts., 1967—, prof. computer sci., 1977—; mem. Ctr. Multivariate Analysis, 1982-87, Ctr. for Parallel and Distributed Intelligent Systems, 1986—96; sabbatical leave Lab. for Info. and Decision Systems, MIT, 1988, Robotics Inst., Carnegie Mellon U., 1999. Mem. sci. adv. com. Horus Therapeutics, Inc., 1995-97. Guest editor: Jour. Cybernetics and Info. Sci., 1979, Computerized Med. Imaging and Graphics, 1991, assoc. editor: Pattern Recognition, 1985—2001, mem. editl. bd.: Internat. Jour. Image and Graphics, 2000—; contbr. articles to profl. jours. Co-recipient cert. of merit Radiol. Soc. N.Am., 1979; rsch. grantee NSF, 1975-81, 85-87, Pa. Dept. Health, 1977-79, We. Pa. Advanced Tech. Ctr., 1983-84, 86-88, Health Rsch. and Svc. Found., 1985-86, Air Force Office Sci. Rsch., 1990-93, Pitts. Digital Greenhouse, Inc., 2000-02. Fellow IEEE (tech. com., com. chmn. 1967—); mem. Biomed. Engring. Soc., AAAS, Pattern Recognition Soc., Sigma Xi, Eta Kappa Nu. Home: 2130 Garrick Dr Pittsburgh PA 15235-5033 Office: U Pitts Dept Elec and Computer Engring Pittsburgh PA 15261 Office Phone: 412-624-9679. Business E-Mail: ccl@engr.pitt.edu.

LI, CHU-TSING, art historian, educator; b. Canton, China, 1920; came to U.S., 1947; m. Yao-wen; children: Ulysses, Amy. BA, U. Nanking, 1943; MA in English Lit., U. Iowa, 1949, PhD in Art History, 1955. Instr. U. Iowa, 1954-55, 56-58, asst. prof., 1958-62, assoc. prof., 1962-65, rsch. prof., 1963—64, prof., 1965-66; prof. art history U. Kans., Lawrence, 1966-78, dept. chmn., 1972-78, Judith Harris Murphy Disting. prof., 1978-90, prof. emeritus, 1990—, dir. NEH summer seminar on Chinese art history, 1975, 78, coord. Mellon faculty seminar, 1979; acting asst. prof. Oberlin Coll., 1955-56; asst. prof. Ind. U., summer 1956; coord. N.Y. state faculty seminar on Chinese Art History, SUNY, 1965; rsch. curator Nelson Gallery of Art, Kansas City, 1966—. Vis. prof. fine arts Chinese U., Hong Kong, 1972-73, summer 1971, leader China visit group, 1973; vis. prof. Grad. Inst. Art History, Nat Taiwan U., 1990; vis. Andrew W. Mellon prof. U. Pitts., 1995; dir. NEH Summer Inst. Modern Chinese Art and Culture, 1991; participant Internat. Symposiums on Chinese Painting, Nat. Palace Mus., Taipei, 1970, Cleve. Mus. Art, 1981, Huangshan Sch. Painters, Hefei, Ahnui, Rep. China, 1984, on Words and Images in Chinese Painting, Met. Mus. Art, N.Y.C., 1985, on the Elegant Brush: Chinese Painting under the Qianlong Emperor, Phoenix Art Mus., 1985, to celebrate 60th anniversary Nat. Palace Mus., Taipei, Taiwan, 1985, on History of Yuan Dynasty, Nanjing U., China, 1986, on art of Badashanren (Chu Ta), Nanchang, China, 1986; on Dunhuang Grottoes, China, 1987; on the Four Monk Painters, Shanghai Mus., 1987; on art of Chang Dai-chien, Nat. Mus. History, Taipei, 1988; Symposium on Contemporary Artistic Development, Nanjing, 1988; Symposium on Chinese Painting of Ming Dynasty Chinese U. Hong Kong, 1988; Symposium on Chinese Painting of the Ming and Qing Dynasties from the Forbidden City, Cleve. Mus. Art, 1989, Symposium on Hist. Studies, since 1911, Nat. Taiwan U., 1989, Symposium on 40th Anniversary of Founding of Liaoning Provincial Mus., Shenyang, China, 1989, Symposium on Painting of Wu Sch., Palace Mus., Beijing, 1990; Internat. Colloquium on Chinese Art History, Nat. Palace Mus. Taipei, 1991, Internat. Symposium on Art of Four Wangs, Shanghai, 1992, VIIeme Colloque Internat. de Sinologie, Chantilly, France, 1992, Symposium Painting at Close Qing Empire, Phoenix, 1992, Symposium on Ming & Qing Painting, Beijing, 1994, Symposium on Art of Zhao Meng-fu, Shanghai, 1995, Symposium on 20th Century Chinese Painting, Hong Kong Mus. Art, 1995, Symposium on Contemporary Chinese Painting, Biennale of Shanghai Art Mus., 1998; spl. cons. Chinese U., Hong Kong, 1971, Symposium on Painting and Calligraphy by Ming Loyalists, Early Ch'ing Period, 1975, Symposium on the Art of Liu Kuo-sung, Mus. of History, Beijing, 2002. Author (books and exhbn. catalogues): The Autumn Colors on the Ch'iao and Hua Mountains, A Painting by Chao Meng-fu, 1254-1322, 1965; author: Liu Kuo-sung: The Development of a Modern Chinese Artist, 1970, A Thousand Peaks and Myriad Ravines: Chinese Paintings in the Charles A Drenowatz Collection, 2 vols., 1974, Trends in Modern Chinese Painting, 1979; co-author: History of Modern Chinese Painting, Part 1: Late Qing, 1998, Part 2: Republican China, 2001, Part 3: Contemporary, 2003; editor: Artists and Patrons: Some Social and Economic Aspects of Chinese Painting, 1990; co-editor: Chinese Scholar's Studio: Artistic Life in Late Ming, Asia Soc., 1987; contbr. articles to profl. jours. Ford Found. Fgn. Area Tng. fellow, 1959-60; grantee Am. Coun. Learned Socs. and Social Sci. Rsch. Coun., 1963-64, NEH, 1975, 78, 91, Com. for Scholarly Communication with People's Republic of China NAS, 1979, Am. Coun. Learned Socs., 1980, Asian Cultural Coun., N.Y., 1981, Kans. U., summers 1966-80; Fulbright-Hayes faculty fellow, 1968-69 Mem. Coll. Art Assn. Am., Assn. for Asian Studies, Midwest Art History Soc., Internat. House of Japan, Min-chiu Soc. Hong Kong, Phi Tau Phi, Phi Beta Kappa (hon.), Phi Beta Delta. Home: 1108 Avalon Rd Lawrence KS 66044-2506 Office: Univ Kans Kress Found Dept Art History Lawrence KS 66045-0001 Personal E-mail: ctsli@earthlink.net. Business E-Mail: ctsli@ku.edu.

LI, DAQI, special education educator; b. Beijing, Feb. 15, 1955; s. Runan and Yiqing Li; m. Jiang Tan, Oct. 10, 1980; 1 child, Xu. MA, Beijing Fgn. Studies U., 1986—86; MEd, Tex. Tech U., Lubbock, 1997, EdD, 2000. Instr. Liaoning Normal U., Dalian, China, 1977—93, assoc. prof., 1993—94; asst. prof. SUNY, Coll., Oneonta, 2000—. Rsch. asst. Tex. Tech U., Lubbock, 1995—2000. Co-author: (books) Road to English World (1989-1991 Liaoning Normal U. Excellent Works Award, 1991); contbr. articles to profl. jours. Mem.: Am. Ednl. Rsch. Assn., The Coun. for Exceptional Children. Home: 27 Wayman Drive Otego NY 13825 Office: SUNY Ravine Pky Oneonta NY 13820 Office Phone: 607-436-2462. Personal E-mail: daqili@yahoo.com.

LI, DAVID WAN-CHENG, cell biologist; b. Heng Shan, Peoples Republic of China, Sept. 2, 1960; came to the U.S., 1986; s. Xi-Lin and Xin-Tao (Guo) L. BS, Hunan Normal U., 1982, MS, 1985; PhD, U. Wash., 1992. Adj. prof. biology Hunan Normal U., Chang Sha, People's Republic of China, 1995—; tchg. asst. U. Alta., Edmonton, Can., 1986; tchg. and rsch. asst. U. Wash., Seattle, 1986-92; rsch. scientist Columbia U., N.Y.C., 1992-95, asst. prof. ophthalmology, 1996-98; asst. prof. molecular biology UMDNJ-Sch. Medicine, Stratford, 1998—. Contbr. articles to profl. jours. Exec. pres. June 4th Found., Seattle, 1990-92, bd. dirs., 1989—. Mem. AAAS, Am. Soc. Cell Biology, Am. Soc. Biochemistry and Molecular Biology, Soc. Devel. Biology, Internat. Soc. Eye Rsch., N.Y. Acad. Sci., Assn. for Rsch. in Vision and Ophthalmology. Achievements include devel. of a set of biol. stds. for the hybrid yue carp and its parents; identification of pair of duplicated genes coding for two different isoelectric forms of insect pigment protein and cloning of these genes; discovery of a common cellular mechanism for stress induced non-congenital cataract formation in humans and animals. Office: U Medicine and Dentistry NJ Dept Molecular Biology 2 Med Ctr Dr Sci Ctr Rm 347 Stratford NJ 08084 E-mail: lidw@umdnj.edu.

LI, DAYUAN, physician, research scientist; s. Shijian and Huanzheng Li; m. Ling Liu, Oct. 1, 1989; children: Jimmy Shuo, Jenny Jia. MD, Bengbu Med. Coll., 1987; PhD, U. Uppsala, 2000. Cert. ECFMG, 2003. Rsch. asst. prof. U. Ark., Little Rock, 2000—, resident, 2004—. Asst. prof. Beijing Med. U., 1994—96. Recipient Young Investigator award, Am. Coll. of Cardiology, Fla., 1997, Astra-Merck Pharm. Co., 1998, Travel award, Merck Losartan, 1998; fellow, U. Fla., Gainesville, 1996—2000, Univ. of Fla. Med. Coll., Divsn. of Cardiology, 1999; grantee, Am. Fedn. Med. Rsch., 1999, AHA Nat. Ctr., 2001—04, AHA Heartland, 2001—03, Astra-Zenic Inc, 2002—04, Takeda Pharmatheutic Inc., 2003—04. Mem.: JCPT (corr.). Achievements include research in Clerified the role of new receptor LOX-1 for oxidized low-density lipoprotein in endothelial injury and atherosclerosis, and described the interaction of ox-LDL and angiotensin in endothelial injury. Office: U Ark Med Sci 4301 W Markham St Mailsot 532 Little Rock AR 72205 Office Phone: 501-686-6724. Office Fax: 501-686-5197. Personal E-mail: lidayuan@uams.edu.

LI, DE-QUAN, medical educator; s. Yao-Jun Li and Sheng-Mei Yu; m. Mei-Fang Jin, Apr. 28, 1976; 1 child, Yinchun. MD, PhD, Shanghai Second Med. U., China. Asst. prof. Baylor Coll. of Medicine, Houston, Tex., 2001—; instr. U. of Miami Sch. of Medicine, Miami, Fla., 1999—2001. Standing com. mem. Baylor Coll. of Medicine, Houston, 2001—. Contbr. articles to profl. jours. Recipient Fisrt award for Med. Rsch., Adminstrn. of Pub. Health in China, 1983, Third award for Med. Rsch., Adminstrn. of Pub. Health in China., 1986, Outstanding Internat. scholar, Nat. Honor Soc. for Internat. Scholars, 1994, Ad Hoc Reviewer Mem. of the NIH Study Sect., NIH, 2004; grantee R03 Rsch. grant, Nei, Nih, 2003—06. Mem.: Internat. Ocular Surface Soc., Tear Film & Ocular Surface Soc., Am. Soc. for Cell Biology, Assn. for Rsch. in Vision and Ophthalmology. Office: Baylor Coll Medicine 6565 Fannin St Houston TX 77030 Office Phone: 713-798-1123. Office Fax: 713-798-1457. Personal E-mail: dequanl@bcm.tmc.edu.

LI, FAN, pianist, music educator; s. Shou Zhen Li and Xue Fan Yang; m. Hong Jiang, June 18, 1995; 1 child, Lushi. MusB, Sichuan Conservatory Music, 1983; MusM, Shanghai Conservatory Music, 1988; artist diploma, Longy Sch. Music, 1992. Piano faculty Sichuan Conservatory Music, Chengdu, China, 1988—90, Manchester Music Sch., NH, 1993—96; piano instr. Fourth Presbyn. Ch., Boston, 1993—98; piano faculty Brookline Music Sch., Mass., 1996—. Bd. mem. New England Piano Tchr. Assn., Boston, 1998—2001. Performer: (CD) Chinese Piano Music, 2003; musician: (solo recitals) Beijing Concert Hall, Jordan Hall, Boston, Weill Recital Hall at Carnegie Hall, N.Y.C., (soloist with orchestra) Carnegie Hall, Lincoln Ctr., N.Y.C., Sanders Theater at Harvard U., Jordan Hall and Boston First Night, author music for mags. and newspapers. Home: 88 Longfellow Rd Newton MA 02462

LI, FUAN, marketing educator, researcher; b. Ning Yang, China, June 7, 1952; came to U.S., 1990; s. Tian You Li and Xiu Fang Ji; m. Bing Lan, Sept. 30, 1977; 1 child, Xiao Yi. BA in Philosophy, Shandong U., Jinan, China, 1982; MBA, Idaho State U., 1994; PhD in Marketing, Fla. Internat. U., 1999. Asst. prof. East China Normal U., Shanghai, 1985-90; vis. prof. St. Olaf Coll., Northfield, Minn., 1990-91; lectr. Fla. Internat. U., Miami, 1997-99; asst. prof. mktg. Mercyhurst Coll., Erie, Pa., 1999—2001; assoc. prof. mktg. William Paterson U., Wayne, NJ, 2002—. Author: Philosophical Logic and Philosophy of Logic, 1989; contbr. articles to profl. jours. Mem. Am. Mktg. Assn. (Doctoral Consortium fellow 1997), Acad. Mktg. Sci., Assn. Consumer Rsch., Soc. Consumer Psychology. Avocations: swimming, hiking, ping pong/table tennis, tai chi. Office: William Paterson U 300 Pompton Rd Wayne NJ 07470-0001 Home: 56 Kiwanis Drive Wayne NJ 07470 E-mail: lif@wpunj.edu.

LI, HANNA WU, music educator; b. Canton, China, Mar. 28, 1934; came to U.S., 1958, naturalized, 1972; d. Yat Chih and Wei Ying (Lo) Wu; m. Ching-Chung Li, June 10, 1961; children: William Wei-Lin, Vincent Wei-Tsin. BA in Piano, Nat. Taiwan Normal U., 1956; MMus in Piano, Northwestern U., 1961. Instr. piano dept. music Nat. Taiwan Normal U., Taipei, 1956—58; instr. piano, prep. sch. dept. music Carnegie-Mellon U., Pitts., 1969—84, dir. piano, prep. sch., 1984—, instr. piano dept. music, 1974—78, artist lectr. in piano, 1979—88, assoc. prof. music, 1988—2005, prof. music, 2005—. Soloist, accompanist chamber music, Taipei, 1954—58; judge Young Musician Audition, Wheeling, W.Va., 1979, 95; adjudicator internat. piano competition Young Keyboard Artist Assn., Ann Arbor, Mich., 1985; judge Chiang Wen Yeh Internat. Young Artist Piano Competition, Washington, 1996; lectr. in U.S. and abroad; piano pedagogy workshop lectr., Shanghai, 93, Zhanjiang, China, 99; mem. com. on future of piano pedagogy World Piano Pedagogy Conf., 1996—; piano pedagogy workshop lectr., Grand Rapids, Mich., 1999; adjudicator Chautauqua (N.Y.) Sch. Music, 1999—; piano pedagogy workshop lectr., Charleston, SC, 1999, 2001. Recipient Presdl. Scholar's Disting. Tchr. award White House, 1997; students have won numerous awards and scholarships. Mem. Am. Music Scholarship Assn. (chmn. ea. region piano contest 1975—), Pitts. Concert Soc. (bd. dirs.), Pi Kappa Lambda. Home: 2130 Garrick Dr Pittsburgh PA 15235-5033 Office: Carnegie-Mellon U Sch Music Pittsburgh PA 15213 Office Phone: 412-268-2376. Business E-Mail: hlzj@andrew.cmu.edu.

LI, HE, political science professor; s. Deren Li and Juhe Huang; m. Naifang Lu, Sept. 2, 1983; 1 child, Bowen. PhD, U. Tex., 1991. Prof. of polit. sci. Merrimack Coll., North Andover, Mass., 1993—. Contbr. articles to profl. jours.; author: From Revolution to Reform: A Comparative Study of China and Mexico, Sino-Latin American Economic Relations. Fulbright fellow, 2004. Mem.: Am. Polit. Sci. Assn. Fax: 978-837-5078. Office Phone: 978-837-5000 4297.

LI, HONG, soil scientist, researcher; b. Lingao, Hainan, China, Aug. 23, 1956; d. Yuchu Wang and Jiwen Fu; m. Tingxian Li, May 23, 1983; children: Annie, Sylvie. BS in Environ. Sci., Zhongshan U., Guangzhou, China, 1982; MS in Land Mgmt., U. Montpellier III, France, 1987; PhD in Soil Sci., Laval U., Quebec City, Can., 1997. Rsch. assoc. Tex. A&M U., Lubbock, 1998—2001; soil scientist N.C. State U., Raleigh, 2001—02, U. Fla., Lake Alfred, 2002—. Rsch. Excellence scholar, Laval U., 1994, Govt. of Que., Can., 1995—97. Mem.: Am. Soc. Agronomy (corr.), Soil Sci. Soc. Am. (corr.). Achievements include research in using GIS and remote sensing technology for optimizing soil water and fertilizer N use in potato, oat, barley, cotton, wheat, soybean and citrus productions; state-space multivariate modeling. Office: U Fla 700 Experiment Staion Rd Lake Alfred FL 33850 Home: 1639 Gaudarville Quebec G2G 2H7 Canada Office Phone: 863-956-4311. Office Fax: 863-956-4631. Business E-Mail: hongli@crec.ifas.ufl.edu.

LI, HONG-JYH, process engineer, researcher; arrived in U.S., 1998; s. Jwao-Shun Li and Shu-Juan Tan; m. Hong-Jyh Li, July 31, 1999; 1 child, John. PhD, U. Tex., 2002; BS in Physics, Nat. Tsinghua U., Taiwan, 1990; MS in physics, Nat. Sun Yat-sen U., Taiwan, 1995. Sr. R&D engr. Philips, Kaohsiung, Taiwan, 1995—98; process engr. Internat. SEMATECH, Austin, Tex., 2002—03; project engr. Infineon Tech., Austin, 2003—. Mem.: IEEE, Material Rsch. Soc. Achievements include patents for surface mounted power chip resistor-process and device manufacturing method; 14 U.S. patents pending. Home: 2201 Desco Dr Austin TX 78748 Office: International SEMATECH 2706 Montopolis Dr Austin TX 78741 Office Phone: 512-356-7556. E-mail: hongjyh@yahoo.com.

LI, HONGZHI, foundation administrator, writer; b. Jilin, China, May 13, 1951; came to U.S., 1996, permanent resident, 1998. m. Li Rui, 1981; 1 child, Li Meige. Qi-gong Master. Founder Falun Dafa, pres. Falun Dafa Inst., Beijing, 1992—; tchr. Falun Gong exercises, 1992-94. Lectr. over 450 on Falun Dafa, China, 1992-94, numerous lectures worldwide, 1995—. Author: China Falun Gong, 1993, Zhuan Falun (Best Selling book 1996, translated in over 20 langs.), 1994, Zhuan Falun II, 1995, Falun Dafa Exposition, 1996, Falun Buddha Law (Essentials for Further Advancement), 1997, Falun Buddha Law (Lecture in U.S.), 1997, Falun Dafa Explication, 1997, The Great Perfection Way of Falun Buddha Law, 1997, Falun Buddha Law (Lecture in Sydney), 1997, Falun Buddha Law (Lecture in European Falun Dafa Conference), 1999, Falun Buddha Law (Lecture in North America), 1999, Falun Buddha Law (Lecture in Changchun), 1999, Falun Buddha Law (Lecture in Singapore), 1999, Falun Buddha Law (Lecture in Switzerland), 1999, Hong Yin, 1999, Falun Buddha Law (Lecture in New Zealand), 2000, Falun Buddha Law (Lecture in Canada), 2000, Falun Buddha Law (Lecture in West America), 2000, Falun Budda Law (lecture in East America), 2000; videos include Falun Dafa 9 Day Lectures, Jinan, 1994, Falun Gong (5 sets) exercise instrn. tape, 1994; music cassette Falun Xuilian Dafa Exercise, 1994, others. Nominated Nobel Peace Prize, 2000, 2001; recipient Award for Advanced Boundary Sci, The Special Gold award, named Qi-gong Master most acclaimed by the masses, Oriental Health Expo., Beijing, 1993, Honor Cert. found. under Ministry of Pub. Security of China, 1993, Award Outstanding Svc., Ill., 1999, over 40 proclamations, resolutions, citations honor Master Li Hongzhi/Falun Dafa including Congl. Recognition of Achievement N.J., N.Y., Pa., Mass., Vt., others, 1999-2001, Internat. Religious Freedom award, Freedom House, U.S., 2001; Hon. Citizen and Goodwill amb., Houston, 1996, Hon. Citizen Atlanta, 1999, Hon. Georgia Citizen, Ga., 2000, Li Hongzhi Day/week proclaimed in over 20 cities, 1996-2001, Falun Dafa or Truth, Compassion, Forbearance day/week/month proclaimed in over 500 cities in U.S., Can., New Zealand, Australia, 1999-2001; honored Courage and Perserverance, N.Y.C., 2000. Avocation: cultivation. Mailing: 136-08 59th Ave Flushing NY 11355-5245

LI, JAMES CHEN MIN, materials science educator; b. Nanking, China, Apr. 12, 1925; came to U.S., 1949; s. Vei Shao and In Shey (Mai) L.; m. Lily Y.C. Wang, Aug. 5, 1950; children: Conan, May, Edward. BS, Nat. Ctrl. U., China, 1947; MS, U. Wash., 1951, PhD, 1953. Rsch. assoc. U. Calif., Berkeley, 1953-55; supr. Mfg. Chemists Assn. project Carnegie Inst. Tech., Pitts., 1955-56; phys. chemist Westinghouse Elec. Co., Pitts., 1956-57; sr. scientist U.S. Steel Corp., Monroeville, Pa., 1957-69; mgr. strength physics Allied Chem. Co., Morristown, N.J., 1969-71; A.A. Hopeman prof. engring. U. Rochester (N.Y.), 1971—. Vis. prof. Columbia U., N.Y.C., 1964-65, adj. prof., 1965-71; adj. prof. Stevens Inst. Tech., Newark, 1971-72; vis. prof. Ruhr U., Bochum, Fed. Republic Germany, 1978-79. Author 1 book; editor 3 books; contbr. 350 articles to profl. jours.; holder 5 patents in 6 countries. Recipient Alexander Von Humboldt award, 1978, Acta Metallurgica Gold medal, 1990, Grad. Teaching award U. Rochester, 1993. Fellow TMS/AIME (Robert F. Mehl medal and lectr. 1978, Champion H. Mathewson Gold medal 1972, Structural Materials Divsn. luncheon spkr. 1993, chmn. phys. mutall. com. 1992-95), ASM Internat. (chmn. materials sci. divsn. 1982-84), Am. Phys. Soc.; mem. ASME, Materials Rsch. Soc., Chinese Soc. Materials Sci. (Lu Tse-Hon medal 1988). Office: U Rochester Dept Mech Engring PO Box 270132 Rochester NY 14627-0133 Office Phone: 585-275-4038. E-mail: li@me.rochester.edu.

LI, JING (TIFFANY), engineering educator; b. Hangzhou, Zhejiang Province, China, 1975; PhD in Elec. Engring., Tex. A&M U., College Station, TX USA, 1999—2002, ME. in Elec. Engring., 1998—99; BS in Computer sci., Peking U., Beijing, China, 1993—97. Certified OS/2 Engineer, IBM Corp., 1996. Asst. prof. Lehigh U., Elec. and Computer Engring. Dept., Bethlehem, Pa., 2003—; rsch. asst. Tex. A&M U., College Station, Tex., 1998—2002; rsch. intern TycoCommunications Lab., Eatontown, NJ, 2001—01, Seagate Rsch. Lab, Pittsburgh, NJ, 2000—00. Assoc. editor for ieee communicatione letters IEEE, 2004—; female faculty retension commitee Lehigh U., 2003—; libr. student adv. com. Tex. A&M U., 2001—02, grad. student coun. officer, 1999—2002; symposia co-chair IEEE Global Comm. Conf. '05, Wireless-Com '05; student paper chair IEEE Sarnoff Symposium '05; poster chair and award com. Wireless and Optical Comm. Conf. '05; tech. com. IASTED Signal Processing Soc., 2004—; tech. program com. IEEE Internat. Conf. on Comm. '05, 2004—05, IEEE Global Comm. Conf. '04, 2003—04; mem. Tchg., Learning and Tech. Roundtable, Lehigh Chpt., 2003—. Author: (book chapter) CRC Handbook of Coding and Signal Proceesing for Recording, Coding, Cryptography and Combinatorics. Recipient Ethel Ashworth-Tsutsui Meml. Award for Rsch., Tex. A&M U., 2001, Third Pl. Prize in Chinese Math. Olympiad, 1993, First Pl. Prize in China Nat. Math. Competition, Chinese Dept. of Edn., 1992, First Pl. Prize in China Nat. Physics Competition, 1992, Third Pl. Prize in 4th Hongzhou Met. Qiushi Cup Physics Competition, Zhejing Province Dept. of Edn., Third Pl. Prize in 4th Hongzhou Met. Qiushi Cup Mathmatics Competition, 1992, First Pl. Prize in Ea. China Six-Province-and-One-Autonomous-City Joint Mathmatics Competition, 1990, Second Pl. Prize China Nat. Math. Competition for Mid. Sch. Students, Chininese Dept. of Edn., 1989, Who's Who Among Students in Am. Universities and Colleges, Tex. A&M U., 2002, Outstanding Honors Sci. Student, Peking U., 1996; fellow SUF Elec. Engring. Fellowship, Tex. A&M U., 2002; grantee Faculty Rsch. Grant, Lehigh U., 2003, Faculty Travel Grant, 2003, 2004, Rsch. grant, NSF, 1994-1996, Army Rsch. Lab., 1994-1995, Pa. Dept. of Cmty. and Econ. Devel., 2003, 2004, 2005, Student Travel Grant, IEEE Internat. Symposium on Info. Theory, 2001, IEEE Internat. Conf. on Comm., 2001; scholar Academic Excellence Scholarship, Peking U., 1994-1995, J. W. Van Dyke Meml. Scholarship for Academic Excellence, Tex. A&M U., TxTEC Scholarship, Tex. Telecom. Engring. Concortium, 2000, Striving Schlolarship, Chinese Acad. of Sci., 1993-1996, Joint-Communications Scholarship, Peking U., 1993-1994, Zhang Pen-Xi Meml. Scholarship, Dept. of Edn., Zhejiang Province, China, 1993. Mem.: Internat. Assn. of Sci. and Tech. for Devel. (tech. com. for signal processing soc. 2004—), SPIE, IEEE (tech. com. for comm. soc. 2004), Pinnacle Nat. Honor Soc. for Grad. and Non-conventional Students, Phi Beta Delta, Xigma Xi. Achievements include patents for Electrodeless Discharge Sodium Lamp, China Patent No. ZL962448184, 1996. Office: Lehigh University 19 Memorial Dr W Bethlehem PA 18015 Office Phone: 610-758-3305. E-mail: tiffanyjingli@ieee.org.

LI, JINLIANG, finance educator; arrived in US, 1997; BS, Tsinghua U.; PhD, Syracuse U., 2001. Chartered fin. analyst CFA Inst. Lectr. Syracuse (N.Y.) U., 2000—01; asst. prof. of fin. Northeastern U., Boston, 2001—. Contbr. articles to fin. jours. (Syracuse U. Doctoral prize, 2002). Recipient Grad. scholarship, Syracuse U., 1997—2001. Mem.: Fin. Mgmt. Assn., Am. Fin. Assn. Avocations: hiking, tennis. Office Phone: 617-821-8547.

LI, JOHN K.H., pathologist, department chairman; b. Nanking, China, Nov. 19, 1932; arrived in U.S., 1949; s. Ti-Tsun and Nora Tsuei (Ju) Li; m. Lorraine L. Yuan, June 29, 1959; children: Dina Wan, Roger M.K. AB, Harvard U., 1954, MD, 1958. Diplomate in anat. pathology and clin. pathology Am. Bd. Pathology. Dir. pathology and labs. Morrisania City Hosp., N.Y.C., 1966—76, North Ctrl. Bronx Hosp., N.Y.C., 1976—92; chmn. dept. pathology L.I. Coll. Hosp., Bklyn., 1992—; assoc. clin. prof. pathology SUNY, Bklyn., 1993—. Pres. Pathologists' Club of N.Y., N.Y.C., 1989, N.Y.C., 90; co-founding physician Chinatown Health Clinic, N.Y.C., 1971—. Contbr. articles to profl. jours. Pres. Chinese Am. Med. Soc., N.Y.C., 1992, 1993. Recipient Cmty. Svc. award, Chinese Am. Med. Soc., 1998, Ann. Recognition award, Othmer Cancer Ctr., 2001. Fellow: Am. Soc. Clin. Pathology, N.Y. Acad. Medicine, Coll. Am. Pathologists. Democrat. Avocations: reading, writing, sailing. Office: LI Coll Hosp 339 Hicks St Brooklyn NY 11201 Office Phone: 718-780-1005. E-mail: johnli@chpnet.org.

LI, JUN, materials scientist, researcher; arrived in U.S., 1988; m. Yi-fen Li, Dec. 11, 1966; children: Owen, Leon. BS, Wuhan U., China, 1987; MS, Princeton U., 1991, PhD, 1994. Post doctoral rsch. assoc. Cornell U., Ithaca, NY, 1994—97; applications scientist Molecular Imaging, Phoenix, 1997—98; rsch. fellow Inst. Materials Rsch. and Engring., Singapore, 1998—2000; sr. rsch. scientist NASA Ames Rsch. Ctr., Moffett Field, Calif., 2000—. Co-founder Integrated Nanosys. Inc., Sunnyvale, Calif., 2000—03; cons. Nanoconduction Inc., Santa Clara, Calif., 2003—; group leader NASA Ames Ctr. for Nanotechnology, Moffett Field. Mem. editl. bd. Mechanics and Chemistry of Biosys., 2004—; contbr. chapters to books. Mem.: Materials Rsch. Soc., Electrochem. Soc., Am. Vacuum Soc. Achievements include invention of bottom-up approach for carbon nanotube interconnects in IC chip; patents for catalyst patterning for nanowire devices; patents pending for nanowire devices and methods of fabrication; signal amplifying targeted reporters for biological and chemical sensor applications; nanoelectrode array for bio- and chemical sensing; nanoengineered carbon nanotube array as thermal interface materials; carbon nanotube arrays for deep brain stimulation and recording. Office: NASA Ames Rsch Ctr MS 229-1 Moffett Field CA 94035 Office Fax: 650-604-5244. E-mail: jli@mail.arc.nasa.gov.

LI, KAI, chemist, research scientist; b. Jiangyin, Jiangsu, China, Aug. 16, 1962; arrived in U.S., 1997; s. Fuxin Li and Xiubao Zhou; m. Linda Yanping Qin, Mar. 4, 1986; children: Tony Zhen, Daniel Lin, Vincent. MSc, Soochow U., Suzhou, China, 1985, U. BC, Vancouver, Can., 1992, Ph.D., 1996. Post-doctoral fellow U. Hawaii at Manoa, Honolulu, 1997—99, U. Wis., Milw., 1999—2000. Sr. rsch. scientist Pharm. Products Devel., Inc, Middleton, Wis., 2000—. Mem.: Am. Chem. Soc. Home: 7625 Sawmill Road Madison WI 53717 Office Phone: 608-827-9400. Home Fax: 608-827-2982; Office Fax: 608-827-8807. Personal E-mail: likai97@gmail.com.

LI, KA-SHING, international entrepreneur; b. Fucheng, Chao'an County, Guangdong Province, 1928; m. Chong Yuet-ming; 2 children. LLD (hon.), U. Hong Kong, 1986, U. Calgary, Can., 1989; D Degree (hon.), Beijing U., 1992; D Social Sci. (hon.), Hong Kong U. Sci. and Tech., 1995; LLD (hon.), Chinese U. of Hong Kong, 1997; D Social Sci (hon.), City U. Hong Kong, 1998; LLD (hon.), Cambridge U., 1999; D Social Sci. (hon.), Open U. Hong Kong, 1999. Salesman toy mfg. co., 1943-49; founder Cheung Kong Plastics Factory, 1950; chmn. Cheung Kong (Holdings) Ltd., Hong Kong, 1971—; founder Li Ka Shing Found. Ltd., 1980; chmn. Hutchison Whampoa Ltd., Hong Kong, 1981—; founder Shantou Univ., 1981; acquired Hong Kong Elec. Holdings, Ltd., 1985; owner, shareholder numerous cos. Mem. drafting com. Basic Law Hong Kong Spl. Adminstrv. Region, 1985—90, mem. prep. com., 1995—97; advisor Hong Kong Affairs, 1992—97. Justice of the Peace, 1981. Decorated knight comdr. Order Brit. Empire, comdr. Order of Crown, Leopold Order (Belgium), Légion d'honneur, France, grand officer Order of Vasco Nuñez de Balboa (Panama); named hon. Citizen, Cities of Shantou, Guangzhou, Shenzhen, Nanhai, Foshan, Zhuhai, Chaozhou, Beijing, Winnipeg, Canada; recipient Entrepreneur of Millennium award, Internat. Disting. Entrepreneur award, Grand Bauhinia Medal of the Hong Kong SAR, 2001. Office: Cheung Kong (Holdings) Ltd 70/F 2 Queen's Rd Ctrl Hong Kong China

LI, NORMAN N., chemicals executive; b. Shanghai, Jan. 14, 1933; naturalized, US, 1969; s. Lieh-wen and Amy H. Li; m. Jane C. Li, Aug. 17, 1963; children: Rebecca H., David H. BSChemE, Nat. Taiwan U., Taipei, 1955; MS, Wayne State U., 1957; PhD, Stevens Inst. Tech., 1963. Sr. scientist Exxon Rsch. and Engring. Co., Linden, NJ, 1963-81; dir. separation sci. and tech. UOP, Des Plaines, Ill., 1981-88; dir. engineered products and process tech. Allied-Signal Inc., Des Plaines, Ill., 1988-92, dir. rsch. and tech., 1993-95; pres., CEO NL Chem. Technology, Inc., 1995—. Mem. NRC, 1985-89; lectr. AIChE, 1975-86. Editor 20 books on separation sci. and tech.; contbr. articles to profl. jours.; patentee in field. Fellow: AIChE (dir. divsn. food, pharms. and bioengring. 1988—91, bd. dirs. 1992—94, Alpha Chi Sigma rsch. award 1988, Ernest Thiele award 1995, Chem. Engring. Practice award 2000, Lifetime Achievement award 2001, Gerhold award in separation tech. 2002); mem.: Acad. Sinica, Chinese Acad. Scis., N.Am. Membrane Soc. (pres. 1991—93, Perkin medalist 2000), Am. Chem. Soc. (Separation Sci. and Tech. award 1988), NAE. Home: 620 N Rolling Ln Arlington Heights IL 60004-5820 Office Phone: 847-824-2888. Personal E-mail: NLChem@aol.com.

LI, PEARL NEI-CHIEN CHU, information technology executive, library director, consultant; b. Jiangsu, China, June 17, 1946; came to U.S., 1968; d. Ping-Yung and Yao-Hwa (Li) Chu; m. Terry Teng-Fang Li, Sept. 20, 1969; children: Ina Ying, Ping Li. BA, Nat. Taiwan U., Taipei, 1968; MA, W.Va. U., 1971; cert. advanced study in info. studies, Drexel U., 1983. Cert. sr. libr., N.J. Instr. Nat. Tchr.'s Coll., Chang-Hua, Taiwan, 1977-78; reference libr. Camden County Libr., Voorhees, NJ, 1981-82; libr. Kulzer and Dipadova, P.A., Haddonfield, NJ, 1982-87; libr. dir. Am. Law Inst., Phila., 1987-92; gen. mgr., info. specialist Unitek Internat. Corp. (Am.), Mt. Laurel, NJ, 1992-96; owner Universal Tech. Inc., Mt. Laurel, 1997—. Tchr. South Jersey Chinese Sch., Cherry Hill, N.J., 1978-82. Editor: CLE Around the Country (annually), 1988-92; contbr. articles to profl. jours. Bus. mgr. Chinese Cmty. Ctr., Voorhees, 1981; mem. N.J. Dept. Commerce and Econ. Devel. for Small and Women and Minority Businesses, City of Phila. Minority/Women and Disadvantaged Bus. Enterprise, Md./D.C. Minority Supplier Devel. Coun., N.Y./N.J. Minority Purchasing Coun., N.Y./N.J. Port Authority Minority Bus. Enterprise. Home: 1132 Sea Gull Ln Cherry Hill NJ 08003-3113 Office: Universal Technology Inc 125 Gaither Dr Ste E Mount Laurel NJ 08054-1706 Fax: 856-235-0590. E-mail: ask@uti8.com.

LI, PETER WAI-KWONG, mathematics professor; b. Hong Kong, Apr. 18, 1952; came to U.S., 1971; s. Chun Tat and Lai Mui (Sum) L.; m. Glenna Marie Seaver, Oct. 30, 1982; children: Tiana, Natasha, Talia. BA, Calif. State U., 1974; MA, U. Calif., Berkeley, 1977, PhD, 1979. Rsch. mem. Inst. for Advanced Study, Princeton, N.J., 1979-80; asst. prof. Stanford (Calif.) U., 1980-83; assoc. prof. Purdue U., West Lafayette, Ind., 1983-85; prof. U. Utah, Salt Lake City, 1985-89, U. Ariz., Tucson, 1989-91, U. Calif., Irvine, 1991—, chmn. math. dept., 1993—96, 1999—2001, Chancellor's prof., 2003—. Editor Rocky Mountain Jour. Math., 1989-91, Procs. of Am. Math. Soc., 1991—; editor-in-chief Comm. in Analysis and Geometry, 1992-2002, editor, 2002—. Named Highly Cited Rschr., ISI, 2003—; NSF grantee, 1980—; Sloan fellow, 1982-83, Guggenheim fellow, 1989-90. Mem. Am. Math. Soc., Phi Beta Kappa. Avocations: swimming, skiing, cooking, wine-tasting. Office: U Calif Irvine Dept Math Irvine CA 92697-3875 Office Phone: 949-824-7049.

LI, QI, research scientist, consultant; b. Fuzhou, Fujian, China, Dec. 26, 1958; arrived in US, 1988; s. Wen Zhang and Li Zhen (Gao) Li; m. Xiumin Xu Li, Mar. 20, 1988; children: Mei, Jeffrey. BS in Chemistry, Hua Chiao U., Chuanchow, China, 1983; PhD in Chemistry, U. Miami, 1993, MS in Computer Info. Sys., 2001. Rsch. asst. Suzhou (China) Rlwy. Tchrs. Coll., China, 1985—86; with China Nat. Chem. Import & Export Corp., Fuzhou, China, 1986—88; postdoctoral U. Miami, Fla., 1994—99; rsch. scientist IVAX Pharm. Corp., Miami, 2000—. Adj. tchg. instr. Fla. Internat. U., Miami, 1997—98; cons. New Span Opto-Tech., Inc., Miami, 2002—; interpreter Berlitz Global Net, Washington, 2002—. Contbr. articles to profl. jours. Recipient Travel award, 1997; fellow, NIH, 1994—96. Mem.: Am. Assn. Pharm. Scientist, US Badminton Assn. Achievements include patents pending in field. Avocation: badminton. Office: IVAX Pharm Corp 50 NW 176th St Miami FL 33169

LI, QIN, news correspondent, reporter, television director, television producer; came to U.S., 1999:; d. Jinkui and Hong Li. BA in Law, Chinese Youth Coll. Polit. Sc., Beijing, 1992; MS in Econs., Chinese Acad. Social Sci., Beijing, 1998; MS in Journalism, Columbia U., 2000. Cert. in pub. affairs. Reporter People's Daily, Beijing, 1992-94, editor, reporter Shanghai, 1994-99; TV anchor, prodr., news reporter Sino TV, Inc., N.Y.C., 2001—. Dep. editor-in-chief New Asia Culture Found. and Pub. House, Hong Kong, 1999—. Prodr.: (TV news documentary) Blue Sky Station: 8th Avenue-New York's 3d Chinatown, 2000 (Emmy award NATAS, 2000); dir., prodr. (TV documentary) A Hole in Chinatown's Heart-Rebuild Chinatown after 9/11, 2003; contbg. author: First-Hand Experience with China's Hope Project in One Hundred Counties, 1991; co-author: Japan: Another Miracle in the 21st

Century?, 1993; contbr. feature stories to internat. publs. Mem. selection com. Internat. Fanzhian Scholarship, Hong Kong, 1998-2001 Recipient Best News award Chinese Nat. Journalists Assn. and Chinese Disability Assn., 1994, Best News award Chinese People's Polit. Consultative Conf., 1993; featured in Selected Works of Outstanding Chinese Editors and Reporters, 1996. Mem. Soc. Profl. Journalists. Office Phone: 212-625-2877. Office Fax: 212-965-8917. E-mail: ql20@columbia.edu.

LI, QIN-BAO, biologist, health facility administrator; b. Fuzhou, jiangxi, China, Jan. 25, 1956; s. Meishou Li and Fuxiang Yang; m. Shan Wu, May 29, 1958; 1 child, Shuang. MS, Lanzhou (China) U., 1984. Asst. prof. Lanzhou U., 1984-91; sr. biol. scientist U. Fla., Gainesville, 1991-99, 1999—. Sr. lab. mgr. U. Fla., Gainesville, 1999—. Contbr. articles to profl. jours. Recipient Honor of Excellence award, Lanzhou U., 1984, 1st Place Advanced award of Sci. and Tech., Gansu Ministry of Edn., 1990, award for excellent paper, Chinese Soc. Plant Physiology, 1990. Home: 5140 NW 30 Ln Gainesville FL 32606 Fax: 352-392-5653. E-mail: qbl@ufl.edu.

LI, QINGDI QUENTIN, physician, research scientist, medical educator; b. Guilin, Guangxi, China, Apr. 18, 1956; m. Li Ding; 1 child, Julie. MA, MD, Guangxi Med. U., 1987; MS, PhD, U. Md., 2000. Microbiologist, immunologist Guangxi Med. U., Nanning, China, 1983—87; dermatologist Sun Yat-sen Univ. Sch. Medicine, Guangzhou, China, 1987—91; postdoctoral fellow Nat. Cancer Inst., Bethesda, Md., 1996—98; rsch. assoc. Balt. VA Med. Ctr., Baltimore, Md., 1998—2000; asst. prof. W. Va. Univ. Health Sci. Ctr., Morgantown, W.Va., 2000—. Rsch. coord. W.Va. U. MBR Cancer Ctr., Morgantown, 2000—; vis. prof. Wuhan (China) U., 2002—, Guangxi Med. U., Nanning, China, 2002—, S.E. U., Nanjing, China, 2003—, Chinese Acad. Mil. Med. Sci., Beijing, 2003—, Tongji Med. Coll., Ctrl. China Univ. Sci. and Tech., Wuhan, 2004—. Recipient Intramural Rsch. Award, Nat. Cancer Inst., 1996-1998, Nat. Svc. Award, NIH, 1998-2000. Mem.: Chinese Soc. Microbiol., Am. Soc. Microbiology, NY Acad. Sci., Am. Assn. Advanced Sci., Am. Assn. Cancer Rsch., Chinese Med. Assn. Home: 216 Watkins Pond Blvd Rockville MD 20850 Office: W Va Univ Health Sci Ctr MBR Cancer Ctr PO Box 9300 Morgantown WV 26506-9300 Office Phone: 304-293-6870. Business E-Mail: qli@hsc.wvu.edu.

LI, RAO, mathematician, computer scientist; b. Fushun, Liaoning, China, May 3, 1965; arrived in U.S., 1993; s. Jingyuan Li and Liangzhi Zhu; m. Yan Wu, Apr. 27, 1966; 1 child, Dorothy. BS, Huaibei Tchr. Coll., 1985; MS, Harbin Inst. Tech., 1988; MA, U. Pitts., 1994; MS in Computer Sci., PhD in Math., U. Memphis, 1999. Asst. prof. Fushun Petroleum Inst., China, 1988—91, lectr., 1991—92; asst. prof. Ga. Southwestern State U., Americus, 1999—2001, U. S.C., Aiken, 2001—. Contbr. articles to profl. jours. Mem.: Assn. for Computing Machinery, Am. Math. Soc. Home: 775 Locks Way Martinez GA 30907 Office: University of South Carolina at Aiken 471 University Parkway Aiken SC 29801

LI, RICHARD T., retired library director, secondary school educator; b. Quidong, Hunan Province, China, Aug. 19, 1929; naturalized, U.S., 1977; s. Town and Pan-Chin Li; m. Felisa T. Tan, Oct. 25, 1964; children: Ray, Joy. BA in English, Tamkang Coll. Arts and Sci., Taipei, Taiwan, 1965; MA in English, S.E. Mo. Coll., 1970; MLS, Kans. State Tchrs. Coll. Emporia, 1971; EdD, U. Kans., 1978. Tchg. cert. Kans. Engring. officer, army capt. Chinese Army, Taiwan, 1954—59; tchr. KW Tech Sch., Taichung, Taiwan, 1959—61, Keelung 5th Mid. Sch., Keelung, Taiwan, 1965—67; tchr., libr. Eastern Heights H.S., Agra, Kans., 1973—74; head libr. media specialist Atchison (Kans.) H.S., 1974—78; asst. prof. Southwestern Okla. State U., Weatherford, 1978—80; Title III project officer Cameron U., Lawton, Okla., 1980—81; asst. dir. learning resources ctr. Tarrant County Jr. Coll., Fort Worth, 1982—97; ret., 1997. Author: Education and Career: An Immigrant's Journey in the Promised Land with Survival Tips, 1999, Where Can I Find It? A Sources Handbook for New Immigrants, 2000, My God, It Missed Me! A Young Soldier's Accounts in the War Torn China 1940-50s, 2002, The Golden Lotus, 2004, Haipin, the student's wife, a common immigrant, a hardworking citizen, 2005. Home: 4554 Rose Tree Ct Fort Worth TX 76137 Personal E-mail: w007745@airmail.net.

LI, SHAOFAN, engineering educator; b. Wuhan, Hubei, China, May 3, 1958; s. Xingjiao Li and Yunzhen Zhang; m. Yan Zhang, Aug. 15, 2003. BS, East China U. Sci. and Tech., Shanghai, 1982; MS, Huazhong U. Sci. and Tech., Wuhan, China, 1989, U. Fla., 1993; PhD, Northwestern U., 1997. Postdoctoral fellow Northwestern U., Evanston, Ill., 1997—2000; asst. prof. U. Calif., Berkeley, 2000—04. Asst. engr. Wuhan Material Protection Inst., 1982—86. Recipient Atanasoff Best Paper award, NASA, 1999, NSF Career award, 2003; Walter P. Murphy Grad. fellow, Northwestern U., 1994, Graham-Cabell fellow, 1996. Mem.: U.S. Computational Mechanics Assn., Sigma Gamma Tau. Achievements include research in computational mechanics and micromechanics. Office: U Calif-Berkeley Dept Civil and Environ Engring 783 Davis Hall Berkeley CA 94720 Office Phone: 510-642-5362. Office Fax: 510-643-8928.

LI, SHUGUANG, mathematics professor, researcher; b. Huhhot, Inner Mongolia, China; m. Meng Zhang; children: Juanchen, Junhao. MS, Sichuan Univeristy, 1985—88; PhD, Univeristy of Ga., Athens, 1992—98. Asst. prof. U. Hawaii, Hilo, 1998—2003, assoc. prof., 2003—. Mem.: Am. Math. Soc. Office: Univ Hawaii at Hilo 200 W Kawili St Hilo HI 96720-4091 Business E-Mail: shuguang@hawaii.edu.

LI, TIEN-SHUN, obstetrician, gynecologist, educator; b. Kaohsiung, Taiwan, Nov. 13, 1932; came to U.S., 1968; MD, Nat. Taiwan U., 1960. Diplomate Am. Bd. Ob-gyn. From intern to resident in ob-gyn. Nat. Taiwan U. Hosp., Taipei, 1961-64; resident in ob-gyn. St. Barnabas Med. Ctr., Livingston, N.J., 1971-73; attending staff Meadowlands Hosp. Med. Ctr., Secaucus, N.J., 1985—; clin. asst. prof. U. Medicine and Dentistry N.J., 1978—; pvt. practice Ft. Lee, N.J., 1978—. Fellow ACOG. Office: 2231 Lemoine Ave Fort Lee NJ 07024-6115 Office Phone: 201-944-1008.

LI, TINGYE, electrical engineer; b. Nanjing, China, July 7, 1931; arrived in U.S., 1953, naturalized, 1963; s. Chao and Lily Wei-peng (Sie) L.; m. Edith Hsiu-hwei Wu, June 19, 1956; children: Deborah Chunroh, Kathryn Dairoh. BSEE, U. Witwatersrand, South Africa, 1953; MS, Northwestern U., Evanston, Ill., 1955, PhD, 1958; DEng (hon.), Nat. Chiao Tung U., Hsinchu, Taiwan, 1991. Mem. tech. staff AT&T Bell Labs., Holmdel, N.J., 1957-67; dept. head repeater techniques research dept. Bell Labs., 1967-76, lightwave media research dept., 1976-84, lightwave systems research dept., 1984-96; dept. head lightwave networks rsch. dept. AT&T Labs.-Rsch., Holmdel, N.J., 1996, divsn. mgr. Middletown, N.J., 1997-98, ret., 1998; ind. cons. Boulder, Colo., 1999—. Hon. prof. Tsinghua U., Shanghai Jiao Tong U., Beijing U. Posts and Telecomms., U. Electronic Sci. and Tech. of China, Qufu Normal U., No. Jiao Tong U., Tianjin U., Nankai U., Fudan U., Nat. Chiao Tung U., Nat. U. Taiwan. Assoc. editor Optics Letters, 1977-78, topical editor, 1989-91; assoc. editor Jour. of Lightwave Tech., 1983-86; editor book series: Optical Fiber Telecommunications IV, Optical Fiber Communications, OSA Trends in Optics and Photonics Series; mem. editl. bd. Procs. IEEE, 1974-83, Microwave and Optical Tech. Letters, 1987-90, Internat. Jour. High Speed Electronics, 1990-95; contbr. articles on microwave antennas and propagation, lasers, coherent optics, optical comms., optical-fiber transmission, systems and networks to sci. jours., chpts. in books; patentee in field. Recipient Alumni Merit award Northwestern U., 1981, Sci. and Tech. medal AT&T, 1997. Fellow IEEE (W.R.G. Baker prize 1975, David Sarnoff award 1979, Photonics award 2004), AAAS, Internat. Engring. Consortium, Photonics Soc. Chinese-Ams. (Achievement award 1998), Optical Soc. Am. (chmn. optical comms. tech. group 1979-80, bd. dirs. 1985-87, chmn. internat. activities com. 1988-90, chmn. photonics divsn. 1991-92, v.p. 1993, pres.-elect 1994, pres. 1995, John Tyndall award 1995, Frederic Ives medal/Quinn Endowment 1997); mem. NAE, Chinese Inst. Engrs. U.S.A. (bd. dirs. 1974-78, Achievement award 1978), Academia Sinica (Taiwan), Chinese Acad. Engring., Chinese Am. Acad. and Profl. Assn. (bd. dirs. 1985-89, Achievement award 1983), Electromagnetics Acad., Sigma Xi, Eta Kappa Nu, Phi Tau Phi (pres. chpt. 1991-93).

LI, TONGCHUAN, pharmacologist, researcher; b. Yongtai, Fujian, China, Oct. 11, 1955; arrived in U.S., 1985; s. Zongyu Li and Suying Lin; m. Xingxian Yan, July 29, 1955; children: Bing, Scion, Louisa, Mark. MD, Fujian Med. U., Fujian, 1982; PhD, U. Minn., 1990. Instr. Fujian Med. U., Fuzhou, China, 1982—85; sr. scientist CytoMed, Cambridge, Mass., 1993—94; project mgr. Cubist Pharms., Inc., Lexington, Mass., 1995—. Guest prof. Fujian Med. U., Fuzhou, 2000. Recipient Bacaner Rsch. award, 1990. Mem.: AAAS, N.Y. Acad.Scis., Am. Soc. Pharmacology and Exptl. Therapeutics, Am. Assn. Fujian Med. U. Alumni (pres. 2002). Achievements include patents for epibatidine and derivatives thereof as cholinergic receptor agonists and antagonists; epibatidine and derivatives thereof as nicotine cholinergic receptor agonists. Home: 4 Doeskin Dr Framingham MA 01701-5016 Office: Cubist Pharms Inc 65 Hayden Ave Lexington MA 02421 Office Phone: 781-860-8366. Business E-Mail: tcli@cubist.com.

LI, TZE-CHUNG, lawyer, educator; b. Shanghai, China, Feb. 17, 1927; came to U.S., 1956; s. Ken-hsiang Li and Yun-hsien (Chang) Li; m. Dorothy In-lan Wang, Oct. 21, 1961; children— Lily, Rose LL.B., Soochow U., Shanghai, 1948; Diploma, Nat. Chengchi U., Nanking, 1949, China Research Inst. of Land Econs., Taipei, 1952; M.C.L., So. Meth. U., Dallas, 1956; LL.M., Harvard U., Cambridge, 1958; MS, Columbia U., N.Y.C., 1965; PhD, New Sch. for Social Research, N.Y.C., 1963. Judge Hwa-lien Dist. Ct., Hwa-lien, Taiwan, Republic of China, 1949-51; dist. atty. Ministry of Justice, Taipei, 1951-52; chief law sect. Ministry of Nat. Def., Taipei, 1952-56; asst. prof. library sci. Ill. State U., Normal, 1965-66; asst. prof. polit. sci., library sci. Rosary Coll., River Forest, Ill., 1966-69, assoc. prof. library sci., 1969-70, 72-74, prof. library sci., 1974-82, dean, prof. Grad. Sch. Library and Info. Sci., 1982-88; prof. Dominican U., River Forest, Ill., 1988-99, dean, prof. emeritus, 2000—; vis. assoc. prof. law Nat. Taiwan U., 1969; vis. assoc. prof. polit. sci. Soochow U., Taipei, 1969; dir. Nat. Central Library, Taipei, 1970-72. Chmn. Grad. Inst. Library Sci., Nat. Central Library, Taipei, 1970-72; commr. Ministry of Examination, Examination Yuan, Taipei, 1971; chmn. com. on library standards, Ministry of Edn., Taipei, 1972; library cons. Soochow U., Nat. Chengchi U., Dr. Sun Yat-sen Meml. Library; mem. library adv. com. Ency. Britannica, 1982-95; hon. prof. library and info. sci. Jiangxi U., People's Republic of China, 1985—; vis. prof. law Suzhou U., Peking U., 1991, Nat. Taiwan U., 1991; hon. cons. univ. library, 1985—; hon. cons. Jiangxi Med. Coll., 1985—; adv. prof. East China Normal U., 1987—; cons. Nova U., 1987-88; mem. ad hoc adv. com. Chgo. Pub. Library Bldg. Planning, 1987-88; CEO LLD Group, 1972—; bd. chmn. Li Ednl. Found., 1977—; legacy leader Nat. Conf. Asian Pacific Am. Librarians, 2001. Author books including: Social Science Reference Sources, 1980, 3d edit., 2000, Mah Jong, 1982, 2d edit., 1991, An Introduction to Online Searching, 1985; also numerous articles in profl., scholarly jours.; founding editor Jour. Library and Info. Sci., 1975-80, mem. editl. bd. 1986-90; founding chmn., mem. editl. bd. Internat. Jour. of Revs., 1984-89; editor: World Libraries, 1996-99. Pres. Chinese Am. Ednl. Found., Chgo., 1968—70. Recipient Govt. Citation Republic of China, 1956, 1972, Philip D. Sang Excellence in Teaching award Rosary Coll., 1971, Disting. Service award Phi Tau Phi, Chgo., 1982, Service award HUD, Chgo. region, 1985, Disting. Service award Chinese Am. Librarians Assn., 1988. Mem. Chinese Am. Librarians Assn. (founding pres. 1976-80), China Assn. Libr. and Info. Sci. Edn. (hon.), Library Assn. China (Taipei), Phi Tau Phi (pres. 1985-87) Roman Catholic. Home: 250 E 54th St 22A New York NY 10022 Business E-Mail: richard@chamonline.org.

LI, VIRGINIA CHENG, public health educator; b. Guangzhou, Guangdong, China, Apr. 2, 1933; arrived in U.S., 1947; d. Han Hun Li and Chu Fang Wu; m. Leonardo Oscar Chait, May 18, 1985; children: Michael Wang, Lawrence Wang, Caroline Wang. BA, Salve Regina Coll., 1954; MA, NYU, 1955; MPH, U. N.C., 1964, PhD, 1968. Health edn. specialist Coop. Ext. Svc. U. Md., College Park, 1968—74; assoc. prof. Johns Hopkins U., Balt., 1975—82; prof. Sch. Pub. Health UCLA, 1982—. Temporary advisor WHO, 1982—89; cons. UN Devel. Program, 1989, Ford Found., 1991—2005. Author: Knowledge From West (3 vols.), 1956—88, (memoir) From One Root Many Flowers, 2003. Fellow: Soc. for Health Edn. Office: UCLA Sch Pub Health PO Box 51772 Los Angeles CA 90095-1772

LI, WEI, engineering educator, researcher; DSc, Chinese Acad. Scis., Beijing, 1994. Assoc. prof. U. of Toledo, Ohio, 2002—. Office: Univ Toledo 2801 W Bancroft St Toledo OH 43606 Office Phone: 419-530-8173. E-mail: wli@eecs.utoledo.edu.

LI, WEI, mechanical engineer, educator; s. Yuen and Shuzhen Li; m. Dongmei Chen; 1 child, Brandon. BS in Precision Engring. and Mechanology, Tsinghua U., Beijing, China, 1990; PhD in Mech. Engring., U. of Mich., 1999. Maint. engr. 301 Gen. Hosp., Beijing, 1990—91; project engr. POME Instrument and Equipment Co. Ltd., Beijing, 1991—92; rsch. asst. Fla. State U., 1994—95, U. Mich., Ann Arbor, 1995—99, rsch. fellow, 1999—2000; asst. prof. U. Wash., Seattle, 2000—. Recipient Faculty Early Career Devel. award (CAREER), U.S. NSF, 2004, Outstanding Young Mfg. Engr. award, The Soc. of Mfg. Engrs., 2002. Mem.: Am. Soc. of Engring. Edn., ASME (assoc.), Soc. of Mfg. Engrs. (assoc.). Achievements include research in open-cell porous polymer; resistance spot welding, control of welding induced distortion. Office: University of Washington Department of Mechanical Engineering Seattle WA 98195-2600 Office Phone: 206-543-5339.

LI, WEIYE, ophthalmologist, educator, biochemist; b. Zhejiang, China, Oct. 10, 1946; arrived in U.S., 1990; s. Zhao-ji and Qin (Yue) Li; m. Xnru Liu, Apr. 12, 1986; 1 child, Yafeng. MD, Peking Second Med. Coll., China, 1970; postgrad., Acad. Med. Scis., China, 1978—80; PhD, U. Pa., 1984. Intern Chao Young Hosp., Peking, 1970—71, resident ophthalmology, 1971—78; rsch. fellow dept. ophthalmology and biochem. grad. sch. Sch. Medicine U. Pa., Phila., 1981—84, postdoctor, asst. prof. dept. ophthalmology Scheie Eye Inst. Sch. Medicine, 1984—85; asst. prof., attending physician ophthalmology Peking Union Med. Coll. Hosp., 1985—86, assoc. prof. ophthalmology, 1986—88, prof. ophthalmology, 1988—, chmn. dept. ophthalmology, 1989—99; prof. ophthalmology, dir. rsch. dept. ophthalmology Hahnemann U., Phila., 1990—; attending ophthalmologist Chrozer Med. Ctr., PA, 2003—. Recipient Rsch. award, Internat. Juvenile Diabetes Found., 1984—86, 1st Class Sci. and Tech. Advances prize, Chinese Ministry Pub. Health, 1988; fellow, Internat. Juvenile Diabetes Found., 1982—84; grantee, NIH, 1981—82, 1986—2000, Fight for Sight Inc., 1982—83, Am. Diabetes Assn., 1990—2001. Mem.: Assn. Chinese Ophthalmology Soc., Assn. Rsch. in Vision and Ophthalmology. Avocations: ping pong/table tennis, bicycling, classical music. Office Phone: 610-892-1708. Business E-Mail: weiye.li@drexel.edu, wl27@drexel.edu.

LI, WEN-HSIUNG, geneticist; b. Pinq-Tung, Taiwan, Sept. 22, 1942; s. Linder and Piau Wang; m. Sue J. Li, Mar. 31, 1975; children: Vivian, Herman, Joyce. BE, Chungyuan Coll. Sci. & Engr., Chung-li, Taiwan, 1965; MS, Nat. Ctrl. U., Mio-li, Taiwan, 1968; PhD in Applied Math, Brown U., Providence, R.I., 1972. Project assoc. U. Wis., Madison, 1972-73; asst. prof. U. Tex.-Houston, 1973-78, assoc. prof., 1978-84, prof., 1984-98, U. Chicago, 1998—. Assoc. editor Genetics, 1984-86; editor Molecular Phylogenetics & Evolution, San Diego, 1991—. Author: Fundamentals of Molecular Evolution, 1991, Molecular Evolution, 1997. Grantee: Nat. Inst. Health, Bethesda, Md., 1983, 96, 87, 98, 99, 00. Fellow AAAS, Soc. for Molecular Biology & Evolution (pres. 2000), George Beadle Prof. Democrat. Avocations: sports, music, movies. Office: Dept Ecology & Evolution 1101 E 57th St Dept Ecology& Chicago IL 60637-1503 Fax: 773-702-9740. E-mail: whli@uchicago.edu.

LI, XIANCHANG, research engineer; b. HeBei, China; PhD, Clemson U., SC, 2000. Rsch. engr. U. New Orleans, 2003—. Mem.: ASME. Achievements include research in single-phase heat transfer or cooling enhanced by mist injection.

LI, XIAOJIE, statistician, researcher; arrived in U.S., 1993; d. Huaru and Menghu Li; m. Hongjian Zhang, Dec. 1988; children: Chenji Zhang, Ruellia Zhang. MS, Chinese Acad. Forestry, Beijing, 1987; PhD in Ecology, U. Ky., 1999; MS in Stats., Calif. State U., Hayward, 2002. Rsch. assoc. Chinese Acad. Forestry, Beijing, 1987—90; postdoctoral rschr. U. Calif., Davis, Salinas, 1999—2000; sr. rsch. assoc. MPR Assocs., Inc, Berkeley, Calif., 2002—. Presenter in field. Contbr. articles to profl. jours. Grad. fellow, U. B.C., Vancover, Can., 1991—92, Calif. State U., Hayward, 2001—02, Heebok Pk. scholar, 2002. Office Phone: 510-665-8240. E-mail: xj93901@yahoo.com.

LI, XIAOYE SHERRY, computer scientist, researcher; m. Suganda Jutamulia, June 9, 1990; children: Ivan Chen Jutamulia, Chen Elaine Jutamulia. PhD, U. of Calif. at Berkeley, 1991—96. Computer systems engr. Lawrence Berkeley Nat. Lab., Calif., 1996—2001, staff computer scientist, 2001—. Cons. Xerox Palo Rsch. Ctr., Palo Alto, Calif., 1994—96. Contbr. articles to profl. jours. Mem.: ASM, IEEE. Achievements include design and implementation of several new algorithms for numerical linear algebra problems, particularly for large sparse linear systems.

LI, XIN, adult education educator; s. Mingzheng Li and Ping Ren; m. Jen Zheng, Sept. 8, 1998; 1 child, Amber. PhD, Princeton U., 2000. Asst. prof. W.Va. U., Morgantown, 2003—; mem. tech. staff Sharp Labs of Am., Camas, Wash., 2000—02. Recipient Best Student Paper award, SPIE Conf. Visual Comm. and Image Proc., 2001; Go Moruo scholar, U. Sci. and Tech. China, 1996. Office: Lane Dept CSEE West Virginia U Morgantown WV 26506 Office Phone: 304-293-0405.

LI, YING, computer scientist, researcher; BS, Wuhan U., 1993; PhD, U. So. Calif.-L.A., 2002. Rsch. staff mem. T. J. Watson Rsch. Ctr. IBM, Hawthorne, N.Y., 2003—. Author: (book) Video content analysis using multimodal information: For movie content extraction, indexing and representation; contbr.: book chpt. Image databases: Search and retrieval of digital imagery, Video mining, Computer science handbook; editor: (article) Jour. Visual Comm. and Image Representation. Mem.: Soc. Photo-Optical Instrumentation Engrs., IEEE. Achievements include patents pending for framework for extracting multiple-resolution semantics in composite media content analysis; systems for adaptively separating foreground from arbitrary background in presentations; scalable video summarization and navigation system and method; scalable video summarization. Office: IBM T J Watson Research Ctr 19 Skyline Dr Hawthorne NY 10532 Business E-Mail: yingli@us.ibm.com.

LI, YONG-GANG FRANK, research scientist, educator; b. Shanghai, China, Jan. 23, 1945; s. Ziping Li and Yueying Wang; m. Yungyung Nancy Wang, Oct. 6, 1973; 1 child, Thomas. BS, Fudan U., 1967, MS, 1968; PhD, U. So. Calif., LA, 1988. Rschr. Inst. of Marine Geology & Geophysics, Shanghai, 1968—81; rsch. assoc. U. So. Calif., LA, 1982—88, rsch. prof., 1989—. Contbr. over 100 sci. articles to profl. jours. Grantee, NSF, 1990—2005. Fellow: Am. Chinese Scholar Assn. So. Calif. (corr.), Fudan U. Alumni Assn. So. Calif. (corr.); mem.: Am. Geophys. Union, Soc. of Exploration Geophysicists, Seismol. Soc. of Am. Achievements include discovery of Fault-Zone Seismic Trapped Waves And Post-Earthquake Fault Healing. Home: 290 Bloom Dr Monterey Park CA 91755 Office: Univ So Calif Dept Earth Scis University Park Los Angeles CA 90089 Office Phone: 213-740-3556. Office Fax: 213-740-8801. E-mail: ygli@usc.edu.

LI, ZHANQING, meteorologist, educator; b. Luoyang, Henan, China, Sept. 17, 1963; s. Zhongtai Li, Bian Liang; m. Fengting Huang; children: Cary, Kelsey. BS, Nanjing Inst. of Meteorology, Nanjing, Jiangsu, China, 1982, MS, 1985; PhD, McGill U., 1991. Rsch. scientist Can. Ctr. for Remote Sensing, Ottawa, Canada, 1992—; prof. U. Md., College Park, 2001—. Team leader Can. Ctr. for Remote Sensing, Ottawa, Ontario, Canada, 1995—2000. Contbr. articles to numerous profl. jours. (4 National Awards received since 1998 (See the award section), 90s). Recipient Earth Sci. merit award, Natural Resource Can., 2000, Head of Pub. Svc. Aaard, Fed. Govt. of Can., 1998, Tech. in Govt. medal, Treasure Bd. Can., 1999, Agatha Bystram Info. award, Coun. Fed. Libr., 1999, Alouette award, Cana. Aero. and Space Inst., 2000, Earth Sci. merit award, Natural Resource Can., 1997. Mem.: Am. Meteorol. Soc., Am. Geophys. Union (atmosheric sci. com. 1992—). Office: ESSIC Univ Md 2207 CSS Bldg College Park MD 20742-2465 Office Phone: 301-405-6699. Office Fax: 301-405-8468. Business E-Mail: zli@atmos.umd.edu.

LI, ZHAOXING, Chinese government official; b. Shandong, People's Republic of China, 1940; married; one son. Grad., Beijing U., 1964; postgrad., Beijing Inst. Fgn. Langs., 1964-67. Staff mem. Chinese People's Inst. Fgn. Affairs, 1967-70; staff mem., attache Chinese Embassy, Kenya, 1970-77; staff mem., dep. divsn. chief info. dept. Chinese Ministry Fgn. Affairs, 1977-83, dep. dir. gen., dir. gen. info. dept., 1985-90; first sect. Chinese Embassy, Kingdom of Lesotho, 1983-85; asst. min. fgn. affairs, 1990-92; permanent rep., amb. extraordinary and plenipotentiary People's Republic China to the UN, 1992-95; vice min. fgn. affairs, 1995-98, 2001—03; amb. extraordinary and plenipotentiary People's Republic China to the U.S., 1998—2001; min. fgn. affairs, 2003—. Guest prof. Beijing U., Nankai U., 1993. Office: Embassy of the Peoples Republic China 2300 Connecticut Ave NW Washington DC 20008-1724 Fax: 202-588-0032. E-mail: webmaster@china-embassy.org.

LI, ZHIGANG, physicist; s. Shuying Mao and Wang Li; m. Beili Li, Aug. 10, 1997; 1 child, Xinyang. PhD, Chinese Acad. of Sci., Changchun Inst. of Optics and Fine Mechanics, 1996—2000. Postdoctoral fellow U. of Pitts., 2001—02; guest rschr. NIST, Gaithersburg, Md., 2002—. Postdoctoral Nankai U., Tianjin City, China, 2000—01. Outstanding Student, Changchun Inst. of Optics and Fine Mechanics, 1995. Mem.: Soc. of Mfg. Engineers, Sigma Xi of Am. (corr.), Optical Soc. of Am. (corr.). Achievements include patents for arthroscopic optical coherence tomography. Office: Nat Inst of Standards and Tech 100 Bureau Dr Stop 8411 Gaithersburg MD 20899-8411 Office Phone: 301-975-3724. Office Fax: 301-208-6937. E-mail: zhigang.li@nist.gov.

LI, ZHILIN, mathematician, educator; b. Nanjing, Jiangsu, China, June 30, 1956; came to U.S., 1989; s. Wenfu Li and Guolan Cang; m. Xiaoyun Wang, Dec. 20, 1983; children: Miyuan Mike, Matthew S. BS in Math., Nanjing (China) Normal U., 1982, MS in Math., 1988; PhD in Applied Math., U. Wash., 1994. Instr. Nanjing Normal U., 1982-89; asst. prof. UCLA, 1994-96, Miss. State U., Starkville, 1996-97; assoc. prof. N.C. State U., Raleigh, 1997—. Recipient Boeing Excellence award, 1991, Oak Ridge Jr. Faculty Enhancement award Oak Ridge Associated Univs., 1997. Mem. Soc. Indsl. and Applied Math., Am. Math. Soc. Office: NC State U Dept Math Box 8205 Raleigh NC 27695 Business E-Mail: zhilin@math.ncsu.edu.

LI, ZIZHONG, research scientist; b. Jinyuan, China, June 25, 1965; s. Changhai Li and Minsu Teng; m. Youwen Xu; 1 child, Qing. BSc, Lanzhou (China) U., 1986, MSc, 1989; PhD, Auburn U., 1997. Rsch. fellow Nat. Lab. Applied Organic Chemistry, Lanzhou U., 1989—93; grad. rsch. asst. Auburn U., 1993—97; rsch. assoc. NIH Isotope Resources Los Alamos (N.Mex.) Nat. Lab., 1997—99; sr. rsch. assoc. med. dept. Brookhaven Nat. Lab., Upton, NY, 1999—2001, asst. scientist Imaging Sci. Group, 2001—03, assoc. scientist, 2003—; prin. scientist. Contbr. articles to profl. jours.; patentee in field. Mem.: AAAS, Am. Chem. Soc., Phi Lambda Upsilon. Home: 14 Circle Dr Shoreham NY 11786

LIACOURAS, PETER JAMES, academic administrator, educator, lawyer, arbitrator; b. Phila., Apr. 9, 1931; s. James Peter and Stella (Lagakos) L.; m. Ann Locke Myers, Sept. 5, 1959; children: Lisa Ann, James Peter, Stephen Myers, Gregory Locke. Student, Coll. William and Mary, 1950-51; BS, Drexel U., 1953; JD, U. Pa., 1956; MA, Fletcher Sch. Law and Diplomacy, 1958; LLM, Harvard U., 1959; postgrad. (Sterling fellow), Yale U. Law Sch., 1964-65; LLD (hon.), Dropsie U., 1982; LHD (hon.), Drexel U., 1984. Bar: Pa. 1957. Atty. Defender Assn. Phila., 1956-57, 59; research assoc. Duke U. Law Sch. Rule of Law Research Center, 1959-63; asst. prof. law Temple U., 1963-65, asso. prof., 1965-67, prof., 1967—, dean Sch. Law, 1972-82, univ. pres., 1982—2000, chancellor, 2000—, prof., 2000—. Spl. dist. atty., Phila., 1969, 70; chmn. Select Commn. on Pa. Bar Exam. Procedures, 1970; co-chmn. sect. legal edn. World Peace Through Law Center, 1973-74; chmn. confidentiality com. Pa. Gov.'s Justice Commn., 1974-78; lectr. law schs., India, 1967, Rome, 1974, 75, Ghana, 1975; lectr. law schs. Hebrew U., Jerusalem, 1975, 76, 77, 78, 79, Tel Aviv, 1981, Greece, 1977, 78, 79, 81, internat. law. Author: The International Court of Justice, 2 vols, 1962; contbr. numerous articles to law jours., 1957— . Abroad residing mem. Acad. Athens, 2003—. Recipient Human Rights award Nat. Conv. Women in Law, 1976, Ann. Human Relations award Am. Jewish Com., Phila., 1978, Disting. Am. award Am. Found. for Negro Affairs, 1987, Great Am. Traditions award, B'nai B'rith, 1999. Mem. ABA (Post-Bakke Task Force 1978-80), Phila. Bar Assn., Acad. Athens. Democrat. Greek Orthodox. Office: Temple University Chancellor's Office Barrack Hall Suite 300 Philadelphia PA 19122*

LIAKHOVITSKI, DIMITRI, organizational effectiveness consultant; arrived in U.S., 1995; s. German Terpugov and Genrieta Liakhovitskaia; m. Alexandra Y. Dimant, Oct. 26, 2001; 1 child, Maia Sarah. BA in Psychology, Freie U., Berlin, 1995; PhD in Indsl. & Orgnl. Psychology, SUNY, Albany, 1999. Lectr. SUNY, Albany, 1998—99; survey cons. The World Bank, Washington, 1999; project dir. Internat. Survey Rsch., Chgo., 1999—2001; sr. rsch. assoc. Mercer Delta Consulting, N.Y.C., 2001—03; orgnl. effectiveness cons. Pfizer, Morris Plains, NJ, 2003—. Contbr. chapters to books. Mem.: Acad. Mgmt., Am. Psychol. Soc., Soc. for Indsl. & Orgnl. Psychology. Office: Pfizer Inc 201 Tabor Rd Morris Plains NJ 07950 Office Phone: 973-385-0508.

LIAN, BONG H., mathematics professor, department chairman; BA, U. Toronto, Can., 1985; PhD in Physics, Yale U., 1991. Math. and sci. tutor Yale Coll. Yale U., 1988—90, postdoctoral fellow dept. math. and physics, 1993; postdoctoral instr. dept. math. U. Toronto, 1991—93; postdoctoral fellow dept. math. Harvard U., 1994—95; asst. prof. dept. math. Brandeis U., Waltham, Mass., 1995—97, assoc. prof., 1997—2001, full prof., 2001—, undergrad. advisor, 1997—99, grad. advisor, 2001—02, chmn. dept. math., 2002—. Vis. assoc. prof. Nat. U. Singapore, 2001. Contbr. articles to profl. jours. Fellow, John Simon Guggenheim Meml. Found., 2003; A.P. Sloan Grad. Dissertation fellow in math., 1990—91. Mem.: Internat. Congress Chinese Mathematicians (sci. com. mem. 1999—), Internat. Sci. Found. Cambridge (sec. 1998—). Achievements include research in representation theory and semi-infinite cohomology; mirror symmetry and Calabi-Yau geometry; string theory. Office: Brandeis Univ Goldsmith Bldg Rm 314 MS 050 415 South St Waltham MA 02454-9110

LIAN, JIE, engineering educator, researcher; b. Jiujiang, Jiangxi, China, July 18, 1973; s. Churen Lian and Yuelan Chen; m. Fan Zhang, Apr. 19, 1980. BS, Yanshan U., China, 1994; M in Engring., Tsinghua U., Beijing, 1998, U. Mich., 2000, DEng, 2003. Rsch. fellow U. Mich., Ann Arbor, 2003—04, asst. rsch. scientist, 2005—. Contbr. over 70 articles to profl. jours. Recipient Travel award, Oak Ridge Associated Univs., 2000, Disting. Scholar award, Microbeam Analysis Soc., 2002, Traveling Poster Exhibit award, Microscopy Soc. of Am., 2004; Rackham Predoctoral Honor fellowship, U. Mich., 2002. Mem.: Materials Rsch. Soc. (corr.), Microbeam Analysis Soc. (corr.), Am. Phys. Soc. (corr.), Alpha Nu Sigma (hon.), Sigma Xi (hon.). Achievements include research in Exceptional contribution for understanding the response behavior of complex ceramics to radiation damage, which has significant implication on the nuclear waste management; Significant contribution to the development of nanotechnology such as carbon nanoube functionalization, self-assembly nanostructure, etc. Office: Univ Mich 2355 Bonisteel Blvd Ann Arbor MI 48109-2104 Office Phone: 734-647-5704. Office Fax: 734-647-5706. Business E-Mail: jlian@umich.edu.

LIAN, YONGSHENG, aerospace scientist; b. Lirzi, ShanDong, China, July 1, 1973; arrived in U.S., 1999; s. Xin-Cong Zhang and Gui-Rong Lian; m. Lihui Bai, Oct. 16, 1973. BS, ShanDong U., Jinan, China, 1995; MS, Chinese Acad. Scis., 1998; M.Phil, Hong Kong U. Sci. and Tech., 1999; PhD, U. Fla., 2003. Sr. rschr. Ohio Aerospace Inst., Cleve., 2003—05; rsch. asst. prof. U. Mich., Ann Arbor, Mich., 2005—. Contbr. articles to profl. jours. Recipient Hua Wei First prize, Chinese Acad. Scis., 1999, Academic Achievement award, U. Fla., 2000, Achievement award, Ohio Aerospace Inst., 2004; fellow, U. Fla., 1999, 2003; grantee, NASA Glenn Rsch. Ctr., 2003. Mem.: AIAA (Outstanding Paper award 2002), Am. Soc. Mechanics Engring. Home: 808 Union Street APT4 Valparaiso IN 46383 Office: University of Michigan 1320 Beal Ave Ann Arbor MI 48109 Office Phone: 734-764-3393.

LIANG, BRYAN ALBERT, law educator, consultant; b. Wilmington, Del., Sept. 8, 1962; s. Charles C. and Anna Rosalyn; m. Shannon Mar Biggs, June 3, 1989. BS, MIT, 1983; PhD, U. Chgo., 1989; MD, Columbia U., 1991; JD, Harvard U., 1995. Med. lic., Hawaii; legal lic., Conn.; diplomate Nat. Bd. Med. Examiners. Clin. pathologist Danbury (Conn.) Hosp., 1991-92; prof. pub. policy studies Sch. Pub. Policy Pepperdine U. Sch. Pub. Policy, Malibu, Calif., 1997-99, prof. law Sch. Law, 1995-99; Arthur W. Grayson Disting. prof. law and medicine So. Ill. U. Sch. Law and Medicine, Carbondale, 1999—. Dir. Am. Bur. for Med. Advancement in China, N.Y.C., 1991—; mem. legal adv. coun. Nat. Legal Ctr. for Pub. Interest, Washington, 1995—. Author: (book) Health Law and Policy, 1999, (monograph) A Zone of Twilight: Executive Orders in the Modern Policy State, 1999. Bd. dirs. Health Alliance Responsibility Project, Santa Monica, Calif., 1996—; grant reviewer Fund for Sci. Rsch., Belgium, 1998—, Cmty. Devel. Work Study Grant Program, Dept. Housing and Urban Devel., Washington, 1999; mentorship advisor Columbia U., Coll. Physicians and Surgeons Alumni/ae Adv. Program, 1995—, Harvard Law Sch. Asian Pacific Am. Alumni/ae, 1996—. Recipient Med., Ednl. and Sci. Found. award for med. writing, 1991; J. Howard Pew Freedom Trust fellow in medicine, arts, and the social scis. U. Chgo., 1986-89, Sheldon Sheevak fellow in law and econs. Harvard Law Sch., 1993-95. Fellow Am. Coll. Legal Medicine (bd. govs. 1998—); mem. Nat. Patient Safety Found. (mem. rsch. program com. 1998—). Home: 1102 W Chautauqua St Carbondale IL 62901-2453 Office: So Ill U Sch Law PO Box 124 Shell WY 82441-0124 Fax: (618) 453-3317. E-mail: baliang@alum.mit.edu.

LIANG, CHENJU, engineering educator; s. Y. T. Liang and Y. H. Tseng; m. C. H. Wang, Jan. 12, 2000; children: T. G., S. G. D of Engring., U. Mass., 2002. Instr. Merrimack Coll., North Andover, Mass., 2003—03; rsch. assoc. U. Mass., Lowell, 2003—04. Cons. Xpert Design and Diagnostics, Stratham, NH, 2003—03, TETRA TECH, Inc., Oak Ridge, Miss., 2003—04. Grantee, Grad. Student Assn., U. of Mass., Lowell, 2000. Achievements include patents for Chemical Oxidation of Organic and Inorganic Contaminants by Chelated Transition Metals Catalyzed Persulfate. Office: National Chung Hsing U 250 Kuo-Kuang Rd Taichung City 402 Taiwan Office Phone: 886-4-22856610. Office Fax: 886-4-22856610. E-mail: cliang@dragon.nchu.edu.tw.

LIANG, CHRISTINE, import company executive; m. Marcel Liang; 2 children. Grad. Tang Ming Coll., Taiwan, 1979. Pres., founder ASI Corp., Fremont, Calif., 1987—. Recipient 17th Top Women Owned Bus., Working Women mag., 1996, 12th Top Women Owned Business, 1997, Number 1 Woman Owned Business, Silicon Valley Bus. Journal, 2002. Office: ASI Corp 48289 Fremont Blvd Fremont CA 94538-6510

LIANG, DANIEL S., surgeon; b. Tientsin, China, Apr. 18, 1926; came to U.S., 1949; divorced; children: Marc, Carol. BS, St. Johns U., 1945, MD, 1949; MS, U. Pa., 1954. Chief urology Pawtucket (R.I.) Meml. Hosp.; clin. asst. prof. urology Brown U., Providence. Author: Facts in Aging. Rsch. grantee NIH, 1962, 67. Fellow ACS, Am. Urol. Soc. Avocations: tennis, bicycling, guitar. Home: 448 Wexford Cir Venice FL 34293-4228

LIANG, EDISON PARKTAK, astrophysicist, educator, researcher; b. Canton, Republic of China, July 22, 1947; came to U.S., 1964; s. Chi-Sen and Siu-Fong (Law) L.; m. Lily K. Yuen, Aug. 7, 1971; children: Olivia, James, Justin. BA, U. Calif., Berkeley, 1967, PhD, 1971. Rsch. scientist U. Tex., Austin, 1971-73; assoc. instr. U. Utah, Salt Lake City, 1973-75; asst. prof. Mich. State U., East Lansing, Mich., 1975-76, Stanford (Calif.) U., 1976-79; physicist, group leader Lawrence Livermore Nat. Lab., Livermore, Calif., 1980-88, assoc. div. leader, 1988-91; prof. space physics and astronomy Rice U., Houston, 1991-2001, Andrew Hays Buchanan prof. astrophysics, 2001—. Mem. NASA Rev. Panels, Washington, 1988—. Editor: (book) Gamma Ray Bursts, 1986. Named Sci. fellow and Anthony scholar U. Calif., Berkeley, 1967-69. Fellow Am. Phys. Soc. (chair topical group in plasma astrophysics 2003); mem. Am. Astron. Soc., Internat. Astron. Union, Phi Beta Kappa, Sigma Xi. Office: Rice U Herman Brown Hall 6100 Main St MS108 Houston TX 77005-1892 Business E-Mail: liang@spacibm.rice.edu.

LIANG, JEROME ZHENGRONG, radiology educator; b. Chongging, China, June 23, 1958; arrived in U.S., 1981; BS, Lanzhou U., China, 1982; PhD, CUNY, 1987. Rsch. instr. Albert Einstein Coll. Medicine, Bronx, NY, 1986—87; rsch. assoc. Duke U. Med. Ctr., Durham, NC, 1987—89, asst. med. rsch. prof., 1990—92; asst. prof. SUNY, Stony Brook, 1992—97, assoc. prof., 1997—2000, prof., 2000—, co-dir. biomed. engring., 1996—. Mem. adv. bd. MDOL, Inc., 1999—; bd. dirs., v.p. R&D, founder Viatronix, Inc., 2000—. Contbr. articles to profl. jours.; mem. editl. bd.: IEEE Transactions on Med. Imaging, 1999—. Recipient NIH awards, 1990—, AHA award, 1996—2001, N.Y. State Biotech. award, 1996—98, E-Z-EM award, 1997—98; grantee, Soc. Thoracic Radiology, 1994—95, ADAC Rsch. Lab., 1994—95. Achievements include development of Bayesian image processing, quantitative emission computed tomography, tissue segmentation from magnetic resonance images, virtual endoscopy, virtual realities in radiology. Avocations: swimming, exercise, tennis. Office: SUNY Stony Brook Dept Radiology 4th Fl Rm 120 Stony Brook NY 11794-8460 Office Phone: 631-444-7837. Business E-Mail: jzl@mil.sunysb.edu.

LIANG, JUNJIEN FELIX, physicist, researcher; s. Chen-Hua Liang and Pu-Chen Pan; m. Yun Wendy Wang, Aug. 5, 1991; 1 child, Linus Hauming. BS, Nat. Tsing Hua U., Hsinchu, Taiwan, 1984; MA, SUNY, Stony Brook, 1989, PhD, 1993. Rsch. assoc. dept. physics U. of Wash., Seattle, 1993—97; sr. rsch. assoc. Oak Ridge Assoc. Univs., Oak Ridge, Tenn., 1997—2000; rsch. scientist dept. physics and astronomy U. of Tenn., Knoxville, 2000—; scientist Physics divsn., Oak Ridge Nat. Lab., Oak Ridge, Tenn., 2000—. Referee Phys. Rev. (jour. of the Am. Phys. Soc.), 1994—, European Phys. Jour., Germany, 2001—, Internal Jour. of Modern Physics, Singapore, 2001—, Nuc. Physics A, 2004—; spkr. in field. Contbr. articles to profl. jours. Recipient Significant Event award, Oak Ridge Nat. Lab., 2003; grantee Seed Money Fund grantee, Lab. Directed R & D Program, 2000, Dir.'s R&D Fund, 2004. Mem.: Am. Phys. Soc. Achievements include research in Discovered enhanced fusion rates in reactions involving exotic nuclei, cited in Science News as a feature story. Office: Physics Divsn MS 6368 Oak Ridge National Laboratory Oak Ridge TN 37831 Office Phone: 865-574-4109. Office Fax: 865-574-1268. Business E-Mail: liang@mail.phy.ornl.gov.

LIANG, JUNXIANG, retired aeronautics and astronautics engineer, educator; b. Hangzhou, Zhejiang, China, Aug. 17, 1932; s. Yigao and Yunruo (Yu) L.; m. Junxian Sun, Jan. 27, 1960; 1 child, Song Liang. Grad., Harbin Inst. Tech., 1960. Head control dept. Shenyang Jet Engine R & D Inst., 1960—70, China Gas Turbine Establishment, Jiangyou, China, 1970—78, assoc. chief engr., 1979—83; vis. scientist MIT, Cambridge, 1984—86; prof. China Aerospace Inst. Sys. Engring., Beijing, 1986—2003; grads. supr. Beijing U. Aero-Astronautics, 1986—2003; chief engr. Full Authority Digital Elec. Engine Control China Aerospace Industry Ministry, Beijing, 1986—93; ret., 2003. Mem. China Aerospace Sci. and Tech. Com., Beijing, 1983-94, Aero-engine R & D Adv. Bd., Beijing, 1991-95; bd. dirs. China Aviation Ency. Editl. Bd., Beijing, 1991-95; tech. support supr., mgmt. info. svc. dir. Am. PC, Inc., Union City, Calif., 1993—. Author: Nonlinear Control System Oscillation, 1964; contbr. articles to Jour. Aeronautics and Astronautics, Jour. Propulsion Tech., Internat. Aviation, Acta Aeronautica et Astronautica Sinica. Recipient Nat. Sci. and Tech. 2d award, China Nat. Sci. and Tech. Com., Beijing, 1965, Sci. and Tech. Progress award, China Aerospace Industry Ministry, 1991, Nat. Outstanding Sci. and Tech. Contbn. award, 1992. Mem. AIAA (sr.), Chinese Soc. Aero. and Astronautical Engine Control (commn. com. 1987—). Achievements include solution of oscillation problem on nonlinear control system; formulation of aircraft overall strategy, study and control of High Thrust/Weight Engine Research Program.

LIANG, QILIAN, engineering educator; PhD, U. of So. Calif., L.A., 2000. Mem. of tech. staff Hughes Network Systems, Inc, San Diego, 2000—02; asst. prof. U. of Tex. at Arlington, 2002. Contbr. articles to profl. jours. Recipient Young Investigator award, U.S. Office of Naval Rsch., 2003; grantee, U.S. Office of Naval Rsch. grantee, 2003—. Mem.: IEEE. Achievements include patents pending for Method, device and computer program product for a demodulator with communications link adaptation; method, device and computer program product for bandwidth utilization and signal strength-based handover initiation in a wireless communications network; method, device and computer program product for MPEG VBR video traffic classification using a nearest neighbor classifier; method, device and computer program product for a demodulator using a fuzzy adaptive filter and decision feedback; rule-based Media Traffic Classifier. Office: University of Texas at Arlington 416 Yates St Rm 518 Arlington TX 76019-0016 Office Phone: 817-272-1339. Office Fax: 817-272-2253. E-mail: liang@uta.edu.

LIANG, YANAN, research scientist; s. Tingying Liang and Yufu Wang; m. Hui Zhou, Sept. 14, 1991. Bachelor, Dalian Rlwy. Inst., China, 1984; Masters, Inst. Metal Rsch., Academia Sinica, Shenyang, China, 1991, PhD, 1995. Post doctoral rschr. Tsinghua U., Beijing, 1995—97; vis. rschr. Sunmoon U., Asan, Republic of Korea, 1997—99; vis. scholar Inst. Ceramics and Glasses, CSIC, Madrid, 1999—2001; vis. prof. U. Oviedo, Gijon, Spain, 2001—03; sci. rschr. Nat. Inst. Stds. and Tech., Gaithersburg, Md., 2003—. Jour. referee WEAR, Cambridge, 2004—, Jour. Materials Sci. and Tech., Shenyang, 2004—. Contbr. articles to sci. publs. and proceedings. Recipient Excellent Paper award, 10th Nat. Conf. Electric Contacts, 1996. Mem.: Soc. Tribologists and Lubrication Engring. (excellent young rschr. in tribology 1996), Soc. Mfg. Engrs., Sigma Xi. Achievements include invention of titanium-nickel alloy foil and sheets materials production.

LIAO, DAIQING, molecular biologist, educator; b. Guiyang, Hunan, China, Nov. 9, 1962; arrived in US, 1987; s. Wanjin Liao and Liuliang Zhu; m. Lisa Yajie Zhao, July 31, 1963; children: Jennifer Xin, Rebecca Ying. BS, Hunan (China) U., 1983; MS, Peking (China) U., 1986; PhD, U. BC, 1993. Postdoctoral assoc. Yale U., New Haven, 1994—97; asst. prof. U. Sherbrooke, Canada, 1997—2000, U. Fla., Gainesville, Fla., 2000—. Grad. coord. U. Fla., 2001—. Contbr. over 20 articles to profl. jours. (Can. Found. Innovation award, 1998). Fellow, Med. Rsch. Coun. Can., 1995—97, Sloan Found., 1992; grantee, NIH, 2001—, Am. Lung Assn., 2003—; scholar, Fonds Rsch. en santé du Québec in Montreal, Can., 1997—2000. Mem.: AAAS, Am. Soc. Cell Biology, Am. Soc. Microbiology. Achievements include research in the fields of genetics, virology and cancer biology; the genetic mechanisms of concerted evolution, and biological functions of tumor suppressors and oncogenes. Home: 10413 SW 17 Place Gainesville FL 32607 Office: University of Florida 1600 SW Archer Road Gainesville FL 32610-0235 Office Phone: 352-294-7976. Home Fax: 352-392-3305. Business E-Mail: dliao@ufl.edu.

LIAO, MEI-JUNE, biopharmaceutical company executive; came to U.S., 1974; BS, Nat. Tsing-Hua U. Taiwan, 1973; MPh, Yale U., 1977, PhD, 1980. Tchg. asst. Nat. Taiwan U., 1973—74, Temple U., Phila., 1974—75, Yale U., New Haven, 1975—76, rsch. asst., 1976—79; postdoctoral assoc. MIT, Cambridge, 1980—83; sr. scientist Interferon Scis., Inc., New Brunswick, NJ, 1983—84; group leader Interferon Scis. Inc., New Brunswick, NJ, 1984—85, dir. cell biology, 1985—87; dir., rsch. & devel. Interferon Scis., Inc., New Brunswick, NJ, 1987—94, v.p., rsch. & devel., 1995—2003; v.p., regulatory affairs and quality Hemispherx Biopharma, Inc., New Brunswick, 2003—. Contbr. articles to profl. jours.; inventor in field. Mem. Am. Soc. Biochemistry and Molecular Biology, Internat. Soc. Interferon and Cytokine Rsch., Internat. Cytokine Soc., Soc. Chinese Bioscientists in Am., N.Y. Acad. Sci. Office: Hemispherx Biopharma Inc 783 Jersey Ave New Brunswick NJ 08901-3660 E-mail: meijuneliao@yahoo.com.

LIAO, PAUL FOO-HUNG, electronics executive; b. Phila., Nov. 10, 1944; s. Tseng Wu and Tung Mei (Lin) L.; m. Karen Ann Pravetz, Aug. 31, 1968; children: Teresa S., Joanna S. BS, MIT, 1966; PhD, Columbia U., 1973. Rsch. assoc. Columbia U., N.Y.C., 1972-73; mem. tech. staff Bell Labs., Holmdel, N.J., 1973-80, dept. head., 1980-83; div. mgr. Bell Communications Rsch., Red Bank, N.J., 1984-89, asst. v.p., 1989-93, gen. mgr., 1993-95, v.p., 1995-96; v.p., chief tech. officer Panasonic Corp. N.Am., 1996—. Co-editor: Academic Press Quantum Electronics Book Series, 1980-96; contbr. over 75 articles to profl. jours.; holder over 12 patents in field. Bd. trustees Brookdale C.C. Fellow IEEE (Millennium medal 2000), Optical Soc. Am. (editor jour.), Am. Phys. Soc.; mem. Lasers and Electro Optic Soc. of IEEE (pres. 1987). Office: Panasonic Corp N Am One Panasonic Way Secaucus NJ 07094

LIAO, SHUTSUNG, biochemist, molecular oncologist; b. Tainan, Taiwan, Jan. 1, 1931; s. Chi-Chun Liao and Chin-Shen Lin; m. Shuching Liao, Mar. 19, 1960; children: Jane, Tzufen, Tzuming, May. BS in Agrl. Chemistry, Nat. Taiwan U., 1953, MS in Biochemistry, 1956; PhD in Biochemistry, U. Chgo., 1961. Rsch. assoc., 1960-63; asst. prof. U. Chgo., 1964-69; assoc. prof. dept. biochemistry and molecular biology Ben May Lab. Cancer Rsch., U. Chgo., 1969-71; prof. depts. biochemistry, molecular and cancer biology Ben May Inst. for Cancer Rsch., 1972—; dir. Tang Ctr. Herbal Medicine Rsch., 2000—02. CEO, chmn. bd., Anagen Therapeutic Co., 2000—; cons. in field. Mem. editl. bd. Jour. Steroid Biochemistry and Molecular Biology, The Prostate, Receptors, Signal Transduction, J. Formosan Med. Assoc., Biomedical Sci.; assoc. editor Cancer Rsch., 1982-89; contbr. over 250 articles to profl jours. V.p. Chgo. Formosan Fed. Credit Union, 1977-79; trustee Taiwanese United Fund in U.S., 1981-85; mem. adv. com. Taiwan-U.S. Cultural Exch. Ctr., 1984-87. Recipient Sci-Tech. Achievement prize Taiwanese-Am. Found., 1983, Pfizer Lecture fellow award Clin. Rsch. Inst. Montreal, 1972, Gregory Pincus medal and award Worcester Found. for Exptl. Biology, 1992, Tzongming Tu award Formosan Med. Assn., 1993, C.H. Li Meml. Lecture award, 1994; NIH grantee, 1962—; Am. Cancer Soc. grantee, 1971-81. Fellow Am. Acad. Art and Scis.; mem. Am. Soc. Biochemistry and Molecular Biology, Am. Assn. Cancer Rsch., Endocrine Soc., N.Am.-Taiwanese Profs. Assn. (pres. 1980-81, exec. dir. 1981—), Nat. Acad. Taiwan. Achievements include discovery of androgen activation mechanism and androgen receptors; cloning and structural determination of androgen receptors and other novel nuclear receptors, and their genes, and receptor gene mutation in hereditary abnormalities and cancers; rsch. on regulation of hormone-dependent gene expression and cell growth, molecular bases of cancer cell growth and progression, chemoprevention, and therapeutic treatment of hormone-sensitive and insensitive cancers and diseases, molecular bases of cholestoral modulation and control in cardiovascular and neurodegenerative diseases and cancer progression. Home: 5632 S Woodlawn Ave Chicago IL 60637-1623 Office: U Chgo Ben May Inst Cancer Rsch 5841 S Maryland Ave Chicago IL 60637-1463

LIAO, THUNSHUN WARREN, manufacturing engineer, educator; b. Huwei, Yunlin, Taiwan, Mar. 19, 1957; s. Soomin Liao and Moodan Lian; m. Chifen Ting, Mar. 7, 1961; children: Allen, Karen. MS, Lehigh U., 1986; BS, Nat. Taipei (China) U. Tech., 1977; PhD, Lehigh U., 1990. From asst. prof. to prof. La. State U., Baton Rouge, 1990—2000, prof., 2000—. Contbr. articles to profl. jours. Fellow, Lehigh U., 1987—89, Army Rsch. Lab., 2000—01; grantee, NSF, 2004. Mem.: Inst. Indsl. Engrs., INFORMS, Soc. Mfg. Engrs. Achievements include research in soft computing and manufacturing. Office: Louisiana State University 3128 Ceba Baton Rouge LA 70803 Office Phone: 225-578-5365. Office Fax: 225-578-5109. Business E-Mail: ieliao@lsu.edu.

LIASSON, MARA, news correspondent; BA in Am. History, Brown Univ. Mng. editor, anchor Calif. Edition; journalist The Vineyard Gazette; gen. assignment reporter, newscaster Nat. Public Radio (NPR), 1985, nat. polit. corr., 1985—, White House corr., 1992—2000, congl. corr., 1989—92; political correspondent FOX News Channel, 1997—. Regular contbr., Special Report with Brit Hume FOX News Channel, panelist, FOX News Sunday. Contbr. reports to All Things Considered and Morning Edition. Recipient Merriman Smith award, White House Correspondents' Assn., 1994, 1995, 1997; fellow Bagehot Fellowship in Economics and Business Journalism. Office: FOX News Channel 400 N Capitol St NW Ste 550 Washington DC 20001*

LIAU, GENE, medical educator; b. Hsing-Chu, Taiwan, Nov. 28, 1954; came to U.S., 1965; BS in Biology, U. N.C., 1977; DPhil, Vanderbilt U., 1982. Postdoctoral fellow Lab. Molecular Biology, Nat. Cancer Inst. NIH, Bethesda, Md., 1982-85; assoc. mem. dept. cell biology Revlon Biotech. Rsch. Ctr., Rockville, Md., 1985-87; scientist I dept. molecular biology Am. Red Cross Jerome H. Holland Lab., Rockville, 1987-90, scientist II, 1990-96, sr. scientist, 1996-98; assoc. prof. dept. anatomy George Washington U. Med. Ctr., Washington, 1995—; unit head metabolic and vascular disease group Genetic Therapy Inc., Gaitersburg, Md., 1998—; adj. prof. molecular biology Holland Lab., 1998—, sr. scientist, 1998—. Mem. AHA Vascular Wall Biology Rsch. Study Com., 1992-96, Pathology A Study Sect. NIH, 1994-98; invited spkr. in field. Contbr. articles to profl. jours. Arthritis Found. fellow, 1982-85; pub. health svc. grantee, 1988—; recipient Nat. Rsch. Svc. award NIH, 1977-81, Rsch. Career Devel. award, 1990-95. Mem. AAAS, Am. Soc. Cell Biology, Am. Heart Assn. Coun. Basic Sci. (Established Investigator 1990, Grant-in-Aid 1992-95, 95-98), Soc. Chinese Bioscientists, Sigma Xi. Office: Genetic Therapy Inc 100 Technology Sq Cambridge MA 02139-3585

LIBA, PETER MICHAEL, Canadian provincial government official, retired communications executive; b. Winnipeg, Man., Can., May 10, 1940; s. Theodore and Rose Liba; m. Shirley Ann Collett, May 4, 1963; children: Jennifer Lacombe, Jeffrey, Christopher. LLD (hon.), U. Manitoba, 2001, Brandon U., 2004. Reporter, news editor The Daily Graphic, The Neepawa Press, Portage la Prairie, Man., 1957-59; reporter The Winnipeg Tribune, 1959-67, city editor, 1967-68; ind. comm. cons. Winnipeg, 1968-73; v.p. pub. affairs CanWest Broadcasting Ltd., Winnipeg, 1974-75, exec. v.p., 1979-97; asst. gen. mgr. Sta. CKND-TV, Winnipeg, 1975-79, mgr., 1980-87, gen. mgr., 1987-92; pres., CEO CKND TV Inc./SaskWest TV Inc., Winnipeg, 1988-94; exec. v.p. CanWest Global Comm. Corp., Winnipeg, 1993—99; lt. gov. Province of Man., Canada, 1999—2004; regional chmn. Can. Forces Liaison Coun., 2004—. Bd. dirs. Global Comm. Ltd., Toronto, CanWest Broadcasting Ltd., Winnipeg, CanWest TV, Inc., Winnipeg, CanWest Prodns., Ltd., Winnipeg, CanWest Properties Ltd., Winnipeg, CanWest Maritime TV, Inc., Halifax, TV 3 Network, New Zealand, Network Ten, Australia; pres. Peli Ventures, Inc., 1975—. Trustee Transcona-Springfield Sch. divsn., Winnipeg, Canada, 1964—67; founding chmn. Variety Club Telethon, Canada; chmn. Winnipeg Conv. Ctr/; bd. dirs. Conv. Ctr. Corp., Winnipeg, 1976—86, chmn. bd. dirs., 1981—84; bd. dirs. Atomic Energy of Can., Ltd., Ottawa, 1981—86, St. Boniface Gen. Hosp., Winnipeg, 1987—99. Named to Can. Broadcasters Hall of Fame, 1998, Spl. Gold Ribbon award 1999. Mem. Broadcasters Assn. Man. (pres. 1981-82), Western Assn. Broadcasters (pres. 1984-85, Broadcaster of Yr. award 1991, Broadcaster of Decade award 1994), Can. Assn.

Broadcasters (chmn. bd. 1990-92, Spl. Gold Ribbon award 1999, named to Can. Broadcasters Hall of Fame, 1998), Variety Club Man. (chief barker 1984-85). Home: 800-237 Wellington Crescent Winnipeg MB R3M OA1 Canada

LIBASSI, FRANK PETER, lawyer; b. NYC, Apr. 20, 1930; s. Frank G. and Mary (Marino) Libassi; m. Mary Frances Steen, July 10, 1954; children: Thomas, Timothy, Jennifer. BA in Polit. Sci. cum laude, Colgate U., 1951; LLB, Yale U., 1954. Bar: N.Y. 1955, Conn. 1980. Enforcement atty. N.Y. State Housing and Rent Commn., 1954-56; regional dir. N.Y. State Commn. Human Rights, Albany, 1956-62; dep. staff dir. U.S. Commn. Civil Rights, 1962-66; spl. asst. to sec., dir. office for civil rights HEW, Washington, 1966-68, gen. counsel, 1977-79; exec. v.p. Urban Coalition, Washington, 1968—71; v.p. Am. City Corp., Columbia, Md., 1971-72; pres., CEO Greater Hartford (Conn.) Process Inc. (Greater Hartford Cmty. Devel. Corp.), 1971-77; ptnr. Verner, Liipfert, Bernhard and McPherson, Washington, 1979-82; sr. v.p. Travelers Corp., Hartford, 1982-93; of counsel Verner, Liipfert, Bernhard & McPherson, Washington, 1993-95; dean Barney Sch. of Bus. and Pub. Adminstrn., U. Hartford, West Hartford, Conn., 1993-96; pres. Children's Fund Conn., Hartford, 1996—2001, Child Health and Devel. Inst. Conn., Hartford, 1997—2001. Mem. Urban Land Inst., 1971—77; v.p. Ctr. Global Bus. Studies, Paris, 1996—97; adv. bd. Bur. Nat. Affairs Housing and Cmty. Devel. Reporter, 1972—77; vis. lectr. Anderson Coll., Chatham Coll., Goddard Coll., Ohio Wesleyan U., 1974—76; adj. faculty Grad. Sch. Bus. and Pub. Adminstrn. U. Hartford, Hartford, 1976—77. Author: The Negro in the Armed Forces, 1963, Family Housing and the Negro Serviceman, 1963, Equal Opportunity in Farm Programs, 1965, Revitalizing Central City Investment, 1977. Mem. nat. consumer adv. com. Am. Health Care Assn., 1985—86; mem. Nat. Retirees Vol. Ctr., 1988—90; chmn. Ct. Cmty. Care, Inc., 1980—86; mem. com. aging soc. NAS, 1982—86; mem. exec. com. Downtown Coun. Hartford, 1983—86, Greater Hartford Arts Coun., 1983—86; chmn. Gov.'s Commn. Financing Long Term Care, 1986—87; mem. com. elderly people living alone Commonwealth Fund, 1985—91; mem. Sec. Bowen's Task Force Long-Term Health Care Policies Health Care Financin Adminstrn., 1986—87; bd. dirs. Alliance Aging Rsch., 1986—91; mem. Pew Commn. Future Health Profls., 1990—93, Pub. Affairs Rsch. Coun. Conf. Bd., 1990—93, United Srs. Health Coop., 1990—91; mem. com. predicting future diseases Inst. Medicine, 1991—93; trustee Conn. Pub. Expenditure Coun., 1991—96; mem. adv. com. health care reform Commonwealth Fund, 1993—98; bd. dirs. Duncaster Cmty., 1993—97, Conn. Health Found., 1999—2004; bus. adv. bd. Conn. Commn. Children, 1998—2004; mem. adv. com. Dem. Nat. Com., 1974—77; bd. dirs. Hartford Sem., 2002—; bd. dirs. legis. com. Am. Coun. Life Ins., 1987—90; bd. dirs., mem. exec. com. Ins. Inst. Hwy. Safety, 1984—88; adv. bd. Nat. Acad. Aging, 1992—96, U. Conn. Sch. Nursing, 1996—2002; bd. dirs. The Bushnel, 1998—; incorporator Inst. Living, 1973—2004, Hartford Hosp., 1973—2004, St. Francis Hosp., 1990—2004, Wheeler Clinic, 1996—. Recipient Superior Performance award, U.S. Commn. Civil Rights, 1963, Meritorious Svc. award, 1965, Sec.'s Spl. citation, 1967, Disting. Svc. award, HEW, 1968, award, Friend La Casa de P.R., Hartford, 1992, Exec. Dirs. award, Conn. Assn. Human Svcs., 1996, John Filer award for Philanthropy, 2004; Woodrow Wilson Sr. fellow, 1973—77. Mem.: Greater Hartford C. of C. (bd. dirs. 1985—93, mem. exec. com.), Am. Assn. Ret. Persons (mem. nat. steering com. new roles in soc. 1987—90), Hartford Club. Office Phone: 860-726-2227. Personal E-mail: libassi@comcast.net.

LIBBIN, ANNE EDNA, lawyer; b. Phila., Aug. 25, 1950; d. Edwin M. and Marianne (Herz) L.; m. Christopher J. Cannon, July 20, 1985; children: Abigail Libbin Cannon, Rebecca Libbin Cannon. AB, Radcliffe Coll., 1971; JD, Harvard U., 1975. Bar: Calif. 1975, U.S. Dist. Ct. (cen. dist.) Calif. 1977, U.S. Dist. Ct. (no. dist.) Calif. 1979, U.S. Dist. Ct. (ea. dist.) Calif. 1985, U.S. Ct. Appeals. (2d cir.) 1977, U.S. Ct. Appeals (5th cir.) 1982, U.S. Ct. Appeals (7th cir.) 1976, U.S. Ct. Appeals (9th cir.) 1976, U.S. Ct. Appeals (D.C. cir.) 1978, U.S. Supreme Ct. 2001. Appellate atty. NLRB, Washington, 1975-78; assoc. Pillsbury Madison & Sutro LLP, San Francisco, 1978-83, ptnr., 1984-99; sr. counsel SBC West Legal Dept., San Francisco, 1999—; dir. Jewish Vocat. Svcs., San Francisco, 2002—. Three Guineas fellow Harvard Law Sch., 1997; dir. Alumnae Resources, San Francisco, 1991-97. Mem. ABA (labor and employment sect.), State Bar Calif. (labor law sect.), Bar Assn. San Francisco (labor law sect.), Radcliffe Club (San Francisco). Office: SBC West Legal Dept 140 New Montgomery St San Francisco CA 94105-3705

LIBBY, DAVID M., internist; b. N.Y.C., Sept. 9, 1947; s. Nathan Libby and Shirley Rebecca State; m. Nancy Ellen Kemeny, May 22, 1977; children: Jacqueline, Laura, Victoria. AB, Columbia U., 1971; MD, Baylor U., 1974. Diplomate Am. Bd. Internal Medicine, Am. Bd. Pulmonary Medicine, Am. Bd. Critical Care Medicine. Attending physician NY Presbyn. Hosp., N.Y.C., 1979—; clin. prof. medicine Weill Med. Coll., Cornell U., N.Y.C., 1979—, bd. dirs. Mem.: AOA, N.Y.C. Physician Golfing Assn. (pres. 2002—03), River Club NY. Avocations: tennis, golf, racquetball, travel. Home: 333 E 67th St New York NY 10021 Office: 407 E 70th St New York NY 10021 E-mail: dmlibby@aol.com.

LIBBY, GARY RUSSELL, museum director emeritus, writer; b. Boston, June 7, 1944; s. Charles W. and Sylvia P. Libby. BA, U. Fla., 1967, MA (NDEA fellow), 1968; MA, Tulane U., 1972. Instr. English Tulane U., 1968-71; asst. prof. Stetson U., Deland, Fla., 1972-77, vis. prof., 1977-86; dir. Mus. Arts and Scis., Daytona Beach, Fla., 1977—2001, dir. emeritus, 2002—. Reviewer Inst. Mus. Svcs.; panelist Mus. Assessment Program; reviewer Accreditation Commn. of Am. Assn. Mus. Author: Two Centuries of Cuban Art, 1985, Cuba: A History in Art, 1997, Coast to Coast: The Contemporary Landscape in Florida, 1998, A Treasury of American Art, 2002; editor: Archipenko: Themes and Variations, 1989, Chihuly: Form From Fire, 1994 (Southeastern Mus. Conf. award, 1994), A Century of Jewelry and Gems, 1995, Celebrating Florida, 1995, Illustrated Dictionary of Florida Art, 2005. Trustee Cuban Found.; mem. artists in edn. panel, visual arts panel, youth and children's mus. panel, sci. mus. panel A.D.A. statewide panel Fla. Arts. Coun.; panelist Challenge Grant Program, Cultural Instns. Program; mem. hist. mus. grants panel Fla. Divsn. History; mem. Halifax Area Advt. Authority, 1999—; mem. adv. bd. Daytona Beach Econ. Devel., 1999—; vice chmn. Mainstreet Redevel. Bd., 2004; mem., chmn. adv. bd. Environ., Cultural, Hist., and Outdoors, 2001—05; mem. Cultural Coun. Volusia County, 2002—03, Main St. Redevel. Agy., 2004—05, Daytona Beach Charter Rev. Mem.: Fla. Cultural and Ednl. Alliance (bd. dirs. 1995), Fla. Assn. Mus. (bd. dirs. 1992-98, 2000—, sec. 1995-96, 96-97, 97-98), Fla. Art Mus. Dirs. Assn. (govt. liaison 1990, pres. 1995-96, 96-97). Home and Office: 723 N Oleander Ave Daytona Beach FL 32118-3826 Business E-Mail: grlibby@moas.org.

LIBBY, LAUREN DEAN, foundation executive; b. Smith Center, Kans., Jan. 9, 1951; s. Dean L. and Elizabeth V. (Hansen) L.; m. June Ellen Hofer, Apr. 29, 1979; 1 child, Grant Lauren. BS in Agrl. Econs., Kans. State U., 1973; MBA, Regis U., 1988. Radio sta. employee, 1968-72; asst. program dir. info. br. Kans. State Extension Svc., Manhattan, 1969-73; economist Howard Houk Assocs., Chgo., 1973-75; asst. to pres. The Navigators, Colorado Springs, Colo., 1975-78, ministry devel. coord., 1979-86, dir. min. advancement, 1986-90, v.p., 1990-97; pres. New Horizons Found., Colorado Springs, 1990—. Bd. dirs. Navigators, Colorado Springs, 1993—; founding bd. dirs. Sta. KTLF-FM/Ednl. Comms. of Colorado Springs, 1987—; cons. 22 listener-supported radio stas., 1989—. Contbr. articles to mags. Bd. dirs. Christian Stewardship Assn., 1995—, ECFA, 1998—, Northwestern Coll. Mem. Nat. Soc. Fundraising Execs., Ctrl. States VHF Soc. (pres. 1995). Avocation: amateur radio. Home: 6166 Del Paz Dr Colorado Springs CO 80918-3004 Office: The Navigators 3820 N 30th St Colorado Springs CO 80904-5000

LIBBY, LEWIS (I. LEWIS LIBBY), federal official; b. 1950; BA magna cum laude, Yale U., 1972; JD, Columbia U., 1975. Legal advisor select com. U.S. Nat. Security and Mil./Comml. Concerns with People's Republic of China (Cox com.) U.S. Ho. of Reps., Washington; mem. policy planning staff office of sec. Paul D. Wolfowitz U.S. Dept. State, Washington, 1981—85, dir. spl. projects bur. East Asian and Pacific Affairs, 1982—85; ptnr. Dickstein, Shapiro, & Morin, Washington, 1985—90; prin. dep. under sec. strategy and resources U.S. Dept. Def., Washington, 1990—92, dep. under sec. for policy, 1992—93; mng. ptnr. Dechert, Price & Rhoads, Washington, 1995—2001; chief of staff to v.p., asst. to v.p. for nat. security affairs The White House, Washington, 2001—. Mem. adv. bd. ctr. Russian and Eurasian studies Rand Corp. Author: (novels) The Apprentice, 1996. Recipient Fgn. Affairs award for Pub. Svc., U.S. Dept. State, 1985, Disting. Svc. award, U.S. Dept. Def., 1993, Disting. Pub. Svc. award, U.S. Dept. Navy, 1993. Mem.: ABA (mem. standing com. on law and nat. security). Office: The White House Office of VP 1600 Pennsylvania Ave NW Washington DC 20500 Office Phone: 204-456-9000.*

LIBBY, WENDY B., academic administrator; m. Richard Libby; children: Glenn, Gregg. BS in Biology, Cornell U., 1972; MBA, Johnson Grad. Sch. of Mgmt. at Cornell U., 1977; PhD in Ednl. Adminstrn., U. Conn., 1994. Dir. adminstrv. ops. Coll. of Architecture, Art and Planning, Ithaca, NY, 1979—84; dir. adminstrn. pub. mgmt. program Johnson Grad. Sch. of Mgmt. at Cornell U., Ithaca, NY, 1979—84; adminstrv. mgr. Coll. Edn. Ohio State U., Columbus, 1984—85, adminstrv. assoc. Office of Fin., 1984—85; asst. dir. U. Conn. Med. Ctr. John Dempsey Hosp., Farmington, Conn., 1985—87, asst. to assoc. exec. dir., 1985—87; spl. asst. to pres. and sr. human resources officer U. Hartford, Conn., 1987—89; chief fin. and bus. officer Westbrook Coll., Portland, Maine, 1989—95; v.p. bus. affairs and CFO Furman U., Greenville, SC, 1995—2003; pres. Stephens Coll., Columbia, Mo., 2003—. Founding bd. mem. Tuition Plan Consortium, Caribbean Inst. of Tech. Bd. mem. Greenville Literacy Assn., mem. fund raising com. Mem.: Soc. Coll. and U. Planning, So. Assn. of Coll. and U. Bus. Officers, Ea. Assn. of Coll. and U. Bus. Officers (bd. dirs.), Nat. Assn. of Coll. and U. Bus. Officers. Office: Stephens Coll 1200 E Broadway Columbia MO 65215

LIBERATI, MARIA THERESA, food company executive, cooking expert, writer; b. Phila., July 16, 1965; Student, Laval U., Que., Can., 1984; BS in Fgn. Lang. Edn., Temple U., 1986. Pres., bd. dirs. Sierra Ctr., Feasterville, Pa., 1988—; pres. M.T.L. Prodns., Phila., 1989—; exec. pres. Art of Living, Prima Medin, 2004—. Spokesperson Compassion for Animals, Phila., 1988—. Author: Fashion, Fun and Fitness, 1989, The Model's Guide, 1998; editor mag. Better Nutrition for Today's Living, 1990—. Named Miss Pa., 1985, Miss World, 1986; recipient Merit award Actors and Artists Assn., Rome. Mem. AFTRA, NAFE (adv. bd. 1988—). Avocations: reading, cooking. E-mail: marialib@hotmail.com, marialiberati@liberaticorporation.com, lacucinadimaria@yahoo.com.

LIBERATO, LYNNE, lawyer; b. Pensacola, Fla., Dec. 22, 1953; BS in Journalism, Sam Houston State U.; MS in Journalism, Tex. A&M Commerce; JD, South Tex. Coll. Law. Bar: Tex. 1981, admitted to practice: US Ct. Appeals (5th Cir.) 1982, US Dist. Ct. (So. Dist.) Tex. Reporter/photographer Huntsville (Tex.) Item, 1974-75, Commerce Jour., 1975-76, Sta. KHOU-TV, Houston, 1976; with pub. affairs dept. Shell Oil Co., Houston, 1976-81; ptnr., Civil Appeals Haynes and Boone LLP, Houston. Chief staff atty. First Ct. Appeals, Houston, 1981-90; mem. adminstrv. oversign com. State Bar of Tex., 1995-96, gen. counsel oversight com., 1995-96, adv. com. legal svcs. corp., 1995-96, others; examiner Tex. Bd. Legal Specialization, 1989, appellate adv. bd. 1990-92; sec. Com. for Harris County Benchbook, 1993-97; speaker in field. Contbr. articles to numerous profl. jour.; author: Reason for Reversal in Texas Courts of Appeals (Outstanding Law Rev. Article Award, Tex. Bar Found., 2004). Chmn. Bd. United Way of Tex. Gulf Coast, 1996—, chmn. allocations rev. team, fund distbrn. subcom. 1997, chmn. implementation redesign com. 1996-97, steering com. for fund distbrn. redesign adv.com. 1994-95; mem. torch relay judging com. U.S. Olympics, 1996; v.p. Neighborhood Justice Ctr., 1981-85; mem. adv. bd. U. Houston Inst. for Urban Edn., 1997. Named Comml. Prosecutor of yr. Internat. Comml. Litigation mag., 1997, One of Ten Women on the Move, Houston Post, 1992, Woman of Year in Law, YWCA, 1993, Top Notch Appellate Lawyer, Tex. Lawyer, 2002, True Texan Award, Muscular Dystrophy Assn., 2002, Woman of Yr., United Way of Tex. Gulf Coast, 2004, one of top 100 Tex. Super Lawyers, Top 50 Female Lawyers, Top 100 Houston Lawyers, Tex. Montly Mag., 2003, 2004. Fellow Tex. Bar Found., Houston Bar Found.; mem. Am. Law Inst., Fedn. of Houston Profl. Women (Woman of Excellence 1994), Houston Bar Assn. (pres. 1993-94, editor jour. 1990-91, chmn. campaign for homeless 1991-92, legal edn. com. 1989-90, others), State Bar Tex. (chmn. client security fund com. 1995-96, exec. com. 1994-97, chmn. nominations and elections com. 1997-98, chmn. bd. dirs. 1996-97, pres. 2000-2001), Supreme Ct. Hist. Soc., Tex. Assn. Civil Trial and Appellate Specialists (bd. dirs. 1992-93). Office: Haynes and Boone LLP 1 Houston Ctr 1221 McKinney Ste 2100 Houston TX 77010 Office Phone: 713-547-2017. Office Fax: 713-236-5538. Business E-Mail: lynne.liberato@haynesboone.com.

LIBERMAN, GAIL JEANNE, editor; b. Neptune, N.J., Feb. 26, 1951; d. Si and Dorothy (Gold) L.; m. Alan Lavine, Dec. 20, 1991. BA, Rutgers U., 1972. Youth editor AP, N.Y.C., 1972-73; writer United Feature Syndicate, N.Y.C., 1973; reporter, broadcast editor UPI, Phila. and Hartford, Conn., 1973-75; reporter Courier-Post, Camden, N.J., 1976-80, Bank Advt. News, North Palm Beach, Fla., 1981-82; editor Bank Rate Monitor, North Palm Beach, 1982-97. Author: Improving Your Credit and Reducing Your Debt, 1994 (endorsed Inst. CFPs), The Complete Idiot's Guide to Making Money With Mutual Funds, 1996, Love, Marriage and Money, 1998, Rags to Riches: Motivating Stories of How Ordinary People Achieved Extraordinary Wealth, 2000, Short and Simple Guide to Life Insurance, 2000, More Rags to Riches: All New Stories of How Ordinary People Achieved Extraordinary Wealth, 2002, Rags to Retirement, 2003; columnist: Boston Herald, 1994—, America Online, 1996—, Investor Square, 1996—, Mutual Funds Interactive, 1996—, Quicken, 1998—, Palm Beach Daily News, 1998—, CNBC.com, 2000, Fasttrack mag., 2001, Pitts. Post-Gazette, 2001-; contbr. articles to profl. jours. Mem. Soc. Am. Bus. Editors and Writers. Personal E-mail: mwliblav@aol.com.

LIBERMAN, JUDITH, artist; b. Haifa, Israel, Mar. 4, 1929; arrived in U.S., 1947; d. Abraham and Zina (Kevesh) Weinshall; m. Robert Liberman, Sept. 22, 1953 (dec. Aug. 1986); children: David, Laura. BA, U. Calif., Berkeley, 1950; MA, U. Chgo., 1951, JD, 1954; LLM, U. Mich., 1956. Cert. art tchr. State of Mass. Contbg. artist Art Connection, Boston, 1997—. Author, illustrator: (children's book) The Bird's Last Song, 1976; author, artist: (exhbn. catalog) The Holocaust Wall Hangings, 1992; author, editor, artist (book) Holocaust Wall Hangings, 2002; one-woman shows include Hebrew Coll. Mus., Brookline, Mass., 1989, Jewish Cmty. Ctr., Newton, Mass., 1990, Mishkan l'Omanut Mus., Ein Harod, Israel, 1992, Yad Vashem Mus., Jerusalem, 1992, DeCordova Mus., Lincoln, Mass., 1994, U. Conn., Storrs, 1995, Hatikvah Holocaust Ctr., Springfield, Mass., 1997, Mus. at Stony Brook, N.Y., 1999, Fla. Holocaust Mus., St. Petersburg, Fla., 1999, The William Benton Mus. Art, Storrs, Conn., 2001, The Temple Tifereth Israel, Cleve., 2003, Hebrew Union Coll., Cin., 2003, Fla. Holocaust Mus., St. Petersburg, 2004, The Temple Tifereth Israel, Cleve., 2004, 05; permanent collections include: Yad Vashem Mus., Jerusalem, Haifa (Israel) Mus. Modern Art, Ghetto Fighters House Mus., Kibbutz Lochemai Hagetaot, Israel, DeCordova Mus., Lincoln, Mass., The Jackson Homestead Mus., Newton, Mass., Mus. Our Nat. Heritage, Lexington, Mass., The Temple Mus. Religious Art., Cleve., The William Benton Mus. Art, U. Conn., Storrs, Conn., Fla. Holocaust Mus., St. Petersburg, Archives at the Fine Arts Dept., Boston Pub. Libr. Mem. Nat. Assn. Women Artists, Am. Soc. Contemporary Artists, N.Y. Artists Equity Assn., Order of Coif, Phi Beta Kappa. Home: 18 Van Roosen Rd Newton MA 02459-3541 Personal E-mail: liberman@tiac.net.

LIBERMAN, ROBERT PAUL, psychiatry educator, researcher, writer; b. Newark, Aug. 16, 1937; s. Harry and Gertrude (Galowitz) L.; m. Janet Marilyn Brown, Feb. 16, 1973; children: Peter, Sarah, Danica, Nathaniel, Annalisa. AB summa cum laude, Dartmouth Coll., 1959, diploma in medicine with honors, 1960; MS in Pharmacology, U. Calif., San Francisco, 1961; MD, Johns Hopkins U., 1963. Diplomate Nat. Bd. Med. Examiners, Am. Bd. Psychiatry and Neurology. Intern Bronx (N.Y.) Mcpl. Hosp.-Einstein Coll. Medicine, 1963-64; resident psychiatry Mass. Mental Health Ctr., Boston, 1964-68; postdoctoral fellow in social psychiatry Harvard U., 1966-68, tchg. fellow in psychiatry, 1964-68; mem. faculty group psychotherapy tng. program Washington Sch. Psychiatry, 1968-70; asst. clin. prof. psychiatry UCLA, 1970-72, assoc. clin. prof., 1972-73, assoc. rsch. psychiatrist, 1973-76, rsch. prof. psychiatry, 1976-77, prof. psychiatry, 1977—. With nat. Ctr. Mental Health Svc., Tng. and Rsch., St. Elizabeths Hosp., also mem. NIMH Clin. and Rsch. Assocs. Tng. Program, Washington, 1968-70; dir. Camarillo-UCLA Clin. Rsch. Unit, 1970-97, dir. Clin. Rsch. Ctr. Schizophrenia and Psychiat. Rehab., 1977-2001; chief Rehab. Medicine Svc., West L.A. VA Med. Ctr., Brentwood divsn., 1980-92; cons. divsn. mental health and behavioral scis. edn. Sepulveda (Calif.) VA Hosp., 1975-80; practice medicine specializing in psychiatry, Reston, Va., 1968-70, Thousand Oaks, Calif., 1977—; staff psychiatrist Ventura County Mental Health Dept., 1970-75, Ventura County Gen. Hosp.; mem. med. staff UCLA Neuropsychiat. Inst. and Hosp., 1971—, Ventura Gen. Hosp., Camarillo State Hosp., 1970-97, West L.A. VA Med. Ctr.; dir. Rehab. Rsch. and Tng. Ctr. Mental Illness, 1980-85; prof. psychiatry, dir. psych. rehab. program UCLA Sch. Medicine. Author: (with King, DeRisi and McCann) Personal Effectiveness: Guiding People to Assert Their Feelings and Improve Their Social Skills, 1975, A Guide to Behavioral Analysis and Therapy, 1972, (with Wheeler, DeVisser, Kuehnel and Kuehnel) Handbook of Marital Therapy: An Educational Approach to Treating Troubled Relationships, 1980, Psychiatric Rehabilitation of Chronic Mental Patients, 1987, (with DeRisi and Mueser) Social Skills Training for Psychiatric Patients, 1989, (with Kuehnel, Rose and Storzbach) Resource Book for Psychiatric Rehabilitation, 1990, Handbook of Psychiatric Rehabilitation, 1992, (with Yager) Stress in Psychiatric Disorders, 1993, (with Corrigan) Behavior Therapy in Psychiatric Hospitals, 1994, International Perspectives on Skills Training with the Mentally Disabled, 1998; mem. editl. bd. Jour. Applied Behavior Analysis, 1972-78, Jour. Marriage and Family Counseling, 1974-78, Jour. Behavior Therapy and Exptl. Psychiatry, 1975-2000, Behavior Therapy, 1979-84, Assessment and Intervention in Devel. Disabilities, 1980-85; assoc. editor Jour. Applied Behavior Analysis, 1976-78, Schizophrenia Bull., 1981-87, Internat. Rev. Psychiatry, 1988—, Psychiatry, 1993—; contbr. over 300 articles to profl. jours. and chpts. to books. Bd. dirs. Lake Sherwood Cmty. Assn., 1978—, pres., 1979-81, 90-92, v.p., 1992-95, sec., 1995-97; mem. Conejo Valley Citizens Adv. Bd., 1979-81. Served as surgeon USPHS, 1964-68. Recipient Noyes award for Rsch. in Schizophrenia, 1992, Kolb award in Schizophrenia, 1994, Human Rights award Psychosocial Rehab., Lilly Reintegration prize, Human Rights award WHO, 2000, Reintegration award Eli Lilly, 2000, Disting. Investigator award Nat. Alliance for Rsch. in Schizophrenia and Depression, 2000-01; rsch. grantee NIMH, SSA, NIDA, VA, 1972—. Mem. Assn. Advancement Behavior Therapy (exec. com. 1970-72, dir. 1972-79), Am. Psychiat. Assn. (Hibbs and Van Ameringen awards, Inst. Psychiat. Svcs. Significant Achievement award), Assn. Clin. Psychosocial Rsch. (mem. coun. 1985-98, pres. 1995-97), Phi Beta Kappa. Home: 528 Lake Sherwood Dr Thousand Oaks CA 91361-5120 Office: UCLA Neuropsychiatric Inst 760 Westwood Plz Los Angeles CA 90095

LIBERT, DONALD JOSEPH, lawyer; b. Sioux Falls, S.D., Mar. 23, 1928; s. Bernard Joseph and Eleanor Monica (Sutton) L.; m. Jo Anne Murray, May 16, 1953; children: Cathleen, Thomas, Kevin, Richard, Stephanie. BS magna cum laude in Social Scis., Georgetown U., 1950, LLB, 1956. Bar: Ohio. From assoc. to ptnr. Manchester, Bennett, Powers & Ullman, Youngstown, Ohio, 1956-65; various positions to v.p., gen. counsel and sec. Youngstown Sheet & Tube Co., 1965-78; assoc. group counsel LTV Corp., Youngstown and Pitts., 1979; v.p. and gen. counsel Anchor Hocking Corp., Lancaster, Ohio, 1979-87; pvt. practice Lancaster, 1987—. Served to lt. (j.g.) USN, 1951-54. Mem. Ohio Bar Assn. (former chmn. sr. lawyers com.), Fairfield County Bar Assn. (mem. alt. dispute resolution com.), Lancaster Country Club, Rotary. Republican. Roman Catholic. Home: 2198 William T Cir Lancaster OH 43130-1087

LIBERTO, JOSEPH SALVATORE, retired bank executive; b. Balt., Apr. 26, 1929; s. Cosimo and Anna (Serio) L.; m. Mary Jane Colandro, May 20, 1962; children— Joseph C., Grace Ann. Student, Balt. City Coll., 1945-47; certificate accounting, Balt. Coll. Commerce, 1949; grad., Nat. Assn. Bank Auditors, and Comptrollers Sch. Banking, U. Wis., 1968. With Signet Bank, Md., Balt., from 1954; auditor Union Trust Co. Md., 1963-98, asst. v.p., security officer, 1979-98; ret. Served with AUS, 1951-53, Japan. Mem. Bank Adminstrn. Inst. (pres. Balt. 1968—), Inst. Internal Auditors. Home: 3219 Hiss Ave Parkville MD 21234-4724 Office: Signet Bank Baltimore St Baltimore MD 21202-1603

LIBERTY, JOHN JOSEPH, librarian; b. Sacramento, Dec. 14, 1927; s. John and Josephine (Zobac) L.; m. Irma Elizabeth Madsen, Aug. 25, 1951 (div. Oct. 1979); children: Kristine Elizabeth (dec. Aug. 1970), Marya Liberty. BA, Calif. State U., 1953; MA, U. Denver, 1963. Sr. law clk. Calif. State Libr., Sacramento, 1953-62, acquisitions libr., 1963-64, social sci. libr., 1964-92; faculty Calif. State U. Libr., Sacramento, 1963—; libr. emeritus, adj. faculty, dissent and social change project Calif. State U. Libr., Sacramento, 1992—. Author: Currents on the Left, 1974, Facing Right, 1977, Journals of Dissent and Social Change, 7th edit., 1993. Mem. ACLU. Home: 5231 Carrington St Sacramento CA 95819-1609 Office: Calif State Univ Libr 2000 State University Dr E Sacramento CA 95819-6039

LIBESKIND, DANIEL, architect; b. Poland, 1946; naturalized, U.S., 1965; married; 3 children. Student of music, Israel; degree in architecture, Cooper Union, 1970; postgrad., Sch. of Comparative Studies, Essex, Eng., 1972; doctorate (hon.), Humboldt U., Berlin, 1997, Essex U., England, 1999, U. Edinburgh, 2002, DePaul U., 2002, U. Toronto, 2004. Cert. arch., Germany. Head dept. architecture Cranbrook Acad., 1978—85; head Inst. Architecture and Planning, Milan, 1986—89; architect Berlin, 1990—2003, New York, 2003—. Sr. scholar John Paul Getty Ctr.; scholar Royal Danish Acad.; Louis Sullivan prof., Chgo.; Bannister Fletcher prof. U. London; Louis Kahn prof. Yale U., New Haven; Frank O'Gehry Chair U. Toronto; Cret chair U. Pa.; prof. Hochschule fur Gestaltung, Karlsruhe, Germany; guest prof. Harvard U., Cambridge, Mass., UCLA, Hochschule Weisensee, Germany; writer in field. Prin. works include Jewish Mus. Berlin, 1989—99 (German Architecture prize, 1999), Felix Nussbaum Mus., Osnabrueck, 1995—99, Danish Jewish Mus., 1996—2004, Victoria and Albert Mus. Ext., London, 1996—, Imperial War Mus. North, Manchester, Eng., 1997—2002, Jewish Mus. San Francisco, 1998—, Denver Art Mus. Ext., 2000—, Westside Shopping and Leisure Centre, Brunnen, Switzerland, 2001—, Bar-Ilan U. Wohl Conv. Centre, Tel Aviv, 2002—, German Mil. Mus., Dresden, 2002—, Dali Mus., Prague, 2004, London Met. U. Grad. Student Centre, 2002—04, World Trade Ctr. site, 2003—, responsible for sets, costumes lights, also dir., St. Francis of Assisi Opera, Berlin Opera, 2003, sets and costumes, Tristan, Opera Saarbruеken, 2001; author: Daniel Libeskind: The Space of Encounter, 2001. Recipient Golden Lion, Venice Biennale, 1985, award for architecture, Am. Acad. Arts and Letters, 1996, Citizen of Berlin Culture prize, 1996, Goethe Medallion for Cultural Contbn., 2000, Hiroshima Art prize, 2001; scholar, Am. Israel Cultural Found. Mem.: European Acad. Arts and Letters, Acad. of the Arts, Fedn. German Architects. Office: Studio Daniel Libeskind 2 Rector St 19th Fl New York NY 10006

LIBIN, ALVIN GERALD, professional sports team executive; b. Calgary, Apr. 22, 1931; m. Mona Libin; 1 child, Robert. LLD (hon.), U. Calgary. Pres., CEO Balmon Investments Ltd.; co-owner Calgary Flames - NHL. Chmn. Alta. Ingenuity Fund; dir. Extendicare, Inc. (N.Am.). Named an Officer of the Order of Canada, 2002. Office: 255-5 Ave SW # 3200 Calgary AB Canada T2P 3G6

LIBIN, LAURENCE ELLIOT, curator; b. Chgo., Sept. 19, 1944; s. Aaron L. and Vera Maye (Sugerman) Zimmerman; m. Genevieve Vaughn, July 26, 1970 (div. 1983); m. Kathryn Shanks, Dec. 31, 1988. Mus. B., Northwestern U., 1966; Mus.M., Kings Coll., U. London, 1968; postgrad., U. Chgo.,

1966-67, 68-71. Asst. prof. Ramapo Coll., Mahwah, N.J., 1972-73; curator dept. mus. instruments Met. Mus. Art, N.Y.C., 1973—, endowed chair, 1989—, rsch. curator, 1999—. Freelance profl. harpsichordist, 1964-. Author: American Musical Instruments, 1985; contbr. articles to profl. lit. Travel and rsch. grantee Nat. Mus. Act, 1979-80, Catherine Lorillard Wolfe Fund, Theodore Rousseau Meml. Fund, 1981; rsch. grantee Nat. Endowment for Arts and NEH, 1976-80, 89. Fellow Royal Soc. Arts; mem. Am. Recorder Soc. (editorial bd. 1979-89), Am. Mus. Instrument Soc. (bd. dirs. 1977—, v.p. 1987—), Am. Musicological Soc., Am. Organ Archives (gov. 1993—), Internat. Com. for Mus. and Collections of Musical Instruments. Home: 126 Darlington Ave Ramsey NJ 07446-1443 Office: Met Mus Art Fifth Ave New York NY 10028 Office Phone: 212-570-3919. Business E-Mail: laurence.libin@metmuseum.org.

LIBIN, PAUL, theater producer, theater director; b. Chgo., Dec. 12, 1930; m. Florence Rowe, Sept. 25, 1956; children: Charles, Claire, Andrea. Student, U. Ill.; B.F.A., Columbia U., 1956. Producing dir., v.p. Jujamcyn Theaters, N.Y.C., 1990—. Producer (plays) including The Crucible, 1958, Six Characters in Search of an Author, 1963, Royal Hunt of the Sun, 1965, Circle in the Sq. Theatre, N.Y.C., 1965-90; co-producer (plays) Uncle Vanya, 1973, The Iceman Cometh, 1973, Death of a Salesman, 1975, The Lady from the Sea, 1976, The Night of the Iguana, 1976, The Club, 1976, Tartuffe, 1977, The Inspector General, Man and Superman, Spokesong, Loose Ends, 1978, Major Barbara, Past Tense, The Man Who Came to Dinner, 1979, The Bacchae, John Gabriel Borkman, The Father, Scenes and Revelations, 1980, Candida, MacBeth, Eminent Domain, 1981, Present Laughter, The Queen and the Rebels, The Misanthrope, 1982, The Caine Mutiny Court-Martial, Heartbreak House, Awake and Sing, 1983, Design for Living, 1984, Arms and the Man, Marriage of Figaro, 1985, You Never Can Tell, 1986, Coastal Disturbances, 1987, A Streetcar Named Desire, Juno and the Paycock, 1988, The Night of the Iguana, 1988, The Devil's Disciple, 1988, Ghetto, 1989, Sweeney Todd, 1989, Zoya's Apartment, 1990, The Miser, 1990; producing dir. plays I Hate Hamlet, 1991, Secret Garden, 1991, La Bete, 1991, Two Trains Running, 1992, Jelly's Last Jam, 1992, Tommy, 1993, Angels in America, 1993, My Fair Lady, 1993, Grease, 1994, Love! Valour! Compassion!, 1995, Smokey Joe's Cafe, 1995, My Thing of Love, 1995, Moon Over Buffalo, 1995, Patti LuPone on Broadway, 1995, Seven Guitars, 1996, A Funny Thing Happened on the Way to the Forum, 1996, Present Laughter, 1996, David Copperfield, Dreams and Nightmares, 1996, Annie, 1997, Young Man from Atlanta, 1997, The Sound of Music, 1998, Forever Tango, 1998, The Beauty Queen of Leenane, 1998, Death of a Salesman, 1999, The Civil War, 1999, The Weir, 1999, Swing, 1999, A Moon for The Misbegotten, 2000, Proof, 2000, King Hedley II, 2001, The Crucible, 2002, Sixteen Wounded, 2004, Caroline, or Change, 2004, Gem of the Ocean, 2004. Served with U.S. Army, 1953—55. Recipient Obie award The Club, Village Voice, 1977, Tony award, 1976, 92, 93, 94, 95, medal Eugene O'Neill Soc., 2003, TAO House award Eugene O'Neill Found., 2004. Mem. 2d League Off Broadway Theatres and Producers (pres. emeritus), 1st League Am. Theatres and Producers (officer, exec. com., bd. govs.), Circle in the Square Theatre (owner, operator), Broadway Cares Equity Fights AIDS (pres.). Office: Jujamcyn Theaters St James Theatre 246 W 44th St New York NY 10036-3971

LI-BLEUEL, LINDA, musician, educator; b. Tex. City, Tex., Dec. 6, 1962; d. Tao Ping and Grace Li; m. John Stephen Bleuel, Aug. 21, 1993. MusB, U. Ill., 1985; MusM, U. Wis., 1987; D in Musical Arts, U. Ga., 1998. Assoc. prof. music Clemson (S.C.) U., 1997—. Dir. women's arts festival Clemson (S.C.) U., 2002—. Musician: North/South Consonance Recital Series in New York City, Seventh International Festival of Women Composers, College of Music Society International Conference, San Jose, Costa Rica, American Composers Alliance Concert, College of Music Society International Conference in Limerick, Ireland. Grantee, SC. Humanities Coun., 2002, NEA, 2005. Mem.: Music Teachers Nat. Assn. (v.p. S.C. competitions 2003—04). Home: 1667 Sequoya Way Seneca SC 29672 Office: Clemson University 221 Brooks Center Clemson SC 29634 Office Phone: 864-656-3856. Office Fax: 864-656-1013. E-mail: llibleu@clemson.edu.

LIBNER, MAURICE ALAN, lawyer; b. Ann Arbor, Mich., Mar. 20, 1953; s. Robert and Ruth (Garfunkel) L.; m. Sharon C. Bouchard, July 13, 1980; 1 child, Dena. BS, MIT, 1974; JD cum laude, Boston U., 1977. Bar: Maine 1977, U.S. Dist. Ct., Maine, 1977. Ptnr. McTeague Higbee, Libner, MacAdam, Case & Watson, Topsham, Maine, 1977-95; pvt. practice Brunswick, 1995—. Contbr. articles to profl. jours. Mem. Assn. Trial Lawyers Am. (Maine chpt., Maine bd. govs. 1991-93), Maine Bar Assn. Democrat. Jewish. Office: PO Box G Brunswick ME 04011-0831

LIBOFF, RICHARD LAWRENCE, physicist, researcher; b. N.Y.C., Dec. 30, 1931; s. William and Sarah (Mell) L.; m. Myra Blatt, July 4, 1954; children: David, Lisa. AB, Bklyn. Coll., 1953; PhD, NYU, 1961. Asst. prof. physics NYU, 1961-63; prof. applied physics, applied math. and elec. engring. Cornell U., 1964—2005; prin. investigator Air Force Office Sci. Research, 1978-83, Army Research Office, 1984—; prof. physics U. Ctrl. Fla., Orlando, 2005—. Cons. Batelle Columbus Lab. Author: Introduction to the Theory of Kinetic Equations, 1969, 1979, Russian edit., 1974, Introductory Quantum Mechanics, 1980, Korean edit., 1992, 4th edit., 2003, Waveguides, Transmission Lines and Smith Charts, 1984, Kinetic Theory: Classical, Quantum and Relativistic Descriptions, 1990, 3d edit., 2003, Primer for Point and Space Groups, 2003. Served with Chem. Corps U.S. Army, 1953-55. Recipient Founders Day cert. N.Y. U., 1961; Solvay fellow, 1972; Fulbright scholar, 1984 Fellow Am. Phys. Soc.; mem. Sigma Xi. Office: U Ctrl Fla Physics-Math Bldg Orlando FL 32816-2385 Office Phone: 407-823-5199. Business E-Mail: rll@physics.ucf.edu.

LIBONATI, MICHAEL ERNEST, law educator, writer; b. Chgo., May 25, 1944; s. Roland V. and Jeannette K. Libonati; m. Yvonne M. Barber, Sept. 30, 1967; children: Michael, Emma. LLB, Yale U., 1967, LLM, 1969. Bar: D.C. 1968, Ill. 1975, Pa. 1976. Prof. law Temple U., Phila., 1972-90, Carnell prof., 1990—; cons. U.S. Adv. Commn. Intergovernmental Rels. Vis. prof. law U. Ala., Tuscaloosa, 1976, Cornell U., Ithaca, NY, 1977, Coll. William and Mary, Williamsburg, Va., 1987. Author (with Sands and Martinez): Local Government Law, 4 vols., 1981—82; author: (with Hetzel and Williams) Legis. Law and Statutory Interpretation, 3d edit., 2001; author: Local Govt. Autonomy, 1993, Local Govt. Autonomy, Japanese edit., 1997, Local Govt. Autonomy, Spanish edit., 2000; author: (with Martinez) State and Local Govt. Law, 2000; asst. editor articles: Am. Jour. Legal History, 1971—82. Named Hon. Editor, Temple U. Law Quar., vol. 59, 1986; recipient Williams prize for Excellence in Tchg., 1985, 1990. Mem.: NAS (nat. rsch. bd., mem. trans. law project adv. commn.), Nat. Assn. Atty.'s Gen. (state constitution law project adv. bd.), Am. Law Inst. Office: Temple U Sch Law 1719 N Broad St Philadelphia PA 19122-6002 Office Phone: 215-204-7872. Business E-Mail: michael.libonati@temple.edu.

LIBRETT, JOHN JAMES, epidemiologist; MPH, PhD, U. Utah. Behavioral epidemiologist Utah Dept. Health, Salt Lake City, 1995—2002; health scientist Centers for Disease Control & Prevention, Atlanta, 2002—. Cons. Lance Armstrong Found., Austin, Tex., 2004—. Editor: (editor-in-chief health jour.) Utah's Health; contbr. articles to profl. jours. Chair Fed. Interagency Coun. on Pub. Health and Recreation, 2003—04; exec. dir. Gov.'s Coun. on Phys. Fitness and Sports, Salt Lake City, 1996—96; chair Coalition for Tobacco-Free Utah, 1996; pub. health liaison Ga. Bikes, Atlanta, 2003—04; mem. cmty. outreach edn. and media com. Utah Pub. Health Assn., Salt Lake City, 1992. Recipient Outstanding Team Performance, U.S. HHS, 2002, 2003, 2004, Quality Award, Utah Dept. Health, 1994, Quality award, 1995, 1996, 1997, 1998, 1999, 2000, Disting. Grad. Paper, U. Utah, 1997; scholar Rsch. Paper Award, U.S. HHS, 1998. Mem.: Am. Coll. Sports Medicine (, comm. and pub. info. com. 2005). Achievements include research in Conducted research in the relationship between recreation and public health; design of Designed a teen tobacco cessation program; first to Developed a nationally recognized youth legislative advocacy model; research in Conducted research exploring the relationship between volunteering and individual health; Conducted research on the relationship between physical activity and cancer.

LIBRETTO, JOHN CHARLES, television director; b. N.Y.C., Oct. 16, 1947; s. Charles and Esther (Boccuzzi) LiB.; m. Kristin Stromquist, Sept. 1, 1973; children: Katharine, Charles. BA in History, C. W. Post Coll., 1968. Mgr. NBC TV Network, N.Y.C., 1968-75, assoc. dir., 1975-85; dir. NBC Sports, N.Y.C., 1985-87, NBC News, N.Y.C., 1987-98, 2000—, ABC-TV, N.Y.C., 1998-2000; sr. dir. NBC News, 2000—. Lectr. NATAS, N.Y.C., 1989. Dir.; (TV shows) World Championship Track and Field, 1983 (Monitor award 1984), Wimbledon Preview, 1983-86, Baseball Pre-Game, 1983-86, NFL Football, 1983-88, Donahue, 1985, Internat. Amateur Athletics Fedn. Track and Field, 1986, NBC Nightly News, 1987-88, XXIV Olympics, 1988, Decisions '88, '92, '96, '00 and '04, Today Show and Weekend Today, 1989-98, Rights and Lives, 1989, A Closer Look, 1991, Presidential Debates, 1992,2004, Pope John Paul II in Central Park, 1995, The Faith Daniels Show, Ricki Lake Show, Tempestt, In Person With Maureen O'Boyle, Good Morning America, 1998-99, Dateline NBC, 2000—, Presdl. Innauguration, 2005, convs. and elections, 2000, Upfront Presentations, 2001— Sgt. USAF, 1969-71, Vietnam. Recipient Emmy award, 1984, 88, Emmy award nomination, 1979-80, 88, 96. Mem. NATAS, Dirs. Guild Am. Episcopalian. Avocations: music, travel, sports. Office: NBC 30 Rockefeller Plz New York NY 10112-0036 Office Phone: 212-664-7897. Business E-Mail: john.libretto@nbcuni.com.

LIBUTTI, FRANK, information technology company executive, former federal agency administrator, retired military officer; b. Long Island, N.Y., Apr. 23, 1945; m. Jean Wallace Libutti. Grad., The Citadel, Marine Corps. Office Cand., 1966; Ph.D (hon.), The Citadel, 2001. Advanced through grades to lt. gen. USMC, 1997, ret., 2001; infantry platoon commander 1st Battalion 9th Marines, Vietnam, 1967; chief instr., commanding officer, br. head capt. Officer Cand. Sch., 1969; squadron combat cargo officer Amphibious Squadron Three, San Diego, 1972; infantry co. commander 1st Battalion 2d Marines, Camp Lejeune, N.C., 1972; major Marine Barracks, Naples, Italy, 1977; head of career mgmt. sect. manpower dept. Hdqs. Marine Corps., Washington, 1980; lt. col., asst. sec. of gen. staff Office of the Asst. Commandant and Chief of Staff, 1982-83; sr. marine aide to comdt. USMC, 1983-85; commanding officer 1st reconnaissance Battalion, 1987, Contingency MAGTG 1-88, 1987; asst. chief staff 1st Marine Divsn., Camp Pendleton, 1988-90; brigadier gen., 1992; major gen., commanding gen. 1st Marine Divsn., 1994; asst. chief staff UN Command, Republic of Korea, 1996-97; commdg. gen. III Expeditionary Force, comdr. Marine Corps. bases, comdr. Marine forces, Japan USMC, 1997-99; comdr. Marine Forces Pacific, H.M. Smith, Hawaii, 1999—2001; spl. asst. for homeland security US Dept. Defense, Washington, 2001—02; dep. commr. of counter-terrorism NYC Police Dept., 2002—03; under sec., information analysis & infrastructure protection US Dept. Homeland Security, Washington, 2003—05; vice chmn., dir. Digital Fusion Inc., Huntsville, Ala., 2005—. Decorated Silver Star medal, Def. Superior Svc. medal with two bronze oak leaf clusters, Legion of Merit with gold star, Purple Heart with two gold stars, Navy Commendation medal, Republic of Korea Chonsu medal, Combat Action Ribbon. Office: Digital Fusion Inc 4949 A Corp Dr Huntsville AL 35805*

LICARY, CHERYL ANN, music educator, church musician; d. Wilbur John and Verna Elise Dietzman; m. Nicholas J. Licary, Mar. 25, 1972 (div. June 15, 1985); children: Nunzio, Chiara. BA, Luther Coll., 1972; MST, U. Wis., Whitewater, 1976. Vocal music instr., dept. chmn. Sch. Dist. Beloit, 1973—; ch. musician, 1973—. Clinician, adjudicator, 1975—. Co-author: Beyond Ratings, 2003. Vol. Red Cross, Beloit, 1983—; mem. adv. bd. U. Wis.-Whitwater Sch. Arts and Comms., 2005; organist, choir dir. Our Savior's Luth. Ch. Recipient Silver Star award, Wis. Dept. Recreation, 1995, Tchr. Recognition award, Beloit Rotary, 2001, Contbr. award, Zonta Commn., 2001, award for Excellence in Tchg. Music, Wis. Music Educators Assn., 2001, Great Minds 21st Century, 2003, 2004, 2005, Woman of Yr., Cambridge Blue Book, 2005, Ecolab Visions for Learning award, 2001, 2005. Mem.: Wis. Sch. Music Assn., Am. Guild of Organists, Assn. for Supr. and Curriculum Devel., Wis. Alliance for Arts Edn., Beloit Edn. Assn., Wis. Choral Dir.'s Assn., Wis. Music Educator's Assn. (Wis. award 2003, Gt. Minds 21st Century 2003), Nat. Edn. Assn., Music Educator's Nat. Conf., Am. Choral Dirs. Assn. Lutheran. Home: 1324 11th St Beloit WI 53511 Office Phone: 608-361-3036. Business E-Mail: clicary@sdb.k12.wi.us.

LICATA, ARTHUR FRANK, lawyer; b. NYC, June 16, 1947; BA in English, Le Moyne Coll., 1969; postgrad., SUNY, Binghamton, 1969—71; JD cum laude, Suffolk U., 1976. Bar: Mass. 1977, NY 1985, U.S. Ct. Appeals (1st cir.) 1977, U.S. Dist. Ct. Mass. 1977, admitted Frank B. Murray, Jr. Inns of Ct. 1990-92. Assoc. Parker, Coulter, Daley & White, Boston, 1977-82; prin. Arthur F. Licata P.C., Boston, 1982—. Prin. Ardlee Internat. Trading Co., Ea. and Ctrl. Europe and Russia, 1989-99; del. White House Conf. on Trade and Investment in Ctrl. Europe, Cleve., 1995; lectr. Mass. Continuing Legal Edn., Boston, 1982-2001, mem. trial adv. com., 1984-88; mem. working group on drinking and drunk driving Harvard Sch. Pub. Health Ctr. for Health Comms., 1986; spkr. Conv. Nat. Fedn. Paralegal Assns., Boston, 1987; del. U.S.-China Joint Session on Trade, Investment and Econ. Law, Beijing, 1987; co-sponsor Estonian legal del. visit to Mass. and NH correctional instns., 1990; Boston host former Soviet legal del. visit, 1989; legal advisor Czech Anglo-Am. Bus. Inst., Prague, Czech Republic, 1989—, Russian Children's Fund, 1992-94, Estonia Acad. for Pub. Safety, 1992-94; adv. bd. Ford Found.'s Legal Resource Ctr., Czech Republic, 1994-96; participant U.S.-Russian Investment Symposium, Harvard U.; spkr. Conf. on Proposed Tobacco Settlement and Tort Law, Harvard Law Sch., 1997; guest WGBH-Ch 2, TV, Greater Boston With Emily Rooney, 1999, 2001; chair seminar Mass. CLE, Boston, 2000. Panel mem. sta. WBZ TV, Boston; contbr. articles to profl. jours. U.S. Del. 6th People to People Juvenile Justice Program to USSR, Moscow, 1989; legal advisor Mass. chpt. MADD, Plymouth County, 1984-87; mem. State Adv. Com. Med. Malpractice, Boston, 1985; bd. dirs. Boston Ctr. for the Arts, 1990-94; mem. profl. adv. bd. Mass. Epilepsy Assn., 1986-93; counsel state coord. commn. MADD, Mass., 1984-86; participant Harvard Law Sch. Seminar Program on Negotiation and Mediation, 2000-01; mem. Congress Fellow, Ctr. Internat. Legal Studies, Salzburg, 2004. Recipient Outstanding Citizen award MADD, 1986, Sacred Angelic Imperial Constanian Order of Saint George awarded by the Duke of Parma, Italy, 2000. Fellow Mass. Bar Found. (life); mem. ATLA, Mass. Acad. Trial Attys. (bd. dirs. 1991-99, exec. com. 1997-99), Nat. Bd. Trial Advocacy (bd. cert. civil trial adv. 1992—). Avocation: travel. Office: Fed Res Plz 600 Atlantic Ave 25th Fl Boston MA 02210-2211 Fax: 617-523-7743. Office Phone: 617-523-9977. E-mail: Licata@att.net.

LICATA, KIMBERLY ALYSON, lawyer; d. Robert Michael and Helena Licata; children: Arielle Elena Martinez, Chloe Elizabeth Martinez. BA with distinction, U. Va., 1993; JD with honors, U. N.C., 1996. Bar: N.C. 1996, D.C. 1997. Atty. Dickstein Shapiro Morin & Oshinsky, Washington, 1996—98, Womble Carlyle Sandridge & Rice, PLLC, Research Triangle Park, NC, 1998—. Contbr. articles to profl. jours. Echols scholar, U. Va., 1990—93, Chancellors' scholar, U. N.C., 1993—96. Mem.: ABA, Am. Health Lawyers Assn., N.C. Bar Assn., Phi Eta Sigma, Order of the Coif (U. N.C. chpt.), Phi Delta Phi. Office: Womble Carlyle Sandridge & Rice PLLC Ste 400 2530 Meridian Pkwy Durham NC 27713 Office Phone: 919-484-2381. Office Fax: 919-484-2367. Business E-Mail: klicata@wcsr.com.

LICHATIN, STEPHEN, III, lawyer; b. Hackensack, NJ, Feb. 28, 1950; s. Stephen Jr. and Christine (Smith) L.; m. Susan Mueller, June 9, 1973; 1 child, Eric Stephen. AB, Colgate U., 1972; JD, Rutgers U., 1975. Bar: NJ 1975, RI 1976, US Dist. Ct. RI, US Ct. Appeals (1st cir.), US Supreme Ct. asst. atty. gen. chief of civil divsn. R.I. Dept. of Atty. Gen., Providence; ptnr. Tillinghast Collins & Graham, Providence; mng. ptnr. Peabody & Brown, Providence; ptnr. Nixon Peabody LLP, Providence, 1999—. Mem. Gov.'s Commn. to Reform Ins. Statutes. Trustee RI Sch. of Design, Providence, 1996—; dir. First Night Providence, 1987-94, chmn. bd. dirs.; incorporator The Providence Found.; treasurer bd. dirs Am. Heart Assn., RI Affiliate; mem. bd. trustees RI Chamber of Bus. and Industry. Fellow Brown Humanities Inst.; mem. ABA, Nat. Assn. of Coll. and Univ. Attys., Providence Found. Inc., NJ Bar Assn., RI Bar Assn., Providence Art Club. Office: Nixon Peabody LLP One Citizens Plz Ste 500 Providence RI 02903 Office Fax: 401-454-1030. E-mail: slichatin@nixonpeabody.com.

LICHFIELD, WALTER CURTIS, religious studies educator, writer; b. Utah; s. Robert Clarence and Vinna Haws Lichfield; m. Wilma Jeannette Browning, Apr. 14, 1949; children: Lawrence, Brent, Robert, Lucille, Joseph(dec.), Terry, Curtis, Jonathan, Jeanette, Maybeth. BS in History and Polit. Sci., Utah State U.; MS, postgrad., Brigham Young U. Sales Edison Bros. Co., St. Louis; tchr. LDS Ch., Utah. Sgt. USMC, 1946—49. Mem.: Sons Utah Pioneers, Am. Legion, Phi Alpha Theta. Home: 11772 Corley St Tonopah AZ 85354

LICHLITER, WARREN EUGENE, surgeon, educator; b. Murphysboro, Ill., Jan. 24, 1952; s. Gene Estel and Dorothy Colleen (Williams) L.; m. Carol Jane Loftin, Nov. 3, 1979; children: Gary Edward, Christopher Warren, Adrienne Leigh, Abigail Meredith. BA, U. Tenn., 1974; MD, U. Tex., Galveston, 1978. Intern and resident in gen. surgery Baylor U. Med. Ctr., Dallas, 1979-83, resident in colon rectal surgery, 1983-84, mem. attending staff dept. colon rectal surgery, 1984—, assoc. dir. surg. edn., 1984—, program dir. dept. colon rectal residency, 2000—, chief dept. colon rectal surgery, 2000—; clin. asst. prof. surgery health sci. ctr. U. Tex., Dallas, 1990—. Mem. adv. bd. Am. Cancer Soc., Dallas. Fellow: ACS, Am. Soc. Colon Rectal Surgeons; mem.: Dallas County Med. Soc. (sec.-treas. 2001—02, pres. 2004), Dallas Soc. Surgeons, Tex. Surg. Soc., Alpha Omega Alpha. Avocations: running, bicycling, sailing, kayaking, swimming. Office: 3409 Worth St Ste 500 Dallas TX 75246-2057

LICHSTEIN, EDGAR, cardiologist; b. N.Y.C., Nov. 27, 1936; s. Joseph and Ruth (Weisner) L.; m. Marilyn Dorf, June 19, 1966; children: Adam Robert, Amy Ruth. AB, Columbia Coll., 1957; MD, SUNY, Bklyn., 1961. Diplomate Am. Bd. Internal Medicine, Am. Bd. Cardiovascular Disease. Intern Lenox Hill Hosp., N.Y.C., 1961-62, resident in medicine, 1962-63, NYU, N.Y.C., 1963-64; fellow in cardiology NYU-Nat. Heart Inst., 1964-66; chief cardiology Mt. Sinai Med. Services Elmhurst, N.Y.C., 1971-77; dir. cardiology Maimonides Med. Ctr., Bklyn., 1977-89, chmn. dept. medicine, 1989—; prof. medicine SUNY Downstate, 1980—2004, Mt. Sinai Sch. Medicine, 2004—. Bd. dirs. Maimonides Rsch. and Devel. Found., Bklyn., N.Y. Heart Assn. Author: Hemodynamicst's Reference File, 1971; contbr. articles to profl. jours. Mem. New Rochelle (N.Y.) Sch. Bd., 1977-81; bd. dirs. New Rochelle Youth Soccer League, 1976. Served to capt. USAF, 1966-68. Fellow ACP, Am. Coll. Cardiology, Am. Coll. Chest Physicians, Coun. Clin. Cardiology; mem. N.Y. Heart Assn. (chmn. coun. cmty. programs, bd. dirs. 1983—). Jewish. Avocation: swimming. Office: Maimonides Med Ctr 4802 10th Ave Brooklyn NY 11219-2844 Office Phone: 718-283-7074.

LICHT, RICHARD A., lawyer; b. Providence, Mar. 25, 1948; s. Julius M. Licht and Irene (Lash) Olson; m. Roanne Sragow; children: Jordan David, Jeremy Michael, Jaclyn Rose, Jacob Adam. AB cum laude, Harvard U., 1968, JD cum laude, 1972; LLM in Taxation, Boston U., 1975. Law clk. to chief justice R.I. Supreme Ct., Providence, 1973-74; ptnr. Letts, Quinn & Licht, Providence, 1974-84; mem. R.I. Senate, Providence, 1975-84, chmn. judiciary com. and rules com., 1984; lt. gov. State of R.I., Providence, 1985-89; mng. ptnr. Tillinghast, Licht, Perkins, Smith & Cohen LLP, Providence, 1989—. Former chmn. R.I. Commn. on Racial, Religious and Ethnic Harrassment, Dr. Martin Luther King Jr. Holiday Commn., State Energy and Tech. Study Commn. rules com.; chmn. Coun. of State Govt., Intergovtl. Affairs Com., Nat. Focus Team, Bd. Gov. Higher Edn.; bd. regents Elem. and Secondary Edn.; mem. Pub. Telecom. Authority R.I., Univ. R.I. Found., Community Coll. R.I. Found. Bd. dirs., mem. corp. Roger Williams Hosp.; advisor Community Prep. Sch.; corporator Roger Williams Hosp.; trustee Save the Bay, Inc., Emma Pendleton Bradley Hosp.; bd. dirs. Temple Emanuel, Providence, Jewish Fedn. R.I., Samaritans; chmn. Small Bus. Adv. Council, Task Force on Teenage Suicide Prevention, CD Civil Preparedness Adv. Council, Urban League R.I., 1980-82, John Hope Settlement House, 1976-81; chair Am. Cancer Soc. Ball, 1989, Jewish Fedn. R.I. Passage to Freedom, 1989; chair R.I. chpt. Anti-Defamation League; mem. Women and Infants Corp., Dorcas Place, PARI, UNITAM, NCLG task force of Youth Suicide Prevention, Jewish Home for the Aged of R.I., bd. govs. for the handicapped; active YWCA of Greater R.I., Vols. in Action, Inc., Big Sister Assn. of R.I., Big Bros. R.I.; coordinator vols. gubernatorial campaigns Frank Licht, 1968, 70; active Jewish Community Ctr., Providence, 1975-83, East Side Sr. Citizens Ctr., 1975-76, R.I. Youth Guidance Ctr., Inc., 1987, Block Island Conservancy, Inc., Notre Dame Health Care Corp., 1987; Dem. candidate for U.S. Senate, 1988; chmn. ann. campaign Meeting Street Sch., 1990-91, mem. steering com. for capital fund drive, 1989-92; mem. corp. Womens and Infants Hosp.; Dem. candidate U.S. Senate, 2000. Named an Outstanding Young Man of R.I., R.I. Jaycees, 1979; recipient David Ben Gurion award State of Israel Bonds, 1977, Outstanding Pub. Service award Temple Torat Yisrael, 1985, Disting. Services to the Hispanic Community award Casa Puerto Rico, 1985, Hon. Pub. Service award Meeting St. Sch., 1986, Recognition award R.I. Day Care Dirs. Assn., 1986, award of Appreciation Child Care/Human Services, 1986, Govtl. Services award Ocean State Residences for the Retarded, 1987. Mem. R.I. Bar Assn., Hosp. Assn. R.I. (bd. dirs. 1997). Democrat. Office: Tillinghast Licht LLP 10 Weybosset St Providence RI 02903-2818 Fax: 401-456-1210. E-mail: rlicht@tllaw.com.

LICHT, ROBERT H., ceramics engineer; b. Newark, June 19, 1950; s. Sam and Lenora Licht; m. Susan Hollowell, May 19, 1985; children: Eric S, Andrew W. BS, Rutgers U., New Brunswick, N.J., 1972; MS, Pa. State U., 1974. Mem.,tech. staff GTE Labs., Waltham, Mass., 1974—78; rsch. supr./rsch. engr. Norton Co., Worcester, Mass., 1978—85, mgr. prototype and devel. ops. Northboro, Mass., 1985—89; mgr. govt. programs group Saint-Gobain/Norton, Northboro, 1989—. Chmn. U.S. Advanced Ceramics Assn., Washington, 2001—03, chmn., govt. affairs com., 1998—2001. Recipient Outstanding Leadership award, U.S. Advanced Ceramics Assn., 2004. Mem.: Am. Ceramic Soc. Achievements include patents for Grinding Wheel for Grinding Titanium; Resin Bonded Grinding Wheel with Fillers. Avocation: history. Home: 48 Emerson Rd Northborough MA 01532 Office: Saint-Gobain Ceramics & Plastics Inc 9 Goddard Rd Northborough MA 01532 Office Phone: 508-351-7815. Business E-Mail: robert.h.licht@saint-gobain.com.

LICHTBLAU, JOHN H., economist; b. Vienna, June 26, 1921; came to U.S., 1939; s. Ernst and Alice (Fischer) Lichtblau-Lind; m. Charlotte M. Adelberg, Apr. 12, 1944; 1 child, Claudia L. Payne. B in Social Sci., CCNY, 1949; postgrad., NYU, 1950-53. Economist U.S. Dept. Labor, Washington, 1951-53, Conf. Bd., N.Y.C., 1953-54, Walter J. Levy Assocs., N.Y.C., 1955-56; research dir. Petroleum Ind. Research Found. Inc., N.Y.C., 1956-61, exec. dir., 1961-72, chmn., 1972—, PIRA Energy Group, N.Y.C., 1977—. Bd. mem. The Energy Forum NYU. Contbr. articles to profl. jours., book chpts. Served with U.S. Army, 1944-47, ETO. Mem. Am. Petroleum Inst., Nat. Petroleum Coun., 1965-2002, Am. Econ. Assn., Internat. Assn. for Energy Economics (5th Ann. award for outstanding contbns. 1986), Coun. on Fgn. Rels. Office: Petroleum Industry Rsch Found 3 Park Ave New York NY 10016-5902 Personal E-mail: jlichtblau@nyc.rr.com.

LICHTE, ARTHUR J., career military officer; b. Bronx, N.Y., Jan. 20, 1949; BS in Bus. Adminstrn., Manhattan Coll., 1971; M in Systems Mgmt., U. Southern Calif., 1978; student, Nat. War Coll., 1989, JFK Sch. Govt., 1994, Naval Postgraduate Sch., 2002. Commd. 2d lt. USAF, 1971, advanced through grades to lt. gen., 2003; pilot, EC-121 552nd Airborne Early Warning and Control Wing, McClellan AFB, Calif., 1972-75; co-pilot, aircraft comdr., flight comdr. 380th Air Refueling Squadron, Plattsburgh AFB, N.Y., 1975-81; various positions Hdqrs. Strategic Air Command, Offutt AFB, Nebr., 1981-85; KC-10A flight comdr., ops. officer to comdr. 9th Air Refueling Squadron, March AFB, Calif., 1985-88; dep. chief Office of Strategic Forces divsn. Hdqrs. USAF, The Pentagon, Washington, 1989-90, exec. officer, dep. chief of staff for programs/resources, 1990-91; asst. dep. comdr. for ops. 2nd Bombardment Wing, Barksdale AFB, La., 1991-92; comdr. 458th ops. group 22nd Air Refueling Wing, Barksdale AFB, La., 1992-93; exec. officer to comdr. chief U.S. Transp. Command, comdr. Air Mobility Command, Scott AFB, Ill., 1993-95; comdr. 92nd Air Refueling Wing, Fairchild AFB, Wash., 1995-96, 89th Airlift Wing, Andrews AFB, Md., 1996-99; dir. global rsch .Office Asst. Sec. Air Force for Acquisition USAF, Arlington, Va., 1999—2000; dir. plans & programs Hdqs. Air Mobility Command Air Mobility Command, Scott AFB, Ill., 2000—02; vice comdr. USAF Europe USAF Europe, Ramstein AFB, Germany, 2002—05; asst. vice chief of staff USAF, Washington, 2005—. Decorated Legion of Merit with oak leaf cluster, Disting. Svc. medal, Def. Superior Svc. medal, Meritorious Svc. medal with three oak leaf clusters, Nat.Order of Merit Office: 1670 Air Force Pentagon Washington DC 20330*

LICHTEN, WILLIAM L., retired physics professor; b. Phila., Mar. 5, 1928; s. Harold and Goldie (Rosenbaum) L.; m. Susan Lurie, June 18, 1950; children: Michael, Stephen, Julia. BA in Physics, Swarthmore Coll., 1949; MS in Physics, U. Chgo., 1953, PhD in Physics, 1956. Rsch. physicist, postdoctoral fellow Columbia U., N.Y.C., 1956-58; from. asst. prof. to assoc. prof. U. Chgo., 1958-64; prof. Yale U., New Haven, 1964—2003, prof. emeritus, 2003—. Contbr. articles to sci. jours. Fellow Am. Phys. Soc. Office: Dept Physics Yale University PO Box 208120 New Haven CT 06520-8120 E-mail: williamlichten@yale.edu.

LICHTENBERG, ALLAN JOSEPH, science educator; b. Passaic, N.J., Sept. 22, 1930; s. Milton and Ida (Krulewitz) L.; m. Elizabeth Anne Lind, Sept. 15, 1959. AB, Harvard U., 1952; MS, MIT, 1954; PhD, Oxford (England) U., 1961. Asst. prof. U. Calif., Berkeley, 1959-65, assoc. prof., 1965-71, prof. science, 1971—. Rsch. prof. Japan Inst. Fusion Sci., Nagoya, 1991. Author: Phase Space Dynamics of Particles, 1969; co-author: Regular and Stochastic Motion, 1983, Regular and Chaotic Dynamics, 2nd Edition, 1991, Principles of Plasma Discharges and Materials Processing, 1994. Fellow Guggenheim Found., 1965-66, Miller Inst., 1968-69, U.S.-Australia fellow NSF, 1984, 91. Home: 1560 Hawthorne Ter Berkeley CA 94708-1806

LICHTENBERG, BYRON K., futurist, consultant, manufacturing executive, pilot; b. Stroudsburg, Pa., Feb. 19, 1948; s. Glenn John and Georgianna (Bierei) L.; children: Kristin, Kimberly; m. Tamara Miller, Mar. 14, 1997; children: Nathan, Jessanne, Georgiana. ScB, Brown U., 1969; MS, MIT, 1975, ScD, 1979. Rsch. scientist MIT, Cambridge, 1978-84; pres. Payload Systems, Inc., Cambridge, 1984-89, chief scientist, 1989-91; pres., chief exec. officer Omega Aerospace Inc., Virginia Beach, Va., 1991-96; pilot S.W. Airlines, 1994—; pres. Zero Gravity Corp., 1993—2004, chief tech. officer, 2005—. Contbg. author NASA Payload Specialist, 1979-92, Flew on Space Shuttle Mission #9, #45; contbr. articles to profl. jours. Trustee X-Prize Found., 1994—. Served to lt. col. USAF, Mass. Air N.G., 1969-93. Recipient NASA Space Flight award, 1983, 92, Spaceflight award VFW, 1983, Haley Spaceflight award AIAA, 1983. Mem. Assn. of Space Explorers (founder), Tau Beta Pi, Sigma Xi Avocations: golf, racquetball, windsurfing, skiing.

LICHTENBERG, MAGGIE KLEE, publishing company executive; b. N.Y.C., Nov. 19, 1941; d. Lawrence and Shirley Jane (Wicksman) Klee; m. James Lester Lichtenberg, Mar. 31, 1963 (div. 1982); m. William Shaw Jones, July 2, 2000; children: Gregory Lawrence, Amanda Zoe. BA, U. Mich., 1963; postgrad., Harvard U., 1963. Book rev. editor New Woman mag., 1972-73; assoc. editor children's books Parents Mag. Press, 1974; editor, rights dir. Books for Young People, Frederick Warne & Co., N.Y.C., 1975-78; sr. editor Simon & Schuster, N.Y.C., 1979-80; dir. sales promotion Grosset & Dunlap, N.Y.C., 1980-81; ednl. sales mgr. Bantam Books, N.Y.C., 1982-84; dir. mktg. and sales Grove Press, N.Y.C., 1984-86, dir. of sales, 1986-87; dir. sales Weidenfeld & Nicolson, N.Y.C., 1986-87; mktg. dir. Beacon Press, Boston, 1988-95; bus. and pub. coach, 1995—. Writer, freelance critic, 1961—. Contbr. articles, essays, stories, poetry, revs. to mags., newspapers and anthologies. Bd. dirs. Children's Book Council, 1978. Recipient 2 Avery Hopwood awards in drama and fiction, 1962, 2 in drama and poetry, 1963; coll. fiction contest award Mademoiselle mag., 1963; Woodrow Wilson fellow, 1963. Mem. Women's Nat. Book Assn. (past pres. N.Y. chpt.), Internat. Coach Fedn. (cert.), The Coaching Collective, Pubs. Mktg. Assn., N.Mex. Book Assn., PEN N.Mex., Adult Congenital Heart Assn. Home and Office: 4 Cosmos Ct Santa Fe NM 87508-2285 Office Phone: 505-986-8807. Personal E-mail: maggie@maggielichtenberg.com.

LICHTENSTEIN, ELISSA CHARLENE, legal association executive; b. Oct. 23, 1954; d. Mark and Rita (Field) L. AB cum laude, Smith Coll., Northampton, Mass., 1976; JD, George Washington U., 1979. Bar: D.C. 1980, U.S. Dist. Ct. (D.C. dist.) 1980, U.S. Ct. Appeals (D.C. cir.) 1980. Law clk. U.S. EPA, Washington, 1978-79; staff dir. ABA, Washington, 1979—, assoc. dir. pub. svcs. divsn., 1981-85, dir., 1985—. Editor, contbr.: Common Boundary/Common Problems: The Environmental Consequences of Energy Production, 1982, Exit Polls and Early Election Projections, 1984, The Global Environment: Challenges, Choices and Will, 1986, (newsletter) Environ. Law; co-editor, contbr. The Environ. Network; co-editor: Determining Competency in Guardianship Proceedings, 1990, Due Process Protections for Juveniles in Civil Commitment Proceedings, 1991, Environmental Regulation in Pacific Rim Nations, 1993, The Role of Law in the 1992 UN Conference on Environment and Development, 1992, Trade and the Environment in Pacific Rim Nations, 1994, Public Participation in Environmental Decision-making, 1995, Endangered Species Act Reauthorization: A Biocentric Approach, 1996, Sustainable Development in the Americas: The Emerging Role of the Private Sector, 1996, Environmental Priorities in Southeast Asian Nations, 1997, Law School Public Interest Law Programs, 1995, 99, numerous others; prodn. contbg. editor American Justice Through Immigrants' Eyes, 2004, A Judge's Guide to Immigration Law in Criminal Proceedings, 2004. Named Named Outstanding Young Woman of Am., 1982. Mem.: NAFE, ABA, Greater Washington Soc. Assn. Execs., D.C. Bar Assn., Met. Washington Environ. Profls. (pres. 1986—96), Assn. Women in Comms., Am. Soc. Assn. Execs., Environ. Law Inst. (assoc.). Democrat. Jewish. Office: ABA Div Pub Svcs 740 15th St NW 9th Fl Washington DC 20005-1019

LICHTENSTEIN, HARVEY, performing arts association administrator; b. Bklyn., Apr. 9, 1929; s. Samuel and Jennie (Meiner) Lichtenstein; m. Phyllis Holbrook, Nov. 14, 1971; children: Saul, John. BA, Bklyn. Coll., 1951, LHD (hon.), 1986; postgrad., Bennington (Vt.) Coll., 1953; ArtsD (hon.), L.I. U., 1989; MusD (hon.), Mannes Coll. Music, 1989; LHD (hon.), Pratt Inst., 1993, Juilliard Sch., 1999, Bard Coll., 1999; DFA (hon.), Princeton U., 1999. Subscription and group sales mgr. N.Y.C. Ballet, also N.Y.C. Opera, 1965-67; pres., exec. producer Bklyn. Acad. Music, 1967-99; chmn. BAM Local Devel. Corp., N.Y.C., 1999—; Am. dir. Spoleto (Italy) Festival, 1971-73. Decorated officer Legion of Honor France; recipient Disting. Svc. to Arts award, Am. Acad. Arts and Letters, 1999, Nat. Medal of Arts, 1999. Mem.: Century Assn. (N.Y.C.). Office Phone: 718-907-4400.

LICHTENSTEIN, LAWRENCE MARK, immunologist, allergist, educator; b. Washington, May 31, 1934; s. Samuel and Lillian (Colodny) L.; m. Carolyn Eggert, June 15, 1956; children: Elizabeth, Joshua, Rebekah. MD, U. Chgo., 1960; PhD, Johns Hopkins U., 1965. Diplomate Am. Bd. Allergy and Immunology. Intern Johns Hopkins Hosp., 1960-61, resident in medicine, 1965-66; asst. prof. medicine Johns Hopkins U. Sch. Medicine, 1966-70, assoc. prof., 1970-75, prof., 1975—, dir. Johns Hopkins Asthma and Allergy Ctr., 1989—2002. Mem. Nat. Adv. Allergy and Infectious Diseases Coun. Mem. editl. bd.: Clin. Immunology and Pathology, Immunology, Pulmonary, Allergy; editor 15 books; contbr. articles to profl. jours. Fellow ACP; mem. Am. Soc. Pharmacology and Exptl. Therapeutics, Am. Assn. Immunology (sec., treas.), Am. Fedn. Clin. Rsch., Am. Soc. Clin. Investigation, Am. Acad. Allergy and Immunology (past pres.), Am. Soc. Exptl. Pathology, Collegium Internat. Allergologicum (past pres.), Assn. Am. Physicians. Democrat. Jewish. Office: John Hopkins Asthma & Allergy Ctr 5501 Hopkins Bayview Cir Baltimore MD 21224-6821 Office Phone: 410-550-2101.

LICHTENSTEIN, ROBERT JAY, lawyer; b. Phila., Jan. 23, 1948; s. Irving M. and Marjorie J. (Weiss) L.; m. Sandra Paley, Aug. 14, 1971; children: David P., Kate. BS in Econs., U. Pa., 1969; JD, U. Pitts., 1973; LLM in Taxation, NYU, 1974. Bar: Pa. 1974, U.S. Tax Ct. 1978, U.S. Dist. Ct. (ea. dist.) Pa. 1979, U.S. Ct. Appeals (3rd cir.) 1982, U.S. Ct. Appeals (4th cir.) 1987. Assoc. Morgan, Lewis & Bockius, Phila., 1974-78; ptnr., leader employee benefits & exec. compensation practice group Morgan, Lewis & Bockius LLP, Phila., 1988—; ptnr. Saul, Ewing, Remick & Saul, 1978-88; dir. Maritrans Inc. Instr. Main Line Paralegal Inst., Wayne, Pa., 1984-87, Paralegal Inst., Phila., 1987-90; adj. prof. law Villanova U. Sch. Law, 1991—, U. Pa. Sch. of Law, 1999—. Trustee Temple Brith Achim, King of Prussia, Pa., 1986-91. Mem.: ABA, Phila. Bar Assn. Democrat. Avocations: skiing, tennis, reading. Office: Morgan Lewis Bockius LLP 1701 Market St Philadelphia PA 19103-2903 Office Phone: 215-963-5726. Office Fax: 215-963-5001. E-mail: rlichtenstein@morganlewis.com.

LICHTENSTEIN, SALLY (ALI) TUCKER, small business owner, writer, English and women's studies educator; d. A. Richard Tucker and Orenadel Pitney; m. John E. Lichtenstein, May 1982; children: Evan, Jesse, Samar, Eli. BA in Cultural Studies and Philosophy, Vt. Coll., 1999, MA in Rhetoric and Women's Studies, 2001; PhD in Interdisciplinary Arts and Sci., Union Inst. and U., 2005. Founder, dir. Empty Bowl Writers, Marlborough, NH, 1998—. Instr. Keene (N.H.) State Coll., 1999—; chmn. Monadnock Arts in Edn., Keene, 2000—03. Contbr. Mem.: AAUW, Nat. Coun. Tchrs. English, Nat. Women's Studies Assn. Democrat. Avocations: hiking, kayaking, travel, writing, photography. Office: Keene State College 202 Parker Hall 229 Main St MS 1402 Keene NH 03435-1402 Office Phone: 603-358-8888 4176. Business E-Mail: alichten@keene.edu.

LICHTER, ALLEN S., oncology educator, university dean; BS, U. Mich., 1968, MD, 1972. Intern St. Joseph Hosp., Denver; resident U. Calif., San Francisco, 1976; former dir. radiation therapy sect. radiation oncology br. Nat. Cancer Inst.; dir. breast oncology program Comprehensive Cancer Ctr., U. Mich., Ann Arbor, 1984-91, chmn. dept. radiation oncology, 1984-97, interim dean Med. Sch., 1998-99, prof. radiation oncology, 1999—, dean Med. sch., 1999—. Assoc. editor Jour. Clin. Oncology; editl. bd. Jour. Nat. Cancer Inst., Internat. Jour. Radiation Oncology; co-editor Clinical Oncology, 1995, 2d edit., 1999. Mem. Am. Soc. Clin. Oncology (past pres.), Am. Soc. Therapeutic Radiology and Oncology (bd. dirs.). Office: U Mich M4101 Med Science Bldg I-C Wing MSI 0624, 1301 Catherine St Ann Arbor MI 48109

LICHTER, PAUL RICHARD, ophthalmology educator; b. Detroit, Mar. 7, 1939; s. Max D. and Buena (Epstein) L.; m. Carolyn Goode, 1960; children: Laurie, Susan. BA, U. Mich., 1960, MD, 1964, MS, 1968. Diplomate Am. Bd. Ophthalmology. Asst. to assoc. prof. ophthalmology U. Mich., Ann Arbor, 1971-78, prof., chmn. dept. ophthalmology and visual scis., 1978—. Chmn. Am. Bd. Ophthalmology, 1987. Editor-in-chief Ophthalmology jour., 1986-94; assoc. editor Am. Jour. Ophthalmology, 2004—. Served to lt. comdr. USN, 1969-71. Fellow: Am. Acad. Ophthalmology (bd. dirs. 1981—97, pres. 1996, sr. hon. award 1986, Lifetime Achievement award 2001); mem.: Acad. Ophthalmologica Internat. (sec.-gen. 2002—), Internat. Coun. Ophthalmology, Assn. Univ. Profs. Ophthalmology (trustee 1986—93, pres. 1991—92), Mich. Ophthalmol. Soc. (pres. 1993—95), Washtenaw County Med. Soc., Mich. State Med. Soc., Pan Am. Assn.Ophthalmology (bd. dirs. 1988—, sec.-treas. English-speaking countries 1991—95, pres. 1999—2001), Am. Ophthalmol. Soc. (pres. 2000—01), AMA, Alpha Omega Alpha. Office: U Mich Med Sch Kellogg Eye Ctr 1000 Wall St Ann Arbor MI 48105-1912 E-mail: Plichter@umich.edu.

LICHTER, STEPHEN MARC, oncologist; b. N.Y.C., Feb. 13, 1949; MD, Univ. Health Scis./Chgo. Med. Sch., 1975. Diplomate Am. Bd. Internal Medicine, Am. Bd. Med. Oncology. Intern Brookdale Hosp. Med. Ctr., NY, 1975—76, resident, 1976—78, fellow, 1978—80; assoc. chief hematology/oncology Beth Israel Med. Ctr., Bklyn.; asst. clin. prof. mediicine SUNY Health Sci. Ctr., Bklyn. Office: 2558 E 18th St Brooklyn NY 11235 Office Phone: 718-616-0801. E-mail: lichter@hemoncare.com.

LICHTERMAN, MARTIN, history professor; b. N.Y.C., July 18, 1918; s. Joseph Aaron and Esther S. (Schacknowitz) L.; m. Charlotte Rottenberg, Oct. 7, 1945; children: Joshua David, Andrew Marc. BS, Harvard U., 1939, A.M., 1947; PhD, Columbia U., 1952. Instr. Rutgers U., Newark, 1948-51; instr., lectr. Princeton U., 1953-55; mem. research staff Princeton U. (Center for Research on World Polit. Instns.), 1951-53; asst. prof. M.I.T., 1955-60; dir. research to gov. Mass., 1959-60; exec. sec., dir. New Eng. Bd. Higher Edn., Winchester, Mass., 1961-66; dean Center Humanities and Social Scis. Union Coll., Schenectady, 1966-71; acting dean faculty Union Coll., 1971-72, dean faculty, 1972-76; prof. history Center Humanities and Social Scis. Union Coll., 1966-76, distinguished prof. history and higher edn., 1976-78; dean Empire State Coll., 1978-82, prof. history, 1982-83, prof. emeritus, 1983—; pres. Alternative Lifelong Learning, Berkeley, Calif., 1989-91. Cons. 20th Century Fund, N.Y.C., 1955-57, Friends World Coll., 1984-86; mem. Mass. Bd. Collegiate Authority, 1961-66; history docent Oakland Mus. of Calif., 1999—. Author: To the Yalu and Back, 1963; co-author: Political Community in the North Atlantic Area, 1957; contbr. articles to profl. jours. Vice chmn. bd. Mass. Com. Children and Youth, 1963-66, mem. exec. bd., 1961-66; adv. bd. Civil Liberties Mass., 1963-66; chmn. bd. New Eng. Council Advancement Sch. Adminstrn., 1961-63; vice chmn. Capital Dist. Civil Liberties Union, 1966-67; chmn. Freedom Forum, Inc., 1970-71, Schnectady Renewals, Inc., 1972-76; bd. dirs. Suffolk County chpt. N.Y. Civil Liberties Union, 1981-87; bd. dirs. Della Corte Internat., Inc., 1983-88; history docent Oakland Mus. of Calif., 1999—; co-founder Alternative Lifelong Learning Berkeley. Home: 2587 Hilgard Ave Berkeley CA 94709-1104 E-mail: mlichty1@comcast.net.

LICHTIG, LEO KENNETH, health economist; b. Bklyn., Oct. 20, 1953; s. Samuel and Alyne Norma (Strauss) L.; m. Susan Mary Walsh, May 15, 1977; children: Brielle Joy, Danica Jill. BS, MS, Rensselaer Poly. Inst., 1974, PhD, 1976. Asst. prof. SUNY, Albany, 1976-77; project specialist, econometrician N.J. State Dept. Health, Trenton, 1977-82; dir. utilization econs. and rsch. Empire Blue Cross/Blue Shield, Albany, 1982-90; v.p. rsch. and demonstration Health Care Rsch. Found., Albany, 1982-90; v.p. Network, Inc., Randolph, N.J., Latham, sr. v.p., chief info. officer Somerset, NJ, Latham, NY, 1994—2002; v.p. life sci. group Aon Consulting, Inc., Somerset, 2002—. Pvt. practice cons., Latham, 1982-90; mem. nat. diagnosis related group steering com. health care fin. adminstrn. Yale U., Washington, 1979-81; mem. adj. faculty Russell Sage Grad. Sch. Health Adminstrn., Albany, 1986-94, Union Coll. Grad. Mgmt. Inst., Schenectady, N.Y., 1991-92; expert reviewer Health Care Financing Adminstrn., Washington, 1987, 89. Author: Hospital Information Systems for Case Mix Management, 1986; contbg. editor (newsletter) Nat. Report on Computers & Health, 1982-85; contbr. articles to profl. jours. Mem. tech. adv. com. Statewide Planning and Rsch. Coop. Sys., N.Y. State Dept. Health; mem. N.Y. State Universal Data Set Specifications Task Force, 1998-2002, N.Y., State Uniform Billing Com., 2002—, N.Y. State Data Protection Rev. Bd., 2003-. Mem. Assn. for Health Svcs. Rsch., Am. Statis. Assn. (com. on privacy and confidentiality 1981-84, subcom. on quality and productivity measures 1988-90), Acad. for Health Svcs. Rsch. and Health Policy, Healthcare Fin. Mgmt. Assn., Internat. Arthurian Soc. (N.Am. br.), Internat. Soc. for Pharmacoeconomics and Outcomes Rsch. Avocation: arthurian legends. Office: Aon Consulting Inc 270 Davidson Ave Somerset NJ 08873-4140 Office Phone: 732-537-4061. E-mail: lichtl@rpi.edu.

LICHTIN, LEON (JUDAH LEON LICHTIN), pharmacist; b. Phila., Mar. 5, 1924; s. Aaron and Rosa (Rosenberg) L.; m. Beverly I. Cohen, Aug. 6, 1950; children— Benjamin Lloyd, Alan Eli. BS in Pharmacy, Phila. Coll. Pharmacy and Sci., 1944, MS in Pharmacy, 1947; PhD in Pharmacy, Ohio State U., 1950. Asst. prof. pharmacy U. Cin., 1950-51, assoc. prof., 1951-64, prof., 1964-71, Andrew Jergens prof. pharmacy, 1971-91, Andrew Jergens prof. pharmacy emeritus, 1991—. Cons. in cosmetic sci. Composer string music, vocal music, prodr. (CD) JuChriLam in Celebration of Jerusalem 3000, Ezekiel, Chapter 37, Verses 1-14 "The Valley of Dry Bones; contbr. articles to pharm. jours. Past pres. No. Hills Synagogue, Cin. Fellow AAAS, Soc. Cosmetic Chemists; mem. Rho Chi. Achievements include patents in field. Home: 801 Cloverview Ave Cincinnati OH 45231-6017 Business E-Mail: Leon.Lichtin@uc.edu.

LICHTIN, NORMAN NAHUM, chemistry professor; b. Newark, N.J., Aug. 10, 1922; s. James Jechiel and Clara (Greenspan) L.; m. Phyllis Selma Wasserman, May 30, 1947; children— Harold Hirsh, Sara Marjorie Boyd, Daniel Albert. BS, Antioch Coll., 1944; MS, Purdue U., 1945; PhD, Harvard U., 1948. Faculty Boston U., 1947-93, prof. chemistry, 1961-93, prof. emeritus, 1993—, univ. prof., 1973-93, chmn. dept. chemistry, 1973-84, dir. divsn. engring. and applied sci., 1983-87; chief scientist Synlize, Inc., 1987-90, Project Sunrise Inc., 1990-92, Photox Corp., Boston, 1993-97; chief sci. adviser, bd. dirs. NanoTek, Inc., Tucson, 1998—2004. Vis. chemist Brookhaven Nat. Lab., Upton, N.Y., 1957-58, research collaborator, 1958-70; guest scientist Weizmann Inst. Sci., Rehovoth, Israel, 1962-63; vis. prof. Inst. Phys. and Chem. Research, Wako, Japan, 1980, Hebrew U., Jerusalem, 1962-63, 70-71, 75-76, 80; Coochbehar lectr. Indian Assn. Cultivation of Sci., Calcutta, 1980 Assoc. editor Solar Energy, 1976-93; rsch. and publs. on mechanisms of chem. reactions including reaction of atomic nitrogen with organic compounds, influence of high energy radiation on organic compounds and photoredox reactions of dyes; photochem. conversion solar energy, ionization processes and ionic reactions in solutions in liquid sulfur dioxide, photo assisted solid-catalysis; catalytic and photocatalytic decomposition of organic and inorganic pollutants of air and water. Mem. alumni bd. Antioch Coll., 1996—2002. NSF sr. fellow, 1962-63. Fellow AAAS; mem. Am. Chem. Soc., Sigma Xi, Phi Beta Kappa (hon.) Home: 195 Morton St Newton MA 02459-1522 Personal E-mail: norlichtin@aol.com.

LICHTMAN, ALLAN JAY, historian, educator, consultant; b. Bklyn., Apr. 4, 1947; s. Emanuel and Gertrude Louise (Cohen) L.; m. Katherine Martin Crane, June 6, 1970 (div.); 1 child, Kara Martin; m. Shelia Bradford, 1980 (div.); m. Karyn Lynn Strickler, June 8, 1991; 1 child, Samuel Allan. BA magna cum laude, Brandeis U., 1967; PhD, Harvard U., 1973. Dir. forensics Brandeis U., Waltham, Mass., 1968-71, Harvard U., Cambridge, Mass., 1971-72; asst. prof. history The Am. U., Washington, 1973-77, assoc. prof. history, 1977-78, prof. of history, 1978—, assoc. dean faculty and curricular devel. coll. arts & scis., 1985-87, chair dept. history, 1997—. Instr. Brandeis U., 1970; cons. Smithsonian Instn., 1974-79, John Anderson campaign for Pres., 1980, George Washington U., 1983, U.S. Dept. Justice, Washington, 1983—, V.P. Albert Gore, Jr., Washington, 1994-95; advisor Ted Kennedy for Pres. campaign, 1980; cons., commentator NBC spl. project on the history of the Am. Presidency; news cons. CBS; polit. commentator NBC News Nightside, Voice of Am., USIA, Am.'s Talking Cable Network; expert witness Com. for Civil Rights Under Law, 1983—, U.S. Dept. Justice, 1983—, pvt. attys., 1986—, various state, mcpl. and county jurisdictions, 1986—, ACLU, 1987—, So. Poverty Law Ctr., 1990, Legal Def. Fund, 1991, Puerto Rican Legal Def. and Edn. Fund, 1991—, NAACP, 1993-94, Reform Party, 1996, 2000, Reuters News Svc., 1996, 2000; columnist Montgomery Jour., Rockville, Md., 1990-98; columnist Montgomery Gazette, Gaithersburg, Md., 1998—; appeared on various radio and TV programs; spkr. at more than 50 confs. Author: Your Family History: How to Use Oral History, Personal Family Archives, and Public Documents to Discover Your Heritage, 1978, Prejudice and the Old Politics: The Presidential Election of 1928, 1979, The Keys to the White House, 1996; co-author (with Valerie French) Historians and the Living Past: The Theory and Practice of Historical Study, 1978, (with Laura Irwin Langbein) Ecological Inference, 1978; co-editor (with Joan Challinor) Kin and Communities: Families in America, 1979, (with Ken DeCell) The 13 Keys to the Presidency, 1990; series editor: Studies in Modern American History, 2000—; contbr. articles to profl. jours. and popular mags. Tchg. fellow Harvard U., 1969-73; rsch. grantee Am. U., 1978, 82; recipient Outstanding Young Men of Am. award U.S. C. of C. 1979-80, Top Spkr. award Nat. Conv. Internat. Platform Assn., 1983, 84, 87; Sherman Fairchild Distinguished Visiting scholar Calif. Inst. Tech., 1980-81; defeated twenty opponents on TIC TAC DOUGH, 1981. Mem. Am. Historian Assn., Orgn. Am. Historians, Social Sci. History Assn., Fed. City Club, Phi Alpha Phi, Phi Beta Kappa. Democrat. Jewish. Home: 9219 Villa Dr Bethesda MD 20817-3365 Office: The Am Univ Washington DC 20016

LICHTMAN, DAVID MICHAEL, retired military officer, orthopedist, educator, health facility administrator; b. Bklyn., Jan. 14, 1942; s. Harry S. and Frances (Rubin) L.; m. Frances Lubin; children: James Matthew, Elisabeth Jill. Student, Tufts Coll., 1962; MD, SUNY, Bklyn., 1966. Diplomate Am. Bd. Orthop. Surgery. Intern U. Minn. Hosp., 1966-67, Naval Aerospace Med. Inst., Pensacola, Fla., 1967; commd. lt. USN, 1967, advanced through grades to rear adm., 1988, flight surgeon Air Wing 3, 1968-69; mem. staff orthop. svc. Nat. Naval Med. Ctr., Bethesda, Md., 1974-77, chmn. dept. orthop. surgery, head, hand surgery svc., 1984-87, dir. orthop. residency program, 1984-87, asst. chmn. dept. orthop. surgery, 1975-77, chmn. dept. orthop. surgery, head hand surgery svc., dir. orthop. residency program, 1984-87; chmn. dept. orthop. surgery and rehab. Naval Hosp., Oakland, Calif., 1977-83, dir. orthop. residency program/dir. navy hand fellowship, 1977-83, head hand and microsurgery svc., 1977-83, mem. staff orthop. surgery, sr. hand/microsurgery cons., 1988-91, commdg. officer, 1989-91; comdr. San Francisco Med. Command, Oakland, 1988-91; promoted to Rear Adm. (lower half), 1989; Rear Adm. (upper half), 1991; ret. USN, 1994; John Dunn prof. orthop. hand surgery Baylor Coll. Medicine, Houston, 1994-98; chmn. dir. orthop. residency tng. John Peter Smith Hosp., Ft. Worth, 1998—; clin. prof. orthop. Southwestern Coll. of Med., Dallas, 1998—. Cons. orthop. surgery asst. sec. def. for health affairs Dept. Def., Washington, 1988-94; specialty advisor naval surgeon gen. for orthop. surgery and hand surgery Bur. Medicine and Surgery Dept. Navy, Washington, 1983-86; prof. surgery and head divsn. orthop. surgery Uniformed Svcs. U. of Health Scis., Bethesda, 1984-94, ex-officio mem. bd. regents, 1991-94' examiner Am. Bd. Orthopaedic Surgery. Editor: The Wrist and Its Disorders, 1988, 2nd edit., 1997, Hand and Wrist Sect. Current Opinion in Orthopaedics.; contbr. articles to profl. jours. Mem. ACS (bd. govs. 1987-96), Am. Acad. Orthop. Surgeons, Am. Soc. for Surgery of the Hand (coun. 1999-2002, pres. 2005—, AMA del. 2001-), Am. Orthop. Assn. (hon.), Mil. Surgeons U.S. (Philip Hench award 1982), Tex. Med. Assn. (del. Tarrant County 2003), Soc. Naval Flight Surgeons, Soc. Med. Consultants to the Armed Forces (coun. 1994—, pres. 2002-03), Soc. Mil. Orthop. Surgeons (bd. dirs. 1987-90), Orthopaedic RRC of the ACGME. Home: 4958 Overton Woods Ct Fort Worth TX 76109-2433 Office: John Peter Smith Hosp Dept Orthopedic Surgery 1500 S Main St Fort Worth TX 76104-4917 Office Phone: 817-920-6903.

LICHTMAN, DEBBIE, writer, secondary school educator; BA, U. of Fla., 1975; MS, Nova U., Ft. Lauderdale, Fla., 1977. Journalism advisor, cons., Miami, Fla., 1983—94; journalism tchr., advisor Beaverton, Oreg., 1994—2000; tchr. English Folsom, Calif., 2004—. Spkr. in field. Author: (children's book) Don't Pick Your Nose (Endorsement by best-selling author, Don Maruska), What If? (Child Mag. website recommended reading, 2004). Author visitations: children's book readings, presentations, and discussions, 2004. Avocations: travel, art, writing, music, theater. Office: Deb on Air Books PO Box 580055 Elk Grove CA 95758 E-mail: www.debonairbooks.com.

LICHTMAN, DOUGLAS GARY, law educator; b. Conn., Jan. 13, 1972; BSE in Elec. Engring./Computer Sci., Duke U., 1994; JD, Yale U., 1997. Bar: Ill. 1997. Fellow Yale Info. Soc. Project, 1997—98; asst. prof. law U. Chgo. Law Sch., 1998—2002, prof., 2002—; sr. scholar MacLean Ctr. for Clin. Med. Ethics U. Chgo., 2003—. Legal & strategic cons., 1999—; vis. prof. Wuhan U., China, 2003, U. So. Calif. Law Sch., 2005; editor Jour. Law & Economics, 2003—. Office: U Chgo Law Sch 1111 E 60th St Chicago IL 60637 Office Phone: 773-702-7311. E-mail: d-lichtman@uchicago.edu.

LICHTMAN, JUDITH L., lawyer, organization administrator; m. Elliott Lichtman; children: Sarah, Julia. Bachelor's degree, U. Wisconsin, Madison, 1962, LLB, 1965. Worked on sch. desegregation in South US Dept Health, Edn., and Welfare; teacher Jackson State Coll.; with Urban Coalition, US

Commn. Civil Rights; worked on George McGovern's presdl. campaign, 1972; legal advisor Commonwealth of Puerto Rico; pres. Women's Legal Def. Fund (National Partnership for Women & Families since 1998), Washington, 1974—. Bd. mem. Women's Law and Pub. Policy Fellowship Program. Recipient Hubert H. Humphrey award, Leadership Conf. on Civil Rights, 2000.

LICHTMAN, MARSHALL ALBERT, hematologist, educator, medical researcher; b. NYC, June 23, 1934; s. Samuel and Vera Lichtman; m. Alice Jo Maisel, June 23, 1957; children: Susan, Joanne, Pamela. AB, Cornell U., 1955; MD, U. Buffalo, 1960. Diplomate Am. Bd. Internal Medicine. Resident in medicine Strong Meml. Hosp., 1960-63; surgeon USPHS, 1963-65; postdoctoral rsch. assoc. Sch. Pub. Health, U. N.C., 1963-65; chief resident, instr. medicine Strong Meml. Hosp., 1965-66; sr. instr. medicine, rsch. trainee in hematology U. Rochester (NY) Sch. Medicine, 1966-67, asst. prof. medicine, 1968-70, spl. postdoctoral rsch. fellow hematology, 1968-70, assoc. prof. medicine Dept. Biochemistry and Biophysics, 1971-74, prof. medicine, biochemistry and biophysics, 1974—, chief hematology unit dept. medicine, 1975-77, co-chief, 1977-89, sr. assoc. dean for acad. affairs and rsch., 1979-89, dean Sch. Medicine and Dentistry, 1990-95; exec. v.p. rsch. and med. affairs Leukemia & Lymphona Soc., 1996—. Mem. sci. coun. Am. Nat. Red Cross, 1987-95; vis. prof. univs.; lectr. in field. Editor: Abnormalities of Granulocytes and Monocytes, 1975, Hematology for Practitioners, 1978, Hematology and Oncology, 1980, (with W.J. William, E. Beutler, A.J. Erslev) Hematology, 3d edit., 1983, 4th edit., 1990, (with E. Beutler, B. Coller, T.J. Kipps), 5th edit., 1995, 6th edit., 2001 (with E. Beutler, B. Coller, T.J. Kipps, U. Seligsohn), (with H.J. Meiselman and P.L. LaCelle) White Cell Mechanics: Basic Science and Clinical Aspects, 1984, Hematology: Landmark Papers of the Twentieth Century, 2000, (with E. Beutler, T.J. Kipps, W.J. Williams) Williams Manual of Hematology, 2003; contbr. articles to profl. jours.; mem. editl. bd. Blood Cells, 1978-84, Stem Cells, 1981-83, 93—, Blood, 1983-87, Internat. Jour. Cell Cloning, 1983-92, Exptl. Hematology, 1990-93, Blood Cells, Molecules and Diseases, 1995—, editor-in-chief, 2000—, Am. Jour. Hematology, 2000—. Bd. govs. ARC, 1990-96, chair sci. coun., 1987-95. Recipient contracts U.S. Army Rsch., 1972-78, U.S. Dept. Energy, 1972-80; USPHS grantee, 1971-95. Master ACP; mem. NIH (hematology study sect. 1982-86), AAAS, Am. Fedn. Med. Rsch., Am. Soc. Hematology (pres. 1989), Internat. Soc. Hematology, N.Y. Acad. Scis., Am. Soc. Clin. Investigation, Assn. Am. Physicians, Am. Assn. for Cancer Rsch., Am. Physiol. Soc., Soc. Leuk Biology, Am. Soc. Cell Biology. Home: 64 Woodbury Pl Rochester NY 14618-3445 Office: U Rochester Sch Medicine & Dentistry Box 610 601 Elmwood Ave Rochester NY 14642-0001 Office Phone: 585-275-2205. E-mail: mal@urmc.rochester.edu.

LICHTSTEIN, DANIEL M., medical educator; b. N.Y.C., Dec. 12, 1949; s. Milton and Charlotte Louise Lichtstein; m. Shirley Ann Lichtstein, June 6, 1970; children: Jason, Michelle. Diplomate Am. Bd. Internal Medicine. Pvt. practice, West Palm Beach, Fla., 1978-96; assoc. prof. medicine U. Miami Sch. Medicine, 1996—. V.p. for med. affairs Intracoastal Health Sys., West Palm Beach, 1999—. Author: (book) Preparation for Medical Practice, 1998. Mentor Palm Beach County Schs., Palm Beach Gardens, 1994. Fellow ACP. Jewish. Avocations: golf, writing, travel, community mentor.

LICHTWARDT, ROBERT WILLIAM, mycologist; b. Rio de Janeiro, Nov. 27, 1924; s. Henry Herman and Ruth Moyer Lichtwardt; m. Elizabeth Thomas, Jan. 27, 1951; children: Ruth Elizabeth, Robert Thomas. AB, Oberlin Coll., 1949; MS, U. Ill., 1951, PhD, 1954. Postdoctoral fellow NSF, Panama, Brazil, 1954-55; postdoctoral rsch. assoc. Iowa State U., Ames, 1955-57; asst. prof. U. Kans., Lawrence, 1957-60, assoc. prof., 1960-65; sr. postdoctoral fellow NSF, Hawaii, Japan, 1963-64; prof. U. Kans., Lawrence, 1965-94, prof. emeritus, 1994—. Author: The Trichomycetes, Fungal Associates of Arthropods, 1986; contbr. 100 articles to profl. jours. Mem. Mycological Soc. Am. (life, pres. 1971-72, editor-in-chief 1965-70, William H. Weston award for tchg. excellence in mycology 1982, Disting. Mycologist award 1991), Brit. Mycological Soc. (hon.), Japan Mycological Soc. (hon.). Office: U Kans Dept Ecology Evol Biology Lawrence KS 66045-7534 Business E-Mail: licht@ku.edu.

LICHTY, WARREN DEWEY, JR., lawyer; b. Colorado Springs, Dec. 17, 1930; s. Warren D. and Margaret (White) L.; m. Margaret Louise Grupy, Dec. 8, 1962. Student, Chadron State Coll., 1948—50; BS in Law, U. Nebr., 1952, JD, 1954. Bar: Nebr. 1954, U.S. Dist. Ct. Nebr. 1954, U.S. Ct. Appeals (8th cir.) 1973, U.S. Supreme Ct. 1979. Spl. agt. CIC, 1955—58; county judge Dawes County, Nebr., 1958—61; spl. asst. atty. gen. Nebr. Dept. Justice, Lincoln, 1961—69; mng. asst. atty. gen., chief counsel Nebr. Dept. Roads, Lincoln, 1969—97. Lectr. law Chadron State Coll., 1959-60; mem. com. on eminent domain and land use, transp. rsch. bd. NAS,-NRC, 1973-90. Served with U.S. Army, 1954—58. Decorated United Grand Imperial Coun., Red Cross Constantine, Grand Sovereign, 2001-2002. Mem. Nebr. Bar Assn., Lincoln Bar Assn., Am. Assn. State Hwy. and Transp. Ofcls. (subcom. on legal affairs 1969-97), Scottish Rite Rsch. Soc. (pres. 1990-95, bd. dirs.), Am. Legion, Internat. Supreme Coun. (hon., Order DeMolay), Hiram Club (past pres.), Masons (33d degree, grand master Nebr. 1979, vice chmn. conf. Grand Masters N.Am. 1980, bd. dirs. Home Corp. Nebr. 1979-90, pres. George Washington Nat. Meml. Assn. 2002-05), Shriners, Royal Order Scotland, Scottish Rite (Grand Chamberlain, supreme coun. so. jurisdiction, U.S. and sovereign grand insp. gen. in Nebr. 1991—, bd. dirs. Found. Nebr. 1981-90, pres. bd. dirs. Found. Nebr. 1990—) Republican. Episcopalian. Home: PO Box 22559 Lincoln NE 68542-2559 Office Phone: 402-421-1112.

LICK, DALE WESLEY, educational leadership educator; b. Marlette, Mich., Jan. 7, 1938; s. John R. and Florence M. (Baxter) L.; m. Marilyn Kay Foster, Sept. 15, 1956; children: Lynette (dec.), Kitty (dec.), Diana, Ronald. BS with honors, Mich. State U., 1958, MS in Math, 1959; PhD in Math, U. Calif., Riverside, 1965. Research asst. physics Mich. State U., East Lansing, 1958, teaching asst. math., 1959; instr., chmn. dept. math. Port Huron (Mich.) Jr. Coll., 1959-60; asst. to comptroller Mich. Bell Telephone Co., Detroit, 1961; instr. U. Redlands, 1961-63; teaching asst. math. U. Calif., Riverside, 1964-65; asst. prof. math. U. Tenn., Knoxville, 1965-67; postdoctoral fellow Brookhaven Nat. Lab., Upton, N.Y., 1967-68; assoc. prof. U. Tenn., 1968-69; assoc. prof., head dept. math. Drexel U., Phila., 1969-72; adj. assoc. prof. dept. pharmacology Med. Sch., Temple U., Phila., 1969-72; v.p. acad. affairs Russell Sage Coll., Troy, N.Y., 1972-74; prof. math. and computing scis. Old Dominion U., Norfolk, Va., 1974-78; also dean Old Dominion U. (Sch. Scis. and Health Professions); pres., prof. math. and computer sci. Ga. So. Coll., Statesboro, 1978-86; pres., prof. math. U. Maine, Orono, 1986-91, Fla. State U., Tallahassee, 1991-93, univ. prof. Learning Sys. Inst. and Dept. Edn. Leadership, 1993—. Cert. in tng. and cons., mng. orgnl. change. Author: Fundamentals of Algebra, 1970, (with C. Murphy) Whole-Faculty Study Groups: A Powerful Way to Change Schools and Enhance Learning, 1998, (with C. Mullen) New Directions in Mentoring: Creating a Culture of Synergy, 1999, (with C. Murphy) Whole-Faculty Study Groups: Creating Student-Based Professional Development, 2001, Whole-Faculty Study Groups: Creating Professional Learning Communities That Target Student Learning, 2005; contbr. articles to profl. jours. Bd. dirs. Statesboro/Coll. Symphony, 1978-86, Statewide Health Coordinating Coun. Va., 1976-78, United Way of the Big Bend, 1992-98; chmn. higher edn. adv. bd. Cmty. of Christ, 1986-2004; mem. planning com. Bulloch Meml. Hosp., 1979-86; active Coastal Empire coun. Boy Scouts Am., 1982-86, Katalidin coun., 1986-91; bd. dirs. Health Care Ctrs. Am., Virginia Beach, Va., 1978, Ea. Va. Health Systems Agy., 1976-78; chmn., bd. dirs. Assembly Against Hunger and Malnutrition, 1977-78, pres., 1977-78; mem., high priest Cmty. of Christ. Mem. AAUP, AAAS, Am. Math. Soc., Math. Assn. Am., Am. Assn. Univ. Adminstrs., Am. Soc. Allied Health Professions, Am. Assn. State Colls. and Univs. (chmn. com. agr. resources and rural devel. 1981-86), Am. Assn. Higher Edn., Sigma Xi, Phi Kappa Phi, Pi Mu Epsilon (governing coun. 1972-77), Beta Gamma Sigma, Pi Sigma Epsilon. Office: Fla State U Learning Systems Inst C-4600 University Ctr Tallahassee FL 32306-2540 Office Phone: 850-553-4080. Business E-Mail: dlick@lsi.fsu.edu, dlick@mailer.fsu.edu.

LICK, WILBERT JAMES, mechanical engineering educator; b. Cleve., June 12, 1933; s. Fred and Hulda (Sunntag) L.; children— James, Sarah. BAE., Rensselaer Poly. Inst., 1955, MAE., 1957, PhD, 1958. Asst. prof. Harvard, 1959-66; sr. research fellow Calif. Inst. Tech., 1966-67; mem. faculty Case Western Res. U., 1967-79, prof. earth scis., 1970-79, chmn. dept., 1973-76; prof. mech. engring. U. Calif.-Santa Barbara, 1979—, chmn. dept., 1982-84. Home: 1236 Camino Meleno Santa Barbara CA 93111-1007 Office: U Calif Dept Mech & Environ Engring Santa Barbara CA 93106 Office Phone: 805-893-4295. Business E-Mail: willy@engineering.ucsb.edu.

LICKE, WALLACE JOHN, lawyer; b. Bemidji, Minn., Jan. 23, 1945; s. George John and Lois (Sanford) L.; m. Martha Miriam Eddy, Dec. 19, 1969; children: Loriann, Paul. BA, U. Minn., 1967, MA, 1970, JD cum laude, 1973. Bar: Minn. 1973, U.S. Dist. Ct. Minn. 1973, U.S. Ct. Appeals (8th cir.) 1981, U.S. Supreme Ct. 1981. Instr. Itasca C.C., Grand Rapids, Minn., 1968—; assoc. Helgesen, Peterson, Engberg & Spector Attys. at Law (now Peterson, Engberg & Peterson), Mpls., 1972-75; sec., gen. counsel Blandin Paper Co. and UPM-Kymmene Inc., subs. UPM-Kymmene Corp., a Finnish Co., Helsinki, 1975—2002; pvt. practice, 2002—. Bd. dirs. Vol. Atty. Program Super Bd., Judy Garland Mus. and Children's Discovery Mus.; chmn. bus. retention and expansion strategies program U. Minn.; mem. panel of arbitrators Am. Arbitration Assn. Mem. bd. editors Minn. Law Rev. Area rep. Minn. awareness project Minn. Internat. Ctr./World Affairs Ctr.; Bd. dirs., pres. hon. bd. dirs. Itasca County Family YMCA, Itasca County Family YMCA, Grand Grand Rapids; bd. dirs., v.p., pres. Itasca County unit Am. Cancer Soc.; bd. dirs., pres. Myles Reif Performing Arts Ctr.; chmn., sec. post com. computer-small bus. explorer post Boy Scouts Am.; adult leader 4-H program Agrl. Extension Svc. U. Minn., St. Paul; mem. Bass Brook Twp. (Minn.) Econ. Devel. Com.; mem. promotion and prospecting com. Itasca Devel. Corp.; trustee Grand Rapids area community found; chmn. coop. solutions adv. bd. Grand Rapids, Minn.; trustee Libr. Found., Grand Rapids, Minn., bd. dirs.; trustee Cmty. Libr. Found.; class rep. U. Minn. Law Sch.; bd. dirs. Judy Garland Mus. and Children's Discovery Mus., Grand Rapids, Minn. Recipient William Spurgeon III award Boy Scouts Am., 1988; NDEA Title IV fellow, 1967, Paul Harris fellow. Mem. ABA (com. mem.), Fed. Bar Assn., Minn. Bar Assn. (del., planning com.), Itasca County Bar Assn. (past sec., pres.), Minn. 15th Dist. Bar Assn. (com. mem.), Am. Corp. Counsel Assn. (charter), Am. Soc. Corp. Secs., Grand Rapids C. of C. (chmn. com., bd. dirs.), Rotary (bd. dirs., pres., sec. Grand Rapids, dist. rep.), Order of Ski U Mah, Phi Beta Kappa. Office Phone: 218-743-6504. Personal E-mail: john_licke@yahoo.com.

LICKHALTER, MERLIN, architect; b. St. Louis, May 4, 1934; s. Frank E. and Sophia (Geller) L.; m. Harriet Braen, June 9, 1957; children: Debra, Barbara. BArch, MIT, 1957. Registered arch., Mo., Calif., Fla., Man. Ptnr. Drake Partnership, Architects, St. Louis, 1961-77; pres. JRB Architects, Inc., St. Louis, 1977-81; sr. v.p., mng. dir. Stone, Marraccini & Patterson, St. Louis, 1981-93; sr. v.p., dir. Cannon, 1993—2002; pres. Lickhalter & Assocs. LLC, 2003—. Owner, pres. mgmt. program Harvard U. Bus. Sch., 1992; cons. Dept. Def., Washington, 1977-78; lectr. Washington U. Sch. Medicine, 1989—. Prin. projects include The Mayo Clinic, Jacksonville, Fla., Washington U. Med. Ctr., St. Louis, U.S. Army Hosp., Frankfurt, Germany, Nat. AIDS Rsch. Ctr., NIH, Washington, Evanston (Ill.) Hosp., Loma Linda (Calif.) U. Med. Ctr., U. Mo. Health Scis. Ctr., Columbia, St. Louis U. Health Scis. Ctr., Children's Hosp. Rsch. Inst., New Orleans, U. Ala. Birmingham Sch. Medicine, U. Ala. Sch. Optometry. Trustee United Hebrew Congregation, St. Louis, 1980-88, 93-98, 2000—; exec. com. bd. dirs. Arts & Edn. Coun. St. Louis, 1991-2002; pres. Acad. Architecture for Health Found., 2002—; treas., exec. com., bd. dirs. United Arts Coun. Collier County, 2003—. Capt. U.S. Army, 1957-59. Recipient Renovation Design award St. Louis Producers Coun., 1976, USAF Europe Design Award, 1990. Fellow: AIA (pres. nat. acad. arch. for health 1993, bd. dirs. 2003—, exec. com.), Am. Coll. Healthcare Architects; mem.: United Arts Coun. (dir. (Naples, Fla.)), Acad. Arch. for Health Found. (pres., trustee 2000—), Am. Assn. Healthcare Engrs., Am. Hosp. Assn., St. Louis Club. Jewish. Home and Office: 6825 Grenadier Blvd Naples FL 34108 Personal E-mail: mlickhalter.hsfa@comcast.net.

LIDDELL, CHRIS R., computer software company executive, former paper company executive; married; 2 children. BS in engring. with honors, Auckland U., New Zealand; MA in philosophy, Oxford U., England. CFO to CEO Carter Holt Harvey, 1995—2002; v.p., fin. Internat. Paper Co., Stamford, Conn., 2002—03, sr. v.p., CFO, 2003—05; CFO Microsoft Corp., 2005—. Office: Microsoft Corp 1 Microsoft Way Redmond WA 98052

LIDDELL, W. KIRK, specialty contracting company executive; b. Lancaster, Pa., July 24, 1949; m. Pamela E. Trow; four children. AB in Econs. magna cum laude, Princeton U., 1971; MBA, JD, U. Chgo., 1976. Assoc. Covington & Burling, Washington, 1976-80; gen. counsel, v.p. AC and S Inc/Irex Corp., Lancaster, 1980-83; pres., CEO Irex Corp., 1984—. Bd. dirs. High Industries Inc., Splty. Products & Insulation Co., PCI Ins., Inc.; chmn. Lancaster City Partnership, 1986, Lancaster C. of C. and Industry, 1991; pres. Econ. Devel. Co. Lancaster County, 1997—98; chmn. Lancaster Alliance, 2002—04. Campaign chmn. United Way of Lancaster County, 1995. Lt. USAR, 1971—73. Leon Carol Marshall scholar U. Chgo. Grad. Sch. Bus., 1974-76; named Scholar-Athlete Nat. Football Found. Mem.: NAM (bd. dirs., asbestos steering com., exec. com., chmn. legal issues policy com.), Nat. Insulation Assn. (chmn. long range planning 1998—), Pa. C. of C. and Industry (govt. affairs com., vice chmn., chmn.). Office: Irex Corp 120 N Lime St Lancaster PA 17602-2923

LIDDLE, ALAN CURTIS, retired architect; b. Tacoma, Mar. 10, 1922; s. Abram Dix and Myrtle (Maytum) L. B.Arch., U. Wash., 1948; postgrad., Eidgenoissche Technische Hochschule, Zurich, Switzerland, 1950-51. Asst. prof. architecture U. Wash., 1954-55; prin. Liddle & Jones, Tacoma, 1957-67, Alan Liddle (architects), Tacoma, 1967-90, Liddle & Jacklin, Tacoma, 1990-98; ret., 1999. Architect oceanography bldgs. U. Wash., 1967, Tacoma Art Mus., 1971, Charles Wright Acad., Tacoma, 1962, Pacific Nat. Bank Wash., Auburn, 1965. Pres. bd. Allied Arts Tacoma, 1963-64, Civic Arts Commn. Tacoma-Pierce County, 1969; commr. Wash. Arts Commn., 1971; Bd. dirs. Tacoma Art Mus., Tacoma Zool. Soc., Tacoma Philharmonic, Inc. Served with AUS, 1943-46. Fellow A.I.A. (pres. S.W. Wash. chpt. 1967-68); mem. Wash. Hist. Soc., U. Wash. Alumni Assn. (all life) Home: 12735 Gravelly Lake Dr SW Lakewood WA 98499-1459 Office: 703 Pacific Ave Tacoma WA 98402-5207 Office Phone: 253-272-3155.

LIDDLE, JEFFREY L., lawyer; b. Aurora, Ill., Apr. 21, 1949; s. Harry Edward and Vera E. (Trippon) L.; m. Tara Liddle; children: Alexa, Harry. BS, Cornell U., 1971; JD, NYU, 1976. Bar: NY 1977, U.S. Dist. Ct. NY (so. and ea. dist.) 1977, U.S. Ct. Appeals (2d cir.) 1979, U.S. Supreme Ct. 1980, DC 1980, U.S. Tax Ct. 1984, U.S. Dist. Ct. NY (no. dist.) 1993, U.S. Ct. Appeals (sixth cir.) 1995, U.S. Ct. Appeals (first cir.) 1999. Assoc. Baer Marks & Upham, NYC, 1976—79; founding ptnr. Liddle & Robinson LLP (formerly Liddle, McMillin & Henze), NYC, 1979—. Co-author: Labor and Employment in NY: A Guide to New York Laws, Regulations, and Practices; contbr. articles to profl. jours.; lectr. in field. Mem. ABA, Fed. Bar Council, Assn. of Bar of City of NY (mem. arbitration com. 2002-). Office: Liddle & Robinson LLP 685 3rd Ave New York NY 10017-4024

LIDDLE, SIDNEY GEORGE, retired mechanical engineer, researcher; b. Salt Lake City, Feb. 27, 1933; s. Clare Maynard and Rozella (Gater) L.; m. Johanna Funkhouser, May 8, 1987 (dec. Aug. 1988). BSME, U. Utah, 1956; PhD in Mech. Engring., U. N.S.W., Sydney, Australia, 1970. Design engr. Rocketdyne divsn. N.Am Aviation, Canoga Park, Calif., 1956-64; tchg. fellow U. N.S.W., Sydney, 1965-69; sr. engr. Rsch. Lab. GM, Warren, Mich., 1969-77, CalTech, Pasadena, Calif., 1977-85; project engr. Rand Co., Santa Monica, Calif., 1985-89; dir. Calif. Engring. Rsch. Inst., Pasadena, 1989-90; propulsion engr. GE Astro-Space, Princeton, N.J., 1990-92; ret., 1992. Contbr. numerous papers to profl. publs. Mem. ASME, AIAA, Soc. Automotive Engrs., Sigma Xi, Tau Beta Pi, Pi Tau Sigma. Achievements include 5 patents. Home: PO Box 2928 Running Springs CA 92382 E-mail: sidliddle@earthlink.net.

LIDDY, EDWARD M., insurance company executive; b. New Brunswick, NJ, 1945; married. Grad., Cath. U. Am., 1968; MBA, George Washington U., 1972. With Internat. Harvester Co., Ford Motor Co., Ryder Systems Inc., 1968-79; sr. v.p. G.D. Searle & Co., Skokie, Ill., 1979-85; with ADT Inc., NYC, 1985-88, CFO, exec. v.p., dir., 1986-88; CFO Sears, Roebuck and Co., 1988-94; with The Allstate Corp. and Allstate Ins. Co., Northbrook, Ill., 1994—, pres., COO, 1994-98, chmn., pres., CEO, 1999—. Bd. dirs. The Kroger Co., 3M, Ins. Information Inst., Goldman Sachs Group, Inc. Chmn. elect, nat. gov. Boys & Girls Clubs Am.; bd. dirs. Northwestern Meml. Hosp., Jr. Achievement of Chgo. Mem.: Catalyst, Bus. Roundtable, Fin. Svcs. Forum. Office: Allstate Insurance Co 2775 Sanders Rd Northbrook IL 60062-6127

LIDE, DAVID REYNOLDS, editor-in-chief; b. Gainesville, Ga., May 25, 1928; s. David Reynolds and Laura Kate (Simmons) L.; m. Mary Ruth Lomer, Nov. 5, 1955 (div. Dec. 1988); children: David Alston, Vanessa Grace, James Hugh, Quentin Robert; m. Bettijoyce Breen, 1988. BS, Carnegie Inst. Tech., 1949; AM, Harvard U., 1951, PhD, 1952. Physicist Nat. Bur. Stds., Washington, 1954-63, chief molecular spectroscopy sect., 1963-69, dir. std. reference data Gaithersburg, Md., 1969-88; editor-in-chief Handbook of Chemistry and Physics, CRC Press, 1988—. Pres. Com. on Data for Sci. and Tech., Paris, 1986-90. Author: Basic Laboratory and Industrial Chemicals, 1993, Handbook of Organic Solvents, 1995; (with G.W.A. Milne) Handbook of Data on Organic Compounds, 3rd edit., 1993, Names, Synonyms, and Structures of Organic Compounds, 1995; (with H.V. Kehiaian) Handbook of Thermophysical and Thermochemical Data, 1994; (with Milne) Handbook of Data on Common Organic Compounds, 1995, Properties of Organic Compounds and Properties of Organic Solvents Databases, 1996; (with G. L. Trigg and E. R. Cohen) AIP Physics Desk Reference, 2002, A Century of Excellence in Measurements, Standards and Technology, 2001, Handbook of Chemistry and Physics on CD-ROM, 2002; founding editor Jour. Phys. and Chem. Reference Data, 1972-92. Recipient Skolnik award for Chem. Info., Am. Chem. Soc., 1988, Patterson-Crane award, 1991, Presdl. Rank award in sr. exec. svc., 1986. Mem. NAS (nat. assoc.), Internat. Union Pure and Applied Chemistry (pres. phys. chemistry divsn. 1983-87). Achievements include research in microwave spectroscopy for studying molecular structure and hindered internal rotation, explanation of HCN laser, development of electronic databases of physical and chemical properties. Home and Office: 13901 Riding Loop Dr North Potomac MD 20878-3879

LIDE, NEOMA JEWELL LAWHON (MRS. MARTIN JAMES LIDE JR.), poet; b. Levelland, Tex., Apr. 1, 1926; d. Charles Samuel and Juel (Yeager) Lawhon; m. Martin James Lide, Jr., Nov. 12, 1950; children: Martin James, III, Brooks Nathaniel, Gardner Lawhon. Secreterial cert., Draughon's Bus. Coll., 1943; student, U. Tex., 1944-46; R.N., Jefferson-Hillman Sch. Nursing, 1950. Writer column Baldwin Times, Bay Minette, Ala., 1964-68, Shades Valley Sun newspapers, Birmingham, Ala., 1974-75; v.p., sec. Martin J. Lide Assocs., Inc., Birmingham, 1977-81; R.N. supr. St. Martin's in the Pines, 1984. Author: Home Sweet Homecoming, (musical skit), 1954, (poetry) Instead of Sunset, 1973; (narrative) Life of Service-These are My Jewels, 1979; Music in the Wind - The Story of Lady Arlington, 1979, rev., 1980, Brother James Bryan-Hope Lives Eternal, 1981; Music of the Soul, 1982; The Past and Psyche of Arlington, 1983, The Light Side of Life in the American Colonies, 1988, Tha American Woman, 1989, revised, 1992, The Lawhons of Texas, 1995, Addenda, 1996, (compilation) The Ussery Connection, 2000 Mem. Mountain Brook Political Scis. Club, 1954; bd. Leagues of Women Voters, 1954-56; Pride of the Valley Sun Newspaper, 1954; mem. U.D.C. Pelham chpt., Sally Jones chpt., 1950's, Ala. State bd., Children of the Am., Revolution, sr. pres., Reuben Rogers Soc., 1959-65; Good Citizens NSDAR com. chmn., (William Speer chpt.), NSDAR early 1960's, pres. advisory com., Cahaba Girls Scouts coun., 1963-64; mem. def. adv. com. Women in Services, for Ala., 1962-64; coordinator women's activities Nat. Vets. Day, Birmingham, 1962-68; disting. guest, Vets. award Dinner and the World Peace Luncheon, 1963-64; hon. mem. IV U.S. Army Corps, 1964; originator and 1st pres., Women Auxiliary for Patriotic Events, 1968, apptd. liaison Nat. Vets. Day exec. dir., 1968-70, charter mem., 1964; exec. bd. Women's Com. of 100 for Birmingham, 1964-65, 84-85; Best original column divsn., A Ala. Press Assn. better Newspaper Contest, 1964, 65, 66. PTA bd., Cherokee Bend Elementary Sch., 1971-72; spkr. (Poetry), Mountain Brook Junior High Sch., (Videotape shown in English Classes), 1974 spkr. Arlington Hist. Assn., 1983; mem. Gorgas bd. U. Ala., Tuscaloosa, 1959. Recipient citation Merit, Muscular Dystrophy Assn. Am., 1961. Mem. Christian Women's Soc. Mountain Brook (bd. dirs. 1993-95), Nat. Soc. DAR (regent Princess Sehoy chpt. 1983-85, 91-92, chpt. spkr. 1988, 92, chpt. exec. bd. 1991-95), The Salvation Army Women's Auxiliary, Birmingham, 1995-96; Cauldron Club (spkr. 1989, 2d v.p. 1992-93, 95). Home: 3536 Brookwood Rd Birmingham AL 35223-1446

LIDE, VINTON DEVANE, lawyer; b. Greenville, S.C., May 4, 1937; s. Theodore Ellis and Mary Elizabeth (DeVane) L.; m. Carol Jean Keisler, July 8, 1979; children: Wade Patrick, Emily Elizabeth. AB, Davidson Coll., 1959; LLB (now JD), U. Va., 1962. Bar: Va. 1962, S.C. 1962, U.S. Ct. Appeals (4th cir.) 1974, U.S. Ct. Appeals (9th cir.) 2001, U.S. Supreme Ct. 1980. Assoc. Shand & Wilmeth, Hartsville, S.C., 1962-64; ptnr. Shand & Lide, Hartsville, S.C., 1964-78; pub. defender Darlington County, S.C., 1969-76; exec. asst./legal advisor to gov. S.C., 1978-79; asst. atty. gen. State of S.C., 1978-79; gen. counsel S.C. Dept. Social Svcs., 1979-81; chief counsel, staff dir. Com. on the Judiciary, U.S. Senate, Washington, 1981-85; adminstrv. asst. to U.S. Senator Strom Thurmond Washington, 1985—. Mcpl. ct. judge, Hartsville, 1963—69; U.S. atty. Dist. of S.C., 1985—89. Recipient cert. of Appreciation, Drug Enforcement Adminstrn., U.S. Dept. Justice, 1980. Mem. ABA (ho. dels. 1978-82), S.C. Bar Assn., Va. Bar Assn. Republican. Lutheran. Office: Vinton D Lide & Assocs LLC 5179 Sunset Blvd Lexington SC 29072 Office Phone: 803-808-1799. E-mail: dee@lidelaw.com.

LIDGATE, DOREEN WANDA, retired librarian; b. Seattle, Jan. 27, 1925; d. Robert Jesse and Doris Ivy (Giffin) L. BA, U. Wash., 1946, M in Librarianship, 1966. Tchr. music St. Nicholas Sch., Seattle, 1948-70, libr., 1950-70, dean of students, 1968-70; reference libr. depts. edn., sociology, psychology Seattle Pub. Libr., 1971-74; libr. in charge Ratti Perbix Clark, Seattle, 1974-90; ret., 1990. Cons. libr. rsch., 1990—. Mem. The Mountaineers, Wash. Athletic Club (v.p. 1955, associate women's bd. 1954), Beta Phi Mu, Alpha Chi Omega. Avocations: travel, hiking. Home: 992 Woolsey Ct Sequim WA 98382-5058

LIDICKER, WILLIAM ZANDER, JR., zoologist, educator; b. Evanston, Ill., Aug. 19, 1932; s. William Zander and Frida (Schroeter) L.; m. Naomi Ishino, Aug. 18, 1956 (div. Oct., 1982); children: Jeffrey Roger, Kenneth Paul; m. Louise N. DeLonzor, June 5, 1989. BS, Cornell U., 1953; MS, U. Ill., 1954, PhD, 1957. Instr. zoology, asst. curator mammals U. Calif., Berkeley, 1957-59, asst. prof., asst. curator, 1959-65, assoc. prof., assoc. curator, 1965-69; assoc. dir. Mus. Vertebrate Zoology, 1968-81, acting dir., 1974-75, prof. zoology, curator mammals, 1969-89, prof. integrative biology, curator of mammals, 1989-94, prof., curator emeritus, 1994—. Dancer Westwind Internat. Folk Ensemble, 1994-2000, Jubilee Am. Dance Theater, 1999—; contbr. articles to profl. jours. Bd. dirs. No. Calif. Com. for Environ. Info., 1971-77; bd. trustees BIOSIS, 1987-92, chmn., 1992; N.Am. rep. steering com., sect. Mammalogy IUBS, UNESCO, 1978-89; chmn. rodent specialist group Species Survival Commn., IUCN, 1980-89; mem. sci. adv. bd. Marine World Found. at Marine World Africa USA, 1987-98; pres. Dehnel-Petrusewicz Meml. Fund, 1985-97, sec.-treas., 1999. Fellow AAAS, Calif. Acad. Scis., Polish Acad. Scis. (fgn. mem., 50 Yr. Anniversary medal and diploma 2004), Explorers Club; mem. Am. Soc. Mammalogists (dir. 1969—, 2d v.p. 1974-76, pres. 1976-78, C.H. Merriam award 1986, hon. mem. 1995),

Am. Soc. Naturalists, Berkeley Folk Dancers Club (pres. 1969, tchr. 1984—, hon. mem. 2000)., Nat. Folk Orgn. (bd. trustees 2005-). Office: U Calif Mus Vertebrate Zoology Berkeley CA 94720-0001 Business E-Mail: wlidicker@berkeley.edu.

LIDMAN, TOMAS ERIK, national archivist; b. Stockholm, June 30, 1948; s. Ivar and Gunhild (Andersson) L.; m. Kerstin Gårdbro, Aug. 19, 1972; children: Erica, Carl-Fredrik, Charlotte. PhD, U. Stockholm, 1979. Asst. libr. Royal Libr., Stockholm, 1971-79; sr. libr. Stockholm U. Libr., 1979-80; head dept. Delegation for Sci. Info., Stockholm, 1980-84; libr. Nordic Mus., Stockholm, 1984-85; dir. Nat. Libr. Psychology and Edn., Stockholm, 1985-92; libr. Stockholm U. Libr., 1992-95; nat. libr. Royal Libr., Stockholm, 1995—2003, nat. archivist, 2003—. Chmn. U. Borås, 1998—2003, Royal U. Coll. Fine Arts, 2004-; bd. dirs. Nordic Coun. Sci. Info., chmn., 2003. Author: Party Politics in the House of Nobility in the 19th Century, 1979, Libraries in Sweden, 1990, Essays on Books and Libraries, 2003; co-author: Litteratursociologi, 1995; editor: Svenska Antikvariat, 1986. Mem. Swedish Assn. Bibliophiles (pres. 1992-97), Swedish Assn. Rsch. Librs. (pres. 1989-94), Scandinavian Fedn. Rsch. Librs. (pres. 1992-94). Avocations: art, music, sports, travel. Office: Nat Archives PO Box 12541 S-10229 Stockholm Sweden Business E-Mail: tomas.lidman@riksarkivet.ra.se.

LIDSKY, ELLA, retired law librarian; b. Wilno, Poland; arrived in U.S., 1962; d. Leib and Sheina (Izygzon) Cwik; m. Alexander Lidsky, Feb. 20, 1963 (dec. Mar., 1996); 1 son, David Abraham. BA, Pedagogical Inst. Odessa, USSR; MS, Columbia U., 1966, MA, 1973. Cert. Russian and Hebrew lang. tchr. Tchr. high sch., Poland, 1948-51; elem. sch., 1961-62; asst. cataloger Tchrs. Coll. Columbia U., N.Y.C., 1966-68; cataloger Fairleigh Dickinson U., Teaneck, N.J., 1968-69, asst. dir. tech. services Madison, N.J., 1973-84; head cataloger Ramapo Coll., Mahwah, N.J., 1971-73; asst. libr. U.S. Ct. Internat. Trade Law Libr., N.Y.C., 1985-2000. Mem. Am. Assn. Law Libraries, Law Librarians of Greater N.Y., N.Y. Tech. Services Librarians, N.J. Law Librarians Assn. Democrat. Jewish. Avocations: music, travel. Personal E-mail: ella64@rcn.com.

LIDSTONE, HERRICK KENLEY, JR., lawyer; b. New Rochelle, N.Y., Sept. 10, 1949; s. Herrick Kenley and Marcia Edith (Drake) L.; m. Mary Lynne O'Toole, Aug. 5, 1978; children: Herrick Kevin, James Patrick, John Francis. AB, Cornell U., 1971; JD, U. Colo., 1978. Bar: Colo. 1978, U.S. Dist. Ct. Colo. 1978. Assoc. Roath & Brega, P.C., Denver, 1978—85, Brenman, Epstein, Raskin & Friedlob, P.C., Denver, 1985—86; shareholder Brenman, Raskin & Friedlob, P.C., Denver, 1986—94; mem. Friedlob Sanderson Raskin Paulson & Tourtilott, LLC, Denver, 1995—98, Norton Lidstone, P.C., Greenwood Village, Colo., 1998—2002, Burns, Figa & Will, P.C., Englewood, Colo., 2002—. Adj. prof. U. Denver Coll. Law, 1985-2000; spkr. in field various orgns.; mem. state securities bd. Colo. Dept. Regulatory Agys., 1999—, vice chair, 2000-01, 04-05, chair, 2001-02, 04-05 Author: Federal and State Securities Regulation for the General Practitioner in Colorado, 2000; editor U. Colo. Law Rev., 1977-78; co-author: Federal Income Taxation of Corporations, 6th edit.; contbg. author: Legal Opinion Letters Formbook, 1996, supplement, 1999; contbr. articles to profl. jours. Served with USN, 1971-75, with USNR, 1975-81. Mem. ABA (Am. Law Inst.), Colo. Bar Assn., Arapahoe County Bar Assn., Denver Assn. Oil and Gas Title Lawyers. Avocation: fluent Spanish language. Office: Burns Figa & Will PC Ste 1030 6400 S Fiddlers Green Cir Englewood CO 80111 Office Phone: 303-796-2626. Business E-Mail: hklidstone@bfw-law.com.

LIDSTROM, MARY E., chemical engineering professor, microbiology professor; BS in Microbiology, Ore. State Univ., 1973; MS in Bacteriology, Univ. Wis., Madison, 1975; PhD in Bacteriology, Univ. Wis., 1977. Prof., environ. engring. sci. Calif. Tech. Inst.; Frank Jungers Chair, Engring. Univ. Wash., and prof. chem. engring, prof. microbiology, assoc. dean for new initiatives in engring. Rsch. prof. Howard Hughes Med. Inst., 2002—. Editl. bd. Jour. Bacteriology; contbr. articles to profl. journals. Recipient Prather award for Young Women in Sci., CalTech award for Excellence, NSF Faculty award for Women, Howard Hughes Med. Inst. grant, 2002. Fellow: Am. Acad. Microbiology. Office: 263 Benson Univ Wash Box 351750 Seattle WA 98195-1750 Office Phone: 206-616-5282. Office Fax: 206-616-5721. Business E-Mail: lidstrom@u.washington.edu.*

LIDSTROM, NICKLAS, professional hockey player; b. Vasteras, Sweden, Apr. 28, 1970; With Detroit Red Wings, 1991—; player NHL All-Rookie Team, 1992, NHL All-Star Game, 1996, 1998—2004. Recipient Norris Trophy Award, 2001, 2002, 2003, Stanley Cup Champion, 1997, 1998, 2002, Conn Smythe Trophy, 2002. Office: Detroit Red Wings Joe Louis Arena 600 Civic Center Detroit MI 48226

LIDTKE, DORIS KEEFE, retired computer science educator; b. Bottineau County, N.D., Dec. 6, 1929; d. Michael J and Josephine (McDaniels) Keefe; m. Vernon L Lidtke, Apr. 21, 1951. BS, U. Oreg., 1952, PhD, 1979; MEd cum laude, Johns Hopkins U., 1974. Programmer analyst Shell Devel. Co., Emeryville, Calif., 1955—59, U. Calif., Berkeley, 1960—62; asst. prof. Lansing (Mich.) C.C., 1963—68; ednl. specialist Johns Hopkins U., Balt., 1968; assoc. program mgr. NSF, Washington, 1984—85, program dir., 1992—93; sr. mem. tech. staff Software Productivity Consortium, Reston, Va., 1987—88; asst. prof. computer sci. Towson U., Balt., 1968—80, assoc. prof., 1980—90, prof., 1990—2002, prof. emerita, 2002—; adj. accreditation dir. computing ABET Inc., 1999—. V.p. Computing Scis. Accreditation Bd., 1993—96, pres., 1996—97. Fellow: Assn. Computing Machinery (edn. bd. 1980—98, coun. 1984—86, spl. interest group bd. 1985—99, chmn. 1994—98, coun. 1994—98, Recognition Svc. award 1978, 1983, 1985, 1986, 1990, 1991, Outstanding Contbn. award 1995); mem.: Assn. Edn. Data Sys. (named Outstanding Educator 1986), Nat. Edn. Computer Conf. (steering com., vice-chmn. 1983—85, chmn. 1985—89, Outstanding Svc. award 1999, Outstanding Leadership award 1999), Computer Soc. of IEEE (Outstanding Contbn. award 1986, 1992, Golden Core). Home: 4806 Wilmslow Rd Baltimore MD 21210-2328 Office: Towson U Computer and Info Scis Baltimore MD 21252-0001 also: ABET Inc 111 Market Pl Baltimore MD 21202 Office Phone: 410-347-7703. Business E-Mail: lidtke@acm.org.

LIDTKE, VERNON LEROY, history professor; b. Avon, S.D., May 4, 1930; s. Albert William and Aganeta (Boese) Lidtke; m. Doris Eileen Keefe, Apr. 21, 1951. BA, U. Oreg., 1952, MA, 1955; PhD, U. Calif., Berkeley, 1962. Tchr. high sch., Riddle, Oreg., 1953-55; instr. social sci. U. Calif., Berkeley, 1960-62; asst. prof. history Mich. State U., 1962-66, asso. prof., 1966-68; vis. asst. prof. U. Calif., Berkeley, 1963; asso. prof. Johns Hopkins U., 1968-73, prof., 1973—2001, chmn. dept. history, 1975-79, prof. emeritus, 2001—; pres. Friends of the German Historical Inst., Washington, 1991-94. Author: (book) The Outlawed Party: Social Democracy in Germany, 1878-1890, 1966, The Alternative Culture: Socialist Labor in Imperial Germany, 1985; mem ed bd: Jour Modern Hist, 1973—76, Cent European Hist, 1982—89, Int Labor and Working Class Hist, 1984—89; contbr. articles to profl jours. Fellow Fulbright Research, 1959—60, 1966—67, Nat Endowment Humanities, 1969—70, Davis Ctr Hist Studies, Princeton Univ, 1974—75, Wissenschaftskolleg zu Berlin, 1987—88, Max-Planck-Institut für Geschichte, Göttingen, 1996. Mem.: AAUP, Conf Group German Polit (officer 1975—83), Conf Group Cen European Hist (vpres 1985, pres 1986), Col Art Asn, Am Hist Asn (chair modern European sect 1992, Eugene Asher Distinguished Teaching Award 1999), Johns Hopkins Club. Home: 4806 Wilmslow Rd Baltimore MD 21210-2328 Office: Johns Hopkins U Dept History Baltimore MD 21218 Business E-Mail: Lidtke@jhu@edu.

LIEB, ELLIOTT HERSHEL, physicist, educator, mathematician, educator; b. Boston, July 31, 1932; s. Sinclair M. and Clara (Rosenstein) L.; m. Christiane Fellbaum; children: Alexander, Gregory. BSc, MIT, 1953; PhD, U. Birmingham, Eng., 1956; DSc (hon.), U. Copenhagen, 1979; D (hon.), Ecole Poly. Fed. Lausanne, Switzerland, 1995, U. Munich, 2004. With IBM Corp., 1960-63; sr. lectr. Fourah Bay Coll., Sierra Leone, 1961; mem. faculty Yeshiva U., 1963-66, Northeastern U., 1966-68, MIT, Cambridge, 1968-75, prof. physics, 1963-68, prof. math., 1968-73, prof. math. and physics, 1973—, Princeton (N.J.) U., 1975—. Author: (with D.C. Mattis) Mathematical Physics in One Dimension, 1966, (with B. Simon and A. Wightman) Studies in Mathematical Physics, (with M. Loss) Analysis; also articles. Recipient Boris Pregel award chem. physics N.Y. Acad. Scis., 1970, Dannie Heineman prize for mathematical physics Am. Inst. Physics and Am. Phys. Soc., 1978, Prix Scientifique, Union des Assurances de Paris, 1985, Birkhoff prize Am. Math. Soc. and Soc. Indsl. Applied Math., 1988, Max-Planck medal German Phys. Soc., 1992, Boltzmann medal Internat. Union of Pure and Applied Physics, 1998, Onsager medal Norwegian U. Sci. and Tech., 1998, Rolf Schock prize in math. Swedish Acad. Scis., 2001, Levi L. Conant prize of Am. Math. Soc., 2002, Austrian medal Sci. Art, 2002, Poincare prize Internat. Assn. Math. Physics, 2003; Guggenheim Found. fellow, 1972, 78. Fellow AAAS, Am. Phys. Soc.; mem. NAS, Austrian Acad. Scis., Danish Royal Acad., Am. Acad. Arts and Scis., Internat. Assn. Math. Physics (pres. 1982-84, 97-99). Office: Princeton U Jadwin Hall-Physics Dept PO Box 708 Princeton NJ 08544-0001 Business E-Mail: lieb@princeton.edu.

LIEB, PETER, lawyer; BA, Yale U.; JD, U. Mich. Law clk. to Chief Justice Warren Burger U.S. Supreme Ct.; asst. atty. U.S. Dist. Ct. NY (So. dist.); asst. gen. counsel GTE Svc. Corp.; ptnr. Jones, Day, Reavis & Pogue; dep. gen. counsel, chief counsel, various sr. legal positions Internat. Paper, 1998—2003; sr. v.p., gen. counsel, sec. Symbol Technologies, Inc., Holtsville, NY, 2003—. Adj. prof. Fordham U. Office: Symbol Technologies Inc One Symbol Plz Holtsville NY 11742-1300 Office Phone: 631-738-4765. Office Fax: 631-738-5980.

LIEBAU, FREDERIC JACK, JR., investment manager; b. Palo Alto, Calif., Sept. 30, 1963; s. Frederic Jack and Charlene (Conrad) L.; m. Carol Platt. BA, Stanford U., 1985. Press aide Office of V.P., Washington, 1982; intern L.A. Times, 1983; analyst Capital Rsch. Co., L.A., 1984-86; ptnr., portfolio mgr. Primecap Mgmt. Co., Pasadena, Calif., 1986—2003; pres. Liebau Asset Mgmt. Co., LLC, 2003—; owner Liebau Farms. Office: Liebau Asset Mgmt Co LLC 301 E Colorado Blvd Ste 810 Pasadena CA 91101-1901 Office Phone: 626-795-5200. Personal E-mail: liebaufarm@aol.com. Business E-Mail: jack@liebauasset.com.

LIEBELER, SUSAN WITTENBERG, lawyer; b. July 3, 1942; d. Sherman K. and Eleanor (Klivans) Levine; m. Wesley J. Liebeler, Oct. 21, 1971; 1 child, Jennifer. BA, U. Mich., 1963, postgrad., 1963-64; LLB, UCLA, 1966. Bar: Calif. 1967, Vt. 1973, DC 1988. Law clk. Calif. Ct. of Appeals, 1966-67; assoc. Gang, Tyre & Brown, 1967-68, Greenberg, Bernhard, Weiss & Karma, L.A., 1968-70; assoc. gen. counsel Rep. Corp., 1970-72; gen. counsel Verit Industries, 1972-73; prof. Loyola Law Sch., L.A., 1973—85; spl. counsel, chmn. John S. R. Shad, SEC, Washington, 1981-82; commr. U.S. Internat. Trade Commn., Washington, 1984-88, vice-chmn., 1984-86, chmn., 1986-88; ptnr. Irell & Manella, L.A., 1988-94; pres. Lexpert Rsch. Svcs., L.A., 1995—. Vis. prof. U. Tex., summer 1982; cons. Office of Policy Coordination, Office of Pres.-elect, 1981-82; cons. U.S. Ry. Assn., 1975, U.S. EPA, 1974, U.S. Price Commn., 1972; mem. Adminstrv. Conf. U.S., 1986-88. Mem. editl. adv. bd. Regulation mag. CATO Inst.; sr. editor UCLA Law Rev., 1965-66; contbr. articles to profl. jours. Mem. adv. bd. U. Calif. Orientation in USA Law; bd. govs. Century City Hosp., 1992—2002, vice chair, 1997—99, chair, 1999—2001. Stein scholar UCLA, 1966. Mem. State Bar Calif. (treas., vice chair, chair exec. com. internat. law sect.), Practicing Law Inst. (Calif. adv. com.), Washington Legal Found. (acad. adv. bd.), Order of Coif. Jewish. Office Phone: 310-589-5546. Business E-Mail: lexpert@lexpertresearch.com.

LIEBEN, THOMAS GEOFFREY, lawyer; b. Omaha; s. Theodore Jack and Eileen (Brooks) L.; m. Anne C., June 26, 1971; children: Elizabeth, Caroline, Andrew. BA, Creighton U., 1968; JD, NYU, 1971. Bar: Nebr. 1971, U.S. Dist. Ct. Nebr. 1971, U.S. Ct. Appeals (8th cir.) 1972, U.S. Tax Ct. 1972. Ptnr. Fitzgerald & Brown, Omaha, 1971-88; prin. Lieben, Whitted, Houghton, Slowiaczek & Cavanagh, P.C., Omaha, 1988—. Dir. Financial Dynamics Inc., Omaha, 1988-99. Contbr. articles to profl. jours. Recipient Order of the Coif award NYU, 1971; fellow Nebr. Bar Found., Lincoln, 1994; named in Best Lawyers in Am., 1983—. Mem. Omaha Bar Assn., Nebr. Bar Assn., ABA, Omaha Estate Planning Coun., Omaha Pension Coun., Employee Benefits Roundtable. Democrat. Avocation: tennis. Office: Lieben Whitted Houghton Slowiaczek & Cavanagh PC 2027 Dodge St Ste 100 Omaha NE 68102-1238 E-mail: jlieben@liebenlaw.com.

LIEBENDORFER, RICHARD ARTHUR, internist; b. Superior, Wis., Oct. 15, 1927; s. Joe and Nellie Marie (Starboard) L.; m. Priscilla Jean Hotle, Sept. 2, 1951 (dec. Oct. 1981); children: Kim Denise Brummett, Kurt R., Craig T.; m. Carole Lee Henderson, Nov. 18, 1982. BA, U. Iowa, 1949, MD, 1953. Diplomate Am. Bd. Internal Medicine. Intern U.S. Naval Hosp., Charleston, S.C., 1953-54; resident Univ. Hosps. U. Iowa, Iowa City, 1956-59; pvt. practice Tulsa; active staff St. John Med. Ctr., Tulsa, 1959—2003, ret., 2003, pres. med. staff, 1989-90, bd. dirs., 1987-92, hon. staff, 2003—. Med. dir. CompMed/Exel Care, Tulsa, 1994-96; mem. strategic planning com., bd. dirs. St. John Med. Ctr., Tulsa, moral and med. ethics com. Lt. USNR, 1953—56. Fellow ACP; mem. Tulsa County Med. Soc. (pres. 1982), Okla. State Med. Assn. (trustee 1981-83). Avocations: tennis, golf, ranching, reading. Home: 3147 S Lewis Pl Tulsa OK 74105-2331 E-mail: rlieben@cox.net.

LIEBENOW, FRANKLIN EASTBURN, JR., English literature educator; b. Fredericksburg, Va., May 9, 1946; s. Franklin Eastburn and Katherine (Garrison) L.; m. Carolyn Lynch, July 3, 1971. BA, Randolph-Macon Coll., 1968; AM, U. Mich., 1969, PhD, 1984. Tchg. fellow, lectr. U. Mich., Ann Arbor, 1968-73, 74-75, 1978-79; lectr. Johannes Gutenberg U., Mainz, Germany, 1973-74; adj. instr. Rappahannock Coll., Warsaw, Va., 1976-77; tech. writing cons. Naval Surface Weapons Ctr., Dahlgren, Va., 1977; tech. writer UNISYS, Dahlgren, Va., 1984-86; tchr. Latin and German King George (Va.) H.S., 1987; asst. prof. Chgo. State U., 1987-92; assoc. prof., 1992-97; prof., 1997—; dept. asst. chair, 1994-96; grad. advisor, 2002—04. Vis. lectr. in theater Mary Washington Coll. U. Va., Fredericksburg, Va., summer 1970, 71. Contbr. articles and reviews to profl. jours. Seminar fellow NEH, Emory U., 1993. Mem. MLA, Am. Soc. for Eighteenth-Century Studies, Midwestern Am. Soc. for Eighteenth-Century Studies, Eighteenth-Century Scottish Studies Soc., Sigma Upsilon, Eta Sigma Phi, Pi Delta Epsilon, Omicron Delta Kappa. Home: 1524 Carson Dr Homewood IL 60430 Office: Chgo State Univ 9501 S King Dr Chicago IL 60628-1501

LIEBENSON, JEFFREY M., lawyer; b. NYC, Mar. 14, 1953; AB, U. Calif., Berkeley, 1975; JD, NYU, 1978, LLM, 1982. Bar: NY 1979. Ptnr. Katten Muchin Zavis Rosenman, NYC. Mem.: Am. Corp. Counsel Assn., Copyright Soc. of USA, Assn. Bar of City NY. Office: Katten Muchin Zavis Rosenman 575 Madison Ave New York NY 10022 Office Phone: 212-940-8597. Office Fax: 212-894-5597. E-mail: jeff.liebenson@kmzr.com.

LIEBER, CHARLES, chemistry professor, researcher, materials scientist; b. Phila., Pa., 1959; BS in Chemistry, Franklin & Marshall Coll., 1981; PhD in Chemistry, Stanford U., 1985; postdoctoral study, Calif. Inst. Tech., 1985—87. Postdoctoral rsch. California Inst. of Tech., 1986; assist. prof. chemistry Columbia U., 1987—91; prof. chemistry, chemical biology & Mark Hyman prof. chemistry div. of engring. & applied sci. Harvard U., 1991—. Scientific founder and mem. scientific adv. bd. Nanosys, Inc. Author numerous scientific articles in professional journals & mags. including: Jour. of Am. Chemistry Soc., Applied Physics Letters, Scientific American, Jour. of Physical Chemistry, Nature, Science. Named one of Brilliant 10, Popular Sci. mag., 2002; recipient Pure Chemistry award, Am. Chemical Soc., 1992, Creativity award, Nat. Sci. Found., 1996, Feynman award in nanotechnology, 2001, MRS medal, 2002, Harrison-Howe award, 2002, APS McGroddy prize for new materials, 2003, Inventor of the Yr., NY Intellectual Property Law Assn., 2003, World Tech. award in materials, 2003, Scientific American award in nanotechnology & molecular electronics, 2003, Chemistry of Materials award, Am. Chemical Soc., 2004. Fellow: Am. Physical Soc.; mem.: AAAS, NAS. Developed and applied a new chemically sensitive microscopy for probing organic and biological materials at nanometer to molecular scales. Office: Harvard U Dept Chemistry & Chemical Biology 12 Oxford St Cambridge MA 02138 Business E-Mail: cml@cmlliris.harvard.edu.

LIEBER, CHARLES SAUL, internist, educator; b. Antwerp, Belgium, Feb. 13, 1931; came to U.S., 1958, naturalized, 1966; s. Isaac and Lea (Maj) L.; m. M. A. Leo; children: Colette, Daniel, Leah, Samuel, Sarah. Candidate in natural and med. sci., U. Brussels, 1951; MD, 1955. Intern, resident U. Hosp., Brugmann, Brussels, Belgium, 1954-56; research fellow med. found. Queen Elizabeth, 1956-58; research fellow Thorndike Meml. Lab., Harvard Med. Sch., 1958-60, instr., 1961; assoc. Harvard U., 1962; assoc. prof. medicine Cornell U., 1963-68; dir. liver disease and nutrition unit Bellevue Hosp., N.Y.C., 1963-68; chief sect. liver disease, nutrition and alcohol Tng. Program VA Hosp., Bronx, 1968—; prof. medicine Mt. Sinai Sch. Medicine, 1969—, prof. pathology, 1976—, dir. Alcohol Research and Treatment Ctr., 1977—. Assoc. vis. physician Cornell Med. div. Bellevue, Meml., James Ewing hosps., 1964-69; Am. Coll. Gastroenterology disting. lectr., 1978, Henry Baker lectr., 1979 Recipient award of Belgian Govt. for rsch. on gastric secretion, 1956, Rsch. Career Devel. award NIH, USPHS, 1964-68, E.M. Jellinek Meml. award, 1976, A. Boudreau award Laval U., 1977, W.S. Middleton award highest honor for med. rsch. Dept. Vets. Affairs, 1977, Leahy Rsch. award highest honor for outstanding investigator, 1994, first Mark Keller award NIAAA-NIH, 1996, AMA Sci. Achievement award, 1998. Master ACP; fellow AAAS, Am. Soc. Nutritional Sci.; mem. Assn. Am. Physicians, N.Y. Gastroent. Assn. (pres. 1974-75), Am. Soc. Biochemistry and Molecular Biology, Am. Soc. Addictive Medicine (pres. 1974-77, Sci. Achievement award 1989, Disting. Scientist award 1996), Assn. Clin. Biochemists (Kone award 1994), Am. Soc. Clin. Nutrition (McCollum award 1973, pres. 1975-76, Robert H. Herman Meml. award 1993), Am. Soc. Clin. Investigation, Am. Soc. Pharmacol. Exptl. Therapy, Am. Gastroent. Assn. (Disting. Achievement award 1973, Hugh R. Butt award for liver/nutrition 1992), Rsch. Soc. on Alcoholism (pres. 1977-79, Sci. Excellence award 1980, Disting. Svc. award 1992), Am. Coll. Nutrition (Outstanding Achievement award 1990, R. Brinkley Smithers award in rsch. and edn. in alcohol 2003). Home: 6 Johnson Ave Englewood Cliffs NJ 07632-2107 Office: VA Med Ctr 130 W Kingsbridge Rd Bronx NY 10468-3904 Office Phone: 718-741-4244. Personal E-mail: liebercs@aol.com.

LIEBER, CONSTANCE E., medical association administrator; Pres. Nat. Alliance for Rsch. on Schizophrenia & Depression, N.Y.C. Achievements include creation of the Lieber prize for outstanding achievement in schizophrenia research. $50,000 prize is funded annually by the Essel Foundation and awarded by NARSAD Scientific Council members. Office: Natl Alliance Rsch Schizophrenia Dept 60 Cutter Mill Rd Ste 404 Great Neck NY 11021

LIEBER, DAVID LEE, university president; b. Stryj, Poland, Feb. 20, 1925; came to U.S., 1927, naturalized, 1936; s. Max and Gussie L.; m. Esther, June 10, 1945; children: Michael, Daniel, Deborah, Susan. BA, CCNY, 1944; B of Hebrew Lit., Jewish Theol. Sem. Am., 1944, M of Hebrew Lit., 1948, D of Hebrew Lit., 1951; MA, Columbia U., 1947; postgrad., U. Wash., 1954—55, UCLA, 1961—63; LDH (hon.), Hebrew Union Coll., 1982. Ordained rabbi, 1948. Rabbi Sinai Temple, L.A., 1950-54; dir. B'nai B'rith Hillel, Seattle, Cambridge, 1954-56; dean students U. Judaism, L.A., 1956-63, Samuel A. Fryer prof. Bible, pres., 1963-92, Skovron Disting. Svc. prof. Bibl. lit., 1990—, pres. emeritus, 1992—; lectr. Hebrew UCLA, 1957-90; vice chancellor Jewish Theol. Sem., 1972-92. Mem. exec. coun. Rabbinical Assembly, 1966-69, v.p., 1994-96, pres., 1996-98; vice chmn. Am. Jewish Com., L.A., 1972-75; bd. dirs. Jewish Fedn. Coun., L.A., 1980-86. Mem. editl. bd. Conservative Judaism, 1968-70; sr. editor (bibl. commentary) ETZ Hayim. Served as chaplain USAF, 1951-53. Recipient Torch of Learning award Hebrew U., 1984, Simon Greenberg award U. Judaism, 2002, Book of Yr. award Nat. Jewish Book Coun., 2002, Tomech Torah award Nat. Jewish Edn. Assn., 2004. Mem. Assn. Profs. Jewish Studies (dir. 1970-71), Phi Beta Kappa. Office: U Judaism 15600 Mulholland Dr Los Angeles CA 90077-1519 Office Phone: 310-440-1288. Personal E-mail: dllieber@aol.com.

LIEBER, MICHAEL RANDALL, biochemist, educator; b. St. Louis, June 21, 1955; s. John Warren Sr. and Matilda V. Lieber; m. Chih-Lin Hsieh, Jan. 1, 1990. BA, BS, U. Mo., 1977; PhD, U. Chgo., 1981, MD, 1983. Diplomate Am. Bd. Pathology. Resident in pathology NIH, Bethesda, Md., 1983-86, postdoctoral fellow, 1986-89; asst. prof., then assoc. prof. Stanford (Calif.) U., 1989-94; assoc. prof. pathology Washington U., St. Louis, 1994-97; prof. U. So. Calif., 1997—. Editl. bd. Molecular and Cellular Biology, JBC, DNA Repair; contbr. over 120 articles to profl. publs., including Nature, Cell, Sci., EMBO Jour., Genes & Devel. Recipient Faculty Scholar award Leukemia Soc. Am., 1994-99, Ed Heitz Meml. Rsch. Fund award Leukemia Soc. Am., 1998, award Warner-Lambert/Parke-Davis, 1998; Stohlman scholar Leukemia Soc. Am., 1999. Mem. AAAS, Am. Soc. Investigative Pathology. Achievements include patents in field. Home: 245 W Palm Dr Arcadia CA 91007 Office: USC Sch Medicine ME 9176 1441 Eastlake Ave Los Angeles CA 90089-9176

LIEBER, RICHARD LOUIS, biomedical engineering scientist, educator; b. Walnut Creek, Calif., Dec. 14, 1956; s. Richard and Janet Elizabeth (Stone) L.; children: Katelyn Suzanne, Kristin Michelle; m. Dina Lieber, Oct. 2004. BS with honors, U. Calif., Davis, 1978, PhD, 1982. Sr.rsch. career scientist VA Med. Ctr., San Diego, 1983—; prof. orthopaerics & bioengring. U. Calif., 1985—. Cons. Pref Med. Products Inc., 1987—. Contbr. sci. papers to profl. publs.; inventor surgical myometor, 1985, adaptive muscle stimulator, 1987. Faculty advisor Inter-Varsity Christian Fellowship, San Diego, 1984—. Recipient Presdl. award Am. Acad. Cerebral Palsy, 1984, Nicolas Andry award Am. Bone & Joint Inst., 1998; State of Calif. Gov.'s scholar, 1974. Mem. IEEE, Orthopaedic Rsch. Soc., Biophys. Soc. (Talbot award 1981), Rehab. Engring. Soc. N.Am., Soc. Neursci., Am. Soc. Biomechanics, Am. Physiol. Soc. Republican. Achievements include patent for surgical myometer; development of techniques used involving computer controlled muscle contraction and optical sensors for structure monitoring; research on skeletal muscle properties in normal and diseased muscles. Home: 10471 Mira Montana Dr Del Mar CA 92014 Office: U Calif Dept Orthopaedics V 151 San Diego CA 92161-0001 Office Phone: 619-552-8585. E-mail: rliever@ncsd.edu.

LIEBER, ROBERT JAMES, political science professor; b. Chgo. m. Nancy Lieber; 2 children. BA in Polit. Sci. with high honors, U. Wis., 1963; postgrad. in Polit. Sci., U. Chgo., 1963-64; PhD in Govt., Harvard U., 1968. Asst. prof. Polit. Sci. U. Calif., Davis, 1968-72, assoc. prof., 1972-77, chmn. dept. Polit. Sci., 1975-76, 77-80, prof., 1977-81; postdoctoral rschr. St. Antony's Coll. Oxford (Eng.) U., 1969-70; prof. Georgetown U., Washington, 1982—, chmn. dept. govt., 1990-96, acting chmn. dept. psychology, 1997-99. Vis. prof. Oxford U., 1969, Fudan U, Shanghai, 1988; rsch. assoc. Ctr. Internat. Affairs, Harvard U., 1974—75; cons. U.S. Dept. State and Dept. Def., 1975—. Author: British Politics and European Unity, 1970, Theory and World Politics, 1972, Oil and the Middle East War: Europe in the Energy Crisis, 1976, The Oil Decade: Conflict and Cooperation in the West, 1983, No Common Power: Understanding International Relations, 1988, 4th edit., 2001; co-author: Contemporary Politics: Europe, 1976; editor, contbg. author: Eagle Adrift: American Foreign Policy at the End of the Century, 1997, Eagle Rules? Foreign Policy and American Primacy in the 21st Century, 2002; co-editor, contbg. author: Eagle Entangled: U.S. Foreign Policy in a Complex World, 1979, Eagle Defiant: U.S. Foreign Policy in the 1980s, 1983, Eagle Resurgent? The Reagan Era in American Foreign Policy, 1987, Eagle in a New World: American Grand Strategy in the Post-Cold War Era, 1992; editor: Will Europe Fight for Oil?, 1983; contbr. articles to Harper's, Commentary, Politique étrangère, N.Y. Times, Washington Post, Christian Sci. Monitor, L.A. Times, others, and profl. jours. Advanceman nat. campaign staff McCarthy for Pres., 1968; fgn. policy advising presdl. campaigns of Sen. Edward Kennedy, 1979-80, Walter Mondale. 1984, Bill Clinton, 1991-92; coord. Mid. East Issues presdl. campaign Michael Dukakis, 1988. Woodrow Wilson fellow, 1963, fellow NDEA, 1963-64, grad. prize fellow Harvard U.,

1964-68, Social Sci. Rsch. Coun., 1969-70, Coun. Fgn. Rels., 1972-73, Guggenheim fellow, 1973-74, Rockefeller Found., 1978-79, Wilson Ctr. Smithsonian Inst., 1980-81, 99-00, Ford Found., 1981; vis. fellow Atlantic Inst. Internat. Affairs, Paris, 1978-79; guest scholar Brookings Inst., 1981. Mem.: Coun. on Fgn. Rels., Phi Beta Kappa. Office: Georgetown U Dept Of Government Washington DC 20057-1034 Office Phone: 202-687-5920. Business E-Mail: lieberr@georgetown.edu.

LIEBER, STANLEY MARTIN See LEE, STAN

LIEBER, TOM ALAN, painter; b. St. Louis, Mo., 1949; BFA, Univ. Ill., Champaign-Urbana, 1971, MFA, 1974. Exhibitions include Guggenheim Mus. NYC 1983, Gruenebaum Gallery NYC, 1986, Met. Mus. Art NYC, 1988, Galerie Edeling Copenhagen, 1990, Friesen Gallert Seattle, 1994 & 1997, Horwitch LewAllen Gallery Santa Fe, 1995, Margulies Taplin Gallery Coral Gables, 1995, Samuelis Baumgarte Galerie Bielefeld, Germany, 1996, John Berggruen Gallery, S.F., 1996, Hackett Freedman Gallery, S.F., 2004; represented in collections of Guggenheim Mus. NYC, Met. Mus. Art NYC, S.F. Mus. Modern Art, Mus. Contemporary Art L.A., Tate Gallery London, Bowdoin Mus. Art, Cleve. Mus. Art, Cantor Arts Ctr. Stanford Univ., Mt. Holyoke Coll. Mus. Art, Oakland Mus. Art, Portland (Maine) Mus. Art, Newport Mus. Art, Santa Fe Mus. Art, Tucson Mus. Art, Palm Springs Desert Mus. Named an Invited Artist, Trillium Press, 2002; grantee Nat. Endowment for the Arts, 1975. Mem.: NAD (academician 1994—). Mailing: Hackett Freedman Gallery 250 Sutter St San Francisco CA 94108*

LIEBERFARB, WARREN N., digital media pioneer; b. Mar. 1943; BS, U. Penn; MBA, U. Mich. Financial analyst Ford Motor Co.; exec. asst. to pres. Paramount Pictures; v.p., telecommunications 20th Century Fox Film, 1973—75; sr. v.p., sales & mktg. Warner Bros., 1982—84; pres. Warner Home Video, Burbank, Calif., 1984—2002; chmn. Lieberfarb & Assoc.

LIEBERMAN, CAROL, healthcare marketing communications consultant; b. St. Louis, June 14, 1938; d. Norman Leonard and Ethel (Silver) Mistachkin; m. Malcolm P. Cooper, Aug. 25, 1962 (div. June 1977); children: Lawrence, Edward, Marcus; m. Edward Lieberman, Apr. 1992. BS, U. Wis., 1959; MA, N.Y. Inst. Tech., 1992; CTEFL, CTBE, Worldwide Tchr.'s Inst., 2000. Cert. tchr. english as foreign lang., tchr. of bus. english. Media buyer Lennen and Newell, L.A., 1959-61; advt. mgr. Hartfield-Zodys, L.A., 1961-62, Haggarty's, L.A., 1962-63; sales rep. Abbott Labs., Bklyn., 1974-75; edn. dir. N.Y. and NJ Regional Transp. Program, N.Y.C., 1975-78; account exec. Med. Edn. Dynamics, Woodbridge, NJ, 1978-79; dir. program devel. Kallir, Phillips & Ross Info. Media, N.Y.C., 1979-81; exec. v.p. sales and mktg. Audio Visual Med. Mktg., N.Y.C., 1981-85; exec. v.p. Park Row Pubs./John Wiley & Sons Med. Div., N.Y.C., 1985-88; pres., prin. Pk. Row Pub., N.Y.C., 1988-91; healthcare mktg. communications cons., Dix Hills, NY, 1991—; prof. comm. and speech N.Y. Inst. Tech., 1991-95; exec. sec. Cardiopulmonary Bypass Consensus Panel, 1993—; asst. prof. profl. studies Southampton Coll., LI Univ., 2000—03; facilitator U. Phoenix Online, Phoenix, 2001—, instr. specialist, 2003—. Cons. Am. Acad. Physician Asst., Washington, 1986-87, Am. Soc. Anesthesiologists, Chgo., 1986-88, Am. Acad. Family Physicians, 1987-91, Am. Psychiat. Assn., 1988, Am. Coll. Gen. Practitioners, 1988, N.Am. Soc. pacing and Electrophysiology, 1988-91, Internat. Immunocompromised Host Soc., 1996-2003; internet pub. Am. Assn. Thoracic Surgery, 1999-2003. Pub. CME Press. Mem. TESOL, IATEFL, Am. Women in Radio and TV, Soc. Tchr. Family Medicine (cons.), Pharm. Advt. Council, Nat. Council Jewish Women, Hadassah. Avocations: tennis, writing fiction, classical piano. Home and Office: 2 Fathers Ct Dix Hills NY 11746 Personal E-mail: carolli@optonline.net.

LIEBERMAN, CHARLES, economist; b. Landsburg, Bavaria, Germany, July 25, 1948; s. Leo and Tola (Melcer) L.; m. Anne Rosenberg, Aug. 26, 1972; children: David, Michael, Jeremy. BS, MIT, 1970; AM in Econs., U. Pa., 1972, PhD in Econs., 1974. Asst. prof. U. Md., College Park, 1974-79; vis. assoc. prof. Northwestern U., Evanston, Ill., 1978-79; economist Fed. Res. Bank N.Y., N.Y.C., 1979-81; sr. economist Morgan Stanley, N.Y.C., 1981-83; v.p., sr. economist Shearson Lehman Bros., N.Y.C., 1983-86; mng. dir., dir. fin. market rsch. Chem. Securities Inc./Mfrs. Hanover Securities Corp., N.Y.C., 1986-96; chief economist The Global Bank, Chase Manhattan Bank, 1996-97; mng. ptnr. Strategic Investors, N.Y.C., 1997—99; mng. mem. Lieberman Asset Mgmt. LLC, 1999—; chief investment officer Advisors Capital Mgmt., 2001—. Econs. commentator CNBC; bd. dirs. Bookrags, Inc., C3I, Inc. Author: (newsletter) Market Commentary; contbr. articles to profl. jours. Sgt. U.S. Army Res., 1970-76. Sloan fellow, 1973, NSF fellow, 1971. Mem. Forecasters Club N.Y. (treas. 1987-89, v.p. 1990-91, pres. 1991-92), Money Marketeers NYU (bd. govs., v.p., pres. 1992-93). Jewish. Avocations: tennis, skiing, classical music. Office: Advisors Capital Mgmt 115 W Century Rd Paramus NJ 07652 Office Phone: 201-986-1900. *Work hard, play hard, and enjoy life.*

LIEBERMAN, DOUGLAS MARK, lawyer; b. Flushing, N.Y., Aug. 17, 1960; s. Harvey Jack and Sandra Ann (Silver) Lieberman; m. Lori Ilene Nadel, Oct. 18, 1987. BA, SUNY, Plattsburgh, 1981; MA, U. Md., 1983; JD, Hofstra U., 1986. Bar: N.J. 1986, U.S. Dist. Ct. N.J. 1986, N.Y. 1987, U.S. Dist. Ct. (so. and ea. dists.) N.Y. 1987. Assoc. Zane & Rudofsky, N.Y.C., 1986-90; ptnr. Markotsis & Lieberman, Hicksville, NY, 1990—. Editor-in-chief: newspaper Conscience, 1985—86, articles editor: Hofstra Labor Law Jour., 1985—86, assoc. editor: Nassau Lawyer, 2000—02, co-editor-in-chief:, 2002—04, chpt. editor: book Mechanics of Beginning, 1994; contbr. articles to profl. jours.; assoc. editor: Nassau Lawyer, 2004—. Scholar Alumni, Plattsburgh Coll. Found. SUNY, Rotary Club. Mem.: ABA, Nassau County Bar Assn., N.Y. State Bar Assn., Alpha Epsilon Rho, Phi Kappa Phi, Phi Alpha Delta. Democrat. Jewish. Avocations: ice hockey, golf, road racing, stamp collecting/philately. Office: 183 Broadway Ste 210 Hicksville NY 11801-4240

LIEBERMAN, EDWARD JAY, lawyer; b. Evansville, Ind., Apr. 8, 1946; s. Heiman George and Anna Sharp (Blacker) L.; m. Ellen Ackerman Wegusen, June 1, 1969; 1 child: Laura Amy. BSBA, Washington U., St. Louis, 1968, JD, 1971. Bar: Mo. 1971. Jr. ptnr. Bryan Cave, St. Louis, 1972-76; assoc. counsel 1st Nat. Bank in St. Louis, 1976-80; ptnr. Lowenhaupt, Chasnoff, Armstrong & Mellitz, St. Louis, 1980-84, Husch & Eppenberger, LLC, St. Louis, 1984—. Mem. ABA, Mo. Bar, Bar Assn. Met. St. Louis, Am. Coll. Mortgage Attys., Nat. Health Care Lawyers Assn. Office: Husch & Eppenberger LLC 190 Carondelet Plz Ste 600 Saint Louis MO 63105 E-mail: ed.lieberman@husch.com.

LIEBERMAN, GAIL FORMAN, investment company executive; b. Phila., May 26, 1943; d. Joseph and Rita Forman. BA in Physics and Math., Temple U., 1964, MBA in Fin., 1977. Dir. internat. fin. Std. Brands Inc., N.Y.C., 1977-79; staff v.p. fin. and capital planning RCA Corp., 1979-82; CFO, exec. v.p. Scali McCabe Sloves, Inc., 1982-93; v.p. fin., CFO, mng. dir. Moody's Investors Svc., N.Y.C., 1994-96; CFO TFPG Thomson Corp., Boston, 1996-99; CEO Liquid Alternatives Inc., 2000; mng. ptnr. Rudder Capital LLC, 2001—. Bd. dirs I-TRAX Corp. Mem. Fin. Execs. Inst. Office Phone: 917-207-4969. Personal E-mail: liebermang@earthlink.net.

LIEBERMAN, JAMES SANFORD, physiatrist, neurologist; b. Mpls., Apr. 24, 1938; BS, U. Calif., 1960, MD, 1963. Instr., asst. prof. neurology SUNY, Downstate, 1967—71; asst. prof. neurology Columbia U., 1971—72; from asst. prof. to prof. phys. medicine and rehab. and neurology U. Calif., Davis, 1972-91, chmn. phys. medicine and rehab., 1982—91; prof., chmn. rehab. medicine Columbia U., N.Y.C., 1991—, sr. assoc. dean, 1996—, asst. v.p. health sci., 1996—2003, assoc. v.p. health sci., 2003—; prof. divsn. head rehab. medicine Cornell U., N.Y.C., 2000—; physiatrist-in-chief N.Y. Presbyn. Hosp., N.Y.C., 2000—. Mem. NAS Inst. Medicine, Am. Acad. Clin. Neurophysiology, Am. Acad. Neurology, Am. Acad. Phys. Medicine & Rehab. Office: Columbia U 630 W 168th St Unit 38 New York NY 10032-3795 Office Phone: 212-305-4818. Office Fax: 212-305-3916. Business E-Mail: jsl12@columbia.edu.

LIEBERMAN, JANET ELAINE, academic administrator; b. N.Y.C., Oct. 21, 1921; d. Samuel and Ida (Schubert) Rubensohn; m. Allen L. Chase, July 9, 1940 (div. 1954); children: Gary Andrew, Randolph H.; m. Jerrold S. Lieberman, June 30, 1957. Student, Vassar Coll., 1939-40; BA, Barnard Coll., N.Y.C., 1943; MA, City Coll., N.Y.C., 1946; PhD, NYU, N.Y.C., 1965. Asst. prof. Hunter Coll., NYC, 1965-70; prof. LaGuardia C.C., Long Island City, NY, 1970-72, asst. dean faculty, 1972-74, prof. psychology, 1974-86, asst. to pres., 1986—, prof. emeritus, 2005. Recipient Innovation in Higher Edn. award Charles A. Dana Found., N.Y.C., 1989, Break the Mold award U.S. Dept. Edn., Washington, 1992, LaGuardia medal of honor, 2002, Disting. Alumni award NYU, 2003, McGraw Hill Ednl. Achievement award, 2004. Mem. Am. Assn. Higher Edn. Avocation: tennis. Office: LaGuardia CC 31-10 Thomson Ave Long Island City NY 11101-3071

LIEBERMAN, JAY R., orthopedist, surgeon; MD, Albany Med. Coll., N.Y., 1984. Assoc. prof. UCLA Med. Ctr., 1991—. Recipient Cap CURE Rsch. award, Cap CURE, 1998—2001, Frank Stinchfield award, Hip Soc., 1999, Russel Hibbs award, Scoliosis Rsch. Soc., 1998, Sumner Koch award, Am. Soc. for Surgery of the Hand, 1998; fellow ABC Traveling fellow, Am. Orthop. Assn., 1997; grantee Physician Scientist award, NIH, 1994—99. Mem.: Hip Soc. (assoc.), Am. Orthop. Assn. (assoc.). Achievements include research in Development of gene therapy to enhance bone repair; understanding the pathophysiology of bone metastasis; deep vein thrombosis prophylaxis after total joint replacement. Office: UCLA Med Ctr 10945 LeConte Ave Los Angeles CA 90095

LIEBERMAN, JOSEPH I., senator; b. Stamford, Conn., Feb. 24, 1942; s. Henry and Marcia (Manger) L.; m. Hadassah Freilich, Mar. 20, 1983; children: Matthew, Rebecca, Ethan, Hana. BA, Yale U., 1964, JD, 1967. Bar: Conn. 1967. Mem. Conn. Senate, 1971-81, senate majority leader, 1975-81; ptnr. Lieberman, Segaloff & Wolfson, New Haven, 1972-83; atty. gen. State of Conn., Hartford, 1983-89; U.S. senator from Conn., 1989—; chmn. govtl. affairs com. Mem. armed svcs. com., environment and pub. works com., small bus. com.; chmn. Dem. Leadership Coun., 1995-2000. Author: The Power Broker, 1966, The Scorpion and the Tarantula, 1970, The Legacy, 1981, Child Support in America, 1986, In Praise of Public Life, 2000. Candidate for v.p. U.S., 2000 Democrat. Jewish. Office: 706 Hart Senate Office Bldg Washington DC 20510-0001*

LIEBERMAN, LAURENCE, poet, educator; b. Detroit, Feb. 16, 1935; s. Nathan and Anita (Cohen) L.; m. Bernice Clair Braun, June 17, 1956; children— Carla, Deborah, Isaac. BA, U. Mich., 1956, MA in English, 1958; postgrad., U. Calif.-Berkeley. Prof. English Coll. V.I., 1964-68; prof. English and creative writing U. Ill., Urbana, 1968—. U. Ill. Ctr. for Advanced Study Creative Writing fellow, Japan, 1971-72 Author: The Unblinding, 1968, The Achievement of James Dickey, 1969, The Osprey Suicides, 1973, Unassigned Frequencies: American Poetry in Review (1964-77), 1977, God's Measurements, 1980, Eros At the World Kite Pageant, 1983, The Mural of Wakeful Sleep, 1985, (poems) The Creole Mephistopheles, 1989, The Best American Poetry, 1991 (award), New and Selected Poems (1962-92), 1993, The St. Kitts. Monkey Feuds, 1995, Beyond the Muse of Memory: Essays on Contemporary Poets, 1995, Dark Songs: Slave House and Synagogue, 1996, Compass of the Dying, 1998, The Regatta in the Skies: Selected Long Poems, 1999, Flight From the Mother Stone, 2000, Hour of The Mango Black Moon, 2004, Carib's Leap: Selected New Poems, 2005; poetry editor poetry books program U. Ill. Press, 1970—; contbr. poetry to lit. jours., popular mags. Recipient award for Best Poems of 1968, Nat. Endowment for Arts, 1969, Jerome P. Shestack award Am. Poetry Rev., 1986; creative writing fellow U. Ill. Ctr. for Advanced Study, 2000—, Nat. Endowment Arts, 1986-87. Office: U Ill English Dept 608 S Wright St Urbana IL 61801-3630 Office Phone: 217-333-2390.

LIEBERMAN, LESTER ZANE, engineering company executive; b. Newark, July 4, 1930; s. Herman P. and Cecile A. (Ashenfeld) Lieberman; m. Judith Mazor, Aug. 11, 1957; children: Susan, Jane. BSME, Newark Coll. Engring., 1951, postgrad., 1953—58; DHL (hon.), Clarkson U., 1991, U. Medicine and Dentistry NJ, 2005. Registered profl. engr., N.J., Pa. Pres. Crest Engring. Inc., Newark, 1955—60; chmn., pres. Atmos Engring. Co. Inc., Kenilworth, NJ, 1960—78; pres., CEO, Clarkson Industries, Inc., N.Y.C., 1978—90; real estate investment and development Dowel Assoc., 1990—; partner, cons. Construction HVAC, 1990—. Bd. dirs. Lazard Fund, Cives Steel Corp. Chmn. Beth Israel Med. Ctr., Newark, 1970—96, N.J. Healthcare Found., 1996—, Irvington Gen. Hosp., 1992—96; mem. coun. N.J. Performing Arts Ctr., Pub. Health Rsch. Inst., N.J. Med. Sch.; trustee Clarkson U., Potsdam, NY. Named Alumnus of the Yr., Newark Coll. Engring., 1980; recipient Friendship award, Best Friends Newark, 1999, Humanitarian award, St. Barnabas' Burn Found., 1999, Citizens award, N.J. Acad. Medicine, 2000, Cmty. award, Y Camps N.J., 2000, Humanitarian award, United Jewish Cmtys., 2004. Mem.: NSPE, ASHRAE, Am. Acad. Environ. Engrs. (diplomate), N.J. Soc. Profl. Engrs., Morristown Club, Stockbridge Country Club (Mass.), Mountain Ridge Country Club (N.J.), Cornell Club (N.Y.), Masons, Tau Beta Pi (Key award 1982). Jewish. Avocations: skiing, sailing, tennis, golf. Home: Spring Valley Rd Morristown NJ 07960-7011 Office: 25 Lindsley Dr Morristown NJ 07960-4455 Office Phone: 973-401-0070. Personal E-mail: leszl@aol.com.

LIEBERMAN, LOUIS (KARL LIEBERMAN), artist; b. Bklyn., May 7, 1944; s. Abraham and Jeannette (Feinberg) L. BFA, R.I. Sch. Design, 1969; cert., Bklyn. Mus. Art Sch., 1964; BA, Bklyn. Coll., 1966. Adj. lectr. Bklyn. Coll., 1971-78, Lehman Coll., Bronx, N.Y., 1972-75; vis. artist Ill. State U., Normal, 1978, Hamilton Coll., Clinton, N.Y., 1982. One-man shows include Vancouver Art Gallery, B.C., Can., 1969, James Yu Gallery, N.Y.C., 1973, 74, Nina Freudenheim Gallery, Buffalo, 1976, Root Art Ctr., Hamilton Coll., Clinton, N.Y., 1980, Harm Bouckaert Gallery, N.Y.C., 1981, John Davis Gallery, Akron, Ohio, 1983, 85, Columbus Mus. Art, Ohio, 1983, John Davis Gallery, N.Y.C., 1986; group shows include Aldrich Mus. Contemporary Art, Ridgefield, Conn., 1973, 74, Johnson Mus. Art, Ithaca, N.Y., 1981, Fine Arts Mus. L.I., Hempstead, N.Y., 1982, Cleve. Inst. Art, 1982, Met. Mus. Art, N.Y.C., 1983, Byer Mus. Art, Evanston, Ill., 1982, Visual Arts Ctr., Beer-Sheva, Israel, 1985, Kunsthauses, Zurich, Switzerland, McNay Art Mus., San Antonio, Phila. Mus. of Art, 1988, Erie (Pa.) Art Mus., 1988, Art Mus. of Santa Cruz, Calif., 1988, Hunter Mus., Chattanooga, 1989, others; represented in permanent collections including Kenan Ctr., Lockport, N.Y., Aldridge Mus. Contemporary Art, Ridgefield, Conn., Met. Mus. Art, N.Y.C., Phila. Mus. Art, Stamford (Conn.) Mus., Bklyn. Mus., Mus. Fine Arts, Budapest, Hungary, Istvan Kiraly Mus., Budapest, Ackland Art Mus., Chapel Hill, N.C.; art critic N.Y. Arts Jour., 1978-79. Recipient Sculpture award Creative Artist Pub. Service Found., 1971-72, Graphics award Creative Artist Pub. Svc. Found., 1980-81, Graphics award N.Y. Found. Arts, 1984-85; visual arts fellow Nat. Endowment for Arts, 1979-80; Pollack-Krasner Found. fellow, 1987; Adolf and Esther Gottlieb Found. grantee, 1989.

LIEBERMAN, MICHAEL J., lawyer; b. 1951; BA summa cum laude, SUNY Albany, 1972; JD, Harvard U., 1976; LLM, NYU, 1984. Bar: NY 1976, Mass. 1995. Atty., leader Tax Practice Group Fine & Ambrogne; ptnr., chmn. & mgr., Tax Sect. Mintz Levin Cohn Ferris Glovsky & Popeo PC, Boston. Office: Mintz Levin Cohn Ferris Glovsky & Popeo PC One Financial Ctr Boston MA 02111 Office Phone: 617-348-1682. Office Fax: 617-542-2241. Business E-Mail: mlieberman@mintz.com.

LIEBERMAN, NANCY ANN, lawyer; b. N.Y.C., Dec. 30, 1956; d. Elias and Elayne Hildegarde (Fox) L.; m. Mark Ellman, Sept. 6, 1997. BA summa cum laude, U. Rochester, 1977; JD, U. Chgo., 1979; LLM in Taxation, NYU, 1981. Bar: N.Y. 1980. Intern White House, Washington, 1975; law clk. Hon. Henry A. Politz U.S. Ct. Appeals (5th cir.), Shreveport, La., 1979-80; assoc. Skadden Arps Slate Meagher & Flom LLP, N.Y.C., 1981-87, ptnr., 1987—. Trustee U. Rochester, 1994-2004, sr. trustee, 2004—; bd. dirs. Pacific Coun. Internat. Policy, 2003—. Mem. ABA, Assn. Bar City N.Y., Coun. Fgn. Rels., Phi Beta Kappa. Republican. Jewish. Home: 935 Park Ave New York NY 10028-0212 Office: Skadden Arps Slate Meagher & Flom LLP 4 Times Sq New York NY 10036-6595 Office Phone: 212-735-2050. Business E-Mail: nlieberman@skadden.com.

LIEBERMAN, PAMELA FORBES, consumer products company executive; MBA. With Price Waterhouse, 1975—88; v.p. fin. Bunzl Bldg. Supply, 1988—92; v.p., CFO Fel-Pro Inc., 1993—98; CFO Shoptalk, Inc., 1998—2001, TruServ Corp., Chgo., 2001—, COO, 2001—, CEO, 2001—. Office: TruServ Corp 8600 W Bryn Mawr Ave Chicago IL 60631-3505

LIEBERMAN, PHILLIP LOUIS, allergist, educator; b. Memphis, Mar. 20, 1940; m. Barbara; children: Ryan, Lee, Jay. Student, London Sch. Econs., 1961; BA in Sociology, Tulane U., 1962; MD, U. Tenn., 1965. Intern City of Memphis Hosp. U. Tenn., 1965-66, asst. resident internal medicine, 1966-67, assoc. resident internal medicine, 1967-68, chief resident, 1968-69; fellow in allergy, immunology Northwestern U., Evanston, Ill., 1969-71; asst. prof., chief div. allergy, immunology U. Tenn., 1971-74, assoc. prof., chief div. allergy, immunology, 1974-79, prof., chief div. allergy, immunology, 1979—. Instr. internal medicine U. Tenn., 1968-69; mem. exec. bd. Joint Coun. of Allergy & Immunology, 1985-90, AAAI rep., 1990; AAAI rep. Mothers for Asthmatics, 1990. Co-editor: Asthma Edition: Abstract-a-Card System, 1991—; contbr. numerous articles, abstracts to profl. publs.; author numerous presentations in field, book chpts., revs. Exec. bd. dirs. Asthma and Allergy Found. of Am., 1990—, mem. med. scientific coun., 1987, chmn., 1990—. Served to cpt. USAR, 1965-71. Mem. Am. Acad. Allergy (com. on alternative forms of therapy, 1980—), Am. Acad. Allergy and Immunology (exec. com. 1983-91, constitution and by-laws com. 1984-87, also chmn. 1985, undergraduate com. 1985, pres.-elect. 1987-88, pres. 1988-89, nominating com. 1987, also chmn. 1989, program com. 1987), Am. Coll. Allergists, Am. Assn. Allergists (sec. 1985), Am. Assn. Certified Allergists (2d v.p. 1986-87, pres. 1989-90), Am. Bd. Allergy and Immunology. also: Allergy Assocs 920 Madison Ave Ste 909N Memphis TN 38103-3438 Office: 7205 Wolf River Blvd #200 Germantown TN 38138-1746

LIEBERMAN, ROBERT ARTHUR, physicist; b. Grand Rapids, Mich., May 22, 1950; s. Arthur A. and Margaret W. Lieberman; children: Samson Robert, Leah Jaye. BS in Physics, Rensselaer Poly. Inst., 1971, MS in Physics, 1973; PhD in Physics, U. Mich., 1981. Exec. com. local br. AFL-CIO, Ann Arbor, Mich., 1977; postdoctoral fellow biophysics rsch. divsn. U. Mich., Ann Arbor, 1981; tech. staff AT&T Bell Labs., Murray Hill, NJ, 1981—91; from dir. advanced fiber optics to v.p. R&D Phys. Optics Corp., Torrance, Calif., 1991—98; from sr. v.p., chief tech. officer to sr. exec. v.p. Intelligent Optical Systems, Inc., 1999—2003, pres., 2003—; chief tech. officer, pres. Optech Ventures LLC, 2001—, pres., 2002—, Optical Security Sensing LLC, 2002—. Prin. investigator NSF, NIH, NASA, Dept. Energy, U.S. Army, USAF, USN, TSWG. Assoc. editor: Jour. Measurement Sci. Tech., 1994-96, Optical Engring. jour. 1997—; contbr. articles to profl. publs. Recipient Tech Brief award, NASA; Space grantee, 2004. Fellow SPIE (chmn. conf. on chem., biochem. and environ. sensors 1988-99, bd. dirs. 2001-2002); mem. IEEE (sr. mem.), AAAS, ASTM (chmn. subcom. on fiberoptic chem. sensing), Am. Phys. Soc. Achievements include patents for fiber optic sensing, solid state physics, biophysics, integrated optics, plasmon resonance, medical sensors, chemical sensors. Office: Intelligent Optical Systems Inc 2520 W 237th St Torrance CA 90505-5217

LIEBERMAN, ROCHELLE PHYLLIS, research and development company executive; b. Bklyn., June 27, 1940; d. Solomon and Freda (Shapiro) Beller; m. Melvyn Lieberman, June 10, 1961; children: Eric Neil, Marc Evan. BA, Bklyn. Coll., 1961; M.Ed., Duke U., 1977. Tchr. Bklyn. pub. schs., 1961-64; instr. Carolina Friends, Durham, N.C., 1967-70; grad. intern Duke U., Durham, 1974-75, faculty adviser, 1975-76; sales assoc. Kelly Matherly, Durham, 1978-81; pres. Shelli, Inc., Durham, 1981—. Treas. Duke Forest Assn., Durham, 1980—85; pres. Bus. Commn., 2004; mem. Predl. Bus. Commn., 2005, Nat. Rep. Congl. Com., Congl. Bus. Adv. Coun. Named NRCC Businesswoman of Yr., Duke-Durham Campaign, 2003. Mem. LWV, Durham and Chapel Hill Bd. Realtors, Women's Council of Realtors (sec. 1980-81), Duke U. Eye Ctr. (adv. bd.), Kappa Delta Pi. Clubs: Duke Faculty, Duke Campus (Durham). Jewish. Avocations: piano, walking, knitting, writing, reading. Office: Shelli Inc 1110 Woodburn Rd Durham NC 27705-5738 Office Phone: 919-489-8829. Personal E-mail: shelliinc@aol.com.

LIEBERMAN, ZACHARY, artist; BA in Fine Arts, Hunter Coll., CUNY, 2000; MFA in Design and Tech., Parsons Sch. Design, New Sch. U., 2002. Invited lectr. in field. Exhibited in group shows at Mus. of the Future: Hidden Worlds of Noise and Voice, Linz, Austria, 2002, SAPPHIRE'03, Ars Electronics Media Art Lounge, Orlando, Fla., 2003, SAP Interactive Spaces, Berlin, Germany, 2004, Interactions/Art Tech., Am. Mus. of the Moving Image, NYC, 2004, and several others, performances, Messa di Voce at Ars Electronics, Brucknerhaus Theater, Linz, Austria, 2003, Messa di Voce at Inst. for Contemporary Art, London, 2003, Messa di Voce at Ultrasound Huddersfield Media Centre, UK, 2003, and several others. Mailing: 381 Hooper St #23 Brooklyn NY 11211*

LIEBERMAN-CLINE, NANCY, sports commentator, former professional basketball coach, former player; b. July 1, 1958; m. Tim Cline, 1988; 1 child, Timothy Joseph. Grad., Old Dominion U., 1981. Guard WBL's Dallas Diamonds, 1980-86, USBL's L.I. Knights, 1986-87, Washington Generals, 1987-88, Athletes in Action, 1996-97, WNBA - Phoenix Mercury, 1997; head coach, gen. mgr. WNBA - Detroit Shock, 1998—2000; now sports commentator. Women's basketball analyst NBA Broadcasting, ESPN, ABC, ESPN 2, Fox Sports Network, NBC. Recipient Broderick Cup, 1979, 80, Wade Trophy (2), U.S. Olympic Silver medal, 1976; named All- Am., 1978-80, ODU Outstanding Female Athlete of Yr., 1977-80; mem. Women's Am. Basketball Championship team, 1985; Named to Basketball Hall of Fame, 1996. Home: 2636 Creekway Dr Carrollton TX 75010-4227

LIEBERMANN, LOWELL, composer, conductor, pianist; b. N.Y.C., Feb. 22, 1961; D in Musical Arts, Juilliard Sch.; studied with David Diamond, Vincent Persichetti, Jacob Lateiner, Laszlo Halasz. Composer-in-residence Dallas Symphony, 1999-2002. Composer (orchestra) War Songs for Bass Voice and Orch. Op. 7, 1981, Concertino for Cello and Chamber Orch. Op. 8, 1982, Symphony No. 1 Op. 9 (BMI award, 1st prize Juilliard Orch. Competition 1987), 1982, Three Poems of Stephen Crane Op. 11 for baritone, string orch., two horns, harp (Devora Nadworney award Nat. Fed. Music Clubs 1986) 1983, Concerto No. 1 for Piano and Orch. Op. 12, 1983, Sechs Gesaenge Nach Gedichten Von Nelly Sachs Op. 18 for soprano and orch., 1986, The Domain of Arnheim Op. 33, 1990, Concerto No. 2 for Piano and Orch. Op. 36, 1992, Flute Concerto Op. 39, 1992, Revelry for Orch. Op. 47, 1995, Concerto for Flute, Harp, and Orch. Op. 48, 1995; (opera) The Picture of Dorian Gray Op. 45, 1995, (chorus) Two Choral Elegies Op. 2 for SATB a capella (Fred Waring Choral award Nat. Fed. Music 1978), 1977, Missa Brevis Op. 15 for SATB chorus, tenor and baritone solos, organ (3d prize Ch. and Artist Composers Competition 1987), 1985; (piano solo) Piano Sonata Op. 1 (Outstanding Composition award Yamaha Music Found. 1982, 1st prize Nat. Composition Contest Music Tchrs. Nat. Assn. 1978), 1977, Piano Sonata No. 2 Sonata Notturna Op. 10, 1983, Variations on a Theme by Anton Bruckner Op. 19, 1987, Nocturne No. 1 Op. 20, 1987, Four Apparitions Op. 17, 1987, others; (chamber music) Sonata for Violoncello and Piano Op. 3, 1978, Two Pieces for Violin and Viola Op. 4, 1978, Sonata for Viola and Piano Op. 13 (1st Place Victor Herbert/ASCAP awards Nat. Fed. Music Clubs 1986, Brian Israel prize Soc. for New Music 1986), 1984, Sonata for Contrabass and Piano Op. 24, 1987, Fantasy on a Fugue by J.S. Bach Op. 27 for flute, oboe, clarinet, horn, bassoon, piano, 1989, Quintet for Piano and Strings Op. 34 for piano and string quartet, 1989, Concert for Trumpet and Orchestra Op. 64, 1999, Symphony No. 2 Op. 67, 1999, Three Impromptus

Op. 68)Grand prize Van Cliburn Internat. Piano Competition 2001, First Am. Composers Invitational prize); others; recordings: Piano Concerto on Hyperion with pianist Stephen Hough, James Galway plays Lowell Liebermann on BMG Classics; also organ music, voice and piano. Nominee Grammy award for best classical contemporary composition for Piano Concerto No. 2, 1997. Mem. ASCAP, NARAS. Office: c/o Theodore Presser Co 588 North Gulph Rd King Of Prussia PA 19406 Business E-Mail: lowelll@lowellliebermann.com.

LIEBERSBACH, NORBERT JOHN, protective services official; b. Langdon, N.D., July 12, 1956; s. John Peter and Florence Gertrude Liebersbach; m. Susan Lynn Liebersbach, June, 19, 1982. AS, Monterey Peninsula Coll., 1977; BA, Golden Gate U., 1982; grad. FBI Nat. Acad., U. Va., 1993. Cert. C.C. tchr., Calif. Dep. sheriff Monterey County Sheriff's Dept., Salinas, Calif., 1977-80, correctional tng. officer, 1980-83, sgt., 1983-90, lt., 1990—. Sgt. U.S. Army, 1974-77. Recipient Cert. of Recognition, Calif. Bd. Corrections, 1983-91, Mgmt. Cert., peace Officers Stds. and Tng., 1993. Mem. Nat. Sheriff's Assn., Calif. State Sheriff's Assn., FBI Nat. Acad. Assocs., Am. Jail Assn. (cert. jail mgr.), Ctrl. Calif. Jail Mgrs. Assn. (pres. 1999), Monterey County Peace Officer Assn. (pres., bd. dirs. 1988-93), Am. Legion, Elis (Elk of Yr. 1997-98). Republican. Roman Catholic. Avocation: home repair. Home: 18570 Van Buren Ave Salinas CA 93906 E-mail: Liebersbachb@co.monterey.ca.us.

LIEBERSON, JAY B., lawyer; b. Phila., Jan. 7, 1956; s. Martin and Vivian L.; m. Lisa R. Patton, Nov. 27, 1982; children: David Martin, Anne Elizabeth. BA, Temple U., 1976; JD, Dickinson U., 1979. Bar: Pa. 1979, U.S. Dist. Ct. (ea. dist) Pa. 1980. Exec. dir. domestic rels. Schuylkill Co., Pottsville, Pa., 1979-80, sr. staff atty. legal aid, 1980-81; assoc. Curtin & Heefner, Morrisville, Pa., 1981-84; pvt. practice Yardley, 1984—. Pres. scholar Temple U., 1976. Mem. Pa. Bar Assn. (mem. various coms.), Bucks County Bar Assn. (mem. various coms.), Phi Beta Kappa, Phi Alpha Delta. Democrat. Jewish. Avocation: civil war enthusiast. Office: 301 Oxford Valley Rd Ste 303A Yardley PA 19067-7709

LIEBERSON, STANLEY, sociologist, educator; b. Montreal, Que., Can., Apr. 20, 1933; s. Jack and Ida (Cohen) L.; m. Patricia Ellen Beard, 1960; children— Rebecca, David, Miriam, Rachel (dec.). Student, Bklyn. Coll., 1950-52; MA, U. Chgo., 1958, PhD, 1960; MA (hon.), Harvard U., 1988; LHD (hon.), U. Ariz., 1993. Assoc. dir. Iowa Urban Cmty. Rsch. Ctr., U. Iowa, 1959-61, instr., asst. prof. sociology, 1959-61; asst. prof. sociology U. Wis., 1961-63, assoc. prof., 1963-66, prof., 1966-67; prof. sociology U. Wash., 1967-71, dir. Ctr. Studies Demography and Ecology, 1968-71; prof. sociology U. Chgo., 1971-74, assoc. dir. Population Rsch. Ctr., 1971-74; prof. sociology U. Ariz., Tucson, 1974-83, head dept., 1976-79; prof. sociology U. Calif., Berkeley, 1983-88, Harvard U., 1988-91, Abbott Lawrence Lowell prof. sociology, 1991—. Vis. prof. Stanford U., summer 1970; Claude Bissell disting. vis. prof. U. Toronto, 1979-80; Christensen fellow Oxford U., St. Catherine's Coll., 2001; mem. com. on sociolinguistics Social Sci. Rsch. Coun., 1964-70; mem. sociology panel NSF, 1978-81 Author: (with others) Metropolis and Region, 1960, Ethnic Patterns in American Cities, 1963; editor: Explorations in Sociolinguistics, 1967, (with Beverly Duncan) Metropolis and Region in Transition, 1970, Language and Ethnic Relations in Canada, 1970, A Piece of the Pie, 1980, Language Diversity and Language Contact, 1981, Making It Count, 1985, (with Mary C. Waters) From Many Strands, 1988, A Matter of Taste, 2000 (co-winner book award culture sect. Am. Sociol. Assn. 2001, Mirra Komarovsky book award Ea. Sociol. Soc. 2002); assoc. editor: Social Problems, 1965-67, Sociol. Methods and Research, 1971-96; editorial cons. Sociol. Inquiry, 1965-67; adv. editor: Am. Jour. Sociology, 1969-74; editorial bd. Lang. in Society, 1972-74, Internat. Jour. Sociology of Lang, 1974-2000, Canadian Jour. Sociology, 1975-2000, Social Forces, 1980-83; adv. council Sociol. Abstracts, 1972-73, Language Problems and Language Planning, 1984-87; mem. editorial com. Ann. Rev. Sociology, 1992-96. Recipient Colver Rosenberger Ednl. prize, 1960; Guggenheim fellow, 1972-73, fellow Ctr. for Advanced Study in Behavioral Scis., 1995-96, Sackler Inst. for Advanced Study, Tel Aviv U., 1999. Fellow: NAS, Am. Acad. Arts and Scis.; mem.: Ea. Sociol. Soc. (Mirra Komarovsky Book award 2002), Am. Name Soc., Sociol. Rsch. Assn. (exec. com. 1976—81, pres. 1981), Pacific Sociol. Assn. (v.p. 1984—85, pres. 1986—87), Internat. Population Union, Population Assn. Am. (dir. 1969—72), Am. Sociol. Found. (trustee 1992—96), Am. Sociol. Assn. (coun. mem. 1985—87, pres. 1990—91, Disting. Contbn. to Scholarship award 1982, co-winner culture sect. award 2001). Office: Harvard U Dept Sociology William James Hall Cambridge MA 02138 Office Phone: 617-495-3818. E-mail: SL@WJH.harvard.edu.

LIEBERT, PETER SELIG, pediatrician, surgeon, consultant; b. N.Y.C., Feb. 27, 1936; s. Louis M. and Sonia F. (Wolfe) L.; m. Mary Ann Rosenfeld; children: Peter S., Lewis Charles. AB, Princeton U., 1957; MD, Harvard U., 1961. Diplomate Am. Bd. Surgery, Am. Bd. Pediat. Surgery. Intern Peter Bent Brigham Hosp., Boston, 1961-62, resident in surgery, 1962-64; resident in surgery, chief resident Montefiore Hosp., N.Y.C., 1964-66; fellow in pediat. surgery Children's Hosp., Phila., 1966-68; practice medicine specializing in pediat. surgery White Plains, N.Y., N.Y.C., Mt. Kisco and, Greenwich, Conn., 1961—; clin. assoc. prof. surgery Columbia U. Coll. Physicians and Surgeons. Chief pediatric surgery White Plains Med. Ctr.; chmn. bd. dirs. Rx Vitamins, Inc.; bd. dirs. Cadus Pharm. Corp. Author: Color Atlas of Pediatric Surgery; editor: Office and Emergency Pediat., mem. editl. bd. Jour. Pediat. Surgery. Dir. Med. Network for Missing Children; mem. Westchester County Bd. Health, 2001—. Mem.: Westchester County Med. Soc. (pres. 2000—01). Office: 222 Westchester Ave White Plains NY 10604-2906 also: 666 Lexington Ave Mount Kisco NY 10549-3632 Office Phone: 914-428-3533. E-mail: pslmd@nipperhead.com.

LIEBESKIND, RICHARD, lawyer; b. New Haven, Conn., June 11, 1958; AB magna cum laude, Duke Univ., 1980; JD, Columbia Univ., 1984. Bar: NY 1985, DC 2002, US Dist. Ct. (DC, so. & ea. dist. NY), US Ct. Appeals (DC cir.). Assoc. Cravath Swaine & Moore, NYC; trial atty. & asst. chief, antitrust div. U.S. Dept. Justice, Washington; dep. asst. dir. Mergers III div. FTC, Washington, asst. dir. Bureau of Competition; ptnr., chmn. Antitrust & Competition practice Pillsbury Winthrop Shaw Pittman, Washington, 2002—. Contbr. articles to profl. jours. Recipient Rand Dixon award, FTC, 1998; Harlan Fiske Stone scholar. Mem.: ABA. Office: Pillsbury Winthrop Shaw Pittman 1133 Connecticut Ave NW Washington DC 20036 Office Phone: 202-775-9838. Office Fax: 202-833-8491. Business E-Mail: richard.liebeskind@pillsburylaw.com.

LIEBHABER, MYRON I., allergist; b. Dec. 28, 1943; MD, U. Ariz., 1972. Allergist Coll. Hosp., Santa Barbara, Calif. Assoc. vis. clin. prof. UCLA. Office: Sansum Med Found Clinic 215 Pesetas Ln Santa Barbara CA 93110-1416 Office Phone: 805-681-7635. Business E-Mail: mliebhab@sansumclinic.org.

LIEBIG, STEUART ANTHONY, musician, composer; b. Santa Monica, Calif., July 25, 1956; s. Anthony Eshman and Phoebe (Stone) Liebig; m. Leslie Ann Rosdol, Aug. 16, 1986; children: Aron Leonis Rosdol, Anya Sophia Rosdol. MusB, Calif. State U., Northridge, 1983. Musician with Les McCann, 1976—79, Julius Hemphill, 1984—87; founder Bloc, 1983—91, Quartetto Stig, 1993—97, Lane Ends Merge Left, 1997—, Stigtette, 1997—, Mentones, 1999—, Minim, 2000—. Composer: Pienso Oculto, 1997, Kola Suite, 2003, Quicksilver, 2004, On the Cusp of Fire and Water, 2004, Kelpland Serenades, 2005; musician: (albums) Hommages Obliques, 1993, Lingua Oscura, 1995, No Train, 1998, Pomegranate, 2001, Antipodes, 2001, Locustland, 2004, Delta, 2005, Prattica Quartet, 2000—, Meninas Quartet, 2005—. Mem.: ASCAP, Chamber Music Am. Personal E-mail: steubig@aol.com.

LIEBLICH, FREDERICH, real estate consultant; BS, U. Ill.; MBA, U. Chgo. Chief investment strategist SSR Realty Advisors Inc., Morristown, NJ, pres., 2003—. Mem. editl. bd.: Jour. Real Estate Portfolio Mgmt. Office: SSR Realty Advisors Inc 10 Park Ave PO Box 2346 Morristown NJ 07962

LIEBLING, JEROME, photographer, educator; b. N.Y.C., Apr. 16, 1924; s. Maurice and Sarah (Goodman) L.; married, Nov. 11, 1949 (div. 1969); children: Madeline, Tina, Adam, Daniella, Rachel Jane. Student, Bklyn. Coll., 1942, 46, 48, New Sch. for Social Research, N.Y.C., 1948-49; LLD (hon.), Portland (Maine) Sch. Art, 1989. Prof. photography U. Minn., Mpls., 1949-69; prof. SUNY-New Paltz, 1957-58, Yale U., New Haven, 1976-77, Hampshire Coll., Amherst, Mass., 1970—. Author, photographer: Jerome Liebling Photographs (Best of Yr. 1982), Aperture, N.Y.C., 1988, The People Yes, The Photographs of Jerome Liebling, Aperture, 1995; editor: Photography-Current Perspective, 1977, Jerome Liebling: The Minnesota Photographs, 1997, The Dickinsons of Amherst, 2001. Served with U.S. Army, 1942-45, ETO, Africa. Fellow Mass. Arts Found., 1975, Nat. Endowman Arts, 1979, Guggenheim, 1977, 81; recipient Umhoefer prize Arts and Humanities Found., 2002; named The Jerome Liebling Ctr. for Film, Photography andVideo, Hampshire Coll., Amherst, Mass., 2004. Mem.: Soc. Photog. Edn. (named Educator of Yr. 2004). Home: 39 Dana St Amherst MA 01002-2208 Office: Hampshire Coll West St Amherst MA 01002-2954 Office Phone: 413-549-5507. Business E-Mail: rnordstrom@hampshire.edu.

LIEBMAN, DAVID, musician; b. Bklyn., Sept. 4, 1946; s. Leo and Frances Liebman; m. Chris Liebman, Oct. 30, 1986; 1 child, Lydia. BS, NYU, 1968; PhD, Sibelius Acad., 1997. Saxophonist Elvin Jones Group, worldwide, 1971—73, Miles Davis Group, worldwide, 1973—74; band leader Lookout Farm, worldwide, 1974—76, David Liebman Quintet, worldwide, 1979—81, Quest, worldwide, 1982—91, Dave Liebman Group, worldwide, 1991—. Artistic dir., founder Internat. Assn. Schs. Jazz, worldwide, 1989—; bd. mem. Jazz Improv Mag., Pa., 2002—, Jazz Alliance, NJ, 2003—. Author: (books) Self-Portrait of a Jazz Artist, 1986, Developing a Personal Saxophone Sound, 1990, Chromatic Approach to Jazz Melody and Harmony, 1990. Recipient Composers/Performance award, NEA, 1980, 1991, Grammy nomination, NARAS, 1998, Hall of Fame, IAJE, 2000, Indiv. Artist award, Penn. Arts Coun., 2005.

LIEBMAN, JUDITH RAE STENZEL, retired operations research specialist; b. Denver, July 2, 1936; d. Raymond Oscar and Mary Madelyn (Galloup) Stenzel; m. Jon Charles Liebman, Dec. 27, 1958; children: Christopher Brian, Rebecca Anne, Michael Jon. BA in Physics, U. Colo., Boulder, 1958; PhD in Ops. Rsch., Johns Hopkins U., 1971. Successively asst. prof., head indsl. systems, assoc. prof. U. Ill., Urbana, 1972-84, prof., 1984-96, prof. emerita, 1996—, acting vice chancellor for rsch., 1986-87, vice chancellor for rsch., 1987-92, acting dean Grad. Coll., 1987-92, dean, 1987-92. Vis. prof. Tianjin (China) U., 1985; charter mem. Ill. Gov.'s Sci. Adv. Com., Ill. Exec. Com., 1989-92; mem. adv. com. for engring. NSF, 1988-92, chmn., 1991-92; mem. NRC Bd. Engring. Edn., 1997-2001, Army Sci. Bd., 1997-99. Author: Modeling and Optimization with GINO, 1986; author numerous articles in field. Bd. dirs. United Way, Champaign, Ill., 1986-91, U. Colo. Found., 1999-2003; bd. dirs. East Cen. Ill. Health Systems Agy., Champaign, 1977-82, pres., 1980-82; trustee U. Colo. Found., 2003—. Mem. Ops. Rsch. Soc. Am. (pres. 1987-88), INFORMS, Nat. Assn. State Univs. and Land Grant Colls. (exec. bd. 1990-92), Rotary, Sigma Xi, Sigma Pi Sigma, Alpha Pi Mu, Phi Kappa Phi. Home: 110 W Whitehall Ct Urbana IL 61801-6664

LIEBMAN, LANCE MALCOLM, law educator; b. Newark, Sept. 11, 1941; s. Roy and Barbara (Trilinsky) L.; m. Carol Bensinger, June 28, 1964; children: Jeffrey, Benjamin. BA, Yale U., 1962; MA, Cambridge U., 1964; LLB, Harvard U., 1967. Bar: DC 1968, Mass. 1976, NY, 1995. Asst. to Mayor Lindsay, NYC, 1968-70; asst. prof. law Harvard U., 1970-76, prof., 1976-91, assoc. dean, 1981-84; dean, Lucy G. Moses prof. law Columbia U. Sch. Law, NYC, 1991-96, prof., dir. Parker Sch. Fgn. Law, 1996—, Williams S. Beinecke prof. law, 1998—; dir. Am. Law Inst., 1998—. Successor trustee Yale Corp., 1971-83 Office: Columbia U Sch Law 435 W 116th St New York NY 10027-7297 Office Phone: 212-854-5699. E-mail: lliebman@law.columbia.edu.

LIEBMAN, RONALD STANLEY, lawyer; b. Balt., Oct. 11, 1943; s. Harry Martin and Martha (Altgenug) L.; m. Simma Liebman, Jan. 8, 1972; children: Shana, Margot. BA, Western Md. Coll., Westminster, 1966; JD, U. Md., 1969. Bar: Md. 1969, U.S. Dist. Ct. Md. 1970, U.S. Ct. Appeals (4th cir.) 1972, D.C. 1977, U.S. Dist. Ct. D.C. 1982, U.S. Ct. Appeals (D.C. cir.) 1982, U.S. Ct. Appeals (5th cir.) 1985, U.S. Ct. Appeals (2nd cir.) 1988, U.S. Ct. Appeals (11th cir.) 1991, U.S. Ct. Appeals (9th cir.) 1992, U.S. Dist. Ct. (no. dist.) Calif. 1994, U.S. Supreme Ct. 1995, U.S. Ct. Appeals (7th cir.) 1996, U.S. Dist. Ct. (ea. dist.) Tex. 1999, U.S. Ct. Appeals (10th cir.) 2003. Law clk. to chief judge U.S. Dist. Ct. Md., 1969-70; assoc. Melnicove, Kaufman & Weiner, Balt., 1970-72; asst. U.S. atty. Office of U.S. Atty., Dept. Justice, Balt., 1972-78; ptnr. Sachs, Greenebaum & Tayler, Washington, 1978-82; ptnr., Litigation & Dispute Resolution, White Collar Criminal Def. practices Patton Boggs LLP, Washington, 1982—, mem. exec. com. Author: Grand Jury, 1983, Shark Tales, 2000; co-editor: Testimonial Privileges, 1983. Recipient spl. commendation award U.S. Dept. Justice, 1978. Mem. ABA, D.C. Bar Assn., Md. Bar Assn., Sergeants Inn Club (Balt.). Office: Patton Boggs LLP 2550 M St NW Ste 500 Washington DC 20037-1350 Office Phone: 202-457-6310. Office Fax: 202-457-6315. Business E-Mail: rliebman@pattonboggs.com.

LIEBMAN, THEODORE, architect; b. Newark, May 7, 1939; s. Edward and Miriam (Applebaum) Liebman; m. Nina Roskin, Oct. 27, 1968; children: Sophie, Hanna, Tessa. B.Arch., Pratt Inst., 1962; M.Arch., Harvard U., 1963. Registered architect, Mass, NY, Colo, Ind, Fla, NJ, Pa. Project design officer Boston Redevel. Authority, mass., 1963-64; project dir. David A. Crane, Architect, Phila., 1966-69; chief architect N.Y. State Urban Devel. Corp., N.Y.C., 1969-75; prin. urban design and archtl. adviser Harvard Inst. Internat. Devel., Tehran, Iran, 1975-77; pres. HAUS Internat., Inc., N.Y.C., 1977-79, The Liebman Melting Partnership, Architects and Planners, N.Y.C., 1979—. Bd advisers Inst Urban Design, New York, NY, 1980—84; assoc prof urban design Pratt Inst, Brooklyn, NY, 1983—88; land develop mgr Russian Fed Housing Project-World Bank, 1995—96. Mem ed bd: Metropolis, 1981—88; contbr. articles to mags. Fellow, Am Acad, Rome, 1966, Wheelwright Travelling, Harvard Univ, 1971. Fellow: AIA (pres NY chpt 1983—84); mem.: Urban Land Inst (mem int coun). Office: The Liebman Melting Partnership 330 W 42nd St New York NY 10036-6902 Office Phone: 212-239-8080.

LIEBMAN, WILMA B., government agency administrator; b. Phila. BA, Barnard Coll., N.Y.C.; JD, George Washington U., Washington. Staff atty. NLRB, 1974—80; legal counsel Internat. Brotherhood of Teamsters, 1980—89; labor counsel Bricklayers and Allied Craftsmen, 1990—93; asst. to dir. Fed. Mediation and Conciliation Svc., 1994—96, dep. dir.; mem. NLRB, Washington, 1997—. Mem.: Coll. of Labor and Employment Lawyers, Inc. (exec. bd.), Indsl. Rels. Rsch. Assn. (exec. bd.). Office: NLRB 1099 14th St NW Washington DC 20570-0001*

LIEBMANN, GEORGE W(ILLIAM), lawyer; b. N.Y.C., June 20, 1939; s. William Liebmann and Margaret (Hirschman) Cook; m. Anne-Lise Grimstad, Apr. 29, 1967; children: Pamela, George, Franklin. AB, Dartmouth Coll., 1960; JD, U. Chgo., 1963. Bar: Md. 1964, Ill. 1964. With Chaucer Head Book Shop, Inc., N.Y.C., 1958-59; law clk. to chief judge Ct. Appeals Md., 1963-64; with Frank, Bernstein, Conaway and Goldman, Balt., 1964-79; asst. atty. gen. State of Md., Balt., 1967-69; exec. asst. to Gov. Md., Annapolis, 1979-80; prin. Liebmann and Shively, P.A., Balt., 1980—. Lectr. U. Md. Law Sch., 1977—78, Johns Hopkins U., 1991—92; mem. Gov.'s Commn. to Revise Annotated Code Md., 1974—83; alt. mem. State Planning Coun. on Radioactive Waste Mgmt., 1980—82; chmn. Gov.'s Task Force on Local Govt. Antitrust Liability, 1982—83, Gov.'s Commn. Health Care Providers' Profl. Liability Ins., 1983—84; gen. counsel Md. Econ. Devel. Corp., 1985—; vis. fellow U. Salford, England, 1996, Wolfson Coll., Cambridge, 1996, 98, 99, 2002, 03, 05; panelist U.S. Bankruptcy Trustee, 1980—. Author: Maryland District Court Law and Practice, 2 vols., 1976, Maryland Civil Practice Forms, 2 vols., 1984, The Little Platoons: Sub-Local Governments in Modern History, 1995, The Gallows in the Grove: Civil Society in American Law, 1997, Solving Problems Without Large Government, 1999, reprint Neighborhood Futures, 2004, Six Lost Leaders: Prophets of Civil Society, 2001, The Common Law Tradition: A Collective Portrait of Five Legal Scholars, 2005; mng. editor U. Chgo. Law Rev., 1962-63. Trustee Hist. Annapolis Found., 1991—99; exec. dir. Calvert Inst. Policy Rsch., 2001—; sec. Coalition Against the SST, Washington, 1969; Rep. primary candidate U.S. Senate, 1998. Simon indsl. and profl. fellow U. Manchester, Eng., 1993-94. Mem. Am. Law Inst., Fed. Jud. Conf. 4th Cir., Libr. Co. Balt. Bar (bd. dirs. 1967—, pres. 1975-77), Engring. Soc. Md. (assoc.) Office: 8 W Hamilton St Baltimore MD 21201-5020 Office Phone: 410-752-5887. Personal E-mail: george.liebmann2@verizon.net.

LIEBMANN, JEFF S., lawyer; AB cum laude, Princeton Univ., 1971; JD cum laude, Harvard Univ., 1978. Bar: N.Y. 1979. Ptnr. & co-chmn. insurance group Dewey Ballantine LLP, N.Y.C. Mem.: ABA, N.Y. State Bar Assn., Soc. of Actuaries (assoc.). Office: Dewey Ballantine LLP 1301 Ave of the Americas New York NY 10019-6092 Office Phone: 212-259-6230. Office Fax: 212-259-6333. Business E-Mail: jliebmann@dbllp.com.

LIEBMANN, SEYMOUR W., construction executive, consultant; b. N.Y.C., Nov. 1, 1928; s. Isidor W. and Etta (Waltzer) L.; m. Hinda Adam, Sept. 20, 1959; children: Peter Adam, David W. BSME, Clarkson U., 1948; grad., Indsl. Coll. Armed Forces, 1963, U.S. Army Command and Gen. Staff Coll., 1966, U.S. Army War Coll., 1971. Registered profl. engr., N.Y., Mass., Ga. Area engr. constrn. divsn. E.I. DuPont de Nemours & Co., Inc., 1952-54; constrn. planner Lummus Co., Inc., 1954-56; prin. mech. engr. Perini Corp., 1956-62; v.p. Boston Based Contractors, 1962-66, A.R. Abrams, Inc., Atlanta, 1967-74, pres., 1974-78, also bd. dirs. Founder Liebmann Assocs., Inc., Atlanta, 1979—; mem. nat. adv. bd. Am. Security Coun.; mem. steering com. Atlanta Engring. Acad. Author: Military Engineer Field Notes, 1953, Prestressing Miter Gate Diagonals, 1960; contbr. articles to publs. Mem. USO Coun., Atlanta, 1968—, v.p., 1978, mem. exec. com., 1975-79; mem. Nat. UN Day Com., 1975; sr. army coord., judge Sci. Fair, Atlanta Pub. Schs., annually, 1979-88, 92-2004; asst. scoutmaster troop 298 Atlanta area coun. Boy Scouts Am., 1980-87, Explorer advisor, 1982-86, unit commr., 1985, dist. commr. North Atlanta Dist., Atlanta Area Coun., 1988-90, asst. coun. commr., 1990-95, mem. faculty Commrs. Coll., 1985-88, 92, mem. North Atlanta Dist. com., BSA, 1996—; mem. alumni adv. com. Clarkson Coll. Tech., 1981—, alumni bd. govs., 1983-94, Disting. Alumni Golden Knight award, 1983; mem. exec. com., zoning chmn. neighbor planning unit "A" City of Atlanta, 1982—, chmn., 1988, 95-2005, vice-chmn., 1989; pres. West Paces/Northside Neighborhood Assn., 1991—; apptd. civil engr. mem. to City of Atlanta Water and Sewer Appeals Bd., 1992—; apptd. mem. to Mayor's Bond Oversight Com. City of Atlanta, 1995-96; mem. Atlanta, Cobb County regional mil. affairs com., 2001—; chair City of Atlanta Nancy Creek Tech. Tunnel Adv. Com., 2002—; mem. blue ribbon panel Fulton County Juvenile Ct., 2001—; mem. Philmont Fall Adventure Trek, 2002; apptd. mem. Mayor's Svc. Commn., 2002—. Col. AUS Ret. Corps Engrs., 1948-52, Korea, Germany. Decorated Legion of Merit, Meritorious Svc. medal, USAR Achievement medal with oak leaf cluster; named to Old Guard of Gate City Guard, 1979; recipient cert. achievement, Dept. Army, 1978, Bronze DeFleury medal, U.S. Army Engr. Regiment, 1997, USO Recognition award, 1979, Order of Arrow award, Boy Scouts Am., 1983, 1987, Scouters Key, 1988, North Atlanta Dist. Merit award, 1989, Silver Beaver award, 1991, Disting. Commn. award, 1991, Engring. Profl. award, Am. Inst. Plant Engrs., 1987, Hands Across Atlanta award, 1997, Medal of Honor award, Ga. Engring. Found., 2004. Fellow: Soc. Am. Mil. Engrs. (life; program chmn. Atlanta post 1980—81, v.p. 1982, pres. 1983, chmn. readiness com. 1986—2000, bd. dirs. 1986—, program chmn. 1988, nat. meeting, asst. regional v.p. for readiness So. region 1991—, life dir. Atlanta Post 1994, James Lucas Chair Atlanta Post 1994, elected nat. dir. 1994—97, program chmn. S.Ea. regional site tng. conf. 1999, Nat. award of Merit 1982—83, Atlanta Post Leadership award 1988); mem.: NRA, NSPE, ASTM, Internat. Concrete Repair Inst. (awards com. 2000), Internat. Concrete Restoration Inst. (judge awards com. 2002), Am. Arbitration Assn. (panel arbitrators 1979—, constrn. adv. com. 1984—), Engrs. Club Boston, Met. Atlanta Engrs. (chmn. Engrs. Week 2000 and 2001 awards com.), Jt. Ga. Soc. Profl. Engrs. and Am. Counsel of Engring. Cos. (chmn. state licensing com. 2002—, bd. dirs. Buckhead chpt., state ethics com., Engr. of Yr. in Pvt. Practice 1990, Ga. Engr. Yr. 1991, Lifetime Achievement award for engring. excellence 2001), Am. Concrete Inst., Army Engr. Assn. (life), U.S. Army Hist. Found., Atlanta Area Mil. Affairs Com., Vets. of the 1st U.S.Army Engr. Combat Bn., Atlanta Hist. Soc., Ga. Conservancy, Benyton Mackaye Trail Assn., Appalachian Trail Conf., Order of Engr., Mil. Order World Wars, Atlanta C. of C. (mil. affairs com. 1999), Downtown Atlanta Kiwanis, Cobb C. of C., Def. Preparedness Assn., Assn. U.S. Army (v.p. exec. com. local chpt. 1998—2000), Nat. Def. U. Found., Soc. 1st U.S. Inf., U.S. Army War Coll. Alumni Assn. (life), U.S. Army War Coll. Found. (life; Alumni Assn. Disting. Alumni Selection Com. 1997—), Res. Officers Assn. (life), Heros of 76, Civitan, Elks, Nat. Sojourners, Shriners, Masons (32d degree). Republican. Jewish. Office: Liebmann Assocs Inc 1266 W Paces Ferry Rd NW Box 518 Atlanta GA 30327

LIEBOWITZ, DANIEL S.F., retired medical educator; b. N.Y.C., Nov. 26, 1921; s. David and Emily Liebowitz; m. Florence Evans Liebowitz, 1978; children: Peter, Sylvie, Danny P. BA, Columbia U., 1943; MD, NYU, 1946. Diplomate internal medicine. Postgrad. tng. Goldwater Meml. Hosp., NY, Crile V.A. Hosp., Western Res. U., Cleve.; clin. prof. medicine emeritus Stanford U. Sch. Medicine; dir. med. edn. emeritus Sequoia Hosp., Redwood City, Calif. Lectr. in field. *As a captain in the Medical Corps, he spent a year in the Army of Occupation in Germany becoming chief of psychiatry at the 385th Evacuation Hospital in Nuremberg. He has been a member of the Explorer's Club since 1967 and the Royal Geographic Society since 1994.* Author: (novels) The Lion and The Flame, 1992, (biography) The Physician and the Slave Trade, The Livingstone Expeditions and the Crusade Against Slavery in East Africa, 1999; co-author: Cook to Your Heart's Content on a Low Fat Low Salt Diet, 1970; co-author: (with Charles Pearson) The Last Expedition - Stanley's Mad journey Through the Congo, 2005; contbr. articles to profl. jours. Capt. U.S. Army, 1949—50. Fellow: ACP, Royal Geog. Soc.; mem.: AMA, Am. Soc. Gastrointestinal Endoscopy, Am. Gastroenterology Assn., Explorers Club. Avocations: hiking, camping, photography, exploration. Home: 175 Fox Hollow Rd Woodside CA 94062

LIEBOWITZ, NEIL ROBERT, psychiatrist; b. Bklyn., Feb. 5, 1956; s. Harold and Gertrude Liebowitz; m. Judith Linda Ross, Oct. 21, 1952; children: Sarah Michelle, Daniel Geoffery. BA, U. Va., 1978; MD, SUNY, Stony Brook, 1982. Cert. Am. Bd. Psychiatry and Neurology; cert. in clin. psychopharmacology Am. Soc. Clin. Psychopharmacology. Intern Greenwich Hosp. Assn., Greenwich, Conn., 1982-83; psychiatry fellow Yale Dept. Psychiatry, New Haven, 1982-86; chief resident psychiatry Yale New Haven Hosp., 1985-86; dir. consultation liaison psychiatry Newington VA Med. Ctr., Newington, Conn., 1986-87, chief mental hygiene clinic, 1986-88; asst. prof. psychiatry U. Conn., Farmington, 1986-92, asst. clin. prof. psychiatry, 1993—; dir. inpatient psychiatry Newington VA Med. Ctr., 1988-89; dir. ambulatory psychiatry John Dempsey Hosp., Farmington, 1989-91. Cons. psychiatrist Rocky Hill (Conn.) Vets. Home and Hosp., 1987-88; attending New Britain Gen. Hosp., 1992—; dir. Conn. Anxiety & Depression Treatment Ctr., Farmington, 1994—; founding mem., bd. dirs. PsychCare, Inc., 1996-98; bd. dirs. Psych Mgmt. Contbr. articles to profl. jours.; co-investigator clin. research Clin. Psychopharmacology, 1988—; mem. Integrated Neuroscis., Inc., 1999-2002. Mem. Am. Psychiat. Assn., Conn. Psychiat. Soc., Hartford Psychiat. Soc. (pres. 1997), Phi Beta Kappa. Office: Conn Anxiety & Depression Treatment Ctr Farmington CT 06032

LIEBOWITZ, RONALD D., academic administrator; m. Jessica Liebowitz; children: David Heschel, Shoshana. AB, Bucknell U.; PhD in geography, Columbia U., 1985. Instr. geography Middlebury Coll., 1984—88, assoc. prof. geography, 1988—93, prof. geography, 1993—, dean of faculty, 1993—95, v.p., 1995—97, provost, exec. v.p., 1997—2004, acting pres., 2002, pres., 2004—. Editor: Gorbachev's New Thinking: Prospects for Joint Ventures, 1988; co-editor: Perestroika and East-West Economic Relations: Prospects for the 1990s, 1989, Russia and Eastern Europe after Communism: The Search for New Political, Economic and Security Systems, 1996. Fellowship, Nat. Coun. on Soviet and East European Rsch., Internat. Rsch. and Exchange Bd., Social Sci. Rsch. Coun., George F. Kennan Inst., Woodrow Wilson Ctr. for Internat. Scholars. Avocations: world metro/subway riding, reading, squash. Office: Office of Pres Middlebury Coll Middlebury VT 05753

LIEBSON, MILT, sculptor, educator, writer; b. N.Y.C., Dec. 12, 1923; s. Ely and Gertrude (Kern) L.; m. Lila Jacobs, Mar. 5, 1944; children: Richard, Ellen Liebson Porges, Donald. BS, St. John's U., 1948; MS, L.I. U., 1960. Tchr. Mercer Community Coll., West Windsor, N.J., 1987-99, Artworks, Princeton, N.J., 1989-96. One-man shows include Gallery 100, Princeton, N.J., George B. Markle Gallery, Hazelton, Pa., Bergen Mus., Paramus, N.J., Rutgers U., New Brunswick, N.J., Baron Art Ctr., Woodbridge, N.J., Monmouth Mus., Lincroft, N.J., AT&T Corp. Gallery, Hopewell, N.J., Ellarslie Mus., Trenton, N.J., Strand Gallery, Summit, N.J., Trenton City Mus., Mus. of Artists, Moscow, Delann Gallery, Plainsboro, N.J., Golden Door Gallery, New Hope, Pa., The Sculpture Showcase, New Hope, others; represented in various permanent collections; author: Direct Stone Sculpture, 1991, Direct Stone Sculpture II, 1992, Direct Wood Sculpture, 2001, Impressions With Clay, 2004; video: Sculpting in Stone, 1995. With U.S. Army, 1942-44. Mem. Internat. Sculpture Ctr., Trenton Artists Workshop Assn., Allied Artists of Am. (assoc. mem.), Rho Chi. Avocations: tennis, golf, music. Home and Office: 69B Picea Plz Monroe Township NJ 08831-4143 E-mail: njmkt@verizon.net.

LIEDKE, GUY ARTHUR, public administrator; b. Fond du Lac, Wis., May 1, 1954; s. Stanley Liedke and Carlaine Beer; m. Jean A. Pulvermacher, Feb. 9, 1974; children: Jennifer, Geoffery. AAS, C.C. of Air Force, 1988; BS in Sociology summa cum laude, St. Leo Coll., 1992; MPA, Troy State U., 1995. Enlisted USAF, 1972; advanced through grades to master sgt. USMC, 1987, ret., 1992; program specialist U.S. Dept. Vets. Affairs, Tampa, Fla., 1993—. Cons. VISN 8 Homeless Working Group, Fla. Mem. ASPA, Non-Commd. Officers Assn., Air Force Assn. Avocations: bicycling, woodworking, chip carving, reading, music. Office: Homeless Providers Grant and Per Diem Program 13000 B Downs Blvd Tampa FL 33612 Home: PO Box 1587 Valrico FL 33595-1587 Fax: (813) 979-3682. E-mail: Guy.Liedke@med.va.gov.

LIEF, BETH, educational association administrator; b. Huntington, Ill. married; 2 children. BA in Urban Studies, Barnard Coll.; JD, NYU. Counsel Legal Def. and Ednl. Fund NAACP; spl. asst. to Richard Beattie N.Y. Bd. Edn.; staff counsel Pub. Edn. Assn.; exec. dir. Mayor's Commn. on Spl. Edn., 1984—86; dir. Program for Homeless Families and Spl. Projects Edna McConnell Clark Found.; founding pres. New Visions for Pub. Schs., 1989—2000; sr. v.p. strategic rels. Teachscape, 2000—03; cons. N.Y.C. Dept. Edn. Children First Strategic Planning Initiative; nat. fellow Inst. for Learning, Learning R&D Ctr., Pitts., 2003—. Bd. dirs., sec. Pub. Edn. Network, Washington; bd. dirs. New Visions for Pub. Schs.; sr. fellow edn. New Democracy Project. Bd. dirs. Bank St. Coll. Edn., United Cerebral Palsy N.Y.C.; Parent Resource Ctr. Scholar Root-Tilden scholar 2nd cir. Office: Pub Edn Network 601 13th St NW Washington DC 20005

LIEF, HAROLD ISAIAH, psychiatrist; b. NYC, Dec. 29, 1917; s. Jacob F. and Mollie (Filler) L.; m. Myrtis A. Brumfield, Mar. 3, 1961; Caleb B., Frederick V., Oliver F.; children from previous marriage: Polly Lief Goldberg, Jonathan F. BA, U. Mich., 1938; MD, NYU, 1942; cert. in psychoanalysis, Columbia Coll. Physicians and Surgeons, 1950; MA (hon.), U. Pa., 1971. Intern Queens Gen. Hosp., Jamaica, NY, 1942-43; resident in psychiatry LI Coll. Medicine, 1946-48; pvt. practice NYC, 1948-51; asst. physician Presbyn. Hosp., NYC, 1949-51; asst. prof. Tulane U., New Orleans, 1951-54, assoc. prof., 1954-60, prof. psychiatry, 1960-67, U. Pa., Phila., 1967-82, prof. emeritus, 1982—, dir. div. family study, 1967-81; dir. Marriage Council of Phila., 1969-81, Ctr. for Study of Sex. Edn. in Medicine, 1968-82; mem. staff U. Pa. Hosp., 1967-81, Pa. Hosp., 1981—; clin. prof. psychiatry Jefferson Med. U., 1994—. Author: (with Daniel and William Thompson) The Eighth Generation, 1960; Editor: (with Victor and Nina Lief) Psychological Basis of Medical Practice, 1963, Medical Aspects of Human Sexuality, 1976, (with Arno Karlen) Sex Education in Medicine, 1976, Sexual Problems in Medical Practice, 1981, (with Zwi Hoch) Sexology: Sexual Biology, Behavior and Therapy, 1982, (with Zwi Hoch) International Research in Sexology, 1983, Human Sexuality With Respect to AIDS and HIV Infection, 1989; contbr. numerous articles to publ. Mem. La. State Commn. Civil Rights, 1958—67; Bd. dirs., chmn. Ctr. for Sexuality and Religion, 1988—2001; mem. adv. bd. False Memory Syndrome Found., 1992—. Maj. M.C. U.S. Army, 1943—46. Commonwealth Fund fellow, 1963-64; recipient Gold Medal award Mt. Airy Hosp., 1977, Lifetime Achievement award Phila. Psychiat. Soc., 1992, Gold Medal, World Assn. Sexology, 1999; named practitioner of yr. Phila. County Med. Soc., 1998. Fellow Phila. Coll. Physicians, Am. Psychiat. Assn. (50 yr. disting. life), NY Acad. Sci., AAAS, Am. Acad. Psychoanalysis (charter, past pres.), Am. Coll. Psychiatrists (founding), Am. Coll. Psychoanalysts (charter); mem. AMA, Sex Info. and Edn. Coun. US (past pres.), Group Advancement Psychiatry (life), Am. Psychosomatic Soc., Assn. Psychoanalytic Medicine (life), Am. Psychoanalytic Assn. (life), Internat. Psychoanalytic Assn., Internat. Acad. Sex Rsch., Soc. Sci. Study of Sex, Am. Soc. Sex Educators, Counselors and Therapists, Soc. Sex Therapists and Rschr., World Assn. Sexology (past v.p.), Soc. Exploration of Psychotherapy Integration (adv. bd.), Pa. Med. Soc., Phila. Med. Soc., Pa. Psychiat. Soc., Columbia Club, Mich. Club of Greater Phila., Penn Club of NY, Sigma Xi, Alpha Omega Alpha, Phi Eta Sigma, Phi Kappa Phi. Home: 840 Montgomery Ave No 302 Bryn Mawr PA 19010-3344 Office: 987 Old Eagle School Rd Ste 719 Wayne PA 19087-1708 Office Phone: 610-971-0889. E-mail: halief@aol.com. *The conflict between individual gratification and the needs of society, between competition and cooperation, appears to me to be the most fundamental issue confronting mankind. My goal in life has been to steer a course that fosters service to others and to society without undue sacrifice of individual aspirations.*

LIEF, MATTHEW S., urologist; b. N.Y.C., Feb. 9, 1955; s. Joseph and Millicent Lief; m. Dee Haynes, Aug. 7, 1983; children: Heather, Harrison, Hannah. BA, Syracuse U., 1976; MD, U. Noreste, Mexico, 1980, U. NY, 1981. Faculty Rush Med. Ctr., Chgo., 1981—86; house physician Johnson Bowman Ctr., Chgo., 1981—86; physician in charge Nutrisystem Weight Loss, Chgo., 1982—86; dir. Us Too Prostate Cancer, 1995—97; med. dir. Incontinence Support Group, 1996, Fla. Home Health, 1995—97; spl. expert witness Agy. for Health Care, Fla., 1996—. Governing bd. mem. Out Patient Surgery Ctr., Coral Springs, Fla., medicus Lithotripsy, Orlando; exec. com. No. W. Med. Ctr., Margate, Fla.; spkr. in field; clinical trial investigator. Urologist We Too - Care for the Indigent, Palm Beach County, Fla. Fellow: Am. Coll. of Surgeons. Avocations: tennis, skiing, fishing, gardening, family vacations. Office: Matthew S Lief MD PA 9750 NW 33rd St Coral Springs FL 33065 Office Phone: 954-755-3801. E-mail: mldoc9@aol.com.

LIEF, THOMAS PARRISH, sociologist, educator; b. N.Y.C., Oct. 4, 1931; s. Alfred and Zola Nina (Vogel) L. BA, U. N.Mex., 1955, MA, 1961; PhD, Tulane U., 1970. Counselor, archaeology asst. U. N.Mex., Albuquerque, 1959-60, 60-61; tchg. asst. dept. sociology Tulane U., New Orleans, 1961-64; instr. to asst. prof. dept. sociology Loyola U., New Orleans, 1964-69; assoc. prof. to prof. dept. sociology So. U., New Orleans, 1968-98; cons. on curriculum devel. Tuskegee Inst. Drug Abuse Human Svcs. Manpower Devel. Tng., 1973-78; adj. prof. sociology, assoc. grad. faculty mem. U. New Orleans, 1975-76; cons. various orgns., 1981-82; vis. prof. dept. sociology Tulane U., New Orleans, 1986; rev. com. mem. Alcohol, Drug Abuse & Mental Health Adminstrn. Office, 1987—. Bd. dirs. Nat. Assn. Alcoholism and Drug Abuse Counselors, 1990-91; pres. La. Assn. Substance Abuse Counselor and Trainers, 1990-91; adv. bd. Michael Halbrook Recovery Ctr. East Lake Hosp., 1990-92; mem. La. State Bd. Certification for Substance Abuse Counselors, 1988-92, Adv. Com. for Historically Black Colls. and Univs. Program for Substance Abuse Tng., 1987-89; tng. cons. Am. Indian Tng. Inst., Sacramento, 1985—; mem. La. Commn. on Alcohol and Drug Abuse, 1984-90, 97-99; mem. La. Commn. on Addictive Disorders, 1999—; mem. L.A. Drug Control and Violent Crime Policy Bd., 1993-2005; contract cons. Ctr. for Substance Abuse Treatment, 1994-95; contract cons. Office Alcohol and Drug Abuse, Dept. Health and Hosps., 1998-99; founder, bd. dirs. Accreditation Coun.: Alcohol and Drug Counselor Program in Higher Edn.; mem. WWNO Pub. Radio adv. bd.; cons. in field. Contbr. numerous articles to profl. jours.; mem. editl. rev. com. Counselor, 1988; co-author: Academic Linkages Resource Manual. Co-chair La. State-Wide Taskforce Counselor Manpower, 1984-90; pres., founder Nat. Assn. Substance Abuse Trainers and Educators, 1983—; bd. dirs. Cmty. Svc. Ctr., 1972—, Nat. Commn. on Accreditation of Alcoholism and Drug Abuse Counselors, 1982-90, Certification Reciprocity Consortium/Alcohol and Other Drug Abuse, Inc., 1981-82; pres., founder La. Cert. Examining Bd. of La. Assn. Substance Abuse Counselor & Trainers, 1978-82; mem. Child Abuse Com. Dist. Atty.'s Office, 1976-80; co-dir. Insight House Adv. Bd., 1976-80; bass Jefferson Symphony Chorus. Mem. Am. Sociol. Assn., Am. Acad. Polit. and Social Scis., La. Assn. Substance Abuse Counselors and Trainers (founder), Nat. Assn. Substance Abuse Trainers and Educators, Soc. for Applied Anthropology, Soc. for Study of Social Problems, So. Sociol. Soc. Avocations: photography, gourd dancing, short story writing.

LIEFF, ROBERT LAWRENCE, lawyer; b. Bridgeport, Conn., Sept. 29, 1936; BA, U. Bridgeport, 1958; JD, MBA, Columbia U., 1962. Bar: Calif. 1966, U.S. Dist. Ct., No. Dist. Calif. 1969, U.S. Ct. Appeals, Ninth Cir. 1969, U.S. Supreme Ct. 1969, U.S. Ct. Appeals, Seventh Cir. 1972, U.S. Tax Ct. 1974, U.S. Dist. Ct., Dist. of Hawaii 1986. Mem. Lieff, Cabraser, Heimann & Bernstein, LLP. Mem.: ABA (mem. Section on Corp., Banking and Bus. Law), Assn. Trial Lawyers of Am., Consumer Attys. Calif., Calif. Trial Lawyers Assn., San Francisco Trial Lawyers Assn., Lawyers Club of San Francisco, State Bar of Calif., Bar Assn. of San Francisco. Office: Lieff, Cabrasser, Heimann & Bernstein Embarcadero Ctr W 275 Battery St, 30th Fl San Francisco CA 94111 Office Phone: 415-965-1000. E-mail: rlieff@lchb.com.

LIEGLER, ROSEMARY MENKE, dean; b. Fairfield, Iowa, Aug. 21, 1939; d. Vincent Thomas and Catherine Lucille Menke; m. Donald G. Liegler, June 8, 1963; children: Katherine, Jerry. BSN, St. Ambrose Coll., 1961; MS in Nursing, Marquette U., 1962; PhD, Claremont Grad. Sch., 1994. Asst. prof. Miami (Fla.)-Dade Jr. Coll., Georgetown U., Washington, U. Miami; prof., dean Sch. Nursing Azusa (Calif.) Pacific U. Bd. dirs. Huntington East Valley Hosp. Mem. ANA, Calif. Assn. Colls. Nursing, East San Gabriel Valley Vis. Nurses' Assn. (cmty. bd. 1995), Sigma Theta Tau. Home: 3226 E Whitebirch Dr West Covina CA 91791-3037 Office: Azusa Pacific U Sch Nursing 901 E Alosta Ave Azusa CA 91702-2769

LIEM, PHAM H., geriatrician; b. Hue, Vietnam; arrived in US, 1974; MD, U. Saigon Med. Sch., 1973. Former intern, internal med., cardiology and neurology Cho-Ray Hosp., Saigon; former resident, family med. U. Ark. for Med. Sci., chief resident, 1979—80, fellow, geriatric med., 1980—82, Jackson T. Stephens prof. and vice chmn., geriatrics dept., 2004—; assoc. chief of staff, geriatrics and extended care Central Ark. Veteran Health Sys. Named one of Am. Top Doctors, 2000, 2002, 2003. Mem.: Gerontological Soc. of Am., Am. Geriatric Soc. Office: U Ark for Med Sci 4301 W Markham Slot 748 Little Rock AR 72205*

LIEN, JOHN DONOVAN, lawyer; b. LaCrosse, Wis., Dec. 30, 1943; s. Arthur Marvin and Alverda (Larson) L.; m. Kathleen MeHenry, June 17, 1967 (div. Mar. 1983); m. Molly Warner, Apr. 2, 1983. BA, U. Wis., 1965; JD, Harvard U., 1968. Bar: Wis. 1968, Ill. 1972, U.S. Dist. Ct. (no. dist.) Ill. 1972, U.S. Ct. Appeals (7th cir.) 1977. Assoc. Wilson & McIlvaine, Chgo., 1972-77, ptnr., 1978-86, Antonow & Fink, Chgo., 1986-88, Foley & Lardner LLP, Chgo., 1988—, chmn. construction practice group. Trustee Village of Winnetka, Ill., 1997-2001, Winnetka Libr. Dist., 1985-93. Capt. USAF, 1968-72. Republican. Episcopalian. Office: Foley & Lardner LLP One IBM Plz Chicago IL 60611 Office Phone: 312-832-4370. Business E-Mail: jlien@foley.com.

LIEN, TING-TING, music educator; b. Kaohsiung, Taiwan, July 3, 1965; arrived in U.S., 1983; d. Johnny Y.D. and Lily Lien; m. Jun Peng, June 27, 1995; children: Jacquelyn Ting, Charlene Ting. MusB, New Eng. Conservatory of Music, 1989; MusM, Rider U., 1996. Instr. music Westminster Conservatory Music, Princeton, 1992—98; adj. prof. Westminster Choir Coll. Rider U., Princeton, 2001—. Choir dir. Princeton Christian Ch., 1994—98; adjudicator Shore Music Educators Assn., NJ, 2002—, NJ Music Tchrs. Assn., 1998—. Mem.: Kindermusick Nat., N.J. Music Tchrs. Assn., Piano Tchrs. Forum. Home: 6 Walden Pond Way Monmouth Junction NJ 08852-2900 Office Phone: 732-274-9211. Personal E-mail: tinglien@comcast.net.

LIENEMANN, DELMAR ARTHUR, SR., accountant, real estate developer; b. Papillion, Nebr., May 17, 1920; s. Arthur Herman and Dorothea M. (Marth) L.; m. Charlotte Peck, Jun 17, 1944 (dec. Mar. 1995); children: Delmar Arthur Jr., David (dec.), Diane, Douglas, Dorothy, Daniel, Denise. BS, U. Nebr., 1941. CPA, Nebr. Acct. Wickstrom Supply, Lincoln, Nebr., 1941, L.L. Coryell & Sons, Lincoln, 1942, Lester Buckley, CPA, Lincoln, 1943-45; pvt. practice Lincoln, 1945—. Pres., v.p., sec., treas., bldg. chmn., charter mem. Christ Luth. Ch., Lincoln, 1949-70; co-commr. Lancaster County, Lincoln, 1954-58; pres. Lincoln Symphony Orch. Found., 1984—, Ethel S. Abbott Charitable Found. Mem. AICPA, N.E. Soc. CPA, Colo. Soc. CPA, Tex. Soc. CPA, Sertoma (sec.-treas. Lincoln chpt. 1952-68, Internat. Sertoman of Yr. 1962), Hillcrest Country Club, Nebr. Club, Nebr. Chancelors Club, Nebr. Touchdown Club, Nebr. Power Club, Nebr. Rebounders Club. Republican. Avocation: travel. Office: PO Box 81407 Lincoln NE 68501-1407

LIENERT, CHRISTOPH, physical education educator; b. Berlin, Jan. 12, 1963; s. Wolfgang and Marlies L. BA, MA, Free U. Berlin (Germany), 1993, We. Mich. U., Kalamazoo, 1990; PhD, Tex. Woman's U., Denton, Tex., 1998. Cert. tchr. Tex. Asst. prof. U. Maine, Presque Isle, Maine, 1998—2001; assoc. prof. Manhattan Coll., Bronx, NY, 2001—. German lang. editor Internat. Coun. of Health, Phys. Edn., Recreation, Sport and Dance, Reston, Va., 1995—; pres. Maine Task Force on Adapted Phys. Edn., Maine, 2000—01. Recipient Biennial Award for Disting. Contbn., Internat. Coun. for Health, Phys. Edn., Recreation, Sport, and Dance, 1997, Kitty Winter Magee Most Promising Profl. award, Tex. Woman's U., 2001. Mem.: AAHPERD, Internat. Fedn. Adapted Phys. Activity (rep. N.Am. Fedn. on Adapted Phys. Activity 2000—04, Elly D. Friedmann Outstanding Young Profl. award 2001), Coun. Exceptional Children, Internat. Soc. Comparative Phys. Edn. and Sport, Phi Kappa Phi (life). Office: Manhattan Coll 4513 Manhattan College Pkwy Bronx NY 10471 Business E-Mail: christoph.lienert@manhattan.edu.

LIENHARD, JOHN HENRY, IV, mechanical engineer, educator; b. St. Paul, Aug. 17, 1930; s. John Henry and Catherine Edith Lienhard; m. Carol Ann Bratton, June 20, 1959; children: John Henry V, Andrew Joseph. AS, Multnomah Jr. Coll., 1949; BS, Oreg. State Coll., 1951; MSME, U. Wash., 1953; PhD in Mech. Engring., U. Calif., Berkeley, 1961; DHL (hon.), U. Houston, 2002, Sacred Heart U., 2002. Assoc. prof. mech. engring. Wash. State U., Pullman, 1961-67; prof. mech. engring. dept. U. Ky., Lexington, 1967-80; prof. mech. engring. U. Houston, 1980-89, M.D. Anderson prof. mech. engring. and history, 1989—2000, prof. emeritus, 2000—. Clyde chair prof. U. Utah, Salt Lake City, 1981. Author (with C. L. Tien): Statistical Thermodynamics, 1971, 1979; author: (with J. H. Lienhard V) A Heat Transfer Textbook, 1981, 1987; author: (with E. T. Layton) History of Heat Transfer, 1988; author: The Engines of Our Ingenuity, 2000, Inventing Modern, 2003; author, host (radio) The Engines of Our Ingenuity; contbr. articles to profl. jours. Mem.: ASME (hon. Heat Transfer Meml. award, Charles Russ Richards award, Engr. Historian award 1998), Nat. Acad. Engring., Am. Soc. Engring. Edn. (Ralph Coates Roe Tchg. medal). Episcopalian. Home: 3719 Durhill St Houston TX 77025-4006 Office: U Houston Dept Mech Engring Houston TX 77204-4006 Office Phone: 713-743-4518. Business E-Mail: jhl@uh.edu.

LIEPACK, SCOT ALAN, psychologist; b. Pitts., Dec. 26, 1956; s. Louis Liepack and Marlene Cherna Roth. BA in Environ. Studies, Claremont Coll., 1980; MS in Clin. Psychology, U. Miami, 1994, D in Clin. Psychology, 1998. Intern Ctr. Mental Health, Charlotte-Mecklenburg Health Authority, 1995—96; rsch. asst. early childhood spl. edn. U. Miami, 1996—98; fellow Kapi'olani Child Protection Ctr., 1998—99; supr. Parents and Children Together MST Team, 2000; provider Felix Class Therapeutic Svc., 2000—01; clin. psychologist Hawaii Dept. Edn., 2001—04; pvt. practice Kailua-Kona, Hawaii, 2002—. Presenter in field. Bd. dirs. West Hawaii Cmty. Health Ctr. Mem.: APA, Nat. Assn. Edn. Young Children, Hawai Island Psychol. Assn. (pres. 2004), Hawaii Psychol. Assn. (Big Island rep. 2002, gen. divsn. rep. 2003). Office: 75-5751 Kuakini Hwy Ste 2011 Kailua Kona HI 96740-1753

LIEPMANN, DORIAN, engineering educator; b. L.A., Nov. 21, 1957; s. Hans Wolfgang and Dietland (Goldschmidt) L.; m. Kathleen Mary Toups, July 10, 1992; 1 child, Colin Wolfgang. BA, Occidental Coll., 1981; BS, Calif. Inst. Tech., 1981, MS, 1983; PhD, U. Calif., San Diego, 1990. Engr. Jet Propulsion Laboratory, Pasadena, Calif., 1983—84; rsch. scientist Technol. Rsch. Group Sci. Applications Internat. Corp., San Diego, 1984—92; rsch. engineer, Inst. for Non-Linear Sci. U. of Calif. San Diego, 1986—92; asst. prof. mechanical engring. U. of Calif. Berkeley, 1992—98, assoc. prof. departments of bioengineering and mechanical engring., 1998—2003; mem. faculty joint grad. group U. of Calif. Berkeley and U. of Calif. San Francisco, 1993—; Lester John and Lynne Dewar Lloyd Disting. Prof. Bioengineering U. of Calif. Berkeley, 2001—, prof. bioengineering and mechanical engring., 2003—, vice chair undergraduate affairs, dept. bioengineering, 2003—, chair dept. bioengineering, 2004—. Dir. Berkeley Sensor and Actuator Ctr. U. of Calif. Berkeley, 1998—. Mem. ASME, Am. Phys. Soc. Office: U Calif 483 Evans Hall 1762 Berkeley CA 94720-1741

LIES, BETTY BONHAM, writer, poet; b. Mpls., Nov. 25, 1935; d. Clarence Samuel and Bertha Leora (Sherwood) Bonham; m. Thomas A. Lies, Sept. 19, 1959; children: Elaine Margaret, Brian Thomas. BA, Carleton Coll., Northfield, Minn., 1957; MA, U. Wis., 1958. Tchr. St. Claire Shores (Mich.) H.S., 1958-59, Saxe Jr. H.S., New Canaan, Conn., 1959-61; instr. U. Conn., Stamford, 1960; tchr. Stuart Country Day Sch., Princeton, N.J., 1971-96; writer in the schs. N.J. State Coun. on Arts, Trenton, 1996—. Author: The Poet's Pen, 1993, My Ticket to Tomorrow, 1997, Earth's Daughters, 1999; contbr. poetry and articles to profl. jours. Recipient 6 grants/fellowships NEH, Washington, 1985-95, Klingenstein fellowship Tchrs. Coll., Columbia U., N.Y.C., 1988-89, grant for poetry N.J. SCA, Trenton, 1995-96, grant at Vt. Studio Ctr., Geraldine R. Dodge Found., Madison, N.J., 1997; named Disting. Tchr. Artist, N.J. State Coun. on Arts, Trenton, 1999, 2002. Mem. Acad. Am. Poets, Poetry Soc. Am. Democrat. Avocations: music, gardening, travel. E-mail: talies@aosi.com.

LIETZ, JEREMY JON, educational administrator, writer; b. Milw., Oct. 4, 1933; s. John Norman and Dorothy B. (Drew) L.; m. Cora Fernandez, Feb. 24, 1983; children: Cheryl, Brian, Angela, Andrew, Christopher, Jennifer. BS, U. Wis., Milw., 1961; MS, U. Wis., Madison, 1971; EdD, Marquette U., 1980. Tchr. Milw. Pub. Schs., 1961-63, diagnostic counselor, 1968-71, sch. adminstr., 1971-95, hearing panel ombudsman, 1999—, acting student svcs. coord., 1999—; tchr. Madison Pub. Sch., Wis., 1964-65; rsch. assoc. U. Wis., Madison, 1965-67; instr. Marquette U., Milw., 1980-82, Milw. U. Sch., 2000—02. Lectr. HEW Conf. on Reading, Greeley, Colo., 1973, NAESP Conf. on Reading, St. Louis, 1974, various state and nat. orgns.; co-founder, bd. dirs., cons. Ednl. Leadership Inst., Shorewood, Wis., 1980—; dir. Religious Edn. Program, Cath. Elem. East, Milw., 1985-86. Author: The Elementary School Principal's Role in Special Education, 1982; contbr. numerous articles, chpts., tests, revs. to profl. jours. V.p. PTA, 1961-62. With U.S. Army, 1954-56, ETO. Recipient Cert. of Achievement award NAESP, 1974. Mem. AAAS, Assn. Wis. Sch. Adminstrs. (mem. state planning com. 1977-79, lectr. 1982), Adminstrs. and Suprs. Coun. (mem. exec. bd. dist. 1977-79, mem. contract negotiations com. 1991-95), Filipino Am. Assn. Wis., U. Wis. Alumni Assn. (Madison), Milw. Mcpl. Chess Assn., U.S. Chess Fedn., Phi Delta Kappa. Home: 424 Susan Ln Thiensville WI 53092-1451 Office: Ednl Leadership Inst PO Box 11411 Shorewood WI 53211-0411 Personal E-mail: dcphil@prodigy.net.

LIETZAU, WILLIAM KENDALL, career officer, lawyer; b. Annapolis, Md., Nov. 9, 1960; s. Karl Ernest and Janice Mae L.; m. Diane Michelle, May 19, 1984; children: Rachel Anne, Zachary Thomas. BS, U.S. Naval Acad., 1983; JD, Yale U., 1989; LLM, U.S. Army JAG Sch., 1995. Bar: Conn. 1989, Ct. Mil. Appeals 1990, U.S. Supreme Ct. 1995. Rifle co. comdr. USMC, Kaneohe Bay, Hawaii, 1984-87, spl asst. U.S. atty. Jacksonville, N.C., 1989-91, lt. col., 1995; chief prosecutor Camp Lejeune, N.C., 1991-92; chief def. counsel Iwakuni, Japan, 1992-93; dep. sta. judge adv., 1993-95; head law armed conflict br. Navy JAG, Washington, 1996-97; dep. legal counsel to chmn. Joint Chiefs Staff Washington, 1997-99; chief mil. judge Atlantic cir., 1999-2000; cmdg. officer 1st RTBn., San Diego, 2000—02; spl. asst. to Dept. Def. gen. counsel, 2002—. Adj. prof. Georgetown U., Washington, 1998-2000; spkr. in field. Contbr. articles to profl. jours. U.S. del. Ottawa Conv. Banning Landmines, Terrorist Bombing Conv., Nuc. Terrorism Conv., Rome Treaty Internat. Criminal Ct., Hague Cultural Property Protocol. Recipient Major Gen. Pugh award, 1995; named Career Mil. Lawyer of the Yr. Judge Adv. Assn., 1998. Avocations: running, biking, lifting. Office: Rm 4A923 1600 Defense Pentagon Washington DC E-mail: wklietzau@msn.com, lietzauw@osdgc.osd.mil.

LIEWEHR, FREDERICK RUSSELL, endodontist, educator; b. Chgo., June 18, 1951; s. Frank Edward and Mary Elizabeth Liewehr; m. Michelle Bernardette Gonzales, Nov. 27, 1970; children: Scott Christopher, Mary Benedicta Cieslak, Virginia Rose. BS, U. Iowa, Iowa City, 1973, DDS, 1981; MS, Med. Coll. Ga., Augusta, 1993. Cert. in endodontics Am. Bd. Endodontics, 1998. Dental officer U.A. Army, 1981—2003; chmn. dept. endodontics Va. Commonwealth U., Richmond, 2004—. Endodontic cons. McGuire Hunter Holmes VA Med. Ctr., Richmond, 2005—. Col. U.S. Army, 1981—2003, Ft. Gordon, Ga. Decorated Order of Mil. Med. Merit OTSG, US Army, Surgeon General's A Designator, Legion of Merit US Army. Fellow: Internat. Coll. Dentists; mem.: ADA, Am. Acad. Oral Medicine, Am. Assn. Oral Biologists, Am. Assn. Endodontists, Torch Club Internat. R-Consevative. Office: Virginia Commonwealth Univ 520 N 12th St Richmond VA 23298-0566 Office Phone: 804-828-0784. Office Fax: 804-827-1373. E-mail: frliewehr@vcu.edu.

LIEWENDAHL, BO KRISTIAN, pathologist, nuclear medicine physician; b. Helsinki, Aug. 21, 1941; s. Ernst August and Irina (Semenov) Liewendahl; 1 child, Kari Peter Nikolai. MD, U. Helsinki, 1966, PhD, 1968. Diplomate. Resident in clin. chemistry Helsinki U. Hosp., 1966-69, resident in medicine, 1969-72, cons. lab. dept., 1974-82; asst. prof., lectr. U. Helsinki, 1977-96, prof., 1996—; chief physician divsn. nuclear medicine Helsinki U. Hosp., 1983-99; NIH fellow U. Calif., San Francisco, 1972-73. Vis. scientist U. Wis., Madison, U. Va., Charlottesville, 1982; dir. nuc. medicine rsch. group Minerva Inst. Found., Helsinki, Finland, 1977—2002; sec. gen. Minerva Found., 1997—2002, bd. dirs., 2002—; pres. European Nuc. Medicine Congress, Helsinki, 1984, Scandinavian Congress Nuc. Medicine, Helsinki, 1998; chmn. European Congress Clin. Chemistry, Tampere, Finland, 1995; del. nuc. medicine sect. European Union Med. Spltys., 1994—2002; del. European Bd. Nuc. Medicine, 1995—2002. Author, editor: Scandinavian Jour. Clin. Lab. Investigation, 1986—96; mem. editl. bd. European Jour. Nuclear Medicine, 1991—2002; contbr. articles to profl. jours. Recipient J. W. Runeberg prize, Finnish Med. Soc., 1969, Ann. Lecture prize, 1973, T.

Heiskanen Meml. prize, Finnish Radiol. Soc. and Finnish Nuc. Medicine Soc., 1985, Gold medal, Minerva Found., 1989. Mem.: N.Y. Acad. Scis., Soc. Nuc. Medicine N.Y., World Fedn. Nuc. Medicine and Biology (del. 1988—2003, organizing com. 8th World Congress, Santiago, Chile 2002), Finnish Soc. Nuc. Medicine (pres. 1996—98), European Thyroid Assn. (sec. Helsinki congress 1976), European Assn. Nuc. Medicine (del. 1988—95, mem. organizing com. Copenhagen congress 1996, organizing com. Helsinki congress 2004, Congress prize 1991). Lutheran. Achievements include research in thyroid function tests, particularly accurate assays for free thyroid hormone concentrations in blood, nuclear medicine procedures for diagnosis of oncological, hematological and neurological diseases. Avocation: history. Office: Minerva Found Inst Biomedicum Helsinki Haartmansgatan 8 00290 Helsinki Finland

LIFSCHITZ, JUDAH, lawyer; b. N.Y.C., Nov. 28, 1952; s. Morris and Edna (Love) L.; m. Marilyn Feder, Dec. 8, 1974; children: Lisa, Ira, Tamar. BA magna cum laude, Yeshiva U., 1974; JD, George Washington U., 1977. Bar: Md. 1977, D.C. 1978, U.S. Dist. Ct. D.C. 1980, U.S. Claims Ct. 1980, U.S. Ct. Appeals (D.C. cir.) 1980, U.S. Ct. Appeals (4th cir.) 1982, U.S. Ct. Appeals (fed. cir.) 1985, U.S. Supreme Ct. 1985. Assoc. Hudson, Creyke, Koehler & Tacke, Washington, 1980, Epstein, Becker, Borsody & Green, Washington, 1980-83; ptnr., chmn. govt. contracts dept. Washington Perito & Dubuc, Washington, 1983-91; ptnr. Shapiro, Lifschitz and Schram, P.C., Washington, 1991—. Author: Heaven Sent Stories of Faith and Effort, 1977, Stories for Sahuli, 1999, The Klausenberger Rebbe, The War Years, 2003. Washington counsel Nat. Coun. Young Israel, N.Y.C., 1980—95; pres. Yeshiva of Greater Washington, 1985-89; bd. dirs. Jewish Community Coun., Washington, 1980—90, United Jewish Appeal Fedn., Washington, 1985. Recipient Shofar award Nat. Coun. Young Israel, 1980, Kesser Torah award Yeshiva of Greater Washington, 2000. Mem. ABA, Md. State Bar Assn. Office: Shapiro Lifschitz and Schram PC 1742 N Street NW Washington DC 20036

LIFSCHULTZ, PHILLIP, diversified financial services company executive, consultant, lawyer; b. Oak Park, Ill., Mar. 5, 1927; s. Abraham Albert and Frances Rhoda (Siegel) L.; m. Edith Louise Leavitt, June 27, 1948; children: Gregory, Bonnie, Jodie. BS in Acctg., U. Ill., 1949; JD, John Marshall Law Sch., 1956. Bar: Ill. 1956; CPA. Tax mgr. Arthur Andersen & Co., Chgo., 1957-63; v.p. taxes Montgomery Ward & Co., Chgo., 1963-78; fin. v.p., contr. Henry Crown & Co., Chgo., 1978-81; prin. Phillip Lifschultz & Assocs., Chgo., 1981—. Exec. dir. Dodi Orgn., 1987-90; v.p. Altra Travel, Northbrook, Ill., 1975-2004; v.p. Tax Execs. Inst., Chgo., 1977-78; pres. Great Lakes Shoe Co., Deerfield, Ill., 1996—. Adv. coun. Coll. Commerce and Bus. Adminstrn., U. Ill., Urbana-Champaign, 1977-78; chmn. Civic Fedn. Chgo., 1980-82; chmn. adv. bd. to Auditor Gen. of Ill., 1965-73; project dir. Exec. Svc. Corps of Chgo., Chgo. Bd. Edn. and State of Ill. projects, 1980-87. With U.S. Army, 1945-46. Mem. AICPA, Am. Arbitration Assn. (comml. panel 1983-94), Ill. Bar Assn., Chgo. Bar Assn., Ill. CPA Soc., Nat. Retail Merchants Assn. (chmn. tax. com. 1975-78), Am. Retail Fedn. (chmn. taxation com. 1971), Standard Club Chgo. E-mail: papalif@aol.com.

LIFSHITZ, FELICE, historian, educator; b. N.Y.C., Sept. 21, 1959; d. David and Belle Lifshitz; life ptnr. Sheri Franklyn, Feb. 14, 1980; m. Joseph Francis Patrouch, Apr. 15, 1994; 1 child, Daniel Alexander Joseph Patrouch; 1 child, Quinn Bellamy. BA in Medieval studies, Barnard Coll., 1981; MA in History, Columbia U., 1983, PhD in History, 1988. Vis. asst. prof. history Trinity Coll., Hartford, Conn., 1988—89; assoc. prof. of history Fla. Internat. U., Miami, 1989—. Vis. fellow Pontifical Inst. Medieval Studies, Toronto, Ont., Canada, 1993; vis. rschr. Abteilung Landesgeschichte U. Freiburg, Germany, 1997; Alexander von Humboldt fellow, Historisches Seminar U. Frankfurt, Germany, 1998; guest rschr. Forschungstelle Mittelalter Oesterreichische Akademie der Wissenschaften, Vienna, 1999. Translator: Viking Normandy: Dudo of St. Quentin's Gesta Normannorum; mem. editl. bd.: Oxford Dictionary of the Mid. Ages, History Compass, 2005—; editor: Medieval Europe, —; contbr. chapters to books, articles to prof. jours., encys. Recipient Tchg. Incentive Program award, State of Fla., 1994; grantee, Whiting Found., 1987—88, Deutscher Akademischer Austauschdienst, 1997, Fla. Humanities Coun., 2001, 2002; Higher Edn. grantee, Jewish Found. for Edn. of Women, 1982—83, rsch. fellow, Alexander von Humboldt Stiftung, 1998. Mem.: Oxford Dictionary of Mid. Ages (edtl. bd. 2004—), Arbeitskreis fuer Hagiographische Fragen, Soc. Medieval Feminist Scholarship (adv. bd. 2003—, editl. bd. Medieval Feminist Forum 2005—, sect. editor Medieval Europe, History Compass 2005—), The Hagiography Soc., Medieval Acad. Am. (publs. adv. bd. 2001—). Democrat. Jewish. Avocations: exercise, photography, travel. Home: 7330 Ocean Ter # 1203 Miami Beach FL 33141 Office: Florida Internat U Dept History Miami FL 33199 Office Phone: 305-348-3557. E-mail: lifshitz@fiu.edu.

LIFSON, KALMAN ALAN, retired retail executive, bank executive, portfolio manager; b. Mpls., Oct. 15, 1926; s. Maurice Kalman and Gertrude (Shulkin) L.; m. Irene Londer, June 17, 1950 (dec. July 1968); m. Judith Abrams, Sept. 3, 1969; children: Valerie Leftwich, Kip, Ione Spear, Stacey Kivowitz, Grant Dorfman. BS in Naval Tech., U. Minn., 1946, MBA, 1949; PhD in Psychology, Purdue U., 1951. Commd. ensign USN, 1945, lt. (j.g.), 1952; engrng. officer Panama Canal Zone, 1945-46; supr. indsl. engrng. Temco Aircraft, Dallas, 1951-52; mgmt. engrng. officer USN, Washington, 1953-54, resigned; prin. Lifson, Wilson, Ferguson & Winick, Dallas, 1954-94, Pers. Decisions, Inc., Dallas, 1995-99; chmn. Harris'Dept. Stores, San Bernadino, Calif., 1980-94, Tex. Rsch. and Electronic Corp. and successors, Dallas, 1962-94, Electronic Mgmt. Info. Sys., 1970-94; chmn. emeritus B.R. Blackmarr & Assocs., Dallas, 1986-99; ret., 1999; portfolio mgr. Delphi/EMSS Bank Fund, Dallas, 2005—. Chmn. Fed. Home Loan Bank of 9th Dist., Little Rock, 1979-80; portfolio mgr. Delphi Emis Bank Fund, 2005-; spkr. fields of psychology, retailing, banking, ops. rsch. Contbr. articles to profl. jours. Chmn. Congl. Commn. on Guaranteed Student Loans, Washington, 1975, Commn. on Orgn. of U.S. Dept. Labor, Washington, 1976; mem. Tex. Commn. on State Employee Productivity, Austin, Tex., 1985. Mem. APA, World Pres. Orgn., Columbian Club (treas. 1950-54), Crescent Club, Sigma Xi. Jewish. E-mail: klifson906@aol.com. *"Winners" are those who can make the big play, who can turn the game around, who can conceive and institute dramatic changes. Those few of us who have been so endowed and developed must use our winnership to effect significant improvements to the well-being of those within our spheres of influence.*

LIFTIN, JOAN R., photojournalist, educator; b. Teaneck, NJ, Nov. 1, 1933; d. Daniel and Hilda (Newman) Liftin; m. Saul Wolf, 1959 (div. 1961); m. Charles Harbutt, Dec. 22, 1978; stepchildren: Sarah, Charles, Damian. BS, Ohio State U., Columbus, 1956. Modern dancer various companies, 1962—69; photo editor, chief photographer UNICEF, N.Y.C., 1969—75; dir. photo libr. Magnum Photos, N.Y.C., 1975—81; founding ptnr. Archive Pictures, N.Y.C., 1981—90; artist in residence Rochester Inst. Tech., NY, 1987; dir. documentary edn. Internat. Ctr. Photography, N.Y.C., 1988—2000. Author: Drive-Ins, 2004; editor: Kertesz-Harbutt Sympathetic Explorations, 1978, Progreso by Charles Harbutt, 1986, Falkland Road by Mary Ellen Mark, 1981; co-editor (with Inge Morach): Magnum's Paris, 1981; contbr. photos to many collections and publications including: Ctr. Creative Photography, Tucson, Akron Mus. Art, Phila. Mus. Art, Wellsley Coll., Columbia U. and Morehead Mus. Democrat. Avocations: chess, reading, tennis. Home: One Fifth Ave Apt 16G New York NY 10003 Personal E-mail: actuality@aol.com.

LIFTIN, JOHN M., lawyer; b. Washington, June 25, 1943; children: Eric, Hilary, Sam. AB, U. Pa., 1964; LLB, Columbia U., 1967. Bar: N.Y. 1967, D.C. 1974, U.S. Dist. Ct. D.C. 1975, U.S. Ct. Appeals (D.C. cir.) 1975, U.S. Supreme Ct. 1980. Assoc. Sullivan & Cromwell, NYC, 1967-71; spl. counsel to chmn. SEC, Washington, 1971-72, assoc. dir. market reg. div., 1972-74; ptnr. Rogers & Wells, Washington, 1974-85; pres. Quadrex Securities Corp., NYC, 1985-87; sr. v.p., gen. counsel Kidder, Peabody Group Inc., NYC, 1987-96; independent cons. Prudential Fin., Newark, 1997—98; sr. v.p., gen. counsel Prudential Insurance, 1998—2000, Prudential Fin., 2000—05; vice-chmn., gen. counsel Bank of NY, NYC, 2005—. Mem. adv. bd. securities regulation and law reports Bur. Nat. Affairs, Inc., Washington, 1979—; mem. N.Y. Stock Exch. Legal Adv. Com., 2000—. Mem. ABA, Univ. Club. Office: Bank of NY One Wall St New York NY 10286

LIFTON, BARBARA, state legislator, secondary school educator; children: Christine Brouwer, Paul Sylvester. English tchr. Geneseo Ctrl. Sch., 1976—82, Ithaca Schs., 1985—88. Chief of staff Assemblyman marty Luster; mem. Tompkins Co. Dem. Com.; treas 3rd Ward Dem. Com. Mem. Justice for All; founder Coalition for Cmty. Unity, 1988, Democratic Response Group. Democrat. Office: 106 E Court St Ithaca NY 14850

LIFTON, RICHARD P., medical educator; b. 1953; BA, Dartmouth Coll.; MD, Stanford U., 1982, PhD. Diplomate Am. Bd. Internal Medicine. Chief med. resident Brigham and Woman's Hosp., Boston; faculty Harvard Med. Sch.; prof. genetics, medicine and molecular biophysics & biochemistry Yale U., New Haven. Recipient Homer Smith award, Am. Soc. Nephrology, Novartis award, Am. Heart Assn., Med. Rsch. award, Pasarow Found., Earnest H. Starling Disting. lectureship, Am. Physiol. Soc., 2002. Mem.: NAS. Office: Yale U Dept Genetics PO Box 208005 New Haven CT 06520-8005 Business E-Mail: richard.lifton@yale.edu.

LIFTON, ROBERT KENNETH, manufacturing executive; b. NYC, Jan. 9, 1928; s. Benjamin and Anna (Pike) L.; m. Loretta J. Silver, Sept. 5, 1954; children: Elizabeth Gail Lifton Hooper, Karen Grace Lifton Healy. BBA magna cum laude, CCNY, 1948; LLB, Yale U., 1951; doctorate (hon.), Bar Ilan U., Israel, 1993. Bar: N.Y. 1952. Assoc. Kaye, Scholer, Fierman, Hays & Handler, N.Y.C., 1955-56; asst. to pres. Glickman Corp., N.Y.C., 1956-57; pres. Robert K. Lifton, Inc., N.Y.C., 1957-61; chmn. bd. Terminal Tower Co., Inc., Cleve., 1959-63; pres. Transcontinental Investing Corp., N.Y.C., 1961-72, chmn. bd., 1969-72; ptnr. Venture Assocs., 1972-89; pres. Preferred Health Care Ltd., 1983-88; chmn. bd. dirs. Marcade Group, Inc., 1986-91, Medis El, 1993—, Cell Diagnostics, Inc., 1992-99; chmn. bd. dirs., CEO Medis Techs., Ltd., N.Y.C., 1999—. CEO, chmn. bd. dirs. Team Am., Inc., 1983-85; treas. Consol. Accessories Corp., 1980-88, Caron's Connection, Inc., 1985-89; bd. dirs. exec. investment com. Bank Leumi USA, NYC; bd. dirs. Leumi Investment Svcs., Inc., 2005; mem. faculty Columbia U. Law Sch., 1973-78, Yale U. Law Sch., 1972-75; guest lectr. Practicing Law Inst., Yale Law Sch., Pace Inst., NYU; founder Nat. Exec. Conf., Washington, Inc.; chmn. oversight com. for Masters Degree, NYU Real Estate Inst., 1987-88. Author: Practical Real Estate: Legal Tax and Business Strategies, 1978; contbr. articles to profl. jours. and handbooks (Graham and Dodd award for best article Fin. Analyst Jour. 1967). Mem. McGovern econ. adv. com., 1972-73; chmn. parents com. Barnard Coll., 1976-78; mem. com. of the collection Whitney Mus., 1976-79; trustee Yale U. Sch. Fund, 1974-77, NYU Real Estate Inst., 1983-89; chmn., bd. dirs. Fund for Religious Liberty, 1987-88; pres. Am. Jewish Congress, 1988-94; chmn. Internat. Bd. U.S. Mid. East Project coun. fgn. rels., 1994—; pres. Israel Policy Forum, 1994—96, chmn. bd., 1996-97, chmn. emeritus, 1997—; bd. dirs. Builders for Peace, 1993—, Abraham Fund, 1993—, Tel Aviv Mus., 1996—2000, Besa Inst., 1994—, HIAS, 1990-96; mem. exec. com. AIPAC, 1990—93; vice-chmn. NJCRAC, 1994—96; exec. com. AIPAC, 1993-96; trustee Am. Friends of Bar Ilan U., 1996—2002, mem. global bd. trustees, 1997—; bd. dirs. Pub. Health Rsch. Inst., 1996—, vice chmn., 1997-98, chmn., 1998-2004, chmn. emeritus, 2004—; co-chmn. Internat. Ctr. Pub. Health, 1999; trustee Bar Ilan Global, 1997—; bd. dirs. Georgia O'Keeffe Mus., 1999-2002. Served to lt. (j.g.) USN, 1952-55. Recipient Achievement award Sch. Bus. Alumni Soc. CCNY, 1984, James Madison award Fund for Religious Liberty, 1987, Stephen S. Wise award Am. Jewish Congress, 1993; named Tech. Pioneer World Econ. Forum, 2003. Mem. Order of Coif, Beta Gamma Sigma. Home: 983 Park Ave New York NY 10028-0808 Office: 805 3rd Ave New York NY 10022-7513 Office Phone: 212-935-8484. E-mail: robertl@medistechnologies.com.

LIGETT, WALDO BUFORD, chemist; b. Middletown, Ohio, Nov. 2, 1916; s. Waldo Buford and Mabel Louise (Berkley) L.; m. Ann Elizabeth Hartwell, Aug. 29, 1940; children: Robert A., John D., Michael T., Steven D., Daniel L. BS, Antioch Coll., 1939; MS, Purdue U., 1941, PhD, 1944, D.Sc. (hon.), 1965; grad., Advanced Mgmt. Program, Harvard U., 1967. Chemist Eastman Kodak Co., Rochester, N.Y., 1935-38; research supr. Ethyl Corp., Detroit, 1944-51, asst. dir. chem., 1951-52, asso. dir. chem., 1952-62, dir. research and devel., 1962-63; v.p. Celanese Chem. Co., Corpus Christi, Tex., 1963-64, v.p. tech. and mfg., 1964-66; tech. dir. Celanese Corp., N.Y.C., 1966-67, v.p., 1967-72, Franklin Inst., Phila., 1973-81; pres. Franklin Inst. Research Labs., 1975-81. Dir. Franklin-Hahnemann Inst., 1974-81 Mem.: Am. Chem. Soc. Achievements include patents in field. Home: 377 Carolina Meadows Villa Chapel Hill NC 27517-7521

LIGGAN, JOANNE DUNKLEY, realtor; b. Richmond, Va., Sept. 24, 1953; d. Charles Samuel and Mary Heath Dunkley; m. Gerald Wayne Liggan, June 21, 1985; m. Michael Edward Thurston, Sept. 19, 1975 (div. May 0, 1985); m. John Joseph Ferri, Sept. 18, 1971 (div.); children: Dawn Nicole Thurston, Angela Hope Ferri. Office mgr. Liggan Homes, Inc., Mechanicsville, Va., 1984—; realtor Olde Towne Properties of Va., Inc., Mechanicsville, Va., 1985—. Sec./treas., bd. dirs. Liggan Homes, Inc., Mechanicsville, Va., 1985—; owner, DJ Jo's Karaoke; mgr., lead singer Hearts Afire dance band. Author: (novel) Heir of Deception. Spl. music coord. Pole Green Ch. of Christ, Mechanicsville, Va., 2003—04. Mem.: Hanover Writers (founder & facilitator 2003—), Va. Writers Club (pres. 1998—2000, bd. mem. 1998—, treas. 2001—04). R-Conservative. Christian. Avocations: singing, writing. Home: 8201 N Shall Dr Mechanicsville VA 23111 Office: Liggan Homes Inc 8201 N Shall Dr Mechanicsville VA 23111 Personal E-mail: jliggan@comcast.net.

LIGGETT, HIRAM SHAW, JR., retired diversified financial services company executive; b. St. Louis, Jan. 12, 1932; s. Hiram Shaw and Lucille (Gardner) L.; m. Margaret McGinness, Jan. 21, 1961; children: Lucille Gardner, Frances Shelby. BA, Colo. Coll., 1953; LLD (hon.), Maryville U., 1991. Cashier Brown Group, Inc., St. Louis, 1957-64, asst. treas., 1964-68, treas., 1968—, v.p., 1983-86 (ret.). Bd. dirs. Roosevelt Fed. Savs. and Loan, St. Louis Past trustee, vice chmn. bd. dirs. McKendree Coll., Lebanon, Ill., 1980-88; trustee, past chmn. bd. trustees Maryville U., St. Louis, 1982-91; past chmn. Provident Counseling, 1983; past v.p., bd. dirs. Jr. Achievement Miss. Valley, 1983; past dir. bi-state chpt. ARC, 1983; bd. dirs., pres. Cardinal Ritter Inst.; bd. dirs., chmn. devel. bd. Paraquad. Capt. USNR, 1953-79. Mem. Fin. Execs. Inst. (pres., dir. 1983—), St. Louis Coun. Navy League (bd. councilors 1982), Univ. Club (St. Louis, chmn. house com. 1975-78), Strathalbyn Farms Club (chmn. house com., pres. bd. dirs.), Alpha Kappa Psi, Tau Kappa Alpha. Republican. Presbyterian. Home: 64 Chesterfield Lakes Rd Chesterfield MO 63005-5400 Office: Liggett-Black & Co 8000 Bonhomme Ave #320 Saint Louis MO 63105 E-mail: hligg498@aol.com.

LIGGETT, LAWRENCE MELVIN, vacuum equipment manufacturing company executive; b. Denver, June 22, 1917; s. Thomas Harrison and Mary Deacon (Taylor) L.; m. Edith Irene Harris, June 20, 1943; children: Pamela Jane Liggett Schwartz, Betty Sue Liggett Brooks El Gammal. AB, Ctrl. Coll., Pella, Iowa, 1938; PhD in Chemistry, Iowa State Coll., 1943. Rsch. chemist NDRC, Iowa State Coll., 1941-43; plant mgr. Cardox Corp., Claremore, Okla., 1943-48; dir. inorganic rsch. Wyandotte Chems. Corp., 1948-55; dir. rsch., v.p. tech. dir. Airco Speer divsn. Airco, Inc., 1955-70, pres. Airco Electronics divsn., 1970-75; pres. Airco Temescal divsn. BOC Group, Berkeley, Calif., 1975-82; cons. bus. and tech., 1982—. Author; patentee in field. Mem. Am. Chem. Soc., Electronic Industries Assn. Republican. Home: 1856 Piedras Cir Alamo CA 94507-2820

LIGGETT, THOMAS JACKSON, retired seminary president; b. Nashville, May 27, 1919; s. Thomas Jackson and Lola Cleveland (Ballentine) L.; m. Virginia Corrine Moore, Aug. 12, 1941; children: Thomas Milton, Margaret Moore Liggett. AB, Transylvania U., 1940; MDiv, Lexington Theol. Sem., 1944, postgrad., 1950-52; LLD, Interam. U., 1965, Culver-Stockton Coll., 1959, Butler U., 1975; DHL, Transylvania U., 1969; DD, Eureka Coll., 1971, Phillips U., 1989, Christian Theol. Sem., 2002. Ordained to ministry Christian Ch., 1940; pastor in Danville, Ky., 1943-45; missionary Argentina, 1946-57; prof. Union Theol. Sem., Buenos Aires, 1948-57; pres. Evang. Sem. of P.R., 1957-65; exec. sec. for Latin Am. Christian Ch., 1965-67, chmn. div. world mission, 1967-68; pres. United Christian Missionary Soc., 1968-74, Christian Theol. Sem., Indpls., 1974-86, ret., 1986. Del. World Coun. Chs. assembly in Uppsala, 1968, adviser assembly, Nairobi, Kenya, 1975; mem. governing bd. Nat. Council Chs., 1969-75; moderator Disciples of Christ, 1985-87. Author: Where Tomorrow Struggles to be Born, 1970; Editor: Cuadernos Teologicos, 1954-55. Co-chmn. McGovern Task Force on Fgn. Policy in Latin Am., 1972, Democratic precinct committeeman, 1970-72. Mem. Disciples of Christ Hist. Soc. (life), Theta Phi. Home: 522 Bradford Ct Claremont CA 91711 E-mail: tjl22@juno.com.

LIGGETT, TWILA C., academic administrator, broadcast executive; b. Pipestone, Minn., Mar. 25, 1944; d. Donald L. Christensen and Irene E. (Zweigle) Christensen Flesher. BS, Union Coll., Lincoln, Nebr., 1966; MA, U. Nebr., 1971; PhD, 1977; DHL (hon.), Marymount Manhattan Coll., 2000. Dir. vocal and instrumental music Sprague (Nebr.)-Martell Pub. Sch., 1966-67; tchr. vocal music pub. schs., Syracuse, Nebr., 1967-69; tchr. Norris Pub. Sch., Firth, Nebr., 1969-71; cons. fed. reading project pub. schs., Lincoln, Nebr., 1971-72; curriculum coord. Westside Cmty. Schs., Omaha, 1972-74; dir. state program Right-to-Read Nebr. Dept. Edn., 1974-76; asst. dir. Nebr. Commn. on Status of Women, 1976-80; asst. dir. project adminstrn./devel. Great Plains Nat. Instructional TV Libr. U. Nebr., Lincoln, 1980-97, 2002—05; sr. v.p. for edn. Lancit Media Ent., Ltd. a Junior Net Co., NY, 1998—2001; exec. prodr. Nebr. ETV Network/6PN, 1980—98, 2001—05; pres. Twila Liggett Media, Inc., 2005—. Cons. U.S. Dept. Edn., 1981; cons. Far West Regional Lab. Nebr. Edn. TV Network, San Francisco, 1978—79; panelist, presenter in field; Blue Ribbon panelist NATAS, 1991—2005; final judge Nat. Cable Ace Awards, 1991—92, 1997. Author: Reading Rainbow's Guide to Children's Books: The 101 Best Titles, 1994, rev. edit., 1996. Bd. dirs. Planned Parenthood, Lincoln, 1979-81. Recipient Grand award, N.Y., 1993, Gold medal, Internat. Film and TV Festival, 1996, 1999, World Gold medal, N.Y. Internat. Film and TV, 1995, Golden Eagle award, Coun. on Non-theatrical Events, 1995, Image award, NAACP, 1994, 1996, 1999, 2002, 24 Nat. Emmy awards, 9 for Outstanding Children's Series, 1985—2003. Mem. NATAS, Internat. Reading Assn. (panelist, presenter, Spl. award Contbns. Worldwide Literacy 1992), Am. Women in Film and TV, Phi Delta Kappa. Presbyterian. Home: 37 Crescent Pl Matawan NJ 07747 Office Phone: 732-583-7481. Business E-Mail: rrainbow1@aol.com.

LIGGINS, ALFRED C., III, broadcasting company executive; b. Omaha, 1965; MBA, Wharton Sch. Bus. U. Penn, 1995. Pres., treas., CEO Radio One Inc., Lanham, Md., 1996—; chmn. TV One LLC, 2003—. Bd. dirs. iBiquity; mem., adv. com. on diversity for comm. in the digital age FCC. Office: Radio One Inc 8th Floor 5900 Princess Garden Pkwy Fl 8 Lanham Seabrook MD 20706-2925

LIGGIO, CARL DONALD, lawyer; b. N.Y.C., Sept. 5, 1943; AB, Georgetown U., 1963; JD, NYU, 1967. Bar: N.Y. 1967, D.C. 1967, Wis. 1983, Ill. 1998. Cons. Arent, Fox, Kintner, Plotkin & Kahn, Washington, 1968-69; assoc. White & Case, N.Y.C., 1969-72; gen. counsel Arthur Young & Co., N.Y.C., 1972-89, Ernst & Young, N.Y.C., 1989-94; ptnr. Dickinson, Wright, Moon, Van Dusen & Freeman, Chgo., 1995-97, of counsel, 1998-99, McCullough, Campbell & Lane, 1999—; CFO, gen. counsel, dir. Tempico, Inc., 1998—, Ethics Point, Inc., 2002—. Bd. dirs. Fios, Inc.; mem. Brookings Civil Justice Reform Task Force, 1988—. Trustee Fordham Prep. Sch., 1988-96. Mem. ABA, Am. Corp. Counsel Assn. (chmn. bd. dirs. 1984, mem. exec. com. 1982-95), Am. Judicature Soc. (bd. dirs. 1988-92), Coll. Law Mgmt., N.Y. State Bar Assn., Wis. Bar Assn., Ill. Bar Assn., D.C. Bar Assn. Home: 233 E Walton St Chicago IL 60611-1510 Office: 215 N Michigan Ave Chicago IL 60601

LIGGIO, JEAN VINCENZA, adult education educator, artist; b. NYC, Nov. 5, 1927; d. Vincenzo and Bernada (Terrusa) Verro; m. John Liggio, June 6, 1948; children: Jean Constance, Joan Bernadette. Student, N.Y. Inst. Photography, 1965, Elizabeth Seton Coll., 1984, Parsons Sch. of Design, 1985. Hairdresser Beauty Shoppe, N.Y.C., 1947-65; instr. watercolor N.Y. Dept. Pks., Recreation and Conservation, Yonkers, 1985-89, Bronxville (N.Y.) Adult Sch., 1989—. Substitute tchr. cosmetology Yonkers Bd. Edn., 1988-89; tchr. watercolor painting J.V.L. Watercolor Workshop of Fine Arts, Jakes Art Ctr., Mt. Vernon, N.Y. Paintings pub. by Donald Art Co., C.R. Gibson Greeting Card Co., Enesco Corp., 1996; paintings for Avon Calendar, Avon Cosmetics Co., 1994, 96, Avon-Can. Publ., 1996-97; greeting cards published by C.R. Gibson Co. Publ., 1996-1997, boxed notecards by C.R. Gibson; painting on cover of C.R. Gibson Jour., 2000, C.R. Gibson Inspirational Jour.; pub. Friends Jour. Mag., Phila.; exhibitor numerous shows, 1981— (more than 244 awards). Mem.: Art Soc. Old Greenwich, Hudson Valley Art Assn., New Rochelle Art Assn., Scarsdale Art Assn. (publicity chmn. 1984—89), Mt. Vernon Art Assn. (pres. membership com. 1983—). Avocation: antiques. Home and Office: 166 Helena Ave Yonkers NY 10710-2524 Office Phone: 914-779-3882.

LIGGITT, LONNIE ROBERT, music educator, researcher; b. Osceola, Iowa, Sept. 25, 1940; s. Robert and Lois Liggitt; m. Cindy Baldwin, Mar. 21, 1982; children: Eric, Todd, Suzanne Cunningham. MusB, Drake U., 1964; MusM, Syracuse U., 1967. Mem. faculty Syracuse (NY) U.; assoc. condr. Pitts. Civic Light Opera, 1967—69; v.p. Dean Witter, Dallas, 1980—90; mem. faculty Tulsa C.C., 1992—; pres., founder Greenwood Found., Tulsa, 1992—97; owner Greenwood Studios, Tulsa, 1992—; pres. Horace Hopper's Musical Adventures, Inc., Tulsa, 1999—. Pres., founder Tulsa Best and Brightest, 2002—; devel. dir. Tulsa Philharm., 1990—92. Composer: (early education CD) Baby Dance (10 Best Audio/Visual Inst. for Childhood Resources, 2001), (BBC TV film) The Three Princes, (BBC radio drama score) Aubrey Beardsley, (orchestral setting) Amazing Grace, (film score) Dancing with Janet Reno, DSM Publisher, (london weekend television score) Theme IV; conductor (American premier, choral-percussion) Missa Brevis, Antol Dorati, (opera (N.Y.C.) premier) Masque of Angels; author: (children's early education course) Horace Hopper's Musical Adventures (Parent's Choice Silver award, 2000). Music dir. St. Aiden Episcopal Ch., Tulsa, 1996—2003. Grantee, Okla. State Arts Coun., 1993—95; Early Edn. Devel. Rsch. grantee, Barthelmus Found., 2001—02, Rsch., Early Edn. grantee, Kravis Found., 2001, Rsch. grantee for autism and devel. disabilities in Oklahoma City Pub. Schs., Kirkpatrick Found., 2003—04, Tchg. fellow, Syracuse U., 1966—67. Libertarian. Episcopalian. Achievements include research in early education math and language development; first to Horace Hopper Musical Adventures, language math development for autistic and developmentally delayed children. Avocation: jazz piano. Home: 28 Westwind Sand Springs OK 74106 Office: Greenwood Studios 4817 C South Peoria Tulsa OK 74105 Office Phone: 918-748-8898. Personal E-mail: lliggitt@aol.com. E-mail: greenwoodstudios@tulsacoxmail.com.

LIGHT, ALFRED ROBERT, law educator; b. Dec. 14, 1949; s. Alfred M. Jr. and Margaret Francis (Asbury) L; m. Mollie Sue Hall, May 28, 1977; children: Joseph Robert, Gregory Andrew. Student, Ga. Inst. Tech., 1967-69; BA with highest honors, Johns Hopkins U., 1971; PhD, U. N.C., 1976; JD cum laude, Harvard U., 1981. Bar: D.C. 1981, Va. 1982. Tax clk. IRS, 1967; lab technician Custom Farm Svcs. Soils Testing Lab, 1968; warehouse asst. State of Ga. Mines, Mining and Geology, 1970; clk.-typist systems mgmt. divsn., def. contract adminstrv. Def. Supply Agy., Atlanta, 1971; rsch. and teaching asst. dept. polit. sci. U. N.C., Chapel Hill, 1971-74; rsch. asst. Inst. Rsch. in Social Sci., 1975-77; program analyst Office of Sec. Def., 1974; asst. prf. polit. sci., rsch. scientist Ctr. Energy Rsch. Tex. Tech. U., Lubbock, 1977-78; rsch. asst. grad. sch. edn. Harvard U., 1978-79; assoc. Butler, Binion, Rice, Cook & Knapp, Houston, 1980, Bracewell & Patterson, Washington, 1980; Hunton & Williams, Richmond, Va., 1981-89; of counsel, 1989-93, 95-96; assoc. prof. St. Thomas U. Sch. Law, Miami, Fla., 1989-93, prof., 1993—. Interim dean, 1993-94; bd. advisors Toxics Law reporter, Bur.

Nat. Affairs, Washington, 1987—. Contbr. articles to profl. jours. Charter mem. West Broward Cmty. Ch. Capt. USAR, 1971-85. Grantee NSF, Inst. Edn. Rsch., U. Mass., Ctr. Energy Rsch., Tex. Tech. U., 1977-78, U.S. EPA, 2003—; recipient William Anderson award Am. Polit. Sci. Assn., 1977. Mem. ABA (vice-chmn.) tort and ins. practice sect. 1988-97, nat. res. and environ. sect. 1993-95, chmn. 1995-2000), Fed. Bar. Assn., Va. Bar Assn., Richmond Bar Assn., Phi Beta Kappa, Phi Eta Sigma. Democrat. Home: 1042 Woodfall Ct Weston FL 33326-2832 Office: St Thomas U Sch Law 16401 NW 37th Ave Miami Gardens FL 33054-6459 E-mail: alight@stu.edu.

LIGHT, ARTHUR HEATH, bishop; s. Alexander Heath and Mary Watkins (Nelson) L.; m. Sarah Ann Jones, June 12, 1953; children: William Alexander, Philip Nelson, John Page, Sarah Heath. BA, Hampden-Sydney Coll., 1951, DD, 1987; MDiv, Va. Theol. Sem., 1954, DD, 1979, St. Paul's Coll., 1979. Ordained priest Episcopal Ch., 1955. Rector West Mecklenburg Cure, Boydton, Va., 1954-58, Christ Ch., Elizabeth City, N.C., 1958-63, St. Marys Ch., Kinston, N.C., 1963-67, Christ and St. Luke's Ch., Norfolk, Va., 1967-79; bishop Diocese of Southwestern Va., Roanoke, 1979-96; pres. Province III Episcopal Ch., 1984-93. Mem. adv. coun. to presiding bishop, 1985-93; nominating com. 25th presiding bishop of the Episcopal Ch., 1994-97. Author: God, The Gift, The Giver, 1984. Bd. dirs. United Cmty. Fund, 1969-79, Norfolk Seamen's Friends Soc., 1969-79, Tidewater Assembly on Family Life, 1970-79, Friends of Juvenile Ct., 1975-79, Va. Inst. Pastoral Care, 1971-72; bd. dirs., exec. com. Va. Coun. Chs., 1979-97; bd. dirs. Roanoke Valley Coun. Cmty. Svcs., 1980-83, Virginians Organized for Informed Cmty. Effort, 1981-86; bd. dirs. Appalachian People's Svc. Orgn., 1981-91, pres., 1981-85, v.p., 1989-91; bio-med. ethics com. Ea. Va. Med. Sch., 1973-79, Lewis Gale Hosp., Salem, 1988-2003, Cmty. Hosp. Roanoke Valley, 1990-94; trustee Va. Episc. Sch., Lynchburg, 1979-96, Episc. H.S., Alexandria, 1979-96, Boys' Home, Covington, 1979-96, Stuart Hall Sch., Staunton, 1979-96, St. Paul's Coll., Lawrenceville, 1979-88; chmn. com. on continuing edn. Va. Theol. Sem., Alexandria, 1985-96, v.p. bd. trustees, 1987-96; bd. dirs., co-chmn. rural residency program Appalachian Ministries Ednl. Resource Ctr., Berea, Ky., 1985-87; mem. coord. cabinet Va. Coun. Churches, 1988-96, chmn. com. on church and soc., 1989-92; mem. Am. com. Kyosato Ednl. Experiment Project, 1990—2004, v.p., 1991—2004; mem. Gen. Conv. Standing Com. on World Mission, 1988-94, chmn., 1991-94; trustee Kanuga Conf. Ctr., 1991-95; bd. dirs. Conflict Resolution Ctr., 1996-98; cmty. rels. task force City of Roanoke, 1995—; bd. dirs. Habitat for Humanity, 1997-2000, Roanoke Valley Pastoral Counseling Ctr., 1998—2003, pres., 1999-2001; bd. dirs. Nat. Conf. for Cmty. and Justice, 2001—, Regional End of Life Partnership Care Com. Named One of Outstanding Men of Yr., Jaycees, 1961, 63; fellow St. George's Coll., Jerusalem, 1978, 89, fellow in biomed. ethics U. Va., 1989; recipient humanitarian award Nat. Conf. Cmty. and Justice, 2002; Va. State Srs. Tennis Doubles champion, 2001, 04. Democrat. Episcopalian.

LIGHT, BETTY JENSEN PRITCHETT, retired dean; b. Omaha, Sept. 14, 1924; d. Lars Peter and Ruth (Norby) Jensen; m. Morgan S. Pritchett, June 27, 1944 (dec. 1982); children: Randall Wayne, Robin Kay Pritchett Church, Royce Marie Pritchett Bishop; m. Kenneth F. Light, Nov. 23, 1985 (dec. 2003). BS, Portland State U., 1965; MBA, U. Oreg., 1966; Ed.D., Oreg. State U., 1973. Buyer Rodgers Stores, Inc., Portland, Oreg., 1947-62; chmn. bus. div. Mt. Hood Community Coll., Gresham, Oreg., 1966-70, dir. evening coll., 1970-71, assoc. dean instn., 1972-77, dean humanities and behavioral scis., 1977-79, dean devel. and spl. programs, 1979-83, dean communication arts, humanities and social scis., 1983-86. State com. for articulation between cmty. colls. and higher edn., 1976-78; mem. Gov.'s Coun. on Career and Vocat. Edn., 1977-86; owner Effective Real Estate Mgmt., 1982-2002. Author: Values and Perceptions of Community College Professional Staff in Oregon, 1973; contbg. author: The Pritchett Study in Retailing, An Economic View, 1969. Mem. Gresham City Council, 1983-86. Mem.: Oreg. Vocat. Assn., Am. Vocat. Assn., Am. Assn. Higher Edn., Oreg. Bus. Edn. Assn., Danish Brotherhood, N.W. Danish Found., Danish Heritage Soc. Home: 1635 NE Country Club Ave Gresham OR 97030-4432

LIGHT, CHRISTOPHER UPJOHN, freelance/self-employed writer, photographer; b. Kalamazoo, Jan. 4, 1937; s. Richard and Rachel Mary (Upjohn) L.; m. Lilykate Victoria Wenner, June 22, 1963 (div. 1986); children: Victoria Mary, Christopher Upjohn Jr.; m. Margo Ruth Bosker, Jan. 2, 1994. AB, Carleton Coll., 1958; MS, Columbia U., 1962; MBA, We. Mich. U., 1967; PhD, Washington U., St. Louis, 1971. Editor, pub. Kalamazoo Mag., 1963-66; pres. Mich. Outdoor Pub. Co., Kalamazoo, 1965-68; product planner Upjohn Co., Kalamazoo, 1967-68; asst. prof. U. Utah, Salt Lake City, 1971-72; assoc. prof., chmn. fin. dept. Roosevelt U., Chgo., 1975-78; vis. prof. fin. No. Ill. U., 1978-79; freelance writer, computer musician, 1979—. Editor: Charles Dickens' Village Coquettes, 1992; mgr. spl. projects Sarasota Music Archive, 1992-96. Contbr. articles to profl. and microcomputer jours.; composer: Ten Polyrhytmic Etudes, 1991, Piano Sonata #1, 1992, (albums) Apple Compote, One-Man Band, 1985, Ultimate Music Box, Vol. I, 1988, Ultimate Music Box, Vol. II, 1993; Aspects of Flowers, Ann Arbor, Mich., 1996, East Lansing, Mich., 1997, Kalamazoo, 1997, Aspects of Flowers II, Ann Arbor, 1997, Aspects of Flowers III, Fontana Festival, 1998, Portraits of Engines, Kalamazoo, 1998, Aspects of Flowers: Selections, Ann Arbor, 1999, Pathways, Kalamazoo, 1999, Aspects of Flowers IV, 2001, Landscapes, 2001. Trustee Harold and Grace Upjohn Found., 1965-85, 94-2002, pres., 1997-2002; trustee, bd. dirs. Kalamazoo Symphony Orch. Assn., 1990-99; trustee Sarasota Music Archive, 1990-95, Kalamazoo Coll., 1991-93; bd. dirs. Am. Symphony Orch. League, 1992-2000, sec., 1996-99; bd. dirs. Sarasota Concert Assn., 1998—, Fontana Chamber Arts, 2002—. Recipient ann. press award Mich. Welfare League, 1967. Mem. ASCAP, NARAS (voting com.), Fin. Mgmt. Assn., Soc. Profl. Journalists, Univ. Club Chgo., Gull Lake Country Club, Columbia U. Club. N.Y. Office: 151 S Rose St Ste 820 Kalamazoo MI 49007-4715

LIGHT, JANE ELLEN, librarian; b. Crosby, ND, May 4, 1948; d. Ralph W. and Ethel S. (Cady) Johnson; children: Jessica, David. BA, Calif. State U., Sacramento, 1973; MLS, U. Calif., Berkeley, 1974. Project mgr. Peninsula Libr. Sys., San Mateo, Calif., 1974-78, sys. dir., 1979-83; program mgr. Coop. Libr. Authority, San Jose, Calif., 1978-79; asst. libr. dir. Redwood City (Calif.) Pub. Libr., 1983-84, libr. dir., 1984-97; city libr. San Jose Pub. Libr., 1997—. Del. On-line Computer Libr. Ctr. User's Coun., 1993—2000; chair exec. bd. Urban Librs. Coun., 2005—. Bd. dirs. Child Care Coordinating Coun., San Mateo, 1988-97, pres. 1992-93; bd. dirs. YMCA of Santa Clara Valley, 2001—. Mem. ALA, Calif. Libr. Assn., Pub. Libr. Assn., Rotary Club San Jose. Office: San Jose Pub Libr Sys 150 E San Fernando San Jose CA 95112 Office Phone: 408-808-2150. Business E-Mail: jane.light@sjlibrary.org.

LIGHT, JO KNIGHT, stockbroker; b. DeQueen, Ark., Mar. 15, 1936; d. Donald R. and Auda (Waltrip) Knight; m. Jerry T. Light, June 21, 1958 (dec. 1979); m. Victor E. Menefee Jr., Nov. 18, 1981; 1 child, Jerry T. Jr. BA cum laude, U. Ark., 1958. CFP. Travel cons. Comml. Nat. Bank, Little Rock, 1971-76; dist. mgr. Am. Express Co., N.Y.C., 1976-82; fin. advisor and retirement planning specialist Morgan Stanley, N.Y.C., 1982—, registered investment advisor, 1996—, sr. v.p. investments, 1999—. Mem. Jr. League of Little Rock Sustainers; vol. Happiness Singers. Mem. Fin. Planning Assn., Internat. Assn. Fin. Planners (bd. dirs. 1992-98, pres. bd. 1995-96), U. Ark. Alumni Assn. (bd. dirs. 1974-77), Morgan Stanley Pres.'s Club, Morgan Stanley Dir.'s Club, Phi Beta Kappa, Kappa Kappa Gamma. Avocations: music, tennis, sailing, skiing. Office: Morgan Stanley 425 W Capitol Ave Ste 200 Little Rock AR 72201-3440 E-mail: jo.light@morganstanley.com.

LIGHT, JOHN RICHARD, sculptor; b. Kalamazoo, Oct. 11, 1940; s. Richard Light and Rachel Mary (Upjohn) L.; m. Frances Mary Hesser, June 21, 1969; 1 child, Aimee Upjohn. BA, Yale U., 1962. Asst. advt. mgr. Verson Allsteel Press Co., Chgo., 1967-68; pub. relations copywriter Barton Brands, Chgo., 1970; investment cons. Chgo., 1972-86; sculptor, 1986—. Editor: Impact Machining, 1968; exhbns. include Skokie (Ill.) Fine Arts Commn., 1991, Iron Feather Gallery, Sedona, Ariz., 1993, Auburn (Calif.) Art Ctr., 1994, Art Guild, Farmington, Conn., 1995, Art at Parkview Hills, Kalamazoo, 2000; represented in permanent collections Goulandris Mus. Cycladic Art, Athens, Greece, Harvard Med. Sch., Cambridge, Mass., Nat. Gallery Art, Washington, Nat. Mus. Ireland, Dublin, Pushkin Mus. Art, Moscow, U. Chgo., Yale U., New Haven. Bd. dirs. Juvenile Protective Assn., Chgo., 1975—, Kalamazoo Child Guidance Clinic, 1969—, Lakeside Boys and Girls Home, 1979—. Recipient Distinguished Service award Publicity Club Chgo., 1972. Mem. Internat. Sculpture Ctr., Nat. Sculpture Soc., Publicity Club (Chgo.) (dir. 1975-77, mgr. club pubs. 1972-73, chmn. seminar com. 1976-77), Kiwanis (Kalamazoo and Chgo.). Roman Catholic. Home: 4020 Old Field Trl Kalamazoo MI 49008-3339

LIGHT, MARGARET JEAN, music educator; b. Denver, Mar. 23, 1951; d. Donald Montford Eastman McLarty and Jean Elspeth (Gullion) Williams; m. James McAvoy Light. MusB in Edn., U. No. Colo., 1972. Cert. music tchr., Okla., Nev., Tex., Tenn. Music specialsit Arlington Heights (Ill.) Pub. Schs., 1973-75; sbustitute tchr. Seguin (Tex.) Pub. Schs., 1976-79; features writer, columnist, editor Seguin Gazette & Gazette-Enterprise, 1979-80; layout artist, cutomer svc. Pip Printing, Tulsa, 1981-86; purchasing and customer rep. Modern Printing, Tulsa, 1987-89; music scpecialsit Undercroft Montesori Sch., Tulsa, 1989-91; asst. band dir. music Mounds (OKla.) Pub. Schs., 1991-92; music specialsit, coord. Holland Hall Sch., Tulsa, 1992-99; music specialist Clark County Schs., Las Vegas, Nev., 1999—. Workshop presenter in field. Mem. steering com. Tulsa Summer Arts, 1993-99. Mem. ASCD, Am. Orff/Schulwerk Assn., Music Educators Nat. Conf., Tau Beta Sigma. Republican. Mem. Assembly of God Ch. Avocations: sewing, writing. Office: CC Ronnow Elem Sch 1100 Lena Las Vegas NV 89101

LIGHT, RICHARD JAY, statistician, educator; b. N.Y.C., Sept. 10, 1942; s. Solomon Julius and Muriel (Szwarcman) L.; m. Patricia Kahn, June 27, 1965; children: Jennifer Susan, Sarah Elizabeth. BS, U. Pa., 1962, AM, 1964; PhD, Harvard U., 1969; LLD (hon.), U. Winnipeg, Can., 1991. Mem. faculty Harvard U., Cambridge, Mass., 1969—, prof. stats., 1975—. Dir. faculty studies John F. Kennedy Inst. Politics, 1971-76; mem. Bd. on Testing and Assessment, 2000—; mem. panel children's and family policy Nat. Acad. Scis., 1977—, chmn. panel on evaluation, 1982; panel program evaluation Social Sci. Research Council, 1977—; bd. dirs Huron Inst., Cambridge, Mass., 1971—; cons. World Bank, 1975—; dir. Harvard Assessment Seminar, Cambridge, 1986—; bd. testing and assessment Nat. Rsch. Coun. Co-author: Data for Decisions, 1982, Summing Up, 1984, By Design, 1990, Meta-analysis for Explanation, 1992; editor: Learning from Experience, 1982, Evaluation Studies Rev., 1983; author: Making the Most of College, 2001. Trustee Buckingham, Browne and Nichols Sch., Cambridge, 1977—, Wellesley Coll., 1998—; mem. policy adv. group Mass. Office of Children, 1977—; bd. dirs. Fund for Improvement Post-Secondary Edn., 1992-95. N.Y. State Advanced Coll. Teaching fellow, 1965; vis. fellow Ctr. Analysis Health Practices, Harvard U. Sch. Pub. Health, 1977-78; Sr. Research award Spencer Found., Chgo., 1978-84; research fellow Ford Found., N.Y.C., 1981; recipient Paul Lazarsfeld award for contbns. to sci., 1992. Fellow Am. Acad. Arts and Scis.; mem. Am. Assn. Higher Edn. Assn., Am. Ednl. Rsch. Assn., Am. Sociol. Assn., Am. Evaluation Assn. (pres. 1986), Coun. Applied Social Rsch., Evaluation Rsch. Soc. (Paul Lazarsfeld award 1991), Am. Assn. for Higher Edn. (nat. bd.), Fund for Improvement Postsecondary Edn. (nat. bd.). Home: 31 Dunbarton Rd Belmont MA 02478-2458 Office: John F Kennedy Sch Govt Harvard U Cambridge MA 02138 Office Phone: 617-495-1183. Business E-Mail: richard_light@harvard.edu.

LIGHT, RICHARD WAYNE, medical educator; b. Steamboat Springs, Colo., Feb. 9, 1942; s. Roland Wayne and Helen Marie (Long) L.; m. Judith Merino, Jan. 30, 1997; children: Mark, Sandra. BS in Engring. Applied Math., U. Colo., 1964; MD, Johns Hopkins U. Med. Sch., 1968; postgrad., Johns Hopkins Hosp. Intern Osler Svc., 1968-69; resident Johns Hopkins Hosp., Balt., 1969-70; asst. prof. medicine La. State U., Shreveport, 1974-77, assoc. prof. medicine, 1977-78, U. Calif., Irvine, 1978-84, prof. medicine, 1984-97, asst. dean rsch., 1985-93; attending pulmonologist La. State U. Med. Ctr., Shreveport, 1974-78; chief pulmonary diseases VA Med. Ctr., Long Beach, Calif., 1978-86, acting chief staff rsch. and devel., 1984-85, assoc. chief staff, 1985-93, chief pulmonary exercise lab., 1983-97; prof. medicine Vanderbilt U., Nashville, 1997—; dir. pulmonary disease program St. Thomas Hosp., Nashville, 1997—. Contbr. articles to profl. jours. Maj. U.S. Army, 1972-94. Fellow Johns Hopkins U. Sch. Medicine, 1970-71, 71-72; Boettcher scholar U. Colo., 1960-64; VA grantee, 1978-80, 80-85, 85-88, 83-88, 87-89, 89-92, 92-95. Fellow Am. Coll. Chest Physicians (program sel. com. 1981, 82, 83, 84); mem. Am. Thoracic Soc. (program sel. com. 1976, 78, 81, 82, 85, 87, 89, rep. counselor clin. problems assembly 1980-81, sec.-treas. clin. problems assembly 1981-82, liaison 1985-88), Am. Soc. Clin. Rsch., So. Soc. Clin. Investigation. Avocations: tennis, travel, sailing, wine. Home: 9470 Chesapeake Dr Brentwood TN 37027-8704 Office: St Thomas Hosp 4220 Harding Pike Nashville TN 37205-2005 Office Phone: 615-222-3043. Personal E-mail: rlight98@yahoo.com.

LIGHT, TERRY RICHARD, orthopedic hand surgeon; b. Chgo., June 22, 1947; BA, Yale U., 1969; MD, Chgo. Med. Sch., 1973. Cert. Am. Bd. Orthopaedic Surgery 1979, ABOS added qualification 1989, 1999. Asst. prof. Yale U., New Haven, 1977-80, Loyola U., Maywood, Ill., 1980-82, assoc. prof., 1982-88, prof., 1988-90, Dr. William M. Scholl prof., chmn. orthop. surgery and rehab, 1991—. Attending surgeon Hines (Ill.) VA Hosp., 1980—, Shriner's Hosp., Chgo., 1981—, Foster McGaw Hosp., Maywood, 1981—; hand cons. Chgo. White Sox, 1986-2003; bus. mgr. Jour. Hand Surgery, 1995-99. Editor Am. Acad. Orthop. Surgeons Hand Surgery Update, 1999, 2d edit. V.p. Frank Lloyd Wright Home and Studio Found., Oak Park, Ill., 1985-88, pres., 1988-90; chmn. bd. Fairfield Pub. Gallery, Sturgeon Bay, Wis., 1998-99; bd. dirs. Loyola U. Health Sys., 1999—. Fellow: ACS, Am. Acad. Orthop. Surgeons; mem.: Am. Orthop. Assn. (2d v.p. 2004—05, 1st v.p. 2005—), Ill. Orthop. Soc. (v.p. 1995, pres.-elect 1996, pres. 1997), Twenty-First Century Orthop. Assn. (pres. 1979—), Acad. Orthopaedic Soc. (pres. 2001—02), Chgo. Soc. for Surgery of Hand (sec. 1985—87, pres.-elect 1987—88, pres. 1988—89), Am. Assn. Hand Surgery (bd. dirs. 1989—91), Am. Soc. for Surgery of Hand (chair Jour. Hand Surgery com. 1995—99, treas. 1999—2002, v.p. 2002—03, pres. 2004—05), Alpha Omega Alpha. Avocation: collecting American arts and crafts and pottery. Office: Loyola U Med Ctr 2160 S 1st Ave Maywood IL 60153-3304 Personal E-mail: tlight1320@aol.com. Business E-Mail: tlight@lumc.edu.

LIGHT, THEODORE BLAINE, JR., chemical company executive; b. Dayton, Ohio, June 24, 1951; s. Theodore Blaine and Kathleen (Rhea) L.; m. Cynthia Ann Chester, Dec. 28, 1974; children: Theodore Blaine III, William Tyler. BBA, U. Cin., 1974, MBA, 1975, PhD, 1993. Various pos. DuBois Co., Cin., 1975—84, asst. v.p., 1984—87, v.p. corp. mktg., 1987—90; sr. v.p., 1990—91; dir. mktg. DuBois USA, divsn. Diversey Corp., Cin., 1991—, v.p., 1994—2001; program chair, Masters of Mktg. and Commerce Franklin U., Columbus, Ohio, 2001—. Mem. Beta Gamma Sigma. Office: Franklin U 201 S Grant Ave Frasch Hall Columbus OH 43215 Home: 874 City Park Ave Columbus OH 43206-2046

LIGHTBURN, ANITA LOUISE, dean, social work educator; b. San Diego, Jan. 2, 1946; d. Kenneth E. and Ann Lorraine (Rosepiler) Schimp; m. Kenneth Dale Lightburn, Aug. 25, 1973; children: Tiffany, Kara. BA, Wheaton Coll., 1968; MS, Columbia U., 1972, MEd, 1988, EdD, 1989. Social worker Mass. Divsn. Child Guardianship, Boston, 1968-70; supr. psychiat. social work McMahon Meml. Shelter, N.Y.C., 1972-73; lectr. Flinders U., Adelaide, Australia, 1973-85; asst., then assoc. prof. Columbia U., N.Y.C., 1989-94; dean, prof. Sch. Social Work Smith Coll., Northampton, Mass., 1994—. Vis. prof. U. Conn., West Hartford, 1985, Columbia U., N.Y.C., 1986-88; cons., clinician, therapist in field. Author chpts. to books; contbr. articles to profl. jours. Mem. NASW. Home: 22 Main St Hatfield MA 01038-9784 Office: 17 Hillcrest View Hartsdale NY 10530

LIGHTBURN, JEFFREY CALDWELL, corporate communications executive; b. Columbus, Ohio, June 17, 1947; s. Willis Caldwell and Nancy Ellen (Snyder) L.; m. Jeanne Kay McGraw, June 13, 1970; children: Nicole Ann, Benjamin Caldwell. BS, So. Ill. U., 1970. Editor base newspaper Fairchild AFB, USAF, Spokane, Wash., 1970-73; staff writer, reporter News Democrat, Belleville, Ill., 1973-76; editor, pub. rels. specialist Ralston Purina, St. Louis, 1976-78; sr. comm. specialist Frito-Lay, Inc., Dallas, 1978-81; mgr. comm. Curtis Mathes, Dallas, 1981-83; dir. internat. comm. Pizza Hut, Wichita, Kans., 1983-90; sr. dir. comm. Taco Bell, Irvine, Calif., 1990-99, Tricon Global Restaurants, Irvine, 1999—. Mem. bd. edn. Sch. Dist. 118, Belleville, 1976-78. Recipient Excellence award Pub. Rels. Soc. Am., 1996, 97. Mem. Soc. Profl. Journalists - Sigma Delta Chi, Internat. Assn. Bus. Communicators (local chapter officer 1976—, Gold Quill awards 1976, 78, 84, 98). Republican. Methodist. Office: Taco Bell Corp 17901 Von Karman Ave Irvine CA 92614-6221 Home: 61335 Steens Mountain Loop Bend OR 97702-2865 E-mail: jlightbu@tacobell.com.

LIGHTCAP-HEWES, ANGIE M., business educator; d. Mary E. and John W. Lightcap; m. James D. Hewes. BS, Del. State U.; M in Instrn., U. Del. Nat. bd. cert. Bus. edn. tchr. Poly. H.S., Woodside, Del., 1997—2002; bus. mgr. Flying Dragon TaeKwon-Do, Ltd., Smyrna, Del., 1997—; bus. edn. tchr. Smyrna H.S., 2002—. Grantee MBNA Am., 2003, 2004, 2005. Mem.: Bus. Professionals Am. (assoc.; asst. state advisor 2000—05, bd. dirs.). Office Phone: 320-653-8581.

LIGHTER, ERIC AARON, real estate and law enforcement software developer, consultant; b. Chico, Calif., Aug. 6, 1950; s. Bruce Clyde and Katherine Bernice (Stutsman) L.; m. Joan E. Prescott, Feb. 14, 1999. Grad., Realtors Inst., 1973; student, U. Hawaii. Salesman Fin. Security Life, Honolulu, 1970; founder, treas. 3d Eye Prodns., Honolulu, 1974-76; pres. Home Rent Hawaii, Honolulu, 1976, A Lighter Cons., Graphic and Media, Honolulu, 1977—; pres., CEO Lighter Properties Corp., Real Estate and Law Enforcement Software Developers, Honolulu, 1978—. Founder Quality Income Sys., Honolulu, 1983, Save Hawaii's Aloha Spirit Trustee's Assn., co-chair, 1992; CEO Credit Bur. Internat., Inc., 1984—; CEO, founder Constn. Coalition, Christian Tolerance Legal Reform Lobby, 1991—; pres. Wells Fargo Protective Alarm Svc. (White Collar Crime Investigation), 1992—; corp. owner, operator Waikiki Hotel; CEO Honolulu Inn and Volcano Inn, 1986, 96; investigative reporter The Am.'s Bull., Medford, 1992—; mem. Honolulu Realtor Pub. Rels. Com., 1983-84, Constnl. Rev. Forum, nat. dir.; CEO, Credit Bur. Internat., Inc., 1989—; innkeeper Volcano Inn, Hawaii, 1996—. Editor: Ke Alaka'i, 1984. Bd. dirs. Hawaii Alliance for Arts in Edn., 1984, Inst. Human Svcs., Honolulu, 1984; Hawaii Statue of Liberty Program mgr., 1986; pres. Royal Hawaiian Heritage, 1989—; investigator Western Iran-Contragate, 1987-98; founder Diamond Cross Ministries, 1985—; nat. media chmn. Gritz for U.S. Pres., 1992. Mem. Hawaii Assn. Realtors, Bldg. Industry Assn. Hawaii (Parade of Homes award of excellence 1983), Hawaii Jaycees (project initiator Silver Jubilee Project 1983, mgr. Outstanding Hawaii Jaycees program mgr., founding pres. Capital Dist. 182, King of King award 1982, 83), Nat. Assn. Bed and Breakfast, Swiss of Hawaii Club, Constn. Rangers Club (chief grand jury and investigations 1996—), Lions (Honolulu) (various offices including treas.). Avocation: playing gospel guitar. Home: Honolulu Inn 1045 Spencer St Honolulu HI 96822-3749 E-mail: lightere001@hawaii.rr.com.

LIGHTFOOT, DAVID WILLIAM, foundation administrator, linguistics educator; b. Looe, Eng., Feb. 10, 1945; s. William Richard and Peggy May (Stevens) L.; m. Sarah Elizabeth Hairs, Feb. 7, 1946 (div. 1980); children: Kirsten, Heidi; m. Sari Ruth Hornstein, Nov. 24, 1955; children: Eric, Alexander. BA with honors, U. London, 1966; MA, U. Mich., 1968, PhD, 1971. Asst. prof. McGill U., Montreal, Que., Can., 1970-75, assoc. prof., 1975-78; prof. U. Utrecht, The Netherlands, 1978-83, U. Md., College Park, 1983-2001; dean grad. sch. Georgetown U., 2001—05; asst. dir. Social, Behavioral and Econ. Scis. NSF, Arlington, Va., 2005—. Author: Natural Logic and Greek Moods, 1975, Principles of Diachronic Syntax, 1979, Explanation in Linguistics, 1981, The Language Lottery, 1982, How to Set Parameters, 1991, Verb Movement, 1994, The Development of Language, 1999, The Syntactic Effects of Morphological Change, 2002, The Language Organ, 2002, New Languages, 2005. Mem. Linguistic Soc. Am., Linguistic Assn. Gt. Britain. Home: 7208 Heatherhill Rd Bethesda MD 20817-4657 Office: NSF 4201 Wilson Blvd Arlington VA 22230*

LIGHTFOOT, EDWIN NIBLOCK, JR., retired chemical engineering educator; b. Milw., Sept. 25, 1925; married 1949, 5 children. BS, Cornell U., 1947, PhD in Chem. Engring., 1951; D in Tech. (hon.), Tech. U. Norway, 1985, Tech. U. Denmark, 2000. Asst prof., prof. biochem engr. U. Wis., Madison, 1953-80, prof. chem. engr., 1980-95, prof. emeritus, 1995—. Vis. prof. Tech. U. Norway, 1962, Stanford U., 1971, U. Canterbury, New Zealand, 1972. Author 14 books; contbr. articles to profl. jours. Recipient William H. Walker award Am. Inst. Chem. Engrs, 1975, Food, Pharm. and Bioeng award, 1979, Warren K. Lewis award, 1991. Mem. NAS, AAAS, Nat. Acad. Engr., Royal Norwegian Soc. Sci. & Letter, Am. Inst. Chem. Engr., Am. Chem. Soc. (E.V. Murphree award, 1994). Achievements include research on physical separation tech. mass transfer, biomedical engring. Office: U Wis 3639 Engineering Bldg 1415 Engineering Dr Madison WI 53706-1691

LIGHTFOOT, WILLIAM P., JR., lawyer; b. Jan. 3, 1950; m. Cynthiana Lightfoot; children: Ariana, B.J. BA, Howard U., 1972; JD, Wash. U., 1977. Bar: Pa. 1977, DC 1980, US Dist. Ct. Dist. Md., cert.: Nat. Bd. Trial Advocacy. Mng. ptnr. Koonz, McKenney, Johnson, DePaolis & Lightfoot, Washington. Lectr. in field; chairperson DC Cable TV Design Commn., 1983—84; mem.-at-large DC Coun., 1988—96; mem. ABA-ALI Restatement of Law, 1994—; diplomat Nat. Coll. Advocacy. Bd. dirs. Children's Advocacy Ctr.; mem. DC Jury Project, 1998—2000, DC Judicial Tenure and Disabilities Commn. Named Trial Lawyer Yr., Trial Lawyers Assn. Met. Wash. DC, 2003; named one of Am. Top Black Lawyers, Black Enterprise Mag., 2003; recipient Cmty. Svc. award, Leadership Wash., 2002. Mem.: Charlotte Rae Am. Inn Ct., Am. Law Inst., Trial Lawyers Assn. Met. Wash., Assn. Trial Lawyers Am., ABA, Bar Assn. DC, DC Bar. Office: Koonz McKenney Johnson DePaolis & Lightfoot 2020 K St NW Ste 500 Washington DC 20006 Office Phone: 202-659-5500. Business E-Mail: wlightfoot@koonz.com.

LIGHTFOOTE, WILLIAM EDWARD, neurologist; b. Tuskegee, Ala., Oct. 6, 1942; s. William Edward Lightfoote and Mary Cornelia Johnson; m. Marilyn Frances Madry, Oct. 23, 1971; 1 child, Lynne Jan-Maria. BA, Grinnell Coll., 1963; MD, Howard U., 1967. Diplomate Am. Bd. Psychiatry & Neurology. Intern Cleve. Clinic Hosp., 1967—68; resident VA Hosp., Washington, 1968—69, George Washington U., Washington, 1971—75. With USPHS, 1975—79. Fellow: ACP, Am. Acad. Neurology. Home and Office: 2106 Waverly Pkwy #3B Opelika AL 36801-4787 Office Phone: 334-745-6622. E-mail: woodbend@bellsouth.net.

LIGHTFORD, KIMBERLY A., state legislator; BA in Pub. Comm., Western Ill. U.; MPA, U. Ill., Springfield. Mem. ins., labor, appropriations, chair edn., vice-chair fin. instns. Ill. Senate, Springfield, 1998—. Elected chair Ill. Senate Black Caucus; former trustee Village of Maywood. Democrat. also: 1127 S Mannheim Rd Ste 114 Westchester IL 60154 Office Phone: 217-782-8505, 708-343-7444. Business E-Mail: lightford@senatedem.state.il.us.

LIGHTFORD, MELVIN, minister; b. Brockton, Mass., Dec. 14, 1954; BS, U. Mass., 1978. Evangelist Melvin Lightford Ministries, Inc., Brockton, Mass., 1999—; owner Vet. Home Outpatient VA Hosp. Vets. Author: The Core of Faith, The Called Vessel, Song Call, You're the Future, My Injustice, 2005, The Strategist, 2005. Vol. numerous church and civic orgns. Home: 11 Cherry St Brockton MA 02301 Office: Melvin Lightford Minisitries Inc PO Box 1516 Brockton MA 02303 Office Phone: 508-857-3915.

LIGHTHIZER, ROBERT E., lawyer; b. Ashtabula, Ohio, 1947; BA, Georgetown U., 1969, JD, 1973. Bar: DC 1973. Ptnr., practice leader internat. trade and transactions Skadden, Arps, Slate, Meagher & Flom, Washington, practice leader, legislative/lobbying. Chief of staff US Senate Com. Fin., 1981-83; dep. US Trade Rep. rank of amb.; treas. Republican Presdl. Campaign, 1996; spkr. on trade and tax issues, politics and other developments in Washington, DC; bd. dir. for several charitable and polit. groups. Contbr. articles to profl. publs. and jours. Mem. Internat. Bar Assn. Office: Skadden Arps Slate Meagher & Flom 1440 New York Ave NW Ste 600 Washington DC 20005 Office Fax: 202-661-8225. Business E-Mail: rlighthi@skadden.com.

LIGHTMAN, ALAN PAIGE, physics professor, writer; b. Memphis, Nov. 28, 1948; s. Richard Louis and Jeanne (Garretson) L.; m. Jean Greenblatt, Nov. 28, 1976; children: Elyse, Kara. AB, Princeton U., 1970; PhD in Physics, Calif. Inst. Tech., 1974; D of Letters (hon.), Bowdoin Coll., 2005. Postdoctoral fellow Cornell U., Ithaca, N.Y., 1974-76; asst. prof. Harvard U., Cambridge, Mass., 1976-79; staff scientist Smithsonian Astrophys. Obs., Cambridge, 1979-88; prof. sci. and writing MIT, Cambridge, 1988-95, John E. Burchard prof. humanities, 1995—2001, adj. prof. humanities, 2001—. Chair sci. panel NRC Astron. and Astrophys. Survey for 1990s. Author: Problem Book in Relativity and Gravitation, 1974, Radiative Processes in Astrophysics, 1976, Time Travel and Papa Joe's Pipe, 1984, A Modern Day Yankee in Connecticut Court, 1986, Origins: The Lives and Worlds of Modern Cosmologists, 1990, Ancient Light, 1991, Great Ideas in Physics, 1992, Time for the Stars, 1992, Einstein's Dreams, 1993, Good Benito, 1995, Dance for Two, 1996, The Diagnosis, 2000, Reunion, 2003, A Sense of the Mysterious: Science and the Human Spirit, 2005. Recipient Most Outstanding Book in Phys. Sci., Assn. Am. Pubs., 1990 (Origins); Runner up PEN New England/Boston Globe Book Award, 1993 (Einstein's Dreams); Lit. Light of Boston Pub. Libr., 1995; Gemant award Am. Inst. of Physics, 1996, Gyorgy Kepes prize in the arts, MIT, 1998; Finalist Nat. Book Award in Fiction, 2000 (The Diagnosis); Disting. Alumnus Award Calif. Inst. Tech., 2003. Fellow AAAS, Am. Acad. Arts and Scis., Am. Phys. Soc.; mem. Am. Astron. Soc. (chmn. high energy astrophysics divsn. 1991).

LIGHTMAN, HAROLD ALLEN, marketing executive; b. Gloucester, Mass., Oct. 23, 1925; s. Abraham and Gertrude (Chait) L.; m. Irma Shorell, Feb. 19, 1954; children: Timothy, Chip, Stacey. Student, Norwich U., 1943; student, Cambridge U., Eng., 1946; BBA, U. Miami, 1949; postgrad., Oxford (Eng.) U., 1996. Acct. exec. Grant Advt., Miami, Fla., 1948-50; advt. dir. Sears Roebuck & Co., Tampa, Fla., 1950-51; acct. exec. Robert Otto Internat., N.Y.C., 1952-53; acct. exec., field supr. Amos Parish & Co., N.Y.C., 1954-56; acct. exec. Dowd, Redfield & Johnstone, N.Y.C., 1957-59; chmn. bd. dirs. H. Allen Lightman Inc., N.Y.C., 1959—. Bd. dirs. Irma Shorell Inc., N.Y.C.; pres., bd. dirs. Ind. Cosmetic Mfg. and Distbrs. U.S.A., v.p. nat. legis. affairs, 1974—; exec. v.p. Alfin Fragrances, Inc., 1985-87; pres. I.S. Labs. Inc., 1987-2000. Columnist: Seen & Heard, 1965-83; producer: Cable TV program Seen & Heard, 1978-87. Sgt. U.S. Army, 1943-46, ETO. Decorated Purple Heart, Bronze Star, European-African-Mid. Ea. Campaign medal with 3 battle stars, Combat Inf. Badge; recipient Pub. Rels. Gold Key award, 1987, Wisdom award Wisdom Soc. for Advancement of Knowledge, Learning and Rsch. in Edn., 2001; eminent Wisdom fellow of Wisdom Hall of Fame, 2001. Fellow Winston Churchill Meml. Libr., Harry S. Truman Meml. Libr.; mem. Nat. Fedn. Ind. Bus. (del. 1979), Internat. Platform Assn., Alpha Delta Sigma (founder, 1st pres. 1947-48), Miami Jr. C. of C. (publicity, pub. rels. dir. 1948-50), DAV, Am. Legion (vice comdr. 1948-49), Vets. of the Battle of the Bulge, The Jockey Club, Nat. Assn. Cosmetic Entrepreneurs (pres. 1997-98), lifetime character mem. Nat. WWII Meml., Wash. D.C., Tribute to a Generation, 2004. Office: 75 E End Ave New York NY 10028-7909 Office Phone: 212-535-9471.

LIGHTNER, CANDY (CANDACE LYNNE LIGHTNER), non-profit management consultant, advocate; b. Pasadena, Calif., May 30, 1946; d. Dykes Charles and Kathryn Josephine Doddridge; children: Serena, Travis. D (hon.), St. Francis Coll., Pa., 1984, Kutztown (Pa.) U., 1987, Marymount U., N.Y., 1987. With various pvt. offices, 1964-70; real estate salesperson, 1972-80; govt. rels. cons. Washington, 1993-94; owner Candace Lightner & Assocs., Alexandria, Va. Spkr., condr. tng. sessions various orgns. Author: Giving Sorrow Words: How to Cope With Grief and Get On With Your Life, 1990; guest nat. talk shows including Good Morning America, Today, 60 Minutes, MacNeil-Lehrer, Phil Donahue, Nightline, Turning Point. Founder MADD, 1980, chief exec. officer, pres., chmn., 1980-85; mem. adv. bd. Mothers Against Sexual Abuse; bd. dirs. Air Crash Support Network; active Sacramento County Task Force on Drunk Driving, Presdl. Commn. on Drunk and Drugged Driving; bd. dirs. Nat. Commn. on Drunk Driving, 1984-86, Nat. Partnership for Drug Free Use, Nat. Hwy. Safety Adv. Com., Love is Feeding Everyone, 1988-89, others; judge Gleitsman Found.; bd. advisors Bhopal Justice Campaign. Recipient Jefferson award Am. Inst. Pub. Svc., Pres. Vol. Action award, Woman of Yr. award YWCA, Woman of Yr. award Women's Internat. Ctr., award for excellence Film Adv. Bd., Testimonial award Civitan Internat., 1984, Epilepsy Found award, 1984, Woman of Year award Mortar Bd. Soc., Baylor U., 1985, Anti-discriminationaward Am. Anti-descrimination Com., 1985, YWCA Woman of Year award, 1986, Commonwealth award U. Del., 1986, Black and Blue award Thomas Jefferson U. Hosp. Emergency Medicine Soc., Human Dignity award Kessler Inst. for Rehab., Woman of Distinction award Third Nat. Congress Coll. Women Student Leaders and Woman of Achievement, 1987, Disting. Leadership award World Congress of Victimology, 1987, Living Legacy award Women's Internat. Ctr., 1988, Friends of Children award Assn. Childhood Edn. Internat., 1988; Named to Good Housekeeping's Most Admired Woman's Poll, 1986; ranked in Top 25 of Am. most influential people World Almanac and Book of Facts, 1986, one of the original thinkers of the eighties, Life mag., 1990; selected by Johns Hopkins U. to participate in Anglo-Am. Successor Generation program, 1985; honored as one of Seven Who Succeeded, Time Mag., 1985; honored by Edquire mag. as mem. Am.'s New Leadership Class, 1985, others. Mem. Nat. Soc. Fund Raising Execs., Women in Arts, Nat. Bd. Realtors. Avocations: gardening, reading, swimming, travel. Office: 1216 Portner Rd Alexandria VA 22314-1317 E-mail: cd_light2003@yahoo.com.

LIGHTNER, GENE CLEEK, investment banker; b. Staunton, Va., Aug. 19, 1955; BSBA in Fin., Am. U., 1992. Internat. banking Nat. Bank Washington, 1981—90; internat. debt mgmt. cons. Dept. Agr., Washington, 1993—95; chief fgn. exch. trader, group v.p. Riggs Bank N.A., Washington, 1995—. Mem. Defender of Wildlife, North Potomac Citizens Assn. Mem.: Washington Assn. Money Mgrs. Avocations: bicycling, tennis, equestrian. Home: 13340 Bondy Way Darnestown MD 20878

LIGHTSTONE, RONALD, lawyer; b. NYC, Oct. 4, 1938; s. Charles and Pearl (Weisberg) L.; m. Nancy Lehrer, May 17, 1973; 1 child, Dana. AB, Columbia U., 1959; JD, NYU, 1962. Atty. CBS, N.Y.C., 1967-69; assoc. dir. bus. affairs CBS News, N.Y.C., 1969-70; atty. NBC, N.Y.C., 1970; assoc. gen. counsel Viacom Internat. Inc., N.Y.C., 1970-75, v.p., gen. counsel, sec., 1976-80; v.p. bus. affairs Viacom Entertainment Group, Viacom Internat., Inc., 1980-82, v.p. corp. affairs, 1982-84, sr. v.p., 1984-87; exec. v.p. Spelling Entertainment Inc., L.A., 1988-91, CEO, 1991-93; chmn. Multimedia Labs. Inc., 1994-97; CEO, pres. New Star Media Inc., 1997-99, vice chmn., 1999-2000. Lt. USN, 1962—66. Mem. ABA (chmn. TV, cable and radio com.), Assn. of Bar of City of N.Y., Fed. Comm. Bar Assn. Business E-Mail: ron@sagpond.com.

LIGHTY, MICHELLE MCCOWAN, secondary school educator; b. Wilmington, Del., Feb. 4, 1961; d. George Edward and Margaret Jane (Hazlett) McCowan; m. Todd Christopher Lighty; children: Trevor Abel, Hannah Kelsey, Aidan Elizabeth, Tessa Elyse. BA in Spanish, Pa. State U., 1982; teaching cert., SUNY, Brockport, 1985; MEd, Nazareth Coll., 1989. Cert. Spanish tchr., N.Y. Spanish tchr. Penfield H.S., NY, 1985—90, Altmar-Parish-Williamstown Mid. and High Sch., Parish, NY, 1990—99; tchr. Spanish Marist H.S., Chgo., 1999—2000, Peotone H.S., Ill., 2000—; adj. Joliet (Ill.) Jr. Coll., 2003—. Ch. sch. tchr. DeWitt Cmty. Ch., DeWitt, N.Y., 1990-1999. Mem. Am. Fed. of Tchrs., Ill. Coun. Tchrs. of Foreign Lang. Avocations: arts and crafts, reading, gardening. Home: 11410 Swinford Ln Mokena IL 60448-9243 Office Phone: 708-258-3236. Business E-Mail: mlighty@peotune.will.k12.il.us.

LIGOCKI, GORDON MICHAEL, artist, educator; b. Hammond, Ind., Sept. 7, 1943; s. Michael and Regina (Hlodnicki) L.; m. Rita K. Herdaliska, Jan. 25, 1968 (div. June 1980); 1 child, Ian Gabriel; m. Linda Lee Heinsen, Oct. 30, 1994. BFA, Ohio Wesleyan U., 1965; MA in Drawing, U. Iowa, 1967; MFA in Sculpture, U. Ill., 1968; postgrad., Gov.'s State U., 1987, 92. Writer Arts Ind., Indpls., 1987-91; writer, art critic Hammond (Ind.) Times, 1985-93; instr. life drawing Art Barn, Valparaiso, Ind., 1989—; assoc. prof. Purdue U., Hammond, 1992-97; gallery dir., adj. prof. Ind. U. N.W., Gary, 1992—2001; assoc. prof. Valparaiso U., 1990—2001; asst. prof. Ancilla Coll., 2003—. Panelist Ind. Arts Commn., Indpls., 1989; cons. on drawing Collegiate Press, Alta Loma, Calif., 1995; curator individual shows Midwest Mus. of Am. Art, Elkhart, Ind., 1991, No. Ind. Art Assn., Munster, Ind., Gary Comty. Mental Health, Hammond Pub. Libr. One-person shows include R.H. Love Gallery, Chgo., 1992, Herr Chambliss Gallery, Hot Springs, Ark., 1992; contbr. articles to newspapers and profl. publs. Named Friend of the Arts in Edn., Ind. Art Edn. Assn., 1991. Mem.: Internat. Soc. of Visual Sociology. Avocation: gardening. Home: 2142 N 125 E Winamac IN 46996-8520 Office: Tortuga Inn Bed & Breakfast 2142 N 125 E Winamac IN 46996-8520 Office Phone: 574-936-8898 x 256. E-mail: gordonligocki@ancilla.edu.

LIGOCKI, KATHLEEN A., auto parts company executive; BA, Ind. U., 1978; MBA, U. Penn., 1985; doctorate (hon.), Ind. U., 2002. Dir. bus. strategy Ford Motor Co., 1998—2000; pres., CEO Ford Mex., 2000—01; corp. v.p. Can., Mex. and N.Am. strategy Ford Motor Co., 2001—02; corp. officer, v.p. Ford Customer Svc. Divsn., 2002—03; dir. Tower Automotive, Inc., Haggerty, Mich., 2003—, pres., CEO, 2003—. Office: Tower Automotive Inc 27275 Haggerty Rd Novi MI 48377

LIGON, DUKE R., lawyer; b. May 16, 1941; BS, Westminister Coll., 1963; JD, U. Tex., 1969. Bar: Okla. 1969, Dist. of Columbia 1973, U.S. Supreme Ct. 1974, NY 2005. Ptnr. Bracewell & Patterson, Corcoran, Hardesty, Whyte, Hemphill & Ligon, Washington, DC; various positions US Dept of Interior, Dept. of Treas., Dept. of Energy; sr. v.p., mng. dir. for investment banking Bankers Trust Co., N.Y.C., 1985—95; ptnr. Mayer, Brown & Platt, N.Y.C., 1995—97; v.p., gen. counsel Devon Energy Corp., 1997—99, sr. v.p., gen. counsel, 1999—. Mem.: ABA, Phi Alpha Delta. Office: Devon Energy Corp 20 North Broadway Oklahoma City OK 73102-8260 Office Phone: 405-552-4604.

LIGON, WILLIAM AUSTIN, automotive executive; b. Trinidad, Colo., Jan. 27, 1951; s. William Hastings and Rosalie (Ferguson) L.; m. Samornmitr Lamsam; children: Aaron Ng, Nisha Ferguson, Nina Rujiraporn. BA with honors, Univ. Tex., 1973, MA, 1978; MBA, Yale Univ., 1980. Economist U. Tex. Med. Sch., San Antonio, 1976-78; sr. cons. Boston Cons. Group, London, 1980-82; pres. Liglam Devel. Ltd., Bangkok, 1983-84; dir. corp. planning Marriott Corp., Washington, 1984-86, v.p. mktg. Big Boy div., 1986-87, v.p., gen. mgr. Allie's Restaurant divsn., 1987-89; sr. v.p. hotel planning Marriott Hotels, 1989-90; sr. v.p., corp. planning Cir. City Stores, Inc., Richmond, Va., 1991—95, pres. CarMax subsidiary, 1995—2002; pres., CEO CarMax Inc., Glen Allen, Va., 2002—. Named one of Top 50 Corp. Execs. under 35, Bus. Week Mag., 1976. Mem. Yale Club (N.Y.C.), Royal Bangkok Sports Club, Deep Run Hunt Club (Richmond, Va.), Phi Beta Kappa. Clubs: Yale (N.Y.C.); Royal Bangkok Sports. Avocations: hiking, squash. Office: CarMax Inc 4900 Cox Rd Glen Allen VA 23060*

LIGON-BORDEN, BETTY LEE, academic administrator; b. Greensboro, NC, Apr. 13, 1945; d. John Ligon and Jo Anne Bertha Pittenger; m. John Robert Jones, Aug. 10, 1963 (div. Sept. 1990); children: Darrell, Douglas, Derrick, Julie Jones Gill; m. Gordon Trotter Borden, June 4, 1994; stepchildren: Justin, Matthew, Borden. BA (hons.) magna cum laude, Sam Houston State U., 1985; MA, Tex. A&M U., 1987; PhD, Rice U., 1993. Sr. adminstrv. asst. Baylor Coll. Medicine, Houston, 1991-92; sr. editor U. Tex. M.D. Anderson Cancer Ctr., Houston, 1992-95, U. Ark. for Med. Sci., Little Rock, 1995-96; acad. dir., adv. bd. dir. The Phoenix Acad., Houston, 1995—. Charter mem. N.W. Bible Fellowship, Spring, Tex., 1977; editl. cons. Word Rite Editl. Consulting, Houston, 1994—; mem. faculty Baylor Coll. Medicine, Houston, 1997—; adj. faculty U. St. Thomas, Houston, 1999-current, U. Houston Downtown, 1989-99; owner Tapestries, ETC, Houston. Editor (monthly newsletter) Palmer Meml. Episcopal Ch., 1998-2002; mng. editor Seminars in Pediat. Infectious Diseases.guest editor, 2003; guest editor Jour. Neuro-Oncology, 1994, 95; contbr. articles to profl. jour. Discussion leader Bible Study Fellowship, Conroe, Tex., 1978-83; tchg. leader Precept Upon Precept, Houston, 1999-2001; lic. lay chalice bearer/reader Episcopal Ch. Merit scholar Inst. in Brit. and Irish Studies, Dublin, Ireland, 1990. Mem. MLA, Soc. for Tech. Comm., Am. Med. Writers Assn., Rice Alumni Assn. Episcopalian. Avocations: interior decorating, home renovation, theology, James Joyce research, needlepoint, James Joyce Studies. Office: Baylor Coll Medicine One Baylor Plaza TCH A150 Houston TX 77030

LIGORANO, MICHAEL KENNETH, lawyer; b. Morristown, N.J., July 24, 1954; s. Michael Thomas and Virginia J. Ligorano; m. Debra Ann Baumann, Aug. 12, 1978. BA cum laude, Rutgers U., Newark, 1975; JD, Western New Eng. Law Sch., Springfield, Mass., 1978. Bar: N.J. 1978, U.S. Dist. Ct. N.J. 1978, Fla. 1980, U.S. Ct. Appeals (3d cir.) 1980, U.S. Tax Ct. 1980, U.S. Supreme Ct. 1985, N.Y. 1990; lic. real estate sales N.J. Assoc. Charles M. Lee, Washington, N.J., 1978-79, Hogan Folk Mahon & Simms, Flemington, Somerville, N.J., 1979-82, ptnr., 1982-83, Mahon Moeller & Ligorano, Flemington, 1983-84, Schaff Motiuk et al, Flemington, Trenton, 1984-87, Ligorano & Sozansky P.C., Flemington, 1987-98, Archer & Greiner, P.C., Flemington, Princeton, 1998—2001, Norms, McLaughlin & Marcus, Somerville, 2001—. Atty. Mine Hill Twp. Bd. Adjustment, 1978-88; asst. Hunterdon County counsel, 1979-82; legal counsel Hunterdon County Bd. Recreation Commrs., 1980-2000; atty. Alexandria Twp. Bd. Adjustment, 1983-84; spl. counsel Solid Waste, Hunterdon County, 1984; atty. Readington Twp. Planning Bd., 1985-91, Readington Twp., 1991-96, Clinton Twp., 1996, Clinton Twp. Planning Bd., 1997-99, Glen Gardner Bd. Edn., 1996-98; spl. title counsel High Bridge Bd. Edn., 1996; mem. Dist. XIII Ethics Com., 1987-91, chair, 1990-91; mem. Dist. XIII Fee Arbitration Com., 1991-2000; mem. N.J. Supreme Ct. Complementary Disput Resolution Project, 1995-98; instr. N.J. Inst. Continuing Legal Edn., 1995-97; adv. bd. Summit Bank, 1990-92, First Cmty. Bank, 1992-94; gen. counsel The Blue Army, U.S.A., World Apostolate of Fatima, 1999—. Environ. commr. Denville Twp., 1973-75; legis. aide N.J. Assembly, 1974-75; mem. N.J. Natural Areas Coun., 1983-84; mem. Glen Gardner Bd. Health, 1993-95; bd. dirs. Hunterdon chpt. ARC, 1982-84, Glen Gardner Youth Ctr., 1988-90; mem. Hunterdon County Rep. Com., 1983-97; mem. Leukemia Soc. of Am. Team in Tng. Alaska Marathon, 1997, San Diego Marathon, 1999; adv. bd. ARC, 1994—. Recipient Vol. of Yr. award, ARC of NJ, 2004. Mem. N.J. State Bar Assn. (gen. coun. 1993-94, sects. on land use, real property, probate and trust, dispute resolution), N.Y. State Bar Assn. (sect. on real property, probate and trust), The Fla. Bar (sect. on land use, real property, probate and trust), Am. Immigration Lawyers Assn., Hunterdon County Bar Assn. (sec. 1991-92, v.p. 1992-93, pres. 1993-94, trustee 1994-97, equity settlement panel 1994—, chair com. on professionalism 1996—), Hunterdon C. of C. (bd. dirs. 1981-86), Hunterdon/Somerset Realtors Assn., Nat. Geneology Soc., Knights of Columbus. Avocations: genealogy, long distance running. Office: PO Box 1018 Somerville NJ 08876-1018 E-mail: mkligorano@nmmlaw.com.

LIGUORI, PETER, film company executive; Advt. exec. Ogilvy & Mather, Saatchi & Saatchi; v.p. consumer mktg. HBO, v.p. to sr. v.p. mktg. home video divsn.; sr. v.p. mktg. Fox/Liberty Networks News Corps., 1996—98, pres., CEO FX Networks, 1998—2005; pres. entertainment Fox Broadcasting Co., LA, 2005—. Office: Fox Broadcasting Co 10201 W Pico Blvd Los Angeles CA 90035 Office Phone: 310-369-1000. Office Fax: 310-369-1049.*

LIGUORI, ROBERT, lawyer, insurance company executive; b. Bklyn, NY, Jan. 7, 1954; AA, Nassau Cmty. Coll., 1973; BA, SUNY, Binghamton, 1975; JD, Potomac Sch. Law, Washington, 1980. Bar: Ga. 1981, Md. 1982, Mass. 2001, US Dist. Ct. (no. dist. Ga. 1981), US Ct. Appeals (5th cir. 1982), US Tax Ct. 1982. Sr. v.p., co-gen. counsel Mass. Mutual Fin. Group, Springfield, Mass. Mem.: ABA, Md. State Bar Assn., DC Bar, State Bar Ga. Office: Mass Mutual Financial Group 1295 State St Springfield MA 01111 Office Phone: 413-788-8411. Office Fax: 413-744-6114.

LIH, SHYH-SHIUH, aeronautical engineer, researcher; PhD, UCLA, 1992. Mem. sr. engring. staff Jet Propulsion Lab., Pasadena, Calif. Vis. lectr. UCLA, L.A. Recipient Space Act award, NASA, 2002. Achievements include patents for mechanical components and ultrasonic applications.

LIKE, STEVEN, lawyer; b. Vincennes, Ind., Sept. 5, 1956; s. Cameron Keith and Sharon Lee (Smith) L.; m. Jane Elizabeth Lambert, June 2, 1979 (div.); children: Brandon, Christopher, Stephanie. BA in Econs., DePauw U., 1978; JD cum laude, Ind. U., 1981. Bar: Ind. 1981, Mich. 1984, U.S. Dist. Ct. (no. and so. dists.) Ind. 1981, U.S. Ct. Appeals (7th cir.) 1986. Assoc. Warrick, Weaver & Boyn, Elkhart, Ind., 1981-85, ptnr., 1986—95; exec. v.p., gen. counsel Patriot Homes, Inc., 1995—. Bd. dirs. Manufactured Housing Inst. Bd. dirs. United Way Elkhart County, 1982-88; bd. dirs. Assn. for Disabled of Elkhart County, 1984-91, pres., 1989; vice-chmn. MHI Govt. Rels. Com., 2001—; bd. govs. IMHA-RUIC, 1999—, pres., 2002—. Mem. ABA, Ind. Bar Assn., Mich. Bar Assn., Elkhart City Bar Assn. Republican. Methodist. Avocations: boating, fishing, golf, travel. Office: 307 S Main St Ste 200 Elkhart IN 46516-3102

LIKENS, GENE ELDEN, biology and ecology educator; b. Pierceton, Ind., Jan. 6, 1935; s. Colonel Benjamin and Josephine (Garner) L.; m. Phyllis Craig; children: Kathy, Gregory, Leslie. BS, Manchester (Ind.) Coll., 1957, DSc (hon.), 1979; MS, U. Wis., 1959, PhD, 1962; DSc (hon.), Rutgers U., 1985, Plymouth State Coll., U. N.H., 1989, Miami U., 1990; LHD (hon.), Union Coll., 1991; DSc (hon.), U. Bodenkultur, Vienna, Austria, 1993, Marist Coll., 1993, Wageningen Agrl. U., Netherlands, 1998, U. Conn., 2004. Asst. zoology Manchester Coll., 1955-57; grad. tchg. asst. U. Wis., 1957-59, vis. lectr., 1963; instr. zoology Dartmouth Coll., 1961, instr. biol. scis., 1963, asst. prof., then assoc. prof., 1963-69; mem. faculty Cornell U., 1969-83, prof. ecology, 1972-83, Charles A. Alexander prof. biol. scis., 1983, adj. prof., 1983—; v.p. N.Y. Bot. Garden, 1983-93; dir. Inst. Ecosystem Studies, Millbrook, NY, 1983—, pres., 1993—, G. Evelyn Hutchinson chair in ecology, 2000—; dir. Mary Flagler Cary Arboretum, 1983—93; prof. biology Yale U., 1984—; prof. grad. field of ecology Rutgers U., 1985—. Vis. prof. Ctr. Advanced Rsch., dept. environ scis. U. Va., Charlottesville, 1978-79; chmn. New Eng. divsn. task force conservation aquatic ecosystems U.S. Internat. Biol. Program, 1966-67; vis. assoc. ecologist Brookhaven Nat. Lab., 1968; C.P. Snow lectr. Ithaca Coll., 1979, 89; Rilett vis. scholar Ill. State U., 1985; vis. scholar James Madison U., 1988; Class of 1960 vis. scholar, Williams Coll., Williamstown, Mass., 1988; William V. Kaesar Meml. scholar U. Wis., Madison, 1991; vis. disting. ecologist, Colo. State U., 1994; Walker Ames prof., U. Wash., Seattle, 2001; adj. prof. SUNY, Albany; Miegunyah fellow U. Melbourne, Australia; cons., panelist, lectr. in field. Author 15 books; contbr. over 480 articles to sci. jours. Recipient Conservation award Am. Motors Corp., 1969, 75th Anniversary award U.S. Forest Svc., 1980, Disting. Achievement award Lab. Biomed. and Environ. Studies, UCLA, 1982, Regents medal SUNY, 1984, NY Acad. Scis. award, 1986, Internat. ECI prize for Limnetic Ecology, 1989, Disting. Svc. award N.Y. Bot. Garden, 1989, Am. Inst. Biol. Scis., 1990, Lifetime Accomplishment award, 2000, Disting. Svc. award Hudson River Environ. Soc., 1997, The Garden Club Am. Spl. Citation, 1992, Tyler World Environment prize U. So. Calif., 1993, Australia prize, 1994; Sr. fellow NATO, 1969, Guggenheim fellow, 1972-73; grantee NSF, EPA, Dept. Energy, USDA Forest Svc., NOAA, Disting. Svc. award Hudson River Environ. Soc., Inc., 1997, Vollenweider award and lecturship, Canada Ctr. for Inland Waters, Nat. Water Rsch. Inst., 1998, Storm King award Scenic Hudson Inc., 1998, Excellence award Nat. Coun. State Garden Clubs Inc., 1999, Nat. Medal Sci., 2001, Blue Planet prize, 2003; Miequnyah Disting. fellow U. Melbourne, Australia, 2004. Fellow: AAAS; mem.: NAS (chmn. sect. 27 1986—89), Inst. Biology (London), Royal Danish Acad. Sci., Am. Inst. Biol. Scis. (pres. 2002—03, Lifetime Accomplishment award 2000, Huxley medal, Inst. Biology (UK) 2001), Austrian Acad. Scis., Australian Soc. Limnology, Internat. Water Resources Assn. (charter), Internat. Assn. Gt. Lakes Rsch., Freshwater Biol. Assn., Explorers Club, Am. Polar Soc., Royal Swedish Acad. Scis., Internat. Assn. Theoretical and Applied Limnology (v.p. 1998, pres. 2001—03, 2003—, Naumann-Thienemann medal 1995), Am. Soc. Limnology and Oceanography (v.p. 1975—76, pres. 1976—77, 1st G.E. Hutchinson award for excellence in rsch. 1982), Ecol. Soc. Am. (chmn. study com. 1971—74, v.p. 1978—79, pres. 1981—82, Eminent Ecologist award 1995), Am. Acad. Arts and Scis., Brit. Ecol. Soc. (hon.), Am. Water Resources Assn. (hon.), Internat. Water Acad. (life), Sigma Xi, Phi Sigma, Gamma Alpha. Methodist. Office: Inst Ecosys Studies Box AB Millbrook NY 12545 Business E-Mail: likensg@ecostudies.org.

LIKENS, JAMES DEAN, economics professor; b. Bakersfield, Calif., Sept. 12, 1937; s. Ernest LeRoy and Monnie Jewel (Thomas) L.; m. Janet Sue Pelton, Dec. 18, 1965 (div.); m. Karel Carnohan, June 4, 1988 (div.); children: John David, Janet Elizabeth; m. Christine Irons, Feb. 8, 2003. BA in Econs., U. Calif., Berkeley, 1960, MBA, 1961; PhD in Econs., U. Minn., 1970. Analyst Del Monte Corp., San Francisco, 1963; economist 3M Co., Mpls., 1968-71; asst. prof. econs. Pomona Coll., 1969-75, assoc. prof. econs., 1975-83, prof. econs., 1983-85, Morris B. and Gladys S. Pendleton prof. econs., 1989—, dept. chair, 1998-2001. Vis. asst. prof. econs. U. Minn., 1970, 71, vis. assoc. prof., 1976-77; pres., dean Western CUNA Mgmt. Sch., Pomona Coll., 1975—; chmn. bd. 1st City Savs. Fed. Credit Union, 1978—; coord. So. Calif. Rsch. Coun., LA, 1980-81, 84-85; adv. coun. Western Corp. Fed. Credit Union, 1993—; cons. in field. Author: (with Joseph LaDou) Medicine and Money, 1976, Mexico and Southern California: Toward A New Partnership, 1981, Financing Quality Education in Southern California, 1985; contbr. articles to profl. jours. Served with USCG, 1961-67; dir. Centennial, Pomona Coll., 1987-88. Named Dir. of Yr., Calif. Credit Union League, 1997, Credit Union Exec. Soc., 2001; recipient Leo H. Shapiro Lifetime Achievement award, Calif. Credit Union League, 2001, Herb Wegner Lifetime Achievement award, Nat. Credit Union Found., 2005; grantee rsch. grantee HUD-DOT, Haynes Found. Mem.: ABA, Western Econ. Assn., Am. Econ. Assn. Avocations: painting, clarinet, family history, golf. Home: 725 W 10th St Claremont CA 91711-3719 Office: Pomona Coll Dept Econs Claremont CA 91711 Office Phone: 909-621-8998. E-mail: jlikens@pomona.edu.

LIKENS, JOHN DAVID, rehabilitation services professional; b. Upland, Calif., June 19, 1972; s. James Dean and Janet Sue Likens; m. Norma A. Likens, Feb. 17, 2001; 1 child, Victoria Elizabeth. AS, Mt. San Antonio, 2003; BS, U. La Verne, 2004. Cert. addiction treatment specialist. Detox counselor Inland Valley, Upland, Calif., 1999—2000, resident advocate, 2000—03, program dir., coord., 2000—03, dir. of devel., 2003—. Intern supr. Inlan Valley, Upland, Calif., 2000—. Mem.: Calif. Assn. Alcohol/Drug Abuse Counselors, Calif. Assn. Alcohol/Drug Educators, Alpha Chi, Phi Theta Kappa. Republican. Office: Inland Valley 916 N Mountain Ave Ste A Upland CA 91786 Office Phone: 909-932-1069.

LIKINS, PETER WILLIAM, academic administrator; b. Tracy, Calif, July 4, 1936; s. Ennis Blaine and Dorothy Louise (Medlin) L.; m. Patricia Ruth Kitsmiller, Dec. 18, 1955; children: Teresa, Lora, Paul, Linda, Krista. BCE, Stanford U., 1957, PhD in Engring. Mechanics, 1965; MCE, MIT, 1958; PhD (hon.), Lafayette Coll., 1983, Moravian Coll., 1984, Med. Coll. Pa., 1990, Lehigh U., 1991, Allentown St. Francis de Sales, 1993, Czech Tech U., 1993. Devel. engr. Jet Propulsion Lab., Pasadena, Calif., 1958-60; asst. prof. engring. UCLA, 1964-69, assoc. prof., 1969-72, prof., 1972-76, asst. dean, 1974-75, asso. dean, 1975-76; dean engring. and applied sci. Columbia U., N.Y.C., 1976-80, provost, 1980-82; pres. Lehigh U., Bethlehem, Pa., 1982-97, U. Ariz., Tucson, 1997—. Cons. in field. Author: Elements of Engineering

Mechanics, 1973, Spacecraft Dynamics, 1982; Contbr. articles to profl. jours. Mem. US Pres.'s Coun. Advisors Sci. and Tech., 1990-93. Ford Found. fellow, 1970-72; named to Nat. Wrestling Hall of Fame Fellow AIAA; mem. Nat. Acad. Engring., Phi Beta Kappa, Sigma Xi, Tau Beta Pi. Office: U Ariz PO Box 210066 Tucson AZ 85721-0066 Office Phone: 520-621-5511. Business E-Mail: plikins@arizona.edu.

LIKINS, ROSE MARIE, foreign service officer; b. Andrews AFB, Md., Jan. 22, 1959; d. Eugene Aloysius and Merlyn (Houghland) McCartney; m. John Foster Likins, MAy 30, 1981; children: James, Kevin. BA in Internat. Affairs, BA in Spanish, Mary Washington Coll., Fredericksburg, Va., 1981. Joined Fgn. Svc., U.S. Dept. State, Washington, 1981—, previous fgn. svc. assignments Honduras, U.S. amb. to El Salvador, 2000—03. Rm. mother Tuckahoe Elem. Sch., Arlington, Va., 1993-94. Mem. Am. Fgn. Svc. Assn., Mortar Board (pres. chpt. 1980-81), Phi Beta Kappa. Roman Catholic. Achievements include fluent in Spanish and Bulgarian.

LIKOSKY, DONALD, epidemiologist, consultant; BA, Emory U., Atlanta, 1990—94; MS, Dartmouth Coll., Hanover, NH, 1998—99; PhD, Dartmouth Coll., 1999—2002. Postdoctoral rsch. fellow Dartmouth Coll., 2001—04, instr., 2004—; asst. prof. Dartmouth Med. Sch., 2005—. Office: Dartmouth Med Sch Hb 7505 Hanover NH 03756 Business E-Mail: likosky@dartmouth.edu.

LIKOVA MINEVA, LORA T., research scientist; d. Tzvetko T. Likov and Angelina B. Tzvetkova; m. Kristyo N. Mineff; 1 child, Zlatko K. Minev. MSc in Computer Sci., Tech. U., Sofia; PhD in Cognitive Neuroscience, Ctrl. and East-European Ctr. Cognitive Scis., New Bulgarian U., Sofia; postgrad., U. Nat. and World Econs., Sofia; fMRI (functional MRI) tng., MIT/HMS/MGH Ctr. for Biomedical Imaging, Boston. Asst. prof. Ctrl. Inst. of Computer Technique, Sofia, Bulgarian Acad. Scis., Sofia, Inst. for Microprocessing Technique, Sofia; rsch. scientist Smith-Kettlewell Eye Rsch. Inst., San Francisco, postdoctoral fellow; vis. scientist U. Warwick, Coventry, England. Hon. prof. Tech. U., Sofia; head Non-Standard Think Group/Computer Inst. Contbr. articles to profl. jours. Recipient award, Nat. Patent Inst.; fellow fellow for European Conf. on Visual Perception, Oxford, Eng., Brit. Coun.; Rachel C. Atkinson fellow, Smith-Kettlewell Eye Rsch. Inst., San Francisco, fellow European Conf. on Visual Perception, Helsinki, Finland, Soros Open Soc. Found. Mem.: Cognitive Neuroscience Soc., Vision Sci. Soc., Orgn. for Human Brain Mapping, Soc. for Neuroscience. Achievements include patents for magnetic head; discovery of new brain areas: first brain imaging studies (fMRI) on dynamic stereovision; discovering a new brain areas for 3D-motion processing; eye disease diagnosis: discovering a fundamental blind-spot related mechanism and inventing a clinical method (Blue Light Papillometry) for early diagnosis of blinding diseases; depth-motion phenomenon: discovering of a new category of perceived 3D-motion in 3D displays (Monopolar Depth Motion); the transient asynchrony/synchrony is a critical organizational factor in visual perception of dynamic world; for the first time in the human brain a figure/ground mechanism based on top-down suppression of the background representation in retinotopic visual areas. Avocations: philosophy, yoga, hiking, drawing, poetry. Office: Smith-Kettlewell Eye Rsch Inst 2318 Fillmore St San Francisco CA 94115 Office Phone: 415-345-2066. Business E-Mail: lora@ski.org.

LILES, CLIFTON ROY, application developer; b. San Antonio, Jan. 28, 1944; s. Roy Clifton and Lucy Mae Liles. BS in Physics, U. Houston, 1978. Software engr. Tex. Instruments, Richardson, Tex., 1978-90, Unisys, Houston, 1990-96; mem. computer sci. staff, software designer United Space Alliance, Houston, 1996—. With U.S. Army, 1967-71. Mem. IEEE, Assn. Computing Machinery, Am. Geophys. Union. Home: 2310 Longwood Dr Pearland TX 77581 Office: United Space Alliance 600 Gemini Ave Houston TX 77058 Business E-Mail: c.r.liles@ieee.org, lilescr@acm.org.

LILES, JOSEPH MARSHALL, III, artist, educator; b. Wadesboro, N.C., Jan. 25, 1950; s. Joseph Marshall Jr. and Helen Coit L.; m. Carole Elizabeth Crump, May 12, 1979; children: Joseph Marshall IV, Elizabeth Lane B Environ. Design-Landscape Architecture, N.C. State U., 1972; MS in Environ. Edn., U. Mich., 1974. Dir. adult edn. Red Sch. House for Native Americans, St. Paul, 1974-77; art tchr. The Art Sch., Carrboro, N.C., 1978-79, Durham (N.C.) Arts Coun., 1979-80; instr. art N.C. Sch. Sci. and Math., Durham, 1980—; profl. printmaker Durham, 1977—. Mem. summer faculty Woodrow Wilson Inst., Princeton, N.J., 1991; cultural cons. Lac Courte Orielles Ojibway Sch., Hayward, Wis., 1991. Author, illustrator: Chapel Hill Coloring Book, 1972, Powwow Tales, The First Americans Newspaper, 1994, Powwow Tales, News from Indian Country, 1996, A Drumstick's Story, News from Indian Country, 2005; editor, illustrator: The Mishomis Book, 1979, Watts Hospital of Durham, N.C., 1991; illustrator: How to Tell Liars from Statisticians, 1983 Organizer First Native Am. Powwow, Durham, 1992. Recipient Emerging Artist award Durham Arts Coun., 1989, N.C. Gov.'s award of excellence, 1994. Mem. Durham Art Guild, Phi Kappa Phi. Avocations: woodworking, landscaping, fly fishing, Native Am. powwows. Home: 2115 Wilson St Durham NC 27705-3225 Office: NC Sch Sci and Math 1219 Broad St Durham NC 27705-3577 Office Phone: 919-416-2730. E-mail: liles@ncssm.edu.

LILES, KEVIN, music company executive; b. 1968; Mem. group Numarx, 1989—91; co-founder, co-pres. Marx Bros. Records, 1991—92; intern Def Jam Records, 1992, gen. mgr. promotions, 1994—96, gen. mgr., v.p. promotions, 1996—98, pres., 1998—2004; exec. v.p. Island Def Jam Music Group, 2002—04, Warner Music Group, 2004—. Writer: songs Girl You Know It's True (performed by Milli Vanilli). Office: Warner Music Group 75 Rockefeller Plz New York NY 10019*

LILEY, PETER EDWARD, retired engineering educator; b. Barnstaple, North Devon, Eng., Apr. 22, 1927; came to U.S., 1957; s. Stanley E. and Rosa (Ellery) L.; m. Elaine Elizabeth Kull, Aug. 16, 1963; children: Elizabeth Ellen, Rebecca Ann. BSc, U. London, 1951, PhD in Physics, DIC, U. London, 1957. With Brit. Oxygen Engring., London, 1955-57; asst. prof. mech. engring. Purdue U., West Lafayette, Ind., 1957-61, assoc. prof., 1961-72; assoc. sr. researcher Thermophys. Properties Research Ctr., Purdue U., West Lafayette, Ind., 1961-72, prof. mech. engring., 1972-98; sr. rschr. Ctr. for Info. and Numerical Data Analysis and Synthesis, Purdue U., West Lafayette, Ind., 1972-92; ret., 1997. Cons. in field. Author: Sect. 2 Perry's Chemical Engineers Handbook, 7th edit., 1997, (with Hartnett et al.) Handbook of Heat Transfer Fundamentals, 2d edit., 1985, (with others) Marks Mechanical Engineers Handbook, 10th edit., 1996, Schaums 2000 Solved Problems in Mechanical Engineering Thermodynamics, 1988, Tables and Charts for Thermodynamics, 1995, Kutz Mechanical Engineers Handbook, 1998; co-author: Steam and Gas Tables with Computer Equations, 1985, Thermal Conductivity of Nonmetallic Liquids and Gases, 1970, Properties of Nonmetallic Fluid Elements, 1981, Properties of Inorganic and Organic Fluids, 1988; editor, mem. editl. bd. Internat. Jour. Thermophysics, 1980-86; contbr. chpts. to handbooks in field; contbr. articles to profl. jours.; reviewer profl. jours. Served with Royal Corps Signals, Brit. Army, 1945-48. Lutheran. Home: 3608 Mulberry Dr Lafayette IN 47905-3937 E-mail: petereliley@insightbb.com.

LILEY, THOMAS, music educator; b. Topeka, Sept. 29, 1948; B in Music Edn., U. Kans., 1971; MusM in Saxophone, Cath. U., 1974; Mus D in Saxophone, Ind. U., 1988. Cert. Music Tchr.'s Nat. Assn. Yamaha performing artist Yamaha Band and Orch., Grand Rapids, Mich., 1982—. Co-author: (book) Cambridge Companion to the Saxophone, 1998; author: Saxophone Journal, 2001, Saxophone Symposium, 2002, A Brief History of the World Saxophone Congress, 2003. Office: Joliet Jr Coll 1215 Houbolt Joliet IL 60565 Business E-Mail: tliley@jjc.edu.

LILIEN, ROBERT JARRETT, diversified financial services company executive; b. N.Y.C., Feb. 17, 1962; s. Robert David and Georgiana Wethers (Lewis) L. BA in Econs., U. Vt., 1984. Instnl. trader Autronet Inc., N.Y.C., 1984-86; v.p. rsch. sales Paine Webber Inc., N.Y.C., 1986-89; pres., chief operating officer Tiedemann Internat. Rsch. Inc., N.Y.C., 1989—99; chief brokerage officer E Trade Group, 2000—03; pres., COO E Trade Fin. Corp., 2003—. Mem. Princeton Club of N.Y., Devon Yacht Club, Met. Squash and Racquets Assn. (chmn. tournament com. 1987). Avocations: guitar, theater, classic cars. Office: E Trade 135 E 57th St New York NY 10022

LILIENSTERN, O. CLAYTON, lawyer, educator; b. Houston, Nov. 13, 1943; s. Oscar C. and Suzanne (Haughton) L.; children: Robert, Susan, Kelli, Melanie. AB, U. Ala., 1965; JD, U. Houston, 1968, MBA, 1992; LLM, George Washington U., 1972; MTS, So. Meth. U., 2002. Bar: Tex. 1968, U.S. Dist. Ct. (so. dist.) Tex. 1973, U.S. Tax Ct. 1975, U.S. Supreme Ct. 1976, U.S. Dist. Ct. (we. dist.) Tex. 1978, U.S. Dist. Ct. (ea. dist.) Tex. 1987, U.S. Dist. Ct. (no. dist.) Tex. 1988, U.S. Ct. Appeals (5th, 9th, 11th and fed. cirs.); cert. civil trial law Tex. Bd. Legal Specialization. Assoc. Andrews & Kurth, Houston, 1972-79, ptnr., 1979-97, Hicks, Thomas & Lilienstern LLP, Houston, 1997—2001, of counsel, 2001—; asst. head sch. Episcopal H.S., Bellaire, Tex., 2004—. Mem. Leadership Houston, 1989—. Capt. JAGC, U.S. Army, 1968-72. Decorated Joint Svc. Commendation medal; NAIS/E.E. Ford fellow, 2005—. Fellow Tex. Bar Found., Houston Bar Found.; mem. ABA, State Bar Tex., Houston Bar Assn., A.A. White Soc., U. Houston Law Ctr., U. Houston Law Alumni Assn. (pres. 1982-83, life), Houston Law Rev. Alumni Assn. (pres. 1991-92), Jasons Soc., Briar Club (bd. dirs., pres. 2004) Delta Tau Delta, Omicron Delta Kappa, Phi Alpha Delta. Home: 4821 Maple St Bellaire TX 77401-5728 Office: Episcopal HS 4650 Bissonnet Bellaire TX 77401

LILIENTHAL, ALFRED M(ORTON), writer, historian, editor; b. N.Y.C., Dec. 25, 1913; s. Herbert and Lottye (Kohn) L. BA, Cornell U., Ithaca, N.Y., 1934; LLB, Columbia U., 1938, JD, 1969. Bar: N.Y. 1938. With Bennett, House & Couts, N.Y.C., 1939-41, State Dept., 1942-43, 45-48; cons. U.S. del. UN San Francisco Conf., 1945; adminstrv. practice, 1947-50; counsel Am.-Arab Assn. Commerce & Industry, 1960-65; editor, pub. Middle East Perspective (monthly newsletter), 1967-85. Lectr. on Middle East at numerous colls. and clubs throughout U.S. and fgn. countries, 1951-94, frequent guest TV and radio news commentator on Middle East devels., 1951-91; lectr. cultural symposium United Arab Emirates, Libya, Lebanon, Vienna, Baghdad, Prague; polit. columnist daily Al Qabas, Kuwait, 1976-77; accredited corr. to UN; chmn. Am. Coun. on the Middle East; cons. UN Internat. Conf. on Question Palestine, Geneva, 1983; participant Model Internat. Conf. on Middle East, Prague, 1988, 27 Middle East trips including West Bank and Gaza, 1953-94; guest of UN Sec.-Gen. at 50th Commemorative meeting, San Francisco, 1995. Author: Which Way to World Government, 1949, What Price Israel?, 1953, There Goes the Middle East, 1957, Studies in Twentieth Century Diplomacy, 1959, The Other Side of the Coin, 1965, Polish transl., 1966, The Zionist Connection, 1978, The Zionist Connection II, 1982, rev. Czechoslovakian edit., 1989, Japanese edit., 1991, This I Do Believe, 1994; contbr. Zionism-The Dream and the Reality, 1974, Searching Jenin: Eyewitness Accounts of the Israeli Invasion, 2003, monthly commenataries Washington Report on Middle East Affairs, 1988—99, also numerous mag. articles and syndicated newspieces. Pres. Rep. First Voters League, 1940; Fusion Party candidate for N.Y.C. Coun., 1941; leader fight against Communist controlled Am. Youth Congress, 1941. With AUS, 1943-45. Papers housed in archives of Hoover Instn., Stanford, Calif. Mem. Nat. Rep. Club, Univ. Club, Capitol Hill Club, Nat. Press Club, Cornell Club Washington. Home and Office: 800 25th St NW Washington DC 20037-2207 E-mail: alfredlilienthal@aol.com.

LILJEBERG, GENEVIEVE BROCATO, artist; b. Shreveport, La., Dec. 12, 1939; d. Samuel Charles and Rosalie Pittari Brocato; m. Robert Louis Liljeberg, June 4, 1960; children: Roxanne, Robert, Sam, Hans, Heidi. Student, Loyola U., 1957-60. One-woman shows include St. Jude Hosp., Kenner, La., 1989, On Four Gallery, New Orleans, 1991, Sylvia Schmidt Gallery, 1994, 1995, 1998, Entergy Ctr., 1997, Sylvia Schmidt, 1999, Zeigler Mus., Jennings, La., 1993, Beresford Sporting Gallery, Saratoga, N.Y., Collector's Gallery, Lexington, Ky., Linda Howell & Assocs., Oklahoma City, 1996, Sportsman Gallery, Vail, Colo., 1998, Ctr. for the Arts Invitational, Mt. Kisco, N.Y., 1998; featured artist Cadwell Arts Coun., 2000; New Orleans Opera Ball poster, 2003, poster and cover 2003 opera program; contbr. articles. Recipient Best in Show award Mus. of the Horse, 1997. Mem. Am. Acad. Equine Art (assoc.). Republican. Roman Catholic. Avocations: jogging, swimming, volleyball, horse racing, opera. Home: 1506 Milan St New Orleans LA 70115-3825 Studio: 832 Baronne St New Orleans LA 70113-1103 E-mail: rliljeberg@aol.com.

LILJEGREN, FRANK SIGFRID, art association administrator, artist, educator; b. N.Y.C., Feb. 23, 1930; s. Josef Sigfrid and Ester (Davidsson) L.; m. Donna Kathryn Hallam, Oct. 12, 1957. Student, Art Students League, N.Y.C., 1950-55. Instr. painting, drawing, composition Westchester County Ctr., White Plains, N.Y., 1967-77, Art Students League, 1974-75, Wassenberg Art Ctr., Van Wert, Ohio, 1978-80, Wright State U. Br. Western Ohio Campus, Celina, 1981—. Corr. sec. Allied Artists Am., N.Y.C., 1967, exhbn. chmn., 1968-, pres., 1970-72, also bd. dirs. Exhibited at Suffolk Mus., Stonybrook, N.Y., Springfield (Mass.) Mus., Marion Kugler McNay Art Inst., San Antonio, Philbrook Mus., Tulsa, NAD, N.Y.C., New Britain (Conn.) Mus. Art, Ft. Wayne (Ind.) Mus. Art; represented in permanent collections Art Students League, Univ. Mus., S.E. Mo. State U., Cape Girardeau, Manhattan Savs. Bank, N.Y.C., Am. Ednl. Pubs. Inst., N.Y.C., New Britain Mus. Am. Art, Conn., U. St. Francis, Ft. Wayne. With AUS, 1951. Recipient numerous awards for still life oil paintings. Mem. Fine Arts fedn. N.Y, Art Students League (life), Acad. Artists Assn., Coun. Am. Artists Socs., Artists Fellowship, Salmagundi. *The best advice I could give young artists is to first learn their craft to the fullest so that they can then be free to express themselves in what ever style and medium they then choose to work. Last but not least, they should have self-respect and great love for what they are doing.*

LILLARD, JOHN FRANKLIN, III, lawyer; b. Bladensburg, Md., Aug. 2, 1947; s. John Franklin Lillard Jr. and Madeline Virginia (Berg) Lillard; m. Kim Leslie Oliver, June 1, 1991 (div.); 1 child, John Franklin Lillard IV. BA, Washington and Lee U., 1969, JD, 1971. Bar: N.Y. 1972, D.C. 1974, Md. 1975. Assoc. Donovan, Leisure, Newton & Irvine, N.Y.C., 1971-74, Pierson, Ball & Dowd (merged into Reed, Smith,. McClay & Lynch), 1974—76; ptnr. Lillard & Lillard, Washington, 1977—; trial atty. civil div. Dept. Justice, Washington, 1976-77. Instr. Dale Carnegie Course, 1988—97. Notes and comments editor: Washington and Lee Law Rev., 1970. Vice chair Village Coun. Friendship Heights, Chevy Chase, Md., 1975—77; chair Am. Solar Energy Assn.; founding mem. Nat. Adv. Coun. Ctr. for Study of the Presidency, 1970—99, Md. State Adv. Bd. on Spl. Tax Dists., 1976—77; alcoholic beverage adv. bd. Montgomery County, 1977—79; chair Eisenhower Centennial Meml. Com., 1990—97; candidate U.S. Congress 5th dist., Md., 1981. Recipient Eastman award, Am. Arbitration Assn., 1971. Mem.: Anne Arundel County Bar Assn., Prince George's County Bar Assn., Md. Bar Assn., Marlborough Hunt Club, Tred Avon Yacht Club (Oxford, Md.), Met. Club. Republican. Episcopalian. Office: 8 Loudon Ln Annapolis MD 21401-1219 Office Phone: 410-268-1900. Personal E-mail: johnlillard@toad.net.

LILLARD, MARK HILL, III, computer scientist, consultant, retired military officer; b. Jacksonville, Fla., Sept. 1, 1943; s. Mark Hill Jr. and Cornelia Kingman (Callaway) L.; m. Marie-Jacques Le Guyader, June 3, 1972; children: Mark Hill IV, Michael Robert. BA, Bowling Green U., 1965; MS, St. Mary's U., San Antonio, 1976; MBA, Auburn U., 1977. Commd. 2d lt. USAF, 1965, advanced through grades to brig. gen., 1991; ret., 1991; exec. v.p. Pilot Rsch. Assocs., Inc., Vienna, Va., 1991—2001, also bd. dirs.; regional v.p. RCM Technologies, Inc., Bethesda, Md., 2001—04; sr. assoc. Booz Allen Hamilton, McLean, Va., 2004; v.p. Seta Corp., McLean, 2005—. Author: Simulation, 1976. Decorated Legion of Merit, Def. Superior Svc. medal, Def. Meritorious Svc. medal; Samil medal (Republic of Korea). Mem. Air Force Assn., Lions, Kiwanis, Phi Delta Theta. Republican. Avocations: tennis, golf. Home: 9516 Locust Hill Dr Great Falls VA 22066-2021 Office: RCM Technologies Inc 4550 Montgomery AVe Ste 410N Bethesda MD 20814 E-mail: mlillard@seta.com.

LILLEHAUG, DAVID LEE, lawyer; b. Waverly, Iowa, May 22, 1954; s. Leland Arthur and Ardis Elsie (Scheel) L.; m. Winifred Sarah (Smith), May 29, 1982; one child, Kara Marie. BA, Augustana Coll., Sioux Falls, S.D., 1976; JD, Harvard U., 1979. Bar: Minn., 1979, U.S. Dist. Ct. Minn., 1979, D.C., 1981, U.S. Ct. Appeals (8th cir.), 1981, U.S. Dist. Ct. D.C., 1982. Law clk. to presiding judge U.S. Dist. Ct., Mpls., 1979-81; assoc. Hogan and Hartson, Washington, 1981-83, 84-85; issues aide, exec. asst. to Walter Mondale, Washington, 1983-84; assoc. Leonard, Street, and Deinard, Mpls., 1985-87, ptnr., 1988-93, 98-99; U.S. atty. Dist. of Minn., 1994-98; atty. Fredrikson & Byron, P.A., Mpls., 2002—. Candidate, U.S. Senate, 1999-2000. Mondale Policy Forum Fellow, U. Minn., 1990-91. Mem. ABA, Minn. Bar Assn. (past chair constrn. law sect., Author's Award 1990). Lutheran. Avocations: fishing, golf. Office: Fredrikson & Byron PA 200 S Sixth St Minneapolis MN 55402 Home: 6701 Parkwood Ln Edina MN 55436 Office Phone: 612-492-7000. E-mail: dlillehaug@fredlaw.com.

LILLEHEI, KEVIN OWEN, neurosurgeon, educator; b. Mpls., July 6, 1953; m. Anne Cheryl Hofmann; 1 child, Kira Anne. BS, Cornell U., 1975; MD, U. Minn., 1975-79. Diplomate Am. Bd. Neurol. Surgery. Intern in surgery U. Mich., 1979—80, resident, 1980—85; asst. prof. surgery neurosurgery divsn. U. Colo. Health Scis. Ctr., Denver, 1985—2000, prof. neurosurgery, 2000—, chief sect. neuro-oncology, 1990—, vice chmn. dept. neurosurgery, 2001—; chief neurosurgery Denver VA Hosp., 1987-90; interim chair dept. neurosurgery Denver Gen. Hosp., 2004—. Mem. AMA, Rocky Mountain Neurosurg. Soc., Colo. Neurosurg. Soc., Colo. Med. Soc., Colo. Neurosurg. Soc., Denver Med. Soc., Denver Acad. Surgery, Congress Neurol. Surgeons. Office: U Colo Health Scis Ctr 4200 E 9th Ave # 307C Denver CO 80262

LILLEMOEN, HENRY DANIEL, retired writer; b. Pitts., Feb. 25, 1928; s. Daniel and Ella Maria (Kohring) L.; m. Betty Jane Veil, Aug. 19, 1950; children: Daniel, John, Richard, Randi, Erik. BA in Latin Am. Studies, U. Pitts., 1950. Supt. Harcliff Coal Co., East Brady, Pa., 1950-53; asst. mgr. Conn. Gen., Washington, 1953-58; sales mgr. Ward Mfg., Washington, 1958-68; nat. sales mgr. El Dorado Ind., Minneapolis, Kans., 1968-73; pvt. practice mfg. rep. Myrtle Beach, S.C., 1973-92; freelance writer Murrells Inlet, S.C., 1992—. Contbr. articles and short stories to popular mags. Lt. (j.g.) USNR. Mem. VFW, Am. Legion. Avocations: fishing, golf. Home: 763 Nelson Dr Murrells Inlet SC 29576-6305

LILLESAND, THOMAS MARTIN, engineer, educator; b. Laurium, Mich., Oct. 1, 1946; m. Theresa Hofmeister, 1968; children: Mark, Kari, Michael. BS, U. Wis., 1969, MS, 1970, PhD in Civil Engring., 1973. Prof. remote sensing SUNY, Syracuse, 1973-78, U. Minn., 1978-82, U. Wis., Madison, 1982—. Cons., 1973—. Recipient SAIC/Estes Meml. Tchg. award, 2005. Mem. Am. Soc. Photogrammetry and Remote Sensing (pres. 1998-99, Alan Gordon award 1979, 93, Talbert Abrams award 1984, Fennell award 1988, SAIC/Estes Meml. Tchg. award 2005). Office: U Wis Environ Remote Sensing Ctr 1225 W Dayton St Rm 1239B Madison WI 53706-1612

LILLESTOL, JANE BRUSH, performing company executive; b. Jamestown, N.D., July 20, 1936; d. Harper J. and Doris (Mikkelson) Brush; m. Harvey Lillestol, Sept. 29, 1956; children: Kim, Kevin, Erik. BS, U. Minn., 1969, MS, 1973, PhD, 1977; grad. Inst. Ednl. Mgmt., Harvard U., 1984. Dir. placement, asst. to dean U. Minn., St. Paul, 1975-77; assoc. dean, dir. student acad. affairs N.D. State U., Fargo, 1977-80; dean Coll. Human Devel. Syracuse (N.Y.) U., 1980-89, v.p. for alumni rels., 1989-95, project dir. IBM Computer Aided Design Lab., 1989—92; prin. Lillestol Assocs.; emeritus faculty Syracuse (N.Y.) U., 1995—; faculty U. Phoenix, 2002—, curriculum devel. specialist, 2003. Charter mem. Mayor's Commn. on Women, 1986-90; NAFTA White House Conf. for Women Leaders, 1993. Bd. dirs. Univ. Hill Corp. Syracuse, 1983-93; mem. steering com. Consortium for Cultural Founds. of Medicine, 1980-89; trustee Manlius Pebble Hill Sch., 1990-94, Archbold Theatre, 1990-95, N.D. State U., 1992—. Recipient award U.S. Consumer Product Safety Commn., 1983, Woman of Yr. award AAUW, 1984, svc. award Syracuse U., 1992; named among 100 Outstanding Alumni Over Past 100 Yrs., U. Minn. Coll. Human Ecology, 2001. Office: 8046 E Via De Los Libros Scottsdale AZ 85258-3056 E-mail: jane@lillestol.com.

LILLESTOL, MICHAEL JOHN, physician; b. Breckenridge, Minn., Nov. 8, 1947; s. Harvey S. and Mildred M. (Hager) L.; m. Mary L. Forsberg, Apr. 9, 1977; children: Kristopher, Kim, John, Karissa. BS in Pharmacy, N.D. State U., 1970; MD, U. Minn., 1974. Intern and resident Abbott/Northwestern Hosp.-Univ. Minn., Mpls., 1974-77; physician Physicians Clin. Profl. Assn., St. Paul, 1977-83, Internal Med. Assocs., Fargo, N.D., 1983-93, Dakota Heartland Health Sys., Fargo, 1994—2001, Internal Medicine Assocs., Fargo, 2002—. Staff sgt. UWAF, 1970-74. Fellow Am. Coll. Physicians; mem. AMA. Republican. Lutheran. Avocations: golf, tennis, Lionel trains. Office: 1707 Gold Dr South Fargo ND 58103 Office Phone: 701-280-2033. E-mail: mikelillestol@cableone.net.

LILLEY, ALBERT FREDERICK, retired lawyer; b. Harrisburg, Pa., Dec. 21, 1932; s. Frederick Anthony and Jane Sander (Ingham) L.; m. Judith Carter Pennock, Sept. 1, 1956; children: Kirk Anthony, Kristin Sander, James Alexander. AB, Bowdoin Coll., 1954; LLB, U. Va., 1959. Assoc. Milbank, Tweed, Hadley & McCloy, N.Y.C., 1959-67, ptnr., 1967-96; ret., 1997. Trustee No. Highlands Regional H.S., Allendale, N.J., 1964-65; mem. Allendale Bd. Zoning Adjustment, 1965-66; bd. overseers Bowdoin Coll., 1976-88, overseer emeritus, 1988—; trustee Valley Hosp., Ridgewood, N.J., 1978-92, vice chmn. bd., 1985-89, chmn. bd., 1989-92; bd. dirs. Valley Care Corp., 1992-97, Valley Home and Cmty. Health Care, Inc., 1992-97, Chapel Hill-Carrboro Arts Ctr., 2001—; mem. alumni coun. U. Va. Law Sch., 1991-94, U.S. Can. Law Project Adv. Bd., 1990-95. 1st lt. U.S. Army, 1954-56. Mem. ABA, Am. Law Inst., U. Va. Law Sch. Alumni Assn. (class mgr. annual giving campaign), Chapel Hill Rotary Club (vocat. svc. dir. 1998-99, treas. 1999-2000, sec. 2000-01, v.p. 2001-02, pres. 2002-03),. Home: 204 Laurel Hill Rd Chapel Hill NC 27514-4325 E-mail: afl@nc.rr.com.

LILLEY, DAVID, chemicals executive; MA in Chem. Engring., Cambridge U. Former v.p., mem. exec. com. Am. Cyanamid Co.; v.p. Am. Home Products Corp., 1994-97; pres., COO, bd. dirs. Cytec Industries, Inc., West Paterson, N.J., 1997-98, pres., CEO, 1998—, chmn. bd. dirs., 1999—. Office: Cytec Industries 5 Garret Mountain Plz West Paterson NJ 07424*

LILLEY, JOHN MARK, academic administrator; b. Converse, La., Mar. 24, 1939; s. Ernest Franklin and Sibyl Arrena (Geoghagan) L.; children: Sibyl Elizabeth, Myles Durham; m. Geraldine Murphy; stepchildren: Benjamin Murphy, Jason Murphy. B in Music Edn., Baylor U., 1961, MusB, 1962, MusM, 1964; D of Musical Arts, U. So. Calif., 1971. Mem. faculty Claremont McKenna, Harvey Mudd, Pitzer and Scripps Colls., Claremont, Calif., 1966-76; asst. dean faculty Scripps Coll., 1973-76; asst. dean arts and scis. Kans. State U., Manhattan, 1976-80; provost, dean Pa. State U., Erie, 1980—2001; pres. U. Nev., Reno, 2001—. Bd. dirs. Erie Conf., 1997-01; mem. N.W. Pa. Indsl. Resource Ctr., 1987-01, Forum for a Common Agenda, 2001-03, Econ. Devel. Authority of West Nev., 2001-. Condr. 1st performances Kubik, 1972, 76, Ives, 1974, (recording) Kubik, 1974. Bd. dirs., v.p. So. Calif. Choral Music Assn., L.A., 1971-76; mem. Archtl. Commn., Claremont, 1974-76; bd. dirs. Erie Philharm., 1980-86, Reno Philharm., 2004-, Sta. WQLN Pub. Broadcasting of N.W. Pa., 1992-01; bd. dirs. United Way of Erie County, 1981-01, chair, 1998-99; mem. Regents Commn. on Nursing Edn., Kansas City, Kans., 1978-79; pres. Pacific S.W. Intercollegiate Choral Assn., L.A., 1969-70. NEH grantee, 1978. Mem. Am. Assn. Higher Edn., Coll. Music Soc., Am. Choral Dirs. Assn., Am. Assn. State Colls. and Univs. (vice chair confs. and profl. devel. com. 1989, 97, chair 1990, bd. dirs. 1995—, govs. tuition account program adv. bd. 1996—), Rotary (bd. dirs. Manhattan club 1979-80, Erie club 1981-88), Montreux Golf Club, Phi Mu

Alpha Sinfonia, Omicron Delta Kappa. Republican. Presbyterian. Avocation: golf. Home: 3103 Marble Ridge Ct Reno NV 89511-5383 Office: U Nev Reno Office Pres MS 001 Reno NV 89557-0061 Office Phone: 775-784-4805. Business E-Mail: lilley@unr.edu.

LILLEY, VICKIE ROBERTSON, academic administrator; b. Waynesboro, Va., Mar. 8, 1963; d. Hollie Aroar and Elizabeth Mae (Serrett) Robertson; m. Michael Wayne Lilley, Sept. 4, 1982; children: Jonathan Michael, Nathan Lynn. AAS magna cum laude, Blue Ridge C.C.; BBA, James Madison U., 1997, MPA, 2005. Instr. James Madison U., Harrisonburg, Va., 1999—. Mem. employee adv. com. James Madison U. Mem.: Assn. Va. Individualized Studies Adminstrs. (website coord. 1999—, v.p. 2004—), Assn. for Continuing Higher Edn. (Region V newsletter editor 2004—), Coun. for Adult and Exptl. Learning, Golden Key Nat. Honor Soc., Phi Theta Kappa. Office: James Madison Univ Msc 1910 Harrisonburg VA 22807-0001 Office Phone: 540-568-6824. Personal E-mail: mlil453@cs.com.

LILLEY, WILLIAM, III, communications executive, consultant; b. Phila., Jan. 14, 1938; s. William, Jr. and Ida Weaver (Macklin) L.; m. Eve Auchincloss, Mar. 12, 1977; children: Buchanan Morgan, Brooke Carole, Whitman Elisa, Justin Weaver BA magna cum laude, U. Pa., 1959; MA, Yale U., 1961, PhD, 1965. Asst. prof. history Yale U., New Haven, 1962-69; prof. govt. U. Va., Charlottesville, 1977; co-founder, editor Nat. Jour., Washington, 1969-73; dep. asst. sec. HUD, Washington, 1973-75; dep., then dir. Council Wage and Price Stability, Washington, 1975-77; staff dir. Com. on Budget, Ho. of Reps., Washington, 1977-78; v.p. CBS, Inc., Washington, 1980-81, v.p. corporate affairs N.Y.C., 1981-84, sr. v.p. corporate affairs, 1985-86; pres. Am. Bus. Conf., 1986-88, Policy Communications Inc., Washington, 1988-2000; chmn., CEO InContext, Inc., Washington, 1992-2000, iMap Data Inc. (a ChoicePoint Co.)., Washington, 2000—. Bd. dirs. Econ. and Social Rsch. Inst., Stanford U. Social Sci. History Inst., Woodrow Wilson Nat. Fellowship Found Co-author: New Technologies Affecting Broadcasting, 1981, Economic and Social Impacts of Media Advertising, 1989, Impact of Advertising on the Competetive Structure of the Media, 1990, Impact of Media Advertising on International Competetiveness, 1991, Geographic Distribution of U.S. Businesses Which Advertise Heavily, 1991, Almanac of State Legislatures, 1994, State Atlas of Political and Cultural Diversity, 1996, State Legislative Elections: Voting Patterns and Demographics, 1997, The Sports That Make Communities Rich: An Inquiry into the Economics of Professional Sports, 1997, Almanac of State Legislatures: Changing Patterns, 1990-97, 1998, The Economic Impact of the European Grands Prix, 1999; contbr. articles to profl. jours. Recipient U.S. Govt. Disting. Svc. award 1975, 76; Samuel F.B. Morse Rsch. fellowship, 1967-68; George Washington Eggleston prize; Most Disting. PhD Dissertation, humanities divsn., Yale U., 1965; Woodrow Wilson Fellowship, 1959-61. Mem. Yale Club, River Club. Office Phone: 732-659-1073. Business E-Mail: wlilley@imapdata.com.

LILLIE, LLOYD, sculptor; b. Washington, May 20, 1932; s. Alfred Lloyd and Thelma (Folsom) Lillie; m. Barbara Ann Bailey, Dec. 4, 1954; children: Nina L., Warren T., Lisa M. Diploma with highest honors, Boston Mus. Sch.; student, Skowhegan Sch. Painting and Sculpture, Corcoran Sch. Art, Washington, Academia di Belle Arti, Florence, Italy. Mem. faculty Boston U., 1961—95, prof. art, 1974—95, prof. emeritus, 1995—. Camargo Found. fellow, Cassis, France, 1990; Boston Mus. Sch. traveling fellow, 59. One-man shows include St. Botolph Club, Boston, Falmouth (Mass.) Pub. Libr., Bumpus Gallery, Duxbury, Mass., Cambridge Art Assn., Mirsky Gallery, Boston, Mt. Ida Coll., Newton, Mass., Milton (Mass.) Acad., exhibited in group shows at Corcoran Gallery Art, Washington, Nat. Sculpture Soc., N.Y.C., Art Inst. of Boston, Boston Pub. Libr., Palazzo Mediceo, Seravezza, Italy, NAD Invitational, 1998, Forest Hills Cemetery Invitational, Boston, 1998, Forest Lawn Cemetery Invitational, 1999, Nat. Sculpture Soc., 2000, others, Represented in permanent collections Boston Pub. Libr., Am. Embassy, Riyadh, Saudi Arabia, Coll. William and Mary, Va., U. Va., Charlottesville, Jefferson U., Phila. Recipient 1st prize in sculpture, NAD, 1994, Sydney Simon prize in sculpture, 1999, Gov.'s Design award, for Curley Park, Boston, 1st prize in sculpture, Boston Arts Festival, 1991, Bronze medal, Nat. Sculpture Soc., 1991. Mem.: NAD.*

LILLY, CHARLES G., protective services official, consultant; b. Louisville, Aug. 24, 1956; s. Foster Dillard Lilly and Amber Helene Ament. MSc, Radford U., 1981. Pers. analyst Jefferson County Officer Pers. Mgmt., Louisville, 1982-85, City of St. Petersburg (Fla.), 1985-87; pers. examination analyst City of Louisville Civil Svc. Bd., 1987-98; dir. police human resources City of Louisville Divsn. Police, 1998—. Mem. Soc. Human Resource Mgmt., Louisville Soc. Human Resource Mgmt. Office: Louisville Divsn Police 633 W Jefferson St Louisville KY 40202 Fax: 502-574-7680. E-mail: glilly@lpdky.org.

LILLY, EDWARD GUERRANT, JR., retired utilities executive; b. Lexington, Ky., Oct. 29, 1925; s. Edward Guerrant and Elisabeth Read (Frazer) L.; m. Nancy Estes Cobb, Nov. 25, 1961; children: Penelope Read, Edward Guerrant III, Collier Cobb (dec.), Steven Clay. BS, Davidson Coll., 1948; MBA, U. Pa., 1949. Credit analyst Citizens and So. Nat. Bank, Charleston, S.C., 1949-50; asst. v.p. Wachovia Bank and Trust Co., Charlotte, 1952-55, v.p., 1956, v.p., loan adminstrv. officer Wilmington, N.C., 1956-60, sr. v.p., area exec. Kinston, N.C., 1961-62, Durham, N.C., 1963-70, sr. v.p., mgr. trust investment svcs. dept. Winston-Salem, N.C., 1970-71, also bd. dirs., 1971-88; sr. v.p., group exec. Carolina Power and Light Co., Raleigh, N.C., 1971-76, sr. v.p., chief fin. officer, 1976-81, exec. v.p., chief fin. officer, 1981-90, also bd. dirs. Bd. dirs. N.C. Enterprise Corp. Mem. U. N.C. bd. visitors, 1974-87; bd. dirs. Gen. Telephone Co. S.E., 1965-1972, Rsch. Triangle Found., Research Triangle Park, CSC Industries, 1990-95; trustee Davidson Coll., 1976-88, Union Theol. Seminary. Lt. USNR, 1950—52. Mem. Edison Electric Inst. (chmn. fin. group 1979) Lodges: Rotary (Raleigh). Presbyterian.

LILLY, ELIZABETH GILES, small business owner; b. Bozeman, Mont., Aug. 5, 1916; d. Samuel John and Luella Elizabeth (Reed) Abegg; m. William Lilly, July 1, 1976; children: Samuel Colborn Giles, Elizabeth Giles. RN, Good Samaritan Hosp., Portland, Oreg., 1941; student, Walla Walla Coll., Lewis and Clark Coll. Bus., Portland. ARC nurse, tchr. area high schs., Portland; owner Welton Studio Interior Design, Portland; in pub. rels. Chas. Eckelman, Portland, Fairview Farms-Dairy Industry; owner, builder Mobile Park Plaza, Inc., Portland. Del. platform planning com. Rep. Party; mem. Sunnyside Seventh Day Adventist Ch., deaconess. Recipient Svc. award Multnomah County Commrs., 1984. Mem. Soroptimist Internat. (local bd. dirs., bd. dirs. Women in Transition), Rep. Women's Club (pres.), C. of C., World Affairs Coun., Toastmistress (pres.), Oreg. Lodging Assn. (pres. bd. dirs.), Rep. Inner Circle (life). Address: 19825 SE Stark St Portland OR 97233-6039

LILLY, GRAHAM C., law educator; b. Welch, W.Va., 1938; BS, Va. Poly. Inst., 1960; LLB, U. Va., 1963. Bar: Va. 1963, DC 1966. Assoc. Covington and Burling, Washington, 1963-64; asst. prof. U. Va. Sch. Law, Charlottesville, 1967-69, assoc. prof., 1969-71, prof., 1971—, Henry L. and Grace Doherty prof. law, 1980—87, Armistead M. Dobie prof. law, 1987—, Class of 1948 rsch. prof., 1992—95, Thomas F. Bergin chair, 1996—99, assoc. dean academic affairs, 1986—89; exec. dir. U. Va. Law Sch. Found., 1970-73; assoc. provost U. Va., 1989—90. Author: An Introduction to the Law of Evidence, 1978;: An Introduction to the Law of Evidence, 1987. Capt. U.S. Army, Judge Adv. Gen.'s Sch., Charlottesville. Mem. Raven Soc., Omicron Delta Kappa, Phi Kappa Phi. Office: U Va Sch Law 580 Massie Rd Charlottesville VA 22903-1789 Office Fax: 434-924-3609. E-mail: gl@virginia.edu.*

LILLY, J. CRAIG, music educator; b. Columbus, Ohio, Sept. 28, 1955; s. Joseph Ray Lilly and Margaret Ellen Casto; m. Suzanne Marie Bancroft, Apr. 7, 1995; 1 child, Candice Marie. MusM, Miami U., 1978—80; MusB in edn., Ohio State U., 1973—78; D, Boston U., 1991—93. Certificate of Fine Arts Fitchburg State U., 1996. Tchr. Dartmouth Pub. Schools, Mass., 1982—96, East Providence City Schools, RI, 1996—2002, Fall River Pub. Schools, 2002—. Mem.: ASCD (assoc.), Nat. Assn. of Jazz Educators (assoc.), Music Educators Nat. Conf. (assoc.), Percussive Arts Soc. (assoc.; pres. 1990—94), Kappa Kappa Psi. Home: 1049 Main Rd Tiverton RI 02878 Office: Durfee HS Arts Dept 360 Elsbree St Fall River MA 02720 Office Phone: 508-675-8185. Office Fax: 508-675-8186. Personal E-mail: lillyband@att.net.

LILLY, JAMES EDWARD, lawyer; b. Birmingham, Ala., Aug. 5, 1960; s. Joseph Lanahan and Mildred Irene (Gorman) L.; m. Dawn Patrice Lee, June 6, 1981; children: Justin Patrick, Mary Jessica, Kaitlin Elizabeth. BA summa cum laude in Bus. Adminstrn. and Polit. Sci., Birmingham-Southern Coll., 1982; JD with high honors, Duke U., 1985. Bar: NC 1985, Ga. 1991. Joined Womble Carlyle Sandridge & Rice PLLC, Winston-Salem, NC, 1985, mem. Atlanta, Charlotte, NC, leader capital markets practice group, 2001—. Mem.: ABA (sect. bus. law). Republican. Roman Catholic. Avocations: golf, basketball, reading. Office: Winston Carlyle Sandridge & Rice PLLC One Wachovia Ctr Ste 3500 301 S College St Charlotte NC 28202-6037 Office Phone: 704-331-4969. Office Fax: 704-338-7854. Business E-Mail: jlilly@wcsr.com.

LILLY, KRISTINE MARIE, professional soccer player; b. Wilton, Conn., July 27, 1971; BA in Comm., U. N.C., 1993. Midfielder U.S. Women's Nat. Soccer Team, Chgo., 1987—; profl. soccer player Boston Breakers, 2001—03. Named Most Valuable Offensive Player, NCAA Championship, 1989, 1991, MVP, U.S. Women's World Cup, 1991, U.S. Soccer's Female Athlete of Yr., 1993, MVP, U.S. Women's World Cup, 1999, U.S. Nat. Team All-Time Appearance Leader (more than 90 games); named to, World Cup Championship Team, 1999; recipient Hemann Trophy, 1991, Gold medal, Centennial Olympic Games, 1996, Athens Olympic Games, 2004, Silver medal, Sydney Olympic Games, 2000. Achievements include member FIFA Women's World Championship Team, 1991; member World Cup Team, 1999; member U. N.C. NCAA National Championship Teams, 1989-92. Office: US Soccer Fedn 1801 S Prairie Ave Chicago IL 60616-1319

LILLY, LUELLA JEAN, retired academic administrator; b. Newberg, Oreg., Aug. 23, 1937; d. David Hardy and Edith (Coleman) L. BS, Lewis and Clark Coll., 1959; postgrad., Portland State U., 1959-61; MS, U. Oreg., 1961; PhD, Tex. Woman's U., 1971; postgrad., various univs., 1959-72. Tchr. phys. edn. and health, dean girls Cen. Linn Jr.-Sr. High Sch., Halsey, Oreg., 1959-60; tchr. phys. edn. and health, swimming, tennis, golf coach Lake Oswego (Oreg.) High Sch., 1960-63; instr., intramural dir., coach Oreg. State U., Corvallis, 1963-64; instr., intercollegiate coach Am. River Coll., Sacramento, 1964-69; dir. women's phys. edn., athletics U. Nev., Reno, 1969-73, assoc. prof. phys. edn., 1971-76, dir. women's athletics, 1973-75, assoc. dir. athletics, 1975-76; dir. women's intercollegiate athletics U. Calif., Berkeley, 1976-97; ret., 1997. Organizer, coach Lue's Aquatic Club, 1962-64; v.p. PAC-10 Conf., 1990-91. Author: An Overview of Body Mechanics, 1966, 3d rev. edit., 1969. Vol. instr. ARC, 1951; vol. Heart Fund and Easter Seal, 1974-76, Am. Heart Assn., 1991-95, Multiple Sclerosis Soc., 1999-2004; vol. ofcl. Spl. Olympics, 1975; mem. L.A. Citizens Olympic Com., 1984; bd. dirs. Las Trampas, 1993-98, sec. 1996-98. Recipient Mayor Anne Rudin award Nat. Girls' and Women's Sports, 1993, Lifetime Sports award Bay Area Women's Sports Found., 1994, Golden Bear award Vol. of Yr., 1995, Su Stauffer Friend of Edn. award, 2002; inducted Lewis and Clark Coll. Athletic Hall of Fame, 1988; named to U. Calif. First 125 Yrs. Women of Honor, 1995, Athletic Hall of Fame, U. Calif., 2005. Mem. AAHPER (life), AAUW, Nat. Soc. Profs., Women's Sports Found. (awards com. 1994-2004), Nat. Assn. Coll. Women Athletic Adminstrs. (divsn. I-A women's steering com. 1991-92, Lifetime Achievement award 1999), Women's Athletic Caucus, Coun. Collegiate Women Athletics Adminstrs. (membership com. 1989-92), Western Soc. Phys. Edn. Coll. Women (membership com. 1971-74, program adv. com. 1972, exec. bd. 1972-75), Western Assn. Intercollegiate Athletics for Women (exec. bd. dirs. 1973-75, 79-82), Oreg. Girls' Swimming Coaches Assn. (pres. 1960, 63), Ctrl. Calif. Bd. Women Ofcls. (basketball chmn. 1968-69), Calif. Assn. Health, Phys. Edn. and Recreation (chmn.-elect jr. coll. sect. 1970), Nev. Bd. Women Ofcls. (chmn. bd., chmn. volleyball sect., chmn. basketball sect. 1969), No. Calif. Women's Intercollegiate Conf. (sec. 1970-71, basketball coord. 1970-71), No. Calif. Intercollegiate Athletic Conf. (volleyball coord. 1971-72), Nev. Assn. Health Phys. Edn. and Recreation (state chmn. 1974), No. Calif. Athletic Conf. (pres. 1979-82, sec. 1984-85), Soroptimists Club (bd. dirs. 1988-2005, v.p. 1989, 92-93, sec. 1993-95, 2001-02, 1st v.p. 1996-97, 2004-, corr. sec. 1997-98, pres. 1998-2000, Women Helping Women award 1991, Women of Distinction award 2002), Phi Kappa Phi, Theta Kappa. Avocation: swimming. Home and Office: 60 Margrave Ct Walnut Creek CA 94597-2511 Office Phone: 925-934-3868.

LILLY, MARTIN STEPHEN, retired university dean; b. New Albany, Ind., Aug. 31, 1944; s. Raymond John and Amy Elizabeth (Peake) L.; m. Marilyn Ann MacDougall, Jan. 8, 1966; children— Matthew William, Mark Christopher, Rachel Marie, Martin Stephen, Jason Wood BA, Bellarmine Coll., Louisville, 1966; MA, Peabody Coll., Nashville, 1967, Ed.D., 1969. Instr. dept. spl. edn. Peabody Coll., 1967-69; asst. prof. edn. U. Oreg., 1969-71; research coordinator N.W. Regional Spl. Edn. Instructional Materials Center, 1969-71; research coordinator div. research Bur. Edn. for Handicapped U.S. Office Edn., 1971-72; assoc. prof. dept. spl. edn. U. Minn., Duluth, 1972-75; assoc. prof., chmn. dept. spl. edn. U. Ill., Urbana-Champaign, 1975-79, prof., chmn., 1979-81, assoc. dean grad. studies Coll. Edn., 1981-84; dean Coll. Edn. Wash. State U., Pullman, 1984-90, Calif. State U., San Marcos, 1990—2004; ret. Cons. in field; U.S. Office Edn. fellow, 1966-69; pres. Tchr. Edn. Coun. State Colls. and Univs.; bd. dirs. San Diego County Childrens Initiative; commr. Calif. Commn. on Tchr. Credentialing, 2002—. Author: Children with Exceptional Needs: A Survey of Special Education, 1979, (with C.S. Blankenship) Mainstreaming Students With Learning and Behavior Problems, 1981; assoc. editor: Exceptional Children, 1969-79; cons. editor: Edn. Unltd, 1979-81; reviewer: Jour. Tchr. Edn, 1980—; mem. editorial bd. Tchr. Edn. and Spl. Edn, 1980-83, co-editor, 1983-84; contbr. chpts. to books, articles to profl. jours. Trustee Vista (Calif.) Unified Sch. Dist., 2004—. Mem. Coun. for Exceptional Children, Assn. Tchr. Educators, Am. Assn. Colls. Tchr. Edn., Phi Delta Kappa. Democrat. Roman Catholic. Office: Calif State U San Marcos CA 92096-0001 Office Phone: 760-750-4310. Business E-Mail: slilly@csusm.edu.

LILLY, MICHAEL ALEXANDER, lawyer, writer; b. Honolulu, May 21, 1946; s. Percy Anthony Jr. and Virginia (Craig) L.; children: Michael Jr., Cary J., Laura B., Claire F., Winston W. AA, Menlo Coll., Menlo Park, Calif., 1966; BA, U. Calif., Santa Cruz, 1968; JD with honors, U. of Pacific, 1974. Bar: Calif. 1974, U.S. Dist. Ct. (no., so., ctrl. and ea. dists.) Calif. 1974, U.S. Ct. Appeals (9th cir.) 1974, Hawaii 1975, U.S. Dist. Ct. Hawaii 1975, U.S. Ct. Appeals (D.C. cir.) 1975, U.S. Supreme Ct. 1978, U.S. Ct. Appeals (7th cir.) 1979. Atty. Pacific Legal Found., Sacramento, 1974-75; dep. atty. gen. State of Hawaii, Honolulu, 1975-79, 1st dep. atty. gen., 1981-84, atty. gen., 1984-85; ptnr. Feeley & Lilly, San Jose, Calif., 1979-81, Ning, Lilly & Jones, Honolulu, 1985—. Author: If You Die Tomorrow-A Layman's Guide to Estate Planning. Dir. Diamond Head Theatre, U.S.S. Mo. Meml. Assn.; Lt. USN, 1968-71, Vietnam; capt. USN, ret. Named hon. Ky. col.; decorated Legion of Merit medal, 1997. Mem. Nat. Assn. Attys. Gen., Navy Res. Assn. (pres. 14th dist. 1986-89), Navy League (dept. judge adv. to bd. Honolulu coun.), Outrigger Canoe Club. Office: Ning Lilly & Jones 707 Richards St Ste 700 Honolulu HI 96813-4623 Office Phone: 808-528-1100. E-mail: michael@nljlaw.com. *Personal philosophy: Always do what you are afraid to do. Never give up. Forgive your enemies.*

LILLY, THOMAS GERALD, retired lawyer; b. Belzoni, Miss., Sept. 17, 1933; s. Sale Trice and Margaret Evelyn (Butt) Lilly; m. Constance Ray Holland, Dec. 29, 1962; children: Thomas Gerald Jr., William Holland, Carolyn Ray. BBA, Tulane U., 1955; LLB, U. Miss., 1960, JD, 1968. Bar: Miss. 1960. Assoc. firm Stovall & Price, Corinth, Miss., 1960—62; asst. U.S. atty. No. Dist. Miss., Oxford, 1962—66; assoc. Wise Carter Child & Caraway (and predecessor), Jackson, Miss., 1966—67, ptnr., 1967—94, Lilly & Wise, Jackson, 1994—2000, of counsel, 2001—03; ret., 2003. Gen. sec. Salt & Light Min. Found., 2005—. With USNR, 1955—88, rear adm. USNR. Decorated Legion of Merit, Navy Commendation medal. Fellow: Found. Fed. Bar Assn. (life); mem.: FBA (nat. coun. 1972—, rec. sec. 1975—76, gen. sec. 1976—77, 2d v.p. 1977—78, pres.-elect 1978—79, pres. 1979—80), Ulster Geneal. and Hist. Guild, Family Rsch. Assn. Miss. (1st v.p. 2004, pres. 2005), Miss. Geneal. Soc., Democracy Devel. Inst. (bd. dirs. 1995—2003), Miss. Bar Found., Miss. State Bar, Hinds County Bar Assn., Naval Hist. Soc., Jackson Civil War Roundtable, Navy League (pres. Ctrl. Miss. coun. 1993), Naval Order U.S., Naval Res. Assn., Res. Officers Assn. (pres. Miss. dept. 1982—83), Mil. Officers Assn. Am., Navy Supply Corps Assn., Chester Dist. Geneal. Soc., Miss. Com. Employer Support Guard and Res., Internat. Trade Club Miss. (bd. dirs. 1995—96), Nat. Lawyers Club (bd. govs. 1976—81), Scabbard and Blade, Lamar Order, Mil. Order World Wars, Sigma Nu, Phi Delta Phi, Omicron Delta Kappa. United Methodist. Personal E-mail: tomcomlilly@earthlink.net.

LILLY, THOMAS JOSEPH, lawyer; b. Bklyn., Feb. 17, 1931; s. Frank A. and Mary Ellen (Kelly) L.; m. Margaret Mary Doherty, June 28, 1959; children: Thomas J., Mary Jo, Joseph, Sean. BA, St. John's Coll., 1953; JD, Fordham U., 1961; LLM, NYU, 1967. Bar: N.Y. 1962, U.S. Dist. Ct. (ea. and so. dists.) N.Y. 1963, U.S. Ct. Appeals (2d cir.) 1965. Dir. rsch. Office and Profl. Employees Internat. Union AFL-CIO, N.Y.C., 1960-62; asst. U.S. atty. U.S. Dist. Ct. (ea. dist.) N.Y., Bklyn., 1962-66; ptnr. Doran, Colleran, O'Hara, Pollio & Dunne, N.Y.C., 1966-79, Quinn & Lilly, P.C., N.Y.C. and Garden City, N.Y., 1979-89; pvt. practice O'Donnell, Schwartz, Glanstein, & Lilly, Garden City, 1989—. Adj. prof. N.Y. State Indsl. and Labor Rels. Sch., Cornell U., 1980-81; arbitrator U.S. Dist. Ct. (ea. dist.) N.Y.; mem. Nassau County Pub. Employment Rels. Bd., 1994-2002. With USN, 1953-57. Mem. ABA, N.Y. Bar Assn., Nassau County Bar Assn., Sea Cliff Yacht Club, Prestwick Golf Club. Home: 136 8th Ave Sea Cliff NY 11579-1308 Office: 245 Hillside Ave Williston Park NY 11596 Office Phone: 516-794-9460. Business E-Mail: ThomasJLillySr@LillyandAssociates.net.

LILLY, WESLEY COOPER, marine engineer, surveyor; b. Phila., May 23, 1933; s. Richard Gladstone and Margaret Jane Lilly; m. Barbara Joan Newton (div. Nov. 24, 1978); children: Pamela Lynn, Barbara Joan. BS in Engring., Pa. Mil. Coll., 1961. Apprentice machinist Phila. Naval Shipyard, 1951-53, prodn. shipbuilding, 1955-66, planning, design divsn., 1966-68; shipbuilding specifications and testing staff Naval Weapons Svc. Office, 1968—70; procurement prodn. Navy Dept. Navsea, Washington, 1970-86; pres., owner Marine Assocs., Amelia Island, Fla., 1972—; pres., founder Saturn Marine Engring., St. Augustine, Fla., 1986—. Programmer Basic, Fortran, and Cobol rev. bus. computech programs; designer Fast Shuttle Tanker 02, 2002. With U.S. Army, 1953—55. Mem.: Soc. Naval Archs. and Marine Engrs. (chmn. com. for small and medium shipyards/shipbldg.), Christian Motorcycle Assn., Island Motorcycle Assn., Antique Outboard Motor Club (dir., bd. dirs.). Achievements include patents and copyrights in field of marine engineering; co-design of the modern accounting system; design of new fast tanker 02. Avocations: accounting, computers, antique outboard motors, motorcycling. Home: 2757 1st Ave Fernandina Beach FL 32034-2345 Office: Saturn Marine Engineering Fernandina Beach FL 32034 Office Phone: 904-321-2722. Personal E-mail: abcmarine2@hotmail.com.

LILLY, WILLIAM ELDRIDGE, federal official; b. Liberty, Tex., Aug. 25, 1921; s. Lawrence C. and Maude (McKinney) L.; m. Blanche Elizabeth Bromert, Jan. 18, 1944; children: Lizbeth Kristine, William Michael. AB, U. Calif. at Berkeley, 1950, grad. student, 1950-51. Program analyst Naval Ordnance Test Sta., China Lake, Calif., 1950-52; head estimates and analysis Naval Bur. Ordnance, Washington, 1952-54; dep. budget officer Nat. Bur. Standards, 1954-56; asst. dir. plans and programs Navy Polaris program, 1956-60; with NASA, 1960-82, asst. adminstr. for adminstrn., 1967-72, comptroller, 1972-82, ind. cons., 1982—. Pres. Arlington County (Va.) Youth Orgn., 1966-69. Served with USN, 1940-46. Recipient Exceptional Svc. medal NASA, 1965, 69, Disting. Svc. medal, 1973, 81, Presdl. Rank of Disting. Exec., 1980 (series code after 1980). Mem.: Phi Beta Kappa, Pi Sigma Alpha. Home: PO Box 2028 Arlington VA 22202-0028 Office: Ste 1204 L'Enfant Plz N SW Washington DC 20024

LILLYMAN, WILLIAM JOHN, language educator, academic administrator; b. Sydney, Australia, Apr. 17, 1937; came to U.S., 1963, naturalized, 1974; s. John and Christina Mary (Munro) L.; m. Ingeborg Wolz, Sept. 14, 1962; children: Gregory, Christina. AB, U. Sydney, 1959; PhD, Stanford U., 1964. Asst. prof. Stanford (Calif.) U., 1964-67; assoc. prof. U. Calif., Santa Cruz, 1967-72, prof. German Irvine, 1972—, dean humanities, 1973-81, vice chancellor acad. affairs, 1981-82, exec. vice chancellor, 1982-88, 98-00. Author: Otto Ludwig's Zwischen Himmel und Erde, 1967, Otto Ludwig: Romane und Romanstudien, 1977, Reality's Dark Dream The Narrative Fiction of Ludwig Tieck, 1979, Goethe's Narrative Fiction, 1983; co-editor; Probleme der Moderne, 1983, Horizonte Festschrift für H. Lehnert, 1990, Critical Architecture and Contemporary Culture, 1994. Recipient Extraordinarius award, U. Calif.-Irvine, 1988, UCI medal, 2000. Mem. MLA, Am. Assn. Tchrs. German. Office: U Calif Exec Vice Chancellors Office 509 Adminstrn Bldg Irvine CA 92697-1000

LIM, ALEXANDER RUFASTA, neurologist, clinical investigator, clinical neurophysiologist, educator, writer; b. Manila, Philippines, Feb. 20, 1942; s. Benito Pilar and Maria Lourdes (Cuyegkeng) Lim; m. Norma Sue Hanks, June 1, 1968; children: Jeffrey Allen, Gregory Brian, Kevin Alexander, Melissa Gail. AA, U. Santo Tomas, Manila, Philippines, 1959, MD, 1964. Intern Bon Secours Hosp., Balt., 1964-65; resident in internal medicine Scott and White Clinic Tex A&M U., Health Sci. Ctr. Coll. Medicine, Temple, Tex., 1965-67; resident in neurology Cleve. Clinic, 1967-69, chief resident in neurology, 1969-70, fellow clin. neurophysiology, 1970-71; clin. assoc. neurologist Cleve. Clinic Hosp., 1971-72; neurologist-in-chief, co-founder, co-mng. ptnr. Neurol. Clinic, Corpus Christi, Tex., 1972—; pres., CEO Neurology, P.A., Corpus Christi, 1972-92. Chief neurology dept. Meml. Med. Ctr., Corpus Christi, Tex., 1975—90, Spohn Hosp., Corpus Christi, 1974—90, Reynolds Army Hosp., Ft. Sill, Okla., 1990—91; clin. assoc. prof. Sch. Medicine U. Tex. Health Sci. Ctr., San Antonio; cons., reviewer Tex. Medicine, 1995—. Mem. editl. bd. Coastal Bend Medicine, 1988—95, NEURO Ctrl., 1999—. Active mentorship program for gifted and talented srs. South Tex. Area H.S. Lt. col. med. corps U.S. Army, 1990—91, Desert Shield/Desert Storm. Recipient Army Commendation medal, 1991, Nat. Def. medal, U.S. Army, 1991. Mem.: KC, AMA, Tex. Neurol. Soc. (sec. 1986—88, pres. 1989—90), Tex. Med. Assn. (chmn. neurology 1985—86), Am. Acad. Pain Mgmt., So. Electroencephalographic Soc., Soc. Behavioral and Cognitive Neurology, Am. Acad. Immunotherapy, Am. Clin. Neurophysiology Soc., Am. Acad. Clin. Neurophysiology, Am. Epilepsy Soc. (editl. bd. mem. Neurocentral), Am. Acad. Neurology (spkrs. bur.), Internat. Soc. Poets, Acad. Am. Poets, Internat. Platform Assn. Republican. Roman Catholic. Avocations: tennis, stamp collecting/philately, travel, skiing, bonsai. Home: 4821 Augusta Cir Corpus Christi TX 78413-2717 Office: The Neurological Clinic Christus Spohn Med Plaza 1415 3d St Ste 101 Corpus Christi TX 78404-2175 Office Phone: 361-883-1731. Personal E-mail: anlim8@hotmail.com. Business E-Mail: alim@neurological_clinic.neurohub.net. E-mail: anlim68@grandecom.com.

LIM, CHERYL CHEON-AE, music educator; b. Seoul, Korea, Oct. 26, 1953; arrived in U.S., 1980; d. Tae Young and Jeong Soon Lim. BA, Seoul Nat. U., 1977; MusM, Northwestern U., Evanston, Ill., 1985, DMA, 1993. Piano instr. Northwestern U., Evanston, 1989—90; head piano dept. Betty Haag Acad. of Roosevelt U., Arlington Heights, Ill., 1986—; adj. prof. Wheaton Coll., Ill., 1993—. Judge Nat. Guild Audition, 1995—2004, Festivals by Ill. State Music Tchrs. Assn., 1996—2003, Music Festival in Honor of Confucias, Chgo., 1999—2003, Soc. Am. Musicians, 1999, 2004, Nat. Fedn. Music Clubs, 2004. Recipient 1st prize, Korean Cultural Ctrl. Competition, 1978, Roosevelt U. Scholarship Competition, 1981, Tchg. Competition award, Nat. Conf. on Piano Pedagogy, 1990. Mem.: Nat. Guild of Piano Tchrs., Music Tchrs. Nat. Assn. (treas. 1988—), Suzuki Assn. of the Ams. Democrat. Avocations: reading, concerts. Office: Betty Haag Acad

Roosevelt Univ 111 W Campbell Arlington Heights IL 60005 also: Wheaton Coll 501 College Ave Wheaton IL 60187 Home: 5065 Dukesberry Ln Barrington IL 60010 Office Phone: 847-483-9811, 630-752-5518.

LIM, DANIEL VAN, microbiology educator; b. Houston, Apr. 15, 1948; s. Don H. and Lucy (Toy) L.; m. Carol Lee, Sept. 2, 1973. BA in Biology, Rice U., 1970; PhD in Microbiology, Tex. A&M U., 1973. Postdoctoral fellow Baylor Coll. Medicine, 1973-76; asst. prof. U. South Fla., Tampa, 1976-81, assoc. prof. microbiology, 1981-87, chmn. dept. biology, 1983-85, prof., 1987—. Pres. Micro Concepts Rsch. Corp; dir. Inst. Biomolecular Sci., 1988-93; cons. and expert witness in field. Author: Microbiology, 1989, 98, 2003, Introduction to Microbiology, 1995. Recipient Outstanding Contbn. in Sci. and Tech. award Fla. Gov., Christopher Columbus Fellowship Found. award Homeland Security, 2004. Fellow Am. Acad. Microbiology; mem. Inter-Am. Soc. Chemotherapy (v.p. 1983-88), Am. Soc. Microbiology (pres. southeastern br. 1990-91, mem. coun. 2000—, mem. career devel. com., 1999—, Carski award com. 1983-86, Margaret Green Outstanding Tchr. award, P.R. Edwards award, Ivan Roth award). Achievements include invention of bacteriological broth. Office: U South Fla Dept Biology SCA 110 4202 E Fowler Ave Tampa FL 33620-5200 Office Phone: 813-974-1618. Business E-Mail: lim@cas.usf.edu.

LIM, HENRY WAN-PENG, dermatologist; b. Bandung, Indonesia, July 19, 1949; s. Budiman Ruslim and Nietje Tedjasuryani; m. Mamie Wong, July 20, 1975; children: Christopher T., Kevin T. BS in Biochemistry with honors, McGill U., 1971; MD cum laude, SUNY, Bklyn., 1975. Diplomate Am. Bd. Dermatology, Nat. Bd. Med. Examiners. Intern Albert Einstein Coll. Medicine, Bronx, NY, 1975-76; resident dept. dermatology NYU Sch. Medicine, N.Y.C., 1976-79, NIH fellow in dermatology, 1979, Dermatology Found. fellow, 1979-80, from instr. to assoc. prof. dermatology, 1979-93, prof. dermatology, 1993-97, asst. dean vet. affairs, 1993-97; chmn., Clarence S. Livingood chair dermatology Henry Ford Health Sys., Detroit, 1997—, dir. acad. programs, 2002—03, v.p. for acad. affairs, 2003—; assoc. dean Wayne State U./Henry Ford Health Sys., Wayne State U. Sch Medicine, Detroit, 2004—. Chief dermatology svc. N.Y. VA Med. Ctr., N.Y.C., 1985—94, chief staff, 1993—97, staff physician dermatology svc., 1994—97; bd. dirs. Am. Bd. Dermatology, Am. Bd. Med. Specialities, Am. Acad. Dermatology; prof. pathology Sch. Medicine Wayne State U., Detroit, 2003—. Editor: Photodermatology, Photoimmunology & Photomedicine, 2000—03; assoc. editor: Jour. Investigative Dermatology, 2003—; mem. editl. bd. Jour. Am. Acad. Dermatology, 1993—, Jour. Cut Med. Surg., 2000—. Recipient numerous awards; scholar, McGill U., 1968—70. Mem.: AMA, AAAS, Internat. Union Photobiology (v.p. 2004—), Photomedicine Soc. (pres. 1992—99), Am. Assn. Immunologists, Am. Soc. Photobiology (councilor 1998—2001, pres. 2002—03, chair sci. program com. 2003—04), Am. Fedn. for Clin. Rsch., Assn. Profs. Dermatology (bd. dirs. 2000—03), Am. Dermatology Assn. (chair membership com. 2002—03), Dermatology Found. (trustee 2003—), Soc. Investigative Dermatology, Am. Acad. Dermatology (chair environ. com. 2000—04, bd. dirs. 2002—, exec. com. 2004—, v.p. elect 2005—), Alpha Omega Alpha. Avocation: travel. Office: Henry Ford Med Ctr New Ctr One Dept Dermatology 3031 W Grand Blvd Dept Ste 800 Detroit MI 48202-2689 Office Phone: 313-916-4060. Business E-Mail: hlim1@hfhs.org.

LIM, JAE DOEG, systems engineer, researcher; b. Seoul, Korea (South), Oct. 3, 1962; arrived in U.S., 1985; s. Chang Lim, Jung Oh; m. Kon Lim, May 21, 1993; children: Jin, Amy. BS, U. Ala., 1990, MS, 1992, PhD, 1999. Rschr. Korea Telecom, Seoul, 1992—95; mgr. Dacom Corp., Seoul, 1995—96; sr. sys. engr. Samsung Telecomm. Am., Richardson, Tex., 2000—. Cons. Dacom Corp., Tuscaloosa, Ala., 1996—96. Author: Radiation and scattering behavior of thin cylindrical antenna, 1992, Fixed Cell Assignment for Forward Link in Broadband Wireless Networks Supporting Internet Protocol Version 6 Mobility, 1999. Grantee, NSF, 1999, Tchg. Assistantship, U. of Ala., 1996—99, Rsch. Assistantship, 1990—92. Mem.: IEEE. Achievements include invention of method for increasing a data transmission rate in mobile wireles communication channels. Home: 2409 Clear Field Dr Plano TX 75025 Office Phone: 972-761-7452. Personal E-mail: jaedoeglim@hotmail.com.

LIM, JEANETTE J., federal agency administrator; b. July 23, 1940; BS in chem., U. Mich., 1962; MS in med. genetics, U. Wis. Med. Sch., 1965; JD, Temple U. Law Sch., 1978. Spl. asst. to pres. West Chester State U., Pa., 1976—79; spl. asst. Dept. Justice, Washington, 1995—97; acting asst. sec. Office for Civil Rights U.S. Dept. Edn., Washington, 1992—93, atty. Office for Civil Rights, acting asst. sec. Office for Civil Rights, 2000—01, dep. asst. sec. mgmt. and ops, 2002—. Office: US Dept Elem and Secondary Edn 400 Maryland Ave SW FOB-6 Rm 3W314 Washington DC 20202 Office Phone: 202-401-9090. E-mail: jeanette.lim@ed.gov.

LIM, JEFFREY JAMES, internist; b. Manila, Apr. 8, 1963; came to U.S., 1990; s. Henry Co and Emily (Weesit) L. BS in Biology, U. of the Philippines, 1984, MD, 1989. Diplomate Am. Bd. Internal Medicine. Intern SUNY, Bklyn., 1990-91, resident, 1991-93; clin. asst. instr. SUNY Health Scis. Ctr., Bklyn., 1990-93; attending physician Meml. Hosp. of Texas County, Guymon, Okla., 1994—, chief of staff, 2001—. Cons. physician Meml. Hosp. Tex. County Home Health, Guymon, 1994—, chmn. mortality & morbidity com., 1997—, chmn. ICU com., 1997—; clin. instr. U. Okla. Coll. Medicine, 2001—. Mem. ACP, AMA, Am. Soc. Internal Medicine, Soc. Critical Care Medicine, Am. Coll. Chest Physicians, Okla. Med. Assn., Okla. Soc. Internal Medicine. Roman Catholic. Avocations: swimming, basketball. Office: Internal Medicine Clinic 410 NE 12th S Guymon OK 73942

LIM, LEN GUI REMOLONA (MARK LIM), critical care and emergency nurse; b. Mauban, Quezon, Philippines, Mar. 2, 1951; came to U.S., 1978; s. Gui Kui Ama and Teofila (Remolona) L. Diploma, Quezon Meml. Hosp., 1974; BSN, Manila Cen. U., 1978. RN, Calif., N.Y., Ill.; cert. critical care nurse ACLS, mobile intensive care nurse. Staff nurse Mauban Emergency Hosp., Quezon, 1974-78; staff nurse med. surg. Dearborn (Mich.) Med. Ctr., 1978-80; rehab. charge nurse Fresno (Calif.) Community Hosp. and Med. Ctr., 1980-82; emergency dept. charge nurse Mary Thompson Hosp., Chgo., 1983-87; clin. nurse emergency dept. Cook County Hosp., Chgo., 1988-90; staff med. nurse Rush Presbyn. St. Lukes Med. Ctr., Chgo., 1990-91; staff emergency dept. Norwegian-Am. Hosp., Chgo., 1990-95; staff Cook Co. Juvenile Detention Ctr., Chgo., 1993—. Mem. ANA, Ill. Nurses Assn., Philippine Nurses Assn. Chgo., Mauban U.S.A. Home: 1926 W Harrison St Apt 504 Chicago IL 60612-3700

LIM, RALPH WEI HSIONG, finance educator; b. N.Y.C., Oct. 3, 1953; s. Yuen and Huan Lim. BSE, Princeton (N.J.) U., 1975; MBA, U. Pa., Wharton, 1977. CFA. Fin exec. Internat. Paper Co., N.Y.C., 1977-82; cons. Synergy Assocs. LLC, Darien, Conn., 1982—; prof. Sacred Heart U., Fairfield, Conn., 1984—; faculty cons. Charter Oak State Coll., New Britain, Conn., 2000—, mem. acad. coun., 2004—, chmn. bus. com., 2005—. Vis. fellow Yale U., New Haven, 1988—89. Contbr. articles to profl. jours. Mem. CAP, Ark., 1978-80, Conn., 1980—; rep. Darien Town Legis., Darien, 1988-89; commr. Darien Housing Authority, 1991-96. Mem. CFA Inst., Stamford CFA Soc. (bd. dirs. 1995-2001, pres. 1998-99), Fin. Execs. Internat. Republican. Avocations: aircraft pilot, acting. Home: PO Box 938 Darien CT 06820-0938

LIM, RAMON (KHE-SIONG LIM), neuroscience educator, researcher; b. Cebu City, Feb. 5, 1933; came to U.S., 1959, naturalized, 1973; s. Eng-Lian and Su (Yu) L.; m. Victoria K. Sy, June 21, 1961; children: Jennifer, Wendell, Caroline. AB, U. Santo Tomas, Manila, 1953; MD cum laude, U. Santo Tomas, 1958; PhD in Biochemistry, U. Pa., 1966. Diplomate Am. Bd. Psychiatry and Neurology. Rsch. neurochemist U. Mich., Ann Arbor, 1966-69; asst. prof. biochemistry U. Chgo., 1969-76, assoc. prof. Brain Rsch. Inst., 1976-81; prof. dept. neurology U. Iowa, Iowa City, 1981—, dir. divsn. neurochemistry and neurobiology, 1981—. Career investigator VA, 1983; adv. internat. writing program U. Iowa, 2002—. Mem. editl. bd. Internat. Jour. Devel. Neurosci., 1984-91, Neurochem. Rsch., 1997—; contbr. numerous articles to sci. jours. Grantee NIH, 1971—, NSF, 1979—, VA, 1981—; recipient 3d prize Art Assn. Philippines, 1957; named Outstanding Overseas Young Chinese, Fedn. Overseas Chinese Orgns., 1961. Mem. Am. Soc. Biochem. Molecular Biology, Internat. Soc. Neurochemistry (vis. lectureship 1986), Am. Soc. Neurochemistry, Soc. Neurosci., Am. Soc. Cell Biology. Achievements include research in isolation and characterization of regulatory brain proteins; growth and differentiation of brain cells; brain chemistry and molecular biology. Avocations: calligraphy, painting, writing, music. Home: 118 Richards St Iowa City IA 52246-3516 Office: U Iowa Iowa City IA 52242 Office Phone: 319-335-8527. E-mail: ramon-lim@uiowa.edu.

LIM, RUSSELL FUN, psychiatrist; s. Richard and Katherine Lim; m. Sally Lim, Apr. 0, 1995; children: James, Jacqueline. MD, U. Calif., 1990. Diplomate Am. Bd. Psychiatry and Neruology, 1998. Asst. clin. prof. Sch. Medicine U. Calif., Sacramento, 1998—2004, assoc. clin. prof. Sch. Medicine, 2004—. Med. dir. Northgate Point RST, Sacramento, 1998—2004. Editor (chapter author): Cultural Psychiatry for Clinicians: A Handbook for Working with Diverse Populations (Chancellor's Achievement award, 2004). Fellow, Okura Mental Health Leadership Found., 2002. Mem.: APA (assoc.; liaison to coun. nat. affairs 1999—2005), Am. Assn. Cmty. Psychiatrists (chmn. diversity com. 1998—). Democrat. Avocations: movies, theater, photography, reading, travel. Office: Behavioral Health Clinic 2230 Stockton Blvd Sacramento CA 95817 Office Phone: 916-734-2961. Office Fax: 916-734-0849. E-mail: rflim@ucdavis.edu.

LIMA, ADRIANA FRANCESCA, model; b. Salvador, Brazil, June 12, 1982; Signed with Elite Model Mgmt., NYC; appeared on covers of Vogue (Italy), 1997, Vogue (UK), 1998, Marie Claire (Brazil), 1998, Vogue (US), 1999, Marie Claire (Italy), 1999; appeared in Victoria's Secret Catalogues, 2000—; modeled for Anna Sui Jeans, Bebe, Gasoline, Mossimo, BCBG, Keds, XOXO. Actor: (films) The Hire: The Follow, 2001; appearances include The Victoria's Secret Fashion Show, 2001, 2002, 2003. Named Winner Ford Supermodel of Brazil Contest, 1996. Office: Elite Model Mgmt. 111 E 22nd St New York NY 10010*

LIMA, DONALD ROGER, retired computer programmer; b. San Luis Obispo, Calif., Jan. 9, 1935; s. Donald Joseph Lima and Vera Cora Moraga; m. Esther Hardin; 1 child, Gary. BA, Calif. State U., L.A., 1995. Programmer analyst City of L.A., 1975-95; ret., 1995. Author: (book) A Piece Is Missing, 1998; appearance in Theater Americana of Altadena, 1988-90. With U.S. Army, 1953-56. Democrat. Methodist. Avocation: pinochle. Mailing: 8101 Petunia Flower Way Las Vegas NV 89147-7435

LIMA, ROBERT, language educator; b. Havana, Cuba, Nov. 7, 1935; came to U.S., 1945; BA in English and Philosophy, Villanova U., 1957, MA in Theatre Arts and Drama, 1961; PhD in Romance Lit., NYU, 1968. Prof. Spanish and comparative lit. Pa. State U., Univ. Pk., Pa., 1965—2002, prof. emeritus, 2002—. Fellow Inst. for Arts and Humanistic Studies Pa. State U., 1986-2002, fellow emeritus, 2002-; vis. prof. comparative lit. Pontificia U. Cath., Peru; poet-in-residence U. Nat. Mayor de San Marcos, Peru, 1976-77; lectr. Romance langs. and lits. Hunter Coll. CUNY, 1962-65, USIA lectr., Peru, Cameroon, Equatorial Guinea. Author: The Theatre of Garcia Lorca, 1963, An Annotated Bibliography of Ramon del Valle-Inclan, 1972, (poetry) Fathoms, 1981, The Olde Ground, 1985, Mayaland, 1992, Dark Prisms Occultism in Hispanic Drama, 1995, Valle-Inclan. El Teatro de su Vida, 1995, Ramon del Valle-Inclan: An Annotated Bibliography of Ramon del Valle-Inclan, 1999, (poetry) Sardinia/Sardegna, 2000, Tracking The Minotaur, 2003, The Dramatic World of Valle-Inclan, 2003, Stages of Evil Occultism in Western Theatre and Drama, 2005; co-author: Dos Ensayos Sobre Teatro Español de los Veinte, 1984; editor, translator: Borges the Labyrinth Maker (A.M. Barrenechea), 1965, Valle-Inclan: Autobiography, Aesthetics, Aphorism, 1966; editor, contbr. Borges and the Esoteric, 1993, Cauda Pavonis issue on Leonora Carrington, 2000; translator: The Lamp of Marvels, Aesthetic Meditations (Ramon del Valle-Inclan), 1986, Savage Acts: Four Plays (Valle-Inclan), 1993; co-editor Readers Ency. Am. Lit., 1962, Homenaje A--Tribute to Martha T. Halsey, 1995, Texts and Contexts: A Tribute to Beno Weiss, 2001; contbr. articles to profl. jours.; prodr., cons., TV and radio programs Centro de Estudios TV la U. Cath., Lima, Peru, 1976-77, Voice of Am., NYC, 1961-62, Pendulum Prodns., 1960-61. Bd. dirs. Pa. Ctr. for Book. Decorated Knight Comdr. Order Queen Isabel Spain, 2003; recipient Founders Day award NYU, 1968, Play Translation prize Modern Internat. Drama, cert. of merit Writer's Digest Mag., 1982, Disting. Alumnus medal Villanova Univ., 1999; Rsch. grant Fund for Rsch. Pa. State U., Inst. for Arts and Humanistic Studies; Cintas Found. fellow in poetry Inst. Internat. Edn., 1971-72, fellow Commonwealth Speakers Program Pa. Humanities Coun., Sr. Fulbright fellow Coun. Internat. Exch. Scholars, 1976-77; others. Fellow Inst. for Arts and Humanistic Studies, Phi Kappa Phi (hon.), Phi Sigma Iota (hon.); mem. Internat. PEN, Poetry Soc. Am., Am. Assn. Tchrs. Spanish and Portuguese, Archaeol. Inst. Am., Am. Comparative Lit. Assn., Internat. Comparative Lit. Assn., Galician Studies Assn., Internat. Assn. Valleinclanistas, Am. Name Soc., Am. Soc. Sephardic Studies, Poets and Writers, Hermetic Text Soc., Beast Fable Soc., Pa. Humanities Coun. (academician), N.Am. Acad. Spanish Lang., Fulbright Alumni Assn., Enxebre Orden da Vieira, Real Academia Española (corr.), Alpha Psi Omega. Home: 485 Orlando Ave State College PA 16803-3477 Office: Pa State U 211 Burrowes Bldg University Park PA 16802 Business E-Mail: rxl2@psu.edu.

LIMACHER, MARIAN CECILE, cardiologist; b. Joliet, Ill., May 4, 1952; d. Joseph John and Shirley A. (Smith) L.; m. Timothy C. Flynn, May 17, 1980; children: Mary Katherine Flynn, Brian Patrick Flynn. AB in Chemistry, St. Louis U., 1973, MD, 1977. Diplomate Am. Bd. Internal Medicine, Am. Bd. Cardiovascular Diseases. Resident in internal medicine Baylor Coll. Medicine, Houston, 1977-80, cardiology fellow, 1980-83, instr. medicine, 1983-84; dir. cardiology non-invasive labs. Ben Taub Hosp., Houston, 1983-84; asst. prof. medicine U. Fla., Gainesville, 1984-91, assoc. prof., 1991-97, prof., 1997—; dir. non-invasive labs. Gainesville VA Med. Ctr., 1984-99, chief cardiology, 1995-99. Dir. preventive cardiology program U. Fla., 1987—. Author (with others): Cardiac Transplantation: A Manual for Health Care Professionals, 1990, Geriatric Cardiology, 1992, The Role of Food in Sickness and in Health, 1993, Clinical Anesthesia Practice, 1994, Primary Care, 1994; mem. editl. bd.: Clin. Cardiology, 1990—, Preventive Cardiology, 1997—, assoc. editor: Jour. Watch Women's Health, 2001—, Clin. Jour. Women's Health, 2001; contbr. articles to profl. jours. Mem. bioethics comm. Diocese of St. Augustine, Jacksonville, Fla., 1990-94. Recipient Preventive Cardiology Acad. award NIH, 1987-92; grantee for Women's Health Initiative, NIH, 1994—. Fellow: ACP, Coun. Clin. Cardiology, Soc. Geriatric Cardiology (bd. dirs. 1997—, pres. 2002), Am. Coll. Cardiology (chair com. women cardiology 1998—2002, trustee 1999—2004); mem.: Am. Clin. and Climatological Assn., Am. Heart Assn. (pres. Alachua County divsn. 1986—89), Am. Soc. Preventive Cardiology (pres. 1998). Roman Catholic. Avocations: tennis, jogging, skiing, playing piano. Office: U Fla Coll Medicine PO Box 100277 Gainesville FL 32610-0277

LIMATO, EDWARD FRANK, agent; b. Mt. Vernon, N.Y., July 10, 1936; s. Frank and Angelina (Lacerra) L. Grad. high sch., Mt. Vernon. With IFA (formerly Ashley Famous Agency), NYC, 1966—78; sr. exec. William Morris Agy., L.A., 1978—88; with Internat. Creative Mgmt., 1988—, talent agt. NYC, L.A., co-pres. Bd. dirs. Motion Picture and TV Fund, Abercrombie & Fitch, L.A. Conservancy, Am. Cinematheque. Mem. Acad. Motion Picture Arts & Scis. (assoc.). Republican. Roman Catholic. Office: Internat Creative Mgmt 8942 Wilshire Blvd Beverly Hills CA 90211-1934*

LIMBACHER, RANDY L., energy executive; B in petroleum engring., La. State U., 1980. V.p. Burlington Resources Oil & Gas Co., Gulf Coast Divsn., Houston, 1996—98, pres., CEO, 1998—2000, BROG GP Inc., 2000—01; sr. v.p., prod. Burlington Resources, Inc., 2001—02, exec. v.p., COO, 2002—. Mem.: La. State U. Engring. Industry Adv. Bd., Am. Petroleum Inst., Indep. Petroleum Assoc. Am., Soc. Petroleum Engrs., Houston Area Jr. Achievement. Office: Burlington Resources 5051 Westheimer Ste 1400 Houston TX 77210-4239

LIMBAUGH, DAVID, lawyer; b. Cape Girardeau, Mo., Dec. 11, 1952; Student, SE Mo. State Univ, 1971—72; BA in Polit. Sci. (cum laude), Univ. Mo., 1975, JD, 1978. Instr. SE Mo. State Univ., 1977—78; atty. Limbaugh, Russell, Payne & Howard, Cape Girardeau, Mo., 1978—. Syndicated columnist; author: Absolute Power, 2001, Persecution, 2003. With Nat. Guard, 1972—78. Mem.: Mo. Bar Assn. Office: 2027 Broadway PO Box 1150 Cape Girardeau MO 63702-1150 Office Phone: 573-335-3316. Office Fax: 573-335-0621. Business E-Mail: firm@limbaughlaw.com.*

LIMBAUGH, MARK A., federal agency administrator; BS, Idaho U., 1978. Exec. dir. Payette River Water Users Assn.; Payette River watermaster Water Dist. 65 Dept. Water Resources, Idaho; pres. Family Farm Alliance; dir. external and intergovernmental affairs, 2002—05; dep. commr. bur. reclamation US Dept. Interior, Washington, 2003—05, asst. sec. water & sci., 2005—. Office: US Dept Interior 1849 C St NW Rm 6657 Washington DC 20240 Office Phone: 202-208-3186. E-mail: mlimbaugh@usbr.gov.*

LIMBAUGH, RONALD HADLEY, retired historian, cultural organization administrator; b. Emmett, Idaho, Jan. 22, 1938; s. John Hadley and Evelyn E. (Mortimore) L.; m. Marilyn Kay Rice, June 16, 1963; 1 child, Sally Ann. BA, Coll. Idaho, 1960; MA, U. Idaho, 1962, PhD, 1967. Hist. libr. Idaho State Hist. Soc., Boise, 1963-66; instr. Boise Coll., 1964-66; asst. prof. history U. of the Pacific, Stockton, Calif., 1966-71, archivist, curator, 1968-87, prof. history, 1977-2000, Rockwell Hunt chair of Calif. history, 1989-2000; dir. Holt-Atherton Ctr., U. of the Pacific, Stockton, 1984-87. Exec. dir. Conf. of Calif. Hist. Socs., Stockton, 1973-76, 77-78, 82-86, 90-97; dir. John Muir Ctr. for Regional Studies, U. of Pacific, Stockton, 1989-2000; cons., evaluator NEH, 1983-86. Author: Rocky Mountain Carpetbaggers, 1982, John Muir's Stickeen and the Lessons of Nature, 1996; co-author: Calaveras Gold, 2003; co-editor: (microform) John Muir Papers, 1986, (book) Guide to Muir Papers, 1986; contbr. articles to profl. jours. With U.S. Army, 1955-56. NDEA fellow, 1960; grantee Calif. Coun. Humanities, 1976, Nat. Hist. Publs. and Records Commn., 1980-82, NEH, 1983, Inst. European Studies, 1989, Hoover Libr. Assn., 1997. Mem. Western History Assn., Mining History Assn. Christian Humanist. Avocations: hiking, mineralogy. Office: U Pacific 3601 Pacific Ave Stockton CA 95211-0197 Office Phone: 209-946-2145. Business E-Mail: limbaugh@mcn.org.

LIMBAUGH, RUSH HUDSON, III, radio talk show host; b. Cape Girardeau, Mo., Jan. 12, 1951; s. Rush Hudson Jr. and Millie Limbaugh; m. Roxy Maxine McNeely, Sept. 24, 1977 (div. July 10, 1980) m. Marries Michelle Sixta, 1983 (div. 1990), m. Marta Fitzgerald, May 27, 1994. Student Southeast Mo. State U.; Grad., Elkins Inst. Radio & Tech. Disc jockey KQV radio, Pitts., 1971, WHB radio, Kansas City, 1975—78; dir. group sales Kansas City Royals, 1979—83, dir. sales & spl. events; political commentator KMBZ radio, Kansas City, 1983—84; radio talk show host KFBK-AM radio, Sacramento, 1984—88, The Rush Limbaugh Show, NYC, 1988—. Author: The Way Things Ought To Be, 1992, See, I Told You So, 1993; TV syndicated show The Rush Limbaugh Show, 1992-1996, commentator, NFL Countdown, ESPN, 2003; publisher, monthly newsletter, The Limbaugh Letter, 1995—; film appearances: Forget Paris, 1995; TV appearance: Hearts Afire, 1994, The Drew Carey Show, 1998. Named to, Broadcasting Hall of Fame, 1993, Nat. Assn. Broadcasters Hall of Fame, 1998; recipient Marconi Radio award for Syndicated Radio Personality of the Year, Nat. Assn. Broadcasters, 1992, 1995, 2000. Republican. Office: The Rush Limbaugh Show 1270 Ave Americas New York NY 10020 Office Phone: 212-563-9166. E-mail: rush@eibnet.com.*

LIMBAUGH, STEPHEN NATHANIEL, federal judge; b. Cape Girardeau, Mo., Nov. 17, 1927; s. Rush Hudson and Bea (Seabaugh) L.; m. DeVaughn Anne Mesplay, Dec. 27, 1950; children— Stephen Nathaniel Jr., James Pennington, Andrew Thomas. BA, S.E. Mo. State U., Cape Girardeau, 1950; JD, U. Mo., Columbia, 1951. Bar: Mo. 1951. Prosecuting atty. Cape Girardeau County, Mo., 1954-58; judge U.S. Dist. Ct. (ea. and we. dists.) Mo., St. Louis, 1983—. With USN, 1945-46. Recipient Citation of Merit for Outstanding Achievement and Meritorious Service in Law, U. Mo., 1982 Fellow Am. Coll. Probate Counsel, Am. Bar Found.; mem. ABA (ho. of dels. 1987-90), Mo. Bar Assn. (pres. 1982-83). Republican. Methodist. Office: US Dist Ct Thomas F Eagleton Cthse 111 S Tenth St Ste 3 125 Saint Louis MO 63102 E-mail: limbaugh@moed.uscourts.gov.

LIMBAUGH, STEPHEN NATHANIEL, JR., state supreme court justice; b. Cape Girardeau, Mo., Jan. 25, 1952; s. Stephen N. and Anne (Mesplay) L.; m. Marsha Dee Moore, July 21, 1973; children: Stephen III, Christopher K. BA, So. Meth. U., 1973, JD, 1976; LLM, U. Va., 1998. Bar: Tex. 1977, Mo. 1977. Assoc. Limbaugh, Limbaugh & Russell, Cape Girardeau, 1977-78; pros. atty. Cape Girardeau County, Cape Girardeau, 1979-82; shareholder, ptnr. Limbaugh, Limbaugh, Russell & Syler, Cape Girardeau, 1983-87; cir. judge 32d Jud. Cir., Cape Girardeau, 1987-92; judge Mo. Supreme Ct., Jefferson City, 1992—. Mem. ABA, State Bar Tex., Mo. Bar. Office: Supreme Ct Mo 207 W High St Jefferson City MO 65101-1516

LIMEBERRY, JOHN WESLEY, humanities educator; b. Louisville, Ky., July 1, 1962; s. John Wesley and Mary Elizabeth Limeberry; m. Lora Lee Fearnow, July 20, 1991; 1 child, Madilyn Brooke. BA, Ind. U., Kokomo, 1986; MA, Ball State U., 1989. Assoc. prof. humanities Jefferson C.C., Louisville, 1990—. Contbr. articles to profl. jours. Advisor Jefferson County Dem. Party, Louisville, 1992—2000; bd. dirs. Yorktown Sr. Ho., Louisville, 2002—. Mem.: Ky. Comm. Assn. (mem.-at-large 2001—02), Popular Culture Assn. Democrat. Disciples Of Christ. Avocation: songwriting. Office Phone: 502-213-7331. E-mail: john.limeberry@kctcs.edu.

LIMEHOUSE, HARRY BANCROFT, JR., real estate developer, transportation consultant; b. Charleston, S.C., Dec. 3, 1938; m. Frankie Fennell, Jan. 18, 1961; children: Chip, Brien, Barry, Brad. BA in English, The Citadel, 1960, LLD, D in Bus., The Citadel, 1997; D in Hospitality (hon.), Johnson & Wales U., 1995. Lic. real estate broker S.C. Mgmt. trainee Deering-Millikin, 1960-61; agt. Prudential Ins. Co., Charleston, 1962-67, mgr. W. Palm Beach, Fla., 1967-69; dir. campaign mgmt. divsn. Rep. Nat. Com., Washington, 1967-69; pres., founder Limehouse Properties, Charleston, 1970—. Bankruptcy trustee U.S. Trustee's Office, Columbia, SC, 1988—. Mem. Pub. Rys. Commn. S.C., 1989—93, chmn., 1992—93; past pres. Carolina chpt. Real Estate Securities Inst.; charter pres. Charleston chpt. Comml. Income Properties Coun.; founding pres. Palmetto State Games; chmn. So. Govs. Conf., 1992, S.C. Dept. Transp. Commn., 1994—99; Citadel bd. visitors, 2004. Named Hotelier of the Yr., S.C. Hospitality Assn., 1994, Man of the Yr., 1996, S.F. Taxpayers Assn., Conservationist of the Yr., S.C. Wildlife Fedn., 1996—; named to, Order of the Palmetto, 1995, 1998. Mem.: Nat. Assn. Realtors, Hibernian Soc., Aircraft Owners and Pilots Assn., Downtown Athletic Club. Avocation: flying. Office: Limehouse Properties 8 Cumberland St Charleston SC 29401-2602 Office Phone: 843-577-6242 x3.

LIMERICK, PATRICIA NELSON, history professor; b. Banning, Calif., May 17, 1951; BA, U. Calif., Santa Cruz, 1972; PhD, Yale, 1980. Prof. history dept. U. Colo., Boulder. Chmn. bd. dirs. Ctr. Am. West. Author: (books) Desert Passages: Encounters With the American Deserts, 1985, The Legacy of Conquest: The Unbroken Past of the American West, 1987, Something in the Soil: Legacies and Reckonings in the New West, 2000. MacArthur fellow, 1995. Office: U Colo Ctr Am West MAcky 229 282 UCB Boulder CO 80309 E-mail: patricia.limerick@colorado.edu.

LIMONT, NAOMI CHARLES, artist, painter, printmaker, educator; b. Pottstown, Pa., Sept. 13, 1919; d. Frank Charles and Mary Jessica (Madden) Nissley; m. Alexander Walker Limont, June 4, 1955. BFA, Pa. Acad. Fine Arts, 1950; MFA, Tyler Sch. Art, 1965; M in Christian Edn., Bibl. Sem., 1951. Lectr., demonstrator in field, Phila., 1965—. Graphics tchr. Cheltenham Art Ctr., Pa., 1965—84, Abington Art Ctr., Jenkintown, Pa., 1984—85; chmn. print com. Phila. Art Alliance, 1980; artist-in-residence Lock Haven State Coll., 1981, Bethel Coll., North Newton, Kans., 1982; art juror various insts.,

West Delaware Valley. Numerous prints. Cresson Travelling scholar, Pa. Acad. Fine Arts, 1948. Mem.: Fellowship Pa. Acad. Fine Arts, Artist Equity Assn. (Grumbacher medal 1981), Am. Color Print Soc. (pres. 1984—, Drabkin medal 1976). Democrat. Presbyterian. Avocations: antiques, singing, gardening. Home and Office: 249 Papermill Rd Barto PA 19504-9236

LIMPERT, JOHN H., JR., fund raising executive; b. Bklyn., May 14, 1933; s. John H. and Sophia (Douropoulos) L.; A.B., Harvard U., 1955, postgrad., 1955-56; children: Alexandra Michelle, John Harold III. Public relations mgr. Frankfort Distillers Co. div. Seagram, N.Y.C., 1959-63; account exec. McCann-Erickson, Inc., N.Y.C., 1963-65, account dir., 1965-68; v.p. Ted Bates & Co., Inc., N.Y.C., 1968-71; mgr. lectrs. and speakers Keedick Lecture Bur., Inc., N.Y.C., 1971-73; dir. membership and devel. Mus. Modern Art, N.Y.C., 1973-83, dir. devel., 1983-86; v.p. for devel. and mktg. The N.Y. Bot. Garden, 1986-88; v.p. devel. Lincoln Ctr. for the Performing Arts Inc., 1988-89; assoc. fund counsel Charles H. Bentz Assocs., Inc., N.Y.C., 1990—; —; trustee Children's Aid Soc., 1966-74, Festival Orch. and Chorus, 1967-69, Schola Cantorum, 1963-65; bd. dirs. Assoc. Harvard Alumni, 1967-69, 73-74; bd. dirs. Bronx C. of C., 1988-91; vestryman Grace Episcopal Ch., Plainfield, 1992-95; bd. dirs. NY chpt., Nat. Soc. Fund Raising Execs., 1989-93. With U.S. Army, 1956-58. Cert. fund raising exec. Office: 950 Hillside Ave Plainfield NJ 07060-3150

LIMPITLAW, JOHN DONALD, publishing executive, minister; b. N.Y.C., Jan. 4, 1935; s. Robert and Olga (Lang) L.; m. Susan Elizabeth Glover, May 21, 1960; children: Alison, Amy Elizabeth. BA, Trinity Coll., Hartford, Conn., 1956; MA in Religion, Yale U., 1992. With Marine Midland Bank Trust Co. N.Y., N.Y.C., 1956-61, Celanese Corp., N.Y.C., 1961-63; mgr. personnel Westvaco Corp., N.Y.C., 1963-69; v.p. Warnaco Inc., Bridgeport, Conn., 1969-77, Macmillan Inc., N.Y.C., 1977-89; vicar Parish of Christ's Ch., Easton, Conn., 1992-97; bd. dirs. St. Mark's Day Care Ctr., Bridgeport, 1995—. Seminarian Yale Divinity Sch., New Haven, Conn., 1989-92; trustee Episcopal Investment Funds; bd. dirs. Inter-Ch. Residences, Inc., 3030 Park, Inc.; dir. Operation Hope; bd. dirs. Habitat, Easton, Conn., bd. ops., Fairfield, Conn., 1998—. Democrat. Episcopalian. Avocations: sailing, skiing. Home: PO Box 2004 140 Whidah Way Wellfleet MA 02667-7735 also: 6825 Grenadier Blvd Apt 1501 Naples FL 34108-7218 Office Phone: 239-598-1524, 508-349-1190. Personal E-mail: jlimpitlaw@aol.com.

LIMPUS, CHARLES EVERETT, III, non-commissioned officer; b. Fuka oka, Japan, Oct. 29, 1948; s. Charles Everett Limpus Jr. and Dorothy Pierce Limpus. Employment officer VFW, Orlando, 1995, legis. officer, 1995—97, employment officer, 1997, surgeon, 1999, svc. officer, 1997—. With U.S. Army, 1967—70, Vietnam. Mem.: 173rd ABN. BDE Soc., 82nd ABN. Div. Assn., VFW. Republican. Avocations: fishing, art, painting, drawing. Office: VFW 4444 Edgewater Dr Orlando FL 32804

LIN, ALICE LEE LAN, physicist, researcher, educator; b. Shanghai, Oct. 28, 1937; came to U.S., 1960, naturalized, 1974; m. A. Marcus, Dec. 19, 1962 (div. Feb. 1972); 1 child, Peter A. AB in Physics, U. Calif., Berkeley, 1963; MA in Physics, George Washington U., 1974. Statis. asst. dept. math. U. Calif., Berkeley, Calif., 1961-63; rsch. asst. in radiation damage Cavendish Lab. Cambridge U., England, 1965-66; info. analysis specialist Nat. Acad. Sci., Washington, 1970-71; tchng. fellow, rsch. asst. George Washington U., Cath. U. Am., Washington, 1971-75; physicist NASA /Goddard Space Flight Ctr., Greenbelt, Md., 1975-80, Army Materials Tech. Lab., Watertown, Mass., 1980—. Contbr. articles to profl. jours. Mencius Ednl. Found. grantee, 1959-60. Mem. AAAS, N.Y. Acad. Scis., Am. Phys. Soc., Am. Ceramics Soc., Am. Acoustical Soc., Am. Men and Women of Sci., Optical Soc. Am. Democrat. Avocations: computers, art collectibles, opera, ballet, gardening, coin collecting/numismatics. Home: 28 Hallett Hill Rd Weston MA 02493-1753 Office Phone: 781-899-6751. Business E-Mail: plinmarcus@alumni.tufts.edu.

LIN, AMY YUH-MEI, industrial engineer, real estate investor; b. Chuang-Hua, Taiwan, Jan. 22, 1948; Came to U.S., 1973; d. Tu-To and Show-Lan (Wu) Tsai; m. Edward Yih-Ling Lin, Dec. 24, 1975; children: Shirley, Kenneth. BSBA, Cheng Kung U., Taiwan, 1971; MS in Indsl. Engring., W.Va. U., 1975. Supr. Yellow Springs (Ohio) Instrument Corp., 1977-78; indsl. engr. MSI Data Corp., Costa Mesa, Calif., 1978-79; sr. programmer, analyst MAI Basic Four Corp., Tustin, Calif., 1979-81; supr., sr. indsl. engr LH Rsch., Inc., Tustin, 1981-85; sr. indsl. engr. Rockwell Internat., Anaheim, Calif., 1985-90; pres., gen. mgr. Maylyne Creations, Irvine, Calif., 1990—, Fortune Investment & Mgmt., Irvine, 1989—. Sec. Cheng Kung U. Found., 1992, treas. 1994—; v.p., treas. Woodbridge High Sch. Chinese Parent Assn., Irvine, Calif., 1993—. Mem. Cheng Kung U. Alumni Assn. (treas. 1992, v.p. 1994—), Apt. Owners Assn. So. Calif., Internat. Inst. Indsl. Engring. Avocations: tennis, writing, reading, pin pong/table tennis. Office: PO Box 18404 Irvine CA 92623-8404

LIN, CHANGQING, chemical engineer, researcher; b. Huian, Fujian, China, Oct. 15, 1972; arrived in U.S., 1997; s. Mingchun Lin and Shunzhu Chen; m. Yun Xiong. BS in Chem. Engring., U. Zhejiang, Hangzhou, China, 1994; ME in Computer Engring., PhD in Chem. Engring., U. S.C., 2001. Rsch. asst. dept. chem. engring. U. S.C., Columbia, 1997—2001; postdoctoral rsch. assoc. dept. material sci. and engring. U. Va., Charlottesville, 2001; rsch. engr. Microcell, Raleigh, NC, 2001—. Contbr. articles to profl. jours. Mem.: AIChE, Electrochemical Soc. Office: Microcell Ste 153 6003 Chapel Hill Rd Raleigh NC 27607 Office Phone: 919-858-8500 204.

LIN, CHENCHY JEFFREY, research scientist; arrived in U.S., 1987; s. Litang and Chinchu Lin; m. Yifang Sandy Hsueh, June 22, 1989; 1 child, Andrew Newton. BS in Chem. Engring., Nat. Taiwan Inst. Tech., Taipei, 1987; MS in Materials Sci. & Engring., U. Pitts., 1990; PhD in Polymer Sci. & Engring., Poly. U., Bklyn., 1995. Post doctoral fellow Princeton U., NJ, 1995—96; rsch. scientist Bridgestone Ams., Ctr. for Rsch. and Tech., Akron, Ohio, 1996—. Contbr. articles to profl. jour. Recipient Irving Skeist award, Poly. U., 1996, Dir. Award, Bridgestone Am., 1999, Pres. award, Bridgestone/Firestone, LLC, 2001, CEO award, Bridgestone Am., 2003, 2005. Achievements include research in rubber compounds for tire applications; patents in field. Office Phone: 330-379-7353. E-mail: linjeffrey@bfusa.com.

LIN, CHING-SHEN, pathologist; b. Ping-Tong, Taiwan, Republic of China, Sept. 11, 1934; s. Ten-Fu Lin and Chuang Chen; m. Lilly Lin, Nov. 25, 1962; children: John, Judith, Jane. MD, Nat. Taiwan U., 1960. Diplomate Am. Bd. Anatomic and Clin. Pathology. Clin. assoc. prof. pathology SUNY Downstate Med. Ctr., Bklyn., 1988-89; dir. autopsy pathology Mt. Sinai Med. Ctr., N.Y.C., 1989-99, assoc. prof. pathology, 1989-99. Bd. editors Am. Coll. Angiology, 1988—. V.p. Taiwan Ctr., N.Y.C., 1998-99. Ensign Chinese Navy, Taiwan, 1960-61. Fellow Am. Clin. Pathologists, Am. Coll. Angiology; mem. AMA, Nat. Taiwan U. Med. Coll. Alumni Assn. (pres. 1992-93), N.Y. Acad. Sci. Home: 26 Ebbtide Ln Dix Hills NY 11746 Personal E-mail: cslin@mindspring.com.

LIN, CHUN CHIA, research physicist, educator; b. Canton, China, Mar. 7, 1930; s. Yue Hang Lam and Kin Ng. BS, U. Calif., Berkeley, 1951, MA, 1952; PhD, Harvard U., 1955. Asst. prof. physics U. Okla., Norman, 1955-59, assoc. prof. physics, 1959-63, prof. physics, 1963-68, U. Wis., Madison, 1968—. Cons., univ. retainee Tex. Instruments Inc., 1960-68; cons. Sandia Labs., 1976-81; sec. Gaseous Electronics Conf., 1972-73, chmn., 1990-92. Contbr. articles ot profl. jours. Sloan Found. fellow, 1962-66; rsch. grantee NSF and Air Force Office Sci. Rsch. Fellow Am. Phys. Soc. (sec. divsn. electron and atomic physics 1974-77, chair divsn. atomic molecular and optical physics 1994-95, Will Allis prize 1996). Home: 1652 Monroe St Apt C Madison WI 53711-2046 Office: U Wis Dept Physics Madison WI 53706 Office Phone: 608-262-0697.

LIN, DAHANG, medical physicist; arrived in U.S., 1985; s. Meitan Lin and Wenzhen Zhang; m. Qixian Zhang; children: Gang, Xia. Diploma, Tsing Hua U., 1967, MS in Physics, 1982; MA in Physics, Bklyn. Coll., 1989; PhD in Physics, CUNY, 1992. Lic. med. physicist N.Y. Instr. Hubei Coll. Traditional Chinese Medicine, Wuhan, 1974—78, Wuhan Poly. Inst., 1981—85; tchg. asst. Bklyn. Coll., 1985—92; med. physicist, assoc. dir. Elmhurst (N.Y.) Hosp. Ctr., 1992—. Contbr. articles to profl. jours. Bd. dirs. N.Y. Chinese Am. Assn., Flushing, 1998—. Mem.: Am. Assn. Physicists in Medicine, Soc. Nuc. Medicine. Avocations: travel, photography, fishing, sports. Home: 40-11 Murray St Flushing NY 11354 Office: Elmhurst Hosp Ctr 79-01 Broadway Elmhurst NY 11373 Business E-Mail: lind@nychhc.org.

LIN, FANG-HUA, mathematics professor; BS, Zhejing U., 1981; PhD, U. Minnesota, 1985. Prof. Courant Inst. NYU, 1985—87; prof. U. Chicago, 1988—89, NYU, 1989—, Silver prof. mathematics, 2002—. Visiting lecturer Congress of Mathematics, Kyoto, 1990, U. Tennessee, 1995, Tulane U., 1997, NYU, 1997, Rice U., 2004, U. Cincinnati, 2004; editorial bd. mem. Comm. on Pure & Applied Mathematics, 1989—, Calculus of Variations & Partial Differential Equations, 1992—, Comm. in Analysis & Geometry, 2000—, SIAM Jour. of Mathematical Analysis, 2001—, Jour. of Differential Geometry, 2004—, Mathematical Rsch. Letters, 2004—. Author: over 130 rsch. papers and two books of lecture notes. Recipient Presidential Young Investigator award, 1989, Outstanding Rsch. award, NSF - China, 1998, Bocher prize, AMS, 2002; grantee Alfred P. Sloan Rsch. Fellowship, 1989. Fellow: Am. Acad. of Arts & Sciences. Office: Courant Inst Mathematical Sciences 251 Mercer St New York NY 10012*

LIN, FRANK C., computer company executive; Chmn. bd. dirs., pres., CEO Trident Microsys. Inc., Mountain View, Calif. Office: Trident Microsystems 1090 E Arques Ave Sunnyvale CA 94085-4601*

LIN, HAI, physicist; arrived in US, 2001; Attended, Hangzhou Fgn. Lang. Sch., 1991—97; BS, Peking U., Beijing, 2001; MA, Princeton U., 2003. Asst. in instrn. Princeton (NJ) U., 2002—. Mem.: Soc. Indsl. and Applied Math., Am. Chem. Soc., Biophysical Soc., Am. Math. Soc., Am. Phys. Soc., NY Acad. Scis. Achievements include research in quark distribution in nucleons; black hole thermodynamics; bacterial cell communication and chemotaxis; duality between string theory and gauge theory; string theory and quantum gravity. Office: Princeton U Dept Physics Washington Rd Princeton NJ 08544 Personal E-mail: hailin@princeton.edu.

LIN, HAMILTON, investment banker, education educator; s. Jerry and Mary Lin; m. Eileen Chan. BS, NYU Stern, 1996—2000. CFA AIMR, 2003. Investment banking rsch. Goldman Sachs, NYC, 1998—99; fin. analyst Ryan Labs, NYC, 1999—2000; m&a analyst Banc of Am. Securities, NYC, 2000—01; m&a assoc. Hales & Co, NYC, 2001—04, Freeman & Co, NYC, 2004; pres. Wall St. Tng., 2005—. Adj. prof. Hunter Coll. Continuing Edn., N.Y.C., 2002—, Baruch Coll.; fin. panelist, N.Y.C., 2000—04; fin. instr. wallst-training.com, 2001—; dir. strategy Ethical Majority, N.Y.C., 2002—04. Editor (editor-in-chief): (monthly company newsletter) Hales Report. NYU Stern Scholars scholarship, NYU Stern, 1996—2000. Mem.: CFA Inst., New York Soc. Security Analysts (seminar instr. 2003—). Office Phone: 718-360-4942. E-mail: hamilton@hammi.net.

LIN, HENRY BAOHUA, writer, consultant; came to U.S., 1988; s. John Luchen and Mary Chih (Cheng) L. Master, Oreg. State U., 1990. Cons. feng shui design, natural health care methods, and face reading. Author: What Your Face Reveals, 1999 (Libr. award 2000), Chinese Health Care Secrets, 2000, The Art and Science of Feng Shui, 2000. E-mail: henry9us@yahoo.com.

LIN, HUAN, engineering researcher; arrived in US, 1987; s. Wei-Cheng Lin and Show-Jing Dome; m. Liang-I Lai, July 14, 1994; children: YuhEn Krista, Christopher Yuh Hsing. BS, Nat. Cheng-Kung U., Tainan, Taiwan, 1986; MS, Oreg. State U., 1990, PhD, 1995. Rsch. asst. Oreg. State U., Corvallis, 1988—94, rsch. assoc. civil engring., 1995—. Reviewer (tech. jour.) Jour. Sound and Vibration, 2004—; contbr. chapters to books. Mem.: ASME (reviewer tech. jour. 2001—), ASCE (assoc.; reviewer tech. jour. 1996—), Chinese Student Assn. (pres. 1992—93, counselor 1993—94), Structural Engring. Inst. (assoc.), Soc. Naval Archs. and Marine Engrs. (assoc.). Office: Dept Civil Engring Oreg State U Corvallis OR 97331 Office Phone: 541-737-6147. Business E-Mail: linh@engr.orst.edu.

LIN, JAMES CHIH-I, biomedical engineer, electrical engineer, educator; b. Dec. 29, 1942; m. Mei Fei, Mar. 21, 1970; children: Janet, Theodore, Erik. BS, U. Wash., 1966, MS, 1968, PhD, 1971. Engr. Crown Zellerbach Corp., Seattle, 1966-67; asst. prof. U. Wash., Seattle, 1971-74; prof. Wayne State U., Detroit, 1974-80, U. Ill., Chgo., 1980—, head dept. bioengring., 1980-92, dir. robotics and automation lab., 1982-89, dir. spl. projects Coll. Engring., 1992-94, rsch. chair NSC, 1993-97, dir. Ctr. Wireless Tech. and Bioelectromagnetics, 1997—. Vis. prof., Beijing, Rome, Shan Dong, Taiwan Univs.; lectr. short courses, 1974—; cons. Battelle Meml. Inst., Columbus, Ohio, 1973-75, SRI Internat., palo Alto, Calif., 1978-79, Arthur D. Little Inc., Cambridge, Mass., 1980-83, Ga. Tech. Rsch. Inst., Atlanta, 1984-86, Walter Reed Army Inst. Rsch., 1973, 87, 88, Naval Aerospace Med. Rsch. Labs., Pensacola, 1982-83, U.R.S. Corp., San Francisco, 1985-87, CBS Inc., N.Y., 1988, U. Va., 1991-92, ACS Inc., Santa Clara Calif., 1989-90, Luxtron Corp., Mountainview, Calif., 1991-92, Commonwealth Edison, Chgo., 1991-95, Lucent Tech./Bell Labs., 1998-2000; program chmn. Frontiers of Engring. and Computing Conf., Chgo., 1985; chmn., convener URSI Jt. Symposium Electromagnetic Waves in Biol. Sys., Tel Aviv, 1987, Internat. Conf. on Sci. and Tech., 1989-91; chmn. Chinese-Am. Acad. and Profl. Conv., 1993; mem. Congrl. Health Care Adv. Coun., 13th dist., Ill., 1987-99; panelist NSF Presdl. Young Investigator award com., Washington, 1984, 89; mem. NIH diagnostic radiology, 1981-85, chmn. spl. study sect., 1986—2003; mem. U.S. Nat. Commn. for URSI, NAS, 1980-82, 90-99, chair Commn. K., 1990-99, Extremely Low Frequency Field monitoring com., 1995-97; mem. Internat. Commn. on Nonionizing Radiation Protection, 2004—; mem. Pres. Com. Nat. Medal of Sci., 1992-93; mem. Nat. Coun. Radiation Protection and Measurement, 1992—, chmn. radio frequency sci. com., 1995—, v.p. 2005—; chmn. Internat. Union of Radio Scis. Commn., Electromagnetics in Biology and Medicine, 1996-99; chmn. Internat. Sci. Meeting on Electromagnetics in Medicine, 1997; mem. citizens adv. coun. Hinsdale Ctrl. H.S., 1988-93 Author: Microwave Auditory Effects and Applications, 1978, Biological Effects and Health Implications of Radiofrequency Radiation, 1987, Electromagnetic Interaction with Biological Systems, 1989, Mobile Comm. Safety, 1996; editor: Advances in Electromagnetic Fields in Living Systems, 1994—, EMB Mag., 1997—99, Wireless Networks, 1996—97; contbr. articles to profl. jours., columns to mags. Recipient Nat. Rsch. Svcs. award 1982, Disting. Svc. award, Outstanding Leadership award Chinese Am. Acad. and Profl. Assn. MidAm., 1989. Fellow AAAS, AIMBE, IEEE (tech. policy coun. 1990-91, chmn. com. on man and radiation, 1990-91, assoc. and guest editor transactions on biomed. engring., guest editor transaction on microwave theory and techniques, disting. lectr. engring. in medicine and biology 1991—, Transaction Best Paper award 1975); mem. Biomed. Engring. Soc. (sr. mem.), Robotics Internat. (sr. mem.), Am. Soc. Engring. Edn., Bioelectromagnetics Soc. (charter, pres.-elect 1993-94, pres. 1994-95, chmn. ann. meeting 1994, d'Arsonval medal 2003), Electromagnetics Acad., Marconi Found. (sci. com. 1996—), Golden Key, Sigma Xi, Phi Tau Phi (v.p.), Tau Beta Pi. Office: U Ill Coll Engring 1030 SEO MC/154 851 S Morgan St Chicago IL 60607-7042 Office Phone: 312-413-1052. Business E-Mail: lin@uic.edu.

LIN, JIA-LIN, meteorologist; b. Beijing, Oct. 30, 1966; s. Han-Lian Lin and Deng-Qin LinYu; m. Tao-Tao Qian, Jan. 11, 1971. BS, Tsinghua U., Beijing, 1990; MS, Peking U., Beijing, 1993; PhD, SUNY, Stony Brook, 2001. Rsch. scientist NOAA-CIRES Climate Diagnostics Ctr., Boulder, Colo., 2001—. Contbr. articles to profl. jours. Recipient, NASA Goddard Space Flight Ctr., Global Modeling and Assimulation Office grantee, 2004, Guang-Hua award, Peking U., 1992; grantee, US Climate Variability and Predictability Program grantee, 2004—. Mem.: Am. Meteorol. Soc. Achievements include discovery of (with Brian Mapes) the wind shear effects on anvil clouds and cloud radiative forcing in the western Pacific warm pool, which is important for tropical climate. Office: NOAA-CIRES Climate Diagnostics Center 325 Broadway R/CDC1 Boulder CO 80305-3328 Office Phone: 303-497-4341. E-mail: jialin.lin@noaa.gov.

LIN, JIIN-HUEY CHERN, engineering educator; b. Kaoshung, Taiwan, Republic of China, Feb. 19, 1949; d. Fen-Fu and Chung-Lin Lin Chen; m. Luh-Yuan Lin, July 5, 1973; children: Albert Isaac, Alice, Seraphina. BS in Physics, Chung Yuan Christian U., Taiwan, 1970; MS in Physics, N.E. La. U., 1974; PhD in Biomaterials, Northwestern U., 1983. Vis. specialist Nat. Yang-Ming U., Taipei, Tawian, 1984-85; asst. prof. Northwestern U., Chgo., 1985-89, vis. prof., 1996-97, Nat. Cheng-Kung U., Tainan, Taiwan, 1987-88, assoc. prof., 1989-95, prof., 1995—, dir. Ctr. for Biomaterials Rsch., 2002—. Strategic com. Nat. Sci. Coun., Taipei, 1997-99. Jour. reviewer Dental Materials, Liverpool, U.K., 1995—, Jour. of Materials Chemistry and Physics, Liverpool, 1997—, Biomaterials, 2004—; contbr. numerous articles to profl. jours.; inventor in field Grantee Nat. Sci. Coun. of Republic of China, Nat. Health Rsch. Inst., 1994—. Fellow The Acad. of Denal Materials; mem. Soc. of Biomaterials, Soc. of Dental Materials, Chinese Bioengring. Soc., Am. Ceramic Soc. Home: 911 Tower Rd Winnetka IL 60093-1935 Office: Nat Cheng-Kung U Tainan Taiwan Business E-Mail: chernlin@mail.ncku.edu.tw.

LIN, JIZHEN, otolaryngologist, researcher; b. Shaxian, Fujian, China, Sept. 18, 1955; s. Hong-Han Lin and Gui-ying Zhang; m. Min Zheng; children: Di, Xin Zheng. MD, Fujian Med. U., Fuzhou, China, 1982. Lin Jizhen Fujian Med. Coll., 1982. Intern Union Hosp., Fujian Med. Coll., Fuzhou, 1981—82, resident, 1984—86, instr., 1987—91; resident in surgery Saxian (China) Hosp., 1982—84; instr. medicine U. Minn., Mpls., 1997—98, asst. prof. medicine, 1998—, dir. auditory molecular biology lab., 1998—, assoc. grad. faculty, 2000—, advising grad. faculty, 2000—. Guest prof. Fujian Med. U., 2000, Xi'An Jiao-Tong U., 2002. Contbr. articles to profl. jours. Recipient Progress Med. Sci. Tech. award (2d place), Fujian Health Adminstrn., 1990, Progress Med. Sci. Tech. award (3rd place), Chinese Health Adminstrn., Beijing, 1991, Brainstorm Grant award, U. Minn., 2003. Mem.: Assn. Rsch. Otorhinolaryngology (life). Achievements include research in establishment of middle ear and inner ear cell lines and characterization of mucin gene expression in the middle ear diseases; identification of molecular switches for hair cell growth and proliferationcas well as biomarkers for head and neck cancers. Office: U Minn Med Sch 2001 6th St SE Minneapolis MN 55455 Business E-Mail: linxx004@umn.edu.

LIN, JOSEPH PEN-TZE, retired radiologist; b. Foochow, China, Nov. 25, 1932; came to U.S., 1959, naturalized, 1974; s. Tai Shui and Chin Sien Lin; m. Lillian Y. Hsu, Dec. 23, 1959; children: James S., Carol W., Julia W. MD, Nat. Taiwan U., 1957. Diplomate Am. Bd. Radiology. Rotating intern Robert B. Green Meml. Hosp., San Antonio, 1959-60; resident in radiology Santa Rosa Med. Ctr., San Antonio, 1960-61, Bellevue Hosp. Ctr., N.Y.C., 1961-63; fellow in neuroradiology NYU Med. Ctr., N.Y.C., 1963-65, instr. radiology, 1965-67, asst. prof., 1967-70, assoc. prof., 1970-74, prof., 1974-97; dir. neuroradiology sect. Univ. Hosp., N.Y.C., 1974-93; dir. neuroradiology Bellevue Hosp., N.Y.C., 1993-97; ret., 1997. Cons. Manhattan VA Hosp., N.Y.C., 1974-97, Booth Meml. Hosp., N.Y.C., 1978-84, St. Vincent's Hosp., S.I., N.Y., 1978-85, New Rochelle (N.Y.) Hosp., 1978-85. Contbr. articles on neuroradiology to med. jours. Fellow Am. Coll. Radiology, Am. Heart Assn. (stroke coun.); mem. Am. Chinese Med. Soc. (pres. 1978), Am. Soc. Neuroradiology, Radiol. Soc. N.Am., Assn. Univ. Radiologists. Home: 15 Oxford Rd New Rochelle NY 10804-3712 E-mail: linpentz@aol.com.

LIN, JUCHUI RAY (JU-CHUI LIN), polymer scientist; b. Taoyuan, Taiwan, China, Apr. 25, 1947; came to U.S., 1974; s. Pai-Liang and Mai (Wang) L.; m. Jing-Fang Wang, Dec. 24, 1975; children: Amy Monica, Audrey Alice. BS in Chemistry, Nat. Taiwan Normal U., 1972; MS in Chemistry, Southwest Tex. State U., 1977; PhD in Macromolecular Sci., Case Western Res. U., 1985. Tchr. Taipei Gimmei Jr. High Sch., Taiwan, 1971-73; lab. instr. Nat. Ctrl. U., Chungli, Taiwan, 1973-74; chemist Sohio Rsch. Ctr., Warrensville Heights, Ohio, 1983, DPJ Rsch. Ctr., SCM Corp., Strongville, Ohio, 1984-86; sr. scientist Spectrum Control Rsch. Ctr., Erie, Pa., 1986-88; tech. mgr. Koch Membrane Systems, Inc., Wilmington, Mass., 1989-93; mgr. ion-exch. membrane technology Ionics, Inc., Watertown, Mass., 1993—. Author youth sci. books Youth Ency., 1970, also papers in field. Fellow Am. Inst. Chemists; mem. AIChE, Am. Chem. Soc., Soc. Plastics Engrs. Achievements include patents in field of conductive polymers, electrical active polymers, resins and coatings, elastomers, encapsulations for electronics, potting, ceramics, polymer blends, polymer surface modifications, membrane formulations, membrane processes; pioneer and inventor of cobalt chain transfer agents for living free radical polymerization, catalyzed grafting reaction of epoxide onto halogenated vinyl polymers, self-assembly surface coating technology, enzyme immobilization. Office: Ionics Inc 65 Grove St Watertown MA 02472-2882 E-mail: jlin@ionics.com.

LIN, LIANLIAN, management educator; b. Liaoning, China, Aug. 22, 1956; d. Jiang Lin and Jianhua Sun; 1 child, Nika Qiao. BA in Econs., Liaoning U., China, 1982; MA in Internat. Fin., Fudan U., Shanghai, China, 1985; LLM, U. Pa., Phila., 1988; PhD in Bus. Adminstrn., U. Tex., Austin, 1992. Mem. law faculty Fudan U., China, 1985—87; prof. mgmt. Calif. State Poly. U., Pomona, 1992—. Vis. prof. Peking U., Beijing, 2000; pres. Asian Pacific faculty staff and student assn. Calif. State Poly U., Pomona, 2001—02. Contbr. articles to profl. jours, also books. Mem.: Chinese Am. Faculty Assn. So. Calif. (pres. 2002—03, pres. CAFA Scholarship Found. 2005—), Chinese Scholars Assn. So. Calif. (pres. 2004—05), Chinese Am. Faculty Assn. Scholarship Found. (pres. 2005—). Office: Calif State Poly U 3801 W Temple Ave MHR Pomona CA 91768 Office Phone: 909-869-2422. Business E-Mail: LLin2@CSUPomona.edu.

LIN, MARIA C. H., lawyer; b. Kunming, Yunnan, China, Jan. 27, 1942; BSc, Coll. Mount St. Vincent, 1966; MSc, U. Kans., 1970; JD, Fordham U., 1978. Bar: N.Y. 1979, U.S. Dist. Ct. (so. and ea. dists.) N.Y. 1979, U.S. Ct. Appeals (Fed. cir.) 1982, U.S. Patent and Trademark Office, 1979, U.S Supreme Ct. 1985. Ptnr. Morgan & Finnegan, N.Y.C. Internat. Intellectual Propery Soc. (chair 2000—02). Office: Morgan & Finnegan LLP Three World Fin Ctr New York NY 10281-2101 Office Phone: 212-415-8700. E-mail: mclin@morganfinnegan.com.

LIN, MAYA, architect, sculptor; b. Athens, Ohio, Oct. 5, 1959; d. Henry H. and Julia (Chang) L. m. Daniel Wolf; 2 children. BA, Yale U., 1981, MA, 1986, PhD in Fine Arts, 1987. Architectural designer Peter Forbes & Assocs., N.Y.C., 1986-87; pvt. practice N.Y.C., 1987—. Bd. dir. So. Poverty Law Ctr.'s Teaching Tolerance project, Kennedy Mus. Art at Ohio Univ. Prin. work include Vietnam Veterans Meml., Washington, 1981, Civil Rights Meml., Montgomery, Ala., 1986. Author: Boundaries, 2000. Bd. mem. Yale Corp., Natural Resources Def. Fund. Mem.: AAAL. Achievements include submitting the winning design for the Vietnam Veterans Memorial at the age of 21.

LIN, MEI-YING, librarian; b. Fukien Province, China, Dec. 9, 1944; d. Chen-Liu and Shu-Yu (Wu) Lin. BA, Nat. Cheng-Chi U., 1966; MS in Libr. Sci., Wayne State U., 1969. Sr. assoc. libr. Asia Libr., U. Mich., Ann Arbor, 1969—. Contbr. articles to profl. jours. Mem.: ALA, Assn. Asian Studies, Coun. East Asian Librs. Home: 3711 Tanglewood Ct Ann Arbor MI 48105-9575 Office: U Mich Asia Libr 920 N University Ann Arbor MI 48109-1205 Office Phone: 734-764-0406, 734-764-0406. Business E-Mail: mylin@umich.edu.

LIN, MING T., plant pathologist; b. Ping-Tung, Taiwan, Dec. 3, 1942; arrived in U.S., 1967; s. Pian Lin and Rai-mei Chen; m. Ching-shu Huang Lin, June 22, 1969; children: Lihuey, Li Yen, Alberto Idje. BS in Agrl. Sci., Nat. Taiwan U., 1965; MS in Plant Pathology, U. Calif., Davis, 1968, PhD in Plant Pathology, 1971. Postdoctoral fellow U. Calif., Davis, 1971—73; assoc.

prof. U. Brasilia, Brazil, 1973—84; mgr. microbiology Bioplanta Tecnologia de Plantas, Campinas, Brazil, 1985—91; rsch. dir. Formosa Agrl. and Environ. Rsch. Ctr., La Ward, Tex., 1991—. Vis. scientist Iowa State U., Ames, 1981—82; cons. EMBRAPA-CNPF, Goiania, Brazil, 1982—83, Bioplant, Venezuela, 1991. Contbr. articles to profl. jours. Mem. coun. Calhoun Agr. Extension, 1994—99; bd. dirs. Port Lavaca C. of C., Tex., 1992—94, Sr. Citizen Found., 1998. Recipient Internat. Rels. award, Pilot Club of Port Lavaca, 1991, Bus./Profl. Individual award, Calhoun Soil and Water Conservation Dist., Port Lavaca, 1994; scholar Internat. Disting. scholar, Iowa State U., 1981. Mem.: Am. Soc. Microbiology, Am. Phytopathol. Soc. Office: Formosa Agrl & Environ Rsch Ctr Hwy 172 S PO Box 69 La Ward TX 77970 Office Phone: 361-872-4010. E-mail: aerd@tisd.net.

LIN, MING-CHANG, physical chemistry professor, researcher; b. Hsinpu, Hsinchu, Taiwan, Oct. 24, 1936; came to U.S., 1967, naturalized, 1975; s. Fushin and Tao May (Hsu) L.; m. Juh-Huey Chern, June 26, 1965; children: Karen, Linus H., Ellena J. BSc, Taiwan Normal U., Taipei, 1959; PhD, U. Ottawa, Ont., Can., 1966. Postdoctoral rsch. fellow U. Ottawa, 1965-67; postdoctoral rsch. assoc. Cornell U., Ithaca, N.Y., 1967-69; rsch. chemist Naval Rsch. Lab., Washington, 1970-74, supervisory rsch. chemist, head chem. kinetics sect., 1974-82, sr. scientist for chem. kinetics, 1982-88; Robert W. Woodruff prof. phys. chemistry Emory U., Atlanta, 1988—. Mem. adv. bd. Internat. Jour. Chem. Kinetics, 1990-93, Inst. Atomic and Molecular Sci., Taipei, 1991—, Chemistry, Inst. Physics, Taiwan, 2000—, Nat. Ctr. for High-performance Computing, Taiwan, 2002—, Nat. Synchrotron Radiation Ctr., Taiwan, 2002—; mem. young presdl. award com. NSF, Washington, 1990; Nat. Sci. Coun. disting. vis. prof. Nat. Chiao Tung U., Taiwan, 2002-04. Contbr. over 430 articles to profl. jours. 2d lt. Taiwan ROTC, 1960-62. Recipient Civilian Meritorious award USN, 1979, Humboldt award Humboldt Found., 1982, prize in sci. tech. Taiwanese-Am. Found., 1989, The Capt. Robert Dexter Conrad award U.S. Navy, 1998; Guggenheim fellow, 1982. Mem. Am. Chem. Soc. (Hillebrand prize 1975), Combustion Inst., Am. Vacuum Soc., Materials Rsch. Soc., N.Am. Taiwanese Profs. Assn., Sigma Xi (Pure Sci. award 1976 Naval Rsch. Lab. chpt.), Academia Sinica (Taiwan). Achievements include discovery of numerous chemical lasers, use of lasers to elucidate mechanisms of combustion, propulsion and gas-surface reactions; first use of lasers to ionize nonfluorescing radicals and to probe for radicals formed in heterogeneous catalytic reactions. Office: Emory Univ Dept Chemistry 1515 Pierce Dr NE Atlanta GA 30322-1003 Office Phone: 404-727-2825. Business E-Mail: chemmcl@emory.edu.

LIN, PEN-MIN, electrical engineer, educator; b. Liaoning, China, Oct. 17, 1928; came to U.S., 1954; s. Tai-sui and Tse-san (Tang) Lin; m. Louise Shou Yuen Lee, Dec. 29, 1962; children: Marian, Margaret, Janice. BSEE, Taiwan U., 1950; MSEE, N.C. State U., 1956; PhD in Elec. Engring., Purdue U., 1960. Asst. prof. Purdue U., West Lafayette, Ind., 1961-66, assoc. prof., 1966-74, prof. elec. engring., 1974-94, prof. emeritus, 1994—. Author: (with L.O. Chua) Computer Aided Analysis of Electronic Circuits, 1975, Symbolic Network Analysis, 1991, (with R.A. DeCarlo) Linear Circuit Analysis, 1995, 2d edit., 2001. Fellow IEEE (life). Home: 3029 Covington St West Lafayette IN 47906-1107 Office: Purdue Univ Sch Of Elec Engring West Lafayette IN 47907

LIN, PING, mechanical engineer; b. Guangdong Province, China, Feb. 1, 1957; came to U.S., 1990; m. Qing Xiu Zhang, 1985; children: Jeffrey Y., Jessica Y. BS in Engring., Beijing Inst. Tech., 1982; MS in Mechanics, Northeastern U., Boston, 1992. Mfg. engr. Shanghai Machinery Co., 1982-84; mech. engr. People's Bank China, Beijing, 1984-86, engring. mgr., 1987-90; sr. project engr. Watts Regulator Co., North Andover, Mass., 1993-97; group leader MKS Instruments, Inc., Andover, Mass., 1997—2002; engring. mgr. Bio-Chem Valve Inc., Boonton, NJ, 2002—04; contract adminstr. Watts Regulator Co., North Andover, Mass., 2004—. Tchg. asst. Northeastern U., Boston, 1992-93. Recipient Nat. Engring. Excellence award Acad. Conf. Sci. Tech. China, 1986. Mem. ASME, Phi Kappa Phi. Achievements include 3 patents, 1 patent pending; research in fluid dynamics, thermal dynamics, mechanics and materials. Mailing: 7 Lawrence Lane Lexington MA 02421 Office Phone: 978-689-6208. Business E-Mail: linp@wattsind.com.

LIN, PI-TANG, physician; b. Chia-Yi, Taiwan, Feb. 15, 1946; MD, Taiwan U., 1972. Diplomate Am. Bd. Otolaryngology. Intern Hackensack (N.J.) Hosp., 1975-76; resident in surgery CMDNJ-Newark Med. Sch., 1976-77; resident in otolaryngology St. Luke's Hosp. Ctr., N.Y.C., 1977-80; fellow Columbia P&S, N.Y.C., 1977-80; mem. staff Lenox Hill Hosp., N.Y.C.; asst. prof. N.Y. Med. Coll., 1981-92. Mem. AMA, ACS, Am. Acad. Otolaryngology-Head and Neck Surgery. Office: Ste 2C 133-29 41st Rd Ste 2C Flushing NY 11355-3670 Office Phone: 718-939-7750. E-mail: ptlin.md@verizon.net.

LIN, QING, medical educator; arrived in U.S., 1992; MD, Fujian Med. U., Fuzhou, 1980; PhD, Fudan U. (formerly Shanghai Med. U.), 1991. Tchg. asst., rsch. asst. Fujian Med. U., Fuzhou, 1980—83, instr., rsch. assoc., 1986—88, Fudan U. (formerly Shangahi Med. U.), Shanghai, 1991—92; vis. scientist U. Tex. Med. Br., Galveston, assoc. mem., 1995—96, asst. prof., 1996—. Guest prof. Fujian Med. U., Fuzhou, vice-chmn. rsch. ctr. neurobiology. Contbr. articles to profl. jours. Grantee, Nat. Inst. Neurol. Disorders and Stroke, NIH, 2001—05; Sealy Meml. Endowment grantee, 1998—2000. Office: Univ Texas Medical Branch 301 University Blvd Galveston TX 77555 Office Phone: 409-772-2404.

LIN, ROBERT KWANHWAN, language educator, consultant; b. Canton, Kwangtong, China, July 7, 1937; arrived in U.S., 1963; s. Chuan-fu Lin and Hui-Chin Chen; m. Deborah Shieh, Feb. 22, 1964; children: Bryan Hsia-pin, Hsia-Lynn, Hsia-Min. BA, Nat. Taiwan U., Taipei, 1960; MA, U. Okla., 1965, U. Mich., 1971; PhD, U. San Francisco, 1983. Tchr. English Chung-li (Taiwan) H.S., 1961—62; instr. Woodbury U., L.A., 1965—66; instr., assoc. libr. Culver-Stockton Coll., Canton, Mo., 1966—70, assoc. prof. history, 1971—78; assoc. prof. English Nat. Taiwan U., Taipei, 1984—85; pub. Everyman's Bilingual Pub., Taipei, 1985—87; cons. Lin's Bilingual Edn. Consulting, San Fracisco, 1987—. Fellow Yale U., New Haven, 1978; commentator World Jour., Millbrae, Calif., 2000—. Author: (book) English Composition, 1984, Parallels in English, 1985; contbr. articles to profl. jours. Adviser Ministry Econs., Taipei, 1984—85. Fellow, NEH, 1977, Fed. Bilingual, Dept. Edn., 1978—80. Avocations: carpentry, birdwatching, hiking, classical music, reading. Home and Office: 1959 44th Ave San Francisco CA 94116

LIN, SHARON SHIANG CHIEN, librarian; b. Aug. 22, 1933; d. Bins C. and Yinlow (Fan) Chien; m. Duo-Liang Lin, June 8, 1963; children: Jennifer, Kenneth. BA, Nat. Taiwan U., 1956; MA, U. Minn., 1960. Cataloger, sr. cataloger Yale U. Libr., New Haven, 1960—64; head periodicals dept. SUNY, Buffalo, 1965—67; vis. libr. Stanford (Calif.) U. Libr., 1966; vis. staff Oxford U. (Eng.) Libr., 1970; serials cataloger SUNY, Buffalo, 1978—2000; vis. libr. Tsing Hwa U. Libr., Peking, 1978; adj. prof. Northeastern Normal U., Changchun, China, 1988—; vis. scholar Nat. Libr. China, Peking, 1994; ret., 2000. Lectr. numerous librs. and libr. schs., including Nat. Libr., throughout China, 1985, 87, 94. Author (with M. Leung): Chinese Libraries and Librarianship: An Annotated Bibliography, 1986; author: Libraries and Librarianship in China, 1998; contbr. articles to profl. jours. and encys. Grantee, N.Y. State United Univ. Professions, 1985, 1987, 1990, 1994. Mem.: ALA (com. cataloging Asian and African materials 1983—85, officer resources and tech. svcs. divsn.), Assn. Coll. and Rsch. Librs. (western N.Y. chpt.), Chinese-Am. Librn.'s Assn., Internat. Rels. Round Table, Greater Buffalo Chinese Club (treas. 1984—85), Chinese Club of Buffalo (sec. 1979—80). Home: 43534 Puesta Del Sol Fremont CA 94539-5634 Personal E-mail: sclin@buffalo.edu.

LIN, TUNG HUA, civil engineering educator; b. Chungkin, China, May 26, 1911; s. Yao-Ching and Yue (Kuo) L.; m. Susan Z. Chiang, Mar. 15, 1939; childern: Rita P., Lin Wood, Robert P., James P. BS, Tangshan Coll., Chiaotung U., 1933; S.M., MIT, 1936; D.Sc., U. Mich., 1953. Prof. Tsing Hua U., China, 1937-39; chief engr. Chinese 2d Aircraft Co., Nancheun, Szechuan, 1939-44; prodn. mgr. Mfg. Factory, China, 1940-44; mem. tech. mission in charge of jet aircraft design, 1945-49; prof. aero. engring. U. Detroit, 1949-55; prof. engring. and applied scis. UCLA, 1955-78, prof. emeritus, 1978—. Cons.N.Am. Aviation, N.Am. Rockwell, L.A., 1964-74, Atomic Internat., Canoga Park, Calif., 1965-68, ARA Inc., Industry City, Calif., 1964-94. Author: Theory of Inelastic Structure, 1968; contbr. articles to profl. jours.; mem. editorial bd.: Jour. Composite Materials, 1966-75. Named Chinese Nat. fellow, Tsing-Hua U., 1933, prin. investigator, Office Naval Rsch., 1985—93, Air Force Office of Sci. Rsch., 1988—97; recipient medal for design of 1st Chinese twin-engine airplane, 1944, Disting. Svc. award Applied Mechanics Rev., ASME, 1966; grantee NSF, 54-78. Fellow ASME, Am. Acad. Mechanics; mem. ASCE (life, gen. chmn. engring. mechanics conf. 1965, Theodore von Karman award 1988); mem. NAE. Acad.Sinica (China). Achievements include patents in field. Home: 906 Las Pulgas Rd Pacific Palisades CA 90272-2441 Office: UCLA Dept Civil Engring 405 Hilgard Ave Los Angeles CA 90095-9000 Office Phone: 310-825-1679. Business E-Mail: thlin@seas.ucla.edu.

LIN, XIAOBO, research scientist; PhD, Va. Tech, Blacksburg, 2000. Grad. rsch. asst. Va. Tech, Blacksburg, Va., 1997—2000; rsch. asst. Wash. U. Sch. of Medicine, St. Louis, Mo., 2000—04, sr. scientist, 2004—. Contbr. scientific papers pub. to profl. jour. (Pratt Fellowship, 1997). Mem.: Am. Heart Assn., Sigma Xi. Office: Wash Univ Sch of Medicine 660 South Euclid AVE Saint Louis MO 63110

LIN, YUKWENG M., engineer, educator; b. Fuzhou, Fujian, China, Oct. 30, 1923; arrived in U.S., 1954, naturalized, 1964; s. Fa Been and Chi Ying (Cheng) Lin; m. Ying-yuh June Wang, Mar. 29, 1952; children: Jane, Della, Lucia, Winifred. BS, Xiamen U., 1946; MS, Stanford U., 1955, PhD, 1957; D of Engring. (hon.), U. Waterloo, Can., 1994. Tchr. Xiamen U., China, 1946-48, Imperial Coll. Engring., Ethiopia, 1957-58; engr. Vertol Aircraft Corp., Morton, Pa., 1956-57; rsch. engr. Boeing Co., Renton, Wash., 1958-60; asst. prof. U. Ill., Urbana, 1960-62, assoc. prof., 1962-65, prof. aero. and astron. engring., 1965-83; Charles E. Schmidt Eminent scholar chair Coll. Engring., dir. Ctr. for Applied Stochastics Rsch. Fla. Atlantic U., Boca Raton, 1984—. Vis. prof. mech. engring. MIT, 1967-68; sr. vis. fellow Inst. Sound and Vibration Research, U. Southampton, Eng., 1976; cons. Gen. Motors Corp., Boeing Co., Gen. Dynamics Corp., TRW Corp., Brookhaven Nat. Lab. Author: Probabilistic Theory of Structural Dynamics, 1967, Probabilistic Structural Dynamics: Advanced Theory and Applications, 1995, Probabilistic Structural Dynamics, 2004; editor: Stochastic Structural Mechanics, 1987, Stochastic Approaches in Earthquake Engineering, 1987, Stochastic Structural Dynamics, 1990, Stochastic Dynamics and Reliability of Nonlinear Ocean Systems, 1994; contbr. articles to profl. jours. Recipient sr. postdoctoral fellowship, NSF, 1967—68, Alexander von Humboldt Sr. US Scientist award, 2000, J.P. Den Hartog award, ASME, 2001. Fellow: ASCE (Alfred M. Freudenthal medal 1984, Theodore von Karman medal 1998), Am. Acad. Mechs.; mem.: Am. Assn. Wind Engring., Internat. Assn. Structural Safety and Reliability, Russian Acad. Engring. (fgn. mem.), Nat. Acad. Engring., Sigma Xi. Home: 2684 NW 27th Ter Boca Raton FL 33434-6001 Office: Fla Atlantic U Coll Engring Boca Raton FL 33431 Business E-Mail: linyk@fau.edu.

LIN, ZHAOJUN, physics professor, researcher; b. Shijiazhuang, Hebei, China, June 22, 1962; D, Semiconductor Inst. of Chinese Acad. of Sci., Beijing, 1997. Postdoctoral rschr. McMaster U., Hamiton, Canada, 1999—2000, Northwestern U., Evanston, Ill., 2000—02, Ohio State U., Columbus, 2002—03; prof. Sch. of Physics, Shandong U., Jinan, China, 2004—. Achievements include research in Some discoveries on AlGaN/GaN HFET researches. Office: Sch Physics Shandong Univ 27 Shanda South Rd Shandong Jinan 250100 China Office Phone: 86-0531-8363700. Office Fax: 86-0531-8564886. E-mail: linzj2000@mail.yahoo.com.

LIN, ZHIGANG, materials scientist; b. Fujian, China, 1966; arrived in U.S., 1996; s. Jinguo and Shuxiang Lin; m. Limin Lin, 1994; children: Daniel, Jessica. BS, Hefei (China) U. Tech., 1987; MS, Northwestern Poly. U., Xian, China, 1990; PhD, U. Calif., Irvine, 2000. Rsch. asst. Northwestern Poly. U., Xian, 1987—90, U. Calif., Irvine, 1996—2000; rsch. engr. Fujian Machinery Sci. Rsch. Inst., Fuzhou, China, 1990—96; materials scientist IJ Rsch. Inc., Santa Ana, Calif., 2000—. Contbr. articles to profl. jours. Recipient Small Bus. Innovative Rsch. award, U.S. Dept. Def., 2003—05. Mem.: IEEE (sr.), Sigma Xi. Achievements include patents in field.

LINARES, CARLOS, language educator, consultant; b. Cerete, Colombia, Aug. 27, 1952; s. Jesus Garcia and Luisa Matilde Linares; m. Nidia Pulles, Nov. 17, 1953; children: Juan Jesus, Gabriel Andres, Natalia. MA in Spanish, Queens Coll., 1977; MS in Computer Info. Sys., Baruch Coll., 1989. Cert. NetWare 4.11 CNE Novell, 1995. Adj. lectr. LaGuardia C.C., LI, NY, 1984—86; assoc. prof. Borough of Manhattan C.C., N.Y.C., 1986—. Independent. Roman Catholic. Avocation: sailing. Office: Borough of Manhattan Comm College 199 Chambers Street S 146 New York NY 10007 E-mail: clinares@bmcc.cuny.edu.

LINAWEAVER, WALTER ELLSWORTH, JR., physician; b. San Pedro, Calif., Oct. 16, 1928; s. Walter Ellsworth and Catherine Breathed (Bridges) L.; m. Lydia Anne Whitlock, Oct. 5, 1957; children: Catherine Ann, Nancy Alyn, Walter E. III. BA cum laude, Pomona Coll., 1952; MD, U. Rochester (NY), 1956. Diplomate Am. Bd. Allergy and Immunology, Am. Bd. Pediat., Am. Bd. Pediatric Allergy. Intern pediat. Med. Ctr. U. Rochester, 1956-57, resident pediat. Med. Ctr., 1958-59; asst. resident pediat. Med. Ctr. UCLA, 1957-58; fellow allergy and immunology Med. Ctr. U. Colo., Denver, 1959-61, instr. pediat. Sch. Medicine, 1961; pvt. practice Riverside (Calif.) Med. Clinic, 1962—. Asst. clin. prof. pediat. Loma Lida U. Med. Sch., 1965—. Elder Presbyn. Ch. Staff sgt. U.S. Army, 1946-48. Inducted into Athletic Hall of Fame Pomona Coll., Claremont, Calif., 1979. Fellow: L.A. Acad. Medicine, Am. Acad. Pediat., Am. Acad. Allergy, Asthma and Immunology; mem.: AMA, Calif. Med. Assn., Riverside County Heart Assn. (pres. 1965—66), Riverside County Med. Soc. (councilor 1964—66). Republican. Avocations: gardening, american and british military history. Home: 1296 Tiger Tail Dr Riverside CA 92506-5475 Office: Riverside Med Clinic 3660 Arlington Ave Riverside CA 92506-3912 Office Phone: 951-782-3681.

LINBERGER, LARA JANE, marriage and family therapist, music educator; b. Winter Park, Fla., June 9, 1974; d. Frederick and Elizabeth Jane Linberger. AB cum laude, Rollins Coll., 1996, MEd with honors, 1998; MA, Seton Hall U., 2003. Child and family therapist Fla. United Meth. Children's Home, Enterprise, Fla., 2003—04; child and family therapist rmhc Healing Harts, Altamonte Springs, Fla., 2004—; instr. ballroom dance Rollins Coll. Phys. Edn. Dept., Winter Park, Fla., 1995—98; owner Piano Studio, Sanford, Fla., 1998—. Tchr. music Sch. Music Rollins Coll., Winter Park, 1997—98; dir. children's choir, instr, music St. James Cath. Cathedral, Conservatory Performing Arts, Orlando, Fla., 1999—2003; dir. children's choir St. Luke's Cathedral, Orlando, 2000—01. Author: (children's lit.) Anna's New Friend. Vol. Fla. Hosp., Altamonte Springs, Fla., 1989; vol. in criminal investigations, property and evidence, criminal intake, and clerical for dep. chief Orlando Police Dept., Orlando, 1999—99; team leader for re-election Pres. Bush, Sanford, 1999—2004; vol. pianist Goldenrod Bapt. Ch., Winter Park, 1989—92; lay eucharistic min. St. Luke's Cathedral, Orlando, 2003—04, chalice bearer, 2004. Recipient Nat. Spkr. Drill Winner, So. Bapt. Assn., 1992, State Bible Drill Winner, 1989, Southeastern Dance Championship Winner, Fred Astaire Dance Studios, 1992, Nat. Dance Championship Winner, 1994, Southeastern Dance Championship Winner, 1994, Fla. State DanceSport Championship Winner, Triple Crown Dance Events, 2001. Mem.: ACA (assoc.), Am. Coll. Musicians, Assn. for Play Therapy (assoc.), Rep. Nat. Conv. (assoc.), Omicron Delta Kappa (life), Pi Kappa Lambda (life), Kappa Delta Pi (life), Phi Eta Sigma (life). R-Consevative. Anglican. Achievements include development of Created and Developed Rollins College Ballroom Dance program; research in Expressive arts in therapy; Therapeutic Interventions for Posttraumatic Stress Disorder in Children; development of Development of a company (Healing Harts) that integrates child/family therapy and the expressive arts. Avocations: ballroom dance, piano, ballet, fencing, travel. Home: 8101 Via Bonita Str Sanford FL 32771 Office: Healing Harts 251 Maitland Ave Ste 113 Altamonte Springs FL 32701 Office Phone: 407-461-7014. Personal E-mail: tn1ea@msn.com.

LIN CHIEN, CHESTER, electronics executive; BSEE, Taipei (Taiwan) Inst. Tech. Mem. prodn., quality and engring. staff, ops. mgr. Gen. Instruments of Taiwan; products mgr. GE, 1984; with SCI Systems; CEO NatSteel Electronics, 1993—2001; exec. v.p. Solectron Corp., Milpitas, Calif., 2001—, pres. Asia/Pacific region, 2001—. Recipient Stars of Asia award, Bus. Week mag., 1999. Office: Solectron Corp 777 Gibraltar Dr Milpitas CA 95035

LINCICOME, DAVID RICHARD, biomedical scientist, animal scientist; b. Champaign, Ill., Jan. 17, 1914; s. David Rosebery and Olive Iola (Casper) L.; m. Dorothy Lucile Van Cleave, Sept. 1, 1941 (dec. Nov. 1952); children: David Van Cleave, Judith Ann; m. Margaret Stirewalt, Dec. 29, 1953 (dec. Apr. 2003). *David Lincicome's ancestor, Thomas Linthicum, arrived in the Port of Baltimore in 1658 from Great Britain (Wales) and became a wealthy landowner. The family migrated westward settling in what is now southwestern Pennsylvania. They later moved to Noble County, Ohio, where David's grandfather, Nathaniel Webster Lincicome, was born--the surname having been changed somewhere along the line to Lincicome from Linthicum. From Noble County, the family migrated to Brown County, Indiana, where David's father, David Rosebery Lincicome, was born. David has two children: David Van Cleave, who practices law and Judith Ann, who is a registered nurse specializing in paediatric intensive care and in handicapped children needing special care and education.* BS, MS with high honors, U. Ill., 1937; PhD in Tropical Medicine, Tulane U., 1941. Diplomate (emeritus) Am. Bd. Microbiology; diplomate Am. Coll. Animal Physiology; cert. animal scientist Am. Registry Profl. Animal Scientists. Asst. instr. U. Ill., 1937; instr. tropical medicine Tulane U. Med. Sch., 1937-41; asst. prof. parasitology U. Ky., 1941-47, U. Wis. Med. Sch., 1947-49; sr. rsch. parasitologist Du Pont Co., 1949-53; from asst. prof. to full prof. biol. scis. Howard U., 1953-70. Vis. sci. NIH, 1965-66; founder, registrar, Jacob Sheep Conservancy, 1988-96, bd. dirs., 1990-97, pres., 1996; vis. scholar Nat. Agrl. Libr., USDA, 1990-92; guest scientist USDA Exp. Sta., Beltsville, Md., 1978—, Naval Med. Rsch. Inst., 1954-62. Founder, editor Exptl. Parasitology, 1949-76; editor Transactions of the Ky. Acad. Sci., 1946-49, Transactions of the Am. Microscopical Soc., 1970-71, Internat. Rev. Tropical Medicine, 1953-63; founder Virology, 1950, Advances in Vet. Sci., 1952. Lt. col. Med. Svc. Corps, U.S. Army, WWII, PTO. Named Eminent Fellow, Wisdom Hall of Fame, 2001; recipient Anniversary award, Helminthological Soc., 1975, Sir Winston Churchill medal, Wisdom Soc. Advancement of Knowledge, Learning and Rsch. in Edn., 2001, 25th anniversary Genetic Conservation award, Am. Livestock Breeds Conservancy, 2002; grantee, NIH, 1958—68. Fellow: AAAS, Explorers Club; mem.: Am. Soc. Tropical Medicine (emeritus), Va. State Dairy Goat Assn. (founder), Ut Prosim Soc. (Va. Poly. Inst. and State U.), Soc. Exptl. Biology and Medicine (sec. D.C. chpt. 1976, emeritus), Midwestern Conf. Parasitologists (1st sec. 1949, founder), Va. State Dairy Goat Assn. (pres. 1976, founder, Friend of VSDGA award 1999), Am. Livestock Breeds Conservancy (bd. dirs. 1994—97, 25th Anniversary award 2002), Nat. Tunis Sheep Registry (sec. 1991—92, bd. dirs. 1991—93), Jacob Sheep Soc. (Eng.), Jacob Sheep Breeders Assn., Natural Colored Wool Growers Assn. (bd. dirs. 1988—94), Nat. Pygmy Goat Assn. (bd. dirs. 1976—92, pres. 1979, founder), Am. Dairy Goat Assn. (bd. dirs. 1972—87, 1st sec. rsch. found. 1979, founder), Am. Goat Soc. (bd. dirs. 1990—96), Royal Soc. Tropical Medicine (emeritus), Am. Microscopical Soc. (emeritus), Am. Soc. Cell Biology, Am. Soc. Parasitologists, Am. Soc. Zoologists (emeritus), Soc. Invertebrate Zoology (emeritus), Am. Physiol. Soc. (emeritus), Helminthological Soc. (pres. 1958, emeritus), Greater Washington Area Soft-Coated Wheaten Terrier Club, Soft-Coated Wheaten Terrier Club Am., Univ. Ill. Pres. Coun., Univ. Ill. Found., Greater Washington D.C. Area Soft Coated Wheaten Terrier Club (pres. 1991—92, bd. dirs. 1999—2001, founder), Sigma Xi (pres. Howard chpt. 1962), Phi Beta Kappa. Achievements include breeding of two rare and endangered breeds of sheep, Jacob and Tunis, early breeder of West African Pygmy Goats and a rare dog, the Soft-coated Wheaten Terrier; founder and first sec. The Rsch. Found. of the Am. Dairy Goat Assn.; founder Midwestern Conf. of Parasitologists; founder four sci. jours. Exptl. Parasitology, Internat. Rev. Tropical Medicine, Virology, and Advances in Vet. Sci. Office Phone: 860-355-1031. E-mail: wheatens@sbcglobal.net, sheepman@frogmoor.org.

LINCICUM, SHIRLEY JOANNE, librarian; b. Salem, Oreg., Apr. 18, 1971; d. Michael Scott and Bernice Louise (Balcomb) Lincicum; m. John Kyle Banerjee, Mar. 1, 1997. BA in History with high honors, Oberlin Coll., 1993; MS in Libr. and Info. Sci., U. Ill., 1995; MS in Edn., Info. Tech., Western Oreg. U., 2003. Catalog libr./asst. prof. U. Oreg., Eugene, 1995—2000; collection mgmt. libr./assoc. prof. Western Oreg. U., Monmouth, 2000—. Mem.: ALA, Am. Soc. for Info. Sci. and Tech. (chair Pacific N.W. chpt. 1999—2000, Chpt. Event of Yr. award 2000), US Figure Skating Assn., Beta Phi Mu (life), Phi Beta Kappa (life). Avocations: figure skating, music (viola & violin), travel, dogs, architecture (design & historic preservation). Office: Western Oreg Univ 345 N Monmouth Ave Monmouth OR 97361 Office Phone: 503-828-8890.

LINCK, CHARLES EDWARD, JR., English language educator; b. Lowemont, Kans., June 6, 1923; s. Charles Edward and Grace Elizabeth (Miller) L.; m. Alice Eugenie Meyer (div. Feb. 1964); 1 child, Charles Edward Lincoln; m. Ernestine Marie Porcher Sewell, Aug. 23, 1970. AB magna cum laude, St. Benedict's Coll., Atchison, Kans., 1951; MS, Kans. State Coll., 1953; PhD in English, U. Kans., 1962. Prof. English East Tex. State U., Commerce, 1958-91, prof. emeritus, 1991—. Owner, pub. Cow Hill Press; spkr. in field. Author, editor: Edgar Rye: North Central Texas Cartoonist and Journalist, 1972; co-editor: Bibliography of Evelyn Waugh, 1984; editor, pub. Evelyn Waugh in Letters by Terence Greeniage, 1994; editor, pub. Colleen, The Mountain Maid - A Story of War and Feud in Kentucky, 1994; editor: Bokay of Biscuits, 3 vols., 1997. With USN, 1943-46, PTO. Mem. MLA, Tex. Coll. English Assn. (pres. 1972), Am. Studies Assn., Tex. Folklore Soc. (pres. 1984). Democrat. Roman Catholic. Avocations: antique printing, native american indian arts and crafts, photography. Home: Tex A&M U PO Box 3002 Commerce TX 75429-3002

LINCOLN, ALEXANDER, III, financial analyst, lawyer, private investor; b. Boston, Dec. 1, 1943; s. Alexander Jr. and Elizabeth (Kitchel) L.; m. Isabel Fawcett Ross, Dec. 27, 1969. BA, Denver U., 1967; JD, Boston U., 1971. Bar: Colo. 1972, U.S. Ct. Appeals (10th cir.) 1972, U.S. Supreme Ct. 1979. Atty. Dist. Ct. Denver, 1973-78, Colo. Ct. Appeals, Denver, 1978-80; mng. ptnr. Alexander Lincoln & Co., Denver, 1980—. Mem. Colo. Bar Assn. (fin. com. 1975-76), Colo. Soc. Mayflower Descendants (life, bd. dirs. 1975—), Order of Founders and Patriots (life). Republican. Avocations: skiing, mountain climbing, horticulture. Home and Office: 121 S Dexter St Denver CO 80246-1052

LINCOLN, ANNA, publishing executive, language educator; b. Warsaw, Dec. 13, 1932; came to U.S., 1948; d. Wigdor Aron and Genia Szpiro; m. Adrian Courtney Lincoln Jr., Sept. 22, 1951; children: Irene Anne, Sally Linda, Allen, Kirk. Student, U. Calif., Berkeley, 1949-50; BA in French and Russian with honors, NYU, 1965; student, Columbia Tchrs. Coll., 1966-67. Tchr. Waldwick (N.J.) H.S., 1966-69; chmn. Tuxedo Park (N.Y.) Red Cross, 1969-71; pres. Red Cross divsn. Vets. Hosp.; pres. China Pictures U.S.A. Inc., Princeton, N.J., 1994—; prof. fgn. rels. Fudan U., Shanghai, 1994—, prof. English and humanitarian studies, 1996—. Adv. bd. guidance dept. Waldwick (N.J.) H.S., 1966-69; hon. bd. dirs. Shanghai Fgn. Lang. Assn., 1994; hon. prof. Fudan U., Shanghai, 1994; leader seminars, China at top univs., 1996—; pub. spkr., human rels., China, 2003—. Author: Escape to China, 1940-48, 1985, Chinese transl., 1985, The Art of Peace, 1995, Anna Lincoln Views China, 2000; publ.: China Beyond the Year 2000 and the Nature of Love, 1997, Anna Lincoln Views China, 1999; co-dir. (TV docudrama) Escape to China 1941-48, 1998. Hon. U.S. Goodwill amb. for peace and friendship,

China, 1984, 85, 86, 88; founder Princeton-Lincoln Found., Inc., 1985—. Named Woman of Yr. Am. Biog. Soc., 1993; recipient Peace Through the Arts prize Assn. Internat. Mujeres en las Artes, Madrid, 1993. Mem. AAUW, Women's Coll. Club (publicity chmn. 1991-96), Lit. Coll. Princeton, Present Day Club. Avocations: reading, swimming, bridge, seminars, ballroom dancing. Home and Office: China Pictures USA Inc 550 Rosedale Rd Princeton NJ 08540-2315

LINCOLN, BLANCHE LAMBERT, senator; b. Helena, Ark., Sept. 30, 1960; BA, Randolph-Macon Woman's Coll., 1982. Sr. assoc. The Pagonis & Donnelly Group, Inc., 1989-91; mem. U.S. Congress from 1st Ark. dist., 1992-96; U.S. senator from Ark., 1999—. Mem. agr. com., energy and natural resources com., spl. com. on aging; mem. Senate Social Security Task Force. Democrat. Office: US Senate 355 Dirksen Senate Office Bldg Washington DC 20510-0001 also: 912 W Fourth St Little Rock AR 72201*

LINCOLN, EDMOND LYNCH, investment banker; b. Wilmington, Del., Aug. 3, 1949; s. Edmond Earl and Mary Margaret (Lynch) Lincoln; m. Pamela Wick, Sept. 3, 1977; children: Lucy Arms, Emily Lord. BA magna cum laude, Harvard U., 1971, MBA with distinction, 1974. Rare book libr. Henry Francis duPont Winterthur Mus., Del., 1971—72; with Kidder Peabody & Co., Inc., N.Y.C., 1974—94, asst. v.p., 1977—79, v.p., 1979—91, sr. v.p., 1991—94, mgr. govt. agy. fin., 1984—86, transp. group, 1986—94; mng. dir. PaineWebber Inc., N.Y.C., 1994—2000; cons. UBS Warburg LLC, N.Y.C., 2000—03; mng. dir. Hilltower Group, N.Y.C., 2003—; faculty program in the arts NYU, 2004—. Pub. interest dir. Fed. Home Loan Bank of NY, 1987—89. Treas. Fed. Hall Meml. Assocs., 1981—87; mem. vis. com. Harvard Coll. Libr., 1981—86, 1988—94; mem. exec. com. Friends of Harvard U. Track, 1972—, sec., 1976—87. Recipient Washburn History prize, Harvard U., 1971. Fellow: Pierpont Morgan Libr.; mem.: Investment Assn. NY, Soc. Naval Architects and Marine Engrs. (assoc.), Assn. Internat. de Bibliophilie, Friends of Winterthur (trustee 1976—81, 1987—93, sec. 1978—81, Winterthur Mus. acad. affairs com. 1993—, Cert. Recognition 2004), Wilmington Country Club, India House, Grolier Club (coun. mem. 1982—84, 2001—, treas. 2002—), Club of Odd Volumes, Bond Club NY, Harvard Club (NYC), Wilmington Club, Phi Beta Kappa. Republican. Roman Catholic. Home: 161 E 79th St New York NY 10021-0480 Office: Hilltower Group 50 Vanderbilt Ave Ste 9 New York NY 10017 Personal E-mail: edmond_lincoln@yahoo.com.

LINCOLN, HARRY B., musicologist; b. Fergus Falls, Minn., Mar. 6, 1922; s. Harry G. and Helen (Barnard) L.; m. Betty Woelk, Dec. 27, 1947; children: Thomas, Nancy, Sally. BA, Macalester Coll., 1946; MMus, Northwestern U., Evanston, Ill., 1947; PhD, Northwestern U., 1951. Prof. SUNY, Binghamton, 1951-83, disting. svc. prof., 1983-87, emeritus prof., 1987—. Author: (books) The Madrigal Collection L'Amorosa Ero, 1968, Seventeenth Century Keyboard Music in the Chigi Manuscripts of the Vatican Library, 1968; editor: Directory of Music Faculties in Colleges and Universities, 1967-72, The Computer and Music, 1970, The Italian Madrigal Indexes to Printed Collections, 1500-1600, 1988, The Latin Motet. Indexes to Printed Collections, 1500-1600, 1993; co-author: Study Scores of Historical Styles, 2 vols., 1986. Pres. Binghamton Symphony, 1953, 56. Sgt. USAF, 1943-45. Grantee Am. Coun. Learned Socs., NEH, Philos. Soc., U.S. Office of Edn., 1967-90. Mem. Coll. Music Soc. (pres. 1968-70), Am. Musicol. Soc. E-mail: bg0056@binghamton.edu.

LINCOLN, HOWARD, manufacturing company and sports team executive; b. Oakland, Calif., Feb. 14, 1940; married; one child. Grad., U. Calif., Berkeley; JD, U. Calif. Sch. Law. Legal work Nintendo Am., 1981—83, sr. v.p., gen. counsel, 1983—94, chmn., 1994—; chmn., CEO Seattle Mariners. Bd. dirs. Nintendo of Am., Nintendo Co. Ltd. of Kyoto, Japan; chmn. Interactive Digital Software Assn. Instrumental in creating Nintendo's charitable contbns. program, including Starlight Found.; major initiator in Club Mario/after-sch. program with Bellevue, Wash. Boys & Girls Club; trustee Seattle Childrn's Hosp. Found., Washington Roundtable; hi-tech chmn. United Way of King County, Wash., 1999; bd. dirs. Boalt Hall Alumni Assn., U. Calif., Berkeley, The Baseball Club of Seattle, LP, Seattle Mariners, Pacific Sci. Ctr., Corp. Coun. for the Arts, others. Naval officer Judge Advocate Gen. Corps. Office: c/o Seattle Mariners Safeco Field PO Box 4100 Seattle WA 98104*

LINCOLN, THOMAS L., pathologist, educator; b. Pitts., Jan. 4, 1929; s. John J. and Jean Gregg Lincoln; m. Nancy, Apr. 15, 1956 (dec. Feb. 1971); children: Elizabeth, John; m. Catherine Delaprée., May 30, 1972; 1 child, Iris. BS, Yale U., 1955, MD, 1960. Diplomate Nat. Bd. Med. Examiners, Am. Bd. Anat. Pathology. Intern in pathology Yale U., New Haven, 1960-61, resident, 1961-63; rsch. asst. prof. Inst. for Fluid Dynamics and Applied Math., U. Md., 1963-66; assoc. clin. prof., dept. pathology U. So. Calif. Cancer Ctr., L.A., 1975-77, assoc. prof., 1977-87, prof. rsch. pathology, 1987-96; prof. emeritus U. So. Calif.; sr. scientist Sunquest Info. Sys., Tucson, 1995-96, Rand Corp., Santa Monica, Calif., 1967—; prof. Coll. Health and Human Devel. Scis., U. Ill., Chgo., 1997—2000. Vis. prof. dept. clin. epidemiology and social medicine, St. Thomas's Hosp. Med. Sch., London, 1972; cons., rschr. in field. Contbr. articles to profl. jours. Fellow Pathology, Johns Hopkins, 1963—65. Mem. AMA, IEEE, Johns Hopkins Med. Soc., Leukemia Soc. Am. (patient advisor, L.A., 1970-82), Cosmos Club (Washington), Coll. of Am. Pathologists, Am. Informatics Assn., Am. Coll. Med. Informatics, others. Episcopalian. Avocations: history, european politics, calendar algorithms, computers, psychology. Home: 802 Franklin St Santa Monica CA 90403-2318 Office: Rand Corp 1776 Main St Santa Monica CA 90401-3297 Business E-Mail: lincoln@rand.org.

LIND, JUDITH YANKIELUN, library director; b. Elizabeth, N.J., Nov. 2, 1953; d. Norbert Eugene and Emily Martha (Zienkowicz) Y.; m. Peter Eugene Lind, July 14, 1984; 1 child, Michael. BA, Kean Coll. N.J., 1975; MA, Rowan U., 1977, NYU, 1987. Lic. advanced media specialist, profl. libr., elem. tchr. Children's libr. Bloomfield (N.J.) Pub. Libr., 1977-79; head reference dept. Scotch Plains (N.J.) Pub. Libr., 1979-83, Berkeley Heights (N.J.) Pub. Libr., 1983-88; dir. Roseland (N.J.) Free Pub. Libr., 1988—. Cons. Magazines for Libraries, 6th, 7th, 8th. 9th and 10th edits.; contbr. articles and revs. to profl. jours. Mem. ALA, N.J. Libr. Assn. Office: Roseland Free Pub Libr 20 Roseland Ave Roseland NJ 07068-1235 Office Phone: 973-226-8636. Business E-Mail: jlind@nplhub.org.

LIND, NIELS CHRISTIAN, civil engineering educator; b. Copenhagen, Mar. 10, 1930; s. Axel Holger and Karen (Larsen) L.; m. Veronica Claire Hummel, Nov. 29, 1957 (div. 1979); children: Julie Wilhelmina, Peter Christian, Adam Conrad; m. Viriginia Patricia Cano Reynoso, Jan. 26, 1985 (div. 1996); 1 child, Andreas. MSc, Tech. U. Denmark, 1953; PhD, U. Ill., 1959. Design engr. Dominia Ltd., Copenhagen, 1953-54; engr. I Bell Telephone Co., Montreal, 1954-55; field engr. Drake-Merritt, Labrador, Nfld., 1955; asst. prof. U. Ill., Urbana, 1959-60; assoc. prof. civil engring. U. Waterloo, Ont., 1960-62, prof., 1962-91, disting. prof. emeritus, 1992, dir. Inst. Risk Research, 1982-88. Adj. prof. U. Victoria, B.C., 1993-95. Recipient Ostenfeld gold medal, 1978; recipient Cancam award Can. Congress Applied Mechanics, 1981, CERRA award Civil Engring. Reliability and Risk Assn., 1999. Fellow Royal Soc. Can., Am. Acad. Mechanics (pres. 1972-73). Home: 404-1033 Belmont Ave Victoria BC Canada V8S 3T4 Office Phone: 250-598-5914. E-mail: nlind@telus.net.

LIND, ROBERT CHARLES, law educator; b. St. Paul, Feb. 20, 1953; s. Robert Charles Lind Sr. and Lorraine Elizabeth Herold Swanson. B of Elected Studies summa cum laude, U. Minn., 1976; JD, George Washington U., 1979, LLM with highest honors, 1983. Bar: D.C. 1980, Calif. 1981. Lectr. in law George Washington U., Washington, 1979-81; vis. lectr. in bus. Marymount Coll. Va., Arlington, 1980; assoc. prof. law Southwestern U., L.A., 1981-85, prof. law, 1985—, Paul E. Treusch prof. law, 2005—. Mem. spl. adv. com. Calif. State Archives, Sacramento, 1987-89. Author: Newsgathering and the Law, 1997, 3d edit., 2005, Entertainment Law, 2d edit., 1997, 3d edit., 2003, Entertainment Law: Legal Concepts and Business Practices, 2d edit., 1998, Copyright Law, 2002, Trademark Law, 2002, Art and Museum Law, 2002. Mem. Am. Intellectual Property Law Assn., Am. Assn. Museums, Copyright Soc. U.S.A., L.A. Copyright Soc., Phi Kappa Phi, Phi Beta Kappa. Avocation: musician. Office: Southwestern U Sch Law 675 S Westmoreland Ave Los Angeles CA 90005-3905 Office Phone: 213-738-6785. Business E-Mail: rlind@swlaw.edu.

LIND, THOMAS OTTO, barge transportation company executive; b. New Orleans, Apr. 24, 1937; s. Henry Carl Lind and Elinor (Rooney) Messersmith; m. Eugenia Niehaus, June 8, 1963; children: Elinor Ashley, Elizabeth Kelly. BSME, Tulane U., 1959, LLB, 1965. Cert. mech. engr., 1959. Assoc. Jones, Walker, Waechter, Poitevent, Carrere and Denegre, New Orleans, 1965-66; v.p., sec., counsel Ingram Corp., New Orleans, 1966-84; v.p. Gulf Fleet Marine Corp., New Orleans, 1984-85; v.p., regulatory counsel, sec. and asst. treas. New Orleans Pub. Svc., Inc. and La. Power and Light Co., 1985-92; regional counsel for La. Entergy Svcs., Inc., 1993-94; risk mgr. Canal Barge Co., Inc., New Orleans, 1994-97, sec., 1995—, gen. counsel, 1997—. Trustee Metairie Park Country Day Sch., 1991-95; mem. bd. govs. Trinity Sch., New Orleans, 1982-85; vestryman Trinity Ch., New Orleans, 1987-91; active Family of Cmty. and Utility Supporters, New Orleans, 1987-94; bd. dirs. Greater New Orleans (La.) Coun. Navy League U.S., 2004—. Lt. (j.g.) USN, 1959-62; comdr. USNR, 1962-79. Mem. Fed. Energy Bar Assn. (bd. dirs. New Orleans chpt. 1988-92, pres. 1992), La. Bar Assn. (bd. dirs. corp. law sect. 1973-75), La. Assn. Waterways Operators and Shipyards (bd. dirs. 1999—), New Orleans Bar Assn. (bd. dir. 1989-97, 2d v.p. 1989-90, sec. 1992-93, 1st v.p. 1993-94, pres.-elect 1994-95, pres. 1995-96, bd. dirs. New Orleans Pro Bono project 1994-96), La. Orgn. for Jud. Excellence (bd. dirs., sec. 1998-2000, v.p. 2000—), New Orleans Lawn Tennis Club (pres. 1986-88), Am. Bar Assn.(Ho. of Dels. 1996-97). Republican. Episcopalian. Avocation: tennis. Home: 5423 Perrier New Orleans LA 70115-3130 Office: Canal Barge Co Inc 835 Union St Ste 300 New Orleans LA 70112-1469 Office Phone: 504-584-1531. Business E-Mail: tlind@canalbarge.com.

LINDA, GERALD, advertising and marketing executive; b. Boston, Nov. 25, 1946; s. Edward Linda and Anne Beatrice (Lipofsky) Coburn; m. Claudia Wollack, Sept. 24, 1978; children— Jonathan Daniel Rezny, Jessica Simone. BS in Bus. Adminstrn., Northeastern U., 1969, MBA, 1971; postgrad., U. Mich., 1971-75. Faculty U. Ky., Lexington, 1975-77; ptnr. Tatham-Laird & Kudner, Chgo., 1977-80; v.p. Marsteller, Chgo., 1980-84; sr. v.p. HCM, Chgo., 1984-86; pres. Gerald Linda & Assocs., Chgo., 1986-89; prin. Kurtzman/Slavin/Linda, Inc., Chgo., 1990-93, Kapuler Mkgt. Rsch., Chgo., 1993-94; pres. Gerald Linda & Assocs., Glenview, Ill., 1994—. Mem. editorial review bd. Jour. Current Issues and Rsch. in Advt., 1984—. Office Phone: 847-729-3403. Personal E-mail: glinda@gla-mktg.com.

LINDALL, TERRANCE, artist; b. Mpls., Oct. 13, 1944; s. Arnold Walfred and Jessie May Lindall. BA, Hunter Coll., N.Y.C., 1970. Mag. cover illustrator Warren Mag, N.Y.C., 1978—81; story illustrator Marvel's Epic Mag., N.Y.C., NY, 1981. Twilght zone mag. TZ Publ., N.Y.C., 1980; story illustrator Heavy Metal Mag., N.Y.C., 1979—80; pres. Williamsburg Art & Hist. Ctr., Bklyn., 1996—; founder Greenwood Mus., Smyrna, NY, 1986—96; writer 11211 Mag., Bklyn., 2003—. Illus. book, Paradise Lost Illustrated (Soc. of Illustrators Award of Merit, 1981); contbr. articles pub. to profl. jour.; creator (TV series) Brave Destiny. Home: 385 Clinton Ave #2-S Brooklyn NY 11238 Office: Williamsburg Art & Historical Center 135 Broadway Brooklyn NY 11211 Office Phone: 719-486-7372. Personal E-mail: wahcenter@earthlink.net.

LINDARS, LAURENCE EDWARD, retired health care products executive; b. N.Y.C., Oct. 14, 1922; s. Arthur John and Florence Vera (Cunard) L.; m. Mary Gibson Grandy, Jan. 22, 1972; children— John L., William A., Nancy E. Student, Dartmouth Coll., 1943-44; BS, Columbia U., 1947. Sr. auditor Arthur Young & Co., N.Y.C., 1947-51; chief acct. Deering, Milliken & Co., 1951-53; treas., dir. Poloron Products, Inc., New Rochelle, N.Y., 1953-58; controller Atlas Gen., Inc., N.Y.C., 1958-59; controller, treas., dir. fin. planning Pepperidge Farm, Inc., Norwalk, Conn., 1959-67; with C.R. Bard, Inc., Murray Hill, N.J., 1967-88, dir., 1972-92, vice chmn., 1983-88. Mem. adv. bd. of Summit Trust Co., 1970-84 Trustee Overlook Hosp., 1973-79, Found., 1988-91, treas., 1989-90; trustee Epilepsy Found. N.J., 1985-90, pres., 1986-87, chmn., 1988-90. Lt. (j.g.) USNR, 1943-46. Mem. Fin. Execs. Inst., Canoe Brook Country Club, Delta Upsilon. Presbyterian. Home: 199 Woodland Ave Summit NJ 07901

LINDAU, PHILIP, commodities trader; b. 1936; With Pillsbury Co., 1964-93; pres. Pillsbury Flour Milling & Spl. Commodities Ops., Mpls.; pres., CEO Commodity Specialists Co., Mpls. Office: Commodity Specialists Co 400 S 4th St Minneapolis MN 55415-1015 Business E-Mail: csc@world.com.

LINDAUER, ERIK D., lawyer; b. Bklyn., Oct. 1, 1956; s. Albert and Dinah (Epner) L.; m. Lisa Diamond, Aug. 16, 1981; children: Jacob, Samuel. BA, SUNY, Albany, 1978; JD, SUNY, Buffalo, 1981. Bar: NY 1982, US Dist. Ct. (ea. dist.) NY 1982, US Dist. Ct. (so. dist.) NY 1982. Assoc. Sullivan & Cromwell, NYC, 1981-89, ptnr. project fin., 1989—, and coord. corp. reorganization/bankruptcy practice area. Mem.: ABA. Office: Sullivan & Cromwell 125 Broad St New York NY 10004-2489 Office Phone: 212-558-3548. Business E-Mail: lindauere@sullcrom.com.

LINDBERG, CHARLES DAVID, lawyer; b. Moline, Ill., Sept. 11, 1928; s. Victor Samuel and Alice Christine (Johnson) L.; m. Marian J. Wagner, June 14, 1953; children: Christine, Breta, John, Eric. AB, Augustana Coll., Rock Island, Ill., 1950; JD, Yale U., 1953; DHL, Augustana Coll., 2000. Bar: Ohio 1954. Assoc. Taft, Stettinius & Hollister, Cin., 1953-61, ptnr., 1961-85, mng. ptnr., 1985-98, of counsel, 1999—. Bd. dirs. Cin. Bengals Profl. Football Team, 1982—2003; chmn. bd. dirs. Schonstedt Instrument Co., 1994—97. Editor: Nat. Law Jour., 1979—90. Bd. dirs. Taft Broadcasting Co., Cin., 1973-87, Dayton Walther Corp., 1986-87, Gibson Greeting, Inc., 1991-2000; bd. dirs. Augustana Coll., 1978-87, 91-99, 2000—, sec., 1981-82, vice-chmn., 1982-83, chmn., 1983-86; pres. Cin. Bd. Edn., 1971, 74, Zion Luth. Ch., Cin., 1966-69; chmn. policy com. Hamilton County Rep. Com., 1981-90; mem. exec. com. Ohio Rep. Fin. Com., 1989-90; chmn. Tyler Davidson Com., 1999-2000; trustee Greater Cin. Ctr. Econ. Edn., 1976-91, pres., 1987-89, chmn., 1989-91; chmn. law firm divsn. Fine Arts Fund, 1985; trustee Pub. Libr. Cin. and Hamilton County, 1982—, pres., 1989, 96, 01. Mem. Cin. Bar Assn., Greater Cin. C. of C. (trustee 1985, exec. com., vice chmn. govt. and cmty. affairs com. 1989-91), Ohio Libr. Trustees Assn. (bd. dirs. 1986-87), Ohio C. of C. (bd. dirs. 1988-89), Queen City Club (sec. 1989-91), Commonwealth Club, Comml. Club (sec. 1994-96), Optimists. Office: 1800 US Bank Tower 425 Walnut St Cincinnati OH 45202-3923 Office Phone: 513-381-2838. Business E-Mail: lindberg@taftlaw.com.

LINDBERG, DONALD ALLAN BROR, library director, pathologist, educator; b. N.Y.C., Sept. 21, 1933; s. Harry B. and Frances Seeley (Little) L.; m. Mary Musick, June 8, 1957; children: Donald Allan Bror, Christopher Charles Seeley, Jonathan Edward Moyer. AB, Amherst Coll., 1954, ScD (hon.), 1979; MD, Columbia U., 1958; ScD (hon.), SUNY, 1987, U. Health Sci. Med. Informatics and Tech., Austria, 2004; LLD (hon.), U. Mo., Columbia, 1990. Diplomate Am. Bd. Pathology, Am. Bd. Med. Examiners (exec. bd. 1987-91). Rsch. asst. Amherst Coll., 1954-55; intern in pathology Columbia-Presbyn. Med. Ctr., 1958-59, asst. resident in pathology, 1959-60; asst. in pathology Coll. Physician and Surgeons Columbia U., N.Y.C., 1958-60; instr. pathology Sch. of Medicine U. Mo., 1962-63, asst. prof. Sch. of Medicine, 1963-66, assoc. prof. Sch. of Medicine, 1966-69, prof. Sch. of Medicine, 1969-84, dir. Diagnostic Microbiology Lab. Sch. of Medicine, 1960-63, dir. Med. Ctr. Computer Program Sch. of Medicine, 1962-70, staff, exec. dir. for health affairs Sch. of Medicine, 1968-70, prof., chmn. dept. info. sci. Sch. of Medicine, 1969-71; dir. Nat. Libr. of Medicine, Bethesda, Md., 1984—. Adj. prof. pathology U. Md. Sch. Medicine, 1988—, clin. prof. pathology U. Va., 1992—; dir. Nat. Coord. Office for High Performance Computing and Comms., exec. office of Pres., Office Sci. & Tech. Policy, 1992-95; mem. computer sci./engring. bd. Nat. Acad. Sci., 1971-74, chmn. Nat. Adv. Com. Artificial Intelligence in Medicine, Stanford U., 1975-84; U.S. rep. to Internat. Med. Info. Assn./Internat. Fedn. Info. Processing, 1975-84; bd. dirs. Am. Med. Info. Assn., 1992—, Health on the Net Found.; adv. coun. Inst. Medicine, 1992—. Author: The Computer and Medical Care, 1968; The Growth of Medical Information Systems in the United States, 1979; editor: (with W. Siler) Computers in Life Science Research, 1975; (with others) Computer Applications in Medical Care, 1982; editor Methods of Info. in Medicine, 1970-83, assoc. editor, 1983—; editor Jour. Med. Systems, 1976—, Med. Informatics Jour., 1976—; chief editor procs. 3d World Conf. on Med. Informatics, 1980; editorial bd. Jour. of AMA, 1991—; contbr. articles to jours. Simpson fellow Amherst Coll., 1954-55, Markle scholar in acad. medicine, 1964-69; recipient Silver Cord award Internat. Fedn. for Info. Processing, 1980, Walter C. Alvarez award Am. Med. Writers Assn. 1989, PHS Surgeon Gen.'s medallion, 1989, Nathan Davis award AMA, 1989, Presdl. Disting. Exec. Rank award, Sr. Exec. Svc., Outstanding Svc. medal Uniformed Svcs. U. Health Scis., 1992, Computers in Healthcare Pioneer award, 1993, recognition award High Performance Computing Industry, 1995, silver award U.S. Nat. Commn. on Librs. and Info. Scis., 1996, meritorious award Coun. Biol. Editors, 1996, pres.'s award Med. Libr. Assn., 1997, Morris F. Collen, M.D. award of excellence Am. Coll. Med. Informatics, 1997, Info. Frontier award N.Y. Acad. Medicine, 1999, Ranice W. Crosby Disting. Achievement award Johns Hopkins U. Sch. Medicine, 1998, Spl. Recognition award Coll. P&S Columbia U. Alumni, 2001, Lila A. Wallis Women's Health award, Am. Med. Women's Assn., 2005. Fellow: AAAS; mem.: Am. Med. Informatics Assn. (pres. 1988—91), Gorgas Meml. Inst. Tropical and Preventive Medicine (bd. dirs. 1987—), Am. Assn. Med. Systems and Informatics (internat. com. 1982—89, bd. dirs. 1982, editor conf. procs. 1983, 1984), Salutis Initas (Am. v.p. 1981—91), Assn. for Computing Machines, Mo. Med. Assn., Coll. Am. Pathologists (commn. on computer policy and coordination 1981—84), Inst. Medicine of NAS, Cosmos Club (38th Cosmos Club award 2001), Sigma Xi. Democrat. Avocations: photography, riding. Home: 13601 Esworthy Rd Germantown MD 20874-3319 Office: Nat Libr Medicine 8600 Rockville Pike Bethesda MD 20894-0002 Office Phone: 301-496-6221.

LINDBERG, DONNA JEANNE, minister; b. Pontiac, Mich., Oct. 15, 1944; d. Hugo W. and Ina A. (Ballard) L.; children: Richard Ronald, Christopher Charles. BA, Adrian Coll., 1966; ThM, So. Meth. U., 1969. Ordained to ministry Meth. Ch., as deacon, 1967, as elder, 1971. Assoc. pastor Beverly Hills United Meth. Ch., Birmingham, Mich., 1970-72, Port Huron (Mich.) United Meth. Ch., 1972-73, Livonia (Mich.) Newburg United Meth. Ch., 1973-74; pastor Rice Meml. United Meth. Ch., Redford, Mich., 1974-79, Hazel Park (Mich.) First United Meth. Ch., 1979-83, Gaylord (Mich.) First United Meth. Ch., 1983-89, Ann Arbor (Mich.) Dist. Supt. United Meth. Ch., 1989—93, Ishpeming (Mich.) Wesley UMC, 1993—97, pastor first UMC manistique and marquette dist. project dir., 1997—2004, ret., 2004, part time project dir. Marquette dist., 2004—. Del. World Meth. Coun., Honolulu, 1981; cons. Clergy Women, Clergy Couples, Ethnic Min. Clergy Women, Detroit, 1984-88; mem. Jurisdictional Ct. of Appeals United Meth. Ch., Chgo., 1988-92; registrar Detroit Conf. Bd. of Ordained Ministry, 1972-84; counselor Mich. Assn. of Problem Pregnancy Counselors, Birmingham, 1970-75; pres. Clergy Assn., Gaylord, 1984-88. Bd. dirs. Hospice, Gaylord, 1986-88, Big Bros./Big Sisters, Gaylord, 1985-87; mem. Sch. Bd. Adv. Com., Gaylord, 1984-89; reg. marquette dist comm. on ordained ministry, 1994—; treas manistique ministerial assoc., 1998-2004; spiritual coord. Schoolcraft Meml. Hospice, 1998-2004 Recipient Clergy of Yr. award Kiwanis Internat., 1988. Home: 396 Harbor View Dr # 11 Manistique MI 49854-1357 *In a world where war is still a reality, basic human needs are in many places unmet and environmental concerns are pressing, it behooves us to seek the guidance of the One who created and sustains us and to Whom we are accountable.*

LINDBERG, DUANE R., bishop, historian; b. Thief River Falls, Minn., Apr. 16, 1933; s. Edgar and Alice (Amundson) L.; m. E. Mardell Kvitne, June 6, 1954; children: Erik Duane, Karen Kristin Kelle, Karl Stephen, Martha Alice Stone, Kristian John. BS in Chemistry, U. N.D., 1954; MDiv in Theology, Luther Sem., St. Paul, 1961; MA in Am. Studies, U. Minn., 1969, PhD in Am. Studies, 1975. Rsch. chemist DuPont Co., 1954; tchg. asst. chemistry dept. U. Wis., Madison, 1956-57; chemist Minn. Farm Bur. Lab., St. Paul, 1957-59; pastor Epping and Wheelock (N.D.) Luth. Chs., 1961-68; rsch. historian Minn. State Hist. Soc., St. Paul, 1969-71; pastor Zion Luth. Ch., West Union, Iowa, 1971-78; sr. pastor Trinity Luth. Ch., Waterloo, Iowa, 1978-87, Acension Luth. Ch., Waterloo, 1987—98, sr. pastor emeritus, 1998—; nat. ch. body founder, presiding pastor Am. Assn. Luth. Chs., Mpls., 1987-99, presiding pastor emeritus, 1999—; interim pastor St. Luke Luth. Ch., Traer, Iowa, 2003—. Vis. prof. Upper Iowa U., Fayette, 1976-77; adj. prof. Am. Luth. Theol. Sem., St. Paul, 1996-. Author: Uniting Word, 1969, Men of the Cloth, 1980; contbr. articles to profl. jours. Bd. dirs. Palmer Meml. Hosp., West Union, Iowa, 1972-78, Allen Meml. Hosp., Waterloo, 1979—; founder, bd. mem. Buffalo Trails Mus., Epping, N.D., 1964-68; founder, bd. mem. Fayette County Hist. Soc., West Union, 1975-78; dean Decorah Conf. Am. Luth. Ch., 1976-78, exec. com. Iowa Dist., 1976-78; bd. dirs. Great Plains Inst. Theology, 1965-68; pres. Eastern Iowa Luth. H.S. Assn., 1997-04. 1st lt. U.S. Army, 1954-56. Recipient award of commendation Concordia Hist. Inst., St. Louis, 1980, Nehemiah award Abiding World Ministries, Mpls., 1990, award of excellence Allen Meml. Hosp., Waterloo, 1995. Mem. numerous profl. ministerial groups and ch. bds., Rotary, Sons of Norway. Lutheran. Office: Valley Luth HS 4520 Rownd St Cedar Falls IA 50613

LINDBERG, FRANCIS LAURENCE, JR., management consultant; b. Jacksonville, Fla., Mar. 13, 1948; s. Francis Laurence and Mildred Hortense (Parrish) L.; m. Anne Louise Stearns, Dec. 29, 1972 (div.); 1 child, Kristen Anne; m. Alexis Jean Parker, Nov. 12, 1983 (dec. May 1996). Student, Eckerd Coll., 1965-66; BA, Jacksonville U., 1969; MBA, U. North Fla., 1976. CPA, Ga. Actuarial asst. Gulf Life Ins. Co., Jacksonville, 1967-73; asst. actuary Am. Heritage Life, Jacksonville, 1973-77; asst. sec.-treas., prin. acctg. officer Atlantic Am. Corp., Atlanta, 1977-84; assoc. v.p. fin. Security Benefit Group, Topeka, 1985-86; exec. v.p., chief fin. officer Am. Way Group of Cos., Southfield, Mich., 1986-87; prin. Lindberg Consulting Group, Inc. (formerly Lindberg Group), Atlanta, 1987-98, pres., 1998—. V.p. fin Carson-Brooks, Inc., Atlanta, 1991-93; treas., bd. advisors Good News Comm., Inc., 1986-94; dep. receiver USEC Ga., Atlanta, 1995—. Recipient Membership Achievement award, Inst. Mgmt. Accts., 1983, George E. Wilson award Inst. Mgmt. Accts., 1991. Mem. AICPA (MAS, PCPS divs.), Soc. Fin. Examiners, Ga. Soc. CPAs, Brotherhood St. Andrew. Republican. Episcopalian.

LINDBERGH, REEVE, writer, poet; d. Charles A. Lindbergh and Anne Morrow L.; m. Nathaniel Tripp. Graduate, Radcliffe Coll., 1968. Bd. dir. Charles A. and Anne Morrow Lindbergh Found., 1977—, v.p., 1986—95, pres, 1995—2004, hon. chairwoman, 2004—. Author: (memoirs) Under a Wing, 1998, No More Words: A Journal of My Mother, Anne Morrow Lindbergh, 2001, (novels) Moving to the Country, 1983, The Names of the Mountains, 1992, (book of essays) View from the Kingdom, 1987, (children's books) The Midnight Farm, 1987, Benjamin's Barn, 1990, There's a COW in the Road!, 1993, What Is The Sun?, 1994, Grandfather's Lovesong, 1995, The Day the Goose Got Loose, 1995, If I'd Known Then What I Know Now, 1996, Awful Aardvarks Shop for School, 2000, The Circle of Days, 2002, On Morning Wings, 2002, My Hippie Grandmother, 2003, Our Nest, 2004, The Visit, 2005. Office: Charles A and Ann Morrow Lindbergh Foundation Ste 310 2150 Third Ave N Anoka MN 55303-2200*

LINDBLOM, MARJORIE PRESS, lawyer; b. Chgo., Mar. 17, 1950; d. John E. and Betty (Grace) P.; m. Lance E. Lindblom, June 13, 1971; children: Derek, Ian. AB cum laude, Radcliffe Coll., 1971; JD with honors, U. Chgo., 1978. Bar: Ill. 1978, U.S. Dist. Ct. (no. dist.) Ill. 1978, U.S. Ct. Appeals (7th cir.) 1978, U.S. Ct. Appeals (10th cir.) 1983, U.S. Supreme Ct. 1983, U.S. Ct. Appeals (5th cir.) 1984, N.Y. 1995, U.S. Dist. Ct. (so. and ea. dist.) N.Y. 1995, U.S. Ct. Appeals (2d cir.) 1995. Assoc. Kirkland & Ellis, Chgo., 1978-84, ptnr., 1984-94; N.Y.C., 1994—. Asst. dir. fiscal affairs Ill. Bd. Higher Edn., 1973-75; budget analyst Ill. Bur. Budget, Office of Gov., 1972-73; admissions officer Princeton U., 1971-72; adj. prof. Northwestern U., Evanston, Ill., 1994. Comment editor U. Chgo. Law Rev., 1977-78. Bd. dirs. Chgo. Lawyers Com. for Civil Rights Under Law, 1989-94, Pub. Interest Law Initiative, 1989-94. Mem. ABA, Chgo. Coun. Lawyers (bd. govs. 1987-91, legal counsel 1986-87), 7th Cir. Bar Assn., Women's Bar Assn. of Ill., Lawyers Com. for Civil Rights Under Law (co-chair, 2004-2005). Office: Kirkland & Ellis Citicorp Ctr 153 E 53rd St New York NY 10022-4611 Office Phone: 212-446-4868. Office Fax: 212-446-4900. Business E-Mail: mlindblom@kirkland.com.

LINDBLOOM, CHAD M., transportation executive; BS, MBA, Univ. Minn. Staff acct. CH Robinson Worldwide Inc., Eden Prairie, Minn., 1990—98, corp. contr., 1998—99, v.p., CFO, 1999—. Office: CH Robinson Worldwide 8100 Mitchell Rd Eden Prairie MN 55344-2248

LINDE, EDWARD H., real estate manager; BS civil engring., M.I.T., 1962; MBA, Harvard Bus. Sch. Vice-pres., sr. project mgr. Cabot, Cabot & Forbes; co-found. Boston Properties, 1970, pres., CEO, 1997—. Dir. Jobs State Mass.; exec. com. Nat. Assn. Real Estate Investment Trusts. Vice-chmn., chmn. elect Boston Symphony Orchestra; former chmn. Board Beth-Israel Hospital. Mem.: Real Estate Round Table (mem. bd. dir.). Office: Boston Properties 111 Huntington Ave Boston MA 02199-7610 Office Phone: 617-236-3300. Office Fax: 617-536-5087.*

LINDE, HANS ARTHUR, state supreme court justice; b. Berlin, Apr. 15, 1924; came to U.S., 1939, naturalized, 1943; s. Bruno C. and Luise (Rosenhain) L.; m. Helen Tucker, Aug. 13, 1945; children: Lisa, David Tucker. BA, Reed Coll., 1947; JD, U. Calif., Berkeley, 1950. Bar: Oreg. 1951. Law clk. U.S. Supreme Ct. Justice William O. Douglas, 1950-51; atty. Office of Legal Adviser, Dept. State, 1951-53; pvt. practice Portland, Oreg., 1953-54; legis. asst. U.S. Sen. Richard L. Neuberger, 1955-58; from assoc. prof. to prof. U. Oreg. Law Sch., 1959-76; justice Oreg. Supreme Ct., Salem, 1977-90, sr. judge, 1990—. Fulbright lectr. Freiburg U., 1967-68, Hamburg U., 1975-76; cons. U.S. ACDA, Dept. Def., 1962-76; mem. Adminstrv. Conf. U.S., 1978-82, Oreg. Law Commn., 1997—; disting. scholar in residence Willamette U. Coll. Law, Salem, Oreg., 1994—. Author: (with George Bunn) Legislative and Administrative Processes, 1976. Mem. Oreg. Constl. Revision Commn., 1961-62, Oreg. Law Commn., 1997—, Oreg. Commn. on Pub. Broadcasting, 1990-93, Pub. Commn. Oreg. Legislative, 2005-; bd. dirs. Oreg. Pub. Broadcasting, 1993-99. With U.S. Army, 1943-46. Fellow Am. Acad. Arts and Scis.; mem. Am. Law Inst. (council), Order of Coif, Phi Beta Kappa. Office: Willamette U Coll Law Salem OR 97301 Business E-Mail: hlinde@willamette.edu.

LINDE, MAXINE HELEN, lawyer, corporate financial executive, investor; b. Chgo., Sept. 2, 1939; d. Jack and Lottie (Kroll) Stern; m. Ronald K. Linde, June 12, 1960. BA summa cum laude, UCLA, 1961; JD, Stanford U., 1967. Bar: Calif. 1968. Applied mathematician, rsch. engr Jet Propulsion Lab., Pasadena, Calif., 1961—64; law clk. U.S. Dist. Ct. No. Calif., 1967—68; mem. firm Long & Levit, San Francisco, 1968—69, Swerdlow, Glikbarg & Shimer, Beverly Hills, Calif., 1969—72; sec., gen. counsel Envirodyne Industries, Inc., Chgo., 1972—89; pres. The Ronald and Maxine Linde Found., 1989—; vice chmn. bd., gen. counsel Titan Fin. Group, LLC, Chgo., 1994—98. Mem. bd. visitors Stanford Law Sch., 1989—92, law and bus. adv. coun., 1991—94, dean's adv. coun., 1992—94. Mem.: Alpha Lambda Delta, Pi Mu Epsilon, Phi Beta Kappa, Order of Coif.

LINDE, RONALD KEITH, science administrator, investor; b. L.A., Jan. 31, 1940; s. Morris and Sonia Doreen (Hayman) L.; m. Maxine Helen Stern, June 12, 1960. BS with honors, UCLA, 1961; MS (Inst. scholar), Calif. Inst. Tech., 1962, PhD (ARCS scholar, Rutherford scholar), 1964. Cons. Litton Industries, L.A., 1961-63, engr., 1961; materials scientist Poulter Labs., Stanford Rsch. Inst., Menlo Park, Calif., 1964; head solid state rsch. Stanford Rsch. Inst., Menlo Park, Calif., 1965-67; chmn. shock wave physics dept., mgr. tech. svcs. Poulter Labs., 1967, dir. shock and high pressure physics div., 1967-68, chief exec. labs., 1968-69; dir. phys. scis. Stanford Rsch. Inst., 1968-69; chmn. bd., CEO Envirodyne Industries, Inc., Chgo., 1969-89; chmn. bd. The Ronald and Maxine Linde Found., Phoenix, 1989—. Co-chmn. bd. Titan Fin. Group, LLC, Chgo., 1994-98; law and bus. adv. coun. Stanford Law Sch., 1991-94, dean's adv. coun. 1992-94. Contbr. articles to various publs.; patentee in field. Mem. adv. bd. ARCS Found., Chgo., 1993-98; mem. Northwestern U. Assocs., 1978-2005; trustee Calif. Inst. Tech., 1989—, chmn. alumni rels. com., 1997-2002, chmn. audit and compliance com., 2002—, Harvey Mudd Coll., 1989-98, vice chmn., bd. trustees, 1993-98, vice chmn. emeritus, 1998—. Mem. Sigma Xi, Tau Beta Pi, Phi Eta Sigma.

LINDE, SHIRLEY, writer, travel company executive; BS in Zoology, postgrad., U. Cin.; MS in Physiology, U. Mich.; PhD in Nutrition, Internat. Coll. Natural Health Scis.; postgrad., NYU, Northwestern U. Former owner Hilltop Restaurant, Treasure Cay, Bahamas; former Chgo. bur. chief Med. News, Med. Tribune, Tele-Med; former rsch. chemist Andrew Jergens Co.; former rsch. asst. U. Cin. Med. Sch.; former rsch. fellow U. Mich. Med. Sch.; former asst. editor Jour. Internat. Coll. Surgeons; former copy editor Yr. Book Pubs.; former assoc. editor Together Mag.; former chief info. svcs. Northwestern U. Med./Dental Schs.; former pres. Pavilion Pub. Co.; editor SmallShipCruises.com, TheCruiseChef.com, FairWinds, The Cruise Chef; pres. Small Ship Cruises, Inc.; freelance author, editor. Pub. rels. cons. numerous cos.; lectr. Columbia U. Grad. Sch.; mem. workshop faculty Fla. Suncoast Writers Conf., Lake Lotowana Writers Conf. Author: The Big Ditch, Story of the Suez Canal, 1962, Total Rehabilitation of Epileptics, 1962, Heart Attacks That Aren't, 1966, Airline Stewardess Handbook, 1968, Modern Woman's Medical Dictionary, 1968; author: (with H. Rapaport) The Complete Allergy Guide, 1970; author: (with R. Allen) Lifegain, 1970; author: Cosmetic Surgery, What It Can Do For You, 1971; author: (with A. Michele) Orthotherapy, 1971; author: Sickle Cell, A Complete Guide, 1972, The Sleep Book, 1974; author: (with F. Finnerty) High Blood Pressure, 1975; author: (with Gideon Panter) Now That You've Had Your Baby, 1976; author: (with Robert Atkins) Dr. Atkins' Superenergy Diet, 1977; author: The Whole Health Catalogue, 1980, The Joy of Sleep, 1981, How to Beat a Bad Back, 1981, 201 Medical Tests You Can Do at Home, 1983, Directory to Holistic Medicine and Alternate Health Care Services, 1986; author: (with R. Johnson) The Charleston Program, 1990; author: (with P.J. Hauri) No More Sleepless Nights, 1990; author: rev. edit., 2000; author: (with Alfred Bonati) No More Back Pain, 1991; author: (with M. Breecher) Healthy Homes in a Toxic Environment, 1992; author: (with L. Lane) Insiders' Guide to the World's Most Exciting Cruises, 1994; author: The World's Most Intimate Cruises, The Guide to Cruising in Small Ships, 1999; author: (with Victor Hoffstein) No More Snoring, 1999; author: (with P.J. Hauri) No More Sleepless Nights Workbook, 2000; contbr. Great Voyages of the World, 1997; contbg. editor Windows--Inside Views on Dining, Traveling and Lodging, 1989; editor: Radioactivity in Man, 1961, Science and the Public, 1962, Response of the Nervous System to Ionizing Radiation, 1962, Medical Science in the News, 1965, Emergency Family First Aid Guide, 1971, Crash Landing, 1991, Feeling Better, Lookin' Good Newsletter, Medical Bull. on Tobacco, Stay Young Newsletter, Biomagnetism/Health Newsletter; contbr. articles to profl. publs., mags., periodicals. Recipient Comm. award, Brandeis U., Svc. award, Sickle Cell Found., Nat. Youth Movement, Outstanding Women of Tampa Bay award, YWCA. Mem.: AAAS, Soc. Am. Travel Writers, Internat. Food, Wine and Travel Writers Assn., N.Am. Travel Journalists Assn. (v.p., bd. dirs.), Am. Med. Writers Assn. (nat. sec., v.p., chpt. treas., Outstanding Svc. award), East-West News Bur., Nat. Assn. Sci. Writers (nat. exec. com.), St. Petersburg Mus. Fine Arts, Al Downing Tampa Bay Jazz Assn. (bd. dirs.), St. Petersburg Yacht Club. Home: 100 Beach Dr NE Saint Petersburg FL 33701 E-mail: Linde@SmallShipCruises.com.

LINDEGREN, CECILE KEYSER, music educator; b. DeFuniak Springs, Fla., July 1, 1946; d. Charles Renshaw and Ouida (Higdon) Keyser; m. John Emory Lindegren, Feb. 14, 1981; children: Erica Kristen. AA, Pensacola (Fla.) Jr. Coll.; B in Mus. Edn., Fla. State U.; M in Mus. Edn., U. South Miss. Cert. elem. and secondary music tchr., Fla. Choral dir. Pryor Jr. High Sch. (now Pryor Mid. Sch.), Ft. Walton Beach, Fla.; adult choir dir. Hurlburt Field AFB Chapel, 1982—84; choral dir. Pryor Jr. High Sch. (now Pryor Mid. Sch.), Ft. Walton Beach, Fla., Walton Mid. Sch., 1996—; dir. music and youth Mary Esther (Fla.) United Meth. Ch.; owner, instr. Lindegren Music Studio, Ft. Walton Beach; chorus and band dir. Walton Mid. Sch., 2001—. Children's choir dir. Trinity United Meth. Ch. Dir. Ft. Walton Beach Cmty. Chorus; bd. dirs. Mattie Kelly Fine Arts Ctr. Coun. Mem. Okaloosa County Music Tchrs. Assn (pres. 1981-83), Fla. Vocal Assn. (chmn. local dist. 2 terms, music performance assessment adjudicator 1976—), Fla. State Music Tchrs. Assn., Emerald Coast Concert Assn. (sec. 1984-86, 88-89, bd. dirs. 1984-89), Music Educators Nat. Conf., Fla. League of Arts (state pres. 2003—), Fla. Music Educators Assn., Fla. Vocal Assn., Ft. Walton Beach Woman's Club (music dir. 1984-87, 2d v.p. 1984-86), Choctaw Bay Music Club (pres. 1985-86). Democrat. Unitarian.

LINDELL, ANDREA REGINA, dean, nurse; b. Warren, Pa., Aug., 21, 1943; d. Andrew D. and Irene M. (Fabry) Lefik; m. Warner E. Lindell, May 7, 1966; children: Jennifer I., Jason M. B.S., Villa Maria Coll., 1970; M.S.N. Catholic U., 1975, D.N.Sc., 1976; diploma R.N., St. Vincent's Hosp., Erie, Pa. Instr. St. Vincent Hosp. Sch. Nursing, 1964-66; dir. Rouse Hosp., Youngsville, Pa., 1966-69; supr. Vis. Nurses Assn., Warren, Pa., 1969-70; dir. grad. program Cath. U., Washington, 1975-77; chmn., assoc. dean U. N.H., Durham, 1977-81; dean, prof. Oakland U., Rochester, Mich., 1981-90, dean, Schmidlapp prof. nursing U. Cin., 1990—; bd. dirs. CHEMED Corp.; cons. Moorehead U., Ky., 1983. Editor; Jour. Profl. Nursing, 1985; contbr. articles to profl. jours. Mem. sch. bd. Strafford Sch. Dist., N.H., 1977-80; Gov.'s Blue Ribbon Commn. Direct Health Policies, Concord, N.H., 1979-81; vice chmn. New England Commn. Higher Edn. in Nursing, 1977-81; mem. Mich. Assn. Colls. Nursing, 1981— . Named Outstanding Young Woman Am., 1980. Mem. Nat. League Nursing, Am. Assn. Colls. Nursing (pres. 1996—), Sigma Theta Tau. Democrat. Roman Catholic. Avocations: water skiing, roller skating, reading, fishing, camping. Office: College of Nursing & Health 3110 Vine St Cincinnati OH 45221-0001

LINDELL, EDWARD ALBERT, academic administrator, religious organization administrator; b. Denver, Nov. 30, 1928; s. Edward Gustaf and Estelle (Lundin) L.; m. Patricia Clare Eckert, Sept. 2, 1965; children: Edward Paul, Erik Adam. BA, U. Denver, 1950, MA, 1956, Ed.D., 1960, L.H.D. (hon.), 1975; Litt.D. (hon.), Tusculum Coll., 1979; D.H.L. (hon.), Roanoke Coll., 1981; Litt.D (hon.), Christ Coll., Irvine, 1992. Tchr. North Denver High Sch., 1952-61; asst. dean Coll. Arts and Scis., U. Denver, 1961-65, dean, 1965-75; pres. Gustavus Adolphus Coll., St. Peter, Minn., 1975-80, Luth. Brotherhood Mut. Funds, Mpls., 1980—. V.p. Luth. Brotherhood Found., 1980—, also exec. dir. Mem. exec. bd. Rocky Mountain Synod Luth. Ch. Am., 1968—, Luth. Coun. U.S.A., v.p., 1975—; also pres. bd. coll. edn. and ch. vocations; trustee Midland Luth. Coll., Fremont, Nebr., Kans. Wesleyan U., Colo. Assn. Ind. Colls. and Univs., Luth. Med. Center, Wheatridge, Colo., Luth. Sch. Theology, Chgo., 1975—, St. John's U., Minn., 1978—; bd. dirs. Swedish Coun. in Am., 1978—, pres., chmn.-elect, 2001, pres., 2002; adv. bd. Royal Swedish Acad. Scis., 1980; v.p. Am.-Swedish Inst., 1980; exec. v.p. external affairs Luth. Brotherhood, 1981—; pres. Nat. Fraternal Congress Am., 1988—; bd. dirs. Pacific Luth. Theol. Sem., 1978-80, Loretto Heights Coll., Colo., 1978-86, Gettysburg Theol. Sem., 1981-83, Wittenberg U., 1988, Bethany Coll., 1991—, Minn. Orch., 1983—, Am. Scandinavian Found., 1982—, Fairview Hosp., 1982—, Luth. Internat. Congress, 1996-2000; bd. dirs. U.S. Swedish Found. Internat. Sci. Rsch., 1981—, v.p. 1986—; bd. dirs. Habitat for Humanity Internat., 1992—, mem. global leadership com., 2003—; pres. U.S. Wittenberg Found., 1996—. Named Outstanding Faculty Mem. Coll. Arts and Scis., U. Denver, 1964; decorated knight King of Sweden, 1976; recipient Suomi Disting. Svc. award, 1989. Mem. Good Samaritan Soc. (bd. dirs. 1997—, vice-chmn. 98-99, chmn.-elect 1999, chmn. 2000—), Swedish Pioneer Hist. Soc. (dir. 1979—), U. Denver Alumni Assn. (Career Alumni Achievement award 1994), Phi Beta Kappa. Office: Swedish Coun Am 2600 Park Ave S Minneapolis MN 55407 E-mail: 2swedes@outtech.com.

LINDELL, LINDA C., art educator; b. Guyman, Okla., Jan. 23, 1948; d. Clifford Cleo and Eula Mae Carlile; m. Paul Thomas Lindell, Nov. 8, 1979; children: Cynthia Schaffner, Lisa Josey, Chris Mason; 1 child, Cheri Barnes. AA, Howard Coll., 1969; BS, Sul Ross U., 1973; M in music edn., Angelo State U., 1984; DFA, Tex. Tech. U., 1995. Music tchr. Big Spring Independent Sch. Dist., Big Spring, Tex., 1992—. Mem. Big Spring Symphony Bd., Big Spring, Tex., 2000—. Avocations: reading, crafts, walking. Home: 2301 Robb Dr Big Spring TX 79720 Office: Big Spring ISD 708 11th Pl Big Spring TX 79720 Office Phone: 432-264-3641. Office Fax: 432-264-4133. E-mail: llindell@bsisd.esc18.net.

LINDEMAN, BARRY JAMES, internal auditor, nurse, minister; b. Cheverly, Md., July 31, 1952; s. Robert Carlton and Eva Mae Lindeman; m. Hilda Alfreda Edelstein, Sept. 8, 2000. ADN, Calhoun CC, 1974; BS in Org. Mgmt., Tusculum Coll., 2003, MBA in Org. Mgmt. Cert. Managed Healthcare Profl. Health Ins. Assn., 1998; RN; cert. Compliance Profl. Healthcare Fraud & Abuse Compliance Inst., Case Mgr. Various nursing positions, Knoxville, Birmingham, Charleston, Huntsville; adminstr. govt. programs John Deere Healthcare, Moline, Ill., sr. regional auditor, 1994—2001; sr. auditor Covenant Health, Knoxville, Tenn., 2001—. Founding mem. MCO fraud roundtable Tenn. Bur. Investigation, Nashville, 1995—; founding mem. working group OIG East Tenn. Healthcare Fraud, Knoxville, 2000—; mem. Coun. Ethical Orgs., 2003—. Sec. Kiwanis, South Knoxville, 1993; organizer Out of the Box, Knoxville, 2003—; bd. dirs. Kiwanis, South Knoxville, 1990—92. Named Outstanding Internal Auditor, City of Knoxville, 2001. Mem.: Inst. Internal Auditors, Assn. Cert. Fraud Examiners. Office: 1400 Centerpoint Blvd Ste 150 Knoxville TN 37932

LINDEMANN, GEORGE L., gas industry executive; b. NYC, 1936; BS in Econ., Univ. Pa. Pres. Smith, Miller and Patch pharmaceuticals, 1962—72, Vision Cable Comm., 1972—81; founder, chmn., CEO Metrol Mobile CTS Inc. (merged with Bell Atlantic), 1983—92; chmn., CEO Southern Union gas pipelines, Wilkes Barre, Pa., 1990—; also, chmn., CEO Activated Comm. Inc., NYC. Bd. dir. Met. Club, NYC, New Orleans Mus. Art, Internat Class A Yacht Assn., Perto Cervo, Sardinia, Italy. Home: FL Office: Southern Union Co 1 PEI Ctr Wilkes Barre PA 18711 Office Phone: 570-820-2400.*

LINDEMANN, RUTH BURRIDGE, librarian; b. Lake Forest, Ill., Sept. 18, 1960; d. George Shaw and Marge (Opitz) Burridge; m. William Albert Lindemann; children: William, George; m. Eric C. Walters, Oct. 2, 1982 (div. July 1985). BA, U. Ala., 1986, MA, 1988; MS, U. Ill., Champaign-Urbana, 1999, PhD, 1996. Asst. editor Microelectronics Mfg. and Testing Mag., Libertyville, Ill., 1980—82; comm. specialist P.E. LaMoreaux & Assoc., Tuscaloosa, Ala., 1984—89; instr. English dept. U. Ill., Champaign-Urbana, 1996—98; reference and instrnl. libr. Danville (Ill.) Area C.C., 1999—. Mem.: LITA, RUSA, ACRL, ALA. Avocations: writing, Web design. Office: Danville Area Cmty Coll 2000 E Main Danville IL 61821 Business E-Mail: rlinde@dacc.edu.

LINDEN, HENRY ROBERT, chemical engineer, researcher; b. Vienna, Feb. 21, 1922; arrived in U.S., 1939, naturalized, 1945; s. Fred and Edith (Lermer) Linden; m. Natalie Govedarica, 1967; children from previous marriage: Robert, Debra. BS, Ga. Inst. Tech., 1944; MChemE, Poly. U., 1947; PhD, Ill. Inst. Tech., 1952. Chem. engr. Socony Vacuum Labs., 1944-47; with Inst. Gas Tech., 1947-78, various rsch. mgmt. positions, 1947-61, dir., 1961-69, exec. v.p., dir., 1969-74, pres., trustee, 1974-78; various acad. appointments Ill. Inst. Tech., Chgo., 1954-86, Frank W. Gunsaulus Disting. Prof. chem. engring., 1987-90, McGraw prof. energy and power engring. and mgmt., 1990—, interim pres., CEO, 1989-90, interim chmn., CEO Ill. Inst. Tech. Rsch. Inst., 1989-90; COO GDC, Inc., Chgo., 1965-73; CEO Gas Devel. Corp. subs. Inst. Gas Tech., Chgo., 1973-78, also bd. dirs.; pres., dir. Gas Rsch. Inst., Chgo., 1976-87, exec. advisor, 1987-2000; mem. strategic adv. coun. Gas Tech. Inst., Chgo., 2003—. Contbr. articles to profl. jours. Named to Hall of Fame, Ill. Inst. Tech., 1982, Engring. Hall of Fame, Ga. Tech., 1996; recipient award of merit oper. sect., Am. Gas Assn., 1956, Disting. Svc. award, 1974, Gas. Industry Rsch. award, 1982, R & D award, Nat. Energy Resources Orgn., 1986, Homer H. Lowry award for excellence in fossil energy rsch., U.S. Dept. Energy, 1991, award, U.S. Energy Assn., 1993, Walton Clark medal, Franklin Inst., 1972, Bunsen-Pettenkofer-Ehrentafel medal, Deutscher Verein des Gas und Wasserfaches, 1978, Lifetime Achievement award, Energy Daily Jour., 1996, Alumni medal, Ill. Inst. Tech., 1995. Fellow: AAAS, AIChE (Ernest W. Thiele award 2000), Inst. Energy; mem.: Am. Chem. Soc. (chmn. divsn. fuel chemistry 1967, councilor 1969—77, H.H. Storch award), So. Gas Assn. (hon.), NAE. Achievements include patents for fuel technology. Office: Ill Inst Tech PH 135 10 W 33rd St Chicago IL 60616-3730 Office Phone: 312-567-3095. Business E-Mail: linden@iit.edu.

LINDEN, KURT JOSEPH, electronics engineer; s. Fred I. and Ruth B. Linden; m. Susan M. Alpert, July 8, 1962; children: Judith A., Philip A., Benjamin N. BS, U. Utah, 1959; MS, MIT, 1963; PhD, Purdue U., 1966. Group leader Raytheon, Waltham, Mass., 1966-76; mgr. Laser Analytics, Bedford, Mass., 1976-84; dir. electronic materials divsn. Spire Corp., Bedford, Mass., 1983—93, mgr. laser product devel., 1993—2000, sr. scientist, 2001—; dir. ops. Axcel Photonics, 2000—01. Sr. lectr. Northeastern U., Boston, 1976—; lectr. MIT, Cambridge, summers 1980—. Contbr. articles to profl. jours. Mem. IEEE, SPIE, Am. Phys. Soc. Home: 17 Keith Rd Wayland MA 01778-4560 Office: Spire Corp 1 Patriots Park Bedford MA 01730-2396 Office Phone: 781-275-6000 ext 208. Business E-Mail: klinden@spirecorp.com.

LINDEN, MARGARET JOANNE, librarian, administrator; b. Berkeley, Calif., Nov. 20, 1938; d. Arthur William and Johanna Gesina (Zuydhoek) Dickie; m. Roy Joseph Linden, Jan. 6, 1965 (dec. Jan. 1989). BA, Swarthmore (Pa.) Coll., 1960; MLS, U. Calif., Berkeley, 1962. Librarian Grad. Social Scis. library U. Calif., Berkeley, 1961-65, librarian Giannini Found. for Agrl. Econs., 1965-70; social scis. librarian Idaho State U., Pocatello, 1970-71; head cataloguer Chevron Corp. (formerly Standard Oil Co. of Calif.), San Francisco, 1971-74, asst. chief librarian, 1974-77, chief librarian, 1978-81, mgr. corp. library, 1981—92; ret., 1992. Mem. Calif. Library Assn., Spl. Libraries Assn. (editor chpt. bull. 1972-73). Office: Chevron Corp 555 Market St San Francisco CA 94105-2870

LINDEN, PEPPY G., museum director; b. Louisville, Dec. 19, 1949; d. Bernard Sylvan and Helen Novitsky Goldstein; m. Russell Mathew Linden, May 9, 1971 (div. May 1979). BEd, U. Mich., 1971. Cert. elem. tchr. Va. Program coord. Project Cmty., Ann Arbor, Mich., 1971-72; sr. rsch. asst. Inst. for Social Rsch., Ann Arbor, 1972-74; infant educator dept. pediats. U. Va., Charlottesville, 1975-76; pediat. admissions and adolescent coord. Kluge Children's Rehab. Ctr., U. Va. Med. Ctr., Charlottesville, 1976-89; exec. dir. Va. Discovery Mus., Charlottesville, 1990—. Mem. Cable TV Citizens' Adv. Com., Charlottesville, 1992-98; mem. Social Svcs. Adv. Bd., Charlottesville, 1996-2005. Judge Nat. History Day, Charlottesville, 1993-96; bd. dirs. Piedmont Coun. of Arts, Charlottesville, 1989-92, Charlotteville Regional Tourism Coun., 2001-04, Town Coun., 2001-04; regional bd. dirs. Sorensen Inst. for Polit. Leadership, 2001—; sec., chair Charlottesville Electoral Bd., 1993-96; election ofcl. City of Charlottesville, 1991-93; pres., v.p. North Downtown Residents' Assn., Charlottesville, 1986-89; treas. Nat. Host Program, Charlottesville, 1993-94; mem. adv. bd. Piedmont Va. C.C. Dickinson Theater; mem. program com. Paramount Theatre, 2002-04; founding bd. Va./N.C. Nat. Soc. for Arts and Letters, 2003—; mem. state social svc. bd., 2005—. Named Woman of Distinction, Va. Skyline coun., Girl Scouts U.S., 1993, Artist of Yr., Piedmont Coun. of Arts, 2001; named one of Area's Disting. Dozen, 2004. Fellow Sorensen Inst. Polit. Leadership; mem. Leadership Charlottesville Alumni Assn., Nat. Soc. Arts and Letters (founding bd. mem. Va./NC chpt.). Jewish. Avocations: theater, water sports, politics, film. Office: Va Discovery Mus 524 E Main St Charlottesville VA 22902-5336 Office Phone: 434-977-1025.

LINDEN, SUSAN PYLES, marketing executive; b. Mt. Clemens, Mich., Apr. 29, 1954; d. Paul James Pyles and Charlotte Ettalene Snowden. BA cum laude, U. South Fla., 1976. Copywriter, account exec. Denton & French, Tampa, Fla., 1977-81, account exec., 1979-81; account rep. J. Walter Thompson, Atlanta, 1981-82; account exec. Liller Neal, Atlanta, 1982-83, The Bloom Agy., Dallas, 1983-85, sr. account exec., 1985-86, v.p., account supr., 1986-89; sales and mktg. dir. Sta. KSPN-FM, Aspen, Colo., 1989-91, World Wide Ski Corp., Aspen, 1991-93; owner Susan Pyles Mktg., 1993-98; mktg. dir. Aspen Glen, 1999—2003; owner Linden Mktg., 2003—. Mem. Women's Forum, Aspen; bd. mem. Roaring Fork Habitat for Humanity. Mem.: Rotary Club. Avocations: skiing, photography, hiking, bicycling. Office: PO Box 1800 Carbondale CO 81623 Office Phone: 970-704-1747. Business E-Mail: susan@lindenmarketing.net.

LINDENBAUM, SAMUEL HARVEY, lawyer; b. N.Y.C., Mar. 29, 1935; s. Abraham M. and Belle (Axelrad) L.; m. Linda Marion Lewis, June 16, 1957; children: Erica Dale Lindenbaum Tishman, Laurie Ellen. BA cum laude, Harvard U., 1956, JD cum laude, 1959; Fulbright fellow, Oslo U., Norway, 1959-60. Bar: NY 1960. Assoc. Fried, Frank, Harris, Shriver & Jacobson, N.Y.C., 1960-62; mem. Lindenbaum & Young, Bklyn., 1962-74; sr. mem. Rosenman & Colin, N.Y.C., 1974-83, of counsel, 1983—2002; counsel Kramer Levin Naftalis & Frankel, N.Y.C., 2002—. Mem. bd. overseers Albert Einstein Coll. Medicine; chmn. exec. com. Jewish Assn. for Svcs. for the Aged; mem. Counsel Assn. for Better NY; hon. trustee Met. Mus. Art; bd. govs., mem. exec. com., v.p. Real Estate Bd. NY; bd. dirs., chmn. exec. com. Am. Friends Israel Mus. Mem. Bklyn. Bar Assn., Harmonie Club, Harvard Club, Friars Club. Home: 998 5th Ave New York NY 10028-0102 Office: Kramer Levin Naftalis & Frankel 1177 Ave Americas New York NY 10036 Office Phone: 212-715-7840. Business E-Mail: slindenbaum@kramerlevin.com.

LINDENBAUM, S(EYMOUR) J(OSEPH), physicist; b. N.Y.C., Feb. 3, 1925; s. Morris and Anne Lindenbaum; m. Leda Isaacs, June 29, 1958. AB, Princeton U., 1945; MA, Columbia U., 1949, PhD, 1951. With Brookhaven Nat. Lab., Upton, N.Y., 1951-96, sr. physicist, 1963-96, sr. physicist emeritus, 1996—, group leader high energy physics research group, 1954-89; vis. prof. U. Rochester, 1958-59; Mark W. Zemansky chair in physics CCNY, 1970-95, Mark Zemansky prof. emeritus of physics, 1995—. Cons. Centre de Etudes Nucleaire de Saclay, France, 1957, CERN, Geneva, 1962; head CCNY Experimental High Energy and Nuclear Physics Rsch. Group, 1970—; dep. for sci. affairs ERDA, 1976-77 Author: Particle Interaction Physics at High Energies, 1973; scriptwriter, narrator, sci. prodr. (multi-screen, audio-visual slide show) Atom Smashing, Atom Smashers: Fifty Years, Smithsonian Instn. Exhibit, 1977; contbr. articles to profl. jours. Fellow Am. Phys. Soc.; mem. N.Y. Acad. Scis., AAAS. Achievements include discovering nucleon isobars dominated high energy particles interactions, isobar model; inventor on line computer technique in scientific experiments; proved experimentally that Einstein's special theory of relativity was correct down to subnuclear distances one hundredth the radius of a proton; discovered the glueball states predicted by quantum chromodynamics. Office: Brookhaven Nat Lab Dept Physics Bldg 510A Upton NY 11973 *I was always fascinated by the orderly and powerful laws of nature. Thus I decided to concentrate on one of mankind's greatest intellectual endeavours—scientific inquiry into the physical laws which govern our universe.*

LINDENBAUM, SHARON, publishing executive; b. Johannesburg; B., U. Kans.; M in acctg., Wichita State U. Sr. acct. Main Hurdman, Wichita, Kans.; mng. partner Lindenbaum & O'Sullivan, Wichita, Kans.; controller Pennypower Shopping News Inc., Wichita, Kans.; v.p. fin. Kansas City (Mo.) Star, 1995—. Office: Kansas City Star 1729 Grand Blvd Kansas City MO 64108-1458

LINDENBERGER, HERBERT SAMUEL, writer, literature educator; b. L.A., Apr. 4, 1929; s. Hermann and Celia (Weinkrantz) L.; m. Claire Flaherty, June 14, 1961; children: Michael James, Elizabeth Celia. BA, Antioch Coll., Yellow Springs, Ohio, 1951; PhD, U. Wash., Seattle, 1955. From instr. to prof. English and comparative lit. U. Calif., Riverside, 1954-66; prof. German and English, chmn. program comparative lit. Washington U., St. Louis, 1966-69; Avalon prof. humanities Stanford (Calif.) U., 1969—2001, Avalon prof. emeritus, 2001—, chmn. program comparative lit., 1969-82; dir. Stanford Humanities Ctr., 1991-92. Author: On Wordsworth's Prelude, 1963, Georg Büchner, 1964, (play) Lear and Cordelia at Home, 1968, Georg Trakl, 1971, Historical Drama: The Relation of Literature and Reality, 1975, Saul's Fall: A Critical Fiction, 1979, Opera: The Extravagant Art, 1984, The History in Literature: On Value, Genre, Institutions, 1990, Opera in History: From Monteverdi to Cage, 1998, Dogstory: A Memoir in Hypertext, 1999; contbr. chpts. to books, articles to profl. jours. Fulbright scholar Austria, 1952-53; Guggenheim fellow, 1968-69; Nat. Endowment Humanities fellow, 1975-76, 82-83; Stanford U. Humanities Ctr. Fellow, 1982-83 Mem. MLA (pres. 1997), Am. Comparative Lit. Assn.

LINDENFELD, JOANN, physician, educator; b. Benton Harbor, Mich., Feb. 11, 1948; d. Nelson Albert and Viola C. Lindenfield. MD, U. MIch., 1973. Diplomate in internal medicine, cardiology and critical care medicine Am. Bd. Internal Medicine. Asst. prof. medicine U. Colo., Denver, 1980-85, assoc. prof. medicine, 1985-90, prof. medicine, 1990—. Mem. cardiovenal adv. panel FDA, Washington, 1995—; cons. for pharm. firms. Author: Geriatric Internal Medicine, 1995, 99; contbr. articles to profl. jours. Recipient numerous awards U. Colo., Denver. Fellow Am. Coll. Cardiology, Am. Heart Assn. (clin. coun. rep.); mem. Internat. Soc. Heart and Lung Transplant, Am. Soc. Transplant Physicians. Avocations: hiking, poetry, gardening, writing. Office: U Colo Health Scis Ctr 4200 E 9th Ave B130 Denver CO 80262-0001 Office Phone: 303-315-4410. Business E-Mail: joAnn.lindenfeld@uchsc.edu.

LINDENFELD, LORE, fiber artist; b. Wuppertal, Germany, Apr. 27, 1921; came to U.S. 1939; d. Alfred and Frieda (Roos) Kadden; m. Peter Lindenfeld, May 31, 1953; children: Thomas, Naomi. Grad. Cert., Black Mt. (N.C.) Coll., 1948; MEd in Creative Arts Edn., Rutgers U., 1982. Fabric designer Herbert Meyer, Inc., John Walther Fabrics, others, N.Y.C., 1948-58; faculty mem. Visual Arts dept. Middlesex County Coll., Edison, N.J., 1968-86; with Newark Mus., 1990—94; docent Princeton (N.J.) U. Art Mus., 1994—. Numerous exhibits of textiles and fiber art including N.J. State Mus., Am. Craft Mus., N.Y.C., Rutgers U., Mus. Folkwang, Germany Am. Craft Mus., Renwick Gallery, The Newark (N.J.) Mus., Phila. (Pa.) U. Fashion Inst. of Tech.; numerous articles in profl. and craft publs. including Craft Internat., Fiber Arts, Surface Design, Craft Horizons (now Am. Craft), others; works in collections of the N.J. State Mus., Renwick Gallery, Nat. Mus. Am. Art, The Newark (N.J.) Mus., Black Mt. Mus. and Arts Ctr., Fashion Inst. Tech., Josef and Anni Albers Found. N.J. State Coun. on the Arts craft fellow, 1985. Mem. Am. Craft Coun., N.J. Designer-Craftsmen, Textile Study Group. Home and Office: 121 Harris Rd Princeton NJ 08540-3375 Business E-Mail: lindenf@physics.rutgers.edu.

LINDENFELD, PETER, physics professor; b. Vienna, Mar. 10, 1925; came to U.S., 1948, naturalized, 1957; s. Bela and Elda (Lachs) L.; m. Lore Kadden, May 31,1953; children: Thomas, Naomi. Student, U. Man., Can., 1942-43; BASc., U.B.C., Can., 1946, MA Sc., 1948; PhD, Columbia U., 1954. Vis. lectr. Drew U., Madison, N.J., 1952-53; instr. Rutgers U., 1953-55, asst. prof. physics, 1955-61, asso. prof., 1961-66, prof., 1966-99, prof. emeritus, 1999—. Cons. summer inst. AID, Tirupati, India, 1965; regional counselor N.J. Am. Inst. Physics, 1963-71; dir. NSF In-svc. Insts. High Sch. Tchrs., 1964-66; Rutgers Rsch. Coun. fellow and guest scientist Faculte de Scis., U. Paris-Sud, Orsay, France, 1970-71; vis. scholar Kyoto U., Japan, 1982. Contbr. articles to profl. jours. Recipient Warren I. Susman award for excellence in teaching, 1988, Robert A. Millikan Lecture award and medal Am. Assn. Physics Tchrs., 1989, Lifetime award contbn. to Physics Educator, NJ Fellow Am. Phys. Soc.; mem. AAUP, Am. Assn. Physics Tchrs. (hon. mem. N.J. sect., N.J. sect. award for lifetime contbns. to physics tchr. 2004). Home: 121 Harris Rd Princeton NJ 08540-3375 Office: Rutgers U Dept Physics and Astronomy Piscataway NJ 08854-8019 E-mail: lindenf@physics.rutgers.edu.

LINDENMAYER, ELISABETH, international organization administrator; married; 2 children. Degree, U. Paris-Sorbonne, U. Geneva, NYU. Various positions with Office of Human Resources Mgmt., UN, 1977, spl. asst. to the then asst. sec.-gen. for personnel svcs.; provided polit. back-up and support Iraq-Kuwait UN Observation Mission (UNIKOM), UN Hdqs., 1992, UN Ops. in Somalia (UNOSOM I, UNITAF Task Force and UNOSOM II), UN Hdqs., 1992—94, UN Mission in Rwanda (UNAMIR), UN Hdqs., 1994—96, Great Lakes Region, Burundi and Zaire (now the Dem. Rep. of Congo); budget officer Office of Programme Planning, Budget, and Fin.; spl. asst. to the controller UN Hdqs., exec. asst. to sec.-gen., 1997—2004, asst. sec.-gen. to the post of dep. chef de cabinet in the exec. office of the sec.-gen., 2004—. Office: UN Hdqs First Avenue at 46th St New York NY 10017 Office Phone: 212-963-1234. Office Fax: 212-963-4879.

LINDENMAYER, JEAN-PIERRE, psychiatrist; b. Basel, Switzerland, July 25, 1942; came to U.S. 1969; s. Franz and Celina Aries L. Diploma med. & surgery, U. Basel, Switzerland, 1968. Diplomate Am. Bd. Psychiatry and Neurology. Resident in psychiatry Downstate Med. Ctr., Bklyn., 1973; fellow doctor med. sci. program Downstate Med. Ctr., SUNY, 1974; dir. psychiat. inpatient svcs. U. Hosp., Downstate Med. Ctr., Bklyn., 1973-76, Bronx (N.Y.) Mcpl. Hosp., 1977-80; from chief of svc. tng. unit to dir. dept. psychiatry Bronx Psychiat. Ctr., 1981-86; dir. schizophrenia rsch. program Albert Einstein Coll. Med., Bronx, 1987-94; dir. psychopharmacology rsch. Manhattan Psychiat. Ctr., N.Y.C., 1994—, Nathan Kline Inst. for Psychiat. Rsch., 1994—. Asst. prof., SUNY, Bklyn., 1975-77, Albert Einstein Coll. of Med., Dept. Psychiatry, Bronx, 1977-87, assoc. prof., 1987-94., clin. prof., Dept. Psychiatry, N.Y. Univ., 1994—. Co-author: Psychotropic Drugs: Manual for Emergency Management of Overdosage, 1981, Psychiatric Emergencies: Principles and Management of Emergency Medicine, 1985, New Biological Vista of Schizophrenia, 1992; contbr. articles on schizophrenia to profl. jours. Fellow, Am. Psychiatric Assn.; mem. Swiss Med. Assn., Am. Orthopsychiatry Assn. Avocations: photography, skiing, flute. Office: 18 E 77th St New York NY 10021-1722 Office Phone: 212-249-2720. Office Fax: 212-249-4116.

LINDER, BEVERLY L., elementary school educator; b. Kansas City, Mo., Mar. 12, 1951; d. William B. and Una M. (Dishman) Reese; m. John H. Linder, Feb. 24, 1979; 1 child, Elaine M. BSEd, Cen. Mo. State U., 1972; MA in Reading, U. Mo., Kansas City, 1975. Cert. elem. edn., reading. Elem. tchr. Ft. Osage Sch. Dist., Independence, Mo., tchr. 4th grade chpt. I reading. Mem. Internat. Reading Assn., Nat. Coun. Tchrs. Math. Home: 1317 NE Buttonwood Ave Lees Summit MO 64086-8438

LINDER, JACQUES L., music educator, musician; b. Vincennes, Ind., Sept. 25, 1945; s. Walter Perry and Grace Lorene Linder. MusB in Edn., U. Evansville, 1967; MusM in Piano, U. Ill., 1969; pvt. piano instruction, Harriet Shirvan, 1973—78, Gabriel Chodos, 1983—88. Instr. piano Performing Art Sch. Worcester, Mass., 1972—75; pvt. piano tchr. Worcester, 1974—90, St. Petersburg, Fla., 1991—. Instr. piano Clark U., Worcester, 1979—90, instr. primary theory, 1985—86; instr. piano U. South Fla., Tampa, 1990—2000, performance program coord., chairperson piano faculty cmty. music divsn., 1990—95, artistic dir., 1995—2000; founder, co-dir. The Commonwealth Competition for Young Pianists Clark U., Worcester. Musician: (soloist) Ill. Ctr. Orch., 1979, Ill. Ctrl. Orch., 1982, Worcester Consortium Orch., 1982, (solo recital) Belknap Mill Concert Series, 1984, 1986, Worcester Art Mus., 1985, 1986, 1987, Camargo Found., 1988, Colgate U., 1989, U. Md. Coll. Park Contemporary Music Festival, 1989, Fla. So. U., 1992, Eckerd Coll. Festival Performing Arts, 1996, U. South Fla., 1990—2000, (guest soloist) Conf. on Open Structure in 20th Century Music, 1986, (solo performance) Assn. U. Composers Conf., 1988, many others. Home: 816 25th Ave N Saint Petersburg FL 33704

LINDER, JOHN E., congressman, dentist; b. Deer River, Minn., Sept. 9, 1942; s. Henry and Vera Elizabeth Davis L.; m. Lynne Leslee Peterson, 1963; children: Kristine Kerry, Matthew John. BS, U. Minn., 1964, DDS, 1967. Pvt. practice, Atlanta, 1969—82; mem. Ga. Ho. of Reps., 1975-80, 82-90; pres. Linder Fin. Corp., 1977-92; mem. U.S. Congress from 4th Ga. Dist., 1993-97, U.S. Congress from 11th Ga. Dist., 1997—; mem. homeland sec. com., house admin. com. House rules com., subcom. on legis. process, steering com., former mem. Nat. Rep. Congl. Com. exec. com. U.S. Ho. of Reps., chmn. Founder I Care, 1970. Capt. USAF, 1967-69. Mem. ADA, Ga. Dental Assn., No. Dist. Dental Soc., Rotary. Republican. Presbyterian. Office: US House of Reps 1026 Longworth HOB Washington DC 20515-0001*

LINDER, MORTON HOWARD, physician, researcher; b. N.Y.C., Feb. 17, 1929; s. William and Claire (Goldstein) L.; m. Lee D'Andrea, Mar. 2, 1955. BA, NYU, 1950; MD, U. Utrecht, Holland, 1957. Diplomate Am. Bd. Internal Medicine. Rotating intern Queens Hosp. Ctr., Jamaica, N.Y., 1957-58; resident in internal medicine Westchester County Med. Ctr., Valhalla, N.Y., 1958-59, chief resident in internal medicine, 1959-60, rsch. fellow in diabetes and metabolism, 1960-61, former sr. attending physician Diabetes Clinic; sr. attending physician Diabetes Clinic N.Y. Med. Coll., Valhalla, 1961—, asst. clin. prof. medicine, 1961—. Contbr. articles to profl. jours. Fellow ACP; mem. N.Y. Acad. Scis., Am. Fedn. for Clin. Rsch., Westchester Diabetes Assn. (pres. 1966-69). Achievements include research in continuous monitoring of blood glucose.

LINDGREN, CHARLOTTE HOLT, English language educator; b. Ipswich, Mass., Jan. 5, 1924; d. Hilmer Harold and Edith Grace (Whittier) L.; m. Donald James Winslow, Aug. 11, 1978. AB, Boston U., 1945, AM, 1947, PhD, 1961; MA (hon.), Emerson Coll., 1967. Tchr. Pinkerton Acad., Derry, N.H., 1945-46, Medfield (Mass.) H.S., 1947-49; adminstrv. asst. Boston Univ., 1949-60; prof. Emerson Coll., Boston, 1960-89, chmn. english dept., 1965-80, prof. emerita, 1989—. Co-leader Emerson Abroad Program, 1966-78; corporator Lasell Coll., Auburndale, Mass., 1997—. Co-author: William Barnes Dorset Engravings, 1986 (Mansell-Pleydell award 1986), Gerald Warner Brace: Writer, Sailor, Teacher, 1998; editor: The Love Poems and Letters of William Barnes, 1986; contbr. articles to History Today, Dorset Yr. Book, T. Hardy Jour. Mem. Thomas Hardy Soc., William Barnes Soc., Herman Melville Soc., Women in Arts, Phi Beta Kappa. Avocations: photography, book reviewing. Home: 23 Maple St Auburndale MA 02466-2404 E-mail: lindwin24@aol.com.

LINDGREN, D(ERBIN) KENNETH, JR., retired lawyer; b. Mpls., Aug. 25, 1932; s. Derbin Kenneth and Margaret (Anderson) Lindgren; m. Patricia Ann Ransier, Dec. 17, 1955; children: Christian Kenneth, Carol Ann, Charles Derbin. BS, U. Minn., 1954, JD, 1958. Bar: Minn. 1958, U.S. Tax Ct. 1959, U.S. Supreme Ct. 1968, U.S. Ct. Appeals (DC cir.) 1981. Pvt. practice law, Mpls., 1958-99; mem. Larkin, Hoffman, Daly & Lindgren, Ltd., Mpls., 1960-95, of counsel, 1995; ret., 1995. Contbr. articles to profl. jours. Active Ind. Sch. Dist. 274 Bd. Edn., Hopkins, Minn., 1970—76, chmn., 1972—76; active Ind. Sch. Dist. 287 Bd. Edn., 1979—83; trustee Mpls. Soc. Fine Arts, 1982—88, Minn. Landscape Arboretum Found., 1989—99, pres., 1992—95, hon. trustee, 2000; mem. Gov.'s Commn. Reform Govt., 1983; bd. overseers Mpls. Coll. Art and Design, 1980—86, vice-chmn., 1982—83, chmn., 1983—86, trustee, 1988—96; bd. overseers Mpls. Inst. Art, 1986—88. Lt. USAF, 1955—57. Fellow: Am. Coll. Trust and Estate Counsel; mem.: ABA, Hennepin County Bar Assn., Minn. Bar Assn., Troon Country Club (bd. dirs. 2000—03), Interlachen Country Club (bd. dirs. 1981—89, pres. 1987), Phi Delta Phi, Alpha Delta Phi. Presbyterian. Home: 11003 E Desert Vista Dr Scottsdale AZ 85255-8061

LINDGREN, JAMES, law educator; married; 1 child. BA cum laude, Yale U., 1974; JD, U. Chgo., 1977. Prof. law U. Conn. Sch. Law, 1982—85, 1987—90, assoc. dean for academic affairs, 1988—90; Norman and Edna Freehling scholar and professor law Chgo.-Kent Coll. Law, 1990—96, co-founder Legal Theory Workshop, co-chair Faculty Appointments Com., 1991—92, 1992—93, assoc. dean for faculty develop., 1992—93; prof. law Northwestern U. Sch. Law, Chgo., 1996—, dir. Faculty Rsch., 2000—01, Benjamin Mazur Rsch. prof., 1999, Stanford Clinton Sr. rsch. prof., 2001—02, dir. Demography of Diversity Project, 1999—. Vis. prof. U. Va. Sch. Law, 1985—87, U. Tex. Sch. Law, 1992. Contbr. articles tp profl. jours. Recipient Morton-Murphy Prize; vis. scholar Northwestern U. Sch. Law, 1992, U. Chgo. Law Sch., 1992. Mem.: Am. Soc. for Polit. and Legal Philosophy, Am. Soc. Legal History, Am. Law and Econ. Assn. Office: Northwestern U Sch Law 357 E Chicago Ave Chicago IL 60611 Office Phone: 312-503-8374. E-mail: jlindgren@law.northwestern.edu.*

LINDGREN, JAMES MICHAEL, historian, educator; b. Elmhurst, Ill., Sept. 3, 1950; s. Raymond L. and Lorraine M. Lindgren; m. Mary Ann Weiglhofer; children: Brian, Charles. BA, U. Dayton, 1972, MA, 1977; PhD, Coll. of William and Mary, 1984. Prof. SUNY, Plattsburgh, NY, 1984—. Author: Preserving Historic New England: Preservation, Progressivism and the Remaking of Memory, Preserving the Old Dominion: Historic Preservation and Virginia Traditionalism, (historical essay) 'Virginia Needs Living Heroes' (G. Wesley Johnson prize, the Nat. Coun. on Pub. Hist.). Recipient Chancellor's Excellence in Scholarship award, SUNY, 2005. Mem.: Orgn. of Am. Historians, Mass. Hist. Soc. (corr.), Phi Beta Kappa. Independent. Office: SUNY Hist Dept Plattsburgh NY 12901

LINDGREN, WILLIAM DALE, librarian; b. Peoria, Ill., Mar. 8, 1936; s. Hugh Gottfried and Olive Kathryn (Myer) L. BA, Bradley U., 1958, MA, 1959; MSLS, U. Ill., 1967. Tchr. Limestone High Sch., Bartonville, Ill., 1960-68; asst. dir. Learning Resources Ctr. Ill. Cen. Coll., East Peoria, 1968-73, dir., 1973—. Mem. transition bd. merger of four systems, 1993-94; bd. dirs. Alliance Libr. Sys.; mem. Ill. State Libr. Com. on Resolving the Unserved Problem, 1996—. Singer Ephphetha Schola Cantorum Gregoriana, 1996—; singer Carnegie Hall concerts, 2001, 03, European concert tours, 2002, 03. Chmn. East Peoria Oral History Com., 1983-84, Resource Sharing Alliance West Ctrl. Ill. Adv. Coun., 1985—; v.p. Illinois Valley Libr. System, pres. bd., 1988, 90—, treas., 1989, bd. dirs., 1990—; regional chair recruitment com. Am. Heart Assn., 1996—; election judge, 2002—. Mem. ALA, Ill. Libr. Assn. (co-chair cracker barrels program ann. conf. 1989, 90, 91), Assn. Ednl. Media Tech., Assn. Ednl. Media and Tech. Ill., Coun. Libr. Tech., Creve Coeur Club (Peoria).

LINDHEIM, RICHARD DAVID, broadcast executive, director; b. N.Y.C., May 28, 1939; s. Gilbert R. and Pearl (Gruskin) L.; m. Elaine Lavis, Dec. 22, 1963; children: Susan Patricia, David Howard. BS, U. Redlands, 1961; postgrad, U. So. Calif., 1963. Adminstrv. asst. story dept. CBS, L.A., 1962-64; project dir. entertainment testing ASI Market Rsch., L.A., 1964-69; v.p. program research NBC, L.A., 1969-78, v.p. dramatic programs, 1978-79; producer Universal TV, L.A., 1979-81, v.p. current programs, 1981-85, sr. v.p. series programming, 1986-87, exec. v.p. creative affairs, 1987-91; exec. v.p. program strategy MCA TV Group, 1991-92; exec. v.p. Paramount TV Group, 1992-99; exec. dir. Inst. for Creative Techs., U. So. Calif., L.A., 1999—; with ICT, Marina Del Rey, Calif. Asst. prof. Calif. State U.; sr. lectr. U. So. Calif.; lectr. UCLA; reviewer NEH; bd. dirs. Am. Fgn. Svc. Intercultural Program-USA. Author: (with Richard Blum) Primetime: Network Television Programming, 1987, Inside Television Producing, 1991; contbr. articles to profl. jours. Mem. Acad. TV Arts and Scis., Producers Guild Am., Writers Guild Am. Democrat. Jewish. Avocations: model railroading, photography, music, travel. Office: ICT 4676 Admiralty Way Ste 1001 Marina Del Rey CA 90292 Office Phone: 310-574-5706. E-mail: lindheim@ict.usc.edu. *In this sophisticated society there are fewer and fewer opportunities for the individual. Technology has made most tasks too complex for one man. As a result the ability to work with other people and to provide leadership and management to groups of people has become vital. The key ingredients are communication, respect for others, and a feeling of belonging, while working in a relaxed, casual environment, where the leader is responsible and receptive.*

LINDHOLM, DWIGHT HENRY, lawyer; b. Blackduck, Minn., May 27, 1930; s. Henry Nathanial and Viola Eudora (Gummert) L.; m. Loretta Catherine Brown, Aug. 29, 1958; children: Douglas Dwight, Dionne Louise, Jeanne Marie, Philip Clayton, Kathleen Anne. Student, Macalester Coll., 1948-49; BBA, U. Minn., 1951, LLB, 1954; postgrad., Mexico City Coll. (now U. of Ams.), 1956-57. Bar: Minn. 1954, Calif. 1958. Sole practice, Los Angeles, 1958-65, 72-81, 84—; ptnr. Lindholm & Johnson, Los Angeles, 1965-69, Cotter, Lindholm & Johnson, Los Angeles, 1969-72; sole practice Los Angeles, 1972-81; of counsel Bolton, Dunn & Moore, Los Angeles, 1981-84. Mem. Calif. Rep. Ctrl. Com., 1962-63, L.A. Republican County Ctrl. Com., 1962-66; bd. dirs. Family Service L.A., 1964-70, v.p., 1968-70; bd. dirs. Wilshire YMCA, 1976-77; trustee Westlake Girls Sch., 1978-81; hon. presenter Nat. Charity League Coronet Debutante Ball, 1984; bd. dirs. Calif. State U.-Northridge Trust Fund, 1989-93; bd. dirs. Queen of Angels/Hollywood Presbyn. Med. Ctr., 1990-98; chmn., CEO Queen of Angels, Hollywood Presbyn. Found., 1997-2000; bd. dirs., corp. sec. Queen
sCare, 1998-2002. Served as capt. JAG Corps USAF, 1954-56. Recipient Presdl. award Los Angeles Jr. C. of C., 1959 Mem. Calif. Bar Assn., L.A. County Bar Assn., Wilshire Bar Assn. (bd. govs. 1989-91), Internat. Genealogy Fellowship of Rotarians (founding pres. 1979-86), Calif. Club, Ocean Cruising Club Eng. (Newport Harbor port officer), Rotary (dir. 1975-78), Delta Sigma Pi, Delta Sigma Rho, Delta Theta Phi (state chancellor 1972-73). Presbyterian. Avocations: sailing, offshore cruising. Office: 3580 Wilshire Blvd Fl 17 Los Angeles CA 90010-2501

LINDHOLM, RICHARD THEODORE, economics and finance educator; b. Eugene, Oreg., Oct. 5, 1960; s. Richard Wadsworth and Mary Marjorie (Trunko) L. m. Valaya Nivasananda, May 8, 1987. BA, U. Chgo., 1982, MA, 1983, PhD, 1993. Ptnr. Lindholm and Osanka, Eugene, 1986-89, Lindholm Rsch., Eugene, 1995—2001, owner, 1995—, The Lindholm Co., 1995—; ptnr. DBA Lindholm Rsch., Eugene, 2001—. Guest lectr. Nat. Inst. Devel. Adminstrn., Bangkok, Thailand, 1989; pres. Rubicon Inst., Eugene, 1988—; adj. asst. prof. U. Oreg., Eugene, 1988—. Campaign co-chmn. Lane C.C. Advocates, Eugene, 1988; coord., planner numerous state Rep. Campaigns, Oreg., 1988—; campaign mgr. Jack Roberts for Oreg. State Labor Commn., 1994; mem. staff Oreg. Senate Rep. Office, 1989-90; precinct committeeperson Oreg. Rep. Party, 1987-92, 94—; bd. dirs. Rubicon Soc., Eugene, 1987—, pres., 1993-98. Republican. Lutheran. Home: 3335 Bardell Ave Eugene OR 97401-8021

LINDLE, JANE CLARK, education educator; b. Annapolis, Md., Jan. 28, 1954; d. Clifton Bob and Sue Helen Louise Clark; m. Garnett Adrian Lindle Jr., May 29, 1982; children: Rachel, Garnett III. BA, U. N.C., 1976; MS, U. Wis., 1982, PhD, 1983. Chair Student Consumer Action Union, Chapel Hill, N.C., 1974-75; tchr., lifeguard St. John's Episcopal Ch., Charleston, S.C., 1975-76; tchr. Luxemburg (Wis.)-Casco Schs., 1976-81; project asst. U. Wis., Madison, 1981-83; prin. St. Mary of Lake, Waunakee, Wis., 1983-84, Our Lady Queen of Peace, Madison, 1984-87; asst. prof. U. Pitts., 1987-91; prof. U. Ky., Lexington, 1991—2004; dist. prof. Clemson U., 2004—. Editor: Ednl. Adminstrn. Quar., 2002—04. Tchr. N.C. Muscular Distrophy Camp, Raleigh, 1974; co-dir. UK/UL Joint Ctr. Study Edn. Policy, Lexington, 1996-2000. Mem. Am. Ednl. Rsch. Assn. (nominations com. chair 1998-2000), Politics Edn. Assn. (pres. 1994-96), U. Coun. Ednl. Adminstrn. (plenary rep. 1999-2003). Avocations: singing, travel, gardening. Office: Clemson Univ 326 Tillman Hall Clemson SC 29634-0707 Office Phone: 864-656-3484. Business E-Mail: jlindle@clemson.edu.

LINDLEY, CHARLES ALEXANDER, aerospace engineer, consultant; b. Union City, Ind., May 12, 1924; s. Charley Alexander and Thursetta (Hall) Lindley; m. Agnes Stucker, Jan. 17, 1946 (dec. July 1997); children: Susan Marie, Charles A.(dec.). BS and MS in Aero. Engring., Ohio State U., 1949; PhD in Aeronautics, Calif. Inst. Tech., 1956. Instr. Ohio State U., Columbus, 1947—49; compressor aerodynamicist Thompson Aircraft Products, Euclid, Ohio, 1949—52, turbomachinery cons., 1952—55; rsch. cons. The Marquardt Corp., Van Nuys, Calif., 1955—63; vehicle tech. The Aerospace Corp., El Segundo, Calif., 1963—85, sr. scientist threat analysis, 1985—92, cons., 1992—. Guest lectr., cons. UCLA and U. Calif.-Santa Barbara, 1961—78. Contbr. articles to profl. jours. Chmn. bd. dirs. Premier Chorale and San Fernando Valley Master Chorale, L.A., 2001—. 2nd lt. Signal Corps U.S. Army, 1943—46., Guggenheim Fellow, 1952—55. Achievements include over 100 inventions including liquid air cycle, air collection systems, reuseable boosters, scramjets, external burning ramjets, artificial gravity systems, wind & solar energy, space reconnaissance. Avocations: singing, vocal music, model aircraft. Home: 18900 Pasadero Dr Tarzana CA 91356 Personal E-mail: 74537.3706@compuserve.com.

LINDLEY, CHERYL A., artist, writer; b. Ketchikan, Alaska, May 23, 1947; d. Joseph J. Friedmann and Lorraine S. Savin; m. Steven C. Lindley, Mar. 17, 1973 (dec. June 1976); children: Issac David, Jennifer Marie. AA, Cuesta; BA, Chapman U. Founder area groups Smokers Anonymous. With USN, 1971—73.

LINDLEY, F. HAYNES, JR., (FRANCIS HAYNES LINDLEY JR.), foundation executive, lawyer; b. L.A., Oct. 15, 1945; s. Francis Haynes and Grace Nelson (McCanne) L.; 1 child, Anne Hollinger Lindley. BA, Claremont (Calif.) Men's Coll., 1967; MFA, Claremont (Calif.) Grad. Sch., 1972; JD, Southwestern U., L.A., 1976. Bar: Calif. 1976, U.S. Supreme Ct. 1980. Deputy pub. defender Office of Pub. Defender, L.A., 1977-79; staff atty., Dept. Trial Counsel The State Bar of Calif., L.A., 1979-81; pvt. practice, 1981-90; pres. John Randolph Haynes and Dora Haynes Found., L.A., 1987-97, pres. emeritus, 1997—. Trustee John Randolph Haynes and Dora Haynes Found., L.A., 1978—. Mem. bd. dirs. TreePeople, L.A., 1985-87, So. Calif. Assn. Philanthropy, L.A., 1985-89; mem. bd. fellows Claremont (Calif.) U. Ctr. and Grad. Sch., 1987—; mem. bd. dirs. Marin Agrl. Land Trust, 1995—. Recipient Disting. Svc. award The Claremont (Calif.) Grad. Sch., 1994. Avocations: sailing, art history, guitar. Home: PO Box 3058 Sausalito CA 94966-3058 Office: John Randolph Haynes & Dora Haynes Found 888 W 6th St Ste 1150 Los Angeles CA 90017-2737 Office Phone: 213-623-9151.

LINDLEY, JEARL RAY, lawyer; b. Abilene, Tex., Mar. 12, 1934; s. Hardie Lindley and Hope Clement Mourant; m. Annabelle Sim Yee Lindley, May 22, 1954; children: Katheryn Ann, Michael Andrew, Carolyn Elizabeth. BS in Chemistry, N.Mex. State U., 1960; MD, U. Colo., 1964; MS, U. Ill., 1967; JD, South Tex. Coll. of Law, 1997. Asst. clin. prof. of surgery Rush Med. Coll. of Rush U., Chgo., 1969-71, U. Ill. Sch. of Medicine, Chgo., 1969-71; assoc. clin. prof. of surgery Tex. Tech. U. Sch. of Medicine, El Paso, 1976-80; atty., counselor Las Cruces, N.Mex., 1997—. Adj. prof. N.Mex. State U., Las Cruces, 1984-86. Author publs. in field (McNeil Meml. Rsch. award 1967). Bd. dirs. Meml. Gen. Hosp., Las Cruces, 1983, So. N.Mex. Regional Dialysis Ctr., Las Cruces, 1984-89; instr. ACLS, AHA, Las Cruces, 1980-86, ATLS, Am. Coll. Surgeons, Las Cruces, 1980-86; mem. emergency med. svcs. com. Dona Ana Emergency, Las Cruces, 1979, City County Hosp. Bd. Govs., Las Cruces, 1981-83; mem. internat. bd. dirs. N.Mex. State U. Alumni Assn., 1979-81; mem. bd. counselors Citizens Bank, Las Cruces, 1991-93. Named to Outstanding Young Men of Am., 1969, Marine of Yr., Marine Corps League, 1990, Guide to Am.'s Top Surgeons, 2002; commd. Ky. Col., State of Ky., 1989, Am.'s Top Surgeon's Guide, 2002; proclamation of Jearl R. Lindley Day/Mayor of Truth or Consequences, N.Mex., 1990; recipient Disting. Citizen medal Dept. of N.Mex. Marine Corps League. Fellow ACS, Am. Coll. Legal Medicine, Internat. Coll. Surgeons, Southwestern Surg. Congress; mem. Internat. Endovascular Soc., Soc. Clin. Vascular Surgery, AHA, Am. Legion, Marine Corps Assn., Marine Corps Heritage Found., Naval Inst., Marine Meml. Club, Air Force Assn., Marine Corps League (Comdt. Dept. of N.Mex. 1990-91, Dept. Comdt.'s medal 1991, medal with bronze star

1988-90). Republican. Mem. Ch. of Christ. Avocations: shooting, photography, reading, motorcycling. Home: 4566 Mockingbird St Las Cruces NM 88011-9616 Office Phone: 505-437-2874.

LINDLEY, JOYCE E., health facility administrator, real estate appraiser; b. Clinton, Ind., May 29, 1953; d. Clyde M. and Juanita M. Delp; m. James A. Lindley; children: Brian, Richard Neil; m. William R. Travis, July 22, 1972 (div. 1983). Cosmetologist, Harolds Sch. Beauty, Terre Haute, Ind., 1975; real estate profl., Ind. State U., Terre Haute, 1989; real estate appraiser, Ind. U.-Purdue U., Indpls., 1993. Cert. assisted living adminstr. Assisted Living Fedn. Am., 2001. Hairstylist, owner, mgr. Hairbarn I, II and You're Special, Wabash Valley area, 1976—89; real estate appraiser Mike Ofsansky and Assoc., Terre Haute, 1993—98; comml. real estate sales dir. Century 21, Terre Haute, 1989—93; mktg. dir. Lakeview Nursing & Rehab., Terre Haute, 1995—99; exec. dir. Morningside Assisted Living, Terre Haute, 1999—2001; pres. Lindley McVeigh and Assocs., Terre Haute, 2001—; adminstr. Bethesda Gardens, Terre Haute, 2001—. Cons. Lindley Advt., Terre Haute, 1994—99; adv. bd. mem. Vencare Hospice, Terre Haute, 1998—99; chairperson adv. bd. Lakeview Golden Health Unit, Terre Haute, 1997—99. Chairperson United Way, Clark County, Ill., 1999—2000; bd. dirs. ARC, Terre Haute, 2002—, Big Brother / Big Sister, Terre Haute, 1999—. Recipient Above and Beyond award, Bethesda Living Ctrs., 2002. Mem.: C. of C. Greater Terre Haute (amb. 1995—, chairperson 2000—02), Appraisor Assn. (developer mktg. / tng. manuals and classes), Terre Haute Bd. Realtors, Wabash Valley Healthcare Mktg. Group (pres. 1998—99, Outstanding Pres. 1999), Am. Mktg. Assn., Exch. Club Terre Haute (pres. 1999—2001, dist. dir. 2002—03, Outstanding Membership Drive award 2001, Outstanding Pres. 2003). Avocations: professional singing, golf, horticulturist, speaking, songwriting. Home: 7 Lakeview Marshall IL 62441 Office: Bethesda Gardens 1450 E Crossing Blvd Terre Haute IN 47802 Business E-Mail: jlindley@blcmail.com.

LINDNER, CARL H., III, insurance company executive; s. Carl H. Lindner, Jr. and Edith Lindner. With Great Am. Ins. Co. (subs. Am. Fin. Group Inc.), 1975—, various ins. ops. positions, 1987—, now vice chmn., pres.; co-pres., dir. Am. Fin. Group, 1996—2005, co-CEO, pres., 2005—. Office: Am Fin Group Inc 1 E 4th St Cincinnati OH 45202

LINDNER, CARL HENRY, JR., insurance company executive, professional sports team executive; b. Dayton, Ohio, Apr. 22, 1919; s. Carl Henry and Clara (Serrer) Lindner; m. Edyth Bailey, Dec. 31, 1953; children: Carl Henry III, Stephen Craig, Keith Edward. HHD (hon.), Xavier U., 1991. Co-founder United Dairy Farmers, 1940; pres. Am. Fin. Group, Cin., 1959—84, chmn., 1959—, CEO, 1984—2005; owner, CEO Cin. Reds, 1999—. Chmn. Great Am. Fin. Resources, Inc., Great Am. Ins. Group. Bd. advisors Bus. Adminstrn. Coll., U. Cin. Recipient Heritage award, Urban League of Greater Cin., 1997. Republican. Baptist. Office: Am Fin Group 1 E 4th St Cincinnati OH 45202-3717

LINDNER, DEBORAH, writer, illustrator, photographer; b. Bklyn., Feb. 3, 1958; d. Theodore G. and Gloria Balke; m. Joseph G. Lindner, Sept. 15, 1984; 1 child, Jennifer Ann. Student, Cornell, Farmingdale, 1978—79, Nassau C.C., 1983—86. Illustrator Fine Line Illustrations, 1978—84, Vantage Art, 1978—84, Burmar Tech. Corp., 1978—84, Webber & Stevens, Inc., 1978—84, Cold Spring Harbor Lab.; freelance illustrator Cold Spring Harbor Fish Hatchery; founder, owner Colorfully Yours, Inc., 1991—. Author, illustrator: mags. articles. Parent adv. Hicksville (N.Y.) Sch. Dist., 1991—2003. Sgt. USAF, 1981—85, sgt. N.Y. Air Nat. Guard, 1981—85. Decorated Airman of Yr. N.Y. State Air Nat. Guard; nominee fire Safety Educator of Yr., Suffolk County Fire Educators, 2003; named Woman of Yr., Oyster Bay, NY, 2003. Mem.: Soc. Children's Book Writers and Illustrators. Avocations: photography, writing, leather crafting, crafts, hiking. Office: Colorfully Yours Inc 9-11 Grant St Bay Shore NY 11706 Office Phone: 800-230-9661. E-mail: deb.lindner@colorfullyyours.com.

LINDNER, KAREN CARR, psychologist, consultant; b. Seattle, Nov. 13, 1943; d. Edward Lewis Carr and Mildred Ellen (Anderson) Lindner; m. William T. Stough, Oct. 12, 1985. BS, U. Wash., 1972, PhD, 1982. Lic. clin. psychologist, Wash. Psychologist trainee McNeil Island Penitentiary, Steilacoom, Wash., 1978-79; coord. diagnostic svcs. Correctional Edn. and Rsch. Programs, 1980-82; psychotherapist Suicidal Behavior Rsch. Ctr., Seattle, 1985-87; pvt. practice psychology, Bellevue, Wash., 1977-92, Seattle, 1992—. Mem. aux. faculty dept. psychology U. Wash., Seattle, 1991—. Contbg. author: Stress: Anxiety, 1987, Brief Counseling of Suicidal Persons, 1983. Mem. APA, NW Alliance for Psychoanalytical Study, Pacific N.W. Psychoanalytic Soc. (founder). Avocations: cocker spaniel, macintosh computers, parrots. Office: 9730 3rd Ave NE Ste 101 Seattle WA 98115-2023

LINDNER, RICHARD G., telecommunications industry executive; b. St. Louis; BS in Bus. Adminstrn., U. Mo., St. Louis; completed advanced mgmt. program in telecom., UCLA. Audit supr. Peat, Marwick, Mitchell & Co.; sr. v.p., CFO Turco Devel. Co.; controller SBC Comm. Inc., San Antonio; dir., investor rels. SBC, 1990—91; dir., fin. SBC Internat., 1991—92; v.p., CFO SBC Telecom, 1986—90, Southwestern Bell Telephone, San Antonio; pres., CEO Southwestern Bell Wireless; sr. v.p., COO SBC Wireless Inc.; CFO Cingular Wireless, Atlanta, 2000—. Bd. mem. Sabre Holdings Corp., 2002—. Office: Cingular Wireless Glenridge Highlands Two 5655 Glenridge Connector Atlanta GA 30342

LINDNER, S. CRAIG (STEPHEN CRAIG LINDNER), insurance company executive; s. Carl H. Lindner Jr. and Edith Lindner. BBA, U. Cinn., 1977. With Am. Fin. Group Inc., Cin., 1977—, co-pres., 1996—2005, co-CEO, 2005—. Pres., CEO Great Am. Fin. Resources; pres. Am. Money Mgmt. Corp. Office: Am Fin Group Inc 1 E 4th St Cincinnati OH 45202-3717*

LINDO, J. TREVOR, psychiatrist, consultant; b. Boston, Feb. 12, 1925; s. Edwin and Ruby Ianty (Peterson) L.; m. Thelma Elaine Thompson, Sept. 22, 1962. BA, NYU, 1946; cert. in pre-clin. studies, U. Freibourg, Switzerland, 1953; MD, U. Lausanne, Switzerland, 1957. Lic. psychiatrist, N.Y., Conn. Clin. instr. Columbia U., N.Y.C., 1965-75, asst. clin. prof., 1975-82, assoc. clin. prof., 1982-85; attending psychiatrist Bedford-Stuyvesant Cmty. Mental Health Clinic, Bklyn., 1976-86, med. dir., 1986—. Attending psychiatrist Harlem Hosp. Ctr., N.Y.C., 1964-75; vis. psychiatrist Interfaith Hosp., Bklyn., 1976-85; psychiat. cons. Bklyn. Bur. Cmty. Svc., 1980, Marcus Garvey Manor, Bklyn., 1982-86; candidate Nat. Bd. Forensic Examiners, 1995. Co-chairperson com. Dr. Thomas Matthew, N.Y.C., 1974. With U.S. Mcht. Marine, 1947-51. Fellow Am. Coll. Internal Physicians; mem. Nat. Med. Assn., Am. Psychiat. Assn., Provident Clin. Soc. (v.p. 1980-82, parliamentarian 1982—), Bklyn. Psychiat. Soc., Black Psychiatrists of Am. Avocations: travel, african art, sailing, swimming. also: Bedford Stuyvesant Cmty Mental Health Ctr 1406 Fulton St Brooklyn NY 11216-2606

LINDO, STEPHEN T., lawyer; b. Watertown, N.Y., July 30, 1947; AB, Princeton U., 1969; JD, Boston U., 1974; LLM in Taxation, NYU, 1980. Bar: NY 1975. Ptnr., chair Exec. Compensation and Employee Benefits Dept. Willkie Farr & Gallagher LLP, NYC. Mem. ABA, N.Y. State Bar Assn. (co-chmn. nonqualified employee benefits com. tax sect. 1991-94). Office: Willkie Farr & Gallagher 787 Seventh Ave New York NY 10019-6018 Office Phone: 212-728-8442. E-mail: slindo@willkie.com.

LINDOR, KEITH D., gastroenterologist, researcher, hepatologist; b. Morris, Minn., June 21, 1953; m. Noralane Morey Lindor, July 16, 1977; children: Carl (CJ), Rachel. BS in Chemistry, U. Minn., 1975; MD, Mayo Med. Sch., Rochester, Minn., 1979. Diplomate Am. Bd. Internat. Medicine. Resident Bowman Gray Sch. Medicine, Winston-Salem, NC, 1979—82; asst. prof. medicine Mayo Clinic Coll. Medicine, Rochester, Minn., 1986—91, assoc. prof. medicine, 1991—96, assoc. vice chair practice dept. medicine, 1997—99, cons. divsn. gastroenterology/hepatology, 1986—, prof. medicine, 1996—, chair divsn. gastroenterology. hepatology, 1999—, dean Mayo Med. Sch., 2005—. Reviewers res. NIH, Bethesda, Md., 2003—; spkr. in field. Editor: (book) Primary Biliary Cirrhosis: From Pathogenesis to Clinical Treatment, 1997; contbr. articles to profl. jours. Grantee NIH, 2001—06. Mem.: Am. Liver Found. (vice chair med. affairs 1999—), Am. Coll. Physicians, Am. Coll. Gastroenterology, Am. Assn. for Study of Liver Disease (chair edn. com. 1997—99). Avocation: landscape gardening. Office: Mayo Clinic Coll Medicine 200 First St SW Rochester MN 55905

LINDQUIST, ELDA EVELYN, music educator, writer; b. Little Sauk, Minn., Mar. 27, 1927; d. Conrad and Myra (Cooper) Freeberg; m. Donald Rodney Duane Lindquist, May 28, 1949; children: David, Daniel, Douglas, Debra, Denise. Student in banking, Internat. Falls, Minn., 1948—49; student in music, Fergus Falls (Minn.) Jr. Coll., 1969—70. Sec., bank teller, acct. various cos., Alexandria, Minn., 1945—71; pvt. piano tchr. Alexandria, Minn., 1945—; Christmas and nursery tree farmer, 1978—2002; editor Swede Talk, Alexandria, Minn., 1980—; driver Rainbow Rider, Lowry, Minn., 1996—. Mem.: Minn. Music Tchrs. Assn., Minn. Fedn. Music Clubs (editorian, historian), Lions, Scandinavian Club (pres. 1995—), Garden Club (pres. Alexandria chpt.), Harjedal's Nat. Swedish Club (pres. 1988—94, 2000—02), Euterpean Music Club (pres. Alexandria chpt. 1980—81). Luth. Avocations: reading, travel. Home and Studio: 6800 N Lake Mina Rd N Alexandria MN 56308 Office Phone: 320-763-7478.

LINDQUIST, ERIN STEWART, biology professor, researcher; b. Saratoga Springs, N.Y., Sept. 27, 1975; d. John David Lindquist and Shari Louise Stewart; m. Marcelo Luiz Ardon, Nov. 26, 2005. BS in Biology, Cornell U., 1997; PhD in Ecology, U. Ga., 2003. Resident prof. Orgn. for Tropical Studies/Duke U., San José, Costa Rica, 2003—. Author: Field Guide to the Trees of Cabo Blanco Absolute Nature Reserve, Costa Rica. ESL tchr. Cath. Social Svcs., Athens, 2002—03; event organizer, translator People of Hope, Athens, 2002—03. Grantee NSF, 2001—03, Costa Rica- USA Coop. Found., 2002—05, Internat. scholar, Phi Beta Delta Honor Soc., 2002. Mem.: Ecol. Soc. Am. (assoc.), Assn. Tropical Biology and Conservation (assoc.), Blue Key. Liberal. Office: Orgn Tropical Studies/Duke U 410 Swift Ave Durham NC 27705 Office Phone: 011-506-524-0607. E-mail: erinlindquist@hotmail.com.

LINDQUIST, EVAN, artist, educator; b. Salina, Kans., May 23, 1936; s. E.L. and Linnette Rosalie (Shogren) L.; m. Sharon Frances Huenergardt, June 8, 1958; children: Eric, Carl. BS, Emporia State U., 1958; MFA, U. Iowa, 1963. Prof. art Ark. State U., 1963—2003, emeritus prof., 2003—, Presdl. fellow, 1981—82, 1984—85. One-man shows include Mo. Arts Coun., 1973-75, Albrecht Art Mus., St. Joseph, Mo., 1975, 89, S.E. Mo. State U., 1977, Sandzen Gallery, Lindsborg, Kans., 1978, Galerie V. Kunstverlag Wolfbrum, Vienna, 1979, Poplar Bluff, Mo., 1987, Gallery V., Kansas CIty, Mo., 1988, Northwest Mo. State U., 1991, U. Iowa, Iowa City, 1995, WR Harper Coll., Palatine, Ill., 1996, Northwestern Coll., Orange City, Iowa, 1997, Art Ctr. of the Ozarks, Springdale, Ark., 1998, Fowler Ctr., Ark. State U., Jonesboro, 2001, Ark. arts Ctr., Little Rock, 2002, Evan Lindquist and the art of the BruinU. N.C., Wilmington, N.C., 2005; group shows include Benjamin Galleries, Chgo., 1976, City of Venice, 1977, Boston Printmakers, 1971-87, Visual Arts Ctr. of Alaska, Anchorage, 1979, Western Carolina U., 1980, Pa. State U., 1980, Kans. State U., 1980, U. N.D., 1981, 92, Ariz. State U., 1981, 93, Barcelona, Cadaques, Girona, 1990, 93, 94, Tulsa, 1982, Jay Gallery, N.Y.C., 1983, Artists Books, German Dem. Rep., 1984, U. Tenn., Knoxville, 1985, Memphis State U., 1985, Ark. Arts Ctr., 1983, Miss. State U., 1986, Hunterdon Art Ctr., Clinton, N.J., 1986-87, 94, 95, Washington, 1988, Soc. Am. Graphic Artists/Printmakers, 1988-94, Boston, 1989-94, John Szoke Gallery, 1989, Woodstock, N.Y., 1990, 92, Silvermine Guild Galleries, New Canaan, Conn., 1992, 93, Woodstock Artists Assn., Littman Gallery, Portland State U., Galeria Brita Prinz, Madrid, Spain, 1992, U. Nebr., 1992,. Parkside Nat., Kenosha, Wis., 1993, 95, 2000, 2001, Minot, N.D., 1994, Fla. C.C., Jacksonville, 1995, Stonemetal Press, San Antonio, Tex., 1995, San Diego Art Inst., 1995, Schenectady (N.Y.) Mus., 1995, Fla. Printmakers, Jacksonville, 1996, Clemson U., 1996, U. Tex., Tyler, 1996, Old Print Shop, N.Y.C., 1997, Frederick Baker Gall., Chgo., 1997, Krasdale Gall., N.Y., 1998, Memphis Brooks Mus., 1998, Webster U., St. Louis, 1999, Bradley U., Peoria, Ill., 1999, 2001, Soc. of Am. Graphic Artists, New York, 1999, Hunterdon Art Ctr., Clinton, NJ, 1999, Irving Arts Ctr., Irving Tex., 1999, Payne Gall., Bethlehem, Pa., 1999, U. Hawaii, Hilo, 2000; represented in permanent collections Albertina, Vienna, Art Inst. Chgo., Nelson-Atkins, Kansas City, Phoenix Art Mus., Ufizi Gall., Florence, Mcpl. Gall., Dublin, San Francisco Art Mus., Whitney Mus. Am. Art, N.Y.C., St. Louis Art Mus., Museo Reina Sofia, Madrid, others; staff artist Emporia State U., 1958-60; dir. Delta Nat. Small Prints Exhibn. Ark. State U., 1996, 97. Mem. Soc. Am. Graphic Artists, Coll. Art Assn. Am., Mid-Am. Coll. Art Assn.

LINDQUIST, LEE A., geriatrician, educator; BS, Loyola U., Chicago, 1996; MD, Northwestern U. Med. Sch., 2000; MPH, Northwestern U., 2005. Diplomate Am. Bd. Internal Medicine, 2000, cert. Geriatric Medicine Am. Bd. Internal Medicine, 2004. Instr. medicine Northwestern U. Med. Sch., Chgo., 2003—05, asst. prof. medicine, 2005—. Clinical research (geriatric medicine) Assisted Living Alternatives. Mem.: ACP (assoc.), Am. Geriat. Soc. (assoc.). Achievements include development of Cruise Ships as Alternatives to Assisted LIving Facilities; research in Senior Patient Safety. Office: Northwestern Univ Med Sch 675 N St Clair Ste 14-200 Chicago IL 60611 Office Phone: 312-695-4525. Office Fax: 312-695-6060. E-mail: lal425@md.northwestern.edu.

LINDQUIST, LOUIS WILLIAM, artist, researcher, writer; b. Boise, Idaho, June 26, 1944; s. Louis William and Bessie (Newman) L.; divorced; children: Jessica Ann Alexandra, Jason Ryan Louis. BS in Anthropology, U. Oreg., 1968; postgrad., Portland State U., 1974-78. Researcher, co-writer with Asher Lee, Portland, Oreg., 1977-80; freelance artist, painter, sculptor Oreg., 1980-91, 98-99. Sgt. U.S. Army, 1968-71, Vietnam. Mem.: NRA, AAAS, Am. Anthropol. Assn. Republican. Avocations: reading, beachcombing, listening to classical, jazz and native North American music. Home and Office: PO Box 991 Bandon OR 97411-0991

LINDQUIST, MICHAEL ADRIAN, career military officer; b. Cheyenne, Wyo., Nov. 12, 1946; s. Swen George and Beryl Esme (Edwards) L.; m. Frances Eleanor Arnold, Apr. 14, 1968 (div. Aug. 20, 2003); children: Michella, Michael, Patricia. BS in Econs., U. Tampa, 1975; MS in Logistics Mgmt., Fla. Inst. Technology, Melbourne, 1985; EdD in Orgnl. Leadership, U. Sarasota, 2002. Enlisted U.S. Army, 1966, advanced through grades to col., staff officer 3d Support Command Frankfurt, West Germany, 1980-83, exec. officer 8th Maintenance Group Hanau, West Germany, 1983-85, cmdr. 601st Ord BN Aberdeen Proving Ground, Md., 1986-88, dep. dir. tests Test & Evaluation Command, 1988-89, action officer The Joint Staff Pentagon, 1990-93, comdr. Tobyhanna (Pa.) Army Depot, 1993-95, comdr. Combat Equipment Group Asia Charleston, S.C., 1995-97; cons. Adrian Cons., Charleston, 1998—; prof. U. Phoenix, 2002—, lead faculty, area chair, 2003—; former exec. dir. Congl. Medal of Honor Soc. Mem. Assn. U.S. Army, VFW, Ret. Officers Assn., Ordnance Assn., Mil. Order of World Wars. Avocations: golf, coin collecting/numismatics, stamp collecting/philately. E-mail: adrianconsulting@comcast.net, dr_col_mal@earthlink.net.

LINDQUIST, SUSAN LEE, biology and microbiology educator; b. June 5, 1949; BA in Microbiology with honors, U. Ill., 1971; PhD in Biology, Harvard U., 1976. Asst. prof. dept. biology U. Chgo., 1978-84, assoc. prof., 1984-88, Albert D. Lasker prof. med. sciences, 1988—2001, investigator Howard Hughes Med. Inst., 1988—2001; dir. Whitehead Inst. MIT, Cambridge, Mass., 2001—04, prof. biology, 2001—. Mem. com. genetics, com. devel. biology U. Chgo., 1999—; cons. Mus. Sci. & Industry, Chgo., 1983-87; vis. scholar Cambridge U., 1983; cons., prin. in film Lights Breaking, 1985; mem. sci. adv. com. Helen Hay Whitney Found., 1997—; bd. dirs. Johnson & Johnson, 2004-; lectr. in field. Co-editor: The Stress Induced Proteins, 1988, Heat Shock, 1990; assoc. editor The New Biologist, 1991-93; mem. editl. bd. Cell Regulation, 1989—, Molecular and Cell Biology, 1984—, Gene Expression, 1994-95, Cell Stress and Chaperones, 1995—, Current Biology, 1996—, Molecular Biology of the Cell, 1996—; monitoring editor Jour. Cell Biology, 1993—; contbr. articles to profl. jours. Teaching fellow Harvard U., 1973-74, Postdoctoral fellow Am. Cancer Soc., 1976-78; Novartis Drew award, 2000. Fellow Am. Acad. Microbiology, AAAS, NAS, Am. Acad. Arts and Sci.; mem. Am. Soc. Cell Biology, Am. Soc. Microbiology, Fedn. Am. Scientists for Exptl. Biology, Genetics Soc. Am. (elected sec. 1998—), Molecular Medicine Soc. Achievements include research in the impact of protein-conformational changes on diverse processes in cellular and organismal biology. Office: Whitehead Inst Nine Cambridge Ctr Cambridge MA 02142-1479 Office Phone: 617-258-5184. E-mail: lindquist_admin@wi.mit.edu.

LINDROS, ERIC BRYAN, professional hockey player; b. London, Ont., Can., Feb. 28, 1973; s. Carl and Bonnie Lindros. Student, York U., Toronto. With Detroit Compuware, 1989—90, Phila. Flyers, 1992—2000, NY Rangers, 2001—04, Toronto Maple Leafs, 2005—; mem. Team Canada Olympic Hockey Team, 2002. Mem. Can. Hockey Team, 1992, Cup All-Star Team, 1989—90, OHL All-Star Team, 1990—91, NHL All-Star Team, 1992—93; player NHL All-Star Game, 1993—94, 1996—2000. Named MVP, World Jr. Hockey Championships, 1990, Ont. Jr. Hockey Assn., 1991, Player of Yr., Can. Hockey League, 1990—91; recipient Plus/Minus award, 1990—91, Red Tilson Trophy, 1990—91, Eddie Powers Meml. Trophy, 1990—91, Hart Trophy, 1995, Lester B. Pearson award, Nat. Hockey League, 1995, Gold Medal, Olympic Games, 2002. Office: Toronto Maple LEafs Air Canada Ctr 40 Bay St Toronto ON M5J 2X2 Canada*

LINDROTH, JAMES TEODOR, music educator; b. South Weymouth, Mass., Nov. 21, 1968; s. Georg Teodor and June Carol Lindroth; m. Tracey Marie Falardeav, Dec. 19, 1993; children: Andrew James, Matthew Richard. B in Music Edn., U. Lowell, 1992; MA, U. Mass., Lowell, 1994. Cert. tchr. music K-12, cmty. coll. music. Music tchr. Beverly (Mass.) Pub. Schs., 1994—95, Miami (Ariz.) Pub. Schs., 1995—97, Brandon (Fla.) H.S., 1997—. Music dir. Tampa (Fla.) Bay Winds, 2000—. Mem.: Fla. Bandmasters Assn., Music Educators Nat. Conf. Mem. Lds Ch. Avocation: hockey. Office: Brandon High Sch 1101 Victoria St Brandon FL 33510 Business E-Mail: James.Lindroth@sdhc.k12.fl.us.

LINDROTH, LINDA (LINDA HAMMER), artist, writer, curator; b. Miami, Sept. 4, 1946; d. Mark Roger and Mae Lang Hammer; m. David George Lindroth, May 26, 1968 (div. Mar. 1985); m. Craig David Newick, June 6, 1987; 1 child, Zachary Eran Newick. BA in Art, Douglass Coll., 1968; studied with Gordon Matta-Clark, Rutgers U., 1975; studied with Garry Winogrand, N.Y., 1976; MFA in Art, Rutgers U., 1979; master class in non-fiction writing, Yale U., 1997. Adj. asst. prof. art Quinnipiac Coll., Hamden, Conn., 1998—. editor: Co-author, Virtual Vintage: The Insider's Guide to Buyin and Selling Fashion Online. Exhibitions include Aetna Gallery, 1987, 1989, 1991, Franklin Furnace, N.Y.C., 1977, Conn. Commn. Arts, Hartford, 1985, 1996, Aldrich Mus. Contemporary Art, Ridgefield, Conn., 1987, 1987, Downey Mus. Art, Calif., 1989, Zimmerlo Art Mus. Rutgers U., 1989, Wesleyan U. Ctr. for Arts, 1990, Boston Pub. Libr., 1991, John Michael Kohler Art Ctr., Sheboygan, Wis., 1992, Joseloff Gallery U., Hartford, 1994, Artspace, New Haven, 1991, 1992, 1993, 1994, 1995, DeCordova Mus., Lincoln, Mass., 1995, Urban Glass, Bklyn., 1996, U. Conn. Atrium Gallery, 1999, Creative Arts Workship, 1999, New Haven Hist. Soc., 1999, Stedman Gallery, 1999, Rutgers U., 1999, others, Represented in permanent collections The Mus. Modern Art, N.Y.C., The Met. Mus. Art, The Mus. City of N.Y., Internat. Polaroid Collection/Artist Program, N.J. State Mus., Trenton, The Bibliotheque Nationale, Paris, Ctr. Creative Photography, Tucson, The Newark Mus., The Jane Voorhees Zimmerli Art Mus., New Brunswick, N.J., High Mus. Art, Atlanta, Yale U., Mus. d'art et d'histoire, Fribourg, Switzerland; co-author: Out of Bounds, 1994 (1st prize), Virtual Vintage, 2002. Dir. Artspace, Inc., New Haven; mem. Mayor's Task Force on Pub. Art, New Haven. Recipient Ann. Design Rev. award ID Mag., 1990, 91, 93, Honorable Mention, Nat. Peace Garden Design Competition, 1989, Pitts. Corning Archtl. Design Competition, 1988, Individual Artist fellow N.J. State Coun. on Arts, 1974-75, 83-84, Wilmer Shields Rich award Coun. Founds., 1995, Printing Industry Am. award, 1995; grantee Found. for Contemporary Performance Arts, Inc., 1989, 90, Fission Fusion NEA InterArts, 1989, New Eng. Found. for Arts, 1992, Fairfield U., 1995, Ruth Chenven Found., N.Y.C., 1997, Ruth Chevnen Found., 1997; Conn. Commn. Arts fellow, 1995, New Eng. Found. Arts/NEA Regional Photography fellow, 1995-96; Emerging Voices lectr. Arch. League of N.Y., 1996; fellowship grantee in sculpture Conn. Commn. on the Arts, 2000, Te Found. Grant, 2002. Studio: 219 Livingston St New Haven CT 06511-2209

LINDSAY, ARLENE ROSARIO, federal judge; BA, U. Dayton, 1968; JD, NYU Law Sch., 1975. Bar: N.Y. Asst. D.A. Bronx, 1975—78; asst. U.S. atty. Eastern Dist. N.Y., 1978—83; deputy atty. Suffolk County, 1983—88; town atty. Huntington, 1988—90; chief white collar crime and complex litigation sect., D.A. office Suffolk Country, 1990; chief Long Island div. U.S. Atty. office Eastern Dist. N.Y., 1990—94; magistrate judge for ea. dist. N.Y., U.S. Magistrate Ct., Bklyn., 1994—. Adj. prof. Touro Law Sch. Mem.: ABA. Office: Fed Plaza Long Island Federal Courthouse 814 Central Islip NY 11722*

LINDSAY, DIANE MILLER, music educator; d. Dave Harlan and Geraldine Clara Miller; m. Allan Karl Lindsay, Dec. 27, 1986; children: Kayla Jean, Megan Lyn. MusB, U. Wis., Whitewater, 1980. Cert. vocal music K-12 edn. Ill. Soprano Chgo. Symphony Chorus, 1986—99; music tchr. Wood Dale Sch. Dist., 1998—2001, Jefferson Mid. Sch., Naperville, Ill., 2001—02; piano tchr. Diane's Music Studio, Lombard, Ill., 2001—. Mem.: Am. Guild Musical Artists, Music Tchrs. Nat. Assn. Office: Diane's Music Studio 242 S Edgewood Ave Lombard IL 60148-2808 Business E-Mail: dmlindsay@ameritech.net.

LINDSAY, DIANNA MARIE, educational administrator; b. Boston, Dec. 7, 1948; d. Albert Joseph and June Hazelton Raggi; m. James William Lindsay III, Feb. 14, 1981. BA in Anthropology, Ea. Nazarene Coll., 1971; MEd in Curriculum and Instrn., Wright State U., 1973, MA in Social Studies Edn., 1974, MEd in Edn. Adminstrn., 1977; EdD in Urban History, Ball State U., 1976; MA in Counseling, U. Dayton, 2000. Supr. social edn. Ohio Dept. Edn., Columbus, 1976-77; asst. prin. Orange City Schs., Pepper Pike, Ohio, 1977-79; prin. North Olmsted (Ohio) Jr. High Sch., 1979-81; dir. secondary edn. North Olmsted City Schs., 1981-82; supt. Copley (Ohio)-Fairlawn City Schs., 1982-85; prin. North Olmsted High Sch., 1985-89, New Trier High Sch., Winnetka, Ill., 1989-96, Worthington Kilbourne H.S., Columbus, Ohio, 1996-2001; headmaster Columbus Jewish Day Sch., New Albany, Ohio, 2001—03; prin. Ridgefield H.S., Ridgefield, Conn., 2003—. Bd. dirs. Harvard Prins. Ctr., Cambridge, Mass., adj. prof. ednl. adminstrn., Grad. Sch. Edn., U. Dayton, Bexley, OH Contbr. articles to profl. jours. Bd. dirs. Nat. PTA, Chgo., 1987-89 (Educator of Yr. 1989), Found. Human Potential, Chgo.,; bd. trustee Columbus Jewish Country Day Sch. Named Prin. of Yr. Ohio Art Tchrs., 1989, one of 100 Up and Coming Educators, Exec. Educator Mag., 1988, Milken Educator of the Yr. Ohio, 1999; recipient John Vaughn Achievements in Edn. North Cen. Assn., 1988; named Ohio Prin. of Yr. 2000. Mem. AAUW, Ill. Tchrs. Fgn. Lang., Rotary Internat., Phi Delta Kappa. Methodist. Avocations: stained glass, reading, travel, biking, harpist. Office: Ridgefield HS 700 N Salem Rd Ridgefield CT 06877 E-mail: dlindsay@ridgefield.org.

LINDSAY, FRANNIE, academic administrator, writer; b. Princeton, NJ, Feb. 3, 1949; d. Frank Whiteman and Katherine Hamilton Lindsay. BA in English, Russell Sage Coll., 1976; MFA in Creative Writing, U. Iowa, 1979. Coord. grad. studies romance langs. Harvard U., Cambridge, Mass., 1996—. Author: (chapbook) The Harp of the First Day, 1978, The Aerial Tide Coming In, 1979, Where She Always Was, 2004 (May Swenson award); contbr. numerous poems to lit. publs. Lit. fellow, NEA, 1989. Mem.: Acad. Am. Poets (assoc.), New Eng. Poetry Club. Democrat. Avocations: piano, greyhound rescue adoption. Home: 20A Prescott St # 8 Cambridge MA 02138

LINDSAY, GEORGE CARROLL, former museum director; b. Cochranville, Pa., Sept. 28, 1928; s. J. George and M. Elizabeth (Copeland) L.; m. Mary-Edythe Shelley, June 27, 1953. BA, Franklin and Marshall Coll., 1950; student, Dickinson Sch. Law, 1950-53; MA (Wintherthur fellow early Am. culture 1953-55), U. Del., 1955. Asst. to dir. Henry Francis du Pont Wintherthur Mus., Del., 1955-56; asst. curator ethnology Smithsonian Instn., 1956-57, asso. curator cultural history, 1957-58, curator mus. service, 1958-66; dir. mus. services N.Y. State Mus., 1966-81, dir., 1981-83, dir. planning and program devel., 1983-86; exec. dir. Vanderbilt Mus., 1986-89, ret., 1989. Lectr. early Am. decorative arts and architecture; cons. in field; v.p. Alexandria Assn., Va., 1961-62, pres., 1962-63, bd. dirs., 1963-66; bd. dirs. Greater Washington Ednl. TV Assn., 1964-66, mem. programming com., 1965-66; bd. dirs. No. Va. Fine Arts Assn., 1964-66, Mus. Audio-Visual Applications Group, 1962-70; mem. com. furnishing ofcl. reception room State Dept., 1960-75 Bd. dirs. Menands (N.Y.) Pub. Libr., 1970-86, Albany Symphony Orch., 1969-72, ARC, Albany, 1977-86; active Strasburg (Pa.) Borough Coun., 1992-96, pres., 1994-95; mem. planning commn. Strasburg Boro, 1995—2003; trustee Octoraro United Presbyn. Ch., 1993—, Strasburg Heritage Soc., 1997—. Mem. Am. Assn. Mus. (coun. 1969-72, v.p. 1970-71, chmn. profl. rels. com. 1974-80), N.Y. State Assn. Mus. (sec. 1968-77, pres. 1977-79, coun. 1985-89), N.E. Mus. Conf. (bd. govs. 1982-85, chmn. long range planning com. 1983-85), St. Andrew's Soc. (pres. Albany 1983-85), St. Andrew's Soc. Phila. Mem. Soc. Of Friends. Address: 255 Wallingford Rd Strasburg PA 17579-1448

LINDSAY, GEORGE PETER, lawyer; b. Bklyn., Feb. 22, 1948; s. Charles Joseph and Marie Antionette (Faraone) Lindsay; m. Sharon Winnett, Sept. 8, 1973; children: William Charles, Kimberly Michelle. BA, Columbia U., 1969; JD, Harvard U., 1973. Bar: N.Y. 1974, Mass. 1985, U.S. Dist. Ct. (so. dist.) N.Y. 1974, U.S. Ct. Appeals (2d cir.) 1975. Assoc. White & Case, N.Y.C., 1973-82; ptnr. Miller, Wrubel & Dubroff, N.Y.C., 1982-83, Sullivan & Worcester LLP, N.Y.C., 1983—. Mem. ABA, Assn. Bar City of N.Y., N.Y. State Bar Assn., Internat. Bar Assn. Office: Sullivan & Worcester LLP 1290 Avenue of Americas 29th Fl New York NY 10104 Business E-Mail: glindsay@sandw.com.

LINDSAY, JUNE CAMPBELL MCKEE, communications executive; b. Detroit, Nov. 14, 1920; d. Maitland Everett and Josephine Belle (Campbell) McKee; m. Powell Lindsay, Nov. 25, 1967; 1 child, Kristi Costa-McKee. BA in Speech with honors (McGregor Fund Mich. grantee), U. Mich., 1943; cert. in electronics engring., Signal Corps Ground Signal Svc., 1943; postgrad. (Inst. Gen. Semantics grantee), U. Chgo., 1944-45; postgrad. (Armour grantee), NYU, 1945-46; postgrad., Columbia U., 1946-47, Wayne State U., 1960-64, U. Mich., 1964-70, 78—; MA, Specialist-in-Aging Cert., Inst. of Gerontology, 1982. Coord., activator McKee Prodns., Detroit, 1943-56, Being Unltd., Detroit, 1957—, InterBeing Inc., Detroit, 1979—, M.U.T.U.A.L. A.I.D., 1981—. Info. dir. Suitcase Theatre Inc., Lansing and Ann Arbor; cons. Cornelian Corner Detroit Inc., 1957-63, Islamic Ctr. Found. Soc., Detroit, 1959-62, city Ann Arbor Human Rels. Commn., 1966-68, Urban Adult Edn. Inst., Detroit, 1968-69, Mich. Bell Tel. Co., Detroit, 1969, African Art Gallery Founders, Detroit Inst. Arts, 1964, WKAR-TV, Mich. State U., 1971—. Mem. Nat. Caucus, Ctr. for Black Aged; bd. dirs. Mus. Youth Internat., Saline, Mich., Ann Arbor Cmty. Devel. Corp.; chaplain's asst. U. Hosp., Ann Arbor, 1971—72; program dir. People-to-People, Ann Arbor, 1971—72; Suitcase Theatre tour coord. Brit. Empire's Leprosy Relief Assn., 1972—; mem. Baha'i Internat. Health Agy., Inst. for Advancement of Health, Mission Health, Catherine McAuley Health Ctr. Share and Care Support Group; assembly cons. Baha'i Faith, 1960—. Recipient Award for Excellence Mich. Ednl. Assn.,1971, Mich. Assn. Classroom Tchrs., 1972; exec. dir. Powell Lindsay Meml. Program in Theatre and Comm., Louhelen Baha'i Sch. and Residential Coll., U. Mich., Flint, Mott Cmty. Coll., 1988—. Mem.: ACLU, People's Med. Soc., Nat. Assn. Pub. Health Policy, Nat. Coun. Sr. Citizens, Washtenaw County Coun. on Aging, Subarea Adv. Coun., Comprehensive Planning Coun. S.E. Mich., Mich. Soc. Gerontology, Mich. League Human Svcs., Mental Health Assn. Mich., Nat. Inst. Clin. Application of Behavioral Medicine, Internat. Soc. Study of Subtle Energies and Energy Medicine, Assn. Holistic Health, U.S. Assn. Humanistic Psychology, Nat. Coun. on Aging, Mich. Health Coun., Am. Soc. on Aging, Inst. Study Conscious Evolution, Internat. Health Found., Mich. Assn. Holistic Health, Wellness Assocs., Am. Pub. Health Assn., Am. Assn. Adult and Continuing Edn., Am. Women in Radio and TV, Soc. for Individual Responsibility, Age-Groups United Relating On-site Respecting Autonomy (activator, troupe leader, prodr., developer videotape vignettes and revues), UN Assn. of U.S., Orgn. Devel. Inst., Nat. Trust Historic Preservation, World Future Soc., Living Tao Found., Giraffe Soc., Alliance for Democracy and Diversity, Am. Assn. Ret. Persons, Interfaith Coun. Peace and Justice, Assn. Baha'i Studies, Planetary Citizens, Gray Panthers, Internat. Platform Assn. Home: 2339 S Circle Dr Ann Arbor MI 48103-3442

LINDSAY, LAURA F., communications educator; b. Chgo., Sept. 22, 1945; d. Thomas M. and M. Dorothy Fletcher; m. Sherwood J. Leomoine (div.); 1 child, Ashley Elizabeth Lemoine; m. Wendell G. Lindsay Jr., Sept. 7, 1991; stepchildren: Lisa, Julie, Doug, Ned. BA, La.State U., 1967; MA, La. State U., 1969, PhD, 1976. Grad. asst. La. State U., 1967—71; instr. East Tex. State U., Texarkana, 1973—76; asst. prof. dept. speech U. Southwestern La., Lafayette, 1978—79; coord. Govtl. Svcs. Inst., La. State U., Baton Rouge, 1979—80, sr. lectr., dir. comprehensive pub. tng. program, 1980—81; assoc. dean La. State U., 1982—84, dean jr. divsn., 1984—89, assoc. vice chancellor acad. affairs, 1989—97, interim vice provost acad. affairs, 1997, vice provost acad. affairs, 1997—99, prof. mass comm., 1999—, interim provost, vice chancellor acad. affairs, 2002—03; exec. asst. to chancellor, interim dir. Mus. Art, 2003—, prof. mass comm., 2003—. Author: Effective Managerial Communication, 1994; contbr. articles to profl. jours., chpts. to books. Vice chair Shaw Ctr. for Arts, Baton Rouge, 2003—04; chair La. Bd. Regents Elec. Learning Com., 1998—2002; mem. Comm. Human Resource and Social Change, 1994—99. Mem.: So. Assn. Colls. and Schs. (pres.-elect 2004, bd. trustees 2002—04, exec. com. 1997—2000). Home: 3874 Chandler Dr Baton Rouge LA 70808

LINDSAY, LESLIE, packaging engineer; b. Amsterdam, N.Y., Oct. 30, 1960; d. R. Gardner and Dorothy (Loucks) Lindsay. BA in Advt., Mich. State U., 1981, BS in Package Engring., 1982. Registered profl. engr. in packaging. Constrn. inspector N.Y. State Dept. Transp., Albany, 1983; sr. package design engr. Wang Labs., Inc., Lowell, Mass., 1983-90; sr. packaging engr. Apple Computer, Inc., Cupertino, Calif., 1990-97, Bose Corp., Framingham, Mass., 1997—2002; dir. packaging Syratech Corp., East Boston, Mass., 2003—05; tech. bus. mgr. Markson Rosenthal & Co., Maynard, Mass., 2005—. Conf. spkr. Internat. Safe Transit Assn., 1994; judge AmeriStar, 1999, 2000. Staff editor: Packaging Horizons Mag. Recipient Silver Ameristar award for Electronics Packaging, 1993, 2000, ID Mag. Packaging award, 1993, Ameristar Judges award for Merit, 1995; N.Y. State Regents scholar, 1977. Mem.: Molded Pulp Environ. Packaging Assn. (seminar spkr. 1997, founding bd. dirs.), Inst. Packaging Profls. (mem. reduction, reuse, and recycling protective packaging task group, cert.), Women in Packaging, Wang Ultimate Frisbee (social chmn. 1986—89), Am. Contract Bridge League, Boston Women's Rugby Club (tour chmn. 1985). Home: 193 Winter St Framingham MA 01702-2435 Office Phone: 978-420-7061. Personal E-mail: leslie.lindsay@rcn.com.

LINDSAY, MICHAEL ANTHONY, lawyer; b. Omaha, Nebr., May 9, 1958; s. William J. and Mary F. Lindsay. BA summa cum laude, Marquette U., 1980; gen. studies with first class honors, London Sch. Econ., 1980; JD cum laude, U. Chgo., 1983. Bar: Minn. 1985, U.S. Dist. Ct. Minn. 1985. Law clk. to judge Richard Posner U.S. Ct. Appeals, Chgo., 1983-84; assoc. Dorsey & Whitney, Mpls., 1985-90, ptnr., trial practice group, 1991—, and co-chmn., anti-trust group. Adj. prof. Hamline U. Sch. Law, St. Paul, 1988—. Pres. Prevention Alliance, Mpls., 1991—. Mem.: Phi Beta Kappa, Order of Coif. Office: Dorsey & Whitney Ste 1500 50 S Sixth St Minneapolis MN 55402-1498 Office Phone: 612-340-7819. Office Fax: 612-340-2868. Business E-Mail: lindsay.michael@dorsey.com.

LINDSAY, MYRANDA J., special education educator, military officer; d. Edward L. and Kathy S. Wright; m. Benjamin D. Wright, July 12, 2003; 1 child, Rebekah G. Grad. in Spl. Edn., Miss. State U., 2001. Cert. mild/moderate spl. edn. K-12 tchr. Miss., 2003. Tchr. spl. edn. Pontotoc Jr. H.S., Miss., 2003—04, Caledonia H.S., Miss., 2004—. Platoon leader/ops. officer 1687Th Transp. Co., Southaven, Miss., 2003—. Youth intern Bapt. Student Union Missionary, Wilmington, Del., 2000—00; rep. Fellowship Of Christian Athletes, Mississippi State, Miss., 2002—03; Bbible study leader Caledonia Bapt. Ch., Miss., 2004—05. 2d lt. U.S. Army N.G., 2003—05. Recipient Leadership award, Itawamba C.C., 1999 - 2001, Holmes Cultural Diversity Ctr. award, Miss. State U., 2000, scholarship, Res. Officer Tng. Corps, 2001 - 2003. Mem.: Fellowship Of Christian Athletes, Golden Key Honor Soc. Republican. Baptist. Avocations: running, travel. Office Phone: 662-356-2002.

LINDSAY, REGINALD CARL, judge; b. Birmingham, Ala., Mar. 19, 1945; s. Richard and Louise L.; m. Cheryl E. Hartgrove, Aug. 15, 1970. Cert., U. Valencia, 1966; AB in Polit. Sci. cum laude, Morehouse Coll., 1967; JD, Harvard U., 1970; LLD (hon.), New Eng. Sch. Law, 2003. Bar: Mass. 1971, U.S. Ct. Appeals (1st cir.) 1971. Assoc. Hill & Barlow, 1970-75, 78-79, ptnr., 1979-93; judge U.S. Dist. Ct. Mass., Boston, 1994—. Arbitrator, mem. comml. arbitration panel Am. Arbitration Assn., 1994—; commr. Mass. Dept. Pub. Utilities, Boston, 1975-77; pres. adv. bd. Mus. of Nat. Center of Afro-Am. Artists, 1975-81, v.p., 1981—; trustee Thompson Islands Edn. Center, Boston, 1975-81; bd. dirs. United Way of Mass. Bay, 1981-84, Morgan Meml. Goodwill Industries, Boston, 1992—, Ptnrs. for Youth with Disabilities, Boston; mem. Nat. Consumer Law Ctr. (bd. dirs.), Mass. Commn. on Jud. Conduct, 1982-88; trustee Newton (Mass.) - Wellesley Hosp. Recipient Ruffin-Fenwick Trailblazer award Harvard Black Law Students Assn., 1994, Amanda V. Houston cmty. svc. award Boston Coll., 1998, Frederick E. Berry Expanding Ind. award Easter Seals, 1999, Heroes Among Us award Boston Celtics, 2001, Leadership award New Eng. Black Law Students Assn., 2001. Mem. ABA, Nat. Bar Found., Mass. Bar Assn., Boston Bar Assn. (coun. 1977—, citation jud. excellence 1999), Pi Sigma Alpha, Phi Beta Kappa. Office: 1 Courthouse Way Ste 5130 Boston MA 02210-3007

LINDSAY, RICHARD PAUL, artist, jewelry designer; b. Aurora, Colo., Nov. 21, 1945; s. Paul Francis and Geraldine Evelyn (Goulet) L.; 1 child, Jared Nicholas. BA in Polit. Sci., Colo. State U., 1967. Profl. ski patrol Santa Fe (N.M.) Ski Basin, 1974-80; prin. Richard Lindsay Designs, Santa Fe, 1973—. Copyrighted designs include Walking Trout (R), Happy Critters (R), Roadkill Rabbit (R), Kachina Klan (R); exhibited in numerous galleries, N.Y.C., Colo., N.M., Tex., France, also others. Served to 1st lt. U.S. Army, 1968-71, Vietnam. Recipient Design award Silversmith Santa Fe Film Festival, 1983, Best Ad Yr., Colo. Press Assn., 1972, 25th Anniversary Silversmith-Telluride Film Festival; decorated Bronze Star, Army Commendation medal. Mem. Jewelers Bd. of Trade. Avocations: fly fishing, camping, hiking, gardening, drawing. Office: Richard Lindsay Designs 1404 Luisa St Ste 4 Santa Fe NM 87505-4158

LINDSAY, RICHARD THOMAS, music educator; b. Van Wert, Ohio, Dec. 31, 1953; children: Joshua, Rebekah, Benjamin. BS in music, DePaul U., 1976; MS in edn., Ind. U., 1982. Cert. tchg. Idaho, lic. Ind. Band dir. Alexander HS, Albaoy, Ohio, 1977—79, Heritage Mid. Sch., Middlebury, Ind., 1980—83, Northridge HS, Middlebury, Ind., 1983—94, Burley Jr. HS, Burley, Idaho, 1994—2005; instr., jazz studies Coll. of Southern Idaho, Twin Falls, Idaho, 2003—05. Mem.: Coll. Music Soc., Music Educator's nat. Conf. Meth. Avocation: jazz. Home Fax: 208-878-3153. E-mail: linrich@pmt.org.

LINDSAY, ROGER ALEXANDER (BARON OF CRAIGHALL), investment executive; b. Dundee, Scotland, Feb. 18, 1941; s. Archibald Carswell Lindsay and Edith Paterson Bissett. Student, The Morgan Acad., Dundee, U. St. Andrews, Scotland. Asst. acct., office mgr. Andrew G. Kidd Ltd., Dundee, 1964-66; head office acct. Associated British Foods Ltd., London, 1966-71; sec., treas. Wittington Investments, Ltd., Toronto, 1971-95; exec. v.p. Wittington Investments Ltd., Toronto, 1991-95; pres. Fort House Investments, Toronto, 1989. Bd. dirs. United World Coll. Internat. Can., Inc., The W. Garfield Weston Found., Benedictine Heritage Ltd.; past pres. St. John Coun. Ontario. Past moderator Presby. of East Toronto; aide-de camp Lt. Gov. of Ont.; chair bd. govs. Knox Coll. U. Toronto; vice chancellor governance Priory Coun. of Can. Venerable Order of St. John. Decorated comdr. Ven. Order Hosp. St. John. Fellow Chartered Inst. Mgmt., Inst. Dirs., Soc. Antiquaries Scotland; mem. Inst. Chartered Accts. Scotland, Royal Overseas League, The Nat. Club (Toronto), Coral Beach Club (Bermuda). Avocations: heraldry, antique silver, genealogy. Office: Fort House Investments 150 Heath St W Ste 1302 Toronto ON Canada M4V 2Y4 Office Phone: 416-487-9291. E-mail: fhilral@aol.com.

LINDSAY, TWYLA LYNN, music educator; b. Chillicothe, Mo., June 22, 1964; d. Jesse Earl and Linda Louise Dodd; m. Ronald R. Lindsay, Aug. 2, 1986; children: Jesalynn Delores, Ronald Micah. B in Edn. Music, Mo. Western State Coll., 1987; EdM, Lesle Coll., 1998. Music educator Kans. City (Mo.) Sch. Dist., 1987—, program dir., coord. career ladder program, 1999—2003. Sunday sch. tchr., youth worker Concord Bapt. Ch., Kansas City, 1986—2003, dir., musician, 1986—2000. Mem.: Mo. Music Educators Assn. Baptist. Avocations: travel, reading, bowling, singing, piano. Office: Kansas City Mo Sch Dist 1211 McGee Kansas City MO 64109 Office Phone: 816-418-6525.

LINDSAY, WILLIAM KERR, surgeon; b. Vancouver, B.C., Can., Sept. 3, 1920; s. James Arthur and Lottie Mary (Early) L.; m. Frances Beatrice Ferris, Feb. 15, 1945; children— William Arthur, Barbara Susanne, Katherine Mary, Anne Louise. MD, U. Toronto, 1945, BS in Medicine, 1949, MS, 1959. Intern Toronto Gen. Hosp., 1945-46; resident Toronto Gen. Hosp. and Hosp. Sick Children, 1948-51, Montreal Gen. Hosp., 1951-52, Baylor U. Hosp., 1952-53; practice medicine, specializing in plastic surgery Toronto, 1953—; staff surgeon to head divsn. plastic surgery Hosp. for Sick Children, 1953-86, cons., 1965-86; project dir. Research Inst., 1954-85; faculty dept. surgery U. Toronto Faculty of Medicine, 1953-86, prof., 1968-86, chmn. interhospital com. for plastic surgery, 1965-86, prof. emeritus, 1986—. Chmn. med. dental staff com. Bloorview MacMillan Treatment Ctr. (formerly Hugh MacMillan Treatment Ctr. and Ont. Crippled Childrens Treatment Ctr.), 1958-63, cons., 1963—. Trustee McLaughlin Found., 1986-2002. With M.C., Royal Can. Army, 1943-46; surg. lt. Royal Can. Navy, 1946-47. Named Hon Head burn and plastic surgery dept. Gansu Provincial Peoples' Hosp., Lanzhou City, China, 1994—; recipient Arbor award, 1994. Fellow ACS, Royal Coll. Surgeons Can.; mem. Am. Assn. Plastic Surgeons (pres. 1970-71, Hon. award 1995), Can. Soc. Plastic Surgeons (pres. 1963), Easter Seal Soc. Ont. (chmn. med. adv. com. 1957-65, cons. 1952-95, mem. rsch. inst. 1979-95, Gold award 1995, Lifetime Achievement award, 2004), Order of Ontario, Am. Soc. Plastic and Reconstructive Surgeons (Spl. Achievement award 1979), Am. Soc. Surgery of Hand, Am. Cleft Palate Assn., Brit. Soc. Surgery of Hand. Home and Office: 77 Clarendon Ave Apt 202 Toronto ON Canada M4V 1J2 Personal E-mail: wmlinds@aol.com.

LINDSEY, ADA MARIE, dean, nursing educator; b. Dayton, Ohio, May 8, 1937; m. George T. Lindsey. BS in Nursing, Ohio State U., 1959, MS, 1960; PhD, U. Md., 1977. RN. Staff nurse Ohio State U. Hosp., Columbus, 1960; instr. Mt. Carmel Sch. Nursing., Columbus, 1960-65, asst. dir., 1965-68; asst. prof. U. Md., Balt., 1968-77, assoc. prof., asst. dean, 1977-78; assoc. prof. U. Calif., San Francisco, 1979-83, chmn., 1979-86, prof., 1983-86; prof., dean Sch. Nursing UCLA, 1986-95; dean coll. nursing U. Nebr. Med. Ctr., 1995—. Co-editor: Pathophysiological Phenomena in Nursing, 1993 (Book of Yr. award 1986); contbr. articles to profl. jours. Fellow Am. Acad. Nursing; mem. Am. Nurses Assn., Nebr. Nurses Assn., Oncology Nursing Soc., Sigma Theta Tau.

LINDSEY, CASIMIR CHARLES, zoologist, educator; b. Toronto, Ont., Can., Mar. 22, 1923; s. Charles Bethune and Wanda Casimira (Gzowski) L.; m. Shelagh Pauline Lindsey, May 29, 1948. BA, U. Toronto, 1948; MA, U. B.C., Vancouver, 1950; PhD, Cambridge (Eng.) U., 1952. Div. biologist B.C. Game Dept., 1952-57; with Inst. Fisheries, also dept. zoology U. B.C., 1953-66; prof. zoology U. Man., Winnipeg, 1966-79; dir. Inst. Animal Resource Ecology, U. B.C., 1980-85; mem. Fisheries and Oceans Adv. Council, 1981-86; prof. emeritus U. B.C., 1988—. Bd. govs. Vancouver Pub. Aquarium, 1956—66, 1980—95, patron, 1996—2004; external assessor univs., Singapore and Nanyang, 1979—81; cons. in field. Author papers in field. Served with Can. Army, 1943-45. Recipient Publ. award Wildlife Soc., 1972; Saunderson award for excellence in teaching U. Man., 1977; Rh Inst. award, 1979; Nuffield Found. grantee, 1973; Killam sr. fellow, 1985-86. Fellow Royal Soc. Can.; mem. Can. Soc. Zoologists (pres. 1977-78), Can. Soc. Environ. Biologists (v.p. 1974-75), Am. Soc. Ichthyologists and Herpetologists (gov.), Fedn. Can. Artists. Office: U BC Dept of Zoology 6270 University Blvd Vancouver BC Canada V6T 1Z4

LINDSEY, DAVID, writer; married. Former editor small pubs., Tex. Author: Requiem for a Glass Heart, 1996, The Color of Night, Body of Truth, 1992 (Bochumer Krimi Archiv award, 1992), Animosity, numerous other novels. Office: c/o Author Mail Warner Books 1271 Ave of the Americas New York NY 10020

LINDSEY, DAVID HOSFORD, lawyer; b. Kingsville, Tex., July 25, 1950; s. Ernest Truman and Helen Elizabeth (Hosford) L.; m. Marilyn Kay Williams, June 8, 1974; children: Seth Williams, Brooks Daniel. BS in Bus. Adminstrn., U. Mo., 1972; JD, Washburn U., 1975. Bar: Mo. 1975. With trust dept. Commerce Bank, Kansas City, Mo., 1974—75, from asst. v.p. to sr. v.p., 1979—94, chief credit officer, 1989—, exec. v.p., 2000—; mgr., sales dept. Pioneer Pallet, Inc., North Kansas City, Mo., 1976; from asst. cashier to v.p. Nat. Bank, North Kansas City, 1977—79. Vice-chmn. planning and zoning com. City of Liberty, Mo., 1981-93, tax increment fin. commr., 2002—; bd. dirs. Kansas City Met. YMCA. Mem. Mo. Bar Assn., Lawyers Assn. Kansas City, Kansas City Met. Bar Assn., Robert Morris Assn. (bd. dirs. Kansas City chpt.), Kansas City C. of C., Kansas City Alumni Assn. (bd. dirs.), Clayview Country Club, Phi Gamma Delta, Omicron Delta Kappa. Baptist. Home: 602 Camelot Dr Liberty MO 64068-1176 Office: Commerce Bank 1000 Walnut St Ste 1800 Kansas City MO 64106-2123

LINDSEY, EDWARD HARMAN, JR., lawyer; b. Atlanta, Dec. 5, 1958; s. Edward Harman and Mary Dennard Lindsey; m. Elizabeth Green, Dec. 30, 1988; children: Harman, Zack, Charlie. BA, Davidson Coll., 1981; JD, U. Ga., 1984. Bar: Ga. 1984, U.S. Ct. Appeals (11th cir.) 1984, U.S. Dist. Ct. (so., mid., and no. dists.) Ga. 1984. Assoc. McClure Ramsey & Dickerson, Toccoa, Ga., 1984-87, Savell & Williams, Atlanta, 1987-90; ptnr. Goodman, McGuffey, Aust & Lindsey, Atlanta, 1990—. Bd. dirs. Atlanta Vol. Lawyers Found., 1997—; mem. Ga. Ho. Reps., 2005—. Mem. ABA, State Bar Ga., Atlanta Bar Assn., Atlanta Lawyers Club. Office: Goodman McGuffey Aust & Lindsey 2100 Tower Pl 3340 Peachtree Rd NE Atlanta GA 30326-1000 Office Phone: 404-264-1500.

LINDSEY, JOANNE M., flight attendant, poet; b. Peoria, Ill., Aug. 27, 1936; d. George Edward and Elsie Rosetta (Mann) Lindsey; AA, El Camino Coll., Torrance, Calif., 1958. Exec. adminstrv. sec. Space Tech. Labs. (formerly Ramo-Woolridge), Hawthorne, Calif., 1958-64; flight attendant Am. Airlines, L.A., 1964—, Civil Res. Air Fleet Mil. Missions, 2003. Mem. acad. coun. Diplomatic Acad., London; vice consul Internat. Biog. Ctr.; with Airlift Svcs. Solicitation, 2003—. Contbr. poems to anthologies, including Internat. Libr. Poetry, Noble House. Attended People to People Amb. Program's S. African Tour of Women Writers, 1998; active Civil Res. Air Fleet Mil. Missions, 2003; with Airlift Svcs. Solicitation, 2003—. Named to Internat. Libr. Poetry, 1996, 1997, 1998, 2002, 2004, 2005; recipient 7 Poetry Editor's Choice awards in anthologies. Mem.: Internat. Soc. Poets, Audie Murphy Rsch. Found., Acad. Am. Poets. Avocations: gardening, writing, skiing, mountain biking, home refurbishing. Home: 846 American Oaks Ave Newbury Park CA 91320-5572

LINDSEY, JOHN HORACE, insurance agency executive; b. Waxahachie, Tex., July 28, 1922; s. Harry E. and Marie (Smith) L.; m. Sara Houstoun, Aug. 30, 1946; children: Edwin (dec.), David C. BA, Tex. A&M U., 1944. Propr. Lindsey Ins. Agy., Houston, 1953—2002. Past bd. regents Texas A&M U. Sys. Former v.p. Houston Mus. Fine Arts; former pres. Alley Theatre; former bd. dirs. South Tex. Coll. Law, Tex. A&M Rsch. Found., College Station; bd. dirs. George Bush Presdl. Libr. Found.; pres. Tex. A&M U. Alumni, 1964; former vice chmn. bd. visitors U.S. Mil. Acad.; bd. visitors Tex. A&M at Galveston. 1st lt. U.S. Army, WWII. Recipient Disting. Alumni award Tex. A&M U. Home: 3640 Willowick Houston TX 77019-1114 Office: Ste 1100 2001 Kirby Dr Houston TX 77019-6081

LINDSEY, JONATHAN ASMEL, academic administrator, school librarian, educator; b. Bulloch County, Ga., June 9, 1937; s. Joel Wesley and Ethel Iora (Stickland) L.; m. Edythe Annette Loewer, Apr. 3, 1965; children: Julianna Elizabeth, Jonathan Edward AB, George Washington U., 1961; BD, So. Bapt. Sem., Louisville, 1964; PhD, So. Bapt. Sem., 1968; MSLS, U. Ala., 1975. Assoc. prof., libr. Judson Coll., Marion, Ala., 1967-77; assoc. dean, libr. Meredith Coll., Raleigh, NC, 1977-83; libr. Baylor U., Waco, Tex., 1983-89, dir. found. devel., 1989-95, dir. donor info. and recognition, 1995-2001, asst. v.p. donor and info. svcs., 2001—. Author librarianship and profl. fund raising, 1988—. Author: (monographs) Free To Be, 1975, Change and Challenge, 1978, Professional Ethics and Librarians, 1985, Performance Evaluation: A Management Basic, 1986; editor: N.C. Libraries (H.W. Wilson award 1981), 1979-83, contbr. articles and book revs. to profl. publs. Mem. Waco Peace Alliance, PTA. Mem. ALA, Assn. Profl. Rschrs. in Advancement, Assn. Fundraising Profls., Coun. for Advancement and Support of Edn., Tex. Libr. Assn. Home: 8265 Mosswood Dr Waco TX 76712-2407 Office: Baylor U One Bear Pl #97026 Waco TX 76798-7026 Office Phone: 254-710-3801. Business E-Mail: jonathan_lindsey@baylor.edu.

LINDSEY, JOYCE W., secondary school educator; b. Wharton, N.J. d. Charles F.V. and Mae Elizabeth Wakefield; m. Richard Lindsey (div.); children: L. Robin, Leslie Carol. BA, Univ. Del., Newark, Del., 1949. Curator Biochemical Rsch. Found., Newark, Del., 1952—53; sec. to sci. chair Univ. Denver, Newark, Del., 1952—53; data sys. analyst E. dupont de Neourssing, Wilmington, Del., 1954—57; asst. registrar Univ. Del., Newark, Del., 1961—66; english tchr. John Dickinson H.S., Stauton, Del., 1966—89. Curriculm sec. chair Stanton Sch. Dist., Stauton, Del., 1969—70; workshop chaired Lang. Arts Leaner Object, 1975. Vol. Prime Hook Nat. Wild Refuge, Milton, Del., 1990—; pres. Milton Century Club, Milton, Del., 1989—, Broadkill Beach Preservation Assn., Milton, 1993—. Recipient President Bush award, 2004. Mem.: Friends of PrimeHook MWR (founder 1997), Del. State Fedr. Womens Club (conservation chair). Avocations: gardening, politics, reading, quilting. Home: 106 Virgina Ave Milton DE 19968

LINDSEY, LAWRENCE BENJAMIN, economist; b. Peekskill, N.Y., July 18, 1954; s. Merritt Hunt and Helen Ruth (Hissam) Lindsey; m. Susan Ann McGrath, Aug. 28, 1982; 3 children. AB magna cum laude, Bowdoin Coll., Brunswick, Maine, 1976; MA, Harvard U., 1981, PhD, 1985; JD (hon.), Bowdoin Coll., 1993. Economist Coun. Econ. Advisers, Washington, 1981—84; from asst. prof. to assoc. prof. Harvard U., Cambridge, Mass., 1984—90; faculty rsch. fellow Nat. Bur. Econ. Rsch., Mass., 1984—89; from assoc. dir. to spl. asst. to Pres., Office of Policy Devel., The White House, Washington, 1989—91; gov. Fed. Res. Bd., 1991—97; resident scholar Am. Enterprise Inst., 1997—2001; mng. dir. Econ. Strategies, Inc., 1997—2001; asst. to Pres. for econ. policy The White House, Washington, 2001—02, dir. Nat. Econ. Coun., 2001—02; pres., CEO Lindsey Group, 2003—. Author:

The Growth Experiment, 1990, Economic Puppetmasters: Lessons From the Halls of Power, 1999; contbr. articles to profl. jours. Recipient Walter Wriston award, Manhattan Inst., 1988, Disting. Pub. Svc. award, Boston Bar Assn., 1994.

LINDSEY, ROBERTA LEWISE, music researcher, historian; b. Munich, Apr. 23, 1958; d. Fred S. and Elsie E. (White) L. BMus, Butler U., 1980, MMus, 1987; PhD, Ohio State U., 1996. Pres., owner Profl. Typing Svcs., Indpls., 1980-84; mktg. specialist Merchants Mortgage Corp., Indpls., 1985-87; exec. asst. Ind. Arts Commn., Indpls., 1988-90; GTA Ohio State U., Columbus, 1990-94, music libr. asst., 1991-93, student coord. music in Ohio festival, 1993, vol. tutor coord., 1994-95, lectr. Marion, 1995; rsch. editor Ind. High Tech. Directory, 1995-97; lectr. Ind. U. Sch. Music, 1998, vis. asst. prof. Indianapolis, 1999—2001, asst. prof. Indpls., 2001—, advisor music minor program, 2000—. Rep. Susan Porter Meml. symposium Ohio State U., Columbus, 1995; program com. AMS Midwest, 2001—02; vis. rsch. fellow Am. Music Rsch. Ctr., 1997; tchr. of record Digital Music Libr. Grant project Ind. U., 2000—05; reader IUPress, 2004—; presenter and spkr. nat. and internat. confs. Book reviewer Ohioana Jour., 1997—2002, contbg. editor Lenten Devotional, 2000—01; contbr. articles to profl. jours. Reader Ctrl. Ind. Radio Reading, Inc., Indpls., 1985-90; co-founder, Grad. Music Students Assn., Ohio State U., Columbus; multicultural diversity com. Coun. of Grad. Students, Columbus, 1992, orgns. and elections com., 1992, co-chair orientation com., 1993; pre-concert lectr. Carmel Symphony Orch., 1998; active Inst. Rep. for the Arts, 1999—, IUPUI/Eiteljorg; adv. bd. Eiteljorg Mus., 1999—, docent, 2004—. Recipient Grad. Student Alumni Rsch. award, Ohio State U., 1993, Innovative Teaching Recognition award, Ind. U. Sch. Music, 2002; grantee Dena Epstein grantee, 2001, Ind. U. Purdue U. Indpls., 2001. Mem. Soc. Am. Music, Am. Musicol. Soc. (prof. com. 2001—, program com. midwest chpt. 2001-02), Coll. Music Soc. (Gt. Lakes chpt. conv. 2001-02), Soc. Ethnomusicology, Am. Music Rsch. Ctr. Office Phone: 317-278-7868. Business E-Mail: rlindsey@iupui.edu.

LINDSEY, SETH MARK, lawyer; b. L.A., Oct. 18, 1947; s. Seth Rankin and Lela Belle L.; m. Susan Adelaide Badger, June 29, 1968; 1 child, Samantha. BA, U. So. Calif., L.A., 1968; JD, Yale U., 1971. Bar: Calif. 1972, U.S. Supreme Ct. 1984. Honors atty. Housing and Urban Devel., Washington, 1971-72, atty., 1972-76; asst. chief counsel Fed. Railroad Adminstrn., Washington, 1976-86, chief counsel, 1986—, acting adminstr., 1993, 2001. Spl. counsel for Conrail and Union Sta. Redevel. Fed. Railroad Adminstrn., 1984-86. Recipient Silver medal Dept. Transp., 1977, 83, Gold medal, 1984, Presdl. Rank award 2003. Baptist. Office: Dept Transp Fed RR Adminstrn 1120 Vermont Ave NW Ms 10 Washington DC 20590-0001 Office Phone: 202-493-6052. E-mail: mark.lindsey@fra.dot.gov.

LINDSEY, SUSAN LYNDAKER, zoologist; b. Valley Forge, Pa., Aug. 23, 1956; d. Howard Paul and Lillian Irene (Whitman) Lyndaker; m. Kevin Arthur Lindsey, July 17, 1982; children: Ryan Howard, Shannon Marie. BS in Biology, St. Lawrence U., 1978; MA in Zoology, So. Ill. U., Carbondale, 1980; PhD in Zoology, Colo. State U., 1987. Rschr. St. Lawrence U., Kenya, East Africa, 1978; tchr. Beth Jacob H.S., Denver, 1986-87; rschr. mammal dept. Dallas Zoo, 1988-93; exec. dir. Wild Canid Survival and Rsch. Ctr., Eureka, Mo., 1993—. Adj. prof. Cedar Valley Coll., 1992-93, So. Ill. U., Carbondale, 1996—; mgmt. group mem. Red Wolf Species Survival Plan, Tacoma, Wash., 1994—, Mexican Gray Wolf Species Survival Plan, Albuquerque, 1993—, Maned Wolf Species Survival Plan, Washington, 1999—. Author: (with others) The Okapi: Mysterious Animal of Congo-Zaire, 1999; contbr. articles to profl. jours. Docent Denver Zool. Found., Denver Zoo, 1985-88. Recipient Disting. Alumni citation, St. Lawrence U., 2003. Mem. Acad. Sci. St. Louis, Am. Zoo and Aquarium Assn., Am. Behavior Soc., Am. Soc. of Mammalogists, Beta Beta Beta, Phi Beta Kappa, Psi Chi. Avocations: horseback riding, canoeing, gardening, photography, travel. Office: Wild Canid Survival Rsch Ctr Wash U PO Box 760 Eureka MO 63025-0760 Office Phone: 636-938-5900.

LINDSEY, TOMMIE, secondary school educator; BA, U. San Francisco, 1973, BS, 1976. Cert. secondary tchg. U. San Francisco, 1976. Tchr. Alameda County Ct. Schs., 1975—80, El Rancho Verde H.S., 1980—88; tchr., head coach speech and debate team James Logan H.S., Union City, Calif., 1988—. Named MacArthur Fellow, John D. and Catherine T. MacArthur Found., 2004; named to KEY Coch Soc., Nat. Forensic League, 2004. Office: James Logan HS 1800 H St Union City CA 94587*

LINDSTROM, DONALD FREDRICK, JR., priest, counselor, consultant; b. Atlanta, July 18, 1943; s. Donald Fredrick Sr. and Elizabeth (Haynes) Lindstrom; m. Marcia Pace, Dec. 30, 1983; children: Christopher Pennewill, Ashley Pennewill, Ellison Pennewill, Eric. ABJ, U. Ga., 1966; MDiv, Va. Theol. Sem., 1969; JD, Woodrow Wilson Coll. Law, 1977; postgrad., U. West Fla., 1984. Lic. marriage and family therapist, Fla., Ala. Broadcast journalist radio and TV, Atlanta and N.Y.C., 1961-68; priest Episcopal ch., 1969—; detective sgt. Atlanta Police Dept., 1970-75; rector St. Thomas Episcopal Church, Greenville, Ala., 1997—. Ecumenical officer Diocese of Ctrl. Gulf Coast, 1989—91, 2002—05, Miss., 1992—97; mem. standing com. commn. on conflict resolution Eccles. Ct., 2005—; bd. visitors Kanuga Conf. Ctr., 1993—; guest chaplain U.S. Ho. of Reps., 1994; mem. ecumenical staff gen. conv. Episcopal Ch., 1994; bd. dirs. Ecclesiastical Ct., 2005—; pvt. practice marriage and family therapist, Pensacola, Fla., 1983—91, Greenville, Ala., 2004—. Writer, producer The Cry for Help, The Autumn Years; contbr. articles to profl. publs. Chaplain Atlanta Police Dept., 1975-78, Meridian Police Dept., 1995-97, Butler County (Ala.) Area Law Enforcement, 1998—; pres. N.W. Fla. chpt. Nat. Kidney Found., 1987-88; mem. Leadership Atlanta, 1975; bd. dirs. Leadership Pensacola; trustee Fla. Trust for Hist. Preservation. Mem. Am. Assn. for Marriage and Family Therapy (clin.), Mental Health Assn. (life, bd. dirs. Pensacola 1986-88), Internat. Conf. Police Chaplains, Rotary Internat., Navy League, Order of Holy Cross (assoc.), Chambellan Provincial, Bronze star of Excellence, Confrerie de la Chaine des Rotisseurs, Bailli Honoraire, Bailliage de Meridian, FOP, Alpha Tau Omega, Sigma Delta Chi, Di Gamma Kappa. Avocations: music, photography, travel, fly fishing.

LINDSTROM, ERIC EVERETT, ophthalmologist; b. Helena, Mont., Nov. 28, 1936; s. Everett Harry and Nan Augusta (Johnson) L.; m. Nancy Jo Alexander, July 24, 1960; children: Laura Ann, Eric Everett. BS, Wheaton Coll., 1958; MD, U. Md., 1963; MPH, Harvard U., 1966. Diplomate Am. Bd. Preventive Medicine, Am. Bd. Ophthalmology. Intern Madigan Army Med. Ctr., Tacoma, 1963-64; resident in aerospace medicine Sch. Aerospace Medicine, Brooks AFB, Tex., 1966-68; resident in ophthalmology Brooke Army Med. Ctr., Ft. Sam Houston, Tex., 1972-75; surgeon 12th combat aviation group U.S. Army, Vietnam, 1968-69; chief profl. svcs. and aviation medicine Beach Army Hosp., Ft. Wolters, Tex., 1969-72; asst. chief ophthalmology clinic Madigan Army Med. Ctr., Tacoma, 1975-76; with Lindstrom Eye Clinic, 1987—; med. dir. Palo Pinto County (Tex.) Mental Health Clinic, 1970-72; ret. Cons. Tex. State Rehab. Com., 1971-72; chmn. bd. trustees South Ctrl. Regional Med. Ctr., 1982-2001; sr. aviation med. examiner, FAA; flight surgeon Miss. Air N.G. (ret.). Deacon First Bapt. Ch., Laurel, Miss., 1978—; bd. dirs. Laurel Salvation Army, Good Shepherd Clin., Laurel. Decorated Bronze Star, Air medal with 2 oak leaf clusters, Meritorious Svc. medal. Fellow ACS, Am. Coll. Physician Execs., Am. Coll. Preventive Medicine, Aerospace Med. Assn. (pres.), Am. Acad. Ophthalmology; mem. AMA, Am. Acad. Cataract and Refractive Surgery, New Orleans Acad. Ophthalmology, Miss. Med. Assn. (trustee), Miss. Hosp. Assn. (bd. govs.), South Miss. Med. Soc., So. Med. Assn. (councilor), Flying Physicians Assn., Soc. Mil. Ophthalmologists, Soc. USAF and US Army Flight Surgeons, Alliance Air N.G. Flight Surgeons, Aircraft Owners and Pilots Assn., Kiwanis, Nu Sigma Nu. Home: 809 Cherry Ln Laurel MS 39440-1651 Office: Lindstrom Eye Clinic PO Box 407 Laurel MS 39441-0407 Office Phone: 601-426-9454. E-mail: drelindstrom@c-gate.net.

LINDSTROM, GREGORY P., lawyer; b. Hollywood, Calif., Aug. 4, 1953; AB summa cum laude, UCLA, 1975; JD, U. Chgo., 1978. Bar: Calif. 1978. With Latham & Watkins, 1978—, former mng. ptnr., Orange County office, now mng. ptnr., San Francisco office. Fellow Am. Coll. Trial Lawyers; mem. Phi Beta Kappa. Office: Latham & Watkins 505 Montgomery St Ste 2000 San Francisco CA 94111-2552 Office Phone: 415-391-0600. Business E-Mail: gregory.lindstrom@lw.com.

LINDSTRÖM, LARS ERNST SIMON, education educator; b. Lund, Sweden, Sept. 8, 1943; s. Henning and Gunhild (Strindfors) L.; stepmother Ruth (Håkansson) L.; m. Barbara Kucha, July 13, 1996; children: Simon, Amanda. BA, Lund U., 1966, MA, 1970; PhD in Edn., Stockholm U., 1986. Lic. psychologist, Sweden. Lectr. Stockholm Sch. Social Work, Sweden, 1973-76; asst. prof. U. Coll. Arts, Crafts, and Design, Stockholm, 1976-90; rsch. assoc. Stockholm Inst. Edn./Stockholm U., 1990-94; prof. edn. Stockholm Inst. Edn., 1995—. Cons. The Municipality of Stockholm, 1975—80; vis. scholar Harvard U., Cambridge, Mass., 1991; chmn. Nordic Network Rschrs. in Visual Arts Edn., 1994—97; project coord. Comenius 3.1 program European Union, 1997—99; vis. prof. Linköping (Sweden) U., 1999; sci. advisor Nat. Swedish Bd. of Health and Welfare; mem. governing bd. Stockholm Inst. Edn., 2000—03; external evaluator Norwegian Min. Edn., 2001; mem. Swedish Rsch. Coun., 2003—05. Author: Managing Alcoholism, 1992; editor: Nordic Visual Arts Research, 1998, The Cultural Context, 2000, Technology Education in New Perspectives, 2005, Educational Assessment, 2005; mem. editl. bd. Comenius-Jahrbuch, 2002—; contbr. articles to profl. jours. and books. Lutheran. Home: Urbergsvägen 20 SE-16764 Bromma Sweden Office: Stockholm Inst Edn Box 34103 SE-10026 Stockholm Sweden E-mail: Lars.Lindstrom@lhs.se.

LINDSTROM, NAOMI EVA, language educator; b. Chgo., Nov. 21, 1950; d. Frederick and Lora Lindstrom. AB, U. Chgo., 1971; MA, Ariz. State U., 1972, PhD, 1975. Asst. prof. U. Tex., Austin, 1975-82, assoc. prof., 1982-90, prof., 1990—. Mem. adv. bd. Brazilian and L.Am. Study Project Ctr. Jewish History, 2005—. Author: Jewish Issues in Argentine Literature, 1989, Women's Voice in Latin American Literature, 1989, Jorge Luis Borges: A Study of the Short Fiction, 1990, Twentieth-Century Spanish American Fiction, 1994, The Social Conscience of Latin American Writing, 1998, Early Spanish American Narrative, 2004; editor (with C. Virgillo): Woman as Myth and Metaphor in Latin American Literature, 1985; mem. editl. bd. Studies Latin Am. Popular Culture, 1981—, Chasqui, 1995—2005, Studies in 20th and 21st Century Literature, 1996—, L.Am. Heritage Series, 1996—; lit. editor: Rocky Mountain Rev., 1980—87, assoc. editor: Sociol. Inquiry, 1997—, L.Am. Rsch. Rev., 2001—. Fellow, Ariz. State U., 1972—75; grantee, Andrew W. Mellon Found., 1983, 1985, 1990, 1994, 1995; scholar, U. Chgo., 1967—71. Mem.: MLA (mem. exec. com. Sephardic studies 1992—96, chmn. Sephardic studies 1995—96, mem. exec. com. divsn. 20th century L.Am., chmn. 1989—90), L.Am. Jewish Studies Assn. (v.p. 1996—2003, mgr. electronic list 1996—), L.Am. Studies Assn. Home: 2210 Enfield Rd Apt 5 Austin TX 78703-3241 Office: U Tex at Austin Benedict Hall 4 116 Austin TX 78712 Office Phone: 512-232-4527. Business E-Mail: lindstrom@mail.utexas.edu.

LINDVIG, LEONA MINDELL, librarian, educator; b. Bremerton, Wash., Sept. 18, 1946; d. Edward and Adene Mindell (Lynum) Vig; m. James David Selin, Nov. 27, 1969 (div. 1977); 1 child: Korin Nicole; m. Paul Wallace Johnson, May 21, 1977 (div. 2000); children: Gunnar, Turi, Ole-Paul. BA in Psychology, Western Wash. U., 1969; forest technician cert., Peninsula Coll., 1975; MEd, Central Wash. U., 1994. Cert. tchr. K-8, Wash. Forest engr. Crown Zellerbach, Sekiu, Wash., 1975-77; forest tech. U.S. Forest Svc., Cle Elum, Wash., 1978; libr. Roslyn (Wash.) Pub. Libr., 1978-96, Carpenter Meml. Libr., Cle Elum, 1980-81; libr. II Clallam Bay (Wash.) Correctional Ctr., 1990; grad. asst. Ctrl. Wash. U., Ellensburg, Wash., 1992-93, libr. specialist, 1996—2004, libr. media specialist, instr., 2004—. Substitute tchr. Cle Elum (Wash.)-Roslyn Sch., 1994-96. Scholar AAUW, 1992. Office: Cen Wash U Ednl Tech Ctr Library Ellensburg WA 98926

LINDZEN, RICHARD SIEGMUND, meteorologist, educator; b. Webster, Mass., Feb. 8, 1940; s. Abe and Sara (Blachman) L.; m. Nadine Lucie Kalougine, Apr. 7, 1965; children: Eric, Nathaniel. AB, Harvard U., 1960, SM, 1961, PhD, 1964. Research assoc. U. Wash., Seattle, 1964-65; Research asso. U. Oslo, 1965-66; with Nat. Center Atmospheric Research, Boulder, Colo., 1966-68; mem. faculty U. Chgo., 1968-72; prof. meteorology Harvard U., 1972-83, dir. Center for Earth and Planetary Physics, 1980-83; Alfred P. Sloan prof. meteorology MIT, 1983—. Lady Davis vis. prof. Hebrew U., 1979; Sackler prof. Tel Aviv U., 1992; Vikram Sarabhai prof. Phys. Rsch. Lab., Ahmendabad, India, 1985; Lansdowne lectr. U. Victoria, 1993; Haurwitz lectr. Am. Meteorol. Soc., 1997; cons. NASA, Jet Propulsion Lab., others; corr. mem. com. on human rights NAS. Author: Dynamics in Atmospheric Physics; co-author: Atmospheric Tides; contbr. to profl. jours. Recipient Macelwane award Am. Geophys. Union, 1968 Fellow NAS, AAAS, Am. Geophys. Union, Am. Meteorol. Soc. (Meisinger award 1969, councillor 1972-75, Charney award 1985, Haurwitz lectr. 1997), Am. Acad. Arts and Scis., Norwegian Acad. Scis. and Letters; mem. Internat. Commn. Dynamic Meteorology, Institut Mondial des Scis. (founding mem.). Jewish. Office: MIT 54 1720 Cambridge MA 02139

LINEEN, EDWARD M., lawyer, information technology executive; b. 1941; BS, JD, Fordham U. Bar: N.Y. 1971. Atty. IBM, Armonk, NY, 1970—83, counsel sales & distbn., 1983—85, counsel comm. & tech. group, 1985—89, gen. counsel personal computer group, 1989—94, v.p. & assist. gen. counsel products, intellectual property, 1995—2002, sr. v.p., gen. counsel, 2002—. Exec. leader People with Disabilities Exec. Task Force, IBM. Office: IBM 1 New Orchard Rd Armonk NY 10504 Office Phone: 914-499-4836. E-mail: lineen@us.ibm.com.

LINEN, JONATHAN S., diversified financial services company executive; With Am. Express, 1969—; pres., CEO, dir. mktg. group and travelers cheque group Am. Express Co. Travel Related Svcs., 1988-90; pres., CEO Shearson Lehman Bros., 1990—92; pres., COO Am. Express Travel Related Svcs., 1992—93; vice chmn. Am. Express, N.Y.C., 1993—. Office: Am Express 200 Vesey St New York NY 10285-1000

LINETT, DAVID, retired lawyer; b. Perth Amboy, N.J., Apr. 9, 1934; s. Jack K. and Anne L.; children: Jon, Peter, Maren. BA, Yale U., 1956; JD, Harvard U., 1959. Bar: D.C. 1959, N.J. 1960. Law sec. to assignment judge Superior Ct. NJ, 1959—60; assoc. Gross, Weissberger & Linett, New Brunswick, N.J., 1960-62, ptnr., 1962-77; prosecutor Somerset County, N.J., 1977-82; of counsel Lowenstein, Sandler, Brochin, Kohl et al and predecessor, Roseland and Somerville, N.J., 1982-85; ptnr. Gindin & Linett, Bridgewater, NJ, 1985—2004. Chmn. N.J. State Bar Com. on Programs for Law Enforcement Personnel, 1978-80; mem. com. on county dist. cts. N.J. Supreme Ct., 1980-82, mem. Post-Indictment Delay Task Force, 1980, dist. XIII ethics com., 1986-90, chair N.J. Supreme Ct., 1989-90, ethics fin. com., 1990-94, treas., 1992-94; gen. counsel United Heritage Bank, 1997-2004. Mem. N.J. Dem. State Com., 1973-77; bd. dirs. Somerset County Resource Ctr. for Women and Their Families, 1982-83; chmn. bd. trustees, Assn. for Advancement of Mentally Handicapped, 1987-89; commr. N.J. Election Law Enforcement Commn., 1987-2000, vice chair, 1996-2000; mem. Ct. House study com., Somerset County Bd. Freeholders, 1979-82; gen.chmn. Rotary Internat. Task Force on Edn. and Tng., 2001-02. Mem. ABA (corp., real property law sect.), Nat. Dist. Attys. Assn. (nat. treas., exec. com. 1981-82, Pres.'s award for outstanding svc. as chmn. fin. com. 1982), New Brunswick Bar Assn. (pres. 1974), N.J. Bar Assn. (land use sect., real property sect.), Somerset County Bar Assn., Somerset County C. of C. (bd. dirs. 1984-90, Outstanding Citizen of Yr. 1989), Rotary (pres. 1986-87, dist. gov. 1991-92, internat. bd. dirs. 2004—). E-mail: ginlin@aol.com.

LINFANTE, ITALO, preventive medicine physician, educator; b. Matera, Italy, Nov. 12, 1962; came to U.S., 1990; s. Felice Linfante and Carolina Atella. MD with honors, U. Rome, 1987. Diplomate Am. Bd. Psychiatry and Neurology. Vis. assoc. NIH, Bethesda, Md., 1990-94; resident George Washington U., Washington, 1994-95, Baylor Coll. Medicine, Houston, 1995-98; faculty Harvard Med. Sch., Boston, 1998—2002, fellow interventional neuroradiology, 2002—. Mem. Am. Heart Assn., Am. Acad. Neurology, Am. Coll. Radiology, Am. Soc. Interventional and Therapeutic Neuroradiology. Office: Harvard Med Sch BIDMC Palmer 126 330 Brookline Ave Boston MA 02215

LINFORD, RULON KESLER, physicist, electrical engineer; b. Cambridge, Mass., Jan. 31, 1943; s. Leon Blood and Imogene (Kesler) L.; m. Cecile Tadje, Apr. 2, 1965; children: Rulon Scott, Laura Linford Williams, Hilary Linford Henderson, Philip Leon. BSEE, U. Utah, 1966; MSEE, MIT, 1969, PhD in Elec. Engring., 1973. Staff CTR-7 Los Alamos (N.Mex) Nat. Lab., 1973-75, asst. group leader CTR-7, 1975-77, group leader CTR-11, 1977-79, program mgr., group leader compact toroid CTR-11, 1979-80, program mgr., asst. divsn. leader compact toroid CTR divsn., 1980-81, assoc. CTR divsn. leader, 1981-86, program dir. magnetic fusion energy, 1986-89, program dir., divsn. leader CTR divsn. office, 1989-91, program dir. nuc. sys., 1991-93, staff LER, 1993-94; coord. sci. and tech. U. Calif., 1994-97; assoc. vice provost lab. programs Office of the Pres., U. Calif., Oakland, 1997—2001, assoc. vice provost, 2001—03, asst. v.p. lab. programs, 2003—04; ret., 2004. Contbr. articles to profl. jours. Recipient E. O. Lawrence award Dept. of Energy, Washington, 1991. Fellow Am. Phys. Soc. (exec. com. 1982, 90-91, program com. 1982, 85, award selection com. 1983, 84, fellowship com. 1986); mem. AAAS, Sigma Xi. Home: 1055 Aquarius Way Oakland CA 94611-1939 E-mail: cecile.rulon@comcast.net.

LING, JAHJA WANG-CHIEH, conductor; b. Jakarta, Indonesia, Oct. 25, 1951; came to U.S., 1970; s. Bok-Som and Eng-Nio (Kwee) L.; m. Jane Yuan, May 8, 1976 (div.), Jessie Chang, Jan. 1, 2001; children: Gabriel En-Wei, Daniel En-Hao, Priscilla, Stephanie. BMus, Julliard Sch., 1974, MMus, 1975; DMus Arts, Yale U., 1980. Asst. conductor San Francisco Symphony, 1981-83, assoc. conductor, 1983-84, Cleve. Orch., 1984-85, resident conductor, 1985—2003; music dir. Fla. Orch., Tampa, 1988—2002, San Diego Symphony Orch., 2004—. Founding music dir. San Francisco Symphony Youth Orch., 1981-84, Cleve. Orch. Youth Orch., 1986-96; music dir. San Francisco Conservatory Orch., 1981-84; co-dir. Tanglewood (Mass.) Young Artists Orch., 1983-84; guest conductor Boston Symphony, Phila. Orch., Minn. Orch., Nat. Symphony in D.C. Recipient Bronze medal Artur Rubinstein Internat. Piano Competition, 1977, Seaver/NEA Conductors award, 1988; Leonard Bernstein fellow Tanglewood Music Ctr., 1980, Exxon/Arts Endowment conductor Affiliate Artists, 1981-84. Home: 1458 Woodglen Ter Bonita CA 91902-4283 E-mail: jahjaling@yahoo.com.

LING, JIAN, research scientist, consultant; b. Chongqing, China, July 6, 1954; came to the U.S., 1994; s. Guangquan Ling and Shufang Xu; m. Huilian Wu, Dec. 10, 1982; 1 child, Yun. BS, Chongqing U., 1982; MS, Fla. Internat. U., 1996, PhD, 1999. Mech. engr. Jiangyou Power Plant, Sichuan, China, 1982-85; asst. prof. Chongqing U., 1988-94, head tchg. and rsch. divsn. in thermal engring., 1992-94; rsch. asst. Fla. Internat. U., Miami, 1994-97, tchg. asst., 1997-99, rsch. assoc., 1999-2000, rsch. scientist, 2001—. Cons. Jiangyou Power Plant, Sichuan, 1988-94. Co-author: Industrial Steam Turbine, 1994; contbr. articles to profl. jours. Mem. ASME (assoc.). Office: Fla Internat Univ 1261 HCET Bldg 10555 W Flagler St Miami FL 33174-1630 Home: 3771 E Kemper Rd Apt 1 Cincinnati OH 45251-2133 E-mail: jianl@hcet.fiu.edu.

LING, NAM, dean; b. Singapore, Dec. 9, 1956; s. Yu-Chich Ling and Siew-Chee Chen; m. Mei-Yan Lu, Dec. 3, 1994; children: Grace, Sophia. PhD, U. La., 1989. Product, process engr. Hewlett Packard, Singapore, 1981—83; asst. prof. Santa Clara (Calif.) U., 1989—94, assoc. prof., 1994—2001, prof., 2001—, assoc. dean, 2002—. Author: Specification and Verification of Systolic Arrays, 1999; contbr. articles over 90 articles to profl. jours., chapters to books. Interpreter Chinese Ch. in Christ, Mountain View, Calif., 1996—2000. Named IEEE Disting. Lectr., 2002—; recipient Rsch. Initiation award, NSF, 1990—93, Rschr. of Yr. award, 2000, Recent Achievement in Scholarship award, 2002; grantee, Nortel Networks, 2000, New Japan Radio Corp., 1995—97, 1997—99, Medianix Semiconductor, Inc., 1997—98. Mem.: IEEE (sr.; assoc. editor 1990—, tech. com. chair 1993—95), Am. Soc. for Engring. Edn., Assn. for Computing Machinery. Avocation: travel. Office: Santa Clara U Dept Computer Engring 500 El Camino Real Santa Clara CA 95053

LING, TA-YUNG, physicist; b. Shanghai, Feb. 2, 1943; married, 1969; 3 children. BS, Tunghai U., Taiwan, 1964; MS, U. Waterloo, Ont., Can., 1966; PhD in Physics, U. Wis., 1971. Rsch. asst. U. Wis., 1967-71; rsch. assoc. physics U. Pa., Phila., 1972-75, asst. prof., 1975-77; from asst. prof. to assoc. prof. Ohio State U., Columbus, 1977-83, prof. physics, 1983—. Recipient Outstanding Jr. Investigator award Dept. of Energy, 1977. Mem. Am. Phys. Soc. Achievements include research in experimental high energy physics; deep inelastic neutrino-nucleon scattering, neutrino masses and mixing, neutrino oscillations, deep inelastic electron-proton scattering, high energy proton-proton collisions. Office: Dept Physics 191 W Woodruff Ave Columbus OH 43210-1117 E-mail: ling@mps.ohio-state.edu.

LING, VICTOR, oncologist, educator; b. Mar. 16, 1943; BS in Biochemistry, U. Toronto, 1966; PhD in Biochemistry, U. BC, 1971. Staff scientist Ont. Cancer Inst., Toronto, 1971-98, head divsn. molecular and structural biology, 1989-98; asst. dean, prof., dept. biochemistry & molecular biology U Brit Columbia, Vancouver, 1998—, prof., dept. of pathology & lab. medicine, 1998—; v.p., resch.,assoc. vice-chair BC Cancer Rsch Ctr., Vancouver, Canada, 1995—. Prof. med. biophysics U. Toronto, 1983-95, mem. coun. sch. grad. studies, 1984-90, mem. faculty of medicine rsch. com., 1985-95, vice-chmn., 1988—; mem. study sect. of experimental therapeutics Nat. Insts. of Health, USA, 1986—; bd. govs. Wellesly Hosp. Rsch. Inst., 1988-90; mem. MRC scholarship com. Med. Rsch. Coun. of Can., 1988—, bd. sci. advisors Hong Kong Inst. Biotech., 1989—, adv. bd. Internat. Jour. Anti-cancer Drugs, 1990—, external adv. com. U. Wis. Clin. Cancer Ctr., 1990—, bd. sci. counselors divsn. cancer treatment Nat. Insts. of Health, 1990—; bd. dirs. Hosp. for Sick Children Found., 1992—. Assoc. editor Cancer Rsch., 1986—, Jour. Cellular Physiology, 1989—, Jour. Cellular Pharmacology, 1989—, Jour. Molecular Pharmacology, 1992—, Jour. Biomed. Sci., 1992-; contbr. to 180 peer-reviewed publs. Victoria U. Alumni scholar in Life Scis., 1965, Centennial fellow MRC of Can., 1969-71; recipient C. Chester Stock award Meml. Sloan-Kettering Cancer Ctr., 1988, Cancer Rsch. award The Milken Family Med. Found., 1988, Merit award The FCCP (Ont.) Edn. Found., 1989, Internat. award Gairdner Found., 1990, Charles F. Kettering prize GM Cancer Rsch. Found., 1991, Joseph Steiner Cancer Rsch. award, 1991 Fellow Royal Soc. Can.; mem. Am. Assn. Cancer Rsch. (bd. dirs. 1992—, Bruce F. Cain Meml. award 1993), Am. Soc. Cell Biology, Can. Cancer Soc. (bd. dirs. 1992—), Can. Soc. Cell Biology, Can. Biochem. Soc., Genetics Soc. Can., Can. Breast Cancer Rsch. Initiative, Nat. Cancer Inst., Hosp. for Sick Children Found., Toronto; mem. GM Adv. Council, Cancer Rsch. Found. Achievements include revolutionizing cancer therapy and research into chemotherapy resistance with his discovery of the membrane transport protein P-glycoprotein, a protein the resists anti-cancer drugs in 1974. Office: BC Cancer Rsch Ctr 601 West 10th Ave Vancouver BC V5Z 4E6 Canada Address: Dept Biochemistry and Molecular Biology Faculty of Medicine Univ of BC 2010-2146 Health Sciences Mall Vancouver BC V6T 1Z3 Canada Office Phone: 604-877-6010, 604-822-3178, 607-877-6000 2524, 604-877-6151. Office Fax: 604-822-5227, 604-877-6150. Business E-Mail: vling@bccancer.bc.ca.

LING, WALTER, neurologist, psychiatrist; b. Swatow, Canton, China, Apr. 3, 1937; came to U.S., 1964; s. K. H. and Sun (Ngo) L.; m. May Ann, Aug. 14, 1966; children: Pamela, Michelle, Deborah, Kimberly. Pre-med., Chulalonghorn U., Bangkok, Thailand, 1959, MD, 1963. Diplomate Am. Bd. Psychiatry and Neurology. Neurology resident Washington U. Med. Sch., St. Louis, 1965-68, psychiatry resident, 1968-70; assoc. dir. outpatient Malcolm Bliss Mental Health Ctr., St. Louis, 1970-71; chief drug dependence treatemtn ctr. VA Hosp., Sepulveda, Calif., 1971-84; med. dir. Friends Med. Sci. Rsch., Tarzana, Calif., 1976—82, 1990—98; neurologist, psychiatrist pvt. practice

Beverly Hills, Calif., 1971-94; med. dir. Health Care Delivery Svc., Beverly Hills, 1980—89, The Matrix Ctr., L.A.; dir. L.A. Addiction Treatment Rsch. Ctr., 1989—98; prof., chief substance abuse program UCLA Dept. Psychiatry and Biobehavioral Scis., Westwood, Calif., 1994—. Cons. in field; dir. Instnl. Rev. Bd. Contbr. articles to profl. jours. and book to chpt. Fellow Am. Acad. Neurology; mem. AMA, Calif. Med. Assn., L.A. County Med. Assn., Royal Coll. Psychiatrists. Achievements include service as chief of substance abuse treatment program UCLA; cons. for Nat. Inst. Drug Abuse and Nat. Inst. Alcohol Abuse and Alcoholism, U.S. Dept. State Internat. Narcotics Matters. Office: Ste 200 11075 Santa Monica Blvd Los Angeles CA 90025-7539 Office Phone: 310-312-0500. Business E-Mail: lwalter@ucla.edu.

LING, YIHE, medical researcher, educator; b. Ninbo, Zhejiang, China, Sept. 18, 1942; arrived in U.S., 1986; s. Shan Xing Ling and Xiang Yue Zhang; m. Ruoping Lin, Jan. 31, 1970. BS, Chinese Acad. Scis., Shanghai, China, 1966, PhD, 1982. Project investigator M. D. Anderson Cancer Ctr. U. Tex., Houston, 1988—91, asst. pharmacologist, 1991—98; rsch. asst. prof. NYU, N.Y.C., 1998—2001; asst. prof. Albert Einstein Coll. Medicine Yeshiva U., Bronx, NY, 2001—. Mem.: Am. Assn. Cancer Rsch. Office: Yeshiva U Albert Einstein Coll Medicine 1300 Morris Park Ave Bronx NY 10461

LINGEMAN, RICHARD ROBERTS, editor-in-chief, writer; b. Crawfordsville, Ind., Jan. 2, 1931; s. Byron Newton and Vera Frances (Spencer) L.; m. Anthea Judy Nicholson, Apr. 3, 1965; 1 child, Jenifer Kate. BA, Haverford Coll., 1953; postgrad., Yale U. Law Sch., 1956-58, Columbia U. Grad. Sch. Comparative Lit., 1958-60. Exec. editor Monocle mag., N.Y.C., 1960-69; assoc. editor, columnist N.Y. Times Book Review, 1969-78; exec. editor The Nation, N.Y.C., 1978-95, sr. editor, 1995—. Author: Drugs from A to Z, 1969, Don't You Know There's A War On?, 1971, reissued 2003, Small Town America, 1980, Theodore Dreiser: At the Gates of the City 1871-1907, 1986, Theodore Dreiser: An American Journey, 1908-1945, 1990 (Chgo. Sun-Times Book of Yr.), Sinclair Lewis: Rebel from Main Street, 2002, Paperback, 2005, Double Lives, 2006; mem. editl. bd. Dreiser Studies. Pres. 12 W. 96th Street Corp. With U.S. Army, 1953-56. NEH fellow. Mem. PEN, Authors Guild, Soc. Am. Historians, N.Y. Hist. Soc., Phi Beta Kappa. Office: Nation 33 Irving Pl New York NY 10003-2332

LINGENFELTER, SHERWOOD GALEN, academic administrator, retired anthropologist; b. Hollidaysburg, Pa., Nov. 18, 1941; s. Galen Miller and Kathern Margaretta (Rogers) L.; m. Judith Elaine Beaumont, Aug. 10, 1962; children: Jennifer Elaine, Joel Sherwood. BA, Wheaton Coll., 1963; PhD, U. Pitts., 1971. Dir. acad. advising U. Pitts., 1964-66; instr. SUNY, Brockport, 1966-67, asst. prof, 1969-74, assoc. prof., 1974-82, prof. anthropology, 1982-83; NIH predoctoral fellow U. Pitts., 1967-69; prof. Biola U., La Mirada, Calif., 1983-88, provost, sr. v.p., 1988-99; dean Sch. of World Mission Fuller Theol. Sem., Pasadena, Calif., 1999—2002, provost, sr. v.p., 2001—. Cons. in anthropology Summer Inst. Linguistics, Dallas, 1977-2003; tng. cons. Liebenzell Mission Am., Schooleys Mountain, NJ, 1981-89; evaluating cons. Trust Ter. of the Pacific Islands, Saipan, Mariana Islands, 1969-74. Author: Yap: Political Leadership, 1975, The Deni of Western Brazil, 1980, Ministering Cross-Culturally, 1986, Transforming Culture, 1992, 2d edit., 1998, Agents of Transformation, 1996, Teaching Cross-Culturally, 2003; editor: Political Development in Micronesia, 1974, Social Organization of Sabah Societies, 1990. Bd. dirs. Christian Scholars Rev., 1989-95, Grace Brethren Internat. Missions, 1994—; mem. Sr. Accrediting Commn. Western Assn. Schs. and Colls., 2000-. Recipient Disting. Tchg. award Biola U., 1987-88; grantee NSF, 1967-69, 79-81, SUNY Rsch. Found., 1970. Fellow Am. Anthrop. Assn., Soc. for Applied Anthropology, Am. Ethnol. Soc.; mem. Assn. Social Anthropology Oceania, Am. Conf. Acad. Deans. Democrat. Mem. Grace Brethern Ch. Office: Fuller Theol Sem Provost and Sr VP 135 N Oakland Ave Pasadena CA 91182-0001 Office Phone: 626-584-5205. Business E-Mail: provost@fuller.edu.

LINGERFELT, ALAN THOMAS, civil engineer, real estate executive; b. Richmond, Va., Sept. 10, 1954; s. Luther Harold and Mildred Juanita (Corvin) L.; m. Gwendolynn Montes Ferguson, Aug. 9, 1975; children— Jonathan Ryan, Justin Michael, Daniel Kenton, Catherine Elizabeth. BSCE, Va. Poly. Inst., State U., 1976; postgrad. MBA program Va. Commonwealth U., 1980. Cert. profl. engr., Va. Founder, pres. Lingerfelt & Assoc., Inc., Richmond, 1977—, Lingerfelt Devel. Corp., 1978—, founder, pres. Lingerfelt Mgmt. Corp., 1980—. Mem. Children's Hosp. Building Fund Raising Campaign, Nat. Right to Work Com., Am. Security Council, Derbyshire Baptist Ch. Recipient Eagle Scout award Boy Scouts Am., 1972. Mem. Nat. Soc. Profl. Engrs., ASCE (pres. central Va. chpt. 1979, dir. Va. sect. 1982-83), Am. Cons. Engrs. Council, Constrn. Specifications Inst., Am. Water Works Assn., Water Pollution Control Fedn., Am. Pub. Works Assn., Richmond Joint Engrs. Council (found. chmn. 1979), Va. Soc. Profl. Engrs. (chmn. pvt. practice sect. central chpt. 1981-82), Inst. Real Estate Mgmt., Nat. Assn. Indsl. and Office Parks (pres. Va. chpt. 1982, outstanding service award 1982), Nat. Assn. Corp. Real Estate Execs., U.S. C. of C., Va. C. of C. (Entrepreneur of the Yr., 1987), Richmond Real Estate Group. Richmond Board Realtors, Urban Land Inst. W. Richmond Bus. Men's Assn., Jaycees (outstanding young man Am. award 1982). Assoc. Gen. Contractors Va., Inc. Clubs: Westwood Racquet, Downtown (Richmond), Va. Power Boat Assn., Skidmore Hunt, Engrs. (Richmond). Lodge: Rotary Internat. (Paul Harris fellow 1987). Home: 9812 Ridge Meadow Pl Richmond VA 23233-5576 Office: PO Box 12 S 3rd St Richmond VA 23219-3702

LINGERFELT, B. EUGENE, JR., minister; b. Highland Park, Mich., Dec. 18, 1955; s. Beecher Eugene and Nellie Beatrice (Sampson) L.; m. Suzanne Marie Martin, Aug. 7, 1976; children: Austin Stuart, Krystina Marie. BA, Ctrl. Bible Coll., Springfield, Mo., 1976; MDiv, Tex. Christian U., 1980; D of Ministry, Southwestern Bapt. Theol., 1984. Ordained min. Cathedral of Praise Ch., 1984. Assoc. pastor Bethel Temple, Ft. Worth, 1978—82; missionary, guest lectr. East Africa Sch. of Theology, Nairobi, Kenya, 1982—83; marriage enrichment seminar spkr., 1983; founder, sr. pastor Cathedral of Praise, Arlington, Tex., 1984—. Founder Cathedral Christian Acad., 1988—; founder Overcoming Faith TV, 1994—. Author: The Spirit of Excellence, 1994, Compromise in the Modern Church, 1995, God's Very Own Child, 2000; co-author: Money: A Spiritual Force, 1985, You, Me & God, 1999, The God Touch, 2005; contbr. articles to religious jours. Named to Outstanding Young Men of Am., 1980. Republican. Office: Cathedral of Praise PO Box 121234 Arlington TX 76012-1234

LINGL, FRIEDRICH ALBERT, psychiatrist; b. Munich, Apr. 4, 1927; came to U.S., 1957, naturalized, 1962; s. Friedrich Hugo and Marie Luise (Lindner) L.; m. Leonore E. Trautner, Nov. 15, 1955; children— Herbert F., Angelika M. MD, Ludwig-Maxim U., Munich, 1952. Diplomate Am. Bd. Psychiatry and Neurology); cert. mental health adminstr. Intern Edward W. Sparrow Hosp., 1957-58; resident internal medicine City Hosp., Augsburg, Germany, 1953-54; resident psychiatry Columbus (Ohio) State Hosp., 1958-61; supt. Hawthornden State Hosp., Northfield, Ohio, 1963-66; dir. Cleve. Psychiat. Inst., 1966-72; pvt. practice, 1972-92; med. dir. Windsor Hosp., 1976-92, med. dir. emeritus, 1992—. Asst. clin. prof. Case Western Res. U., Cleve., 1970-97. Contbr. articles to med. jours. Fellow Am. Psychiat. Assn. (disting. life); mem. AMA, Ohio Med. Assn., Ohio Psychiat. Assn., Am. Assn. Psychiat. Adminstrs., Cleve. Psychiat. Soc. Address: 40 Farwood Dr Chagrin Falls OH 44022-6848 Personal E-mail: flingl@aol.com.

LINGLE, CRAIG STANLEY, glaciologist, educator; b. Carlsbad, N.Mex., Sept. 11, 1945; s. Stanley Orland and Margaret Pearl (Ewart) L.; m. Diana Lynn Duncan, Aug. 21, 1972; 1 son, Eric Glenn. BS, U. Wash., 1967; MS, U. Maine, 1978; PhD, U. Wis., 1983. Nat. rsch. coun. resident rsch. assoc. Coop. Inst. for Rsch. in Environ. Scis., U. Colo., Boulder, 1983-84, rsch. assoc., 1984-86; program mgr. polar glaciology divsn. polar programs NSF, Washington, 1986-87; cons. Jet Propulsion Lab., Pasadena, Calif., 1987-88; nat. rsch. coun. resident rsch. assoc. NASA Goddard Space Flight Ctr., Oceans and Ice Branch, Greenbelt, Md., 1988-90; rsch. assoc. prof. Geophys. Inst. U. Alaska, Fairbanks, 1990-2000, acting dir. Alaska synthetic aperture radar facility Geophys. Inst., 1997-98, rsch. prof. geophysics Geophys. Inst., 2000—, group leader snow, ice and permafrost Geophys. Inst., 2003—. Contbr. articles to profl. jours. Recipient Antarctic Svc. medal of U.S., NSF, 1987, Rsch. Project of Month award Office of Health and Environ. Rsch., U.S. Dept. Energy, 1990, Group Achievement award NASA, 1992. Mem. AAAS, Internat. Glaciological Soc., Am. Geophys. Union, Sigma Xi. Avocations: downhill and cross-country skiing, canoeing. Office: U Alaska Geophys Inst PO Box 757320 Fairbanks AK 99775-7320 Office Phone: 907-474-7679. E-mail: craig.lingle@gi.alaska.edu.

LINGLE, JOLYNN FLEISHMAN, writer, educator; b. Everett, Wash., June 20, 1938; d. Gustave A. and Sara M. Ruana; m. Ronald Martin Lingle, June 5, 1959; children: Kevin Todd, Gregory Scott. MS, Pepperdine U., Malibu CA, 1979; BA Home Economics, San Diego State U., San Diego CA, 1974. Cert. Childbirth Education U. of Calif., San Diego, 1978. IBM machine operator US Air Force, March AFB, Calif., 1957—59; IBM keypunch/machine operator San Diego State U., 1959—66, sr. clk., 1966—67; educator Pregnant Minor program San Diego Unified Schs., 1977—99; educator San Diego C.C., 1991—99. Adminstrv. intern Twain Jr Sr H.S., San Diego, 1988—89, accreditation writing coord., 1995—97; GED educator San Diego Unified Schs., 1994—99. Author: (feature article) Trailblazer, (directory) Alternative Education, San Diego Unified Schools. Spkr. San Diego Cmty., 1980—99; founder JoLynn Lingle Ann. Pregnant Minor Program Scholarship. A2c US Airforce, 1957—59, March AFB. Recipient Vol. of TheYear, San Diego Cmty. Svc. Assn., 1988-1989, Calif. State Tchr. of The Yr., CA Assn. of Family and Consumer Sciences, 1998, One of Top Ten Teachers In The Nation, Am. Assn. of Family and Consumer Sciences, 1998. Mem.: Am. Assn. of Family and Consumer Scis., Colo. Assn. of Family and Consumer Scis. (home and cmty. sect., state bd. dirs.). Home: 9081A Yarrow Street Westminster CO 80021

LINGLE, LINDA, governor; b. St. Louis, June 4, 1953; BJ, Calif. State U., Northridge, 1975. Mayor County of Maui, Hawaii; chair. Democratic Party of Hawaii; mem. Maui County Coun., 1980—90; mayor Maui County, 1990—98; chmn. Hawaii Republican Party, 1999—2001; gov. State of Hawaii, Honolulu, 2003—. Recipient Evelyn McPhail award, 2000. Republican. Jewish. Office: Off of the Gov State Capitol Executive Chambers Honolulu HI 96813 Address: PO Box 25111 Honolulu HI 96825

LINGLE, MARILYN FELKEL, writer, columnist; b. Hillsboro, Ill., Aug. 16, 1932; d. Clarence Frederick and Anna Cecelia (Stank) Felkel; m. Ivan L. Lingle, Oct. 4, 1950 (dec. Aug. 2001); children: Ivan Dale, Aimee Lee, Clarence Craig. Sec. Ill. State Police, 1950; with welfare dept. Ill. Pub. Aid, Hillsboro, 1951-52; rschr. Small Homes Coun., Champaign, 1952-53; sec. Hillsboro Schs., 1954; office, payroll clk. Eagle Picher Zinc, Hillsboro, 1955—56; continuity dir. Sta. WSMI, Litchfield, 1966—87. Adv. bd. Am. Savs. Bank/Citizens Savs. Bank, vice chmn., 1986-93; founder Dunsford Books, 2004. Author: Configurations, 2004, numerous poems. Cmty. edn. bridge instr. Lincoln Land C.C.; fin. chmn. Hillsboro Hosp. Aux., 1972; lit. vol. Graham Correctional Ctr., Hillsboro, 1986-97; pres., bd. dirs. Montgomery Players and Encore Play Theatre, 1954-70. Recipient Vol. of Yr. award Graham Correction Ctr., 1995, award of Merit Ill. State Bd. Edn., 1994-95. Mem. Cousteau Soc., Internat. Wildlife Fedn., Nat. Wildlife Fedn., Natural Resources Def. Coun., Phi Theta Kappa Internat., Hillsboro Country Club, Hillsboro Book Club, Red Hat Soc. Democrat. Lutheran. Avocations: bridge, golf, gardening, travel, reading. Office Phone: 217-532-2532.

LINGLE, SARAH ELIZABETH, research scientist; b. Woodland, Calif., July 22, 1955; d. John Clayton and Dorothy Adelaide (Dubois) L.; m. Thomas Pratt Washington IV, May 20, 1989. BS, U. Calif., Davis, 1977; MS, U. Nebr., 1978; PhD, Wash. State U., 1982. Lab. asst. U. Calif., Davis, 1975-77; rsch. asst. U. Nebr., Lincoln, 1977-78; rsch., teaching asst. Wash. State U., Pullman, 1979-82; rsch. assoc. Agrl. Rsch. Svc., USDA, Fargo, N.D., 1982-84, supr. plant physiologist Weslaco, Tex., 1984-97, acting rsch. leader, 1991-92, plant physiologist New Orleans, 1997—. Assoc. editor Crop Sci., 1991-97; contbr. articles to profl. jours., chpts. to 2 books. Fellow Am. Soc. Agronomy; mem. AAAS, Am. Soc. Plant Physiologists, Crop Sci. Soc. Am., Sigma Xi. Episcopalian. Achievements include research in biochemistry and physiology of sugar deposition in sucrose-storing plant tissues. Office: USDA Agrl Rsch Svc 1100 Robert E Lee Blvd New Orleans LA 70124 Office Phone: 504-286-4488. Business E-Mail: slingle@srrc.ars.usda.gov.

LINHARDT, ROBERT JOHN, medicinal chemistry educator; b. Passaic, N.J., Oct. 18, 1953; s. Robert J. and Barbara A. (Kelley) L.; m. Kathryn F. Burns, May 31, 1975; children: Kelley, Barbara. BS in Chemistry, Marquette U., 1975; MA in Chemistry, Johns Hopkins U., 1977, PhD in Organic Chemistry, 1979; postgrad., Mass. Inst. Tech., 1979-82. Rsch. assoc. Mass. Inst. Tech., Cambridge, 1979-82; asst. prof. U. Iowa, Iowa City, 1982-86, assoc. prof., 1986-90, prof. medicinal and natural products chemistry, 1990—2003, prof. chem. and biochem. engring., 1996—2003, F. Wendell Miller Disting. prof., 1996—2003, prof. chemistry, 1999—; constellation chair in biocatalysis and metabolic engring. Rensselaer Poly. Inst., Troy, NY. Cons. in field.; interacad. exchange scientist to USSR NAS, 1988. Mem. editl. bd. Applied Biochemistry and Biotech., 1985—, Carbohydrate Rsch., 1990—, Jour. Carbohydrate Chemistry, 1995—, Jour. Biol. Chem., 1995-2000, Analytical Biochemistry, 1991-97, 2001—; contbr. numerous articles to profl. jours. Johnson and Johnson fellow MIT, 1981; NIH grantee, 1982—. Mem. AAAS, AACP (Volwiler award 1999), Am. Chem. Soc. (Horace S. Isbell award Carbohydrate Chemistry 1994, Claude S. Hudson award in carbohydrate chemistry 2003), Soc. Glycobiology. Office: Rensselaerp Poly Inst 110 8th St Troy NY 12180 Home: 214 Lancaster St Albany NY 12210-1132 E-mail: linhar@rpi.edu.

LINHARES, JUDITH YVONNE, artist, educator; b. Pasadena, Calif., Nov. 21, 1940; m. Philip E. Linhares June 15, 1961 (div. July, 1971); 1 child, Amanda Linhares Mason. Student, LA Otis Art Inst., 1960, San Francisco Art Inst., 1963; BFA, Calif. Coll. Arts & Crafts, 1964, MFA, 1970. Art tchr. San Francisco State Coll., 1969-71, San Jose City Coll., 1971-72, U. Calif., Davis, Berkeley, 1979, U. San Francisco, San Francisco Art Inst. other univs., Calif., N.Y., La., 1978—, Sch. of Visual Arts, N.Y.C., 1981—, NYU, 1990—. Lectr. at univs. and art insts. nationwide, 1974— One-woman shows include include Berkeley Gallery, San Francisco, 1972, one-woman shows include San Francisco Art Mus., 1976, Paule Anglim Gallery, San Francisco, 1978, 1980, 1982, 1984, 1988, 1989, 1994, 2003, Nancy Lurie Gallery, Chgo., 1981, 1989, 1990, Concord Gallery, N.Y.C., 1982, 1983, Ruth Siegel Gallery, 1985, Mo David Gallery, 1985, L.A. Louver Gallery, Venice, Calif., 1988, Julie Sylvester Edition, N.Y.C., 1989, The Gaibreath Gallery, Lexington, Ky., 1993, Greenville (S.C.) County Mus. of Art, 1994 (survey exhibition 1971-93), Sonoma (Calif.) State U., 1994, Edward Thorp Gallery, N.Y.C., 1997, 2001, exhibited in group shows at San Francisco Art Inst., 1973, Indpls. Mus. Art, 1984, Peninsula Mus., Monterey, Calif., 1987, Michael Walls Gallery, N.Y., 1987, Rosenberg Gallery, N.Y.C., 1992, pub. collections including, Greenville (S.C.) County Mus. Art, pub. collections, Oakland (Calif.) Mus., Butler Inst. Am. Art, Youngstown, Ohio, Crocker Art Mus., Sacramento, Calif., San Francisco Mus. Modern Art, San Francisco Airport Commn., Whitney Mus. Am. Art. Recipient Adeline Kent award San Francisco Art Inst., 1976; grantee Nat Endowment for Arts, 1979, 87, 93-94, Gottlieb grantee, 1993; Guggenheim fellow, 1997, Anonymous Was a Woman Found. grantee, 1999-2000. E-mail: judithlinhares@aol.com.

LINHART, JOSEPH WAYLAND, retired cardiologist, educational administrator; b. N.Y.C., Feb. 7, 1933; s. Joseph and Myrla Watson (Wayland) L.; m. Marilyn Adele Voight, Sept. 1, 1956; children: Joseph, Mary-Ellen, Richard, Jennifer, Donna-Lisa, Daria. BS, George Washington U., 1954, MD, 1958. Diplomate Am. Bd. Internal Medicine with subspecialty in cardiovascular diseases. Intern Washington Hosp. Ctr., 1958-59; resident George Washington U. Hosp., Washington, 1959-60, Duke U. Hosp., Durham, N.C., 1961, fellow, 1960, 62-63, Nat. Heart Inst./Johns Hopkins Hosp., Bethesda/Balt., Md., 1963-64; asst. prof. medicine U. Fla., Gainesville, 1964-67; clin. assoc. prof. U. Miami, Fla., 1967-68; assoc. prof. medicine U. Tex., San Antonio, 1968-71; prof., dir. cardiology Hahnemann Med. Coll., Phila., 1971-75; prof., chmn. dept. medicine Chgo. Med. Sch., 1975-79, Oral Roberts U., Tulsa, 1979-83; prof. medicine U. South Fla., Tampa, 1983-92; prof., regional chmn. medicine Tex. Tech. U., Odessa, 1992-93; prof. medicine La. State U., Shreveport, 1993-97; chief med. svc. VA Med. Ctr., Shreveport, 1993-97, acting chief of staff, 1996-97; ret., 1997. Cons. in cardiology and med./legal questions. Contbr. articles to profl. jours.; author 4 books. Mem. med. adv. com. YMCA, Niles, Ill., 1976-79; bd. govs. Phila. Heart Assn., 1972-75; mem. rsch. coun. Okla. Heart Assn., Tulsa, 1980-83. Fellow ACP, Am. Coll. Cardiology; mem. AAAS, Planetary Soc., Nat. Space Soc., Astron. Soc. of Pacific, Alpha Omega Alpha. Republican. Avocations: astronomy, history, model building, organ playing, music. Home: 625 Red Cedar Ct NE Saint Petersburg FL 33703-6203

LINHART, LETTY LEMON, editor; b. Pittsburg, Kans., Sept. 22, 1933; d. Robert Sheldon and Lois (Wise) Lemon; m. Robert Spayde Kennedy, June 8, 1955 (div. 1978); children: Carole Shea, Nancy Schrimpf, Nina Woodward; m. Daniel Julian Linhart, June 9, 1986. BS, BA in English and Journalism, U.Kans., 1955; MS in Journalism, Boston U., 1975. Reporter Leavenworth (Kans.) Times, 1954; editor Human Resources Rsch. Office George Washington U., Washington, 1955-56; editor Behavior Rsch. Lab. Harvard Med. Sch., Boston, 1956-58; instr. Boston YMCA, 1960-64; freelance writer and columnist, 1975—; editor Somerville (Mass.) Times, 1975-77; pub. rels. dir. Lettermen of Lexington, Mass., 1978; instr. English Rollins Coll., Winter Park, Fla., 1978-79, Valencia Community Coll., Orlando, Fla., 1978-82, U. Cen. Fla., Orlando, 1979-82; tech. writer Kirschman Software, Altamonte Springs, Mass., 1980-81, Dynamic Control Software, Winter Park, Fla., 1981-82; editor Fla. Specifier, Winter Park, 1982-85, Mobile Home News, Maitland, Fla., 1985-86; instr. English Seminole C.C., Sanford, Fla., 1986-94; Elderhostel instr. Canterbury Rsch. Ctr., 1994—98; editor Oviedo (Fla.) Voice, 1994-95, 96, Tuscawilla Today Monthly Mag., 2000—01; columnist Oviedo Voice, Oviedo, Fla., 2001; reporter North County Times, Vista, Calif., 2001—. Resource person Am. on Line, 1996—. Author: Are These Extravagant Promises, 1989, Clues for the Clueless, 1996, Bits and Bytes of Recovery, 1998, Turn Your Eyes, 2002, In The End it's Faith, 2003, The Minister Made Macramé, 2004; editor: The Cascadian Vista, 2004—; author: The Alcoholic Fish, 2005; contbr. articles to profl. jours. Pres. MIT Dames Boston, 1958-59, Boston Alumnae of Delta Delta Delta, 1959-62; dist. pres Delta Delta Delta, Tex., 1962-65; svc. provider, content provider, cmty. leader Am. On Line Careers and Work Forum, 1996—; cmty. leader media & journalism, AOL, 2000-. Named Outstanding Collegiate Delta Delta Delta, 1955. Mem. NAFE, Ctrl. Fla. Jazz Soc. (bd. dirs. 1983-93), Internat. Platform Soc., Soc. Women Execs., Altrusa Club (publicity com. 1980-83), Orlando Press Club (bd. dirs.), Mortar Bd., Phi Beta Kappa (Belmont, Mass. pres. 1965-78), Theta Sigma Phi, Sigma Delta Chi, Delta Sigma Rho. Avocations: swimming, singing, jazz. Home and Office: 1600 E Vista Way # 5 Vista CA 92084-1020 Personal E-mail: vistaletty@aol.com.

LINICK, ANDREW S., direct marketing expert; b. 1945; PhD in Indsl. Psychology, NYU, 1972. Chmn. bd. dirs. Linick Group Inc., Middle Island, NY. Office: Linick Group Inc The Linick Bldg PO Box 102 Middle Island NY 11953-0102 Office Phone: 631-924-3888. Business E-Mail: LinickGrp@att.net.

LINIGER, DAVE, real estate company executive; Student, U. Ind. Realtor; co-founder RE/MAX Internat., Inc., Denver, 1973—, chmn. bd.; co-owner Sanctuary Golf Course, Sedalia, Colo., 1997—. Co-founder The Wildlife Experience, Denver. With USAF. Avocations: golf, horse breeding, commercial pilot, NASCAR driving. Office: RE/MAX International Inc 8390 E Crescent Pkwy Ste 500/600 Greenwood Village CO 80111-2800 Home: PO Box 3907 Englewood CO 80155-3907

LINK, DAVID THOMAS, dean, lawyer; b. 1936; BS magna cum laude, U. Notre Dame, 1958, JD, 1961; postgrad., Georgetown U., 1965—66. Bar: Ohio 1961, Ill. 1966, Ind. 1975, U.S. Supreme Ct. 1965. Trial atty. Office of Chief Counsel, IRS, 1961—66; ptnr. Winston, Strawn, Smith & Patterson, Chgo., 1966—70; prof. U. Notre Dame Law Sch., Notre Dame, Ind., 1970—99, dean, 1975—99, dean, prof. emeritus, 1999—; pres. vice chancellor U. Notre Dame, Australia, 1990—92, pres., vice chancellor emeritus, bd. trustees, bd. govs., 1992—; founding dep. vice chancellor, provost St. Augustine U. Coll., South Africa, 1999—; pres., CEO Internat. Ctr. Healing and Law, 2001—; assoc. coun. Office Ind. Counsel. Cons. to GAO. Author (with Soderquist): Law of Federal Estate and Gift Taxation, Vol. 1, 1978, Vol. 2, 1980, Vol. 3, 1982, Healing and the Law, 2 vols., 2004. Mem. Ind. Gov.'s Com. on Individual Privacy; mem. pres.' task force New Methods for Improving the Quality of Lawyers' Svcs. to Clients; chair Ind. State Ethics Commn., 1988—90, Pub. Officers' Compensation Adv. Commn., 2004—; acad. coun., provost's adv. com., athletic affairs, acad. affairs, faculty affairs coms. of bd. trustees U. Notre Dame Ctr. for Civil and Human Rights. Served to lt. comdr. USN. Mem.: ABA (coun. on sci. and tech., com. on advt., sect. on legal edn., com. on professionalism 1993—97), Future of Russia Found., Woodrow Wilson Internat. Ctr. for Scholars, Miracle of Nazareth Internat., World Law Inst., Soc. for Values in Higher Edn. Office Phone: 269-353-0592. E-mail: link@healingandthelaw.org.

LINK, GEORGE HAMILTON, retired lawyer; b. Sacramento, Calif., Mar. 26, 1939; s. Hoyle and Corrie Elizabeth (Evans) L.; m. Betsy Leland; children— Thomas Hamilton, Christopher Leland. AB, U. Calif., Berkeley, 1961; LLB, Harvard U., 1964. Bar: Calif. 1965, U.S. Dist. Ct. (no., ea., ctrl. and so dists.) Calif. 1965, U.S. Ct. Appeals (9th cir.) 1965. Assoc. Brobeck, Phleger & Harrison, San Francisco, 1964-69, ptnr., 1970—2001, mng. ptnr. L.A., 1973-93, mng. ptnr. firmwide, 1993-96; ret., 2001. Chmn. Pacific Rim Adv. Coun., 1992-95. Bd. regents U. Calif., 1971-74; trustee Berkeley Found., Jr. Statesmen Am.; bd. govs. United Way, 1979-81; trustee, v.p. Calif. Hist. Soc., 1987—; bd. dirs. Ancient Egypt Rsch. Assocs. Fellow Am. Bar Found.; mem. ABA, Calif. Bar Assn., L.A. Bar Assn., U. Calif. Alumni Assn. (pres. 1972-75), Calif. Club, Bohemian Club, Jonathan Club. Republican. Methodist. Office Phone: 310-476-1836. Personal E-mail: georgehlink@msn.com.

LINK, ROBERT O., JR., lawyer; b. Ottumwa, Iowa, Dec. 4, 1954; BS with highest honors, U. Tenn., 1977, MBA, JD, 1980. Bar: Tenn. 1980, Ga. 1982, NY 1985. Assoc. Cadwalader, Wickersham & Taft, N.Y.C., 1987—90, ptnr., 1990—, chmn., mng. ptnr., mem. mgmt. com. & chmn. Capital Markets Dept. Mem. N.Y.C. Olympic 2012 Legal Adv. Com.; mem. adv. council Dean of Coll. Bus. Adminstrn., Univ. Tenn.; bd. dir. Wall St. Rising. Recipient Am. Jurisprudence awards. Mem.: Mortgage Bankers Assn., N.Y. State Bar Assn., Order of Coif. Office: Cadwalader Wickersham & Taft LLP 1 World Fin Ctr New York NY 10281 Office Phone: 212-504-6172. Office Fax: 212-504-6666. Business E-Mail: robert.link@cwt.com.

LINK, SCOTT J., lawyer; b. Kankakee, Ill., Oct. 16, 1961; BS with honors, Ea. Ill. Univ., 1983; JD magna cum laude, No. Ill. Univ., 1986. Bar: Fla. 1986, US Dist. Ct. (no., so., middle dist. Fla.), US Ct. Appeals (11th cir.). Ptnr. Gunster Yoakley & Stewart, 1986—96; founding ptnr., bus. & securities litigation Ackerman Link & Sartory, West Palm Beach, Del., 1996—. Mem. NASD Nat. Arbitration & Mediation Com. Named one of Fla. Legal Elite, Fla. Trend mag., 2004. Mem.: ABA, Fla. Bar, Palm Beach County Bar Assn. Office: Ackerman Link & Sartory LLP Ste 1250 Esperante 220 Lakeview Ave West Palm Beach FL 33401 Office Phone: 561-838-4100. Office Fax: 561-838-5305. Business E-Mail: slink@alslaw.com.

LINKER, ARTHUR S., lawyer; b. N.Y.C., May 20, 1947; s. Jack and Gertrude (Reibeisen) L.; m. Diane Spanier, June 4, 1973; children: Beth, Jennifer, Michael, Anne. AB summa cum laude, Columbia U., 1968, MA, 1970; JD cum laude, Harvard U., 1974. Bar: NY, US Dist. Ct. (so. and ea. dists.) NY, US Ct. Appeals (2d cir.) 1975, (4th cir.) 1989, (8th cir.) 1990, (9th cir.) 2000; US Supreme Ct. 1979. Ptnr. Rosenman & Colin LLP, N.Y.C., 1974—2002, Katten Muchin Rosenman LLP, N.Y.C., 2002—. Mem. ABA,

N.Y. State Bar Assn., Assn. Bar City N.Y. Avocations: computers, astronomy. Office: Katten Muchin Rosenman LLP 575 Madison Ave Fl 26 New York NY 10022-2585 Office Phone: 212-940-7007. Business E-Mail: arthur.linker@kattenlaw.com.

LINKLATER, RICHARD, film director, actor, screenwriter; b. Houston, July 30, 1960; Student, Sam Houston State U., U. Tex. Founder Detour Filmprodn., Austin, Tex. Dir., prodr., writer, cinematographer, editor: It's Impossible to Learn to Plow by Reading Books, 1988; dir., prodr., writer, actor: Slacker, 1991; dir., prodr., writer: Dazed and Confused, 1993, Before Sunset, 2004; dir., prodr.: Bad News Bears, 2005; writer, dir.: Before Sunrise, 1995 (Berlin Film Festival Silver Bear for Best Dir. 1995), The Newton Boys, 1998; dir.: Suburbia, 1997, School of Rock, 2003; actor: The Underneath, 1995, Scotch and Milk, 1998, Spy Kids, 2001; dir., prodr. actor (animated film) Waking Life, 2001 (NY Film Critics Cir. award 2001, Nat Soc. Film Critics award 2001). Founder, artistic dir. Austin Film Soc.*

LINKLATER, WILLIAM JOSEPH, lawyer; b. Chgo., June 3, 1942; s. William John and Jean (Connell) L.; m. Dorothea D. Ash, Apr. 4, 1986; children: Erin, Emily. BA, U. Notre Dame, 1964; JD, Loyola U., 1968. Bar: Ill. 1968, U.S. Dist. Ct. (no. dist.) Ill. 1968, U.S. Ct. Appeals (7th cir.) 1971, U.S. Supreme Ct. 1971, U.S. Ct. Appeals Wash. 1978, Calif. 1981, U.S. Dist. Ct. (cen. dist.) Calif. 1981, U.S. Tax Ct. 1982, U.S. Dist. Ct. (no. dist.) Calif. 1983, U.S. Dist. Ct. (ea. dist.) Mich. 1989, U.S. Ct. Appeals (6th cir.) 1990, U.S. Dist. Ct. Hawaii 1992. Atty. Fed. Defender Project, Chgo.; assoc. Baker & McKenzie, Chgo., 1968-75, ptnr., 1975—, dir. profl. responsibility. Contbr. articles to profl. jours. Named one of World's Leading White Collar Crime Lawyers, Euromoney, World's Leading Competition and Antitrust Lawyers. Mem.: FBA, ABA (past co-chmn. com. on internat. criminal law criminal justice sect., mem. criminal practice and procedure com. antitrust sect., others), Nat. Assn. Criminal Def. Lawyers, Am. Bd. Criminal Lawyers, Am. Coll. Trial Lawyers, Colo. Bar Assn., Calif. Bar Assn., Chgo. Bar Assn. (pres. 2000—01, bd. mgrs. 1997—2002, past v.p. jud. candidates evaluation com., chmn. large law firm com.), 7th Cir. Bar Assn., Ill. Bar Assn., Wong Sun Soc. San Francisco (internat. proctor), Chgo. Inn of Ct., Alpha Sigma Nu. Office: Baker & McKenzie LLP 130 E Randolph Dr Ste 2500 Chicago IL 60601 Office Phone: 312-861-2794.

LINKLETTER, ARTHUR GORDON, radio and television broadcaster; b. Moose Jaw, Sask., Can., July 17, 1912; s. Fulton John and Mary (Metzler) L.; m. Lois Foerster, Nov. 25, 1935; children: Jack, Dawn, Robert (dec.), Sharon, Diane (dec.). AB, San Diego State Coll., 1934. Program dir. Sta. KGB, San Diego, 1934; program dir. Calif. Internat. Expn., San Diego, 1935; radio dir. Tex. Centennial Expn., Dallas, 1936; San Francisco World's Fair, 1937-39; pres. Linkletter Prodns.; ptnr., co-owner John Guedel Radio Prodns. Chmn. bd. Linkletter Enterprises; owner Art Linkletter Oil Enterprises. Author: theme spectacle Cavalcade of Golden West, 1940; author and co-producer: theme spectacle Cavalcade of Am, 1941; writer, producer, star in West Coast radio shows, 1940-55; former star, writer: People Are Funny, NBC-TV and radio, Art Linkletter's House Party, CBS-TV and radio; Author: People Are Funny, 1953, Kids Say The Darndest Things, 1957, The Secret World of Kids, 1959, Confessions of a Happy Man, 1961, Kids Still Say The Darndest Things, 1961, A Child's Garden of Misinformation, 1965, I Wish I'd Said That, 1968, Linkletter Down Under, 1969, Oops, 1969, Drugs at My Door Step, 1973, Women Are My Favorite People, 1974, How to be a Super Salesman, 1974, Yes, You Can!, 1979, I Didn't Do It Alone, 1979, Public Speaking for Private People, 1980, Linkletter on Dynamic Selling, 1982, Old Age is not for Sissies, 1988; co-host (with Bill Cosby) series Kids Say the Darnedest Things, 1998—; lectr. convs. and univs. Nat. bd. dirs. Goodwill Industries; commr. gen. to U.S. Exhibit at Brisbane Expo 88, Australia, 1987; commr. gen. to rank of U.S. amb. to The 200th Anniversary Celebration, Australia, 1987—; bd. regents Pepperdine U.; chmn. bd. Ctr. on Aging, UCLA; chmn. bd. French Found. for Alzheimers Rsch. Recipient numerous awards. Mem.: United Srs. Assn. (pres.). Address: 8484 Wilshire Blvd Ste 205 Beverly Hills CA 90211-3213

LINKONIS, SUZANNE NEWBOLD, probation officer, counselor; b. Phila., Aug. 24, 1945; d. William Bartram and Kathryn (Taylor) Newbold; m. Bertram Lawrence Linkonis, May 29, 1966; children: Robert William, Deborah Anne, Richard Anthony. AA in Psychology, Albany (Ga.) Jr. Coll., 1979; BA in Psychology, Albany (Ga.) State U., 1981; MS in Indsl. Psychology, Va. Commonwealth U., 1986. Office mgr., media buyer Long Advt. Agy., Richmond, Va., 1981-84; media mgr. Clarke & Assocs., Richmond, 1984-85; human resources asst. Continental Ins., Richmond, 1985; rsch. assoc. Signet Bank, N.A., Richmond, 1986-87; program coord. Med. Coll. Va., Richmond, 1988; personnel mgr. Bur. Microbiology, Richmond, 1988-89; pers. specialist Va. State Dept. Corrections, Richmond, 1989-90; human rights adv. Va. State Dept. Youth and Family Svcs., Richmond, 1990-92, rehab. counselor, 1992-94, sr. rehab. counselor, 1994; pre-trial case mgr./counselor Henrico County Govt., Richmond, 1994-97, cmty. corrections case mgr., counselor, 1997-2000, sr. county probation officer, counselor, 2001—. Future dir., cons. Mary Kay Cosmetics, Springfield, Va., 1975-77. Republican. Roman Catholic. Avocations: networking, walking, reading. Home: 401 Saybrook Dr Richmond VA 23236-3621 Office: 8600 Dixon Powers Dr Richmond VA 23273-7032 Office Phone: 804-501-4124. Business E-Mail: lin04@co.henrico.va.us.

LINKOUS, WILLIAM JOSEPH, JR., lawyer; b. Roanoke, Va., July 17, 1929; s. William Joseph and Mary Virginia (Lester) L.; m. Anita Marie Stedronsky, Oct. 15, 1960; children— William Joseph III, Brian Keith BA, Roanoke Coll., Salem, Va., 1951; MA in Econs., U. Va., 1954, JD, 1956. Bar: Va. 1956, Ga. 1957. Assoc. Powell, Goldstein, Frazer & Murphy, Atlanta, 1956-62, ptnr., 1962-79, 85—, mng. ptnr., 1979-85. Trustee Holy Innocents Episcopal Sch., Atlanta, 1974-80, Roanoke Coll., 1980-95, emeritus 1995—. Fellow Am. Coll. Trust and Estate Counsel, Am. Bar Found.; mem. State Bar Ga. (past chmn. fiduciary sect., chmn. Ga. trust law revision com. 1988-91, 2003—, chmn. Ga. probate code revision com. 1991-97, chmn. Ga. guardianship code revision com.1997-2003), Va. State Bar, Am. Law Inst., Internat. Acad. Estate and Trust Law, Atlanta Estate Planning Coun. (pres. 1983-84). Avocation: tennis. Office: Powell Goldstein LLP One Atlantic Ctr Fourteenth Fl 1201 West Peachtree St NW Atlanta GA 30309-3488 Office Phone: 404-572-6610. Business E-Mail: wlinkous@pogolaw.com.

LINKS, ROBERT DAVID (BO LINKS), lawyer; b. San Francisco, Aug. 25, 1949; s. Milton Arnold and Roslyn (Morris) L.; 1 child, Alexis Jade. AB in Journalism, U. Calif., Berkeley, 1971; JD, UCLA, 1974. Bar: Calif. 1974, U.S. Dist. Ct. (no. dist.) Calif. 1974, U.S. Ct. Appeals (9th cir.) 1979, U.S. Supreme Ct. 1978. Assoc. Jacobs, Blanckenburg, May & Colvin, San Francisco, 1974-79; ptnr. Colvin Martin & Links, 1979-85; assoc. Harold S. Dobbs, 1985, Dobbs, Berger, Molinari, Casalnuovo, Vanelli & Nadel, 1985-86, ptnr., 1986-89, Dobbs, Berger, Molinari, Vanelli, Nadel & Links, 1989-94; spl. counsel Berger, Nadel & Vannelli. Student intern, Justice Mathew O. Tobriner, Calif. Supreme Ct., 1973. Editor: Toward Social Change, 1971, California Civil Practice Civil Rights Module, 1994—; author: Follow the Wind, 1995, Riverbank Tweed & Roadmap Jenkins, 2001. Bd. dirs. San Francisco-Bay area chpt. Am. Jewish Com., 1982—. Mem. Am. Arbitration Assn., Calif. Bar Assn., San Francisco Bar Assn., San Francisco Trial Lawyers Assn., Lake Merced Golf Club, Phi Beta Kappa. Democrat. Avocations: golf, photography, creative writing. Office: Berger Nadel & Vannelli 650 California St Fl 25 San Francisco CA 94108-2702 Personal E-mail: bolinks@sbcglobal.net.

LINN, BRIAN M, education educator; BA with honors, U. of Hawaii at Manoa, 1978; MA, Ohio State U., 1981, PhD, 1985. Vis. asst. prof. U. Nebr., Dept. of History, 1986—87, Old Dominion U., Dept. of History, 1987—89; asst. prof. Tex. A&M U., Dept. History, 1989—95, assoc. prof., 1995—98; prof. history Tex. A&M U., 1998—. Harold K. Johnson vis. prof. of mil. history Army War Coll., 1999—2000; grad com. Tex. A&M U., 1997—99, grad. com., 2000—, Asian history search com., 1997—98; dir. Mil. Studies Inst., 2001; co-chair, program com. Soc. for Mil. History Ann. Conf., 2001—02; awards com. Soc. for Mil. History, 2001—. Mem. editl. bd. Jour. of Mil. History, 1998—2001. Recipient U.S. Army Mil. History Inst. Advanced Rsch. Assoc., 1982; fellowship, John Simon Guggenheim Meml. Found., 2003, grant, Tex. A&M U., 1993, 1997, Faculty Develop. grant, 1995—96, Susan Louise Dyer Peace fellowship, Hoover Inst. on War, Revolution and Peace, Stanford U.1993, 1993—94, John M. Olin postdoctoral fellowship, Yale U., 1990—91, Rsch. and Grad Studies Faculty Mini-Grants, Tex. A&M U., 1992, 1993, Mil. Studies Inst. Summer Rsch. grant, 1991, Rsch. and Grad Studies Faculty Mini-Grants, 1992, Nat. Endowment for the Humanities Summer Stipend, 1989, grant, U.S. Marine Corps Hist. Ctr. Rsch. grant, 1986—87, U.S. Army Ctr. of Mil. History Visiting Rsch. Fellow, 1984—85. Mem.: Inter-Univers Seminar on Armed Forces and Soc., Philippine Hist. Assn., U.S. Commn. on Mil. History, Soc. for Mil. History. Office: Tex A&M U 200A History Bldg College Station TX 77843-4236

LINN, DIANA PATRICIA, elementary school educator; b. Perth, Australia, Dec. 31, 1943; came to U.S., 1948; d. Evan Andrew and Grace Henrietta (Springhall) Jarboe; m. Jim F. Erlandsen, July 9, 1966 (div. Mar. 1989); children: Rebecca, Tim, Jenny; m. Richard George Linn, Mar. 31, 1990; 1 stepchild, Cristal. AA, Olympic Coll., 1963; BA in Elem. Edn., Western Wash. U., 1965; MA, U. Ariz., 1969. Cert. tchr., Wash. Tchr. Neomi B. Willmore Elem., Westminster, Calif., 1965-66; tchr. English and sci. Sunnyside Jr. H.S., Tucson, 1966-70; tchr. kindergarten All Seasons Sch., Tucson, 1972-74; tchr. St. Cyril's Sch., Tucson, 1974-77; elem. tchr. Grace Christian Sch., Tucson, 1977-80; kindergarten and elem. tchr. Ridgeview Christian Ctr., Spokane, Wash., 1983-85, Spokane Christian Schs., 1985-87; dir. Ridgeview Christian Learning Ctr., Spokane, 1987-88; tchr. kindergarten Arlington Elem. Sch., Spokane, 1988-96, Grant Elem. Sch., Spokane, 1996—2005. Mem. curriculum study com. Sunnyside Sch. Dist., Tucson, 1967-68; chmn. accreditation and sch. bd. St. Cyril's Sch., Tucson, 1976-77; chair faculty involvement group, chair staff devel., chair wellness com. Arlington Elem., Spokane, 1992-93, sch. reporter, 1994-95; instr. reading readiness Family Learning Fair, Home Schooling Seminar, Spokane Falls C.C., Spokane, 1988; chair, coord. pre-sch. coop. Arlington Elem. with Spokane Falls C. C. of Spokane C.C., 1992-93; chair faculty involvement group, Arlington Elem., Spokane, 1995-96, Grant Elem. Sch., 1996-97, also wellness chair, 1996-2001, site coun. faculty rep. 2001-05, strategic plan equity com. Arlington Elem., Spokane, 1995-96, pres. site coun., 2003-04. Coord. Christian edn. Valley Foursquare Ch., Spokane, 1982-87; coord. children's ch. Victory Faith Fellowship, Spokane, 1993-2003; Brownie troop leader Willmore Elem., Westminster, 1965-66; ednl. restructuring rep. for Arlington Elem., Spokane Sch. Dist. 81, 1992-93; mem. equity com., 1996-99, mem. early childhood com., 1996-2004, mem. strategic planning com., 1998-2003, wellness chmn., 1998-2000, mem. instrnl. team, 1999-2003; primary rep. Site Coun. Grant Elem., 2002, pres. site coun., 2003-04. Scholar Naval Officer's Wives Club, 1961-62; recipient Eisenhower grant, 1990, 94, 96-97. Mem. ASCD, NEA, Wash. Edn. Assn., Spokane Edn. Assn. (Arlington Elem. rep. 1991-93), CPA Wives Club (sec., ball chair 1983-84), Alpha Delta Kappa (membership chair 1994-95, corr. sec. 1996-99). Republican. Avocations: collecting dolls, plates, swimming, quilt-making. Home: 1324 S Perry St Spokane WA 99202-3572 Office: Grant Elem Sch 1300 E 9th Ave Spokane WA 99202-2499 E-mail: dianaL.@sd81.k12.wa.us.

LINN, MARCIA CYROG, education educator; b. Milw., May 27, 1943; d. George W. and Frances (Vanderhoof) Cyrog; m. Stuart Michael Linn, 1967 (div. 1979); children: Matthew, Allison; m. Curtis Bruce Tarter, 1987 (div. 2003). BA in Psychology and Stats., Stanford U., 1965, MA in Ednl. Psychology, 1967, PhD in Ednl. Psychology, 1970. Prin. investigator Lawrence Hall Sci. U. Calif., 1970-87, prin. investigator Sch. Edn., 1985—, asst. dean Sch. Edn., 1983-85, prof., 1989—; prin. investigator NSF Funded Ctr.- Tech.-Enhanced Learning in Sci. (TELS), 2003—08; chancellor's prof., 2003—. Fulbright prof. Weizmann Inst., Israel, 1983; exec. dir. seminars U. Calif., 1985-86, dir. instnl. tech. program, 1988-96, chair cognition and devel., 1996—98; cons. Apple Computer, 1983—; mem. adv. com. on sci. edn. NSF, 1978—85, Ednl. Testing Svc., 1986—, Smithsonian Instn., 1986—, Fulbright Program, 1983-86, Grad. Record Exam. Bd., 1990-94, adv. com. edn. and human resources directorate, NSF; chair Cognitive Studes Bd. McDonell Found., 1994-97; mem. computing svcs. adv. bd. Carnegie Mellon U., 1991-99; mem. steering com. 3d Internat. Math. and Sci. Study, U.S., 1991-2002. Author: Education and the Challenge of Technology, 1987; co-author: The Psychology of Gender--Advances Through Meta Analysis, 1986—, Designing Pascal Solutions, 1992—, Designing Pascal Solutions with Data Structures, 1996, Computers, Teachers, Peers-Science Learning Partners, 2000, Internet Environments for Science Education, 2004; contbr. articles to profl. jours. Sci. advisor Parents Club, Lafayette, Calif., 1984-87; mem. Internat. Women's Forum, Women's Forum West, 1992—, membership com., 1995-98; bd. dirs. Nat. Ctr. for Sci. Edn., 1997—, GIS and edn. com., 2000—; mem. bd. on behavioral, cognitive and sensory scis. Nat. Rsch. Coun., 1997-2005, mem. com. on info. tech. literacy, computer sci. and telecomms., 1997-2000; mem. nat. adv. bd. Nat. Ctr. for Improving Student Learning and Achievement in Math. and Sci., 1997—; mem. com. on info. tech. fluency and H.S. grad. outcomes NRC, 2004-05. Recipient fellow Ctr. for Adv. Study in Behavior. Scis. 1995-96, 2001-02, Excellence Ednl. Rsch. award Coun. Sci. Soc. Pres., 1998. Fellow AAAS (bd. dirs. 1996-2001, chair-elect edn. sect. 2005—), APA, AAUW (mem. commn. tech. and gender 1998-2001), Am. Psychol. Soc.; mem. Nat. Assn. Rsch. in Sci. and Teaching (bd. dirs. 1983-86, assoc. editor jour., Outstanding Paper award 1978, Outstanding Jour. Article award 1975, 83, Disting. Contbns. to Sci. Edn. Through Rsch. award 1994), Am. Ednl. Rsch. Assn. (chmn. rsch. on women and edn. 1983-85, Women Educators Rsch. award 1982, 88, edn. in sci. and tech. 1989-90, ann. mtg. program com. 1996, Willystine Goodsell award 1991), Internat. Soc. Learning Svcs. (bd. dirs. 2005—), Nat. Sci. Tchrs. Assn. (mem. rsch. agenda com. 1987-90, task force 1993-94), Soc. for Rsch. in Child Devel. (editl. bd. 1984-89), Soc. Rsch. Adolescence, Sierra Club. Avocations: skiing, hiking. Office: U Calif Grad Sch Edn 4611 Tolman Hl Berkeley CA 94720-0001

LINN, RICHARD, federal judge; b. Bklyn., Apr. 13, 1944; BEE, Rensselaer Poly. Inst., 1965; JD, Georgetown U., 1969. Bar: Va., D.C. 1970, N.Y. 1994. Patent examiner U.S. Patent Office, 1965—68; patent agent U.S. Naval Research Lab., 1968—69; assoc. Brenner, O'Brien, Guay, Connors, 1970—71; patent advisor U.S. Naval Air Systems Command, 1971—72; assoc. Stepno & Neilan, 1972—73; partner Stepno, Schwabb & Linn, 1973—74, Imirie, Smiley & Linn, 1974—77, Marks & Murase, L.L.P., 1977—97, exec. comm., 1987—97; partner, pract. group leader intellectual prop. dept Foley & Lardner, 1997—99; judge U.S. Ct. Appeals (fed. cir.), Washington, 1999—. Lecturer Geo. Washington Sch. of Law, 2001—; mem. Intellectual Property Adv. Bd., GWU Sch. of Law. Recipient Rensselaer Alumni Assn Fellows award, 2000.*

LINN, STUART MICHAEL, biochemist, educator; b. Chgo., Dec. 16, 1940; s. Maurice S. and Pauline Linn; children: Matthew S., Allison D., Meagan S. BS in Chemistry with honors, Calif. Inst. Tech., 1962; PhD in Biochemistry, Stanford U., 1967. Asst. prof. biochemistry U. Calif., Berkeley, 1968-72, assoc. prof., 1972-75, prof., 1975-87, head divsn. biochemistry and molecular biology, 1987-90, 1995-2000. Mem. editl. bd. Nucleic Acids Rsch., 1974—, Jour. Biol. Chemistry, 1975—80, Molecular and Cellular Biology, 1987—91; contbr. articles to profl. jours., chapters to books. Helen Hay Whitney fellow, 1966—68, John Simon Guggenheim fellow, 1974—75, Merit grantee, USPHS, 1988—97. Mem.: AAAS, Am. Soc. Microbiologists, Am. Soc. Biol. Chem. Molecular Biol., Am. Acad. Arts and Scis. Office: U Calif Divsn Biochem & Molec Bio Barker Hall Berkeley CA 94720-3202

LINN, TERRY ANN NOFFSINGER, secondary school educator; b. Fort Belvoir, Va., July 14, 1950; d. Terrell Limuel and Juanita Noffsinger; m. Joseph Linn; children: Joseph Christopher, Tara, Renee, Steven Eric Orders. BS, East Carolina U., N.C., 1972. Nat. Bd. Cert. Tchr. Nat. Bd. Prof. Tchg. Stds., 2002. Math. tchr. Eleanor Roosevelt HS, Greenbelt, Md., 1984—2000, 2002—; math. tchr., dept. chair Charles Herbert Flowers HS, Springdale, Md., 2000—02. Recipient Outstanding Math. Tchr., Md. Coun. of Math., 2000. Mem.: Nat. Coun. Tchrs. of Math. Office: Eleanor Roosevelt HS 7601 Hanover Pkwy Greenbelt MD 20770 Personal E-mail: linnmath@aol.com.

LINNÉA, SHARON, writer, playwright; d. William Diderichsen and Marilynn Joyce Webber; m. Robert Owens Scott; children: Jonathan Brendan Scott, Linnéa Juliet Scott. Student, Wheaton Coll., 1974-76; BA, NYU, 1978. With editl. dept. various titles William Morrow and Co., N.Y.C., 1977-78, Taplinger and Assocs., N.Y.C., 1978-80, Flying Magazine, N.Y.C., 1982-83; features editor Scholastic Voice, N.Y.C., 1983-85; staff writer Guideposts Mag., N.Y.C., 1985-91, contbg. editor, 1991—99, Angels on Earth, 1995—99; prodr. Inspiration Beliefnet.com, 1999—2002; head writer New Morning Show Hallmark Network, 2002. V.p. Imagining Things Enterprises, N.Y.C.; spkr. in field. Producer (film) Knowing Lisa, 1991 (Silver award Worldfest/Houston film festival); author: (study guide) Romeo and Juliet by William Shakespeare, 1984, Hedda Gabbler and A Doll's House by Henrik Ibsen, 1985, (book) Raoul Wallenberg: The Man Who Stopped Death, 1993 (Best Book of 1993 Jewish World, Dayton Jewish Chronicle, The Speaker), Princess Ka'iulani: Hope of A Nation, Heart of A People, 1999 (Carter G. Woodson award), (with Jeff Meyer) America's Famous and Historic Trees, 2001, Chicken Soup from the Soul of Hawaii, 2003, (plays), Clown of God, 1977, The Singer, 1978, A Matter of Time, 1981, Tales from the Vermont Woods, 1982, (screenplays) Missouri, Ma Cheri, Tomorrow Is My Dancing Day; ghostwriter articles in Reader's Digest and Guideposts Mag.; profile biographer World of Heroes Sch. Curriculum; psychology columnist Beliefnet.com; freelancer Marvel Comics, Children's TV Workship, Hallmark Hall of Fame; freelance editor Chicken Soup for the Soul; contbr. to book pubs. including From the Ashes, 2001, Big Book of Angels, 2002; contbr. articles to popular publs. Recipient Storytelling World award, 2004. Mem.: Authors Guild. Avocations: latching rugs, public speaking. Office: Imagining Things Enterprises 36 Crystal Farm Rd Warwick NY 10990-2862

LINNEBUR, SUNNY A, pharmacist; m. Scott Linnebur. PharmD, U. of Kans., 1993—99. Bd. cert. pharmacotherapy specialist Bd. of Pharm. Specialties, 2002. Asst. prof. U. of Colo. Health Sciences Ctr., Denver, 2001—. Rsch. funding grant, Sankyo Pharma, 2004. Mem.: Am. Coll. of Clin. Pharmacy (ambulatory care prn chair, chair task force pharmacy and the elderly 2004—). Achievements include research in in involving hyperlipidemia, dementia, osteoporosis, anticoagulation. Office: Univ of Colo Health Sci 4200 East Ninth Ave Box C238 Denver CO 80262

LINNELL, ROBERT HARTLEY, editor-in-chief; b. Kalkaska, Mich., Aug. 15, 1922; s. Earl Dean and Constance (Hartley) L.; m. Myrle Elizabeth Talbot, June 17, 1950; children: Charlene LeGro, Lloyd Robert, Randa Ruth, Dean Maxfield. BS, U. N.H., 1944, MS, 1948; PhD, U. Rochester, 1950. Asst. instr. U. N.H., 1942-44, instr., 1947; asst. prof. chemistry Am. U., Beirut, 1950-52, assoc. prof., chmn. chemistry dept., 1952-55; v.p. Tizon Chem. Corp., Flemington, N.J., 1955-58; assoc. prof. chemistry U. Vt., 1958-61; dir. Scott Research Labs., Plumsteadville, Pa., 1961-62; program dir. phys. chemistry NSF, 1962-65, planning assoc., 1965-67, program mgr. departmental sci. devel., 1967-69; dean Coll. Letters, Arts and Scis., U. So. Calif., Los Angeles, 1969-70; dir. Office Instl. Studies U. So. Calif., 1970-82, chmn. safety sci. dept., 1982-85, prof. emeritus, 1985—; pres. Harmony Inst., 1985-92. Cons. Reheis Corp., 1958-61, Coll. Chemistry Cons. Service, 1970-76, EPA, 1971-73, Lake Erie Environment Program, 1971-73 Author: Graduate Student Support and Manpower Resources in Graduate Science Education, 1968, Air Pollution, 1973, Hydrogen Bonding, 1971, Dollars and Scholars, 1982, Meeting The Needs of The Non-Smoking Traveler, 1986, Ignition Interlock Devices: An Assessment of Their Application to Reducing DUI, 1991; editor: my-oped.com, 1999—; contbr. articles to profl. jours. Mem. traffic adv. com. Auto Club So. Calif., 1985-93; treas. Norwich Congl. Ch., 1995-96, chair bus. com. 1996-98; coord. Concord Coalition, Upper Valley, N.H. and Vt., 1995-2000; mem. devel. bd. Upper Valley Tchr. Tng. Program, 1995-97; mem. scholarship com. Upper Valley Cmty. Found., 1996—; bd. overseers Dartmouth Hitchcock Med. Ctr., 1997-2002; bd. dirs. Upper Valley Habitat for Humanity, 1993-95; Dem. candidate for Pre. U.S., N.H. Primary, 2004. Recipient Outstanding Achievement award Coll. Tech., U. N.H., 1969 Mem. AAUP, Am. Chem. Soc. (program chmn. Washington 1968, divsn. chem. edn. 1971), Assn. Instl. Rsch., Am. Lung Assn. of Ctrl. Calif. (bd. dirs. 1986-92, pres. 1991-92), Rotary. Achievements include patents in chemistry field. Home: 121 Mascoma St # 238 Lebanon NH 03766 Office Phone: 603-448-6074. E-mail: rhllinn@valley.net.

LINNEN, THOMAS FRANCIS, international strategic management consulting executive; b. Carbondale, Pa., Sept. 29, 1925; s. John Joseph and Marie Dolores (Fitzpatrick) L.; m. Mary Joanne, Dec. 28, 1951; children: Nancy, Paula, Michele, Thomas F. Jr., Mary J. Jr. BS in Fgn. Svc., Georgetown U., 1949; postgrad., Am. U., Washington, 1951—52, U. Rochester, Sch. Bus., 1988. Writer Congl. News Reports, Washington, late 40's; congl. press asst. Washington, 1949; asst. for pub. relations office of pres. Georgetown U., 1950; officer U.S. Army Aide Office, sect. army and psychol. spl. ops., Ft. Bragg, NC, 1951—53; mgr. Retail Credit Company, Atlanta, 1953-56, 59-72; various managerial assignments GM Equifax Inc., Chgo., 1972-80; regional mgr. ops. and sales Equifax Inc., Upstate, N.Y., 1980-89; pres. The NORAM Group Ltd., Buffalo, 1990-94, chmn., 1992; pres. Am. Auto. Exports Inc., Russia, 1993; chmn. AIG, Moscow, ABC, Moscow; pres. Thomas F. Linnen & Assocs., 1998—99. Bd. dirs. Gaflin Comm. Group, Inc., Chgo.; on spl. assignment CIA, 1956-59; cons. to Russian govtl. units on market economy transition. Pub. Russian internat. bus. newsletter "The Ural Region Focus"; contbr. articles to jours. and mags. Mem. adv. bd. Barat Coll., Internat. Inst. Buffalo, Chgo. Coun. Fgn. Rels.; chmn. United Way, Crusade of Mercy, Heart Fund Campaigns and other civic orgns.; chairmanship role in John F. Kennedy, Jimmy Carter and Jack Kemp and George W. Bush campaigns for the Presidency; bd. trustees Pulmonary Hypertension Assn., Media Rsch. Ctr., President's Club (exec. com.), Heritage Found., Acton Inst. coun., Maj. USAR ret. Mem. Res. Officers Assn. U.S. (former nat. officer), Am. Legion (life), Disabled Vet. Am. Republican. Roman Catholic. Home: 404 Clearwater Dr Ponte Vedra Beach FL 32082-4170 *Democracy, with all its warts and imperfections, remains the best form of government known to man. Yet, democracy, eroded by unbridled freedom and corrupt self-interests, lethally turns in upon itself. Freedom, devoid of individual responsibility and in mindless confrontation with man's God, will, over time, kill the democratic body politic itself.*

LINNERT, TERRENCE GREGORY, lawyer; b. Cleve., Oct. 16, 1946; s. Ralph Marshall and Mary Gertrude (Gessner) L.; m. Susan Kay Chesnes, Jan 25, 1969; children: Michael, Patrick, Terrence, Timothy. BSEE, U. Notre Dame, 1968; JD, Cleve. State U., 1975. Bar: Ohio 1975. Engr. Cleve. Electric Illuminating, 1968-77, corp. counsel, 1977-84, sr. corp. counsel, 1984-86, Centerior Energy Corp., Independence, Ohio, 1986-87; prin. counsel Centerior Service Co., Independence, Ohio, 1987; asst. gen. counsel Centerior Svc. Co., Independence, Ohio, 1988-89; gen. counsel Centerior Energy Corp., Independence, 1989-92, v.p., legal & govtl. affairs, 1992-95; sr. v.p. & gen. counsel B.F. Goodrich Co., Charlotte, NC, 1995—, sec., CFO, 2000—. Mem. Citizens' League, Cleve; pres. St. Gabriel's Parents' Assn., Concord, Ohio, 1984-85, v.p. parish coun., 1986-87; pres. Lake Cath. Edn. Commn., Mentor, Ohio, 1991-92. Mem.: ARC, Econ. Am., Leadership Cleve. & Akron. Roman Catholic. Home: 14521 Nolen Ln Charlotte NC 28277-1576 Office: BF Goodrich Co Four Coliseum Center 2730 W Tyvola Rd Charlotte NC 28217-4578 Office Phone: 704-423-7000. Office Fax: 704-423-5540. Business E-Mail: terry.linnert@goodrich.com.

LINNEY, BEVERLY See HALLAM, BEVERLY

LINNEY, LAURA, actress; b. NYC, Feb. 5, 1964; d. Romulus Linney and Ann Leggett Perse; m. David Adkins, 1995 (div. 2000). BFA, Brown U., 1986; grad., Juilliard Sch., 1989. Motion picture and T.V. actress. Films include Lonrenzo's Oil, 1992, Searching for Bobby Fischer, 1993, Blind Spot, 1993, Dave, 1993, A Simple Twist of Fate, 1994, Congo, 1995, Primal Fear, 1996, The Truman Show, 1998, Absolute Power, 1998, Lush, 1999, You Can

Count on Me, 2000, The House of Mirth, 2000, Running Mates, 2000, Maze, 2000, The Laramie Project, 2002, The Mothman Prophecies, 2002, The Life of David Gale, 2003, Mystic River, 2003, Love Actually, 2003, P.S., 2004, Kinsey, 2004, The Squid and the Whale, 2005, The Exorcism of Emily Rose, 2005, (TV films) Tales of the City, 1993, More Tales of the City, 1998, Love Letters, 1999, Wild Iris, 2001; theatre prodn.: The Crucible, 2002 (Tony nominee). Office: c/o CAA 9830 Wilshire Blvd Beverly Hills CA 90212-1804*

LINNEY, ROMULUS, author, educator; b. Phila., Sept. 21, 1930; s. Romulus Zachariah Linney and Maitland (Thompson) Clabaugh; m. Laura Callanan; children: Laura, Susan. BA, Oberlin Coll., 1953, LittD (hon.), 1994; MFA, Yale U., 1958; DLitt. (hon.), Applachian State U., 1995, Wake Forest U., 1998. Prof. Actors Studio MFA New Sch., N.Y.C. Lectr. U. N.C., Chapel Hill, Raleigh, U. Pa., Bklyn. Coll., Conn. Coll., Princeton U., Hunter Coll., Columbia U. Author: (novels) Heathen Valley, 1962, Slowly, By Thy Hand Unfurled, 1965, Jesus Tales 1980, (plays) The Sorrows of Frederick, 1968, Democracy and Esther, and the Love Suicide at Schofield Barracks, 1973, Holy Ghosts, and The Sorrows of Frederick, 1977, Old Man Joseph and His Family, 1978, The Captivity of Pixie Shedman, 1981, Tennessee, 1981 (Obie award), Childe Byron, 1981, The Death of King Philip, 1983, Laughing Stock, 1984, Sand Mountain, 1985, A Woman Without a Name, 1986, Pops, 1987, Juliet, Yancy and April Snow, 1989, Three Poets, 1989, Unchanging Love, 1990, '2', 1990, Ambrosio, 1991 (Obie award Sustained Excellence in Playwriting), Spain, 1993, True Crimes, 1995, Oscar Over Here, 1995, Mock Trial, 1996, Mountain Memory, 1996, A Christmas Carol (from Dickens), 1996, Gint (from Ibsen), 1998, A Lesson Before Dying (from novel by Ernest J. Gaines), 1998, The Unwritten Song (from a book by Willard R. Trask), 1999, Hisself, Goodbye, Oscar, 1999, others. Mem. Coll. of the Fellows of the Am. Theatre. With U.S. Army, 1954-56. Grantee NEA, Guggenheim Found., Rockefeller Found., others; recipient Lit. award AAAL, 1984, Award of Merit, 1999. Mem.: Fellowship of So. Writers, Ensemble Studio Theatre, Acad. Arts & Letters, Am. Acad. Arts & Sci., Corp. of Yaddo (bd. dirs.). Address: 289 Dales Bridge Rd Germantown NY 12526-5222 E-mail: romuluslinney@msn.com.

LINO, MARISA ROSE, retired diplomat; d. Luigi and Vida (Bego) L. BA in Polit. Sci., Portland State U., 1971; MA in Internat. Affairs, George Washington U., 1972; postgrad., U. Zagreb, Yugoslavia, 1972-73; cert. in advanced engring. studies, MIT, 1982. Rotational officer Dept. State, Lima, Peru, 1975-77, watch officer ops. ctr. Washington, 1977-78, staff asst. policy planning staff, 1978-79, econ./comml. officer Baghdad, Iraq, 1979-81, info. systems officer, 1982-83, adminstrv. officer Rome, 1983-85, econ. counselor Damascus, Syria, 1986-88, refugee coord. Islamabad, Pakistan, 1988-90, consul gen. Florence, Italy, 1990-93, mem. sr. exec. seminar, 1993-94, dep. exec. sec. of state, 1994-96; U.S. amb. Republic of Albania, 1996-99; sr. inspector Office Inspector Gen., Washington, 1999-2000; sr. negotiator for base access and burden sharing Polit. Mil. Affairs Bur., Washington, 2000—03; dir. Johns Hopkins U. Sch. Advanced Internat. Studies, Bologna Ctr., Italy, 2003—. Exhibited in group show of watercolor monotypes, Province of Florence, 1993. Mem. Am. Fgn. Svc. Assn. Avocations: tennis, sailing, hiking. Office: Via Belmeloro 11 40126 Bologna Italy

LINOWES, DAVID FRANCIS, finance educator, corporate financial executive; b. N.J., Mar. 16, 1917; m. Dorothy Lee Wolf, Mar. 24, 1946; children: Joanne Linowes Alinsky, Richard Gary, Susan Linowes Allen (dec.), Jonathan Scott. Founder, ptnr. Leopold & Linowes (now BDO Siedman), Washington, 1946-62; cons. sr. ptnr. Leopold & Linowes, Washington, 1962-82; nat. founding ptnr. Laventhol & Horwath, 1965-76; chmn. bd, CEO Mickleberry Comm. Corp., 1970-73; chmn., CEO Perpetual Investment Co., Inc., 1950-88; dir. Horn & Hardart Co., 1971-77, Piper Aircraft, 1972-77, Saturday Rev./World Mag., Inc., 1972-77, Chris Craft Industries, Inc., 1958—2004; prof. polit. economy, pub. policy, bus. adminstrn. U. Ill., Urbana, 1976—2000, Boeschenstein prof. emeritus, 1987—. Cons. DATA Internat. Assistance Corps., 1962-68, U.S. Dept. State, UN, Sec. HEW, Dept. Interior; chmn. Fed. Privacy Protection Commn., Washington, 1975-77, U.S. Commn. Fair Market Value Policy for Fed. Coal Leasing, 1983-84, Pres.'s Commn. on Fiscal Accountability of Nation's Energy Resources, 1981-82; chmn. Pres.' Commn. on Privatization, 1987-88; mem. Council on Fgn. Relations; cons. panel GAO; adj. prof. mgmt. NYU, 1965-73; Disting. Arthur Young Prof. U. Ill., 1973-74; emeritus chmn. internat. adv. com. Tel Aviv U.; headed U.S. State Dept. Mission to Turkey, 1967, to India, 1970, to Pakistan, 1968, to Greece, 1971; U.S. rep. on privacy to Orgn. Econ. Devel. Intergovtl. Bur. for Informati cs, 1977-81, cons., N.Y.C., 1977-81; U.S. State Dept. mission to Chile, Argentina and Uruguay, July, 1988, Yugoslavia, May, 1991. Author: Managing Growth Through Acquistion, Strategies for Survival, Corporate Conscience; commn. report Personal Privacy in Information Society, Fiscal Accountablility of Nation's Energy Resources; editor: The Impact of the Communication and Computer Revolution on Society, Privacy in America, 1989, Creating Public Policy, 1998, Living Through 50 Years of Economic Progress with 10 Presidents-The Most Productive Generation in History 1946-1996, 2000; contbr. articles to profl. jours. Trustee Boy's Club Greater Washington, 1955-62, Am. Inst. Found., 1962-68; assoc. YM-YWHA's Greater N.Y., 1970-76; chmn. Charities Adv. Com. of D.C., 1958-62; emeritus bd. dirs. Religion in Am. Life, Inc.; former chmn. U.S. People for UN; chmn. citizens com. Combat Charity Rackets, 1953-58. 1st lt. Signal Corps, AUS, 1942-46. Recipient 1970 Human Relations award Am. Jewish Com., U.S. Pub. Service award, 1982, Alumni Achievement award U. Ill., 1989, CPA Distinguished Pub. Svc. award, Washington, 1989. Mem. AICPA (v.p. 1962-63), U. Ill. Found. (emeritus bd. dirs. 1), Coun. Fgn. Rels., Cosmos Club, Phi Kappa Phi (nat. bd. dirs.), Beta Gamma Sigma. Home (Summer): 5630 Wisconsin Ave 801 Chevy Chase MD 20815

LINS, DEBRA, bank executive; BA magna cum laude, Lakeland Coll., 1979; MBA, U. Wis., 1984. Loan officer Farm Credit Svcs., Baraboo, Wis., 1979—83; v.p., sr. lender M&I Bank So. Wis., Sauk City, Wis., 1983—90, First Bus. Bank Madison, Wis., 1990—93; pres. Cmty. Bus. Bank, Sauk City, 1994—, CEO, 1993—, dir., 1993—. Bd.dir. Badger Chpt. ARC; bd. dirs. Sauk Prairie Area C. of C.; bd. dir. Sauk Prairie Meml. Hosp., 1992—98, Sauk Prairie United Way, Inc., 1996—2001, benedictine Life Found. Wis., Inc., 2000—02. Named Disting. Woman in Banking, N.W. Fin. Rev., 1994, Outstanding Entrepreneurial Woman in Dane County, The Bus. Forum, 1997, Outstanding Woman in Agr., Assn. Women in Agr., 1998, Wis. Woman of Century, Wis. Woman Mag., 2000, One of 25 Most Powerful Women in Banking, U.S. Banker Mag., 2003. Mem.: Am. Banker's Assn. (mem. cmty. bankers Coun.). Office: Community Business Bank 1111 Sycamore St PO Box 636 Sauk City WI 53583-0636

LINSENMEIER, CAROL VINCENT, music educator; b. Manchester, Conn., Feb. 5, 1952; d. Donald Scott and Alys (Campbell) Vincent; m. John Andrew Linsenmeier, Dec. 28, 1979; children: Andrew, Thomas. B Music Edn., Coll. of Wooster, Ohio, 1974; M Music Edn., U. Ga., Athens, 1978; PhD in Spl. Edn., Kent State U., 2004. Strings specialist Greenville (S.C.) County Schs., 1974—76; Suzuki coord. U. Ga., Athens, 1977—80; violin/viola tchr. The Sch. of Fine Arts, Willoughby, Ohio, 1980—, chair music dept., 1988—2005. Adj. prof. violin and viola Lake Erie Coll., Painesville, Ohio, 2005—. Arranger: children's musical How Big Is Your Circle, 2000. Rschr., bd. trustees No. Ireland Cmty. Cooperation Initiative, Mentor, Ohio, 1999—2003; sec., bd, trustees Svcs. for Ind. Living, Cleve., 1998—; treas., trustee Suzuki Assn. No. Ohio, Stow, Ohio, 2001—. Mem.: Suzuki Assn. of the Americas, Kappa Lambda, Kappa Delta Pi, Phi Kappa Phi. Avocations: Irish fiddling, Traditional Am. fiddling, needlepoint. Office: The Fine Arts Assn 38660 Mentor Ave Willoughby OH 44094 E-mail: carollinsenmeier@mac.com.

LINSENMEYER, JOHN MICHAEL, lawyer; b. Columbus, Ohio, June 20, 1940; s. John Cyril and Ruth Theresa (Motz) L.; m. Barbara Panish, Aug. 12, 1961; children: Ann Elizabeth Linsenmeyer Nelson, Thomas More, Barbara Mary Linsenmeyer Malone. AB, Georgetown U., 1961, JD, 1964. Bar: Va. 1964, N.Y. 1965, U.S. Supreme Ct.1967, D.C. 1975. Assoc. Cravath, Swaine & Moore, N.Y.C., 1966-75; ptnr. Forsyth, Decker, Murray & Broderick, N.Y.C., 1975-80, Morgan, Lewis & Bockius, N.Y.C., 1980—. Columnist Southern Conn. Newspapers, Greenwich, 1984—; contbr. articles to profl. jours. Police officer, sgt. Greenwich Police Dept. Spl. Divsn., 1966-87; cons. firearms Presdl. Commn. on the Causes and Prevention of Violence, 1968-69; bd. dirs. Fairfield County Fish and Game Agy., Newtown, Conn., 1973-77; ordained deacon Roman Cath. Diocese of Bridgeport, 2004, for pastoral work St. Agnes Roman Cath. Parish, Greenwich, Conn. Mem. N.Y. State Bar Assn., N.Y.C. Fed. Bar Coun., Univ. Club (N.Y.C.), Squadron A (N.Y.C.), Rocky Point Club (Old Greenwich, Conn.), Royal Can. Mil. Inst. (Toronto.). Republican. Roman Catholic. Avocations: theology, hunting, shooting, military history. Home: 9 Hendrie Ave Riverside CT 06878-1808 Office: Morgan Lewis & Bockius 101 Park Ave Fl 43 New York NY 10178-0002 E-mail: jlinsenmeyer@morganlewis.com.

LINSENMEYER, TODD ALAN, medical educator, physician; Student, Whittier (Calif) Coll., 1971-72; BS with honors, Stanford U, 1975; MD, U. Hawaii, 1979. Diplomate Am. Bd. Spinal Cord Medicine, Am. Bd. Urology, Am. Bd. Phys. Medicine and Rehab. Surg. intern Queen's Hosp., Honolulu, 1979-80; resident urology Tripler Amy Med. Ctr., Honolulu, 1980-84; resident physical medicine and rehab. Stanford (Calif.) Med. Ctr., 1986-89; clin. asst. prof. surgery U. Medicine and Dentistry/N.J. Sch. Medicine, Newark, 1989-95, asst. prof. rehab. medicine, 1989-97, asst. prof. surgery, 1995—, assoc. prof. rehab. medicine, 1996—, assoc. prof. surgery, 1997—; asst. chief urology 98th Gen. U.S. Army Hosp., Nuremberg, Germany, 1984-86; dir. urology Kessler Inst. Rehab. Medicine, West Orange, N.J., 1989—. Cons. urodynamics Dept. Vets. Affairs Med. Ctr., East Orange, 1991—; vis. prof. phys. medicine and rehab. Stanford U., 1992; reviewer Male Spinal Cord Injury Fertility Program: Miami Project for Cure of Paralysis, 1994; mem. sci. adv. bd. Paralyzed Vets. Am., 1995—; mem. grant rev. com. NIH, 1991, 92; mem. adv. com. Spinal Cord Injury Practice Consortium, 1995—, mem. steering com., 1995—; chmn. autonomic dysreflexia practice parameter guideline com. SCI Practice Parameter Consortium, 1995—; presenter various meetings, orgns., confs. Contbr. articles to profl. jours., chpts. to books. Maj. M.C. U.S. Army, 1980-87. Recipient 2nd pl. award paper competition ACS, Honolulu, 1984; grantee Sprague Dawley Rat Eastern Paralyzed VA, 1992-93, NIH, 1992-95, VA, 1995-98, Am. Paraplegia Soc., 1995-96. Mem. AMA, Am. Paraplegia Soc. (bd. dirs. 1993—, membership com. 1990, chmn. membership com. 1992-94, chmn. clin. practice parameter com. 1995—, pres. 2003—), Am. Spinal Cord Injury Assn. (mem. urology com. sexuality and disability 1991—, mem. program com., publs. com. 1994-99), Am. Acad. Phys. Medicine and Rehab., Am. Congress Rehab. Medicine (mem. nat. task force on sexuality and disability 1988—), Am. Urodynamics Soc. (assoc.), Assn. Acad. Physiatrists, Am. Urol. Assn. Office: Kessler Inst Rehab 1199 Pleasant Valley Way West Orange NJ 07052-1499

LINSK, MICHAEL STEPHEN, real estate company executive; b. LA, Apr. 20, 1940; s. Abe P. and Helen Linsk; m. Wilma M. Stahl, Aug. 11, 1979; children from previous marriage: Cari E., Steven D. BSBA, U. So. Calif., 1965, MBA, 1969. CFO Larwin Group, Inc., Encino, Calif., 1970-75; v.p. fin., dir. Donald L. Bren Co., LA, 1976-78; v.p., CFO, treas., dir. Wilshire Mortgage/Wilshire Diversified, Burbank, Calif., 1980-81; pres., dir. subs. Wilshire Mortgage Corp., Burbank, 1981-84; pres., dir. Wilshire Realty Investments, Burbank, 1981-84, Glenfed Investments Inc., subs. Glendale Fed. Savs., 1982-84; pres. Eastern Pacific Fin. Group, LA, 1984-85; sr. v.p. Leisure Tech., Inc., LA, 1985-87; CEO Investec Realty Group, Inc., Encino, 1987-88; sr. v.p. LA Land Co., 1988-91; mng. dir. FTI Consulting (formerly Price Waterhouse Coopers), 1992—. Bd. dirs. Savs. Bank, Jewel City Ins., Verdugo Svcs., Inc. Treas., bd. dirs. Am. Theater Arts; bd. dirs. North Hollywood Cultural Ctr., Inc., Cmty. Friends, Inc., 1998—; trustee Temple Judea, Tarzana, Calif., 1981—83, treas., 1982—83. Mem.: AICPA, Urban Land Inst., Calif. Soc. CPAs, Bldg. Industry Assn. (bd. dirs. LA chpt. 1981—88), Beta Gamma Sigma. Office: FTI Consulting Inc 633 W 5Th St Ste 1600 Los Angeles CA 90071-2030 Office Phone: 213-452-6009. Business E-Mail: michael.linsk@fticonsulting.com.

LINSKY, MARTY, public policy educator, consultant; b. Brookline, Mass., Aug. 28, 1940; s. Harold Max and Ruth Doran L.; m. Helen Roberts Strieder, Dec. 10, 1964 (div. Jan. 1979); children: Alison, Sam; m. Lynn H. Staley, July 7, 1979; 1 child, Max. BA, Williams Coll., Williamstown, Mass., 1961; JD, Harvard U., 1964. Asst. atty. gen. Commonwealth of Mass., Boston, 1967, chief sec. to the gov., 1992-95; mem. and asst. minority leader Mass. Ho. of Reps., Boston, 1967-72; editorial writer and reporter The Boston Globe, 1973-75; editor-in-chief The Real Paper, Cambridge, Mass., 1975-79; asst. dir. Inst. of Politics, John F. Kennedy Sch., Cambridge, 1981-85; instr. in law Boston Coll., Newton, Mass., 1973-85; lectr. in pub. policy John F. Kennedy Sch. of Govt. at Harvard, Cambridge, 1985-92, 95—; co-founder, prin. Cambridge Leadership Assocs., 2002—. Coord. seminars Ethics Ctr., Poynter Inst. for Media Studies, St. Petersburg, Fla., 1987-88, dir. ownership and leadership project, 1995-97; project dir. Revson Found., N.Y.C., 1982-85. Author: Impact: How the Press Affects Federal Policy Making, 1986, How the Press Affects Federal Policy Making: 6 Case Studies, 1986, (with Ed Grefe) The New Corporate Activism, 1995, (and Ronald Heifetz) Leadership on the Line: Staying Alive Through the Dangers of Leading, 2002; consulting editor: (books) Getting to Yes, 1981, Beyond the Hotline, 1985. Bd. dirs., selection com. Cavallo Found., Cambridge, 1988-96; bd. dirs. Ford Hall Forum, Boston, 1989-92; regular polit. commentator Monitor Network, Boston, 1992, WHDH-TV, CBS affiliate, Boston, 1990; trustee Gaudino Meml. Fund, Williams Coll., 1992-2002, chair, 1999-2002; chair selection com. William Bulger Excellence in Legis. Leadership award, 1999—. Recipient cash prize, second place essay competition, Woodrow Wilson Ctr. for Media Studies, Washington, 1990. Mem. Inst. for Alternative Journalism (bd. dirs. 1983-95, chair 1992-95), Poynter Inst. for Media Studies (bd. advisors 1981-97). Avocations: running, mexican food, collecting baseball cards. Home: 333 Central Park W Apt 26 New York NY 10025-7104 Office: John F Kennedy Sch Govt Harvard Univ Cambridge MA 02138 Office Phone: 617-576-5766. Business E-Mail: marty@cambridge-leadership.com. E-mail: mahty@pipeline.com.

LINSLER VALENTINE, CONNIE FRANCES, performing company executive; b. Ellicottville, N.Y., Oct. 12, 1960; d. James Paul Linsler and Eunice Margaret Feldman; m. Alan Darrell Valentine, July 21, 2002. BS, SUNY, Oswego, 1982. Intern, tel. subscription sales campaign mgr. Syracuse Symphony Orch., NY, 1981; Orch. Mgmt. Fellow Am. Symphony Orch. League, Washington, 1982—83; asst. mgr. Midland-Odessa Symphony & Chorale, Tex., 1983—85, exec. dir., 1985—90, Greater Akron Music Assn., Ohio, 1991—98, Savannah Symphony, Ga., 1998—99; cons. Fla. Philharm., Fort Lauderdale, 1999—2000, exec. dir., 1999—2001; exec. dir. and CEO Nashville Chamber Orch., 2002—. Participant ASOL Orch. Acad. Artistic Leadership Seminar, Aspen, Colo., 1999; exec. com. Odessa Cultural Coun., Odessa, Tex., 1983—90; chmn. Awesome Apr. campaign Nashville Conv. and Vis. Bur., Nashville, 2004—05; exec. com. Akron Area Arts Alliance, Ohio, 1992—98, sec., 1995—98; exec. com. Arts Assembly of Midland, Tex., 1983—90. Exec. prodr.: (recording) Kid Pan Alley- Nashville; prodr.: American Voices; prodr.: (recording) All-Bernstein with Florida Philharmonic; prodr.: (recording) The Music of Copland. Participant Leadership Midland, Midland, Tex., 1988—89, Leadership Akron, Akron, Ohio, 1991—92; bd. mem. Children's Services Bd., Akron, Ohio, 1995—98; dir. Ohio Young Scholars, Ohio, 1995—98. Mem.: Am. Symphony Orch. League (mgr. divsn. 6 1989—91, chmn. 1989—91, sec. 1994—95, mem. policy group B 1994—96, vice chmn. 1995, mgr. divsn. 5 1995, sec. 1998—99, mgr. divsn. 4 1998—99, mem. policy A mgr. com. 1998—99, vice chmn. 2003—, mgr. divsn. 6 2003—). Avocations: volleyball, reading, music. Home: 208 Summit Oaks Pl Nashville TN 37221 Office: Nashville Chamber Orch 2002 Blair Blvd Nashville TN 37212 Office Phone: 615-256-6546. Office Fax: 615-467-7023. E-mail: clinsler@nco.org.

LINSTER, MICHELLE LYNN, education educator, consultant; d. John Bufer, Sr. and Susie Graves Linster; m. George Thalma Glenn, Oct. 19, 1985 (div. Dec. 16, 2001); children: George Thalma Glenn III, Mari-Michele Linster Glenn, Jonathan Maxwell Linster Glenn. Masters, U. of N.C., 1981, PhD, 1985. Practicing Psychologist N.C. Psychology Bd., 1990. Adj. faculty Ctr. for Creative Leadership, Greensboro, NC, 1994—; asst. prof. Winston-Salem State U., NC, 1997—. Asst. prof. Bennett Coll., Greensboro, NC, 1986—91, chair psychology dept., 1990—91; practicing psychologist Pvt. Practice, Greensboro, NC, 1992—98. Mem. Jr. League, Greensboro, NC, 1989—2003; steering com. mem. Com. of 100, Greensboro, NC, 1994—99; bd. mem. Greensboro Montesorri Sch., Greensboro, NC, 1996—99; mem. APA, Washington, 1994—2000; co-chair outreach Super Computing Conf. 2003, 2002—03; evaluation specialists Super Computing Global 2003, 2002—03; mem. N.C. Psychol. Assn., Greensboro, NC, 1994—98. Scholar Fulbright Hayes Short Term Scholarship, Fulbright Found., 1990. Mem.: Southeastern Psychol. Assn., Am. Psychol. Soc., Jr. League, Jack and Jill, Inc. (sec. 2001—), Psi Chi (advisor wssu chpt. 2001—03), Delta Sigma Theta Sorority. Conservative. Baptist. Avocations: reading, writing, volunteering. Office: NC A&T State U 303 Gibbs Hall Greensboro NC 27412 Office Phone: 336-350-7970. Personal E-mail: linsterglenn1@msn.com. E-mail: mllinste@ncat.edu.

LINSTONE, HAROLD ADRIAN, management consultant, educator; b. Hamburg, Fed. Republic Germany, June 15, 1924; came to U.S., 1936; s. Frederic and Ellen (Seligmann) L.; m. Hedy Schubach, June 16, 1946; children: Fred A., Clark R. BS, CCNY, 1944; MA, Columbia U., 1947; PhD, U. So. Calif., 1954. Sr. scientist Hughes Aircraft Co., Culver City, Calif., 1949-61, The Rand Corp., Santa Monica, Calif., 1961-63; assoc. dir. planning Lockheed Corp., Burbank, Calif., 1963-71; prof. Portland (Oreg.) State U., 1970—. Pres. Systems Forecasting, Inc., Santa Monica, 1971-98; cons. 1973—. Author: Multiple Perspectives for Decision Making, 1984, Decision Making for Technology Executives, 1999; co-author: The Unbounded Mind, 1993, The Challenge of the 21st Century, 1994; co-editor The Delphi Method, 1975, Technological Substitution, 1976, Futures Research, 1977; editor-in-chief Technol. Forecasting Social Change, 1969—. Recipient Disting. Svc. award World Future Soc., 2003; NSF grantee, Washington, 1976, 79, 85. Mem. Inst. Mgmt. Scis., Ops. Rsch. Soc., Internat. Soc. Systems Scis. (pres. 1993-94). Avocation: photography. Office: Portland State U PO Box 751 Portland OR 97207-0751 Personal E-mail: linstoneh@aol.com.

LINSTROTH, TOD BRIAN, lawyer; b. Racine, Wis., Feb. 19, 1947; s. Eugene and Gloria L.; m. Jane Kathryn Zedler, June 23, 1972; children: Kathryn, Krista, Kassandre, Kyle. BBA in Acctg., U. Wis., 1970, JD, 1973. Bar: Wis. Assoc. Michael, Best & Friedrich, Madison, Wis., 1973-79, ptnr., 1980—, chair firm mgmt. com., 2003—05. Chmn. Wis. Tech. Coun., Inc., 2001—. Bd. visitors Univ. Wis. Sch. Bus., 1991-94; mem. Wis. Gov.'s Sci. and Tech. Coun., Madison, 1993-95; pres. Madison Repertory Theatre. Mem. Greater Madison Area C. of C., Wis. Venture Fair (chair Steering Com. 1997—), Wis. Tech. Coun. (chair 2001—). Avocations: skiing, sailing, reading. Office: Michael Best & Friedrich 1 S Pinckney St Ste 700 Madison WI 53703-4236 Office Phone: 608-257-3501. Business E-Mail: TBLinstroth@michaelbest.com.

LINTINGER, GREGORY JOHN, electrical engineer, educator; b. New Orleans, Oct. 8, 1946; s. Emile John Jr. and Lucy (Perez) L.; m. Barbara Gaudet, Mar. 14, 1965 (div. Sept. 1981); children: Gregory John Jr., Melissa Anne; m. Brenda Celeste Wambsgans, Dec. 12, 1981; 1 child, Emily Celeste. BS in Elec. Engring., U. New Orleans, 1985. Registered profl. engr., La., Tenn., Miss., Ark. Office mgr. Upper City Electric Co., New Orleans, 1967-72, elec. estimator, 1972-76, elec. designer, estimator, 1976-87, v.p. elec. design/estimating, 1987—; mgr., elec. and instrumental engring. dept. Wink Engring., New Orleans, 1994—. Instr. Associated Builders and Contractors, New Orleans, 1975-95. Pres. Young Men's Bus. Club of Greater New Orleans, 1975. Recipient Bush award Young Men's Bus. Club, New Orleans, 1973-75, Colomb award, 1975; named U. New Orleans Disting. Engring. Alumni, 1999. Mem. Illuminating Engrs. Soc. (sec. 1987-88), Inst. Electronic Engrs., Industry Application Soc. (exhibits chair 1997 annual meeting), Kiwanis (treas. 1986-87), A.B.C. (bd. dirs. New Orleans chpt. 1986-87). Republican. Roman Catholic. Avocations: piano, computers, music, philanthropy. Home: 639 Labarre Dr Metairie LA 70001-5442 Office: Wink Engineering Elect & Instrumental Engring Dept 4949 Bullard Ave Ste 100 New Orleans LA 70128-3147

LINTON, DONNA JOAN, foreign language educator, dean; b. Yonkers, N.Y., Aug. 13, 1953; d. Edward Howard and Marjorie Charlotte (Witthaus) L.; m. Roy Stuart Chustek, Dec. 5, 1981; children: Ian, Alison. BA in French, U. Houston, 1975; MA in French Lit., NYU, 1981. Coord. divsns. and discussion groups MLA, N.Y.C., 1978-79; tchr. French and Spanish Trevor Day Sch., N.Y.C., 1979—, dean of students, 1982-96. Coord. human sexuality edn. and life issues program Trevor Day Sch., N.Y.C., 1982-97; dir. Fgn. Lang. project, 1996—98, chmn., 1998—; presenter in field; conf. chmn., 1999—. Fulbright Teaching fellow French Govt., Montreuil, 1976-77. Mem. Assn. Tchrs. Independent Schs. (presenter, 1997, 98), Am. Assn. Tchrs. of French, Nat. Network Early Lang. Learning. Office: Trevor Day Sch 4 E 90th St New York NY 10128-0603 Business E-Mail: dlinton@trevornet.org.

LINTON, FRED ERNEST JULIUS, mathematics professor, department chairman; b. Genova, Italy, Apr. 8, 1938; arrived in US, 1940; s. Martin and Melitta (Joel) L.; m. Barbara Mikolajewska, Dec. 18, 1990. BA, Yale U., 1958; MA, Columbia U., 1959, PhD, 1963; MA (hon.), Wesleyan U., Middletown, Conn., 1972. Asst. prof. Wesleyan U., Middletown, 1963-68, assoc. prof., 1968-72, prof. math., 1972—, chmn. math. dept., 1975. Mem.: Math Assn. Am., Am. Math Soc. Home: 36 Everit St New Haven CT 06511-2208 Office: Wesleyan U Dept Math Middletown CT 06459-0001

LINTON, JACK ARTHUR, lawyer; b. N.Y.C., May 29, 1936; s. Paul Phillip and Helen (Feller) L.; div.; children: Ann Deborah Linton Wilmot, James Paul, John Michael. BA, Albright Coll., 1958; JD, NYU, 1961, LLM in Taxation, 1966. Bar: Pa. 1962, N.Y. 1963, U.S. Tax Ct. 1966, U.S. Dist. Ct. (ea. dist.) Pa. 1978, U.S. Ct. Appeals, 1984. Assoc. DeLong, Dry & Binder, Reading, Pa., 1961-63; asst. house counsel Bob Banner Assocs., Inc., N.Y.C., 1963-66; ptnr. DeLong, Dry, Cianci & Linton, Reading, 1967-70, Williamson, Miller, Murray & Linton, Reading, 1970-72, Gerber & Linton, P.C., Reading, 1972-88, Linton, Giannascoli, Barrett & Distasio, P.C., Reading, 1989-97, Linton, Giannascoli, Distasio & Adams, PC, Reading, 1997-98, Linton, Distasio, Adam & Kauffman, PC, Reading, 1998—2001, Linton, Distasio, Adams & Palanga, P.C., Reading, 2001—04, Linton, Distasio, Adams & Edwards, P.C., Reading, 2004—. Solicitor Reading Parking Authority, 1967-76, City of Reading, 1980-96, City of Reading Officers and Employees Retirement Bd., 1996—; solicitor, contr. County of Berks, 2002—; bd. dirs. The Group, Inc., Small Bus. Coun. Am., Inc., chmn. polit. action com., 1988—, numerous med. profl. corps., Reading area; lectr. nat. seminars on tax problems for small bus.; co-founder, mem. Estate Planning Coun. Berks County, 1978—. Editor Tax Law Rev., 1965-67; contbr. articles to profl. jours. Pres. Berks County Mental Health Assn., 1968-69, Reading Jewish Community Ctr., 1980-82; mem. Mental Health/Mental Retardation Bd. Berks County, 1974-80; treas., bd. dirs. Reading-Berks Youth Soccer League, 1982-85; bd. dirs. Gov. Mifflin Sch. Dist., Shillington, 1985-93, Exeter Township Sch. Dist., 1999-, v.p., 2000-. Kenneson fellow, NYU Sch. Law, 1965—67. Mem. ABA (mem. personal svc. orgn. com., tax sect. 1981—, chairperson task force for repeal top-heavy rules 1987-89, vice chmn. personal svc. orgn. com. 1990-92, chmn. personal svc. orgn. com. 1992-94), Pa. Bar Assn., Berks County Bar Assn. (treas. 1969-72), Berks County C. of C. (mem. govt. affairs com.). Democrat. Jewish. Avocations: sports, reading. Office: Linton Distasio Adams & Edwards PC PO Box 461 1720 Mineral Spring Rd Reading PA 19602-2231 Office Phone: 610-374-7320. Business E-Mail: linton@ldaklaw.com.

LINTON, JOY SMITH, primary school educator; b. Scranton, Pa., Dec. 9, 1952; d. Burnley J. and Josephine (Sbaraglia) Smith; m. William Howard Linton Jr., May 28, 1972; children: Kristy, David, Shelby, Jonathan. BSEd, West Chester State Coll., 1973. Minister St. Leo the Great Parish, Lancaster, Pa.; tchr. Hempfield United Meth. Preschool, Lancaster. Bio-med. ethics com., bio-med. edn. com. Ephrata Cmty. Hosp; subcom. med. and legal affairs Lancaster County Bar Assn. Mem. nat. bd. dirs., head family affairs commn. Nat. Coun. of Cath. Women, 1994-96 (pub. in Cath. Woman mag., submissions pub. in Bulletin Bd. publ.). Named St. Leo Woman of Yr., 1993; Hannah Kent Shopf Meml. scholar; Pa. Higher Edn. grantee. Mem. Nat. Assn. Edn. Young Children, Lancaster Assn. Edn. Young Children, Zeta Tau Alpha. Home: 808 Hillaire Rd Lancaster PA 17601-2221 E-mail: joy.linton@att.net.

LINTON, MICHAEL ALAN, retail company executive; b. East Cleveland, Ohio, Dec. 7, 1956; s. Ralph Edwin and Katherine (Vodanoff) L. BSBA, Bowling Green State U., 1978; MBA, Duke U., 1980. Brand asst. Proctor & Gamble, Cin., 1980-81, asst. brand mgr., 1982-83, brand mgr., 1983-87; mktg. mgr. Progressive Ins., Cleve., 1987-88, ops. adn ins. svcs. mgr., 1988-89, gen. mgr., asst. v.p., 1989-93; v.p. James River Corp., 1993-97; sr. v.p., strategic mktg. Best Buy Co., Inc., Eden Praire, Minn., 1999—2002, chief mktg. officer, EVP, consumer and brand marketing Richfield, Minn., 2002—. Bd. dirs. The Walker Mus. Contemp. Art, Peet's Coffee & Tea. Avocations: sports, travel, current events, biking. Office: Best Buy Co Inc 7601 Penn Ave S Richfield MN 55423 Office Phone: 612-291-5171.

LINTULA, MARGARET M., elementary and secondary school educator; b. Duluth, Minn., June 19, 1941; d. Yule Porter Eaton and Catherine Gurine Fleming Eaton Berg; m. John Elias Lintula, Aug. 17, 1963; 1 child, Maija Gurine Lintula Alexandrou. BS, U. Minn., 1963; MS, U. Wis., Superior, 1975. Lic. elem. tchr., K-12 reading specialist, Wis. Tchr. grade 4 Lakeside Elem. Sch., Duluth, 1963-66; tchr. grades 3-4 Boze Elem., Tacoma, 1967-71; tchr. English grades 7-8 Drummond (Wis.) Sch., 1971—2002, K-12 dist. reading specialist, 1976—2002; ret., 2002. Del. Dem. Nat. Conv., N.Y.C., 1992, state convs., 1988—, vice-chmn. Dem. party, Bayfield County, 1986-02. Named Secondary Tchr. of Yr., Wis. Congress Parents & Tchrs. Inc., 1989—90. Mem. NEA (bd. dirs. 1991-98, mem. women's issues com. 1998-02), Wis. Edn. Assn. Coun. (bd. dirs. 1976-82, 88-98), Drummond Edn. Assn. (pres., chief negotiator 1980-01), Wis. State Reading Assn., Internat. Reading Assn., Lions Club (Cable, Wis. chpt.). Democrat. Avocations: poetry, biking, painting, reading, travel. Home: PO Box 136 Drummond WI 54832-0136

LINTZ, BERNADETTE CELESTINE, French educator; b. Alsace, France; came to the U.S., 1977; Lic., U. Strasbourg, France, 1975; MA in English, U. Strasbourg, 1977; MA in French, Rice U., 1982, PhD in French, 1984. Tchg. fellow Rice U., Houston, 1979-81, instr., 1981-82; asst. prof. Colgate U., Hamilton, N.Y., 1983-89, assoc. prof., 1989—. Vis. assoc. prof. U. Mich., Dearborn, 2001—. Co-editor: Victor Hugo! Oeuvres et Critique (1981-83), 1992, The French Novel from Lafayette to Desvignes, 1995; contbr. articles to profl. jours. Grad. fellow Rice U., 1978-81; ACLS travel grantee, 1985; Sr. Picker Rsch. fellow Colgate U., 1990, Mellon grantee, 1999. Mem. MLA, Nineteenth Century French Studies Assn., Am. Assn. Tchrs. French, Assn. Internat. Zola Naturalism, Internat. Soc. Interdisciplinary Study, Groupe Inter-Univ. Victor Hugo. Avocations: travel, movies, photography. Office: Colgate U Dept Romance Langs & Lit 13 Oak Dr Hamilton NY 13346 E-mail: blintz@mail.colgate.edu.

LINTZ, ROBERT CARROLL, retired financial holding company executive; b. Cin., Oct. 2, 1933; s. Frank George and Carolyn Martha (Dickhaus) L.; m. Mary Agnes Mott, Feb. 1, 1964 (dec.); children— Lesa, Robert, Laura, Michael. B.B.A., U. Cin., 1956. Staff accountant Alexander Grant, Cin., 1958-60; dist. mgr. Uniroyal, Memphis, 1960-65; v.p. Am. Fin. Corp., Cin., 1965—2002; dir. Rapid-American Corp., McGregor Corp., Faberge Inc., all N.Y.C., H.R.T. Industries Inc., Los Angeles. Fisher Foods Inc., Cleve., Am. Agronomics, Tampa, Fla. Trustee, St. Francis-St. George Hosp., Cin., 1974-81. Served to capt. U.S. Army, 1956-58, 61-62. Republican. Roman Catholic. Home: 5524 Palisades Dr Cincinnati OH 45238-5620 Office: Am Fin Corp 1 E 4th St Cincinnati OH 45202-3717

LINVILL, JOHN GRIMES, engineering educator; b. Kansas City, Mo., Aug. 8, 1919; s. Thomas G. and Emma (Crayne) L.; m. Marjorie Webber, Dec. 28, 1943; children: Gregory Thomas, Candace Sue. AB, William Jewell Coll., 1941; SB, Mass. Inst. Tech., 1943, SM, 1945, ScD, 1949; D of Applied Sci., U. Louvain, Belgium, 1966; DSc, William Jewell Coll., 1992. Asst. prof. elec. engring. Mass. Inst. Tech., 1949-51; tech. staff Bell Telephone Labs., 1951-55; assoc. prof. elec. engring. Stanford U., 1955-57, prof., dir. solid-state electronics lab., 1957-64, prof., chmn. dept. elec. engring., 1964-80, prof., dir. Center for Integrated Systems, 1980-90—, Canon USA prof. engring., 1988-89, prof. emeritus, 1989—; co-founder, dir. Tele Sensory Corp., 1971-2000; dir. Read-Rite Corp., 1992-2000. Author: Transistors and Active Circuits, 1961, Models of Transistors and Diodes, 1963; inventor Optacon reading aid for the blind. Recipient citation for achievement William Jewell Coll., 1963, John Scott award for devel. of Optacon, City of Phila., 1980, Medal of Achievement Am. Electronics Assn., 1983, Louis Braille Prize Deutscher Blindenverband, 1984. Fellow IEEE (Edn. medal 1976), AAAS; mem. Nat. Acad. of Engring., Am. Acad. of Arts and Scis. Office: Stanford U Dept Elec Engring Stanford CA 94305 Home: 325 Sharon Park Dr 205 Menlo Park CA 94025 also: 620 Sand Hill Rd Apt 122 F Palo Alto CA 94304 Business E-Mail: linvill@ee.stanford.edu.

LINVILLE, RAY PATE, educational association administrator, retired military officer, editor, writer; b. Winston-Salem, N.C., Feb. 27, 1946; s. Clyde Burton and Nellie Pearl (Helm) L.; m. Mary Ann Slordal, July 30, 1970; children: Russell Pate, Rachel Ann. BA in Journalism, U. N.C., 1967; MS in Logistics Mgmt. with distinction, Air Force Inst. Tech., 1973. Commd. 2d lt. USAF, 1967, advanced through grades to col., 1989, materials mgr. Madrid, 1973-76; mem. staff Tactical Air Command, Hampton, Va., 1976-79; plans officer UN Command, Seoul, Korea, 1980-81; staff analyst USAF, Washington, 1981-85; rsch. fellow Harvard U., Cambridge, Mass., 1985-86; chief combat support analysis Joint Chiefs of Staff, Washington, 1986-89; dir. logistics plans Strat. Air Command, Omaha, 1989-92; chief logistics plans and programs Air Combat Command, Hampton, 1992-93; ret. USAF, 1994; rsch. fellow Logistics Mgmt. Inst., McLean, Va., 1993-2000. Adj. prof. U. Va., Falls Church, 1986—88; grad. prof. Webster U., Washington, 1988—2000; adj. grad. prof. U. So. Calif., L.A., 1981; mgr. alumni edn. U. N.C. Gen. Alumni Assn., 2000—; English instr. Wake Tech. C.C., Raleigh, NC, 2003, Sandhills C.C., Pinehurst, NC, 2004—. Author: (monograph) Command and Control of Forces..., 1987; editor, asst. editor, mem. rev. bd. Logistics Spectrum, 1990-2000; contbr. articles to profl. jours. Dir., v.p., treas. Danbury Forest Com. Assn., Springfield, Va., 1982-84; youth group advisor, deacon Presbyn. Ch., Omaha and Fairfax, Va., 1986-99. Decorated Legion of Merit; recipient Outstanding Young Man of Am. award U.S. Jaycees, 1978. Mem. Internat. Soc. Logistics (sr., life, cert. profl. logistician, chpt. chmn. 1990-91, Bronze award 1991, Pres.'s award for Merit 1996, 97, 99), Air Force Assn. (life), U. N.C. Gen. Alumni Assn. (life), U.S. Chess Fedn. (life), Sigma Iota Epsilon. Avocations: writing, golf, piano, chess. Home: 845 St Andrews Dr Pinehurst NC 28374-9621 Office: U NC Gen Alumni Assn PO Box 660 Chapel Hill NC 27514-0660 Business E-Mail: linville@carolina.net.

LINXWILER, LOUIS MAJOR, JR., retired finance company executive; b. Blackwell, Okla., Mar. 7, 1931; s. Louis Major and Flora Mae (Horton) Linxwiler; m. Susan Buchanan, July 27, 1963 (dec.); children: Louis Major III, Robert William. BS, Okla. State U., 1953. Mgr. credit dept. Valley Nat. Bank, Tucson, 1957-60; sales rep. Vega Industries, Syracuse, NY, 1960-62; program dir. Am. Cancer Soc., Phoenix, 1962-67; v.p., mgr. credit dept. United Bank Ariz., Phoenix, 1967-76; dean edn. Am. Inst. Banking, Phoenix, 1976-80; cons. United Student Aid Funds Inc., Phoenix, 1980—81, U. Phoenix, 1981; founder, pres., CEO, bd. dirs. Ariz. Student Loan Fin. Corp., 1981—88; founder, chmn., CEO Western Loan Mktg. Assn., Phoenix, 1984-90; pres. Precision Design and Engring., Inc., Phoenix, 1993—, Circulator Motor Co., Phoenix, 1996—; organizer, mng. ptnr. Energy Transition Products, L.L.C., 1998—. Organizer, v.p. Pollution Free Planet Found., Alternative Energy Sys., LLC. Editor: Money and Banking, 1978, The Solar Hydrogen Civilization, 2003. Pres. bd. dirs. Phoenix YMCA, 1974—75; v.p. N. Mountain Behavioral Inst., Phoenix, 1975—77; pres. City Commn. Sister Cities, Phoenix, 1986—87, Am. Inst. Banking, Phoenix, 1973—74. Served to 1st lt. U.S. Army, 1954—56. Mem.: Rotary (bd. dirs. 1982—83, 1993—94, 1996—97, 2003—04, 2005—), Shriners, Beta Theta Pi. Republican. Presbyterian. Avocations: restoring automobiles, WWII history, hydrogen fuel research. Home: 222 S 54th Pl Mesa AZ 85206-1406 Personal E-mail: loulinx@cox.net.

LINZ, ANTHONY JAMES, osteopathic physician, consultant, educator; b. Sandusky, Ohio, June 16, 1948; s. Anthony Joseph and Margaret Jane (Ballah) Linz; m. Kathleen Ann Kovach, Aug. 18, 1973; children: Anthony Scott, Sara Elizabeth. BS, Bowling Green State U., 1971; D.O., Des Moines U., 1974. Diplomate Nat. Bd. Osteo. Examiners; bd. cert., diplomate Am. Osteo. Bd. Internal Medicine, Internal Medicine, Med. Diseases of Chest and Critical Care Medicine. Intern South Pointe Hosp. Brentwood Hosp., Cleve., 1974-75; resident in internal medicine South Pointe Hosp. Cleve. Clinic Sys., 1975-78; chief resident Brentwood Hosp., 1977-78; subsplty. fellow in pulmonary diseases Riverside Meth. Hosp., Columbus, Ohio, 1978-80; med. dir. pulmonary svcs. Sandusky (Ohio) Meml. Hosp., 1980-85; med. dir. cardio-pulmonary svcs. Firelands Community Hosp., Sandusky, 1985—. Cons. staff dept. medicine Good Samaritan Hosp., 1982—85, sect. internal medicine specializing pulmonary diseases; cons. pulmonary, critical care and internal medicine Firelands Regional Med. Ctr., 1985—, active staff sect. internal medicine, chmn. dept. medicine, head div. pulmonary medicine, 1985—; cons. pulmonary, critical care, and internal medicine Providence Hosp., Sandusky, Mercy Hosp., Willard, Ohio; clin. prof. pulmonary and critical care med.,internal med. Ohio U. Coll. Osteo. Medicine; clin. prof. medicine Univ. Health Scis. Coll. Osteo. Medicine, Kansas City, Mo.; clin. asst. prof. med. Med. Coll. of Ohio at Toledo; adj. prof. applied scis. Bowling Green State U., mem. respiratory tech. adv. bd. Firelands Campus, 1983—, med. dir. respiratory care tech. program, 1984—; clin. prof. pulmonary and critical care med. Des Moines U.; rep. Pub. Health Adminstrn., 2001—; exec. bd. pub. health student orgn. N.W. Ohio Consortium for Pub. Health; cons. physician O.E. Meyer Corp., 2003—. Contbr. articles and abstracts to profl. jours. Water safety instr. ARC, 1965—; med. dir., clin. rsch. investigator Camp Superkid Asthma Camp, 1984-97; bd. trustees Stein Hospice, 1986-90, chmn., 2000--; mem. adv. bd. Ams. with Disabilities Act, City of Sandusky, Ohio, chmn., 2001--; med. dir. in residence Camp Superkids Asthma Camp, 1984-97 Recipient Edward Ruff Comty. Svc. award Am. Lung. Assn., 1985, Master Clinician award Ohio U. Coll. Osteopathic Medicine, 1987, Golden Rule award J.C. Penney, 1990, Disting. Alumna/Alumnus award Firelands Coll., Bowling Green State U., 1995. Fellow: ACP-Am. Soc. Internal Medicine (Ohio chpt.), Am. Coll. Osteo. Internists (master) (Grover Gillum Soc. Master Fellows), Am. Coll. Critical Care Medicine, Am. Coll. Chest Physicians; mem.: AAAS, Ohio Lung Assn. (N.W. regional adv. bd.), Found. Critical Care (mem. Founder's Cir.), Ohio Pub. Health Assn., Am. Soc. Internal Medicine, So. Critical Care Medicine, Ohio Soc. Respiratory Care (med. adviser/dir. 1982—), Nat. Assn. Med. Dirs. Respiratory Care, Sandusky Yacht Club (corr.), Am. Lung Assn. (bd. dirs. Ohio's So. Shore sect. 1984—, pres., 1st v.p., exec. bd. dirs., med. adv. bd. chmn., bd. dirs. Ohio Norwest Region), Ohio Thoracic Soc., Am. Thoracic Soc., Am. Heart Assn., Ohio Osteo. Assn. (past pres., past v.p., past sec.-treas., acad. trustees 5th dist. acad.), Am. Osteo. Assn., European Thoracic Soc., Phi Kappa Phi, Atlas Med. Fraternity, Pi Kappa Alpha, Beta Beta Beta, Alpha Epsilon Delta. Roman Catholic. Office Phone: 419-626-7400. Office Fax: 419-621-0642. Personal E-mail: doclinz@aol.com.

LINZ, WERNER MARK, international publishing executive; b. Cologne, Germany, Apr. 6, 1935; came to U.S., 1959, naturalized, 1976; s. George A. and Catherine B. (Wegener) L.; m. Helen Ruth Baumler, July 27, 1959; children: Julia, Alice. Student, U. Frankfurt, Germany, 1954-57, NYU, 1958. Successively treas., mktg. v.p., exec. v.p. Herder & Herder Pub. Co., N.Y.C., 1958-71; pub., gen. mgr. Herder div. McGraw-Hill Book Co., 1971-73; pres., chief exec. officer Seabury Press, N.Y.C., 1973-80; founder, chmn., CEO Continuum Pub. Co. and Crossroad Pub. Co., N.Y.C., 1980-92; chmn., CEO Continuum Pub. Group, N.Y.C., 1992-2000; co-founder, v. chmn. Continuum Internat. Pub. Group, London and N.Y.C., 2000—; dir. Am. U. Press, Cairo, 1995—. Adj. prof. mktg. NYU, City U., Pace U. Charter mem. nat. adv. com. Ctr. for the Book Libr. of Congress; mem. Nat. Com. on Higher Edn. and Libr. Programs; bd. dirs. Peterson's, Princeton, N.J., Aperture Found., Jung Found., N.Y.C. Mem. Assn. Am. Pubs. (bd. dirs., chmn. edn. com.), Soc. Scholarly Pub. (charter) Clubs: University (N.Y.C.); Am. Yacht (Rye, N.Y.). Home: 230 Stuyvesant Ave Rye NY 10580-3115 Office: Am U in Cairo 420 Fifth Ave New York NY 10017 also: Continuum International Pub Group 15 E 26th St 17 New York NY 10010-1505

LINZEY, JAMES FRANKLIN, minister, military officer, vocalist; b. San Diego, Sept. 26, 1958; s. Stanford Eugene and Verna May (Hall) L. BA in Religion, Vanguard U. So. Calif., 1979; MDiv, Fuller Theol. Sem., 1983; DD, Kingsway Theol. Sem., 2000. Ordained Assemblies of God Internat. Fellowship, 1977. Pastor of youth First Assembly of God, Huntington Park, Calif., 1979-80, assoc. pastor Sun Valley, Calif., 1982-83; telephone clk. World Vision Hdqrs., Pasadena, Calif., 1983; tchr. Santa Ana (Calif.) Unified Sch. Dist., 1983-85; commd. 1st lt. USAF, Norton AFB, Calif., 1985-89, advanced through grades to capt., 1989; Protestant chaplain USAFR, Norton AFB, 1985—94, Vandenburg AFB, Calif., 1994-95, USAF, Laughlin AFB, Tex., 1995-98, 244th Quartermaster Bn., Ft. Lee, Va., 1998-2001, 249th Signal Bn. U.S. N.G., Dallas, 2001—. Tchr. L.A. Unified Sch. Dist., 1985-93, La Mirada-Norwalk Unified Sch. Dist., 1993-95; sr. pastor Cornerstone Cmty. Ch., Anaheim, Calif., 1986-88; chaplain Full Gospel Businessmen's Fellowship Internat., Knott's Berry Farm Chpt., Buena Park, Calif., 1992-94, v.p., 1992-94. Rec. artist (tape) Who Am I, 1993, (CD) You Were Always There, 1994, When the World Turns to God, 1995, Narrow Road, 2000; author: A Divine Appointment in Washington, D.C., 1999, The Holy Spirit, 2004; host: Operations Freedom on Vision Channel, Europe, 2004-05, Prime Time Christian Broadcasting, 2004-05 and Angel One, Phillipines. contbr. articles to jours. Choir dir. First United Meth. Ch., La Palma, Calif., 1983-84; assoc. pastor Messenger Fellowship, Norwalk, Calif., 1985-86; state chaplain U.S. Res. Officers Assn. Calif., 1991-94. Commd. Capt. Chaplain U.S. Army, 2000, advanced through grades to Major, 2002. Decorated Air Force Commendation medal with oak leaf cluster, Army Commendation medal with oak leaf cluster. Mem. Nat. Assn. Evangelicals, Res. Officers Assn. (state chaplain 1991-94), Gospel Music Assn. Republican. Achievements include chaplain for largest mobilization mission in U.S. for Operation Iraqi Freedom. Avocations: golf, volleyball, chess. Home: 22 White Sands Missile Range White Sands Missile Range NM 88002

LINZEY, VERNA MAY, minister, writer; b. Coffeyville, Kans., May 17, 1919; d. Carey Franklin Hall Jr. and Alice May (Hart) Hall-Doyle; m. Stanford Eugene Linzey Jr., July 13, 1941; children: Gena May English, Janice Ellen Mathis, Stanford Eugene III, Virginia Darnelle Lemons(dec.), Sharon Faye, George William, Vera Evelyn Clark, Paul Edward, David Leon, James Franklin. Student, Southwestern Assembly of God U., Waxahachie, Tex., 1938—39, Fuller Theol. Sem., Pasadena, Calif., 1980—. Lic. Minister Assembly of God, 1945. Asst. minister First Assembly of God, Baldwin Park, Calif., 1953—54; co-founder Holy Spirit Evangelism, Escondido, Calif., 1976—. Cons. Holy Spirit Evangelism, Escondido, Calif., 1976—; leader Pentecostal Movement Worldwide, 1976; TV interviews/appearances PBS, 2004, Prime Time Christian Broadcasting Netwokk, 2004. Songwriter: O Blessed Jesus, 2004; author: The Baptism with the Holy Spirit, 2004; contbr. articles to religious publs., 2001—02. Mem. adv. bd. Operation Freedom, 2003—; mem. nat. com. Dem. orgn., 1943—45, Republican Orgn., 1946—. Recipient Cert. of Recognition, Mayor of Escondido, Calif., 2001, Congressional Proclamation Rev. Dr. Verna May Linzey Day April 29th, 2001. Avocations: gardening, piano, photography, genealogy, singing. Home: 1641 Kenora Dr Escondido CA 92027 Office: Verna M Linzey 354 E Washington Ave Ste A Escondido CA 92025 Office Phone: 760-743-3913. Personal E-mail: vlinzey@aol.com.

LINZNER, JOEL, lawyer; b. Phila., May 11, 1952; BA, Brandeis U., 1974; JD, U. Calif., Berkeley, 1977. Bar: Calif. 1977, U.S. Ct. Appeals (9th cir.) 1979, U.S. Supreme Ct. 1987. Former ptnr. Crosby, Heafey, Roach & May P.C., Oakland, Calif.; v.p. worldwide bus. affairs Electronic Arts, Calif., 1999—2002, sr. v.p. worldwide bus. affairs, 2002—04, sr. v.p. legal & bus. affairs, 2004—. Adj. prof. Sch. Law Santa Clara U., 1990, 92-93. Contbr. articles to profl. jours. Mem. ABA, State Bar Calif., Bar Assn. San Francisco. Office: Crosby Heafey Roach & May PC PO Box 2084 Oakland CA 94604-2084

LIO, YUHLONG, mathematician, educator; s. Ren-Fu Lio and Shwu-Jen Lee; m. Biying Lee Lio, Feb. 14, 1982; children: Vicky, Wilber. BS, Nat. Cheng-Kung U., Tai-Nan, Taiwan, 1977; MS, Nat. Ctrl. U., Chung-Li, Taiwan, 1979; PhD, U. S.C., 1987. Instr. math. and engring. U. Chung-Yuan, Taiwan, 1979—83; tchg. asst. U. S.C., Columbia, 1983—87; asst. prof. math. U. S.D., Vermillion, 1987—91, assoc. prof., 1991—97, prof., 1997—. Adj. prof. Calif. Nat. U., 1993—; vis. scholar Harvard U., 1994; supported by USAF Office Sci. Rsch., 1984—87, Hughes Med. Inst., 1995, 1996—97; presenter in field; referee various math. jours. Contbr. articles to profl. jours. Grantee, SD Dept. Correction, 1989, Rsch. Office U. SD, 1998, Gov. of SD, 2001. Mem.: Inst. Math. Stats., Am. Statis. Assn., Math. Assn. Am., Pi Mu Epsilon. Office: U SD 414 E Clark St Vermillion SD 57069 Office Phone: 605-677-5991. Business E-Mail: ylio@usd.edu.

LION, LINDA N., retired federal agency administrator; b. Brookline, Mass., Feb. 18, 1949; m. Donor M. Lion, Sept. 29, 1978; 2 children. BA in Biology, Wheaton Coll., 1970; PhD, MIT, 1975; grad., Nat. Def. U., Ft. Lesley J. McNair, Washington, 1990. Instr. human nutrition MIT, Cambridge, 1975-76; ind. nutrition cons. Haiti, Dominican Republic, Ghana, Bolivia, 1976-77; regional health and nutrition adviser Health & Nutrition Divsn. Office Devel. Resources Bur. Latin Am. and Caribbean USAID, Washington, 1977-78; dir. Office Health, Population & Nutrition USAID, Jamaica, 1978-79; health devel. officer, officer policy devel. & program rev. Bur. Policy and Program Coord. USAID, Washington, 1979; dir. Office Health Population & Nutrition USAID, Guyana, 1979-81, dir. Office Project Devel. & Monitoring Pakistan, 1981-85; chief Mid. East Divsn. Office Project Devel. Bur. Asia and Near East USAID, Washington, 1985-86; chief Capital Devel. Project Divsn. USAID, Peru, 1986-87, dir. Office Human Resources, 1987-89, dep. dir. Office Info. Resources Mgmt. Bur. Mgmt. Washington, 1990-94, mission dir. regional support mission for East Asia Bangkok, 1994-96, dep. asst. adminstr. human resources Bur. Mgmt. Washington, 1996—2000, dep. asst. adminstr. global programs, 2000—02. Avocations: golf, bridge. Office: 6600 Baymeadow Ct Mc Lean VA 22101

LIONAKIS, GEORGE, architect; b. West Hiawatha, Utah, Sept. 5, 1924; s. Pete and Andriani (Protopapadakis) L.; student Carbon Jr. Coll., 1942-43, 46-47; BArch., U. Oreg., 1951; m. Iva Oree Braddock, Dec. 30, 1951; 1 dau., Deborah Jo. With Corps Engrs., Walla Walla, Wash., 1951-54; architect Liske, Lionakis, Beaumont & Engberg, Sacramento, 1954-86, Lionakis-Beaumont Design Group, 1986—. Mem. Sacramento County Bd. Appeals, 1967—, chmn., 1969, 75, 76; pres. Sacramento Builders Exchange, 1976. Served with USAAF, 1943-46. Mem. AIA (pres. Central Valley chpt., 1972—), Constrn. Specifications Inst. (pres. Sacramento chpt., 1962; nat. awards, 1962, 63, 65), Sacramento C. of C. (code com., 1970—). Club: North Ridge Country (pres. 1987). Lodge: Rotarian (pres. East Sacramento 1978-79). Prin. works include Stockton (Calif.) Telephone Bldg., 1968, Chico (Calif.) Main Telephone Bldg., 1970, Mather AFB Exchange Complex Sacramento, 1970, Base Chapel Mather AFB, Sacramento, 1970, Woodridge Elementary Sch., Sacramento, 1970, Pacific Telephone Co. Operating Center Modesto, Calif., 1968, Sacramento, 1969, Marysville, Calif., 1970, Red Bluff, Calif., 1971, Wells Fargo Banks, Sacramento, 1968, Corning, Calif., 1969, Anderson, 1970, Beale AFB Exchange Complex, Marysville, 1971, Cosumnes River Coll., Sacramento, 1971, base exchanges at Bergstrom AFB, Austin, Tex., Sheppard AFB, Wichita Falls, Tex., Chanute AFB, Rantoul, Ill., McChord AFB, Tacoma, Wash., health center Chico State U., Sacramento County Adminstrn. Center, Sacramento Bee Newspaper Plant. Home: 160 Breckenwood Way Sacramento CA 95864-6968 Office: Lionakis Beaumont Design Group 1919 19th St Sacramento CA 95814-6714

LIONE, GAIL ANN, lawyer; b. NYC, Oct. 22, 1949; d. James G. and Dorothy Ann (Marsino) L.; 1 child, Margo A. Peyton. BA in Polit. Sci., magna cum laude, U. Rochester, 1971; JD, U. Pa., 1974. Bar: Pa. 1974, Ga. 1975, D.C. 1990, N.C. 1998. Atty. Morgan, Lewis & Bockius, Phila., 1974-75, Hansell & Post, Atlanta, 1975-80; v.p. 1st Nat. Bank of Atlanta, 1980-86; sr. v.p., corp. sec., gen. counsel Sun Life Group of Am., Inc., Atlanta, 1986-89; v.p. Md. Nat. Bank, Balt., 1989-90; gen. counsel, sec. U.S. News & World Report, L.P., Applied Graphics Technologies, Atlantic Monthly Co., Washington, 1990—97; v.p., gen. counsel, sec. Harley-Davidson, Inc., Milw., 1997—. Bd. mgrs. U. Pa. Law Sch., 1982-85. Sec., dir., com. chair State Bar Ga. (Young Lawyers Sect.), 1976-84; Chmn. bd. Spl. Audiences, Inc., 1983-85, bd. dirs., 1975-89; trustee Client Security Fund State Bar Ga., 1985-89; vice chmn. Metro Atlanta United Way Campaign, 1986-87; chmn. bd. Atlanta Ballet, 1985-86, bd. dirs., 1975-89; mem. Atlanta Legal Aid Soc., 1981-89; bd. mgrs. U. Pa. Law Sch., 1982-85; mem. U. Rochester Trustee Coun., 1994—; bd. dirs. YMCA Balt., 1989-90; past bd. dirs. Metro YMCA, Atlanta, Sudden Infant Death Syndrome Inst., Atlanta Cmty. Food Bank; mem. Leadership Atlanta, 1988; mem. fin. com. Nat. Symphony Ball, 1995; adv. bd. Cardiovascular Ctr. Medical Coll. Wis., 1999-2002; mem., bd. dirs. Bradley Ctr. Sports & Entertainment Corp., 2003-; Milw. Art Mus., 2004-, Outstanding Atlanta award, TOYPA, 1982, outstanding Vol. Golden Rule award, 1984; named Top 40 Under 40 Atlanta Mag., 1984, Top 20 Women in Atlanta by Atlanta Bus. Chronicle, 1987; teaching fellow Salzburg Inst., 1989. Mem. ABA (mem. ho. delegates, 1980-84, chmn. standing com. comm. on assn. comms., 1993-96, co-chair. litig. sect. com. fed. legis. 1994—96, regional co-chair forum on comms. law, 1996—98, standing com. on publishing oversight and strategic comms., 1996-2000), Copywright Soc. USA (trustee 1996-99), Manufacturing Inst., 2002-, Nat. Assn. Manufacturers, Phi Beta Kappa Office: Harley Davidson 3700 W Juneau Ave PO Box 653 Milwaukee WI 53201-0653 Office Phone: 414-343-4044.

LIOTTA, LANCE ALLEN, pathologist; b. Cleve., July 12, 1947; married; 2 children. BA in Gen. Sci. and Biology, Hiram Coll., 1969; PhD in Biomed. Engring. and Biomath., Case Western U., 1974, MD, 1976. Cert. basic life support Am. Heart Assn., advanced life support Am. Heart Assn. Instr. pathology for inhalation therapists dept. pathology St. Luke's Hosp., Cleve., 1972-74; sr. instr. pulmonary pathology Phase I and Phase II, Sch. Medicine Case Western Reserve U., 1973-74; USPHS resident physician Lab. Pathology, Nat. Cancer Inst. NIH, Bethesda, Md., 1976-78, pathologist, expert/cons. Lab. Pathophysiology, Nat. Cancer Inst., 1978-80, sr. investigator, pub. health svc. officer Lab. Pathophysiology and Pathology, Nat. Cancer Inst., 1980-82, chief tumor invasion and metastases sect. Lab. Pathology and Lab. Pathology, Nat. Cancer Inst., 1982—, dir. anatomic pathology residency program Lab. Pathology, Nat. Cancer Inst., 1982—, dep. dir. intramural rsch., 1992-93. Adj. clin. prof. pathology Sch. Medicine George Wash. U.; mem. adj. faculty Sch. Medicine Georgetown U.; invited faculty mem. Rockefeller U., 1979; speaker in field. Author: (with others) Cancer Invasion and Metastasis, 1977, Pulmonary Metastasis, 1978, Metastatic Tumor Growth, 1980, Bone Metastasis, 1981, Cell Biology of Breast Cancer, 1980, New Trends in Basement Membrane Research, 1982, Tumor Invasion and Metastasis, 1982, Progress in Clinical and Biological Research, 1982, Growth of Cells in Hormonally Defined Media, 1982, Understanding Breast Cancer: Clinical and Laboratory Concepts, 1983, The Role of Extracellular Matrix in Development, 1984, Basic Mechanisms and Clinical Treatment of Tumor Metastasis, 1985, Hemostatic Mechanisms and Metastasis, 1984, Biological Responses in Cancer, vol. 4, 1985, The Cell in Contact: Adhesions and Junctions as Morphogenetic Determinants, 1985, Rheumatology, vol. 10, 1986, Progress in Neuropathology, vol. 6, 1986, Cancer Metastasis: Experimental and Clinical Strategies, 1986, Biochemistry and Molecular Genetics of Cancer Metastasis, 1986, Basement Membranes, 1985, 1986 Year Book of Cancer, New Concepts in Neoplasia as Applied to Diagnostic Pathology, 1986, Head and Neck Management of the Cancer Patient, 1986, Cancer Metastasis: Biological and Biochemical Mechanisms and Clinical Aspects, 1988, Important Advances in Oncology, 1988, Breast Cancer: Cellular and Molecular

Biology, 1988, Cancer: Principles and Practice of Oncology, vol. 1, 3d edit., 1989, Molecular Mechanisms in Cellular Growth and Differentiation, 1991, Peptide Growth Factors and Their Receptors, 1990, Molecuar Genetics in Cancer Diagnosis, 1990, Cancer Surveys-Advances & Prospects in Clinical, Epidemiological and Laboratory Oncology, vol. 7, no. 4, 1988, Genetic Mechanisms in Carcinogenesis and Tumor Progression, 1990, Molecular and Cellular Biology, Host Immune Responses and Perspectives for Treatment, 1989, Origins of Human Cancer: A Comprehensive Review, 1991, Cancer and Metastasis Reviews, vol. 9, 1990, Comprehensive Textbook of Oncology, 1991, Textbook of Internal Medicine, 2d edit., vol. 2, 1992, Molecular Foundations in Oncology, 1991, Genes, Oncogenes, and Hormones: Advances in Cellular and Molecular Biology of Breast Cancer, 1991, Cell Motility Factors, 1991, Oncogenes and Tumor Suppressor Genes in Human Malignancies, 1993, Principles and Practice of Gnecologic Oncology, 1992, Cancer Medicine, 3d edit., 1993; contbr. articles to profl. jours. NIH Pre-doctoral fellow; recipient Arthur S. Flemming award, 1983, Flow award lectureship Soc. Cell Biology, 1983, Nat. award and lectureship Am. Assn. Clin. Chemistry, 1987, Rsch. award Susan G. Komen Found., 1987, Disting. Lectr. award Rush Cancer Ctr., 1987, George Hoyt Whipple award and lectureship Sch. Medicine U. Rochester, 1988, Karen Grunebaum Symposium award lectureship Hubert H. Humphrey Cancer Rsch. Ctr., 1988, Cancer Rsch. award Milken Family Med. Found., 1988, William M. Shelly Meml. award and lectureship Centennial Johns Hopkins Med. Inst., 1989, Josef Steiner Cancer Found. prize, 1989, Basic Rsch. award Am. Soc. Cytology, 1989, Officer's Recognition award Equal Employment Opportunity, 1990, John W. Cline Cancer Rsch. award and lectureship U. Calif., 1990, Herman Pinkus award lectureship Am. Soc. Dermatology, 1990, Simon M. Shubitz award U. Chgo. Cancer Ctr., 1991, Stanley Gore Rsch. award, 1991, Lila Gruber Cancer Rsch. award Am. Acad. Dermatology, 1991, Am.-Italian Found. Cancer Rsch. award, 1992, Scie. Achievement medal U.S. Surgeon Gen., 1994. Mem. Am. Assn. Cancer Rsch. (bd. dirs., 6th Ann. Rhoads Meml. award 1985), Am. Assn. Pathologists (Warner-Lambert/Parke-Davis award 1984), Am. Soc. Cell Biology, Am. Soc. Clin. Investigation, Internat. Acad. Pathology, Internat. Assn. Metastasis Rsch. (pres. 1990-93), Sigma Xi, Phi Beta Kappa. Achievements include patents for method and device for determining the concentration of a material in a liquid, method for isolating bacterial colonies, test method for separating and/or isolating bacteria and tissue cells, device and method for detecting phenothiazine-type drugs in uring, in vitro assay for cell invasiveness, enzyme immunoassay with two-zoned device having bound antigens, metalloproteinase peptides, matrix receptors role in diagnosis and therapy of cancer, genetic method for predicting tumor aggressiveness, therapeutic application of an anti-invasive compound; patents for role of tumor motility factors in cancer diagnosis, role of tumor metalloproteinases in cancer diagnosis, peptide inhibitor of metalloproteinases, protein inhibitors of metalloproteinases, autotaxin motility stimulating proteins diagnosis and therapy, motility receptor protein and gene diagnosis and therapy. Office: Lab of Pathology Nat Cancer Inst 9000 Rockville Pike Bethesda MD 20892-0001

LIOTTA, RAY, actor; b. Newark, Dec. 18, 1955; s. Alfred and Mary Liotta; m. Michelle Grace Liotta, Feb. 15, 1997 (div. 2004); 1 child. Grad., U. Miami. Actor (TV appearances: series and films) Another World, NBC, 1978-81, Hardhat & Legs, CBS movie, 1980, Crazy Times, ABC pilot, 1981, Casablanca, NBC, 1983, Our Family Honor, NBC, 1985-86, Women and Men: Stories of Seducation, 1990, Women and Men 2: In Love There Are no Rules, 1991, Point of Origin, 2002; (films) The Lonely Lady, 1983, Something Wild, 1986, Arena Brains, 1987, Dominick and Eugene, 1988, Field of Dreams, 1989, Goodfellas, 1990, Article 99, 1992, Unlawful Entry, 1992, No Escape, 1994, Corrina, Corrina, 1994, Operation Dumbo Drop, 1995, Unforgettable, 1996, Turbulence, 1997, Copland, 1997, Phoenix, 1998 (also co-prodr.), The Rat Pack, 1998, Forever Mine, 1999, Muppets From Space, 1999, Pilgram, 2000, A Rumor of Angels, 2000, Hannibal, 2001, Heartbreakers, 2001, Blow, 2001, Narc, 2002 (also prodr.), John Q, 2002, Identity, 2003, The Last Shot, 2004, Control, 2004, Revolver, 2005, Slow Burn, 2005 (also co-exec. prodr.); guest appearances include St. Elsewhere, 1983, Mike Hammer, 1984, Frasier, 1995, Family Guy (voice), 2001, Just Shoot Me!, 2001, 2002; Saturday Night Live (host), 2003, Punk'd, 2003, ER, 2004 (Creative Arts Primetime Emmy awards for guest actor in a drama, 2005). Mem. SAG, AFTRA. Office: Endeavor Talent Agy 9701 Wilshire Blvd Beverly Hills CA 90212*

LIOU, FUE-WEN FRANK, engineering educator; b. Taichung, Taiwan, Sept. 24, 1957; came to U.S., 1982; s. Fun-Nien and Jay-Yu (Lay) L.; m. Min-Yu Liao, July 14, 1987; children: Jonathan, Connie. BS, Nat. Cheng-Kung U., Tainan, Taiwan, 1980; MS, N.C. State U., 1984; PhD, U. Minn., 1987. Asst. prof. mech. engring. U. Mo., Rolla, 1987-93, rsch. assoc. intelligent sys. ctr., 1991-93, rsch. investigator intelligent sys. ctr., 1993-97, assoc. prof. mech. engring., 1993-99, prof. mech. engring., 1999—, sr. rsch. investigator intelligent sys. ctr., 1997—, interim program coord. mfg. engring., 1998—. Boeing A.D. Welliver faculty fellow Boeing Co., Wichita, Kans., 1997; chair exec. com. Mfg. Edn. Program, Rolla, Mo., 1998—, dir., 2000—. Contbr. over 100 articles to profl. jours. Major Rsch. Equipment grantee NSF, 1998. Mem. ASME, Am. Soc. Engring. Edn., SAE (faculty advisor 1989-94, advisor 1994). Office: U Mo 121 Me Anx Rolla MO 65409-1350 Office Phone: 573-341-4603. Business E-Mail: liou@umr.edu.

LIPAN, HOWARD KENNETH, information technology executive; b. NYC, June 17, 1939; s. Irving and Rose Lipan; m. Nanci Lee Youngerman, May 28, 1971 (div. Feb. 1986); m. Marjorie Ann Morris, May 29, 1988. BS, Columbia U., 1966, postgrad., 1967-68. Computer programmer Met. Life, N.Y.C., 1968-69; sys. analyst Western Union, N.Y.C., 1969-71; project leader, sys. architect E.F. Shelley & Co., N.Y.C., 1971-75; dir. applications and sys. devel. NYU, N.Y.C., 1975-76; pres. Digital Automation Enterprises, N.Y.C., 1977-82; sr. cons., founding mem. The Yourdon Cons. Group, N.Y.C., 1983-85; mng. cons. James Martin Assocs., Reston, Va., 1985; sr. cons., instr. McDonnell Douglas/Gane & Sarson IST, St. Louis, 1985-91; prin. cons., owner DAE LLC, NYC, 1991—. Cons. Inst. Mus. Svcs., Washington, 1979-80. Author course books and articles. Cadet CAP, Island Park, N.Y., 1950s; computer advisor Orpheus Chamber Orch., N.Y.C., 1994; mem. jr. com. N.Y.C. Ballet, 1995-98; mem. Ovation Soc. Carnegie Hall, N.Y.C., 1996—; founding mem. Nat. Campaign for Tolerance, 2001. Mem. AAAS, IEEE Computer Soc., Assn. for Computing Machinery, Am. Mgmt. Assn., Data Adminstrn. Mgmt. Assn., N.Y. Acad. Scis., Alumni Fedn. of Columbia U. Achievements include mentoring and leading the business innovation and technology transformation for the new senior managemet team to turn around the fortunes of a near failing regional bank (US Bancorp); to become the 8th largest financial holding company in the U.S. with $189 billion in assets; Proved the feasibility of segmentation and asset swapping between internal business units that satisfied state insruance regulations requiring external, non-segmentated operations; Pioneered the use of opeations research models in the grants award process. Avocations: travel, photography, sailing, sculpture, tennis. Office: DAE LLC 300 E 71st St Ste 17E New York NY 10021-5242

LIPAN, PETRUTA E., semiotician, curator, artist; b. Braila, Romania, Oct. 18, 1957; d. Ene and Maria C. L. BFA, Washington Univ., 1991; MFA, PhD in Semiotic Studies, Ind. Univ., 1995. Instr. sculpture Ind. U., Bloomington, 1993-94, instr. 3-dimensional design, 1994-95; instr. sculpture Laumeyer Sculpture Mus., St. Louis, 1995-96; prof. art appreciation St. Louis U., 1996, assoc. curator S. Cuples House and McNamee Gallery, 1996—; mem. faculty Washington U., St. Louis, 1996-99; prof. art history St. Louis U., 1999-2000. Vis. artist Laumeier Sculpture Park, 1997, 1996, artist in residence, 1996; assisted in curating, organization and mktg. of shows including Edward Boccia: The Eye of the Painter, 1996, Ads With A Conscience, 1997, A Voice of Their Own, 1997, Mev Puelo: Witness to Life, 1997, Iridescence, 1998; curator Enduring Light: Fragility and Persistence, 1998, Passion for Color: Frederick Carder at Steuben Glass Works, 1999; presenter 5th Argentinian congress on Color, APHRA Behn Soc., Phila., 1999, Can. Semiotic Assn. Conf., Que., 1999, 7th Congress of IASS-AIS, Dresden, Germany, 1999, Math. Connections in Art, Music, and Sci., Winfield, Kans., 1999. Group exhibitions include Sioux City Art Ctr., 1997, Ind. Univ., 1996, Centre Interculturel Strathearn, 1996, The Editions Limited Gallery of Art, 1995, The Carver Cultural Ctr., 1995, Ind. Univ. Art Mus., 1995, Ind. Univ., 1993, 94, 95, San Diego Art Inst., 1993, Steinberg Gallery, 1991, Bixby Gallery, 1991, South Grand Gallery, 1986, numerous others. Mem. Nat. Sculpture Soc., Internat. Assn. for Semiotic Studies (presenter at confs.), Semiotic Soc. Am., Am. Assn. Mus., Assn. for Art History, Internat. Assn. for Visual Semiotics, Midwest Art History Soc. Home: 1129 Olivaire Ln Saint Louis MO 63132-3010 E-mail: lipanp@yahoo.com.

LIPCHIK, RANDOLPH J., physician; MPH, U. Minn., 1980; MD, CM, McGill U., Montreal, 1984. Diplomate Am. Bd. of Internal Medicine. Prof. medicine Med. Coll. Wis., Milwaukee, 1990—. Fellow: ACP, Am. Coll. Chest Physicians; mem.: Wis. Thoracic Soc., Am. Thoracic Soc. Office: Med Coll Wis 9200 W Wisconsin Ave Milwaukee WI 53226 Office Phone: 414-456-7040.

LIPCSEI, MARIANNE, administrative assistant, writer; b. Highland Park, Mich., June 23, 1952; d. John Dominic and Martha Victoria Cesare; m. James Laurie Heath (div.); children: Jason Laurie Neal Heath, Christina Elaine Heath; m. Frank James Lipcsei, July 15, 1989. Student, Oakland CC, Farmington Hills, Mich., 1971—72, U. Windsor, Ontario, Can., 1987—88. Fin. counselor Botsford Gen. Hosp., Farmington Hills, Mich., 1971—75; bookdealer Gale Rsch. Co., Detroit, 1977—79; receptionist, sales, sec. Elmara Constrn., Windsor, 1981—83; owner, operator Crossroad Constrn., Windsor, 1983—85; sr. payroll clk. U. Windsor, 1984—95; payment specialist Med. Accts. Mgmts., Grand Haven, Mich., 1996—2003; office mgr. Dr. Zelenka-Rauch DC LLC, Grand Haven, 2004—. Author: numerous poems. Sr. payroll clk. Can. Payroll Assoc., 1994—95; vol. Grand Haven Jaycees, 1995—2004; mentor Central and Mary A. White Elem. Schs., 2000—04; deacon First Presbyn. Ch., Grand Haven, 2001—04, facilitator Alpha course. Recipient cert. appreciation, Grand Haven Area Jaycees, 1996, cert., Women's Incentive Ctr., Windsor, 1994. Mem.: Order of St. Luke (spirituality and discilesip com. mem. 2004—, prayer min. 2004—). Avocations: rollerblading, bicycling, hiking, reading. Office: Jennifer Zelenka-Rauch DC LLC 950 Taylor Ave Ste 170 Grand Haven MI 49417 Office Phone: 616-842-8999. E-mail: tremors@chartermi.net.

LIPELES, ENID SANDRA, secondary chemistry educator; b. N.Y.C., Aug. 28, 1942; d. Aaron and Pauline (Seltzer) Singer; m. Ralph M. Lipeles, June 16, 1962; children: Brett, Charles, Jennifer. AB, CUNY, 1963, postgrad.; MS, U. Bridgeport, 1969. Chemistry and physics tchr. Mamaroneck (N.Y.) High Sch., 1963, Paul D. Schreiber High Sch., Port Washington, N.Y., 1963-65, Masuk High Sch., Monroe, Conn., 1965—; prof. chemistry Sacred Heart U., Fairfield, Conn., 1980-90; also chair dept. sci. Masuk High Sch., Monroe, Conn. Pres. Am. Field Svc., Monroe, 1970-77, treas., 1977—; mem. Monroe Zoning Bd. Appeals, 1988—; chmn. Monroe Town Coun. 2000—, chair, 2001— Named Outstanding Tchr., Chem. Mfrs. Am., 1980; Toshiba Am. Internat. grantee. Mem. LWV (exec. bd. Monroe chpt. 1988—, editor 1988—), New Eng. Assn. Chemistry Tchrs. (editor newsletter 1977-88, 90—, exec. bd. 1980-87, 90—, scholar 1976, 85), Maine Edn. Assn. (editor newsletter 1989—, v.p. 1988—), Monroe Tennis Assn. (pres. 1980-86, 90—), Jewish Women's Club of Monroe (pres. 1972-76, 90—, Monroe Tchr. of Yr. 1990-91), Delta Kappa Gamma. Republican. Avocations: tennis, reading. Home: 69 Ridgedale Rd Monroe CT 06468-1244

LIPEZ, KERMIT V., federal judge, former state supreme court justice; b. Phila., 1941; BA, Haverford Coll., 1963; LLB, Yale Law Sch., 1967; LLM, Univ. Va. Law Sch., 1990. Staff atty., civil rights divsn. US Dept. of Justice, 1967—68; spec. asst. & legal counsel Gov. Kenneth M. Curtis, Maine, 1968—71; legis aide US Sen. Edmund Muskie, 1971—72; ptnr. Curtis, Thaxter, Lipez, Stevens, Broder & Micoleau, 1975—85; judge Maine Superior Ct., 1985—94; assoc. justice Supreme Jud. Ct. of Maine, Portland, 1994—98; judge U.S. Ct. Appeals (1st cir.) Maine, Portland, 1998—. Mem. fed.-state jurisdictional com. Jud. Conf. Mem.: Am. Law Inst., Cumberland County Bar Assn. (chair justice action group), Maine Bar Assn. Office: 156 Federal St Portland ME 04101-4152*

LIPFORD, ROCQUE EDWARD, lawyer; b. Monroe, Mich., Aug. 16, 1938; s. Frank G. and Mary A. (Mastromarco) L.; m. Marcia A. Griffin, Aug. 5, 1966; children: Lisa, Rocque Edward, Jennifer, Katherine. BS, U. Mich., 1960, MS, 1961, JD with distinction, 1964. Bar: Mich. 1964, Ohio 1964. Instr. mech. engring. U. Mich., 1961-63; atty. Miller, Canfield, Paddock & Stone, Detroit, 1965-66; asst. gen. counsel Monroe Auto Equipment Co., 1966-70, gen. counsel, 1970-72, v.p., gen. counsel, 1973-77, Tenneco Automotive, 1977-78; ptnr. firm Miller, Canfield, Paddock & Stone, Detroit, 1978—, mng. ptnr., 1988-91. Bd. dirs. La-Z-Boy Inc., MBT Fin. Mem.: Knights of Malta, Legatus, Mich. Bar Assn., Mariner Sands Golf and Country Club, Monroe Golf and Country Club, North Cape Yacht Club, Otsego Ski Club, Pi Tau Sigma, Tau Beta Pi. Home: 1065 Hollywood Dr Monroe MI 48162-3045 Office: Miller Canfield Paddock & Stone 214 E Elm Ave Ste 100 Monroe MI 48162-2682 Office Phone: 734-243-2000. Business E-Mail: lipford@mcps.com.

LIPIN, JOAN CAROL, healthcare executive, consultant, lawyer; b. Denver, Aug. 25, 1947; d. Theodore and Kathe (Pardo) Lipin. BA, NYU, 1969; postgrad., MIT, 1973-74; MBA, Boston U., 1977; JD, N.Y. Law Sch., 2005. Adminstrv. staff MIT, Boston, 1969, tech. asst., 1977; adminstr. Mass. Gen. Hosp., Boston, 1975-76, mgmt. cons., 1976; dept. head N.Y. Hosp., N.Y.C., 1977-80; exec. v.p. Gordon-Keeble, N.Y.C., 1980-83; owner, pres. Thor Sci., N.Y.C., 1983-86; sr. mgr. health svcs. ARC in Greater N.Y., 1986-88; cons. to pres. Nat. Inst. Life Threatening Illness and Loss, 1988-91; owner, pres. Thor Rsch., N.Y.C., 1989—; asst. to sr. atty. Arthur M. Wisehart, N.Y.C., 1990—. Cons., mem. rev. bd. Ind. Testing Lab., N.Y.C., 1981-85, Forum Corp. Responsibility, 1981-82. Pub. poet; Libr. of Congress/Poetry Guild. Exec. mem., officer Lexington Dem. Club, 1993-2003; judicial del.-alt., 1995-2003; mem. county com. Dem. Party County of N.Y., 1994—; mem. Nat. Def. Counsel, Drs. Without Borders, Physicians for Social Responsibility; charter mem. So. Law Poverty Ctr., 2000; founding mem. Nat. Campaign for Tolerance, Earth Justice Legal Def. Fund.; mem. Women's Action Coun., 2001—; charter mem. women's action coun., Amnesty Internat., 2001—. Student mem. ATLA, ABA (jud. divsn., judicial performance and evaluation exec. com. 2003-04—), N.Y. State Bar Assn. (com. on atty. professionalism 2002—, com. profl. responsibility of ins., 2003—), N.Y. Acad. Sci., Am. Soc. Zoologists, Union Concerned Scientists, Amnesty Internat., Audubon Soc., World Wildlife Fund, Thanatology Found. (steering com., spl. asst. to pres. 1988-91), Amnesty Internat. (charter), Nat. Inst. Life (co-chair Threatening Illness and Loss symposium 1991), Pre-Hosp. Care Providers, Sierra Club, Nat. Wildlife Fund. Home: 45 E 89th St Apt 14G New York NY 10128-1229 Office: Thor Sci Rsch PO Box 1257 New York NY 10028-0009 Personal E-mail: jclipin@aol.com.

LIPIN, S. BARRY, business executive, investor; b. Chgo., Oct. 7, 1920; s. Bernard and Mary (Schrier) L.; m. Priscilla Richter, Oct. 7, 1952; m. 2d, Rachel Kucheck, Nov. 21, 1976 (dec. Apr. 1992). Student Ill. Inst. Tech., 1939-41, DePaul U. Commerce, 1943-44, DePaul Coll. Law, 1944-45. Founder/owner new and used automobile sales co., Chgo., 1945—, U.S. Auto Leasing Co., Chgo., 1954; chmn., chief exec. officer Lipin Enterprises Inc. (U.S. Auto Leasing Co., Lipin Rent-A-Car, Automobile Corp. N.Am., Rifco Auto Leasing Co., Modern Cars Inc.), Chgo., 1982—; chmn., chief exec. officer Presdl. Car Rental, Ltd. (and predecessors), Chgo., 1986—, Presdl. Limousine, Ltd., 1986—; pres., chief exec. officer Paul-Sey Investment Corp.; founder S. Barry Lipin LLC, Denver, 2004—; mem. gov.'s adv. coun. State of Ill., 1988—; mem. allied industries coun. City of Hope. Bd. dirs. Am. Hearing Research Found., Lipin Found., Michael Reese Hosp. Med. Research Inst. Council, Jewish Vocat. Service; trustee internation hdqs. Inst. Crit. Care, Palm Springs, Calif., 1993. Recipient State of Israel Bonds award, 1980; Automotive Industry-Leasing Div. Man of Yr. award; Spirit of Life award City of Hope, 1983, Humanitarian award Holocaust Meml. Found. Ill., 1987. Mem. Am. Automotive Leasing Assn., Automotive and Allied Industries Council (pres.), Chgo. Assn. Commerce and Industry, Ill. C. of C., Phi Kappa Tau. Clubs: Variety; Canyon Country (Palm Springs, Calif.); Covenant, Mid-America, Executive. Office: 1800 N Ashland Ave Chicago IL 60622-1206

LIPINSKI, ANN MARIE, editor; b. Trenton, Mich. m. Steve Kagan; 1 child, Caroline. B in Am. Studies, U. Mich. Joined Chgo. Tribune, 1978, named head investigative team, 1990, assoc. mng. editor met. news., 1991—93, dep. mng. editor, 1994—95, mng. editor, 1995—2000, v.p. & exec. editor, 2000—01, sr. v.p. & exec. editor, 2001—. Juror Puliter Prize, 2001, 02; mem. Pulitzer Prize Bd., 2003—. Bd. visitors Poynter Inst., U. Mich. Journalism Fellows program, Stanford U. Journalism Fellows program. Recipient Pulitzer Prize for investigative reporting, 1988; Nieman Fellowship Harvard U., 1989-90. Office: Chgo Tribune 435 N Michigan Ave Chicago IL 60611-4066*

LIPINSKI, DANIEL, congressman; b. Chgo., July 15, 1966; s. William and Marie Lipinski; m. Judy Lipinski. BS, Northwestern Univ., 1988; MA, Stanford Univ., 1989; PhD in polit. sci., Duke Univ., 1998. Assoc. prof. Notre Dame Univ., 2000—01, Univ. Tenn., 2001—04; mem. U.S. Congress from 3d Dist Ill., 2005—; mem. sci. com., small bus. com. U.S. Ho. of Reps. Democrat. Roman Catholic. Office: 1217 Longworth House Office Bldg Washington DC 20515 Office Phone: 202-225-5701.*

LIPINSKI, TARA KRISTEN, retired professional figure skater; b. Phila., June 10, 1982; Prof. figure skater Stars On Ice, 1998—. Nat. spokesperson Campaign for Tobacco-Free Kids. Tara Lipinski's A Night of Skating Champions, Houston, 2003; actor(TV appearance): 7th Heaven, 2003, The Wayne Brady Show, 2003. Recipient Mary Lou Retton award, U.S. Olympic Festival, 1994, 2nd Place, Skate Can., 1996, 1st (team), Postal Svc. Challenge, 1996, 2nd Place, Nations Cup, 1996, 3rd Place, Trophy Lalique, 1996, 1st Place, Hershey's Kisses Challenge, 1997, World Championships, 1997, Champion Series Final, 1997, 1998, 1st Nat. Sr., 1997, 2nd Place, Nat. Championship, 1998, 1st Place, Rattle and Roll, 1998, Gold Medal, Winter Olympic Games, 1998. Achievements include youngest Olympic Festival gold medalist at age 12. Avocations: reading, cooking, tennis.

LIPINSKI, WILLIAM OLIVER, former congressman; b. Chgo., Dec. 22, 1937; s. Oliver and Madeline (Collins) L.; m. Rose Marie Lapinski, Aug. 29, 1962; children: Laura, Daniel. Student, Loras Coll., Dubuque, Iowa, 1957-58. Various positions to area supr. Chgo. Parks, 1958-75; alderman Chgo. City Coun., 1975-83; mem. 98th-108th Congresses from 5th (now 3rd) Dist. Ill., 1983—2005, mem. transp. and infrastructure com. Dem. ward committeeman, Chgo., 1975—; del. Dem. Nat. Midterm Conv., 1974, Dem. Nat. Conv., 1976, 84, 88; pres. Greater Midway Econ. and Community Devel. Com.; mem. Chgo. Hist. Soc., Art Inst., Chgo., pres.'s coun. St. Xavier Coll.; mem. Congl. Competitive Caucus, Congl. Caucus for Women's Issues, Congl. Hispanic Caucus, Congl. Human Rights Caucus, Congl. Populist Caucus, Dem. Study Group, Export Task Force, Inst. for Ill., Maritime Caucus, N.E.-Midwest Congl. Coalition, Urban Caucus. Named Man of Yr. Chgo. Park Dist. 4, 1983; recipient Archer Heights Civic Assn. award 1979, 23d Ward Businessmen and Mchts. award Chgo., 1977, Garfield Ridge Hebrew Congregation award Chgo., 1975-77, Installing Officer award Vittum Park Civic Assn., 23d Ward Minuteman award, Friends of Vittum Park Polish award, Nathan Hale Grand award from S.W. Liberty Soc., S.W. Am. Edn. and Recreation program award, Sentry of Yr. award Stars & Stripes Soc., Ill. State Minuteman award 1991. Mem. Polish Nat. Alliance, Kiwanis (Disting. Svc. award, pres., Peace Through Strength Leadership award 1991). Democrat. Roman Catholic.

LIPINSKY DE ORLOV, LUCIAN CHRISTOPHER, consultant; b. N.Y.C., Feb. 21, 1962; s. Lino Sigismondo and Leah Safier (Penner) L.; m. Ann Marie Coffey, Aug. 23, 1986. BS in Computer Sci., SUNY, Binghamton, 1984, MS in Advanced Tech., 1985. Ptnr., cons. Computer Solutions Unltd., Johnson City, N.Y., 1983-85; programmer IBM Corp., Tarrytown, N.Y., 1985, assoc. info. ctr. analyst, 1986-87; mktg. rep. IBM Media Br., N.Y.C., 1987-90, account mktg. rep. U.S. mktg. and svcs., 1990-92, large sys. mgmt. cons., 1992; programmer Integrated Sys. Solutions Corp., 1992-93, advisory programmer, 1993-94, project mgr., 1994-95; dir. transmillennium svcs. Cap Gemini Am., 1995-98; prin. cons. Year 2000 practice IBM Global Svcs., 1998—. Editor: IBM Corp. Hdqtrs. Info. Systems Jour., 1985—, IBM Corp. Hdqtrs. Info. Products and Software Services Product Catalogue, 1985—; contbr. to profl. newsletter. Bus. adv. coun. Norman Thomas High Sch., N.Y.C., 1988—; mem. Katonah-Bedford Hills (N.Y.) Vol. Ambulance Corps, 1979-85, North Salem (N.Y.) Vol. Ambulance Corps, 1985—, line officer 1988-89; vol. Caramoor Ctr. for Music and the Arts, Katonah, 1976—, head usher, 1978; bd. dirs., bus. adv. coun. Norman Thomas H.S., N.Y.C. Bd. Edn., 1988-92; adminstrv. advisor AIS Hudson Valley Support Group, Pomona, N.Y., 1988-92; judge Distributed Edn. Clubs Am. Northeast Regional Mktg. Competition Finals, N.Y.C., 1989-90. Recipient Bernard V. Deutchman Bus. Person of Yr. award Norman Thomas H.S., 1991. Mem. IEEE, Assn. Computing Machinery, Soc. Am. Magicians, Internat. Brotherhood Magicians, Nat. Eagle Scout Assn. (life), Mensa, N.Y. State Emergency Med. Technicians, Aircraft Owners and Pilots Assn. Avocations: magic, photography, skydiving, aviation. Home: 53 Tod Hill Cir Goldens Bridge NY 10526

LIPKIN, DAVID, chemist; b. Phila., Jan. 30, 1913; s. William and Ida (Zipin) L.; m. Silvia Stantic Alvarez, Nov. 10, 1973; children— Jeffrey Alan, Edward Walter. BS, U. Pa., 1934; PhD, U. Calif., Berkeley, 1939. Research chemist Atlantic Refining Co., Phila., 1934-36; research fellow U. Calif., Berkeley, 1939-42; research chemist Manhattan Project, Berkeley, 1942-43; research chemist, group leader Los Alamos Sci. Lab., 1943-46; mem. faculty Washington U., St. Louis, 1946—81, prof. chemistry, 1948-66, chmn. dept., 1964-70, William Greenleaf Eliot prof., 1966-81, emeritus, 1981—. Sr. vis. fellow Agrl. Research Council, Cambridge, Eng., 1960; vis. research scientist John Innes Inst., Norwich, Eng., 1971, 78; trustee Argonne Univs. Assn., 1969-71; cons. in field. Author; patentee in field. Guggenheim fellow, 1955-56 Mem. Am. Chem. Soc. (St. Louis award 1970), AAUP, Sigma Xi, Tau Beta Pi, Pi Mu Epsilon. Office: Washington Univ Chemistry Dept Saint Louis MO 63130 Home: 1 McKnight Pl Apt 259 Saint Louis MO 63124-1971

LIPKIN, DAVID LAWRENCE, physician; b. Bklyn., Mar. 9, 1938; s. Herman and Celia (Granate) Lipkin; m. Nicole Van Laere, Sept. 23, 1962; children: Lawrence, Elline, Diane. AB in Biology, Clark U., Worcester, Mass., 1957; MD, Catholic U. Louvain, Belgium, 1964. Diplomate Am. Bd. Phys. Medicine and Rehab. Intern Lutheran Med. Ctr., Bklyn., 1963—64; resident in pediat. N.J. Coll. Medicine, Jersey City, 1964—66; resident rehab. medicine Albert Einstein Coll. Medicine, Bronx, NY, 1966—68, chief resident, 1968—69; clin. instr. U. Miami, 1974—80, clin. asst. prof. dept. rheumatology, 1980—84, clin. assoc. prof. dept. orthopedics and rehab., 1992—96. Med. dir. rehab. Pkwy. Regional Med. Ctr. Humana Hosp., Biscayne, Fla., 1974—88; med. dir. Bon Secours Hosp., North Miami, Fla., 1984—88; chief dept. rehab. medicine Sinai Med. Ctr.; cons. in field. Chmn. stroke com. Am. Heart Assn., Monroe and Dade Counties, Fla., 1980—82; bd. dirs. Multiple Sclerosis Soc., Dade, 1987, Villa Maria Nursing Ctr., 1986. NIH fellow, 1966—69. Mem.: So. Soc. Phys. Medicine and Rehab., Am. Acad. Phys. Medicine and Rehab. Fla. Rheumatology Soc., Am. Rheumatism Assn., Fla. Soc. Phys. Medicine and Rehab. (pres. 1976—78, 1989—91), Fla. Med. Assn., Dade County Med. Assn.

LIPKIN, MARTIN, medical educator, research investigator; b. N.Y.C., Apr. 30, 1926; s. Samuel S. and Celia (Greenfield) L.; m. Joan Schulein, Feb. 16, 1958; children: Richard Martin, Steven Monroe. AB, NYU, 1946, MD, 1950. Diplomate Nat. Bd. Med. Examiners. Mem. staff N.Y. Hosp., Meml. Hosp. for Cancer and Allied Diseases, 1972-96; prof. medicine Cornell U. Med. Coll., 1978—, prof. Grad. Sch. Med. Scis., 1978—, mem. and attending physician Meml. Sloan-Kettering Cancer Ctr., 1985-96; dir. clin. rsch. Strang Cancer Prevention Ctr., N.Y.C., 1996—. Vis. physician Rockefeller U. Hosp., 1981—; nominator Nobel Prize for Physiology and Medicine, 1982; Chao disting. lectr. U. Calif., 2000 (Elise Shang L'Esperance Leadership award,

2005); bd. dirs., officer The Med. Ednl. and Sci. Found. of N.Y.; bd. dirs. Internat. Soc. Cancer Chemoprevention; chmn. bd. Irving Weinstein Found. Mem. editl. bd. Internat. Jour. Oncology, World Jour. Gastroenterology; editor: Gastrointestinal Tract Cancer, 1978, Inhibition of Tumor Induction and Development, 1981, Gastrointestinal Cancer: Endogenous Factors, 1981, Calcium, Vitamin D and Prevention of Colon Cancer, 1991, Cancer Chemoprevention, 1992; contbr. articles to profl. jours. Served as officer USN, 1953-55. Recipient NIH career devel. award, 1962-71; Albert F.R. Andresen award N.Y. State Med. Soc., 1971, medallion Nat. Cancer Ctr. Rsch. Inst., Tokyo, 1976, U. Padua, Italy, 1978, Elise Strang L'Esperance Leadership awrd 2005 Fellow: ACP, Am. Coll. Gastroenterology; mem.: Am. Gastroenterol. Assn., Am. Assn. Cancer Rsch., Am. Physiol. Soc., Am. Soc. Clin. Investigation, Med. Soc. State of NY (chmn. sci. program com. 1990—91, chmn. edn. com. 1991—99). Achievements include research in the first human intervention study of dietary calcium as a chemopreventive agent against colon cancer. Office: 1230 York Ave New York NY 10021-6307 Business E-Mail: lipkin@rockefeller.edu.

LIPKIN, SEYMOUR, musician, conductor, educator; b. Detroit, May 14, 1927; s. Ezra and Leah (Vidaver) L.; m. Catherine Lee Bing, Dec. 27, 1961 (div. 1983); 1 son, Jonathan Michael; m. Ellen Werner, 2003. MusB, Curtis Inst. Music, 1947; studied piano with, David Saperton, 1938-41, Rudolf Serkin, Mieczyslaw Horszowski, 1941-47; conducting with, Serge Koussevitzky, Berkshire Music Center, 1946, 48-49. Piano tchr. Juilliard Sch. Music, N.Y.C., 1986—. Faculty Manhattan Sch. Music, 1965-70, 72-86, NYU, 1980-86; piano faculty Curtis Inst. Music, 1969—, New Eng. Conservatory, 1984-86, faculty music dept. Marymount Coll., Tarrytown, N.Y., 1963-72, chmn. music dept., 1968-71. Condr. Bklyn. Coll. Orch., 1973-74; Ford Found. commn. to perform concerto by Harold Shapero, 1959; debut with Detroit Civic Orch., 1937; apprentice condr. to George Szell, Cleve. Orch., 1947-48; appearances as pianist other U.S. orchs. including Boston Symphony in Tanglewood; ann. tours including soloist, Buffalo and Nat. Symphony, soloist, asst. condr. N.Y. Philharm. tour, Europe and Russia, 1959; conducting debut Detroit Symphony, 1944; recitalist, 92d St YMHA, N.Y.C., 1981, 83, soloist N.Y. Philharm., N.Y.C., 1983, participant in chamber music, Spoleto Festivals, 1982, 83, co-condr. Curtis Inst. Orch., 1952-53, asst. condr. Goldovsky Opera Co. on tour, 1953, condr. N.Y.C. Opera Co., 1958, 1 of 3 asst. condrs. New York Philharm., 1959-60; mus. dir. Teaneck Symphony, N.J., 1961-70, L.I. Symphony, 1963-79, Scarboro Chamber Orch., N.Y., 1964-65, Joffrey Ballet, N.Y. City Center, 1966-68, 1972-79, prin. guest condr., 1968-72; artistic dir. Kneisel Hall Summer Chamber Music Sch. and Festival, 1987— (performed cycle of 32 Beethoven Sonatas 1988-90, Gardner Mus., Boston, 1996-99, Beethoven Soc., N.Y., 1997—, 10 Beethoven Violin Sonatas with Andrew Dawes 1995, Uto Ughi, Santa Cecilia, Rome, 1995, 5 cello sonatas with David Soyer 1989, Laurence Lesser, 1996, 5 piano concertos with Santa Fe Symphony 1993, complete sonatas of Schubert at Kneisel Hall, Gardner Mus., Boston, Kaye Playhouse, N.Y.C.); appearances as opera condr. Curtis Inst., Teatro Petruzzelli, Bari, Italy, 1986-87; participant in chamber music Norfolk Fest., 1984-85, Marlboro Fest., 1986; recorded Stravinsky Piano Concerto and Capriccio with N.Y. Philharm., Bernstein, Grieg, Saint-Saens, Strauss sonatas with Aaron Rosand (violin), Grieg, Dohnanyi, Weiner sonatas with Oscar Shumsky (violin), Franck Sonata, Chausson Concerto with Rosand, Beethoven Sonatas op. 106 and 109, Schubert Works and Weber Sonatas with Arnold Steinhardt (violin), 32 Beethoven piano sonatas; tour of China, recitals and master classes, 2004; artistic dir. internat. piano festival and William Kapell competition U. Md., 1988-92. Recipient 1st prize Rachmaninoff Piano Competition, 1948. Home: 420 West End Ave New York NY 10024-5708 Office: Perform Artist Internat 4417 Dunwick Ln Ste 300 Fort Worth TX 76109-2508

LIPKOWITZ, STAN, physician; s. Leo and Elaine Lipkowitz; m. Ellen Patricia Kenny, June 10, 1984; children: Katherine Anne, Sarah Elizabeth. AB, Cornell U., Ithaca, N.Y., 1973—77; MD, PhD, Cornell U. Med. Coll., N.Y.C., 1977—84. Diplomate in Oncology Am. Bd. Internal Medicine, 1989, in Internal Medicine Am. Bd. Internal Medicine, 1987. Investigator Lab. of Cellular and Molecular Biology, CCR, NCI, Bethesda, Md., 1997—; assoc. prof. Uniformed U. Health Scis., Bethesda, Md., 1997—. Assoc. editor Clin. Cancer Rsch. Jour., 2001—04. Comdr. Pub. Health Svc., 1991—98, Bethesda, Md. Mem.: AAAS, Am. Soc. Clin. Oncology, Am. Assn. for Cancer Rsch. Office: Nat Cancer Inst 37 Convent Dr Bethesda MD 20892 Office Phone: 301-402-4276. Office Fax: 301-496-8479. Personal E-mail: slipkowitz@comcast.net. E-mail: lipkowitz@nih.gov.

LIPMAN, FREDERICK D., lawyer, writer, law educator; b. Phila., Nov. 16, 1935; s. Charles S. and Beatrice (Sanderow) Lipman; m. Gail Heller, July 25, 1965; children: L. Keith, Darren A. AB, Temple U.; LLB, Harvard Law Sch. Bar: Pa. 1960, N.Y. Practitioner, Phila., 1960-62; corp. counsel AEL Industries, Inc., Colmar, Pa., 1962-69; ptnr. Blank Rome LLP, Phila., 1970—. Lectr. U. Pa. Law Sch., 1989—98, Temple U. Law Sch., 1989—94, Wharton Sch. Bus., 1998—2003. Author: Going Public, 1994, How Much is Your Business Worth, 1996, Venture Capital and Junk Bond Financing, 1998, Financing Your Business with Venture Capital, 1998, Complete Going Public Handbook, 2000, Audit Committees, 2001, The Complete Guide to Employee Stock Options, 2001, The Complete Guide to Valuing and Selling Your Business, 2001, Valuing Your Business, 2005. Bd. dirs. Walnut St. Theatre, 1997—99, Phila. Geriatric Ctr., Penjerdel, Phila. Ch. Bezalel, 1989—91. Scholar, Temple U., 1953, Harvard Law Sch., 1957. Mem.: Harvard Law Sch. Assn. Greater Phila. (pres. 1988—89), Greater Phila. C. of C. (bd. dirs., mem. exec. com. 1980—90, chmn. tech. coun. 1983—85), Masons. Democrat. Jewish. Avocation: tennis. Office: Blank Rome LLP 1 Logan Sq Fl Three Philadelphia PA 19103-6998 Office Phone: 215-569-5518. Business E-Mail: lipman@blankrome.com.

LIPMAN, IRA ACKERMAN, security service company executive; b. Little Rock, Nov. 15, 1940; s. Mark and Belle (Ackerman) L.; m. Barbara Ellen Kelly Couch, July 5, 1970; children: Gustave K., Joshua S, M Benjamin. Student, Ohio Wesleyan U., 1958-60; LLD (hon.), John Marshall U., Atlanta, 1970; LLD (Hon.), Northeastern U., Boston, 1996. Salesman, exec. Mark Lipman Svc. Inc., Memphis, 1960-63; v.p. Guardsmark, Inc., Memphis, 1963-66, pres., 1966—, CEO, 1968—, chmn. bd., 1968—. Bd. dirs. Nat. Coun. on Crime and Delinquency, 1975—, exec. com., 1976—, chmn. fin. com., treas., 1978-79, vice chmn. bd. dirs., 1982-86, chmn. exec. com., 1986-93, chmn. bd. dirs., 1993-94, chmn. emeritus, 1993—, hon. chmn. 1997—; bd. dirs. Greater Memphis Coun. Crime and Delinquency, 1976-78, entrepreneurial fellow Memphis State U., 1976; mem. environ. security com., pvt. security adv. coun. Law Enforcement Assistance adminstrn., 1975-76; mem. conf. planning com. 2d Nat. Law Enforcement Explorer Conf., 1980. Author: How to Protect Yourself From Crime, 1975, 4th edit., 1997; contbr. numerous articles to profl. jours., mags. and newspapers. Bd. dirs. Memphis Jewish Cmty. Center, 1974, Memphis Shelby County unit Am. Cancer Soc., 1980-81, Memphis Orchestral Soc., 1980-81, Memphis Jewish Fedn., 1974-83; chmn. Shelby County com. U.S. Savs. Bonds, 1976; mem. president's coun. Memphis State U., 1975-79;, mem. visual arts coun., 1980-82; Memphis met. chmn. Nat. Alliance Businessmen, 1970-71; mem. task force Reform Jewish Outreach, Union Am. Hebrew Congregations, 1979-83; mem. young leadership cabinet United Jewish Appeal, 1973-78, mem. S.E. regional campaign cabinet, 1980; exec. bd. Chickasaw council Boy Scouts Am., 1978-81; bd. dirs., exec. com. Tenn. Ind. Coll. Fund, 1979; trustee Memphis Acad. Arts, 1977-81; mem. president's club Christian Bros. Coll., 1979-89; bd. dirs. Future Memphis, 1980-83, 83-86; nat. trustee NCCJ, 1980-92, exec. com., 1981-92, nat. Jewish co-chmn., 1985-88, nat. chmn., 1988-92, hon. chmn., past nat. chmn. Nat. Conf. Christians and Jews, 1992—; bd. dirs. Memphis chpt., 1980-85, life bd. dirs. Memphis chpt. 1985—; group II chmn. for 1982 campaign United Way Greater Memphis, 1981; v.p. exec. com. Internat. Coun. Christians and Jews, 1992-94; bd. govs. United Way of Am., 1992-99, bd. gov.'s liaison, 1991-92, chmn. ethics com., 1992-97, mem. exec. com., 1992-97, co-chmn. vol. involvement com., 1992—, mem. strategic planning com., 1994-96, diversity com., 1997-99; chmn. UWLC steering com. 1995-96; mem. Alexis de Tocqueville Sóc. Nat. Leadership Coun., 1992-97, mem. emeritus, 1998—, mem. Second Century Initiative Vol. Involvement com., 1987-91; chair Task Force on Critical Markets, 1987-91, mem. exec. cabinet, 1990-91; trustee Memphis Brooks Mus. Art, 1980-83, Yeshiva U. of L.A., 1982-; trustee Simon Wiesenthal Ctr., 1982—, chmn. nominating com., 2004-, chmn. campaign com., 1983-92, mem. fin. and audit com., 1993-2004, exec. com., 1994—, co-chmn. budget and fin. com. Jerusalem Project, 1999-2004; bd. dirs. Nat. Alliance against Violence, 1983-85, Nat. Ctr. Learning Disabilities, 1989-94, gen. campaign chmn., 1985-86; founder, bd. overseers B'nai B'rith, 1980; bd. dirs. Tenn. Gov.'s Jobs for High Sch. Grads. Program, 1980-83; trustee Ohio Wesleyan U., 1988-97; vice chmn. spl. task force on endowment growth Ohio Wesleyan U., 1990-97; mem. bd. overseers Wharton Sch., U. Pa., 1991-2004, devel. com., 1995-2004, exec. adv. bd. Zicklin Ctr. Bus. Ethics Rsch., 1997—; assoc. trustee U. Pa., 1991—; mem. adv. bd. ctr. bus. ethics Bentley Coll., 1996-; mem. Northeastern U. Corp., 1997-; mem. Dean's Coun., Mt. Sinai Sch. Medicine, 2004-; mem. exec. com. Am. Israel Pub. Affairs Com., 1991-2001, 2004-; bd. trustees Com. for Economic Devel., 1999—; adv. bd. dirs., Tenn. Titans, 1999-2000; mem. Hillel Internat. Bd. Govs., 2001-2003; bd. trustees, Fifth Ave. Synagogue, 2001—; Nat. Campaign Against Youth Violence (founding bd. mem.) 1999-2002; mem. Coun. on Fgn. Rels., 2002-, Chmn.'s adv. coun., 2004-, corp. affairs com., 2003-; founding mem. Homeland Security Project, 2004-; bd. dirs. Ligue Internationale des Sociétés de Surveillance, 2004-; adv. bd. Ctr. Values Based Leadership Sacred Heart U., 2002-03, Ctr. Bus. Ethics Bentley Coll., 1996—, Libr. of Congress, James Madison Coun., 2004-. Named one of Best Corp. Chief Exec. of Achievement, Gallagher Pres.'s Report, 1974; recipient Humanitarian of Yr. award, NCCJ, 1985, Outstanding Cmty. Sales award, Sales and Mktg. Execs. Memphis, 1987, Jr. Achievement Master Free Enterprise award, 1987, Alexis de Tocqueville Soc. award, 1995, Corp. Citizenship award, Com. for Econ. Devel., 2002, Stanley C. Pace award leadership in ethics, Ethics Resource Ctr., 2002, Dean's Medal, Wharton Sch., U. Pa., 2004. Mem. Internat. Assn. Chiefs Police, Am. Soc. Criminology, Internat. Soc. Criminology, Am. Soc. Indsl. Security (cert. protection profl.), 100 Club, B'nai B'rith, Econ. Club (bd. dirs. 1980-86, v.p. 1983-84, pres. 1984-85, chmn. exec. com. 1984-85), Bus. Execs. Nat. Security. Republican. Office: Guardsmark LLC Attn: Lorie Clayton 10 Rockefeller Plz 12th Fl New York NY 10020-1903

LIPMAN, RICHARD PAUL, pediatrician; b. Cambridge, Mass., Aug. 1, 1935; s. Hyman Zelig and Betty (Likovsky) L.; m. Mary Alice Wilcox, Aug. 25, 1963; children: Gregory, Susan; m. Lora H. Higgins, July 6, 1996; children: Sarad, Michael Tomlinson. AB magna cum laude, Harvard U., 1957; MD cum laude, Tufts U., 1961. Diplomate Am. Bd. Pediatrics. Intern Boston Floating Hosp., 1961-62, jr. resident, 1962-63, sr. resident, 1963-64, chief resident, 1964; rsch. fellow infectious disease Med. Sch. U. N.C., Chapel Hill, 1967-69; practice pediatrics Peabody and Salem, Mass., 1969—. Mem. staff North Shore Children's Hosp., Salem, Mass., assoc. chief of staff, 1974-76, pres., chief of staff, 1976-79, chief of medicine, 1979-83, trustee, 1980-84, corporator, 1985-86; mem. staff Tufts-New Eng. Med. Ctr., Boston, Boston Children's Hosp., North Shore Children's Hosp., Beverly Hosp., Melrose-Wakefield Hosp., Salem Hosp.; clin. instr. pediatrics Tufts U. Sch. Medicine, Boston, 1969-74, asst. clin. prof., 1974-78, assoc. clin. prof., 1978—; bd. dirs. Tufts Assoc. Health Maintenance Orgn., 1988-95, North Shore Health Systems, Inc., 1995-96. Contbr. articles to profl. jours. Capt. M.C., AUS, 1964-66. Fellow Am. Acad. Pediatrics; mem. AMA, Am. Soc. Microbiology, Mass. Med. Soc., Tufts Alumni Assn., Nat. Assn. Watch and Clock Collectors. Office: 10 Centennial Dr Peabody MA 01960

LIPNICK, ANNE RUTH, advocate; b. Cambridge, Mass., Aug. 9, 1943; d. Henry and Celia Florence (Weinberg) Goldberg; m. Robert Louis Lipnick, June 11, 1967; children: Deborah Ellen Lipnick Bort, David Henry. BA, Brandeis U., 1965; MSW, U. Minn., 1972. Rsch. asst. Brandeis U., Waltham, Mass., 1965—66; social worker Divsn. Child Guardianship, Boston, 1966—68, Jewish Family Svc., St. Paul, 1968—70, Family and Children's Svcs., Stamford, Conn., 1974—78; coord. spl. edn. parent resource ctr. Alexandria (Va.) City Pub. Schs., 1989—. Study group chair Children Together, Alexandria, 1999—; mem. Early Intervention Interagency Coordinating Coun., Alexandria. Exec. com. Brookville-Seminary Valley Civic Assn., Alexandria, 2002—03; v.p. for youth svcs. Agudas Achim Congregation, Alexandria, 1999—2001. Recipient Riggs-ARC Ednl. Leadership award, Assn. for Retarded Citizens No. Va., 1991, John Duty Collins III Outstanding Adv. for Persons with Disabilities award, Alexandria Commn. on Persons with Disabilities, 1996. Mem.: NASW (cert. 2005). Home: 5308 Pender Ct Alexandria VA 22304 Office Phone: 703-706-4552. Business E-Mail: alipnick@acps.k12.va.us.

LIPNICK, ROBERT LOUIS, chemist, toxicologist; b. Balt., Sept. 9, 1941; s. David Aaron and Dorothy (Moss) L.; m. Anne Ruth Goldberg, June 11, 1967; children: Deborah Ellen Lipnick Bort, David Henry. BS in Chemistry, U. Md., 1963; PhD in Organic Chemistry, Brandeis U., 1969. Postdoctoral fellow dept. chemistry U. Minn., Mpls., 1968-72; rsch. assoc. Sloan-Kettering Inst. Cancer Rsch., Rye, N.Y., 1974-79; leader, structure activity group U.S. EPA, Washington, 1980—85, sr. chemist, 1985—; com. sci. fellow U.S. Dept. of State, Washington, 1993—94. Vis. lectr. various African univs., 1973-74, 125th anniversary of Pharmacological Inst. U. Marburg, Germany, 1992; Crafoord Found. vis. scientist Pharm. Inst., U. Lund, Sweden, summer 1989; Umweltbundesant vis. scientist Borstel Rsch. Inst., Fed. Republic of Germany, summer 1986; co-organizer EPA workshop on structural properties determining mechanisms of toxic action, 1988; invited lectr. on quantitative structure-activity relationships in environ. chemistry and toxicology Commn. of European Communities, Ispra, Italy, 1990; invited sci. specialist, 1992; mem. internat. sci. com. 4th Internat. Workshop on Quantitative Structure-Activity Relationships Environ. Toxicology, Netherlands, 1990, 5th, Duluth, Minn., 1991; invited speaker Rekker Symposium, Netherlands, 1993. Author: (with others) Probing Bioactive Mechanisms, 1989, Comprehensive Medicinal Chemistry, 1990; editor: C.E. Overton's Studies of Narcosis, 1991; mem. editorial bd. Xenobiotica, Quantitative Structure Activity Relationships; co-editor Persistent Bioaccumulative and Toxic Chemicals, 2000, Chemicals in the Environment: Fate, Transport, and Remediation, 2002; assoc. editor Spl. Publs., Soc. Environ. Toxicology and Chemistry; contbr. 72 sci. pubs., articles to profl. jours., chapters to books. Bd. dirs., v.p. Friends of Marshlands, Rye, 1977-79; bd. dirs. Dowden Terr. Recreation Assn., Alexandria, Va., 1984-85; mem. publs. com. Wood Libr.-Mus. of Anesthesiology, 1993—94; mem. validation and tech. transfer com. Johns Hopkins U. Ctr. for Alternatives to Animal Testing; mem. Interagency Regulatory Alternatives Group; U.S. rep. sound mgmt. group chem. working group, Trilateral CEC. Mem. Am. Chem. Soc. (mem. environ. chem. divsn. exec. com.), Soc. Environ. Toxicology and Chemistry (charter), QSAR Soc. Jewish. Home: 5308 Pender Ct Alexandria VA 22304-1937 Office Phone: 202-564-7632. Business E-Mail: lipnick.robert@epa.gov.

LIPNIKOV, KONSTANTIN, mathematician; b. Yaroslavl, Russia, July 8, 1967; s. Nikolay Lipnikov and Zinaida Lipnikova. MS in Applied Math., Moscow Inst. Physics & Tech., 1990; PhD in Math., U. Houston, 2002. Postdoc Los Alamos Nat. Lab., N.Mex., 2002—04, staff mem., 2005—. Contbr. articles to profl. jour. Mem.: Soc. Indsl. and Applied Math. (assoc.). Achievements include research in theory of mimetic finite difference methods on polyhedral meshes; theory of error estimates on anisotropic adaptive meshes. Office: Los Alamos Nat Lab Ms B284 Los Alamos NM 87545 Office Phone: 505-667-1719. Office Fax: 505-665-5757. E-mail: lipnikov@lanl.gov.

LIPOVETSKY, STAN (STANISLAV LIPOVETSKY), statistician, mathematician; b. Moscow, Jan. 13, 1947; s. Simeon Eliezer Lipovetsky and Rebecca Abraham Sandalova; m. Natalia J. Smoliannikova, Oct. 24, 1994; 1 child, Steven J.; m. Olga N. Tarasova, Dec. 19, 1970 (div. May 1, 1990); children: Lena, Daniel. MSc in Theoretical Physics, Moscow U., 1971, PhD in Math. Methods in Econs., 1989. Prof. faculty mgmt. Tel Aviv U., 1990—95; rsch. mgr. Custom Rsch. Inc., Mpls., 1998—. Mem. adv. bds.: internat. jour. on ops. rsch.; contbr. articles to profl. jours. Mem.: Internat. Soc. on Multiple Criteria Decision Making, Inst. Ops. Rsch. and Mgmt. Scis., Math. Assn. Am., Am. Statis. Assn. Office: Custom Research Inc 8401 Golden Valley Rd Minneapolis MN 55427 E-mail: lipovetsky@customresearch.com.

LIPOVSKY, ROBERT P., marketing executive; b. Chgo., Apr. 15, 1950; s. Rudoplh John and Anna Mary (Nemec) L.; m. Sharon Sue Zelienka, July 1, 1972; children: Katherine Michelle, Robert Paul. BS, Western Ill. U., 1972. Dist. mgr. W.R. Grace and Co., Peoria, Ill., 1972-78; mktg. mgr. Doane Agrl. Svc., St. Louis, 1978-82; v.p., div. mgr. Maritz Mktg. Rsch. Inc., St. Louis, 1982—, pres., Maritz Performance Improvement Co., Fenton, Mo. Mem. Nat. Agrl. Mktg. Assn. Republican. Lutheran. Avocations: golf, hunting, sports, trap and skeet shooting. Office: Maritz Performance Improvement Co 14 S Hwy Dr Fenton MO 63099-0001

LIPP, ROBERT I., insurance company executive; b. 1938; married. Grad., Williams Coll.; grad. in bus., Harvard U.; JD, NYU, 1969. With Chem. Bank, NYC, 1963-86, sr. trainee, 1963-65, office asst. control div., 1965-66, asst. controller, 1966-67, asst. v.p. corp. planning, 1967-69, corp. sr. v.p., dep. head ops., 1972-74, exec. v.p., head ops. div., 1974-77, exec. v.p., head met. div., 1977-79, corp. sr. exec. v.p., head met. div., 1979, sr. exec. v.p., 1979-83, pres., 1983-86; v.p. corp. planning, treas. Chem. NY Corp., 1969-70, dep. mgr. ops. div., 1970-72; exec. v.p. for consumer fin. services group Comml. Credit Co., Balt., 1986-89, chmn. consumer fin. svcs., 1999; exec. v.p. consumer fin. svcs. Primerica Corp. (parent co.), NYC, 1988; exec. v.p., chmn., CEO Travelers Aetna Property, Hartford, Conn., 2001—04; exec. chmn. St. Paul Travelers Cos., Inc., Minn., 2004—. Bd. dirs. Greater N.Y. Fund; mem. mgmt. team Comml. Credit Corp., San Antonio. Trustee Jackie Robinson Found. Office: St Paul Travelers 385 Washington St Saint Paul MN 55102*

LIPPA, CAROL FRANCES, neurologist; b. Erie, Pa., Aug. 19, 1955; d. John Winn and Dorothy Marie (Zarembski) Ryan; m. Robert Leo Lippa, July 1982; children: Sara Marie, Alex Mitchell, Adam Lee. BA, McGill U., 1978; MD, U. Mass., 1983. Diplomate Am. Bd. Psychiatry and Neurology, Am. Bd. Neurorehab. Intern St. Vincent Hosp., Worcester, Mass., 1983—84; resident in neurology U. Mass. Med. Ctr., Worcester, 1984—86, chief resident, 1986—87, resident in neuropathology, 1987—88, fellow neurobiology of aging, 1988—89, asst. prof. neurology, 1989—95, dir. brain donation program, 1993—, investigator clin. drug trials, 1992—; physician neurorehab. svc. Fairlawn Rehab. Hosp., 1992—96; prof. neurology Drexel U. Coll. Medicine, Phila., 1996—; chief neurology svc. Med. Coll. Pa.-Hahnemann U., Phila., 2000—03, dir. Memory Disorders Ctr., 1996—. Contbr. more than 150 abstracts and articles to profl. jours. Recipient 2d prize residents and fellows presentation, Boston Soc. Neurology and Psychiatry, 1985. Mem.: Phila. Neurol. Soc. (pres. 2004—05), Am. Neurol. Assn., Am. Soc. Neurorehab., Soc. Neurosci., Am. Acad. Neurology, Alpha Omega Alpha. Home: 16 Radcliff Rd Bala Cynwyd PA 19004-2631 Office: Hahnemann Hosp Mailstop 423 245 N 15th St Philadelphia PA 19102

LIPPARD, LUCY ROWLAND, writer, educator, critic, curator; b. N.Y.C, Apr. 14, 1937; d. Vernon William and Margaret Isham (Cross) L.; m. Robert Tracy Ryman, Aug. 19, 1961 (div. 1968); 1 child, Ethan Isham Ryman. BA, Smith Coll., 1958; MA in Art History, NY Inst. Fine Arts, 1962; DFA (hon.), Moore Coll. Art, 1972, San Francisco Art Inst., 1984, Maine Coll. Art, 1994, Mass. Coll. Art, 1998, Art Institute of Chgo., 2003. Freelance writer, lectr., curator, 1964—; rsch. assoc. Mus. N.Mex./Mus. of Indian Arts and Culture, Office of Cultural Affairs, Sante Fe, N.Mex. Prof. Sch. Visual Arts, N.Y.C., Williams Coll., Queensland U., Brisbane, Australia, U. Colo., Boulder; mem. adv. bd. Franklin Furnace, N.Y.C., 1979—; co-founder, bd. dirs. Printed Matter, N.Y.C.; bd. dirs. Ctr. Study Polit. Graphics, L.A., Time & Space Ltd., Hudson, NY, Sustainable Settings, Woody Creek, Colo., Earth Works Inst., Santa Fe; co-founder W.E.B., Ad Hoc Women Artist's Com., Artists Meeting for Cultural Change, Heresies Collective and Jour., Artists Call Against US Intervention in Ctrl. Am., Polit. Art Documentation/Distbn.; lectr. in field. Author: Pop Art, 1966, The Graphic work of Philip Evergood, 1966, Changing: Essays in Art Criticism, 1971, Tony Smith, 1972, Six Years: The Dematerialization of the Art Object, 1973, From the Center: Feminist Essays on Women's Art, 1976, Eva Hesse, 1976, Sol Le Witt, 1978, (with Charles Simonds) Cracking (Brüchig Werden), 1979, Issue: Social Strategies by Women Artists, 1980, Intricate Structure, 1980, Ad Reinhardt, 1981, Collected Visions: Work by Women Artists Living in Rural New York State, 1982, Overlay: Contemporary Art and the Art of Prehistory, 1983, Get the Message? A Decade of Art for Social Change, 1984, Jerry Kearns, 1987, Mixed Blessings: New Art in a Multicultural America, 1990, Secrets, Dialogues, Revelations: The Art of Betye and Alison Saar, 1990, A Different War: Vietnam in Art, 1990, The Pink Glass Swan: Selected Feminist Essays on Art, 1995, Michael Lucero:Sculpture, 1996, Defining Eye: Women Photographers of the 20th Century, 1997, The Lure of the Local: Senses of Place in a Multicentered Society, 1997, Florence Pierce: In Touch With Light, 1998, On the Beaten Track: Tourism, Art and Place, 1999, (with Alfred Barr and James Thrall Soby) The School of Paris, 1965, (novel) I See/You Mean, 1979; author, editor: Partial Recall: Photographs of Native North Americans, 1992; editor: Surrealists on Art, 1970, Dadas on Art, 1971; contbg. editor: Art in Am.; founding editor El Puente de Galisteo, 1997—; contbr. monthly columns Village Voice, 1981-85, In These Times, Z Mag., also numerous articles to mag., anthologies, and mus. catalogs, 1964—; curator 50 exhbns.; perfomer in guerilla and street theater. Mem. Santa Fe County Open Lands and Trails Planning and Advisory Committee (COLTPAC), 1999. Recipient Frederick Douglass award North Star Fund, 1994, Frank Jewett Mather award for criticism Coll. Art Assn., 1974, Claude Fuess award for pub. svc. Phillips Andover Acad., 1975, curating award Penny McCall Found., 1989, citation NYC mayor David Dinkins, 1990, Smith Coll. medal, 1992, Athena award RISD, 2004; Guggenheim fellow, 1968, ArtTable award, 1999; grantee Lannan Found., 2000. Avocations: hiking, rock art, local history. Home and Office: 14 Avenida Vieja Lamy NM 87540-9783 Office Phone: 505-466-1276.

LIPPARD, THOMAS EUGENE, lawyer; b. Pitts., 1943; Student, Haverford Coll., 1960—64; BA, U. Pitts., 1965; JD, U. Chgo., 1968. Bar: Pa. 1968, U.S. Dist. Ct. (we. dist.) Pa. 1968, U.S. Ct. Appeals (3d cir.) 68, U.S. Tax Ct. 1984. From assoc. to ptnr. Houston, Cooper, Speer & German, 1968—74; ptnr. Cohen, Cohen & Lippard, 1974—76, Houston, Cohen, Harbaugh & Lippard, PC, Pitts., 1976—85, Thorp Reed & Armstrong, 1986—96, of counsel, 1997—99; sr. v.p. fin. and adminstrn., gen. counsel Tube City LLC, Glassport, Pa., 1997—2001, exec. v.p. fin. and adminstrn., gen. counsel, 2002—; v.p., gen. counsel Tube City IMS Corp., 2005—. Mem.: ABA (chmn. com. devel. law union adminstrn. and procedure sect. labor law 1975, mgmt. co-chmn. formulation and editing com. report com. law union & ad 1980—85, procedure sect. labor and employment law 1980—85), Pa. Bar Assn., Allegheny County Bar Assn. Office: Tube City LLC 12 Monongahela Ave Glassport PA 15045-1397 E-mail: tlippard@tubecity.com.

LIPPE, PHILIPP MARIA, neurosurgeon, educator, academic administrator; b. Vienna, May 17, 1929; came to U.S., 1938, naturalized, 1945; s. Philipp and Maria (Goth) L.; m. Virginia M. Wiltgen, 1953 (div. 1977); children: Patricia Ann Marie, Philip Eric Andrew, Laura Lynne Elizabeth, Kenneth Anthony Ernst; m. Gail B. Busch, Nov. 26, 1977. Student, Loyola U., Chgo., 1947-50; BS in Medicine, U. Ill. Coll. Medicine, 1952, MD with high honors, 1954. Diplomate Am. Bd. Neurol. Surgery, Nat. Bd. Med. Examiners, Am. Bd. Pain Medicine. Rotating intern St. Francis Hosp., Evanston, Ill., 1954-55; asst. resident gen. surgery VA Hosp., Hines, Ill., 1955, 58-59; asst. resident neurology and neurol. surgery Neuropsychiat. Inst., U. Ill. Rsch. and Ednl. Hosps., Chgo., 1959-60, chief resident, 1962-63, resident in neuropathology, 1962, postgrad. trainee in electroencephalography, 1963; resident in neurology and neurol. surgery Presbyn.-St. Luke's Hosp., Chgo., 1960-61; practice medicine, specializing in neurol. surgery/pain medicine San Jose, Calif., 1963—; clin. prof. neurosurgery Stanford U., Calif. Instr. neurology and neurol. surgery U. Ill., 1962-63; clin. instr. surgery and neurosurgery Stanford U., 1965-69, clin. asst. prof., 1969-74, clin. assoc. prof., 1974-96, clin. prof., 1996—; staff cons. in neurosurgery O'Connor Hosp., Santa Clara Valley Med. Ctr., San Jose Hosp., Los Gatos Cmty. Hosp., El Camino Hosp. (all San Jose area); chmn. divsn. neurosurgery Good Samaritan Hosp., 1989-97, chmn. dept. clin. neurosci., 1997-99; founder, exec. dir. Bay Area Pain Rehab. Ctr., San Jose, 1979—; clin. adviser to Joint Commn. on Accreditation of Hosps.; mem. dist. med. quality rev. com. Calif. Bd. Med. Quality Assurance,

1976-87, chmn., 1976-77; cons., med. expert Med. Bd. Calif., 1996—. Assoc. editor Clin. Jour. Pain; contbr. articles to profl. jours. Capt. USAF, 1956-58. Fellow ACS, Am. Coll. Pain Medicine (bd. dirs. 1991-94, v.p. 1991-92, pres. 1992-93, exec. med. dir.); mem. AMA (ho. of dels. 1981—, CPT editl. panel 1995-99, sr. adv. panel Guides to the Evaluation of Permanent Impairment 1997—), Am. Coll. Physician Execs., Calif. Med. Assn. (ho. of dels. 1976-80, sci. bd., coun. 1979-87, sec. 1981-87, Outstanding Svc. award 1987), Santa Clara County Med. Soc. (coun. 1974-81, pres. 1978-79, Outstanding Contbn. award 1984, Benjamin J. Cory award 1987), Chgo. Med. Soc., Congress Neurol. Surgeons, Calif. Assn. Neurol. Surgeons (dir. 1974-82, v.p. 1975-76, pres. 1977-79, Pevehouse Disting. Svc. award 1997), San Jose Surg. Soc., Am. Assn. Neurol. Surgeons (chmn. sect. on pain 1987-90, dir. 1983-86, 87-90, Disting. Svc. award 1986, 90), Western Neurol. Soc., San Francisco Neurol. Soc., Santa Clara Valley Profl. Stds. Rev. Orgn. (dir., v.p., dir. quality assurance 1975-83), Fedn. Western Socs. Neurol. Sci., Internat. Assn. for Study Pain, Am. Pain Soc. (founding mem.), Am. Acad. Pain Medicine (sec. 1983-86, pres. 1987-88, Philipp M. Lippe Disting. Svc. award 1995, exec. med. dir. 1996—), Am. Bd. Pain Medicine (pres. 1992-93, exec. v.p. 1994—), Am. Soc. Law, Medicine, and Ethics, Alpha Omega Alpha, Phi Kappa Phi. Achievements include pioneer med. application centrifugal force using flight simulator. Office: PO Box 41217 San Jose CA 95160-1217 Address: Am Acad Pain Medicine 4700 W Lake Glenview IL 60025 Office Phone: 408-927-0803. Fax: 877-734-8750. E-mail: pmlippe@att.net.*

LIPPER, KENNETH, investment banker, film producer, writer; b. NYC, June 19, 1941; s. George and Sally L.; m. Evelyn Rebecca Gruss, June 12, 1966 (div. 2000); children: Joanna Helene, Daniella, Tamara, Julie BA, Columbia U., 1962; JD, Harvard U., 1965; LLM, NYU, 1966; postgrad., Faculté de Droit et Economique, Paris, 1967. Bar: NY 1965. Assoc. Fried, Frank, Harris, Shriver & Jacobson, NYC, 1967-68; dir. industry policy Office Fgn. Direct Investment, Washington, 1968-69; assoc., ptnr. Lehman Bros., NYC, 1969-75; mng. dir., ptnr. Salomon Bros., NYC, 1976-82; dep. mayor City of NY, 1983-85; chmn. Lipper & Co., 1986—2004; sr. adviser Cushman & Wakefield, NYC, 2004—. Adj. prof. internat. affairs Sch. Internat. and Pub. Affairs, Columbia U., NYC, 1976-83; mem. adv. bd. Fed. Res. Bank NY, 1994-2003, J.P. Morgan Chase Manhattan Bank, 1994—. Author: (novel) Wall Street, 1987 and chief tech. advisor movie, 1987; author, screenwriter, prodr. City Hall, 1996; prodr. film and play The Winter Guest, 1997; prodr. The Last Days, 1998 (Acad. award 1999); pub. Lipper Viking Penguin Biograph. Series, 1997—. Mem. exec. com. Harvard U. Resources, 1994—; bd. dirs. Case New Holland N.V., 1997—, Sundance Inst., 1997-2005. Recipient medal of distinction City of NY, 1985; John Harvard fellow, 2001. Mem. Internat. Inst. Strategic Studies, Coun. Fgn. Rels., Econ. Club NY, Century Assn., Phi Beta Kappa Office: Cushman & Wakefield 51 W 52nd St 12th Fl New York NY 10019 Office Phone: 212-841-5906. Business E-Mail: ken.lipper@lipper.com.

LIPPERT, NELS T., lawyer; b. Plainfield, N.J., Oct. 21, 1943; BS, Bethany Coll., 1965; JD, Case-Western Reserve U., 1968. Bar: N.Y. 1970, U.S. Patent & Trademark Office. Atty. White & Case, N.Y.C.; ptnr., vice chmn. Intellectual Property dept., mem. exec. com. Wilmer Cutler Pickering Hale & Dorr, NYC, 2000—. Adj. prof. Benjamin N. Cardozo Sch. Law, NYC. Contbr. articles to profl. jours. Mem. ABA, Am. Intellectual Property Law Assn., Internat. Trademark Assn., WIPO Domain Name Panel of Neutrals. Office: Wilmer Cutler Pickering Hale & Dorr 399 Park Ave New York NY 10022 Office Phone: 212-937-7201. Office Fax: 212-230-8888. Business E-Mail: nels.lippert@wilmerhale.com.

LIPPERT, WERNER D., history professor, researcher; b. Karlsruhe, Germany, May 8, 1972; s. Werner H. and Elke Lippert; m. Carola Simon, Oct. 16, 1993; 1 child, Katharina Michelle. MEd, Johnson (Vt.) State Coll., 1995; MA in History, U. NC, Wilmington, 2002; PhD, Vanderbilt U., 2005. Cert. in tchg. Vt. State Bd. Edn., 1994. Adj. prof. German U. NC, Wilmington, 2001; assoc. prof. history Ind. U. Pa., 2005—. Recipient Dissertation Fellowship award, German Am. Academic Exch. Program, Bonn, 2004—05. Mem.: Am. Hist. Assn. (assoc.). Avocation: hiking. Personal E-mail: wdl@rocketmail.com.

LIPPES, GERALD SANFORD, lawyer; b. Buffalo, Mar. 23, 1940; s. Thomas and Ruth (Landsman) Lippes; children: Tracy E, David S, Adam F. Student, U. Mich., 1958-61; JD, U. Buffalo, 1964. Bar: NY 1964. Sr. ptnr. Lippes, Mathias, Wexler Friedman LLP, Buffalo, 1964—; sec., dir., gen. counsel Mark IV, Industries, Inc., Amherst, NY, 1969-2000. Chmn. Del. Photographic Products, Buffalo, 1970—88, Ingram Micro-D, Buffalo, 1982—86, Abels Bagels, Inc., Buffalo, 1972—75; bd. dirs. Gilbraltar Industries, Inc., Protective Industries, LLC, Gilbraltar Inds., Inc., Hamister Group Cos. Bd dirs. Buffalo Fine Arts Acad., U. Buffalo Found., U. Buffalo Coun., N.Y. State Arts Coun.; chmn. bd dirs. Kaleida Health Sys., 2001—02. Named Entrepreneur of the Yr, 1993; recipient Distinguished Alumni Award, Univ Buffalo Law Sch, Citation Award, Nat Conf Christians and Jews, 1997, Jaeckle Award, SUNY, Bufflo. Mem.: Am Soc Corp Secys, Erie County Bar Asn, NY State Bar Asn. Office: Lippes Mathias Wexler Friedman 665 Main St Ste 300 Buffalo NY 14203

LIPPES, RICHARD JAMES, lawyer; b. Buffalo, Mar. 18, 1944; s. Thomas and Ruth (Landsman) L.; m. Sharon Richmond, June 4, 1972; children: Amity, Joshua, Kevin. BA, U. Mich., 1966; JD cum laude, SUNY, Buffalo, 1969. Bar: N.Y. 1970, U.S. Dist. Ct. Md. 1970, U.S. Ct. Appeals (4th cir.) 1970, N.Y. 1971, U.S. Dist. Ct. (we. dist.) N.Y. 1971, U.S. Ct. Appeals (2d cir.) 1971, U.S. Dist. Ct. (no. dist.) N.Y. 1973, U.S. Dist. Ct. (so. dist.) N.Y. 1985. Clk. to presiding justice U.S. Ct. Appeals (4th cir.), Balt., 1970; exec. dir. Ctr. for Justice Through Law, Buffalo, 1971; pvt. practice, Buffalo, 1971-77; ptnr. Moriarity, Allen, Lippes & Hoffman, Buffalo, 1977-79, Allen & Lippes, Buffalo, 1979—. Adj. prof. SUNY, Buffalo, 1978, 79, 2004; lead counsel and spl. environ. counsel for hazardous waste, mass toxic tort cases. Contbr. articles to profl. jours. Chmn. Atlantic chpt. Sierra Club, 1978-82; chmn. Buffalo chpt. Am. Jewish Com., 1986-88; chmn. lawyers com. Niagara Frontier chpt. N.Y. Civil Liberties Union, 1971, chpt. chmn., 1972-74; chmn. Buffalo Environ. Mgmt. Commn., 1987-96; bd. dirs. N.Y. State Preservation League; chmn. Buffalo Task Force, 1986-87; pres. Erie County Preservation Coalition, 1998—. Urban and Environ. Law fellow, 1969. Mem. Erie County Bar Assn (former chmn. pub. interest law com. and prepaid legal svcs. com.). Democrat. Office Phone: 716-884-4800. E-mail: rlippes@concentric.net.

LIPPINCOTT, JAMES ANDREW, retired biochemistry and biological sciences educator; b. Cumberland County, Ill., Sept. 13, 1930; s. Marion Andrew and Esther Oral (Meeker) L.; m. Barbara Sue Barnes, June 2, 1956; children— Jeanne Marie, Lisa Ellen, John James. AB, Earlham Coll., 1954; A.M., Washington U., St. Louis, 1956, PhD, 1958. Lectr. botany Washington U., 1958-59; Jane Coffin Childs Meml. fellow Centre Nat. de la Recherche Scientifique, France, 1959-60; asst. prof. biol. scis. Northwestern U., Evanston, Ill., 1960-66, assoc. prof., 1966-73, prof., 1973-81, prof. biochemistry, molecular biology and cell biology, 1981-94, prof. emeritus Evanston, Ill., 1994—, assoc. dean biol. scis., 1980-83; ret., 1994. Vis. assoc. prof. U. Calif., Berkeley, 1970-71; vis. prof. Inst. Botany U. Heidelberg (Germany), 1974. Contbr. articles to profl. jours. Grantee NIH, NSF, Am. Cancer Soc., USDA Mem. Am. Soc. Biol. Chemists, Am. Soc. Plant Physiologists, Bot. Soc. Am., Am. Soc. Microbiology

LIPPINCOTT, JONATHAN RAMSAY, healthcare executive; b. Cin., Dec. 26, 1946; s. Morss d'Isay and Virginia Yvonne (Peugnet) L.; m. Nancy Todd Smith, Feb. 22, 1975; children: Jonathan J.E., Michael R.T. BA, Yale U., 1968; MLitt, Oxford U., 1972. Program research analyst human resources adminstrn. City of New York, 1973-76; exec. asst. to dir. med. ctr. U. Cin. Med. Ctr., 1977, asst. sr. v.p., 1977-84; fellow in HMO planning policy & mgmt. Harvard Community Health Plan, Brookline, Mass., 1985-86; assoc. sr. v.p. U. Cin. Med. Ctr., 1984-94; assoc. dir. U. Cin. Hosp., 1993-94; sr. v.p., chief strategic officer Health Alliance Greater Cin., 1994-97, exec. v.p., chief strategic officer, 1997—; exec. dir. bus. devel. Alliance Ptnrs., 1996-2000, bd. dirs., 2000—. Chmn., bd. Southwestern Ohio Sr. Svcs. Inc., Maple Knoll Village, 1993-96, trustee, 1988-97; bd. dirs., sec., treas. Univ. Health Maintenance Orgn., Inc., 1989-93; exec. bd. dirs. The Health Initiative, Cin.; co-dir. U. Cin. Inst. Health Policy and Health Svcs. Rsch., 1993-96, fellow, 2002—. Contbr. articles to cons. and acad. mags. Pres., bd. trustees Little Miami, Inc., Cin., 1984-85; steering com., chmn. health & human svcs. session Leadership Cin., 1983-84; vice chmn. Cin. Transp. Study Com., 1984-85. Mem. Am. Assn. Med. Colls. (midwest regional chmn. group on inst. planning 1991-93), Am. Coll. Health Care Execs., Cin. C. of C. (health care com.), Cin. Yale Club (exec. com.). Office: Health Alliance Greater Cin 3200 Burnet Ave Cincinnati OH 45229-3099

LIPPINCOTT, JOSEPH P., photojournalist, educator; b. Somerset, Pa., Mar. 12, 1940; s. Joseph Britton and Louise Frances (Picking) L.; widowed; children: Douglas B., David S.; m. Karen L. Krause, 1999. BA in Journalism, U. Iowa, 1968. Staff photographer The Miami (Fla.) Herald, 1964-67; pub. rels. dir. Lock Haven (Pa.) State Coll., 1967-68; mag. editor Caterpillar Tractor Co., Peoria, Ill., 1968-69; photo editor, photographer The Detroit Free Press, 1969-75; photo advisor The State News Mich. State U., East Lansing, 1975-84; instr. Lansing C.C., 1977-84; photo editor The Detroit News, 1984-87, The Patriot Ledger, Quincy, Mass., 1988-95; lectr. Boston U., 1990—. Author: An Introduction to Camera Maintenance, 1980, Care and Repair of Classic Cameras for Photographers and Collectors, 1999. Mem. Nat. Press Photographers Assn. (chmn. nat. portfolio critique 1994-96, Pictures of the Yr. awards). Avocation: unique photographic equipment. Home: 95 Old Colony Ave # 291 Quincy MA 02170-2629

LIPPINCOTT, PHILIP EDWARD, retired paper products company executive; b. Camden, NJ, Nov. 28, 1935; s. J. Edward and Marjorie Nix (Spooner) L.; m. Naomi Catherine Prindle, Aug. 22, 1959; children: Grant, Kevin, Kerry. BA, Dartmouth Coll., 1957; MBA with distinction, Mich. State U., 1964. With Scott Paper Co., Phila., 1959-94, staff v.p. corp. planning, 1971, div. v.p., consumer products mktg., 1971-72, corp. v.p., mktg., 1972-75, sr. v.p., mktg., 1975-77, v.p., group exec. packaged products div., 1977—79, dir., 1978-94, pres., COO, 1980-94, chief exec. officer, 1982-94, chmn., 1983-94; ret., 1994. Chmn. bd. Campbell Soup Co., 1999-2001; bd. dirs. Campbell Soup Co., Exxon Mobil Corp., Oryon Tech., LLC; trustee Penn Mut. Life Ins. Co. Trustee Fox Chase Cancer Ctr., Phila., 1981—, chmn. bd. trustees, 1995-2003; active Bus. Coun. Capt. U.S. Army, 1957-59. Mem. Pine Valley Golf Club, Quail West Golf and Country Club, Park Meadows Country Club, Kappa Kappa Kappa, Pi Sigma Epsilon, Beta Gamma Sigma. Mem. Society Of Friends. E-mail: lipper66@msn.com.

LIPPINCOTT, WALTER EDWARD, law educator; b. Bronxville, N.Y., Aug. 15, 1959; s. Walter Edwin and Helen (Patterson) L.; m. Andrea Pratt, July 30, 1983; children: Brittany Marie, Matthew, Anna. BS, Roger Williams Coll., 1981; JD, Western New Eng. Coll., 1984; MS, Fla. Inst. Tech., 1995. Bar: Conn. 1984, D.C. 1985. Prosecutor State of Conn. Judicial Dept., Hartford, 1990-93; prof. Naugatuck Valley Cmty. Coll., Waterbury, Conn., 1993—, U. Conn., Storrs, 1996-97. Col. U.S. Army, 1985-90, USAR, 1990—. Mem. ABA, Conn. Bar Assn., D.C. Bar Assn. Home: 1167Highland Ave Torrington CT 06790-4410

LIPPINCOTT, WALTER HEULINGS, JR., publishing executive; b. Phila., Jan. 16, 1939; s. Walter Heulings and Helen B. (Howe) L.; m. Caroline Seebohm, June 8, 1974 (div. June 1993); children: Sophie, Hugh. AB, Princeton U., 1960. With Morgan Guaranty Trust Co., N.Y.C., 1960-63; coll. traveler Harper & Row Pubs., 1963-65, editor, 1965-70, editor-in-chief, coll. dept., 1970-74; editorial dir. Cambridge Univ. Press, N.Y.C., 1974-81; assoc. dir. Cornell Univ. Press, 1982, dir., 1983-86, Princeton U. Press, N.J., 1986—. Mem.: Knickerbocker (N.Y.C.), Century (N.Y.C.). Home: 1 River Knoll Dr Titusville NJ 08560-1308 Office: Princeton U Press 41 William St Princeton NJ 08540-5237 Business E-Mail: whl@pupress.princeton.edu.

LIPPMAN, LAURA, writer; b. Atlanta; BS in Journalism, Northwestern Univ. Reporter Waco Tribune-Herald, Tex., 1981—83, San Antonio Light, 1983—89, Balt. Evening Sun, 1989—91, Balt. Sun, 1991—2001. Author: (novels) Baltimore Blues, 1997, Charm City, 1997 (Edgar award, Shamus award, Anthony award nominee), Butchers Hill, 1998 (Agatha award, Anthony award, Edgar, Shamus, Macavity awards nominee), In Big Trouble, 1999 (Anthony award, Shamus award, Edgar, Agatha awards nominee), The Sugar House, 2000 (Best PI Novel of Yr. nominee, Romantic Times), In a Strange City, 2001 (NY Times Notable Book), The Last Place, 2002, Every Secret Thing, 2003 (Anthony award, Barry award, Nero Wolfe award), By a Spider's Thread, 2004 (Edgar Award nominee for best novel, 2005), To the Power of Three, 2005. Recipient Mayor's award for lit. excellence, Balt. Mailing: c/o Author Mail William Morrow 10 E 53rd St New York NY 10022 Home: Baltimore*

LIPPMAN, SHARON ROCHELLE, art historian, filmmaker, art therapist; b. NYC, Apr. 9, 1950; d. Emanuel and Sara (Goldberg) L. Student, Mills Coll., Columbia U., 1968; BFA, New Sch. Social Rsch., 1970, CCNY, 1972; MA in Cinema Studies, NYU, 1976, postgrad., 1987. Cert. secondary tchr., N.Y.; cert. in nonprofit orgn. mgmt. Instr., dir., founder Sara Sch. of Creative Art, Sayville, N.Y., 1976-85; founder, exec. dir., tchr. Art Without Walls, Inc., Sayville and N.Y.C., 1985—; curator art exhbn. Mus. Without Walls Heckscher State Park, East Islip, NY, 1985-87; exec. dir., curator Profl. Artist Network for Artists Internationally, 1991—; founder Art Without Walls, Inc., 1985—, Mus. Without Walls, Ctrl. Park, N.Y.C., 2005. Organizer Profl. Artist Network for Nat./Internat. Artists, 1994; curator Pub. Art in Pub. Spaces; instr. art therapy sessions Maryhaven Ctr., Port Jefferson, N.Y., 2004; head art therapy project Mary Haven Ctr., Port Jefferson, N.Y., 2004; origami zoo art therapist Southside Hosp., Bayshore, N.Y., 2005. Author: Patterns, 1968, College Poetry Press Anthology, 1970, America at the Millennium, 2000; exhibited in group shows at L.I. Children's Mus., Garden City, N.Y., 1995-97, Suffolk County Legislature, Hauppauge, N.Y., 1997, Bayport-Bluepoint Libr., 1997, East Islip Libr., 1997-98, U.S. Dept. Interior, Ft. Wadsworth, N.Y., 2001, Ellis Island Immigration Mus., N.Y., 2002, West Islip Libr., 2000-01, Battery Park, N.Y.C., 2002, Central Park, N.Y.C., 2003, Spirit Walk Gallery, Sayville, N.Y., 2003, Within These Walls, Nassau County Detetion Ctr., Westbury, N.Y., 2003, By Land or By Sea, South St. Seaport, N.Y.C., 2004, Southside Hosp., Bayshore, N.Y., 2005, West Islip (N.Y.) Libr., 2005, South Country Libr., Bellport, N.Y., 2005, Mus. Without Walls-Central Park, N.Y.C., 2005, South County Libr., Bellport, N.Y., 2005, others; art exhbn. By Land or By Sea, So. Street Seaport, N.Y.C., 2004; pub. art mural History of L.I. Baymen, 1987, Immigration on the NYS Waterways, 2001, Art Therapy Program and Exhbn. at Leadership Tng. Inst., Hempstead, N.Y., 2003, Nassau County Detention Ctr., 2003, Southside Hosp., Bay Shore, N.Y., 2004; represented in permanent collection Devel. Disabilities Inst., Suffolk County Legis. Bldg., Polish Consulate, N.Y., West Islip Pub. Libr., East Islip Pub. Libr., Ctrl. Park Zoo, Coll. Art Assn. Bull. Conv. N.Y., Robert Moses State Park, N.Y., Smith Haven Mall Lake Grove, Garden City Mall, N.Y., Southside Hosp., Bayshore, N.Y., Southside Hosp., Bayshore, N.Y.; art therapy program and exhbn. Leadership Tng. Inst., 2003, Suffolk Outreach Project, Art Therapy Wellness Program, 2003, Mary Haven Ctr., Port Jefferson Station, NY, 2004. Vol. Good Samaritan Hosp., 1984, Southside Hosp., 1983, U. Stony Brook Hosp., 1985, Schneider Children's Hosp., New Hyde Park, N.Y., 1992, New Light-AIDS Patients, Smithtown, N.Y., 1993, Helen Keller Svcs. for the Blind, Hempstead, N.Y., 1993-94, St. Charles Hosp. and Rehab. Ctr., 1996, Nat. Health Bill Pub. Forum, Sayville Mid. Sch., 1996, Art Puzzles-Art Therapy Geriatrics Ward, Brookhaven (N.Y.) Meml. Hosp., 1990, Art Therapy Program Original Dept. Disabilities, Suffolk County, N.Y., 1988, Din-o-Soar Art Therapy Southside Hosp.-Pediatrics Ward, Bayshore, N.Y., 1999, Art Box-Art Therapy, Pediat. Ward Southside Hosp., Bayshore, 2000, It Takes Two Art Therapy, St. Charles Hosp., Port Jefferson, N.Y., 2000; mem. Whitney Mus., Guggenheim Mus., Mus. Modern Art, Met. Mus. Art, Jewish Mus., Mus. of the City of N.Y., Art in Am., Art News, Am. Artist; trustee Sayville Libr. Bd., 1996; bd. dirs. Friends of the Arts St. Joseph's Coll., N.Y., 1997. Recipient Suffolk County New Inspiration award, 1990, Am. Artist Art Svc. award Am. Artists mag., 1993, Suffolk County Legis. proclamation, 1993, Newsday Leadership Vol. award Newsday newspaper, 1994, Nat. Women's Month award Town of Islip, 1996, Disting. Women's award Town of Islip, 1996, Nat. Poetry Press award, 1996, Cmty. Action award Suffolk County Ret./Sr. Vol. Program, 2002; named to L.I. Vol. Hall of Fame for Cultural Arts, 2004. Mem. Orgn. Through Rehab. and Tng., Coll. Art Assn., Met. Mus. Art, Mus. Modern Art Univ. Film Assn., Sayville C. of C. Avocations: fine art, books, cinema, political science, inventions. Office: Art Without Walls Inc PO Box 2066 Sayville NY 11785-2066 also: Art Without Walls Inc PO Box 341 Sayville NY 11782 Office Phone: 631-567-9418. Business E-Mail: artwithoutwalls@webtv.net.

LIPPMAN, WILLIAM JENNINGS, investment company executive; b. N.Y.C., Feb. 13, 1925; s. Henry J. and Fanny (Schapira) L.; m. Doris Kaplan, July 11, 1948; children— Howard Mark, Deborah Ellen. BBA cum laude, Coll. City N.Y., 1947; MBA, N.Y.U., 1957. Marketing mgr. Pavelle Color, Inc., N.Y.C., 1947-50; sales mgr. Terminal Home Sales Corp., N.Y.C., 1950-55; div. mgr. King Merritt & Co., Inc., Englewood, N.J., 1955-60; pres., dir. Pilgrim Distbrs. Inc., Ft. Lee, N.J., 1960-86; pres. L.F. Rothschild Managed Trust L.F. Rothschild Fund Mgmt. Inc., N.Y.C., 1986-88, also dir.; pres. Franklin Managed Trust, New York, 1988—. Mem. faculty Fairleigh Dickinson U. Sch. Bus. Adminstrn., 1957-69; bd. govs. Investment Co. Inst. Contbg. author: Investment Dealer Digest. Mem. Nat. Assn. Securities Dealers (investment cos. com.) Home: 18 Daniel Dr Englewood NJ 07631-3736 Office: Franklin Managed Trust 1 Parker Plz Fort Lee NJ 07024-2937 Office Phone: 201-592-6700.

LIPPMANN, JANET GURIAN, artist, art gallery owner; b. Bklyn., May 10, 1936; d. William and Gertrude (Shukovsky) Gurian; m. Morton Lippmann, Nov. 24, 1956; children: Amy, Stanley, David. BA in Art and Edn., CUNY, 1956, MA in Art and Edn., 1960. Permanent cert. art tchr., N.Y. Tchr. art pub. schs., N.Y.C., Cin., Westchester, N.Y., 1956-74; founder, tchr. Children's Art Workshop, Mt. Vernon, N.Y., 1964-76; pres., dir. The River Gallery, Irvington-on-Hudson, N.Y., 1974-89, Janet Lippmann Fine Arts, Irvington-on-Hudson, 1989—. One-woman shows include River Gallery, 1986, 1988, Nat. Arts Club, 1991, 1994, 1998, 2002, Newington Cropsey Mus., 2003, Irvington Pub. Libr., 2005, represented in many pvt. collections including, The Reader's Digest Collection; contbr. articles to profl. jours. Recipient award for pastel, Art Spirit Found., 2003. Mem.: Art Du Pastel En France, Hudson Valley Art Assn. (award winner), Pastel Soc. of Am., Pen & Brush, Salmagundi Club, Nat. Arts Club. Studio: 15 Gramercy Park S New York NY 10003-1705 Office: 8 N Dutcher St Irvington NY 10533-1518 Office Phone: 914-591-9240. E-mail: jlippmann@earthlink.net.

LIPPOLD, ROLAND WILL, retired surgeon; b. Staunton, Ill., May 1, 1916; s. Frank Carl and Ella (Immenroth) L.; m. Margaret Cookson, June 1, 1947; children: Mary Ellen Lippold Elvick, Catherine Anne Lippold Rolf, Carol Sue Lippold Webber. BS, U. Ill., 1940, MD, 1941. Diplomate Am. Bd. Surgery. Intern Grant Hosp., Chgo., 1941-42, resident in surgery, 1942-43, 47-48, St. Francis Hosp., Evanston, Ill., 1946-47; fellow in pathology Cook County Hosp., Chgo., 1947-48, resident in surgery, 1949-50; practice medicine specializing in surgery Chgo., 1950-53; also asst. in anatomy U. Ill., Chgo., 1950-53; practice medicine specializing in surgery Sacramento, 1953-68; chief med. officer No. Reception Ctr.-Clinic, Calif. Youth Authority, Sacramento, 1954-68, chief med. services, 1968-79; ret. Cons. in med. care in correctional instns.; cons. Calif. State Personnel Bd. Contbr. articles to med. publs. Chmn. Calif. Expn. Hall of Health, 1971-72. Comdr. M.C., USNR, 1943-73, PTO. Mem. Sacramento Surg. Soc., Sacramento County Med. Soc., Calif. Med. Assn., AMA, Sacramento Hist. Soc. (life). Republican. Lutheran. Home: 1811 Eastern Ave Sacramento CA 95864-1724

LIPPOLD, SCOTT A., corporate financial executive, consultant; b. Silvertoin, Oreg., Nov. 1, 1967; s. Roland John and Barbara Ann Lippold. AA, Mt. Hood C.C., Gresham, Oreg., 1992; BSBA, Portland State Univ., Portland, Oreg., 1994. Radioman petty officer third class U.S. Navy, Various, Fla., 1985—89; office adminstr. Bell's Constrn. and Drafting, Portland, Oreg., 1990—93; office coord. Portland Vet Ctr., Portland, Oreg., 1992—94; mgr. Marsee Baking, Portland, Oreg., 1994—95; dir. of mktg. Naegeli & Assoc., Portland, Seattle, Oreg., 1995—98; account exec. Robert Half Internat., Portland, Oreg., 1998—99; area mgr. Smith Johnson & Assoc., Vancouver, Wash., 1999—2000; oreg. market mgr. Spherion, Portland, Oreg., 2000—. Rm3 USN, 1985—89, San Diego, Iceland, Florida, Persian Gulf. Decorated Armed Forces Expeditionary medal U.S. Navy, Salior of the Day. Mem.: SHRMA (assoc.). Home: 12507 NE 36th Ave Vancouver WA 98685 Office Phone: 503-296-1126. Office Fax: 503-296-1126. Business E-Mail: scottlippold@spherion.com.

LIPPS, DELORIS JEAN, secondary school educator; b. Buckhannon, W.Va., Jan. 27, 1949; d. Kenna Monroe and Martha Jane (Pringle) L. BA in Edn., Glenville State Coll., 1971; MS in Teaching, U. N.H., 1978; postgrad., Marshall U., 1973, 74, W.Va. U., 1976-77, 82. Cert. secondary tchr., W.Va. Math. tchr. Wirt County High Sch., Elizabeth, W.Va., 1971—, head math. dept., 1979—. County math. adminstr. Wirt County Schs., Elizabeth, 1978—, dir. math. field day, 1980-2000; dir. math. field day W.Va. Region V., 1990-91, 2005—. Editor: Wirt County Math Field Day Manual, 1988, WVCTM History Update, 1991; (newsletter) Math News, 1987-2000 Recipient Presdl. award for Excellence in Math. Teaching, NSF, 1987. Mem. Nat. Coun. Tchrs. of Math., W.Va. Coun. Tchrs. of Math. (historian 1987-92), W.Va. Acad. Sci., Coun. Presdl. Awardees in Math., Delta Kappa Gamma (chapt. treas. Mu, 1996-2002, sec. 2002-2004, pres. 2004—). Methodist. Avocations: embroidery, bead crafts, reading. Home: PO Box 124 Elizabeth WV 26143-0124 Office: Wirt County High Sch PO Box 219 Elizabeth WV 26143-0219 Business E-Mail: dlipps@access.k12.wv.us.

LIPPS, JERE HENRY, paleontology educator; b. L.A., Aug. 28, 1939; s. Henry John and Margaret (Rosaltha) L.; m. Karen Elizabeth Loeblich, June 25, 1964 (div. 1971); m. Susannah McClintock, Sept. 28, 1973; children: Jeremy Christian, Jamison William. BA, UCLA, 1962, PhD, 1966. Asst. prof. U. Calif., Davis, 1967-70, assoc. prof., 1970-75, prof., 1975-88, Berkeley, 1988—, prof. paleontology, 1988-89, prof. integrative biology, 1989—; dir. Mus. Paleontology, Berkeley, 1989-97. Dir. Inst. Ecology U. Calif., Davis, 1972-73, chmn. dept. geology, 1971-72, 79-84, chmn. dept. integrative biology, Berkeley, 1991-94. Contbr. articles to sci. publs. Dir. Micropaleontology Project Cushman Found., pres., 1983—84, 2002—03. Recipient U.S. Antarctic medal NSF, 1975, Darwin award NCSE, 2002; Lipps Island, Antarctica named in his honor, 1979. Fellow: Com. for the Sci. Investigation of Claims of the Paranormal, AAAS, Cushman Found. (pres. 1983—84, 2001—02), Geol. Soc. Am., Calif. Acad. Scis.; mem.: Coun. for Media Integrity, Paleontol. Soc. (pres. 1996—97). Avocation: scuba diving. Office: U Calif Mus Paleontology #4780 1101 Valley Life Sciences Bldg Berkeley CA 94720-4780 Business E-Mail: jlipps@berkeley.edu.

LIPSCHUTZ, MICHAEL ELAZAR, chemistry professor, consultant, researcher; b. Phila., May 24, 1937; s. Maurice and Anna (Kaplan) L.; m. Linda Jane Lowenthal, June 21, 1959; children: Joshua Henry, Mark David, Jonathan Mayer. BS, Pa. State U., 1958; S.M., U. Chgo., 1960, PhD, 1962. Gastdocent U. Bern, Switzerland, 1964-65; from asst. prof. chemistry to assoc. head dept. Purdue U., West Lafayette, Ind., 1965—93, prof. chemistry, 1973—, assoc. head dept. of chemistry, 1993—2001; dir. chemistry ops. Purdue Rare Isotope Measurement Lab. (PRIME), 1990—2002. Vis. assoc. prof. Tel Aviv U., 1971-72; vis. prof. Max-Planck Inst. fuer Chemie, Mainz, Fed. Republic Germany, 1987; mem. panel space sci. experts Com. on Space Rsch., Space Agy. Forum of the Internat. Space Yr., Internat. Coun. Sci. Unions, 1990-92; cons. in field. Assoc. editor 11th Lunar and Planetary Sci. Conf., 3 vols., 1980; fin. editor Meteoritics and Planetary Sci., 1992-2000; contbr. numerous articles to profl. jours. Served to 1st lt. USAR, 1958-64. Recipient Cert. of Recognition, NASA, 1979, Cert. of Spl. Recognition, 1979, Group Achievement award, 1983, Cert. Appreciation, Nat. Commn. on Space, 1986; postdoctoral fellow NSF, 1964-65, NATO, 1964-65; Fulbright fellow, 1971-72 Fellow Meteoritical Soc. (treas. 1978-84, mem. joint com. on pubs. of Geochem. and Meteoritical Socs. 1985-93, fin. officer 1985-93, chmn. 1988-90); mem. AAAS, Am. Chem. Soc., Am. Geophys. Union, Planetary Soc., Internat. Astron. Union (U.S. rep. 1988—), Sigma Xi. Achievements include having minor planet named in honor of Lipschutz by Internat. Astron. Union, 1987, Cert. of Recognition, Dept. Def., 1999. Office: Purdue U Dept Chemistry West Lafayette IN 47907 Office Phone: 765-494-5326. Business E-Mail: rnaapuml@purdue.edu.

LIPSCOMB, GARY HESTON, obstetrician, gynecologist, academic administrator; b. Lawrenceburg, Tenn., Jan. 13, 1955; s. Charles Allen and Doris Gean Lipscomb; m. Lori Lynn Green, June 7, 1985; children: Jessica Nicole, Rebecca Jeanne. MD, U. Tenn, 1981. Cert. Am. Bd. Med. Speciaties Am. Bd. Ob-Gyn, 1987. Dir. divsn. Dept Ob-Gyn., U. Tenn., Memphis, 1996—, vice-chmn. clin. affairs, 2003—. Contbr. New England Jourl. Medicine. Recipient Nat. Faculty Award for Excellence in Clin. Tchg., U. Tenn., 1997. Fellow: ACS, Am. Coll. Ob-Gyn. Office: Univ Tenn 853 Jefferson Ave Memphis TN 38163 Office Phone: 901-448-5819.

LIPSCOMB, JAMES CHAPMAN, film producer; b. Tulsa, Mar. 8, 1926; s. Joseph Karnes and Ethel Chapman Lipscomb; 1 child, John Harris. BA, U. Miami, 1947; MFA, U. Iowa, 1951. Instr. U. Miami, 1952; editor Life Mag., N.Y.C., 1953—61; prod., dir. Drew Assoc., N.Y.C., 1961—67, James Lipscomb Inc., N.Y.C., 1967—. Prodr.: (TV films) Polar Bear Alert (Emmy award), Tall Ship: High Sea Adventure (Emmy award), Life's First Feelings (Media First pize APA, Blue Ribbon award Am. Film Festival), (dir., photographer) Carrier: Fortress at Sea (Emmy award, 1994). Air cadet USN, 1944—45. Avocations: tennis, sail racing. Home: 58 Heritage Hill Tarrytown NY 10591 Office: James Lipscomb Inc 31 E 31st Apt 10C New York NY 10016 Office Phone: 212-689-5044. Office Fax: 212-689-1566.

LIPSCOMB, JAMES LOUIS, lawyer; b. Albany, N.Y., Feb. 14, 1947; s. Eric and Vinel Lee (Motley) L.; m. Nancy Angela Moore; children: Kathryn, Julie, Angela. AAS, Hudson Valley Community Coll., Troy, N.Y., 1967; BA, Howard U., 1969; JD, Columbia U., 1972; LLM, NYU, 1977. Bar: N.Y. 1973, Calif. 1980, U.S. Dist. Ct. (so. dist.) N.Y. 1975, U.S. Dist. Ct. (no. dist.) Calif. 1980, U.S. Ct. Appeals (2d cir.) 1975. Atty. Met. Life Ins. Co., NYC, 1972-79, asst. gen. counsel San Mateo, Calif., 1979-81, assoc. gen. counsel Foster City, Calif., 1981-88, v.p., assoc. gen. counsel, 1988, head mortgage portfolio in real estate investments dept., 1992—98, head corp. planning and strategy, 1998—2000, sr. v.p., dep. gen. counsel NYC, 2001—03, exec. v.p., gen. counsel, 2004—; pres., CEO Conning Corp., a former MetLife subs., 2000—01. Dir. MetLife Found., Life Ins. Coun. N.Y. Author: Structuring Complex Real Estate Transactions, 1988. Treas. Emmanuel Bapt. Ch., San Jose, Calif., 1984—, stewardship chmn., 1987—; vice chair Citizens Budget Commn.; bd. dirs. N.Y. Citizens Crime Commn. Mem. Am. Coll. Real Estate Lawyers (mem. bd. govs., editor ACREL papers), Calif. State Bar Assn. (real property law sect. 1981—), ABA (mem. real property, probate and corp. law sects.), Assn. of Life Ins. Counsel, Am. Council Life Ins., City of N.Y. Bar Assn. (treas., mem. exec. com.), N.Y. Bar Assn. Avocations: racquetball, painting. Office: Gen Counsel MetLife Inc 1 Madison Ave New York NY 10010-3690

LIPSCOMB, OSCAR HUGH, archbishop; b. Mobile, Ala., Sept. 21, 1931; s. Oscar Hugh and Margaret (Saunders) Lipscomb. STL, Gregorian U., Rome, 1957; PhD, Cath. U. Am., 1963. Ordained priest Roman Cath. Ch., 1956, consecrated bishop 1980. Asst. pastor, Mobile, 1959—65; tchr. McGill Inst., Mobile, 1959—62; vice chancellor Diocese of Mobile-Birmingham, 1963—66, chancellor, 1966—80; pastor St. Patrick Parish, Mobile, 1966—71; lectr. history Spring Hill Coll., Mobile, 1971—72; asst. pastor St. Matthew Parish, Mobile, 1971—79, Cathedral Immaculate Conception, Mobile, 1979—80; adminstr. sede vacante Archdiocese of Mobile, 1980, archbishop, 1980—. Pres. Cath. Housing Mobile, Mobile Senate Priests, 1978—80; chmn. com. on doctrine Nat. Conf. Cath. Bishops, 1988—91. Contbr. articles to profl. jours. Chmn. NCCB Com. on Ecumenical and Interreligious Affairs, 1993—96, Cath. Common Ground Initiative, 1996—, chmn. com. on the liturgy, 1999—; mem. Mixed Internat. Commn. for Theol. Dialogue Between the Cath. Ch. and the Orthodox Ch., 1999—2002, Vox Clara commn. Congregation for Divine Worship, Rome, 2002—; Chmn. bd. dirs. Mobile Mus., 1966—88, Ala. Dept. Archives and History, 1979—, chmn., 1999—; chmn. bd. dirs. Cath. U. Am., Washington, 1983—98, Spring Hill Coll., Mobile, 1982—; chmn. bd. govs. N.Am. Coll., Rome, 1982—85. Mem.: Am. Cath. Hist. Assn., Ala. Hist. Assn., So. Hist. Assn. (pres. 1971—72, exec. com. 1981—88), Hist. Mobile Preservation Soc., Lions. Roman Catholic. Address: 36633 400 Government St PO Box 1966 Mobile AL 36633-1966*

LIPSCOMB, THOMAS HEBER, III, media company executive; b. Washington, Sept. 12, 1938; s. Thomas Heber and Louise Buchanan (Heiss) L.; children: Peter Scott, Adrienne Clare. BA, Coll. William and Mary, 1961; MA, Ind. U., 1965. Editor Bobbs-Merrill Co., 1965-67, Stein & Day Pubs., 1967-69; sr. editor Prentice-Hall, Inc., 1969-70; exec. editor, editor-in-chief Dodd, Mead & Co., 1970-73; pres. Mason & Lipscomb Pubs., 1973-74; ptnr. Hamilton Assocs., 1974-76; pres., CEO Times Books (N.Y. Times Book Co.), 1976-81; chmn. bd. New Capital Publs., Inc., 1981-85; pres. Delphi Assocs., N.Y.C., 1985-87; pres., CEO Cryptologics Internat., 1988-91, Infosafe Sys., Inc., N.Y.C., 1992-96, chmn., 1996-97, Ctr. for the Digital Future, 1997—. Chmn. bd. Atlantech Aquaculture Ltd., chmn. Cardiact, Inc., 1999-2004. Contbr. articles to profl. jours. including N.Y. Times, Wall St. Jour., Washington Post, Chgo. Sun-Times, others; patents in digital tech. Mem. exec. bd. Am. Ctr. PEN, 1973-79; trustee Internat. Ctr. for Econ. Growth, Robert Coll., Istanbul, Turkey, 1973-81; panel of advisors George Polk Award, 1977—, Mus. Digital Licensing Collection; chmn. NY Vietnam Vet.'s Leadership Program, 1985-88; dir. Giraffe Project, 1989—, NYU Ctr. Copyright in New Media. Lt. U.S. Army, 1961-64. Fellow Digital Copyright Forum; mem. Coun. on Fgn. Relations, Internat. Broadcast Inst., East-West Inst. Security Studies, Gibraltar-Am. Coun., St. Nicholas Soc., N.Y. Acad. Scis., Holland Lodge, Mid-Atlantic Club, Nat. Press Club. Office: 1360 York Ave Ste 3D New York NY 10021 E-mail: tom@digitalfuture.org.

LIPSCOMB, WILLIAM NUNN, JR., retired chemistry professor; b. Cleve., Dec. 9, 1919; s. William Nunn and Edna Patterson (Porter) Lipscomb; m. Mary Adele Sargent, May 20, 1944; children: Dorothy Jean, James Sargent; m. Jean Craig Evans, 1983; 1 child, Jenna. BS, U. Ky., 1941, DSc (hon.), 1963; PhD, Calif. Inst. Tech., 1946; DSc (hon.), U. Munich, 1976, L.I. U., 1977, Rutgers U., 1979, Gustavus Adolphus Coll., 1980, Marietta Coll., 1981, Miami U., 1983, U. Denver, 1985, Ohio State U., 1991, Transylvania U., 1992; DSc h.c. (hon.), Mahidol U., Bangkok, Thailand, 2003. Phys. chemist Office of Sci. R&D, 1942—46; faculty U. Minn., Mpls., 1946—59, asst. prof., 1946—50, assoc. prof., 1950—54, acting chief phys. chemistry divsn., 1952—54, prof. and chief phys. chemistry divsn., 1954—59; prof. chemistry Harvard U., Cambridge, Mass., 1959—71, Abbott and James Lawrence prof., 1971—90, prof. emeritus, 1990—. Mem. U.S. Nat. Commn. for Crystallography, 1954—59, 1960—63, 1965—67; chmn. program com. 4th Internat. Congress of Crystallography, Montreal, 1957; mem. sci. adv. bd. Robert A. Welch Found.; mem. adv. bd. Mich. Molecular Biology Inst.; mem. adv. com. Inst. Amorphous Studies; mem. sci. adv. com. Nova Pharms., Daltex Med. Sci., Gensia Pharms., Binary Therapeutics. Author: The Boron Hydrides, 1963; author: (with G.R. Eaton) NMR Studies of Boron Hydrides and Related Compounds, 1969; assoc. editor: Jour. Chem. Physics, 1955—57; contbr. articles to profl. jours. Clarinetist, mem. Amateur Chamber Music Players. Named Robert Welch Found. lectr., 1966, 1971, Howard U. disting. lecture series, 1966, George Fisher Baker lectr., Cornell U., 1969, centenary lectr., Chem. Soc., London, 1972, lectr., Weizmann Inst., Rehovoth, Israel, 1974, Evans award lectr., Ohio State U., 1974, Gilbert Newton Lewis Meml. lectr., U. Calif., Berkeley, 1974, lectr., Mich. State U., 1975, U. Iowa, 1975, Ill. Inst. Tech., 1976; recipient Harrison Howe award in chemistry, 1958, Disting. Alumni Centennial award, U. Ky., 1965, Disting. Svc. in advancement inorganic chemistry, Am. Chem. Soc., 1968, George Ledlie prize, Harvard, 1971, Nobel prize in chemistry, 1976, Disting. Alumni award, Calif. Inst. Tech., 1977, First Outstanding Alumni award, U. Ky., 1999, Sr. U.S. Scientist award, Alexander von Humboldt-Stiftung, 1979, award lecture, Internat. Acad. Quantum Molecular Sci., 1980; fellow Guggenheim, Oxford U., Eng., 1954—55, Cambridge U., Eng., 1972—73, NSF sr. postdoctoral fellow, 1965—66, Overseas fellow, Churchill Coll., Cambridge, Eng., 1966, 1973. Fellow: Am. Acad. Arts and Scis.; mem.: NAS, Academie Europeenne des Scis., des Arts et des Lettres, The Netherlands Acad. Arts and Scis. (fgn.), Royal Soc. Chemistry (hon.), Assn. Bioinorganic Scientists (hon.), Am. Crystallographic Assn. (pres. 1955), Am. Chem. Soc. (chmn. Minn. sect. 1949—50, Peter Debye award phys. chemistry 1973), Phi Mu Epsilon, Sigma Pi Sigma, Phi Lambda Upsilon, Alpha Chi Sigma, Sigma Xi, Phi Beta Kappa. Office: Harvard U Dept Chemistry & Chem Biol 12 Oxford St Cambridge MA 02138-2902 Business E-Mail: lipscomb@chemistry.harvard.edu.

LIPSEY, CHARLES E., lawyer; b. Pensacola, Fla., Nov. 27, 1950; BChE, Ga. Inst. Tech., 1972; JD with high honors, George Washington U., 1977, LLM in Patent and Trade Regulation Law with highest honors, 1981. Bar: Va. 1977, D.C. 1979, U.S. Ct. Appeals (fed. cir.) 1979, U.S. Patent and Trademark Office. Ptnr. Finnegan, Henderson, Farabow, Garrett & Dunner, Washington. Tech. advisor to Assoc. Judge Giles S. Rich, U.S. Ct. Customs and Patent Appeals, 1976-78; profl. lectr. law George Washington U., 1984-89; cons. U.N. Indsl. Devel. Orgn.; expert cons. Implications Advances in Genetic Engring. for Developing Countries, Vienna, 1981. Co-author: Patent Law Perspectives, 1982-88. Recipient Joseph Rossman Meml. award, 1979; named one of best lawyers in intellectual property law, Best Lawyers in Am., 2005. Mem. ABA, Am. Intellectual Property Law Assn., Va. State Bar, D.C. Bar, Bar Assn. D.C., Tau Beta Pi, Order of Coif. Office: Finnegan Henderson Farabow Garrett & Dunner LLP Two Freedom Sq 11955 Freedom Dr Reston VA 20190-5675 Office Phone: 571-203-2700. Office Fax: 202-408-4400. Business E-Mail: charles.lipsey@finnegan.com.

LIPSEY, HOWARD IRWIN, lawyer, educator; b. Providence, Jan. 24, 1936; s. Harry David and Anna (Gershman) L.; children: Lewis Robert, Bruce Stephen. BA (hon.), Providence Coll., 1957; JD, Georgetown U., 1960. Bar: R.I., 1960; U.S. Dist. Ct. R.I., 1961; U.S. Supreme Ct., 1972. Assoc. Edward I. Friedman, 1963-67, Kirshenbaum and Kirshenbaum, 1967-72; ptnr. Abedon, Michaelson, Stanzler, Biener, Skolnik, and Lipsey, 1972-83, Lipsey and Skolnik Esquires, Ltd., Providence, 1983-93; assoc. justice R.I. Family Ct., Providence, 1993—. Lectr. trial tactics Nat. Coll. Adv., 1986, U. Bridgeport, Yale U., U. Denver, Suffolk U.,1987—; adj. prof. U. Houston ., 1994-98; adj. prof. family law Roger Williams U., 1996-2000; co-chair R.I. Supreme Future of the Courts Com., 2004, chair, 2005; chair R.I. Supreme Ct. Permanent com. Women and Minorities in the Courts, 2005—; chair adv. com. on women and minorities in the courts R.I. Supreme Ct. Contbg. author: Valuation and Distribution of Marital Property, 1984; bd. editors Georgetown U. Law Jour. Capt. JAGC, USAR, 1960-71. Fellow: Am. Acad. Matrimonial Lawyers, Am. Coll. Trial Lawyers; mem.: ATLA, ABA (chair trial advocacy inst. 1994—97, coun. 1995—2001, sec. family law sect. 2002—03, bd. edit. Family Advocate, vice chair 2003—04, chair-elect 2004—), Family Law Inn of Ct. (counselor), R.I. Bar Assn., B'nai B'rith. Office: RI Family Ct 1 Dorrance Plz Providence RI 02903-3922 Office Phone: 401-458-5310.

LIPSEY, JOSEPH, JR., wholesale distribution executive; b. Selma, Ala, Sept. 12, 1934; s. Joseph and Anna (Bendersky) L.; m. Betty Fay Willan, June 5, 1960; children: Debora, Joseph III, Elizabeth, Tami. BA, La. State U., 1955, LLB, 1957; grad. Owner/Pres. Mgmt. Program, Harvard Grad. Sch. Bus., 1985. Bar: La. 1957, U.S. Dist. Ct. La. 1957, Korea 1959, Ryukyu Islands 1958. Ptnr. Howell & Lipsey, Baton Rouge, 1960—65; v.p. Wellan's, Inc., 1965—81, Lipsey's Wholesale, Baton Rouge, 1965—81; pres. Palais Royal, Inc., Shraveport, La., 1986—89. Pres. Wellan's, Inc., Alexandria, La., 1981-89, Palis Royal, Inc., Shraveport, La. and Fla., 1986—, So. Media Rsch. Co., Monroe, La., 1984-92, mng. ptnr. Rapides Interests, Inc., Alexandria, 2003—; chmn. Composite Analysis Group, Inc., Alexandria, 1989—; CEO Lipsey Mountain Spring Water, Atlanta, 1990—, Nantahalla Spring Water Bottling Co., Highlands, NC, 1994—; chmn., sec.-treas. EAS Pub. Co., Inc., 1994—; bd. dir., ind. dir. Weingarten Golden State, Inc., Houston, Tex., 2001—; spkr. OPM 10 Harvard U., 1985; lectr. La. State U. Law Sch., Baton Rouge, 1961-63, Freeman Sch. Bus., Tulane U.; mem. chancellor's bd. Paul M. Hebert Law Ctr., La. State U., 2001-04; chmn. Fashion Mcht. Conf., NYC, 1977-81. Mem. exec. com. Com. for a Better La., Baton Rouge, 1971-86; mem. La. State U. Found., 1975—, pres., 1980-81. Capt. USAF, 1957-60. Inducted into La. State U. Law Sch. Hall Fame, 1987. Mem. La. State C. of C. (pres. 1973-75), Alexandria C. of C. (pres. 1971-72), Bus. Exec. for Nat. Security, Rotary. Democrat. Jewish. Office Phone: 770-449-0001. Business E-Mail: lipsey@lipseywater.com.

LIPSEY, RICHARD GEORGE, economist, educator; b. Victoria, BC, Can., Aug. 28, 1928; s. Richard Andrew and Faith Thirell (Ledingham) L.; m. Diana Louise Smart, Mar. 17, 1960; children: Mark Alexander (stepson), Mathew Richard, Joanna Louise, Claudia Amanda. BA with honours, U. BC, 1950, LLD (hon.), 1999, McMaster U., 1984, Victoria U., 1985, Carleton U., 1986, Queens U., 1990, U. Western Ont., 1994, U. Essex, 1996; MA, U. Toronto, 1953; PhD, London Sch. Econs., 1958; DSc (hon.), Toronto U., 1992; DLitt (hon.), Guelph U., 1993. Rsch. asst. B.C. Dept. Trade and Industry, 1950-53; from asst. lectr. to prof. econs. London Sch. Econs., 1955-63; prof. econs., chmn. dept., dean Sch. Social Studies, U. Essex, Eng., 1965-69; vis. prof. U. B.C., 1969-70, U. Colo., 1973-74; Irving Fisher vis. prof. Yale U., 1979-80; Sir Edward Peacock prof. econs. Queens U., Kingston, Ont., 1970-87; prof. Simon Fraser U., Vancouver, B.C., 1989-97, prof. emeritus, 1997—. Sr. rsch. advisor C.D. Howe Inst., 1983-89; dir. rsch. into growth in U.K. Nat. Econ. Devel. Coun. U.K., 1961-63; mem. coun. and planning com. Nat. Inst. Econ. and Social Rsch. U.K., 1962-69; mem. bd. Social Sci. Rsch. Coun. U.K., 1966-69. Author: An Introduction to Positive Economics, 10th edit, 2003, The Theory of Customs Unions: A General Equilibrium Analysis, 1971; co-author: An Introduction to a Mathematical Treatment of Economics, 3d edit, 1977, Economics, 12th edit., 1999, Mathematical Economics, 1976, An Introduction to the U.K. Economy, 1983, 4th edit., 1993, Common Ground for the Canadian Common Market, 1984, Canada's Trade Options in a Turbulent World, 1985, Global Imbalances, 1987, First Principles of Economics, 1988, 3d edit., 1996, Evaluating the Free Trade Deal, 1988, The NAFTA, What's In, What's Out, What Next, Business Economics, 1997, A Structuralist Assessment of Innovation Policies, 1998, Economic Transformations: General Purpose Technologies and Long Term Economic Growth, 2005; editor: Rev. Econ. Studies, 1962-64. Decorated officer Order of Can.; Can. Inst. for Advanced Rsch. fellow, 1989—2002. Fellow Econometric Soc., Royal Soc. Can., Can. Inst. for Advanced Rsch., IC2 Soc. (Austin, Tex.); mem. Royal Econ. Soc. (council 1967-71), Econ. Study Soc. (chmn. 1965-69), Am. Econ. Assn., Can. Econ. Assn. (pres. 1980-81), Atlantic Econ. Soc. (chmn. 1986-87). Office Phone: 604-947-9714. Personal E-mail: rlipsey@sfu.ca.

LIPSEY, ROBERT EDWARD, economist, educator; b. NYC, Aug. 14, 1926; s. Meyer Aaron and Anna (Weinstein) L.; m. Sally Irene Rothstein, Nov. 24, 1948; children: Marion (Mrs. William Greenlee), Carol (Mrs. William Hersh), Eleanor (Mrs. William Ho). BA, Columbia U., 1944, MA, 1946, PhD, 1961. Rsch. asst. Nat. Bur. Econ. Rsch., NYC, 1945-53, rsch. assoc., 1953-60, sr. rsch. staff, 1960—, v.p. rsch., 1970-75, dir. internat. studies, 1975-78, dir. NY Office, 1978—. Lectr. econs. Columbia U., 1961-64; prof. econs. Queens Coll. and Grad. Ctr., CUNY, 1967-95, prof. emeritus, 1995—; cons. Dept. Commerce, Fed. Res. Bd., UN, World Bank; mem. Pres. Adv. Bd. on Internat. Investment, 1977-78; bd. dirs. Rsch. Found. CUNY, 1994-95; exec. com. European Union Studies Ctr., CUNY, 1994—. Author: Price and Quantity Trends in the Foreign Trade of the U.S, 1963, (with Raymond W. Goldsmith) Studies in the National Balance Sheet of the U.S, 1963, (with Doris Preston) Source Book of Statistics Relating to Construction, 1966, (with Irving B. Kravis) Price Competitiveness in World Trade, 1971, (with Phillip Cagan) Financial Effects of Inflation, 1978, (with Irving B. Kravis) Saving and Economic Growth: Is the U.S. Really Falling Behind, 1987, (with Magnus Blomström and Lennart Ohlsson) Economic Relations Between the U.S. and Sweden, 1989, Measures of the Transnationalization of Economic Activity, United Nations, New York and Geneva, 2001; editor: (with Helen Stone Tice) The Measurement of Saving, Investment and Wealth, 1989, (with Robert E. Baldwin and J. David Richardson) Geography and Ownership as Bases for Economic Accounting, 1998, (with Alan Heston) International and Interarea Comparisons of Income, Output, and Prices, 1999, (with Jean-Louis Mucchielli) Multinational Firms and Impacts on Employment, Trade, and Technology, 2002, (with Heinz Herrmann) Foreign Direct Investment in the Real and Financial Sector of Industrial Countries, 2003; assoc. editor Rev. of Econs. and Stats., 1989-92; mem. editl. bd. Rev. of Income and Wealth, 1992—, Internat. Trade Jour., 1998—, Contemporary Econ. Policy, 2000—; contbr. articles to profl. jours. Fellow Am. Statis. Assn., NY Acad. Scis.; mem. Acad. Internat. Bus., Nat. Assn. for Bus. Econs., Am. Econ. Assn., Internat. Assn. for Rsch. in Income and Wealth, Conf. on Rsch. in Income and Wealth, Econometric Soc., Internat. Trade and Fin. Assn. (pres. 1997), Western Econ. Assn. (bd. dirs. 1996-99), European Econ. Assn. Office: National Bureau Of Economic Research 365 5th Ave Fl 5 New York NY 10016-4309 Office Phone: 212-817-7961. E-mail: rlipsey@gc.cuny.edu.

LIPSHULTZ, STEVEN EDWARD, pediatrician, cardiologist; b. Englewood, N.J., Mar. 25, 1954; s. Harry and Anita Lois Lipshultz; m. Tracie Lea Miller, May 19, 1984; children: Hannah, Zachary, Emma and Sarah. BA, U. Pa., 1976, MA, 1980; MD, Dartmouth Med. Sch., 1981. Lic. physician Ohio, Mass., N.Y., Fla., diplomate Am. Bd. Pediatrics. Assoc. cardiology Harvard Med. Sch., Children's Hosp., Boston, 1984—2000; rsch. assoc. prof. Boston U., 1987—95; prof. pediat., chief cardiology U. Rochester Sch. Medicine, NY, 1996—2003; prof., chmn. dept. pediat., prof. epidemiology and medicine U. Miami Sch. Medicine, Fla., 2003—. Dir. Pediatric Cardomyopathy Registry, Miami, Fla., 1994; dir. med. adv. bd. Children's Cardiomyopathy Found., Tenafly, NJ, 2001—; mem. exec. com. Assn. Med. Sch. Dept. Chairs, Chapel Hill, NC, 2004—. Editor: 2 books, 7 jour. issues; mem.: 3 editl. bds.; contbr. over 350 articles to profl. jours. Recipient Cardiology Rsch. Achievement award, MD Anderson, 2004; numerous Rsch. grants including, NIH. Fellow: Am. Acad. Pediatrics; mem.: Greater Miami Pediatric Soc. (bd. dirs. 2003—), Assn. Fla. Children's Hosps. (bd. dirs. 2003—), Fla. Pediatric Soc. (bd. dirs. 2003—), Am. Heart Assn. (bd. dirs. 2004—), Am. Pediatric Soc., Soc. for Pediatric Rsch. Office: Univ Miami Sch Medicine Dept Pediat PO Box 016820 Miami FL 33101

LIPSHUTZ, LAUREL SPRUNG, psychiatrist; b. Easton, Pa., Dec. 11, 1946; d. Joseph A. and Helen A. (Rochlin) S.; m. Robert M. Lipshutz, June 15, 1975; 1 child, Jonathan. BA, U. Pa., 1968; MD, Albany Med. Coll. of Union U., 1972. Diplomate Am. Bd. Psychiatry and Neurology. Resident in psychiatry Johns Hopkins Hosp., Balt., 1972-75; unit chief psychiat. inpatient unit Phila. Gen. Hosp., 1975-77; dir. psychiat. inpatient svc. Pa. Hosp., Phila., 1977-96; assoc. dir. residency tng. Inst. of Pa. Hosp., Phila., 1983-96; coord. psychiat. clerkship for U. Pa. med. students Pa. Hosp., Phila., 1982-95. Sr. examiner Am. Bd. Psychiatry and Neurology, 1979—; sr. attending psychiatrist Inst. Pa. Hosp., Phila., 1989-97, psychiatrist, 1984—; clin. assoc. prof. psychiatry U. Pa. Sch. Medicine, Phila., 1997—, Thomas Jefferson Med. Coll., Phila. 1994-97. Fellow Am. Psychiat. Assn. (disting.); mem. Am. Soc. Psychoanalytic Physicians, Pa. Psychiat. Assn. (com. on women), Phila. Psychiatry Soc., Assn. Acad. Psychiatry (region III Excellence in Tchg. award 1995). Office: 210 W Washington Sq Ste 750 Philadelphia PA 19106-3514 Office Phone: 215-923-7851. Office Fax: 215-592-7853.

LIPSHUTZ, ROBERT JEROME, lawyer, former government official; b. Atlanta, Dec. 27, 1921; s. Allen A. and Edith (Gavronski) L.; m. Barbara Sorelle Levin, Feb. 16, 1950 (dec.); children: Randall M., Judith Ann, Wendy Jean, Debbie Sue; m. Betty Beck Rosenberg, Feb. 10, 1973; stepchildren: Robert, Nancy Fay. JD, U. Ga., 1943. Bar: Ga. 1943, D.C. 1980. Practice in, Atlanta, 1947-77, 79—; ptnr. firm Lipshutz, Greenblatt & King, 1979—. Counsel to Pres. U.S., Washington, 1977-79 Past vice chmn. Ga. Bd. Human Resources; treas., legal counsel Jimmy Carter Presdl. campaign com., 1976; trustee The Carter Ctr.; adv. com. Jimmy Carter Libr. Lt. AUS, 1943-46. Mem. Am., Ga., Atlanta, D.C. bar assns., Atlanta Lawyers Club, Atlanta., B'nai B'rith (past pres., Disting. Svc. award). Jewish (past pres. The Temple). Office: Lipshutz Greenblatt & King Harris Tower 233 Peachtree St Ste 2400 Atlanta GA 30303-1504 Office Phone: 404-688-2300.

LIPSIG, ETHAN, lawyer; b. N.Y.C., Dec. 11, 1948; s. Daniel Allen and Haddassah (Adler) L. BA, Pomona Coll., 1969; postgrad., Oxford U., 1969-70; JD, UCLA, 1974. Bar: U.S. Dist. Ct. (cen. dist.) Calif. 1974, U.S. Ct. Appeals (9th cir.) 1974, U.S Tax Ct. 1978. Ptnr. Paul, Hastings, Janofsky & Walker LLP, L.A. Author: Individual Retirement Arrangements, 1980, Downsizing, 1996. Mem.: Calif. C. of C., Nat. Assn. Pub. Pension Attys., State Bar Calif., tax sect. (chmn. employee benefits com. 1981—84), Am. Coll. Employee Benefits Counsel (charter mem.), ABA, sect. taxation (com. employee benefits), ABA, sect. labor & employment law, employee benefits com. (sub-com. fed, preemption 1978—79, sub-com. investments & funding 1981), L.A. Men's Garden Club, Soc. Fellows of Huntington Libr., Order Coif. Avocations: travel, horticulture, wine, music, art. Office: Paul Hastings Janofsky & Walker LLP 515 S Flower St Fl 25 Los Angeles CA 90071-2280 Office Phone: 213-683-6304. Office Fax: 213-627-0705. Business E-Mail: ethanlipsig@paulhastings.com.

LIPSITT, LEWIS PAEFF, psychology professor; b. New Bedford, Mass., June 28, 1929; s. Joseph and Anna Naomi (Paeff) L.; m. Edna Brill Duchin, June 8, 1952; children: Mark, Ann. BA, U. Chgo., 1950; MS, U. Mass., 1952; PhD, U. Iowa, 1957. Lic. Psychologist RI, 1965. Instr. dept. psychology Brown U., Providence, 1957, asst. prof., 1958-61, assoc. prof., 1961-66, prof., 1966-96, dir. Child Study Ctr., 1967-92, Wriston lectr., 1993—, prof. emeritus psychology, med. sci. and human devel., 1996—, rsch. prof. psychology, 1996—. Mem. Gov.'s Adv. Commn. on Mental Retardation, 1963-66; cons. Nat. Inst. Health; edn. task force Model Cities Program, Providence, 1969-71; fellow Stanford Ctr. for Advanced Study in Behavioral Scis., 1979-80; vis. scientist Nat. Inst. Mental Health, 1986-87; chair steering com. nat. child care project Nat. Inst. for Child Health and Human Devel., 1994-99, adv. com., 1999-2001. Co-author: Child Development, 1979; founder, editor: Infant Behavior and Devel., 1978-82; founding co-editor: Advances in Child Development and Behavior, 1963-70, 78-82; co-editor: Research Readings in Child Psychology, 1963, Experimental Child Psychology, 1971, Advances in Infancy Research, 1981-99, Self-regulatory Behavior and Risk Taking, 1991, Progress in Infancy Research, 1991—; contbr. articles to profl. jours. Bd. dirs. Providence Child Guidance Clinic, 1960-63, RI Kid Count, 2003-04, chmn., 2004—; trustee Butler Hosp., Providence, 1965-84; mem. bd. sci. counselors Nat. Ins. Child Health and Human Devel., 1984-88; nat. co-dir. Lee Salk Family Ctr., Kidspeace, Allentown, Pa., 1993—; participant White House Conf. on Child Care, 1998. With USAF, 1952—54, clin. psychologist USAF, 1952—54, Lackland AFB. Recipient Mentor award for lifetime achievement, AAAS, 1995, Profl. Achievement citation, U. Chgo., 1995; USPHS Spl. Rsch. fellow, 1966, Guggenheim fellow, 1972—73, USPHS fellow, 1973. Fellow AAAS (Lifetime Mentor award 1994), APA (exec. com. divsn. devel. psychology 1967-70, pres. divsn. devel. psychology 1980-81, bd. sci. affairs 1985-88, exec. dir. for sci. 1990-91, sci. officer 1991-92, Nicholas Hobbs award 1990, exec. com. divsn. gen. psychology 1997-2001, coun. of reps. 1997-2000, pres. divsn. gen. psychology 1999-2000, exptl. psychology coun. of reps. 2001-06, Ernest R. Hilgard award for life achievement in gen. psychology 2004, Urie Bronfenbrenner award for studies in child devel. 2004); mem. AAUP, Soc. Rsch. in Child Devel., Internat. Soc. Study Behavioral Devel. (membership sec. 1981-83, exec. com. 1984-89), Am. Psychol. Soc. (founding mem., charter fellow, bd. dirs. 1989-90), Can. Inst. for Advanced Rsch. (chair adv. com. human devel. group 1995-2003, mem. adv. com. human devel. and population health 2000-04), RI Psychol. Assn. (bd. dirs. 1995-98, Mental Health Svc. award 1998). Jewish. Office Phone: 401-863-2332. Business E-Mail: Lewis_Lipsitt@brown.edu.

LIPSKY, BURTON G., lawyer; b. Syracuse, N.Y., May 29, 1937; s. Abraham and Pauline (Leichtner); m. Elaine B. Mannheimer, July 27, 1967; 1 child, Erika S., m. Carol S. Samberg, Feb. 4, 1973; 1 child, Andrew H. BBA, U. Mich., 1959; JD summa cum laude, Syracuse U., 1962. Bar: N.Y. 1962, U.S. Supreme Ct. 1967. Trial atty. U.S. Dept. Justice, Washington, 1962-67; assoc. Kaye, Scholer, Fierman, Hays & Handler, N.Y.C., 1967-72; ptnr. Delson & Gordon, N.Y.C., 1972-87, Lipsky & Stout, N.Y.C., 1991-96; pvt. practice, N.Y.C., 1996—. Mem. bd. visitors Syracuse U. Coll. of Law,

1989—; sec.-treas., dir. Robert Mapplethorpe Found., Inc., 1988—. Mem. ABA, N.Y. Bar Assn., Order of Coif, Justinian Soc., Am. Contract Bridge League (life master). Office: 100 Park Ave 33rd Floor New York NY 10017-5586 Office Phone: 212-370-0747. Personal E-mail: BurtLip@aol.com.

LIPSKY, IAN DAVID, biotechnologist, director; b. Bklyn., May 26, 1957; s. Eugene Herman and Janet Dorothy (Heller) Lipsky; m. Cheryl Joy Weinberg; 1 child, Ethan Maxwell. BS in Marine Engring., Maine Maritime Acad., 1979; MBA, U. San Francisco, 2000. Lic. eng contractor, Calif; US Coast Guard, Merchant Mariners Document steam & motor vessels. Third asst. engr. Interlake Steamship Co., Cleve., 1979-81; port engr. Exxon Internat. Co., Florham Park, NJ, 1981-84; prodn. supr. Alfred Conhagen Inc. Calif., Hercules, 1984-87, gen. mgr., 1987-89, v.p., 1989-2000; sr. mgr. facilities svcs. dept. Genentech, Inc., South San Francisco, 2001—, assoc. dir., head of facilities biochem. mfg., 2003—. Pres. No. Calif. alumni chpt. Maine Maritime Acad., 2003—. Mem.: NSPE, Port Engrs. San Francisco, Inst. Marine Engrs. (London), Marine Port Engrs. NY, Soc. Naval Architects and Marine Engrs., U. San Francisco MBA Alumni Soc. (bd. dirs. 2003—). Democrat. Jewish. Avocations: golf, running, bicycling, drums. Office: Genentech Inc 1 DNA Way South San Francisco CA 94080-4990 Home: 34 Madera Del Presidio Dr Corte Madera CA 94925-2068 Personal E-mail: idlipsky@yahoo.com.

LIPSKY, PAT, artist; b. NYC, Sept. 21, 1941; d. Bernard G. and Bernice D. (Brown) Sutton; children: David Lipsky, Jonathan Lipsky. BFA, Cornell U., 1963; postgrad., Bklyn. Mus. Art Sch., 1960-61, Art Student's League, 1963; MA, Hunter Coll., 1968. Faculty Fairleigh Dickinson U., 1968-69, Hunter Coll., 1972, San Francisco Art Inst., 1974; assoc. prof. U. Hartford, 1983—2002. Guest lectr. Hirshhorn Mus., 1975, Va. Commonwealth U., Bennington Coll., 1977, U. Pitts., 1974, NYU, 1983, SACI, Florence, 1986, Springfield Mus., 1987-88, U. Miami, 1992, Pollock-Krasner House and Study Ctr., East Hampton, L.I., N.Y., 1995, Am. U., 1997, Muhlenberg Coll., 1999; guest lectr. Parsons Sch. Design, 1990, lectr., 1982-83, 90; instr. SUNY, Purchase, 1980-81; adv. coun. Cornell U. Coll. Art and Architecture, 1988—. One-woman shows include Andre Emmerich Gallery, N.Y.C., 1970, 72, 74, 75, Deichter O'Reilly Gallery, 1976, Medici-Berenson Gallery, 1976, Everson Mus., 1970, Gloria Luria Gallery, Miami, 1988, Slater-Price Gallery, NYC, 1986, Hartell Gallery Cornell U., 1989, Andre Zarre Gallery, 1991, Virginia Miller Gallery, Coral Gables, Fla., 1994, Bookstein Fine Arts, N.Y.C., 1997, The Kitchen, 1999, Elizabeth Harris Gallery, 1999, 2001, 03, 04, Piltzer Gallery, Barbizon, France, 2002, L.I.C.K. Ltd. Fine Art, Long Island City, NY, 2003, Elizabeth Harris Gallery, 2004, New Monotypes, Aurobora Press Gallery, San Francisco, 2005, others; exhibited in group shows at Whitney Mus. Am. Art, 1971, Hirshhorn Mus. and Sculture Garden, 1975, Promenade Gallery, Hartford, 1984, U. Mass. Art Gallery, Amherst, 1987, Gloria Luria Gallery, 1988, 92, Andre Zarre Gallery, 1990, 95, Denise Renè Gallery, Paris, 1993, Gallery One, Toronto, Can., 1996, Snyder Fine Art, NYC, 1996, Lori Bookstein/Fine Arts, 1997, Am. Acad. Arts & Letters, 2001, DC Moore Gallery, 2004, Am. Embassy, Sarajero, Bosnia, 2005; represented in permanent collections Herbert Johnson Mus., Ithaca, NY, Witney Mus., Hirshhorn Mus., Walker Art Ctr., Hunter Coll., Fogg Art Mus., Harvard U., San Francisco Mus. Art, Bklyn. Mus., Blanton Mus. Art, U. Tex., Austin, Wadsworth Atheneum, Hartford, Portland Mus. Art, Mus. Fine Arts, Houston; stage designer (play) Custody, Westbeth Theatre, N.Y.C., 1991; works include silkscreen and poster edit. Lincoln Ctr./List Great Performers Series, 2004. Recipient Childe Hassam Purchase prize AAAL, 2001; grantee N.Y. State Coun., 1972, N.Y. Found. Arts, 1992, Jerome Found., 1999, Adolph & Esther Gottlieb Found., 1999, Pollock-Krasner Found., 2000; sponsorship from Winsor and Newton Paint Co., 1992; fellow Va. Ctr. for Creative Arts, 1986, 93, Tyrone Guthurie Centre, Co., Moneghan, Ireland, 1996. Home: 410 W 24th St New York NY 10011-1303 Studio: 526 W 26th St Rm 1011 New York NY 10001-5541 Personal E-mail: pslipsky@aol.com.

LIPSMAN, RICHARD MARC, lawyer, educator; b. Bklyn., Aug. 17, 1946; s. Abraham W. and Ruth (Weinstein) L.; m. Geri A. Russo, 1979; children: Eric, Dara Briana. BBA, CCNY, 1968; JD, St. John's U., Jamaica, NY, 1972; LLM in Taxation, Boston U., 1976. Bar: NY 1973, Mass. 1975, US Dist. Ct. (ea. and so. dists.) NY 1977, US Supreme Ct. 1978, US Tax Ct. 1979; CPA, NY, Mass. Tax atty. Arthur Young & Co., NYC, 1972-74; assoc. Gilman, McLaughlin & Hanrahan, Boston, 1974-76, Lefrak, Fischer & Meyerson, NYC, 1976-77; ptnr. Tarnow, Landsman & Lipsman, NYC, 1978; pvt. practice NYC, 1979—. Adj. faculty Baruch Coll. CUNY, 1984-86, curriculum specialist Rsch. Found. CUNY, 1977-78; adj. faculty Pratt Inst., Bklyn., 1974, Queensboro Coll., Bayside, NY, 1978-80. Author, producer book/cassette program Learning Income Taxes, 1978—. Mem. ABA, AICPA, NY State Bar Assn., Assn. Bar City NY, NY State Soc. CPA's. Jewish. Office Phone: 212-532-7700. Personal E-mail: rmlny@pipeline.com.

LIPSON, ABIGAIL, psychologist; b. Washington, Mar. 6, 1956; d. Leon Samuel and Dorothy Ann (Rapoport) L.; m. Craig Nicholson, 1996. BA, Hampshire Coll., 1977; PhD, Duke U., 1981. Lic. clin. psychologist. Instr., teaching asst. Duke U., Durham, NC, 1977—79; staff psychotherapist Duke Psychol. Svcs., Durham, NC, 1977—81; clin. psychology intern Harvard U., Cambridge, Mass., 1981—82; sr. counselor Harvard U. Bur. Study Counsel, Cambridge, Mass., 1982—97; pvt. practice Cambridge, Mass., 1983—97; dir. psychol. svcs. Am. U., Washington, 1997—2005; dir. Bur. of Study Counsel Harvard U., 2005—. Vis. faculty Cambridge Coll., 1984, Kennedy Sch. Govt., Cambridge, 1985, 91; NIMH rsch. assoc. U. Mass., Amherst, 1989-91. Co-author: BLOCK, 1990; contbr. articles to psychology and edn. jours. Mem. APA, Am. Ednl. Rsch. Assn., Mass. Psychol. Assn. Office Phone: 617-495-2581.

LIPSON, ALLEN S., entertainment company executive, lawyer; b. N.Y.C., Dec. 15, 1942; BS, U. Wis., 1964; JD, Columbia U., 1967. Bar: N.Y. 1968, U.S. Dist. Ct. (so. dist.) N.Y. 1968, Conn. 1989. Assoc. Casey, Lane & Mittendorf, N.Y.C., 1967-72; asst. gen. counsel Textron, Inc., Providence, 1972-77; corp. counsel BIC Corp., Milford, Conn., 1977-88; gen. counsel, v.p. adminstrn., sec. Remington Products, Inc., Bridgeport, Conn., 1988—96, v.p. adminstrn., gen. counsel, sec., 1996—99; exec. v.p. bus. & legal affairs, sec. Marvel Enterprises, Inc., NYC, 1999—2003, CEO, pres., 2003—. Office: Marvel Enterprises Inc 10 E 40th St New York NY 10016

LIPSON, BARRY J., lawyer, columnist; b. NYC, May 30, 1938; s. Sidney J. and Irene (Abrams) L.; m. Lois J., June 7, 1975; children: Steven J., David J. Grad., Wharton Sch., 1956—59; BS in Econ., U. Pa., 1959; JD, Columbia U., 1962; LLM in Trade Regulation, NYU, 1968; post grad., Oxford U., 1982, Harvard U. Sch. Law Sch., 1984. Bar: NY 1962, Pa. 1970, US Supreme Ct. 1967. Dep. asst. atty. gen. State of NY, 1963-64, asst. atty. gen., 1964-67; assoc. counsel, asst. sec. Block Drug Co., Inc. and Reed & Canrick, 1968-69; asst. sec., counsel, trade regulation counsel Koppers Co., Inc., Pitts., 1969-81; v.p., gen. counsel, sec. Elkem Metals Co., Elkem Group, 1982-85; head of corp. divsn. Weisman, Goldman, Bowen & Gross, Pitts., 1985—2004; CEO, exec. dir. CorpLaw Ctr., 2004—. Adj. settlement judge US Dist. Ct. (we. dist.) Pa., 1995—, arbitrator, 1995—; arbitrator, master Pa. Ct. Common Pleas, Allegheny County, 1970—; arbitrator, mediator Am. Arbitration Assn., Better Bus. Bur., Arbitration Forums, Inc., EEOC; guest lectr. George Washington U. Sch. Law, 1979-83; mem. Bus. Roundtable Lawyers Adv. Com., 1978-82; mem. Pa. C. of C. Antitrust Adv. Com., 1978-85; mem. Indsl. Functional Adv. Com. on Internat. Stds., US Dept. Commerce and Office of US Trade Rep., 1980-88, columnist, 1985—, CorpLaw Commentaries, Federally Speaking, published in the Lawyers Jour., Small Bus. Legal Report, Fed. Legal Forum, Pa. Law-Jour. Reporter, LA Daily Jour. Report, Pitts. Legal Jour., Pitts. Bus. Times, Pitts. Neighbors, Cin. Downtowner, Allegheny Bus. News; lectr. in field Contbg. author NY Law Jour., 1965-67, Antitrust Law Jour., 1982, LA Daily Jour. Report, 1983, 86, The Practical Lawyer and The Practical Lawyer's Manual on Trade Regulation, 1967- 1985, Pa. Law Jour.-Reporter, 1983-87, Antitrust for Bus., 1989, Advising Small Bus., 1992—; founding editor Sherman's Summations, 1979-82; interviewee Off the Bench and Off the Cuff, 1987; contbr. articles to profl. jour. Vice-chmn. Pitts. chpt. ACLU, 1977-78, 93-94, bd. dir., 1972-2000, chmn. legal com., 1975-77; bd. dir. Pa. ACLU, 1977-84, 91-94, nat. biennial del., 1995; pres. Allegheny County Transit Coun., 1996-97, legis. chair, 1993-94, v.p., 1994-96, chief counsel, 1995-99, exec. com., 1993-99; mem. adv. panel Southwestern Pa. Regional Planning Commn., 1993-98; pres. Beth Samuel, 1990-92; dir. United Synagogue, Western Pa. Region, 1989-97; organizer, mem. steering com. Nat. Conf. Peacemaking and Conflict Resolution, 1996-97, Pitts. Mediation Ctr., Cultural Competency Com., 2005—; counselor Score, Counselors to Am's Small Bus., 2005—; instr. Sr. Net, 2005—. Lt. comdr. JAGC, USNR, 1965-75. Mem.: ABA (chmn. monopolization taskforce 1976—79, chmn., lectr. monopolization program 1978, vice chmn. Sherman Act com. 1979, chmn. monopolization subcom. 1979—82, chmn. antitrust compliance counseling taskforce 1979—82, faculty Nat. Inst. 1980), Fed. Bar Asn. (v.p. nat. del. Pitts. chpt. 1987—93, democracy devel. initiative com. 1990—, nat. rules com. 1993—95, founding pres. western Pa. chpt. 1994—98, Nat. Mem. Com. 1995—98, 3d cir. v.p. 1998—2004, chmn. nat. chptr. activity fund 2002—04, Nat. Spl. Recognition award 1995), Am. Corp. Counsel Asn. (founding western pa. chpt. dir., sec. 1984—86), Allegheny County Bar Asn. (founding mem., chmn. antitrust and class action com. 1980—82, vice chmn. hdqs. com. 1983—85, alt. dispute resolution com. 1992—, ADR Players 1995, writer ACBA Players 1997—99, chmn. Unauthorized Practice of Law Com. 1998—2000, publ. com. 2002—), Boy Scouts Am. (troop com. chair 1993—97, coun. com. chair 1995—98, Masonic Boy Scout award, Shofar award), Blue Lodge, Elks, York Rite Masons (St. Clair chpt., Most Excellent High Priest 1994), Grotto (past masters unit, ritual team), Tall Cedars (grand tall cedar, Al-O-Mon Forest 2002, pres. past officers assn. 2003, prest. dist. 2005), Shriners (pres. Syria Temple Luncheon Club 1993, pres. West Hills Caravan 1997, Oriental Guide Ritual Team, former Syria temple asst. solicitor, chmn. Heinz Hall spectacular, judge adv. Legion of Honor, provost guard, Knights of Mecca, v.p. dep. unit), Scottish Rite (32d degree, commander, legion of honor 1999—2000, Sovereign Prince, Princes of Jerusalem 2000—01, 32d degree, Dads and Sons Soc. 2001—, Charter Chancellor, King Cyrus Ritual Team), Masons (mem. Doric Hall Assn. 1990—97, worshipful master Germania Lodge #509 2001, charter mem. Pa. Lodge Rsch. 2001—), Kiwanis (pres. number 3, Pitts. club 1991—92, chair Bill of Rights project, Internat. Del., Internat. Meritorious award, Kiwanian of Yr.), Forty and Eight (Chevaux), Am. Legion (judge advocate, former adjutant). Achievements include owner, federally registered trademark CorpLaw. Office: CorpLaw Ctr 102 Christler Ct Moon Township PA 15108-1359 Office Phone: 412-264-9417. Business E-Mail: bjlipson@gmail.com.

LIPSON, CHARLES HENRY, political scientist, educator; b. Clarksdale, Miss., Feb. 1, 1948; s. Harry Mason Jr. and Dorothy (Kohn) L.; m. Susan Linda Bloom, July 13, 1980; children: Michael H., Jonathan S. BA, Yale Coll., 1970; MA, Harvard U., 1974, PhD, 1976. Rsch. assoc. Harvard Ctr. for Internat. Affairs, Cambridge, Mass., 1976-77; asst. prof. U. Chgo., 1977-84, assoc. prof., 1984—2002, prof., 2003—. Vis. scholar Harvard Ctr. for Internat. Affairs, 1979-80; founding dir. program on internat. politics, econs. and security U. Chgo., 1987—, chair com. on internat. rels., 1992-95; vis. fellow London Sch. Econs, 1988-89; mem. Chgo. Com.; ptnr. Capstone Entertainment. Author: Standing Guard: Protecting Foreign Capital in the 19th and 20th Centuries, 1985, Reliable Partners: How Democracies Have Made a Separate Peace, 2003, Doing Honest Work in College, 2004; editor: Theory and Structure in International Political Economy, 1999, Issues and Agents in International Political Economy, 1999, Rational Design of International Institutions, 2004; mem. bd. editors Internat. Orgn., 1984-90, 96-2001, World Politics, 1998—, How to Write a BA Thesis, 2005; contbr. articles to profl. jours. Bd. dirs. Newberger Hillel Found. U. Chgo., 1990—, exec. com., 1993—, chmn. bd. dirs., 1994-99; bd. dirs. K.A.M. Isaiah Israel Congregation, Chgo., 1992-2001. Recipient Faculty Achievement award Burlington-No. Found., 1986; grantee German Marshall Fund U.S., 1983-84; fellow Rockefeller Found., 1979-81. Mem. Am. Polit. Sci. Assn. (sec. 1990-91), Brit.-Am. Project, Chgo. Com., Chgo. Coun. on Fgn. Rels., Internat. Inst. for Stratetic Studies, Internat. Studies Assn., Royal Inst. for Internat. Affairs. Jewish. Home: 5809 S Blackstone Ave Chicago IL 60637-1855 Office: U Chgo Dept Polit Sci 5828 S University Ave Dept Polit Chicago IL 60637-1515 Office Phone: 773-702-8053. Business E-Mail: c-lipson@uchicago.edu.

LIPSON, MELVIN ALAN, technology and business management consultant; b. Providence, R.I., June 1, 1936; s. Nathan and Esta (Blumenthal) L.; m. Jacqueline Ann Barclay, July 2, 1961; children: Donna, Robert, Michelle, Judith. BS, U. R.I., 1957; PhD, Syracuse U., 1963. Chemist ICI Organics, Providence, 1963, Philip A. Hunt Chem. Co., Lincoln, R.I., 1964-67, rsch. mgr., 1967-69; tech. dir. Dynachem div. Morton Thiokol Inc., Tustin, Calif., 1969-72, v.p., 1979-82, sr. v.p., 1972-82, 1982-85, exec. v.p., 1985-86, pres., 1986-89; v.p. tech. devel. Morton Internat. Inc., Chgo., 1989-92; pres. Lipson Assocs., Newport Beach, Calif., 1993—. Chmn. bd., CEO Aurelon, Inc., Huntington Beach, Calif., 1993-96, Pivotech., Inc., Newport Beach, Calif., 1996-98; CEO Meltex, Inc., Huntington Beach, Calif., 1998—. Home and Office: 14 Belcourt Dr Newport Beach CA 92660 Office Phone: 949-644-2403. Personal E-mail: mellipson@yahoo.com.

LIPSON, PAMELA, information scientist; m. Pawan Sinha. BA, Harvard U., 1989; MS, MIT, 1993, PhD, 1996. Postdoctoral rschr. Artificial Intelligence Lab., MIT, 1996—97; co-founder, pres., CEO, Imagen, Inc., 1997—. Achievements include development of technology for encoding alphanumeric and graphical information with high density on crystalline substrates. Office: Imagen Inc 955 Massachusetts Ave # 351 Cambridge MA 02139

LIPSON, STEVEN MARK, clinical virologist, microbiologist, environmental scientist, educator; b. Bklyn., May 25, 1948; s. Jonas and Ana (Rogers) L.; m. Heleen P. Bleiweiss, Apr. 25, 1971; children: Tracy J., Jennifer B. BS in Biology, L.I. U., 1967; MS in Microbiology and Marine Sci., C.W. Post Coll., 1972; PhD in Cell Biology and Microbiology, NYU, 1981. Cert. dir. in virology and immunology N.Y. State Dept. Health, in virology Am. Soc. Clin. Pathologists, lic. in biology and health edn. N.Y. State Dept. Edn.; cert. radioactive materials N.Y. State Dept. Health. Tchr. biology Erasmas Hall HS, N.Y., 1967—74; rsch. assoc. hematology/oncology Bklyn. Hosp.-Caladonian Hosp., 1980-82; rsch. assoc. immunology lab. dept. neoplastic diseases Mt. Sinai Sch. Medicine, N.Y.C., 1982-84; chief virology lab., assoc. dir. divsn. microbiology Nassau County Med. Ctr., East Meadow, NY, 1984-90; dir. virology lab., rsch. asst. prof. microbiology/medicine North Shore U. Hosp.-NYU Sch. Medicine, Manhasset, NY, 1990-00; acting dir. Flow Cytometry/Cellular Immunology Lab. North Shore U. Hosp.-NYC Sch. Medicine, Manhasset, NY, 1995-97; chief Virology Lab., Columbia-Presbyn. Med. Ctr., N.Y.C., 2000; asst. prof. pathology Columbia U. Coll. Physicians and Surgeons, N.Y.C., 2000; with Virology Cons., Inc., Bklyn., N.Y.C., 2000—; assoc. prof. biology dept. St. Francis Coll., Bklyn. Heights, NY, 2002—. Adj. prof., L.I. U., NY, 1987—2001; asst. prof. dept. biology NYC Tech. Coll., CUNY, 2001—02; mem. profl. adv. panel Med. Lab. Advisor, 1994—; tchg. hosp. edn. specialist clin. microbiology lab. dept. pathology SUNY, Stony Brook, 2001—05; rsch. scientist DVA, Northport, NY, 2001—02; invited reviewer grants rsch. profl. staff congress CUNY, 2004—; lectr. in field; presenter over 80 abstracts at sci. meetings. Contbr.: Clinical Microbiology Procedures Manual (Virology), 1993, guest edtl. bd.: Clin. Rev. in Microbiology, 1995, Manual of Clin. Microbiology, 1995, Jour. Infectious Disease, Arch. Path. Lab. Med., European Jour. Epidemiology, mem. editl. bd.: Med. Sci. Monitor, assoc. editor: Diagnostic Microbiol. Infectious Disease; contbr. articles to 68 profl. peer reviewed publs., over 100 abstract presentations. Vol. lectr. Kiwanis Club, Long Island, 1985-90; vol. N.Y. Hall of Sci., Queens, 1996. Grantee, Am. Cranberry Inst., 2005. Mem.: Met. Assn. Col. Univ. Biology, Long Island Infectious Disease Soc., N.Y. Infectious Diseases Soc., Am. Soc. for Microbiology (nat. and N.Y. City br.), Ind. Order Odd Fellows (noble grand 2005—), Borough Park Lodge. Achievements include research in anti-viral effects of cranberr juice. Avocations: fine dining, stamp collecting/philately, travel, motorcycling, scuba diving. Office: Biology Dept St Francis College 180 Reman St Brooklyn NY 11201 E-mail: montmor@aol.com.

LIPSTEIN, ROBERT A., lawyer; b. Wilmington, Del., Dec. 6, 1954; s. Eugene Joseph and Leona (Feld) L.; m. Cheryl A. Artibee-Wedlake, July 30, 1978; children: Rebecca Lynn, Matthew Wedlake. BA in Econs., Stanford U., 1975; JD, Stanford Law Sch., 1978. Bar: D.C. 1978, U.S. Dist. Ct. D.C., 1979, U.S. Ct. Appeals (D.C. cir.) 1980, U.S. Ct. Internat. Trade, 1984, U.S. Ct. Appeals (fed. cir.), U.S. Supreme Ct. 1990. Assoc. Morgan, Lewis & Bockius, Washington, 1978-84, Coudert Bros., Washington, 1984-86, ptnr., 1987-94; mng. ptnr. Lipstein, Jaffe & Lawson, L.L.P., 1994—2003; ptnr. Crowell & Masing LLP, 2003—. Mem. ABA (antitrust sect., law practice mgmt. sect.), D.C. Bar Assn., Phi Beta Kappa. Avocations: golf, wood working, tae kwon do (3d degree black belt). Home: 511 Stonington Rd Silver Spring MD 20902-1545 E-mail: rlipstein@crowell.com.

LIPTAK, DAVID, composer; b. Pitts., Dec. 18, 1949; m. Pia Terndrup, Aug. 15, 1998; 1 child, Carena. DMA, Eastman Sch. of Music, Rochester, New York, 1973—76. Asst. prof. Mich. State U., East Lansing, Mich., 1976—80; assoc. prof., asst. prof. U. of Ill., Urbana, 1980—87; prof. Eastman Sch. of Music, U. of Rochester, Rochester, NY, 1987—, prof., dept. chair, 1987—. Composer: Janus Variation (1998) - clarinet, violin, cello, and piano, Rhapsodies (1992) (Reader's Digest Consortium Commn.), The Moon Singer (1998) - chamber opera (Hanson Inst. for Am. Music Commn.), Commedia (2001) - clarinet, violin, and piano, Ancient Songs (1992), Trumpet Concerto (1995) (Fromm Found. Commn.), The Passing of Memory (2003), String Quartet No. 2 (2002) (Barlow Endowment Commn.), Northern Light (1997), Serenade for Alto Saxophone and Strings (2001), Broken Cries (2001), String Quartet No. 1 Chaconne (2000). Recipient Acad. Award in Music, AAAL, 2002, Commn., Barlow Endowment for Music Composition, 2002, Elise L. Stoeger Prize, Chamber Music Soc. of Lincoln Ctr., 1995. Office: Eastman Sch of Music 26 Gibbs St Rochester NY 14604

LIPTON, BRONNA JANE, marketing communications executive; b. Newark, May 10, 1951; d. Julius and Arlene (Davis) L.; m. Sheldon Robert Lipton, Sept. 23, 1984. BA in Spanish, Northwestern U., 1973. Tchr. Spanish Livingston (N.J.) H.S., 1973-78; profl. dancer Broadway theater, film, TV, N.Y.C., 1978-82; v.p., mgr. Hispanic mktg. svcs. Burson-Marsteller Pub. Rels., N.Y.C., 1982-89; exec. v.p. Lipton Comm. Group, Inc., N.Y.C., 1989-99, Latin Reports, 1996-99; v.p. Bienestar LCG Comm., Inc., 1999—2003; prin. Cmty. Direct, N.Y.C., 2003—. Mem. minority initiatives task force Am. Diabetes Assn., Alexandria, Va., 1987-90, mem. pub. rels. com., 1990-91, mem. visibility and image task force, 1991-92, bd. dirs. N.Y. Downstate affiliate, chmn. visibility and image com., 1992-93. Mem. rev. panel Hispanic Designers, Inc. Recipient Pinnacle award Am. Women in Radio and TV (N.Y. Chpt.), 1984, Value Added awards Burson-Marsteller, N.Y.C., 1982, 83, 84. Avocations: ballet, jazz dance, tennis, foreign travel, birding. Home: 1402 Chapel Hill Rd Mountainside NJ 07092-1405 Office Phone: 212-966-8222. Business E-Mail: blipton@gocommunitydirect.com.

LIPTON, CHARLES, public relations executive; b. N.Y.C., May 11, 1928; s. Jack B. and Bertha (Lesser) Lipton; m. Audrey Williams, Nov. 11, 1951; children: Susan, Jack. AB, Harvard U., 1948. Market rschr. Cecil & Presbury, Inc., N.Y.C., 1948—49; spl. events dir. 20th Century Fox Film Corp., N.Y.C., 1949—52; account exec. Ruder & Finn, Inc., N.Y.C., 1953—58, v.p., 1958—63, sr. v.p., 1963—69, vice-chmn., 1969—95; sr. counsel, bd. dirs., 1995—. Guest lectr. Boston U., 1967—68. Mem. coun. Ctr. for Vocat. Arts, Norwalk, Conn., 1966—74; treas., mem. exec. com. Norwalk Symphony Soc., 1972—85; chmn. parents coun. Washington U., St. Louis, 1976—77, trustee, 1977—; chmn. Wycliffe Charities Found., 1998—; trustee Norwalk Jewish Ctr., 1966—70. Mem.: Nat. Investor Rels. Inst., Nat. Emphysema Soc. (trustee), USIA (pub. rels., pvt. sector com. 1988—93), Internat. Pub. Rels. Assn., Am. Soc. Colon and Rectal Surgeons (trustee), Harvard Varsity Club, Harvard Club. Home: 4502 Hazleton Ln Lake Worth FL 33467-8633 Office: Ruder Finn Inc 301 E 57th St Fl 3 New York NY 10022-2900 Personal E-mail: audles@aol.com.

LIPTON, JACK PHILIP, lawyer; b. N.Y.C., Apr. 23, 1952; BA, UCLA, 1973; MA, Calif. State U., Northridge, 1975; PhD, U. Calif., Riverside, 1979; JD, U. Ariz., 1988. Bar: Calif., 1989. Faculty Humboldt State U., Arcata, Calif., 1979-80, Union Coll., Schenectady, N.Y., 1980-85, U. Ariz., Tucson, 1985-88; clk. U.S. Ct. Appeals, Phoenix, 1988-89; assoc. Irell & Manella, L.A., 1989-92; pvt. practice law $, Beverly Hills, Calif., 1992-98; ptnr. Burke, Williams & Sorensen, LLP, L.A., 1998—. Contbr. articles to profl. jours. Mem. APA. Office: Burke Williams & Sorensen 611 W 6th St Fl 25 Los Angeles CA 90017-3101

LIPTON, JACKIE F., artist, educator; b. N.Y.C., Jan. 23, 1950; d. Victor Samuel and Helen Duberstein Lipton; m. John Christopher Bolton, Oct. 17, 1990. BA, Fordham U., 1978; postgrad., Sch. Visual Arts, N.Y.C., 1993-94; MFA, Milton Avery Grad. Sch. Arts, Annandale-on-Hudson, N.Y., 1994. Art educator in spl. edn. P35, N.Y.C., 1994—. One person shows include Art Resources Transfer Gallery, 2001, 02; exhibited in group shows West Chelsea Open Art Studio Festival, 1997, 98, 99, Drawings at the Westbeth Gallery, N.Y.C., 1999, Art Resources Transfer Gallery, 1999, 2000, 01, Gale-Martin Fine Art, N.Y.C. 2001-02, Gallery Boreas, N.Y.C., 2003, 04, others; peer studio artist Art Resources Ctr. of Whitney Mus. Am. Art, N.Y.C., 1973-75; gallery artist Condeso/Lawler, 1983-88, Gale-Martin Fine Art, N.Y.C. 2001-03. Grantee Pollock-Krasner Found., 1985-86, 86-87, 99-2000; fellow Macdowell Colony, 1988, Cummington Cmty. of the Arts, 1990, Va. Ctr. for Creative Arts, 1991, 93, 95, 97, 99-2000. Home: 55 Bethune St Apt A515 New York NY 10014-2010 Studio: 526 W 26th St Rm 619 New York NY 10001-5523 E-mail: jaaris@nyc.rr.com.

LIPTON, JAMES, television personality; b. Detroit, Sept. 19, 1926; s. Lawrence Lipton; m. Nina Foch, 1954 (div. 1959). Former dean Actors Studio Drama Sch. New Sch. U., NYC. Bd. dirs. The Actors Studio. Prodr.: (Broadway plays) The Mighty Gents; co-prodr.: Ain't Misbehavin'; writer: TV series The Edge of Night, 1956, head writer: TV series Another World, 1964, The Best of Everything, 1970, Return to Peyton Place, 1972, writer, exec. prodr.: TV films Happy Birthday, Bob, 1978, writer, prodr.: novel, TV show Mirrors, 1985, writer: TV films Copacabana, 1985; host, exec. prodr.: (TV series) Inside the Actors Studio, 1994—; actor: (films) The Big Break, 1953; (TV series) The Guiding Light, 1952—62, (guest appearance): (films) Bewitched, 2005; (TV series, voice) The Simpsons, 2002; (TV series) Arrested Development, 2004, Cold Squad, 2005; author: (books) Exhalation of Larks, 1991, Exhalation of Home and Family, 1993, Exhalation of Business and Finance, 1993, (musical lyrics) Sherry!. Mem.: Aircraft Onwers and Pilots Assn. Office: Actors Studio Drama Sch New Sch Univ 66 W 12th St New York NY 10011*

LIPTON, JEFFREY M., physician; b. N.Y.C., Apr. 27, 1947; s. Alfred and Thelma Lipton; m. Linda C. Rudolph, July 6, 1968; children: David, Joshua. BA, Queens Coll., CUNY, 1967; PhD, Syracuse U., 1972; MD, St. Louis U., 1975. Asst. in medicine Children's Hosp., Boston, 1979-84; asst. prof. pediats. Harvard Med. Sch., 1979—84; assoc. attending Columbia Presbyn. Med. Ctr., N.Y.C., 1984-87; assoc. prof. pediats. Columbia U. Coll. Phys. and Surg., 1984—87; chief pediatric hematology/oncology Mt. Sinai Med. Ctr., N.Y.C., 1987-99; prof. pediatrics Albert Einstein Coll. Medicine, N.Y.C., 2001—; chief pediatric hematology/oncology and stem cell transplantation Schneider Children's Hosp., New Hyde Park, N.Y., 1999—. Advisor The Bone Marrow Found.-Resource and Ednl. Ctr., 1999—. Author more than 100 articles and book chpts. Mem. Am. Soc. Pediatric Hematology/Oncology (sec.-treas. 2002—), Soc. for Pediatric Rsch., Am. Soc. Hematology, Am. Soc. for Blood and Marrow Transplantation, N.Y. Soc. Study of Blood (pres. 1998), Pediatric Oncology Group/Children's Oncology Group (chair bone marrow transplant com. 1990-2003), Alpha Omega Alpha. Office: Schneider Children's Hosp 269-01 76th Ave New Hyde Park NY 11040-1434 Business E-Mail: jlipton@lij.edu.

LIPTON, JOAN ELAINE, advertising executive; b. NYC, July 12, 1927; 1 child, David Dean. BA, Barnard Coll., 1948. With Young & Rubicam, Inc., NYC, 1948-52, Robert W. Orr & Assocs., NYC, 1952-57, Benton & Bowles, Inc., NYC, 1957-64; asso. dir. Benton & Bowles, Ltd., London, 1964-68; with McCann-Erickson, Inc. (advt. agy.), NYC, 1968-85, v.p., 1970-79, sr. v.p., creative dir., 1979-85; pres. Martin & Lipton Advt. Inc., 1985—. Mem. Bus. Coun. UN Decade Women, 1977-78; bd. vis. PhD program bus. CUNY, 1986—. Recipient Honors award Ohio U. Sch. Journalism, 1976, Matrix award, 1979, YWCA award women achievers, 1979, Clio Classic award; named Woman Yr., Am. Advt. Fedn., 1974, Advt. Woman Yr., 1984; named Matrix Hall Fame, 1998. Mem. Advt. Women NY (1st v.p. 1975-76, v.p. Found. 1977-78), Women's Forum (bd. dirs. 1988-90), Women Comm. (pres. NY chpt. 1974-76, named Nat. Headliner 1976). Office: 163 E 62nd St New York NY 10021-7613 Office Phone: 212-832-3049. Personal E-mail: joanlipton@nyc.rr.com.

LIPTON, LESTER, ophthalmologist, entrepreneur; b. N.Y.C., Mar. 14, 1936; s. George and Rita (von Steinbaum) L.; m. Harriet Arfa, June 25, 1960; children: Sherri, Brandi, Shawn BA, NYU, 1959; MD, Chgo. Med. Sch, 1964. Rsch. fellow Chgo. Med. Sch., 1959-60; intern Brookdale Hosp. Ctr., Bklyn., 1964-65; resident Harlem Eye and Ear Hosp., N.Y.C., 1965-68; assoc. attending Polyclinic French hosps., N.Y.C., 1968-75; asst. attending physician, ophthalmologist, surg. instr. St. Clare's Hosp., N.Y.C., 1975—; attending ophthalmologist Cabrini Med. Ctr., N.Y.C., 1982—, St. Vincent's Hosp., N.Y.C., 1995—. Founder Lipton Eye Clinic, N.Y.C., 1981—; v.p. Van Arfa Realty, N.Y.C., 1984-88; pres. H&L Realty, Suffern, N.Y., 1981—; mem. bd. dirs. Salisbury (Conn.) Pub. Health Nursing Assn. Mem. U.S. Congl. Adv. Bd.; mem. bd. deacons Congregationalist Ch. With AUS, 1956-58. Named Internat. Amigo, OAS; recipient Presdl. Citation for outstanding community svc., 1991 Mem. N.Y. Med. Soc., Am. Assn. Individual Investors, Bronx High Sch. Sci. Alumni Assn., Sharon Country Club, United Shareholders Assn., Internat. Platform Assn., Wider Quaker Fellowship, Vanderbilt U. Cabinet Club. Republican. Home: 55 Interlaken Estates Box 1923 Lakeville CT 06039 Office: Lipton Eye Clinic 51 E 90th St New York NY 10128-1205 Mailing: PO Box 1923 Lakeville CT 06039 Office Phone: 212-427-2422. E-mail: hslipton@sbcglobal.net.

LIPTON, LOIS JEAN, lawyer; b. Chgo., Jan. 14, 1946; d. Harold and Bernice (Reiter) Farber L.; m. Peter Carey, May 30, 1978; children: Rachel, Sara. BA, U. Mich., 1966; JD summa cum laude, DePaul Coll. Law, Chgo., 1974; postgrad., Sheffield (Eng.) U., 1966. Bar: Ky. 1974, U.S. Dist. Ct. (we. dist.) Ky. 1974, U.S. Ct. Appeals (6th cir.) 1974, Ill. 1975, U.S. Dist. Ct. (no. dist.) Ill. 1975, U.S. Ct. Appeals (7th cir.) 1976. Staff counsel Roger Baldwin Found. of ACLU, Inc., Chgo., 1975-79, dir. reproductive rights project, 1979-83; atty. McDermott, Will & Emergy, Chgo., 1984-86, G.D. Searle, Skokie, Ill., 1988-90; sr. atty. AT&T, Chgo., 1990—. Del. White House Conf. on Families, Mpls., 1980; chmn. elect Chgo. Found. for Women. Recipient Durfee award, 1984, Roger Baldwin Lifetime Achievement award 2004. Mem. ACLU (v.p.), ABA, Chgo. Coun. Lawyers. Office: AT&T # R15 222 W Adams St Chicago IL 60606-5017 Office Phone: 312-230-2667. Personal E-mail: llipton@att.com.

LIPTON, MARTIN, lawyer; b. Jersey City, N.J., June 22, 1931; s. Samuel D. and Fannie L.; m. Susan Lytle, Feb. 17, 1982; children: James, Margaret, Katherine, Samantha BS in Econs., U. Pa., 1952; LLB, NYU, 1955. Bar: N.Y. 1956. Founding ptnr., corp. dept. Wachtell Lipton Rosen & Katz, N.Y.C., 1965—. Spec. counsel City of N.Y., 1975—78, U.S. Dept. Energy, 1979—80; acting gen. counsel U.S. Synthetic Fuels Corp., 1980; counsel NYSE Com. on Market Structure, Governance & Ownership, 1999—2000. Chmn. Bd. Trustees NYU 1998-; trustee, NYU Sch. Law 1972-, chmn. 1988-98; co-chmn. Partnership for N.Y.C.; chmn. Legal Adv. Com., NYSE, 2002-2004; bd. dirs. Inst. Jud. Adminstrn. Mem.: ABA, Assn. Bar City of N.Y., N.Y.C. Lawyers Assn., Am. Law Inst. (council mem.), Am. Acad. Arts and Scis. Office: Wachtell Lipton Rosen & Katz 51 W 52nd St Fl 29 New York NY 10019-6150 Office Phone: 212-403-1200. Office Fax: 212-403-2200. Business E-Mail: mlipton@wlrk.com.

LIPTON, ROBERT STEVEN, lawyer; b. NYC, May 12, 1946; s. Max and Mildred (Goodman) Lipton; m. Stephanie F. Kass, Aug. 8, 1971. BA, NYU, 1967, JD, 1971. Bar: NY 1972, US Ct. Appeals (2d cir.) 1972, US Dist. Ct. (so. dist.) NY 1973, US Supreme Ct. 1975. Assoc. Curtis, Mallet-Prevost, Colt, and Mosle, NYC, 1971—80, ptnr., 1980—2001, of counsel, 2001—. Editor: NYU Law Rev., 1969—71. Mem.: ABA, NYC Bar Assn., NY State Bar Assn., Fed. Bar Coun., India House, NYC, Phi Beta Kappa. Office: Curtis Mallet-Prevost Colt and Mosle 101 Park Ave Fl 34 New York NY 10178-0061 Business E-Mail: rlipton@cm-p.com.

LIPTON, STUART ARTHUR, neuroscientist; b. Danbury, Conn., Jan. 11, 1950; s. Harold and Evelyn Ruth (Stein) L.; m. Elisabeth Kay Ament, Aug. 10, 1980; children: Jennifer Ann, Jeffrey Harris. BA, Cornell U., 1971; MD, PhD, U. Pa., 1977; postgrad., Cornell U., 1971, Harvard U., 1974-76. Diplomate Am. Bd. Psychiatry and Neurology. Intern Beth Israel Hosp. and Harvard Med. Sch., Boston, 1977-78; resident in neurology Beth Israel, Brigham and Women's, Children's Hosp., Boston, 1978-80, chief neurology resident, 1980-81; research fellow in neurobiology Harvard Med. Sch., Boston, 1980-83, instr. in neurology, 1981-83, asst. prof. neurology and neurosci., 1983-87, assoc. prof. neurology and neurosci., 1987-97, dir. cellular and molecular neurosci. Children's Hosp., 1987-97; chief Cerebrovasc. and Neurosci. Rsch. Inst. Brigham and Women's Hosp., Harvard Med. Sch., 1997-99. Neurologist Mass. Gen. Hosp., Brigham and Women's Hosp., Beth Israel Hosp., Children's Hosp., Boston, 1981-99; prof., dir. Ctr. Neurosci. and Aging, The Burnham Inst., La Jolla, Calif.; adj. prof. The Salk Inst., Scripps Rsch. Inst., U. Calif., San Diego. Contbr. articles to profl. jours.; patentee in field; composer of popular songs including one that sold 1.5 million copies, 1968. Established investigator Am. Heart Assn., 1988-93. Hartford Found. fellow, 1981, 82, 83, 84, NIH fellow, 1984, 85, 86, 87, 88, 89; NIH grantee, 1984—; recipient Pattison award, 1989; Nobel Found. lectr. Karolinska Inst., 1994, Ernst Jung prize, 2001. Mem. AAAS, Am. Acad. Neurology, Am. Neurol. Assn., Soc. for Neurosci., Assn. for Rsch. in Vision and Opthalmology, Biophys. Soc., Phi Beta Kappa, Alpha Omega Alpha. Avocations: musical composition, soccer. Office: Ctr Neurosci and Aging The Burnham Inst 10901 N Torrey Pines Rd La Jolla CA 92037-1005 E-mail: slipton@burnham-inst.org.

LIPTZIN, BENJAMIN, psychiatrist; b. N.Y.C., Sept. 17, 1945; s. David Murray and Mollie (Brody) L.; m. Sharon Leslie Rothstein, June 10, 1968; children: Shoshanna, Daniel, Deborah. BA, Yale U., 1966; MD, U. Rochester, N.Y., 1971. Diplomate Am. Bd. Psychiatry and Neurology. Resident in psychiatry U. Va. Hosp., Charlottesville, 1971-74; med. officer NIMH, Rockville, Md., 1974-78; dir. geriatric psychiatry McLean Hosp., Belmont, Mass., 1978-89, asst. gen. dir., 1989-90; chief dept. psychiatry Baystate Med. Ctr., Springfield, Mass., 1990—; prof., dep. chmn. dept. psychiatry Tufts U. Sch. Medicine, 1990—. Contbr. articles to profl. jours. With USPHS, 1972-78. Recipient Acad. award NIMH, 1983. Fellow Am. Psychiat. Assn. (trustee-at-large 1992-95); mem. AMA, Am. Coll. Psychiatrists. Democrat. Jewish. Office: Baystate Med Ctr Dept Psychiatry 759 Chestnut St Springfield MA 01199-1001 Office Phone: 413-794-4235. E-mail: benjamin.liptzin@bhs.org.

LIPUT, ANDREW LAWRENCE, lawyer, educator; b. Trenton, NJ, June 28, 1962; s. Andrew and Bernice Helen L.; m. Jacquelyn Anne Liput, Jan. 11, 1997; children: Mallory, Sloane, Scarlett. BA, Drew U., 1984; JD, Fordham U., 1987. Bar: N.J., 1987, N.Y., 1988, Conn., 1996. V.p., gen. cousel Parssine Group, Inc., NYC, 1988-91, Marjam Supply Co., Inc., Bklyn., 1993-96; v.p., gen. counsel US Mortgage Corp., 2004—; sr. lawyer Hartman, Buhrman & Winnicki, Paramus, NJ, 1991-93; ptnr. Liput, Ricca, Donner LLP, Huntington, NY, 1996—2004; adj. prof. Felician Coll., Lodi, NJ, 1994-97; assoc. prof. Suffolk C.C., Long Island, NY, 1998—, Briarcliff Coll., Bethpage, NY, 2001—; prof. St. Joseph's Coll., 2001—. Trust officer, Neighborhood Cleaners Assn., NYC, 1998-, Met. Package Store Assn., Westchester, NY, 1997-03. Author: Long Lost Tales of the Legendary Snarfdoodle, 2001, Last Train to Vladivostoky, 2003; contbr. articles to profl. jours. Pres., dir. Bridge the Gap!, Long Island, 1998—, councilman, No. Plainfield, NJ, 1988-89. Mem. US Rowing Assn., Aircraft Owners & Pilots Assn., NY State Bar Assn., NJ State Bar Assn., Conn. Bar Assn., NC Bar Assn. Republican. Avocations: rowing, flying, reading, world travel. Home: 134 Old Turnpike Rd Port Murray NJ 07865 Office: US Mortgage Corp PO Box 2014 19D Chapin Rd Pine Brook NJ 07058 Office Phone: 973-244-7100 ext. 1173. Office Fax: 973-276-5371. Business E-Mail: aliput@usmtg.com.

LIRO, JOSEPH R., diversified financial services company executive; BA in Monetary Econs., MA in Monetary Econs., Am. U.; PhD in Econs., Syracuse (N.Y.) U. Staff rschr. Fed. Res. Sys.; prof. Sch. Mgmt. U. Mass.; sr. economist Fin. Control Bd., 1984—86; chief economist S.G. Warburg & Co., 1986—95, CIBC Oppenheimer Corp., 1995—98; v.p. Stone & McCarthy Rsch. Assocs., Skillman, NJ, 1998—, equity strategist, 1998—. Office: Stone & McCarthy Rsch Assocs 101 Business Park Dr Skillman NJ 08558

LISAK, ROBERT PHILIP, neurologist, researcher, educator; b. Bklyn., Mar. 17, 1941; s. Irving Arthur and Sylvia Lillian (Kadish) L.; m. Deena Freda Penchansky, Aug. 2, 1964; children: Ilene Ann, Michael Loren. BA, NYU, 1961; MD, Columbia U., 1965; MA (hon.), U. Pa., 1976. Diplomate Am. Bd. Neurology. Intern in medicine Montefiore Hosp. and Med. Ctr., Bronx, 1965-66; rsch. assoc. NIMH, Bethesda, Md., 1966-68; resident in medicine Bronx Mcpl. Med. Ctr., 1968-69; resident in neurology Hosp. of the U. of Pa., Phila., 1969-72; with Sch. of Medicine U. Pa., Phila., 1972-87, prof. neurology Sch. of Medicine, 1980-87, vice chmn. dept. neurology Sch. of Medicine, 1985-87; prof., chmn. dept. neurology Sch. of Medicine Wayne State U., Detroit, 1987—. Mem. adv. bd. Guillain-Barre Syndrome Internat., Wynnewood, Pa., 1985—; mem. med. adv. bd. Myasthenia Gravis Found., Mpls., 1988—, Nat. Multiple Sclerosis Soc., N.Y.C., 1988—. Co-author: Myasthenia Gravis, 1982; mem. editl. bd. Jour. Neuroimmunology, 1984-98, Muscle and Nerve Jour., 1981-86, 92-95, 98—, Neurology, 1981-86, Annals of Neurology, 1990-95, Jour. Peripheral Nervous Sys., Clin. Neuropharm., 1997—; editor-in-chief Jour. Neurol. Sci., 1998—; contbr. articles to profl. jours. With USPHS, 1966-68. Fulbright rsch. scholar, London, 1978-79; recipient Disting. Teaching award U. Pa., 1985, Drs. award Myasthenia Gravis Found., 1991. Fellow Am. Acad. Neurology (sci. issues com. 1987-93); mem. Am. Neurol. Assn. (membership com. 1989-91, chmn. 1990-91, sci. program com. 1994-96, councillor 2002—), Internat. Soc. Neuroimmunology (exec. com. 1987-91, 95-2001, sec.-treas. 1991-95), Am. Assn. Immunologists, Soc. for Neurosci., Norwegian Neurol. Assn., Royal Soc. Medicine. Office: Wayne State U Sch Medicine 8DE-UHC 4201 St Antoine Detroit MI 48201 Office Phone: 313-577-1249. Business E-Mail: rlisak@med.wayne.edu.

LISAN, PHILIP, medical educator; b. Phila., Oct. 5, 1919; s. Manuel F. and Rose (Kolinsky) L.; m. Selma A. Balaban, Aug. 3, 1988; children: Ronald M., David A. BA, U. Pa., 1940; MD, Hahnemann U., 1951. Diplomate Am. Bd. Internal Medicine. Intern Hahneman U., 1951-52, resident, 1952-54, cardiology fellow, 1954-55; prof. medicine Hahnemann U., Phila., 1957—; cons. Guardian Life Ins. Co., Bethlehem, Pa. Assoc. prof. medicine Med. Coll. Pa., Phila., 1972-75; med. dir. JFK Meml. Hosp., Phila., 1972-76. Contbr. chpts. in books and articles to profl. jours. Capt. USAF, 1955-57. Fellow ACP, Am. Coll. Cardiology, Coll. Physicians. Home: 10159 Diamond Lake Dr Boynton Beach FL 33437-5534

LISANDRELLI, ELAINE SLIVINSKI, secondary school educator; b. Pittston, Pa., July 11, 1951; d. Leo Joseph and Gabriella Alexandra (Sharek) Slivinski; m. Carl A. Lisandrelli, June 20, 1980. BA, Marywood U., Scranton, Pa., 1973, MS, 1976. Cert. secondary tchr. English and counselor, Pa. Tchr. English North Pocono Mid. Sch., Moscow, Pa., 1973—. Part-time instr. Marywood U., 1986-2000; ednl. cons., Pa., 1988-93. Author: Maya Angelou: More Than a Poet, 1996 (Carter G. Woodson honor), Bob Dole: Legendary Senator, 1997, Ida B. Wells-Barnett: Crusader Against Lynching, 1998, Ignacy Jan Paderewski: Polish Pianist and Patriot, 1999, Jack London: A Writer's Adventurous Life, 1999; co-author: Creating Lifelong Learners: Strategies for Success in Creativity and Innovation in Content Area Teaching, 2000; contbr. articles to lit. mags. Named to the Young Adult's Choice List, 1998. Mem. Nat. Coun. Tchrs. English, Soc. Children's Book Writers and Illustrators, Pa. Edn., Assn., Kosciuszko Found., Polish Arts and Cultural Found. Avocations: aerobics, reading, researching, movies. Home: 3501 Lawrence Ave Moosic PA 18507-1729 Office: North Pocono Mid Sch Church St Moscow PA 18444

LISBAKKEN, JAMES ROBERT, lawyer; b. Washington, June 25, 1945; s. Robert Benjamin and Genevieve Louise (Roberts) L.; m. Linda Jean Alvey, Jan. 2, 1982; children: Kelly, Benjamin. BS, Oreg. State U., 1967; JD, U. Oreg., 1975. Bar: Wash. 1975, U.S. Dist. Ct. Wash. 1975. Engr. Westinghouse Electric Nuclear Power Div., Monroeville, Pa., 1967-70; assoc. Perkins Coie, Seattle, 1975-81, ptnr., 1981-83; dir., exec. v.p., sec., gen. counsel Genetic Systems Corp., Seattle, 1983-85; ptnr., Bus. Law Practice Area Perkins Coie, Seattle, 1985—. Mem. Mcpl. League, Seattle, 1976-80; organizing com. Northwest Biotech. Series. Mem. ABA, Wash. Bar Assn., Seattle King County Bar Assn., Phi Delta Phi, Tau Beta Pi, Wash. Athletic Club. Republican. Presbyterian. Avocations: tennis, skiing, mountain climbing, sailing. Office: Perkins Coie 1201 Third Ave Ste 4800 Seattle WA 98101-3099 Office Phone: 206-359-8660. Office Fax: 206-359-9000. Business E-Mail: jlisbakken@perkinscoie.com.

LISBOA-FARROW, ELIZABETH OLIVER, public and government relations consultant; b. N.Y.C., Nov. 25, 1947; d. Eleuterio and Esperanza Oliver; m. Jeffrey Lloyd Farrow, Dec. 31, 1980; 1 child, Hamilton Oliver Farrow; 1 stepchild, Maximillian Robbins Farrow. Student pvt. schs., N.Y.C. With Harold Rand & Co. and various other pub. rels. firms, N.Y.C., 1966—75; dir. pub. rels. N.Y. Playboy Club and Playboy Clubs Internat., 1975—79; pres., CEO Lisboa Assocs., Inc., N.Y.C., 1979—; founder, pres. Lisboa Prodns., Inc., Washington, 1994—. Counselor Am. Woman's Devel. Corp. Sec. Nat. Acad. Concert and Cabaret Arts; mem. nat. adv. coun. SBA, 1980-81, apptd., 1994—; exec. dir. Variety Club of Greater Washington Children's Charity, Inc., 1985-90; bd. dirs. Variety Myoelectric Limb Bank Found., 1990-91, Comcast, 2001, Hispanic Radio Network, 2001, Group hosp. and Med. Svcs., Inc. d/b/a Carefirst Blue Cross Blue Shield, 2005; trustee Hispanic Coll. Fund, 1995—, vice chair, 1996—; chair bd. trustees Southeastern U., 1997-2004; mem. adv. bd. Indsl. Bank, N.A., 1996. Named Pub. Rels. Woman of Yr., Women in Pub. Rels., 1992, Empresaria del Milenio, Duodecimo Encuentro Empresarian, P.R., 2001, Hispanic Bus. Woman of Yr., Nat. Hispanic Bus. Coun., 1996, Hispanic of Yr. in Bus., La Nacion Newspaper, 1997, Entrepreneur of Yr., Hispanic Mag., 1999, Bus Woman of Yr., N.Y. State Hispanic Chambers Commerce; recipient Disting. award of Excellence, SBA, 1992, Women Bus. Enterprise award, U.S. Transp. Nat. Hwy. Transp. Safety Adminstrn., 1994, Civic Cmty. Achievement, Black Bus. and Profls. Network, 1999, Excellence in Entrepreneurship award, Dialogue on Diversity, Inc., 1995, Women of Distinction award, Nat. Conf. Coll. Women Student Leaders, 2000, Applause award, Women's Bus. Enterprise Nat. Coun., 2000, Imagen award, San Juan, P.R., 2001, Presdl. medal, Sistema U. Ana G. Mendez, U. Metropolitana, San Juan, 1999, Internat. Leadership award, Mex. Am. C. of C., 2001. Mem. U.S. Hispanic C. of C. (bd. dirs. 1998-2004, Nat. Hispanic Businesswoman of Yr. 1996, vice chair 1999, chair 2000-02), D.C. C. of C. (pres. 2000), Small Bus. Adv. Coun., U.S. C. of C. (Blue Chip Enterprise award 1993), Advt. Coun., Am. Heart Assn., Hispanic Bus. and Profl. Women's Assn., Ibero-Am. C. of C. (bd. dirs. 1993, v.p. 1995, pres. 1997, 1998, adv. chair 1999, Small Bus. award 1993, Corp. of Yr. award 2000), Nat. Edn. Assn. Found. (bd. dirs. 2004). Office: 1112 16th St NW Washington DC 20036 Office Phone: 202-737-2622. E-mail: elisboa@lisboa.com.

LISENBY, DORRECE EDENFIELD, realtor; b. Sneads, Fla., Dec. 2, 1942; d. Neal McLendon and Linnie (McCroan) Edenfield; m. Wallace Lamar Lisenby, Nov. 18, 1961; children: Pamela Ann, Wallace Neal. BS in Tech. Bus. magna cum laude, Athens (Ala.) State Coll., 1991. Stenographer State of Fla., Tallahassee and Miami, Fla., 1960-62, Gulf Oil Corp., Coral Gables, Fla., 1962-64, Gulf Power Co., Pensacola, Fla., 1965-68; loan svc. asst. First Fed. Savs. and Loan Assn., Greenville, S.C., 1969-70; various real estate positions Greenville, 1978-85; adminstrv. asst. Charter Retreat Hosp., Decatur, Ala., 1986-91; broker/salesperson Ferrell Realty Plus, Inc., Tallahassee, Fla., 1995-2001; broker, owner Lisenby Realty, Inc., 2001—. Mem.: P.E.O. Sisterhood, Tallahassee C. of C., Econ. Club Fla., Tallahassee Symphony Soc., Killearn Ladies Club (pres.), Taylor's Garden Club (prs. Taylor's chpt. 1975—76), Avondale Forest Cmty. Club (pres. Taylors, S.C. chpt. 1969), Am. Legion (Citizenship award 1957). Republican. Baptist. Avocations: reading, music, bridge, gardening. Home: 2925 Shamrock St S Tallahassee FL 32309-3226 Office Phone: 850-383-7567. Business E-Mail: lisenby@lisenbyrealty.com.

LISETTI, CHRISTINE LAETITIA, computer scientist, educator; b. Nice, France; PhD, Fla. Internat. U., 1995. Postdoctoral rsch. fellow Stanford (Calif.) U., 1996—98; asst. prof. U. South Fla., Tampa, 1998—2001, U. Ctrl. Fla., Orlando, 2001—. Contbr. articles to profl. jours. Recipient Individual Rsch. Svc. award, NIH, 1998, Nils Nilsson award for integrating AI techs., 2000; grantee, Intel Corp., 1998, Interval Rsch. Corp., 1998—99, Office of Naval Rsch., 2000—, U.S. Army Simulation, Tng. and Instrumentation Command, 2002—. Mem.: Emotion Rsch. Soc., IEEE Soc. on Social Implications of Tech., IEEE Computer Soc., Assn. Computing Machinery, Am. Assn. Artificial Intelligence. Office: U Ctrl Fla Sch EECS Dept Computer Sci University Blvd CSB Orlando FL 32816-2362 Business E-Mail: lisetti@cs.ucf.edu.

LISH, BRUCE JARED, dentist; b. June 27, 1969; s. Jerome and Marion Lish; m. Cindy Michelle Rosenblum-Lish, Aug. 15, 1993; children: Matthew, Jessica. BA Biology, NYU, 1991, DDS, 1994. Cert. dental oral surgery Brookdale U. Hosp. Med. Ctr. Pvt. practice gen. dentistry, Bklyn., 1995—; clin. asst. prof. NYU Coll. Dentistry, N.Y.C., 1996—98; residency dir. gen. practice program Brookdale U. Hosp. Ctr., Bklyn., 1998—2000; dir. divsn. dentistry St. Luke's-Roosevelt Hosp., N.Y.C., 2000—. Creator: (ednl. dental program) Dr. Molar Magic Show, 1993—; pub.: Magic Builder's Monthly, 2000. Performer, provider cmty. svc. Clown Dr. Program, 1994—; bd. dirs. Hebrew Ednl. Soc., Bklyn., 1998—2003. Mem.: Am. Soc. Dentistry for Children (sec./treas. 2000—01), Am. Acad. Implant Dentistry, Soc. Am. Magicians (chpt. pres. 1998). Jewish. Office: 7224 Ave T Brooklyn NY 11234 Office Phone: 718-763-1817. E-mail: blish@chpact.org.

LISHER, JAMES RICHARD, lawyer; b. Aug. 28, 1947; s. Leonard B. and Mary Jane (Rafferty) L.; m. Martha Gettelfinger, June 16, 1973; children: Jennifer, James Richard II. AB, Ind. U., 1969, JD, 1975. Bar: Ind. 1975, U.S. Dist. Ct. (so. dist.) Ind. 1975, U.S. Supreme Ct. 2000. Assoc. Rafferty & Wood, Shelbyville, Ind., 1975, Rafferty & Lisher, Shelbyville, Ind., 1976-77; dep. prosecutor Shelby County Prosecutor's Office, Shelbyville, 1976-78; ptnr. Yeager, Lisher & Baldwin, Shelbyville, 1977-96; pvt. practice, Shelbyville, 1996—. Pros. atty. Shelby County, Shelbyville, 1983-95, pub. defender, 1995—, chief pub. defender, 2000—. Speaker, faculty advisor Ind. Pros. Sch., 1986. Editor: (manual) Traffic Case Defenses, 1982, First Law Office, 1998. Bd. dirs. Girls Club of Shelbyville, 1979-84, Bears of Blue River Festival, Shelbyville, 1982-2002; pres. Shelby County Internat. Rels. Coun., 1997-2003. With USNR, 1969—75. Recipient Citation of Merit, Young Lawyers Assn. Mem. ATLA, VFW, Nat. Assn. Criminal Def. Lawyers, Ind. Pub. Defender Assn., Ind. State Bar Assn. (bd. dirs. young lawyer sect. 1979-83, bd. dirs. gen. practice sect. 1996-98, treas. 1997-98, vice-chmn. 1998-99, chmn. 2000-01), Shelby County Bar Assn. (sec.-treas. 1986, v.p. 1987, pres. 1988), Ind. Prosecuting Attys. Assn. (bd. dirs. 1985-95, sec.-treas. 1987, v.p. 1988, pres. 1990), Masons, Elks, Lions. Home: 106 Western Trce Shelbyville IN 46176-9765 Office: 407 S Harrison St Shelbyville IN 46176-2170 Office Phone: 317-392-2500. Personal E-mail: vettelaw@sbcglobal.net.

LISI, ANTHONY JAMES, chiropractor, educator; b. Bklyn., July 12, 1962; s. Bernard James and Lucille Marie Lisi; m. Jennifer Ann Hartko, Oct. 28, 1988; children: Mark Andrew, John Matthew. DC, Palmer Coll. of Chiropractic West, San Jose, 1996. Assoc. faculty Palmer Ctr. for Chiropractic Rsch., Davenport, Iowa, 1999—; asst. prof. U. of Bridgeport, Bridgeport, 2003—; staff chiropractor VA Conn. Healthcare Sys., West Haven, 2004—. Grantee, Found. for Chiropractic Edn. and Rsch., 2003—04. Office: VA Conn Healthcare Sys 950 Campbell Ave West Haven CT 06516 Office Phone: 203-932-5711. E-mail: anthony.lisi@med.va.gov.

LISI, MARY M., federal judge; BA, U. R.I., 1972; JD, Temple U., 1977. Tchr. history Prout Meml. H.S., Wakefield, RI, 1975-76; law clk. U.S. Atty., Providence, 1976, Phila., 1976-77; asst. pub. defender R.I. Office Pub. Defender, 1977-81; asst. child adv. Office Child Adv., 1981-82; also. pvt. practice atty. Providence, 1981-82; dir. office ct. apptd. spl. adv. R.I. Family Ct., 1982-87; dep. disciplinary counsel office disciplinary counsel R.I. Supreme Ct., 1988-90, chief disciplinary counsel, 1990-94; U.S. Dist. judge Dist. Ct., Providence, Dist. R.I. (1st cir.), Providence, 1994—. Mem. Select Com. to Investigate Failure of R.I. Share and Deposit Indemnity Corp., 1991-92. Recipient Providence 350 award, 1986, Meritorious Svc. to Children of Am. award, 1987. Office: Fed Bldg and US Courthouse 1 Exchange Ter Providence RI 02903-1744

LISIO, DONALD JOHN, historian, educator; b. Oak Park, Ill., May 27, 1934; s. Anthony and Dorothy (LoCelso) Lisio; m. Susznne Marie Swanson, Apr. 22, 1958; children: Denise Anne, Stephen Anthony. BA, Knox Coll., 1956; MA, Ohio U., 1958; PhD, U. Wis., 1965. Mem. faculty overseas div. U. Md., 1958-60; from asst. prof. history to prof. emeritus Coe Coll., Cedar Rapids, Iowa, 1964—2002, prof. emeritus, 2002—. Author: (book) The President and Protest: Hoover, Conspiracy, and the Bonus Riot, 1974, Hoover, Blacks, and Lily-Whites: A Study of Southern Strategies, 1985; contbg. author: book The War Generation, 1975; contbr. articles to hist. jours. Mem. exec. com. Cedar Rapids Com. Hist. Preservation, 1975—77. With U.S. Army, 1958—60. Fellow William F. Vilas Rsch., U. Wis., 1963—64, NEH, 1969—70, Rsch., 1984—85, Am. Coun. Learned Socs., 1977—78; grantee, 1971—72, Rsch., U.S. Inst. Peace, 1990. Mem.: AAUP, Am. Hist. Assn., Orgn. Am. Historians. Roman Catholic.

LISK, PENELOPE TSALTAS, artist; b. N.Y.C., June 16, 1959; d. Theodore-Theodosios and Margaret (Owen) Tsaltas; m. Douglas Crumback Lisk, July 7, 1990; children: Christina Margaret, Douglas Lloyd. AB in Fine Arts, Bryn Mawr Coll., 1981; MFA, Cranbrook Acad. Art, 1985. Tchr., intern Phila. Mus. Art, 1983; gallery asst. Noël Butcher Gallery, Phila., 1985—87; account mgr. Archibald Allan Assocs., West Conshohocken, Pa., 1987—91; artist Media, Pa., 1985—. Asst. organizer alumnae exhbn. Baldwin Sch., Bryn Mawr, 1989. One-woman shows include The Chilton Co., Radnor, Pa., 1990, Cabrini Coll., Radnor, 1988, Quisset, Haverford, Pa., 1987, Wayne (Pa.) Hotel, 1986, The Epis. Acad., 2001, Betsy Meyer Meml. Exhbn. MainLine Art Ctr. (Constanza award); group shows include ARTREACH/AURA Soc., Villanova U., Phila., 1991, Villanova U., 1990, The Baldwin Sch., Bryn Mawr, Pa., 1989, Sishuan Inst. Fine Art, Tin Sin U., China, 1986, Cranbrook Acad. Art, Bloomfield Hills, Mich., 1985, The Art League, 2002-03, Del. County C.C., 2003; work represented in collections at Detroit Inst. of Art, Nelson Atkins Mus., Newport Harbor Mus. Recipient 2d prize painting, Villanova U., purchase price/Nat. Drawing 1987, Trenton (N.J.) State Coll. Mem. Artists Uniting Religion and Art, Print Club, Pa. Arts Coalition, Main Line Art Ctr., Chester Springs Studio Cmty. Art Ctr. Republican. Episcopalian.

LISKO (DOZER), BONNIE LEE, education educator; b. Zanesville, Ohio, Dec. 15, 1924; d. Carl Raymond Dozer and Luanna Faye Swingle; m. Andrew Lisko, Aug. 1, 1953; children: Karen Luann, Daniel Andrew, Margaret Lee. BA, Capital U., Columbus, Ohio, 1946; MA in Sch. Langs., Middlebury (Vt.) Coll., 1952. Cert. tchr. Ohio, 1946. Tchr. French I, II, English I, II, Sci., drama

Bryan HS, Yellow Springs, Ohio, 1946—47; tchr. French, Spanish, ESL, dean of women Concordia Jr. Coll., Bronxville, NY, 1947—51; tchr. French and Spanish, head resident Berea (Ky.) Coll., 1951—52; asst. dean of women, tchr. modern lang. dept. Capital Univ., Columubs, Ohio, 1952—87; pvt. French tchr. Interpreter Gov. Richard Celeste, Country Club, Cols. and Pres. of Senegal, 1987. Recipient award, Am. Luth. Ch., 1942, French Govt. to Middlebury Sch. French, 1948, Fulbright award, 1952. Mem.: AAUP (state pre.), Am. Assn. Tchrs. French (pres.). Presbyterian. Avocations: reading, swimming, fishing. Home: 805 Pleasant Ridge Ave Columbus OH 43209 Office: Campus Learning Ctr Modern Lang Dept Columbus OH 43209 Home (Summer): RR #1 Peterborough Canada K9J 6X2

LISKOW, FREDERIC CULLEN (RIC), printing company executive; b. Apr. 26, 1960; m. Beth Liskow; 5 children. B in Polit. sci., Rice U., 1982; JD, So. Meth. U. With Jenkens & Gilchrist, PC, Ins. Group, Ft. Worth; sr. v.p., gen. counsel Citigroup's Am. Health and Life, Citigroup, Inc./Assocs. First Capital Corp., 1993—2002; with Kinko's, Dallas, 2002—, sr. v.p., gen. counsel, sec., 2003—. Office: Kinkos 13155 Noel Rd Ste 1600 Dallas TX 75240

LISLE, LAURIE, author; b. Providence, R.I., Sept. 11, 1942; d. Laurence Lisle and Adeline Cole Simonds; m. Robert I. Kipniss, Dec. 17, 1994. BA in English, Ohio Wesleyan U., 1965. Rschr. Newsweek mag., N.Y.C., 1970-78; assoc. prof. Southampton Coll. of L.I. U., 1981-82; ind. scholar So. Conn. Libr. Coun., Hamden, 1989—2002; spkr. N.Y. Coun. for the Humanities, N.Y.C., 2000—02. Author: Portrait of an Artist: A Biography of Georgia O'Keeffe, 1980, Louise Nevelson: A Passionate Life, 1990, Without Child: Challenging the Stigma of Childlessness, 1996, Four Tenths of an Acre: Reflections on a Gardening Life, 2005. Mem.: The Authors Guild, The Century Assn., Am. Pen Ctr. Democrat. Unitarian Universalist. Mailing: PO Box 170 Ardsley On Hudson NY 10503 Address: c/o Charlotte Sheedy Literary Agy 65 Bleeker St New York NY 10012 Business E-Mail: readermail@laurielisle.com.

LISMON, GREGORY LAMONTE, SR., minister; b. Indpls., Aug. 22, 1961; s. James Scruggs and Sylvia Victoria Lismon-Bryant; m. Valencia O. Martin-Lismon, Apr. 24, 1995; children: Alexander Marcus Green, Gregory Lamont, Jr., Tiffany Christine, Jannelle A. Moniguette, Tyerelle Lamonte, Vincent Omar Lamonte. Traffic mgmt. diploma, USMC, 1984; grad. barber, Lovelle Barber Sch., 2000; B of Pastorial Theology, Beulah Bible Coll. and Sem., 2001. Min., Ind., 1978—; lifeguard Fall Creek YMCA, Indpls., 1988—90; aquatic mgr. Riverside Recreational Ctr., Indpls., 1990—91; aquatic dir. Atkins Boys and Girls Club., Indpls., 1992—93; barber Cuts by Gregory at the Hair Emporium, South Bend, Ind., 2000—01. CEO The Lords Kitchen, New Testament Ministries Worldwide, 1997; exec. bd. dirs. Southside Cmty. R Ross, Indpls., 1998—99; Chaplain King Park Area Neighborhood Orgn., Indpls., 1995—96. Lt. cpl. USMC, 1980—84. Republican. Baptist. Avocations: aquatics, coaching, lifeguarding, administration, mentor. Home: 3119 Moller Rd Indianapolis IN 46227-2101

LISNEK, MARGARET DEBBELER, artist, educator; b. Covington, Ky., Sept. 26, 1940; d. Aloysius Frank and Mary Elizabeth (Haubold) Debbeler; m. Schiller William Lisnek, June 26, 1966 (dec. May 1995); 1 child, Kimberly Anne. AA with honors, Mt. San Antonio Coll., 1985; BA in Art with honors, Calif. State U., Fullerton, 1991. Cert. substitute tchr., Calif. Freelance artist, 1985—; tchr. art Rorimer Elem. Sch., La Puente, Calif., 1992-93, City of Walnut (Calif.) Recreation Svcs., 1992-96, Christ Luth. Sch., West Covina, Calif., 1993-98, Los Molinos Elem. Sch., Hacienda Heights, Calif., 1993-98, Los Altos Elem. Sch., Hacienda Heights, 1993-98. Mem. Getty Inst. Insvc. Resource Team. One-woman shows include Calif. State U., Fullerton, 1990; exhibited in group shows. Sec., treas., social chair PTA, Los Altos Elem. Sch., Hacienda Heights, 1972-73; membership and social chair Friends of Libr., Hacienda Heights, 1974-75; active Nat. Mus. Women in the Arts, L.A. County Art Mus., Norton Simon Mus., Pasadena, Calif. Mem. Calif. Art Edn. Assn. Avocations: world travel, art history, collecting stamps, foreign languages, dance.

LISONI, GAIL MARIE LANDTBOM, lawyer; b. San Francisco, Mar. 11, 1949; d. William A. and Patricia Ann (Cruden) Landtbom; m. Joseph Louis Lisoni, Mar. 24, 1984. BA, Dominican Coll., Calif., 1971; JD, U. West L.A., 1978, cert. paralegal, 1974. Bar: Calif. 1979. Campaign treas. Calif. for Lisoni, Arcadia, 1979-81; assoc. Joseph Lisoni, Esq., L.A., 1981, Arnold S. Malter, Esq., L.A., 1982; ptnr. Lisoni & Lisoni, L.A., 1983—. Lead atty. nat. class action recall on Firestone. Co-chair Dems. for James Rogan, 1996, 98; eucharistic minister St. Andrew's Ch., Huntington Meml. Hosp.; vol. Union Sta. Found. Homeless Shelter, Legal Aid Clinic. Mem. ABA, Assn. Trial Lawyers Am., Attys. Assn. L.A., Italian Am. Lawyers Assn., Sons of Italy, Centinela Valley Lodge. Roman Catholic. Office Phone: 626-440-1333. Personal E-mail: lisoni@earthlink.net.

LISOVICZ, SUSAN, anchor, correspondent; Degree in comm., William Paterson Coll. Prodr., writer Sta. WABC-TV, N.Y.C.; anchor, corr. CNBC, Ft. Summit, N.J., 1991-97, CNN Fin. News, N.Y.C., corr. The Moneyline Newshour with Lou Dobbs. Mem. N.Y. Fin. Writers Assn. (pres.). Office: CNN 5 Penn Plz Fl 20 New York NY 10001-1810

LISOWSKI, JOSEPH ANTHONY, language educator, poet, writer; s. Anthony Francis and Harriet L.; m. Linda Rose Tucker, Dec. 6, 1980; 1 child, Jozef. PhD, SUNY, Binghamton, NY, 1969—74. Prof. of english U. Vi., St. Thomas, 1986—96; chair divsn. arts and scis. Mercyhurst Coll., North East, Pa., 2001—02; assoc. prof. English Elizabeth City State U., Elizabeth City, NC, 2002—. Poetry editor New Works Rev., Chgo., 1999—2002. Author: (novels) Looking for Lisa, Looking for Lauren (P.T.T. Bradshaw award, 1996), poems. Home: 915 Woodruff Ave Elizabeth City NC 27909 Office: Elizabeth City State Univ Weeksville Road Elizabeth City NC 27909 Personal E-mail: jalisowski@mail.ecsu.edu.

LISS, ARTHUR YALE, lawyer; b. Detroit, July 12, 1946; s. George R. and Rose B. Liss; m. Beverly Bein, Jan. 16, 1972; children: Jeremy Seth, Lindsay Audra, Zachary Jonathan. BSBA, Wayne State U., 1968, JD, 1972. Bar: Mich., U.S. Dist. Ct. (ea. dist.) Mich., U.S. Ct. Appeals (6th cir.), U.S. Supreme Ct. Prin. Liss & Assocs., Bloomfield Hills, Mich., 1972—. Dir. Anestesia and Ctrl. Care Rsch. Found., Chgo., 1998—; cons. and lectr. in field. Fellow Million Dollar Advocates Assn.; mem. Mich. Trial Lawyers Assn. (bd. dirs. 1999—), Am. Trial Lawyers Assn. (bd. dirs. 1975—). Avocations: travel, scuba diving, golf. Office: Liss & Assocs PC 39400 Woodward Ave Ste 200 Bloomfield Hills MI 48304

LISS, HERBERT MYRON, communications educator; b. Mpls., Mar. 23, 1931; s. Joseph Milton and Libby Diane (Kramer) L.; m. Barbara Lipson, Sept. 19, 1954; children: Lori-Ellen, Kenneth Allen, Michael David. BS in Econs., U. Pa., 1952. With mktg. mgmt. Procter & Gamble Co., Cin., 1954-63, Procter & Gamble Internat., various countries, 1963-74; gen. mgr. Procter & Gamble Comml. Co., San Juan, P.R., 1974-78; v.p., mgr. internat. ops. InterAm. Orange Crush Co. subs. Procter & Gamble Co., Cin., 1981-84; pres. River Cities (Ohio) Comm. Inc, 1985—; pub. The Downtowner newspaper and others, Cin., 1985-96. Lectr. MBA and undergraduate bus. program Xavier U., Ohio, 1998—. Bd. dirs. Charter Com., Cin., 1958-63, Promotion and Mktg. Assn. US, 1978-81, Jr. Achievement, Cin., 1980-87, Inst. for Learning in Retirement, 1998—, Downtown Coun., Cin., 1985-94, treas., 1991-92; bd. dirs. Downtown Cin. Inc., 1995-98, mem. DCI retail mktg. com., 1995-98. Mem. Manila Yacht Club, Manila Polo, Club Escuela de Equitación De Somos Aquas (Madrid), Rotary Club. (Cin.), Sycamore Cmty. Band (clarinet). Home: 8564 Wyoming Club Dr Cincinnati OH 45215-4243

LISS, JEFFREY FRED, lawyer, educator; b. Balt., June 10, 1951; s. Solomon and Gertrude (Nadich) L.; m. Susan Michelson, July 30, 1972; children: Joanna M., Harrison S. BA, U. Mich., 1972, MA, JD, 1975. Bar: D.C. 1975, Md. 1981. Law clk. Judge Charles R. Richey, U.S. Dist. Ct., Washington, 1975-77; from assoc. to ptnr. Wald, Harkrader & Ross, Washington, 1977-85; ptnr. Piper & Marbury (now DLA Piper Rudnick Gray Cary US LLP), Washington, 1985—99; COO Piper & Marbury (now DLA Piper Rudnick Gray Cary LLP), Washington, 1999—2004, co-mng. ptnr., 2005—. Adj. prof. U. Mich. Law Sch., 1996, 02, 04, Georgetown Law Sch., 1985—, Am. U. Sch. Law, 1978-85; spl. govt. employee, Office of White House Counsel, 1996-97. Co-author: Remedies in Business Torts Litigation, 1992; contbr. articles to profl. jours. Bd. dirs. Washington Lawyers Com. for Civil Rights, Washington, 1992-98; pro bono counsel numerous orgns., Washington, 1977—; treas., Friends of Lt. Gov. Kathleen Kennedy Townsend, Md., 1996-2002. Recipient Judge Learned Hand award, Am. Jewish Com., 2003. Fellow Am. Bar Found.; mem. Am. Law Inst., D.C. Cir. Hist. Soc. (bd. dirs.), Balt. Symphony Orch. (sec., exec. com., bd. dirs.). Democrat. Jewish. Avocations: baseball, reading, piano. Office: DLA Piper Rudnick Gray Cary LLP 1200 19th St NW Washington DC 20036-2412 Office Phone: 202-861-3940. Office Fax: 202-223-2085. Business E-Mail: Jeffrey.Liss@dlapiper.com.

LISS, NORMAN, lawyer; b. N.Y.C., May 7, 1932; m. Sandra Hirsch, Feb. 28, 1959. BS, NYU, 1952, LLB, 1955. Bar: N.Y. 1955, U.S. Dist. Ct. (so. dist.) N.Y. 1961, U.S. Dist. Ct (ea. dist.) N.Y. 1962. Assoc. Booth, Lipton & Lipton, New York, 1956-57, Seymour Detsky, New York, 1957-58; pvt. practice New York, 1958—. Cons. to Portugal Re-Cultural Events in U.S.; jour. chair UJA Trial Lawyers USCG Acad. Law Day, 1987, 89, 94, 98. Contbr. articles to profl. jours. Chmn. Bronx County Bar divsn. United Jewish Appeal, Hist. Documents Exhbn., Operation Sail, 1986, USCG Acad. Law Day, 1987, 89; chmn. devel. Ellis Island Restoration Commn.; counsel N.Y. State Statue of Liberty Centennial Com., Mayor's Handicapped Citizens Adv. Bd., N.Y.C., Coun. on Arts; mem. Bronx County 350 Commn., N.Y.C. Commn. for Presdl. Conv.; rep., counsel N.Y.C. Com. on Bicentennial of U.S. Constitution; cons. Soc. Congl. Medal of Honor; commd. lt. col. N.Y. Guard Judge Advocate Gen. Unit; exec. com. Am. Jewish Congress; trustee Am. Jewish Hist. Soc.; co-chmn. 350th Ann. of 1st Jewish Am. Settlement in U.S.; Def. of Liberty 9/11, N.Y. Recipient Disting. Humanitarian award Inst. of Applied Human Dynamics, Meritorious Pub. Svc. award USCG, 1989, 9/11 Def. of Liberty medal N.Y. Guard; named Man of Yr. Am. Jewish Congress, Man of Yr. Kinneret Sch., 1985. Mem. ABA, N.Y. Bar Assn., Bronx County Bar Assn., Am. Arbitration Assn. (panel arbitrators), Assn. Trial Lawyers Am., Law Day Outreach Com., NYU Alumni Assn. (adv. coun.). Home: 2727 Palisade Ave Bronx NY 10463-1018 Office: 200 W 57th St New York NY 10019-3211 Office Phone: 212-586-6165. E-mail: lisslaw@earthlink.net.

LISSAUER, JACK JONATHAN, astronomy educator; b. San Francisco, Mar. 25, 1957; s. Alexander Lissauer and Ruth Spector. SB in Math., MIT, 1978; PhD in Applied Math., U. Calif., Berkeley, 1982. NAS-NRC resident rsch. assoc. NASA-Ames Rsch. Ctr., Moffett Field, Calif., 1983-85; asst. rsch. astronomer U. Calif., Berkeley, Calif., 1985, vis. rschr. dept. physics Inst. for Theoretical Physics Santa Barbara, Calif., 1985-87; asst. prof. astronomy program dept. earth and space sci. SUNY, Stony Brook, 1987-93, assoc. prof., 1993-96; space scientist NASA Ames Rsch. Ctr., 1996—. Rep. Univs. Space Rsch. Assn., SUNY, Stony Brook, 1987-96; vis. scholar dept. planetary sci. and lunar and planetary lab. U. Ariz., Tucson, 1990; guest prof. dept. physics U. Paris VII et Observatoire Paris, Meudon, France, 1990; mem. Lunar and Planetary Geoscis. Rev. Panel, 1989, 91, 99; vis. asst. rsch. physicist Inst. for Theoretical Physics, U. Calif., Santa Barbara, 1992, organizer Program on Plant Formation, 1992; rsch. assoc. Inst. d'Astrophysique, Paris, 1993; vis. scholar dept. astronomy U. Calif., Berkeley, 1994-95; adj. assoc. prof. SUNY, Stony Brook, 1996-2002; Yuval Ne'eman Disting. lectr. geophysics, atmosphere and space sci. Tel Aviv U., 2001, cons. prof. dept. geology and environ. sci. Stanford U., 2002—. Planetary sci. editor New Astronomy Reviews; contbr. numerous articles on planet and star formation, extrasolar planets, spiral density wave theory, rotation of planets and comets to profl. jour. including Nature, Astron. Jour., Icarus, Sci., Astrophys. Jour. Letters, Astrophys. Jour., Jour. Geophys. Rsch., Astron. Astrophysics, Ann. Rev. Astron. Astrophysics, Revs. of Modern Physics. Textbook author "Planetary Sciences" Cambridge Univ. Press, NASA Grad. student fellow, 1981-82, Alfred P. Sloan Found. fellow, 1987-91. Mem. Am. Astronomical Assn. (divsn. planetary sci., divsn. dynamical astronomy, Harold C. Urey prize divsn. planetary sci. 1992), Internat. Astronomical Union, Am. Geophys. Union. Achievements include research in planetary accretion, extrasolar planets, dynamics of planetary rings, cratering, binary and multiple star systems, circumstellar disks, resonances and chaos. Office: NASA Ames Rsch Ctr Space Sci Artrobiology Divsn 245-3 Moffett Field CA 94035 Business E-Mail: lissauer@ringside.arc.nasa.gov.

LISSKA, ANTHONY JOSEPH, humanities educator, philosopher; b. Columbus, Ohio, July 23, 1940; s. Joseph Anthony and Florence (Wolfel) L.; m. Marianne Hedstrom, Mar. 16, 1968; children: Megan Catherine, Elin Elizabeth. BA in Philosophy cum laude, Providence Coll., 1963; AM in Philosophy, St. Stephen's Coll., Dover, Mass., 1967; PhD in Philosophy, Ohio State U., 1971; Cert., Harvard U., Cambridge, 1979. Asst. prof. Denison U., Granville, Ohio, 1969-76, assoc. prof., 1976-81, dean of coll., 1978-83, prof. philosophy, 1981—, dir. honors program, 1987—2002, Charles and Nancy Brickman disting. svc. chair, 1998-2001, Maria Theresa Barney chair in philosophy, 2004—. Vis. scholar U. Oxford, Eng., 1984; Aquinas lectr. Providence Coll., 2002; Suarez lectr. Fordham U., 2004; honors lectr. Okla. State U., 2004; project reviewer NEH, Washington, 1979-90, evaluator; adv. bd. Midwest Faculty Seminar, Chgo., 1981-90; mem. scholarship com. Sherex Chem. Co., Dublin, Ohio, 1984-92; cons. Franklin Pierce Coll., Ringe, N.H., 1991, Hampden-Sydney (Va.) Coll., 1998, Luther Coll., 2005; referee various philosophy jours. Author: Philosophy Matters, 1977, Aquinas's Theory of Natural Law, 1996, paperback edit. 1997, 2002; co-editor: The Historical Times, 1988-, Bi-centennial History of Granville, 2004; contbr. numerous articles to profl. jours., chpts. to books. Bd. mgmt. Granville Hist. Soc., 1987-2002; precinct rep. Dem. Party, Granville, 1994—; convener Civil War Roundtable, Granville, 1989-95; v.p. The Granville Found., 2003-, pres. 2004; mem. Granville Bicentennial Commn., 1996—. Named Carnegie Prof. of Yr., Carnegie Found., 1994, Sears Found. Teaching award, 1990; NEH grantee, 1973, 77, 85; R.C. Good fellow, 1990, 96, 2002. Mem. Am. Philos. Assn. (program com. 2003, Tchg. award 1994), Am. Cath. Philos. Assn. v.p.-elect 2004-05, pres.-elect), Nat. Collegiate Honors Coun., Soc. for Ancient Greek Philosophy, Soc. for Medieval and Renaissance Philosophy, Internat. Thomas Aquinas Soc. Democrat. Roman Catholic. Avocations: local history, photography. Home: 285 Burtridge Rd Granville OH 43023-1214 Office: Denison U Dept Philosophy Knapp Hall Granville OH 43023 Office Phone: 740-587-5616. Business E-Mail: lisska@denison.edu.

LIST, DOUGLASS WILLIAM, management consultant, investment advisor, civil engineer; b. Phila., Nov. 27, 1955; s. Harold Adams and Marie Laura (Fisher) L.; m. Sherri Elisabeth Anderson, June ll, 1982; children: Brittany Anderson, Peyton Elizabeth. BSCE, MSCE, U. Va., 1977; MBA, Harvard U., 1982. Chartered fin. analyst. Ops. analyst So. Ry., Atlanta, 1977-78; svc. analyst Union Pacific R.R., Omaha, 1979-80; cons. Merrimac Transport Assocs., Newburyport, Mass., 1980-81, McKinsey & Co., Atlanta and Boston, 1982-85; v.p. mktg. and strategic planning CSX Equipment Co., Balt., 1986-87; pres. List & Co., Inc., Balt., 1988—; gen. mgr. Ry. Engring. Assocs., Balt., 1988-92, chmn., pres., 1992—; pres. Moorgate, Inc., Balt., 1997—; v.p. Boston Cons. Group, N.Y.C., 1999—. Bd. dirs. IQ Systems, Inc. Contbr. articles on mgmt. of r.r. equipment to profl. jours. Mus. dir. Redeemer Theatre Co., Balt., 1987-92; chair strategic mgmt. com. United Way, 1989-94; bd. dirs. B&O Rd. Mus., 1997—; adv. com. Johns Hopkins U. Sch. Continuing Studies Downtown Campus. Baker scholar Harvard U., 1982. Mem. Transp. Rsch. Forum (nat. bd. 1989-94), Am. Mktg. Assn., Am. Rwy. Engring. Assn., ASME, Harvard Bus. Sch. Club Md., Balt. Security Analysts Soc. Episcopalian. E-mail: list.douglass@bcg.com.

LIST, ERICSON JOHN, environmental engineering science educator, consultant; b. Whakatane, New Zealand, Mar. 27, 1939; came to U.S., 1962; s. Ericson Bayliss and Freda Helen (Sunkel) L.; m. Olive Amoore, Feb. 3, 1962; children: Brooke Meredith, Antonia Michael. B.E. with honors, U. Auckland, N.Z., 1961, B.Sc., M.E., U. Auckland, N.Z., 1962; PhD, Calif. Inst. Tech., 1965. Registered profl. engr., Calif., S.C., N.C., Ga., Fla., Nev. Sr. lectr. U. Auckland, 1966-69; asst. prof. Calif. Inst. Tech., Pasadena, 1969-72, assoc. prof., 1972-78, prof. environ. engring. sci., 1978-97, exec. officer, 1980-85, prof. emeritus, 1997; with Flow Sci. Inc., Pasadena, 1997—. Bd. dirs. Environ. Def. Scis., Pasadena; bd. chmn. Flow Sci. Inc., Pasadena, 1983-; cons. So. Calif. Edison, Rosemead, Calif., 1973-, City and County of San Francisco, 1974-. Author: (with Hugo B. Fischer et al), Mixing in Inland and Coastal Waters, 1979, (with W. Rodi) Turbulent Jets and Plumes, 1982, (with Roscoe Moss Co.) Handbook of Ground Water Development, 1990. Mem. Blue Ribbon Commn. City of Pasadena, 1976-78. Recipient Spl. Creativity award NSF, 1982 Fellow ASCE (life, editor Jour. Hydraulic Engring. 1984-89, Athenaeum (Pasadena) (chmn. wine com. 1981-83). Republican. Office: Flow Sci Inc 723 E Green St Pasadena CA 91101-2111 Home: 196 Wandolea Dr Mount Pleasant SC 29464-2524 Office Phone: 843-856-8925. Business E-Mail: ejlist@flowscience.com.

LISTENGART, JOSEPH, lawyer; b. June 2, 1968; BA econ., Stanford U., 1990; JD magna cum laude, Boston U. Sch. Law, 1994; MBA, Boston U., 1995. Atty. Hitchens, Wheeler & Dittmar, 1995—98; v.p., gen. counsel Kinder Morgan Energy Ptnrs., Houston, 1999—2001, v.p., gen. counsel, sec., 2001—. Office: Kinder Morgan Energy Ptnrs 500 Dallas St Houston TX 77002

LISTER, EARLE EDWARD, retired research executive; b. Harvey, N.B., Can., Apr. 14, 1934; s. Earle Edward and Elizabeth Hazel (Coburn) L.; m. Teresa Ann Moore, June 4, 1983. BSc in Agriculture, McGill U., Montreal, Can., 1955, MSc in Animal Nutrition, 1957; PhD in Animal Nutrition, Cornell U., 1960. Feed nutritionist Ogilvie Flour Mills, Montreal, 1960—65; rsch. scientist rsch. br. Animal Rsch. Ctr. Agriculture Can., Ottawa, 1965—74, dep. dir. rsch. br. Animal Rsch. Ctr., 1974—78, program specialist ctrl. region rsch. br., 1978—80, dir. gen. Atlantic region rsch. br. Halifax, Canada, 1980—85, dir. gen. plant health and plant products and pesticides, food prodn. and inspection br. Ottawa, 1985—87, dir. rsch. br. Animal Rsch. Ctr., 1987—91; dir. Ctr. Food and Animal Rsch., 1991—92; cons., 1992—2001; chmn. Can. Found. for Conservation Farm Animal Genetic Resources, 1996—; hon. dir. Can. Farm Animal Genetic Resource Found. Presenter seminars in India, Hong Kong, Taiwan; mem. Can. del. to gen. FAO meetings. Co-chmn. United Way/Health Ptnrs. for Agriculture Can., Ottawa, 1991; former dir. N.S. Inst. Agrologists. McGill U. scholar, 1953-55; recipient Nat. Rsch. Coun. Post Grad. Spl. scholarship Cornell U., 1957-59. Fellow: Agrl. Inst. Can.; mem.: Ont. Inst. Agrologists, Can. Soc. Animal Sci. (life; former dir.). Achievements include research in the determination of nutrient requirements of beef cattle, determination of protein and energy levels and appropriate sources of nutrients for dairy calves; development of intensive feeding system for raising high quality beef from Holstein male calves. Home: 6929 Lakes Pk Dr Greely ON Canada K4 P1M6 E-mail: elister@rogers.com.

LISTER, GEORGE, pediatrician; b. Miami, May 8, 1947; BA in psychology/religious studies, Brown U., 1969; MD, Yale U. Sch. Medicine, 1973. Intern Yale-New Haven Hosp., 1973—74, resident in pediat., 1974—75; fellow in pediat. cardiology and neonatology U. Calif., 1975—78; asst. to full prof. pediat. and anesthesiology Yale U. Sch. Medicine, 1978—2003, section chief pediat. critical care medicine, 1978—2003, dir. pediat. intensive care unit, 1978—2003; Robert L. Moore chair pediat. and prof. pediat. Southwestern Med. Sch., Dallas, 2003—. Former editor-in-chief Pediat. Rsch.; sr. editor Rudolph's Pediat.; editor Rudolph's Pediat. Online. Named one of Best Doctors Am., 1992—; recipient Established Investigator award, Am. Heart Assn., 1985; fellow, Fulbright. Mem.: Soc. Pediat. Rsch. (past pres., Maureen Andrew Mentor award 2004), Internat. Pediat. Rsch. Found., Am. Pediat. Soc., Am. Acad. Pediat. (chmn. 2004, Disting. Career award, section on critical care 1999). Office: UT Southwestern Med Ctr Dallas Pediat 5323 Harry Hines Blvd Dallas TX 75390-9063 Office Phone: 214-648-3563.

LISTER, HARRY JOSEPH, financial company consultant; b. Teaneck, N.J., Jan. 27, 1936; s. Harry and Arline L.; m. Erika Anna Maria Englisch, Sept. 3, 1960; children: Harry Joseph Jr., Karen P. Lister Lawson, Leslie M. Lister Fidler, Andrea A. Lister Lytle, Michael P. BS in Fin. and Econs., Lehigh U., 1958. Rsch. analyst Calvin Bullock, Ltd., N.Y.C., 1959-61, assoc. dir. estate planning, 1961-65, dir. estate planning., 1965-72, asst. v.p., 1969-72; v.p. N.Y. Venture Fund, Inc., N.Y.C., 1970-72; registered rep. Johnston, Lemon & Co., Inc., Washington, 1972—2004, dir., 1978-90, v.p., 1978-83, from corp. sec. to sr. v.p., 1978-90; v.p. Wash. Mgmt. Corp., 1972-81, corp. sec., 1978-81, exec. v.p., 1981-85, pres., CEO, 1985—2004, dir., 1978—; pres. JL Fin. Svcs., Inc., Washington, 1975-90, Washington Mut. Investors Fund, Inc., Washington, 1972—; dir., former pres., vice chmn. The Growth Fund of Washington, Inc. (now JP Morgan Value Opportunities Fund), 1985—2005; vice chmn., bd. dirs., former pres. Washington Funds Distbrs., Inc., 1985-93. Former pres., vice chmn. bd. trustees The Tax Exempt Fund of Md. and The Tax Exempt Fund of Va., 1986—; vice chmn., bd. dirs. Washington Investment Advisers, Inc., 1991-2001; cons. Johnston, Lemon Group, Inc., 2004—, Capital Group, Inc., L.A., 1972-2002; regent Coll. for Fin. Planning, Denver, 1979-84, mem. exec. com., 1980-84, chmn. bd. regents, 1981-83. Author: Your Guide to IRAs and 14 Other Retirement Plans, 1985. Bd. dirs. ctrl. Bergen chpt. ARC, Hackensack, N.J., 1968-72, chmn. exec. com., 1970-72; bd. dirs. Westwood (N.J.) Planning Bd., 1969-72, vice chmn., 1970-72; bd. dirs. Westwood Zoning Bd. Adjustment, 1970-72; bd. dirs. ICI Edn. Found., 1996—, chmn., 1997—. Mem.: Nat. Assn. Securities Dealers, Inc. (investment cos. com. 1984—87, bd. arbitrators 1987—98), Investment Co. Inst. (pension com., chmn. 1976—81, tax com., rsch. com., dirs. svc. com.), Mt. Vernon Ladies Assn. (mem. adv. com. 2001—), Lowes Island Club, Univ. Club, Met. Club. Home: Spinnaker Ct Reston VA 20191

LISTER, MICHAEL C., music educator; b. Ashtabula, Ohio, Feb. 15, 1971; s. Darryl Damon and Carol Eleanor Lister. BA, Mt. Vernon Nazarene U., 1993; MusM, Ind. U., 1995. Piano faculty Otterbein Coll., Westerville, Ohio, 1996—97; dir. choral activities Cuyahoga Falls (Ohio) Chrisitian Acad., 1997—2003; music dir. Hudson (Ohio) Cmty. Chapel, 1998—2005. Music minister Delaware (Ohio) Ch. of Nazarene, 1996—97; mem. Cleve. Orch. Chorus, 2001—05; accompanist Reach Out and Dance, Cuyahoga Falls, 2003—04; accompanist, vocal dir. Akron (Ohio) Lyric Opera, 2003—05; mem. Voices on Canton, Inc., Ohio, 2004. Vol. House of Rest, Akron, 2004. Mem.: Am. Choral Dir.Assn., Alpha Chi.

LISTER, THOMAS EDWARD, lawyer; b. Columbus, Ohio, Apr. 19, 1948; s. Richard Elwyn and Jean (Nelson) L.; m. Sarah Gray Robinson, July 25, 1970; children: Matthew Thomas, Joshua Capps. BA, DePauw U., 1970; JD, U. Wis., 1973. Bar: Wis. 1973, U.S. Dist. Ct. (we. dist.) Wis. 1973. V.p. Coll. Mktg. and Rsch. Corp., Indpls., 1969-70; staff criminal appeals unit Wis. Dept. Justice, 1971-73; ptnr. Sherman, Stutz & Lister, Black River Falls, Wis., 1973-83; dist. atty. Jackson County, Wis., Black River Falls, 1975-80, corp. counsel, 1975-78; mem. firm Stutz & Lister, S.C., Black River Falls, 1983—. Guest lectr. U. Wis., Madison, 1988; pres. Wis. Global Tech. Ltd., 1992—; chmn. ThermoSense Co., LLC, 1998—; vice chmn., dir., v.p. legal affairs Hyperformance Materials, Inc., Greensboro, N.C.; corp. dir. Lunda Constrn. Co., Black River Falls, Wis., 2000—. Chmn. S.W. Coun. on Criminal Justice, 1979-82; mem. Wis. Coun. on Criminal Justice, 1982-83, Wis. County Forest Adv. Coun., 1982-84; bd. dirs. Tri-County Cmty. Mental Health, Alcohol and Drug Abuse Bd, 1976-82, Black River Falls Youth Hockey, 1983-84; co-founder, dir. Black River Falls Area Found., 1986-88; chmn. Mayor's Commn. Golf Course Expansion Fundraising, 1988-90, Wazee Lake Recreation Commn., 1991-96; commencement spkr. Black River Falls H.S., 1992; mem. com., presenter All-Am. City Finalist Competition, Charlotte, N.C., 1992; chmn. adminstrv. coun. United Meth. Ch., Black River Falls, 1992-93, bldg. commn., co-chair fundraising, 1992-94; mem. cmty. rels. com. Wis. Dept. Corrections, 1993—. Mem. ABA, ATLA, Wis. Acad. Trial Lawyers (bd. dirs. 1984-90), Wis. Bar Assn., Tri-County Bar Assn. (pres. 1991-92), Black River Falls C. of C. (bd. dirs.), Rotary (bd. dirs., past pres. youth exch.

officer), Black River Recreation Assn., Skyline Golf Club (bd. dirs., pres. 1993). Home: N6570 Riverview Dr Black River Falls WI 54615-9207 Office: Stutz & Lister SC PO Box 370 Black River Falls WI 54615-0370 Office Phone: 715-284-7453. E-mail: tom@tlister.com.

LISTER-SINK, BARBARA ANN, musician, education educator; b. Lexington, NC, Jan. 18, 1947; d. Bright Immanuel Sink and Annie Lee Fitzgerald. BA, Smith Coll., 1969; Prix d'excellence in piano, Utrecht Conservatory, Netherlands, 1977; vocal studies, Amsterdam Conservatory, Netherlands. Pianist NH Music festival, 1979—83, NC Symphony, 1976—79; piano instr. Muzick Lyceum, Amsterdam, 1973—75; keyboardist Royal Concertgebouw Orch., Amsterdam, 1971—75; vis. lectr. Duke U., Durham, NC, 1975—76; assoc. prof. Eastman Sch. of Music, Rochester, NY, 1979—86; dean sch. of mus. Salem Coll., Winston-Salem, NC, 1986—92; artist in residence, prof. piano Salem Coll., Winston-Salem, NC, 1992—; piano faculty Brevard Music Ctr., NC, 2001—. Concert pianist self employed; dir. instr. Wingsound. Prodr.: (video) Freeing the Caged Bird, 1997; (documentaries). Mem.: European Tchrs. Ach., Am. Liszt Soc., Music Tchrs. Nat. Assn. Democrat. Avocations: singing, art, gardening. Office: Salem Coll Winston Salem NC 27108 Business E-Mail: swallow@salem.edu.

LISTON, HELEN J., retired minister; b. Joplin, Mo., Nov. 2, 1932; d. Kenneth Harold Latta and Erma Nadine Latta - Pieffer; m. Dan R. Liston, Jan. 2, 1954 (dec. July 31, 1999); children: Diane, Dan, Del, Darin, Darci. BA, Kans. U., Lawrence, 1981; MDiv, St. Paul Sch. Theology, Kans. City, Mo., 1991. Kalaidescope staff Hallmark Cards, Kansas City, Mo., 1987—91; min. Asbury United Meth. Ch., Prairie Village, Kans., 1990—93, Leawood United Meth. Ch., Kans., 1995—2003; chaplain Heartland Hospice, Kansas City, Mo., 1998—2004. Author: (book) The Dime Store, 2002; presenter Kans. City Hist. Soc., 1998—2004, Women's Wisdom Week, Crete, Greece; contbr. articles to periodicals. Home: 8731 Walmer Overland Park KS 66212 E-mail: hliston@kc.rr.com.

LISTORTI, IRENE M., music educator; b. Williamantic, Conn., Nov. 30, 1944; d. Louis Robert and Viola Mary (White) Berthelson; m. John Joseph Listorti; children: Joyce, John Jr., Thomas, Christopher. AA, Univ. Bridgeport, Conn., 1965. Pvt. piano tchr., Stratford, Conn., 1964—68, Old Saybrook, Conn., 1969—; organist St. Anthony's, Bridgeport, Conn., 1961—68, Our Lady of Sorrows, Essex, Conn., 1972—; music tchr. St. John Cath. Sch., Old Saybrook, Conn., 1999—. Mem.: Conn. State Music Tchrs. Assn. (v.p. 2002—, pres. 2004—, sec.), Our Lady of Sorrows Womans Guild (founder). Home: 62 Coulter St Old Saybrook CT 06475

LITAN, ROBERT ELI, lawyer, economist; b. Wichita, Kans., May 16, 1950; s. David and Shirley Hermine (Krischer) Litan. BS in Econs., U. Pa., 1972; MPhil in Econs., Yale U., 1976, JD, 1977, PhD in Econs., 1987. Bar: (D.C.) 1980. Rsch. asst. Brookings Instn., 1972-73; instr., then lectr. econs. Yale U., 1975-76; energy cons. NAS, 1975-77; regulation and energy specialist Pres.'s Coun. Econ. Advs., 1977-79; assoc. Arnold & Porter, Washington, 1979-82; assoc., then ptnr. and counsel Powell, Goldstein, Frazer & Murphy, Washington, 1982-90; sr. fellow Brookings Instn., Washington, 1984-92, dir. Ctr. for Econ. Progress, 1987-93; dep. asst. atty. gen. Dept. Justice, Washington, 1993-95; assoc. dir. Office of Mgmt. and Budget, Washington, 1995-96; v.p., dir. econ. studies Brookings Inst., Washington, Cabot family chair in econs., 1996—2003; v.p. rsch. and policy The Kauffman Found., Kans. City, Mo., 2003—. Cons. Inst. Liberty and Democracy, Lima, Peru, 1985—88; vis. lectr. Yale U. Law Sch., 1985—86; mem. Presdl. Congl. Commn. Causes of Savs. and Loan Crisis, 1991—92; cons. U.S. Dept. Treasury, 1996—97, 1999—2000; v.p. rsch. and policy The Kauffman Found., 2003—; sr. fellow The Brookings Inst., 2003—. Author: Energy Modeling for an Uncertain Future, 1978, Reforming Federal Regulation, 1983, Saving Free Trade: A Pragmatic Approach, 1986, What Should Banks Do?, 1987, Liability: Perspectives and Policy, 1988, American Living Standards: Threats and Challenges, 1988, Blueprint for Restructuring America's Financial Institutions, 1989, Banking Industry in Turmoil, 1990, The Revolution in U.S. Finance, 1991, The Liability Maze, 1991, Down in the Dumps: Administration of the Unfair Trade Laws, 1991, The Future of American Banking, 1992, Growth With Equity, 1993, Assessing Bank Reform, 1993, Verdict, 1993, Financial Regulation in a Global Economy, 1994, Footing the Bill for Superfund Cleanups, 1995, American Finance for the 21st Century, 1997, Globaphobia: Confronting Fears of Open Trade, 1998, None of Your Business: World Data Flows and the European Privacy Directive, 1998, The GAAP Gap, 2000, Beyond the Dot.Coms, 2001, Sticking Together: The Israeli Experiment in Pluralism, 2002, Protecting the American Homeland, 2002, Following the Money: Corporate Disclosure After Enron, 2003, Financial Statecraft, 2005; contbr. articles to profl. jours. Recipient Class of 1964 award, U. Pa., W. Gordon award, 1972, Albert A. Berg award, 1971, 1972, Felix S. Cohen award, Yale U., 1976, Silver medal, Royal Soc. Arts, 1972; fellow Thouron, Eng., 1972. Mem.: ABA, Coun. on Fgn. Rels., Am. Econs. Assn. Democrat. Home: 5437 Mohawk St Fairway KS 66205-2732 Office: The Kauffman Found 4801 Rockhill Rd Kansas City MO 64110 Office Phone: 816-932-1179. Business E-Mail: rlitan@brook.edu, rlitan@kauffman.org.

LITES, JAMES R., professional hockey team executive; b. Pentwater, Mich. m. Denise Lites; children: Brooke, Samuel. BA with highest honors, U. Mich., 1975; JD cum laude, Wayne State U., 1978. Exec. v.p. Detroit Red Wings, 1982—93; COO Olympia Arenas, Inc; v.p. Little Caesar's Internat., Inc.; pres. Dallas Stars, 1993—2002, 2002—, Phoenix Coyotes, 2002, Texas Rangers, Arlington, 1999—2002. Team rep. bd. govs. NHL. Office: Dallas Stars Dr Pepper Star Ctr 211 Cowboys Pkwy Irving TX 75063-5931*

LITEWKA, ALBERT BERNARD, publishing executive, entertainment executive; b. NYC, Feb. 5, 1942; s. Joel and Leah L. BA summa cum laude, UCLA, 1964; postgrad., U. Calif., Berkeley, 1964-65. Mgr. purchasing McGraw-Hill Book Co., N.Y.C., 1965-67; pres. Mktg. Innovations, Inc., N.Y.C., 1967-69; v.p. Westinghouse Leisure Time Industries, N.Y.C., 1972-75; exec. v.p. mktg. The Baker & Taylor Co. (W.R. Grace & Co.), N.Y.C., 1975-77; pres. Pix of Am. (W. R. Grace & Co.), N.Y.C., 1978; v.p. consumer services group W.R. Grace & Co., N.Y.C., 1977-79; pres. Macmillan Gen. Books div., N.Y.C., 1980-82; sr. v.p. Macmillan Pub. Co., Inc., 1980-82; pres. Warner Software, Inc., 1982-85; chmn., CEO Air Creative Group, Los Angeles and N.Y.C., 1986-98, Creative Domain, Inc., Los Angeles, Calif., 1991—. Author: Warsaw: A Novel of Resistance, 1989. Chmn. bd. trustees Oakwood Sch. Internat. Ladies Garment Workers Union Nat. scholar, 1959-64, U. Calif. Regents scholar, 1959-64; Woodrow Wilson Nat. Grad. fellow, 1964-65; recipient 1st prize Acad. Am. Poets, 1964. Mem. Am. Film Inst., Third Decade Coun., Authors Guild, Authors League Am., Acad. TV Arts & Scis. Office: Creative Domain Inc 9000 W Sunset Blvd Fl 9 Los Angeles CA 90069-5801 E-mail: alitewka@creativedomain.com.

LITFIN, A. DUANE, academic administrator; b. Mich. m. Sherri Litfin; 3 children. B in Bibl. Studies, Phila. Coll. of the Bible, 1966; ThM, Dallas Theol. Seminary; PhD in Interpersonal Comm., Purdue U.; DPhil in N.T. Studies, Oxford U. Tchr. Purdue U., Ind. U.; pastor Metea Bapt. Ch., Lucern, Ind.; assoc. prof. pastoral ministries Dallas Theol. Sem., 1974—84; sr. pastor First Evang. Ch., Memphis, 1984—93; pres. Wheaton Coll., Ill., 1993—. Author: Public Speaking: A Handbook for Christians, 1992, St. Paul's Theology of Proclamation, 1994. Office: Wheaton Coll 501 College Ave Wheaton IL 60187-5593 Office Phone: 630-752-5002. E-mail: Duane.Litfin@wheaton.edu.

LITHERLAND, ALBERT EDWARD, physics professor; b. Wallasey, Eng., Mar. 12, 1928; emigrated to Can., 1953, naturalized, 1964; s. Albert and Ethel (Clement) L.; m. Anne Allen, May 12, 1956; children: Jane Elizabeth, Rosamund Mary. B.Sc., U. Liverpool, Eng., 1949, PhD, 1955; DSc (hon.), U. Toronto, 1998. Rutherford scholar Atomic Energy of Can., Chalk River, Ont., 1953-55, sci. officer, 1955-66; prof. physics U. Toronto, 1966-79, Univ. prof., 1979-93, Univ. prof. emeritus, 1993—. Contbr. articles to profl. jours. Recipient Rutherford medal Inst. Physics, London, 1974, Silver medal for accelerator-based dating techniques Jour. Applied Radiation and Isotopes, 1980; Guggenheim fellow, 1986-87. Fellow Royal Soc. Can. (Henry Marshall Tory medal 1993), Royal Soc. London, AAAS, Am. Phys. Soc.; mem. Can. Assn. Physicists (Gold medal for achievement in physics 1971) Home: Apt 801 120 Rosedale Valley Rd Toronto ON Canada M4W 1P8 Office: 60 St George St Toronto ON Canada M5S 1A7

LITHGOW, JOHN ARTHUR, actor, film director; b. Rochester, N.Y., Oct. 19, 1945; s. Arthur and Sarah L.; m. Jean Taynton, Sept. 10, 1966 (div.); 1 child, Ian; m. Mary Yeager, 1981; children: Phoebe, Nathan. Grad. magna cum laude, Harvard U., 1967; postgrad., London Acad. Music and Dramatic Art, 1967-69. Printmaker, founder Lithgow Graphics. Actor (movies) Obsession, 1976, The Big Fix, 1978, Rich Kids, 1979, All That Jazz, 1979, Blow Out, 1981, I'm Dancing as Fast as I Can, 1982, The World According to Garp, 1982, Twilight Zone: TheMovie, 1983, Terms of Endearment, 1983, 2010: The Year We Make Contact, 1984, Footloose, 1984, Adventures of Buckaroo Banzai Across the 8th Dimension, 1984, Santa Claus, 1985, Mesmerized, 1986, The Manhattan Project, 1986, Harry and the Hendersons, 1987, Distant Thunder, 1988, Out Cold, 1989, Memphis Belle, 1990, At Play in the Fields of the Lord, 1991, Richochet, 1991, Raising Cain, 1992, Cliffhanger, 1993, The Pelican Brief, 1993, Good Man in Africa, 1994, Silent Fall, 1994, Princess Caraboo, 1994, Hollow Point, 1995, Special Effects: Anything Can Happen (voice), 1996, Officer Buckle and Gloria, 1998, Johhny Skidmarks, 1998, Homegrown, 1998, A Civil Action, 1998, Portofino, 1999, (voice) Rugrats in Paris: The Movie-Rugrats II, 2000, C-Scam, 2000, (voice) Shrek, 2001, Orange County, 2002, The Life and Death of Peter Sellers, 2004, Kinsey, 2004; (Broadway plays) Sweet Smell of Success, 2000-03 (Tony for Best Male Actor 2002), The Retreat from Moscow, 2004, Dirty Rotten Scoundrels, 2005; (TV series and movies) Mom, the Wolfman and Me, 1983, Not in Front of the Children, 1982, The Day After, 1983, The Glitter Dome, 1984, Resting Place, 1986, Baby Girl Scott, 1987, Traveling Man, 1989, Ivory Hunters, 1990, The Boys, 1991, The Wrong Man, 1993, Love, Cheat and Steal, 1993, Then There Were Giants, 1994, American Cinema, 1994, World War II: When Lions Roared, 1994, The Tuskegee Airmen, 1995, My Brother's Keeper, 1995, Redwood Curtain, 1995, Christmas in Washington, 1996, 3rd Rock from the Sun, 1996-2001 (Emmy for Outstanding Lead Actor in a Comedy Series 1996, 97, 99, Golden Globe award for Best Actor in a TV Series Musical and Comedy 1996), Don Quixote (miniseries), 1999; TV guest appearances include Amazing Stories, 1985 (Emmy for Outstanding Guest Performer in a Drama Series 1986), Tales from the Crypt, 1989, Cosby, 1996; singer (song) Singing in the Bathtub, 1999; author (children's books) The Remarkable Farkle McBride, 2000, Marsupial Sue, 2001, I'm a Manatee, 2003, Carnival of the Animals, 2004.*

LITKE, DONALD PAUL, acquisition executive, retired military officer; b. Denver, Nov. 7, 1934; s. Walter Monroe and Alice Vivian (Fowler) L.; m. Myrna Kay McDonald, July 1, 1956; children— Bradley, Susan, Lisa BS in Econs., Colo. A&M U., 1956; MS in Internat. Affairs, George Washington U., 1966. Ops. and staff positions U.S. Air Force, 1956-79; vice comdr. Oklahoma City Air Logistics Ctr., 1979-81; dep. dir. logistics and security assistance U.S. European Command, Stuttgart, Germany, 1981-83; comdr. U.S. Logistics Group, Ankara, Turkey, 1983-85; dep. dir. Def. Logistics Agy., Alexandria, Va., 1985-86; pres. Bus. Devel. Internat., Alexandria and Niceville, Fla., 1986—2004. Contbr. articles to profl. jours. Mem. Air Force Assn. (Middle Mgr. of Yr. 1970, award of excellence 1977), Alpha Tau Omega Methodist. Avocations: auto restoration, racquetball. Home and Office: 2422 Edgewater Dr Niceville FL 32578-2305 E-mail: dnklitke@cox.net.

LITMAN, BERNARD, electrical engineer, consultant; b. N.Y.C., Oct. 26, 1920; s. Nathan and Gussie (Friedman) L.; m. Ellen Ann Kaufman, Feb. 27, 1949; children— Barbara, Richard. BS in Elec. Engring, Columbia U., 1941, PhD, 1949; MS, U. Pitts., 1943. Design engr. energy equipment Westinghouse Electric Co., Pitts., 1941-47; with AMBAC Industries div. United Tech. Corp., Garden City, N.Y., 1949-83, tech. dir. guidance equipment Atlas inter-continental missile, 1962-63, chief engr. systems devel. and research, 1964-83; dir. advanced tech. Gull Electronics Systems Div., Parker Hannifin Corp., 1983-93; tech. cons., 1994-96; ret., 1996. Westinghouse lectr. U. Pitts., 1944; lectr. Adelphi U., Garden City. Co-author: Gyroscopics, 1961; patentee rotary amplifiers, axial motors, gravity pendulums, inductors, 2 axis accelerometers, ballistic missile safety devices, gyro attenuators, thrust retainers. William Petit Trobridge fellow, 1948 Asso. fellow Am. Inst. Aeros. and Astronautics (Achievement award L.I. sect. 1966); mem. IEEE (sr.), Am. Automatic Control Council, N.Y.-N.J. Trail Conf., Sigma Xi. Jewish. Home: 228 Wagon Wheel Ln Columbus NJ 08022-1119

LITMAN, GEORGE IRVING, physician, educator; b. Mass., Oct. 15, 1939; children: Scott, Amy, Kimberly, Megan. BS, Boston Coll., 1960; MD, Boston U., 1964. Intern Phila. Gen. Hosp., 1964-65; resident Univ. Hosp., Boston, 1965-66, Boston Vet.'s Hosp., 1966-67; fellow cardiology Emory U., Atlanta, 1967—69; unit head cardiology Genessee Hosp., Rochester, N.Y., 1969-71; assoc. physician Morton F. Plant Hosp., Clearwater, Fla., 1971-72; chief cardiology Akron Gen. Med. Ctr., Akron, Ohio, 1972—, med. dir. The Heart Ctr., 2002—; prof. medicine NE Ohio U., Rootstown, Ohio, 1982—. Recipient Disting. Svc. award Ohio Heart Assn., 1988. Fellow Am. Coll. Cardiology, ACP, Am. Coll. Chest Physicians; mem. AMA, Summit County Med. Soc., Am. Heart Assn. (trustee Ohio 1974—, research rev. com. 1975—, chmn. 1981-83), Ohio Heart Assn. (Disting. Service award 1983), Akron Heart Assn. (Sauvageot Vol. Services award 1984). Office: Akron Gen Med Ctr 400 Wabash Ave Akron OH 44307-2463 Office Phone: 330-344-2132. E-mail: glitman@agmc.org.

LITMAN, HARRY PETER, lawyer, educator; b. Pitts., May 4, 1958; s. S. David and Roslyn M. (Margolis) L.; m. Julie Roskies, Sept. 21, 2003; children: David, Lila. BA, Harvard U., 1981; JD, U. Calif., Berkeley, 1986. Bar: Calif. 1987, U.S. Ct. Appeals (D.C. cir.) 1987, Pa. 1988, D.C. 1989, U.S. Ct. Appeals (9th cir.) 1990, U.S. Dist. Ct. (so. dist.) Tex. 1992, U.S. Supreme Ct. 1992, U.S. Dist. Ct. (ea. and we. dists.) Pa. 1993, U.S. Ct. Appeals (7th cir.) 1994, U.S. Dist. Ct. (ea. dist.) Va. 1997. Prodn. asst. feature films, N.Y.C., 1980-82; newsman, clk. baseball desk AP, N.Y.C., 1982-83, sports reporter, 1983-86; law clk. to Hon. Abner J. Mikva U.S. Ct. Appeals (D.C. cir.), 1986-87; law clk. to Hon. Thurgood Marshall U.S. Supreme Ct., Washington, 1987-88, law clk. to Hon. Anthony M. Kennedy, 1989; asst. U.S. atty., dep. chief appellate sect. Dept. Justice, San Francisco, 1990-92, dep. assoc. atty. gen. Washington, 1992-93, dep. asst. atty. gen., 1993-98; U.S. atty. Western Dist. of Pa., 1998—2001; of counsel Phillips & Cohen, Washington, 2001—, San Francisco, 2001—. Adj. prof. Boalt Hall Sch. Law U. Calif., Berkeley, 1990-92, Georgetown U. Law Ctr., 1996-99, U. Pitts. Law Sch., 1999—, Rutgers Law Sch., 2003—; disting. visitor, fellow law and pub. affairs Princeton U., 2001-03; gen. counsel for Pa., Kerry-Edwards Campaign, 2004. Editor-in-chief Calif. Law Rev., Vol. 73; writer (TV show) Without a Trace; contbr. articles to profl. jours. Presdl. scholar, 1976. Mem. Pa. Bar Assn., State Bar Calif., D.C. Bar, Order of Coif.

LITMAN, JACK THEODORE, lawyer; b. N.Y.C., July 26, 1943; s. Charles Louis and Sarah G. (Hornblas) L.; m. Helena Dunica, Aug. 25, 1968; children: Sacha F., Benjamin S. BA, Cornell U., 1964; LLB, Harvard U., 1967; diploma, Inst. of Criminology, Paris, 1968. Bar: N.Y. 1968, U.S. Dist. Ct. (so. and ea. dists.) N.Y. 1973, U.S. Ct. Appeals (2d cir.) 1973, U.S. Supreme Ct. 1975. Asst. dist. atty. N.Y. County, N.Y.C., 1968-74; sr. trial asst., dep. chief Homicide Bur., 1968—74; sr. ptnr. Litman, Asche, & Gioiella LLP, N.Y.C., 1974—. Adj. prof. law NYU, N.Y.C., 1970—93. Editor: Criminal Trial Advocacy, 1975; contbr. articles to profl. jours. Fulbright scholar, 1967-68. Mem. N.Y. State Bar Assn. (mem. exec. com. criminal justice sect. 1983—, named Outstanding Practitioner of Yr. 1986), Assn. of Bar of City of N.Y. (mem. com. criminal courts and law procedure 1975-78), N.Y. Criminal Bar Assn. (pres. 1987—89, bd. dirs.), Nat. Assn. Criminal Def. Lawyers (bd. dirs.), N.Y. State Assn. Criminal Def. Lawyers (bd. dirs., pres. 1990-91) Democrat. Jewish. Avocations: chess, movies, sports, number theory. Office: Litman Asche & Gioiella 45 Broadway Atrium New York NY 10006-3007

LITMAN, RICHARD CURTIS, lawyer; b. Phila., May 2, 1957; s. Benjamin Norman and Bette Etta (Saunders) L.; m. Cheryl Lynn Goldstein, May 28, 1989; children: Amanda Rose, Jessica Brooke, Daniel Grant, Victoria Grace. BS, Union Coll., 1973; JD cum laude, U. Miami, 1979; LLM in Patent and Trade Regulation, George Washington U., 1980; M of Forensic Sci., Antioch Sch. Law, 1981. Bar: D.C. 1979, Fla. 1979, Pa. 1979, Va. 1980, Md. 1984, U. Ct. Appeals (fed. cir.), U.S. Patent and Trademark Office, U.S. Supreme Ct. Pvt. practice, Arlington, Va., 1983—. Instr. continuing legal edn.; organizer, dir. James Monroe Bank. Contbr. articles to profl. jours. Fellow Food and Drug Law Inst., 1979-80; named Small Bus. of Yr. Arlington C. of C., 1995. Mem. ABA, Fed. Bar Assn., Am. Acad. Forensic Scis., Am. Intellectual Property Law Assn.(chair), Arlington County Bar Assn., DC Bar (co-chair intellectual property law section), Econ. Devel. Commn. (chair), Masons (32d degree Scottish Rite), Shriners. Office: Litman Law Offices Ltd Patent Law Bldg 3717 Columbia Pike Arlington VA 22204-4255 E-mail: litman@4patent.com.

LITMAN, ROBERT BARRY, physician, writer, television and radio commentator; b. Phila., Nov. 17, 1947; s. Benjamin Norman and Bette Etta (Saunders) L.; m. Niki Thomas, Apr. 21, 1985; children: Riva Belle, Nadya Beth, Caila Tess, Benjamin David. BS, Yale U., 1968, MD, 1970, MS, MPhil in Anatomy, 1972. Diplomate Am. Bd. Family Practice, cert., recert. Am. Bd. Family Practice. Postdoct. rsch. fellow Am. Cancer Soc. Yale U., New Haven, 1970-73, USPHS fellow, 1974-75; resident in gen. surgery Bryn Mawr (Pa.) Hosp., 1973-74; pvt. practice in medicine and surgery Ogdensburg, N.Y., 1977-93, San Ramon, Calif., 1993—; mem. staff A. Barton Hepburn Hosp., 1977-93, John Muir Med. Ctr., 1993—, San Ramon Regional Med. Ctr., 1993—, also chmn. med. edn., chmn. dept. family practice, 1998-99, chmn. med. edn., 2004—. Commentator Family Medicine Stas. WWNY-TV and WTNY-Radio, TCI Cablevision, Contra Costa T.V.; moderator Ask the Dr.; clin. preceptor dept. family medicine State U. Health Sci. Ctr., Syracuse, 1978—. Author: Wynnefield and Limer, 1983, The Treblinka Virus, 1991, Allergy Shots, 1993; contbr. articles to numerous profl. jours. Pres. No. N.Y. chpt. AHA. Fellow Life Ins. Med. Rsch. Fund, U. Coll. Hosp., U. London, 1969-70; recipient We. Access Video Excellence award, 1998, 2001, Bay Area Cable Excellence award, 1999, Telly award, 1999-2005. Fellow Am. Coll. Allergy, Asthma, and Immunology, Am. Acad. Family Physicians; mem. AMA (Physicians Recognition award 1970—), Calif. State Med. Assn., Alameda-Contra Costa County Med. Assn., Joint Coun. Allergy and Immunology, Nat. Assn. Physician Broadcasters (charter), Acad. Radio and TV Health Communicators, Book and Snake Soc., Gibbs Soc. Yale U. (founder), Sigma Xi, Nu Sigma Nu, Alpha Chi Sigma. Home and Office: PO Box 1857 San Ramon CA 94583-6857 Office Phone: 925-866-7007.

LITMAN, ROSLYN MARGOLIS, lawyer; b. N.Y.C., Sept. 30, 1928; d. Harry and Dorothy (Perlow) Margolis; m. S. David Litman, Nov. 22, 1950; children: Jessica, Hannah, Harry. BA, U. Pitts., 1949, JD, 1952. Bar: Pa. 1952; approved arbitrator for complex comml. litigation and employment law. Practiced in Pitts., 1952—; ptnr. firm Litman Law Firm, 1952—; adj. prof. U. Pitts. Law Sch., 1958—. Permanent del. Conf. U.S. Circuit Ct. Appeals for 3d Circuit; past chair dist. adv. group U.S. Dist. Ct. (we. dist.) Pa., 1991-94, mem. steering com. for dist. adv. group, 1991—; chmn. Pitts. Pub. Parking Authority, 1970-74; mem. curriculum com. Pa. Bar Inst., 1986—, bd. dirs., 1972-82. Bd. dirs. United Jewish Fedn., 1999—, cmty. rels. com., co-chair ch./state com.; bd. dirs. City Theatre, 1999—. Recipient Roscoe Pound Found. award for Excellence in Tchg. Trial Advocacy, 1996, Disting. Alumnus award U. Pitts. Sch. Law, 1996, Disting. Svc. award Acad. Trial Lawyers, 2004; named Fed. Lawyer of Yr., We. Pa. Chpt. FBA, 1999. Mem. ABA (del., litigation sect., anti-trust health care com.), ACLU (nat. bd. dirs., Marjorie H. Matson Civil Libertarian award Greater Pitts. chpt. 1999), Pa. Bar Assn. (bd. govs. 1976-79), Allegheny County Bar Assn. (bd. govs. 1972-74, pres. 1975, Woman of Yr. 2001), Allegheny County Acad. Trial Lawyers (charter), Order of Coif. Home: 5023 Frew St Pittsburgh PA 15213-3829 Office: One Oxford Centre 34th Fl Pittsburgh PA 15219 Office Phone: 412-456-2000. Business E-Mail: rlitamn@Litman-Law.com.

LITOFF, JUDY BARRETT, history professor; b. Atlanta, Dec. 23, 1944; d. John and Dorothy (Woodall) Barrett; children: Nadja Barrett, Alyssa Barrett. BA, Emory U., Atlanta, 1967; MA, Emory U., 1968; PhD, U. Maine, 1975. Asst. prof. history Bryant U., Smithfield, RI, 1975-81, assoc. prof. history, 1981-87, prof. history, 1987—. Scholarly reader U. Ga. Press, Greenwood Press, U. Ill. Press, Prentice Hall, Univ. Press of Ky., Univ. Press of Colo.; project dir. U.S. Info. Agy. Grant, Minsk, Belarus, 1997-2000, higher edn. support program, Grant, Minsk, 1999. Author: American Midwives, 1978, American Midwife Debate, 1986; co-author: Miss You, 1990, Since Your Went Away, 1991, Dear Boys, 1991, We're In This War, Too, 1994, European Immigrant Women, 1994, American Women in a World at War, 1997, Dear Poppa, 1997, What Kind of World Do We Want?, 2000, Fighting Fascism in Europe, 2003; contbr. articles to profl. jours.; book reviewer many profl. jours. Bd. dirs. R.I. Hist. Soc.; bd. dirs., chair Goff Inst. for Ingenuity and Enterprise, 1998—2003; bd. dirs. R.I. Com. for Humanities, 1982-86; bd. overseers The Lincoln Sch., Providence, 1982-88, The Moses Brown Sch., Providence, 1984-93; leader Girl Scouts R.I., 1978-87. Recipient Disting. Faculty award Bryant Faculty Fedn., 1988, Bryant Alumni Assn., 1989, James Madison prize Soc. for History in Fed. Govt., 1994, Bryant U. Rsch. and Pub. award, 1997, 2005; Ford Career scholar Emory U., 1965-67. Mem. Orgn. Am. Historians, Am. Hist. Assn., So. Hist. Assn., R.I. Hist. Soc., R.I. Black Heritage Soc. (bd. dirs. 2004—), Humanities Forum R.I. (bd. dirs. 2000—), Coordinating Com. on Women in the Hist. Profession, So. Assn. Women Historians, Phi Kappa Phi, Phi Alpha Theta. Avocations: skiing, hiking. Home: 248 Morris Ave Providence RI 02906-2424 Office: Bryant Univ 1150 Douglas Pike Smithfield RI 02917-1291 Office Phone: 401-232-6248. E-mail: jlitoff@bryant.edu.

LITRENTA, FRANCES MARIE, psychiatrist; b. Balt., June 25, 1928; d. Frank P. and Josephine (DeLuca) L. AB, Coll. Notre Dame Md., 1950; MD, Georgetown U., 1954. Diplomate Am. Bd. Psychiatry and Neurology. Intern St. Agnes Hosp., Balt., 1954-55, asst. resident in psychiatry, 1955-56; fellow psychiatry Univ. Hosp., Balt., 1956-57; fellow child psychiatry Georgetown U. Hosp., Washington, Washington, 1957-59; clin. instr. psychiatry Med. Ctr. Georgetown U., Washington, 1959-63, clin. asst. prof. Med. Ctr., 1963-72, clin. assoc. prof. psychiatry Med. Ctr., 1972-87; pvt. practice Balt., 1959—. Cons. St. Vincent's Infant Home, Balt., 1965-75; mem. coun. to dean Georgetown U. Sch. Medicine, 1977-93. Recipient Georgetown U. Alumni Assn. John Carroll award, 1998. Fellow Am. Acad. Child and Adolescent Psychiatry, Am. Orthopsychiat. Assn. (life); mem. Am. Psychiat. Assn. (life), Md. Psychiat. Soc. (life), Georgetown Med. Alumni Assn. (nat. comm. chair 1987-90, class co-chair 1974-87, class comm. chair 1987—, bd. dirs. 1989—, gov. 1989-95, senator 1995—), Georgetown U. Alumni Assn. (Founder's award 1994, John Carroll award 1998). Office: 6110 York Rd Baltimore MD 21212-2697 Office Phone: 410-435-6340.

LITROWNIK, ALAN JAY, psychologist, educator; b. Los Angeles, June 25, 1945; s. Irving and Mildred Mae (Rosin) L.; m. Hollis Merle, Aug. 20, 1967; children: Allison Brook, Jordan Michael BA, UCLA, 1967; MA, U. Ill., Champaign-Urbana, 1969, PhD, 1971. Psychologist Ill. Dept. Mental Health, Decatur, 1970-71; asst. prof. psychology San Diego State U., 1971-75, assoc. prof., 1975-78, prof., 1978—, chmn. dept. psychology, 1981-87, assoc. dean for curriculum and acad. planning, North County Campus, 1987-88; co-dir. Ctr. for Behavioral and Community Health Studies, San Diego, 1989—2004. Cons. San Diego County Dept. Edn. Program Evaluation, 1975-81; project dir. Self-Concept and Self-Regulatory Processes in Developmentally Disabled Children and Adolescents, 1975-78; co-dir. Child Abuse Interdisciplinary Tng. Program, 1987-2002; project dir. tobacco use prevention in youth orgns., 1989-92. Research, publs. in field. Contbr. chpts. to books Mem. San

Diego County Juvenile Justice Commn., 1989-92; mem. juvenile systems adv. group San Diego County Bd. Suprs., 1989-91. Grantee U.S. Office Edn., 1975-78, 80-81, Nat. Ctr. Child Abuse, 1987—, Calif. Dept. Health, 1989-92, U. Calif. Tobacco-Related Disease Rsch. Program, 1992-94. Office Phone: 858-966-7703 7146.

LITSCHGI, A. BYRNE, lawyer; b. Charleston, S.C., Dec. 31, 1920; s. Albert William and Mary Catherine (Byrne) L.; m. Mary Elaine Herring, Sept. 13, 1952. BBA, U. Fla., 1941; JD, Harvard U., 1948. Bar: Fla. 1948, D.C. 1950. Atty. Office Gen. Counsel, Treasury Dept., Washington, 1949-52; legis. asst. to U.S. senator, 1952; mem. firm Hedrick & Lane, Washington, 1953-60, Coles, Himes & Litschgi, Tampa, Fla., 1960-62, Shackleford, Farrior, Stallings & Evans, 1962-87, Dykema Gossett, Tampa, Fla., 1988-92; chmn. SL Industries, Inc., 1976-92; mem. firm Holland & Knight, Tampa, 1992—. Incorporator, dir. Communications Satellite Corp., 1962-64; mem. Fla. Jud. Council, 1965-68, U.S. Internal Revenue Commn. Adv. Group, 1967-68 Mem. Harvard Law Sch. Assn. (nat. council 1956-61), ABA (chmn. excise and miscellaneous tax com. tax sect. 1956-59), Fla. Bar, Bar Assn. D.C. Office: Holland & Knight PO Box 1288 Tampa FL 33601-1288

LITSCHGI, RICHARD JOHN, computer manufacturing company executive; b. St. Louis, July 1, 1937; s. William J. and Mary F. (Eynatten) L.; m. Christine Ewert, Aug. 21, 1968. BS, St. Louis U., 1959; MS, U. Okla., 1964. Cert. meteorology St. Louis U./USAF. Supr. Bellcomm, Inc., Washington, 1964-67; mgr. Computer Scis., Brussels, 1967-68, Intranet Computing Co., L.A., 1968-71, Xerox Corp., El Segundo, Calif., 1971-76; dir. Honeywell Info. Sys. Inc., L.A., 1976-80, v.p. Phoenix, 1980-85, Mpls., 1985-87, Honeywell Bull, Inc., 1987-88, Bull HN, Inc., Boston, 1988-89, Groupe Bull, Boston and Paris, 1990-93, Vanguard Automation, Inc., Tucson, 1993-94; ret., 1994. Bd. dirs. Arizonians for Cultural Devel., 1981-85; trustee Phoenix Art Mus., 1982-85. Capt. USAF, 1959-62. Home: 24 Tupelo Rd Falmouth MA 02540-1945

LITT, MITCHELL, chemical engineer, educator, bioengineer; b. Bklyn., Oct. 11, 1932; s. Saul and Mollie (Steinbaum) L.; m. Zelda Sheila Levine, Sept. 6, 1955; children: Ellen Beth, Steven Eric. AB, Columbia U., 1953, BS in Engring, 1954, MS, 1956; D.Engring. Sci., Columbia, 1961. Research engr. Esso Research and Engring. Co., 1958-61; faculty U. Pa., 1961—, assoc. prof. chem. engring., 1965-72, prof., 1972—, prof. bioengring., 1977—2001, chmn. dept. bioengring., 1981-90, prof. bioengring. emeritus, 2001—. Vis. prof. environ. medicine Duke, 1971-72; vis. prof. Weizmann Inst., Israel, 1979; v.p. research and devel. KDL Med. Techs. Inc., 1984-95; v.p. rsch. & devel. BioFlo Systems, Inc., 1995—. Co-editor: Rheology of Biological Systems, 1973; asso. editor: Biorheology; contbr. articles to profl. engrs. Mem. IEEE (engring. in medicine and biology soc.), Am. Inst. Chem. Engrs., Am. Soc. Engring. Edn., Am. Chem. Soc., Biomed. Engring. Soc., Internat. Soc. Biorheology, N.Am. Soc. Biorheology, Am. Inst. Med. Biol. Engring., Phi Beta Kappa, Sigma Xi, Tau Beta Pi, Phi Lambda Upsilon, Theta Tau. Achievements include spl. research biorheology transp. processes, chemically reacting systems, med. aspects engring. Home: 2420 Spruce St Philadelphia PA 19103-6423 Office: Univ Pa Dept Bio Engring Philadelphia PA 19104 Personal E-mail: mitchlitt@comcast.net.

LITT, ROBERT S., lawyer; b. Dec. 29, 1949; BA, Harvard Univ., 1971; MA, Yale Univ., 1973, JD, 1976. Bar: N.Y. 1978, D.C. 1980, Md. 1998. Law clk. Judge Edward Weinfeld, US Dist. Ct., So. N.Y. Dist., 1976—77, Justice Potter Stewart, US Supreme Ct., 1977—78; asst. U.S. atty., So. Dist. N.Y. U.S. Dept. Justice, 1978—84; spec. adv. U.S. Dept. of State, Washington, 1993—94; dep. asst. atty. gen. U.S. Dept. Justice, Washington, 1994—97, prin. assoc. dep. atty. gen., 1997—99; ptnr., White Collar Practice Group Arnold & Porter, Washington, 1999—. Mem.: ABA (past chmn. White Collar Crime Com., Criminal Justice Sect.). Office: Arnold & Porter 555 Twelfth St NW Washington DC 20004-1260 Office Phone: 202-942-6380. Office Fax: 202-942-5999. Business E-Mail: robert.litt@aporter.com.

LITTELL, MARCIA SACHS, Holocaust and genocide studies professor; b. Phila., 1937; d. Leon Harry Sobel and Selma Lipson; children: Jonathan R., Robert L. Jr., Jennifer; m. Franklin H. Littell, Mar. 23, 1980. BS in Edn., Temple U., 1971, MS in Edn., 1975, EdD, 1990. Internat. exec. dir. Anne Frank Inst., Phla., 1981-89; exec. dir. Ann. Scholars' Conf. on the Holocaust & the Chs., Merion, Pa., 1980—; prof. Holocaust and genocide studies, founding dir. MA program Holocaust & genocide studies The Richard Stockton Coll. N.J., 1997—. Adj. prof. Temple U., Phila., 1990-97; vis. prof. Phila. C.C., 1974-76; dir. Phila. Ctr. on the Holocaust, Genocide and Human Rights, 1989—; exec. com. Remembering for the Future, Oxford, Eng. and Berlin, 1986—; mem. edn. com. U.S. Holocaust Meml. Mus., Washington, 1987-89, chmn.'s adv. com., 1985. Mem. editl. bd. Holocaust & Genocide Studies, Oxford U. Press, 1987—, Bridges: An Interdisciplinary Journal of Theology, Philosophy, History and Science, 1995—; editor: Holocaust Education: A Resource for Teachers and Professional Leaders, 1985, Liturgies on the Holocaust: An Interfaith Anthology, 1986, rev. edit., 1996 (Merit of Distinction award), The Holocaust: Forty Years After, 1989, The Netherlands and Nazi Genocide, 1992, From Prejudice to Destruction: Western Civilization in the Shadow of Auschwitz, 1995, Remembrance and Recollection: Essays on the Centennial Year of Martin Neimoller and Reinhold Niebuhr, 1995, The Uses and Abuses of Knowledge: The Holocaust and the German Church Struggle, 1997, The Holocaust: Lessons For the Third Generation, 1997, Holocaust and Church Struggle: Religion, Power and the Politics of Resistance, 1996, Confronting the Holocaust: A Mandate for the 21st Century, part 1, 1997, part 2, 1998, A Modern Prophet, 1998, Hearing the Voices: Teaching the Holocaust to Future Generations, 1999, Women in the Holocaust, 2001, The Century of Genocide, 2002, The Genocidal Mind, 2005. Exec. com. YM/YWHA Arts Coun., Phila., 1980—; adv. bd. Child Welfare, Montgomery County, 1975-80, Am. Friends the Ghetto Fighters House; bd. govs. Lower Merion Scholarship Fund, 1972-80. Named Woman of the Yr., Brith Sholom Women, Phila., 1993; recipient Eternal Flame award Anne Frank Inst., 1988; named to Hall of Fame Sch. Dist. of Phila., 1988. Fellow Nat. Assn. Holocaust Educators, Assn. of Holocaust Orgns. (founding sec. 1985-88), Nat. Coun. for the Social Studies. Democrat. Jewish. Avocations: walking, travel, reading. Office: PO Box 10 Merion Station PA 19066-0010 Office Phone: 609-652-4418. Business E-Mail: marcia.littell@stockton.edu.

LITTENBERG, MICHAEL RICHARD, lawyer; b. N.Y.C., Sept. 27, 1965; BS, Ind. U., 1987; JD, Tulane U., 1990. Bar: N.Y. 1991. Ptnr. Schulte Roth & Zabel LLP, N.Y.C., 1996—. Contbr. articles to profl. jours. Mem.: Manhattan C. of C. (bd. dirs. 2001—). Office: Schulte Roth & Zabel LLP 919 Third Ave New York NY 10022 E-mail: michael.littenberg@srz.com.

LITTENEKER, REBECCA ULFERS, lawyer; b. Fairbury, Ill., Oct. 6, 1958; d. Warren and Mary Ann (Hild) Ulfers; m. Randall John Litteneker, Aug. 9, 1980; 1 child, Alan Ulfers Litteneker. BA in Sociology magna cum laude, U. Utah, 1979; JD, U. Calif., San Francisco, 1983. Bar: Calif. 1983, U.S. Dist. Ct. (no. dist.) Calif. 1983, U.S. Dist. Ct. (ea., ctrl. and so. dists.) Calif., U.S. Ct. Appeals (9th cir.) 1984. Law clk. U.S. Ct. Appeals, San Francisco, 1983-84, Charles E. Wiggins, U.S. Ct. Appeals, San Francisco, 1984-85; assoc. Murphy Weir & Butler, San Francisco, 1985-90; v.p., counsel The Bank of Calif., N.A., 1990-95; spl. counsel Severson & Werson, 1995—. Co-author: California Title Insurance Practice, 1997. Mem. ABA (vice chair loan workouts and bankruptcy subcom. banking law com. 1993-98, chair 1998—), State Bar Calif., Bar Assn. San Francisco, San Francisco Barristers Club (co-chair comml. law and bankruptcy com. 1989-90), Commonwealth Club. Office: Severson & Werson 1 Embarcadero Ctr Fl 25 San Francisco CA 94111-3714

LITTIG, LAWRENCE WILLIAM, psychologist, educator; b. Madison, Wis., June 30, 1927; s. Lawrence Victor and Elsie Louise (Rosanske) L.; m. Iris Mark, June 15, 1957; children— Eve Alexandra, Amy Victoria, Sharon Elizabeth. BS, U. Wis., 1950, MS, 1955; PhD, U. Mich., 1959. Instr. dept. psychology U. Mich., Ann Arbor, 1958-59; asst. prof. psychology U. Buffalo, 1959-62; asst. program dir. instl. programs NSF, Washington, 1962-63; social psychologist W.E. Upjohn Inst. Employment Research, Washington, 1963-65; prof. social psychology Howard U., Washington, 1965-92, prof. emeritus social psychology, 1992—; prof. psychology Md. Inst. Coll. of Art, Balt., 1993—. Fulbright prof. U. Nottingham, 1961-62; vis. scholar U. London, 1971-72; cons. Brookings Instn., 1968-70, Dept. Labor, 1968-70; vis. prof. U. Wis., 1970 Cons. editor: Jour. Cross Cultural Psychology, 1969-74; contbr. articles to profl. jours. Mem. Annapolis Bd. Port Wardens, 1994—. U.S. Office Edn. grantee, 1965-70; NIMH research grantee, 1968-69; NSF research grantee, 1961-62; Nat. Inst. Child Health and Human Devel. grantee, 1971-73 Fellow: APA, AAAS, Soc. for Personality and Social Psychology, Am. Psychol. Soc.; mem.: Brit. Psychol. Soc., Psychonomic Soc., Annapolis bd. Port Wanders, Chesapeake Area Profl. Capts. Assn., Fleet Reserve Club, Cosmos Club (Washington), Eastport Yacht Club (Annapolis, Md.), Annapolis Yacht Club, Amateur Fencing Club (London), Sigma Xi. Home: 2 Wells Lndg Annapolis MD 21403-2316 Office: Howard U Dept Psychology Washington DC 20059-0001 Personal E-mail: llittig@comcast.net.

LITTLE, ALAN BRIAN, gynecologist, educator; b. Montreal, Que., Can., Mar. 11, 1925; emigrated to U.S., 1951, naturalized, 1959; s. Herbert Melville and Mary Lizette (Campbell) L.; m. Nancy Alison Campbell, Aug. 20, 1949 (div.); children: Michael C. (dec.), Susan MacF. and Deborah MacF. (twins), Catherine E., Jane A., Mary L.; m. Bitten Stripp, Mar. 31, 1983 BA, McGill U., 1948, MD, CM, 1950. Intern Montreal Gen. Hosp., 1950-51; resident Boston Lying-in and Free Hosp. for Women, 1951-55, asst. obstetrician, asso. obstetrician and gynecologist, 1955-65; teaching fellow, asst. prof. Harvard Med. Sch., 1952-65; prof. ob-gyn, then Arthur H. Bill prof. ob-gyn Case Western Res. U. Sch. Medicine, Cleve., 1965-82, chmn. dept. reproductive biology, 1972-82; prof. gynecology McGill U., Montreal, 1983—, chmn. dept. ob-gyn., 1983-94; clin. prof. ob-gyn. U. Medicine and Dentistry N.J., Newark, 1994—. Dir. dept. ob-gyn. Univ. Hosps., Cleve., to 1982, Royal Victoria Hosp., Montreal, 1983-94; mem. adv. com. Nat. Inst. Child Health and Human Devel. Author: (with B. Tenney) Clinical Obstetrics, 1962; editor: (with others) Gynecology and Obstetrics-Health Care for Women, 1975, 2d edit., 1982; (with D. Tulchinsky) Maternal Fetal Endocrinology, 2d edit., 1994; contbr. articles to profl. jours. Served with RCAF, 1943-45. Fellow: ACS, Am. Coll. Obstetricians and Gynecologists, Royal Coll. Surgeons Can.; mem.: Soc. Ob-Gyn. Can., Soc. Gynecol. Investigation, Assn. Profls. Ob-Gyn., Am. Gynecol. and Obstet. Soc. Office: UMDNJ MSB E506 185 S Orange Ave Newark NJ 07103-2757 Business E-Mail: littleb1@umdnj.edu.

LITTLE, ALEX G, thoracic surgeon, educator; b. Atlanta, Aug. 24, 1943; s. Alex G. and Roline (Adair) L.; m. Louise Rogers, June 7, 1975; children: Ashley Suzanne, Jody Louise. AB, U. N.C., 1965; MD, Johns Hopkins U., 1974. Diplomate Am. Bd. Surgery and Am. Bd. Thoracic Surgery. Intern in surgery Johns Hopkins Hosp., Balt., 1974-75, resident, 1975-76; resident in gen. and thoracic surgery U. Chgo., 1977-81, asst. prof. dept. surgery, 1981-84, assoc. prof., 1984-87; prof., chmn. dept. U. Nev., Las Vegas, 1988—2003; prof., chmn. Wright State Dept. Surgery, 2003—. Editor: Lung Cancer and Diseases of Esophagus, Vol. 1, 1987, Vol. 2, 1990; contbr. over 100 articles to sci. jours., 50 chpts. to books. Fellow ACS (editl. bd. Jour. 1999), Am. Coll. Chest Physicians (pres. 1991-92), Soc. Thoracic Surgeons, Am. Assn. for Thoracic Surgery, Soc. for Surgery Alimentary Tract, Am. Surg. Assn.; mem. Phi Beta Kappa, Alpha Omega Alpha. Avocation: tennis. Home: 5408 Spice Bush Lane Dayton OH 45429 Office: Wright State Dept Surgery One Wyoming St WCHE 7000 Dayton OH 45409 Office Phone: 937-208-3771.

LITTLE, BRIAN KEITH, music educator; b. Bellflower, CA, Apr. 16, 1969; BS, U. So. Calif., L.A., 1991. Cert. tchr. 1993. Tchr. L.A. Sch. Dist., L.A., Calif., 1993—. Singer: (alternative rock band) Reciprocal of Ancient Ruins, 1999.

LITTLE, BRUCE WASHINGTON, professional society administrator; b. Feb. 22, 1936; m. Nancy J. Mains; children: Elizabeth, Thomas, David. BS, Kans. State U., 1963, DVM, 1965. Pvt. practice assoc., Normal, Ill., 1965-69; pvt. practice Americana Animal Hosp., Bloomington, Ill., 1969-85; asst. exec. v.p. AVMA, Schaumburg, Ill., 1986-96, exec. v.p., 1996—. Rabies control officer McLean County, Ill., 1968-72; instr. U. Ill. Extension Svc., 1974, adv. Mclean County Bd. of Health, 1980-85; pres., ops. mgr. Blooming Grove Farm, Inc., Bloomington, 1983-86; bd. dirs. Assn. Forum Chicagoland, 2003-04, Am. Vet. Med. Found., 1996-, Nat. Commn. of Vet. Econ. Issues, 1998-; spkr. in field. Contbr. articles to profl. jours. Coach, Ill. 4-H Equine Judging Teams, 1974-76; bd. dirs. Mclean County Assn. Commerce Industry, 1983-85, Assn. Forum Chicagoland, 2003—, Am. Vet. Med. Found., 1996—, Nat. Commn. on Vet. Econ. Issues, 1999—; v.p. Ill. State U. Athletic Booster Club, 1980-82, pres., 1982-84. With U.S. Army, 1955-57. Named an alumni fellow, Kans. State U., 1998. Mem. AVMA, Ill. State Vet. Med. Assn., Chgo. Vet. Med. Assn., Rotary (Paul Harris Fellow), Alpha Zeta. Avocations: sports, golf, reading, horse breeding. Office: Am Vet Med Assn 1931 N Meacham Rd Schaumburg IL 60173-4364

LITTLE, CHARLOTTE LOUISE, poet, writer; b. Scotia, Calif., May 9, 1948; d. Henry Author East and Melva Berniece Clifford; m. Stanley Lee Little, July 30, 1966; 1 child, Stan Lee; 1 child, Rhonda Meichelle. Diploma, John A. Rowland, Rowland Heights, Calif., 1966. Poet, writer, Riverside, Calif. Author: numerous poems; contbr. poetry to poethunter.com. Deacon Solid Rock Ch. Internat. Named to Internat. Poetry Hall of Fame, 1996; recipient Diamon Homer trophy, Famous Poet Soc., 1996, Shakespeare Trophy of Excellence award, 2003, Poet of Yr. Medallion, 2003. Mem.: Internat. Soc. Poets (disting. mem., Internat. Poet of Merit award 1996). Avocations: writing, guitar, crafts, Bible reading, gardening. Personal E-mail: st9lt@aol.com, stanleylittle@charter.net.

LITTLE, DANIEL EASTMAN, philosopher, educator, director; b. Rock Island, Ill., Apr. 7, 1949; s. William Charles and Emma Lou (Eastman) L.; m. Ronnie Alice Friedland, Sept. 12, 1976 (div. May 1995); children: Joshua Friedland-Little, Rebecca Friedland-Little. BS in Math. with highest honors, AB in Philosophy with high honors, U. Ill., 1971; PhD in Philosophy, Harvard U., 1977. Asst. prof. U. Wis.-Parkside, Kenosha, 1976-79; vis. assoc. prof. Wellesley (Mass.) Coll., 1985-87; vis. scholar Ctr. Internat. Affairs Harvard U., 1989-91, assoc. Ctr. Internat. Affairs, 1991-95; asst. prof. Colgate U., Hamilton, N.Y., 1979-85, assoc. prof., 1985-92, prof., 1992-96, chmn. dept. philosophy and religion, 1992-93, assoc. dean faculty, 1993-96; v.p. academic affairs Bucknell U., Lewisburg, Pa., 1996-2000, prof. philosophy, 1996-2000; chancellor U. Mich., Dearborn, 2000—, prof. philosophy, 2000—; faculty assoc. Inter-U. Consortium for Social and Political Rsch., 2000—. Teaching fellow Harvard U., 1973-76; participant internat. confs. Ctr. Asian and Pacific Studies, U. Oreg., 1992, Social Sci. Rsch. Coun./McArthur Found., U. Calif., San Diego, 1991, Budapest, Hungary, 1990, Morelos, Mex., 1989, Rockefeller Found., Bellagio, Italy, 1990, U. Manchester, Eng., 1986; mem. screening com. on internat. peace and security Social Sci. Rsch. Coun./MacArthur Found., 1991-94; manuscript reviewer Yale U. Press, Cambridge U. Press, Princeton U. Press, Oxford U. Press, Westview Press, Harvard U. Press, Can. Jour. Philosophy, Philosophy Social Scis., Synthese, Am. Polit. Sci. Rev.; grant proposal reviewer NSF, Social Sci. Rsch. Coun., Nat. Endowment for Humanities; tenure and promotion reviewer U. Tenn., Bowdoin Coll., Duke U., U. Wis.; faculty assoc. Inter-Univ. Consortium for Social and Polit. Rsch., 2000—. Author: The Scientific Marx, 1986, Understanding Peasant China: Case Studies in the Philosophy of Social Science, 1989, Varieties of Social Explanation: An Introduction to the Philosophy of Social Science, 1991 (Outstanding Book award Choice 1992), On the Reliability of Economic Models, 1995, Microfoundations Method and Causation: On the Philosophy of the Social Sciences, 1998, The Paradox of Wealth and Poverty: Mapping the Ethical Dilemmas of Global Development, 2003; contbr. articles to profl. jours., books. Social Sci. Rsch. Postdoctoral fellow MacArthur Found., 1989-91, Rsch. grantee NSF, 1987, Woodrow Wilson Grad. fellow, 1971-72. Mem. Am. Philos. Assn., Assn. Asian Studies, Internat. Devel. Ethics Assn., Social Sci. History Assn., Soc. for the History of Tech., Phi Beta Kappa. Office: Chancellor U Mich Dearborn 4901 Evergreen Rd Dearborn MI 48128 E-mail: delittle@umich.edu.

LITTLE, FREED SEBASTIAN, retired petroleum equipment manufacturing company executive; b. Ft. Smith, Ark., May 4, 1926; s. Jess Edward and Floy Kimbrough (Witt) Little; m. Jana V. Jones, Dec. 9, 1951 (div.); 1 child, Mark McKenna. BA, U. Ark., 1950. With Gilbarco Inc., Houston, 1964—90, ctrl. area mgr. Chgo., 1969—73, Western regional mgr. Houston, 1974—85, Western/Pacific regional mgr., 1986—90; founder, pres. Little and Assocs., Inc. Mgmt. cons., outsourcing placement specialist, 1990; bd. dirs. Wall St. Svcs., Inc., San Antonio, Waterhouse Fin. Mgmt. Group, Inc., San Antonio. Bd. dirs. Post Oak Family YMCA, Houston, 1990—95; patron Houston Mus. Fine Arts. Served with USAAF, 1944—46. Mem.: Am. Mgmt. Assn., Petroleum Equipment Inst., Am. Petroleum INst., Huguenot Soc., Oxford Club, Houston City Club, Am. Legion, Sigma Alpha Epsilon. Presbyterian.

LITTLE, GEORGE DANIEL, clergyman; b. St. Louis, Dec. 18, 1929; s. Henry and Agathe Cox (Daniel) L.; m. Joan Phillips McCafferty, Aug. 22, 1953; children: Deborah Philips, Cynthia McCafferty (dec.), Alice Annette, Daniel Ross, Benjamin Henry. AB, Princeton U., 1951; MDiv, McCormick Theol. Sem., Chgo., 1954; LLD (hon.), Huron Coll., 1977. Ordained to ministry Presbyn. Ch., 1954; pastor East London Group Ministry, Presbyn. Ch. Eng., 1954-56, Friendship Presbyn. Ch., Pitts., 1956-62; assoc. dir. dept. urban ch., planning assoc. Bd. Nat. Missions, United Presbyterian Ch. U.S.A., N.Y.C., 1962-72; assoc. for budgeting Gen. Assembly Mission Council, 1973-76, exec. dir. council, 1976-84; pastor First Presbyn. Ch., Ithaca, N.Y., 1984-93; interim pres. McCormick Theol. Sem., Chgo., 1993-94; pastor-in-residence Village Presbyn. Ch., Prairie Village, Kans., 1995-96, Westminster Presbyn. Ch., Mpls., 1997-99, 2002; ret., 1999. Presbyterian. Home: 13 Julia Cir Madison WI 53705-1033 E-mail: danglittle@aol.com.

LITTLE, GEORGE L., lawyer; b. Winston-Salem, Sept. 14, 1942; s. George Lester and Jean (Misenheimer) L.; m. Susan Pollard, June 19, 1965; children: George L., Sara Lee. BA, Davidson (N.C.) Coll., 1964; JD with hons., U. N.C., 1967. Bar: N.C. 1967, U.S. Supreme Ct., U.S. Ct. Appeals (4th, 9th, 11th and Fed. cir.), U.S. Dist. Ct. (ea., middle, we. dist.) N.C. Assoc. Petree Stockton & Robinson, Winston-Salem, 1971-75; ptnr. Kilpatrick Stockton LLP, Winston-Salem, 1976—. Author: The Antitrust Health Care Handbook, 1988. Mem. Winston-Salem Forsyth County Util. Commn.; bd. & exec. com. mem. Piedmont Opera Theatre; past pres. St. Andrew's Soc. N.C., Inc., Pinehurst; bd. mem. Winston-Salem Alliance, Idealliance; past chmn. Greater Winston-Salem C. of C., Winston-Salem Bus. Inc.; past mem. exec. com. Piedmont Triad Partnership; v.p., dir. Winston-Salem Symphony Assn., 1987-89, United Way of Forsyth County, Winston-Salem, 1976-82. Capt. U.S. Army, 1967-71. Mem. ABA, Internat. Trademark Assn. (mem. disting. panel neutrals), NC Bar Assn., Oldtown Club, Rotary Club, Piedmont Club. Democrat. Presbyterian. Avocations: wine, gardening, opera, sailing, scottish heritage. Office: Kilpatrick Stockton LLP 1001 W 4th St Winston Salem NC 27101-2400 Office Phone: 336-607-7300. Office Fax: 336-734-2620. Business E-Mail: glittle@kilpatrickstockton.com.

LITTLE, JOHN BERTRAM, radiologist, educator, researcher; b. Boston, Oct. 5, 1929; s. Bertram Kimball and Nina (Fletcher) L.; m. Francoise Cottereau, Aug. 4, 1960; children: John Bertram, Frederic Fletcher AB in Physics, Harvard U., 1951; MD, Boston U., 1955. Diplomate Diplomate Am. Bd. Radiology. Intern Johns Hopkins Hosp., Balt., 1955—56; resident in radiology Mass. Gen. Hosp., Boston, 1958-61; fellow Harvard U., Cambridge, Mass., 1961-63; from instr. to assoc. prof. radiobiology Harvard Sch. Pub. Health, Boston, 1963-75, prof., 1975—, chmn. dept. physiology, 1980-83, James Stevens Simmons prof. radiobiology, 1987—, chmn. dept. cancer cell biology, 1997—2002, dir. Ctr. for Radiation Scis. and Environ. Health, 1998—; dir. Kresge Ctr. Environ. Health, Boston, 1982-98. Cons. radiology Mass. Gen. Hosp., Boston, 1965—, Brigham and Women's Hosp., Boston, 1968—; chmn. bd. sci. counsellors Nat. Inst. Environ. Health Sci., 1982—84; bd. sci. counsellors Nat. Toxicology Program, 1988—92; mem. sci. coun. Radiation Effects Rsch. Found., Hiroshima, Japan, 1992—98, chmn., 1996—98; bd. dirs. on radiation effects rsch. NAS, 1992—98, chmn., 1996—98; mem. Coun. Internat. Assn. for Radiation Rsch. Mem. editorial bd. numerous nat. and internat. jours.; contbr. chpts. to books and articles to profl. jours. Mem. coun. Nat. Coun. on Radiation Protection and Measurements, 1993—; trustee various hist. and cultural orgns. Capt. U.S. Army, 1956-58. Named one of Outstanding Investigator grantee, Nat. Cancer Inst., 1988—; recipient numerous rsch. and tng. grants, NIH, 1968—; grantee, Am. Cancer Soc., 1965—68. Mem. AAAS (coun. in med. scis. 1988-91), Radiation Rsch. Soc. N.Am. (pres.-elect 1985, pres. 1986-87), Am. Assn. Cancer Rsch., Am. Physiol. Soc., Health Physics Soc., Am. Soc. Photobiology, Internat. Assn. Radiation Rsch. (coun.). Natl. Assoc. mem., Natl. Acad. of Sci. Avocations: music, architectural history. Office: Harvard U Dept Cancer Cell Biology 665 Huntington Ave Boston MA 02115-6021

LITTLE, JOHN DUTTON CONANT, finance educator; b. Boston, Feb. 1, 1928; s. John Dutton and Margaret (Jones) L.; m. Elizabeth Davenport Alden, Sept. 12, 1953; children: John Norris, Sarah Alden, Thomas Dunham Conant, Ruel Davenport. SB in Physics, MIT, 1948, PhD, 1955; PhD (hon.), U. Liege, Belgium, 1992, Cath. U. of Mons, 1997; PhD (hon.), U. London, 2002. Engr. Gen. Electric Co., Schenectady, 1949-50; asst. prof. ops. research Case-Western Res. U., 1957-60, assoc. prof., 1960-62; research asst. MIT, 1951-54, assoc. prof. mgmt., 1962-67, prof., 1967-78, George M. Bunker prof. mgmt., 1978-89, Inst. prof., 1989—, dir. Ops. Research Ctr., 1969-76, head mgmt. sci. group Sloan Sch. Mgmt., 1972-82, head behavioral and policy scis. area, 1982-88, chmn. undergrad. program, 1990—; pres. Mgmt. Decision Systems, Inc., 1967-80, chmn. bd. dirs., 1967-85; dir., advisor to bd. dirs. Info. Resources, Inc., 1985—2003. Cons. ops. rsch. indsl. govtl. orgns., 1958—; vis. prof. mktg. European Inst. Bus. Adminstrn., Fontainebleau, France, fall 1988; researcher math. programming, queuing theory, mktg., traffic control, decision support systems, e-commerce; bd. dirs. InSite Mktg. Technology, Inc., 1997-99. Assoc. editor: Mgmt. Sci, 1967-71; contbr. articles to profl. jours. Trustee Mktg. Sci. Inst., 1983-89. Served with AUS, 1955-56. Fellow AAAS (mem. coun. 2000—03); mem. NAE, Ops. Rsch. Soc. Am. (coun. 1970-73, pres. 1979-80), Inst. Mgmt. Scis. (v.p. 1976-79, pres. 1984-85), Fellow Inst. for Ops. Rsch. and the Mgmt. Scis. (pres. 1995), Am. Mktg. Assn., Sigma Xi. Home: 37 Conant Rd Lincoln MA 01773-3912 Office: MIT Sloan Sch Mgmt Cambridge MA 02142-1347

LITTLE, JOHN WILLIAM, plastic surgeon, educator; b. Indpls., Mar. 12, 1944; s. John William Jr. and Naida (Jones) L.; m. Patricia Padgett Lea, May 26, 1969 (div. 1974); m. Teri Ann Tyson, Feb. 28, 1981 (div. 1982). AB, Dartmouth Coll., 1966, B in Med. Scis., 1967; MD, Harvard U., 1969. Diplomate Am. Bd. Med. Examiners, Am. Bd. Surgery, Am. Bd. Plastic Surgery. Intern Case Western Res. U., Cleve., 1969-70, resident in surgery, 1970-74, resident in plastic surgery, 1973-75; fellow in plastic surgery U. Miami, 1975-77; asst. prof. Georgetown U., Washington, 1977-82, assoc. prof., 1982-87, prof., 1987-92, clin. prof., 1992—, dir. div. plastic surgery, residency tng. program, plastic surgeon-in-chief univ. hosp., 1979-92; dir. Nat. Capital Tng. Program in Plastic Surgery affiliated hosps. Georgetown U. and Howard U., 1988-92; dir. Georgetown Plastic Surgery Fellowship in Breast and Aesthetic Surgery, 1990-92; pvt. practice Washington, 1992—. Prof. postgrad. edn. in plastic surgery Internat. Soc. Aesthetic Plastic Surgery, 1999—; chief plastic surgery Medlantic Ctr. for Ambulatory Surgery, Inc., 1993—, mem. med. adv. bd., 1993—; cons. Nat. Cancer Inst., NIH, Bethesda, Md., 1977-92, Washington VA Med. Ctr., 1981-92, Reach to Recovery program Nat. Capital chpt. Am. Cancer Soc., 1981—, RENU program in breast reconstrn., 1982; specialist site visitor plastic surgery residency rev. com. Accreditation Coun. for Grad. Med. Edn., 1982-95; vis. lect. various insts.; bd. govs. Nat. Endowment for Plastic Surgery, 1995—. Adv. editor Plastic and Reconstructive Surgery, 1997—, manuscript reviewer Plastic and Reconstructive Surgery, Annals of Plastic Surgery; assoc. editor Surgery of the Breast: Principles and Art, 1998; contbr. numerous articles to med. jours., numerous chpts. to books. Bd. dirs. Triann reconstructive surgery teams to

Caribbean and S.Am., Georgetown Tissue Bank, 1986-88, Operation Luz del Sol; founder, pres., med. dir. Reconstructive Surgeons Vol. Program; bd. dirs. Washington Summer Opera Theater; trustee Washington Opera, 1993—, artistic com., 1994—; Domingo Circle, 1995—, Laureates' medal, 1999. Recipient Laureate medallion Domingo Cir., 1999, Mem. AMA, ACS (coord. plastic surgery audiovisual program Ann. Clin. Congress 1988-90, 92-93, bd. govs., Met. Washington chpt. councillor 1985-94, chmn. sci. program com. 1990-91, v.p. 1991-92, pres. 1992-93, bd. govs. 1998—), Nat. Capital Soc. Plastic Surgeons (sec. treas. 1982-83, pres. 1984-85), Am. Soc. Plastic Surgeons (audiovisual program dir. ann. meeting 1984-86, strategic planning com. 1987-96, fin. com. 1989-94, conv. policy com. 1993-96, ops. com. 1993-96, chmn. 1994-95, spokesperson network steering com. 1994-96, bd. dirs. 1994-96, exec. com. 1995-96, spokesperson 1998—, rep. to IPRAS 1999—), Am. Assn. Plastic Surgeons (co-chmn. various coms.), Plastic Surgery Ednl. Found. (bd. dirs. 1985-97, devel. com. 1991—, chmn. 1997-2000, chmn. various coms., rep. to Coun. Plastic Surg. Orgns. 1989-95, parliamentarian 1992-93, v.p. 1993-94, pres. adv. coun. 1993-96, commr. various commns., pres.-elect, 1995, pres. 1995-96, Maliniac fellow 1998—, Disting. Svc. award, 2000), Med. Soc. D.C. (chmn. plastic surgery sect. 1985), D.R. Millard Surg. Soc. and Ednl. Found. (pres. 1985-87), Am. Cleft Palate Assn., Am. Soc. Maxillofacial Surgeons, Washington Acad. Surgeons (coun. 1988-90), Am. Soc. Aesthetic Plastic Surgery (In Chun Sung award philanthropic svc. 2000), NE Soc. Plastic Surgeons (chmn. various coms., v.p. 1991-92, pres. 1992-93, historian 1994-99), Internat. Soc. Aesthetic Plastic Surgery (chmn. bylaws com. 1990-93, 95-97, parliamentarian 1992-93, mem. membership com. 1993-97, chmn. 1993-95, sec. gen. 1997-2000, rep. to IPRAS 1997-2000, prof. postgrad. edn. in aesthetic plastic surgery, others), Am. Alpine Workshop in Plastic Surgery (founder, pres. 1991-92, historian 1995—), Internat. Confedn. Plastic Reconstructive and Aesthetic Surgery (mem. exec. com. 1997-2000, coun. dels. 1999—), Nat. Endowment Plastic Surgeons (bd. govs. 1995—), Internat. Plastic, Reconstructive and Aesthetic Surgery Found. (bd. dirs. 1999—, ednl. program com. chmn. 1999—, vice chmn. devel. com. 1999—, publs. and videotape com.), European Assn. Plastic Surgeons (corr.), Turkish Soc. Plastic Surgeons (hon.), Argentine Soc. Plastic, Reconstructive and Aesthetic Surgeons (assoc.), Atlantic Soc. Plastic Surgeons (hon.), Soc. Am. and Italian Plastic Surgeons (founding mem. 1988—), Turkish Soc. Plastic Surgeons (hon. mem. 1996—), Argentina Soc. Esthetic Plastic Surgery and Repair (corr. mem. 1999—), European Assn. Plastic Surgeons (corr. mem 2000—), Atlantic Soc. Palstic Surgeons (hon. mem. 2000—), Mediterranean Soc. Plastic and Aesthetic Surgery (active mem. 2001—); fellow Am. Israeli Plastic Surgeons (charter mem. 1997—), Republican. Presbyterian. Home: 3030 K St NW Ph 212 Washington DC 20007-5107 Office: 1145 19th St NW Ste 802 Washington DC 20036-3700

LITTLE, JOSEPH HUGH, plastic surgeon; b. Dayton, Ohio, July 10, 1945; s. Robert Hugh and Miriam Therese Little; m. Jean Paulette Little, May 24, 1975; children: Gregory Douglas, Elisabeth, Joseph. AB, U. Calif., Berkeley, 1967; MD, UCLA, 1972. Diplomate Am. Bd. Plastic Surgery. Pvt. practice plastic surgery, Dallas and Plano, Tex., 1980—. Maj. USAF, 1976—78. Mem.: Am. Soc. Plastic Surgeons. Avocations: golf, swimming, reading. Office: 1600 Coit Rd # 205 Plano TX 75075 Office Phone: 972-985-0065. Office Fax: 972-985-0076.

LITTLE, KEVIN GERARD, lawyer; b. N.Y.C., Feb. 25, 1966; s. Henry Leroy Little, Jr. and Bertha Marie Little; m. Virna Liza Santos, Aug. 18, 1990; 1 child, Enrique Raymond Santos. BA cum laude, Harvard U., 1987, JD cum laude, 1990. Bar: Calif. 1990, U.S. Supreme Ct. 1994, U.S. Ct. Appeals (all circuits) 1994, U.S. Ct. Fed. Claims 1994, U.S. Dist. Ct. (cen. dist.) Calif. 1990, U.S. Dist. Ct. (ea. dist.) Calif. 1995, U.S. Dist. Ct. (no. dist.) Calif. 1998, U.S. Dist. Ct. P.R., U.S. Dist. Ct. (we. dist.) Tex. Assoc. O'Melveny & Myers, L.A., 1991—92; law clk. Hon. Consuelo B. Marshall, L.A., 1991—92, Hon. Cecil F. Poole, San Francisco, 1992—93; solo practitioner San Juan, PR, 1993—95; atty. Frampton, Williams & Little, Fresno, Calif., 1995—2001; solo practitioner Fresno, Calif., 2001—. Vis. atty. Boalt Hall Sch. Law, Berkeley, Calif., 2001; guest spkr. Ea. Dist. Calif. Law Enforcement Summit, Squaw Valley, 2002, Bay Area Police Watch, San Francisco, 1999—2000. Sponsor Big Bros./Big Sisters, Fresno, 1996—; participant Campaign Against Prop 209, Fresno, 1997. Named one of most tenacious litigators in Calif., Calif. Lawyers Mag.; recipient Svc. award, Helping Our Own Destiny, Fresno, 1997, San Joaquin Coll. Law, 1998—. Democrat. Office: 1275 E Province Fresno CA 93780 Office Phone: 559-486-5730. E-mail: fwllaw@aol.com.

LITTLE, LOREN EVERTON, musician, ophthalmologist; b. Sioux Falls, S.D., Oct. 28, 1941; s. Everton A. and Maxine V. (Alcorn) L.; m. Christy Gyles; 1 child, Nicole Moses; children from previous marriage: Laurie, Richard. BA, Macalester Coll., 1963; BS, U. S.D., 1965; MD, U. Wash., 1967. Prin. trumpeter Sioux Falls Mcpl. Band, 1956-65; trumpeter St. Paul Civic Orch., 1960-62; leader, owner Swinging Scots Band, St. Paul, 1960-63; trumpeter Edgewater Inn Show Room, Seattle, 1966-67, Jazztet-Arts Council, Sioux Falls, 1970-71, Lee Maxwell Shows, Washington, 1971-74; residency in ophthalmology Walter Reed Med. Ctr., Washington, 1974; co-leader, trumpeter El Paso (Tex.) All Stars, 1975; freelance trumpeter, soloist various casinos and hotels, Las Vegas, Nev., 1977—. Trumpeter (album) Journey by R. Romero Band, 1983, Sizenter, 1997; soloist for numerous entertainers including Tony Bennett, Burt Bacharach, Jack Jones, Sammy Davis Jr., Henry Mancini, Jerry Lewis Telethon, for video Star Salute to Live Music, 1989; with Stan Mark Band Nat. Pub. Radio Broadcast, 1994, 95; soloist on video Stan Mark Live at the 4 Queens Hotel, Las Vegas; pres. S&L Music, S&L Records; prodr. Carl Saunders Debut Album Out Of the Blue, 1996, Eclecticism, 2000. Trustee Nev. Sch. of the Arts, Las Vegas, 1983—; pres. S&L Music SNL Rec. Served to lt. col. U.S. Army, 1968-76, Vietnam. Decorated Silver Star, Purple Heart, Bronze Star, Air medal; fellow Internat. Eye Found., 1974; Dewitt Wallace scholar Readers Digest, 1963-65. Fellow ACS, Am. Acad. Ophthalmology; mem. Am. Fedn. Musicians, Nat. Bd. Med. Examiners. Presbyterian. Avocations: history, music, medicine, sports, skiing.

LITTLE, POLLY ANN, artist; b. St. Joseph, Mo., Nov. 13, 1954; d. Thomas Lee and Adeline Hope (Ketzscher) L.; m. Mark Leo Lavatelli, Apr. 6, 1975; children: Anna Chiaretta, Zoe Elizabeth. BFA, Mo. Western State U., 1976; BFA in Painting, U. N.Mex., 1978, MA, 1980. Teaching asst., lithography asst. U. N.Mex., Albuquerque, 1978-80; asst. dir. Mattingly Baker Gallery, Dallas, 1980-82; adj. asst. prof. Tex. Women's U., Denton, Tex., 1983-84, North Lake Community Coll., Irving, Tex., 1985-88; teaching artist Arts in Edn. of Western N.Y., Buffalo, 1990—. Artist Gallery 44, Boulder, Colo., 1987—, Ruth Wiseman Gallery, Dallas, 1985—. One-person exhibitions include Ruth Wiseman Gallery, Dalls, 1989, 500X Gallery, Dallas, 1986, North Lake Gallery, Irving, Tex., 1986, AKAS, Hot Springs, Ark., 1985, Mattingly Baker Gallery, Dallas, 1984, Tex. Christian Univ., Ft. Worth, 1983, ASA Gallery, Albuquerque, 1980; exhibited in group shows including Hallwalls Gallery, 1991, Niagara Power Project, 1990, Gallery 44, 1990, The Artists' Gallery, 1989, Clary-Miner Gallery, 1989, Conduit Gallery, 1988, Edith Baker Gallery, 1987 and others. Recipient Lift grant Arts Coun. of Buffalo & Erie County, 1989, Ford Found. grant, 1978, 79, Cash award Mixed Media, 1st Place Niagara Falls Art Coun., 1990, 89. Mem. Hallwalls Gallery, Albright Knox Art Gallery, Dallas Mus. Fine Arts, Coll. Art Assn. Home: 749 Richmond Ave Buffalo NY 14222-1160

LITTLE, R. DONALD, real estate entrepreneur; b. Gastonia, N.C., Mar. 18, 1937; s. Coy Marshall and Stella May (Pruett) L.; m. Jacqueline Beatrice Mandel, June 10, 1967 (dec. Mar. 1995); Linda Lee Stoner; Sept. 7, 1999; children by previous marriage: Tina June Whitman, Diana Dawn Little, Laura Marie Van Meel; stepchildren: Keith, Don. BA, U. Md., 1972; BS in Architecture, Cath. U. Am., 1981, MArch, 1983. Ordained, chartered non-denominational minister, 1998. Blood bank and med. technologist Dr. Oscar B. Hunter Meml. Lab., Washington, 1961-66; biol. lab. technologist Naval Med. Rsch. Inst., Bethesda, Md., 1966-68; blood bank and med. technologist, supr. Ctrl. Lab. Doctor's Hosp., Washington, 1959-79; jr. architect VVKR Inc., University Park, Md., supr. architect; br. head design divsn. Naval Surface Weapons Ctr., Silver Spring, Md., 1981-87; supr. architect, chief facility engring. br. Agrl. Rsch. Svc., USDA, 1987-96; area adminstrv. officer BARC Rsch. Svc., USDA, Beltsville, Md., 1996—2002; ret., 2002; real estate entrepreneur, 2002—. With USN, 1956—61. Mem. Am. Assn. Blood Banks, Am. Soc. Med. Technologists. Home: 148 Williams Way Lewes DE 19958-4376 Office: Long and Foster Realtors 720 Rehoboth Ave Rehoboth Beach DE 19971 Office Phone: 302-236-1373. E-mail: coolsummerbreeze@aol.com.

LITTLE, RICHARD ALLEN, mathematics professor, computer science educator; b. Cochocton, Ohio, Jan. 12, 1939; s. Charles M. and Elsie Leanna (Smith) L.; children from previous marriage: Eric, J. Alice, Stephanie; m. Laura Ann Novosel, June 15, 1991. BS in Math. cum laude, Wittenberg U., 1960; MA in tchg., Johns Hopkins U., 1961; EdM in Math., Harvard U., 1965; PhD in Math. Edn., Kent State U., 1971. Tchr. Culver Acad., Ind., 1961-65; instr., curriculum cons. Harvard U., Cambridge, Mass. and Aiyetoro, Nigeria, 1965-67; from instr. to assoc. prof. Kent State U., Canton, Ohio, 1967-75; from assoc. prof. to prof. Baldwin-Wallace Coll., Berea, Ohio, 1975—, dept. chair, 1978-83. Mathematician/educator Project Discovery Ohio Bd. Regents, 1992-96; vis. prof., math. Ohio State U., Columbus, 1987-88, 92-95; pres. Cleve. Collaborative on Math. Edn., 1986-87; policy bd. Ohio Resource Ctr. for Math. Sci. and Reading, 2000—, exec. com. policy bd., 2001—, chair exec. com., 2002-03; vis. prof., dept. math. and stats. Bowling Green State U., 2004-05; lectr. in field. Contbr. articles to profl. jours. Bd. dirs. Canton Symphony Orch., 1973-75; Sunday sch. tchr. Bethany English Luth. Ch., Cleve., 1991—; bd. deacons Holy Cross Luth. Ch., Canton, 1968-74, chmn., 1971-74. Recipient Strosacker Excellence in Tchg. award and Student Senate Faculty Excellence award Baldwin-Wallace Coll., 1999. Mem. Nat. Coun. Tchrs. Math. (profl. devel. and status adv. com. 1987-90, program com. ann. meeting 1997), Ohio Coun. Tchrs. Math. (pres. 1974-76, v.p. 1970-73, sec. 1982-84, dir. state math. contest 1983-92, Christofferson-Fawcett award 1990), Ohio Math. Educators Leadership Coun. (pres. 1990-91, bd. dirs. 1988-92), Greater Canton Coun. Tchrs. Math. (pres. 1969-70), Math. Assn. Am. (pres. Ohio sect. 1983-84, editor 1977-83). Avocations: hiking, tennis, handball. Office: Baldwin-Wallace Coll Dept Math & Computer Sci 275 Eastland Rd Berea OH 44017-2005 Office Phone: 440-826-2006. Business E-Mail: rlittle@bw.edu.

LITTLE, ROBERT DAVID, library science professor; b. Milw., July 11, 1937; s. Kenneth Edwin and Grace Elizabeth (Terwilleger) L. BA, U. Wis., Milw., 1959; MA, U. Wis., 1964, PhD, 1972. Tchr., sch. librarian Sevastapol Pub. Schs., Sturgeon Bay, Wis., 1959-62; sch. librarian Highland Park (Ill.) High Sch., 1962-63; supr. sch. libraries Sevastapol/Gilbraltor Pub. Sch., Sturgeon Bay, 1963-65; state sch. library supr. Wis. Dept. Pub. Instrn., Madison, 1965-69, program adminstr., 1969-70; asst. prof. libr. sci. U. Wis., Milw., 1970-71, acting dir. Sch. Libr. Sci., 1971; assoc. prof. libr. sci. Ind. State U., Terre Haute, 1971-77, prof., 1977-97, chmn. dept., 1971-93. Cons. Ind. Nat. Network Study, Terre Haute, 1978-79; cons., researcher Nat. Ctr. Edn. Stats., Washington, 1978-79; mem. Ind. State Libr. Adv. Coun., Indpls., 1981-91. Co-author: Public Library Users and Uses, 1988; editor: Cataloging, Processing, Administering AV Materials, 1972; contbr. articles to profl. jours. Pres. West Cen. Ind. chpt. Ind. Civil Liberties Union, 1988-92. Edn. Act fellow U. Wis., Madison, 1967, 68. Mem. ALA, Am. Assn. Sch. Librs., Assn. Ind. Media Educators (pres. 1981-82, Peggy Leach Pfeiffer Svc. award 1987). Methodist. Avocations: reading, travel. Home: 500 W 43rd St Apt 22H New York NY 10036-4335

LITTLE, ROBERT EUGENE, engineering educator; b. Enfield, Ill., May 24, 1933; s. John Henry and Mary (Stephens) L.; m. Barbara Louina Farrell, Feb. 4, 1961; children: Susan Elizabeth, James Robert, Richard Roy, John William. BSME, U. Mich., 1959; MSME, Ohio State U., 1960; PhDME, U. Mich., 1963. Asst. prof. mech. engring. Okla. State U., Stillwater, 1963-65; assoc. prof. U. Mich., Dearborn, 1965-68, prof., 1968—. Author: Statistical Design of Fatigue Experiments, 1975, Probability and Statistics for Engineers, 1978, Mechanical Reliability Improvement, 2003. Mem. ASTM, Am. Statis. Assn. Home: 3230 Pine Lake Rd West Bloomfield MI 48324-1951 Office: U Mich 4901 Evergreen Rd Dearborn MI 48128-1491

LITTLE, STEPHANIE ANN, psychology professor, researcher; b. Canton, Ohio, Aug. 7, 1967; d. Richard Allen Little and Gail Koons Dailey; m. Matthew Lee Arntz, Feb. 3, 1967; children: Sophia Ellen Arntz children: Abigail LeeAnn Arntz. BA, Smith Coll., 1989; MA, PhD, Vanderbilt U., 2000. Predoctoral fellow in devel. psychopathology NIMH/Vanderbilt U., Nashville, 1994—96; statistician Vanderbilt U., Nashville, 1999—2002; asst. prof. Wittenberg U., Springfield, Ohio, 2002—. Clin. intern Vanderbilt U. Med. Ctr., Nashville, 1998—99. Contbr. articles to profl. jours. Vol. CASA, Nashville, 2000—01. Mem.: APA, Soc. for Rsch. in Child Devel., Phi Beta Kappa, Psi Chi, Sigma Chi (assoc.). Avocations: reading, crafts, movies, travel. Home: 3575 Queen Victoria Ct Beavercreek OH 45431 Office: Wittenberg Univ Psychology Dept Ward St at N Wittenberg Ave Springfield OH 45501-0720 Office Phone: 937-327-7484. Office Fax: 937-327-7481. Personal E-mail: slittle@wittenberg.edu.

LITTLE, STEVEN GILBERT, psychologist, director; b. Quincy, Mass., Aug. 24, 1954; s. George Ervin and Irene Ursula Little; m. Karen Angeleque Akin, May 21, 1998. BS, Tulane U., New Orleans, 1972—76; MS, U. New Orleans, 1977—79; PhD, Tulane U., New Orleans, 1983—87. Lic. psychologist State of N.Y., 2003, State of Calif., 2005. Asst. prof. Hofstra U., Hempstead, NY, 1987—91, assoc. prof., 1999—2002; asst. prof. Calif. State U., Northridge, 1991—93, No. Ill. U., DeKalb, 1993—97; assoc. prof. U. Ala., Tuscaloosa, 1997—99, SUNY, Albany, 2002—03; prof., dept. chair U. of the Pacific, Stockton, Calif., 2003—. Treas. Coun. of Dirs. of Sch. Psychology Programs, 1998—2003. Contbr. articles to profl. jours. Fellow: APA (pres., divsn. sch. psychology 2002); mem.: Am. Ednl. Rsch. Assn., Nat. Assn. Sch. Psychologists. Home: 5743 Westchester Cir Stockton CA 95219 Office: Univ of the Pacific Dept of Ednl and Sch Psychology Stockton CA 95211 Office Phone: 209-946-3276. Office Fax: 209-946-2380. E-mail: slittle@pacific.edu.

LITTLE, THOMAS M., public relations executive; b. Columbus, Ohio, Dec. 21, 1935; s. John William and Eulalia Josephine (Mayer) L.; m. Susan Mulford, Sept. 29, 1959; children: Carin Andrea, Debora Mayer, Sharon Mulford, Patricia Anne. BS in Journalism, Northwestern U., 1958; postgrad., Bradley U., 1958. Account supr. Philip Lesly Co., Chgo., 1962—65; v.p., account supr. Burson-Marsteller, N.Y.C., 1966—76; v.p. Foote Cone & Belding, Inc., N.Y.C., 1977-78; pres. FCB Pub. Rels., N.Y.C., 1978-81, Bus. Orgn., Inc. divsn. Carl Byoir & Assocs., N.Y.C., 1982, Tracy-Locke/BBDO Pub. Rels., Dallas, 1983-85; exec. v.p., gen. mgr. Manning, Selvage & Lee, N.Y.C., 1986; pres. T.J. Ross & Assocs., N.Y.C., 1986-87; pres., gen. mgr. Golin/Harris Communication, N.Y., 1987-91; pub. rels. cons., 1992—. Bd. dirs. Damon Runyon-Walter Winchell Cancer Fund, N.Y.C. Lt. (j.g.) USN, 1959-62. Mem. Am. Mktg. Assn., Pub. Rels. Soc. Am. (S.C. and Ga. chpts.), Hilton Head Island C. of C., Publicity Club N.Y.C., Mt. Kisco (N.Y.) Country Club, Sea Pines Country Club (Hilton Head Island), Lotos Club (N.Y.C.), Sigma Alpha Epsilon. Roman Catholic. Home and Office: PO Box 1959 43 Village E Rd Wilmington VT 05363-1959 Office Phone: 802-464-2767. Personal E-mail: littlevthh@aol.com.

LITTLE, W(ILLIA)M A(LFRED), language educator, researcher, musicologist; b. Boston, July 28, 1929; s. Wm. A. and Myrle A. (Holmes) L. BA, Tufts U., 1951; LTCL, Trinity Coll., London, 1952; MA, Harvard U., 1953; PhD, U Mich., 1961. Asst. prof. Williams Coll., Williamstown, Mass., 1957-63; assoc. prof., chair Tufts U., Medford, Mass., 1963-66; chair U. Va., Charlottesville, 1966-72, prof., 1966-95, prof. German and music emeritus, 1995—. Vis. prof. musicology U. Rochester, N.Y., 1996. Author: G.A. Bürger, 1974; editor: Mendelssohn-Complete Organ Works, 5 vols., 1987-90; editor The German Quarterly, 1970-78; contbr. articles to profl. jours. Cpl. U.S. Army, 1953-55. Sesquicentennial fellow U. Va., 1972-73, 78-79, 88-89. Mem. MLA (chair comp. lit. 1970-72), Am. Assn. Tchrs. German (nat. exec. coun. 1968-78), Am. Guild Organists (registrar Mass. chpt. 1949-53, dean Charlottesville chpt. 1977-78, registrar, archivist Ctrl. Fla. chpt. 1995-99, nat. com. profl. edn. 1990-2002), Am. Mus. Soc., Orgn. Hist. Soc., Am. Bach Soc., Neue Bachgesellschaft (Leipzig). Home: 245 Terrell Rd West Charlottesville VA 22901 E-mail: wal@virginia.edu.

LITTLE, WILLIAM ARTHUR, physicist, researcher; b. South Africa, Nov. 17, 1930; came to U.S., 1958, naturalized, 1964; s. William Henry and Margaret (Macleod) L.; m. Annie W. Smith, July 15, 1955; children— Lucy Claire, Linda Susan, Jonathan William. PhD, Rhodes U., S. Africa, 1953, Glasgow (Scotland) U., 1957. Faculty Stanford, 1958—, prof. physics, 1965-94; prof. emeritus, 1994—. Cons. to industry, 1960—; co-founder, chmn. MMR Techs. Inc., 1980—, 3L&T, Inc., 1999—. Recipient Deans award for disting. teaching Stanford U., 1975-76, Walter J. Gores award for excellence in teaching, Stanford U., 1979, IR-100 award Indsl. Rsch. and Devel., 1981; NRC Can. postdoctoral fellow Vancouver, Can., 1956-58, Sloan Found. fellow, 1959-63, John Simon Guggenheim fellow, 1964-65, NSF sr. postdoctoral fellow, 1970-71 Fellow Am. Phys. Soc.; mem. Am. Chem. Soc. Achievements include spl. research low temperature physics, superconductivity, neural network theory, cryogenics; holder 14 patents in area of cryogenics and med. instrumentation. Home: 15 Crescent Dr Palo Alto CA 94301-3106 Office: Stanford U Dept Physics Stanford CA 94305 Business E-Mail: bill@mmr.com.

LITTLE, WILLIAM GRADY (GRADY LITTLE), professional baseball coach; b. Abilene, Tex., Mar. 30, 1950; m. Debi Little. Player-coach Yankee orgn., 1971—73; coach Ea. League, West Haven, Conn., 1974; minor league coach Balt., 1980, FSL, Miami; mgr. Appalachian League Oriole's Blufield rookieclub; mgr. minor league Atlanta, 1980—95, mgr., 1986, Richmond, 1993—95; coach bullpen Nat. League West Divsn. Championships, San Diego, 1996; bench coach Indians; bench coach, instr. Boston Red Sox, 1997—99, mgr., 2002—03; asst. gen. mgr. Chicago Cubs, 2004—. Named Mgr. of Yr., Richmond, 1994; recipient Mgr. of Yr. awards, Baseball Am., Sporting News, 1992. Office: c/o Chicago Cubs 1060 W Addison St Chicago IL 60613-4397

LITTLEFIELD, DANIEL CURTIS, historian, educator, researcher; b. Denison, Tex., Sept. 29, 1941; s. Elroy Littlefield and Ophelia Marie Williams; m. Valinda Whitted, June 23, 1990. AB, Sacramento State U., 1964; MA, Johns Hopkins U., 1973, PhD, 1977. Instr. York Coll. CUNY, N.Y.C., 1973-77; asst. prof. Va. Commonwealth U., Richmond, 1977-78; assoc. prof. La. State U., Baton Rouge, 1978-88; prof. U. Ill.-Urbana, Urbana-Champaign, 1988-99; Carolina prof. U. S.C., Columbia, 1999—. Coun. Omohandro Inst. Early Am. History and Culture, Williamsburg, Va., 1996-99. Author: Rice and Slaves, 1981, Revolutionary Citizens, 1997. Mem. Am. Hist. Assn., So. Hist. Assn. (mem. exec. coun. 1998-2000), South Caroliniana Soc., Orgn. Am. Historians. Office: U SC Dept History Columbia SC 29208 Office Phone: 803-777-0810.

LITTLEFIELD, DAVID, professional sports team executive; Degree, U. Mass. Scout Detroit (Mich.) Tigers, 1989—91; with Montreal (Can.) Expos, 1991—96, dir. player devel., 1996—98; v.p., asst. gen. mgr. Fla. Marlins, 1998—2001; gen. mgr. Pitts. (Pa.) Pirates, 2001—. Mailing: 115 Federal St Pittsburgh PA 15212

LITTLEFIELD, JOHN WALLEY, geneticist, cell biologist, pediatrician; b. Providence, Dec. 3, 1925; s. Ivory and Mary Russell (Walley) Littlefield; m. Elizabeth Lascelles Legge, Nov. 11, 1950; children: Peter P., John W., Elizabeth I. MD, Harvard U., 1947; MHS, Johns Hopkins U., 1992. Diplomate Am. Bd. Internal Medicine. Intern Mass. Gen. Hosp., Boston, 1947-48, resident in medicine, 1948-50, staff, 1956-74, chief genetics unit children's service, 1966-73; assoc. in medicine Harvard U. Med. Sch., 1956-62, asst. prof. medicine, 1962-66, asst. prof. pediatrics, 1966-69, prof. pediatrics, 1970-73; prof., chmn. dept. pediatrics Johns Hopkins U. Sch. Medicine, Balt., 1974-85; pediatrician-in-chief Johns Hopkins U. Hosp., 1974-85; prof., chmn. dept. physiology Johns Hopkins U. Sch. Medicine, Balt., 1985-92. Author: Variation, Senescence and Neoplasia in Cultured Somatic Cells, 1976. With USNR, 1952—54. Fellow Guggenheim, 1965—66, Josiah Macy Jr. Found., Oxford U., 1979. Mem.: NAS, Assn. Am. Physicians, Am. Pediatric Soc., Am. Soc. Human Genetics, Soc. Pediatric Rsch., Tissue Culture Assn., Am. Soc. Clin. Investigation, Am. Soc. Biol. Chemists, Am. Acad. Arts and Scis., Phi Beta Kappa, Delta Omega, Alpha Omega Alpha. Home: 304 Golf Course Rd Owings Mills MD 21117-4114 Office: Johns Hopkins U Sch Medicine Dept Physiology Baltimore MD 21205 E-mail: jlittlef@jhmi.edu.

LITTLEFIELD, LAUREN MONTENEGRO, psychologist, educator; b. Bethesda, Md., June 21, 1969; d. Robert Alfred and Joyce Marie Montenegro; m. Paul Anton Littlefield, Aug. 17, 1996; children: Joseph Cameron, Matthew Anton. BA, Washington Coll., 1991; MS, Drexel U., 1994, D of Clin. Neuropsychology, 1997. Lic. clin. psychologist 2001. Postdoctoral fellow Woodrow Wilson Rehab. Ctr. U. Va., Fishersville, Charlottesville, 1997—98; assoc. prof. Washington Coll., Chestertown, Md., 1998—. Clin. neuropsychologist Dept. Juvenile Justice, Md., 2001—. Contbr. chpts. in books, articles to profl. jours. Vol. Upper Shore Cmty. Mental Health Ctr., Chestertown, 1998—. Recipient Alumni award for disting. tchr., Washington Coll., 2004; grantee, Carl Pacifico Found., 1996. Mem.: APA, Ea. Psychol. Assn., Sigma Xi. Republican. Lutheran. Office: Washington Coll 300 Washington Ave Chestertown MD 21620 Office Phone: 410-810-7152. Business E-Mail: llittlefield2@washcoll.edu.

LITTLEFIELD, PAUL DAMON, retired management consultant; b. Cambridge, Mass., June 8, 1920; s. W. Joseph and Sally Pastorius (Damon) L.; m. Emmy Farnsworth Neiley, June 19, 1943 (dec. Apr. 9, 1982); children: Diane Neiley Littlefield Ritsher, Elizabeth Damon Littlefield Lehman, Paul Damon Jr.; m. Lucy Jean Boyd, Dec. 30, 1983. AB, Harvard U., 1942, MBA with distinction, 1948. Assoc. Freeport Minerals Co., N.Y.C., 1948-50, 52-62, treas., 1956-62; v.p. fin., treas. Arthur D. Little, Inc., Cambridge, 1962-73, sr. v.p., CFO, 1973-85, cons., 1985—; pres. Brynmere Assoc., Inc., 1991-92. Asst. to pres. Coty, Inc., 1951-52; bd. mem. Cambridge Trust Co., 1965-2000. Hon. trustee, past chmn. Old Sturbridge Village, mem. investment com. With destroyers and submarines to Lt. cmdr., 1942, USNR, 1945. Baker scholar, Harvard U., 1948. Mem. Fin. Execs. Inst., Harvard Bus. Sch. Assn. Boston (past pres.), Treas.' Club of Boston, Cape Ann Hist. Assn. (bd. mgrs.). Home: 15 Norwood Heights Annisquam Gloucester MA 01930

LITTLEFIELD, ROBERT STEPHEN, communications educator, training consultant; b. Moorhead, Minn., June 21, 1952; s. Harry Jr. and LeVoyne Irene (Berg) L.; m. Kathy Mae Soleim, May 24, 1974; children: Lindsay Jane, Brady Robert. BS in Edn., Moorhead State U., 1974; MA, N.D. State U., 1979; PhD, U. Minn., 1983. Tchr. Barnesville (Minn.) Pub. Schs., 1974-78; teaching asst. N.D. State U., Fargo, 1978-79, lectr., 1979-81; teaching assoc. U. Minn., Mpls., 1981-82; instr. N.D. State U., Fargo, 1982-83, asst. prof., chmn., 1983-89, assoc. prof., chmn., 1989-90, interim dean, 1990-92, assoc. prof., chmn., 1992-94, prof., 1994—; dir. Inst. for Study of Cultural Diversity, 1992-97. Owner KIDSPEAK Co., Moorhead, 1987-97. Author/co-author: (series) KIDSPEAK, 1989-92; lyricist (centennial hymn) Built on a Triangle with Faith in the Triune, 1989; contbr. more than 50 articles to profl. jours. Vol. forensic coach Fargo Cath. Schs. Network, 1992—; mem. N.D. dist. com. Nat. Forensic League, 1995—; advisor to exec. coun. Nat. Jr. Forensic League, 1995—. Recipient Burlington No. award N.D. State U., 1988-89; named Outstanding Speech Educator, Nat. Fedn. High Sch. Activities Assn., 1990-91. Mem. Am. Forensic Assn. (sec. 1990-92), N.D. Speech and Theatre Assn. (historian 1989—, pres. 1985-87, Hall of Fame 1989, Scholar of Yr. 1989), N.D. Multicultural Assn., Speech Comm. Assn., Pi Kappa Delta (nat. coun. 1983—, nat. pres. 1991-93, nat. sec.-treas. 1993—), Fargo Lions Club (pres. 1990-91). Democrat. Lutheran. Office: ND State U 321G Minard Hall Fargo ND 58105

LITTLEFIELD, ROY EVERETT, III, association executive, law educator; b. Nashua, NH, Dec. 6, 1952; s. Roy Everett and Mary Ann (Prestipino) L.; m. Amy Root; children: Leah Marie, Roy Everett IV, Christy Louise. BA, Dickinson Coll., 1975; MA, Catholic U. Am., 1976, PhD, 1979. Aide U.S. Senator Thomas McIntyre, Democrat, N.H., 1975-78, Nordy Hoffman, U.S. Senate Sergeant-at-arms, N.H., 1979; dir. govt. rels. Nat. Tire Dealers and Retreaders Assn., Washington, N.H., 1979-84; exec. dir. Svc. Sta. and Automotive Repair Assn., Washington, NH, 1984—2003; exec. v.p. Svc. Sta. Dealers of Am., 1994—2003, Tire Industry Assn., 2003—. Faculty Cath. U. Am., Washington, 1980—; cons. Internat. Tire and Rubber Assn., 1984-2003, now exec. v.p. Author: William Randolph Hearst: His Role in American Progressivism, 1980, The Economic Recovery Act, 1982, The Surface: Transportation Assistance Act, 1984; editor Nozzle mag.; contbr. over 3300 articles to acad., profl. and legal jours. Mem. Nat. Dem. Club, 1978—. Mem. Am. Soc. Legal History, Md. Hwy. User's Fedn. (pres.), Am. Hwy. User's Alliance (treas., sec.), Nat. Capitol Area Transp. Fedn. (v.p.), N.H. Hist. Soc., Kansas City C. of C., Capitol Hill Club, Phi Alpha Theta. Roman Catholic. Home: 1707 Pepper Tree Ct Bowie MD 20721-3021 Office: 1532 Pointer Ridge Pl Ste G Bowie MD 20716-1883 Office Phone: 800-876-8372. Personal E-mail: royel3@aol.com.

LITTLEFIELD, WARREN, television executive; b. Lincoln, Neb. m. Theresa Littlefield; 2 children. Student, Am. U., Washington; grad. in psychology, Hobart Coll., Geneva, N.Y. With Westfall Prodns., N.Y.C.; dir. comedy devel. Warner Bros. TV, 1979; mgr. comedy devel. NBC, 1979—81, v.p. current comedy programs, 1981—85; sr. v.p series, spls. and variety programming NBC Entertainment, 1985—87, exec. v.p. prime time programs, 1987—90, pres., 1990—98; founder, prodr. Littlefield Co., 1999—; head programming Sony Pictures Entertainment, Inc., Culver City, Calif.; with Paramount Network TV, 2001—05, Touchstone TV, 2005—. Bd. dirs. Lauch Media, Inc. Prodr.: (TV films) The Last Giraffe, 1979; exec. prodr.: (TV series) Do Over, 2002, Like Family, 2003—04, Keen Eddie, 2003—04, Repo Cohen, 2004, Harry Green and Eugene, 2004, Foody Call, 2005—, Love, Inc., 2005—, others. Address: Launch Media Inc 2700 Pennsylvania Ave Santa Monica CA 90404-4066*

LITTLEJOHN, DAVID, writer; b. San Francisco, May 8, 1937; s. George Thomas and Josephine Mildred (Cullen) Littlejohn; m. Sheila Beatrice Hageman, June 10, 1963; children: Victoria, Gregory David. BA, U. Calif., Berkeley, 1959; MA, Harvard U., 1961, PhD, 1963. Asst. prof. English, U. Calif., Berkeley, 1963-69, assoc. prof. journalism, 1969-76, prof., 1976-97, vice chmn. acad. senate, chmn. senate policy com., 1984-86, assoc. dean Grad. Sch. Journalism, 1974-78, 85-86, 87-89, prof. emeritus, 1997—. Arts critic Sta. KQED-TV, San Francisco, 1965-75, PBS nationwide, 1971-72; critic and corr. London Times, 1975-89, Architecture mag., 1984-89, Wall Street Jour., 1990—. Author: Architect: The Life and Work of Charles W. Moore, 1984, The Ultimate Art: Essays Around and About Opera, 1992, The Fate of the English Country House, 1997, The Real Las Vegas, 1999, 11 other books; contbr. over 350 articles and 200 TV programs. Fulbright lectr., Montpellier, France, 1966-67; Am. Coun. Learned Socs. rsch. fellow, London, 1972-73, Berkeley fellow, 2004; NEH grantee 1976-77. Mem.: Am. Inst. Arch. (hon.), Arts Club Berkeley (sec.). Democrat. Roman Catholic. Home and Office: 719 Coventry Rd Kensington CA 94707-1403 Office Phone: 510-527-1554.

LITTLEJOHN, KENT OSCAR, lawyer; b. Terre Haute, Ind., Oct. 3, 1945; s. Elmer O. and Evelyn P. (Shawver) L.; m. Brenda K. Swisher Littlejohn, Apr. 2, 1966; children: Douglas, Jessica, Gregory. BS in Bus. Adminstrn., Ind. State U., 1966; JD, Ind. U., 1969. Bar: U.S. Supreme Ct. Nebr. 1969, U.S. Dist. Ct. Nebr. 1969, U.S. Tax Ct. 1972, U.S. Ct. Appeals 1972, U.S. Ct. Claims, 1977. Assoc. Baird, Holm, McEachen, Pedersen, Hamann & Strasheim, Omaha, 1969-72, ptnr., 1972—, mng. ptnr., 1991—. Dir. Great Plains Fed. Tax Inst., Lincoln, Nebr., 1972-2000, Nebr. Continuing Legal Edn. Svc., Lincoln, Nebr., 1975-84. Fellow Am. Coll. Tax Counsel, Nebr. State Bar Found., Nebr. Bar Assn., Omaha Bar Assn. Office: Baird Holm McEachen Pedersen Hamann & Strasheim 1500 Woodmen Tower Omaha NE 68102 E-mail: KLittlejohn@bairdholm.com.

LITTLEPAGE, GLENN E., social psychology educator; b. Dallas, Nov. 21, 1946; s. Gordon Ray and Mary Lucille Littlepage; 1 child from previous marriage, Nick; m. Anna Littlepage, June 1, 1986; 1 child, Morgan A. Jones. BS, U. N.Mex., 1969; MS, Kans. State U., 1971, PhD, 1974. Rsch. psychologist U.S. Army Retraining Brigade, Ft. Riley, Kans., 1971—73; prof. psychology dept. Mid. Tenn. State U., Murfreesboro, 1973—. Cons. editor Jour. Personality and Social Psychology, 2000-2001; assoc. editor Group Dynamics, 2001—. Contbr. articles to profl. jours. Mem. Soc. Exptl. Social Psychology, Soc. Personality and Social Psychology, Soc. for Indsl. and Orgnl. Psychology. Avocations: bass fishing, woodworking, stained glass, motorcycling. Office: Mid Tenn State U Box 534 Murfreesboro TN 37132

LITTLER, GENE ALEC, professional golfer; b. San Diego, Calif., July 21, 1930; s. Stanley Fred and Dorothy (Paul) L.; m. Shirley Mae Warren, Jan. 5, 1951; children: Curt Michael, Suzanne. Student, San Diego State Coll. Mem. U.S. Ryder Cup Team, 61, 63, 65, 67, 69, 71, 75. Served with USN, 1951-54. Achievements include winning Nat. Jr. Championship, 1948, Calif. State Open, 1953, Calif. State Amateur, 1953, Nat. Amateur Championship, 1953, also winning 29 PGA tour events including San Diego Open (as an amateur), 1954, U.S. Open, 1961, Canadian Open, 1965, Tournament of Champions, 1955, 56, 57, World Series of Golf, 1966, Taheiyo Masters, Japan, 1974, 75, Australian Masters, 1980, 15 sr. tour titles and Coca Cola Grand Slam, Japan, 1983, Fuji Elec. Grand Slam, Tokyo, Japan, 1987.

LITTLE RICHARD, (RICHARD WAYNE PENNIMAN), recording artist, pianist, songwriter, minister; b. Macon, Ga., Dec. 5, 1932; s. Bud and Leva Mae Penniman; m. Ernestine Campbell, 1957 (div.). BA, Oakwood Coll. Sem., Huntsville, Ala., 1961. Ordained to ministry Seventh Day Adventist Ch., 1961 (performed marriage of Bruce Willis and Demi Moore, Las Vegas). Began singing and dancing on streets of Macon, Ga., 1942; won talent shows in Atlanta, 1943 and 1951; toured with Dr. Hudson's Medicine Show and other shows, 1949-51; worked with own band doing dances and clubs, 1951-52, with Tempo Toppers in New Orleans, 1953-54; recording artist Peacock Records, Houston, 1953-54, Splty. Records, 1955-58, 64; toured in Big 10 Package shows, U.S., Australia and Gt. Brit., 1957-58; recording artist Veejay Records, 1964-65. Songs include Long Tall Sally, Tutti Frutti, Slippin' and Slidin', Rip it Up, Ready Teddy, Lucille, Send Me Some Lovin', Jenny, Jenny, Miss Ann, Keep A-Knockin', Good Golly Miss Molly, Baby Face, True Fine Mama, Kansas City, Bama Lama Bama Loo, Freedom Blues, Greenwood Mississippi; albums include Here's Little Richard, 1958, Little Richard 2, 1958, The Fabulous, 1959, Well Alright, 1959, Sings Gospel, 1964, Coming Home, 1964, Sings Freedom Songs, 1964, King of Gospel Songs, 1965, Wild & Frantic, 1965, The Explosive, 1967, The Explosive & Roy Orbison, 1970, The Rill Thing, 1971, King of Rock N Roll, 1971, Second Coming, 1971, All Time Hits, 1972, Rock Hard Rock Heavy, 1972, The Very Best Of, 1975, Georgia Peach, 1980, Get Down With It, 1982, Ooh! My Soul, 1983, Lucile, 1984, Shut Up, 1988, The Specialty Sessions, 1990, Greatest Songs, 1995, Mega-Mix, 1995; film appearances include The Girl Can't Help It, 1956, Don't Knock the Rock, 1957, She's Got It, 1957, Mr. Rock and Roll, 1957, Jimi Plays Berkeley, 1970, Let the Good Times Roll, 1973, Jimi Hendrix, 1973, Down and Out in Beverly Hills, 1985 Chuck Berry Hail! Hail! Rock 'n' Roll, 1987, Purple People Eater, 1988, Scenes from the Class Struggle in Beverly Hills, 1989, Magic Years, Vols. 1-3, 1989, Sunset Heat, 1991, The Naked Truth, 1992, The Last Action Hero, 1993, The Pickle, 1993, The History of Rock 'n' Roll, Vol. 1, 1995, Why Do Fools Fall in Love, 1998, Mystery, Alaska, 1999; TV appearances include Tonight Show, Merv Griffin Show, Mike Douglas Show, Smothers Brothers Show, American Bandstand, Glen Campbell Good Time Hour, Tom Jones Show, Midnight Special, Donny & Marie Show, The Godess of Love, 1988, Mother Goose Rock 'n' Rhyme, 1990, Happy Birthday Bugs!: 50 Looney Years, 1990, Columbo: Columbo & the Murder of a Rock Star, Sinatra: 80 Years My Way, 1995, The Late Shift, 1996, The Fifties, 1997, Motown 40: The Music is Forever, 1998, Hollywood Squares, 1998; stage appearances include Paramount Theatre, The Felt Forum, Wembley Stadium, Hollywood Paladium. Inducted Rock & Roll Hall of Fame, 1986. Achievements include being referred to as the Architect of Rock 'n Roll.

LITTLETON, HARVEY KLINE, artist; b. Corning, N.Y., June 14, 1922; s. Jesse Talbot and Bessie (Cook) L.; m. Bess Toyo Tamura, Sept. 6, 1947; children: Carol Louise Littleton Shay, Thomas Harvey, Kathryn Tamra (dec.), Maurine Bess, John Christopher. Student, U. Mich., 1939-42, B in Design, 1947; MFA, Cranbrook Acad. Art, 1951; DFA (hon.), Phila. U. of the Arts, 1982, RISD, 1996, U. Wis., 2000; Docorate (hon.), N.C. State U., Raleigh, 2004. Instr. ceramics Toledo Mus. Art, 1949-51; prof. art U. Wis., Madison, 1951-77, chmn. dept., 1964-67, 69-71, prof. emeritus, 1977—; curator Littleton Studios. Author: Glass Blowing - A Search for Form, 1971; one- and two-man exhbns. include Lee Nordness Galleries, N.Y.C., 1969-70, Maison de Culture, Liege, Belgium, 1974, J & L Lobmeyr, Vienna, 1974, Brooks Meml. Art Gallery, Memphis, 1975, Contemporary Art Glass Gallery, N.Y.C., 1977, 78, 79, Habatat Gallery, Detroit, 1980, 81, Heller Gallery, N.Y.C., 1980, 81, 82, 83, 84, 85, Glasmuseum Ebeltoft, Sweden, 1989, Royal Copenhagen Gallery, 1989, Finnish Glasmuseum, Riihimaki, Finland, 1989, Kunsthaus am Mus., Cologne, Germany, 1990, Immenhausen, Germany, 1990, Glasmuseum, Frauenau, Germany, 1992, Yokohama (Japan) Mus. Art, 1995, retrospective exhbn. originated by High Mus. Art, Atlanta, 1984, traveling to the Renwick Gallery, Am. Craft Mus., Iowa State U., Milw. Art Mus. and Portland (Maine) Mus. Art, originated at Mint Mus. Craft & Design, Charlotte, N.C., 1999-2000, traveling to Ark. Art Ctr. Decorative Arts Mus., Little Rock, St. John's Mus. Art, Wilmington, N.C., Hunter Mus. Art, Chattanooga, Elvehjem Art Ctr., Madison, Wis.; represented in permanent collections, Victoria and Albert Mus., London, museums in, Germany, Holland, Switzerland, Belgium, Austria and, Czechoslovakia, also, Met. Mus. Art, N.Y.C., Mus. Modern Art, N.Y.C., Am. Craft Mus., N.Y.C., L.A. County Mus. Art., L.A., Corning Mus. of Glass, Toledo Mus. Art, Detroit Art Inst., Milw. Art Center, Smithsonian Instn., Washington, High Mus. Art, Atlanta, Chrysler Mus., Norfolk, Va., U. Mich., U. Ill., Ohio State U., Phila. Mus. Art, The White House, Washington, numerous other pub. and pvt. collections. Bd. dirs. Penland Sch., N.C., pres. bd. dirs., 1986-88; pres., chmn. Littleton Co., Inc., Spruce Pine, N.C., 1981—. With Signal Corps U.S. Army, 1942-45, ETO. Recipient diploma of honor Glass Mus. Frauenau, Germany, Fine Arts award Gov. N.C., 1987, Master of Medium award James Renwick Alliance, 1997, Disting. Alumnus award U. Mich. Sch. Art, Wis. Visual Art Lifetime Achievement award, 2004, honor for contbn. and leadership to Studio Glass Movement Nat. Am. Glass Club, 2005; named Living Treasure, State N.C.; Rsch. grantee U. Wis., 1954, 57, 62, 73, 75, Toledo Mus. Art, 1962, grantee Louis Comfort Tiffany Found. grantee, 1970-71, Corning Glass Works, 1974, Nat. Endowment for Arts, 1978-79. Fellow Wis. Acad. Arts and Scis., Am. Crafts Coun. (trustee 1957, 61-64, trustee emeritus, gold medal 1983), Corning Mus. Glass (Rakow award for excellence in art of glass); mem. Nat. Coun. for Edn. in Ceramic Arts (hon.), Glass Art Soc. (hon. life, lifetime achievement award 1993), Am. Ceramic Soc. (hon. life), Nat. Assn. Schs. Art and Designs (Disting. Svc. in Visual Arts citation 1996, Urbanglass award for Lifetime Achievement in Glass 1998). Office Phone: 772-595-9845. E-mail: glassman@vol.com, hklittle@bellsouth.net.

LITTLETON, ISAAC THOMAS, III, retired library director; b. Hartsville, Tenn., Jan. 28, 1921; s. Isaac Thomas Jr. and Bessie (Lowe) L.; m. Dorothy Etta Young, Aug. 12, 1949; children— Sally Lowe Littleton Phillips, Thomas Young, Elizabeth Ann BA, U. N.C., 1943; MA, U. Tenn., Knoxville, 1950; MSLS, U. Ill., Champaign-Urbana, 1951, PhD, 1968. Circulation librarian, asst. librarian U. N.C., Chapel Hill, 1951-58; asst. dir. then dir. libraries N.C. State U., Raleigh, 1959-87, emeritus dir. libraries, 1987—. Mem. N.C. Libr. Networking Steering Com., Raleigh, 1982-85; bd. dirs. Southeastern Libr. Network, Atlanta, 1973-74, 83-86, chmn., 1985-86; chmn. Assn. Southeastern Rsch. Librs., 1969-71; mem. com. Gov.'s Conf. on Libr. and Info. Svcs., 1990. Author: The Literature of Agricultural Economics, 1969, State Systems of Higher Education and Libraries, 1977, D.H. Hill Library: An Informal History, 1993; editor: N.C. Union List of Scientific Serials, 1967. Bd. dirs., treas. Theater in Park, Raleigh, 1982-85, Friends of Wake County Pub. Librs.; sec. N.C. State U. Friends of Libr., Raleigh, 1964-87, bd. dirs., 1990-94, life mem. 1988; pres. Friends of N.C. Libr. for Blind and Physically Handicapped, 1989-93, bd. dirs. 1993-94; v.p. Wake County UN Assn., 1994-95, sec., 1999-2000, pres., 2001-04. Lt. (j.g.) USN, 1943-46, PTO. Council on Library Resources fellow, Washington, 1975-76 Mem. Southeastern Libr. Assn. (exec. bd. 1974-78), N.C. Libr. Assn. (exec. bd. 1969-71, hon. life), Torch Club (pres. Raleigh 1974-75), Raleigh Golden K Kiwanis Club (pres. 2001-02). Mem. Community United Ch. of Christ. Avocations: theater, reading. Home: 4813 Brookhaven Dr Raleigh NC 27612-5706 E-mail: littletons@mindspring.com.

LITTLETON, JESSE TALBOT, III, radiology educator; b. Corning, N.Y., Apr. 27, 1917; s. Jesse Talbot and Bessie (Cook) L.; m. Martha Louise Morrow, Apr. 17, 1943 (dec. 1994); children: Christine, Joanne, James, Robert, Denise; m. Mary Lou Durizch, Mar. 25, 1995. Student, Emory and Henry Coll., 1934-35, Johns Hopkins U., 1935-39; MD, Syracuse U., 1943. Diplomate Am. Bd. Radiology. Intern Buffalo Gen. Hosp., 1943; resident in medicine, surgery and radiology Robert Packer Hosp., Sayre, Pa., 1946-51, assoc. radiologist, 1951-53, chmn. dept. radiology, 1953-76; prof. radiology U. South Ala., Mobile, 1976-87, prof. emeritus, 1987—. Cons. in field. Author 4 textbooks; contbr. chpts. to books and articles to profl. jours., sci. exhibits to profl. confs. Served with M.C., U.S. Army, 1944-46, PTO. Fellow Am. Coll. Radiology; mem. AMA, Radiol. Soc. N.Am., Am. Roentgen Ray Soc., Ala. Acad. Radiology, Med. Assn. Ala., French Soc. Neuroradiology, Country Club of Mobile, Sigma Xi, Alpha Omega Alpha. Republican. Methodist. Achievements include research on conventional tomography, physical principles, equipment development and testing and clinical applications; transportation and radiology of acutely ill and traumatized patient; development of patient litter with removable top leading to placement of backboards in ambulances; development of dedicated trauma x-ray machine; angiography, development of first sheet film serialograph; development of equipment for sectional radiographic anatomy with Durizch. Home: 5504 Churchill Downs Ave Theodore AL 36582-9601 Office: U South Ala Med Ctr 2451 Fillingim St Mobile AL 36617-2238 Office Phone: 251-471-7674. E-mail: littletonjtandml@aol.com.

LITTLETON, TAYLOR DOWE, humanities educator; b. Birmingham, Ala., Mar. 14, 1930; s. M. Taylor and Florence (Longcrier) L.; m. Lucy Williams, Aug. 7, 1954; children: Dowe, George, Franklin, Mary Wood. BS, Fla. State U., 1951, MA, 1952, PhD, 1960. Tchg. fellow Fla. State U., Tallahassee, 1954-57; from instr. to prof. dept. English Auburn U., Ala., 1957—, dean undergrad. studies, 1968-71, v.p. for acad. affairs, 1972-83, W. Kelly Mosley prof. sci. and humanities, 1983—. Author: Advancing American Art: Painting, Politics, and Cultural Confrontation at Mid-century, 1989, 2d edit., 2005, Athletics and Academe: An Anatomy of Abuses and a Prescription for Reform, 1991, The Color of Silver: William Spratling, His Life and Art, 2000; author, editor: To Prove A Villain: The Case of King Richard III, 1964, The Idea of Tragedy, 1965; editor: multi-vol. series The Franklin Lectures in Sci. and Humanities: Approaching the Benign Environment, 1970; The Shape of Likelihood, 1974, A Time To Hear and Answer, 1977, The Rights of Memory, 1985; assoc. editor So. Humanities Rev., 1967-70. With U.S. Army, 1952—54. Mem. So. Atlantic MLA, Phi Kappa Phi, Omicron Delta Kappa, Phi Beta Kappa. Democrat. Episcopalian. Home: 415 Norman Cir Auburn AL 36830-6307 Office: Auburn U Dept English & Humanities Haley 9030 Auburn AL 36830

LITTLEWOOD, DOUGLAS BURDEN, brokerage house executive; b. Buffalo, Sept. 24, 1922; s. Frank and G. Joan (Burden) L.; m. Jevene Hope Baker, July 2, 1949; children— Douglas Baker, Dean Houston, Laurie Littlewood Vogelsang BS in Mech. Engring, Rensselaer Poly. Inst., 1945; MBA, Harvard, 1947. Sales engr. Otis Elevator Co., 1948-49; asst. to sec. Nat Gypsum Co., Buffalo, 1949-52, sec., 1952-67; investment banker Hornblower & Weeks, 1967-68; pres. Littlewood Assocs., Inc., 1968-95, chmn. bd., 1995—. Past pres. Greater Niagara Frontier coun. Boy Scouts Am.; active Buffalo YMCA, United Fund; bd. dirs. Presbyn. Homes of Western N.Y.; bd. dirs., chmn. emeritus Salvation Army; v.p. N.E. region Boy Scouts Am. Served to lt. (j.g.) USNR, 1943-46. Recipient Silver Beaver, 1965; recipient Silver Antelope, 1978, Disting. Eagle, 1979 Mem. Country Club of Sebring, Buffalo Jr. C. of C. (past dir., chmn. bd.), Am. Soc. Corp. Secs., Buffalo Canoe Club (past commodore), Buffalo Country Club. Home: 1121 Lakeview Dr Sebring FL 33870-4938 Office: 22 Dawnbrook Ln Buffalo NY 14221-4930 E-mail: lotawood22@aol.com. *If you truly believe you are happy and successful then, and only then, you truly are.*

LITTMAN, DAN R., microbiologist; MD, PhD, U. Wash., 1980. Helen L. and Martin S. Kimmel prof. molecular immunology, prof. pathology and microbiology NYU Sch. Medicine; dir. molecular pathogenesis program, Skirball Inst. NYU; investigator Howard Hughes Med. Rsch. Inst. Mem.: Nat. Acad. Scis. Office: Skirball Inst Biomolecular Medicine 2nd Fl Lab 17 540 First Ave New York NY 10016 Business E-Mail: dan.littman@med.nyu.edu.

LITTMAN, EARL, advertising and public relations executive; b. Jan. 29, 1927; s. David and Cele Littman; m. Natalie Carol Jacobson, Dec. 21, 1948; children: Erica Humphrey, Bonnie Likover, Michael L. Littman. BS, NYU, 1948. With George N. Khan, N.Y.C., 1948-50, Jones & Brown, Pitts., 1950-52; chmn., CEO Goodwin, Dannenbaum, Littman & Wingfield Inc., Houston, 1952-92; pres. The Advertizing Firm, Inc., 1992, Two Nerds and a Suit, Inc., 1994; chmn., CEO Point of Purchase Broadcasting Co. Founder, inventor new wireless advtsg. in-store P.O.P. Broadcasting Co., 2003—. Bd. dirs. Ctr. for Am. History, U. Tex., mem. Chancellor's Coun.; chmn. Anti-Defamation League, Tex., 1984; bd. dirs. Am. Heart Assn., Houston, Glassell Sch, Houston chpt. World Pres. Orgn., Ctr. for Am. History, U. Tex.; active End Hunger Network, Houston, 1984; active NCCJ; founder, exec. dir. Drugs Kill Prevention/Edn. Program, 1997; exec. dir. Drugs Kill. With USN, 1944-45. Recipient Silver medal Am. Advt. Fedn., 1989, Outstanding Vol. award Savvy, 1990, Anti-Defamation League Popkin award, 1990, End Hunger Network award, 1992; Am. Heart Assn. honoree, 1988, John McMahon award Am. Heart Assn., 1996; Heritage award Am. Women in Radio and TV, 1992, Cmty. Champion award Tex. Commn. Alcohol and Drug Abuse, 2000; named Mktg. Man of Yr., Am. Mktg. Assn., 1999. Mem.: Am. Advtsg. Agy. Assn. (gov. Houston chpt. 1990, Paul Dudley White award 1991), Marathon Assn., Winedale Hist. Assn. (former pres.), Houston Advt. Fedn. (Living Legend award 1993, Heritage award), Affiliated Advt. Agys. Internat. (pres. 1979—80). Office Phone: 713-621-7678. Personal E-mail: papaearl@hotmail.com. E-mail: earl@popbroadcasting.com.

LITTMAN, HOWARD, chemical engineer, educator; b. Bklyn., Apr. 22, 1927; s. Morris and Gertrude (Goldberg) L.; m. Arline F. Caruso, July 3, 1955; children— Susan Joy, Vicki Kim, Paul William. BChemE, Cornell U., 1951; PhD, Yale U., 1956. Asst., then assoc. prof. Syracuse U., 1955-65; on leave to Brookhaven Nat. Lab., summer 1957, Argonne Nat. Lab., 1957-59; faculty Rensselaer Poly. Inst., Troy, N.Y., 1965—, prof. chem. engring., 1967—2001, rsch. prof. emeritus, 2001—. Vis. prof. Imperial Coll., London, 1971—72, Chonn'am Nat. U., Kwangju, Republic of Korea, 1988; Fulbright lectr. U. Belgrade, Yugoslavia, 1972. Patentee in field; contbr. articles to profl. jours. A founder Onondaga Hill Free Library, 1961, trustee, 1961-65, pres., 1965; a founder Onondaga Library System, 1962, trustee, 1962-65, v.p., 1965; trustee Capital Dist. Library Council, 1969-75, pres., 1970, 73. Served with USN, 1945-46. IREX grantee U. Belgrade, summer 1973; recipient Disting. Faculty award Rensselaer Poly. Inst., 1988. Mem. Am. Inst. Chem. Engrs., Am. Chem. Soc., Sigma Xi. Home: 7 Tulip Tree Ln Schenectady NY 12309-1837 Office: Rensselaer Poly Inst Troy NY 12180-3590 Office Phone: 518-276-6039.

LITTMAN, MARLYN KEMPER, information scientist, educator; b. Mar. 26, 1943; d. Louis and Augusta (Jacobs) Janofsky; m. Bennett I. Kemper, Aug. 1, 1965 (dec. June 1987); children: Alex Randall, Gari Hament, Jason Myles; m. Lewis Littman, Apr. 22, 1990. BA, Finch Coll., 1964; MA in Anthropology, Temple U., 1970; MA in Info. Sci., U. South Fla., 1983; PhD in Info. Sci., Nova Southeastern U., 1986. Dir. Hist. Broward County Preservation Bd., Hollywood, Fla., 1979—87; automated systems libr. Broward County Main Libr., Ft. Lauderdale, Fla., 1984—86; assoc. prof. info. sci. Nova U., Ft. Lauderdale, Fla., 1987—94, dir. info. sci. doctoral program, 1987—94; prof. info. sci. Nova Southeastern U., Ft. Lauderdale, Fla., 1995—. Weekly columnist Ft. Lauderdale News, 1975—79; contbg. editor Hyper Nexus-Jour. Hypermedia and Multimedia Studies, 1996—2000; assoc. editor Jour. On-Line Learning, 1997—2002. Author: A Comprehensive Documented History of the City of Pompano Beach, 1982, A Comprehensive History of Dania, 1983, A Comprehensive History of Hallandale, 1984, A Comprehensive History of Deerfield Beach, 1985, A Comprehensive History of Plantation, 1986, A Comprehensive History of Davie, 1987, Networking: Choosing a LAN Path to Interconnection, 1987, Building Broadband Networks, 2002; author: (with others) Mosaics of Meaning, New Ways of Learning, 1996; contbr. articles to profl. jours., chapters to books. Pub. info. officer Broward County Hist. Commn., 1975—79; vice chmn. Broward County Adv. Bd., 1987—92; bd. dirs. Ctrl. Agy. Jewish Edn., 1992—94. Recipient Judge L. Clayton Nance award, 1977, Broward County Hist. Commn. award, 1979. Mem.: IEEE, Assn. Computing Machinery, Info. Resources Mgmt. Assn. Internat., Phi Kappa Phi, Beta Phi Mu, Upsilon Pi Epsilon. Home: 2845 NE 35th St Fort Lauderdale FL 33306-2007 Office: Nova Southeastern U Grad Sch Computer and Info Sci 3301 College Ave Fort Lauderdale FL 33314 Office Phone: 954-262-2078. Business E-Mail: marlyn@nova.edu.

LITTMAN, RICHARD ANTON, psychologist, educator; b. NYC, May 8, 1919; s. Joseph and Sarah (Feinberg) L.; m. Isabelle Cohen, Mar. 17, 1941; children— David, Barbara, Daniel, Rebecca. AB, George Washington U., 1943; postgrad., Ind. U., 1943- 44; PhD, Ohio State U., 1948. Faculty U. Oreg., 1948—, prof. psychology, 1959—, chmn. dept., 1963-68, vice provost acad. planning and resources, 1971-73, prof. emeritus, 1990. Vis. scientist Nat. Inst. Mental Health, 1958-59 Contbr. articles to profl. jours. Sr. postdoctoral fellow NSF, U. Paris, 1966-67; sr. fellow Nat. Endowment for Humanities, U. London, 1973-74; Ford Found. fellow, 1952-53; recipient U. Oreg. Charles H. Johnson Meml. award, 1980. Mem. APA, Western Psychol. Assn., Am. Psychol. Soc., Soc. Research and Child Devel., Psychonomics Soc., Animal Behavior Soc., Soc. Psychol. Study of Social Issues, Internat. Soc. Developmental Psychobiology, History of Sci. Soc., Am. Philos. Assn., AAUP, Sigma Xi. Home: 3625 Glen Oak Dr Eugene OR 97405-4736 Office: U Oreg Dept Psychology Eugene OR 97403 E-mail: rlittman@darkwing.uoregon.edu.

LITTON, ANDREW, musical director; b. N.Y.C., May 16, 1959; BS, MBA, Juilliard Sch. Music; Doctorate (hon.), Univ. Bournemouth. Music dir. Dallas Symphony, 1994—. Recipient Sanford Medal for musical achievement, Yale Univ. Office: Morton H Meyerson Symphonic Ctr 2301 Flora St Ste 300 Dallas TX 75201-2404*

LITTOOY, FRED NELSON, peripheral vascular surgeon; b. Kansas City, Mo., May 6, 1943; s. Fred Clyde and Helen Virginia (Johnson) L.; children: Fred Cameron, Heather Lynn, Chandra Renee, Stephanie Amber; m. Karla Van Drunen Evans, Sept. 1, 1996. AB, U. Kans., 1965, MD, 1969. Intern, resident U. Calif., San Francisco, 1969-72, 74-76, wound healing rsch., 1972-74, fellow in peripheral vascular surgery, 1976-77; from asst. prof. to prof. surgery Loyola U. Med. Ctr., Maywood, 1977—2000, program dir. peripheral vascular surgery, 1997—2005; staff physician, chief divsn. peripheral vascular surgery Hines (Ill.) VA Med. Ctr., 1983—. Mem. editl. bd. Vascular Surgery, 1995—. Fellow ACS; mem. Soc. for Vasc. Surgery, Western Surg. Assn., Midwestern Vascular Surg. Soc. (treas. 1985-88, pres. 1991). Avocations: travel, classical and jazz music, photography, hiking. also: Hines VA Med Ctr Vascular Surgery Divsn Hines IL 60141 Office Phone: 708-202-8387 21720. Business E-Mail: fred.littooy@med.va.gov. E-mail: flittooy@sbcglobal.net.

LITUCHY, GREGG, dentist; b. NYC, Mar. 31, 1959; BA in Biology, SUNY, Binghamton, 1980; DDS, Columbia U., 1984. Gen. practice intern L.I. Coll. Hosp., 1984—85; pvt. practice cosmetic dentistry Lowenberg and Lituchy, N.Y.C., 1985—. Cons. ABC's Extreme Makeover; guest Oprah Winfrey Show, Good Morning Am., The View; former spokesman Listerine mouthwash; formerspokesman Crest toothpaste. Mem.: ADA, Dental Soc. State of N.Y., Am. Acad. Implant Dentistry, Internat. Congress of Oral Implantologists, Am. Acad. Cosmetic Dentistry, Acad. Gen. Dentistry. Office: Lowenberg and Lituchy 230 Central Park S New York NY 10019 Office Phone: 212-586-2890. Office Fax: 212-586-2889.

LITVACK, SANFORD MARTIN, lawyer; b. Bklyn., Apr. 29, 1936; s. Murray and Lee M. (Korman) L.; m. Judith E. Goldenson, Dec. 30, 1956; children: Mark, Jonathan, Sharon, Daniel. BA, U. Conn., 1956; LLB, Georgetown U., 1959. Bar: N.Y. 1964, D.C. 1979. Trial atty. antitrust div. Dept. Justice, Washington, 1959-61, asst. atty. gen., 1980-81; assoc. firm Donovan, Leisure, Newton & Irvine, NYC, 1961-69, ptnr., 1969-80, 81-86, Dewey, Ballantine, Bushby, Palmer & Wood, NYC, 1987-91; vice chmn. bd. The Walt Disney Co., Burbank, Calif., 1991—2001, also bd. dirs.; ptnr. Quinn, Emanuel, Urquhart, Oliver & Hedges, 2001. Bd. dirs. Bet Tzedek. Fellow Am. Coll. Trial Lawyers; mem. ABA, Fed. Bar Coun., N.Y. State Bar Assn. (sec. antitrust sect. 1974-77, chmn. antitrust sect. 1985-86), Va. Bar Assn., Calif. Inst. of Arts (bd. dirs.), Am. Arbitration Assn. (bd. dirs.).

LITVIN, INESSA ELIZABETH, piano educator; b. Gorky, Russia, Sept. 13, 1939; came to U.S., 1980; d. Aron J. and Elizabeth I. (Shapiro) Frenkel; m. Edward J. Litvin, Aug. 22, 1975. MA in Piano Performing magna cum laude, Conservatory, Leningrad, Russia, 1965. Prof. music Ctrl. Music Sch., Leningrad, 1965-79; pvt. instr. piano Encinitas, Calif., 1980—. Recipient prize Shostakovich Piano Competition, Leningrad, 1964, recognition for exceptional artistic achievements of students Nat. Found. Advancement in Art, Miami, Fla., 1999. Mem. Calif. Assn. Profl. Music Tchrs., Music Tchrs. Assn. Calif. Home: 1632 Jerrilynn Pl Encinitas CA 92024-4757 E-mail: ielitvin@adelphia.net.

LITVINE, VLADIMIR A., research scientist, physicist; b. Dnepropetrovsk, Ukraine, June 7, 1969; s. Andrei and Olga Litvine; m. Olena Kuznyetsova, Aug. 6, 2004. BA, Moscow Inst. of Phsyics and Tech., 1993; MS in Physics, Moscow Inst. of Physics and Tech., 1993. Scientist Moscow Inst. of High Energy Physics, Protvino, Russia, 1993—99; sr. engr. in high energy physics Calif. Inst. of Tech., Pasadena, Calif., 1999—. Mem. of editl. bd., Electronic Mag. Insider - Computing Security, Calif., 1998—99; program com. mem. Confs. Digital Librs., 2000—. Contbr., articles to profl. and sci. jours. Mem.: NY Acad. Scis. Achievements include research in Monte Carlo simulation of Higgs diphoton decays for CMS at LHC; Monte Carlo study of RS-1 graviton diphoton decay channel for CMS at LHC; calibration of electromagnetic caolrimeter for CMS at LHC; Grid-enabled highly distributed cross-cluster computing system for High energy physics; Multi-scaling analysis in scaling behaviour in transition economies; Highly distributed cross-platform automatic job submission system in multi-cluster environment; Grid - enabled physics analysis for CMS at LHC; Multi-scaling analysis and scaling behaviour of economies in transition. Office: Calif Inst Tech 1200 E California Blvd MC 256-48 Pasadena CA 91125 Office Phone: 626-395-6659. Personal E-mail: litvin@hep.caltech.edu.

LITVINOFF, SAUL, law educator, lawyer; b. Buenos Aires, Mar. 15, 1925; m. wife deceased, 1 daughter AB, Univ. Buenos Aires, 1944, LLB, 1949, SJD, SCD, Univ. Buenos Aires, 1956; LLM, Yale Univ., 1964. Assoc. Ibero Berenguer & Assoc., Buenos Aires, 1949—54, ptnr., 1954—59; sr. ptnr. Merlino Litvinoff & Rodriguez, Buenos Aires; vis. prof. Univ. Puerto Rico, 1963—65, La. State Univ., 1965—67, assoc. prof., 1967, prof., 1970—85; Boyd prof. La State Univ., 1985—93; Boyd prof. & Stockwell prof. La. State Univ., 1993—; dir. Ctr. Civil Law Studies, La. State Univ., 1977—. Vis. prof. Universite Catholique de Louvain, Belgium, 1986—94. Author: of 17 books on banking & finance laws; contbr. articles to prof. jour. Recipient Medaille Henri Capilant, France, Order Jose Cecilio del Valle, Honduras, Sauberan medal, Argentina, James William Rivers award, Univ. Southwestern La., Year 2000 Prof. Law award, La. Bar Found. Mem.: Argentine Bar, La. State Bar Inst., Honduras Bar (hon.), Costa Rica Bar (hon.), Argentine Nat. Acad. Legal Sci., Order of the Coif. Office: Louisiana State University Hebert Law Center Baton Rouge LA 70803

LITVINOV, DMITRI, engineering educator; b. Donetsk, Ukraine, July 5, 1970; s. Alexander Litvinov and Natalia Litvinova; m. Julia Novikov; children: Mitchell children: Alexandra. BS in Gen. and Applied Physics, Moscow Inst.Physics and Tech., Dolgoprudny, Moscow Dist., Russia, 1992; MS in Physics, U. Miami, Coral Gables, Fla., 1994; MS in Elec. Engring., U.Michigan, Ann Arbor, 1997, PhD, 1999. Rsch. asst. Inst. Solid State Physics, Chernogolovka, 1990—92, U. Miami, Coral Gables, Fla., 1992—94, U. Mich., Ann Arbor, 1994—97, Horace H. Rackham fellow, 1998; vis. scientist Carnegie Mellon U., Pitts., 1999—2000; rschr. Seagate Rsch., Pitts., 1998—2003; assoc. prof. elec. and computer engring. U. Houston, 2003—. Peer reviewer Am. Inst. Physics, Argonne, 1997—; peer reviewer Elsevier Publs., Amsterdam, Netherlands, 1998—, Publs. IEEE Magnetics Soc., Pitts., 1999—; co-chair North Am. Perpendicular Magnetic Rec. Conf., Coral Gables, 2001—02; adj. prof. U. Miami, Coral Gables, Fla., 2001—; co-chair Joint N.Am. Perpendicular Magnetic Rec. Conf. and Japanese Perpendicular Magnetic Rec. Conf., Monterey, Calif., 2002—, IEEE Conf. on Nanoscale Devices and Sys. Integration, Miami, Fla., 2004. Author: (Research) Cubic Boron Nitride, 1999 (Horace H. Rackham Fellowship, 1998); contbr. articles to profl. jours. Mem.: IEEE (publs. chair Transactions on Magnetics 2001—, guest editor "Nano-technology"), Am. Phys. Soc., Materials Rsch. Soc. Achievements include 98 provisional patents filed in data storage field, 1999-; 30 utility patent applications filed Magnetic Rec. Tech., 1997-; 3 issued U.S. patents; research in gen. contbns. to materials and device engring. Office: Univ Houston Dept Elec & Computer Engring N 308 Engring Bldg 1 Houston TX 77204-4005 Personal E-mail: dmitri.litvinov@ieee.org.

LITWACK, GERALD, biochemistry researcher, educator, administrator; b. Boston, Jan. 11, 1929; s. David and Edith Jean (Berkman) Lytell; m. Patricia Lynn Gorog, Feb., 1956 (div. 1973); 1 child, Claudia; m. Ellen Judith Schatz, Aug. 31, 1973; children: Geoffrey Sandor, Katherine Victoria. BA, Hobart Coll., 1949; MS, U. Wis., 1950, PhD, 1953. Postdoctoral fellow Biochem. Labs. U. Paris, 1953-54; asst. prof. Rutgers U., New Brunswick, NJ, 1954-60; trainee Oak Ridge Inst. Nuc. Studies, 1955; assoc. prof. U. Pa., Phila., 1960-64; Carnell prof., dep. dir. Fels Inst., Sch. of Medicine Temple U., Phila., 1964-91; prof., chair dept. pharmacology Thomas Jefferson U., Phila., 1991-96, also dep. dir. Kimmel Cancer Inst., 1991-97; assoc. dir. for basic sci. Kimmel Cancer Ctr., Phila., 1992-97, prof., chmn. dept. biochemistry and molecular pharmacology, 1996—2003, emeritus, 2003, dir. Ctr. Apoptosis Rsch., assoc. dean sci. affairs, 1996-2001, vice dean for rsch., 2001—03; vis. scholar Dept. Biol. Chemistry David Geffen Sch. Medicine UCLA, 2004—. Chmn. adv. com. am. Cancer Soc., NYC, 1977-80; mem. adv. panel NSF, Washington, 1980-84; mem. ad hoc panels NIH, Bethesda, 1985, 89, reviewer, 1977, 84, 91, cons. Nat. Inst. Environ. Health Sci., 1982; mem. ad hoc panels Israel Cancer Rsch. fund Sci. Rev. Panel, 1992-93, US Army Breast Cancer Study Sect., 1994; mem. US Army Neurotoxicology and Neurodegeneration Study Sect., 1997, NIH, NIDDK, subcom. B Study Sect.,1998, NIH, NIDDK Spl. Emphasis Panel, Primary Reviewer Molecular Endocrinology,2003, others; councilor Soc. for Exptl. Biology and Medicine, NYC, 1984-88; cons. Franklin Inst., 1976, Georgetown U., 1980; reviewer Haverford Coll., 1976, NIH programs, 1984, 91; mem. adv. bd. Diabetes Rsch. Ctr. U. Pa., 1996—; mem. joint steering com. for pub. policy Rockville, Md., 1997—; evaluator Roswell Park Meml. Inst., 1978; mem. sci. adv. bd. Norris Cotton Cancer Ctr. Dartmouth Med. Sch., 1984—; Jefferson rep. U. Catania, Sicily, 1994— 2001, U Naples, Italy, 2001--; mem. subcom. B study sect. NIH, NIDDK, 1998; mem. subcom. on rsch. Sharpe-Strumia Found., 1998—; external reviewer NICHD, NIH, 1999; vis. prof. U. Calif., Berkeley, 1956, U. Calif., San Francisco, 1972; hon. prof. biochemistry Rutgers U., 1957-60; vis. scientist Courthauld Inst. Biochemistry, U. London, 1971; mem. study sect. SPORE breast and prostate cancer rsch., NIH and NCI, 2000-01; vis. scholar dept. biol. chemistry David A. Geffen Sch. Medicine at UCLA, 2004—. Bd. dirs. Sharpe-Strumia Found. Bryn Mawr Hosp., 1997—2003. Recipient Rsch. Career Devel. award NIAMD, NIH, 1963-69, Pub. Svc. award Chapel of Four Chaplains, 1977, Faculty Rsch. award Temple U., 1987. Mem. Endocrine Soc. (program com. 1991-93, sci. and edn. com. 1992-93, ann. meeting steering com. 1990-93, com. on sci. and ednl. programs 1992-93), Am. Soc. Biochemistry and Molecular Biology, Am. Soc. Pharmacology and Exptl. Therapeutics, Am. Assn. Cancer Rsch. (chair task force on endocrinology 1995, endocrinology and signal transduction subcom., program com., 1995-96, Tellers Com., 2002), Am. Chem. Soc., Assn. of Am. Med. Coll. (GREAT group 1997—2003, congl. liaison 1998-2003), Assn. for Med. Sch. Pharmacology, Assn. of Med. and Grad. Dept. of Biochemistry. Achievements include discovery and identification of the glucocorticoid receptor; co-discovery of ligandin (glutathione S-Transferase family) mechanism of glucocorticoid receptor activation, studies in apoptosis, immunophilin signal transduction, basic studies in asthma, glucocorticoid induced gene expression. Office: 4610 Ledge Ave Toluca Lake CA 91602 Business E-Mail: gerry.litwack@mail.tju.edu.

LITWACK, LEON FRANK, historian, educator; b. Santa Barbara, Calif., Dec. 2, 1929; s. Julius and Minnie (Nitkin) L.; m. Rhoda Lee Goldberg, July 5, 1952; children: John Michael, Ann Katherine. BA, U. Calif., Berkeley, 1951, MA, 1952, PhD, 1958. Asst. prof., then assoc. prof. history U. Wis., Madison, 1958-65; mem. faculty U. Calif., Berkeley, 1965—, prof. history, 1971—, Alexander F. and May T. Morrison prof. history, 1987—; dir. NDEA Inst. Am. History, summer 1965. Vis. prof. U. S.C., 1975, Colo. Coll., Sept. 1974, 79, La. State U., 1985; Fulbright prof. Am. history U. Sydney, Australia, 1991, Moscow (USSR) State U., 1980; Wentworth scholar-in-residence U. Fla., Spring 1983; mem. Nat. Afro-Am. History and Culture Commn., 1981-83; mem. screening com. Fulbright Sr. Scholar Awards, 1983-86; bd. acad. advisors The American Experience Sta. WGBH-TV, 1986—, Africans in America, WGBH-TV, 1990-98; Ford Found. prof. So. studies U. Miss., 1989; mem. exec. com. of dels. Am. Coun. of Learned Socs., 1993-96; lectr. in field. Author: North of Slavery: The Negro in the Free States, 1790-1860, 1961, Been in the Storm So Long: The Aftermath of Slavery, 1979, Trouble in Mind: Black Southerners in the Age of Jim Crow, 1998; (film) To Look for America, 1971; co-author: The United States, 1981, rev. edit., 1991, Without Sanctuary: Lynching Photography in America, 2000; editor: American Labor Movement, 1962; co-editor: Reconstruction, 1969, Black Leaders in the Nineteenth Century, 1988, Harvard Guide to African American History, 2001. Mem. Bradley Commn. on History in Schs., 1987-90, Schomburg Commn. for the Preservation of Black Culture; trustee Nat. Coun. for History Edn., 1990-96, mem. steering com. 1994 NAEP History Consensus Project; chair U. Calif. Acad. Senate Libr. Com. 1995-97. Served with AUS, 1953-55. Recipient Excellence in Teaching award U. Calif., Berkeley, 1967, 95, Disting. Tchg. award, 1971, 95 Mem. Orgn. Am. Historians (chmn. nominations bd. 1975-76, exec. bd. 1983-85, pres. 1986-87), Am. Hist. Assn. (chmn. program com. 1980-81), So. Hist. Assn. (bd. dirs. 2003—), Soc. Am. Historians, Am. Acad. Arts and Scis., Am. Antiquarian Soc., U. Calif. Alumni Assn., Assn. for the Study African Am. Life and History, PEN Am. Ctr. Office: U Calif Dept History 3229 Dwinelle Hall Berkeley CA 94720-2550

LITWILLER, ROGER W., anesthesiologist, medical association executive; MD, Univ. Fla. Coll. Medicine, Gainesville. Diplomate Am. Bd. Anesthesiology. Resident in anesthesiology Case Western Reserve Univ., Cleveland, Univ. Va., Charlottesville; staff anesthesiologist, past chief anesthesia svc. Carilion Roanoke Mem. Hosp., Va. Fellow: Am. Coll. Anesthesiologists; mem.: Am. Soc. Anesthesiologists (1st v.p. 2002, pres. elect 2003, pres. 2004), Va. Soc. Anesthesiologists (pres. 1986—88). Office: 3001 Burnleigh Rd SW Roanoke VA 24014 Office Phone: 540-345-0289.

LITWIN, BURTON HOWARD, lawyer; b. Chgo., July 26, 1944; s. Manuel and Rose (Boehm) L.; m. Nancy I. Stein, Aug. 25, 1968; children: Robin Litwin Levine, Keith Harris, Jill Stacy. BBA with honors, Roosevelt U., 1966; JD cum laude, Northwestern U., 1970. Bar: Ill. 1970, U.S. Dist. Ct. (no. dist.) Ill. 1970, U.S. Tax Ct. 1971, U.S. Ct. Fed. Claims 1983; CPA, Ill. Sr. counsel Neal, Gerber & Eisenberg, Chgo., 2002—. Author chpts. of books; contbr. articles to profl. jours. Recipient Gold Watch award Fin. Execs. Inst., Chgo., 1965. Mem. ABA (chmn. nonfiler task force for No. Ill. 1992-94), Chgo. Bar Assn. (chmn. adminstrv. practice subcom., fed. taxation subcom. 1982-83) Avocations: roses, painting, photography. Office: Neal Gerber & Eisenberg Two N LaSalle St Ste 2200 Chicago IL 60602-3801 Office Phone: 312-269-5986. Business E-Mail: blitwin@ngelaw.com. E-mail: gosox13@aol.com.

LITWIN, PAUL JEFFREY, lawyer; b. Boston, May 4, 1955; s. Robert I. and Tamara D. L.; m. Robin Gile, June 28, 1986; children: Peter Hill, Alexander James. BA with honors, U. Wis., 1977; JD cum laude, Suffolk U., 1983. Paralegal Hale and Dorr, Boston, 1979-80; clk. to presiding justice Mass. Superior Ct., Boston, 1983-84; staff atty. Mass. Supreme Ct., Boston, 1984-85; sports, entertainment atty. Bob Woolf Assocs., Boston, 1985-86; ptnr. entertainment law practice Shames & Litwin, Boston, 1986—; asst. prof. entertainment law Berklee Coll. Music, Boston, 1990-97, Emerson Coll., Boston, 1995-96. Comml. arbitrator Am. Arbitration Assn., Boston, 1991-97. Co-chmn. Brookline, Mass. Dem. Com., 1984-86; mem. Concord, Mass. Dem. Com., 1986—; del. Mass. State Dem. Conv., 2004. Mem. ABA, Mass. Bar Assn., Boston Bar Assn. (founder, chmn. sports and entertainment com. 1987-89, del. to Mass. State Democratic Convention, 2004). Democrat. Avocations: skiing, sailing, tennis, travel. Home: 23 Wright Farm Concord MA 01742-1528 Office: Shames & Litwin 10 St James Ave Boston MA 02116 Office Phone: 617-305-2016. Business E-Mail: plitwin@shames-litwin.com.

LITWINOWICZ, ANTHONY, information scientist, researcher; b. Jelenia Gora, Poland, July 29, 1952; came to U.S., 1978; s. Anthony and Anna (Zdrojewski) L.; m. Catherine Veronica Gajdos, June 30, 1979; children: Catherine, Anthony, John Paul, Peter. MA in History and Philosophy, Lodz U., Poland, 1976; MS in Info. Studies, Drexel U., 1984, postgrad., 1985-90. Cert. in info. mgmt. Sr. info. specialist Laventhol & Horwath CPAs, Phila., 1984-89; instr. info. sci. Delaware Valley Coll., Doylestown, Pa., 1989-91; dir. Info. Ctr. Samsung Electronics, Ridgefield Park, N.J., 1992—. Author: Nazi Occupation of Poland, 1978; contbr. articles to profl. jours. Mem.: Soc. Competitive Intelligence Profls., Assn. Independent Info. Profls., Spl. Librs. Assn., Nat. Assn. Investigative Specialists. Republican. Roman Catholic. Avocations: collecting antiques, reading, martial arts. Home: Ste 3 287 Parker Ave Clifton NJ 07011 Office: Samsung Electronics Am 105 Challenger Rd Ridgefield Park NJ 07660-2113 Personal E-mail: elcidpa@yahoo.com. Business E-Mail: johndoenj@hotmail.com. E-mail: t.litwinow@sumaung.com.

LITYNSKI, DANIEL MITCHELL, engineering educator, retired military officer; b. Amsterdam, N.Y., Mar. 13, 1943; s. Mitchell Peter and Stella Agnes Litynski; m. Dianne Helene Miller, Dec. 28, 1963; children: Laura Ann Ropelis, James Mitchell, John Thomas. BS in Physics, Rensselaer Poly. Inst., 1965; MS in Optics, U. Rochester, 1971; PhD in Physics, Rensselaer Poly. Inst., 1978. National Defense University, Industrial College of the Armed Forces US Dept. of Def., 1989, US Army Command & General Staff College US Army, 1974, US Army Ordnance Officer Advanced Course US Army, 1969, US Army Mechanical Maintenance Officer Course US Army, 1967, US Army Airborne School US Army, 1965, US Army Armor Officers Course US Army, 1965. Commd. officer U.S. Army, 1965, advanced through grades to brig. gen., exec. officer HHC USA Armor & Engr. Bd. Ft. Knox, Ky., 1965—65, platoon leader B Co, 2nd Bn., 34th Armor Ft. Irwin, Calif., 1966—66, exec. officer B Co, 2nd Bn., 34th Armor Vietnam, 1966—67, commdg. officer 551st Light Maintenance Co., 1967—67, commdg. officer HHC USA Ordnance Ctr. and Sch. Aberdeen Proving Ground, Md., 1967—68, rsch. physicist Ballistic Rsch. Labs., 1969—69, materiel officer 19th Maintenance Bn. Vietnam, 1971—72, optical physicist Ballistic Rsch. Labs. Aberdeen Proving Ground, Md., 1972—73, rsch. officer physics U.S. Mil. Acad. West Point, NY, 1974—75, instr. physics U.S. Mil. Acad., 1975—76, asst. prof. physics U.S. Mil. Acad., 1976—78, exec. officer 79th Maintenance Bn. Germany, 1978—80, assoc. prof. elec. engring. U.S. Mil. Acad. West Point, NY, 1980—86, prof., dept. head elec. engring. U.S. Mil. Acad., 1986—89, prof. U.S. Mil. Acad., dept. head elec. engring. and computer sci., 1989—90, prof. U.S. Mil. Acad., head elec. engring. and computer sci., 1990—99, ret., 1999; dean engring. and applied scis. Western Mich. U., Kalamazoo, 1999—2002, provost and v.p. for academic affairs, 2002—, interim pres., 2003. Mem. internat. adv. com. internat. faculty engring. Tech. U. Lodz, Poland, 1992—93; rev. panel chair and mem. NSF, Washington, 1993—97; conf. co-chair FIE 2001 Frontiers in Edn. Conf., Reno, 2000—02; presenter in field. Contbr. chapters to books, articles to profl. jours. Commd. second lt. (2LT), 1965, advanced to brig. gen. (BG), 1999. Decorated U.S. Army Commendation medal U.S. Govt., Bronze Stars, US Army Meritorious Svc. medal, DSM U.S. Army; recipient Order Merit, Tech. U. Lodz, 1994, Cavalier Cross of Merit, Pres. of the Republic of Poland, 2002; scholar, Rensselaer Poly. Inst., 1960—63; N.Y. State Regents Engring. scholar, N.Y. State, 1960—64, USMA fellow to the Nat. Def. U. Indsl. Coll. of the Armed Forces, U.S. Army, 1988—89. Mem.: Edn. Soc. IEEE (v.p. 2002—03), IEEE, Am. Soc. Engring. Educators, Armed Forces Comm. and Electronics Assn., Assn. for Computing Machinery, Soc. Photo-Optical Instrumentation Engrs., Optical Soc. Am., Rotary Internat., Sigma Xi, Phi Kappa Phi, Eta Kappa Nu, Sigma Pi Sigma, Upsilon Pi Epsilon, Tau Beta Pi, Sigma Phi Epsilon (life; pres., nyd 1963). Roman Catholic. Achievements include patents for Photonic Analog-to-Digital Converter Based on Temporal and Spatial Oversampling Techniques, 2003. Avocations: sailing, golf, skiing, travel, genealogy. Home: 1430 Long Rd Kalamazoo MI 49008-1320 Office: Western Mich Univ 1903 West Michigan Ave Kalamazoo MI 49008-5204 Personal E-mail: ddlitynski@msn.com. E-mail: dan.litynski@wmich.edu.

LITZAU, MARK D., secondary school educator; s. Albert John and Mary Ann Litzau; m. Andrea N. Desiato, July 1, 1995; children: Grace Ann, Carmen J. BA, U. No. Colo., 1995; MEd, U. Denver, 2005. Tchr., instrnl. coach Jefferson County Schools, Golden, Colo., 1995—. Mem.: Assn. Supervision and Curriculum Devel. Office: Ralston Valley High Sch 13355 W 80th Ave Arvada CO 80005 Office Phone: 303-982-5611. Office Fax: 303-982-5601.

LITZSINGER, RICHARD MARK, retail executive; b. Houston, Sept. 7, 1955; s. Paul Richard and Dona Lucy (Follett) L. BFA, Tex. Christian U., 1978. Mgmt. trainee Saddleback C.C. Bookstore, Mission Viejo, Calif., 1978, Follett Coll. Stores, Elmhurst, Ill., 1978-79; bookstore mgr. U. Ill., Champaign, 1979-81, Northwestern U., Evanston, Ill., 1981-83; dir. of mktg. Follett Coll. Stores, Elmhurst, Ill., 1983-85, spl. asst. to pres., 1985-88; dir. of devel. Follett Corp., Chgo., 1989—91, also bd. dirs., pres. Custom Acad. Pub. Co., 1991—98, vice chmn., 1998—2001, chmn., 2001—. Trustee Follett Ednl. Found. Republican. Presbyterian. Avocations: tennis, skiing, running, paddle tennis, golf. Home: 120 E Sheridan Pl Lake Bluff IL 60044-2633 Office: Follett Corp 2233 N West St River Grove IL 60171-1895

LIU, AGNETE MEI-CHENG, retired librarian; b. Sept. 17, 1937; came to U.S., 1961; BA, Nat. Cheng Kung U., Tainan, Taiwan, 1960; MA in Libr. Sci., Peabody Tchr.s Coll., 1963. Children's libr. Chgo. Pub. Libr., 1963-64; libr. dir. Escanaba (Mich.) Pub. Libr., 1966-67; head of catalog dept. No. Mich U. Libr., Marquette, Mich., 1967-69; head of tech. processing McAllen (Tex.) Meml. Libr., 1974—2004; ret., 2004. Home: 311 S Cypress Cir Pharr TX 78577-5950

LIU, AIMEE E., writer; b. Conn., 1953; d. Maurice and Jane Liu. BA, Yale U., 1975. Instr. UCLA Ext., 1999—; v.p. PEN Ctr. USA West, L.A., 1998—2001, pres., 2002—03; lectr. in field. Author: Solitaire, 1979; co-author (with Drs. Art Ulene and Steve Shelov): Bringing Out the Best in Your Baby, 1986; co-author: (with Dr. Stan J. Katz) False Love and Other Romantic Illusions, 1988, Success Trap, 1990; author: The Academy Book of Childcare, 1991; co-author (with Dr. Stan J. Katz): The Codependency Conspiracy, 1991; author: Face, 1994, Cloud Mountain, 1997; contbr. numerous articles to mags. and jours. including Lear's, Glamour, Self, New Woman, Footwear News, Entrepreneur, Aim Plus, Feeling Great, Cabletime, Cosmopolitan, others; author: Flash House, 2003. Mem.: Authors Guild, Yale Club of So. Calif. Office: c/o Richard Pine & Assocs 250 W 57th St New York NY 10019

LIU, BEDE, electrical engineering educator; b. Shanghai, Sept. 25, 1934; arrived in U.S., 1954, naturalized, 1960; s. Henry and Shan (Yao) L.; m. Maria Agatha Sang, Jan. 31, 1959; 1 child, Beatrice Agatha. BS in Elec. Engring., Nat. Taiwan U., 1954; MEE, Poly. Inst. Bklyn., 1956, DEE, 1960. Equipment engr. Western Electric Co., N.Y.C., 1954-56; intermediate engr. A.B. DuMont Lab., Clifton, NJ, summer 1956; mem. tech. staff Bell Telephone Labs., Murray Hill, NJ, 1959-62, summers 1957, 58, 66; mem. faculty Princeton U., 1962—, prof. elec. engring., 1969—; dept. chmn., 1994-97. Vis. prof. Nat. Taiwan U., 1970—71, U. Calif., Berkeley, 1971, Shanghai Jiao Tong U., 1979; hon. prof. Acad. Sinica, Beijing, 1988, Chinese U. Electronics, Sci. and Tech., Chengdu, 1997. Co-author: (Book) Digital Signal Processing, 1976, Multamedia Data Hiding, 2002; editor: Digital Filters and the Fast Fourier Transform, 1975. Mem.: IEEE (pres. Cir. and Systems Soc. 1982, bd. dirs. 1984—85, Centennial medal 1984, Achievement award Signal Processing Soc. 1985, Edn. award Cir. and Systems Soc. 1988, Soc. award Signal Processing Soc. 1997, Mac Van Valkenburd award Cir. and Systems Soc. 1997, Millenium medal 2000), Nat. Acad. Engring. Achievements include patents in field. Office: Princeton Univ Dept Elec Engring Princeton NJ 08540 E-mail: liu@princeton.edu.

LIU, BEN-CHIEH, economist; b. Chungking, China, Nov. 17, 1938; came to U.S., 1965, naturalized, 1973; s. Pei-juang and Chung-su L.; m. Jill Jyh-huey, Oct. 2, 1965; children— Tina Won-ting, Roger Won-jung, Milton Won-ming. BA, Nat. Taiwan U., 1961; MA, Meml. U. Nfld., 1965, Washington U., St. Louis, 1968, PhD, 1971. Economist Chinese Air Force and Central Customs, Taiwan, 1961-63; resource economist Canadian Land Inventory and Forest Services, Nfld., 1963-65; research project dir. St. Louis Regional Indsl. Devel. Corp., 1968-72; prin. econs. Midwest Research Inst., Kansas City, Mo., 1972-80; mgr. Energy and Environ. Systems Div., Argonne (Ill.) Nat. Lab., 1980-81. Prof. econs., assoc. dir. rsch. Oklahoma City U., 1981-82; prof. mgmt., mktg. and info. systems Chgo. State U., 1982—; pres. Liu & Assocs., Inc., 1982—; vis. prof. econs. U. Mo., 1970-78, Nat. Taiwan U., 1991-92; Fulbright prof., dir. Internat. Enterprises Inst., Nat. Dong-Hwa U., Taiwan, 1997-98; dean Coll. Bus., Chung-Yuan Christian U., Taiwan, 2000-01; cons. UN, NSF; mem. Gov. Thompson's Adv. Com. on Agrl. Export, 1985-87, Congressman Fawell's Adv. Com. on Sci. and Tech., 1985-98; commr. Nat. Commn. on Librs. and Info. Svcs., 1991-94. Author: Interindustrial Structure Analysis: An Input-Output Study for St. Louis Region, 1968, The Quality of Life in the United States, 1970, Rating, Index and Statistics, 1973, Quality of Life Indicators in U.S. Metropolitan Areas, 1975, Physical and Economic Damage Functions for Air Pollutants by Receptors, 1976, Earthquake Risk and Damage Functions, An Integrated Model, 1981, Income, Energy and Quality of Life: An Information Systems Approach to Decisions, 1988; mem. editorial bd.: Internat. Jour. Math. Social Sci, Am. Jour. Econs. and Sociology, Hong Kong Jour. Bus. Mgmt., Internat. Jour. of Bus.; Internat. Jour. Mgmt.; contbr. articles to profl. jours. Recipient rsch. study award, Am. Indsl. Devel. Coun., 1969—, Fulbright scholar awards, 1992, 1996, Faculty Meritorious awards, Chgo. State U., 1983, 1986, 1989, 1990, 2002, Disting. Prof. Advancement Increase awards, 1990, 1996, 2003, Outstanding Rsch. award, Nat. Sci. Coun., 1997—98; U.S. Econ. Devel. Adminstrn. fellow, 1967—68, Korean Govt. scholar, 1963—65, Fulbright scholar, Mgmt. Devel. Inst., Delhi U., 1992. Fellow Am. Statis. Assn. (com. mem.); mem. Am. Econ. Assn. (com. mem.), Econometric Soc., Royal Econ. Soc., Internat. Statis. Instn., Assn. for Social Econs. (com. mem.), Tax Inst. Am., Chinese Acad. and Profl. Assn. (pres. 1984-85), Chinese Econ. Assn. in N.Am. (pres. 1988-90), Chinese Am. Profs. Assn. (pres. 1996—). Home: 5360 Pennywood Dr Lisle IL 60532-2032 Office: Chgo State U Chicago IL 60628 Personal E-mail: liuasso1982@yahoo.com. E-mail: bencliu678@hotmail.com. *The joy of living may temporarily rest on present or past glory, but it is the immersion in planning for the future— the living ahead of one's time— which ensures* *permanently the flourishing of the joy of life. In a commonwealth society, happiness does not come from doing what we like to do, but from liking what we have to do for the less-well-to-do-ones.*

LIU, CAROL, state representative; b. Berkeley, Calif., Sept. 12, 1940; m. Michael Peevey; children: Darcie, Maria, Jared. BA, San Jose State Coll., 1963; student, U. Calif., Berkeley, 1964, student, 1978. Tchr. Richmond Unified Sch. Dist., 1964—77, adminstr., 1978—84; mem. La Cañada Flintridge City Council, 1992—96; mayor La Cañada Flintridge, Calif., 1996—99; mem. Calif. State Assembly, 2000—. Co-chair Asian Pacific Islander Legislative Caucus; mem. Women's Legislative Caucus, Calif. Seismic Safety Commn.; mem. transportation and govt. org. com., higher edu. com., budget com. Calif. State Assembly. Pres. La Canada H.S. PTA; coun. pres. Mus. Contemporary Art; co-chair capital campaign Pasadena City Coll., pres. found. bd., co-chair phys. edn. campaign; trustee U. Calif., Berkeley; bd. dirs. Child Care Info. Svcs., Five Acres; mem. exec. bd. Women's Leadership Network. Democrat. Office: State Capital PO Box 942849 Rm 4112 Sacramento CA 94249*

LIU, CEJUN, science educator, researcher, program analyst; s. Chengxong Liu and Shuqiu Li; m. Qun Wang, Jan. 22, 1969; 1 child, Kun. Diploma, Xiangtan Normal U., Hunan, 1982; BS, Hunan Ednl. Inst., China, 1987; MS, PhD, U. Ga., 2002. Assoc. prof. physics, cert. lectr. physics. Physics instr. Xiangtan Tech. Sch., Xiangtan, 1982—85; lectr. physics South China Agrl. U. Ga., Guangzhou, 1991—95; head and assoc. prof. of physics physics divsn. South China Agrl. U., 1996—97; grad. rsch. asst. Ctr. Simulational Physics, U. Ga., Athens, 1997—. Author: (book) General Physics, 1985, General Physics Experiment, 1986; contbr. scientific papers to profl. jours. Named Excellent Grad. Student, Ministry of ShangHai Higher Edn., 1991, Excellent Young Tchr., GuangDong People's Govt., 1996. Mem.: Am. Phys. Soc., Am. Statis. Assn. Home: D102 107 College Station Rd Athens GA 30605 Office: U Ga Ctr for Simulational Physics Athens GA 30602 Home: 2564 Chain Bridge Rd #204 Vienna VA 22181 Personal E-mail: liu@physast.uga.edu.

LIU, CHI TSIEH, aerospace scientist, researcher; b. Kung-shin, Honan, China, Aug. 8, 1939; arrived in U.S., 1964, naturalized, 1973; s. Mo En and Da Jen Liu; m. Lien-Yu Chang Liu, Jan. 30, 1965; children: Patricia Meng-Fu, Jeffrey Chia-Perng, Michael Chia-Hriang. BS, Cheng-Kung U., Tainan, Taiwan, 1962; degree in engring., Columbiz U., 1968; PhD, Va. Polytech. State U., 1975. Stress analyst Fairchild Rep. Co., Farningdale, NY, 1968—72; aerospace engr. Naval Ordinance Sta., Indian Head, Md., 1975—77; rsch. mech. engr. U. S. Dept. Transp., Washington, 1977—78; aerospace engr. Naval Engring. Support Office, Alameda, Calif., 1978—80, NASA Ames Rsch. Ctr., Moffett Field, Calif., 1980—81; prin. rsch. engr. Air Force Rsch. Lab, Edwards AFB, Calif., 1981—2001; sr. scientist So. Ill. U., Carbondale, 2001—, advisor materials tech. ctr., 1998—. Cons. various orgns., 1981—. Contbr. articles to profl. jours. Recipient Star Team award, Air Force Office Sci. Rsch., 1991, Harold Brown Award, Air Force. Fellow: Soc. Expl. Mechanics. Avocations: fishing, swimming. Office: Air Force Rsch Lab AFRL/PRSM 10 E Saturn Blvd Edwards Afb CA 93524-7680

LIU, CHIU, transportation engineer, educator; b. Bo Luo, Canton, China, Oct. 25, 1964; came to U.S., 1984; parents Cho-hung Liu and Yan Jiang; m. Yan-hong Cheng, Aug. 7, 1996. BS, Calif. State U., 1986; PhD in Physics, U. Tex., 1993, MSCE, 1994, PhD in Civil Engring., 1997. Tchg. asst. U. Tex., Austin, 1987-93, 95; rsch. eng. asst. Ctr. Transportation Rsch., Austin, Tex., 1995-97, rsch. engr. assoc., 1997; mem. staff Dept. Civil Engring., El Paso, Tex., 1998; transportation engring. dir. Tex. Ctrs. Border Econ. Devel., El Paso, Tex., 1998—. Adv. panel Tex. Dept. Transportation, Austin, 1998—; com. mem. Nat. Rsch. Coun., Washington, 1998—. Contbr. articles to profl. jours. including Jour. Transportation Engring., Transportation Rsch. Record, others. Adv. panel Metropolitan Planning Org., El Paso, 1998; coord. NAFTA Inst., El Paso, 1998. Fellow Advanced Inst. Transportation Engring., U. Tex., Austin, 1995-97. Mem. Nat. Soc. Profl. Engrs., Am. Soc. Civil Engrs., Am. Physical Soc., Sigma Xi. Achievements include development of sound theoretical frameworks for understanding the dynamic response of layered structures, eg. road structure to response tovehicle-road interaction, sound theoretical framework for predicting the evolution of surface profile of a layered road structure by linking together the vehicle dynamic characteristics, road surface characteristics and dynamic material properties of the road structures, a sound theoretical framework for rehabilitating road surfaces; rsch. in the control of vehicle flow, the geometric and physical design of roads, the theory of traffic flow, the transportation planning, and the evolution of pavement distress due to vehicle loading. Office: Tex Ctrs for Border Economic Devel Univ Tex El Paso TX 79968-0001 Personal E-mail: uilcc@hotmail.com. E-mail: chiu.liu@villanova.edu.

LIU, CYNTHIA, pathologist, hematologist; MD, Jinzhou Med. Coll., 1982; PhD, U. South Fla., 1995. Cert. Anatomic Pathology/Clin. Pathology Am. Bd. Pathology, 2002, Hematologist Am. Bd. Pathology, 2003. Asst. prof. pathology Sch. Medicine NYU, 2003—. Fellow: Am. Soc. Clin. Pathologist; mem.: Can. Acad. Pathology, U.S. Acad. Pathology.

LIU, DAVID RUCHIEN, biochemist; b. Riverside, Calif., June 12, 1973; BA in chemistry summa cum laude, Harvard Coll., 1994; PhD in organic chemistry, U. Calif., Berkeley, 1999. Asst. prof. chemistry Harvard U., 1999—2003, John L. Loeb prof. chemistry and chem. biology, 2003—. Editl. adv. bd. ChemBioChem, Chemical Reviews. Contbr. articles to profl. jour. Named one of Top 100 Young Innovators, MIT Tech. Review, 2004; recipient Career award, NSF, 2001, Rsch. Scholar, Am. Cancer Soc., 2001, Genome-related Pilot Rsch. award, Merck, 2003, Excellence in Chemistry award, AstraZeneca Pharm., 2003, Arthur C. Cope Young Scholar award, ACS, 2004, Chemistry Scholarship award, Glaxo-Smith-Kline, 2004, Camille Dreyfus Tchr.-Scholar award, 2004, "Brilliant 10" recognition, Popular Sci., 2004; Rsch. Fellow, Alfred P. Sloan Found., 2002. Office: Harvard U Dept Chemistry and Chem Biology 12 Oxford St Cambridge MA 02138 Business E-Mail: liu@chemistry.harvard.edu.

LIU, DAVID SHIAO-KUNG, research scientist, consultant; b. Chung King, China, Aug. 27, 1940; s. Chen and Betty Shih Liu; m. Emily Tsai; children: John, Jeffrey, Joanne. BSc, Nat. Cheng Kung U., Taiwan, 1962; MS, U. Calif., Berkeley, 1965; PhD, NYU, 1972. Registered profl. engr., N.Y., civil engr., Calif. Sr. scientist RAND Corp., Santa Monica, Calif., 1971—91; pres. Gen. Sys., Malibu, Calif., 1990—. Sr. adv. sci. adv. bd. Office Prime Min., Taipei, Taiwan, 1987—2000; sr. cons. RAND Corp., Santa Monica, 1995—2000; prof. oceanographic engring. Nat. Cheng-Kung U., Tainan, Taiwan, 1980—87; adj. assoc. prof. U. So. Calif., L.A., 1977—85; sr. cons. Ministry of Econ. Affairs, Taipei, Taiwan, 1989—2000; sr. advisor Cen. Weather Bur., Taipei, Taiwan, 1986—2000; sr. cons. Coun. Econ. Devel., Taiwan, 1994—97, Naval Hydrographic Bur., Taiwan, 1981—96. 2d lt. mil. police, 1962—63, Taiwan. Achievements include development of 3-dimensional numerical model, water quality of N.Y. Harbor. Home: 3706 Oceanhill Way Malibu CA 90265-5640 E-mail: davidskliu@charter.net.

LIU, DAVID T., retired librarian; b. Zhong-shan City, China, Dec. 6, 1936; came to U.S., 1961; s. Chung-Ling and Ging-Wa (Vong) L.; m. Agnete M.C. Shih, Dec. 15, 1962; children: Nadine, Austin W.T. Student, Tamkang English Coll., Taipei, Taiwan, 1954-55; BA, Nat. Taiwan U., Taipei, 1959; postgrad., Nat. Normal U., Taipei, 1960-61, U. Wash., 1962; MA in Libr. Sci., George Peabody Coll. for Tchrs., 1963. Interpreter, officer Chinese Air Force Hdqrs., Taipei, 1960-61; cataloger Chgo. Pub. Libr., 1963-64; chief adult svcs., reader's advisor Joliet (Ill.) Pub. Libr., 1964; head libr., asst. prof. polit. sci. Bay de Noc C.C., Escanaba, Mich., 1964-73; libr. dir. Pharr (Tex.) Meml. Libr., 1973—2002, ret., 2002. Pres. libr.'s adv. coun. Hidalgo County Libr. System, McAllen, Tex., 1980. Author: Taiwan Revisited, 1985. Recipient 25-Yr. Disting. Svc. award City of Pharr, 1998. Mem. ALA, Chinese-Am. Librs. Assn. (pres. 1981-82), Asian/Pacific-Am. Librs. Assn. (chair recruitment & scholarship com. 1993-94). Avocations: study of french and spanish, fishing, translating/writing, interpretations and analyses of international affairs & chinese literary classics. Home: 311 S Cypress Cir Pharr TX 78577-5950

LIU, DON H., lawyer; b. Seoul, Korea, 1961; BA magna cum laude, Haverford Coll.; JD, Columbia U. Bar: Pa., 1986. Law clerk NJ Supreme Ct.; atty. Richards & O'Neil, N.Y.C., Simpson Thacher & Bartlett, N.Y.C.; v.p., dep. chief legal officer Aetna US Healthcare, 1992—99; sr. v.p., gen. counsel Ikon Office Solutions Inc, Malvern, Pa., 1999—. Mem. ABA, Nat. Asian Pacific Am. Bar Assn. Office: Ikon Office Solutions Inc 70 Valley Stream Pkwy Malvern PA 19355-1453*

LIU, GANG-YU, chemist, educator; b. Zhengzhou, Henan, China, Apr. 19, 1964; came to U.S., 1986; parents Zhen Kun and Quan Xian (Guo) L.; m. Xiaoyuan Li, Dec. 1, 1987. BS, Peking (China) U., 1988; MS, Princeton U., 1990, PhD, 1992. Postdoctoral assoc. U. Calif., Berkeley, 1992-94; asst. prof. chemistry Wayne State U., Detroit, 1994—99. Camille and Henry Dreyfus fellow, 1994-99, Miller Rsch. fellow The Miller Inst. for Basic Rsch. in Sci., 1992-94, Harold W. Dodds Honorific fellow Princeton U., 1991-92, CGP fellow Ministry of Edn., China, 1986-87. Mem. AAAS, Am. Chem. Soc., Am. Phys. Soc., Am. Vacuum Soc. Office: U Cal Dept Chem 1 Shields Ave Davis CA 95616

LIU, GUOLIANG, electrical engineer; s. Yongyuan Liu and Jiying Wang; m. Ruqian Teng, Oct. 6, 1974; 1 child, Andrew Teng. BS, Peking U., 1992, MS, 1996; MS in Engring., U. Tex., 2000, PhD, 2003. Grad. rsch. asst. Tex. Materials Inst., Austin, Tex., 1997—2001; elec. engr. Dallas Semiconductor, 2001—. Manuscripts reviewer Jour. Materials Rsch. Contbr. scientific papers. Mem.: IEEE (sr.; tech. com. auto test sys., IEEE Instrumentation and Measurement Soc.). E-mail: gliu@ieee.org.

LIU, HANLI, biomedical engineer, educator; b. Beijing, Mar. 6, 1960; d. Li-ya Wang and Zhongcheng Liu; m. Anqi Wu, July 6, 1957; children: Eric Wu, Rodney Wu. PhD in Physics, Wake Forest U., Winston-Salem, N.C., 1994. Rsch. assoc. U. City Sci. Ctr., Phila., 1992—96; post-doctoral fellow U. of Pa, Phila., 1994—96; asst. prof. of biomed. engring. U. of Tex., Arlington, 1996—2001, assoc. prof. of biomedical engring., 2001—. Adj. faculty mem. joint program in biomed. engring. U. Tex. Southwestern Med. Ctr., Dallas, 1996—. Recipient Outstanding Young Scientist award, Houston Soc. for Engring. in Medicine and Biology, 1998, Outstanding Young Faculty Award, Coll. of Engring., U. of Tex., Arlington, 1999, Univ. Outstanding Rsch. Achievement award, U. Tex. Arlington, 2004. Mem.: IEEE, Internat. Soc. for Optical Engring., Optical Soc. of Am. Home: 1211 Hillary Ln Arlington TX 76012 Office: Univ Tex Arlington PO Box 19138 Arlington TX 76019 Office Phone: 817-272-2054. Business E-Mail: hanli@uta.edu.

LIU, HAOZHE, research scientist; arrived in U.S., 2001; s. Ying and Jiuzhi (Li) Liu; m. Luhong Wang, Sept. 30, 1994; children: Elizabeth Meimei children: Hubang. BS, Jilin U., 1991, MS, 1994; PhD, Inst. Metal Rsch., Chinese Acad. Scis., Shenyang, Liaoning, 1997. Postdoctoral rsch. fellow Inst. of Physics, Chinese Acad. Scis., Beijing, 1997—99; vis. scholar Max Planck Inst. Solid State Rsch., Stuttgart, Germany, 2000—01; rsch. scientist Mineral Physics Inst., SUNY, Stony Brook, 2002—03, High Pressure Collaborative Access Team, Advanced Photon Source, Argonne, Ill., 2003—. Mem.: European Geophys. Soc. and the European Union of Geoscis., European Geoscis. Union, Am. Geophys. Union. Office: HPCAT Argonne Nat Lab Bldg 434E 9700 S Cass Ave Argonne IL 60439 Office Phone: 630-252-4058.

LIU, HONGYU, atmospheric scientist; b. Jiangyan, Jiangsu, China; m. Xiaojing Xu; children: Eric children: Sarah. BSc in atmospheric physics, Peking U., China, 1990; MSc in atmospheric physics, Peking U., 1993; PhD, Hong Kong Poly. U., 1998; PhD in geophysics, Harvard U., 2003. Spl. rsch. asst. Hong Kong Poly. U., 1994—97; grad. rsch. asst. Harvard U., Cambridge, Mass., 1997—2002; staff scientist ICASE - NASA Langley Rsch. Ctr., Hampton, Va., 2002, Nat. Inst. of Aerospace, Hampton, Va., 2003—04, sr. staff scientist, 2004—. Contbr. articles various profl. jours. Mem.: Am. Meteorol. Soc., Am. Geophys. Union. Achievements include research that first linked observations of enhanced tropospheric ozone amounts with biomass burning over continental Southeast Asia (Liu et al., Atmospheric Environment, 33, 2403-2410, 1999). Avocations: music, reading. Office: Nat Inst of Aerospace 100 Exploration Way Hampton VA 23666-6147 Office Phone: 757-325-6904. E-mail: hyl@nianet.org.

LIU, HUAN, education educator; PhD, U. of So. Calif., 1985—89. Sr. engr. Telecom Australia Rsch. Labs, Clayton, Australia, 1989—93; assoc. prof. Nat. U. of Singapore, 1994—99, Ariz. State U., 2000—. Author: (book) Feature Selection for Data Mining and Knowledge Discovery. Mem.: IEEE, ACM, AAAI. Office Phone: 480-727-7349.

LIU, HUI (ROBIN LIU), principal scientist, consultant, author; s. Shao W. Liu and Zhong J. Cheng; m. Mui Cheung, July 20, 1993; children: Vick C., Benjamin C. PhD, U. Ill., 2000. Prin. scientist, sect. mgr. Motorola Labs, Tempe, Ariz., 2000—. Cons. Neah Power Systems Inc., Bothell, Wash., 2002—; assoc. dir. Applied NanoBioSci. Ctr., Tempe, 2002—; mem. sci. com. 2nd Ann. Internat. IEEE-EMBS Conf. on Microtechs. in Medicine and Biology, Madison, Wis., 2002; mem. internat. steering com. 2001 Internat. MEMS Workshop Conf., 2001; mem. industry adv. bd. Berkeley Sensor and Actuator Ctr. U. Calif., Berkeley, 2001—02; mem. sci. com. symposium on MEMS Internat. Conf. on Materials for Advanced Techs., 2002—. Author: Microfluidics and BioMEMS Applications; contbr. articles to profl. jours. Grantee, Nat. Inst. Stds. and Tech., Def. Advanced Rsch. Projects Agy. Mem.: ASME, IEEE, Internat. Optical Engring. Soc. (assoc. editor SPIE Jour. Microlithography, Microfabrication and Micros 2001—). Achievements include patents pending for an autonomous self-regulating microfluidic system; hybridization enhancement using oscillation flow in DNA array channel; integrated DNA amplification and detection microfluidic system; enhanced mixing in microfluidic devices; fluidic valve having a bi-phase valve element; microfluidic device with built-in high gradient magnetic separation microchannels; highly parallel integrated microfluidic biochannel arrays; thermopneumatically actuated PDMS microvalve; application of in-line chaotic micromixer for biological sample processing; microfluidic integrated circuit for biological applications; cell capture and DNA isolation using two-bead method. Office: Motorola Inc 7700 S River Pky Tempe AZ 85284 Home: 12726 72Nd Dr Se Snohomish WA 98296-7692 Personal E-mail: Robin.Liu@asu.edu.

LIU, JUANYU, civil engineer, researcher; arrived in U.S., 2000; d. Fuxiang Liu and Lanying Su. BS, Tongji U., Shanghai, China, 1995; MS, Tex. A&M U., College Station, 2001, PhD, 2005. EIT Tex. Bd. Profl. Engineers, 2002; cert. in bus. Mays Bus. Sch. Tex. A&M U., 2004. Rsch. asst. State Key Lab. Concrete Materials Rsch., Shanghai, 1995—99; tchg. asst. dept. civil engring. Tex. A&M U., College Station, 2000—01; rsch. asst. Tex. Transp. Inst. Tex. A&M U., 2001—. Author conf. proceedings; contbr. scientific papers, articles to profl. jours.; author: (software) Strategic Analysis of Pavement Evaluation and Repair Beta version 2.0; reviewer: 8th Internat. Conf. on Concrete Pavements. Fellow: Grad. Tchg. Acad.; mem.: ASCE, Internat. Soc. Concrete Pavements, Transp. Rsch. Bd., Inst. Transp. Engrs. (assoc.), Am. Concrete Inst. Achievements include research in crushed gravel in concrete paving; repair and rehabilitation of concrete pavement; fracture properties of high-strength Ccncrete; fractal characteristics and statistical features of fracture surface of concrete. Office: Tex Transp Inst Rm 501H CE/TTI Bldg TAMU College Station TX 77843-3135 E-mail: liujuanyu@neo.tamu.edu.

LIU, KAI-LIH, epidemiologist; b. Hualien, Taiwan, Apr. 24, 1964; s. Bao-Chong Liu and Eng-Lian Chen. MPH, Nat. Taiwan U., Taipei, 1988; PhD, Yale U., 1995. Rsch. asst. Nat. Taiwan U., Taipei, 1986—88; epidemiologist R.I. Dept of Health, Providence, 1996—98; rsch. fellow/scientist Columbia U., N.Y.C., 1998—99; city rsch. scientist N.Y.C. Dept. of Health and Mental Hygiene, 2000—. Cons. R.I. Dept of Health, Providence, 1996—96. Postdoctoral fellowship, NIMH, 1998—99. Mem.: APHA, Internat. AIDS Soc. Achievements include research in Evaluation of Rhode Island Syringe Exchange Program for HIV prevention; Conducting data analyses for various CDC-funded HIV research projects on perinatally infected children/adolescents, HIV patients, gay men, and transgenders in New York City. Office: NYC Dept of Health & Mental Hygiene 346 Broadway Rm 701 Box 44 New York NY 10013 Office Phone: 212-513-7340. E-mail: kliu@health.nyc.gov.

LIU, KEH-FEI FRANK, physicist, researcher; b. Beijing, Jan. 11, 1947; came to U.S., 1969; s. Hsien-Chang and Juihua (Wang) L.; m. Yao-Chin Ko, Apr. 6, 1974; children: Helen, Alexander. BS, Tunghai U., Taichung, Taiwan, 1968; MS, SUNY, Stony Brook, 1972, PhD, 1975. Vis. scientist C.E.N. Saclay France, Paris, 1974-76; from rsch. assoc. to adj. asst. prof. UCLA, 1976-80; assoc. prof. U. Ky., Lexington, 1980-86, prof. physics, 1986—. Vis. prof. SUNY, Stony Brook, 1985-86, 1990; univ. rsch. prof. U. Ky., 1992. Editor: Chiral Solitons, 1987; assoc. editor World Scientific Pub. Co., Singapore, 1985—; contbr. articles to profl. jours. Recipient First Prize in Theoretical Physics Academia Sinica, China, 1987, Grand Challenge award DOE, 1988, 1989, Alexander Von Humboldt Sr. Scientist award Humboldt Found., Germany, 1990. Fellow Am. Phys. Soc.; mem. European Phys. Soc., Overseas Chinese Physicists Assn. (pres. 2003—). Office: U Ky Dept Physics & Astronomy Lexington KY 40506-0001

LIU, KEVIN H., research scientist, software architect; b. Beijing, Jan. 23, 1970; B Engring., Beijing U. Sci. and Tech., 1991; grad. diploma in computer sci., Royal Melbourne Inst. Tech., Australia, 1992; M Bus. Sys., Monash U., Melbourne, 1993; PhD in Computer Sci., Victoria U. Tech., Melbourne, Australia, 1997. Rsch. asst. Victoria U. Tech., 1994-96, lectr., 1996-97; mem. rsch. faculty Rutgers U., New Brunswick, N.J., 1997-98; rsch. scientist Telcordia Techs., Red Bank, NJ, 1998—2002; software arch. QOptics Inc., Portland, Oreg., 2002—. Mem. tech. program com. IEEE Internat. Conf. on Computer Comm. and Networks, 2000-02. Contbr. articles to profl. jours., including IEEE Transactions on Comms., IEEE Jour. Lightwave Tech., IEEE Jour. on Selected Areas in Comm., IEEE Network Mag., others; author: IP over WDM, 2002. Mem. IEEE, Assn. for Computing Machinery. Business E-Mail: kliu@ieee.org.

LIU, LIANG, engineering educator; s. Ying-Tao and Yueh-Kwei Chung Liu; m. Sylvia Y. Liu; children: Claire Y., Darren. BS in Civil Engring., Nat. Chiao-Tung U., Tsin-Chu, 1982; MS in Constrn. Mgmt., U. Mich., 1987, PhD in Civil Engring., 1991. Rsch. asst. U. Mich., Ann Arbor, 1987—90; engr. PMA Cons., Inc., Ann Arbor, 1990—92; v.p. Champaign Engring. and Technologies, Champaign, Ill., 1997—2000; asst. prof. U. Ill., Champaign-Urbana, 1992—97, assoc. prof. dept. civil engring., 2000—. Advisor student chpt. Assoc. Gen. Contrs. of Am., Urbana, 1992—. Planner Habitat for Humanity, Ann Arbor, 1990; vol. Arcadia Chamber Players, Champaign, 1999—. Recipient Coll. Engring. Tchg. award, U. Ill., 2003; scholar W.E. O'Neal Faculty scholar, 2001. Mem.: ASCE, Sigma Xi. Avocations: golf, fly fishing. Office: Univ of Illinois 205 N Mathews Ave Urbana IL 61801 Office Phone: 217-333-6951. E-mail: lliu1@uiuc.edu.

LIU, LIZHONG, physicist; b. Dongguang, Hebei, China, Feb. 3, 1964; s. Qishan Liu and Lianzhi Li; m. Dongxia Jiang, Sept. 24, 1985; children: Peggy Jie Liu, Linda Jacqueline Liu. BS, Beijing U., 1982; MS, U. Pitts., 1984; PhD, U. Mich., 1991. Cert. Therapeutic Radiol. Physicist Am. Bd. Radiology, 1998. Postdoctoral assoc. Yale Univ., New Haven, 1991-93, postdoctoral fellow, 1993-94; radiol. physicist Yale-New Haven Hosp., 1994—97; asst. prof. U. UT, Salt Lake City, 1997—99; assoc. prof. SUNY Upstate Med. U., Syracuse, NY, 1999—. Contbr. articles to profl. jours. Mem. Am. Assn. Physicists in Medicine. Office: SUNY Upstate Medical Univ 750 E Adams St Syracuse NY 13210 Business E-Mail: liul@upstate.edu.

LIU, LUCY, actress; b. Queens, N.Y., Dec. 2, 1968; Student, NYU; BA in Chinese Lang. and Culture, U. Mich., 1990. Actor: (TV series) Beverly Hills, 90210, 1991, L.A. Law, 1993, Coach, 1994, Home Improvement, 1995, Hercules: The Legendary Journeys, 1995, ER, 1995, The X-Files, 1996, Nash Bridges, 1996, High Incident, 1996, The Real Adventures of Johnny Quest, 1997, NYPD Blue, 1997, Michael Hayes, 1997, Sex and the City, 2001, (voice only) King of the Hill, 2002, Jackie Chan Adventures, 2004, Pearl, 1996—97, Ally McBeal, 1998—2002, (voice only) Game Over, 2004,: (TV films) Riot, 1997; (films) Ban wo zong heng, 1992, Protozoa, 1993, Bang, 1995, Jerry Maguire, 1996, Gridlock'd, 1997, City of Industry, 1997, Guy, 1997, Flypaper, 1997, Love Kills, 1998, Payback, 1999, True Crime, 1999, Molly, 1999, The Mating Habits of the Earthbound Human, 1999, Play It to the Bone, 1999, Shanghai Noon, 2000, Charlie's Angels, 2001, Hotel, 2001, Ballistics: Ecks vs. Sever, 2002, Cypher, 2002, Chicago, 2002, Charlie's Angels: Full Throttle, 2003, Kill Bill: Vol. 1, 2003, Kill Bill: Vol. 2, 2004. Office: William Morris Agy One William Morris Pl Beverly Hills CA 90212

LIU, MARGARET C., music educator; b. Canton, China, Aug. 10, 1947; arrived in U.S., 1972; d. Man-Hymn Wong and Shau-Chung Ng; m. John Pui-Chee, July 28, 1973; children: Amos Tao-Peng, Deborah Tao-En. BA, Hong Kong Bapt. U., 1970; M in Ch. Music, Southwestern Bapt. Theol. Sem., 1975. Freelance vocal and keyboard performer, various cities, 1972—; pvt. music tchr., 1975; music dir. 1st Chinese Bapt. Ch., Atlanta, 1976-80, 85-89, Chinese Bapt. Ch., College Park, Md., 1980-83; pres., CEO Cambridge Acad. Music and Arts, Atlanta, 1999—. Bd. mem. Alliance Theatre Edn. Adv. Coun., Atlanta, 1996-99; pres. North Dekalb Music Tchrs. Assn., Atlanta, 1997-99; Ga. local rep. Associated Bd. of the Royal Schs. Music, London, 1997—. Deacon Hanley Rd. Bapt. Ch., St. Louis, 1984, Briarcliff Bapt. Ch., Atlanta, 2003-. Mem. Music Tchrs. Nat. Assn., Music Educators Nat. Conf., Nat. Guild Piano Tchrs., Kindermusik Educators Assn.

LIU, MAW-SHUNG, physiologist, dentist; b. Taiwan, Republic of China, Feb. 2, 1940; came to U.S., 1968; s. Chao-Tung and Chian (Hwang) L.; m. Min-Chau Chang, Sept. 15, 1966; 1 child, Chien-Ye. DDS, Kaohsiung Med. U., Taiwan, 1964; PhD, U. Ottawa, Can., 1976. Cert. by Coun. Nat. Bd. Dental Examiners. Intern in pathology U. Ky., Lexington, 1968-69; instr. physiology La. State U. Med. Ctr., New Orleans, 1974-76, asst. prof., 1976-78; assoc. prof. Sch. of Medicine, Wake Forest U., Winston-Salem, N.C., 1978-82; prof. St. Louis U. Sch. Medicine, 1982—. Vis. prof. Beijing Med. U., 1984-, Zhejiang Med. U., 1986, Kaohsiung Med. U., 1989-, Chang Gung Med. U., 1989-; mem. surgery, anesthesiology and trauma study sect. NIH, 1988—92. Mem. editl. bd. Circulatory Shock, 1982-93, Shock, 1993—; contbr. over 90 articles and 90 papers to profl. jours. Named hon. prof. Nanjing Med. Univ., 1984, Hunan Med. Univ., 1988; grantee Nat. Heart Lung and Blood Inst., Inst. Gen. Med. Sci., 1977—. Mem. Internat. Soc. Heart Rsch., Am. Physiol. Soc., The Shock Soc. Achievements include first to significant contribution to the understanding of molecular pathogenesis of myocardial and hepatic dysfunction during shock, sepsis and trauma. Office: St Louis U Sch Medicine Dept Pharm and Physiol Sci 1402 S Grand Blvd Saint Louis MO 63104-1004 E-mail: Lium@slu.edu.

LIU, NIAN, neuroscientist; b. Yangchun, Guangdong, China; m. Jane Wang, Nov. 23, 1993; children: Andrew, Grace. PhD, U. Louisville, 1997. Postdoctoral rsch. assoc. Cornell U. Med. Coll., White Plains, NY, 1997—2000; software engr. Flooz.com, Inc., N.Y.C., 2000—01; postdoctoral fellow Yale U., New Haven, 2001—05, assoc. rsch. scientist, 2005—. Contbr. articles various profl. jours. Research-in-Aid grant, Sigma Xi Sci. Soc., 1997, Rsch. grant, Nat. Parkinson's Found., 2000, NIH, 2005. Mem.: AAAS, Assn. for Chemoreception Scis., Soc. for Neuroscience, Am. Med. Informatics Assn. Office: Yale U 300 George St Ste 501 New Haven CT 06511 Office Phone: 203-737-2934. E-mail: nian.liu@yale.edu.

LIU, PAUL ISHEN, pathologist, educator; b. Taipei, Taiwan, Nov. 23, 1932; arrived in U.S., 1964; s. Shueh Fu Liu and Yu Chow Hsu; m. Jaojen Grace Chung, Sept. 15, 1936; 1 child, Spencer Spin. MD, Nat. Taiwan U., Taipei, 1960; PhD, St. Louis U., 1969; DMS, Hiroshima (Japan) U., 1974. Lic. physician Calif. Med. Bd., diplomate Am. Bd. Pathology. Assoc. prof. pathology Med. Coll. Ga., Augusta, 0197—1976; prof. lab. medicine Med. U. S.C., Charleston, 1976—80; prof. pathology and medicine U. South Ala., Mobile, 1981—90; prof., chair pathology Olive View-UCLA Med. Ctr. UCLA Affiliated Med. Ctr., Sylmar, 1992—; prof., vice-chair dept. pathology and lab. medicine UCLA, 1992—. Mem. editl. bd.: Annals of Clin. and Lab. Sci., 1985—90, Chang Gung Med. Jour., 1981—90, guest editl. bd.: Jour. Formosa Med. Assn., 1990—; author: (textbook) Blue Book of Diagnostic Tests, 1986, Clinical and Laboratory Diagnosis, 1988. Capt. USNR, 1983—96. Recipient Outstanding Achievement in Promoting Sino-Am. Culture award, Sun-Yet-Shen Inst., Chgo., 1980, Outstanding Cmty. Svc. award, Sickle Cell Anemia Assn., 1984. Master: Internat. Assn. Chinese Pathologists (founding pres. 1990—92); fellow: ACP, Am. Soc. Clin. Pathologists, Am. Coll. Pathologists. Republican. Presbyterian. Home: 1032 S Del Mar Ave San Gabriel CA 91776 Office: Olive View-UCLA Med Ctr 14445 Olive View Dr Sylmar CA 91342-1438 E-mail: piliu@ucla.edu.

LIU, PENG, information scientist, educator; s. Quanwu Liu and Guijin Xing; m. Qing Liu, June 18, 1996. BS, U. Sci. and Tech. of China, Hefei, 1993; MS, U. Sci. and Tech. of China, Beijing, 1996; PhD, George Mason U., 1999. Asst. prof. of info. systems U. Md., Balt., 1999—2002; asst. prof. info. scis. and tech. Pa. State U., University Park, 2002—. Dir. cyber security lab. Pa. State U., University Park, 2002—, rsch. dir. Pa. State Ctr. for Info. Assurance, 2003—; chair internat. workshops; lectr. and presenter in field. Contbr. articles and conf. procs. Recipient Outstanding Grad. Rsch. award, George Mason U., 2000, Early Career Prin. Investigator award, US Dept. of Energy, 2002-2005; grantee Capacity Bldg. in Info. Assurance grantee, NSF, 2004-06; 1st prize scholarship for best student, U. of Sci. and Tech. of China, 1991-1992, ZhangZongZhi fellow, 1993, Measuring Quality of Info. Assurance grant, Def. Advanced Rsch. Project Agy., 2002, Rsch. grantee, NSF, 2002-2005, 2003-2006, Info. Assurance scholar, USA Dept. of Def., 2004-05. Mem.: IEEE, Assn. Computing Machinery. Achievements include design and implementation of the first intrusion tolerant database system in the world; development of fundamental frameworks and technologies for online attack recovery; ITDB: a prototype intrusion tolerant database system that contains about 35, 000 lines of source code; design of self-healing workflow systems; development of proactive worm containment technologies; view-free XML access control technologies based on query-rewriting; a framework for privacy-preserving semantic interoperation and access control of heterogeneous databases; ESVT: An Internet Security Experiment Specificaton and Visualization Toolkit; efficient key management schemes for wireless data broadcast applications. Office: Pa State Univ 313G IST Bldg University Park PA 16802 Office Phone: 814-863-0641. Home Fax: 815-865-6426; Office Fax: 814-865-6426. Personal E-mail: pliu@ist.psu.edu.

LIU, RHONDA LOUISE, librarian; b. Honolulu; d. David Yuk Fong Liu and Shirley May Chong Liu. BA, U. Hawaii at Manoa, Honolulu, 1974, M of Libr. Info. Studies, 1991; grad., FBI Citizens Acad., 1998. Remote regions/homework ctrs. outreach libr. Alu Like Native Hawaiian Libr. Project, Hawaii, 1992; libr. II Hawaii State Libr., Hawaii, 1992; fgn. expert libr. studies in English program Beijing Fgn. Studies U., 1992—93; info. specialist Savs. & Cmty. Bankers of Am., Washington, 1993—94; staff specialist III Md. State Dept. Edn., Md. State Libr. for Blind and Physically Handicapped, Balt., 1995—99; asst. project mgr. Serial Record Holdings Conversion Project/LSSI Libr. of Congress, Washington, 2000; reference libr. George Washington U. at Mt. Vernon Coll., Washington, 2000—01; sr. technician, serial record divsn. Libr. of Congress, Washington, 2001—02, serials control specialist, serial record divsn., 2002—03, sr. technician cataloguing in pub. div., 2003—04, cataloguer, history and lit. cataloguing divsn., children's lit. team, 2004—. Libr. asst. State of Hawaii Legis. Reference Bur. Libr., 1989-90; asst. rschr. State of Hawaii Legis. Info. Sys. Office, 1984-85; ESL tutor Keimei Gakuen, Tokyo, 1979; exhibit facilitator Smithsonian Instn., 1999. Active Friends of the Md. State Libr. for Blind and Physically Handicapped, 1994-99, Md. State Dept. Edn. Employees Adv. Coun., 1998-99; sec. Coalition Opposed to Violence and Extremism, State of Md., 1997-99; v.p., sec. U. Hawaii Sch. Libr. and Info. Studies, 1990-91; program chair Libr. Congress Asian Assn., 2004—, poster coord., 2005. Alu Like Native Hawaiian Libr. fellow, 1990-91; Kamehameha Sch./Bishop Estate scholar, 1991. Mem.: Libr. Congress Asian Assn. (program chmn. 2004—05, Asian Pacific Am. heritage month planning com. 2005), Libr. Congress Profl. Assn., Lung Kong Kung Shaw Soc., Kamehameha Schs. Alumni Assn. (East Coast region), U. Hawaii Sch. Lib. and Info. Studies Alumni Assn., U. Hawaii Alumni Assn., Libr. Congress Cooking Club. Business E-Mail: rliu@loc.gov.

LIU, SHENGZHONG (FRANK LIU), chemist, researcher; b. China, 1963; came to U.S., 1989; BSc, Shaanxi Tchrs. U., 1983; MSc, Lanzhou U., 1986; PhD, Northwestern U., 1992. Tchg., rsch. fellow Lanzhou U., China, 1986—89; material chemist Argonne Nat. Lab., Ill., 1992—94; sr. scientist QQC, Inc., Dearborn, Mich., 1994—97; scientist SI Diamond Tech. Inc., 1997—98; sr. scientist BP Solar, Toano, Va., 1998—. Contbr. articles to Sci., Nature. Recipient R&D 100 award. Mem. ASM Internat., Materials Sci. Soc., Am. Chem. Soc., Minerals, Metals, Materials Soc. Achievements include patents for synthesis of diamond and related materials, methods of joining metal components, preparation of nanoscale materials. Home: 2154 Kennedy Dr Rochester MI 48309-2900 Business E-Mail: fliu@uni-solar.com.

LIU, SI-KWANG, veterinary pathologist; b. Kwangsi, China; came to U.S., 1959; s. Yeeshao and Shinmei (Yeh) L.; m. Sing-ping Chueh, Dec. 20, 1961; children: Davis, Ernest, Diana, Phillip. DVM, Chinese Vet. Coll., Anshun Kweichow, 1950; PhD, U. Calif., Davis, 1964. Chief veterinarian Taitung Agrl. Rsch. Sta., Taiwan, 1951-56; instr., chief Nat. Taiwan U. Vet. Hosp., Taipei, 1956-59; rsch. asst. U. Calif. Sch. Vet. Med., Davis, 1959-64; pathologist, sci. fellow N.Y. Zool. Soc., Bronx, 1964-88, 88—; pathologist, chief, sr. staff mem. Animal Med. Ctr., N.Y.C., 1964-97; fellow in pathology VA Gen. Hosp., Bronx, 1965-68; sr. pathologist, chmn. dept. pathology Animal Med. Ctr., N.Y.C., 1997-98; from asst. assoc. prof. to prof. N.Y. Med. Coll., N.Y.C., 1966-90; sr. pathologist, assoc. dir. Caspary Rsch. Inst., N.Y.C., 1998—. Cons. Pig Rsch. Inst., Taiwan, 1984—; vis. expert Nat. Sci. Coun., Taipei, 1976, 83, 88, 91; vis. prof. Nat. Taiwan U., Taipei, 1976, 88, 91, Nat. Chung Hsing U., Taichung, Taiwan, 1983; adj. prof. medicine Cornell U. Med. Coll., N.Y.C., 1998—; condr. some 300 lectrs., acad. presentations, and discussions in biomed. and sci. confs., U.S. and abroad. Author: An Atlas of Cardiovascular Pathology, 1989; contbr. more than 250 articles to Jour. Vet. Med. Assn., Am. Jour. Pathology, others. Elder Presbyn. Ch. of Newtown, Elmhurst, N.Y., 1970-80. Recipient rsch. award Ralston Purina Co., 1982, Feline Disease award Cornation, 1984, Rsch. Excellence award Beecham, 1986, comparative pathology award Chinese Pathology Soc., 1989, Outstanding Svc. award N.Y.C. Vet. Assn., 1991, Outstanding Svc. award N.Y. State Vet. Medicine Soc., 1991, Rsch. award Japanese Vet. Cardiol. Soc., 1992, Rsch. and Svc. award Chinese Vet. Med. Assn., 1992, award Chinese Vet. Med. Assn., 1993, 95, Postgrad. Edn. award Chinese Vet. Med. Assn., 1995, Rsch. Excellence in Cardiovasc. Diseases award Pig Rsch. Inst., Taiwan, 1995, Disting. Svc. award Animal Med. Ctr., 1999. Mem. Internat. Acad. Pathology, Internat. Skeletal Soc., Internat. Cardiovascular Pathology Soc., N.Y. Acad. Scis., Am. Vet. Med. Assn., Vet. Med. Assn. N.Y.C. (hon.), N.Y. State Vet. Medicine Soc. Office: Animal Med Ctr 510 E 62nd St New York NY 10021-8314

LIU, TAOSHENG, neuroscientist; b. Lanzhou, Gansu, China; s. Zhongyuan Liu and Guizhi Zhang; m. Lily Yan; 1 child, Sophia. PhD, Columbia U., 2001. Postdoctoral fellow Johns Hopkins U., Baltimore, Md., 2001—03; rsch. scientist NYU, N.Y.C., NY, 2003—. Grad. Rsch. fellow, Columbia U., 1996. Mem.: Soc. for Neuroscience. Achievements include research in brain mechanisms of visual attention. Office: NYU 6 Wash Pl 8th Fl New York NY 10003 Office Phone: 212-998-8233.

LIU, XIAO, ophthalmologist, neurobiologist; b. Shanghai, Feb. 11, 1967; s. Benren Liu and Ke Hu. MD, Shanghai Med. U., 1990; PhD, Kyoto U., 1999. Ophthalmologist Huadong Hosp., Shanghai, 1990—94, Nagata Eye Hosp., Ikoma Gen. Hosp., Japan, 1995—98; predoctoral rsch. fellow Northwestern U. Med. Sch., Chgo., 1998—99; postdoctoral rsch. fellow Doheny Eye Inst. U. So. Calif. Keck Sch. Medicine, L.A., 1999—2001; rsch. fellow dept. ophthalmology U. Calif., San Francisco, 2001—. Recipient Eye Rsch. award Meml. Eye Rsch. Fund, Tokyo, 1994, Travel award Japan Med. Assn., 1995, Toyobo Bio-tech. Travel award, Tokyo, 1997, Eye Rsch. award, China-Japan Med. Assn., 1998. Mem. AAAS, N.Y. Acad. Sci., Assn. Rsch. in Vision and Ophthalmology, Assn. Online Ophthalmologists, Fedn. Am. Soc. for Exptl. Biology, Am. Assn. Anatomists. Achievements include research in cataract, glaucoma and retina surgery; cell adhesion study; transgenic mice study; nerve regeneration and growth cone study. Office: UCSF Beckman Vision Ctr Dept ophthalmology 10 Kirkham St San Francisco CA 94143 Office Phone: 415-476-4135. Personal E-mail: xiaoliu98@yahoo.com. Business E-Mail: xiaoliu@itsa.ucsf.edu.

LIU, XIAO, physicist, researcher; b. Shanghai, Nov. 7, 1963; arrived in U.S.A., 1995; s. Shuxian Liu and Linli Shen; m. Hong Chen, Jan. 13, 1990; children: Ray Hui, Jing Jean. BS, Tongji U., Shanghai, China, 1986, MS, 1989; D rerum naturalium, U. Karlsruhe, Germany, 1995. Rsch. asst. Tongji U., Shanghai, 1989—91; rsch. academia U. Karlsruhe, Germany, 1991—95; postdoctoral assoc. Cornell U., Ithaca, NY, 1995—98; rsch. physicist SFA, Inc., Largo, Md., 1998—2003, Naval Rsch. Lab., Washington, 2003—. Contbr. scientific papers, articles to profl. jours. Recipient Alan Berman Rsch. Publs. award, Naval Rsch. Lab., 2002. Mem.: Am. Physics Soc. Achievements include research in low temperature solid state physics. Office: Naval Rsch Lab 4555 Overlook Ave SW Washington DC 20375 Office Phone: 202-404-8065. Business E-Mail: xiao.liu@nrl.navy.mil.

LIU, XIAOHANG, research scientist; b. Linquan, Anhui, China, Oct. 21, 1966; s. Wencai Liu and Shizhen Yu; m. Wei Dai, May 10, 1992; 1 child, Jessica. BS, Nanjing U., China, 1986, MS, 1989, PhD, 1992. Postdoctoral Chinese Acad. Scis., Beijing, 1992—94; rsch. scientist Brandenburg Tech. U., Berlin, 1994—95; Humboldt Rsch. fellow Fraunhofer Inst., Garmisch-P., Germany, 1995—97; rsch. prof. Chinese Acad. Scis., Beijing, 1997—99; rsch. fellow U. Mich., Ann Arbor, 1999—2002, rsch. scientist, 2000—. Contbr. over 30 articles to profl. jours. Mem.: Am. Meteorol. Soc., Am. Geophys. Union. Office: Univ Mich Dept Atmos Oceanic and Space Scis 2455 Hayward St Ann Arbor MI 48109

LIU, XINRU, history professor, researcher; b. Changsha, China; arrived in U.S., 1980; d. Xiangwen Liu and Yinglei Duan; m. Weiye Li, Apr. 12, 1986; 1 child, Yafeng Li. PhD, U. Pa., 1985. Sr. rschr. Chinese Acad. Social Scis., Beijing, 1979—; part-time faculty mem. Coll. of N.J., Ewing, 1998—2005, faculty mem., 2005—. Rsch. fellow Am. Inst. Indian Studies, New Delhi, 1985; vis. prof. Beijing U., 1988—89; rsch. fellow Woodrow Wilson Ctr., Washington, 1990—91; vis. prof. U. Tex., Austin, 1991, 94; rsch. fellow Indian Coun. Social Sci., New Delhi, 1994; vis. fellow Princeton U., 1997—98; rsch. fellow Maison des Scis. de l'homme, Paris, 1998. Author: Ancient India and Ancient China, 1988 (award Chinese Acad. Social Scis., 1991), Silk and Religion, 1996, (pamphlet) The Silk Road, 1998. Grantee AAUW, 1984, Woodrow Wilson Internat. Ctr. for Scholars, 1990. Mem.: World History Assn., Am. Hist. Assn., Am. Assn. Asian Studies. Avocations: photography, gardening. Home: 17 Henley Rd Wynnewood PA 19096 Office: Coll of NJ History Dept PO Box 7718 Ewing NJ 08628 Office Phone: 609-771-2341.

LIU, XINSHENG, chemist; b. Jilin, China, Dec. 24, 1953; came to U.S., 1990; s. Hongru Liu and Gaoqin Wei; m. Xianying Meng, Feb. 2, 1978; children: Lei, Dan. MS, Jilin U., 1981; PhD, U. Cambridge, Eng., 1986. Lectr., assoc. prof. Jilin U., Changchun, China, 1977-90; vis. scholar U. Cambridge, 1990; rsch. assoc., rsch. prof. U. Notre Dame, Ind., 1990-96; sr. chemist, rsch. assoc. Engelhard Corp., Iselin, NJ, 1996—. Contbr. articles to profl. jours. Grantee Chinese Nat. Sci. and Tech. Com., 1988. Mem. Am. Chem. Soc., Chinese Chem. Soc. (Solid State Chemistry divsn. com.). Achievements include discovering a galliation method for introducing gallium into structures of zeolites; synthesizing for the first time gallosilicate zeolite, and titanosilicate molecular sieves using solid TiO_2, finding surface structure of alumina, SCR catalysts for NOx. Home: 6 Ventnor Dr Edison NJ 08820-2734 Office: Engelhard Corp 101 Wood Ave S Iselin NJ 08830-2703 Office Phone: 732-205-7038. E-mail: xinsheng_liu@englehard.com.

LIU, XIUFENG, science educator; PhD, U. BC, 1993. Asst., assoc. prof. St. Francis Xaiver U., Antigonish, Canada, 1992—98; assoc. prof. U. Prince Edward Island, Charlottetown, 1998—2002, SUNY, Buffalo, 2002—. Presenter over 30 referred confs. Author: 1 edited book; contbr. over 25 referred jour. articles. Mem.: Nat. Assn. Rsch. Sci. Tchg., Am. Ednl. Rsch. Assn. Office: SUNY at Buffalo Flint Rd Buffalo NY 14260-1000

LIU, YING, research scientist; b. Chengdu, Sichuan, China; d. Guanghou Liu and Jinyun He; m. Larry Zhao, Sept. 24, 1999; 1 child, Lily J Zhao. B.S., West China U. Med. Sciences, 1990; M.S., U. Scis. Phila., 1999, Ph. D., 2002. Rsch. assoc. Anti-parasitic Disease Inst. of Sichuan Med. Acad., Chengdu, China, 1990—95; vis. scientist Fox Chase Cancer Ctr., Philadelphia, Pa., 1995—96; rsch. scientist West Pharm. Services, Lionville, Pa., 2002—. Abraham Glaser fellow, U. Scis. Phila., 1996—2002. Mem.: Americal Assn. of Pharm. Scientists, Rho Chi. Office: West Pharm Svcs 101 Gordon Dr Lionville PA 19341 Office Phone: 610-594-3935. Office Fax: 610-594-3007. E-mail: ying.liu@westpharma.com.

LIU, YONG, computer scientist, researcher; b. Lichuan County, China, Dec. 5, 1971; s. Erming Liu and Jinxian Pan; m. Yuancheng Tu, June 6, 1997. B in Engring., Tsinghua U., Beijing, 1994, M in Engring., 1997; M in Computer sci., PhD, U. Ill., 2001. Cert. Microsoft profl. Rsch. programmer U. Ill., Urbana, 2001—. Author: (software) BIODDPMS, Ill. Microarray Database; contbr. articles to profl. jours. Grantee, Nat. Ctr. Supercomputing Applications, 2003. Mem.: Internat. Soc. Environ. Info. Scis., Am. Geophys. Union, Soc. Indsl. and Applied Math., Assn. Computing Machinery. Achievements include development of computationally efficient multiscale algorithm for large scale optimal design of bioremediation.

LIU, YOUCHENG, research scientist, educator; s. Shangrong Liu and Zaihua Wang. MD, Nanjing Med. U., China, 1983; MPH, Beijing Med. U., China, 1987; MS, Harvard U., 1994, DSc, 1997. Rschr. Yale U., New Haven, 1999—, asst. prof. medicine, 2003—, lectr. pub. health, 2004—. Adv. com. mem. Harvard U. Sch. of Pub. Health, Boston, 2004—. Contbr. articles in field. Mem.: Internat. Soc. Exposure Analysis, Am. Conf. Govtl. Indsl. Hygienist, Am. Indsl. Hygiene Assn. Office: Yale U Sch Medicine 135 College St New Haven CT 06510 Home: 1240 Whitney Ave Hamden CT 06517 Office Phone: 203-785-5969. Office Fax: 203-785-7391. Business E-Mail: youcheng.liu@yale.edu.

LIU, YUE, research scientist; b. Yibin, China, Aug. 13, 1959; s. Bangzhou Liu and Gouying Gao; m. Chang Lam, Jan. 17, 1998; children: Amy, Ella. BS in Chem. Physics, Sichuan (China) U., 1985; PhD, SUNY, Buffalo, 1995. Sr. rsch. scientist Ciba Splty. Chems., Tarrytown, NY, 1996—2004; sr. computer scientist Ferro Corp, Penn Yan, NY, 2004—. Recipient 1st prize in math. competition, Sichuan U., 1982. Mem.: Am. Chem. Soc. Achievements include patents for CMP Slurry Formulation. Home: 30 Burncoat Way Pittsford NY 14534

LIU, YULIANG, industrial designer, educator; arrived in U.S., 1995; s. Zhongtao Liu and Guixiang Shen; m. Wei Su, June 9, 1992; children: Sujing, Sujia, Sufang. B in Applied Linguistics, Hengyang Normal Coll., China, 1984; MEd, NW Normal U., Gansu, China, 1990; PhD, Tex. A&M U., 2000. Classroom tchr. Hengyang Mid. Sch., Hengyang, China, 1984—87; rsch. assoc. Changsha Ednl. Inst., Changsha, China, 1990—95; asst. prof. So. Ill. U., Edwardsville, Ill., 2000—. Program dir. of instrnl. tech. So. Ill. U., Edwardsville, Ill., 2003. Contbr. chapters to books, articles to profl. jours. Recipient Alumni Amb. Award, Tex. A&M University-Commerce, 2003; grantee, Ill. Bd. of Higher Edn., 2002, So. Ill. Collegiate Common Market and Southwestern Ill. Higher Edn. Consortium, 2001, Ill. Gen. Assembly, 2000, Sch. of Edn., So. Ill. U., 2001, Grad. Sch., So. Ill. U., 2001, 2003, 2004, 2005. Mem.: Soc. of Internat. Chinese in Ednl. Tech. (corr.), Assn. for the Advancement of Computing in Edn. (corr.), Am. Edn. Rsch. Assn. (corr.), Assn. for Ednl. Comm. and Tech. (corr.). Mem. Citizens Party. Achievements include research in designing and developing an online course entitled research methods in education; conducted various comparative studies between online and traditional education. Home: 7060 Stallion Drive Edwardsville IL 62025 Office: Campus Box 1125 Southern Illinois University Edwardsville IL 62026 Office Phone: 618-650-3293. Office Fax: 618-650-3808. Personal E-mail: yliu63@gmail.com. E-mail: yliu@siue.edu.

LIU, ZI-KUI, materials engineering educator; b. Xiang Dong Tungsten Mine, Cha-Ling Hunan, China, Jan. 21, 1963; came to the U.S., 1996; s. Kecai Liu and You Ling Song; m. Weiming Huang; children: Erik, David. BS, Ctrl. South U. Tech., Changsha, China, 1982; MS, U. Sci. and Tech., Beijing, 1985; PhD, Royal Inst. Tech., Stockholm, 1992, docent, 1996. Tchg. staff U. Sci. and Tech., Beijing, 1985—87; rschr. Royal Inst. Tech., Stockholm, 1992—96; rsch. assoc. U. Wis., Madison, 1996—98; sr. rsch. scientist Questek Innovations LLC, Evanston, Ill., 1998; asst. prof. Pa. State U., University Park, 1999—2003, assoc. prof., 2003—. Editor-in-chief: CALPHAD; contbr. articles to profl. jours. Bd. mem. Chinese Lang. Sch., Madison, 1996-98. Recipient 3rd prize China Nat. Key Projects, Ministry Metallurgy, China, 1988; China State Coun. expert lecturing scholar, 1998, Career award NSF, 1999. Mem. The Mineral, Metals and Materials Soc. (TMS Young Leader 1998), Am. Soc. Metals, Materials Rsch. Soc., Sigma Xi. Avocations: tennis, skiing, squash, golf. Office: Pa State Univ 209 Steidle Bldg University Park PA 16802-5006 Business E-Mail: zikui@psu.edu.

LIVA, EDWARD LOUIS, eye surgeon; b. Lyndhurst, N.J., Aug. 30, 1925; s. Paul Francis and Lucy Agnes (Andreozzi) L.; m. Dorothea Lucille Carter, Aug. 29, 1946; children: Edward Jr., Bradford, Douglas, Jeffrey, Elaine. SB, Harvard U., 1946, MD, 1950. Diplomate Am. Bd. Ophthalmology. Intern Med. Coll. Va., Richmond, 1950-51; fellow in eye pathology Mass. Eye and Ear, Boston, 1951; resident Brooklyn Eye and Ear, N.Y., 1952-53; chief ophthalmic examiner Workman's Compensation Bd., N.Y.C., 1957-63; sr. ophthalmic surgeon Hackensack (N.J.) Med. Ctr., 1957—, Valley Hosp., Ridgewood, N.J., 1963-99; sr. ophthalmic surgeon, resident instr. oculoplastics Manhatten Eye, Ear and Throat, N.Y.C., 1957-96, emeritus, 1996—. Pres. Bergen Surg. Ctr., Paramus, N.J., 1991—, Eye Inst. of Paramus, 1987—. Author: Advances in Ophthalmic Plastic, 1983. Active Rep. Club, Ridgewood, 1960—. Capt. USAF, 1955-57. Fellow AMA, Am. Acad. Ophthalmology, Internat. Coll. of Surgeons, Am. Soc. of Ophtalmic Plastic and Reconstructive Surgery (chartered). Republican. Roman Catholic. Achievements include development of new lid flaps oculoplastics, prototype of lid canal laceration repair, major modification of ptosis surgical procedures widely used, disproved Trichromatic theory of color vision in 1952. Office: Liva Eye Ctr One West Ridgewood Ave Paramus NJ 07652 Home: # Lph 2600 S Ocean Blvd Boca Raton FL 33432-8385 Personal E-mail: eliva@mac.com.

LIVAUDAIS, MARCEL, JR., federal judge; b. New Orleans, Mar. 3, 1925; m. Carol Black (dec.); children: Julie, Marc, Durel. BA, Tulane U., 1945, JD, 1949. Bar: La. 1949. Assoc. Boswell & Loeb, New Orleans, 1949-50, 52-56; ptnr. Boswell Loeb & Livaudais, New Orleans, 1956-60, Loeb & Livaudais, 1960-67, 71-77, Loeb Dillon & Livaudais, 1967-71; U.S. magistrate, 1977-84; judge U.S. Dist. Ct. (ea. dist.) La., New Orleans, 1984-96, sr. judge, 1996—. Mem. Am. Judicature Soc. Office: US Dist Ct C-405 US Courthouse 500 Camp St New Orleans LA 70130-3313*

LIVELY, CAROL A., retired professional society administrator; b. Chgo., Sept. 2, 1935; d. William Mann and Lillian (Juske) Haycock; m. E. Raymond Platig; children: Richard B., Laura Jean. L.P.N., Los Angeles Sch. Nursing, 1953; student, Columbia U., 1954, Boston U., 1956-57. Program dir. United Fund, Pittsfield, Mass., 1966-71; exec. dir. Western Mass. Health Council, 1971-74; asst. exec. dir. Genesse Health Council, Rochester, N.Y., 1974-76; dir. devel. Shimer Coll., Mt. Carroll, Ill., 1976-77; assoc. dir. Am. Hosp. Assn., Chgo., 1977-80; dir. health div., v.p. Smith Bucklin Assn., Washington, 1980—96, ret., 1996. Mem. Achievement Rewards Coll. Scientists, Washington, 1980-96, Meridan House, 2000—, Black Tie Club, Inc., 1993—; cons. Dept. Health Rep. Haiti, Washington, 1976— Contbg. author: Politics of Health Planning, 1962; contbr. articles to profl. jours. Bd. dirs. Jacobs Pillow Dance Theatre, Pittsfield, 1968, Albany Regional Med. Program, N.Y., 1971-74. Symphony Soc.; v.p. Symphony Guild; mem. Jr. League, 1965—; mem. Commn. Drug Abuse Council, Boston, 1971-74; mem. women's bd. Washington Ballet, 1998-2001; trustee Shimer Coll.; mem. Fla. Internat. Music Festival Guild, Mus. Arts and Sci., Daytona Beach. Recipient Woman of Yr. award Bus. and Profl. Women, 1971 Fellow Am. Coll. Nuclear Physicians; mem. New Eng. Pub. Health Assn., Mass. Council on Aging, Am. Soc. Hosp. Planning, Am. Pub. Health Assn., Nat. Rehb. Hosp. Bd. Assn. Home: 1 Old Trl Ormond Beach FL 32174-4312

LIVELY, CARTER CUNNINGHAM, museum director; b. Portsmouth, Va., Aug. 25, 1953; s. Warren Powell and Sarah Frances (Gayle) L.; m. Cathy Lynn Spitler, June 3, 1976. BA, James Madison U., 1976. Historian George Washingtons Grist Mill State Park, Alexandria, Va., 1977; mgr. Luray (Va.) Caverns Corp., 1977-86; asst. dir. Belle Grove Plantation, Middletown, Va., 1986-92; exec. dir. Liberty Hall Hist. Site, Frankfort, Ky., 1992—. Bd. dirs. Blue Grass Places, Bluegrass Region, Ky.; v.p. Hist. Confederation Ky., 1994. Pres. Am. Cancer Soc., Page County, Va., 1987. Named Ky. Col., Gov. of Ky., 1994. Mem. Ky. Hist. Soc., Historic Homes Found., Mus. Early So. Decorative Arts, Friends of Shakertown, Civil War Roundtable, Filson Club. Episcopalian. Avocations: archtl. history and design, decorative arts. Home: 106 Evon Ct Severna Park MD 21146-1914 Office: Liberty Hall Historic Site 218 Wilkinson St Frankfort KY 40601-1826

LIVELY, PIERCE, retired federal judge; b. Louisville, Aug. 17, 1921; s. Henry Thad and Ruby Durrett (Keating) L.; m. Amelia Harrington, May 25, 1946; children: Susan, Katherine, Thad. AB, Centre Coll., Ky., 1943; LL.B., U. Va., 1948. Bar: Ky. 1948. Individual practice law, Danville, Ky., 1949—57; mem. firm Lively and Rodes, Danville, 1957—72; judge U.S. Ct. Appeals (6th cir.), Cin., 1972—, chief judge, 1983—88, sr. judge, 1988—97, ret., 1997. Trustee Centre Coll. With USNR, 1943—46. Mem.: ABA, Am. Judicature Soc., Raven Soc., Order of Coif, Omicron Delta Kappa, Phi Beta Kappa. Presbyterian.

LIVENGOOD, SCOTT A., former food products executive; b. Salisbury, NC, Aug. 11, 1952; BS, U. N.C., 1974. With Krispy Kreme Doughnuts Inc., 1977—2005, COO, 1992—98, pres., 1992—2005, CEO, 1998—2005, chmn., 1999—2005, dir., 1994—2005. Mem. exec. com. U. N.C. Chapel Hill Ednl. Found.; advisor Carolina First Campaign Com., Winston-Salem, NC.

LIVENGOOD, VICKIE YVONNE, broadcast executive; b. Prosser, Wash. d. Gail Frances Flint; m. Victor Scott Livengood, Mar. 18, 2000; children: Daniel, Jeremy, Dustin, Andrew, Charles, Bryce, Victoria. Lic. and ordained minister 2002. Gen. mgr. KRLB-TV, Richland, Wash., 2001—. Pub. spkr., filmmaker. Youth mentor. Mem.: IFM. Christian. Avocation: autocross. Office: KRLB-TV 704 Symons St Richland WA 99352 Business E-Mail: info@rlb.org.

LIVERIS, ANDREW N., chemical company executive; b. Darwin, Australia; married; 3 children. BS in Chemical Engring., U. Queensland, 1976. Joined Dow Chem. Co., 1976, gen. mgr. all ops., 1989—92, group bus. dir. Midland, Mich., 1992—93, gen. mgr., 1993—94, v.p., 1994—95, pres., Dow chem. pacific Hong Kong, 1995—98, v.p. splty. chems. Midland,

1998—2000, bus. group pres., 2000—04, pres., 2003—, COO, 2003—04, CEO, 2004—. Bd. mem., exec. com. OPTIMAL Group, Malaysia; bd. dirs. Dow Corning Corp., Dow Chemical Co., 2004—; bd. trustees Herbert H. and Grace A. Dow Found. Bd. mem. Lake Huron Area Coun., Boy Scouts Am. Mem.: Am. Chemistry Coun., Soap and Detergent Assn., Comerica Bank (Midland advisory bd. mem.), Inst. Chem. Engrs. (UK) (corp. mem.), Midland Ctr. for the Arts (bd. mem.). Office: The Dow Chem Co 47 Building Midland MI 48667

LIVERMORE, ANN M., computer company executive; b. Greensboro, N.C., Aug. 23, 1958; BA in Econ., U. N.C., Chapel Hill, 1980; MBA, Stanford U., 1982. Various mgmt. positions Hewlett-Packard Co., Palo Alto, Calif., 1982-1995, corp. v.p., 1995—, pres., CEO enterprise computing divsn., 1998—2003, pres. tech. solutions group, 2003—. Bd. dirs. UPS; bd. visitors Kenan-Flagler Bus. Sch., bd. visitors. Named an Most Powerful Women, Forbes mag., 2005. Office Phone: 650-691-5565.

LIVERMORE, BETH ANNE, journalist, photographer; b. Waterbury, Conn., Jan. 10, 1962; d. Robert Allen and Anne Elizabeth (DeGrote) L. BJ, U. Mo., 1986. Writer, editor Health mag., N.Y.C., 1987-90; assoc. editor Sea Frontiers, Miami, Fla., 1993-96. Contbr. numerous articles to Sea Frontiers (1st place award 1991, 93), Smithsonian, Glamour, Self, Destination Discovery, Omni, Nat. Geog. World, Travel Holiday, E: The Environ. Mag., Popular Sci., Snow Country, Mademoiselle. Recipient gold award Nat. Health Info. Awards, 1995; internat. enrichment scholar, 1985, Virginia McElroy Schwartz journalism scholar, 1986, Nat. Arts Club, 1992; sci. writing fellow Marine Biol. Labs., 1990, APA, 1996. Mem. Am. Soc. Journalists and Authors, Nat. Press Photographers Assn., Soc. Environ. Journalists, Nat. Assn. Sci. Writers, N.Y. Newswomen's Assn. Avocations: scuba diving, horseback riding, skiing, biking, ballet.

LIVERS, CATHERINE MCGHEE, writer; b. Indpls., June 11, 1953; d. Martha McGhee, Phillip McGhee; m. Fred L. Livers, Aug. 11, 1973; children: Shereka, Marcus, Victoria. AA, Rehoboth Christian Coll., Indpls., 1998. Instr. Hebrew and Greek langs. Rehoboth Christian Coll., Indpls., 1995—99; instr. Greek lang. Simmons Bible Coll., Indpls., 1998—99. Dir. Shahar Inst., Indpls., 1997—; CEO Shahar Pub., Indpls., 1999—. Author: Biblical History of Black Mankind, 1999 (Merit award Writers Digest, 2000, Book of Yr. award UBUS Comms. Sus., 2000, Meet the Artist XII award Indpls. Marion County Pub. Libr., 2001), Biblical History of Mankind, 2004. Mem.: Nat. Coun. Negro Women, Ind. African-Am. Genealogy Group, African Am. Authors Helping Authors. Office: Shahar Publishing 8605 Allisonville Rd #283 Indianapolis IN 46250 Office Phone: 317-577-0392. Business E-Mail: shaharpublishing@hotmail.com.

LIVERSAGE, RICHARD ALBERT, cell biologist, educator; b. Fitchburg, Mass., July 8, 1925; s. Rodney Marcellus and Hazel Mildred (Huntting) L.; m. June Patricia Krebs, June 19, 1954; children: John Walter, Robert Richard, James Keith, Ross Andrew. BA, Marlboro Coll., 1951; A.M., Amherst Coll., 1953, Princeton U., 1957, PhD, 1958. Fellow Bowdoin Coll., Brunswick, Maine, 1953-54; instr. Amherst Coll., 1954-55, Princeton, 1958-60; mem. faculty U. Toronto, 1960—, prof. zoology, 1969—, grad. sec. dept., 1975-77, asso. chmn. grad. affairs dept., 1978-84, acting chmn., 1980-81. Investigator Huntsman Marine Lab., St. Andrews, N.B., Can., 1968-71; vis. prof. Strangeways Rsch. Lab., Cambridge, Eng., 1972. Contbr. numerous articles on role of nerves and endocrine secretions and the genetic basis of vertebrate appendage regeneration to sci. jours. Served as flight engr. USAAF, 1943-45. Recipient 5 decorations. Mem. Royal Can. Inst., Sigma Xi (exec. com., v.p., pres. U. Toronto chpt.). Home: PO Box 651 RR 3 Bobcaygeon ON Canada K0M 1A0 Office: U Toronto Ramsay Wright Zool Lab Toronto ON Canada M5S 3G5 Office Phone: 416-978-3476. Business E-Mail: liversage@zoo.utoronto.ca.

LIVESAY, THOMAS ANDREW, museum director, educator; b. Dallas, Feb. 1, 1945; s. Melvin Ewing Clay and Madge Almeda (Hall) L.; m. Jennifer Clark, June 15, 1985 (div.); 1 child, Russell; m. Amanda Haralson, Nov. 12, 1994; children: Heather Marie, Seth Stover. BFA, U. Tex., Austin, 1968, MFA, 1972; postgrad., Harvard U. Inst. Arts Adminstrn., 1978. Curator Elisabet Ney Mus., Austin, 1971-73; dir. Longview (Tex.) Mus. and Arts Ctr., 1973-75; curator Amarillo (Tex.) Art Ctr., 1975-77, dir., 1977-80; asst. dir. for adminstrn. Dallas Mus. Fine Arts, 1980-85; dir. Mus. of N.Mex., Santa Fe, 1985-2000, Whatcom Mus. History and Art, Bellingham, Wash., 2000—. Mem. touring panel Tex. Commn. Arts; mem. panel Nat. Endowment Arts, Inst. Mus. Svcs.; adj. prof. U. Okla., Coll. Liberal Studies, 1992—, U. N.Mex., 1992—; chmn. N.Mex. State Records and Archives Commn., 1986—. Author: Young Texas Artists Series, 1978, Made in Texas, 1979; editor: video tape American Images, 1979, Ruth Abrams, Paintings, 1940-85, NYU Press. Served with U.S. Army, 1969-71. Mem. Am. Assn. Mus. (coun. 1986-89, commn. on ethics 1992—, accreditation commn. 1994—, chmn. accreditation commn. 1997-2003, bd. dirs. 2004—), Tex. Assn. Mus. (v.p. 1981, pres. 1983), Rotary. Presbyterian. Office: Whatcom Mus History & Art 121 Prospect St Bellingham WA 98225 Office Phone: 360-676-6981 x210. Business E-Mail: tlivesay@cob.org.

LIVI, IVAN DAVID, retired educational administrator; b. Belle Vernon, Pa., June 17, 1920; s. Attilio Ausilio and Maria (Lazzari) L.; m. Annabelle Rigotti, Apr. 14, 1945; 1 child, Darla. Student, U. Pitts., 1958-64. Technician Mid-States Aviation, Northbrook, Ill., 1945-51; instr. Pitts. Inst. of Aero., 1951-54, dir. tng., 1954-64, v.p., 1964-72, exec. dir., 1972-78, pres., 1978—93; ret., 1993. Pres. Aviation Tech. Edn. Coun., Harrisburg, Pa., 1975-77. Contbr. articles to profl. jours. Recipient Award of Excellence FAA, 1989, Clifford Ball award Aero Club of Pitts., 1990, Award of Excellence Profl. Aviation Maint. Assn., 1991. Mem. Pa. Assn. Pvt. Sch. Adminstrs. (pres. 1977-79). Avocations: music, science, astronomy. Home: 210 Melvin Dr Pittsburgh PA 15236-1432 E-mail: ivan.livi@verizon.net.

LIVICK, STEPHEN, fine art photographer; b. Leeds, Yorkshire, Eng., Feb. 11, 1945; arrived in Can., 1947; Student, Sir George Williams U., Montreal, Can., 1963-66. Self employed artist, 1970—. One man shows include Centaur Gallery, Montreal, 1972, London Art Gallery, Ont., 1973, George Eastman House, Rochester, N.Y., 1975, David Mirvish Gallery, Toronto, 1976, 77, Photography Gallery, Bowmanville, Ont., 1976, 77, Balt. Mus. Art, 1978, Lunn Graphics, Washington D.C., 1978, Gallery Graphics, Ottawa, 1978, Jane Corkin Gallery, Toronto, 1979, 80, 81, U. Western Ont., London, 1981, 93, George Dalsheimer Gallery, Balt., 1982, MacDonald Stewart Art Ctr., Guelph, 1983, 94, New Brunswick Craft Sch., Fredericton, 1986, Winnipeg Photographers Group, 1987, Galerie Sequence, Quebec, 1988, U .Sherbrooke, 1990, Can. Mus. Contemporary Photography, Ottawa, 1992, MacKenzie Art Gallery, Regina, 1994, Meml. U. Art Gallery, St. John's, 1994, Beaverbrook Art Gallery, Fredicton, 1995, Art Gallery Windsor, 1995, Columbia U., N.Y., 1996, Tokyo Art Gallery, Ginza, Japan, 1998; travelling exhibitions include George Eastman House, 1978-81, London Regional Art Gallery, 1976-77, Nat. Film Bd., 1976-84, Art Gallery Ont., 1980, 81, Can. Mus. Contemporary Photography, 1986, 87; exhibited in group shows at Nat. Art Gallery, Ottawa, 1975, London Pub. Art Gallery, 1976, Nat. Film Bd., Ottawa, Can., 1977, Mendal Art Gallery, Saskatoon, Can., 1977, Neikrug Galleries, N.Y.C., 1978, Banff-London Exchange, Alberta, Can., 1978, Smithsonian Instn., Washington, 1981, Carpenter Ctr. Visual Arts, Cambridge, Mass., 1981, U. Calgary, 1982, Saidy Bronfman Mus., Montreal, 1984, Photographers Gallery, London, Eng., 1984, Presentation House, Vancouver, B.C., 1985, Photo Union Gallery, Hamilton, Ont., 1986, Film In The City, St. Paul, 1989, Corcoran Gallery Art, Washington, 1989, London (Can.) Regional Art Mus., 1990, Can. Mus. Contemporary Photography, Ottowa, 1992, others; represented in permanent collections Nat. Art Gallery Can., Can Mus. Contemporary Photography, Art Gallery Ont., Can. Art Bank, Nat. Archives Can., Mus. Modern Art, N.Y., George Eastman House, Rochester, N.Y., Carnegie Mus. Art, Pitts., Mus. Fine Arts, Houston, Fogg Art Mus., Cambridge, Mass., Balt. Mus. Art, George Washington U., Washington, Norton Gallery Art, West Palm Beach, Fla., Syracuse (N.Y.) U., Middlebury (Vt.) Coll., Hickory (N.C.) Mus. Art, U. Iowa Mus., U. No. Iowa, Art Gallery Hamilton, Can., High Mus. Art, Atlanta, Ga., London Regional Art Gallery, Corcoran Gallery Art, Washington, Queens U., Kingston, Can., Winnipeg (Can.) Art Gallery, Sarnia (Ont.) Art Gallery, U. Western Ont., London, Macdonald Stewart Art Ctr., Guelph, Ont., numerous pvt., corp. collections. B level grantee Can. Coun., Ottawa; sr. grantee Ont. Arts Coun., Toronto. Home and Office: 22A Maitland St Studio London ON N6B 3L2 Canada N6B 3L2 Office Phone: 519-672-2011. E-mail: slivick@livick.com.

LIVINGOOD, WILSON S., protective services official; b. Phila., Oct. 1, 1936; s. Clarence S. and Louise S. L.; m. Mari Louise Vatter, Feb. 21, 1998; stepchildren: Sarah, Elizabeth, Anne. BS in Police Adminstrn., Mich. State U., 1961. Spl. agt. U.S. Secret Svc., Dallas, 1961-69, spl. agt. in charge, 1969-86, deputy asst. dir., 1986-89, exec. asst. to dir., 1989-95; sgt. at arms U.S. Ho. of Reps., Washikngton, 1995—. Bd. dirs. Fed. Law Enforcement Tng. Ctr., Glynco, Ga. With USN, 1954-57. Mem. Nat. Sheriffs Assn., Internat. Assn. Chiefs of Police (exec. com. 1993-2001), Belle Haven Country Club (past bd. dirs.). Episcopalian. Avocations: tennis, running, skiing, sailing, golf. Office: US Ho of Reps H-124 The Capitol Washington DC 20515-0001

LIVINGSTON, BOB (ROBERT LINLITHGOW LIVINGSTON JR.), lawyer, retired congressman; b. Colorado Springs, Colo., Apr. 30, 1943; s. Robert L. and Dorothy (Godwin) Livingston; m. Bonnie Robichaux, Sept. 13, 1965; children: Robert Linlithgow III, Richard Godwin, David Barkley, SuShan Alida. BA in Econs., Tulane U., 1967, JD, 1968; postgrad., Loyola Inst. Politics, 1973. Bar: La. 1968. Ptnr. Livingston & Powers, New Orleans, 1976—77; asst. U.S. atty., dep. chief criminals divsn. U.S. Attys. Office, 1970—73; chief spl. prosecutor, chief armed robbery divsn. Orleans Parish Dist. Atty.'s Office, 1974—75; chief prosecutor organized crime unit La. Atty. Gen.'s Office, 1975—76; mem. 95th-106th Congresses from 1st La. Dist., 1977—99; chair appropriations com., 1996—98; founder The Livingston Group, Washington, 1999—. Bd. dirs. Holcim, Inc., 2000—. Bd. suprs. Smithsonian Inst., 1995—98; bd. dirs. Internat. Rep. Inst., 1993—2003, Ctr. for Democracy, 1996—2003, Medal of Honor Found., Shakespeare Theatre, Washington, 2004—, Internat. Found. for Election Security, 2003—; bd. trustees Am. U. Central Asia, Kyrgyzstan, 2001—. Named Outstanding Asst. U.S. Atty., 1973. Mem.: ABA, New Orleans Bar Assn., La. Bar Assn., Fed. Bar Assn., Am. Legion, Navy League. Roman Catholic. Office: The Livingston Group 499 S Capitol St SW Ste 600 Washington DC 20003 Home: 7703 Northdown Rd Alexandria VA 22308-1333

LIVINGSTON, BRADFORD LEE, lawyer; b. Detroit, Apr. 15, 1954; s. L. Clayton and Helen Barbara (Grudzien) L.; m. Kathleen Ann Holuj, Mar. 9, 1980; children: Clayton Thomas, Amy Catherine. BA, U. Mich., 1976, JD, 1979. Bar: Ill. 1979, Wis. 1988, U.S. Dist. Ct. (no. dist.) Ill. 1980, U.S. Dist. Ct. (ea. dist.) Wis. 1980, U.S. Ct. Appeals (7th cir.) 1983, U.S. Dist. Ct. (cen. dist.) Ill. 1987, U.S. Dist. Ct. (ea. dist.) Mich. 1987, U.S. Ct. Appeals (3d cir.) 1994, U.S. Supreme Ct. 1998. Assoc. Seyfarth Shaw LLP, Chgo., 1979-87, ptnr., 1987—. Assoc. editor: Practice and Procedure in Labor Arbitration, 1991; contbg. author Global Counsel Handbooks Labour and Employee Benefits, 2004-05. Mem. ABA (labor and employment law and litigation sect.), Ill. State Bar Assn., Wis. Bar Assn., Chgo. Bar Assn., Internat. Bar Assn. (employment and indsl. rels. com.), Phi Delta Phi. Roman Catholic. Home: 408 Fuller Rd Hinsdale IL 60521-3621 Office: Seyfarth Shaw LLP 55 E Monroe St Ste 4200 Chicago IL 60603-5863 Office Phone: 312-296-8880. Business E-Mail: blivingston@seyfarth.com.

LIVINGSTON, DAVID MORSE, internist, biomedical researcher; b. Cambridge, Mass., Mar. 29, 1941; s. Arthur Joshua and Phyllis Freda (Kanters) Livingston; m. Jacqueline Gutman, June 23, 1963 (div. 1983); m. Emily Rabb, Jan. 25, 1986; children: Catherine Ellen, Julie. AB cum laude, Harvard U., 1961; MD magna cum laude, Tufts U., 1965. Diplomate Am. Bd. Internal Medicine. Intern, resident Peter Bent Brigham Hosp., Boston, 1965—67; rsch. assoc., sr. staff fellow, sr. investigator NCI-NIH, Bethesda, Md., 1967—69, 1971—73; rsch. fellow in biol. chemistry Harvard Med. Sch., Boston, 1969—71, asst. prof. medicine, 1973—76, assoc. prof. medicine, 1976—82, prof. medicine, 1982—92, Emil Frei prof. medicine, 1992—; v.p. Dana-Farber Cancer Inst./Harvard Med. Sch., Boston, 1989—91, dir., physician-in-chief, 1991—95, dep. dir., mem. exec. com., 1999—; Emil Frei prof. medicine and genetics Harvard Med. Sch., Boston, 1998—, chmn. exec. com. rsch., 1995—2000. Mem. edit. bd. Virology, 1989—97, MOI & Cell Biology, 1998—2000; editor: BBA Revs. on Cancer, 1988—2001; contbr. articles to profl. jours. Vice chmn. sci. adv. com. Pezcoller Found., Trento, Italy, 1994—; mem. sci. adv. bd. Inst. Cancer Rsch., Fox Chase, Pa., 1991—96, Lineburger Comprehensive Cancer Ctr., U. N.C., Chapel Hill, 1993—95, MIT Cancer Ctr., 1994—; mem. ext. adv. com. Fred Hutchinson Cancer Rsch. Ctr., 1992—96, Ctr. Cancer Rsch. MIT, 1994—; chmn. bd. sci. advisers, mem. exec. com. NCI/NIH, 1995—99; mem. sci. adv. com. Damon Runyan-Walter Winchell Cancer Fund, NYC, 1988—92, chmn. sci. adv. com., 1989—92, bd. dirs., 1992—97, bd. dirs., vice-chmn. sci. programs; pres. bd. Cancer Rsch. Fund, 1997—. Comdr. USPHS, 1967—73. Recipient Claire & Richard Morse award for Rsch., Dana-Farber Cancer Inst., 1991, Baxter award, AAMC, 1997, Brinker award, Susan Komen Found., 1997, Lila Gruber award, 2001, Clowes award, AACR C.H.A, 2005. Fellow: Am. Acad. Arts and Scis.; mem.: NAS, Am. Acad. Microbiology, Inst. Medicine of NAS, Am. Soc. Virology, Am. Soc. Biol. Chemistry and Molecular Biology, Assn. Am. Physicians, Am. Soc. for Clin. Investigation, Harvard Club (N.Y.C., Boston), St. Botolph Club, Met. Club Washington, Alpha Omega Alpha. Achievements include discovery of important aspects of the neoplastic transforming process and of the mechanisms governing control of the mammalian cell cycle. Office: Dana-Farber Cancer Inst 44 Binney St Smith Bldg Rm 870 Boston MA 02115-6084 Office Phone: 617-632-3074. Office Fax: 617-632-4381. Business E-Mail: david_livingston@dfci.harvard.edu.

LIVINGSTON, DEBRA A., law educator; BA, Princeton U., 1980; JD, Harvard U., 1984. Law clk. to Hon. J. Edward Lumbard US Ct. of Appeals (2nd cir.), 1984—85; assoc. Paul, Weiss, Rifkind, Wharton & Garrison, 1985—86, 1991—92; asst. US atty. gen. So. Dist. NY, 1986—91; faculty mem. U. Mich. Law Sch., 1992—94, Columbia Law Sch., NYC, 1994—, Paul J. Kellner prof. law. Legal cons. UN High Commr. for Refugees, Bangkok, 1982—83; commr. NYC Civilian Complaint Review Bd., 1994—2003. Co-author: Comprehensive Criminal Procedure. Office: Columbia Law Sch 435 W 116th St New York NY 10027 Office Phone: 212-854-2527. Office Fax: 212-854-7946. E-mail: sissac@law.columbia.edu.

LIVINGSTON, DONALD RAY, lawyer; b. Oak Ridge, Tenn., Jan. 11, 1952; s. Tally R. and Pansy L. (Heiskell) L.; m. Anne Davis, May 2, 1992; children: John Tally, Elizabeth Davis. AB in Econs., U. Ga., 1974, JD, 1977. Bar: Ga. 1977, U.S. Dist. Ct. (no. dist.) Ga. 1977, U.S. Dist. Ct. (mid. dist.) Ga. 1978, U.S. Dist. Ct. (no. dist.) Calif. 1984, U.S. Dist. Ct. (no. dist.) N.Y. 1994, U.S. Ct. Appeals (5th cir.) 1978, U.S. Ct. Appeals (4th and 11th cirs.) 1981, U.S. Ct. Appeals (6th cir.) 1984, U.S. Supreme Ct. 1983. Assoc. Adair, Goldthwaite, Stanford & Daniel, Atlanta, 1977-79; ptnr. Adair, Goldthwaite & Daniel, Atlanta, 1979-87; exec. asst. to gen. counsel EEOC, Washington, 1987-90, acting gen. counsel, 1990-91, gen. counsel, 1991-93; ptnr., head labor and employment practice group Akin, Gump, Strauss, Hauer & Feld, Washington, 1993—. Lectr. seminars on employment law, 1987—. Author: EEOC Litigation & Change Resolution, 2005; contbr. articles to profl. jours. Mem. ABA, Ga. Bar Assn. (chair labor law sect. 1985-86), D.C. Bar Assn. Office: Akin Gump Strauss Hauer & Feld Ste 400 1333 New Hampshire Ave NW Washington DC 20036-1564 Office Phone: 202-887-4242. Office Fax: 202-955-7806. Business E-Mail: dlivingston@akingump.com.

LIVINGSTON, DOUGLAS MARK, lawyer; b. Lawton, Okla., Nov. 2, 1945; s. Oscar Calloway and Irene (Norton) L.; m. Vicki Sue Ratts, Dec. 21, 1969; children: Lisa Marie, Stephen Mark, Anna Lee, Micah James. BS, Okla. Christian Coll., 1967; MPH, U. Okla., 1969, JD, 1980; MEd, Wayne State U., 1981; Grad., USAF War Coll., 1994, U.S. Army War Coll., 1998. Bar: Okla. 1980, U.S. Dist. Ct. (we. dist.) Okla. 1987, U.S. Army Ct. Mil. Rev. 1989, U.S. Ct. Appeals for Armed Forces 1995, U.S. Ct. Appeals (fed. cir.) 1995, U.S. Supreme Ct. 2000. Intern Cleveland County Dist. Atty., Norman, Okla., 1979-80; gen. counsel, dir. Delphi Devel., Ltd., Norman, 1980-81, Pepco Devel., Inc., Norman, 1981-85; gen. counsel Pepco, Inc., Norman, 1981-85; owner, ptnr. Payne, Livingston & Harold, P.C., Oklahoma City, 1985-86, Livingston Law Office, Norman, 1986-92, 93-94; staff atty. U.S. Dept. of Army, Ft. Sill, Okla., 1992-93, labor atty., 1994-2000; atty.-advisor Dept. Air Force, Tinker AFB, Okla., 2000—. Ptnr. Concord Investments, Ltd., Norman, 1982-88; team dir. 33d judge adv. gen. detachment, Oklahoma City, 1988-91, 29th judge adv. gen. detachment, Tulsa, 1991-93; staff judge adv. 4003d U.S. Army Garrison, Ft. Chaffee, Ark., 1993-95, 122nd USAR Command, North Little Rock, Ark., 1995; comdr. 1st Legal Support Orgn., San Antonio, 1995-98; staff judge adv. 90th Regional Support Command, North Little Rock, Ark., 1998-2001. Editor coll. newspaper Talon, 1966; note editor Am. Indian Law Rev., 1979-80. Bd. dirs. Big Bros./Big Sisters, Norman, 1983-85, Rock Creek Youth Camp, Norman, 1985-94; Rep. precinct chmn., Oklahoma City, 1971. Capt. U.S. Army, 1973-77; col. USAR. Named one of Outstanding Young Men of Am., 1973. Mem. Okla. Bar Assn., Fed. Bar Assn., Cleveland County Bar Assn., Res. Officers Assn., Assn. U.S. Army., Sr. Army Res. Comdr.'s Assn., U.S. Army JAG Sch. Alumni Assn., U.S. Army War Coll. Alumni Assn. Mem. Ch. of Christ. Avocations: family activities, reading, running. Home: 911 S Lahoma Ave Norman OK 73069-4509 Office: Office of Staff Judge Adv 7460 Arnold St Sewing Tinker Afb OK 73145-9002 E-mail: douglas.livingston@tinker.af.mil.

LIVINGSTON, JAMES BRISTOL, educational services owner, writer, retired secondary school educator, education educator, writer; s. J. Clarke and Nancy W. Livingston; children: Andrew Clarke, Erica Brooke, Lawrence Russel, James Paul. BA in Philosophy, U. Minn., Mpls., 1967; M in Philosophy, Bryn Mawr Coll., Pa., 1969; MEd, U. St. Thomas, St. Paul, Minn., 1987. Cert. Tchr.'s Lic. Grades 7-12 Minn., Sci. Tchr.'s Lic. all grades. Sci. tchr. Archdiocese of Mpls./St. Paul, 1970—79; sci., math. tchr. Spring Lake Park schs., 1979—80; substitute tchr. Mpls. Pub. Schs., Minn., 1989—98; sci., math. tchr. West Bank HS, Mpls., 1998—99; instr. Century CC, Minn., 2000, Arts Inst. Internat., Mpls., 2002, North Hennepin CC, Bklyn. Ctr., Minn., 2002; facilitator HS for Recording Arts, St. Paul, 2000—01; sci. tchr. Ctr. Sch., Mpls., 2002—04; owner Livingston Ednl. Support Svcs., Mpls., 1998—; pres. Livingston Arts Presentation Svcs., Mpls., 2000—. Editor: (mag.) MINED, 2000, 2001; author: Sci. Tchr., 1989, (book) We Have Cried So Many Times Before, 2002; contbr. 60 poems in 50 jours.; writer, prodr., dir., actor: Trans State, writer, pub.: Marginalia, Lavander Dandelions. Actor Midtown YWCA Theatre, Mpls., 2003, 2004; founder, facilitator Southside Writers' Studio, Eagan, 1985—96; mem. Bd. and Com. Seward Neighborhood, Mpls., 1996—99; vice chmn. Parents of East Africans, Mpls., 1997—99. Recipient Artist Recognition award, VSA Arts, 1997, Minn. Playwrights' Discovery award, 1999. Mem.: Minn. Sci. Tchrs. Assn., Minn. Ctr. Book Arts, SASE: Write Pl. (Mentorship award 2004). Democrat. Buddhist. Avocations: dance, camping.

LIVINGSTON, JAMES DUANE, physicist, researcher; b. Bklyn., June 23, 1930; s. James Duane and Florence (Boullee) L.; m. Nancy Lee Clark, June 27, 1953 (div. 1976); children: Joan, Susan, Barbara; m. Sharon Hood Penney, Mar. 30, 1985. B in Engring. Physics, Cornell U., 1952; PhD in Applied Physics, Harvard U., 1956. Physicist R & D GE, Schenectady, N.Y., 1956-89; sr. lectr. dept. material sci. and engring. MIT, Cambridge, 1989—. Author: Driving Force: The Natural Magic of Magnets, 1996, Electronic Properties of Engineering Materials, 1999; co-author: A Very Dangerous Woman: Martha Wright and Women's Rights, 2004; author, co-author over 100 publs. in field. Coolidge Fellow Gen. Electric Corp. R & D, 1987; recipient Disting. Career award Hudson-Mohawk chpt. AIME, 1986. Fellow Am. Soc. Metals, Am. Phys. Soc.; mem. Nat. Acad. Engring., IEEE, AAAS, Materials Rsch. Soc., The Minerals, Metals and Materials Soc. Democrat. Unitarian Universalist. Achievements include 7 patents; advanced research in superconducting, ferromagnetic, and mechanical properties of materials. Home: 90 Albee Dr Braintree MA 02184-8252 Office: MIT 16-206 Cambridge MA 02139 Business E-Mail: jdliv@mit.edu.

LIVINGSTON, JO ELLEN BROOKS, music educator; b. Beckley, W.Va., Dec. 4, 1953; d. Henry Edward and Ramona Ann Brooks; m. James M Livingston, Oct. 3, 1981. BS in music edn., Concord Coll., 1971—77; MusM, U. of So. Miss., 1977—80. Music educator St. Francis de Sales Sch., Beckley, 1980—81; music dir. Theatre W.Va., Beckley, 1981—90, Curtain Callers, Mt. Hope, W.Va., 1981—94; music educator Raleigh County Pub. Schools, Beckley, W.Va., 1981—94, Prince William County Pub. Schools, Manassas, Va., 1995—; music dir. Ctr. for the Arts, Manassas, 1995—, Rooftop Players, Manassas, 2003—. Music curriculum com. Prince William County Pub. Schools, Manassas, 2001; min. of music Meml. Bapt. Ch., Beckley, 1992—94; performer Gary Matheny Trio, Athens, W.Va., 1971—77, Commanders Big Band, Athens, 1972—77; percussionist Hattiesburg Light Opera Co., Hattiesburg, Miss., Opera South, Jackson, Miss., Miss. Ballet Orch., Jackson, Jackson Symphony Orch., Tupelo (Miss.) Symphony Orch., Meridian (Miss.) Symphony Orch., Miss. Opera Co., Jackson; string solo and ensmble chair Prince William County Schools, Manassas, 2002—; percussionist W.Va. Symphony Orch., Charleston; mid. sch. honor choir chair Prince William County, Manassas; Prince William County Mid. Sch. honors orch. chair Prince William County Schools, Manassas; dist. mid. sch. honor choir chair Va. Music Educators Assn., Manassas; dist. 9 honor bands audition chair VBODA, District 9, Va.; region i chair W.Va. Music Educators Assn., Region I, all-state h.s. honors chorus chair, Charleston; auditorium mgr. Woodrow Wilson H.S., Beckley, 1988—90. Mem. Curtain Callers, Mt. Hope, W.Va. Recipient Gilbert award, U. of So. Miss. Theater, Governor's Citation for Musical Contributions, State Of W.Va. Mem.: Nat. Educators Assn. (assoc.; state del. and sch. rep.), Va. Music Educators Assn. (assoc.), Omicron Delta Kappa (assoc.), Mu Phi Epsilon (assoc.; v.p. 1978). Avocation: painting. Home: 9301 Battle St Manassas VA 20110 Office: Parkside Middle School 8602 Mathis Ave Manassas VA 20110 Office Phone: 703-361-3106. Personal E-mail: jbldiva@comcast.net. E-mail: livingjb@pwcs.edu.

LIVINGSTON, JOHN H., retired engineer, retired military officer; b. Mo., Sept. 8, 1912; s. Alfred W. Livingston and Ida Catherine Fink; m. Sarah Hester Eilyeen Broyles, Apr. 3, 1943 (dec. Apr. 30, 1998); children: John H. Jr., Joseph W., Mary E. BSCE, Mo. Sch. Mines, 1939; graduate, Command and Gen. Staff Coll., Ft. Leavenworth, Kans., 1943; MSCE, Tex. A&M U., 1948; graduate, Air Force Inst. Tech., 1969. Served to lt. col. U.S. Army, 1939—49; engr. State of Mo., 1949; civilian engr. Strategic Air Command, Barksdale AFB, La., 1951—71. Mem. Phelps County Heritage Soc., Rolla, Mo.; donator South Bossier Vol. Fire Dept.; donator 3,000 books Centenary Coll., Shreveport, La. Recipient Purple Heart, U.S. Army, Bronze Star, Commendation Ribbon. Mem.: VFW, Army Engr. Assn., Alumni Adv. Bd. Found., Soc. Am. Mil. Engrs. (pres.), Heroes of '76, La. Engring. Soc., Retired Officers Assn. (life), Mil. Order of Purple Heart (life), Am. Legion, Atkins Lodge. Home: PO Box 178 Elm Grove LA 71051-0178

LIVINGSTON, JOHNSTON REDMOND, manufacturing executive; b. Foochow, China, Dec. 18, 1923; s. Henry Walter V and Alice (Moorehead) Livingston; m. Caroline Johnson, Aug. 17, 1946 (dec.); children: Henry, Ann, Jane, David; m. Patricia Karolchuck, Sept. 4, 1965. BS in Engring. with honors, Yale U., 1947; MBA with distinction, Harvard U., 1949. With Mpls.-Honeywell Regulator Co., 1949-55; with Whirlpool Corp., 1956-66, v.p., until 1966, Redman Industries, Dallas, 1966-67; dir. Constrn. Tech., Inc., Dallas, 1967—, pres., chmn. bd. dirs. Denver, 1974-89; chmn. bd. dirs. Enmark Corp., Denver, 1979-90. Pres. Marcor Housing Sys., Inc., Denver, 1971-74. Past mem. industry adv. com. Nat. Housing Ctr.; bd. dirs., past pres. Nat. Home Improvement Coun.; pres., chmn. bd. dirs. Denver Symphony Assn., 1977-81; bd. dirs., past chmn. bd. dirs. Rocky Mountain Regional Inst. Internat. Edn.; trustee, chmn. emeritus, bd. dirs. Bonfils-Stanton Found., Denver, 1979—; hon. trustee Inst. Internat. Edn., N.Y. Recipient Internat. Leadership award Rocky Mountain Regional Inst. Internat. Edn., 2003; Baker scholar, Harvard U., 1949. Mem. Rocky Mountain World Trade Assn. (bd.

dirs., past chmn. bd. dirs.), Denver Country Club, Yale Club N.Y., Sigma Xi, Tau Beta Pi. Home: 2800 S University Blvd No 27 Denver CO 80210 Office: 5070 Oakland St Denver CO 80239-2724

LIVINGSTON, KIMBERLY R., elementary school educator; b. Columbia, S.C., June 9, 1968; d. Larry L. and Angeline R. Rankin; m. James P. Livingston, May 20, 1990; children: Taylor K., James P. Jr., Samuel H. III. BA in Psychology, U. S.C., Aiken, 2000; MEd, U. S.C., 2005. Cert. tchr. elem. edn. S.C. Tchr. Aiken County Pub. Schs., Ridge Spring, SC, 1995—. Team capt. Relay for Life, Samoa, 2005; bd. dirs. 1st Steps S.C., Samoa, 2000—01. Mem.: Nat. Coun. Tchrs. English, Internat. Reading Assn., Alpha Tau. Republican. Baptist. Avocations: horses, Japanese gardening, mosaics. Home: 429 Murphy Farm Rd Ridge Spring SC 29129 Office: Ridge Spring Elem 422 Hazzard Cir Ridge Spring SC 29129 Office Phone: 803-685-2000. Office Fax: 803-685-2008. E-mail: klivingston@aiken.k12.sc.us.

LIVINGSTON, LEE FRANKLIN, real estate consultant, financial consultant; b. Boston, Feb. 20, 1942; s. William and Frances (Turner) L.; m. Elaine Wiesenfeld, June 9, 1968; children: Eli, Jed. Student, Sch. Visual Arts, 1959-62, Georgetown U., 1964. Mem. staff pub. rels. and promotion dept. Newsweek, N.Y.C., 1965-70; mng. dir., sec., treas. Anasarca Corp., North Brunswick, 1971—. Pres. Imperial Cons., Inc.; ptnr. Bess & Co., Phila. Stock Exch.; cons. on charitable fund raising to various charities, 1971—. Active charities for retarded citizens and women and children victims of abuse, also Spl. Olympics; trustee, pres. Anshe Emeth Meml. Temple; treas. Jewish Social Svcs.; bd. dirs. Women Aware. With C.E., U.S. Army, 1962-64. Recipient Am. Svc. award Girl Scouts U.S., Bronze Svc. award Spl. Olympics, Svc. award Spl. Edn., 1989, 91, N.J. Person of Yr. award, 1992. Mem. Greenacres Country Club, Phila. Stock Exch. Club. Democrat. Home: 12 Derby Ln # 4 North Brunswick NJ 08902-4729 also: 3300 S Ocean Blvd Palm Beach FL 33480-5637 Office: 850 Us Highway 1 New Brunswick NJ 08902-3312

LIVINGSTON, LOUIS BAYER, lawyer; b. N.Y.C., Dec. 12, 1941; s. Norman and Helen (Bayer) L.; m. Mari Livingston, Apr. 6, 1968; children: Diana, Alex, Ann. BA, Yale U., 1963; LLB, Harvard U., 1966. Bar: N.Y. 1967, Oreg. 1971. Atty. NLRB, Memphis, 1967-68, Poletti, Freidin et al., N.Y.C., 1968-71; ptnr. Miller Nash LLP, Portland, Oreg., 1971—. Office: Miller Nash LLP 111 SW 5th Ave Ste 3400 Portland OR 97204-3699

LIVINGSTON, MYRAN JAY, author, film writer, director and producer; b. N.Y.C., Mar. 19, 1934; s. Myran Jabez and Anne Josephine (White) L.; m. Elizabeth Rasmussen, July 28, 1956 (div. May 1971); 1 child, Lisa Browning; m. Bernice Helen Beck, Nov. 8, 1971; children: Simon Jabez, Sarah Gustine. Student, Kenyon Coll., 1952-56, U.C.L.A., 1957-58. Writer/dir. CBS TV Network, L.A., 1956-64, McCann-Erickson, San Francisco, 1965-71, Eastman Kodak, Rochester, N.Y., 1980-83; owner, operator Promethean Prodns., L.A., 1983-96. Guest lectr. Coll. of Marin, San Franciso, 1972-73, Loyola Marymount U., L.A., 1979, Rochester Inst. of Tech., 1982. Author: (novels) The Prodigy, 1979, The Synapse Function, 1985, Tchr. in comml. prodn. San Francisco Women in Advertising, 1976, The Del Monte Corp., San Francisco, 1970, Van Nuys (Calif.) H.S., 1980, Mira Catalina Sch., Palos Verdes, Calif., 1986. Recipient 7 Golden Eagle awards Coun. on Internat. Theatrical Events, 1982-84, 1st place Gold Camera award U.S. Indsl. Film Festival, 1984, CLIO for "Most Beautiful Spot" award Bullocks, 1978, 4 Telly Silver and Bronze awards 14th and 17th Ann. Competition, 1993,96. Mem. Writer's Guild of Am., The Author's Guild. Episcopalian. Avocations: classical piano, songwriting. Home and Office: 12475 Centerville Rd Chico CA 95928 Personal E-mail: mjayliv@direcway.com.

LIVINGSTON, PAMELA A., corporate image and marketing management consultant; b. Richmond Hill, N.Y., Nov. 21, 1930; d. Paul Yount and Anna Margaret (Altland) L. BA, Adelphi U., 1951; postgrad., NYU, 1952, Columbia U., 1959, Am. Acad. Dramatic Art, 1954, IBM Sys. and Mktg. Schs., 1967-70, Brandon Sch. Electronic Data, 1973, Pa. State U., 1993. Pers. and pub. rels. depts. Am. Can Co., N.Y.C., 1951-60; exec. sec. to pres. York (Pa.) divsn. Borg-Warner Corp., 1962-65; freelance writer, 1965-67; mktg. ofcl. IBM Corp., 1967-70; rsch. analyst, dir. new EDP bus. Ins. Co. N.Am., 1971-74; asst. to v.p. corp. affairs IU Internat., Phila., 1974-75; comm. and mktg. mgmt. cons. specializing in corp. identity, 1975—. Corp. image cons., 1984—; freelance writer, spkr. on identity, 1994—. Contbr. articles to tech jours. Recipient various journalism awards, award in mktg. and sales IBM, 1969-70, award for innovative product application, 1969. Mem. AAUW, Sales/Mktg. Execs. Internat., Art Alliance, Pub. Rels. Soc. Am., Econs. Club of York C. of C., Phila. Club Advt. Women, Phila. Acad. Fine Arts, World Affairs Coun., English-Speaking Union, Kappa Kappa Gamma. Home and Office: 108 S Rockburn St York PA 17402-3467

LIVINGSTON, ROBERT GERALD, historian, journalist; b. N.Y.C., Nov. 17, 1927; s. Robert Teviot and Geraldine (Gray) L.; m. Jeanne Andrée Nettel, May 12, 1955; children: Catherine Schuyler Livingston Fernandez, Robert Eric. AB, AM, Harvard U., 1953, PhD, 1959. Fgn. svc. officer U.S. Dept. State, Washington, 1956-74; v.p. German Marshall Fund U.S., Washington, 1974-77, pres., 1977-81; writer Washington, 1981-83; acting dir. Am. Inst. for Contemporary German Studies, Johns Hopkins U., Washington, 1983-87, dir. Am. Inst. for Contemporary German Studies, 1987-94, chief devel. officer, 1995-96; sr. vis. fellow German Hist. Inst., Washington, 1997—. Commentator "Deutsche Welle" and other German radio stas., 1997—. Co-author, editor The Federal Republic in the 1980s, 1983, West German Political Parties, 1986; contbr. over 300 articles to polit. jours. and newspapers. Sgt. U.S. Army, 1946-49. Mem. German Studies Assn. U.S., Coun. on Fgn. Rels., N.Y. Soc. Sons of the Cincinnati, Cosmos Club, Chevy Chase Club, Barnstable Yacht Club (Mass.), Phi Beta Kappa. Democrat. Episcopalian. Avocations: hiking, swimming. Office: German Historical Inst 1607 New Hampshire Ave NW Washington DC 20009-2562 E-mail: jliving844@aol.com.

LIVINGSTON, VERNON, retired health facility administrator; b. Phila., Oct. 29, 1942; s. Lee and Orietta (Lawton) Livingston; m. Shirley Livingston, Jan. 25, 1965; 1 child, Crystal. Student, Temple U. Hosp., 1964—65. Map maker U.S. Govt.: Aero. Corp., Phila., 1962—63; dir. respiratory therapy Meth. Holistic Hosp., Phila.; supr. Temple U., 1965—66; dept. supr. U. Pa. Hosp., 1966—67, health facility adminstr., 1967—89; ret., 1989. Achievements include invention of standardly-used oxygen mask.

LIVINGSTON, WILLIAM SAMUEL, academic administrator, political scientist, educator; b. Ironton, Ohio, July 1, 1920; s. Samuel G. and Bata (Elkins) L.; m. Lana Sanor, July 10, 1943; children: Stephen Sanor, David Duncan. BA, MA, Ohio State U., 1943; PhD, Yale U., 1950. Asst. prof. U. Tex., Austin, 1949-54, assoc. prof., 1954-61, prof. govt., 1961—, chmn. dept. govt., 1965-69, Jo Anne Christian centennial prof. Brit. studies, 1982-95, asst. dean Grad. Sch., 1954-58, chmn. Grad. Assembly, 1965-68, chmn. faculty senate, 1973-79, chmn. comparative studies program, 1978-79; v.p., dean grad. studies U Tex., Austin, 1979-95, acting pres., 1992-93, sr. v.p., 1995—; vice chancellor acad. programs U. Tex. Sys., 1969-71. Vis. prof. Yale U., 1955-56, Duke U., 1960-61; sec.-treas. Assn. Grad. Schs., 1982-85; bd. dirs. Coun. Grad. Schs. in U.S., 1983-86. Author: Federalism and Constitutional Change, 1956; contbg. author: World Pressures on American Foreign Policy, 1962, Teaching Political Science, 1965, Federalism: Infinite Variety in Theory and Practice, 1968, Britain at the Polls 1979, 1981; editor: The Presidency and Congress: A Shifting Balance of Power, 1979; co-editor: Australia, New Zealand and the Pacific Islands Since the First World War, 1979; editor, contbr. author: Federalism in the Commonwealth, 1963, A Prospect of Liberal Democracy, 1979, The Legacy of the Constitution: An Assessment for the Third Century, 1987; book rev. editor: Jour. Politics, 1965-68, editor-in-chief, 1968-72; mem. editl. bd. Publius: Jour. of Federalism, 1971-95; mem. bd. editors: P.S, 1976-82, chmn., 1978-82. Served to 1st lt. FA AUS, 1943-45. Decorated Bronze Star, Purple Heart.; Recipient Tchg. Excellence award, 1959; Ford Found. fellow, 1952-53; Guggenheim fellow, 1959-60; USIS lectr. in U.K. and India, 1977. Mem. Am. Polit. Sci. Assn. (exec. coun. and adminstrv. com. 1972-74, chmn. nominating com. 1973-74, 78-79), So. Polit. Sci. Assn. (exec. coun. 1964-67, pres. 1974-75), Southwestern Polit. Sci. Assn. (pres. 1973-74), Hansard Soc. (London), Philos. Soc. Tex., Tex. Coun. for the Humanities, Austin Soc. for Pub. Adminstn. (pres. 1973-74), Southwestern Social Sci. Assn. (pres. 1977-78), Phi Beta Kappa, Omicron Delta Kappa, Phi Gamma Delta, Pi Sigma Alpha (nat. coun. 1976-84, nat. pres. 1980-82). Home: 3203 Greenlee Dr Austin TX 78703-1621 Office: U Tex Office Sr VP Austin TX 78712 Office Phone: 512-471-3266. Business E-Mail: wsl@po.utexas.edu.

LIVINGSTONE, JOHN LESLIE, accountant, economist, management consultant, educator; b. Johannesburg, Aug. 29, 1932; m. Trudy Dorothy Zweig, Aug. 7, 1977; children: Roger Miles, Adrienne Jill, Graham Ross, Robert Edward. B of Commerce, U. Witwatersrand, South Africa, 1956; MBA, Stanford U., 1963, PhD, 1966. CPA, N.Y., Tex.; cert. in bus. valuation. Budget dir. Edgars Stores Ltd., South Africa, 1958-61; asso. prof. Ohio State U., Columbus, 1966-69, Arthur Young Disting. prof., 1970-73; Fuller E. Callaway prof. Ga. Inst. Tech., Atlanta, 1973-78, mem. exec. bd., 1976-78; ptnr. Coopers & Lybrand, N.Y.C., 1978-81; prin., v.p. Mgmt. Analysis Center, Inc., Cambridge, Mass., 1975-90; prof., chmn. div. acctg. and law Babson Coll., 1985-89, adj. prof., 1990-99. Cons. FPC, SEC, HEW, also maj. corps. Author 12 books including Accounting for Changing Prices: Replacement Cost and General Price Level Adjustments, 1976, Management Planning and Control, 1987, The Portable MBA: Finance and Accounting, 1992, 3d edit., 2002; assoc. editor: Decision Scis., 1973-78; mem. editl. bd. The Acctg. Rev., 1969-72, 76-78, Acctg., Orgns. and Socs., 1975-78, Jour. Acctg. and Pub. Policy, 1983-95; contbr. numerous articles to profl. jours. Mem. AICPA, Fla. Inst. CPAs, N.Y. Soc. CPAs, Inst. Bus. Appraisers, Nat. Assn. for Forensic Econs., Nat. Assn. Bus. Economists, Am. Arbitration Assn. (arbitrator comml. panel), Tex. Soc. CPAs, Pres. Country Club (West Palm Beach). Office: 2300 Palm Beach Lakes Blvd Ste 312 West Palm Beach FL 33409-3303 E-mail: les561@hotmail.com.

LIVINGSTONE, SUSAN MORRISEY, management consultant, former federal agency administrator; b. Carthage, Mo., Jan. 13, 1946; d. Richard John II and Catherine Newell (Carmean) Morrisey; m. Neil C. Livingstone III, Aug. 30, 1968. AB, Coll. William and Mary, 1968; MA, U. Mont., 1973; postgrad., Tufts U., 1972—73, Fletcher Sch. Law and Diplomacy, 1973—. Rschr. Senator Mark O. Hatfield, Washington, 1969-70; chief legis. and press asst. Congressman Richard H. Ichord, Washington, 1973-75, adminstrv. asst., 1975-81; cons. Congressman Wendell Bailey, Washington, 1981; exec. asst. VA, Washington, 1981-85, assoc. dep. adminstr. logistics and mgmt., 1985-86, sr. procurement exec., 1985-89, assoc. dep. adminstr. logistics, 1985—89; asst. sec. Army U.S. Dept. of Def., Washington, 1989-93; v.p. health and safety svcs. ARC, Washington, 1993-97; cons. mgmt., 1997-2001; under sec. of Navy U.S. Dept. Navy, Washington, 2001—03; mem. return-to-flight task group NASA, 2003—. Mem interagy. com. on women's bus. enterprise The White House, 1985-89; mem. Pres.'s Coun. on Mgmt. Improvement, 1985-86; cons. Def. Sci. Bd., 1998, 2000; mem. adv. bd. Martin Inst. U. Idaho, 2000-01; mem. nat. security studies bd. advs., Maxwell Sch. Syracuse U., 2003—; bd. dirs. The Atlantic Coun., 2004; mem. adv. subcom. on naval history Sec. of Navy, 2004—. Vice chair White House Commn. on Nat. Moment of Remembrance, 2002—03; bd. dirs. The Army Hist. Found. Inc., 2005—. Mem. Procurement Round Table (bd. dirs. 1994-01, 03-), Assn. U.S. Army (bd. dirs. 1994-, coun. trustees 1996-01, CEO, dep. chmn. 2000-01), Women in Internat. Security (mem. adv. bd. 1994-97). Episcopalian.

LIVNE, NAVA LEVIA, psychologist, researcher; b. Haifa, Israel, Aug. 12, 1952; arrived in U.S., 2002; d. Moshe Yitzchak and Guta Tova Meiri; m. Giora Livne, Jan. 2, 1978; children: Oren, Nilly. Student, U. Ill., Chgo., 1972—73; BA in Advanced Studies in Psychology (disting. scholar), Hebrew U., Jerusalem, 1977; MSc in Social Psychology (disting. scholar), Bar Ilan U., Ramat Gan, Israel, 1996; PhD in Ednl. Psychology (Excellence in Rsch. scholar), Tel Aviv U., 2002. Lic. psychologist Israel. Mentor Hebrew U., Jerusalem, 1974—75; mentor, advisor to highly gifted children Israel, 1978—95; dir. extended learning program City of Kiryat Motzkin, Israel, 1982—89, City of Kiryat Yam, Israel, 1989—91; dir. unit rsch. and assessment Sch. Edn. Bar Ilan U., Ramat Gan, 1996—98; dir. workshops Ctr. Advancement Tchg. Tel Aviv U., 1998—2002; rsch. specialist U. Calif., Irvine, 2002—04; postdoctoral fellow U. N.Mex, Albuquerque, 2004; ednl. rschr. and program dir. U. Utah, Salt Lake City, 2005—. Contbr. scientific papers to profl. jours. Vol. tchr. Jewish Sch. Congregation Kol Ami, Salt Lake City, 2005. With Isreali Def. Force, 1970—72. Recipient Excellence in Rsch. award, Am. Mensa, 1999; Jr. Faculty fellow, NSF, 2004. Mem.: APA, Internat. Soc. Learning Scis., World Coun. Gifted and Talented, Am. Ednl. Rsch. Assn., Alpha Delta Lambda (life). Avocations: hiking, symphonic concert, opera, lectures, reading. Office: U Utah 1901 S Central Campus Dr Rm 3490 Salt Lake City UT 84112 Office Phone: 801-587-5835, 801-587-5835. Business E-Mail: nlivne@aoce.utah.edu.

LIVNE, OREN, property manager; b. Israel, 1974; s. Micha and Joanna Livne. BS in chem. engring., Rutgers U., 1992—96. Patent Agent: US Patent and Trademark Office 2000. Howard hughes med. inst. rsch. fellow Rutgers U., Piscataway, NJ, 1995—95; tchg. and rsch. asst. U. of Calif., Berkeley, 1997; cofounder OfficeWorkout.com, Alameda, Calif., 1999—2001; tech. writer U. of Calif., Office of Tech. Transfer, Oakland, 1998—2000, licensing officer, 2000—04; patent mgr. U. of Calif., Santa Barbara, 2004—. Contbr. articles to profl. jours. Recipient Hoechst Celanese Excellence award Recipient, Rutgers U., 1994, 1995, Recognition of Excellence, Rutgers Alumni Assn., 1996; Hewlett Found. fellow, U. of Calif., Berkeley, 1996—97. Mem.: Assn. of U. Tech. Managers, Licensing Executives Soc., Tau Beta Pi, Nat. Engring. Achievements include patents for gift item candle with falling sections; patents pending for candle with connector for securing attachments; development of a new type of hatching candle. Avocation: Aikido. Home: 1560 Douglas Dr El Cerrito CA 94530

LIVSEY, ROBERT CALLISTER, lawyer; b. Salt Lake City, Aug. 7, 1936; s. Robert Frances and Rosezella Ann (Callister) L.; m. Renate Karla Guertler, Sept. 10, 1962; children: Scott, Rachel, Daniel, Benjamin. BS, U. Utah, 1962, JD, 1965; LLM, NYU, 1967. Bar: Utah 1965, Calif. 1967. Prof. Haile Selassie U., Addis Abbaba, Ethiopia, 1965-66; spl. asst. to chief counsel IRS, Washington, 1977-79; assoc., then ptnr. Brobeck, Phleger & Harrison, San Francisco, 1967—2003; of counsel Morgan, Lewis & Bockius, San Francisco, 2003—. Adj. prof. U. San Francisco Law Sch., 1970-77; mem. adv. com. IRS Dist. Dirs., 1986-89; mem. western region liason com IRS (chmn. 1989). Research editor U. Utah Law Rev., 1964-65; editor Tax Law Rev., 1966-67; contbr. articles to profl. jours. Bd. dirs. Gilead Group, 1986-88, East Bay Habitat for Humanity, 1987-88, Morning Song, 1992-94. Mem. ABA (chmn. subcom. real estate syndications 1981-84), State Bar Calif. (chmn. taxation sect. 1984-85), San Francisco Bar Assn. (chmn. taxation sect. 1982), Am. Coll. Tax Counsel, Am. Law Inst., Tax Litigation Club (pres. 1986-87), Order of Coif, Beta Gamma Sigma. Democrat. Mem. Evangelical Covenant Ch. Club: Commonwealth (San Francisco). Home: 128 La Salle Ave Piedmont CA 94610-1233 Office: Morgan Lewis & Bockius 1 Market Plz Fl 31 San Francisco CA 94105-1100 Office Phone: 415-442-1230. E-mail: rlivsey@morganlewis.com.

LIVULPI, CHRISTINE J., elementary school educator; b. Queens Village, N.Y., Dec. 25, 1966; d. Matthew A. and Patricia R. Solano; m. Eugene Livulpi, Sept. 15, 1990; children: Jennifer C., Nicolette P. MSED, LI U., Westchester, 1999. Elem. tchr. Kent Elem. Sch., Carmel, NY, 2000—. Office: Kent Elem Sch 1091 Rte 52 Carmel NY 10512 Office Phone: 845-225-5029.

LIXEY, ELIZABETH VOULGARAKIS, secondary school educator; b. Erie, Pa., Jan. 28, 1952; d. Paul Thomas Voulgarakis and Irene Elizabeth Gourgonis-Voulgarakis; m. William Henry Lixey, Dec. 16, 1978; children: Heather Elizabeth, Jennifer Laura. AA in Theatre Arts, Am. River Coll., 1971; BA in Drama, Calif. State U., 1973; MEd, Jacksonville (Ala.) State U., 1991. Cert. tchr. Ala., 1991, Dept. of Def. Dependents Schs., 1992, profl. cert. Pa., 1995, provisional edn. cert. Mich., 1998, cert. profl. educator Mich., 2004. Social Security Adminstrn. benefit authorizer HHS, San Francisco, 1974—79, Social Security Adminstrn. tech. advisor Richmond, Calif., 1979—81, Social Security Adminstrn. svc. rep. Roseville, Mich., 1981—82; mid. and secondary lang. arts educator Taegu Am. H.S., Camp George, Republic of Korea, 1992—93; adj. English prof. Keimyung U., Taegu, Republic of Korea, 1993, Hyosung U., Hayang, Republic of Korea, 1993—94; liturgy and chapel comm. coord. Holy Family Parish, Maxwell AFB, Ala., 1995—96; outreach program coord. U.S. Army Cmty. Svcs., Ft. McClellan, Ala., 1996; secondary lang. arts educator Hale (Mich.) Area H.S., 1998—. Advisor drama club Hale H.S., 1998—, co-advisor English club, 1999—, co-chair sch. improvement team, 2000—, advisor Nat. Honor Soc., 2001—05. Sta. chmn. ARC, Ft. McClellan, 1997—98, teen program dir., 1997; chem. spouses sr. leader Chem. Sch., Ft. McClellan, 1996—98; catechist, lector, eucharistic min. Holy Family Parish, East Tawas, Mich., 1999—. Decorated Outstanding Civilian Svc. medal Dept. of the Army; recipient Comdr.'s award for pub. svc., 1994, 1998; fellow Nat. Writing Project, Jacksonville State U., 1997. Mem.: Nat. Collegiate Players Honorary Dramatic Soc., Hale Fedn. Tchrs. (HS Tchr. of Yr. 2005), Quota Club Internat., Kappa Delta Pi, Delta Kappa Gamma Soc. Internat. Republican. Roman Catholic. Avocations: photography, creating computer media, boating, golf, reading. Home: 2706 Lixey Beach Rd East Tawas MI 48730 Office: Hale Area HS 415 E Main Hale MI 48739 Office Phone: 989-728-2861. Personal E-mail: eagleteacher98@hotmail.com.

LIZIK, ANDREA NOREEN, elementary school educator; b. Pitts., Mar. 28, 1953; d. Andrew Thomas and Leona Geraldine (Biesuz) L. BS in Elem. Edn., Edinboro State Coll., 1974; MS in Edn., Duquesne U., 1977. Cert. elem. edn. tchr., Pa. Tchr. St. James Elem. Sch., Apollo, Pa., 1975-78, Kiski Area Sch. Dist., Vandergrift, Pa., 1978—, head tchr., 1980—, mentor, 1991—. Fellow Marconi Ladies Aux., 1985—, Assumption Ladies Guild, 1982—. Fellow NEA, Pa. State Edn. Assn., Kiski Area Edn. Assn. (rep. coun. 1978—, tchr. of yr. 1991, faculty award 1991), Delta Kappa Gamma. Home: 194 Fitzgerald St Leechburg PA 15656-8399 Office: Kiski Area Sch Dist 200 Poplar St Vandergrift PA 15690-1466 Office Phone: 724-845-2032.

LJUBIMOV, ALEXANDER V., molecular biologist, cell biologist, researcher; b. Moscow, Oct. 27, 1952; s. Vladimir V. Ljubimov and Margarita S. Ljubimova; m. Julia Y. Savchenko, Apr. 1, 1989; children: Anna A. Ljubimova, Vladimir A. PhD, Russian Cancer Rsch. Ctr., Moscow, 1977. Staff scientist Russian Cancer Rsch. Ctr., 1979—93; rsch. scientist Cedars Sinai Med. Ctr., L.A., 1993—2002, dir. Ophthalmology Rsch. Labs., 2002—; prof. UCLA Sch. Medicine, 2003—. Mem. editl. bd.: Frontiers in Biosci., Exptl. Eye Rsch.; mem. editl. bd. Investigative Ophthalmology and Visual Science; contbr. articles to profl. jours. Grantee, NIH, 1998—. Mem.: European Acad. Scis., Internat. Soc. Eye Rsch., Am. Diabetes Assn., Assn. Rsch. in Vision and Ophthalmology, Assn. UICC Fellows. Achievements include patents for cancer research and angiogenesis (2 U.S.S.R., 2 U.S.). Office: Cedars Sinai Med Ctr Ste D2025 8700 Beverly Blvd Los Angeles CA 90048 Office Phone: 310-423-7645. E-mail: ljubimov@cshs.org.

LJUNGQVIST, ALEXANDER, finance educator; arrived in US, 2000; s. Peter Jans and Cecilia Ljungqvist. MSc, Lund U., Sweden, 1989—92; MPhil, Oxford U., Eng., 1992—94; PhD, Oxford U., 1992—96, MA, 1995. Fin. fellow Merton Coll., Oxford, England, 1995—2000; lectr. mgmt. studies Oxford (England) U., 1995—2000; asst. prof. fin. NYU, 2000—05, assoc. prof. fin., 2005—, dir. Berkley Ctr., 2005—. Assoc. cons. Oxera Ltd., Oxford, 1996—2000; program dir. Salomon Ctr. NYU, 2003—; dir. rsch. Berkeley Ctr. NYU. Author: (monograph) Going Pub. Recipient CDC award, NYU, 2002, Glucksman prize, 2002, 2003; scholar Michael Hansen stipendium, Michael Hansen Kollegium, 1990-1992; Eric Nylander scholar, Utlandsvenskarnas Foerening, 1989—90, Citicorp scholar, Citicorp, 1992—94, Wallenberg scholar, Wallenberg Found., Sweden, 1993—94, Nuffield Coll. scholar, Nuffield Coll., Oxford, 1995, Charles Schaefer Family fellow, NYU, 2003—. Mem.: Western Fin. Assn., Am. Fin. Assn., Oxford and Cambridge Club. Office: NYU Suite 9-160 44 W 4th St New York NY 10012 Office Phone: 212-998-0304. Business E-Mail: aljungqv@stern.nyu.edu.

LLAURADO, JOSEP G., nuclear medicine physician, researcher; b. Barcelona, Catalonia, Spain, Feb. 6, 1927; s. José and Rosa (Llaurado) Garcia; m. Catherine D. Entwistle, June 28, 1958 (dec.); m. Deirdre Mooney, Nov. 9, 1966; children: Raymund, Wilfred, Mireya. BS, BA, Balmes Inst., Barcelona, 1944; MD, Barcelona U., 1950, PhD in Pharmacology, 1960; MSc in Biomed. Engring., Drexel U., 1963. Diplomate Am. Bd. Nuclear Medicine. Resident Royal Postgrad. Sch. Medicine, Hammersmith Hosp., London, 1952-54; fellow M.D. Anderson Hosp. and Tumor Inst., Houston, 1957-58, U. Utah Med. Coll., Salt Lake City, 1958-59; asst. prof. U. Otago, Dunedin, New Zealand, 1954-57; sr. endocrinologist Prizer Med. Rsch. Lab., Groton, Conn., 1959-60; assoc. prof. U. Pa., Phila., 1963-67; prof. Med. Coll. Wis., Milw., 1970-82, Marquette U., Milw., 1967-82; clin. dir. nuc. medicine svc. VA Med. Ctr., Milw., 1977—82; chief nuc. medicine svc. VA Hosp., Loma Linda, Calif., 1983—; prof. dept. radiation scis. Loma Linda U. Sch. Medicine, 1983—. U.s. rep. symposium dynamic studies with radioisotopes clin. medicine and rsch. IAEA, Rotterdam, Netherlands, 1970, Knoxville, Tenn., 74. Hon. editor: Internat. Jour. Biomed. Computing, dep. editor: Mgmt. Environ. Quality; contbr. articles to profl. jours. Merit badge counselor Boy Scouts Am., 1972—; pres. Hales Corners (Wis.) Hist. Soc., 1981—83. Recipient Commendation cert., Boy Scouts Am., 1980, Joan d'Alos prize, Cardiovasc. Ctr. St. Jordi, Barcelona, 1999, XII Batista-Roca prize, Inst. Exterior Projection Catalan Culture, 2000. Fellow: Am. Coll. Nutrition; mem.: IEEE (life), Calif. Med. Assn. (mem. sci. adv. panel nuc. medicine 1993—), Soc. Catalana Biologia, Am. Soc. Nuc. Cardiology, Endocrine Soc., Soc. Math. Biology (founding), Am. Soc. Pharmacology and Exptl. Therapeutics, Am. Physiol. Soc., Biomed. Engring. Soc. (charter), IEEE Medicine and Biology Soc. (mem. nat. adminstrv. com. 1986—89), Soc. Nuc. Medicine (computer and acad. couns.), Royal Acad. Medicine Catalonia/Barcelona, Casal dels Catalans Calif. (pres. 1989—91). Roman Catholic. Office: VA Hosp Nuclear Med Svc Rm 115 11201 Benton St Loma Linda CA 92357-0001 Office Phone: 909-583-6102.

LL COOL J, (JAMES TODD SMITH), rap artist, actor; b. Bayshore, NY, Jan. 14, 1968; s. Jimmy Nunya; m. Symone Smith Aug. 1995; 4 children. Albums: Radio, 1984, Bigger and Deffer, 1987, Walking with A Panther, 1989, Mama Said Knock You Out (Grammy award Best Rap Vocal), 1991, 14 Shots To The Dome, 1993, Mr. Smith, 1996, All World-Greatest Hits, 1996, Phenomenon, 1997, The G.O.A.T, 2000, The DEFinition, 2004; actor: (films) Krush Groove, 1984, The Hard Way, 1991, Toys, 1992, The Right to Remain Silent, 1996, Woo, 1997, BAPS, 1997, Caught Up, 1998, Halloween: H20, 1998, Deep Blue Sea, 1999, In Too Deep, 1999, Any Given Sunday, 1999, Kingdom Come, 2001, Rollerball, 2002, Deliver Us from Eva, 2003, Rugrats Go Wild (voice), 2003, S.W.A.T., 2003, Mindhunters, 2004, Slow Burn, 2005; (TV series) In the House, 1995-1999, Oz, 1997; (TV movie) Wildcats, 1986. Grammy nomination (Best Rap Solo, 1994) for "Stand By Your Man". Office: Def Jam Recording Simmons 89 Bradhurst Ave New York NY 10039-3314*

LLEWELLYN, JOHN SCHOFIELD, JR., former food company executive; b. Amsterdam, N.Y., Jan. 10, 1935; s. John S. and Dorothea (Breedon) L.; m. Mary Martha Pallotta, June 9, 1962; children: Mary M., John S. III, Robert J., James P., Timothy J. AB, Holy Cross Coll., 1956; MBA, Harvard U., 1961. With mktg. Gen. Foods Corp., White Plains, N.Y., 1961-69, Sunshine Biscuit div. Am. Brands, N.Y.C., 1973-77; exec. v.p. Morton Frozen Foods div. ITT Continental Baking Co., Charlottesville, Va., 1977-79; gen. mgr. Continental Kitchens ITT Continental Baking Co., Rye, 1980-81; sr. v.p. Ocean Spray Cranberries Inc., Plymouth, Mass., 1982-86, exec. v.p., chief operating officer, 1986-87, pres., chief exec. officer, 1988-97; ret., 1997. Bd. dirs. Dean Foods Co. Trustee St. Sebastian's Country Day Sch., Needham, Mass., 1991—; bd. dirs. Mass. Environ. Trust, 1991—; mem. bd. advisors Boardroom Consultants; Sr. Corps Ret. Execs. counselor. Capt. USMC, 1957-63. Mem. Nat. Food Processors Assn. Roman Catholic. Home: Steamboat Ln Hingham MA 02043 E-mail: jsllewe@comcast.net.

LLEWELLYN, LEONARD FRANK, real estate broker, investment company executive; b. Harlowton, Mont., Oct. 31, 1933; s. Ralph Emory and Frances Louise (Ewing) L.; m. Patricia Lockrom, Aug. 16, 1951 (div. 1955); m. Corrie J. Spruit, Apr. 21, 1974 (div. 1995); m. Anna N. McKinney, 1997. BSEE, Eastern Mont. Coll. Edn., 1955. Enlisted USMC, 1957, advanced through grades to capt., 1960, ret., 1967; owner Capitol Fla. Assn., Inc., Alexandra, Va., 1966-74; pres., owner Fla. Properties, Inc., Balt., 1968-74; chmn. Marco Beach Realty, Inc., Marco Island, Fla., 1975-82, 82—, Cons., Inc. of S.W. Fla., Marco Island, 1982—; mng. dir., founding ptnr. Capital Mgmt. Co., 1999—. Served as presdl. pilot for presidents Kennedy and Johnson, 1963-66; bd. dirs. Founders Nat. Bank and Trust Co.; mem. adv. bd. Founding Ptnrs. Capital Mgmt. Co., co-mng. dir., 1999—. Author: (manual) Aero-Gunnery Tactics, 1958. Bd. dirs. Collier County Conservancy, 1978-83; trustee Naples (Fla.) Cmty. Hosp., 1980-83, Cmty. Found. Collier County, 1990-94; sheriff's commr., Collier County, Fla., 1990—. Named Top Gun, USN, USMC, 1958, Citizen of Yr. Marco Island N.Y. Times and Marco Island Eagle, 1982. Mem. Marco Island Bd. Realtors (pres. 1982), Marco Island C. of C. (pres. 1981-82, pres. emeritus 1984), Naples Forum (pres. 1985-86), Nat. Aviation Club, Nat. Assn. Sales Masters, Rotary Club. Republican. Office: Newgate Ctr Ste 119 5100 N Tamiami Trail Naples FL 34103 Home: 5251 FM 2946 Emory TX 75440 Office Phone: 239-514-2900. Personal E-mail: lenllew@yahoo.com.

LLEWELLYN, MARYANN C., school system administrator; b. Bklyn., May 22, 1949; d. Thomas Raymond and Genieve Justina (Roche) Costello; m. Richard Llewellyn, Nov. 23, 1974. BA, LI U., 1970; MA, C.W. Post, 1990. Cert. tchg. K-6, 7-12 Social Studies SDA. Elem. tchr. Riverhead Sch. Dist., Riverhead, NY, 1973—85, adminstrv. asst. to supt., 1985—88; dir. curriculum Garden City Sch. Dist., Garden City, NY, 1988—91; supt. East Quogue Sch. Dist., East Quogue, NY, 1991—95; elem. prin. Glen Cove Sch. Dist., Glen Cove, NY, 1995—98; supt. curriculum instn. Nassau Boces, Garden City, 1998—2004; asst. supt. curriculum Uniondale Pub. Schs., Uniondale, NY, 2004—. Edn1. cons. Independent, NY, 1970—2005. Eucharist min. Roman Cath. Ch., Syosset, NY, 1976—2005, lector, 1976—2005. Named Educator of Yr., Dioceses of Rockville Ctr., 1990; recipient Elem. Prin. award, Nassau County Elem. Assoc., 1999. Mem.: Assn. of Curriculum Devel., Nat. Cound. of Tchrs. of English, Assn. Edn. Rsch. Cath. Avocations: reading, travel, gardening. Office: Uniondale Pub Schs 933 Goodrich St Uniondale NY Office Phone: 516-560-8824. Office Fax: 516-560-8917. E-mail: mllewellyn@uniondaleschools.org.

LLEWELLYN, RALPH ALVIN, physics professor; b. Detroit, June 27, 1933; s. Ralph A. and Mary (Green) L.; m. Laura Diane Alsop, June 12, 1955; children: Mark Jeffrey, Rita Annette, Lisa Suzanne, Eric Matthew. BS in Chem. Engring. with high honors, Rose-Hulman Inst. Tech., 1955; PhD in Physics, Purdue U., 1962. Mem. faculty Rose-Hulman Inst. Tech., Terre Haute, Ind., 1961-70, assoc. prof. physics, 1964-68, prof., 1968-70, chmn. dept. physics, 1969-70; prof., chmn. dept. Ind. State U., Terre Haute, 1970-72, 74-80; dean Coll. of Arts and Scis. U. Ctrl. Fla., Orlando, 1980-84, prof., 1980—, chmn. dept. physics, 2003—. Exec. sec. Energy Bd., staff officer environmental Studies Bd. NAS/NRC, Washington, 1972-74; vis. prof. Rensselaer Poly. Inst., Troy, N.Y., 1964; cons. Commn. on Coll. Physics, 1987-89, NSF, 1965-66; mem. Ind. Lt. Gov.'s Sci. Adv. Coun., 1974-80; adv. bd. Ind. Gov.'s Energy Extension Svc., Fla. Solar Energy Ctr., policy coun. Fla. Inst. Govt., Fla. Radon Adv. Coun., 1988-96; mem. environ. adv. com. Fla. Inst. Phosphate Rsch.; mem. grievance com. Fla. Bar, nat. adv. coun. Nat. Commn. on Higher Edn. Issues, 1982. Author: (with others) Physics 3E, 1991, Elementary Modern Physics, 1992, Modern Physics 3E, 1999, Modern Physics 4E, 2003; contbr. articles to profl. jours.; producer instructional films and TV. Trustee Merom (Ind.) Inst. Recipient Tchg. Incentive award Fla. State Univ. Sys., 1994, 97; NSF Coop. fellow, 1959-60, Am. Coun. Edn. Acad. Adminstrn. Internship Program fellow. Fellow Ind. Acad. Sci. (chmn. physics divsn. 1969-70, Spkr. of Yr. award 1975, pres.-elect 1980); mem. AAAS, AAUP, Am. Phys. Soc., Am. Assn. Physics Tchrs. (pres. Ind.), N.Y. Acad. Scis., Fla. Acad. Scis. (endowment com.), Internat. Oceanographic Found., Ind. Acad. Sci., Sigma Xi, Tau Beta Pi. Home: 1463 Palomino Way Oviedo FL 32765-9304 Office: U Cen Fla Dept Physics Orlando FL 32816-0001 Business E-Mail: ral@physics.ucf.edu.

LLINAS, RODOLFO RIASCOS, neuroscientist, researcher; b. Bogota, Colombia, Dec. 16, 1934; came to U.S., 1959, naturalized, 1973; s. Jorge Enrique (Llinas) and Bertha (Riascos) L.; m. Gillian Kimber, Dec. 24, 1965; children: Rafael Hugo, Alexander Jorge. BS, Gimnasio Moderno, Bogota, 1952; MD, U. Javeriana, Bogota, 1959; PhD, Australian Nat. U., 1965; MD (hon.), U. Salamanca, Spain, 1985; PhD (hon.), U. Barcelona, Spain, 193, U. Nacional Bogota, Colombia, 194; D, Univ. Complutense, Madrid, 1997. Research fellow Mass. Gen. Hosp.-Harvard U., 1960-61; NIH research fellow in physiology U. Minn., Mpls., 1961-63, assoc. prof., 1965-66; assoc. mem. AMA Inst. Biomed. Research, Chgo., 1966-68, mem., 1970, head neurobiology unit, 1967-70; assoc. prof. neurology and psychiatry Northwestern U., 1967-71; guest prof. physiology Wayne State U., 1967-74; professorial lectr. pharmacology U. Ill.-Chgo., 1967-68, clin. prof., 1968-72; prof. physiology, head neurobiology div. U. Iowa, 1970-76; prof., chmn. physiology and biophysics NYU, N.Y.C., 1976—, Thomas and Suzanne Murphy prof. neurosci., 1985—. Mem. neurol. sci. research tng. com. Nat. Inst. Neurol. Diseases and Stroke, NIH, 1971-73; mem. neurology A study sect. div. research grants NIH, 1974-78; assoc. neurosci. research program MIT, 1974-83; mem. U.S. Nat. Com. for IBRO, 1978-81; acting chmn. U.S. Nat. Com. For IBRO, 1982, chmn., 1983-89, exec. com., 1985—; mem. sci. adv. bd. Max-Planck Inst. for Psychiatry, Munich, 1979-83; professorial lectr. Coll. de France, Paris, 1979, Nat. Poly. Inst., Mexico City, 1981; IBRO internat. lectr., S.Am., 1982; McDowall lectr. King's Coll., London, 1984 Author: (with Hubbard and Quastel) Electrophysiological Analysis of Synaptic Transmission, 1969; editor: Neurobiology of Cerebellar Evolution and Development, 1969, (with W. Precht) Frog Neurobiology: A Handbook, 1976; chief editor: Neurosci., 1974—1999; mem. editorial bd.: Jour. Neurobiology, 1980—; mem.: Pfluegers Archives, 1981—, Jour. Theoretical Neurobiology, 1981—. Recipient John C. Krantz award U. Md., 1976, Einstein Gold medal UNESCO, 1991, Signoret award in cognition, Fondation Ipsen La Salpâtrière, Paris, 1994. Mem. NAS, Soc. For Neurosci. (council 1974-78), Am. Physiol. Soc. (Bowditch Lectr. 1973), Am. Soc. Cell Biology, Biophys. Soc., Harvey Soc., Internat. Brain Research Orgn., N.Y. Acad. Scis., Am. Acad. Arts & Scis., Am. Philosophical Soc., Real Academia Nacional de Medicina, Nat. Deafness and Other Communication Disorders, Nat. Inst. of Health (adv. coun.), Alpha Omega Alpha (hon.), French Acad. Scis. Office: NYC Sch Med 550 1st Ave New York NY 10016-6402

LLORENS, MERNA GEE, elementary school educator, retired music educator; b. Ofahoma, Miss., Oct. 4, 1939; d. Junior McKinley and Birdie Rose Smith; m. Ramon James Llorens Sr., Oct. 1, 1960; children: Regina Llorens Shamburger, Ramon James Llorens Jr. BS, Western Mich. U., 1971. Sec. Follet Pub. Co., Chgo., 1960-62, Mohawk Tablet Co., Chicago Heights, Ill., 1963-65; elem. tchr. St. Basil Cath. Sch., South Haven, Mich., 1965-79, South Haven Pub. Schs., 1979—2004, ret., 2004. Chair Jubilee 100th Ann. St. Basil Ch., Faith and Vision campaign com. Mem.: South Haven Edn. Assn. (chair courtesy com. 1985—2000), Black History Leadership Soc. (charter, treas., publicity/program chair, Spl. Tribute Role Model of Yr. award 2001), St. Basil Altar Rosary Women's Svc. Guild (treas. 2002—, Woman of Yr. 1990), Lions Club (sgt.-at-arms 2004, dist. 11-82 Region 1 Zone chmn. 2005—, 1st v.p., named Lion of Yr. Covert Township chpt. 2003, pres. Covert Township chpt. 2004—05), Delta Sigma Theta (pres. 1999—2001, sgt. at arms 2002, Benton Harbor/St. Joseph Alumnae chpt.). Democrat. Roman Catholic. Avocations: crafts, camping, gardening, Minnie Pearl impersonation. Home: 67556 County Rd 338 South Haven MI 49090-8372 Office Phone: 269-637-1418. Personal E-mail: mergee@aol.com.

LLOYD, ALEX, lawyer; b. Atlantic, Iowa, Aug. 13, 1942; s. Norman and Ruth (R.) L.; m. Jacqueline Roe, Aug. 24, 1963 (dec.); children: Erin, Andrea, John, Peter. BA in Econs., Colby Coll., 1964; LLB, Yale U., 1967. Bar: Conn., U.S. Dist. Ct. Conn., U.S. Ct. Appeals (2d cir.), U.S. Tax Ct., U.S. Supreme Ct. Assoc. Shipman & Goodwin, 1967-72, ptnr., 1972—, chmn. mgmt. com., 1985-96. Bd. dirs. Hartford Hosp., Conn. Health Sys., Inc. Recipient Dist. Svc. award, Conn. Legal Svcs. Fellow Am. Bar Found., Conn. Bar Found. (bd. dirs.); mem. ABA, Am. Soc. of Hosp. Attys., Conn. Bar Assn. (Charles J. Parker award). Avocations: golf, boating, fishing, raquet sports, piano. Office: Shipman & Goodwin One Constitution Plz Hartford CT 06103-2833 Office Phone: 860-251-5102. Business E-Mail: alloyd@goodwin.com.

LLOYD, BOARDMAN, investment company executive; b. Concord, N.H., Jan. 8, 1942; s. Francis Vernon and Elisabeth (Boardman) L.; m. Barbara Horwich, Mar. 20, 1966 (div. 1999); children: Pamela, Amy, Emily; m. Lyn C. Farro, May 21, 2005. BA, Yale U., 1964; JD, U. Chgo., 1967. Bar: N.Y. 1968, Mass. 1971. Assoc. Casey, Lane & Mittendorf, N.Y.C., 1967-69, Choate, Hall & Stewart, Boston, 1969-76, ptnr., 1976-90; pres. Harris & Lloyd Inc., Belmont, Mass., 1991—. Chmn. Cambridge United Way, 1975-82, Yale U. Parents Com., 1986-90, com. mem., 1986-90, chmn., 1989-90; bd. dirs. Greater Boston Legal Svcs., 1986—; trustee First Night, Boston, 1987-90, Shady Hill Sch., Cambridge, 1980-84; trustee Coydog Found., 1996—. Mem. N.Y. Bar Assn., Boston Bar Assn. Office: Harris & Lloyd Inc 2 Brighton St 2d Fl Belmont MA 02478

LLOYD, CHARLES JOSEPH, lawyer; b. Spokane, Wash., Feb. 15, 1961; s. George Brearley and Vivian McLaughlin L.; m. Mary Elizabeth Wahl, Feb. 3, 1990; children: George, Thomas, Catherine. BA honors, Gonzaga U., Spokane, Wash., 1983; JD, U. Minn., 1986. Bar: Minn., U.S. Dist. Ct. Minn., U.S. Dist. Ct. (no. dist.) Calif., U.S. Ct. Appeals (8th and fed. cirs.), U.S. Supreme Ct. Law clk. to Justice Glenn E. Kelley Minn. Supreme Ct., St. Paul, 1986-87; assoc. Lindquist & Vennum, Mpls., 1987-92, ptnr., 1993—. Contbg. author: The Minnesota Justices Series: The Judicial Career of Glenn E. Kelley, 1993. Mem. ABA, Minn. State Bar Assn., Vol. Lawyers Network, Legal Rights Ctr. (bd. dirs.).

LLOYD, CHRISTOPHER, actor; b. Stamford, Conn., Oct. 22, 1938; Actor, Neighborhood Playhouse, N.Y.C.; actor: summer stock and off-Broadway, including title roles in Kaspar, 1973 (Obie award, Drama Desk award), Trumbo, 2003; Broadway appearances include Red, White and Maddox, Macbeth, Twelfth Night, Mornings at Seven, N.Y. Shakespeare in the Park; films include Butch and Sundance, 1969, Three Warriors, One Flew Over the Cuckoo's Nest, 1975, Goin South, 1978, The Onion Field, 1979, The Black Marble, 1980, The Legend of the Lone Ranger, 1981, Mr. Mom, 1983, To Be or Not to Be, 1983, Star Trek III, 1984, Adventures of Buckaroo Banzai, 1984, Joy of Sex, 1984, Back to the Future, 1985, Clue, 1985, Who Framed Roger Rabbit, 1988, Walk Like a Man, 1987, Eight Men Out, 1988, Track 29, 1988, Why Me, The Dream Team, 1989, Back to the Future, Part II, 1989, Back to the Future, Part III, 1990, The Addams Family, 1991, Suburban Commando, 1991, Dennis the Menace, 1993, Twenty Bucks, 1993, Addams Family Values, 1993, Angels in the Outfield, 1994, The Pagemaster, 1994, Camp Nowhere, 1994, The Radioland Murders, 1994, Things To Do in Denver When You're Dead, 1995, Changing Habits, 1996, Cadillac Ranch, 1996, Quicksilver Highway, 1997, Real Blonde, 1997, Anastasia, 1997, My Favorite Martian, 1999, Man on the Moon, 1999, Baby Geniuses, 1999, Wit, 2001, Interstate 60, 2002; dependent film appearance: Flakes; TV films: Lacy and the Mississippi Queen, 1978, The Word, 1978, Stunt Seven, 1979, Money on the Side, 1982, September Gun, 1983, Avonlea, 1991 (Emmy award, Best Actor in a Drama Series, 1992), Dead Ahead: Exxon Valdez, 1992, T-Bone N Weasel, 1992, Rent-A-Kid, 1995, The Ransom of Red Chief, 1996, The Right to Remain Silent, 1996, Alice in Wonderland, 1999; TV appearances as a regular in Taxi, 1978-83 (Best Supporting Actor Emmy award 1982, 83), Stacked; guest spots: Cheers, 1982, Road to Avonlea, 1992 (Best Actor Emmy), Back to the Future, 1991-92, Deadly Games, 1995, Spin City, 1996, Ed, 2000, Malcolm in the Middle, 2000, The Tick, 2002, Tremors, 2003, The West Wing; TV movie Amazing Stories, 1985; TV series: Clubhouse, 2004-. Office: The Gersh Agency c/o Bob Gersh 252 N Canon Dr Beverly Hills CA 90210-5302 also: Andy Freedman, Mgr 20 Ironsides St Venice CA 90292

LLOYD, DAVID LIVINGSTONE, JR., lawyer; b. Butler, Pa., Aug. 28, 1952; s. David Livingstone and Jean Marie (Basher) L.; m. Dana L. Kadison, June 26, 1983; children: John Gabriel, Margaret Kadison. BS, AB, U. Pa., 1974, JD, 1977. Bar: N.Y. 1977. Assoc. Dewey Ballantine, N.Y.C., 1977-85, ptnr., 1986-93; sr. counsel Financing and transactions GE Aircraft Engines, Cin., 1993—. Office: GE Aircraft Engines 1 Neumann Way # F17 Cincinnati OH 45215-1915

LLOYD, DOUGLAS SEWARD, physician, public health administrator; b. Bklyn., Oct. 16, 1939; s. Heber Hughes and Virginia Seward (Chamberlin) L. AB in Chemistry, Duke U., 1961, MD, 1971; postgrad., Old Dominion U., 1965-67; MPH in Health Planning, U. N.C., 1971. Diplomate Am. Bd. Preventive Medicine. Intern Duke U., Durham, N.C., 1971-72, clin. scholar, 1972, resident in family practice, 1972-73; commr. health Conn. Dept. Health Services, 1973-87; assoc. med. dir. Nat. Med. Rsch. Corp., Hartford, Conn., 1987-89; pres. Doug Lloyd Assocs., Farmington, Conn., 1989-92; dir. Ctr. Pub. Health Practice Health Resources and Svcs. Adminstrn., Rockville, Md., 1992-98; with Assn. Schs. Pub. Health, Washington, 1999—. Lectr. Yale U., Conn., 1973-87; chmn. bd. Pub. Health Found., 1984-87. Contbr. articles to profl. jours. Capt. USNR, ret. Recipient Lange Publ. award, 1971, McCormick award for excellence in pub. health, 1987, Ervin award for creative vision, The Pub. Health Found., 2001. Fellow Am. Coll. Preventive Medicine; mem. AMA, Am. Pub. Health Assn., Assn. State and Territorial Health Ofcls. (past pres.). Home: 10804 Bird Song Path Columbia MD 21044-3693 Office: Ctr for Pub Health HRSA Parklawn 8-103 5600 Fishers Ln Rockville MD 20857 E-mail: dLloyd@hrsa.gov.

LLOYD, EUGENE WALTER, retired construction company executive; b. Bklyn., Apr. 9, 1943; s. Walter Vincent and Mary Regina L.; m. Julia Ann Bain Menzies, May 6, 1967; children: Deborah Ann, Doreen Marie. AA in Constrn., N.Y. Tech. Coll., 1960-63. With Stephen H. Falk & Assocs., Great Neck, N.Y., 1962-65, Builder's Estimating Service, N.Y.C., 1965-67; estimator Humphreys & Harding, Inc., N.Y.C., 1967-68; chief estimator, corp. sec. Conforti & Eisele, Inc., N.Y.C., 1968-76; exec. v.p. Torcon, Inc., Westfield, N.J., 1976-93; v.p., dir. The Henderson Corp., Raritan, N.J., 1994-98; contract mgr. Huber, Hunt & Nichols, Inc., Indpls., 1998; ret., 1998. Served with U.S. Army, 1963-69. Republican. Roman Catholic. Home: 6910 E Bobwhite Way Scottsdale AZ 85262-8526 Personal E-mail: Eugenewlloydaz@aol.com.

LLOYD, GERALD JOSEPH, music educator; b. Lebanon, Ohio, Sept. 6, 1938; s. Joseph Eben and Nina Lydia Lloyd; m. Jeannie Elizabeth Church, May 23, 1940. PhD, Eastman Sch. Music U. Rochester, 1967. Asst. prof. We. Mich. U., Kalamazoo, 1963—69; asst. dean Fine Arts Drake U., Des Moines, 1971—75; dean Conservatory Music Capital U., Columbus, Ohio, 1975—80; dir. Sch. Music Ohio U., Athens, 1980—83; prof. music U. Mass. Lowell, 1999—. Dean Conservatory Music Capital U., Columbus, Ohio, 1975—80; dir. Sch. Music Ohio U., Athens, Ohio, 1980—83; dean Fine Arts U. Mass. Lowell, 1983—99, prof. music, 1999—. Composer (consultant, producer): (compositions) Misc. For Orchestra, Chamber. Accreditor evaluator Nat. Assn. Schs. Music, Reston, Va., 1986—90. Home: 447 Princeton Blvd Lowell MA 01851 Office: University Massachusetts Lowell Wilder St Lowell MA 01854 Personal E-mail: gjlloyd@attbi.com. E-mail: gerald_lloyd@uml.edu.

LLOYD, HUGH ADAMS, lawyer; b. Pine Apple, Ala., Oct. 5, 1918; s. James Adams and Kate (Compton) L.; m. Lydia Douglas, Sept. 18, 1942; children: Kathryn Lloyd Allen, Sally Douglas (Mrs. Charles Proctor), Elizabeth Anne (Mrs. Thomas Goodman), Hugh Adams Jr. Student, Oglethorpe U., 1936-37; AB, U. Ala., 1941, LL.B., 1942. Bar: Ala. 1942, U.S. Supreme Ct 1958. Adjudicator VA, Montgomery, Ala., 1946-47; ptnr. Lloyd, Dinning, Boggs & Dinning, Demopolis, Ala., 1947—2000; mem. Lloyd & Dinning LLC, Demopolis, 2001—. Active Boy Scouts Am.; chmn. Demopolis Indsl. Devel. Com., 1970; mem. Regional Com. Juvenile Delinquency, 1970; chmn. Marengo County Devel. Bd., 1972-73; mem. Demopolis City Coun., 1974; chmn. Indsl. Devel. Bd. Marengo County, 1980; pres. Marengo County Port Authority, 1987—, Demopolis City Schs. Found., 1995—; trustee Judson Coll., Marion, Ala., 1981, vice-chmn. bd., 1989, chmn., 1991; bd. dirs. Judson Coll.-Marion Inst. Joint Found.; Sunday sch. tchr. Bapt. Ch., 1950—; past chmn. ch. bd. deacons bylaws com. Ala. State Bapt. Conv., 1997. With AUS, 1943-45. Decorated Bronze Star; recipient Silver Beaver award Boy Scouts Am., 1972, Paul Harris Fellow award Rotary Found., 1998, award for cmty. svc. West Ala. Mental Health Bd., 1998, Demopolis Citizen of Yr. award, 1998. Mem. ABA, Am. Judicature Soc., Ala. Bar Assn., 17th Jud. Circuit Bar Assn. (pres.), Marengo County Hist. Soc. (v.p. 1980), Demopolis C. of C. (pres., Citizen of Yr. 1998, Lifetime Achievement award 2002), Ala. Law Inst. (coun.), Bus. Coun. Ala. (dir. 1995), Ala. Safety Coun. (past bd. dirs.), Demopolis Country Club (pres. 1967-68), Kiwanis (dist. gov. 1967, chmn. internat. com. Key clubs 1969, internat. com. on boys and girls work 1972, dist. chmn. laws and regulations com. Ala. dist. 1979). Home: 1408 Colony Dr Demopolis AL 36732-3443 Office: PO Drawer 740 501 N Walnut Ave Demopolis AL 36732-2037 Office Phone: 334-289-0556. Business E-Mail: hlloyd@westal.net.

LLOYD, JAMES D., federal agency administrator; b. Granville, N.Y., Oct. 5, 1947; BSME with honors, Union Coll., 1969; M Indsl. Engring., Tex. A&M U., 1970. Safety engr. U.S. Army Aviation Sys. Command, St. Louis; prin. safety engr., chief program evaluation U.S. Army Materiel Command, Alexandria, Va., dir. field safety activity, 1979—87; with NASA Hdqrs., Washington, 1987—, dir. product assurance, dir. safety and risk mgmt. divsn. Office of Safety and Mission Assurance, 1993—2003, Deputy Chief office of safety and mission assurance, 2003—; dir. product assurance Space Station Program, 1988—93. Office: NASA Hdqrs Mail Ste 5039 300 E St SW Washington DC 20546

LLOYD, JAMES F., public relations executive; m. Jackie Lloyd. BA, Stanford U.; MA, U. So. Calif. Polit. sci. prof. Mount San Antonio Coll., 1970-73; mem. U.S. Ho. of Reps., 1974; mem. armed svcs., sci. and aging coms.; assoc. Foley Govt. Rels., Potomac, Md. Mayor, councilman West Covina, Calif. Office: PO Box 61303 Potomac MD 20859

LLOYD, JAMES ROBERT, scientist; b. Pitts., June 8, 1948; s. James Robert and Agnes (Marzovac) L.; m. Susan Jean Ogurian, Aug. 18, 1984; children: James Edson, Stephanie Patricia. BS, Stevens Inst. Tech., 1970, MS, 1973, PhD, 1978. Engr., AMAX Base Metals, Carteret, N.J., 1970-73; engr. IBM, Hopewell Junction, N.Y., 1978-88; adj. prof. Poly. Inst., Bklyn., 1979-88; engring. cons. Digital Equipment Corp., 1988—; bd. dirs. Ralph Stegmeier Inst., Fishkill, N.Y., 1982-88; mentor Semiconductor Rsch. Corp. Contbr. over 50 articles to profl. jours.; editor: Electromigration, 1985; co-editor: Materials Reliability in Microelectronics, 1991, 92. Recipient Invention Achievement award IBM, 1980, 83, Best Paper award, 1983, award N.J. Aviation Hall of Fame Mus., pilot Vin Fiz Reenactment Flight, 1986; named Hon. Texan, Gov. Tex., 1986. Mem. Materials Rsch. Soc., Sigma Xi. Avocations: soccer, aviation. Home: PO Box 194 Stow MA 01775-0194

LLOYD, JEAN, retired early childhood educator; b. Montgomery, Ala., Mar. 3, 1935; d. James Jack and Dorothy Gladys (Brown) L.; 1 child, Jamie Angelica. BA, Queens Coll., 1957; MA, NYU, 1960, PhD, 1976. Tchr. jr. HS NYC Bd. of Edn., 1961, dir. head start ctr., 1966, 67 summer, tchr. early childhood, 1961-69, tchr. kindergarten, 1984—2004; instr., asst. prof. U. Coll. Rutgers U., Newark, 1969-83; ret., 2004. Cons. Bd. Examiners, N.Y.C., 1982, Dept. of Pers., N.Y.C., 1985; rsch. cons. Seymour Laskow CPA, 1983; chmn. bd. dirs. Your Family Inc., N.Y.C., 1989-2004; prodr. New Ventures cable TV show (Manhattan), 1987-2004. Author: Sociology and Social Life, 1979; contbr. over 10 articles to profl. jours. Recipient Ed Press award Ednl. Press Assn., 1968; Project Synergy fellow Tchrs. Coll., Columbia, 1991-93. Mem. ASCD, United Fedn. of Tchrs., Delta Kappa Gamma. Democrat. Methodist. Avocations: writing poetry and feature articles, singing in church choir. Home: 180 W End Ave New York NY 10023-4902

LLOYD, JOHN RAYMOND, mechanical engineering educator; b. Mpls., Aug. 1, 1942; s. Raymond Joseph and Wilma Mable (Epple) L.; m. Mary Jane Whiteside, Dec. 20, 1963; children: Jay William, Stephanie Christine. BS in Engring., U. Minn., 1964, MSME, 1966, PhDME, 1971; D in Tech. Sci. (hon.), Russian Acad. Scis., 2000. Devel. engr. Procter & Gamble Co., Cin., 1966-67; prof. mech. engring. U. Notre Dame, South Bend, Ind., 1970-83; disting. prof. Mich. State U., East Lansing, 1983—, chmn. dept. mech. engring., 1983-91, dir. Inst. Global Engring. Edn., 1997—2001. Cons. LeRoy Troyer & Assocs., Mishawaka, Ind., 1980—90, Azdel Inc., Shelby, NC, 1987—90; advisor NSF, Washington, 1987—90; Nat. Bur. Stds. assessment panel NRC, Washington, 1987—93; sci. coun. Internat. Ctr. Heat and Mass Transfer, Yugoslavia, 1986—; chmn. Midwest Energy Consortium, 1993—2000; adv. editor McGraw Hill, Inc., 1990—. Adv. editor Internat. Jour. Heat and Fluid Flow, 1985—, Jour. Engring. Physics and Thermodynamics, 1993—; contbr. over 100 articles to profl. jours., chpts. to books. Recipient Outstanding Faculty award U. Notre Dame, 1975, 82, Ralph R. Teetor Ednl. award Soc. Automotive Engrs., 1986. Fellow: ASME (nat. bd. comm. 1983—90, rsch. and tech. devel. bd. 1985—99, editor Jour. Heat Transfer 1989—95, coun. on edn., critical techs. com. 1991—93, sr. v.p. engring. 1999—2002, v.p. rsch. 1995—98, Outstanding Paper award 1977, Melville medal 1978, Heat Transfer Meml. award 1995, Dedicated Svc. award 1999). Office: Mich State U Dept Mech Engring 2242 Engring Bldg East Lansing MI 48824 E-mail: lloyd@egr.msu.edu.

LLOYD, JUNE BURK, retired librarian, archivist; b. York County, Pa., June 7, 1939; d. Wiley A. Burk and Olive M. Shelley; m. Ronald E. Lloyd, Aug. 14, 1956; children: Lisa A., Linda S. BA summa cum laude, York Coll., Pa., 1995; MA in Am. Studies, Pa. State U., 1999. Asst. libr. Kaltreider Meml. Libr., Red Lion, Pa., 1980—89; libr. York County Heritage Trust, York, Pa., 1989—2005, archivist, 1989—2005; ret., 2005. Author: Faith and Family, 2001; curator (exhibitions) Faith and Family in Fraktur, 2001. Named libr. Emerita. Mem.: Palatines to Am., Pa. German Soc. Lutheran. Avocation: history. Office: York County Heritage Trust 250 E Market St York PA 17403

LLOYD, LEONARD EDWARD, marriage and family therapist, consultant; b. San Francisco, Calif., 1934; s. Donald DeHart and Josephine Mary (Museo) Lloyd; m. Gretchen Anne Brentlinger (div.); m. Stephanie Stewart; children: Barbara, Kathleen, Karen, Cynthia. Degree in Sociology and Psychology, San Jose (Calif.) State U., 1962; degree in Counseling Psychology, Calif. State U., 1976. Cert. marriage and family therapist Calif., 1978. Unit supr., dep. probation officer Alameda County Probation Dept., Oakland, Calif., 1962—78; project dir. Social Advocates Youth, San Francisco, 1978—80; mgr. Horizens Family Counseling Livermore (Calif.) Police Dept., 1981—2001. Mem. local planning coun. Comprehensive Youth Svc., Oakland, Calif., 1998—; mem. steering com. Juvenile Justice Study, Oakland, 2002—04; mem. allocations com. Tri-Valley Cmty. Found., Pleasanton, Calif., 2001—. Author: Deinstitutionalization of Status Offenders, 1980. Chief petty officer USCG, 1957—99. Named Friend of Edn., Livermore (Calif.) Bd. Edn., 1999; recipient Disting. Svc. award, Tri-Valley Cmty. Fund, 1997, Cmty. Svc. award, Tri-Valley Cmty. Champions, 2000. Mem.: Calif. Assn. Marriage and Family Therapists. Avocations: motorcycling, wetlands restoration, politics. Office: Psychological Svcs 7567 Amader Valley Blvd 202 Dublin CA 94568

LLOYD, MARGARET ANN, psychologist, educator; b. Weiser, Idaho, Sept. 14, 1942; d. Laurance Henry and Margaret Jane (Patch) L. BA, U. Denver, 1964; MS in Edn., Ind. U., 1966; MA in Psychology, U. Ariz., 1972, PhD in Psychology, 1973. Asst. prof. psychology Suffolk U., Boston, 1973-76, assoc. prof., 1976-79, prof., 1979-88, chair dept., 1981-88; prof. Ga. So. U., Statesboro, 1988—2004, head dept., 1988—93, prof. emerita and chair, 2004—. Author: Adolescence, 1985; author: (with others) Psychology Applied to Modern Life, 1991, 1994, 1997, 2000, 2003; contbr. articles to profl. jours. Mem. AAUP, APA (bd. ednl. affairs 2000-2002, sec.-treas. divsn. 2 1990-93, pres. 1994-95, coun. rep. 2003—), New Eng. Psychol. Assn. (steering com. 1984-86), Mass. Psychol. Assn. (sec. 1979-81, chair bd. acad.

and. sci. affairs 1981-82), Coun. Undergrad. Psychology Programs (chmn. 1990-91). Home: 805 Shelter Pointe Rd Statesboro GA 30458-9113 Business E-Mail: mlloyd@georgiasouthern.edu.

LLOYD, PATRICK M., dental educator, dean; B in Mathematics, Marquette U., 1974; DDS, Marquette U. Sch. Dentistry, 1978; MS, Marquette U. Grad. Sch., 1989. Cert. in Prosthodontics Vet. Adminstrn. Med. Ctr., 1981. Chief dental geriatrics VA Med. Ctr., Milwaukee, 1981—85; nat. coord. geriatric dental programs Dept. Vet. Affairs, 1985—92; head, Special Patient Care Clinic Marquette U. Sch. Dentistry-, 1992—96; head dept. family dentistry U. Iowa Coll. Dentistry, 1996—2003; dean U. Minn. Sch. Dentistry, 2004—. Editor-in-chief: Journal of Prosthodontics, 1993—. Fellow: Gerontological Soc. Am., Clin. Med. Sect. (mem. fellowship com. 1998—), Am. Coll. Prosthodontics (pres. elect); mem.: Internat. Coll. Prosthodontics (co-pres. 2001—03). Office: U Minn Sch Dentistry Moos Health Sciences Tower 515 Deleware St SE Minneapolis MN 55401

LLOYD, PRISCILLA ANN, finance educator; b. Defuniak Springs, Fla., June 21, 1946; d. Thomas Sherman and Leona Campbell Brown; m. Leroy Lloyd, Aug. 15, 1969; 1 child, Leroy Erison. BS, U. Okla., 1974, EdM, 1975. Cert. adminstrn. and supervision U. of Ctrl. Fla. Tchr. bus. H.B. Plant H.S., Tampa, Fla., 1975—78, Meadowbrook Jr. H.S., Orlando, Fla., 1978—84, Apopka (Fla.) H.S., 1984—90, Cypress Creek H.S., Orlando, 1990—93; coord. bus. programs Orange County Sch. Dist., Orlando, 1993—96; instr., adminstr. asst. program Mid Fla. Tech, Orlando, 1996—. Pres. Orange County Bus. Edn. Assoc., Orlando, 1991—92, Fla. Bus. Edn. Assn., Orlando, 1992—94; dist. dir. Future Bus. Leaders Am., Orlando, 1992—93. Named Outstanding Tchr., Fla. Bus. Edn. Assn., 1993, Outstanding Educator, Orange County Vocat. Assoc., 1994. Mem.: Fla. Bus. Edn. Assoc. Conf. (chmn. 44th annual conf.), Family Christian Athletic Assn. (bd. mem. 2002—03). Catholic Orthodox. Avocations: reading, writing, photography, travel. Home: 7202 Jonquil Dr Orlando FL 32818 Office Phone: 407-293-6635.

LLOYD, RAY DIX, health physicist; b. Mar. 10, 1930; s. Ray Ernest and Dixie (Penrose) L.; m. Louise Mortensen, July 10, 1954; children: Thomas R., Janna L. Brady, Alan T., Christopher R., Heather L. Smith. BS, U. Utah, 1954, MS, 1956, PhD, 1974; postgrad., U. Southwestern La., 1959, La. State U., 1960. Diplomate Am. Bd. Health Physics. From rsch. asst. radiobiology divsn. to rshc. prof. U. Utah, 1961—84, rsch. prof. dept. pharmacology, radiobiology divsn., 1984-92; part-time rsch. prof. U. Utah Sch. Medicine, 1992—. Adj. asst. prof. dept. mech. engring. U. Utah, 1975-90; adj. prof. engring. U. Utah, 1997—, rsch. prof. radiology, 1998—; cons. in field; mem. Nat. Coun. Radiation Protection and Measurements, 1980-92, consociate mem., 1992—; mem. radiol. health adv. com. Utah State Divsn. Health. Assoc. editor: (jour.) Health Physics, 1990-92; (book) Delayed Effects of Bone Seeking Radionuclides; reviewer: Radiation Rsch., Health Physics, Radiat. Protection, Internat. Jour. Radiation Biology, others; contbr. articles to profl. jours., chpts. to books; patentee radiation detector. Master sgt. U.S. Army, 1951—52, Korea. Fellow Health Physics Soc.; mem. Am. Acad. Health Physics, Radiation Rsch. Soc., Health Physics Soc. (Great Salt Lake chpt.), Utah br. Am. Assn. for Lab. Animal Sci., Internat. Radiation Protection Assn., Sigma Xi, Phi Kappa Phi, Gamma Theta Upsilon. Office: U Utah Radiobiology 729 Arapeen Dr 2334 CAMT Salt Lake City UT 84108-1218 Office Phone: 801-581-6810. Business E-Mail: ray.lloyd@hsc.utah.edu.

LLOYD, ROBERT BLACKWELL, JR., lawyer; b. York, Pa., July 20, 1926; s. Robert Blackwell and Grace Irene (Dunkelberger) L.; m. Mary Ruth Hall, May 29, 1951; children— Lisa, Robert Bradford. A.B., Harvard Coll., 1947; LL.B., Duke U., 1950, J.D., 1971. Bar: N.C. 1950. Assoc. Norman Block, Greensboro, N.C., 1950-52; ptnr. Block, Meyland & Lloyd, Greensboro, 1952-80; sec. treas. Block, Meyland & Lloyd, P.A., Greensboro, 1981—91; with Turner Enochs & Lloyd, Greensboro, 1991-2002, Lloyd Miller & Assoc., Greensboro, 2002—. Bd. dirs. Eastern Music Festival, Greensboro, 1976—80; bd. dirs. N.C. Symphony Soc., 1974-76; dist. chmn. Gen. Greene council Boy Scouts Am., 1962-65; deacon, elder, chmn. bd. deacons, clk. session Starmount Presbyterian Ch. Served with USNR, 1944-61. Fellow Am. Coll. Probate Counsel (N.C. state chmn, 1985-86, practice com., editl. bd. 1996—); mem. ABA, N.C. Bar Assn. (chmn. sect. probate and fiduciary law 1980-81), Greensboro Bar Assn., N.C. State Bar (vice chmn. splty. com. on estate planning and fiduciary law of bd. of specialization 1984—), 4th Fed. Circuit Jud. Conf. Democrat. Clubs: Lions, Greensboro City, Starmount Forest Country, 100 Club. Office: Lloyd Miller & Assoc PA PO Box 29247 Greensboro NC 27429-9247 Office Phone: 336-373-5991. E-mail: rbl@lloydmillerlaw.com.

LLOYD, R.W., psychiatrist; AB, Princeton U., 1968; PhD, U. S.C., 1975; MD, U. Ariz., 1986. Diplomate Am. Bd. Psychiatry and Neurology. Resident and intern U. Ariz. Affiliated Hosps., Tucson, 1986-90; clin. asst. prof. psychiatry, Coll. Medicine U. Ariz., 1991—95; chief in patient psychiatry Tucson VA Med. Ctr., 1990—94, chief substance abuse treatment unit, 1992—94.

LLOYD, SETH, physicist; b. Boston, Aug. 2, 1960; s. Robert Andrew and Susan Margaret (McIntosh) L. AB, Harvard U., 1982; M.Phil, Cambridge U., 1984; PhD, Rockefeller U., 1988. Rsch. fellow Calif. Inst. Tech., Pasadena, 1988-91, Los Alamos (N.Mex.) Nat. Lab., 1991—94; prof. mech. engring. and engring systems Mass. Inst. Tech., Cambridge, Mass., 1994—, prin. investigator rsch. lab. electronics. Adj. faculty Santa Fe Inst., 1988—. Mem. ASME, Am. Phys. Soc. Achievements include research in complex systems and foundations of quantum mechanics. Office: Mass Inst Tech 77 Massachusetts Ave Bldg 3-160 Cambridge MA 02139-4307 Office Phone: 617-252-1803. Business E-Mail: slloyd@mit.edu.

LLOYD, TONYA RAINA, elementary school educator; b. Augusta, Ga., Jan. 22, 1972; d. Floyd and Joanne Lloyd; m. Timothy Lamont Moore, Feb. 7, 1996; 1 child, Alexis Nikia Moore. M in Curriculum and Tech., U. Phoenix, 2005. Tchr. McCormick County Schs., SC, 2000—04, Aiken County Pub. Schools, SC, 2004—. Recipient McCormick Elementary Tchr. of Yr. award; grantee, SC. Dept. Edn., 2001—02. Mem.: NEA (assoc.). Baptist. Avocations: gardening, arts and crafts, travel. Home: 2905 Loren Street Aiken SC 29801 Personal E-mail: tonyalloyd@yahoo.com.

LLOYD, WILLIAM F., lawyer; b. Youngstown, Ohio, Dec. 27, 1947; AB magna cum laude, Brown U., 1969; JD cum laude, U. Chgo., 1975. Bar: Ill. 1975, U.S. Supreme Ct. 1980, US Dist. Ct. (no. dist.) Ill. 1975, (no. dist.) Calif. 1986, US Ct. of Appeals, 7th cir. 1978, DC cir., 1980, 3rd cir. 1988, 10th cir. 1988, 8th cir. 1993, 5th cir. 2004. Assoc. Sidley & Austin, Chgo., 1975—82; ptnr. and head, securities and fin. litig. group Sidley Austin Brown & Wood LLP, Chgo., 1982—, mem. exec. com. Mem. ABA (mem. litigation and bus. sects.), Chgo. Bar Assn., Legal Club Chgo. Office: Sidley Austin Brown & Wood LLP Bank One Plz 10 S Dearborn St Chicago IL 60603 Office Phone: 312-853-7736. Office Fax: 312-853-7036. Business E-Mail: wlloyd@sidley.com.

LLOYD-CALDWELL, MARIAN JEAN, business owner; b. Detroit, June 19, 1942; d. Junius and Ada Mae (Thomas) L.; m. Julius James Caldwell. BA, U. Windsor, Ont., Can., 1978; cert., Marygrove Coll., 1987; grad. Dale Carnegie course, 1987. Employment recruit State of Mich., Detroit, 1981-82; job developer Greater Orgn. Indsl. Ctr., Detroit, 1982-83; dist. mgr. State of Mich. Bur. of Lottery, Detroit, 1984—; owner J. Brandon Co., Detroit, 1986—. Lectr. Lakeview High Sch., St. Clair Shores, Mich., 1972; TV producer Employment Svcs. of Mich., St. Clair Shores, 1981; producer, writer J. Brandon Co., Detroit, 1986—, pub. rels com., 1986—. Author: MARJEAN, 1977, What Becomes of the Watermelon Seeds, 1997 (Voices of Civl Rights Recognition, 2005); editor: newsletter The Calvary Advocator, 1980; playwright play Not Yet Lord, 1989. Founder. Library Tribute to Black Am., Detroit, 1975; campaign mgr. Dem. candidate for office, Detroit, 1982; pres. local sch. community orgn., Detroit, 1986-89. Recipient Outstanding Recognition, 1986, 87, 90, Voices of Civil Rights Recognition Am. Civil Rights Movement, 2005. Mem. NAFE, Gamma Phi Delta. Avocations: public speaking, choirs, bowling, travel. Office: 19410 Livernois Ave Detroit MI 48221-1760 E-mail: marjohn19@yahoo.com.

LLOYD-JONES, DADIVA BOCOBO, nursing assistant, writer; b. Tarlac, Philippines, Nov. 7, 1931; arrived in U.S., 1989; d. Alfredo Santiago Perez and Inez Dupitas Bocobo; m. Bernardo Villanueva Aperocho, Aug. 27, 1951 (div.); children: Butch Aperocho(dec.), Darius, Norman, Noel, Rey(dec.); m. Leon Thomas Lloyd-Jones, Mar. 12, 1992. BS in Edn., U. of the East, Manila, Philippines, 1955; MA, Ateneo de Manila, 1964; EdD, U. Pangasinan, Dagupan, Philippines, 1977. Cert. nursing asst., Wash. H.S. English tchr. Gerona Inst., Tarlac, 1956—64; prof. Feati U., Manila, 1964—71, U. Pangasinan, 1971—81; speech and drama tchr. Ramon Magsaysay, Manila, 1981—89; home health aide Olympic Peninsula Home Health, Wash., 1991—94, nursing asst., 1995—97, Dynamic Corp., L.A., 1995—. Co-author: Speech and Drama, 1988; author: (poems) Of Tears and Flowers, 1999, Heart and Soul, 2000. Recipient Editor's Choice awards (4), Internat. Libr. Poetry, 1998—2000, Editor's Choice awards (6), Nat. Libr. of Poetry, 1998—99. Mem.: Internat. Soc. Poets. Avocations: writing poems and essays, piano, singing. Home: 2621 Midvale Ave Los Angeles CA 90064-4213

LLOYD-JONES, SIR (PETER) HUGH (JEFFERD), writer; b. St. Peter Port, Guernsey, Sept. 21, 1922; s. William and Norah Leila (Jefferd) Lloyd-J.; m. Frances E. Hedley, 1953 (div. 1981); children: Edmund Stephen, Ralph Alexander, Antonia; m. Mary R. Lefkowitz, 1982. MA, Oxford (Eng.) U., 1947; DHL (hon.), U. Chgo., 1970; PhD (hon.), U. Tel Aviv, 1984, Thessalonica U., 1999, U. Göttingen, 2002. Author: The Justice of Zeus, 1971, 2d edit., 1983, Blood for the Ghosts, 1982, Classical Survivals, 1982, (with P.J. Parsons) Supplementum Hellenisticum, 1983, (with N.G. Wilson) Sophoclis Fabulae, 1990, (with N.G. Wilson) Sophoclea, 1990, Academic Papers, 2 vols., 1990, 3 vols., 2005, Greek in a Cold Climate, 1991, Sophocles, 3 vols., 1994-96, (with N.G. Wilson) Sophocles: Second Thoughts, 1997, Supplementation Supplements Hellenistici, 2005; others; translator Oresteia (Aeschylus), 1970. With Brit. Army, 1942—46. Fellow Jesus Coll., Cambridge (Eng.) U., 1948-54; fellow and E.P. Warren praelector in classics Corpus Christi Coll., Oxford, 1954-60; Regius prof. Greek, Oxford U., 1960-89; vis. prof. Yale U., 1964, 67, U. Chgo., 1972, Harvard U., 1976; Sather prof. U. Calif., Berkeley, 1969. Fellow: Acad. Athens, Brit. Acad.; mem.: Am. Philos. Soc., Bayerische Acad., Lettere e Belle Arti, Accademia di Archeologia Naples, Nordrhein-Westfälische Acad., Am. Acad. Arts and Scis. Address: 15 W Riding St Wellesley MA 02482-6914 also: Christ Ch Oxford OX1 1DP England E-mail: mlefkowitz@wellesley.edu.

LLOYD WEBBER, LORD ANDREW (BARON OF SYDMONTON), composer; b. London, Mar. 22, 1948; s. William Southcombe and Jean Hermione (Johnstone) Lloyd-Webber; m. Sarah Jane Tudor Hugill, July 24, 1971 (div. 1983); children: Imogen Lloyd-Webber, Nicholas Lloyd-Webber; m. Sarah Brightman, Mar. 1984 (div. 1990); m. Madeleine Astrid Gurdon, Feb. 1, 1991; children: Alastair Adam Lloyd-Webber, William Richard Lloyd-Webber, Isabella Aurora Lloyd-Webber. Ed., Westminster Sch., Magdalen Coll., Oxford U.; FRCM, Royal Coll. Music, 1988. Composer: (Broadway plays) Joseph and the Amazing Technicolor Dreamcoat, 1968, 1973, 1991 (Tony nom. best original score, 1982), 2003; prodr.: (Broadway plays) Joseph and the Amazing Technicolor Dreamcoat, 1973, 1974, 1978, 1980, 1991; composer, orchestrator (Broadway plays) Jesus Christ Superstar, 1970 (Tony nom. best original score, 1972), composer, prodr., 1996, 1998; composer: (Broadway plays) Jeeves, 1975; composer, prodr. (Broadway plays) By Jeeves (revision of Jeeves), 1996; prodr.: Jeeves Takes Charge, 1975; composer, orchestrator (Broadway plays) Evita, 1976, (stage version Broadway plays), 1978; composer: Tell Me on a Sunday, 1980, 2003; composer, prodr. (Broadway plays) Cats, 1981 (Tony award best original score, 1983), Song and Dance, 1982 (Tony nom. best musical, 1986, Tony nom. best original score, 1986), Starlight Express, 1984 (Tony nom. best original score, 1987), The Phantom of the Opera, 1986 (Tony nom. best book of a musical, 1988, Tony nom. best original score, 1988), Aspects of Love, 1989 (Tony nom. best book of a musical, 1990, Tony nom. best original score, 1990), Sunset Boulevard, 1993 (Tony award best book of a musical, 1995, Tony award best original score, 1995), Whistle Down the Wind, 1996, 1998; composer: The Beautiful Game, 2000, The Woman in White, 2004; prodr., orchestrator (films) Jesus Christ Superstar, 1973, Evita, 1996 (Tony award best original score, 1980); prodr.: (films) The Phantom of the Opera, 2004; composer: (films) Gumshoe, 1971, The Odessa File, 1974, Starlight Express 3D, 2003, (other musical works) The Toy Theatre Suite, 1959, Variations, 1977, Requiem, 1985, (TV series) The South Bank Show, 1978, Watership Down, 1999; prodr.: (Broadway plays) Bombay Dreams, 2002, Daisy Pulls It Off, 1983, The Hired Man, 1984, On Your Toes, 1984, Café Puccini, 1986, The Resistable Rise of Arturo Ui, 1987, Lend Me a Tenor, 1988; (Broadway plays) Shirley Valentine, 1989, La Bête, 1992; author (with Timothy Rice): Evita, 1978; author: Cats: the book of the musical, 1981; author: (with Timothy Rice) Joseph and the Amazing Technicolor Dreamcoat, 1982; author: The Complete Phantom of the Opera, 1987, The Complete Aspects of Love, 1989, Sunset Boulevard: from movie to musical, 1993. Named a Living Legend Grammy, 1989, created knight in Queen's Honours Birthday List, 1992, elevated to peerage in New Yrs. Honours list, 1997; named one of The Top 200 Collectors, ARTnews Mag., 2004; recipient Grammy awards, 1980, 1983, 1985, Triple Play award, ASCAP, 1988, City and Music Ctr. of L.A., 1991, Praemium Imperiale award for music, 1995, Richard Rodgers award for contbn. to musical theatre, 1996, Bernard Delfont award for contbn. to show bus., 1997, Acad. award, 1997. Fellow: Royal Coll. Music. Achievements include awards include Acad. award (Oscar), Golden Globe, Tony, Drama Desk, and Grammy. Avocations: architecture, Collector of 18th to 20th century paintings, especially the Pre-Raphaelites. Office: 22 Tower St London WC2H 9NS England

LNENICKA, WADE SHERIDAN, purchasing agent, councilman; b. Kansas City, Mo., Nov. 1, 1951; s. William Joseph and Georgia Marie (Ericksen) L.; m. Robin Ann Brown, June 22, 1985. BS in Mgmt., Ga. Inst. Tech., 1973; MBA, U. Mich., 1978; grad. with honors, U.S. Army Command and Gen. Staff Coll., 1983; grad., Nat. Def. U., 1991. Cert. purchasing mgr. Nat. Assn. Purchasing Mgmt., Inc. Bus. mgr. Wink Davis Equipment Co., Inc., Atlanta, 1978-79; order control supr. Printpack Inc., Atlanta, 1980-82, purchasing supr., 1982-87, purchasing mgr., 1987-2000; mem. Smyrna City Coun., Ga., 1988—2003; mayor pro tem City of Smyrna, 2003—; v.p. purchasing CPG-Pepsi Bottlers, Inc., Atlanta, 2000—05. Mem. civic adv. com. Emory-Adventist Hosp. Home Health, 1997—2003; mem. Emory-Adventist Hosp. Sr. Oasis, 1998—2000; mem. adv. bd. Small Cities newsletter, 1998—; bd. dirs. Ridge Assisted Living, Inc. at Ridgeview Inst., 1998—. 1st lt. U.S. Army, 1973—76, maj. USAR, 1976—95. Mem. Am. Legion, Vets. Meml. Assn. of Smyrna, Ga., Inc., U.S. Intercollegiate Lacrosse Assn., U.S. Lacrosse, Cobb Mcpl. Assn. (sec. 1992, treas. 1993, v.p. 1994, pres. 1995). Avocations: bridge, lacrosse, military history, politics. Home: 3950 Glenhurst Dr SE Smyrna GA 30080-5896

LO, BERNARD, medical educator; BA summa cum laude, Harvard Univ., 1966; MA, Univ. Sussex, England, 1968; AM, Harvard Univ., 1970; MD, Stanford Univ., 1975, postdoctoral fellow, 1978—80. Internship, residency UCLA, 1975—77; residency Stanford Univ., 1977—78; asst. prof. Univ. Calif., San Francisco, 1980—87, assoc. prof., 1987—93, co-dir. UCSF-Stanford Robert Wood Johnson Clinical Scholars prog., 1989—96, dir. prog. in Medical Ethics, 1989—, prof. medicine, 1993—. Author: Resolving Ethical Dilemmas: A Guide for Clinicians; contbr. articles to profl. jours. Mem.: Am. Soc. of Law Medicine & Ethics (bd. dir.), Inst. Medicine (mem., bd. of health sci. policy), Am. Assoc. Physicians, We. Soc. for Clinical Investigation, Phi Beta Kappa. Office: U Calif Dept Medicine PO Box Cc-126 San Francisco CA 94143-0001

LO, CHESTER C.H., research scientist; b. Hong Kong, 1970; arrived in U.S., 1998; s. Hin W. Lo and Shun S. Leung. PhD, U. Oxford, Eng., 1998. Post doctoral rsch. fellow Ames lab. Iowa State U., Ames, 1998—2000, assoc. scientist Ctr. Nondestructive Evaluation, 2000—. Presenter at internat. profl. confs.; cons. Gillette Advances Tech., USA. Contbr. chapters to books, scientific papers to profl. jours. Recipient Hetherington prize, U. Oxford, 1996; fellow, NSF-NATO, 2000; grantee, NSF, 2000, 2001, 2004, Midwest Forensics Rsch. Resource Ctr., 2002, Roy J. Carver Charitable Trust, 2002, 2004; scholar, Croucher Found., Hong Kong, 1994—97. Achievements include patents pending in field. Office: Iowa State Univ Rm 205 Metals Devel Ames IA 50010 Office Phone: 515-294-4312.

LO, FU-CHEN, economist, educator, ambassador; b. Chia-yi, Taiwan, May 8, 1935; s. Chian-Tien and Tan-Baih Lo; m. Vickie Chin-fun Mao, June 15, 1962; children: Theadore Tse-shin, David Tse-yen. BA, Nat. Taiwan U., 1958; MA, Waseda U., Tokyo, 1963; PhD, U. Pa., 1968. Chief comparative studies UN Ctr. Regional Devel., Nagoya, Japan, 1973-80; sr. rsch. fellow East-West Ctr., Honolulu, 1981-82; affiliated faculty U. Hawaii, Honolulu, 1981-84; rsch. coord. Asia and Pacific Devel. Ctr., Kuala Lumpur, Malaysia, 1985-89; prin. acad. officer UN U., Tokyo, 1990-95, dep. dir./prof. Inst. Advanced Studies, 1995-2000, prof. emeritus Inst. Advanced Studies, 2000—; dir. Modern Culture Found., 2000—; Taiwan ambassador to Japan. Vis. prof. U. Pa., Phila., 1982-84; founder, organizer Future of Asian-Pacific Economy Conf., 1985-89; bd. dirs. Taiwan Soc., 1991-94; founder, pub. Taiwan Tribune, N.Y., 1981-87. Author: Growth Pole Strategy and Regional Development Policy, 1978, Asian and Pacific Economy Toward the Year 2000, 1987, Global Adjustment and the Future of Asia-Pacific Economy, 1989, Emerging World Cities in Pacific Asia, 1995. Founding mem., ctr. com. mem. World United Formosans for Independence, N.Y., Taipei, 1970—; bd. dirs. Amnesty Internat., Tokyo, 1975-77; founding mem., bd. dirs. Formosan Assn. for Pub. Affairs, 1982. Grantee Toyota Found., 1977-78, Internat. Devel. Ctr. Japan, 1993-94, Environment Agy. of Japan, 1995-96. Mem. Am. Econ. Assn., Japan Soc. for Internat. Devel. (founding mem.), Internat. Geog. Union (founding mem., mem. working group on urbanization in developing countries). Office: Association East Asian Relations 4th Fl Yu Ming Mansion No 7 section 1 Roosevelt Rd Taipei Taiwan

LO, JIEN-CHUNG, electrical engineer; b. Taichung, Taiwan, Dec. 27, 1960; s. Chang-Kuei Lo and Yu-Shuang Lo-Kuo; m. Suh-Ying Suhng, July 15, 1985; children: Wenchau Albert, Wenyen Agatha. PhD, U. La., 1989. Field svc. engr. Digital Equipment Corp. Taiwan, Taipei, 1983—85; asst. prof. U. R.I., Kingston, 1989—94, assoc. prof., 1994—99, prof., 1999—. Dir. Lab. Electronic Testing, Kingston, 1999—; patentee in field. Editor: IEEE Transactions on Computers, 2001; author: An Introduction to the Fundamentals of Fault-Tolerant Computing, 1994; contbr. articles to profl. jours. Recipient, Champlin Found., 1999, State of R.I. and Cherry Semiconductor Inc., 1999—2000; fellow, NSF and Global Collaboration Program, Japan, 1996; grantee, Office of Naval Rsch., 1994—96, NSF, 1999—2001. Mem.: IEEE (gen. chair North Atlantic workshop 1999, gen. chair symposium defect and fault tolerance in VLSI sys. 2001). Office: Dept Electrical & Computer Engring 4 E Alumni Ave Kingston RI 02881 Office Phone: 401-874-2996. Office Fax: 401-782-6422. Business E-Mail: jcl@ele.uri.edu.

LO, KWOK-YUNG KWOK YUNG, astronomer, educator, researcher; b. Nanking, Jiangsu, China, Oct. 19, 1947; came to U.S., 1965; s. Pao-Chi and Ju-Hwa (Hsu) Lu; m. Helen Bo Kwan Chen Lo, Jan. 1, 1973; children: Jan Hsin, Derek. BS in Physics, MIT, 1969, PhD in Physics, 1974. Rsch. fellow Calif. Inst. Tech., Pasadena, 1974-76, sr. rsch. fellow, 1978-80, asst. prof., 1980-86; prof. U. Ill., Urbana, 1986-2000, assoc. Ctr. for Advanced Study, 1991-92, chmn. astronomy dept., 1995-97; dir., disting. fellow Inst. Astronomy and Astrophysics, Academia Sinica, Taipei, Taiwan, 1997—2002, disting. rsch. fellow, 1997—2002, elected academician, 1998—2002; prof. physics Nat. Taiwan U., 1998—2002; sr. scientist, dir. Nat. Radio Astronomy Obs., 2002—. Chmn. vis. com. to Haystack Obs., Westford, Mass., 1991—92; chmn. adv. panel Academic Sinica Inst. Astronomy and Astrophysics, Taipei, Taiwan, 2002—; mem. AUI vis. com. for Nat. Radio Astronomy Obs., 1993—97; mem. steering com. Australia Telescope Nat. Facility, 1999—2001. Contbr. articles to profl. jours.; mem. editl. bd.: Chinese Jour. Astronomy & Astrophysics, 2001—. Recipient Alexander von Humboldt award, 1995; grantee NSF, 1977-96; Miller fellow U. Calif., Berkeley, 1976-78, James Clerk Maxwell telescope fellow U. Hawaii, 1991. Mem. Am. Astron. Soc., Internat. Astron. Union, Acad. Sinica. Achievements include identification of accretion of ionized gas in center of Galaxy, size measurement of compact radio source at Galactic Center, first suggestion of circumnuclear H2O masers in active galaxies, and conditions of star formation in galaxies; observation of cosmic microwave background. Office: Nat Radio Astronomy Observatory 520 Edgemont Rd Charlottesville VA 22903-2475 Business E-Mail: flo@nrao.edu.

LO, PATRICK PUNCHUK, physician; b. Hong Kong, Nov. 26, 1952; came to U.S., 1972; s. Yuen and City-Yu (Cheung) L.; m. Daisy Yawluan Sim, Dec. 19, 1982; 1 child, Jeffrey. BS in Pharmacy, U. Okla., 1977; DO, Okla. State U., 1982. Diplomate Am. Bd. Osteo. Gen. Practice; registered pharmacist, Okla. Intern Hillcrest Health Ctr., Oklahoma City, 1982-83; physician Corn Med. Clinic, Oklahoma City, 1983—. Mem. Am. Osteo. Assn., Okla. Osteo. Assn., Am. Coll. Gen. Practice, Lions. Office: Corn Med Clinic 1506 S Agnew Ave Oklahoma City OK 73108-2432 Office Phone: 405-235-3933.

LO, YEE ON, composer; b. Chong Qing, Si Chuan, China, Sept. 29, 1945; came to U.S., 1966; p. Kei-Pak and Bih-Tang Lo. AB, U. Calif., Berkeley, 1972, MS, 1979; PhD, Stanford U., 1987. Composer Wings II: Portrait, aka Portrait of Timbre as a Wild Wooddove, performed worldwide, 1994—, Chile, 2000, Spain, 2001, Can. 2002; Dream I - Shattered, When That Call Shudders 'cross..., Duo Concertant - Le Conte du Troubador, The Interrupted Serenade, Three Postludes, Dreams-Sequence, River Through Time, Night Space. Recipient Program Music prize Bourges Concours Internat., Bourges, France, 1997 . Mem. ASCAP (awards 1997, 98, 99), Home and Office: PO Box 62 Palo Alto CA 94302-0062 Personal E-mail: acoustic@panix.com.

LOACKER, LYNN J., lawyer; AB, Stanford Univ., 1974; JD Order of the Coif, Hastings College of Law, 1979. Bar: Wash., New York. Atty., shareholder Heller, Ehrman, White, & McAuliffe, New York, NY, 1999—, Co-Chair, Corp. Finance. Office: Heller Ehrman 120 West 45th St New York NY 10036 Office Phone: 212-847-8647. Office Fax: 212-447-0849. E-mail: lloacker@hewm.com.

LOADER, JAY GORDON, retired utilities executive; b. Plainfield, NJ, Aug. 3, 1923; s. Carl and Madalyn (Wright) L.; m. Joan Merrell, Aug. 19, 1965; children: Michael Jay, Sandra Lee, Gigi Ann. BS, U. Ala., 1951. C.P.A., Ga. Auditor Arthur Andersen & Co., Atlanta, 1951-55; with Fla. Power Corp., St. Petersburg, Fla., 1955-82, asst. sec., asst. treas., 1960-67, sec.-treas., 1967-82, v.p., 1980-89; v.p., sec. Fla. Progress Corp., St. Petersburg, 1983-89; ret., 1989. Served with AUS, 1943-44. Mem. AICPA, Am. Soc. Corp. Secs., Fin. Analysts Soc. Ctrl. Fla., U. Ala. Alumni Assn., St. Petersburg Yacht Club, Phi Eta Sigma, Beta Gamma Sigma, Beta Alpha Psi. Home: 1236 SW 14th St Boca Raton FL 33486

LOAR, PEGGY ANN, foundation administrator, museum administrator; b. Cin., May 14, 1948; d. Jerome Vincent and Elizabeth (Ranz) Wahl; m. Bartholomew Voorsanger, 2004. BA in History of Art, U. Cin., 1970, MA in History of Art, 1971; student in Bus., Stanford U., 2003. Summer intern Met. Mus. Art, N.Y.C., 1968; curator edn. Indpls. Mus. Art, 1971-76, asst. to the dir., 1974-75, asst. dir., 1975-77; asst. dir. programs and policy Inst. Mus. Svcs., 1977-80; dir. Smithsonian Inst. Traveling Exhbn. Svc., Washington, 1980-87; founding dir. Wolfsonian Found., Miami, Fla., 1987—96, Genoa, Italy, 1987—96; dir. Voorsanger Architects, N.Y.C., 2005—. Lectr. art history U. Cin., 1970-71; lectr. art appreciation and criticism Ind. U., Purdue U., 1975-77; mem. women's health adv. com. Stanford U., 2002—; guest lectr. in field. Project dir.: The Art of Cameroon Exhibition and Catalog, 1984, Treasures from the Smithsonian Inst. Exhibition and Catalog, 1984, Paris Style 1900: Art Noveau Bing, 1986, Hollywood: Legend & Reality Exhibition Catalog, 1988. Travel grantee Japan Found., 1984; Swedish Inst. grantee; Aspen Inst. Humanistic Studies fellow, 1986-87, recipient Smithsonian Gold

Medal for Disting. Service, 1987. Mem. Am. Assn. Museums (mus. ethics com. 1980-98), Internat. Coun. Museums (pres. U.S. nat. com., 1996-2002), Com. Internat. Musees d'Art Moderne. Avocations: biking, hiking, dogs, gardening, wine. Office: COPIA Am Ctr Wine Food & Arts 500 1st St Napa CA 94559 Address: 845 UN Plaza 11H New York NY 10017

LOARIE, THOMAS MERRITT, healthcare executive; b. Deerfield, Ill., June 12, 1946; s. Willard John and Lucile Veronica (Finnegan) L.; m. Stephanie Lane Fitts, Aug. 11, 1968 (div. Nov. 1987); children: Thomas M., Kristin Leigh Soule. BSME, U. Notre Dame, 1968; Student, U. Minn., 1969-70, U. Chgo., 1970-71, Columbia U., 1978. Registered profl. engr., Calif. Prodn. engr. Honeywell, Inc., Evanston, Ill., 1968-70; various positions Am. Hosp. Supply Co., Evanston, Ill., 1970-83, pres. Heyer-Schulte divsn., 1979-83; pres. COO Novacor Med. Corp., Oakland, Calif., 1984-85, also bd. dirs.; pres. ABA Bio Mgmt., Danville, Calif., 1985-87; chmn., CEO Keravision, Inc., Fremont, Calif., 1987-2001; founder, chmn., med. device CEO Roundtable, 1993—2002; founder, chmn., CEO Learnings, Danville, Calif., 2001—; co-founder, chmn. CardioProfile, Inc., Berkeley, Calif., 2002—04, Adams Merritt, Inc., Danville, 2003—; chmn., CEO Enos Bionics, Inc., San Leandro, Calif., 2005—. Asst. prof. surgery Creighton U. Med. Sch., Omaha, 1986-94; guest lectr. Anderson Sch. Mgmt., UCLA, 2001-2003, Haas Sch. Bus., U. Calif., Berkeley, 2002-03; bd. dirs. Bay Tec, Oakland, Calif., 2003—04; trustee Grad. Theol. Union, Berkeley, Calif., 2003—; mem. adv. bd. Uptake Med., Inc., Seattle, 2005—, Occulogix, Inc., Tampa, 2001-05; mem. adv. bd. Uptake Med., Inc., Seattle; spkr. in field. Contbr. articles on med. tech. and pub. policy to Wall St. Jour., Jour. Retractive Surgery, others. Bd. dirs. Marymount Sch. Bd., 1981-84; bd. dirs. United Way Santa Barbara, 1981-84, assoc. chairperson, 1982-83, treas., 1983; trustee Grad. Theol. Union, U. Calif., Berkeley, 2003—. Named One of 50 Rising Stars: Exec. Leaders for the 80's Industry Week mag., 1983. Mem. Assn. for Rsch. in Vision and Ophthalmology, Contact Lens Assn. Ophthalmology, Health Industry Mfrs. Assn. (spl. rep. bd. dirs. 1993-96, bd. dirs. 1997-2001, exec. com. 1997-2001, treas. 1998-2000, chmn.-elect 2000-01), Am. Entrepreneurs for Econ. Growth, Med. Tech. Leadership Forum, Calif. Healthcare Inst. (bd. dirs. 1998-2001, exec. com. 1999-2001), Diablo Venture Alliance Roman Catholic. Achievements include leading development of Intacs corneal ring segments for treatment of nearsightedness (named One of Top 10 Medical Advances by Health Magazine/CNN 1999). Office Phone: 925-525-0272. Personal E-mail: tloarie@aol.com.

LOAYZA, DIEGO, cell biologist, educator; b. N.Y.C., Dec. 31, 1965; s. Luis Loayza and Rachel Guerne; m. Naima Ismaili, July 10, 2002; 1 child, Raphael. MA, Princeton U., 1993; PhD, Johns Hopkins U., 1997; student, U. Geneva, 1984—88. Fellow Rockefeller U., N.Y.C., 1998—. Fellow, Am. Cancer Soc., 2000—02. Achievements include research in cell biology and biochemistry of cancer cells; genetics. Office Phone: 212-327-8148.

LOBALBO, ANTHONY CHARLES, music educator, protective services official; b. Bronx, N.Y., Oct. 27, 1949; s. Charles Francis and Marian Elizabeth (Salanitro) LoBalbo. Student, SUNY Crane Sch. of Music, Potsdam, N.Y., 1967—71, U.di Pisa, Italy, 1970—71, Manhattan Sch. of Music, 1971—73, N.Y.U. S.E.A.N.A.P., 1973—82. Assoc. prof. St. John's U., Jamaica, NY, 1976—; dep. sheriff Duchess County Sheriff's Office, Poughkeepsie, 1989—; police officer Town of Lewisboro Police Dept., South Salem, NY, 1999—. Instr. Zone 14 Police Acad. Sheriff's Office, Dutchess County, NY, 1999—2005. Pianist for benefit recital Newman Theatre, Pleasantville, NY, 2001, No. Westchester Coun. for the Arts, Mt. Kisco, NY, 2002, South Salem Libr., NY, 2004. Mem.: Fraternal Order of Police, Film Music Soc. Home: 400 Stormville Mt Rd Stormville NY 12582 Office: St John's Univ 800 Utopia Pkwy Jamaica NY 11439 Office Phone: 718-990-5411. Office Fax: 895-878-3305. Personal E-mail: Anth1654@aol.com. Business E-Mail: lebalboa@stjohns.edu.

LOBANOV-ROSTOVSKY, OLEG, management consultant; b. San Francisco, July 12, 1934; s. Andrei and Grace S. (Pope) L-R.; m. Susan Waters, Sept. 8, 1979; 1 child, Alexandra; children by previous marriage: Christopher, Nicholas. BA, U. Mich., 1956. Cmty. concert rep. Columbia Artists Mgmt. Inc., 1958-59; mgr. Columbus (Ohio) Symphony Orch., 1959-62, Hartford (Conn.) Symphony Orch., 1962-65, Balt. Symphony, 1965-69; program officer div. humanities and arts Ford Found., 1969-75; exec. dir. Denver Symphony Orch., 1975-76; mng. dir. Nat. Symphony Orch., Washington, 1977-80; cons. Fed. Coun. on Arts, 1980-81; exec. dir. Del. Ctr. for Performing Arts, 1981-82; from exec. v.p., mng. dir. to pres. Detroit Symphony Orch., 1982-89; ind. cons., 1989-90; mng. ptnr. Middle Am. divsn. Jerold, Panas, Young & Ptnrs. Inc., Chgo., 1990-91; pres. Calif. Ctr. for the Arts, Escondido, Calif., 1991-96; sr. ptnr. Jerold Panas, Linzy & Ptnrs., Inc., Chgo., 1996—2004; v.p. fund devel. and mktg. Cath. Relief Svcs., Balt., 2004—.

LOBAY, IVAN, mechanical engineering educator; b. Koltuny, Ukraine, Oct. 4, 1911; came to U.S., 1961, naturalized, 1968; s. Stephan and Clementina (Maret) Lobay; m. Halyna Makarenko, Apr. 25, 1943; children: Maria Ivanna, Halyna Blahoslava. Mech. Engr., Inst. Tech., Brno, Czechoslovakia, 1940, Cen. U. Venezuela, Caracas, 1956. Registered profl. engr., Conn. Engr., designer Erste Bruenner Maschinenfabriksgesellschaft, Brno, 1940-41; asst. prof. dept. mech. engring. Inst. Tech., Lviv, Ukraine, 1942-43, sci. asst. dept. mech. engring. Brno, 1943-45; engr. san. and civil engring. Ministry San. Affairs, Caracas, Venezuela, 1948-59; prof. dept. civil engring. U. Santa Maria, Caracas, 1957-60; prof., chmn. divsn. tech. machines & prodn Cen. U. Venezuela Mech. Engring. Sch., Caracas, 1956-62; prof. dept. mech. engring. U. New Haven, West Haven, 1963-77, 83-84, prof. emeritus, 1984—; prof. gas sect. Inst. Algerien du Petrole, Boumerdes, Algeria, 1977-82. Cons. Ministry of Edn., Ukraine, Kyiv, 1993. Author: Lecciones de Elementos de Maquinas, No. 3, 1960, No. 2, 1961, Estudio Sobre Descarga de Aguas de Lluvia, 1962, Free Lateral Discharge from an Open Triangular Channel, 1993, Education of Engineering Squads in USA, 1996, Workload of University Professors in USA, 1996, Faculty in Higher Education in USA, 1997, Governance in Higher Education in USA, 1999, Memoirs, 1999. With U.S. Army, 1945-47. Decorated Hramota and Cross of Merit Bukovynian Battalion, 1995; recipient Hramota award Govt. in Exile of Ukrainian Nat. Republic, 1992. Mem. AAUP, AAAS, ASME, NSPE, Conn. Soc. Profl. Engrs., N.Y. Acad. Scis., Ukrainian AAUP, Ukrainian Engrs. Soc. Am., Coll. Engrs. Venezuela, Assn. Profs. U. Ctrl. Venezuela, Acad. Engring. Scis. Ukraine. Home: 873 Orange Center Rd Orange CT 06477-1712

LOBB, WILLIAM ATKINSON, financial services executive; b. Arlington, Pa., Apr. 21, 1951; s. Anthony William and Annamarie (Hilpert) L.; m. Maureen Veronique O'Hagan, July 7, 1977; children: William Atkinson III, Anthony Hagan. BS, Georgetown U., 1977. Account exec. Johnston Lemon, Washington, 1977-78; sr. account exec. Merrill Lynch, Alexandria, Va., 1979-83; asst. v.p. E.F. Hutton, Washington, 1983-85; mng. dir., ptnr.-in-charge Oppenheimer, Inc., Atlanta, 1985—. Bd. trustees Madison Morgan Cultural Ctr.; bd. dirs. Atlanta Charity Clays, Atlanta Opera, Ferst Books Found. Mem. Nat. Securities Traders Assn., Ga. Securities Assn., Univ. Club, Burge Plantation Hunt Club, Piedmont Driving Club, Nairn Golf Club (Scotland). Avocation: squash. Office: Oppenheimer Inc 1200 Monach Plz 3414 Peachtree Rd NE Atlanta GA 30326-1153 Office Phone: 404-262-5355. E-mail: will.lobb@opco.com.

LOBB, WILLIAM K., dean, dental educator; Student, Notre Dame U., Nelson, BC, U. Calgary, 1970—72; DDS, U. Alberta, Edmonton, 1977; MS in orthodontics, U. Mich., Ann Arbor, 1981. Resident in dentistry U. Alberta Hosp., Edmonton, Canada; pvt. orthodontics practice Edmonton; mem. faculty U. Alberta, Edmonton, 1981—89; chair dept. orthodontics Dalhousie U., Halifax, 1989—94; assoc. dean acad. affairs Sch. Dentistry Marquette U., 1994—97, dean, 1997—. Recipient W.W. Wood award for excellence in dental edn., Assn. Can. Faculties Dentistry. Fellow: Internat. Coll. Dentists, Pierre Fachard Acad., Am. Coll. Dentists; mem.: ADA, Wis. Dental Assn., Omicron Kappa Upsilon. Office: Marquette Univ Sch Dentistry 1801 W Wisconsin Ave Milwaukee WI 53233 Business E-Mail: william.lobb@marquette.edu.

LOBDELL, DAVID HILL, pathologist; b. Erie, Pa., July 9, 1930; s. Webster Alexander Lobdell, Christine (Kern) Lobdell. AB, Kenyon Coll., 1952; MD, U. Mich., 1956. Diplomate Am. Bd. Pathology 1961. Resident Pathology Bellevue-NYU Med. Ctr., 1956—60; pathologist St. Vincent's Med. Ctr., Bridgeport, Conn., 1960—63, chair Dept. Lab. Medicine, 1963—95, sr. pathologist, 1996—. Asst. clin. prof. Pathology NYU Sch. Medicine, 1961—69; assoc. clin. prof. Allied Health U. Conn., Storrs, 1984—95. Sec., bd. dirs. St. Vincent's Med. Found., Bridgeport. Fellow: Am. Soc. Clin. Pathology, Coll. Am. Pathologists (del. House of Dels. 1991—97); mem.: Conn. Soc. Pathologists (pres. 1982—83), Alpha Omega Alpha, Phi Beta Kappa. Avocation: stamp collecting/philately. Office: St Vincent Med Ctr 2800 Main St Bridgeport CT 06606

LOBDELL, FRANK, artist; b. Kansas City, Mo., 1921; m. Ann Morency, 1952; children: Frank Saxton, Judson Earle; m. Jinx Rowan, 1996. Studied, St. Paul Sch. Art, 1938-39, Calif. Sch. Fine Arts, 1947-50, Academie de la Grande Chaumiere, Paris, France, 1950-51. Tchr. Calif. Sch. Fine Arts, 1957-65; prof. art, Stanford, 1965—. One man shows, Lucien Labaudt Gallery, 1949, Martha Jackson Gallery, 1958, 60, 63, 72, 74, de Young Meml. Mus., San Francisco, 1959, Ferus Gallery, 1962, Pasadena Art Mus., 1961, San Francisco Mus. Art, 1969, Benador Gallerie, Geneva, Switzerland, 1964, Gallerie Anderson-Mayer, Paris, 1965, Smith-Anderson Gallery, San Francisco, 1982, Oscarsson Hood Gallery, N.Y.C., 1983, 84, 85, John Berggruen Gallery, San Francisco, 1987, Campbell-Thiebaud Gallery, San Francisco, 1988, 90, 92, 95, Printworks Gallery, Chgo., 1988-96, Stanford Mus. Art, 1988, Hackett Freedman Gallery, 2002, Charles Cowles Gallery, N.Y.C., 2002, The Palace of the Legion of Honor, San Francisco, 2003, Hackett-Freedman Gallery, San Francisco, 2003, 04, Portland Art Mus., 2004, Fresno Art Mus., 2004, San Jose Mus. Contemporary Art, 2005, retrospective show, Pasadena Art Mus. and Stanford Mus., 1966, San Francisco Mus. Modern Art, 1983, Stanford Mus., 1993, Saint Mary's Coll., 1998, Western Mich. U. Art Gallery; exhibited group Shows, Salon du Mai, Paris, 1950, III Sao Paulo Biennial, 1955, Whitney Mus. Am. Art, 1962-63, 72, Guggenheim Mus., N.Y.C., 1964, Van Abbemuseum, Eindhoven, Holland, 1970, Corcoran Gallery Art, Washington, 1971, U. Ill., 1974, 15 Calif. Modernists, Fresno Art Mus., 1995; represented in permanent collections, San Francisco Mus. Art, Oakland Mus. Art, L.A. County Mus., Nat. Gallery Washington, others. Served with AUS, 1942-46. Recipient Nealie Sullivan award San Francisco Art Inst., 1960, award of merit AAAL, 1988.

LOBDELL, R MARTIN, psychology professor; b. Seattle, Wash., May 11, 1947; s. George Ulyssis and Norma Eileen Lobdell; m. Elizabeth A Scott, Jan. 4, 2004; m. Nancy Jean Houck (div.); children: Beth Jean, Kris Martin. AA, Highline Cmty. Coll., 1967; BS, W.W.U., 1969, MA, 1971. Psychology prof. Pierce Coll., Lakewood, Wash., 1971—. Chmn. Pierce County Rope Relief, Tacoma, 1983—85; bd. mem. Greater Lakes Mental Health, Lakewood, Wash., 1990—94; faculty pres. Pierce Coll., Lakewood, Wash., 1989—90. Democrat. Avocations: skiing, hiking, bicycling, kayaking. Office: Pierce Coll 9401 Farwest Dr SW Lakewood WA 98498 Business E-Mail: mlobdell@pierce.ete.edu.

LO BELLO, JOSEPH DAVID, bank executive; b. Northampton, Mass., Feb. 5, 1940; s. Joseph Vincenzo and Marie (Mandella) Lo B.; m. Karen Suzanne Martin, June 21, 1969; children: Mark, Kara, Kimberly. BS, Babson Coll., 1961; MBA, U. Mass., 1963; postgrad., Harvard Bus. Sch., 1987. Loan officer Third Nat. Bank Hampden County, Springfield, Mass., 1963-65, v.p., 1965-75, sr. v.p., 1975-81; exec. v.p. Bank of New Eng. West, N.A., Springfield, 1981-90; regional pres. Bank of New Eng. N.A., Springfield, 1990-92; pres., chief exec. officer Peoples Savs. Bank, Holyoke, Mass., 1992—. Dir. Mass. Indsl. Fin. Agy., Boston, 1987, Conn. Online Computer, 1994, Credit Data Svcs., Inc., 1993; treas., trustee Basketball Hall of Fame, Springfield, 1985; trustee Springfield Coll., 1984; chmn. Baystate Health System, Springfield, 1983. Mem. Rotary Club. Avocations: golf, hiking, theater, travel. Home: 152 Meadowbrook Rd Longmeadow MA 01106-1341

LOBELLO, PETER, artist; b. New Orleans, Nov. 18, 1933; Attended, Tulane U. Sch. Arch.; ind. study, Sicily, Tunisia, Libya, Egypt, and Iran; artist-in-residence, Rome, 1967—68. Prin. works include Grand Hyatt Hotel, NYC, 1978—80, New Istana Palace, Capital City Bandar Seri Begawan, Brunei (Borneo) Southeast Asia, 1984, Madison Equities and Grey Advt., NYC, 1985, Poydras Plz., New Orleans, 1986, Gates Commn., Seattle, 1994—97, Legier & Matherne, New Orleans, 1996—97, Connecticut Ballet, Stamford, 1998, Represented in permanent collections Aldrich Mus. Contemporary Art, Ridgefield, Connecticut, Geneva Mus. Art, Switzerland, New Mus., NYC, Miriam Walmsley Gallery, New Orleans, Sadruddin Aga Kahn, Collonge Bellerive, Geneva, Victor Emmanuel and Marina Savoia, Heckler Corp., NYC, Foster White Gallery, Seattle, Bumper Collection, Calgary, Alberta, Miller Orgn., NYC, U. Minn., BHF-Bank, NYC, Frankfurt, one-man shows include Hugo de Pagano Gallery, N.Y., 1998, exhibited in group shows at Sarah Y. Rentschler Gallery, N.Y.C., 1984, Galerie Les Hirondelles, Geneva, 1987, 1989. Home: 71 Grand St New York NY 10013-2219

LOBENFELD, ERIC JAY, lawyer; b. Bklyn., Aug. 18, 1950; s. Samuel J. and Ruth E. (Rifkin) L.; m. Patricia L. McCarron, May 3, 1981; children: Claire A., Margot R. BA, SUNY, Binghamton, 1971; JD, Bklyn. Law Sch., 1975. Bar: N.Y. 1976. Assoc. Donovan, Leisure, Newton and Irvine, N.Y.C., 1975-84, ptnr., 1984-86, Dewey Ballantine, N.Y.C., 1987-91, 92-94; v.p., chief litigation counsel Reliance Group Holdings, Inc., N.Y.C., 1991-92; ptnr. Chadbourne & Parke, N.Y.C., 1994—, Hogan & Hartson LLP, N.Y.C., dir. litig. practice group. Adj. assoc. prof. Bklyn. Law Sch., 1984-90; lectr. Practising Law Inst., N.Y.C., 1987-90. Mem. N.Y. State Bar Assn., Fed. Bar Coun., Internat. Intellectual Property Assn., N.Y. Intellectual Property Assn., Nat. Inst. for Trial Advocacy (faculty mem.). Republican. Avocations: stamp collecting/philately, music, sports. Home: 174 Clarence Rd Scarsdale NY 10583-6318 Office: Hogan & Hartson LLP 875 Third Ave New York NY 10022 Office Phone: 212-918-8202. Office Fax: 212-918-3100. Business E-Mail: ejlobenfeld@hhlaw.com.

LOBER, IRENE MOSS, educational consultant; b. NYC, Aug. 1, 1927; d. David and Beckie Moss; m. Solomon William Lober, Oct. 25, 1947; children: Clifford Warren, Richard Wayne, Lori Ann. BS in Edn., CCNY, 1948; MA, George Washington U., 1967; EdD, Va. Poly. Inst. and State U., 1974. Registered sch. bus. adminstr. Formerly tchr., libr.; prin. staff devel. Fairfax County Pub. Schs., Va., 1965—77; supt. University City (Mo.) Pub. Schs., 1977—81, Danbury (Conn.) Pub. Schs., 1981—85; prof. SUNY, New Paltz, 1985—98, chmn. dept. ednl. adminstrn., 1990—98, dir. EdD program, 1993—95, coord. distance learning programs, 1995—98, cons. ednl. adminstrn., 1998—. Guest lectr. Washington U., George Washington U., Va. Poly. Inst. and State U., U. Va., Fordham U., C.W. Post Coll., L.I. U.; mem. bus. adv. coun. Datahr, Inc., 1982—85; pres. N.Y. State Coun. for Advancement of Depts. of Ednl. Adminstrn., 1994; cons. in field; founding incorporator Sci. Horizons, Inc., Danbury, 1984—85, COMPUtourney, Inc., 1990—98; designated disting. expert and peer reviewer Asst. Sec. Edn. Chester Finn, 1987—89; spkr./presenter various internat., nat. and state confs. and convs.; book reviewer Tchrs. Coll. Press, Columbia U., 2004. Author: Promoting Your School, 1993; contbr. articles to profl. jours.; book reviewer: Teacher's Coll. Press, 2004. Mem. legal and govt. studies group Nat. Inst. Edn. Dept. HEW; nat. adv. bd. U. Wis. R & D Ctr., 1978—80; chairperson Mo. Instrnl. TV Coun., 1981; lay adv. bd. St. Louis Met. Med. Soc., 1980—81; bd. advisors St. Joseph's Inst. Deaf, 1980—81; apptd. supt. in residence Western Conn. State U., 1984; divsn. chairperson United Way Campaign, 1982—86; mem. bd. edn. Poughkeepsie City Sch. Dist., 1993—96; mem. instl. rev. bd. M.D. Anderson Cancer Ctr., Orlando, 2002—04; pres. Lake Mary chpt. AARP, 2001—03; bd. dirs. Temple Israel, Longwood, Fla., 2005—; pres. Rishona-Chavaret group, Orlando chpt. Hadassah, 2005—, co-pres., 2004—05; pres. adv. cabinet Greater St. Louis coun. Girl Scouts U.S., 1980—81, bd. dirs. Southwestern Conn. Coun., 1981—85; bd. dirs. Fairfield coun. Boy Scouts Am.; bd. dirs. Danbury region Jr. Achievement, 1981—86, Regional Hospice, Danbury, 1984—86, Danbury Coun. Am. Heart Assn., 1985—86; exec. bd., trustee United Way No. Fairfield County; trustee, bd. dirs. United Way, Danbury, 1982—85; bd. dirs. TRIAD Seminole County, Fla., 2001—, Meals on Wheels Inc. Seminole County, Fla., 2000—04. Recipient Townsend Harris medal, CCNY Alumni Assn., Nat. Leadership award, Hadassah, 2005; IDEA fellow, Ford Found. grantee, 1977—78. Mem.: NEA, ASCD, Authors League, Authors Guild, Nat. Assn. Secondary Sch. Prins. (chair profs. secondary sch. adminstrn. com.), Assn. Sch. Bus. Ofcls. Internat. (nat. chmn. maintenance and ops. rsch. com. 1985—89), N.Y. State Assn. Sch. Bus. Ofcls., N.Y. State Coun. Sch. Supts., Ednl. Rsch. Svc., Sch. Adminstrs. Assn. N.Y. State, Am. Assn. Sch. Adminstrs. (nat. chmn. higher edn. com. 1987—89, chmn. membership svcs. com. 1995—96), Pi Lambda Theta (publs. adv. bd. 1981—84), Phi Kappa Phi, Phi Delta Kappa (pres. New Paltz chpt. 1991—93). Personal E-mail: loberim@bellsouth.net.

LOBER, LIONEL M., scriptwriter, film producer; b. Alexandria, Egypt, Nov. 13, 1933; s. Louis and Eva (Horowitz) L.; m. Mati Elpern, June 20, 1961 (dec. Nov. 1983); children: Sharon Nadine, Alma Nora. BA in Theater, English, Brandeis U., 1955. Assoc. prodn. mgr., asst. to Otto Preminger Exodus, 1960; exec. asst. to exec. v.p. United Artists Corp., N.Y.C., 1961-63; v.p. European prodn. Metro-Goldwyn-Mayer, 1963-65; exec. in charge of prodn. D.E.A.R. Studios, Rome, 1965-70; v.p. Prodigal Prodns., Paris, 1970-75; writer, producer Warner Bros. TV, United Artists Corp., Cannon Films, N.Y.C., Los Angeles, London, 1975-78. Lectr. on film writing and prodn. Calif. State U., Northridge. Screenwriter: A Candle for the Dead, 1969, Black Madonna, 1972, Who Stole Irving, 1975, The Second Coming, 1979, He and She, 1983, Slit Throat, 1987, The Corsican Brothers, 1987, Final Scream, 1988, Danger Girl, 1989, Cop Out, 1990, Checkmate, 1991, Double Impact, 1992, Turnabout, 1994, An Ideal Husband, 1995, (play) Shadow of Guilt, 1996, Lost Soul, 1998, With A Bang!, 1999, Kiss and Run, 2004. Capt. USMC, 1956-60. Mem. Writers Guild Am. West, Brit. Acad. Film and TV Arts (L.A.). Democrat. E-mail: loberlionel@hotmail.com.

LOBIG, JANIE HOWELL, special education educator; b. Peoria, Ill., June 10, 1945; d. Thomas Edwin and Elizabeth Jane (Higdon) Howell; m. James Frederick Lobig, Aug. 16, 1970 (dec. Dec. 2001); 1 child, Jill Christina. BS in Elem. Edn., So. Ill. U., 1969; MA in Spl. Edn. Severely Handicapped, San Jose State U., 1989. Cert. elem. tchr., Calif., Mo., Ill., handicapped edn., Calif., Mo.; ordained to ministry Presbyn. Ch. as deacon, 1984. Tchr. trainable mentally retarded children Spl. Luth. Sch., St. Louis, 1967-68; tchr. trainable mentally retarded and severly handicapped children Spl. Sch. Dist. St. Louis, 1969-80, head tchr., 1980-83; tchr. severly handicapped children San Jose (calif.) Unifed Sch. Dist., 1983-86; tchr. autistic students Santa Clara County Office Edn., San Jose, 1986—; tchr. Suzanne Dancers, 1991-92. Vol. Am. Cancer Soc., San Jose, 1986—89, 1992, Am. Heart Assn., 1985—, Multiple Sclerosis Soc., 1990—, Wildlife Ctr. Silicon Valley, 1998—; moderator bd. deacons Evergreen Presbyn. Ch., 1986—89. Mem. Council for Exceptional Children, Assn. for Severly Handicapped, Nat. Edn. Assn., Calif. Tchrs. Assn. Avocations: golf, motor home travel, bridge, needlecrafts. Office: James Franklin Smith Elem Sch 2220 Woodbury San Jose CA 95121 Home: 3211 Bracciano Ct San Jose CA 95135 Office Phone: 408-270-6368. Personal E-mail: JanieAngel@aol.com.

LOBINSKE, RICHARD JOHN, entomologist; b. Chanute AFB, Rantoul, Ill., Sept. 4, 1963; s. Walter H. and Ingrid I. Lobinske; m. Louise M. Pare, Apr. 1, 1987. AA, Lake-Sumter C.C., Leesburg, Fla., 1983; BS, U. Ctrl. Fla., Orlando, 1984, MS, 1995; PhD, U. Fla., 2001. Biol. scientist U. Fla. Inst. Food Agrl. Scis., Mid Fla. Rsch. and Edn. Ctr., Apopka, 1985—2001, sr. biol. scientist, 2001—05; supt. Leon County Mosquito Control Dist., Tallahassee, 2005—. Mem.: Fla. Mosquito Control Assn., Am. Mosquito Control Assn., Fla. Acad. Sci., Fla. Entomol. Soc., Entomol. Soc. Am. Office: Leon County MosquitoControl Dist 501 Appleyard Dr Ste H Tallahassee FL 32304 Personal E-mail: rlobinske@aol.com. Business E-Mail: rjlobinske@ifas.ufl.edu.

LOBIONDO, FRANK A., congressman; b. Bridgeton, NJ, May 12, 1946; m. Tina Ercole; children: Adina, Amy. BA in Bus. Adminstrn., St. Joseph's U., 1968. Ops. mgr. LoBiondo Bros. Motor Express, Inc., Rosenhayn, N.J., 1968-94; mem. Cumberland County Bd. Chosen Freeholders, 1985-88; mem. First Legis. Dist. N.J. Gen. Assembly, 1988-94; mem. U.S. Ho. Reps. from 2nd N.J. dist., 1995—; mem. house transp. & infrastructure com. and house armed svcs. com. U.S. Ho. Reps., 1995—. Pres. Cumberland County Guidance Ctr., 1982—84; founder Cumberland County Environ. Health Task Force, 1987; chmn. Cumberland County chpt. Am. Heart Assn., 1989—90; hon. chmn. ann. fund raising drive Cumberland County Hospice, 1992; bd. dirs. YMCA, trustee, 1981—84, 1990—94. Republican. Office: US House Reps 225 Cannon Ho Office Bldg Washington DC 20515-3002*

LOBL, HERBERT MAX, lawyer, writer; b. Vienna, Jan. 10, 1932; s. Walter Leo and Minnie (Neumann) L.; m. Dorothy Fullerton Hubbard, Sept. 12, 1960; children: Peter Walter, Michelle Alexandra. AB magna cum laude, Harvard U., 1953, LLB cum laude, 1959, Avocat honoraire, 1993. Bar: N.Y. 1960, U.S. Tax Ct. 1963, French Conseil Juridique 1973; French avocat. mem. Paris bar, 1992, avocat hon., 1993. Assoc. Davis, Polk & Wardwell, N.Y.C., 1959-90, N.Y.C. and Paris, 1963-69, ptnr., 1969-92, sr. counsel, 1993—; assoc. counsel to Gov. Nelson Rockefeller Albany, N.Y., 1960-62. Lectr. law Columbia U., N.Y.C., 1993—95; mem. supervisory bd. CII-HB Internationale, Amsterdam, Netherlands, 1977—82. Author: Welcome to West Berlin, 2002, A Tender Offer, 2004. Gov. Am. Hosp. Paris, 1981-83, 88-93; bd. trustees Am. Libr., Paris, 1969-81, Nantucket (Mass.) Cottage Hosp., 1996-99, dir. Nantucket Arts Coun., 2000-02. Served to 1st lt. USAF, 1954—56. Fulbright scholar, U. Bonn, Germany, 1954. Mem.: Am. C. of C. (bd. dirs. France 1988—90), Harvard Club, Univ. Club. Office: Davis Polk & Wardwell 450 Lexington Ave New York NY 10017-3911 Address: 3 Westview The Springs Purchase NY 10577 Office Phone: 212-450-4665. E-mail: d-h-lobl@earthlink.net.

LOBLE, LESTER HENRY, II, lawyer; b. Helena, Mont., Nov. 14, 1941; s. Henry and Grayce E. Loble; m. Arlene Loble, Mar. 1967 (div. 1975); 1 child, Rachel; m. Teryle L. Loble, Feb. 12, 1978; children: Jason, Jeremie. AB, Stanford U., 1963; JD, U. Mont., 1966. Bar: Mont. 1966, U.S. Dist. Ct. Mont. 1966, N.D. 1987, U.S. Dist. Ct. N.D. 1987. Atty.-advisor U.S. Dept. Interior, Washington, 1966-67; pres. Loble & Pauly, P.C., Helena, 1967-87; gen. counsel, sec. MDU Resources Group, Inc., Bismarck, N.D., 1987—. Contbr. articles to profl. jours. Recipient Community Svc. award Carroll Coll., 1987; named Outstanding Freshman Legislator, Mont. State Legislature, 1969-71. Mem. ABA, Am. Gas Assn. (mem. mng. com. legal sect. 1987—), State Bar Mont (pres. young lawyers sect. 1970-71), State Bar N.D. (mem. atty. standards com. 1991—), Big Muddy Bar Assn. (pres. 1991-92). Lutheran. Avocations: backpacking, alpine skiing, gourmet cooking. Office: MDU Resources Group Inc 400 N 4th St Bismarck ND 58501-4092

LOBLEY, ALAN HAIGH, retired lawyer; b. Elkhart, Ind., Aug. 26, 1927; s. Frederick Askew and Eva May (Haigh) L.; m. Kathleen Covert Nolan, Mar. 2, 1957; children: James, Sarah. BSChemE, Purdue U., 1949; JD, Ind. U., 1952. Bar: Ind. 1952, U.S. Dist. Ct. (so. dist.) Ind. 1955, U.S. Ct. Appeals (7th cir.) 1963, U.S. Supreme Ct. 1971, U.S. Ct. Appeals (6th cir.) 1979. From assoc. to ptnr. Ice, Miller, Donadio & Ryan (formerly Ross, McCord, Ice & Miller), Indpls., 1955-97; ret., 1997. Commr. Indpls. Hist. Preservation Comm., 2001-; 1st lt. USAF, 1952-54. Mem. ABA, Am. Arbitration Assn., Ind. Bar Assn., Indpls. Bar Assn., Indpls. Rowing Ctr. (bd. dirs.). Democrat. Avocations: photography, music, sculling. Home: 4535 N Park Ave Indianapolis IN 46205-1836

LOBO, BOBBY LEONARD, pharmacologist, educator; b. Great Yarmouth, England, June 22, 1963; s. Simon Hyacinth and Beverly M Lobo (Stepmother); m. Melanie McPhail McPhail, Aug. 16, 1990; children: Eryn Ashton, Ethan Alexander. PharmD, U. Nebr., 1988. Cert. pharmacotherapist Bd. Pharm. Specialties, 1993. Resident U. Tenn., Memphis, 1988—89; pharmacist Meth. U. Hosp., 1989—91; clin. pharmacist VA Hosp., 1991—. Assoc. prof. Coll. Pharmacy U. Tenn., Memphis, 2000—; cons. in field. Author: Clinical Pharmacy Services: Successful Practices in Community Hospitals, 2005. Vestryman St. George's Episcopal Ch., Germantown, Tenn., 2000—04. Recipient Team award, Meth. Pursiut Perfection Quality Expo, 2003; scholar, Sandoz Pharmaceuticals, 1985, Plough Pharmaceuticals, 1986. Mem.: Am. Soc.Cons. Pharmacists (assoc.), Am. Soc. Health-Sys. Pharmacists (assoc.), Am. Coll. Clin. Pharmacy (assoc.), Mid-South Coll. Clin. Pharmacy (assoc.; pres. 1999—2000), Rho Chi (hon.). Avocation: running. Office: Methodist University Hospital 1265 Union Ave Memphis TN 38104 Office Phone: 901-516-8170.

LOBO, REBECCA, professional basketball player; b. Hartford, Conn., Oct. 6, 1973; BA in Polit. Sci., U. Conn., 1995. Basketball player USA Women's Nat. Team, N.Y. Liberty, 1997—2001, Houston Comets, 2001—02, Conn. Sun, Uncasville, 2003—. Mem. U.S. Olympic Festival East Team, 1992, Jr. World Championship Qualifying Team, 1992, USA Jr. World Championship Team, 1993. Co-author: The Home Team, 1996. Founder Ruth Ann & Rebecca Lobo scholarship in allied health U. Conn., 2001. Named Big East Conf. Player of Yr., Nat. Player of Yr., Naismith, U.S. Basketball Writers Assn., 1995, Big East Tournament Most Outstanding Player, 1994, Big East Conf. Women's Basketball Scholar Athlete of Yr., 1995, Female Athlete of Yr., AP, 1995; named to All-Am. 1st team, Kodak, 1994, 1995; recipient Wade trophy. Office: c/o Conn Sun 1 Mohegan Sun Blvd Uncasville CT 06382*

LOBO, ROGERIO A., obstetrician, gynecologist; b. Hong Kong, 1949; MD, Georgetown U., 1974. Diplomate Am. Bd. Ob-Gyn. Intern U. Chgo. Hosps., 1974-75, resident in obstetrics, 1975-78; fellow in reproductive endocrinology L.A. County-U. So. Calif. Med. Ctr., 1980; physician Presbyn. Hosp., NYC, 1995—; dir. Sloane Hosp. for Women, Columbia Univ. Med. Ctr., NYC, 1995—2002; Willard C. Rappleye prof. and chmn. ob-gyn. Columbia Coll. Physicians and Surgeons, NYC, 1995—2002. Editor Jour. Soc. for Gynecol. Investigation, 1993—. Mem. ACOG, Am. Soc. Reproductive Medicine, Endocrine Soc., Soc. Gynecol. Investigation (past pres.). Office: Columbia Univ Med Ctr 622 W 168th St Rm 16 69 New York NY 10032-3720 Office Phone: 212-305-6337.

LOBRON, BARBARA L., speech educator, editor, photographer, writer; b. Phila., Mar. 19, 1944; d. Martin Aaron and Elizabeth (Gots) L. Student, Pa. State U., 1962—63; BA cum laude, Temple U., Phila., 1966; student art therapy, Erika Steinberger, N.Y.C., 1994—2003; MS, Coll. Mt. St. Vincent, 2001. Reporter, writer Camden (N.J.) Courier-Post, 1966-68; editl. asst. Med. Insight mag., N.Y.C., 1970-71; mng. editor Camera 35 mag., N.Y.C., 1971-75; also assoc. editor photog. anns. U.S. Camera/Camera 35, 1972, 73; freelance editor as Word Woman N.Y.C., 1975-77, 79-99; acct. exec. Bozell & Jacobs, N.Y.C., 1977-79; copy editor Camera Arts mag., N.Y.C., 1981-83; editl. coord. Ctr. mag. Nat. Ctr. Health Edn., 1985; editl. coord. Popular Photography mag., 1986-95; assoc. editor Sony Style, 1995; tchr. speech improvement N.Y.C. Bd. Edn., 1995—. Contbg. editor: Photograph; participant 3M Editor's Conf. (1st woman), 1972; photography group exhbns. include Internat. Women's Art Festival, N.Y.C., 1975, Rockefeller Ctr., N.Y.C., 1976, Photograph Gallery, N.Y.C., 1981; acrylic painting exhbns. Tchrs. Coll., N.Y.C., 1994, Warwick Hotel, N.Y.C., 1995; represented in collection Libr. Calif Inst. Arts, Valencia; copy editor: The Complete Guide to Cibachrome Printing, 1980, The Popular Photography Question and Answer Book, 1979, The Photography Catalog, 1976, Strand: Sixty Years of Photography, 1976, You and Your Lens, 1975; contbr. articles to comml. publs., chpts. to books. Tchr. Sch. Vol. Program, N.Y.C. Recipient 1st pl. honors Dist. 1, Internat. Assn. Bus. Communicators, 1977. Mem. Soka Gakkai Internat. Buddhist. Avocations: dance, reading, photography, origami, walking. Home: 85 Hicks St Apt 7 Brooklyn NY 11201-6825 E-mail: barbaralobron@hotmail.com.

LOCATELLI, PAUL LEO, academic administrator; b. Santa Cruz, Calif., Sept. 16, 1938; s. Vincent Dino and Marie Josephine (Piccone) L. BS in Acctg., Santa Clara U., 1961; MDiv, Jesuit Sch. Theology, 1974; DBA, U. So. Calif., 1971. CPA, Calif.; ordained priest Roman Cath. Ch., 1974. Acct. Lautze & Lautze, San Jose, Calif., 1960-61, 73-74; prof. acctg. Santa Clara (Calif.) U., 1974-86, assoc. dean Bus. Sch., 1976—78, acad. v.p., 1978—86, pres., 1988—. Campus Compact Assn. Jesuit Colls. and Univs., JV:SV Network, Am. Leadership Forum Silicon Valley, Silicon Valley Mfg. Group, NCCJ; trustee Jesuit Sch. Theology, Berkeley; exec. com. Ind. Colls. and Univs. of Calif.; pres. coun. Assn. Governing Bds. Co-author: (assessment) The New Curriculum: A Guide to Professional Accounting, 1995. Adv. coun. John Gardner Ctr. for Youth and Their Cmtys., Proyecto Pastoral; mem. acad. adv. bd. Panetta Inst. Mem. AICPA, Calif. Soc. CPAs (Disting. Prof. of the Yr. award 1994), Am. Acctg. Assn., Commonwealth Club Silicon Valley. Democrat. Office: Santa Clara U 500 El Camino Real Santa Clara CA 95053-0015

LOCHBIHLER, FREDERICK VINCENT, lawyer; b. Chgo., Jan. 30, 1951; s. Frederick Louis and Marion Helen (Rutkauskas) L.; m. Darlene Gotfryde Wantuch, Nov. 8, 1952; 1 child, Frederick Karlman. AB in Govt. summa cum laude, U. Notre Dame, 1973; JD with honors, U. Chgo., 1976. Bar: Ill. 1976, U.S. Dist. Ct. (no. dist.) Ill. 1977, U.S. Ct. Appeals (7th cir.) 1980, U.S. Ct. Appeals (8th cir.) 1981, U.S. Supreme Ct. 1982, U.S. Dist. Ct. (ctrl. dist.) Ill. 1983, U.S. Dist. Ct. Ariz. 1991, U.S. Ct. Appeals (Fed. cir.) 2001, U. S. Dist. Ct. (so. dist.) Ind. 2002. Assoc. Chapman and Cutler, Chgo., 1976-84, ptnr., 1984—. Mem. Phi Beta Kappa, Order of Coif. Avocations: military history, literature, travel. Office: Chapman and Cutler 111 W Monroe St Ste 1700 Chicago IL 60603-4006 Office Phone: 312-845-3705. E-mail: lochbihl@chapman.com.

LOCHER, CHRISTOPHER PHILLIP, vaccinologist, director, researcher; s. Phillip Carroll and Diane Dolores Locher; m. Nicole Locher, May 27, 2000; 2 children children: Ryan John Phillip. PhD, U. Hawaii, 1992. Vis. scientist Prince Leopold II Inst. Tropical Medicine, Antwerp, Belgium, 1993; rsch. fellow U. Calif., San Francisco, 1994—98, rsch. virologist, 1998—2001; project leader Maxygen, Redwood City, Calif., 2002—. Recipient award, Merck and Co., 1992, Roche Laboratories award, Nat. Student Rsch. Forum, 1992, Joseph E. Alicata award, U. Hawaii, 1992; fellow, Damien Found., 1993. Achievements include research in vaccine strategies for HIV, malaria and Alphaviruses; synthetic and molecular adjuvant formulations and evaluation; discovery of new lead pharmaceuticals for malaria and new vaccine molecules for malaria and alphaviruses. Office: Maxygen Inc 515 Galveston Dr Redwood City CA 94063 Office Phone: 650-298-5487.

LOCHER, RICHARD ALFRED, JR., operating engineer, musician; b. Joliet, Ill., Dec. 12, 1950; s. Bertha Locher and Richard Alfred Locher, Sr.; 1 child, Beth L. Smith. Ch. organist, Joliet, Ill., 1963—; oper. engr. Local 150, Joliet, Ill., 1969—. Vol. C. of C., Frankfort, Ill., 1990—; docent Ill. Philharm. Orch., Park Forest, Ill. Mem.: Fox Valley Chpt. of the Am. Guild of Organists. Home: 3900 Buck Ave Joliet IL 60431 Personal E-mail: iplayorgan@comcast.net.

LOCHRIDGE, LLOYD PAMPELL, JR., lawyer; b. Austin, Tex., Feb. 3, 1918; s. Lloyd Pampell and Franklin (Blocker) Lochridge; m. Frances Potter, Jan. 23, 1943; children: Anne, Georgia, Lloyd P. III, Patton G., Hope N., Frances P. AB, Princeton U., 1938; LLB, Harvard U., 1941. Bar: DC 1942, Tex. 1945, U.S. Ct. Appeals (5th cir.), U.S. Supreme Ct. Assoc. Law Office Vernon Hill, Mission, Tex., 1945-46; ptnr. Hill & Lochridge, Mission, 1946-49, Hill, Lochridge & King, Mission, 1949-59, McGinnis, Lochridge & Kilgore, Austin, 1959—. Mem. adv. bd. Salvation Army, Austin, 1962—; trustee Austin Lyric Opera, 1986—; mem. vestry Ch. Good Shepherd, Austin, 1968—73. Comdr. USNR, 1941—46, ETO. Mem.: ABA (bd. govs. 1989—92), Hidalgo County Bar Assn. (pres. 1954—55), Travis County Bar Assn. (pres. 1970—71), State Bar Tex. (pres. 1974—75). Episcopalian. Avocations: tennis, squash, sailing. Office: McGinnis Lochridge and Kilgore Capitol Ctr 919 Congress Ave Ste 1300 Austin TX 78701-2499 Business E-Mail: llochridge@mcginnislaw.com.

LOCHRIDGE, PATTON G., lawyer; b. McAllen, Tex., Dec. 30, 1949; s. Lloyd and Frances (Potter) L.; m. Candy Lundgren, June 28, 1975; children: Eleanor, Patton, Joe, Lloyd. BA, U. Tex., 1972, JD, 1976. Bar: Tex. 1976, U.S. Dist. Ct. (no., so., ea. and we. dists.) Tex., U.S. Ct. Appeals (5th cir.), U.S. Supreme Ct. Law clk. to Hon. Joseph T. Sneed U.S. Ct. Appeals (9th cir.), San Francisco, 1976-77; assoc. to ptnr., comml. litig. McGinnis Lochridge & Kilgore LLP, Austin, Tex., 1977—, mng. ptnr., 2000—. Chmn. com. ct. adminstrn. US Dist Ct. we. dist. Tex., 1986—97, chmn. admissions com., 1995—. Trustee Salvation Army, Austin, St. Andrews Episc. Sch. Austin. Fellow: Am. Coll. Trial Lawyers; mem.: ABA, Am. Bd. Trial Advocates, Travis County Bar Assn., Phi Delta Phi, Order of the Coif. Office: McGinnis Lochridge & Kilgore Ste 1300 919 Congress Ave Austin TX 78701 Office Phone: 512-495-6044. Office Fax: 512-505-6344. Business E-Mail: plochridge@mcginnislaw.com.

LOCHTE, RICHARD SAMUEL, writer; b. New Orleans, Oct. 19, 1946; s. Richard Samuel and Eileen Helen (Carbine) L.; m. Jane Bryson, July, 1989. BA, Tulane U., 1968. Theater critic Los Angeles mag., 1975-95. Screenwriter: Escape to Athena, 1979, Sleeping Dog, 1988; author: Sleeping Dog (Nero Wolfe award 1985), Laughing Dog, 1988, Blue Bayou, 1992, The Neon Smile, 1995, (with C. Darden) The Trials of Nikki Hill, 1999, Lucky Dog and Other Tales of Murder, 2000, (with C. Darden) L.A. Justice, 2001, (with C. Darden) The Last Defense, 2004; book columnist L.A. Times, 1996—. Served to lt. comdr. USCG, 1976. Recipient spl. award Mystery Writers of Am., 1986. Mem. Writers Guild of Am., L.A. Drama Critics Circle (v.p. 1986), Nat. Book Critics Circle, Authors Guild Am., Am. Crime Writers League (pres. 1999-2000_. Mystery Writers Am. (bd. dirs. 1988), Pvt. Eye Writers Am., Internat. Crime Writers. Avocations: tennis, archery. Office: PO Box 5413 Santa Monica CA 90409-5413

LOCICERO, JOSEPH, thoracic surgeon, researcher; b. Chgo., Nov. 1, 1948; s. Joseph and Inez LoCicero; m. Martha Jane Slater, July 19, 1948; 1 child, John Paul. BS, Tulane U., 1966, MD, 1973. Diplomate Am. Bd. Surgery, Am. Bd. Thoracic Surgery. Chief thoracic surgery Med. Sch. Northwestern U., Chgo., 1984—91; chief thoracic surgery Deaconess Hosp., Boston, 1991—97, Beth Israel Deaconess Hosp., Boston, 1997—2001; chmn. surgery Chgo. Med. Sch., 2001—02, U. S. Ala., Mobile, Ala., 2002—. Capt. U.S. Army, 1975—77. Mem.: Am. Surg. Assn. Office: U So Ala 2451 Fillingim St Mobile AL 36617 Office Phone: 251-471-7993. Business E-Mail: jlocicero@usouthal.edu.

LOCIGNO, PAUL ROBERT, public relations executive; b. Cleve., Sept. 17, 1948; s. Paul Robert and Anna Mae (Zingale) L.; m. Ki Cho Rim; children: Paul III, Tammy, Robert. AA, Cuyahoga C.C., Parma, Ohio, 1974; BA, Case We. Res. U., 1976; postgrad., Cleve. State U., 1977—78. Part-time faculty Cuyahoga C.C., 1979—83; vice-chmn. Presdl. Inaugural Labor Com., Washington, 1980—81; vice-chmn. labor com. Presdl. Inaugural Com., Washington, 1984—85; legis. agt. Internat. Brotherhood of Teamsters, Washington, 1977—90, dir. govt. internat. affairs, 1983—89, dir. Asian/Pacific br. Taipei, Taiwan, 1985—88; spl. rep. of chmn. Hill & Knowlton Pub. Affairs Worldwide, Washington, 1989—91; pres., founding ptnr. Rollins Internat. Ltd., Alexandria, Va., 1997—2004; CEO Ganeden Biotech Inc., San Diego, 2004—; pres. Locigno Internat. Inc., 2004—. Bd. dirs. Nanjing Ya Dong Corp. Mem. Pres.'s Export Coun., 1988-89; mem. Asia adv. com. Bicentennial of U.S. Constitution, 1990; bd. govs. Am. League for Exports and Security Assistance, 1989; mem. Nat. Commn. for Employment Policy, Washington, 1981-86; bd. dirs. Children's Right Coun., Washington, 1997-2002; mem. zoning ordinance rev. com. Prince William County, Va. With USMC, 1968-70, Vietnam. Republican. Roman Catholic. Avocations: archery, golf, fishing. Home: 3650 Secret Grove Ct Dumfries VA 22025

LOCK, ALBERT LARRY, JR., finance company executive; b. St. Louis, Nov. 20, 1947; s. Albert Larry and Bernadine Helen (Syron) L.; m. Barbara Ann Harding, Feb. 13, 1971; children: Brian C., Sean M. Student, U. Mo., St. Louis, 1966-68; AA, Northwest Mo. State U., 1975; MS in Fin. Svcs., The Am. Coll., 1998. CLU, 1979, ChFC, 1983. Ins. agt. Western and So. Life, St. Louis, 1970-74; field underwriter Home Life of N.Y., St. Louis, 1975—84; owner, fin. advisor Universal Fin. Group Inc., St. Louis, 1984—. Cons. fin. planning workshop St. Louis C.C., 1983-90; mem. broker/dealer Pres.'s Coun. Mutual Svc. Corp., 1992--; bd. dirs., legis. chmn. St. Louis Assn. Ins. and Fin. Advisors, mem. Top-of-the-Table Million Dollar Round Table. Pres. St. Paul Sch. Bd., 1990-91; bd. dirs. Bishop DuBourg H.S., 1997—, Marianist Retreat Ctr., St. Louis, 1997--. Sgt. U.S. Army, 1968-70, Vietnam. Decorated Bronze star, Air medals. Mem. St. Louis Soc. Fin. Svcs. Profls. (pres. 1988-89. chair fin. counseling sects.), Nat. Assn. Securities Dealers (registered prin.), Million Dollar Round Table. Roman Catholic. Avocation: racquetball. Office: Universal Fin Group Inc 7751 Carondelet Ave Saint Louis MO 63105-3316

LOCK, EDOUARD, performing company executive; b. Casablanca, Morocco, Mar. 3, 1954; Founder Lock-Danseurs now La La La Human Steps, 1980. Artistic dir. performances include those at N.Y.'s Dance Theatre Workshop (Bessie award for choreography, 1986), dir., co-conceived David Bowie's Sound and Vision world tour; also dir. films. associated with prodn., 1989, showcased in the documentary Inspirations by Michael Apted, photographer (exhibitions) included in cities such as Stockholm, Los Angeles and Amsterdam, (private collections) Universite du Quebec a Montreal and Air Canada. Named Officer of the Order of Can., 2002; named one of Quebec's 10 most influential personalities; named to Chevalier de l'Ordre National du Quebec; recipient Chalmers Nat. Dance prize, 2001, Nat. Arts Ctr. prize. Office: La La La Human Steps 5655 ave du Parc Ste 206 Montreal PQ H2V 4H2 Canada*

LOCK, GERALD SEYMOUR HUNTER, retired mechanical engineering educator; b. London, June 30, 1935; arrived in Can., 1962, naturalized, 1973; s. George and Mary (Hunter) L.; m. Edna Burness, Sept. 19, 1959; children: Graeme, Gareth, Grenville. B.Sc. with honors, U. Durham, Eng., 1959, PhD, 1962. Asst. prof. mech. engring. U. Alta. (Can.), Edmonton, 1962-64, assoc. prof., 1964-70, prof., 1970-93, dean interdisciplinary studies, 1976-81; cons. mech. engr., Edmonton, 1993—. Chmn. Internat. Arctic Sci. Commn. Regional Bd., 1993-96. Vice chmn. Alta. Manpower Adv. Coun., 1979-84, chmn., 1984-89; chmn. Salvation Army Red Shield Appeal, 1980-82; bd. govs. Alta. Coll., chmn., 1982-85; founding pres. Alta. Poetry Festival Soc., 1981. Recipient Queen Elizabeth II Silver Jubilee medal, 1977 Fellow Engring. Inst. Can, Can. Soc. Mech. Engring. (pres. 1977-78), ASME; mem. Sci. Coun. Can., Can. Polar Commn. Mem. Progressive Conservative Party. Anglican. Home: 11711 83rd Ave Edmonton AB Canada T6G 0V2 Office: U Alta Edmonton AB Canada T6G 2G3

LOCK, RICHARD WILLIAM, packaging company executive; b. N.Y.C., Oct. 5, 1931; s. Albert and Catherine Dorothy (Magnus) L.; m. Elizabeth Louise Kenney, Nov. 2, 1957; children— Albert William, Dorothy Louise Lock Kuhl, John David. BS, Rutgers U., 1953; MBA, N.Y. U., 1958. Acct. Gen. Electric Co., 1953-54, Union Carbide Co., N.Y.C., 1956-58; div. controller St. Regis Paper Co., Houston, 1959-62, Owens-Illinois, Inc., Toledo, 1962-64, supr. programmer office methods and data processing, 1964-65, asst. mgr. data processing procedures, 1965-67, mgr. systems analysis and devel., 1967-68, mgr. corp. systems analysis and devel., 1968-70, dir. corp. systems and data processing, 1970-72, gen. mgr. electro/optical display, 1972-75, treas., 1975-80, v.p., dir. corp. planning, 1980-84, v.p., asst. chief fin. officer, treas., 1984-88; mng. dir. Magnus Assocs., 1989—. Mem. adv. bd. Toledo Salvation Army, 1973—, chmn., 1974-77; pres. Toledo Area Govtl. Rsch. Assn., 1978-79; bd. dirs. Riverside Hosp. Found., Toledo, 1982—. Served with USAF, 1954-56. Mem. Fin. Execs. Inst., Am. Soc. Corp. Secs., Phi Beta Kappa. Clubs: Toledo. Republican. Lutheran.

LOCKAMY, ARCHIE, III, operations management educator; b. El Paso, Tex., July 24, 1957; s. Archie Jr. and Corrine Ann Lockamy; m. Vicki G. Glover, Dec. 19, 1981. B of Chem. Engring., Ga. Inst. Tech., 1979; MBA, Atlanta U., 1983; PhD, U. Ga., 1990. Cert. in prodn. and inventory mgmt.; cert. fellow in prodn. and inventory mgmt.; acad. Jonah. Corp. mgmt. intern TRW, Inc., Cleve., 1983-85; prodn. supt. TRW Motor Divsn., Dothan, Ala., 1985-87; asst. prof. ops. mgmt. U. Mich., Ann Arbor, 1990-92; interim asst. v.p. for acad. affairs Fla. A&M U., Tallahassee, 1996-97, prof. ops. mgmt., 1992-2000, Samford U., Birmingham, Ala., 2000—. Mem. bd. examiners Malcolm Baldridge Nat. Quality Award, 1997-2002; acad. quality improvement project design cons. North Cen. Assn. Colls. and Schs., 1999-2000. Co-author: (book) Reengineering Performance Measurement, 1994; contbr. articles to profl. jours.; mem. editl. rev. bd. Benchmarking: An Internat. Jour., 1995—. Jour. Ops. Mgmt., 1994—; referee Mfg. Rev., 1991, Internat. Jour. Prodn. Rsch., 1992—, Jour. Sys. Improvement, 1994—, Ann. Advances in Bus. Cases, 2000—, Prodn. and Inventory Mgmt. Jour., 2000—; contbr. APICS Dictionary, 1992-97. Bd. dirs. Innovation Investment Program, Tallahassee, 1996, APICS E&R Found., 1998-2000, sec., 1999, v.p., 2000. Recipient Cert. of Appreciation for Outstanding Svc. to the Nation, U.S. Dept. Commerce, 1997-2002. Mem. APICS, AIChE, Decision Scis. Inst., Prodn. and Ops. Mgmt. Soc., Performance Measurement Assn., Beta Gamma Sigma (pres. Sanford U. chpt. 2001-03). Avocations: chess, racquetball, music. Office: Samford U 800 Lakeshore Dr Birmingham AL 35229 Office Fax: 205-726-2464. E-mail: aalockam@sanford.edu.

LOCKART, DAVID R., music educator, composer; b. Seattle, Dec. 5, 1955; s. Royce Z. Lockart and Mary L. Nightingale; m. Linda C. Caldwell, Sept. 29, 1959; children: Jason M., Heather L. MusB in Edn., Westminster Choir Coll.; MusM, U. Ill. Tchr. music North Hunterdon H.S., Annandale, NJ, 1980—90; supr. music North Hunterdon Voorhees HS Dist, 1990—. Cons., music theory com. mem. The Coll. Bd., 1998—2004; dir. NJ. Young Composers Festival, Princeton, NJ, 1996—2002. Composer: (choral music) Various (Ithaca Choral Composition Contest Finalist), (cantata) Passing; Cantate Music Pub.; author: AP Music Theory Teacher's Guide, 2005. Recipient AP Music Theory Recognition award, The Coll. Bd., 1992, Best Practices award, NJ Dept. Edn. Mem.: Am. Choral Directors Assn., Music Educators Nat. Conf. Achievements include Led Five European Concert Tours. Office: North Hunterdon Voorhees HS District 1445 Route 31 Annandale NJ 08801 Office Phone: 908-713-4165. Personal E-mail: dlockart@nhvweb.net.

LOCKE, CARL EDWIN, JR., academic administrator, engineer, educator; b. Palo Pinto County, Tex., Jan. 11, 1936; s. Carl Edwin Sr. and Caroline Jane (Brown) L.; m. Sammie Rhae Batchelor, Aug. 25, 1956; children: Stephen Curtis, Carlene Rhae. BSChemE, U. Tex., 1958, MSChemE, 1960, PhD-ChemE, 1972. Rsch. engr. Continental Oil Co., Ponca City, Okla., 1959-65; prodn. engr. R.L. Stone Co., Austin, Tex., 1965-66; prodn. rsch. engr. Tracor Inc., Austin, 1966-71; vis. assoc. prof. U. Tex., Austin, 1971-73; from asst. prof. to prof., dir. chem. engring. U. Okla., Norman, 1973-86; dean engring. U. Kans., Lawrence, 1986—2002, prof. chem. and petroleum engring., 1986—. Co-author: Anodic Protection, 1981; contbr. articles to profl. jours. Recipient Disting. Engring. Svc. award U. Kans. Sch. Engring., 2002; named Disting. Engring. grad. U. Tex., 1993, Kansas Engr. of Yr. Kansas Engring. Soc., 1996. Fellow AIChE, NSPE; mem. ASTM, Nat. Assn. Corrosion Engrs. (regional chair 1988-89, Eben Junkin award South Cen. region 1990), Am. Soc. Engring. Edn. (vice-chair engring. deans coun. 1999-2001, chair 2001-02), Lawrence C. of C., Rotary (pres. 2001-02). Democrat. Presbyterian. Office: U Kans Sch Engring 1530 W 15th St Rm 4006 Lawrence KS 66045-7526 E-mail: lok@ku.edu.

LOCKE, CATHY J., art director, artist; d. Charles Stanley and Nora Lou Locke; m. James Hodge, May 1, 1993. BFA, Art Ctr. Coll., Pasadena, Calif., 1985. Ptnr. Locke Veach Comm., Sausalito, Calif., 1987—97; pres. Studio North, Novato, Calif., 1997—. Chair mktg. Legal Mktg. Assn., San Francisco, 2004. Recipient Best of Show award, Pastel Soc. of the West Coast, 2005. Mem.: Indian Valley Artists, Women Artists of West (assoc.), Portrait Soc. Am. (assoc.), Pastel Soc. Am. (assoc.), Calif. Art Club (assoc.). Office: Studio North 560 Trumbull Ave Novato CA 94947 Office Phone: 415-893-9292. Office Fax: 415-893-9464. E-mail: cathy@cathylocke.com.

LOCKE, CYNTHIA MILBURN, lawyer; b. Indpls., May 11, 1949; d. Theodore Laurence and Jean Cameron (Pickett) L; children: Karen, Peter, Christopher. Student, Hillsdale (Mich.) Coll., 1967-71; BA, Butler U., Indpls., 1981; JD, Ind. U., Indpls., 1985. Bar: Ind. 1985, U.S. Dist. Ct. (no. and so. dists.) Ind. 1985, U.S. Ct. Appeals (7th cir.) 1994, U.S. Supreme Ct. 1996. Law clk. Ind. Ct. Appeals, Indpls., 1984-86; atty. White & Raub, LLP, Indpls., 1986—, ptnr., 1995—2004, mng. ptnr., 2002—04; ptnr. Stewart & Irwin, P.C., Indpls., 2004—. Mem. Jr. League of Indpls., 1974-84; crisis line vol. Marion County Mental Health Assn., 1978-84; pres. Mental Health Assn. Hamilton County, Ind., 1991-92. Mem. ABA, Ind. State Bar Assn., Indpls. Bar Assn., Def. Rsch. Inst., Def. Trial Counsel of Ind. Office: Stewart & Irwin PC 251 E Ohio St Ste 1100 Indianapolis IN 46204 Office Phone: 317-639-5454. Business E-Mail: clocke@silegal.com.

LOCKE, EDWIN ALLEN, III, retired psychologist, educator; b. N.Y.C., May 15, 1938; s. Edwin Allen and Dorothy (Clark) Locke; m. Cathy Durham, Apr. 13, 2001. BA, Harvard U., 1960; MA, Cornell U., 1962, PhD, 1964. Assoc. research scientist Am. Inst. Research, 1964-66, research scientist, 1966-70; asst. prof. psychology U. Md., College Park, 1967-69, assoc. prof., 1969-70, assoc. prof. bus., mgmt. and psychology, 1998—2001, dean's prof. of leadership & motivation, 1984—96; chmn. faculty mgt. and orgn. Coll. Bus. and Mgmt. U. Md., College Park, 1984-96, prof. emeritus, 2001. Author: A Guide to Effective Study, 1975, The Prime Movers: Traits of the Great Wealth Creators, 2000; co-author: Goal Setting: A Motivational Technique That works, 1984, A Theory of Goal Setting and Task Performance, 1990, The Essence of Leadership, 1991; editor: Generalizing from Laboratory to Field Settings, 1986, Handbook of Principles of Organizational Behavior, 2000, Postmodernism in Management: Pros Cons and the Alternative, 2003; contbr. articles to profl. jours. Office Naval Research grantee, 1964, 79; NIMH grantee, 1967; Army Rsch. Inst. grantee, 1993. Fellow APA, Acad. Mgmt., Am. Psychol. Soc., Soc. Indsl. and Orgnl. Psychology (Disting Scientific Contbn. award 1993). E-mail: elocke@rhsmith.umd.edu. *The most important literary/philosophical influence in my life has been Ayn Rand. Her philosophy of Objectivism demonstrates that man's highest moral purpose is the achievement of his own happiness and that reason is his only means to achieve it. Her novels, which portray man as an heroic being, are an inspiration to every man to achieve the best within him.*

LOCKE, ELIZABETH HUGHES, retired foundation administrator; b. Norfolk, Va., June 30, 1939; d. George Morris and Sallie Epps (Moss) Hughes; m. John Rae Locke, Jr., Sept. 13, 1958 (div. 1981); children: John Rae III, Sallie Curtis. BA magna cum laude, Duke U., 1964, PhD, 1972; MA, U. N.C., 1966; DHum (hon.), Furman U., 2004. Instr. English U. N.C., Chapel Hill, 1970-72; dir. univ. pubs. Duke U., Durham, NC, 1973-79; corp. contbns. officer Bethlehem Steel Corp., Pa., 1979-82; dir. edn. divsn. & comm. Duke Endowment, Charlotte, NC, 1982-96, exec. dir., 1996-97, pres., 1997—2004; ret., 2004. Vis. prof. English Duke U., 1972—73. Editor: Duke Encounters, 1977, prospectus for Change: American Private Higher Education, 1985, (mag) Issues, 1985-96. Pres. Angier B. Duke Meml., Inc., 1997-2005, Duke Endowment, 1997-2005, Nanaline H. Duke Fund, 1997-2005, Doris Duke Trust, 1998, Jr. League, Durham, 1976, Hist. Preservation Soc., Durham, 1977, Charlotte Area Donors Forum; past pres. Comm. Philanthropy, Washington, Sch. of Arts, Charlotte; mem. legis. com. Coun. on Founds., 1997-, Washington, 1995; trustee Southeastern Coun. of Founds., 1997—, Wing Haven Found.; commr. So. Assn. Colls. & Schs., 1998—; bd. vis. Davidson Coll., Charlotte County Day Sch., Duke U., Johnson C. Smith U.; trustee Winghaven Found. Recipient Leadership award Charlotte C. of C., 1984;

Danforth fellow, 1972. Mem. Nat. Task Force, English Speaking Union, The Most Venerable Order of St. John of Jerusalem (officer sister), Colonial Dames Am., Charlotte City Club (bd. govs.), Phi Beta Kappa. Democrat. Episcopalian. Office: 100 N Tryon St Ste 3500 Charlotte NC 28202-4001 Personal E-mail: betsL@earthlink.net.

LOCKE, GARY F., lawyer, former governor; b. Wash., Jan. 21, 1950; s. James and Julie Locke; m. Mona Lee, Oct. 15, 1994; children: Emily Nicole, Dylan James, Madeline Lee. BA in Polit. Sci., Yale U., 1972; JD, Boston U., 1975. Dep. prosecuting atty. State of Wash., King County; mem. Wash. State Ho. of Reps., Olympia, 1983—94; gov. State of Wash., Olympia, 1996—2005; ptnr. Davis Wright Tremaine LLP, Seattle, 2005—. Cmty. rels. mgr. U.S. West; chief exec. King County, 1994—97; bd. dirs. Safeco Corp., Seattle, 2005—. Named First in effectiveness among Puget Sound area lawmakers Seattle Times, 1990. Democrat. Became first Chinese-Am. gov. in US history when elected gov. of Washington in 1996. Office: Davis Wright Tremaine LLP 2600 Century Sq 1501 4th Ave Seattle WA 98101*

LOCKE, GENE L., lawyer; b. Conroe, Tex., 1947; BA, U. Houston, 1965; JD, South Tex. Coll. Law, 1981. Bar: Tex. 1981, US Dist. Ct. (So. Dist.) Tex., US Dist. Ct. (No. Dist.) Tex., US Dist. Ct. (Ea. Dist.) Tex., US Dist. Ct. (We. Dist.) Tex., US Ct. Appeals (5th Cir.), US Supreme Ct. Adminstrv. asst., legal counsel US Congressman Mickey Leland, 1983-85; assoc. mcpl. judge City Houston, 1986-89, city atty., 1995—; mng. ptnr. Nelson & Locke PC, Houston, 1985-95; ptnr. Mayor, Day, Caldwell & Keeton, Houston, 1995—; ptnr., Pub. Law Practice Andrew Kurth LLP, Houston, mem. mgmt. com. Adj. prof. govt. U. Houston, 1981-83; presenter in field. Fellow Am. Leadersip forum, 1991—; bd. trustees Houston Cmty. Coll. Sys., 1989-95, chmn. 1989-90; bd. dirs. U. Houston Alumni Assn., 1989-92; chmn. bd. dirs. SHAPE Cmty. Ctr., 1985-88. Recipient Freedom award outstanding svc. NAACP, 1993, Outstanding Alumnus award U. Houston Black Alumni Assn., 1995, Disting. Alumnus award South Tex. Law Sch., 1996. Mem. ABA, Nat. Bar Assn., State Bar Tex. (govt. sect.), Tex. Bar Found., Assn. Trial Lawyers Am., Houston Bar Assn. (bd. dirs. 1993—), Houston Bar Found., Houston Lawyers Assn. Office: Andrews Kurth LLP 600 Travis St Ste 4200 Houston TX 77002-3090 Office Phone: 713-220-3956. Office Fax: 713-238-7294. Business E-Mail: genelocke@andrewskurth.com.

LOCKE, GREGORY DUANE, evangelist; b. Donelson, Tenn., May 18, 1976; s. Judy Lynelle Sumner; m. Melissa Kay Biggers, Apr. 24, 1971; 1 child, Hudson-Taylor Kemle. Grad. in Theology, Amb. Bapt. Coll., Lattimore, N.C., 1998; B in Bibl. Studies, Bapt. Theol. Sch. New Eng., Pascoag, R.I, 2000, M in Bibl. Studies, 2001, DD, 2004. Ordained Somerville Bapt. Ch., AL., 1998, lic. Somerville Bapt. Ch., AL., 1998. Pres. and evangelist Greg Locke Ministries, Murfreesboro, Tenn., 1996—. Chaplain Rutherford County Sheriffs Dept., Murfeesboro, 2004—; founder and pres. Hudson Bible Coll., Benin City, Nigeria, 2004—. Author: Revival: Then Fire Of The Lord Fell, Blinded By Benny, The Trap Of Christian Rap. Coop. bd. mem. Good Shepherd Children's Home, Murfreesboro, Tenn., 2003—. Recipient Pastors award, Franklin Rd. Bapt. Ch., 1995, Outstanding Preacherboy award, Franklin Rd. Christian Sch., 1995, Golden Web award, Internet Assn. Webmasters and Designers, 2003, Innovative Contbn. award, Earle C. Job Corps, 2003; scholarship, Chick fil a Restaraunt, 1997. Achievements include crusades in forty states and a dozen foreign countries. Avocation: travel. Home: 212 Woodcraft Rd Murfreesboro TN 37127 Office: Greg Locke Ministries PO Box 1099 Murfreesboro TN 37133 Office Phone: 615-405-1665. Personal E-mail: greg@greglockministries.com.

LOCKE, J. DUANE, poet, painter, photographer; b. Vienna, Ga., Dec. 29, 1921; s. Julius Guy and Finis Taylor Locke; PhD, U. Fla., 1958. Poet in residence, creative writing and lit. tchr. U. Tampa, Fla., 1958—82. Author: Watching Wisteria, 1995, numerous poems; exhibitions include U. Fla., one-man shows include Tampa Pyramid Gallery, 2003. Recipient Walt Whitman award, Poetry Soc. Am., 1974, Charles Agnoff award, Lit. Rev., 1974, Edna St. Vincent Miller award, Smith Publ., 1974. Democrat. Avocations: philosophy, opera, birdwatching. Home: 400 S Florida Ave Apt 1011 Lakeland FL 33801 Personal E-mail: duanelocke@netzero.net.

LOCKE, MICHAEL, zoology educator; b. Nottingham, Eng., Feb. 14, 1929; came to U.S., 1961; s. R.H. and K.N. L.; m. J. V. Collins; children by previous marriage, Vanessa, John, Timothy, Marius. BA, Cambridge U., 1952, MA, 1955, PhD, 1956, Sc.D., 1976. State scholar, found. scholar St. John's Coll., 1949-56; lectr. zoology Univ. Coll. W.I., 1956-61; guest investigator Rockefeller Inst., N.Y.C., 1960; assoc. prof. biology Case Western Res. U., Cleve., 1961-67, prof. biology, 1967-71; prof., chmn. dept. zoology U. Western Ont., London, Can., 1971-85, prof. zoology, 1985-94; prof. emeritus, 1994—. Raman prof. U. Madras, India, 1969; vis. dir. rsch. Internat. Ctr. Insect Physiology and Ecology, Nairobi, Kenya, 1977-81; chmn. Gordon Conf. on Lysosomes, 1970. Editor Monographs on Ultrastructure, 1970—; mem. editorial bd. Tissue and Cell, 1968—, Jour. Insect Physiology, 1978—, Insect Sci. and Its Applications, 1979-89; former editor: Growth Soc. Symposia; editor, contbr. vols. 11 A, B, C, Insecta-Microscopic Anatomy of Invertebrate, 1998; contbr. over 200 articles to profl. jours. Served with No. 3 Med. Parachute Team RAF, 1947—49. Recipient Disting. Internat. award in insect morphology and embryology gold medal, 1988, Wigglesworth medal and lectr., Internat. Entomol. Congress, Brazil, 2000, Cert. of Distinction, 2000, Helmuth Prize, U.W.O., 2001;, Killam fellow, 1988—90. Fellow Royal Soc. Can., AAAS, Am. Soc. Entomol. (hon.), Royal Entomol. Soc. London (hon.); mem. Am. Soc. Cell Biology. Avocations: lapidary, gemologist, bone, ivory, horn antiquities. Office: U Western Ont Dept Biology London ON Canada N6A 5B7 Business E-Mail: mlocke@uwo.ca.

LOCKE, NORTON, hotel management and construction company executive; b. Mpls., May 22, 1927; s. Ben and Harriet (Markus) L.; m. Peggy Jane Smith, Nov. 6, 1959; children: Alexandria, Jonina, Elizabeth, Victoria. BS, U. Wis., 1951; MBA, Mich. State U., 1957, cert. food and beverage exec., 1984, cert. hotel adminstr., 1986, cert. food service profl., 1988. Corp. dir. food and beverage Kahler Corp., Rochester, Minn., 1970; gen. mgr., chief exec. officer Carolando Corp., Orlando, Fla., 1971-74; also dir.; gen. mgr. Radisson Muehlebach Hotel, Kansas City, Radisson Cadillac Hotel, Detroit, 1974-79; v.p., gen. mgr. White Co. Hospitality Div., Merrillville, Ind., 1979-80; dist. dir. I.D.M. Mgmt. Co., Chgo., 1980-83; v.p., gen. mgr. Skirvin Plaza Hotel, Oklahoma City, 1983-87; v.p., dir. ops. SBI Mgmt. Co., Oklahoma City, 1987-91; v.p., gen. mgr. Anaheim (Calif.) Plz. Hotel, 1991-93; corp. dir. Midwest Hospitality Mgmt., Anaheim, Calif., 1993-99. Faculty Vallencia Coll., 1971-74; adj. prof. Oklahoma City C.C., 1983-89, Century Coll., San Diego, 1996-98, ITT Tech. Coll., San Diego, 1997-99 Author: Hard Times Cook Book, World Without Milk Cookbook, Land of Milk and Honey, Heritage, A Taste of Tradition. Bd. dirs. U. Minn. Tech. Coll., 1970-75, Am. Hotel and Motel Assn. Sch., 1975-79, Detroit Conv. and Visitors Bur. Served with inf. AUS, 1944-46. Mem. Internat. Food Service Execs. Assn. (dir. 1971-74), Am. Hotel and Motel Assn. (cert.), Am. Chefs Assn., Mich. and Ind. Hotel Assn., Nat. Restaurant Assn., Hotel Sales Mgrs. Assn., Am. Fisheries Inst. (dir. 1970-71), Okla. State Hotel Assn. (Innkeeper of Yr. 1985, Bd. Mem. of Yr. 1986) Clubs: Masons (Scottish Rite 32 degree), Shriners, Rotary, SKAL Internat, Toastmasters Internat. Republican.

LOCKE, VIRGINIA OTIS, writer; b. Tiffin, Ohio, Sept. 4, 1930; d. Charles Otis and Frances Virginia (Sherer) L. BA, Barnard Coll., 1953; MA in Psychology, Duke U., 1972, postgrad. Program officer, asst. corp. sec. Agrl. Devel. Coun., N.Y.C., 1954-66; staff psychologist St. Luke's-Roosevelt Med. Ctr., N.Y.C., 1973-75; freelance writer and editor N.Y.C., 1976-85; writer-editor Cornell U. Med. Coll./N.Y. Hosp. Med. Ctr., N.Y.C., 1986-89; sr. editor humanities and social scis. coll. divsn. Prentice Hall, Upper Saddle River, N.J., 1989-96; profl. writer behavioral scis., 1996—. Co-author: (coll. textbook) Introduction to Theories of Personality, 1985, (book) The Agricultural Development Council: A History, 1989, (coll. textbook) Child Psychology: A Contemporary Viewpoint, 1999 6th edit., 2005; co-editor: The Life and Work of Arthur T. Mosher, 2001. Founder Help Our Neighbors Eat Yearround (H.O.N.E.Y.), Inc., N.Y.C., chmn., 1983-87, vol., 1987-99, newsletter editor, 1992-97; reader Recording for the Blind, N.Y.C., 1978-84; vol. Reach to Recovery program Am. Cancer Soc., Bergen County, N.J., 1990-96. Recipient Our Town Thanks You award, N.Y.C., 1984, Mayor's Vol. Svc. award, N.Y.C., 1986, Cert. of Appreciation for Community Svc. Manhattan Borough, 1986, Jefferson award Am. Ins. Pub. Svc., Washington, 1986. Home and Office: 9316 Bocina Ln # G Atascadero CA 93422 Personal E-mail: volwriter@mindspring.com.

LOCKE, WILLIAM, retired endocrinologist; b. Morden, Man., Can., Mar. 16, 1916; s. Corbet and Ruby Louise (Brown) L.; m. Katherine Elizabeth Acer Russell, Sept. 29, 1945 (dec.). MD, U. Man., Winnipeg, 1938; MS in Medicine, U. Minn., 1947. Diplomate Am. Bd. Internal Medicine. Intern Winnipeg (Man., Can.) Gen. Hosp., 1937-38; fellow in medicine Mayo Found., Rochester, Minn., 1938-40, 46-48; rsch. fellow Harvard U., Boston, 1948-50; staff Ochsner Clinic, New Orleans, 1950-2000, sr. cons., 1987-2000; clin. prof. medicine Tulane U., New Orleans, 1968-86, prof. emeritus, 1986—, ret., 2000. Sec. Alton Ochsner Med. Found., New Orleans, 1976—81; pres. med. staff Ochsner Found. Hosp., New Orleans, 1954—55, trustee, 1978—2003, councillor, 2003—, cons. in endocrinology, 1998—. Author, co-editor: Hypothalmus and Pituitary in Health and Disease, 1972; contbr. chpts. to books and articles to profl. jours. Lt. comdr. RCNVR, 1940-46. NIH grant, 1958-62. Fellow ACP; mem. Am. Diabetes Assn., Endocrine Soc., Sigma Xi. Republican. Episcopalian. Home: 150 Broadway St Apt 1104 New Orleans LA 70118-7612 Office: Ochsner Clinic 1514 Jefferson Hwy New Orleans LA 70121-2483 E-mail: wmlocke@bellsouth.net.

LOCKE LLOYD, JENNIFER C., elementary school educator, consultant; b. Chgo., Apr. 22, 1951; d. Aldridge and Dorothy Locke; m. Carlton (Tony) Carpenter, Sept. 21, 1976 (div. July 1978); children: Rachel C., Carleton Carpenter II; m. John Lloyd, July 1995; 1 child, Rachel. BA, Chgo. State U., 1974; MEd, Nat. Louis U., 2000. Art tchr. Chgo. Bd. Edn., 1975-98, primary sch. tchr., 1989—; pres. Arts n' Us Fine Gifts, Chgo., 1998—. Artists cons. Locke Lloyd Prodns., Chgo., 1995—; planner spl. events. Artist, face painter, body artist, sculptor; creator masks for plays; presenter folktales and drama sems. Mem. South Shore Art Coalition, 1995-2001, Coalition for Improvement of Edn. in south Shore, 2001. Tchr. Incentive grantee Oppenheimer Fund, 1985-87; equipment grantee Chgo. Bd. Edn. Cultural Arts Dept., 1997-99; grantee Chgo. Found. for Edn., 1989. E-mail: lockelloyd@aol.com.

LOCKETT, LANDON JOHNSON, retired linguist; b. Ft. Benning, Ga., May 22, 1929; s. Landon Johnson and Roberta Blye (Davies) Lockett; m. Carol Yvonne Ramsay, Aug. 11, 1990. BA, U. Tex., 1954, LLB, 1957, PhD, 1968; M in Comparative Law, So. Meth. U., 1959. Bar: Tex. Atty. Raymond M. Hill and Assocs., Houston, 1957-61; NDEA fellow U. Tex., Austin, 1962-65, instr. Portuguese, 1965-69, asst. prof. Portuguese lang. & linguistics, 1969-75; assoc. prof. linguistics Univ. Fed. Rio Grande North, Natal, Brazil, 1982-83, ret., 1983—. Vis. prof. linguistics Pontificia U. Cath. Rio Grande S., Porto Allegre, Brazil, 1970, U. Autonoma Guadalajara, Mexico, 1976—77, U. Fed. Rio Grande N., 1978—82; conservation rschr., adv. Author: O Uso do Infinitivo num Corpus de Portugues Coloquial Brasileiro, 1969; contbr. articles to profl. jours. Cadet U.s. Cadet Corps, 1948—50. Recipient Nancy Benedict Meml. award, Native Plant Soc. Tex., 1994, Pres.'s award for Rsch. and Writing, Sabal Mexicana Native Plant Soc. Tex., 2003. Mem.: Tex. State Hist. Assn. Achievements include discovery of wild population of Sabal mexicana palm trees 200 miles north of what was believed to be northern limit of range; led successful effort to protect, by creation of a 46 acre preserve, a unique population of Sabal palm trees of an as yet undetermined taxonomic status. Home: 3210 Stevenson Ave Austin TX 78703-2242 Office Phone: 512-476-1951. Personal E-mail: lockett@ev1.net.

LOCKETT, SANDRA ANITA JOHNSON BOKAMBA, librarian; b. Hutchinson, Kans., Nov. 18, 1946; d. Herbert Wales and Dorothy Bernice (Harrison) Johnson; children: Eyenga Marthe Bérénice Bokamba, Madeline Bernice. BS, U. Kans., 1968; MLS, U. Ind., 1973. Spl. assignments libr. Public Libr., Gary, Ind., 1973—74; libr. Alcott Br., Gary, 1974—76; asst. dir. pub. rels. and programming Pub. Libr., Gary, 1976—78, head extension svcs. and pub. rels., 1978—79; head govt. documents dept. U. Iowa Law Libr., Iowa City, 1979—84; br. mgr. Ctr. St. Libr. Milw. Pub. Libr., 1984—88, extension svcs. coord., 1988—91, asst. city libr., 1991—. Mem.: NAACP (sec 1980—81), ALA (Black Caucus), Wis. Black Librs. Network, Pub. Libr. Fundraising Assn. (mem. alternative edn. and IRS tax forms distbn. coms.), Wis. Libr. Assn., Iowa Libr. Assn. (vice chmn., chmn. elect govt. docs. divsn. 1980—83), Mid-Am. Law Libr. Assn., Am. Assn. Law Librs., The Links, Inc. (past pres. Milw. chpt.), Alpha Kappa Alpha (past pres. Upsilon Mu Omega chpt., past pres.). Democrat. Roman Catholic. Home: 7748 W Heather Ave Milwaukee WI 53223-2504 Office: Milwaukee Pub Library 814 W Wisconsin Ave Milwaukee WI 53233-2309 Office Phone: 414-286-3023.

LOCKETTE, DAPHNEY D., elementary school educator; b. N.Y.C., Sept. 30, 1973; BA, Va. State U., 1995; M in Elem. Edn., Fairleigh Dickinson U., 2001; postgrad. studies in instructional tech., Farleigh Dickinson U., Teaneck, N.J., 2001—; postgrad. in human svcs., 2003—. Technology coord. Americorps/Project First, N.Y.C., 1995—97; substitute tchr. Bergen County Bd. of Edn., Englewood, NJ, 1997; adminstrv. asst. Silver Palate, Cresskill, NJ, 1997; kindergarten tchr. My Friend's Day Sch., Teaneck, NJ, 1997—99; tchr. asst. First Grade Englewood on the Palisades Charter Sch., Englewood, NJ, 1999—. Tutor computer tech. and lang. arts Esteem Acad., Englewood. Author: Secrets from the Depths of My Soul, 2000, From Pain to Passion, 2003. Treas., Praise Ministries, 2000—. Mem. Alpha Kappa Alpha.

LOCKEY, RICHARD FUNK, allergist, immunologist, educator; b. Lancaster, Pa., Jan. 15, 1940; s. Stephen Daniel and Anna (Funk) L.; m. Carol Lee Madill, July 3, 1982; children: Brian Christopher, Keith Edward. BS, Haverford Coll., 1961; MD, Temple U., 1965; MS, U. Mich., 1972. Diplomate Am. Bd. Internal Medicine, Am. Bd. Allergy and Immunology. Intern Temple U. Med. Sch., Phila., 1965-66; asst. resident internal medicine Univ. Hosp. U. Mich., Ann Arbor, 1966-67, resident, 1966-68, fellow in allergy and immunology, 1969-70; asst. prof. medicine U. South Fla. Coll. Medicine, Tampa, 1973-77, assoc. prof. medicine, 1977-83, asst. dir. divsn. allergy and immunology, 1979-82, dir. allergy and immunology, 1982—, prof. medicine, 1983—, prof. pediat., 1983—, prof. pub. health, 1987—; asst. chief sect. allergy and immunology VA Hosp., Tampa, 1973-82, chief sect. allergy and immunology, 1983—, Joy McCann Culverhouse endowed chair allergy and immunology, 1997. Mem. allergenic adv. com. FDA, 1985-89. Editor: Allergy and Clinical Immunology, 1980; co-editor: (with S.C. Bukantz) Fundamentals of Immunology and Allergy, 1987, (with S.C. Bukantz) Principles of Immunology and Allergy, 1987, JAMA Primer on Allergic and Immunologic Diseases, 1987, (with S. C. Bukantz) Allergen Immunotherapy, 1991, (with M. Levine) Monograph on Insect Allergy, 1995, (with S. Bukantz) Allergens and Allergen Immunotherapy, 1999, (with D. Ledford) Immunotherapy: A Practical Review and Guide, 2000, (with S. Kemp) Diagnostic Testing of Allergic Disease, 2000, (with S. Bukantz) Allergens and Allergen Immunotherapy Allergic Diseases, 4th edit., 2004, (with M. Levine) Insect Allergy, 4th edit., 2004; mem. editl. bd. Jour. on Allergy and Immunology, 1999-04; contbr. more than 500 articles to profl. jours. and chpts. to books; author monographs. Hon. chmn. R.I. chpt. Asthma and Allergy Found., 2004. Served to maj. USAF, 1971-73. Named Outstanding Med. Specialist, Town and Country Mag., 1989, Claude P. Brown Meml. lectr. Assn. Clin. Scientists, ADA, 1981, Disting. Visitor Ann. Meeting of Coll. of Medicine, Republic of Costa Rica, 1979, spl. mem. Internat. Sci. Bd. Pharmacia Allergy Rsch. Found., 1992—; recipient Alumni Achievement award Temple U. Sch. of Medicine Alumni Assn., 1990, Outstanding Leadership in Chpt. Devel. and Patient Support, Nat. Asthma and Allergy Found. of Am. award, 1992, Cert. of Appreciation Fla. Med. Assn., 1992, medalist Fla. Acad. Scis., 2000, Disting. Svc. award Univ. S. Fla., 2001. Fellow ACP, AAAS, AMA, Am. Coll. Chest Physicians, Am. Acad. Allergy and Immunology (chmn. com. on insects 1978-81, chmn. undergrad. and grad. edn. com. 1982-88, com. on occupl. lung disease 1982—, chmn. com. on standardization of allergenic extracts 1983-86, exec. com. mem. at large 1986-88, historian 1988-89, sec. 1989-90, treas. 1990-91, pres.-elect 1991-92, pres. 1992-93, Am. Bd. Allergy and Immunology (bd. dirs. 1993-98), World Allergy Assn. (bd. dirs. 1997—), Internat. Assn. Allergology (clin. immunology bd. dirs.), Soc. Allergy and Immunology of Cordoba, Argentina (hon.), John M. Sheldon U. of Mich. Allergy Soc. (councilor 1977-80, pres. 1980-82), Fla. Allergy and Immunology Soc. (sec.-treas. 1979-80, pres. 1981-82, Disting. Svc. award 2002), Southeastern Allergy Assn., Hillsborough County Med. Assn., Joint Coun. Allergy and Immunology, Clin. Immunology Soc., Fla. Thoracic Soc., Univ. Club, Aliva Country Club, Tampa Yacht Club. Avocations: antique cut glass, antique tools, hunting, fishing. Home: 2708 W Marlin Ave Tampa FL 33611 Office: U So Fla VA Hosp #502 13801 Bruce B Downs Blvd Tampa FL 33613-3946

LOCKHART, CLAUDIA JO, adult education educator, department chairman; d. Roy Oscar and Helen Mary Eckberg; life ptnr. Charles William Houseman; 1 child, Jennifer Ann Buttram. BFA, U. Long Beach, 1967. Secondary Teaching Degree Dept. Edn. Calif., 1970. Educator, dept. chair Anaheim (Calif.) Sch. Dist., 1968—69, Inglewood (Calif.) Cmty. Adult Sch., 1971—. Grant writing certification L.A. Sch. Grant Writing, 1988—; staff devel. coord. Inglewood Cmty. Adult Sch., 1988—96, mem. chair steering com., 1997—99. Artist, cmty. coord. Art Impacts Day. Recipient Halo awards, Bd. Suprs. L.A., 1982—89. Independent. Achievements include development of principles of alphabet literacy program. Avocations: art, sailing, reading, house design, travel. Office: Inglewood Cmty Adult Sch Ste 350 106 E Manchester Blvd Inglewood CA 90301 Personal E-mail: cjlcwh@aol.com.

LOCKHART, GREGORY GORDON, prosecutor; b. Dayton, Ohio, Sept. 2, 1946; s. Lloyd Douglas and Evelyn (Gordon) L.; m. Paula Louise Jewett, May 20, 1978; children: David H., Sarah L. BS, Wright State U., 1973; JD, Ohio State U., 1976. Bar: Ohio 1976, U.S. Dist. Ct. (so. dist.) Ohio 1977, U.S. Ct. Appeals (6th cir.) 1988, U.S. Supreme Ct. 1993. Legal advisor Xenia and Fairborn (Ohio) Police Dept., 1977-78; asst. pros. atty. Greene County Prosecutor, Xenia, 1978-87; ptnr. DeWine & Schenck, Xenia, 1978-82, Schenck, Schmidt & Lockhart, Xenia, 1982-85, Ried & Lockhart, Beavercreek, Ohio, 1985-87; asst. U.S. atty. (so. dist.) OH US Dept. Justice, Columbus, 1987-2001, U.S. atty. (so. dist.) Ohio, 2001—. Adj. prof. Coll. Law U. Dayton, 1990—, Wright State U., Dayton, 1979—. Co-author: Federal Grand Jury Practice, 1996. Pres. Greene County Young reps., Xenia, 1977-79. With USAF, 1966-70; Vietnam. Mem. Fed. Bar Assn. (chpt. pres. 1994-95), Dayton Bar Assn., Kiwanis (pres. 1983-84, lt. gov. 1986-87), Jaycees (pres. 1976-79), Am. Inns of Ct. (master of bench emeritus). Methodist. Avocations: golf, tennis, hiking, camping. Office: US Attorney Federal Bldg 200 W 2d St Rm 602 Dayton OH 45402 Office Phone: 937-225-2910. E-mail: gregory.lockhart@usdoj.gov.

LOCKHART, JAMES BICKNELL, III, federal agency administrator; b. White Plains, N.Y., May 13, 1946; s. James Bicknell Jr. and Mary Ann (Riegel) L.; m. Carolyn Strahan Zoephel, June 17, 1972; children: James Bicknell IV, Grace Strahan. BA, Yale U., 1968; MBA, Harvard U., 1974. Asst. treas. Gulf Oil (E.H.), London, 1979-80; fin. dir. Gulf Oil Belgium, Brussels, 1980-81; sr. mgr. Gulf Oil Corp., Pitts., 1981-82, asst. treas., 1982-83; v.p., treas. Alexander and Alexander Services, N.Y.C., 1983-89; exec. dir. Pension Benefit Guaranty Corp., Washington, 1989-93; mng. dir., head pvt. fin. group Smith Barney, Inc., N.Y.C., 1993-95; sr. v.p. fin. Nat. Reins. Corp., 1996; mng. dir., CFO NetRisk, Greenwich, Conn., 1997—2001; dep. commr., COO Social Security Adminstrn., Washington, Balt., 2002—. Contbr. articles to profl. jours. Served to lt. (j.g.) USNR, 1969-72. Fellow Assn. Corp. Treas. (Eng.); mem. Assn. Pvt. Pension and Welfare Plans (bd. dirs. 1993-95). Office: Social Security Admin 500 E St SW Washington DC 20254

LOCKHART, JOHN MALLERY, management consultant; b. Mellen, Wis., May 17, 1911; s. Carl Wright and Gladys (Gale) L.; m. Judith Anne Wood, Feb. 26, 1938 (dec. June 1991); children: Wood Alexander, Gale, Thomas. BS, Northwestern U., 1931; JD, IIT, 1938. CPA, Ill. Teaching fellow Northwestern U., 1931; asst. v.p. Welsh, Davis & Co. (investment bankers), Chgo., 1935-41; treas. Transcontinental & Western Air, Inc., Kansas City, Mo., 1941-47; exec. v.p., CEO TACA Airways, S.A., 1944-45; v.p., dir. The Kroger Co., 1947-71, exec. v.p., 1961-71; pres. Kroger Family Ctr. Stores, 1969-71, Lockhart Co. (mgmt. cons.), 1971—; v.p. corp. fin. Gradison & Co., 1973-86. Chmn. bd. dirs., CEO Ohio Real Estate Investment Co., Ohio Real Estate Equity Corp., 1974-76; bd. dirs. Employers Mut. Cos., Des Moines, Witt Co.; chmn. bd. dirs. Autotronics Systems, Inc., 1976-78; bd. dirs. Vectra Internat., Inc., Hamilton Mut. Ins. Co. Chmn. Hamilton County Hosp. Commn., 1965-84; mem. adv. bd. Greater Cin. Airport, 1961-86. Mem. Comml. Club, Cin. Country Club, Conquistadores del Cielo Club. Home and Office: 2770 Walsh Rd Cincinnati OH 45208-3425

LOCKHART, KEITH ALAN, conductor, musician, teacher; b. Poughkeepsie, NY, Nov. 7, 1959; s. Newton Frederick and Marilyn Jean (Woodyard) Lockhart. BA summa cum laude in German, MusB summa cum laude Piano Performance, Furman U., 1981; MFA in Orch. Conducting, Carnegie-Mellon U., 1983; D, Boston Conservatory, 1996; D (hon.), Northeastern U., 1998, Furman U., 2000; Doctorate (hon.), Boston Conservatory. Mem. condrs. faculty Carnegie-Mellon U., 1983-89; music dir. Pitts. Civic Orch., 1987-90; asst. condr. Akron Symphony Orch., 1988-90, Cin. Symphony Orch., Cin. Pops Orch., 1990-92, assoc. condr., 1992-95; music dir. Cin. Chamber Orch., 1992-99, Boston Pops Orch., 1995—, Utah Symphony Orch., 1998—. Guest condr. Chgo. Symphony Orch., Cleve. Orch., L.A. Philharm., L.A. Chamber Orch., Toronto Symphony, Mont. Symphony Orch., Indpls. Symphony, N.Y. Philharm., Phila. Orch., Houston Symphony, Milw. Symphony, Dallas Symphony, Orch. Sinfonica de Tucuman, Argentina, New Japan Philharm.; mem. adv. bd. Music Educators Nat. Conf.; pres. nat. adv. bd. Brevard Music Ctr., 1996—. Co-editor (arranger performance edit. opera): John Gay: The Beggar's Opera, 1985. Mem.: Condr.'s Guild Am., Symphony Orch. League, Am. Fedn. Musicians. Avocations: reading, cooking, skiing, racquetball, outdoor sports. Office: The Boston Pops Orchestra 301 Massachusetts Ave Symphony Hall Boston MA 02115 E-mail: klockhart@bso.org.*

LOCKHART, MADGE CLEMENTS, educational organization executive; b. Soddy, Tenn., May 22, 1920; d. James Arlie and Ollie (Sparks) Clements; m. Andre J. Lockhart, Apr. 24, 1942 (div. 1973); children: Jacqueline, Andrew, Janice, Jill. Student, East Tenn. U., 1938-39; BS, U. Tenn., Chattanooga and Knoxville, 1955, MEd, 1962. Elem. tchr. Tenn. and Ga., 1947-60, Brainerd H.S., Chattanooga, 1960-64, Cleveland (Tenn.) City Schs., 1966-88; owner, operator Lockhart's Learning Ctr., Inc., Cleveland and Chattanooga, 1966-2003; co-founder, pres. Hermes, Inc., 1973-79; co-founder Dawn Ctr., Hamilton County, Tenn., 1974; apptd. mem. Tenn. Gov.'s Acad. for Writers. Author numerous poems, short stories; contbr. articles to profl. jours. and newspapers. Pres. Cleveland Assn. Retarded Citizens, 1970, state v.p., 1976; pres. Cherokee Easter Seal Soc., 1973-76, Cleveland Creative Arts Guild, 1980; bd. dirs. Tenn. Easter Seal Soc., 1974-77, 80-83; chair Bradley County Internat. Yr. of Child; mem. panel for grants Coun. Govts. S.E. Tenn. Devel. Dist., 1990-92; mem. Internat. Biog. Centre Adv. Coun., Cambridge, Eng., 1991-92; mayor's com. Mus. for Bradley County, Tenn., 1992—. Recipient Service to Mankind award Sertoma, 1978, Gov.'s award for service to handicapped, 1979; mental health home named in her honor, Tenn., 1987. Mem. NEA (life), Tenn. Edn. Assn., Am. Assn. Rehab. Therapy, S.E. Tenn. Arts Coun., Cleveland Edn. Assn. (Service to Humanity award 1987). Mem. Ch. of Christ. Clubs: Byliners, Fantastiks. Home: 3007 Oakland Dr NW Cleveland TN 37312-5281 Office Phone: 423-476-3066.

LOCKHART, MICHAEL D., manufacturing executive; b. Muncie, Ind., Mar. 25, 1949; s. Roy Eugene and Marjorie Ilene (Thornburg) L.; children: Jennifer, Jessica, Kathleen Coleman. MBA, U. Chgo., 1975. Systems analyst Needham Harper & Steers, Chgo., 1969-74; v.p. Boston Consulting Group, 1975-81, GE Credit Corp., 1981-83, GE Corp. Exec. Office, Fairfield, Conn., 1984-85, GE Turbine Bus. Ops., Schenectady, NY, 1985-87, GE Aircraft Engines, Cin., 1987-88, GE Transp. Systems, Erie, Pa., 1989-91; v.p., gen.

mgr. GE Aircraft Engines, Cin., 1992-94; pres. Gen. Signal Corp., Stamford, Conn., 1994-99, chmn., CEO, Armstrong Holdings Inc., Lancaster, Pa., 2000—. Mem. Beta Gamma Sigma. Office: 2500 Columbia Ave Lancaster PA 17603-4117

LOCKHART, SHARON, artist; b. Norwood, Mass., 1964; MFA, Art Ctr. Coll. Design, Pasadena, Calif. One-woman shows include Art Ctr., Pasadena, 1994, Neugerriemschneider, Berlin, 1994, 1996, Friedrich Petzel Gallery, N.Y., 1994, 1996, 1998, Kunstlerhaus Stuttgart, Germany, 1995, Blum and Poe, Santa Monica, 1996, 1998, John Spotten Cinema, Toronto, 1997, S.L. Simpson Gallery, 1997, Cinema Paris, Berlin, 1997, Pacific Film Archive, Berkeley Art Mus., 1997, Wako Works Art, Tokyo, 1998, Brit. Coun. Cinema, Daniel Buckholz Gallery, Cologne, 1998, Mus. Contemporary Art, Tokyo, 1998, L.A., 1998, Galerie Yvon Lambert, Paris, 1998, Kemper Mus. Contemporary Art, Kansas City, Mo., 1998, exhibited in group shows at Bliss House, Pasadena, 1992, Merz Acad., Stuttgart, 1993, Margo Leavin Gallery, L.A., 1994, Galerie Paul Andriesse, Amsterdam, 1995, Studio Guenzani, Milan, Italy, 1996, L.A. County Mus. Art, 1996—97, Armand Hammer Mus. Art, L.A., 1997, Le Magasin, Grenoble, 1998, Inst. Contemporary Arts, London, 1998, Mus. Modern Art and the Film Soc. Lincoln Ctr., N.Y., 1998, Fondazione Sandretto Re Rebaudengo, Torino, Italy, 1998, Torino, 2001, Stedelijk Van Abbemuseum, Eindhoven, 1999, Neugerriemschneider, Berlin, 1999, Galerie für Zeitgenossische Kunst Leipzig, 1999, Art Gallery Ont., Toronto, 2000, Chac Mool Gallery, L.A., 2001, MCA Chgo., 2001, 2003, Galerie Volker Diehl, Berlin, 2001, Mus. für Neue Kunst, Karlsruhe, Germany, 2003, Barbara Gladstone Gallery, N.Y.C., 2003, Vedanta Gallery, Chgo., 2003, Whitney Biennial, Whitney Mus. Am. Art, 2004, ICA Boston, 2004, Represented in permanent collections Boijmans van Beuningen Mus., Rotterdam, Eli Broad Family Found., Santa Monica, Calif., L.A. County Mus., MCA Chgo., Yokohama (Japan) Mus. Art, Henry Art Gallery, Seattle, Fondazione Sandretto Re Rebaudengo, Torino, Italy, Mus. Contemporary Art, San Diego, L.A., Whitney Mus. Am. Art, N.Y., Albright-Knox Gallery, Buffalo, The Israel Mus., Jerusalem, St. Louis Art Mus., Mus. Contemporary Art, Chgo., Walker Art Ctr., Mpls., Worcester (Mass.) Art Mus. Film/Video/Multimedia fellow, Rockefeller Found., 2000, Film Making fellow, John Simon Guggenheim Meml. Found., 2001. Fax: 212-431-6638.*

LOCKHEAD, GREGORY ROGER, psychology professor; b. Boston, Aug. 8, 1931; s. John Roger and Ester Mae (Bixby) L.; m. Jeanne Marie Hutchinson, June 9, 1957; children: Diane, Elaine, John. BS, Tufts U., 1958; PhD, Johns Hopkins, 1965. Psychologist rsch. staff IBM Research, Yorktown Heights, N.Y., 1958-61; rsch. assoc., instr. Johns Hopkins U., Balt., 1961-65; asst. prof. psychology Duke U., Durham, N.C., 1965-68, assoc. prof., 1968-71, prof., 1971-2001, chmn. dept. exptl. psychology, 1991-97, prof. dept. psychol. and brain scis., 2001—. Scholar Stanford U.; rsch. assoc. U. Calif., Berkeley, 1971-72; fellow Wolfson Coll., Oxford (Eng.) U., 1980-81; scholar Fla. Atlantic U., 1981; cons. in human engring. Cons. editor: Perception and Psychophysics, 1972-92; contbr. articles to profl. jours., co-author, editor chpts. in books. With USN, 1951-55. NSF grantee, 1966-69, 79-84, USPHS grantee, 1963-69, 70-79, Air Force Office Sci. Rsch., 1983-91. Fellow APA, Am. Psychol. Soc., Soc. Exptl. Psychologists; mem. Psychonomic Soc., Internat. Soc. Psychophysics, Sigma Xi, Phi Beta Kappa (hon.). Home: 2900 Montgomery St Durham NC 27705-5638 Office: Duke U Dept Psychology and Brain Scis Durham NC 27708

LOCKLEAR, ARLINDA FAYE, lawyer; b. Ft. Bragg, N.C., Sept. 9, 1951; d. Edsel Locklear and Mary Elizabeth (Revels) Joyce; m. Gilbert Leon Hall, June 12, 1983; children, Garret & Rachel. BA, Coll. of Charleston, 1973; JD, Duke U., 1976; DHL (hon.), SUNY, 1990. Bar: N.C. 1976, D.C. 1978, Md., U.S. Supreme Ct. 1982. Staff atty. Native Am. Rights Fund, Boulder, Colo., 1976-77, Washington, 1977—87; atty., private practice Jefferson, Md., 1987—; of counsel, Native Am. Affairs, Public Policy practices Patton Boggs LLP, Washington. Guest lectr. Harvard Inst. Politics, Boston, 1983, NYU Law Sch., 1986, Colgate U., Hamilton, N.Y., 1986. Contbr. articles to profl. jours. Bd. dirs. ACLU, N.Y.C., 1984-88; Inst. for Development of Indian Law; trustee Univ. N.C. Pembroke; mem. bd. adv. Ency. of Native Am. in the 20th Century; mem. adv. panel, Winds of Change (PBS series); mem. Lumbee tribe, Cheraw Indians. Recipient Am. Heroine award Ladies Home Jour., 1984; named one of Young Women of Promise Good Housekeeping Mag., 1985; Outstanding Woman of Color award, Nat. Inst. for Women of Color, 1987; Julian T. Pierce award, Pembroke State Univ. 1994; Carpathian Award for Speaking Out, N.C. Equity, 1995. Democrat. Office: Patton Boggs LLP 2550 M St NW Washington DC 20037-1350 Office Fax: 202-457-6000, 202-457-6315. Business E-Mail: alocklear@pattonboggs.com.

LOCKLEAR, HEATHER, actress; b. Westwood, Calif., Sept. 25, 1961; d. Bill and Diane L.; m. Tommy Lee, May 10, 1986 (div. Aug. 16, 1993); m. Richie Sambora, Dec. 17, 1994, 1 child, Eva Elizabeth. Student, UCLA. Appeared in (TV series) Dynasty, 1981-89, T.J. Hooker, 1982-87, Going Places, 1990, Melrose Place, 1993-99, Spin City, 1999-2002, LAX, 2004; (films) Firestarter, 1986, Return of the Swamp Thing, 1990, The Big Slice, 1991, Wayne's World 2, 1993, A Dangerous Woman, 1993, The First Wives Club, 1996, Double Tap, 1997, Money Talks, 1997, Uptown Girls, 2003, Looney Toons: Back in Action, 2003, The Perfect Man, 2005; (TV movies) Twil, 1981, City Killer, 1984, Blood Sport, 1986, Rock 'n' Roll Mom, 1988, Rich Men, Single Women, 1990, Her Wicked Ways, 1991, Dynasty: The Reunion, 1991, Highway Heartbreaker, 1992, Body Language, 1992, Fade to Black, 1993, Texas Justice, 1995, Shattered Mind, 1996, Too Many Lovers, 2003, Once Around the Park, 2003.*

LOCKLEDGE, JACK E., retired principal; b. West Pittston, Pa., Oct. 6, 1928; s. Louis Frank Lockledge and Edna Mae Curnow; m. Mary Anne Potter, Aug. 10, 1957 (div. June 1984); children: David Evans, Jeffrey Carleton, Scott Potter. BA in Psychology, U. Ariz., 1954; BA in Fgn. Trade, Am. Inst. Fgn. Trade, 1955; MS in Edn., Hofstra U., 1960; student, Lehigh U., 1962-63; EdD, Nova U., 1982. Fgn. trade salesperson E.I. Dupont de Nemours, Wilmington, Del., 1955-56; tchr. Porterville (Calif.) Union H.S., 1956-57, Newbridge Rd. Sch., East Meadow, N.Y., 1958-61, Linden Sch., Doylestown, Pa., 1961-62, Hancock Elem. Sch., Norristown, Pa., 1962-63; prin. Ichabod Crane Ctrl. Schs., Kinderhook, N.Y., 1963-65, Highland (N.Y.) Ctrl. Sch., 1965-67, Canton (Pa.) Area Sch. Dist., 1967-86; headmaster St. Andrew's Elem. and Middle Sch., Annapolis, Md., 1986-91; ret., 1992. Founder Open Space Sch., 1968; bd. dirs. Land Hollow Cmty. Assn., 2005. With USN, 1946-49. NDEA Inst. Fgn. Langs. scholar Pa. State U., U. Kans., 1962, 63. Mem. Md. Child Care Assn. (legis. com.), Wyo. Camp Meeting Assn., Masons, Rotary (past pres.), Venice Opera Guild (grant officer), Lambda chpt. Phi Delta Epsilon (past pres.), Gamma Epsilon, Kappa Alpha (past pres.). Republican. Episcopalian. Avocations: hiking, swimming, opera, furniture refurbishing, painting and sculpting. Home: 225 Laurel Hollow Dr Nokomis FL 34275-4014 Personal E-mail: jlockledge@aol.com. E-mail: jack@lockledge.com.

LOCKLIN, GERALD, language educator, poet, writer; b. Rochester, NY, Feb. 17, 1941; s. Ivan and Esther Locklin. BA, St. John Fisher Coll., 1961; MA, U. Ariz., 1963, PhD, 1964. Instr. Calif. State U., L.A., 1964-65, prof. English Long Beach, 1965—. Author: Down and Out, 1999, Go West, Young Toad: Selected Writings, 1999, A Simpler Time A Simpler Place: Three Mid-Century Stories, 2000, Candy Bars: Selected Stories, 2000, The Life Force Poems, 2002, The Pocket Book: A Novella and Nineteen Short Fictions, 2003; (novella) The Case of the Missing Blue Volkswagen, 1984; (short stories) The Gold Rush, 1989; co-editor: A New Geography of Poets, 1992; featured in The Oxford Companion to Twentieth Century Literature in English, 1996; author numerous poems, short stories Mem.: Western Lit. Assn., Assoc. Writing Programs, Hemingway Soc., E.E. Cummings Soc., PEN USA/West. Avocations: swimming, jazz, travel, yankees, lakers. Office: Calif State U English Dept Long Beach CA 90840-0001 Office Phone: 562-985-5285. Business E-Mail: glocklin@csulb.edu.

LOCKLIN, WILBERT EDWIN, management consultant; b. Washington, Apr. 2, 1920; s. Wilbert Edwin and Margaret Mae (Franklin) L.; m. Olga Maria Osterwald, June 28, 1947; children: Kenneth, Patricia, Randall. BS, Johns Hopkins U., 1942; LLD, George Williams Coll., 1966; DHum, Springfield Coll., 1994. Vice-pres. Nat. Bur. Pvt. Schs., N.Y.C., 1947-49; account exec. Reuel Estill & Co., N.Y.C., 1949-51; asst. dir. admissions Johns Hopkins, 1945-47, asst. to pres., 1955-65; v.p. Johns Hopkins Fund, 1960-65; pres. Springfield (Mass.) Coll., 1965-85, Locklin Mgmt. Services, 1985—. Chmn. bd. dirs., mem. exec. com., salary com., charitable funds com.; chmn. trust com. Bay Bank Valley Trust Co., 1966-91; mem. exec. com. Assn. Ind. Colls. and Univs. in Mass., 1971-83; founding mem. Cooperating Colls. of Greater Springfield.; pres. Cooperating Colls. of Greater Springfield, 1982-83; mem. exec. com., bd. dirs. Business Friends of Arts. Bd. dirs. Springfield Symphony Orch., 1973-83; campaign dir. Elms Coll., 1992-94; sr. advisor Mass. Soc. for Prevention of Cruelty to Animals, 1995-99, Loomis Communities, 1998—. Served with USAAF, 1942-45. Decorated DFC, Air medal. Home: 2400 S Ocean Dr Apt 7242 Fort Pierce FL 34949-8082 Home (Summer): 150 White Birch Ln Hinsdale MA 01235-0445

LOCKMAN, STUART M., lawyer; b. Jersey City, July 18, 1949; s. Albert Korey and Edna Sally (Easton) Lockman; m. Deena Laurel Young, Dec. 27, 1970; children: Jeffrey, Alison Susan, Stephen, Karen. BA, U. Mich., 1971, JD, 1974. Bar: Mich. 1974, Fla. 1991; bd. cert. health law specialist, Fla. Ptnr. Honigman Miller Schwartz and Cohn LLP, Detroit, 1974—. Office: Honigman Miller Schwartz & Cohn 2290 1st National Bldg Detroit MI 48226 Office Phone: 313-465-7500. E-mail: sml@honigman.com.

LOCKNER, VERA JOANNE, farmer, rancher, state legislator; b. St. Lawrence, S.D., May 19, 1937; d. Leonard and Zona R. (Ford) Verdugt; m. Frank O. Lockner, Aug. 7, 1955; children: Dean M., Clifford A. Grad., St. Lawrence (S.D.) High Sch., 1955. Bank teller/bookkeeper First Nat. Bank, Miller, SD, 1963-66, Bank of Wessington, SD, 1968-74; farmer/rancher Wessington, 1955-2000. Sunday sch. tchr. Trinity Luth. Ch., Miller, 1968-72; treas. Trinity Luth. Ch. Women, 2005—; treas. PTO, Wessington, 1969-70; treas., vice chmn., chmn., state com. woman Hand County Dems., Miller, 1978-2003, SD state legislator, 1992-2000; mem. S.D. Eem. Exec. Bd., 1997-2000. Named one of Outstanding Young Women of Am., Women's Study Club, Wessington, 1970. Mem. Order of Ea. Star (warder, marshall, chaplain 1970-2002). Democrat. Avocations: painting, crafts, gardening, photography. Home and Office: 301 3rd St NW Saint Lawrence SD 57373-2324

LOCKSHIN, MICHAEL DAN, rheumatologist; b. Columbus, Ohio, Dec. 9, 1937; s. Samuel Dan and Florence (Levin) L.; m. Jane Toby Roberts, Sept. 2, 1965; 1 child, Amanda. AB, Harvard U., 1959, MD, 1963. Diplomate Am. Bd. Internal Medicine. From asst. prof. to prof. Cornell U. Med. Coll., N.Y.C., 1970-89; attending physician Hosp. for Spl. Surgery and N.Y. Hosp., N.Y.C., 1970-89; dir. extramural program Nat. Inst. Arthritis & Musculoskeletal Skin Diseases/NIH, Bethesda, Md., 1989-97, acting dir., 1994-95; dir. Barbara Volcker Ctr. Hosp. for Spl. Surgery, N.Y.C., 1997—. Prof. Cornell U. Med. Coll., N.Y.C., 1997—. Editor: Arthritis & Rheumatism, 2005-; contbr. over 150 articles to jours., chpts. to books. Mem. Am. Rheumatism Assn. (2d v.p. 1984-85), La Sociedad Chilena de Reumatologica (hon.), Alpha Omega Alpha. Office: 535 E 70th St New York NY 10021-4872 Office Phone: 212-606-1461. Business E-Mail: volckerctr@hss.edu.

LOCKTON, DAVID BALLARD, entrepreneur, information technology executive; b. Indpls, Mar. 28, 1937; s. Richard Curtis and Violet (Ballard) L.; m. Mary Shullenberger, Aug. 1961 (div. Dec. 1969); children: Jennifer Anne Barker, Mary Wendell Marshall; m. Kathy Austin, Apr. 3, 1971; 1 child, Richard A. BA, Yale U., 1959; JD, U. Va., 1962; postgrad. in Bus., Stanford U., 1972. Ptnr. Lockton and Scopelitis, Inc., Indpls., 1965-70; founder, pres., chief exec. officer Ontario Motor Speedway, Calif., 1968-71; chief exec. off., publisher, owner Calif. Bus. Mag., LA, 1972-75; pres., chief exec. officer Lola Grand Prix, Ltd., LA, 1976-79; founder, chief exec. officer Data Broadcasting, Inc., San Mateo, Calif., 1980-85; chmn., founder, CEO Interactive Network, Inc., 1986-99; pres. Lockton Ventures, 1996—; founder AirPlay Network, Inc., 2004—. Co-founder, bd. dir. A.Z.L. Resources, Inc., 1964-75; creator, developer Internat. Race of Champions TV Racing Series, 1972—, co-founder, chmn. Repair Shop Systems, Inc., 1986; lectr. on entrepreneurship and info. tech. Patentee in interactive TV and wireless data. Dir. U.S. Auto Club, 1967-70; mem. bud. adv. coun. U. Va. Law Sch., 1997—. Recipient Meritorious Svc. award Soc. Automotive Engr., 1970. Mem. Crooked Stick Golf Club (co-founder) (Indpls.), Carmel Valley Ranch, Penrod Soc. (co-founder, Indpls.). Republican. Episcopalian. Avocations: jazz organ, golf. Office: Lockton Ventures Suite 389 225 Cross Roads Blvd Carmel CA 93923-8649 Office Phone: 831-620-5800. E-mail: dlockton@aol.com.

LOCKWOOD, BERT BERKLEY, JR., law educator; b. Utica, N.Y., Feb. 12, 1944; s. Bert Berkley and Mildred (Dowling) L.; m. Lynn Grigoli, Dec. 23, 1979; children: Matthew, Dylan, Courtney, Meredith. BA, St. Lawrence U., 1966; JD, Syracuse U., 1969; LLM, U. Va., 1971. Bar: Ohio 1981. Exec. dir. Procedural Aspects of Internat. Law Inst., N.Y.C., 1980-89; asst. dir., sr. fellow Ctr. for Internat. Studies NYU, N.Y.C., 1971-74; program dir. World Peace Through Law Ctr., Washington, 1974-76; assoc. dean Am. U. Law Sch., Washington, 1976-79; assoc. prof. U. Cin. Law Sch., 1979-86, prof., 1986—, dir. Urban Morgan Inst. for Human Rights, 1979—; vis. scholar U. Essex, Colchester, U.K., 1994. Adv. bd. Internat. Human Rights Law Group, Washington, 1978—, Can. Found. on Human Rights, Montreal, Quebec, Can., 1984—. Editor in chief Human Rights Quar., 1982—, Amnesty Internat. USA Legal Support Network Newsletter, 1990-93; series editor Pennsylvania Studies in Human Rights, 1988—. Coord. Group 86 Amnesty Internat., Cin., 1984—; adv. bd. Diana Project, 1994—. Recipient Sol Feinstein Alumni award St. Lawrence U., 1990; honoree Cin. chpt. ACLU, 1991. Mem. ABA, Cin. Bar Assn., Am. Soc. Mag. Editors, Internat. Law Assn. (human rights com. 1982—). Office: U Cincinnati Coll of Law Urban Morgan Institute PO Box 210040 Cincinnati OH 45221-0040

LOCKWOOD, CHRIS A., business educator, consultant; b. Hollywood, Calif., Sept. 17, 1946; s. Glenn LaVerne Lockwood and B. Ernestine (Ivy) Harris; m. Christina Elizabeth Bishop, Oct. 8, 1965 (div. Apr. 1970); children: Brenda, Tristan, Kerri; m. Elaine Kay Judeman, Aug. 26, 1972 (div. July 1981); one child, John; m. Faye Ann Pluhar, Jan. 3, 1985; children: Ryan, Wendy, Anthony. B in Gen. Studies, Chaminade U., 1980; MBA, Ariz. State U., 1982, PhD, 1991. With USN, 1964-80; mem. faculty, dir. MBA program No. Ariz. U., Flagstaff, 1987—. Contbr. articles to profl. jours.; co-author (with Carla C. Carter): Making Measurement Work, 2000. Judge Ariz. Gov.'s award for Quality, 1996—; cons., bd. dirs. The Guidance Ctr., Ariz., 1995-96. Mem. Acad. Mgmt., Am. Soc. Quality, Decision Scis. Inst. Avocation: computer technology. Home: 1622 W Natal Ave Mesa AZ 85202-7436 Office: No Ariz U Flagstaff AZ 86011

LOCKWOOD, FRANK STEPHEN, real estate investor, venture capitalist; b. Washington, Feb. 11, 1943; s. Fred Stark and Helen (Day) L.; m. Linda Pickhardt, June 25, 1966; children: Amy Helen, Rebecca Elizabeth. BS, Ripon Coll., 1965; MBA, Emory U., 1969. Registered rep. Smith Barney, Chgo., 1969-74; v.p. Blunt, Ellis & Loewi, Barrington, Ill., 1974-78; pres. Barrington Trading, 1978-83, Thermal Services, Barrington, 1984—, FSL Enterprises Inc., Barrington, 1983—. Bd. dirs., chief fin. officer, sec. Patriot Health Cos., Inc., Barrington; treas., sec. Patriot Life Ins. Co., Tampa, Fla., Modern Pioneers Life Ins. Co., Phoenix, Sharp Concepts, Inc., Barrington; pres. Lockwood Group, Inc., Barrington; ptnr. Corporetum Towers Ltd. Ptnrship., Lisle, Ill., 1985—. Served to 1st lt. U.S. Army, 1965-67. Mem.: Union League (Chgo.). Republican. Office: Lockwood Group Inc PO Box 450 Barrington IL 60011-0450

LOCKWOOD, GARY LEE, lawyer; b. Woodstock, Ill., Dec. 3, 1946; s. Howard and Luella Mae (Behrens) L.; m. Cheryl Lynn Wittrock, Jan. 5, 1967; children: Jennifer, Lee, Cynthia. BA magna cum laude, Iowa Wesleyan Coll., 1969; student, Albert Ludwig U., Freiburg in Breisgau, Fed. Republic Germany, 1968-69; JD, Northwestern U., 1976. Bar: Ill. 1976, U.S. Dist. Ct. (no. dist.) Ill. 1976, U.S. Ct. Appeals (7th cir.) 2000, U.S. Ct. Appeals (9th cir.) 2002. Assoc. Lord, Bissell & Brook, Chgo., 1976-85, ptnr., 1985—2005; ptnr., founder Walker, Wilcox, Matousek LLP, 2005—. Bd. dirs. McHenry Sch. Dist. 15, Ill., 1974-85, pres., 1979-80. Served to sgt. U.S. Army, 1970-72. Mem. ABA (bus. and ins. com. 1985—). Methodist. Avocation: sports. Home: 333 N Canal St Chicago IL 60606 Office: Walker Wilcox Matousek LLP 225 West Washington St Ste 2400 Chicago IL 60606 Office Phone: 313-244-6701. Business E-Mail: glockwood@wwmlawyers.com.

LOCKWOOD, HELSHI, advertising executive; b. East Orange, NJ, May 18, 1941; d. Warren Sewell and Ann Frances (Gleason) L.; m. Bertram A. Tunnell Jr., Dec. 13, 1969 (div. Oct. 1976); children: Bertram A. III, Tory Lockwood; stepchildren: John, Mark, Tracy, Wendy, Jan, Kate; m. William B. Hewson Jr., May 30, 1981; 1 child, Charles W.; stepchildren: William B. III, Andrew L., Elizabeth S. BA, Pa. State U., 1963. Promotion asst. Vogue Mag., London, 1963-64; advt. sales rep. Brides Mag., London, 1964-65; west coast mgr. Status Mag., L.A., 1965-67, asst. advt. mgr. N.Y.C., 1968-69; advt. sales rep. Eye Mag., N.Y.C., 1967-68; N.Y. mgr. Phil. and Boston Mags., N.Y.C., 1969-76; v.p. Metro Mag., N.Y.C., 1976-78; exec. v.p., ptnr. Catalyst Communications, N.Y.C., 1978-80; account mgr. Dun's Rev., N.Y.C., 1980-82; ea. advt. dir. Dun's Bus. Month, N.Y.C., 1982-84, advt. dir., 1984-85; dir. nat. accounts Chgo. Mag., N.Y.C., 1986; from ea. advt. mgr. to v.p., mng. dir. Mediatex Nat. Sales, N.Y.C., 1987—98; pres. Emmis Pub. Nat. Sales (acquired by Emmis Comm.), NYC, 1998—2003; assoc. mag. pub. Atlanta Mag. Emmis Comm., Atlanta, 2003—, assoc. mag. pub. LA Mag. LA, 2003—. Deacon Brick Ch., N.Y.C., 1983. Mem. Advt. Women N.Y. Republican. Presbyterian. Home: 8 Hanson Rd Darien CT 06820-2502 Office: Emmis Publ 60 E 42d St Ste 1103 New York NY 10165 Office Phone: 212-986-7647. E-mail: hlockwood@emmis.com.

LOCKWOOD, PAUL TIMOTHY, actor, writer, film director; b. Joliet, Ill., Jan. 23, 1959; s. Doris and Ronald George Lockwood. BA in Journalism, Comm., U. St. Francis, 1981; MFA in Creative Writing, Sarah Lawrence Coll., 2000. Dir. mktg. York Group, Pitts., 2002—03; dir. comm. Adam Filippo & Assoc., Pitts., 2000—01; events coord. Ohio State U. Sch. Music, 2004—. Pres. Worthington Civic Theatre, 2005—; v.p. First UU Interweave, 2005—. Author: (novels) A Hill Without Reason, (screenplays) The Quiet Storm (Sundance Screenwriting Semifinalist, 1999), Soul Searchers; musician: (albums) Positive (#1 Single & Album, Nat. Gay & Lesbian Music Charts, 2000); author: (plays) Running From Paramus. Pres. Worthington Civic Theater Bd., 2005—; comm. chair Friendship Preservation Group, Pitts., 2001—03. Mem.: Guild of Italian Am. Actors, Nat. Trust for Hist. Preservation. Office Phone: 614-262-0707. Personal E-mail: enzowalker@aol.com.

LOCKWOOD, ROBERT W., management consultant; b. Boise, Idaho, June 11, 1924; s. Walter Thomas and Elizabeth C. (Chamberlain) L.; m. Lois M. Minely, Feb. 19, 1945; children— Linda Kay Lockwood Johnson, Craig H. BS, U. Calif., Berkeley, 1949, MBA, 1950; LL.D. (hon.), Northrop U., 1971. Civilian chief mgmt. Los Angeles procurement dist. U.S. Army, 1955-56; cons. Booz Allen and Hamilton, Los Angeles, 1956-58; v.p. United Calif. Bank, Los Angeles, 1958-75; v.p. acad. affairs Northrop U., 1975-76; asst. to pres. Bradston Hurricane, 1979-80; pres. Diversified Baby Products Internat., West Covina, Calif., 1980—. Grad. prof. mgmt. Northrop U., Nat. U., San Diego. Served to 1st lt. USAR, 1942-45. Fellow Am. Inst. Indsl. Engrs. (pres. 1971-72) Clubs: Masons.

LOCKWOOD, THEODORE DAVIDGE, retired academic administrator; b. Hanover, N.H., Dec. 5, 1924; s. Harold John and Elizabeth (Van Campen) L.; m. Elizabeth Anne White, Apr. 13, 1944 (dec. Feb. 1980); children: Tamara Jane Lockwood Quinn, Richard Davidge, Mavis Ferens Borak, Serena Katherine; m. Lucille LaRose Abbot, Sept. 7, 1980. BA, Trinity Coll., 1948, LittD (hon.), 1981; MA, Princeton, 1950, PhD, 1952; LHD, Concord Coll., 1968; LLD, Union Coll., 1968, U. Hartford, 1969; LHD, Wesleyan U., Middletown, Conn., 1970. Instr. great issues Dartmouth, 1952-53; asst. prof. history Juniata Coll., Huntingdon, Pa., 1953-55, MIT, 1955-60; dean faculty Concord Coll., Athens, W.Va., 1960-64; provost, dean faculty Union Coll., Schenectady, 1964-68; pres. Trinity Coll., Hartford, Conn., 1968-81, Armand Hammer United World Coll. of Am. West, Montezuma, N.Mex., 1981-93. Chmn. Greater Hartford Consortium for Higher Edn., 1972-81. Author: Mountaineers, 1945, Studies in European Socialism, 1960, Our Mutual Concern: The Role of the Independent College, 1968, Dreams and Promises: The Story of the Armand Hammer United World College, 1997. Bd. dirs. Vols. Internat. Tech. Assistance, 1965-85, chmn., 1966-71; Bd. fellows Trinity Coll., 1962-64, trustee, 1964-81; corporator Hartford Hosp., 1978-81, Hartford Pub. Libr., 1969-81; bd. dirs. Inst. for Living, 1969-81, Edn. Commn. of States, 1969-71, Am. Coun. on Edn., 1977-81; trustee Northwood Sch., Lake Placid, N.Y., 1969-78; dir. adv. coun. Audubon Soc. Expdn. Inst., 1978-90; bd. dirs. Harry Frank Guggenheim Found., 1979—, Nepal adv. com. World Wildlife Fund, 1985-95; dir. Ars Publica, 1989-95. With U.S. Army, 1943-45. Belgian-Am. Fellow, 1959 Mem. Assn. Am. Colls. (dir. 1973-78, chmn. 1976-77, mem. project on undergrad. edn. 1981-85), Greater Hartford C. of C. (dir. 1977-81), Phi Beta Kappa, Pi Gamma Mu. Unitarian Universalist.

LOCKWOOD, WILLIAM BYRON, physician; b. Knoxville, Oct. 24, 1944; s. William Byron and Estelle (Ghormley) L. BA, Ctr. Coll. Ky., 1966; PhD, U. Louisville, 1971, MD, 1975. Intern pathology U. Louisville (Ky.) Affiliated Hosps., 1975-76, resident pathology, 1976-78; clin. lab. dir. VA Med. Ctr., Louisville, 1978-86; pres. Qualimetrix, Inc., Louisville, 1987-98; med. dir. ARC Blood Svcs., Louisville, 1988—99; pres. Lockwood and Assocs., Inc., Cordon, Ind., 1998—; dir. transfusion svcs. and tissue/bone bank U. Louisville, 1999—, Norton-Kosair Children's Hosp., Louisville, 1999—. Grantee Alliant Health Sys., Louisville, 1992-94, 96—. Mem. Am. Assn. Blood Banks, Ky. Assn. Blood Banks (pres. 1993-94), Ky. Med. Assn., Tenn. Assn. Blood Banks, Jefferson County Med. Soc. Democrat. Baptist. Office: U Louisville Hosp 530 S Jackson St Ste CIR06 Louisville KY 40202 Office Phone: 502-852-5857.

LOCKWOOD-BENET, MILDRED M., language educator; b. Mo., Dec. 24, 1962; d. William Lockwood and Ilia Irma Benet; m. Juan Fernandez-Gonzalez, Feb. 13, 1988; children: Camila, Guillermo, Marilia. BA in Elem. Edn., Boston Coll., 1984; M, Columbia U., 1987; EdD, U. P.R., 2003. Prof. English U. P.R., Guaynabo, PR, 1988—. Cons. Coll Bd., PR, Santillana Docentes, PR, First Hosp. Corp. Health Svcs., PR. Mem.: TESOL, Am. Ednl. Rsch. Assn. Avocations: reading, pilates, sewing. Home: S-21 California St Urb Mallorca Guaynabo PR 00969 Office: Univ PR Coll Gen Studies English Dept PO Box 23323 San Juan PR 00931 Office Phone: 787-764-0000 2186.

LOCKYER, BILL, state attorney general; b. Oakland, Calif., May 8, 1941; children: Lisa, Diego. BA in Polit. Sci., U. Calif., Berkeley; cert. in sec. tchg., Calif. State U., Hayward; JD, U. of the Pacific. Past tchr., San Leandro, Calif.; Mem. Calif. State Assembly, 1973; state senator State of Calif., 1982; pres. pro tem, chmn. senate rules com., chmn. senate jud. com. Calif. State Senate, 1994—98; atty. gen. State of Calif., 1999—. Active San Leandro Sch. Bd., 1968—73. Past chair Alameda County Dem. Ctrl. Com. Named Legislator of Yr., Planning and Conservation League, 1996, Calif. Jour., 1997. Democrat. Office: Office Atty Gen Dept Justice PO Box 944255 Sacramento CA 94244-2550 Office Phone: 916-322-3360. Business E-Mail: piu@doj.ca.gov.

LOCRICCHIO, MATTHEW, actor, writer; s. Paul P. and Virginia Mary Locricchio; life ptnr. Richard Keohane Farley. Student, Ea. Mich. U., 1967—69, No. Mich. U., 1966—67, Macomb County C.C., Warren, Mich., 1965—66. Theater/film/TV actor, San Francisco, 1971—81; actor/playwright N.Y.C., 1982—99; author Marshall Cavendish Corp., Tarrytown, NY, 1998—2004. Nominating com. SAG, N.Y.C., 2002—03. Author: (book) Internat. Cookbook for Kids, 2004, (plays) Fabric of a Vision, 1993, The Legend of Sleepy Hollow, 1993; actor: (plays) Largo Desolato, 1986, Ghetto,

1992, When You Comin' Back, Red Ryder?, 1976, Of Mice and Men, 1987, (TV movie) Stone Pillow, 1985. Fund raiser Nat. AIDS Meml. Grove, San Francisco, 1996—97. Named Best Actor, San Francisco Chronicle, 1977; recipient The Yr. of Thomas Cole award, Gov. of N.Y., 1993; Michael O'Sulllivan scholar, Am. Conservatory Theatre, 1972. Mem.: AFTRA, SAG, Actors Equity, Slow Food USA (assoc.). Avocations: carpentry, New York history, gardening, interior decorating.

LODDE, GORDON MAYNARD, health physics consultant; b. Lafayette, Ind., Aug. 19, 1933; s. Herman Morris and Eva Grace (Robinson) Lodde; m. Nancy Jean Caldwell, Aug. 21, 1955; children: Gordon A., Bruce C., Melissa J. BS, Purdue Univ., 1958; MS, Univ. Rochester, 1964. Health physist U.S. Army, 1959-79; health physics cons. Porter Cons., Ardmore, Pa., 1979-84; cons. engr. GPU Nuclear, Middletown, Pa., 1984-94; health physics cons. Mt. Joy, Pa., 1994—. Contbr. Handbook for Management of Radiation Protection Programs, 1992. Scoutmaster Boy Scouts Am., White Sands, N.Mex., 1967—70, Edgewood, Md., 1975—79, post adv., 1976—80. With Med. Svc. Corp U.S. Army, 1959—79. Decorated Commendation medal with two oak leaf clusters, Legion of Merit; recipient Merit award, Boy Scouts Am., 1976, Silver Beaver award, 1978. Mem.: N.Y. Acad. Scis., Am. Assn. Physicists in Medicine, Am. Indsl. Hygiene Assn., Am. Conf. of Gov. Hygienists, Am. Nuc. Soc., Health Physics Soc. Home and Office: 742 Ferndale Rd Mount Joy PA 17552-9384 E-mail: gml-hpc@msn.com.

LODE, TRYGVE TENNYSON, entrepreneur, actor; b. Mankato, Minn., Feb. 3, 1963; s. Tenny Dahlin and Jane (Bosch) Lode. Attended, U. Denver, 1981. Owner Lode Data Corp., Denver, 1982—; pres., bd. dirs. Nyx Net, Littleton, Colo., 1997—; owner The Midgard Corp., Littleton, 1998—, Warriorquest Internat., Denver, 2000—, Valkyrie Illumination, Littleton, 2000—, Asgard Entertainment, Denver, 2001—. Exec. prodr. Inferno Film Prodns., Littleton, 1999—. Actor: (films) Dragon and the Hawk, The Shadow Walkers. Achievements include writing The Design Assistant which became the industry standard for broadband communication systems design. Avocations: weightlifting, bicycling, humor writing. Home: 6529 Lakeside Cir Littleton CO 80125-9615 Home Fax: 303-470-1011. Personal E-mail: trygve@trygve.com.

LODEN, RACHEL, poet, consultant; d. Howard Joshua and Cynthia Ulrich Edelson; m. Jussi Antero Ketonen, May 14, 1973; 1 child, Skye Miranda Ketonen. Contbg. editor Pushcart Prize anthology series, Wainscott, NY, 2002—; freelance poetry manuscript cons., Palo Alto, Calif., 1995—. Author: Hotel Imperium (winner contemporary poetry series competition U. of Ga. Press, 1999), My Domain, Affidavit, The Richard Nixon Snow Globe, The Last Campaign (winner poetry chapbook competition Hudson Valley Writers' Ctr., 1998); contbr. poetry to numerous lit. mags. and anthologies. Named one of Ten Best Poetry Books of 2000, San Francisco Chronicle Book Rev., 2000; recipient Poetry Book Club selection, Acad. Am. Poets, 2000, award in poetry shortlist, Bay Area Book Reviewers Assn., 2000, Pushcart Prize in Poetry, 2002; Poetry fellow, Calif. Arts Coun., 2001—02. Mem.: Poets and Writers (listed writer), Acad. Am. Poets, Poetry Soc. Am., PEN Am. Ctr. Home: 3072 Stelling Dr Palo Alto CA 94303-3968 Personal E-mail: rloden@gmail.com.

LODER, DAVID E., lawyer; b. New Haven, Conn., Apr. 22, 1954; BA, Wesleyan U., 1977; JD, U. Pa., 1981; LLM in Internat. Law, London Sch. Economics, 1982. Bar: Pa. 1981, US Dist. Ct. Ea. Dist. Pa., US Ct. Appeals 3rd Cir., Supreme Ct. Pa. Assoc. Duane Morris LLP, Phila., 1982—88, ptnr., 1989—, mem. firm partners bd., 1999—, co-chair firm health law dept., 2000—. Gen. counsel Hosp. & Health Sys. Assn. Pa., Health Partners Phila., Pa. Trauma Systems Found. Co-trustee Dolfinger-McMahon Found., Lindback Found.; bd. mem. World Affairs Coun. Phila., 1996—2004, U. Sciences, Phila., 1998—; mem. exec. com. Wilma Theater, 2001—. Mem.: ABA, Pa. Soc. Healthcare Attorneys, Am. Soc. Internat. Law., Phila. Bar Assn., Pa. Bar Assn. Office: Duane Morris LLP One Liberty Pl Philadelphia PA 19103-7396 Office Phone: 215-979-1834. Office Fax: 215-979-1020. Business E-Mail: deloder@duanemorris.com.

LODER, VICTORIA KOSIOREK, information broker; b. Batavia, N.Y., May 27, 1945; d. Leon Stanley and Jennie Joann (Amatrano) Kosiorek; m. Ronald Raymond Loder, Nov. 6, 1965. BS in Bus. Mgmt., Roberts-Wesleyan Coll., Rochester, N.Y., 1989; MLS, SUNY, Buffalo, 1992; postgrad. in Religious Study, Liberty U., Lynchburg, Va., 1993—; postgrad., Faith Bible Bapt. Coll., Medina, N.Y., 1999—2002. Tech. info. specialist Eastman Kodak Co., Rochester, 1985-92; reference libr. Xerox Corp., Webster, N.Y., 1993-95, mgr. XPS strategy and integration libr. Fairport, N.Y., 1995-97, mgr. PSG Strategy and Bus. Info. Resource Ctr., 1997-99. V.p., treas. Victron Design Svc. USA, Kent, N.Y., 1988—; pres., owner Alpha Omega Info Source, Kent, N.Y., 1993—. Avocations: clothing design/construction, horticulture/landscape design, floral design.

LODEWICK, PHILIP HUGHES, equipment leasing company executive; b. Bklyn., Dec. 31, 1944; s. Robert John and Louise Mary (Bockhold) L.; m. Christine Helen Lobeck, July 5, 1969; children: Alyssa Erin, Kendra Blythe. BS, U. Conn., 1966, MBA, 1967. With sales dept. IBM Corp., N.Y.C., 1969-71; officer Boothe Fin. Corp., San Francisco, 1971-80; pres. The Tradewell Corp., equipment leasing co., Ridgefield, Conn., 1980—. Gen. ptnr. Sierra Assoc. IV, San Francisco, 1981-88; CFO Wicklo's Maple Hill Farm, Ridgefield, 1983-; bd. dirs. Ancora Coffee Roasters Inc., U. Conn. Found.; chmn., bd. dirs. Project Graphics, Inc.; bd. overseers U. Conn. Bus. Sch.; chmn. bd. trustees U. Conn. Found. Trustee U. Conn. Found.; bd. dirs. St. Andrew's Luth. Ch., Ridgefield, 1979—; mem. Conn. Refugee Resettlement Commn., 1985-88; bd. dirs., treas. Family Y in Ridgefield, 1985-89; founder, dir. Discovery Ctr., 1986—; founder, pres. A Better Chance in Ridgefield, 1987—; founding dir. Internat. Forgiveness Inst., Madison, Wis. With AUS, 1967-69, Korea. Mem. Computer Lessors and Dealers Assn., Golden Bridge Hounds, L.I. Golden Retreiver Club (pres. 1979-80), Golf Club on the Internet (bd. dirs.). Republican. Lutheran. Avocations: golf, tennis, basketball, travel, reading. Home and Office: Tradewell Corp 201 Spring Valley Rd Ridgefield CT 06877-1229

LODGE, ARTHUR SCOTT, mechanical engineering educator; b. Waterloo, Lancashire, Eng., Nov. 20, 1922; arrived in US, 1968, naturalized, 1973; s. Wilfred Claude and Jean Dea (Scott) L.; m. Helen Catherine Bannatyne, July 18, 1945; children: Keith Bannatyne, Alison Mary Shambrook, Timothy Patrick. BA, U. Oxford, 1945, MA, D.Phil., U. Oxford, 1948. Jr. sci. officer Admiralty, Eng., 1942-45; theoretical physicist NRC, Montreal, Que., Can., 1945-46, Brit. Rayon Research Assn., Manchester, Eng., 1948-60; sr. lectr. Math Inst. Sci. and Tech., U. Manchester, 1961-68; prof. dept. engring. mechanics U. Wis., Madison, 1968-91, Hougen vis. prof., 1991, prof. emeritus, 1991—; v.p. Bannatek Co., Inc., Madison, 1981—2001. Author: Elastic Liquids, 1964 (citation classics award 1981), Body Tensor Fields..., 1974, An Introduction to Elastomer Molecular Network Theory, 1999; contbr. articles to profl. jours.; patentee stressmeter. Recipient Byron Bird award U. Wis.-Madison, 1980; grantee U.S. govt. agys. Fellow Inst. Physics London; mem. NAE, Soc. Rheology (Bingham medal 1971), Brit. Soc. Rheology (Gold medal 1983). Republican. Avocation: piano playing. E-mail: aslodge@wisc.edu.

LODGE, GEORGE C(ABOT), business administration educator; b. Boston, July 7, 1927; s. Henry Cabot Jr. and Emily (Sears) L.; m. Nancy Kunhardt, Apr. 23, 1949 (dec. Feb. 1997); children: Nancy Lodge Burmeister, Emily Lodge Pingeon, Dorothy Lodge Peabody, Henry, George Jr., David; m. Susan Alexander Powers, Aug. 2, 1997. AB cum laude, Harvard U., 1950; hon. doctorate, INCAE, 1994. Polit. reporter, columnist Boston Herald, 1950-54; dir. info. U.S. Dept. Labor, Washington, 1954-58, asst. sec. labor for internat. affairs, 1958-61, U.S. del. to ILO, chmn. governing body, 1960-61; lectr. Grad. Sch. Bus. Adminstr., Harvard U., Boston, 1961-68, assoc. prof., 1968-72, prof. bus. adminstrn., 1972-91, Jaime and Josefina Chua Tiampo prof. bus. adminstrn., 1991-98, prof. emeritus, 98—. Author: Spearheads of Democracy: Labor in the Developing Countries, 1962, Engines of Change: United States Interests and Revolution in Latin America, 1970, The New American Ideology, 1975 (Ann. Book award Am. Acad. Mgmt. 1995), The American Disease, 1984, Perestroika for America, 1990, Comparative Business-Government Relations, 1990, Managing Globalization in the Age of Interdependence, 1995; co-author: Ideology and National Competitiveness, 1987; editor: U.S. Competitiveness in the World Economy, 1984. Rep. candidate U.S. Senate, Mass., 1962; vice-chmn. Inter-Am. Found., 1970-77. With USN, 1945-46. Named one of 10 Outstanding Youn Men in U.S., U.S. Jr. C. of C., 1961; recipient Arthur S. Fleming award, 1961, McKinsey award Harvard Bus. Rev., 1970, 74, Disting. Svc. award Harvard Bus. Sch., 2001; Lee Kuan Yew fellow Gov. of Singapore, 1991. Mem. Coun. Fgn. Rels., Carnegie Endowment for Internat. Peace (emeritus trustee), Robert F. Kennedy Meml. (trustee). Office: Harvard U Bus Sch Soldiers Fld Boston MA 02163-1317 E-mail: glodge@hbs.edu.

LODGE, HENRY SEARS, physician; b. Oct. 20, 1958; BA, U. Pa., 1981; MD, Columbia U., 1985. Diplomate Am. Bd. Internal Medicine. Intern Columbia U. Presbyterian Med. Ctr., N.Y.C., residency; attending physician N.Y. Presbyterian Hosp., 1988—; asst. clin. prof. Coll. Physicians and Surgeons Columbia U., N.Y.C., 1989—; pvt. practice specializing internal medicine and prevention N.Y.C. Chmn., CEO N.Y. Physicians LLP; past pres. Presbyn. Hosp. Alumni Assn., N.Y. Clin. Soc., Soc. Practitioners of Columbia Presbyn. Med. Ctr. Mem. Am. Coll. Physicians. Office: 635 Madison Ave New York NY 10022-1009

LODGE, J. RICHARD, lawyer; b. Franklin County, Tenn., June 16, 1949; BA cum laude, U. of the South, 1971; JD, Vanderbilt U., 1974. Bar: Tenn. 1974. Asst. atty. gen. State of Tenn., 1974-76; legis. dir. U.S. Senator Jim Sasser, 1977-78; mem. Willis & Knight, Nashville, 1977—85; mem., litig. practice Bass, Berry & Sims, Nashville, 1985—. Chmn. Tenn. Dem. Party, 1983—88, Sports Authority Nashville-Davidson County, Tenn., 1995—2000. Chmn. Nashville Legal Aid, 1981—82; mem. bd. regents U. of South at Sewanee. Named one of Power 100, Nashville Post, 2002—03. Fellow Nashville Bar Found.; mem. ABA, Tenn. Bar Assn, Nashville Bar Assn. Office: Bass Berry & Sims Suite 2700 AmSouth Ctr 315 Deaderick St Nashville TN 37238-3001 Office Phone: 615-742-6254. Office Fax: 615-742-2754. Business E-Mail: dlodge@bassberry.com.

LODGE, PATTI ANNE, state senator; b. Pitts., July 29, 1942; m. Edward J. Lodge; children: Mary Jeanne, Edward, Anne Marie. BA, Maryhurst U., 1964. Edn. media specialist Caldwell Sch. Dist., 1968-99, edn. media coord., 1980-97; pres. Windridge Vineyards, 1987—; mem. Idaho State Senate, Idaho, 2000—. Vice chair health and welfare com., jud. and rules com.; mem. commerce and human resources com., e-commerce interim com., tech. interim com., drug court coord. interim com.; del. Nat. Rep. Platform Com., 1996; cons. St. Paul's Sch., Our Lady of the Valley, 1999—. Nat. Fedn. GOP Women Resolutions, 1997—99; chair Miss Rodeo Caldwell Com., 1964—80, Canyon County Reps., 1986—88; bd. dirs. Day at the Legislature, 2000; dir. Idaho H.S. Rodeo Dist. 3, 1970—78; precinct chair Canyon County Rep. Com. 22, 1980—2000; pres. Idaho Fedn. Rep. Women, 1991—96; chair Idaho Rep. Gala Celebration, 2000; vol. Latino Voter Registration, 2000; chair bd. dirs. West Valley Med. Ctr., 1986; bd. dirs. Idaho Cath. Found., 1992—. Roman Catholic. Office: Idaho State Senate State Capitol 700 W Jefferson Boise ID 83720-0081 also: PO Box 83720 Boise ID 83720-0003 Fax: 208 459-7199.

LODICO, CHERYL MADELINE, secondary school educator; b. Bklyn., Aug. 24, 1944; d. Philip and Helen (Kutner) Miller; m. Nicholas Joseph Micucci, Feb. 13, 1969 (dec. Aug. 1987); m. Emanuel Joseph Lodico, Jan. 15, 1989; stepchildren: Diana Lynn, William Maurice. BA, Cortland State Coll., 1966; MS in Edn. in English, Queens Coll., 1971. Permanent cert. to teach English grades 7-12. English tchr. grade 9 Jerusalem Ave. Jr. H.S. North Bellmore, L.I., N.Y., 1966; English tchr. grades 7, 8, 9, also grade 6 gifted Lawrence Middle Sch., L.I., 1966-96; ret., 1996; tchr. ECC Acad., Bayside, N.Y., 1997-98; writer, 1998—. Sponsor, editor Creative Writing Club. Contbr. articles to profl. jours.; author of poetry. Mem. Nat. Coun. Tchrs. English. Home: 14712 15th Dr Whitestone NY 11357-2509

LODISH, LEONARD MELVIN, finance educator, entrepreneur; b. Cleve., Ohio, Aug. 1, 1943; s. Nathan H. and Sylvia (Friedman) L.; m. Susan Joyce Fischer, July 11, 1965; children: Max, Jacob, Chaim. AB magna cum laude, Kenyon Coll., 1965, LLD (hon.), 1999; PhD, MIT, 1968. Asst. prof. mktg. U. Pa., Phila., 1968-71, assoc. prof., 1971-75, prof. mktg., 1975-87, chmn. mktg. dept., 1984-88, Samuel R. Harrell prof., 1988—, vice dean Wharton West, 2001—; founding dir. Evergreen Health Group, Inc., 1984-91; founder, chmn. The Wharton Global Cons. Practicum, 1995—. Bd. dir. Franklin Electronic Pub. Inc., Mt. Holly, N.J., J&J Snack Foods, Inc., Pennsauken, N.J., 1995-2005; co-founder, prin. Mgmt. Decisions Sys., Inc., Waltham, Mass., 1967-85; co-founder, dir. Shadow Broadcast Svcs., Bala Cynwyd, Pa., 1991-98. Author: The Advertising and Promotion Challenge: Vaguely Right or Precisely Wrong?, 1986, Entrepreneurial Marketing: Lessons from Wharton's Pioneering MBA Course, 2001; mem. editl. bd. Mgmt. Sci., Jour. Mktg. Sci., Jour. Advt. Rsch., Jour. Personal Selling and Sales Mgmt.; contbr. articles to profl. jours. Pres. Temple Beth Hillel/Beth El, Wynnewood, Pa., 1983-85, bd. dir. 1975-98, 99, trustee, 1995—. Recipient Odell award for best impact article, 2000. Mem. Inst. Mgmt. Scis. (Franz Edelman award 1987), Ops. Research Soc. Am., Am. Mktg. Assn. (winner 1st Paul E. Green award 1996), Phi Beta Kappa. Jewish. Home: 301 Kent Rd Wynnewood PA 19096-1814 Office: U Pa Wharton Sch Dept Mktg Philadelphia PA 19104

LODOR, MARCI ANN, dietician; b. Pitts., Pa., Aug. 2, 1965; d. Anthony Nicola Minucci and Julia Anna Renac; m. John Anthony Lodor Jr., June 1, 2002. BS in Clin. Dietetics, Univ. Pitts., 1988. Registered dietitian Am. Dietetic Assn. Asst. food svc. dir. Morrisons & Wightman, Squirrel Hill, Pa., 1988—91; clin. dietitian Mc Keesport (Pa.) Hosp., 1991—95; cons. dietitian Pvt. Practice, Pitts., 1996—97; food svc. dir. various long term care facilities, Pitts., 1997—2000; regional dietitian Extendicare, We. & Ctrl. Pa., 2000—02; registered dietitian HCR Manorcare, North Hills, Pa., 2003; nutritionist Greater Pitts. Cmty. Food Bank, Duquesne, 2004—05; cmty. connections program coord., nutrition specialist Luth. Svc. Soc., Bellevue, 2005—. Registered dietitian cons. Three Rivers Family Hosp., White Oak, Pa., 1996—. Bd. dir. White Oak Animal Safe Haven, 2002—. Avocations: skating, dance, flea markets, reading, theater. Home: 612 Park St Mc Keesport PA 15132 Office Phone: 412-460-3663 ext. 217.

LODOWSKI, CHARLES ALAN, trade association administrator, lobbyist; b. Dallas, May 10, 1945; s. Charles Harry and Genevieve (Gowaty) L.; m. Patricia Anne Snead, May 27, 1967; children: Charles, Tracy, Amy. BBA in Fin., U. Tex., 1968. Pres. East Tex. Citizens Credit Union, Palestine, Tex., 1978-86; dist. rep. Nat. Fedn. Ind. Bus., Nashville, 1987-88, regional tng. mgr., 1991-93, div. mgr., 1989-90, 94-96, dir. sales ops., 1996—2002; pres. BLTN, Inc., Brentwood, Tenn., 2002—. Republican. Avocations: woodworking, gardening. Office: BLTN Inc PO Box 1164 Brentwood TN 37024-1164 Home: 6132 Brentwood Chase Dr Brentwood TN 37027-4443 Office Phone: 615-641-3450.

LODWICK, GWILYM SAVAGE, radiologist, educator; b. Mystic, Iowa, Aug. 30, 1917; s. Gwylim S. and Lucy A. (Fuller) Lodwick; m. Maria Antonia De Brito Barata; children from previous marriage: Gwilym Savage III, Philip Galligan, Malcolm Kerr, Terry Ann. Student, Drake U., 1934—35; BS, State U. Iowa, 1942, MD, 1943. Resident in pathology State U. Iowa, 1947—48, resident in radiology, 1948—50; fellow, sr. fellow radiologic and orthop. pathology Armed Forces Inst. Pathology, 1951; asst., then assoc. prof. State U. Iowa Med. Sch., 1951—56; prof. radiology, chmn. dept. U. Mo. at Columbia Med. Sch., 1956—78, rsch. prof. radiology, 1978—83, interim chmn. dept. radiology, 1980—81, chmn. dept. radiology, 1981—83, prof. bioengring., 1969—83, acting dean, 1959, assoc. dean, 1959—64; assoc. radiologist Mass. Gen. Hosp., 1983—88, radiologist, 1988—91, hon. radiologist Boston, 1991—; vis. prof. dept. radiology Harvard Med. Sch., 1983—93. Vis. prof. Keio U. Sch. Medicine, Tokyo, 1974; chmn. sci. program com. Internat. Conf. on Med. Info., Amsterdam, 1983; trustee Am. Registry Radiologic Technologists, 1961—69, pres., 1964—65, 1968—69; mem. radiology tng. com. Nat. Inst. Gen. Med. Scis., NIH, 1966—70; com. radiology NAS-NRC, 1970—75; chmn. com. computers Am. Coll. Radiology, 1965, Internat. Commn. Radiol. Edn. and Info., 1969—73; cons. to health care tech. divsn. Nat. Ctr. for Health Svcs., Rsch. and Devel., 1971—76; dir. Mid-Am. Bond Tumor Diagnostic Ctr. and Registry, 1971—83; adv. com. mem. NIH Biomed. Image Processing Grant Jet Propulsion Lab., 1969—73; nat. chmn. MUMPS Users Group, 1973—75; mem. radiation study sect. divsn. rsch. grants NIH, 1976—79, mem. study sect. on diagnostic radiology and nuc. medicine divsn. rsch. grants, 1979—82, chmn., 1980—82; mem. bd. sci. counselors Nat. Libr. Medicine, 1985, chmn., 1987—89; dir. radiology Spaulding Rehab. Hosp., 1986—92; cons. in field. Adv. editl. bd.: Radiology, 1965—86, cons. to editor:, 1986—91, adv. editl. bd.: Current/Clin. Practice, 1972—88, mem. editl. bd.: Jour. Med. Systems, 1976—, Radiol. Sci. Update divsn. Biomedia, Inc., 1975—83, Critical Revs. in Linguistic Imaging, 1990, mem. cons. editl. bd.: Skeletal Radiology, 1977—92, Contemporary Diagnostic Radiology, 1978—80, assoc. editor: Jour. Med. Imaging, 1988—. Served to maj. U.S. Army, 1943—46, ETO. Decorated Sakari Mustakallio medal Finland; named Most Disting. Alumnus in Radiology, State U. Iowa Centennial, 1970; recipient Sigma Xi Rsch. award, U. Mo., Columbia, 1972, Gold medal, XIII Internat. Conf. Radiology, Madrid, 1973, Founder's Gold medal, Internat. Skeletal Soc., 1990, Disting. Alumni Achievement award, U. Iowa, 2002. Fellow: AMA (radiology rev. bd. coun. med. edn., coun. rep. on residency rev. com. for radiology 1969—74), Am. Coll. Radiology (co-chmn. ACR-NEMA standardization com. 1983—90, NEMA Med. Tech. Leadership award 1995); mem.: Phila. Roentgen Ray Soc., Ind. Roentgen Soc., Tex. Radiol. Soc., Salutis Unitas, Mo. Radiol. Soc. (1st pres. 1961—62), Finnish Radiol. Soc. (hon.), Portuguese Soc. Radiology and Nuc. Medicine (hon.), Assn. Univ. Radiologists, Radiol. Soc. N.Am. (3d v.p. 1974—75, chmn. ad hoc com. representing assoc. scis. 1979—87, chmn. assoc. scis. com. 1981—87), Nat. Acad. Practice in Medicine, Am. Coll. Med. Informatics (founding), NAS Inst. Medicine, Cosmos, Harvard of Boston Club, Rotary, Alpha Omega Alpha. Home: 3900 Galt Ocean Dr Apt 307 Fort Lauderdale FL 33308-6622 E-mail: lodwickmd@aol.com.

LODWICK, JUDITH LYNNE, nursing educator; b. New Orleans, Feb. 20, 1954; d. Frank Tillman Jr. and Grace Evelyn (Hilty) L. BSN, La. State U., 1976. RN, La.; cert. CPR, ACLS instr., advanced trauma life support coord., med.-surg. nurse, cert. emergency nurse. Head nurse hemotology-oncology endocrinology Ochsner Found. Hosp., New Orleans, 1978-82, unit instr., head nurse Ochsner emergency dept., 1983-88, staff nurse emergency dept., 1989-91; staff nurse, relief charge nurse, preceptor E. Jefferson Gen. Hosp., Metairie; clin. instr. post ICU East Jefferson Gen. Hosp., Metairie, 1991-96, supr. post ICU, 1996-98. Coord. orientation workshops and preceptorships, affilate faculty Charity Delgado Sch. of Nursing, 1996-97, educator N.A. advancement PCT program; chairperson universal chart order post ICU flowsheet East Jefferson Gen. Hosp. Mem. Nat. Oncology Soc., Emergency Nursing Assn. (sec. emergency dept. quality assurance program com.), Critical Care Nurses Assn. (chmn. post ICU quality assurance com, competency based edn. com.), Nursing Edn. Com., Policy and Procedure Com., ICU flowsheet com. (chmn.). Home: 2056 Lafitte St La Place LA 70068-2029

LODWICK, MICHAEL WAYNE, lawyer; b. New Orleans, Sept. 21, 1946; s. Frank Tillman Jr. and Grace Evelyn (Hilty) L.; children: Sarah Peirce, Jane Durborow, Elizabeth Hilty; m. Mary League, June 15, 1991. BA, La. State U., 1968; MA, Tulane U., 1972, PhD, 1976; JD, Loyola U., New Orleans, 1981. Bar: La., U.S. Dist. Ct. (ea. dist.) La. 1981, U.S. Ct. Appeals (5th cir.) 1981, U.S. Ct. Appeals (D.C. cir.) 1982, U.S. Ct. Appeals (11th cir.) 1986, U.S. Ct. Appeals (9th cir.) 1990, U.S. Ct. Appeals (2d cir.) 1996, U.S. Ct. Appeals (4th cir.) 1996, U.S. Supreme Ct., 1987, Calif. 1990, U.S. Dist. Ct. (ctrl., no. and so. dists.) Calif. 1990. Instr. to asst. prof. Tulane U., New Orleans, 1976-78; assoc. Barham & Churchill, New Orleans, 1981-83, O'Neil, Eichin & Miller, New Orleans, 1983-87, ptnr., 1987-89, Fisher & Porter, 1989-97, Porter, Groff & Lodwick, 1997—. Editor, co-founder and pub. Plantation Soc. in Americas jour., 1979-83, 86—; editor-in-chief Loyola Law Rev., 1980-81; contbr. articles to profl. jours. Mem. New Orleans Symphony Chorus, 1985-89, Pacific Chorale, 1989—. Tulane U. fellow, 1970-72; recipient Loyola U. Law Rev. Honor award, 1981, Loyola Law Alumni award, 1981. Mem. ABA, La. State Bar Assn., State Bar Calif., Fed. Bar Assn., Assn. Transp. Law, Logistics and Policy, Maritime Law Assn. U.S. Home: 20241 Seashell Cir Huntington Beach CA 92646-4436

LÖE, HARALD, retired dentist, educator, researcher; b. Steinkjer, Norway, July 19, 1926; s. Haakon and Anna (Bruem) Löe; m. Inga Johansen, July 3, 1948; children: Haakon, Marianne. DDS, U. Oslo, 1952; D in Odontology, 1961; hon. degree, U. Gothenburg, 1973, Royal Dental Coll., Aarhus, 1980, U. Athens, 1980, Cath. U., Leuven, 1980, U. Lund, 1983, Georgetown U., 1983, U. Bergen, 1985, U. Md., 1986, Med. U. N.J., 1987, Royal Dental Coll., Copenhagen, 1988, U. Toronto, 1989, U. Detroit, 1990, S.C. Med. U., 1990, U. Helsinki, Finland, 1992, Pacific U., 1993, U. Milan, Italy, 1994. Instr. Sch. Dentistry, Oslo U., 1952-55; rsch. assoc. Norwegian Inst. Dental Rsch., 1956-62; Fulbright rsch. fellow, rsch. assoc. dept. oral pathology U. Ill., Chgo., 1957-58; Univ. rsch. fellow Oslo U., 1959-62, asso. prof. dept. periodontology, 1960-61; prof. dentistry, chmn. dept. periodontology Royal Dental Coll., Aarhus, Denmark, 1962-72, asso. dean, dean-elect, 1971-72; prof., dir. Dental Rsch. Inst., U. Mich., Ann Arbor, 1972-74; dir. Nat. Inst. Dental Rsch. Nat. Inst. Dental Rsch., Bethesda, Md., 1983-96; dean, prof. periodontology U. Conn. Health Ctr. Sch. Dental Medicine, Farmington, 1974-82, univ. prof., 1994-97; vis. prof. U. Bern, Switzerland, 1997—. Vis. prof. periodontics Hebrew U., Jerusalem, 1966—67; hon. prof. Med. Scis. U. Beijing, 1987; cons. FDA, WHO, NIH; lectr. in field. Contbr. over 350 articles to sci. pubis. With Norwegian Army, 1944—48. Decorated knight of Danebrog, comdr. Royal Norwegian Order of Merit; recipient 75th Anniversary award, Norwegian Dental Assn., 1958, prize, Aalborg Dental Soc., 1965, William J. Gies Periodontology award, 1978, Alfred C. Fones medal, U.S. Surgeon Gen.'s medal and Exemplary award, 1988, Internat. award, Swedish Dental Assn., 1989, Harvard medal, 1992, Scandinavian Pub. Health award, 1994. Mem.: ADA (Gold medal 1994, Callahan medal 1995, Spenadel medal 1995, U. Conn. medal 2003, Pierre Fauchard medal 2003), AAAS, Mass. Dental Soc. (Internat. award), Am. Soc. Preventive Dentistry (Internat. award), Scandinavian Assn. Dental Rsch., Danish Dental Assn., Am. Acad. Periodontology, Am. Coll. Dentists, Inst. Medicine NAS, Internat. Assn. Dental Rsch. (pres. 1980, Basic Rsch. in Periodontology award 1969), Internat. Coll. Dentists, Am. Assn. Dental Rsch. (hon.).

LOEB, BEN FOHL, JR., retired law educator; b. Nashville, May 15, 1932; s. Ben Fohl and Frances (Paysinger) L.; m. Anne Nelson, Sept. 23, 1961 (div. 1982); children: Charles Nelson, William Nelson. BA, Vanderbilt U., 1955, JD, 1960. Bar: Tenn. 1960, NC 1975, US Supreme Ct. 1966. Law clk. Office of Sec. of Navy, 1959; assoc. Crownover, Branstetter & Folk, Nashville, 1960-64; asst. dir. Inst. Govt. U. N.C., Chapel Hill, 1964—, prof. pub. law and govt. Sch. Govt., 1972—, prof. emeritus, 2004—. Counsel to N.C. legis. coms. on motor vehicle law and transp., Raleigh, 1973-83; cons. on alcohol beverage control, 1985-89; cons. on wildlife, natural and scenic areas, 1989-93; mem. U. N.C. Faculty Coun., 1994-97. Author: Traffic Law and Highway Safety, 1970, Alcohol Beverage Control Law, 1971, Motor Vehicle Law, 1975, Legal Aspects of Dental Practice, 1977, Eminent Domain Procedure, 1984, Punishments for Crimes and Motor Vehicle Offenses, 1999; assoc. editor Vanderbilt Law Rev., 1959-60. 1st lt. U.S. Army, 1955-57. Mem. ABA, Tenn. Bar Assn., Phi Beta Kappa, Phi Delta Phi, Pi Kappa Alpha (chpt. pres. 1954-55), Carolina Club (Chapel Hill). Democrat. Baptist. Home: 17 Bluff Trail Chapel Hill NC 27516-1603 Personal E-mail: benloeb@bellsouth.net.

LOEB, G. HAMILTON, lawyer; b. New Orleans, June 22, 1951; s. Ferdinand M. and Margaret (Gibbs) L.; m. Bonnie Schlitz, June 9, 1973; children: Miller Anne, Maxwell Lazard. BA, U. Va., 1973; JD magna cum laude, Harvard U., 1978. Bar: Calif. 1979, D.C. 1980, U.S. Ct. Appeals (9th cir.) 1979, U.S. Ct. Appeals (D.C. cir.) 1980, U.S. Dist. Ct. D.C. 1981. Legis. asst. to Hon. Robert Steele U.S. Ho. Reps., Washington, 1973-74; law clerk to Hon. James Browning U.S. Ct. Appeals, San Francisco, 1978-79; assoc. Wald, Harkrader & Ross, Washington, 1981-82; ptnr. Paul, Hastings, Janofsky & Walker, LLP, Washington, 1982—, mng. ptnr. Washington Office, 1997—, vice chairperson litig. dept. Author, editor: North American Free Trade Agreement, 1993; articles editor Harvard Law Review., 1977-78. Chair, pres. Washington Area Lawyers for the Arts, 1986-92; mem. exec. com. Netherlands Am. Amity Trust, 1987—. Echols scholar U. Va., 1973. Jewish. Home: 3802 Gramercy St NW Washington DC 20016-4226 Office: Paul Hastings Janofsky & Walker LLP 875 15th St NW 10th Fl Washington DC 20005 Business E-Mail: hamiltonloeb@paulhastings.com.

LOEB, JAMES ALAN, lawyer; s. Sheldon and Loretta K. Loeb; m. Lisa Ellen Witt, Aug. 7, 1988; 2 children. BA, Ohio State U., 1985, JD, 1988. Bar: Ohio 1988, US Dist. Ct. (no. dist. Ohio) 1988. Tchg. asst. Ohio State U. Coll. Law, Columbus, 1986; jud. extern Fed. Judge George W. White US Dist. Ct. No. Dist. Ohio, 1986; ptnr., lawyer Baker & Hostetler LLP, 1988—. Chmn. Family Law Sect. Cleve. Bar Assn., 2004; lectr. in field. Office: Baker & Hostetler LLP Nat City Ctr 1900 E 9th St Ste 3200 Cleveland OH 44114 Office Phone: 216-621-0200. Office Fax: 216-696-0740. Business E-Mail: jloeb@bakerlaw.com.

LOEB, JANE RUPLEY, academic administrator, educator; b. Chgo., Feb. 22, 1938; d. John Edwards and Virginia Pentland (Marthens) Watkins; m. Peter Albert Loeb, June 14, 1958; children: Eric Peter, Gwendolyn Lisl, Aaron John. BA, Rider Coll., 1961; PhD, U. So. Calif., 1969. Clin. psychology intern Univ. Hosp., Seattle, 1966-67; asst. prof. ednl. psychology U. Ill., Urbana, 1968-69, asst. coord. rsch. and testing, 1968-69, coord. rsch. and testing, 1969-72, asst. to vice chancellor acad. affairs, 1971-72, dir. admissions and records, 1972-81, assoc. prof. ednl. psychology, 1973-82, assoc. vice chancellor acad. affairs, 1981-94, prof. edn. psychology, 1982—. Author: College Board Project: the Future of College Admissions, 1989; co-editor: Academic Couples: Problems and Promises, 1997. Chmn. Coll. Bd. Coun. on Entrance Svcs., 1977-82; bd. govs. Alliance for Undergrad. Edn., 1988-93; active charter com. Coll. Bd. Acad. Assembly, 1992-93. HEW grantee, 1975-76. Mem. APA, Am. Ednl. Rsch. Assn., Nat. Coun. Measurement in Edn., Harvard Inst. Ednl. Mgmt. Avocation: the french horn. Home: 1405 N Coler Ave Urbana IL 61801-1625 Office: U Ill 1310 S 6th St Champaign IL 61820-6925

LOEB, JOHN LANGELOTH, JR., investment counselor, consultant; b. N.Y.C., May 2, 1930; s. John Langeloth and Frances (Lehman) L.; children: Nicholas, Alexandra. Grad., Hotchkiss Sch., 1948; AB cum laude, Harvard, 1952, MBA, 1954; LL.D. (hon.), Georgetown U. With Loeb, Rhoades & Co., N.Y.C., from 1956, gen. ptnr., mem. mgmt. com., 1964-73, mng. ptnr., pres., 1971-73, ltd. ptnr., 1973-84; chmn. bd. Holly Sugar Co., Colo., 1969-71; amb. to Denmark Copenhagen, 1981-83; chmn. John L. Loeb, Jr. Assocs., N.Y.C., 1984—. U.S. del. to 38th session Gen. Assembly of UN; spl. advisor environ. matters to Gov. Nelson A. Rockefeller, 1967-73; chmn. Gov. N.Y. Coun. Environ. Advisors, 1970-75, Langeloth Found. 1996-2001, trustee 1978-; chmn. Winston Churchill Found. 2003-; pres. 1981-2003, trustee 1975-1981; trustee Ednl. Testing Svc., Princeton, N.J., 1986-93; bd. dirs. Am.-Scandinavian Found. Bd. trustee Monefiore Hosp. and Med. Ctr., Mus. City, NY, 1962—94; bd. trustees John and Frances L. Loeb Found., 1957—98; mem. Harvard Vis. Com. Loeb Drama Ctr., 1988—94, N.Y. State Coun. on the Arts, 1996—; pres. John L. Loeb Jr. Found., 1963—; bd. dirs. Am.-Scandinavian Found., 2002—. Lt. USAF, 1954—56. Lord of the Manor of Brinsley; Decorated Grand Cross of the Order of Dannebrog (Denmark); recipient Lee Max Friedman award Am. Jewish Hist. Soc., Disting. Patriot award SAR; Hon. Comdr. of the Most Excellent Order of the Brit. Empire. Mem. Downtown Assn. (N.Y.C.), Harvard Club, Century Country Club, Sleepy Hollow Club (Westchester, N.Y.), Buck's Club, Brooks's Club, Hurlingham Club (London), Royal Danish Yacht Club (Copenhagen), Royal Swedish Yacht Club (Stockholm), Lyford Cay Club (Nassau, Bahamas), Soc. Colonial Wars, NY. Home: Ridgeleigh 194 Anderson Hill Rd Purchase NY 10577-2101 Office: John L Loeb Jr Assocs Inc 50 Broad St Rm 1137 New York NY 10004-2307 Office Phone: 212-509-1500. E-mail: johnloeb@aol.com.

LOEB, JOHN NICHOLS, physician, educator; b. N.Y.C., Dec. 17, 1935; s. Robert Frederick and Emily Guild (Nichols) L. AB summa cum laude, Harvard Coll., 1957; MD summa cum laude, Harvard Med. Sch., 1961. Diplomate Am. Bd. Internal Medicine. Intern in medicine Mass. Gen. Hosp., Boston, 1961-62; asst. resident in medicine Presbyn. Hosp., N.Y.C., 1962-63, chief resident in medicine, 1965-66, asst. physician, 1966—67, asst. attending physician, 1967-73, assoc. attending physician, 1973-79, attending physician, 1979—98, secy. medical bd., 1976—77; attending physician N.Y.-Presbyn. Hosp., 1998—; rsch. assoc. lab. of molecular biology Nat. Inst. Arthritis and Metabolic Diseases, NIH, Bethesda, Md., 1963-65; NIH trainee in metabolism Columbia U. Coll. Phys. and Surg., 1966—67; asst. prof. medicine Columbia U., N.Y.C., 1967-73, assoc. prof. medicine, 1973-79, prof. medicine, 1979—2004, prof. emeritus medicine, 2005—, spl. lectr. in medicine, 2005—, assoc. chmn. rsch. dept. medicine, 1997—2003, vice chmn. for acad. affairs, 2003—04. Vis. chief resident Mass. Gen. Hosp., Boston, Mass., 1966; asst. vis. physician Harlem Hosp., N.Y.C., 1968-73; adj. asst. prof. Rockefeller U., N.Y.C., 1970-75, adj. assoc. prof., 1975-83; vis. prof. dept. internal medicine Pahlavi U., Shiraz, Iran, 1974, 77; vis. prof. dept. medicine U. Cape Town, 1982; sec. med. bd. Presbyn. Hosp., 1976-1977; mem. Med. Coun. of the Iran Found., 1974-75; councillor Harvard Med. Alumni Assn., 1982-85; dir. Royal Soc. Medicine Found., N.Y., 1984-95; praktikant Friedrich Miescher Inst., Basel, Switzerland, 1986 Contbr. articles to profl. jours. Elder Presbyn. Ch., 1982—; ruling elder Madison Ave. Presbyn. Ch., N.Y.C., 1983-88; mem., bd. dirs. Amateur Chamber Music Players, Inc., 1984-99, vice chmn., 1985-99, mem. adv. coun., 1999—. Lt. comdr. grade surgeon USPHS, 1963-65 Recipient Boylston medal Harvard U., 1961, P&S Club Tchg. award, 1969, Career Scientist award Irma T. Hirschl Charitable Trust, 1973-77, Disting. Tchr. award Coll. of Physicians and Surgeons, Columbia U., 1974, Tchg. award citation, 1975, House Staff Recognition award Presbyn. Hosp., 2004; grantee NIH, 1988-98. Fellow AAAS, ACP, N.Y. Acad. Medicine, Royal Soc. Medicine; diplomate Am. Bd. Internal Medicine; mem. Assn. Am. Physicians, Practitioners' Soc. N.Y. (sec. 1973, 74, pres. 1985, 86), Am. Soc. Clin. Investigation, Am. Fedn. for Clin. Rsch., Harvey Soc., Am. Clin. and Climatological Assn., Century Assn., Soc. for Exptl. Biology and Medicine, Endocrine Soc., Soc. Gen. Physiologists, Peripatetic Club (councillor 1987-94), Interurban Clin. Club, Charaka Club (pres. 1984-85), Am. Philos. Soc., Phi Beta Kappa, Alpha Omega Alpha. Presbyterian. Achievements include research in mechanisms of hormone action, physical chemistry of receptor-ligand interactions and their quantitative relationship to biological response, and regulation of glucose and monovalent cation transport. Home: 80 Haven Ave New York NY 10032-2617 Office: Columbia Univ Dept Medicine 630 W 168th St New York NY 10032-3702

LOEB, LARRY MORRIS, communications company executive; b. Morgan City, La., Oct. 13, 1940; s. Richard Levy and Pauline Endler (Forgotston) L.; m. Maria-Luisa Elvira Achino, Apr. 5, 1968; children: Maddalena, Leonora. BA, Tulane U., 1962; postgrad., Columbia U., 1962-63, JD, 1966. Bar: NY 1967. Staff atty. ABC, Inc., NYC, 1966—68, gen. atty., 1968—80; v.p., dir. bus. affairs ABC Video Enterprises Inc., NYC, 1980—86; v.p. legal and bus. affairs Video Enterprises and Pub. Capital Cities/ABC, Inc., NYC, 1986—93; v.p. cable and internat. devel., legal ABC, Inc., NYC, 1993-97; sr. counsel Hearst Corp., NYC, 1998—. Mgmt. com. A & E Networks, NYC, 1981-96, Lifetime, 1983-85; adv. coun. TMM (RTL2), 1996-97; mng. dir. Hearst Enterprises, B.V., 2000-2003; bd. dirs. SCMP Hearst Pubs., Hong Kong, Edimer Ltd., Cyprus. Bd. dirs. Theater for a New Audience, N.Y.C., 1981—. Woodrow Wilson fellow, 1962-63. Mem. N.Am. Nat. Broadcasters Assn. (pres. 1996-97), European Broadcasting Union (legal com. 1973-97). Democrat. Jewish. Avocations: piano, theater, reading, travel, languages. Home: 164 W 94th St New York NY 10025-7015 Office: The Hearst Corp 959 8th Ave New York NY 10019-3795 Office Phone: 212-649-2027. Business E-Mail: lmloeb@hearst.com.

LOEB, LISA, singer, lyricist; b. Bethesda, Md., 1968; BA in Comparative Lit., Brown U., 1990; student, Berklee Sch. Music. Founder Lisa Loeb and Nine Stories, 1990. Singer, musician: (albums) Tails, 1995, Firecracker, 1997 (Grammy nomination), Cake and Pie, 2002, Hello Lisa, 2002; (single): Stay (Reality Bites soundtrack), 1994 (Grammy nomination, 1994, Critic's Choice award, 1995), (children's albums): Catch the Moon (with Elizabeth Mitchell), 2004; co-host: (TV series) Dweezil & Lisa, 2004. Office: Artemis Records 130 5th Ave 7th Fl New York NY 10011

LOEB, MARSHALL ROBERT, journalist; b. Chgo., May 30, 1929; s. Monroe Harrison and Henrietta (Benjamin) L.; m. Elizabeth Peggy Loewe, Aug. 14, 1954; children: Michael, Margaret. BJ, U. Mo., 1950; postgrad., U. Goettingen, Germany, 1950-51. Reporter Garfield News and Austinite, Chgo., 1944-45; reporter, columnist Garfieldian and Austin News, Chgo., 1946-47, 49-51; reporter Columbia Missourian, 1948-50; staff corr. UP, Frankfurt, Germany, 1952-54; reporter St. Louis Globe-Democrat, 1955-56; contbg. editor Time mag., 1956-61, assoc. editor, 1961-65, sr. editor, 1965-80, econs. editor and columnist, 1978-80; mng. editor Money Mag., 1980-84; editor Time Inc. Mag. Devel., 1984-86; mng. editor Fortune, 1986-94, editor-at-large, 1994-95, columnist, 1996; editor Columbia Journalism Rev., 1997-99; columnist, adv. bd. mem. Marketwatch website, 1999—. Daily commentator CBS Radio Network; assoc. fellow Yale U., Berkeley Coll., 1977—; bd. dirs. priceline.com. Author (with William Safire): Plunging Into Politics, 1962; author: Marshall Loeb's Money Guide, 1983, ann. edits., 1985—94, Money Minutes, 1986, Lifetime Financial Strategies, 1996, 52 Weeks to Financial Fitness, 2001; editor (with Andrew Leckey): Best Business Stories of the Year, 2001. Bd. dirs. Nat. Neurofibromatosis Found., Recording for the Blind and Dyslexic; bd. advisors Knight-Bagehot Fellowship. Recipient Gerald M. Loeb award UCLA Sch. Mgmt., 1974, Lifetime Achievement award, 1996, Journalism medal U. Mo., 1988, TJFR Bus. Journalism Luminaries award 1990, 2000, Disting. Achievement award Soc. Am. Bus. Editors and Writers, 1998. Mem. Econ. Club of N.Y., Coun. Fgn. Rels., Am. Soc. Mag. Editors (pres. 1988-90), Overseas Press Club Am. (v.p.). Jewish. Home: 31 Montrose Rd Scarsdale NY 10583-1129 Office: MarketWatch dot com 1697 Broadway New York NY 10019-2925 Office Phone: 212-975-8694. Business E-Mail: mloeb@marketwatch.com.

LOEB, SUSANNA, education educator; BSCE, BA in Polit. sci., Stanford U., 1988; MPP in Pub. Policy studies, U. Mich., 1994, PhD in Econs., 1998. Rsch. asst. U. Mich. Sch. Edn., 1991—93; rsch. asst. dept. econs. U. Mich., 1993—96; rsch. fellow Population Studies Ctr., U. Mich., 1995—; rsch. asst. U. Mich. Sch. Edn., 1996—; asst. prof. U. Calif., Davis, 1998—99; asst. prof. edn. Stanford (Calif.) U., Calif., 1999—. Rsch. cons. Inst. for Rsch. on Women and Gender, U. Mich., 1997—. Office: Stanford U Sch Edn 485 Lasuen Mall Stanford CA 94305-3096*

LOEFFLER, FRANK JOSEPH, physicist, educator; b. Ballston Spa, NY, Sept. 5, 1928; s. Frank Joseph and Florence (Farrell) L.; m. Eleanor Jane Chisholm, Sept. 8, 1951; children: Peter, James, Margaret, Anne Marie. BS in Engring. Physics, Cornell U., 1951, PhD in Physics, 1957. Research asso. Princeton U., 1957-58; mem. faculty Purdue U., Lafayette, Ind., 1958-97, prof. physics, 1962-97; prof. emeritus, 1997—; vis. prof. Hamburg U., Germany, 1963-64, Heidelberg U., Germany, CERN, Switzerland, 1971, Stanford U. Linear Accelerator Ctr., 1980-83. Trustee, exec. com., chmn. high energy com. Argonne Univs. Assn., 1972-76, 78-79, com. on fusion programs, 1979-80; vis. prof. U. Hawaii, 1985-86. Contbr. articles to profl. jours. Recipient Antarctic Svc. medal NSF/USN, 1990, Ruth and Joel Spira award for outstanding tchg., 1992. Fellow Am. Phys. Soc., Sigma Xi, Tau Beta Pi. Achievements include developing and manufacturing undergraduate physics laboratory experiments and lecture demonstration apparatus. Exptl. research in astrophysics, high energy gamma ray astronomy, high energy particle interactions and on-line data acquisition-processing systems. Established gamma ray astronomy lab. at South Pole, Antarctica, 1989, 91, 92. Home: 341 Hokulani St Makawao HI 96768-8612 Office: Purdue U Dept Physics Lafayette IN 47907 Office Phone: 808-572-8804. Personal E-mail: fjloef@aol.com.

LOEFFLER, JAMES JOSEPH, lawyer; b. Evanston, Ill., Mar. 7, 1931; s. Charles Adolph and Margaret Bowe L.; m. Margo M. Loeffler, May 26, 1962; children— Charlotte Bowe, James J. BS, Loyola U.; JD, Northwestern U. Bar: Ill. 1956, Tex. 1956. Assoc. Fulbright & Jaworski, Houston, 1956-69, ptnr., 1969—82, sr. ptnr., 1982—86, Chamberlain, Hrdlicka, White, Johnson & Williams, Houston, 1986-90; pvt. practice law Houston, 1990-2000. Mem. Ill. Bar Assn., Tex. Bar Assn., Houston Country Club.

LOEFFLER, MARTIN H., communications executive; Chmn., pres., CEO Amphenol. Office: Amphenol 358 Hall Ave Wallingford CT 06492 Office Phone: 203-265-8900. Fax: 203-265-8516.

LOEHLE, CRAIG, mathematical ecologist; b. Chgo., Oct. 23, 1952; s. Richard and Betty (Barnes) L.; m. Neda Samadani, July 5, 1980; children: Sholeh, Gloria, Niki. BS in Forest Sci. cum laude, U. Ga., 1976; MS in Forest Mgt., U. Washington, 1978; PhD in Math. Ecology, Colo. State U., 1982. Rsch. assoc. Colo. State U., Ft. Collins, 1978-82; scientific programmer SPSS, Inc., Northfield, Minn., 1982-84; postdoctoral fellow U. Ga., Athens, 1984-87; rsch. ecologist Westinghouse Savannah River Lab., Aiken, S.C., 1987-91; scientist Argonne (Ill.) Nat. Lab., 1991-98; sr. scientist Nat. Coun. Air & Stream Improvement, 1998—. Cons. Office of Environment Baha'i Internat. Community, N.Y.C., 1990—. Author: Thinking Strategically, 1996, On the Shoulders of Giants, 1994; contbr. over 90 articles to profl. jours. Mem. Ecol. Soc. Am., Internat. Soc. Ecol. Modeling. Mem. Baha'i Faith. Achievements include research in ecosystem structure and dynamics, catastrophe theory, life history theory, fractals in ecology, environmental impact analysis.

LOEHLIN, JOHN CLINTON, psychologist, educator; b. Ferozepore, India, Jan. 13, 1926; s. Clinton Herbert and Eunice (Cleland) L.; m. Marjorie Leafdale, Jan. 2, 1962; children: Jennifer Ann, James Norris. AB, Harvard U., 1947; PhD, U. Calif., Berkeley, 1957. With rsch. dept. McCann-Erickson, Inc., Cleve., 1947-49; instr. to asst. prof. psychology U. Nebr., Lincoln, 1957-64; mem. faculty U. Tex., Austin, 1964—, prof. psychology and computer scis., 1969-92, prof. emeritus, 1992—. Author: Computer Models of Personality, 1968, Latent Variable Models, 1987, Genes and Environment in Personality Development, 1992; co-author: Race Differences in Intelligence, 1975, Heredity, Environment and Personality, 1976, Introduction to Theories of Personality, 1985. With USNR, 1945-47, 51-53. Fellow Ctr. Advanced Study Behavioral Scis., 1971-72. Fellow Am. Psychol. Soc.; mem. Behavior Genetics Assn., Soc. Multivariate Exptl. Psychology. Home: 304 Almarion Dr Austin TX 78746-5644 Office: U Tex Dept Psychology 1 U Station A8000 Austin TX 78712-0187 Office Phone: 512-475-7008. E-mail: loehlin@psy.utexas.edu.

LOEHR, MARLA, chaplain; b. Cleve., Oct. 7, 1937; d. Joseph Richard and Eleanore Edith (Rothschuh) L. BS, Notre Dame Coll., South Euclid, Ohio, 1960; MAT, Ind. U., 1969; PhD, Boston Coll., 1988; Degree (hon.), Notre Dame Coll. Ohio, 1995. Cert. high sch. tchr., counselor, Ohio; cert. spiritual dir., pastoral min. Dean students Notre Dame Coll., South Euclid, Ohio, 1972-85, acting acad. dean, 1988, pres., 1988-95; chaplain Hospice of Western Res., Cleve., 1995—, spiritual dir., 1997—. Author: Mentor Handbook, 1985; co-author: Notre Dame College Model for Student Development, 1980. Hon. mem. Leadership Cleve. Class of 1990; v.p., trustee SJ Wellness Ctr., 1999; mem. leadership coun. Future Ch., Diocese of Cleve. Recipient Career Woman of Achievement award YWCA, 1992; named One of 100 Cleve.'s Most Powerful Women. Mem. Spiritual Dirs. Internat., Nat. Hospice Assn., Alpha Sigma Nu, Kappa Gamma Pi. Avocations: photography, hiking, reading, sports. Office: Hospice Western Res 29101 Health Campus Dr Ste 400 Westlake OH 44145-5268 E-mail: marlajlo@cs.com.

LOEHRER, PATRICK J., SR., internist, oncologist, educator; b. Chgo., Sept. 22, 1953; s. William Phillip and Marian (Greene) L.; m. Deborah Elaine Nell, June 7, 1975; children: Patrick Jr., Andrew, Elizabeth. MD, Rush Med. Coll., Chgo., 1975; BSME, Purdue U., 1978. Diplomate Am. Bd. Internal Medicine, Am. Bd. Oncology. From intern to resident in internal medicine Rush-Presbyn.-St. Luke's Hosp., Chgo., 1978-81; fellow in med. oncology Ind. U., Indpls., 1981-83, prof. internal medicine, 1993—. Chmn. Hoosier Oncology Group, Indpls., 1984—. Mem. ACP, Am. Soc. Clin. Oncology, Am. Fedn. Clin. Rsch.

LOEHRL, TODD A., otolaryngologist, surgeon; MD, Med. Coll. of Wis., 1991. Diplomate Am. Bd. of Otolaryngology. Rhinology/sinus surgery instr., fellow Johns Hopkins U., Balt., 1998—99; assoc. prof. Med. Coll. Wis., Milw., 1999—; chief otolaryngology head and neck surgery Zablocki VA Med. Ctr., Milw., 2001—. Contbr. articles to profl. jours. Cons. Am. Rhinologic Soc., 2003—05. Fellow: Am. Acad. Otolaryngology. Achievements include research in role of autonomic nervous system dysfunction in rhinosinusitis. Office: Med Coll Wis Dept Otolaryngology 9200 W Wisconsin Avenue Milwaukee WI 53226 Office Phone: 414-805-5585. Office Fax: 414-805-7936.

LOEHWING, LORD RUDI CHARLES, JR., publicist, radio broadcasting executive, journalist; b. Newark, July 26, 1957; s. Rudy Charles Sr. and Joan Marie (Bell) L.; m. Claire Popham, Sept. 4, 1987; children: Aspasia Joyce, Tesia Victoria, Rudi Douglas, Anna Marie, Samantha Diane, Ian Ryan. Student, Biscayne U., 1975, Seton Hall U., 1977, Hubbard U., 1980. Announcer radio sta. WHBI FM, N.Y.C., 1970-72; producer Am. Culture Entertainment, Belleville, N.J., 1973-74, exec. producer Hollywood, Calif., 1988-94; CEO Broadcaster's Network Internat., La Crescenta, Calif., 1989—, U.K., 1989—. Co-founder BNI Comms., L.A., 1989; bd. dirs. First Break, Hollywood, also U.K., 1988—. Author: Growing Pains, 1970; dir. exec. producer TV documentaries and comml. advertisements, 1983; patentee in field. Bd. dirs. Civic Light Opera of South Bay Cities, 1998—, L.A. Civic Light Opera, Tax Edn. Assn., Just Say No to Drugs, L.A., 1989, Hands Across the Atlantic, Internat. Country Top 10, The Rock of Russia, Job Search, Hollywood, U.K. and Russia. Named Youngest Comml. Radio Producer and Announcer for State of N.Y., Broadcaster's Network Internat., 1972 Mem. Nat. Press Club, Broadcasters Network Assn. (bd. dirs. 1977—), Profl. Bus. Comms. Assn. (founder 1989), BNI News Bur. (chmn. 1991—), Civic Light Opera of South Bay Cities (bd. dirs. 1996—), Friar's Club. Avocations: music, writing, photography, martial arts (recipient awards). Home: Leicester House 11487 Mt Gleason Ave Tujunga CA 91042-1229 Office: Broadcasters Netowrk Internat. Ltd Leicester House 11417 Mt Gleason Ave Tujunga CA 91042 Office Phone: 818-951-7933, 818-294-2885. Business E-Mail: rudil@bnicomm.com.

LOENGARD, JOHN BORG, photographer, editor; b. N.Y.C., Sept. 5, 1934; s. Richard Otto and Margery (Borg) L.; m. Eleanor Sturgis, Aug. 25, 1963 (div. 1987); children: Charles, Jennifer, Anna BA, Harvard Coll., 1956. Staff photographer Life mag., N.Y.C., 1961-72, picture editor, 1973-87; freelance photographer, 1987—; columnist Popular Photography mag., N.Y.C., 1987, Am. Photographer, N.Y.C., 1988—. Author: Pictures Under Discussion, 1987, Life Classic Photographs: A Personal Interpretation by John Loengard, 1988, Life Faces: Commentary by John Loengard, 1991, Celebrating the Negative, 1994, Georgia O'Keeffe at Ghost Ranch, 1995, Life Photographers: What They Saw, 1998; cons. editor: The Great Life Photographers, 2004; essays in Life mag., The Shakers, 1967, Georgia O'Keeffe, 1968, Vanishing Cowboys, 1970, Photographers Over 80, 1982, Henry Moore, 1983, Interstate 80, 1989. Recipient Ansel Adams award Am. Soc. Mag. Photographers, 1987, Lifetime Achievement award Photog. Adminstrs., Inc., 1996, Henry Luce Lifetime Achievement award Time Inc., 2004. Home: 20 W 86th St New York NY 10024-3604 E-mail: loenpics@aol.com.

LOENGARD, RICHARD OTTO, JR., lawyer; b. N.Y.C, Jan. 28, 1932; s. Richard Otto and Margery (Borg) L.; m. Janet Sara Senderowitz, Apr. 11, 1964; children: Maranda C., Philippa S.M. AB, Harvard U., 1953, LLB, 1956. Bar: N.Y. 1956, U.S. Dist. Ct. (so. dist.) N.Y. 1958. Assoc. Fried, Frank, Harris, Shriver & Jacobson, predecessor firms, N.Y.C., 1956-64, ptnr., 1967-97; of counsel Fried, Frank, Harris, Shriver & Jacobson, N.Y.C., 1997—; dep. tax legis. counsel, spl. asst. internat. tax affairs U.S. Dept. Treasury, Washington, 1964-67. Mem. Commerce Clearing House, Riverwoods, Ill. Editl. bd. Tax Transaction Libr., 1982-94; contbr. articles to profl. publs. Fellow Am. Coll. Tax Counsel; mem. ABA, N.Y. State Bar Assn. (exec. com. tax sect. 1984—, sec. 1994-95, vice chair 1995-97, chair 1997-98), Assn. Bar City N.Y. Office: Fried Frank Harris Shriver & Jacobson 1 New York Plz New York NY 10004-1980 Business E-Mail: loengri@ffhsj.com.

LOENING-BAUCKE, VERA, pediatrician, educator; MD, U. Erlangen, Germany, 1967. Prof. pediat. U. Iowa, Iowa City, 1992—2004. Author: Children With Constipation/encopresis (Fulbright Sr. Award, 1998). Office: U Iowa 200 Hawkins Dr Iowa City IA 52242 Office Phone: 319-356-1832. Office Fax: 319-356-4855.

LOEPERE, CAROL COLBORN, lawyer; b. Mpls., Oct. 6, 1959; BA in history, Radcliffe Coll., Harvard U., 1981; JD, NYU, 1984. Bar: Md. 1985, DC 1985, US Ct. Appeals 7th Cir. 1986. Assoc. Reed Smith LLP, Washington, 1984—92, ptnr., 1992—, also head health care group. Mem.: Women's Bar Assn. of DC, Am. Health Lawyers Assn., DC Bar Assn. Office: Reed Smith LLP 1301 K St NW, Ste 1100 - East Tower Washington DC 20005 Office Phone: 202-414-9216. Office Fax: 202-414-9299. Business E-Mail: cloepere@reedsmith.com.

LOERKE, WILLIAM CARL, art historian, educator; b. Toledo, Aug. 13, 1920; s. William Carl and Anna Louisa (Stallbaum) L.; m. Helen Trautmann, 1944; children— Anna Hurd, Timothy, Eric, Alison, Lisa Huff, Ellen, Martha. BA, Oberlin Coll., 1942; M.F.A., Princeton U., 1948, PhD, 1957. Acad. positions history of art Brown U., 1949-59; assoc. prof. Bryn Mawr Coll., 1959-64; prof. art history U. Pitts., 1964-71, chmn. fine arts dept., 1964-69; prof. Byzantine art Harvard U., Dumbarton Oaks Research Library, 1971-88, prof. emeritus, 1988—; dir. studies Ctr. Byzantine Studies, 1971-77; vis. prof. Cath. U. Am., 1978-88. Vis. prof. U. Md., 1988-92; mem. adv. bd. Ctr. for Advanced Study in Visual Arts, Nat. Gallery Art, Washington, 1979-82, 89-92, 97-2000. Co-author: The Place of Book Illumination in Byzantine Art, Princeton, 1975, Monasticism and the Arts, 1984, Codex Rossanensis, Commentarium, Rome, 1987, Architecture: Fundamental Issues, N.Y., 1990; contbr. Byzantine East, Latin West: Art Historical Studies in Honor of Kurt Weitzman, 1995; contbr. articles to profl. jours.; contbr. Dictionary of Byzantium, 1991. Served with USNR, 1943-46. Jr. fellow Princeton U., 1946-48, Dumbarton Oaks Harvard U., 1948-49, Danforth Tchr. fellow, 1956-57; Fulbright Rsch. scholar Am. Acad. Rome, 1952-53; recipient A.K. Porter prize Coll. Art Assn., 1961. Mem. Coll. Art Assn., Medieval Acad. Am., Soc. Fellows, Am. Acad. at Rome, Internat. Ctr. Med. Art. Home: 3004 Northridge Rd C504 Ellicott City MD 21043 E-mail: bloerke@aol.com.

LOESCH, KATHARINE TAYLOR, communication and theatre educator; b. Berkeley, Calif., Apr. 13, 1922; d. Paul Schuster and Katharine (Whiteside) Taylor; m. John George Loesch, Aug. 28, 1948; 1 child, William Ross. Student, Swarthmore Coll., 1939-41, U. Wash., 1942; BS, Columbia U., 1944, MA, 1949; grad., Neighborhood Playhouse Sch., 1946; postgrad., Ind. U., 1953; PhD, Northwestern U., 1961. Instr. speech Wellesley (Mass.) Coll., 1949-52, Loyola U., Chgo., 1956; asst. prof. English and speech Roosevelt U., Chgo., 1957, 62-65; assoc. prof. comm. and theatre U. Ill., Chgo., 1968-87, assoc. prof. emeritus, 1987—. Contbr. articles to profl. jours.; author numerous poems; performer of poetry. Active ERA, Ill., 1975-76. Grantee, Am. Philos. Soc., 1970, U. Ill., Chgo., 1970; Fgn. Travel grantee, 1983, Dylan

Thomas scholar. Mem. MLA, Am. Soc. for Aesthetics, Linguistic Soc. Am., Chgo. Linguistic Soc. (co-chmn. 1954-56), Nat. Comm. Assn. (chair interpretation divsn. 1979-80, Golden Ann. award 1969), Celtic Studies Assn. N.Am., Pi Beta Phi. Episcopalian. Home: 2129 N Sedgwick St Chicago IL 60614-4619 Office: U Ill Dept Performing Arts M/C 255 1040 W Harrison St Chicago IL 60607-7130 Office Phone: 312-996-0954. E-mail: dpa@uic.edu.

LOESCHER, RICHARD ALVIN, gastroenterologist; b. Brockton, Mass., Feb. 6, 1940; s. Vernon Alvin and Anna Marie (Good) L.; m. Linda Rockwell Clifford Loescher, June 5, 1965 (div. Jan. 1982); children: Steven Clifford Loescher, Laura May Loescher. BA, De Pauw U., 1961; MD cum laude, Harvard U., 1965. Diplomate Am. Bd. Internal Medicine, 1972, Am. Bd. Gastroenterology, 1973. Chief Med. Svc. U.S. Pub. Health Svc. Hosp., Lawton, Okla., 1967-69; chief Med. Staff, 1968-69; svc. unit dir., 1969; attending physician Seattle, 1970-71, U. Hosp., Seattle, 1970-71; active staff Sacred Heart Med. Ctr., Eugene, Oreg., 1973—, Eugene (Oreg.) Hosp., 1972-88; courtesy staff McKenzie-Williamette Hosp., Springfield, Oreg., 1982—2004. Recipient Rector scholarship DePauw U., 1957-61, Maimonides award Harvard Med. Sch., 1965. Mem. AMA, ACP-Am. Soc. Internal Medicine, Lane County Med. Soc., Oreg. Med. Assn., Am. Soc. for Gastrointestinal Endoscopy, Am. Acad. Med. Acupuncture, Alpha Omega Alpha, Phi Beta Kappa. Democrat. Unitarian Universalist. Avocations: physical fitness, personal growth, magic, outdoor activities. Home: 2345 Patterson St Apt 34 Eugene OR 97405-2974 Office: 1162 Willamette St Eugene OR 97401-3568 Office Phone: 541-687-6271.

LOESER, HANS FERDINAND, lawyer; b. Kassel, Germany, Sept. 28, 1920; s. Max and Cecilia H. (Erlanger) Loeser; m. Herta Lewent, Dec. 14, 1944; children: Helen, Harris M., H. Thomas. Student, CCNY, 1940—42, U. Pa., 1942—43; LLB magna cum laude, Harvard U., 1950. Bar: Mass. 1950, U.S. Supreme Ct. 1968. Assoc. Foley, Hoag & Eliot, Boston, 1950—55, ptnr., 1956—. Hon. consul-gen. Republic of Senegal, 1970—85; former mem. Mass. Bd. Bar Overseers; trustee Vineyard Open Land Found., Martha's Vineyard, Mass.; mem. exec. com., nat. bd. Lawyers' Com. for Civil Rights Under Law; steering com., past chmn. Lawyers Com. for Civil Rights Under Law of Boston Bar Assn.; founder, dir., treas. Lawyers Alliance for World Security, Washington. Corporator Mt. Auburn Hosp., Cambridge, Mass. Capt. U.S. Army, 1942—46. Decorated Bronze Star, Purple Heart; hon. fellow, U. Pa. Law Sch., 1978—79. Fellow: Mass. Bar Found., Am. Bar Found.; mem.: ABA, Boston Bar Assn., Mass. Bar Assn., Cambridge Club. Office: Foley Hoag LLP 155 Seaport Blvd Boston MA 02210-2600 Office Phone: 617-832-1139. Business E-Mail: hloeser@fhe.com.

LOESS, HENRY BERNARD, psychology educator; b. Chgo., June 24, 1924; s. Henry William and Alice Cecilia (Mansfield) L.; m. Frances Mary Van Horn, May 26, 1951; children— Kurt, Karin, Andrew, Alan. BS, Northwestern U., 1949, MS, 1950; PhD, U. Iowa, 1952. Prof. psychology, chmn. dept. Lake Forest (Ill.) Coll., 1952-58, Wooster (Ohio) Coll., 1958-88, prof. emeritus, 1988—; vis. lectr. Ohio State U., 1958-63; vis. research scholar U. Calif. at Berkeley, 1963-64, Cambridge (Eng.) U., 1968-69, U. Mich., 1973-74, Yale U., 1980-81. Vis. scientist Ohio Acad. Sci., 1962-92; regional coord. Am. Inst. Rsch. Project Talent, 1961-69; assoc. North Ctrl. Assn. Colls. and Secondary Schs., 1970-86; bd. dirs. Habitat for Humanity, Wayne County, 1989—, Hospice of Wayne County, 1990—, Wayne County Bd. Mental Retardation and Devel. Disabiliies, 1978-86, 93—. Author articles in field; cons. editor: Memory and Cognition, 1971-85. Served with USAAF, 1943-46. Mem. Am., Midwestern, Eastern psychol. assns., Psychonomic Soc., AAAS, Am. Assn. U. Profs., Sigma Xi. Home: 5410 Lehr Rd Wooster OH 44691-9288 E-mail: hloess@bright.net.

LOETE, STEVEN DONALD, pilot; b. Tacoma, Aug. 21, 1959; s. Donald Kenneth and Ida Lorraine (Buck) L.; m. Jodi Christine Barnett, 1998; children: Samantha, Tiffani, Joshua, Taylor. BA, Pacific Luth. U., 1984. Pilot contracting office USAF, Williams AFB, Ariz., 1985; flight instr. Clover Park Tech. Coll., Tacoma, 1986, 99; charter pilot Stellar Exec., Chandler, Ariz., 1986-87; pilot, airline capt. Maui Airlines, Guam, 1987; airline capt., checkairman Westair Airlines, Fresno, Calif., 1987-98; airline pilot Air Wis., 1998—; owner Northwestern Properties; corp. pilot Exec. Jet Mgmt., Cin., 1999—2004; pilot Aerodynamics, Inc., 2004—. Contbr. Save the Children, 1988-90; mem. Angel Flight, U. Puget Sound, 1981-83; bd. dirs. aviation adv. com. Clover Park Tech. Coll., 1991—. 1st lt. USAF, 1983-93. Mem. Airline Pilots Assn. (chmn. organizing com. 1989, chmn. coun. 1989-91). Republican. Methodist. Avocations: racquetball, fishing. Home and Office: Box 760 Spanaway WA 98387 Office Phone: 253-906-2000. E-mail: northwesternproperties@comcast.net.

LOEVINGER, JANE, psychologist, educator; b. St. Paul, Feb. 6, 1918; d. Gustavus and Millie (Strouse) L.; m. Samuel I. Weissman, July 13, 1943; children: Judith, Michael B. BA in Psychology, U. Minn., 1937, MS in Psychometrics, 1938; PhD. in Psychology, U. Calif., Berkeley, 1944. Instr. psychology and edn. Stanford (Calif.) U., 1941-42; lectr. psychology U. Calif., Berkeley, 1942-43; part-time instr. in stats. and sociology Washington U., St. Louis, 1946-47, research psychologist and cons. air force projects, 1950-53, research assoc. prof. child psychiatry, 1960-64, research assoc. prof., Grad. Inst. Edn., 1964-71, research assoc., Social Sci. Inst., 1964-70, research prof., 1971-74, prof., 1974-88, Stuckenberg prof. human values and moral devel., 1984-88, prof. emeritus dept. psychology, 1988—; rsch. assoc. Jewish Hosp., St. Louis, 1954-60. Mem. personality and cognition research rev. com. NIMH, 1970-74; ad hoc reviewer U. Witwatersrand, Johannesburg, Republic of South Africa, 1985, NSF, NIMH, various other orgns.; mem. various coms. Washington U.; lectr. in field. Author: (with R. Wessler) Measuring Ego Development 1: Construction and Use of a Sentence Completion Test, 1970, (with R. Wessler and C. Redmore) Measuring Ego Development 2: Scoring Manual for Women and Girls, 1970, Ego Development: Conceptions and Theories, 1976, Scientific Ways in the Study of Ego Development, 1979, Paradigms of Personality, 1987; cons. editor: Psychol. Rev., 1983—, Jour. Personality and Social Psychology, 1984—, Jour. Personality Assessment 1987—; contbr. articles to profl. jours., book revs., letters and abstracts. Recipient Research Sci. award NIMH, 1968-73, 74-79; Ednl. Testing Service Disting. Vis. scholar, 1969; Margaret M. Justin fellow, 1955-56, NIMH grantee, 1956-79. Fellow Am. Psychol. Assn. (pres. Div. 5 1962-63, mem. com. on tests, mem. policy and planning bd. 1969-72, mem. policy task force on psychologists in criminal justice system 1976-77, pres. Div. 24 1982-83, com. on early career award in personality 1985), Phi Beta Kappa, Sigma Xi (assoc.). Democrat. Home: 6 Princeton Ave Saint Louis MO 63130-3136 Office: Washington U Dept Of Psychology PO Box 11251 Saint Louis MO 63105-0051 Business E-Mail: jloeving@artsci.wustl.edu.

LOEVINGER, ROBERT, retired research physicist; b. St. Paul, Minn., Jan. 31, 1916; BA, U. Minn., 1936; MA, Harvard Coll., 1938; PhD, U. Calif., Berkeley, 1947. Asst. physicist The Mt. Sinai Hosp., N.Y.C., 1947-56; asst. prof. Stanford U. Med. Sch., Palo Alto, Calif., 1957-65; chief dosimetry sect. Internat. Atomic Energy Agy., Vienna, 1965-68; dosimetry group leader Nat. Inst. Stds. and Tech., Washington, 1968-88. Recipient William D. Coolidge award Am. Assn. Physicists in Medicine, 1995. Home: 316 New Mark Esplanade Rockville MD 20850-2734

LOEW, FRANKLIN MARTIN, academic administrator, biologist, consultant; b. Syracuse, N.Y., Sept. 8, 1939; s. David Franklin and Sarah (Adelaide) Loew; children: Timothy, Andrew. BS, Cornell U., 1961, DVM, 1965; PhD, U. Sask., 1971; DHL, Becker Coll., Worcester, Mass., 1998. Cert. Lic. veterinarian. Rsch. asst. Tulane U., New Orleans, 1966—67; prof. U. Sask., Saskatoon, 1967—77; dir. comparative medicine Johns Hopkins U., Balt., 1977—82; dean Sch. Vet. Medicine, Tufts U., Boston, 1982—95, Henry and Lois Foster prof. comparative medicine, 1985—95; v.p. Tufts U. Devel. Corp. Inc., Boston, 1991—95; dean Coll. Vet. Medicine Cornell U., Ithaca, 1995—97; pres., CEO Med. Foods, Inc., Cambridge, Mass., 1997—98; pres. Becker Coll., Worcester, Mass., 1998—. Cons. Can. Coun. Animal Care, Ottawa, 1969—84; mem. life scis. com. Nat. Acad. Sci., Washington, 1981—88; N.B. Lectr. Am. Soc. Microbiology; mem. nat. adv. bd. Ctr. on Bioethics Lit., Kennedy Inst. Georgetown U., 1986—; Scholfield lectr. U. Guelph, Canada; Smith lectr. U. Saskatachwen; Schalm lectr. U. Calif.; univ. lectr. Tex. A&M U.; bd. dirs. Mass. Health Resources Inst.; sci. and tech. avd. com. State of Mass., 1988—92; mem. Sec.'s Avd. Com. nat. Rsch. Initiative USDA, 1992—95; trustee Marine Biol. Lab., 1990—94, New Eng. Aquarium, 1991—98, Guys Drug Rsch. Unit., England; mem. panel animal health Nat. Rsch. Coun., 1992—; mem. Tuskegee Bioethics Adv. Com., 1998—; vis. scientist MIT, 1998—; chmn. Med. Foods, Inc., Cambridge, 1998—. Author: (novels) Vet in the Saddle, 1978; editor Laboratory Animal Medicine, 1984; contbr. numerous articles to profl. jours. Chmn. bd. trustees Boston Zool. Soc., 1984—88; trustee Worcester Acad., 1984—90, 1999—; Humane Soc. U.S., 1999—; mem. adv. coun. Nat. Ctr. Rsch. Resources, NIH, Blue Ribbon USDA, 1987—91; bd. dirs. Mass. SPCA, 1996—; mem. bus. bd. Pharmacia & Upjohn, 1996—98. Decorated Queen Elizabeth II Jubilee medal Gov.-Gen. Can.; named Vet. of Yr., Mass. SPCA, 1989; recipient Charles River prize, Am. Vet. Med. Assn., 1988, Disting. Svc. award, Mass. Vet. Med. Assn., 1992; grantee Med. Rsch. Coun. Can. fellow, 1969—71. Mem.: Am. Antiquarian Soc., Am. Socs. for Exptl. Biology, Assn. Am. Vet. Colls. (pres. 1985—86), Am. Inst. Nutrition, AAAS, NAS/Inst. Medicine. Office: Becker Coll 61 Sever St Worcester MA 01609-2165 E-mail: floew@beckercollege.edu.

LOEWEN, JAMES WILLIAM, sociologist; b. Decatur, Ill., Feb. 6, 1942; s. David F. and Winifred (Gore) L.; divorced, 1975; children: B. Nicholas, Lucy C. BA in Sociology cum laude with distinction, Carleton Coll., 1964; MA in Sociology, Harvard U., 1967, PhD in Sociology, 1968. From asst. prof. to assoc. prof. sociology Tougaloo Coll., 1968-75, chmn. dept. sociology-anthropology, 1969-72, chmn. social sci. divsn., 1972-74; assoc. prof. sociology U. Vt., 1975-83, prof. sociology, 1983—95. Vis. prof. sociology La Trobe U., Melbourne, Australia, 1981; adj. prof. Millsaps Coll., 1969-74; asst. prof. Harvard U., 1969; expert witness in voting and civil rights cases; speaker and presenter in field. Author: The Mississippi Chinese, 1971, 88, Social Science in the Courtroom, 1982, The Truth About Columbus, 1992, Lies My Teacher Told Me, 1994, Sundown Towns: A Hidden Dimension of Segregation in America, 2005; author, editor: Mississippi: Conflict and Change, 1975 (Lillian Smith award for best Southern nonfiction 1976). NSF postdoctoral fellow, 1975, Fulbright fellow, 1981, sr. postdoctoral fellow Smithsonian Instn., 1990-91, 93. Mem. Am. Sociol. Assn. (Sidney Spivack award 1978), Am. Studies Assn., Am. Edn. Rsch. Assn. Unitarian Universalist. Avocations: whitewater canoeing, wild mushrooming. Address: Jodi Solomon Speakers Ste 112 325 Huntington Ave Boston MA 02115

LOEWENBERG, GERHARD, political science professor; b. Berlin, Oct. 2, 1928; came to U.S., 1936, naturalized, 1943; s. Walter and Anne Marie (Cassirer) L.; m. Ina Perlstein, Aug. 22, 1950; children: Deborah, Michael. AB, Cornell U., 1949, A.M., 1950, PhD, 1955. Mem. faculty Mount Holyoke Coll., 1953-69, chmn. dept. polit. sci., 1963-69, acting academic dean, 1968-69; prof. polit. sci. U. Iowa, Iowa City, 1970—2003, U. Iowa Found. Disting. prof. emeritus, 2003—, chmn. dept., 1982-84, dean Coll. Liberal Arts, 1984-92, dir. Comparative Legis. Research Center, 1971-82, 92—; vice chair East-West Parliamentary Practice Project, 1990-2000. Vis. assoc. prof. Columbia, UCLA, 1966, U. Mass. summer session at Bologna, Italy, 1967, Cornell U., 1968; mem. council Inter-Univ. Consortium for Polit. Research, 1971-74, chmn., 1973-74 Author: Parliament in the German Political System, 1967, Parlamentarismus im politischen System der Bundesrepublik Deutschland, 1969, Modern Parliaments: Change or Decline, 1971; co-author: Comparing Legislatures, 1979; co-editor: Handbook of Legislative Research, 1985, Legis. Studies Quar., Legislatures: Comparative Perspectives on Representative Assemblies, 2002; contbr. articles to profl. jours. Trustee Mt. Holyoke Coll., 1971-84, chmn., 1979-84. Fulbright fellow, 1957-58; Rockefeller fellow, 1961-62; Social Sci. Research Council faculty research fellow, 1964-65; Guggenheim fellow, 1969-70 Fellow Am. Acad. Arts & Scis.l; mem. Am. Polit. Sci. Assn. (coun. 1971-73, v.p. 1990-91, Frank J. Goodnow award 2001), Midwest Polit. Sci. Assn., Phi Beta Kappa, Phi Kappa Phi, Pi Sigma Alpha. Office: U Iowa 336 Schaeffer Hall Iowa City IA 52242-1409 Office Phone: 319-335-2345. Business E-Mail: g-loewenberg@uiowa.edu.

LOEWENSTEIN, GEORGE F., education educator; m. Donna Harsch; children: Max, Rosa. PhD, Yale U., 1985. Asst. Inst. for Advanced Study, Princeton, 1984—85, fellow Berlin, 1994—95; prof. grad. sch. bus. U. Chgo., 1985—90; prof. Carnegie Mellon U., Pitts., 1990; fellow Ctr. for Advanced Study Beh Sci., Stanford, Calif., 1997—98. Vis. scholar Russell Sage Found., NYC, 1988—89. Office: Carnegie Mellon Univ Dept Social & Decision Sci Pittsburgh PA 15213 Office Phone: 412-268-8787. Office Fax: 412-268-6938. Business E-Mail: gl20@andrew.cmu.edu.

LOEWENSTEIN, WALTER BERNARD, nuclear energy industry executive; b. Gensungen, Hesse, Germany, Dec. 23, 1926; arrived in U.S., 1938; m. Lenore C. Pearlman, June 21, 1959; children: Mark Victor, Marcia Beth. BS, U. Puget Sound, 1949; postgrad., U. Wash., 1949-50; PhD, Ohio State U., 1954. Registered profl. engr., Calif. Rsch. asst., fellow Ohio State U., Columbus, 1951-54; rsch. asst. Los Alamos Nat. Lab., 1952-54; sr. physicist, divsn. dir. Argonne (Ill.) Nat. Lab., 1954-73; dept. dir., dep. divsn. dir. Electric Power Rsch. Inst., Palo Alto, Calif., 1973-89, profl. cons., 1989—, mem. large aerosol containment experiment project bd., 1983-87. Mem. Marviken project bd. Studsvik Rsch. Ctr., Stockholm, 1978-85; mem. LOFT project bd. Nuc. Energy Agy., Paris, 1982-89; mem. tech. adv. com. nuc. safety Ontario Hydro Corp., 1990-98; mem. nuc. engring. dept. adv. com. Brookhaven Nat. Lab., 1992-96; mem. advanced tech. divsn. adv. com. Los Alamos Nat. Lab., 1994-99; mem. nuc. engring. dept. adv. com. U. Calif., Berkeley, 1994-2003. With USNR, 1945-46. Recipient Alumnus Cum Laude award U. Puget Sound, 1976. Fellow Am. Phys. Soc., Am. Nuc. Soc. (v.p., pres. 1988-90); mem. Am. Assn. Engring. Socs. (sec., treas. 1990), Nat. Acad. Engring. Jewish. Avocations: history, golf. Home and Office: 515 Jefferson Dr Palo Alto CA 94303 Personal E-mail: wblo3@aol.com.

LOEWENTHAL, NESSA PARKER, intercultural communications consultant; b. Chgo., Oct. 13, 1930; d. Abner and Frances (Ness) Parker; m. Martin Moshe Loewenthal, July 7, 1951 (dec. Aug. 1973); children: Dann Marcus, Ronn Carl, Deena Miriam; m. Gerson B. Selk, Apr. 17, 1982 (dec. June 1987). BA in Edn. and Psychology, Stanford U., 1952. Faculty Stanford Inst. for Intercultural Communication, Palo Alto, Calif., 1973-87; dir. Trans Cultural Svcs., San Francisco, 1981-86, Portland, Oreg., 1986—. Dir. dependent svcs. and internat. edn. Bechtel Group, San Francisco, 1973-81, internat. edn. cons., 1981-84; mem. adv. com. dept. internat. studies Lesley Coll., Cambridge, Mass., 1986—; mem. Oreg. Ethics Commns., 1990—; mem. Bay Area Ethics Consortium, Berkeley, 1985-90; chmn. ethics com. Sietar Internat., Washington, 1987—, mem. governing bd., 1992-95; mem. faculty Summer Inst. for Internat. Comms., Portland, Oreg., 1987-97; core faculty Oreg. Gov.'s Sch. Svc. Leadership, Salem, 1995-97. Author: Professional Integration, 1987, Update: Federal Republic of Germany, 1990, Update: Great Britain, 1987; author, editor book series Your International Assignment, 1973-81; contbr. articles to profl. jours. Mem. equal opportunity and social justice task force Nat. Jewish Coun. on Pub. Affairs; bd. dirs. Kids on the Block, Portland, Portland Jewish Acad., 1996—, Portland Ashkalon Sister City Assn., Portland Jewish Fedn., 1999—, Coalition to Eliminate Bias and Hate Crimes in Oreg., 1999—; bd. dirs., co-chair ethics com. Soc. Humanistic Judaism, 1996-99; task force on Racism and Violence, Portland, Oreg.; mem. Lafayette (Calif.) Traffic Commn., 1974-80; bd. dirs. Ctr. for Ethics and Social Policy, 1988-91; mem. exec. bd. and planning com. Temple Isaiah, Lafayette, 1978-82; bd. dirs. Calif. Symphony, Orinda, 1988-90; mem. exec. com. overseas schs. adv. com. U.S. Dept. State, 1976-82; bd. dirs. Jewish Fedn. Oregon; mem. cmty. rels. com. Portland Jewish Fedn.; mem. Nat. Jewish Cmty. Rels.; mem. Task Force on Racism, Ethnicity and Pub. Policy, 1998—. Named Sr. Interculturalist, Sietar Internat., 1986. Mem. ASTD (exec. bd. internat. profl. performance area 1993-97, 99), Soc. for Intercultural Edn. Tng. and Rsch. (chmn. 1986-87, nomination com. 1984-86, co-chmn. 1989-90, chmn. ethics com. 1989-98, governing bd. 1992-95), World Affairs Coun. Democrat. Avocations: photography, swimming. Office: PO Box 6526 Bend OR 97708-6526 E-mail: nessa@transport.com.

LOEWENTHAL, STEVEN RICHARD, lawyer; b. Beverly Hills, Calif., July 11, 1973; s. William Julius and Martha Rotler Loewenthal. BS in Criminology, U. Tampa, 1996; JD, Stetson U., 1999. Intern Fed. Pub. Defenders Office, Tampa, 1998, Hillsborough County States Atty., 1998; assoc. Moye, O'Brien, O'Rourke, Orlando, 1999—2000; atty pvt. practice, Tampa, 2000—. Office: 209 S Howard Tampa FL 33606 E-mail: attorney@tampabay.rr.com.

LOEWY, ROBERT GUSTAV, aerospace transportation executive, engineering educator; b. Phila., Feb. 12, 1926; s. Samuel N. and Esther (Silverstein) L.; m. Lila Myrna Spinner, Jan. 16, 1955; children: David G., Esther Elizabeth, Joanne Victoria, Raymond Matthew. B in Aero. Engring., Rensselaer Poly. Inst., 1947; MS, MIT, 1948; PhD, U. Pa., 1962. Sr. vibrations engr. Martin Co., Balt., 1948-49; assoc. rsch. engr. Cornell Aero. Lab., Buffalo, 1949-52, prin. engr., 1953-55; staff stress engr. Piasecki Helicopter Co., Morton, Pa., 1952-53; chief dynamics engr., then chief tech. engr. Vertol divsn. Boeing Co., Essington, Pa., 1955-62; from assoc. prof. to prof. mech. and aerospace scis. U. Rochester, 1962-73, dean Coll. Engring. and Applied Sci., 1967—73; dir. Space Sci. Ctr., 1966-71; v.p., provost Rensselaer Poly. Inst., Troy, NY, 1973—78, inst. prof., 1978-93; dir. Rotorcraft Tech. Ctr., 1982-93; chmn. sch. aerospace engring. Ga. Inst. Tech., 1993—, Wm. R.T. Oakes prof., 2000—. Chief scientist USAF, 1965-66; cons. govt. and industry, 1959—; mem. aircraft panel Pres.'s Sci. Adv. Coun., 1968-72; mem. Air Force Sci. Adv. Bd., 1966-75, 1978-85, vice chmn., 1971, chmn., 1972-75, chmn. aero. systems div. adv. group, 1978-84; mem. Post Office Rsch. and Engring. Adv. Coun., 1966-68; mem. rsch. and tech. adv. com. on aeros. NASA, 1970-71, mem. rsch. and tech. adv. coun., 1976-77, chmn. aero. adv. com., 1978-83; mem. aerospace engring. bd. NRC, 1972-78, 1988-93, mem. bd. on army sci. and tech., 1986-90; mem. naval studies bd. NAS, 1979-82; chmn. tech. adv. com. FAA, 1976-77; bd. dirs. Vertical Flight Found. Contbr. articles to profl. jours. Served with USNR, 1944-46. Recipient NASA Disting. Pub. Svc. award, 1983; Gotshall-Powell scholar Rensselaer Poly. Inst., 1946; USAF Exceptional Civilian Svc. awards, 1966, 75, 85, Spirit of St. Louis medal ASME, 1996. Fellow AAAS; hon. fellow AIAA (Lawrence Sperry award 1958, Dryden lectr. 1999), Am. Helicopter Soc. (pres. 2002-03, tech. dir. 1963-64, chmn. bd. 2003-04, Nikolsky lectr. 1984); mem. Am. Soc. Engring. Edn., Nat. Acad. Engring., Sigma Xi, Sigma Gamma Tau, Tau Beta Pi. Achievements include research on unsteady rotor aerodynamics first showing it to be fundamentally different from fixed wing. Home: 3420 Wood Valley Rd NW Atlanta GA 30327-1518 Office: Ga Inst Tech Sch Aerospace Engring Atlanta GA 30332-0001 Office Phone: 404-894-3002. Business E-Mail: robert.loewy@ae.gatech.edu. *Looking back, I was fortunate to have known somehow, from an early age, that I would be an aeronautical engineer. That profession, through positions in industry, research and education, has provided challenge, satisfaction and valued associations.*

LOFGREN, CHARLES AUGUSTIN, historian, educator; b. Missoula, Mont., Sept. 8, 1939; s. Cornelius Willard and Helen Mary (Augustin) L.; m. Jennifer Jenkins Wood, Aug. 6, 1986. AB with great distinction, Stanford U., 1961; AM, 1962, PhD, 1966. Instr. history San Jose State Coll., 1965-66; asst. prof. Claremont McKenna Coll., 1966-71; assoc. prof., 1971-76; prof., 1976—; prof. Am. history and politics, 1976—. Author: Government from Reflection and Choice, 1986, The Plessy Case, 1988, Claremont Pioneers, 1996; contbr. articles to profl. jours. Served with USAR, 1957-63. Mem. Am. Soc. Legal History, Orgn. Am. Historians, Am. Hist. Assn. Republican. Roman Catholic. Office: Claremont McKenna Coll Dept History 850 Columbia Ave Claremont CA 91711-6420 Business E-Mail: clofgren@mckenna.edu.

LOFGREN, CHRISTOPHER B., trucking executive; BS in Indsl. and Mgmt. Engring., MS in Indsl. and Mgmt. Engring., Mont. State U.; PhD in Indsl. and Systems Engring., Georgia U. Tech. V.p. Schneider Logistics, Green Bay, Wis., 1994—2000, chief info. officer; COO Schneider Nat., Inc., Green Bay, Wis., 2000—. Office: Schneider Nat Inc PO Box 2545 3101 S Packerland Dr Green Bay WI 54306-2545

LOFGREN, KARL ADOLPH, surgeon, educator, retired surgeon; b. Killeberg, Sweden, Apr. 1, 1915; s. Hokan Albin and Teckla Elizabeth (Carlsson) L.; m. Jean Frances Taylor, Sept. 12, 1942; children: Karl Edward, Anne Elizabeth. Student, Northwestern U., 1934-37; MD, Harvard U., 1941; MS in Surgery, U. Minn., 1947. Diplomate Am. Bd. Surgery. Intern U. Minn. Hosps., Mpls., 1941-42; Mayo Found. fellow in surgery, 1942-44, 46-48; asst. surgeon Royal Acad. Hosp., Uppsala, Sweden, 1949; asst. to surg. staff Mayo Clinic, Rochester, Minn., 1949-50, cons. sect. peripheral vein surgery, 1950-81; instr. in surgery Mayo Grad. Sch. Medicine, 1951-60, asst. prof. surgery, 1960-74; comdg. officer USNR Med. Co. Mayo Clinic, 1963-67, head sect. peripheral vein surgery, dept. surgery, 1966-79, sr. cons., 1980-81. Assoc. prof. surgery Mayo Med. Sch., 1974-79, prof., 1979-81, emeritus prof., 1982—; cons. surg. staff Rochester Meth. Hosp., St. Mary's Hosp. Contbr. chpts. to textbooks, articles to profl. jours. Mem. adv. bd. Salvation Army, Rochester, 1959-81, 82—, pres., 1962-63. Served to capt. M.C. USNR, 1944-46. Decorated Bronze Star Fellow ACS; mem. Soc. Vascular Surgery, Midwestern Vascular Surgery Soc., Internat. Cardiovascular Soc., Minn. Surg. Soc., Swedish Surg. Soc. (hon.), Swiss Soc. Phlebology (co-worker), So. Minn. Med. Assn. (pres. 1972-73), Scandinavian Soc. Phlebology (hon.), Am. Venous Forum, Rotary Club, Sigma Xi. Baptist. Office: Mayo Clin Rochester MN 55905-0001 Home: 211 2nd St NW Apt 1916 Rochester MN 55901

LOFGREN, RONALD RICHARD, music educator; b. Nov. 8, 1952; m. Lauran Lofgren, Aug. 15, 1975; children: Kathryn Willis, Elisabeth. BA magna cum laude, Bethany Coll., 1974; MusM in Choral Conducting, M in Sacred Music, So. Meth. U., 1979; D of Musical Arts, U. Kans., 1989. Music instr. Unified Sch. Dist. #354, Claflin, Kans., 1975—77; vocal music instr. Unified Sch. Dist. #400, Lindsborg, Kans., 1980—84; grad. tchg. asst. U. Kans., Lawrence, 1985—89; asst. prof. music St. Mary of the Plains Coll., Dodge City, Kans., 1989—92; assoc. prof. music William Penn Coll. (now U.), Oskaloosa, Iowa, 1992—97; dir. vocal/choral activities Southwestern Mich. Coll., Dowagiac, Mich., 1997—2000; assoc. prof. music Wayne (Nebr.) State Coll., 2000—. Condr./clinician in field; adjudicator in field. Pulpit supply various Luth. Churches in NE, IA, KS, 1970—2004; mem. Wayne Cmty. Theater Bd. Mem.: Nat. Assn. Tchrs. Singing, Music Educators Nat. Conf., Internat. Assn. for Jazz Edn., Coll. Music Soc., Chorus Am., Am. Choral Dirs. Assn. (life), Pi Kappa Lambda, Phi Mu Alpha Sinfonia, Beta Tau Sigma. Office: Wayne State College 1111 Main Wayne NE 68787 Office Phone: 402-375-7358. Business E-Mail: rolofgr1@wsc.edu.

LOFGREN, ZOE, congresswoman; b. Palo Alto, Calif., Dec. 21, 1947; d. Milton R. and Mary Violet Lofgren; m. John Marshall Collins, Oct. 22, 1978; children: Sheila Zoe Lofgren Collins, John Charles Lofgren Collins. BA in Polit. Sci., Stanford U., 1970; JD cum laude, U. Santa Clara, 1975. Bar: Calif. 1975, D.C. Adminstrv. asst. to Congressman Don Edwards, San Jose, Calif., 1970-79; ptnr. Webber and Lofgren, San Jose, 1979-81; mem. Santa Clara County Bd. Suprs., 1981-94, U.S. Congress from 16th Calif. dist., 1995—, Homeland Security com., House Adminstrn. com. and Judiciary com., Joint com. on Libr. Mem. com. on stds. of ofcl. conduct, jud. com., sci. com.; part-time prof. law U. Santa Clara, 1978-80. Exec. dir. Cmty. Housing Developers, Inc., 1979-80; trustee San Jose C.C. Dist., 1979-81; bd. dirs. Cmty. Legal Svcs., 1978-81, San Jose Housing Svc. Ctr., 1978-79; mem. steering com. sr. citizens housing referendum, 1978; del. Calif. State Bar Conv., 1979-82, Dem. Nat. Conv., 1976; active Assn. Immigration and Nationality Lawyers, 1976-82, Calif. State Dem. Ctrl. Com., 1975-78, Santa Clara County Dem. Ctrl. Com., 1974-78, Notre Dame H.S. Blue Ribbon Com., 1981-84, Victim-Witness Adv. Bd., 1981-94. Recipient Bancroft-Whitney award for Excellence in Criminal Procedure, 1973. Mem. Santa Clara County Bar Assn. (trustee 1979—), Santa Clara County Women Lawyers Com. (exec. bd. 1979-80), Santa Clara Law Sch. Alumni Assn. (v.p.

1977, pres. 1978), Nat. Women's Polit. Caucus, Assn. of Bay Area Govts. (exec. bd. 1981-86). Democrat. Office: US Ho Reps 102 Cannon Ho Office Bldg Washington DC 20515-0516 also: 635 N 1st St Ste B San Jose CA 95112-5110

LOFLAND, GARY KENNETH, cardiac surgeon; b. Milford, Del., Mar. 5, 1951; s. Joseph Sudler and Doris Louise (Peters) L.; m. Janice Marie Show, Feb. 3, 1979; children: Kiernan Sudler, Glennis Kathleen. BA cum laude, Boston U., 1969, MD cum laude, 1975. Diplomate Am. Bd. Surgery, Am. Bd. Thoracic Surgery; lic. physician, Va., N.Y., Mont., N.C. Intern, jr. asst. resident in surgery Duke U. Med. Ctr., Durham, N.C., 1975-81, rsch. fellow dept. surgery, 1979-81, sr. asst. resident in surgery, 1981-84, chief resident in surgery, 1984-85, teaching scholar in cardiac surgery, 1985-86; sr. registrar in cardiothoracic surgery Hosp. for Sick Children, London, 1986-87; dir. cardiovascular surgery Children's Hosp. of Buffalo, 1987-88; asst. prof. surgery SUNY, Buffalo, 1987-88; assoc. prof. surgery/pediatrics, Med. Coll. Va., Richmond, 1988-94, dir. pediatric cardiac surgery/med. dir. cardiac surgery ICU, 1988-94; clin. prof. surgery Georgetown U., Washington, 1994-97; dir. Columbia/HCA Ctr. Congenital Heart Disease, Richmond, 1994-97; dir. cardiovascular surgery Children's Mercy Hosp., Kansas City, Mo., 1997—; prof. surgery U. Mo. Kansas City Sch. Medicine, 1997—, Joseph Boon Gregg chair sect. cardiac surgery. Editor (in chief): Progress in Pediat. Cardiology, 2002—; mem. editl. rev. bd.:, —, Year Book of Thoracic Surgery, —; contbr. articles to profl. jours. Pres. Am. Heart Assn., Richmond; mem. bd. trustees Transplant Found. Lt. comdr. USPHS, 1977-79. Recipient Univ. Hosp. Trustees award, Boston, 1975; HEW/USPHS commendation medal, 1979. Mem. AMA, Am. Heart Assn., Am. Assn. Thoracic Surgery, Assn. for Acad. Surgery, Internat. Soc. for Heart Transplantation, Med. Soc. Va., Richmond Acad. Medicine, Richmond Surg. Soc., So. Thoracic Surg. Assn., Soc. for Thoracic Surgeons, Congenital Heart Surgeons Soc., Alpha Omega Alpha. Home: PO Box 126 Crozier VA 23039-0126 Office: Children's Mercy Hosp Divsn Cardiovascular Surgery 2406 Gillham Rd Kansas City MO 64108 Office Phone: 816-234-3580. Business E-Mail: glofland@cmh.edu.

LOFQUIST, VICKI L., journalist; b. Des Moines, Aug. 2, 1949; d. Edgar William and Gwendolyn Marjorie Lofquist; m. Craig Peter Thiesen, May 23, 1997. Student, St. Andrews (Scotland) U., 1969—70; BA, Grinnell Coll., 1971; MA, U. Minn., 1976. Cert. fund raising exec. 2004. Prodr. Sta. KUOM Radio U. Minn., Mpls., 1974—85, 1989—91; cons., ind. radio prodr. Mpls., 1992—96; devel. dir. Minn. Internat. Ctr., Mpls., 1997—2000, Books for Africa, St. Paul, 2000—; devel. officer Children's Home Soc. and Family Svcs., St. Paul, 2001—04; alumni rels., ann. fund coord. Metro. State U., St. Paul, 2004—. Prodr.(writer): (radio documentaries) Leading to Beijing: Voices of Global Women (Clarion Award, Women In Communication, 1996, Hon. Mention, Internat. Assn. of Women in Radio & T.V., 1997), Science Lives: Women & Minorities in the Sciences, Sound Studies in Psychology, a CPB/Annenberg Project. Bd. dirs. St. Paul LWV, 2002—. Grantee Bicentennial Swedish-Am. Exch. Fund, Swedish Inst., Stockholm, Sweden, 1991. Office: Metro State Univ 700 E 7th St Saint Paul MN 55106 Office Phone: 651-793-1810.

LÖFSTEDT, LEENA (MAIJA LEENA LÖFSTEDT), Romance philology educator; b. Helsinki, Finland, July 17, 1937; came to U.S., 1967; d. Paavo and Maire Anelma (Sormunen) Kekomäki; m. Bengt Torkel Magnus Löfstedt, Oct. 15, 1961 (dec.); children: Ragnar, Torsten, Ritva, Ingvar. MA, Helsinki U., 1960, PhD, 1966. Assoc. prof. Romance philology U. Helsinki, 1976-78, periodical tchg. of Romance philology, 1980—; prof. Romance philology U. Jyväskylä, Finland, 1978-81; rsch. assoc. Ctr. for Medieval and Renaissance Studies, UCLA, 1989—. Mem. Adv. Coun. Romance Philology, Berkeley, Calif., 1996—; mem. Com. Sci., RLiR, Nancy, France, 1998-2004; adv. coun. Neuphilologische Mitteilungen, Helsinki, 2001—. Author: Les expressions du commandement et de la défense en latin, 1966, Textual criticism: editions of Old French translations of Vegetius by Jean de Meun, 1979, Jean de Vignay, 1982, the anonymous of 1380, 1989, and the editio princeps of an Old French translation of Gratian's Decretum, 1992, 93, 96, 97, 2001, (with Bengt Löfstedt) Maturin Cordier, De Corrupti sermonis emendatione, 1989; contbr. numerous articles to profl. jours. Mem. Société Néophilologique, Medieval Acad. Am., Academia Scientiarum Fennica, N.Y. Acad. Scis. Lutheran. Avocations: family activities, hiking, gardening. Business E-Mail: leenal@ucla.edu.

LOFTFIELD, ROBERT BERNER, biochemistry professor; b. Detroit, Dec. 15, 1919; s. Sigurd and Katherine (Roller) L.; m. Ella Bradford, Aug. 24, 1946 (dec. Dec. 1990); children: Lore Loftfield DeBower, Eric, Linda, Norman, Bjorn, Curtis, Katherine, Earl, Allison Dinsdale, Ella-Kari. BS, Harvard U., 1941, MA, 1942, PhD, 1946. Research assoc. MIT, Cambridge, 1946-48; research assoc. to sr. research assoc. Mass. Gen. Hosp., Boston, 1948-64; asst. to assoc. prof. biochemistry Harvard U. Sch. Medicine, Boston, 1948-64; prof. biochemistry Sch. Medicine U. N.Mex., Albuquerque, 1964-90, chmn. dept. biochemistry, 1964-71, 78-90, prof. emeritus, 1990—. Contbr. articles on protein biosynthesis and enzymology to profl. jours. Served as corp. U.S. Army, 1945-46. Fellow Damon Runyon Fund, 1952-53, Guggenheim Found., 1961-62; Fulbright fellow, 1977, 83; sr. fellow NIH, 1971-72. Mem. AAAS, Am. Soc. Biol. Chemists, Am. Chem. Soc., Am. Assn. Cancer Rsch., Biophys. Soc., Marine Biol. Lab. Lutheran. Avocations: sailing, hiking, camping, skiing. Home: 707 Fairway Rd NW Albuquerque NM 87107-5718 Office: U NMex Sch Medicine Dept Biochemis & Molecular Biology Albuquerque NM 87131-0001 Office Phone: 505-272-8452.

LOFTIS, JOHN, JR., (JOHN CLYDE LOFTIS JR.), language educator; b. Atlanta, May 16, 1919; s. John Clyde and Marbeth (Brown) L.; m. Anne Nevins, June 29, 1946; children: Mary, Laura, Lucy. BA, Emory U., 1940; MA, Princeton U., 1942, PhD, 1948. Instr. English Princeton, 1946-48; instr., then asst. prof. English UCLA, 1948-52; faculty Stanford U., 1952-81, prof. English, 1958-81, Bailey prof. English, 1977-81, Bailey prof. emeritus, 1981—, chmn. dept., 1973-76. Author: Steele at Drury Lane, 1952, Comedy and Society from Congreve to Fielding, 1959, La Independencia de la Literatura Norteamericana, 1961, The Politics of Drama in Augustan England, 1963, The Spanish Plays of Neoclassical England, 1973, (with others) The Revels History of Drama in English, Vol. V, 1976, Sheridan and the Drama of Georgian England, 1977, Renaissance Drama in England and Spain: Topical Allusion and History Plays, 1987; editor: (Steele) The Theatre, 1962, Restoration Drama: Modern Essays in Criticism, 1966, (with V.A. Dearing) The Works of John Dryden, Vol. IX, 1966, (Sheridan) The School for Scandal, 1966, (Nathaniel Lee) Lucius Junius Brutus, 1967, (Addison) Essays in Criticism and Literary Theory, 1975, The Memoirs of Anne, Lady Halkett and Ann, Lady Fanshawe, 1979, (with D.S. Rodes and V.A. Dearing) The Works of John Dryden, Vol. XI, 1978, (with P.H. Hardacre) Colonel Bampfield's Apology, 1993; co-editor Augustan Reprint Society, 1949-1952, English Literature, 1660-1800: A Current Bibliography, 1951-56; gen. editor: Regents Restoration Drama Series, 35 vols, 1962-81; mem. editorial bd.: Studies in English Literature, 1966-76, Huntington Library Quar., 1968-76, Wesleyan Edit. Works Henry Fielding, 1970-83, Augustan Reprint Soc., 1985-90. Served with USNR, 1942-46, PTO. Fellow Fund Advancement Edn., 1955-56; Fulbright lectr. Am. studies Peru, 1959-60; Guggenheim fellow, 1966-67; fellow Folger Shakespeare Library, 1967; NEH fellow, 1978-79 Mem. MLA, Phi Beta Kappa, Kappa Alpha. Home: 7 Arastradero Rd Portola Valley CA 94028-8012 Office: Stanford Univ Dept English Stanford CA 94305

LOFTIS, ROBERT G., ambassador; b. Fayetteville, N.C., Nov. 1956; married; 2 children. BA in Polit. Sci., Colo. State U., 1979. Various positions with Fgn. Svc., 1980—2001; various to dep. dir. Office of Peacekeeping and Humanitarian Affairs, Dept. State, 1993—95; counselor for polit. and specialized agy. affairs U.S. Mission, Geneva, 1995—99; dep. chief of mission U.S. Embassy Maputo, Maputo, Mozambique, 1999—2001; U.S. amb. to Lesotho, 2001—. Recipient Meritorious Honor award, Dept. State, 1988, Superior Honor award, 1986, 1993, 1995. Office: DOS Amb 2340 Maseru Pl Washington DC 20521

LOFTON, KEVIN EUGENE, medical facility administrator; b. Beaumont, Tex., Sept. 29, 1954; BS, Boston U., 1976; M Health Care Adminstrn., Ga. State U., 1979. Adminstrv. resident Meml. Med. Ctr., Corpus Christi, Tex., 1978-79; adminstr. emergency svcs. Univ. Hosp., Jacksonville, Fla., 1979-80, adminstr. material mgmt., 1980-81, asst. exec. dir. ambulatory care, 1981-82, asst. v.p. ambulatory svcs., 1982-83, v.p. profl. svcs., 1983-86; exec. v.p. Univ. Med. Ctr., Jacksonville, 1986-90; exec. dir. Howard Univ. Hosp., Washington, 1990-93, U. Ala. Hosp., Birmingham, 1993-98; group pres. Cath. Health Initiative, Louisville, 1998-99, COO Denver, 1999—. Contbr. articles to profl. publs. Fellow Am. Coll. Health Care Execs. (R.S. Hudgens award 1993); mem. Am. Hosp. Assn. (bd. dirs.), Nat. Assn. Health Svcs. Execs. (past pres., bd. dirs.). Office: Catholic Health Inti 2000 Warrington Way #163 Louisville KY 40222-6467

LOFTON, THOMAS MILTON, lawyer; b. Indpls., May 12, 1929; s. Milton Alexander and Jane (Routzong) L.; m. Betty Louise Blades, June 20, 1954; children: Stephanie Louise, Melissa Jane. BS, Ind. U., 1951, JD, 1954, LLD (hon.), 2000, Wabash Coll., 2001. Bar: Ind. 1954, U.S. Ct. Appeals (7th cir.) 1959, U.S. Supreme Ct. 1958. Law clk. to justice U.S. Supreme Ct., Washington, 1954-55; ptnr. Baker & Daniels, Indpls., 1958-91. Dir. Ind. U. Found., Bloomington, 1978-91, Clowes Fund, 1980-2001; chmn. bd. Lilly Endowment, Indpls., 1991—; mem. bd. visitors Ind. U. Law, Bloomington, 1976—. Editor-in-chief Ind. Law Jour., 1953. Trustee Earlham Coll., 1988—91; dir. Allen Whitehill Clowes Charitable Found., 1990—. 1st lt. U.S. Army, 1955—58. Recipient Peck award Wabash Coll., 1982, Disting. Alumni Svc. award Ind. U., 1997. Mem.: Ind. Acad., Masons, Order of Coif, Sigma Nu, Beta Gamma Sigma. Republican. Presbyterian. Home: 9060 Pickwick Dr Indianapolis IN 46260-1714 Office: Lilly Endowment 2800 N Meridian St Indianapolis IN 46208-4713

LOFTUS, EDWARD VINCENT, JR., gastroenterologist; b. Phila., Aug. 29, 1962; s. Edward Vincent Loftus, Sr. and Nancy Burke; m. Beth Bravante, Nov. 10, 1990; children: Sarah, Laura. BS, Villanova U., 1984; MD, U. Pa., 1988. Diplomate Internal Medicine Am. Bd. of Internal Medicine, 1991, Gastroenterology Am. Bd. of Internal Medicine, 1995. Resident internal medicine Temple U. Health Sciences Ctr., Phila., 1988—91; gen. med. officer Indian Health Svc. U.S. Pub. Health Svc., Harlem, Mont., 1991—92; fellow gastroenterology Mayo Sch. of Grad. Medicine, Rochester, Minn., 1992—95; instr. medicine Mayo Med. Sch., Rochester, 1996—98, asst. prof. medicine, 1998—2002, assoc. prof. medicine, 2002—. Assoc. editor Am. Jour. Gastroenterology, 2003—. Chair, patient edn. com. Crohn's and Colitis Found. of Am., N.Y.C., 2002—; chair, chpt. med. adv. com. Crohn's and Colitis Found. of Am., Minn. Chpt., St Paul, 2001—. Fellow: ACP, Am. Coll. of Gastroenterology (Aux. Award 2001); mem.: Upper Midwest Regional Endoscopy Soc. (pres. 2003—05), Crohn's and Colitis Found. of Am., Am. Soc. for Gastrointestinal Endoscopy, Am. Gastroent. Assn. Office: Mayo Clinic 200 First St SW Rochester MN 55905 Office Phone: 507-266-0873.

LOFTUS, THOMAS DANIEL, lawyer; b. Nov. 8, 1930; s. Glendon Francis and Martha Helen (Wall) L. BA, U. Wash., 1952, JD, 1957. Bar: Wash. 1958, U.S. Ct. Appeals (9th cir.) 1958, U.S. Dist. Ct. Wash. 1958, U.S. Ct. Mil. Appeals 1964, U.S. Supreme Ct. 1964. Trial atty. Northwestern Mut. Ins. Co., Seattle, 1958—62; sr. trial atty. Unigard Security Ins. Co., Seattle, 1962—68, asst. gen. counsel, 1969—83, govt. rels. counsel, 1983—89; of counsel Groshong, LeHet & Thornton, 1990—98; mem. Wash. Commn. on Jud. Conduct (formerly Jud. Qualifications), 1982—88, vice-chmn., 1987—88; self-employed arbitrator, mediator, 1998—; judge pro tem Seattle Mcpl. Ct., 1973—81; mem. nat. panel of mediators Arbitration Forums, Inc., 1990—; pvt. practice arbitrator, mediator, 1998—. 1st lt. U.S. Army, 1952-54, col. Res., 1954-85; nat. committeeman Wash. Young Rep. Fedn., 1961-63, vice-chmn., 1963-65; pres. Young Reps. King County, 1962-63; bd. dirs. Seattle Seafair, Inc., 1975; v.p. Salvation Army Adult Rehab. Ctr., 1979-86; pres., bd. dirs. Vis. Nurse Svcs., 1979-88; Sec., trustee Seattle Opera Assn., 1980-91; pres., bd. dirs., gen. counsel Wash. Ins. Coun., 1984-86, sec., 1986-88, v.p., 1988-90; bd. dirs. Arson Alarm Found., 1987-90; Am. Mediation Panel Mediators, 1990-96; bd. visitors Law Sch. U. Wash., 1993-98. Fellow Am. Bar Found.; mem. Am. Arbitration Assn. (nat. panel arbitrators 1965—, nat. panel mediators 2000—), Am. Arbitration Forums, Inc. (nat. panel arbitrators 1992), Nat. Assn. Security Dealers (bd. arbitrators 1997—), Am. Mediation Panel, Wash. Bar Assn. (gov. 1981-84), Seattle King County Bar Assn. (sec., trustee 1977-82), ABA (ho. of dels. 1984-90), Internat. Assn. Ins. Counsel, U.S. People to People (del. Moscow internat. law-econ. conf. 1990), Def. Rsch. Inst., Wash. Def. Trial Lawyers Assn., Wash. State Trial Lawyers Assn., Am. Judicature Soc., Res. Officers Assn., Judge Advocate Gen.'s Assn., Assn. Wash. Gens., U. Wash. Alumni Assn., Coll. Club Seattle, Wash. Athletic Club, Masons, Shriners, English Spkg. Union, Ranier Club, Pi Sigma Alpha, Delta Sigma Rho, Phi Delta Phi, Theta Delta Chi. Republican. Presbyterian. Home: 3515 Magnolia Blvd W Seattle WA 98199-1841 Office: Coll Club Bldg 505 Madison St Ste 300 Seattle WA 98104-1123 Office Phone: 206-622-1264.

LOGA, SANDA, physicist, researcher; b. Bucharest, Romania, June 13, 1932; came to U.S., 1968; d. Stelian and Georgeta (Popescu) L.; m. Karl Heinz Werther, Mar. 1968 (div. 1970); m. Radu Zaciu, 1996. MS in Physics, U. Bucharest, 1955; PhD in Biophysics, U. Pitts., 1978. Asst. prof. faculty medicine and pharmacy, Bucharest, 1963-67; rsch. asst. Presbyn./St. Luke's Hosp., Chgo., 1968-69; assoc. rsch. scientist Miles Labs., Elkhart, Ind., 1969-70; rsch. asst. U. Pitts., 1971-78; rsch. assoc. Carnegie-Mellon U., Pitts., 1978-80; health physicist VA Med. Ctr., Westside, Chgo., 1980; med. physicist, VA Med. Ctr. N. Chgo, 1980-97. Assoc. prof. Chgo. Med. Sch., N. Chgo., 1985-2004. Mem. Am. Assn. Physicists in Medicine, Health Physics Soc. Office: Chgo Med Sch U Health Scis 3333 Green Bay Rd North Chicago IL 60064-3037 Business E-Mail: sanda.loga@rosalindfranklin.edu.

LOGAN, BEN H., III, lawyer; b. Medina, Ohio, 1951; BA magna cum laude, Duke U., 1973; JD, Stanford, 1976. Bar: Calif. 1976, US Dist. Ct. (Ctrl. Dist. Calif.) 1978, DC 1984, US Dist, Ct. (No. and So. Dists. Calif.) 1986, US Dist. Ct. (Dist. Ariz) 1990, US Dist. Ct. (Ea. Dist. Calif.) 1991, US Ct. Appeals (2nd Cir.) 1991, US Ct. Appeals (9th Cir.) 1994. Ptnr. O'Melveny & Myers LLP, Los Angeles. Mem. Stanford Law Review, 1974—76; editor: Stanford Law Review, 1975—76. Mem. ABA, State Bar Calif. (mem., debtor/creditor rels. and bankruptcy subcommittee, comml. law and bankruptcy sect.1986-91), LA County Bar Assn. (mem. bankruptcy com. 1989-92), Phi Beta Kappa; fellow Am. Coll. Bankruptcy. Office: O'Melveny & Myers 400 S Hope St Los Angeles CA 90071-2899 Office Phone: 213-430-7704. Office Fax: 213-430-6407. Business E-Mail: blogan@omm.com.

LOGAN, DAN, investor, writer; b. Chgo., Dec. 10, 1946; s. David S. and Reva (Frumkin) L.; m. Gloria Jean Blasz, July 8, 1973; children: Elizabeth, Andrew. BA, Knox Coll., 1969. Sr. speechwriter, asst. Ill. Gov. Daniel Walker, Springfield, Ill., 1975-76; spl. asst. U.S. Sen. Joseph Biden, Jr., Washington, 1977; speechwriter, cons. U.S. Rep. Max Baucus Senate campaign, Washington, 1978; speechwriter Charles Ferris, chmn. FCC, Washington, 1980; exec. dir. Free Men, Inc., Washington, 1980-87; co-founder Nat. Congress for Fathers and Children, Washington, 1981. Ptnr. Mercury Investments, Chgo., 1988—. Contbr. articles to newspapers. Founder Save Jazz 90, 1997; bd. dirs. Reva and David Logan Found., 1998—, WPFW Radio, 2004. Recipient Vol. Svc. award, 1984. Mem. Nat. Writers Union. Unitarian Universalist.

LOGAN, DAVID BRUCE, health facility administrator, nurse; b. Grand Rapids, Mich., Jan. 30, 1942; s. Wesley Goldsmith and Ernestine (Sovereen) L.; m. Joann Fern Jordan, Nov. 5, 1961; children: Jennifer, Julie, Jeanine, David II, Douglas, Dean. MusB, U. Mich., 1964; B Zoology with honors, Mich. State U., 1970; MBA, U. Ill., 1978. Tchr. sci. Flint (Mich.) Pub. Schs., 1970-71; health care adminstr. USAF, Mpls., 1971-75; asst. chief, med. adminstrn. svc. trainee VA, Mpls., 1975-76, asst. chief med. adminstrn. svc. Danville, Ill., 1976-78; asst. med. dist. coord. VA Med. Dist. 15, Indpls., 1978-80; med. dist. coord. VA Med. Dist. 8, Durham, N.C., 1980-87; nat. disaster med. system mgr. VA, Salisbury, N.C., 1987-99, ret. Dir. choir Kirk of Kildaire Presbyn. Ch., 1981-85; asst. scoutmaster, scoutmaster Boy Scouts Am., 1978-94. Capt. USAF, 1964-68, lt. col. Res. ret. Fellow Am. Coll. Healthcare Execs., Soc. Air Force Res. Med. Officers, Air Force Assn., Res. Officers Assn. (bd. dirs. Minn. 1973-74, jr. v.p. for air 1974-75).

LOGAN, EARL STEVEN, artist; b. South Bend, Ind., Oct. 20, 1956; s. Earl and Barbara Jean L. BS in Bus., Ind. U., 1985. Real estate agt. Cressy and Everett Better Homes and Gardens, Mishawaka, Ind., 1985-89; quality control supr. Qualex, South Bend, 1990; retail assoc. Montgomery Ward, South Bend, 1991; retail specialist L.S. Ayres, Mishawaka, 1992—. Exhibited in group shows at Colfax Cultural Ctr., South Bend, Ind., 1995, Mus. Sci. and Industry, Chgo., 1995, 96, Elkhart Regional Juried Art Competition, 1995, 96, 99, 17th Ann., 1995 (Makielski Merit award), 18th Ann., 1996 (Best Drawing), 21st Ann., 1999 (Best Painting, Louise J. Anes Meml. Purchase award 1999), Midwest Mus. Am. Art, Elkhart, Spring Salon, 2003, Limner Gallery, N.Y.C. Avocations: reading, astronomy, basketball, meditation.

LOGAN, FRANCIS DUMMER, retired lawyer; b. Evanston, Ill., May 23, 1931; s. Simon Rae and Frances (Dummer) Logan; m. Claude Riviere, Apr. 13, 1957; children: Carolyn Gisele, Francis Dummer. BA, U. Chgo., 1950; BA Juris, Oxford U., 1954; LLB, Harvard U., 1955. Bar: N.Y. 1956, Calif. 1989. Assoc. Milbank, Tweed, Hadley & McCloy, N.Y.C., 1955-64, ptnr. N.Y.C. and L.A., 1965-96, chmn., 1992-96. Commr. Burbank-Glendale-Pasadena Airport Authority. Mem.: N.Y. State Bar, Pacific Coun. Internat. Policy, Am. Law Inst., Coun. Fgn. Rels., Calif. State Bar. Home: 1726 Linda Vista Ave Pasadena CA 91103-1132

LOGAN, HENRY VINCENT, transportation executive, consultant; b. Phila., Nov. 7, 1942; s. Edward Roger and Alberta L.; m. Mary Genzano, Sept. 28, 1963; children: Michele Leah, Maureen Laura, Monica Lynn. BS in Commerce, DePaul U., 1975; M in Mgmt., Northwestern U., 1984. Successively supr. corp. acctg., asst. mgr. gen. acctg., mgr. gen. acctg., dir. corp. acctg. and taxes TTX Co., Chgo., 1962-70, contr., 1970-78, dir. fin. planning, 1978-83, mng. dir., fin. adminstr., 1983-85, CFO, v.p., 1985-88, sr. v.p. fleet mgmt., 1988—2001; cons., 2001—. Bd. dirs. Calpro, Co., Mira Loma, Calif Treas. TTX Co. Polit. Action Com., Chgo., 1980; vol Sch. Dist. 87 Task Force, Glen Ellyn, Ill., 1986. Hon. fellow U. Denver Intermodal Transp. Inst., 1999. Mem. Nat. Freight Transp. Assn., Intermodal Assn. N.Am. (chmn. legis. com. 1992-94), Rlwy. Supply Assn. (bd. dirs., treas., sec., v.p., chmn. fin. com., pres. 2001), Union League Club (mem. reception com. 1987-92, fin. com. 1993-95), Willoughby Golf Club, Fla. (membership com. 2003, green com., 2004). Republican. Roman Catholic. Avocations: golf, music, reading, bicycling.

LOGAN, J. MURRAY, investment manager; b. Balt., Mar. 15, 1935; s. Lloyd and Helen Mildred (Gilbert) L.; m. Mary Page Cole, June 19, 1987 (dec. Sept. 1993); 1 child by previous marriage, Maria Charlotte. BA, Johns Hopkins U., 1959. Securities analyst Merrill Lynch Pierce Fenner & Smith, N.Y.C., 1959-62; ptnr. Wood Struthers & Winthrop, N.Y.C., 1962-70; v.p. EFC Mgmt. Corp., L.A., 1970-73, Faulkner, Dawkins & Sullivan, Inc., N.Y.C., 1973-75; chmn. investment policy com. Rockefeller & Co., Inc., N.Y.C., 1975-97; mng. ptnr. L-R Global Ptnrs., N.Y.C. Bd. dirs. World Trust Fund, Luxembourg, Berkshire Opera Co., Camphill Found., Camphill Village, U.S.A., past pres. Trustee Johns Hopkins U., Balt., 1984-91. With USCG, 1954-56. Mem.: Mashomack, The Leash, Racquet and Tennis Club. Office: 430 Park Ave 7th Fl New York NY 10022

LOGAN, JAMES KENNETH, lawyer, retired judge; b. Quenemo, Kans., Aug. 21, 1929; s. John Lysle and Esther Maurine (Price) Logan; m. Beverly Jo Jennings, June 8, 1952; children: Daniel Jennings, Amy Logan Sliva, Sarah Logan Sherard, Samuel Price. AB, U. Kans., 1952; LLB magna cum laude, Harvard U., 1955. Bar: Kans. 1955, Calif. 1956. Law clk. U.S. Cir. Judge Huxman, 1955—56; with firm Gibson, Dunn & Crutcher, LA, 1956—57; asst. prof. law U. Kans., 1957—61, prof., dean Law Sch., 1961—68; ptnr. Payne and Jones, Olathe, Kans., 1968—77; judge U.S. Ct. Appeals (10th cir.), 1977—98; pvt. practice Logan Law Firm LLC, Olathe, 1998—2001, Foulston Siefkin LLP, Overland Park, Kans., 2002—. Ezra Ripley Thayer tchg. fellow Harvard Law Sch., 1961—62; vis. prof. U. Tex., 1964, Stanford U., 1969, U. Mich., 1976; sr. lectr. Duke U., 1987, 91, 93; commr. U.S. Dist. Ct., 1964—67; mem. U.S. Jud. Conf. Adv. Com. Fed. Rules of Appellate Procedure, 1990—97, chair, 1993—97. Author (with W.B. Leach): Future Interests and Estate Planning, 1961; author: Kansas Estate Administration, 5th edit., 1986; author: (with A.R. Martin) Kansas Corporate Law and Practice, 2d edit., 1979; author: The Federal Courts of the Tenth Circuit: A History, 1992, also articles. Candidate for U.S. Senate, 1968. Served with U.S. Army, 1947—48. Recipient Disting. Svc. citation, U. Kans., 1986, Francis Rawle award, ABA-ALI, 1990; scholar Rhodes Scholarship, 1952. Mem.: ABA, Kans. Bar Assn., Order of Coif, Phi Delta Phi, Alpha Kappa Psi, Pi Sigma Alpha, Omicron Delta Kappa, Beta Gamma Sigma, Phi Beta Kappa. Democrat. Presbyterian. Office Phone: 913-498-2100. Business E-Mail: jlogan@foulston.com.

LOGAN, JAMES SCOTT, SR., federal agency administrator; b. Stanford, Ky., June 18, 1948; s. James M.H. and Lillian Elizabeth (Givens) L.; m. Rose Marie Helm, Aug. 31, 1968; children: James Matthew, Tasha Marie. AA, Columbia (Mo.) Coll., 1990, BS/BA cum laude, 1992; postgrad., U. Colo., 1992—. Unit adminstr. USAR, Lakewood, Colo., 1972-82; continuity of govt. planner Fed. Emergency Mgmt. Agy. Region VIII, Lakewood, 1983-90, tech. hazards program specialist, 1991-92, sr. tech. hazards program specialist, 1992-95, team leader state and local programs, 1995—; emergency analyst Office of Regional Dir., Denver, 1995—, dir. preparedness tng. and exercises divsn., 1998—2000, dir. readiness, response and recovery divsn., 2001—, dir. nat. preparedness divsn., 2003—. Chmn. bd. dirs. Rocky Mountain Human Svcs. Coalition, 1995-99, bd. dirs. 1998—, pres., 1998-99. Mem. NAACP, Denver, 1992; mem. NCOA NCO Assn., Denver, 1979-2004; mem. citizen's adv. com. polit. sci. dept. U. Colo., Denver; chmn. bd. dirs. Rocky Mt. Human Svcs. Coalition, 1995—, pres., 1998-99; bd. dirs. City Club Denver, 2000. With U.S. Army, 1968-71, Vietnam, USAR, 1972. Decorated Legion of Merit. Mem. VFW, Am. Legion, Order Ky. Cols. (hon.), Denver City Club, Pi Sigma Alpha. Democrat. Baptist. Avocations: reading, computers, political science. Home: 16952 E Bates Ave Aurora CO 80013-2243 Office: FEMA Region VIII PO Box 25267 Bldg 710A Denver CO 80225-0267 Business E-Mail: scott.logan@dhs.gov.

LOGAN, JANET LOUISE, retired elementary school educator; b. St. Louis, Nov. 2, 1945; d. Charles Hubert and Evelyn I. (Curtis) Cornwell; m. Dean Hugh Logan, July 27, 1968; 1 chld, David. BS in Edn., Northeast Mo. State U., 1967; MA in Curriculum and Instrn., William Woods U., 1998. Cert. elem. tchr., Mo. Tchr. North Kansas City (Mo.) Sch. Dist., 1967-68, Oskaloosa (Iowa) Sch. Dist., 1968-69, Centerville (Iowa) Sch. Dist., 1969-71, Chillicothe (Mo.) II Schs., 1974—79, 1986—2005, ret., 2005. Bd. deacons Presbyn. Ch., Chillicothe, 1985-88, trustee, 1992-95; bd. dirs. RSVP, Chillicothe, 1978-80 Mem. Internat. Reading Assn., Mo. State Tchrs. Assn., Nat. Assn. Edn. of Young Children, Alpha Tau Sigma, Beta Sigma Phi (treas. 1988-89, v.p. 1990-91). Avocations: reading, crafts, quilting. Home: 2121 Oaklawn Dr Chillicothe MO 64601-3552 Office: Dewey Elementary School 905 Dickinson Chillicothe MO 64601

LOGAN, JOHN A., III, hospital administrator; b. Dec. 16, 1937; BS, Western Ky. U., 1958; MD, Vanderbilt U., 1961. Intern Toledo Hosp., 1961-62; pvt. practice Henderson, Ky., 1962-86; chief of staff Meth. Hosp., Henderson, 1967-86, med. dir., 1986—. Author: Innovation, 1992. Pres. YMCA, Henderson. Named Citizen of Yr., Henderson C. of C., 1993. Mem. Rotary (pres.). Address: 1305 N Elm St # 48 Henderson KY 42420-2783 Office Phone: 270-827-7353. Business E-Mail: jalogan@methodisthospital.net.

LOGAN, JOHN ARTHUR, JR., retired foundation executive; b. Chgo., Dec. 8, 1923; s. John Arthur and Dorothea (Halstead) L.; m. Ann Orr deForest, Aug. 30, 1960. Grad., Taft Sch., Watertown, Conn., 1942; BA, Yale, 1949, MA, 1951, PhD, 1954; LL.D., Western Md. Coll.; L.H.D., Hollins Coll. Faculty Yale, 1949-61, asst. prof. history, 1958-61; pres. Hollins Coll., 1961-75, Ind. Coll. Funds Am., N.Y.C., 1975-86. Vis. lectr. Salzburg Seminar in Am. Studies, 1961. Author: No Transfer: An American Security Principle, 1961. Served to capt. AUS, 1942-46. Fellow Saybrook Coll., Yale, 1950— Mem. Phi Beta Kappa. Clubs: Elizabethan (New Haven); Century Assn. (N.Y.C.), Yale (N.Y.C.). Home: 88 Notch Hill Rd Apt 353 North Branford CT 06471-1853

LOGAN, KENNETH RICHARD, lawyer; b. N.Y.C., Dec. 26, 1944; s. John S. and Hazel (Mathias) L.; m. Grace Winter-Durennel, Aug. 12, 1967; children: Finlay, Emily. BA, Princeton U., 1967; JD, U. Pa., 1972. Bar: N.Y., U.S. Dist. Ct. (so. dist.) N.Y., U.S. Ct. Appeals (2nd cir.). Assoc. Simpson Thacher & Bartlett, N.Y.C., 1972-79, ptnr., 1979—, mem. exec. com. Served with U.S. Army, 1969-70. Office: Simpson Thacher & Bartlett 425 Lexington Ave Fl 15 New York NY 10017-3954 Office Phone: 212-455-2650. Office Fax: 212-455-2502. Business E-Mail: klogan@stblaw.com.

LOGAN, LEE ROBERT, orthodontist; b. L.A., June 24, 1932; s. Melvin Duncan and Margaret (Seltzer) L.; m. Maxine Nadler, June 20, 1975; children: Chad, Casey. BS, UCLA, 1952; DDS, Northwestern U., 1956, MS, 1961. Diplomate Am. Bd. Orthodontics. Gen .practice dentistry, Reseda, Calif., 1958—59; practice orthodontics Northridge, Calif., 1961—; pres. Lee R. Logan DDS Profl. Corp. Mem. med. staff Northridge Hosp.; owner Maxine's Prodn. Co.; owner Maxine's Talent Agy.; guest lectr. dept. orthodontics UCLA, U. So. Calif. Contbr. articles to profl. jours. Achievements include patent and licensing agreement with 3M for a device to attach braces, 2001. Served to lt. USNR, 1956-58. Named 1st Pl. winner, Autistic Jogathon, 1981—2001, (with wife) Couple of Yr., Autistic Children Assn., 1986; recipient Nat. Philanthropy award, 1987. Mem. ADA, San Fernando Valley Dental Assn. (pres. 1998), Am. Assn. Orthodontists, Pacific Coast Soc. Orthodontists (dir., pres. so. sect. 1974-75, chmn. membership 1981-83), Foudn. Orthodontic Rsch. (charter mem.), Calif. Soc. Orthodontists (chmn. peer rev. 1982-93), G.V. Black Soc. (charter) Angle Soc. Orthodontists (pres. 1981-82, bd. dirs. 1982—, nat. pres. 1985-87), U. S.C. Century Club Fraternity, Xi Psi Phi, Chi Phi. Home: 4830 Encino Ave Encino CA 91316-3813 Office: 18250 Roscoe Blvd Northridge CA 91325-4226 E-mail: orthologan@aol.com.

LOGAN, MARIANNE MCNEIL, poet; b. Sturgis, S.D., Sept. 12, 1929; d. John Frederick and Elleene (Allison) McFarland; m. Grant Smith McNeil, Mar. 3, 1950 (dec. Apr. 19910); m. Claude Herman Logan, Mar. 23, 1994. Organizer cowboy poets for Old West Days celebration, Amarillo, Tex., 1986, monthly Cowboy Poetry Breakfasts, Amarillo, 1991, monthly cowboy poetry programs Barnes and Noble bookstores, Amarillo; spkr. writer and poets' confs. SW; foudned, moderated Amarillo Sr. Citizens Writers' Groups; established Tri-State Lit. Contests. Author: (rhyming poetry) Celebration for Sonneteers (Crossroads Poetry Chapbook Cmpetition, Pegasus award, Pulitzer nominee), 1986, Girls Write Poetry Too (Nat. league Am. Pen Women Book Contest, nominated Acad. Western Artists), 1990, Designed by Heritage, 1998; author (with Vivian Ramsey Stewart): Singing Songs of Friendship in the Vivienne Pattern, Singing Songs of Inspiration in the Marianne Pattern. Recipient Tex. winner for arts Col. Sanders Super Achiever Nat. Contest, 1996, United Poet Laureate Internat. Congress Contest 1st pl. award, Plainview, 2005, Long Rhymed Poetry 1st pl. award Frontiers in Writing Tri-State Conf., 2005. Mem. Poetry Soc. Tex. (councilor-at-large, Hilton Ross Greer Outstanding Svc. award), S.W. Cowboy Poets Assn. (organizer, coord. 1991—, Outstanding Svc. award 2004), Hi-Plains Soc. (pres. 1998—), Writers Assn. Golden Spread Moderator 1999), Amarillo Sr. Citizens Writers's Group (organizer, coord.), Panhandle Profl. Writers (lifetime award 1998). Republican. Presbyterian. Avocations: reading, playing pool, dance, travel.

LOGAN, MARIE-ROSE VAN STYNVOORT, literature educator, publishing executive, writer; b. Brussels, May 26, 1944; d. Jean Stevo and Marie-Rose (Mabille) Van Stynvoort; m. John Frederick Logan, Sept. 7, 1968 (div. 1997); 1 child, Franklin. Licence, U. Brussels, 1966; MA, Yale U., 1970; MPhil, 1972, PhD, 1974. Instr. Yale U., New Haven, 1972-74; asst. prof. Columbia U., N.Y.C., 1974-83; assoc. prof. Rice U., Houston, 1983-93, Goucher Coll., Balt., 1993-96; assoc. prof. dept. English Temple U., Phila., 1996—; vis. prof. Columbia U., 2003—; prof. European and comparative literature Soka U. Am., 2005. Gen. editor Annals of Scholarship Quar. in Humanities and Social Scis., 1994—; assoc. editor Columbia Dictionary in European Lit., N.Y., 1978-81; lectr. in field. Editor: Contending Kingdoms, 1992, Gerard Genette Figures of Literary Discourse, 1981; author: Michel de Ghelderode, 1996; contbr. over 100 articles to profl. jours. Pres. Annals of Scholarship, Inc., 1995—. Recipient Chevalier de l'Ordre des Palmes Academiques Govt. of France, 1980; Nat. Endowment of Humanities fellow, 1981-88, Harvard U. fellow, 1975-76, Inst. for Advanced Study in Humanities fellow U. Edinburgh, 1989. Mem. Soc. Fellows in Humanities Columbia U., Elizabethan Club Yale U. Home: 4041 Ridge Ave # 4-416 Philadelphia PA 19129-1550 Office: Temple U Coll Arts and Scis Dept English Philadelphia PA 19129 E-mail: ml2322@columbia.edu.

LOGAN, MATHEW KUYKENDALL, journalist; b. Norman, Okla., Aug. 19, 1933; s. Leonard Marion and Floy-Elise (Duke) L.; m. Linda Dianne Elderkin, Dec. 31, 1964. BA in Journalism, U. Okla., 1955. Reporter UPI, 1957—58; city editor Daily Oklahoman, 1958—69; asst. mng. editor Houston Post, 1969—76, mng. editor, 1976—83, Sta. KHOU-TV, 1984—87; asst. dean for community affairs Med. Sch. U. Tex., 1987—92; v.p. pub. affairs and mktg. Hermann Hosp., 1992—97; v.p. corp. comm. Meml. Hermann Healthcare Sys., 1997—2002; vis. prof. journalism Sam Houston State U., Huntsville, 2002—05. Served with AUS, 1957. Mem. UPI Editors Tex. (pres. 1977), Tex. AP Mng. Editors Assn. (pres. 1983), Sigma Chi. Methodist. Home: 24 Sunlit Forest Dr The Woodlands TX 77381-2986 Fax: 281-367-2686. E-mail: dlogan@houston.rr.com.

LOGAN, NANCY ALLEN, library media specialist; b. Rochester, NY, Mar. 27, 1933; d. Warren William and Dorothea Amelia (Pund) Allen; m. Joseph Skinner Logan, Dec. 29, 1952; children: Joseph Skinner Logan Jr., Susan, Annette Logan Miller, Jennifer Logan Haber. Student, Middlebury Coll., 1951-52; BA, Cornell U., 1955; MLS, SUNY, Albany, 1967; cert. legal asst., Marist Coll., 1983. Cert. libr. media specialist, social studies tchr. NY. Libr. media specialist Hyde Park (NY) Sch. Dist., 1971-93. Editor: Dear Friends, 1989; editor: (newsletter) Sch. Libr. Media Specialists, 1984—85, Jamestown Hist. Soc., 1997—2001. Arts chmn. Jr. League, Poughkeepsie, NY, 1967—69; dir. Jr. Arts Ctr., 1967—69, edn. chmn., 1970—71; sec. bd. dirs. Poughkeepsie Tennis Club, 1973—79; indexer periodicals Dutchess County Hist. Soc., Poughkeepsie, 1979—93; county rep. Sch. Libr. Media Specialists, 1982, exhibits chmn. ann. meeting, 1983, 1984; indexer Jamestown (RI) Press, 1993—; bd. dirs. Friends Jamestown Philomenian Libr., 1994—97, trustee, 1999—, v.p, treas. bd. trustees, 2004—; mem. Jamestown Planning Commn., 1999; stewardship chair Conanicut Island Land Trust, 2002. Mem.: Beavertail Lighthouse Assn. (bd. dirs. 1994—97). Avocation: reading, sailing, swimming, travel, bicycling. Home: 149 Seaside Dr Jamestown RI 02835-3117

LOGAN, PAULA M., entertainment company executive, accountant; b. Bklyn., Nov. 23, 1971; d. Charles L. Price and Vyris Logan; 1 child, Tyrone T. BS in Acctg. and Econs., L.I. U., 1999. Account exec. Blanksteen Cos., N.Y.C., 1990-93, property and casualty ins. broker, 1993; account exec. Rude Boy Internat. Sounds, Bklyn., 1989—, Vy's Bake Shop, Bklyn., 1989—, Lady P's Party Cons. Co., Bklyn., 1989-93, v.p., 1993—; mem. N.Y.C. Special Enforcement Unit, 2002—. Cons. Macy's East Herald Square Bridal Registry, 2002. Vol. income tax assistance program, IRS, Bklyn., 1997—; youth counselor St. Mary's Ch. of Christ, 1993—. Mem. AICPAs, Lions. Democrat. Pentecostal. Avocations: collecting teddy bears and porcelain dolls, stamps and coins, reading, dance. Office: Lady P's Party Cons 166 St Marks Ave Brooklyn NY 11238 E-mail: PLoganGrant@netscape.net, Lady_P_01@hotmail.com.

LOGAN, SHARON BROOKS, lawyer; b. Nov. 19, 1945; d. Blake Elmer and Esther N. (Statum) Brooks; children: John W. III, Troy Blake. BS in Econs., U. Md., 1967, MBA in Mktg., 1969; JD, U. Fla., 1979. Bar: Fla. 1979. Ptnr. Raymond Wilson, Esq., Ormond Beach, Fla., 1980, Landis, Graham & French, Daytona Beach, Fla., 1981, Watson & Assocs., Daytona Beach, 1982—84; prin. Sharon B. Logan, Esq., Ormond Beach, 1984—. Legal adv. to paralegal program Daytona Beach CC, 1984—. Sponsor Ea. Surfing Assn., Daytona Beach, 1983—, Nat. Scholastic Surfing Assn., 1987—; bd. dir. Ctr. for Visually Impaired, 1991—. Recipient Citizenship award, Rotary Club, 1962—63; fellow Woodrow Wilson, U. Md., 1967. Mem.: ABA, Daytona Beach Area Bd. Realtors, Volusia county Estate Planning Coun., Fla. Supreme Ct. Hist. Soc., Volusia County Real Property Coun., Inc. (bd. dirs. 1987—, sec. 1987—88, v.p. 1988—89, pres. 1989—90, sec. 1990—91, 1991—97, pres. 1997—98, 1998—), Volusia County Bar Assn. (bd. dir.), Fla. Bar Assn. (real property and probate sect., cert. real estate atty. 1996), Beech Mountain Country Club, Univ. Ctr. Club (Tallahassee), Daytona Boat Club, Ducks Unlimited, Mus. Arts and Scis., Ormond Beach C. of C., Gator Club, Halifax Club, Tomoka Oaks Country Club, Md. Club, Sigma Alpha Epsilon, Delta Delta Delta (Scholarship award 1964), Omicron Delta Epsilon, Phi Kappa Phi, Alpha Lamba Delta, Beta Gamma Sigma. Democrat. Episcopalian. Avocations: golf, cooking, sewing, tennis, aerobics. Office: Sharon B Logan Esq 180 Vining Ct PO Box 4258 Ormond Beach FL 32175-4258 Office Phone: 386-673-5787. E-mail: sloganpa@cfl.rr.com.

LOGAN, THADDEUS SUMNER, III, architect; b. Arlington, Va., June 7, 1955; s. Thaddeus Sumner Jr. and Mary Gertrude (Boehling) L.; m. Patricia Ruth Eisemann, Oct. 6, 1984; children: Thaddeus Sumner IV, Devitt August Henry. BS in Arch., U. Va., 1977; MS in Urban Planning, Columbia U., 1982. Lic. arch., N.Y. Project mgr., planner N.Y. City Dept. Ports and Terminals, 1981-84, dir. port and aviation devel., 1984-86; project mgr. Coopers & Lybrand, N.Y.C., 1986-93; dir. property mgmt. The Bank of N.Y., N.Y.C., 1994—2002, sr. v.p., 2002—. Co-author: Hatton Grange Mill, 1976. Mem. parish coun. Holy Innocents Parish, Pleasantville, N.Y., 1992-93; mem. phase I, II citizens com. Pleasantville Sch. Bd., 1998; chmn. Pleasantville Parking Task Force, 2002-03. William Kinne fellow Columbia U., 1981; recipient Outstanding Student award Am. Planning Assn., 1981. Mem. Real Estate Bd. N.Y. (mem. institutional owners com. 1995-97). Roman Catholic. Office: The Bank of NY 75 Park Pl New York NY 10286

LOGAN, VERYLE HUDSON, retail executive, realtor; b. St. Louis, Oct. 24; d. Benjamim Bishop and Eddie Mae (Williams) Logan. BS, Mo. U., 1968; postgrad., Wayne State U., 1974, 76, U. Mich., Detroit, 1978, 80. Cert. residential specialist. With Hudson Dept. Store, Detroit, 1968-84, Dayton Hudson, Mpls., 1984-86, divsn. mdse. mgr., 1980-84, retail exec. divsn. mdse. mgr. coats and dresses, 1984-86; pres. Ultimate Connection, Inc., Mpls., 1987—. Mem. Golden Valley Black History Month Com., 1987—, co-chair, 1991-92. also bd. dirs., 1993-95; trustee Harry Davis Found., 1988-94, mem. exec. bd., 1991, v.p., 1991-92; chair equal opportunity com. Mpls. Bd. Realtors, also bd. dirs., 1993-96. Named Woman of Yr., Am. Bus. Women, 1984. Mem. Grad. Realtors Inst., Am. Bus. Womens Assn. (v.p. 1983-84, named Woman of Yr. 1984), Minn. Black Networking (exec. bd. 1985-90), Delta Sigma Theta (life, Mpls.-St. Paul alumnae chpt., recording sec. 1985-87, chmn. arts and letters, corr. sec. 1987-88, chmn. heritage and archives 1988-89, 1st v.p. 1991-93, pres. 1993-95, named Delta of the Yr. 1988), M.L. King Tennis Buffs Club. Office: Coldwell Banker Burnet Realty Minn Lakes 3033 Excelsior Blvd Ste 100 Minneapolis MN 55416-4678 Office Phone: 612-925-8428. E-mail: vlogan@cbburnet.com, verylej@aol.com.

LOGAN-SUTTON, FLORETTA R., elementary school educator; b. Elizabeth City, N.C., Mar. 13, 1930; d. Ivy Hillard and Rosa Lillian (Stewart) Roach; m. Chester C. Sutton, Sept. 19, 1949 (dec. 1988); children: Gwen Omari, Chester Jr., Karen Bailey, Fred, Renee, Verona Dunn; m. Ben L. Logan; stepchildren: Tyrone, Karen Graham, Kathy, Darryl, Victor, Christopher. BA, Elizabeth City State U., 1955; MA, Glassboro (N.J.) State Coll., 1962. Tchr. grades 1-5 Bd. Edn., Atlantic City, N.J., tchr. basic skill improvement program. Contbr. rsch. to profl. jours. Mem. NEA, NAACP, Internat. Assn. Ministers' Wives and Ministers' Widows, Inc., N.J. Ret. Edn. Assn. Atlantic County, N.J. Edn. Assn., Atlantic City Edn. Assn., Phi Delta Kappa, Alpha Bettes. Home: #A 6025 College Dr Suffolk VA 23435-2019

LOGEMANN, JERILYN ANN, speech pathologist, educator; b. Berwyn, Ill., May 21, 1942; d. Warren F. and Natalie M. (Killmer) L. BS, Northwestern U., 1963; MA, 1964, PhD, 1968. Grad. asst. dept. communicative disorders Northwestern U., 1963-68; instr. speech and audiology DePaul U., 1964-65; instr. dept. communicative disorders Mundelein Coll., 1967-71; rsch. assoc. dept. neurology and otolaryngology and maxillo, 1970-74; asst. prof., 1974-78; dir. clin. and rsch. activities of speech and lang., 1975—; assoc. prof. depts. neurology, otolaryngology and comm. scis, 1978-83; prof., 1983; chmn. dept. comm. scis. and disorders, 1982-96; Ralph and Jean Sundin Prof. of Comm. Scis. and Disorders, 1995—; mem. assoc. staff Northwestern meml. Hosp., 1976—; N. Chgo. VA Hosp., 1983—; Evanston (Ill.) Hosp., 1988—. Cons. in field; assoc. dir. cancer control Ill. Comprehensive Cancer Coun., Chgo., 1980-82; mem. rehab. com. Ill. divsn. Am. CAncer Soc., 1975-79, chmn., 1979—; mem. upper aerodigestive tract organ site com. Nat. Cancer Inst., 1986-89; postdoct. fellow Nat. Inst. Neurologic Disease, Communicative Disorders and Stroke,Northwestern U., 1968-70. Author: The Fisher-Logeman Test of Articulation Competence, 1971, Evaluation and Treatment of Swallowing Disorders, 1983, 2nd edit., 1998, Manual for the Videofluorographic Evaluation of Swallowing, 1985, 93; assoc. editor: Jour. Speech and Hearing Disorders, Jour. Head Trauma Rehab., Dysphagia Jour., 1978—. Fellow Inst. Medicine Chgo., 1981—; grantee Nat Cancer Inst., 1975—, Am. Cancer Soc., 1981-82, Nat. Inst. Dental Rsch., 1996—, Nat. Inst. Deafness and Other Comm. Disorders, 1997—; recipient Honors award Conn. Speech Lang. Hearing Assn., 1995, Am. Acad. Otolaryngology-Head Neck Surgery, 1997, Appreciation award Coun. Grad. Prgrams in Comms. Scis. and Disorders, 1995, Cellular One award Vanderbilt U., Am. Special Lang. Hearing Assn., 2003. Fellow Speech, Lang. and Hearing Assn. (pres. 1994, 2000, Honors award 2003), Inst. Medicine; mem. Internat. Assn. Logopedics and Phoniatrics, AAUP, Acoustic Soc. Am. (program com. Chgo. regional chpt.), Linguistic Soc. Am., Speech Comm. Assn., Am. Cleft Palate Assn., Ill. Speech and Hearing Assn. (DiCarlo award 1988), Chgo. Heart Assn., Chgo. Speech Therapy and Auditory Soc. Office: Northwestern U Med Sch 303 E Chicago Ave Chicago IL 60611-3072 also: Northwestern U Dept Comm Sci and Disorder 2240 Campus Dr Evanston IL 60208-0001 Office Phone: 847-491-2490.

LO GERFO, FRANK WILLIAM, surgeon; b. Middletown, N.Y., Sept. 15, 1940; MD, U. Rochester, 1966. Diplomate Am. Bd. Surgery. Intern Boston U. Hosp., 1966-67, resident in surgery, 1967-71; chief vascular surgery Beth Israel Deaconess Med. Ctr., Boston, 1987—. Prof. surgery Boston U., 1973-87, Harvard U. Med. Sch., 1991—. Maj. USMC, 1971-73. Fellow Am. Coll. Surgeons; mem. Am. Surg. Assn., Internat. Soc. Cardiovascular Surgery, Soc. Univ. Surgeons, Soc. Vascular Surgeons, Am. Bd. Surgery (dir.). Office: Beth Israel Deaconess MC 110 Francis St Ste 5-B Boston MA 02215-5501 Office Phone: 617-632-9955. E-mail: flogerfo@biomc.harvard.edu.

LOGGIE, JENNIFER MARY HILDRETH, retired medical educator, retired physician; b. Lusaka, Zambia, Feb. 4, 1936; arrived in U.S., 1964, naturalized, 1972; d. John and Jenny (Beattie). M.B., B.Ch., U. Witwatersrand, Johannesburg, South Africa, 1959. Intern Harare Hosp., Salisbury, Rhodesia, 1960-61; gen. practice medicine Lusaka, 1961-62; sr. pediatric house officer Derby Children's Hosp., also St. John's Hosp., Chelmsford, Eng., 1962-64; resident in pediatrics Children's Hosp., Louisville, 1964, Cin., 1964-65; fellow clin. pharmacology Cin. Coll. Medicine, 1965-67; mem. faculty U. Cin. Med. Sch., 1967—, prof. pediatrics, 1975-98, assoc. prof. pharmacology, 1972-77, prof. emeritus pediatrics, 1998—; ret., 1998. Contbr. articles to med. publs.; editor Pediatric and Adolescent Hypertension, 1991. Grantee, Am. Heart Assn., 1970—72, 1989—90. Mem. Am. Pediatric Soc. (Founder's award 1996), Midwest Soc. Pediatric Rsch. Episcopalian. Home: 1133 Herschel Ave Cincinnati OH 45208-3112 Personal E-mail: jennlog@webtv.net.

LOGIE, JOHN HOULT, former mayor, lawyer; b. Ann Arbor, Mich., Aug. 11, 1939; s. James Wallace and Elizabeth (Hoult) Logie; m. Susan G. Duerr, Aug. 15, 1964; children: John Hoult Jr., Susannah, Margaret Elizabeth. Student, Williams Coll., 1957-59; BA, U. Mich., 1961, JD, 1968; MS, George Washington U., 1966; D of Pub. Svc. (hon.), Ferris State U., 2004. Bar: Mich. 1969, U.S. Dist. Ct. (we. and ea. dists.) Mich. 1969, U.S. Ct. Appeals (6th cir.) 1987. Assoc. Warner, Norcross & Judd, Grand Rapids, Mich., 1969-74, ptnr., 1974—2001, of counsel, 2002—; mayor City of Grand Rapids, 1991—2003. Instr. U.S. Naval Acad., 1964—66; chmn. civil justice adv. group U.S. Dist. Ct. (we. dist.) Mich., 1995—99; bd. vis. Sch. Bus. and Pub. Mgmt. George Washington U., 1995—2004; program coord. condemnation law sect. Inst. CLE; guest lectr. Grand Rapids CC, Grand Valley State U., Western Mich. U., Mich. State U. V.p., bd. dirs. Am. Cancer Soc., Grand Rapids, 1970—81; pres. Grand Rapids PTA Coun., 1971—73; pres., trustee Heritage Hill Assn., 1971—84, pres., 1976; v.p., bd. dirs. Goodwill Industries, Grand Rapids, 1973—79; chmn. Grand Rapids Urban Homesteading Commn., 1975—80, Grand Rapids Hist. Commn., 1985—90, Grand Rapids/Kent County Sesquicentennial Com., 1986—88, Clarke Hist. Libr., Ctrl. Mich. U., 2000—; pres., trustee Hist. Soc. Mich., 1984—90; mem. Headlee Blue Ribbon Commn., 1993—94, Mich. Workforce Devel. Bd., 2002—04; trustee Grand Valley State U. Found., 1998—. Lt. USN, 1961—66. Recipient Lifetime Achievement award, Mich. Hist. Preservation Network, 2000, Emeritus award, Aquinas Coll., 2002, Lifetime Achievement award, Econ. Club, 2004, Disting. Trustee award, Leadership Grand Rapids, 2005, Disting. Cmty. Trustee award, Grand Rapids C. of C., 2005. Mem.: ABA (mem. forum com. healthlaw 1980—), Mich. Soc. Hosp. Attys. (pres. 1976—77), Grand Rapids Bar Assn. (dir. young lawyers sect. 1970, Worsfold Lifetime Svc. award 2004), Mich. Bar Assn. (chmn. condemnation com. real property sect. 1985—88), Am. Health Lawyers Assn., Univ. Club (dir. 1979—82, pres. 1980—82). Avocations: motor cruising, hunting, fishing. Home: 601 Cherry St SE Grand Rapids MI 49503-4726 Office: Warner Norcross and Judd 111 Lyon St NW Ste 900 Grand Rapids MI 49503-2487 Office Phone: 616-752-2111. Business E-Mail: jlogie@wnj.com.

LOGOGLU, OSMAN FARUK, ambassador; b. Ankara, Turkey, 1941; BA, Brandeis U., 1963; MA, Princeton U., 1966, PhD, 1970. First sec. at European Union, 1973—76; with Turkish Ministry of Fgn. Affairs, Dhaka, Bangladesh, 1976—78; counselor to Turkish Permanent Del. at UN NYC, 1980—84; consul gen. Turkish Consulate, Hamburg, Germany, 1986—89; dep. dir. gen. Dept. of Bilateral Polit. Affairs, Greece, 1989—93; dep. undersecretary of Polit. Affairs Ministry of Fgn. Affairs, Turkey, 1998—2000, undersecretary, 2000—01; Turkish amb. to Denmark, 1993—96, to Azerbaijan, 1996—98, to the U.S., 2001—. Lectr. in Polit. Sci. Middlebury Coll., Vt., 1969—70. Author: (books) Ismet Inonu and the Making of Modern Turkey. Office: Embassy of Turkey 2525 Mass Ave NW Washington DC 20008 Office Phone: 202-612-6712.

LOGSDON, RICHARD M., English language educator, magazine editor; b. Boise, Idaho, June 2, 1948; s. Richard M. and Eula Jane (Randall) L.; m. Juliet Anne de Neufuille, Dec. 27, 1968; children: Tobias, Heather. BA, U. Oreg., 1970, MA, 1972, PhD, 1976. English prof. C.C. So. Nev., Las Vegas, 1975—. Author: (textbooks) Community College Reader, 1984, 4th edit., 1991, Red Rock Reader, 2003; editor-in-chief Red Rook Rev., 1995—; editor: In the Shadow of the Strip, 2003; author: (short stories) Alex the Wolfgod, 1999, Valley of the Shadow, 2000, Sweet Darkness, 2002. Coach boys and girls teams Nev. State Youth Soccer, 1981-93; head soccer coach men's team Las Vegas Premiere Soccer League, 1991—, coll. men's team, 1999—. Avocations: coaching soccer, writing fiction, fishing, sports. Home: 3090 El Camino Rd Las Vegas NV 89146-6620 Office: CC So Nev 3200 E Cheyenne Ave North Las Vegas NV 89030-4228 E-mail: RandJLogsdon@aol.com.

LOGSDON-CONRADSEN, SUSAN CAROL, psychology professor; b. Darien, Conn., Apr. 6, 1970; d. Jorgen Peter and Conny B. Conradsen; m. Damond Joseph Logsdon, June 8, 1995; 1 child, Annalise. BA, U. Ga., 1992; MA, U. Louisville, 1996, PhD, 1998. Lic. psychologist Ga. Resident Med. Coll. Ga., Augusta, 1997—98; fellow Emory U., Atlanta, 1998—99; assoc. prof. Berry Coll., Mt. Berry, 1999—. Contbr. articles to profl. jours. Mem. social justice com. Unitarian Ch., Roswell. Mem.: APA, Ga. Psychol. Assn. (grantee), Sierra, Phi Betta Kappa, Phi Kappa Phi. Democrat. Avocations: gardening, reading, hiking, writing. Office: Berry Coll Psychology Dept Mount Berry GA 30149

LOGSTROM, BRIDGET A., lawyer; b. 1958; BS magna cum laude, Univ. Minn., 1980; JD magna cum laude, William Mitchell Coll. Law, 1983. Bar: Minn. 1983. Assoc. Dorsey & Whitney LLP, Mpl.s, 1983—90, ptnr, individual, estate & trust svcs. group, 1983. Fellow: Am. Coll. of Trust and Estate Counsel; mem.: Hennepin County Bar Assn., Minn. State Bar Assn. Office: Dorsey & Whitney LLP Ste 1500 50 S Sixth St Lake Elmo MN 55042-1498 Office Phone: 612-343-7945. Office Fax: 601-340-8827. Business E-Mail: logstrom.bridget@dorsey.com.

LOGUE, DENNIS EMHARDT, finance educator, consultant, dean; b. Bklyn., Mar. 28, 1944; s. Joseph Paul and Helen Rose (Emhardt) L.; m. Marcella Julia Watson, June 11, 1966; children: Dennis E. Jr., Patrick G. AB, Fordham U., 1964; MBA, Rutgers U., 1966; PhD, Cornell U., 1971. Asst. prof. Ind. U., Bloomington, 1971-73; sr. economist U.S. Treasury, Washington, 1973-74; prof. bus. Tuck Sch., Dartmouth Coll., Hanover, 1974—2001, Steven Roth prof. mgmt., former assoc. dean; dean Michael F. Price Coll. Bus. Univ. Okla., Fred E. Brown chair Price Coll. Bus., 2001—. Founding bd. dirs. Ledyard Nat. Bank; bd. dirs. Sallie Mae (GSE), Waddell and Reed Fin. Inc., Abraxas Petroleum Corp. Grad. Mgmt. Admissions Coun., Duckwell ALCO Stores. Author: Legislative Influence on Corporate Pension Plans, 1979, The Investment Performance of Corporate Pension Plans, 1988, Managing Pension Plans, 1998; editor: Handbook of Modern Finance, 1998; co-editor Fin. Mgmt., 1978-81. Former pres. bd. trustees Crossroads Acad.; founding mem. Josiah Bartlett Ctr. for Pub. Policy Rsch. Served to 1st lt. U.S. Army, 1966-68. Mem. Am. Econ. Assn., Am. Fin. Assn. (bd. dirs. 1981-84), Fin. Mgmt. Assn. (bd. dirs., pres. 1995-96), Knights of Malta, Equestrian Order Holy Sepulchre; fellow Fin. Mgmt. Assn., Fin. Econ. Roundtable, Beta Gamma Sigma. Republican. Roman Catholic. Office: Price Coll Bus Adams Hall Univ Okla Norman OK 73019 Home: 1000 Riviera Dr Norman OK 73072-7623 Office Phone: 405-325-0100. Business E-Mail: dlogue@ou.edu.

LOGUE, JAMES NICHOLAS, epidemiologist; b. Duryea, Pa., June 18, 1946; s. James and Lucille (Polen) L.; m. Mary Frances Carey, Nov. 25, 1972; children: Melissa, Jimmy, Jeffrey. BS, Kings Coll., 1968; MPH, U. Mich., 1971; DrPH, Columbia U., 1978. Statistician Warner Lambert Co, Morris Plains, N.J., 1969-70, 71-73; sr. med. biostatistician Ciba-Geigy Co., Summit, N.J., 1973-78; epidemiologist GEOMET Technologies, Inc., Rockville, Md., 1978-80; supervisory epidemiologist US FDA, Rockville, 1980-82; dir. divsn. environ. health epidemiology Pa. Dept. Health, Harrisburg, 1982—; acting dir. Bur. Epidemiology, 2004—05. Office: Pa Dept Health PO Box 90 Harrisburg PA 17108-0090

LOGUE, JOSEPH CARL, electronics engineer, consultant; b. Phila., Dec. 20, 1920; s. Percival J. and Mathilda (Moser) L.; m. Jeanne Martha Neubecker, Mar. 31, 1943; children: Raymond, Marilyn, Paul. BEE, Cornell U., 1944, MEE, 1949. Instr. Cornell U., Ithaca, N.Y., 1944-49, asst. prof., 1949-51; engr. IBM, Poughkeepsie, N.Y., 1951-86, dir. rsch. divsn. Yorktown Heights, N.Y., 1986; CEO Lorex Industries Inc., Poughkeepsie, 1986—. 30

patents in field; contbr. papers to profl. publs. IBM fellow. Fellow IEEE, AAAS; mem. NAE, Rsch. Soc. Am. Avocations: scuba diving, photography. Home: 52 Boardman Rd Poughkeepsie NY 12603-4228

LOGUE, JUDITH FELTON, psychoanalyst, educator, professional coach; b. Phila., Aug. 21, 1942; d. Martin and Laura (Goldman) Kirshenbaum; m. Stephen Felton, Feb. 8, 1966 (div. Aug. 1989); 1 child, Jane Jennifer; m. A. Douglas Logue, Feb. 14, 1990. AB in Govt., Wheaton (Mass.) Coll., 1963; MSW, Rutgers U., 1966, PhD, 1983; grad., N.Y. Ctr. Psychoanalytic Tng., 1978. Diplomate Am. Bd. Psychotherapy, Am. Bd. Forensic Medicine, Am. Bd. Examiners Clin. Social Worker, Am. Bd. Forensic Examiners, Am. Bd. Psychol. Specialties, cert. profl. coach, mentor coach. Clin. social worker VA, Newark, 1967; psychotherapist Santa Barbara (Calif.) Mental Health Svcs., 1967-69; supr. Santa Barbara Counselling Ctr., 1967-69; pvt. practice psychoanalysis, 1969—. Psychoanalyst, therapist Fifth Ave. Ctr. for Psychotherapy, NYC, 1969-72; instr. Marymount Manhattan Coll., 1971; psychotherapy supr. clin. faculty, dept. psychiatry Rutgers Med. Sch., New Brunswick, NJ, 1972-75, tchg. asst. Grad. Sch. Social Work, 1974-76; vis. lectr. Bryn Mawr Coll. Sch. Social Work and Social Rsch., 1980; faculty NY Ctr. for Psychoanalytic Tng., 1980—, NJ Inst. Psychoanalysis and Psychotherapy, 1982—; adv. bd. Am. Bd. Forensic Social Workers, 1999, chair adv. bd., 2000; pres. Goldilox Co., Inc., ShAIRing, Inc.; faculty So. NJ Psychoanalytic Inst., Brigantine, 2004—, bd. dirs. Mem. editl. bd. jour Current Issues in Psychoanalytic Practice, 1983-93; contbr. articles to profl. jours. Bd. dirs. N.Y. Ctr. for Psychoanalytic Tng., Inst. for Psychoanalysis and Psychotherapy N.J. Faculty, 1982—. Recipient Disting. Faculty award Atlantic County Psychoanalytic Soc., 1987; NIMH fellow, 1965. Fellow N.J. Soc. for Clin. Social Work; mem. AAUP, NASW, APA, Conf. Psychoanalytic Psychotherapists, Nat. Assn. for Advancement of Psychoanalysis, Acad. Cert. Social Workers, Soc. for Psychoanalytic Tng. (bd. dirs. 1983-90, dir. social sci. program 1983-86), Am. Coll. Forensic Examiners (mem. editl. bd. jours. 1999—, Outstanding Svc. award 2000), Internat. Coach Fedn.; mem. APA (pres. div. 39 sec. III, 2003-04), Am. Psychoanalytic Assn. (com. on psychotherapist assocs. 2003—), Am. Coll. Forensic Social Workers (chair 2000-01), Women in Aviation Internat, 99's Internat. Orgn. Women Pilots, Nat. Bus. Aviation Assn, Rutgers U. Alumni Assn. (bd. dirs., 2003—), So. NJ Psychoanalytic Inst. (faculty and bd. mem. 2004-). Home and Office: 159 Valley Rd Princeton NJ 08540-3442 Office Phone: 609-921-0828. Personal E-mail: judith@judithlogue.com.

LOGUE, KYLE D., law educator; BA summa cum laude, Auburn U.; JD, Yale U. Law clk. for Hon. Patrick E. Higginbotham US Ct. Appeals (5th cir.); atty. Sutherland, Asbill & Brennan, Atlanta; prof. law U. Mich. Law Sch., Ann Arbor. Vis. prof. U. Va. Sch. Law. Contbr. articles to law jours. Nat. Harry S. Truman Scholar, Olin Scholar. Office: U Mich Law Sch 408 Hutchins Hall 625 S State St Ann Arbor MI 48109 Office Phone: 734-936-2207. Office Fax: 734-764-8309. E-mail: klogue@umich.edu.*

LOGUE, RONALD E., corporate financial executive; BS, Boston Coll., 1967, MBA, 1974. Head mutual fund custody divsn. State Street Corp., Boston, 1990—92, head global investor svcs. group, 1992—99, vice chmn., 1999—2001, COO, pres., 2001—04, chmn., CEO, 2004—. Office: State Street Corp 225 Franklin St Boston MA 02110

LOGUE, SUSAN, dean, educator; d. Arthur A. and Effie Vera (Newberry) Logue; m. Keith E. VanCleave, July 10, 1960; 1 child, Michelle Suzanne Jacobs. BS Advanced studies Photography, Music, So. Ill. U., Carbondale, 1992; MS in Libr. and Info. Sci., U. Ill., Urbana, 1994. Supr. bindery preparation libr. affairs So. Ill. U., Carbondale, 1983—88, preservation unit coord. libr. affairs, 1989—98, asst. instrnl. support services libr., libr. affairs, 1995—99, dir., instrnl. support svcs., libr. affairs, 1999—2001, assoc. dean libr. affairs, 2001—. Spkr. numerous confs. and presentations. Author: (book) Instructional Support Services, ARL, OMS, SPEC Kit #265, Washington, DC, Role of Libraires in Distance Education. ARL, OMS, SPEC Kit #216, Washington, DC, (web publication) Library Affairs Showcase, Freedom of the Press Bibliography. Troup leader Girl Scouts Am., Makanda, Ill., 1993—99; pres. Midland Hills Country Club, Makanda, 2003—05, 1995—96. Recipient Outstanding Faculty award, Libr. Affairs, So. Ill. U., 2001. Mem.: ALA (chair, program coordinating com. 2003—05), Libr. and Info. Tech. Assn. (chair, distance learning interest group 1997—2000, nat. forum planning com. mem. 1999—2000, leadership devel. com. mem. 1999—2003, coord., interest group chairpersons 1999—2003, chair, web-based continuing edn. task force 2001—01). Office: Libr Affairs So Ill Univ 605 Agriculture Dr Carbondale IL 62901 Office Phone: 618-453-2522. Home Fax: 618-453-3440; Office Fax: 618-453-3440. Personal E-mail: slogue@lib.siu.edu.

LOGUE-KINDER, JOAN, financial planner, consultant; b. Richmond, Va., Oct. 26, 1943; d. John T. and Helen (Harvey) Logue; m. Lowell A. Henry Jr., Oct. 6, 1963 (div. Sept. 1981); children: Lowell A. Henry III, Catherine D. Henry, Christopher Logue Henry; m. Randolph S. Kinder, Dec. 13, 1986 (div. Nov. 1995). Student, Wheaton Coll., 1959-62; BA in Sociology, Adelphi U., 1964; cert. in edn., Mercy Coll., Dobbs Ferry, N.Y., 1971; postgrad., NYU, 1973; cert. in edn., St. John's U., 1974. Asst. to dist. mgr. U.S. Census Bur., N.Y.C., 1970; tchr. and adminstr. social studies Yonkers (N.Y.) Bd. Edn., 1971-75; dir. pub. rels. Nat. Black Network, N.Y.C., 1976-83; corp. v.p. NBN Broadcasting (formerly Nat. Black Network), N.Y.C., 1984-90; sr. v.p. The Mingo Group/Plus, N.Y.C., 1990-91; v.p. Edelman Pub. Rels. Worldwide, N.Y.C., 1991-93; dep. asst. sec. pub. affairs U.S. Dept. Treasury, Washington, 1993-94, asst. sec. pub. affairs, 1994-95; dir. corp. comm. programs The Seagram Co., N.Y.C., 1995-96; v.p. Save the Children, Westport, Conn., 1997-98; sr. v.p., dir. mktg. and comm. Lynch, Jones & Ryan, N.Y.C., 1998—99; v.p. investment devel. Overseas Pvt. Investment Corp., Washington, 1999—2001; dir. comm. Office of the Mayor of D.C., 2001. Mem. alumnae recruitment coun. Wheaton Coll.; mem. Nigerian-Am. Friendship Soc., 1978-81; bd. dirs. Westchester Civil Liberties Union, 1974-77, Greater N.Y. coun. Girl Scouts U.S.A., 1985-93, Operation PUSH, 1985-93; del. White House Conf. on Small Bus.; active polit. campaigns, including Morris Udall for U.S. Pres., Howard Samuels for Gov.; sr. black media advisor Dukakis/Bentsen presdl. campaign, 1988; conv. del. N.Y. State Women's Polit. Caucus, 1975, pres. black caucus, 1976-77. Recipient Excellence in Media award Inst. New Cinema Artists, 1984. Mem. World Inst. Black Comm. (bd. dirs. 1983-91). Address: 5703 Woodcrest Ave Philadelphia PA 19131-2224 Office Phone: 610-457-8077, 215-878-1001. E-mail: Joan.Logue-Kinder@dc.gov, jlk45plus@msn.com.

LOGUERCIO, MATTHEW, actor, film producer, film director; b. Queens, NY, Jan. 27, 1961; s. Anthony Michael LoGuercio and Marilyn Comiskey; m. Alison Leiko Hong, Aug. 13, 2004; children: Alexander Loguercio, Gregory Loguercio, Michael Loguercio. BA in English and Polit. sci., L.I. U., 1984; MPA in Labor Rels., NYU, 1989. Law clk. Sanora & McKay, N.Y.C., 1985—90; v.p. adminstrn. Prudential Securities, N.Y.C., 1990—2000; actor, 1999—; owner Sleeping Dog Entertainment, LLC, Bedford Hills, NY, 1999—. Mem. adv. bd. Covenant House, N.Y.C., 1990—92. Author: Digital Filmmaking for the Masses, 2004; dir., writer: (film) The More Things Change, 2004; asst. prodr. (TV program) An Evening with: Gabriel Byrne; An Evening with: Jim Sheridan; editor: Latino Entertainment Report; prodr. (documentary) Habitat for Humanity; prodr.: DVD Justin Hayward; prodr.: (various commls.). Vol. Ronald McDonald House, N.Y.C., 1990—2000, dir. food fund, 1992—98; vol., v.p. bd. dirs. Victims for Victims, N.Y.C., 1989—95; vol., advisor Achiles Track Club, N.Y.C., 1996—99; co-coach NYU Men's Ice Hockey Club; mem. alumni bd. dirs. Southampton Coll., L.I. U.; fund raiser Oxfam Am., Amfar; young exec. support mem. Young Exec. Support; vol. NY Cares; bd. govs. St. Aid-St. News; mem. benefit com. Barrow Group; vice chmn. bd. dirs. Mint Theater Co. Named Vol. of Yr., City of NY, 1993; recipient, Filmmakers Mag., 2004. Mem.: SAG, Prodrs. Guild Am. Roman Catholic. Avocations: golf, running, photography, movies, reading. Home: 25 Woodland Rd Bedford Hills NY 10507 Office Phone: 917-854-2953.

LOH, ARTHUR TSUNG YUAN, finance company executive; b. Shanghai, People's Republic of China, Dec. 2, 1923; came to U.S., 1948; s. Chengor and Kwei N. (Wang) L.; m. Monica K.L. Chen, Apr. 16, 1955; children: Stephanie T.L., Pamela T.K. BA, St. John's U., Shanghai, 1945; MS, U. Ill., 1949, PhD, 1952. V.p., co-owner R.W. Pressprich & Co., N.Y.C., 1952-69; exec. v.p. fin. GAC Corp., Allentown, Pa., 1970-71; v.p., co-owner N.Y. Securities Co., N.Y.C., 1972-74; sr. v.p., chief fin. officer Govt. Employees Ins. Co., Criterion Ins. Co., Washington, 1974-80; chief fin. officer Rotary Internat., Evanston, Ill., 1981-88; founder, chmn. Loh Assocs., Greenwich, Conn., 1988—. Chmn. bd. GAC Securities Co., Ft. Lauderdale, Fla., 1973-74. Chmn. devel. com. Travelers Aid Soc., N.Y.C.; active Rep. Nat. Com., Washington, Heritage Found.; dir. Mid. Patent Rural Cemetery. Mem. Assn. for Investment Mgmt. and Rsch., Internat. Soc. Security Analysts, Am. Econ. Assn., Fin. Execs. Inst., Inst. Chartered Fin. Analysts (chartered), N.Y. Soc. Security Analysts, Wall Street Club, Bankers Club Am., Windmill Club, Greenwich Polo Club, Rotary, Downtown Assn. (N.Y.C.), City Midday Club (N.Y.C.). Methodist. Avocations: tennis, swimming, skiing, travel. Home: 9 North Ln Armonk NY 10504-2238 also: East of Rte 7 Danby VT 05739 Office: Loh Assocs 2001 W Main St Stamford CT 06902-4501 E-mail: atyloh@aol.com.

LOH, HORACE H., pharmacology educator; b. Canton, Republic China, May 28, 1936; BS, Nat. Taiwan U., Taipei, Republic China, 1958; PhD, U. Iowa, 1965. Lectr. dept. pharmacology U. Calif. Sch. Medicine, San Francisco, 1967; assoc. prof. biochem. Wayne State U., Detroit, 1968-70; lectr., rsch. assoc. depts. psychiatry, pharmacology Langley Porter Neuropsychiatric Inst. U. Calif. Sch. Medicine, San Francisco, 1970-72, assoc. prof. depts. psychiatry, pharmacology Langley Porter Neuropsychiatric Inst., 1972-75, prof. depts. psychiatry, pharmacology Langley Porter Neuropsychiatric Inst., 1975-88; prof., head dept. pharmacology U. Minn. Med. Sch., Mpls., 1989—, Frederick and Alice Stark prof., head dept. pharmacology, 1990—. Chmn. ann. meeting theme com. on receptors Fedn. Am. Socs. for Exptl. Biology, 1984; mem. exec. com. Internat. Narcotic Rsch. Conf., 1984—87, chair sci. program ann. meeting, 1986; mem. adv. com. Nat. Tsing Hua U. Inst. Life Scis., Taiwan, China, 1985—89; mem. exec. com. Com. on Problems of Drug Dependence, Inc., 1985—88; mem. sci. adv. com. Nat. Found. for Addictive Diseases, 1987—; cons. U.S. Army R & D Dept. Def., 1980—84. Contbr.;, editor (1 book); contbr. Recipient Career Devel. award, USPHS, 1973—78, 1978—83, Rsch. Scientist award, 1983—88, 1989—94, Humboldt award for sr. U.S. scientists, 1977. Mem.: We. Pharmacology Soc. (councilor 1980—83, pres. 1984—85), Soc. Chinese Bioscientists in Am. (pres. 1985—86), Am. Soc. Pharmacology and Exptl. Therapeutics (program com. 1976—86, trustee bd. publs. 1987—93, com. on confs. 1990—93), Am. Coll. Neuropsychopharmacology (honorific awards com. 1988—). Office: U Minn Med Sch Dept Pharm 6-120 Jackson Ha 321 Church St SE Minneapolis MN 55455-0250 Office Phone: 612-626-4460, 612-625-9997. Business E-Mail: lohxxool@mmn.edu.

LOH, ROBERT N. K., engineering educator; b. Lumut, Malaysia; arrived in Can., 1962, came to U.S., 1968; m. Annie Loh; children: John, Peter, Jennifer. BSc in Engring., Nat. Taiwan U., Taipei, 1961; MSc in Engring., U. Waterloo, Ont., Can., 1964, PhD, 1968. Asst. prof. U. Iowa, Iowa City, 1968-72, assoc. prof., 1973-78; prof. Oakland U., Rochester, Mich., 1978—, John F. Dodge prof., 1984—, assoc. dean, 1985-98, dir. Ctr. for Robotics and Advanced Automation, 1984—. Mem. editorial bd. Info. Systems, 1975—, Jour. of Intelligent and Robotic Systems, 1987—, Asia-Pacific Engring. Jour., 1990—; contbr. over 190 jour. publs. and tech. reports. Recipient numerous research grants and contracts from Dept. Def., NSF and pvt. industry. Mem. IEEE, Soc. Machine Intelligence (bd. dirs. 1985—), Assn. Unmanned Vehicle Systems, 1987—, Sigma Xi, Tau Beta Pi. Office: Oakland U Ctr for Robotics and Advanced Automation Dodge Hall Engring Rochester MI 48309-4401

LOHAN, LINDSAY, actress; b. NYC, July 2, 1986; d. Michael and Dina Lohan. Former model. Actor: (TV series) Another World, 1996—97, Bette, 2000; (TV films) Life-Size, 2000, Get A Clue, 2002; (films) The Parent Trap, 1998, Freaky Friday, 2003, Confessions of a Teenage Drama Queen, 2004, Mean Girls, 2004, Herbie: Fully Loaded, 2005; singer: (albums) Speak, 2004. Office: Creative Artists Agy 9830 Wilshire Blvd Beverly Hills CA 90212*

LOHF, KENNETH A., librarian, writer; b. Milw., Jan. 14, 1925; s. Herman A. and Louise (Krause) Lohf. AB, Northwestern U., 1949; AM, Columbia U., 1950, MS in Library Sci., 1952. Asst. librarian spl. collections Columbia U., N.Y.C., 1957-67, librarian rare books and manuscripts, 1967-92. Author: Thirty Poems, 1966, Conrad at Mid-Century: Editions and Studies, 1957, The Achievements of Marianne Moore: A Bibliography, 1958, Yvor Winters: A Bibliography, 1959, Frank Morris: A Bibliography, 1959, Sherwood Anderson: A Bibliography, 1960, An Index to the Little review, 1914-1929, 1961, The Collection of Books, Manuscripts and Autograph Letters in the Library of Jean and Donald Stralem, 1962, Indices to Little Magazines, 1953—64, The Literary Manuscripts of Hart Crane, 1967, The Jack Harris Samuels Library, 1974, The Centenary of John Masefield's Birth, 1978; author: (poems) Seasons, 1981, Arrivals, 1987, Fictions, 1990, Passages, 1991, Places, 1992, Endings/Beginnings, 1994; editor: Hart Crane, Seven Lyrics, 1966, Collections and Treasures of the Rare Book and Manuscript Library of Columbia University, 1985, Poets in a War, 1995, Hours, 1996, Moon and Sun, 1997, Columbia Library Columns, 1981—92, A Hymn of Simon Peter, 1998, Red Unto White, 1999, The Book of Twelve, 2000; contbr.; author: (novels) East West, 2002. Sec.-treas. Friends of Columbia U. Librs., 1973—92; mem. coun. Am. Mus. Britain; mem. vestry St. Thomas Ch. of Fifth Ave. 1st lt. USAF, 1943—46. Mem.: Coun. Fellows Pierpont Morgan Libr., Order of St. John of Jerusalem, Grolier Club (coun., sec. 1987—90, pres. 1990—94), Century Club, Knickerbocker Club. Episcopalian. Home: c/o Dewey Ballantin 1301 Ave of the Americas #Fl 33 New York NY 10019-6022

LOHMAN, GORDON RUSSELL, retired manufacturing executive; b. 1934; BS, MIT, 1955. Rsch. metallurgist, project engr. Amsted Industries, Inc., Chgo., 1958-61; project engr. Amsted Rsch. Labs., Chgo., 1961-67; dir. rsch. Amsted Industries, Inc., Chgo., 1967-68, pres. rsch., 1968-76, pres. MacWhyte divsn., 1976-78, v.p., 1978-87, exec. v.p., then pres., 1987-88, pres., COO, 1988-90, pres., CEO, 1990-1999; ret., 1999. Trustee Ill. Inst. Tech.; bd. dirs. Fortune Brands Inc., Ameren. Lt. USAF, 1955—58.

LOHMAN, JANETTE MASSIE, lawyer, educator; b. Washington, Mo., Oct. 14, 1955; d. Helen Sudie Williams Lohman; m. Douglas Kevin Rush, Feb. 14, 1983. BA summa cum laude in Polit. Sci. and Bus., William Jewell Coll., 1977; JD, St. Louis U. Sch. Law, 1981; MBA, St. Louis U. Sch. Bus. Adminstrn., 1982; LLM in Taxation, Wash. U., St. Louis, 1985. CPA Mo. State Bd. Accountancy, 1982; bar: Mo. 1981. Sr. mgr. tax dept. Touche Ross & Co., St. Louis, 1985—87; asst. gen. counsel, dir. tax planning McDonnell Douglas Corp., St. Louis, 1987—93; dir. revenue Dept. Revenue, State of Mo., Jefferson City, 1993—97; ptnr. Blackwell Sanders Matheny Weary & Lombardi LP, Kansas City, 1998, Blackwell Sanders Peper Martin LLP, St. Louis, 1998—2003, Thompson Coburn LLP, St. Louis, 2003—. Asst. adj. prof. St. Louis U. Sch. Law, 1998—. Editor: (property tax publication) American Bar Association/Institute of Professionals in Taxation Property Tax Desk Book, (tax periodical) Journal of Multistate Taxation and Incentives. V.p., trustee Mo. Citizens for the Arts, St. Louis, 1999. Named one of Best Lawyers in Am., Woodward White, 2005—; recipient Citation for Achievement, William Jewell Coll., 1995. Mem.: ABA (assoc.; exec. com. 2004, state and local tax subcommittee). Home: 9 Lenox Pl Saint Louis MO 63108 Office: Thompson Coburn LLP One US Bank Plz Ste 3500 Saint Louis MO 63108 Office Phone: 314-552-6161. Office Fax: 314-552-7161. E-mail: jlohman@thompsoncoburn.com.

LOHMANN, GEORGE YOUNG, JR., neurosurgeon, health facility administrator, artist; b. Scranton, Pa., Aug. 9, 1947; s. George Young Lohmann and Elizabeth (Nichols) Frantzen; m. Joette Calabrese, May 15, 1973 (div. 1981); m. Rosemary Ei-Ling Ma, Sept. 24, 1988 (div. 1998); 1 child, Norelle Christa Victoria. AB in Chemistry with honors, Hobart Coll., 1968; MD, SUNY, Buffalo, 1972. Diplomate Am. Bd. Neurol. Surgeons, Am. Acad. Pain Specialists, Am. Bd. Forensic Medicine, Am. Acad. Disability Analysts. Resident gen. surgery Wesley Meml. Hosp., Chgo., 1972-73; asst. med. dir. West Side Orgn., Chgo., 1973-74; emergency physician St. James Hosp., Chicago Heights, Ill., 1973-74; from jr. resident to chief resident neurosurgery Georgetown U. Hosp., Washington, 1975-79; chief resident neurosurgery Washington Vets. Hosp., 1978; pvt. practice Baton Rouge, 1979-81, 81-84; dir. dept. neurosurgery Brookdale Hosp. Med. Ctr., Bklyn., 1984-93; pres. Bklyn. Neurosurg. Svcs., Inc., 1985—; pvt. practice Midland, Tex., 1994-96; founding pres. Dragongate Adoption Cons., Inc., 1999—. Mem. Med. Dir. Com., Risk Mgmt. Com., Exec. Quality Assurance Com., 1987-93; mem. Med. Bd. Com., 1985-93, Exec. Bd. Com., 1984-93, Pain Mgmt. Com., 1988-91; regional dir. Tex. Physicians Resource Coun., 1996-97. Contbr. articles to profl. jours.; actor: (in amatur theatre). Mem. adv. bd. Ctr. Latin Affairs, Baton Rouge, 1982-84; mem. Senatorial Inner Cir., 1988, mem. presdl. roundtable, 1991; mem. Presdl. Roundtable, 1992; trustee Christian Victory Ctr., Hempstead, N.Y., 1986-88; vol. Appalachian Project, 1970; mem. transition team for Pres. Ronald Reagan, 1980-81. Named to Compton-Connolly Guide to Best Physicians in the N.Y. Met. Area; selected by peers as one of Best Doctors in America Ctrl. Region, 1996-97. Fellow ACS, Am. Coll. Pain Mgmt., Am. Coll. Forensic Examiners, Am. Coll. Disability Analysts; mem. AMA, Am. Assn. Neurol. Surgeons (sect. intensive care), Christian Med. and Dental Soc., Am. Assn. Neurologic Surgeons, N.Y. State Neurosurg. Soc., N.Y. Soc. Neurosurgery, Congress Neurologic Surgeons (spine sect., sect. on trauma, sect. on intensive care), Tex. State Med. Soc., So. Med. Soc. Presdl. Roundtable (presdl. transition team 1980-81), NRA (life), West Tex. Cigar Soc., Physicians Resource Coun. (Tex. regional dir.), Argentier Honoraire Confrerie de la Chaine des Rotisseurs, Bailli Foundateur de Midland-Confrerie de la Chaine des Rotisseurs, Midland Confrerie de la Chaine des Rotisseurs (Bailli Honoraire), Chaine des Rotisseurs (comdr.), Consul de L'Ordre Mondial des Gourmets Degustateurs, Brilliat-Savarin Soc., Shanhai Tiffin Club, Donyin Sister City Assn., Midland Arts Assn., Midland C. of C., Midland-Odessa Symphony and Choral Soc. Achievements include patents in field. Avocations: skiing, painting, poetry, music, cooking.

LOHMANN, KEITH HENRY OSKAR, police department official, consultant; b. Dec. 26, 1955; s. Henry August and June Dorothy (Friberg) L.; m. Margaret Lynch, Mar. 31, 1984; 1 child, Katarina. AS in Law Enforcement, Guilford Coll., 1977, BS in Adminstrn. of Justice, 1981; M in Pub. Affairs, U. N.C., 1987. Ops. mgr. H. Lohmann and Son, Brookhaven, 1973-75, 81-82; ops. supr. Powers Detective and Patrol, Greensboro, N.C., 1975-81; pub. safety officer Chapel Hill (N.C.) Police Dept., 1982-84, police planner, 1984-87; coord. law enforcement dist. N.H. U.S. Dept. Justice, Concord, 1987-89; spl. asst. U.S. Atty., Washington, 1989-92; prof. criminal justice N.H. Tech. Inst., 1992-93; lt. N.H. Police Stds. & Tng. Coun., Concord, 1993-95, maj., 1996—2003, dir., 2003—. Security cons. Hotel Europa, Inc., Chapel Hill, 1982-83. Mem. Nat. Coun. Law Enforcement Edn. and Tng., Internat. Assn. Dirs. of Law Enforcement Stds. and Tng., N.H. Assn. Chiefs of Police, Internat. Assn. Chiefs of Police. Lutheran. Avocations: golf, tennis, skiing. Office: NH Police Stds & Tng Coun 17 Institute Dr Concord NH 03301-7413 Office Phone: 603-271-2133.

LOHMULLER, MARTIN NICHOLAS, retired bishop; b. Phila., Aug. 21, 1919; s. Martin Nicholas and Mary Frances (Doser) L. BA, St. Charles Borromeo Sem., Phila., 1942; D.Canon Law, Cath. U. Am., 1947. Ordained priest Roman Cath. Ch., 1944. Officialis Diocese Harrisburg, Pa., 1948—63; vicar for religious Diocese of Harrisburg, 1958—70; pastor Our Lady of Good Counsel Parish, Marysville, Pa., 1954—64, St. Catherine Laboure Parish, Harrisburg, 1964—68; consecrated Bishop of Ramsbury, 1970; vicar gen. Archdiocese Phila., 1970—94; aux. bishop of Phila., 1970—94; pastor Old St. Mary's Parish, Phila., 1976—89, Holy Trinity Parish, Phila., 1976—89; ret., 1994. Roman Catholic. E-mail: bishiplo@adphila.org.

LOHNER, HENNING, composer, filmmaker; b. Bremen, Germany, July 17, 1961; s. Edgar Lohner and Marlene Clewing; m. Ariane Riecker. MA, Johann Wolfgang Goethe U., Germany, 1987. Artist in residence Inst. for New Media, Frankfurt, Germany, 1994—96; composer in residence Media Ventures, Santa Monica, Calif., 1996—. Guest lectr. Film Akademie Baden-Württemberg, Ludwigsburg, Germany, 2003—. Exhibition, audio & video installation, Raw Material, Vol. 1 - 11; dir.: (film) The Revenge of the Dead Indians (Input TV Conf., 1993), Peefeeyatko (1st Internat. Music Film awards, Cannes, 1991), One11 And 103 (Silver Apple, Nat. Edn. awards, 1993); composer: (concert for prepared piano & orchestra) Orlac's Hands, (orchestral soundtrack) Mimic Sentinel, (orchestral suite) Catching the Stars for World Expo, 2000, (orchestral soundtrack) Der Große Bagarozy, (orchestral soundtracks) Hellraiser: Deader, 2003, Incident at Loch Ness, 2003, Santa's Slay, 2004, (concert for 2 percussionists and orch.) Ring 2, 2005, Bloodrayne, 2005. Office: Remote Control Prodns / Lohneranger 1547 14th St Santa Monica CA 90404 Office Phone: 310-349-9975.

LOHNES, WALTER F. W., German language and literature educator; b. Frankfurt, Germany, Feb. 8, 1925; came to U.S., 1948, naturalized, 1954; s. Hans and Dina (Koch) L.; m. Claire Shane, 1950; children: Kristen, Peter, Claudia. Student, U. Frankfurt, 1945-48, Ohio Wesleyan U., 1948-49, U. Mo., 1949-50; PhD, Harvard U., 1961. Asst., Inst. German Folklore, U. Frankfurt, 1947-48; instr. German U. Mo., 1949-50; head dept. German, Phillips Acad., Andover, Mass., 1951-61; asst. prof. Stanford (Calif.) U., 1961-65, assoc. prof., 1965-68, prof., 1969-95, prof. emeritus, 1995—, dir. NDEA Inst. Advanced Study, 1961-68, chmn. dept. German studies, 1973-79, dir. Inst. Basic German, 1975-95, prin. investigator NEH grant, 1978-80. Vis. prof. Woehler-Gymnasium, Frankfurt, 1956-57, Middlebury Coll., 1959, U. N.Mex., 1980, 81, 86, U. Vienna, 1990, Coll. de France, Paris, 1992; mem., chmn. various coms. of examiners Ednl. Testing Svc. and Coll. Bd.; chmn. German Grad. Record Exam. Author: (with V. Nollendorfs) German Studies in the United States, 1976, (with F. W. Strothmann) German: A Structural Approach, 1968, 4th rev. edit., 1988; (with E.A. Hopkins) Contrastive Grammar of English and German, 1982, (with Martha Woodmansee) Erkennen und Deuten, 1983, (with J.A. Pfeffer) Grunddeutsch, Texte zur gesprochenen deutschen Gegenwartssprache, 3 vols., 1984, (with D. Benseler and V. Nollendorfs) Teaching German in America: Prolegomena to a History, 1988; contbr. numerous articles to profl. jours.; editor: Unterrichtspraxis, 1971-74 Bd. dirs. Calif. Youth Symphony, 1977-78, Oakland (Calif.) Symphony Youth Orch., 1978-80, Peninsula Dem. Coalition, 1998—. Decorated Fed. Order of Merit (Germany); Medal of Honor in Gold (Austria); German Govt. grantee, 1975, 76, 78. Mem. MLA, Am. Assn. Tchrs. German (v.p. 1961-62, 70-71, Outstanding Educator award 1994; hon. 1995), Am. Assn. Applied Linguistics, Am. Coun. on Teaching Fgn. Langs., German Studies Assn., Internat. Vereinigung Germanische Sprach und Literaturwissenschaft. Home: 733 Covington Rd Los Altos CA 94024-4903 Office: Stanford U Dept German Studies Stanford CA 94305-2030

LOHOKARE, SAURABH K., process engineer, research scientist; s. Krishna S. and Seema K. Lohokare. BEE, U. Nagpur, Nagpur, India, 1998; MEE, PhD in Elec. and Computer Engring., U. Del., Newark, Del., 2004. Sr. process engr. Intel Corp., Chandler, Ariz., 2004—; rsch. scientist U. Del., Newark. Tech. cons. Astropower, Inc, Newark, 2000—04. Contbr. scientific papers pub. to profl. jour. Cmty. svc. vol., Phoenix, Ariz., 2004—05. Scholar Grad. Rsch. Asst., USNR, 1999-2004. Achievements include patents for A novel fabrication process for conductive polymer based flip-chip interconnects.

LOHR, DENNIS E., research scientist, education educator; life ptnr. Nita J. Dagon. BA chemistry, Beloit Coll., 1965; PhD biochemistry, U.NC, Chapel Hill, 1970. Postdoctoral Oreg. State U., 1972—77, rsch. asst. prof., 1978—79; asst. prof. Ariz. State U., 1979—84, assoc. prof., 1984—89, prof., 1989—. Grant rev. panels NIH, Washington, 1981—88; grant rev. panel NSF, Arlington, Va., 2001—03. Contbr. over 40 articles to profl. jours. Vol. tchr. Peace Corps., Kenya, 1970—71. Recipient Rsch. Career Devel. award, NIH, 1984—89; rsch. grants, 1978—. Achievements include research in discovering nucleosome structure; unraveling basic structure of chromosomes; first to characterize nucleosome structure of single copy eukaryotic gene. Office: Arizona State U Chemistry & Biochemistry Box 871604 Tempe AZ 85287-1604 E-mail: dlohr@asu.edu.

LOHR, HAROLD RUSSELL, retired bishop; b. Gary, SD, Aug. 31, 1922; s. Lester Albert and Nora Helena (Fossum) L.; m. Theola Marie Kottke, June 21, 1947 (div. Dec. 1973); children: Philip Kyle, David Scott, Michael John; m. Edith Mary Morgan, Dec. 31, 1973. BS summa cum laude, S.D. State U., 1947; PhD, U. Calif.-Berkeley, 1950; MDiv summa cum laude, Augustana Theol. Sem., Rock Island, Ill., 1958. Ordained to ministry Augustana Luth. Ch., 1958; installed as bishop, 1980. Research chemist Argonne Nat. lab., Lemont, Ill., 1950-54; pastor Luth. Ch. of Ascension, Northfield, Ill., 1958-70; assoc. exec. Bd. Coll. Edn., N.Y.C., 1970-73; dir. research Div. Profl. Leadership, Phila., 1973-77, assoc. exec., 1977-80; synodical bishop Luth. Ch. in Am., Fargo, N.D., 1980-87, Evang. Luth. Ch. in Am., Moorhead, Minn., 1988-91, ret., 1991. Mem. exec. council Luth. Ch. in Am., N.Y.C., 1982-87; mem. commn. of peace and war, 1983-85. Contbg. author: Growth in Ministry, 1980; also articles to sci. jours. Bd. dirs. Gustavus Adolphus Coll., 1980-87, Luther Northwestern Sem., St. Paul, 1980-87, Concordia Coll., Moorhead, Minn., 1988-91; mem. ch. coun. Evang. Luth. Ch. in Am., Chgo., 1990-91, disciplinary hearing officer, 1992-97, interim dir. synodical rels., 1993-94; mem. bd. govs. Chgo. Ctr. Religion and Sci., 1987-99, Zygon Ctr. Religion and Sci., Chgo., 1999-2003; mem. Summit on Environ., Joint Appeal in Religion and Sci., Washington, 1992; mem. adv. bd. Ctr. for Faith and Sci. Exch., Concord, Mass., 1995-99, mem. exec. bd., 1999-2001; mem. diocesan rev. com. Roman Cath. Diocese of Worcester, Mass., 2003—. Recipient Suomi award Suomi Coll., 1983. Mem. Phi Kappa Phi. Democrat. Home: 47 Brook Ln Berlin MA 01503-1671 Personal E-mail: hrlohrs@aol.com.

LOHR, JACOB ANDREW, pediatrician, educator; b. Lexington, N.C., Aug. 15, 1940; s. Dermot and Blanche (Grimes) L.; m. Elizabeth Waite, June 19, 1967 (div. 1978); m. Lura Galloway, Nov. 27, 1993; children: Jason Merrill, Lara Jane Parker (dec.), Jonathan Waite, Elizabeth Brice. AB, U. N.C., 1962, MD, 1967. Diplomate Am. Bd. Pediats. Chief resident dept. pediat. U. Va., Charlottesville, 1969-70, prof., 1984-90, divsn. chief, assoc. chair, 1976-90; prof. dept. pediat. U. N.C., Chapel Hill, 1990—, divsn. chief, assoc. chair, 1990-98, vice chair dept. pediat., 1998-2000; pediatrician-in-chief N.C. Children's Hosp., Chapel Hill, 1999-2000, sr. clinician, 2000—; exec. dir. Gov.'s Inst. Alcohol and Substance Abuse, 1998—. Cons. to task force on urinary tract infections Am. Acad. Pediats., 1992-99, WHO Com. on Hospitalized Children at Risk, Geneva, 1999-2000; McLemore Birdsong disting. prof. U.Va., 1984-90. Editor: Pediatric Outpatient Proceedings, 1992, Guidelines for Nurse Practitioners, 1994, 5th edit., 1999, Essence of Pediatrics, 2000; med. editor Am. Bd. pediats., 1996—; contbr. articles to profl. jours. Bd. dirs. Head Start, Charlottesville, 1973-76, Ronald McDonald House, 1980-82, Orange County Ptnrship. for young Children, Chapel Hill, 1994-96; trustee Bowman Fund, U. Va., 1972—. Lt. comdr. USN, 1970-72. Recipient H. Fleming Fuller award, U. NC Healthcare Sys. Fellow Am. Acad. Pediats.; mem. Am. Soc. for Microbiology, Ambulatory Pediat. Assn., Pediat. Infectious Disease Soc., Infectious Disease Soc. Lutheran. Avocations: golf, boating. Office: U NC Dept Pediat 5041 Bioinformatics Bldg Chapel Hill NC 27599-0001 Business E-Mail: jlohr@med.unc.edu.

LOHR, MICHAEL F., judge; BA cum laude, U. Md., 1974, JD cum laude, 1977; LLM summa cum laude, George Wash. U., 1984. With office gen. coun. USN; clk. State Dist. Ct. Md.; def. counsel, sr. trial counsel, adminstrv. atty. Naval Legal Svc. Office, San Francisco; staff judge advocate USS Coral Sea USN, 1981, with internat. law divsn. office judge advocate gen., 1984—87, asst. spl. counsel to chief naval ops., 1987, sr. def. counsel Naval Legal Svc. Office Wash., 1987—88, internat. law atty., commander-in-chief U.S. Pacific Fleet, staff judge advocate to comdr. U.S. Naval Forces Ctrl. Command Pearl Harbor, 1988—89, fleet judge advocate U.S. Second Fleet Norfolk, 1989—91, with U.S. Seventh Fleet Yokosuka, Japan, 1991—93; dep. legal counsel to chmn. Joint Chiefs of Staff Pentagon, 1993—96, legal counsel to chmn., 1997—2000; comdr. Mid-Atlantic USN, Norfolk, 1996—97, dep. JAG, comdr. U.S. Legal Svc. Command, 2000—02, JAG, 2002—04; counsel The Boeing Co., Arlington, Va., 2005—. Rep. ocean policy affairs Dept. Def. Decorated Def. Superior Svc. Medal with oak leaf cluster, Legion of Merit, Meritorious Svc. Medal (three awards), others; recipient Disting. Svc. medal, 2004. Office: The Boeing Co 1200 Wilson Blvd Arlington VA 22209

LOHR, WALTER GEORGE, JR., lawyer; b. Balt., Mar. 3, 1944; s. Walter George and Janet Louise (Cartee) L.; children: Lila Meredith, Walter George III, Frederick Boyce. AB, Princeton U., 1966; LLB, Yale U., 1969. Bar: Md. 1969. Law clk.to Hon. Harrison L. Winter U.S. Cir. Ct., Richmond, Va., 1969-70; assoc. Piper & Marbury, Balt., 1970-74, ptnr., 1977-88, Hogan & Hartson, Washington, 1992—; asst. atty. gen. State of Md., Balt., 1974-76; prin. Walter G. Lohr Jr., Balt., 1988-92. Bd. dirs. Danaher Corp., Washington, Cmty. of Sci., Inc., Balt., iSky, Inc., Laurel, Md., chmn.; mem. adv. bd. Prudential Venture Ptnrs., N.Y.C., 1985-93. Trustee Balt. Mus. Art, 1985-1998, 2000—. Office: Hogan & Hartson 111 S Calvert St Ste 1600 Baltimore MD 21202-6191 E-mail: wglohr@hhlaw.com.

LOIACONO, JOHN P., information technology executive; BA in Comm., Fresno State U. With Sun Microsystems, Santa Clara, Calif., 1987—, chief mktg. officer, sr. v.p. operating platforms group, exec. v.p. software group. Office: Sun Microsystems Inc 4150 Network Cir Santa Clara CA 95054 Office Phone: 650-960-1300, 800-555-9786. Office Fax: 408-276-3804.

LOIELLO, JOHN PETER, diplomat; b. Oceanside, N.Y., Aug. 16, 1943; s. Rosario Paul and Mary Agnes (Butler) L.; m. Elaine Margaret Robinson, June 14, 1944. BA in History, Fordham U., 1965; MA in History, SUNY, Buffalo, 1973; PhD in African History, U. London, 1980. Tchr. history The Gow Sch., South Wales, N.Y., 1967-71; instr. U. Md. (U.K.), London, 1976-78; exec. dir. Dem. Party Com. Abroad, Washington and London, 1978-80; sr. cons. Assn. Am. Chambers of Commerce in Latin Am., Washington, 1980; spl. asst. to chmn. NEH, Washington, 1978-82; assoc. dir. Democracy Prog., Washington, 1982-83; founding exec. dir. Nat. Dem. Inst. for Internat. Affairs, Washington, 1983-85; pres. Gowran Internat., Washington, 1985-93, 2000—; assoc. dir. ednl. and cultural affairs U.S. Info. Agy., Washington, 1994-98, sr. advisor to dir., 1999-2000. Pres. Alcide de Gaspari Found. (USA), Washington, 1987-89. Contbr. articles to profl. jours. Commr. Commn. on Platform Accountability, Dem. Nat. Com., Washington, 1981-85, chmn. fgn. policy subcom., 1980, platform com., 1980; sec. Tax Equity for Ams. Abroad, London, 1977-79; sec. Dems. Abroad, London, 1976-79. Recipient Commdr. of Order of Lion Senegal, 1999; African Studies scholar, U. London, 1974-78, grantee, 1975. Mem. Nat. Italian Am. Found., Royal African Soc. Democrat. Roman Catholic. Avocations: travel, reading, swimming.

LOIOCANO, BARBARA J., language educator; b. Dunkirk, N.Y., Feb. 13, 1953; d. Carl Russell and Jean Eleanor (Bowker) Loiocano. BS in Edn., SUNY, Fredonia, 1975; MS in Edn., SUNY, Plattsburgh, 1980; CAS, SUNY, New Paltz, 1993. Cert. tchr. Spanish edn. and bilingual edn., sch. adminstr./supr., sch. dist. adminstr. N.Y. Spanish tchr. Delaware Valley Ctrl. Sch., Callicoon, NY, 1984-85, Monticello (N.Y.) Ctrl. Sch., 1985-86; bilingual tchr. Otisville (N.Y.) Correctional Facility, 1986—. Bilingual tchr. Marist Coll., Poughkeepsie, NY, 1987; Spanish tchr. Mercy Coll., Dobbs Ferry, NY, 1988; adult edn. tchr. Sullivan County Bd. Coop. Ednl. Svcs., Liberty, NY, 1985, Liberty, 1989—90; acting edn. supr. Otishill Sch., 1989—94; sec. literacy coun. Otisville Correctional Facility, 1992—, supr. literacy vols., 1992—93. Mem.: State Assn. Bilingual Edn., N.Y. State Assn. Fgn. Lang. Tchrs., Nat. Assn. Bilingual Edn., Am. Legion Aux. Office: Otisville Correctional Facility PO Box 8 Otisville NY 10963-0008

LØJ, ELLEN MARGRETHE, ambassador; b. Gedesby, Denmark, Oct. 17, 1948; Grad. econs., Copenhagen U., 1973. Joined Ministry Fgn. Affairs, 1973; first sec. Permanent Mission to the UN Ministry Fgn. Affairs, N.Y.C., 1977—80, counsellor Permanent Representation of Denmark to the European Cmty. Brussels, 1982—85, head dept., 1986—89; amb. to Israel Ministry Fgn. Affairs, 1989—92; under-sec. multilateral affairs, South Group Ministry Fgn. Affairs, 1992—94, under-sec. bilateral affairs South Group, 1994—96, state sec. South Group, 1996—2001, permanent rep. of Denmark to the UN, amb., 2001—. Mem. supervisory bd. The Investment Fund Ctrl. and Ea. Europe, 1994—96, The Industrialization Fund for Developing Countries, 1994—96, Scandlines AG and Scandlines A/S, 1998—2001; participant Danish dels. to several internat. meetings and U.N. confs. Office: Permanent Rep of Denmark to the UN One Dag Hammarskjöld Plaza 885 Second Ave 18th Fl New York NY 10017-2201 Office Phone: 212-705-4968.

LOK, JOAN MEI-LOK, community affairs specialist, artist; b. Hong Kong, Apr. 2, 1962; d. Chi Hong Stephen Pan and Mui Kan Teresa Chan; m. David Tai-Wai Lok, Jan. 11, 1986; children: Wesley Kevin, Gary Alexander. B in Tourism and Hotel Mgmt., Hong Kong Poly. U., 1983; BBA, Baruch Coll., 1988; MBA, Strayer U., 2005. Commd. compliance examiner FDIC, 1999. Cmty. affairs specialist FDIC, Balt., 1999—, Chinese money smart transl. mgr., 2002—, compliance examiner Holyoke, Mass., 1997—99, affordable housing specialist Hartford, Conn., 1994—97, bank liquidation specialist South Brunswick, NJ, 1988—94. V.p. Lingnam Art Assn. of Am., NYC, 1992—94; nat. pres. Sumi-e Soc. of Am., Inc., Washington, 2002—; mem. Md. Gov.'s Commn. on Asian Pacific Am. Affairs, 2003—, Md. Gov.'s Citation Outstanding Cmty. Svc., 2004. Recipient Artist's Alternative award, Ea. Arts Connection, 1994, First Pl., Glastonbury Art Guild, 1995, Best in Watercolors award, Audubon Soc. of Conn. in Glastonbury, 1996, Diana Kan award, Sumi-e Soc. of Am., 1997, Grumbacher Gold metal, 1998, Cheng Dia Chien award, 1999, Blue Heron award, 2002, 2004, Benefactors of the Soc. award, 2003, Artist of the Yr. award, Edison Arts Soc., 2000, Gardens of Edison award, 2002, Svc. to Am. medal, Partnership for Pub. Svcs., 2003, Md. Gov. citation for outstanding cmty. svc., 2004, Nat. Cherry Blossom Festival Art contest, 2005; fellow, Walt Disney World, 1983—84; scholar, Hong Kong Hotel Assn., 1982. Mem.: Edison Arts Soc., Glastonbury Art Guild, Internat. Soc. of Lingnam Artists (dir. of pub. rels. 2003—), Assn. of Chinese Calligraphy in Am. Achievements include initiated the first virtual juried exhibition of sumi-e art in the Sumi-e Society of America's 39 years history; first Chinese-American to be elected national President of the Sumi-e Society of America in its 40 years history; first female executive of a Chinese cultural club in New York Chinatown in 1992. Office: FDIC 8850 Stanford Blvd Ste 3000 Columbia MD 21045 Business E-Mail: jlok@fdic.gov.

LOKE, JOAN TSO FONG, respiratory therapist; b. Hong Kong, Nov. 29, 1950; d. Choong Shee and Elsie L.C. Loke; m. Fabian Chan, Dec. 2, 1975 (div. July 1993); children: Jeffrey Chan, Jeremy Chan. BS in Biology, U. Puget Sound, 1973, BS in Med. Tech., 1974; AS in Respiratory care, Kapiolani C.C., 1995. Cert. respiratory therapy technician, registered respiratory technologist. Med. technologist Harborview Med. Ctr., Seattle, 1975—76; EKG technologist St. Francis, Honolulu, 1987—94, oxygen technologist, 1994—95, respiratory therapist, 1995, Kapiolani Med. Ctr., Honolulu, 1995—2002, Kaiser Permanent, Honolulu, 1995—, Tripler Med. Ctr., Honolulu, 2002—. Mem.: AARC (pact team mem. 2002—03, pub. rels. chair 2002—03), HSRC (v.p. 2000, bd. dirs. 2000, pres. 2001—03). Avocations: Karate (black belt), swimming, tennis, piano, singing. Home: 965 Prospect St #605 Honolulu HI 96822 Office: Kaiser Permanente 3288 Moanalua Rd Honolulu HI 96819 E-mail: catnap@hawaii.rr.com.

LOKEN, BARBARA, marketing educator, social psychologist; b. Owatonna, Minn., Aug. 22, 1951; d. Gordon Keith and June Rosaline (Iverson) Anderson; 1 child, Elizabeth Loken Diebel. BA in Psychology magna cum laude, U. Minn., 1973; MA, NYU, 1976; PhD in Social Psychology, U. Ill., 1981. Rsch. and statis. asst. Nat. Soc. Prevention Blindness, N.Y.C., 1974-76; rsch. asst. dept. psychology U. Ill., 1976, 78-80, instr., 1977-78; NIMH trainee in measurement, 1979-80; asst. prof. dept. mktg. U. Minn., 1980-86, assoc. prof., 1986-92, prof., 1992—. Co-dir. edn. evaluation Minn. heart health project Sch. Pub. Health, 1982-88, adj. assoc. prof. dept. psychology, 1987-92, adj. prof., 1992—; vis. assoc. prof. mktg. UCLA, 1988. Assoc. editor: Jour. Consumer Rsch., 1996-99; contbr. articles to profl. jours. Rsch. grantee Sch. Mgmt., U. Minn., 1981-84, 86, 88-2005. Mem. Am. Psychol. Assn., Am. Mktg. Assn., Assn. Consumer Rsch., Assn. for Consumer Rsch. 2000 (treas.).

LOKEN, JAMES BURTON, federal judge; b. Madison, Wis., May 21, 1940; s. Burton Dwight and Anita (Nelson) Loken; m. Caroline Brevard Hester, July 30, 1966; children: Kathryn Brevard, Kristina Ayres. BS, U. Wis., 1962; LLB magna cum laude, Harvard U., 1965. Law clk. to Hon. J. Edward Lumbard U.S. Ct. Appeals (2d Cir.), N.Y.C., 1965—66; law clk. to assoc. justice Byron White U.S. Supreme Ct., Washington, 1966—67; assoc. atty. Faegre & Benson, Mpls., 1967—70, ptnr., 1973—90; gen. counsel Pres.'s Com. on Consumer Interests, Office of Pres. of U.S., Washington, 1970; staff asst. Office of Pres. of U.S., Washington, 1970—72; judge U.S. Ct. Appeals (8th cir.), St. Paul, 1990—, chief judge, 2003—. Editor: Harvard Law Rev., 1964—65. Mem.: Am. Law Inst., Phi Beta Kappa, Phi Kappa Phi. Avocations: golf, running. Office: US Courthouse 300 S 4th St Ste 11W Minneapolis MN 55415-0848 also: US Ct Appeals 8th Cir 111S 10th St Rm 24-32 Saint Louis MO 63102*

LOKENSGARD, JERROLD PAUL, chemist, educator, organic chemist; b. Saskatoon, Saskatchewan, Canada, July 30, 1940; s. Bernhard Oliver and Eleanor Ruth Lokensgard; m. Elizabeth Ann Hopkins, Aug. 14, 1965; children: Michael John, Ann-Marie. BA, Luther Coll., Decorah, Iowa, 1962; MA, U. Wis., 1964, PhD, 1967. Post-doctoral rsch. fellow Iowa State U., Ames, Iowa, 1967; asst. prof. chemistry Lawrence U., Appleton, Wis., 1967—75, assoc. prof. chemistry, 1976—89, prof. chemistry, 1989—, Robert McMillen prof. chemistry, 1993—, chair dept. chemistry, 1992—96, 1998—. Rsch. assoc. U. Toronto, Ont., Canada, 1973—74; vis. assoc. prof. chemistry Cornell U., Ithaca, NY, 1980—81. Contbr. articles to profl. jours. Charter mem. White Heron Chorale, Appleton, Wis. Grantee, various orgns. including NSF, 1968—, NSF and the Hewlett Packard Co., 1973—; scholar, Nat. Merit Scholarship Corp., 1958—62; Grad. fellow, Danforth Found., 1962—67, NSF, 1962—64, Postdoctoral fellow, NIH, 1967. Mem.: AAAS, Am. Chem. Soc. (local sect. chair 1972). Evangelical Lutheran. Achievements include research in synthetic and physical organic chemistry. Home: 614 E Roosevelt St Appleton WI 54911 Office: Lawrence Univ PO Box 599 Appleton WI 54912-0599 Office Phone: 920-832-6726. E-mail: jerrold.p.lokensgard@lawrence.edu.

LOKER, ELIZABETH ST. JOHN, newspaper executive; b. Leonardtown, Md., Jan. 1, 1948; d. William Meverell and June Whiting (Farner) L.; m. Donald Scott Rice, Sept. 11, 1980 BA, George Washington U., 1969. Analyst Met. Washington Council Govt., 1973-74; analyst, programmer Washington Post, 1974-75, mgr. systems research, 1976, dir. data processing, 1976-78, asst. to pub., 1979, v.p. advanced systems, 1979—, v.p. sys. and engring., 1992—. Contbr. chpt. to book Trustee Greater Washington Research Ctr., also mem. exec. com.; bd. dirs. Copyright Clearance Ctr.; bd. dirs. Washington Chamber Symphony. Mem. Newspaper Systems Group (past pres.), Assn. for Computing Machinery, Soc. Info. Mgmt. Avocations: antiques, gardening, historic preservation. Office: Washington Post Co 1150 15th St NW Washington DC 20071-0002

LOKER, ROBIN LEE, music educator; b. NYC, Jan. 16, 1951; d. Victor Ronald and Evelyn Sylvia Chirco; m. Eric Samuel Loker, June 9, 1973; children: Ryan Douglas, Kristin Mara. BMus, Ithaca Coll., N.Y., 1969—73. Cert. tchr. N.Mex., 1998. Music tchr. Elwell Elem. Sch., Belleville, Mich., 1973—74, St. Cecilia Elem. Sch., Ames, Iowa, 1975—78; orch. tchr. Albany Pub. Schs., Oreg., 1979—83; violin tchr. Va. Commonwealth U. Cmty. Music Sch., Richmond, 1983—84; orch. tchr. Albuquerque Pub. Schs., 1985—. Recipient Classroom Tchr. of Yr., N.Mex Am. String Teachers Assn., 2005. Mem.: Nat. Teachers Fedn., Music Educators Nat. Orgn., Am. String Teachers Assn. (treas. 2002—04). Office Phone: 505-268-3961. Personal E-mail: loker@aps.edu.

LOKKEN, STEVEN LEE, chiropractor, internist, nutritionist; b. Thief River Falls, Minn., Apr. 1, 1950; s. Leroy Albert and Delores May (Johnson) L.; m. Kathryn Ann Ehret, Feb. 5, 1977; children: John, Ryan, Shane, Stephanie. D of Chiropractic, Palmer Coll. Chiropractic, Davenport, Iowa, 1972. Diplomate Am. Bd. Chiropractic Internists, Am. Bd. Clin. Nutrition; cert. clin. nutritionist; bd. cert. naturopathic physician., Calif., 1973-92; pvt. practice Colorado Springs, Colo., 1993—. Fellow Am. Acad. Chiropractic Physicians; mem. Am. Chiropractors Assn. (mem. coun. internal diagnosis and family practice), Am. Diabetes Assn., Am. Assn. Clin. Nutritionists, Internat. Assn. Clin. Nutritionists, Am. Acad. Anti-Aging Medicine, Am. Naturopathic Med. Assn. Avocations: ultramarathon running, mountain biking, fly fishing, four-wheeling. Office: 815 E Platte Ave Colorado Springs CO 80903-3546 Office Phone: 719-633-8112. E-mail: slkol@adelphia.net.

LOKMER, STEPHANIE ANN, international business development consultant; b. Wheeling, W.Va., Nov. 14, 1957; d. Joseph Steven and Mary Ann (Mozney) Lokmer. BA in Comm., Bethany Coll., 1980; cert., U. Tübingen, Germany, 1980, Sprach Inst., Tübingen, 1980; MGC in Negotiation, Georgetown U., 2003; degree in nat. security telecom., George Washington U., 2003. V.p. Wheeling Coffee and Spice, W.Va., 1981—; pres. Lokmer & Assocs., Inc., McLean, W.Va., 1986-2000; v.p. strategic devel. Telia Internat. Carrier, Inc., 2000—04; cons. internat. bus. Lokmer & Assocs., 2004—. Bd. dirs. Am. Found. of Ivory Coast. Mem.: Internat. Assn. Tech. of No. Va., Counselors Acad., World Affairs Coun., Pub. Rels. Soc. Am., Fed. City Club, Zeta Tau Alpha. Republican. Avocations: tennis, reading. Office Phone: 202-744-4740. Personal E-mail: slokmer@attglobal.net.

LOLAS, ANTHONY JOSEPH, SR., health and environmental business executive; b. Detroit, Mar. 27, 1942; s. Charles and Doris (Rutkowski) L.; m. Marilyn Ruth Hickey, June 7, 1967 (div. Jan. 1989); children: Anthony J. Jr., Nicole E.; m. Patricia Smith Dod, Dec. 9, 1995. BS in Engring. Mgmt., USAF Acad., 1967; MBA in Bus. Ops. Analysis, UCLA, 1968; EdS in Adminstrn. and Supervision, Troy State U., 1980; PhD in Adminstrn. and Leadership, U. S.C., 1994. CEO Bus. Svcs., Charleston, S.C., 1980-91; chief bus. mgmt. S.C. Dept. Health and Environ. Control, Columbia, 1992—. Cons. various cos., Charleston, 1973-89; adj. prof. computer resource mgmt. Webster U., 1993—. Author: (books) Education Objectives, 1980, Crisis in Confidence, 1994. Cons., advisor Future Bus. Leaders, Charleston, 1994-96. Lt. col. USAF, 1967-90. Decorated D.F.C., Meritorious Svc. medal, 4 Air medals. Mem. S.C. Govt. Assn. Purchasing Ofcls., S.C. Fleet Mgmt. Assn., Profl. Risk Mgmt. Assn., Judo Assn. Am. (life), Mensa, S.C. C. of C. (issues com.). Home: 4700 Carter Hill Dr Columbia SC 29206-4604 Office: DHEC Bus Mgmt 2600 Bull St Columbia SC 29201-1797

LOLLEY, WILLIAM RANDALL, minister; b. Troy, Ala., June 2, 1931; s. Roscoe Lee and Mary Sara (Nunnelee) L.; m. Clara Lou Jacobs, Aug. 28, 1952; children: Charlotte, Pam. AB, Samford U., 1952, DD (hon.), 1980; BD, Southeastern Sem., 1957, ThM, 1958; ThD, Southwestern Sem., 1962; DD (hon.), Wake Forest U., 1971, U. Richmond, 1984; LLD (hon.), Campbell U., 1986; LittD (hon.), Mercer U., 1988. Ordained to ministry So. Bapt. Conv., 1951. Pastor First Bapt. Ch., Winston-Salem, N.C., 1962-74; pres. Southeastern Bapt. Theol. Sem., Wake Forest, N.C., 1974-88; pastor First Bapt. Ch., Raleigh, N.C., 1988-90, Greensboro, N.C., 1990-96, ret., 1996. Author: Crises in Morality, 1963, Bold Preaching of Christ, 1979, Servant Songs, 1994. Mem. Coop. Bapt. Fellowship, Rotary. Democrat. Baptist. Home: 11508 Old Creedmoor Rd Raleigh NC 27613-6910 E-mail: louran@earthlink.net.

LOLLI, DON R(AY), lawyer; b. Macon, Mo., Aug. 9, 1949; s. Tony and Emma Naomi (Gerlich) Lolli; m. Deborah Jo Mrosek, May 29, 1976; children: Christina Terese, Joanna Elyse, Anthony Justin. BA in Econs., U. Mo., 1971, JD, 1974. Bar: Mo. 1974, U.S. Dist. Ct. (we. dist.) Mo. 1974, U.S. Ct. Appeals (8th cir.) 1976, U.S. Ct. Appeals (10th cir.) 1979, U.S. Supreme Ct. 1979, U.S. Tax Ct. 1981, U.S. Ct. Appeals (3d cir.) 1992, U.S. Dist. Ct. (ea. dist.) Mo. 1996, U.S. Dist. Ct. Kans. 1998. Assoc. Beckett & Steinkamp, Kansas City, Mo., 1974-79; mem. Beckett, Lolli and Bartunek, Kansas City, 1980-96, Swanson, Midgley, LLC, Kansas City, 1997—2003, Dysart, Taylor, Lay, Cotter & McMonigle, P.C., Kansas City, 2003—. Lectr. CLE seminar U. Mo. Sch. Law, Kansas City, 1984—89. Vol. coach Visitation Sch.; co-chair St. Teresa's Acad. Fundraising, Rockhurst HS Fundraising. Mem.: ABA, Lawyers Assn. Kansas City, Kansas City Bar Assn., Mo. Bar Assn., U. Mo. Alumni Assn., Rotary, Phi Delta Phi (pres.), Beta Theta Pi (asst. gen. sec. 1997—2003, Tiedman Inn 1973—74, merit cert. 1974). Roman Catholic. Home: 645 W 62nd St Kansas City MO 64113-1501 Office: Dysart Taylor Lay Cotter & McMonigle PC 4420 Madison Ave Kansas City MO 64111 Office Phone: 816-931-2700. Business E-Mail: dlolli@dysarttaylor.com.

LOLLMAN, MATTHEW TOBIAS, music educator; b. Kansas City, Mo., Mar. 17, 1971; s. Kenneth Michael and Karel Ann Lollman. BA in Edn., Northeastern St. U., 1995. Cert. Tchr. Okla., 1995. Band dir. Valliant Pub. Sch., Valliant, Okla., 1995—99, Vinita Pub. Sch., Vinita, Okla., 1999—. Band dir. after sch. program Vinita Pub. Sch., 2001—, dir. four yr. plan com., 2001. Musician, composer: (albums) Pyramid, 1994. Named Tchr. of Yr., Valliant Pub. Schs., 1997. Mem.: NEA, Okla. Edn. Assn., Okla. Music Educators Assn., Music Educators Nat. Conf., Northeastern Band Dir. Assn. (sec. 2000—). Conservative. Methodist. Avocations: camping, music, sports. Home: 914 W North Avenue Vinita OK 74301 Office: Vinita Public Schools 226 N Miller Vinita OK 74301 Personal E-mail: bandman95@cableone.net.

LOMAN, MARY LAVERNE, retired mathematics professor; b. Stratford, Okla., June 10, 1928; d. Thomas D. and Mary Ellen (Goodwin) Glass; m. Coy E. Loman, Dec. 23, 1944; 1 child, Sandra Leigh Loman Easton. BS, U. Okla., 1956, MA, 1957, PhD, 1961. Grad. asst., then instr. U. Okla., Norman, 1956-61; asst. prof. math. U. Ctrl. Okla., Edmond, 1961-62, assoc. prof., 1962-66, prof., 1966-93, prof. emeritus, 1993—. NSF fellow, 1965-67. Mem. Math. Assn. Am., Nat. Coun. Tchrs. Math., Okla. Coun. Tchrs. Math. (v.p. 1972-76), Higher Edn Alumni Coun. Okla., VFW Aux., Delta Kappa Gamma. Home: 2201 Tall Oaks Trl Edmond OK 73003-2325 Personal E-mail: laverneL2@cox.net. *Strive to do each task to the best of your ability. Then don't look back, saying "If only I had ...", but look forward to the next, knowing you gave your very best effort.*

LOMAS, LYLE WAYNE, agricultural research administrator, educator; b. Monett, Mo., June 8, 1953; s. John Junior and Helen Irene Lomas; m. Connie Gail Frey, Sept. 4, 1976; children: Amy Lynn, Eric Wayne. BS, U. Mo., 1975, MS, 1976; PhD, Mich. State U., 1979. Asst. prof., animal scientist S.E. Agrl. Rsch. Ctr., Kans. State U., Parsons, 1979-85, assoc. prof., 1985-92, prof., 1992—, head, 1985—. Contbr. articles to refereed sci. jours. Mem. Am. Soc. Animal Sci., Am. Registry Profl. Animal Scientists, Am. Forage and Grassland Coun., Rsch. Ctr. Adminstrs. Soc. (bd. dirs. 1993—, sec. 1999-2000, 2d v.p. 2000-01, v.p. 2001-02, pres. 2002-03), Rotary (bd. dirs. Parsons 1992—96 v.p. 1994-95, pres. 1995-96), Phi Kappa Phi, Gamma Sigma Delta. Presbyterian. Achievements include research in ruminant nutrition, forage utilization by grazing stocker cattle. Home: 24052 Douglas Rd Dennis KS 67341-9014 Office: Kans State U SE Agrl Rsch Ctr PO Box 316 Parsons KS 67357-0316 Office Phone: 620-421-4826. Business E-Mail: llomas@oznet.ksu.edu.

LOMAX, ELISABETH LOUISE, music educator; d. Robert Donald and Faye Simmons Lomax. D in Musical Arts, U. Mo., Kansas City, 1990. Composer: (intermediate piano arrangements) 21st Century Americana.

LOMAX, JOHN PHILLIP, history professor; b. Omaha, May 9, 1952; s. John Phillip and Mary Eleanor Lomax; children: Hannah Chloe Lomax-Vogt, Madeleine Claire Lomax-Vogt. BA, Nebr. Wesleyan U., 1970—74; MA, U. Chgo., 1974—75; PhD, U. Kans., 1975—87. Vis. instr. history U. Nebr., Omaha; lectr. history U. Tex., Austin, Tex., 1987—88; prof. history Ohio No. U., Ada, Ohio, 1988—. Contbr. articles to historical publs. Radioman second class US Coast Guard Res., 1978—90. Fellow Fulbright-Hays Grant, Inst.

Internat. Edn., 1984-1985. Mem.: Soc. Medieval Canon Law, Am. Hist. Assn., Medieval Acad. Am. Roman Catholic. Avocations: walking, gardening, reading. Home: PO Box 35 Ada OH 45810-0035 Office: Ohio Northern U 525 S Main St Ada OH 45810 Office Phone: 419-772-2088. Business E-Mail: j-lomax@onu.edu.

LOMAX, MICHAEL LUCIUS, non-profit association administrator; b. LA, Oct. 2, 1947; m. Pearl Cleage, 1969 (div. 1979); 1 child, Deignan; m. Cheryl Ferguson Lomax, 1986; children: Michele, Rachel. BA in English, Morehouse Coll., 1968; MA in English lit., Columbia U.; PhD in Am. and Afro-Am. lit., Emory U., 1984. Mem. faculty Morehouse Coll., Spelman Coll.; dir. parks, librs., and cultural and internat. affairs Atlanta, 1975—78; bd. commrs. Fulton County, Ga., 1978—93, bd. chair, 1981—93; pres., CEO Nat. Faculty, Atlanta, 1994—97; pres. Dillard U., New Orleans, 1997—2004; pres., CEO United Negro Coll. Fund, Inc., Fairfax, Va., 2004—. Vis. prof. Emory U., Ga. Inst. Tech., U. Ga. Founding chmn. Nat. Black Arts Festival, 1988; bd. dirs. Studio Mus. in Harlem, Emory U. Carter Ctr., United Way of Am., Teach for Am.; mem. Presdl. Adv. Bd. on Historically Black Colls. and Univs., 2002-; mem. Nat. Mus. African Am. History and Cultural Plan for Action Presdl. Commn. Office: United Negro Coll Fund 8260 Willow Oaks Corp Dr Fairfax VA 22031

LOMBARD, JOHN JAMES, JR., lawyer, writer; b. Phila., Dec. 27, 1934; s. John James and Mary R. (O'Donnell) L.; m. Barbara Mallon, May 9, 1964; children: John James, William M., James G., Laura K., Barbara E. BA cum laude, LaSalle Coll., 1956; JD, U. Pa., 1959. Bar: Pa. 1960. Ptnr. Obermayer, Rebmann, Maxwell & Hippel, Phila., 1959-84; mgr. personal law sect. Morgan Lewis & Bockius LLP, Phila., 1985-90, vice-chair personal law sect., 1990-92, chair, 1992-99; spl. counsel McCarter & English LLP, Phila., 2000—. Sec., dir. Airline Hydraulics Corp., Phila., 1969-2000; adv. com. on decedents estates laws Joint State Govt. Commn., 1992—, mem. subcom. on powers of atty., 1993—; co-chair So. Jersey Ethics Alliance, 1993-97. Co-author: Durable Powers of Attorney and Health Care Directives, 1984, 3d edit. 1994; contbr. articles to profl. jours. Bd. dirs. Redevel. Authority Montgomery County, Pa., 1980-87, Gwynedd-Mercy Coll., Gwynedd Valley, Pa., 1980-89, LaSalle Coll. H.S., Wyndmoor, Pa., 1991-97. Recipient Treat award Nat. Coll. Probate Judges, 1992, Disting. Estate Planner award Phila. Estate Planning Coun., 2002. Mem. ABA (chmn. com. simplification security transfers 1972-76, chmn. mem. com. 1972-82, mem. coun. real property, probate and trust law sect. 1979-85, sec. 1985-87, divsn. dir. probate div. 1987-89, chair elect 1989-90, chair 1990-91, co-chair Nat. Conf. Lawyers & Corp. Fiduciaries), Pa. Bar Assn. (ho. of dels. 1979-81), Phila. Bar Assn. (chmn. probate sect. 1972), Am. Coll. Trust and Estate Counsel (editor Probate Notes 1983, bd. regents 1986-91, mem. exec. com. 1988-91, elder law com. 1993—, pres. found., 2005-06), internat. Acad. Estate and Trust Law (exec. com. 1984-88, 90-94), Am. Bar Found., Internat. Fish and Game Assn., Union League Club (Phila.), Ocean City Club (N.J.), Marlin and Tuna Club, Ocean City Yacht Club. Office: McCarter & English LLP Mellon Bank Ctr Ste 700 1735 Market St Philadelphia PA 19103

LOMBARD, KENNETH T., food products executive; Pres. Johnson Develop. Corp., Magic Johnson Theatres, 1992—2004; sr. v.p., pres. Starbucks Entertainment Starbucks Corp., Seattle, 2004—. Office: Starbucks Corp 2401 Utah St Seattle WA 98134*

LOMBARD, MARJORIE ANN, financial officer; b. Stoughton, Mass., Feb. 25, 1956; d. John Joseph and Marie Josephine (Hopkins) Lombard; children: Katie Marie Burt, Elizabeth Ann Burt. BSBA with honors, Northeastern U., 1979; MBA, Suffolk U., 2000. Acctg. trainee HEW Audit, Boston, 1976-78; staff acct. Etonic, Inc., Brockton, Mass., 1979-81; ops. acct. Foxboro Co., East Bridgewater, Mass., 1981-82, 86-87; chief acct. New Eng. Structures, Inc., Avon, Mass., 1983-84; bus. mgr. Mutron Corp., Brockton, Mass., 1988-92; contr. Connector Tech. Corp., Warwick, R.I., 1992-94; bus. mgr. Cath. Charities-Laboure Ctr., South Boston, Mass., 1994-97; contr. Cath. Charities, Boston, 1997-98, CFO, 1998-2000; bus. adminstr. Carver (Mass.) Pub. Schs., 2000—05; CFO, Action for Boston Cmty. Devel., 2005—. Tchr. confraternity Christian doctrine program St. Thomas Aquinas Ch., Bridgewater, 1988-94; keyperson Old Colony United Way, Brockton, 1988-91, mem. funds allocation com., 1991—; vol. tchr. You and Me drug prevention program, Bridgewater, 1990-92, Parents for Edn., Bridgewater, 1990-97; vol. Am. Electronics Assn.-Brockton Jr. High Sch. Alliance, 1990-92; mem. Bridgewater Parents Collaborative, 1991-97. Mem. Am. Electronics Assn., Small Bus. Assn. New Eng. Roman Catholic. Avocations: reading, writing, crafts, interior decorating, walking.

LOMBARD, RICHARD SPENCER, lawyer; b. Panama Canal Zone, Jan. 28, 1928; s. Eugene C. and Alice R. (Quinn) L.; m. Arlene Olson, Dec. 27, 1952; children: Anne, James. AB, Harvard U., 1949, JD, 1952. Bar: N.Y. 1953, Tex. 1971. Assoc. Haight, Gardner, Poor & Havens, N.Y.C., 1952-55; mem. law dept. Creole Petroleum Corp., Caracas, Venezuela, 1955-65, mgr., 1963-65; gen. counsel Esso Chem. Co., N.Y.C., 1966-69; assoc. gen. counsel Humble Oil & Refining Co., Houston, 1969-71; asst. gen. counsel Exxon Corp., N.Y.C., 1971-72, assoc. gen. counsel, 1972-73, gen. counsel, 1973-93, v.p., 1980-93; counsel Baker & Botts, Dallas, 1993-96. Trustee Parker Sch. Fgn. and Comparative Law, Columbia U., 1977—, chmn. bd. trustees, 1985-2003. Author: American-Venezuelan Private International Law, 1965. Served with USAAF, 1946-47. Fellow Am. Bar Found.; mem. Am. Law Inst., Am. Arbitration Assn. (bd. dirs., chmn. bd. 1983-86), Assn. Bar City of N.Y., State Bar of Tex., Univ. Club (N.Y.C.).

LOMBARDI, CORNELIUS ENNIS, JR., lawyer; b. Portland, Oreg., Feb. 12, 1926; s. Cornelius Ennis and Adele (Volk) L.; m. Ann Vivian Foster, Nov. 24, 1954; children— Cornelius Ennis, Gregg Foster, Matthew Volk. BA, Yale, 1949; JD, U. Mich., 1952. Bar: Mo. Since practiced in, Kansas City, Mo.; mem. firm Blackwell, Sanders, Peper, Martin, 1957-92, of counsel. Former pres. Kansas City Mus. Assn., Estate Planning Coun. of Kansas City; trustee Pembroke Country Day Sch.; chmn. soc. of fellows Nelson Gallery Found.; bd. dirs., Mo. Parks Assn. Mem.: Kansas City Country Club, Order of Coif, Phi Alpha Delta. Home: 5049 Wornall Rd Kansas City MO 64112-2423 Office: 408 Main St Ste 1000 Kansas City MO 64112 Office Phone: 816-983-8000.

LOMBARDI, DAVID ENNIS, JR., lawyer, educator, arbitrator; b. Mar. 5, 1940; s. David E. and Ruth Harriet (Harrison) L.; m. Susanna C. Woodbury, June 20, 1970; children: Sara Ennis, Eric David. BA, U. Calif., Berkeley, 1962; postgrad., U. Florence, Italy, 1964; JD, Yale U., 1966. Bar: Calif. 1966. John woodman Ayer fellow at law U. Calif., Berkeley, 1963; assoc. Brobeck, Phleger & Harrison, San Francisco, 1967-73; adj. prof. bus. law U. Md., NATO Hdqrs., Belgium and Italy, 1974-75; sr. atty. Crown Zellerbach Corp., San Francisco, 1975-76; sr. ptnr. Lombardi & Lombardi, San Francisco, 1976-83, Steinhart & Falconer, San Francisco, 1983-92; spl. counsel Bianchi, Engel, Keegin & Talkington, San Rafael, Calif., 1992. Chief cir. mediator U.S. Ct. Appeals (9th cir.), San Francisco, 1992—; lectr. on negotiation, mediation U. Calif. Sch. Law, Davis, U. San Francisco Sch. Law, U. Santa Clara Sch. Law, Stanford Law Sch., U. Wash. Sch. Law, U. Cairo Faculty of Law, Sch. Law Nat. U. India, Coll. Law U. Calcutta, others; chancellor's com. for univ. affairs U. Calif. 1962-63; cons. on law reform and mediation for Ministry of Justice, Egypt, India, Israel, Hawaii, others; alumni adv. com. U. Calif., 1968-69. Trustee Head Royce Sch., 1983-86, San Domenico Sch., 1986-90, Kentfield Schs. Found., 1985-90. Mem. ABA, Calif. Bar Assn. (prin. referee Calif. State Bar Ct. 1977-86), San Francisco Bar Assn., Am. Soc. Internat. Law, Yale U. Law Sch. Alumni Assn. (pres. No. Calif. 1989-2003), Olympic Club, Fgn. Svc. Assn. No. Calif. Home: 1650 Lake St San Francisco CA 94121-1343 Office: US Ct Appeals PO Box 193939 San Francisco CA 94119-3939 Business E-Mail: david_lombard@ca9.uscourts.gov.

LOMBARDI, DOMENIC JOSEPH, manufacturing engineer; b. Orange, N.J., Sept. 16, 1928; s. Domenic Lewis and Margaret Lombardi; m. Antoinette Felicia Pavone, Apr. 19, 1953; children: Domenic, Diane, Maryann, Kathleen, Gary. Student, Lincoln Inst., Cleve. Stockhander Nevins Ch. Press, Glen Ridge, NJ; pressman Union Camp Corp., Clifton, NJ, supr. Cpl. U.S. Army, 1951—52, Korea. Named to Hon. Order Ky. Cols., 1989. Mem.: NRA, VFW, KC. Roman Catholic. Avocations: golf, home projects, coin collecting/numismatics, stamp collecting/philately, miniature cars. Home: 52 E Madison Ave Florham Park NJ 07932-2635

LOMBARDI, EUGENE PATSY, retired conductor, musician, educator; b. North Braddock, Pa., July 7, 1923; s. Nunzio C. and Mary (Roberto) L.; m. Jacqueline Sue Davis, Mar. 1955; children: Robert, Genanne. BA, Westminster Coll., 1948; MA, Columbia U., 1948; Edn. Specialist, George Peabody Coll., 1972; MusD, Westminster Coll., 1981. Band dir. Lincoln H.S., Midland, Pa., 1948-49; orch. dir. Du Pont Manual H.S., Louisville, 1949—50, Male H.S., Louisville, 1949-50, Phoenix Union H.S., 1950-57; orch. dir., prof. Ariz. State U., Tempe, 1957-89; ret., 1989. Condr. Phoenix Symphonette, 1954-61, 70-73, Phoenix Symphony Youth Orch., 1956-66, Phoenix Pops Orch., 1971-83, Fine Arts String Orch., Phoenix, 1995-97 With USAAF, 1943-46. Decorated Bronze Star; recipient Alumni Achievement award Westminster Coll., 1976, gold medal Nat. Soc. Arts and Letters, 1973, Disting. Tchr. award Ariz. State U. Alumni, 1974, Phoenix appreciation award, 1983 Mem. Music Educators Nat. Conf., Am. String Tchrs. Assn. (pres. Ariz. unit 1965-67), Am. Fedn. Musicians, Ariz. Music Educators Assn. (pres. higher edn. sect. 1973-75, Excellence in Teaching Music award 1989), Ind. Order Foresters, Phi Delta Kappa, Phi Mu Alpha, Alpha Sigma Phi. Republican. Methodist. Home: 920 E Manhatton Dr Tempe AZ 85282-5520 E-mail: lomsemiquaver@gbronline.com.

LOMBARDI, FREDERICK MCKEAN, lawyer; b. Akron, Ohio, Apr. 1, 1937; s. Leonard Anthony and Dorothy (McKean) L.; m. Margaret J. Gessler, Mar. 31, 1962; children: Marcus M., David G., John A., Joseph F. BA, U. Akron, 1960; LLB, Case Western Res., 1962. Bar: Ohio 1962, U.S. Dist. Ct. (no. and so. dists.) Ohio 1964, U.S. Ct. Appeals (6th cir.) 1966. Prin., shareholder Buckingham, Doolittle & Burroughs, Akron, 1962—, chmn. comml. law and litigation dept., 1989-99. Bd. editors Western Res. Law Rev., 1961-62. Trustee, mem. exec. com., v.p. Ohio Ballet, 1985-93; trustee Walsh Jesuit H.S., 1987-90; life trustee Akron Golf Charities, NEC World Series of Golf; bd. mem. Summa Health Sys. Found., Downtown Akron Partnership, St. Hilary Parish Found. Mem. Ohio Bar Assn. (coun. of dels. 1995-97), Akron Bar Assn. (trustee 1991-94, 97-2000, v.p., pres.-elect 1997-98, pres. 1998-99), Case Western Res. U. Law Alumni Assn. (bd. govs. 1995-98, bd. dirs. 2003—), Case Western Res. Soc. Benchers, Fairlawn Swim and Tennis Club (past pres.), Portage Country Club, Pi Sigma Alpha. Democrat. Roman Catholic. Office: Buckingham Doolittle & Burroughs 50 S Main St Akron OH 44308-1828 Office Phone: 330-376-5300. E-mail: flombardi@bdblaw.com.

LOMBARDI, JOHN LANG, research and development company executive; s. Robert Paul Lombardi and Jacqueline Lang Lombadri. BS, Worcester Polytech. Inst., 1990; MS, U. Ariz., 1994, PhD, 1996. Rsch. engr., tech. Norton Co., Worcester, Mass., 1989—90; pres. J.L. Lombardi & Assocs., Tucson, 1992—95; sr. rsch. specialist Advanced Ceramics Rsch., Inc., 1996—2002; CEO Ventura Rsch., 2002—. Sec., bd. dirs. Las Familias Charity, Tucson, 1998—2000; philanthropic chair Active 20-30 Club So. Ariz., 1997. Recipient Rsch. award, Materials Rsch. Soc., 1994. Mem.: Am. Chem. Soc. Avocations: scuba diving, travel, book collecting. Office: Ventana Rsch Corp 2702 S 4th Ave Tucson AZ 85713

LOMBARDI, JOHN V., academic administrator, historian; b. Los Angeles, Aug. 19, 1942; s. John and Janice P. Lombardi; m. Cathryn Lee; children: John Lee, Mary Ann. BA, Pomona Coll., 1963; MA, Columbia U., 1964, PhD, 1968. Prof. contratado Escuela de Historia, Universidad Central de Venezuela, Caracas, 1967; lectr. history Ind. U. S.E., Jeffersonville, 1967-68, asst. prof., 1968-69; vis. asst. prof. Ind. U., Bloomington, 1968-69, from asst. prof. history to dean, 1969—85, dean Coll. Arts and Scis., 1985—87; prof. history Johns Hopkins U., 1987-89, provost, vp. for acad. affairs, 1987-89; pres. U. Fla., Gainesville, 1989-99, prof. history, dir. The Ctr., 1999—; prof. history, chancellor Univ. of Mass., Amherst, Mass., 2002—. Author: (with others) Venezuelan History: A Comprehensive Working Bibliography, 1977, People and Places in Colonial Venezuela, 1976, Venezuela: Search for Order, Dream of Progress, 1982; Mem. editorial bd.: (with others) UCLA Statis. Abstracts Latin Am, 1977—; contbr. (with others) articles to profl. jours. Fulbright-Hayes research fellow, 1965-66 Mem. Am. Hist. Assn., Latin Am. Studies Assn., Pan Am. Inst. Geography and History, Academia Nacional de la Historia (corr. mem .) Office: Univ Mass Amherst Chancellor's Office Amherst MA 01003

LOMBARDI, JOSEPH J., retail executive; BA, Cornell U.; MBA, U. Mich. CPA. V.p., controller Toys 'R' Us, Inc.; ptnr. Ernst & Young Consumer Products Practice; CFO The Mus. Co. Inc.; v.p., controller Barnes & Noble, N.Y., 2002—03, CFO, 2003—. Office: Barnes & Noble 122 Fifth Ave New York NY 10011

LOMBARDI, MARK OWEN, academic administrator, international relations educator; b. Providence, Dec. 14, 1960; s. Martin Thomas and Betty Natalie (Owen) L.; m. Judy Rollins Downs, Dec. 31, 1993; stepchild, Richie Downs. BA, Purdue U., 1982; MA, Ohio State U., 1986, PhD, 1989. Asst. Consortium for Internat. Edn., Columbus, Ohio, 1983-85; grad. asst. Ohio State U., Columbus, 1983-86; vis. instr. Wittenberg U., Springfield, Ohio, 1987-88; asst. prof. through prof., dept. chmn., dept. of govt., history & sociol. Univ. Tampa, Fla., 1988—2001, dir. Baccalaureate Experience, office of internat. programs & develop., 1992—2001; v.p. academic & student affairs Coll. of Santa Fe, N.Mex., 2001—04, provost, 2004—05, interim pres., 2005—. Polit. cons. WTOG News, Tampa, 1989-95; advisor Vision Quest, Tampa, 1994-95. Author: The Unfolding Legacy of 9/11, 2004; editor: Perspectives on Third World Sovereignty, 1995; contbr. chpt. to book and articles to profl. jours. Umpire S.E. Umpires Assn., Tampa, 1991-93. Dana Found. grantee U. Tampa, 1989, 91, 93, 95; Social Sci. grantee U. Toledo, 1992. Mem. Internat. Studies Assn., African Studies Assn., Acad. Polit. Sci., Pi Gamma Mu (advisor), Pi Sigma Alpha. Avocations: golf, reading, walking, jogging. Office: College of Santa Fe Office of the President 1600 St Michael's Dr Santa Fe NM 87505*

LOMBARDO, ANN MARIE, special education educator, writer, artist; b. Melrose, Mass., Jan. 10, 1955; d. James William Pike, II and Mary Ann (Duncan) Pike; m. Steven Edward Lombardo, Sept. 11, 1982; children: Nicholas Michael, Kali Ann. Student, Plymouth State Coll., 1973; BA, Rivier Coll., 1978. Freelance tchr. arts and crafts, Hollis, NH, 1972—73, 1975; art tchr. Hollis (N.H.) Elem. and Secondary Schs., Hollis, NH, 1978; proprietor, asst. Jameson Fine Arts Gallery, La Jolla, Calif., 1978—79; graphic artist, tech. writer J.M. Yurick Assocs., Smersworth, NH, 1980—87; spl. needs educator Winthrop Elem. Sch., Ipswich, Mass., 1995—. Freelance artist, writer, 1983—92; presenter, cons. in field. Author (artist & correspondent): (column) The Portsmouth (N.H.) Herald, 1988—93; Yonder Mountain (A Cherokee Legend), 1999, one-woman shows include Link Art Gallery, Rowley, Mass., 2002; columnist: Annadotes; radio commentary WERZ talk radio. Tchr. arts and crafts Nashua (N.H.) Orphanage, 1970; cook, distributor The Food Kitchen Shelter, San Diego, 1988; rschr., artist Ea. Bank Cherokees, Qualla Bouundary, NC, 1999—2001. Recipient Outstanding Regional Art award, 1973. Mem.: Newburyport Art Assn., San Diego (Calif.) Art Assn. Avocations: painting furniture, cross country skiing, hiking, camping. Home: 101 Leslie Rd Rowley MA 01969 Mailing: PO Box 124 Ipswich MA 01938

LOMBARDO, FREDRIC ALAN, pharmacist, educator; b. New Castle, Pa., May 11, 1948; s. Valentine Frank and Clara Eleanor (Cugini) Lombardo; m. Loretta D. Patts, May 22, 1971; children: Alan John, Lauren Beth, Leslie Anne. BS in Pharmacy, Duquesne U., 1971, PharmD, 1974; MS, Fla. Inst. Tech., 1979. Lic. pharmacist Pa., Va., D.C., Tex., cert. Am. Coll. Clin. Pharmacists. Resident in hosp. pharmacy Mercy Hosp., Pitts., 1973; commd. 2nd lt. U.S. Army, 1974, advanced through grades to lt. col., 1993; chief clin. pharmacy support svc. Brooke Army Med. Ctr., Ft. Sam Houston, Tex., 1980-85; chief outpatient pharmacy svc. Walter Reed Army Med. Ctr., Washington, 1985-86, chief cancer treatment sect., chief hematol.-oncol. pharmacy, 1986-92; resigned active duty entered U.S. Army reserve, 1993; sr. clin. pharmacy supr. Nat. Heart, Lung and Blood Inst., NIH, Bethesda, Md., 1992-95; asst. prof. clin. and adminstrv. pharmacy sci. Howard U., Washington, 1995—, asst. prof. psychiatry Coll. Medicine, assoc. prof. cmty. medicine and family practice; asst. prof. U. Md. Asst. prof. pharmacology Cath. U., Washington, 1995—, H. Lee Med. Sch., USUHS, Bethesda, Md., 1995—; asst. prof. pharmacology Cancer Ctr., Ctr. Sickle Cell Disease Howard U., 1995—, asst. dir. Cancer Ctr., 1997; prof. Found. Advancement Edn. Sci., Grad. Sch. NIH, 1996—; mem. Mid-Atlantic Oncology Adv. Group, Washington, 1997; mem. coun. experts com. Oncologic Diseases USP; mem. faculty, cons. Comprehensive AIDS Tng. Initiative and Nat. Minority AIDS Edn. and Tng. Ctr.; cons. faculty Nat. Minority AIDS Edn. and Tng. Ctr. Faculty Comprehensive AIDS Tng. Inst. Co-host Ask the Pharmacy Doctor program Sta. WRC-980, Washington, 1997—, guest various TV and radio programs. Active Urban Health U., Urban Family Inst., Washington, 1996—97. Lt. col. USAR, 1993—. Grantee Rsch., Ortho-McNeil Pharm., Washington, 1996—97. Fellow: Am. Soc. Cons. Pharmacists; mem.: Nat. Pharm. Assn., Am. Soc. Health Professions, Am. Pharm. Assn. (bd. cert. in pharmacotherapy nutrition support, oncology, psychopharmacology, and geriatrics), KC, Am. Legion. Democrat. Roman Catholic. Avocations: military history, mathematics. Home: 13503 Apple Barrel Ct Herndon VA 20171-4006 Office: Howard U Sch Pharmacy and Coll Medicine 2300 4th St NE Washington DC 20002 Business E-Mail: flombardo@howard.edu.

LOMBARDO, MARY JO, artist; b. Stamford, Conn., May 4, 1959; d. Augustus Clarence Lombardo and Josephine Rose Correnty Lombardo; m. K. Dean Hubbard, Jr.; children: Jesse Lombardo Hubbard, Maya Lombardo Hubbard. BA, Mt. Holyoke Coll., South Hadley, Mass., 1981. Dir. of devel. & adminstrn. Ctr. For Contemporary Printmaking, Norwalk, Conn., 2002—03; co-president Women's Caucus For Art - CT Chpt., Conn., 2002—04. Represented in permanent collections moveable mural, Mid. Ch. Today, A Women's Wailing Wall, So. Conn State Univ., altar piece, Baptism., Reform Ch. of Am., N.Y.C. Arts outreach Mid. Collegiate Ch., N.Y., 1999—2004. Mem.: Graphic Artists Guild, Portrait Soc. of Am., Am. Soc. of Portrait Artists.

LOMBARDO, MICHAEL JOHN, lawyer, educator; b. Willimantic, Conn., Mar. 25, 1927; s. Frank Paul and Mary Margaret (Longo) Lombardo; children: Nancy C., Claire M. BS, U. Conn., 1951, MS, 1961, JD, 1973. Bar: Conn. 1974, U.S. Dist. Ct. Conn. 1975, U.S. Supreme Ct. 1979, U.S. Ct. Appeals (2d cir.) 1980. Div. controller Jones & Laughlin Steel Corp., Willimantic, 1956-67; adminstrv. officer health ctr. U. Conn., Hartford, 1968-69; dir. adminstrv. svcs. South Central Community Coll., New Haven, 1969-70; asst. dir. adminstrn. Norwich (Conn.) Hosp., 1970-77; asst. atty. gen. State of Conn., Hartford, 1977-92; pvt. practice Willimantic. Adj. asst. prof. U. Hartford, 1961-70; adj. prof. bus. Old Dominion U., 1973-81; adj. lectr. in law and bus. Ea. Conn. State U., 1973-2000, disting. adj. faculty, 1990. Vol. Windham Ctr. (Conn.) Fire Dept. Sgt. U.S. Army, 1945-46, 1st lt. USAFR, 1951-53, col. USAFR, 1953-87, col. USAF ret., 1987. Decorated Air Force Meritorious Svc. medal, 1980; named Disting. Mil. Grad., U. Conn., 1950. Mem. AAUP, VFW, ATLA, Internat. Platform Assn., Retired Officers Assn., Conn. Bar Assn., Windham County Bar Assn., Assn. Trial Lawyers Am., Mensa Internat., Am. Legion, Lions (bd. dirs. Willimantic chpt. 1960-64). Home: 14 Mansfield Ave Willimantic CT 06226-2018 E-mail: ecsuprof@aol.com.

LOMBARDO, PHILIP JOSEPH, broadcasting company executive; b. Chgo., June 13, 1935; s. Joseph Pete and Josephine (Franco) L.; m. Marilyn Ann Tellefsen, June 22, 1963; children: Dean, Jeffrey. Student, U. Ill., 1953-55; BA in Speech, Journalism and Radio/TV, postgrad. speech, U. Mo., 1958; grad. advanced mgmt. program, Harvard U., 1976. Account exec. Sta. WWCA, Ind., 1959-60; producer-dir. Sta. WBBM-TV, Chgo., 1960-65; program mgr., acting gen. mgr. Sta. WLWT, Cin., 1965-67; v.p., gen. mgr. Sta. WGHP-TV, N.C., 1968-73; pres., chief exec. officer Corinthian Broadcasting Corp., N.Y.C., 1973-82; chmn., pres., chief exec. officer Champlain Communications Corp., N.Y.C., 1982-84; mng. gen. ptnr. Citadel Communications Co. Ltd., N.Y.C., 1982—; chmn., pres., chief exec. officer Citadel Communications, Co. Ltd., C.C.C. Communications Corp., Lombardo Communications II, Inc., P.J.L. Investments, Inc., N.Y.C., 1984—; mng. gen. ptnr., nat. sales rep. U.S. and Can. TV stas. Can. Communications Co., Toronto, 1985—; mng. gen. ptnr. Coronet Communications Co., N.Y.C., 1985—, Capital Comm. Co., Inc., 1994—, Citadel Comm., LLC, 1995—. Bd. dirs. The Gabelli Group, The Lynch Corp., N.Y.C., ABC-TV Affiliate Assn.; chmn. Nat. Assn. Broadcasters, Broadcasters' Found. Mem. adv. bd. Salvation Army; com. budget, bd. dirs. United Fund; mem. com. High Point (N.C.) United Schs.; 1st vice chmn. Central Carolina chpt. Nat. Multiple Sclerosis Soc., 1968-73; bd. dirs. High Point Arts Council, 1968-73; mem. Columbus Citizens Found., Inc. Served with AUS, 1959, 62. Recipient Disting. Svc. award Freedom Found., Am. Legion, High Point (N.C.) Youth Coun. Mem. Dirs. Guild Am., Internat. Radio and TV Soc. (bd. govs.). Clubs: Winged Foot Golf, Marco Polo, Board Room, Bronxville Field, Chgo. Press, Rotary, Kiwanis, Siwanoy Country Club, Longboat Key Club. Home: 24 Masterton Rd Bronxville NY 10708-4804 Office: Citadel Comm Co 99 Pondfield Rd Bronxville NY 10708-3902 Office Phone: 914-793-3400. Personal E-mail: citnyltd@aol.com.

LOMET, DAVID BRUCE, computer scientist; b. Neptune, N.J., Aug. 2, 1939; s. Pierre and Helen (Foster) L.; m. Charlotte Jean Vandermark, Aug. 15, 1964; children: Bruce, Kevin. BS in Physics, Lafayette Coll., 1961; MS in Math., George Washington U., 1966; PhD in Computer Sci., U. Pa., 1969. Mem. rsch. staff IBM Corp., Yorktown Heights, NY, 1969—85; vis. rschr. U. Newcastle (UK upon Tyne), 1975—76; prof. computer sci. Wang Inst. Grad. Studies, Tyngsboro, Mass., 1985—87; sr. info. cons. Digital Equipment Corp., Nashua, NH, 1987—89, sr. cons. engr. and mem. rsch. staff Cambridge, Mass., 1989—94; sr. rschr., mgr. database rsch. group Microsoft Corp., Redmond, Wash., 1995—. Chmn. program com. FODO93; vice-chmn. program com. ICDE, 1995, 96, 98, co-chmn. program com., 2000, conf. co-chmn., 01, mem. conf. steering com., 2001—, vice chmn. program com., 2002, 03, 04. Editor IEEE Data Engring. Bull., Parallel and Distributed Database Sys. Jour., ACM SIGMOD Digital Revs; contbr. over 80 articles to profl. publs. Mem., v.p. Bd. Edn., Yorktown Heights, N.Y., 1980-85. Recipient 2 Best Paper awards SIGMOD Conf.; IBM resident grad. fellow, 1966. Fellow IEEE (life, Outstanding Contbn. award, Golden Core Meritorious Svc. award), ACM (editor Transactions on Database Sys., assoc. editor ACM SIGMOD Anthology, SIGMOD Digital Reviews); mem. AAAS, Phi Beta Kappa. Democrat. Achievements include over 26 patents; research in database systems, programming languages, computer architecture and distributed systems. Office: Microsoft Rsch One Microsoft Way Redmond WA 98052

LOMICKA, WILLIAM HENRY, investor; b. Irwin, Pa., Mar. 9, 1937; s. William and Carabel Lomicka; m. Carol L. Williams, Feb. 14, 1979; 1 child, Edward W. BA, Coll. Wooster, Ohio, 1959; MBA, U. Pa., 1962. Sr. securities analyst Guardian Life Ins. Co., N.Y.C., 1962-65; treasury svcs. mgr. L. B. Foster Co., Pitts., 1966-68, Welch Foods Co., Westfield, N.Y., 1969-70; asst. treas. Ashland Oil, Inc., Ky., 1970-75; sr. v.p. fin. Humana Inc., Louisville, 1975-85; pres., fin. cons. Old South Life Ins. Co., Louisville, 1985-87; sec. econ. devel. Commonwealth of Ky., 1987-88; acting pres. Citizens Security Life Ins. Co., Louisville, 1988-89; pres. Mayfair Capital, Inc., Louisville, 1989-99; chmn. Coulter Ridge Capital, Tucson, 1999—. Bd. dirs. Pomeroy IT Solutions, Inc., Counsel Corp. Bd. trustees Ariz.-Sonora Desert Mus. With USAR, 1962—63. Home and Office: 7406 N Secret Canyon Dr Tucson AZ 85718-1435

LOMKE, EVANDER, publishing executive; b. Mt. Vernon, N.Y., Sept. 6, 1953; s. Lester and Leah Polizzotti L.; m. Fotini Stavros, Nov. 29, 1980; 1 child, Elizabeth Leah. BA, CCNY, 1975; MA, U. Toronto, 1976. Assoc. editor Frederick Ungar Publishing, N.Y.C., 1982—86; assoc. mng. editor

Crossroad/Ungar/Continuum, N.Y.C., 1986—87; mng. editor Continuum Pub. Group, N.Y.C., 1987—95, v.p., mng. editor, 1995—2002; v.p., sr. editor Continuum Internat. Pub. Group, N.Y.C., 2002—. Editor: We Will Prevail: President George W. Bush on War, Terrorism, and Freedom, 2003. Bd. dirs., chmn. editl. com. Am. Mental Health Found. William Bradley Otis fellow CCNY, 1975. Mem. PEN, Phi Beta Kappa. Home: 3215 Arlington Ave Apt 6H Bronx NY 10463-3334 Office Phone: 212-953-5858 x 104. Business E-Mail: evander@continuum-books.com.

LOMON, EARLE LEONARD, physicist, educator, consultant; b. Montreal, Nov. 15, 1930; came to U.S., 1951, naturalized, 1965; s. Harry and Etta (Rappaport) L.; m. Ruth Margaret Jones, Aug. 4, 1951; children: Martha Glynis, Christopher Dylan, Deirdre Naomi. B.Sc., McGill U., Montreal, 1951; PhD, MIT, 1954. NRC Can. overseas research fellow Inst. Theoretical Physics, Copenhagen, 1954-55; fellow Weizmann Inst., Rehovoth, Israel, 1955-56; research assoc. lab. nuclear studies Cornell U., Ithaca, N.Y., 1956-57; assoc. prof. theoretical physics McGill U., Montreal, 1957-60; assoc. prof. physics MIT, Cambridge, 1960-70, prof., 1970-99, prof. emeritus, 1999—; program dir. NSF, 2002—. Vis. staff mem. Los Alamos Nat. Lab., 1968—; project dir. Unified Scis. and Math. for Elem. Schs., Cambridge, 1970-77; adj. prof. U. Louvain-la-Neuve, Belgium, 1980; vis. prof. U. Paris, 1979-80, 86-87, UCLA, 1983, U. Wash., 1985, Nanjing U., 2002; vis. rschr. Kernforschungsanlage Jülich, 1986-92, U. Geneva, 1993, CERN, Geneva, 1994, IPN, Orsay, 1994; Lady Davis vis. prof. Hebrew U., Jerusalem, 1993-94; vis. rschr. U. Tübingen, 1997; vis. fgn. scientist KEK (Tanashi br.), Tokyo, 1999-2000, vis. rschr. and lectr. Nanjing U., 2002. Contbr. articles to profl. jours. Guggenheim Meml. Found. fellow CERN, Geneva, 1965-66; Dupont fellow, 1952-53; Ossabaw Island Project fellow (Ga.), 1978; Sci. Research Council fellow U. London, 1980 Fellow Am. Phys. Soc.; mem. Can. Assn. Physicists Office: MIT 6-302 77 Mass Ave Cambridge MA 02139-4307 Business E-Mail: lomon@lns.mit.edu.

LOMONOSOFF, JAMES MARC, marketing professional; b. Van Nuys, Calif., Apr. 29, 1951; s. Boris Marc and Eileen Fairfax (Thomson) Lomonosoff; m. Elisabeth Maas, June 12, 1982; children: Marc Frederik, James Forrest. BA in Econs., Colgate U., 1973; MBA in Gen. Mgmt., U. Va., 1975. With Saatchi and Saatchi Advt., N.Y.C., 1975-93, v.p., account supr., 1975-85, sr. v.p., mgmt. supr., 1986-87, exec. v.p., mgmt. dir., 1987-93, pres. Collateral Plus divsn., 1987-90; CEO, pres. Saatchi & Saatchi Specialized Comm., 1991-92; account dir. VDB/Compton B.V., Amsterdam, Netherlands, 1980-83; acct. dir. Saatchi and Saatchi Compton S.A., Madrid, 1983-84; regional acct. dir. Saatchi and Saatchi Compton Worldwide, London, 1984-86; mng. dir., CEO BSB/Saatchi and Saatchi, Prague, 1992-93; v.p. internat. mktg. Walt Disney Attractions Inc., Lake Buena Vista, Fla., 1994-98, v.p. internat. mktg. and sales L.Am. Coral Gables, Fla., 1999; sr. v.p. mktg. Celebrity Cruises Inc., Miami, Fla., 1999—2001; pres. Lomonosoff Ptnrs., Inc., Miami, Fla., 2001—. Mem.: Beta Theta Pi. Republican. Home: 4211 Monserrate St Coral Gables FL 33146-1207 Office Phone: 305-666-7019. Personal E-mail: jameslomonosoff@netscape.net.

LONABAUGH, ELLSWORTH EUGENE, retired lawyer; b. San Diego, Feb. 24, 1923; s. Alger Wellman and Marion G. (Bailey) L.; m. Carol W. Marr, Dec. 29, 1949 (div. June 1965); children: Marr, Ellsworth, Carol; m. Jean LaValle Miterenga, Dec. 29, 1967; 1 child, Jason. JD, U. Colo., 1950. Bar: Wyo. 1950, Tex. 1951, U.S. Dist. Ct. (so. dist.) Tex. 1951, U.S. Dist. Ct. (fed. dist.) Wyo. 1953, U.S. Ct. Appeals (10th cir.) 1963, U.S. Supreme Ct. 1971. Assoc. Williams & Thornton, Galveston, Tex., 1951-53; ptnr. Lonabaugh & Lonabaugh, Sheridan, Wyo., 1953-71; sr. ptnr. various law firms, Sheridan, 1971-79, Lonabaugh & Riggs, Sheridan, 1980-98, of counsel, 1998-2001. Mem. uniform state laws commn. State of Wyo., 1963-77; city atty. City of Sheridan, 1957; mem. Wyo. Ho. of Reps., Cheyenne, 1955-56, 67-71; pres. Sheridan Investment Co., 1995-2001. Commr. Wyo. Bar, 1972-74; sr. warden St. Peter's Episcopal Ch., 1962-63; chmn. county ctrl. com. Rep. Party, 1966-70. Staff sgt. U.S. Army, 1942-45, ETO. Decorated Bronze Star; recipient Spl. 76 award Sheridan County Commrs., 1976. Mem. Am. Bar Found. (life), Sheridan County Bar Assn. (pres. 1960-61), Sheridan County C. of C. (pres. 1974-75, named Man of Yr., 1975), Am. Legion, DAV, Sheridan Country Club (sec. 1955-59, Rotary (pres. local chpt. 1972-73), Shriners, Sigma Chi (pres. 1946-47), Phi Delta Phi. Episcopalian. Avocations: golf, sports. Home (Winter): 56 Durango Circle Rancho Mirage CA 92270 Office: PO Dr 5059 Sheridan WY 82801

LONBORG, JAMES REYNOLD, dentist, former professional baseball player; b. Santa Maria, Calif., Apr. 16, 1942; s. Reynold H. and Ada (Ryan) L.; m. Rosemary Irene Feeney, Nov. 21, 1970; children: Phoebe Lea, Claire Elizabeth, Nicholas James, Nora Kathleen, John Bartholomew, Jordon Michael. BA, Stanford U., 1964; D.MD, Tufts U. Dental Sch., 1983. Baseball player Boston Red Sox, 1965-71, Milw. Brewers, 1972; pitcher Phila. Phillies, 1973-79; gen. dentist, 1979—. Asst. to adminstr. New Eng. Rehab. Clinic, Woburn, Mass., 1972-74 Mem. sports medicine com. U.S. Olympic Com., 1997. Recipient Cy Young award, 1967 Achievements include recording 1000th maj. league strikeout, Aug. 19, 1973; career record 157 wins, 137 losses. Home: 498 First Parish Rd Scituate MA 02066-3201 Office: 105 Webster St Hanover MA 02339-1227 Office Phone: 781-871-4039.

LONCHYNA-LISOWSKY, MARIA, music educator; b. Munich, Sept. 26, 1945; d. Bohdan Ivan and Irene Lonchyna; m. Bohdan Lisowsky, May 31, 1969; children: Mykola Lisowsky, Danylo Lisowsky, Taras Lisowsky, Petro Lisowsky. Diploma of Artistic Merit, Ukrainian Music Inst. Am., Detroit, 1967; BA, U. Detroit, 1967; MMus, Wayne State U., 1969. Cert. tchr. piano Mich. Music Tchrs. Assn., 2001. Piano soloist various venues, 1960—99; piano tchr. Ukrainian Music Inst. Am., Detroit, 1967—, dir., 2001—. Accompanist Suzuki workshops, Troy, Mich., 1984—98, Mich. Sch. Band and Orch. Assn. Solo and Ensemble Festivals, Troy, 1984—98, 2004, 05, Trembita Chorus, Detroit, 1975—77, others, 2004—; music dir. Luna Ensemble, Warren, Mich., 1977—83; pianist Ukrainian Music Inst. Trio, Detroit, 1965—67; accompanist Immaculate Conception Ukrainian Cath. H.S. Chorus and Orch., Hamtramck, Mich., 1959—63; accompanist for nat. edn. com. Ukrainian Nat. Women's League Am., Inc. Musician: Listen and Sing Along - Ukrainian Christmas Carols, 1981, Ukrainian Stories for Children, 1976, Listen and Sing Along, 1979. Librarian Detroit Symphony Civic Orch., Detroit, 1996—98. Recipient Alumna of Yr. award, Parents Club of Immaculate Conception Ukrainian Cath. H.S., 1991. Mem.: Ukrainian Arts Soc. (pres. 1996—), Ukrainian Ednl. Assn. (treas. 1985—86, pres. 1986—92, treas. 1992—97), Plast, Inc. (corr. sec. Detroit region 1964—69, subscription chair, sr. divsn. 1984—92, dues, sr. divsn. 1984—92, subscriptions 1992—96, pres. 2005—06, Recognition award 1999), Met. Detroit Musicians League (sec. 2001—04, pres. 2005—, Tchr. of the Yr. 2003—04), Ukrainian Nat. Women's League of Am. (ednl. com. chair chpt. 53 1976—78, rec. sec. chpt. 53 1978—80, corr. sec. 1980—84, pres. chpt. 53 1995—97, corr. sec. regional coun. 1997—99, press sec. Ukrainian lang. 2003—05, corr. sec. 2004, corr. sec. regional coun. 2004—05, mem. audit com. 2005, 2005, Recognition award 1998).

LOND, HARLEY WELDON, editor, publishing executive; b. Chgo., Feb. 5, 1946; s. Henry Sidney and Dorothy (Shaps) L.; m. Marilyn Moss, Aug. 20, 1981; 1 child Elizabeth. BA in Journalism, Calif. State U., L.A., 1972. Adminstrv. dir. Century City Ednl. Arts Project, L.A., 1972-76, hon. dir., 1982—; founder, editor Intermedia mag., L.A., 1974-80; prodn. mgr. Film-Row Publs., L.A., 1981; assoc. editor Box Office mag., Hollywood, Calif., 1981-84, editor, assoc. pub., 1984-94; dir. publs. Entertainment Data, Inc., 1994-95; pres. CyberPod Prodns., 1995—; asst. news editor The Hollywood Reporter, 1995-2000, news editor, 2000—. Syndicated columnist Continental Features, Washington, Tel-Aire Publs., Dallas, 1986—; hon dir. Monterey (Calif.) Film Festival, 1987; mem. media adv. bd. Cinetex Internat. Film Festival, 1988; cons. Take 3 Info. Svc.; web architect-master, OnVideo website, 1995—. Editor: Entertainment Media Electronic Info. Svc.; contbg. editor: (video) Family Style Mag.; contbr. articles to profl. publs. Calif. Arts Council grantee, 1975, Nat. Endowment for Arts grantee, 1976-77. Mem. MLA, Soc. Profl. Journalists, Assn. for Edn. in Journalism and Mass Communication, Speech Communication Assn., Soc. for Cinema Studies. Home and Office: PO Box 17377 Beverly Hills CA 90209-3377 Personal E-mail: harleyl@earthlink.net.

LONDEN, JACK W., lawyer; b. Feb. 11, 1953; married; 3 children. BA magna cum laude, Harvard U., 1975; JD, Yale U., 1978. Bar: Calif. 1979, Ariz. 1979. Law clerk to Hon. William W. Schwarzer U.S. Dist. Ct. (no. dist.) Calif., 1979-80; mem. Morrison & Foerster, San Francisco, 1980—. Named one of Top Ten Lawyers in Bay Area, San Francisco Chronicle, 2003. Office: Morrison & Foerster 425 Market St San Francisco CA 94105-2482 Office Phone: 415-268-7415. Business E-Mail: jlonden@mofo.com.

LONDON, ALAN E., lawyer; b. Pitts., Mar. 13, 1945; AB magna cum laude, Yale Univ., 1967, JD, 1972. Bar: Pa. 1972, US Dost. Ct. we. Pa. dist. Assoc. to ptnr. fin. svc., capital markets practices Reed Smith LLP, Pitts., 1972—. Mem. Phi Beta Kappa. Office: Reed Smith LLP 435 6th Ave Pittsburgh PA 15219-1886

LONDON, ANDREW BARRY, film editor; b. Bronx, N.Y., Jan. 1, 1949; s. Max Edward and Nellie (Steiner) L. BA in Cinema magna cum laude, U. So. Calif., 1970. Prin. works include: (features) Big Eden, 2000, The Meteor Man, 1993, F/X 2, 1991, Rambo III, 1988, Planes, Trains and Automobiles, 1987, Link, 1986, Cloak & Dagger, 1984, Psycho II, 1983, The True Story of Eskimo Nell, 1975; (TV shows) The Soul Collector, 1999, A Memory in My Heart, 1999, Murder at 75 Birch, 1999, Before He Wakes, 1997, Perfect Crime, 1997, Divided By Hate, 1997, The Crying Child, 1996, Evil Has a Face, 1996, Don't Talk to Strangers, 1994, Day of Reckoning, 1993, Mortal Sins, 1992, Running Delilah, 1992, True Tales, 1992, Sweet Poison, 1991, Tales from the Crypt, 1989-90, Beauty and the Beast Pilot, 1987, The Christmas Star, 1986; sound editor: Wolfen (MPSE Golden Reel award 1982), Hammett, Roadgames, Psycho II, I'm Dancing As Fast As I Can, Perfect, Protocol, Coal Miner's Daughter, The Long Riders, others. Mem. Phi Beta Kappa. Office: 3085 St George St #5 Los Angeles CA 90027-2532

LONDON, CHARLOTTE ISABELLA, secondary school educator; b. Guyana, S.Am., June 11, 1946; came to U.S., 1966, naturalized, 1980; d. Samuel Alphonso and Diana Dallett (Daniels) Edwards; m. David Timothy London, May 26, 1968 (div. May 1983); children: David Tshombe, Douglas Tshaka. BS, Fort Hays State U., 1971; MS, Pa. State U., 1974, PhD, 1977. Elem. sch. tchr., Guyana, 1962-66; secondary sch. tchr., 1971-72; instr. lang. arts Pa. State U., University Park, 1973-74; reading specialist/ednl. cons. N.Y.C. C.C., 1975; dir. Skills Acquisition and Devel. Ctr. Stockton (N.J.) State Coll., 1975-77; reading specialist Pleasantville (N.J.) Pub. Schs., 1977—, supr. English dept., supr. gifted and talented program, 1999—, supr. world langs., 2002—. Ind. specialist United Nations Devel. Programme, Guyana, 1988—; v.p. Atlantic County PTA, 1980-82; del. N.J. Gov.'s Conf. Future Edn. N.J., 1981; founder, pres. Guyana Assn. Reading and Lang. Devel., 1987. Sec. Atlantic County Minority Polit. Women's Caucus. Mem. Internat. Reading Assn., Nat. Coun. Tchrs. English, ASCD, AAUW, Pi Lambda Theta, Phi Delta Kappa (sec.). Mem. African Meth. Episcopal Ch. Home: 6319 Crocus St Mays Landing NJ 08330-1107 Office: Pleasantville Pub Schs W Decatur Ave Pleasantville NJ 08232

LONDON, CRAIG, electronics executive; BS in Physics, U. Calif., Berkeley, Calif.; MBA, Pepperdine U. With AT&T, Pacific Telephone, Electronic Sys. Assocs., Rockwell Internat. Telecomms., Nortel Networks; pres., CEO Diva Comms., Inc.; exec. officer, mng. dir. tech. products Safeguard Scientifics, Inc.; exec. v.p. to pres. Tech. Solutions Solectron Corp., 2002, exec. v.p., strategy, mktg., global svcs., corp. devel., 2002—. Bd. dirs. Boy Scouts Am.-Am.-Pacific Skyline Coun., The San Francisco (Calif.) Zool. Soc. Office: Solectron Corp 777 Gibraltar Dr Milpitas CA 95035

LONDON, DAVID BRUCE, psychiatrist; b. Chgo., Sept. 25, 1948; AB, George Washington U., 1970, MD, 1974. Diplomate Am. Bd. Psychiatry and Neurology, Am. Bd. Adolescent Psychiatry. Intern in internal medicine George Washington U., Washington, 1974-75; fellow in psychiatry Yale U., New Haven, 1975-78; clin. and research fellow Yale Psychiat. Inst., New Haven, 1978-80; forensic fellow in psychiatry Yale U., New Haven, 1984-86; sr. staff psychiatrist Inst. of Living, Hartford, Conn., 1980-82; pvt. practice Madison, Conn., 1982-99, Waterford, Conn., 1984—. Cons. in psychiatry Waterford Country Sch., 1983—, Madison (Conn.) Youth Svcs., 1987-90, Norwich (Conn.) Ct. Diagnostic Clinic, 1988-96; med. dir. Chem. Addiction Recovery Enterprise, New London, Conn., 1987-91, asst. clin. prof. psychiatry Yale U., New Haven, 1987; cons. psychiatrist Act Team Gilead House, Middletown, Conn., 1994-95. Contbr. articles to profl. jours. Mem. Am. Psychiat. Assn., Am. Acad. Med. Acupuncture. Office: 567 Vauxhall Street Ext Ste 320 Waterford CT 06385-4341 Office Phone: 860-443-5822.

LONDON, HERBERT IRA, humanities educator, academic administrator; b. NYC, Mar. 6, 1939; s. Jack and Esta (Epstein) L.; m. Joy Weinman, Oct. 13, 1942 (div. 1974); children: Staci, Nancy; m. Vicki Pops, Nov. 18, 1950; 1 child, Jaclyn. BA, Columbia U., 1960, MA, 1961; PhD, N.Y. U., 1966; DL, U. Aix.-Marseille, Aix-en-Province, France, 1982, Grove City Coll., 1993. Teaching fellow N.Y. U., N.Y.C., 1963-64, instr., 1964-65, asst. prof., 1967-68, univ. ombudsman, 1968-69, assoc. prof., 1969-73, prof., 1973—, dean Gallatin div., 1972-92, John M. Olin U. Prof. Humanities, 1992—; instr. New Sch. for Social Research, N.Y.C., 1964-65; research scholar Australian Nat. U., Canberra, Australia, 1966-67; pres. Hudson Inst., 1997—. Bd. overseers Ctr. for Naval Analysis, Washington, 1983-93; trustee Hudson Inst., Indpls., 1979—, research fellow 1974—; sr. fellow Nat. Strategy Info. Ctr. Created TV programs: Myths That Rule America, The American Character; contbr. numerous articles to profl. jours. Bd. dirs., former chmn. Nat. Assn. Scholars, N.Y.C., 1986; bd. advisors Coalition for Strategic Def. Initiative, Washington, 1986; candidate for mayor of N.Y.C., 1989; conservative candidate for gov., N.Y., 1990, 94; candidate for comptroller of N.Y. State, 1994. Named Danford Assoc., Danford Found., 1971; recipient Anderson award, NYU, 1965, Fulbright award, U.S. Govt., 1966—67, Def. Sci. award, Def. Sci. Jour., 1985, Martin Luther King award, Congress of Racial Equality, 1995, Peter Shaw Meml. award, Exemplary Writing Nat. Assn. Scholars, 1996, Jacques Maritain Humanitarian award, Am. Maritain Assn., 1996, Ellis Island Medal of Honor, 2000, Am. Jewish Congress award, 2001, Libery and Media award, 2002. Mem. Freedom House, Am. Hist. Assn., Edn. Excellence Network, Heritage Found (assoc. scholar 1983—), Ethics and Pub. Policy Ctr. (assoc. scholar 1985—), Nat. Strategy Info. Ctr., Coun. Fgn. Rels. Republican. Jewish. Avocations: writing, tennis. Home: 10 West St New York NY 10004 Office: NYU 90 Broad St New York NY 10004 Office Phone: 212-232-8722. E-mail: herb@hudson.org.

LONDON, IRVING MYER, physician, educator; b. Malden, Mass., July 24, 1918; s. Jacob A. and Rose (Goldstein) London; m. Huguette Piedzicki, Feb. 27, 1955; children: Robert L.J., David T. B in Jewish Edn., Hebrew Coll., 1938; AB summa cum laude, Harvard U., 1939, MD, 1943; DSc (hon.), U. Chgo., 1966. Sheldon Traveling fellow Harvard U., 1939—41, Delamar research fellow med. sch., 1940—41; intern Presbyn. Hosp., N.Y.C., 1943, asst. resident, 1946—47, asst. physician, 1946—52, assoc. attending physician, 1954—55; Rockefeller fellow in medicine Coll. Physicians and Surgeons, Columbia U., 1946—47; instr. Columbia U., 1947—49; asso. in medicine Coll. Phys. and Surg., Columbia U., 1949—51; asst. prof. Coll. Phys. and Surg., Columbia, 1951—54, assoc. prof., 1954—55; prof., chmn. dept. medicine Albert Einstein Coll. Medicine, N.Y.C., 1955—70, vis. prof. medicine, 1970—; prof. biology MIT, 1969—89, prof. emeritus, 1989—; vis. prof. medicine Harvard Med. Sch., 1969—72, prof. medicine, 1972—89, prof. emeritus, 1989—; dir. div. health scis. and tech. Harvard and MIT, 1969—85, prof. medicine, 1972—, Grover M. Hermann prof. health scis. and tech., 1977—89, prof. emeritus, 1989—; dir. Whitaker Coll. Health Scis., Tech. and Mgmt., MIT, 1978—83; dir. med. service Bronx Mcpl. Hosp. Center, 1955—70. Delta Epsilon lectr. U. Colo., 1962, Harvey lectr., 61; Jacobaeus lectr., Stockholm, 64; vis. scientist Pasteur Inst., Paris, 1962—63; Commonwealth Fund fellow, 1962—63; Alpha Omega Alpha lectr. Yale, Boston U., Columbia, SUNY Downstate Med. Ctr., U. Chgo.; Harry L. Alexander vis. prof. Washington U., St. Louis, 1968; Alpha Omega Alpha vis. prof. Johns Hopkins U., 1970; Eugene A. Stead Jr. vis. lectr. Duke Med. Ctr., 1970; cons. to Surgeon Gen. AUS, 1957—60; chmn. metabolism study sect. USPHS, 1961—63; Med. fellowship bd. NAS, NRC, 1955—64; mem. bd. sci. cons. Sloan Kettering Inst., 1960—72; bd. sci. counselors Nat. Heart Inst., 1964—68; exec. com. Health Rsch. Coun., City N.Y., 1958—63; mem. sci. adv. coun. Pub. Health Rsch. Inst., N.Y.C., 1958—63; mem. adv. com. to dir. NIH, 1966—70, nat. cancer adv. bd., 1972—76; physician Brigham and Women's Hosp., 1972—83, sr. physician, 1983—; chmn. rsch. group Nat. Commn. on Arthritis, 1975—76; chmn. adv. com. Divsn. Health Scis., Inst. Medicine, 1979—82; mem. Bd. Sci. Counselors, NIADDK, 1979—83; bd. dirs., cons. Johnson and Johnson, 1982—89; founder Genetix Pharms., 1996. Assoc. editor: Jour. Clin. Investigation, 1952—57, mem. editl. bd.: Am. Jour. Medicine, 1965—79. Bd. trustees Hebrew Coll., 2000—; bd. dirs. Philippe Found. Capt. U.S. Army, 1944—46. Recipient Bloomfield medal and lectr., Lady Davis Inst., 1986. Fellow: Am. Acad. Arts and Scis., Am. Assn. Advanced Scis. (Theobald Smith award in med. scis. 1953); mem.: NAS (med. bd. medicine 1967—70, founding mem. Inst. Medicine 1970), Assn. Am. Physicians, Internat. Soc. Hematology, Am. Soc. Hematology, Am. Soc. Clin. Investigation (pres. 1963—64), Am. Soc. Biol. Chemists, Alpha Omega Alpha, Phi Beta Kappa. Office: Harvard U-MIT Div Health Scis and Tech 77 Massachusetts Ave Cambridge MA 02139-4301 E-mail: imlondon@mit.edu.

LONDON, JAN, small business owner, writer; b. Brookline, Mass., Apr. 4, 1946; d. George and Irene London. B in Liberal Arts., Long Beach State U., 1968. Cert. Federated Gemological Assn., Sri Lanka, 1982. Asst. to leading macrobiotic and taoist leader, Hong Kong, Japan, 1983—95; pub. JL Books, 2001—. Author: (cookbook) Happy Stomach-The Stevia Natural Foods Cookbook, Coconut Cuisine featuring Stevia; contbr. columns in newspapers. Personal E-mail: jan@happystomach.com.

LONDON, JESSICA MARIE, elementary school educator; b. Wolfe City, Tex., June 28, 1981; d. Tommy C and Pam A London. BSc in interdisciplinary studies magna cum laude, Tex. A&M U., 2004. Tchr. Wolfe City (Tex.) Elem. Sch. Dist., 2002—. Mem. Site Based Decision Mktg. Co., Wolfe City, Tex., 2004—05. Mem.: Alpha Chi. Home: 6336 Hwy 34N Wolfe City TX 75496 Office: Wolfe City Elem 505 W Dallas Wolfe City TX 75496

LONDON, JILL S., artist, educator; b. L.A., Jan. 19, 1959; d. Lawrence London and Shirley Ruth Kestenbaum. BA, Temple U., 1981. Apprentice Robert Kulicke Studio, N.Y., 1986—93; freelance gilder, painter, 1991—. Adj. prof. Fashion Inst. Tech., N.Y., 2004—; tchr. The Lower East Side Printshop, N.Y., 2003—; master gilder Apprentice Alliance, 1991—95. Mus. Arch., Cuenca, Spain, 1986—90, de Young Mus., San Francisco, Calif., 2000, Appearances Mag., 2000, exhibited in group shows at Pierogi 2000, Bklyn., N.Y., exhibitions include Va. Commonwealth Gallery, Qatar, 2004, TRIBES Gallery, N.Y., 2004, Wingspread Gallery, N.E. Harbor, Maine, 2004, Kentler Drawing Space, N.Y., 2004, Miranda Fine Arts, 2004, Mahattanville Coll. Gallery, 2004. Vol. gardner Green Thumb Le Petite Versailles, N.Y., 1997—. Mem.: Bay Area Art Conservation Guild, Am. Inst. Conservation Hist. and Artistic Works, Soc. Gilders (edn. chmn. 2000—, sec. 2002—). Democrat. Jewish. Avocation: tai chi. Home: 227 E 2nd St 2B New York NY 10009 Personal E-mail: jill@londongild.com.

LONDON, JUSTIN JOSHUA, entrepreneur, writer; b. Royal Oak, Mich., Jan. 26, 1973; s. Leon Arthur and Leslie Ann London. BA in econ. and math. cum laude with distinction, U. Mich., 1995, MA in applied econ., 1996, MS in fin. engring., 1997, MS in math., 1998; MS in computer sci., U. Mich.-Dearborn, 2001; postgrad., John Marshall Law Sch. Cert. java programmer Sun Microsystems. CEO, founder Global Max Trading Corp., Chgo., 1997—; adj. prof. Oakland Cmty. Coll., Farmington Hills, Mich., 1999—2000; sr. developer Compuwave Corp., Farmington Hills, 2000—02; sr. cons. London Quant Adv., Chgo., 2002—03; sr. portfolio mgr., analyst Bank of Montreal, Chgo., 2003—04; CEO, founder Global Max Auctions, Chgo., 2003—; also bd. dirs. Bd. dirs. Global Max Trading, Chgo. Author: Modeling Derivatives in C++, 2004. Mem.: Internat. Assn. of Fin. Engineers, Variety Club Children's Charity. Achievements include invention of global system trading technology, live auction technology. Avocations: golf, rollerblading, computer programming. Business E-Mail: jlondon@ameritech.net.

LONDON, MARTIN, lawyer; b. Glen Cove, N.Y., Apr. 4, 1934; children: Jesse, Lizbeth; m. Doris Wilke, July 28, 1983. AB, Cornell U., 1955; LLB, NYU, 1957. Bar: N.Y. 1958, U.S. Dist. Ct. (so. dist.) N.Y. 1962, U.S. Tax Ct. 1968, U.S. Dist. Ct. (ea. dist.) N.Y. 1969, U.S. Ct. Appeals (2d cir.) 1969, U.S. Dist. Ct. D.C. 1970, U.S. Supreme Ct. 1971, U.S. Ct. Appeals (6th and 7th cirs.) 1982, U.S. Ct. Appeals (4th cir.) 1990. Assoc. Gallop, Climenko & Gould, N.Y.C., 1958-61, Paul, Weiss, Rifkind, Wharton & Garrison, N.Y.C., 1962-68, ptnr., 1969—. Spl. counsel judiciary relations com. First Judicial Dept., 1973-74, counsel gov.'s judicial nomination com., 1975-82, chmn. deptl. disciplinary com., 1980-85; spl. trial counsel Ct. on the Judiciary, 1977. Served as sgt. U.S. Army, 1957-58, 61-62. Mem. Am. Coll. Trial Lawyers, Assn. of Bar of City of N.Y., Fed. Bar Council, Am. Arbitration Assn. (nat. panel arbitrators). Avocations: deep sea fishing, skiing. Office: Paul Weiss Rifkind Wharton & Garrison LLP Ste 2613 1285 Avenue Of The Americas New York NY 10019-6064 Office Phone: 212-373-3197. E-mail: mlondon@paulweiss.com.

LONDON, MICHAEL, retail executive; married; 2 children. BA in Psychology, Duke U., 1970. Former sr. v.p., gen. mktg. mgr. Lechmere; former exec. v.p. Ctrl. Tractor Farm & Country; former sr. v.p. retail and comml. sales NordicTrack; v.p. gen. merchandise Best Buy Co., Inc., 1996—98, sr. v.p., 1998—, exec. v.p., gen. merchandise mgr., 1998—. Bd. dirs. Citizen's Scholarship Found. Am.

LONDON, STEVE NORMAN, obstetrician, gynecologist, educator; b. Ardmore, Okla., Apr. 22, 1952; MD, U. Okla., 1977. Bd. cert. in ob-gyn.; subspecialty in reproductive endocrinology. Asst. prof., dir. divsn. reproductive endocrinology U. Ark. Health Sci. Ctr., Little Rock, 1986-90; assoc. prof., dir. divsn. reproductive endocrinology U. Ky., Lexington, 1990-94; prof., chmn. dept. ob-gyn. La. State U. Health Sci. Ctr., Shreveport, 1994—2003, program dir. ob-gyn. residency, 1998—2003; med. dir. N.W. La. Coalition for the Health of Women and Children, 2003—. Examiner Am. Bd. Ob-Gyn., Dallas, 1994—. Author: (book) Menopause Clinical Concepts, 3d edit., 1999. Bd. trustees Noel Meth. Ch., Shreveport, 1997—; scoutmaster Boy Scouts Am., Shreveport, 1994—. Fellow ACOG; mem. Soc. for Reproductive Endocrinology, Am. Soc. Reproductive Endocrinology. Avocations: gardening, camping. Office: La State U Dept Ob-Gyn 1501 Kings Hwy Shreveport LA 71103-4228 E-mail: slondo@lsuhsc.edu.

LONDON OWENS, GEORGETTE, artist; b. Paris, Aug. 28, 1930; came to U.S., 1950; d. Louis and Marie Isabelle (London) Patreaux; m. Frank Xavier; children: Frank, Gail May. BA, U. Sorbonne, 1949. Pres. Alliance of Women Artists, San Francisco, 1988—. Jewelry designer Pierre Cardin, Paris; artist comml. designs for new products. Exhibited in group shows at Mus. of Art, Cleve., 1957, Mus. of Modern Art, Cin., 1958, N.Y.C., 1959, Modern Art Gallery, N.Y., 1960, Arts from France, N.Y.C., 1966, George Wiener Gallery, N.Y.C., 1966, 70, 73, 76, Marumo Galler, L.A., 1985, Marin County Civic Ctr., San Francisco, 1988, Bay Model Ctr., Sausalito, 1990, in group shows in France G. Cauvin Galerie, Nice, France, 1986, Biennale des Femmes, Grand Palais, Paris, 1990, others; one woman shows 150 paintings, 50 drawings Vinciguerra Gallery, L.A., 2005, Tondinelli Galleria, Rome, 2005 Recipient Lifetime Achievement award, 1998. Home: 165 1/2 Lower Via Casitas Greenbrae CA 94904-2200

LONDRAVILLE, KATHRYN JORDAN, middle school educator; b. Potsdam, N.Y., July 19, 1953; d. Leon Edward and Dorothy Helen (O'Neil) Jordan; m. Mark Richard Londraville, July 2, 1977; children: Jordan David,

Michael Francis, Erin Ashley. BA in Elem. Edn., SUNY, Potsdam, 1975, MS in Reading, 1979. Lic. tchr., N.Y. Tchr. A A Kingston Mid. Sch., Potsdam, N.Y., 1975—. Mem., chairperson Bldg. Planning Team, Potsdam, 1987-90. Mem. Potsdam Hosp. Guild; chairperson St. Mary's Religious Formation Com., Potsdam, 1992-93. Recipient Outstanding Sponsor Teacher award Phi Delta Kappa, 1994. Mem. Am. Fedn. Tchrs., N.Y. State United Tchrs., N.Y. State Reading Assn., North County Coun. of Internat. Reading Assn. (hon., pres. 1979-80), Delta Kappa Gamma (chair scholarship com.). Democrat. Roman Catholic. Home: 127 Regan Rd Potsdam NY 13676-3207 Office: A A Kingston Mid Sch Outer Lawrence Ave Potsdam NY 13676

LONDRÉ, FELICIA MAE HARDISON, theater educator; b. Ft. Lewis, Wash., Apr. 1, 1941; d. Felix M. and Priscilla Mae (Graham) Hardison; m. Venne-Richard Londré, Dec. 16, 1967; children: Tristan Graham, Georgianna Rose. BA with high honors, U. Mont., 1962; MA, U. Wash., 1964; PhD, U. Wis., 1969. Asst. prof. U. Wis. at Rock County, Janesville, 1969-75; asst. prof., head theatre program U. Tex. at Dallas, Richardson, 1975-78; assoc. prof. U. Mo., Kansas City, 1978-82, prof. theatre, 1982-87, curators' prof., 1987—; women's chair in humanistic studies Marquette U., 1995. Dramaturg Mo. Repertory Theatre, Kansas City, 1978-2001, Nebr. Shakespeare Festival, 1990—; guest dramaturg Gt. Lakes Theater Festival, 1988; mem. archives task force Folly Theatre, 1982-83; artistic advisor New Directions Theatre Co., 1983-90; hon. lectr. Mid.-Am. State Univs. Assn., 1986-87; mem. U.S.-U.S.S.R. Joint Commn. on Theatre Historiography, 1989; mem.adv. bd. Contemporary World Writers, 1991—; lectr. univs. Budapest, Pecs, Debrecen, Hungary, 1992; vis. prof. Hosei U., Tokyo, 1993; vis. scholar Wabash Coll., 2003, lectr. U. Rouen, Caen, Paris, 2003; Geske lectr. U. Nebr., Lincoln, 2005. Author: Tennessee Williams, 1979, Tom Stoppard, 1981, Federico Garcia Lorca, 1984, Love's Labour's Lost: Critical Essays, 1997; (play) Miss Millay Was Right, 1982 (John Gassner Meml. Playwriting award 1982), The History of World Theater: From the English Restoration to the Present, 1991 (Choice Outstanding Acad. Book award 1991), Chow Chow Pizza, 1995 (Kansas City Gorilla Theatre First Prize, winner Stages '95 Competition, Dallas); (opera libretto) Duse and D'Annunzio, 1987; (with Daniel J. Watermeier) The History of North American Theater: The United States, Canada, and Mexico from Pre-Columbian Times to the Present, 1998; co-editor: Shakespeare Companies and Festivals: An International Guide, 1995; book rev. editor: Theatre Jour., 1984-86; assoc. editor: Shakespeare Around the Globe: A Guide to Notable Postwar Revivals, 1986; mem. editl. bd. Theatre History Studies, 1981-87, 89—, Studies in Am. Drama, 1945 to the present, 1984-93, 19th Century Theatre Jour., 1984-95, Bookmark Press, Tennessee Williams Rev., 1985-87, Jour. Dramatic Theory and Criticism, 1986—, On-Stage Studies, The Elizabethan Rev., 1992-99, Theatre Symposium, 1994—, The Oxfordian, 1998—, Estreno Contemporary Spanish Plays, 1998—, So. Ill. U. Press Theater in the Americas series, 2000—, Eugene O'Neill Rev., 2005—; contbr. articles to profl. jours. Hon. co-founder Heart of Am. Shakespeare Festival, bd. dirs., 1991-2004, v.p., 2000-04; bd. dirs. Edgar Snow Meml. Fund, 1993-2002; active UMKC Grad. Coun., 2001-04, acad. stds. com. Coll. Arts and Scis., 2001-04; elected Nat. Theatre Conf., 2001, trustee, 2004—; sec. Coll. Fellows Am. Theatre, 2001-03. Fulbright grantee U. Caen, Normandy, France, 1962-63, NEH grantee, 1971, 80, Faculty Rsch. grantee U. Mo., 1985-86, 90-91, tchr. seminar grantee Mo. Humanities Coun., 1993, 96; recipient Disting. Alumni award U. Mont., 1998, winner Amy and Eric Burger Essay on Theatre Competition, U. Wyo., 2003; grad. fellow U. Wis., 1966-67, Trustees fellow U. Kansas City, 1987-88; inductee Coll. Fellows Am. Theatre. Fellow Mid-Am. Theatre Conf. (chair grad. rsch. paper competition 1985); mem. Am. Soc. Theatre Rsch. (exec. com. 1984-90, program chair 1995), Shakespeare Theatre Assn. Am. (sec. 1991-93), Internat. Fedn. for Theatre Rsch. (del. gen. assembly 1985), Am. Theatre Assn. (commn. on theatre rsch. 1981-87, chmn. 1984-86), Theatre Libr. Assn., Dramatists Guild, Literary Mgrs. and Dramaturgs Am., Shakespeare Oxford Soc., Am. Theatre and Drama Soc. (v.p. 1995-97, pres. 1997-99), Nat. League of Am. PEN Women (v.p. 2002-04, pres. 2004—, bd. dirs. Kansas City-Westport br.), Assn. for Theatre in Higher Edn. (v.p. for awards 2001-03, Outstanding Tchr. award 2001), Internat. Al Jolson Soc., Lewis and Clark Heritage Found. Roman Catholic. Avocations: travel, theater, continental cuisine. Home: 528 E 56th St Kansas City MO 64110-2769 Office: Dept Theatre 4949 Cherry St Kansas City MO 64110-2499 Office Phone: 816-235-2781. Business E-Mail: londref@umkc.edu.

LONDRIGAN, THOMAS FOSTER, lawyer; b. Springfield, Ill., May 10, 1937; s. Joseph Aloysius and Bridgett Loretta (Foster) L.; m. Carol Ann Fish, Aug. 31, 1963; children: Joseph, Patrick, Thomas Jr., Genevieve. AB, U. Notre Dame, 1959; LLB, U. Ill., 1962. Bar: Ill. 1962. Asst. U.S. Atty., Springfield, 1963-65; law clerk 4th Dist. Appellate Ct., Springfield, 1965-66; sr. ptnr. Londrigan, Potter & Randle, Springfield, 1966—. Contbr. articles to profl. jours. Activities chmn. Illini for Kennedy, Champaign, Ill., 1960; pres. U. of Ill. Young Dems., Champaign, 1961; co-chair Ill. Dems. for Reagan, Springfield, 1980. Mem. ABA, Internat. Acad. Trial Lawyers, Ill. Bar Assn. (co-chair Com. on Uniform Circuit Ct. Rules 1974-75), Sangamon County Bar Assn., Assn. of Trial Lawyers of Am. (bd. mem. 1988-90). Am. Coll. of Trial Lawyers, Ill. Trial Lawyers Assn. (pres. 1983-84), Soc. of Trial LAwyers, 7th Cir. Ct. of Appeals Bar Assn. Democrat. Roman Catholic. Avocation: competitive sailing. Office: Londrigan Potter & Randle P O Box 399 Springfield IL 62705-0399

LONEGAN, THOMAS LEE, retired restaurant corporation executive; b. Kansas City, Mo., July 4, 1932; s. Thomas F. and Edna L. (Payton) L.; m. Donna F. Ednie, Apr. 11, 1958; children: Timothy L., John M. BSME, Gen. Motors Inst., 1955; MS in Mgmt., USN Post Grad Sch., 1963; grad., Indsl. Coll. Armed Forces, Washington, 1970; postgrad., Calif. State U., Long Beach, 1979-83; grad., Coll. for Fin. Planning, Denver, 1984. Registered profl. engr., Mass.; CFP. Commd. ensign USN, 1956, advanced through grades to comdr., 1978; dir. pub. works, officer in charge of constrn. Naval Weapons Sta., Seal Beach, Calif., 1974-78; ret., 1978; dir. cen. staff McAthco Enterprises, Inc., Camarillo, Calif., 1985, exec. v.p., CFO, 1986-90, pres., CEO, 1991-93, exec. v.p., CFO, 1994-95; ret. Bd. dirs. McAthco Enterprises; exec. v.p. engring. Orange County Engring. Coun., 1977-78. Author: Analysis and Attenuation of Air Borne Noise in Industrial Plants, 1955, Formalized Training of Maintenance Personnel, 1963. Vol. various couns. Boy Scouts Am., 1968-76. Decorated Bronze Star with combat device, Meritorious Svc. medal, Jt. Svcs. Commendation medal, Navy Achievement medal; decorated Order of Chamoro (Guam); named Sr. Engr./Arch. Yr. Naval Facilities Engr. Command, 1972; recipient Silver medal Boy Scouts Am., 1974. Fellow Soc. Am. Mil. Engrs., Mil. Officers Assn. Am., GM Inst. Robots Honor Soc.; mem. Beta Gamma Sigma. Avocations: reading, theater, music. E-mail: tomlonegan@socal.rr.com.

LONERGAN, ROBERT A., lawyer; m. Marsha Lonergan. AB in English Lit., Fordham Coll.; JD, Forham U., 1975; grad. fin. for sr. exec. program, Harvard U., 1997. With Cadwalader, Wickersham & Taft, N.Y.C.; counsel Bethlehem (Pa.) Steel Corp.; v.p., gen. counsel, sec. Kusan, Inc., Brentwood, Tenn.; v.p., gen. counsel, sec., bd. mem. Kennecott Corp., Salt Lake City; sr. v.p., gen. counsel, sec. Pegasus Gold, Inc., Spokane, Wash., 1995—99; v.p., gen. counsel, corp. sec. Rohm and Haas Co., Phila., 1999—, corp. sec., 2002—. Bd. dirs. Inst. for Law and Econs., U. Pa., Phila. Mus. Art, Nat. Assn. Mfrs., Walnut St. Theatre, Com. of Seventy. With U.S. Army, Vietnam. Mem.: Greater Phila. C. of C. (bd. dirs.). Office: Rohm and Haas Co 100 Independence Mall West Philadelphia PA 19106-2399

LONEY, GLENN MEREDITH, theater educator; b. Sacramento, Dec. 24, 1928; s. David Merton and Marion Gladys (Busher) L. BA, U. Calif., Berkeley, 1950; MA, U. Wis., 1951; PhD, Stanford U., 1953. Teaching asst. U. Calif., Berkeley, 1949-50, Stanford U., Calif., 1952-53; instr. San Francisco State U., 1955-56, U. Nev., Las Vegas, 1956; prof. U. Md., Europe, N. Africa, Middle East, 1956-59; instr. Hofstra U., Hempstead, N.Y., 1959-61, Adelphi U., Garden City, N.Y., 1959-61; prof. speech and theater Bklyn. Coll. and City U. Grad. Ctr., 1961-71, prof. theater, 1971—. Author: Briefing and Conference Techniques, 1959, Peter Brook Midsummer Night's Dream, 1974, The Shakespeare Complex, 1974, Young Vic Scapino, 1980, The House of Mirth-The Play of the Novel, 1981, Twentieth Century Theatre, 1983, California Gold Rush Drama, Musical Theatre in America, 1984, Unsung Genius, 1984, Creating Careers in Music Theatre, 1988, Staging Shakespeare, 1990, Peter Brook: Oxford to Orghast, 1997; editor: The Modernist; chief correspondent N.Y. Theatre-Wire and N.Y. Museums.com, Curator's Choice on Internet, 1996—, founding editor, project dir., Modern Theatre Online, NYU. Served with AUS, 1953-55. Fellow Am. Scandinavian Found.; mem. AAUP, Am. Theatre Critics Assn., Am. Dance Critics, Outer Critics Circle (sec.), Am. Music Critics Assn., Am. Soc. Theatre Research, Internat. Fedn. Theatre Research, Theatre Library Assn., Theatre Hist. Soc., Internat. Assn. Theatre Critics, Phi Beta Kappa, Alpha Mu Gamma, Phi Eta Sigma, Phi Delta Phi. Democrat. Office: 3 E 71st St New York NY 10021-4154 Office Phone: 212-879-5386.

LONEY, MARY ROSE, former airport administrator, aviation industry consultant; b. Ohio, 1952; B in Sociology and Philosophy, U. Pitts., 1973; MPA, U. Nev., Las Vegas, 1983. Ticket sales staff Grand Canyon Airlines, 1973—75; mgr. Lucky's Grocery Stores, 1976—78; planning svcs. mgr. McCarran Internat. Airport, Las Vegas, Nev., 1979-84; asst. aviation dir. Albuquerque Internat. Airport, 1984-86; asst. dir. aviation San Jose (Calif.) Internat. Airport, 1986-89; first dep. commr. aviation Chgo. Airport Sys., 1989-92; dep. exec. dir. fin. and adminstrn. Dallas/Ft. Worth Internat. Airport, 1992-93; dir. aviation Phila. Internat. Airport, 1993-96; commr. aviation Chgo. Airport Sys., 1996—99; pres. Travelways, Inc., NJ, 1999—2000; pres., CEO The Loney Group, Satellite Beach, Fla., 2000—. Bd. dirs. Chgo. Tourism and Visitors Bur., 1993—2000, Phila. Conv. and Visitors Bur., 1993—2000, Chgo.-Gary Airport Authority, 1996—2000; bd. mem. Chgo. Econ. Devel. Commn., 1996—2000. Trustee St. Joseph's U., Phila., 1994—97; bd. dirs. Chgo. Pub. Art Commn., 1996—2000. Named Santa Clara County Woman of Achievement, 1988, Woman of Yr., Phila. Customs Brokers and Freight Forwarders Assn., 1994, one of State Pa. Honor Roll of Women, 1996; recipient YWCA's Tribute to Women in Industry award, 1989, Bus. Woman of Yr. award Great Valley Regional C. of C., 1994, Transp. award March of Dimes, 1995. Mem. FAA (appointed rsch. engring. and devel. adv. com.), Am. Assn. Airport Execs. (accredited airport exec., nat. bd. dirs. 1995-97, chmns. award 1994), St. Joseph's U. (bd. trustees). Office: The Loney Group LLC Oceancrest Ctr 1290 Highway A1A Ste 204 Satellite Beach FL 32937

LONG, ALAN K., research administrator; b. Burlington, Vt., June 19, 1950; married; 2 children. BS, Yale U., 1971; MA, Harvard U., 1976, PhD, 1979. From rsch. assoc. to lab. dir. depts. chem. and earth sci. Harvard U., Cambridge, Mass., 1979—, asst. dean for rsch. fins. and sys. Faculty Arts and Scis., 2002—. Mem. Am. Chem. Soc. Office: Harvard U Faculty Arts and Scis 1414 Massachusetts Ave # 430 Cambridge MA 02138

LONG, ALFRED B., retired oil industry executive; b. Aug. 4, 1909; s. Jessie A. and Ada (Beckwith) L.; m. Sylvia V. Thomas, Oct. 29, 1932; 1 child, Kathleen Sylvia (Mrs. E.A. Pearson, II). Student, S. Park Jr. Coll., 1928-29, Lamar U., 1947-56, U. Tex., 1941; grad., Citizens Police Acad. With Sun Oil Co., Beaumont, Tex., 1931-69, driller geophys. dept., surveyor engring. dept., engr. operating dept., engr. prodn. lab., 1931-59, regional supr., 1960-69; ret., 1969; cons. Sun Oil Co., Beaumont, Tex., 1969—. Inventor oil well devices. Sr.'s bd. dirs. Bapt. Hosp., Beaumont; chaplain sr.'s vols. bd. dirs. S.E. Tex. Rehab. Hosp., Beaumont, Srs.-Lawmen Coun.; chaplain; Jefferson County Program Planning Com., 1964; tech. adv. group Oil Well Drilling Inst., Lamar U., Beaumont. Recipient Nat. Jefferson award for Outstanding Pub. Svc. Am. Inst. for Pub. Svc., 1992, Cmty. Svc. award Quarter Century Wireless Assn., 1994, Sensational Srs. of the U.S. honor CBS TV, 1994, Hometown Heroes Sta. CH6TV, 1995, Nat. CBS Cable The Best of US, 1997, Eye on the People, 1997 Ageless Hero Cmty. Involvement Year 2000 award Blue Cross-Blue Shield; Olympic Torch bearer, 1996, Police 100 Club (life mem. 1998), Pub. Svc. award Beaumont Police Dept., 2000, Julie Rogers Gift of Life Spirit of Love award, 2005., Pub. Svc. award Beaumont, 2005 Mem. IEEE, Soc. Petroleum Engrs. (Legion of Honor 2004), Am. Petroleum Inst., Am. Assn. Petroleum Geologists, Houston Geol. Soc., Gulf Coast Engring. and Sci. Soc. (treas. 1962-65), U.S. Power Squadron, Soc. Wireless Pioneers, Citizen Police Acad. (life), Sheriffs Assn. Tex, Tex. Police Assn., Proclamation County of Jefferson Tex. Pub. Svc., 2005

LONG, ALLEN FLOYD, music educator, minister; b. Clovis, Calif., May 7, 1951; s. Allen Jackson and Donna Leah Long; m. Nancy A. Nice, June 7, 1975; children: Heather A. Englebretson, Daniel P. BA, Calif. State U., Fullerton, 1975; ThM, Dallas Theol. Sem., 1981; M Music Edn., So. Meth. U., 2005. Ordained Richland Bible Fellowship, 1982. Staff pastor Richland Bible Fellowship Ch., Richardson, Tex., 1981—92; min. worship and music Trinity Fellowship Ch., Richardson, 1992—. Piano tchr. Allen Long Piano Studio, Garland, Tex., 1984—, accompanist, 1990—. Composer: (song) A Song of Confession (Psalm 51), 1996, Psalm 3, 2004, (congregational hymn) My Song Is Love Unkown, 2001; musician (co-arranger): (H.S. string orch. arrangement) Ballade - Debussy, 1997, Danse - Debussy, 1997, All Is Well, 1997, (H.S. string orchestra arrangement) Gigue - J. S. Bach, 1998; composer: (choral anthem) Praise the Lord! To God Be the Glory!, 1999, King of Heaven, (congregational hymn), 1999. Mem.: The Hymn Soc. of the U.S. and Can., Tex. Choral Dirs. Assn., Am. Choral Dirs Assn., Music Tchrs. Nat. Assn., Tex. Music Tchrs. Assn., Phi Kappa Lambda, Richardson Music Teachers Assn. (yr. book editor 1990—2005). Avocations: reading, gardening, cooking, music. Office: Trinity Fellowship Ch 932 S Greenville Ave Richardson TX 75081 Office Phone: 972-690-9535. Personal E-mail: musicman@trinityfellowship.org.

LONG, ANN MARIE, health facility administrator; b. Hartford, Conn., Oct. 9, 1945; d. John and Bridie (Griffin) O'Connell; m. Michael T. Long, Sept. 9, 1967; children: Michael, Maura, Deirdre. Diploma, St. Francis Hosp., Hartford, 1966; BSN magna cum laude, U. Hartford, 1978; M in Health Care Mgmt., The Hartford Grad. Ctr., 1987. RN, Conn.; cert. in advanced continuity of care; cert. in nursing adminstrn.; cert. in case mgmt. Critical care staff nurse St. Francis Hosp. and Med. Ctr., Hartford, 1966-67, continuing care coord., 1978-83, nursing supr., 1983-90, dir. continuing care, 1990—, Mt. Sinai Hosp., Hartford, 1992—; nursing instr. St. Francis Sch. Nursing, Hartford, 1967-68; dir. of continuing care St. Francis Hosp. and Med. Ctr., Mt. Sinai Hosp., 1992-95; dir. divsn. continuum of care mgmt. St. Francis Hosp. and Med. Ctr., 1995. Profl. adv. com. Vis. Nurses Assn. Farmington Valley. Justice of the Peace, Simsbury, Conn. Mem. Conn. Nurses Assn., Conn. Hosp. Assn. (continuing care coords. conf.), Conn. Assn. Continuity Care, Case Mgmt. Soc. Am., Case Mgmt. Soc. New Eng., Am. Orgn. Nurse Execs., Sigma Theta Tau, Alpha Chi. Home: 38 Old Mill Ct Simsbury CT 06070 Business E-Mail: along@stfranciscare.org.

LONG, ANTHONY ARTHUR, classics educator; b. Manchester, Eng., Aug. 17, 1937; came to U.S. 1983; s. Tom Arthur and Phyllis Joan (LeGrice) L.; m. Janice Calloway, Dec. 30, 1960 (div. 1969); 1 child, Stephen Arthur; m. Mary Kay Flavell, May 25, 1970 (div. 1990); 1 child, Rebecca Jane; m. Monique Marie-Jeanne Elias, Mar. 22, 1997. BA, U. Coll. London, 1960; PhD, U. London, 1964. Lectr. classics U. Otago, Dunedin, N.Z., 1961-64; lectr. classics U. Nottingham, Eng., 1964-66; lectr. Greek and Latin U. Coll. London, 1966-71; reader in Greek and Latin U. London, 1971-73; Gladstone prof. Greek U. Liverpool, Eng., 1973-83; prof. classics U. Calif., Berkeley, 1982—; pub. orator U. Liverpool, Eng., 1981-83; Irving Stone prof. lit. U. Calif., Berkeley, 1991—, chmn. dept. classics, 1986-90. Mem. Inst. Advanced Study, Princeton, N.J., 1970, 79; vis. prof. U. Munich, 1973, Ecole Normale Supérieure, Paris, 1993, 2001; Cardinal Mercier prof. philosophy U. Louvain, Belgium, 1991; Belle van Zuylen prof. philosophy, U. Utrecht, Netherlands, 2003. mem. Mellon Fellowships Selection Com., 1984-90; mem. selection com. Stanford U. Humanities Coun., 1985-86; Corbett lectr. U. Cambridge, 1998-99; Faculty Rsch. lectr. U. Calif., Berkeley, 1999-2000; Brackenridge lectr., U. Tex., San Antonio, 2003. Author: Language and Thought in Sophocles, 1968 (Cromer Greek prize 1968), Problems in Stoicism, 1971, 96, Hellenistic Philosophy, 1974, 2d edit., 1986, (with Fortenbaugh and Huby) Theophrastus of Eresus, 1985, (with Sedley) The Hellenistic Philosophers, 1987, (with Dillon) The Question of Eclecticism, 1988, 96, (with Bastianini) Hierocles, 1992, (with others) Images and Ideologies, 1993, Stoic Studies, 1996, 2d edit., 2001, Cambridge Companion to Early Greek Philosophy, 1999, Epictetus, 2002-04; editor: Classical Quar., 1975-81, Classical Antiquity, 1987-90; gen. editor: (with Barnes) Clarendon Later Ancient Philosophers, 1987-. Served to lt. Royal Arty., Eng., 1955-57 Named hon. citizen City of Rhodes, Greece; sr. fellow humanities coun. Princeton U., 1978, short-term fellow, 2002, Bye fellow Robinson Coll., Cambridge, 1982, Guggenheim fellow, 1986-87, sr. fellow Ctr. for Hellenic Studies, 1988-93, fellow NEH, 1990-91, Wissenschaftskolleg fellow, Berlin, 1991-92, William Evans fellow U. Otago, New Zealand, 1995. Fellow Am. Acad. Arts and Scis., Brit. Acad. (corr.); mem. Classical Assn., Aristotelian Soc., Am. Philol. Assn., Phi Beta Kappa (hon.). Avocations: music, walking, travel, bridge. Home: 32 Sunset Dr Kensington CA 94707-1139 Office: U Calif Dept Classics Berkeley CA 94720-0001 E-mail: aalong@berkeley.edu.

LONG, BOB EUGENE, music educator, director; b. Kansas City, Mo., Nov. 28, 1958; s. John Moore (Stepfather) and Mary Catherine Michael; m. Judith Kay Pearman, July 1, 1964; children: James Alexander, Hanna Christina. BME in Instrumental Music, Truman State U., Kirksville, Mo., 1982, MA in Music Edn., 1984. Instr. music Truman State U., Kirksville, Mo., 1984—85; doctoral grad. tchg. asst. U. Mo. Conservatory of Music, Kansas City, 1985—88; asst. band dir. Hoover H.S., Des Moines, 1989—92; adj. instr. saxophone William Penn U., Oskaloosa, Iowa, 1991—95; coord. jazz studies Valley H.S., West Des Moines, 1992—2004; tchg. artist saxophone Drake U., Des Moines, 1996—2002; dir. jazz studies Mo. Western State Coll., St. Joseph, 2004—. Sec. Iowa Jazz Championships, 1994—2004; clinician Drake Honor Band Festival, Des Moines, 1997—2001, Iowa Music Educators Assn. State Conf., Ames, 1999, Nebr. State Bandmasters Assn. Summer Band Clinic, 2000, Mo. Bandmasters Assn. Clinic, 2003; guest condr. Cmty. Jazz Ctr./Drake Honor Jazz Band Festival, Des Moines, 1992, Des Moines All-Metro Jazz Ensemble, 1996, Mid-America All Star Jazz Ensemble, St. Joseph, Mo., 2002—03, Ctrl. Mo. Music Educators All-District Jazz Ensemble, Jefferson City, 2003. Musician: (recordings) Des Moines Big Band Featuring Bobby Shew, 1992, Des Moines Big Band In The Red, 1996, Des Moines Big Band, Being There featuring Walter White, 1998, Ashanti, Sin Fronteras, 2003, Des Moines Big Band, Let's Play One, 2003, Ashanti, Dyos Bo'otik, 2004. Named to Disneyland All-American Coll. Band, Disney Entertainment, 1981; recipient Outstanding Grad. Achievement award, Conservatory of Music U. Mo. Kansas City, 1986, Outstanding Jazz Educator award, The Nat. Band Assn., 1996. Mem.: Internat. Assn. Jazz Educaators (bd. dirs. Iowa chpt. 1996—2004). Home: 1920 Eugene Field Ave Saint Joseph MO 64505 Office: Mo Western State Coll 4525 Downs Dr Saint Joseph MO 64507 Office Phone: 816-271-4430.

LONG, CEDRIC WILLIAM, health facility administrator; b. Mpls., Mar. 4, 1937; s. Tracy Steven and Clarice Cecilia (Robertson) L. BA, UCLA, 1960, MA, 1962; PhD, Princeton U., 1966. Postdoctoral fellow U. Calif., Berkeley, 1966-68; instr. NYU Med. Sch., N.Y.C., 1968-70; lab. chief Flow Labs., Rockville, Md., 1970-76, Litton Industries, Frederick, Md., 1976-80; preclin. chief NIH, Nat. Cancer Inst., DCT, Bethesda, Md., 1980-86; gen. mgr. Nat. Cancer Inst.- Frederick Cancer R & D Ctr., 1986-97; spl. asst. to dir. Nat. Cancer Inst. - Divsn. Extramural Activities, 1997-2000, asst. dir., 2000—. Home: 2 Basildon Cir Rockville MD 20850-2724

LONG, CHARLES FRANKLIN, retired corporate communications executive; b. Norman, Okla., Jan. 19, 1938; s. James Franklin and Mary Katherine (Nemecek) L.; m. Joan Hampton, Sept. 16, 1961; children: Charles Franklin, David Hampton, Stephen Andrew. BA, U. Okla., 1961. Sports writer San Angelo (Tex.) Standard-Times, 1961-62; news reporter Norman Transcript, 1962-63; asso. editor Sooner mag., U. Okla., 1963-66; news editor Quill mag., Chgo., 1967-71, editor, 1971-80; sr. editor Cahners Pub. Co., Des Plaines, Ill., 1981-83; mgr. internal communications Beatrice Cos., Inc., Chgo., 1983-86, dir. communications, 1986-88; dir. corp. communications Tellabs, Inc., Lisle, Ill., 1989-99. Author: With Optimism for the Morrow, 1965. Bd. dirs. Wheaton (Ill.) Youth Outreach, 1988-94, Western DuPage Spl. Recreation Assn. Found., 1994-98; chmn. exec. com. Wheaton Grand Theatre, 1999-00, bd. dirs. 2005— Named to Okla. Journalism Hall of Fame, 1979, We. DuPage Spl. Recreation Assn. Found. Hall of Fame, 2003. Mem. Internat. Assn. Bus. Communicators (Spectra Excellence award Chgo.), Soc. Profl. Journalists-Sigma Delta Chi, Beta Theta Pi. United Methodist. Home: 1106 N Washington St Wheaton IL 60187-3860 Personal E-mail: clsooner@hotmail.com. *My parents, through gentle persuasion and by their own example, taught their sons to be curious and conscientious. I suppose it was those principles which eventually led me into a career in journalism and to come to realize that the supreme test of any good journalism is the measure of its public service— to serve the truth; to subscribe to ethical standards; to enlighten the public as to the nature and meaning of journalistic pursuits, especially in how those efforts support the American people's stake in their First Amendment to the Constitution.*

LONG, CHARLES THOMAS, lawyer, history professor; b. Denver, Dec. 19, 1942; s. Charles Joseph and Jessie Elizabeth (Squire) L.; m. Susan Rae Kircheis, Aug. 9, 1967; children: Brian Christopher, Lara Elizabeth, Kevin Charles. BA, Dartmouth Coll., 1965; JD cum laude, Harvard U., 1970; PhD in History, George Washington U., 2005. Bar: Calif. 1971, U.S. Dist. Ct. (cen. dist.) Calif. 1971, U.S. Ct. Appeals (9th cir.) 1975, D.C. 1980, U.S. Dist. Ct. D.C. 1981, U.S. Ct. Claims 1995. Assoc. Gibson, Dunn & Crutcher, Los Angeles, 1970-77, ptnr., 1977-79, Washington, 1979-83; dep. gen. counsel Fed. Home Loan Bank Bd., Washington, 1984-85; ptnr. Jones, Day, Reavis & Pogue, Washington, 1985-98; grad. tchg. asst. hist. dept. George Washington U., 1998—2002, tchg. fellow, asst. professorial lectr., 2003—. Bar: Calif. 1971, U.S. Dist. Ct. (ctrl. dist.) Calif. 1971, U.S. Ct. Appeals (9th cir.) 1975, D.C. 1980, U.S. Dist. Ct. 1981, U.S. Ct. Fed. Claims 1995. Contbr. articles to profl. jours. Mem. Chesapeake Bay Maritime Mus., Friends of the Nat. Maritime Mus., Greenwich, Eng.; pres. Leigh Mill Meadows Assn., Great Falls, Va., 1980. Served to lt. USNR, 1965-67. Mem. ABA, Calif. Bar Assn., D.C. Bar Assn., Coun. for Excellence in Govt., Women in Housing and Fin., Dartmouth Lawyers Assn., Herrington Harbour Sailing Assn. (sec.-treas. 1996), Soc. for Mil. History, N.Am. Conf. on Brit. Studies, Navy Records Soc. (London), U.S. Naval Inst., Am. Hist. Assn., Orgn. Am. Historians, Omohundro Inst. Early Am. History and Culture, Chesapeake Bay Maritime Mus., Friends of the Nat. Maritime Mus. (Greenwich, Eng.), Westwood Country Club (Vienna, Va.). Republican. Methodist. Avocations: sailing, photography, computers, naval history.

LONG, CLARENCE DICKINSON, III, lawyer; b. Princeton, N.J., Feb. 7, 1943; s. Clarence Dickinson and Susanna Eckings (Larter) L.; children: Clarence IV, Andrew, Amanda, Victoria, Stephen. BA, Johns Hopkins U., 1965; JD, U. Md., 1971; postgrad., Judge Adv. Gen.'s Sch., 1979-80. Bar: Ct. Appeals Md. 1972, U.S. Dist. Ct. D.C. 1972, U.S. Ct. Mil. Appeals 1975, U.S. Supreme Ct. 1976, N.C. 1978, U.S. Ct. Claims 1982, U.S. Ct. Appeals (fed. cir.) 1990. Asst. state's atty., Balt., 1973-74; trial atty., trial team chief Office Chief Trial Atty. Contract Appeals Divsn., U.S. Army, Washington, 1980-84; chief atty. Def. Supply Svc., Washington, 1984-87; trial team chief contract appeals divsn. U.S. Army, Washington, 1987-92; sr. atty. USAF, Washington, 1992—. Contbr. articles on Am. Civil War to various periodicals. Lt. col. U.S. Army. Decorated Silver Star, Soldier's medal, Bronze Star, Purple Heart (2), Meritorious Svc. medal (2), Army Commendation medal (2), Cross of Gallantry with gold star, Combat Infantryman's badge, Legion of Merit. Mem. D.C. Bar Assn., N.C. Bar Assn., BCA Bar Assn. (editor), Federalist Soc., Grant Monument Assn. (trustee). Home: 5328 Danbury Forest Springfield VA 22151-1702 Office Phone: 703-696-9085. E-mail: longc@pentagon.af.mil.

LONG, CLARENCE WILLIAM, accountant; b. Hartford City, Ind., Apr. 17, 1917; s. Adam and Alice (Weschke) L.; m. Mildred Bernhardt, Aug. 8, 1940; children: William Randall, David John, Bruce Allen. BS, Ind. U., 1939. With Ernst & Young, Indpls., 1939-78, ptnr., 1953-78, ret., 1978. Mem. econ. exec. com. Gov. Ind., 1968-73. Mem. nat. budget and consultation com.

United Way of Am., 1968-70; bd. dirs. United Fund Greater Indpls., 1966—, treas., 1968—; bd. dirs. Jr. Achievement, Ind., 1966-67; mem. exec. com. Nat. Jr. Achievement, 1966-67; mem. fin. com. Indpls. Hosp. Devel. Assn., 1966-67; trustee Ind. U., 1975-84; trustee Art Assn. Indpls., pres., 1977-86; mem. adv. com. to dir. NIH, 1986-92. Mem. Am. Inst. C.P.A.'s (council 1959-62), Ind. Assn. C.P.A.'s, Nat. Assn. Accountants, Ind. C. of C. (dir.), Delta Chi, Beta Alpha Psi, Alpha Kappa Psi. Clubs: Woodstock (Indpls.) (dir. 1958-60), Columbia (Indpls.) (dir. 1971-77, pres. 1976), Royal Poinciana Golf Club (Naples, Fla.). Republican. Lutheran. Home: 607 Somerset Dr W Indianapolis IN 46260-2924 Office: 1 Indiana Sq Indianapolis IN 46204-2004

LONG, DAVID MICHAEL, JR., biomedical researcher, cardiothoracic surgeon; b. Shamokin, Pa., Feb. 26, 1929; s. David Michael and Elva (Christ) L.; m. Donna Rae Long, Feb. 26, 1954; children: Kurt, Raymond, Carl, Grace, Carolyn, Ruth. BS magna cum laude, Muhlenberg Coll., Allentown, Pa., 1951; MS, Hahnemann U., Phila., 1954, MD, 1956; PhD, U. Minn., 1965. Lic. physician, Calif.; diplomate Nat. Bd. Med. Examiners, Am. Bd. Surgery, Am. Bd. Thoracic Surgery; cert. trauma provider, advanced life support; advanced cardiac life support. Intern Hahnemann U. Hosp., Phila., 1956-57; resident in surgery U. Minn., Mpls., 1957-65, fellow in surgery, 1957-61, 63-65, fellow in physiology, 1959-61; pres., chmn. bd. Long Labs., San Diego, 1984-85; chmn., dir. rsch. Fluoromed Pharm., Inc., San Diego, 1985-89; chmn., dir. sci. Alliance Pharm. Corp., La Jolla, Calif., 1989-91; pres., chmn. Abel Labs., Inc., Spring Valley, Calif., 1991—; CEO, chmn. Biofield Corp., Spring Valley, 2000—. Mem. faculty Hahnemann U., 1953-54, U. Calif., San Diego, 1973-92, U. Minn., 1959-61, 63-64, Naval Med. Sch., 1962, Chgo. Med. Sch., 1965-67, Cook County Grad. Sch. Medicine, 1965-73, U. Ill., 1967-73; cons. Chgo. State Tuberculosis Sanitarium, 1967-72; asst. dir. dept. surg. rsch. Hektoen Inst. for Med. Rsch. of Cook County Hosp., 1965-68, dir., 1968-73, assoc. attending staff, 1965-73; attending staff West Side VA Hosp., 1966-73, U. Ill. Hosp., 1967-73, Villa View Hosp., 1973-85, AMI Valley Med. Ctr., 1973-85, Grossman Dist. Hosp., 1973-85, Alvarado Cmty. Hosp., 1973-85, Sharp Meml. Hosp., 1973-84; head divsn. cardiovasc. and thoracic surgery U. Ill., 1967-73; cons. continuing med. edn. com. Grossmont Dist. Hosp., 1985—; mem. continuing med. edn. com. Sharp Healthcare Sys., 1994—; cons. Docent Corp., 1975-76; com. mem. consensus devel. com. Thrombolytic Therapy in Thrombosis, NIH/FDA, 1980; trustee N.Y. Acad. Art, N.Y.C., 1997—; bd. govs., chmn. Hahnemann U. Hosp./Tenet Healthcare, Phila., 1999—. Contbr. numerous articles and abstracts to profl. jours., chpts. to books; editl. bd. Current Surgery, 1967-89; co-editor Hematrix, 1982-85. Bd. dirs. Rsch. Assocs. of Point Loma Nazarene Coll., San Diego, chmn., 1984-85; trustee Muhlenberg Coll., Allentown, Pa., 1992-2002, chmn., 1994-2002; bd. dirs. Grossmont Hosp. Found., Grossmont Hosp., La Mesa, Calif., 1992—; co-chmn. Calif. divsn. of campaign of Muhlenberg Coll., 1992-93; chmn. Campaign of Grossmont Hosp. Found. for David and Donna Long Cancer Treatment Ctr. and Cardiac Diagnosis Ctr., 1992-94; co-chmn. Campaign for Health Ctr., Point Loma Nazarene Coll., San Diego, 1992-94. Rsch. fellow Heart Assn. Southeastern Pa., 1953-54, Student Senate of Hahnemann U., 1955; trainee Nat. Cancer Inst., 1957-58, Nat. Heart Inst., 1958-60, 63-64; spl. rsch. fellow Nat. Heart Inst., 1960-61; established investigator Minn. Heart Assn, 1964-65; Muhlenberg Coll. scholar, 1947-51, Hahnemann U. scholar, 1952-55, Luth. Brotherhood Leadership scholar, 1951 Fellow ACS, Am. Coll. Chest Physicians (sec. cardiovascular surgery com. 1976-78), Am. Coll. Cardiology; mem. AAAS, AMA, Am. Assn. Thoracic Surgery, Am. Assn. Anatomists, Internat. Cardiovascular Surgery Soc., Internat. Soc. for Artificial Cells and Immobilization Biotechnology, Am. Heart Assn., Am. Physiol. Soc., Am. Thoracic Soc., Assn. for Advancement of Med. Instrumentation, Cajal Soc. Neuroanatomy, Calif. Med. Assn., Internat. Soc. Surgery, Internat. Soc. Hemorheology (founding mem.), N.Y. Acad. Sci., San Diego County Med. Soc., Soc. Thoracic Surgeons, Soc. Univ. Surgeons, Warren H. Cole Soc., Western Thoracic Surg. Soc. Lutheran. Achievements include 17 U.S. patents and 11 fgn. patents. Office: Abel Laboratories Inc 2737 Via Orange Way Ste 108 Spring Valley CA 91978-1750

LONG, DAVID R., food products executive; BA in Agrl. Econs. with distinction, Cornell U., 1965; MS in Agrl. Econs., Ohio State U., 1970, PhD in Agrl. Econs., 1972. Ptnr. family farm, Albion, NY, 1965-68; policy planning analyst U.S. Dept. Agr., Washington, 1972-76; bus. analyst Ill. Grain Co., Bloomington, Ill., 1976-78; mgr., dir., to v.p., gen. mgr. Anheuser Busch Co., Inc., St. Louis, 1978-87; v.p. transp. Staley Continental, Inc., Decatur, Ill., 1987-89; pres., CEO Rice Growers Assn. Calif., Sacramento, 1989-93; pres. Calif. Pear Growers Assn., Sacramento, 1994-96; pres., CEO Snokist Growers, Inc., Yakima, Wash., 1996—2000; with Signature Fruit Co., Modesto, Calif., 2002. Bd. dirs. Rice Millers Assn., 1989-93; mem. Am. Agrl. Econs. Assn., 1968-93, U.S.D.A. Fed. Grain Inspection adv. com., 1986-91. Mem. Boy Scouts Am.; bd. trustees Sacramento Valley Open Space Conservancy, 1992—. Mem. Rotary, Phi Kappa Phi. Address: 18 W Mead Ave Yakima WA 98902-6026 Office: Signature Fruit Co LLC 2260 Tenaya Dr Modesto CA 95354

LONG, DAVID W., lawyer; b. Punxsutawney, Pa., Feb. 18, 1942; AB, Duke U., 1964; JD, U. N.C., 1967. Bar: N.C. 1967, U.S. Ct. Appeals (4th cir.) 1970, U.S. Tax. Ct. 1972, U.S. Supreme Ct. 1979. Asst. U.S. atty. U.S. Dist. Ct. (ea. dist.) N.C., 1969-71; mem., litig. practice Poyner & Spruill, Raleigh, NC. Mem. com. on local rules practice and procedure U.S. Dist. Ct. (ea. dist) N.C., mem. magistrate merit selection panel, 1985; mem. Fed. Bar Adv. Coun., 1988-93, chmn., 1991-92; mem. merit screening com. Fed. Pub. Defender, 1991; chmn. Ea. Dist. N.C. Adv. Group under Civil Justice Reform Act 1990. Fellow Internat. Soc. Barristers; assoc. Am. Bd. Trial Advocates; mem. ABA, Nat. Assn. Criminal Def. Lawyers, NC Bar Assn., NC Acad. Trial Lawyers, Wake County Bar Assn. (bd. dirs. 1979-80, 88-89), 10th Jud. Dist. Bar Assn. (pres. 1997). Office: Poyner & Spruill PO Box 10096 3600 Glenwood Ave Raleigh NC 27605-0096 Office Phone: 919-783-2808. Office Fax: 919-783-1075. Business E-Mail: dwlong@poynerspruill.com.

LONG, DEBORAH JOYCE, lawyer; b. Oct. 26, 1953; d. Thomas C. and Margaret N. (Falks) Long; m. William Daniel Sockwell, May 26, 1979; 1 child, Daniel Long Sockwell. BA, Auburn U., 1975; JD, U. Ala., 1980. Bar: Ala. 1980, U.S. Ct. Appeals (5th cir.) 1980, U.S. Ct. Appeals (11th cir.) 1981, U.S. Dist. Ct. (no. dist.) Ala. 1981. Law clk. U.S. Ct. Appeals for 5th Cir., Montgomery, Ala., 1980-81; assoc. Cabaniss, Johnston, Gardner, Dumas & O'Neal, Birmingham, Ala., 1981-84, Maynard, Cooper & Gale, P.C., Birmingham, 1984—94; mem.; sr. v.p., gen. counsel Protective Life Corp., Birmingham, Ala., 1994—. Recipient Cert. of Appreciation, Ala. Bar Assn., Montgomery. Mem. Farrah Soc., Ala. State Bar (bd. bar examiners 1987-92, bd. editors 1991-94), Birmingham Bar Assn. (bd. editors 1989-90), Assn. Life Ins. Counsel (pres. 2005) Office: Protective Life Corp 2801 Highway 280 S Birmingham AL 35223-2488

LONG, DONLIN MARTIN, surgeon, educator; b. Rolla, Mo., Apr. 14, 1934; s. Donlin M. and Davene E. (Johnson) L.; m. Harriett Page, June 13, 1959; children: Kimberley Page, Elisabeth Merchant, David Bradford. Student, Jefferson City Jr. Coll., 1951-52; MD, U. Mo., 1959; PhD in Neuroanatomy, U. Minn., 1964. Diplomate Am. Bd. Neurol. Surgery. Intern U. Minn. Hosps., Mpls., 1959-60; resident in neurol. surgery U. Minn. Health Sci. Ctr., Mpls., 1960-64, Peter Bent Brigham and Children's Hosp. Med. Center, Boston, 1965; practice medicine specializing in neurosurgery Balt., 1973—; asst. prof. dept. neurosurgery U. Minn. Hosps., 1967-70, neurosurgeon, 1967-73, assoc. prof., 1970-73; neurosurgeon-in-chief dept. neurosurgery Johns Hopkins Hosp., 1973-2000; prof. and chmn. dept. neurosurgery Johns Hopkins U., 1973—, mem. prin. staff Applied Physics Lab., 1976—. Cons. neurosurgery Mpls. VA Hosp., 1967-73, John F. Kennedy Inst., 1977, Balt. City Hosp., 1973— Contbr. numerous articles on neuropathology and surgery to profl. jours.; contbr. to book chpts. in field. Served with USPHS, 1965-67. Mem. Soc. Neurosci., Am. Assn. Neuropathologists, Soc. Neurol. Surgeons, AAAS, AMA, Balt. Neurol. Soc., Internat. Assn. Study of Pain, Internat. Soc. Pediatric Neurosurgery, William T. Peyton Soc., Congress Neurol. Surgeons, Johns Hopkins Med. and Surg. Assn., Electron Microscopy Soc. Am., Md. Neurosurg. Soc., Am. Acad. Neurosurgery, Am. Assn. Neurol. Surgery, Neurol. Soc. Am., Cajal Club, Sigma Xi, Omicron Delta Kappa, Alpha Omega Alpha, Phi Eta Sigma, Pi Mu Epsilon, Mystical 7. Home: 9 Blythewood Rd Baltimore MD 21210-2401 Office: Johns Hopkins Hosp Dept Neurosurgery 600 N Wolfe St Carnegie 466 Baltimore MD 21287-7709 Fax: 410-955-6407. Office Phone: 410-614-3536. Business E-Mail: dmlong@jhmi.edu.

LONG, EDWARD ARLO, management consultant, retired manufacturing executive; b. Detroit, May 5, 1927; s. Arlo Russell and Florence Viola (Magown) L.; m. Lorraine Ruth Nordin, May 21, 1947; children: Karin Louise Long Schelke, Marian Elizabeth Long Benton. BS, Wayne State U., 1956, MBA, 1964. Mfg. mgr. Ex-Cell-O Corp., Detroit, 1950-68; v.p. mktg. Colonial Broach & Machine, Warren, Mich., 1968-70; group v.p. Blue Bird Body Co., Fort Valley, Ga., 1970-75; pres. tool equipment div. Chgo. Pneumatic Tool, Franklin, Pa., 1975-77; group v.p. Joy Mfg. Co., Pine Bluff, Ark., 1977-87; v.p., gen. mgr. Wheeling Machine Products Co./Cooper Industries, Pine Bluff, 1987-94; ret., 1994. Dir. Security Nat. Bank, Wheeling, W.Va. Bd. dirs. Franklin Hosp., 1976-76, Oglebay Inst., Wheeling, 1981-83, Ohio Valley Hosp. Trust, Wheeling, 1982-83, Ark. Ind. Colls., 1984, Jefferson County Indsl. Found., 1985; pres. Pine Bluff Fifty for the Future, 1985, Pine Bluff Symphony Orch., 1987, Leadership Pine Bluff, 1990; apptd. zoning commr., Pine Bluff, 1995. Served with USCG, 1945-46. Scholar Nat. Office Mgmt. Assn., 1952, Beta Gamma, Detroit, 1953 Mem. AIME, Am. Petroleum Inst., Duquesne (Pitts.) Club, Rotary, Alpha Kappa Psi, Psi Chi, Sigma Iota Epsilon. Democrat. Roman Catholic. Home and Office: 7409 S Laurel St Pine Bluff AR 71603-8121 Fax: 870-534-3321. E-mail: longtrapper2@sbcglobal.net.

LONG, EDWIN TUTT, surgeon; b. St. Louis, July 23, 1925; s. Forrest Edwin and Hazel (Tutt) L.; m. Mary M. Hull, Apr. 16, 1955; children: Jennifer Ann, Laura Ann, Peter Edwin. AB, Columbia U., 1944, MD, 1947. Diplomate Am. Bd. Surgery, Am. Bd. Thoracic Surgery. Rotating intern Meth. Hosp., Bklyn., 1947—48; surg. intern U. Chgo. Clinics, 1948-49, resident in gen. surgery, 1952-55, resident in thoracic surgery, 1955-57; asst. prof. surgery U. Chgo., 1957-59; thoracic and cardiovasc. surgeon Watson Clinic, Lakeland, Fla., 1960-69, chief surgery dept., 1969; dir. Watson Clinic Rsch. Found., 1965—69; assoc. prof. surgery U. Pa., Phila., 1970-73; attending thoracic and cardiovasc. surgeon Allegheny Cardiovasc. Surg. Assocs., Pitts., 1973-88; exec. v.p. Mailings Clearing House and Roxbury Press, Inc., 1988-90, pres., 1990-96, chmn. bd. dirs., 1991—. Disting. lectr., curriculum advisor Healthcare Leadership Program, Helzberg Sch. Mgmt., Rockhurst U., 2001—; nat. adv. panel Ctr. for Practical Health Reform, 2003—, regional co-chair Kansas City chpt., 2003—. Capt. USAF, 1950—52. Pressure Vectorography rsch. grantee Alfred P. Sloan Found., 1963; Nelson-Atkins Mus. fellow, 1997—. Mem. AMA, ACS, Am. Coll. Cardiology, Soc. for Vascular Surgery, Nat. Assn. Pacing and Electrophysiology (charter), Allegheny Vascular Soc. (pres. 1987), Ea. Vascular Soc. (founding mem.), Soc. Thoracic Surgery (founding mem.), Ctr. for Practical Bioethics, Kansas City Concensus, Woodside Club, Rotary, Sigma Xi, Beta Theta Pi. Achievements include patents for gas sterilizer. Home: 4550 Warwick Blvd # 1204 Kansas City MO 64111-7725 Office: 4550 Warwick Blvd # 1209 Kansas City MO 64111 also: Roxbury Press Inc 601 E Marshall St Sweet Springs MO 65351-0295 Office Phone: 816-753-0089. E-mail: elongmd@kc.rr.com.

LONG, ELAINE, writer, editor; b. Sterling, Colo., Jan. 12, 1935; d. Guy William and Evelyn Irene (Simpson) Mullenax; m. Thomas John O'Rourke, Aug. 17, 1963 (dec. Feb. 1965); 1 child, Mary Kendall; m. Arthur Warren Long, Oct. 4, 1969 (dec. Jan., 2003). BA, U. Colo., 1955. Tchr. Portland (Oreg.) Pub. Schs., 1955-57, Denver Pub. Schs., 1957-58, U.S. Civil Svc., Upper Heyford, Eng., 1958-59; copywriter KBOL Radio, Boulder, Colo., 1959-61; ranch hand Guy Mullenax, Gillette, Wyo., 1961-62; copy and feature writer, traffic mgr. KKAR Radio, Pomona, Calif., 1962-63; freelance writer Denver, 1966—. Editor Boulder, Buena Vista, Colo., 1974—. Author: Jenny's Mountain, 1987, Bittersweet Country, 1991; cons. editor: Separate Lives: The Story of Mary Rippon, 1999, Dancing with Principle: Hanya Holm in Colorado, 1941-1983, 2001, A Texas Tragedy: Orphaned by Bootleggers, 2001, Behind the Badge: 125 Years of the Boulder Police Department, 2003, Out of the Shadows, 2004, author short stories; contbr. articles to profl. jours. Mem. Western Writers Am. (Spur awards chmn. 1993, 2005, Svc. award 1994-95, 2005, bd. dirs. 1994-95), Aircraft Owners and Pilots Assn., Women Writing the West, Author's Guild NY, Colo. Authors' League (bd. dirs. 1987-88). Avocations: flying, songwriting, singing, hiking, reading. E-mail: elainelong@chaffee.net.

LONG, EUGENE THOMAS, III, philosophy educator, administrator; b. Richmond, Va., Mar. 16, 1935; s. Eugene Thomas and Emily Joyce (Barker) L.; m. Carolyn Macleod, June 25, 1960; children: Scott, Kathryn. BA, Randolph-Macon Coll., 1957; BD, Duke U., 1960; PhD, U. Glasgow, Scotland, 1964. Asst. prof. philosophy Randolph-Macon Coll., 1964-67, assoc. prof., 1967-70, U. S.C., Columbia, 1970-73, prof., 1973—2002, prof. emeritus, 2002—, chmn. dept., 1972-87. Author: Jaspers and Bultmann, 1968, Existence, Being and God, 1985, Twentieth Century Western Philosophy of Religion, 1900-2000, 2000; contbr., editor: God, Secularization & History, 1974, Experience, Reason and God, 1980, Prospects for Natural Theology, 1992, God, Reason and Religions, 1995; editor: Handbook of Contemporary Philosophy of Religion, 1995—; editor-in-chief Internat. Jour. for Philosophy of Religion, 1990—; assoc. editor Internat. Jour. Philosophy of Religion, 1975-90, So. Jour. Philosophy, 1978-83; contbr., co-editor: God and Temporality, 1984, Being and Truth, 1986; mem. editl. bd. The Works of William James, 1974-88, Correspondence of William James, 1988—; editor, contbr. Issues in Contemporary Philosophy of Religion, 2001; contbr. articles to profl. jours. Mem. S.C. Com. for Humanities, 1980-85; mem. adv. bd. The Franklin J. Matchette Found., 1992—. Recipient Rsch. award NEH, 1968, Duke U./U. N.C. Coop. Program in Humanities, 1968-69. Mem. Soc. Philosophy in Religion (pres. 1980-81), Metaphys. Soc. Am. (sec. treas. 1977-81, exec. coun. 1991-94, v.p./pres.-elect 1996-97, pres. 1997-98), So. Soc. Philosophy and Psychology (exec. coun. 1976-79), Am. Philos. Assn. (sec. treas. eastern divsn. 1985-94). Office: U SC Dept Philosophy Columbia SC 29208-0001 Office Phone: 803-777-4166. Business E-Mail: longq@sc.edu.

LONG, FRANCIS MARK, retired electrical engineer; b. Iowa City, Nov. 10, 1929; s. Frank B. and Hilda B. (Rohret) L.; m. Mary Ann Coyne, June 8, 1964 (dec. Apr. 1994); children: Ann Brett, Mary Bronwyn, Thomas Martin Carver, Caitlin Frances. BS, U. Iowa, 1953, MS, 1956; PhD, Iowa State U., 1961. With Collins Radio Co., Cedar Rapids, Iowa, summers 1952, 55, Douglas Aircraft Co., Santa Monica, Calif., summer 1953, USNAMTC, Point Mugu, Calif., summer 1956, Good All Electric Co., Ogallala, Nebr., summer 1957, Lawrence Radiation Lab., Livermore, Calif., summer 1967, Globe Union Co., Milw., summer 1975, Naval Rsch Lab., Washington, 1988, 89, 91; instr. U. Wyo., Laramie, 1956-58, prof. elec. engring., 1960-95, prof. emeritus, 1995—, head elec. engring. dept., 1977-87; instr. Iowa State U., 1958-60. Dir. Wyo. Biotelemetry, Inc., Rocky Mountain Bioengring. Symposium; pres. Alliance for Engring. in Medicine and Biology, 1983, 84, mem. exec. com., 1979-89; conf. chmn., procs. editor 1st, 2d, 3d and 5th Internat. Conf. on Wildlife Biotelemetry; adj. prof. Univ. Denver, 1996—, Colo. Tech. Univ., 1997—, U. Colo., Denver, 1999—. Author: (with E.M. Lonsdale) Introductory Electrical Concepts, 1967, rev. edit., 1977; co-author: (with R.G. Jacquot) Introduction to Engineering Systems, 1988. Trustee St. Paul's Newman Center Parish, 1969-72; mem. City of Laramie Planning Commn., 1970-72. Served CE U.S. Army, 1953—55. Decorated citation Republic of Korea Army C.E.; recipient G.D. Humphrey Outstanding Faculty award U. Wyo., 1973, Western Electric Fund award for engring. teaching, 1978 Mem. IEEE (life, edn. activities com. chmn. Denver sect. 1997), Am. Soc. Engring. Edn. (v.p., dir., 1st Outstanding Biomed. Engring. Educator award biomed. engring. divsn. 1981, chmn. Elec. Engring. divsn. 1986-87), Internat. Soc. for Hybrid Microelectronics (v.p. Rocky Mountain chpt. 1996-97, pres. 1998), Sigma Xi. Republican. Home: 1888 S Jackson St Apt 701 Denver CO 80210-3918 E-mail: flong30989@aol.com.

LONG, FRANK WESLEY, JR., chemist; b. Springfield, Ill., Aug. 26, 1925; s. Frank Wesley and Elizabeth Margaret (Franke) L.; m. Thelma Elizabeth Keil Long, Nov. 17, 1951; children: Stephen Wesley, William Douglas, Valerie Elizabeth Long Feiss. BS, U. Ill., 1946; PhD in Organic Chemistry, State U. Iowa, 1950. Grad. asst. State U. Iowa, Iowa City, 1946-50; lab. chemist 3M Co., Mpls., summer 1948, Ethyl Corp., Ferndale, Mich., summer 1949, GAF Corp., Easton, Pa., 1950-52; project mgr. textile dyeing and finishing U.S. Army Quartermaster, Phila., 1952-53; sec. mgr. sales devel. Hooker Electrochem. Co., Niagara Falls, N.Y., 1953-64; dir. product devel. Princeton (N.J.) Chem. Rsch. Inc., 1964-67; product dir. ARCO Chem. Co. (subsidiary of Atlantic Richfield Co.), Phila., 1967-83; owner Riverside Assocs., Princeton, 1983—; dir. bus. devel. Princeton Advanced Tech., Princeton, 1991—. Expert witness in field. Contbr. chpts. to books: Chemicals in Plastics, 1967, U.S. Petrochemical Industry, 1974, Fundamentals of the U.S. Petroleum Industry, 1980. Pres. elem. sch. PTA, Niagara Falls, 1963. Mem. Comml. Devel. Assn. (bd. dirs. 1976-78, Golden C award 1991), Am. Chem. Soc. (bd. dirs. chem. mktg. divsn. 1974-76), Am. Assn. Textile Chemists and Colorists, Chem. Cons. Network, John Priestley Soc. of Chem. Heritage Found., Princeton Ind. Cons., Chemist's Club, Old Guard of Princeton. Achievements include development of flame retardant chemicals and plastics, heat resistant plastics, petrochemicals. Home and Office: Riverside Assocs 292 Riverside Dr Princeton NJ 08540-5432

LONG, GREGORY ALAN, lawyer; b. San Francisco, Aug. 28, 1948; s. William F. and Ellen L. (Webber) L.; m. Jane H. Barrett, Sept. 30, 1983; children: Matthew, Brian, Michael, Gregory. BA magna cum laude, Claremont Men's Coll., Calif., 1970; JD cum laude, Harvard U., 1973. Bar: Calif. 1973, U.S. Dist. Ct. (ctrl. dist.) Calif. 1973, U.S. Ct. Appeals (9th cir.) 1976, U.S. Supreme Ct. 1977, U.S. Ct. Appeals (fed. cir.) 1984. Assoc. Overton, Lyman & Prince, L.A., 1973-78, ptnr., 1978-87, Sheppard, Mullin, Richter & Hampton, L.A., 1987—. Arbitrator L.A. Superior Ct. Fellow Am. Bar Found.; mem. ABA (young lawyers divsn. exec. coun. 1974-88, chmn. 1984-85, ho. of dels. 1983-89, exec. coun. litigation sect. 1981-83), Calif. Bar Assn. (del. 1976-82, 87-88), L.A. County Bar Assn. (exec. com. 1979-82, trustee 1979-82, barristers sect. exec. coun. 1976-82, pres. 1981-82, exec. coun. trial lawyers sect. 1984-88, chair amicus briefs com. 1989-92). Office: Sheppard Mullin Richter & Hampton 333 S Hope St Los Angeles CA 90071-1406 Office Phone: 213-617-5443. Business E-Mail: glong@smrh.com.

LONG, HILDA EDELINA, nursing administrator; b. Burlington, Wash., Feb. 21, 1967; d. Maria Ramona Villalobos; children: Nathan Ryan, Christopher Steven, Lauren Elizabeth. Grad. in Nursing, Tex. State Tech. Inst., 1991. Edn. resource specialist III, Meml. Hermann NW, Houston, 1992—97; performance improvement coord. Meml. Hermann Rehab. Hosp., Houston, 1997—2000, Meml. Hermann Continuing Care Corp., Houston, 2000—02; quality mgmt. dir. Triumph Hosp. North Houston, 2002—. Bd. treas. Wainwright Elem. PTA, Houston, 2003—04. Home: 5303 Saxon Dr Houston TX 77092 Office: Triumph Hosp N Houston 7407 N Freeway Houston TX 77076 Office Phone: 832-200-6035. Office Fax: 832-200-5713. Personal E-mail: speciallongh@aol.com. Business E-Mail: hlong@triumph-healthcare.com.

LONG, HOWARD CHARLES, retired physics professor; b. Seizholtzville, Pa., Dec. 12, 1918; s. Howard William and Isabella Geneva (Reese) L.; m. Frances Monroe Hoke, Apr. 16, 1945; children— Howard Charles, David William, Carol Joyce. BA, Northwestern U., 1941, postgrad., 1941-42; PhD, Ohio State U., 1948. Asst. prof. physics Washington and Jefferson Coll., 1948-51; head Electromagnetism Influence Fields sec., U.S. Naval Ordnance Lab., 1951-52; assoc. prof., dept. chmn. physics Am. U., 1952-53; prof. physics, chmn. dept. Gettysburg Coll., 1953-59; prof. physics Dickinson Coll., 1959-81, chmn. dept., 1963-75, Joseph Priestley Chair of Natural Philosophy, 1973, prof. emeritus, 1981—. Cons. physicist Naval Ordnance Lab., White Oak, Md., 1952-73, McCoy Electronics Co., Mt. Holly Springs, Pa., 1958-59 Contbr. articles to ednl. jours. Active Boy Scouts Am. Served with USNR, 1944-45. Mem. Am. Assn. Physics Tchrs. (sec.-treas. Central Pa. sect. 1958-59, v.p. 1959-60, pres. 1960-61), A.A.U.P. (sec.-treas. Dickinson chpt. 1963-64, v.p. 1964-65, pres. 1965-66), A.A.A.S., Am. Phys. Soc., Cumberland Conservancy. Methodist (chmn. adminstrn. bd. 1961-62, chmn. ofcl. bd. 1957-59, mem. conf. bd. edn. 1971-73). Home: 240 Belvedere St Carlisle PA 17013-3501 Office: Dickinson Coll Carlisle PA 17013

LONG, JEANINE HUNDLEY, retired state legislator; b. Provo, Utah, Sept. 21, 1928; d. Ralph Conrad and Hazel Laurine (Snow) Hundley; m. McKay W. Christensen, Oct. 28, 1949 (div. 1967); children: Cathy Schuyler, Julie Schulleri, Kelly M. Christensen, C. Brett Christensen, Harold A. Christensen; m. Kenneth D. Long, Sept. 6, 1968. AA, Shoreline C.C., Seattle, 1975; BA in Psychology, U. Wash., 1977. Mem. Wash. Ho. of Reps., 1983-87, 93-94, mem. Inst. Pub. Policy; mem. Wash. Senate, Dist. 44, Olympia, 1995—2003. Ranking mem. Human Svcs. and Corr. com. Wash. Senate, 1995-96, 99-2002, chair, 1997-98; vice-chair Rep. Caucus, 1997-98; mem. Braam panel to monitor Dept. Social and Health Svcs., 2005—. Mayor protem, mem. city coun. City of Brier, Wash., 1977-80. Republican. Office: PO Box 40482 Olympia WA 98504-0482 E-mail: long_je@leg.wa.gov.

LONG, JOHN BROADDUS, JR., economist, educator; b. Bklyn., Feb. 28, 1944; s. John Broaddus and Katharine Lumpkin (Wicker) L.; m. Carol Elaine Stephens, Aug. 6, 1966; children: Jennifer Tipton, Owen Rosser, John McCauley BA, Rice U., 1966; PhD, Carnegie-Mellon U., 1971. Asst. prof. U. Rochester, N.Y., 1969-74, assoc. prof., 1974-84, prof., 1984—. Editor Jour. Fin. Econs., 1982-96, adv. editor, 1996-98; contbr. articles to profl. jours. Office: U Rochester William E Simon Grad Sch Bus Adminstrn Wilson Blvd Rochester NY 14627 Business E-Mail: long@simon.rochester.edu.

LONG, JOHN D., historian, museum director; b. Roanoke, Va., Oct. 5, 1966; s. Stanley W. and Helen Frankenfield Long; m. Candace Kile Long, June 28, 2003; children: Caitlynne, Sarah, John. BA, Roanoke Coll., 1989; MA, U. Va., 1991. Sr. lectr. Roanoke Coll., Salem, Va., 1993—. Adj. prof. Radford (Va.) U., 0194—1998; curator Salem Mus. and Hist. Soc., 1998—2002, dir., 2002—. Author: South of Main: A History of the Water Street Community of Salem, Va., 2000. Pastoral asst. New Testament Bapt. Ch., Va., 1993—; asst. scoutmaster Boy Scouts Am., Roanoke, 1999—. Baptist. Office: Salem Mus and Hist Soc 801 E Main St Salem VA 24153 Business E-Mail: long@salemmuseum.org.

LONG, JOHN EDD, military officer, researcher, management consultant; b. Ardmore, Okla. s. Edd and Lola Williams Long; m. Armanda Jane Beavers, Dec. 8, 1956; children: John Edd III, Pamela Ann. BA in History, U. Okla., 1956; MA in Pub. Adminstrn., Shippensburg (Pa.) U., 1974. Commd. lt. U.S. Army, 1956, advanced through grades to maj. gen., ret., 1990; pres. Fiesta Foods, Dallas, 1990—91, Pace-Weil, Inc., Irving, Tex., 1991—92; ptnr. L&R Consulting, Inc., Ft. Worth, 1992—. Mem.: Ft. Worth (Tex.) Symphony League, Ft. Worth (Tex.) Breakfast Club. Avocations: fly fishing, stamp collecting/philately. Home: 3315 Bellaire Park Ct Fort Worth TX 76109 Office: L&R Consulting Inc 4802 Hwy 377 South Fort Worth TX 76116

LONG, JOHN PAUL, pharmacologist, educator; b. Albia, Iowa, Oct. 4, 1926; s. John Edward and Bessie May L.; m. Marilyn Joy Stookesberry, June 11, 1950; children: Jeff, John, Jane. BS, U. Iowa, 1950, MS, 1952, PhD, 1954. Research scientist Sterling Winthrop Co., Albany, N.Y., 1954-56; asst. prof. U. Iowa, Iowa City, 1956-58, asso. prof., 1958-63, prof. pharmacology, 1963—, head dept., 1970-83. Author 315 research publs. in field. Served with U.S. Army, 1945-46. Recipient Abel award Am. Pharm. Assn., 1958; Ebert award Pharmacology Soc., 1962 Mem. Am. Soc. Pharm. Exptl. Therapy, Soc. Exptl. Biol. Medicine. Republican. Home: 1817 Kathlin Dr Iowa City IA 52246-4617 Office: U Iowa Coll Medicine Dept Pharmacology Iowa City IA 52242

LONG, KAREN DRAUT, librarian; b. Middletown, Ohio, Aug. 25, 1939; d. Arthur William and Estelle (Lowe) Draut; m. Kenneth Robert Long, Feb. 2, 1962; children: Kristin E., Keith T. BA, Ohio Wesleyan U., 1961; MA, U. Ill., 1962; MLS, U. Pitts., 1988. Dir. Childhood League Nursery Sch., Columbus, Ohio, 1963; asst. dean of women Ohio Wesleyan U., Delaware, Ohio, 1964, lectr. in politics and govt., 1965; tchr. Oxford (Ohio) City Schs., 1967, Highline Pub. Schs., Washington, 1967-70; freelance calligrapher Pitts., 1973-87; head fgn. lit. Cleve. Pub. Libr., 1990—; owner Quilts by Karen. Mem. Play Readers, Cleve., 1988; libr. St. Paul's Episcopal Ch., Wash. Mem. ALA, Ohio Libr. Coun. (action coun. 1992—), Pub. Libr. Assn., Mortar Bd. Soc. Phi Beta Kappa, Beta Phi Mu. Avocations: calligraphy, needlecrafts. Home: 100 Lands End Ln Port Townsend WA 98368-9221

LONG, KATHY JEAN, special education educator; b. Barberton, Ohio, Sept. 2, 1951; d. John Henry and Mary (Momchilov) Schake; m. Gary William Long, June 19, 1976; children: Kristin Michelle, Sean Gary, Jennifer Kathryn. BA in French, U. Akron, 1974, BA in Secondary Edn., 1990, Certification in Spl. Edn., 1999. Cert. French, spl. edn. tchr. Ohio. Bookstore mgr. Waldenbooks, Akron, Ohio, 1976—77; spl. edn. tutor, intervention specialist Green (Ohio) Local Schs., 1995—99, spl. edn. tchr., 1999—, French enrichment instr., 2003—04. Author: (novel) Oklahoma's Gold, 2004, A Pleasant View, 2005. Recipient Walter Horn Achievement award, North Ea. Ohio Spl. Edn. Regional Resource Ctr., 2005. Mem.: NEA, Green Edn. Assn., North Ea. Ohio Edn. Assn. Avocations: playing guitar, writing song lyrics, reading, tennis. Office: Green HS PO Box 218 Green OH 44232 Office Phone: 330-896-7575.

LONG, KENNETH MAYNARD, chemistry educator; b. Nappanee, Ind., July 10, 1932; s. G. Maurice and Mabel A. (Bechtel) L.; m. Nancy Y. Long, Aug. 27, 1952; children: Gregory, Steven, Jeffrey, Kristen, Kevin. BS, Goshen Coll., 1954; MAT, Mich. State U., 1960; PhD, Ohio State U., 1967. Tchr. Bethel Springs Sch., Culp, Ark., 1954-56, Lakeshore H.S., Stevensville, Mich., 1956-61; rsch. asst. Whirlpool Corp., St. Joseph, Mich., 1961; instr. Westminster Coll., New Wilmington, Pa., 1962-65, asst. prof., 1967-70, assoc. prof., 1970-79, prof., 1979—2002, chair chemistry, 1983-99, asst. dean, 1971-75, prof. emeritus. Bd. overseers Goshen (Ind.) Coll., 1972-81; vis. scholar Northeastern U., Shenyang, China, 1988-89. Contbr. articles to profl. jours. Mem. Am. Chem. Soc., Nat. Speleological Soc., Field Conf. Pa. Geologists, Sigma Xi. Mennonite. Avocations: geology, caving, hiking, gardening. Office: Dept Chemistry Westminster Coll New Wilmington PA 16172-0001 E-mail: longkm@westminster.edu.

LONG, KIM MARTIN, language and literature educator; b. Denton, Tex., Oct. 23, 1955; d. William Matheson Martin and Wando Jo (Foster) Sparks; m. Mark Dale Mayo, Aug. 13, 1977 (div. June 1987); children: Scott, Bryan, Kyle; m. David Harrison Long, Feb. 14, 1988. BA in English, U. North Tex., Denton, 1978, MA in English, 1986, PhD in English, 1993. Cert. secondary English and history tchr. Tchr. Irving (Tex.) Ind. Sch. Dist., 1978-90; instr. North Lake Coll., Irving, 1992-93; teaching fellow U. North Tex., Denton, 1990-93; instr. Tex. Woman's U., Denton, 1991-94, U. Tex.-Dallas, Richardson, 1992-94; tchr. Nimitz H.S. Irving Ind. Sch. Dist., 1993—95; assoc. prof. English Shippensburg (Pa.) U., 1995—. Author: American Eve, 1993. Mem. MLA, Am. Lit. Assn., Coll. English Assn., Melville Soc., Poe Soc., Nat. Coun. Tchrs. English, Multi-Ethnic Lits. of U.S. (treas.) Democrat. Home: 217 E King St Shippensburg PA 17257-1426 Office: 1871 Old MainDr Shippensburg PA 17257 Office Phone: 717-477-1215. Business E-Mail: kmlong@ship.edu.

LONG, LARRY, state attorney general; b. Martin, S.D. m. Jan Long; 2 children. Grad., S.D. State U., 1969; JD, U. S.D., 1972. Pvt. practice, Martin, 1972—73; state's atty. Bennett County, 1973—90; chief dep. atty. gen. SD, 1991—2002; atty. gen. State of SD, 2003—. With U.S. Army. Republican. Office: 500 E Capitol Pierre SD 57501-5070

LONG, LELAND TIMOTHY, geophysics educator, seismologist; b. Auburn, N.Y., Sept. 6, 1940; s. Walter K. and Carmalita Rose Long; m. Sarah Alice Blackard, Mar. 1970; children: Sarah Alice, Katherine Rose, Amy Virginia. BS in Geology, U. Rochester, 1962; MS in Geophysics, N.Mex. Inst. Mining and Tech., 1964; PhD in Geophysics, Oreg. State U., 1968. Registered profl. geologist, Ga. From asst. to assoc. prof. Sch. Earth and Atmosphere Scis. Ga. Inst. Tech., Atlanta, 1968-81, prof., 1981. Cons. in seismology, near-surface seismic imaging, seismic road vibrations, blast vibrations and gravity data analysis. Contbr. articles to profl. jours. Office: Ga Inst Tech Earth And Atmospheric Scis Atlanta GA 30332-0340 Business E-Mail: tim.long@eas.gatech.edu.

LONG, LINDA ANN, lawyer; b. Durham, N.C., Feb. 8, 1952; d. Grover Cleveland and Ellen (Parnell) L. BA, U. Del., 1974; JD, Widener U., 1979. Bar: D.C. 1989. Lobbyist Legis. Svcs., Inc., Dover, Del., 1977-79; campaign staff Connally for Pres., Arlington, Va., 1979-80; exec. dir. Reagan-Bush Com. Del., Wilmington, 1980; asst. for legis. affairs Gov. Pierre S. duPont IV, Dover, 1981; regional rep. pub. affairs Gulf Oil Corp., Phila., 1981-83, dir. GULFPAC, area dir. pub. affairs Pitts., 1983-85; pres. Long Cons. Inc., Washington, 1985-89; dir. press & pub. liaison with NASA for Christa McAuliffe Challenger 51-L Mission, Wash., 1985-86, Johnson Space Ctr., Houston, Kennedy Space Ctr., Cape Canaveral, Fla.; atty. Montgomery, McCracken, Walker & Rhoads, Washington and Houston, 1989-94, Blank, Rome, Comisky & McCauley, Washington, 1994-96; pvt. practice Wilmington, 1996—. State and fed. legislation regulatory affairs, and non profit advisor to state senate campaigns, Del., 1998; adv. to Del. gubernatorial candidate, 1998—; counsel Pa. House Legis. Redistricting, 1991; gen. counsel Women Execs. in State Govt., 1990-95; counsel Nat. Policy Forum, 1993-96; lectr. Internat. Rep. Inst., election law for Macedonia Parliamentary Party Mem., 1992; del. Internat. Observer Mission-Romania Parliamentary and Presdl. Elections, 1992; mem. comml. space transp. adv. com. U.S. Dept. Transp., 1988-90; bd. dirs., exec. com. Air and Space Heritage Coun., 1987—; loaned exec. pub. affairs dept. NASA, 1984-85; sr. adv. to conv. mgr. Rep. Conv., 1992; lectr. press rels. to state ofcls. Mem. Rep. Bus. Coun. Del., 1982-83; cons., asst. to chmn. Rep. Nat. Com., 1986-89, dep. polit. counsel, 1987-89, dep. to gen. counsel, 1992-96, life mem.; mem. women's adv. bd. Internat. Rep. Inst.; mem. Gov.'s Commn. Status of Women Spkrs. Bur., 1981-83; mem. Wright Meml. Dinner Com., 1985; dir. contract negotiations-ops. 1989 Am. Bicentennial Presdl. Inaugural Com.; mem. Del. Lawyers for George W. Bush for Pres. Mem. Women in Govt. Rels., Am. Petroleum Inst. (com. pub. rels. 1981-84), Rep. Nat. Lawyers Assn. (bd. dirs. 1993—), U.S. Dept. Transp. Comml. Space Transp. (adv. com. 1988-90), Charter 100, Capitol Hill Club. Office: 32 Harlech Dr Greenville DE 19807 E-mail: lalong1@aol.com.

LONG, MADELEINE J., mathematics and science educator; b. N.Y.C. d. Harry L. and Irma (Silverman) L. BA, Queens Coll., 1960; M.Ed., Harvard U., 1963; Ed.D., Columbia U., 1967. Tchr. Westbury (N.Y.) Sch. System, 1960-61; teaching fellow Harvard U., 1962-63; prof. edn. L.I. U., asst. to dean, 1967-69, chmn. dept., 1969-76, dir. div. edn., dir. grad. programs at Westchester br. campus, 1977-83, dir. Inst. Advancement Math. and Sci., 1983-91; program officer (on leave from L.I. U.) NSF, Washington, 1991-96; v.p. The Implementation Group, 1996-99; program dir. math., sci., tech. and extended day programs AAAS, 1999—. Vis. scientist, spl. asst. comprehensive design planning NSF, 1992-93, sr. program officer Urban Systemic Initiative, 1993-96, reader, 1973, 77, 79, 85, 88, 90, career access panelist and chair, 1988; dir. summer tng. programs N.Y.C. Bd. Edn., 1978, 79, 81; reader Fund for Improvement Postsecondary Edn., 1984, 85, 87, N.J. Bd. Higher Edn., Minority Instns. Sci. Improvement Program; cons. to various univs. and sch. sys.; lectr. in field; apptd. coun. on excellence and equity in math. and sci. edn. N.Y. State, 1986-91; v.p. The Implementation Group, 1996-99; mem. adv. bd. L.A. Collaborative Tchr. Edn., 1997—, Tchrs. Am. Math. & Sci. Programs, 1996—. Mem. editorial bd. Jour. Coll. Sci. Teaching, 1986-89; contbr. articles to profl. jours. Mem. edn. subcom. Mayor's Commn. on Sci. and Tech., 1989-91. Columbia U. fellow, 1963-64, grantee NSF, 1972, 78, 79, 80, 81, 84-87, 87-91, 91-94, Career Edn., 1975, Fund for Improvement Postsecondary Edn., 1983-87, Title II Edn. for Econ. Security Act N.Y. State. Fellow Philosophy of Edn. Soc.; mem. AAAS (chair sect. Q, Sci. Edn., chmn. edn. section, program dir. 1999—), Assn. Supervision and Curriculum Devel., N.Y. Acad. Sci., Nat. Sci. Tchrs. Assn., Nat. Coun. Tchrs. Math., Am. Ednl. Rsch. Assn., Kappa Delta Pi. Office: NSF 4201 Wilson Blvd Arlington VA 22230-0001

LONG, MAXINE MASTER, lawyer; b. Pensacola, Fla., Oct. 20, 1943; d. Maxwell L. and Claudine E. (Smith) M.; m. Anthony Byrd Long, Aug. 27, 1966; children: Deborah E., David M. AB, Bryn Mawr Coll., 1965; MS, Georgetown U., 1971; JD, U. Miami, 1979. Bar: Fla. 1979, U.S. Ct. Appeals (5th cir.) 1980, U.S. Dist. Ct. (so. dist.) Fla. 1980, U.S. Ct. Appeals (11th cir.) 1981, U.S. Dist. Ct. (mid. and no. dists.) Fla. 1987. Law clk. to U.S. dist. judge U.S. Dist. Ct. (so. dist.) Fla., Miami, 1979-80; assoc. Shutts & Bowen, Miami, 1980-90, of counsel, 1990-92, ptnr., 1992—. Mem. Fla. Bar Assn. (cert. bus. litigator, mem. bus. litigation cert. com. 1995-99, vice chair, 1996-97, past chair bus. litigation com., chair bus. law sect. 2004-2005) Dade County Bar Assn. (mem. fed. cts. com., recipient pro bono award/Vol. Lawyers for the Arts 1989). Office: Shutts & Bowen 201 S Biscayne Blvd Ste 1500 Miami FL 33131-4308 Office Phone: 305-358-6300. Business E-Mail: mlong@shutts-law.com.

LONG, MICHAEL ALAN, musician, writer; b. Chgo., Oct. 14, 1945; s. Irving Robert and Libby (Zasser) L.; m. Isola Charlayne Jones, Aug. 3, 1989 (div. Oct. 1995). BA in English, Ariz. State U., 1967; MusM, Phila. Inst. Music, Kharkov Ukraine, 1993; Mus D, Philharm. State Inst. Music, Kharkov, Ukraine, 1997. Artist in residence Ariz. State U., Tempe, 1968-73; investment banker Bancom Fin. Corp., Phoenix, 1972-83. Edn. dir. U.S. Office Econ. Opportunity, Phoenix, 1969-72; pres. Solaris Classics, Phoenix, 1997—; internat. mgr. Russian Fed. Orch., Moscow, 1995-00; artist adv. U.S. Coun. of the Arts, Phoenix, 1970-75; cons. Ministry of Culture of Republic of Ukraine; vis. prof. Philharm. Inst., Kharkov, 1997-00; internat. mgr. State Symphony of Russian Republic; cons. concerts in field, worldwide. Classical recordings include Hovhaness Symphony for Guitar, Music of the Royal Courts, Hovhaness Mystery of the Holy Martyrs, Tristeza de Amor, Partitas of J.S. Bach; writer, prodr., performer Mr. Cobb's Corner, 1978, PBS TV series In Concert, CBS series Perimeter; dramatist: Il Valentino, 1996, Don Carlos, 1997. Recipient Best Documentary Sound Track, U.S. Coun. of the Arts, 1969, Internat. Gold medal Swedish Arabian Horse Assn., Stockholm, 1982, Gold Medal Premio Roma, 5 Grammy award nominations. Jewish. Avocations: weightlifting, collecting books and art, ancient numismatics, breeding horses. Office: 3550 N Central Ave Ste 701 Phoenix AZ 85012-2109

LONG, MICHAEL ELDON, government and history educator; b. Charleston, W.Va., Aug. 15, 1950; s. Roy Eldon and Alice Mae (Leonard) Long; m. Marilyn Sue Branscome, May 25, 1970 (div. Sept. 1997); children: Lisa Michelle, Michael Brent. BA, U. Charleston, 1973; postgrad., George Washington U., 1974—75, U. Hawaii-Manoa, 1983; MS, Cen. Mich. U., 1985; postgrad., Marshall U., 1999, U. S. Fla., 2002. Enlisted U.S. Army, 1977, commd. officer, 1978—97; maj. (ret.) USAR, 1997; asst. prof. history and polit. sci. Pasco-Hernando C.C., 2001—. Adj. prof. govt. and history Southside Va. C.C., 1992—93, St. Petersburg Jr. Coll., Fla., 1999—2001, U. Charleston, W.Va., 1999, Pasco-Hernando C.C., Fla., 2000—01, Fla. Met. U., Tampa, 2000—01; cons. Discussant Southwestern Polit. Sci. Assn., 2001. Manuscript/book reviewer: Jour. Politics, White Ho. Studies, Fla. Hist. Qur., W.Va. History, Richmond Times-Dispatch, Mil. Rev. Dir. Ft. Scammon Hist. Assn., South Charleston, W.Va., 1964—65; seasonal ranger-historian Nat. Pk. Svc., Petersburg Nat. Battlefield, Va., 1972; curator divsn.hist. preservation Fairfax County Pk. Authority, Annandale, Va., 1973—75; participant Woodlawn Conf. Hist. Site Adminstrn., Mt. Vernon, Va., 1974; curator collection and exhibits Hist. Bethlehem, Inc., Pa., 1975—76; exec. dir. Parkersburg (W.Va.) Arts Ctr., 1976—77; bd. dirs. Meherrin River Arts Coun., Emporia, Va., 1990—91, South Charleston Mus. Found., 1998—99. Mem.: So. Polit. Sci. Assn. (panel chair 2001), Am. Polit. Sci. Assn., Acad. Polit. Sci., Am. Hist. Assn., Assn. U.S. Army Club (Suncoast chpt.), Am. Legion. Republican. Roman Catholic. Avocation: historic preservation. Home: 9222 Foremast Ave #3812 Port Richey FL 34668 Office Phone: 727-816-3255. Business E-Mail: longm@phcc.edu.

LONG, NANCY ELLEN, writer, lawyer; b. Springfield, Va., Feb. 27, 1960; d. Richard Vincent and Margaret Patricia Long. BBA, Coll. of William and Mary, 1982; JD, George Mason Law Sch., 1990. Cert. journalist Nat. Journalism Ctr., 1983; bar: Va. 1990, D.C. 1992. Asst. editor Policy Rev., Washington, 1983-84; editor U.S. Agy. for Internat. Devel., Washington, 1986-93; dir. pub. rels. and comm. Agrl. Coop. Devel. Internat./Vols. Overseas Coop. Assistance, Washington, 1995—. Editor: World Report, 1997—2002. Mem. Nat. Press Club, Va. Bar Assn., D.C. Bar Assn. Republican. Roman Catholic. Avocations: jogging, reading, travel, photgraphy. Office: ACDI/VOCA 50 F St NW Ste 1075 Washington DC 20001-1532 E-mail: nancy.long@acdivoca.org.

LONG, PETER AVARD CHIPMAN, retired military officer; b. Montreal, Que., Can., Feb. 19, 1944; m. Janet Elaine Hall; children: Melinda, David. BS, U.S. Naval Acad., 1967; MS in Pers. Mgmt., Naval Postgrad. Sch., Monterey, Calif., 1972; PhD in Learning Tech., Nova Southeastern U., Ft. Lauderdale, 1991. Commd. ensign U.S. Navy, 1967, advanced through grades to rear adm., 1994; main propulsion asst., damage control asst. USS Dennis J. Buckley, 1967-69; engr. officer USS Hepburn, 1972-75; comdg. officer USS Moctobi, Pearl Harbor, Hawaii, 1975-76; exec. officer USS Albert David, 1980-81; comdg. officer USS David R. Ray, 1985-87, USS Reeves, 1991-93; rear adm. Cruiser-Destroyer Group 5, Kitty Hawk Battle Group, 1994—. Additional shore duties include: exec. officer Navy Recruiting Dist., San Diego, Placement Office and Detailer at Naval Mil. Pers. Command, Washington, CNO Chair Indsl. Coll. of the Armed Forces, commdg. officer Naval Sta., Mayport, Fla.; commdg. officer Naval Sta., Pearl Harbor, Hawaii, comdr. Logistics Group We. Pacific, Singapore, dep. chief of staff for shore installation mgmt., U.S. Pacific Fleet; provost Naval War Coll., 1998-2000; pres. Valley Forge Mil. Acad. and Coll., 2000—. Decorated Navy DSM, Legion of Merit with 4 gold stars, Navy Commendation medal with gold star; recipient Navy Achievement medal. Office: Valley Forge Mil Acad 1001 Eagle Rd Wayne PA 19087-3613 Office Phone: 610-989-1201. E-mail: plong@vfmac.edu.

LONG, PHILLIP CLIFFORD, museum director; b. Tucson, Oct. 11, 1942; s. Hugh-Blair Grigsby and Phyllis Margaret (Clay) L.; m. Martha Whitney Rowe, Aug. 26, 1972; children— Elisha Whitney, Charlotte Clay, Elliot Sherlock BA, Tulane U., 1965. Sec. Fifth Third Bancorp, Cin., 1974-94; sr. v.p., sec. Fifth Third Bank, Cin., 1988-94; dir. Taft Mus. Art, Cin., 1994—. Trustee Contemporary Arts Ctr., 1974-84, Art Acad. Cin., 1980-94, Cin. Symphony Orch., 1981-87, Cin. Nature Ctr., 1982-88, Taft Mus., 1987-94, Cin. Country Day Sch., 1991-97; trustee, treas. Cin. Music Hall, 1981-92, Convalescent Hosp. for Children, 1989—, Cin. Assn. for Arts, 1992—. Mem. The Camargo Club, Queen City Club. Home: 4795 Burley Hills Dr Cincinnati OH 45243-4007 Office: Taft Mus Art 316 Pike St Cincinnati OH 45202-4293

LONG, RALPH STEWART, clinical psychologist; b. Pitts., Feb. 23, 1926; s. Ralph S. and Virginia (Hawk) L.; m. Vera Lazorchak, June 16, 1951; children: Karen Virginia, Brian Reed, Lauri Michelle. BS, Lock Haven U., 1950; MEd, Pa. State U., 1951; PhD, Washington U., St. Louis, 1965. Lic. psychologist, Tex. Commd. 2d lt. med. svc. corp USAF, 1951, clin. psychologist to chief clin. psychology svcs. hosp. Sampson AFB, NY, 1951—55; chief psychology svc. hosp. Warren AFB, Wyo., 1955—57; Inst. Tech. scholar, Wash. U. USAF, St. Louis, 1957—61, chief psychology dept. med. ctr. Andrews AFB, DC, 1961—62, dir. psychol. svcs. Scott AFB, Ill., 1962—65, dir. psychol. svcs. regional med. ctr. Sheppard AFB, Tex., 1965—67, dir. psychol. svcs. hosp. Wiesbaden, Germany, 1967—70, dir. psychol. svcs. regional med. ctr. Sheppard AFB, Tex., 1970—71, advanced through grades to lt. col., 1968; ret., 1971; dir. psychol. svcs. Cmty. Ctr. Mental Health, Mental Retardation, Wichita Falls, Tex., 1971-72; psychol. cons. Family Counseling Ctr., Wichita Falls, 1972-74; dir. psychol. svcs. Nueces County Mental Health-Mental Retardation Cmty. Ctr., 1974-77; dir. Corpus Christi Counseling Ctr./Physicians-Surgeons Hosp., Tex., 1977-79, Psychol. Cons., Corpus Christi, 1979-82; exec. dir. Personal Dynamics Inst., Corpus Christi, 1982—, dir., 1988—2005, emeritus, 2005—. Instr. dept. psychology McKendree Coll., Lebanon, Ill., 1962-63; instr. So. Ill. U., 1962-64; adj. prof. human rels. Webster U., Webster Groves, Mo., 1976-79, 88-93; adj. prof. psychology Del Mar Coll., Corpus Christi, 1977-83, adj. prof. bus. adminstrn., 1991-93; cons. Tex. Dept. Corrections, 1988-90; bd. dir. Ctr. Creative Living; cons., trainer Crisis Svc., 1980-2005; profl. adv. bd. North Tex. Regional Coun. Alcoholism, 1971-74, Mental Health Assn. Coastal Bend, 1974-83, Wichita Mental Health Assn., 1965-67, 70-74; adj. prof. Embry-Riddle U., Corpus Christi, 1991-93; clin. dir. Shoreline Chem. Dependency Treatment Ctr., 1989-92; consulting psychologist Nueces County Juvenile Justice Ctr., Corpus Christi, 1992-2005, Warm Springs Rehab. Ctr., Corpus Christi, 1992-2005, MCC Managed Behavioral Care, Inc., Eden Prairie, Minn., 1992—, Champus Provider, 1972-2005; presenter in field. Active Tex. chpt. ARC; founding mem. Nat. Campaign for Tolerance; charter sponsor Air Force Meml. Found., Statue of Liberty-Ellis Island Found.; mem. Nat. Com. to Preserve Social Security and Medicine; charter mem. Citizens Against Govt. Waste. With USN, 1944—51, Pacific Theater WWII. Named Am. Man Sci., 1962. Fellow: Soc. Air Force Clin. Psychologists; mem.: VFW, DAV, APA, Air Force Meml. Found. (charter sponsor), Military Officers Assn. of Am., Anti-Defamation League, Prescribing Psychologists Register, Nat. Air and Space Soc. (founding), US Naval Inst., Nat. Register Health Svc. Providers in Psychology, Air Force Assn., Tex. Assn. Mental Health, Tex. Assn. Mental Health (exec. com. 1980—83), Libr. of Congress (charter), Am. Inst. Hypnosis, U.S. Navy Meml. (charter mem.), Nat. D-Day Mus. (charter), Mil. Officers Assn. Am., Am. Air Mus. in Britain (charter), US Holocaust Meml. Mus. (charter), Am. Assn. Ret. Persons, Ret. Officers Assn., Am. Mil. Soc., Common Cause, Citizens Against Govt. Waste (charter), WWII Meml. Soc. (charter), Earth Justice Legal Def. Fund., Nat. Arbor Day Found., United Srs. Assn., Theosophical Soc. Am., Nat. Wildlife Fedn., Nat. Mus. Am. Indian (charter), F.D. Roosevelt Meml. (founding), Nat. Trust Hist. Preservation, National Audubon Soc., Smithsonian, Sierra Club, Shriners, Masons, Am. Legion, Sigma Xi. Avocations: painting, writing, travel, camping, fishing.

LONG, REGINALD ALAN, lawyer, educator; b. Pitts., Jan. 9, 1960; s. William Bryant and Betty (Holmes) L.; m. Lisa D. Love, Apr. 26, 1987; children: Reginald Alan Jr., Bryant A. BS, California (Pa.) State Coll., 1981; MBA, Fordham U., 1990; JD, N.Y. Law Sch., 1996. Bar: N.Y. 1997, N.J. 1998, U.S. Dist. Ct. (no. dist.) N.J. 1998. Sys. analyst Pa. Dept. Transp., Harrisburg, 1981-84; bus. analyst Pa. Blue Shield, Camp Hill, 1984-87; assoc. dir. TIAA-CREF, N.Y.C., 1987-98; ptnr. Love and Long, L.L.P., Newark, 1997—. Adj. prof. real estate Rutgers U. Grad. Sch. Bus., Newark, 1998—. Mentor Youth Emergency Ctr., Newark, 1987; counselor, vol. Youth Crisis Ctr., Newark, 1987; mem. Bro. to Bro. Mentor Program, East Orange, N.J., 1998. Mem. ABA, N.Y. Bar Assn., Omega Psi Phi (Man of Yr. award 1993). Avocations: winemaking, basketball, golf. Home: 338 Warwick Ave South Orange NJ 07079-2445 Office: Love & Long LLP 108 Washington St Newark NJ 07102-3024

LONG, ROBERT C., retired military officer, management consultant; b. Phila., June 12, 1945; s. Claude Adam Long and Teresa Masgai; m. Janet V. Long, Dec. 7, 1963; children: Tracy, Robert, Gina. AS in Electronics, Chulo Vista (Calif.) C.C., 1973; BS in Bus., U. N.Y., 1985; MS in Bus. Adminstrn., Ctrl. Mich. U., 1995. Commd. ensign USN, 1963, advanced through grades to commdr., ret., 2003, electronics officer USS Kitty Hawk, 1987—89, ops. officer USS Constellation, 1989—93, comdg. officer Naval Brig. Phila., 1993—95, comms. officer New Orleans, 1995—97, chief staff Norfolk, Va., 1997—98; prin. cons. PriceWaterHouseCoopers, Fairfax, Va., 1998—2000; mgr. smart ship Nausses Phila., 2000—. Decorated 3 Meritorious Svc. awards USN, 5 Commendation medals, 2 Achievement awards, 3 Gold Conduct awards; recipient Outstanding Civil Svc. award, 1996. Mem.: Naval Inst., Navy League, Shriners. Avocation: antique auto restoration. Home: 2575 Gallaway Rd Bensalem PA 19020

LONG, ROBERT EMMET, author; b. Oswego, N.Y., June 7, 1934; s. Robert Emmet and Verda (Lindsley) L. BA, Columbia Coll., 1956; MA, Syracuse U., 1964; PhD, Columbia U., 1968. Instr. SUNY, Cortland, 1962-64; asst. prof. Queens Coll., CUNY, N.Y.C., 1968-71; writer, 1971—. Author: The Great Succession: Henry James and the Legacy of Hawthorne, 1979, The Achieving of the Great Gatsby, 1979, Henry James: The Early Years, 1983, John O'Hara, 1983, Nathanael West, 1985, Barbara Pym, 1986, James Thurber, 1988, James Fenimore Cooper, 1990, The Films of Merchant Ivory, 1991, 2d revised edit., 1997, Ingmar Bergman: Film and Stage, 1994, Broadway, the Golden Years: Jerome Robbins and the Great Choreographer-Directors, 2001, First Impressions: Observations on Theater and Books, 2003, An Enlarging Vision: Early Essays and Stories, 2004, James Ivory in Conversation: How Merchant Ivory Makes Its Movies, 2005, Gallagher House, 2005; editor numerous books, including John Huston: Interviews, 2001, George Cukor: Interviews, 2001; contbr. articles to profl. jours. and popular mags. Democrat. Episcopalian. Avocations: films, theater, ballet, jazz, travel. Address: 254 S 3rd St Fulton NY 13069-2356

LONG, ROBERT EUGENE, banker; b. Yankton, S.D., Dec. 5, 1931; s. George Joseph and Malinda Ann (Hanson) L.; m. Patricia Louise Glass, June 19, 1959; children: Malinda Ann, Robert Eugene, Jennifer Lynn, Michael Joseph. BS in Acctg., U. S.D., 1956; MBA, U. Mich., 1965; grad., Madison Grad. Sch. Banking, 1973, Nat. Comml. Lending Grad. Sch., U. Okla., 1977. Cert. comml. lender. Financial analyst Chrysler Corp., 1958-59; supr. finance Ford Motor Co., 1966-67; with First Wis. Bankshares Corp., Milw., 1967—, v.p. fin., 1973—; exec. v.p. 1st Wis. Fond du Lac, 1978—; dir. 1st Wis. Nat. Bank of, Southgate, Waukesha and Fond du Lac; exec. v.p., dir. West Allis State Bank, 1979-81, pres., dir., 1981—, chief exec. officer, 1983—; sr. v.p. adminstrn. Park Banks, 1987—; chmn., pres., CEO Robert E. Long & Assoc., L.L.C., 2002—. Speaker/chmn. banking seminars Am. Mgmt. Assn., 1970—. Pres. local br. Aid Assn. Luth., 1970—, corp. bd. dirs., 1982—, vice chmn. bd., 1989—; pres. Mt. Carmel Luth. Ch., Milw., 1972; team capt. Re-elect Nixon campaign, 1972; bd. dirs. Luth. Social Svcs. of Wis. and Upper Mich., 1978—, chmn. bd., 1983—; bd. dirs. Luther Manor, 1981, Luther Manor Found., 1984, pres. bd. dirs. United Luth. Program for Aging, 1986—; bd. dirs. Wis. Inst. Family Medicine, 1985, pres., 1992—, elected corp. adv. coun., 1996; vice chmn. adv. coun. West Allis Meml. Hosp., 1993—; bd. dirs. Luth. Sem. Theology at Chgo., 1997. With USAF, 1951-52. Recipient Good Citizenship award Am. Legion, 1948 Mem. Wis. Assn. Family Practice (bd. dirs. 1992—), Wauwatosa C. of C. (bd. dirs. 1992—), Alpha Tau Omega. Clubs: Western Racquet (Elm Grove, Wis.) (dir. 1976—); Bluemound Golf and Country; Elmbrook Swim (pres. 1977-78). Lodges: Masons, Shriners, Jesters, Scottish Rite. Lutheran. Home and Office: N21w24052 Dorchester Dr Unit 6D Pewaukee WI 53072-4692 E-mail: PattyLou4@aol.com.

LONG, ROBERT LEROY, retired utilities executive, consultant; b. Renovo, Pa., Sept. 9, 1936; s. John Leroy and Mary Geraldine (Olmstead) L.; m. Ann Gullborg, Sept. 2, 1957; children: Beth, Jeff, Mark. BSEE, Bucknell U., 1958; MS in Engring., Purdue U., 1959, PhD in Nuclear Engring., 1962. Rsch. assoc. exp. reactor physics Argonne Nat. Lab., 1960-62; reactor specialist nuclear effects br. White Sands (N.Mex.) Missile Range, 1962-65; from asst. prof. to prof. nuclear engring. U. N.Mex., Albuquerque, 1965-78, asst. dean., 1972-74, chmn. chem. and nuc. engring. dept., 1974-78; with GPU Service Corp. (name now GPU Nuc. Corp.), Parsippany, N.J., 1978-96, mgr. generation productivity dept., 1978-79, dir. reliability engring. dept., 1979-80, dir. tng. and edn., 1980-82, v.p. nuclear assurance Parsippany, N.J., 1982-87, v.p. planning and nuclear safety, 1987-89; v.p. corp. svcs. GPU Nuc. Corp., Parsippany, 1989-93, v.p. svcs., 1993-95, v.p. nuclear svcs., 1995-96; recovery officer, v.p. human resources N.E. Nuc. Energy Co., 1998—. With rsch. partic. Sandia Corp., 1965-78; cons. White Sands Missile Range Fast Burst Reactor Facility, 1965-78, Sandia Lab., Albuquerque, 1965-70, Con Edison, N.Y.C., 1970-73, Electric Power Rsch. Inst., Palo Alto, Calif., 1976-78, NSF, U.S. Dept. Energy, others; rsch. assoc. nuc. rsch. divsn. Atomic Weapons Rsch. Estab., Eng., 1966-67; mem. Nuc. Stewardship, LLC. Contbr. articles to profl. jours. Served to capt. U.S. Army, 1962-64. AEC fellow, 1958-59; recipient Disting. Engring. Alumnus award Purdue U., 1993. Fellow Am. Nuc. Soc. (chmn. edn. divsn. 1974-75, chmn. nuc. engring. dept. heads com. 1975-76, chmn. No. N.J. chpt. 1986-87, 88-89, v.p., pres.-elect 1990-91, pres. 1991-92, Pioneer in Nuc. Tng. award 1999); mem. Nuc. Energy Inst., Profl. Reactor Operators Soc. Presbyterian. Avocations: church school teaching, woodworking, reading, choir, model garden railroading. Home: 9615 Elena Dr NE Albuquerque NM 87122-3866

LONG, ROBERT RADCLIFFE, fluid mechanics engineer, educator; b. Glen Ridge, N.J., Oct. 24, 1919; s. Clarence D. and Gertrude (Cooper) L.; m. Cristina Nersing, 1962; children: John Radcliffe, Robert William. AB in Econs, Princeton, 1941; MS in Meteorology, U. Chgo., 1949, PhD, 1950. Meteorologist U.S. Weather Bur., Paris, France, 1946-47; asst. prof. Johns Hopkins U., Balt., 1951-56, assoc. prof., 1956-59, prof. fluid mechanics, 1959-88, prof. emeritus, 1988—, dir. hydrodynamics lab., 1951-88. Assoc. dept. aero. and mech. engring. Ariz. State U. Author: Mechanics of Solids and Fluids, 1960, Engineering Science Mechanics, 1964; also articles in field. Home: 3989 Myrtle St Sarasota FL 34235-5157 Personal E-mail: rrlong4@comcast.net.

LONG, ROBERT RICHARD, banker; b. Atmore, Ala., Mar. 4, 1937; s. Robert Richard and Vivian (Crook) L.; m. Jane Hamilton Hancock, June 22, 1968; children: Robert Richard, Caroline Tison. BS, Auburn U., 1959; MBA, Harvard U., 1967. With Merchants Nat. Bank, Mobile, Ala., 1961-65, Sun Trust Bank, Atlanta, 1967—; controller Trust Co. Bank, Atlanta, 1972-73, group v.p., 1973-74, exec. v.p. Savannah, Ga., 1974-77, sr. v.p. Atlanta, 1977-78, exec. v.p., 1978-85, pres., 1985—, pres., chmn. and CEO, 1995—, also bd. dirs. Vice pres. Am. Cancer Soc., Atlanta City unit, 1983, pres., 1985; treas. Atlanta Arts Alliance, 1984-87; trustee Morris Brown Coll., 1984—, bd. dirs. 1998—; bd. Atlanta C. of C., 1997—; bd. dirs. C. of C., 1996—; Served to 1st lt. U.S. Army, 1959-61, Korea. Clubs: Piedmont Driving (Atlanta); Oglethorpe (Savannah). Home: 119 Brighton Rd NE Atlanta GA 30309-1539 Office: SunTrust Bank, Atlanta 25 Park Pl NE Atlanta GA 30303-2900

LONG, ROGER LEONARD, artist; b. Jackson, Tenn., Oct. 26, 1978; s. Roger Long, Linda Marie Long; m. Athena Adele Wilson, May 22, 1999. Owner, artist Portrait Phenomena, Ridgeland, Miss., 1998—; art, dance instr. Smarty Pants Ednl. Svcs., Jackson, Miss., 2000; art, dance instr./asst. mgr. Basic Skills Learning Ctr., Madison, Miss., 2001. Owner, choreographer Go Long Prodns., Ridgeland, Miss., 2001—; instr., choreographer Choreorobics, Jackson, Miss., 2001—; dir., cons. Artual Minds, Jackson, 2001—; choreobics instr. prime-of-life program City of Ridgeland, 2001—. Uncle, 1993 (Scholastic award, 1994), Elvis, 1993 (Clarion Ledger Elvis Drawing Contest award, 1993); choreographer performer Tribute to a Young Man, 2001. Min. Christian Congregation Jehovah's Witness, Jackson, 1995—. Avocation: Avocations: dancing, drawing, writing, music. Office: Go Long Prodns 526 Evergreen St Ridgeland MS 39157 Home: 526 Evergreen St Ridgeland MS 39157 Office Phone: 601-853-7480.

LONG, RUSSELL CHARLES, academic administrator; b. Alpine, Tex., Oct. 9, 1942; s. Roy Joel and Lovis Lorene (Graham) L.; m. Elaine Gresham, May 8, 1964 (div. Jan. 1986); 1 child, Mark Roy; m. Natrelle Hedrick, Mar. 28, 1986. BS, Sul Ross State U., Alpine, 1965; MA, N.Mex. State U., 1967; PhD, Tex. A&M U., 1977. Assoc. prof. Schreiner Coll., Kerrville, Tex., 1967-69; instr. Tarleton State U., Stephenville, Tex., 1969-72, asst. prof., 1972-77, assoc. prof., 1977-85, prof., 1985-92, asst. v.p. acad. adminstrn., 1987-90, chair dept. English and Lang., 1990-92; provost and v.p. acad. adminstrn. West Tex. A&M U., Canyon, 1992-94, interim pres., 1994-95, pres., 1995—. Office: West Texas A&M Univ Wt Sta 2501 4th Ave Canyon TX 79016-0001 Business E-Mail: rlong@mail.wtamu.edu.

LONG, SARAH ANN, librarian; b. Atlanta, May 20, 1943; d. Jones Lloyd and Lelia Maria (Mitchell) Sanders; m. James Allen Long, 1961 (div. 1985); children: Andrew C., James Allen IV; m. Donald J. Sager, May 23, 1987. BA, Oglethorpe U., 1966; M in Librarianship, Emory U., 1967. Asst. libr. Coll. of St. Matthias, Bristol, Eng., 1970-74; cons. State Libr. Ohio, Columbus, 1975-77; coord. Pub. Libr. of Columbus and Franklin County, Columbus, 1977-79; dir. Fairfield County Dist. Libr., Lancaster, Ohio, 1979-82, Dauphin County Libr. Sys., Harrisburg, Pa., 1982-85, Multnomah County Libr., Portland, Oreg., 1985-89; sys. dir. North Suburban Libr. Sys., Wheeling, Ill., 1989—. Chmn. Portland State U. Libr. Adv. Coun., 1987-89, bd. dirs. Am. Libr., Paris, 2000-02. Contbr. to weekly column in Daily Herald; monthly cable show Whats New in Libraries; contbr. articles to profl. jours. Bd. dirs. Dauphin County Hist. Soc., Harrisburg, 1983-85, ARC, Harrisburg, 1984-85; pres. Lancaster-Fairfield County YWCA, Lancaster, 1981-82; vice chmn. govt. and ednl. divsn. Lancaster-Fairfield County United Way, Lancaster, 1981-82; sec. Fairfield County Arts Coun., 1981-82; adv. bd. Portland State U., 1987-89; mentor Ohio Libr. Leadership Inst., 1993, 95. Recipient Dir.'s award Ohio Program in Humanities, Columbus, 1982; Sarah Long Day established in her honor Fairfield County, Lancaster, Bd. Commrs., 1982. Mem. ALA (pres. 1999-2000, elected coun. 1993-97, chair Spectrum fund raising com. 2001-02), Pub. Libr. Assn. (pres. 1989-90, chair legis. com. 1991-95, chair 1998, nat. conf. com. 1995-98), Ill. Libr. Assn. (pub. policy com. 1991-97, Librarian of Yr. award 1999), Ill. Libr. Sys. Dirs. Orgn. (pres. 2000—), Libr. Cmty. Found. (bd. dirs. 1995-2005). Office: N Suburban Libr Systems 200 W Dundee Rd Wheeling IL 60090-4750 Business E-Mail: slong@nsls.info.

LONG, SARAH ELIZABETH BRACKNEY, physician; b. Sidney, Ohio, Dec. 5, 1926; d. Robert LeRoy and Caroline Josephine (Shue) Brackney; m. John Frederick Long, June 15, 1948; children: George Lynas, Helen Lucille Corcoran, Harold Roy, Clara Alice Lawrence, Nancy Carol Sieber. BA, Ohio State U., 1948, MD, 1952. Intern Grant Hosp., Columbus, Ohio, 1952-53; resident internal medicine Mt. Carmel Med. Ctr., Columbus, 1966-69, chief resident internal medicine, 1968-69; med. cons. Ohio Bur. Disability Determination, Columbus, 1970—. Physician student health Ohio State U., Columbus, 1970-73; sch. physician Bexley (Ohio) City Schs., 1973-83; physician advisor to peer rev. Mt. Carmel East Hosp., Columbus, 1979-86, med. dir. employee health, 1981-96; physician cons. Fed. Black Lung program U.S. Dept. Labor, Columbus, 1979-98. Mem.: AMA, Gerontol. Soc. Am., Columbus Med. Assn., Ohio State Med. Assn., Ohio Hist. Soc., Phi Beta Kappa, Alpha Epsilon Delta. Home: 2765 Bexley Park Rd Columbus OH 43209-2231 Personal E-mail: jfsblong@sbcglobal.net.

LONG, SARAH SUNDBORG, pediatrician, educator; b. Portland, Oreg., Oct. 31, 1944; MD, Jefferson Med. Coll., 1970. Diplomate Am. Bd. Pediat. Intern St. Christopher Hosp. for Children, Phila., 1970-71, resident, 1971-73, fellow pediat. and infectious diseases, 1973-75, staff, 1975—2002; prof. pediat. Drexel U. Coll. Medicine, 2002—. Chief editor: Principles and Practice of Pediatric Infectious Diseases, 1997; assoc. editor Jour. Pediatrics, 1997—; contbr. over 100 articles to med. jours. Mem. Am. Acad. Pediat., Soc. for Pediat. Rsch., Am. Pediat. Soc., Pediatric Diseases Soc. (pres. 1999-2001). Office: St Christopher Child Hosp Sect Infectious Diseases Erie Ave at Front St Philadelphia PA 19134 Office Phone: 215-427-5204.

LONG, SHARON RUGEL, dean, molecular biologist, educator; b. Mar. 2, 1951; d. Harold Eugene and Florence Jean (Rugel) Long; m. Harold James McGee, July 7, 1979; 2 children. BS, Calif. Inst. Tech., 1973; PhD, Yale U., 1979. Rsch. fellow Harvard U., Cambridge, Mass., 1979-81; from asst. prof. molecular biology to prof. Stanford U., Palo Alto, Calif., 1982-92, prof. biol. scis., 1992—, William C. Steere, Jr.-Pfizer Inc. prof. biological scis., Vernon R. & Lysbeth Warren Anderson dean Sch. Humanities and Scis., 2001—. Investigator Howard Hughes Med. Inst., 1994—; adv. bd. Jane Coffin Childs Meml. Fund; bd. dirs. Ann. Revs. Inc. Assoc. Editor Jour. Bacteriology; assoc. editor Jour. Plant Physiology, 1992—; mem. editl. bd. Devel. Biology; editl. com. Ann. Review Cell Biology. Recipient award NSF, 1979, NIH, 1980, Shell Rsch. Found. award 1985, Presdl. Young Investigator award NSF, 1984-89; grantee NIH, Dept. Energy, NSF; MacArthur fellow, 1992-97, Georges Morel fellow I.N.R.A., France, 1998; fellow Noble Found. Fellow Assn. Women in Sci.; mem. NAS, Genetics Soc. Am., Am. Soc. Plant Physiology (Charles Albert Shull award 1989), Am. Soc. Microbiology, Soc. Devel. Biology. Office: Sch of Humanities and Scis Off of Dean Bldg 1 - Main Quad Stanford CA 94305-2070 also: Dept Biol Scis 371 Serra Mall Stanford CA 94305-5008 Office Fax: 650-723-3235. E-mail: srl@stanford.edu.*

LONG, STEPHEN CARREL MIKE, lawyer; b. Roswell, N.Mex., Sept. 22, 1951; s. R.E. (Mike) and Evelyn Marie (Row) Long; m. Barbara I. Lowe, July 19, 1980; children: Jennifer Long Wilson, Joel Raymond Matthew. BBA with honors, N.Mex. State U., 1973; JD, U. N.Mex., 1977; MDiv, Golden Gate Theol. Sem., 2004. Bar: N.Mex. 1977, U.S. Dist. Ct. N.Mex. 1977, U.S. Tax Ct. 1977, U.S. Ct. Appeals (10th cir.) 1977, U.S. Supreme Ct. 1982, U.S. Ct. Mil. Appeals 1982. Pvt. practice, Albuquerque, 1977-82, 85-87; assoc. Wheeler, Nye, McElwee & Martone, Albuquerque, 1982-84; v.p. Wheeler, McElwee, Sprague & Long, P.C., Albuquerque, 1984-85; pres. Long Law Firm, P.A., Albuquerque, 1987-90; dir. Long & Thomas, P.A., Albuquerque, 1990-91; pvt. practice Placitas, N.Mex., 1992-94; assoc. Ron Koch, P.A., Albuquerque, 1994-2001, Bill Gordon & Assocs., Albuquerque, 2001—. Staff judge adv. N.Mex. Dept. Mil. Affairs, 1980—92; adj. prof. Wayland Bapt. U., 1999—2000. Author: Consumer Bankruptcy Law in New Mexico, 3d edit., 1991; editor Nat. Resources Jour., 1976-77; staff N.Mex. Law Rev., 1975-76; contbr. articles to profl. jours. Trial coach N.Mex. Law Related Edn. Project, 1983-88, 99-2000; bd. dirs., Christian Legal Aid & Referral Svcs., Inc., Albuquerque, 1982-88; chmn., bd. dirs., Hosanna, Inc., Albuquerque, 1986-94; assoc. pastor Sierra Vista Bapt. Ch., 1995-99; tchg. pastor First Bapt. Ch., Bosque Farms, N.Mex., 2000-01, Mission Valley Ch., 2001-03; pastor Tender Mercy Bapt. Ch., 2004—; clk., mem. exec. com. Ctrl. Bapt. Assn., 1996-2003; instr. CLD program Golden Gate Baptist Theol. Sem., 2001-. Served to col., N.Mex. Dept. Mil. Affairs. Mem.: N.Mex Trial Lawyers Assn., N.Mex. Criminal Def. Lawyers Assn. (bd. dirs. 2004—), N.Mex. State Bar Assn. (bd. dirs. bankruptcy sect. 1990—94, chmn. 1994), Nat. Assn. Criminal Def. Lawyers, Sigma Pi, Delta Theta Phi. Republican. Baptist. Avocation: cowboy. Office: 2501 Yale SE Ste 204 Albuquerque NM 87106 Office Phone: 505-265-1000. Business E-Mail: steve@billgordon.com.

LONG, STEPHEN R., lawyer; b. Hackensack, NJ, 1951; BA, Seton Hall Univ., 1973, JD, 1980. Bar: NJ 1980. Assoc. Drinker Biddle & Reath LLP, 1980—88, ptnr., litig., 1988—, and vice chair, litig. dept., mem. labor, employment practice group Florham Park, NJ. Arbitrator US Dist. Ct., Dist. NJ. Frequent writer, lectr. in field. Mem.: ABA, NJ Bar Assn., Trial Attys. NJ, Assn. Fed. Bar NJ. Office: Drinker Biddle & Reath LLP 500 Campus Dr Florham Park NJ 07932-1047 Office Phone: 973-549-7280. Office Fax: 973-360-9831. Business E-Mail: stephen.long@dbr.com.

LONG, SUSAN ELIZABETH, lawyer; b. Hannibal, Mo., Oct. 22, 1964; d. Richard Dean and Evalyn Elizabeth (VanWinkle) L.; children: Taylor Elizabeth Ortiz, Jordan Frances Hall BA in English, U. Mo., Kansas City, 1987, JD, 1989. Bar: Mo. 1989, U.S. Dist. Ct. (we. dist.) Mo. 1989, Kans. 1990, U.S. Dist. Ct. Kans. 1990. Assoc. Cochran, Oswald et al, Blue Springs, Mo., 1989—91, T. K. Thompson & Assocs., Liberty, Mo., 1991—97, Withers, Brant, Igoe & Mullenix, Liberty, 1997—2002, Blessing & Long LLC, Liberty, 2002—. Contbg. author: Missouri Practice Vol. 21, 1990. Tng. coord. Ea. Jackson County Youth Ct., Grain Valley, Mo., 1996-99. Mem. Clay County Bar Assn. (exec. com., bd. dirs. 1996-2004, pres. 2004) Avocations: volleyball, softball. Office: Blessing & Long LLC 2 S Main St Liberty MO 64068-2323 E-mail: susan@blessinglong.com.

LONG, TERESA C., city health department administrator; m. Tom Denune; 1 child, Katherine. MD, U. Calif., San Francisco; MPH, U. Calif., Berkeley. Med. dir., asst. health commr Columbus Health Dept., Ohio, 1986—2002, commr., 2002—; clin. assoc. prof. Ohio State U., Coll. Medicine and Pub. Health. Chair Ctrl. Ohio Med. Dirs. Coalition, Columbus Area Asthma Coalition; co-chair Healthy Columbus Adv. Bd. Recipient Elizabeth Blackwell award for Pioneering Efforts to Improve Women's and Cmty. Health. Mem.: Columbus Med. Assn. (past pres., past pres., bd. trustees found.). Office: Columbus Health Dept 240 Parsons Ave Columbus OH 43215

LONG, TERESA LOZANO, foundation administrator, educator; BA, MA in Edn., U. Tex., Austin, PhD, 1965. Rsch. assoc. Tex. Edn. Agency, cons. Div. Compensatory Edn.; rsch. assoc. Tex. Govs. Com. Pub. Sch. Edn.; cons. Migrant Edn. and Head Start Prog. US Office of Edn.; founder Long Found., Austin, 1999—. Mem. Nat. Coun. Arts, Nat. Endowment for Arts, 2002—. Mem. bd. dirs. Austin Lyric Opera, Umlauf Sculpture Mus., Austin Cmty. Found., Austin Urban League, Laguna Gloria Art Mus., Austin Volunteer Coun., Ballet Austin, Umlauf Sculpture Garden, Tex. Com. for Nat. Mus. of Women in Arts, Intercholastic League Found., U. Tex. Chancellor's Coun. Office: The Long Found 40 N IH 35, Ste 7C2 Austin TX 78701 Office Phone: 512-479-4080.*

LONG, THAD GLADDEN, lawyer; b. Dothan, Ala., Mar. 9, 1938; s. Lindon Alexander and Della Gladys (Pilcher) L.; m. Carolyn Frances Wilson, Aug. 13, 1966; children: Louisa Frances Stockman, Wilson Alexander. AB, Columbia U., 1960; JD, U. Va., 1963. Bar: Ala. 1963, U.S. Dist. Ct. (no. dist., so. dist., mid. dist.) Ala., U.S. Ct. Appeals (11th cir., 5th cir.), U.S. Supreme Ct. Assoc. atty. Bradley, Arant, Rose & White, Birmingham, Ala., 1963-70, ptnr., 1970—. Adj. prof. U. Ala., Tuscaloosa, 1988—2002, Samford U., Birmingham, Cumberland Law Sch., 1999—2002. Co-author: Unfair Competition Under Alabama Law, 1990, Protecting Intellectual Property, 1990; mem. editl. bd. The Trademark Reporter; contbr. articles to profl. jours. Chmn. Columbia U. Secondary Schs. Com. Ala. Area, 1975—, pres., chmn., Greater Birmingham Arts Alliance, 1977-79; trustee, pres. Birmingham Music Club, 2000-03; trustee Oscar Wells Trust for Mus. Art, Birmingham, 1983—, Canterbury Meth. Found., 1993-2002, sec., 1993—; chmn. Entrepreneurship Inst. Birmingham, 1989; vice chmn., trustee Sons Revolution Found., Ala., 1994-2002; pres. Birmingham-Jefferson Hist. Soc., 1995-97; trustee Birmingham Music Club Endowment, 1995—, Birmingham-Jefferson History Mus., 2004—; mem. Birmingham Com. Fgn. Rels. Fellow: Ala. Bar Found.; mem.: U.S. Patent Bar, Internat. Trademark Assn., Am. Law Inst., Ala. Law Inst., Birmingham Legal Aid Soc., Ala. Bar Assn. (chmn., founder bus. torts and antitrust sect.), Biotechnology Assn. of Ala., Inc. (sec. 1998—2001), Am. Arbitration Assn., S.R. (pres. 1994—95), U. Va. Law Alumni (chmn. Birmingham chpt. 1984—89), Gen. Soc. S.R. (gen. solicitor 1994—2000), Soc. Colonial Wars, Order of the Coif, Omicron Delta Kappa. Republican. Methodist. Avocations: travel, writing, ping pong/table tennis. Home: 2880 Balmoral Rd Birmingham AL 35223-1236 Office: One Federal Place Birmingham AL 35203 Office Phone: 205-521-8259. E-mail: tlong@bradleyarant.com.

LONG, THOMAS LESLIE, lawyer; b. Mansfield, Ohio, May 30, 1951; s. Ralph Waldo and Rose Ann (Cloud) L.; m. Peggy L. Bryant, Apr. 24, 1982. AB in Govt., U. Notre Dame, 1973; JD, Ohio State U., 1976. Bar: Ohio 1976, U.S. Dist. Ct. (so. dist.) Ohio 1976, U.S. Dist. Ct. (no. dist.) Ohio 1977, U.S. Ct. Appeals (6th cir.) 1978. Assoc. Alexander, Ebinger, Fisher, McAlister & Lawrence, Columbus, Ohio, 1976-82, ptnr., 1982-85, Baker & Hostetler, Columbus, 1985—. Mem. ABA, Ohio Bar Assn., Columbus Bar Assn., Fed. Bar Assn., Assn. Trial Lawyer Am. Clubs: Capitol (Columbus). Democrat. Roman Catholic. Home: 2565 Leeds Rd Columbus OH 43221-3613 Office: Baker & Hostetler 65 E State St Ste 2100 Columbus OH 43215-4260

LONG, THOMAS MICHAEL, investment banker; b. Tulsa, June 30, 1943; s. Thomas Marvin Long and Marcia Acosta; m. Catherine Howell, Dec. 30, 1964; children: Jane Alexander Long-Gering, Hampton Howell. BA in Govt. cum laude, Harvard U., 1965; MBA with distinction, Harvard U., Boston, 1971. Dir., Ohio Plan Ohio U., Athens, 1966-68; with Boston Cons. Group, 1968-69; ptnr. Brown Bros. Harriman & Co., pvt. bankers, N.Y.C., 1971—; co-mgr. 1818 Fund, L.P., 1818 Fund II, L.P., 1989-98, 1818 Fund, III, L.P., 1998—; mem. investment com. The 1818 Mezzanine Fund, L.P., The 1818 Mezzainine Fund II, L.P. Bd. dirs. HCA Inc., Nashville, CMS Inc., St. Louis, Vaalco Energy, Inc., Houston, Medsource Techs., Inc., Mpls., Picis, Inc., Boston, Genesee & Wyoming, Inc., Greenwich. Contbr. articles on mergers and acquisitions and banking industry consolidation to Am. Banker, Bankers Mag., Investment Dealers Digest Trustee Greenwich Country Day Sch., 1987-92, The Healthcare Chaplaincy, Inc., N.Y.C., 1992-98, Upper Can. Coll. Ednl. Found., 1996—, Ithaca Coll., 2003—. Corning Glass traveling fellow Harvard U., 1965-66 Mem. Knickerbocker Club (N.Y.C.), India House (N.Y.C.), Country Club Litt Rock, The Spring Island Club (Beaufort County, S.C.), The Grad. Fly Club (Cambridge, Mass.), The Quantuck Club (Quogue, L.I.). Roman Catholic. Home: 3 Old Mill Rd Greenwich CT 06830-3342

LONG, TIMOTHY SCOTT, chemist, consultant; b. Racine, Wis., Dec. 20, 1937; s. Leslie Alexander and Esther (Sand) L.; m. Karen M. Koniarski, July 13, 1985; children by previous marriage: Corinne, Christine. BS in Chemistry, Winona State U., 1975. Staff chemist IBM, Rochester, Minn., 1962-77, adv. chemist Harrison, N.Y., 1977-80, IBM Instruments, Inc., Danbury, Conn., 1980-81, mgr. Midwest Instrument Ctr. Chgo., 1981-85; mgr. corp. environ. engring. IBM, Stamford, Conn., 1985-89, industry cons. White Plains, N.Y., 1989-92; environ. cons. Geraghty & Miller, Inc., Rochelle Park, N.J., 1992-94, Indpls., 1994-97. Mem. World Environ. Ctr., N.Y.C., 1985-89; adv. bd. Coop. Ctr. Rsch. in Hazardous and Toxic Substances, Newark, 1985-89. Author: Testing for Prediction of Material Performance, 1972, Methods for Emissions Spectrochemical Analysis, 1977, 2d edit., 1982; contbr. articles to Applied Spectroscopy, Plating, Polymer Engring. and Sci. Mem. ASTM (com. emission spectroscopy), Soc. Applied Spectroscopy (chmn. Minn. sect. 1976-77), Soc. Plastics Engrs. (bd. reviewers 1975-76). Achievements include demonstration of world's first application using ion chromatography in the analysis of indsl. waste water. Home: 2 Calle Final Placitas NM 87043-9214

LONG, VIRGINIA, state supreme court justice; m. Jonathan D. Weiner; 3 children. Grad., Dunbarton Coll. of Holy Cross; JD, Rutgers U., 1966. Dep. atty. gen. State of NJ; assoc. Pitney, Hardin, Kipp and Szuch; dir. NJ Divsn. Consumer Affairs, 1975; commr. NJ Dept. Banking, 1977-78; judge NJ Superior Ct., 1978-84, Appellate Divsn. NJ Superior Ct., 1984-95, presiding judge, 1995-99; assoc. justice NJ Supreme Ct., 1999—. Office: Supreme Ct NJ PO Box 970 Trenton NJ 08625-0970

LONG, W. MICHAEL, real estate company executive; Pres., CEO The Continuum Co., Inc., CSC, 1996—97; CEO Healtheon Corp., 1997—99; chmn. bd., dir. WebMD Corp., 1999—2001; CEO Homestore Inc., Westlake Village, Calif., 2002—, bd. dirs. Office: Homestore Inc 30700 Russell Ranch Rd Westlake Village CA 91362

LONG, WILLIAM ALEXANDER, JR., retired pediatrician, retired medical educator; Attended, Millsaps Coll., 1948, U. Miss., 1949; BS, Tulane U., 1951, MD, 1955. Lic. MD Miss., Colo., diplomate Nat. Bd. Medical Examiners, Am. Bd. Pediatrics. Intern Colo. Gen. Hosp., Denver, 1955—56, pediatrics residency, 1965—66, fellow adolescent medicine, 1966—67; attending physician U. Hosp., Jackson, Miss., 1969—2000; pvt. practice Gulfport, Miss., 1958—61, Denver, 1961—65; pvt. practice in general pediatrics & adolescent medicine, 1967—69; pvt. practice in adolescent medicine Jackson, 1969—95. Lectr. pediatrics U. Colo. Sch. Nursing, 1966—67; asst. pediatrics U. Colo. Sch. Medicine, 1966—67, instr. pediatrics, 1967—69; clin. instr. pedicatrics U. Miss. Sch. Medicine, 1969—74, clin. asst. prof. pediatrics, 1974—83, clin. assoc. prof. pediatrics, 1983—95, emeritus clin. assoc. prof. pediatrics, 1995—2000; adj. prof. The Union for Experimenting Colls. & Univs., Cin., 1986—87; mem. pier review panel Miss. Found. Medical Care, Alaska, 1975—77, 1983—85; chief dept. medicine Doctors Hosp. Jackson, 1975—76; sec. dept. pediatrics St. Dominic Hosp., 1976; spkr., lectr. in field. Contbr. articles to profl. jours. Mem. juvenile delinquency advisory council Miss. State Law Enforcement Assistance Divsn., 1969—71; chmn. exec. bd. Youth Crisis Ctrs., Inc., 1971—75; deacon First Presbyterian Ch., Jackson, 1971—75, ruling elder, 1975—99; bd. dirs. United Givers Fund, 1972—74, Willowood Devel. Ctr., 1975—79. Flight surgeon USAF, 1957—58, Fairbanks, Ark. Recipient Liberty Bell award, Hinds County Jr. Bar Assn., 1971, Svc. to Mankind award, SW Sertoma Club, Jackson, 1972, Sertoma Internat., Miss. Dist., 1972. Fellow: Soc. Adolescent Medicine (ad hoc com. on improved pub. & profl. image 1986—92, chmn. adolescent medicine nominations com. 1992—94, Mead Johnson Tchg. award for major contributions in tchg. of adolescent health care 1982), Am. Acad. Pediatrics (chmn. youth com. 1968—69, chmn. youth com.-Miss. chpt. 1969—90, adolescence com. 1977—80, chmn. com. adolescence 1980—83, adolescent health secct. nominations com. 1983—84, adolescent health exec. com. 1986—88, chmn. adolescent health exec. com. 1988—90, task force on future role of the pediatrician 1989—90, chmn. adolescent health nominations com. 1990—92, Adele Dellenbaugh Hofmann award 1993); mem.: AMA, Soc. Adolescent Medicine (exec. coun. 1973—75, chmn. nominations com. 1975, pvt. practice com. 1976—77, chmn. pvt. practice com. 1977—81, chmn. ad hoc com. on fellowship status 1981—83, nominations com. 1982—83), Ctrl. Medical Soc. (exec. bd. 1971), State Medical Assn. (mental health com. 1971—74), Hinds County Assn. Mental Health (profl. advisory com. 1970—77), Miss. State Medical Assn. (Robins award for outstanding cmty. svc. by a physician 1973), Ctrl. Medical Soc., Jackson Rotary Club (bd. dirs. 1972—73, chmn. youth com. 1972—73, 1976—77), Alpha Omega Alpha, Alpha Epsilon Delta, Phi Eta Sigma, Phi Chi, Phi Delta Theta.

LONG, WILLIAM ALLAN, retired forest products company executive; b. Columbus, Ohio, Aug. 25, 1928; s. Allan C. and Dorothy (Crates) L.; m. Ann Cors, Aug. 27, 1954; children: Leslie, David, Steven, Jeffrey. BA, Ohio Wesleyan U., 1951. Vice pres. Diamond Internat., N.Y.C., 1951-70; exec. v.p. Overhead Door Corp., Dallas, 1970-75; v.p. St. Regis Paper Co., N.Y.C., 1975-79; group v.p. Inland Container Corp., Indpls., 1979-93; ret., 1993. Sgt. U.S. Army, 1946-47. Republican. Presbyterian. Home: 8073 Clymer Ln Indianapolis IN 46250

LONG, WILLIAM MCMURRAY, physiology educator; b. Greenville, S.C., Nov. 9, 1948; s. William McMurray and Cecile Mae (Ariail) L.; m. Kathleen Webb, Mar. 18, 1971 (dec. Oct. 1990); m. Marianne Castrén, July 22, 1992. BA, Tulane U., 1970, BS, 1974; PhD, La. State U., 1980. Rsch. assoc. Med. Ctr. La. State U., New Orleans, 1974-75; pathology extern Charity Hosp. of La., New Orleans, 1975-80; Nat. Rsch. Svc. Award fellow Pa. State Med. Ctr., Hershey, 1980-82; rsch. assoc. Mt. Sinai Med. Ctr., Miami Beach, Fla., 1983-89; rsch. physiologist VA Med. Ctr., Miami, Fla., 1982-89; asst. prof. medicine U. Miami, 1982-89; asst. prof. physiology U. N.D., Grand Forks, 1989-94; CFO OBI Lab. Co., 1994-2000, dir., 2000—. Cons. VA Med. Ctr., Miami, 1991; ad hoc reviewer Am. Jour. Physiology, Bethesda, Md., 1990-91, Va. Ctrl. Office, 1987-90; dir. Minority Access to Rsch. Careers, U. N.D., Ah'jo'gun to the Baccalaureate. Author: Non-Steriodal Agents in Sepsis Syndrom, 1989, (with others) Airways: Asthma, Bronchietasis and Emphysema, 1992; contbr. articles to profl. jours. Chmn. Nat. Letter-In Com., New Orleans, 1968, Cliff Solar Fund, New Orleans, 1973; cood. Spring Jazz Festival, New Orleans, 1970. Recipient Rsch. award Bush Found., 1990, Nat. Rsch. Svc. award NIH, 1980-82; grantee NIH, 1986-89, Fla. Lung Assn., 1984-85, VA, 1986-90, Am. Heart Assn. Dakota affiliate, 1991-93, Nat. Inst. Gen. Med. Scis., 1992—. Mem.: Am. Physiol. Soc., Am. Thoracic Soc., N.Y. Acad. Scis., Da Vinci Soc. (sec. 1987—88). Achievements include research in modification of cardiac proteolysis with amino acid methyl esters, in inefficacy of steroids in treatment of septic shock syndrome, in differentiation of histamine effects on bronchial flow and bronchomotor tone, on protein profiles in differentiating mechanisms of pulmonary edema, in role of bronchial blood flow in allergic airway disease and pharmacologic modification of that response; establishment of research and science education program for minorities and statewide tribal colleges; differential accumulation in brain of radon daughters in Alzheimer's Disease and Parkinson Disease. Office: OBI Labs 1339A Clara Brown Rd PO Box 718 Prosperity SC 29127-0718

LONG, WILLIS FRANKLIN, electrical engineering educator, researcher; b. Lima, Ohio, Jan. 30, 1934; s. Jesse Raymond and Cerelda Elizabeth (Stepleton) L.; m. Ginger Carol Miller; children: Andrew Mark, Kristin Kay, David Franklin. BS in Engring. Physics, U. Toledo, 1957, MSEE, 1962; PhD, U. Wis., 1970. Registered profl. engr., Wis. Project engr. Doehler Jarvis div. Nat. Lead Co., Toledo, 1957, 59-60; instr. U. Toledo, 1962-66; mem. tech. staff Hughes Rsch. Labs., Malibu, Calif., 1969-73; asst., then assoc. prof. depts. extension engring. and elec. engring. U. Wis., Madison, 1973-80, prof., chair dept. extension engring., 1980-83, prof. depts. engring., profl devel. and elec. and computer engring., 1985—, prof. emeritus, 2001—; dir. ASEA Power System Ctr., New Berlin, Wis., 1983-85. Prin. Long Assocs., Madison, 1973—; cons. Dept. Energy, Washington, 1978—, ABB Power Systems, Raleigh, N.C., 1985—. Editor EMTP Rev., 1987-91; contbr. articles to profl. jours.; patentee power switching. Mem. adv. com. energy conservation Wis. Dept. Labor, Industry and Human Rels., 1976-77; mem. rural energy mgmt. coun. Wis. Dept. Agrl., Trade and Comsumer Protection, 1999-2001; chmn. Wis. chpt. Sierra Club, 1977; pres. bd. dirs. Madison Urban Ministry, 1993-95. 2d lt. Signal Corps., U.S. Army, 1958. Recipient Disting. Engring. Alumnus award U. Toledo, 1983, award of excellence U. Wis.-Extension, 1987; Sci. Faculty fellow NSF, 1966. Fellow IEEE (life, Meritorious Achievement in Continuing Edn. award 1991); mem. Internat. Coun. on Large Electric Systems (expert advisor 1979—). Mem. United Ch. of Christ. Avocation: canoeing. Home: 125 N Hamilton St #906 Madison WI 53703 Office: U Wis 432 N Lake St Rm 737 Madison WI 53706-1415

LONGABERGER, TAMI, home decor accessories company executive; BSBA in Mktg., Ohio State U., 1984. Joined Longaberger Co., Newark, Ohio, 1984, pres., 1994, CEO, 1998. Chair bd. trustees Ohio State U.; mem. 60th commn. human rights United Nation; bd. dirs. Woodrow Wilson Internat. Ctr. Scholars, John Glenn Inst. for Pub. Svc. and Pub. Policy.

LONGAKER, MARK, gallery critic, writer; Gallery views writer Georgetowner. Office: Georgetowner 1054 Potomac St Washington DC 20007 Office Phone: 202-338-4833. Office Fax: 202-342-0751.*

LONGAKER, RICHARD PANCOAST, retired political science professor; b. Phila., July 1, 1924; s. Edwin P. and Emily (Downs) L.; m. Mollie M. Katz, Jan. 25, 1964; children— Richard Pancoast II, Stephen Edwin, Sarah Ellen, Rachel Elise. BA in Polit. Sci, Swarthmore Coll., 1949; MA in Am. History, U. Wis., 1950; PhD in Govt, Cornell U., 1953. Teaching asst. Cornell U., 1950-53, vis. asso. prof., 1960-61; asst. prof. Kenyon Coll., 1953-54, asso. prof., 1955-60; asst. prof. U. Calif., Riverside, 1954-55, faculty Los Angeles, 1961-76, chmn. dept. polit. sci., 1963-67, prof., 1965-76, dean acad. affairs grad. div., 1970-71; prof. Johns Hopkins U., Balt., 1976-87, provost and v.p. for acad. affairs, 1976-87, prof. emeritus, cons. western states office Santa Monica, Calif., 1987—; prof. in residence UCLA, 2001—. Author: The Presidency and Individual Liberties, 1961; co-author: The Supreme Court and the Commander in Chief, 1976, also articles, revs. Served with AUS, 1943-45. Mem. Am. Polit. Sci. Assn. Office: 16550 Chalet Ter Pacific Palisades CA 90272-2344 Business E-Mail: longaker@ucla.edu.

LONGAN, GEORGE BAKER, III, real estate company executive; b. Kansas City, Mo., Apr. 20, 1934; s. Benjamin Hyde and Georgette Longan O'Brien; divorced; 1 child, Nancy Ann Longan LaPoff. BSBA, U. Ariz., 1956; postgrad., U. Kans., 1956-57. Cert. real estate broker. Sr. v.p., gen. mgr. Paul Hamilton Co., Kansas City, 1963-84; pres. Eugene D. Brown Co., Kansas City, 1984-93; v.p. J.C. Nichols Real Estate, 1993-94. Bd. dirs. Genesis Relocation Network, N.J. Served to staff sgt. USAF, 1958-62. Mem. Nat. Real Estate Assn. (bd. dirs. 1991-94, 99, 2000), Mo. Real Estate Assn. (bd. dirs. 1987-90), Ariz. Real Estate Assn. (bd. dirs. 1999, 2000), Real Estate Bd. Kansas City (bd. dirs. 1987-90), Met. Kansas City Real Estate Bd. (pres. 1992), Beta Sigma Psi, Sigma Chi. Episcopal. Avocations: antique collecting, swimming. Office: Long Realty Co 5683 N Swan Rd Tucson AZ 85718-4565

LONGAN, SUZANNE M., retired elementary school educator; b. San Francisco, June 8, 1936; d. Walter Emerson Murfee and Ferne Inez Nelson; m. George B. Longan III, Aug. 27, 1958 (div. June 7, 1965); 1 child, Nancy Ann. BA with distinction, U. Ariz., 1958; postgrad., Calif. State U., 1987—89. Elem. sch. tchr. Johnson County Sch. Dist., Leawood, Kans., 1958—60; corp. sec., CEO Villa Chartier-Lanai, Inc., San Mateo, Calif., 1965—84. Dir. San Mateo County Hotel and Restaurant Assn., 1971—79. Treas. Pre-Sch. for the Visually Handicapped, Kans. City, Mo., 1961—62, chmn. advisory bd., 1963—65; div. chmn. Heart of Am. United Campaign, Kans. City, 1962; chair sch. solicitation Johnson County (Kans.) United Funds, 1963; mem. adv. bd. Children's Mercy Hosp., Kans. City, 1963—65; treas. Music in the Mountains, Nev. City, Calif., 1986—90; mem. bd. trustees Foothill Theatre Co., Nev. City, Calif., 1990—92; treas. Nev. County Land Trust, Nev. City, 1995—97; mem. Emmanuel Episc. Ch. Choir, Grass Valley, Calif., 1981—91; treas., CFO Emmanuel Episc. Ch., Grass Valley, Calif., 1988—91; mem. bd. dirs. Twin Cities Concert Assn., Grass Valley, 1984—86. Named Vol. Nurse Aide, Am. Red Cross, 1964, Concessionaire Extraordinaire, Foothill Theatre Co., 1986—87, Master Gardener, U. Calif., 1990; recipient Cmty. Svc. award, United Funds Coun., Inc., 1963. Mem.: Jr. League, Gamma Phi Beta. Republican. Episcopalian. Avocations: gardening, wildlife habitat maintenance. Home: 13350 Wildwood Heights Dr Penn Valley CA 95946

LONGDEN, ROBERT EDWARD, JR., lawyer; b. Jersey City, July 18, 1949; s. Robert Edward and Eileen (Kelly) L.; m. Joanna R. Longden, June 2, 1979; children: Timothy Charles, Carolyn Mary. BA, Boston Coll., 1971; JD, Suffolk U., 1975. Bar: Mass. 1975, U.S. Dist. Ct. Mass. 1975. Mng. ptnr. Bowditch & Dewey, Worcester, Mass., 1975—. Mem. Mass. Bar Assn. (ho. of dels. 1998—), Worcester County Bar Assn. (exec. com. 1990—, pres . 1994-95), Mass. Bar Found. (life), Worcester County Bar Found. (trustee 1995—, pres. 1995-96). Office: Bowditch & Dewey 311 Main St Worcester MA 01608-1552 E-mail: rlongden@bowditch.com.

LONGENBAUGH, JOHN TODD THOMAS, playwright, director; b. Sitka, Alaska, Feb. 16, 1965; s. Dee and George Harley Longenbaugh. BA in Classical Civilization and English, U. Kent, Canterbury, Eng., 1985—88; MA in Turn of the Century Fiction, U. York, Eng., 1988—90; Advanced Directing Degree, Ctrl. Sch. Speech and Drama, London, 1992—93. Artistic dir. Ursa Maj. Theatre Co., Seattle, 1993—, Theatre Babylon, Seattle, 2003—05. Mem., faculty Freehold Theatre Studio, Seattle, 2004—. Author: (plays) Argus, 1989, Scotch and Donuts, 1998, The Eternal Vaudeville, 2000, The Man Who Was Thursday, 2002 (Playwrights Horizons Finalist, 2000), Little White Pill, 2002, How to be Cool, 2003, Influence, a Theatre Comedy, 2005. Pres. NW Playwrights Guild, Seattle, 1995—99. Recipient Communicator of Excellence, Wash. Press Assn., 1996, Excellence in Journalism, First Pl., Soc. of Profl. Journalists, 1999. Mem.: Theatre Puget Sound. Liberal. Home: 906 E John St #201 Seattle WA 98102 Office Phone: 206-720-1942. Personal E-mail: jlongenb@blarg.net.

LONGENECKER, MARK HERSHEY, JR., lawyer; b. Akron, Ohio, Feb. 16, 1951; s. Mark Hershey and Katrina (Hetzner) L.; children: Emily Irene, Mark Hershey III; m. Marcie Garrison, June. 5, 2004. BA, Denison U., 1973; JD, Harvard U., 1976. Bar: Ill. 1976, Ohio 1979. Atty. Lord, Bissell & Brook, Chgo., 1976-79; ptnr. Frost Brown Todd LLC (and predecessor firms), Cin., 1979—2002, chmn. bus.-corp. dept., 1996—2002; mem. Greenebaum, Doll & McDonald, PLLC. Dir. ST Media Group Internat., HealthPro Brands, Inc. Bd. govs. Ohio Fair Plan Underwriting Assn., Columbus, 1989-92; dir. Salvation Army, Cin., 2000—. Mem. Cin. Country Club, Gyro Club, Harvard Club (Cin. pres. 1993-94). Office: Greenebaum Doll McDonald PLLC 2800 Chemed Ctr 255 E Fifth St Cincinnati OH 45202 Home: 7708 Chumani Ln Cincinnati OH 45243 Business E-Mail: mhl@gdm.com.

LONGENECKER, MARTHA W., museum director; BA in Art, UCLA; MFA, Claremont Grad. Sch.; studied with Millard Sheets, Shoji Hamada, Tatsuzo Shimaoka. Owner ceramics studio, Claremont, Calif.; prof. art, now prof. emerita San Diego State U.; founder, dir. Mingei Internat. Mus., San Diego. Coord. editing, design and prodn. of exhbn. documentary publs.; condr. tours. Contbr. chpts. to books; developer videotapes; exhibited at Dalzell Hatfield Galleries. San Diego State U. Found. grantee, 1967, Calif. State U. Rsch. grantee, 1978; recipient Disting. Alumna award Claremont Grad. Sch., 1980, Essence of Life award ElderHelp of San Diego, 1993, Living Legacy award Women's Internat. Ctr., 1994, Women of Distinction award Soroptimist Internat. of La Jolla, 1994, Headliner of Yr. Art, San Diego Press Club, 1998, Disting. Svc. medal, San Diego State U., 1998, Reischauer Internat. Edn. award, Japan Soc. San Diego and Tijuana, 1999, San Diego Women Who Mean Bus. award, Foley Vardner Attys. at Law, San Diego Bus. Jour., 2000, Gold Rays with Rosette, Order of Rising Sun, Emperor of Japan, 2003, Golden Hanger Spl. award, Fashion Careers of Calif. Coll., 2004. Office: Mingei Internat Mus Balboa Park 1439 El Prado San Diego CA 92101-1617 also: Mingei Internat Mus PO Box 553 La Jolla CA 92038-0553

LONGFELLOW, DAVID, administrator; b. Akron, Ohio, Nov. 16, 1942; married, 1965; 2 children. BS, Lynchburg Coll., 1964; PhD, Johns Hopkins U., 1972. Tech., mgr. urology rsch. lab. animal facility Georgetown U., Washington, 1963-64; tech. lab. viral oncology NIH, Bethesda, Md., 1965-66, rsch. biologist, 1975-76, biologist, 1976-78, asst. chief chem. & phys. carcinogenesis br., 1979-83, acting chief chem. and phys. carcinogenesis br., 1983-84, chief chem. and phys. carcinogenesis br., 1984-95, acting spl. asst. environ. cancer, 1994-95, chief chem. and phys. carcinogenesis br., 1995—2003, sr. coord. for carcinogenesis, 2003—. Damon Runyon fellow, 1972-74, NCI fellow, 1974-75. Mem. Chi Beta Phi, Iota Beta Gamma. Office: NCI Divsn Cancer Biology Ste 5000 MSC 7398 6130 Executive Blvd Bethesda MD 20892-7398 Office Phone: 301-496-9448.

LONGFIELD, WILLIAM HERMAN, health products executive; b. Chgo., Aug. 8, 1938; s. William A. and Elizabeth (Beringer) L.; m. Nancy Shofstall, June 10, 1961; children: William, Scott. BS, Drake U., 1960; grad. bus. mgmt. program, Northwestern U., 1972. Pres. Convertors divsn. Am. Hosp. Supply, Evanston, Ill., 1961-82; exec. v.p., dir. Lifemark, Inc., Houston, 1982-83; pres., CEO Cambridge Group, Inc., Dallas, 1983-89; chmn., CEO C.R. Bard, Inc., Murray Hill, NJ, 1989—2003, also bd. dirs.; ret., 2003. Bd. dirs. Atlantic Health Sys., Manor Care, Inc., Toledo, West Pharm. Svcs., Pa., Horizon Health Corp., Dallas; bd. dirs. Internat. Non-Wovens Assn., N.Y.C., 1975-82; chmn. AdvaMed; bd. dirs. Applera. Chmn., bd. dirs. Deerfield (Ill.) Youth Orgn., 1975-80. Recipient Pres.' award Nat. Nurse Cons. Assn., 1980. Mem. Baltrusol Golf Club, Metedeconk Country Club, Hamilton Farm Golf Club, Bull Bay Golf Club. Republican. Presbyterian. Avocations: golf, tennis. Office: C R Bard Inc 328 Springfield Ave Summit NJ 07901

LONGHOFER, GORDAN ALLEN, art educator, performance artist; b. Wichita, Kans., May 14, 1960; s. Donald Eugene and Erma Maxine Longhofer; m. Karen Lynn Byrd, Aug. 16, 1983; children: Blake, Dean, Luke, Abby. MusB, MusB in Edn., Okla. Bapt. U., 1983; MusM, U. Okla., 1984. Educator's cert. Fla., Okla., Kans. Vocal music instr. Carnegie (Okla.) Pub. Schs., Carnegie, Okla., 1984—87, Barber County N. USD #254, Medicine Lodge, Kans., 1987—88, Palm Beach County Sch. Dist., West Palm Beach, Fla., 1988—91, 1999—2001; instr. voice Palm Beach Atlantic Coll., West Palm Beach, 1991—97; lead instr. Palm Beach Opera, West Palm Beach, 1998—2001, edn. and outreach coord., 2001—. Condr., messiah Barber County Choral Soc., Medicine Lodge, 1988; music dir. Santaluces Cmty. H.S., Lantana, 1990. Singer: (Operas) Tosca, 1990, 1998, Madama Butterfly, 1991, 1997, La traviata, 1992, 1996, Aïda, 1992, Rigoletto, 1993, 1997, 2001, Il barbiere di Siviglia, 1994, 2001, 2000, Il trovatore, 1993, La Bohème, 1993, 1998, 2000, Carmen, 1994, Salome, 1995, Eugene Onegin, 1996, The Merry Widow, 1996, 2001, Turandot, 1996, Così fan tutte, 1995, 1997, Manon, 1999, Un ballo in maschera, 2000, Der Fliegende Holländer, 2000, Norma, 2001, Luisa Miller, 2001; singer: (bass soloist) (oratorio) Mozart Requiem, 1985, 1991, Messa di Gloria, 1993, Petite Messe Solennelle, 1994, Messiah, 1990, 1995, 1997, Creation, 1987, 1991, 1995, 1996, 1997, Mass in C Major by Beethoven, 1990, 2000; actor: (musical) "M" Madeline and Merlin's Magic at Midnight, 2001. Deacon Westside Bapt. Ch., Boynton Beach, Fla., 1994—97; mem. cultural edn. com. Palm Beach County Cultural Coun., West Palm Beach, 2001—02; mental health month planning com. Mental Health Assn. of Palm Beach County, West Palm Beach, 2002—02. Named Nat. Finalist Stewart Awards Operatic Voice Competition, Okla. Symphony Orch., 1986, Semi-Finalist, Luciano Pavarotti Internat. Voice Competition, 1995; recipient Encouragement award, Tulsa Dist. Met. Opera Nat. Coun., 1985, Most Promising Singer award, 1986; scholar Benton-Schmidt Vocal, U. Okla., 1983-1984. Mem.: NEA, Fla. Edn. Assn., Fla. Vocal Assn., Fla. Music Educators Assn., Music Educators Nat. Conf. Avocations: golf, reading, fishing. Office: Palm Beach Opera 415 S Olive Ave West Palm Beach FL 33401

LONGHOFER, RONALD STEPHEN, lawyer; b. Junction City, Kans., Aug. 30, 1946; s. Oscar William and Anna Mathilda (Krause) L.; m. Elizabeth Norma McKenna; children: Adam, Nathan, Stefanie. BMus, U. Mich., 1968, JD, 1975, MBA, 2004. Bar: Mich. 1975, U.S. Dist. Ct. (ea. dist.) Mich., U.S. Ct. Appeals (6th cir.), U.S. Supreme Ct.; cert. chartered fin. analyst, fraud examiner. Law clk. to judge U.S. Dist. Ct. (ea. dist.) Mich., Detroit, 1975-76; ptnr. Honigman, Miller, Schwartz & Cohn, Detroit, 1976—2003, chmn. litigation dept., 1993-96; dir. Stout, Risius, Ross, Inc., 2004—. Co-author: Courtroom Handbook on Michigan Evidence, 2005, Michigan Court Rules Practice, 1998, Michigan Court Rules Practice-Evidence, 2002, Introducing Evidence at Trial, 2003; author: Courtroom Handbook on Michigan Civil Procedure, 2005, Michigan Court Rules Practice, 2004; editor Mich. Law Rev., 1974-75. Served with U.S. Army, 1968-72. Mem. ABA, Detroit Bar Assn., Fed. Bar Assn., Oakland County Bar Assn., CFA Detroit, CFA Inst., Assn. Cert. Fraud Examiners, Inst. Bus. Appraisers, U. Mich. Pres.' Club, Order of Coif, Phi Beta Kappa, Phi Kappa Phi, Pi Kappa Lambda, Beta Gamma Sigma. Home: 974 Penniman Ave Plymouth MI 48170 Office: Stout Risius Ross Inc 32255 Northwestern Hwy Ste 201 Farmington Hills MI 48334 Office Phone: 248-432-1321. Business E-Mail: rlonghofer@gosrr.com.

LONGHURST, ROBERT RUSSELL, retired secondary school educator; b. Montgomery, Ala., Feb. 28, 1921; s. Lawrence Alston and Margaret Earlene (King) L.; m. Anne McMahon, Nov. 26, 1952 (div. 1982). Student, Vanderbilt U., 1942; BA in Econs., Peabody Coll., 1949, MA, 1950. Cert. tchr., Tenn. Various positions Stinson Aviation & Consol.-Vultee Aircraft Corp., 1940-43; tech. rep. Lockheed Overseas Corp., British Isles, 1943-44; tchr. Nashville Bd. Edn., 1950-77, coordinator vocat. edn., 1977-87; ret., 1987. Nat. defense course in aeronautics, Vanderbilt U., 1942. Served as petty officer USNR, 1944-46, PTO. Mem. NEA, Tenn. Edn. Assn., Met. Nashville Edn. Assn., Am. Vocat. Assn., Am. Legion, Pi Gamma Mu. Mem. Ch. of Christ. Avocations: woodworking, music, financial planning, investing. Home: 2421 Eastland Ave Nashville TN 37206-1101

LONGIN, THOMAS CHARLES, retired academic administrator; b. Lewistown, Mont., Nov. 17, 1939; s. Charles Otto and Anne Dorothy (Vavrovsky) L.; m. Nancy Tillinghast; children: Kevin C., Teresa L., Karl T., Anne M. BA in History, Carroll Coll., 1962; MA in History, Creighton U., 1965; PhD in Am. History, U. Nebr., 1970. Instr. Carroll Coll., Helena, Mont., 1965-67; asst. prof. Va. Poly. Inst. and State U., Blacksburg, 1970-73; asst. prof., then assoc. prof. Ithaca (N.Y.) Coll., 1973-82, dean humanities and scis., 1976-82, provost, 1985-96; v.p. acad. affairs Seattle U., 1982-85; v.p. programs and rsch. Assn. of Governing Bds., Washington, 1997—2002, ret., 2002. Cons. in field. Exec. editor Planning in Higher Education, 2004—. Home: 10452 Courtney Dr Fairfax VA 22030 Personal E-mail: tomlongin@cox.net.

LONGLEY, MARJORIE WATTERS, newspaper executive; b. Lockport, N.Y., Nov. 2, 1925; d. J. Randolph and Florence Lucille (Craine) Watters; m. Ralph R. Longley, Oct. 1, 1949 (dec.). BA in English with highest honors cum laude, St. Lawrence U., 1947. Sports editor, feature writer Lockport Union Sun and Jour., 1945; with N.Y. Times, N.Y.C., 1948-88, asst. to v.p. consumer mktg., 1975-78, circulation sales mgr., 1978-79, sales dir., 1979-81, dir. pub. affairs, 1981-88; pres. Gramercy Internat., Inc. (mktg. and pub. rels.), N.Y.C., 1988—; assoc. pub. The Earth Times, N.Y.C., 1996—. Dir. pub. affairs and pub. info., N.Y.C. Off-Track Betting Corp., 1990-94; mem. Nat. Newspapers' Readership Coun., 1979-82; mem. adv. coun. API, 1980-85. Author: America's Taste, 1960. Trustee St. Lawrence U., 1969-75, 77—; chmn. bd. dirs. Am. Forum for Global Edn., 1977-98, chmn. emerita, 1999—; pres. N.Y. City Adult Edn. Coun., 1974-77, Grmercy Pk. Lot Owners Assn., Inc., 1995—; mem. N.Y. State Adv. Coun. for Vocat. Edn, 1976-81, postsecondary edn., 1978-81, Mayor's Coun. Environment of N.Y.C., 1983-96; bd. dirs. Nat. Charities Info. Bur., 1983-96, Literacy Ptnrs., Inc., 1996—; chmn. 42d St. Edn., Theatre, Culture, 1984-88, chmn. emeritus, 1988—. Mem. Nat. Inst. Social Scis., Am. Mgmt. Assn. (nat. mktg. coun. 1972-89, bd. dirs. 1986-88), Nat. Arts Club, Overseas Press Club, Phi Beta Kappa. Democrat. Baptist. Office: Gramercy Internat Inc 34 Gramercy Park E New York NY 10003-1731

LONGLEY, MICHAEL CHARLES H., spine surgeon; b. Hakare, Zimbabwe, Oct. 12, 1961; MD, U. Cape Town, South Africa, 1984. Intern McCords Zulu Hosp., Durban Natal, South Africa, 1985-86; resident Royal U. Hosp.-U. Saskatchewan, Saskatoon, Can., 1986-90, fellow, 1990, Victoria Hosp.-U. Western Ont., London, Can., 1990-91, Minn. Spine Ctr., Mpls., 1991-92; staff Immanuel Med. Ctr., Omaha, 1992—, Bergan Mercy Hosp., Omaha, 1992—, U. Nebr. Med. Ctr., Omaha, 1992—; instr. U. Nebr., Omaha, 1992—. Mem. RCSC, Am. Acad. Orthop. Surgeons, ABOS, MOMS. Office: 11819 Miracle Hills Dr Ste 102 Omaha NE 68154-4428

LONGMAN, ANNE STRICKLAND, special education educator, consultant; b. Metuchen, N.J., Sept. 17, 1924; d. Charles Hodges and Grace Anna (Moss) Eldridge; m. Henry Richard Strickland, June 22, 1946 (dec. 1960); m. Donald Rufus Longman, Jan. 20, 1979 (dec. 1987); children: James C., Robert H. BA in Bus. Adminstrn., Mich. State U., 1945; teaching credentials, U. Calif., Berkeley, 1959; postgrad., Stanford U., 1959-60; MA in Learning Hand, Santa Clara U., 1974. Lic. educator. Exptl. test engr. Pratt & Whitney Aircraft, East Hartford, Conn., 1945-47; indsl. engr. Marchant Calculators, Emeryville, Calif., 1957-58; with pub. rels. Homesmith, Palo Alto, Calif., 1959-62; cons. Right to Read Program, Calif., 1978-79; monitor, reviewer State of Calif., Sacramento, 1976-79; tchr. diagnosis edn. Cabrillo Coll., Aptos, Calif., 1970-79; lectr. edn. U. Calif., Santa Cruz, 1970-79; cons. Santa Cruz Bd. Edn., 1970-79; reading rschr. Gorilla Found., Woodside, Calif., 1982—. Bd. mem. Western Inst. Alcoholic Studies, L.A., 1972-73; chmn. Evaluation Com., Tri-County, Calif., 1974; speaker Internat. Congress Learning Disabilities, Seattle, 1974; ednl. cons. rsch. on allergies, 1993—; artist-in-residence Yosemite, 1998-2004 Author: Word Patterns in English, 1974-92, Cramming 3D Kids, 1975—, 50 books for migrant students, 1970-79; artist Watsonville Pajaronian; contbr. articles on stress and alcoholism and TV crime prevention for police, 1960-79. Founder Literacy Ctr., Santa Cruz, 1968-092; leader Girl Scouts U.S.A., San Francisco, 1947-50; vol. Thursday's Child, Santa Cruz, 1976-79, Golden Gate Kindergarten, San Francisco, 1947-57; vol. Yosemite Nat. Pk.; judge art Santa Creeg County Fair Recipient Fellowships Pratt & Whitney Aircraft, 1944, Stanford U., 1959 Mem. Internat. Reading Assn. (pres. Santa Cruz 1975), Santa Clara Valley Watercolor Soc., Artists Equity, Arts Habitat, Los Altos Art Club (v.p. 1992), Eichler Swim and Tennis Club. Republican. Episcopalian. Avocations: drawing, watercolor, watercolor painting, travel, drama. Home and Office: 651 Sinex Ave #J211 Pacific Grove CA 93950

LONGMAN, GARY LEE, accountant; b. Kewanee, Ill., Apr. 25, 1948; s. Howard L. and Dorothy (Wenk) L.; m. Ruth Ann Biesboer; children: Gregory, Rebecca. AA, Joliet (Ill.) Jr. Coll., 1968; BS in Acctg., No. Ill. U., 1970. CPA, Ill. Staff acct. KPMG Peat Marwick, Chgo., 1970-72, sr. acct., 1972-74, mgr., 1974-80, ptnr., 1980-91, ptnr.-in-charge Chgo. office mfg. practice, 1991-93, ptnr.-in-charge Chgo. audit dept., 1991-93, midwest ptnr.-in-charge info., comm. & entertainment, 1993-96, midwest ptnr.-in-charge mfg., retailing, and distbn., 1996-98; ptnr.-in-charge Assurance Chgo./Milw., 1998-2000. Bus. adv. coun. Dept. Commerce, DePaul U., 1991-95; bd. dirs. Jr. Achievement, Chgo., SunnyRidge Family Svcs., 1998—; bd. exec. advisors Coll. Bus. No. Ill. U., 1998—; treas. 1st Congl. Ch. Western Springs, 2001—. Mem. AICPAs, Ill. Soc. CPAs, LaGrange Country Club, Westmoor Country Club, Five Seasons Country Club, Econ. Club of Chgo.

LONGMAN, STANLEY VINCENT, retired performing arts educator; b. Iowa City, Iowa, Aug. 14, 1938; s. Lester Duncan and Florence Brown Longman; m. Ruth Helen Farstrup, Aug. 11, 1961; children: Alexander Marius, Eric Anders, Ian Duncan. BA, U. Iowa, 1960, MA, 1962; PhD, U. of Iowa, Iowa City, 1971. Asst. prof. Buena Vista Coll., Storm Lake, Iowa, 1965—68; prof. & dept. head U. Ga., Athens, 2000—04; ret., 2004. Author: (books) Composing Drama for Stage and Screen, Page and Stage: an Approach to Scipt Analysis; editor: Drama as Rhetoric/Rhetoric as Drama, Theatre at the Crossroads: East and West; translator: (plays) Our Fathers, Six Characters in Search of an Author, Mistress of the Inn. Named to Iowa Hall of Fame, U. Iowa Dept. of Drama, 1996; recipient Medal of Excellence, Am. Coll. Theatre Festival, 1978, Sr. Tchg. Fellow, U. Ga., 1992—93, Tchg. Acad. award, 1999; Fulbright Fellowship, govt., 1963—64, Fellowship, NDEA., 1961—63, fellow, Phi Kappa Phi U. Ga. chpt., 2003. Mem.: Internat. Fedn. Theatre Rsch., Am. Coll. Theatre Festival (nat. chair playwriting 1979—81), Southeastern Theatre Conf. (v.p. 1974—76), Assn. for Theatre in Higher Edn., Am. Soc. for Theatre Rsch. Home: 475 Millstone Circle Athens GA 30605 Office: Department of Drama and Theatre University of Georgia Athens GA 30602-3154 Personal E-mail: rflsvl@aol.com. Business E-Mail: longman@uga.edu.

LONGMIRE, VENUS DELOYSE, minister; b. Greenville, Ala., July 21, 1945; d. James Wilbert and Estelle Golson Longmire; m. Melvin Robinson II, July 22, 1966 (div. Nov. 1975); 1 child, Melvin Longmire Robinson III; m. Amon Olugbala Ra, July 28, 2000. BS, Livingstone Coll., 1965; MSW, Ind. U., 1970; M in Theology, Emory U., 1982; D in Theology (hon.), U. Life Ch. Inst., San Fafael, Calif., 1989; PhD, Columbia Pacific U., 1989; D in Divinty (hon.), New Covenant Inst., 1995. Family svcs. supr. City of Atlanta Housing Authority, 1973—76; v.p. contract develop. Longmire Coal Corp., Knoxville, Tenn., 1976—86; dir. religious develop. Ala. State U., Montgomery, 1987—90; med. social worker State of Ala. Dept. Pub. Health, Hayneville, 1991—92; dir. min. The Sisterhood, Inc., Greenville, 1992—. Grant writer cons., 1965—; cons. energy develop. Del Kijaico Inc., Wilmington, Del., 1990—2002. Author: (prose) As We Are, So Is Our World, 1982; author, editor: Mother's Voice: Lost Writings of Mary, 2003. Mem. Hist. Perservation Soc., Montgomery, 1999—2003; advisor, sponsor Saving Our Cmty. & Kids, Greenville High, Ala. Named Cmty. Advocate, City of Atlanta, 1975; named one of Women in Bus., Knoxville Jour., 1983; recipient Ala. Treasure Forestry award, Forestry Commn., USDA, 2003. Mem.: So. Proverty Law Ctr., Coun. on Aging (lobbyist 1995—), Nat. Assn. Social Workers (lobbyist 1983—). Democrat. Methodist. Avocations: running, chess. Home: 101 N Haardt Dr Montgomery AL 36105 Office: New Covenant Inst Human Svc Ministries 236 W Commerce St Greenville AL 36037 Office Phone: 334-657-9467. E-mail: venuslongmire@aol.com.

LONGNECKER, DAVID EUGENE, anesthesiologist, educator; b. Kendallville, Ind., 1939; MD, Ind. U., 1964, MA in Anesthesiology, 1968. Diplomate Am. Bd. Anesthesiology. Intern Blodgett Meml. Hosp., Grand Rapids, Mich., 1964—65; resident in anesthesiology U. Ind., 1965—69; asst. prof. dept. anesthesiology U. Mo., 1970—73; assoc. prof. dept. anesthesiology U. Va., Charlottesville, 1974—78, prof., 1978—88; Robert D. Dripps prof., chmn. dept. anesthesia U. Pa., Phila., 1999—2002, sr. v.p., corp. chief med. officer, 2002—04, Robert D. Dripps prof. anesthesia emeritus, 2005—; dir. AAMC, 2005—. With USPHS, 1968—70. Mem.: Inst. Medicine, Am. Soc. Anesthesiologists. Office: AAMC 2450 N St NW Washington DC 20037-1127 Office Phone: 215-662-3145, 202-862-6113. E-mail: dlongnecker@aamc.org.

LONGO, DAN LOUIS, internist, researcher, oncologist; b. St. Louis, Apr. 25, 1949; s. Dominic L. and Alene V. (Bratcher) L.; m. Nancy Kay Schiffman, May 29, 1971; children: Jennifer Alene, Adam Daniel, Paul Anthony. AB,

Washington U., St. Louis, 1970; MD cum laude, U. Mo., 1975. Diplomate Am. Bd. Internal Medicine, Am. Bd. Oncology, Nat. Bd. Med. Examiners. Resident in medicine Peter Bent Brigham Hosp., Boston, 1975-77; fellow in oncology Nat. Cancer Inst., Bethesda, Md., 1977-78; postdoctoral fellow in immunology Nat. Inst. Allergy and Infectious Diseases, Bethesda, 1978-80; sr. investigator Medicine Br. Nat. Cancer Inst., Bethesda, 1980—85; assoc. dir. Biolog. Response Modifiers Program Nat. Cancer Inst., Frederick, Md., 1985-95; sci. dir. Nat. Inst. on Aging, Balt., 1995—. Mem. editl. bd. Critical Reviews in Oncology/Hematology; editor: Clin. Oncology Alert, 1985—2000, Cancer Chemotherapy and Biol. Response Modifiers Annual, 1987—2000, Harrison's Principles of Internal Medicine, 1995—; asst. editor Am. Jour. Clin. Nutrition, 1981—91, assoc. editor Jour. Nat. Cancer Inst., Clin. Cancer Rsch., Jour. Immunology, Clin. Immunology, Blood; contbr. chpts. to textbooks, over 700 articles to profl. jours. Rear adm. USPHS, 1977—. Recipient Harvard Book award, 1965, Young Physician award U. Mo. Alumni Assn., Citation of Merit, 1997, Tovi Comet-Walerstein award Bar-Ilan Univ., Israel, 1992. Fellow: AAAS, ACP (MKSAP IX Oncology Subsplty. Com. 1989—91, MKSAP 12 1999—2001, MKSAP 13 2002—04), Molecular Medicine Soc.; mem.: N.Y. Acad. Scis., Assn. Am. Physicians, Clin. Immunology Soc. (councilor 1987—90), Am. Soc. Cell Biology, Am. Soc. Clin. Investigation, Am. Soc. Hematology (subcom. on Neoplasia 1989—91, chmn. 1990, program com. 1994), Am. Assn. Cancer Rsch. (program com. 1986), Am. Assn. Immunologists, Am. Soc. Clin. Oncology (edn. com. 1992—94), Am. Soc. Clin. Nutrition (award com. 1989—91, program com. 1990), Am. Inst. Nutrition, Am. Soc. Microbiology, Am. Fedn. Clin. Rsch., Alpha Omega Alpha, Phi Kappa Phi, Sigma Xi. Office: Nat Inst Aging GRC 5600 Nathan Shock Dr Baltimore MD 21224-6825 Office Phone: 410-558-8110. Business E-Mail: longod@grc.nia.nih.gov.

LONGO, LAWRENCE DANIEL, physiologist, educator, obstetrician, gynecologist; b. LA, Oct. 11, 1926; s. Frank Albert and Florine Azelia (Hall) L.; m. Betty Jeanne Mundall, Sept. 9, 1948; children: April Celeste, Lawrence Anthony, Elisabeth Lynn, Camilla Giselle. BA, Pacific Union Coll., 1949; MD, Coll. Med. Evangelists, Loma Linda, Calif., 1954. Diplomate Am. Bd. Ob-Gyn. Intern L.A. County Gen. Hosp., 1954-55, resident in ob-gyn., 1955-58; asst. prof. ob-gyn UCLA, 1962-64; asst. prof. physiology and ob-gyn U. Pa., 1964-68; prof. physiology and ob-gyn Loma Linda U., 1968—; dir. ctr. for perinatal biology Loma Linda U. Sch. Medicine, 1974—. Perinatal biology com. Nat. Inst. Child Health, NIH, 1973-77; co-chmn. reprodn. scientist devel. program NIH; NATO prof. Consiglio Nat. delle Rsch., Italian Govt. Editor: Respiratory Gas Exchange and Blood Flow in the Placenta, 1972, Fetal and Newborn Cardiovascular Physiology, 1978, Charles White and A Treatise on the Management of Pregnant and Lying-in Women, 1987; co-editor: Landmarks in Perinatology, 1975-76, Classics in Obstetrics Gynecology, 1993, Dearest G..., Yours W.O., William Osler's Letters from Egypt to Grace Revere Osler, 2003, William Osler's Man's Redemption of Man, 2003, Our Lords the Sick..., 2004; editor classic pages in ob-gyn. Am. Jour. Ob-Gyn.; contbr. articles to profl. jours. Served with AUS, 1945-47. Founder Frank A. and Florine A. Longo lectureship in faith, knowledge, and human values Pacific Union Coll., 1993. Fellow Royal Coll. Ob-Gyns., Am. Coll. Ob-Gyns.; mem. Am. Assn. History Medicine (coun.), Am. Osler Soc. (bd. govs., sec.-treas., pres.), Am. Physiol. Soc., Assn. Profs. Ob-Gyn., Perinatal Rsch. Soc., Soc. Gynecologic Investigation (past pres.), Neurosci. Soc., Royal Soc. Medicine. Adventist. Office: Loma Linda U Sch Medicine Ctr Perinatal Biology Loma Linda CA 92350-0001 Office Phone: 909-558-4325. Business E-Mail: llongo@llu.edu.

LONGO, M. ROSS, lawyer; b. Jefferson, La., Oct. 1, 1976; s. Gary Richard and Beverly Jovett Longo. BA in History cum laude, Tex. Christian U., 1999; JD, Tex. Tech. U., 2002. Bar: Tex. 2002, U.S. Dist. Ct. (so. dist.) Tex. 2003. Assoc. Abbott Simses Kuchler APLC, Houston, 2002—05, McFall, Sherwood & Breitbeil, PC, Houston, 2005—. Mem. Houston World Affairs Coun., Tex., 2003—, Young Texans Against Cancer, 2005—. Mem.: ABA, Young Texans Against Cancer, Houston Bar Assn., Tex. Bar Assn. Avocations: travel, running, tennis. Office: McFall Sherwood & Breitbeil PC 1331 Lamar Ste 1250 Houston TX 77010 Office Phone: 713-590-9300. Office Fax: 713-590-9399.

LONGO, PAUL ALBERT, retired industrial engineer, consultant; b. N.Y.C., May 30, 1916; s. Anthony and Theresa (DeFranco) L.; m. Frances Abruscatto, Sept. 24, 1939; children: Robert, Virginia Lorey, Dennis, James, Dina Miller. Student, NYU, 1942-43, Columbia U., 1953-54, Indsl. Coll. Armed Forces, 1954-55; diploma, U.S. Army Logistics Mgmt. Ctr., 1958, U.S. Army Chem. Corps Sch., 1965. Registered profl. engr., cert. mfg. engr. Field project engr. Dept. Def., N.Y.C., 1940-65; supervisory indsl. engr. Aberdeen Proving Grounds, Edgewood, Md., 1966-70, programs mgr., 1970-71, chief indsl. ops., 1971-75, disposal engr., 1975-77. Chmn. indsl. planning coun. Dept. Def. Munitions Bd., 1954-58; chmn. Armed Svcs. Indsl. Readiness Coun., 1954-56; bd. dirs., v.p. Sci. Experiments Corp., N.Y.C., 1956-58; chief field engr. Jones Engring., Towson, Md., 1978-79; engring. cons. ICI Ams., Inc., Wilmington, Del., 1979-81; tech. instr. Harford C.C., Bel Air, Md., 1968; mil. instr. Army Chem. Sch., Ft. McClellan, Ala., 1968; tech. advisor Dept. Def., 1965-70. Author books, 1986-90; co-author: Fundamentals of Tool Design, 1983-84; contbr. articles to profl. jours.; editor: Jigs and Fixture Design, 1983; developer integrated Cad-Cam system for transition of design of army chem. ordnance to manufacturing, 1966-70; patentee in field. Dir.-at-large Beach Pkwy. Civic Assn., Cape Coral, Fla., 1991-97. Lt. col. ret. U.S. Army Res., 1949-69. Recipient Dept. Def. Meritorious Civilian Svc. award Army Chem. Corps, 1945, Meritorious Svc. medal U.S. Army, 1969, 1st pl. trophy award Ralph H. Landes Indsl. Mgmt. Soc., Chgo., 1970, 2d pl., 1973, multiple merit awards Soc. Mfg. Engrs., Dearborn, Mich., 1960-79. Mem. Ret. Officers Assn. (life), Engring. Soc. Cape Coral, Md. Res. Officers Assn. (pres. Edgewood chpt. 1965), Internat. Soc. Mfg. Engrs. Tech. (sem. chmn. 1969). Republican. Roman Catholic. Avocations: golf, boating, swimming, tennis, fishing. Home and Office: 1907 SE 40th Ter Cape Coral FL 33904-8007

LONGO, ROBERT, artist, film director; b. Bklyn., Jan. 7, 1953; BFA, SUNY, Buffalo, 1975. One-man shows include Metro Pictures, N.Y., 1981, Stedelijk Mus., Amsterdam, 1985, U. Art Mus., Calif. State U., 1986, Contemporary Arts Mus., Houston, 1986, L.A. County Mus. Art, L.A., 1989, Mus. Contemporary Art, Chgo., 1989, Wadsworth Atheneum, Hartford, 1989, Galerie Daniel Templon, Paris, 1990, Galerie Daniel Templon, Galerie Antoine Candau, Galerie Thaddaeus Ropac, A.B. Galleries, Galerie Gordon Pym et Fils, 1991, The Isetan Mus. Art, Tokyo, 1995, Ashikaga City Mus., Kirin Plaza Art Space, Osaka, Japan, 1995, Mus. Fridericianum, Kassel, Germany, 1996, Kunsthalle Tubingen, Germany, 1997, Kunsthal Rotterdam, The Netherlands, 1997, Kunsthalle Bielefeld, Germany, 1997, exhibited in group shows at Documenta 7, Kassel, 1982, Doumenta 8, 1987, Whitney Mus. Am. Art, N.Y.C., 1983, 1997, Tate Gallery, London, 1983, Laforet Mus., Tokyo, 1985, Tochigi (Japan) Prefectural Mus. Fine Arts, 1985, Tazaki Hall Espace Media, Kobe, Japan, 1985, Mus. Contemporary Art, L.A., 1989, Mus. Modern Art, N.Y.C., 1992, La Biennale di Venezia: XLVII Esposizione Internat. d'Arte, Venice, Italy, 1997, LipanjePuntin Artecontemporanea, Trieste, Italy, 2000, Galerie Burkhard Eikelmann, Essen, Germany, 2001, Galerie Six Friedrich Lisa Ungar, Munich, 2002, DaimlerChrysler Contemporary, Berlin, 2003, Represented in permanent collections Art Inst. Chgo., Guggenheim Mus., N.Y., L.A. County Mus. Art, Mus'e d'Art Contemporain, Montreal, Can., Mus. Modern Art, N.Y.C., Saatchi Collection, London, Stedelijk Mus., Amsterdam, Tate Gallery, London, Walker Art Ctr., Mpls., Whitney Mus. Am. Art, N.Y.C.; dir.: (films) Arena Brains, 1988, Johnny Mnemonic, 1995; (TV series, episode) HBO's Tales from the Crypt, 1989, (music videos) REM's The One I Love and New Order's Bizarre Love Triangele; co-dir., set designer, costume designer: (Operas) Lucio Silla, Mozart Festival, Salzburg, Austria, 1992, 1993; Lucio Silla, Frankfurt Opera House, 1995.*

LONGO, VINCENT, art educator, painter, printmaker; b. N.Y.C., Feb. 15, 1923; s. Salvatore and Margaret (Stigliano) L.; m. Pat Adams (div. 1969); children: Matthew, Jason; m. Kathleen Davis, Nov. 27, 1972. Diploma, Cooper Union, 1946. Instr. painting and prints Bklyn. Mus. Art Sch., 1955-57, Bennington (Vt.) Coll., 1957-67; prof. art Hunter Coll., CUNY, 1967—2001; ret., 2001. Asst. dir. Yale U. Summer Art Sch., Norfolk, Conn., 1955-59, dir., 1969. Represented in permanent collections Bklyn. Mus., Corcoran Gallery, Washington, Detroit Inst. Art, Fogg Mus., Libr. of Congress, Met. Mus. Art, N.Y. Mus. Fine Arts, Boston Mus. Modern Art; one-person shows Alfred Univ., 1978, Andrew Crispo, N.Y.C., 1980, Adam Gimbel Gallery, N.Y.C., Condeso/Lawler Gallery, N.Y.C., 1984, 85, 87, 89, 90, 93, Hunter Coll. Art Galleries, Career Retrospective, 2003; group exhibitions Boca Raton Ctr., Fla., 1984, The Whitney Mus. Am. Art, N.Y.C., 1982, others. Recipient profl. achievement citation Cooper Union, 1973; Fulbright scholar, 1951; Guggenheim fellow, 1971; grantee Nat. Endowment for Arts, 1973. Mem. Am. Abstract Artists, NAD (academician).*

LONGOBARDI, DAVID, editor-in-chief; b. 1962; AB, Harvard Univ., 1984; M journalism & mass comm., NYU. Editl. dir. Water's Info. Svs., 1990—96; pub., editl. dir. Securities Industry News, 1996—99; editor-in-chief Am. Banker Mag., 1999—. Office: Am Banker Mag 1 State St Plz 27th Fl New York NY 10004

LONGOBARDO, ANNA KAZANJIAN, engineering executive; b. N.Y.C. d. Aram Michael and Zarouhy (Yazejian) Kazanjian; m. Guy S. Longobardo, July 12, 1952; children: Guy A., Alicia. Student, Barnard Coll., 1947; BSME, Columbia U., 1949, MSME, 1952. Sr. systems engr. Am. Bosch Arma Corp., Garden City, N.Y., 1950-65; rsch. sect. head Sperry Rand Corp., Gt. Neck, N.Y., 1965-68, rsch. sect. head systems mgmt., 1968-73; mgr. engring. personnel utilization Sperry Corp., Gt. Neck, 1973-77, mgr. systems mgmt. program planning, 1977-81, mgr. planning systems mgmt. group, 1981-82, dir. tech. svc. sys. devel., 1982-89, dir. field engring., 1989-93; dir. strategic initiatives Unysis Corp., Gt. Neck, 1993-95; bd. dirs. Engring. Found. Gateway Engring. Edn. Coalition, 1998—, also bd. dirs.; vice chmn. Engring. Conf. Found. Bd., 2001—04. Chmn. exec. compensation com. Woodward-Clyde Group, Denver, 1989-97. Contbr. articles to profl. publs. Trustee Columbia U., N.Y.C., 1990-96, trustee emerita, 1996—; mem. Columbia Engring. Coun., 1987—, chmn., 1987-91; vice chmn. Bronxville (N.Y.) Planning Bd.; chmn. Bronxville Design Rev. Com., 1993—; pres. Soc. Columbia Grads., 1998-2000. Recipient hon. citation Wilson Coll. Centennial, 1970, Alumni medal for conspicuous svc. Columbia U., 1980, Egleston medal for disting. engring. achievement Columbia U., 1997; named One of 100 N.Y. Women of Influence, New York Woman mag., 1986. Fellow Soc. Women Engrs. (founder, pioneer); mem. AIAA (sr.), ASME (sr.), Columbia U. Engring. Alumni Assn. (pres. 1977-81), Columbia U. Alumni Fedn. (pres. 1981-85), Bronxville Field Club.

LONGOBARDO, GUY ALFRED, lawyer; b. N.Y.C., May 9, 1961; s. Guy S. and Anna Grace (Kazanjian) L.; children: Alice Elisabeth, Anne Abigail. BA cum laude, Williams Coll., 1982; JD, Columbia U., 1985. Bar: N.Y. 1986. Assoc. Milbank, Tweed, Hadley & McCloy, N.Y.C., 1985-95; mng. dir., chief adminstrv. officer, orgn. and adv. HSBC Securities, Inc., 1995-97, mng. dir., head of corp. fin., 1997-98; gen. counsel, v.p. bus. devel. AMNEX, Inc., New Rochelle, NY, 1998—2001; CEO, ETS Payphones, Inc., Lithia Springs, Ga., 2001—. Dep. village counsel Village of Bronxville, 1991-96. Mem. long range planning com. Village of Bronxville; mem. com. for non-partisan nomination and election of sch. trustees Bronxville, N.Y., 1995-96, coach Eastchester Youth Soccer Assn., 1995-98; gov. Bronxville Field Club, 2000-; pres. Bronxville Field Club, 2003-; dir. Am. Pub. Comm. Coun., 2001-. Harlan Fiske Stone scholar Columbia U., 1983. Mem. Bronxville Field Club (gov. 2000-, pres. 2003-), Am. Pub. Comm. Coun. (dir. 2001-). Christian Scientist. Avocations: tennis, skiing, platform tennis. Home: 22 Greenfield Ave Bronxville NY 10708 Office: ETS Payphones Inc 1490 Westfork Dr Ste G Lithia Springs GA 30122 E-mail: glongbard@aol.com.

LONGORIA, EVA (EVA JACQUELINE LONGORIA, EVA LONGORIA CHRISTOPHER), actress; b. Corpus Christi, Tex., Mar. 15, 1975; m. Tyler Christopher, Jan. 20, 2002 (div. Jan. 19, 2005). BS in Kinesiology, Tex. A&M-Kingsville. Actress (TV series) The Young and the Restless, 2001—03 (ALMA award for Outstanding Actress in a Daytime Drama), L.A. Dragnet, 2003, Desperate Housewives, 2004— (co-recipient, Outstanding Performance by an Ensemble in a Drama Series, Screen Actors Guild award, 2005), (video) Snitch'd, 2003, Señorita Justice, 2004, (TV films) The Dead Will tell, 2004, actress, co-prodr. (films) Carlita's Secret, 2004, co-prodr., performer (variety show, video) Hot Tamales Live: Spicy, Hot and Hilarious, 2003; performer: (Broadway plays) What the Rabbi Saw; guest appearances Beverly Hills, 90210, 2000. Named Miss Corpus Christi, 1998; named one of Ten New Faces to Watch, Variety, 2004, Fall's TV's Hot 11, USA Today, 2004, New Faces of Fall, TV Guide, 2004, Hot 100 for 2004, Maxim Mag., 2004, 25 Most Beautiful People, People en Espanol's. Address: Desperate Housewives Touchstone Televison 100 University City Plaza Bldg 2128 Ste Universal City CA 91608*

LONGORIA, STEVE, security firm executive, consultant; b. Madera, Calif., July 8, 1961; s. Stefano D. and Armida A. Longoria; 1 child, Steven Alexander. BS in Edn. and Tng., So. Ill. U., 1997; cert. in hazardous materials mgmt., U. Calif., Davis, 1998; cert. in indsl. safety, U. Wash., Spokane, 1999. Project mgr., BrainBench Inc., 1998; counterterrorism planner Israeli Def. Forces, 1994, cert. homeland security profl. level III. Enlisted USAF, 1980, advanced through grades to master sgt., site security chief Aviano Air Base, Italy, 1980—83, antiterrorism mgr. Grand Forks Air Force Base, ND, 1983—87, Aviano Air Base, 1987—92, Sembach Air Base, Germany, 1992—94, supt. law enforcement tng. Travis Air Force Base, Calif., 1994—96, chief of safety, 1996—97, ret., 1997; CEO Aanko Technologies Inc., Vacaville, Calif., 2001—; pres. LifeLong Learning Systems, Vacaville, 1997—2001. Sec. Solano C.C. Edml. Found., Fairfield, Calif., 2002—. Author: (book) Defense Against Terrorist Aggression, 1986, (antiterrorism training course) Security Surveys: Audit, Analysis and Reporting. Dir. Streetwise-Booksmart Project, Fairfield, 1995—2000; fund raiser Solano County Bus. and Edn. Alliance, Vallejo, Calif., 1999—99; campaign mgr. Sch. Bd., Vacaville, 2000—00. Decorated Meritorious Svc. medal U.S. Congress; named NCO of the Yr., Calif. Air Force Assn., 1997; recipient Commandant's award, Kisling NonCommissioned Officer Acad., 1993; Eagle grantee, USAF, 1996. Mem.: Am. Soc. for Indsl. Security. Achievements include Only person in Department of Defense History selected as top professional in three different career classifications: Antiterrorism (1994); Security (1994) and Safety (1997). Home: Ste 191 607 Elmira Rd Vacaville CA 95687 Office: Aanko Technologies Inc Ste 207 419 Mason St Vacaville CA 95688 Business E-Mail: steve.longoria@aanko.com.

LONGSTREET, SUSAN CANNON, lawyer; b. Washington, July 18, 1944; d. Price Watkins and Martha Virginia (Cannon) L.; m. Harrison Fargo McConnell II, Sept. 4, 1965 (div. July 1974); 1 child, Catherine Dianne. Student, Duke U., 1962-64; BA in Econs., George Washington U., 1967; JD, Coll. of William and Mary, 1984. Bar: Va., 1984, D.C. 1985. Counsel Shaw Pittman, Washington, 1984-2000; ptnr. Winston & Strawn, Washington, 2000—. Mem. ABA, Va. State Bar Assn., D.C. Bar Assn. Home: 5831 Berkshire Ct Alexandria VA 22303-1630 Office: Winston & Strawn 1400 L St NW Ste 800 Washington DC 20005-3508

LONGSTREET, WILMA S., retired education educator; b. NYC, July 3, 1935; d. Hyman Steinberg and Estelle Rosa; widowed; stepchildren: Patricia, Robert, Richard Engle. BA, Hunter Coll., 1956; MS, Ind. U., 1968, PhD, 1970. Cert. tchr., N.Y.C. Asst. prof. U. Ill., Champaign/Urbana, 1970-72; from assoc. prof. to prof. edn. U. Mich., Flint and Ann Arbor, 1972-78; dean, prof. edn. DePaul U., Chgo., 1978-82; dean edn. U. New Orleans, 1982-85, prof. curriculum and instrn., 1982—2004. Mem. Coll. and Univ. Faculty Assembly, 1970—, pres., 1999; with online doctoral program Walden U., 2004—; cons. in field Author: Aspects of Ethnicity, 1978, The Leaders and the Led, 1979; co-author: A Design for Social Education, 1972, (with Shirley H. Engle) Curriculum for a New Millennium, 1993; contbr. over 70 articles to profl. jours. Mem. Profs. of Curriculum (factotum, chair nominating com. 2001), Phi Delta Kappa. Democrat. Unitarian-Universalist. Home: 49 Gull St New Orleans LA 70148 E-mail: wlongstr@walden.edu.

LONGSTRETH, BEVIS, lawyer; b. N.Y.C., Jan. 29, 1934; s. Alfred Bevis and Mary Agnes (Shiras) L.; m. Clara Seymour St. John, Aug. 10, 1963; children: Katherine Shiras, Thomas Day, Benjamin Hoyt. BS cum laude, Princeton U., 1956; LL.M., Harvard U., 1961. Bar: N.Y. 1962. Assoc. Debevoise & Plimpton, N.Y.C., 1962-70, ptnr., 1970-81; commr. SEC, Washington, 1981-84; ptnr. Debevoise & Plimpton, 1984-97, of counsel, 1997—2000. Lectr. Columbia U. Law Sch., N.Y.C., 1975-81, adj. prof., 1994-99; cons. Ford Found., 1971-72; cons. to Comptroller Gen. of U.S.; mem. pension fin. com. World Bank, 1987-95; bd. govs. Am. Stock Exch., 1992-98; bd. dirs. AMVESCAP, plc, Coll. Ret. Equities Fund. Author books, numerous articles on investment, securities and law. Trustee Nathan Cummings Found., 1991-97, 1999—, The Textile Mus., New Sch. U., 1987—; mem. fin. com. Rockefeller Family Fund, 1986—; chmn. Fund for Independence in Journalism, 2004—. Lt. USMC, 1956-58. Mem. Am. Law Inst., Assn. of Bar of City of N.Y., Coun. Fgn. Rels. Democrat. Home: 322 Central Park W New York NY 10025-7629 Office: Debevoise & Plimpton 919 3rd Ave New York NY 10022-6225 Office Phone: 212-909-6651. E-mail: blongstreth@mindspring.com, blongstreth@debevoise.com.

LONGSTRETH, RICHARD WASHINGTON, education educator, consultant; b. Pasadena, Calif., Mar. 4, 1946; s. Thaddeus and Lucy Washington (Norton) Longstreth; m. Lucinda Edwards Train Longstreth; 1 child, Elizabeth Edwards Train. AB in arch., U. of Pa., 1964—68; PhD, U. of Calif., 1971—77. Archtl. historian R.I. Hist. Preservation Commn., 1975—76; asst. prof. Kansas State U., 1976—83; prof. of Am. studies George Wash. U., Washington, 1983—. Beinecke-Reeves disting. vis. chair U. Fla., 2001; pres. Soc. of Archtl. Historians, 1998—2000; v.p. Vernacular Arch. Forum, 1989—91; bd. mem. Nat. Bldg. Mus., 1988—94, Adirondack Archtrl. Heritage, 1998—; adminstrn. mem. Nat. Register of Peer Profls., Gen. Svcs., Adminstrn., 2002—. Author: (book) The Buildings of Main Street: A Guide to American Commercial Architecture, 1987, On the Edge of the World: Four Architects in San Francisco at the Turn of the Century, 1989, The Drive In, the Supermarket..., 1999, City Center to Regional Mall, 1997 (Abbott Lowell Cummings award, 1998, Lewis Mumford prize, 1997, Spiro Kostof award, 1999); mem. editl. bd. (journal) Washington History, 1992—. Mem. Nat. Hist. Landmarks Com., Nat. Pk. Svc., 1989—94; chair Md. Nat. Register Rev. Bd., 1997—. Lt. USN, 1968—71. Recipient Rsch. award, Graham Found., 1998—2003, Ctr. for Wash. Area Studies, 1994, 1997, Renchard prize, Hist. Soc. of Wash., 1991—. Avocation: photography. Office: Am Studies Dept George Wash U Washington DC 20052

LONGSWORTH, ROBERT MORROW, language educator; b. Canton, Ohio, Feb. 15, 1937; s. Robert H. and Margaret Elizabeth (Morrow) L.; m. Carol Herndon, Aug. 16, 1958; children: Eric D., Margaret W., Ann E. AB, Duke U., 1958; MA, Harvard U., 1960, PhD, 1965. Asst. prof. Oberlin Coll., 1964-70, assoc. prof., 1970-75, prof. English, 1975—, emeritus prof., 2001—, dean Coll. Arts and Scis., 1974-84. Author: The Cornish Ordinalia, 1967, The Design of Drama, 1972 A Decade of Campus Language at Oberlin College, 2003; contbr. articles to profl. jours. Danforth Found. fellow Fellow Am. Coun. Learned Socs., Nat. Humanities Ctr.; mem. MLA, Medieval Acad. Am., Cornwall Archaeol. Soc., Phi Beta Kappa.

LONGSWORTH, SUSAN KAY, elementary school educator; b. Ft. Wayne, Ind., Mar. 6, 1949; d. Gastao Firmino and Dorothy Marie (Johnson) de Azevedo; m. Richard E. Longsworth, July 1, 1972; children: John, Jim, Jennifer, Jeff. BS in Elem. Edn., Ind. U., 1971; MS in Elem. Edn., Ind. U., Ft. Wayne, 1972. Cert. tchr., Ind. Tchr. grades 3, 4 Ft. Wayne Community Schs., 1971-75; substitute tchr. SW Allen County Schs., Ft. Wayne, 1986-87; tchr. grade 4 St. Vincent de Paul Sch., Ft. Wayne, 1987—2000; tchr. grade 3 St. Joseph-St. Elizabeth Sch., 2000—. Mem. Internat. Reading Assn., Nat. Cath. Educators Assn., Pi Lambda Theta, Alpha Lambda Delta. Home: 3723 Winterfield Run Fort Wayne IN 46804-2660 Office: 2211 Brooklyn Ave Fort Wayne IN 46802

LONGUET, GREGORY ARTHUR, automation engineer, consultant; b. Pensacola, Fla., Nov. 1, 1945; s. Harry Charles and Gretchen (Gregory) L.; m. Elaine Gail Shuler, July 11, 1970; children: Ondreja N., Courtney E. BS, Ga. State U., 1974; MS in Mech. Engring., Ga. Inst. Technology, 1975. Cert. mfg. specialist. Toolmaker GM, Doraville, Ga., 1970-74; mfg. engr. Gen. Dynamics Corp., Ft. Worth, 1974-79; automation engr., cons. IBM, Lexington, Ky., 1979-91, design team cons., rep., 1985-91, mfg. consulting engr. Ala., Miss. trading area Montgomery, Ala., 1991-94; sr. mfg. info. sys. cons., mgr. Tech. Consulting, Inc., Louisville, 1994—. Dir. ops. sys. Gen. Cable Corp., Highland Heights, Ky. Elder Presbyn. Ch., Lexington, 1980—; mem. Habitat for Humanity, Girl Scouts U.S., South Ctrl. Ala. Capt. U.S. Army, 1966-70, Vietnam. Mem. Am. Prodn. and Inventory Control Soc., Soc. Mfg. Engrs., Nat. Mgrs. Assn., Masons, Beta Phi Gamma. Avocations: sports cars, aircraft, astronomy. Office: Tech Consulting Inc 1800 Meidiogen Tower Louisville KY 40202

LONGWELL, HARRY J., oil industry executive; b. Bunkie, La., July 20, 1941; BS in Petroleum Engring., La. State U., 1963. Joined Exxon, 1963; engr. drilling Exxon Co., U.S.A., New Orleans, mgr. ops. Corpus Christi, 1974, L.A., 1974—77, divsn. mgr., 1977—80, mgr. ops. dept. prodn. Houston, 1980—83, v.p. dept. prodn., 1983—86; v.p. exploration and prodn. in Europe Exxon, London, 1986; exec. asst. to chmn. Exxon Corp., N.Y.C., 1986; v.p. exploration and prodn. Exxon Co., Internat., Florham Park, NJ, 1987—88, sr. v.p., 1988—90, exec. v.p., 1990—92; pres. Exxon Co., U.S.A., 1992—95; sr. v.p., dir. Exxon Corp. (now Exxon Mobil Corp.), Irving, Tex., 1995—2001; exec. v.p., dir. Exxon Mobil Corp., Irving, Tex., 2001—. Mem. exec. com., bd. dirs. Nat. Action Coun. for Minorities in Engring.; chmn. bd. trustees U. Dallas; mem. bd. visitors U. Tex. M.D. Anderson Cancer Ctr.; mem. adv. bd. Dallas Area Habitat for Humanity. Office: Exxon Mobil Corp 5959 Las Colinas Blvd Irving TX 75039-4202 Office Phone: 972-444-1976. E-mail: hjlongwell@exxonmobil.com.

LONGWORTH, RICHARD COLE, journalist; b. Des Moines, Mar. 13, 1935; s. Wallace Harlan and Helen (Cole) L.; m. Barbara Bem, July 19, 1958; children: Peter, Susan. BJ, Northwestern U., 1957; postgrad., Harvard U., 1968-69. Reporter UPI, Chgo., 1958-60, parliamentary corr. London, 1960-65, corr. Moscow, 1965-68, Vienna, 1969-72, diplomatic corr. Brussels, 1972-76; econ. and internat. affairs reporter Chgo. Tribune, 1976-86, bus. editor, econ. columnist, 1987-88, chief European corr., 1988-91, sr. writer, 1991—2002, sr. corr., 2002—03; internat. affairs commentator Sta. WBEZ-FM, Chgo., 1984—; exec. dir. Global Chgo. Ctr. of Chgo., Coun. on Fgn. Relations, 2003—. Adj. prof. Northwestern U., 1998—, guest scholar, 2001. Author: Global Squeeze: The Coming Crisis for First-World Nations, 1998, Global Chicago, 2000. With U.S. Army, 1957-58. Nieman fellow, 1968-69; recipient award for econ. reporting U. Mo., 1978, 80, John Hancock, 1978, 79, 82, Gerald Loeb award for econ. reporting, 1979, Media award for econ. understanding Dartmouth Coll., 1979, award Inter-Am. Press Assn., 1979, Peter Lisagor award Sigma Delta Chi, 1979, Sidney Hillman award, 1985, Lowell Thomas award for travel writing, 1985, Beck award for fgn. corr., 1986, Domestic Reporting award, 1987, Overseas Press Club award, 1994, 97, Alumni Merit award Northwestern U., 2000, finalist, Pulitzer prize, 1979, 2003 Mem. Coun. Fgn. Rels. N.Y., Chgo. Com. of Council Fgn. Rels., Assn. Am. Corrs. in London, Internat. Music Found. (dir.), Ednl. Found. for Nuclear Sci. (dir.). Office: Chgo Coun on Fgn Relations 332 South Michigan Ave 11th Fl Chicago IL 60604 Office Phone: 312-821-7508. Business E-Mail: rlongworth@ccfr.org.

LONIGAN, PAUL RAYMOND, language professional, educator; b. New York, May 27, 1935; s. William Raymond Maloy and Irene Rita (Hickman) Lonigan; m. Cynthia Ann (Hartley), June 5, 1965; children: Jennifer, Cynthia. BA (hon.), Queens Coll., N.Y., 1960; PhD, Johns Hopkins U., 1967. Instr. Russell Sage Coll., Troy, NY, 1963-65; assoc. prof. State Univ. of N.Y., Oswego, NY, 1965—67, Queens Coll., City Univ. of N.Y. Grad. Ctr., N.Y.C., 1967-83, prof., 1983—, dep. exec. officer PhD program in French, 1969-72, coord. French program, 1982-85, 91-96. Author: Gormont et Isembart, 1976; Chrétien's Yvain, 1978; The Early Irish Church, 1989; The Druids, 1996;

Studies on: Hagiographic Literature, The Song of Roladn, Chretien De Troyes, Rabelais Montaigne, The Classics and The French Renaissance, Francios Villon, Latin American Poetry, Shamanism in the Old Irish Tradition, Women in the Middle Ages, The Magi Napoleon; editor: Respuetas del Corazón, 1999, Fragmentos de Una Tarde by Maria Carreño, 2004; contbg. editor: Oidhreacht. Sponsor Le Cercle Français. Served in U.S. Marine Corps, 1954-62. Decorated chevalier L'Ordre Des Palmes Académiques (France), Internat. Order of Merit; recipient Commemorative medal of Honor. Mem. Phi Beta Kappa, and Delta Phi Alpha. Avocations: coin collecting/numismatics, stamp collecting/philately, poetry, hunting, fishing. Office: Queens Coll King 207 6530 Kissena Blvd Flushing NY 11367

LONNQUIST, GEORGE ERIC, lawyer; b. Lincoln, Nebr., Mar. 29, 1946; s. John Hall and Elizabeth Claire (Hanson) L.; m. Wendi Ann McDonough; children: Alethea, Courtenay, Barrett. BS, U. Tenn., 1968; JD, U. Nebr., 1971; LLM, NYU, 1974. Bar: Calif. 1983, Oreg. 1972, Nebr. 1971. Law clerk Oreg. Supreme Ct., Salem, 1971-72; dep. legis. counsel Oreg. Legislature, Salem, 1972-73; ptnr. Meysing & Lonnquist, Portland, 1974-78; v.p., assoc. gen. counsel Amfac, Inc., Portland and San Francisco, 1978-84; sr. v.p., gen. counsel Homestead Fin. Corp., Millbrae, Calif., 1984-91, Homestead Savs., Millbrae, 1984-93; pvt. practice, San Francisco, 1993—. Democrat. Roman Catholic. Avocation: woodcarving. Home: 1945 Beach Park Blvd Foster City CA 94404-1326 Office: 4000 E 3rd Ave Foster City CA 94404-4805 Office Phone: 650-235-2861. Business E-Mail: lonn@legacypartners.com.

LONSBERG, JOHN V., lawyer; BA summa cum laude, U. Notre Dame, 1976; JD cum laude, U. Mich., 1979. Bar: Mo. 1979. Ptnr., group leader Internat. Bryan Cave LLP, St. Louis. Mem.: Pi Sigma Alpha, Phi Beta Kappa. Office: Bryan Cave LLP One Metropolitan Square 211 N Broadway, Ste 3600 Saint Louis MO 63102 Office Phone: 314-259-2251. E-mail: jvlonsberg@bryancave.com.

LOO, BEVERLY JANE, publishing company executive; b. L.A. d. Richard Y. and Bessie E. Sue Loo. BA, U. Calif., Berkeley. Dir. subs. rights Prentice-Hall, Inc., N.Y.C., 1957—59; fiction editor McCall's mag., 1959—62; exec. editor and dir. subs. rights, gen. books div. McGraw-Hill Book Co., N.Y.C., 1962—82; pres. Beverly Jane Loo Assocs., Inc., N.Y.C., 1982—85; sr. editor, dir. subs. rights World Almanac Pharos Books, N.Y.C., 1985—88; dir. mktg. and subs. rights Paragon House, N.Y.C., 1988—91; dir. mktg. and sales Thomasson-Grant, Charlottesville, Va., 1991—93; dir. pub. and comm. inst. U. Va. Sch. Continuing Edn. and Profl. Studies, Charlottesville, 1993—2004; asst. prof., dir. Masters of Profl. Studies in Pub. George Washington U., Coll. Profl. Studies, Washington, 2005—. Mem.: U. Va. Faculty Club, Va. Writers Club, Overseas Press Club (N.Y.C.), Arts Club (London). Home: Lewis & Clark Sq # 701 250 W Main St Charlottesville VA 22902-5072 Office: George Washington U Coll Profl Studies 805 21st St NW Ste 301 Washington DC 20052 Office Phone: 202-994-3004. Business E-Mail: bevloo@gwu.edu.

LOO, LYNN (YUEH-LIN), chemical engineer; BSE in materials sci. and engring., BSE in chemical engring., U. Pa., 1996; MA in chemical engring., Princeton U., 1998, PhD in chemical engring., 2001. Asst. prof. dept. chemical engring. U. Tex., Austin, Ctr. Nano-and Molecular Sci. and Tech., Tex. Materials Inst. Contbr. articles to profl. jour. Named one of Top 100 Young Innovators, MIT Tech. Review, 2004; recipient Frank J. Padden award for excellence in polymer rsch., APS, 2000, Camille & Henry Dreyfus New Faculty award, 2002, DuPont Young Prof. award, 2003, Career award, NSF, 2004; Porter Ogden Jacobus fellow, Princeton U., 2000. Office: U Tex Dept Chemical Engring CPE 4422 1 University Station C0400 Austin TX 78712-1062 Business E-Mail: lloo@che.utexas.edu.

LOO, MARCUS HSIEU-HONG, urologist, physician, educator; b. N.Y.C., Aug. 12, 1955; s. David Wei and Patricia (Pai) L.; m. Donna C. Wingshee, Oct. 3, 1987; children: Christopher, Courtney. BSEE with distinction, Cornell U., 1977, MD, 1981. Diplomate Am. Bd. Urology. Asst. attending urologist NY Hosp.-Cornell Med. Ctr., NYC, 1988—; clin. asst. prof. urology Cornell U. Med. Coll., NYC, 1994-2000, clin. assoc. prof. urology, 2000—. Admissions com. Cornell U. Med. Coll.; mem. univ. coun. Cornell U.; mem. operating bd. Columbia Cornell Care, LLC.; cons. Chinatown Health Cilnic; clin. dir. Asian Am. Cancer Awareness Rsch. and Tng. grant. Author: The Prostate Cancer Source Book, 1998. Mem. Univ. Coun. Cornell U., 2002—, trustee, 2003—. Fellow: ACS; mem.: IEEE, AMA, Fedn. Chinese Am. and Chinese Can. Med. Socs. (bd. dirs., v.p.), Chinese Am. Med. Soc. (pres., bd. dirs. 1990—97), Soc. Internat. d'Urologie, Am. Urological Assn., Am. Assn. Clin. Urologists, Cornell U. Med. Coll. Alumni Assn. (bd. dirs.), Tau Beta Pi, Phi Tau Phi, Eta Kappa Nu. Office: 449 E 68th St New York NY 10021-4941 Office Phone: 212-925-8388.

LOO, NANCY, newscaster; b. Hong Kong; m. Brian Jenkins; 2 children. BA in Broadcast Journalism, U. Oreg. Former journalist English-language news stations, Hong Kong and Japan, NY 1 News, NYC, 1992—94; former news anchor, reporter WABC-TV, NYC, 1994—2001; anchor morning and noon newscasts WFLD-TV (Fox Chicago), 2001—. Named Reporter/Anchor of the Yr., Women in Cable, 1994; recipient Emmy awards, NY Gov.'s award of excellence, 1992. Office: Fox Chicago WFLD-TV 205 N Michigan Ave Chicago IL 60601*

LOO, WILSON M.N., lawyer, judge; b. N.Y.C., July 20, 1954; m. Janice M. T. Luke, Aug. 24, 1982; children: Jaclyn, Kristin, David. BA cum laude, CCNY, 1977; JD, Rutgers U., 1980. Bar: Hawaii 1980, U.S. Dist. Ct. Hawaii 1980, U.S. Ct. Appeals (9th cir.) 1981, U.S. Supreme Ct. 1985, High Ct. of Trust Ter. of Pacific 1985. Dep. pros. atty. City and County of Honolulu, 1980-84; jud. clk. to Hon. Harold M. Fong, U.S. Dist. Ct. Hawaii, 1982-83; ptnr. Torkildson, Katz, Honolulu, 1984—. Per diem dist. judge 1st cir. ct. State Hawaii, 1995—. With U.S. Army, 1971-73. Named one of Best Lawyers of Am., Best Lawyers Consumer Guide. Mem. ABA (internat. bus. law com., fgn. investment in U.S. subcom.), Am. Arbitration Assn. (internat. arbitration panel 1990—), Hawaii Bar Assn., Chinese C. of C., Waialae Country Club, Phi Alpha Delta (Humanitarian award). Republican. Roman Catholic. Avocation: golf. Office: Torkildson Katz Topa Financial Ctr 700 Bishop St 15/F Honolulu HI 96813-4124 Office Phone: 808-523-6000. E-mail: wml@torkildson.com.

LOOCKERMAN, WILLIAM DELMER, retired educational administrator; b. Phila., Feb. 24, 1939; s. William Delmer and Kathleen (Cullen) L.; m. Alice Clara Winnemore, June 9, 1962; 1 child, Alice B. BS in Health and Phys. Edn., West Chester (Pa.) State U., 1962, MS in Health and Phys. Edn., 1967; EdD in Phys. Edn., Temple U., 1970; cert. sch. dist. adminstr., Niagara U., 1974. Tchr. Upper Darby (Pa.) Schs., 1965-68; tchg. assoc. Temple U., Phila., 1968-70; asst. prof. SUNY, Buffalo, 1970-73; dir. health, phys. edn. and recreation Orchard Park (NY) Ctrl. Schs., 1973-81; registered sch. bus. adminstr. Springville (NY) Griffith Inst. Ctrl. Sch. Dist., 1981-2001, ret., 2001, adminstr. emeritus, 2001—. Adj. asst. prof. Niagara U., Niagara Falls, NY, 1975—77; adj. prof. Canisius Coll., Buffalo, 1979—81; statewide rep. Group 491 Ins. Safety Program, Albany, NY, 1983—2001, trustee, 1991—2001, mem. exec. com., 1991—2001, chair, 1996—2001; spkr. local, state, nat. and internat. meetings. Contbr. articles to profl. jours. Mem. Springvile Cmty. Choir, 1997. Capt. USNR ret. Recipient spl. honor award NY State Coaches Assn., 1980, honor award NY State Assn. Health, Phys. Edn. and Recreation, 1979, conf. dedication, 1980; Colden Sch. gymnasium named in his honor, 2001. Mem. Internat. Assn. Sch. Bus. Ofcls. (mem. choir 1989—, song leader Opening Gen. Session 1997, appreciation award 1990, 94), NY State Sch. Bus. Ofcls. (chpt. exec. com. 1983-85), AMVETS, Naval Order U.S. (chpt. comdr. 1987-96, 2000-01, companion to gen. coun. 1997-99, Naval Res. Assn. (chpt. pres., nat. budget/fin. com. 1995—, nat. v.p. 1997-99, 2001-03, nat. treas. 1999-2001, mem. nat. adv. com . 1987—, mem. nat. investment oversight com. 1995—, chmn., 2003—, chair 50th ann. com. 2004, Nat. award of Merit 2001, Nat. Pres.'s award 2004), Am. Legion (WNY Armed Forces Week com. 1980—, post 1st vice comdr. 2003-2005, bd. dirs. 2002-05, chmn. 2003-04), Navy League of U.S. (exec. v.p. coun. 2004—, pres. coun. 2005—). Republican. Episcopalian. Avocation: woodworking. Home: 7643 Lewis Rd Holland NY 14080-9625 Personal E-mail: wloockerman@aol.com.

LOOK, ALICE, journalist, television producer; b. N.Y.C., Aug. 2, 1952; d. Walter F. W. and Soak Har (Ho) L.; m. Donald (Sandy) Forbes McGill Jr., May 26, 1984; 1 child, Ian Look McGill. BA, NYU, 1974. Producer, news writer NBC Radio, N.Y.C., 1976-77, WNBC TV, N.Y.C., 1977-87, reporter, 1987; owner LOOK TV, Darien, Conn., 1991—; reporter, prodr. Business Now, 1999—. Bd. dirs. YWCA of Darien (Conn.)-Norwalk, 1991-93, pub. rels. cons., 1990-93. Writer, prodr., dir. A Yankee Passion, 1995 (Best Original Videotape, Conn. Press Club 1996). Pres., bd. trustees Darien Libr., 1997-99; TV host Darien Dateline, 1991; coord. Christmas In April Program, Darien YWCA, 1992. Recipient Emmy for best news broadcast NATAS, 1983-84. Mem. ITVA, Conn. Press Club (1st Pl. award 1996), Nat. Fedn. of Press Women. Home and Office: 36 Walmsley Rd Darien CT 06820-5129

LOOK, DAVID CHARLES, research physicist, consultant; b. St. Paul, Dec. 19, 1938; s. Oliver Ardell and Hyacinth Harriet (Hanson) L.; m. Rita Marie Beatty, Oct. 19, 1968; children— James Wesley, Christine Marie. B.Physics, U. Minn., 1960, M.S., 1962; Ph.D., U. Pitts., 1966; M.S., U. Dayton, 1978. Research physicist U. Dayton, Ohio, 1969-71, sr. research physicist, 1971-80; sr. research physicist Wright State U., Dayton, 1980—; pres. DCL Semiconductor Co., Dayton, 1984—; chmn. 1st Internat. Workshop on Zinc Oxide, Dayton, 1999. Author: Semi-Insulating III-V Materials, 1984, Electrical Characterization of FaAs Materials and Devices; contbr. 400 articles to jours.; patentee Toneburst NMR Relaxation. Leader Spinning Rd. Baptist Ch., Dayton, 1972— . Served to capt. USAF, 1966-69. Andrew W. Mellon fellow, 1962; NSF fellow, 1963. Fellow Am. Phys. Soc.; mem. Am. Sci. Affiliation, IEEE, Electrochem. Soc. Avocations: tennis, volleyball. Home: 1851 Stonewood Dr Dayton OH 45432-4002 Office Phone: 937-255-1725. E-mail: david.look@wright.edu.

LOOK, PAUWILO, media specialist, architectural engineer; b. Honolulu, Dec. 22, 1964; m. Stanley James Wilson, Aug. 22, 1987 (div. Sept. 1992); 1 child, Raelyn; Carlson Chun Ping Look, May 22, 1995; children: BrayDn, Sarah Champayn, LonDyn Sydney. Degree in Comms., Honolulu C.C./U. Hawaii; grad. with honors, Columbia Sch. Broadcasting. Sales asst., spl. events prodr. KHON-TV 2, Honolulu, 1992-94; news dir. KCCN AM and FM/KINE Radio, Honolulu, 1994-95; live events prodr., promotions coord. Oceanic Cable, a Time Warner affiliate, Mililani, Hawaii, 1995-98; telethon host Muscular Dystrophy Assn. Hawaii, Honolulu, 1998—; mktg. specialist Coca-Cola Bottling Co. of Hawaii, 2000—01; account exec. CompUSA, Inc., 2002—; premise account rep. Verizon Info. Svcs., 2003—. Prodr., writer, voiceover Taste Hawaii with Hari, 1999; prodr., writer, host ann. TV spls. Road to Fame Talent Search, 1995—, Kiddieoke Kids Talent Search, 1995—; prodr., writer, narrator ann. TV spl. Christmas Mele, 1995—. Bd. dirs. Coalition for a Drug-Free Hawaii, Honolulu, Crimestoppers, Honolulu. Named Internat. Queen of Queens, Ms. Profl. Woman Internat., 1998, Ms. Asia Profl. Woman Internat., 1999, Ms. Hawaii Am. Achievement, 1998, 99, Ms. US Internat. Beauty, 2000-01, 01-02, Ms. World Internat. Beauty, 2002-03, Mrs. Asia Pacific Universal Achievement, 2001, Ms. Hawaii, 2001; recipient award Mother-Dau. Hawaii World of Pageants, 1998, Mrs. Am. Achievement Nat. Career award, 2000. Mem. NAFE, Assn. Broadcasters, Hawaii Music Awards. Avocation: pageants. Office: PO Box 970306 Waipahu HI 96797-0306 E-mail: go@lookhawaii.com.

LOOMAN, JAMES R., lawyer; b. Vallejo, Calif., June 5, 1952; s. Alfred R. and Jane M. (Halter) L.; m. Donna G. Craven, Dec. 18, 1976; children: Alison Marie, Mark Andrew, Zachary Michael. BA, Valparaiso U., 1974; JD, U. Chgo., 1978. Bar: Ill, 1978, U.S. Dist. Ct. (no dist.) Ill. 1978, U.S. Claims Ct. 1979. Ptnr. Sidley Austin Brown & Wood, Chgo., 1986—. Assoc. gen. counsel Comml. Fin. Assn., 2002—. Fellow Am. Coll. Comml. Fin. Lawyers; mem. ABA, Chgo. Bar Assn. (chmn. comml. and fin. transactions com. 1996-97, 2002-03), Chgo. Athletic Assn., Skokie Country Club, Mid-Day Club. Lutheran. Office: Sidley Austin Brown & Wood Bank One Plz Chicago IL 60603-2003 Office Phone: 312-853-7133. E-mail: jlooman@sidley.com.

LOOMER, GERALD EARL, secondary school science educator; b. Hot Springs, S.D., May 5, 1947; s. Myron Henry and Pauline Ann (Miller) L.; m. Lynn Clar Lilevjen, June 7, 1974 (div. Dec. 1993); children: Michael Franklin, Myra Francine. BS in Physics, St. John's U., 1969; MS in Physics, S.D. Sch. Mines and Tech., 1972. Cert. tchr., S.D., Minn., W.Va., Tex. Physics instr. S.D. Sch. Mines and Tech., Rapid City, 1969-72; tchr. sci. Philip (S.D.) H.S., 1972-74, Lakefield (Minn.) H.S., 1974-78, 2000—, Rapid City (S.D.) Ctrl. H.S., 1978—87, 2001—; tchr. geology, phys. scis. Rapid City Stevens H.S., 1988—2000, 2000—; tchr. physics, chemistry, biology TI-IN Network, San Antonio, 1987-88. Contbr. articles to profl. jours. and mags.; co-author conf. procs. Internat. Conf. on Thermal Conductivity; host Kids Quest - Fill Your Mind with Space TV program, 2005. Precinct chmn., state del. Rep. Party, Rapid City, 1982-87, 2000—; parish rep. MayFest, Rapid City, 1984-86. Named S.D. Tchr. of Yr., S.D. Dept. Edn., 1983; recipient Presdl. award for excellence in sci. tchg. U.S. Dept. Edn., 1984, Alumni Achievement award St. John's U., 1985; Tchr. in Space finalist NASA, 1985;, NASA Educator Astronaut Network, 2004—, Christa McAuliffe fellow U.S. Nat. Sci. Found., 1987-88; named to 100 Top Grads., S.D. Sch. of Mines and Technology, 1985; recipient Mines award for Tchg. and Leadership, S.D. Sch. of Mines and Technology, 1994; Radio Shack/Tandy Tech. scholar, 2000. Mem. S.D. Sci. Tchrs. Assn. (pres., newsletter editor 1978-87, Outstanding Svc. award 1994), Nat. Edn. Assn. (v.p. Uniserve 1978—, S.D. Tchr. of Yr.), S.D. Education Assn. (state bd. dirs., EPIC com. del. NEA rep. assembly), KC (chancellor, lector 1975—), S.D. Edn. Assn. (bd. dirs., del., EPIC com., state elections com. del.), NEA Rep. Assembly, Phi Delta Kappa (pres., v.p., sec., Pres.' award 1991, 75 Outstanding Leaders in Edn. award 1980), Am. Assoc. Phys. Tchrs. (phys. tchrs. resource agent, 1985—), Promise Keepers. Roman Catholic. Avocations: travel, hunting, playing cards. Home: 435 Viking Dr Apt WWE5 Rapid City SD 57701-9558 Office: 433 N Mt Rushmore Rd mail Stop WWAE Rapid City SD 57701 Office Phone: 605-394-4001 239.

LOOMIS, CAROL J., journalist; b. Marshfield, Mo., June 25, 1929; d. Harold and Mildred (Case) Junge; m. John R. Loomis, Mar. 19, 1960; children: Barbara, Mark. Student, Drury Coll., 1947-49; B in Journalism, U. Mo., 1951. Editor Maytag News, Maytag Co., Newton, Iowa, 1951-54; rsch. assoc. Fortune mag., N.Y.C., 1954-58, assoc. editor, 1958-68, mem. bd. editors, 1968—. Office: Fortune Mag 1271 Avenue Of The Americas New York NY 10020-1300*

LOOMIS, HOWARD KREY, banker, director; b. Omaha, Apr. 9, 1927; s. Arthur L. and Genevieve (Krey) L.; m. Florence Porter, Apr. 24, 1954; children: Arthur L. II, Frederick S., Howard Krey, John Porter. AB, Cornell U., 1949, MBA, 1950. Mgmt. trainee Hallmark Cards Inc., Kansas City, Mo., 1953-56; sec., contr., dir. Mine Svc. Co. Inc., Ft. Smith, Ark., 1956-59; contr., dir. Electra Mfg. Co., Independence, Kans., 1959-63; v.p., dir. The Peoples Bank, Pratt, Kans., 1963-65, pres., 1966-2001, chmn., dir., 1998—. Pres., dir. Gt. Plains Leasing Inc., Pratt, 1966-80, Ctrl. States Inc., Pratt, 1970-76; pres. Krey Co. Ltd., Pratt, 1978-99, chmn., dir. 1999—; fin. chmn. Econ. Lifelines, Topeka; chmn. bd. dirs. All Ins. Inc., Pratt. Past pres. Pratt County United Fund, Kanza coun. Boy Scouts Am.; past chmn. Cannonball Trail chpt. ARC; bd. dirs., past comdg. gen. Kans. Cavalry; past dir. Kans. Wildscape Fedn. With U.S. Army, 1950-52. Mem. Kans. C. of C. and Industry (past transp. chmn., dir., v.p.), Pratt Area C. of C. (past pres., bd. dirs.), Kans. Bankers Assn. (past bd. dirs.), Fin. Execs. Inst., Park Hills Country Club (past pres.), Elks, Rotary, Sigma Delta Chi, Chi Psi. Republican. Presbyterian. Home: 502 Welton St Pratt KS 67124-0928 Office: Krey Co Ltd 118 East Third St Pratt KS 67124-0928

LOOMIS, JAMES COOK, Olympic team official, mathematician, cyberneticist, writer, educator, navigator; b. Long Beach, Calif., Sept. 22, 1935; s. Joseph Gray and Elizabeth Cook L.; children: Gannon, Megan Leslie Loomis Powers. BS, U. Calif., 1958, MA, 1961; postgrad., U. Mich., 1962. Dept. head math. Culver City (Calif.) H.S., 1962-70; dir. Cetacean Rels. Soc., Maui, Hawaii, 1976-98, Planetary Healing Pageants, Maui, Hawaii, 1976—2005. Fellowship., Mental Health Rsch. Inst., Prisoner's Dilemma, under Dr. Merril Flood, Genetic Algorithms, under John Holland and dir. J.G. Miller, Living Systems; spkr., U Hawaii Matsunaga Peace Inst., 1st Global Peace Rsch. Conf., 1994, SHE PEACE: A World Peace Beadgame; Creating Future Friendly ECO-GEO-CEO's; capt., Proj. Jonah Grant, 1976, Deep Breathold diving Dolphin Entertainer; creator, Y2Kaper FOANA-TUNUP-HAS Flags of All Nations and The United Nations Underwater Parade Honoring All Species for the Global Millenium Television network 2001, 24 hr. Broadcast. Author: Saving The Cosmos ('il Tuesday), 1995, Strange Fluke, 1990 (1st prize Maui Writers Conf. 1994); creator Psydic Balm. Address: PO Box 790958 Paia HI 96779-0958 E-mail: loomis@dnitalspecies.net.

LOOMIS, REBECCA C., psychologist; b. New London, Conn., Nov. 9, 1959; d. Aubrey Kingsley and Marillyn Louise (Dirks) Loomis; m. DeWitt Montgomery Smith, Nov. 24, 1984 (div. Sept. 1997); children: Adrienne Kingsley Smith, Walker Loomis Smith. BA in Sociology and Polit. Sci., Vanderbilt U., 1981; MEd, U. Houston, 1990, PhD in Counseling Psychology, 2004. Group rep. Home Life Ins., Houston, 1981—83; sr. account exec. CNA Ins. Co., Houston, 1983—87; rsch. asst. dept. ednl. psychology U. Houston, 1988—90, 1991—93, tchg. asst., 1993, rsch. asst. Clearwater, Tex., 1993, rsch. assoc., 1999—; acad. advisor Montclair (N.J.) State U., 2001—02; psychology intern Assn. Help of Retarded Children, N.Y.C., 2002—03; prin. investigator Manhattan Ctr. for Pain Mgmt./St. Luke's-Roosevelt Hosp., NYC, 2001—04; clinician Assn. for Help of Retarded Children, NYC, 2003—. Group facilitator children div. parents, counselor Houston Child Guidance, 1990; counselor learning support svcs. U. Houston, 1990, counselor counseling and testing svcs., 1994—95; facilitator mentorship program Wildwood Elem. Sch., Mountain Lakes, NJ, 1996. Contbr. articles to various profl. jours. Hospice aid Casa de Ninos Hospice, Houston, 1986—87; vol. Houston Area Women's Ctr., 1992—93, 1994—95; cmty. aid Mountain Lakes, 1999—; vol. organizer grief workshop for September 11, 2001 attacks Cmty. Ch. Mem.: APA, N.J. Psychol. Assn. Democrat. Home and Office: 82 Briarcliff Rd Mountain Lakes NJ 07046 E-mail: beckyloomis@earthlink.net.

LOOMIS, ROBERT DUANE, publishing company executive, author; b. Conneaut, Ohio, Aug. 24, 1926; s. Kline C. and Louise C. (Chapman) L.; m. Gloria Colliani, Apr. 12, 1956 (div.); 1 dau., Diana Rachel; m. Hilary Paterson Mills, Sept. 18, 1983; 1 child, Robert Miles. BA, Duke U., 1950. Assoc. editor Rinehart & Co., N.Y.C., 1956-58; v.p., exec. editor Random House, Inc., N.Y.C., 1958—. Author: Story of the U.S. Air Force, 1959, Great American Fighter Pilots, 1961, All About Aviation, 1964. Served with USAF, 1945. Recipient Roger Klein award for creative editing, 1977 Home: 68 W 11th St New York NY 10011-8673 Office: Random House Inc 1745 Broadway New York NY 10019

LOOMIS, SALORA DALE, psychiatrist; b. Peru, Ind., Oct. 21, 1930; s. S. Dale Sr. and Rhea Pearl (Davis) L.; m. Carol Marie Davis, Jan 3, 1959; children: Stephen Dale, Patricia Marie. AB in Zoology, Ind. U., 1953, MS in Human Anatomy, 1955, MD, 1958. Diplomate Am. Bd. Psychiatry and Neurology. Intern Cook County Hosp., Chgo., 1958-59; resident in psychiatry Logansport (Ind.) State Hosp., 1959-60, Ill. State Psychiat. Inst., Chgo., 1960-62; staff psychiatrist Katharine Wright Psychiat. Clinic, Chgo., 1962-65, dir., 1965-92. Cons. Ill. Youth Commn. 1962-64; instr. psychiatry Northwestern U. Med. Sch., Chgo., 1962-64, assoc. 1964-67; asst. dir. Northwestern U. Psychiat. Clinics, Chgo., 1963-65; attending psychiatrist St. Joseph Hosp., Chgo., 1964—; lectr. psychiatry and neurology Loyola U. Med. Sch. Chgo., 1964-65, assoc. 1965, asst. prof. 1965-73, lectr. 1980-89, clin. assoc. prof., 1989-2002, clin. prof., 2002—; psychiat. cons. Ill. Dept. Pub. Health, 1967-92; sr. attending psychiatrist, chmn. dept. psychiatry Ill. Masonic Med. Ctr., Chgo. 1970-92, chmn. emeritus, 1992—; clin. assoc. prof. psychiatry U. Ill. Coll. Medicine, Chgo., 1973—. Fellow Am. Coll. Psychiatrists, Am. Psychiat. Assn. (disting. life), Acad. Psychosomatic Medicine; mem. AMA, Ill. State Med. Soc. (chmn. council on mental health and addiction 1974-75, chmn. joint peer rev. com. 1975-76), Ill. Psychiat. Soc. (chmn. ethics com. 1974-75, chmn. peer rev. com. 1976-78), Chgo. Med. Socs. Office Phone: 630-232-2331. Personal E-mail: sdaleloomis@mac.com.

LOOMIS, SUSAN KRAUSS, humanities and communication educator; b. Boston, May 19, 1945; d. Raymond A. and Rose M. (Malomo) Krauss; children: John Todd, David Krauss. AS, Aquinas Coll., 1965; BA, Regis Coll., 1971; MA, U. Maine, 1976. English tchr. Randolph (Mass.) H.S., 1971-72; English prof., chmn. dept. of arts and scis. Maine Maritime Acad., Castine, 1976-80, prof. humanities and comms., dir. Coll. Writing Ctr., 1985—; cons. Maine Dept. Edn. and Cultural Svcs., Augusta, 1980-84. Founding trustee, assoc. dir. Bagaduce Music Lending Libr., Blue Hill, Maine, 1983—; bd. dirs. Maine Ctr. Arts, Orono. Mem. AAUW, Nat. Coun. Tchrs. English, Castine Arts Assn. (founder, hon. chair). Democrat. Avocations: tennis, music, reading. Office: Maine Maritime Acad Dept Humanities Castine ME 04420-0001 Office Phone: 207-326-2345.

LOONEY, CLAUDIA ARLENE, healthcare administrator; b. Fullerton, Calif., June 13, 1946; d. Donald F. and Mildred B. Schneider; m. James K. Looney, Oct. 8, 1967; 1 child, Christopher K. BA, Calif. State U., 1969. Dir. youth YWCA No. Orange County, Fullerton, Calif., 1967-70; dir. dist. Camp Fire Girls, San Francisco, 1971-73, asst. exec. dir. L.A., 1973-77; asst. dir. cmty. resources Childrens Hosp., L.A., 1977-80; dir. cmty. devel. Orthopaedic Hosp., L.A., 1980-82; sr. v.p. Saddleback Meml. Found./Saddleback Meml. Med. Ctr., Laguna Hills, Calif., 1982-92; v.p. planning and advancement Calif. Inst. Arts, Santa Clarita, Calif., 1992-96; pres. Northwestern Meml. Found., Chgo., Ill., 1996-99; sr. v.p. Childrens Hosp., L.A., 1999—. Instr. U. Calif., Irvine, Univ. Irvine; mem. steering com. U. Irvine. Steering com. United Way, L.A., 1984-86, bd. mem. Woodmark Forum, 2004—. Recipient Orange County Woman of Achievement award, YWCA, 2004. Fellow Assn. Healthcare Philanthropy (nat. chair-elect, chmn. program Nat. Edn. Conf. 1986, regional dir. 1985-89, 98, fin. com. 1988—, pres., com. chn. 1987—, Give To Life com. chmn. 1987-91, mid-west regional conf. chmn. 1998, Orange County Fund Raiser of Yr. 1992, L.A. County fund raiser of yr. 1996); mem. Nat. Soc. Fund Raising Execs. Found. (cert., vice chmn. 1985-90, chair 1993—, mem. Chgo. conf. com. 1997, 98), So. Calif. Assn. Hosp. Devel. (past pres., bd. dirs.), Profl. Ptnrs. (chmn. 1986, instr. 1988—), Philanthropic Ednl. Orgn. (past pres.), Assn. for Healthcare Profls. (regional conf. co-chmn. 2003), Assn. Fundraising Profls. (mem. internat. ethics com. 2003—), Orange County Women of Achievement. Avocations: swimming, sailing, photography. Office: Children's Hosp LA 4650 Sunset Blvd Ste 29 Los Angeles CA 90027

LOONEY, GERALD LEE, medical educator, administrator; b. Bradshaw, W.Va., Nov. 22, 1937; s. Noah Webster and Anna Belle (Burris) L.; m. Linda Louise Pluebell, Oct. 19, 1962 (div. Apr. 1975); children: Deborah Lynn, Catherine Ann, Karen Marie, Kelli Rachelle. AB, Johns Hopkins U., 1959, MD, 1963; MPH, Harvard U., 1968. Diplomate Am. Bd. Preventive Medicine, Am. Bd. Pediatrics. Resident pediatrics Tufts-New Eng. Med. Ctr., Boston, 1965-67; physician-in-chief Kennedy Meml. Hosp., Boston, 1969-71; asst. prof. family and cmty. medicine U. Ariz. Coll. Medicine, Tucson, 1971-72; asst. prof. emergency medicine U. So. Calif. Sch. Medicine, L.A., 1972-77; assoc. clin. prof. medicine U. Calif., Irvine, 1991—; emergency dept. dir. Glendale (Calif.) Adventist Med. Ctr., 1978-84, Orthopaedic Hosp., L.A., 1985-88; urgent care dir. Bay Shore Med. Group, Torrance, Calif., 1988-93; med. dir. Surecare and LAX Clinics Centinela Hosp., Inglewood, Calif., 1993-95; dir. med. svc. Boeing Co. Mil. Aircraft, Long Beach, Calif., 1996—. Bd. dirs. Beach Cities Health Dist., Redondo Beach, Calif., 1992-93. Avocation: history. Office Phone: 310-962-6616. E-mail: docger@hotmail.com.

LOONEY, WILLIAM FRANCIS, JR., lawyer; b. Boston, Sept. 20, 1931; s. William Francis Sr. and Ursula Mary (Ryan) L.; m. Constance Mary O'Callaghan, Dec. 28, 1957; children: Willam F. III, Thomas M., Karen D., Martha A. AB, JD, Harvard U. Bar: Mass. 1958, D.C. 1972, U.S. Supreme Ct. 1972, U.S. Dist. Ct. (ea. dist.) Mich. 1986. Law clk. to presiding justice Mass. Supreme Jud. Ct., 1958-59; assoc. Goodwin, Procter & Hoar, Boston, 1959-62; chief civil divsn. U.S. Attys. Office, 1964-65; ptnr. Looney & Grossman, Boston, 1965-94, sr. counsel, 1995—. Asst. U.S. atty. Dist. Mass., 1962-65; spl. hearing officer U.S. Dept. Justice, 1965-68; mem. Mass. Bd. Bar Overseers, 1985-91, vice-chmn., 1990-91; corp. mem. Greater Boston Legal Svcs., Inc., 1994—; spl. asst. Atty. Gen., Commonwealth of Mass., 2002—. Mem. Zoning Bd. of Appeals, Dedham, Mass., 1971-74; bd. dirs. Boston Latin Sch. Found., 1981-85, pres. 1981-84, chmn. bd. dirs., 1984-86; trustee Social Law Libr., 1994-97; chmn. ADR adv. com. U.S. Dist. Ct., 1998—; spl. asst. atty. gen. Commonwealth of Mass., 2003— Fellow Am. Coll. Trial Lawyers (state com. 1996-2001); mem. Mass. Bar Assn. (co-chmn. standing com. lawyers responsibility for pub. svc. 1987-88, chmn. fed. ct. adv. com. Alternative Dispute Resolution 1998—), Boston Bar Assn. (pres. 1984-85, coun. 1985-90, chmn. sr. lawyers sect. 1992-94, Maguire award for professionalism 1995), Nat. Assn. Bar Pres.'s, Boston Latin Sch. Assn. (pres. 1980-82, life trustee 1982—, Man of Yr. 1985), USCG Found. (bd. dirs. 1987-2000, dir. emeritus 2000—), Norfolk Golf Club, Harvard Club, Harvard U. Alumni Assn. (bd. dirs. 2001-04). Democrat. Roman Catholic. Home: 43 Coronation Dr Dedham MA 02026-6230 Office: 101 Arch St Fl 9 Boston MA 02110-1112 Office Phone: 617-951-2800. Business E-Mail: wlooney@lgllp.com. E-mail: h.wlooney@socialaw.com.

LOONEY, WILLIAM R., III, career military officer; b. Norman, Okla., Mar. 5, 1949; BS, USAF Acad., 1972; student, Squadron Officer Sch., 1977; M in Mgmt., Ctrl. Mich. U., 1979; student, Armed Forces Staff Coll., 1983, Nat. War Coll., 1990, Exec. Warfare Course, 1993, Joint Flag Officer Warfighting Course, 1997, Joint Force Air Component Comdr. Course, 1997, Undergraduate Space & Missile Training Staff Course, 1998, Nat. & Internat. Security Seminar, 1999. Commd. 2d lt. USAF, 1972, advanced through grades to gen., 2005, AC-130 gunship pilot Udon Royal Thai AFB, Thailand, 1973-74; instr. pilot 50th Flying Tng. Squadron, Columbus AFB, Miss., 1975-78; air staff tng. program Directorate of Pers. Plans, The Pentagon, Washington, 1978-79; instr. pilot, flight comdr. and asst. ops. officer 94th Tactical Fighter Squadron, Langley AFB, Va., 1980-83; aide-de-camp to dep. comdr. in chief U.S. European Command, Stuttgart, West Germany, 1983-85; chief of wing plans 36th Tactical Fighter Wing, Bitburg AB, West Germany, 1985-86; ops. officer to comdr. 22nd Tactical Fighter Squadron, Bitburg AB, 1986-89; conventional negotiations br. chief Directorate of Strategic Plans and Policy, The Pentagon, Washington, 1990-92; vice comdr. Air Forces Iceland, Keflavik Naval Air Sta., Iceland, 1992-93; comdr. 33rd Fighter Wing, Eglin AFB, Fla., 1993-95, 1st Fighter Wing, Langley AFB, Va., 1995-96; comdt. Armed Forces Staff Coll., Norfolk, Va., 1996—98; comdr. Space Warfare Ctr., Schriever AFB, Colo., 1998-99; dir. ops. USAF, Peterson AFB, Colo., 1999—2000; comdr. 14th Air Force & Component Comdr. US Space Command, Vandenberg AFB, Calif., 2000—02; comdr. Aero. Systems Ctr. Air Force Material Command, Hanscom AFB, Mass., 2002—03, Wright Patterson AFB, Ohio, 2003—05; comdr. Air Edn. & Training Command, Randolph AFB, Tex., 2005—. Decorated Disting. Svc. medal with oak leaf cluster, Def. Superior Svc. medal, Def. Meritorious Svc. medal with oak leaf cluster, Legion of Merit with oak leaf cluster, Air medal, Aerial Achievement medal, Air Force Commendation medal with oak leaf cluster, Air Force Achievement medal, Combat Readiness medal with oak leaf cluster, Global War on Terrorism medal with oak leaf cluster, Humanitarian Svc. medal, Air & Space Campaign medal. Office: Air Edn & Training Command 12FTW/PA Randolph Afb TX 78150*

LOOP, FLOYD D., retired healthcare executive; b. Lafayette, Ind., Dec. 17, 1936; s. Floyd Addison and Marie D. L.; m. Bernadine P. Healy, Aug. 17, 1985; children: Alison, Frederick, Kendall, Bartlett, Marie. BS, Purdue U., 1958; MD, George Washington U., 1962. Diplomate: Am. Bd. Surgery, Am. Bd. Thoracic Surgery. Intern, resident in gen. surgery George Washington U., 1962-64, chief resident, 1967-68; fellow in cardiac surgery Cleve. Clinic Found., 1968-70, staff surgeon thoracic and cardiovascular surgery, 1971-75, chmn. dept. thoracic and cardiovascular surgery, 1975-89, chmn. bd. govs., CEO, 1990—2004, ret.; bd. dirs. Tenet Healthcare, Santa Barbara. Trustee Healthcare Leadership Coun. Mem. Editorial bd. Jour. Thoracic and Cardiovascular Surgery, 1979-85, Am. Jour. Cardiology, 1978-83, Am. Heart Jour, 1980, Clin. Cardiology, Jour. Cardiac Surgery, Jour. Cardiothoracic Anesthesia, Cleve. Clinic Jour. Medicine, Perfusion. With M.C. USAF, 1964-66. Decorated Brazilian Order of Merit Fellow ACS (adv. council for cardiothoracic surgery), Am. Coll. Cardiology (Theodore and Susan B. Cummings Humanitarian award 1975); mem. Am. Assn. Thoracic Surgery (treas., mem. council), Am. Surg. Assn., Soc. Thoracic Surgeons, Am. Coll. Chest Physicians, Thoracic Surgery Dirs. Assn., Am. Heart Assn. (exec. com. of council on cardiovascular surgery, Paul Dudley White citation for internat. service 1980), Am. Soc. Artificial Internal Organs Soc. Vascular Surgery.

LOOPER, DONALD RAY, lawyer; b. Ft. Worth, Sept. 4, 1952; s. Rudolph Winnard and Margie Lee (Nix) L.; m. Cara Shoen, Oct. 17, 1992; children: Scott Aaron, Cory Michael, Jonathan Reed, L. Quinn. BBA with honors, U. Tex., Austin, 1974, M in Profl. Acctg., 1976; JD cum laude, U. Houston, 1979. Bar: Colo. 1979, Tex. 1981; cert. arbitrator. Assoc. Cohen, Brame, Smith & Krendl, Denver, 1979-81; dir. Reynolds, Allen & Cook, Houston, 1981-85, head tax sect., 1984-85; dir. Looper, Reed & McGraw, Houston, 1985—. Lectr. Houston Soc. CPA's, 1984; acquisition negotiations in Europe, Asia, U.S. and OPEC Countries, 1987—. Coach national champion Women's Softball Team, Houston, 1981-90. Named one of Outstanding Young Men Am., 1980, 84. Mem. ABA, Tex. Bar Assn. (seminar speaker l983-85, divorce tax com. 1985-86, lectr. tax sect. 1983-86), Houston Bar Assn. (tax sect. coun. l985-87), Phi Delta Phi (province pres. l984-86). Republican. Presbyterian. Avocations: tennis, softball, backpacking, coaching. Office: Looper Reed & McGraw 1300 Post Oak Blvd Ste 2000 Houston TX 77056-8000 Home: Apt 321 2345 Bering Dr Houston TX 77057-4752

LOOPER-WILSON, LEAH MARIE, human resources specialist, controller, interior designer; d. Gary Wendell and Jacqueline McCraw Looper; m. Shane Forrester Lasseter, Dec. 31, 2002; 1 child, Rebekkah Synclaire Wilson. BA, So. Wesleyan U., 1995; AA in Criminal Justice, Greenville (S.C.) Tech. Coll., 1995. Residence counselor Greenville Hosp. Sys., 1995—99; interior designer/sales cons. Grand Home Furnishings, Greenville, 1997—99; dir. human resources, contr., fin. mgr., v.p. Byte Software LLC, Mauldin, SC, 2000—. Choreographer Banjo Fantasy Dance, 1991. Active Peace Ctr. for Performing Arts, Greenville, 2001—; mem. Encore Soc. Greenville Symphony Orch., 2001—; mem., supporter Centre Stage, Greenville, 2002—, S.C. Children's Theatre, Greenville, 2001—. Named Miss Pickens, Miss S.C. Pageant, 1992. Mem.: Upstate Visual Arts, Commerce Club. Office: Byte Software LLC 317 Neely Ferry Rd Mauldin SC 29662 Personal E-mail: leah.wilson@byte-software.com.

LOORY, STUART HUGH, journalist; b. Wilson, Pa., May 22, 1932; s. Harry and Eva (Holland) L.; m. Marjorie Helene Dretel, June 19, 1955 (div. July 1995); children: Joshua Alan, Adam Edward, Miriam Beth; m. Nina Nikolaevna Kudriavtseva, Aug. 17, 1995. BA, Cornell U., 1954; MS with honors, Columbia U., 1958; postgrad., U. Vienna, Austria, 1958. Reporter Newark News, 1955-58, N.Y. Herald Tribune, 1959-61, sci. writer, 1961-63, Washington corr., 1963-64, fgn. corr. Moscow, 1964-66; sci. editor Metromedia Radio Stas., 1962-64, Moscow corr., 1964-66; sci. writer N.Y. Times, 1966; White House corr. Los Angeles Times, 1967-71; fellow Woodrow Wilson Internat. Center for Scholars, Washington, 1971-72; exec. editor WNBC-TV News, 1973; Kiplinger prof. pub. affairs reporting Ohio State U., Columbus, 1973-75; assoc. editor Chgo. Sun-Times, 1975-76, mng. editor, 1976-80; v.p., mng. editor Washington bur. Cable News Network, 1980-82, Moscow bur. chief, 1983-86, sr. correspondent, 1986, exec. producer, 1987-90; exec. dir. internat. rels. Turner Broadcasting System, Inc., Atlanta, 1988—; editor-in-chief CNN World Report, 1990-91; v.p. CNN, 1990-95; exec. v.p. Turner Internat. Broadcasting, Russia, 1993-97; v.p., supervising prodr. Turner Original Prodns., 1995. Lee Hills chair in free press studies U. Mo., Columbia, 1997—; lectr. in field. Author: (with David Kraslow) The Secret Search for Peace in Vietnam, 1968, Defeated: Inside America's Military Machine, 1973, (with Ann Imse) Seven Days That Shook the World: The Collapse of Soviet Communism, 1991; Editor IPI Report (Internat. Press Inst.), 1998-1999, IPI Global Journalist, 1999—; contbr. articles mags. and encys. Recipient citation Overseas Press Club, 1966; Raymond Clapper award Congl. Press Gallery, 1968; George Polk award L.I.U., 1968; Du Mont award U. Calif. at Los Angeles, 1968; Distinguished Alumni award Columbia, 1969; 50th Anniversary medal Columbia Sch. Journalism, 1963; Edwin Hood award for diplomatic corr. Nat. Press Club, 1987; Pulitzer traveling scholar, 1958. Jewish. Office: U Mo Sch Journalism 132A Neff Annex Columbia MO 65211-1200 Office Phone: 573-884-1599. Business E-Mail: loorys@missouri.edu.

LOOS, JOHN THOMPSON, business owner; b. West Palm Beach, Fla. s. John T. and Margaret (Browning) L.; children: Amy, John, Melissa. BSBA, U. Fla. Co-founder, v.p., bd. dirs. Am. Mktg. and Mgmt., Inc., Ft. Lauderdale, Fla., 1970-78; pvt. practice real estate investor Ft. Lauderdale, 1978—. Pres. First Lauderdale Investments-Di-Mar Properties. Active Ft. Lauderdale Riverwalk Com., 1987-91, Jud. Nominating Commn., Broward County, Fla., 1988-92; bd. dirs. Broward County YMCA, 1982—, past pres.; bd. dirs., vice-chmn., chmn. North Broward Hosp. Dist., 1989-93; bd. dirs., vice chmn. Downtown Devel. Authority, Ft. Lauderdale, 1990, 93, 96, 03, chmn., 1990-94, active, 1988-2000, 2001-2005; chmn. Cmty. Svcs. Bd., Ft. Lauderdale, 1986-90; bd. dirs. North Lauderdale-Progreso Devel. Dist., 1990-91, Broward County Planning Coun., 1993-95, Broward County Charter Rev. Com., 1994-96, Broward County Partnership for the Homeless, 1997-98; bd. dirs. Downtown Coun., Fort Lauderdale Transp. Mgmt. Authority. Named Downtowner of Yr., Ft. Lauderdale, 1997, Person of Yr., Ft. Lauderdale Riverwalk, 2002. Mem.: Lauderdale Yacht Club. Republican. Home: PO Box 399 Fort Lauderdale FL 33302-0399

LOOS, RANDOLPH MEADE, financial planner; b. Warren, Ohio, May 22, 1954; s. Donald Ambert and Kathleen Jean (Woods) L.; m. Jolene Lora Turkoc, Aug. 3, 1985. BSBA, U. Fla., 1977. CFP. Rsch. cons. Fla. State U., Tallahassee, 1977—78; exec. sec. Chi Phi Fraternity, Atlanta, 1978—79, nat. dir., 1979—80; sys. rep. Burroughs Corp., Chgo., 1980—81, sr. sys. rep., 1981—82; account exec. Prudential-Bache Securities, Charlotte, NC, 1982—84; investment broker A. G. Edwards & Sons, Clearwater, Fla., 1984—, sr. investment broker, 1991—92, v.p. investments, 1992—2000, sr. v.p. investments, 2001—, trust specialist, 1995—. Trustee Harmony Found., 2001—, chmn. bd. dirs., 2004—; musical dir. Toast of Tampa Show Chorus, 1986—97, internat.champions, 1994; musical dir. Tampa Bay Heralds of Harmony, 2003—05. Republican. Avocations: golf, barbershop harmony, wine collecting. Office: A G Edwards & Sons Inc 28100 Us Highway 19 N Ste 500 Clearwater FL 33761-2686 Office Phone: 727-669-4909. E-mail: randyl999@aol.com.

LOOS, WILLIAM H(ENRY), librarian, consultant; b. North Tonawanda, N.Y., Feb. 26, 1937; s. William R. and Hildegarde Ida (Nickel) Loos; m. Judylee Rita Matesick, Feb. 17, 1979. BA in History, SUNY, Buffalo, 1965; MA in Libr. Sci., Syracuse U., 1968. Cert. pub. libr. Libr. trainee City of Tonawanda, 1965—67; reference libr. Buffalo (N.Y.) & Erie County Pub. Libr., 1968—70, cataloger, 1970—72, curator Grosvenor Rare Book Rm., founder, 1972—2002; ret., 2002; pres., trustee Western N.Y. Heritage Press, Cheektawoga, NY, 2001—. Cons. Western N.Y. Libr. Resources Coun., Buffalo, 1969—77; mem. N.Y. State Libr. Adv. Coun. on Preservation and Conservation, 1985—88; lectr. in field. Author: Negro Exhibit at the Pan American Exposition 1901, 2001; co-editor: Western New York Union List of Serials, 1970; contbr. libr. periodicals. Pres. Salisbury Club, Buffalo, 1975—77. Pub. Libr. Tng. grantee, N.Y. State, 1967. Mem.: ALA (rare books and manuscripts sect.), Bibliographical Soc. Am., Manuscript Soc., Am. Printing Hist. Assn., Beta Phi Mu. Republican. Mem. United Ch. Of Christ. Achievements include playing a leading role in the recovery of the first half of the manuscript of Mark Twain's Adventures of Huckleberry Finn missing for 105 years. Avocation: collecting fine books, prints and maps. Home: 119 Colvinhurst Dr Tonawanda NY 14223-1469

LOOSE, D. SCOTT, music educator; b. Ephrata, Pa., Oct. 1, 1958; s. Larry and Rebecca Loose; m. Debra Vierling, Apr. 14, 1979; children: Ryan, Michael. B in Music Edn., Wittenberg U., Springfield, Ohio, 1980; MusM, West Chester U., Pa., 1988. Cert. music K-12 Pa., 1980. Dir. Am. Music Abroad European Tour. Mem.: Cavalcade Judges Assn. (music caption chief 1990—2000), Music Educators Nat. Conf. (local pres. 1995—97), Phi Beta Mu. Republican. Methodist. Avocation: golf. Home: 245 Pleasant View Dr Strasburg PA 17579 Office: Lampeter-Strasburg PO Box 428 Lampeter PA 17537 Personal E-mail: getzenman@verizon.net. E-mail: scott_loose@l-spioneers.org.

LOOSEMORE, PAULA M., literature and language educator; m. Michael John Loosemore, Apr. 16, 1977; children: Michael Paul, Allysen Marie. BA in English, Worcester State Coll., 1974, MEd, 1979. Cert. educator Mass., 1974. Tchr. English Bartlett Jr. Sr. H.S., Webster, Mass., head English dept., 2002—. Webster rep. Ctrl. Mass. H.S. Alliance, Worcester, 2001—. Mem. Auburn Woman's Club. Mem.: NEA, Mass. Reading Assn., Nat. Coun. Tchrs. English, Webster Tchrs. Assn. Office: Bartlett Jr Sr High Sch 52 Lake Pky Webster MA 01570 Office Phone: 508-943-8552.

LOOSER, DEVONEY KAY, English literature educator; b. St. Paul, Apr. 11, 1967; d. LeRoy Joseph and Sharon Lee Ann (Sarslow) Looser; m. George Lewis Justice, 1996; 1 child, Carl Anchor Justice. BA, Augsburg Coll., 1989; PhD, SUNY, Stony Brook, 1993. Instr. English SUNY, Stony Brook, 1989-93; asst. prof. English Ind. State U., Terre Haute, 1993-98, acting dir. women's studies, 1997-98; asst. prof. women's studies U. Wis., Whitewater, 1998-2000; vis. asst. prof. English Ariz. State U., 2000-2001; asst. prof. English La. State U., 2001—02, U. Mo., Columbia, 2002—, assoc. prof. English, 2004—. Author: British Women Writers and the Writing of History, 1670-1820, 2000 (Choice Outstanding Acad. Title award 2001); editor: Jane Austen and Discourses of Feminism, 1995; co-editor: (with E. Ann Kaplan) Generations: Academic Feminists in Dialogue, 1997, Jour. for Early Modern Cultural Studies, 2004—; contbr. articles to profl. jours. Fellow, NEH, 1994, Nat. Humanities Ctr. Inst., 2003, Huntington Libr., 2004, King's Coll., London, 2004, Spencer Libr., U. Kans., 2004, Newberry Libr., 2005. Mem. MLA (exec. com. late eighteenth century divsn. 2004—, exec. com. Midwestsect. 2004—), Am. Soc. Eighteenth Century Studies, Jane Austen Soc. N.Am. (bd. dirs. 2000-02), Nat. Women's Studies Assn., N.Am. Soc. Study of Romanticism. Office: U Mo Columbia Dept English Columbia MO 65211 Office Phone: 573-884-7791. Business E-Mail: looserd@missouri.edu.

LOOSER, DONALD WILLIAM, academic administrator; b. Lufkin, Tex., June 14, 1939; s. William E. and Mildred H. (Wageneck) L.; m. Elsa Jean Albritton, Aug. 20, 1966; 1 child, William Gregory. MusB, Baylor U., 1962; MusM, Northwestern U., 1963; PhD, Fla. State U., 1972. Instr. Miss. Coll., Clinton, 1963-64; asst. prof. Houston Bapt. U., 1964-68, asst. to pres., 1968-72, dean gen. edn., 1972-77, v.p. adminstrv. affairs, 1977-83, v.p. acad. affairs, 1983—. Pres. Conf. Deans Faculties and Acad. V.P.s, 1985-86; mem Harvard U. Inst. Edn. Mgmt., 1985; pres. Nat. Conf. Acad. Deans, 1990-91. Contbr. articles to profl. jours.; rec. artist A Jubilant Song, 1983. Mem. adv. bd. Houston Symphony Orch., Houston Grand Opera, pianist Tallowood Bapt. Ch., 1965-88; pianist Second Bapt. Ch., Houston, 1988-98. Mem. Am. Assn. Higher Edn., Houston Philos. Soc., Rotary, Phi Delta Kappa, Omicron Delta Kappa, Pi Kappa Lambda, Kappa Delta Pi. E-mail: dlooser@hbu.edu.

LOOSER, WILLIAM GREGORY, lawyer; b. Houston, July 24, 1969; BA, JD, Baylor U., 1991. Bar: Tex. 1994, U.S. Dist. Ct. Tex. (No. dist.) 1995, U.S. Dist. Ct. Tex. (So. dist.) 1996. V.p., gen. counsel, sec. Pride Internat., Inc., Houston. Mem.: ABA, Am. Corp. Counsel Assn., Internat. Assn. Def. Counsel, Houston Young Lawyers Assn. (co-chair profl. devel. com. 1997), State Bar Tex., Houston Bar Assn., Nat. Order Barristers, Phi Delta Phi. Office: Pride Internat Inc 5847 San Felipe Ste 3300 Houston TX 77057

LOOTS, JAMES MASON, lawyer; b. Iowa City, May 24, 1958; s. Robert James and Mary (Ladd) L.; children: Mason S., Karl R. BSJ, Northwestern U., Evanston, Ill., 1980; JD cum laude, Mich. Law Sch., 1984. Bar: D.C. 1984, U.S. Dist. Ct. D.C. 1985, U.S. Dist. Ct. Md., 1992, U.S. Ct. Appeals (D.C. cir.) 1985, U.S. Tax Ct. 1990, U.S. Ct. Fed. Claims 1998, U.S. Ct. Appeals (4th cir.) 2000. Assoc. Skadden, Arps, Slate, Meagher & Flom, Washington, 1984-89, Jones, Day, Reavis & Pogue, Washington, 1989-92; ptnr. Barrymore & Loots, Washington, 1992-95, Perry, Simmons & Loots, Washington, 1995-99, Goldstein & Loots, Washington, 1999—2002, Ford & Harrison LLP, Washington, 2002—. Treas. Worldly Goods, Inc., Washington, 1988-94; adj. prof. Am. U. Wash. Coll. Law, 1990-96. Editorial Bd. Mich. Law Rev., 1982-84. Vol. VISTA, Baton Rouge, 1980-81; v.p. Bedford Springs (Pa.) Festival, 1987-89; adv. bd. Washington Legal Counsel for the Elderly, 1988-97; mem. D.C. Small Bus. Adv. Bd., 1990-99; chmn. D.C. Commn. Human Rights, 1991-2001; bd. dirs. Capitol Hill Assn. Merchants & Profls., 1994-97. Mem. D.C. Bar Assn. (Pro Bono Lawyer of Year, 1988), Washington Coun. Lawyers. Office: Ford & Harrison LLP 1300 19th St NW # 700 Washington DC 20036 Mailing: PO Box 76852 Washington DC 20013 Office Phone: 202-359-0442. Business E-Mail: jloots@lootslaw.com.

LOOYENGA, ROGER L., insurance company executive; BS, Minot State Coll. CLU, CPCU. Exec. v.p. Auto-Owners Ins. Co., Lansing, Mich., 1999—2004, chmn., CEO, 2004—. Trustee Am. Inst. for CPCU, 2004—, Ins. Inst. Am., 2004—. Office: Auto Owners Insurance Co 6101 Anacapri Blvd Lansing MI 48917*

LOPACH, JAMES JOSEPH, political science professor; b. Great Falls, Mont., June 23, 1942; s. John Ernest and Alma Marie (Schapman) L.; div. Dec. 10, 1991; children: Christine, Paul. AB in Philosophy, Carroll Coll., 1964; MA in Am. Studies, U. Notre Dame, 1967, MAT in English Edn., 1968, PhD in Govt., 1973. Mgr. Pacific Telephone, Palo Alto, Calif., 1968-69; adminstr. City of South Bend, Ind., 1971-73; prof. U. Mont., Missoula, 1973—, chmn. dept. polit. sci., 1977-87, assoc. dean Coll. Arts and Scis., 1987-88, acting dir. Mansfield Ctr., 1984-85, spl. asst. to the univ. pres., 1988-92, assoc. provost, 1992-95, spl. asst. to provost, 1995-96. Cons. local govts., state agys., tribal govts., law firms, 1973—; expert witness. Author, editor: We the People of Montana, 1983, Tribal Government Today, 1990, 98, Planning Small Town America, 1990, Jeannette Rankin: A Political Woman, 2005; contbr. articles to profl. jours. Roman Catholic. Office: U Mont Dept Polit Sci Missoula MT 59812-0001 Office Phone: 406-243-4829. E-mail: james.lopach@umontana.edu.

LOPAT, ROMALDA REGINA, publisher, editor; b. Bridgeport, Conn., Aug. 2, 1954; d. Francis George and Susan Jane (Hermenze) L.; m. Larry R. Sorensen (div. 1983); m. John Dobyns Drummond, June 11, 1988; children: Danielle Ferree, Leah Michelle. BA, U. Conn., 1976; M Urban Planning & Policy, U. Ill., Chgo., 1979. Dir. programs Ill.-Ind. Bi-State Commn., Chgo., 1979-80, dep. dir., 1981; dir. pub. & cmty. rels. Chgo. Dept. Aviation, 1981-85; prin. R. Lopat Comm., 1985—. Dep. dir. Chgo. Econ. Devel. Commn., 1986-89. Pub. Weedpath Gazette, 1992-2003, Operates Weedpatch-.com, 2002-. Recipient Recognition cert. FAA, 1985. Mem. Ill.-Ind. Bi-State Commn. (hon.), Garden Writers Assn. (Best Newsletter 2001). Avocations: gardening, historic preservation, landscape design, land conservation.

LOPATA, VASILI IVANOVICH, artist; b. Nova Basan, Ukraine, Apr. 28, 1941; s. Ivan Mykolayovich and Hanna Antonivna Lopata; m. Regina V. Lopata, Sept. 23, 1969; 1 child, Olga V. Lopata. MA, Acad. Arts Kyiv, 1970; PhD, USSR Acad. Arts, 1972. Cons. Radyansky Pismennik, Kyiv, 1967, Radyanska Shcola, Kyiv, 1968-89, Dnipro, Kyiv, 1970-88, Veselka, Kyiv, 1970-93, Tavria, Simpheropol, Ukraine, 1972, Melbourne, Australia, 1974, Molodaya Gvardiya, Moscow, 1976, Voronezh, Russia, 1980; author design of Ukrainian currency Govt. of Ukraine, 1991-92. Illustrator, designer Pobratimy, 1972 (2d prize 1972), Poltava, 1980 (2d prize 1980), Ballady, 1982 (2d prize 1982), Topolya, 1984 (1st prize 1984), Slovo o Polku Igorevim, 1986, 1989 (1st prize 1986), History of Ukraine, 1993 (1st prize 1993), The Lord is the Strength of His People, 1996; over 600 woodcuts, linocuts and etchings; artist portrait John Paul II, 1993 (Privet Gift from his holyness 1993); painter numerous oils, pastels, watercolors; author: Somewhere Within My Heart, Hope and Disappointment; contbr. articles to profl. jours.; work collected in numerous museums. With Soviet Army, 1961—64. Named honored citizen, City Hall of Winnipeg, Can., 1990, City Hall of Brundon, Can., 1990, honored artist of Ukraine, 1979, Order of Honor, Govt. of Ukraine, 1988, nat. artist, 2001; recipient First Pl. Book-Plate Competition, London, 1989, Shevchenko prize laureate, Govt. of Ukraine, 1992, First prize, Prominvestbank, 1998. Mem.: Union of Artists of Ukraine. Avocation: collector old and new prints and books. Home: 1800 22nd Ave Apt 103 San Francisco CA 94122-4449 E-mail: vilopata@yahoo.com.

LOPATE, PHILLIP, language educator, writer; b. N.Y.C., Nov. 16, 1943; s. Albert and Frances (Berlow) L.; m. Carol Ascher, Jan. 15, 1964 (div. 1968); m. Cheryl Cipriani, Dec. 31, 1990; 1 child. BA, Columbia U., 1964; PhD, Union Grad. Sch., 1979. Edn. dir. Tchrs. & Writers Collaborative, N.Y.C., 1968-80; assoc. prof. English U. Houston, 1980-88; adj. prof. English Columbia U., 1988-92; prof. English Bennington (Vt.) Coll., 1992-93, Hofstra U., Hempstead, N.Y., 1993—. Author: Being With Children, 1975, Bachelorhood, 1981, The Rug Merchant, 1987, Against Joie de Vivre, 1989, Portrait of My Body, 1996, Getting Personal, 2003, Waterfront, 2004,; editor (anthology) The Art of the Personal Essay, 1994. Juror Pulitzer Prize, N.Y.C., 1984, Nat. Book Award, N.Y.C., 1990, Associated Writing Programs, 1993; various coms. Mcpl. Arts Soc., N.Y.C., 1989—. Recipient Best Non-Fiction Book award Tex. Inst. Letters, 1981, grant NEA, 1978, 85, fellowship John Simon Guggenheim Found., 1988. Mem. Authors Guild, Tchrs. & Writers Collaborative (bd. dirs. 1980—), PEN. Home and Office: 402 Sackett St Brooklyn NY 11231-4704

LOPATIN, ALAN G., lawyer; b. New Haven, May 25, 1956; s. Paul and Ruth (Rosen) L.; m. Debra Jo Engler, May 17, 1981; children: Jonah Adam, Asa Louis. BA, Yale U., 1978; JD, Am. U., 1981. Bar: D.C. 1981, U.S. Supreme Ct. 1985. Law clk. FMC, Washington, 1980-81; counsel com. on post office and civil svc. U.S. Ho. of Reps., Washington, 1981-82, counsel com. on budget, 1982-86, dep. chief counsel, 1986-87, counsel temp. joint com. on deficit reduction, 1986, dep. gen. counsel com. on post office and civil svc., 1987-90, gen. counsel com. on edn. and labor, 1991-94; pres. Ledge Counsel, Inc., Washington, 1995—; exec. dir. Nat. and Cmty. Svc. Coalition, 1995-99; ptnr. Valente Lopatin & Schulze, Washington, 1998—2002; of counsel Valente and Assoc., Washington, 2003—. Mem. presdl. task force Health Care Reform, Washington, 1993. Mem. ABA, D.C. Bar Assn., Nat. Assn. Thrift Savs. Plan Participants (pres. 1999—), Nat. Dem. Club, Yale Club (Washington). Democratic. Jewish. Home: 4958 Butterworth Pl NW Washington DC 20016-4354 Office: Ledge Counsel Inc 4958 Butterworth Pl NW Washington DC 20016-4354 Office Phone: 202-244-2244. Business E-Mail: alan@ledgecounsel.com.

LOPATIN, CAROL KEESLER, artist; b. Spring Valley, N.Y., Oct. 16, 1934; d. Irving Verdin and Jessie Louise (Day) Keesler; m. Milton Lopatin, Apr. 5, 1963; 1 child, John David. BS, Skidmore Coll., 1956. Artist mem. Spectrum Gallery, Washington, 1985-93, Touchstone Gallery, Washington, 1996-2000, 2002—; juried studio artist Arlington (Va.) Art Ctr., 1984-93, Torpedo Factory Art Ctr., Alexandria, Va., 1988—; participating artist Women in Art and Culture, Beijing, 1995. One-woman shows Spectrum Gallery, Washington, 1988, 91, 93, 20th Century Gallery, Williamsburg, Va., 1989, 95, Charles County C.C., La Plata, Md., 1992, Arlington (Va.) Art Ctr., 1993, Holden Gallery, Warren Wilson Coll., Swannanoa, N.C., 1996, Art Assn. Harrisburg, Pa., 1996, Touchstone Gallery, Washington, 1997, 99, 2002, Warm Springs (Va.) Gallery, 1998, 99, Del. Ctr. for Contemporary Arts,

Wilmington, 2000; exhibited in group shows Art League Gallery, Alexandria, Va., 1985-2002, Chrysler Mus., Norfolk, Va., 1990, 92, Strathmore Hall Found. Inc., Rockville, Md., 1991, 92, 94, 99, 2002, Assoc. Artists and Milton Rhodes Galleries, Winston-Salem, N.C., 1992, Greater Reston (Va.) Arts Ctr., 1992, 94, 95, 97, Delaplaine Visual Arts Ctr., Frederick, Md., 1994, 95, 97, Adirondacks Art Ctr., Old Forge, N.Y., 1995, 97, Foothills Art Ctr., Golden, Colo., 1995, 96, 97, 99, Global Focus, Beijing, 1995, Gadsden (Ala.) Ctr. for Cultural Arts, 1995, Olin Fine Arts Gallery, Washington, Pa., 1996, Moss-Thorns Gallery Art, Ft. Hays U., Hays, Kans., 1996, others; represented in permanent collections McGraw-Hill Cos., No. Va. C.C., George Washington U. Med. Coll., also corp. and pvt. collections. Recipient purchase award Watercolor Soc. Ala., 1995, 99. Mem. Nat. Acrylic Painters Assn. (signature mem.), Nat. Watercolor Soc. (signature mem., 1st Combined award 1995, Past Pres. award 1999, award 2002), Pa. Watercolor Soc. (signature mem.), Watercolor Soc. Ala. (signature mem.), Artists Equity (1st place award 1992, juror's award 1994), Art League Alexandria (numerous awards), Greater Reston Art Ctr. Presbyterian. Office: Torpedo Factory Art Ctr 105 N Union St Ste 301 Alexandria VA 22314-3217

LOPER, CARL RICHARD, JR., metallurgical engineer, educator; b. Wauwatosa, Wis., July 3, 1932; s. Carl Richard S. and Valberg (Sundby) Loper; m. Jane Louise Loehning, June 30, 1956; children: Cynthia Louise Loper Koch, Anne Elizabeth. BS in Metall. Engring., U. Wis., 1955, MS in Metall. Engring., 1958, PhD in Metall. Engring., 1961; postgrad., U. Mich., 1960. Metall. engr. Pelton Steel Casting Co., Milw., 1955-56; instr., rsch. assoc. U. Wis., Madison, 1956-61, asst. prof., 1961-64, assoc. prof., 1964-68, prof. metall. engring., 1968-88, prof. materials sci. and engring., 1988-2001, ret. prof. materials sci. and engring., 2001, assoc. chmn. dept. metall. and mineral engring., 1979-82; pres. CRL Corp., 1979—. Rsch. metallurgist Allis Chalmers, Milw., 1961; adj. prof. materials U. Wis., Milw., 2002—; cons., lectr. in field. Author: (book) Principles of Metal Casting, 1965; contbr. articles to profl. jours. Chmn. 25 Anniversary Ductile Iron Symposium, Montreal, Canada, 1973; pres. Ygdrasil Lit. Soc., 1989—90. Recipient Adams Meml. award, Am. Welding Soc., 1963, Howard F. Taylor award, 1967, Svc. citation, 1969, 1972, others, Silver medal award, Sci. Merit Portuguese Foundry Assn., 1978, medal, Chinese Foundrymen's Assn., 1989, E.J. Walsh Award, 2002; fellow Foundry Ednl. Found., 1953—55, Wheelbrator Corp., 1960, Ford Found., 1960. Fellow: AIM, Am. Soc. Metals (chmn. 1969—70); mem.: Yedrasil-Norwegian-Am. Lit. Soc., Tau Beta Pi, Foundry Ednl. Found. (E.J. Walsh award 2002), Korean Inst. Metals and Materials (hon.), Am. Welding Soc., Am. Foundrymen's Soc. (bd. dirs. 1967-70, 76-79, Foundry Ednl. Found. dirs. award 1994, Best Paper award 1966, 67, 85, John A. Penton gold medal 1972, Hoyt Meml. lectr. 1992, Aluminum Divsn. award sci. merit 1995), Blackhawk Country Club, Torske Klubben (bd. dirs., co-founder 1978—, Foundry Hall of Honor 2001), Gamma Alpha, Alpha Sigma Mu, Sigma Xi. Lutheran. Achievements include significant contributions to understanding the solidifcation and metallurgy of ferrous and non-ferrous alloys; recognized authority of solidification and cast iron metallurgy, and on education in metallurgy and materials science. Office Phone: 608-836-1296.

LOPER, DAVID ERIC, geophysicist, mathematician; b. Oswego, N.Y., Feb. 14, 1940; married, 1966; 4 children. BS, Carnegie Inst. Tech., 1961; MS, Case Inst. Tech., 1964, PhD in Mech. Engring., 1965. Sr. scientist Douglas Aircraft Corp., 1965-68; from asst. prof. to assoc. prof. Fla. State U., Tallahassee, 1968-77, prof. math., 1977-97, prof. geology and math., 1997—2003; dir. Geophysical Fluid Dynamics Inst., 1994—2002. Nat. Ctr. Atmospheric Rsch. fellow, 1967-68, sr. vis. fellow U. Newcastle-upon-Tyne, Eng., 1974-75, Cambridge U., Eng., 1990; H.C. Webster fellow U. Queensland, Australia, 1983. Fellow Am. Geophys. Union; mem. Sigma Xi. Achievements include research on boundary layers in rotating, stably stratified, electrically conducting fluids; evolution of the earth's core including stratification, heat transfer, solidification and particle precipitation; karst hydrology. Office: Fla State U Geophys Fluid Dynamics Inst 18 Keen Bldg Tallahassee FL 32306 E-mail: loper@gfdi.fsu.edu.

LOPER, JOHNNY M., lawyer; b. Forest, Miss., July 25, 1952; BS with highest distinction, Miss. State U., 1974, MBA, 1975; JD magna cum laude, U. Miss. Sch. Law, 1983. Bar: Miss. 1983, admitted to practice: US Ct. Appeals (4th Cir.), US Dist. Cts. (Ea., Mid. and Western Dists., NC), No. and So. Dists. Miss. Summer assoc. Brunini, Grantham, Grower & Hewes, Jackson, Miss., 1981—82, assoc., 1983—87; ptnr. bus. litig. dept. Womble Carlyle Sandridge & Rice PLLC, Raleigh, NC, mem. mgmt. com., recruiting com., budget com., tech. com., personal resources com., office pro bono coord. Lectr. in field. Mng. editor Miss. Law Jour., 1983. Mem., pub. info. com. Adminstrn. of justice Task Force; mem. Pub. Speakers Bur. Mem.: 10th Jud. Dist. Bar Assn., NC State Bar Assn., NC Bar Assn. (mem., litig. sect.). Office: Womble Carlyle Sandridge & Rice PLLC 150 Fayetteville St Mall Ste 2100 Raleigh NC 27601 Mailing: Womble Carlyle Sandridge & Rice PLLC PO Box 831 Raleigh NC 27602 Office Phone: 919-755-2116. Office Fax: 919-755-6056. Business E-Mail: jloper@wcsr.com.

LOPER, JOYCE E., plant pathologist, educator; BS in Biol. Scis., U. Calif., Davis, 1974, MS in Plant Pathology, 1978; PhD in Plant Pathology, U. Calif., Berkeley, 1983. Prof. dept. botany and plant pathology Oreg. State U., 1987—; rsch. plant pathologist USDA-Agrl. Rsch. Svc., rsch. leader Hort. Crops Rsch. Lab., 2000—. Mem. agr. bd. NRC, ecologically-based pest mgmt.: new solutions for a new century panel NAS, Washington, 1992-95, sci. adv. panel NSF Ctr. Microbial Ecology Mich. State U., 1992-96; councilor-at-large Am. Phytopathol. Soc., 1997-2000. Sr. editor Am. Phytopathol. Soc. Press, 1990-93; assoc. editor Molecular Plant-Microbe Interactions, 1996-99; mem. editorial com. Ann. Reviews of Phytopathology, 1996—; mem. editorial bd. European Jour. Plant Path., 1995—. Recipient CIBA GEIGY award Am. Phytopathological Soc., 1995. Fellow Am. Phytopathol. Soc. Office: USDA ARS Hort Crops Lab 3420 NW Orchard Ave Corvallis OR 97330-5014

LOPER, LINDA SUE, library director; b. Wakefield, RI, Jan. 28, 1945; d. Delmas Field and Dora Belle (Hanna) Sneed; children: Matthew Lee Mathany, Amanda Virginia Mathany Van DerHeyden, Morgan Lynnclare Loper. BA, Peabody Coll., Nashville, 1966, MLS, 1979; EdD in Ednl. Adminstrn., Vanderbilt U., Nashville, 1988. Tchr. Parkway Sch., Chesterfield, Mo., 1966-68, Charlotte Mecklenburg Schs., Charlotte, N.C., 1968-71; dir. city libr. Jackson George Regional Libr. System, Pascagoula, Miss., 1979-82; media ctr. specialist Pascagoula Mcpl. Sch. Dist., 1982-83, Moore County Sch. System, Lynchburg, Tenn., 1983-91; ref. libr. Motlow State C.C., Tullahoma, Tenn., 1983-85; dir. learning resource ctr. Columbia (Tenn.) State C.C., 1991-99; CEO Grant Seekers, Inc., 1996-99, Loper Literary Agy., 1999—2001; accounts svcs. mgr. E.B. Stephens Co. (EBSCO), 1999-2001; spl. collections divsn. mgr. Nashville Pub. Libr., 2001—05; libr. dir. Germantown (Tenn.) Cmty. Libr., 2005—; dir. ops. Wolf River Libr. Consortium, Germantown, 2005—. Presenter TLA Ann. Conv., Knoxville, 1998, 2005, Am. Assn. Women in C.C.s Regional Conf., 1997, LEAP State Dept. Edn. Conf. for Libr., Chattanooga; career ladder participant Tenn. Edn. Dept. Level II; TIM trainer Dept. Edn., Nashville; exec. dir. Tenn. Bd. of Regents Media Consortium, 1993-96; chair profl. staff orgn. Columbia State C.C., 1998-99; presenter, judge 6th Ann. Cumberland Writers Conf., Cookeville, Tenn. Author: Bibliography for Tennessee Commission on Status of Women, 1979; contbr. article to profl jour. Pres. Moore County Friends of Libr., Lynchburg, Tenn., 1991; bd. dirs. Moore County Hist. and Geneal. Soc., Lynchburg, 1991; mem. Tenn. Bicentennial Com., Giles County, 1996; co-dir. So. Tapestry, a Bicentennial oral history project; sec., mem. exec. bd. Hope Ho. Domestic Violence Shelter, 1993—96, mem. adv. bd., 1996—99; mem. steering com. Bus., Industry, Edn. Partnership, 1994—99; mem. adv. bd. Nashville Pub. TV Cmty., 2003—05; Emmy judging panel Cultural Programming Mid-East Divsn., 2004. Recipient Gov.'s Acad. award State Dept. of Edn., U. Tenn., 1988, Inst. for Writing Tenn. History, U. Tenn., 1990, Gov.'s Conf. on Info. Sci., Nashville, 1990. Mem. ASCD, Am. Info. Assn. (Mid. Tenn. chapter), S.E. Libr. Assn., Tenn. Libr. Assn. (co-chair strategic planning com. 1996-99), TENNSHARE (chair collection devel. com. 1996-99), Moore County Edn. Assn. (treas., chair tchrs. study coun., chair polit. action commn. 1989-91), Giles County Edn. Found. UDC, DAR, Tenn. Acad. Libr. Collaborative (exec. coun. 1996-99), Soc. of Tenn. Archivists, Phi Delta Kappa, Beta Phi Mu, Delta Kappa Gamma. Democrat. Episcopalian. Avocations: cross stitch, sewing, reading, gardening. Office: Germantown Cmty Libr 1925 Exeter Rd Germantown TN 38138 Business E-Mail: sloper@readgermantown.org.

LOPES, DAVEY, former professional baseball manager; b. Providence, May 3, 1946; 1 child, Vanessa Lin. Grad., Washburn U., Topeka, 1969. Profl. baseball player Dodgers, Athletics, Cubs, Astros, 1972-87; dugout and first base coach Tex. Rangers, 1988-91; mgr. Ariz. Fall League; first base coach Balt. Orioles, 1992-94, San Diego Padres, 1995-99; mgr., head coach Milw. Brewers Baseball Club, 1999—2002.

LOPES, JAMES LOUIS, lawyer; b. Watsonville, Calif., Feb. 1, 1947; s. Allen M. and Norma Maxine (McElroy) L.; m. Gail R. Lopes, Mar. 24, 1979; children: Elizabeth, Jane. BS, U.Calif., Davis, 1969; JD, U. Pacific, 1974; LLM, Harvard U., 1975. Bar: Calif. 1974, U.S. Ct. Appeals (9th cir.), U.S. Dist. Ct. (no., ea., ctrl. dists.) Calif. Assoc. Gendel, Raskoff, Shapiro & Quittner, L.A., 1975-78; ptnr. Gordon, Peitzman & Lopes, San Francisco, 1978-81, Howard, Rice & Nemerovski, San Francisco, 1982—. Adv. com. bankruptcy/creditors' rights Practicing Law Inst., 1992—. Fellow Am. Coll. Bankruptcy, Calif.; mem. Bankruptcy Forum (bd. dirs. 1990-93), Calif. State Bar Assn. Avocations: flying, contract bridge. Office: Howard Rice & Nemerovski 3 Embarcadero Ctr Ste 7 San Francisco CA 94111-4074 Office Phone: 415-434-1600. E-mail: jlopes@howardrice.com.

LOPES, JERRY, broadcast executive; b. Providence; m. Rhonda Wade. Attended, Boston U. With Armed Forces Radio & Television service, 1970—73; news dir. WILD, Boston, 1974—75; with WHDH/ WCOZ, Boston, 1975—80; news dir. Sheridan Broadcasting Network, Washington, 1980—90, v.p. programming & ops. Pitts., 1990—92; exec. v.p. programming Am. Urban Radio, Pitts., 1992—93, pres., 1993—. Office: Am Urban Radio Networks 960 Penn Ave Ste 200 Pittsburgh PA 15222-3811

LOPES, ROSALY MUTEL CROCCE, astronomer, planetary geologist; b. Rio de Janeiro, Jan. 8, 1957; came to U.S., 1989; d. Walmir Crocce and Atir (Mutel) Lopes; m. Thomas Nicholas Gautier, III, Nov. 17, 1990 (div.); 1 child, Thomas N. Gautier. BSc in Astronomy, U. London, 1978, PhD in Physics, 1986. Curator Old Royal Obs., Greenwich, Eng., 1985-88; rsch. assoc. Vesuvius Obs., Naples, Italy, 1989; NRC rsch. assoc. Jet Propulsion Lab., Pasadena, Calif., 1989-91, rsch. scientist Galileo Project, 1990—2002, rsch. scientist Cassini Project, 2002—04, prin. scientist Cassini Project, 2004—. Mem. Volcanic Eruption Surveillance Team, U.K., 1981. Author: Volcanic Worlds, 2004, The Volcano Adventure Guide, 2005, numerous other works in sci. field. Recipient Latinas in Sci. award Commn. Feminil Mexicana Nat., L.A., 1990; named Woman of the Yr. in Sci., Gems TV, 1997. Fellow Explorers Club; mem. Internat. Astron. Union, Am. Astron. Soc. (Carl Sagan medal 2005), Am. Geophys. Union. Office: Jet Propulsion Lab Mail Stop 183-601 4800 Oak Grove Dr Pasadena CA 91109-8001 Office Phone: 818-393-4584. Business E-Mail: rosaly.m.lopes@jpl.nasa.gov.

LOPEZ, BARRY HOLSTUN, writer; b. Port Chester, NY, Jan. 6, 1945; s. Adrian Bernard and Mary Frances (Holstun) L.; m. Sandra Jean Landers, June 10, 1967 (div. Jan. 16, 1999). BA cum laude, U. Notre Dame, 1966, MA in Teaching, 1968; postgrad., U. Oreg., 1968-69; LHD (hon.), Whittier Coll., 1988, U. Portland, 1994, Tex. Tech. U., 2000; LHD in Environ. Studies (hon.), Utah State U., 2002. Free-lance writer, 1970—. Assoc. Media Studies Ctr. at Columbia Univ., N.Y.C., 1985—; mem. U.S. Cultural Delegation to China, 1988; residency fellow Lannan Found., 1999, Bernadine Kielty Scherman fellow MacDowell Colony, 2004. Author: Desert Notes, 1976, Giving Birth to Thunder, 1978, Of Wolves and Men, 1978 (John Burroughs Soc. medal 1979, Christophers of N.Y. medal 1979, Pacific Northwest Booksellers award in nonfiction 1979), River Notes, 1979, Winter Count, 1981 (Disting. Recognition award Friends Am. Writers in Chgo. 1982), Arctic Dreams, 1986 (Nat. Book award in nonfiction Nat. Book Found. 1986, Christopher medal 1987, Pacific Northwest Booksellers award 1987, Frances Fuller Victor award in nonfiction Oreg. Inst. Literary Arts 1987), Crossing Open Ground, 1988, Crow and Weasel, 1990 (Parents Choice Found. award), The Rediscovery of North America, 1991, Field Notes, 1994 (Pacific Northwest Booksellers award in fiction 1995, Critics' Choice award 1996), Lessons From the Wolverine, 1997, About This Life, 1998, Apologia, 1998, Light Action in the Caribbean, 2000, Vintage Lopez, 2004, Resistance, 2004; also numerous articles, essays and short stories; contbg. editor Harper's mag., 1981-82, 84—, N.Am. Rev., 1977—, Ga. Rev., 2000—; works translated into Japanese, Swedish, German, Dutch, Italian, French, Norwegian, Chinese, Finnish, Slovak, Spanish, Arabic. Recipient award in Lit., Am. Acad. Arts and Letters, 1986, Antarctic Svc. medal U.S. Congress, 1989, Gov.'s award for Arts, 1990, Lannan Found. award, 1990, Internat. Environ. award Prescott Coll., 1992, John Hay award, The Orion Soc., 2002, St. Francis of Assisi award DePaul U., 2002; HEA Title V fellow, 1967, John Simon Guggenheim Found. fellow, 1987; grantee NSF, 1987, 88, 91, 92, 99; vis. disting. vis. scholar Tex. Tech U., 2003—. Fellow Explorers Club; mem. PEN Am. Ctr., PEN Ctr. USA West, Authors Guild, Poets and Writers, Amnesty Internat., Nature Conservancy (hon. life), Arctic Inst. N.Am. (life). Achievements include archive purchased for The James Sowell Family Collection in Literature, Community and the Natural World, Tex. Tech. U., 2000.

LOPEZ, CAROLYN CATHERINE, physician; b. Chgo., Oct. 13, 1951; d. Joseph Compean and Angela (Silva) L. BS, Loyola U., Chgo., 1973; MD, U. Ill., 1978. Diplomate Am. Bd. Family Practice. Intern, resident Rush/Christ Hosp., Chgo., 1978-81; med. dir. Wholistic Health Ctr., Oak Lawn, Ill., 1981-82; clin. dir. Anchor HMO, Oak Brook, Ill., 1982-84, assoc. med. dir., 1984-87; med. dir. Chgo. Pk. Dist., 1987-91; v.p. Rush Access HMO, Chgo., 1992-93; asst. dean Rush Med. Coll., 1990-93; med. dir. Rush Access HMO, Chgo., 1991-93, v.p., 1992-93; v.p. for profl. affairs Rush Anchor HMO, 1993; sr. v.p. and chief med. officer Rush-Prudential Health Plans, 1993-95; chair dept. family practice Cook County Hosp., 1996—. Mem. Chgo. Bd. Health, 2004—; bd. govs. Inst. Medicine, Chgo., 2003—. Primary Care Policy fellow USPHS, 1993. Fellow Inst. Medicine of Chgo. (bd. govs. 2003—); mem. AMA, APHA, Am. Acad. Family Physicians (alt. del. 1992-95, del. 1996-99, vice-spkr. 1999-2002, spkr. 2002-04), Am. Coll. Physicians Execs., Ill. Acad. Family Physicians (bd. dirs. 1987-89, speaker 1990-91, bd. chair 1990-91, pres.-elect 1991-92, pres. 1992-93), Am. Med. Women's Assn. Roman Catholic. Avocations: swimming, cooking. Office: Cook County Hosp Dept Family Practice 1900 W Polk St Chicago IL 60612-3736

LOPEZ, CHESTER HENRY, JR., lawyer; b. Yarmouth, Maine, Aug. 2, 1936; s. Chester Henry and Betty (Kinney) L.; m. Mary Lillian Jordan, Sept. 6, 1958; children: Steven Greg, Gary Allen, Susan Ellen. BA, Colby Coll., 1958; JD, U. Chgo., 1961. Bar: N.H. 1961, U.S. Dist. Ct. N.H. 1965, U.S. Ct. Appeals (1st cir.) 1970. Atty., mng. dir. Hamblett & Kerrigan, Nashua, N.H., 1961—; also dir. trustee Southern N.H. Med. Ctr., 1981-89. Trustee Southern N.H. Med. Ctr., 1981-89, pres. 1984-86; trustee Andover Newton Theol. Sch., 1984-85; bd. dirs. United Way of Greater Nashua, 1995—. Mem. ABA, N.H. Bar Assn., Nashua Bar Assn. (pres. 1984), Nashua C. of C. (bd. dirs. 1975-77). Clubs: Nashua Country (bd. govs., v.p. 1985-86, pres. 1986-87), Rotary (pres. 1980-81)(Nashua, N.H.). Republican. Baptist. Home: 99 Walden Pond Dr Nashua NH 03064-2877 Office: 146 Main St Nashua NH 03060-2731 E-mail: clopez@hamker.com.

LOPEZ, DAVID, lawyer; b. N.Y.C., May 9, 1942; s. Damaso and Carmen (Gonzalez) L.; m. Nancy Mary Cea, Aug. 29, 1964; children: David, Jonathan. AB, Cornell U., 1963; JD, Columbia U., 1966. Bar: N.Y. 1966. Assoc. firm Leon, Weill & Mahoney, N.Y.C., 1966-67, Bressler & Meislen, 1967-70; pvt. practice N.Y.C., 1970—. Chmn. bd. A.T.I. Adv. Svcs., Inc., 1979—; dir. Nancy Lopez, Inc., Southampton, N.Y. Mem. ABA, N.Y. State Bar Assn., Suffolk County Bar Assn., Barrel Hill Conservancy, Inc. Office: 171 Edge of Woods Rd PO Box 323 Southampton NY 11969-0323 Office Phone: 631-287-5520. Personal E-mail: davidlopezesq@aol.com.

LOPEZ, DAVID TIBURCIO, lawyer, educator, arbitrator, mediator; b. Laredo, Tex., July 17, 1939; s. Tiburcio and Dora (Davila) L.; m. Romelia G. Guerra, Nov. 20, 1965; 1 child, Vianei López Robinson. Student, Laredo Jr. Coll., 1956-58; BJ, U. Tex., 1962; JD summa cum laude, South Tex. Coll. Law, 1971. Bar: Tex. 1971, U.S. Dist. Ct. (so. dist.) Tex. 1972, U.S. Ct. Appeals (5th cir.) 1973, U.S. Dist. Ct. (we. dist.) Tex. 1975, U.S. Ct. Claims 1975, U.S. Ct. Appeals (fed. cir.) 1975, U.S. Supreme Ct. 1976, U.S. Dist. Ct. (ea. dist.) Tex. 1978, U.S. Dist. Ct. N.Mex. 2000, U.S. Ct. Appeals (11th cir.) 1981, U.S. Ct. Appeals (9th cir.) 1984; cert. internat. com. arbitrator Internat. Ctr. for Arbitration; mediator tng. Atty.-Mediator Inst. Reporter Laredo Times, 1958-59; cons. Mexican Nat. Coll. Mag., Mexico City, 1961-62; reporter Corpus Christi (Tex.) Caller-Times, 1962-64; state capitol corr. Long News Svc., Austin, Tex., 1964-65; publs. dir. Interam. Regional Orgn. of Workers, Mexico City, 1965-67; nat. field rep. AFL-CIO, Washington, 1967-71, publs. dir. Tex. chpt. Austin, 1971-72; pvt. practice Houston, 1971—. Adj. prof. U. Houston, 1972-74, Thurgood Marshall Sch. Law, Houston, 1975-76; mem. adv. com. nat. Hispanic ednl. rsch. project One Million and Counting Tomas Rivera Ctr., 1989-91; mem. adv. bd. Inst. Transnat. Arbitration; charter mem. Resolution Forum Inc.; mem. adv. bd. South Tex. Ctr. Profl. Responsibility; mem. nat. panel of neutrals JAMS/ENDISPUTE, 1996-2000. Mem. bd. edn. Houston Ind. Sch. Dist., 1972—75; bd. dirs. Pacifica Found., N.Y.C., 1970—72, Houston C.C., 1972—75, FM Radio Sta., 2000—02. With U.S. Army. Mem. ABA, FBA, Tex. Bar Assn. (com. on pattern jury changes), Houston Bar Assn. (com. on alternative dispute resolution), Internat. Bar Assn., Interam. Bar Assn., Bar of U.S. Fed. Cir., Mex.-Am. Bar Assn., Inter-Pacific Bar Assn., Tex.-Mex. Bar Assn., Hispanic Bar Assn., World Assn. Lawyers (chair internat. lab. sect.), Am. Judicature Soc., Indsl. Rels. Rsch. Assn., Am. Arbitration Assn., Sigma Delta Chi, Phi Alpha Delta. Democrat. Roman Catholic. Home: 28 Farnham Ct Houston TX 77024 Office: 3900 Montrose Blvd Houston TX 77006-4959 Office Phone: 713-523-3900. Business E-Mail: dtlopez@lopezlawfirm.com.

LOPEZ, ERIC JOSEPH, psychology educator, consultant; s. Jose López, Jr. and Maria Julia López; m. Eva Menchaca, July 14, 2001. BA, Tex. A&M U., 1991; EdS, U. Iowa, 1995, PhD, 1997. Lic. level 3 sch. psychologist N.Mex Pub. Edn. Dept., 1999, level 3 ednl. diagnostician N.Mex Pub. Edn. Dept., 1999, nat. cert. sch. psychologist NASP, 1997, nat. cert. bd. mem. NASP, 2005. Bilingual sch. psychologist Las Cruces Pub. Schs., N.Mex., 1996—99; asst. prof. N.Mex State U., Las Cruces, 1999—2005, chmn. Hispanic faculty/staff caucus, 2001—02, assoc. prof., 2005—. Cons. López, PhD and Menchaca-López, LLC, Las Cruces, 2003—. Asst. dir. Fruto De La Vid Spanish Choir, Dona Ana, N.Mex., 2004. Named Outstanding Young Men of Am., 1995. Mem.: NASP, Nat. Assn. Educating Young Children (consulting editor 2002—05), N.Mex Assn. Sch. Psychologists (pres. 2001—02). Home: PO Box 4165 Las Cruces NM 88003 Office: NMex State U PO Box 30001 MSC 3SPE Las Cruces NM 88003 Home Fax: 505-382-4492; Office Fax: 505-646-7712. Personal E-mail: ericlopezphd@msn.com.

LOPEZ, GEORGE, actor, comedian; b. Mission Hills, Calif., Apr. 23, 1961; m. Ann Serrano, 1993. Radio show host MEGA 92.3 (KCMG), Los Angeles, 2001; co-founder The George & Ann Lopez-Richie Alarcon Care Found. Actor: (films) Fist of Fear, Tough of Death, 1980, Ski Patrol, 1990, Fatal Instinct, 1993, Bread and Roses, 2000, Real Women Have Curves, 2002, Outta Time, 2002, Ali G In Da House, 2002; appearances (TV specials) Latino Laugh Festival, 1997, 2nd Annual Latino Laugh Festival, 1998, host Loco Comedy Jam, 4th Annual Latin Grammy Awards, 2003, 5th Annual Latin Grammy Awards, 2004, correspondent (TV series) Inside the NFL, HBO, 2003—; actor: (TV miniseries) Fidel, 2002; actor, co-creator, writer, prodr. George Lopez, 2002—, comedian (headliner) ARCO Arena, Sacramento, Shoreline Amphitheater, San Francisco, Majestic Theatre, Dallas, San Antonio, Wiltern Theatre, Los Angeles, HBO US Comedy Arts Festival, Aspen; performer: (live comedy albums) Team Leader, 2003 (Grammy nom. best comedy album, 2003), Right Now Right Now, 2004; author: Why You Crying?: My Long, Hard Look at Life, Love, and Laughter, 2004. Spokesperson Stop the Violence program, Los Angeles Police Dept. Named one of 25 Most Influential Hispanics, Time Mag., 2005; recipient Nat. Hispanic Media Coalition Impact award, Community Spirit award, Manny Mota Found., Artist of the Yr. award, Harvard Found. for Intercultural & Race Relations, 2004. Achievements include first Latino to headline a morning radio show on an English-language station in Los Angeles. Office: c/o Ron DeBlasio SDM Inc 740 N La Brea Ave Los Angeles CA 90039

LOPEZ, GERALD P., law educator; b. 1948; BA, U. So. Calif., 1970; JD, Harvard U., 1974. Bar: Calif. 1974. Law clk. to Hon. Edward J. Schwartz US Dist. Ct. So. Dist. Calif., San Diego, 1974-75; pvt. practice law San Diego, 1975-79; asst. prof. Calif. Western Sch. Law, San Diego, 1976-78; vis. prof. UCLA, 1978-79, acting prof., 1979-83, prof., 1983-85; vis. prof. Harvard U., Cambridge, Mass., 1983-84, Stanford U., 1984-85, prof., 1985—94, UCLA, 1994—2000; prof. clin. law NYU Sch. Law, 2000—, founder, dir. Ctr. Cmty. Problem Solving, 2003—. Author: Rebellious Lawyering, 1992. Office: NYU Sch Law 5th Fl 245 Sullivan St New York NY 10012 Office Phone: 212-998-6469.*

LOPEZ, J. BLANCA O., school system administrator; d. Tomas Lopez and Olga Sanchez. BS, U. Tex., 1993, M in Edn., 1997; postgrad., N.Mex. State U., 1997—. Bilingual tchr. El Paso Ind. Sch. Dist., 1993—96; math and sci. mentor Ysleta Ind. Sch. Dist., El Paso, 1996—2004, tchr. recruiter, 2004—. Named Tchr. of Tchrs., U. Tex. El Paso, 1997; scholar All Am. scholar, U.S. Achievement Acad., 1996, Hispanic Scholar Fund, 1999—2000. Mem.: Am. Ednl. Rsch. Assn., Gamma Beta Phi. Roman Catholic. Avocations: reading, writing, music, exercise. Office: Ysleta Ind Sch Dist 9600 Sims El Paso TX 79925 Office Phone: 915-434-0410.

LOPEZ, JENNIFER, actress, singer, dancer; b. Bronx, NY, July 24, 1970; d. David and Guadalupe Lopez; m. Ojani Noa, Feb. 22, 1997 (div. Jan. 1, 1998); m. Cris Judd, Sept. 29, 2001 (div. Jan. 26, 2003); m. Marc Anthony, June 5, 2004. Launched clothing line J-Lo by Jennifer Lopez, 2001, lingerie line, 2004; released signature fragrance Glow, 2002, Still, 2004, Miami Glow, 2005; owner Madre's restaurant, Pasedena, 2002-. Won dance competition and was hired as dancer for TV series In Living Color, 1991-93; actor (TV series) Second Chances, 1993-94, South Central, 1994, Hotel Malibu, 1994; actor (films) Money Train, 1995, Jack, 1996, Blood and Wine, 1996, Anaconda, 1997 (ALMA award 1998), Selena, 1997 (ALMA award 1998), My Family, 1995, U-Turn, 1997, Antz (voice), 1998, Out of Sight, 1998 (ALMA award 1999), Thieves, 1999, Pluto Nash, 1999, The Cell, 2000 (Blockbuster Entertainment award for favorite actress, MTV Movie award for best dressed), The Wedding Planner, 2001, Angel Eyes, 2001, Enough, 2002, Maid in Manhattan, 2002, Gigli, 2003, Jersey Girl, 2004, Shall We Dance?, 2004, Monster-in-Law, 2005, An Unfinished Life, 2005; actor (TV guest appearances) Will & Grace, 2004; singer (albums) On the 6, 1999, J.Lo, 2001, J to Tha L-O!: The Remixes, 2002, This Is Me...Then, 2002, Rebirth, 2005. Recipient ALMA Female Entertainer Yr. award 2000, Lasting Image award 1998, Lone Star Film and TV award 1998; named one of 50 Most Beautiful People in the World, People mag., 1997; voted #1 in 100 Sexiest Women list, FHM, 2000, 2001; named one of 25 Most Influential Hispanics, Time Mag., 2005. Office: Endeavor c/o Patrick Whitesell 9701 Wilshire Blvd, 10th Fl Beverly Hills CA 90212*

LOPEZ, JORGE LUIS, lawyer; b. Havana, Cuba, Apr. 21, 1961; s. Luis and Sarah Lopez; m. Mercedes L Rodriguez, Oct. 26, 1996. BA magna cum laude in Polit. Sci., St. Thomas U., 1983, MBA, 1985; JD cum laude, U. Miami, 1987. Bar: Fla. 1987, U.S. Supreme Ct. Fla. 1987. Dir. intergovernmental affairs Miami-Dade County, Fla., 1982—84; of counsel Shutts & Bowen, LLP, Miami, 1996—98; mng. shareholder Verner Liipfert, Bernhard, McPherson and Hand, Miami, 1998—2001; ptnr. Steel Hector & Davis LLP, Miami, 2001—. Mem. exec. com. Beacon Coun., Miami, 2002—. Contbr. articles to profl. jours. including U. Miami Internat. Am Law Rev. Fundraiser Nat. Rep. Fin. Com., Washington, 2000, Pres. George W. Bush Fin. and Inaugural Coms., Austin, Tex., 2000, Gov. Jeb Bush Fin. and Inaugural Coms., Tallahassee, 1998; mem. president's adv. coun. St. Thomas U., Miami, 2001; mem. cabinet United Way, Miami, 2002; mem. Vizcaya and Gardens Trust, Miami, 1998; dir. Carlos Albizu U., Miami, 2002. Mem.: Soc. Bar and Gavel (life), Soc. Wig and Robe (life), Omicron Delta Kappa (life). Catholic. Avocations: golf, reading, racquetball, basketball, reading. Office: Steel Hector & Davis LLP 200 S Biscayne Blvd Ste 4000 Miami FL 33131-2398 E-mail: jlopez@steelhector.com.

LOPEZ, JOSE JAVIER, geographer, educator; b. San Juan, P.R., Feb. 19, 1969; s. Carlos Lopez-Feliciano and Gloria Jimenez-Normandia; m. Marimigda Medina, Jan. 8, 1994; children: Ariana Diane, Naomi Maureen. BA, U. P.R., 1991; MS, U. Akron, 1993; PhD in Geography, Ind. State U., 1998. Grad. tchg. asst. Ind. State U., Terre Haute, Ind., 1996—97; instr. St. Mary Woods Coll., 1997; assoc. prof. Minn. State U., Mankato, 1998—. Mentor Minn. State U., 2003—04, instr. McNair scholars, 2004, coord. geography grad. program, 1999—2004; bd. dirs. L.A.M.A.N.O., Inc. Contbr. articles to profl. jours. Reviewer grant applications U.S. Dept. Housing, 2000—03. Recipient Benjamin Moulton award, Ind. State U., 1997; scholar, U. P.R., 1994. Mem.: Nat. Coun. Geographic Edn., Assn. Am. Geographers. Avocation: scuba diving. Home: 304 Ridgewood St Mankato MN 56001 Office: Minn State U Geography Dept 07 Armstrong Hall Mankato MN 56001 Office Phone: 507-389-2617.

LOPEZ, JOSEPH R., lawyer; BA, U. Ill., 1978; JD, Chgo. Kent U., 1983. Bar: State of Ill. Supreme Ct. 1984, U.S. Dist. Ct. for No. Dist. Ill. 1985, U.S. Ct. of Appeals for 7th Circuit 1985, U.S. Dist. Ct. for No. Dist. Ind. 1986, U.S. Dist. Ct. for Ea. Dist. Wis. 1988, U.S. Ct. Appeals for 2d Circuit 1989, U.S. Dist. Ct. for Ctrl. Dist. Ill. 1989, U.S. Ct. of Appeals for 8th Circuit 1990, U.S. Dist. Ct. for Western Dist. Mich. 1988, U.S. Ct. Appeals 5th Circuit 2003. Atty. pvt. practice, Chgo., 1984—. Recipient Outstanding Atty. of Yr., Pan Am. Civic Alliance, 2002. Mem.: Nat. Assn. Criminal Def. Lawyers. Office: Joseph R Lopez LTD 53 W Jackson Ste 1122 Chicago IL 60604 Office Fax: 312-922-7920.

LOPEZ, LINDA CAROL, social sciences educator; b. N.Y.C., Dec. 26, 1949; d. Ralph B. and Miriam (Tayor) L. BA, U. Wis., 1972; MA, Ohio State U., 1974, PhD, 1976. Vis. asst. prof. U. Wis., Eau Claire, 1976-77; instr., asst. prof. SUNY, Oneonta, 1977-83; assoc. prof. Rockford (Ill.) Coll., 1983—89; prof. dept. social scis. Western N.Mex. U., Silver City, 1989—, dir. field experience, 1989—91. Contbr. articles to profl. jours., including Psychol. Reports, Internat. Jour. Addiction, Hispanic Jour. Behavioral Scis., Jour. Genetic Psychology, Jour. Employment Counseling, Perceptual and Motor Skills, Reading Improvement, Counseling and Values, Social Studies Jour. Recipient Best Paper award New Eng. Ednl. Rsch. Orgn., 1979; postdoctoral faculty fellow Northeastern U., Boston, 1980-81. Mem.: Ill. Psychol. Assn., Am. Assn. Behavioral and Social Scis., Phi Delta Kappa. Avocations: walking, reading, travel. Home: PO Box 1479 Bayard NM 88023 Office: Western NMex U Dept Social Scis 1000 W College Ave Silver City NM 88062

LOPEZ, M. EDWARD, small business owner; b. Ft. Bragg, N.C., Feb. 16, 1968; s. Manuel and Maria Rosario Lopez; m. Lisa T. Palmer, Dec. 22, 1990; children: Diana, Alexandra, Gabriella. BA in Govt., S.W. Tex. State U., 1990. Spl. asst. to Senator Lloyd Bentsen U.S. Senate, Tex., 1990—92; presdl. transition team Clinton Transition Team, Washington, 1992—93; mgr. pub. affairs H.B. Zachary Co., San Antonio, 1993—95; dir. govt. affairs San Antonio Water Sys., 1995—96; owner Office M. Edward Lopez, San Antonio, 1996—. Mem.: Tex. Lyceum Assn. (dir. 2000—), S. Side C. of C. (adv. mem. 2001—), San Antonio Hispanic C. of C. (bd. dirs. 2000—02). Independent. Roman Catholic. Avocations: golf, song writing.

LOPEZ, MANUEL, immunology and allergy educator; b. Bucaramanga, Colombia, Sept. 30, 1939; came to U.S., 1964. married; 4 children. BS, Colegio San Pedro Claver, Bucaramanga, 1956; MD, Univ. Javeriana, Bogota, Colombia, 1963. Diplomate Am. Bd. Allergy and Immunology, Am. Bd. Diagnostic Lab. Immunology. Intern Hosp. San Juan De Dios, Bucaramanga, 1962-63, resident, 1963-64, med. dir., 1969-71; clin. and rsch. fellow dept. medicine allergy unit Harvard U. and Harvard Med. Sch. at Mass. Gen. Hosp., Boston, 1964-68; dir. med. rsch. Univ. Indsl. De Santander, Bucaramanga, 1968-69; dir. immunology svc. lab. La. State Med. Ctr., New Orleans, 1971-74; asst. prof. medicine med. ctr. La. State U., New Orleans, 1971-74; from clin. asst. prof. to assoc. prof. med. sch. Tulane U., New Orleans, 1974-89, prof., 1989—, dir. immunology diagnostic lab. med. sch., 1974-83, dir. clin. immunology labs., 1983—99, program dir. allergy and immunology tng. program, 1990—98, acting chief sect. allergy and clin. immunology, 1990-91, chief sect. clin. immunology, allergy & rheumatology, 1991—. Mem. med.-sci. adv. com. Asthma and Allergy Found. Am., 1986-89; ad hoc mem. immunological sci. study sect. NIH, 1987, allergy and clin. immunology spl. reviewer immunology and transplantation rsch. com., 1988, mem. gen. clin. rsch. ctrs. com., 1993-94; reviewer merit rev. grants VA, 1988, 89, 90; grant program reviewer Ctrs. of Excellence, Dept. Health and Human Svcs., 1991; mem. allergic products adv. com. FDA, 1993-96; mem. spl. rev. com. Nat. Inst. Allergy and Infectious Diseases, 1993; presenter in field. Mem. editl. bd. Jour. Allergy and Clin. Immunology, 1986-94, reviewer, 1987—; mem. editl. bd. Annals of Allergy, 1998—2003; contbr. articles to profl. jours. and chpts. to books. Fellow John Simmon Guggenheim Meml. Found., 1964-66. Fellow Am. Acad. Allergy and Clin. Immunology (mem. internat. com. 1986-89, mem. immunotherapy of asthma com. 1987-88, mem. Latin Ctrl. and South Am. com. 1987—, chmn. internat. grant aids 1988-89, mem. continuing med. edn. com. 1992-94, chmn. EOD interest sect. 1999-01); mem. Am. Assn. Immunologists, Am. Fedn. Clin. Rsch., Am. Thoracic Soc., U.S.-Colombian Med. Assn. (pres. IX Congress 1989), La. Allergy Soc. (pres. 2003-04), N.Y. Acad. Scis., Southeastern Allergy Assn., Internat. Assn. Aerobiology, Cordoba Allergy Soc. (hon.), Hispanic Am. Med. Assn. La. (pres. 2001-03). Office: Tulane U Med Sch Clin Immunology Sect 1700 Perdido St SL-57 New Orleans LA 70112-1210

LOPEZ, NANCY, former professional golfer; b. Torrance, Calif., Jan. 6, 1957; d. Domingo and Marina (Griego) Lopez; m. Ray Knight, Oct. 25, 1982; children: Ashley Marie Knight, Erinn Shea Knight, Torri Heather Knight. Student, U. Tulsa, 1976-78. Founder and Principal Nancy Lopez Golf Company. Player U.S.A. Solheim Cup, 1990. Author: (book) The Education of a Woman Golfer, 1979. Named first victory winner, Bent Tree Classic, Sarasota, Fla., 1978, AP Athlete, 1978, Rolex Rookie of the Yr., 1978, Rolex Player of the Yr., 1978, 1979, 1985, winner, LPGA Championship, 1978, 1985, Mazda LPGA Championship, 1989, others; named to LPGA Hall of Fame, 1987, PGA World Golf Hall of Fame, 1989; recipient Vare Trophy, 1978. Mem.: LPGA (Player and Rookie of the Yr. 1978). Republican. Achievements include winning 48 LPGA Tour events, 3 maj. championships. Office: care Internat Mgmt Group 1360 E 9th St Ste 100 Cleveland OH 44114-1715

LOPEZ, PEDRO FELIPE, social worker, educator, playwright, writer; b. Havana, Cuba, Aug. 23, 1938; s. Pedro Lopez and Josefa Margarita Bravo. D of Pedagogy, Santa Clara U., Cuba, 1959. Cert. Tchr. of Spl. Edn., Enseñanza Diferenciada, Cuba 1962. Med. social worker N.Y.C. HHC, 1968—2001. Trainer child abuse and maltreatment recognition Lincoln Med. and Mental Health Ctr., N.Y.C., 1991—2001. Home: 452 Fort Washington Avenue Apt # 40 New York NY 10033-4618

LOPEZ, RALPH IVAN, pediatrics educator; b. San Juan, PR, Jan. 3, 1942; s. Ralph and Aida (Miranda) L.; m. Paula, July 30, 1964; 1 child, Abigail AB cum laude, Fordham Coll., 1963; MD, NYU, 1967. Intern pediatrics NYU Bellevue Hosp., N.Y.C., 1967-68, resident pediatrics, 1968-69, Boston Children's Hosp., Harvard Med. Ctr., 1969-70; asst. prof. pediatrics N.Y. Hosp., N.Y.C., 1973-79, assoc. prof. pediatrics, 1979-83, clin. assoc. prof. pediatrics, 1983—. Cons. physician Dalton Sch., NYC, 1973-86, Nightingale Bamford, NYC, 1986-90. Editor: Adolescent Medicine Topics, 1976, 2d edit. 1980; author: The Teen Health Book, 2002; contbr. articles to profl. jours. Bd. dirs. Louis August Jones Found., Rhinebeck, NJ, 1973-91, chmn. bd. dirs., 1990—; bd. dirs. Covenant House, NYC, 1990-92; chmn. Ind. Doctors of NY; nominating com. Girl Scouts U.S., NYC, 1991. Lt. comdr. USNR, 1971-73 Mem. Phi Beta Kappa. Office: 418 E 71st St New York NY 10021-4894 Office Phone: 212-772-8989.

LOPEZ, RAMON ROSSI, lawyer; b. Vallejo, Calif., Aug. 14, 1950; s. Louis and Katherine Rita (Rossi) L.; m. Jamie Gray, May 26, 1973; children: James Louis, Matthew Ramon, Scott Nicholas, Katherine Joan. BS, Loyola U., L.A., 1972, JD, 1978. Bar: Calif. 1979, U.S. Dist. Ct. (so. dist.) Calif. 1979. Sales rep. Eaton Labs., L.A., 1972-75; claims rep. Chubb/Pacific Indeminity, L.A., 1975-78; assoc. Cummins, White, Robinson & Robinson, L.A., 1979-80, Robinson & Robinson, Newport Beach, Calif., 1981-82; ptnr. Barth & Lopez, Newport Beach, 1982-87, Barth, Lopez & Hodes, Newport Beach, 1987-90, Lopez & Hodes, Newport Beach, 1991-98; mng. ptnr. Lopez, Hodes, Restaino, Milman, Skikos & Poles, Newport Beach. Co-lead counsel, mem. plaintiffs exec. com. Rezulin Litigation; co-lead counsel PPA, State Ct. Litigation. Bd. dirs. Newport Nat. Little League, 1988, Our Lady Queen of Angels Sch., 1989-90, Am. Youth Soccer Assn., 1988—. Fellow Internat. Soc. Barristers; mem. ATLA, Consumer Attys. Calif., L.A. Trial Lawyers Assn., Orange County Bar Assn., Consumer Lawyers Calif. (plaintiffs steering com., breast implant litigation, plaintiff exec./mgmt. com., diet drugs litigation, bd. mem.), Balboa Bay Club. Democrat. Roman Catholic. Home: 5 Canyon Ct Newport Beach CA 92660-5918 Office: Lopez Hodes Restaino Et Al 450 Newport Center Dr 2d Fl Newport Beach CA 92660-7617

LOPEZ, ROBERT, composer, lyricist; Attended, BMI Lehman Engel Musical Theater Workshop, 1999. Composer children's musicals Theatreworks/USA; composer various songs The Disney Channel. Composer, lyricist (with Jeff Marx) (Broadway plays) Avenue Q, 2003 (Lucille Lortel award for best musical, 2003, Tony award best musical score, 2004), (plays) Kermit, Prince of Denmark (Ed Kleban award). Office: John Golden Theatre 252 W 45th St New York NY 10010

LOPEZ, SOLEDAD, actress; d. Primitivo Lopez and Mariana Hernandez; m. Angel Gil Orrios, Feb. 22, 1980; children: Sebastian Gil-Lopez, Mariana Gil-Lopez. Cert. acting The Real Stage, Ny, 1985. Actor: (plays) Jaime Salom's Almost a Goddess (Best Actress award, ACE, 2005), Renaldo Ferradas' La Visionaria, Alegre Cudos' Verde Doncella Asalta Un Cine, Don Juan Por Los Siglos De Los Siglos (Best Actress award, Golden Age Festival, El Paso, 1989), Alegre Cudos' La Madre Que Te Pario, Calderon de la Barca's The Purgatory of Saint Patrick, Garcia Lorca's The Audience & Play Without A Title, Almodovar/Cabal's Dark Habits, Sartre's No Exit, Espriu's Piel de Toro, La Pasion De Cristo, Ramos Perea's We Women Do It Better (Best Actress award, ACE and Hola, 2004), Tiempo Del 98, Santiago Moncada's Caprichos, Carlos Fuentes' The One-eyed Man Is King, Jardiel Poncela's Brake Four Hearts, Picasso's Guernica, Calderon de la Barca's The Great Theatre of the World (Best Actress award, Hola, 2001), Miguel Sierra's Palomas Intrepidas (Best Actress award, ACE, 1996), Santiago Moncada's Entre Mujeres (Best Actress award, ACE, 1995), Martin Descalzo's Las Prostitutas Os Precederan en el Reino de los Cielos (Best Actress award, ACE, 1994). Recipient Vermeil medal, French Acad. Arts, Scis. and Letters, Paris, 2005. Mem.: Hispanic Orgn. Latin Actors (Best Actress award 2001, 2003). Personal E-mail: soledad@thaliatheatre.org.

LOPEZ-ALVAREZ, CARMEN A., language educator; b. Ponce, PR, Mar. 8, 1964; d. Miguel Angel López-Rodríguez and Carmen Dolores Alvarez-Matos; m. Jason Aaron Feingold, May 22, 1993 (div. Nov. 14, 1997); 1 child, Jacob Adán Feingold-López; m. Melvin Hiram Rodríguez-Vélez, Apr. 3, 1998; 1 child, Laura Beatriz Rodríguez-López. BA in Polit. Sci., U. P.R., 1986; MPA, Syracuse U., 1987; BA in Spanish, U. P.R., 1990; MA in Spanish, Pa. State U., 1991, PhD in Spanish, 1995. Tchg. asst. Pa. State U., University Park, 1991—94, editl. coord. Estreno, 1993—95, lectr. Spanish, 1994—95; asst. prof. Spanish Alvernia Coll., Reading, Pa., 1995—96, U. PR, Ponce, 1996—2001, assoc. prof. Spanish, 2001—. Cons. in field; writer Coll. Bd., San Juan, PR, 2002—, Advanced Placement reader, NJ, 2004—. Editor: (handbook) I Am Graduating: What Should I Do?, 1998, Towards a New Millennium, 1999, www.success.com, 2000; author: Law 51, 2003. Assn. for Pub. Policy Analysis and Mgmt. fellow, Alfred P. Sloan Found., 1985, Minority Scholars fellow, Pa. State U., 1990—91. Mem.: MLA, Am. Coun. on Tchg. of Fgn. Langs., Am. Assn. Tchrs. Spanish and Portuguese. Methodist. Avocations: reading, music, writing, travel, Internet. Home: Urb La Rambla 3059 Calle San Judas Ponce PR 00730 Office: U PR Po Box 7186 Ponce PR 00732 Office Phone: 787-844-8181. Business E-mail: calaupr@hotmail.com.

LOPEZ-FITZSIMMONS, BERNADETTE MARIA, librarian; b. NYC, Dec. 24, 1955; d. Edward Joseph Fitzsimmons and Serafina Sagrario Lopez Cueto. BA in English and Spanish magna cum laude, Iona Coll., 1973—77; MA in Spanish, Queens Coll., 1977—80, MLS with honors, 1996—2000; cert., Tech. and Librarianship, 2000—; continuing profl. edn. classes, 2000—01. Libr. cert. in cataloging Rutgers U., New Brunswick, NJ, 2002. Instr. Am. lang. Bergen County Cmty. Coll., Paramus, NJ, 1985—88; instr. ESL Passaic County Cmty. Coll., 1986—88, Eugenio Maria de Hostos Cmty. Coll., Bronx, 1986—90; instr. spanish Borugh Manhattan Cmty. Coll., 1991—; libr. asst. Art Library Queens Coll., Flushing, 1996—2000; reference asst. Rosenthal Libr. Queens Coll., 1997—2000; reference libr. Spanish World Langs., Donnell Ctr., NY Pub. Libr., 2000; cataloger libr. O'Malley Libr., Manhattan Coll., 2000—, coord. migration, new libr. sys., 2003—04. Com. mem. Friends of Zarzuela, 1994—; mem. ALDEEU, 1998—2000; mem. faculty rsch. com. Manhattan Coll., 2001—, mem. pub. com., 2002—03, mem. faculty tech. com., 2003—, mem. athletics com., 2005—; mem. Middle States Acad. Integrity Task Force, 2001; tech. svc. com. WALDO-WELD, 2000—04, migration planning com., 2002—04, mem. sys. planning com., 2002, sec., 2004—; com. mem. WALDO Endeavor Libr. Dels., 2004—; coord. NYLINK Connexion, 2004—; Webex moderator Voyager MS Access/Reporter Client Tng., 2005. Contbr. reviews to profl. jours. Mem. Healthy Heart Program, St. John's Hosp., St. Vincent's Med. Ctr., 2002—03. Mem.: MLA, Med. Libr. Assn., ALA. Avocations: travel, painting, walking, reading, writing, yoga, writing, pilates, meditation. Office: O'Malley Libr Manhattan Coll 4513 Manhattan Coll Pkwy Bronx NY 10471 Office Phone: 718-862-7982.

LOPEZ-GARCIA, ESTHER, public health service officer, researcher; b. Toledo, Spain; arrived in U.S., 2003; d. Pedro Lopez-Gabanas and Teresa Garcia-Vazquez. PharmD, Complutense U., 1998; MPH, Autonoma U., 2000, DPH, 2001. Fellow Rutonomib U., Madrid, 1999—2001, rschr., 2001—02; rschr. Sch. Pub. Health Harvard U., Boston, 2003—. Tchr. Butonomd U., 1999—2003. Contbr. articles to profl. jours. Fellow, Fulbright Found., 2002; grantee, Ministry Edn., Spain, 2004. Mem.: Am. Heart Assn. (Trudy Bush fellow 2004). Roman Cath. Avocations: running, reading, music.

LOPEZ HEREDIA, HUBERT, artist; b. Oran, France, Sept. 15, 1936; m. Andree Lopez Heredia, Sept. 29; children: Jean Marc, Sandrine. BA, Ecole Des Beaux Arts, France, 1952. Creator of the flower abstraction and the expansion movement. Officer Spl. Troops, 1955—63, Algerie. Decorated Croix De La Valeur Militaire. Achievements include patents for floral abstract art (Patent 16553 -5/21/75). Office Phone: 561-633-9395. Personal E-mail: lopezheredia@artmls.com.

LOPEZ-MORILLAS, FRANCES M., translator; b. Fulton, Mo., Sept. 3, 1918; d. Erwin Kempton and Laura (Hinkhouse) Mapes; m. Juan López-Morillas, Aug. 12, 1937; children: Martin Morell, Consuelo, Julian. BA, U. Iowa, 1939, MA, 1940. Translator Collins Radio Co., Cedar Rapids, Iowa, 1940-43; tchr. Spanish Lincoln Sch., Providence, 1943-44; tchr. French and Spanish Mary C. Wheeler Sch., Providence, 1951-64; tchr. ESL Internat. Inst., Madrid, 1957-58; freelance translator, 1964—. Co-editor: (with E.K. Mapes) J.J. Fernandez de Lizardi, El periquillo sarniento, 1952; translated more than 25 books and numerous articles including Journey to the Alcarria: Travels through the Spanish Countryside, 1964, Miguel de Unamuno, 1966, An Economic History of Spain, 1969, Spain in the Fifteenth Century, 1971, Tales of Potosí, 1975, The Krausist Movement and Ideological Change in Spain, 1981, Torquemada, 1986, Understanding Spain, 1990, The Medieval Heritage of Mexico, 1992, Castaways: The Narrative of Alvar Núñez Cabeza de Vaca, 1993, Selected Writings of Andrés Bello, 1997, Natural and Moral History of the Indies, 2002. Grantee NEH, 1984, NEA, 1986; recipient translation prize Tex. Inst. Letters, 1991. Mem. Internat. Assn. Hispanists, Am. Literary Translators Assn., Phi Beta Kappa. Home: 355 Blackstone Blvd Providence RI 02906-4946 Personal E-mail: fmorillas@aol.com.

LOPEZ-MUNOZ, MARIA ROSA P., real estate development company executive; b. Havana, Cuba, Jan. 28, 1938; came to U.S., 1960; d. Eleuterio Perfecto and Bertha (Carmenati Colon) Perez Rodriguez; m. Gustavo Lopez-Munoz, Sept. 9, 1973. Student, Candler Coll., Havana, 1951-53, Sch. Langs., U. Jose Marti, 1954-55. Lic. interior designer, real estate broker. Pres. Fantasy World Acres, Inc., Coral Gables, Fla., 1970-84, pres., dir., 1984—; sec. Sandhills Corp., Coral Gables, 1978-85, dir., 1978—. Treas., Am. Cancer Soc., Miami, Fla., 1981, sec. Hispanic bd., 1987, pres. Hispanic divsn., 1989, bd. dirs., aux. treas.; bd. dirs Am. Heart Assn., Miami, 1985, chmn. Hispanic divsn.; bd. dirs. YMCA, Young Patronesses of Opera, Miami, 1985, Lowe Mus. of U. Miami, 1986—, Linda Ray Infant Ctr.; former pres. Ladies Aux. Little Havana Child Care Ctr.; trustee Ronald McDonald House, sec. exec. bd., 1992; mem. exec. bd., rec. sec. Young Patronesses of the Opera; mem. Fla. Grand Opera; mem. cabinet Children's Cardiac Found., New Horizons Cmty. Devel., Transplant Ctr. Sch., Medicine, U. Miami-Jackson Meml. Hosp., 1992; bd. dirs. Cultura Italiana, Inc.; pres. Messengers of Peace, 2002; amb. 1999 Alpine Ski Championships, Vail, Colo. Recipient Merit award Am. Cancer Soc., 1980, 81, 82, 83, 84, Dynamic Woman award, 1992; Woman with Heart award Am. Heart Assn., 1985, Merit awards, 1980-84, Woman of Yr., 1986, Outstanding Lady award Greater Miami Opera, 1992, Cultural Star of the Millennium award Vizcaya Mus., 1999; named Woman of Yr., Children's Hosp., 1993; named to Great Order José Martí, 1988; named Leading Miami's Beautiful Couples for ACS, 1995. Mem. Real Estate Bd. Realtors, Coral Gables Real Estate Assn., Vail 50 Club, Ocean Reef Club (Key Largo, Fla.), Opera Guild Miami, YPO, Key Biscayle Yacht Club, Regine's Internta. Bath Club (Miami Beach). Republican. Roman Catholic. Avocations: yachting, skiing, scuba diving, guitar, piano. Office Phone: 305-299-5179.

LOPEZ-MURPHY, RICARDO HIPOLITO, economist; b. Buenos Aires, Aug. 10, 1951; s. Juan Jose Lopez-Aguirre and Brigida Murphy; m. Norma Ruiz Huidobro; children: Pablo, Analia, Ezequiel. MA, U. Chgo., 1980. Prof. U. La. Plata (Argentina), 1975—; cons. IMF, Buenos Aires, 1984-88; chief economist, rsch. economist FIEL, Buenos Aires, 1990—; min. of defense Govt. of Argentina, Buenos Aires, 2000-01, min. of economy, 2001—; Presdl. candidate, 2003. Mem. Assn. Argentina Economics. (sec. 1995). Roman Catholic. Office: FIEL Cordoba 637 Fl 40 1054 Buenos Aires Argentina Office Phone: 5411 4314 1990. E-mail: ricardo@fiel.org.ar.

LOPGUE, RONALD, finance company executive; BS, MBA, Boston Coll. Sr. v.p. State St. Corp., 1991; systems develop. and operation areas former Bank of New England; programmer/analyst Johnson & Johnson Co. Mem. bd. dirs. State Street Corp.; dir. Boston Fin. Data Services; mem. bd. dirs. Met. Boston Housing Partnership; former chmn. bd. dirs. State St. Bank Europe Ltd., State St. Cayman Trust Co., Ltd.

LOPICCOLO, JOSEPH, psychologist, educator, author; b. L.A., Sept. 13, 1943; s. Joseph E. and Adeline C. (Russo) Lo P.; m. Leslie Joan Matlen, June 20, 1964 (div. 1978); 1 child, Joseph Townsend; m. Cathryn Gail Pridal, Dec. 20, 1980; 1 child, Michael James. BA with highest honors, UCLA, 1965; MS, Yale U., 1968, PhD, 1969. Lic. psychologist, Mo. Asst. prof. U. Oreg., Eugene, 1969-73; assoc. prof. U. Houston, 1973-74; prof. SUNY, Stony Brook, 1974-84, Tex. A&M U., College Station, 1984-87; prof. psychology U. Mo., Columbia, 1987—, chmn. dept., 1987-90. Vis. scholar Cambridge (Eng.) U., 1991. Author: Becoming Orgasmic, 1976, 2d edit., 1988, also book chpts.; editor: Handbook of Sex Therapy, 1978; contbr. numerous articles to profl. jours. Woodrow Wilson Found. fellow; NIH rsch. grantee, 1973-84 Fellow Am. Psychol. Assn.; mem. Internat. Acad. Sex Rsch., Soc. for Sci. Study of Sex (pres. 1983-84, Alfred Kinsey Meml. Rsch. award), Soc. for Sex Therapy and Rsch. (Masters and Johnson Rsch. award 1997), Phi Beta Kappa, Sigma Xi. Office: U Mo Dept Psychology 210 Mcalester Hall Columbia MO 65211-2500 Office Phone: 573-882-7752. Business E-Mail: LoPiccoloJ@missouri.edu.

LOPPNOW, MILO ALVIN, clergyman, former church official; b. St. Charles, Minn., Jan. 13, 1914; s. William and Doretta (Penz) L.; m. Gertrude Stoltz, Feb. 6, 1942; children— Donald, Bruce, David. BA, Moravian Coll., 1937; M.Div., Moravian Theol. Sem., 1940, D.D., 1970. Ordained to ministry Moravian Ch. in Am., 1940; pastor congregations nr. Wisconsin Rapids, Wis., 1940-41, Waconia, Minn., 1941-53, Lakeview Ch., Madison, Wis., 1953-64; dist. pres. Western Dist. Moravian Ch., Madison, 1965-78; elected bishop, 1970. Chmn. Youth Commn., Madison, 1957-63; Trustee Moravian Coll., 1954-78, Moravian Theol. Sem., Bethlehem, Pa.; former chaplain, dir. devel. Marquardt Meml. Manor, Watertown, Wis. Mem. Moravian Ch. E-mail: malopp@GDInet.com.

LOPREATO, JOSEPH, evolutionary sociologist, writer; b. Stefanaconi, Italy, July 13, 1928; arrived in U.S., 1951; s. Frank and Marianna (Pavone) L.; m. Carolyn H. Prestopino, July 18, 1954; (div. 1971); children: Gregory F., Marisa S. Schmidt; m. Sally A. Cook, Aug. 24, 1972 (div. 1978). BA in Sociology and Anthropology, U. Conn., 1956; MA in Sociology, Yale U., 1957, PhD in Sociology, 1960. Asst. prof. sociology U. Mass., Amherst, 1960-62; vis. lectr. U. Rome, 1962-64; assoc. prof. U. Conn., Storrs, 1964-66; prof. sociology U. Tex., Austin, 1968-98, chmn. dept. sociology, 1969-72. Vis. prof. U. Catania, Italy, 1974, U. Calabria, Italy, 1980; steering com. Council European Studies, Columbia U., 1977-80; chmn. sociology com. Council for Internat. Exchange Scholars, 1977-79; mem. Internat. Com. Mezzogiorno, 1986-88; Calabria Internat. Com., 1988-90. Author: Italian Made Simple, 1959, Vilfredo Pareto, 1965, Peasants No More, 1967, Italian Americans, 1970, Class, Conflict and Mobility, 1972, Social Stratification, 1974, The Sociology of Vilfredo Pareto, 1975, La Stratificazione Sociale negli Stati Uniti, 1945-1975, 1977, Human Nature and Biocultural Evolution, 1984, Evoluzione e Natura Umana, 1990, Mai Più Contadini, 1990, Crisis in Sociology: The Need for Darwin, 1999; contbr. articles to profl. jours. Mem. Nat. Italian-Am. Com. for U.S.A. Bicentennial; mem. exec. com. Congress Italian Politics, 1977-80. Served to cpl. U.S. Army, 1952-54. Fulbright faculty research fellow, 1962-64, 73-74; Social Sci. Research Council faculty research fellow, 1963-64; NSF faculty research fellow, 1965-68; U. Tex. Austin research fellow, 1973-74, spring 1985, spring 1993; Guido Dorso award for U.S.A., Italy, 1992. Mem.: AAAS (behavioral sci. rsch. prize com. 1992—94), Internat. Soc. Human Ethology, So. Sociol. Soc. (assoc. editor Am. Sociol. Rev. 1970—72, Social Forces 1987—90, Jour. Polit. and Mil. Sociology 1980—90), Evolution and Behavior Soc., European Sociobiol. Soc., Internat. Sociol. Assn. Catholic-Episcopalian. Home and Office: 115 Yellowstone Rd Georgetown TX 78628 Office Phone: 512-869-8479. Personal E-mail: lopreato@mail.la.utexas.edu. E-mail: jlopreato@cox.net.

LOPREST, FRANK JAMES, chemist; b. N.Y.C., Jan. 8, 1929; s. John and Josephine Celeste (Lisitano) L.; M. Jane Anne Stables, Jan. 23, 1960; children— Frank James, Lorraine Jo, Pamela Jane, Amy Marie, Elizabeth Anne. B.S., St. John's U., 1950; M.S., NYU, 1952, Ph.D., 1954. Research chemist Oak Ridge Nat. Lab., Tenn., 1954-56; research supr. Thiokol Chem. Corp., Denville, N.J., 1956-65; mgr. research and devel. GAF Corp., Binghamton, N.Y., 1965-77; dir. research Am. Can. Co., Princeton, N.J., 1977-83; assoc. dir. research Colgate Palmolive Co., Piscataway, N.J., 1983—

. Patentee in field. Mem. Am. Chem. Soc., AAAS, Am. Soc. for Metals, Sigma Xi. Democrat. Roman Catholic. Avocations: tennis; literature. Home: 838 Winthrop Dr Morrisville PA 19067-4317

LOPRETE, JAMES HUGH, lawyer; b. Detroit, Sept. 17, 1929; s. James Victor and Effie Hannah (Brown) LoP.; m. Marion Ann Garrison, Sept. 11, 1952; children: James Scott, Kimberly Anne, Kent Garrison, Robert Drew. AB, U. Mich., 1951, JD with distinction, 1953. Bar: Mich. 1954. Practiced law, Detroit, 1954—; atty. Chrysler Corp., Detroit, 1953; assoc. Monaghan, LoPrete, McDonald, Yakima, Grenke & McCarthy, P.C. and predecessor firms, Detroit, 1954, mem. firm, 1966—2001, pres., 1979—2001. Bd. dirs. Drake's Batter Mix Co.; instr. legal writing Wayne State U., Detroit, 1955-57. Trustee scholarship fund U. Mich. Club of Detroit, 1961, pres., 1982—; trustee Samuel Westerman Found., 1971—, pres., 1984; trustee John R. and M. Margrite Davis Found.; pres., dir. Louis and Nellie Sieg Found., 2000—, Frank G. and Gertrude Dunlap Found., 2001—. Fellow Am. Coll. Trust and Estate Counsel (litig. com. 1997—), Internat. Acad. Estate and Trust Law; mem. ABA, Oakland County Bar Assn., State Bar Mich. (chmn. probate and estate planning sect. 1977), Detroit Athletic Club (dir. 1983-88, sec. 1986-88), Orchard Lake Country Club, U. Mich. of Greater Detroit (pres. 1966). Home: 2829 Warner Dr Orchard Lake MI 48324-2449 Office: Monaghan LoPrete McDonald et al 40700 Woodward Ave Ste A Bloomfield Hills MI 48304-5110 Office Phone: 248-642-5770. Business E-Mail: jhloprete@monaghanpc.com.

LORANDOS, DEMOSTHENES ANISTASIOS, lawyer, psychologist; b. San Francisco, Apr. 30, 1946; s. George and Jewell (Honey) Lawrence; m. Edeline Delva Lorandos, Nov. 15, 1971 (div. Jan. 1981); children: Orestes, Xorgeos; m. Patricia R. Allen, Sept. 3, 1993. B in Psychology, San Francisco State U., 1969; M in Psychology, New Sch. Social Rsch., N.Y.C., 1972; D in Clin. Psychology, Union Grad. Sch., Cin., 1978; JD, U. Detroit, 1991. Bar: Mich. 1993, Calif. 1995, U.S. Dist. Ct. (ea. dist.) Mich. 1993, U.S. Dist. Ct. (we. dist.) Mich. 1994; diplomate Am. Med. Psychotherapy Assn. Psychology trainee Synanon House, Marin County, Calif., 1965-67; cons. Castalia Cons., N.Y.C., 1969-71; treatment dir. Delos-No. Ill. Mental Health Ctr., South Bend, Ind., 1975-76, Bay Area Social Inter. Svc., Bay City, Mich., 1977-79; cons. psychologist Tri-City Assessment Inc., Bay City, 1979-80, Bay Psychoil. Assn., Bay City, 1980-81; pres., psychologist Mich. Psychol. Svc., Saginaw, 1981-89; atty., psychologist Family Advocacy Svcs., Ann Arbor, Mich., 1989-93; pvt. practice law and psychology Ann Arbor, 1994—. Contbr. articles to profl. jours. Grad. faculty scholar New Sch. Social Rsch., N.Y.C., 1971, tng. grant Comprehensive Employment and Tng. Act, Bay City, 1977, rsch. grant Skillman Found., Saginaw, 1982. Fellow Am. Ortho-Psychiat. Assn. Office: 214 N 4th Ave Ann Arbor MI 48104-1404 E-mail: lorandos@psychlaw.net.

LORANGER, STEVEN R., industrial manufacturing company executive; BA, MA, Colo. U. Sales mgr. mil. power sys. Garret Turbine Engine Co., 1984—87; v.p. comml. aux. power AlliedSignal Inc., pres. Bendix Truck Brake Group, pres., CEO AlliedSignal Engines; pres., CEO engines, systems and svcs. Honeywell Internat. Inc., 1999—2002; exec. v.p., COO Textron, Inc., 2002—04; pres., CEO ITT Industries Inc., White Plains, NY, 2004—. With USN, 1975—81. Mem.: Congl. Medal of Honor Bd., Nat. Assn. Mfrs., Aerospace Industries Assn. Office: ITT Industries Inc Four West Red Oak Ln White Plains NY 10604

LORBER, BARBARA HEYMAN, communications executive, television producer; b. N.Y.C. d. David Benjamin and Gertrude (Meyer) Heyman. AB in Polit. Sci., Skidmore Coll.; MA, postgrad., Columbia U. Asst. dir. young citizens divsn. Dem. Party; exec. asst. to dean Albert Einstein Coll. Medicine, Bronx, NY; exec. asst. to v.p. devel. Vanderbilt U., Nashville; spl. projects dir. Am. Acad. in Rome, N.Y.C.; pub. affairs dir. Met. Opera, N.Y.C.; sr. v.p. Hill and Knowlton, N.Y.C.; pres. Lorber Group, Ltd., N.Y.C.; v.p. comms. and planning N.Y.C. Partnership and C. of C.; sr. v.p. major events and promotions NYC & Company. Guest lectr. Arts and Bus. Coun., N.Y.C., Internat. Soc. Performing Arts Adminstrs., Columbia U. Tchrs. Coll., N.Y.C., NYU Sch. Continuing Edn., Nat. Media Conf., Nat. Soc. Fund Raising Execs., N.Y.C.; exec. prodr., prodr., writer N.Y. Internat. Festival Arts, N.Y.C., 1988; team leader, 2002 Salt Lake Olympic Torch Relay to N.Y.C., 2004 Athens Olympic Torch Relay in N.Y.C; spl. projects cons. NYC 2012 Olympic Games Bid Com. Contbr. chpts. to book; contbr. articles to profl. jours. Office: NYC & Company/Major Events 810 7th Ave 3d Fl New York NY 10019-5818

LORBER, MORTIMER, retired physiology educator; b. NYC, Aug. 30, 1926; s. Albert and Frieda (Levin) L.; m. Eileen Segal, May 20, 1956; children: Kenneth, Stephanie. BS, NYU, 1945; DMD cum laude, Harvard U., 1950, MD cum laude, 1952. Diplomate Nat. Bd. Med. Examiners. Rotating intern A.M. Billings Hosp., 1952-53; resident in hematology Mt. Sinai Hosp., N.Y.C., 1953-54, asst. resident in medicine, 1957; asst. resident medicine Georgetown U. Hosp., Washington, 1958; instr., asst. prof. dept. physiology and biophysics Georgetown U., Washington, 1959-68, assoc. prof., 1968-97; ret., 1997. Lectr. physiology U.S. Naval Dental Sch., Bethesda, Md., 1962-70, Walter Reed Army Inst. Dental Rsch., Washington, 1963-70; guest scientist Naval Med. Rsch. Inst., Bethesda, 1978-83. Contbr.: The Merck Manual, 14th-17th edits., 1982, 87, 92, 99; contbr. articles to profl. jours. Lt. USNR, 1954-56. Recipient Lederle Med. Faculty award Lederle Co., Pearl River, N.Y., 1960-63, USPHS Rsch. Career Devel. award Nat. Inst. Dental Rsch., Bethesda, 1963-70; grantee Am. Cancer Soc., USPHS. Mem. Am. Physiol. Soc., Am. Soc. Hematology, Assn. Rsch. in Vision and Ophthalmology, Internat. Assn. Dental Rsch. Jewish. Achievements include discovery that the ground substance is masked but not lost in calcification, removal of spleen is followed by a reticulocytosis that is permanent in dogs, dogs have many more young reticulocytes in their blood than man, stretching of skin increases mitoses in the rat showing physical factors can modulate DNA and cell division, adult Gaucher cells contain iron secondary to erythrophagocytosis, the spleen protects against insecticide-induced hematoxicity, biological armature provides internal stability to exocrine glands, rat lacrimal glands are stretched by their attachments and contain somatostatin, mastication reflexly increases gastroduodenal motility. Home: 5823 Osceola Rd Bethesda MD 20816-2032 Personal E-mail: melorber@aol.com.

LORBERBAUM, JEFFREY S., textiles executive; With Aladdin Mills, Inc., Calhoun, Ga., 1976-86, v.p. ops., 1986-94; pres., CEO Mohawk Industries, Inc., Calhoun, Ga., 1994—, mem. bd. dir., 1994, now chmn., 2004—. Office: Mohawk Industries Inc 160 S Indsl Blvd Calhoun GA 30701

LORCH, ERNEST HENRY, lawyer; b. Frankfurt, Germany, Oct. 11, 1932; came to U.S., 1940; s. Alexander and Kate (Freundt) L. AB, Middlebury Coll., 1954; JD, U. Va., 1957; LLD (hon.), Fairfield U., 1987. Bar: N.Y. 1958. Assoc. Olwine, Connelly, Chase, O'Donnell & Weyher, N.Y.C., 1957-65, ptnr., 1965-84; pres., chief oper. officer Dyson-Kissner-Moran Corp., N.Y.C., 1984-90, pres., chief exec. officer, 1990-91; chmn., chief exec. officer, 1991-92; ret., 1992; of counsel Whitman, Breed, Abbott & Morgan, N.Y.C., 1992—. Chmn. bd. dirs. Varlen Corp., Chgo.; bd. dirs. Tyler Corp., Dorsey Trailers, Inc. Dir. various inner city athletic assns., N.Y.C., 1959—; The DYSM Found., N.Y.C., 1985-92; trustee, officer, dir. The Riverside Ch., N.Y.C., 1961—; treas., dir. Wheelchair Charities Inc., Religion in American Life, 1993-96. Mem. ABA, N.Y. State Bar Assn.

LORCH, KENNETH F., lawyer; b. Indpls., July 24, 1951; BSBA, Washington U., 1973; JD, John Marshall Sch. Law, 1976. Bar: Ill. 1976, U.S. Dist. Ct. (no. dist.) Ill. 1977; CPA, Ill. Ptnr. Hamilton Thies Lorch & Hagnell LLP, Chgo. Mem. planned giving adv. coun. Chgo. Symphony Orch.; chair Chgo. bd. Am. Technion Soc.; sec. Chgo. Coun. on Planned Giving; v.p. Coun. for Jewish Elderly; mem. profl. adv. com. Chgo. Cmty. Trust. Mem. Chgo. Bar Assn. (exec. com., Cook County Probate Ct. rules and forms com., mem. legis. com., mem. probate practice com. 1991, mem. trust law com., chmn. estate planning com., mem. young lawyers sect. 1983-85), Chgo. Estate Planning Coun., Jewish Fedn. Chgo. (past chair profl. adv. com.). Office: Hamilton Thies Lorch & Hagnell LLP 200 S Wacker Dr Ste 3800 Chicago IL 60606 Office Phone: 312-650-8640. Business E-Mail: lorch@wildmanharrold.com.

LORCH, MARISTELLA DE PANIZZA, writer, educator; b. Bolzano, Italy, Dec. 8, 1919; came to U.S., 1947, naturalized, 1951; d. Gino and Giuseppina (Cristoforetti) de Panizza Inama von Brunnenwald; m. Claude Bové, Feb. 10, 1944 (div. 1955); 1 child, Claudia; m. Edgar R. Lorch, Mar. 25, 1956; children: Lavinia Edgarda, Donatella Livia. Ed., Liceo Classico, Merano, 1929-37; Dott. in Lettere e Filosofia, U. Rome, 1942; DHL (hon.), Lehman Coll., CUNY, 1993. Prof. Latin and Greek Liceo Virgilio, Rome, 1941-44; assoc. prof. Italian and German Coll. St. Elizabeth, Convent Station, N.J., 1947-51; faculty Barnard Coll. and Columbia U., 1951-90; prof. Barnard Coll., 1967—, chmn. dept., 1951-90, co-founder, chmn. medieval and renaissance program, 1972-90; vice chmn. emeritus prof. Columbia U., 2005—, v.p. ERIC emeritus, 2005—. Founder, dir. Ctr. for Internat. Scholarly Exch., Barnard Coll., 1980-90; dir. Casa Italiana, Columbia U., 1969-76, chmn. exec. com. Italian studies, 1980-90, founding dir. Italian Acad. Advanced Studies in Am., 1991-96, founding dir. emerita and dir. external rels., 1996—. Author: Critical edit. L. Valla, De vero falsoque bono, Bari, 1970, (critical edit.) Michaelida (with W. Ludwig), 1976, On Pleasure (with A. K. Hieatt), 1981, A Defense of Life: L. Valla's Theory of Pleasure, 1985, Folly and Insanity in Renaissance Literature, 1986, (with E. Grassi) All' America, 1990, Italy at the Millennium, 2001, (novel) Mamma in Her Village, 2005; editor: Il Teatro Italiano del Renascimento, 1981, Humanism in Rome, 1983, La Scuola, New York, 1987; mem. editorial bd. Italian jour. Romanic Review; also articles on Renaissance lit., philosophy and theater. Chmn. Am. Ariosto Centennial Celebration, 1974; trustee Lycée Française NY, 1986—2004, mem. adv. bd., 2004—; adv. bd. Marconi Found., 1998; chmn. bd. trustees La Scuola NY, 1986—92. Decorated cavaliere della Repubblica Italiana, commendatore della Repubblica Italiana, grande ufficiale della Repubblica Italiana; recipient AMITA award for Woman of Yr. in Italian Lit., 1973, Columbus '92 Countdown prize of excellence in humanities, 1990, Elen Cornaro award Sons of Italy Woman of Yr., 1990, Father Ford award, 1994, hon. mem. Legendary Women, 1997, founding dir. emeritus Italian Acad. in Advance Studies in Am., Columbia U. Mem. Medieval Acad. Am., Renaissance Soc. Am., Am. Assn. Tchrs. Italian, Am. Assn. Italian Studies (hon. pres. 1990-91), Internat. Assn. for Study of Italian Lit. (Am. rep., assoc. pres. 8th Congress 1973), Acad. Polit. Sci. (life), Pirandello Soc. (pres. 1972-78), Arcadia Acad. (Asteria Aretusa 1976). Home: 445 Riverside Dr New York NY 10027-6801 Office: Columbia Univ Italian Acad Adv Study Casa Italiana New York NY 10027 Office Phone: 212-854-8640. Business E-Mail: ML48@columbia.edu.

LORCH, ROBERT K., corporate financial executive; V.p. global picture tube bus. Thomson Multimedia; sr. v.p., CFO Marmon Group, 2002—. Exec. positions GE, RCA Corp.; with mgmt., fin., global gen. mgmt., sales and mktg., and strat. planning. Office: Marmon Group 225 Washington St Ste 1900 Chicago IL 60606

LORD, ALBERT L., finance company executive; BS in Bus., Pa. State U., 1967. With Student Loan Mktg. Assn., 1981—90, exec. v.p., COO, 1990—94; pres., founder LCL, Ltd., 1994—97; vice chmn., CEO SLM Corp. (Sallie Mae), Reston, Va., 1997—2005, chmn., 2005—. Bd. dirs. SLM Corp., 1995—, SS&C Technologies, Inc, 2001—, BearingPoint, Inc., 2003—, Nat. Acad. Found., Student Loan Mktg. Assn, Va Found. Ind. Coll., Va Ballet Theatre; mem. advisory bd. Abington Coll-Pa. State U. Office: SLM Corp 12061 Bluemont Way Reston VA 20190

LORD, CAROLYN MARIE, artist; b. L.A., Oct. 6, 1956; m. Robert Bryce Anglin, Nov. 1, 1980; 1 child, Devin Lord Anglin. BA, Principia Coll., 1978. Artist, 1978—. Instr. workshops Calif., Oreg., Ariz., Tex, Italy; juror shows. One-woman shows include Maybeck Gallery, Elsah, Ill., 1978-83, Fireside Gallery, Carmel, Calif., 1978-92, Northeastern Nev. Mus., Elko, 1985, 90, Art e Espaco, Aracatuba, Brazil, 1988, Ojai (Calif.) Gallery and Design Studio, 1990, Stary-Sheets Fine Art Galleries, Laguna Beach, Calif., 1983-2000, Banaker Gallery, San Francisco, 1993-96, Maynard Dixon County Art Festival, 1999-2005, Laguna Plein Air, 2003—, Carmel Art Festival, 2001, 03-05; represented in permanent collections Principia Coll., Millard Sheets Family Collection, Scripps Coll., The Buck Collection, Beringer Vineyards, Ventura County Mus., L.A. Atheletic Club; contbr. articles to mags. including Am. Artist, Watercolor, Watercolor Magic. Mem.: Nat. Watercolor Soc., Calif. Lawyers for Arts, Calif. Art Club. Christian Scientist.

LORD, EVELYN MARLIN, mayor; b. Melrose, Mass., Dec. 8, 1926; d. John Joseph and Mary Janette (Nourse) Marlin; m. Samuel Smith Lord Jr., Feb. 28, 1948; children: Steven Arthur, Jonathan Peter, Nathaniel Edward, Victoria Marlin, William Kenneth. BA, Boston U., 1948; MA, U. Del., 1956; JD, U. Louisville, 1969. Bar: Ky. 1969, U.S. Supreme Ct. 1973. Exec. dir. Block Blight Inc., Wilmington, Del., 1956—60; mem. Del. Senate, Dover, 1960—62; administrv. asst. county judge Jefferson County, Louisville, 1968—71; corr. No. Ireland News Jour. Co., Wilmington, 1972—74; legal adminstr. Orgain, Bell & Tucker, Beaumont, Tex., 1978—83; v.p. Tex. Commerce Bank, Beaumont, 1983—84; councilman City of Beaumont, 1980—82, mayor pro tem, 1982—84, mayor, 1990—94, 2002—05. Tourism chmn. U.S. Conf. Mayors, 1994, adv. bd., chmn. arts, culture and recreation, 1992—94, 2002—05; sr. counselor Ky. Bar, 2002—; adv. bd. U.S. Com. Mayors, 2002—05. Trustee United Way, Beaumont, 1990—, pres., 1994, 1997; mem. adv. bd. Boy Scouts Am., Three Rivers, 1978—84, 1989—94, mem. exec. bd., 2000—; mem. (life) Girl Scouts U.S.A., pres. Kentuckiana coun., 1966—70; trustee Lamar U. Found., 1999—2003; pres. Tex. Energy Mus., 1995—2001; bd. dirs. Symphony Soc. S.E. Tex., 1990—98, 2002—05, Evelyn M. Lord Teen Ct., 1993—, Found. S.E. Tex., 1990—, Lincoln Inst., 1994—2001, Beaumont Pub. Schs. Found., 1993—99, Ptnrs. for Children, Child Protective Svcs.; chmn. Spindletop 2001 Com. Named Citizen of Yr., Sales and Mktg. Assn., 1990, Beaumont Man of the Yr., 1993, Woman with Heart, Am. Heart Assn., 2000, Free Ent. Person of the Yr., Assn. Bldg. Contrs., 2000, Newsmaker of the Yr., Press Club Jefferson County, 2001, Hurricane Evelyn, ARC, 2001, Disting. Law Alumni, U. Louisville, 2002, Woman of Yr., Quota Club Internat., 2002; recipient Silver Beaver award, Boy Scouts Am., Beaumont, 1979, Disting. Alumni award, Boston U., 1983, Disting. Leadership award, Nat. Assn. Leadership Orgns., Indpls., 1991, Labor-Mgmt. Pub. Sector award, 1991, Disting. Grad. award, Leadership Beaumont, 1993, Rotary Svc. Above Self award, 1994, Excellency award, Tex. State Hist. Commn., 2001, Cmty. Builder award, Grand Masonic Lodge of Tex., 2003, Athena award, Beaumont C of C, 2003, Mrs. S.E. Tex. award, Dogwood Festival, 2004, Regional Leadership award, S.E. Tex. Regional Planning Commn., 2005. Mem.: DAR, LWV (Del. state pres. 1960—62, bd. dirs. Tex. 1978—80), Bus. and Profl. Women Assns. (Woman of Yr. 1983), Colonial Dames (Citizenship award 2004), Soc. Mayflower Descs., Rotary, 100 Club (pres. 1995—97). Avocations: writing, reading, african violets, genealogy. Home: 1240 Nottingham Ln Beaumont TX 77706-4316 Office Phone: 409-880-3736. Personal E-mail: evelynlord@aol.com. Business E-Mail: elord@ci.beaumont.tx.us. *Basically - I believe in "blooming where you're planted". Life with my husband has taken me all over the world but we've always managed to be "at home" wherever we've been able to give a bit of ourselves.*

LORD, GEORGE DEFOREST, language educator; b. NYC, Dec. 2, 1919; s. George deForest and Hazen (Symington) L.; m. Ruth Ellen du Pont, Mar. 22, 1947 (div. 1978); children: Pauline, George deForest Jr., Edith (dec.), Henry; m. Louise Robins Hendrix, 1978 (div. 1992); m. Marcia Adkisson Babbidge, 1993. BA, Yale U., 1942, PhD, 1951. Instr. English Yale U., New Haven, 1947-66, prof., 1966—. Master Trumbull Coll., 1963-66, dir. directed studies, 1968-70, acting chmn. English dept., 1983-86; dir. Fiduciary Trust, N.Y., 1969-91; cons. PBS TV program Transformations of Myth Through Time, 1982-90; lectr. in field. Author: Homeric Renaissance: the "Odyssey" of George Chapman, 1956, Poems on Affairs of State, 1963, Andrew Marvell, Complete Poetry, 1968, rev. edit., 1985, Andrew Marvell: A Collection of Critical Essays, 1968, Anthology of Poems on Affairs of State, 1975, Heroic Mockery: Variations on Epic Themes from Homer to Joyce, 1977, Trials of the Self: Heroic Ordeals in the Epic Tradition, 1983, Classical Presences in Seventeenth-Century English Poetry, 1987 (Outstanding acad. book 1987 Choice mag.); gen. editor Poems on Affairs of State: Augustan Satirical Verse: 1660-1714, 7 vols., 1963-75; contbr. articles, revs. to acad. jours. Trustee Winterthur Mus., 1952-80, Mary Holmes Coll., West Point, Miss., 1971-80, Fair Haven Housing, 1972-78; trustee, advisor Outward Bound USA, 1977-92; vestryman Calvary Episcopal Ch., Stonington, Conn., 1986-89. Morse fellow 1954-55, NEH sr. fellow, 1982. Mem. MLA, English Inst., Renaissance Soc. Am., Am. Acad. in Rome, The Century Assn. Home: 3 Diving St Stonington CT 06378-1405 Office: Yale U Dept English New Haven CT 06520 Office Phone: 860-535-3946. E-mail: glor63452@earthlink.net.

LORD, JERE JOHNS, retired physics professor; b. Portland, Oreg., Jan. 3, 1922; s. Percy Samuel and Hazel Marie (Worstel) L.; m. Miriam E. Hart, Dec. 30, 1947; children— David, Roger, Douglas. Physicist U. Calif. Radiation Lab., Berkeley, 1942-46; research asso. U. Chgo., 1950-52; asst. prof. physics U. Wash., Seattle, 1952-57, assoc. prof., 1957-62, prof., 1962-92, prof. emeritus, 1992—. Fellow AAAS, Am. Phys. Soc.; mem. Am. Assn. Physics Tchrs. Home: 720 Seneca St Apt 1004 Seattle WA 98101 Office: U Wash Dept Physics Box 351560 Seattle WA 98195-1560

LORD, JEROME EDMUND, education administrator, secondary school educator, writer; b. Waterbury, Conn., Dec. 24, 1935; s. James Andrew and Mary Frances (Hayes) L.; m. Eleanor Louise Collins, Apr. 22, 1967; children: Hayes Alexander FitzWarin, Stavely Hampston deHodnet, Savile Collins de Montenay, Dorian Warfield d'Amours, Wallis Jennings dePantulf. BA, Georgetown U., 1957; MA, Boston Coll., 1962, Columbia U., 1963, PhD, 1969; diploma (hon.), U. Madrid, 1962. Tchr. The Taft Sch. Peekskill Mil. Acad., 1957—60; editor, lang. recs. supr. Allyn and Bacon Inc., Boston, 1961—62; adminstrv. assoc. internat. programs and services Tchrs. Coll. Columbia U., N.Y.C., 1963—65, assoc. in higher edn., 1965—66; asst. prof. edn., exec. asst. to dean acad. devel. CUNY, 1965—67, assoc. prof. edn., exec. asst. to vice chancellor exec. office, 1967—69; dir. rsch. Ford and Carnegie Study of Fed. Politics of Edn. Brookings Instn., Washington, 1969—70; program officer Nat. Ctr. for Ednl. Tech., U.S. Dept. Edn., Washington, 1971—73; sr. assoc. Nat. Inst. Edn., Washington, 1973—86, Office Ednl. Rsch. and Improvement, Washington, 1986—2002, Office Inst. Edn. Scis., Dept. Edn., Washington, 2002—. Pres. Jerome Lord Enterprises, Inc., Washington; advisor to vol. edn. policy group Office Dir. Def. Edn., U.S. Dept. Def., 1975-76; chmn. Fed. Interagy. Panel for Rsch. on Adulthood; founder Nat. Soc. Aesthetics and Competitive Gargless Am., 2005; mem. World Affairs Coun., Washington, other various nat. panels and coms.; cons. in field; lectr. in field. Playwright: Teresa, 1971, The Election, 1972, Audition!, 1973, Decent Exposure, 1979, Amazing Grace, 1987, Heads You Win, 1991, Making Believe, 1996, My One and Only, 1997, Susie of Chicago, 2005; Dear Minerva, 2005; author: Perfectly Proper, 1993, Teacher Training Abroad: New Realities, 1993, Adult Literacy Programs: Guidelines for Effectiveness, 1995; contbr. articles to profl. jours. Trustee St. John's Child Devel. Ctr., Washington, 1978-83; mem. nat. bd. sponsors Protestant and Orthodox Ctr., N.Y. World's Fair, 1964; mem. adv. bd. N.Y.C. Urban Corps, 1965-69, others; mem. coun. of friends Folger Shakespeare Libr.; sponsor Nat. Symphony Orch.; mem., donor reception rooms Dept. State. Named Coakley scholar, 1953-57, M.T. Runyan scholar, 1967-68; fellow W.T. Kellogg Found., 1968-69, Rinehart Found., 1970-71, others. Mem. Nat. Soc. Aesthetic and Competitve Garglers Am. (founder, grand-garglemaster protem, 2005, Soc. Friends St. George's and Desc. Knights of Garter, Acad. Am. Poets, Pilgrims of the U.S., World Affairs Coun., The Lansdowne Club (London), Met. Club, Kappa Delta Pi, Phi Delta Pi, Eta Sigma Phi. Episcopalian. Avocations: historic preservation, music, art history, architecture, antiques. Office: 555 New Jersey Ave NW Washington DC 20001-2029 Home: 2500 S Ocean Blvd Palm Beach FL 33480 Personal E-mail: jeromeelord@aol.com.

LORD, JOHN WILLIAM, educational materials developer, writer; b. Pitts., Dec. 13, 1938; s. John William and Helen Scott (Hardie) L.; m. Carol Diane Bodey, 1970; children: Jennifer K., Benjamin Alexander. BA, Harvard U., 1961; MA, UCLA, 1965. Dir. product devel. Film Assocs. Calif., L.A., 1964-69; pres. Paideia, Santa Monica, Calif., 1970-79, 89—; editor-in-chief Enterprise for Edn., Santa Monica, 1979-89. Author: Sizes, 1995; curriculum materials. Office: PO Box 1583 Santa Monica CA 90406-1583 Office Phone: 310-395-6165. E-mail: jwl@johnlord.com.

LORD, JONATHAN T. (JACK LORD), medical association administrator; BS in Chemistry cum laude, U. Miami, 1973, MD, 1978. Diplomate Nat. Bd. Med. Examiners, Am. Bd. Pathology; cert. Am. Bd. Quality Assurance and Utilization Rev. Physicians. Commd. officer USNR, 1978, advanced through grades to comdr.; intern pathology Naval Regional Med. Ctr., San Diego, 1978-79, resident anatomic and clin. pathology, 1979-82; fellow forensic pathology Armed Forces Inst. Pathology, Washington, 1982-83; command forensic pathologist, physician advisor risk mgmt. Naval Hosp., Portsmouth, Va., 1984-85; physician dir. profl. stds. br. Naval Med. Command, Washington, 1985-86; clin. profl. healthcare profl. implementation group Sec. of the Navy, Dept. of the Navy, Washington, 1986-87, spl. asst. for med. staff matters to dept. dir., 1986-87; med. dir. for quality assurance and staff pathologist Naval Hosp., Bethesda, Md., 1987-88; dir. quality assurance divsn. Naval Med. Command, Office Surgeon Gen., Washington, 1988-89; sr. v.p. for med. staff affairs, exec. sec. med. staff Anne Arundel Med. Ctr., Annapolis, Md., 1989-92, exec. v.p., 1994-95, SunHealth, Charlotte, N.C., 1992-94; sr. advisor for clin. affairs Am. Hosp. Assn., Washington, 1994-97, COO, 1997—; sr. v.p. & chief medical officer Humana, 2000; sr. v.p. & chief clin. strategy and innovation officer, 2001—. Chief resident dept. lab. medicine Naval Regional Med. Ctr., San Diego, 1982; clin. assoc. prof. dept. forensic scis. George Washington U. Grad. Sch., Washington, 1982-83; asst. prof. dept. pathology Ea. Va. Med. Sch., Norfolk, 1984-85; clin. faculty Joint Commn. on Accreditation of Healthcare Orgns., Chgo., 1987-94; adj. assoc. prof. dept. preventive medicine and biometrics Uniformed Svcs. U. Health Scis., Bethesda, 1987—; adj. prof. cmty. and family medicine Dartmouth Med. Coll., 1998-99; designated pathologist Commonwealth Va., 1983-85; med. advisor Hosp. Assn. N.Y. State, Albany, 1990-92; cons., surveyor Hosp. Accreditation Svcs., Joint Commn. on Accreditation of Healthcare Orgns., Chgo., 1990-94; mem. governing bd., editl. bd. The Quality Letter, Bader and Assocs., Rockville, Md., 1989—, Md. Hosp. Edn. Inst., Md. Hosp. Assn., Lutherville, 1992-93; vice chmn. Am. Hosp. Pub., Inc., Chgo., 1997; chmn. Am. Hosp. Assn.-Ins. Resources Inc., Chgo., 1998—, Health Forum, Chgo., 1998—; lectr. and presenter in field. Author: (with D.R. Longon, K.R. Ciccone) Integrated Quality Assessment: A Model for Concurrent Review, 1989; contbg. author: Integrated Quality Assessment, 1988; contbr. chpts. to books and articles to profl. jours. Decorated Navy Commendation medal, 1985, Navy Achievement medal, 1985, Meritorious Svc. medal 1987, 88, 89; NSF scholar, 1972-73; Nat. Psoriasis Found. fellow, 1975, Nat. Program for Dermatology fellow, 1975. Mem. AMA, Am. Coll. Physician Execs., Sigma Xi. Home: 205 Coralberry RD Louisville KY 40207-5712 Fax: 410-544-6033. E-mail: jlord1@aha.org.

LORD, LANCE W., career military officer; BSc in Edn., Otterbein Coll., 1968; MA in Indsl. Mgmt., U. N.D., 1972; Disting. grad., Air Command & Staff Coll., Maxwell AFB, 1979; student, Air War Coll., 1987—88; nat. fellow, Syracuse U., 2004. Commd. 2d. lt. USAF, 1969, advanced through grades to gen., 2002; Minuteman II combat crew mem. 321st Strategic Missile Wing, Grand Forks AFB, ND, 1969-73; Minuteman II evaluation mem. 3901st Strategic Missile Evaluation Squadron, Vandenberg AFB, Calif., 1973-75; missile ops. staff officer, Air Staff Training Program, Directorate of Ops. USAF, Washington, 1975—76, missile ops. staff officer, Air Staff Training Program, Directorate of Ops. & Readiness, 1976—78; military asst. to dir. Net Assessment Office of the Sec. of Defense, Washington, 1979-82; air force rsch. assoc. Ohio State U., Columbus, 1982-83; comdr. 10th Strategic Missile Squadron, Malmstrom AFB, Mont., 1983—84; dep. comdr. 341st

Combat Support Group, Malmstrom AFB, Mont., 1984—85; dir. Ground-Launched Cruise Missile Program Mgmt. Office, dep. chief of staff plans & programs USAF, Ramstein AFB, Germany, 1985-87; vice comdr. 351st Strategic Missile Wing, Whiteman AFB, Mo., 1988-89; comdr. 321st Strategic Missile Wing, Grand Forks AFB, ND, 1989-90; comdt. Squadron Officer Sch., Maxwell AFB, Ala., 1990—92; comdr. 90th Missle Wing, Warren AFB, Wyo., 1992—93, 30th Space Wing & Western Range, Vandenberg AFB, Colo., 1993-95; dir. plans Air Force Space Command, Peterson AFB, Colo., 1995—96; comdr. 2nd Air Force, Keesler AFB, Miss., 1996—97, Air Force Space Command, Peterson AFB, Colo., 1997—99, Air U., Maxwell AFB, Ala., 1999—2001; asst. vice chief of staff USAF, Washington, 2001—02; commdr. Air Force Space Command, Peterson AFB, Colo., 2002—. Decorated Distinguished Svc. medal, Legion of Merit with two oak leaf clusters, Defense Meritorious Svc. medal, Meritorious Svc. medal with oak leaf cluster, Air Force Commendation medal with oak leaf cluster, Air Force outstanding Unit award with oak leaf cluster, Air Force Orgnl. Excellence award with two oak leaf clusters, Combat Readiness medal, Nat. Defense Svc. medal with svc. star; Sec. of the Air Force Leadership award, 1988, Gen. Thomas D. White Space trophy, Air Force Assn., 1999. Office: Air Force Space Comm (SPACECOM) 150 Vandenburg St Ste 1105 Peterson Afb CO 80914

LORD, M. G., writer; b. La Jolla, Calif., Nov. 18; d. Charles Carroll and Mary (Pfister) L.; m. Glenn Horowitz, May 19, 1985 BA, Yale U. Editl. cartoonist, columnist Newsday, N.Y.C., 1979-94. Cartoons syndicated L.A. Times Syndicate, 1984-89; column syndicated Copley News Svc., 1989-94; resident humanities fellow U. Mich., 1986-87. Author: Mean Sheets, 1982, Prig Tales, 1990, Forever Barbie: The Unauthorized Biography of a Real Doll, 1994, Astro Turf, The Private Life of Rocket Science, 2005. Knight-Wallace fellow U. Mich., 1986-87. Office: care Eric Simonoff Janklow & Nesbit Assoc 445 Park Ave New York NY 10022-2606

LORD, MARVIN, apparel company executive; b. N.Y.C., Sept. 22, 1937; s. Harry and Irene (Taub) L.; m. Joan Simon, Aug. 5, 1961; children— Elisa Anne, Michael Harris BS, Long Island U., Bklyn., 1959. Mdse. mgr. Oxford Industries, Inc., N.Y.C., 1964-66, gen. mdse. mgr., 1966-70, v.p., gen. mgr., 1970-73; pres. Holbrook Co., Inc. Div Oxford Industries, Inc., N.Y.C., 1970-85; pres., chief exec. officer Crystal Brands, Inc.-Youthwear Group, N.Y.C., 1985—; pres. Cluett Shirtmakers, N.Y.C., 1988—, M.L. Enterprises, Roslyn Heights, N.Y., 1990—; pres., chief oper. officer Sanyo Fashion House, N.Y.C., 1991—; pres., CEO MAternity Resources Inc., N.Y.C., 1994—; exec. v.p. E.A. Hughes & Co., N.Y.C., 1996—. Chmn. Fathers Day Coun., N.Y.C., 1984—; bd. dirs. Nat. Conf. Cmty. and Justice, 1997, Fashion Inst. of Tech., 1997. Recipient Disting. Alumni award L.I. U., 1987. Mem. Mens Fashion Assn., Young Menswear Assn. Jewish. Avocation: tennis. Home: 53 Parkway Dr Roslyn Heights NY 11577-2705 Office: E A Hughes & Co 245 Fifth Ave New York NY 10016-3108 Business E-Mail: mlord@eahughes.com.

LORD, PENNY, writer; b. N.Y.C., Sept. 23, 1928; d. Richard and Lillian Macaluso; m. Bob Lord, Dec. 21, 1958; children: Clare, Joseph, Luz Elena, Richard. Grad., Am. Acad. Dramatic Arts, N.Y.C. TV host Eternal Word TV Network, Birmingham, Ala., 1986—; TV prodr. Journeys of Faith, Morrilton, Ark., 1990—, pilgrimage dir., 1983—, lectr., 1986—; pub. Good Newsletter, Morrilton, 1989—. Co-founder Holy Family Mission, Morrilton, 2000—. Co-author: 23 books, 1986—, This is My Body, This is My Blood: Miracles of the Eucharist, Book I, 1986, Book II, 1994, The Many Faces of Mary, Book I, 1987, Book II, 2003, Super Saints, Book I-III, 1998, (TV series) Miracles of the Eucharist, 1988, Many Faces of Mary, 1992, Super Saints, 1996—. Recipient Award for Excellence in Edn. and Catechetics, Internat. Cath. Film Festival, Niepakalanow, Poland, 1995, Poverello award, Franciscan U., Steubenville, Ohio, 2001. Republican. Roman Catholic. Office: Journeys of Faith 65 Holy Family Mission Dr Morrilton AR 72110 Office Phone: 501-354-6100.

LORD, ROBERT, writer; b. N.Y.C., Sept. 9, 1935; s. Theodore Charles Lord and Agnes Cecilia Lyne; m. Penny Lord, Dec. 21, 1958; children: Clare, Joseph, Luz Elena, Richard. Grad., Am. Acad. Dramatic Arts. Pilgrimage dir. Journeys of Faith, Morrilton, Ark., 1983—, TV prodr., 1990—, lectr., book pub., 1986—, newspaper pub., 1989—; TV host Eternal Word TV Network, Birmingham, Ala., 1986—. Co-founder Holy Family Mission, Morrilton, 2000—. Co-author: 23 books, This is My Body, This is My Blood: Miracles of the Eucharist, Book I, 1986, Book II, 1994, The Many Faces of Mary, Book I, 1987, Book II, 2003, Super Saints, Book I-III, 1998, (TV series) Miracles of the Eucharist, 1988, Many Faces of Mary, 1992, Super Saints, 1996—. Cpl. U.S. Army, 1954—56. Recipient Award for Excellence in Edn. and Catechetics, Internat. Cath. Film Festival, Niepakalanow, Poland, 1995, Poverello award, Franciscan U., Steubenville, Ohio, 2001. Republican. Roman Catholic. Office: Journeys of Faith 65 Holy Family Mission Dr Morrilton AR 72110 Office Phone: 501-354-6100.

LORD, ROBERT JOSEPH, retired priest; b. Waterbury, Conn., Mar. 9, 1934; s. James Andrew Lord and Mary Frances Hayes. Ordained priest Roman Cath. Ch. Assoc. pastor St. Augustine Ch., North Branford, Conn., 1960—62, St. Vincent de Paul Ch., East Haven, Conn., 1962—68, St. Paul Ch., Kensington, Conn., 1968—73; co-pastor St. Rita Ch., Hamden, Conn., 1973—81; campus min. Ctrl. Conn. State U., New Britain, Conn., 1982—94; ret., 1994. Founder Rev. Robert J. Lord Trust, Ctrl. Conn. State U., New Britain, 1994, founder James A. and Mary Hayes Lord scholarship, 1985; founder Rev. Robert Lord Spkr.'s Trust Cath. Campus Ministers Assn., Cin., 1999. Recipient Archbishop Paul Hallinan award, Cath. Campus Ministers Assn., 2000. Mem.: Walter Camp Football Found., Seagrape Tower Assn. Avocations: art, antiques, reading, gardening. Home: PO Box 4097 Milford CT 06460-1297 Home (Winter): 5460 N Ocean Dr # 12D West Palm Beach FL 33404-0503

LORD, VALERIE ARLENE, music educator, musician; b. Niskayuna, NY, Oct. 22, 1955; d. David Calhoun and Betty McEldowney Lord. MusB Edn., Crane Sch. Music, SUNY, 1973—77. K-12 music edn. NY, 1977. Music tchr. Bolton Ctrl. Sch., Bolton Landing, NY, 1977—80, Ballston Spa H.S., NY, 1980—. Camp coord. Lake George Opera Summer Camp, Saratoga Springs, NY, 2004—; singer, music dir. various theatres/operas, NY. Mem.: NYSSMA, NYSUT, ACDA, AFM, MENC. D-Liberal. Avocations: travel, gardening, voluntary research assistance, theatre criticism.

LORDE-ROLLINS, ELIZABETH, obstetrician, gynecologist; b. N.Y.C., Mar. 16, 1963; d. Edwin Rollins and Audre Lorde. BA, Harvard-Radcliffe Coll., 1985; MD, Columbia U., 1993. Clin. instr. Harlem Hosp., NYC, 1997—98; attending phys. Women's Health Care N.E. Pa., Honesdale, 1998—2001, Mt. Sinai Adolescent Health, NYC, 2002—. Fellow: ACOG; mem.: Physicians for Social Responsibility, Nat. Med. Assn., Am. Assn. Gynecol. Laparoscopists. Avocations: bicycling, writing, woodworking.

LORDI, KATHERINE MARY, lawyer; b. Jersey City, Mar. 24, 1949; d. Peter G. and Hilde E. (Illy) Lordi. AB, Trinity Coll., Washington, 1971; JD, Fordham U., 1975. Bar: N.J. 1975, U.S. Dist. Ct. N.J. 1975, U.S. Supreme Ct. 1983, U.S. Ct. Appeals (3d cir.) 1989. Clk. Friedman & D'Allesandro, East Orange, NJ, 1974-75, assoc., 1975-76; pvt. practice Bloomfield, NJ, 1976—. Adj. instr. Coll. St. Elizabeth, Convent Station, NJ, 1978—86, adj. prof., 1986—; legal adviser Mcpl. Ct. Clks. Assn., 1977—84. Notes editor: Fordham Urban Law Jour., 1974—75. Trustee Cath. Family and Cmty. Svcs., 1980—, v.p., 1986—; mem. adv. bd. Acad. St. Elizabeth, Convent Station, 1980—84; mem. Essex County Adv. Bd. Status Women, 1983—92, chmn., 1985—88, co-chair, 1990—92; trustee New Sch. Arts, 1988—89, Family Svc. League, Inc., 1986—2000, pres., 1991—94; trustee Bloomfield C. of C., 1986—94, v.p. legis., 1990—94. Fellow: Soc. Encouragement Arts, Manufactures and Commerce; mem.: ABA, Essex County Bar Assn., N.J. Bar Assn., Bloomfield Lawyers Club. Roman Catholic. Office: 54 Fremont St Bloomfield NJ 07003-3428 Office Phone: 973-743-0050. E-mail: k.lordi@worldnet.att.net.

LORD MARSHALL OF KNIGHTSBRIDGE, See LORD MARSHALL, COLIN

LORD OF CURSONS, See RAWL, ARTHUR

LORE, MARTIN MAXWELL, lawyer; b. Milw., June 13, 1914; s. Michael and Jean (Dinerstein) L.; m. Doris Silver, Mar. 19, 1944; children: Amy L. Kovner, Dr. Cathy Jo. BA, U. Wis., 1934, LLB, 1936; LLM, Harvard, 1937; BCS, Strayer Coll. Accountancy, 1939. Bar: Wis. 1936, N.Y. 1946, D.C. 1947, Fla. 1977, U.S. Supreme Ct. 1939; CPA, D.C. Assoc. Rubin, Zabel & Ruppa, Milw., 1936-37; with Office Undersec. Treasury, 1937-38; spl. atty. office chief counsel, bur. IRS, 1938-40; trial counsel IRS (New Eng. div. tech. staff), 1940-42, IRS (N.Y. div.), 1945-47; tax counsel S.J. Foosaner, Newark, 1947-48; pvt. law practice N.Y.C., 1948-72; mem. firm Zissu Lore Halper & Robson, N.Y.C., 1972-76, counsel, 1976-80; ptnr. Lore & Levy, N.Y.C., 1981—. Pres. bd. Fed. Tax Forum, Inc.; lectr. Tax Workshop, 1953-55, law sch. St. John's U., 1954, Fairleigh Dickinson U., 1955-56; specialist fed. tax matters, lectr. taxation NYU, 1946-50, 65, Practising Law Inst., 1947-48, Tax Inst., 1948, Pa. State Coll., 1949-50, U. W.Va., U. San Francisco, 1951, SUNY, Stony Brook, 1978-79; tax cons. Med. Econs.; pres. Estate Planning Coun. N.Y.C., 1968-69; part-time employee Melnik & Karan, Milw., 1933-36. Author: The Administration of The Federal Income Tax Through the United States Board of Tax Appeals, 1937, How to Win a Tax Case, 1955, Thin Capitalization, 1958; co-editor: Jour. of Taxation; chmn. bd. editors: How To Work with the Internal Revenue Code of 1954; contbr. articles to legal and accounting jours. Lt. comdr. Office Gen. Counsel, USNR, 1942-44. Mem. ABA (com. income taxation estates and trusts), N.Y. State Bar Assn., Assn. Bar City of N.Y. (taxation com., com. on trusts, estates and surrogate's cts.), FBA (chmn. com. fed. taxation), AICPA (sec. fed. tax lawyers com.), D.C. Accts., County Lawyers Assn. (taxation com.), Seawane Club (bd. govs.), Lawyers Club (N.Y.C.), Harvard Club (N.Y.C.), Barristers (Washington). Home: 46 Broome Ave Atlantic Beach NY 11509-1214

LOREE, JAMES M., consumer products company executive; BA in Econ., Union Coll. With fin. mgmt. staff Stanley Works, New Britain, Conn., 1980—99, exec. v.p. fin. and strategic planning, CFO, 1999—. Office: Stanley Works 1000 Stanley Dr New Britain CT 06053

LOREFICE, LAURENCE SANTO, psychiatrist; b. N.Y.C., May 11, 1950; s. Lawrence Salvatore and Gemma (Patrone) L.; m. Mary Ellen Foulds; children: Jeanne, Kristine, Luke. BA, Johns Hopkins U., 1971; MD, U. Pa., 1975; MPH, Harvard U., 1979. Diplomate Am. Bd. Psychiatry and Neurology; cert. psychopharmacology. Internship and resident in psychiatry Mass. Gen. Hosp., Boston, 1975-78, fellow in social and community psychiatry, 1978-79; chief resident Outpatient Clinic Erich Lindemann Mental Health Ctr., Boston, 1977-78; clin. fellow psychiatry Med. Sch. Harvard U., 1975-79; chief psychiatrist Day Treatment Program, mem. staff Mt. Sinai Med. Ctr., N.Y.C., 1979-80; dir. Intermediate Care Treatment Unit Westchester County (N.Y.) Med. Ctr., 1980-82; dir. Washington Heights Outpatient Clinic N.Y. State Psychiat. Inst., 1982-84; assoc. chief dept. psychiatry Stamford (Conn.) Hosp., 1986-96; instr. N.Y. Med. Coll., Valhalla, 1980-82, clin. asst. prof. psychiatry, 1985-96; asst. clin. prof. psychiatry Coll. Physicians and Surgeons Columbia U., N.Y.C., 1982-95; pvt. practice Old Greenwich, Conn., 1978—. Contbr. articles to profl. jours. Fellow Am. Psychiat. Assn. (disting., Tchg. award). Office: 404 Sound Beach Ave Old Greenwich CT 06870-2222

LORELL, BEVERLY H., medical products executive; BA with distinction, Stanford U., 1971; MD, Stanford Sch. Medicine, 1975. Intern to resident physician Stanford U. Hosp.; clin. rsch. fellowship, cardiology Mass. Gen. Hosp., Harvard Med. Sch.; dir., program in heart failure Besth Israel Deaconess Med. Ctr.; prof., medicine Harvard U. Med. Sch.; v.p., chief med. tech. officer Guidant, Indpls., 2003—. Mem.: Besth Israel Intervention Cardiology Team, Am. Coll. Cardiology, Heart Failure Soc. of Am., Am. Heart Assn., Guidant Compass Bd. Office: Guidant 111 Monument Cl 2900 Indianapolis IN 46244 Mailing: PO Box 44906 Indianapolis IN 46244

LORELLI, MICHAEL KEVIN, consumer products company executive; b. NYC, Apr. 17, 1951; s. Domenic and Effie (Stankevich) L.; m. Nancy Buck; children: Karen, Elizabeth. BE, NYU, 1972, MBA in Mktg., 1973. Dir. mktg. Clairol Co., N.Y.C., 1973-81, v.p., gen. mgr. divsn. Almay cosmetics, 1983-84; v.p., gen. mgr. internat. div. Playtex, Stamford, Conn., 1981-84; v.p. mktg. Apple Computer, Cupertino, Calif., 1984-85; exec. v.p. Pepsi-Cola Co., Somers, NY, 1985-88; pres. Pepsi-Cola East, Somers, NY, 1989-92, Pizza Hut Internat., 1993-95; pres. America's divsn. Tambrands, Inc., White Plains, NY, 1995-96; ptnr. Bryant Ptnrs. L.L.C., 1997-99; v.p., chief devel. officer Air Express Internat., Darien, Conn., 1999-2001; pres., CEO Lens Express, Inc., Yonkers, NY, 2001—02; pres. Latex Internat., Shelton, 2003—. Author: Traveling Again, Dad?. Bd. dirs. Trident Internat., Inc., Closure Inc., Keep Am. Beautiful, Rosenbluth Travel; trustee Sarah Lawrence Coll., Madison Sq. Boys and Girls Club. Mem.: Inst. Cancer Prevention. Republican. Roman Catholic. Avocations: flying, golf, running. Office Phone: 203-924-0700 ext. 400. Personal E-mail: miklorelli@aol.com.

LOREN, ALLAN Z., business information company executive; Grad., Queens Coll., N.Y., Stanford U. Various positions including chief info. officer, chief adminstrv. officer Cigna Corp., 1971-87; chief info. officer, then pres. Apple Computer, 1987-91; pres., CEO Galileo Internat., 1991-94; exec. v.p., chief info. officer Am. Express Co., 1994-2000; chmn., CEO Dun & Bradstreet, Short Hills, NJ, 2000—. Bd. dirs. Dun & Bradstreet Corp., U.S. Cellular Corp., Hershey Foods Corp., Reynolds & Reynolds Co., Venator Group, Inc., First Knowledge Ptnrs. Inc.; mem. adv. bd. eCustomers.com. Office: Dun & Bradstreet 103 John F Kennedy Pkwy Short Hills NJ 07078-2708

LOREN, DONALD PATRICK, naval officer; b. N.Y.C., Mar. 17, 1952; s. Nicholas A. and Helen T. (Carrado) L.; m. Maureen M. Lynch, Jan. 12, 1991. BS in Ops. Analysis, U.S. Naval Acad., 1974; MS in Edn., Old Dominion U., 1983; postgrad., Harvard U., 1993-94, MIT, 1994-95. Commd. ens. USN, 1974, advanced through grades to rear adm., combat sys. officer, Destroyer Squadron Thirty-One, 1978; ops. officer USS Peterson, 1979-80; ops. and readiness officer Destroyer Squadron Two Staff, 1981-82; asst. chief of staff for comms. Cruiser Destroyer Group Eight Staff, 1983-85; exec. officer USS John Hancock, 1985-86; flag sec. to comdr. in chief U.S. Naval Forces, Europe, 1986-88; NATO policy officer Strategic Plans and Policy Directory, Joint Staff, 1989-91; comdg. officer USS Elrod FFG-55, 1991-93; doctrine devel. officer Naval Doctrine Command, 1993; fed. exec. fellow Ctr. for Internat. Affairs Harvard U., Cambridge, Mass., 1993-94; profl. staff mem. Ind. Commn. on Roles and Missions of Armed Forces, 1993-94; comdr. Destroyer Squadron Twenty-eight, Norfolk, Va., 1995-97; dep. dir. strategy and policy divsn. Office the the Chief of Naval Ops., 1997-98; exec. asst. to comdr. in chief U.S. Naval Forces Europe, 1998—2001; and comdr. in chief Allied Forces So. Europe, 1998—2001; exec. asst., prin. advisor to operational comdr. NATO Combat Forces, 1999—2001; dep. dir. surface ships Office of the Chief of Naval Ops., 2001—03; dep. dir. politico-mil. affairs Europe, NATO and Russia, The Joint Staff, 2003—. Fellow MIT, Seminar XXI, fgn. politics, internat. rels. and the nat. interest, 1994-95; fellow nat. security studies Maxwell Sch., Syracuse U., 2003; fellow Nat. Def. Coll., Rome, 2004; fellow sr. execs. in nat. and internat. security program Harvard U. JFK Sch. Govt., 2004. Author: Shape Up! A Shipboard Program for Physical Fitness, 1981; contbr. articles to profl. publs. Mem. Phi Kappa Phi, Sigma Iota Epsilon. Avocations: jogging, weight training, classical music, ballet, opera. Office: 6504 John Thomas Dr Alexandria VA 22315 Office Phone: 703-697-8591. Business E-Mail: donald.loren@js.pentagon.mil.

LOREN, SOPHIA, actress; b. Rome, Sept. 20, 1934; d. Riccardo Scicolone and Romilda Villani; m. Carlo Ponti, Apr. 12, 1967; children: Carlo Ponti, Edoardo. Student, Scuole Magistrali Superiori. Films include E Arrivato l'Accordatore, 1951, Africa sotto i Mari, La Favorita, La Tratta Delle Bianche, 1952, Aida, Tempi Nostri, Ci Troviamo in Gellera, La Domenica Della Buona Genti, Il Paese dei Campanelli, Un Giorno in Pretura, Due Notti con Cleopatra, Pelegrini d'Amore, Attila, Carosello Napoletano, 1953, Miseria e Nobilta, Gold of Naples, Woman of the River, Too Bad She's Bad (Best Actress award Buenos Aires Festival), 1954, Lucky To Be A Woman, Sign of Venus, The Millers Wife, Scandal in Sorrento, 1955, Pride and Passion, Boy on a Dolphin, Legend of The Lost, 1957, Desire Under the Elms, Houseboat, The Key (Best Actress award Japan), 1958, That Kind of Woman, Black Orchid, 1959 (Best Actress Venice Festival, David Di Donatello award Italy, Victoire Popularity award France), Heller in Pink Tights (Best Actress Rapallo Festival Italy), It Started in Naples, A Breath of Scandal, The Millionaires, 1960, Two Women, (11 Best Actress awards including Oscar, Hollywood, Di Donatello award, Cannes Film Festival, N.Y. Critics, Golden Globe, Brit. Film Acad., others from Ireland, Japan, Belgium, Spain, France, W. Ger., also other awards), El Cid, Madame, Bocaccio 70, 1961, The Condemned of Altona, Five Miles to Midnight, 1962, Yesterday, Today and Tomorrow, (Best Actress Di Donatello award, Golden Globe award), 1963, The Fall of the Roman Empire, Marriage Italian Style, 1964 (Best Actress Di Donatello award, Golden Globe award, Alexander Korda award Brit. Film Inst., others), Operation Crossbow, Lady L, Judith, 1965, Arabesque, A Countess From Hong Kong, 1966, Happily Ever After, Ghosts, Italian Style (Best Fgn. Actress Diploma USSR), 1967, More Than A Miracle, (Ramo d'Oro award Italy, other awards), 1968, Sunflower (Best Actress Di Donatello award), 1969, The Priest's Wife, 1970, Lady Liberty, White Sister, 1971, Man of La Mancha, 1972, The Voyage (Di Donatello award), 1973, Brief Encounter, The Verdict, 1974, The Cassandra Crossing, A Special Day, 1977, Firepower, 1978, Brass Target, 1979, Blood Feud, 1981, Ready to Wear (Prêt-à-Porter), 1994, Grumpier Old Men, 1995, Messages, 1996, Soleil, 1997, Destinazione Verna, 1999, Between Strangers, 2002, Too Much Romance.It's Time for Stuffed Peppers, 2004; TV film appearances include Sophia Loren: Her Own Story, 1980, Angela, 1982, Aurora, 1985, Mother Courage, 1986, The Fortunate Pilgrim (Best Actress of Yr. for TV mini-series), 1987, La Ciociara, 1989. Recipient numerous awards including Nastro d'Argento, Italy, 14 Bambi and Bravo Popularity awards, Fed. Republic Germany, 3 Prix Uilenspigoel Fiamingo award, Belgium, Popularity awards Am. Legion, Tex. Cinema Exhibitors, 4 Snosiki Popularity awards, Finland, 2 Best Actress awards Bengal Film Journalists Assn., India, Box-Office Favourite Medal, Italy, Helene Curtis award, U.S.A., Simpatia Popularity award, Italy, Rudolph Valentino Screen Svcs. award, Italy, Best Actress award Moscow Film Festival, Hon. Acad. award, 1990; named Most Popular Actress in Italy. Address: c/o La Concordia Ranch 1151 Hidden Valley Ranch Rd Thousand Oaks CA 91361

LORENCZ, MARY, public relations executive; BA in English, Mich. State U.; M in Public Relations, Wayne State U. Various positions to dir. corp. media rels. Kmart Corp., Troy, Mich., 1985—2003; sr. counselor John Bailey & Associates, Inc. Public Relations, 2003—. Mem.: Internat. Assoc. Bus. Communicators, Detroit Chap. (past pres.).

LORENO, NINA LOUISE, elementary school educator; b. Mpls., Sept. 16, 1972; d. Francis and Roberta Kay Loreno; m. Eric Andrew Cook, June 19, 2004. BA in Speech and Comms., U. Minn., 1995, BA in English, 1999; cert. tchr., U. St. Thomas, 2000, MA in Edn., 2001. Ednl. asst. Mpls. Pub. Schs., 1998—2000, mid. sch. tchr., 2001—. Avocations: running, reading. Office: Cityview Cmty Sch 3350 4th St N Minneapolis MN 55412

LORENSEN, GUNNHILDUR S., librarian; b. Flateyri, Iceland, Aug. 1922; arrived in U.S., 1943; d. Snorri Sigfusson and Gudrun Johannesdottir; m. Lyman E. Lorensen, 1950; children: Gudrun, Ingrid, Gilda. BS, Am. U., 1946; MS, Cornell U., 1949; MLS, U. Calif., Berkeley, 1968. Rsch. asst. Icelandic Dept. Edn., Reyjavik, 1949—50; sch. libr. Martinez (Calif.) Sch. Sys.; hon. consul of Iceland Icelandic Govt., Orinda, Calif., 1989—97. Libr. Orinda Cmty. Ch., 1989—99; mem. San Francisco Consular Corps, 1989—97. Mem.: AAUW, Icelandic Soc. No. Calif. (co-founder 1956, pres. 1956—66, v.p. 1999). Democrat. Avocations: gardening, reading, singing. Home: 9 Broadview Terr Orinda CA 94563-3101

LORENZ, HANS ERNEST, photographer; b. Karlsbad, Czechoslovakia, Sept. 11, 1940; came to U.S., 1950; naturalized, 1954. s. Hugo and Maria (Gareis) L.; m. Pamela Marie Carswell, May 27, 1978; 1 child, April Nicole. BA, Okla. Bapt. U., 1962. Tchr. pub. schs., Prince George County, Va., 1964-65; sr. curatorial photographer Colonial Williamsburg (Va.) Found., 1965—. Writer, lectr. 19th Century photographic history. Contbr. photographs to numerous books on 18th Century antiques. Mem. Am. Photographic Soc., Nat. Stereoscopic Assn., Am. Numismatic Assn. Baptist. Home: 116 Walnut Hills Dr Williamsburg VA 23185-3433 Office: PO Box 1776 Williamsburg VA 23187-1776 E-mail: hlorenz@cwf.org.

LORENZ, HUGO ALBERT, retired insurance executive, consultant; b. Elmhurst, Ill., July 5, 1926; s. Hugo E. and Linda T. (Trampel) L. BS, Northwestern U., 1949; LL.B., Harvard U., 1952. Bar: Ill. 1954. Mem. patent staff Bell Telephone Labs., Murray Hill, N.J., 1952-53; atty. First Nat. Bank Chgo., 1954-58; gen. counsel N.Am. Life Ins. Co. of Chgo., 1958-73; dir., v.p., gen. counsel, sec. Globe Life Ins. Co., Chgo., 1973-95; v.p. Union Fidelity Life Ins. Co., Chgo., 1993-96; sec. Gt. Equity Life Ins. Co., Chgo., 1977-80, Pat Ryan & Assos. Inc., Va. Surety Co., Chgo., 1977-96. Bd. dirs. Sr. Ctrs. Met. Chgo., 1977-93, pres., 1983-85; trustee Hull House Assn., 1983-88. With USNR, 1944-46. Mem. Assn. Life Ins. Counsel, Connoisseurs Internat (bd. dirs. 1972—2004, pres. 1980-95), Internat. Wine and Food Soc. Chgo. (gov. and oenologist 1980—). Unitarian Universalist. Home: 950 N Clark St # A Chicago IL 60610-8701

LORENZ, JOHN GEORGE, librarian, consultant; b. N.Y.C., Sept. 28, 1915; s. John W. and Theresa T. (Wurtz) L.; m. Josephine R. Trumbull, Oct. 1, 1944; children: Laurence T., Janice R. BS (Library fellow), CCNY, 1939; BS in L.S, Columbia U., 1940; MS in Pub. Adminstrn., Mich. State U., 1952. With Queens Borough (N.Y.) Library, then Schenectady Pub. Library, 1940-44; chief reference div. Grand Rapids Pub. Library, 1944-46; asst. librarian Mich. State Library, 1946-56; with U.S. Office Edn., 1957-65, dir. div. library services and ednl. facilities, 1964-65; dep. librarian of congress Library of Congress, Washington, 1965-76; exec. dir. Assn. Research Libraries, 1976-80; library cons., 1980—; interim dir. libraries Cath. U. Am., 1982-83; liaison mem. com. sci. and tech. info. exec. office, 1966-73; interim dir. CAPCON, 1985; spl. asst. to librarian Georgetown U. Library, 1985-87; interim dir. Washington Research Library Consortium, 1987-88; coord. libr. stats. program Nat. Commn. on Librs. and Inf. Sci., 1988-97. Exec. com. Nat. Book Com., 1968-74 Author numerous articles in field; contbr. to books. Presdl. appointee Nat. Hist. Publs. and Records Commn., 1979-83; bd. dirs. Pitts. Lifetime Care Cmty. Recipient Superior Svc. award HEW. Mem. ALA (coun. 1960-64, 69-73, chmn. panel UNESCO 1965-70, exec. bd. 1970-75, Lippincott award 1993), D.C. Libr. Assn., Internat. Fedn. Libr. Assn. (mem. program devel. group 1974-78), Am. Nat. Stds. Inst. (treas. libr. stds. com. 1980-88), Cosmos Club. Home: 100 Norman Dr Apt 311 Cranberry Township PA 16066-4229

LORENZ, LEE SHARP, cartoonist; b. Hackensack, N.J., Oct. 17, 1932; s. Alfred Lloyd and Martha (Castagnetta) L.; children: Matthew, Martha, Ava. Student, Carnegie Inst. Tech., 1950-51; BFA, Pratt Inst., 1954. Staff cartoonist New Yorker mag., 1958—, art editor, 1973—97. Author: The Art of the New Yorker, 1995, The World of William Steig, 1998, The Essential George Booth, 1999, The Essential Charles Barsott, 1999, The Essential Jack Ziegler, 2001. Trustee Swann Coll. of Cartoon and Caricature, 1978—; dir. Mus. for African Art. Mem. Cmty. Church. Home: PO Box 117 Easton CT 06612-0117

LORENZ, MICHAEL DUANE, veterinary medicine educator, dean; m. Velda Clark. BS, Okla. State U., DVM, 1969. Diplomate Am. Coll. Vet. Internal Medicine. Formerly with U. Ga. Coll. Vet. Medicine, Athens; dean Kans. State U. Coll. Vet. Medicine, Manhattan, 1988-94, Okla. State U. Coll. Vet. Medicine, Stillwater, Okla. Mem. Nat. Acads. of Practice in Vet.

Medicine. Office: Okla State U Coll Vet Medicine Office of the Dean 205 McElroy Hall Stillwater OK 74078-2007 Office Phone: 405-744-7672. Office Fax: 405-744-6633. Business E-Mail: mlorenz@okstate.edu.

LORENZ, RODNEY ALAN, physician, educator; b. Decatur, Ill., Aug. 12, 1945; s. Ralph B. and Natalia W. Lorenz; m. Karin Lee Cross, Sept. 2, 1972; children: Matthew, Kathlynn, Rebekah. BA, Wash. U., St. Louis, 1967; MD, Vanderbilt U., Nashville, 1971. Cert. Nat. Bd. Med. Examiners, 1972, Am. Bd. Pediat., 1979, Am. Bd. Pediat. Endocrinology, 1986. Asst. resident, chief resident Vanderbilt U., Nashville, 1971—74; epidemic intelligence svc. mem. CDC, Atlanta, 1974—76; fellow, pediat. endocrinology Vanderbilt U., Nashville, 1976—79, asst. prof., 1979—86, assoc. prof., prof., 1986—99; prof., chair, pediat. U. Ill. Coll. Medicine, Peoria, 1999—2005, dean, 2005—. Bd. dirs. Tenn. Camp for Diabetic Children, 1980—99; mem., behavioral medicine study section NIH, Bethesda, Md., 1985—91; chair, Tenn. diabetes adv. bd. Tenn. Dept. Health, 1995—99; acting chair Nat. Diabetes Edn. Program, 1999—2000, chair, expert panel on diabetes in schs., 2000—04; chair, Coun. on Diabetes in Youth Am. Diabetes Assn., Arlington, Va., 1999—2001. Contbr. articles to profl. jours., chapters to books. Lt. cmdr. USPHS, 1974—76. Fellow: Am. Acad. Pediats.; mem.: Am. Diabetes Assn., Lawson Wilkins Pediat. Endocrine Soc., Alpha Omega Alpha. Avocations: poetry, backpacking, gardening. Office: Univ Ill Coll Medicine One Illini Dr Peoria IL 61649 Office Phone: 309-671-8402.

LORENZ, RONALD THEODORE, manufacturing executive; b. Chgo., Apr. 9, 1936; s. Raymond W. and Olga (Hagel) L.; m. Elizabeth L. Lehning, Nov. 26, 1960 (div. 1970); children: Dane B., Drenna D.; m. Phyllis J. Scordato, May 5, 1972 (div. May 1989); children: Amy J., Adam R. Cert. stationary engr. Asst. engr. Conrad Hilton Hotel, Chgo., 1953-55, engr., 1957-59, Kemper Ins. Co., Chgo., 1959-67; pres. Capitol Music Ctrs., Elgin, Ill., 1967-81, Rapco Internat., Jackson, Mo., 1982-91, Allied Industries, Cape Girardeau, Mo., 1992—. Served with U.S. Army, 1955-57. Mem. Jackson C. of C. (officer 1987-88), Nat. Assn. Music Mchts. (officer trade show com. 1987-90). Republican. Avocations: music, walking, boating, swimming. E-mail: roncapt@cableone.net.

LORENZEN, KRISTINA ANNE, psychologist; b. Glendale, Ariz., May 11, 1976; d. David Frank and Karen Anne Tisdale; m. Richard James Lorenzen, June 26, 1999. BS in Edn., No. Ariz. U., 1998; MA in Edn., U. No. Iowa, 2002, EdS, 2004. Nationally cert. sch. psychologist. Tchr. North Tama Sch. Dist., Traer, Iowa, 1999—2001; sch. psychologist Area Edn. Agy. 267, Cedar Falls, Iowa, 2003—04, El Paso County Sch. Dist. 8, Fountain, Colo., 2004—. Grad. asst. Integrating Techs. Into Methods of Edn., Cedar Falls, Iowa, 2001—02, Tchr. Edn. Addressing Minority-Lang. Spkrs., Cedar Falls, Iowa, 2002—03. Named Outstanding Jr. scholar, No. Ariz. U., 1997; recipient Laura Clark Student of Yr. award, Iowa Sch. Psychologist Assn., 2003. Mem.: Nat. Assn. Sch. Psychologists, Phi Eta Sigma. Avocations: reading, travel, shopping, dance.

LORENZEN, ROBERT FREDERICK, ophthalmologist; b. Toledo, Ohio, Mar. 20, 1924; s. Martin Robert and Pearl Adeline (Bush) L.; m. Lucy Logdson, Feb. 14, 1970; children: Roberta Jo, Richard Martin, Elizabeth Anne. BS, MD, Duke U., 1948; MS, Tulane U., 1953. Intern Presbyn. Hosp., Chgo., 1948-49; resident Duke U. Med. Ctr., 1949-51, Tulane Grad. Sch., 1951-53; practice medicine specializing in ophthalmology Phoenix, 1953—. Bd. dirs. St. Vincent de Paul Eye Clinic; mem. staff St. Joseph's Hosp., St. Luke's Hosp., Good Samaritan Hosp., Surg. Eye Ctr. of Ariz. Pres. Ophthalmic Scis. Found., 1970-73; chmn. bd. trustees Rockefeller and Abbe Prentice Eye Inst. of St. Luke's Hosp., 1975—. Editor in chief Ariz. Medicine, 1963-66, 69-70. Named to Honorable Order of Ky. Colls.; recipient Gold Headed Cane award, 1974. Fellow ACS, Internat. Coll. Surgeons, Am. Acad. Ophthalmology and Otolaryngology, Pan Am. Assn. Ophthalmology; mem. Am. Assn. Ophthalmology (sec. of ho. of dels. 1972-73, trustee 1973-76), Ariz. Ophthal. Soc. (pres. 1966-67), Ariz. Med. Assn. (bd. dirs. 1963-66, 69-70), Royal Soc. Medicine, Rotary (pres. Phoenix 1984-850). Republican. Office: 3333 E Camino Sin Nombre Paradise Valley AZ 85253

LORENZO, MICHAEL, engineer, real estate broker, government official; b. Newton, N.J., 1920; m. Anastasia Hackett; 5 children. BS in Chemistry and Physics, Pa. State U., 1947; MEA, George Washington U., 1956, postgrad., 1975-78, USDA Grad. Sch. Registered profl. engr., D.C., Md.; cert. Internat. Property Specialist, FIPC; lic. real estate broker, Md., Va., D.C. Field instrumentation engr. Fischer and Porter Co., Harboro, Pa., 1947-52; aerospace engr. Dept. Def., 1952-65; with Westinghouse Electric Corp., Friendship, Md., 1965-81; mgr. Air Resources Westinghouse Mgmt. Services, Inc., 1966-70, dir. environ. quality control, 1970-73; founder, pres. Tech. Protection Engring. Co., 1982—; dep. under-sec. def. Washington, 1981-82; founder, prin. broker First Lady Realty Corp., 1986—. Author: (with others) Chemical Equipment Costs, 1950; assoc. editor: Missile and Rockets, 1958-61; contbr. articles to profl. jours.; patentee stall surge sonic sensor. Rear Admiral AC USN, World War II, Korea. Decorated D.S.M., D.F.C. (2), Air medals (7) Mem. Profl. Tennis Registry. Office: First Lady Realty Corp 3126 Shadeland Dr Falls Church VA 22044-1726 Office Phone: 703-534-7920. *Healthy mind requires healthy body and vice versa. Per Winston Churchill "A Democracy is one of the worst forms of Government invented, except for all the others." It's my time in life to give back. You don't get a second chance to make a good first impression.*

LORI, WILLIAM E., bishop; b. Louisville, May 6, 1951; BA, St. Pius X Sem., Covington, Ky., 1973; MA, Mount St. Mary's Sem., Emmitsburg, Md., 1977; STD, Cath. U. Washington, 1982. Ordained priest Roman Cath. Ch. 1977. Sec. to James Cardinal Hickey, 1983-94; chancellor/vicar gen., moderator of Curia, 1994-95; titular bishop Diocese of Bulla, 1995-2001; aux. bishop, vicar gen./moderator of Curia, Archdiocese of Washington, 1995-2001; bishop of Bridgeport, Conn., 2001—. Chmn. Archdiocesan Commn. for Ecumenical and Interreligious, 1982—86; theol. advisor to Archbishop, 1982—94; mem. com. in edn. USCC, 1996, mem. com. on human values, 96; trustee Cath. U. Am., 1997—, chmn. bd. trustees, 2003—, chair acad. affairs com., 1998—; mem. USCCB Commn. on Doctrine, 2001, USCCB Com. on Pro Life Activities; chmn. bd. trustees Sacred Heart U., Fairfield, Conn., 2001—; bd. dirs. St. Luke Inst., Silver Spring, Md., Blessed Pope John XXIII Sem., Boston. Roman Catholic. Office: 238 Jewett Ave Bridgeport CT 06606

LORIA, JEFFREY H., sports team executive; b. N.Y.C. 3 children. Grad., Yale U., 1962; MBA, Columbia U. Owner Oklahoma City 89ers, 1989-93; chmn., CEO Montreal Expos, 1999—2002; owner Florida Marlins, 2002—; internat. art dealer. Author: Collecting Original Art, What's It All About Charlie Brown. Former bd. dirs. Art Dealers Assn. Am. Named Am. Assn. 1992 Exec. of Yr. Office: Pro Player Stadium 2267 Dan Marino Blvd Miami FL 33028

LORIE, JAMES HIRSCH, business administration educator; b. Kansas City, Feb. 23, 1922; s. Alvin J. and Adele (Hirsch) L.; m. Sally Rosen, June 16, 1948 (div. 1953); 1 child Susan; m. Nancy A. Wexler, June 19, 1958 (dec. 1966); stepchildren: Katherine Wexler, Jeffrey Wexler; m. Vanna Metzenberg Lautman, Aug. 27, 1967; stepchildren: Erika Lautman, Victoria Lautman, Karl Lautman. AB, Cornell U., 1942, A.M., 1945; PhD, U. Chgo., 1947. Research asst. Cornell U., Ithaca, N.Y., 1944-45; mem. staff seminar Am. civilization Salzburg, Austria, 1947; mem. faculty U. Chgo. Grad. Sch. Bus., 1947-92, prof. bus. adminstrn., asso. dean, 1956-61; dir. Center Research in Security Prices, 1960-75. Cons. divsn. rsch. and statistics bd. govs. Fed. Res. Sys., 1950-52; cons. U.S. Treas. Dept., 1973-74; bd. dirs. Thornburg Mortgage Co., Inc., Chgo.; mem. Nat. Market Adv. Bd., 1975-77. Author: (with Harry V. Roberts) Basic Methods of Marketing Research, 1951, (with Richard A. Brealey) Modern Developments in Investment Management, 1972, (with Mary T. Hamilton) The Stock Market: Theories and Evidence, 1973; Contbr. articles to profl. jours. Served with USCGR, 1942-44. Mem. Mont Pelerin Soc., Nat. Assn. Securities Dealers (dir. 1972-75), Phi Beta Kappa. Clubs: Arts (Chgo.); Quadrangle (U. Chgo.).

LORIMER, LINDA KOCH, university educator; children: Katharine Elizabeth, Peter Brailler. AB, Hollins Coll., 1974; JD, Yale U., 1977; DHL (hon.), Green Mountain Coll., 1991, Washington Coll., 1992, Randolph-Macon Coll., 1992. Bar: N.Y. 1978, Conn. 1982. Assoc. Davis Polk and Wardwell, N.Y.C., 1977-78; asst. gen. counsel Yale U., New Haven, 1978-79, assoc. gen. counsel, 1979-84, assoc. provost, 1983-87, acting assoc. v.p. human resources, 1984-85; prof. law, pres. Randolph-Macon Woman's Coll., Lynchburg, Va., 1987-93; v.p., sec. Yale Univ., New Haven, 1993—. Lectr. Yale Coll. Undergrad. Seminars, 1980, 83; bd. dirs. Sprint, McGraw Hill, Yale-New Haven Hosp.; mem. corp. Yale U., 1990-93, chair Virginia Rhodes scholarship com., 1991-93; trustee HollinsU., Berkeley Divinity Sch. Chair editorial bd. Jour. Coll. and Univ. Law, 1983-87. Former trustee Hollins Coll., Berkeley Div. Sch.; mem. com. on responsible conduct rsch. Inst. Medicine, NAS, 1988; bd. dirs. Norfolk Acad.; cabinet mem. United Way of Greater New Haven. Mem. Nat. Assn. Coll. and Univ. Attys. (exec. bd. 1981-84), Nat. Assn. Schs. and Colls. United Meth. Ch. (1st v.p.), Am. Assn. Colls. and Univs. (pres. bd.), Assn. Am. Colls.,(pres. bd. dirs., chmn. bd.), Am. Assn. Theol. Schs. (bd. dirs.), Mory's Assn., Phi Beta Kappa. Episcopalian. Office: Woodbridge Hall PO Box 208230 Yale Univ New Haven CT 06520-8230

LORING, ARTHUR, lawyer, diversified financial services company executive; b. N.Y.C., Oct. 13, 1947; s. Murray and Mildred (Rogers) Loring; m. Vicki Hootstein, June 4, 1978. BS in Commerce, Washington and Lee U., 1969; JD cum laude, Boston U., 1972. Bar: Mass. 1972. Atty. Fidelity Mgmt. & Rsch. Co., Boston, 1972-98, sr. legal counsel, 1980-82, v.p., gen. counsel, 1983—93, sr. v.p., gen. counsel, 1993-98; v.p.-legal FMR Corp., Boston, 1982-98; sec. Fidelity Group of Funds, Boston, 1982-98; dir. Fidelity Capital Publs. Inc., 1991-98; v.p. Fidelity Distbr. Corp., Boston, 1984-98; sr. v.p., gen. counsel Fidelity Investments Instnl. Svcs., Inc., 1994-98; mng. dir. Cypress Holding Co., 1998-2000; mng. dir., mem. exec. com. Spyglass Investments LLC, Boston, 2000—04. Bd. govs. Investment Co. Inst., 1988—90; chmn. ICI SEC Rules Com., 1990—95; mem. adv. bd. Fund Directions, 1993—98; bd. dirs., chmn. audit com. New River, Inc., 1998—; dir. Global Alliance Value Investors, Ltd., 1999—2000, Advantage Bank, bd. dirs., chmn. investment com., 2000—03; bd. dirs. 1st United Bank, 2005—. Case editor: Boston U. Law Rev., 1971—72. Bd. dirs. Tradition of the Palm Beaches, 2004—, pres., 2004—; bd. dirs. Jewish Fedn. Palm Beach, 2001—, chmn. found. com., 2001—03, mem. exec. com., 2002—, v.p., 2004—; bd. dirs. Kramer Sr. Svc. Agy., 2000—; mem. adv. bd. Sch. Commerce, Washington and Lee U., 1996—; bd. dirs. Morse Geriatric Ctr., 2001—, pres. found., 2001—, v.p., 2002—04, pres., 2004—. Mem.: Palm Beach Country Club (bd. dirs. 2002—), Pine Brook Country Club (bd. gov. 1996—, v.p. 2000—02, pres. 2002—04), Cavendish Club (bd. dirs. 1981—84), Boston Chess Club (pres. Brookline, Mass. 1981—83). Republican. Jewish. Avocations: golf, bridge, exercise, poker. Home: 622 N Flagler Dr #1001 West Palm Beach FL 33401

LORING, DENIS WALLACE, actuary; b. Flushing, N.Y., May 28, 1947; s. S. Jerome and Helen Paula (Kuhnberg) L. BA, Harvard U., 1969; SM, MIT, 1971. Actuary John Hancock Mut. Life Ins. Co., Boston, 1971-81; sr. v.p. Equitable Life Assurance Soc. U.S., N.Y.C., 1981—. Editor: Monographs on Varieties of United States Large Cents 1795-1803, 1976. Fellow Soc. Actuaries; mem. Am. Acad. Actuaries. Democrat. Jewish. Avocations: numismatics, backgammon, running. Home: 15 W 72nd St Apt 33-F New York NY 10023-3473 Office: Equitable Life Assurance Soc 787 7th Ave Fl 38 New York NY 10019-6018

LORING, GLORIA JEAN, vocalist; b. N.Y.C., Dec. 10, 1946; d. Gerald Louis and Dorothy Ann (Tobin) Goff; m. Alan Willis Thicke, Aug. 22, 1970 (div. 1986); children: Brennan Todd, Robin Alan; m. Christopher Beaumont, June 18, 1988 (div. 1993); m. René Lagler, Dec. 20, 1994. Grad. high sch. Owner Glitz Records, L.A., 1984—; pres. Only Silk Prodns., L.A., 1985-90; owner Silk Purse Prodns., 1992—. Began profl. singing, Miami Beach, 1965; appeared in numerous TV shows; featured singer: Bob Hope's Ann. Armed Forces Christmas Tour, 1970; featured several record albums; featured actress: Days of Our Lives, 1980-86; composer: TV themes Facts of Life, 1979, Diff'rent Strokes, 1978; author: Days of Our Lives Celebrity Cookbook, 1981, Vol. II, 1983, Living the Days of Our Lives, 1984, Kids, Food and Diabetes, 1986, Parenting a Diabetic Child, 1991, The Kids Food and Diabetes Family Cookbook, 1991, Parenting a Child with Diabetes, 1999. Celebrity chmn. Juvenile Diabetes Rsch. Found. Recipient Humanitarian of Yr. award Juvenile Diabetes Rsch. Found., 1982, 88, Lifetime Commitment award Juvenile Diabetes Rsch. Found., 1999, Woman of Achievement award Miss Am. Orgn., 1999. E-mail: gloria@glorialoring.com. *Life is a constant amazement!.*

LORING, JOHN ROBBINS, artist, writer; b. Chgo., Nov. 23, 1939; s. Edward D'Arcy and China Robbins (Logeman) L. BA, Yale U., 1960; postgrad., Ecole Beaux Arts, Paris, 1960-63; D in Arts (hon.), Pratt Inst., 1996. Disting. vis. prof. U. Calif., Davis, 1977; bur. chief Archtl. Digest mag., N.Y.C., 1977—78; mem. acquisitions com. dept. prints and illustrated books Mus. Modern Art, N.Y.C., 1990—99. Contbg. editor: Arts mag., 1973-79, Archtl. Digest mag., 2000—; books include: The New Tiffany Tablesettings, 1981, Tiffany Taste, 1986, Tiffany's 150 Years, 1987, The Tiffany Wedding, 1988, Tiffany Parties, 1989, The Tiffany Gourmet, 1992, A Tiffany Christmas, 1996, Tiffany's 20th Century, 1997, Tiffany Jewels, 1999, Paulding Farnham, Tiffany's Lost Genius, 2000, Magnificent Tiffany Silver, 2001, Louis Comfort Tiffany at Tiffany & Co., 2002, Tiffany Flora/Tiffany Fauna, 2003, Tiffany in Fashion, 2003, Tiffany Timepieces, 2004, Greetings from Andy, 2004, Tiffany Diamonds, 2005, Tiffany's Palm Beach, 2005; one-man exhbns. include Balt. Mus. Art, 1972, Hundred Acres Gallery, N.Y., 1972, Pace Edits., 1973, 77, Long Beach Mus. Art, 1975, A.D.I. Gallery, San Francisco, 1976; group exhbns. include Phila. Mus. Art, 1971, N.Y. Cultural Ctr., 1972, Biennale graphic Art, Ljubljana, Yugoslavia, 1973, 77, Intergrafia 74, Cracow, Poland, 1974, Bklyn. Mus. Nat. Print Exhbn., 1974, Art Inst. Chgo., 1975, R.I. Sch. Design, 1976; represented in permanent collections Mus. Modern Art, N.Y.C., Whitney Mus. Am. Art, Chgo. Art Inst., Boston Mus. Fine Arts, R.I. Sch. Design, Balt. Mus. Art, Yale U. Art Gallery; commd. by U.S. Customhouse, N.Y.C., Prudential Ins. Co. Am. Eastern Home Office, Woodbridge, N.J., City of Scranton, Pa., Western Savs., Phila., Tivoli Garden, Copenhagen. Recipient Edith Wharton award Design & Art Soc., 1988, Distinction in Design award Fashion Group Internat., 1996, Legends award Pratt Inst., 2002, Dallas Fashion award, 2004, Lifetime Achievement award Mus. Art and Design, NYC, 2005. Office: Tiffany & Co 600 Madison Ave New York NY 10022-2580 also: Harry N Abrams 100 5th Ave Fl 6 New York NY 10011-6903 Office Phone: 212-230-5339. *I look on whatever talents I may have as natural resources to be given freely wherever needed. A lot has been given out; a lot has come in.*

LORIZZO, ROBERT P., science administrator; BS in Physics, St. Johns U., 1962. From mgr. advanced programs to gen. mgr. navy avionics divsn. Northrop Grumman Corp., LA, 1984—91, gen. mgr. space divsn., 1992—97, v.p., gen. mgr. command, control, comm., intelligence and naval sys. divsn., 1997—2001, corp. v.p., pres. electronic sys., 2001—. Contbr. articles to profl. jours. Recipient Henry A. Rosenberg Sr. Disting. Citizen award, Balt. Area coun. BSA, 2003. Mem.: Assn. Naval Aviation, Air Force Assn. Exec. Forum, Navy League, Nat. Space Club (bd. govs.). Achievements include patents for laser techniques. Office: Northrop Grumman Corp 840 Century Park E Los Angeles CA 90067-2199 also: PO Box 17319 Mail Stop A-255 Baltimore MD 21203-7319

LORMAN, BARBARA K., retired state senator; b. Madison, Wis., July 31, 1932; 3 children. Student, U. Wis., Whitewater and Madison. Pres. Lorman Iron and Metal Recycling Co., Ft. Atkinson, Wis., 1979—87; mem. Wis. Senate, Madison, 1980—94. Formerly chair edn. com.; mem. health, human svc. and aging com., mem. fin. insts. and cultural affairs com., mem. select com. on healthcare reform; sec. Legis. Coun., also chmn. spl. com. on farm safety, mem. spl. com. on women offenders in correctional system; mem. spl. com. study sch. aid formula; commr. Edn. Commn. of States. bd. mem. Ft Atkinson Health Svcs., Auril; bd. mem. Ft. Healthcare Ptnrs. Bd. dirs. Rainbow Hospice Care, Inc., Ft. Atkinson (Wis.) Devel. Coun., Ft. Atkinson Meml. Hosp., Madison Area Tech. Coll., Wis. Pub. Radio Assn., past pres.; bd. dirs., past pres. Ft. Atkinson Hist. Soc., Ft. Atkinson Cmty. Found.; mem. exec. bd. Sinissippi coun. Boy Scouts Am.; mem. Wis. Gov.'s Commn. USS Wisconsin; mem. bd. visitors U. Wis. Extension; active Wis. Rep. Com.; chmn. spl. projects com. City of Ft. Atkinson. Mem.: Rotary. Address: 1245 Janette St Fort Atkinson WI 53538-1526

LORNE, SIMON MICHAEL MICHAEL, lawyer; b. Hampton, Eng., Feb. 1, 1946; arrived in U.S., 1952, naturalized, 1961; s. Henry Thomas and Daphne Mary (Brough) Lorne; children: Christopher, Michele, Allison, Nathan James, Katrina. AB cum laude, Occidental Coll., 1967; JD magna cum laude, U. Mich., 1970. Bar: Calif. 1971. Assoc. firm Munger, Tolles & Olson, L.A., 1970—72, ptnr., 1972—93; gen. counsel U.S. SEC, 1993—96; mng. dir. Salomon Bros. Inc., 1996—. Vis. assoc. prof. law U. Pa., 1977—78; acting dir. Ctr. Study of Fin. Instns., 1977—78; lectr. in law, corp. fin. U. So. Calif., 1986—88. Author: (book) Acquisitions and Mergers: Negotiated and Contested Transactions, 1985. Served with USMCR, 1967—68. Mem.: ABA, L.A. County Bar Assn., Calif. (exec. com. bus. and corps. law sect., chmn. 1984—85), L.A. Area C. of C. (leadership mission to People's Republic of China 1980, exec. com., internat. commerce com.), Jonathan Club. Republican. Roman Catholic.

LORO, ANTONIO, artist; b. Nove, Italy, May 6, 1934; came to U.S., 1949; s. Giuseppe and Evelina (Menegotto) L.; m. Gretchen; children: Brooks, Clark. PhD in Humanities, Occidental U. St. Louis, 1978; PhD in Art Sci., Greenwich U., 1991. Founder, dir. St. Mark Acad. Art Conservation Sci., Houston, Caribbean Fine Arts Sch., P.R., First Mus. Art Aguadilla; vis. prof. emeritus U. Ariz. Art restorer. Executed murals Hall Ford Motor Co., Gral Pacheco, Argentina, Adminstrn. Bldg. U. P.R., Arecibo Regional Libr. Coll. U. P.R., Borinquen Internat. Airport, Coliseum Aguadilla, Hall BMW, Houston, Assumption Cath. Ch., Houston; exhibited in group shows at Met. Mus. Fine Art, N.Y.C. Recipient Silver, Gold medals Nat. Salon Arts, Grand Prize of Honor, Argentina, Internat. Grand Mcpl. prize, Italy, Cross and Title Cavalier, Pres. Italian Republic, City Hall Recognition, City of Nove, Italy, 1998. Mem. Appraisers Assn. Am., Am. Chem. Soc., Am. Inst. Conservation Historic Artistic Works, Internat. Inst. Conservation Restoration, Scottish Soc. Conservation Restoration, Internat. Assn. Conservation Books Ppaer Archival Material, Australian Inst. Conservation Cultural Material, Internat. Soc. Fine Arts Appraisers (sr.). Address: 1612 W Alabama St Houston TX 77006-4102

LORRAINE, ACKER DONNA, dean; d. Frankie and Delores Acker. BS, SUNY, Brockport, 1999; MS, Western Ill. U., 2001. Resident dir. U. Ill., Champaign, 2002—05; asst. dean students U. NC, Charlotte, 2005—. Mem.: Am. Coll. Pers. Assn. Internat. (CMA liasion standing com. GLBT awareness 2004—). Office: U NC Charlotte 9201 Univ Blvd Charlotte NC 28223 Office Phone: 704-687-2375. E-mail: bkprtgrad@yahoo.com.

LORRAINE, RICHARD, chemicals executive; b. N.Y.C. BS in Acctg., NYU, 1976. With Westinghouse Electric Corp., 1963—78, Clark Equipment Co., 1978—80; CFO Fluid Tech. Group ITT Automotive, 1980—84, CFO, 1984—90; pres. ITT Automotive Aftermarket Group, 1990—95; exec. v.p., CFO Occidental Chem. Corp., 1995—2003; CFO Eastman Chemical, Kingsport, Tenn., 2003—. Office: Eastman Chemical PO Box 1975 Kingsport TN 37662-2000

LORTON, LEWIS, dentist, researcher; b. N.Y.C., Nov. 3, 1939; s. Frederick S. and Rosell (Engel) L.; divorced; children: Elizabeth, Mark, Michael S.; m. Jacqueline Carol Andor, Aug. 3, 1982; children: Michael E., Erin. BA, Brandeis U., 1960; DDS, U. Pa., 1964; MSD, Ind. U., 1978. Pvt. practice, West Medway, Mass., 1964-66; commd. lt. U.S. Army, 1966, advanced through grades to col., 1983, rschr., tchr., 1976—2005; ret., 2005. Cons. Armed Forces Inst. Pathology, Washington, 1986-97; chief info. mgr. Henry M. Jackson Found., 1989-91; v.p. Klemm Analysis Group, Inc., 1991-92; pres. Lorton Assoc., 1992-94; exec. dir. Health Care Open Systems & Trials, Inc., 1994-98, mng. ptnr. Intersect Assocs., LLC, 1998-2000; adminstr. Forum on Privacy and Security in Healthcare, 1998-2002; chmn., founder HIPAA-Docs Corp. Contbr. numerous articles to profl. jours. Recipient Carl Schlack award Assn. Mil. Surgeons U.S., 1988. Fellow Am. Forensic Soc.; mem. Am. Med. Informatics Assn., Health Info. Mgmt. ys. Soc. Avocations: bicycling, computers, fly fishing, squash. Personal E-mail: llorton@comcast.net.

LO RUSSO, DIANE, radiologist; b. N.Y.C., NY, Apr. 22, 1946; MD, SUNY, 1969. Cert. diagnostic radiology 1974. Intern Brookdale Hosp. Med. Ctr., Bklyn., 1969—70; resident Montefiore Med. Ctr., Bronx, 1971—74; radiologist Rye Radiology Assoc., Rye Brook, NY, 1974—. Office: Rye Radiology Assoc 30 Rye Ridge Plz Rye Brook NY 10573-2830

LOS, CORNELIS ALBERTUS, risk analyst, economist, finance educator; b. Purmerend, Netherlands, Dec. 14, 1951; arrived in U.S., 1977, naturalized, 1994; s. Klaas and Adriaantje (Nieuwland) Los; m. Diane Nichols, June 10, 1979 (div. 1984); 1 child, Francesca R. E.; m. Elizabeth M. Ten Houten, June 18, 1986 (div. 1991); 1 child, Marguerita E. A.; m. Rose Lee Haubenstock, May 5, 1994. Candidatus cum laude (BA Hon), U. Groningen, 1974, Doctorandus (MPhil), 1976; diploma, Inst. Social Studies, The Hague, 1977; MPhil, Columbia U., 1980, PhD, 1984. Tchg. asst. Columbia U., N.Y.C., 1978-80, preceptor, 1979, instr., 1980-81; economist Fed. Res. Bank of N.Y., N.Y.C., 1981-85, sr. economist, 1985-87, Nomura Rsch. Inst. (America) Inc., 1987—90; chief U.S. economist NMB Postbank Group/ING Bank/ING Capital, N.Y.C., 1991-93; assoc. prof. banking and fin. Nanyang Tech. U., Singapore, 1995-99; assoc. prof. fin. U. Adelaide, Australia, 2000; vis. assoc. prof. fin. Deakin U., 2001; assoc. prof. fin. Kent State U., 2001—. Adj. lectr. Hunter Coll., N.Y.C., 1980, CCNY, 1980—81; adj. prof. Baruch Coll., N.Y.C., 1985—86; rsch. assoc. Ctr. Math. Sys. Theory U. Fla., Gainesville, 1986—92; pres. EMEPS Assocs. Inc., 1986—; lectr. numerous profl. confs., U.S. and fgn. countries; cons. Worldbank, 1994—, Inter-Am. Devel. Bank, 1994—, Asian Devel. Bank, 1996—. Author: Computational Fin.-A Sci. Perspective, 2001, Financial Market Risk: Measurement & Analysis, 2003, Solutions Manual to Accompany Computational Finance, 2004, Solutions Manual to Accompany Financial Market Risk, 2004; contbr. articles to profl. jours., chapters to books. Mem. acad. bd. Nanyang Tech. U., 1997—99; bd. dirs. The Netherland-Am. Found., Inc., 1991—95. Recipient Lady Van Renswoude of The Hague Found. awards, 1974—75, MAOC Countess Van Bylandt Found. award, 1976, Scholten Cordès Found. awards, 1976—77; Fulbright-Hays scholar, 1977. Fellow: Soc. Columbia Scholars, Australasian Inst. Banking and Fin., Am. Coll. Forensic Examiners (life); mem.: CFA Inst., IEEE (sr.), European Fin. Mgmt. Assn., Bachelier Fin. Soc., N.Y. Acad. Sci., Am. Math. Soc., Am. Fin. Assn., Am. Econ. Assn., Am. Statis. Assn., Internat. Assn. Math. and Computer Modeling, Internat. Assn. Fin. Engrs., Econometric Soc., Math. Assn. Am., Friends of New Netherland, London Goodenough Trust, World Coun. Alumni Internat. Ho. (N.Y.C.), Grad. Faculties Alumni Columbia U., Contemporary Long Rifle Assn., Co. Mil. Historians, Nat. Muzzle Loading Assn., Columbia U. Club (Singapore) (found. treas.), Nat. Econ. Club. Republican. Avocations: history, travel, target shooting with flintlocks, photography. Office: Kent State U Coll Bus Adminstrn & Grad Sch Mgmt Dept Fin Rm 416 Kent OH 44242-0001 Office Phone: 330-672-1207. Business E-Mail: clos500@cs.com.

LOS, MARINUS, retired agrochemical researcher; b. Ridderkerk, The Netherlands, Sept. 18, 1933; arrived in U.S., 1960; s. Cornelis and Neeltje (Zoutewelle) Los; m. Lorraine Betty Lowe, May 11, 1957; children: Simon, Sija, Michael, Martin(dec.). BS, Edinburgh U., Scotland, 1955, PhD, 1957. Sr. rsch. chemist Am. Cyanamid Co., Princeton, NJ, 1960—71, group leader, 1971—84, sr. group leader, 1984—86, mgr. crop protection chems., 1986—88, assoc. dir. crop scis., 1988-92, rsch. dir. crop scis., 1992—96; ret., 1996. Recipient Disting. Inventor of 1990 award, Intellectual Property Owners, Inc., Washington, 1990, Thomas Alva Edison Patent award, R&D Coun. of N.J., 1991, Nat. Medal of Tech., NSF, 1993, Achievement award, Indsl. Rsch. Inst. Inc., 1994. Mem.: AAAS, Plant Growth Regulator Soc., Am.

Chem. Soc. (Perkin medal 1994, Creative Invention award 1995, Heroes of Chemistry 1999, Internat. award for rsch. in agrochemicals 2002). Achievements include patents in field. E-mail: mar6lor2000@yahoo.com.

LOSADA-ZARATE, GLORIA, psychologist; b. Havana, Cuba, Apr. 20, 1957; came to U.S., 1962; BA, Fla. Internat. U., 1980; D Psychology, Nova U., 1984. Lic. psychologist, Conn. Pre-doctoral pyschology fellow Yale U., New Haven, 1983-84; dir. treatment program for mentally retarded offenders Southbury Tng. Sch., Stat of Conn., 1984—86; clin. psychologist State of Conn. Dept. Mental Retardation New Haven Ctr., New Haven, 1986-88; dir. psychol. svcs. State of Conn. Dept. Mental Retardation Region 6, Waterford, Conn., 1988-92; clin. psychologist State of Conn. Dept. of Mental Health and Addiction Svcs., Middletown, 1997—2002; supervising psychologist Conn. Dept. Children and Families, Middletown, 2002—. Pvt. practice psychology, 1986—. Mem. APA. Democrat. Roman Catholic. Avocations: ballet, classical music, jazz, contemporary dance. Office: 95 E Main St Ste B-15 Meriden CT 06450

LOSANOFF, JULIAN EMIL, surgeon, educator; b. Sofia, Bulgaria, June 26, 1961; s. Emil Krumov and Margarita Hristova (Stambolieva) L.; m. Krassimira Sabeva Ivanoff, Nov. 12, 1987; 1 child, Christian Julian. MD, Med. U., Sofia, 1987; Diploma, Higher Inst. Econs., 1996. Diplomate Bulgarian Bd. Gen. Surgery. Gen. med. practice, Drenovets, Bulgaria, 1987-91; clin. fellow Tokushukai Med. Corp., Japan, 1997; resident in gen. surgery Mil. Med. Acad., Sofia, 1991-99, surgeon, asst. prof., 1991-2000; rsch. assoc. dept. surgery U. Mo., Columbia, 2000—01, rsch. instr., 2001—04; fellow divsn. transplantation U. Chgo., 2004—. Contbr. articles to profl. jours. With Bulgarian Army, 1979-81. Mem. N.Y. Acad. Scis., Internat. Soc. Surgery, Nat. Geog. Soc., Sofia Surg. Soc. (sec.), Bulgarian Med. Assn., Bulgarian Mil. Med. Soc. (sec.), European Soc. Emergency Medicine. Greek Orthodox. Avocations: painting, graphics. E-mail: jelosanoff@yahoo.com.

LOSCALZO, JOSEPH, cardiologist, biochemist; b. Camden, N.J., Oct. 26, 1951; s. Joseph and Dolores Rita (Ventura) L.; m. Anita Beth Sendrow, Mar. 10, 1974; children: Julia, Alexander. AB summa cum laude, U. Pa., 1972, MD and PhD, 1978. Diplomate in internal medicine and cardiovasc. disease Am. Bd. Internal Medicine. Postdoctoral fellow U. Pa., Phila., 1978; resident in internal medicine Brigham and Women's Hosp., Boston, 1978-81, clin. fellow cardiology, 1981-83, chief med. resident, 1983-84, instr. medicine, 1983-85, chair, dept med., physician chief, 2005—, physician-in-chief, 2005—; clin. fellow medicine Harvard Med. Sch., Boston, 1978-81, asst. prof. medicine, 1985-88, assoc. prof., 1989-93, hersey prof., 2005—; chief cardiol. sect. Brockton West Roxbury VA Med. Ctr., Boston, 1989-93; prof. biochemistry Boston U., 1994—2005, disting. prof. medicine, 1994—97, dir. Whitaker Cardiovasc. Inst., Sch. Medicine, 1994—2005, vice chmn. dept. medicine, chief cardiovasc. medicine, 1994-96, Wade prof., chmn. dept. medicine, 1997—2005; Hersey prof. theory and practice medicine Med. Sch. Harvard U., 2005—, chmn. Dept. Medicine, 2005—. Mem. rsch. rev. com. Am. Heart Assn., 1988—, chmn., 2000—02; rsch. rev. coms. Nat. Heart, Lung and Blood Inst., Bethesda, Md., 1990—, mem. bd. sci. counselors, 2000—04, chair, 2001—04; dir. NIH Specialized Ctr. Rsch. in Ischemic Heart Disease, 1995—2005; chair cardiovsasc. disease bd. Am. Bd. Internal Medicine, 1999—2003. Author, or editor 22 books on vascular biology, medicine, thrombosis and hemostasis; editor-in-chief Circulation, 2004—; assoc. editor New Eng. Jour. Medicine, 1995-2004; contb. mem. editl. bd. Circulation, Circulation Rsch., Jour. Am. Coll. Cardiology, Jour. Thrombosis and Thrombolysis, Vascular Medicine, Am. Jour. Cardiology, Jour. Am. Coll. Cardiology; contbr. over 400 articles to profl. jours. Recipient med. scientist tng. award NIH, 1972-77, rsch. career devel. award, 1989-94, Clin. Scientist award Am. Heart Assn., 1983-88, Disting. Scientist award 2004. Fellow ACP, Am. Coll. Cardiology; mem. Am. Fedn. Clin. Rsch., Am. Soc. Clin. Investigation, Assn. Am. Physicians, Assn. Univ. Cardiologists, Am. Soc. Biol. Chemistry, Phi Beta Kappa, Alpha Omega Alpha. Achievements include 25 patents related to nitric oxide congeners. Office: Brigham and Womens Hosp 75 Francis St Boston MA 02115

LOSCHEN, EARL LEE, psychiatrist, educator; b. Minden, Nebr., Jan. 10, 1944; s. Herman George and Agnes Anna (Garrelts) L.; m. Marilyn Jean Reinhardt, June 15, 1974; children: Rebecca, Elizabeth. BS, Midland Luth. Coll., 1966; MD, U. Nebr., Omaha, 1970; MS in Edn., So. Ill. U., 1988. Diplomate Am. Bd. Psychiatry and Neurology. Asst. prof. U. Nebr., Omaha, 1973-74, So. Ill. U., Springfield, 1974-80, assoc. prof., 1980-95; prof., 1995—2002; prof. emeritus So. Ill. U., 2002—, asst. chmn. dept. psychiatry Springfield, 1980-92, chmn. dept. psychiatry, 1992—2002. Cons. Ill. Dept. Pub. Health, Springfield, 1976-88, Ill. Dept. Rehab. Services, Springfield, 1977-88, Aid to Retarded Citizens, Springfield, 1981—, Macoupin County Mental Health, Carlinville, Ill., 1974-95; mem. psychiat. panel Health Care Financing Adminstrn., 1986—. Contbr. chpts. to books. Mem. com. rights of minors Ill. Commn. Children, 1974-77, com. youth and law, 1977-79; del. 1980 Ill. White House Conf. on Children, 1980, Ill. Conf. Children's Priorities of 1980's, 1981; bd. dirs. ARC-IL, 2002—, treas., 2003—; mem. Ill. Task Force on Autism, 2004—. Fellow Am. Psychiat. Assn. (disting. life); mem. AMA, NADD (bd. dirs. 2000-01), ARC (bd. dirs. Ill. chpt. 2002—), Nat. Assn. Rural Mental Health (bd. dirs. 1985-91, pres. 1988-89), Ill. State Med. Soc. (coun. mental health and addiction 1985-88, com. on drugs and therapeutics 1995-2005), Ill. Psychiat. Soc. (downstate counselor 1996-2001, pres.-elect 2001-02, pres. 2002-2003), Am. Assn. Mental Retardation Avocations: photography, gardening.

LOSCHI, RICHARD PAUL, middle school educator; b. Medford, Mass., Feb. 18, 1949; s. Leo Francis and Frances Rita (Forti) L. BS in Edn., U. Mass., 1970, MAT, 1971. Elem. tchr. grades 4-6 West Elem. Sch., Andover, Mass., 1971-88; mid. sch. tchr. West Middle Sch., Andover, 1988—, team leader grade 6, 1989—2004, team leader grade 7, 2004—, social studies curriculum advisor, 2003—. Mem. NEA, Andover Edn. Assn., Mass. Tchrs. Assn., Nat. Soccer Coaches Assn., Ea. Mass. Soccer Coaches Assn. (treas., Coach of Yr. 1987, 95, 99, 2001), Mass. State Soccer Assn. (treas.). Roman Catholic. Avocations: golf, hockey, soccer, travel. Home: 40 Lowell St Andover MA 01810 Office: West Middle Sch Shawseen Rd Andover MA 01810 E-mail: Rloschi@aps1.net.

LOSCHIAVO, FRANCESCA, set designer; Set decorator (films) E la nave va, 1983, Der Name der Rose, 1986, (TV miniseries) The Secret of the Sahara, 1987, (films) The Adventures of Baron Munchausen, 1988, La Voce della luna, 1990, Hamlet, 1990, Interview with the Vampire: The Vampire Chronicles, 1994, Kundun, 1997, Gangs of NY, 2002, Cold Mountain, 2003, The Aviator, 2004 (Academy award for best art direction, 2005). Mailing: c/o Miramax Film Corp 375 Greenwich St New York NY 10013*

LOSCHIAVO, LINDA BOSCO, library director; b. Rockville Ctr., N.Y., Aug. 31, 1950; d. Joseph and Jennie (DelRegno) Bosco; m. Joseph A. LoSchiavo, Sept. 7, 1974. BA, Fordham U., 1972, MA, 1990; MLS, Pratt Inst., 1974. Picture cataloguer Frick Art Reference Libr., N.Y.C., 1972-75; sr. cataloguer Fordham U. Libr., Bronx, N.Y., 1975-87, head of retrospective conversion, 1987-90, systems libr., 1990-91, dir. libr. at Lincoln Ctr., 1991—. Libr. cons. Mus. Am. Folk Art Libr., N.Y.C., 1985-90; indexer Arco Books, N.Y.C., 1974. Editor: Macbeth, 1990, Julius Ceasar, 1990, Romeo and Juliet, 1990. Mng. producer Vineyard Opera, N.Y.C., 1981-88. Mem. ALA, N.Y. Tech. Svcs. Librs., Beta Phi Mu, Alpha Sigma Nu. Home: 317 Collins Ave Mount Vernon NY 10552-1601 Office: Fordham Univ Library 113 W 60th St New York NY 10023-7404

LOSEE, JOHN FREDERICK, JR., manufacturing executive; b. Milw., Apr. 27, 1951; s. John Frederick and Helen (Joslyn) L.; m. Jane Agnes Trawicki, Aug. 25, 1973; children: Nicole Marie, John Michael. BSME, Marquette U., 1973, MS in Indsl. Engring., 1982. Registered profl. engr., Wis.; cert. numerical control mgr., Wis. Mfg. engr. OMC-Evinrude div. Outboard Marine Corp., Milw., 1975-78, mfg. engr. supr., 1978-80, mgr. tool engring., 1980-85, mgr. process and tool engring., 1985-86, dir. mfg. engring., 1986-88; v.p. ops. Rytec Corp., Jackson, Wis., 1988-90; v.p. adminstrn. Custom Products Corp., 1990-91; part-owner Nat. Mfg. Co. Inc., Milw., 1991-96; owner JFL Mfg., Inc., Sussex, Wis., 1996—. Mem. Numerical Control Soc., Soc. Mfg. Engrs., Computer and Automated Systems Assn. Republican. Roman Catholic. Home: W264 N6565 Hillview Dr Sussex WI 53089-3452 Office Phone: 262-820-9090. Personal E-mail: jflmfg27@aol.com.

LOSEE, MICHAEL PATRICK, music director; b. Milton, Fla., July 26, 1955; s. Patrick J. and Anne Melvin Losee. AA, Pensacola Jr. Coll., 1978; BA, U. W. Fla., 2000. Lic. cosmetologist Dept. Rehab. Svcs., State of Fla., 1984. Dir. music East Side Bapt. Ch., Milton, Fla., 1984—88; deptl. acct. U. W. Fla., Pensacola, 1996—98, opera scenes accompanist, 1997—98; dir. music St. Sylvester Cath. Ch., Gulf Breeze, Fla., 2000—01, St. Rose of Lima Cath. Ch., Milton, Fla., 2001—. Accompanist Pensacola Little Theatre, 1994; dir. music Emerald Coast Chorale, Pensacola, 1999—2001; music dir. Chamber Ensemble St. Sylvester Cath. Ch., Pensacola. Mem. Santa Rosa County Rep. Party, Milton. Named All-Am. Scholar, All-Am. Collegiate Soc., 1998—; scholar Gittenstein scholar, U. W. Fla., 1997, Maude Kelly scholar, 1998. Mem.: Fla. Music Tchrs. Assn., Music Tchrs. Nat. Assn., Coll. Music Soc., Golden Key, Delta Omicron. Roman Catholic. Office: St Rose of Lima Cath Ch 6451 Park Ave Milton FL 32570 Personal E-mail: farrosee@juno.om. Business E-Mail: loseem@ptdiocese.org.

LOSER, JOSEPH CARLTON, JR., dean, retired judge; b. Nashville, June 16, 1932; s. Joseph Carlton and Pearl Dean (Gupton) L.; m. Mildred Louise Nichols, May 25, 1972; 1 child, Joseph Carlton III. Student, U. Tenn., 1950-51, Vanderbilt U., 1952-55; LLB, Nashville YMCA Night Law Sch., 1959. Bar: Tenn. 1959. Pvt. practice, 1959-66; judge Gen. Sessions Ct., Davidson County, Tenn., 1966-69, Cir. Ct. 20th Jud. Dist. Tenn., 1969-86; dean Nashville Sch. Law, 1986—. Mem. ABA, Tenn. Bar Assn., Nashville Bar Assn., Am. Legion, Masons, Shriners, Sigma Delta Kappa, Kappa Sigma.

LOSEY, BEVERLEY BROWN, lawyer; b. Seattle, July 25, 1948; d. Frederick Sherwood and M. Doris (Grimes) Brown; m. Robert F. Losey, Jr., Feb. 12, 1982. BS in Nursing, U. Md., 1970; JD, U. Puget Sound (Seattle U.), 1984. Bar: Wash. 1984, U.S. Dist. Ct. (we. dist.) Wash. 1984. Community health nurse Dept. Army, Tex., S.C., Fed. Rep. Germany, 1970-77; dist. nursing supr. Wyo. Nursing Svcs., Buffalo, 1977-81; pvt. practice Seattle and Tacoma, Wash., 1984—. Mem. ABA, Wash. State Bar Assn., Res. Officers Assn. (v.p. Tacoma chpt. 1986), Zeta Tau Alpha (bd. dirs., treas. Psi chpt. 1986-87). Episcopalian. Office: 1001 4th Ave Ste 3200 Seattle WA 98154 Office Phone: 206-625-2200. Business E-Mail: bbhoseyjd@abanet.org.

LOSEY, RALPH COLBY, lawyer; b. Daytona Beach, Fla., May 26, 1951; s. George Spar and Alix (Colby) L.; m. Molly Isa Friedman, July 7, 1973; children: Eva Merlinda, Adam Colby. Student, Inst. European Studies, Vienna, Austria, 1971; BA, Vanderbilt U., 1973; JD cum laude, U. Fla., 1979. Bar: Fla. 1980, U.S. Dist. Ct. (mid. dist.) Fla. 1980. Assoc. Subin, Shams, Rosenbluth & Moran, Orlando, Fla., 1980-84; ptnr. Katz, Kutter, Alderman, Bryant & Yon, P.A., Orlando, Fla., 1984—2004; shareholder Akerman Senterfitt, Orlando, Fla., 2004—. Author: Laws of Wisdom, 1994, Your Cyber Rights and Responsibilities: Using the Internet, 1996; contbr. articles to profl. jours. Pres. Prima Sounds Found. Mem. Fla. Bar Assn., Orange County Bar Assn., Computer Law Assn. Democrat. Avocations: computers, golf, music, philosophy, reading. Home: 1661 Woodland Ave Winter Park FL 32789-2774 Office: Akerman Senterfitt PO Box 231 Orlando FL 32802-0231 Office Phone: 407-843-7860.

LOSH, SUSAN CAROL, education educator, researcher; b. Detroit, May 30, 1946; d. Rubin Losh and Naomi Lois Hendelman; m. Neil Bernard Betten, Aug. 18, 1984; 1 child, Reuben Losh-Betten. BA Psychology, U. Mich., 1968, MA Sociology, PhD Sociology, U. Mich., 1973. Asst. prof. sociology Fla. State U., Tallahassee, 1973—78, assoc. prof. sociology, 1978—2000, assoc. professor ednl. psychology, 2000—, program leader learning and cognition, 2001—. Cons. United Faculty of Fla., Tallahassee, 1984—, program leader, learning and cognition, 2001—. Contbr. over 30 articles to profl. jours., over 80 contbns. to various confs. (awards for tchg. and tech. innovation in tchg.). Cons. AAUW, Tallahassee, 2001—, City of Tallahassee, 1975—81; sec. Tallahassee Area Shetland Sheepdog Assn., Tallahassee, 1995—; exec. com. mem. Southern Sociological Soc., Atlanta, 1980—82. Rsch. fellow, Am. Statis. Assn., NSF, 2003, various grants. Achievements include development of historical data archive of the NSF survey of pub. understanding of sci. and tech; tripled the number of graduate student majors. Avocation: Shetland Sheepdogs, Housing Renovation. Office: Fla State U Ednl Psychology and Learning Sys Tallahassee FL 32306-4453 Business E-Mail: slosh@garnet.acns.fsu.edu.

LOSI, MAXIM JOHN, medical communications executive; b. Jersey City, Dec. 27, 1939; s. Maxim Fortune and Carrie (Rivoli) Losi; m. Mary Ann De Grandis, May 30, 1968; children: Christopher, Benjamin. AB, Princeton U., 1960; postgrad., N.Y. Med. Coll., 1960-61, Albert Einstein Coll. Medicine, 1961-62; PhD in English, NYU, 1972. Lectr. English C.W. Post Coll., Greenvale, NY, 1965-67; instr. English, Centenary Coll. for Women, Hackettstown, N.J., 1967-71, chmn. dept., 1970-71; med. abstractor, indexer Coun. for Tobacco Rsch., N.Y.C., 1972-73; freelance med. writer, 1973-74; sr. clin. info. scientist Squibb Inst. Med. Rsch., Princeton, N.J., 1974-77, project team leader, 1975-77; chief med. writer ICI Ams., Wilmington, Del., 1977-79; dir. biomed. comm. Revlon Health Care Group, Tuckahoe, N.Y., 1979-86; exec. dir. documentation mgmt. and regulatory submissions Covance Clin. and Peri-Approval Svcs. Inc., Princeton, 1987-97; v.p. regulatory affairs Scirex Corp., Blue Bell, Pa., 1997-98; pres. Max Losi Assocs. Pharm. Regulatory Cons. & Comm., Trenton, NJ, 1998—; cons. med. writer Rsch. Pharm. Svcs. Inc., 2002—. FDA cons. Microbiol. Assocs., Bethesda, Md., 1973; mgmt. cons. Robert S. First Assocs., N.Y.C., 1974; vis. lectr. med. writing techniques St. George U. Med. Sch., Grenada, W.I., 1977; adj. asst. prof. English, Rider U., Lawrenceville, N.J., 1999—. Mem.: Drug Info. Assn., Am. Med. Writers Assn. (pres. N.Y. chpt. 1984—85, nat. pres. 1987—88). Roman Catholic.

LOSICK, RICHARD M., biology professor; BA in Chem., Princeton Univ.; PhD in Biochem., MIT. Past. chmn., dept. molecular, cellular biology Harvard Coll., Maria Moors Cabot prof., biology. Former vis. scholar Phi Beta Kappa Soc.; sci. adv. bd. Tularik Tex. Corp., 1995—; chair, sci. adv. bd. Cumbre; rsch. prof. Howard Hughes Med. Inst., 2002—. Editl. bd. Science, Cell. Recipient Howard Hughes Med. Inst. grant, 2002. Fellow: Am. Acad. Microbiology, AAAS, Am. Acad. Arts and Sci.; mem.: NAS. Office: Biology Dept Harvard Coll Rm 3023 16 Divinity Ave Cambridge MA 02138 Office Phone: 617-495-4905. Business E-Mail: losick@mcb.harvard.edu.*

LOSKEN, ALBERT, medical educator; m. Elizabeth Losken. MD, Harvard Med. Sch., 1996. Cert. Plastic Surgery Am. Bd. Of Plastic Surgeons, 2003. Asst. prof. surgery Emory Plastic Surgery, Atlanta, Ga., 2002—. Chief of plastic surgery Egleston Childrens Hosp., Atlanta VA Hosp., Atlanta, 2002—. Contbr. articles various profl. jours. Recipient Rsch. and Tchg. award, 2001-2003. Office: Emory Plastic Surgery 550 Peachtree St Ste 84300 Atlanta GA 30308 Office Phone: 404-686-8143.

LOSONCZY, MARTA ELIZABETH, psychologist, educator; b. Budapest, Hungary, June 1, 1956; arrived in U.S., 1961; d. John Ambrosio and Martha Ambrosio Losonczy. BA in Philosophy, Salisbury U., 1978; MA in Clin. Psychology, Towson U., 1986; PhD in Devel. Psychology, George Washington U., 2001. Early childhood tchr. Relay Children's Ctr., Md., 1979—86; psychologist Balt. Assn. Retarded Citizens, 1986—88; instr. psychology Wor-Wic C.C., Salisbury, Md., 1992—94; bereavement counselor Coastal Hospice, Salisbury, 1993—94; lectr. Salisbury U., 1994—2001, asst. prof., 2001—. Bereavement support group facilitator Coastal Hospice, Salisbury, 1994—2002. Vol. Joseph Ho. Ministries, Salisbury, 1993—95; religious edn. tchr. St. Francis De Sales Ch., Salisbury, 1994—95, eucharistic min., 1997—2005, sacristin, 1999—2005. Grantee, Fulton Sch. Liberal Arts, 2000, 2002, 2003. Mem.: World Assn. Infant Mental Health, Internat. Soc. Study Behavioral Devel., Internat. Soc. Infant Studies, Soc. Rsch. Child Devel., N.Y. Acad. Scis. Democrat. Roman Catholic. Achievements include research in emotional development in infants. Avocations: fishing, hiking, reading, knitting, needlepoint. Office: Salisbury U Psychology Dept 1101 Camden Ave Salisbury MD 21801 Office Phone: 410-543-6444. E-mail: melosonczy@salisbury.edu.

LOSS, MARGARET RUTH, lawyer; b. Phila., June 17, 1946; d. Louis and Bernice Rose (Segaloff) L.; 1 child, Elizabeth Loss Johnson. BA, Radcliffe Coll., 1967; LLB, Yale U., 1970. Bar: Conn. 1970, N.Y. 1973. Assoc. Sullivan & Cromwell, N.Y.C., 1971-77; with Equitable Life Assurance Soc. U.S., N.Y.C., 1977-88, asst. gen. counsel, 1979-85, v.p. and counsel, 1985-88; counsel LeBoeuf, Lamb, Greene & MacRae, N.Y.C., 1988-98. Mem. com. Yale Law Sch. Fund. Mem. ABA, Am. Law Inst., Conn. Bar Assn., Assn. of Bar of City N.Y. Home and Office: 201 E 80th St # 12A New York NY 10021-0516 Office Phone: 212-717-6132. E-mail: margaretloss@cs.com.

LOSSING, WALLACE WILLIAM, inventor, minister; b. Quinn, S.D., Dec. 12, 1932; s. Burnie Wilder and Alpha (Jarvis) L.; children: Gary Michael, Kenneth James, Elaine J. Lossing Grathwol, Kristina H. Lossing Schultz, Jonathan W. Grad., Blackduck (Minn.) H.S., 1950. Cert. orthotist, hypnotherapist; ordained to ministry, Metaphysical Universal Ministries, 1997. Pres. Lossing Orthopedic, Mpls., 1965-95, VMG Med., Staunton, Va., 1993—; min. Metaphys. Universal Ministries, Allentown, Pa., 1997—. Advisor Curative Workshop, Mpls., 1970-74, N.W. C.C., Mpls., 1972-76; instr. Total Body Concepts, Staunton, 1986—, Spiritual Phys. Healing, Staunton, 1997—. Inventor (registered) Neck-trac, facil-a-trac, (trademark) My Pillow, Trac-A-Cise; developer, co-inventor (registered) Sister Kenny Gravity Lumbar Reduction System, (trademark) Geisha Back, Backtrac. Home: 246 Caldwell Ln Fishersville VA 22939-9639 Office: VMG Med 542 Walnut Hills Rd Staunton VA 24401-6936 Office Phone: 540-836-9085. Business E-Mail: wwl@vmgmed.com.

LOTAN, RACHEL, education educator; BA in English Lit. and French Lang., Lit. and Civilization, Tel Aviv U., 1971; MA in Edn., Stanford U., 1981, MA in Sociology, 1983, PhD in Edn., 1985. Tchr. jr. and sr. h.s., 1969—80; rsch. asst. Ctr. for Ednl. Rsch., Stanford U., Calif., 1982—85; assoc. prof. edn. Stanford (Calif.) U., 1999—, and dir., tchr. edn. program. Vis. asst./assoc. prof. Inst. for Advancement of Social Integration in Schs., Bar-Ilan U., Israel, 1986—91. Mem. editl. bd.: European Jour. for Intercultural Edn. Office: Stanford U Sch Edn 485 Lasuen Mall Stanford CA 94305-3096*

LOTAS, JUDITH PATTON, advertising executive; b. Iowa City, Apr. 23, 1942; d. John Henry and Jane (Vandike) Patton; children: Amanda Bell, Alexandra Vandike. BA, Fla. State U., 1964. Copywriter Liller, Neal, Battle and Lindsey Advt., Atlanta, 1964-67, Grey Advt., N.Y.C., 1967-72; creative group head SSC&B Advt., N.Y.C., 1972-74, assoc. creative dir., 1974-79, v.p., 1975-79, sr. v.p., 1979-82, exec. creative dir., 1982-86; founding ptnr. Lotas Minard Patton McIver, Inc., N.Y.C., 1986—. Fundraiser Nat. Coalition Homeless, N.Y.C., 1986—; mem. creative rev. bd. Partnership Drug-Free Am.; rep. Afghan Am. Peace Corp.; bd. dirs. Samuel Wasman Cancer Rsch. Found., N.Y.C., 1981—88, Women's Venture Fund, 1995—; active scholarship fund raising, 2004. Named Woman of Achievement, YWCA; named one of Advt.'s 100 Best Women, Ad Age, 1989; recipient Clio award, Venice Film Festival award, Graphics award, Am. Inst. Graphic Artists, 1970, Effie award, Grad. of Distinction award, Fla. State U., 1993. Mem.: Ad. Coun. (mem. creative rev. bd. 1994—, bd. dirs. 1995—), Advt. Women N.Y. (bd. dirs. 1981—87, 1st v.p. 1984—87, Advt. Woman of the Yr. 1993), Kappa Alpha Theta. Democrat. Office Phone: 212-288-5676. E-mail: jlotas@earthlink.net, jlotas@lpny.com.

LOTHIAN, JAMES ROBERT, economist, educator; b. Queens, NY, Apr. 23, 1945; s. James Robert and Margaret Virginia Lothian; m. Judith Ann McLaughlin, June 21, 1969; children: James Robert, Mary Nora Gibbons, John Andrew, Ann Ruth, Elizabeth Julia. BA Cum Laude, Cath. U. Am., 1967; MA, U. Chgo., 1969, PhD, 1973. Economist Citibank, New York, NY, 1972—76, asst. v.p., 1976—78, v.p., 1978—87; vis. prof. NYU, N.Y.C., 1988—90; prof. Fordham U., N.Y.C., 1990—97, disting. prof. fin., 1997—. Vis. scholar Fed. Res. Bank. Atlanta; cons. Nat. Bur. Econ. Rsch., N.Y.C., 1976—78, rsch assoc., 1978—82; vis. scholar Internat. Monetary Fund, Washington, 1978—82; mem. editl. bd. Jour. of Internat. Money and Fin., 1982—86, editor, 1986—; North Am. corr. Brandsma Rev., Dun Llaoghaire, Ireland, 1996—; vis. scholar Maastricht U., Netherlands, 1998; sci. com. Internat. Tor Vergata Conf. on Banking and Fin., Rome, 2001—; vis. lectr. U. Coll. Dublin, 2004. Author: The Internat. Transmission of Inflation; contbr. articles to profl. jours. Recipient mem., Phi Beta Kappa, 1966, Gladys and Henry Crown Faculty Excellence award, Fordham U. Grad. Sch. Bus., 1998; fellow Richard Weaver, Intercollegiate Studies Inst., 1968, 1969. Mem.: Mont Pelerin Soc., Cliometric Soc., Fin. Mgmt. Assn., Am. Econ. Assn. Office: Fordham U Sch Bus 113 West 60th St New York NY 10023 Office Phone: 212-636-6147. Personal E-mail: jrmlothian@aol.com. Business E-Mail: lothian@fordham.edu.

LOTHROP, JOY D., corporate compliance officer; d. George and Rose Lothrop. Nursing diploma, Children's Hosp. Med. Ctr., Boston, 1976; BSBA in Mgmt./Fin., Northeastern U., 1987; MBA in Fin., Bentley Coll., 1989. RN Mass., cert. profl. utilization rev. Patient care svcs., adminstrv. supr. Santa Maria Hosp., Cambridge, Mass., 1984—89; DON Lake Highlands Nursing Ctr., Clermont, Fla., 1994—95, Southlake Nursing and Rehab., Jacksonville, Fla., 1995; Medicare specialist Horizon Healthcare, Albuquerque, 1996—97; Medicare cons. Premiere Mgmt. Assn., Deltona, Fla., 1997—98, Sun Healthcare, Albuquerque, 1998—99, The MCR Group, Orlando, Fla., 1999—2000; dir. corp. compliance Ctrl. Vt. Med. Ctr., Berlin, 2000—. Mem.: Healthcare Compliance Assn. (region I steering com. 2001—), Healthcare Fin. Mgmt. Assn., Am. Healthcare Lawyers Assn., Assn. Fraud Examiners. Avocations: gardening, painting. Office: Ctrl Vt Med Ctr Fisher Rd Barre VT 05641 Office Phone: 802-371-5955.

LOTITO, NICHOLAS ANTHONY, lawyer; b. Neptune, NJ, June 19, 1949; s. Nicholas and Grace (Pascazio) L. BA, Emory U., 1971; JD, U. Va., 1975. Bar: Ga. 1975, U.S. Dist. Ct. (no. dist.) Ga., U.S. Ct. Appeals (4th, 5th, 11 cirs.), U.S. Supreme Ct., 2001. Atty. FTC, Atlanta, 1975-76; trial atty. Antitrust Div. U.S. Dept. Justice, Atlanta, 1976-82; of counsel Fierer & Westby, Atlanta, 1983-89; ptnr. Davis, Zipperman, Kirschenbaum & Lotito, Atlanta, 1989—. Chmn. World Literacy Initiative, Inc., 2002—. Contbr. articles to profl. jours. Chairperson World Literacy Initiative, inc., 2002—. Mem. NACDL, ABA (criminal and antitrust sects.), Ga. Assn. Criminal Def. Lawyers (past pres., exec. com., chmn. amicus com.), Lamar Inn of Ct. Democrat. Avocations: sports, writing. Home: 1055 Alta Ave NE Atlanta GA 30307-2512 Office: Davis Zipperman Kirschenbaum & Lotito 918 Ponce De Leon Ave NE Atlanta GA 30306-4212 Office Phone: 404-688-2000. E-mail: nick@dzkl.com.

LOTKO, WILLIAM, engineering educator; m. Mary K. Hudson; 2 children. B in engring. physics, U. Kans.; M in engring. physics, U. Mo.; PhD in plasma physics, UCLA, 1981. Mem. faculty Dartmouth Coll. Thayer Sch. Engring., 1984—, prin. investigator Sun-Earth Connection Theory program, co-investigator Ctr. for Integrated Space Weather Modeling, sr. assoc. dean, 1999—2004, interim dean, 2004—. Mem. bd. NH Space Grant Consortium, 1991—; vis. scientist Max Planck Institut for Extraterrestrische Physik, Germany, Space Sciences Lab., U. Calif., Berkeley, Los Alamos Nat. Lab. Author: numerous articles and papers; contbg. author (book) Auroral Plasma Physics, 2003. Mem.: IEEE, Am. Soc. Engring. Edn., Am. Geophys. Union, AAAS. Office: Thayer Sch Engring Dartmouth Coll 8000 Cummings Hall Hanover NH 03755-8000

LOTLIKAR, SAROJINI DATTARAM, retired university librarian; b. Bombay, Hindu, India, Apr. 26, 1930; arrived in USA, 1969; d. Dattaram V. and Laxmibai D. Lotlikar. BA with honors, Bombay U., India, 1951; diploma libr. sci., Bombay Lib. Assn., 1966; MSLS, Villanova U., Pa., 1970; student, Internat. Grad. Summer Sch., Aberystwyth, Wales, UK, 1985. Asst. libr. Khalsa Coll., Bombay, 1966—69; cons. Balodyan sch. libr., 1966—; catalog libr. Ganser Libr., Millersville U., Pa., 1971—; ret., 1997. Emerita asst. prof. librarianship Millersville Univ., Pa. Contbr. chapters to books Program Souvenir of Cultures, 1992. Grantee grant, State Sys. Higher Edn., 1994. Mem.: Phila. Area Rsch. Librs. Exch., Assn. Pa. Coll., Univ. Prof., Rsch. Libr., ALA. Office: Helen Ganser Libr N George St Millersville PA 17551

LOTMAN, ARLINE JOLLES, lawyer; b. Phila., Feb. 5, 1937; d. Samuel Clearsfeld and Sarah (Shiffrin) Jolles; married, Sept. 27, 1959 (deceased); 1 child, Maurice. BA, Temple U., 1960, JD, 1977, MA in Comm., 1984. Bar: Pa. 1977, D.C. 1980, U.S. Dist. Ct. (ea. dist.) Pa. 1983, U.S. Ct. Appeals (3d cir.) 1987, U.S. Supreme Ct. 1997. Exec. dir. gov.'s office Commonwealth of Pa., Harrisburg, Pa., 1972-74; assoc. Adler Barish Levin & Creskoff, Phila., 1978-80; pvt. practice pvt. practice, 1980—. Lectr. in field; spl. counsel Greitzer and Locks, 1998-2000; mem. merit selection panel for magistrate judge appointment for U.S. Dist. Ct. (ea. dist.) Pa., 2003-04. Commr. Home Rule Charter Commn., Phila., 1993—95. Mem. ABA (ho. of dels. 1992-94, standing com. on election law 1997-2000), Phila. Bar Assn. (chair jud. commn. 1991-92, chair bar news media com. 2004), Pa. Bar Assn. (ho. of dels. 1988-91, zone 1), DC Bar Assn., Nat. Assn. Bond Lawyers (nat. bond opinion com.), Temple Law Alumni Assn. (pres. 1993-95). Home and Office: 3 Pkwy Ste 1320 1601 Cherry St Philadelphia PA 19102 Office Phone: 215-825-1469. E-mail: ajlotman@aol.com.

LOTOCKY, WALTER LUBOMYR, music educator; b. Manhattan, N.Y., Jan. 29, 1959; s. Michael Lotocki and Rose Wasylyna Motruk; m. Anna Mary Maksymowich, Nov. 14, 1987; children: Kathryn, Tatiana, Daria, Taisa, Sonya, Wolodymyr. BS in Music, Mercy Coll., 1981; BS in Music, Westchester Conservatory Music, White Plains, N.Y., 1981. Rt. sales assoc. Haagen-Dazs, Miami, Fla., 1992—99; account exec. Lynk Sys., Inc., Ft. Lauderdale, Fla., 1999—2000; tchr. music Pompano Beach H.S., Fla., 2001—. Fellow: Assn. Women in Sci.; mem.: APHA (Profl. Merit award statistics sect. 1993), Am. Statis. Assn., Biometric Soc. (pres. ENAR 1991), Caucus for Women in Stats. (pres. 1993—94), Soc. Clin. Trials. Ukrainian Catholic. Avocations: scuba diving, swimming, fishing, boating. Home: 9015 SW 51 Pl Cooper City FL 33328 Office: Pompano Beach HS 1400 NE 6th St Pompano Beach FL 33060 Personal E-mail: wlotocky@yahoo.com.

LOTSTEIN, JAMES IRVING, lawyer; b. Steubenville, Ohio, Jan. 27, 1944; s. Jack and Dorothy (Nach) L.; m. Paulette L. Gutcheon, June 25, 1972; children: Melissa A., Amanda J. BSBA, Northwestern U., 1965; JD, U. Conn., 1968. Bar: Conn. 1969, U.S. Ct. Appeals (2d cir.) 1971, U.S. Supreme Ct. 1972. From assoc. to ptnr. Hoppin, Carey & Powell, Hartford, Conn., 1969-86; ptnr. Cummings & Lockwood, Hartford, 1986—96, ptnr.-in-charge, 1988-95, chmn. dept. Mergers and Acquisitions Practice Group, 2001—03; ptnr. Edwards & Angell, LLP, Hartford, Conn., 2003—. Adv. bd. Conn. chpt. Nat. Assn. Corp. Dirs.; adv. com. Hartford (Conn.) chpt. Am. Soc. Corp. Secs. Author: An Introduction to the Connecticut Business Corporation Act, 1994, Ten Things You Can Do Now to Prepare for the New Connecticut Business Corporation Act, Connecticut Business Corporation Act Sourcebook, New Indemnification Provisions of the Connecticut Business Corporation Act, 1997, Why Choose Connecticut? Advantages of the Connecticut Business Corporation Act Over the Delaware General Corporation Law, 2000, Update on Connecticut Corporation Law, Corporate Governance of Connecticut Nonprofit Corporations, 2002, Amendments to the Connecticut Business Corporation Act, 2003, Commonly Negotiated Provisions in Business Acquisitions, 2005. Trustee Conn. Pub. Broadcasting, Inc.; mem. adv. bd. Conn. chpt. Nat. Assn. Corp. Dirs.; mem. adv. com. Hartford chpt. Am. Soc. Corp. Secs.; mem. Sec. of State's bus. adv. com. State of Conn.; active Am. Coll. Investment Counsel; mem. Econ. Devel. Agy., Canton, Conn., 2001— 1st lt. JAGC, USAR, 1968-74. Mem. ABA (chmn. dirs. and officers task force 1996-2002, mem. corp. laws com. 1992), Conn. Bar Assn. (chmn. mcpl. law and govtl. svc. com. 1981-82, chmn. bus. law sect. 1990-92, co-chmn. Conn. bus. corp. act task force 1993-98). Office: Edwards & Angell LLP 90 State House Sq 9th Fl Hartford CT 06103

LOTT, ALFRED DAVIS, assistant city manager; b. Detroit, Mar. 7, 1954; s. George Edward Jr. and Muriel Davis L.; children: Alfred Davis II, Ingrid Nicole; m. Carolyn Gibson Lott, May 15, 1999. BS in Polit. Sci., Tuskegee U., 1976; MPA, U. Ctrl. Tex., 1994. Commd. 2nd lt. U.S. Army, 1976, advanced through grades to lt. col., 1998; comdr. Aviation Tng. Co., Fort Rucker, Ala., 1985-86; ops. officer Aviation Bn. Fort Hold, Killeen, Tex., 1991-92; divsn. chief aviation divsn. U.S. Army III Corps, Killeen, Tex., 1993; chief pub. affairs WWII com. Dept. Def. Pentagon, Washington, 1993-95; chief pub. affairs U.S. Army, L.A., 1995-97; pub. affairs plans officer Dept. Def. Pentagon, Washington, 1997-98; asst. city mgr. City of College Park, Md., 1998—2002; pub. works dir. City of Takoma Park, Md., 2002—. Active Neighborhood Watch, College Park, 1998—. Mem. Am. Legion, Internat. Assn. Bus. Communicators, Ret. Officers Assn., ICMA. Democrat. Methodist. Avocation: chess. Office: Pub Works Dept 7500 Maple Ave Takoma Park MD 20910

LOTT, BRET, literature and language professor, writer; b. Hawthorne, Calif., Oct. 8, 1958; s. Wilman Sequoia and Barbara John (Holmes) L.; m. Melanie Kai Swank, June 28, 1980; children: Zebulun Holmes, Jacob Daynes. BA in English, Calif. State U., Long Beach, 1981; MFA in Creative Writing, U. Mass., 1984. Instr. Ohio State U., Columbus, 1984-86; prof. English, Coll. of Charleston, SC, 1986—2004. Mem. faculty Vt. Coll., Montpelier, 1994-2000, dir. faculty, 2000—. Author: (novels) The Man Who Owned Vermont, 1987, Stranger's House, 1988, Jewel, 1991 (Oprah Book Club selection 1999), Reed's Beach, 1993, The Hunt Club, 1998, A Song I Knew By Heart, 2004, The Difference Between Women and Men, 2005, (memoir) Fathers, Sons and Brothers, 1997; editor, The Southern Review, 2004-. Cubmaster Boy Scouts Am., Mt. Pleasant, S.C., 1990-97; mem. James Island Christian Sch. Bd., Charleston, 2000—. Recipient Pushcart prize Pushcart Press, 2000, Chancellor's medal U. Mass., 2000, Nat. Media award Nat. Down Syndrome Congress, 2000. Mem. Assoc. Writing Programs. Republican. Baptist. Avocations: golf, fine cigars. Office: Southern Review La State Univ Baton Rouge LA 70803*

LOTT, CHERYL LYNN, special education educator; b. San Antonio, Jan. 1, 1958; d. Waymond Maurice and Yvonne Pearl Wilson; children: Charmaine Yvette, Courtney Brichelle, Kia Yvonne. BA in Edn., Incarnate Word Coll., San Antonio, 1983. Cert. tchr. in elem. spl. edn./speech Tex. Resource tchr. San Antonio Sch. Dist., 1985—. Mem. campus leadership team San Antonio Ind. Sch. Dist. Author: (children's book) My Firefly Friend, 2003. Democrat. Baptist. Avocations: art, skating, dance, writing, stamp collecting/philately. Home: # 3402 2554 NE Loop 410 San Antonio TX 78217 Office: San Antonio Sch Dist 1717 W Magnolia St San Antonio TX 78201 Office Phone: 210-732-4741.

LOTT, MARLEY, lawyer; b. Greenwood, Miss., Aug. 27, 1947; BA with honors, Hollings Coll., 1969; JD cum laude, Harvard U., 1977. Bar: Tex. 1978. Ptnr., global projects & mem. exec. com. Baker & Botts L.L.P., Houston. Bd. dir. Contemporary Arts Mus., Houston; mem. exec. com. & vice-chmn. projects Friends of Herman Park, Houston. Named a Texas Super Lawyer, Texas Monthly mag. & Law & Politics mag., 2003—04. Mem. ABA, State Bar Tex., Houston Bar Assn., Phi Beta Kappa. Office: Baker Botts LLP One Shell Plz 910 Louisiana St Houston TX 77002-4995 Office Phone: 713-229-1666. Office Fax: 713-229-7766. Business E-Mail: marley.lott@bakerbotts.com.

LOTT, R(OBERT) ALLEN, musicologist; b. San Antonio, Feb. 26, 1956; s. John Claude Lott and Katie Pearl Little; m. Carolyn Ann Armstrong, July 25, 1987 (dec. Aug. 14, 1999); 1 child, Andrew Emory. MusB in Piano, Trinity U., San Antonio, 1977; PhD in Musicology, CUNY, 1986. Rsch. asst. Bklyn. Coll., 1984—86; prof. Southwestern Bapt. Theol. Sem., Ft. Worth, 1986—. Author: From Paris to Peoria: How European Piano Virtuosos Brought Classical Music to the American Heartland, 2003; contbr. articles to profl. jours. Mem.: Am. Musicological Soc., Soc. for Am. Music (sec. 2003—). Office: Southwestern Baptist TheologicalSeminary PO Box 22390 Fort Worth TX 76122-0390 Office Phone: 817-923-1921 3250.

LOTT, RONNIE (RONALD MANDEL LOTT), retired professional football player, television broadcaster; b. Albuquerque, May 8, 1959; BS in Pub. Adminstrn., U. So. Calif., 1981. With San Francisco 49ers, 1981—90, L.A. Raiders, 1991—93, N.Y. Jets, 1993—94, Kansas City Chiefs, 1994—95; analyst NFL Fox Broadcasting Co., Beverly Hills, Calif., 1996—. Founder All Stars Helping Kids, 1989. Named to Sporting News Coll. All-Am. team, 1980, Pro Bowl team, 1981—84, 1986—91, Sporting News All-Pro team, 1981, 1987, 1990.*

LOTT, TRENT, senator; b. Grenada, Miss., Oct. 9, 1941; s. Chester P. and Iona (Watson) L.; m. Patricia E. Thompson, Dec. 27, 1964; children—Chester T., Jr., Tyler Elizabeth. B.P.A., U. Miss., 1963, JD, 1967. Bar: Miss. 1967. Assoc. Bryan & Gordon, Pascagoula, Miss., 1967; adminstrv. asst. to Congressman William M. Colmer, 1968-72; mem. 93d-100th Congresses from 5th Miss. dist., 1973-89; Rep. whip 97th-100th Congresses from 5th Miss. dist., mem. Ho. Rules com.; U.S. senator from Miss., 1989—; majority whip 104th Congress, 1995—96; majority leader 104th-105th Congress, 1996—2002; mem. Senate armed svcs. com., budget com., energy, natural resource. Field rep. for U. Miss., 1963-65; acting alumni sec. Ole Miss Alumni Assn., 1966-67; named as observer from House to Geneva Arms Control talks; chmn. Commerce, Sci. & Transp.; mem. Senate Republican Policy Com., Commerce, Fin. Com., 1996, Rules Com., 1996. Author: (autobiography) Herding Cats, A Lifetime in Politics, 2005. Recipient Golden Bulldog award, Guardian of Small Bus. award. Mem. ABA, Jackson County Bar Assn., Sigma Nu, Phi Alpha Delta. Lodges: Mason. Republican. Baptist. Office: 487 Russell Senate Office Bldg Washington DC 20510-0001 also: Ste 127 911 Jackson Ave Oxford MS 38655*

LOTTA, TOM (ANTHONY TOM LOTTA), artist; b. Rochester, N.Y., Mar. 28, 1924; s. Joseph and Julia (Roncone) L.; m. Rosemary Alionello, June 18, 1949; children: Tom, Karen. AS, Rochester Inst. Tech., 1950. Freelance artist, Rochester, 1951—. Committeeman Rep. Cen. Com., Greece, N.Y., 1970—. Sgt. U.S. Army, 1943-45. Named to, Boxing Hall of Fame, Can., 1977, Rochester Boxing Hall of Fame; recipient numerous awards for paintings, 58 awards in the arts. Mem. Am. Watercolor Soc., Soc. Illustrators, Rochester Art Club (pres. 1976-77). Roman Catholic. Studio: 1337 Beach Ave Rochester NY 14612-1846

LOTTER, CHARLES ROBERT, retired lawyer; b. 1937; married. BA in Math., St. Johns U., 1959, JD, 1962; LLM, NYU, 1969. With anti-trust div. U.S. Dept. Justice, 1962-65; with Revere Copper & Brass, Inc., 1965-69, Del E. Webb Corp., 1969-70, Louis O. Kelso, 1970-71; joined J.C. Penney Co. Inc., LA, 1971, gen. atty. Washington, 1974—84, NYC, 1984—85, assoc. gen. counsel Plano, Tex., 1985—87, sr. v.p., sec., gen. counsel, 1987—93, exec. v.p., sec., gen. counsel, 1993—2005. Mem. legal affairs coun. U.S. C. of C.; bd. dirs. Legal Svcs. of No. Tex. Inc.; mem. adv. bd. Inst. Internat. and Comparative Law Ctr. Am. and Internat. Law; bd. dirs. Eckerd Corp., 1996—, J.C. Penney Corp. Inc., 2002—. Mem. adv. bd. Corp. Counsel Law Review Symposium So. Methodist U., Corp. Counsel Inst. Georgetown U. Law Ctr.; with USAFR, 1962—64, USNR, 1964—70. Mem.: Texas Bar Assn., State Bar of Tex., State Bar of Calif., State Bar of Ariz., NY State Bar, DC Bar, Am. Corp. Counsel. Assn. (corp. governance com.), ABA.

LOTTIE, ADRIAN JEROME, public information officer, consultant; s. Arthur Julius and Lou Willie Lottie. BA Psychology, BA Economics, Wayne State U., Detroit, 1985, MA Economics, 1988, PhD, 1996. Asst. prof. Ea. Mich. U., Ypsilanti, Mich., 1992—2002; pres. Adrian J. Lottie & Assocs. Bus. & Econ. Consultants, Detroit, 1996—; assoc. dir. Inst. Diversity and Bus. Ea. Mich. U., Ypsilanti, Mich., 1996—2002, assoc. dir. African Am. Ctr. for applied rsch. and svcs., 2000—, assoc. prof., 2002—. Cons. Assoc. Gen. Contractors of Am. Greater Detroit Br. Workforce Devel./Edn. Com., Southfield, Mich., 1997—, Gt. Lakes Constrn. Alliance, Detroit, 1999—, Mich. Econ. Devel. Corp. Office of Econ. Independence and Entrepreneurship, Detroit, 2000—02; evaluation cons. Mich. Inst. for Nonviolence Edn., Detroit, 2002—. Contbr. articles to profl. jours. Bd. dirs. Internat. Inst. of Met., Detroit, 1997—, pres., 2001—02, Erma Henderson Found., Detroit, 2001—02. Specialist 5 U.S. Army, 1966—68, Ft. Knox, Ky. Fellow Minority Grad. Fellow, Skillman Found., 1985- 1988; grantee Project Start, New Detroit Inc., 1996-1999, Project Connect, Bank One, 1996-2001, Rsch. Excellence Fund, Ea. Mich. U., 1996-2003. Mem.: Am. Soc. Pub. Administrators, Acad. Polit. Sci., Am. Econ. Assn., Am. Polit. Sci. Assn. Independent. Protestant. Avocations: travel, swimming, hiking, golf, reading. Office: Eastern Michigan Univ 601-R Pray-Harrold Ypsilanti MI 48197 Office Phone: 313-231-4114. Personal E-mail: AdrianLottie@aol.com. E-mail: adrian.lottie@emich.edu.

LOTWIN, STANFORD GERALD, lawyer; b. NYC, June 23, 1930; s. Herman and Rita (Saltzman) L.; m. Judy Scott, Oct. 15, 1994; children: Lori Hope, David. BS, Bklyn. Coll., 1951, LLB, 1954, LLM, 1957. Bar: N.Y. 1954, U.S. Supreme Ct. 1961, Pa. 1986. Ptnr. Blank Rome LLP, N.Y.C., 1987—. Served with U.S. Army, 1954-56. Fellow Am. Acad. Matrimonial Lawyers (bd. of mgrs. 1984—); mem. NY State Bar Assn. (family law sect.), NY County Trial Lawyers (lectr. 1980—), Internat. Acad. Matrimonial Attys. (referee Commn. on Judicial Conduct). Office: 405 Lexington Ave New York NY 10174-0002 E-mail: slotwin@blankrome.com.

LOTZ, DENTON, minister, church official; b. Flushing, N.Y., Jan. 18, 1939; s. John Milton and Adeline Helen (Kettell) L.; m. Janice Robinson, Mar. 15, 1970; children: John-Paul, Alena, Carsten. BA, U. N.C., 1961; STB, Harvard Div. Sch., 1966; ThD, U. Hamburg, Fed. Republic Germany, 1970; DD (hon.), Campbell U., 1982, Ea. Bapt. Sem., 1991, Alderson-Broadus, 1995, Dallas Bapt. U., 2000, Moscow Theol. Sem., 2004; DD, Ctrl. Baptist Theol. Sem., 2005; DD (hon.), Internat. Baptist Sem., Prague, 2005. Prof. mission Bapt. Sem., Ruschlikon, Switzerland, 1972-80; dir. evangelism Bapt. World Alliance, McLean, Va., 1980-88, gen. sec., 1988—. Fraternal rep. Am. Bapt. Internat. Ministries To Ea. Europe, Valley Forge, Pa., 1970-80. Author, editor: Baptists in the USSR, 1987; editor: Spring Has Returned to China, 1987. V.p. CARE, N.Y.C., 1981. 1st lt. USMC, 1961-63. Mem. Internat. Religious Liberty Assn. (pres. 1990-91, 96-97, 03-). Office: Bapt World Alliance 405 N Washington St Falls Church VA 22046

LOTZ, GEORGE MICHAEL, retired computer company executive, graphics designer, photographer; b. Balt., Aug. 28, 1928; s. Michael Henry and Mina Catherine Lotz; m. Anna Mae Carlson, July 21, 1951; 1 child, Georgeanna. Student, Md. Inst. Art, 1956-58, Johns Hopkins U., 1957-58, Catonsville C.C., 1975, Essex C.C., 1976-78. Mech. draftsman, designer Sinclair Scott Canning House Machinery Co., Balt., 1948-50; illustrator, designer Comm. divsn. Bendix Corp., Towson, Md., 1950-69, supr. graphic arts, photography, 1969-73, supr. computer graphics and drafting, 1972-81, mgr. tech., publs., engring. libr., transformer design, multilith dept., spl. svcs. lab., engring. print dept. graphic arts & photography depts., 1981-83; mgr. elec. pub. & tech. svcs. depts. Allied Signal Co. (formerly Bendix Corp.), Towson, 1983-93, ret., 1993; owner George M. Lotz Designer/Photographer, 1993—. Art dir., pres. Glen Arm Graphic, 1963-74; advisor Md. State Dept. Art Edn., 1973-78, U. Md. Coll. Human Ecology, 1981—, Essex C.C. Computer Graphics, 1981—, C.C. Balt. Graphics, 1978—, Goucher Coll., 1991—; mem. panel Nat. Endowment Arts, 1977-78; conf. chmn. Indsl. Graphics Internat., U. Md., 1974, adv. Coll. of Human Ecology & Art Design, 1981—; advisor graphic arts C.C. Balt., 1978—, Essex C.C., 1981—; tchr. tech. writing Goucher Coll.; guest spkr. various locals colls., 1973, 77, profl. groups, 1967-78. Contbr. articles on graphic art and edn. to profl. jours. Judge Jr. Miss. Pagent, Reisterstown, Md., 1971, 72. With USNR, 1947-48. Recipient 38 nat. awards for art direction, graphics design including 1st pl. newsletter design Nat. Assn. Indsl. Artists, 1970, 1st pl. award Assoc. Printing Industries Am., 1976, award of excellence Printing Industries Md., 1978, 79, 1st pl. in photography 1982 World's Fair Design Competition. Mem. Indsl. Graphics Internat. (pres. 1975-77, exec. dir. 1980—, award of merit 13th ann. design competition for promotional photography Vancouver, B.C., Can., 1986), Coun. Comm. Soc. (dir. 1984-85), Advt. Assn. Balt. (dir. 1971-78), Soc. Tech. Comm. (1st place award 1977), Bendix Emblem Club, Bendix Mgmt. Club (pres. 1982-83), Balt. Camera Club. Home and Office: 11212 Old Carriage Rd Glen Arm MD 21057-9415

LOTZE, BARBARA, retired physicist; b. Jan. 4, 1924; came to U.S., 1961, naturalized, 1967. d. Matyas and Borbala (Toth) Kalo; m. Dieter P. Lotze, Oct. 6, 1958 (dec. Dec. 1987); m. Herbert L. Retcofsky, July 1998. Applied Math. Diploma with honors, Eotvos Lorand U. Scis., Budapest, Hungary, 1956; PhD, Innsbruck (Austria) U., 1961. Mathematician Hungarian Cen. Statis. Bur., Budapest, 1955-56; tchr. math. Iselsberg, Austria, 1959-60; from asst. prof. physics to assoc. prof. to prof. Allegheny Coll., 1963-90, prof. emeritus, 1990—, chmn. dept., 1981-84. Lectr. in history of physics; spkr. to civic groups. Editor: Making Contributions: An Historical Overview of Women's Role in Physics, 1984; co-editor: The First War Between Socialist States: The Hungarian Revolution of 1956 and Its Impact, 1984; contbr. articles to profl. jours. Mem. AAUW, Am. Phys. Soc. (mem. com. internat. freedom of scientists 1993-95), Am. Inst. Physics (mem. adv. com. history of physics 1994-97), Am. Assn. Physics Tchrs. (coun., sect. rep. Western Pa. 1978-86, chmn. com. on women in physics 1983-84, com. internat. physics edn. 1991-93, com. history and philosophy of physics 1996-98, Disting. Svc. award 1986, cert. of appreciation 1988), Am. Hungarian Educators Assn. (pres. 1980-82). Home: 2269 Watchfield Dr South Park PA 15129-8977

LOTZENHISER, GEORGE WILLIAM, musician, educator, academic administrator, composer; b. Spokane, Wash., May 16, 1923; m. Kathryn Tuttle, 1944; children: William (dec.), Jon. BA cum laude, Ea. Wash. U., 1946, BEd in Social Sci., 1947; MusM, U. Mich., 1948; EdD, U. Oreg., 1956. Prof. music U. Ariz., Tucson, 1948-60; prof. Ea. Wash. U., Cheney, 1960-83, dir. H.S. creative arts summer series, 1960-83; dean Ea. Wash. U. Sch. Fine Arts, Cheney, 1960-83, dean emeritus, 1983—. Cons. and lectr. in field; tchg. fellow U. Mich., 1947-48, U. Oreg., 1955-56. Author: A Study of Faculty Loads in Member Schools of the National Association of Schools of Music, 1963, A Study of the Selection Process of Administrators of the Fine Arts in Colleges and Universities in the U.S., 1970, Music 200: A Programmed Music Theory Text; numerous solo and ensemble compositions; contbr. articles to profl. jours.; profl. condr./trombonist symphony, opera, musical theatre, ballet, circus, etc. Mem. Wash. State Music Adv. Com., 1967-83, exec. com. Alliance for Arts Edn., 1972-83; mem. Spokane Riverfront Festival of the Arts, 1976-78, Allied Arts of Wash. State, 1977-83. Served to rear adm. USNR, 1942-82. Decorated Legion of Merit; named Disting. Eagle Scout, Boy Scouts Am. Mem. ASCAP, Nat. Assn. Schs. Music (accreditation com. chmn. 1960—), Nat. Music Educators Research Council, N.W. Assn. Accreditation Com., Western Assn. Schs. and Colls. Com. Congregationalist. Home: PO Box 1528 Coupeville WA 98239-1528 E-mail: glotz@whidbey.net.

LOU, HANQING, research scientist; b. Beijing, Dec. 26, 1973; arrived in U.S., 2000; d. Yuannien Lou and Weixiang Li; m. Huiyong Liao, Oct. 1, 2001. BS, Beijing U., 1997, MS, 2000; postgrad., U. Del., 2005—. Tchg. asst. Beijing U., 1997—2000, Tex. A&M U., College Station, 2000—01; rsch. asst. U. Del., Newark, 2001—. Contbr. articles to profl. jours. Mem.: IEEE. Avocations: music, ping pong/table tennis, reading, cooking. Office Phone: 302-831-3610.

LOU, JANET, electrical engineer, researcher; BS, MIT, 1989—93; MS in Engring., U. Mich., 1993—95, PhD, 1995—2000. Rsch. physicist SFA, Inc., Largo, Md., 2000—. Contbr. numerous articles to sci. jours. and conferences. Grantee Horace H. Rackham Travel Grant, Rackham Sch. Grad. Studies, U. Mich., 1997—2000; NSF Sci. and Tech. Ctr. fellowship, U. Mich., 1993—94. Mem.: Lasers and Electro-Optics Soc., Inst. for Elec. & Electronics Engrs. Achievements include two patent applications being processed: (with Thomas F. Carruthers) High speed electro-optic clock recovery circuit, filed 2001; (with Thomas Clark, Marc Currie, Thomas Carruthers) Multiple wavelength pulsed source, filed 2002.

LOU, JIANZHONG, chemical engineer, educator; arrived in U.S., 1987; s. Zongshi Liu and Huixin Lou; m. Hong Yin, Apr. 21, 1991; children: Bob, Lily. BS in Chem. Engring., Zhejiang U. Tech., 1982; PhD in Chem. Engring., U. Utah, 1994. Sr. rsch. staff Clopay Plastics Co., Cin., 1999—2001; supr. staff engr. Tate & Lyle N.Am., Arabi, La., 1994—99; assoc. prof. mech. and chem. engring. N.C. Agrl. and Tech. State U., Greensboro, NC, 2001—. Recipient Excellence in Mentoring award, NASA SHARP Program, 2003—04; grantee, NSF, 2003, USDA, 2003; scholar, Am. Soc. for Engring. Edn., 2002. Mem.: AIChE (pres. 2002—03, John J. McKetta grants 2002—03, Planning grant 2002—03), Piedmont Coun. Engring. and Tech. Socs. (treas. 2003—05), Soc. Plastics Engrs. (founder and advisor 2003—04), Greensboro (N.C.) Chinese Assn. (v.p. 2004—05). Achievements include invention of ultrahigh selectivity filled polymer membranes; discovery of rheological percolation in filled polymers. Home: 2802 Norwell Ct Oak Ridge ND 27310 Office: 1601 E Market St Greensboro NC 27411 Office Phone: 336-334-7620. Personal E-mail: jlou888@yahoo.com. E-mail: lou@ncat.edu.

LOU, LIZA, artist; Student, San Francisco Art Inst. One-woman shows include Santa Monica Mus. Art, Bass Mus. Art, Miami, Kemper Mus. Contmporary Art, Kansas City, Ctr. Estudis Art Contemporani, Barcelona, exhibited in group shows at New Mus., NYC, Heinie Onstad Kunstenter, Norway, Victoria and Albert Mus., London, Fondation Cartier, Paris. Fellow MacArthur Found. fellow, 2002; grantee MacArtur Found. Office: c/o Elizabeth Schwartz/Deitch Projects 76 Grand St New York NY 10013*

LOU, WENJING, engineering educator; arrived in U.S., 1999; B Engring., Xi'an (China) Jiaotong U., 1993, M Engring., 1996; PhD, U. Fla., 2003. Rsch. engr. Nanyang Technol. U., Singapore, 1997—99; asst. prof. Worcester (Mass.) Poly. Inst., 2003—. Contbr. articles to profl. jours., chpts. to books. Mem.: IEEE, Tau Beta Pi. Office: Worcester Poly Inst 100 Institute Rd Worcester MA 01609 Office Phone: 508-831-5338.

LOU, YIMING, chemical engineer; B in engring., Zhejiang U., 1993—97, M in engring., 1997—2000; PhD, UCLA, 2000—04. Rsch. assoc. Dept. Chem. Engring. UCLA, 2000—04; sr. engr. Advanced Projects Rsch. Inc., 2004—. Presenter in field. Contbr. scientific papers. Recipient O. Hugo Shuck Best Paper award, Am. Automatic Control Coun., 2004; U. Fellowship, UCLA, 2000, Rockwell scholarship, Rockwell, 1997. Mem.: IEEE, Am. Inst. Chem. Engrs., Sigma Xi. Home: 1140 Golden Springs Dr Unit A Diamond Bar CA 91765 Office: Advanced Projects Rsch Inc 1925 McKinley Ave Ste B La Verne CA 91750 Office Phone: 909-392-1103. Personal E-mail: louyiming@yahoo.com. E-mail: yiming.lou@advancedprojects.com.

LOUARD, RITA JEAN, endocrinologist, educator; b. N.Y.C., June 15, 1954; d. Vernon Benjamin and Agnes Anthony L. AB, Bryn Mawr Coll., 1976; MD, Columbia U., 1981. Diplomate Am. Bd. Internal Medicine and Endocrinology. Intern, then resident Boston City Hosp., 1981-84; clin. instr. Peninsula Hosp., Far Rockaway, N.Y., 1984-85; attending physician Harlem Hosp., N.Y.C., 1985-86; instr. clin. medicine Columbia U. Coll. Physicians and Surgeons, N.Y.C., 1985-86; fellow in endocrinology Yale U., New Haven, 1986-89, assoc. rsch. scientist, 1989-94; med. dir. eastern blind rehab. svc. West Haven (Conn.) VA Med. Ctr., 1992-94; dir. Comprehensive Diabetes Care Ctr., assoc. prof. Med. Coll. Ga., Augusta, 1994-2000, clin. assoc. prof., 2000—; attending physician Atlanta Med. Ctr., 2000—, sect. chief endocrinology, dir. diabetes metabolic ctr., 2001—. Chair diabetes adv. coun., Ga. Diabetes Adv. Coun., 2000—; instr. Nat. Diabetes Ednl. Initiative, 1997-99. Mem. editl. bd. Diabetes Lifeline, 1997-2000, Ethnicity and Disease, 1997—. Hannah E. Longshure Meml. Med. scholar Bryn Mawr Coll., Pa., 1977, JB Johnson Meml. lectr., 2003; named Healthcare Profl. of 2003, Am. Legacy Mag., named Top Physician of 2003, Consumers Rsch. Coun. Am. Fellow Am. Coll. Endocrinology; mem. ACP, Internat. Soc. Study Hypertension in Blacks, Am. Diabetes Assn. (bd. dirs. South Coastal region 1999, pres. 2002-, nat. com. 2000--), Am. Women's Med. Assn., Endocrine Soc., Am. Assn. Clin. Endocrinologists, Alpha Omega Alpha. Democrat. Episcopalian. Avocation: quilting. E-mail: rita.louard@etenethealth.com.

LOUARGAND, MARC ANDREW, real estate executive, financial consultant; b. San Francisco, July 3, 1945; s. Andrew Louargand and Edna Antoinette McNeil (dec.); m. Elizabeth A. Warner, June 18, 1966 (div. Oct. 1978); m. J. R. McDaniel, Feb. 14, 1986. BA, U. Calif., Santa Barbara, 1967; MBA, UCLA, 1974, PhD, 1982. Asst. prof. Calif. State Polytech. U., Pomona, 1975-77; assoc. prof. Calif. State U., Northridge, 1977-83, U. Mass., Boston, 1983-88; sr. lectr. Ctr. for Real Estate Devel. MIT, Cambridge, 1986-93; 2d v.p., sr. officer Mass. Mut. Life Ins. Co., Springfield, Mass., 1993-94; mng. dir., co-founder Cornerstone Real Estate Advisors, 1993—. Chmn. Mile Square Farm Inc., Vt. Only of Mile Square Farm; cons. in field. Author: CRE2000: Managing the Fifth Strategic Resource, Study Guide to Financial Management, 1986, (with others) Principles and Techniques of Appraisal Review, 1980, Handbook of Real Estate Portfolio Management; co-editor Jour. Real Estate, Portfolio Mgmt.; assoc. editor Jour. Real Estate Lit., Jour. Corp. Real Estate (UL), Briefings in Real Estate Fin., (UK); contbr. articles to profl. jours. Bd. dirs. Beverly Glen Assn., Bel Air, Calif., 1973-77, Citronia Homeowners Assn., Northridge, Calif., 1978-83; chmn. Carlisle (Mass.) Bd. Assessors, 1985-93. Fellow, Homer Hoyt Inst. Fellow Am. Real Estate Soc. (v.p., program chair, dir., counselor of real estate); mem. Nat. Coun. Real Estate Investment Fiduciaries (chair portfolio strategy com.). Republican. Avocations: tree farming, skiing, building restoration.

LOUBE, SAMUEL DENNIS, physician; b. Rumania, Aug. 26, 1921; came to U.S., 1922, naturalized, 1927; s. Harry and Rebecca (Pollack) L.; m. Emily Wallace, Apr. 14, 1976; children— Julian M., Jonathan B., Susan C., Karen E., Patricia A., Pamela B., Brian R. AB, George Washington U., 1941, MD cum laude, 1943. Diplomate: Am. Bd. Internal Medicine. Intern, then resident in medicine Gallinger Municipal Hosp., Washington, 1943-46; physician USPHS, 1946-48; postdoctoral fellow NIH, 1948-50; research fellow in endocrinology Michael Reese Hosp., Chgo., 1948-49; research fellow in metabolism and endocrinology May Inst. Jewish Hosp., Cin., 1949-50; mem. faculty George Washington U. Med. Sch., 1950-89, clin. prof. medicine, 1975-89, prof. emeritus, 1989. Practice medicine specializing in endocrinology and metabolic diseases, Washington, 1950-88, mem. Washington Internal Medicine Group, 1965-88; former chmn. dept. medicine, chief sect. endocrinology Sibley Meml. Hosp. Contbr. articles to med. jours. Fellow ACP; mem. AMA, Am. Diabetes Assn., Endocrine Soc., Am. Soc. Internal Medicine, Diabetes Assn. D.C. (past pres.), Jacobi Med. Soc. (past pres.). Jewish.

LOUCK, JAMES DONALD, physicist, researcher; b. Grand Rapids, Mich., Dec. 13, 1928; m. Margaret Carolyn Marsh, 1960; children: Samuel, Thomas, Joseph. BS, Ala. Poly. Inst., Auburn, 1950; MS, Ohio State U., 1952, PhD, 1958. Staff mem. Los Alamos (N.Mex.) Sci. Lab., 1958-60, 63-83, lab. fellow, 1983-90; assoc. rsch. prof. Auburn (Ala.) U., 1960-63, lab. assoc., ret. fellow, 1991—; adj. prof. Nankai U., Tianjin, China, 1996—, hon. dir. ctr. combinatorics, 1998—; pres. Nicholas C. Metropolis Math. Found., 1998—. Co-author: Quantum Theory of Angular Momentum, 1981, The Racah-Wigner Algebra in Quantum Theory, 1981, Symbolic Dynamics of Trapezoidal Maps, 1986; mem. editl. bd.: Jour. Molecular Spectroscopy, 1975—85, Jour. Math. Physics, 1989—91, Annals of Combinatorics, 1996—, Internat. Sch. Theoretical Physics, 1996—; contbr. articles to profl. jours. Lt. (j.g.) USN, 1952—55. Mem.: AAAS, Am. Phys. Soc. Achievements include discovery and development of mathematical advances in physical applications of symmetry methods and their combinatorial interpretations. Avocation: gardening. Home: 54 Wildflower Way Santa Fe NM 87506-2116

LOUCKS, ALLEN FRAZIER, prosecutor, lawyer; b. Huntington Park, Calif., Oct. 31, 1957; married; 1 child. BA, U. Rochester, 1979; MA, Columbia U., 1980; JD, George Washington U., 1985. Bar: Md. 1985, D.C. 1986, U.S. Ct. Appeals (4th cir.) 1986. Assoc. Venable, Baetter & Howard, Balt., 1985-87, Murphy & McDaniel, Balt., 1987, Smith Somerville & Case, Balt.; asst. US atty. chief civil divsn. (dist. Md.) US Dept. Justice, 2001—, interim US atty., 2005. Adj. prof. law U. Balt., 1989—. Office: US Atty 101 W Lombard St Ste 6625 Baltimore MD 21201*

LOUCKS, DANIEL PETER, environmental systems engineer; b. Chambersburg, Pa., June 4, 1932; s. Emerson Hunsberger and Eleanor Wright (Johnson) L.; m. Marjorie Ann Grant, June 24, 1967; children: Jennifer Lee, Susan Louise. BS, Pa. State U., 1954; MS, Yale U., 1955; PhD, Cornell U., 1965. Asst. prof. environ. engring. Cornell U., Ithaca, N.Y., 1965-70, assoc. prof., 1970-74, prof., 1974—, chmn. dept., 1974-80, assoc. dean research and grad. studies Coll. Engring., 1980-81. Rsch. fellow Harvard U., Cambridge, Mass., 1968; economist IBRD, Washington, 1972-73; vis. prof. MIT, Cambridge, 1977-78; rsch. scholar Internat. Inst. for Applied Sys. Analysis, 1981-82; vis. disting. prof. U. Colo., 1992, U. Adelaide, 1992, Tech. U. Aachen, Germany, 1993, U. Tech., Delft, The Netherlands, 1995; Maass/White fellow U.S. Army C.E. Inst. for Water Resources, 2002; cons. NATO, UN, WHO, FAO, UNESCO, IRBD on water resources and regional devel. projects in Asia, Western and Eastern Europe, Africa and L.Am., 1970—, EPA on water quality planning USSR, 1975-77; vis. prof. Internat. Inst. Hydraulic and Environ. Engring., Delft, 1976-80, 86—; environ. adv. bd. U.S. Army Corps Engrs., 1994-98, chmn. 1996-98; dir. NATO Advanced Rsch. Workshops, 1990, 95. Contbr. articles to jours. and books on math. models. for mng. water resources systems and environ. quality. Bd. dirs. Wilderness Corp., Plymouth, Vt., 1968-96, treas., 1987-96; pres. Cmty. Improvement Assn., Ithaca, 1976-77, 99-2000. Capt. USNR, 1956—81. Recipient U.S. Sr. Rsch. award Alexander von Humboldt Found., 1992, Joy Wyatt Challenge (EDUCOM) award, 1991, Disting. Lecture award Nat. Rsch. Coun. Taiwan, 1990, 99, Warren A. Hall medal Univs. Coun. Water Resources, 2000, Cannes Internat. grand prize Network Rsch. Founds., 2005; Fulbright-Hayes fellow Yugoslavia, 1975. Fellow Am. Geophys. Union; mem. ASCE (hon., Walter Huber rsch. award 1970, Julian Hinds award 1986), NAE, Internat. Water Resources Assn., Am. Water Resources Assn., Internat. Assn. Hydraulic Rsch., Internat. Assn. Hydrologic Scis., Sigma Xi. Home: 116 Crest Ln Ithaca NY 14850-2704 Office: Cornell U Hollister Hall Ithaca NY 14853 Office Phone: 607-255-4896. Business E-Mail: DPL3@cornell.edu.

LOUDA, J. WILLIAM, chemist, biochemist, educator; b. Cin., Apr. 20, 1947; s. Joseph John and Jeanne Helen (Haeufle) Louda; m. Deborah Ann Wernander, May 1, 1993. BS in Biology, Wright State U., 1971; MS in Biology, Fla. Atlantic U., 1978; PhD in Marine Sci., U. South Fla., 1993. Rsch. assoc. Wright State U., Dayton, Ohio, 1970—71; rsch. asst. Fla. Atlantic U., Boca Raton, 1971, tchg. asst. in marine biology, invertebrate zoology, animal physiology, 1972—74, from rsch. assoc. to sr. lab. specialist, 1978—99, asst. scientist, 1999—2003, assoc. scientist, 2003—; rsch. asst. Aquatic Scis., Boca Raton, 1972. Vis. instr. dept. chemistry Fla. Atlantic U., Boca Raton, 1987—88, adj. faculty dept. chemistry and biochemistry, 1995—99; presenter in field. Contbr. articles to profl. jours. Grantee, South Fla. Water Mgmt. Dist., 1995—98, 2002—05, US Dept. Commerce Nat. Marine Fisheries Divsn., 2001—02, U. Miami, 2003. Mem.: AIChE, Coastal Edn. and Rsch. Found., Estuarine Rsch. Fedn., Am. Soc. Limnology and Oceanography, Latin-Am. Assn. Organic Geochemistry, Fla. Acad. Scis. (chmn. environ. and chem. scis. sect. 2000—01), European Assn. Organic Geochemists, Am. Chem. Soc., Ocean Conservancy, Nature Conservancy, Nat. Geographic Soc., Audubon of the Everglades, Loxahatchee Groves Landowners Assn. (pres. 1996—2004, bd. dirs., planning com.), Audubon Soc., Sierra Club, Phi Eta Tau. Avocations: fishing, skeet shooting, canoeing. Home: PO Box 1238 Loxahatchee FL 33470 Office: Fla Atlantic Univ 777 Glades Rd Boca Raton FL 33431 Office Phone: 561-297-3309. Business E-Mail: blouda@fau.edu.

LOUDERBACK, KEVIN WAYNE, business owner; b. Mt. Vernon, Ill., Mar. 10, 1971; s. Richard Lynn and Wilberta Maxine (Anderson) L. Draftsman, civil engr. Finley Engring. Co., Inc., Lamar, Mo., 1988-91; civil engr. GTE North, Sun Prairie, Wis., 1991-92; with Empiregas Corp., Lebanon, Mo., 1992-93; EMT-A Breech Paramedics Ambulance Svc., Lebanon, Mo., 1993-94; EMT Lake of the Ozarks Ambulance Svc., 1994—; owner, chmn., pres. Ozark Jerky Co., Inc., Conway, 1992—; v.p., CFO J&K Enterprises, Inc., 1997—; owner, ptnr. Ecclectic Collections, ltd., Lebanon, 1997—. Vol. EMT-P Conway Rescue Group, 1993-95, EMT-P Dallas County Rescue, 1995—. Vol. fireman Barton County Alert Squad, Lamar, 1989-92; mem. Barton County Disaster Team, 1989-92, Barton County Haz-Mat Squad, 1988-92, Mo. Emergency Preparedness Assn., 1989-92; dir. Dallas County First Responders, 1995—. Baptist. Avocations: flying private planes, golf, photography, travel. Office: 2011 S Jefferson Ave Lebanon MO 65536-4285

LOUDERBACK, PETER DARRAGH, accountant, consultant; b. July 16, 1931; s. Darragh and Constance (Clemens) L.; m. Roberta Wildow, Jan. 7, 1978; children by previous marriage: John, Jim, Susan, Tom. BA, U. Vt., 1955. With Bell Telephone of Pa., Phila., 1955-61, supr. revenue acctg., 1959-61; cons. Peat, Marwick, Mitchell & Co., Newark, 1962-71, ptnr. in charge comml. bank cons. practice, 1979-81, dir. fin. instns. cons. practice, 1981-85; prin., owner earnings performance group Newark, 1985-90; dir. fin. svcs. cons. AGS Info. Svcs., 1990-91; owner Cons. Cooperative, Inc., 1991—. CEO Spatial Decision Mgmt. Windermere, Fla., 1994-97; dir., cons. svcs. Medici Tech., Inc., Lebanon, N.H., 1997-98; ind. bank cons., 1999—. Served to capt. U.S. Army, 1961. Republican. Episcopalian. Home: 2 Bayberry Ln Nantucket MA 02554-2800 Office Phone: 508-228-3368. Personal E-mail: peter@louderback.com.

LOUDERMILK, JOEY M., insurance company executive, lawyer; b. Warner Robins, Ga., Apr. 4, 1953; BS cum laude, Ga. State U., 1975; JD, U. Ga., 1978. Bar: Ga. 1978, US Dist. Ct. Mid. and No. Districts Ga. 1978, US Ct. Appeals 11th Cir. 1981. Assoc. Moore & Worthington, Columbus, Ga., 1981—83; dir. legal dept. AFLAC Inc., Columbus, Ga., 1983—2000, dir. govt. rels., 1988—2000, sr. v.p., corp. counsel, 1989—91, sr. v.p., gen. counsel, 1991—2000, exec. v.p. legal and govt. affairs, gen. counsel, 2000—, corp. sec. Bd. dirs. Ga. Pub. Policy Found. Pres. Rotary Club, Columbus, Ga.; elder Edgewood Bapt. Ch.; bd. dirs. Ga. State U. Law Sch., Columbus Regional Med. Found., Ga. Humanities Coun. Mem.: Am. Soc. Corp. Secretaries, Am. Corp. Counsel Assn., State Bar Ga. Office: AFLAC Inc 1932 Wynnton Rd Columbus GA 31999

LOUDON, CRAIG MICHAEL, video specialist; b. Chgo., June 23, 1950; s. Howard Edgar and Laverne Anne (McKeeta) L. BS in Broadcast Prodn., So. Ill. U., 1976. Lic. radiotelephone operator, FCC. Announcer, engr. Sta. WGSB, St. Charles, Ill., 1976-77, Sta. WVVX-AM-FM, Highland Park, Ill., 1977; video tape operator, editor, cameraman ABC-TV, Chgo., 1977-84; video tape operator, editor Sta. KABC-TV, Hollywood, Calif., 1984, The Video Tape Co., North Hollywood, Calif., 1985-86, Bluth Video Systems, Burbank, Calif., 1986-87; video tape operator NBC-TV, 1987-89, Paramount Pictures, Hollywood, 1989—2002, Prime Post, L.A., 2002—03; video tape quality control oper Studio Svcs. Internat., Burbank, 2003—; mastering coord. The Walt Disney Co., 2004. Avocations: volleyball, coin collecting/numismatics. Home: PMB 194 9135-A Reseda Blvd Northridge CA 91324 E-mail: winwoodie@aol.com.

LOUGANIS, GREG E. (GREGORY EFTHIMIOS LOUGANIS), retired Olympic athlete, actor; b. San Diego, Jan. 29, 1960; s. Peter E. and Frances I. (Scott) Louganis. Student, U. Miami, 1978—80; BA in Drama, U. Calif., 1983. Former mem. US Nat. Diving Team; ret., 1989. Color commentary US Olympic Festival, 1985, US Diving Championships, 1985, Circus of the Stars, 1986, US Diving Nats., 1990; coach Hill-Nickleodeon Sport Theater, 1997. Author: Breaking the Surface, 1995, For the Life of Your Dog, 1999; prodr.: (video diary) Breaking the Surface; actor: (plays) Working, 1978; (plays, Camelot), 1978; (plays) Carousel, 1978, Equus, 1980, Dance Kaliedescope, 1987, Cinderella, 1989, The Boyfriend, 1990, Jeffrey, 1994, The Only Thing Worse You Could Have Told Me..., 1995, Just Say No, 1999, Nunsense A-Men, 1999; (TV series) Battle of the Sexes, 1979, 1981, The Brain, 1985, NBC Superstars, 1985, Battle of the Network Stars, 1985, Circus of the Stars, 1986, Hollywood Sqs., 1986, 2000, 1987; host (TV series) Where Are They Now?, 1997; actor: (films) 16 Days of Glory, 1985, 1989, Dirty Laundry, 1985, Object of Desire, 1990, Mighty Ducks II, 1992, It's My Party, 1995, Touch Me, 1997. Named winner 47 U.S. Nat. Diving Titles, winner 5 World Diving Championships (platform and springboard), 1986; named to Olympic Hall of Fame, 1985; recipient Silver medal, Olympic Games, 1976, 2 Gold medals, 1984, 1988, James E. Sullivan award, 1984, Jesse Owens award, 1987, Gold medal, Pan Am. Games, 1979, 1983, 1987, Gold medal (platform and springboard), Seoul Olympic Games, 1988, Maxwell House/US Olympic Com. Spirit award, Olympic Games, 1988. Home: PO Box 4130 Malibu CA 90264-4130 Office: IMG c/o Jamie O'Connor 825 7th Ave 8th Fl New York NY 10019*

LOUGEE, DAVID LOUIS, lawyer; b. Worcester, Mass., Mar. 20, 1940; s. Laurence H. and Erma Virginia (MacAllister) L.; m. Mary Anne Strebb, July 15, 1979; children: Adam, Sara, Barbara, Laurence. AB, Bates Coll., 1962; LLB, Duke U., 1965. Bar: Mass. 1965. Ptnr. Mirick O'Connell, DeMallie & Lougee, Worcester, 1965—, mng. ptnr., 1985—2001. Bd. dirs. The Protector Group, Inc. Named Woodward White, The Best Lawyers in Am. Mem.: Tatnuck Country Club (bd. govs. and sec.). Office: 100 Front St Worcester MA 01608-1425 Office Phone: 508-791-8500. E-mail: dllougee@prodl.com.

LOUGHEED, PETER, lawyer, former Canadian premier; b. Calgary, Alta., Can., July 26, 1928; s. Edgar Donald and Edna (Bauld) L.; m. Jeanne Estelle Rogers, June 21, 1952; children— Stephen, Andrea, Pamela, Joseph. BA, U. Alta., 1950, LL.B., 1952; MBA, Harvard U., 1954. Bar: Alta 1955. With firm Fenerty, Fenerty, McGillivray & Robertson, Calgary, 1955-56; sec. Mannix Co., Ltd., 1956-58, gen. counsel, 1958-62, v.p., 1959-62, dir., 1960-62; individual practice law, from 1962; formerly mem. Alta. Legislature for Calgary West; formerly leader Progressive Conservative Party of Alta., 1965-85; premier of Alta., 1971-85; ptnr. Bennett Jones, Calgary, 1986-99, counsel, 1999—. Named an inductee, Canadian Med. Hall of Fame, 2001. Office: Bennett Jones LLP 855 2nd St SW 4500 Bankers Hall Calgary AB Canada T2P 4K7

LOUGHLIN, JOHN P., publishing executive; BA, St. Lawrence U.; MBA, Harvard U. With NY Times Co., 1985—93; v.p., bus. mgr. Family Circle, 1988—91, sr. v.p., group pub., 1991—93; v.p., pub. dir., mag. group Meredith Inc., 1993—97, pres. broadcasting group, 1997; pres., CEO Primedia Consumer Media and Mag. Group, NYC; exec. v.p. Primedia Inc.; pres. TV Guide Publishing Group, Gemstar-TV Guide Internat., Inc., NYC, 2002—. Office: 4th Fl 1211 Avenue of the Americas New York NY 10036*

LOUGHLIN, LORI, actress; b. N.Y., July 28, 1965; m. Mossimo Giannuli, 1997; children: Isabella Rose, Olivia Jade 1 stepchild, Gianni. Actor (films) Amityville 3-D, 1983, The New Kids, 1985, Secret Admirer, 1985, RAD, 1986, Back to the Beach, 1987, The Night Before, 1989, Critical Mass, 2000; (TV films) Too Far to Go, 1979, The Tom Swift and Linda Craig Mystery Hour, 1983, North Beach and Rawhide, 1985, Babies Having Babies, 1986, Brotherhood of Justice, 1986, A Place to Call Home, 1987, No Means No, 1988, Tales from the Hollywood Hills: The Old Reliable, 1988, Doing Time on Maple Drive, 1992, Empty Cradle, 1993, Sidney Sheldon's A Stranger in the Mirror, 1993, One of Her Own, 1994, Abandoned and Deceived, 1995, In the Line of Duty: Blaze of Glory, 1997, Tell Me No Secrets, 1997, The Price of Heaven, 1997, Medusa's Child, 1997, Eastwick, 2002; (TV series) The Edge of Night, 1980-83, Full House, 1988-95, Hudson St., 1995, Summerland, 2004; TV appearances include Green Acres, 1969, Matt Houston, 1982, The Equalizer, 1986, 87, The Larry Sanders Show, 1997, Suddenly Susan, 1997, Seinfeld, 1997, Cursed, 2001, Spin City, 2001, Wednesday 9:30 (8:30 Central), 2002, Birds of Prey, 2002, The Drew Carey Show, 2002.

LOUGHRAN, JAMES NEWMAN, philosopher, educator, academic administrator; b. Bklyn., Mar. 22, 1940; s. John Farley and Ethel Margaret (Newman) L. AB, Fordham U., 1964, MA, 1965, PhD in Philosophy, 1975; PhD (hon.), Loyola Coll., Balt., 1985; PhD (hon.), Mt. St. Mary's Coll., 2002. Joined S.J., 1958; ordained priest Roman Catholic Ch., 1970. Instr. philosophy St. Peter's Coll., Jersey City, 1965-67; asst. dean Fordham U., Bronx, N.Y., 1970-73, tchr. philosophy, 1974-79, 82-84, dean, 1979-82; pres. Loyola Marymount U., L.A., 1984-91; acting pres. Bklyn. Coll., 1992; Miller Prof. Philosophy John Carroll U., Cleve., 1992-93; interim pres. Mount St. Mary's Coll., Emmitsburg, Md., 1993-94; interim acad. v.p. Fordham U., Bronx, N.Y., 1994-95; pres. St. Peter's Coll., 1995—. Contbr. numerous articles and revs. to popular and scholarly jours. Mem. (ex-officio) N.J. Commn. for Higher Edn., 2000—02; trustee St. Peter's Coll., Jersey City, 1972—78, 1994—, Xavier U., Cin., 1981—84, Canisius Coll., Buffalo, 1994—2001, Fordham U., 2000—, Coll. Mt. St. Vincent, Bronx, NY, 2004—; chair N.J. Presidents' Coun., 2000—02. Mem. Am. Philos. Assn. Avocation: tennis. Office Phone: 201-915-9014. Business E-Mail: jloughran@spc.edu.

LOUGHRAN, PETER J., lawyer; b. Feb. 22, 1964; BA, Georgetown U., 1986; JD, Columbia U., 1989. Bar: NY 1990, Conn. 1990. With Debevoise & Plimpton LLP, NYC, 1989—, ptnr., mem Securities Practice Group. Mem.: Assn. Bar of City NY. Office: Debevoise & Plimpton LLP 919 Third Ave New York NY 10022 Office Phone: 212-909-6375. Office Fax: 212-909-6836. E-mail: pjloughran@debevoise.com.

LOUGHREY, F. JOSEPH, manufacturing executive; b. Holyoke, Mass., Oct. 27, 1949; s. F. Joseph and Helen T. (Barrett) Loughrey; m. Deborah Jane Welsh, July 23, 1988; 1 stepchild, Blair Edward Bochmer. BA in Econs., African Studies, U. Notre Dame, 1971. Pres. AIESEC-U.S. Inc., N.Y.C., 1971-73; mgr. corp. employment Cummins Engine Co., Columbus, Ind., 1974-75, mgr. internat. personnel, 1975-79, dir. personnel (mktg.), 1979-81, dir. personnel (mktg. and subs.), 1981-83, dir. internal mgmt., 1983-84; mng. dir. Holset Engring. Co. Ltd., Huddersfield, Eng., 1984-86; v.p. employee rels. Cummins Engine Co., Columbus, Ind., 1986-87, from. v.p. So. Ind. ops. to v.p. heavy duty engines, 1988-90, group v.p. worldwide ops., 1990-95, exec. v.p., group pres. indsl. and chief tech. officer, 1996-99, pres.-engine bus., 1999—, pres., COO, 2005—. Sr. mem. nat. adv. bd. Tauber Mfg. Inst. U. Mich.; mem. adv. coun. coll. arts and letters U. Notre Dame; pres. bd. disr. Developmental Svcs., Inc.; bd. dirs. Tower Automotive, Inc., Sauer-Danfoss, Inc., Cummins Found., Columbus Learning Ctr., 2003—, Cummins Inc. Fellow: Brit. Inst. Mgmt.; mem.: NAM (bd. dirs. 2002—), AIESEC Internat. (sr.). Democrat. Roman Catholic. Office: Cummins Inc PO Box 3005 Columbus IN 47202-3005 Office Phone: 812-377-5123. Business E-Mail: joe.loughrey@cummins.com.

LOUGHRIDGE, JOHN HALSTED, JR., lawyer; b. Chestnut Hill, Pa., Oct. 30, 1945; s. John Halsted Sr. and Martha Margaret (Boyd) L.; m. Amy Claire Booe, Aug. 3, 1980 (div. Apr. 1995); 1 child, Emily Halsted. AB, Davidson Coll., 1967; JD, Wake Forest U., 1970. Bar: N.C. 1970, U.S. Dist. Ct. 1970, U.S. Ct. Mil. Appeals 1986, U.S. Supreme Ct. 2002. Divsn. head, v.p., counsel Wachovia Mortgage Co., Winston-Salem, N.C., 1971-79; sr. v.p., counsel Wachovia Corp. and Bank, Winston-Salem, NC, 1980—. UCC Article 5 drafting com. NC Gen. Statues Commn., 1999. Mem. cabinet, chair profl. divsn. United Way Forsyth County, 1994; mem. Rep. Nat. Com.; Rep. Presdl. Victory Team leader, 2004; hon. chmn. bus. adv. coun. Nat. Repub. Congl. Com., 2004, 2005, GOP Attys. Com.-Help Am. Vote Act, 2004. Col. JAGC, USAR, 1970-2000. Recipient Ronald Reagan Rep. Gold Medal award, Nat. Rep. Congl. Com., 2004. Mem.: ABA (corp. banking and bus. law sect. 1970—, internat. law and practice sect. 1999—2002), Dept. of Def. N.C. Com. for Employer Support of the Guard and Reserve, N.C. Bar Found. (continuing legal edn. program planner 2000—01), Mortgage Bankers Assn. Am. (legal issues com. 1982—92, fin. affiliates com. 1988—92), Assn. Corp. Counsel (bd. dirs. N.C. chpt. 1988—98, 2001—04, v.p.), Forsyth County Bar Assn., N.C. Coll. Advocacy, N.C. State Bar (bar examination candidate interviewer 2001, 2002), N.C. Bar Assn. (real property sect. 1971—, bus. law sect. 1971—, internat. law sect. 1984—, fin. instns. com. 1995—, governing coun. real property sect. 1988—91, corp. counsel sect. 1989—, real property curriculum com. 1990—93, governing coun. corp. coun. sect. 1992—98, treas. 1999—2000, bus. law curriculum com. 1999—2001, corp. coun. sect. sec. 2000—01, vice chair 2001—02, chmn. 2002—03, mem. nominating com. 2003—05), Res. Officers Assn. (chpt. pres. 1996—97, sec. 1997—), Davidson Coll. Alumni Assn. (bd. dirs. 2001—03), Rotary, Forsyth Country Club, Twin City Club (sec. 1990—97, gov. 1994—, pres. 1997—2001), Union League Phila., Phi Delta Theta, Phi Delta Phi. Republican. Presbyterian. Avocations: golf, tennis. Home: 615 Arbor Rd Winston Salem NC 27104 Office: Wachovia Corp 301 S College St Charlotte NC 28288-0630 Office Phone: 704-374-3191. Business E-Mail: john.loughridge@wachovia.com.

LOUGHRIDGE, MARK, computer company executive; b. Leadville, Colo., 1953; BSME, Stanford U.; MBA, U. Chgo. Joined IBM Corp., Armonk, NY, 1977, various key fin. positions, 1988—91, v.p., controller, 1998—2002, sr. v.p., gen. mgr. personal systems group, 2002—04, CFO, sr. v.p., 2004—. Office: IBM Corp 1 New Orchard Rd Armonk NY 10504

LOUIE, DAVID MARK, lawyer; b. Oakland, Calif., Oct. 8, 1951; s. Paul and Emma (Woo) L.; m. Johanna C. Chuan, Sept. 6, 1986; children: Ryan David, Jenna Rachel. AB cum laude, Occidental Coll., 1973; JD, U. Calif., Berkeley, 1977. Bar: Calif. 1977, U.S. Dist. Ct. (no. Dist.) Calif. 1977, U.S. Ct. Appeals (9th cir.) 1977, Hawaii 1978, U.S. Dist. Ct. Hawaii 1978. Ptnr. Case & Lynch, Honolulu, 1977-88; sr. ptnr. Roeca, Louie & Hiraoka, Honolulu, 1988—. Faculty mem. Profl. Edn. Systems, Inc. (PESI) Seminars: Hawaii Ins. & Tort Update, 1995, 1996, Depositions (Strategies, Tactics & Mechanics), 1990, Nat. Bus. Inst. (NBI) Seminars: Arbitrating and Trying the Automobile Injury Case in Hawaii, 1993, Ins. Litigation in Hawaii, 1992, Pacific Law Inst. (PLI) Seminars: Premises Liability, 1995, Hawaii State Bar Assn. Depositions, 1997, Mediation Techniques, 2001, miscellaneous seminars: Hawaiian Bitumuls & Paving Co., Job Site Accidents, 1994, Hawaiian Dredging Construction Co., Job Site Accidents, 1993; mem. Def. Rsch. Inst., 1990—. Contbg. author: Going Back, 1972, Hawaii Tort Liability Issues in Work Site Accident Cases, 1989, Trying the Automobile Accident Case, 1991, Hawaii Tort Law Update, 1992, 94. Bd. dirs. Jr. Achievement Hawaii, Honolulu, Aloha Tower Devel. Corp., 1998—, chmn., 1999—; Sec., v.p., dir. Ohana Ins. Co. Hawaii, Inc., 1994-95. Mem. ABA (sects. on tort and ins. practice litigation 1978—, minority couns. demonstration program 1994), Hawaii State Bar Assn. (bd. dirs. 1994-98, v.p. 2000, pres. 2001), Calif. State Bar Assn., Hawaii Def. Lawyers Assn. (bd. dirs. 1990—, sec.-treas. 1994-99), Nat. Asian Pacific ABA (Hawaii chpt. pres. 1992-95, bd. dirs. 1996—), Mensa, Pacific Club. Home: 4122 Pakolu Pl Honolulu HI 96816-3930 Office: Roeca Louie & Hiraoka 841 Bishop St Ste 900 Honolulu HI 96813-3917

LOUIE, STEVEN GWON SHENG, physics professor, researcher; b. Canton, China, Mar. 26, 1949; came to U.S., 1961; s. Art and Kam Shui (Lau) L.; m. Jane Yuk Wong, Aug. 3, 1975; children: Jonathan S., Jennifer Y., Sarah W. AB in Math. and Physics, U. Calif., Berkeley, 1972, PhD in Physics, 1976. IBM postdoctoral fellow IBM Watson Rsch. Ctr., Yorktown Heights, N.Y., 1977-79; mem. vis. tech. staff AT&T Bell Labs., Murray Hill, N.J., 1979; asst. prof. U. Pa., Phila., 1979-80; NSF postdoctoral fellow physics dept. U. Calif., Berkeley, 1976-77, assoc. prof., 1980-84, prof., 1984—, Miller rsch. prof., 1986, 95. Faculty scientist Lawrence Berkeley Lab., 1980-93, sr. faculty scientist, 1993—; cons. Exxon Rsch. & Engring. Co., Annandale, N.J., 1981-87. Editor Solid State Comm., 1994—; contbr. over 360 articles to sci. jours. Recipient sustained outstanding rsch. in solid state physics award Dept. Energy, 1993, Feynman prize Foresight Inst., 2003; fellow A.P. Sloan Found.,

1980, Guggenheim fellow, 1989. Fellow Am. Phys. Soc. (Aneesur Rahman prize 1996, Davisson-Germer prize 1999); mem. Materials Rsch. Soc. Baptist. Achievements include patents in field. Avocations: gardening, skiing, tennis. Office Phone: 510-642-1709.

LOUIS, GLENN, music educator; b. Brooklyn, May 3, 1951; B, Juilliard Sch., 1973. Lic. tchr. N.Y. Clk. IRS, Holtsville, NY, 1976; music tchr., 1973—. Mem.: Am. Fedn. Musician. Avocations: golf, tennis. Home: 2928 Ruddell Rd #123 Lacey WA 98503-7829

LOUIS, KENNETH R.R. GROSS, academic administrator; m. Diana Louis; children: Amy Katherine, Julie Jeannette. BA, Columbia U., 1959, MA, 1960; PhD, U. Wis., 1964. Asst. prof. Ind. U., 1964—67, assoc. prof. English and Comparative Lit., 1967—73, prof., 1973—, assoc. chmn. comparative lit. dept., 1967—69, assoc. dean arts and scis., 1970—73, chmn. English dept., 1973—78, dean arts and scis., 1978—80, v.p. acad. affairs, 1980—2001, chancellor Bloomington, 1980—2001, sr. v.p. for acad. affairs, chancellor, 2004—. Active Friends of the Lilly Libr.; chair Com. on Instnl. Cooperation, 1986—2000; active Commn. for Downtown Revitalization, Inc., NEH Commn. Humanities and the Am. People. Mem.: AAUP, MLA, Coun. for Acad. Affairs, Nat. Assn. Univs. and Land Grant Colls., Monroe County Libr. Assn., North Ctrl. Assn., Nat. Coun. Tchrs. English, Christianity and Lit., Woodburn Guild, Univ. Club, Phi Beta Kappa. Office: Ind Univ Bloomington Bryan Hall 100 107 S Indiana Ave Bloomington IN 47405-7000 Office Phone: 812-855-9011. E-mail: grosloui@indiana.edu.

LOUIS, LESTER See BROWN, LES

LOUIS, PAUL ADOLPH, lawyer; b. Key West, Fla., Oct. 22, 1922; s. Louis and Rose Leah (Weinstein) L.; m. Nancy Ann Edgeworth Lapof, Dec. 28, 1971; children: Louis Benson, IV, Connor Cristina and Marshall Dore (twins). BA, Va. Mil. Inst., Lexington, 1947; LL.B., U. Miami, Fla., 1950, JD, 1967. Bar: Fla. 1950, U.S. Dist. Ct. (so. dist.) Fla. Asst. state atty., 1955-57; atty. Beverage Dept. Fla., 1957-60; spl. asst. atty. gen. State of Fla., 1970-71; partner firm Sinclair, Louis, Heath, Nussbaum & Zavertnik (P.A.), Miami, 1960—; mem. Fed. Jud. Nominating Commn., 1977-80; mem. peer rev. com. U.S. Dist. Ct. for So. Dist. Fla., 1983-85. Author: Defamation, How Far Can You Go, Trial and Tort Trends, 1969; contbr.: chpts. to Fla. Family Law, 1967, 72. Founder mem. Palm Springs Gen. Hosp. Scholarship Com., 1968; mem. Dade County Health Facilities Authority, 1979-82; trustee Fla. Supreme Ct. Hist. Soc., 1994—. Served to 1st lt. USAAF, 1943-45, ETO, maj. USAF Res., 1962. Decorated Air medal with three oak leaf clusters, Bronze Star (7), Purple Heart. Mem. ABA, Fla. Bar (bd. govs. 1970-74), Dade County Bar Assn. (dir. 1954-55, 66-69), Am. Judicature Soc., Va. Mil. Inst. Alumni Assn. Clubs: Miami, Bath. Democrat. Jewish. Home: 4411 Palm Ln Miami FL 33137-3346 Office: 1125 A I duPont Bldg 169 E Flagler St Miami FL 33131-1210

LOUIS, VIRGIE LEE, secondary school educator; b. New Orleans, May 27, 1945; d. John Reddick and Marguerite (LaFrance) Reddick-Ragas; m. Alfred James Louis I, Dec. 24, 1966; children: Alfred, Tyra. BS, Grambling State U., 1969; postgrad., Creighton U., 1972-73, U. Nebr., 1973-75, 1982, U. Calif.; MS in Classroom Tech., Lesley U., 2000. Instr. Omaha Pub. Schs., 1969—2003; operator Northwestern Bell Tel., Omaha, 1970; educator Ceta Youth Program, Omaha, 1982-84, asst. dir., 1985; tchr. gen. ednl. devel. Omaha Pub. Schs., 2003—, intergenerational mentor program for edn. majs., 2004—. Mem. Citizens for Mature Leadership, Omaha, 1985—; curriculum developer Career Edn. Workshop, Omaha; host family to fgn. exch. students, 1988-99; sponsor Golden Viking's Vikettes Pom Pons, 1986-91; del. 1992 Dem. Nat. Conv., 1996 Dem. Nat. Conv.; dist. 2 Nebr. Dem. Women's Caucus rep.; Douglas County Dem. exec. bd.; mem. Nebr. State Pers. Bd., 1993-2005; dist. 11 legis. co-chair, 1992; Family Svcs. mentor, 1992; mem. met. dist. bd. Pub. Affairs, chair, 1997—; bd. dirs., chair Charles Drew Health Ctr., 1996-2000. Recipient Nebr.'s Favorite Tchr's award Nebr. State PTA, 1988. Mem. NEA, Omaha Edn. Assn., Nebr. Edn. Assn., Nebr. Bus. Edn. Assn., Nat. Bus. Edn. Assn., Assn. Mary Immaculate (missionary), Assn. Supervision & Curriculum Devel. Democrat. Roman Catholic. Avocations: reading, travel, workshops. Home: 3818 N 34th Ave Omaha NE 68111-2815 Office: Omaha Pub Schs Skinner Magnet Ctr 4410 N 33d St Omaha NE 68111-2207

LOUIS, WILLIAM CHARLES, III, physicist; b. Chgo., July 24, 1951; s. William Charles Jr. and Clementina Scott (Ransom) L.; m. Catherine Ann Gribler, July 4, 1980. BS, Ga. Inst. Tech., Atlanta, 1973; PhD, U. Mich., 1978. Lic. physicist. Rsch. assoc. Rutherford Lab., Chilton, U.K., 1978-81; asst. prof. Princeton (N.J.) U., 1981-87; mem. staff Los Alamos (N.Mex.) Lab., 1987--. Contbr. numerous articles to profl. jours. Named Jr. Investigator, U.S. Dept. Energy, 1984-87. Mem. Am. Pys. Soc. Office: Los Alamos Nat Lab Ms H846 Los Alamos NM 87545-0001 Office Phone: 505-667-6723. E-mail: louis@lanl.gov.

LOUIS, WILLIAM ROGER, historian; b. Detroit, May 8, 1936; s. Henry Edward and Bena May (Flood) L.; m. Dagmar Cecilia Friedrich; children: Antony Andrew, Catherine Ann. BA, U. Okla., 1959; MA, Harvard U., 1960; DPhil, Oxford U., 1962, DLitt, 1979; DLitt (hon.), Westminster Coll., 1998. Asst. prof., then assoc. prof. history Yale U., 1962-70; prof. history U. Tex., Austin, 1970-85, dir. Brit. Studies, 1975—, Kerr chair English history and culture, 1985—, disting. teaching prof., 1998—. Supernumerary fellow St. Antony's Coll., U. Oxford, Eng., 1986-96, hon. fellow, 1996—; fellow Brit. Acad., 1993—; Chichele lectr. All Souls Coll., U. Oxford, Eng., 1990, 2002, 2003; Disting. lectr. London Sch. Econs., 1992; Cust lectr. Nottingham (Eng.) U., 1995; Brit. Acad. Elie Kedourie Meml. lectr., 1996; Churchill Meml. lectr., 1998; history faculty lectr. U. Oxford, Eng., 2001; disting. vis. prof. Am. U. in Cairo, 2001; Kalb lectr. Rice U., 2001, Fusco lectr. U. Conn., 2001, Costa lectr. U. Ohio, 2002; dir. summer seminars NEH, 1985, 88, 90, 91, 96, 2000; Antonius lectr. Oxford U., 2002, Leonard Stein lectr. Balliol Coll., Oxford U.; chmn. planning com. Nat. History Ctr. U.S. State Dept. Hist. Adv. Com. Author: Ruanda-Urundi, 1963, Germany's Lost Colonies, 1967, (with Jean Stengers) The Congo Reform Movement, 1968, British Strategy in the Far East, 1919-1939, 1971, Imperialism at Bay, 1977 (History Book Club), British Empire in the Middle East, 1984 (George Louis Beer prize Am. Hist. Assn. and Tex. Inst. Letters award), In The Name of the God Go! Leo Amery and the British Empire in the Age of Churchill, 1992; editor British Documents on the End of the Empire, 1988—; editor-in-chief Oxford History of the British Empire, 1992—; editor: (with P. Gifford) Britain and Germany in Africa, 1967, France and Britain in Africa, 1971, The Origins of the Second World War: A.J.P. Taylor and His Critics, 1972, National Security and International Trusteeship in the Pacific, 1972, Imperialism: The Robinson and Gallagher Controversy, 1976, (with William S. Livingston) Australia, New Zealand and the Pacific Islands Since the First World War, 1979, (with P. Gifford) The Transfer of Power in Africa, 1982, (with R. Stookey) End of the Palestine Mandate, 1986, (with H. Bull) The Special Relationship: Anglo-American Relations Since 1245, 1986, (with P. Gifford) Decolonization and African Independence, 1988, (with James Bill) Musaddiq, Iranian Nationalism and Oil, 1988, (with Roger Owen) Suez 1956: The Crisis and Its Consequences, 1989, (with Robert A. Fernea) The Iraqi Revolution of 1958, 1991, (with Robert Blake) Churchill, 1993, Adventures with Britannia, 1995, More Adventures with Britannia, 1998, Still More Adventures with Britannia, 2003, (with Michael Howard) The Oxford History of the Twentieth Century, 1998, (with Judith Brown) The Oxford History of the British Empire: The Twentieth Century, 1999, (with Ronald Hyam) The Conservative Government and the End of Empire, 1957-64, 2000, Festschrift: The Statecraft of British Imperialism: Essays in Honor of William Roger Louis, 1999, (with Roger Owen) A Revolutionary Year: The Middle East in 1958, 2002. Decorated comdr. Brit. Empire; Woodrow Wilson fellow Harvard U., 1959-60, Marshall scholar Oxford U., 1960-62, NEH fellow, Am. Inst. Indian Studies fellow, Guggenheim fellow, vis. fellow All Souls Coll., U. Oxford, Balliol Coll., Oxford U., overseas fellow Churchill Coll., U. Cambridge, Eng., fellow Woodrow Wilson Internat. Ctr.; guest scholar Brookings Instn.; disting. visitor hist. dept. Peking U., Beijing, 1999. Fellow Royal Hist. Soc.; mem. Am. Hist. Assn. (pres. 2001-02), Coun. on Fgn. Rels. (N.Y.C.), Tex. Inst. Letters, Reform Club (London), Century (N.Y.C.), Met. Club (Washington). Democrat. Office: U Texas Dept History Austin TX 78712

LOUISA, ANGELO JOSEPH, social studies educator, researcher; b. Bridgeville, Pa., Oct. 12, 1951; s. Joseph Peter and Anna Maria Louisa; m. Pamela Lynn Acre, June 19, 1976. BA magna cum laude, St. Vincent Coll., Latrobe, Pa., 1973; MA, Duquesne U., Pitts., 1975; PhD, U. Minn., Mpls., 1985. Cert. temp. tchr. social studies Pa., 1973. Tchg. asst. dept. history Duquesne U., Pitts., 1973—75, U. Minn., Mpls., 1975—79, reader-grader dept. history, 1978—79, instr., 1979; cmty. faculty mem. Met. State U., St. Paul, 1982—87; instr. dept. history Concordia Coll., Moorhead, Minn., 1983, Lakewood C.C., White Bear Lake, Minn., 1985; asst. prof. Met. State U., St. Paul, 1987—88; lectr. dept. history U. Nebr., Omaha, 1994—96, asst. prof., 1996—97, lectr., 1997—99, asst. prof., 1999—2000; lectr. dept. history Creighton U., Omaha, 1999—2002, asst. prof., 2002—03, lectr., 2003—04, asst. prof., 2004—05, lectr., 2005—. Editl. assoc. Historicus, Lawrence, Kans., 1979—81; asst. to the Minn. state dir. Nat. History Day program, Mpls., 1979—83; exec. and fin. dir. The Coll. Football Stats. Quar., Omaha, 1989—94; judge Omaha metro area competition Nat. History Day program, Omaha, 1997—, judge Nebr. state competition, Lincoln, 1999, Lincoln, 2001; co-founder and mem. steering com. Rose and Thistle Soc. U. Minn.; co-founder and mem. steering com. Medieval/Renaissance Studies minor program U. Nebr., Omaha; coord., chair, lectr. academic confs. Co-creator Maj. League Brief 'n' Brisk Baseball Game; contbr. articles to ency., to profl. jours. Mem. Nebr. State Hist. Records Adv. Bd., Lincoln, Nebr., 2001—04, 2004—. Named Outstanding Faculty, Order of Omega, Creighton U., 2003; recipient Student Assn. award, St. Vincent Coll., 1973, Grad. Student Assn. award in History, Duquesne U., 1975; McMillan Travel grant, U. of Minn., 1979. Mem.: Soc. for Am. Baseball Rsch., Am. Hist. Assn., The Robert W. Maxwell Football Club, Pi Gamma Mu, Omicron Delta Kappa, Phi Kappa Phi, Phi Alpha Theta (scholarship 1979). Avocations: music, reading, walking, baseball history, movies. Home: 10327 Fieldcrest Ct #311 Omaha NE 68114 Office: Creighton Univ Dept of History 2500 Calif Plaza Omaha NE 68178

LOUIS-DREYFUS, JULIA, actress; b. N.Y.C., Jan. 13, 1961; d. William and Judith Louis-Dreyfus; m. Brad Hall, 1987; children: Henry, Charles. Attended, Northwestern U. Former mem. Second City and the Practical Theatre Company, Chicago, Ill. TV appearances include Saturday Night Live, 1982-85, Day by Day, 1986-89, The Art of Being Nick, 1986, Seinfeld, 1989-98 (Emmy award supp. actress, 1996, Emmy nom., 1992, 93, 94, 95, 97, 98, Amer. Comedy award best supp. actress, 1993, 94, 95, 97, 98, Golden Globe award supp. actress, 1994, SAG award, 1997, 98), Animal Farm (voice), 1999, Gepetto, 2002; actor, prodr. Watching Ellie, 2002-2003; TV guest appearances include Family Ties, 1988, Dinosaurs, 1991, The Single Guy, 1995, Hey Arnold, 1997, Curb Your Enthusiasm, 2000, 01, The Simpsons (voice), 2001, Arrested Development, 2004; films Soul Man, 1986, Troll, 1986, Hannah and Her Sisters, 1986, National Lampoon's Christmas Vacation, 1989, Jack the Bear, 1993, North, 1994, Father's Day, 1997, (TV movie) London Suite, 1996, Deconstructing Harry, 1997, A Bug's Life (voice) 1998, Gilligan's Island, 1999, Speak Truth to Power, 2000. Office: Jonas PR 240 26th St Ste 3 Santa Monica CA 90402 also: Hofflund/Polone 9465 Wilshire Blvd Beverly Hills CA 90212

LOUISE, LYNETTE, counselor, writer; b. Calgary, Alberta, Canada, Apr. 2, 1957; d. Robert Joseph and Amy Elizabeth Cyr; m. Timothy McMillin, Aug. 6, 2000; children: Tsara Delinda Shelton, Jady Deandra Shelton, Brandessa Dawn Shelton, Khiya Diree Shelton, Dar Alexander Shelton, Cash Anthony Shelton, Chance Andrew Shelton, Rye Adam Shelton. Student, Herzing Career Coll., 1980—81. Option Process Mentor Counsellor/Child Facilitator Option Inst. and Fellowship, Mass., 2003, cert. EEG Spectrum, MIT Cambridge, Mass., 2005. Bookkeeper Singer Sewing Machine, Winnipeg, Canada, 1974—74; stand-up comedian Clubs and Univs. across N.Am., Toronto, 1989—94; singer Player's Lounge, Toronto, 1989—95; children's entertainer Clowns, Characters and Critters, Houston, 1995—98; romance, sex therapist Self-employed, 1996—98; option process mentor, counselor, child facilitator Option Inst. and Fellowship, Sheffield, Mass., 2003—; d.j., news reporter KYCX, Mexia, Tex. Spkr. Mother Craft, Toronto, 1992—93; seminar leader Parentimes, Houston, 1996—98. Actor: (films) Indigo, South Pacific, 1942, Severe, No Angel, Dorp, Inner City, A Fashion Disaster; actor, writer, dir. (plays) 101 Ways to Flush a Toilet, host (national television series) Cross Country Cookin'; actor: (documentaries) Ghosts, ID. Please, History of Manners; (TV series) Divorce Court, The Marriage Counsellor; (plays) Dangerous Obsession, Amateur Night Fever; composer: (albums) Sing Me A Song Please; host (radio interview show) Just A Mom; contbr. articles to magazines; author: Jeff: A Sexually Realized Spiritual Odyssey of Stepping into Love, 2003. Fund raiser Giant Steps Sch. Autism, Toronto, 1991—92. Named winner, Yuk Yuk's Nat. Comedy Search, 1991; Music Pub. grantee, Ont. Grants Arts, 1995. Achievements include patents pending for Card-O-Dex business card organizer. Avocations: dance, reading, writing (poetry), hiking. Office Phone: 877-LYN-ETTE. Personal E-mail: lynette@lynettelouise.com.

LOUIZOS, ANNA ALEXANDRA, set designer; b. Marysville, Calif., June 24, 1957; d. Evangelos and Dianna (Marenakis) L.; m. Andrew Brian Farber, Sept. 21, 1984 (div. Apr. 1989). Student, Mills Coll., 1975-77; BFA, NYU, 1980, MFA, 1989. Assoc. designer Regional Theatre/Off Broadway, 1983-93; art dir. The Tony Awards, N.Y.C., 1990-93; asst. designer The Cosby Show, N.Y.C., 1989-90, Broadway plays My Fair Lady, 1993, The Red Shoes, 1993, Birdie Blue, 2005; assoc. designer A Christmas Carol, N.Y.C., 1994, (game show) Snakes and Ladders, 1996, Whistle Down the Wind, 1996, The Scarlet Pimpernel, 1997; interior designer Passport Mex. Restaurant, 1991, Sharaku Japanese Restaurant, 1993. Recipient The Irving Goldman award The Friars Club, 1988. Mem. Acad. TV Arts and Scis. (Emmy award nominee 1993, Tony award for art direction 1992), United Scenic Artists. Democrat. Avocations: music writing, singing. Home: 207 E 5th St Apt 12 New York NY 10003-8540 Office: 648 Broadway Ste 507A New York NY 10012-2301

LOUMIET, JUAN P., lawyer; b. Havana, Cuba, Aug. 5, 1948; BA cum laude, Yale Univ., 1971; JD magna cum laude, Univ. Miami, 1973. Bar: Fla. 1974. Shareholder Greenberg Traurig LLP, Miami, Fla., and co-chair Miami real estate dept., 2001—. Founding chmn., adv. bd. mem. Cuban Oral History Project and Ctr., St. Thomas Univ.; v.p. Performing Arts Ctr.Trust of Dade County; dir. Miami City Ballet. Office: Greenberg Traurig 1221 Brickell Ave Miami FL 33131 Office Phone: 305-579-0500. Office Fax: 305-579-0717. Business E-Mail: loumietj@gtlaw.com.

LOUNDMON-CLAY, JUANITA L., academic administrator, educator, dean; b. Charleston, W.Va., Aug. 11; d. Albert D. and Mattie L. (Collins) L.; m. Earl Clay Jr. (dec.); children: Pamela Clay-Mitchell, Kimberly Clay-Clay, Dana Clay-Braddock. BA, W.Va. State Coll.; MSW, W.Va. U.; MA, Ind. U.; PhD, Fla. State U., 1978. Psychologist Navistar Corp., Indpls., 1978-80; pvt. practice psychology, Indpls., 1980-84; clin. psychologist Lakeview Mental Health Ctr., Pensacola, Fla., 1984-85; pvt. practice A Better Way Christian Counseling Ministry, Tallahassee, Fla., 1985-88; prof. Regent U., Virginia Beach, Va., 1988-89; assoc. prof. Am. U. of Les Cayes, Haiti, 1989-91; mental health cons. to Christian Orgns., Ft. Wayne, Ind.; pres., CEO A Better Way Counseling and Cons. Agy., Ft. Wayne; v.p. student affairs, assoc. prof. Bluefield State Coll. Cons. Washington Project, 1989—, Haiti Mins. Conf., Port-Au-Prince, 1989; founder, dir. first group treatment home for adolescent girls in State of Ind.; founder A Better Way Counseling and Diagnostic Agy. Author: New Career Development Strategies For The Black Working Poor, 1977; prodr. Black-on-Black Pub. Svc. TV Program. Precinct chmn. Rep. Exec. Com., Tallahassee, 1987-88; bd. mem. City Coun. EEO Commn., Tallahassee, 1987-89, Bluefield Cmty. Ctr., 2000-01; former pres. Ind. Conf. Social Welfare, Indpls.; bd. dirs. Cmty. Action of N.E. Ind., Ft. Wayne Ballet, Old Fort br. YMCA; life mem. NAACP, mem. cmty. access network TV, Martin Luther King Breakfast Club Inc.; candidate Ind. Legislature, 1996; vol. docent Lincoln Mus.; spkr., motivator Christian Women's Groups. Fla. U. Systems grantee, 1976; named one of Outstanding Young Women Am., 1978; recipient Cmty. Svc. award City of Pensacola, 1974, YMCA, C. of C., Ft. Wayne, Ind., 1970, Ebony in Excellence award, 1997. Mem. Am. Assn. Counseling and Devel., Va. Assn. Counseling and Devel., Ind. Psychology Assn. (life), Kiwanis Internat. Office: 219 Rock St Bluefield WV 24701 E-mail: JCandJesus@Juno1.com.

LOUNSBERRY, JOYCE BEVERLY, psychologist, nurse; b. Cloquet, Minn., Jan. 31; d. Eino Harold and Lempi Maria (Maijala) Halmet-Sohn; m. Richard Harrington Lounsberry, Mar. 17; children: Teresa, Mark, Kenneth. BA, U. Redlands, 1981; MA, U. Phoenix, 1992, Inst. Transpersonal Psychology, 1995, PhD, 2001. RN, Minn.; cert. occupl. health nurse, holistic nurse, creative expression. Instr. Lawton Sch. Med. Assts., 1968-73; occupl. health nurse, pers. generalist Teledyne Semiconductor, 1973-78; corp. dir., occupl. health cons. Calif. Indsl. Med. Clinic, Inc., 1978-84; pres. Lounsberry Cons. Svcs., Cupertino, Calif., 1984—; instr. Inst. Transpersonal Psychology, assoc. prof., 2004—. Occupl. health cons. Digital Equipment Corp., 1988-92. Sec. Santa Clara (Calif.) Vanguard, 1979-81; bd. dirs. Prince of Peace Ch., Saratoga, Calif., 1993-94; ambassador People to People, China and Mongolia, 1994. Recipient Occupl. Health Nurse award Schering Corp., 1989. Mem. AAOHN (past chmn. coms., bd. dirs.), Am. Holistic Nurses Assn., Calif. Assn. Occupl. Health Nurses (2d v.p., chmn. coms.), Western Assn. Occupl. Health Nurses (pres., v.p., bd. dirs. mem. coms.), El Camino Real Assn. Occupl. Health Nurses (bd. dirs., v.p. chmn. com.), Assn. Transpersonal Psychology. Avocations: reading, travel, ballroom dancing. Home and Office: 1211 NE 146th St Vancouver WA 98684

LOUNSBURY, HELEN MARIE, education educator, consultant; d. Joseph and Helen Golden; m. Patrick Lounsbury Sr.; children: Patrick Jr., Elaine, Amy BS with distinction, SUNY, 1960; MA in Lit., Vt. Coll., 1993. Tchr. Mohanasen Ctrl. Sch., Rotterdam, N.Y., 1960-62, Berne-Knox-Westerlo Ctrl. Sch., Berne, N.Y., 1962-96; clin. edn. regional supr. SUNY, Oneonta, 1996—; instr. Coll. St. Rose, Albany, N.Y., 1996-98; themes advisor Albany Sch. Humanities, 1997—2001; scorer Nat. Eral Svc., 2001—; clin. edn. supr. SUNY Potsdam, 2003—; clin. edn. regional supr. SUNY, Potsdam, NY, 2003—. Cons. U.S. Dept. Edn.; pres. bd. edn. Berne-Knox-Westerlo Ctrl. Sch. Dist.; reviewer N.Y. State Dept. Edn., 1997—, CTB McGraw-Hill, 1999--, WESTAT, 1998-; mem. NY Dept. Ed. Commnr. Dist. Adv. Com., 1998-; scorer N.Y. State Tchr. Cert. Exams, NES, 2000—; scorer SAT essay Pearson Edn., 2005—; presenter in field. Co-author: DeBeers, A Factory Family, 1985, Chances Are: Investigations in Probability, 1995. Bd. dirs. Hilltown Cmty. Rsch. Ctr., Berne, 1982-94, Albany County (N.Y.) Rural Housing Alliance, 1984-99, Albany City Reading Coun.; coord. Arts Connection Learning Partnership, Albany, 1992-95, coord. BERNE Heritage Days, 2003; trustee Libr., Berne, N.Y., 2005—. Named N.Y. Tchr. of Excellence, 1993; grantee NEH Masterworks Study, 1995, N.Y. Found. of the Arts, 1993, 94, Pioneering Partner Found., 1996, 98, NY Coun. Humanities, 2003. Mem. ASCD, PTA (hon. life, Disting. Svc. award 1996)), N.Y. State Reading Assn., N.Y. State Math. Assn., Internat. Reading Assn., Assn. Math. Tchrs. N.Y. State, N.Y. State English Tchrs., Hodge Podge Soc., Civil War Roundtable, Kiwanis, Kappa Delta Pi. Avocations: travel, reading, genealogy. Office: Lounsbury Cons East Berne NY 12059

LOUNSBURY, STEVEN RICHARD, lawyer; b. Evanston, Ill., July 26, 1950; s. James Richard and Reba Jeanette (Smith) L.; m. Dianne Louise Daley, Apr. 16, 1983; children: Jimson, Cody Summer, Richard. BA, U. Calif., Santa Barbara, 1973; JD, U. West L.A., 1977. Bar: Calif. 1979, Oreg. 1997, U.S. Dist. Ct. (cen. dist.) Calif. 1979, U.S. Dist. Ct. Oreg. 1999. Pvt. practice, L.A., 1979-83; contract atty. FAA, L.A., 1981; trial atty. Hertz Corp., L.A., 1983-86; mng. counsel 20th Century Ins. Co., Woodland Hills, Calif., 1986-94; mng. atty. Lounsbury and Assocs., Brea, Calif., 1986-94; sr. trial atty. Bollington, Lounsbury and Chase, Brea, 1994-99; asst. Coos County counsel, Coquille, Oreg., 1999—2002; county counsel Coos County, 2002—04, Clackamas County, Oregon City, Oreg., 2004—. Arbitrator Orange County Superior Ct., Santa Ana, Calif., 1992-99. Mem. Calif. Bar Assn., Oreg. Bar Assn., Oreg. County Counsel Assn. (legis com 2004—), Oreg. State Bar (mem. govt. law sect.), Clackamas County Bar Assn. Avocations: music, flute, saxophone. Home: PO Box 217 Camas Valley OR 97416 Office: Office of County Counsel Clackamas County Pub Svcs Bldg 2051 Kaen Rd Oregon City OR 97045 Personal E-mail: lounsbury@mbol.us. Business E-Mail: stevenlou@co.clackamas.or.us.

LOURIE, ALAN DAVID, federal judge; b. Boston, Jan. 13, 1935; AB, Harvard U., 1956; MS, U. Wis., 1958; PhD, U. Pa., 1965; JD, Temple U., 1970. Bar: Pa. 1970. Chemist Monsanto Co., St. Louis, 1957-59; lit. scientist, chemist, patent agt. Wyeth Labs., Radnor, Pa., 1959-64; counsel Smith Kline Beecham Corp., Phila., 1964-90, successively as patent agt., atty., dir. corp. patents, asst. gen. counsel, v.p. corp. patents; cir. judge U.S. Ct. Appeals (fed. cir.), Washington, 1990—. Mem. Judicial Conf. Com. on Financial Disclosure, 1990-98; mem. U.S. del. to Diplomatic Conf. on Revision of Paris Conv. for Protection of Indsl. Property, 1982, 84; vice chmn. industry functional adv. com. to U.S. Trade Rep. and Dept. Commerce, 1987-90; chmn. U.S. group of U.S.-Japan Bus. Coun. Task Force on Patents. Bd. visitors Law Sch., Temple U. Mem. Phila. Patent Law Assn. (pres. 1984-85), Am. Intellectual Property Law Assn. (bd. dirs. 1982-85), Assn. Corp. Patent Counsel (treas. 1987-89), Pharm. Mfrs. Assn. (chmn. patent com. 1981-86), Am. Chem. Soc., Cosmos Club, Harvard Club Washington. Office: US Ct Appeals Fed Cir 717 Madison Pl NW Washington DC 20439-0002

LOUX, GORDON DALE, religious organization administrator; b. Souderton, Pa., June 21, 1938; s. Curtis L. and Ruth (Derstine) L.; m. Elizabeth Ann Nordland, June 18, 1960; children: Mark, Alan, Jonathan. Diploma, Moody Bible Inst., Chgo., 1960; BA, Gordon Coll., Wenham, Mass., 1962; BD, No. Bapt. Sem., Oak Brook, Ill., 1965, MDiv, 1971; MS, Nat. Coll. Edn., Evanston,Ill., 1984; LHD (hon.), Sioux Falls Coll., 1985. Ordained to ministry, Bapt. Ch., 1965. Assoc. pastor Forest Park (Ill.) Bapt. Ch., 1962-65; alumni field dir. Moody Bible Inst., Chgo., 1965-66, dir. pub. rels., 1972-76; dir. devel. Phila. Coll. Bible, 1966-69; pres. Stewardship Svcs., Wheaton, Ill., 1969-72; exec. v.p. Prison Fellowship Ministries, Washington, 1976-84, pres., CEO, 1984-88, Prison Fellowship Internat., Washington, 1979-87; pres. Internat. Students, Inc., Colorado Springs, Colo., 1988-93, Gordon D. Loux & Co., LLC, Colorado Springs, 1994—, Trinity Cmty. Found., 1996—. Author: Uncommon Courage, 1987, You Can Be a Point of Light, 1991; contbg. author: Money for Ministries, 1989, Dictionary of Christianity in America, 1989. Bd. dirs. Evang. Coun. for Fin. Accountability, Washington, 1979-92, vice chmn., 1981-84, 86-87, chmn., 1987-89; vice chmn. Billy Graham Greater Washington Crusade, 1985-85; bd. dirs. Evang. Fellowship of Mission Agys., 1991-94, Ctr. for Christian Jewish Dialogue, Colorado Springs, 1996—, Hope and Home, Colorado Springs, 1998—, C2ure, Mechanicsburg, Pa., 1999—, Global Leaders Initiative. Named Alumnus of Yr., Gordon Coll., 1986. Mem. Broadmoor Golf Club (Colo. Springs). Republican. Home: 740 Bear Paw Ln N Colorado Springs CO 80906-3215 Office: PO Box 38898 Colorado Springs CO 80937-8898 Personal E-mail: louxco@aol.com.

LOUX, JONATHAN DALE, business development consultant; b. Oak Park, Ill., Mar. 23, 1966; s. Gordon Dale and Elizabeth (Nordland) L.; m. Jan Mary Peters, July 22, 1989; children: Kara Leigh, Kurtis Dale, Kenton Stanley, Kourtney Grayce. BS, Eastern Coll., St. Davids, Pa., 1988. CPA, Ill. Acctg. supr. Capin, Crouse, LLP, Wheaton, Ill., 1989-93; supr. internal audit Select Beverages, Ind., Darien, Ill., 1993-94; pres. Gordon D. Loux Co., LLC, Colorado Springs, Colo., 1994—, Loux Group, LLC, Colorado Springs, 1996—2005; v.p. Cure Internat., Lemoyne, Pa., 2002—05; assoc. program dir. RDV Corp., Grand Rapids, Mich., 2005—. Trustee Eastern Coll., St. Davids, Pa., 2000—. Republican. Presbyterian. Home and Office: 1003 4th St New Cumberland PA 17070

LOVAAS, JOHN L., foreign aid executive, community activist; b. Washington, Mar. 27, 1943; s. Lloyd C. and Mary Alyce Lovaas; m. Frances C. Andersen, July 31, 1965; children: Deron, Terrence, Jennifer. BS, U. Md.,

1967. Chief program officer U.S. AID, Tegucigalpa, Honduras, 1974-79, dep. dir. Niamey, Niger, 1981-83, Panama, Panama, 1983-86, asst. dir. Office Caribbean Affairs Washington, 1986-88, dir. ops. task force humanitarian assistance Ctrl. Am., 1988-89, dep. dir. Office Ctrl. Am. Affairs, 1989-90, dep. mission dir. San Salvador, El Salvador, 1990-94; v.p. Cambridge Consulting Corp., McLean, Va., 1996-98; spl. asst. to pub. Connection Newspapers, McLean, 1998—. Cons. World Bank, Tegucigalpa, 1996. Prodr.: (TV series) Reston Impact, 2001—; host:, 1991—. V.p. Reston Assn., 1996—99; pres. Alliance Better Cmty., Reston, 1997, Reston Citizens Assn., 1999—2000; market master Reston Homegrown Farmers Market, 1997—; chmn. Reston 2000 Transp. Com., 1998—; mem. steering com. ARC Fairfax County, Herndon, Va., 2001—03; vol. Rucker Homeless Shelter, 2001—, FISH, 2001—04; bd. govs. Reston Cmty. Ctr., 2002—04; vice chair Fairfax County Dem. Com., Falls Church, Va., 1995—96; mem. ctrl. com. Va. Dem. Party, 1998—; co-chair Hunter Mill Dist. Dem. Com., Reston, 1997—98. Mem.: Sierra Club. Avocations: travel, gardening, theater, reading. Home: 11437 Washington Plaza W Reston VA 20190 Office: Connection Newspapers 7913 Westpark Dr Mc Lean VA 22102 Office Phone: 703-917-6405. E-mail: jlovaas@aol.com.

LOVE, APRIL GAYE MCLEAN, librarian; b. San Jose, Calif., Apr. 28, 1947; d. Frederick F. and Geneva A. (Gmelin) McL.; m. Glen Bolinger, 1974 (div. 1984). B.A., U. Oreg., 1969, M.L.S., 1970, M.A. in Biology, 1976, BA in Dance, U. Calif., Irvine, 1989. Rsch. asst. Oreg. State U., Corvallis, 1972-74; sci. illustrator Smithsonian Inst., La Jolla, Calif., 1974; sci. bibliographer U. Calif.-Irvine, 1975-94; phys. scis. reference librarian, phys. sci. bibliographer dept. collection and devel., also mem. percussion ensemble, Sch. Fine Arts, U. Calif.-Irvine Symphony Orch., 1986-94; libr. phys. sci. Univ. Calif., Irvine, Calif., 1994-2004; libr. sci. and engring. libr. U. Utah, Salt Lake City, Utah, 2004—. Co-dir. classical music Sta. KUCI-radio, 1983-2000. Mem. ALA (conf. attendant, 1981, 87), Calif. Acad. Research Librarians, Sci. and Engring. Academic Librarians (chair program com., sec. so. br., 1988—), So. Calif. Botanists, Orange County Library Assn; attended confs. in field. Choreographer: Everyone Gets the Blues, 1980; contbr. article to popular mag. Office: Univ Utah J Willard Marriott Libr Sci and Engring 295 South 1500 East Salt Lake City UT 84112-0860 Office Phone: 801-581-7533. Business E-Mail: april.love@library.utah.edu.

LOVE, BEN HOWARD, retired organization executive; b. Trenton, Tenn., Sept. 26, 1930; s. Ben Drane and (Whitehead) Virginia; m. Ann Claire Hugo, Mar. 4, 1933; children: Ben H. Jr., Phillip H.(dec.), Leigh Anne, Mark E. BS, Lambuth Coll., 1955, HHD (hon.), 1986; Dr. Philanthropy (hon.), Pepperdine U., 1987; LHD (hon.), Montclair State U., 1991. With Boy Scouts Am., 1955—, dist. exec. Jackson, Tenn., 1955-60, scout exec. Delta area council, Clarksdale, Miss., 1960-64, dir. Nat. council, North Brunswick, N.J., 1964-68, scout exec. Longhorn council, Ft. Worth, 1968-71, scout exec. Sam Houston council, Houston, 1971-73, dir. Northeast region, Dayton, N.J., 1973-85, chief scout exec. Nat. council, Irving, Tex., 1985-93. Bd. dirs. AIG Valic I, Valic II. Served with U.S. Army, 1951-52. Recipient Gold medal SAR, Bronze Wolf award World Scout Orgn. Republican. Presbyterian. Avocations: tennis, golf, swimming, reading, spectator sports. Office: 1327 Anna Ct Cedar Park TX 78613 Office Phone: 512-250-8156.

LOVE, CHARLES MARION, III, lawyer; b. Charleston, W.Va., Mar. 23, 1939; s. Charles Marion Jr. and Naomi (Nale) L.; m. Sally Biddle McCue, Oct. 21, 1965; children: Charles M. IV, John Lewis Biddle, Peter Stuart McKinley. AB, W.Va. U., 1963, LLB, 1965. Bar: W.Va. 1965, U.S. Supreme Ct. 1969, U.S. Tax Ct. 1980. Assoc. Dayton, Campbell & Love, Charleston, W.Va., 1965-66; asst. U.S. atty. U.S. Atty.'s Office, Charleston, W.Va., 1966-69; assoc. Stone Bowles Kauffelt & McDavid, Charleston, W.Va., 1969-71; ptnr. Bowles Rice McDavid Graff & Love LLP, Charleston, W.Va., 1971—. Mem. jud. conf. for U.S. Ct. Appeals, 4th cir. Chmn., CEO W.Va. Housing Devel. Fund, Charleston, 1981—2003; past mem. former officer bd. trustees Herbert J. Thomas Meml. Hosp. Fellow ABA, W.Va. State Bar Assn. (chmn. legal ethics com. 1991-94, mem. ethics com. 1988-94, mem. bd. trustees, pres. 2004-); mem. W.Va. Bar Assn. (mem. exec. coun., pres.) Kanawha County Bar Assn., Am. Bd. Trial Advocates, W.Va. State Bar (pres., 2004-05), W.Va. Bar Assn. (pres., 2004-2005), Phi Delta Phi. Democrat. Home: 920 Newton Rd Charleston WV 25314-1413 Office: Bowles Rice McDavid Graff & Love PLLC PO Box 1386 600 Quarrier St Charleston WV 25301-2121 Office Phone: 304-347-1104. Office Fax: 304-347-1746. Business E-Mail: clove@bowlesrice.com.

LOVE, CHRISTINE E., artist; b. Memphis, Jan. 29, 1953; Studied with Billie Price-Hosmer, 1961-64; student, Memphis Acad. Arts, 1971-72. Owner C. Love Studio/Gallery, Carmel Valley, Calif., 1988—. Lectr., spkr. in field. One-woman shows include Local Color Gallery, Pacific Grove, Calif., 1980, Licsko Gallery, Carmel, Calif., 1992, Three Sisters Gallery, Carmel Valley, Calif., 1993, Marjorie Evans Gallery, Carmel, 1995; exhibited in group shows at Sacramento (Calif.) State Fair, 1981, Licsko Gallery, 1991, Corona del Sol Gallery, Carmel, 1993, Van Gaurd Gallery, Carmel, 1994, Carl Cherry Found., Carmel, 1994, Glamour Con, L.A., 1994, Fingerhut Gallery, Sausalito, Calif., 1995; permenant collections include Elan's Lodge at Pebble Beach, Calif., Three Swans Publ., San Diego, Quail Mountain Herbs, Santa Cruz, Calif., Mongomery Securities, San Francisco, Arcadian Winery, Carmel Valley, Monterey Plaza Hotel, Calif., Hall, Kinion & Assoc.; represented in pvt. and pub. collections; illustrator The Masters Manual of Pa Kua Chang, 1984. Recipient 1st prize Gouache Watercolor Fine Arts, Monterey County, 1980-81. Avocations: instruction, counseling, writing, psychology. Studio: PO Box 2436 Carmel Valley CA 93924-2436

LOVE, COURTNEY, singer, actress; b. San Francisco, July 9, 1964; d. Hank Harrison and Linda Carroll; m. James Moreland, 1989 (div. 1989), m. Kurt Cobain, Feb. 1992 (dec.); 1 child, Frances Bean. Singer, writer, musician Hole, 1989—2002. Albums with Hole include Pretty on the Inside, 1991, Live Through This, 1994, Celebrity Skin, 1998; Solo album includes America's Sweeteart, 2004; actress (films) Sid and Nancy, 1986, Straight to Hell, 1987, Tapeheads, 1988, Basquiat, 1996, Feeling Minnesota, 1996, The People vs. Larry Flynt (Best Supporting Actress award, NY Film Critics Cir., Boston Soc. of Film Critics), 1996, Not Bad For a Girl, 1996 (also co-prodr.), Man on the Moon, 1999, 200 Cigarettes, 1999, Beat, 2000, Julie Johnson, 2001, Trapped, 2002; television appearance on MTV Unplugged, 1995.

LOVE, DANA FRANCIS IGNATIUS, telecommunications industry executive; b. Hartford, Conn., Dec. 1, 1969; d. Francis Henry and Alice Glick Love; m. Faith Ellen Moser, Sept. 25, 1968. BS, U. Richmond, 1988; MBA, Harvard U., 1992; PhD in Econs., Chelsea U., 2004. V.p. Radnet, Inc., Cambridge, Mass., 1995—98; prin. investigator, internet protocol comm. GTE, Waltham, Mass., 1998—99; exec. v.p. Metacloud Comm., Vienna, Va., 1999—2000; v.p., gen. mgr. ADC Telecom., Washington, 2000—01; exec. v.p., sales and mktg. Prosodie Interactive, Washington, 2001—03; cons. Radnet Sys., Boyds, Md., 2003; pres. Astyra Corp., Richmond, Va., 2003—. Adv. bd. Sonim Tech., Inc., Redwood City, Calif., 2002—, Gerson Lehrman Group, N.Y.C., 2003—. Editor: Connecting to the Internet: A Practical Guide about LAN-Internet Connectivity, 1998, Frame Relay: Technology and Practice, 1999. Mem.: Conferie Chaine Rotisseurs, Bailliage des Etats-Unis (chevalier 2002). Republican. Roman Catholic. Achievements include patents pending for sys. and method for monitoring packet telephony network with in-band custom quality of svc; enhanced telephone svc. sys. with packet telephony sys. and out-of-band routing tools; apparatus and method for determining quality of svc. on an arbitrary packet telephony network using in-band signaling. Home: 11413 Braidstone Ln Chesterfield VA 23838 Office Phone: 202-262-1608. Personal E-mail: me@danalove.com.

LOVE, DAVIS MILTON, III, professional golfer; b. Charlotte, NC, Apr. 13, 1964; m. Robin; children: Alexia, Davis IV. Student, U. N.C. Profl. golfer PGA, 1985—; mem. Ryder Cup Team, 1993, 1995, 1997, 1999, 2002, 2004; winner Buick Invitational Calif., 1996. Winner The Internat., 1990, MCI Heritage Classic Champion, 1987,91 & 92, 1998, 2003; The Players Championship, 1992; KMart Greater Greensboro Open, 1992; Infiniti Tournament of Champions, 1993; Las Vegas Invitational, 1993; Freeport-McMoran Classic, 1995; Buick Invitational, 1996; PGA Championship, 1997; Buick Challenge, 1997; Buick Invitational, 2002; AT&T Pebble Beach Nat. Pro-Am, 2001; WGC-Accenture Match Play Championship, 2002, 2003; International, 2003 Achievements include ranks 4th on the all-time PGA list with over $30 million in earnings.

LOVE, EDITH HOLMES, theater producer; b. Boston, Oct. 17, 1950; d. Theodore Rufus and Mary (Holmes) L. Student, Denison U., 1968-72; BFA, U. Colo., 1973. Freelance designer various orgns., Atlanta, 1974-75; costumer Atlanta Children's Theatre, 1975-77; prodn. acct. David Gerber Co., L.A., 1980-81; bus. mgr. Alliance Theatre/Atlanta Children's Theatre, 1977-79, adminstrv. dir., 1981-83, gen. mgr., 1983-85, mng. dir., 1985-96, Dallas Theater Ctrn., 1997—2003, Portland (Oreg.) Ctr. Stage, 2003—. Adv. bd. Stage Hands, Inc., Atlanta, 1983-89; mem. exec. com. Prodn. Valves, Inc., Atlanta, 1985-89; mem. adv. com. arts mgmt. program Carnegie Mellon U.; panelist Nat. Endowment for Arts, 1994-96; vis. prof. Yale Sch. Drama, 1997. Active Cultural Olympiad Task Force, 1996 Summer Olympic Games, 1992-96, Met. Atlanta Arts Fund Bd., 1992-97; bd. dirs. Atlanta Convention and Vistor's Bur., 1993-95, Arts Dist. Friends, Theatre Comm. Group; exec. com. Dallas Theatre League, 1999—. Recipient Deca award for Outstanding Bus. Women in Atlanta, 1992. Mem. League Resident Theatres (treas. 1987-97, v.p. 1997-2000), Atlanta Theatre Coalition (exec. com. 1987-91, pres. 1989), Atlanta C. of C. (bd. dirs. bus. coun. for arts 1988-97), Leadership Atlanta, Charter 100 Dallas, Bd. Arts Dist. Found. Home: 4109 NE Thompson St Portland OR 97212-5432 Office: Portland Center Stage 1111 SW Broadway Portland OR 97212

LOVE, GAY MCLAWHORN, manufacturing executive; m. J. Erskine Love (dec. 1987); children: Dennis, Jimmy, Bill, Keith, David; 1 child, Carol Anne Love Jennison. Grad., Duke U. Chair PrintPack Inc., Atlanta, 1987—. Co-founder The Gay and Erskine Love Found., 1976. Named an honorary alumnus, Georgia Tech., 1989. Office: PrintPack Inc PO Box 43687 Atlanta GA 30336-0687

LOVE, GAYLE MAGALENE, school system administrator; b. New Orleans, July 25, 1953; d. Lowell F. Sr. and Nathalie Mae (Adams) L.; children: Nathanael Dillard, Raphael. BMEd, Loyola U., New Orleans, 1975, MMEd, 1981; postgrad., U. New Orleans, Nova Southeastern U. Cert. learning disabled, emotionally disturbed, gifted-talented, adult edn., mild-moderate, elem.-secondary vocal music, prin., spl. sch. prin., parish/city sch. supr. instrn., supervision of student tchg., supr. adult edn. & spl. edn., child search coord. Asst. prin., dean student svcs. Jefferson Parish Sch. Bd., Harvey, La., chmn. spl. edn. dept., 1990-94; adult educator instr. Chmn. Sch. Bldg. Level Com., 1994-96, 97; presenter St. Joseph the Worker Cath. Ch., 2005, Very Spl. Arts Week Jefferson founder, pres. Good Morning God Found.; presenter in field if sch. improvement. Author: Good Morning, God: Prayers and Reflections and Meditations for Early Morning, 2003. Mem. adv. bd. Jefferson Parish Litter; mem. parish coun. St. Joseph Worker, Grand Lady Knights Peter Claver; mem. Hazel Rhea Hurst Scholarship Com., City Citizens Involved with Today's Youth. Recipient Trailblazer award, Jefferson Parish, La., 2003. Mem.: ASCD, La. Assn. of Sch. Adminsitrs. of Federally Assisted Programs, Jefferson Alliance of Black Sch. Educators, Jefferson Assn. Pub. Sch. Adminstrs., La. Assn. Sch. Execs. Home: 1740 Burnley Dr Marrero LA 70072-4522

LOVE, JAMES SANFORD, III, communications executive; b. Jackson, Miss., Aug. 4, 1944; s. James Sanford Jr. and Jo Ellis (Buie) L.; m. Barbara Ann Harris, June 11, 1966 (div. Oct. 1981); children: James S. IV, Caroline E., Gillian M. BBA in Bus. and Govt., U. Miss., 1966; MBA, U. Va., 1968. Acct. exec. J. Walter Thompson, N.Y.C., 1968-70; rsch. analyst, asst. v.p. Dean Witter Co., N.Y.C., 1970-73; chmn., CEO Love Broadcasting Co., Biloxi, Miss., 1972-91, Lakewood Meml. Pk., Jackson, Miss., 1972-91; rsch. analyst Baker Weeks & Co., N.Y.C., 1973-75; rsch. analyst, v.p. Paine Webber & Co., N.Y.C., 1975-77; chmn., CEO Love Comm. Co., Jackson, 1991—. Cosn. Norberg Capital, N.Y.C., 1979-97; co-founder Millsaps Buie House Bed and Breakfast Inn, 1987—; owner White House Hotel, Biloxi, Miss., 1989—. Exec. prodr.: Miss. News Tonight, 1991-92. Trustee Millsaps Coll., Jackson, 1989—, Land Trust for the Miss. Coastal Plain, Miss. chpt. Nature Conservancy, 1990—, chmn. bd. trustees, 1996—97; chmn. leadership bd. Boys and Girls Club of Miss. Gulf Coast, 1994—96; mem. adv. bd. Salvation Army, 1997—. Named to All-Am. Rsch. Team, Instl. Investor Mag., 1974-75; recipient George Foster Peabody award U. Ga., 1989, regional Emmy award, 1990, 50th Anniversary Hero award The Nature Conservancy Miss. Chpt. Mem. Boston Club (New Orleans), Windance Country Club (Gulfport, Miss.), Univ. Club (Jackson), Biloxi Yacht Club. Episcopalian. Avocations: gardening, photography, salt water fishing, history. Home: 12137 Hickman Rd Biloxi MS 39532-9429 Office: Love Comm Co 240 Eisenhower Dr Bldg C Biloxi MS 39531-3601

LOVE, JOSEPH L., history professor, former cultural studies center administrator; b. Austin, Tex., Feb. 28, 1938; s. Joseph L. Sr. and Virginia (Ellis) L.; m. Laurie Reynolds, Dec. 23, 1978; children: Catherine R., David A.; children from previous marriage: James A., Stephen N. AB in Econs. with honors, Harvard U., 1960; MA in History, Stanford U., 1963; PhD in History with distinction, Columbia U., 1967. From instr. to prof. U. Ill., Urbana-Champaign, 1966—, dir. ctr. Latin Am. and Caribbean studies, 1993-99. Rsch. assoc. St. Antony's Coll. Oxford U.; vis. prof. Pontifical Cath. U., Rio de Janeiro, 1987; presenter in field. Author: Rio Grande do Sul and Brazilian Regionalism, 1882-1930, 1971, Sao Paulo in the Brazilian Federation, 1889-1937, 1980, Crafting the Third World: Theorizing Underdevelopment in Rumania and Brazil, 1996; editor: (with Robert S. Byars) Quantitative Social Science Research on Latin America, 1973, (with Nils Jacobsen) Guiding the Invisible Hand: Economic Liberalism and the State in Latin American History, 1988, (with Werner Baer) Liberalization and its Consequences: A Comparative Perspective on Latin America and Eastern Europe, 2000; bd. editors Latin Am. Rsch. Rev., 1974-78, Hispanic Am. Hist. Rev., 1984-89, The Americas, 1995-99; contbr. articles to profl. jours. Fulbright-Hays Rsch. grantee; fellow Social Sci. Rsch. Coun., IREX, Guggenheim; vis. scholar U. São Paulo, Inst. Ortega y Gasset, Madrid, U. Nova, Lisbon; sr. rsch. fellow NEH, others; sr. univ. scholar U. Ill., 1993-96. Mem. Am. Hist. Assn., Conf. Latin Am. History (chair Brazilian studies com. 1973, mem. gen. com. 1983, Conf. prize 1971), Latin Am. Studies Assn. Unitarian Universalist. Office: U Ill Dept History 309 Gregory Hall 810 S Wright St Urbana IL 61801-3644 Office Phone: 217-333-3182. Business E-Mail: j-love2@uiuc.edu.

LOVE, KEITH SINCLAIR, communications executive; b. Apr. 26, 1947; s. James and Ruth L. BA, NYU, 1980. Editor N.Y. Times, N.Y.C., 1973-79; editor, polit. writer L.A. Times, 1979-90; asst. to v.p. ops. McClatchy Newspapers, Inc., 1990-92; pub. Ellensburg (Wash.) Daily Record, 1992-98; comm. dir. Gov. State of Washington, Olympia, 1998-99; v.p. comm. St. Michelle Wine Estates, Woodinville, Wash., 1999—. Office: Stimson Lane Vineyards State Wash PO Box 1976 Woodinville WA 98072-1976

LOVE, LAURA, singer, songwriter; Mussician grunge rock bands; performer Carnegie Hall, 1994; rec. artist Z Therapy, 1990, Helvetica Bold, 1990, Pangaea, 1992, Jo MIller and Laura Love Sing Bluegrass and Old-Time Music, 1995, Laura Love Collection, 1995, Octoroon, 1997, Shum Ticky, 1998.

LOVE, LEEANN, elementary school educator; b. Rock Island, Ill., Feb. 14, 1949; d. Larry Vernon and Betty June Burchfield; m. James Stuart Love, Aug. 1, 1978; children: Patrice, Jeff, Will. BA, Rockford Coll., 1972. Health educator Winnebago (Ill.) Dept. Pub. Health; tchr. Byron Sch., Winnebago Sch. Dist. Home: 12195 Tower Rd Byron IL 61010 Address: Jean McNair Elem Sch 304 E McNair Rd Winnebago IL 61088

LOVE, MARY ANN E., state legislator; b. West Pittston, Pa., Feb. 21, 1940; married; 2 children. Grad., Wilkes-Barre (Pa.) Bus. Sch., 1959. State legis. dist.32 Md. Ho. Reps., Annapolis, 1993—, mem. econ. matters com. Chmn. Anne Arundel County Delegation, 1999—. Bd. dirs. Providence Ctr., Hospice of the Chesapeake, North Arundel Hosp. Recipient County Achievement award Nat. Assn. Counties, 1986-89, Anne Arundel Trade Coun. Legis. of Yr. award, 1997. Mem. No. Anne Arundel County C. of C. (Pres.'s award 1996). Office: Md Ho of Reps 214 Lowe House Office Bldg Annapolis MD 21401

LOVE, MARY SUE, finance educator, researcher; b. Mex., Mo., Oct. 23, 1966; d. Robert Carroll and Gloria Sue Love; 1 child, Austin L. Stuart. BBA, Univ. Mo., Kans. City, Mo., 1988, MBA, 1993; PhD, Univ. Mo., Columbus, Mo., 2001. PR rep. Prudential, Kans. City, Mo., 1989—90; underwriter Farmers Ins. Group, Overland, Kans., 1990—94; grad. asst. Univ. Mo., Columbia, Mo., 1994—99; asst. prof. Maryville Univ., St. Louis, 1999—2001, So. Ill. Univ., Edwardsville, Ill., 2001—. Contbr. articles pub. to profl. jour. Mem.: Acad. of Mgmt. Office: SIUE Box 1100 Edwardsville IL 62026 Office Phone: 618-650-2733. Business E-Mail: marlove@siue.edu.

LOVE, MILDRED ALLISON, retired secondary school educator, historian, writer, volunteer; b. Moultrie, Ga., Mar. 12, 1915; d. Ulysees Simpson Sr. and Susie Marie (Dukes) Allison; m. George Alsobrook Love, Aug. 24, 1956 (dec. 1978). BSEd, U. Tampa (Fla.), 1941; MS in Home Econs., Fla. State U., 1953; MA in History, U. Miami, Coral Gables, Fla., 1969. Cert. tchr., Fla. Vocat. home econs. tchr. Hamilton County Pub. Schs., Jasper, Fla., 1941-43, Pinellas County Pub. Schs., Tarpon Springs, Fla., 1946-51, Dade County Pub. Schs., Miami, Fla., 1951-61, history tchr., 1961-73; supr. food svcs. Ft. Jackson (S.C.), 1944-46. Chmn. subcoun. for crime prevention Brickell Area, City of Miami, 1983-87; mem. Crisis Response Team, Miami Police Dept., 1983—; vol. VA Hosp., Miami, 1987—; historian, vol. vets affairs VFW Aux., Miami, 1988-89; precinct worker presdl. election, 1976, 80; sponsor history honor soc. Miami Edison Sr. H.S., 1961-73; mem. Mus. of Sci., St. Stephen's Episc. Ch., Coconut Grove, Fla.; mem. Dade Heritage Trust; charter mem. Libr. Congress Assocs.; mem. Arthritis Found., Consumer Union. Mem. AAUW, VFW (aux. post 471 Miami, Fla.), Am. Assn. Ret. Persons, Hist. Assn. S. Fla., U. Miami Alumni Assn., Fla. Ret. Educators Assn., Nat. Wildlife Fedn., Am. Legion (aux. post 29 Miami, Fla.), Nat. Trust Hist. Preservation, Coll. of Arts and Scis. Assn. U. Miami, Fla. Vocat. Home Econs. Tchrs. (pres. 1947), Fla. Vocat. Home Econs. Assn. (pres. 1948-49), Dade Heritage Trust, Woman's Club of Miami Beach, Sierra Club, Phi Alpha Theta. Democrat. Episcopalian. Avocation: foreign languages. Home: 2411 S Miami Ave Miami FL 33129-1527

LOVE, RICHARD EMERSON, retired equipment manufacturing company executive; b. NYC, Dec. 15, 1926; s. Emerson C. and Ruth A. (Mealley) L.; m. Margaret A. Lloyd, June 24, 1950; children— Mary-Ann, Nancy, Jane, Thomas. Grad., N.Y. State Maritime Coll., 1946; AAS, Hofstra Coll., 1955. Group v.p. Crane Co., N.Y.C., 1967—72, U.S. Filter Co., N.Y.C., 1972—75; group pres. Peabody Internat. Corp., Stamford, Conn., 1975—77, exec. v.p., 1978—85; group v.p. Pullman Co. (merged with Peabody Internat. Corp.), Stamford, 1985—87; v.p. ops. Hosokowa Micron Internat. Inc., N.Y.C., 1987—93; dir., cons. Hosokawa Micron Internat., N.Y.C., 1993—95; ret., 1995. Pres. Internat. Area Mgmt., Hilton Head, S.C., 1995—. Served with USN, 1948-49. Mem. ASME, Instruments Soc. Am. Office: Internat Area Mgmt 16 Old Fort Dr Hilton Head Island SC 29926-2698

LOVE, ROBERT, editor; b. 1952; BA, SUNY, Stony Brook. Managing editor Rolling Stone Magazine, NYC, 1997—2002; editor-in-chief Rollingstone.com; editor-at-large Playboy, 2003—. Bus. reporter Chem. Mktg. Reporter; assoc. editor Saga Mag.; asst. editor NY Mag.; adj. faculty, grad. sch. journalism Columbia U., NYC, 2004—. Editor: The Best of Rolling Stone: 25 Years of Journalism on the Edge, 1993, Tattoo Nation, 2002, George Harrison, 2002.

LOVE, ROBERT LYMAN, retired education educator, consultant; b. Oswego, N.Y., July 28, 1925; s. Robert Barnum and Marion Alberta (Peavy) L.; m. Janet May Fuller, June 26, 1948; children: Robert H., Andrew L., Charles D., Cynthia S. Student, U. Rochester, 1943-44; AB, Syracuse U., 1945, postgrad., 1946-48, MEd, 1949; postgrad., Cornell U., 1963-64. Sci. tchr. Middlesex Valley Central Sch., Rushville, N.Y., 1949-53; mem. faculty Agrl. and Tech. Coll., SUNY-Alfred, 1953-81; prof., dean Agrl. and Tech. Coll., SUNY (Sch. Allied Health Techs.), until 1981, dean emeritus, 1981—; pres. Edn. Cons. Services, Alfred Station, NY, 1981—. Former mem. bd. dirs. Nat. Tech. Inst. Deaf Med. Records program; program evaluation steering com. AMA; allied health reviewer HEW; mem. health sub-com. 39th Congl. Dist. Author: He and She, An Introduction to Human Sexuality and Birth Control, 1970; editor: Upward Mobility for Lab Personnel, 1970. Literacy vol.; pres., bd. dirs. Genesee Valley Habitat for Humanity, Inc., 1993—95, treas., 1995—96, Allegany County Office for Aging Handyman's Svc.; fin. sec., mem. adminstrv. bd. Alfred United Meth. Ch., bd. dirs. presch. and day care ctr., 1992—2003, pres., 1998—2003; mem. Roving Vols. in Christ's Svc., 1982—91, bd. dirs., 1984—86, 1989—91, chmn. bd. dirs., 1989—90; mem. Selected Vols. in Christ's Svc., 1987—88; chaplain vol. Thompson Meml. Hosp., Canandaigua, NY, 2004—, M.M. Ewing Continuing Care Ctr., Canandaigua, 2004—. Fellow Sci. Tchrs. Assn. N.Y. State, Am. Soc. Allied Health Professions; mem. Gideons Internat. (past pres. Hornell Camp), Literacy Vols. Am. (bd. dirs. Allegany County chpt. 1990-93), Masons, Order Eastern Star. Republican. Office: Loves Angels Stained Glass and Edn Cons Svc 171 Deseyn Dr Canandaigua NY 14424 Personal E-mail: rlove4@rochester.rr.com. *Having had the opportunity to work with young people has kept me young and knowing the Lord has saved me.*

LOVE, SAMMIE L., administrative assistant, writer; b. Jefferson, Tex., Sept. 22, 1961; d. Felix P. Love and Lessie M. Mitchell; m. Melvin Earl Grant, July 28, 1980 (div. July 23, 2002); children: Derion Terell Grant, Derion Terell Grant. Cert., Inst. Children's Lit., West Redding, Conn., 1996; BS, U. Phoenix, Dallas, 2001. Safety mgr. Environ., Health & Safety Coun., 1998. Safety mgr. Internat. Paper Co., Jefferson, 1995—2001; adminstrv. asst. Nationwide Tech. Svcs., Inc., Dallas, 2002—. Author: (poetry) Through Love's Eyes (Editor's Choice Award, 1999), Thrown Away Love (Editor's Choice Award, 1999). Hospitality mem. Agape Christian Fellowship, Arlington, Tex., 2001, choir mem., 2001. Mem.: Internat. Soc. Poets (Merit award 1999, 2000, 2001, 2002, 2003). Avocations: volleyball, softball, writing, reading, puzzles. Office: Nationwide Tech Svcs Inc 4010 LaReunion Pkwy Ste 160 Dallas TX 75212 Personal E-mail: gracegiven41@netzero.net. E-mail: slove@ntecserv.com.

LOVE, SHARON IRENE, elementary school educator; b. Pontiac, Mich., July 27, 1950; d. James and Ethlyn (Cole) M.; div.; 1 child, Sheralyn Reneé. BS, Western Mich. U., 1964; postgrad., Oakland U., Rochester, Mich. Cert. elem. educator, early childhood educator, Mich. Tchr. kindergarten Pontiac Bd. Edn., 1964-69, 76-83, 87—, tchr. 1st grade, 1965-66, tchr. 4th grade, 1983-84, tchr. 2d grade, 1984-87. Tchr. trainer triple I.E. classroom instruction Emerson Elem. Sch., Pontiac, 1988-89; trainer Math Their Way, Pontiac Sch. Sys., 1989, leadership, 1990; trainer Mich. Health Model Oakland Schs., Waterfort, 1987; co-chair com. for developing and writing new Fine Arts curriculum for Pontiac Sch. Dist., 1993-94; chmn. coordinating coun. Webster Elem. Sch., 1994-95; head tchr. kindergarten pilot Bethune Elem. Sch., 1995-96. Co-author: kindergarten sci. curriculum for Pontiac Sch. Dist., 2000—02. Chair coord. coun. Walt Whitman Elem. Schs., Pontiac, 1987-91; mem. PTA, 1970-90; chair coord. coun. Webster Elem. Sch., 1993-94, Bethune Elem. Sch., 1999-2000, mem. sch. improvement com., 1999-2000, mem. tech. com., 1999-2000. Creative Art grantee Pontiac PTA, 1965; recipient cert. Appreciation Pontiac Blue Ribbon Com., 1991, cert. for outstanding educator Mich. Gov. Engler, 1991, Mark Twain Elem. cert. for excellence, 2001, AIDS Awareness cert. City of Pontiac, 2001, named to Wall of Tolerance, 2004. Mem. NAACP, Mich. Edn. Assn., Pontiac Edn. Assn. (del. 1965-66). Avocations: art, poetry, sewing. Office: Pontiac Bd Edn 350 Wide Track Dr E Pontiac MI 48342-2243

LOVE, SUSAN MARGARET, surgeon, educator, writer; b. NJ, Feb. 9, 1948; d. James Arthur and Margaret Connick (Schwab) L.; life ptnr. Helen Sperry Cooksey, Sept. 8, 1982; 1 child, Katherine Mary Love-Cooksey. BS, Fordham U., 1970; MD, SUNY, NYC, 1974, DSc (hon.), 1998; MBA, UCLA, 1998; DSc (hon.), Northeastern U., 1991, Trinity Coll., 1999; D of Humane Sci. (hon.), Simmons Coll., 1992; LHD (hon.), U. R.I., 1997. Surgery intern Beth Israel Hosp., Boston, 1974—75, surgical resident, 1975—79, chief resident, 1979, clin. fellow in pathology, 1980, asst. in surgery, 1980—87, dir. breast clinic, 1980-88, assoc. surgeon, 1987—92; clin. fellow in surgery Harvard Med. Sch., Boston, 1977-78, clin. instr. in surgery, 1980-87, asst. clin. prof. surgery, 1987-92; clin. assoc. in surg. oncology Dana Farber Cancer Inst., Boston, 1981-92; dir. Faulkner Breast Ctr. Faulkner Hosp., Boston, 1988-92; assoc. prof. clin. surgery UCLA Med. Sch., 1992-96, adj. prof. divsn. gen. surgery, 1996—2002; dir. Revlon/UCLA Breast Ctr., 1992-96; clin. prof. divsn. gen. surgery David Geffen Sch. Medicine, UCLA, 2002—. Prin. investigator Nat. Surg. Adjuvant Breast and Bowel Project, 1985—96; adv. com. Women's Health Initiative Program, Washington, 1993—95; adv. coun. Breast and Cervical Cancer Program and Breast Cancer Early Detection Program, State of Calif. DHS, 1994—98; mem. Pres.'s Nat. Action Plan on Breast Cancer, DHHS, 1994—2000; co-chair Biol. Resources Working Group, 1994—98; mem. Nat. Cancer Adv. Bd., 1998—2004; nat. adv. environ. health sci. coun. NIH, 2003—04; med. dir. Dr. Susan Love Rsch. Found. (formerly Santa Barbara Breast Cancer Inst., 1983-2000, The Susan Love MD Breast Cancer Research Foundation, 2000-04), 1995—; pres. bd. dirs. Dr. Susan Love Rsch. Found.; founder, sr. ptnr., dir. LLuminari, Inc., 2000—; bd. dirs. Sanarus Med.; cons. Cytyc Health Corp., 2002—04. Author: Dr. Susan Love's Breast Book, 1990, 4th edit., 2005, Dr. Susan Love's Menopause and Hormone Book, 1997, 2nd edit., 2003; Atlas of Techniques in Breast Surgery, 1996; contbr. chpts. to books, articles to profl. jours. Founder, bd. dirs. Nat. Breast Cancer Coalition, 1991—; bd. dirs. Lesbian Health Found., 1992—, Soc. Menstrual Cycle Rsch., 2000—, Y-ME Nat. Breast Cancer Orgn., 2001—. Recipient Rose Kushner award, Am. Med. Writers Assn., 1991, Achievement award, Am. Assn. Physicians for Human Rights, 1992, Women Making History award, U.S. Senator Barbara Boxer, 1993, Woman of Yr. award, YWCA, 1994, Frontrunner award, Sara Lee Corp., 1994, Spirit of Achievement award, Albert Einstein Coll. of Yeshiva U., 1995, Abram L. Sachar medallion, Brandeis U., 1996, Bicentennial honoree, U. Louisville, 1997, Walker prize, Boston Mus. Sci., 1998, Radcliffe medal, 2000, Humanitarian of Yr. award, Western U. Health Sci., Pomona, Calif., 2001, Excellence in Cancer Awareness award, Cancer Rsch. Found. Am., 2002, Dir.'s award, Nat. Cancer Inst., 2004; grantee, Dept. of Def., 1994, 1996. Mem. Am. Med. Women's Assn. (pres. br. 39 1987, Lila Wallis Women's Health award 2004), Soc. for Study of Breast Disease, Am. Soc. Preventive Oncology, Southwestern Oncology Group (women's health and breast com. 1992-96, surg. rep. 1992-96), L.A. Med. Soc., Boston Surg. Soc., N.Am. Menopause Soc., Am. Assn. Cancer Rsch., Am. Coll. Women's Health Physicians, Assn. Women Surgeons. Office: Dr Susan Love Rsch Found PO Box 846 Pacific Palisades CA 90272-0846 Office Phone: 310-230-1712. Business E-Mail: slove@earthlink.net.

LOVE, WILLIAM EDWARD, lawyer; b. Eugene, Oreg., Mar. 13, 1926; s. William Stewart and Ola A. (Kingsbury) L.; m. Sylvia Kathryn Jaureguy, Aug. 6, 1955; children: Kathryn Love Petersen, Jeffrey, Douglas, Gregory. BS, U. Notre Dame, 1946; MA in Journalism, U. Oreg., 1950, JD, 1952. Bar: Oreg. 1952. Newspaper reporter Eugene Register Guard, 1943-44, 47-52; asst. prof. law, asst. dean Sch. Law U. Wash., Seattle, 1952-56; ptnr. Cake, Jaureguy, Hardy, Buttler & McEwen, Portland, Oreg., 1956-69; pres., chmn., CEO Equitable Savs. & Loan, Portland, 1969-82; sr. ptnr. Schwabe, Williamson & Wyatt, Portland, 1983—. Chmn. Oreg. Savs. League, 1976; dir. Portland Gen. Electric, 1976-83, Fed. Home Loan Bank of Seattle, 1976-79, 85-96, adv. coun. Fed. Nat. Mortgage Assn., Washington, 1978-80; exec. dir. Oreg. Facilities Authority, 1990—. Author (with Jaureguy): Oregon Probate Law and Practice, 2 vols., 1958; contbr. articles to profl. jours. Commr., past chmn. Oreg. Racing Commn., 1963-79; pres. Nat. Assn. State Racing Commrs., 1977-78; commr. Port of Portland, 1979-86, pres. 1983; referee Pac-10 football, 1960-81, Rose Bowl, 1981; active United Way, Boy Scouts Am., Portland Rose Festival, polit. campaigns; mem. adv. coun. Jockey's Guild, Inc., 1990-2001. Served to lt. (j.g.) USN, 1944-47. Mem. Oreg. Bar Assn., Multnomah County Bar Assn., Multnomah Athletic Club, Golf Club (Portland). Republican. Home: 421 SW 70th Terr Portland OR 97225-4356 Office: Schwabe Williamson & Wyatt 1211 SW 5th Ave Ste 1800 Portland OR 97204-3713 Office Phone: 503-222-9981.

LOVEJOY, C. OWEN, education educator, researcher; b. Puducah, Ky., Feb. 11, 1943; s. Claude Kildow and Barbara S. Lovejoy; m. Melanie A. McCollum, Mar. 30, 1965. MS, Case Inst. Tech., 1967; PhD, U. Mass., 1970. Prof. Kent (Ohio) State U., Ohio, 1968—. Tech. adv. Cuyahoga County Coroner's Office, Cleve., 1985—; prof. N.E. Ohio Coll. Medicine, Rootstown, Ohio, 1985—2001. Contbr. articles to profl. jours. Recipient Gov. cert., 2000. Home: 7437 Knoll Rd Kent OH 44240 Office: Kent State Univ Hilltop Dr Kent OH 44242 Personal E-mail: olovejoy@aol.com. Business E-Mail: olovejoy@kent.edu.

LOVEJOY, GEORGE MONTGOMERY, JR., real estate company executive; b. Newton, Mass., Apr. 15, 1930; s. George Montgomery and Margaret (King) L.; m. Ellen West Childs, June 30, 1956; children: George Montgomery III, Edward R., Philip W., Henry W. BA, Harvard U., 1951. V.p. Minot, DeBlois & Maddison, Boston, 1955-72; from exec. v.p. to chmn. Meredith & Grew, Inc., Boston, 1972—95; chmn. Fifty Assoc., Boston, 1988-94, pres., 1994—2001. Trustee various Scudder Kemper Inc. mut. funds, 1975-2000. Mem. Weston (Mass.) Planning Bd., 1961-68, chmn., 1965-67; mem. Bd. Selectmen, 1968-71, chmn., 1970-71; bd. dir. Boston Mcpl. Rsch. Bur., 1966—, chmn., 1982-84; mem. com. Fund for Preservation Wildlife and Natural Areas, 1985-94, chmn., 1992-94; trustee New Eng. Aquarium, 1969-2002, overseer, 2002—, pres. 1992-94, chmn. 1994; trustee Radcliffe Coll., 1987-95; mem. Corp. Northeastern U., 1983-2002; bd. dir. Pioneer Inst. for Pub. Policy Rsch. Mem. Counselors of Real Estate (past pres., bd. dir.), Greater Boston Bldg. Owners and Mgr. Assn. (past pres.), Inst. Real Estate Mgmt. (past pres. New Eng. chpt.), Greater Boston Real Estate Bd. (past pres.), Mass. Assn. Realtors, Nat. Assn. Realtors, Nature Conservancy (mem. Mass. adv. bd., chmn. 1994-97), Harvard Club Boston (past pres.). Avocations: outdoor activities, land conservation. Home: 54 Beacon St Boston MA 02108-3531 Office: 50 Congress St Ste 543 Boston MA 02109-4002

LOVEJOY, JEAN HASTINGS, social services counselor; b. Battle Creek, Mich, July 1, 1913; d. William Walter and Elizabeth (Fairbank) H.; m. Allen Perry (dec. 2003); children: Isabel L. Best, Linda L. Ewald, Elizabeth L. Fulton, Margaret L. Baldwin, Helen L. Battad. BA, Mt. Holyoke Coll., So. Hadley, Mass., 1935. Traveling sec. Student Vol. Movement, NYC, 1935; bookkeeper Hartford Consumers Co-op, Conn., 1944; tchr. Pre-School, Congl. Ch., West Hartford, Conn., 1944-45; instr. St. John's U., Shanghai, 1947—49; tchr. Edn., 1st Congl. Ch., Berkeley, Calif., 1958-59; instr. Tunghai U., Taiwan, 1960-63; sec. Pres. Tunghai U., Taichung, Taiwan, 1960-63. Pres. Ecumenical Assn. for Housing, San Rafael, 1971, 78-80; founding mem. Hospice of Havasu, 1982, pres. bd. dir., 1985-87, vol. trainer, 1987-92; bereavement vol. Cmty. Hospice, Tucson, 1993-96; vol. friendly visitor N.W. Interfaith Ctr., Tucson, 1995-98; vol. libr. La Rosa Health Ctr., Tucson, 1998—. Recipient OACC Sr. Achievement award, 1991; named Vol. of Yr., Marin County, Calif., 1970, 79; street named Lovejoy Way in her honor Novato (Calif.) City Coun., 1980. Mem. LWV (program v.p. Pierce County, Wash.chpt. 1967, pres. cen. Marin County chpt. 1973-75, legis. analyst land use 1979-80, Calif. chpt.). Mem. United Ch. of Christ (Stephen min.) Home: Apt 8208 7500 N Calle Sin Envidia Tucson AZ 85718-7363

LOVEJOY, PAUL ROBERT, lawyer; b. Rochester, NY, Jan. 30, 1955; s. V. Paul and Jean M. Lovejoy; m. Susan Seyfarth, Dec. 30, 1978; 1 child, Kate Hightower. BA summa cum laude, New Eng. Coll., 1977; JD, Case Western Reserve U., 1981. Bar: Ohio 1981, NY 1988. Assoc. Squire, Sanders & Dempsey, Cleve., 1981—89, ptnr., 1989—90; asst. gen. counsel Texaco Inc., White Plains, NY, 1990—99; ptnr. Weil, Gotshal & Manges, NYC, 1999—2003; sr. v.p., gen. counsel, sec. UAL Corp., Chgo., 2003—. Trustee New Eng. Coll., Henniker, NH, 1993—2002; bd. dirs. S.W. Legal Found., Dallas, 1990—2003. Office: UAL Corp 1200 E Algonquin Rd Elk Grove Village IL 60007

LOVELACE, ELDRIDGE HIRST, retired landscape architect, city planner; b. Kansas City, Kans., Mar. 16, 1913; s. Charles Wilson and Eva (Hirst) L.; m. Marjorie Van Evera, May 15, 1937; children: Jean (Mrs. William C. Stinchcombe), Richard. B.F.A. in Landscape Architecture, U. Ill., 1935. Registered profl. engr., Mo. With Harland Bartholomew & Assocs., Inc., St. Louis, 1935— 81, mem., 1943-79, chmn. bd., 1979— 81; master plans for naval facilities Hawaiian Islands and P.I. Vice pres. Internat. Fedn. Landscape Architects, 1975-77, sec. gen., 1980—81; cons. in field. Author: Harland Bartholomew: His Contributions to American Urban Planning. Mem. bd. commrs. Tower Grove Park, 1971—, pres. 1986-94. Fellow Am. Soc. Landscape Architects (past sec.), ASCE; mem. Am. Inst. Cert. Planners. Home: 8600 Delmar Blvd Saint Louis MO 63124-1973 E-mail: marjorielovelace@aol.com.

LOVELACE, GAIL T., human resources specialist; married. Various positions Gen. Svcs. Adminstrn., Washington, 1979—98, chief people officer, 1998—. Chief Human Capital Officers Coun. Recipient Presdl. Rank award, 2002, Sr. Exec. Svc. Disting. Exec. award, 2001. Mem.: Internat. Personnel Mgmt. Assn. Office: 1800 F St NW Washington DC 20405*

LOVELACE, JULIANNE, former library director; b. Jackson, Miss., July 30, 1941; d. Benjamin Travis and Julia Elizabeth (Knight) Robinson; m. William Frank Lovelace, July 6, 1963 (div. Mar. 17, 1972); 1 child, Julie Lynn. BA in History, So. Meth. U., 1963; MLS, U. North Tex., 1970. Clk. Dallas Pub. Libr., 1963-64, children's libr. asst., 1964-66, children's libr., 1966-69; libr. Richardson (Tex.) Pub. Libr., 1971-72, supr. pub. svcs., 1972-87, dir., 1987-2001; CFO 4womenShopping, Inc., 2000—. Active Richardson Adult Literacy Ctr., Altrusa Internat., Inc. Richardson, Leadership Richardson Alumni Assn., Friends of the Richardson Pub. Libr., Richardson Regional Med. Ctr., Women's Adv. Coun.; bd. dirs. Richardson Regional Med. Ctr. Found.; mem. exec. steering com. Wildflower Arts & Music Festival. Named one of 21 for the 21st Century, Collin County Bus., 2000. Mem.: Rotary. Avocation: blackjack. Personal E-mail: jl3430@swbell.net.

LOVELACE, RICHARD VAN EVERA, education educator, research scientist; s. Eldridge Hirst and Marjorie Van Evera Lovelace; m. Marina M. Romanova, Oct. 11, 1997; children: Jennifer B., Evera U., Alisa Blinova, Alena Blinova. BS, Wash. U., 1961—64; PhD, Cornell U., 1964—70. Rsch. assoc. Cornell U. Lab. of Plasma Studies, 1970—73; asst. prof. Cornell U. Dept. of Applied and Engring. Physics, 1974—80, assoc. prof., 1980—86; prof. Cornell U., Dept. of Applied and Engring. Physics and Dept. of Astronomy, 1986—. Guggenheim fellowship, Guggenheim Found., 1989, Churchill Coll. Overseas fellow, Churchill Coll., Cambridge U., 1994, Orsan Anderson fellow, Los Alamos Nat. Lab., 2000. Fellow: Am. Phys. Soc.; mem.: Internat. Astron. Union. Office: Cornell Univ Dept Astronomy 410 Space Science Building Ithaca NY 14853-6801

LOVELACE, ROSE MARIE SNIEGON, federal space agency administrator; b. Sweet Hall, Va., Feb. 19, 1937; d. Adolph and Annie (Mickel) Sniegon; m. William Wayne Lovelace, Aug. 11, 1962. Degree in bus., Longwood Coll., 1957. Adminstrv. aide Dept. of Navy, Washington, 1957-60; adminstrv. asst. Joint Blood Coun.-Pvt., Washington, 1960-63; exec. staff NASA, Washington, 1963-73, program analyst-specialist, 1973-80, chief adminstrv. ops. and Congl. affairs br., 1980-92; ret., 1992. Cons. NASA, 1992—. Editor, author: (pamphlet) Space Operations, 1989, (video) Space Communications, 1991. Pres. Jr. Achievement Co., 1953-55, Kettering Recreation Coun., Largo, Md., 1974-76; league coord. U.S. Tennis Assn., Anne Arundel County, Md., 1989-91, team capt., 1984-99, 2001, 04, 05; active Hospice Cup Regatta (sponsor 2000-), Hospice Beacon Hope Gala Com. Fundraiser, 2004, 05, Hospice Circle of Care Soc., 2005-; active LWV, Hospice Planned Giving Coun. Recipient Jr. Achievement Exec. award and Nat. Speakers award, 1954, Gold medal Parks and Planning, Prince Georges County, Md., 1976, Exceptional Svc. award NASA, 1983, Exceptional Svc. medal NASA, 1992. Mem.: Hospice Cir. of Care Soc., Heritage Soc. Anne Arundel Med. Ctr., Historic Annapolis Found., Annapolis Opera, Inc., Am. Heart Assn. (Heart Ball com. fundraiser 2000), Anne Arundel County Tennis Assn., Sportfit Racquet and Fitness Club, Severn Town Club (pres. 1996—98, chair Holly Ball fundraiser 1998—99). Republican. Methodist. Avocations: tennis, gardening, flower arranging, organizing social and tennis events, designing and painting wearable art.

LOVELAND, EUGENE FRANKLIN, retired gas industry executive; b. Anderson, Ind., Sept. 11, 1920; s. Irving Eugene and Clare (Macfarlane) L.; m. Joan King, Aug. 4, 1944; children: Jeffrey, David C. and Peter F. (twins), Mark, Laurie E. BA, Wesleyan U., Middletown, Conn. With Shell Oil Co., 1946-80, v.p. central mktg. region, 1968-71, v.p. oil products Houston, 1972-80; pres. Transworld Oil USA, Inc. (formerly T.W. Oil Inc.), Houston, 1981—; chmn., chief exec. officer T.W. Oil Inc., 1983-89, ret., 1989. Bd. dirs. Transworld Oil Ltd., Bermuda. Bd. dirs. Lyric Theatre, Houston, Am. Dance Cos.; chmn. Houston Ballet Found., Combined Arts Corp., Campaign, Houston, Greater Houston Skating Coun., vice chmn. Better Bus. Bur., Houston; hon. counsul gen. Republic of Malta in Tex.; dir. Cultural Arts Coun. Houston, 1989-93; chmn. Greater Houston Ice Skating Coun., 1989—; mem. exec. com. Houston Internat. Festival, 1992; chmn. devel. commn. Fay Sch., 1992. With USNR, 1943-45. Decorated D.F.C., Air medal (2); recipient Disting. Alumnus award Wesleyan U., 1993, Nat. Order of Merit, Country of Malta, 2003. Mem. Mil. and Hospitaller Order St. Lazarus Jerusalem.

LOVELAND, JOHN BIGELOW, small business owner; b. N.Y.C., Apr. 17, 1934; s. John Howland Gibbs and Daphne Tilton Pell; m. Ellen Pell (dec.); children: John D. Pell, William B. Pell, Daphne C. Pell; m. Bara H. Fischer, July 2, 2001. BA in philosophy, SUNY, 1991. Securities analyst John H.G. Pell & Co., N.Y.C., 1957—60; workshop investigator N.Y.C., 1960—62; bookkeeper, gen. assoc. Pell Gallery, N.Y.C., 1963—75; reg. rep. First Investors Corp., N.Y.C., 1978—79; v.p. Wall St. Mgmt. Corp., N.Y.C., 1980—84; compliance assoc. Morse, Williams & Co., N.Y.C., 1984; ins. agt. Equitable Fin. Svcs., N.Y.C., 1985; proofreader, dispatcher Fact Typographers, N.Y.C., 1986; terminal operator Cosmos Commn., N.Y.C., 1987—88; typesetter Cardinal Type Svc., N.Y.C., 1987; editor Beauty Fashion, Inc., N.Y.C., 1988—89; pres., founder New Earth Found., Sedona, Ariz., 1997—; founder, pres., CEO Earth Cmty. Rsch. Corp., Beaver Creek, Ariz., 2000—. Pres., trustee Ft. Ticonderogo Assn., Ticonderoga, NY, 1988—94. Contbr. articles to profl. jours. With U.S. Army, 1954—56, Germany. Recipient Nat. Leadership award, Nat. Rep. Congrl. Com., 2003. Mem.: Am. Assn. Ret. Persons, Coop Am., Ft. Ticonderoga Assn. Democrat. Episcopal. Avocations: hiking, squash, gardening, opera, piano, reading, plays. Home and Office: Earth Cmty Rsch PO Box 5214 Lake Montezuma AZ 86342 Personal E-mail: jlpell@earthlink.net.

LOVELESS, DARCY E., lawyer; d. Curtis M. and Paula J. Loveless; m. John C. Rentz, Aug. 18, 2001. BA in Criminal Justice, Am. U., DC, 1996; JD, Baylor U., Waco, Tex., 1999. Bar: Tex. 1999, bd. cert. family law: 2005. Atty. Loveless & Loveless, Attys. at Law, LP, Denton, Tex., 1999—. Lectr. in field. Contbr. articles in field. Mem.: Denton County Bar Assn. Family Law Sect. (sec., treas. 2001—02, chair-elect 2002—03, chair 2003—04), Tex. Bar Assn., Denton County Bar Assn. (courts com. mem. 2000—02, dir. 2002—04, chair, fee arbitration com. 2002—, dir. 2004—), Tex. Young Lawyer's Assn., Greater Denton County Young Lawyer's Assn. (dir. 2000—02, sec., treas. 2002—03, pres.-elect 2003—04, pres. 2004—05, chair, reading power com. 2000—02). Office: Loveless Loveless Attorneys at Law LP 218 N Elm Denton TX 76201 Office Phone: 940-387-9776. Fax: 940-898-0196.

LOVELESS, EDWARD EUGENE, education educator, musician; b. Lafayette, Ind., July 29, 1919; s. Benjamin Moses and Belva Lucille (Bowles) L.; m. Jean Evelyn Skinner, May 18, 1941; children: Linda Louise Loveless Reeder, Kathleen Beal Loveless Bodine, Stephen Edward, Melissa Jane Loveless Campbell, Benjamin Warwick. BS, Purdue U., 1940, MS, 1941; Ed.D., Stanford U., 1960. Tchr., prin., supt. public schs., Ind., 1941-57; asst. Stanford U., 1957-60; prin. public schs. Palo Alto, Calif., 1961-65; asst. prof. sch. adminstrn. San Francisco State Coll. and assoc. prof. San Jose State Coll., 1960-65; assoc. prof. U. Nev., Reno, 1965-72, prof., 1972-85, prof. emeritus, 1986—. Vis. prof. Purdue U., summers 1965, 68, 75; prof. exec. devel. program USAF, Crete, spring 1973. Author: (with Frank Krajewski) The Teacher and School Law: Cases and Materials in the Legal Foundations of Education, 1974, (with J. Clark Davis) The Administrator and Educational Facilities, 1982; contbr. over 70 articles to profl. jours.; editor: Who's Who in Northern Nevada Education, 1976; spkr. on sch. vandalism; clarinetist, saxaphonist, vocalist Jean and Ed (musical duo), 1984—; musical tours Ms World Discoverer, Singapore, The South Seas, New Guinea, Western Samoa, Tonga, Fiji, Tahiti, others, 1984-85; performance South Pacific Coll., Stanford U. Alumni Assn., 1985; royal command performance King Tauf-ahau Tupou IV, Tonga, 1985; commd. performance Trident submarine USS Nev., 1986; concert U.S. Embassy, Geneva, 1987; recs. include Songs of the 30's and 40's, The Gershwin Bros., The Best of Irving Berlin, Jerome Kern Favorites, Hoagy & Benny Revisited, An Evening with Cole Porter, We Like Rodgers & Hart, The Genius of Duke Ellington, Easy Listening, Songs of Jule Styne, A Tribute to Jimmy Van Heussen, A Geriatric Jam with Jean, Ed and Nancy Wilson, 1998, Rodgers and Hammerstein Music, 1989, cassette tape series for Wickenburg (Ariz.) Hist. Mus., 1989, Golden Anniversary performance Purdue U., 1990, 74th Birthdays Cassette, 1993, Nat King Cole Songs, 1996. Performer, concert artist for retirement homes and hosps., Palo Alto, Calif., 1990—. Recipient Commendations for providing benefit concerts and performances Sierra Health Care Ctr., 1985, Salvation Army Family Emergency, 1986, VA Hosp., 1988, Daus. of Norway, 1988, Westwood Retirement Home, 1989, State of Nev. Employees Assn., 1989; recipient Certs. of Appreciation Riverside Hosp., 1986, Carson Convalescent Ctr., 1987, Reno Lions Club, 1987, Thank-U-Gram Physicians Hosp., 1988, Manor at Lakeside, 1988, award Washoe County Sr. Citizens Ctr., 1989, Sharon Heights Convalescent Hosp., Palo Alto, Calif., 1993. Mem. NEA, Nev. Edn. Assn., Internat. Soc. Gen. Semantics, Nat. Soc. Profs., Navy League, Kappa Sigma, Phi Delta Kappa (cert. for disting. service 1974, placque of appreciation Gamma Psi chpt. 1976) Democrat. Presbyterian (elder). Home: 2170 Princeton St Palo Alto CA 94306-1325 *Providing musical entertainment for retired and/or hospitalized people has a therapeutic effect that medicine cannot provide. Wynton Marsalis says that "music washes away the dust of everyday life from your feet".*

LOVELESS, GEORGE GROUP, retired lawyer; b. Baldwinsville, N.Y., Sept. 16, 1940; s. Frank Donald and Mayme (Lont) L.; m. Shirley Morrison, Nov. 27, 1965; children: Michael, Peter. BS, Cornell U., 1962, MBA, 1963; JD, U. Md., 1968. Bar: Pa. 1969, U.S. Dist. Ct. (ea. dist.) Pa., U.S. Ct. Appeals (3d cir.). Ptnr. Morgan, Lewis & Bockius LLP, Phila., 1968-2000; ret., 2000. With USAFR, 1963-68. Republican. Presbyterian. Home: 11 Rose Valley Rd Media PA 19063-4217 Office: Morgan Lewis & Bockius LLP 1701 Market St Philadelphia PA 19103-2921 Office Phone: 610-566-1132. E-mail: GGL1@cornell.edu.

LOVELESS, PATTY (PATTY RAMEY), country music singer; b. Pikeville, Ky., Jan. 4, 1957; m. Terry Lovelace (div.); m. Emory Gordy, Jr., Feb. 1989. Recording artist MCA, 1985-93, Sony Music, 1993—. Albums: Patty Loveless, 1987, If My Heart Had Windows, 1988, Honky Tonk Angel, 1988 (gold), On Down the Line, 1990, Up Against My Heart, 1991, Only What I Feel, 1993, Greatest Hits, 1993, When Fallen Angels Fly, 1994, The Trouble With the Truth, Sings Songs of Love, 1996, Long Stretch of Lonesome, 1997, Classics, 1999, Strong Heart, 2000, 20th Century masters: The Millenium Collection, 2000, Mountain Soul, 2001, Bluegrass & White Snow, 2002, On Your Way Home, 2003; # 1 hit singles Timber, I'm Falling in Love, Chains. Named Favorite New Country Artist by Am. Music Awards, 1989, Album of Yr. Country Music Awards, 1995, Top Female Vocalist Acad. Country Music, 1996, Female Vocalist of Yr. Country Music awards, 1996, Vocal Event of Yr., Country Music awards, 1993, 98, 99; recipient TNN Music City News Country Award, Female Artist, 1990, Country Music Awards' Album of the Yr.; co-recipient Grammy award for Best Country Collaboration with Vocals, 1998; inductee Grand Ole Opry, 1988.

LOVELL, CARL ERWIN, JR., lawyer; b. Riverside, Calif., Apr. 12, 1945; s. Carl Erwin and Hazel (Brown) L.; mchildren: Carl Erwin III, Timothy C., Tishia R., Ashley P., Garrett T., Christopher C. BA, Vanderbilt U., 1966, JD, 1969. Bar: Nev. 1969, D.C. 1971, U.S. Supreme Ct. 1973. Jr. editor Land and Water Law Rev., 1973-89; instr. bus. law U. Nev., Las Vegas, Clark County C.C.; city atty. City of N. Las Vegas, 1970-73; elected city atty. City of Las Vegas, 1973-77; v.p., sec.-treas., legal counsel Circus Circus Hotels, Inc., Las Vegas, 1977-83; sr. ptnr. Lovell, Bilbray & Potter, Las Vegas, 1984-89; pvt. practice Las Vegas, 1989—; ptnr. Loven & Lovell, 2000—03, Mitchelson & Lovell, Calif., 2001—; v.p., dir. Air Nev. Airlines, Inc. Chmn. Nat. Inst. Mcpl. Law Officers Consumer Protection Adv. Com., 1973-77, Nev. Crime Commn. Bd., 1974-77; U.S. rep. to China-U.S. Internat. Trade and Law Talks, Beijing, 1987; arbitrator, AAA, 1989—. Bd. dirs., v.p. BBB, 1983-91; chmn. NCCJ; pres. Clark County Young Dems., 1971-72; bd. dirs. Nat. Kidney Found.; pres., trustee Nev. Donor Network, Inc., 1992-96. Mem. ABA, ATLA, Nev. State Bar, Nev. Trial Lawyers Assn., Elks (justice Las Vegas chpt. 1985-88). Office: 2801 S Valley View Blvd Ste 1B Las Vegas NV 89102-0116 Office Phone: 702-362-7922. Business E-Mail: carl@lovell-lovell.com.

LOVELL, EDWARD GEORGE, mechanical engineering educator; b. Windsor, Ont., Can., May 25, 1939; s. George Andrew and Julia Anne (Kopacz) Lovell; m. Roxann Engelstad; children: Elise, Ethan. BS, Wayne State U., 1960, MS, 1961; PhD, U. Mich., 1967. Registered profl. engr., Wis. Project engr. Bur. Naval Weapons, Washington, 1959, Boeing Co., Seattle, 1962; test engr. Ford Motor Co., Troy, Mich., 1960; instr. U. Mich., Ann Arbor, 1963-67; design engr. United Tech., Hartford, Conn., 1970; prof. engring. U. Wis., Madison, 1968—, chmn. dept. engring. mechanics and astronautics, 1992-95, assoc. chmn. dept. of mech. engring., 1999—. Cons. structural engring. to govt. labs., indsl. orgns., maj. textbook pubs., 1968—. Contbr. numerous articles to profl. jours. Postdoctoral research fellow Nat. Acad. Sci., 1967; NATO Sci. fellow, 1973; NSF fellow, 1961 Mem. Wis. Fusion Tech. Inst., Wis. Ctr. for Applied Microelectronics, Sigma Xi, Tau Beta Pi, Phi Kappa Phi Office: U Wis Dept Mech Engring 1513 University Ave Madison WI 53706-1572

LOVELL, EMILY KALLED, retired journalist; b. Grand Rapids, Mich., Feb. 25, 1920; d. Abdo Rham and Louise (Claussen) Kalled; m. Robert Edmund Lovell, July 4, 1947. Student, Grand Rapids Jr. Coll., 1937-39; BA, Mich. State U., 1944; MA, U. Ariz., 1971. Copywriter, asst. traffic mgr. Sta. WOOD, Grand Rapids, 1944-46; traffic mgr. KOPO, Tucson, 1946-47; reporter, city editor Alamogordo (N.Mex.) News, 1948-51; Alamogordo corr., feature writer Internat. News Svc., Denver, 1950-54, El Paso Herald-Post, 1954-65; Alamogordo news dir., feature writer Tularosa (N.Mex.) Basin Times, 1957-59; co-founder, editor, pub. Otero County Star, Alamogordo, 1961-65; newscaster KALG, Alamogordo, 1964-65; freelance feature writer Denver Post, N.Mex. Mag., 1949-69; corr. Electronic News, N.Y.C., 1959-63, 65-69; Sierra Vista (Ariz.) corr. Ariz. Republic, 1966; freelance editor N.Mex. Pioneer Interviews, 1967-69; asst. dir. English skills program Ariz. State U., 1976; free-lance editor, writer, 1977—2003; ret., 2003. Part-time tchr., lectr. U. Pacific, 1981-86; part-time interpreter Calif., 1983-91, Interpreters Unlimited, Oakland, 1985-91; sec., dir. Star Pub. Co., Inc., 1961-64, pres., 1964-65, 3d v.p., publicity chmn. Otero County Cmty. Concert Assn., 1950-65; mem. Alamogordo Zoning Commn., 1955-57; mem. founding com. Alamogordo Ctrl. Youth Activities Com., 1957; vice chmn. Otero County chpt. Nat. Found. Infantile Paralysis, 1958-61; charter mem. N.Mex. Citizens Coun. for Traffic Safety, 1959-61; pres. Sierra Vista Hosp. Aux., 1966; pub. rels. chmn. Ft. Huachuca chpt. ARC, 1966; mem. nat. bd. Hospitalized Vets. Writing Project,

1972-99; vol. instr. autobiography and creative writing, 1991-2002. Author: A Personalized History of Otero County, New Mexico, 1963, Weekend Away, 1964, Lebanese Cooking, Streamlined, 1972, A Reference Handbook for Arabic Grammar, 1974, 77; contbg. author: The Muslim Community in North America, 1983. Recipient 1st Pl. awards N.Mex. Press Assn., 1961, 62, Pub. Interest award Nat. Safety Coun., 1962, 1st Pl. award Nat. Fedn. Press Women, 1960, 62; named Woman of Yr. Alamogordo, 1960, Editor of Week Pubs. Aux., 1962, adm. N.Mex. Navy, 1962, col. A.D.C. Staff Gov. N.Mex., 1963, Woman of Yr., Ariz. Press Women, 1973. Mem. N.Mex. Press Women (past sec.), Ariz. Press Women (past pres.), N.Mex. Fedn. Womens Clubs (past dist. pub. rels. chmn., hon. life Alamogordo), N.Mex. Hist. Soc. (life), N.Mex. Fedn. Bus. and Profl. Womens Clubs (past pres., hon. life Alamogordo), Pan Am. Round Table Alamogordo, Theta Sigma Phi (past nat. 3d v.p.), Phi Kappa Phi. Democrat. Moslem. Home: Apt 222 1925 Possum Hollow Rd Slidell LA 70458-8318 *Personal philosophy: You have to live with yourself...an idle grouch is bad company.*

LOVELL, JOHN A., music educator; b. Hopkinsville, Ky., Aug. 16, 1976; s. Ed and Margaret Lovell; m. Cara Lovell, May 20, 2000; 1 child, Landon Allen. BS, Ausin Peay State u., 2000. Band dir. and chair music Todd County H.S., Elkton, Ky., 2001—. Chairperson 3rd Dist. Band Dir. Assoc., 2004—. Mem.: Music Educators Nat. Conf., Phi Mu Alpha. Mem. Ch. Of Christ. Home: 209 Andrew Dr Hopkinsville KY 42240

LOVELL, MALCOLM READ, JR., public information officer, educator, retired trade association administrator, retired federal official; b. Greenwich, Conn., Jan. 1, 1921; s. Malcolm Read and Emily (Monihan) L.; m. Celia Coghlan, 1978; children by previous marriage: Lucie, Sara. Annette, Caroline. Student, Brown U., 1939-42; I.A., Harvard U., 1943; MBA, Harvard, 1946. With Ford Motor Co., Dearborn, Mich., 1946-58; mgr. employee services Am. Motors Corp., Detroit, 1958-61; chmn. State Labor Mediation Bd., Detroit, 1963; dir. Mich. Office Econ. Opportunity, 1964, Mich. Employment Security Commn., Detroit, 1965-69; exec. asso. Manpower, Urban Coalition, 1969; dep. asst. sec. of labor and manpower adminstr., 1969-70; asst. sec. of labor for manpower, 1970-73; pres. Rubber Mfrs. Assn., 1973-81; asst. dir. Office Policy Coordination and Econ. Affairs, Office Pres.-Elect, 1980; undersec. Dept. Labor, Washington, 1981-83; vis. scholar Brookings Instn., Washington, 1983-85; disting. vis. prof. govt. and dir. Labor Mgmt. Inst., George Washington U., 1985-92, 99—; pres. Nat. Policy Assn., 1992-99; sr. fellow Hudson Inst., 1985-88; exec. Exec. Coaching Network, 1999—; exec. in residence George Washington U. Sch. Bus. and Pub. Mgmt., 1999—. Mem. Nat. Adv. Coun. on Vocat. Edn., 1975-79, Nat. Commn. for Manpower Policy, 1977-79; chmn. sec. labor Task Force on Econ. Adjustment and Worker Dislocation, 1985-86; mediator Collective Bargaining Forum, 1983-2000; adj. prof. Sch. Bus., George Washington U. V.p. Birmingham (Mich.) Sch. Bd., 1956-60; bd. dirs. Nat. Alliance Bus., 1984—; bd. dirs. Travelers Aid of Washington, 1983-86, pres., 1985-86. Lt. USNR, 1943-46. Sr. fellow Hudson Inst., 1985-88. Mem. Clean Plate (Washington), Cosmos Club (Washington), Alpha Delta Phi.

LOVELL, MICHAEL C., economics professor; b. Cambridge, Mass., Apr. 11, 1930; s. Reginald Ivan and Rose Mary (Chittenden) L.; m. Adrienne Goolkasian, June 21, 1959; children: Leslie Rosemary, Stacie Alice, George Ivan, Martin Benjamin BA, Reed Coll., 1952; MA, Stanford U., 1954; PhD, Harvard U., 1959. Instr. Yale, 1958-59, asst. prof., 1959-63; mem. staff Cowles Found., 1958-63; assoc. prof. Grad. Sch. Indsl. Adminstrn., Carnegie-Mellon U., 1963-66, prof., 1966-69; prof. econ. Wesleyan U., Middletown, Conn., 1969—, chmn. dept., 1973—75, 1994—96; prof. Chester D. Hubbard/Soc. Sci., 1996—2002. Vis. prof. Sch. Mgmt. Yale U., 1981-82, 86, 88; cons. Pres.'s Coun. Econ. Advisors, 1964, 67; sr. adviser Brookings Panel on Econ. Activity, 1974-90. Author: (with Albert Hirsch) Sales Anticipations and Inventory Behavior, 1969, Macroeconomics: Measurement, Theory and Policy, 1975, (with Attila Chikan) The Economics of Inventory Management, 1988, Economics With Calculus, 2004; assoc. editor Econometrica, 1965-68, Jour. Econs. and Bus., 1983-86, Jour. Econ. Behavior and Orgn., 1987-98, Rev. Econs. and Stats., 1991-92, Social Sci. Computer Rev., 1993-99; fgn. editor Rev. Econ. Studies, 1968-70. With U.S. Army, 1953-55. Recipient 1st prize Joint Council Econ. Edn., Kazanjian Found. awards program for teaching econs., 1973-74; Ford Found. Faculty Research fellow, 1964-65; Social Sci. Research Council Tng. fellow, 1957-58; Earhart Found. fellow, 1956-57; Harvard Grad. Sch. fellowship, 1955-56; W.H. Robinson fellowship, 1952-53; NSF research grantee, 1962-64, 66-68, 70-72 Fellow Econometric Soc.; mem. Am. Econ. Assn. (chmn. publs. com. 1975-78), Am. Statist. Assn. (assoc. editor Jour. 1975-78), Internat. Soc. Inventory Rsch. (exec. com., chmn. inventories and nat. economy sect. 1982—, pres. 1992-94) Home: 121 Paterson Dr Middletown CT 06457 E-mail: mlovell@wesleyan.edu.

LOVELL, THEODORE, electrical engineer, consultant; b. Paterson, N.J., May 10, 1928; s. George Whiting and Ethel Carol (Berner) L.; m. Wilma Syperda, May 8, 1948 (div. Oct. 1961); m. Joyce Smelik, July 15, 1962; children: Laurie, Dorothy Jane, Valerie, Cynthia, Karen, Barbara. BEE, Newark Coll. Engring., 1948; postgrad., Canadian Inst. Tech., 1950. Exec. dir. Lovell Electric Co., Franklin Lakes, N.J., 1955-82; ptnr., exec. dir. Lovell Design Services, Swedesboro, N.J., 1982—. Author engring. computer software, 1982. Bd. dirs., treas. Contact "Help" of Salem County, 1991-93; pres. Bloomingdale Bd. Edn., N.J., 1970-82; mem. Mcpl. Planning Bd., Bloomingdale, 1980-82, Swedesboro/Woolwich Bd. Edn., 1987-94, v.p., 1990-92, pres. 1993-94; mayoral candidate Borough of Bloomingdale, 1982; v.p. Woolwich Twp. Rep. Club, 1996—; chmn. Woolwich Twp. Bus. Adv. Com., 1997—; mem. Gloucester County Econ. Devel. Coun., 1998-2002, chmn., Woolwich Township Nike Base Com., 2004-. Recipient Outstanding Service award Lake Iosco Co., Bloomingdale, 1985, 20 Yr. Svc. award N.J. Sch. Bd. Assn., 1994. Fellow Radio Club Am.; mem. Soc. Engring. Technicians, Dickinson Theater Organ Soc. (corp. sec., bd. dirs.). Presbyterian. Avocations: Lincoln history, theatre organ music. Home: 16 Liberty Ct Woolwich Township NJ 08085-3010 Office: Lovell Design Svcs PO Box 366 Swedesboro NJ 08085-0366 Office Phone: 856-467-2578. *It has become apparent to me, slowly perhaps that as I progress through life, the things that bring lasting joy and satisfaction are not personal achievements, but those things that help others.*

LOVELL, TOBIN RYAN, psychologist, educator; b. Marion, Ohio, June 5, 1975; s. Gary Lee and Linda Jean Lovell. BA in Psychology and Polit. Sci., Ohio U., 1997; PsyD, Wright State U., 2002. Lic. psychology Ga. Staff psychologist Ga. So. U., Statesboro, 2003—. Home: 103 Valley Rd #13 Statesboro GA 30458

LOVELL, WALTER BENJAMIN, secondary education educator, radio broadcaster; b. Cottonwood, Ariz., Jan. 7, 1947; s. Walter William Lovell and Mary Katherine (MacDonald) Bruce; m. Patsy Nichols, July 16, 1965 (div. Nov. 1986); children: Katherine Vi, Walter Kenneth, Karen Jennifer, Kristin Diane; m. Karen Lynn Bird, Mar. 3, 1990. AA, Ea. Ariz. Coll., 1966; B of Music Edn., No. Ariz. U., 1969, MusM, 1975; PhD in Music Edn., Hamilton U., 2002. Dir. of bands Kingman (Ariz.) High Sch., 1968-70; asst. dir. bands Phoenix Union High Sch., 1970-71; dir. bands Carl Hayden High Sch., Phoenix, 1971-73, Mohave High Sch., Bullhead City, Ariz., 1973-78, Elko (Nev.) High Sch., 1978—. Condr. competitive performances with Elko H.S. Band, including Grand Champions Holiday Bowl Parade, Field and Jazz competition, 1994, Nat. Freedom Bowl, Anaheim, Calif., 1988, 90, Disneyland Parade, Anaheim, 1990, Weber State U., Ogden, Utah, 1990-97, 2002, U. Utah, 1995, Boise (Idaho) State U., 1990-97, 2000-01, U. Nev.-Las Vegas Band Competition, 1988, Fiesta Bowl Parade, Phoenix, 1985, Tournament of Roses Parade, Pasadena, 1983, 95, 99, Presdl. Inaugural Parade, Washington, 1981, No. Nev. Youth Band Tour of Great Britain, 1982, Macy's Thanksgiving Day Parade, 1979, 2000, Performances in Washington, 1981, 2000, Hollywood Christmas Parade, 2002, 6ABC/Boscov's Thanksgiving Day Parade, Phila., 2004; assoc. dir. All-Ariz. Bi-Centennial Band, 1976. Composer: (concert band compositions) Suite for Band, 1975, Tranquility, 1988. Recipient Gubernatorial Proclamation for Elko H.S. Band, 1981, 83, 86, 88, 90, 92, 94, 96, 98, Proclaimed The Pride of Nev., 1995, 96, 2000, 2002, Proclaimed Nev.'s Mus. Amb., 1998, 2000; Gubernatorial Proclamation No. Nev. Youth Band, 1982, Nat. Sch. Band Achievement awards, 1981, 82; recipient Disting. Svc. award U. Nev.-Reno Bands, 1986, Citation of Excellence Nat. Band Assn., Nev. State Bd. Edn., 1983, Disting. Bandmaster of Am. award, 1981, Nev. State Marching Band Champion award, 1983-86, 92-94, 97, 99, 2001, Holiday Bowl Jazz Festival Grand Champion award, 1992, Nev. Music Educator of Yr., 1999; named to Nev. Broadcasters Hall of Fame, 2001; regional finalist Bands of Am., 1999, Class AA Regional Champion, 2001. Mem. Nat. Band Assn. (citation of Excellence 1987), Am. Sch. Band Dirs. Assn., Nev. Music Educators Assn., Music Educators Nat. Conf., Ariz. Band and Orchestra Dir.'s Assn., Internat. Assn. Jazz Educators, Nat. Assn. Jazz Educators, Ariz. Music Educators Assn. Office: Elko High Sch 987 College Ave Elko NV 89801-3419 E-mail: bandguy@frontiernet.net.

LOVELL, WHITFIELD, artist; b. N.Y.C., 1959; BFA, Cooper Union Sch. Art, 1981. Artist-in-residence Mousem D'Asilah, Morocco, 1988, Art Awareness, Lexington, NY, 1991, Warhol Mus., Pitts., 1998, U. North Tex., 1999, Hand Workshop Art Ctr., Richmond, Va., 2000, Ctr. for Documentary Studies, Duke U., Durham, NC, 2001, Contemporary Art Ctr. Va., 2002; Diebenkorn fellow San Francisco Art Inst., 2003. One-man shows include Interchurch Ctr., N.Y., 1982, Galeria Morivivi, 1984, John Jay Coll., 1985, Harlem Sch. Arts, 1987, Jersey City Mus., 1988, Lehman Coll. Art Gallery, N.Y., 1993, Southeastern Ctr. Contemporary Art, Winston-Salem, 1997, D.C. Moore Gallery, N.Y., 1997—2000, 2002, The Andy Warhol Mus., Pitts., 1998, U. North Tex. Art Gallery, Denton, 1999, Studio Mus., Harlem, N.Y., 2000, Neuberger Mus. Art, N.Y., 2000, Montclair (N.J.) Art Mus., 2001, Tubman African Am. Mus., Ga., 2001, Jones Ctr. Contemporary Art, Tex., 2000, Knoxville Mus., Tenn., 2001, Boston U. Art Gallery, 2001, Hand Workshop, Richmond, Va., 2001, Evansville (Ind.) Mus., 2002, U. Wyo. Art Mus., Laramie, 2002, Columbus (Ga.) Mus., 2002, Thomasville Cult Ctr., Ga., 2002, Black History Mus., Va., 2002, Cont. Art Ctr., 2002, Hurston Nat. Mus., Fla, 2003, Art Mus. S.E. Tex., 2003, Bronx Mus., N.Y., 2003, Flint (Mich.) Inst. Arts, 2003, Mus. Contemporary Art, Sydney, 2004, others, exhibited in group shows at AIR Gallery, N.Y., 1981—82, ABC No Rio, 1982, Cayman Gallery, 1983, one-man shows include Flint Inst., Mich., 2003, exhibited in group shows at Kenkeleba Gallery, N.Y.C., 1984—85, Howard U. Gallery of Art, Washington, 1985, Bronx River Art Gallery, N.Y.C., 1985, Longwood Arts Gallery, 1986, Met. Life Gallery N.Y., 1987, Alijira Gallery, Newark, 1988, Cinque Gallery, N.Y., 1989, Snug Harbor Cultural Ctr., 1990, Pepsico Gallery, 1991, Boston Mus. Fine Arts, 1991, Allen Meml. Art Mus., Miami, Fla., 1992, Intar Gallery, N.Y., 1993, Agustin Barrios Gallery, Asuncion, Paraguay, 1994, 450 Broadway Gallery, N.Y., 1994, Puffin Found., N.Y.C., 1994, Exit Art, 1995, Ark. Arts Ctr., Little Rock, 1995, DC Moore Gallery, N.Y., 1995, 1996, 1998, Round 3 Inst. Project Row Houses, Houston, 1996, Atrium Gallery, Morristown, N.J., 1997, David Klein Gallery, Birmingham, Mich., 1997, Sexta Biennial, Havana, Cuba, 1997, Craven Gallery, West Tisbury, Mass., 1998, Bronx Mus. Art, 1999—2000, Nat. Mus. Am. Art, Washington, 1999, Seattle Art Mus., 2000, Yale U. Art Gallery, New Haven, 2000, Megura Mus., Tokyo, 2001, Hunter Coll., N.Y., 2000, Bronx Mus., 2000, Colby Coll., Maine, 2001, Met. Mus. Art, N.Y.C., 2003, Corcoran Gallery, Washington, 2003, others, Represented in permanent collections The Libr. of Congress, Washington, Met. Mus. Art, N.Y.C., New Sch. Social Rsch., Seattle Art Mus., Yale U. Art Gallery, Neuberger Mus. Art, N.Y.C., Nat. Mus. Am. Art, Washington, Hunter Mus. Art, Tenn., The Promise of Learnings Collection, N.Y.C., Ark. Arts Ctr., Bronx Mus., Chrysler Mus., Va., Flint Inst. Arts, Mich., Greenville Co. Mus., S.C., Harvard Bus. Sch., MA, Montclair Mus., N.J., Whitney Mus., N.Y., Corcoran Gallery, Washington, Met. Mus. Art, NY, Montclair (NJ) Art Mus., Ark. Arts Ctr., Little Rock. Fellow Jerome Found. fellow, Robert Blackburn Printmaking Workshop, 1982, Regional fellow, Mid-Atlantic Nat. Endowment Arts, 1992; scholar Eastman scholar, Skowhegan Sch. Painting and Sculpture, 1985; Joan Mitchell Found. grantee, 1996, Robert Blackburn Printmaking Workshop fellow, 1985, N.Y. Found. Arts fellow, 1997, N.Y. State Coun. Arts grantee, 1986—87, Penny McCall Found. grantee, 1990, Artists Homeless Shelter Collaborative grantee, 1991, N.Y. Found. Arts grantee, 1991. Office: care DC Moore Gallery 724 5th Ave New York NY 10019-4106

LOVELY, RANDY, editor; b. Tennessee; Grad., Central Mich. Univ. Asst. managing editor News-Press, Fort Myers, Fla.; managing editor The Times, Shreveport, La., 1997—2000; exec. editor Desert Sun, Palm Springs, Calif., 2000—02; managing editor Arizona Republic, 2002—. Office: c/o Arizona Republic 200 E Van Buren Street Phoenix AZ 85004

LOVEMAN, GARY W., gaming company executive; BA in Econs., Wesleyan U., 1982; PhD in Econs., MIT, 1989. Assoc. prof. bus. adminstrn. Harvard U., 1989—98; cons. Harrah's Entertainment, Inc., exec. v.p., 1998—2001, COO, 1998—2003, pres., 2001—, CEO, 2003—, also chmn. Co-author: The Evolving Role of Small Business and Some Implications for Employment and Training Policy, 1990; author: An Assessment of the Productivity Impact of Information Technologies, 1994; co-author: Starting Over in Eastern Europe: Entrepreneurship and Economic Renewal, 1995. Recipient Apgar award for Excellence and Innovation in Tchg., Harvard Bus. Sch.; Alfred Sloan Doctoral Dissertation fellow. Mem.: Phi Beta Kappa. Office: One Harrahs Ct Las Vegas NV 89119 Office Phone: 702-407-6316.

LOVEN, ANDREW WITHERSPOON, environmental engineering company executive; s. Andrew Witherspoon Loven and Annie Laura (Crowell) Stewart; m. Elizabeth Joann DeGroot, June 20, 1959 (dec.); children: Laura Elizabeth, James Edward. BS, Maryville Coll., 1957; PhD in Chemistry, U. N.C., 1962. Registered profl. engr., Colo., Ga., La., Md., N.C., S.C., D.C., Ohio, Fla., Mich., Va. Rsch. assoc. U. N.C., Chapel Hill, 1962-63; sr. rsch. chemist Westvaco Corp., Charleston, S.C., 1963-66, mgr. carbon devel., 1966-71, mgr. wastewater cons. svc., 1967-71; mgr. engring. concepts Engring.-Sci. Inc., McLean, Va., 1971-74, v.p., regional mgr. Atlanta, 1974-80, group v.p., 1980-86; pres., CEO Engring. Sci. Inc., Pasadena, Calif., 1986-95, also chmn. bd. dirs.; exec. v.p. Parsons Engring. Sci. Inc., Pasadena, Calif., 1995; pres., CEO Millennium Sci. & Engring., Inc., McLean, Va., 1995—. Contbr. articles to profl. jours. NSF grantee, 1958-59; recipient Maryville Coll. Alumni Citation award, 1992. Mem. AIChE, NSPE, Am. Acad. Environ. Engrs. (diplomate, membership com. 1985—), Water Environment Fedn., Am. Water Works Assn., Am. Pub. Works Assn., Constrn. Industry Pres. Forum, Country Club Roswell, Sigma Xi, Alpha Gamma Sigma. Avocations: golf, hiking. Home: 1512 Barksdale Ct Kennesaw GA 30152 Office: Millennium Sci & Engring Inc 6145 Barfield Rd Ste 110 Atlanta GA 30328

LOVENTHAL, MILTON, writer, playwright, lyricist; b. Atlantic City; s. Harry and Clara (Feldman) L.; m. Jennifer McDowell, July 2, 1973. BA, U. Calif., Berkeley, 1950, MLS, 1958; MA in Sociology, San Jose State U., 1969. Researcher Hoover Instn., Stanford, Calif., 1952-53, spl. asst. to Slavic Curator, 1955-57; librarian San Diego Pub. Library, 1957-59; librarian, bibliographer San Jose (Calif.) State U., 1959-92. Tchr. writing workshops, poetry readings, 1969-73; co-producer lit. and culture radio show Sta. KALX, Berkeley, 1971-72; editor, pub. Merlin Press, San Jose, 1973—, Lipstick & Toy Balloons Publ. Co., 1978—, Abbie & Dolley Records, 2003—. Author: Books on the USSR, 1951-57, 57, Black Politics, 1971 (featured at Smithsonian Inst. Special Event, 1992), A Bibliography of Material Relating to the Chicano, 1971, Autobiographies of Women, 1946-70, 72, Blacks in America, 1972, The Survivors, 1972, Contemporary Women Poets an Anthology, 1977, Ronnie Goose Rhymes for Grown-Ups, 1984; co-author: (Off-Off-Broadway plays) The Estrogen Party to End War, 1986, Mack the Knife, Your Friendly Dentist, 1986, Betsy & Phyllis, 1986, The Oatmeal Party Comes to Order, 1986, (plays) Betsy Meets the Wacky Iraqi, 1991, Bella and Phyllis, 1994; co-writer (mus. comedy) Russia's Secret Plot to Take Back Alaska, 1988; lyricist Intern Girl, 1998, Smithsonian, 2002; (musical revs., CD) She, A Tapestry of Women's Lives (Found. award Calif. State U. ERFA, 2004). Recipient Bill Casey Award in Letters, 1980; grantee, San Jose State U., 1962—63, 1984. Mem. Assn. Calif. State Profs., Calif. Alumni Assn., Calif. Theatre Coun., Am. Assn. for Advancement of Slavic Studies, Soc. for Sci. Study of Religion. Office: PO Box 5602 San Jose CA 95150-5602 Office Phone: 800-889-8305. E-mail: jeditorphd@earthlink.net.

LOVERICH, BARBARA LOUISE, secondary school educator; b. Gary, Ind., July 3, 1949; d. Charles Carroll and Edith Ruth (Siewert) Gibson; m. Richard James Loverich, Jan. 24, 1970; children: Derek, Melissa. BS in Edn., Ind. U., 1972; MALS in History, Valparaiso U., 1976; postgrad., Ind. U.-Purdue U., Indpls., 1989, Taylor U., Upton, Ind., 1990, Valparaiso U., 1989, St. Mary of Woods, 1989, Earlham, 1991. Tchr. social studies Portage (Ind.) High Sch., 1972-79, Bishop Noll Inst., Hammond, Ind., 1981-85; asst. dir. adminstrn. LaLumiere, La Porte, Ind., 1987-88; tchr. social studies Hobart (Ind.) High Sch., 1988—, dept. chair, 2003—. Tchr. cons. Geographers Edn. Network, Ind., 1989—. Recipient Outstanding Secondary Educator, C. of C., 2003. Mem. APA, Geographers Edn. Network of Ind., Ind. Coun. Social Studies, Nat. Coun. Social Studies, Tchrs. psychology in Secondary Schs., Nat. Geographers Assn. Democrat. Roman Catholic. Avocations: soccer, volleyball, crocheting, reading, knitting. Office: Hobart High Sch 36 E 8th St Hobart IN 46342-5196 Office Phone: 219-942-8521 357.

LOVERIDGE, B. CLARK, mathematician, educator; b. Kalamazoo, Mich., Dec. 3, 1949; s. Benjamin Clark and Margaret Mae (Wright) Loveridge; m. Lee H. Friedman, Nov. 10, 2002; children: Daniel B. Friedman, Victor C. Freidman. BA in Math., Western Mich. U., Kalamazoo, 1973; MA in Stats., U. Mich., Ann Arbor, 1975; MA in Math., Temple U., Phila., 1993, PhD in Math., 2002. Clk. U. Mich., Ann Arbor, 1975—78, Robin's Book Store, Phila., 1978—82; math instr. C.C. Phila., 1982—. Mem. negotiating team Am. Fedn. Tchrs. local 2026, Phila., 1984—85; mem. math awards com. C.C. Phila., 1999—. Vol. Movement New Society, Phila., 1979—88. Mem.: Am. Fedn. Tchrs., Math. Assn. Am., Am. Math. Soc. Avocations: folk dancing, folk music, bicycling. Office: CC Phila 1700 Spring Garden St Philadelphia PA 19130 Office Phone: 215-751-8689.

LOVERIDGE-SANBONMATSU, JOAN MEREDITH, communication studies and women's studies educator, poet; b. Hartford, Conn., July 5, 1938; d. Gilbert Thomas and Rosabel Frances (Nowry) Loveridge; m. Akira Sanbonmatsu, Aug. 29, 1964; children: James Michael, Kevin Yosh. BA, U. Vt., 1960; MA, Ohio U., 1963; PhD, Pa. State U., 1971. Writer, programming radio/tv WRUV, WCAX, Burlington, Vt., 1956-60, WOUB, Athens, Ohio, 1962-63, AFKN, Korea, 1960-61; unit head ARC, Japan, Korea, 1960-61; asst. prof. SUNY, Brockport, 1963-77, prof. comm. studies and women's studies Oswego, 1977-98, prof. emerita, 1999—, instr. intensive English summer program, 1993—2001, co-coord. women's studies program, 1978-80, 82, instr. internat. studies infusion program, 1985-91. Vis. prof. Rochester (N.Y.) Inst. Tech., 1971; assoc. adj. prof. Monroe C.C., Rochester, 1972-76; instr. Pa. State, State College, 1966-67; cons. for oral history project ARC Overseas Assn., 1994—; cons. Cazenovia Coll., N.Y., 1988-89; pres. bd. dirs. Woman's Career Ctr. Inc., Rochester, 1975-76; invited Japan Lecture Tour, 1997. Author: Winged Odyssey: Poems and Stories, 2002; co-author: Feminism and Woman's Life, 1995; contbg. author: Women Public Speakers in the US, 1925-1993, Vol. 2, 1994, Life in a Fishbowl: A Call to Serve, 2003; poetry editor/editl. bd. Lake Effect, 1985-92; contbr. articles to profl. jours., poetry to lit. publs. Religious edn. team tchr. May Meml. Unitarian Universalist Soc., Syracuse, 1979-81; mem. adv. parent com., Oswego H.S., 1986-87. Recipient Unsung Heroine award Ctrl. N.Y. NOW, Syracuse, 1987; presdl. citation for social change ARC Overseas Assn., 1998, Creative Contbn. award, 2005; rsch. grantee Pa. State U., 1970, SUNY, Oswego, 1978, 91, 92, 94, 95, 96, N.Y. State United Univ. Professions Profl. Devel. and Quality of Working Life grantee, 1985, 87, 93, 94, 98, SUNY Oswego Women's Ctr. award, 1996, 98, SEED award for outstanding work with disabled students, 1998, Internat. Awareness and Peace award Coalition for Peace Edn., 2000, Student award ESL, 1995, 96, 98, Syracuse Poster Project award, 2005; fellow U. Ill., Chgo., 1983. Mem. N.Y. Asian Studies Assn., Nat. Comm. Assn. (women's caucus job placement dir., exec. bd. 1977-78), Ea. Comm. Assn., N.Y. Nat. Comm. Assn., Soc. for Intercultural Edn., Tng. and Rsch., Nat. Women's Studies Assn., Speech Comm. Assn. P.R., N.Y. State Women's Studies Assn., ARC Overseas Assn. (v.p. 1999-2001), Nat. Assn. Poet and Writers, Inc. Avocations: Spanish, walking. Home: 23 McCracken Dr Oswego NY 13126-6011

LOVERINK, VIRGINIA LOUISE, retired elementary school educator; b. Newton, Iowa, Apr. 21, 1940; d. Chester and Ruth Helen (Fennema) VanZee; m. Gene Edwin Loverink, July 6, 1962; children: David Mark, Elizabeth Louise. BA, Ctrl. Coll., Pella, Iowa, 1962. Cert. tchr., Iowa. Tchr. kindergarten Grinnell Sch. Sys., Iowa, 1962—66, Norwalk Sch. Sys., Iowa, 1966—67; tchr. pre-sch. Wakonda Christian, Des Moines, 1974—75; tchr. Susuki piano Des Moines, 1981—84; tchr. pre-sch. St. Andrews, Des Moines, 1985—93; dir. pre-sch. West Des Moines Christian Ch., 1993—95; ret., 2004. Piano tchr., 1986—2004; asst. tchr. pre-sch. Farmer in the Dell Pre-Sch., 1996—97, lead tchr., 1997—2001. PTA bd. dirs. Olmstead Sch., 1980-83; curriculum com. Park Ave Presbyn. Ch., Des Moines, 1978, ch. sch. tchr., 1975-79, Reformed Ch., Des Moines, 1983-88; hospitality chmn. Bankers Wives of Des Moines, 1983, corr. sec., 1982, sec., 1984, 2d v.p., 1985; v.p. Reformed Ch. Women, Des Moines, 1984-85, pres. 1985-86; camp chmn. TTT Women's Soc. (chpt. CC), 1982-84. Avocations: sewing, needlecrafts, gardening, camping. Home: 5055 Windsor Cir Pleasant Hill IA 50327-0908

LOVETT, CLARA MARIA, academic administrator, historian; b. Trieste, Italy, Aug. 4, 1939; came to U.S., 1962; m. Benjamin F. Brown. BA equivalent, U. Trieste, 1962; MA, U. Tex., Austin, 1967; PhD, U. Tex., 1970. Prof. history Baruch Coll. CUNY, N.Y.C., 1971-82, asst. provost, 1980-82; chief European divsn. Libr. of Congress, Washington, 1982-84; provost, v.p. acad. affairs George Mason U., Fairfax, Va., 1988-93; on leave, dir. Forum on Faculty Roles and Rewards Am. Assn. for Higher Edn., 1993-94; pres. No. Ariz. U., Flagstaff, 1994-2001, pres. emerita, 2001—; sr. fellow, dir. Ctr. for Competency-Measured Edn. The Oquirrh Inst., 2002—03; pres., CEO Am. Assn. for Higher Ed., 2003—05. Vis. lectr. Fgn. Svc. Inst., Washington, 1979-85. Author: Democratic Movement in Italy 1830-1876, 1982 (H.R. Marraro prize, Soc. Italian Hist. Studies); Giuseppe Ferrari and the Italian Revolution, 1979 (Phi Alpha Theta book award); Carlo Cattaneo and the Politics of Risorgimento, 1972 (Soc. for Italian Hist. Studies Dissertation award), (bibliography) Contemporary Italy, 1985; co-editor: Women, War, and Revolution, 1980, (essays) State of Western European Studies, 1984; contbr. sects. to publs., U.S., Italy. Organizer Dem. clubs Bklyn., 1972-76; mem. exec. com. Palisades Citizens Assn., Washington, 1985-87; vestry mem. St. David's Episc. Ch., Washington, 1986-89; bd. dirs. Blue Cross Blue Shield Ariz., 1995—; trustee Western Govs. U., 1996—; mem. Ariz. State Bd. Edn., 1999-2001. Fellow Guggenheim Found., 1978-79, Woodrow Wilson Internat. Ctr. for Scholars, 1979 (adv. bd. West European program), Am. Coun. Learned Socs., 1976, Bunting Inst. of Radcliffe Coll., 1975-76, others; named Educator of Yr. Va. Fedn. of Bus. and Profl. Women, 1992. Mem. Am. Assn. Higher Edn. (cons. 1979—), Soc. for Italian Hist. Studies, Assn. Am. Coll. and Univs. (bd. dirs. 1990-93). Avocations: choral singing, swimming. Business E-Mail: clara.lovett@nau.edu.

LOVETT, JOHN ROBERT, retired chemical company executive; b. Norristown, Pa., June 17, 1931; s. James and Margaret (Creighton) L.; m. Sandra Miller, May 26, 1956; children: Judy, Jackie, John Robert Jr. BS, Ursinus Coll., 1953; MS, U. Del., 1955, PhD, 1957. Rsch. chemist Exxon Rsch., Linden, N.J., 1957-64; lab. dir. Exxon Rsch./Exxon Chem., Linden, 1964-70; v.p. Paramins Exxon Chem., Houston, 1970-74, tech. mgr. Linden, 1974-76; v.p. rsch. Air Products and Chems., Inc., Allentown, Pa., 1976-81; pres. Europe Air Products and Chems., Inc., Hersham, Eng., 1981-88; group v.p. chems. Air Products and Chems., Inc., Allentown, 1988-92, exec. v.p. gases & equipment, 1992-93, exec. v.p. strategic planning and tech., 1993-96. Mem. AICE, Chem. Mfrs. Assn. (bd. dirs. 1990-95), Am. Chem. Soc., Soc. Chem. Industry. Home: 2830 W Liberty St Allentown PA 18104-4748

LOVETT, KEITH W., retail executive; B in Polit. Sci., Willamette U., 1965; JD, Coll. of Law, Willamette U., 1968. Labor rels. mgr. Alberston's Inc., Boise, Idaho, 1974—84; sr. v.p. human resources Eagle Food Centers Inc., Milan, Ill., 1988—92; sr. v.p., human resources Fred Meyer, Inc., 1992—2000; sr. v.p. human resources Rite Aid Corp., Camp Hill, Pa., 2000—. Office: Rite Aid Corporation 30 Hunter Lane Camp Hill PA 17011

LOVETT, LAURENCE DOW, retired real estate and steamship executive; b. Jacksonville, Fla., Apr. 13, 1930; s. William Radford and Agnes Nisbet (Dow) L. BA, Harvard U., 1951, LL.B., 1954. Vice pres. Eric Boulton, Inc., N.Y.C., 1958-60; vice pres. Eastern Steamship Lines, Miami, Fla., 1960-65, Suwanee Steamship Co., N.Y.C., Jacksonville, 1965-78; pres. Burgoyne Properties, 1978-85; v.p. Piggly Wiggly Corp., 1965-82. Chmn. bd. dirs. Met. Opera Guild, 1979-86; mem. bd. dirs. Met. Oprea Assn., 1979-93; chmn. Save Venice Inc., 1987-98, Venetian Heritage, Inc., 1998—; chmn. bd. dirs. Chamber Music Soc. of Lincoln Ctr., 1989-93. Served with AUS, 1955-57. Mem.: Knickerbocker. Address: 11 Ave Princess Grace Monte Carlo 98000 Monaco

LOVETT, MELENDY, semiconductor company executive; BS in mgmt. and mgmt. info. systems, Tex. A&M; MS in acctg., U. Tex., Dallas. CPA. Former sr. mgr. Coopers & Lybrand; former v.p. human resources Tex. Instruments Inc., sr. v.p. Dallas, 2004—, pres. ednl. and productivity solutions bus., 2004—. Office: Tex Instruments Inc 12500 TI Blvd Dallas TX 75243 Office Phone: 972-995-2011. Office Fax: 972-995-4360.

LOVETT, MILLER CURRIER, retired management educator, minister, educator; b. Lynn, Mass., Mar. 18, 1923; s. Charles William and Phoebe Frances (Miller) L.; m. Dorothy Johnsen, Feb. 14, 1946 (div.); children: Anne E., Celeste M., Peter W., Rebecca J.; m. Virginia Lavelli, May 26, 1979. BSBA, Boston U., 1944, STB, 1946, PhD, 1964; postgrad., MIT, Boston U., 1970-72. Pastor Wesley United Meth. Ch., Medford, Mass., 1946-52; sr. pastor United Meth. Ch., Ellensburg, Wash., 1952-62, Congl. Ch., Laconia, N.H., 1965-70; assoc. prof. bus. adminstrn. Belknap Coll., Center Harbor, N.H., 1970-73; prof. bus. adminstrn. Bunker Hill Community Coll., Charlestown, Mass., 1973-77; assoc. prof. mgmt. Boston State Coll., 1977-82, U. Mass., Boston, 1982—2002; ret., 2002. Founder, exec. dir. Social Ventures Trust, Lexington, Mass., 1985—; cmty. econ. devel. projects, Peru, USA, 1985-97, Boston, 1990-2002, NH, 1995—. Contbr. articles to profl. jours. Co-chair space needs com. Town of Meredith, NH, 2003-04, trustee of trust funds, 2003—, capital improvement com., 2004—; bd. dirs. Linkage Com. Greater Meredith Program, 2003—. Lt. col. CAP USAF, 1955— Recipient Disting. Svc. award Ellensburg Jr. C. of C., 1956. Mem. Mass. Tchrs. Assn., Masons. Avocation: stamp and coin collecting. Home: PO Box 1669 25 Spindle Point Rd Meredith NH 03253-6748 Office Phone: 781-718-3553.

LOVETT, RADFORD DOW, marine terminal real estate and investment company executive; b. Jacksonville, Fla., Sept. 6, 1933; s. William Radford And Agnes (Dow) L.; m. Katharine R. Howe, June 25, 1955 (dec. Jan. 1991); children: Katharine, William Radford, Philip, Lauren; m. Susan Wylie Rogers, June 16, 1995; children: Nick, Peter, Teddy Rogers. With Merrill Lynch, Pierce, Fenner & Smith Inc., N.Y.C., 1958-78; mng. dir. Capital Markets Group, 1975-78; pres. Piggly Wiggly Corp., Jacksonville, Fla., 1978-82; chmn. bd. Commodores Pt. Terminal Corp., Jacksonville, 1978—. Chmn. Southcoast Capital Mgmt. Corp., Jacksonville, 1995—; bd. dirs. Wachovia Corp., Fla. Rock Industries Inc., Patriot Transp., Inc., Winn-Dixie Stores, Inc. Trustee Drew U., 1976-79, St. Vincent's Found., Jacksonville Zool. Soc. Lt. F.A. U.S. Army, 1955-57. Mem. Coastal Conservation Assn. Fla. (bd. dirs.). Episcopalian. Office: Ste 1600 One Independent Dr Jacksonville FL 32202-5009

LOVETT, RICHARD, talent agency executive; b. Wis. m. Brittany Lovett. Attended, U. Wis.-Madison. Began as mailroom employee and advanced from agent trainee to agent Creative Artists Agency, pres., 1995—. Tchr. Venice H.S., 1994—; co-founder Creative Artists Agency Found., 1996; bd. dirs. Artists Rights Found. Named one of 50 Most Powerful People in Hollywood, Premiere mag., 2004—05; recipient City of Angels Helen Bernstein award, David Niven award, 2000, Champion of Children award, Fulfillment Fund, 2002, Amb. for Humanity award, Shoah Found., 2004. Avocations: sports, yoga. Office: Creative Artists Agency 9830 Wilshire Blvd Beverly Hills CA 90212-1825*

LOVETT, ROBERT G., lawyer; b. York, Pa., Aug. 17, 1944; BA, U. Pitts., 1966; JD, Duquesne U., 1969. Bar: Pa. 1970. Ptnr. Lovett Bookman Harmon Marks, LLP, Pitts. Past chmn. real property, probate and trust law Penn. Bar Assn.; past mem. Estate Planning Coun. Pitts.; trustee Univ. Pitts., Bellefield Ednl. Trust, Pressley Ridge Schools. Contbr. articles to numerous legal jours. Office: Lovett Bookman Harmon Marks LLP Fifth Ave Pl Suite 2900 120 Fifth Ave Pittsburgh PA 15222

LOVETT, WENDELL HARPER, architect, educator; b. Seattle, Apr. 2, 1922; s. Wallace Herman and Pearl (Harper) L.; m. Eileen (Whitson), Sept. 3, 1947; children: Corrie, Clare. Attended, Pasadena Jr. Coll., 1943-44; BArch, U. Wash., 1947; MArch, M.I.T., 1948. Arch., designer Naramore, Bain, Brady, and Johanson, Seattle, 1948; arch. assoc. Bassetti and Morse, Seattle, 1948-51; instr. architecture U. Wash., 1948-51; pvt. practice, arch. Seattle, 1951—; asst. prof. U. Wash., 1951-60, assoc. prof., 1960-65, prof., 1965-83, prof. emeritus, 1983—. Lectr. Technische Hochschule, Stuttgart, 1959-60. Prin. works include nuclear reactor bldg., U. Wash., 1960; Villa Simonyi Medina, Wash., 1989; patentee in field. Pres. Citizen's Planning Coun., Seattle, 1968-71; bd. dir. Seattle Baroque Orch., 1998-2002. Served in AUS, 1943-46. Recipient 2d prize Progressive Architecture U.S. Jr. C. of C., 1949; Internat. design award Decima Triennale di Milano, 1954; Arch. Record Homes awards, 1969, 72, 74; Interiors award, 1973; Sunset-AIA awards, 1959, 62, 69, 71; Fulbright grantee, 1959; AIA fellow, 1978 Mem. AIA (sec. Wash. chpt. 1953-54, bd. dirs. Found. Seattle chpt. 1991-92, Seattle chpt. medal 1993, pres. sr. coun. 1991-92, Plestcheeff Inst. bd. dir. 1992; bd.dir., Soc. of Architectural Historians, MDRC, 2002-03. Home and Office: 420 34th Ave Seattle WA 98122-6408 Office Phone: 206-329-3275.

LOVETT, WILLIAM ANTHONY, law and economics educator; b. Milw., Sept. 2, 1934; AB, Wabash Coll., 1956; JD, NYU, 1959; PhD in Econs., Mich. State U., 1969. Bar: N.Y. 1960. Atty. U.S. Dept. Justice, Washington, 1962; economist FTC, Washington, 1963-69; prof. Tulane U., New Orleans, 1969—, dir. internat. law, trade and fin. program, 1985—. Joseph Merrick Jones prof. law and econs., 1991—. Author: Inflation and Politics, 1982, Banking and Financial Institutions Law, 1984, 5th edit., 2001, World Trade Rivalry, 1987, U.S. Shipping Policies and the World Market, 1996, U.S. Trade Policy, 1999, 2d edit., 2003. Root-Tilden scholar, 1956-59. Mem. ABA, Am. Econs. Assn., Am. Soc. Internat. Law, Phi Beta Kappa. Office: Tulane Law Sch New Orleans LA 70118 Office Phone: 504-865-5960.

LOVETT, WILLIAM LEE, surgeon; b. Natchez, Miss., June 12, 1941; s. Frank Lee and Lucille (Mullen) L.; m. Martha Lynn Gray, Aug. 15, 1964; children: Shelby Elizabeth Lovett Cuevas, Heather Lee Lovett Dunn, Michael Gray. BA, U. Miss., Oxford, 1963; MD, U. Miss., Jackson, 1967. Diplomate Am. Bd. Surgery, Am. Bd. Hand Surgery. Intern in surgery U. Va. Med. Ctr., Charlottesville, 1967-68, jr. asst. resident in surgery, 1968-69, sr. asst. resident in surgery, 1970-72, co-chief resident in surgery, 1972-73; fellow surg. rsch. dept. surgery U. Va., Charlottesville, 1969-70; physician S.W. Hand Surgeons Ltd., Phoenix, 1983—; vice chief of staff St. Joseph's Hosp., Phoenix, 1990-93, rep. orthopedic surgery com., 1990—, vice chair dept. orthopedics, 1991-92, chief of staff, 1996-98; physician S.W. Hand Surgeons Ltd., Phoenix; med. dir., med. staff adminstrn. St. Joseph's Hosp. and Med. Ctr., Phoenix, 2002—. Mem. sports medicine adv. team Ariz. State U., 1991-95; presenter in field. Contbr. articles to profl. jours. Mem. Sch. Bd. Xavier High Sch., 1983-87, v.p., 1985-86, pres., 1986-87; chief Webelos den Roosevelt coun. Boy Scouts Am., Phoenix, 1992-93, asst. scoutmaster, 1993—. Comdr. USN, 1974-76. Fellow ACS (pres. Ariz. chpt. 1983-84); mem. AMA, Am. Soc. for Surgery of the Hand, Ariz. Med. Assn. (del. 1985), Phoenix Surg. Soc. (pres. 1985-86), Muller Surg. Soc., Scottsdale Mounted Posse. Avocations: horseback riding, fly fishing, quail hunting, canoeing. Home: 6049 N 5th Pl Phoenix AZ 85012-1219 Office: St Josephs Hosp and Med Ctr 350 W Thomas Phoenix AZ 85013 Office Phone: 602-406-4095. Personal E-mail: L5hand@cox.net. Business E-Mail: wlovett@chw.edu.

LOVETTE, LILLIE FAYE, education educator; b. Magee, Miss., May 18, 1951; d. Barnett L. and Margaret Smith AA, Hinds Community Coll., 1978; B of Edn., U. Miss., 1980, M of Social Sci., 1981. Social worker, tchr. Sunnybrook Children's Home, Ridgeland, Miss., 1982-83; prof. Holmes Community Coll., Ridgeland, Miss., 1983—. Co-author: (with Dr. Leroy Gruner) Sociology: As You Like It, 1988, Interaction, Conflict and Change, 1989. State coord. Miss. humanities coun. Smithsonian Mus. on Main St., 2004—05; coord. Miss. humanities coun. Victory on Home Front exhibit. Fulbright scholar, 1989; NEH fellow; recipient Internat. Fulbright Rsch. award, 1985, Pub. Achievement award Miss. Humanities, 2003; named Outstanding Educator Miss. Legis., Jackson, 1990, Outstanding Coll. Educator Madison County Chamber of Conn., Ridgeland, 1991. Mem. Am. Sociol. Assn., Ala.-Miss. Sociol. Assn Episcopalian. Avocation: florist. Home: 204 Royal St Edwards MS 39066-8943 Office: Holmes Community Coll 412 W Ridgeland Ave Ridgeland MS 39157-1815

LOVEWELL, MARJORIE KLINGENSMITH, secondary school educator; b. Mpls., Aug. 19, 1938; d. Medford Shirley and Margaret Isabel (Jepson) Klingensmith; m. Hubart S. Lovewell Jr., Aug. 6, 1960 (div. Dec. 1981). BS, U. Minn., 1960; MEd, U. Ga., 1974. Cert. secondary edn. tchr., Minn., Ga. Tchr. Ind. Sch. Dist. #281, Robbinsdale, Minn., 1961-69, Dekalb County Bd. Edn., Decatur, Ga., 1969—2002; ret., 2002. Curriculum writer State Dept. Edn., Atlanta, 1989-90; bd. dirs. Ida's Cove, (sec. 2003-). Bd. dirs. Ga. chpt. Myasthenis Gravis Found., 1999—. Mem.: Brain Injury Assn. Ga. (bd. dirs. 2000—03), Ga. Assn. Family and Consumer Sci. (dist. M treas. 1996—), Am. Assn. Family and Consumer Scis. (cert. 1990—), Atlanta Alliance Theater Guild (corr. sec. 2001—02), Alpha Sigma (chpt. pres. 2003—), Delta Kappa Gamma (state scholarship found. com. 2003—), Delta Zeta Found. (sec. 1989—93, treas. 1993—95, v.p. 1995—97, pres. 1997—2001, spl. advisor 2001—), Delta Zeta Sorority (alumnae pres. Atlanta chpt. 1974, delegate 2004). Episcopalian. Home: 96 The Prado NE Atlanta GA 30309-3370

LOVEWELL, MARK ALAN, journalist; b. May 9, 1952; s. John Sherman and Beth Davis Lovewell; m. Teresa Yuan, July 20, 1974 (div. July 20, 1998); children: Mark Alan, Emma Rose. BA in Journalism, Empire State Coll., SUNY, 1978. Reporter, photographer Vineyard Gazette, Edgartown, Mass., 1979—. Contbr. chapters to books; musician: (albums) Sea Songs of Martha's Vineyard, 2002, 2004, Martha's Vineyard Folksongs, 2005. Mem.: Masons. Home: 35 Lagoon Pond Rd PO Box 2034 Vineyard Haven MA 02568-2034 Office Phone: 508-627-4311 x 121. Personal E-mail: mark@markalanlovewell.com.

LOVICK, NORMAN, accountant; b. Wilson, NC, July 10, 1942; s. Henry J. and Ella (Lovick) Webb; children: Norman Lovick Jr., Michael D. BS, Durham (N.C.) Coll., 1963; AA, N.C. Cen. Coll., Durham, 1961; MS, Am. U., 1964; Adv. Deg., USDA Grad. Sch., Washington, 1971. Acctg. analyst U.S. Dept. Treasury, Washington, 1967-76; fin. analyst Midland Nat. Corp., Wheaton, Md., 1976-78; tax cert. fin. planner Lovick's Fin. Assocs., Hyattsville, Md., 1978-88, chief exec. officer, pres., 1985—. Gen. agt. Bankers United, Cedar Rapids, Iowa, 1977-79; notary pub. With U.S. Army, 1965—67. Mem. Nat. Assn. Accts., D.C. Life Underwriters Assn., Nat. Assn. Life Underwriters, Nat. Soc. Pub. Accts., Am. Inst. Profl. Bookkeepers, D.C. Soc. Ind. Accts., Am. Mgmt. Assn., Masons (32 deg., chaplain). Democrat. Pentecostal Ch. Avocations: fishing, boating, reading, dance. Office: Lovick's Fin Assoc Inc 3601 Hamilton St Ste 201 Hyattsville MD 20782-3946 Office Phone: 301-927-5630. Personal E-mail: nlovick@aol.com, nlovick@verizon.net.

LOVIN, KEITH HAROLD, retired academic administrator, philosopher, educator; b. Clayton, N.Mex., Apr. 1, 1943; s. Buddie and Wanda (Smith) L.; m. Marsha Kay Gunn, June 11, 1966; children: Camille Jenay, Lauren Kay BA, Baylor U., 1965; postgrad., Yale U., 1965-66; PhD, Rice U., 1971. Prof. philosophy Southwest Tex. State U., San Marcos, 1970-77, chmn. dept. philosophy, 1977-78, dean liberal arts, 1978-81; provost, v.p. acad. affairs Millersville U., Pa., 1981-86; provost, v.p. acad. and student affairs U. So. Colo., Pueblo, 1986-92; pres. Maryville U. St. Louis, 1992—2005, pres. emeritus, 2005—. Adv. bd. Southwest Studies in Philosophy, 1981—90. Contbr. articles to profl. jours. Bd. dirs. St. Louis Symphony Orch., 1995-2001, United Way Greater St. Louis, 1992-99, Boys Hope, Jr. Achievement Mississippi Valley, Inc., 1992-2001, Nat. Coun. Alcohol and Drug Abuse Adv. Bd., St. Louis Intercollegiate Athletic Conf., Higher Edn. Coun., St. Luke's Hosp., vice-chmn., 2001-03, chmn., 2003—; bd. dirs., pres. Ind. Colls. and Univs. Mo., 1999-2002, vice chair, 2002-03; mem. pres.'s adv. com. Mo. Coordinating for Bd. Higher Edn., 2002-05; trustee KETC Channel 9, 2003—05. Mem.: Chesterfield C. of C., Gov. Bus. Edn. Roundtable, St. Louis Club. Avocation: fly fishing. Home: 3006 Hawthorne Cove Georgetown TX 78628 Office Phone: 512-869-2053. Personal E-mail: klovin@yahoo.com.

LOVIN, ROBIN WARREN, clergy member, educator; b. Peoria, Ill., Mar. 22, 1946; s. Harvey Gifford and Irene Warren Lovin. BA, Northwestern U., Evanston, IL, 1964—68; BD, Harvard Div. Sch., Cambridge, MA, 1968—71; PhD, Harvard U., Cambridge, MA, 1974—77. Ordained United Meth. Ch., 1970. Faculty Div. Sch., U. of Chgo., Chicago, Ill., 1978—91; dean, Theol. Sch. Drew U., Madison, NJ, 1991—94; dean, Sch. of Theology So. Meth. U., Dallas, 1994—2002, prof. ethics, 2002—. Editor-at-large The Christian Century, Chicago, Ill., 1991—. Author: (book) Reinhold Niebuhr and Christian Realism, Christian Ethics: An Essential Guide, (articles) Journal of Religious Ethics. Grantee John Simon Guggenheim Fellowship, Guggenheim Found., 1987. Mem.: Soc. of Christian Ethics (pres. 1999—2000). Methodist. Office: Southern Methodist University Box 317 Dallas TX 75275-0317 Office Phone: 214-768-4134. Business E-Mail: rlovin@smu.edu.

LOVING, CHARLES ROY, museum director, curator; b. Waukesha, Wis., June 2, 1957; s. Wesley E. and Ruth A. (Zieskie) L.; m. Annick P. Gendre, Apr. 28, 1984. BFA, U. Wis., 1980; MFA, U. Utah, 1982, MA, 1985. Asst. coord. Utah Arts Coun., Salt Lake City, 1982-84; asst. dir. Utah Mus. of Fine Arts, Salt Lake City, 1984—, Snite Mus. Art, U. Notre Dame, dir., curator modern sculpture, 1999—. Juror Park City (Utah) Arts Festival, 1985-90; grants reviewer Inst. Mus. Svcs., Washington, 1988-89. Curator (exhibit) Power Dressing, 1989; co-curator (exhibit) Recent Fires, 1990. Bd. dirs. Utah Citizens for the Arts, Salt Lake City, 1984-88, Salt Lake City Art Design Bd., 1987—, Moab (Utah) Arts Ctr., 1990—. Mem. Am. Assn. Mus. (state rep.), Utah Fundraising Svc. Office: Snite Mus Art U Notre Dame PO Box 368 Notre Dame IN 46556-0368 E-mail: loving.1@nd.edu.*

LOVING, DEBORAH JUNE PIERRE, lawyer, real estate broker; b. Omaha, Jan. 21, 1953; d. Thomas Eukis and June (Dawson) L.; children: La Shaun, Ronald, Mignion. BA, Mills Coll., 1977; JD, U. Iowa, 1979. Bar: Hawaii 1987, U.S. Dist. Ct. (no. dist.) Calif. 1987, U.S. Dist. Ct. Hawaii 1987, U.S. Ct. Mil. Appeals 1987; lic. real estate broker, Calif.; tchg. credential Calif. C.C. Pvt. practice, Oakland, Calif., 1987—. Real estate developer, Cancun, Mex. and U.S., 1991—; officer, bd. dirs. Cmty. Based Developers, Oakland, 1992—; mem. adv. bd. Bayview Med. Group, Vallejo, Calif., 1995—. Mem. Oxford Club. Avocations: sailing, travel, tennis, art. Office: 2000 Powell St 1500 Emeryville CA 94608 Office Phone: 510-420-8787. E-mail: pierre@jps.net.

LOVING, SUSAN BRIMER, lawyer, former state official; m. Dan Loving; children: Lindsay, Andrew, Kendall. BA with distinction, U. Okla., 1972, JD, 1979. Asst. atty. gen. Office of Atty. Gen., 1983-87, 1st asst. atty. gen., 1987-91; atty. gen. State of Okla., Oklahoma City, 1991-94; ptnr. Lester, Loving & Davies, Edmond, Okla., 1995—. Master Ruth Bader Ginsburg Inn of Ct., 1995-97. Mem. Pardon and Parole Bd., 1995—96, 2003—, vice-chmn., 1995, chmn., 2004; mem. Gov.'s Commn. on Tobacco and Youth, 1995—97; mem. med. steering com. Partnership for Drug Free Okla., Inst. for Child Advocacy, 1996—97; bd. dirs. Bd. for Freedom of Info., Okla. Inc., 1995—2001, Legal Aid Svcs. of Okla., 2002—03, Legal Aid of West Okla., 1995—2001. Recipient Nat. Red Ribbon Leadership award Nat. Fedn. Parents, Headliner award, By-liner award Okla. City and Tulsa Women in Comm., First Friend of Freedom award, Freedom of Info., Okla., Dir. award Okla. Dist. Attys. Assn. Mem.: Oklahoma County Bar Assn. (bd. dirs. 2001—), Okla. Bar Assn. (mem. ho. dels. 1996—97, task force on professionalism and civility 1999—, mem. ho. dels. 2001—04, past chmn. adminstrv. law sect., chmn. adminstrn. of justice com., chmn. profl. responsibility commn., Spotlight award 1997), Phi Beta Kappa. Office: Lester Loving & Davis PC 1701 S Kelly Ave Edmond OK 73013-3623 Office Phone: 405-844-9900. Business E-Mail: sloving@lldlaw.com.

LOVINGER, WARREN CONRAD, emeritus university president; b. Big Sandy, Mont., July 29, 1915; s. Wilbur George and Ruth Katherine (Hokanson) L.; m. Dorothy Blackburn, Aug. 14, 1937; children— Patricia Mae, Jeanie, Warren Conrad. BA, U. Mont., 1942, MA, 1944; EdD, Columbia U., 1947. Tchr., prin. Pub. Schs. Mont., 1937-43; instr. history U. Mont., Missoula, 1943-44; pres. No. State U., Aberdeen, S.D., 1951-56, Central Mo. State U., Warrensburg, 1956-79, pres. emeritus, 1979—. Exec. sec. Am. Assn. Colls. for Tchr. Edn., 1947-51, nat. pres., 1963-64; nat. pres. Am. Assn. State Colls. and Univs., 1974-75; mem. del. to study effects of Marshall Plan on Western Europe, 1950; leader study of tchr. edn. in Fed. Republic of Germany, 1964; leader del. People's Republic of China, 1975; mem. comparative study tour of Republic of China, 1976 Author: General Education in Teachers Colleges, 1948; contbr. articles to profl. jours. Served as lt. USNR, 1944-46, ETO Recipient Silver Beaver award Boys Scouts Am., 1970; Outstanding Civilian Service award Dept. Army, 1979 Mem. Mo. Tchrs. Assn., Am. Assn. Sch. Adminstrs., Mo. Assn. Sch. Adminstrs., Columbia U. Alumni Assn., Stover C. of C., Am. Legion, Gideons Internat., Phi Kappa Phi, Phi Delta Kappa, Kappa Delta Pi, Lodges: Masons, Shriners, Rotary, Lions. Baptist. Avocations: travel, writing, fishing, farming.

LOVINS, AMORY BLOCH, physicist, energy consultant; b. Washington, Nov. 13, 1947; s. Gerald Hershel and Miriam (Bloch) L.; m. L. Hunter Sheldon, 1979 (div. 1999). Student, Harvard U., 1966—67, student, 1964—65, Magdalen Coll., Oxford, Eng., 1967—69; MA, Oxford U., Oxford, 1971; DSc (hon.), Bates Coll., 1979; DSc (hon.), Williams Coll., 1981, Kalamazoo Coll., 1983; DSc (hon.), U. Maine, 1985; LLD (hon.), Ball State U., 1983; D of Environ. Sci. (hon.), Unity Coll., 1992; D of Pub. Serv. (hon.), Northfield Coll., 2001. Jr. research fellow Merton Coll., Oxford, England, 1969-71; Brit. rep., policy advisor Friends of the Earth, San Francisco, 1971-84; regent's lectr. U. Calif., Berkeley and Riverside, 1978, 81; CEO, CFO and dir. Rocky Mountain Inst., Old Snowmass, Colo., 1982—. Govt. and indsl. energy cons., 1971—; vis. prof. Dartmouth Coll., 1982; disting. vis. prof. U. Colo., 1982, U. St. Gallen, Switzerland, 1999; prin. tech. cons. E Source, 1989-99; prin. The Lovins Group, 1994-99; mem. Def. Sci. Bd. panel U.S. Sec. Def., 1999-2001; chmn., dir. Hypercar Inc., Basalt, Colo., 1998—. Author (also layout artist and co-photographer): Eryri, The Mountains of Longing, 1971; author: The Stockholm Conference: Only One Earth, 1972, Openpit Mining, 1973, World Energy Strategies: Facts, Issues, and Options, 1975, Soft Energy Paths: Toward a Durable Peace, 1977; co-author (with J. Price): Non-Nuclear Futures: The Case: The Case for an Ethical Energy Strategy, 1975; co-author: (with L.H. Lovins) Energy/War: Breaking the Nuclear Link, 1980; co-author: Brittle Power: Energy Strategy for National Security, 1982; co-author: (with L.H. Lovins, F. Krasue and W. Bach) Least-Cost Energy: Solving the CO2 Problem, 1982; co-author: (with L.H. Lovins, F. Krause and W. Bach), 1989; co-author: (with L.H. Lovins, sr. author and S. Zuckerman) Energy Unbound: A Fable for America's Future, 1986; co-author: (hardware reports) The State of the Art: Lighting, 1988, The State of the Art: Drivepower, 1989; co-author: The State of the Art: Appliances, 1990, The State of the Art: Water Heating, 1991, The State of the Art: Space Cooling and Air Handling, 1992; co-author: (with Paul Hawkena and L.H. Lovins) Natural Capitalism, 1999, author numerous poems; contbr. articles to profl. jours., reports to tech. jours. Co-founder, treas. Windstar Land Conservancy, Colo., 1996-2000. Recipient Right Livelihood award Right Livelihood Found., 1983, Sprout award Internat. Studies Assn., 1977, Pub. Edn. award Nat. Energy Resources Orgn., 1978, Pub. Svc. award Nat. Assn. Environ. Edn., 1980; Mitchell prize Mitchell Energy Found., 1982, Delphi prize Onassis Found., 1989, Nissan prize Internat. Symposium Automotive Tech. and Automation, 1993, Award of Distinction, Rocky Mountain chpt. AIA, 1994, Heinz award 1997, Lindbergh award 1999, World Tech. award 1999, Happold medal U.K. Construction Industries Coun., 2000, Heroes for the Planet award Time, 2000; MacArthur fellow John D. and Catherine T. MacArthur Found., Chgo., 1993. Fellow: AAAS, Lindisfarne Assn., World Acad. Art and Sci.; mem.: Internat. Orgn. Found., World Bus. Acad., Internat. Assn. Energy Econs., Am. Solar Energy Soc., Soc. Automotive Engring., Am. Phys. Soc., Fedn. Am. Scientists. Achievements include patents in field. Home and Office: 1739 Snowmass Creek Rd Snowmass CO 81654-9115 E-mail: ablovins@rmi.org. *Personal philosophy: Devotion to efficient and sustainable use of resources as a path to global security, with emphasis on how advanced technologies, market economics, and Jeffersonian politics can provide new solutions to old problems, or better still, avoid them altogether.*

LOVINS, L. HUNTER, public policy institute executive, consultant, educator; b. Middlebury, Vt., Feb. 26, 1950; d. Paul Millard and Farley (Hunter) Sheldon; m. Amory Bloch Lovins, Sept. 6, 1979 (div. 1999). BA in Sociology, BA in Polit. Sci., Pitzer Coll., 1972; JD, Loyola U., L.A., 1975; LHD, U. Maine, 1982. Bar: Calif. 1975. Asst. dir. Calif. Conservation Project, L.A., 1973-79; policy advisor Friends of the Earth, 1979—81; co-CEO, co-founder Rocky Mountain Inst., Snowmass, Colo., 1982—2002; co-chair Natural Capitalism Group, Snowmass, 2000—; pres. Natural Capitalism Solutions, 2004—. Vis. prof. U. Colo., Boulder, 1982; Henry R. Luce vis. prof. Dartmouth Coll., Hanover, N.H., 1982; prof. sustainable mgmt. Presidio World Coll., 2003—; pres. Nighthawk Horse Co., 1993; bd. dirs. EcoStructure Fin. Co-author: Brittle Power, 1982, Energy Unbound, 1986, Least-Cost Energy Solving the CO2 Problem, 2d edit., 1989, Factor Four, 1997, Green Development, 1998, Natural Capitalism, 1999, The Natural Advantage of Nations, 2005. Bd. dirs. Basalt and Rural Fire Protection Dist., 1987-2000, Nighthawk Horse Co., Rocky Mountain Inst., 1982-2002, Windstar Land Conservancy, 1996-2002, Internat. Ctr. Sustainable Devel., 2004-; vol. EMT and firefighter, Engrs. Without Borders, 2003, bd. dirs., 2003-; advisor Energy Ministry Afghanistan, 2004—. Recipient Mitchell prize Woodlands Inst., 1982, Right Livelihood Found. award, 1983, Best of the New Generation award Esquire Mag., 1984, Nissan prize, 1995, Lindbergh award, 1999, Bd. Govs.' award Loyola Law Sch., 2000, LOHAS award for svc. to bus., 2001, Shingo Prize for Excellence in Mfg. Rsch., 2001, Leadership in Bus. award, 2001; named Hero of Planet, Time Mag., 2000. Mem. Calif. Bar Assn., Am. Quarter Horse Assn., Am. Polocrosse Assn. Avocations: rodeo, fire rescue, polocrosse. Office: Natural Capitalism Solutions PO Box 3125 Eldorado Springs CO 80025 Office Phone: 303-554-6550.

LOVITZ, JON, actor, comedian; b. Tarzana, Calif., July 21, 1957; Attended, U. Calif.-Irvine; studied acting, Film Actors Workshop. Began performing in comedy improvisation with the Groundlings, L.A.; TV work includes (series) Foley Square, 1985, Saturday Night Live, NBC, 1985-90, The Critic (voice), 1994-95; feature films include The Last Resort, 1986, Ratboy, 1986, Jumpin' Jack Flash, 1986, Three Amigos, 1986, Big, 1988, My Stepmother is an Alien, 1988, Brave Little Toaster (voice), 1989, Mr. Destiny, 1990, An American Tail: Fievel Goes West (voice), 1991, A League of Their Own, 1992, Mom and Dad Save the World, 1990, Coneheads, 1993, National Lampoon's Loaded Weapon I, 1993, City Slickers II: The Legend of Curley's Gold, 1994, North, 1994, Trapped in Paradise, 1994, High School High, 1996, Matilda, 1996, The Great White Hype, 1996, Happiness, 1998, The Wedding Singer, 1998, Happiness, 1998, Lost & Found, 1999, Small Time Crooks, 2000, Little

Nicky, 2000, Sand, 2000, 3000 Miles to Graceland, 2001, Cats & Dogs (voice), 2001, Rat Race, 2001, Good Advice, 2001, Eight Crazy Nights (voice), 2002, Dickie Roberts: Former Child Star, 2003, The Stepford Wives, 2004.

LOVOY, JOSEPH T., investment advisor; b. Birmingham, Ala., Apr. 8, 1932; s. Brace M. and Mary C. (Ciravolo) L.; m. Lynne B. Bass, Feb. 14, 1963; children: Steve, Kenneth, Thomas, Amy, Jon. BS, U. Ala., 1953. CMFC fin. advisor Nat. Endowment for Fin. Edn. Fin. advisor Am. Express Fin. Advisors, Mpls., 1964—. Cons. Escambia County Utility Authority, Pensacola. Chmn. Pensacola (Fla.) Opera Co., 19987-88, Am. Diabetes Assn., Pensacola, 1988-91, Found. Bd. for Pub. TV, Pensacola, 1992—. Recipient Nat. Pub. Broadcasting Svc. award Nat. Pub. Broadcasting, Pensacola, 1998. Office: C-104 744 E Burgess Rd Ste C104 Pensacola FL 32504-6361 Fax: 850-476-0261.

LOW, ANDREW M., lawyer; b. N.Y.C., Jan. 1, 1952; s. Martin Laurent and Alice Elizabeth (Bernstein) L.; m. Margaret Mary Stroock, Mar. 31, 1979; children: Roger, Ann. BA, Swarthmore Coll., 1973; JD, Cornell U., 1976. Bar: Colo. 1981, U.S. Dist. Ct. Colo. 1981, U.S. Ct. Appeals (10th cir.) 1986. Assoc. Rogers & Wells, N.Y.C., 1977-81, Davis Graham & Stubbs LLP, Denver, 1981-83, ptnr., 1984—. Editor: Colorado Appellate Handbook, 1984, 94. Pres. Colo. Freedom of Info. Coun., Denver, 1990-92, Colo. Bar Press Com., 1989, appellate practice subcom. Colo. Bar Assn. Litig. Coun., 1994—; bd. dirs. CLE in Colo., Inc., 1993-96; trustee 9 Health Fair, Denver, 1988—; mem. Colo. Superior Ct. Joint Com. on Appellate Rules, 1993—. Avocations: skiing, golf, fly-fishing. Office: Davis Graham & Stubbs LLP Ste 500 1550 17th St Denver CO 80202 E-mail: andrew.low@dgslaw.com.

LOW, ANTHONY, language educator; b. San Francisco, May 31, 1935; s. Emerson and Clio (Caroli) L.; m. Pauline Iselin Mills, Dec. 28, 1961; children: Louise, Christopher, Georgianna, Elizabeth, Peter, Catherine, Nicholas, Alexandra, Michael, Frances, Jessica, Edward, Charlotte. AB, Harvard U., 1957, MA, 1959, PhD, 1965. Mem. faculty Seattle U., 1965-68; mem. faculty NYU, N.Y.C., 1968—; prof. English lit., 1978—; chmn. dept. English, 1989-95. Vis. scholar Jesus Coll., Cambridge, Eng., 1974-75. Author: Augustine Baker, 1970, The Blaze of Noon, 1974, Love's Architecture, 1978, The Georgic Revolution, 1985, The Reinvention of Love, 1993, Aspects of Subjectivity, 2003; editor: Urbane Milton, 1984. Pres. Conf. on Christianity and Lit., 1996-99. Pew Evangelical fellow, 1995; Milton scholar, 1996. Mem. Milton Soc., Donne Soc., MLA, Renaissance Soc., Phi Beta Kappa. Home: 748 Kent Hill Rd East Calais VT 05650 Office: NYU Dept English 19 University Pl New York NY 10003-4556 E-mail: low@compuserve.com.

LOW, BOON CHYE, physicist; b. Singapore, Feb. 13, 1946; came to U.S., 1968; s. Kuei Huat and Ah Tow (Tee) Lau; m. Daphne Nai-Ling Yip, Mar. 31, 1971; 1 child, Yi-Kai. BSc, U. London, Eng., 1968; PhD, U. Chgo., 1972. Scientist High Altitude Observatory Nat. Ctr. for Atmospheric Rsch., Boulder, Colo., 1981-87, sect. head, 1987-90, 97—, acting dir., 1989-90, sr. scientist, 1987—. Mem. mission operation working group for solar physics NASA, 1992-94; vis. sr. scientist Princeton Plasma Physics Lab., 1998-99; mem. Living With a Star steering com. for targeted rsch. and tech. NASA, 2004; mem. Theoretical Inst. for Advanced Rsch. in Astrophysics, Taiwan, 2004—. Mem. editl. bd. Solar Physics, 1991—. Named Fellow Japan Soc. for Promotion of Sci., U. Tokyo, 1978, Sr. Rsch. Assoc., NASA Marshall Space Flight Ctr., 1980. Mem. Am. Physical Soc., Am. Astron. Soc., Am. Geophysical Union. Office: Nat Ctr for Atmosph Rsch PO Box 3000 Boulder CO 80307-3000 Office Phone: 303-497-1553. Business E-Mail: low@ucar.edu.

LOW, FREDERICK EMERSON, language educator; b. Oct. 25, 1943; AA, Am. Coll., Paris, France, 1967; BA, Queens Coll., 1969, MLS, 1976; MA, CUNY, 1972. Prof. La Guardia Comm. Coll., CUNY, Long Island City, N.Y., 1978-95; dir. Asia World Learning Ctr., Inc., Flushing, NY, 1996—2001, Asian-Am. Ctr. for Edn. of N.Y., Inc., Flushing, 1998—2001; pvt. tchr., rschr., 2001—. Home: 15 Croyden St New Hyde Park NY 11040 Personal E-mail: fredelow@yahoo.com.

LOW, HARRY WILLIAM, judge; b. Oakdale, Calif., Mar. 12, 1931; s. Tong J. and Ying G. (Gong) L.; m. May Ling, Aug. 24, 1952; children: Larry, Kathy, Allan. AA, Modesto Jr. Coll., 1950; AB Polit. Sci. with honors, U. Calif., Berkeley, 1952, JD, 1955. Bar: Calif. 1955, U.S. Ct. Appeals (9th cir.) 1955. Commr. Worker's Compensation Commn., 1966; teaching assoc. Boalt Hall, 1955-56; dep. atty. gen. Calif. Dept. Justice, 1956-66; judge Mcpl. Ct., San Francisco, 1966-74, presiding judge, 1972-73; judge Superior Ct., San Francisco, 1974-82; presiding justice Calif. Ct. Appeals, 1st dist., 1982-92; commr. Calif. Ins. Dept., San Francisco, 2000—03; arbitrator/mediator JAMS, 2003—. Pres. San Francisco Police Commn., 1992-96; pres. San Francisco Human Rights Commn., 1999-2000, 2003; mem. Jud. Arbitration and Mediation Svcs., 1992-2000, 2003-, Commn. on Future of Cts., 1991-94; Calif. Ins. Commr., 2000-03, BAJI-Jury Instrn. Com. Contbr. articles to profl. jours. Chmn. bd. Chinese-Am. Internat. Sch., 1979-99; bd. visitors U.S. Mil. Acad., 1980-83; bd. dirs. Friends of Recreation and Parks, Salesian Boys Club, World Affairs Coun., 1979-85, NCCJ, San Francisco chpt. St. Vincent's Boys Home, Coro Found., 1970-76, San Francisco Zool. Trust, 1987, Union Bank Calif., 1993-2000, Calif. Health Plan Found., 2003—; pres. San Francisco City Coll. Found., 1977-87, Inst. Chinese Western History U. San Francisco, 1987-89. Mem. ABA (chmn. appellate judges conf. 1990-91, commr. on minorities, Spirit of Excellence award, 2002), San Francisco Bar Assn., Chinese Am. Citizens Alliance (pres. San Francisco chpt. 1976-77, nat. pres. 1989-93), Calif. Judges Assn. (pres. 1978-79), Calif. Jud. Coun., State Bar Calif. (rsch. editor publs. 1958-76, pub. affairs com. 1987-90, exec. bd. 1992-94), Calif. Conf. Judges (editor jour. cts. commentary 1973-76), Calif. Judges Assn. (exec. bd. 1976-79), Asian Bus. League (dir. 1986-93), Nat. Ctr. State Cts. (bd. dirs. 1986-91), San Francisco Bench Bar Media Commn. (chmn. bd. dirs. 1987-92), Boalt Hall Alumni Assn. (Distinguished Svc. award 1992, Judge Lowell Jensen award 2000), Phi Alpha Delta. Office Phone: 415-982-5267. *Try to enjoy whatever task you are doing and enjoy the good company of those with whom you associate. Be an active part of the community and try to improve it. Keep busy and try to understand and respect others.*

LOW, JAMES A., physician; b. Toronto, Ont., Can., Sept. 22, 1925; s. Donald M. and Doris V. (Van Duzer) L.; m. Margery Una, Oct. 5, 1952; children: Donald E., Margeret P., Norman I. MD, U. Toronto, 1949. Intern Toronto Gen. Hosp., 1949-50; resident in ob-gyn U. Toronto, 1950-54; fellow ob/gyn Duke U., 1955; clin. instr. dept. ob-gyn U. Toronto, 1955-65; prof. and chmn. dept. ob-gyn Queens U., Kingston, Ont., Can., 1965-85, prof., 1985—. Exec. dir. Mus. Health Care at Kingston, 1995—. Mem. editl. bd. Ob-Gyn., 1986-89, Am. Jour. Ob-Gyn., 1995-99. Served with Can. Navy, 1943-45. Fellow: Royal Coll. Physicians and Surgeons Can. (chmn. splty. com. 1976—82, chmn. manpower com. 1984—92); mem.: Am. Acad. Cerebral Palsy, Can. Soc. Clin. Investigation, Soc. Obstetricians and Gynecologists Can., Soc. Gynecol. Investigation, Am. Gynecol. and Obstet. Soc., Assn. Profs. Ob-Gyn. Can. (sec.-treas. 1972—80, pres. 1983—84). Home: 185 Fairway Hills Kingston ON Canada K7M 2B5 Office: Queens U Dept Ob Gyn Kingston ON Canada K7L 3N6 Office Phone: 613-549-6666 ext. 4094. Business E-Mail: lowj@kgh.kari.net.

LOW, JOHN WAYLAND, lawyer; b. Denver, Aug. 7, 1923; s. Oscar Wayland and Rachel E. (Stander) L.; m. Merry C. Mullan, July 8, 1979; children: Lucinda A., Jan W. BA, Nebr. Wesleyan U., 1947; JD cum laude, U. Denver, 1951. Bar: Colo. 1951, U.S. Dist. Ct. (Colo. dist.) 1951, U.S. Ct. Appeals (10th cir.), U.S. Supreme Ct. 1960. Ptnr. Sherman & Howard LLC, Denver, 1951-93, counsel, 1993—. Trustee U. Denver, 1987—; chmn. bd. Denver Symphony Assn., 1989-90; vice chmn. Colo. Symphony Assn., 1990-96; pres. Colo. Symphony Found., 1995—, Mesa Verde Found., 1997-2003; chmn. Colo. Alliance of Bus., Denver, 1983-87; pres. First Plymouth Found, 1982—; dir. Public Edn. and Bureau Coalition, 1995—. 1st lt. U.S. Army, 1942-46, CBI. Recipient Learned Hand award Am. Jewish Com., 1989, Outstanding Law Alumni award U. Denver, 1994, Evans Disting. Svc. award U. Denver, 2001. Mem. ABA, Colo. Bar Assn., Denver Bar Assn., University Club of Denver, Garden of Gods Club (Colorado Springs). Republican. Mem. United Ch. of Christ. Office: Sherman & Howard 633 17th St Ste 3000 Denver CO 80202-3665 Office Phone: 303-299-8148. Business E-Mail: jlow@sah.com.

LOW, KATHLEEN R., primary school educator; d. Harry and Monica Low. BA, Calif. State U., Fresno, 1976; MA in Edn., Calif. State U. Stanislaus, Turlock, 2004. Specialist Credential-Learning Handicapped Commn. on Tchr. Credentialing, Calif., 1978, Multiple Subjects Credential Commn. on Tchr. Credentialing, 1980, Resource Specialist Certificate of Competence Commn. on Tchr. Credentialing, 1983, Language Development Specialist Certificate Commn. on Tchr. Credentialing, 1991, Reading Credential Commn. on Tchr. Credentialing, 2004. Tchr. resource specialist Lodi (Calif.) Unified Sch. Dist., 1978—85, tchr. third grade, 1985—99, literacy resource tchr., 1999—2000, literacy coach/dist. staff developer, 2000—03, tchr. second grade, 2003—. Mem.: ASCD, Calif. Reading Assn., Internat. Reading Assn., Phi Delta Kappa. Avocations: gardening, sandhill crane docent, travel. Office: Lodi Unified School District Lodi CA 95240 Office Phone: 209-953-8301.

LOW, MALCOLM JAMES, research scientist; b. Edinburgh, Scotland, Aug. 25, 1955; s. George Duncan Low and Jessie Forbes Morton; m. Gaye Thomas, Dec. 26, 1981; children: Nicholas Duncan Thomas-Low, Jacob Armon Thomas-Low. BS, Rensselaer Poly. Inst., 1975; MD, Albany Med. Coll., 1979; PhD, Tufts U., 1987. Diplomate Am. Bd. Internal Medicine, 1982, Am. Bd. Endocrinology and Metabolism, 1985. Intern, resident in internal medicine Michael Reese Hosp., Chgo., 1979—82; neuroendocrinology fellow New Eng. Med. Ctr., Boston, 1982—85; asst. prof. medicine Tufts U., Boston, 1986—89; asst. scientist Oreg. Health & Sci. U., Portland, 1990—94, asst. prof. biochemistry and molecular biology, 1991—95, scientist, 1995—, assoc. prof. biochemistry and molecular biology, 1996—2002, prof. behavioral neurosci., 2002—, sr. scientist, 2003—. Mem. endocrinology and IPOD study sect. Ctr. for Sci. Rev., NIH, Bethesda, Md., 2001—. Contbr. articles to profl. jours. Recipient Pfizer Scholar award, Pfizer Pharmaceuticals, 1988—90; fellow Individual Nat. Rsch. Svc. award, NIH, 1983—84, Physician-Scientist award, 1984—89; grantee s, 1988—2003. Mem.: AAAS, Pituitary Soc., Soc. Neurosci., Endocrine Soc., Alpha Omega Alpha (life). Achievements include patents for mammalian melanocortin receptors and uses; development of transgenic mice with fluorescent proopiomelanocortin neurons for physiological studies of neuronal function; patents pending for upstream control elements of the proopiomelanocortin gene and their use; modification of feeding behavior; assessment of neurons in the arcuate nucleus to screen for agents that modify feeding behavior; invention of ß-endorphin knockout mice; dopamine D2 receptor knockout mice; dopamine D4 receptor knockout mice; human follicle stimulating hormone ß-subunit transgenic mice; immortalized pituitary melanotroph cell line. Avocations: travel, model railroading. Office: Vollum Inst Oreg Health & Sci Univ L-474 3181 SW Sam Jackson Park Rd Portland OR 97239-3098 Office Phone: 503-494-4672. E-mail: low@ohsu.edu.

LOW, MARY LOUISE (MOLLY LOW), documentary photographer; b. Quakertown, Pa., Jan. 3, 1926; d. James Harry and Dorothy Collyer (Krewson) Thomas; m. Antoine Francois Gagné, Nov. 3, 1945 (div.); children: James L., David W., Stephen J., Jeannie Wolff-Gagné; m. Paul Low, July 11, 1969 (dec. July 1991). Student, Oberlin Conservatory of Music, 1943-44, Oberlin Coll., 1944; cert., Katharine Gibbs Sec. Sch., 1945; degree in psychiat. rehab. work, Einstein Coll. Medicine, 1968-70. Sec. Dept. Store, N.Y.C., 1945; sec., treas. Gagné Assocs., Consulting Engrs., Binghamton, N.Y., 1951-66; psychiat. rsch. asst. Jacobi Hosp., Bronx, 1969-70; asst. to head of sch. Brearley Sch., N.Y.C., 1976-78; pvt. practice San Diego, 1984—. Contbr. articles to profl. jours. Pres., bd. trustees Unitarian-Universalist Ch., 2005—. Recipient Dir.'s award for excellence Area Agy. on Aging, San Diego, 1993, Citizen Recognition award County of San Diego, Calif., 1993. Avocations: singing, documentary photography, writing, travel. Office: Molly Low Photography 5576 Caminito Herminia La Jolla CA 92037-7222 Personal E-mail: molly@mollylow.com.

LOW, MERRY COOK, civic worker; b. Uniontown, Pa., Sept. 3, 1925; d. Howard Vance and Eleanora (Lynch) Mullan; m. William R. Cook, 1947 (div. 1979); m. John Wayland Low, July 8, 1979; children: Karen, Cindy, Bob, Jan. Diploma in nursing, Allegheny Gen. Hosp., Pitts., 1946; BS summa cum laude, Colo. Women's Coll., 1976. RN, Colo. Dir. patient edn. Med. Care and Rsch. Found., Denver, 1976-78. Contbr. chpt. to Pattern for Distribution of Patient Education, 1981. DuArt bd. dirs. U. Denver, 1998—2004; docent Denver Art Mus., 1979—99, vol. exec. bd., 1988—94, nat. docent symposium com., 1991, chair collectors' choice benefits, 1988, pres. vols., 1988—90; co-chair art auction Colo. Alliance Bus., 1992—93, com., 1994—97; founding chair Rocky Mountain Conservation Ctr., 1989; trustee ch. coun., chair invitational art show 1st Plymouth Congl. Ch., Englewood, Colo., 1981—84; bd. dirs. women's libr. assn. U. Denver, 1982—, vice chmn., 1985—86, chair, 1986—87, co-chair spl. event, 1992; bd. dirs. Humanities Inst., 1993—, pres., 1999; bd. dirs. Rocky Mountain Conservation Ctr., 1999—2000, co-chair Founder's Day com., 1994—, chair Culturefest, 1995—96; bd. dirs. Lamont Sch. Music Assocs., 1990—96. Recipient Disting. Svc. award U. Denver Coll. Law, 1988, King Soopers Vol. of Week award, 1989, Citizen of Arts award Fine Arts Found., 1993, Outstanding Vol. Colo. Alliance of Bus., 1994, U. Denver Cmty. Svc. award, 1996. Mem. Am. Assn. Mus. (vol. meeting coord. 1990-91), P.E.O. (pres. Colo. chpt. DX 1982-84), U. Denver Alumni Assn. (bd. dirs., sec. 1996-98), Welcome to Colo. (sec. 2004—), Women for Profit Investment Club (sec. 1999-2002, co-presiding ptnr. 2003-05). Republican. Congregationalist. Home: 2552 E Alameda Ave Apt 11 Denver CO 80209-3324 Personal E-mail: merrylow@aol.com.

LOW, MICHAEL CHRISTOPHER, secondary school educator, researcher; b. Atlanta, Apr. 7, 1979; s. Michael Chester and Edwina Harris Low; m. Cari Elizabeth Evans, Aug. 28, 1979. BS in Secondary Social Sci. Edn., State U. West Ga., 2001. Cert. social sci. tchr. Ga. Profl. Standards Commn., Ga., 2001. Tchr. world studies Avondale Mid. Sch., Avondale Estates, Ga., 2001—04; grad. rsch. asst. history dept. Ga. State U., Atlanta, 2004—. Contbr. berkshire encyclopedia of world history. Scholar Promise Tchrs. scholar, State of Ga., 1999—2001, Joe McGiboney scholar, State U. West Ga., 2000—01, Ga. State U. Dept. History, 2004—05; Fubright-Hays grantee, U.S. Dept. Edn., Kennesaw State U., 2004, Hope scholar, State of Ga., 1997—2001, Carroll-Heard Ret. Tchr. scholar, State U. West Ga., 1999—2001. Mem.: Am. Hist. Assn., World History Assn., Phi Kappa Phi, Phi Alpha Theta. Liberal. Agnostic. Avocations: history of British Empire in India, Islamic studies, travel, hiking. Home: 633 Moreland Ave Unit 1 Atlanta GA 30307 Personal E-mail: chrislow@earthlink.net.

LOW, MORTON DAVID, retired neuroscientist, educator, claims consultant; b. Lethbridge, Alta., Can., Mar. 25, 1935; s. Solon Earl and Alice Fern (Litchfield) L.; m. Cecilia Margaret Comba, Aug. 22, 1959 (div. 1983); children— Cecilia Alice, Sarah Elizabeth, Peter Jon Eric; m. Barbara Joan McLeod, Aug. 25, 1984; 1 child, Kelsey Alexandra MD, C.M., Queen's U., 1960, M.Sc. in Medicine, 1962; PhD with honors, Baylor U., 1966. From instr. to asst. prof. Baylor Coll. Medicine, Houston, 1965-68; assoc. prof. medicine U. B.C., Vancouver, Can., 1968-78, prof. medicine, 1978-89, clin. assoc. dean, 1974-76, assoc. dean rsch. and grad. studies, 1977-78, coord. health scis., 1985-89, creator Health Policy Rsch. Unit, 1987; Alkek-Williams Disting. Prof. and pres. U. Tex. Health Sci. Ctr., Houston, 1989-2000, disting. mem. faculty Grad. Sch. Biomed. Scis., 1989—2004, dir. Health Policy Inst., 1990—; Rockwell chair in soc. and health, dir. Ctr. Soc./Population U. Tex., Houston, 2000—04; prof. neurology U. Tex. Med. Sch., Houston, 1989—2001; prof. health policy and mgmt. Sch. Pub. Health U. Tex., 1989—2004, prof. emeritus, 2005—. Adj. prof. psychology Simon Fraser U., Vancouver, Can.; cons. in neurology U. Hosp. Shaughnessy site, Vancouver, 1971-89, U. B.C. site, Vancouver, 1970-89; dir. dept. diagnostic neurophysiology Vancouver Gen. Hosp., 1968-87; cons. in EEG, 1987-89; exec. dir. Rsch. Inst., 1981-86; med. sci. adv. com. USIA, 1991-93; adj. prof. Health Informatics Sch. Allied Health Scis.; adj. prof. psychology Simon Fraser U., 2005—; mem. Premier's Adv. Coun. on Health, Alta., Can., 2000-2002; strategic adv. Calgary Regional Health Auth., 2002—. Mem. editorial bd. numerous jours.; contbr. articles to profl. jours. Bd. dirs. Tex. Inst. for Rehab. and Rsch. Found., Greater Houston Ptnrship., 1994-2000, Episcopal Health Charities Found., 1997-2004, Houston Ind. Sch. Dist. Found., 2002-04; governing bd. Houston Mus. Natural Sci., 1991-97; trustee Kinkaid Sch., Houston, 1991-2004, Meml.-Herman Hosp. Sys., 1997-2000. Med. Rsch. Coun. Can. grantee, 1968-80; recipient Tree of Life award Jewish Nat. Fund, 1995, Caring Spirit award Inst. Religion, 1995. Fellow Am. EEG Soc., Royal Coll. Physicians (Can.), Royal Soc. Medicine (London); mem. AMA, Tex. Med. Assn. (coun. on med. edn. 1990-2000), Tex. Found. Soc. & Health (founding chmn. 1999), Can. Soc. Clin. Neurophysiology, Internat. Fedn. Socs. for EEG and Clin. Neurophysiology (rules com. 1977-81, sec. 1981-85), Assn. Acad. Health Ctrs. (task force on access to care and orgn. health svcs. 1988-95, chmn. 1992, task force on instnl. values 1989-95), Harris County Med. Soc., Am. Coun. Edn., Forum Club of Houston. Avocations: sailing, photography, soccer, skiing, flying. E-mail: mdlow@shaw.ca.

LOW, PETER W., law educator; b. Springfield, Mass., May 17, 1937; s. George W. and Doris J. Low; m. Carol Randolph, Sept. 10, 1960; children: Cathryn E., Diana R. AB, Princeton U., 1959; LLB, U. Va., 1963. Bar: Va. 1963, U.S. Supreme Ct. 1970. Law clk. to Chief Justice Earl Warren U.S. Supreme Ct., Washington, 1963—64; mem. faculty U. Va. Law Sch., Charlottesville, 1964—, asst. dean, 1965—69, assoc. dean, 1969—76, 1989—94, Hardy Cross Dillard prof. law, 1975—, v.p., provost, 1994—2001, Earle K. Shawe prof., 2003—. Vis. prof. Inst. Criminology, Cambridge, England, 1970, Salzburg Seminars in Am. Studies, 1972, U. Pa. Law Sch., 1974—75, Stanford Law Sch., 1977; cons. FBI Acad., Quantico, Va., 1972—99. Author: Federal Criminal Law, 2d edit., 2003; author: (with Jeffries) Federal Courts and the Law of Federal-State Relations, 5th edit., 2003; author: others. Mem.: Va. Bar Assn., Am. Law Inst., Order of Coif. Office: U Va Sch Law 580 Massie Rd Charlottesville VA 22903-1789 E-mail: pwl@virginia.edu.*

LOW, RANDALL, internist, cardiologist; b. San Francisco, June 24, 1949; s. Huet Hee and Betty Tai (Quan) L.; m. Dorothy Fung, May 4, 1975; children: Audrey, Madeleine, Jennifer. AA, City Coll., San Francisco, 1969; BA, U. Calif., Berkeley, 1971; MD, U. Calif., Davis, 1975. Diplomate Am. Bd. Internal Medicine, Nat. Bd. Med. Examiners, Am. Bd. Cardiovascular Diseases. Intern Hosp. of Good Samaritan, L.A., 1975-76, resident, 1976-77, chief med. resident, 1977-78, fellow in cardiology, 1979-81; mem. staff St. Francis Meml. Hosp., San Francisco, 1981—, chmn. dept. cardiology, 1995—; pvt. practice internal medicine and cardiology San Francisco, 1981—; mem. staff Chinese Hosp., San Francisco, 1981—, chief of medicine, 1991-92; asst. clin. prof. U. Calif., San Francisco, 1994-2000. Mem. courtesy staff St. Mary's Hosp., San Francisco, 1981—, Calif. Pacific Med. Ctr., San Francisco, 1990—; cardiology cons. Laguna Honda Hosp., San Francisco, 1981—. Mem. home health quality assurance com. Self Help for Elderly, San Francisco, 1991—; bd. trustees San Francisco Health Authority, 2000—; bd. dirs. Youth Advocates, San Francisco, 1992-99. Recipient Hearst Pub. Svc. award U. Calif.-Berkeley, 1970, 6th ann. homecare recognition award Self Help for Elderly, 1993. Mem. ACP, Am. Soc. Internal Medicine, Am. Coll. Cardiology, Am. Heart Assn. (bd. govs. 1983-90), Calif. Acad. Medicine, Calif. Med. Soc., San Francisco Med. Soc. (bd. dirs. 1999—), Assn. Chinese Cmty. Physicians (sec.-treas. 1986-89), Chinese Cmty. Health Care Assn. (pres. 1991-96, 99-2002). Office: 909 Hyde St Ste 501 San Francisco CA 94109-4853

LOW, RICHARD H., broadcasting executive, producer; b. Union City, N.J., Feb. 20, 1927; s. Irving and Regina (Krieger) L.; 1 dau., Jennifer A. Student, U. Mich., 1947-49; JD, Columbia U., 1952. With CBS News, 1952-56, CBS-TV Network, 1956-62, dir. contracts, facilities and program sales, 1959-62; with Young & Rubicam, 1962-84, v.p. TV-radio dept., 1970-72, v.p. programming, 1972-73, sr. v.p., 1973-81, responsible for network TV programming and purchasing, 1973-84, includes cable TV, 1980-84, exec. v.p., dir. broadcast programming and purchasing, 1981-84; pres. Manticore Prodns., Inc. 1985—. Pres. Universal Holding Co.; advisor LWV presdl. TV debates, 1980; judge N.Y. World TV Festival, 1979-80, Internat. Emmy awards, 1981-83; panelist Nat. Assn. TV Programming Execs. Conf., 1981; keynote spkr. 25th Anniversary seminar Broadcasters Promotion Assn., 1981; presenter S.I. Newhouse Sch. Pub. Comm., Syracuse U., 1981; discussant Ctr. for Comm., 1982; mem. Task Force on Pub. Broadcasting, 1983. Mem. task force Nat. Coun. Arts, 1977, Aspen Inst., 1973; v.p., trustee Am. Mus. Immigration; trustee Town Hall Found.; bd. dirs. U.S. Comm. 1983 Bicentennial of Air and Space; advisor Ramsey Clark for U.S. Senate, 1976. With U.S. Army, 1945-46. Office: 1056 5th Ave New York NY 10028-0112 Office Phone: 212-722-6600. *In the beginner's mind, there are many possibilities.*

LOW, RUSSELL NORMAN, physician; b. Stockton, Calif., Apr. 11, 1953; s. Loren Irving and Rose Low; m. Carolyn Hesse-Low, Apr. 27, 1980; children: Ryan, Robert. BS, U. Calif., Santa Barbara, 1975; DDS, U. Calif., L.A., 1979; MD, U. Calif., San Diego, 1990. Resident diagnostic radiology U. Calif., 1986—90; fellow body imaging Stanford U. Med. Ctr., Palo Alto, Calif., 1990—91; physician San Diego Diagnostic Radiology, San Diego, 1991—. Med. dir. Sharp and Children's MRI Ctr., Calif., 1992—. Contbr. 40 articles to profl. and med. jours. on clin. applications for MRI of the abdomen and pelvis. Named David Carroll Med. Intern of Yr., St Mary's Med. Ctr. San Francisco, 1986, One of Best Drs. in Am., Best Drs. Inc., 2003. Mem.: Internat. Soc. Magnetic Resonance in Medicine, Am. Coll. Radiology (bd. cert. 1990), Radiologic Soc. N.Am., Phi Beta Kappa. Office: Sharp and Children's MRI Ctr 7901 Frost St San Diego CA 92123

LOW, STEPHEN, foundation administrator, educator, retired diplomat; b. Cin., Dec. 2, 1927; s. Martin and Margaret (Friend) L.; m. Helen Sue Carpenter, Oct. 9, 1954; children: Diego, Rodman, Jesse. BA, Yale U., 1950; MA, Fletcher Sch. Law and Diplomacy, Tufts U., 1951, PhD, 1956. With Dept. State, various locations, 1956-74; sr. staff mem. NSC, 1974-76; U.S. ambassador to Zambia, 1976-79; U.S. ambassador to Nigeria, 1979-81; dir. Fgn. Service Inst. Dept. State, 1982-87; dir. Bologna (Italy) Ctr. Sch. Advanced Internat. Studies Johns Hopkins U., 1987-92; pres. Assn. Diplomatic Studies and Tng., 1992-97; retired, 1997; pres. Fgn. Affairs Mus. Coun., 2000—. Served with AUS, 1946-47. Address: 2855 Tilden St NW Washington DC 20008-3820

LOWANCE, MASON I., American literature educator; b. Atlanta, June 2, 1938; s. Mason I. and Kathleen Bowden Lowance; m. Susan Coltrane, July 19, 1963; children: Susan Radclifee, Margaret Elizabeth Lowance Rorick. AB cum laude, Princeton U., 1960; BA with honors, Oxford (Eng.) U., 1964, MA with honors, 1966; PhD, Emory U., 1967. Instr. in English and religion Punahou Sch., Honolulu, 1960-61; instr. in English Morehouse Coll., Atlanta, 1964-67; asst. prof. U. Mass., Amherst, 1967-71, assoc. prof., 1971-75, prof. Am. lit., 1975—. Vis. prof. Tufts U., 1971, Corpus Christi Coll., 1979-80, Oxford U., 1979-80, Clark U., 1988, Harvard U., 1981—; cons. U.S. Office Edn., Washington, 1965-78; dir. NEH seminars for coll. tchrs. Newberry Libr., 1982, 95, Brown U., 1976. Author: Increase Mather, 1974, Massachusetts Broadsides of the American Revolution, 1976, The Language of Canaan, 1980, The Typological Writings of Jonathan Edwards, 1993, The Stowe Debate: Rhetorical Strategies in Uncle Tom's Cabin, 1994, Against Slavery: An Abolitionist Reader, 2000, A House Divided: The Antebellum Slavery Debates in America, 1776-1865, 2003. Fellow NEH, 1976, Nat. Humanities Inst., 1982-83, Guggenheim Found., 1982-83. Mem. Rotary, St. Botolph's Club, Harvard Faculty Club, U. Mass. Faculty Club. Democrat. Episcopalian. Avocations: sailing, travel, golf. Office: U Mass Dept Am Lit Amherst MA 01003 Office Phone: 413-545-2332. Business E-Mail: masonl@english.umass.edu.

LOWBER, JOHN M., communications executive; b. 1950; Sr. mgr. KPMG Peat Marwick; CFO Gen. Comm., Inc., Anchorage, 1987—, sec., treas., 1988—, CFO, sr. v.p., 1989—. Office: Gen Comm Inc Ste 1000 2550 Denali St Anchorage AK 99503 Office Fax: 907-265-5076.

LOWDEN, JOHN L., retired manufacturing executive; b. Yakima, Wash., Oct. 29, 1921; s. Roy Ruben and Hildegarde Annie (Grommesch) L.; m. Janet Katherine Langan, Jan. 21, 1961; children: Susan Elizabeth, Jonathan Roy, Andrew Matthias. BA, U. Nev., 1949. Account supr. Campbell-Ewald Advt., 1951-57, Erwin, Wasey Advt., 1957-59; advt. dir. Gen. Dynamics Corp., 1959-61; account supr. Foote, Cone & Belding, 1961-63; with ITT Corp., 1963-84, v.p. corp. rels. and advt., 1977-84. Author: Silent Wings at War, 1992. Served with USAAF, 1941-45. Decorated Air medal with oak leaf cluster, Presdl. Unit Citation, Bronze Arrowhead of initial assault troops, 4th degree Knight Order of William Netherlands. Catholic.

LOWE, AISHA NONI, social sciences educator; d. Richard and Theodosia Ann Lowe. BA in Psychology, Stanford U., 1999, MA in Sociology, 2004, postgrad. in Edn., 2000—. Exec. dir. East Palo Alto Stanford Acad., Stanford, Calif., 1996—99; prof. Pierce Coll., Woodland Hills, 2004—. Co-chair bd. trustees Fellowship Acad., San Francisco, 2000—04. Recipient James Lyons Svc. award, Stanford U., 1999. Mem.: APA, Am. Ednl. Rsch. Assn., Stanford U. Alumni Assn. (life). Achievements include research in Stereotype Threat, Self-Relevence, and African American 4th Graders; An Investigation of School Culture; Stereotype Threat, Racial Identity, and School Culture. Home: 9101 National Blvd Unit 2 Los Angeles CA 90034 Personal E-mail: aisha@stanford.edu.

LOWE, ANTHONY S., information technology executive; BA in Internat. Polit. Sci. cum laude, U. Wash.; JD, U. Santa Clara; MDiv, Va. Union U.; Exec. M in Bus., George Mason U. Bar: Washington, DC, Pa., Wash., US Ct. Internat. Trade, US Dist. Ct. We. Dist. Wash., US Ct. Appeals Ninth Circuit. Sr. trade intern Internat. Trade Adminstrn., Fgn. and Comml. Svc., US Dept. Commerce, Seattle, 1983—84; leg. asst. US Senator Slade Gorton, Washington, 1988—90; legal counsel Wash. State Senate, Majority Office of Legal Counsel and Policy Devel., Olympia, 1991—92; jud. extern US Ct. Appeals Ninth Circuit, Judge Robert R. Beezer, Seattle, 1991; assoc. dir. Internat. Ctr. Econ. Growth and Internat. Ctr. Self-Governance Programs, Inst. Contemporary Studies, Washington, 1991; dep. prosecutor King County Prosecutor's Office, Seattle, 1992—97; sr. leg. counsel US Senate Jud. Com. Subcommittee on Antitrust, Competition, and Bus. Rights, Washington, 1997—2002; CEO, dir. IT Risk Solutions, Inc., 2002—; dir. mitigation divsn., fed. ins. adminstr. US Fed. Emergency Mgmt. Agy., Dept. Homeland Security, 2002—04. TV polit. and legal commentator. Coach full impact program J.C. & Frankie Watts Found.; former Redmond Planning commr.; former trustee Children's Home Soc.; mem. Leadership Tomorrow Program Greater Seattle C. of C.; mem. Redmond C. of C.; assoc. minister Antioch Baptist Ch. Mem.: Bellevue Breakfast Rotary Club.

LOWE, CALVIN W., university president; B in Physics, N.C. A&T; M in Physics, M in Physics, PhD in Physics, MIT. Former asst. prof. physics U. Ky.; former asst. and assoc. prof., chair dept. physics Hampton U., former v.p. for rsch., dean grad. coll.; former chair dept. physics Ala. A&M; pres. Bowie (Md.) State U. Office: Bowie State U Office of Pres 14000 Jericho Park Rd Henry Admin Bldg Rm 206 Bowie MD 20715-9465

LOWE, CAMERON ANDERSON, dentist, endodontist, educator; b. Alcester, S.D., Dec. 19, 1932; s. Richard Barrett and Emma Louise Lowe; m. Doris Teresita Franquez, Dec. 23, 1957; children: Barrett, Steven, Leslie. Student, George Washington U., 1951-53, U. Va., 1955-56; DDS, Georgetown U., 1956-60; cert. residency in endodontics, U.S. Naval Dental Sch., 1967-69. Commd. lt. (j.g.) U.S. Navy Dental Corps, 1960, advanced through grades to capt., 1976, ret., 1978; pvt. practice endodontist Newport News, Va., 1978-81; assoc. prof. dentistry emeritus Old Dominion U., Norfolk, Va., 1991, asst. chair Sch. Dental Hygiene, 1985-89. Adj. asst. prof. Med. Coll. Va.-Va. Commonwealth U. Sch. Dentistry, Richmond, 1979-81. Contbr. articles to profl. jours. and to book: Oral Pathology, 3d edit., 1989. Tutor adult literacy, 1994-99; coord. Neighborhood Watch, 1994-98; pack and troop chmn. Boy Scouts Am., Guam, 1969-72, Virginia Beach, Va., 1972-78. With USN, 1953-55. Mem. Assn. Mil. Surgeons of U.S., Am. Assn. Endodontists, Am. Acad. Oral Medicine, Am. Dental Assn., Va. Acad. Endodontics, USN Assn. Endodontists, Peninsula Dental Soc., Sigma Alpha Epsilon, Delta Sigma Delta, Sigma Phi Alpha (Dental Hygiene Honor Soc.). Methodist. Avocations: tennis, drawing, carving, reading, sculpting. Home: 1497 Wakefield Dr Virginia Beach VA 23455-4541

LOWE, CLAYTON KENT, radio film critic, educator; b. Endicott, N.Y., July 10, 1936; s. Clayton Edwin and Loretta Arlene (Terry) L.; m. Janet E. Snider, 1957 (div. 1977); children: Steven Scott, Kim Ann Parker, David William, Rebecca Michelle Sobel; m. Robin S. McKell, 1980 (div. 1993). BA, Bethany Coll., 1958; MS, Butler U., 1967; PhD, Ohio State U., 1970; BD, Christian Theol. Sem., Indpls., 1962. Pastor Bellaire (Ohio) Christian Ch., 1957-58, Beallsville (Ohio) Christian Ch., 1958, Russellville (Ind.) Christian Ch., 1958-60, Montclair (Ind.) Christian Ch., 1960-61; youth dir. St. Paul United Ch. of Christ, Columbus, 1967-70; asst. prof. journalism U. Ga., 1970-72; asst. prof. comm. Ohio State U., Columbus, 1972-73, asst. prof. photography and cinema, 1973-74, assoc. prof., 1974—, chairperson photography and cinema, 1974-78, assoc. prof. emeritus, 1992—. Comml. TV prodr., dir., writer Sta. WISH-TV, 1960—66, Sta. WLWI-TV, 1966—67, Sta. WOSU-TV, 1967—70; moderator World Film Classics, Educable TV-25, 1991—97, also bd. dirs.; part-time faculty Franklin U., 2000—; film critic It's Movie Time WCBE FM, 2001—; part-time faculty Denison U., 2003. Editor: The Movies on Media Catalog, 1995, 2000, Movies on Media Video Collection. Bd. dirs. Columbus Friends of the Libr.; trustee Met. Libr., 1997—2002. Nominee Regional Emmy award, Lucasville, 1970, High Street, 1975; recipient Casper award for A Thing Called Hope, WISH-TV, 1966, Regional Emmy award for A Tribute to Dr. King, 1968, Leadership award, Ohio State U. Outstanding Alumni Soc., 1997, Communicator award of excellence for It's Movie Time New Yr.'s Spl., Sta WCBE-FM, 2002, Silver Microphone award, It's Movie Time, 2002, 2003; grantee, Eli Lilly Found., 1961—63, Ohio State U. Devel. of media on media Study Collection, 1985, Ohio Humanities Coun., 1996—97, 1999. Mem.: Ohio State U. Dept. Photography and Cinema Alumni Assn. (pres. 1994—95, 2001—02, bd. dirs. 1994—). Home: 68 Walhalla Rd Columbus OH 43202-1441 Office Phone: 614-262-3284. Personal E-mail: claytonlowe@hotmail.com. *If these were my last words, I would write of the beauty that has filled me and that I in turn have filled. I would look past the darkness and pain, toward those radiant spots of light when family and friends were most open and life was at its wondrous best.*

LOWE, DAVID ALAN, epidemiologist; b. Boston, May 6, 1945; s. Charles and Anne Lowe; m. Rosanne Minard, June 6, 1971; children: Darren, Jaime. MD, Harvard Med. Sch., Boston, 1967—71; BA, U. of Mass., Amherst, 1963—67. Cert. infectious diseases Am. Bd. of Internal Medicine, 1976, internal medicine Am. Bd. of Internal Medicine, 1974. Infectious disease cons. Kent Hosp., Warwick, RI, 1976—, epidemiologist, 1981—, pres. of the med. staff, 2002—, v.p. of med. staff, 2000—02, dir. of travel clinic, 1991—; cons. in tropical medicine Foster Parents Plan Internat., Warwick, 1984—94; clin. instr. of medicine Brown U. Sch. of Medicine, Providence, 1979—93; chief, dept. of medicine Kent Hosp., Warwick, 1987—89; asst. prof. of medicine U. of Vt. Coll. of Medicine, Burlington, 1976—77. Author: (novel) The Rope. Mem.: Infectious Disease Soc. of Am. Avocations: writing, landscape photography. Office: 615 Jefferson Blvd Warwick RI 02886 Office Phone: 401-885-5409. Personal E-mail: pasteur@aol.com.

LOWE, DOUGLAS HOWARD, architect; b. Akron, Ohio, Nov. 1, 1952; s. Howard Bernard and Dorothy Rachael (Nowag) L.; m. Mary Louise Folk, Jan. 1, 1975; children: Ashley Marie, Austin Douglas, Andrea Catherine. BA in Pre Architecture with honors, Clemson U., 1974, MArch, 1976. Registered profl. architect, Tex., Va., interior designer, Tex. Archtl. programmer Lockwood, Andrews, Newnam, Houston, 1978-80; sr. assoc. Planning Design Research Corp., Houston, 1980-82; v.p., head interior architecture and programming 3D/Internat., San Antonio, 1982-88, exec. v.p., chief ops. officer 3D/M subs., 1988-92; founder, pres. Facility Programming and Consulting, San Antonio, 1992—; co-founder, v.p. Facility Consulting Group, San Antonio, 1994-95. Mem. Design-Build Inst. of Am., First Presbyn. Ch., San Antonio; mem. legis. com. Alamo Heights Ind. Sch. Dist. Mem. AIA, Tex. Soc. Archs., Internat. Facility Mgmt. Assn., Nat. Coun. Archtl. Registration Bds., Nat. Trust Hist. Preservation, Soc. for Coll. and Univ. Planning, Rotary Club San Antonio, Soc. Coll. & Univ. Planning, Town Club San Antonio, Phi Kappa Phi, Tau Sigma Delta. Republican. Presbyterian. Avocations: remodeling homes, golf. Office: Facility Programming & Cons 100 W Houston St Ste 1100 San Antonio TX 78205-1457

LOWE, FRANKLIN C., urologist, educator; s. Irwin and Edna I. Lowe; m. Lauren Silbert, May 27, 1979; children: Logan S., Jensen R. BA, PrincetonU., 1975; MD, MPH, Columbia U., 1979. Lic. MD MD, 1981, Pa., 1984, NY, 1985, Mass., 1996, cert. urology 1997. Asst. chief of svc.-urology Johns Hopkins Hosp., Balt., 1985; asst. dir. urology St. Luke's Roosevelt Hosp., N.Y.C., NY, 1985—; prof. clin. urology Columbia U., Coll. of Physicians and Surgeons, N.Y.C., 2003—. Bd. dirs. guidelines panel Am. Urological Assn., Balt., 1996—2004, chmn. alternative medicine, 2001—. Editor (assoc. editor): (jour.) Urology, 1999—; editl. bd.: jour. Prostate Cancer and Prostate Diseases, 2000—. Exec. bd. Manhattan Soccer Club, N.Y.C., 1999—2003; co-chair alumni selective com. Princeton U., Bronx, NY, 2002—; cert. referee US Soccer Federation. Named Best Doctors in NY, NY Mag., 1998, Best Doctors in Am., Calle and Connolly, 2001, Tchr. of Yr., Columbia Coll. of Physicians and Surgeons, 2001. Fellow: NY Acad. of Medicine, Sectum Urology (pres. 2000—01), Am. Coll. of Surgeons. Avocation: racquetball. Office: St Lukes Roosevelt Hosp Urology Dept 425 W 59th St 3A New York NY 10019

LOWE, GREGG A., semiconductor company executive; b. Cleveland; BS in elec. engring., Rose Hulman Inst. Tech., 1984; grad., Stanford Exec. Program, Stanford U. Field sales Tex. Instruments, 1984—89, dir. European automotive sales teams (led teams in Germany, Italy, England, and Spain), 1989—94, mgr. microcontroller orgn., 1994—98, mgr. ASIC orgn., 1998—2001, mgr. high speed comm. and controls, High Performance Analog Unit Dallas, 2001, sr. v.p., mgr. High Performance Analog Bus. Unit, 2001—. Office: Tex Instruments Inc 12500 TI Blvd Dallas TX 75243 Office Phone: 972-995-2011. Office Fax: 972-995-4360.

LOWE, IDA BRANDWAYN, library administrator, systems administrator; b. Bogota, Colombia, Oct. 5, 1946; came to U.S., 1964; d. Jacobo and Donna (Ghelman) Brandwayn; m. Fredric Robert Lowe, Aug. 16, 1970; children: Evin, Laurence. BA, Cornell U., 1968; MA, New Sch. Social Rsch., 1971; MSLS, Columbia U., 1972; MBA, Baruch Coll., 1988. Cataloger Baruch Coll. Libr., N.Y.C., 1973-80, mgr. info. svcs., 1981-86, asst. dean, 1987, coord. for systems, 1988-94, dep. dir., 1990-97, dir. network techs., 1994-97; mgr. network systems Thomson Fin. Svcs., N.Y.C., 1997-2000, dir. ops., user support svcs., 2000—. Cons. UN Ctr. on Transnational Corp., Ethiopia, 1990-91, UN Devel. Prog., N.Y.C., 1989, Telecom & Network Tng., Colombia and Ecuador, 1993, various librs., 1987— various corps., 1986—, UNDP Mozambique, 1993. Contbr. articles to profl. jours. Recipient Baruch/CUNY award for disting. svc., 1993. Home: 45 Strathmore Ln Westport CT 06880-4715 Office: Thomson Fin Svcs 195 Broadway New York NY 10007

LOWE, IRVING JACK, physics professor; b. Woonsocket, R.I., Jan. 4, 1929; s. Louis H. and Frieda (Angel) L.; m. Irene Povlish; children: Rachel, Marc, Margo. BEE, Cooper U., N.Y.C., 1951; PhD, Washington U., St. Louis, 1957. Postdoc. fellow Washington U., St. Louis, 1956-58; asst. prof. U. Minn., Mpls., 1958-62; assoc prof., prof. U. Pitts., 1962—. Contbr. over 200 papers in field. Office: Dept Physics Univ Pittsburgh Pittsburgh PA 15260

LOWE, J. ALLEN, minister; b. Midland, Tex., Dec. 20, 1945; s. Homer Allen and Theresa (Lowry) L.; m. Shirley Christy, Apr. 9, 1965; children: Robert Allen, John David, Steven Scott. BS, Howard Payne U., 1968; MDiv, Tex. Christian U., 1976; postgrad, Princeton Theol., 1990, postgrad., 2002. Cert. secondary tchr.; ordained to the ministry Christian Ch., 1976. Instr. Biblical history Midland (Tex.) Ind. Sch. Dist., 1968-74; assoc. min. First Christian Ch., Denison, Tex., 1974-76; campus min. United Campus Ministries, Ctrl. Mo. State U., Warrensburg, 1976-78; nurture min. Meml. Christian Ch., Midland, Tex., 1978-84; assoc. min. 1st Christian Ch., Corpus Christi, Tex., 1984-91; sr. min. South Shore Christian Ch., Corpus Christi, 1991-2000, First Christian Ch., Richardson, Tex., 2000—. Chmn. Cen. Area Youth Coun., Tex., 1980-84; moderator Youth Ministry Coun. S.W., 1984-87, Bluebonnet Area Youth Coun., 1986-93; advisor Gen. Youth Coun., U.S. and Can., 1985-87; vice moderator Bluebonnet Area of Christian Ch. in S.W., 1994-95. Mem. IMPACT, 1974-82; charter mem. Nat. Peace Acad., 1973-78; coach YMCA basketball, 1980-81, Little League, Youth Flag Football teams, Denison and Midland, 1967-68, 70, 74; mem. ethics commn. City of Corpus Christi, 1994-2000; active City League Youth Basketball, Corpus Christi, 1995-97; mem. com. on the ministry Christian Ch. in the S.W., 1997-2000, 2002-2006; mem. North Tex. Area Youth Min. Coun., 2001-2004; spkr. Christian Youth Confs., 1980—; advisor internat. youth coun. Disciples of Christ Ch., U.S. and Can Recipient Friend of Youth City award, 1989; O.H. Karr Ministerial scholar Tex. Christian U., 1975-76. Home: 2722 Laurel Oaks Dr Garland TX 75044 Office: First Christian Ch 601 E Main St Richardson TX 75081-3521 Office Phone: 972-235-3583. Business E-Mail: office@fccrichardson.org. *My guiding principle is that Christianity is a relationship. Therefore, it must be lived as a relationship-we experience the love of God only in relationship to another (others) and thus only in relationship can we teach Christianity. In short, the slogan "Preach the Gospel, use words if necessary".*

LOWE, JAMES ALLISON, lawyer, educator; b. Cleve., July 15, 1945; s. Allison S. and Betty B. (Bernstein) L.; m. Jacalyn S. Scholss, June 24, 1967 (div.); children: David, Joseph, Jeremiah; m. Teresa L. DiPuccio, Aug. 13, 1989; 1 child, Alison. BA, U. Pa., 1967; JD cum laude, Cleve. State U., 1972. Bar: Ohio 1972, U.S. Dist. Ct. (no. dist.) Ohio 1973, U.S. Ct. Appeals (6th cir.) 1981, U.S. Supreme Ct. 1979; cert. civic trial adv. Nat. Bd. Trial Advocacy. Assoc. Berkman, Gordon & Kancelbaum, Cleve., 1972—74; sole practice Cleve., 1974—76; ptnr. Sindell, Lowe & Guidubaldi Co., L.P.A., Cleve., 1976—96, Lowe Eklund Wakefield Co., LPA, Cleve., 1996—2000, Lowe Eklund Wakefield & Mulvihill Co., LPA, Cleve., 2000—. Instr. law Cleve. State U., 1974-77, Case Western Res. U., 1979-92. Author: Products Liability Litigation: Pretrial Practice, 1988, Product Liability in Ohio After Tort Reform, 1988. Active Jewish Cmty. Fedn.; fellow Roscoe Pound Found. Fellow Internat. Soc. Barristers, Am. Bd. Trial Advs., Am. Coll. Trial Lawyers; mem. ABA, ATLA (chmn. products liability adv. com., chmn. products liability sect., dir. products liability sect.), Ohio Acad. Trial Attys. (chmn. products liability sect. 1987-89, trustee 1990—), Ohio Bar Assn., Cleve. Acad. Trial Attys. (bd. dirs. 1988—, v.p. 1990—), Greater Cleve. Bar Assn., Attys. Info. Exch. Group, Am. Bd. Trial Advocates. Office: Lowe Eklund Wakefield & Mulvihill Co LPA 610 Skylight Office Tower 1660 W 2nd St #610 Cleveland OH 44113-1454 Office Phone: 216-781-2600. Business E-Mail: Jlowe@lewm.com.

LOWE, JAMES EDWARD, JR., plastic and reconstructive surgeon; b. Warsaw, N.C., Dec. 5, 1950; s. James Edward and Alice Mae (Gavin) L.; m. Philamina Lucy Lozado, Oct. 7, 1989; children: James III, Jesse, Joseph. BS, Livingstone Coll., 1971; MD, Meharry Med. Coll., 1975. Diplomate Am. Bd. Plastic Surgery. Intern Downstate Med. Ctr., Bklyn., 1975—76, resident in surgery, 1975—78, Luth. Med. Ctr., Bklyn., 1978—82; resident in plastic surgery Lenox Hill Hosp., N.Y.C., 1982—84, pvt. practice, 1984—, assoc. attending surgeon, 1984—99, Good Hope Hosp., Erwin, NC, 1999—. Student mentor Purchase (N.Y.) Coll., 1996—; elder Presbyn. Ch., Scarborough, N.Y., 1998—; student tutor Highland Presbyn. Ch., Fayetteville, N.C., 2003. Health Career scholar Harvard U. Med. Sch., Boston, 1970. Mem.: NAACP, AMA (Physicians Recognition award 2005—), Cumberland County Med. Soc., Nat. Med. Soc., Lenox Hill Plastic Surgery Soc., The Morestin Soc., Phi Beta Sigma. Office: 4155 Ferncreek Dr Ste 102 Fayetteville NC 28314 E-mail: jameselowe@msn.com.

LOWE, JASON DAVID, music educator; b. Detroit, June 4, 1972; s. Richard Dennis and Carolyn Ethel Lowe; m. Sharon Lynn Abramovich, Aug. 15, 1973; children: Duncan Richard children: Annika Mae. Bachelor of Gen. Studies, U. Mich., 1994—94. Instrumental music tchr. North Farmington High Sch., Farmington Hills, Mich., 1998—2003; dir. of bands Beal City Pub. Schs., Mount Pleasant, Mich., 2003—. Recipient Tchr. Yr., North Farmington High Sch., 2002. Mem.: Music Educators Nat. Conf., Mich. Sch. Band and Orch. Assn. Office: Beal City Pub Sch 3117 Elias Rd Mount Pleasant MI 48858-9734 Office Phone: 989-644-3944. Personal E-mail: jdlowe@provide.net.

LOWE, JOHN, III, consulting civil engineer; b. N.Y.C., Mar. 14, 1916; s. John and Rose Marie (Jahoda) L.; m. Jeanne Wright, June 19, 1943; children: Jonathan Alan, Barbara Jean, Heather Ellen. BS in Engring., CCNY; MSC.E., MIT. Registered profl. engr., N.Y., La., PR., Calif. Instr. U. Md., College Park, 1937-40, MIT, Cambridge, Mass., 1941-44; physicist David Taylor Model Basin, Carderock, Md., 1945; chief soils engr. Tippetts-Abbett-McCarthy-Stratton, N.Y.C., 1945-55, assoc. ptnr., 1956-62, ptnr., 1962-83; pvt. practice geotech. and dam engring., 1984—. Adj. assoc. prof. NYU, 1949-51; lectr. soil mechanics CCNY, 1953-60; 8th Terzaghi lectr., 1971, 4th Nabor Carrillo lectr., 1978, 2d U.S. Com. on Large Dams lectr., 1982, Marty Kapp lectr., 1986; keynote address Roller Compacted Concrete II, 1988, Mueser/Rutledge lectr., 1997; cons. Corps. Engrs., Washington, 1962-80; dam constrn. projects in many countries including U.S., Turkey, Taiwan, Morocco, Pakistan, Brazil, Greece. Contbr. chpts. to 4 books, 38 articles in field to profl. jours. Decorated comdr. Order of Alouites (Morocco); recipient Townsend Harris medal Alumni CCNY, 1982. Fellow ASCE; mem. NAE, U.S. Com. Large Dam (chmn. 1977-78), Nat. Com. Soil Mechanics and Found. Engring., Moles, Univ. Club, Bronxville Field Club. Personal E-mail: jloweiii@aol.com.

LOWE, JOHN BURTON, medical association administrator, molecular biologist, educator, pathologist; b. Sheridan, Wyo., June 13, 1953; s. Burton G. and Eunice D. Lowe. BA, U. Wyo., 1976; MD, U. Utah, 1980. Diplomate Am. Bd. Pathology. Asst. med. dir. Barnes Hosp. Blood Bank, St. Louis, 1985-86; instr. Sch. of Medicine Washington U., St. Louis, 1985, asst. prof. Sch. of Medicine, 1985-86; asst. investigator Howard Hughes Med. Inst., Ann Arbor, Mich., 1986-92, assoc. investigator, 1992-96, investigator, 1997—2005; asst. prof. Med. Sch. U. Mich., Ann Arbor, 1986-91, assoc. prof. Med. Sch., 1991-95, prof. Med. Sch., 1995—2005; Henry Willson Payne prof. and chair dept. pathology Case Western Res. U. Sch. Medicine, Cleve., 2005—, prof., chmn. dept. pathology, 2005. Dep. editor Jour. Clin. Investigation, 1997—2002, mem. editl. bd. European Jour. Biochemistry, 2001—; contbr. articles to profl. jours. including Jour. Biol. Chemistry, Genes and Devel., Nature, Cell Sci. Fellow: AAAS; mem.: Am. Assn. Physicians, Am. Soc. Clin. Investigation. Office: Dept Pathology Case We Reserve Univ Sch Medicine 10900 Euclid Ave Cleveland OH 44106-7288

LOWE, JOHN THOMAS, JR., church and concert musician; b. Lynchburg, Va., Sept. 1, 1970; s. John Thomas Lowe and Evelyn G. Lowe-Woody. BS in Organ Performance, Liberty U., 1993; MusM, U. Ala., 1996; MusD, Ind. U., 2005. Organist United Meth. Ch. World Conf. Ctr., Lake Junaluska, NC, 1993; organist, choirmaster Canterbury Chapel Episcopal Ch. and Student Ctr., Tuscaloosa, Ala., 1993—96; full-time music intern West End United Meth. Ch., Nashville, 1996—98; music dir., organist Congregation Micah, Nashville, 1996—98, The Ch. of the Nativity (Episcopal), Indpls., 1998—2003; dir. of music, organist 1st United Meth. Ch., Ocala, Fla., 2003—; condr., artistic dir. Ctrl. Fla. Master Choir, Ocala, 2004—. Organist: CD Singing Hymns and Spiritual Songs, 1998. Finalist organ performance competition, Deerfield, Ill., 1991, undergrad. competition in organ performance, Ottumwa, Iowa, 1991, 1992; recipient 1st prize nat. student auditions, Nat. Fedn. Music Clubs, 1995, 2d prize organ performance competition, San Marino, Calif., 1996. Mem.: Fellowship of United Methodists in Music and Worship Arts, Chorister's Guild (Ruth Kribbel Jacobs Meml. scholar 1999—2000), Am. Choral Dirs. Assn., Am. Guild English Handbell Ringers, Am. Guild Organists (Ocala chpt. dean 2004—05, 1st prize regional competition for young organists 1991, 2d prize 1993), Organ Hist. Soc., Phi Mu Alpha (life). Home: 3240 SW 34th St #231 Ocala FL 34474 Office: 1st United Meth Ch 1126 E Silver Springs Blvd Ocala FL 34470 Office Phone: 352-622-3244. Office Fax: 352-732-9701. Personal E-mail: johntlowejr@aol.com. E-mail: john@fumcocala.org.

LOWE, JONATHAN WAYNE, lawyer; b. Miami, Dec. 15, 1947; BS, U. Pa., 1970; JD, Harvard U., 1975. Bar: U.S. Dist. Ct. (no. dist.) Ga. 1975. Assoc. Alston & Bird, Atlanta, 1975-82, ptnr., corp. health care & technology group, 1982—. Trustee Paideia Sch., Atlanta, 1986—; mem. Leadership Atlanta, 1989. 1st lt. U.S. Army QMC, 1970-72. Recipient Spl. Vol. award Gov. of State Ga., 1985. Mem. Ansley Golf Club. Office: Alston & Bird One Atlantic Ctr 1201 W Peachtree St NW Ste 4200 Atlanta GA 30309-3449 Office Phone: 404-881-7555. Office Fax: 404-881-7777. Business E-Mail: jlowe@alston.com.

LOWE, JUDITH, music educator; b. Lincoln, N.H., Aug. 17, 1947; B in Organ Music, U. of the Arts, Phila., 1970; M in Choral Conducting, U. Md., 2000. Cert. profl. arts mgr. PAMI. Dir. Delaware County Music Sch., Media, Pa., 1970—76; mem. faculty, staff Settlement Music Sch., Phila., 1976—89; dir., adminstr. Judith Lowe and Assocs., 1989—2000, N.Y.C., 2001—. Dir. music various chs., Phila. area, 1963—2001; cons. Cath. Social Svcs., Phila., 1983—89; elected faculty rep. Settlement Music Sch., Phila., 1985—89; univ. organist, vis. lectr. Lincoln U., Pa., 1986—89; founder, dir. Challenge Summer Performing Arts Camps for Children, NYC, 2002—; dir. music and arts Episcopal and Luth. chs., Queens, 2003—, Challenge Arts Programs, NYC, 2001—. Dir. Narberth Cmty. Chorus, 1987—95; founder Narberth Cmty. Harvest for the Homeless, 1986—96; vol. Narberth Cmty. Meml. Day and 4th of July, 1988—2000; bd. dirs., vol. cook Human Understanding and Growth, N.Y.C., 2002—; bd. dirs. Lower Merion Narberth Coalition on Aging, Bryn Mawr, 1987—93. Recipient award for outstanding cmty. svc., Olney H.S., 1965, award for outstanding svc. to religious cmty., Lincoln U., 1987, award for cmty. svc., Grace Ch. and Sch., N.Y.C., 2003; scholar Phila. Bd. Edn., 1960. Mem.: Chorus Am., Am. Guild Organists, Greenpeace. Democrat. Lutheran. Avocations: cooking, gardening, medieval religious drama and opera. Office: Judith Lowe and Assocs PO Box 863240 Ridgewood NY 11385 Office Phone: 718-456-0187.

LOWE, KATHLENE WINN, lawyer; b. San Diego, Dec. 1, 1949; d. Ralph and Grace (Rodes) Winn; m. Russell Howells Lowe, Oct. 7, 1977; 1 child, Taylor Rhodes. BA in English magna cum laude, U. Utah, 1971, MA in English, 1973, JD, 1976. Bar: Utah 1976, U.S. Dist. Ct. Utah 1976, U.S. Ct. Appeals (10th cir.) 1980, Calif. 1989, U.S. Dist. Ct. (ctrl. dist.) Calif. 1990. Assoc. Parsons, Behle & Latimer, Salt Lake City, 1976-80, ptnr., 1980-84; v.p. law Skaggs Alpha Beta Inc., Salt Lake City; ptnr. Brobeck, Phleger & Harrison, Newport Beach, Calif.; ptnr.-in-charge, So. Calif. Dorsey & Whitney LLP, Irvine, Calif. Contbg. editor Utah Law Rev., 1975-76. Mem. ABA, Utah Bar Assn., Salt Lake City Bar Assn., Phi Kappa Phi. Avocations: fly fishing, reading, skiing, golf, travel. Office: Dorsey & Whitney LLP 38 Technology Dr Irvine CA 92618-5310 Office Phone: 714-424-5555. Office Fax: 714-424-5554. Business E-Mail: lowe.kathlene@dorsey.com.

LOWE, KEVIN BRIAN, finance company executive; b. Louisville, Ky., June 5, 1958; s. Charles Edward Lowe and Betty Sue Doyle; m. Sharon Elaine Huskey, Nov. 19, 1983; children: Tara, Rachel. BS, U. Louisville, 1980, MBA, Stetson U., 1982; PhD in Bus. Adminstrn., Fla. Internat. U., 1997. Fin. analyst Am. Hosp. Supply, Miami, Fla., 1982—85; fin. forecasting specialist Fla. Power & Light, Miami, 1985—87; asst. prof. Shorter Coll.,

Rome, Ga., 1987—90; assoc. prof. U. N.C., Greensboro, 1996—. Cons. Orgnl. Performance Dimensions, Miami, 1995—97, ConocoPhillips, Houston, 1997—2004, Ctr. Cteative Leadership, Greensboro, 1998—2003; vis. fellow U. Western Australia, 2002, 04; faculty fellow U. NC, Greensboro, 2001—05. Author: High Performance Work Organizations, 1999; contbr. articles to profl. jours. (Leadership Qtrly. Best Paper award, 1996, 2000). Recipient Outstanding Reviewer award, Western Acad. Mgmt., N.Mex., 2002, Best Congress Paper award, Australia and N.Z. Acad. Mgmt./Internat. Fedn. Scholars in Mgmt., 2002. Avocations: golf, travel. Home: 205 Erskine Dr W Greensboro NC 27410 Office: Univ NC Greensboro Greensboro NC 27402 Office Phone: 336-334-3055. Business E-Mail: kblowe@uncg.edu.

LOWE, LOUIS ROBERT, JR., lawyer; b. Indpls., May 30, 1937; BSCE, Purdue U., 1959; LLD, Ind. U., 1967. Bar: U.S. Dist. Ct. (so. dist.) Ind. 1967, U.S. Tax Ct. 1977; lic. profl. engr. Engr. various cons. engring. cos., Indpls., 1960-64, Ind. Hwy Needs Study, Indpls., 1966-67; ptnr. Lowe, Gray, Steele & Darko, Indpls., 1967—2002, Bose McKinney & Evans, LLP, Indpls., 2003—. Contbr. articles to profl. jours. Sec. English Speaking Union, Indpls., 1967—; trustee Hanover Coll.; elder and trustee Second Presbyn. Ch., Indpls. Fellow Indpls. Bar Found.; mem. Ind. Bar Assn., Purdue U. Alumni Assn., Indpls. Purdue Assn. (pres. 1968-69), Contemporary Club (pres. 1986-87), Columbia Club (bd. dirs. 1993-96), Columbia Club Found. (pres. 1995-97), Gyro Club (bd. dirs. 1982-85). Home: 535 Pine Dr Indianapolis IN 46260-1452 Office: 2700 First Ind Plz 135 N Pennsylvania St Indianapolis IN 46204 Office Phone: 317-684-5351. E-mail: rlowe@boselaw.com.

LOWE, MARVIN, artist, educator; b. Bklyn., May 19, 1922; m. Juel Watkins, Apr. 1, 1949; 1 dau., Melissa. Student, Julliard Sch. Music, 1952-54; BA, Bklyn. Coll., 1956; MFA, U. Iowa, 1961. Prof. fine arts Ind. U., Bloomington, 1968-92, prof. emeritus, 1992—. Vis. artist-lectr., 1970-91. Exhibited in 64 one-person shows; over 200 group and invitational exhbns.; participated in U.S. info. exhbns. in Latin Am., Japan, USSR, and most European countries; represented in 84 permanent collections including Phila. Mus. Art, Bklyn. Mus., Smithsonian Instn., Brit. Mus., Japan Print Assn., N.Y.C. Pub. Libr., Calif. Palace Legion of Honor, San Francidso, Boston Pub. Libr., Columbia U., Libr. of Congress, Indpls. Mus. Art, Ringling Mus., Honolulu Acad. Art, Ft. Wayne Mus. Art, Purdue U. Mus. Fine Art, Springfield, Mass, Retrospective exhbn. Ind. U. Art Mus., 1998 Served with USNR, 1942-45. Fellow Nat. Endowment for Arts, 1975; fellow Ford Found., 1979, Ind. Arts Commn., 1987; recipient numerous Purchase awards, 1960—; grantee: Ind. Arts. Commn., 1997, Florsheim, 1997. Office: Ind U Sch Fine Arts Bloomington IN 47405 *As a visual artist, I have tried to refrain from making public statements about my work which ultimately must speak for itself.*

LOWE, MARY FRANCES, federal official; b. Ft. Meade, Md., Apr. 15, 1952; d. Benno Powers and Peggy Catherine (Moore) L. BA, Coll. William and Mary, 1972; MA, Fletcher Sch. Law and Diplomacy, 1974, MA Law and Diplomacy, in 1975; diplome, Grad. Inst. Internat. Studies U. Geneva, Switzerland, 1975; M.P.H. in epidemiology, Johns Hopkins Sch. Hygiene and Pub. Health, 1986. External collaborator ILO, Geneva, 1974; legis. asst. to U.S. Senator Richard S. Schweiker Washington, 1975-76; profl. staff mem. health and sci. rsch. subcom. U.S. Senate Com. Labor and Human Resources, Washington, 1976-81; exec. sec. U.S. Dept. HHS, Washington, 1981-85; sr. asst. to commr. program policy FDA, 1985-89; sr. asst. pesticide programs EPA, 1989-96; asst. Office Environ. Policy U.S. Dept. State, Washington, 1997-99; program advisor pesticide program govt. and internat. svcs. EPA, Washington, 1999—. Rep. U.S. delegations World Health Assemblies, Geneva, NAFTA and WTO Coms., 1995—98; alt. trustee Woodrow Wilson Internat. Ctr. Scholars. Mem. Soc. for Epidemiologic Rsch., Am. Assn. World Health, Exec. Women in Govt., Soc. for Chem. Hazard Comm., Soc. Risk Analysis, Washington World Affairs Coun., Delta Omega. Home: 7920 Spotswood Dr Alexandria VA 22308-1125 Office: US EPA 1200 Pennsylvania Ave NW Washington DC 20460-0001 Office Phone: 703-305-5689. Business E-Mail: lowe.maryfrances@epa.gov.

LOWE, MARY KATHERINE, technology company executive, writer; b. Dayton, Ohio; d. Carl and Lucille A. Gross; m. Paul R. Lowe; children: David C., Benjamin P. Degree in psychology, U. of Dayton, 1997. Pres., CEO Nuovo Techs. Inc., Indpls., 1999—. Author: (novels) Paige's Reunion, 2001. Mem.: Psi Chi (assoc.). Avocations: writing, reading, travel, art, music. Home: 10455 Courageous Dr Indianapolis IN 46236 Office: 10455 Courageous Dr Indianapolis IN 46236 Personal E-mail: marylowe@comcast.net.

LOWE, PATRICIA A., psychologist, educator; b. Landstuhl, Germany, July 31, 1957; (parents Am. citizens); d. Gerald H. and Hazel C. Lowe. BS magna cum laude, Boise State U., 1980; PhD, Tex. A&M U., 2000. Lic. psychologist Idaho, cert. sch. psychologist Idaho, Kans. Grad. rsch./tchg. asst. Tex. A&M U., College Station, 1995—99; psychology intern Warm Springs Counseling Ctr. and Tng. Inst., Boise, Idaho, 1999—2000, post-doctoral resident, 2000—01; prof. U. Kans., Lawrence, 2001—. Cons. for tech. initiative grant The Ind. Sch. Dist. of Boise City, 1999—2000; cons./tech. advisor to Nat. Ctr. on Learning Disabilities U. Kans., Lawrence, 2002—, clin. supr. Assoc. editor: book Encyclopedia of School Psychology; co-author: (test manual) Adult Manifest Anxiety Scale, (test) Adult Manifest Anxiety Scale-Elderly Version, Adult Manifest Anxiety Scale-Adult Version, Adult Manifest Anxiety Scale-College Version, (book) Clinical Applications of Continuous Performance Tests: Measuring Attention and Impulsive Responding in Children and Adults, Encyclopedia of School Psychology, (test) Test Anxiety Inventory for Children and Adolescents; contbr. chapters to books, articles to profl. jours.; mem. editl. bd. profl. jours. Faculty rep. U. Kans. Cir. K Svc. Orgn., Lawrence, 2001—03; univ. trainer Kans. Assn. Sch. Psychologists, 2001—02. Recipient Alumni award, Boise State U., 1980, cert. of achievement, Kans. Assn. Sch. Psychologists; Lechner Grad. Merit fellow, Tex. A&M U., 1995—96, Rsch. grantee, U. Kans., 2002, 2003. Mem.: APA, NASP, Psi Chi, Kappa Delta Phi, Phi Kappa Phi. Achievements include test development. Avocations: skiing, tennis, racquetball, swimming, running. E-mail: tlowe@ku.edu.

LOWE, PETER STEPHEN, non-profit company executive; b. Lahore, Pakistan, Oct. 23, 1958; s. Eric and Margaret Winnifred (Bradshaw) L.; m. Tamara Angela Forte, May 9, 1987. BA, Carleton U., Ottawa, Ont., Can., 1986. Pres. Lifemasters Tng. Co., Vancouver, B.C., Can., 1981-87, Global Achievers, New Orleans, 1987-90; pres., chief exec. officer Peter Lowe Internat., Inc., Tampa, Fla., 1990—; CEO LifeWin, Inc., Tampa, 2002—. Mem. Nat. Spkrs. Assn. Office: 4710 Eisenhower Blvd Ste C4 Tampa FL 33634

LOWE, RANDALL B., lawyer; b. Englewood, N.J., Nov. 20, 1948; BA, U. R.I., 1970; JD, Washington U., 1973. Bar: Ill. 1973, Conn. 1975, D.C. 1976, U.S. Ct. Appeals (2d and D.C. cirs.) 1976, N.J. 1977, U.S. Dist. Ct. N.J. 1977, U.S. Ct. Appeals (3d cir.) 1977, U.S. Ct. Appeals (9th cir.) 1979, N.Y. 1980, U.S. Dist. Ct. (ea. and so. dists.) N.Y. 1980. Atty. Callis & Filcoff, Granite City, Ill., 1973-75, AT&T, Washington and N.Y.C., 1975-78, ITT Corp, 1978-83, Surrey & Morse, Washington, 1983-86; ptnr. Jones, Day, Reavis & Pogue, Washington, 1986-94, Piper & Marbury, Washington, 1994-99, of counsel, 1999-2000; exec. v.p./chief legal officer Prism Comms. Svcs., 1999-2001; ptnr. Davis Wright Tremaine, Washington, 2001—. Office: 1500 K St NW Ste 450 Washington DC 20005-1272 Office Phone: 202-508-6621. Business E-Mail: randylowe@dwt.com.

LOWE, ROB, actor; b. Charlottesville, Va., Mar. 17, 1964; m. Sheryl Berkoff, July 22, 1991; 2 children. Appeared in films including The Outsiders, 1983, Class, 1983, The Hotel New Hampshire, 1984, Oxford Blues, 1984, St. Elmo's Fire, 1985, Youngblood, About Last Night..., 1986, Square Dance, 1987, Illegally Yours, Masquerade, 1988, Bad Influence, 1991, The Dark Backward, 1991, Wayne's World, 1992, Frank and Jesse (also prodr.), 1994, Billy the Third, 1995, First Degree, 1995, Eye of the Storm, 1995, Tommy Boy, 1995, Mullholland Falls, 1996, Crazy Six, 1997, Austin Powers: International Man of Mystery, 1997, Living in Peril, 1997, Contact, 1997, Hostile Intent, 1997, One Hell of a Guy, 1998, Crazy Six, 1998, Under Pressure, 1999, Statistics, 1999, Dead Silent, 1999, Austin Powers: The Spy Who Shagged Me, 1999, Proximity, 2000, Proximity, 2001, Austin Powers in Goldmember, 2002, View from the Top, 2003; appearances include (TV series) A New Kind of Family, The West Wing, 1999-2003, The Lyon's Den, 2003-04, Dr. Vegas, 2004 (also prodr.); (mini-series) Atomic Train, 1998, Beach Girls, 2005, (TV films) Thursday's Child, A Matter of Time, Schoolboy Father, Stephen King's The Stand, On Dangerous Ground, 1995, Midnight Man, 1995, Outrage, 1998; (stage) A Few Good Men, London, 2005; writer, dir. (TV films) Desert's Edge, 1997, Jane Doe, 2001, Framed, 2002, Salem's Lot, 2004; TV guest appearances include The Larry Sanders Show, 1992, The Naked Truth, 1995. Office: Brillstein Grey 9150 Wilshire Blvd Ste 350 Beverly Hills CA 90212-3453

LOWE, ROBERT CHARLES, lawyer; b. New Orleans, July 3, 1949; s. Carl Randall and Antonia (Morgan) L.; m. Theresa Louise Acree, Feb. 4, 1978; 1 child, Nicholas Strafford. BA, U. New Orleans, 1971; JD, La. State U., 1975. Bar: La. 1975, U.S. Dist. Ct. (ea. dist.) La. 1975, U.S. Ct. Appeals (5th cir.) 1980, U.S. Dist. Ct. (we. dist.) La. 1978, U.S. Supreme Ct. 1982. Assoc. Sessions, Fishman, Rosenson, Boisfontaine, and Nathan, New Orleans, 1975-80, ptnr., 1980-87, Lowe, Stein, Hoffman, Allweiss and Hauver, New Orleans, 1987—. Author: Louisiana Divorce, West Pub. Co., 1984; mem. La. Law Rev., 1974-75; contbr. articles to profl. jours. Named one of Best Lawyers in Am. ann., 1983—. Mem. ABA, La. State Bar Assn. (chmn. family law sect. 1984-85), La. Assn. Def. Counsel, New Orleans Bar Assn. (chmn. family law sect. 1991-92), La. State Law Inst., La. Trial Lawyers Assn., Order of Coif, Phi Kappa Phi. Republican. Home: 9625 Garden Oak Ln New Orleans LA 70123-2005 Office: 701 Poydras St Ste 3600 New Orleans LA 70139-7735 Office Phone: 504-581-2450.

LOWE, ROBERT STANLEY, lawyer; b. Herman, Nebr., Apr. 23, 1923; s. Stanley Robert and Ann Marguerite (Feese) L.; m. Anne Kirtland Selden, Dec. 19, 1959; children: Robert James, Margaret Anne. AB, U. Nebr., 1947, JD, 1949. Bar: Wyo. 1949. Ptnr. McAvoy & Lowe, Newcastle, 1949—51, Hickey & Lowe, Rawlins, 1951—55; county and pros. atty. Rawlins, 1955—59; pvt. practice, 1959—67; assoc. dir. Am. Judicature Soc., Chgo., 1967—74; gen. counsel True Oil Co. and affiliates, 1974—98, of counsel, 1998—99. Bd. dirs. Hilltop Nat. Bank, Casper, sec., 1981—; legal adv. divsn. Nat. Ski Patrol Sys., 1975-88; city atty. City of Rawlins, 1963-65; atty., asst. sec. Casper Mountain Ski Patrol, 1988—. Chmn. mil. affairs com. Casper C. of C., 1995-2000; mem. Wyo. Ho. of Reps., 1952-54; bd. dirs. Vols. in Probation, 1969-82; leader lawyer del. to China, People to People, 1986; mem. Wyo. Vets. Affairs Commn., 1994-2003, chmn., 1996-2003; mem. legis. com. United Vets. Coun. Wyo., 1993—; trustee Troopers Found., Inc., 1994—, pres., 1994-99; pres. Casper WWII Commemorative Assn., 1995-96; dir. Vets.' History Project, 2003— Recipient Dedicated Cmty. Worker award Rawlins Jr. C. of C., 1967, Yellow merit star award Nat. Ski Patrol System, 1982, 85, 87, 88, Small Bus. Administrate Vet. Adv. award, 1998, Disting. Svc. award Disabled Am. Vets. Dept., 1994, Commendation award Joint Resolution Wyo. Legis., 2003, Medal of Excellence award N.G. Assn., 2003, R. Stanley Lowe Adminstrv. award, 2004; proclaimed R. Stanley Lowe Day, City of Casper, Oct. 11, 2003 Fellow Am. Bar Found. (life); mem. VFW (life mem.; post adv. 1991-96, nat. aide-de-camp 1993-94, 98-99, judge adv. dist. 3 Dept. Wyo., 1994-2001, mil. order of cootie grand judge adv. 1994-2001), ABA (sec. jud. adminstrn. divsn. lawyers conf., exec. com. 1975-76, chmn. 1977-78, chmn. judicial qualification and selection com. 1986-93, coun. jud. adminstrn. divsn. 1977-78, mem. com. to implement jud. adminstrn. stds. 1978-83, Ho. of Dels. state bar del. 1978-80, 86-87, state del. 1987-93, Assembly del. 1980-83, mem. standing com. on the fed. judiciary 1997-99, ad hoc com. state justice initiatives 1997-99), Am. Judicature Soc. (dir. 1961-67, 85-89, bd. editors 1975-77, Herbert Harley award 1974), Wyo. State Bar (chmn. com. on cts. 1961-67, 77-87), Nebr. State Bar Assn., Ill. State Bar Assn., D.C. Bar, Selden Soc., Navy League (Wyo. coun. pres. 1997-2000, state pres. 2000-03, pres. Rocky Mountain North Area, 2003-04, nat. dir. 2003—, nat. merchant marine and legis. coms., 2005—), Rocky Mountain Oil and Gas Assn. (legal com. 1976-99, chmn. 1979-82, 90-91), Rocky Mountain Mineral Law Found. (trustee 1980-94), Am. Law Inst. (life), Order of Coif, Delta Theta Phi (dist. chancellor 1982-83, chief justice 1983-93, assoc. justice 1993—; Percy J. Power Meml. award 1983, Gold Medallion award 1990), Am. Legion (chmn. Americanism com. 1993-2003, post 2d vice comdr. 2003-04, post comdr. 2004—, nat. merchant marine and legis. coms.), Casper Rotary Club (pres. 1985-86), Casper Rotary Found. (dir. 1990—, sec. 1990-2000), Internat. Skiing Fellowship of Rotarians (sec., bd. dirs. 1994-98, bd. dirs. 1998-2001, Appreciation plaque 2004) Mem. Ch. Of Christ. Home and Office: 97 Primrose Casper WY 82604-4018 Business E-Mail: rolowe@trib.com.

LOWELL, ABBE DAVID, lawyer; b. N.Y.C., Apr. 28, 1952; s. Armand A. and Sylvia (Newman) L.; m. Rhonda F. Kleiner; children: Alizah, Elana. BA magna cum laude, Columbia U., 1974, JD, 1977. Bar: N.Y. 1978, D.C. 1981, Md. 1984, Md. Fed. 1981, Conn. Fed. 2001, U.S. Supreme Ct. 1981, U.S. Ct. Appeals D.C. Cir. 1981, U.S. Ct. Appeals 4th cir. 1981, U.S. Ct. Appeals 2nd cir. 1986, U.S. Dist. Ct. Md. 1981, U.S. Dist. Ct. D.C. 1981, U.S. Dist. Ct. So. N.Y. 2001. Trial atty. U.S. Dept. Justice, Washington, 1977-78, spl. asst. to atty. gen., 1979—81, spl. asst. U.S. atty., 1978-79; assoc. Venable, Baetjes, Houdl & Ciulletti, Washington, 1982-83; founding and mng. ptnr. Brand & Lowell, Washington, 1983—99; D.C. mng. ptnr., head white collar and spl. investigations practice group Manatt Phelps & Phillips, LLP, Washington, 1999—2003; ptnr. Chadbourne & Parke, Washington, 2003—. Mem. nat. adv. bd. Ctr. Nat. Policy, Washington; adj. prof. law Georgetown U., Washington, 1984—; counselor to UN High Commr. for Human Rights 1994-95, spl. counselor 1995-96; chief minority counsel of Pres. Clinton to U.S. Ho. Rep. 1998-99. Editor, Columbia Law Review; contbr. articles to profl. jours. Mem. Dem. Cen. Com. Montgomery County, Kensington, Md., 1982—; bd. dirs. Jewish Community Ctr., Rockville, Md., 1982— (gen. counsel 1986—); bd. trustee, The Shakespeare Theatre at the Landsburgh. Named one of Top 10 Most Successful Trial Lawyers, Nat. Law Jour., 2002, 75 Best Lawyers in Washington, Washingtonian Mag., 2002, Top Lawyers in Washington, 1989, 1992, 1997, 2002, 2004; Harlan Fiske Stone Scholar. Mem. ABA (former chair, com. on rules, white collar crime sect.), Nat. Assn. of Criminal Def. Lawyers, Phi Beta Kappa. Avocations: writing, tennis, jogging. Office: Chadbourne & Park 1200 New Hampshire Ave NW Washington DC 20036 Business E-Mail: adlowell@chadbourne.com.*

LOWELL, FREDERICK K., lawyer; b. NYC, Aug. 9, 1948; BA, Columbia U., 1971; JD, U. Va., 1975. Bar: Va. 1975, Calif. 1975. Assoc. then ptnr. Pillsbury, Madison & Sutro, San Francisco, 1975—2001; (Pillsbury Madison & Sutro merged with Winthrop, Stimson, Putnam and Roberts, 2001); ptnr., govt. relations & polit. law Pillsbury Winthrop LLP, San Francisco, 2001—05; (Pillsbury Winthrop LLP merged with Shaw Pittman LLP, 2005); ptnr., govt. relations & polit. law, chair polit. law group Pillsbury Winthrop Shaw Pittman LLP, San Francisco, 2005—. Author: The Regulation of Politics in Calif. Mem. Calif. Rep. State Central Com.; chair Lincoln Club of No. Calif.; Calif. delegate Nat. Rep. Convention, 1992, 1996, 2000, 2004; volunteer counsel Bush 2000 Campaign, Bush-Cheney 2004 Campaign. Mem.: ABA, San Francisco Bar Assn., Va. State Bar Assn., Calif. State Bar Assn., Calif. Polit. Atty. Assn. (former pres.). Office: Pillsbury Winthrop Shaw Pittman LLP 50 Fremont St San Francisco CA 94105 Office Phone: 415-983-1585. Office Fax: 415-983-1200. Business E-Mail: frederick.lowell@pillsburylaw.com.

LOWELL, HOWARD PARSONS, archivist, federal agency administrator; b. Rockland, Maine, May 10, 1945; s. Chauncey Vernon Lowell and Delia Coffin (Parsons) Morey; m. Marica Barrell, Feb. 15, 1969 (div. 1980); m. Charlesa Ann Gatson, July 27, 1985 (dec. Oct. 2003); 1 stepchild, Garrett Timmons. BA, U. Maine, Orono, 1967; MS, Simmons Coll., 1974. Adminstrn. svcs. officer Maine State Archives, Augusta, 1968-72; ednl. specialist Mass. Bur. Libr. Ext., Boston, 1974-75; dir. Revere (Mass.) Pub. Libr., 1975-76; freelance cons. Salem, Oreg., 1976-81, Denver, 1976-81; adminstr. resources br. Okla. Dept. Librs., Oklahoma City, 1981-89; archivist, records adminstr. State of Del., 1990-2000; dep. asst. archivist records svcs. Washington Nat. Archives and Records Adminstrn., College Park, Md., 2000—. Acting dir. N.E. Document Conservation Ctr., Andover, Mass., 1978. Commr. Nat. Hist. Publs. and Records Commn., 1997—2000. Mem.: Nat. Assn. Govt. Archives and Records Adminstrs. (bd. dirs. 1985—87, 1995—96, pres. 1992—94), Acad. Cert. Archivists, Phi Beta Kappa, Beta Phi Mu, Phi Alpha Theta, Phi Kappa Phi. Democrat. Unitarian. Office: Nat Archives for Records Adminstrn 8601 Adelphi Rd College Park MD 20740-6001 Business E-Mail: howard.lowell@nara.gov.

LOWELL, J(AMES) DAVID, geological consultant, cattle rancher; b. Nogales, Ariz., Feb. 28, 1928; s. Arthur Currier and Lavina (Cumming) L.; m. Edith Walmisly Sykes, Mar. 30, 1948; children: Susan, William, Douglas. BS in Mining Engring., U. Ariz., 1949, E.Geol., 1959; MS in Geology, Stanford U., 1957; D. Hon. Causa, U. N at. Mayor de San Marcos, Peru, 1998; Dsc (hon.), U. Ariz, 2000. Registered profl. engr., Ariz. Mining engr. to mine foreman Asarco, Chihuahua City, Mex., 1949-51; field geologist to dist. geologist AEC, Grand Junction, Colo., 1951-54; chief geologist to v.p. S.W. ventures Ventures Ltd. and subs., Denver, Tucson, 1955-59; dist. geologist Utah Internat., San Francisco, Tucson, 1959-61; geol. cons. Lowell Mineral Exploration, Tucson, 1961—, pres. Chile, 1985—, Acuarios Mineral, Peru, 1991-96; chmn. Areguipa Resources Ltd., Can., 1993-96; pres. Exploraciones Mineras Lowell SA de CV, Mex., 1998—, Lowell Mineral Exploration LLC, Ariz., 1998—; chmn. Bear Creek Mining Co., 2002—, Peru Copper Inc., 2004—. Mem. bd. dirs. Soc. Econ. Geologists Found., 1986-91; Thayer Lindsley disting. lectr. Soc. Econ. Geologists, 1978; disting. exch. lectr. Soc. Econ. Geologists, 2000-02; cons. to 120 other oil and mining cos., U.S. and fgn. countries, 1961—, to nat. govt. orgn., U.S.; cons. retainer Bechtel Corp., San Francisco, 1976-1980; dir. Nat. Mining Hall of Fame, 2000-. Assoc. editor Econ. Geology, New Haven, 1970-75. Recipient Disting. Citizen award U. Ariz., 1974, Soc. Econ. Geol. Thayer Lindsley Dist. Lectr., 1977, Silver Medal Soc. Econ. Geologists, 1983, Medal of Merit Am. Mineral Hall of Fame, 1994; named Can. Mining Man of Yr., No. Miner, 1999; inductee Am. Mining Hall of Fame, 2002. Mem. NAE, Ariz. Geol. Soc. (pres. 1965-66), Soc. Econ. Geologists, Am. Inst. Mining Engrs. (pres. Yavapai sect. 1957, Daniel Jackling award 1970, Robert Dreyer award 2000, Earll McConnell award 2000), Can. Inst. Mining and Metall. Engrs. (disting. lectr. 1972), Internat. Assn. on Genesis of Ore Deposits, Mining and Metallurgy Soc. Am. (gold medal award 2001, Soc. Econ. Geologists Penrose medal 2004), Mining Club S.W. (dir. 1969-70), Prescott Country Club. Republican. Episcopalian. Home: 789 Avenida Beatriz Rio Rico AZ 85648-2200 Office: Lowell Mineral Exploration 789 Avenida Beatriz Rio Rico AZ 85648-2200 Office Phone: 520-281-8271. Business E-Mail: davidlowell@perucopper.com.

LOWELL, LAURETTA JANE, craftsman, poet; b. Gunnison, Colo., 1946; d. Howard and Linnia Lowell; m. Robert Campbell, 1994. Assoc. Gen. Studies, Pikes Peak C.C., 1987; student, Mesa State Coll., 1991, 99. Nurses aide St. Francis Hosp., Colorado Springs, Colo., 1978-85; owner Light in Leather/Green Knight PUb., Delta, Colo., 1996—2001; home care provider Adult Home Care, Delta, Colo., 1991—. Author, pub.: Selected Poems of A Religious Nature, 1996, Sample a Poetry Treat, 1997; included in Best Poems of 1998, Rhyme and Reason, 2001, Best Poems and Poets of 2003 (editors awards); lyricist Summer Song, 1998; editor, pub. Columbian Notes, 1998— Organizer reunion 1264th Army Engineer Battalion, Delta, 1991-93; leader 4-H, Colorado Springs and Delta, 1984-90; advocate for mental health issues Colo. Health Networks, Colorado Springs, 1996-98; advocate Delto Columbine Plan, 1992—, established The Delta Columbine Plan, 2004—. Phi Theta Kappa scholar, 1985, Colo. State Coll. scholarship, 1965. Fellow United Meth. Women; mem. Internat. Soc. Poets (life mem., Poetry Hall of Fame 1996). Avocations: camping, fishing, sewing, cooking, writing. Home: 114 W 6th St Delta CO 81416-1806 E-mail: LaurellaLowell@yahoo.com.

LOWELL, VIRGINIA LEE, librarian; b. San Jose, Calif., Nov. 21, 1940; d. Earnest S. and Dorothy (Givens) Greene; children: Michael Edward, Christopher Scott. Student, Reed Coll, 1958-61; BA, U. Calif., Berkeley, 1963; MSLS, Western Res. U., 1964. Cataloger Wittenberg U., Springfield, Ohio, 1965-66, John Carroll U., Cleve., 1966-68, Cuyahoga Community Coll., Cleve., 1968-70, cons., instr., 1970; head catalog dept. Cuyahoga County Pub. Library, Cleve., 1976-78; dir. tech. svcs. Cuyahoga County Pub. Libr., Cleve., 1979-89; dir. Jackson (Mich.) Dist. Libr., 1989—98; state libr. State of Hawaii, 1998—. Chmn. bd. trustees Ohionet, Columbus, 1987-89. Mem. ALA, Ohio Libr. Assn. (coord. automation and tech. div. 1988—), No. Ohio Tech. Svc. Librs. (chmn. 1988-89), Ohio Women Librs. (treas. 1987-89), Am. Mgmt. Assn., Mich. Libr. Assn. Democrat. Roman Catholic. Avocation: choral singing. Office: 465 S King St Rm B-1 Honolulu HI 96813

LOWEN, ROBERT MARSHALL, plastic surgeon; b. Detroit; MD, U. Mich. Med. Sch., 1971. Diplomate Am. Bd. Plastic Surgery. Internship Pacific Presbyn., San Francisco, 1971-72; resident general surgery Stanford U. Med. Ctr., 1983-85; resident plastic surgery U. Okla. HSC, Okla. City, 1985-86; fellow hand surgery U. Colo. HSC, Denver, 1986-87, resident plastic surgery, 1987-88; pvt. practice Mountain View, Calif., 1988—; mem. staff El Camino Hosp., Mountain View, Calif., 1988—, Sequoia Hosp., Redwood City, Calif., 1988—. Mem. Am. Soc. Plastic Surgeons, Am. Soc. Lasers in Medicine and Surgery, Calif. Med. Soc., Santa Clara County Med. Assn., Am. Soc. for Aesthetic Plastic Surgery. Home and Office: 305 South Dr Ste 1 Mountain View CA 94040-4207 Office Phone: 650-965-7888.

LOWENBERG, GEORGINA GRACE, retired elementary school educator; b. El Paso, Tex., Feb. 15, 1944; d. Eduardo Antonio and Grace Elizabeth (Fletcher) Orellana; m. Edward Daniel Lowenberg, June 14, 1968, (div. 1985); 1 child, Jennifer Anne. BSEd, U. Tex., El Paso, 1965, postgrad., 1965-66, U. St. Thomas, 1983. Permanent profl. teaching cert., Tex. Tchr. 5th grade El Paso Pub. Sch. Dist., 1965-70; tchr. 3d grade gifted, talented Ysleta Ind. Sch. Dist., El Paso, 1980—2002. Mem. com. Tex. State Textbook Selection Com., Austin, 1984-85, Tex. State TEAMS Math Adv. Com., Austin, 1986-87; sci. presentor Silver Burdett, Albuquerque, 1985-86; critic reader Scott-Foresman, Dallas, 1986; pres., v.p. Scotsdale Elem. Sch. PTA, El Paso, 1976-83; v.p. Eastwood Middle Sch. PTA, El Paso, 1984-85; mem. Eastwood Heights Elem. Sch. PTA, 1980-2002; sec. Eastwood High Sch. Band Boosters, El Paso, 1985-89, Speech Boosters, 1986-88; life mem. Tex. State PTA, 1981—. Troop leader Brownie and Jr. Girl Scouts Am., El Paso, 1977-82; dir. Eaglette Dance. Team, 1994—; libr. asst. Eastwood Heights Libr., 2004— Named Tchr. of Yr., Eastwood Heights Elem., 1983, Top Ten Dist. Tchr. of Yr., 1983. Mem. Assn. Tex. Profl. Educators (regional treas. 1987-88), Ysleta and Tex. Ret. Tchrs. Assn. (chmn. Hall of Fame 2002—). Roman Catholic.

LOWENBERG, MARC GREGORY, dentist; b. NYC, Mar. 2, 1946; m. Joan Levy. BA in psychology, Am. U., Washington, DC, 1968; DDS, NYU, 1972. Gen. practice intern Met. Hosp., NYC, 1972—73; pvt. practice cosmetic dentistry Lowenberg and Lituchy, NYC, 1973—. Cons. ABC's Extreme Makeover; adv. bd. cancerandcareers.org; guest Oprah Winfrey Show, Good Morning Am., The View. Mem.: ADA, Dental Soc. State NY, Am. Acad. Implant Dentistry, Internat. Congress Oral Implantologists, Am. Acad. Cosmetic Dentistry, Acad. Gen. Dentistry. Office: Lowenberg and Lituchy 230 Central Park S New York NY 10019 Office Phone: 212-586-2890. Office Fax: 212-586-2889.

LOWENBERG, MICHAEL, lawyer; b. Bklyn., Mar. 6, 1943; s. Leo and Edna (Hanft) L.; m. Julie Goldberg, June 13, 1965; children: Daniel, Frances, Anthony. BA, Bklyn. Coll., 1963; LLB, Harvard U., 1966. Bar: Tex. 1966, U.S. Dist. Ct. (no. dist.) Tex. 1966, U.S. Ct. Appeals (5th cir.) 1967. Assoc. Akin, Gump, Strauss, Hauer & Feld, L.L.P., Dallas, 1966-71; ptnr. Akin, Gump, Strauss, Hauer & Feld, Dallas, 1972—2002; of counsel Gardere Wynne Sewell LLP, Dallas, 2003—. Pres. Dallas Legal Services Found., 1972; chmn. Dallas chpt. Am. Jewish Com., 1973-74. Mem. ABA, Tex. Bar Assn., Bar Assn. of 5th Cir. (past pres., bd. dirs.), Dallas Bar Assn., Dallas Bar Found., Tex. Bar Found., Coll. of State Bar Tex., Tex. Appleseed (bd.

dirs.). Democrat. Home: 5321 Drane Dr Dallas TX 75209-5501 Office: Gardere Wynne Sewell LLP 3000 Thanksgiving Twr 1601 Elm St Dallas TX 75201-4761 E-mail: mlowenberg@gardere.com.

LOWENFELD, ANDREAS FRANK, law educator; b. Berlin, May 30, 1930; s. Henry and Yela (Herschkowitsch) L.; m. Elena Machado, Aug. 11, 1962; children: Julian, Marianna. AB magna cum laude, Harvard U., 1951, LLB magna cum laude, 1955. Bar: NY 1955, US Supreme Ct. 1961. Assoc. Hyde and de Vries, NYC, 1957-61; spl. asst. legal adv. US State Dept., 1961-63, asst. legal adviser econ. affairs, 1963-65, dep. legal adviser, 1965-66; fellow John F. Kennedy Inst. Politics Harvard U., Cambridge, Mass., 1966-67; prof. law Sch. Law NYU, NYC, 1967—, Charles L. Denison prof. law, 1981-94, Herbert and Rose Rubin prof. internat. law, 1994—. Arbitrator internat. comml. panels Internat. C. of C., Am. Arbitration Assn., Internat. Ctr. Settlement Investment Disputes. Author (with Abram Chayes and Thomas Ehrlich): Internat. Legal Process, 1968—69; author: Aviation Law, Cases and Materials, 1972, 2d edit., 1981, Internat. Economic Law, vol.I, 1975, 3d edit., 1997, vol. II, 1976, 2d edit., 1982, vol. III, 1977, vol. IV, 1977, 2d edit., 1984, vol. VI, 1979;: 2d edit., 1983, Conflict of Laws, Fed., State and Internat. Perspectives, 1986, 2d rev. edit., 2002, Internat. Litig. and Arbitration, 1993, 2d edit., 2002, Internat. Litig.: The Quest for Reasonableness, 1996, The Role of Govt. in Internat. Trade: Essays Over Three Decades, 2000, Internat. Econ. Law, 2002, Lowenfeld on International Arbitration, 2005; editor, co-author Expropriation in the Americas: A Comparative Law Study, 1971; assoc. reporter: Am. Law Inst. Restatement on Foreign Relations Law; co-reporter Am. Law Inst. Project on Internat. Jurisdiction and Judgments; contbr. articles to profl. jours. Mem.: ABA, Internat. Acad. Comparative Law, Inst. de Droit Internat., Coun. Fgn. Rels., Am. Law Inst., Am. Arbitration Assn. (arbitrator), Am. Soc. Internat. Law, Assn. Bar City NY, Gray's Inn (assoc.). Home: 5776 Palisade Ave Bronx NY 10471-1212 Office: NYU Sch Law Sch Law 40 Washington Sq S New York NY 10012-1005 Office Phone: 212-998-6208. E-mail: andreas.lowenfeld@NYU.edu.

LOWENFELS, FRED M., lawyer; b. Richmond, Va., Mar. 22, 1944; s. Fred C. and Joan (Weber) L.; m. Joan Roberta Brafman, June 10, 1974; children: Erica Anne, Helene Beth. AB, Harvard U., 1965, JD, 1968; postgrad., Univ. Libre de Bruxelles, 1968-69. Bar: N.Y. 1969. Assoc. Wolf, Haldenstein, Adler, Freeman & Herz, N.Y.C., 1970-74; sr. v.p., gen. counsel Transammonia Inc., N.Y.C., 1974—. Trustee Jewish Home & Hosp. Lifecare Sys., N.Y.C., 1974—, chmn. bd. trustees, 2001—. Mem. Assn. Bar. City of N.Y., Am. Corp. Counsel Assn., Harvard Club N.Y.C. Office: Transammonia Inc 320 Park Ave New York NY 10022-6815

LOWENFELS, LEWIS DAVID, lawyer; b. N.Y.C., June 9, 1935; s. Seymour and Jane (Phillips) L.; m. Fern Gelford, Aug. 15, 1965; children: Joshua, Jacqueline. BA magna cum laude, Harvard U., 1957, LLB, 1961. Bar: N.Y. 1961, (lic. corp. and securities atty.). Ptnr. Tolins & Lowenfels, N.Y.C., 1967—. Adj. prof. Seton Hall U. Law Sch; lectr. Practicing Law Inst., Southwestern Legal Found., U. Minn. Fed. Bar Assn., 1972; pub. gov. Am. Stock Exch., 1993-96. Co-author: Bromberg and Lowenfels on Securities Fraud and Commodities Fraud, 7 vols., 2004; contbr. articles to profl. jours. With USAR, 1957—63. Mem. ABA (fed. regulation of securities com. 1978—, lectr.), N.Y. County Lawyers Assn. (securities and exchanges com. 1974—), Phi Beta Kappa, Harvard Club. Avocations: reading, writing, athletics. Office: Tolins & Lowenfels 747 3d Ave 19th Fl New York NY 10017-1028 Office Phone: 212-421-1965. Business E-Mail: lew@tolinslowenfels.com.

LOWENGRUB, MORTON, academic administrator; BA, NYU; MA, Calif. Inst Tech. Faculty Duke U., N.C. State U., Wesleyan U., Ind. U., dean Coll. Arts and Scis., 1988—99; v.p. for acad. affairs Yeshiva U., N.Y.C., 1999—. Contbr. articles to profl. jours. Office: Yeshiva Univ Office VP Wilf Campus 500 W 185th St New York NY 10033-3201

LOWENHAUPT, CHARLES ABRAHAM, lawyer; b. St. Louis, May 19, 1947; s. Henry Cronbach and Cecile (Koven) L.; m. Rosalyn Lee Sussman, Dec. 28, 1969; children: Elizabeth Anne, Rebecca Jane. BA cum laude, Harvard U., 1969; JD magna cum laude, U. Mich., 1973. Bar: Mo. 1973, U.S. Dist. Ct. (ea. dist.) Mo. 1975, U.S. Ct. Appeals (8th cir.) 1975, U.S. Tax Ct. 1975, U.S. Ct. Claims 1975, U.S. Supreme Ct. 1987. Law clk. to presiding justice U.S. Tax Ct., Washington, 1973-75; ptnr. Lowenhaupt, Chasnoff, Armstrong & Mellitz, St. Louis, 1977-94; mem. adv. faculty Inst. for Pvt. Investors, 1991-93; mem. Lowenhaupt & Chasnoff, LLC, St. Louis, 1994—; emeritus mem. adv. faculty Inst. for Pvt. Investors, St. Louis, 1995—. Spkr. Nat. Assn. Ind. Schs., St. Louis Assn. Legal Assts., Washington U. Bus. Sch., Inst. for Pvt. Investors, numerous others; mem. adv. bd. dirs. Textile Mus., Washington; cmty. outreach adv. coun. St. Louis Coll. Pharmacy, 1998—; lectr. law dept. Fudan U., Shanghai, 1999; spkr. Beijing U. Law Sch. Contbg. author: The Deal, 2003; co-author: Estate Planning, 2001, Wealthy and Wise, 2002. Bd. dirs. Ctrl. West End Assn., Inc., St. Louis, 1976-80, Temple Emanuel, St. Louis, 1982-89, Butterfly Ho., St. Louis, sec., 1995—; bd. dirs. Craft Alliance St. Louis, 1987-90, Helicon Found., San Diego, St. Louis Met. Assn. for Philanthropy, St. Louis Regional Med. Ctr. Found., 1993-98, chmn. bd. dirs., 1995-98; bd. dirs., Grand Ctr., 2002-; bd. dirs. Crown Ctr. St. Louis sect., Nat. Coun. Jewish Women, 1994-96, St. Louis Zoo Found., 1993-99, sec., 1995-98; mem. St. Louis Zool. Subdist. commn., 1989-92; bd. govs. Clements Libr. Assocs., U. Mich., 1997—; mem. St. Louis Cmty. Sch. Assn., 1981-89; pres. Assn. St. Louis U. Librs., Inc., 1982-83; mem. exec. com. U.S.-China C. of C. Midwestern Regional Office; mem. George W. Warren Brown Sch. Social Work nat. coun. Washington U., 2000—; com. chair, Alliance for Bldg. Capacity, Washington U., 2002-; bd. dirs. Found. for Fiduciary Studies, Pitts., 2000—; mem. campaign cabinet Cath. Cmty. Svcs. and Archbishops Commn. on Cmty. Health, 2001. Recipient St. Louis Argus Disting. Citizen award, 2001, Cmty. Svc. award, Young Dems. of St. Louis, 1996. Mem. ABA (tax section, estate and gift section, real property section, probate and trust law, task force legal financial planning, chmn. generation-skipping transfer tax subcom., estate and gift tax com. tax sect. 1995-2004), Mo. Bar Assn. (tax section, probate and trust section), Bar Assn. of Met. St. Louis (tax section, real property and development sect.), Order of the Coif, St. Louis Estate Planning Coun., Mo. Athletic Club, Harvard Club of N.Y.C., Noonday Club, The Racquet Club, Harvard Club of St. Louis (pres. 1991-92, chmn. schs. and scholarshop com. 1989-91). Home: 801 S Skinker Blvd Saint Louis MO 63105-3269 Office: Lowenhaupt & Chasnoff LLC 10 S Broadway Ste 600 Saint Louis MO 63102-1733

LOWENSTEIN, ALAN VICTOR, lawyer; b. Newark, Aug. 30, 1913; s. Isaac and Florence (Cohen) L.; m. Amy Lieberman, Nov. 23, 1938; children: John, Roger, Jane Lowenstein Forsyth. AB, U. Mich., 1933; MA, U. Chgo., 1935; LLB, Harvard U., 1936. Bar: N.J. 1936. Practiced in Newark and Roseland, 1936—; sr. partner Lowenstein, Sandler, PC, 1961—. Assoc. atty. Temporary Nat. Econ. Com., 1938-39; asst. prof. Rutgers U. Law Sch., 1951-57; chmn. N.J. Corp. Law Revision Commn., 1959-72; spl. hearing officer Dept. Justice, 1961-65; chmn. bd. United Steel & Aluminum Corp., 1976-96. Pres. Jewish Community Council Essex County, 1950-53, United Way Essex and West Hudson, 1953-55; chmn. Newark Charter Commn., 1953, Newark Citizens Com. Mcpl. Govt., 1954-58, Newark Community Survey, 1959-60; v.p. Council Jewish Fedns., 1965-68, assoc. treas., 1981; pres. N.J. Symphony Orch., 1971-73, chmn. bd., 1973-76; mem. adv. council Rutgers U. Sch. Social Work, 1955-64; vice chmn. Liberty State Park Devel. Corp., 1984—; bd. overseers Rutgers U. Found., 1994-2000. Recipient Brotherhood award Nat. Conf. Christians and Jews, 1972, Trustees award for Disting. Community Service, N.J. Inst. Tech., 1984, Equal Justice award Legal Services N.J./N.J. State Bar Assn., 1988. Mem. ABA, N.J. Bar Assn., Essex County Bar Assn. (Pro-Bono Achievement award 1994), Am. Judicature Soc., Order of Coif, Phi Beta Kappa (v.p. N.J. 1951-52), Phi Kappa Phi, Tau Kappa Alpha. Home: 1872 Arnold Bay Rd Panton VT 05491-9152 Office: Lowenstein Sandler PC 65 Livingston Ave Ste 9 Roseland NJ 07068-1725 E-mail: alowenstein@lowenstein.com.

LOWENSTEIN, ARLENE JANE, nursing educator, health facility administrator; b. Phila., Oct. 10, 1936; d. Nathan Morris and Rae (Greenburg) Needleman; m. Manfred Lowenstein, June 9, 1957; children: Jay David, Russell Scott. Diploma in nursing, Hosp. of U. Pa., Phila., 1957; BSN, Fairleigh Dickinson U., 1969; MA, NYU, 1974; PhD, U. Pitts., 1985. Staff and tchg. nurse Albert Einstein Med. Ctr., Hosp. U. Pa., 1957-59; instr. Middlesex County Coll., Edison, NJ, 1969-71; staff nurse Vis. Nurse Svc., N.Y.C., 1970-72; supr. obstet. and pediat. Middlesex Gen. Hosp., New Brunswick, NJ, 1972-74; dir. ambulatory & cmty. health Peter Bent Brigham Hosp., 1974-79, dir. nurse practitioner program, 1974-81; dir. surg. nursing Brigham and Women's Hosp., Boston, 1980—81; acting dir. nursing Peter Bent Brigham Hosp., Boston, 1978-80; assoc hosp. dir., dir nursing svc. U. Ky. Med. Ctr., Lexington, 1981-83; asst. prof. U. Pitts., 1983-85; prof. nursing, dept. chair. Med. Coll. Ga., Augusta, 1985-95; prof., dir. grad. program in nursing Mass. Gen. Hosp. Inst. of Health Professions, Boston, 1995—2003, prof. emeritus, 2003—. Contbr. articles to profl. jours. Bd. dirs. Sr. Citizens Coun. of Ctrl. Savannah River Area, Augusta, 1982-95. Mem. ANA, Coun. Grad. Edn. for Nursing Adminstrs. (chair 1990-92), Sigma Xi, Sigma Theta Tau. Avocations: opera, music, art. Home: 312 Lewis Wharf Boston MA 02110-3905 Business E-Mail: alowenstein@mghihp.edu.

LOWENSTEIN, DEREK IRVING, physicist; b. Hampton Court, Eng., Apr. 26, 1943; came to U.S., 1946; s. Siegfried and Ilse (Mildenberg) L.; m. Elaine Hartmann, July 6, 1968; children: Jessica R. Lowenstein-Leif, Peter D. BS, CCNY, 1964; MS, U. Pa., 1965, PhD, 1969. Postdoctoral fellow U. Pa., Phila., 1969-70; research assoc. U. Pitts., 1970-73; asst. physicist Brookhaven Nat. Lab., Upton, N.Y., 1973-75, assoc. physicist, 1975-77, physicist, 1977-83, sr. physicist, 1983—, head Exptl. Planning and Support div., 1977-84, dep. chmn. accelerator dept., 1981-84, chmn. Alternating Gradient Synchrotron dept., 1984-99, chmn. collider accelerator dept., 1999—; prin. investigator NASA Space Radiation Lab., 2003—. Assoc. mem. U.S.-Russia Joint Coordinating Commn. on Fundamental Properties of Matter, 1983—, U.S.-Japan Commn. on High Energy Physics, 1984—; mem. Dept. of Energy High Energy Physics Adv. Panel, 1993-96; prin. investigator NASA Space Radiation Lab., 1993-; mem. Tech. Adv. Group (LANL/LLNL), 2001-03. Contbr. articles on particle and accelerator physics to profl. jours. Fellow Am. Phys. Soc.; mem. AAAS, N.Y. Acad. Scis., Sigma Xi. Office: Brookhaven Nat Lab Collider-Accelerator Dept Upton NY 11973 E-mail: lowenstein@bnl.gov.

LOWENSTEIN, JAMES GORDON, former diplomat, international consultant; b. Long Branch, NJ, Aug. 6, 1927; s. Melvyn Gordon and Katherine Price (Goldsmith) L.; children: Laurinda Vinson (Douglas), Price Gordon. Grad., Loomis Sch., 1945; BA, Yale U., 1949; postgrad., Harvard Law Sch., 1955—56. With Office Spl. Rep. in Europe, Econ. Cooperation Adminstrn., Paris, 1950—51; mem. US Spl. Mission to Yugoslavia, Sarajevo, 1951; fgn. svc. officer Bur. European Affairs Dept. State, 1957—58; fgn. svc. officer Am. Embassy, Colombo, 1959—61, Belgrade, 1961—64; cons. Fgn. Rels. Com., US Senate, Washington, 1965—74; prin. dep. asst. sec. state for European affairs Washington, 1974—77; amb. to Luxembourg, 1977—81; with Bur. European Affairs, Dept. State, 1981—82; ptnr. IRC Group, Washington, 1982—87; sr. cons. APCO Assoc., Washington, 1988—99; sr. advisor Heller and Rosenblatt, Washington, 2000—. Mem. internat. observer group Sri Lanka elections, 1993, 94, sr. elections adv. Osce Mission to Bosnia, 1996, 97; chmn. bd. dirs. The Ukraine Fund; trustee Lafarge (U.S.) Holdings Trust; past sec. bd. Emerging Eastern European Fund; past chmn. Baltic Investments; past dir. AIS Worldwide Fund; co-founder, bd. dirs. French-Am. Found.; past bd. dirs. Refugees Internat.; past mem. adv. coun. Sch. Advanced Internat. Studies and Bologna (Italy) Ctr. Johns Hopkins U. Lt. (j.g.) USNR, 1952-55, staff Naval War Coll., 1954-55. Decorated officier Légion d'Honneur (France); Grand Croix de la Couronne de Chene (Luxembourg). Mem. Coun. Fgn. Rels., Internat. Inst. Strategic Studies, French Inst. Internat. Rels., Met. Club, Century Assn., Knickerbocker Club, Explorers Club, Travellers Club, Racing Club de France. Home: 3139 O St NW Washington DC 20007-3117 also: 52 Rue de Varenne 75007 Paris France Office: Heller & Rosenblatt Ste 205 1101 15th St NW Washington DC 20005-5002 Office Phone: 202-466-4700. Personal E-mail: jamesglowen@aol.com.

LOWENSTEIN, LOUIS, law educator; b. N.Y.C., June 13, 1925; s. Louis and Ralphina (Steinhardt) L.; m. Helen Libby Udell, Feb. 12, 1953; children: Roger Spector, Jane Ruth, Barbara Ann. BS, Columbia, 1947, LL.B., 1953; M.F.S., U. Md., 1951. Bar: N.Y. 1953. Pvt. practice law, N.Y.C., 1954-78; Assoc. Judge Stanley H. Fuld, N.Y. Ct. Appeals, 1953-54; assoc., then partner Hays, Sklar & Herzberg, 1954-68; partner Nickerson, Kramer, Lowenstein, Nessen, Kamin & Soll, 1968-78; Simon H. Rifkind prof. emeritus law and fin. Columbia U. Law Sch., 1980—, project dir. Instl. Investor Project, 1988-94; pres. Supermarkets Gen. Corp., Woodbridge, N.J., 1978-79. Bd. dirs. Liz Claiborne, Inc. 1988-96; mem. pub. oversight bd. Panel on Audit Effectiveness, 1998-2000. Author: What's Wrong with Wall Street, 1988, Sense and Nonsense in Corporate Finance, 1991; contbr., co-editor: Knights, Raiders and Targets, 1988; editor in chief Columbia Law Rev., 1951-53. V.p., mem. exec. com. Fedn. Jewish Philanthropies N.Y.; pres. Jewish Bd. Family and Children's Svcs. N.Y., 1974—78; trustee Beth Israel Med. Ctr., N.Y.C., 1975—81; dir. Goddard-Riverside Cmty. Ctr., 1996—2002; mem. Citizens Budget Commn., 2003—; chmn. bd. dirs. Coalition for the Homeless, 1997—2004. Mem. ABA, Assn. of Bar of City of N.Y., Am. Law Inst, N.Y. State Commn. Public Authority Reform. Home: 5 Oak Ln Larchmont NY 10538-3917 Office: Columbia U Law Sch 435 W 116th St New York NY 10027-7297

LOWENSTEIN, PETER DAVID, lawyer; b. N.Y.C., Dec. 31, 1935; s. Melvyn Gordon and Katherine Price (Goldsmith) L.; m. Constance Cohen; children from previous marriage: Anthony, Kate E., Christopher. BA, Trinity Coll., 1958; LLB, Georgetown U., 1961. Bar: Conn. 1962, N.Y. 1963. With SEC, Washington, 1961-63; assoc. Whitman & Ransom, N.Y.C., 1963-70, ptnr., 1970-83; sec., gen. counsel Value Line, Inc., N.Y.C., 1983-87; v.p., sec., gen. counsel Service Am. Corp., Stamford, Conn., 1988-90; ptnr. O'Connor, Morris & Jones, Greenwich, Conn., 1990-92; pvt. practice, Greenwich, 1992—. Legal counsel Value Line Mutual Funds. Bd. dirs. Grand St. Settlement, N.Y.C., 1970-92, Greenwich Health Assn., Conn., 1978-85; bd. dirs. Greenwich chpt. ARC, 1989-94, vice chmn., 1991-93. Mem.: Yale Club of N.Y., Greenwich Field Club, Nantucket Yacht Club. Home: 496 Valley Rd Cos Cob CT 06807-1627 Office: Two Sound View Dr Ste 100 Greenwich CT 06830-5436 Personal E-mail: PDLOW@aol.com.

LOWENSTEIN, RALPH LYNN, university dean emeritus; b. Danville, Va., Mar. 8, 1930; s. Henry and Rachel (Berman) L.; m. Bronia Grace Levenson, Feb. 6, 1955; children: Joan, Henry. BA, Columbia U., 1951, MS in Journalism, 1952; PhD in Journalism, U. Mo., 1967. Reporter Danville (Va.) Register, 1952, El Paso Times, 1954-57; asst. prof. journalism U. Tex. at El Paso, 1956-62, assoc. prof., 1962-65; publs. editor Freedom of Info. Ctr., Columbia, Mo., 1965-67; vis. prof., head journalistic studies Tel Aviv U., 1967-68; assoc. prof. Sch. Journalism, U. Mo., Columbia, 1968-70, prof., 1970-76, chmn. news-editorial dept., 1975-76; press critic CBS Morning News, 1975-76; dean Coll. Journalism and Communications, U. Fla., Gainesville, 1976-94. Author: Bring My Sons from Far, 1966, Pragmatic Fund-Raising, 1997; author: (with John C. Merrill) Media, Messages and Men, 2d edit., 1979; author: Macromedia, 1990; editor (with Paul Fisher): Race and the News Media, 1967. Served with Israeli Army, 1948; AUS, 1952-54. Named to Fla. Freedom of Info. Hall of Fame, 1997; recipient Disting. Svc. award, Columbia Journalism Alumni, 1957, 30th Anniversary award, State of Israel, 1978, Freedom Forum Journalism Adminstr. of Yr. award, 1994. Mem.: Soc. Profl. Journalists (Rsch. in Journalism award 1971), Assn. Edn. in Journalism and Mass Comm. (pres. 1990—91). Home: 1705 NW 22nd Dr Gainesville FL 32605-3953 Office Phone: 352-392-6525. Business E-Mail: rlowenstein@jou.ufl.edu.

LOWENTHAL, ABRAHAM FREDERIC, international relations educator; b. Hyannis, Mass., Apr. 6, 1941; s. Eric Isaac and Suzanne (Moos) L.; m. Janet Wyzanski, June 24, 1962 (div. 1983); children: Linda Claudina, Michael Francis; m. Jane S. Jaquette, Jan. 20, 1991. AB, Harvard U., 1961, MPA, 1964, PhD, 1971; postgrad., Harvard Law Sch., 1961—62. Tng. assoc. Ford Found., Dominican Republic, 1962-64, asst. rep. Lima, Peru, 1969-72; asst. dir., then dir. of studies Coun. Fgn. Rels., N.Y.C., 1974-76; dir. Latin Am. program Woodrow Wilson Internat. Ctr. for Scholars, Washington, 1977-83; exec. dir. Inter-Am. Dialogue, Washington, 1982-92; prof. Sch. Internat. Rels., U. So. Calif., L.A., 1984—; dir., ctr. internat. studies U. So. Calif., 1992-97; pres. Pacific Coun. Internat. Policy, L.A., 1995—2005; v.p. Coun. Fgn. Rels., L.A., 1995—2005. Vis. fellow, rsch. assoc. Ctr. Internat. Studies, Princeton U., 1972-74, lectr., 1974; vis. lectr. polit. sci. Cath. U. Santiago, Dominican Republic, 1966; spl. cons. Commn. U.S.-L.Am. rels., N.Y.C., 1974-76; mem. internat. adv. bd. Ctr. U.S.-Mex. Rels., U. Calif.-San Diego, 1981-94; mem. internat. adv. bd. Helen Kellogg Inst., 1984-95; cons. Ford Found., 1974-90. Author: The Dominican Intervention, 1972, 2nd edit., 1995, Partners in Conflict: The United States and Latin America in 1990s, 1991; editor, contbg. author: The Peruvian Experiment: Continuity and Change Under Military Rule, 1975, Armies and Politics in Latin America, 1976, Exporting Democracy: The United States and Latin America, 1991; co-editor, contbg. author: The Peruvian Experiment Reconsidered, 1983, The California-Mexico Connection, 1993; editor Latin Am. and Caribbean Record, vol. IV, 1985-86, vol. V, 1986-87, Latin America in a New World, 1994, Constructing Democratic Governance: Latin America, 1996; mem. editl. bd. Jour. Inter-Am. Studies and World Affairs, 1980-97, New Perspectives Quarterly, 1984—, Hemisphere, Internat. Security, 1977-85, Wilson Quar., 1977-83; contbr. articles to profl. jours. Mem. nat. adv. coun. Amnesty Internat., 1977-83, Ctr. for Nat. Policy, 1986—. Mem. Internat. Inst. Strategic Studies, Am. Polit. Sci. Assn. (coun. 1979-81), Latin Am. Studies (exec. coun. 1979-81), Coun. Fgn. Rels. Democrat. Jewish. Office: Univ So Calif Los Angeles CA 90089-0035 Office Phone: 213-740-6954. Business E-Mail: afl@usc.edu.

LOWENTHAL, CONSTANCE, art historian, consultant; b. N.Y.C., Aug. 29, 1945; d. Jesse and Helen (Oberstein) L. BA cum laude, Brandeis U., 1967; AM, Inst. Fine Arts, NYU, 1969; PhD, Inst. Fine Arts, NYU, N.Y.C., 1976. Mem. faculty Sarah Lawrence Coll., Bronxville, N.Y., 1975-78; asst. mus. educator Met. Mus. Art, N.Y.C., 1978-85; exec. dir. Internat. Found. Art Research, N.Y.C., 1985-98; dir. Commn. for Art Recovery World Jewish Congress, N.Y.C., 1998-2001; cons. art ownership disputes N.Y.C., 2001—. Bd. dirs. Ctr. for Edn. Studies, Inc. Regular contbr. Art Crime Update column Wall Street Jour., 1988-97; mem. editl. bd.: The Spoils of War, World War II and Its Aftermath: The Loss, Reappearance and Recovery of Cultural Property, 1997; contbr. articles to Mus. News and other profl. publs. Office Phone: 212-876-3140. Business E-Mail: cl@lowenthal.inc.com.

LOWENTHAL, DAVID, historian, geographer; b. N.Y.C., Apr. 26, 1923; s. Max and Eleanor (Mack) L.; m. Mary A. Lamberty, Oct. 16, 1970. BA, Harvard U., 1943; MA, U. Calif., Berkeley, 1950; PhD, U. Wis., 1953. Rsch. analyst U.S. State Dept., Washington, 1945-46; asst. prof. history Vassar Coll., Poughkeepsie, N.Y., 1952-56; rsch. assoc. Am. Geog. Soc., N.Y.C., 1958-72; with U. of the West Indies, Jamaica, 1956-70, history lectr., rsch. assoc., cons. to vice chancellor; with Inst. of Race Rels., London, 1961-72; prof. geography U. Coll., London, 1972-85, hon. rsch. fellow, 1986—; vis. prof. heritage studies St. Mary's U. Coll. Strawberry Hill, U.K., 1995-2000. Mem. bd., contbg. editor Internat. Ency. Social Scis., 1964-68; U.S., U.K. del. Internat. Coun. on Monuments and Sites, mem. gen. assembly, 1981, 87, cons. hist. landscapes and site authenticity, 1994—. Author: George Perkins Marsh: Versatile Vermonter, 1958, West Indian Societies, 1972, The Past is a Foreign Country, 1985 (Univ. and Profl. Pub. award 1986), The Heritage Crusade and the Spoils of History, 1996, George Perkins Marsh, Prophet of Conservation, 2000 (J.B. Jackson award, finalist Brit. Acad. prize). Georgian Group del. Harrow Conservation Area Adv. Com., 1987—97; sec., dir. Crown St. and Area Residents Assn., Harrow, 1974—2001. With U.S. Army, 1943—45. Recipient Victoria medal, Royal Geog. Soc., 1997, Cullum Geog. medal, Am. Geog. Soc., 1999, medal, Royal Scottish Geog. Soc., 2004; fellow, Leverhulme emeritus, 1992—93, John Simon Guggenheim Found., 1965—66, Brit. Acad., 2001; Landes Sr. fellow, Rsch. Inst. the Study of Man, 1992—93. Mem. AAAS (councilor 1964-71), Soc. for Caribbean Studies (founding chair 1977-79), Landscape Rsch. Group (vice chair 1979-84, chair 1984-89), Internat. Cultural Property Soc. (editl. bd. 1989—). Office: Univ Coll London London England Home: 22 Heron Place 9 Thayer St London W1U 3JL England also: 1401 LeRoy Ave Berkeley CA 94708 E-mail: D.Lowenthal@ucl.ac.uk.

LOWENTHAL, HENRY, retired greeting card company executive; b. Frankfurt, Germany, Oct. 26, 1931; came to U.S., 1940, naturalized, 1945; s. Adolf and Kella (Suss) L.; m. Miriam Katzenstein, June 29, 1958; children—Sandra, Jeffry, Joan Chana, Benjamin, Avi. BBA cum laude, City U. N.Y., 1952, MBA, 1953; JD, N.Y. U., 1962. CPA. Lectr. acctg. Baruch Coll., N.Y.C., 1952-53; auditor Price Waterhouse & Co., N.Y.C., 1955-62; v.p., contr. Am. Greetings Corp., Cleve., 1962-68, contr., 1966-68, sr. v.p., CFO, 1977-95, sr. v.p., 1995-97. V.p. fin., treas. Tremco Inc., Cleve., 1968-77; mem. adv. bd. Case We. Res. U. Dept. Accountancy, 1986-97. Chmn. bd. dirs. Rabbinical Coll. Telshe, 1974-77, v.p., 1977-90; v.p. Hebrew Acad. Cleve., 1977-97; pres. Agudath Israel of Cleve., 1978-95, treas., 1995-97; v.p. Agudath Israel Am., 1989—, chmn. regional v.p.s, 1996—; bd. dirs. Jewish Cmty. Fedn., Cleve., 1979-88, 90-95, chmn. audit com., 1992-95; trustee Mt. Sinai Med. Ctr., Cleve., 1992-96; chmn. citizens rev. com. Cleveland Heights-Univ. Heights Sch., 1972-73, mem. lay fin. com., 1974-79; mem. Cleveland Heights Citizens Adv. Com. for Cmty. Devel., 1976-79; mem. com. Jewish edn. Jewish Cmty. Fedn., Balt., 1997—, bd. advisors job link, 1997—; dir. victim svcs. Northwest Citizens Patrol, 1998-2001; bd. dirs. Beth Medrash Govoha Rabbinical Coll., Lakewood, N.J., Bnos Yisroel Sch., Balt., Shearith Israel Congregation, treas. Mended Hearts Chpt., 2001-2002. With AUS, 1953-55. Mem. AICPA, Assn. of Publicly Traded Cos. (budget & fin. com. 1986-97, bd. dirs. 1987-97, treas. 1990-97), Fin. Execs. Inst. (sec. N.E. Ohio chpt. 1979-80), Ohio Soc. CPA, Greater Cleve. Growth Assn., Beta Gamma Sigma, Beta Alpha Psi. Home: 6115 Biltmore Ave Baltimore MD 21215-3601 Personal E-mail: henrylow@aol.com.

LOWENTHAL, RICHARD MARK, neurologist; b. Cin., July 14, 1942; s. Gerson and Irma May (Pushin) L.; m. Toni Louise Ach, June 16, 1967 (dec. 1982); children: Sarah, Anna; m. Barbara K. Goodspeed Chen, Nov. 23, 1986; stepchildren: Christian Chen, Marisa Chen. AB cum laude, Harvard U., 1964; MD, U. Chgo., 1968. Diplomate Am. Bd. Psychiatry and Neurology (examiner 1984—). Med. intern U. Chgo. Hosps., 1968-69; resident neurology U. Calif., San Francisco, 1971-74, rsch. fellow, 1974-75, instr., 1975-76; asst. clin. prof. U. So. Calif., L.A., 1980-83, assoc. clin. prof., 1983—; neurologist Sansum Med. Clinic, Santa Barbara, 1976-97; dir. Calif. Neurol. Inst., Santa Barbara, 1997—. Chmn. dept. neurology Cottage Hosp., Santa Barbara, 1979-82, vice chmn., 1990-92, chmn. dept. neurology and neurosurgery, 1992-94; bd. dirs. Nat. Multiple Sclerosis Soc. Channel Islands, 1980—, chmn. profl. adv. com., 1980—; dir. Muscular Dystrophy Assn. Clinic, Santa Barbara. Lt. commdr. USPHS, 1969-71. Recipient L.J. Henderson prize Harvard Coll., 1964. Fellow Am. Acad. Neurology (mem. edn. com. 1984-90). Avocations: automobile mechanics, soccer. Office: 2431 Castillo St Santa Barbara CA 93105

LOWENTHAL, STEVEN R., lawyer; BS, U. Calif., Berkeley, 1979; JD, Stanford U., 1982. Bar: Calif. 1982, admitted to practice: US Ct. Appeals (9th Cir.), US Dist. Ct. (No. and Ctrl. Dists. Calif.), Ct. Fed. Claims, Washington, DC. Ptnr. Farella Braun & Martel LLP, San Francisco, chmn. litig. dept., former mem. exec. com., former mem. strategic advisory bd., chmn., 2005—. Faculty, trial advocacy program Stanford Law Sch. Advocacy Skills Workshop; taught trial advocacy U. San Francisco Law Sch. Mem.: Assn. Bus. Trial Lawyers (bd. gov.). Office: Farella Braun & Martel LLP Russ Bldg 235 Montgomery St San Francisco CA 94104-3105 Office Phone: 415-954-4405. Office Fax: 415-954-4480. Business E-Mail: slowenthal@fbm.com.*

LOWENTHAL, SUSAN, realtor, artist; b. Munich, Nov. 30, 1946; came to U.S., 1949; d. Jerry and Gertrude (Wiestreich) L.; m. Alex J. Stolitzka, Oct. ll, 1987. BA, Bklyn. Coll., 1969. Exec. dir. Manhattan Girls Club, N.Y.C., 1969-73; conf. coord. Orton Soc., N.Y.C., 1973-77; v.p. Gemtique, N.Y.C., 1977-81; broker Prudential Bache, N.Y.C., 1981-83, Smith Barney, N.Y.C., 1983-85; pres., CEO Lowenthal Fin. Svcs., Inc., NYC, 1985—89, fin. cons., money mgr. N.Y.C., 1990-98; realtor, exclusive buyer agt. March Buyers Realty, 1995—. Designer/artist works sold in museum gift shops and pub. in nat. mags.; guest appearances on cable TV shows; pres. AcScents! Naturally. Artist, designer; designs published in maj. nat. mags. Jewish. Avocations: skiing, reading, bridge. Personal E-mail: susan@susanlowenthal.com.

LOWER, GEORGE FRANCIS, JR., musician, director; b. Killeen, Tex., June 7, 1967; s. George Francis Lower and Barbara Ann Stilwell-Lower; m. Cynthia Marie Nepper, Dec. 6, 1989; children: Spencer Ryan, Haley Lauren, Dylan Scott, Logan Tyler, Evan Michael. BS in Social Studies Edn., U. South Fla., 1993. Tchr. sci. Acad. at the Lakes Day Sch., Land O' Lakes, Fla., 1994—98; dir. religious edn. St. Patrick Cath. Ch., Tampa, Fla., 1998—99; dir. music ministries Holy Name Jesus Ch., West Palm Beach, Fla., 1999—. Composer (prodr., musician): (albums) Of Saints and Angels; composer: (songs) We Praise Your Holy Name. With U.S. Army, 1988—90. Decorated Expert Inf. Badge U.S. Army. Mem.: Nat. Pastoral Musicians Assn. Republican. Roman Catholic. Avocations: genealogy, travel. Office: Holy Name of Jesus Church 345 South Military Trail West Palm Beach FL 33415 Office Phone: 561-683-3555. Office Fax: 561-683-1051. Personal E-mail: guitplyr@adelphia.net.

LOWER, ROBERT CASSEL, lawyer, educator; b. Oak Park, Ill., Jan. 8, 1947; s. Paul Elton and Doris Thatcher (Heaton) L.; m. Jean Louise Lower, Aug. 24, 1968 (dec. Aug. 1985); children: David Elton, Andrew Bennett, James Philip Thatcher; m. Cheryl Bray, July 26, 1986. AB magna cum laude with highest honors, Harvard U., 1969, JD, 1972. Bar: Ga. 1972. Assoc. Alston & Bird, Atlanta, 1972-78; ptnr., e-commerce, healthcare, privacy area Alston & Bird LLP, Atlanta, 1978—. Adj. prof. Emory U., 1978-85, 92. Contbr. articles to profl. jours. Co-founder, pres. Ga. Lawyers for the Arts, Inc., 1975—79; chmn. Fulton County (Ga.) Arts Coun., 1979—87; trustee Woodruff Arts Ctr., 1988—95, Piedmont Coll., Ga. Found. Ind. Colls. Mem. Ga. Bar Assn., Atlanta Bar Assn., Midtown Bus. Assn. (bd. dirs. 1988-90), Author's Ct. Harvard Club (Ga.), Ansley Golf Club, Phi Beta Kappa. Presbyterian. Avocations: running, music, bonsai. Office: Alston & Bird LLP 1 Atlantic Ctr 1201 W Peachtree St NW Atlanta GA 30309-3400 Office Phone: 404-881-7455. E-mail: rlower@alston.com.

LOWERY, CHARLES DOUGLAS, historian, educator, dean; b. Greenville, Ala., May 8, 1937; s. Reuben F. and Frances Louise (Jordan) L.; m. Sara Bradford, June 24, 1961; children: Thomas Bradford, Douglas Trenton, Charles Daniel. BA, Huntingdon Coll., 1959; MA, Fla. State U., 1961; PhD, U. Va., 1966. Asst. prof. history Ball State U., Muncie, Ind., 1964-66; from asst. prof. to prof. Miss. State U., Starkville, 1966—, head dept. history, 1985—, asst. dean Coll. Arts and Scis., 1971-74, assoc. dean, 1974-81, dir. Inst. for Humanities, 1981-85. Author: James Barbour: The Biography of A Jeffersonian Republican, 1984, (with others) America: The Middle Period, 1973, Encyclopedia of African-American Civil Rights: From Emancipation to the Present, 1992, The Greenwood Encyclopedia of African-American Civil Rights, 2004; contbr. articles to profl. jours. Mem. Miss. Com. for Humanities, Jackson, 1986-88; vice chmn. Miss. Humanities Coun., Jackson, 1988-89; active Habitat for Humanity. Grantee NEH, 1980, 81, 84, Miss. Humanities Coun., 1983, 84, 88. Mem. Orgn. Am. Historians, Soc. Historians of Early Am. Rep., So. Hist. Soc., Miss. Hist. Soc. (com. chmn. 1989-90). Democrat. Presbyterian. Avocations: camping, travel, fishing, historical preservation, woodworking. Home: 609 Sherwood Rd Starkville MS 39759-4009 Office: Miss State U Dept History Drawer H Mississippi State MS 39762 Personal E-mail: charsue36@excite.com. E-mail: cdl2@ra.msstate.edu.

LOWERY, DAVID J., lawyer; b. Belleville, Ill., Dec. 3, 1953; BBA cum laude, So. Meth. U., 1975, JD, 1978. Bar: Tex. 1978. Mem. Jones, Day, Reavis & Pogue, Dallas; now ptnr., co-chair real estate practice worldwide Jones Day, Dallas. Editorial bd. Briefings in Real Estate Fin. Mem.: Nat. Assn. Real Estate Investment Trusts, State Bar of Tex. Office: Jones Day 2727 N Harwood St Dallas TX 75201-1515 Office Phone: 214-969-3710. Office Fax: 214-969-5100. Business E-Mail: djlowery@jonesday.com.

LOWERY, KATHLEEN ANN, elementary school educator; b. Oswego, N.Y., Aug. 28, 1949; d. Joseph Harold and Mary Agnes (Mulcahey) Lowery. BS, SUNY, Oswego, 1971. Art tchr. Little Falls (N.Y.) City Sch. Dist., 1971—73, kindergarten tchr., 1973—. Mem. early childhood adv. com. Herkimer (N.Y.) County C.C., 1993—. Mem.: NY State United Teachers, Little Falls Tchrs. Assn. Avocations: art, sports, crafts. Home: 305 Lansing St Herkimer NY 13350 Office: Benton Hall Acad 1 Ward Sq Little Falls NY 13365 Office Phone: 315-823-1400 ext. 1416.

LOWERY, ROBERT (ARTIE) ARTHER, technical education educator; b. Fort Meade, Md., Jan. 17, 1958; s. Bob and Ilene Lowery; m. Barbara Ann Smith, Nov. 14, 1957; children: Robert Andrew, Roger Anthony, Rodney Alexander. BS in indsl. arts edn., Ctrl. State U., 1986. Tchg. Cert Okla. State Dept. of Edn., 1992. Tech. edn. tchr. Putnam City West H.S., Oklahoma City, Okla., 1992—. Viste project pilot site NC State U. Viste Project, 2003—. Mem.: Okla. Tech. Edn. Assn. (assoc.), Okla. Assn. of Career and Tech. Edn. (assoc.), Internat. Tech. Edn. Assn. (assoc.), Assn. of Career and Tech. Educators (assoc.), Epsilon Pi Tau (hon.). Bapt. Home: 8428 NW 85th ST Oklahoma City OK 73132 Office: Putnam City W HS 8500 NW 23 st Oklahoma City OK 73127 Office Phone: 405-787-1140 2461. Personal E-mail: pcwtechie@yahoo.com. E-mail: alowery@putnamcityschools.org.

LOWERY, ROBERT CHESLEY, thoracic surgeon, educator; b. Columbus, Ohio, Oct. 7, 1949; s. Robert Lowery and Rutha Mae Whiteside; m. Nancy Lowery, July 19, 1986 (div. Dec. 9, 2002); 1 child, Jason. At, State U. of Calif. at LA, 1969—72; MD, U. Calif., San Francisco, 1976. Cert. Nat. Bd. of Med. Examiners, 1978, Am. Bd. of Surgery, 1984, Am. Bd. of Thoracic Surgery, 1986. Dir. sickle cell screening and testing, student nat. med. ctr. U. Calif., San Francisco, 1974—75; acting chief divsn. of cardiothoracic surgery Howard U., Washington, 1987—88; chmn. med. adv. com. Washington Regional Transplant Consortium, 1987—89; co-founder Cardiovasc. and Thoracic Surgery Assoc., Washington, 1994; prof. surgery SUNY Downstate Sch. of Medicine, Bklyn., 2002—; chief divsn. of cardiothoracic surgery, Downstate Sch. of Medicine SUNY, Bklyn., 2002—. Pvt. practice, Washington, 1989—; pres. Stillwild Photography, Washington, 1995—; mem. bd. med. dirs. Life Link MD, Washington, 2000—. Contbr. articles to profl. jours. Fundraiser DC Pub. Sch., Washington, 2002. Recipient commendation, NY Health and Hosp. Corp., 1979, Patient Choice award, Washington Hosp. Ctr., 1997—2001, Top Dr., Washingtonian mag., 1999. Mem.: Cosmos Club, Sigma Alpha, Epsilon Boulé chpt. Roman Catholic. Achievements include development of new vascular procedure. Avocations: skiing, scuba diving, photography, hiking, wine collecting. Office: SUNY Downstate Med Ctr 450 Clarkson Ave Brooklyn NY 11203 Office Phone: 718-270-1981. Business E-Mail: rlowery@downstate.edu.

LOWERY, WILLA DEAN, obstetrician, gynecologist; b. Caryville, Fla., Apr. 16, 1927; d. Ernest and Nadine (Fowler) L. BS in Chemistry, Stetson U., 1948; MS in Microbiology, U. Fla., 1952; MD, U. Miami, 1959; MPH, U. Pitts., 1963; MDiv in Theology, Pitt. Theol. Sem., 1995. Diplomate Am. Bd. Ob-Gyn.; ordained to ministry Presbyn. Ch. Microbiologist Fla. Dept. Pub. Health, Jacksonville, 1948-52, pub. health officer, 1959-65; microbiologist U. S. Operation Mission to Brazil, Belém, 1952-55; rotating intern Jackson Meml. Hosp., Miami, Fla., 1959-60; resident in ob-gyn. Magee Women's Hosp., Pitts., 1965-68; asst. prof. ob-gyn. Sch. Medicine, U. Pitts., 1968-69; pvt. practice Pitts., 1970-88; pastor Presbyn. Ch. So. Ind. County Parish, 1995—. Cons. Med. Mission in Brazil, Teresina, 1986-89; mem. Ethics Bd. of Chldns. Hosp U. Pittsburgh, 1998. Contbr. articles to profl. jours. Recipient Disting. Alumni award, Stetson U., 2003. Mem. AMA, ACOG, Pa. State Med. Soc., Allegheny County Med. Soc. Home: 119 Sunnyhill Dr Pittsburgh PA 15237-3666

LOWERY, WILLIAM HERBERT, lawyer; b. Toledo, June 8, 1925; s. Kenneth Alden and Drusilla (Pfanner) L.; m. Carolyn Broadwell, June 27, 1947; children: Kenneth Latham, Marcia Mitchell; m. Janice Gamble Gerrie, Dec. 28, 2002. PhB, U. Chgo., 1947; JD, U. Mich., 1950. Bar: Pa. 1951, U.S. Supreme Ct. 1955. Assoc. Dechert Price & Rhoads, Phila., 1950-58, ptnr., 1958-89, mng. ptnr., 1970-72; mem. policy com., chmn. litigation dept., 1962-68, 81-84; of counsel Dechert, Phila., 1989—; counsel S.S. Huebner Found. Ins. Edn., Phila., 1970-89. Faculty Am. Conf. of Legal Execs., Pa. Bar Inst.; permanent mem. com. of visitors U. Mich. Law Sch. Author: Insurance Litigation Problems, 1972, Insurance Litigation Disputes, 1977. Pres. Strafford Civic Assn., 1958; chmn. Tredyffrin Twp. Zoning Bd., Chester County, Pa., 1959—75; bd. dirs. Paoli Meml. Hosp., 1964—89, chmn., 1972—75; bd. dirs. Main Line Health, Radnor, 1984—89; permanent mem. Jud. Conf. 3d Cir. Ct. 2n lt. USAF, 1943—46. Mem. ABA (chmn. life ins. com. 1984-85, chmn. Nat. Conf. Lawyers and Life Ins. Cos. 1984-88), Order of the Coif, Royal Poinciana Golf Club (bd. dirs. 1997-2003, sec. 1997-2000, v.p. 2000-03), Phi Gamma Delta, Phi Delta Phi. Home: 1255 Gulf Shore Blvd N Apt 6-South Naples FL 34102 Office: Dechert 4000 Bell Atlantic Tower 1717 Arch St Philadelphia PA 19103-2793

LOWERY, WILLIAM ODELL, personnel services executive; b. Winston-Salem, Aug. 1, 1935; m. Lucienne Lowery, Mar. 3, 1962. BS in Polit. Sci., Trenton State Coll., 1987. Commd. 2d lt. U.S. Army, advanced through grades to maj., 1974, pers. action specialist hdqrs. 24th divsn. Augsburg, Germany, 1962-65, 65-66, pers. mgmt. specialist hdqrs. The Pentagon Washington, 1967-70; pers. staff officer to set up operation to deactivate 4th Inf. Divsn., An Khe, Vietnam, 1970-71; pers. hdqrs. DA U.S. Army, Heidelberg, Germany, 1971-74, pers. staff Ft. Ben Harrison, Ind., 1974-79; mail carrier U.S. Postal Svc., New Hope, N.J., 1979-80; pers. specialist Civilian Pers. Office, Ft. Dix, 1980-94; FECA program adminstr. Dept. of Def. Police, Ft. Dix, NJ, 1996—2002. Instr. eng. OCS U.S. Army, Ft. Belvoir, Va., 1965-67. Publisher: autobiographical book Life, Goals, Beyond with Am. Lit. Press. Program spkr. AARP Spkr. Bureau of NJ, 2003—05. Decorated Army Commendation medal (2), Meritorious Svc. medal (2), Bronze Star medal, Vietnam Svc. medal. Mem.: Vietnam Veterans of Am. NJ Chpt. Home: 37 E Chestnut St Bordentown NJ 08505-2063 Office Phone: 609-298-3286.

LOWEY, NITA M., congresswoman; b. N.Y., July 5, 1937; m. Stephen Lowey, 1961; children: Dona, Jacqueline, Douglas. BS, Mt. Holyoke Coll., 1959. Community activist, prior to 1975; asst. sec. state State of N.Y., 1975-87; mem. U.S. Congress from 20th N.Y. dist., 1989-92, U.S. Congress from 18th N.Y. dist., 1993—. Mem. appropriations com., 1993—. Democrat. Office: US Ho of Reps 2329 Rayburn Ho Office Bldg Washington DC 20515-0001*

LOWI, ALVIN, JR., mechanical engineer, consultant; b. Gadsden, Ala., July 21, 1929; s. Alvin R. and Janice (Haas) L.; m. Guillermina Gerardo Alverez, May 9, 1953; children: David Arthur, Rosamina, Edna Vivian, Alvin III. BME, Ga. Inst. Tech., 1951, MSME, 1955; PhD in Engring., UCLA, 1956-61. Registered prof. engr., Calif. Design engr. Garrett Corp., Los Angeles, 1956-58; mem. tech. staff TRW, El Segundo, Calif., 1958-60, Aerospace Corp., El Segundo, 1960-66; prin. Alvin Lowi and Assocs., San Pedro, 1966—; pres. Terraqua Inc., San Pedro, Calif., 1968-76; v.p. Daeco Fuels and Engring. Co., Wilmington, Calif., 1978—, also bd. dirs.; pres. Lion Engring., Inc. Vis. research prof. U. Pa., Phila., 1972-74; sr. lectr. Free Enterprise Inst., Monterey Park, Calif., 1961-71; bd. dirs. So. Calif. Tissue Bank; research fellow Heather Found., San Pedro, 1966--. Contbr. articles to profl. jours.; patentee in field. Served to lt. USN, 1951-54, Korea. Fellow Inst. Humane Studies; mem. ASME, NSPE, Soc. Automotive Engrs., Soc. Am. Inventors, So. Bay Chamber Music Soc., Scabbard and Blade, Pi Tau Sigma. Jewish. Avocations: chamber music, jazz, photography, classic automobiles, motor sports, philosophy of science. Home and Office: 2146 W Toscanini Dr Palos Verdes Peninsula CA 90275-1420

LOWI, THEODORE JAY, political science professor; b. Gadsden, Ala., July 9, 1931; s. Alvin R. and Janice (Haas) L.; m. Angele M. Daniel, May 11, 1963; children: Anna Amelie, Jason Daniel. BA, Mich. State U., 1954; MA, Yale U., 1955, PhD, 1961; HLD (hon.), Oakland U., 1972; LittD (hon.), SUNY, Stony Brook, 1988; Doctorate (hon.), Nat. Found. Polit. Scis., Paris, 1992. Mem. faculty dept. govt. Cornell U., Ithaca, NY, 1959—65, 1972—, asst. prof., 1961-65, John L. Senior prof. Am. instns., 1972—; assoc. prof. U. Chgo., 1965—69, prof., 1969—72. Fellow Ctr. Advanced Study in Behavioral Scis., 1977-78; chair Am. civilization U. Paris, 1981-82. Author: At the Pleasure of the Mayor, 1964, The End of Liberalism, 1969, 2d edit., 1979, Japanese edit., 1981, French edit., 1987, The Politics of Disorder, 1971, Incomplete Conquest: Governing America, 1981, The Personal President: Power Invested, Promise Unfulfilled, 1985, The End of the Republican Era, 1995, La Scienza del Politiche, 1999; author: (with others) Poliscide - Big Government, Big Science, Lilliputian Politics, 1976, 1991, Nationalizing Government: Public Policies in America, 1981, with others: Spanish edit., 1993; author: (with B. Ginsberg and Kenneth Shepsle) American Government: Power and Purpose, 1990, 8th edit., 2004; author: (with B. Ginsberg) Embattled Democracy, 1995; author: (with B. Ginsberg and M. Weir) We the People, 1997, 5th edit., 2005; author: (with J. Romance) A Republic of Parties? Debating the Two-Party System, 1998; author: (with Robert Kennedy) The Pursuit of Justice, 1964. Recipient Richard Neustadt award for Best Book on Presidency, 1986; Social Sci. Rsch. Coun. fellow, 1963-64; Guggenheim Found. fellow, 1967-68; NEH fellow, 1977-78; Ford Found. fellow, 1977-78; Fulbright 40th Anniversary Disting. fellow, 1987. Mem. Am. Polit. Sci. Assn. (v.p. 1985-86, pres. 1991), Am. Acad. Arts and Scis., Policy Studies Orgn. (pres. 1977), Internat. Polit. Sci. Assn. (1st v.p. 1994-97, pres. 1997-2000). Home: 101 Delaware Ave Ithaca NY 14850-4707 Office Phone: 607-255-6766. E-mail: TJL7@cornell.edu. *If there is a how-to of success it is this: a passion for work, an ethic of workmanship, and an idea of what, in the end, is a good product.*

LOWINGER, FREDERICK CHARLES, lawyer; b. Chgo., July 18, 1955; s. Alexander I. and Muriel (Rosencranz) L.; m. Lynn T. Wollins, July 12, 1981; Lauren, Daniel, Stephen. BS in Acctg., MS in Acctg., U. Pa., 1977; JD, U. Chgo., 1980. CPA. Bar: Ill. 1982. Law clk. to Judge J. Skelly Wright US Ct. Appeals (DC cir.), Washington, 1980-81; clk. to Justice William J. Brennan Jr. US Supreme Ct., Washington, 1981-82; assoc. Sidley & Austin (now Sidley Austin Brown & Wood LLP), Chgo., 1982—88; ptnr. Sidley Austin Brown & Wood LLP, Chgo., 1988—, and mem. exec. com., 1996—, head, Chgo. office corp. group, 1999—. Dir. Jewish Vocat. Svc., Chgo., 1993-98. Mem. ABA, Chgo. Bar Assn., The Law Club. Avocations: golf, skiing. Office: Sidley Austin Brown & Wood LLP Bank One Plz 10 S Dearborn St Chicago IL 60603 Office Phone: 312-853-7238. Office Fax: 312-853-7036. Business E-Mail: flowinger@sidley.com.

LOWITT, RICHARD, history professor; b. N.Y.C., Feb. 25, 1922; s. Eugene and Eleanor (Lebowitz) L.; m. Suzanne Catharine Carson, Sept., 1953; children: Peter Carson, Pamela Carson Bennett. BSS., CCNY, 1943; MA, Columbia U., 1945, PhD, 1950. Instr. U. Md., College Park, 1948-52; asst. prof. U. R.I., Kingston, 1952-53; faculty mem. Conn. Coll., New London, 1953-66, prof. history, 1966, Fla. State U., Tallahassee, 1966-68, U. Ky., Lexington, 1968-77; prof., chmn. dept. history Iowa State U., Ames, 1977-87, prof., 1987-89, U. Okla., Norman, 1990-97; Regents prof. Univ. Sci. and Arts, Okla., Chickasha, 1998—. Mem. Iowa Humanities Bd., 1987-89; mem. Okla. Humanities Bd., 1995-2001; vis. prof. U. Colo., summer 1953, Yale U., 1961-62, Brown U., 1965-66, U. Chattanooga, summer 1965, Emory U., Atlanta; Sutton prof. U. Okla., 1989-90; Regents prof. U. Sci. and Arts of Okla., Chickasha, 1998—. Author: A Merchant Prince of the 19th Century, 1954, George W. Norris, 3 vols., 1963, 71, 78; editor: Nils Olsen and the Bureau of Agricultural Economics, 1980; co-editor: One Third of a Nation-Lorena Hickok Reports on the Great Depression, 1981, The New Deal and the West, 1984, Letters From An American Farmer: The Eastern European and Russian Correspondence by Roswell Garst, 1987, Henry A. Wallace's Irrigation Frontier: On the Trail of the Cornbelt Farmer, 1990, Bronson M. Cutting, Progressive Politican, 1992, Politics in the Postwar American West, 1995, Fred Harris: His Journey From Liberalism to Populism, 2002 (Outstanding Book Okla. History award Hist. Soc. Okla., 2002), The Standing Bear Controversy: Prelude to Indian Reform, 2003. Trustee Pub. Libr., Lexington, 1973-77. NEH sr. fellow, 1974, John Simon Guggenheim Found. fellow, 1957; grantee Social Sci. Rsch. Coun., 1958, Am. Coun. Learned Socs., 1962, Am. Philos. Soc., 1964, Huntington Libr., 1986; recipient Gaspar Perez de Villagra award Hist. Soc. N.Mex., 1993, Muriel H. Wright award Hist. Soc. Okla., 1995. Fellow Agrl. History Soc. (exec. com. 1973-75, pres. 1991-92); mem. Am. Hist. Assn., So. Hist. Assn. (membership com. 1973, Ramsdell prize com. 1975, program com. 1983, nominating com. 1990), Western History Assn. (bd. editors 1986-88, program com. 1995, merit award 1992), Orgn. Am. Historians (nominating com. 1970, Turner prize com. 1972-76, bd. editors 1985-87). Democrat. Office: Univ Okla Dept History Norman OK 73019-0001 Office Phone: 405-325-6001. Business E-Mail: richard.lowitt-1@ou.edu.

LOWMAN, JOHN D., JR., physical therapist, researcher; s. John D. Lowman Sr. and Carol W. Smith, Sandra S. Lowman (Stepmother) and Bobby M. Canode (Stepfather), Robert A. Smith (Stepfather); m. Mary (Beth) E. Lindsay, Aug. 17, 1996. BS in Edn., Va. Poly. Inst. and State U., 1993; MS, Duke U., 1995; PhD, Va. Commonwealth U., 2004. Lic. Physical Therapist N.C. Bd. Phys. Therapy Examiners, 1995, cert. Cardiovascular and Pulmonary Physical Therapy Clinical Specialist Am. Bd. Phys. Therapy Specialties, 1999. Phys. therapist Vencor Hosp., Greensboro, NC, 1995—96, Interim Healthcare, Durham, 1996—97, Duke U. Med. Ctr., 1996—2005; grad. rsch. and tchg. asst. Va. Commonwealth U., Richmond, 2000—04; postdoctoral assoc. Va. Commonwealth U. Med. Ctr., Richmond, 2005—; asst. prof. dept. phys. therapy U. Ala., Birmingham, 2005—. Phys. therapist asst. exam. devel. com. Fedn. State Bds. Phys. Therapy, Alexandria, Va., 2004—; cardiovasc. and pulmonary specialization acad. content experts Am. Bd. Phys. Therapy Specialties, 2003—06; adj. instr. New River C.C., Dublin, 1993. Asst scoutmaster Boy Scouts Am. Troop 45, Dublin, 1989—93, Boy Scouts Am. Troop 430, Richmond, 2001—02; asst. scoutmaster Boy Scouts Am. Troop 736, Glen Allen, Va., 2003—05. Recipient Disting. Svc. award, Va. Tech., Cardiac Therapy and Intervention Ctr., 1992, Outstanding Sr. of Yr., Va. Tech Coll. Edn., 1992—93, Paul Gunsten Leadership award, Va. Tech., Health and Phys. Edn. Dept., 1993, Outstanding Acad. Achievement award, Va. Tech., Coll. Edn., 1993, U. Outstanding Svc. award, Va. Commonwealth U., 2004, U. Outstanding Leadership award, 2004; scholar, Va. Tech., Health and Phys. Edn. Dept., 1993, Found. Phys. Therapy, 2003—04; Andrea Walnes Meml. scholar, Va. Tech., Coll. Edn., 1992—93. Mem.: Am. Assn. Cardiovasc. and Pulmonary Rehab., Am. Physiol. Soc., Am. Phys. Therapy Assn. Achievements include patents pending for Thermostatic Animal Platform for Intravital Microscopy and/or Contractile Measurement in Skeletal Muscle. Avocations: bicycling, hiking, backpacking, rock climbing. Office: U Ala Dept Phys Therapy Sch Health Related Pro 1530 3d Ave S Birmingham AL 35294-1212 Office Phone: 205-934-3566. Office Fax: 205-975-7787. Personal E-mail: lowma001@duke.edu. E-mail: jdlowman@vcu.edu.

LOWMAN, JOY RAE, disposal dog diaper company executive; b. Crockett, Tex., Apr. 15, 1951; d. Raymond Y. Rains and Betty Genois (Bartee) Carroll; m. David Pittman Lowman, May 5, 1988; 1 child, Jonathan David. Student, Durham Bus. Coll., Houston, Houston C.C. Pres. Diapette Corp., Stafford, Tex., 1989—. Contbr. to poetry anthology; inventor lst commercially produced disposable dog diaper. Republican. Avocations: writing, interior design, poetry. Office: Diapette Corp 16727 Tranquil Dr Sugar Land TX 77478-1981

LOWMAN, ROBERT PAUL, psychology professor, academic administrator; b. Lynwood, Calif., Jan. 23, 1947; s. Hubert Alden and Martha Guynn (Howard) L.; m. Kathleen Marie Drew, June 25, 1972; children: Sarah Guynn, Amy Katherine. AB, U. So. Calif., 1967; MA, Claremont U., 1969, PhD, 1973. Asst. prof. U. Wis., Milw., 1972-76; adminstrv. officer APA, Washington, 1976-81; asst. dean Kans. State U., Manhattan, 1981-86, assoc. dean grad. sch., 1986-90, assoc. vice provost, 1990-91; dir. rsch. svcs. U. N.C., Chapel Hill, 1991—2002, adj. assoc. prof. psychology, 1991—, assoc. vice chancellor for rsch., 1994-96, 2001—, assoc. vice provost for rsch., 1996-2001. Editor: APA's Guide to Rsch. Support, 1981; contbr. over 30 articles to profl. jours. Recipient numerous grants. Mem. APA (sec. bd. sci. affairs 1976-81, sec. com. on internat. rels. in psychology 1978-81), AAAS, Am. Psychol. Soc., Soc. for Psychologists in Mgmt. (newsletter editor 1994-96, bd. dirs. 1996-2001, pres. 2000), Nat. Coun. Univ. Rsch. Adminstrs., Soc. Rsch. Adminstrs., Phi Beta Kappa, Phi Kappa Phi, Phi Eta Sigma, Psi Chi. Democrat. Methodist. Home: 104 Chesley Ln Chapel Hill NC 27514-1459 Office: Univ NC Office of Vice Chancellor for Rsch CB # 4100 Chapel Hill NC 27599-4100 E-mail: lowman@unc.edu.

LOWMAN, TYRONE DAVID, entrepreneur; b. Newark, June 14, 1978; s. Elliott Lowman and Joyce Mabine. At, Dover Bus. Coll. Clk. Phillip Van Hensen, Bridgewater, NJ; investor Sterling Funding, Inc., Newark; freelance writer TDL LLC, Newark; mktg. Clifford J. Scott, Ea. Orange, NJ. Asst. promotions V.E.M. Young Entrepreneurial Merchants, 1997; assoc. Prepaid Legal, 1998, ICR Svcs., 2000. Author: (books) The Reasons Why They are Rich and You are Not, 2001, What are We Afraid of, 2002. Achievements include owning 7 houses by age 22, writing first book by 21 and doing a booksigning at age 22. Home: 123 Norman Street East Orange NJ 07017 Office: Phillip Van Hensen 1001 Frontier Rd Bridgewater NJ 08807

LOWNDES, JOHN FOY, lawyer; b. Jan. 1, 1931; s. Charles L. B. and Dorothy (Foy) L.; m. Rita Davies, Aug. 18, 1983; children: Elizabeth Anne, Amy Scott, John Patrick, Joseph Edward, Jennifer Susanne. BA, Duke U., 1953, LLB, 1958. Bar: Fla. 1958. Pvt. practice, Daytona Beach, Fla., 1958, Orlando, Fla., 1959-69; sr. ptnr., chmn. bd. dirs. Lowndes, Drosdick, Doster, Kantor & Reed, P.A., Orlando, 1969—. Chmn. U. Ctrl. Fla. Found.; mem. Fla. Constl. Rev. Commn., 1998. Former chmn. bd. trustees Orlando Mus. Art, Winter Park Meml. Hosp.; bd. visitors Duke U. Law Sch. Capt. USMCR, 1953-61, ret. Republican. Home: 1308 Green Cove Rd Winter Park FL 32789-2549 Office: Lowndes Drosdick Doster Kantor & Reed 215 N Eola Dr Orlando FL 32801-2095 Office Phone: 407-843-4600. E-mail: jfloundes@aol.com.

LOWNEY, TIMOTHY JAY, lawyer; b. Boston, Nov. 27, 1973; s. Charles William and Irene (Medieros) Lowney. BA, Boston Coll., 1996; JD, Suffolk U., 1999. Bar: Mass. 99. Law clk. Karol & Karol, Milton, Mass., 1996—99, assoc., 1999—2000, Roberson & Assocs., Hyde Park, Mass., 2000—01, Lawyers Unltd., Hyde Park, 2001—. Mem. warrant com. Town of Milton, Milton, 2001—02, mem. town meeting, 1999—; v.p. Mass. Recreation and Park Assn., 2000—01. Mem.: ATLA, ABA, Mass. Assn. Trial Attys. Office: Lawyers Unltd 1234 Hyde Park Ave Ste 102 Boston MA 02136 E-mail: atty.lowney@verizon.net.

LOWRANCE, MURIEL EDWARDS, program specialist; b. Ada, Okla., Dec. 28, 1922; d. Warren E. and Mayme E. (Barrick) Edwards; B.S. in Edn., East Central State U., Ada, 1954; 1 dau., Kathy Lynn Lowrance Gutierrez. Accountant, adminstrv. asst. to bus. mgr. East Central State U., 1950-68; grants and contracts specialist U. N.Mex. Sch. Medicine, Albuquerque, 1968-72, program specialist IV, dept. orthopaedics, 1975-86; asst. adminstrv. officer N.Mex. Regional Med. Program, 1972-75. Bd. dirs. Vocat. Rehab. Center, 1980-84. Cert. profl. contract mgr. Nat. Contract Assn. Mem. Am. Bus. Women's Assn. (past pres. El Segundo chpt., Woman of Yr. 1974), AAUW, Amigos de las Americas (dir.). Democrat. Methodist. Club: Pilot (Albuquerque) (pres. 1979-80, dir. 1983-84, dist. treas. 1984-86, treas. S.W. dist., 1984-86, gov.-elect S.W. dist. 1986-87, gov. S.W. dist. 1987-88). Home: 3028 Mackland Ave NE Albuquerque NM 87106-2018

LOWRIE, JEAN ELIZABETH, librarian, educator; b. Northville, Oct. 11, 1918; d. A. Sydney and Edith (Roos) L. AB, Keuka Coll., 1940, LLD (hon.), 1973; B.L.S., Western Res. U., 1941, PhD, 1959; MA, Western Mich. U., 1956. Childrens librarian Toledo Pub. Library, 1941-44; librarian Elementary Sch., Oak Ridge, Tenn., 1944-51; exchange tchr., libr. Nottingham, England, 1948—49; campus sch. librarian Western Mich. U., Kalamazoo, 1951-56; asso. prof. Western Mich. U. (Sch. Librarianship), 1958-61, prof., 1962-83, dir. sch., 1963-81. Mem. faculty summer U. Ky., 1951, U . Calif., Berkeley, Calif., 1958; chmn. Internat. Steering Com. for Devel. Sch. Librs.; del. meetings World Conf. Orgns. Tchg. Profn., Paris, 1964, Vancouver, 67, Dublin, 98, Abidjan, 69, Sydney, 70; pres. Internat. Assn. Sch. Librarianship, 1971—77, exec. sec., 1978—96; mem. exec. bd. Internat. Fedn. Libr. Assns. and Instns.; pres. Jensen Beach Friends of Libr., 1997—2005; chair Martin County Libr. Br. Coun., 1998—2004. Author: Elementary School Libraries, rev. edit., 1970, School Libraries: International Developments, 1972, 2d edit., 1991, also articles.; adviser: filmstrip Using the Library, 1962. Recipient Dutton-Macrae award ALA, 1957, Profl. Achievement award Keuka Coll. Alumni, 1963 Mem. ALA (pres. 1973-74), Mich. Library Assn., Assn. Libr. & Info. Sci. Educators, Am. Assn. Sch. Librarians (dir., past pres., 1st President's award 1978), Fla. Libr. Assn., Altrusa Club (Kalamazoo), Delta Kappa Gamma, Beta Phi Mu. Home: 1235 NE Oceanview Cir Jensen Beach FL 34957-3715

LOWRIE, PAMELA BURT, artist, educator; b. Geneva, Ill., May 12, 1937; d. Morris Nathan and Helyn (Beetlestone) B.; children: Edmund Gale, Matthew Burt; m. Michael Hammer, Aug. 14, 1982. BA, U. Mich., 1959; MS in Edn., No. Ill. U., DeKalb, 1970; MA, Claremont Grad. Sch. (Calif.), 1979. Art cons. Sch. Dist. 41, Glen Ellyn, Ill., 1970-72; prof. art Coll. DuPage, Glen Ellyn, 1972-94; ret., 1994; curator Olcott Gallery, Wheaton, Ill., 1994—. Dir., staff Nat. Great Tchrs. Seminars, Williams Bay, Wis., 1976-94; staff Calif. Great Tchrs. Seminar, Santa Barbara, 1979, Hawaii Great Tchrs. Seminar, 1990; vis. prof. Christ Ch. Coll., Canterbury, Eng., 1990. One-woman shows include Loyola U. Gallery, Chgo., U. Ill. Med. Ctr. Gallery, 1978, Elmhurst (Ill.) Coll. Gallery, 1980, Kankakee (Ill.) Coll. Gallery, 1982, The Edge Gallery, Villa Park, Ill., 1984, Gahlberg Gallery Coll. of DuPage, 1986, 87, 92, Elmhurst Art Mus., 1994, Am. Hdqs. of Theosophical Soc., Wheaton, Ill., 1995, 2000, 2005, Schafer Gallery, 1995, NICOR, Naperville, Ill., 1996, 97, 2001, Olcott Gallery, Wellness Ctr., 1997, Zurich AM Bldg., Schaumberg, Ill., 1998, DuPage Art League, Wheaton, Ill., 1999, Unilever Corp. Office, Rolling Meadows, Ill., 1999, City Hall, Wheaton, Ill., 2000, Roosevelt U., Schaumburg, Ill., 2001, Olcott Gallery, The Theosophical Soc., Wheaton, 2005; group shows include Five Women Artists from Ill., Notre Dame U., 1979, Springfield (Ill.) Art Assn. Gallery, 1981, Am. Cultural Ctr., Taipei, Taiwan, 1982, Campanille Gallery, Chgo., 1986, Limelight-Abstract Art, Riverwalk Gallery, Naperville, 1987, David Adler Cultural Ctr., Libertyville, Ill., Norris Gallery, St. Charles, Ill., Gov. State U., Park Forest, Ill., 1982-91, Woman Made Gallery, Gallery Egg, Chgo., Claremont Grad. Sch. Gallery, Calif., 1994, Kohn Turner Gallery, L.A., 1995, N.W. Cultural Coun. Corp. Gallery, 1996-97, Helene Curtis Corp. Ctr., 1997, Unilever Corp., 2000, 2002, Bloomigdale Art Mus., 2001, Roosevelt U., 2001, TLD Design Ctr. and Gallery, 2001, Zurich AM Bldg., 2002, Am. Hdqs. of Theosophical Soc., 2002, 2003, DePaul U., Naperville, Ill., 2004; represented in permanent collections Coll. DuPage, Glen Ellyn, AT&T, Naperville, Eastman Pharms., Malvern, Pa., Getty Synthetic Fuel, Chgo., Monte Christo Condominiums, Fla., Nara Jr. Coll., Japan, No. Trust Bank, Chgo., Plan Corp., Wheaton, Nat. Hdqs. Theosophical Soc., Wheaton, Zurich-Am. Ins. Co., Schaumberg, Assurance Agy., Ltd., Rolling Meadows, Ill. Bd. dirs. Fine Arts Rev. Com., DuPage County, Ill., 1982. Home: 926 N Scott St Wheaton IL 60187-3862 E-mail: pmblowrie@aol.com.

LOWRIE, WILLIAM G., former oil company executive; b. Painesville, Ohio, Nov. 17, 1943; s. Kenneth W. and Florence H. (Strickler) L.; m. Ernestine R. Rogers, Feb. 1, 1969; children: Kristen, Kimberly. BChemE, Ohio State U., 1966. Engr. Amoco Prodn. Co. subs. Standard Oil Co. (Ind.), New Orleans, 1966-74, area supt., Lake Charles, La., 1974-75, div. engr., Denver, 1975-78, div. prodn. mgr., Denver, 1978-79, v.p. prodn., Chgo., 1979-83; v.p. supply and marine transp. Standard Oil Co. (Ind.), Chgo., 1983-85; pres., Amoco Can., 1985-86; sr. v.p. prodn., Amoco Prodn. Co., 1986-87, exec. v.p. USA, 1987-88; exec. v.p. Amoco Oil Co., Chgo., 1989-90, pres., 1990-92; pres. Amoco Prodn. Co., 1992-94; exec. v.p. E&P sector Amoco Corp., 1994-95, pres. 1996-98, dep. CEO BP Amoco. Bd. dirs. Jr. Achievement, Northwestern Meml. Corp.; trustee, bd. dirs. Nat. 4-H Coun. Named Outstanding Engring. Alumnus, Ohio State U., 1979, Disting. Alumnis Ohio State U., 1985. Mem. Am. Petroleum Inst., Soc. Petroleum Engrs., Mid-Am. Club (Chgo.). Republican. Presbyterian. Home: 24 Eagle Island PL Sheldon SC 29941-3015

LOWRY, DAVID BURTON, lawyer; b. Bronxville, N.Y., Nov. 6, 1943; s. Burton S. and Virginia Evelyn (Ford) L. BA, U. Ariz., 1966, JD, 1969. Bar: Ariz. 1969, Oreg. 1973. Legal aid atty., Tucson and Coolidge, Ariz. and Hillsboro, Oreg.; asst. atty. gen. Oreg.; dep. dist. atty. Marion County, Oreg.; dep. pub. defender Mohave County, Ariz.; pvt. practice Portland, Oreg., 1989—. Mem. Oreg. State Bar Assn., Ariz. State Bar Assn., Am. Mgmt. Assn., Assn. Trial Lawyers Am., Alpha Delta Sigma, Phi Alpha Delta, Alpha Sigma Phi. Republican. Home: 13490 SW Genesis Loop Tigard OR 97223-3959 Office Phone: 503-245-6309. Business E-Mail: summary@integraonline.com.

LOWRY, DOUGLAS A., dean, composer, conductor; s. Mildred Lowry; m. Marcia J Rhoads, Dec. 28, 1971; children: Jennifer A, Melanie J, Timothy J. MusB, U. Ariz., 1974; MusM, U. So. Calif., 1978. Assoc. dean Thornton Sch. of Music U. So. Calif., L.A., 1992—2000; dean Conservatory Music U. Cin., Cin., 2000—. Composer: (songs) Christen the Voyage. Bd. dirs. Cin. (Ohio) Symphony Orch., 2000. Recipient Article of the Yr. award, Am. Music Tchr., 2004. Office: University of Cincinnati / CCM PO Box 210003 Cincinnati OH 45221-0003 Office Phone: 513-556-3737. Office Fax: 513-556-3330.

LOWRY, EDWARD FRANCIS, JR., lawyer; b. L.A., Aug. 13, 1930; s. Edward Francis and Mary Anita (Woodcock) L.; m. Patricia Ann Palmer, Feb. 16, 1963; children: Edward Palmer, Rachael Louise. Student, Ohio State U., 1948—50; AB, Stanford U., 1952, JD, 1954. Bar: Ariz. 1955, D.C. 1970, U.S. Supreme Ct. 1969. Camp dir. Quarter Circle V Bar Ranch, 1954; tchr. Orme Sch., Mayer, Ariz., 1954—56; trust rep. Valley Nat. Bank Ariz., 1958—60; pvt. practice Phoenix, 1960—; assoc. atty. Cunningham, Carson & Messinger, 1960—64; ptnr. Carson, Messinger, Elliott, Laughlin & Ragan, 1964—69, 1970—80, Gray, Plant, Mooty, Mooty & Bennett, 1981—84, Eaton, Lazarus, Dodge & Lowry Ltd., 1985—86; exec. v.p., gen. counsel Bus. Realty Ariz., 1986—93; pvt. practice, Scottsdale, Ariz., 1986—88; ptnr. Lowry & Froeb, Scottsdale, 1988—89, Lowry, Froeb & Clements, P.C., Scottsdale, 1989—90, Lowry & Clements P.C., Scottsdale, 1990, Lowry, Clements & Powell, P.C., Scottsdale, 1991—. Asst. legis. counsel Dept. Interior, Washington, 1969-70; mem. Ariz. Commn. Uniform Laws, 1972—, chmn., 1976-88; judge pro tem Ariz. Ct. Appeals, 1986, 92-94; mem. Nat. Conf. Commrs. on Uniform State Laws, 1972-97, life mem., 1997—. Chmn. Coun. of Stanford Law Socs., 1968; bd. dirs. Scottsdale Prevention Inst., 1999-2003; vice chmn. bd. trustees Orme Sch., 1972-74, treas., 1981-83; trustee Heard Mus., 1965-91, life trustee, 1991—, pres., 1974-75; bd. visitors Stanford Sch. Law; magistrate Town of Paradise Valley, Ariz., 1976-83, town councilman, 1998-2004, mayor, 1998-2004; juvenile ct. referee Maricopa County, 1978-83. Capt. USAF, 1956-58. Fellow Ariz. Bar Found. (founder); mem. ABA, Maricopa County Bar Assn., State Bar Ariz. (chmn. com. uniform laws 1979-85), Stanford Law Soc. Ariz. (past pres.), Scottsdale Bar Assn. (bd. dirs. 1991—, v.p. 1991, pres. 1992-95), Ariz. State U. Law Soc. (bd. dirs.), Delta Sigma Rho, Alpha Tau Omega, Phi Delta Phi. Home: 7600 N Moonlight Ln Paradise Valley AZ 85253-2938 Office: Lowry Clements & Powell PC 4200 N 82d St Ste 2001 Scottsdale AZ 85251-2771 Office Phone: 480-423-1200.

LOWRY, GEORGE S., art appraiser; Owner Swann Galleries, NYC, 1970—, pres., 1970—2001, chmn., 2001—. Author: Autographs: Identification & Price Guide, 2004. Mem.: Antiquarian Booksellers' Assn. Am., Universal Autograph Collectors Club, Manuscript Soc. Office: Swann Galleries 104 E 25th St New York NY 10010 Office Phone: 212-254-4710. Office Fax: 212-979-1017. Business E-Mail: glowry@swanngalleries.com.*

LOWRY, GLENN DAVID D., art museum director; b. N.Y.C., 1954; s. Warren and Laure (Lynn) L.; m. Susan Chambers, Aug. 24, 1974; children: Nicholas, Alexis, William. BA, Williams Coll., 1976; MA, Harvard U., 1978, PhD, 1982; PhD (hon.), Penn. Acad. Fine Arts, 2000. Asst. curator Fogg Art Mus., Harvard U., Cambridge, Mass., 1978-80; rsch. asst. Archeol. Survey of Mediterranean Town of Amalfi, Italy, 1980; curator Oriental art Mus. Art, R.I. Sch. Design, Providence, 1981-82; dir. Joseph and Margaret Muscarelle Mus. Art, Williamsburg, Va., 1982-84; curator Nr. Ea. art Arthur M. Sackler and the Freer Gallery Art, Smithsonian Instn., Washington, 1984-90, curatorial coord., 1987-89; dir. Art Gallery Ont., Toronto, Can., 1990-95, Mus. Modern Art, N.Y.C., 1995—. Mem. adv. coun. dept. art history and archaeology Columbia U., Smithsonian Coun.; steering com. Aga Kahn Arch. award. Co-author: Fatehpur-Sikri: A Source Book, 1985, From Concept to Context: Approaches to Asian and Islamic Calligraphy, 1986, An Annotated Checklist of the Vever Collection, 1988, A Jeweler's Eye: Art of the Book from the Vever Collection, 1988, Timur and the Princely Vision: Persian Art and Culture in the Fifteenth Century, 1989, Europe and the Arts of Islam: The Politics of Taste, 1991. Trustee Metro Toronto Conv. and Visitors Assn. Recipient Inst. Turkish Studies Travel award Smithsonian Instn., 1980, Spl. Exhbns. award, 1987, Scholarly Studies award, 1990., Officer of Order Arts & Letters award, Govt. France. Mem. Assn. Am. Art Mus. Dirs., Coll. Art Assn., Am. Acad. Arts & Scis. Mailing: Mus Modern Art 11 W 53rd St New York NY 10019-5498 Office Phone: 212-708-9773.

LOWRY, HAROLD, writer; Tchr. Spkr. in field. Author: 34 Books (Nat. Best Seller list USA Today). Mem.: Romance Writers of Am. (adv., nat. bd. dir., Regional Svc. award 1993, Nat. Svc. award 1993). Office: Romance Writers of America 16000 Stuebner Airline Rd #140 Spring TX 77379-7389

LOWRY, JAMES HAMILTON, management consultant; b. Chgo., May 28, 1939; s. William E. and Camille C. Lowry; m. Doris Davenport; 1 child, Aisha. BA, Grinnell Coll., 1961; M in Polit. and Instnl. Adminstrn., U. Pitts., 1965; diploma in mgmt., Harvard U., 1973. Assoc. dir. Peace Corps, Lima, Peru, 1965-67; spl. asst. to pres., project mgr. Bedford-Stuyvesant Restoration Corp., Bklyn., 1967-68; sr. assoc. McKinsey & Co., Chgo., 1968-75; pres. James H. Lowry & Assocs., Chgo., 1975-2000; v.p. Boston Consulting Group, 2000—. Mem. Small Bus. Adv. Com.; bd. dirs. Ill. Coalition, Holland Trust Fund. Mem. vis. com. Harvard U.; adv. bd. J.L. Kellogg Grad. Sch. Mgmt., Northwestern U., also adj. prof.; trustee Grinnell Coll.; bd. dirs. Chgo. United, Northwestern Hosp., Chgo. Pub. Libr., Chgo. Fgn. Affairs; chmn. City of Chgo. Durban/Chgo. Sister City Program; chmn. bd. trustees Sengstacke Enterprises. John Hay Whitney fellow, 1963-65; co-chmn. Chgo. United. Mem. Harvard Alumni Assn. (dir., vis. com.), Inst. Mgmt. Cons., Econ. Club, Univ. Club, Comml. Club Chgo. Home: 3100 N Sheridan Rd Chicago IL 60657-4954 Office: 200 S Wacker Dr Chicago IL 60606 Office Phone: 312-993-3300. E-mail: lowry.james@bcg.com.

LOWRY, LARRY LORN, engineering company executive; s. Frank William and Viola L.; m. Jean Carroll Greenbaum, June 23, 1973; 1 child, Alexandra Kristin BSEE, MIT, 1969, MSEE, 1970; MBA, Harvard U., 1972. Mgr. Boston Consulting Group, Menlo Park, Calif., 1972—80; sr. v.p., mng. ptnr. Booz, Allen & Hamilton Inc, San Francisco, 1980—2000, McKinsey & Co., 2001—03; chmn. Demand Tec Inc., 2004—. Western Electric fellow, 1969, NASA fellow, 1970 Mem. Sigma Xi, Tau Beta Pi, Eta Kappa Nu Home: 137 Stockbridge Ave Atherton CA 94027-3942

LOWRY, LOIS (LOIS HAMMERSBERG), writer; b. 1937; Author: A Summer to Die, 1977, Find A Stranger, Say Goodbye, 1978, Anastasia Krupnik, 1979, Autumn Street, 1980, Anastasia Again, 1981, Anastasia at Your Service, 1982, The One Hundredth Thing About Caroline, 1983, Taking Care of Terrific, 1983, Anastasia, Ask Your Analyst, 1984, Us and Uncle Fraud, 1984, Anastasia on Her Own, 1985, Switcharound, 1985, Anastasia Has the Answers, 1986, Anastasia's Chosen Career, 1987, Rabbie Starkey, 1987, All About Sam, 1988, Number the Stars, 1989 (John Newbery medal 1990), Your Move, J.P.!, 1990, Anastasia at This Address, 1991, Attaboy, Sam!, 1992, The Giver, 1993 (John Newbery medal 1994), Anastasia Absolutely, 1995, See You Around, Sam!, 1996, Stay! Keeper's Story, 1997, Looking Back, 1998, Zooman Sam, 1999, Gathering Blue, 2000, Gooney Bird Greene, 2002, The Silent Boy, 2003, Messenger, 2004, Gooney Bird and the Room Mother, 2005. Recipient Chgo. Tribune Young Adult Book prize, 2003. Address: 205 Brattle St Cambridge MA 02138-3345 Office: care Houghton Mifflin 222 Berkeley St Boston MA 02116-3748

LOWRY, MARILYN JEAN, horticultural retail company executive; b. Greensburg, Pa., Oct. 19, 1932; d. Clifford Henry and Martha McCune (Whitehead) Bushyager; m. John Cathcart Lowry, June 14, 1958; children: Martha Kim Hultberg, John Ryan, Nancy Lynn. BS, Ind. U. of Pa., 1954; MEd, Pa. State U., 1958. Tchr. Jeannette (Pa.) pub. schs., 1954-57; grad. asst. Pa. State U., University Park, 1957-58; demonstration sch. tchr. Towson (Md.) U., 1958-59; sec.-treas. Lowry & Co., Inc., Phoenix, Md., 1964—, 1987—. Master flower show judge Nat. Council State Garden Clubs, Inc., St. Louis, 1987—, landscape design critic, 1985—; master gardener U. Md. Extension Svc., 1984—. Mem. Lutherville Garden Club (pres. 1979—), Am. Assn. Nurserymen Aux. (pres. 1972), Federated Garden Clubs Md. (dir. dist. III 1981-83), Am. Nursery and Landscape Assn. (chmn. wholesale plant sales profls. 1999—). Republican. Presbyterian.

LOWRY, MONTECUE JUDSON, military historian; b. Ft. Worth, Tex., Feb. 23, 1930; s. Mark and Susan Olivia (Hall) Lowry; m. Jo Gail Tuttle, June 4, 1955 (div. Mar. 1985); 1 child, Mary; m. Jennifer Lynn Gunlock, Dec. 27, 1985; children: Jeremy, Montecue J. II. BS, U.S. Mil. Acad., West Point, N.Y., 1953; BA, U. So. Miss., 1958; MS, U.S. Naval Postgrad. Sch., Monterey, Calif., 1965; MA, U. So. Miss., 1967; PhD in Physics, Tex. Christian U., 1977; PhD in History, U. North Tex., 1988. Officer U.S. Army, 1953-73; chief quality control Vinnell Corp., Riyadh, Saudi Arabia, 1982-83; instr. history U. North Tex., Denton, 1983-86; mil. analyst CIA, Washington, 1986-88; assoc. prof. history Liberty U., Lynchburg, Va., 1988-89; assoc. prof. physics Houston Bapt. U., 1990-96; mil. historian, 1996—. Author: (book) Forge of West German Rearmament, 1990, Glasnost, 1991, Great Captains of the Faith, 2002; contbr. articles to profl. jours. Neighborhood commr. Boy Scouts Am., Fulda, Germany, 1960—62; pres. PTA, Fulda, 1961—62. Mem.: Soc. Mil. History. Avocations: bicycling, weightlifting, classical music, reading. Home: 7402 Redding Rd Houston TX 77036-5542

LOWRY, NICHOLAS D., art appraiser; b. NYC, 1968; s. George S. Lowry. BA in Art Hist., Cornell Univ., 1990. Tchr. English, Prague; journalist; dir., poster dept. Swann Galleries, NYC, 1995—, pres., prin. auctioneer, 2001—. Appraiser Antiques Roadshow, WGBH-PBS. Named one of 100 Most Eligible Bachelors, Gotham Mag., 2004. Office: Swann Galleries 104 E 25th St New York NY 10010 Office Phone: 212-254-4710. Office Fax: 212-979-1017. Business E-Mail: nlowry@swanngalleries.com.*

LOWRY, RALPH JAMES, SR., retired history educator; b. Pitts., Dec. 30, 1928; s. Robert William and Elizabeth (Carter) L; 1 son. AB with hons., Lincoln U. of Pa., 1955; MA, Temple U., 1957; PhD, U. N.Mex., 1972; postgrad., Carnegie-Mellon U., 1980. History tchr. William Penn High Sch. for Girls, Phila., 1957-58; asst. prof. dept. history So. Univ., Baton Rouge, La., 1959-64, Md. State U., Princess Anne, 1965-69; tchr. sixth grade John Marshall Elem. Sch., Albuquerque, 1969-70; assoc. prof. dept. history/geography Va. State U., Petersburg, 1970-78; tchr. English/social studies Schenley High Sch., Pitts., 1978-80; assoc. prof. history and geography Bishop Coll., Dallas, Tex., 1980-83; asst. prof. philosophy and history Alcorn State U., Lorman, Miss., 1983-90; assoc. prof. history and geography Lincoln Univ., Pa., 1991; ret. Lincoln Univ. of Pa., Pa., 1995. Adj. prof. Black history, John Tyler C.C., Chester, Va., 1971-72, U. Va., Danville, 1972-74; substitute tchr. Dallas Ind. Sch. System, 1983; history scholar U.S. Mil. Acad., West Point, N.Y., summer 1985. Contbr. articles to profl. jours./publs. With USN, 1948-52, Korea. John Hay Whitney fellow, Jessie Smith Noyes scholar, others. Mem. Am. Hist. Soc., Miss. Polit. Sci. Assn., Western Pa. Psychiat. Clinic, Smithsonian Assocs., Western Pa. Rsch. and Hist. Soc., Phi Delta Kappa, Phi Alpha Theta, Alpha Phi Omega, Beta Sigma Tau, Pi Gamma Mu, Alpha Kappa Mu, Alpha Mu Gamma, Shriners. Democrat. Episcopalian. Home: # 425 4511 Walnut St Philadelphia PA 19139-4559

LOWRY, RICH, editor; BA in English, Univ. Va., 1990. Joined National Review, 1992—, articles editor, 1994—97, editor, 1997—. Syndicated columnist; contbr. articles NY Times, Washington Post, Wall St. Jour.; polit. analyst Fox News, CNN, MSNBC, McLaughlin Group. Address: King Features Syndicate 235 E 45th St New York NY 10017 Office: National Review 4th Fl 215 Lexington Ave New York NY 10016 Office Phone: 212-679-7330.*

LOWRY, ROBERT DUDLEY, lawyer; b. Washington, Apr. 12, 1949; s. Robert Newton and Mary (Dudley) L.; m. Becky Jo Kangas, Aug. 3, 1974; children: Samuel Robert, Joseph Houston. BA in Biology, U. Oreg., 1971, postgrad., 1971-73, JD, 1980. Bar: Oreg. 1980, U.S. Dist. Ct. Oreg. 1980, U.S. Claims Ct. 1987, U.S. Supreme Ct. 1991, U.S. Ct. Appeals (9th cir.) 1991, U.S. Ct. Appeals (fed. cir.) 1992. Law clk. Oreg. Supreme Ct., Salem, 1980-81; ptnr. Jaqua & Wheatley, Eugene, 1981-91; prin. Robert D. Lowry, Atty. at Law, Eugene. Past chmn. Regional Trauma Adv. Bd., Oreg.; legal counsel Boy Scouts Am., Eugene, 1984—, March of Dimes; past chair Lawyer Reps. to 9th Cir. Jud. Conf., U.S. Cts. Dist. Oreg.; chair Lawyers Reps. Jud. Conf. U.S. Cts. for 9th Cir. Mem. ABA (chmn. joint state med.-legal com. 1988-89), ATLA, Lane County Bar Assn. (chmn. fed. ct. com. 1985-88, med. legal com. 1986-87), Oreg. Assn. Def. Counsel, Def. Rsch. Inst., Nat. Health Lawyers Assn., Phi Delta Phi. Democrat. Episcopalian. Home: 2875 Emerald St Eugene OR 97403-2504 Office: PO Box 12010 975 Oak St Ste 790 Eugene OR 97401-3121

LOWTHER, FRANK EUGENE, research physicist; b. Orrville, Ohio, Feb. 3, 1929; s. John Finger and Mary Elizabeth (Mackey) Lowther; m. Elizabeth E Koons, Apr. 21, 1951; children: Cynthia E, Victoria J, James A, Frank Eugene. BS Engring. Physics, Ohio State U., Columbus, 1952; postgrad., Boston U., 1952-54. Scientist missile divsn. Raytheon Corp., Boston, 1952-57, GE, Syracuse, N.Y., Daytona Beach, Fla., 1957-65; adv. to pres. Gen. Railway Signal, Rochester, N.Y., 1965-67; chief sci. Purification Sci., Inc., 1967-72; mgr. ozone R & D W.R. Grace Co., Curtis Bay, Md., 1972-75; sr. engring. assoc. Linde divsn. Union Carbide Corp., Tonawanda, N.Y., 1975-80; scientist Atlantic Richfield-Energy Conversion and Materials Lab., L.A., 1980—83; prin. scientist Atlantic Richfield-Corp. Tech., L.A., 1983-85, sci. advisor, 1985-88, rsch. advisor Plano, Tex., 1988-93, cons. tech. advisor, 1993—2001. Advisor Energy Sci Inc, Canandaigua, NY, 1993—, Custom Technology Creations Inc, Canandaigua, NY, 1993—, World Ecol Inc, Geneva, 1999—. Named to Wall of Honor, Nat Aviation and Space Exploration, 2001; recipient Inventor of the Yr Award, Patent Law Assn and Tech Socs Coun, 1976. Fellow: AIAA; mem.: AAAS, IEEE (life), NY Acad Scis, Masons. Achievements include patents for ozone technology, plasma generators, solid state power devices, internal combustion engines, electrodesorption, oil field technology, chemical and physical reactors, weapons, others. Home and Office: 4965 Adams Dr Canandaigua NY 14424-4200

LOWTHER, FREDERICK M., lawyer; b. Sewickly, Pa., Dec. 28, 1943; AB magna cum laude, Brown U., 1965; JD with honors, Yale U., 1968. Bar: NY 1969, Pa. 1970, DC 1973, US Supreme Ct. 1977. Law clk. to Hon. Caleb M. Wright US Dist. Ct., Dist. Del., Wilmington, 1968—69; assoc. Pepper Hamilton & Scheetz, Phila., 1969—71; atty. U.S. Maritime Adminstrn., 1971-72; dir. Office of Energy Programs U.S. Dept. Commerce, 1972-73; atty. Dickstein, Shapiro & Morin, Washington, 1973—82; ptnr. Dickstein, Shapiro Morin & Oshinsky LLP, Washington, 1982—, mng. ptnr., 1982—89, group leader, Corp. & Fin. Practice Group. Bd. dir. J. Makowski Corp., 1986—94, Yankee Energy Sys., 1992—98, Poseidon Resources Corp., 1995—, EEX Corp., 1997—, Shell Tech. Ventures Inc., 1996—99, Gulf Midstream Svcs., 1998—2000, Northeast Gas Markets, 1998—, KeySpan Energy Develop. Corp., 1998—. Mem.: US-Russian Coun., Pa. Bar Assn., NY State Bar Assn., DC Bar, Fed. Energy Bar Assn., ABA, Phi Beta Kappa, Phi Kappa Psi. Office: Dickstein Shapiro Morin & Oshinsky LLP 2101 L St NW Washington DC 20037-1526 Office Phone: 202-828-2208. Office Fax: 202-887-0689. Business E-Mail: lowtherf@dsmo.com.

LOWTHER, GERALD HALBERT, lawyer; b. Slagle, La., Feb. 18, 1924; s. Fred B. and Beatrice (Halbert) L.; children by previous marriage: Teresa, Craig, Natalie, Lisa. AB, Pepperdine Coll., 1951; JD, U. Mo., 1951. Bar: Mo. 1951. Since practiced in, Springfield; ptnr. firm Lowther, Johnson, Joyner, Lowther, Cully & Housley. Mem. Savs. and Loan Commn. Mo., 1965-68, Commerce and Indsl. Commn. Mo., 1967-73; lectr. U. Tex., 1955-57, Crested Butte, Colo., 1958-59 Contbr. articles law jours. Past pres. Ozarks Regional Heart Assn.; Del., mem. rules com. Democratic Nat. Conv., 1968; treas. Dem. Party Mo., 1968-72, mem. platform com., 1965, 67, mem. bi-partisan commn. to reapportion Mo. senate, 1966; Bd. dirs. Greene County Guidance Clinic, Ozark Christian Counseling Service, Greene County, Mo.; past pres. Cox Med. Center. Served with AUS, 1946-47; Col. staff of Gov. Hearnes 1964, 68, Mo. Mem. ABA, Mo. Bar Assn., Greene County Bar Assn., Def. Orientation Conf. Assn., Internat. Assn. Ins. Counsel, Def. Rsch. Inst., Springfield C. of C. Clubs: Kiwanian (pres. 1962), Quarterback (pres. 1958), Tip Off (pres. 1960). Office: 540 Foggy River Rd Hollister MO 65672 Home: 350 S John Q Hammons Pkwy Springfield MO 65806-2505

LOWTHER, JOHN MARTIN, writer; b. Pullman, W. Va., Nov. 14, 1921; s. Jesse Reh and Enid Elaine Lowther; m. Sarah Brenner Lowther, Sept. 7, 1950; children: Rex, Jocelyn, Geoffrey, Linda, Alan. BA, Syracuse U., 1951. Scheduler Ford Motor Co., Ypsilanti, Mich., 1955—57; writer Chrysler Missile Sterling Twp., Hazel Park, Mich., 1957—60, Marshall Space Ctr. (Chrysler), Huntsville, Ala., 1960—62, Kennedy Space Ctr. (Chrysler), Cocoa Beach, Fla., 1962—71; pub. affairs dir. Alfred U., Alfred, NY, 1971—74; planner Fla. Dept. Aging, Tallahassee, 1974—87; ret., 1987. Dir., found. Sr. Smarts Program, Fla. Author: (novel) Having Fun With God, 2005, plays, co-author 2 monographs. Radioman USN, 1940—45. Mem.: Scottish-Israelite Soc. (charter mem. 1970—), Internat. Toastmasters (spkr. 1963—68), VFW. Democrat. Avocations: table tennis, walking, fishing, reading, writing.

LOW-WESO, DENISE LEA, writing educator; b. Emporia, Kans., May 9, 1949; d. William Francis and Dorothy Lea (Bruner) Dotson; m. Donald Andrew Low, Jan. 10, 1972 (div.); children: David Andrew, Daniel Lee; m. Anthony Thomas Allard, Dec. 18, 1983 (div.); m. Thomas Francis Weso, Dec. 7, 1994. BA in English, U. Kans., 1971, MA in English, 1974; MFA in Creative Writing, Wichita State U., 1984; PhD in English, U. Kans., 1997. Part-time instr. Kans. State U., Manhattan, 1975-77; lectr. U. Kans., Lawrence, 1977-84, 88, Washburn U., Topeka, 1982, 84; instr. Haskell Indian Nations U., Lawrence, 1984—; vis. prof. U. Richmond, 2005. Editor, reader Cottonwood Press, Lawrence, 1977—84; bd. dirs. Woodley Meml. Press, Topeka, 1986—; vis. prof. U. Richmond, Va., 2005. Author: Dragon Kite, 1981, Spring Geese, 1984, Starwater, 1988; editor: Kansas Poems of William Stafford, 1990, Tulip Elegies: An Alchemy of Writing, 1993, Touching the Sky: Essays, 1995, New and Selected Poems, 1999, Thailand Journal, 2003, Word Alchemy: Essays, 2005; editor: (with Thomas Weso) Langston Hughes in Lawrence, 2004. Recipient Poetry Prize Roberts Found., 1989; fellow Nat. Endowment Humanities, 1987, 90; recipient Kans. Arts Commn. Lit. fellow, 1991. Mem. MLA, Associated Writing Programs. Democrat. Congregationalist. Office: Haskell Indian Nations U Lawrence KS 66046 E-mail: dlow@haskell.edu.

LOWY, DOUGLAS RONALD, oncologist; b. N.Y.C., 1942; MD, NYU, 1968. Intern Stanford Med. Ctr., Calif., 1968—69, resident in internal medicine, 1969—70; rsch. assoc. lab. viral diseases Nat. Inst. Allergy and Infectious Diseases, NIH, 1970—73; resident in dermatology Yale-New Haven Med. Ctr., 1973—75; with Lab. Cellular Oncology, Nat. Cancer Inst., Bethesda, Md., 1975—83, chief of lab., 1983—; dep. dir. divsn. basic scis. Nat. Cancer Inst., 1996—. Recipient Wallace Rowe award for virus rsch. Mem.: Inst. of Medicine, 2004. Office: Nat Cancer Inst Lab Cellular Oncology Bldg 36 Rm 1D-32 Bethesda MD 20892-4040

LOWY, FREDERICK HANS, academic administrator, psychiatrist; b. Grosspetersdorf, Austria, Jan. 1, 1933; arrived in Can., 1944; s. Eugen and Maria (Braun) Lowy; m. Anne Louise Cloudsley, June 25, 1965 (dec. 1973); children: David, Eric, Adam; m. Mary Kathleen O'Neil, June 1, 1975; 1 child, Sarah. BA, McGill U., Montreal, Can., 1955, MD, 1959, LLD, 2001, U. Toronto, Can., 1998. Intern, resident in internal medicine Royal Victoria Hosp., Montreal, Canada; resident in psychiatry U. Cin. Hosp., Cin. VA Hosp.; psychoanalytic tng. Montreal Psychoanalytic Inst.; psychiatrist Allan Meml. Inst.-Royal Victoria Hosp., Montreal-McGill U. Faculty Medicine, 1965-70; psychiatrist-in-chief Ottawa Civic Hosp., Canada; prof. dept. psychiatry U. Ottawa, 1971-74; prof. psychiatry, chmn. dept. U. Toronto, dir. Clarke Inst. Psychiatry, 1974-80, dean Sch. Medicine, 1980-87, dir. Ctr. for Bioethics, 1989-95; pres., vice chancellor Concordia U., Montreal, 1995—. Co-editor: (book) A Method of Psychiatry, 1980, Alzheimer's Disease Research, 1991; contbr. articles to profl. jours. Decorated officer Order of Can. Fellow: Am. Coll. Psychiatrists, Royal Coll. Physicians and Surgeons; mem.: Am. Psychiat. Assn., Can. Psychiat. Assn. (editor jour. 1972—76), Internat. Psychoanalytic Assn. Office: Concordia U Office of President 1455 de Maisonneuve Blvd W Montreal PQ Canada H3G 1M8 E-mail: lowyfh@concordia.ca.

LOWY, GEORGE THEODORE, lawyer; b. N.Y.C., Oct. 6, 1931; s. Eugene and Elizabeth Lowy; m. Pier M. Foucault, Sept. 7, 1957. BA cum laude, LLB cum laude, NYU. Bar: N.Y. 1955, U.S. Dist. Ct. (so. dist.) N.Y. 1958, U.S. Supreme Ct. 1972, U.S. Ct Appeals (2d cir.) 1975. Assoc. Cravath, Swaine and Moore, N.Y.C., 1957-65, ptnr., 1965—81, sr. coun., 1982—. Trustee NYU Law Ctr. Found.; bd. dirs. Equitable Life Assurance Soc. U.S., Eramet, Paris, Axa Fin., U.S.; adj. prof. NYU Law Sch., 1983—88; bd. overseers Brandeis U. Grad. Sch. Internat. Econs. and Fin. Fellow ABA; mem. Am. Law Inst., Assn. of Bar of City of N.Y. (chmn. com. on corp. law), Internat. Bar Assn., Union Internat. des Avocats, Cercle Interallie Paris. Home: 580 Park Ave New York NY 10021-7313 Office: Cravath Swaine & Moore World Wide Pla 825 8th Ave Fl 43 New York NY 10019-7416 E-mail: glowy@cravath.com.

LOWY, PETER, executive; Exec. dir. Westfield Mgmt. Ltd., 1986, Westfield Holdings Ltd., 1987, Westfield Am. Mgmt. Ltd., 1996, mng. dir. LA, 1997—, bd. dir. Bd. gov. Nat. Assn. of Real Estate Investment Trusts; bd. dir. Lowy Inst. for Internat. Policy. Office: Westfield Corp Inc 11601 Wilshire Blvd 11th Fl Los Angeles CA 90025-1748 Office Phone: 310-478-4456. Office Fax: 310-478-1267.

LOY, FRANK ERNEST, retired federal agency administrator; b. Nuremberg, Germany, Dec. 25, 1928; arrived in U.S., 1939; s. Alfred Loewi and Elizabeth (Loeffler) L.; m. Dale Haven, 1963; children: Lisel, Eric Anthony. BA, UCLA, 1950; LLB, Harvard U., 1953. Bar: DC 1953, Calif. 1954. With O'Melveny & Myers, L.A., 1954-65; spl. asst. to adminstr. FAA, 1961-63; spl. cons. to adminstr. AID, 1963-64; dep. asst. sec. state for econ. affairs, 1965-70; sr. v.p. Pan Am. World Airways, Inc., N.Y.C., 1970-73; pres. Pennsylvania Co., Washington, 1974-79, Penn Ctrl. Corp., 1978-79; dir. Bur. Refugee Programs, Dept. State, Washington, 1980-81; pres. German Marshall Fund of U.S., 1981-95; chmn. League Conservation Voters, Washington, 1993-98, pres., 1995-96; chmn. Found. Civil Soc., 1997-98; under sec. of state for Global Affairs U.S. Govt., Washington, 1998—2001. Chmn. U.S. delegation to Climate Change Conf., The Hague, The Netherlands, 2000; dir. Nat. Gallery of Art, 1998—2001; vis. lectr. Yale Law Sch., 1996; dir. Pharm. Product Devel., Inc., 1995—98. Chmn. bd. trustees Goddard Coll., Vt., 1976-78, Environ. Def. Fund, 1983-90, Washington Ballet, 1991-94; U.S. mem. Bd. Regional Environ. Ctr. for Ctrl. and Ea. Europe, Budapest, Hungary, 1990-97; chair Environment 2004, 2003-; vice chair Resources for the Future, 2002-. With U.S. Army, 1953-55. Personal E-mail: loyfrank@aol.com.

LOYA, RANALDO, senior physician assistant; b. Whittier, Calif., July 1, 1954; s. Bernard Romero and Nora (Valverde) L. AA in Gen. Edn., Rio Hondo Coll., Whittier, Calif., 1980; BS in Health Sci., Calif. State U., Dominguez Hills, 1982; MHA, U. LaVerne, 1997. Cert. primary care physician asst.; cert. physician's asst.; cert. personal trainer IFPA; cert. sports nutritionist. Emergency med. technician, ambulance driver, attendant Adams Ambulance Co., South Gate, Calif., 1974-75; emergency room technician, clerk Maywood-Bell Cmty. Hosp., Bell, Calif., 1975; sr. physician asst. Physician Asst. Svcs., L.A., 1981-94; physician asst. urgent care Ball-Taft Med. Clinic Ctr., Anaheim, Calif., 1984-85; sr. physician asst., corp. v.p., admin. Signal Med. Mgmt., Long Beach, Calif., 1985-88; sr. physician asst. U. Calif. Irvine Med. Ctr., Orange, Calif., 1988-90, U. So. Calif. Emergency Med. Assoc., L.A., 1989-90, U. Calif. Mt. Zion Med. Ctr., San Francisco, 1990-94, La Clinica Esperanza Mission Neighborhood Health Ctr., San Francisco, 1991-94. Fellow: Am. Acad. Physician Assts., Washington, 1982—; Calif. Acad. Physician Assts., Anaheim, 1982—; past mem. instl. review bd., Project Inform, San Francisco, 1991-92. Contbr. New England Journal of Medicine, 1990; mem. editl. bd. Clinician Reviews. Human rights commr., City of Palm Springs, Calif., 1996—; mem. Long Beach Pride, Inc., 1987-90, past v.p.; mem. Human Rights Campaign Fund, Washington, 1996—; mem. Orange County Gay and Lesbian Comm. Svcs. Ctr., Garden Grove, Calif., 1987-88; mem. adv. bd. The Desert Sun Newspaper Cmty.; mem. Dr. Martin Luther King Commemorative Day Com., Amnesty Internat. With USN, 1975-79, Hawaii. Recipient Meritorious Mast, USN, 1978. Fellow Physicians Assts. Latino Heritage; mem. NAACP, Nat. Assn. Mulitcultural Edn., Calif. Acad. Physician Assts. (minority affairs com.), Calif. Assn. Human Rels. Orgns., Nat. Trust for Hist. Preservation, Internat. AIDS Soc., Drew U. Med. Sch. Alumni Assn., Hispanic C. of C. Democrat. Mem. Unity Ch. Avocations: reading, public speaking, weightlifting. Home: 1179 N Calle Rolph Palm Springs CA 92262-4938

LOYD, JOYCE SCHENCK, elementary school educator; b. Ridley Park, Pa., July 27, 1955; d. Robert Crowley and Janet Mae Schenck; m. William Bell Loyd, Oct. 6, 1984. BS in Elem. Edn., Slippery Rock U., 1977; MA in Elem. Edn., Austin Peay U., 1981, postgrad., 1990—91. Cert. tchr. Ky. Tchr. multi-age grades 2-3 Ft. Campbell (Ky.) Schs., 1977—83, tchr. multi-age grades 4-5, 1983—86, mid. sch. tchr. grade 6, 1986—97, tchr. 5th grade, 1997—. Named Tchr. of the Yr., Dept. Def. Edn. Activity, 2004, Model Tchr. for Reading, Nat. Renaissance Reading, 2001, 2003, Ky. Dist. Tchr. of the Yr., Dept. of Def. Ky. Sch. Dist., 2004; recipient Supt.'s People Helping People award, Ft. Campbell Sch. Dist. Supt., 1984. Mem.: PTO, ASCD, Nat. Coun. Tchrs. Math., Phi Delta Kappa (pres., v.p., sec., historian 1983—2004). Methodist. Avocations: collecting rabbits, travel, reading, collecting wine glasses. Home: 112 Beulah Blvd Pleasant View TN 37146 Office: Lucas Elem Sch 2115 Airborne St Fort Campbell KY 42223 Office Phone: 931-431-7711. Personal E-mail: hoptoit@worldnet.att.net. Business E-Mail: joyce.loyd@am.dodea.edu.

LOYD, MARTHA ROSE, forester; b. Sanford, Fla., Oct. 24, 1951; d. Charles W. and Geraldine (Greer) Rose; m. Randall Allen Loyd, Oct. 1, 1983 (div. Oct. 1998); children: Erin Leslie, Matthew Allen. BS in Forestry, U. Fla., 1978. Unit mgr. Scott Paper Co., Monroeville, Ala., 1978—86, regional mgr., 1986—93; mgr. silvicultural ops. Kimberly-Clark, Monroeville, 1993—99; divsn. forester Molpus Timberlands Mgmt., Huxford, Ala., 1999—2002; pres. Southeast Timberlands Mgmt., Monroeville, 2003—. Founder Monroeville Bus. Women, 1985; bd. dirs. YMCA, Monroeville, 1998—99. Mem.: Ala. Forestry Assn. (com. chairperson 1991—93). Avocations: gardening, travel, yoga, home improvement projects. Home: 456 Overlook Dr Monroeville AL 36460 Office: Southeast Timberlands Mgmt PO Box 477 Monroeville AL 36461

LOYD, WARD EUGENE, lawyer, state legislator; b. Henderson, Ky., Feb. 8, 1943; s. Ward Beecher Loyd and Maxine Watkins; m. Suzanne Keeler, Dec. 29, 1966; children: Katherine Marie, Keele Suzanne. BA, Southwestern Coll., 1965; JD with honors, Washburn U., 1968. Bar: Kans. 1968, U.S. Dist. Ct. Kans. 1968, U.S. Ct. Appeals (10th cir.) 1969. Pvt. practice, Garden City, Kans., 1968—; mem. Kans. Ho. of Reps., 1998—. Gen. counsel Garden City Urban Renewal Agy., 1969-75, Garden City Pub. Sch. Sys., 1972-91, Garden City C.C., 1971-, S.W. Kans. Area Coop., Ensign, 1995—; chmn. Kans. Criminal Justice Recodification, Rehab. and Restoration Commn., 2004—; mem. Kans. Supreme Ct. Stds. Com., Topeka, 1980, Kans. Supreme Ct. Client Protection Fund Commn., 2000-, mem., child support guidelines adv. commn., 2002-; bd. dirs. Western State Bank, Garden City. Comments editor Washburn Law Jour., 1967-68. City commr. City of Garden City, 1985-89, 90-94, 97, mayor, 1986, 88; mem. Cmty. Congl. Ch. Garden City; past bd. mem., past pres. Cmty. Day Care Ctr.; past mem. Kans. League Municipalities. Recipient Award of Merit, Garden City Area C. of C., 1992, Outstanding Pub. Official of Yr., Kans. Assn. Addition Profls., 2003. Fellow Kans. Bar Found.; mem. Nat. Assn. Sch. Bds. (coun. sch. attys.), Kans. Bar Assn. (mem. ethics com. 1978-82), S.W. Kans. Bar Assn. (pres. 1986-88, sec. 1992-93, dir.), Kans. Sch. Attys. Assn. (regional dir. 1980-84), Kans. Assn. Def. Counsel, Finney County Bar Assn., Garden City C. of C. (bd. dirs. 1990-92), Phi Alpha Delta (justice 1968). Republican. Home: 2203 Center Garden City KS 67846-3525 Office: Ward Loyd Law Office LLC PO Box 834 118 W Pine St Garden City KS 67846-5444 Office Phone: 620-275-1415. E-mail: loyd@gcnet.com.

LOYEVSKY, MARK MICHAEL, biochemist, parasitologist, researcher; b. Kharkov, Ukraine, Oct. 11, 1952; arrived in U.S., 1995; s. Michael Peter and Rachel Mark Loyevsky; m. Violetta Semion Ilstein, July 9, 1976; 1 child, Konstantin. MS in Biochemistry, State U. Kharkov, 1977; PhD in Biochemistry, Inst. Cryobiology, Ukrainian Acad. Sci., Kharkov, 1985. Rsch. assoc. Inst. Cryobiology, Kharkov, 1981—91; postdoctoral rschr. Hebrew U., Jerusalem, 1991—95; adj. scientist NIH, Bethesda, Md., 1997—2005; rsch. scientist George Washington U., Washington, 1995—99; asst. prof. microbiology Howard U., Washington, 1999—2004; dir. parasitology Sanaria, Inc., Rockville, Md., 2004—. Contbr. articles to profl. jours. Rsch. grantee, Israel Ministry Sci., 1991, Novartis Pharma AG, 1999. Mem.: Internat. BioIron Soc., Am. Soc. Tropical Medicine and Hygiene. Achievements include research in iron-regulatory pathways in the malaria parasite, Plasmodium falciparum; working on the development of live, attenuated sporozoite antimalarial vaccine. Avocations: soccer, cats, art galleries. Home: 12408 Benjamin Hill Ln Fairfax VA 22033 Office: Sanaria Inc 12115 Parklawn Dr Ste L Rockville MD 20852 Office Phone: 301-770-3222. E-mail: mloyevsky@sanaria.com.

LOZANO, ALFREDO, language educator; b. Monterrey, Nuevo Leon, Mexico, Dec. 3, 1965; s. Alfredo Lozano and Norma Lopez; m. Lina Garza; children: Alfredo, Angel. MD, Hosp. Universitario Uanl, Mex., 1988. Plastic Surgeon Plastic, Aesthetic, And Reconstructive Surgery Mexican Coun., 1994; Bilingual Educator State Bd. Of Educators In Tex., 2002. Chief of residents plastic and reconstructive surgery svc. UANL, Mexico, 1993—94; head of the capacitation and rsch. dept. Sec. Of Health, Salamanca, Mexico, 1995—96, mcpl. dir. Uriangato, Mexico, 1996—99, Yuriria, Mexico, 1999—2001; bilingual educator Ft. Bend Isd, Houston, 2004—. Bd. mem. Med. Collegiate Assn., Moroleon, Guanajuato, Mexico, 1998—99. Mem. Mcpl. Devel. Coun., Uriangato, Mexico, 1996—98; founding mem. Nat. Campaign of Tolerance, 2005; founder The Wall Tolerance Civil Rights Meml. Ctr., Montgomery, Ala., 2005. Mem.: AASCD, Tex. Coun. Elem. Sci., Sci. Tchrs. Assn. Tex., Nat. Coun. Tchrs. Math., NY Acad. Sci. Avocations: travel, photography. Personal E-mail: apll65@msn.com.

LOZANO, JOSE, nephrologist; b. San Vicente, El Salvador, Feb. 11, 1941; came to U.S., 1968; s. Jose E. and Transito Maria (Mendez) L.; m. Hilda Berganza, Jan. 27, 1965; children: Jose E., Claudia Maria. MD, U. El Salvador, 1965. Diplomate Am. Bd. Internal Medicine, Am. Bd. Nephrology. Rotating intern Nat. Med. Ctr., San Salvador, El Salvador, 1963-64; asst. resident in internal medicine Rosales Hosp., San Salvador, 1965-66, resident in internal medicine, 1966-67, chief resident in internal medicine, 1967-68; resident in internal medicine Baylor U. Affiliated Hosps., Houston, 1968-70, fellow in nephrology, 1970-71, 73-74; asst. prof. medicine U. El Salvador, 1971-72; internist and nephrologist Social Security Hosp., San Salvador, 1971-72; instr. in medicine Baylor Coll. Medicine, Houston, 1974-75, asst. prof. medicine in nephrology, 1975-76, clin. asst. prof. medicine, 1976-80; mem. staff internal medicine St. Elizabeth Hosp., Beaumont Med./Surg. Hosp., Bapt. Hosp., Beaumont, Tex., 1976; med. dir. Golden Triangle Dialysis Ctr., Beaumont, 1977-98, BMA Jasper, Jasper, Tex., 1986-98, BMA Orange, Orange, Tex., 1987-90. Med. dir. Jasper Dialysis Ctr., 1986-98; mem. Kidney Health Care Adv. Com., 1981-82; pesenter in field. Contbr. articles to profl. publs. Fellow ACP, Am. Soc. Nephrology; mem. AMA, Internat. Soc. Nephrology, Tex. Med. Assn., Harris County Med. Soc., Jefferson County Med. Soc., Physicians for A Nat. Health Plan. Office: 3150 Medical Ctr Dr Ste 3 Beaumont TX 77701 E-mail: bmtnp410@aol.com. *In terms of health care we need a system that provides easy, uncomplicated access to primary care services. We urgently need a health care system that provides universal and comprehensive access to health care without considerations given to the ability to pay, race, gender, religion or sexual orientation. We need a system that is independent of employment, in which people with existing conditions are not restricted from free and adequate access to health care. The creation of a universal health care system is in the best interests of all citizens of this country.*

LOZANO, RAMIRO C., music educator, director; b. San Benito, Tex., Nov. 28, 1962; s. Yolanda De La Cerda Garcia Moreno. MusB, Tex. A&I U., 1987. Cert. music educator Tex. Edn. Assn., 1987. Tchr. music O'Grady Elem. Sch., Mission, Tex., 1987—90; dir. choir Zapata (Tex.) City Ind. Sch. Dist., 1990—94, Castro Elem. Sch., Mission, 1994—98, Dr. Garza Elem., San Benito, Tex., 1998—2003, Berta Cabaza MS, San Benito, Tex., 2003—. Pvt. music instr., 2001. Cantor, organist St. Benedict Roman Cath. Ch., San Benito, Tex., 1986—88, dir. schola cantorum, 2003—05; dir. music liturgy Our Lady of Guadalupe Roman Cath. Ch., Mission, Tex., 1994—98; dir. music litrugy Our Lady of Lourdes Roman Cath. Ch., Zapata, Tex., 1990—94; dir. music liturgy Our Lady Queen of Universe Roman Cath. Ch., San Benito, 1998—99; diocesan chorister Corpus Christi (Tex.) Cathedral, 1991—94; cantor, organist Our Lady of Sorrows Roman Cath. Ch., McAllen, Tex., 1988—89. Named Elem. Tchr. of Yr., San Benito City Ind. Sch. Dist., 2001. Mem.: Tex. Music Educatiors Assn. Democrat. Roman Catholic. Avocations: organ, schola cantorum, religious education, travel, movies. Home: 25345 Pennsylvania Ave San Benito TX 78586 Office: Berta Cabaza Choral Department 2901 Shafer Rd San Benito TX 78586 Office Phone: 956-361-6628. Office Fax: 956-361-6608. Personal E-mail: ramloz@msn.com. E-mail: rlozano2@mail.sanbenito.k12.tx.us.

LOZANO-CENTANINO, MONICA CECILIA, publishing executive; b. L.A., July 21, 1956; d. Ignacio Eugenio and Marta Eloisa (Navarro) Lozano; m. Marcelo Centanino, Sept. 27, 1987; 1 child, Santiago Alberto. Student, U. Oreg., 1974—76; student San Francisco City Coll.; LHD (hon.), Occidental Coll., 1999. Mgr. Copy-Copia, Inc., San Francisco, 1980—85; mng. editor La Opinion, L.A., 1985—89, assoc. pub., 1989—91, assoc. pub., exec. editor, 1991—2000, pres., COO, 2000—04, pub., CEO, 2004—; pub. El Eco del Valle, San Fernando, Calif., 1990—91; v.p. Lozano Comm., 2000—04; sr. v.p. ImpreMedia LLC, 2004—. Bd. dirs. The Walt Disney Co., Union Bank Calif., Calif. Health Care Found., Tenet Healthcare Corp., Nat. Coun. La Raza; trustee SunAm. Asset Mgmt. Corp. Trustee U. So. Calif.; mem. bd. regents U. Calif., 2000—; bd. dirs. L.A. County Mus. Art, Venice Family Clinic, Ctrl. Am. Resource Ctr. Recipient Humanitarian award, Cen. Am. Refugee Ctr., L.A., 1989, Outstanding Achievement, Mex. Am. Opportunities Found., L.A., 1989. Mem. Nat. Assn. Hispanic Pubs., Nat. Assn. Hispanic Journalists, Calif. Hispanic Pubs., Am. Soc. Newspaper Editors, Calif. Chicano News Assn., Nat. Network Hispanic Women. Avocations: photography, reading, water sports. Office: La Opinion 411 W Fifth St Los Angeles CA 90013

LOZANSKY, EDWARD DMITRY, physicist, consultant, writer; b. Kiev, Ukraine, Feb. 10, 1941; arrived in U.S., 1977; s. Dmitry R. and Dina M. (Chizhik) Lozansky; m. Tatiana I. Yershov, Feb. 27, 1971; 1 child, Tania. MS, Moscow Phys. Engring. Inst., 1966; PhD, Inst. Atomic Energy, Moscow, 1969; LHD, Waynesburg Coll., 1995. Asst. prof. Moscow State U., 1969-71; assoc. prof. Mil. Tank Acad., Moscow, 1971-75; prof. U. Rochester, NY, 1977-80, Am. U., Washington, 1981-83, L.I. U., Bklyn., 1983-87; pres. Independent U., Washington, 1987-91, Russia House, Inc., 1991—, Am. U. Moscow, 1992—, Am. Univs. in Russia, Ukraine and New Independent States, 1994—. Author: Theory of the Spark, 1976, Mathematics, 1976, For Tatiana, 1984, Andrei Sakharov, 1986, Mathematical Competitions, 1988, Democracy: USA-Russia, 1994, Winning Solutions, 1996, Russia: Experience in Democracy, 1997, Foundations of Free Society, 1998, Sociology of Politics: Comparative Study of the American and Russian Realities, 2001, Society, Power, Politics, 2003, Russian Lobby in America, 2004. Mem.: Russian Acad. Soc. Scis. Avocations: skiing, chess, lecturing on Russia. Office: Russia House 1800 Connecticut Ave NW Washington DC 20009-5731 Office Phone: 202-986-6010. Personal E-mail: lozansky@aol.com.

LOZITO, GILDA LELIA, artist, painter; b. N.Y.C., Dec. 20; d. Massimo and Concetta (D'Amico) Greco; m. Rocco Jerome Lozito, Aug. 19, 1941. Student, Bono Hall Acad Fine Arts, 1937-41, Norton Sch. Art, 1949-53, Palm Beach Community Coll., 1960. Art instr. nat. Youth Adminstrn. Art Ctr., N.Y.C., 1939-41; Fed. Civil Svc., Eglin Field, Fla., 1942-45, Morrison Field, Fla., 1946; Architect Agnes Ballard, West Palm Beach, Fla., 1947-52; art instr. pvt. practice West Palm Beach, Fla., 1953—; artist Bagatelle Art Shop, Palm Beach, Fla., 1960-65; art consignments Gallery Gemini, Palm Beach, Fla., 1962-69; art judge City of West Palm Beach, 1968; lectr., cons. Fla., 1953—. Cons. in art Pub. Civic Activities, 1970s; dir. exhbns. Nat. League of Am. Pen Women, Palm Beach, 1980s; art instr. in pvt. practice, 1996-99. One woman shows at Norton Mus. Art, West Palm Beach, 1954, Hobbelink Kaastra Art Gallery, Palm Beach, 1955, Upstairs Art Gallery, Palm Beach, 1959, 1st Nat. In Palm Beach, 1970, 71, 72, 73, 74, 76, 90, 91, 92, 93, 94; exhibited in group shows at Palm Beach Coun. Arts, Soc. Four Arts Contemporary Juried Exhbn., Northwood Inst. Art, West Palm Beach, 1997, Palm Beach (Fla.) Garden Gallery Rest., 1998; contbr. illustrations to mags. and jour., art reprodns. for book covers, art revs. in Palm Beach Today, Palm Beach's Pictorial P.B. with photograph, Palm Beach Daily News, Photo. of Paintings; portrait in oil installation wall of City Hall, West Palm Beach, 1995; honored in Heart Ball mag., 2000; portrait St. Edward's Ch., Palm Beach, 2004. Chairperson 20th Anniversary Celebration of Nat. League of Arts & Pen, 1985. Recipient Hon. Diploma awarded in the 2,000 Women of Achievement, 1972, First Prize award Palm Beach Art League Juried Art Exhibition, 1953, First Prize award Lake Worth Art League, 1954, Awards of merit Norton Sch. of Art, 1951, 52, Award of Merit, Palm Beach Nat. League of Art & Pen Women, 1975. Mem. Fla. Artists Group Inc., Soc. Four Arts, Fla. Fedn. Art, Artists Equity Nat., Nat. League Am. Arts and Pen Women (pres.), Palm Beach Quills and Artists, Northwood's Women Aux. in Arts, Nat. Mus. Women Artists, Nat. Mus. Women in the Arts (charter), Fla. Watercolor Soc., Nat. League Am. Women (pres. Palm Beach branch 1985, chairperson anniversary celebration), Norton Mus. Art, Il Circolo Cultural Assn., Nat. League Am. Pen-Arts Women (art presentation for exhbn., lectr. 2003). Avocations: poetry, ceramics, sculpture, calligraphy, gardening. Home and Office: 307 Cordova Rd West Palm Beach FL 33401-7907

LOZOFF, BETSY, pediatrician; b. Milw., Dec. 19, 1943; d. Milton and Marjorie (Morse) L.; 1 child, Claudia Brittenham. BA, Radcliffe Coll., 1965; MD, Case Western Res. U., 1971, MS, 1981. Diplomate Am. Bd. Pediat. From asst. prof. to prof. pediatrics Case Western Res. U., Cleve., 1974-93; prof. pediatrics U. Mich., Ann Arbor, 1993—, dir. Ctr. for Human Growth and Devel., 1993—. Recipient Rsch. Career Devel. award Nat. Inst. Child Health and Human Devel., 1984-88. Fellow Am. Acad. Pediatrics; mem. Soc. for Pediatric Rsch., Soc. Rsch. in Child Devel. (program com. 1991-97), Soc. Behavioral Pediatrics (exec. com. 1985-88), Ambulatory Pediatric Soc. Office: Univ Mich Ctr Human Growth and Devel 300 N Ingalls St Ann Arbor MI 48109-2007

LU, ADOLPH, physicist, researcher; b. Chengdu, Sichuan, China, Feb. 19, 1942; U.S.1965; s. Frank Chao and Jean Wang Lu; m. Karen Wenfeng Liu, Mar. 10, 1993. BS, Queen's U., Kingston, Can., 1964; MA, U. Toronto, Can., 1965; PhD, U. Calif., Berkeley, 1973. Rsch. physicist U. Paris, 1973—75; rsch. faculty U. Calif., Santa Barbara, 1976—2002, Berkeley, 2002—. Jour. referee IEEE Procs., 1998—. Contbr. articles to more than 400 profl. pubs. Mem.: Am. Phys. Soc. Avocations: skiing, kayaking, calligraphy, guitar. Home: 117 Eagle Trace Dr Half Moon Bay CA 94019 Office: Univ Calif Physics Dept 301 LeConte Hall Berkeley CA 94720

LU, BING, medical researcher, educator; b. Juancheng, Shangdong, China, Oct. 14, 1967; m. Jing Zhou, June 19, 1999. MD, China Med. U., Shenyang, 1991; MPH, Chinese Ctr.Disease Control and Prevention, Beijing, 1997; MS, U. NC, 2002—02, DPH, 2002—. Rsch. assoc. Jinan (China) Ctr. Disease Control, 1991—94; asst. prof. Chinese Ctr. Disease Control and Prevention, 1997—99; rsch. asst. U. NC, Chapel Hill, 1999—. Fellow NIH. Mem.: Am. Statis. Assn. (hon.). Home: 618 S LaSalle St Apt 6H Durham NC 27705 Office: U NC-Chapel Hill 123 W Frankin St Chapel Hill NC 27516

LU, BO, medical educator; s. Lu and Zhang; 1 child, Brian. Cert. Radiation Oncology Am. Bd. of Radiology, 2004. Asst. prof. Vanderbilt U., Nashville, Tenn., 2002—. Rsch. grant, Dept. of Def. Office: Vanderbilt U 1301 22nd Ave S TVC B902 Nashville TN 37232 Office Phone: 615-343-9233. Office Fax: 615-343-0161.

LU, CAI-CHENG, engineering educator, researcher; m. Cheryl Pan; 1 child, Cynthia. BS, Beijing U. Aeronautics and Astronatics, 1983, MS, 1986; PhD, U. Ill., 1995. Rsch. scientist Ctr. for Computational Electromagnetics, Urbana, Ill., 1995—97, Demaco, Inc., Urbana, 1997—99; assoc. prof. U. Ky., Lexington, 1999—. Recipient Younger Investigator award, Office of Naval Rsch., 2000—03, CAREER award, NSF, 2001—. Mem.: IEEE, Phi Kappa Phi. Achievements include pioneering study and implementation of multilevel fast multipole algorithms in computational electromagnetics. Office: U Ky 453 Anderson Hall Lexington KY 40506 Office Fax: 859-257-3092.

LU, DAVID JOHN, historian, writer; b. Keelung, Taiwan, Sept. 28, 1928; arrived in U.S., 1950, naturalized, 1960; s. Ming and Yeh (Lai) Lu; m. Annabelle Compton, May 29, 1954; children: David John, Daniel Mark, Cynthia King, Stephen Paul. BA in Econs, Nat. Taiwan U., 1950; postgrad., Westminster Theol. Sem., Phila., 1950-52; M. Internat. Affairs, Columbia, 1954; certificate, East Asian Inst., 1954, PhD, 1960. Editor Prentice-Hall, Inc., 1956-60; instr. Rutgers U., 1959; asst. prof. history Bucknell U., Lewisburg, Pa., 1960-64, assoc. prof., 1964-69, prof., 1969-94, prof. emeritus, 1994—, dir. Ctr. for Japanese Studies, 1965-94. Cons. on global edn. Pa. Dept. Edn., 1961—62, 1978, U.S. Dept. Edn., 1973—85; resident dir. associated Kyoto program Doshisha U., 1987—88. Author: From the Marco Polo Bridge to Pearl Harbor, 1961; author: (Japanese edit.) Taiheiyo Senso e no Dotei, 1967; author: Sources of Japanese History, 1974, Bicentennial History of the United States, 1976, The Life and Times of Matsuoka Yosuke, 1880-1946, 1981, Inside Corporate Japan: The Art of Fumble-Free Management, 1987, Japan: A Documentary History, 1997, Agony of Choice, Matsuoka Yosuke and the Rise and Fall of the Japanses Empire, 2002; translator: The China Quagmire, 1983, What is Total Quality Control? The Japanese Way, 1985, Kanban, Just-in-Time at Toyota, 1986, Total Quality Control for Management: Strategies and Techniques from Toyota and Toyoda

Gosei, 1987, TQC (Total Quality Control), The Wisdom of Japan, 1988; contbr. Sekai to Nippon, (The World and Japan) weekly, Tokyo. Fulbright-Hays scholar Japan, 1966—67. Presbyterian. Home: 1303 Mazeland Dr Bel Air MD 21015-6358

LU, EDWARD TSANG, astronaut; b. Springfield, Mass., July 1, 1963; s. Charlie and Snowlily Lu. BSEE, Cornell U., 1984; PhD in Applied Physics, Stanford U., 1989. Vis. scientist High Altitude Observatory, Boulder, Colo., 1989—92; postdoctoral fellow Inst. Astronomy, Honolulu, 1992—95; mission specialist NASA, Houston, 1995—. Astronaut Space Shuttle Atlantis, 1997, 2000, International Space Station, 2003. Fellow, Hughes Aircraft Co.; scholar Presdl. scholar, Cornell U. Mem.: Am. Astronomical Soc., Exptl. Aircraft Assn., Aircraft Owners & Pilots Assn. Avocations: aerobatic flying, coaching wrestling, piano, tennis, surfing. Office: Astronaut Office CB NASA Johnson Space Center Houston TX 77058*

LU, GUIYANG, electrical engineer; b. Guiyang, China, May 10, 1946; arrived in U.S., 1982; s. Wen and Yunqiu Deng; m. Jing Du; 1 child, Jia. Degree in elec. engring., Tsing Hua U., Beijing, 1970; postgrad., South China U. Tech., Guangzhou, 1980-81; MA in Math., Calif. State U., Fresno, 1984; MSEE, Poly. U., N.Y.C., 1986. Instr. in elec. engring. South China U. Tech., Guangzhou, 1973-80; v.p. engring. Kawahara Corp., N.Y.C., 1986-88; H.S. math. tchr. N.Y.C. Bd. Edn., 1988-90; engring. cons. Measurement and Control Sys., N.Y.C., 1989-90; sr. R&D engr. Avid Inc., Norco, Calif., 1991-98; sr. RF engr. Securay Key, Chatsworth, Calif., 1998—2002; rsch. assoc. Avery Dennison, Irwindale, Calif., 2002—04; dir. R&D Avid Identification Sys., Norco, Calif., 2004—. U.S. patentee in field. Mem.: IEEE. Home: 1718 Eastgate Ave Upland CA 91784-9210 Office: Avid Identification Sys 3185 Hamner Ave Norco CA 92860 Personal E-mail: gylu@aol.com.

LU, HAO, quantitative researcher; s. Yibing Lu and Yulian Yang; m. Li Chang, Jan. 27, 1974. PhD, Columbia U., 2001. Assoc. Morgan Stanley, NYC, 2000; v.p. Thales Fund Mgmt., LLC, 2001—. Adj. asst. prof. Columbia U., NYC, 2001. Contbr. acad. rsch. articles to profl. jours. Recipient First prize, Chinese Nat. Math. Competition, 1990; Disting. Student scholar, Nankai U., China, 1991-1995. Mem.: Am. Statis. Assn., Am. Fin. Assn. Achievements include research in Bayesian statistics and computational finance. Office: Thales Fund Mgmt LLC 140 Broadway 45th Fl New York NY 10005 Office Phone: 212-509-3111. Office Fax: 212-509-3722. Personal E-mail: luhao0@gmail.com. E-mail: hlu@thales.com.

LU, HONG LIANG, telecommunications industry executive; b. Taiwan; BS civil engring., Univ. Calif., Berkeley. COO Unison World Inc., pres., CEO, 1983—86, Kyocera Unison, 1986—91, Unitech Telecom, 1991—95; chmn. pres., CEO UTStarcom, Alameda, Calif., 1995—. Mem. strategic adv. bd. Pacrim Venture Partners. Office: UTStarcom 1275 Harbor Bay Pkwy Alameda CA 94502*

LU, HUANQING, computer scientist, educator; m. Hui Ma. B in Civil Engring., Tianjin U., China, 1992, M in Project Mgmt., 1997; M in Computer Sci., PhD, U. Fla., 2002. Asst. prof. East Carolina U., Greenville, NC, 2003—. Mem.: ASCE. Personal E-mail: luh@mail.ecu.edu.

LU, JOHN KUEW-HSIUNG, physiology educator, endocrinologist; b. Miaoli, Taiwan, Republic of China, Sept. 16, 1937; came to U.S., 1967; s. En-Gie and Jan-Mei (Wu) L.; m. Marianne Mann Wang, Dec. 29, 1969; children: Judith Maria, John Lawrence. BS, Nat. Taiwan Normal U., Taipei, 1961; MS, Nat. Taiwan U. Med. Sch., 1967; PhD, Mich. State U., 1972. Postdoctoral fellow U. Pitts., 1972-74; rsch. assoc. Mich. State U., East Lansing, 1974-75; asst. prof. U. Calif.-San Diego, La Jolla, 1975-77; asst. prof. depts. ob-gyn. and neurobiology UCLA Sch. Med., 1977-82, assoc. prof., 1982-88, prof., 1988—. Mem. biochem. endocrinology study sect. NIH, Bethesda, 1990-94, Health Reviewers Res., NIH, 1994-98. Mem. editl. bd. Procs. Soc. Exptl. Biology and Medicine, N.Y.C., 1987—93, mem. publ. com., 1996—2001; contbr. articles to profl. jours., chpts. to books. Recipient Methods to Extend Rsch. in Time award, NIH, 1987—97, Cert. Commendation, D. Geffen Sch. Medicine, UCLA, 2003—04, Rsch. grantee on reproductive senescence, Nat. Inst. Aging, 1980—91, Rsch. grantee on oocyte physiology, NICHD, 2003—. Mem. Soc. for Study Reprodn., Endocrine Soc., Am. Physiol. Soc., Soc. for Gynecologic Investigation, Soc. Exptl. Biology and Medicine. Home: 1129 Iliff St Pacific Palisades CA 90272-3830 Office: D Geffen Sch Medicine at UCLA Dept Ob-Gyn 22-172 CHS 10833 Le Conte Ave Los Angeles CA 90095-1740 Office Phone: 310-206-8915. E-mail: jlu@mednet.ucla.edu.

LU, MI, computer engineer, educator; b. Chongqing, Sichuan, China, July 22, 1949; d. Chong Pu Lu and Shu Sheng Fan. MS, Rice U., 1984, PhD, 1987. Registered profl. engr. From asst. prof. to assoc. prof. Tex. A&M U., Coll. Sta., 1987-98, prof., 1998—. Stream chmn. 7th Internat. Conf. Computing and Info., Peterborough, Ont., Can., 1995; conf. chmn. 5th Internat. Conf. Computer Sci. and Informatics, 2000, 6th Internat. Conf., 2002. Assoc. editor Jour. Computing and Info., 1995—, Info. Sci., 1996-97. 2002--; contbr. articles to profl. jours. Mem. Computer Soc. of IEEE (sr.). Office: Tex A&M U Dept Elec Engring College Station TX 77843

LU, MILTON MING-DEH, plastic surgeon, consultant; b. Chengtu, China, Nov. 12, 1919; came to U.S., 1946; naturalized, 1955. s. Yow-Cheng and Su-Cheng (Cheng) L.; m. Hiltrud Marie M. Reineke, Dec. 27, 1963; children: Barbara Ann, Winifred, Rita Doreen, Oliver. DDS, W. China Union U., 1943, MD, 1951; MS, U. Rochester, 1952. Resident Strong Meml. Hosp., Rochester, N.Y., 1947-51; fellow in plastic surgery St. Louis, 1952-56; asst., instr. Strong Meml. Hosp.-Sch. Medicine and Dentistry U. Rochester, 1946-50; asst. plastic surgeon Barnes Hosp.-Wash. U., 1952-56; gen. surgeon VA Hosp., Lebanon, Pa., 1956-58; plastic surgeon St. Joseph's Hosp., Lancaster, Pa., Lancaster Gen. Hosp. Cons. Good Samaritan Hosp., Lebanon, Pa. Contbr. articles to profl. jours. Served to maj. Med. Unit, Chinese Army, 1945. Recipient Disting. Svc. award VA Hosp. Fellow Internat. Coll. Dentists, Royal Coll Health, ACS; mem. Robert Ivy Soc. Plastic Surgeons, AMA, Pa. Med. Soc., Lancaster County Med. Soc., Am. Trauma Soc. (founder mem.), Am. Burn Assn. Mem. Soc. Of Friends. Home: 2114 Oregon Pike Lancaster PA 17601-4605

LU, MINGYU, electrical engineer, researcher; arrived in U.S., 1997; s. Daozhong Lu and Zhang. BSs, Tsinghua U., 1995; PhD, U. Ill., 2002. Postdoctoral rsch. assoc. U. Ill., Urbana-Champaign, Ill., 2002—. Co-author: Review of Radio Science, 2002; contbr. scientific papers, articles to profl. jours. Mem.: IEEE (First Pl. Student Paper award 2001). Achievements include research in computational electromagnetics. Home: 408 East Stoughton St Apt 11 Champaign IL 61820 Office: University of Illinois 1406 West Green St Room #447 Urbana IL 61801

LU, NATALIE, federal agency administrator; PhD, U. Md., 1995. Rsch. assoc. Johns Hopkins U., Balt., 1995—98; program mgr. Dept. Justice, Washington, 1998—. Achievements include patents pending for Monoclonal antibody specific for crack cocaine metabolites, a cell line producing the same, and crack cocaine conjugates. Personal E-mail: nat518@yahoo.com.

LU, NINGPING, environmental chemist; b. Sichuan, China, June 18, 1941; d. Yiungdi and Jinghua (Liu) L.; m. Li Pin-Fun, July 23, 1964 (div. 1990); children: Ying, Nin. BS in Biophysics, Sichuan U., 1964; MS of Soil Chemistry, Auburn U., 1990, PhD in Environtl. Soil Chemistry, 1993. Dir. Atomic Agrl. Ins., Sichuan, 1983; rsch. assoc. Fertilizer Ins., Sichuan, 1985-86; postdoctoral rsch. assoc. Auburn U., 1993-94, Los Alamos Nat. Lab., 1994-97, tech. staff mem., 1997—. Vis. scientist Purdue U., West Lafayette, Ind., 1983-84, Auburn U., 1984-85; cons. UN Devel. Program in China, Beijing, 1997—. Contbr. over 70 articles to profl. publs. Mem. Agronomy Soc. of Am., Soil Sci. Soc. of Am., Am. Chem. Soc., N.Y. Acad. of Sci., Phi Kappa Phi. Achievements include development of remedial processes of radionuclide (e.g. uranium-238, cesium-137, plutonium-239, strontium-90, Americium-241, american-241, strantium-90) contaminated soils, surface water and ground water; utlization of municipal solid wastes on agricultural land; research in remediation of radionuclide contaminated soil, water and sites; actinide interactions with colloids of metal oxides, clays and silica; transport of radio-colloids in groundwater; stability, solubility and speciation of actinides at nuclear waste repository sites. Office: E-ET Los Alamos Nat Lab Ms J514 Los Alamos NM 87545-0001 E-mail: ningping@lanl.gov.

LU, SHIH-PENG, history educator; b. Kao-Yu, Chiang-Su, China, Sept. 16, 1928; s. Ch'un-Tai and Chu-Yin (Chia) L.; m. Wei-Chun Julia Lee; children: Ting Ting, Shin. BA, Nat. Taiwan U., Taipei, 1952. Cert. full prof., Ministry of Edn., Taiwan. Tchg. asst. Taiwan U., Taipei, 1953-55; rsch. asst. Acad. Sinica, Taipei, 1955-58; lectr. Tunghai U., Taichung, Taiwan, 1958-63, assoc. prof., 1963-67, prof., 1967—. Vis. scholar Harvard U., Cambridge, Mass., 1961-63; rsch. fellow Yale U., New Haven, 1980-81; dir. evening divsn. Tunghai U., 1972-81, chmn. dept. history, 1981-87, dean Coll. Arts, 1988-94; dir. Chinese Culture Monthly, Taichung, 1988—. Author: Vietnam During the Period of Chinese Rule, 1964 (Nat. Sci. Coun. Publ. award 1965), The Modern History of China, 1979 (World Books Co. Authors award 1979), The Contemporary History of China, 1991 (Ministry of Edn. Outstanding Textbook award 1992); editor Chinese Culture Monthly, 1979— (Ministry of Edn. Best Jour. award 1991). 2nd lt. ROTC, Chinese Mil., 1952-53. Named Outstanding Youth, China Youth Corps, Taiwan, 1952, Outstanding Prof., Ministry of Edn., 1992. Mem. Assn. Modern History (chairperson bd. overseers 1994-96), Chinese Hist. Assn. (bd. dirs. 1983-94), Taiwan U. Alumni Assn. (chmn. 1987-89), Assn. for Ming Studies (exec. dir. 1995-97). Avocations: reading, classical music, ping pong/table tennis, jogging, chinese opera. Home: 19-8A Tunghai Rd 407 T'aichung Taiwan Office: Tunghai Univ Dept History 407 Taichung Taiwan

LU, SHIYONG, engineering educator; s. Weibin Lu and Aiqin Hu; m. Shuyun Xu, Mar. 18, 1996; children: Emily, Kevin. PhD, SUNY, Stony Brook, 1996—2002. Asst. prof. Wayne State U., Detroit, 2002—. Author: (exhibition) People of Detroit: a Living Project. Mem.: IEEE (life), ISCA (life), ACM (life), Ais Sigsemis (life). Office: Wayne State Univ 5143 Cass Ave Detroit MI 48202

LU, TAIJIN, physical chemist, researcher; b. P.R, Jiangsu, China, Aug. 1, 1959; arrived in U.S.A., 1997; s. Tieru Lu and Jizhen Zhou; m. Lian Li; 1 child, Joanna Da. DSc, Tohoku U., Sendai, Japan, 1989. Spl. rschr. Inst. of Physical and Chem. Rsch. (RIKEN), Wako, Japan, 1990—92; rsch. & tchg. fellow Nat. Univ. of Singapore (NUS), Singapore, 1992—96; rsch. scientist Gemological Inst. Am., Carlsbad, Calif., 1997—. Mem.: Optical Engring. Soc. Home: 1913 Triumph Street Vista CA 92083 Office: Gemological Institute of America (GIA) 5355 Armada Drive Carlsbad CA 92008 Personal E-mail: taijinlu@hotmail.com. Business E-Mail: tlu@gia.edu.

LU, YEN-CHIAO ANGEL, medical researcher; b. Pingtung, Taiwan; d. Han-Chang Lu and Yu-Hui Pan; m. Tony Hung; 1 child, Ryan Hung. BSN, U. Dubuque, 1995; MS, U. Utah, 2000; MBA, U. Balt., 2004. RN Md., 2005. Nursing informatics specialist Chung Shan Med. U. Hosp., Taichung, Taiwan, 2000—01; grad. rsch. asst. U. Md., Balt., 2002—. Mem.: Am. Med. Informatics Assn., Capital Area Rountable on Informatics in Nursing, Healthcare Informatics and Mgmt. Systems Soc., Beta Gamma Sigma, Sigma Theta Tau. E-mail: angellu01@gmail.com.

LU, YI, chemistry professor; BS, Beijing Univ.; PhD, UCLA; postdoctoral rsch., Calif. Inst. Tech. Assoc. prof., dept. chem., dept. biochem. and computational biology Univ. Ill. Urbana-Champaign. Faculty Environ. Coun., Ctr. for Nanoscale Sci., Tech., Univ. Ill. Urbana-Champaign; rsch. prof. Howard Hughes Med. Inst., 2002—. Adv. bd. Jour. of Biological Inorganic Chemistry; contbr. articles to profl. journals. Recipient Nat. Sci. Found. Career award, Arnold and Mabel Beckman Young Investigator award, 1996, Rsch. Corp. Cottrell Scholars award, 1997, Alfred P. Sloan Rsch. Fellowship, 1998, Camille Dreyfus Teacher-Scholar award, 1999, Howard Hughes Med. Inst. grant, 2002. Office: Dept Chem A322 Chem & Life Sci Univ Ill 600 S Mathews Ave Urbana IL 61801 Office Phone: 217-333-2619. Office Fax: 217-333-2685. Business E-Mail: yi-lu@uiuc.edu.*

LUBAND, CHARLES, lawyer; b. Boston, Dec. 18, 1967; s. Leonard J. and Marian S. Lubinsky; m. Robin J. Rittenband, Jan. 2, 1999; children: Max R., Ruby T. BA in Pub. Policy & Am. Instns., Brown U., 1990; JD, Harvard Law Sch., 1996; MPP, Kennedy Sch. of Govt., 1996. Clk. for Herbert J. Wilkins, Chief Justice Mass. Supreme Jud. Ct., Boston, 1996—97; ptnr., assoc. Powell Goldstein LLP, Wash., 1997—. Mem.: Am. Health Lawyers Assn. Jewish. Office: Powell Goldstein LLP 901 New York Ave NW Third Floor Washington DC 20001 Office Fax: 202-624-7222. Business E-Mail: cluband@pogolaw.com.

LUBAR, JEFFREY STUART, journalist, trade association executive; b. Rockville Centre, N.Y., Apr. 15, 1947; s. Sidney and Rose (Grupsmith) L.; m. Barbara Ruth Bigelman; children— Debra, Adam, Rachel. BA, Am. U., 1969. Dir. Washington News Bur., Susquehanna Broadcasting Co., 1969-86; v.p. pub. affairs Nat. Assn. Realtors, Washington, 1987-99; dir. comms. Mortgage Ins. Cos. of Am., 2000—. Mem. exec. com. of corrs. Radio-TV Assn. (U.S. Congress), 1974-75 Served with AUS, 1969-75. Mem.: Nat. Press Club. Jewish. Home: 6307 Karmich St Fairfax Station VA 22039-1622 Office: 1425 K St NW Washington DC 20005 Office Phone: 202-682-2683. E-mail: jeff@micadc.org.

LUBARS, DAVID, advertising executive; b. Bklyn. s. Walter Lubars; m. Cindy Bost; children: Alex, Michael. BA in comm., Boston U., 1980. With Leonard Monahan Saabye (name changed to Leonard, Moniker, Lubars, and Kelly), Providence, 1982—85, Chiat/Day, Calif., 1985—87; ptnr., exec. v.p., creative dir. Leonard, Moniker, Lubars, and Kelly, Providence, 1988—93; exec. v.p., exec. creative dir. BBDO West, LA, 1993—94, pres., exec. creative dir., 1994—98; creative dir. Mpls. office Fallon Worldwide, 1998—99, co-pres., exec. creative dir. Mpls. office, 1999—2004, pres., exec. creative dir. N. Am., 2002—04; chmn., chief creative officer BBDO N. Am., NYC, 2004—. Named Creative Dir. Yr., Adweek, 2000. Office: BBDO Worldwide 1285 Ave Am New York NY 10019 Office Phone: 212-459-5000.

LUBATTI, HENRY JOSEPH, physicist, researcher; b. Oakland, Calif., Mar. 16, 1937; s. John and Pauline (Massimino) L.; m. Catherine Jeanne Berthe Ledoux, June 29, 1968; children: Karen E., Henry J., Stephen J.C. AA, U. Calif., Berkeley, 1957, AB, 1960; PhD, U. Calif., 1966; MS, U. Ill., 1963. Research assoc. Faculty Scis. U. Paris, Orsay, France, 1966-68; asst. prof. physics MIT, 1968-69; assoc. prof., sci. dir. visual techniques lab. U. Wash., 1969-74, prof., sci. dir. visual Techniques lab., 1974-98. Vis. lectr. Internat. Sch. Physics, Erice, Sicily, 1968, Herceg-Novi, Yugoslavia Internat. Sch., 1969, XII Cracow Sch. Theoretical Physics, Zapokane, Poland, 1972; vis. scientist CERN, Geneva, 1980-81; vis. staff Los Alamos Nat. Lab., 1983-86; guest scientist SSC Lab., 1991-93; mem. physics editl. adv. com. World Sci. Pub. Co. Ltd., 1982-93; guest scientist Fermilab., 1999-2000; vis. scientist U. Rome, summers 2001-04. Editor: Physics at Fermilab in the 1990's, 1990; contbr. numerous articles on high energy physics to profl. jours. Alfred P. Sloan research fellow, 1971-75 Fellow AAAS, Am. Phys. Soc.; mem. Sigma Xi, Tau Beta Pi. Office: Elem Particle Experiment Group U Wash PO Box 351560 Seattle WA 98195-1560 Office Phone: 206-543-8964. E-mail: lubatti@u.washington.edu.

LUBAWSKI, JAMES LAWRENCE, healthcare consultant; b. Chgo., June 4, 1946; s. Harry James and Stella Agnes (Pokorny) L.; m. Kathleen Felicity Donnellan, June 1, 1974; children: Kathleen N., James Lawrence, Kevin D., Edward H. BA, Northwestern U., 1968, MBA, 1969, MA, 1980. Asst. prof. U. Northern Iowa, Cedar Falls, 1969-72; instr. Loyola U., Chgo., 1974-76; dir., market planning Midwest Stock Exchange, Chgo., 1976-77; dir. mktg. Gambro Inc., Barrington, Ill., 1977-79; mktg. mgr. Travenol Labs., Deerfield, Ill., 1979-82; dir. mktg. Hollister Inc., Libertyville, Ill., 1982-84; pres., chief exec. officer Neomedica Inc., Chgo., 1984-86; v.p. bus. devel. Evangl. Health Svcs., Oak Brook, Ill., 1986-87; pres., chief exec. officer Cath. Health Alliance Met. Chgo., 1987-95; mng. dir. Ward Howell Internat., Chgo., 1995-98; v.p. A.T. Kearney, Chgo., 1998-2000; pres. Zwell Internat., Chgo., 2000—02; founder Lubawski & Assocs., Northfield, 2002—. Author: Food and Man, 1974, Food and People, 1979; co-editor: Consumer Behavior in Theory and in Action, 1970. Dir. Crossroads Coun. Girl Scouts Am., Libertyville, Ill., 2003—. Mem. Evanston Golf Club (pres. 2000-02), Equestrian Order of Knights of Holy Sepulchre. Avocations: golf, fishing. Office: 1765 Maple St Ste 15 Northfield IL 60093 Personal E-mail: Jim@Lubawski.com.

LUBBEN, DAVID J., lawyer; b. Cedar Rapids, Iowa, 1951; BA, Luther Coll., 1974; JD, U. Iowa, 1977. Bar: Minn. 1977. Atty to ptnr. Dorsey & Whitney LLP, Mpls., 1977—96; gen. counsel, sec. UnitedHealth Group, Minnetonka, Minn., 1996—. Office: UnitedHealth Group 9900 Bren Rd E Minnetonka MN 55343-9664

LUBBERS, AREND DONSELAAR, retired academic administrator; b. Milw., July 23, 1931; s. Irwin Jacob and Margaret (Van Donselaar) L.; m. Eunice L. Mayo, June 19, 1953 (div.); children— Arend Donselaar, John Irwin Darrow, Mary Elizabeth; m. Nancy Vanderpol, Dec. 21, 1968; children— Robert Andrew, Caroline Jayne. AB, Hope Coll., 1953; AM, Rutgers U., 1956; LittD, Central Coll., 1977; DSc, U. Sarajevo, Yugoslavia, 1987; LHD, Hope Coll., 1988; DSc, Akademia Ekonomiczna, Krakow, Poland, 1989, U. Kingston Univ., Eng., 1995. Rsch. asst. Rutgers U., 1954-55; rsch. fellow Reformed Ch. in Am., 1955-56; instr. history and polit. sci. Wittenberg U., 1956-58; v.p. devel. Central Coll., Iowa, 1959-60, pres., 1960-69, Grand Valley State U., Allendale, Mich., 1969-2001; ret., 2001. Mem. Am. Assn. State Colls. and Univs. seminar in India, 1971, Fed. Commn. Orgn. Govt. for Conduct Fgn. Policy, 1972; USIA insp., Netherlands, 1976; mem. pres.'s commn. NCAA, 1984-87, 89—, chmn. pres.'s commn., 1998-2002; bd. dirs. Grand Bank, Grand Rapids, Mich., Macatawa Bank; cons. in field. Sudent Cmty. amb. from Holland (Mich.) to Yugoslavia, 1951; bd. dirs. Grand Rapids Symphony, 1976-82, 99, Butterworth Hosp., 1988; chmn. divsn. II NCAA Pres.'s Commn., 1992-95, 98-99, mem. pres.'s coun., 1997; mem. Michigan Cmty. Svc. Commn., 2001--. Recipient Golden Plate award San Diego Acad. Achievement, 1962, Golden-Emblem Order of Merit Polish Peoples Republic, 1988, trustee's award cmty. leadership Aquinas Coll., 1998, Lifetime Achievement award Econ. Club Grand Rapids, 2001; named 1 of top 100 young men in U.S. Life mag., 1962. Mem. Mich. Coun. State Univs. Pres. (chmn. 1988, 2000—), Grand Rapids World Affairs Council (pres. 1971-73), Phi Alpha Theta, Pi Kappa Delta, Pi Kappa Phi. Home: 4195 N Oak Pointe Ct Grand Rapids MI 49525 Office Phone: 616-331-6607. Personal E-mail: njdelta@aol.com. Business E-Mail: lubbers@gvsu.edu.

LUBCHENCO, JANE, marine biologist, educator, science association director; b. Denver, Dec. 4, 1947; married; 2 children. BA, Colo. Coll., 1969; MS, U. Wash., 1971; PhD in Ecology, Harvard U., 1975; DSc (hon.), Princeton U. Asst. prof. ecology Harvard U., Cambridge, Mass., 1975—77; rsch. assoc. Smithsonian Inst., 1978—; from asst. prof. to assoc. prof. Oreg. State U., Corvallis, 1978—88, prof. zoology, 1988—, disting. prof., 1993—, Wayne and Gladys Valley prof. marine biology, 1995—; pres.-elect Internat. Coun. for Sci., Paris, 2001—02, pres., 2002—. Prin. investigator NSF, 1976—; mem. UN Environment Programme Scientific & Tech. Advisory Panel, 1993—; adv. forum on Environment & Natural Resources White House Office of Sci. & Tech. Policy, 1994; mem. Nat. Sci. Bd., 1994, 2000; mem. Ecosystem Principles Advisory Panel Nat. Marine Fisheries Service, 1997—; mem. President's Council of Advisors on Sci. & Tech., 1997—98; mem. Technical Advisory Com. Nat. Geographic Soc. Sustainable Seas Expeditions, 1998—. Named Oreg. Scientist of Yr., Oreg. Acad. Scis., 1994; recipient Heinz Environmental award, 2002; fellow, John D. and Katherine T. MacArthur Found., 1993—98; Pew Scholar in conservation and environment, 1992, MacArthur fellow, 1993. Mem.: NAS, AAAS (pres. 1995—98), Am. Inst. Biol. Sci., Am. Soc. Zoologists, Am. Soc. Naturalists, Phycological Soc. Am. (nat. lectr. 1987—89), Ecol. Soc. Am. (mem. coun. 1982—84, chair awards com. 1983—86, nominating com. 1986, George Mercer award 1979). Achievements include research in population and community ecology, plant-herbivore and predator-prey interactions, competition, marine ecology, algal ecology, agal life histories, biogeography and chemical ecology. Office: Oreg State U Dept Zoology Cordley 3029 Corvallis OR 97331 also: Internat Council Sci 51 Bd de Montmorency 75016 Paris France

LUBECK, MARVIN JAY, ophthalmologist; b. Cleve., Mar. 20, 1929; s. Charles D. and Lillian (Jay) L. A.B., U. Mich., 1951, M.D., 1955, M.S., 1959. Diplomate Am. Bd. Opthamology; m. Arlene Sue Bitman, Dec. 28, 1955; children: David Mark, Daniel Jay, Robert Charles. Intern, U. Mich. Med. Ctr., 1955-56, resident ophthalmology, 1956-58, jr. clin. instr. ophthalmology, 1958-59; pvt. practice medicine, specializing in ophthalmology, Denver, 1961—; mem. staff Rose Hosp., Porter Hosp., Presbyn. Hosp., St. Luke's Hosp. With U.S. Army, 1959-61. Fellow ACS; mem. Am. Acad. Ophthalmology, Denver Med. Soc., Colo. Ophthalmol. Soc. Home: 590 S Harrison Ln Denver CO 80209-3517 Office: 1666 South University Blvd Denver CO 80210

LUBELL, ELLEN, writer; b. Bklyn., Apr. 7, 1950; d. Edward and Sonia Lubell. BA in Fine Arts, SUNY, Stony Brook, 1971. Contbg. editor Arts Mag., N.Y.C., 1972-79; founder, editor Womanart Mag., Bklyn., 1976-78; columnist Soho Weekly News, N.Y.C., 1977-79; contbr. Art in Am., N.Y.C., 1981-85; dir. pub. rels. Gerstman & Meyers Inc., N.Y.C., 1984-89; freelancer, columnist, publicist The Village Voice, N.Y.C., 1984-91; columnist, freelancer N.Y. Newsday, 1988—89; dir. comm. Inform, Inc., N.Y.C., 1991-95; comm. dir. Child Care Action Campaign, N.Y.C., 1995-99; freelance writer Star-Ledger, Newark, 1996-97; dir. pub. rels. The Childrens Aid Soc., N.Y.C., 1999—. Art Critics fellow, Nat. Endowment for the Arts, 1978.

LUBELL, MICHAEL STEPHEN, physicist, educator; b. N.Y.C., Mar. 25, 1943; s. Richard M. and Lillian (Aronoff) L.; 1 child, Karina B. BA, Columbia U., 1963; MS, Yale U., 1965, PhD, 1969. Postdoctoral fellow Yale U., New Haven, 1970, instr., 1971—72, asst. prof., 1972—77, assoc. prof., 1977—80, CUNY, 1980—82, prof., 1983—, chmn. dept. physics, 1999—. Advisor basic rsch. U.S. Army, 1980-84; mem. exec. com. Internat. Conf. on Physics of Elec. and Atomic Collisions, 1983-91, co-chmn. local organizing com., 1989; vis. scientist Brookhaven Nat. Lab., 1986-87; chmn. com. on atomic and molecular sci. NRC, 1988-90; mem. adv. com. on pub. info. Am. Inst. Physics, 1988-90, adv. com. on media and govt. relations, 2003; mem. steering com. Sci. Coalition, 2003-; vis. lectr. Inst. Theoretical Physics, U. Calif., Santa Barbara, 1990; vis. prof. U. Tex., Austin, 1990, U. Bielefeld, 1993; cons. in field; sci. and tech. policy columnist APS News. Sci. and sci. policy spokesman, radio and TV and print media; contbr. articles to profl. jours. and books. Sci., tech. adv. U.S. Sen. Christopher J. Dodd, Washington, 1980—; chmn. Dem. Town com., Westport, Conn., 1986-91; del. Dem. Nat. Conv., 1984. Rsch. grantee and contracts NSF, Dept. Energy, Dept. Def., 1974—; fellow AEC, 1970, Alfred P. Sloan Found., 1980-84 Fellow AAAS, Am. Phys. Soc. (panel on pub. affairs 1983-84, co-organizer Congl. Day 1991-92, dir. pub. affairs 1995—); mem. N.Y. Acad. Scis., Sigma Xi. Home: PO Box 188 Westport CT 06881-0188 Office: CUNY City Coll Dept Physics Convent Ave New York NY 10031 Office Phone: 202-662-8700. E-mail: lubell@aps.org.

LUBEN, DELMA, writer; b. Soda Springs, Idaho, Jan. 6, 1925; d. Delbert John and Madge Butler Panting; m. Robert Lee Luben, Aug. 26, 1945 (dec.); children: Hal R., Lyn D. Student, Weber Coll., 1992—93. Tech. writer U.S. Army Comm. Command, Ft. Huachuca, Ariz., 1957—63, chief, adminstrn., 1963—67; exec. editor Sierra Vista Daily Dispatch, Ariz., 1968—69; chief, protocol World Wide Comm. Command, Ft. Huachaca, 1970—76; contbng. editor Writers World Mag., Big Stone Gap, Va., 1979—83. Writing tchr. in field. Author: The Protocol Officer Handbook, 1976, Poems for Poets &

Writers, 1990, The Universal Experience, 1995, The Freedom Nation, 1996, The Writing World, 2003, Glorious Autumn, 2005; prodr., host (TV series) The Writing World, Tucson, 1980—83, (radio series) Poetry for the Public, Phoenix, 1985—88. Recipient Fed. Womens Award, U.S. Dept. Def., 1972, 1974. Mem.: Internat. Soc. Poets for Peace, Soc. Southwestern Authors (publicity dir., historian 1980—83). Avocations: history, philosophy, travel.

LUBENOW, WILLIAM CORNELIUS, historian, educator; b. Freeport, Ill., July 28, 1939; s. Paul and Martha (Dorst) Lubenow. BA, Ctrl. Coll., Pella, Iowa, 1961; MA, U. Iowa, 1962, PhD, 1968. Assoc. prof. history Ctrl. Coll., Pella, 1962—71; prof. history Stockton Coll., Pomona, NJ, 1971—. Vis. fellow Wolfson Coll., Cambridge, England, 1987—2004. Author: Politics of Government Growth, 1972, Parliamentary Politics and Irish Home Rule, 1988, Cambridge Apostles 1820-1914, 1998. Warden Grace Ch., Haddonfield, NJ, 2000—02, 2005—. Fellow: Royal Hist. Soc. London; mem.: Social Sci. History Soc., Am. Hist. Assn., Bredon Soc. (Cambridge), Middle Atlantic Conf. Brit. Studies (pres. 2002—), N.Am. Conf. Brit. Studies (v.p. (pres.-elect) 2003—), Vesper Club (Phila.), Reform Club (London). Avocations: music, hiking, cooking. Office: Stockton Coll Dept History Pomona NJ 08240 Office Phone: 609-652-4436. Business E-Mail: william.lubenow@stockton.edu. E-mail: wclubenow@aol.com.

LUBER, THOMAS J(ULIAN), lawyer; b. Louisville, Feb. 16, 1949; s. John J. and Martha E. (Cotton) L.; m. Dorothy Ann Carter, Dec. 19, 1975; children: Katharine Ann, Allison Julia. BS in Acctg., U. Louisville, 1972, JD with honors, 1976; LLM in Taxation, NYU, 1977. Bar: Ky. 1976. Agt. IRS, Louisville, 1972-73; assoc. Fahey & Gray, Louisville, 1977-79; from assoc. to ptnr. Wyatt, Tarrant & Combs and predecessor firms, Louisville, 1979—, chmn. tax sect., 1983—. Lectr. U. Louisville, 1978-80; speaker in field; bd. advisors Jour. Multistate Taxation. Contbr. articles to profl. jours. Bd. dirs. Univ. Pediatrics Found., Louisville, Univ. Ob-gyn. Found., Louisville, Assumption High Sch., Louisville. With USAF, 1967-69. Mem. ABA, Ky. Bar Assn. (chmn. tax sect. 1983-84), Louisville Bar Assn., Ky. Inst. Fed. Taxation (mem. planning com. 1981—, chmn. 1984—), Jefferson Club, Big Spring Country Club. Democrat. Roman Catholic. Avocations: hiking, working out. Home: 2324 Saratoga Dr Louisville KY 40205-2021 Office: Wyatt Tarrant & Combs 2800 Citizens Plz Louisville KY 40202-2898 E-mail: tluber@wyattfirm.com.

LUBET, STEVEN, law educator; b. 1949; JD, U. Calif., Berkeley, 1973. Staff atty. Legal Asst. Fedn., Chgo., 1973-75; vis. asst. prof. Northwestern U. Sch. Law, Chgo., 1978—81, asst. prof., 1976—78, assoc. prof., 1978—81, prof. law, 1981—, dir. Program on Advocacy and Professionalism, prof. comparative literary studies; designated consumer rep. FTC, 1977—78; spl. edn. hearing officer Ill. Office of Edn., 1978—81; instr., asst. team leader, tchg. team leader Midwest Regional Trial Advocacy Program Nat. Inst. Trial Advocacy, 1978—86, dir. Expert Witness Program, 1982—98, dir. Midwest Deposition Program, 1988—99. Lectr. DePaul U., 1974—75; vis. prof. law Emory U. Sch. Law, 1987—88. Co-author: Judicial Conduct and Ethics, 1990; author: Modern Trial Advocacy, 1997; co-author: Evidence in Context, Exercises and Problems in Professional Responsibility, Problems and Materials in Evidence and Trial Advocacy, Arbitration Advocacy, Expert Testimony: A Guide for Expert Witnesses and the Lawyers Who Examine Them, 1998; contbr. articles to profl. jours. Fellow: Am. Judicature Soc. Office: Northwestern U Sch Law 357 E Chicago Ave Chicago IL 60611-3059 E-mail: slubet@law.northwestern.edu.*

LUBETSKI, EDITH ESTHER, librarian; b. Bklyn., July 16, 1940; m. Meir Lubetski, Dec. 23, 1968; children: Shaul, Uriel, Leah. BA, Bklyn. Coll., 1962; MLS, Columbia U., 1965; MA in Jewish Studies, Yeshiva U., 1968. Judaica libr. Stern Coll. Yeshiva U., N.Y.C., 1965-66, acquisitions libr., 1966-69, head libr., 1969—. Author (with Meir Lubetski): (book) Building a Judaica Library Collection, 1983; author: The Jewish Woman: Recent Books, 1995; contbr. articles to profl. jours. Mem. exec. bd. Jewish Book Coun., 1998—. Mem.: ACRL, ALA, N.Y. Libr. Assn., Assn. Jewish Librs. (corr. sec. 1980—84, pres. N.Y. chpt. 1984—86, nat. v.p. 1984—86, nat. pres. 1986—88, Fanny Goldstein Merit award 1993, Life Membership award 2003). Office: Yeshiva U Hedi Steinberg Libr 245 Lexington Ave New York NY 10016-4605 Office Phone: 212-340-7720. E-mail: Lubetski@ymail.yu.edu.

LUBIC, BENITA JOAN ALK, travel executive; b. Green Bay, Wis., May 18, 1936; d. Isadore George and Marion (Segal) Alk; m. Robert Bennett Lubic, May 31, 1959; children: Wendy Alison, Bret David, Robin Kimberly Lubic Bliss. BBA, U. Wis., 1958. Cert. Travel Cons. Inst. Cert. Travel Agts. Pres., owner Transeair Travel, Inc., Washington, 1959—. Instr. Internat. Travel Tng. Sch., 1982-91; lic. Cuba Travel Svc. Provider, 2000—. Contbr. articles on incentive travel to mags. Mem. SKAL, Washington; mem. adv. bd. Braniff Airlines, Republic Airlines, Sonesta Hotel Corp. Mem. Am. Soc. Travel Agts. (pres. Washington sub chpt. 1985-88, bd. dirs. 1979-96), Prost Exec. Women in Travel (v.p. 1982-83, treas. 1984-85, bd. dirs., 1985—), Internat. Fedn. Women's Travel Orgns. (dir. 1993-94, 1999—). Democrat. Jewish. Avocations: golf, tennis, swimming, bicycling, travel. Home: 2813 McKinley Pl NW Washington DC 20015-1104 Office: Transeair Travel Inc 2813 McKinley Pl NW Washington DC 20015-1104 Office Phone: 202-362-6100. Personal E-mail: blubic@aol.com.

LUBIC, ROBERT BENNETT, law educator; b. Pitts., Mar. 9, 1929; s. H. Murray and Rose M. (Schwartz) L.; m. Benita Joan Alk, May 18, 1959; children: Wendy, Bret, Robin. AB, U. Pitts., 1950, JD, 1953; LLM in Patent Law, Georgetown U., 1959. Bar: Pa. 1953, U.S. Ct. Appeals (D.C.) cir. 1958, U.S. Supreme Ct. 1958, U.S. Patent Office, 1959, U.S. Dist. Ct. D.C. 1964. Atty., advisor FCC, Washington, 1957-59; pvt. practice, Pitts., 1959-63; asst. prof. law Duquesne U. Law Sch., Pitts., 1963-65; prof. law Am. U. Law Sch., Washington, 1965-2000, prof. emeritus, 2000—, assoc. dean, 1970-71. Cons. Embassy Republic of Georgia; pres. Stas. WRGI-AM-FM, Naples and Marco Island, Fla., 1974-77; vis. prof. U. P.R. Law Sch., 1993, Internat. Christian U., Tokyo, 1988-89, East China U. Politics and Law, 1994, U. Warsaw, Poland, 1995, U. Turin, Italy, 1997; CEO GlobalMedArb LLC, 2000—; panel conciliators and arbitrators of Internat. Ctr. of Investment Settlement Disputes of World Bank; permanent panel arbitrator U.S. Postal Sys., Washington, 1978—, U.S. Dept. Labor, Washington, 1982—; arbitrator Pub. Employee Rels. Bd. D.C., Washington, 1984—, Pub. Employee Rels. Bd. V.I., 1982—, Met. Washington Airports Authority, 2001—; hearing examiner Libr. of congress, 2001—; dir. Labor Disputes Resolution Seminar, Hamilton, Bermuda, 1982-83, Nassau, Bahamas, 1983; labor cons. Govt. of Bermuda, 1985; creator, dir. Ea. European Summer Law Program, Moscow and Warsaw, 1979-81, Chinese Am. Summer Law Program, Beijing, Shanghai and Hong Kong, 1984-86; co-dir. Mid. East Summer Law Program, Jerusalem, 1976, 78. With U.S. Army, 1953—55. Recipient Outstanding Tchr. award Am. U. Student Bar Assn., 1981. Mem.: DC Bar Assn., Fed. Comm. Bar Assn. Democrat. Jewish. Home: 2813 McKinley Pl NW Washington DC 20015-1104 Office: GlobalMedArb LLC 2813 McKinley Pl NW Washington DC 20015-1104 Office Phone: 202-966-1880. E-mail: lubic@globalmedarb.com.

LUBIC, RUTH WATSON, health facility administrator, nurse midwife; b. Bucks County, Pa., Jan. 18, 1927; d. John Russell and Lillian (Kraft) Watson; m. William James Lubic, May 28, 1955; 1 child, Douglas Watson. Diploma, Sch. Nursing Hosp. U. Pa., 1955; BS, Columbia U., 1959, MA, 1961, EdD in Applied Anthropology, 1979; cert. in nurse midwifery, SUNY, Bklyn., 1962, DSc (hon.), 1993; LLD (hon.), U. Pa., 1985; DSc (hon.), U. Medicine and Dentistry, N.J., 1986; LHD (hon.), Coll. New Rochelle, 1992, Pace U., 1994. Staff nurse through head nurse Meml. Hosp. for Cancer and Allied Disease, N.Y.C., 1955-58; clin. assoc. Grad. Sch. Nursing N.Y. Med. Coll., N.Y.C., 1962-63; parent educator, cons. Maternity Ctr. Assn., N.Y.C., 1963-67, gen. dir., 1970-95, dir. clin. projects, 1995-97; project dir. Nat. Assn. of Childbearing Ctrs., Washington, 1997-99; pres., CEO D.C. Developing Families Ctr., 1998—2002, founder, pres. emeritus, 2003—, also bd. dirs.; pres., CEO, bd. dirs. D.C. Birth Ctr., 1998—. Cons. in midwifery, nursing and maternal and child health Office Pub. Health and Sci. HHS, 1995—97; adj. prof. divsn. nursing NYU, 1995—; bd. dirs., v.p. Am. Assn. World Health U.S. Com. WHO, 1975—94, pres. Am. Assn. World Health U.S. Com., 1980—81; mem. bd. maternal child and family health NRC, 1974—80; mem. Commn. Grads. Fgn. Nursing Schs., 1979—83, v.p., 1980—81, treas., 1982—83; bd. govs. Frontier Nursing Svc., 1982—92; bd. dirs. Pan Am. Health Edn. Found., pres., 1987—88; vis. prof. King Edward Meml. Hosp., Perth, Australia, 1991; Kate Hanna Harvey vis. prof. cmty. health nursing Frances Payne Bolton Sch. Nursing Case Western Res., 1991; Lansdowne lectr. U. Victoria, B.C., Canada, 1992; adj. prof. Sch. Nursing, Georgetown U., 1997—; Therese Dondero lectr. Am. Coll. Nurse-Midwives Found., 1995; Andrea Printy Meml. lectr. U. Minn., 1998; Kemble lectr. Sch. Nursing, U. N.C., Chapel Hill, 2000; Hugh P. Davis lectr. Emory U. Sch. Nursing, 2004. Author (with Gene Hawes): (book) childbearing: A Book of Choices, 1987; contbr. articles to profl. jours. Named Maternal-Child Health Nurse of the Yr., ANA, 1985, Disting. Alumna, U. Pa., 1992; named to Nursing Hall of Fame, 1999; recipient Letitia White award, Florence Nightingale medal, 1955, Nursing Practice award, U. Pa., 1980, Rockefeller Pub. Svc. award, 1981, Hattie Hemschemeyer award, 1983, Alumnae award, Sch. Nursing U. Pa., 1986, McManus medal, Tchrs. Coll. Columbia U., 1992, Disting. Svc. award, Francis Payne Bolton Sch. Nursing, 1993, Hon. Recognition, N.Y. State Nurses Assn., 1993, Nurse-Midwifery Faculty award, Columbia U., 1993, Spirit of Nursing award, Vis. Nurses Svc. N.Y., 1994, Maes-Macinnes award, Divsn. Nursing NYU, 1994, Hon. Recognition, ANA, 1994, Carola Warburg Rothschild award, Maternity Ctr. Assn., 1997, Healthy Babies Project award, 1998, Woman of Distinction award, Nat. Assn. Women in Edn., 1999; Irving Harris vis. scholar, Coll. Nursing U. Ill., 1999, MacArthur fellow, 1993. Fellow: AAAS, Soc. for Applied Anthropology, Am. Acad. Nursing (Living Legend award 2001); mem.: APHA (mem. com. on internat. health, sec. maternal and child health coun. 1982, mem. governing coun. 1986—89, mem. nominating com. 1987, mem. action bd. 1988—90), Vis. Nurse Svc. of N.Y. (Lillian Wald award 2003), Herman Biggs Soc. (sec.-treas. 1989—90), Am. Assn. Colls. Nursing (McGovern lectr. 1997), Nat. Assn. Childbearing Ctrs. (pres. 1983—91), Inst. of Medicine of NAS (Lienhard award 2001), Am. Coll. Nurse Midwives (v.p. 1964—66, pres.-elect 1969—70), N.Y. Acad. Medicine, Alpha Omega Alpha (hon.). Personal E-mail: Rlubic@aol.com. *As a professional nurse-midwife and public health scientist, the guiding principles of my professional life are to listen carefully to the families to be served and to combine their needs with proven scientific knowledge in constructing models for care. It is my belief that the primary purpose of maternal and child health programs is to assist families to achieve a sense of self-confidence about their ability to bring forth and rear offspring in conjunction with, but not dependent upon, professional guidance.*

LUBICK, DONALD CYRIL, lawyer; b. Buffalo, Apr. 29, 1926; s. Louis and Minna D. (Nabith) L.; m. Susan F. Cohen, June 5, 1960; children: Jonathan, Caroline, Lisa. BA summa cum laude, U. Buffalo, 1945; JD magna cum laude, Harvard U., 1949. Bar: N.Y. 1950, Fla. 1974, D.C. 1981; lic. fgn. law cons. Ont., 1989. Teaching fellow Harvard U. Law Sch., 1949-50; lectr. law U. Buffalo, 1950-61; assoc., then ptnr. Hodgson, Russ, Andrews, Woods & Goodyear, Buffalo and Washington, 1950-61, 64-77, 81-94; tax legis. counsel Treasury Dept., Washington, 1961-64, asst. sec. for tax policy, 1977-81, dir. tax adv. program for countries of Ctrl. and Ea. Europe and former Soviet Union Paris, 1994-96, from acting to asst. sec. for tax policy, 1996-99. Adj. prof. of law Washington Coll. Law, Am. U., 2002—. Author: (with Hussey) Basic World Tax Code and Commentary, 1992, 95. Chmn. Tax Revision Com., City of Buffalo, 1958; mem. adv. com. to select Com. on Election Reform, N.Y. State Legislature, 1974, mem. adv. group to commr. internal revenue, 1976. Served with USAAF, 1945-46. Harvard Internat. Tax Program sr. fellow, 1991—. Mem. ABA, Am. Law Inst., Am. Bar Found., N.Y. State Bar Assn., Fla. Bar Assn., Erie County Bar Assn. Democrat. Jewish. E-mail: donaldlubick@msn.com.

LUBIN, DANIEL C., venture capitalist; BS in fgn. svc. cum laude, Georgetown U. Sch. Fgn. Svc.; MBA with honors, Harvard Bus. Sch. Co-founder Cambridge Heart, Inc.; spl. asst. to chmn. Ctr. Strategic and Internat. Studies; lending officer Mfrs. Hanover Trust Co.; co-founder, mng. dir. KBL Healthcare Inc.; pres., COO KBL Healthcare Acquisitions Corp.; dir. investment banking divsn. Schroder Wertheim & Co.; co-founder, mng. ptnr. Radius Ventures, LLC, 1997—. Bd. dirs. Phylogix, Inc., EyeTel Imaging, Inc. Office: Radius Ventures LLC 400 Madison Ave 8th Fl New York NY 10017 Office Phone: 212-897-7778. Office Fax: 212-397-2656.

LUBIN, DONALD G., lawyer; b. N.Y.C., Jan. 10, 1934; s. Harry and Edith (Tannenbaum) L.; m. Amy Schwartz, Feb. 2, 1956; children: Peter, Richard, Thomas, Alice Lubin Spahr. BS in Econs., U. Pa., 1954; LLB, Harvard U., 1957. Bar: Ill. 1957. Ptnr. Sonnenschein Nath & Rosenthal LLP, Chgo., 1957—, chmn. exec. com., 1991-96. Former mem. exec. com., fin. com., chmn. nominating and corp. governance com. McDonald's Corp.; bd. dirs., sr. dir. Molex, Inc.; bd. dirs. Daubert Industries Inc., Charles Levy Co., Tennis Corp. Am.; founding bd. dirs. Lake County Cmty. Trust. Former mem. Navy Pier Redevel. Corp., Highland Park Cultural Arts Commn., Chgo. Bicentennial Commn.; life trustee, former chmn. bd. Highland Park Hosp., Ravinia Festival Assn.; chmn. Chgo. Metropolis 2020, Anchor Cross Soc., New Schs. for Chgo.; trustee, mem. exec. com. Rush-Presbyn.-St. Luke's Med. Ctr.; life trustee Chgo. Symphony Orch.; bd. dirs., v.p. Ronald McDonald House Charities, Inc., Chgo. Found. for Edn.; mem. Evanston Northwestern Healthcare Found.; former dir. Smithsonian Inst., Washington; pres., bd. dir. The Barr Fund; former bd. dirs., v.p., sec. Ragdale Found.; bd. govs. Art Inst. Chgo.; former mem. Chgo. Lighthouse for the Blind; mem. citizens bd. U. Chgo.; mem. coun. Children's Meml. Hosp.; former bd. overseers Coll. Arts and Sci., U. Pa.; former dir. Nat. Mus. Am. History, Washington. Woodrow Wilson vis. fellow Fellow Am. Bar Found., Ill. Bar Found., Chgo. Bar Found.; mem. Chgo. Bar Assn., Civic Com. (mem. steering com.), Lawyers Club Chgo., Chgo. Hort. Soc. (past bd. dirs.), Comml. Club (mem. exec. com.), Std. Club, Lakeshore Club, Beta Gamma Sigma. Home: 2269 Egandale Rd Highland Park IL 60035-2501 Office: Sonnenschein Nath & Rosenthal 233 S Wacker Dr Ste 8000 Chicago IL 60606-6491 Office Phone: 312-876-8007. Personal E-mail: dlubin@sonnenschein.com.

LUBIN, MICHAEL FREDERICK, physician, educator; b. Phila., Mar. 20, 1947; BA, Johns Hopkins U., 1969, MD, 1973. Resident Emory U. Affiliated Hosp., Atlanta, 1973-76; asst. prof. medicine Emory U. Sch. Medicine, Atlanta, 1976-82, assoc. prof. medicine, 1982—2001, dir. div. gen. medicine, 1989-95; dir. preoperative clinic Grady Hosp., Atlanta, 1995—; chmn. housestaff evaluation com. dept. medicine Emory U. Sch. Medicine, 1985—2001, dir. geriatrics assessment clinic, 1998—, prof. medicine, 2001—. Chmn. univ. adv. coun. tchg. Emory U., 2004—05. Editor: Medical Management of the Surgical Patient, 1982; editor: (3d rev. edit.), 1995; editor: Med. Rounds, 1988—90; contbr. to Med. Knowledge Self Assessment Program X, 1994. Chmn. univ. adv. coun. on tchg. Emory U.; mem. alumni coun. Johns Hopkins U., 1995—2001; mem. Cmty. Supporters of Atlanta Symphony Orch., 1996—98, bd. dirs., 1996—97. Scholar Hartford scholar in Geriatrics, UCLA, 1984—85, Ctr. for Medicare & Medicaid Svcs. Health Policy scholar, 2003. Fellow: ACP, Phi Beta Kappa (bd. dirs. Met. Atlanta chpt. 1996—2000, v.p. 2000—); mem.: Soc. Gen. Internal Medicine (edn. com. 2003—), Am. Geriat. Soc., Alpha Omega Alpha, Fellows of Phi Beta Kappa (bd. dirs. 2002—), Phi Lambda Upsilon. Office: Emory U Sch Medicine 49 Jesse Hill Jr Dr Atlanta GA 30303 Office Phone: 404-778-1607.

LUBIN, STANLEY, lawyer; b. May 7, 1941; children: David Christopher, Jessica Nicole; m. Barbara Ann Lubin. AB, U. Mich., 1963, JD with honors, 1966. Bar: D.C. 1967, U.S. Ct. Appeals (D.C. cir.) 1967, U.S. Ct. Appeals (4th cir.) 1967, Mich. 1968, U.S. Ct. Appeals (6th cir.) 1968, U.S. Supreme Ct. 1970, Ariz. 1972, U.S. Ct. Appeals (9th cir.) 1976, U.S. Ct. Appeals (fed. cir.) 1985, Tex. 2002, U.S. Ct. Appeals (5th cir.) 2002, U.S. Dist. Ct. (ctrl. and so. dist.) Tex. 2005. Atty. NLRB, Washington, 1966-68; asst. gen. counsel UAW, Detroit, 1968-72; assoc. Harrison, Myers & Singer, Phoenix, 1972-74, McKendree & Tountas, Phoenix, 1975; ptnr. McKendree & Lubin, Phoenix and Denver, 1975-84; shareholder Treon, Warnicke & Roush, P.A., 1984-86; pvt. practice Law Offices Stanley Lubin, Phoenix, 1986-95, The Law Offices of Stanley Lubin, P.C., 1996-98, Lubin & Enoch, P.C., 1999—. Mem. Ariz. Employment Security Adv. Coun., 1975—77. Co-author: Union Fines and Union Discipline Under the National Labor Relations Act, 1971. Active ACLU, dir. Ariz. chpt., 1974-81; vice chair Ariz. State Cen. Com. Dem. Party, 1986-91, 93-2004, sec., 1991-92, mem. state exec. com., 1986-2004, Ariz. Dem. Coun., 1987-99, chmn., 1988-93, Thomas Jefferson Forum, 1987-99, chmn., 1988-93. Mem.: Ariz. Indsl. Rels. Assn. (exec. bd. 1973—, pres. 1979—80, 1984), Indsl. Rels. Rsch. Assn., Maricopa County Bar Assn., State Bar Ariz. Home: 7520 N 9th Pl Phoenix AZ 85020-4138 Office: 349 N 4th Ave Phoenix AZ 85003 also: 1450 Empire Ctrl Ste 170 Dallas TX 75247 Office Phone: 602-234-0008, 214-951-9666. Business E-Mail: stanley.lubin@azbar.org.

LUBIN, STEVEN, concert pianist, musicologist; b. N.Y.C., Feb. 22, 1942; s. Jack and Sophie Lubin; m. Wendy Lubin, June 2, 1974; children: Benjamin, Nathaniel. AB in Philosophy, Harvard U., 1963; MS in Piano, Juilliard Sch. Music, 1965; PhD in Musicology, NYU, 1974. Mem. faculty Juilliard Sch. Music, N.Y.C., 1964-65, Aspen (Colo.) Music Sch., 1965; Mem. faculty Vassar Coll., Poughkeepsie, N.Y., 1970-71; coordinator grad. music theory program Cornell U., Ithaca, N.Y., 1971-75; prof. Conservatory of Music, SUNY, Purchase, 1975—; founding mem. The Mozartean Players, 1978—. Mem., NYU Electronic Composers Workshop, 1967-68; concert pianist tours in U.S. and Europe, 1976—; appeared as fortepiano soloist and condr. in Authentic-Instrument concert series, N.Y.C., 1981—; rec. artist Decca, Arabesque Records, Harmonia Mundi; filmed solo performances for Brit. documentary TV in London and Vienna, 1986; soloist in complete Beethoven piano concertos for London/Decca Records, 1987; performed complete cycle Beethoven concertos, London, 1987; solo recordings (new series) Decca including Beethoven Sonatas, 1991; contbr. articles to N.Y. Times, Keyboard Classics, others. Martha Baird Rockefeller grantee, 1968. Mem. Am. Mus. Soc., Soc. Music Theory.

LUBINIECKI, GREGORY MICHAEL, physician; b. Pitts., Nov. 18, 1972; s. Anthony Stanley and Robin Lea Lubiniecki; m. Min Lubiniecki, Aug. 30, 2003. SB, MIT, 1994; MD, Johns Hopkins U., 1998. Diplomate in internal medicine and oncology Am. Bd. Internal Medicine. Resident physician Mayo Clinic, Rochester, Minn., 1998-2001; fellow hematology, oncology U. Pa., Phila., 2001—04, clin. asst. prof. medicine, 2004—. Lector Roman Cath. Ch., 1988-2003. Mem.: ACP, AMA, Am. Soc. Hematology, Am. Soc. Clin. Oncology, Sigma Xi, Phi Beta Kappa, Alpha Chi Sigma. Avocations: bicycling, literature. Home: 695 Barton Run Blvd Marlton NJ 08053 Office: Presbyn Med Ctr U Pa Med Arts Bldg Rm 103 Presbyn Med Ctr 39th and Market Sts Philadelphia PA 19104 Office Phone: 215-662-8947. Business E-Mail: luber@alum.mit.edu.

LUBIT, BEVERLY WEISS, lawyer, science educator; b. N.Y., Aug. 23, 1950; d. Milton and Charlotte Weiss; m. Fredric Alan Lubit, Jan. 30, 1971; children: Amanda, Ryan. BA, NYU Univ. Heights, Bronx, N.Y., 1972; MA, Columbia U., 1974, MPhil, 1975; PhD, Columbia Univ. Graduate Sch. Arts & Scis., N.Y., 1977; MBA, Fairleigh Dickinson Univ., Teaneck, N.J., 1992; JD, N.Y. Law Sch., N.Y., 1998. Bar: NJ 1999, N.Y. 1999, patent 2001. Post doctoral fellow Columbia U., N.Y.C., 1977—81; asst. prof. U. Medicine and Dentistry NJ, Newark, 1981—86; pres. Starbased Tech. Inc., Kinnelon, NJ, 1986—95; assoc. Orrick Herrington & Sutcliffe, NYC, 1998—99, Sullivan & Cromwell, NYC, 1999—2001, Greenberg, Traurig, NYC, 2001—04; counsel Lowenstein Sandler, LLC, NJ, 2004—. Contbr. articles pub. to profl. jour. Mem.: AIPLA, BIO2005, Sigma Xi, Phi Beta Kappa. Office: Lowenstein Sandler PC 65 Livingston Ave Roseland NJ 07068 Office Phone: 973-597-6170. Business E-Mail: blubit@lowenstein.com.

LUBKIN, GLORIA BECKER, physicist; b. Phila., May 16, 1933; d. Samuel Albert and Anne (Gorrin) B.; m. Yale Jay Lubkin, June 14, 1953 (div. Apr. 1968); children: David Craig, Sharon Rebecca. AB, Temple U., 1953; MA, Boston U., 1957; postgrad., Harvard U., 1974—75. Mathematician Fairchild Stratos Co., Hagerstown, Md., 1954, Letterkenny Ordnance Depot, Chambersburg, Pa., 1955-56; physicist TRG Inc., N.Y.C., 1956-58; acting chmn. dept. physics Sarah Lawrence Coll., Bronxville, N.Y., 1961-62; v.p. Lubkin Assocs., electronic cons., Port Washington, N.Y., 1962-68; assoc. editor Physics Today Am. Inst. Physics, N.Y.C., 1963-69, sr. editor, 1970-84, editor, 1985-94, editl. dir., 1994-00, editor-at-large, 2001—03, editor emerita, 2004—. Cons. in field; mem. Nieman adv. com. Harvard U., 1978-82; co-chmn. search/adv. com. Theoretical Physics Inst., U. Minn., 1987-89, co-chmn. oversight com. 1989—; mem. mng. com. Westinghouse Sci. Writing Prizes, 1988-91; mem. selection com. Knight Fellowships, 1990. Contbr. articles to profl. publs. Gloria Becker Lubkin Professorship of Theoretical Physics established in her honor U. Minn., 1990; Nieman fellow, 1974-75. Fellow: AAAS (chair nominating com. for sect. B physics 1989, nominating com. for sect. B physics 2003—), Am. Phys. Soc. (founding mem. com. on status of women in physics 1971—72, exec. com. forum on physics and soc. 1977—78, exec. com. history of physics divsn. 1983—86, 1992—95, 1998—, coun. mem. 1998—, exec. bd. 2000—01, com. on coms. 2000—02, chair Lilienfeld prize com. 2002, com. on coms. 2004—, audit com. 2004); mem.: Com. Concerned Journalists, DC Sci. Writers Assn., Nat. Assn. Sci. Writers, NY Acad. Scis. (mem. The Scis. pub. com. 1992—93), Sigma Pi Sigma. Jewish. Office: Am Inst Physics One Physics Ellipse College Park MD 20740 Office Phone: 301-209-3050. Business E-Mail: glubkin@aip.org.

LUBLINSKI, MICHAEL, lawyer; b. Eskilstuna, Sweden, Sept. 11, 1951; came to U.S., 1956; s. Walter and Dora L. BA magna cum laude, CCNY, 1972; JD, Georgetown U., 1975. Bar: N.Y. 1976, Calif. 1980, D.C. 2001, Ct. Internat. Trade 1981, U.S. Dist. Ct. (cen. dist.) Calif. 1981, U.S. Dist. Ct. (so. dist.) N.Y. 1981, U.S. Ct. Appeals (D.C. cir.) 1982. Atty. U.S. Customs Service, Washington, 1975-79, U.S. Dept. Commerce, Washington, 1980; assoc. Mori & Ota, L.A., 1980-84, Kelley Drye & Warren LLP, L.A., 1984-85, ptnr., mem. intellectual property practice group, 1986—2003. Panel moderator Calif. continuing edn. of bar Competitive Bus. Practices Inst., Los Angeles and San Francisco, 1984. Mem. ABA, Calif. Bar Assn., Los Angeles County Bar Assn. (arbitrator 1981-82, chmn. customs law sect. 1986), N.Y. State Bar Assn., D.C. Bar Assn., Phi Beta Kappa. Avocations: travel, movies. Office: 548 York Hill Blvd Thornhill ON L4J 5K7 Canada Office Phone: 905-764-2544. E-mail: mlublinski@bellnet.ca.

LUBNAU, THOMAS EDWIN, II, lawyer; b. Laramie, Wyo., Dec. 12, 1958; s. Thomas Edwin and Cynthia L'Vere (Kirkland) L. BS in Fin., U. Wyo., 1981, JD, 1984. Bar: Wyo. 1984, U.S. Dist. Ct. Wyo. 1984, U.S. Ct. Appeals (10th cir.) 1984, U.S. Supreme Ct. 1995. Mem. Lubnau, Bailey & Dumbrill, P.C., Gillette, Wyo., 2000—. Chmn. Wyo. Bd. CLE, Cheyenne, 1990-92; trustee Rocky Mountain Mineral Law, Denver, 1992-95; legal counsel Wyo. Jaycees, Gillette, 1986-94, Campbell County Rep. Party, Gillette, 1989—. Contbr. to Land and Water Law rev., 1984. Bd. dirs. Campbell County Libr. Found.; chalice bearer, lay reader Holy Trinity Episcopal Ch., Campbell County Rep. Party (state committeeman 1988-89), Campbell County C. of C. (chmn. 1993-94). Mem. ABA, Assn. Trial Lawyers Am., Campbell County C. of C. (bd. dirs.), Gillette Rotary (bd. dirs.), Wyo. State Bar (commnr. 1998-2001, v.p. 2001-02, pres.-elect 2002-03), Cambell County Bar Assn. (pres. 2000-01), Gov.'s Probate Com. (1984-90), Bd. Continuing Ed. (chmn. 1988-91), Rocky Mtn. Mineral Law Found. (trustee 1992-95), Atty.'s Assistance Com. (co-chair, 1995-96). Republican. Avocations: woodworking, photography, writing. Office: Lubnau Bailey & Dumbrill PC PO Box 1028 Gillette WY 82717-1028

LUBORSKY, FRED EVERETT, research physicist; b. Phila., May 14, 1923; s. Meyer and Cecelia (Miller) L.; m. Florence R. Glass, Aug. 25, 1946; children— Judith, Mark, Rhoda BS, U. Pa., 1947; PhD, Ill. Inst. Tech., 1952. Teaching-research asst. Ill. Inst. Tech., Chgo., 1947-51; research assoc. Gen. Elec. Co., Schenectady, 1951-52, West Lynn, Mass., 1952-58, research physicist Schenectady, 1958-92. Gen. chmn. 2d Joint Internat. Magnetism and Magnetic Materials Conf., 1979; chmn. adv. com. Conf. on Magnetism and Magnetic Materials, 1980 Editor: Amorphous Metallic Alloys, 1984; mem. editorial bd. Internat. Jour. Rapid Solidification, 1984—; mem. editorial adv.

bd. Internat. Jour. Magnetism, 1972—; contbr. articles to profl. jours.; patentee in field Served with USN, 1944-46 Recipient citation achievement in indsl. sci. AAAS, 1956; Brit. Sci. Research Council fellow, 1977; Coolidge fellow in research and devel. Gen. Elec. Corp., 1978 Fellow IEEE (editorial bd. Transactions on Magnetics jour. 1968—, editor-in-chief 1972-75, editorial bd. Spectrum jour. 1972-73, Centennial medal 1984, mem. Fellows com. 1993—), Am. Inst. Chemists, N.Y. Acad. Scis.; mem. Nat. Acad. Engring., Magnetics Soc. of IEEE (pres. 1975-77, named disting. lectr. 1979, achievement award 1981), Am. Chem. Soc., Materials Research Soc. Home: 137 Glen Eddy Dr Schenectady NY 12309

LUBOVITCH, LAR, dancer, choreographer; b. Chgo. Student, Art Inst. Chgo., U. Iowa, Juilliard Sch. Music, Am. Ballet Theatre Sch., Martha Graham, Anthony Tudor. Dancer debut with Pearl Lang Dance Co., 1962, with modern cos. Glen Tetley, John Butler, Sophie Maslow and Donald McKayle, Manhattan Festival Ballet, Santa Fe Opera, Harkness Ballet, formed Lar Lubovitch Dance Co., 1968; guest choreographer Bat-Dor Dance Co., Gulbenkian Ballet, Dutch Nat. Ballet, Ballet Rambert, Pa. Ballet, Am. Ballet Theatre, Royal Danish Ballet, Bejart Ballet XX Century, Alvin Alley Am. Dance Theater, John Curry Ice Dancing Co., Les Grandes Ballets Canadiens, Stuttgart Ballet, N.Y.C. Ballet, Pacific N.W. Ballet, Paris Opera Ballet, White Oak Dance Project, ballets choreographed include Blue, 1968, Freddie's Bag, 1968, Journey Back, 1968, Greeting Sampler, 1969, Whirligogs, 1969, Unremembered Time-Forgotton Place, 1969, Variations and Theme, 1970, Ecstasy, 1970, Sam Nearlydeadman, 1970, The Teaching, 1970, Some of the Reactions, 1970, The Time Before, 1971, Clear Lake, 1971, Air, 1972, Joy of Man's Desiring, 1972, Chariot Light Night, 1973, Scherzo for Massah Jack, 1973, Three Essays, 1974, Zig Zag, 1974, Avalanche, 1975, Rapid Transit, 1975, Session, 1975, Eight Easy Pieces, 1975, Girl on Fire, 1975, Marimba, 1976, Les Noches, 1976, Scriabin Dances, 1977, Exultate Jubilate, 1977, North Star, 1978, Valley, 1978, Tiltawhirl, 1979, Up Jump, 1979, Mistral, 1980, Cavalcade, 1980, American Gesture, 1981, Beau Danube, 1981, Big Shoulders, 1983, Tabernacle, 1983, Adagio and Rondo, 1984, A Brahms Symphony, 1985, Concerto Six Twenty-Two, 1986, Blood, 1986, Of My Soul, 1987, Musette, 1988, Rhapsody in Blue, 1988, Fandango, 1989, Just Before Jupiter, 1990, Hautbois, 1990, Sinfonia Concertante, 1991, Waiting for the Sunrise, 1991, American Gesture, 1992, So In Love, 1994, Touch Me, 1996, Bach Adagio, 1996, Gershwin Variations, 1996, I'll Be Seeing You, 1996, Othello, 1997, Thus is All, 1998, Yiddish Songs of Love and Wonder, 1999, Meadow, 1999, All Ye Need to Know, 2000, Men's Stories, 2000, My Funny Valentine, 2001, Smile with my Heart, 2002, Artemis, 2003; choreographer Pentimento, 2004, Do You Be, 2004, Love Stories, 2005, (TV films) Sleeping Beauty (WGBH-TV), 1987, (TV series) The Planets, A&E-TV, 1994, (TV films) Othello, WNET-TV, 2003, (Broadway plays) Into the Woods, 1987, Salome, 1992, The Red Shoes, 1993, The King and I, 1998, High Society, 1998, The Hunchback of Notre Dame, Berlin, 1999. Recipient Tony award nominee, 1988, Astaire award, 1993—94, Elan award, 2004; Guggenheim fellow, CAPS grantee, NEA grantee. Address: care Lubovitch Dance Co 229 W 42d St 8th Fl New York NY 10036 Office Phone: 212-221-7909. Personal E-mail: Lubovitch@aol.com.

LUBS, HERBERT AUGUSTUS, genetics educator, administrator; b. Jan. 7, 1929; BA, Washington and Lee U., 1950; MD, Yale U., 1954. Diplomate Am. Bd. Internal Medicine, Am. Bd. Med. Genetics. Intern Yale-New Haven Hosp., 1954-55, resident in medicine, 1957-59, chief resident, 1959-60; clin. assoc., endocrinology br. Nat. Cancer Inst., USPHS, Bethesda, Md., 1955-57; spl. trainee in rsch. and genetics NIH, Dept. of Human Genetics, U. Mich. and Dept. Biology, Yale U., 1957-63; instr. in Medicine Yale Sch. Medicine, New Haven, 1959-63, asst. prof. Medicine, chief sect. medicine genetics, 1963-67; clin. investigator VA Hosp., West Haven, Conn., 1960-63; dir. Yale Pvt. Diagnostic Clinic, New Haven, 1964-66; assoc. prof. dept. pediatrics U. Colo. Med. Ctr., Denver, 1968-79, assoc. prof. dept. biophysics and genetics, 1973-79; prof. dept. pediatrics, dir. genetics div., Mailman Ctr. for Child Devel. U. Miami Sch. Medicine, Fla., 1979—; prof. genetics U. Tromsø, Norway, 1992-99. Lectr. numerous med. schs. and meetings; sci. presentations at nat. and internat. meetings; mem. human subjects rev. com., 1980-83, U. Miami Sch. Medicine, dean's task force on genetics, 1982-84, human subjects exec. rev. com., 1984—. Editor: Computers in Biology and Medicine; editor Am. Jour. Med. Genetics, BioEssays (corr.), Birth Defects Ency. Chmn. Com. on Environ. Hazards, Am. Soc. of Human Genetics, NICHD sponsored meeting genetic counseling, 1979; cons. Standing Com. on Chromosome Nomenclature; mem. Med. Adv. Com. to Indor Radon Study, Grand Junction, Colo., 1975-79, Gov.'s Adv. Coun. on Radiation, Colo., 1979; co-chmn. NIH mtg. on Marker X, 1983; chmn. Am. Soc. of Human Genetics Genetic Svcs. subcom. on Cytogeneticvs Lab. Proficiency Testing and Quality Assurance; steering com. NICHD Collaborative Study on Chorionic Villus Sampling and Amniocentesis, 1984—; mem. various NIH site visit coms. and ad hoc rev. coms., 1979—. Recipient VA clin. investigatorship, 1960-63, USPHS Career Devel. award, 1963-73, Joseph P. Kennedy Jr. Internat. award for rsch. in mental retardation, 1986. Mem. Am. Soc. of Human Genetics (bd. dirs., Genetic Svcs. Com. 1985—, Travel Com. 1986, Tissue Culture Soc.), Am. Fed. for Clin. Rsch., Soc. for Study of Social Biology, So. Soc. for Pediatric Rsch., Alpha Omega Alpha, Phi Beta Kappa. Office: U Miami Dept Pediatrics PO Box 016820 Miami FL 33101-6820 Home: 31374 Nandua DR Painter VA 23420-3113 E-mail: hlubs@peds.med.miami.edu.

LUBY, ELLIOT DONALD, psychiatrist, educator; b. Detroit, Apr. 3, 1924; m. Ideane Maura Levenson, June 28, 1950; children: Arthur, Howard, Joan. Student, U. Chgo., 1943-44; BS, U. Mo., 1945-47; MD, Wash. U., St. Louis, 1947-49. Clin. dir. Lafayette Clinic, Detroit, 1957-74; chief psychiatry Harper Hosp., Detroit, 1978-91. Prof. psychiatry and law Wayne State U., 1965—, pres. Comprehensive Psychiatry Services, Southfield, Mich., 1972-98. Contbr. numerous articles to various publs., also several book chpts. Served to lt. USPHS, 1950-52. Recipient Gold Medal award Am. Acad. Psychosomatic Medicine, 1962. Fellow Am. Psychiat. Assn. (life), Am. Coll. Psychiatrists; mem. AMA, N.Y. Acad. Sci., Sigma Xi. Jewish. Office: 28800 Orchard Lake Rd Ste 250 Farmington Hills MI 48334-2922 Home: 27540 Lakehills Dr Franklin MI 48025-1742

LUCÀ-MORETTI, MAURIZIO, research scientist, medical researcher, nutritionist, researcher; b. Rome, June 2, 1945; came to U.S., 1995; s. Giuseppe and Elena (Moretti) L.; m. Anna Grandi, Jan. 2, 1974; 1 child, Elena. BS, Ministry of Edn., Caracas, Venezuela, 1969; PhD in Allied Health Scis., DSc in Human Nutrition, Pacific Western U., 1990; MD (hon.), Universidad Santo Tomas, La Paz, Bolivia, 1994; MPH (hon.), Inst. Superiore di Studi Sanitari, Rome, 1995. Rschr. Inst. Italiano di Terapia Fisica e Medicina Interna, Rome, 1974-76, sr. rschr., 1976-78, dir. rsch., 1978-80, Caracas, Venezuela, 1980-88; dir. human nutrition rsch. program and AIDS rsch. program InterAm. Med. and Health Assn., Boca Raton, Fla., 1989—, pres., 1989—; gen. sec. World Acad. Medicine, 1992—; prof. emeritus Pacific Western U., New Orleans, 1992; dir. rsch. Internat. Nutrition Rsch. Ctr., 1995—. Invited prof. Univ. di Chiete, Italy, 1991, Univ. de Asuncion, Paraguay, 1992, Univ. di Roma, Rome, 1995; hon. prof. Univ. de Granada, Spain, 1994, Univ. Nacional Pedro Enrique Ureña, Santo Domingo, Dominican Rep., 1994, Inst. Superiore di Studi Sanitari, 1996, Univ. Catolica Santo Domingo, Dominican Rep., 1996, St. Thomas U., Miami, 1998. Recipient medal Univ. Asuncion, Paraguay, 1992, medal Univ. Granada, Spain, 1993; decorated Cruz de Alfonso X el Sabio, Spani, 1997. Fellow NAS (Dominican Rep.), Royal Nat. Acad. Medicine Spain, Royal Acad. Scis. Spain, Royal Acad. Medicine Salamanca, Royal Acad. Medicine Granada, Royal Acad. Medicine Valencia, Royal Acad. Medicine of Zaragoza, Nat. Acad. Medicine Bolivia, Nat. Acad. Medicine Ecuador, Nat. Acad. Medicine Paraguay, Nat. Acad. Medicine Dominican Rep., Acad. Medicine Maracaibo, Reial Acad. Medicina Catalunya. Achievements: discovery of the Master Amino Pattern (MAP); discovery of the Dietary Protein Engring. (DPE); also patents in nutritional amino acids formulations with extremely high human Net Nitrogen Utilization (NNU). Home: 3025 Saint James Dr Boca Raton FL 33434-3370 Office: Internat Nutrition Rsch Ctr 7900 Los Pinos Cir Coral Gables FL 33143 Office Phone: 305-740-7480. E-mail: inrc@msn.com.

LUCAS, ALEXANDER RALPH, child psychiatrist, educator, writer; b. Vienna, July 30, 1931; came to U.S., 1940, naturalized, 1945; s. Eugene Hans and Margaret Ann (Weiss) L.; m. Margaret Alice Thompson, July 6, 1956; children: Thomas Alexander, Nancy Elizabeth Watson, Alexander Eugene, Peter Clayton. BS, Mich. State U., 1953; MD, U. Mich., 1957. Diplomate Am. Bd. Psychiatry and Neurology (psychiatry and child and adolescent psychiatry), Am. Bd. of Med. Specialties. Intern U. Mich. Hosp., 1957-58; resident in child psychiatry Hawthorn Ctr., Northville, Mich., 1958-59, 61-62, staff psychiatrist, 1963-65, sr. psychiatrist, 1965-67; resident in psychiatry Lafayette Clinic, Detroit, 1959-61, rsch. child psychiatrist, 1967-71, rsch. coord., 1969-71; asst. prof. psychiatry Wayne State U., 1967-69, assoc. prof., 1969-71; cons. child and adolescent psychiatry Mayo Clinic, 1971-97; assoc. prof. Mayo Med Sch., 1973-76, prof., 1976-97; emeritus prof., 1998—; head sect. child and adolescent psychiatry Mayo Clinic, Rochester, Minn., 1971-80, emeritus cons., 1998—. Dir. com. on certification in child and adolescent psychiatry Am. Bd. Psychiatry and Neurology, 1997-2001; residency rev. com. Accreditation Coun. for Grad. Med. Edn., 1999-2001. Author (with C. R. Shaw): The Psychiatric Disorders of Childhood, 1970; author: Demystifying Anorexia Nervosa, 2004, Preventing and Overcoming Bulemia and Obesity, 2005. Recipient Eating Disorders Scientific Achievement award, 1998. Fellow Am. Acad. Child and Adolescent Psychiatry (life, editl. bd. jour. 1976-82), Am. Orthopsychiat. Assn. (life), Am. Psychiat. Assn. (life); mem. Minn. Soc. Child and Adolescent Psychiatry (pres. 1993-95, chair Mayo clinic emeritus staff, 2004-05), Soc. Profs. Child and Adolescent Psychiatry (pres. 2000-2002), Sigma Xi Achievements include research in biol. aspects of child psychiatry, psychopathology, psychopharmacology, eating disorders, psychiat. treatment of children, adolescents, and young adults. Office: Mayo Clinic 200 1st St SW Rochester MN 55905-0002 Office Phone: 507-284-2691.

LUCAS, AUBREY KEITH, retired university president; b. State Line, Miss., July 12, 1934; s. Keith Caldwell and Audelle Margaret (Robertson) L.; m. Ella Frances Ginn, Dec. 18, 1955; children: Margaret Frances, Keith Godbold (dec.), Martha Carol Pittman, Alan Douglas, Mark Christopher. BS, U. So. Miss., 1955, MA, 1956; PhD, Fla. State U., 1966; DHL, Miss. Coll., 1997. Instr. Hinds Jr. Coll., Raymond, Miss., 1956-57; pres. Delta State U., Cleveland, Miss., 1971-75; asst. dir. reading clinic U. So. Miss., Hattiesburg, 1955-56, dir. admissions, 1957-61, registrar, 1963-69, dean Grad. Sch., 1969-71, pres., 1975-96, pres. emeritus, prof. higher edn., 1997—2004. Bd. dirs. Miss. Power Co., 1983-2004. Author: The Mississippi Legislature and Mississippi Public Higher Education, 1890-1960; contbg. author: A History of Mississippi, 1973. Bd. dirs. Africa U., 1997-, treas., 1999—; bd. dirs. Pine Burr Area coun. Boy Scouts Am., 1990-2003, Miss. Inst. Tech. Devel., 1984-96, Miss. Assn. Coll., 1979-80, Miss. Arts Commn., 1977-87; bd. dirs. Salvation Army, chmn., 2000-02; gen. bd. Global Ministries, United Meth. Ch., 1984-92, gen. bd. higher edn. and ministry, 1992-2000, investment com., 2002-; chmn. Miss. Arts Commn., 1983-85; campaign chmn. Forrest United Way, 1979, So. U. Conf., 1995-96; state chmn. Am. Cancer Soc., 1978; mem. Commn. on Nat. Devel. Postsecondary Edn., 97th Congress; pres. Miss. Econ. Coun., 1982-83; lay leader Miss. Meth. Conf., 1980-88, 2004—; bd. visitors Air U., 1990-94, chmn., 1991-92; exec. bd. Commn. on Colls. of So. Assn. Colls. and Schs., 1990-93. Mem. Hattiesburg C. of C., Miss. Forestry Assn., Newcomen Soc. N.Am., Am. Assn. State Colls. and Univs. (bd. dirs. 1982-86, chmn. 1984-85), Am. Coun. Edn. (bd. dirs. 1984-86), Miss. Inst. Arts and Letters (pres. 1999-2000), Hattiesburg Cmty. Found., Hattiesburg Conv. Ctr. Commn., Lauren Rogers Mus. Art (pres. bd. trustees, chmn. 2001—04), Red Red Rose Club, Sigma Phi Epsilon, Omicron Delta Kappa, Phi Kappa Phi, Pi Gamma Mu, Pi Tau Chi, Kappa Delta Pi, Phi Delta Kappa, Kappa Pi. Home: 3200 Jamestown Rd Hattiesburg MS 39402-2333 Office: U So Miss 118 College Dr # 5164 Hattiesburg MS 39406-0001 Office Phone: 601-266-4351. Business E-Mail: aubrey.lucas@usm.edu.

LUCAS, BARBARA B., electrical equipment manufacturing executive; b. 1945; BA magna cum laude, U. Md., 1967; MA, Johns Hopkins U., 1968. V.p., sec. Equitable Bancorp, 1977-85; sr. v.p. pub. affairs, corp. sec. Black & Decker Corp., Balt., 1985—96, sr. v.p., pub. affairs, 1996—, corp. sec., 1996—. Bd. dirs. Provident Bankshares; chair bd. dirs. Greater Balt. Med. Ctr., Balt. Named one of The 100 Women to Watch in Corp. Am., Bus. Month. Mem.: Am. Soc. Corp. Secretaries (pres. Mid-Atlantic Regional chpt., nat. dir.). Office: Black & Decker Corp 701 E Joppa Rd Baltimore MD 21286-5502

LUCAS, C. PAYNE, development organization executive; b. Spring Hope, N.C., Sept. 14, 1933; s. James Russell and Minnie (Hendricks) L; m. Freddie Emily Myra Hill, Aug. 29, 1964; children: Therese Raymonde, C. Payne Jr., Hillary Hendricks. BA in History, U. Md.; LLD (hon.), U. Md., 1975; MA in Govt., Am. U. Asst. dir. Peace Corps, Togo, 1964, dir., 1965-67, dir. Africa region, 1967-71; pres. Africare, Washington, 1971—. Lectr. in field. Author: (with Kevin Lowther) Keeping Kennedy's Promise--The Peace Corps: Unmet Promise of the New Frontier, 1978; contbr. articles to profl. publs. Bd. dirs. Coun. Fgn. Rels., Overseas Devel. Coun. World Resources Inst., InterAction, Population Action Internat., Kagiso Trust USA, Nat. Planning Assn.; bd. dirs., chmn. Reach & Teach USA; bd. dirs., founding mem. Corp. Coun. on Africa. Recipient Disting. Fed. Svc. award Pres. Lyndon B. Johnson, Presdl. Hunger award for Outstanding Achievement, Pres. Ronald Reagan, 1984, Aggrey medal Phelps-Stokes Fund, 1986, Order of Disting. Svc. award Pres. Kenneth Kaunda of Zambia, 1986, Recognition awards Nat. Order of Rep. Niger, 1988, Zambia, Cote D'Iroire, Senegal, Benin, Disting. Bicentennial award Land Grant Coll., 1990, Hubert H. Humphrey Pub. Svc. award APSA, 1991. Mem. Cosmos Club, Omega Psi Phi. Office: Africare 440 R St NW Washington DC 20001-1935 E-mail: cplucas@africare.org.

LUCAS, DOINA C., librarian; b. Berlin, Oct. 9, 1945; d. Katharina E. and Emile G. Nedila; children: David B., Christopher D.J. BA, Albertus Magnus Coll., Conn., 1967; MEd, U. Ga., 1971; MLS, So. Conn. State U., 1977. Wash. post indexer Rsch. Publs., Woodbridge, 1982—86; head info. svcs. Miller Meml. Libr., Hamden, Conn., 1987—; lectr. Ctrl. Conn. State U., New Britain, 1996—. Chair Reference Round Table, Hamden, Conn., 1987—88; bd. mem., officer So. Conn. Libr. Coun., Wallingford, 1987—90; sect. chair exec. bd. Conn. Libr. Assn., 1989—96. Editor: (address directory) Addressbuch der Direktoren und Aufsichtsraete. Mem.: AAUP, Conn. Libr. Assn., ALA. Liberal. Lutheran. Avocations: travel, hiking, reading. Office: Miller Meml Libr 2901 Dixwell Ave Hamden CT 06518 Office Phone: 203-287-2680.

LUCAS, DONALD LEO, investor; b. Upland, Calif., Mar. 18, 1930; s. Leo J. and Mary G. (Schwamm) L.; m. Lygia de Soto Harrison, July 15, 1961; children: Nancy Maria Lucas Thibodeau, Alexandra Maria Lucas Ertola, Donald Alexander Lucas. BA, Stanford U., 1951, MBA, 1953. Assoc. corp. fin. dept. Smith, Barney & Co., N.Y.C., 1956-59; gen., ltd. ptnr. Draper, Gaither & Anderson, Palo Alto, Calif., 1959-66; pvt. investor Menlo Park, Calif., 1966—. Bd. dirs. Cadence Design Systems, San Jose, Calif., Oracle Corp., Redwood Shores, Calif., Macromedia, San Francisco, PDF Solutions, San Jose, 51job Inc., Shanghai. Mem. bd. regents Bellarmine Coll. Prep., 1977-2002; regent emeritus U. Santa Clara, 1980—. 1st lt. AUS, 1953-55. Mem. Am. Coun. Capital Formation (dir.), Stanford U. Alumni Assn., Stanford Grad. Sch. Bus. Alumni Assn., Order of Malta, Stanford Buck Club, Menlo Circus Club (Atherton, Calif.), Bighorn Country Club, Calif., Zeta Psi. Office: 3000 Sand Hill Rd Ste 3-210 Menlo Park CA 94025-7119 Home: 449 Selby Ln Atherton CA 94027-5411 Office Phone: 650-854-4223.

LUCAS, DONALD RICHARD, psychologist, educator; b. Elmhurst, Ill., Sept. 21, 1967; s. Leon Jack and Velma Marie McClelland; m. Lisa Marie Lucas; children: Sember Ann, Rayen Marie. BS in Psychology, Ill. State U., 1989; PhD in Psychology/Neurosci. and Behavior, No. Ill. U., 1994. Assoc. scientist Ctr. Family Violence and Sexual Assault Rsch., No. Ill. U., DeKalb, 1996—98; postdoctoral rsch. assoc. Smith-Kettlewell Eye Rsch. Inst., San Francisco, 1994—95; rsch. cons. JBP Engring., San Antonio, 1999—2003; instr. NW Vista Coll., San Antonio, 2000—03, asst. prof., 2003—. Presenter in field. Contbr. articles to profl. publs.;, author monographs in field. Mem.: APA (assoc.), Southwestern Psychol. Assn. Achievements include invention of fluorescent-lighted four post bed. Office: NW Vista Coll 3535 Ellison San Antonio TX 78251

LUCAS, FRANK D., congressman; b. Cheyenne, Okla., Jan. 6, 1960; m. Lynda L. Bradshaw, 1988; 3 children. BS, Okla. State U., 1982. Mem. Okla. Ho. of Reps., 1989-94, U.S. Congress from 3rd Okla. Dist. (formerly 6th), 1994—; mem. agrl., banking and fin. svcs. and sci. coms.; chmn. agrl. subcommittee on conservation, credit, rural devel., and rsch. Mem.: Okla. Farmer's Union, Okla. Farm Bur. Republican. Baptist. Home: RR 2 Box 136A Cheyenne OK 73628-9802 Office: US Ho of Reps 2342 Rayburn Ho Office Bldg Washington DC 20515-3606*

LUCAS, FRANK EDWARD, architect; b. Charleston, S.C., Oct. 31, 1934; m. Edith R. Dority; children: Susan R. Lucas Tezza, Kelly E., Julie C. Lucas Rodenberg. BArch, Clemson U., 1959. Registered architect, S.C., Fla., N.C., W.Va., Ala., Ga., Va., Ky. Founder, architect Lucas and Stubbs Assocs. (now LS3P Assocs. Ltd.), Charleston, S.C., 1964—; chmn. bd. dirs. LS3P Architects Ltd. (now LS3P Assocs. Ltd.). Mem. Charleston County Bd. Rev., Bldg. and Elec. Codes, 1972-85; mem. St. Philip's Episcopal Ch., former vestryman, sr. warden, lay reader St. James Episcopal Ch.; trustee Cities in Schs., Charleston, 1990-94; past pres. nine county region Girl Scouts Am., 1988-90; affiliate S.C. Sch. Bds. Assn.; pres. adv. coun. Clemson U., mem. bd. visitors; mem. Trident Tech. Coll. Found., Coll. Charleston Found.; dir. Cmty. Firstbank, Charleston Recipient Elizabeth O'Neill Verner award S.C. Arts Commn., 1990; featured in exhibit at Gibbes Art Gallery titled 20 Yrs. of Design Excellence, 1988. Fellow AIA (mem. jury of fellows); mem. S.C. AIA (pres. 1970, Disting. Svc. award), S.C. Econ. Developers Assn., Soc. Am. Mil. Engrs., Charleston Trident C. of C. (pres. 1990-91, Jos. P. Riley Leadership award 1996), Preservation Soc. Charleston, S.C. Hist. Soc., Carolina Art Assn., S.C. Arts Found. (bd. dirs.), Executives Assn. Greater Charleston (pres. 1983), Greater Charleston Real Estate Bd., Clemson Archtl. Found. (bd. dirs. 1967-73, 77-81, 86—, pres. 1975, 81, 89), Hibernian Soc. (mng. com. 1984-96, chmn. managing com. 1996-97, v.p. 1998-99, pres. 2000-2002), Hibernian Soc. Found. (v.p. 1990-92, pres. 1992-94), Country Club of Charleston (bd. dirs. 1976-79, exec. com. 1991), S.C. State C. of C. (bd. dirs. 1989-98, com. to reorganize state govt. 1990, exec. com. 1992), S.C. Arts Commn. (bus. and arts awards adv. com.), Assn. of Citadel Men, IPTAY Clemson U., Clemson Alumni Assn. (Disting. Alumni), Clemson Low Country Assn., Palmetto State Tchrs. Assn. (affiliate), Carolina Yacht Club, Rotary (N. Charleston chpt., Paul Harris fellow), Country Club Charleston (bd. dirs. 1973-76), Health Scis. Found. (bd. dirs.), The Harbor Club (Charleston, founding dir.). Home: 607 N Shore Dr Charleston SC 29412-4213 Office: LS3P Assoc Ltd 205 1/2 King St Charleston SC 29401-3129 E-mail: lucas@ls3p.com.

LUCAS, GENE, academic administrator; BS, U. Calif., Santa Barbara, 1973; MS, MIT, 1975, ScD, 1978. Joined faculty U. Calif., Santa Barbara, 1978, exec. vice chancellor, 2003—. Office: Exec Vice Chancellor 5105 Cheadle Hall Univ Calif Santa Barbara CA 93106 Office Phone: 805-893-2126. Business E-Mail: gene.lucas@evc.ucsb.edu.

LUCAS, GEORGE WALTON, JR., film director, film producer, scriptwriter; b. Modesto, Calif., May 14, 1944; Student, Modesto Jr. Coll.; BA, U. So. Calif., 1966. Chmn. Lucasfilm Ltd., San Rafael, Calif., 1971—. Mem. TV bd. councilors U. So. Calif.; chmn. George Lucas Ednl. Found., Artists Rights Found., Joseph Campbell Found., Film Found. Asst. to Francis Ford Coppola The Rain People, 1969, creator short film, dir., co-writer THX-1138:4EB, 1970, THX-1138, 1971, dir., co-writer American Graffiti, 1973, dir., author screenplay Star Wars, 1977 (earned seven Acad. awards); exec. prodr.: More American Graffiti, 1979, The Empire Strikes Back, 1980, Raiders of the Lost Ark, 1981, Indiana Jones and the Temple of Doom, 1984, Labyrinth, 1986, Howard the Duck, 1986, Willow, 1988, Tucker, 1988, Radioland Murders, 1994, (co-author screenplay): Return of the Jedi, 1983; co-exec. prodr. Mishima, 1985; co-author (co-exec. prodr.): Indiana Jones and the Last Crusade, 1989; exec. prodr.(TV series): The Young Indiana Jones Chronicles, 1992—93; author (dir., exec. prodr.): Star Wars: Episode I The Phantom Menace, 1999, Star Wars: Episode II Attack of the Clones, 2002, Star Wars: Episode III Revenge of the Sith, 2005. Mem. adv. bd. Sci. Fiction Mus. and Hall of Fame. Recipient Irving G. Thalberg Meml. award, Academy of Motion Picture Arts and Sciences, 1991, Lifetime Achievement award, Am. Film Inst., 2005. Office: Lucasfilm Ltd PO Box 2009 San Rafael CA 94912-2009

LUCAS, GEORGES, retired physicist, researcher; b. Marosvasarhely, Transylvania, Rumania, Dec. 11, 1914; arrived in France, 1933; s. Emeric and Hermine (Grun) Lukacs; m. Irene Weingrow, Jan. 10, 1948. Degree in Chem. Engring., U. Strasbourg, France, 1938; postgrad., Ecole Normale Superieure, Paris, 1938-40; PhD, U. Paris, Sorbonne, 1955. Rsch. assoc. astrophysics Centre Nat. de la Recherche Scientifique Observatory, Meudon, France, 1953-55; with rsch. dept. Tidewater Oil Co., Avon, Calif., 1956-65, Elf-Aquitaine, Paris, 1965-77, ret., 1977. Author: Transfer Theory for Trapped Electromagnetic Energy, 1983; contbr. articles to profl. jours., abstracts to profl. proceedings; patentee in field. Mem. Am. Phys. Soc., Am. Soc. Photobiology, European Photochemistry Assn., European Soc. Photobiology, N.Y. Acad. Scis. Avocation: drawing. Home: 83-85 rue Saint Charles 75015 Paris France

LUCAS, GWENDOLYNN SUE, principal, farmer; b. Elizabethtown, Ky., Jan. 7, 1972; d. Bernard L. and Shirley Jane Lucas. BA, Western Ky. U., 1994, MA, 1998, postgrad. Cert. tchr. Tchr. agr. Ctrl. Hardin H.S., Cecilia, Ky., 1994—2004; prin. Hardinsburg (Ky.) Elem. Sch., 2004—. Mem.: Ky. Vocat. Tchrs. Assn., Ky. Farm Bur., Ky. Assn. Sch. Adminstrn., Ky. Future Farmers Am. Alumni Assn. Baptist. Avocations: boating, fishing, gardening, singing, travel. Office: Hardinsburg Elem Sch 519 E 3rd St Hardinsburg KY 40143

LUCAS, HENRY CAMERON, JR., information scientist, educator, writer; b. Omaha, Sept. 4, 1944; s. Henry Cameron and Lois (Himes) L.; m. Ellen Kuhbach, June 8, 1968; children: Scott C., Jonathan G. BS in Indsl. Adminstrn. magna cum laude, Yale U., 1966; MS, MIT, 1968, PhD, 1970. Cons. Arthur D. Little, Inc., Cambridge, Mass., 1966-70; asst. prof. computer and info. systems Stanford (Calif.) U., 1970-74; assoc. prof. computer applications and info. systems NYU, 1974-78, prof., chmn. dept. info. systems, 1978-84; on leave IBM European Systems Rsch. Inst., Belgium, 1981; INSEAD Fontainebleau, France, 1985; prof. info. systems NYU, 1985-2000; Shaw Found. Prof. Nat. Tech. U., Singapore, 1997-98; Robert H. Smith prof. info. sys. Robert H. Smith Sch. Bus. U. Md., 2000—; co-dir. Ctr. for Electronic Markets and Enterprises, 2001—04. Author: The T-Form Organization, 1996 Computer-Based Information Systems in Organizations, 1973, The Information Systems Environment, 1980 (with F. Land, T. Lincoln and K. Supper) Casebook for Management Information Systems, 3d edit., 1985, The Analysis, Design and Implementation of Information Systems, 4th edit., 1992, Information Technology for Management 7th edit., 2000, Coping with Computers: A Manager's Guide to Controlling Information Processing, 1982, Introduction to Computers and Information Systems, 1986, Managing Information Services, 1989, Information Technology and Productivity Paradox: Assessing the Value of Investing in IT, 1999, Strategies for Electronic Commerce and the Internet, 2002, (with G. Anandalingam) Beware the Winner's Curse: Victories that can Sink You and Your Company, 2004; editor Indsl. Mgmt., 1967-68; mem. editl. bd. Sloan Mgmt., Rev., 1975-91; assoc. editor MIS Quar., 1977-83; editor-in-chief Systems, Objectives, Solutions, 1980—, v.p. publs. Assn. for Info. Systems, 1996-98; editor-in-chief Jour. and Comms. of AIS, 1998-2001; contbr. articles to profl. jours. Recipient award for excellence in tchg. NYU Sch. Bus., 1982. Fellow Assn. Info. Sys.; mem. IEEE, Publs. Assn. (v.p. 1995—), Assn. Computing Machinery, Phi Beta Kappa, Tau Beta Pi. Home: 871 Coach Way Annapolis MD 21401-6481 Office: Smith Sch Bus U Md 4337 Van Munching Hall College Park MD 20742-1106 Office Phone: 301-405-0100. Business E-Mail: hlucas@rhsmith.umd.edu.

LUCAS, JAMES E(VANS), operatic director; b. San Antonio, Mar. 15, 1933; s. Mason Harley and Nora Norton (Evans) L. BA, Hiram Coll., 1951; postgrad., Stanford U., 1951-52, Juilliard Sch. Music, 1952-53. Faculty Temple U., 1965-71, Mannes Coll. Music, 1964-70, Manhattan Sch. Music, 1970-78, Carnegie-Mellon U., 1977-79; prof. music, stage dir. Ind. U., 1987-94; vis. prof. Seoul Nat. U., 1996, Dartmouth Coll., 1997. Free-lance operatic stage dir.; worked for opera cos. in U.S., Can. including, Met. Opera, San Francisco Opera, N.Y.C. Opera, Can. Opera Co.; dir. for various summer festivals. Mem. Am. Guild Musical Artists, Am. Fedn. Musicians, Can. Actors Equity. Home and Office: 201 W 85th St New York NY 10024-3907

LUCAS, JAMES RAYMOND, finance company executive, consultant; b. St. Louis, Mar. 9, 1950; s. James Earl and Anna LaVerne (Ryan) L.; m. Pamela Kay Petersen, June 10, 1972; children: Laura Christine, Peter Barrett, David Christopher, Bethany Gayle. BS in Engring. Mgmt., U. Mo., 1972, postgrad., 1978, Regent Coll. Vancouver, 1999. Registered profl. engr., Mo., Kans. Product analyst The Lee Co., Westwood, Kans., 1971—73; mgr. planning Black & Veatch, Kansas City, Mo., 1973—79; dir. constrn. Hallmark Cards, Kansas City, Mo., 1979—81; project mgr. The Pritchard Corp., Kansas City, Mo., 1981—83; gen. mgr., pres., CEO EPIC Mfg., Kansas City, Mo., 1984—86; pres. and CEO Luman Cons. Internat., Overland Park, Kans., 1983—; exec. dir. Relationship Devel. Ctr., 1992—. Prof. Rockhurst U., 2000—; sr. mem. seminar faculty, faculty adv. com. Am. Mgmt. Assn., 1994—; pub., pres. Quintessential Books, 1993—. Author: Weeping in Ramah, 1985, The Parenting of Champions, 1989, Noah: Voyage to a New Earth, 1991, Proactive Parenting, 1993, Walking Through the Fire, 1996, Fatal Illusions: Shredding a Dozen Unrealities That Can Keep Your Organization From Success, 1997, 2001, Balance of Power: Feuling Employee Power Without Relinquishing Your Own, 1998, 2002, The Passionate Organization: Igniting the Fire of Employee Commitment, 1999, 1001 Ways to Connect With Your Kids, 2000, 2003, A Perfect Persecution, 2001, Am I the One?: Clues to Finding and Becoming a Person Worth Marrying, 2002, The Paradox Principle of Parenting, 2003, Knowing the Unknowable God, 2003, Think: How World-Class Leaders Merge Competing Ideas, 2005, Broaden the Vision and Narrow the Focus: Managing in a World of Paradox, 2005. Pres. Mother and Unborn Baby Care, Overland Park, 1990; elder Living Faith Ch., 1985-96. Mem. ASTD, Soc. Mfg. Engrs. (sr.), Am. Assn. Christian Counselors (charter), Am. Mgmt. Assn., Christian Leaders and Spkrs. Soc. Avocations: piano, writing music, reading, travel. Home: 7303 Rosewood Shawnee Mission KS 66208-2458 Office: Luman Cons Internat 6320 Lamar Ste 230 Overland Park KS 66202 Office Phone: 913-248-1733. E-mail: jlucas@lumanconsultants.com.

LUCAS, JAMES WALTER, federal official; b. Frankfort, Ind., Oct. 20, 1940; s. Walter Kenneth and Hester (Kesterson); m. Sara Sue Stewart, Feb. 17, 1962; 1 child, Catherine Anne Lucas Fulkerson. BS, Ball State U., 1963, MA, 1964; postgrad., Am. U., 1977, Harvard U., 1990; DA, George Mason U., 1995. Asst. dir. intelligence coordination Nat. Security Council, Washington, 1975-76; exec. asst. to dep. dir. CIA, Washington, 1976-77, dep. exec. sec., 1977-79; CIA program budget officer Intelligence Community Staff, 1979-81; dep. asst. sec. U.S. Dept. Air Force, 1981-82, prin. dep. asst. sec., 1982-83; dir. crisis mgmt. planning staff Nat. Security Council, 1983-85; Disting. prof., dean Def. Intelligence Coll., Washington, 1985-93; assoc. dir. liaison Def. Intelligence Agy., 1993-96; dep. dir. Open Source Info., CIA, 1996-97; prof. Nat. Def. U., Washington, 1997—2003. Adj. prof. U. Md.-Far East divsn., 1970-71, Def. Intelligence Coll., 1974-83; guest lectr. Am. U., Washington, 1971-77; cons. Pres.'s Fgn. Intelligence Adv. Bd. 1981-85. Author: Intelligence and National Security in the Nixon Administration, 1972, Simulation and Strategic Intelligence Analysis, 1973, Information Needs of Presidents, 1989, Organizing the Presidency: The Role of the Director of Central Intelligence, 1995. Pres. Muncie Young Republican's Club, Ind., 1959-64; pres. Students for Goldwater, 1964; mem. Reston Rep. Assn. With USAF, 1965-77, brig. gen. USAF Res., 1977-96. Decorated Legion of Merit, Bronze Star medal, Meritorious Svc. medal, Republic of Vietnam Gallantry Cross with palm. Mem. Am. Polit. Sci. Assn., Air Force Assn., Nat. Mil. Intelligence Assn., Assn. Former Intelligence Officers, Res. Officers Assn., Pi Sigma Alpha, Phi Gamma Mu, Sigma Chi Lodges: Masons. Office: Nat Def Univ Washington DC 20319-0001 E-mail: jwlucas@erols.com.

LUCAS, JOAN DAWSON, music educator; b. Olney, Tex., May 2, 1949; d. Edwin Luel and Norma Lucille Dawson; m. William Roy Lucas, May 2, 1970; 1 child, David William. BM, Tex. Tech U., 1970, MusM, 1972; PhD, La. State U., 1978. Grad. tchg. asst. Tex. Tech U., Lubbock, 1970—72; piano and theory prof. East Tenn. State U., Johnson City, 1973—76, La. Coll., Pineville; pvt. piano tchr. Midland, Tex., 1985—. Organist St. Nicholas' Episcopal Ch., Midland, Tex., 1985—92, First United Meth. Ch., Midland, 1992—. Mem.: Midland Music Tchrs. Assn. (v.p. 1988—89). Methodist.

LUCAS, JOAN M., education educator; B, Cornell U., 1982; PhD, Princeton U., 1987. Assoc. prof. SUNY, Brockport, 1990—. Office Phone: 585-395-2196.

LUCAS, JOHN ALLEN, lawyer; b. Washington, Aug. 1, 1943; s. George Luther and Opal (McCollum) L.; m. Carol Kaine, June 7, 1969; children: John Christian, Helen Elizabeth, David Marshall, Kerri Christine. BS, U.S. Mil. Acad., 1969; JD, U. Tex., 1977. Bar: Va. 1978, Tenn. 1984, N.Y. 1986. Assoc. Hunton & Williams, Richmond, Va., 1977-83, ptnr. Knoxville, Tenn., 1984—. Prof. law U. Richmond, 1979-80; lectr. various legal seminars, 1979—. Contbr. articles to profl. jours. Bd. dirs. Knoxville Boys Club, 1984-88; bd. dirs. Tenn. Juvenile Diabetes Assn., 1989-92; pres. West Point Soc. of E. Tenn., 1999-. Capt. U.S. Army, 1969-74. Fellow Tenn. Bar Found., Knoxville Bar Found.; mem. Va. Bar Assn., Tenn. Bar Assn. Roman Catholic. Avocations: mountain climbing, sport parachuting, white-water kayaking, triathlons, motorcycling. Office: Hunton & Williams PO Box 951 Knoxville TN 37901-0951

LUCAS, JOSH (JOSH MAURER), actor; b. Little Rock, Ark., June 20, 1971; Actor: (films) Alive, 1993, Father Hood, 1993, McGregor, 1993, Thinner, 1996, True Blue, 1996, Minotaur, 1997, The Definite Maybe, 1997, Harvest, 1998, Restless, 1998, You Can Count on Me, 2000, American Psycho, 2000, Drop Back Ten, 2000, The Dancer, 2000, The Weight of Water, 2000, The Deep End, 2001, When Strangers Appear, 2001, Session 9, 2001, A Beautiful Mind, 2001, Coastlines, 2002, Sweet Home Alabama, 2002, Four Reasons, 2002, Hulk, 2003, Secondhand Lions, 2003, Wonderland, 2003, Around the Bend, 2004, Stealth, 2005, An Unfinished Life, 2005; (TV films) Child of Darkness, Child of Light, 1991, Class of '61, 1993, In the Heat of the Night: A Matter of Justice, 1994; (TV series) Snowy River: The McGregor Saga, 1993, (TV appearances) True Colors, 1990, Life Goes On, 1990, Parker Lewis Can't Lose, 1991, Jake and the Fatman, 1991, (off-Broadway play) Corpus Christi, 1998. Office: Internat Creative Mgmt 8942 Wilshire Blvd Beverly Hills CA 90211-1934*

LUCAS, JUDITH ANN, secondary school educator; b. Waterloo, Iowa, Aug. 12, 1939; d. Edward Newton and Ona Norine (Carter) Foster; m. Paul Robert Lucas, Apr. 14, 1962 (dec.); children: Rebecca Ann, Robert Corydon. BA, Simpson Coll., 1962; MS, Ind. U., 1982. Cert. English and Spanish tchr., Minn., English and Reading tchr., Ind. English and Spanish tchr. Mpls. Pub. Schs., 1962-67, Monroe County Pub. Schs., Bloomington, Ind., 1967-69; English tchr. Richland-Bean Blossom Cmty. Schs., Ellettsville, Ind., 1978—2003; ret., 2003; supv. student tchrs. Ind. U. Sch. Edn., Bloomington. Recipient Shining Star award for Excellence in Teaching, Sta. WTHR-TV and Star Fin. Bank Indpls., 1994, Prentice Hall/Nat. Mid. Sch. Teaching Team award, 1995; Tchr. Creativity fellow Lilly Endowment, Inc. Mem. NEA, Nat. Coun. Tchrs. English, Ind. Coun. Tchrs. English, Nat. Mid. Sch. Assn., Ind. State Tchrs. Assn., Richland Bean Blossom Tchrs. Assn. (negotiation team 1985-95). Avocations: music, piano, painting. Home: 2125 White Tail Run Bloomington IN 47401-4593

LUCAS, KAREN, music educator; d. Clemon Willis and Celina Lucas. BS, Nazareth Coll., 1984; M in Music Edn., Mansfield U., 1986. Cert. music tchr. K-12 N.Y., 1990. Dir. bands Olinville Jr. H.S., Bronx, 1987—87, Kensington H.S., Buffalo, 1987—94; tchr. dist. wide music Geneva Mid. Sch., 1994—2001; dir. band Geneva H.S., 2001—03; tchr. dist. wide music Geneva Mid. Sch., 2003—. Playground supr. Geneva Recreation Dept., 1998—2001; unit supr. Nassau County AHRC, Hunter, 1989—90, athletic dir., 1987—89, camp counselor, Hunter, 1985—87. Guest conductor Rochester All City Elem. Band, Finger Lakes Concert Band. Bd. mem. Boys & Girls Club of Geneva, 2001—; commr. Geneva Human Rights Commn., 2003—. Mem.: N.Y. State Music Adminstrs., N.Y. State Music Educators Assn., Finger Lakes Music Educators Assn., Music Educators Nat. Conf., N.Y. State Band Dirs. Assn. Baptist. Avocations: music, softball, bicycling, camping, golf. Home: 188 High St Geneva NY 14456 Office: Geneva Mid Sch 63 Pulteney St Geneva NY 14456-2307 Office Phone: 315-781-2093. Personal E-mail: lucask@usadatanet.net.

LUCAS, KRISTINA PETERSON, literature and language professor; b. Watertown, S.D. d. Warren Duane and Karen Martha (Lerdall) P.; m. Thomas F. Lucas, May 4, 1985; children: Marissa Lynn, Dylan Thomas. MA in Teaching, Edn., U. N.H., 1989. Adj. prof. dept. English N.H. Tech. Inst., Concord, 1999—. Academic advisor N.H. Tech. Inst., Concord; writng tutor. Mem. editl. bd.: N.H. Tech. Inst. Pedagogy Jour. Mem. Jr. Svc. League, Concord, NH, Equal Ptnrs. Investment Club. Avocations: travel, skiing, hiking, reading. Home: 14 Saltmarsh Cir Bow NH 03304-3824

LUCAS, M. FRANCES, university administrator; b. Jackson, Miss., Oct. 24, 1956; d. Aubrey and Ella Lucas; children: Michael, Anna Catherine. BA in Comms., Miss. State U., 1978; MA in Higher Edn. Adminstrn., U. Ala., 1980, PhD in Higher Edn. Adminstrn., 1985; postgrad., Harvard U., 1989. Resident life coord. U. Ala., Tuscaloosa, 1979-83; asst. dean for student life Miss. State U., Starkville, 1983-86; v.p. for student affairs Baldwin-Wallace Coll., Berea, Ohio, 1986-92; v.p., sr. v.p. for campus life Emory U., Atlanta, 1992—. Faculty mem. Nat. Housing Tng. Inst., Gainesville, 1993, Mid-Mgrs. Inst., 1991-93, 94-95. Author: NASPA Journal, 1990, 91, College Student Affairs Journal, 1994, About Campus Journal, 1996. Mem. Nat. Assn. of Student Pers. (Greek rels. chair 1985—), The Nat. V.P.'s Group, So. Assn. of Coll. Student Affairs, Nat. Interfraternity Conf., Am. Coll. Pers. Assn., Assn. of Fraternity Advisors, Nat. Assn. of Student Pers. Adminstrs. (assoc. dir. Mid-Mgrs. Inst. 1993-94), Omicron Delta Kappa. Office: Emory U Campus Life 605 Asbury Cir Atlanta GA 30322-1006

LUCAS, PAUL DAVID MARK, lawyer; b. Hartford, Jan. 24, 1943; s. Albert Joseph and Helené Rita Lucas; m. E. Jean Lucas, Aug. 10, 1979; children: Terry, Anthony, Timothy. BA, San Diego State U., 1961—65, MA, 1965—67; JD, U. of Fla., 1973—76. Bar: Fla., D.C., U.S. Dist. Ct. (so. and mid. dists.) Fla., U.S. Ct. Appeals (5th and 11th cirs.); cert. law, history, English and bus. tchr. Calif., A-V Rated Atty. Martin-Dale Hubbel. Atty. Hamilton, James, Merke, etc., West Palm Beach, 1977—81, 1982—83, Graham, Phillips and Lea Pa., Orlando, 1983—85, Cramer, Hoffman and Haber Pa., Orlando, 1985—87, Baskin and Sears PC, Miami, 1986—87; pvt. practice Miami, 1987—89, Wellington, Pa., 1989—94; ins. sales Life of Va., Ft. Lauderdale, 1989—90; atty. Gary, Williams, Parenti, Finney, Lewis, Watson, et al, Stuart, 1990—. Brand asst. Proctor and Gamble, United States, 1972—73; with Palmer-Smith, Palmer-Lucas Co. Mem. Rotary Club Internat., 2001—. Exec. officer Ops., Comm., Intelligence USN, 1968—71. Mem.: Phi Delta Phi Alumni Assn., Lamda Chi Alpha Alumni Assn., Am. Inns Ct. (St. Lucie and Martin Counties, Fla.), Martin County Bar Assoc. (Fla. Profl. and Litig Com.), Am. Bar Assoc., Assoc. of Trial Lawyers, Am., Acad. of Fla. Trail Lawyers, Fed. Bar Assn., Am. Coll. Legal Medicine (assoc.). Lutheran. Avocations: gardening, collect Indian art, porcelains, western travel.

LUCAS, ROBERT EMERSON, JR., economist, educator; b. Yakima, Wash., Sept. 15, 1937; BA, U. Chgo., 1959, PhD, 1964; PhD (hon.), U. Paris-Dauphine, 1992, Athens U. Econ. and Bus., 1994; DSc (hon.), Technion-Israel Inst. Tech., 1996; PhD (hon.), U. Montréal, 1998. Lectr. U. Chgo., 1962-63; asst. prof., economics Carnegie-Mellon U., Pittsburgh, 1963-67; assoc. prof., 1967-70; prof., 1970-75; prof., economics U. Chgo., 1975-80, vice chmn. Dept. Econs., 1975—83, John Dewey Disting. Svc. prof., 1980—, chmn. Dept. Econs., 1986—88. Ford Found. vis. rsch. prof. U. Chgo., 1974-75; vis. prof. econ. Northwestern U., Chgo., 1981-82. Author: Studies in Business-Cycle Theory, 1981, Models of Business Cycles, 1987, Lectures on Economic Growth, 2001; co-author: Recursive Methods in Economic Dynamics, 1989; co-editor: Rational Expectations and Econometric Practice, 1981; assoc. editor Jour. Econ. Theory, 1972-78, Jour. Monetary Econs., 1977—; editor Jour. Polit. Theory, 1978-81, 1988-; contbr. articles to profl. jours. Woodrow Wilson fellow, 1959-60, Brookings fellow, 1961-62, Woodrow Wilson Dissertation fellow, 1963, Ford Found. Faculty fellow, 1966-67, Guggenheim Found. fellow, 1981-82; Proctor and Gamble scholar, 1955-59; recipient Nobel Prize in Econ., 1995. Fellow AAAS, Econometric Soc. (2nd v.p. 1995, pres. 1997), Am. Acad. Arts and Scis.; mem. NAS, Econometric Soc. (2nd v.p., v.p. 1995, pres. 1997), Am. Econ. Assn. (v.p. 1987, pres. 2001), European Acad. Arts, Scis. and Humanities, Am. Philosophical Soc., Phi Beta Kappa. Achievements include developing and applying the hypothesis of rational expectations, and thereby having transformed macroeconomic analysis and deepened out understanding of economic policy. Office: U Chgo Dept Econs 1126 E 59th St Chicago IL 60637-1580*

LUCAS, ROY EDWARD, JR., minister; b. Shawnee, Okla., Dec. 19, 1955; s. Roy Edward Sr. and Shirley Ann (Padgett) L.; m. Roberta Lee Duncan, Feb. 28, 1975; children: Jonathon Edward, Jerebeth Glenae. BA, Okla. Bapt. U., 1978, BA in Edn., 1979; MDiv, Southwestern Bapt. Theol. Sem., Ft. Worth, 1984, MRE, 1985, PhD, 1993. Ordained to ministry So. Bapt. Conv., 1978; cert. elem. tchr., Okla. Assoc. pastor Temple Bapt. Ch., Shawnee, 1975, Calvary Bapt. Ch., Shawnee, 1975-79; pastor Brandon (Tex.) Bapt. Ch., 1982-85, Fox (Okla.) Bapt. Ch., 1985-90, Union Hill Bapt. Ch., Purcell, Okla., 1990-99; prof. New Testament Cleer Creek Baptist Bible Coll., Pineville, Ky., 1999—. Instr. Sem. Ext.-Enon Assn., Ardmore, Okla., 1986-89; teaching fellow Southwestern Bapt. Sem., 1989; adj. prof. Ministry Tng. Inst. Okla. Bapt. U., 1996-97. Home and Office: Clear Creek Bapt Bible Coll 300 Clear Creek Rd #410 Pineville KY 40977-9752 E-mail: rlucas@ccbbc.edu.

LUCAS, SANDRA J., psychologist; b. Lawrence, Mass., Jan. 29, 1945; d. Leonard J. and Claire R. (Hart) L. BA in Polit. Sci., U. Mass., 1978, MEd, CAGS, 1997. Cert. sch. psychologist grades K-12, Commonwealth Mass. Dept. Edn. Owner, operator Video Images, Shrewsbury, Mass., 1983-93; substitute tchr. grades K-12 Shrewsbury Sch. Sys., 1992—, cons., 1998—. Grad. student counselor divsn. counseling and psychol. svcs. U. Mass., Amherst, 1996, grad. admissions com. dept. edn., 1997; sch. psychology intern Paton Elem. Sch., Shrewsbury, 1996-97. Election poll worker, Shrewsbury, 1984—; town meeting mem., Shrewsbury, 1985—; vol. Shrewsbury H.S. Alumni, 1994—; campaign worker State Rep. Ron Gauch, 1995. Mem. Nat. Orgn. Sch. Psychologist, Mass. Sch. Psychologist Assn., Phi Delta Kappa (U. Mass. chpt.). Roman Catholic. Avocations: golf, sailing, volleyball. Home: 58 Hillside Dr Shrewsbury MA 01545-5814 E-mail: LUCASSJ@AOL.COM.

LUCAS, STEVEN MITCHELL, lawyer; b. Ada, Okla., Jan. 19, 1948; s. John Dalton and Cherrye (Smith) Lucas; m. Lori E. Seeberger (dissolved); children: Steven Turner, Brooke Elizabeth, Sarah Grace. BA, Yale U., 1970; JD, Vanderbilt U., 1973. Bar: DC 1973, U.S. Ct. Mil. Appeals 1974, U.S. Dist. Ct. DC 1979, U.S. Ct. Appeals (DC cir.) 1979, U.S. Supreme Ct. 1979. Assoc. Shaw, Pittman, Potts & Trowbridge, Washington, 1978-82, ptnr., 1983-92; ptnr., head fin. instns. practice Wiley, Rein & Fielding, Washington, 1992-93, Winston & Strawn, Washington, 1993-97; pvt. practice Washington, 1997—. Cons. internat. rels. Rockefeller Found., N.Y.C., 1978; mem. negotiating team Panama Canal Treaty, Washington, 1975—77; legal advisor Dept. Def. Panama Canal negotiations working group; presdl. apptd. U.S. panelist Internat. Ctr. Settlement Investment Disputes, ICSID-World Bank, 2002—; mem. panel of arbitrators Nat. Arbitration Forum, 2004—; sr. cons. Iraq Reconstrn. Mgmt. Office, Dept. of State, 2004—. Editor-in-chief: Vanderbilt U. Jour. Transnational Law, 1972—73. Capt. JAGC U.S. Army, 1974—77. Republican. Episcopalian. Home and Office: 1001 Jigger Ct Annapolis MD 21401 E-mail: lucassm@state.gov.

LUCAS, WILLIAM RAY, aerospace scientist, consultant; b. Newbern, Tenn., Mar. 1, 1922; married 1948; 3 children. BS, Memphis State U., 1943; MS, Vanderbilt U., 1950, PhD in Chem. Metallurgy, 1952; L.H.D. (hon.), Mobile Coll., 1977; D.Sc. (hon.), Southeastern Inst. Tech., 1980, U. Ala., Huntsville, 1981. Instr. chemistry Memphis State U., 1946-48; chemist guided missile devel. div. Redstone Arsenal, 1952-54, chief chem. sect., 1954-55; chief engr. material sect. Army Ballistic Missile Agy., 1955-56, chief engr. material br., 1956-60; with Marshall Space Flight Center, NASA, 1960—, chief engring. materials br., 1960-63, material div., 1963-66, dir. propulsion and vehicle engring. lab., 1966-68, dir. program devel., 1968-71, dep. dir., 1971-74, dir., 1974-86; pvt. practice aerospace cons. Hunstville, Ala., 1986—2002; ret. Served as lt. USNR, 1943-46. Recipient Exceptional Sci. Achievement medal NASA, 1964, 2 Exceptional Service medals, 1969, Disting. Service medal, 1972, Disting. Service award, 1981, 86; Presdl. rank Disting. Exec., 1980; Roger W. Jones award for outstanding exec. leadership Am. U., 1981; Space award for outstanding contbns. in field of space VFW, 1983; Disting. Alumni award Memphis State U., 1984; Aubrey D. Green award Lions Club Ala., 1986; named one of Tenn. Outstanding Scientists and Engrs., Tenn. Tech. Found., 1986; named to Ala. Engring. Hall of Fame, 1990. Fellow Am. Soc. Metals, Am. Astronautical Soc. (Space Flight award 1982), AIAA (Oberth award 1965, Holger N. Toftoy award 1976, Elmer A. Sperry group award 1986); mem. Nat. Acad. Engring., Am. Chem. Soc., Sigma Xi, Tau Beta Pi Achievements include research in materials engring. metallurgy, inorganic chemistry, environ. effects on materials, especially space environ. effects.

LUCCA, LOUIS ANTHONY, academic administrator; s. Louis and Freda Habib Lucca. BA in Modern Langs., Seton Hall U.; MA in TESOL, NYU, 1992, PhD in Applied Linguistics, 2002. Internat. acct. rep. McGraw Hill, Inc., NYC, 1980—86, asst. mgr. std. and poor's ratings group, cash sys., 1986—91; tutor MAC Testing and Cons., Inc., Red Bank, NJ, 1980—92; instr. CUNY, NYC, 1992—95, instr. English Lang. Inst., 1992—95, coord. speech. comm. Media Studies and The Speech Ctr., 2000—. Presenter in field. Mem.: ASCD, Tchrs. English Spkrs. Other Langs., Nat. Comm. Assn., Modern Lan. Assn., Internat. Comm. Assn. Home: 9728 Third Ave # 341 Brooklyn NY 11209 Office: FH Iaguardia C C 31-10 Thomson Ave Long Island City NY 11101

LUCCHESI, BRUNO, sculptor; b. Lucca, Toscana, Italy, July 31, 1926; came to U.S., 1958; s. Giovanni and Natalina (Magnani) L. Maestrodarte, Art Institute, Lucca, 1949. Art instr. U. Florence, Italy, 1950-57, New Sch. for Soc. Res., N.Y.C., 1960-70, Nat. Acad. of Design, N.Y.C., 1970-80. Art seminars: U. Utah, George Washington U., Marshal U., Hartford U. Author: Terracotta, 1976, Modelling Head, 1977, Modelling Figure, 1980. Recipient of Lion of S. Marco award Holion Cultural Soc., N.Y.C., 1981.*

LUCCHESI, LIONEL LOUIS, lawyer; b. St. Louis, Sept. 17, 1939; s. Lionel Louis and Theresa Lucchesi; m. Mary Ann Wheeler, July 30, 1966; children: Lionel Louis III, Marisa Pilar. BSEE, Ill. Inst. Tech., 1961; JD, St. Louis U., 1969. Bar: Mo. 1969. With Emerson Electric Co., 1965-69; assoc. Polster, Polster & Lucchesi, St. Louis, 1969-74, ptnr., 1974—. City atty. City of Ballwin, Mo., 1979—85, 1992—. Mem. Zoning Commn., 1971—77; alderman City of Ballwin, 1977—79. Recipient Am. Jurisprudence award, St. Louis U., 1968—69; scholar NROTC, 1957—61. Mem.: ATLA, ABA, Newcomen Soc. N.Am., St. Louis Met. Bar Assn. (exec. com., pres.-elect 1984, pres. 1985—86), Am. Patent Law Assn., Superstition Mountain Club, Forest Hills Club, Rotary (pres.-elect St. Louis 1991—92, pres. 1992—93). Republican. Roman Catholic. Office: 12412 Powers Ct Dr Saint Louis MO 63131 Office Phone: 314-238-2400. E-mail: llucchesi@patpro.com.

LUCCHINO, LAWRENCE, sports team executive, lawyer; b. Pitts., Sept. 6, 1945; s. Dominic A. and Rose (Rizzo) L. AB cum laude, Princeton U., 1967; JD, Yale U., 1972. Bar: Calif. and Pa. 1973, D.C. 1975. Counsel Impeachment Inquiry, House Judiciary Commn., Washington, 1974; assoc. Williams & Connolly, Washington, 1975-79, ptnr., 1979—; pres., CEO Balt. Orioles, 1988-93, San Diego Padres, 1995—. Sec., bd. dirs., gen. counsel Washington Redskins Football Club, 1978-85; bd. dirs., gen. counsel Balt. Orioles Baseball Club, from 1979, v.p., 1982-88, pres., CEO, 1988-93; CEO San Diego Padres Baseball Club, 1994—; bd. dirs. Army Times, Springfield, Va. Trustee Nat. Found. on Counseling, Princeton, N.J., 1984—; bd. dirs. Nat. Aquarium Natl., Balt. Symphony, Princeton Electronic Bd., Babe Ruth Mus. Mem. ABA Democrat. Roman Catholic. Office: San Diego Padres PO Box 2000 San Diego CA 92112-2000 also: Williams & Connolly 725 12th St NW Washington DC 20005-3901

LUCCI, DOROTHY ANN, educational consultant, psychologist; d. Brantisio and Mary Lucci. BE, Wheelock Coll., 1978; MEd, U. Mass., Boston, 1989, Cert. in Advanced Grad. Study, 1990. Cert. tchr. elem. edn. Dept. Edn., Commonwealth Mass., 1978, tchr. moderate spl. needs Dept. Edn., Commonwealth Mass., 1978, sch. psychology Dept. Edn., Commonwealth Mass., 1990. Tchr. children with autism League Sch. Boston, 1978—81; rsch. assoc. Boston U., U. Conn., 1981—90; ednl. cons. Ednl. and Psychol. Consultation Svcs., Framingham, Mass., 1983—; sch. psychologist READS Collaborative, Middleboro, Mass., 1990—93; dir. Autism Support Ctr., Danvers, Mass., 1993—95; consulting psychologist Wellesley Pub. Schs., Mass., 1995—. Bd. mem. human rights com. May Ctr., Arlington, Mass., 1995—2000; bd. mem. Asperger's Assn. New Eng., Watertown, Mass., 1997—; instr. Framingham State Coll., 2004—; therapeutic group leader YouthCare Mass. Gen. Hosp., Wellesley, 2004—. Contbr. chapter to book, 12 articles to profl. jours. Parent and sibling trainer North Shore Arc, Danvers, 1993—95; mem. First Spiritual Temple, Brookline, Mass., 1999—2005. Mem.: NASP, ASCD (assoc.), Autism Soc. Am., Mass. Tchrs. Assn., Mass. Assn. Sch. Psychologists. Avocations: kayaking, snowshoeing, hiking, bicycling, yoga. Office: Ednl and Psych Consultation Svcs 130 Dennison Ave Framingham MA 01702 Office Phone: 508-872-6331. Business E-Mail: dotepcs@aol.com.

LUCCI, SUSAN, actress; b. Scarsdale, N.Y., Dec. 23, 1946; d. Victor and Jeanette L.; m. Helmut Huber, 1969; children: Liza Victoria, Andreas Martin. BA, Marymount Coll., 1968. Portrays Erica in TV series All My Children, 1970—; appearances in other series include: Fantasy Island, The Love Boat, The Fall Guy; TV films: Invitation to Hell, 1985, Mafia Princess, 1985, Ebbie, 1995, Seduced and Betrayed, 1995, (mini-series) Anastasia: The Mystery of Anna Anderson, 1986, Haunted by Her Past, 1988, Lady Mobster, 1988, The Bride in Black, 1990, The Women Who Sinned, 1991, Double Edge, 1992, Between Love and Hate, 1993, French Silk, 1994, Blood on Her Hands, 1998; host of spl. with Tony Danza 99 Ways to Attract the Right Man. Recipient 20 Emmy nominations and 1 Emmy award for best actress in daytime drama series, numerous other awards. Office: All My Children 320 W 66th St New York NY 10023-6397

LUCCO, JAMES PERRY, writer; b. Jamestown, N.Y., Nov. 2, 1946; s. James Perry and Josephine Helen Lucco; m. Gail Catherine Frazier, July 14, 1986. BA, Columbia U., 1971. Asst. to pres. P&A Ent., Miami, Fla., 1972—74; sr. hearing officer State of N.J., Trenton, 1975—77; comptroller Tiger Mgmt., N.Y.C., 1985—97; asst. to pres. Empire Rubbish & Ash, N.Y.C., 1993—96, Moyer Plating, Newark, 1992—95; bus. assoc. T.W. Alexander Esq., Elizabeth, NJ, 1995—. Founder The Urban Triangle Enterprise, 2002. Author: (plays) A Pagans Wine, 1968, The Last Tiger, 2004, (novels) New York City Garbage Wars, 2000, Old Soldiers, 2003, Luca, 2005. Bd. dir.

South Orange Sr. Citizens, South Orange, NJ, 1992—2004; bd. dirs. La Cosa Nova, 2005. Mem.: Lions (dir. pub. rels. 1998—2004). Roman Catholic. Avocation: golf. Home: 376 Williamson St #8 Elizabeth NJ 07202 Office Phone: 908-209-4701.

LUCE, CHARLES FRANKLIN, retired utilities executive, lawyer; b. Platteville, Wis., Aug. 29, 1917; s. James Oliver and Wilma Fisher (Grindell) L.; m. Helen G. Oden, Oct. 24, 1942; children: James O., Christine Mary, Barbara Anne, Charles Franklin; m. Margaret E. Richmond, Nov. 9, 2001. BA, LL.B., U. Wis., 1941; Sterling fellow, Yale U., 1941-42. Bar: Wis. 1941, Wash. 1946, Oreg. 1945, N.Y. 1981. Law clk. Justice Hugo L. Black, U.S. Supreme Ct., 1943-44; gen. practice law Walla Walla, Wash., 1946-61; adminstr. Bonneville Power Adminstrn., Dept. Interior, Portland, Oreg., 1961-66; under sec. interior Washington, 1966-67; chmn. bd. Consol. Edison Co. of N.Y., Inc., 1967-82, chief exec. officer, 1967-81, chmn. emeritus, 1982—; ptnr. Preston, Thorgrimson, Ellis & Holman, Portland, Oreg., 1982-86; spl. counsel Met. Life Ins. Co., 1987-94. Dir. emeritus UAL and Met. Life Ins. Co.; trustee Henry M. Jackson Found.; trustee emeritus Columbia U., N.Y.C. Mem. Wis. Bar Assn., Phi Beta Kappa, Order of Coif. Episcopalian. Office: Consol Edison 4 Irving Pl New York NY 10003-3502

LUCE, DONALD SANDERS, social worker; b. East Calais, Vt., Sept. 20, 1934; s. Collins Andrew and Margaret Sanders L. BS, U. Vt., 1957; MS, Cornell U., 1959. Vol. Internat. Vol. Svcs., Vietnam, 1958—59, dir., 1960—67; rsch. assoc. Cornell U., Ithaca, NY, 1967—68; rsch. dir. World Coun. Chs., Vietnam, 1969—71; dir. Asia Resource Ctr., Washington, 1971—90; pres., CEO Internat. Vol. Svcs., Washington, 1991—96, AIDS prevention coord., 1997—98; dir. devel. Cmty. Missions, Niagara Falls, NY, 1998—. Co-author: Viet Nam: The Unheard Voices, 1968, Hostages of War, 1972. Bd. dirs. Am. Friends Svc. Com., Phila., 1971-91; AIDS prevention activist Western NY Peace Ctr., Buffalo, 1985—. Recipient Peace award War Resistors League, NYC, 1990, Gold medal NY Film Festival, NYC, 1985, Medal of Honor, Govt. Vietnam, 2004. Mem. United Ch. of Christ. Avocation: poetry. Office Phone: 716-285-3404 2226.

LUCE, EDWARD ANDREW, plastic surgeon; b. Syracuse, NY, Mar. 5, 1940; s. Edward Andrew and Constance Faith (Jones) L.; m. Rebecca Sue Wall (div.); children: Darcie, Michael, Caitlin. BS, U. Dayton, 1961; MD, U. Ky., 1965. Diplomate Am. Bd. Surgery, Am. Bd. Plastic Surgery (chmn. 1990-91). Resident in surgery Barnes Hosp., St. Louis, 1965-71; resident in plastic surgery Johns Hopkins Hosp., Balt., 1971-73, asst. prof. plastic surgery, 1973-75; assoc. prof. plastic surgery U. Ky., Lexington, 1975-87, prof. plastic surgery, 1987-95, chief plastic surgery, 1975-95, VA Hosp., 1975-95; Kiehn-DesPrez prof. surgery Case Western Reserve U., Cleve., 1995—; chief plastic surgery U. Hosps. of Cleve., 1995—, VA Hosp., Cleve., 1995—. Attending plastic surgeon St. Joseph Hosp., Lexington, 1975-95, Good Samaritan Hosp., Lexington, 1978-95, Humana Hosp., Lexington, 1982-95; Kiehn-DesPrez Prof. and Chief of Plastic Surgery, Case Western Reserve U. and Univ. Hosps. of Cleveland; pres. Assn. Acad. Chmn. of Plastic Surgery, 1989-90, Am. Soc. Maxillofacial Surgeons (pres. 1990-91), Southeastern Soc. Plastic and Reconstructive Surgeons (pres. 1992-93). Pres. U. Ky. Med. Alumni Assn., 1977-78; pres. John Hoopes Plastic Surgery Found., 1993. Recipient Clinician of Yr., Am. Assn. Plastic Surgeons, 1990. Mem. Plastic Surgery Ednl. Found. (pres. 1993-94), Am Coll. Surgeons, Am. Surg. Assn., So. Surg. Assn., Am. Assn. Plastic Surgeons (pres. 2000-2001), Am. Soc. Plastic and Reconstructive Surgeons (pres. 2001-2002), Soc. Head and Neck Surgeons. Avocations: clinical photography, military history of small, obscure wars, collecting old and rare medical books. Office: Plastic Surgery Group 6027 Walnut Grove Ste 216 Memphis TN 38120 Office Phone: 901-761-9030. Personal E-mail: edluce@yahoo.com.

LUCE, Mrs. HENRY See HADLEY, LEILA

LUCE, PRISCILLA MARK, public relations executive; b. NYC, Feb. 4, 1947; d. S. Carl and Patricia (Greenfield) Mark; m. Robert Warren Luce, July 19, 1969; children: James Warren, David Mark. BA, U. Pa., 1968. Adminstrv. asst. Phila. Mus. Art, 1968-69; asst. dir. pub. info. Mt. Holyoke Coll., South Hadley, Mass., 1969-71; v.p. Barnes & Roche, Inc., Phila., 1971-82; mgr. civic programs TRW Inc., Cleve., 1982-85, mgr. cmty. rels., 1985-88, mgr. external comm., 1988-90, dir., pub. affairs and advt., 1990-92, v.p. TRW info. sys. and svcs. comms., 1992-94, v.p. mktg. and orgn. comm., 1994—2001, v.p. corp. comm., 2001—03. Trustee New Orgn. for the Visual Arts, Cleve., 1983—97, pres., 1984—86; trustee Cmty. Info. Vol. Action Ctr., Cleve., 1984—86, Albert M. Greenfield Found., Phila., 1989—, pres., 1999—; trustee Cleve. State U. Found., 1996—, chmn. devel. com., 1998—, vice-chmn., 1999—2004, chmn., 2004—; trustee Bus. Vols. Unltd., Cleve., 1998—2003, WVIZ/PBS, WCPN Radio, 1997—, chmn. pub. rels. com., 1998—2001; chmn. media and mktg. com. Cleve. Today, 1999—2001; trustee Ohio Chamber Orch., Cleve., 1986—92, chmn. devel. com., 1987—88, chmn., trustee, 1991—92, exec. v.p., 1990—91; mem. steering com. Cleve. Art Festival, 1983—84, Mayor's Cultural Arts Planning Task Force, 1985—87; trustee Ret. Sr. Vol. Prog., 1991, Western Res. Hist. Soc., 1999—2002; leadership devel. prog. participant United Way Svcs., Cleve., 1983, cons., 1983—85; steering com. Bus. Volunteerism Coun. of Cleve., 1984—92; comm. adv. com. Work in NE Ohio Coun., 1991—94. Recipient Woman of Profl. Excellence award, YWCA of Cleve., 1990. Mem.: Nat. Assn. Mfrs. Commns. Coun., Arthur W. Page Soc. Republican.

LUCE, R(OBERT) DUNCAN, psychology professor; b. Scranton, Pa., May 16, 1925; s. Robert Rennselaer and Ruth Lillian (Downer) L.; m. Gay Gaer, June 6, 1950 (div.); m. Cynthia Newby, Oct. 5, 1968 (div.); m. Carolyn A. Scheer, Feb. 27, 1988; 1 child, Aurora Newby. BS, MIT, 1945, PhD, 1950; MA (hon.), Harvard U., 1976. Mem. staff research lab electronics MIT, 1950-53; asst. prof. Columbia U., 1953-57; lectr. social relations Harvard U., 1957-59; prof. psychology U. Pa., Phila., 1959-69; vis. prof. Inst. Advanced Study, Princeton, 1969-72; prof. Sch. Social Scis., U. Calif., Irvine, 1972-75; Alfred North Whitehead prof. psychology Harvard U., Cambridge, Mass., 1976-81, prof., 1981-83, Victor S. Thomas prof. psychology, 1983-88, Victor S. Thomas prof. emeritus, 1988, chmn., 1988-94; disting. prof. cognitive sci. U. Calif., Irvine, 1988-94, dir. Irvine Rsch. Unit in math. behavioral sci., 1988-92, disting. rsch. prof. cognitive sci. and rsch. prof. econs., 1994—; dir. Inst. for Math. Behavioral Sci., 1992-98. Chmn. assembly behavioral and social scis. NRC, 1976-79 Author: (with H. Raiffa) Games and Decisions, 1957, Individual Choice Behavior, 1959, (with others) Foundations of Measurement, I, 1971, II, 1989, III, 1990, Response Times, 1986, (with others) Stevens Handbook of Experimental Psychology, I and II, 1988, Sound & Hearing, 1993, Utility of Gains and Losses, 2000. Served with USNR, 1943-46. Ctr. Advanced Study in Behavioral Scis. fellow, 1954-55, 66-67, 87-88, NSF Sr. Postdoctoral fellow, 1966-67, Guggenheim fellow, 1980-81; recipient Disting. award for Rsch. U. Calif., Irvine, 1994, medal, 2001, gold medal award for achievement in sci. psychology Am. Psychol. Found., 2001, Daniel G. Aldrich, Jr. Disting. Svc. award U. Calif., Irvine, 2003, Ramsey medal Soc. for Decision Analysis, 2003, Norman Anderson award for lifetime achievement Soc. Exptl. Psychologists, 2004, Nat. medal of Sci., 2003. Fellow: Am. Psychol. Soc. (bd. dirs. 1989—91), APA (bd. sci. affairs 1993—95, exec. com. divsn. I 2000, disting. sci. contbn. award 1970), AAAS (chair elect psychology sect. 1998—99, chair 1999); mem.: Soc. Math. Psychology (pres. 1979), Psychonomic Soc., Psychometric Soc. (pres. 1976—77), Fedn. Behavioral Psychol. and Cognitive Scis. (pres. 1988—90), Math. Assn. Am., Am. Math. Soc., Nat. Acad. Scis. (chmn. sect. psychology 1980—83, class behavioral and social scis. 1983—86), Am. Philos. Soc., Am. Acad. Arts and Sci., Tau Beta Pi, Phi Beta Kappa, Sigma Xi. Home: 20 Whitman Ct Irvine CA 92617-4057 Office: U Calif Social Sci Plz Irvine CA 92697-5100 Office Phone: 949-824-6239. Business E-Mail: rdluce@uci.edu.

LUCE, THOMAS WARREN, III, federal agency administrator; b. Dallas, June 18, 1940; s. Thomas Warren and Ruth (Hardy) L.; m. Phoebe Ann McCain; children: Ken, Ellen Luce Tucker, Susan. Student, Va. Mil. Inst.; BBA in Acctg., So. Meth. U., 1963, LLB, 1966. Bar: Tex. 1966, U.S. Dist. Ct. (no. dist.) Tex. 1966, U.S. Supreme Ct. 1971, U.S. Ct. Appeals (2d cir.) N.Y. 1976, U.S. Ct. Appeals (5th cir.) La. 1981, U.S. Ct. Appeals (11th cir.) Ga. 1981. Assoc. McKenzie & Baer, Dallas, 1966-67; assoc. then ptnr. Jenkens, Spradley & Gilchrist, Dallas, 1968-73; founding ptnr. Hughes & Luce, Dallas, 1973—97, of counsel, 1997—2005; chief justice pro tempore Tex. Supreme Ct., Dallas, 1988; asst. sec., office of planning evaluation & policy develop. US Dept. Edn., Washington, 2005—. Bd. dir. Dell Inc.; chmn. Nat. Ctr. for Ednl. Accountability; chief of staff Tex. Select Com. of Pub. Edn.; delegate Edn. Commn. of the States 1995-98; dir. Libr. Congress Trust Fund; chmn. & founder Just for the Kids 1995-; trustee So. Meth. U., Dallas; bd. dirs., founding mem. Episcopal Sch. Dallas; bd. dirs. Dallas Citizen Council; chmn. Tex. Nat. Rsch. Lab. Commn., 1987-89. Mem. ABA, Tex. Bar Assn., Dallas Bar Assn. Clubs: Salesmanship of Dallas. Office: US Dept Edn Rm 8022 1990 K St NW Washington DC 20006 Office Phone: 202-502-7950.*

LUCERO, ANNE, critical care nurse; b. Lynwwod, Calif., Aug. 21, 1954; d. Kenneth and Dorothy Irene (Berkland) Boulter; m. Emmett Ronald Lucero, Jan. 15, 1977 (div. June 1993); children: Christina Marie, Kathleen Anne. BSN, Calif. State U., Chico, 1976; MSN in Nursing Edn., Calif. State U., San Jose, 2001. RN, 1976, CCRN 1983, ACLS. Staff nurse Watsonville Cmty. Hosp., Calif., 1977-78, staff nurse/relief charge critical care, 1979-2000, 2005—; part-time faculty Sch. Nursing, Cabrillo Coll., Aptos, Calif., 1992-2000, full-time faculty, 2000—. Leader Campfire Boys and Girls, Santa Cruz Co., 1984-90, Bethel Guardian Internat. Order Jobs Daughters, 1993-98. Mem. Calif. Nurses Assn. (nurse rep. 1979-83, bd. dirs. 1980-91, political action com. 1989-91, legis. laison congressman, 1982-92), Am. Nurses Assn. (delegate 1990-92), Calif. Tchrs. Assn., Sigma Theta Tau. Avocations: golf, walking, bike riding, reading. E-mail: lucerolady@aol.com.

LUCERO, CARLOS, federal judge; b. Antonito, Colo., Nov. 23, 1940; m. Dorothy Stuart; 1 child, Carla. BA, Adams State Coll.; JD, George Washington U., 1964. Law clk. to Judge William E. Doyle U.S. Dist. Ct., Colo., 1964—65; pvt. practice Alamosa, Colo., 1966—95; sr. ptnr. Lucero, Lester & Sigmund, Alamosa, Colo.; judge U.S. Ct. Appeals (10th cir.), 1995—. Mem. Pres. Carter's Presdl. Panel on Western State Water Policy. Bd. dirs. Colo. Hist. Soc., Sante Fe Opera Assn. of N.Mex. Recipient Outstanding Young Man of Colo. award, Colo. Jaycees, Disting. Alumnus award, George Washington U.; fellow Paul Harris, Rotary Found. Fellow: Internat. Soc. Barristers, Internat. Acad. Trial Lawyers, Colo. Bar Found. (pres.), Am. Coll. Trial Lawyers, Am. Bar Found.; mem.: ABA (mem. action com. to reduce ct. cost and delay, mem. adv. bd. ABA jour., mem. com. on the availability of legal svcs.), Colo. Rural Legal Svcs. (bd. dirs.), Colo. Hispanic Bar Assn. (profl. svc. award), Nat. Hispanic Bar Assn., San Luis Valley Bar Assn. (pres.), Colo. Bar Assn. (pres. 1977—78, mem. ethics com.), Order of the Coif. Office: US Ct Appeals 1823 Stout St Denver CO 80257*

LUCEY, JEROLD FRANCIS, pediatrician; b. Holyoke, Mass., Mar. 26, 1926; s. Jeremiah F. and Pauline A. (Lally) L.; m. Ingela Barth, Oct. 7, 1972; 1 child, Patrick; children by previous marriage: Colleen, Cathy, David. AB, Dartmouth Coll., 1948; MD, NYU, 1952. Intern Bellevue Hosp., N.Y.C., 1952-53; resident in pediat. Columbia-Presbyn. Med. Ctr., 1953-55; rsch. fellow Harvard-Children's Hosp., 1955-56; rsch. fellow in biochemistry U. Vt., 1956-60, from asst. prof. to prof. pediat., 1961-74, prof., 1974—95, Harry Wallace prof. of neonatology, 1995—. Rsch. fellow in biol. chemistry Harvard Coll., 1960—61; cons. NIH; vis. prof. Royal Soc. Medicine, England, 1980; mem. senate U. Vt., 2000—. Editor-in-chief Pediatrics, 1974—; contbr. articles on neonatology, phototherapy and transcutaneous oxygen to profl. jours. With USN, 1944—46. Recipient Humbolt Sr. Scientist award, 1978, United Cerebral Palsy Rsch. award, 1984, McDonald prize, 1991, Apgar award, 1993; Markel scholar, 1960-65, Humbolt scholar, 1978, Univ. scholar, 1991, Columbia Alumnus of Yr. award, 1995, Vt. Physician of Yr., 2005. Fellow Am. Acad. Pediat. (Grulee award 1988, Lifetime Achievement award 1997); mem. Royal Soc. Medicine, World congress on Perinatal Medicine (pres. 1993), Indian Pediat. Soc. (hon., Gold medal 1994, Perinatal Edn. award 1997), Inst. Medicine, Finnish Pediat. Soc. (hon.). Home: 52 Overlake Park Burlington VT 05401 Office: Given Bldg D201 89 Beaumont Ave Burlington VT 05405-0068 Office Phone: 802-656-5248.

LUCEY, MICHAEL RONAN, gastroenterologist; b. Dublin, Dec. 29, 1952; s. Michael Lucey and Mary Frances Ronayne; m. Patricia A.M. Hughes; children: Catherine, Aidan, Rory, Emer. MB BCh BA, U. Dublin, 1976, MD, 1985. Intern The Meath Hosp., Dublin, 1976—77; resident Fed. Dublin Vol. Hosps., 1977—79; registrar St. Vincent's Hosp., 1979—80; asst. prof. gastroent. U. Mich., Ann Arbor, 1987—92, assoc. prof. gastroent., 1992—95; assoc. prof. dept. medicine U. Pa., 1995—99, prof. dept. medicine, 1999—2001, U. Wis., Madison, 2001—, chief sect. gastroent. and hepatology, 2001—. Mem. liver transplant evaluation com. U. Mich., 1987—95, mem. transplantation task force, 1990—95, mem. transplant program data mgmt. com., 1990—95, med. dir. liver transplant program, 1991—95; assoc. chief divsn. gastroent., dir. hepatology, med. dir. liver transplant program U. Pa., 1995—2001, interim chief divsn. gastroent., 1997—98, mem. rev. bd. gen. clin. rsch. ctr., 1998—2001, co-chair quality improvement com. digestive and liver ctr., 1996—2001; mem. ept. medicine exec. com. U. Wis., 2002—, mem. med. found. fin. com., 2002—. Mem. editl. bd.: Hepatology, 1992—96, Jour. Clin. Gastroent., 1992—98, Liver Transplantation, 1993—, Am. Jour. Gastroent., 2002—; editor: Graft, 1997—2001, Am. Jour. Transplantation, 2000—01; contbr. articles to profl. jours., chpts. to books. Named Physicians of Yr., Del. Valley chpt. Am. Liver Found., 1997; recipient Jr. Clin. prize, The Meath Hosp., 1974, PEter Beckett Meml. prize Psychiatry, 1975, Sr. Clin. prize, The Meath Hosp., 1976, Sir John Banks medal, U. Dublin, 1983; fellow, St. Bartholomew's Hosp., London, 1980—83, Kings Coll. Hosp., London, 1983—85, U. Mich., Ann Arbor, 1985—87. Fellow: Coll. Physicians Phila., Royal Coll. Physicians Ireland (William Stokes Traveling scholar 1980); mem.: European Assn. Study of Liver, Am. Soc. Transplantation (manpower com. 1993—94, mem. liver and intra-abdominal organs com. 1993—95, pub. policy com. 1993—96, ad-hoc com. organ donation 1994—96, chair liver and intra-abdominal organs com. 1995—96, ann. meeting planning com. 1997—2001, mem. governing coun. 1997—, awards com. 1997—, edn. com. 2000—, sec.-treas. 2001—02, pres. elect 2002—03), Am. Gastroent. Assn. (patient care com. 1995—96, clin. practice/practice econs. 1996—99, UNOS rep. 2000—), Am. Assn. Study Liver Diseases (clin. com. 1993—95, strategic alliance task force 1997—2000, clin. guidelines com. 2002—). Office: U Wis-Madison Med Sch Sect Gastroen and Hepatology H6/515 Clin Rsch Ctr 600 Highland Ave Madison WI 53792

LUCHAK, FRANK ALEXANDER, lawyer; b. Alta., Can., Feb. 19, 1950; came to US, 1956; s. George and Elizabeth (Szilagyi) Luchak. BA in Economics, Princeton U., 1972; JD, SUNY, Buffalo, 1978. Bar: Pa. 1978, NJ 1979, US Dist. Ct. NJ 1979, US Dist. Ct. Ea. Dist. Pa. 1980, US Ct Appeals 3rd Cir., US Supreme Ct. 1986. With internat. divsn. Bank of Montreal, Quebec, Canada, 1972—75; assoc. Harvey, Pennington, Herting & Renneisen, Ltd., Phila., 1977-81, Duane, Morris & Heckscher (now Duane Morris LLP), 1981-86, ptnr., 1986—, mng. ptnr. Marlton/Cherry Hill office, 1992—2004, mng. ptnr. Princeton office, 2004—, team member partners bd., 1998—. Mem. life, health, accident and disability ins. com. Def. Rsch. Inst. Mem. ABA, NJ State Bar Assn., Camden County Bar Assn., Burlington County Bar Assn. Office: Duane Morris LLP PO Box 5203 Princeton NJ 08543-5203 Office Phone: 609-631-2444. Office Fax: 609-631-2401. Business E-Mail: luchak@duanemorris.com.

LUCHINI, JOSEPH S., lawyer; b. 1948; BS in aerospace engrng. with high honors, W.Va. U., 1970; JD, Georgetown U., 1973. Bar: Va. 1973, DC 1990, US Ct. Appeals for Armed Forces 1974. Served in Judge Adv. Gen.'s Office USAF, 1973—79; with Hazel & Thomas, PC (combined with Reed Smith in 1999), 1979—99; ptnr. Reed Smith LLP, Falls Church, Va., 1999—, Va. practice group leader litig. group. Office: Reed Smith LLP 3110 Fairview Park Dr, Ste 1400 Falls Church VA 22042 Office Phone: 703-641-4274. Office Fax: 703-641-4340. Business E-Mail: jluchini@reedsmith.com.

LUCHINS, DANIEL JONATHAN, psychiatrist; b. N.Y.C., July 1, 1948; s. Abraham Samuel and Edith (Hirsch) L.; children: Kerith, Matthew. BSc, McGill U., Montreal, Que., Can., 1971, MD, 1973. Diplomate Am. Bd. Psychiatry and Neurology; cert. geriatric psychiatry. Vis. scientist NIMH, Washington, 1977-81; assoc. prof. U. Chgo., 1981—; med. coord. mental health Ill. Dept. Mental Health, Chgo., 1989-91; chief of adult psychiatry U. Chgo., 1991-93; chief for clin. svcs. . Office of Mental Health, Ill. Dept. Human Svcs., Chgo., 1995—; chief pub. psychiatry U. Chgo., 1996. Contbr. articles to profl. publs. Recipient A.E. Bennett award Soc. Biol. Psychiatry, Geriatric Mental Health acad. award NIMH, 1984-87, Exemplary Psychiatrist award NAMI, 1998. Fellow Am. Psychiat. Assn.; mem. Ill. Psychiat. Assn. (councillor 1989-91, pres. 1995, Am. Psychiat. Assn. rep.). Jewish. Achievements include development of criteria for hospice care for demented patients. Office: U Chgo Dept Psychiatry 5841 S Maryland Ave Chicago IL 60637-1463 Office Phone: 773-702-9716. Business E-Mail: danl@yoda.bsd.uchicago.edu.

LUCHT, JOHN CHARLES, management consultant, writer; b. Reedsburg, Wis., June 1, 1933; s. Carl H. and Ruth A. (Shultis) L.; m. Catherine Ann Seyler, Dec. 11, 1965 (dv. 1982). BS, U. Wis., 1955, LLB, 1960. News dir. Sta. WISC-AM/FM, Madison, Wis., 1952-55; merchandising dir. The Bartell Group (radio and TV stas.), Milw., 1955-56; instr. U. Wis. Law Sch., 1959-60; TV contracts exec., account exec. J. Walter Thompson Co., N.Y.C., 1960-64; product mgr., new products supr., dir. new product mktg. Bristol-Myers Co., N.Y.C., 1964-69; dir. mktg. W.A. Sheaffer Pen Co., Ft. Madison, Iowa, 1969-70; gen. mgr. Tetley Tea div. Squibb Beech-Nut Inc., N.Y.C., 1970-71; v.p. Heidrick & Struggles, N.Y.C., 1971-77; pres. The John Lucht Consultancy, Inc., N.Y.C., 1977—, The Viceroy Press Inc., 1987—, RiteSite.com, 1998—. Lectr. in field. Author: Rites of Passage at $100,000 to $1 Million Plus, The Insiders's Guide to Executive Job-Changing, Executive Job-Changing Workbook, Insights for the Journey—Navigating to Thrive, Enjoy and Prosper in Senior Management. Mem. Soc. Am. Bus. Editors and Writers, Internat. Assn. Corp. and Profl. Recruiters, State Bar Wis., N.Y. Bd. Trade, Assn. Exec. Search Cons., N.Y. Acad. Scis., Overseas Press Club, Met. Club, Can. Club, Phi Beta Kappa, Phi Eta Sigma, Phi Kappa Phi, Phi Delta Phi, Sigma Alpha Epsilon. Office: Worldwide Plaza West Ste 8-B 350 W 50th St New York NY 10019 Office Phone: 212-259-9211.

LUCIA, MARILYN REED, physician; b. Boston; m. Salvatore P. Lucia, 1959, (dec. 1984); m. C. Robert Russell, (dec. 2000); children: Elizabeth, Walter, Salvatore, Darryl. AB with highest honors, U. Calif., Berkeley, 1951; MD, U. Calif., San Francisco, 1956. Cert. in psychiatry and child psychiatry Am. Bd. Psychiatry and Neurology. Intern Stanford U. Hosp., 1956-57; NIMH fellow, resident in psychiatry Langley Porter, U. Calif., San Francisco, 1957-60; NIMH fellow, resident in child psychiatry Mt. Zion Hosp., San Francisco, 1964-66; NIMH fellow, in cmty. psychiatry U. Calif., San Francisco, 1966—68, clin. prof. psychiatry, 1982—. Founder, cons. Marilyn Reed Lucia Child Care Study Ctr., U. Calif., San Francisco; cons. Craniofacial Ctr., U. Calif., San Francisco; No. Calif. Diagnostic Sch. for Neurologically Handicapped Children; dir. children's psychiat. svc. Contra Costa County Hosp., Martinez. Fellow Am. Psychiat. Assn. (disting. life), Am. Acad. Child Psychiatry; mem. Am. Cleft Palate Assn., San Francisco Med. Soc., Phi Beta Kappa. Office: 350 Parnassus Ave Ste 602 San Francisco CA 94117-3608

LUCIAN, JOHN, lawyer; s. Joseph and Mary Lucian. JD, U. Md., 1998. Bar: Md. 1998, Va. 1999, Fla. 1999, Pa. 2004. Atty. Linowes & Blocher LLP, Bethesda, 1995—99; assoc. Blank Rome LLP, Philadelphia, Pa., 1999—. Contbr. articles to profl. jours. Gen. counsel Cath. Faith Alive!, Inc., Md.; bd. of visitors Ave Maria U. Sch. of Law, Ann Arbor, Mich. Recipient, Hattie Strong Found. award, 1997; scholar Senatorial scholar, Md. Senate, 1997. Mem.: Va. Bar Assn., Bankruptcy Bar Assn. for the Dist. of Md. Office: Blank Rome LLP One Logan Sq Philadelphia PA 19103 Office Phone: 215-569-5500. Office Fax: 215-569-5555. E-mail: lucian@blankrome.com.

LUCIANO, ROSELLE PATRICIA, advertising executive, editor; b. Bklyn., Feb. 10, 1921; d. Giacomo Roberto and Francesca Rosa (Ruvolo) Rubino; m. Anthony Vincenzo Luciano, Nov. 24, 1946; 1 child, Nino Vincenzo Luciano. Attended, NYU. College shop mgr. Abraham & Straus, Bklyn., 1939-41, advtg. copywriter, 1941-44; fashion editor Syndicated MB Reports, N.Y.C., 1945-48; advtg. mgr., fashions copywriter Macy's 34th St., N.Y.C., 1949-54; publicist, adminstr. Fun With Prodns., N.Y.C., 1959-69; chair, adminstr. U.U. Plandome Forum, Manhasset, N.Y., 1970-78, UU Veatch Found., Manhasset, N.Y., 1979-84; dir. devel. IALRW Literacy For Women Program, Great Britain and India, 1984—. Coord. numerous workshops in field for various orgns.; served as spkr., editor, writer, publicist, 1984—. Operator political booth Democratic Party, Garden City, 1984, 88, 92; founder R.P.L. Literacy Fund for Women, 1996—. Recipient Best Advtg. Ad of the Yr. award Women's Wear Daily, 1954, Citizen of the Yr. award Carle Place Schs., 1965, award for outstanding leadership and encouragement for working women Women-On-the-Job, Inc., N.Y., 1987, Susan B. Anthony award U. U. Women;s Fedn., 1997. Unitarian Universalist. Avocations: environmental activism, opera, ballet, theater, travel.

LUCID, ROBERT FRANCIS, language educator; b. Seattle, June 25, 1930; s. Philip Joseph and Nora May (Gorman) L.; m. Joanne K. Tharalson, Sept. 18, 1954; 1 son, John Michael. BA, U. Wash., 1954; MA, U. Chgo., 1955, PhD, 1958. Faculty U. Chgo., 1957-59, Wesleyan U., Middletown, Conn., 1959-64; mem. faculty U. Pa., Phila., 1964—, prof. English, 1975-96, emeritus, 1996—, chmn. dept. English, 1980-85, 90-91, chmn. faculty senate, 1976-77, master Hill Coll. House, 1979-96; master Gregory Coll. House, 1998—. Editor: Journal of Richard Henry Dana, 1968, The Long Patrol, 1971, Norman Mailer, the Man and His Work, 1971. Served with USAF, 1951-53. Recipient Lindback award U. Pa., 1975, Abrams award, 1986; Yaddo fellow, 1970 Mem. MLA, AAUP, PEN (exec. bd. 1987-93), Am. Studies Assn. (exec. sec. 1964-69), Penn Club (N.Y.C.). Office: U Pa Dept English Philadelphia PA 19104 E-mail: rlucid@dept.english.upenn.edu.

LUCID, SHANNON W., biochemist, astronaut; b. Shanghai, Jan. 14, 1943; d. Joseph Oscar and Mary Wells; m. Michael F. Lucid, 1968; children: Kawai Dawn, Shandara Michelle, Michael Kermit. BS in Chemistry, U. Okla., 1963, MS in Biochemistry, 1970, PhD in Biochemistry, 1973. Sr. lab. technician Okla. Med. Rsch. Found., 1964-66, rsch. assoc., from 1974; chemist Kerr-McGee, Oklahoma City, 1966-68; astronaut NASA Lyndon B. Johnson Space Ctr., Houston, 1979—, mission specialist flights STS-51G and STS-34, mission specialist on Shuttle Atlantis Flight, 1991, mission specialist flight STS-58, 1993, mission specialist flight STS 76 & 79, 1996, mgmt., astronaut office Houston, 2003—; mission specialist stationed on Space Station Mir, 1996; chief scientist NASA Hdqs., Washington, 2003—03. Recipient Space award Aviation Week and Space Tech., 1997; first woman to fly on the shuttle three times; remained aloft 188 days in shuttle Mir. Address: NASA Johnson Space Ctr CB-Astronaut Office Houston TX 77058

LUCIER, P. JEFFREY, publishing executive; b. Manchester, NH, June 20, 1941; s. Paul A. and Elaine (Wilson) Fraser L.; m. Judith Margaret Akers, Dec. 21, 1963 (div. 1975); children— Kathryn Elizabeth, Amy Wilson; m. Velma Lee Frye, Nov. 27, 1976 (div. 1981); m. Susan Elizabeth Hess, May 25, 1985; children: Madalyn Antonette, Caitlin Elaine. BA, Union Coll., N.Y., 1963; MA, U. Chgo., 1964. Instr. English, Northwestern U., Evanston and Chgo., 1967-69; registered rep. Paine Webber, Akron, Ohio, 1969-71; asst. to pres. Banks-Baldwin Law Pub., Cleve., 1971-74, v.p. editorial, 1974-76, exec. v.p., 1977-78, pres., editor-in-chief, 1978-96; CEO, Pegasus Techs. Ld., Painesville, Ohio, 1996-98, All-Stater Pub. LLC, Columbus, Ohio, 1997-2000; chmn. STACK LLC, 2005—. Pres. The Banks-Baldwin Found.; bd. dirs. JumpStart, Inc., Hawken Sch. Pres. Cleve. Music Sch. Settlement; bd. dirs. Cleve. Bot. Garden, Mus. Contemporary Art Cleve., Cleve. Shakespeare Festival, ECity, Cleve. affiliate of Nat. Found. for Tchg. Entrepreneurship. Mem.: Cleve. Playhouse Club, Cleve. City Club. Democrat. Roman Catholic. Office Phone: 216-570-4863. E-mail: pjl@en.com.

LUCIUS, RANDALL H., psychologist; b. Atlanta, Feb. 19, 1968; PhD in Applied Psychology, U. Ga., 1997. Rsch. dir. Turknett Leadership Group, Atlanta, 1998—2000, Fitability Sys., Atlanta, 2000—03; sr. cons. Applied Psychol. Tech., Atlanta, 2003—. Pres. Atlanta Soc. Applied Psychology, 2000. Author (creator): (personality assessment) Fitablity 5 & Profiler, 1998, 2001. Mem.: APA, Soc. Human Resource Mgmt., Soc. Indsl./Orgnl. Psychology (chairperson 2002—). Achievements include development of Profiler personality assessment used by over 200,000 and worldwide; Fitability5 personality assessment used by over 10,000 job applicants and 500 hiring managers. Office: Applied Psychol Tech 315 W Ponce deLeon Ave Ste 701 Decatur GA 30030

LUCK, DENNIS NOEL, biologist, educator, researcher; b. Durban, Natal, South Africa, Dec. 8, 1939; s. Peter Burvill and Eva Annie (Taylor) L.; m. Joan Burchall, Jan. 18, 1969; 1 child, Roy Burvil. BSc, U. Natal, South Africa, 1961, MSc, 1963; DPhil, Oxford U., Oxford, Eng., 1966. Lectr. in biochemistry U. Natal, South Africa, 1966-69; vis. asst. prof. Baylor Coll. Medicine, Houston, 1969-70; asst. prof. zoology U. Tex., Austin, 1970-72; asst. prof., assoc. prof. biology Oberlin Coll., Ohio, 1972-82, prof., 1982—, chmn., 1995-98. Cons. Gilford Instrument Labs., Oberlin, 1980-82, The Oberlin Sci. Co., 1989-90. Contbr. more than 20 articles to profl. jours. including Nature, Molecular Endocrinology, DNA, Procs. NAS, Biochimica et Biophysica Acta, Protein Engring.; speaker at maj. sci. meetings, 1988, 90, 94. Recipient Eleanor Roosevelt Internat. Cancer fellowship Internat. Union Against Cancer, Geneva, Switzerland, 1978-79; grantee NSF, 1975-80, 1984-98. Fellow Ohio Acad. Sci.; mem. Endocrine Soc., Biochem. Soc. London, Am. Soc. for Microbiology, Am. Soc. for Biochemistry and Molecular Biology. Achievements include a structure-function analysis of bovine prolactin. Home: 240 Oak St Oberlin OH 44074-1518 Office: Dept Biology Science Ctr 119 Woodland St Oberlin OH 44074 E-mail: dennis.n.luck@oberlin.edu.

LUCK, JAMES I., foundation executive; b. Akron, Ohio, Aug. 28, 1945; s. Milton William and Gertrude (Winer) L.; children: Andrew Brewer, Edward Aldrich. L. BA, Ohio State U., 1967; MA, U. Ga., 1970. Caseworker Franklin County Welfare Dept., Columbus, Ohio, 1967-69; dir. forensics Tex. Christian U., Ft. Worth, 1970-74; assoc. dir. Bicentennial Youth Debates, Washington, 1974-76; exec. dir. Nat. Congress on Volunteerism and Citizenship, Washington, 1976-77; fellow Acad. Contemporary Problems, Columbus, Ohio, 1977-79; exec. dir. Battelle Meml. Inst. Found., Columbus, 1980-82; pres. Columbus Found., 1981—2001, pres. emeritus, 2001—; exec. dir. Columbus Youth Found. and Ingram-White Castle Funds, 1981—2001; chmn. Am Resource Devel., LLC, Columbus, 2002—; pres., CEO Global 3E, 2003—. Co-chmn. Task Force on Citizen Edn., Washington, 1977; mediator Negotiated Investment Strategy, Columbus, 1979; chmn. Ohio Founds. Conf., 1985; cons. HEW, Peace Corps., U. Va. Author: Ohio-The Next 25 Years, 1978, Bicentennial Issue Analysis, 1975; editor: Proceedings of the Nat. Conf. on Argumentation, 1973; contbr. articles to profl. jours. Trustee Godman Guild Settlement House, Columbus, 1979-81, Am. Diabetes Assn., Ohio, 1984-88; chmn. spl. com. on displacement Columbus City Coun., 1978-80; bd. dirs. Commn. on the Future of the Professions in Soc., 1979. Mem. Donors Forum Ohio. Clubs: Capital, Columbus Club, Columbus Met., Kit-Kat. Lodges: Rotary. Avocations: travel, reading. Home: 799 Pinecliff Pl Worthington OH 43085-1906 Office: Am Resources Devel LLC 1650 Watermark Dr Ste 100 Columbus OH 43215 Office Phone: 614-364-7111. E-mail: jluck@ard501.cm.

LUCKE, ROBERT VITO, investment company executive; b. Kingston, Pa., July 26, 1930; s. Vito Frank and Edith Ann (Adders) L.; m. Jane Ann Rushin, Aug. 16, 1952; children: Thomas, Mark, Carl. BS in Chemistry, Pa. State U., 1952; MS in Mgmt., Rensselaer Polytech Inst., 1960. Polymer chemist Uniroyal Naugatuck (Conn.) Chem. Div., 1954-60; comml. devel. engr. Exxon Enjay Div., Elizabeth, N.J., 1960-66; gen. mgr. Celanese Advanced Composites, Summit, N.J., 1966-70; bus. mgr. polymer div. Hooker Chem., Burlington, N.J., 1970-74; gen. mgr. Oxy Metal Industries Environ. Equipment. Divs., Warren, Mich., 1974-79; v.p., gen. mgr. Hoover Universal Plastic Machinery Divs., Manchester, Mich., 1979-84; pres. Egan Machinery, Somerville, N.J., 1984-87; pres., chief exec. officer Krauss Maffei Corp., Cin., 1987-93; pres. Adventa Global LLC, Cin., 1990—. Instr., Chem. Market Rsch. Assn., 1974. Author: (with others) Plastics Handbook, 1972; inventor, 2 patents in field. 1st lt. Corp Engrs., 1952-54, Korea. Senatorial scholar, Pa. State U., 1948-52. Mem. Am. Chem. Soc., Soc. Plastics Engrs. (sect. engr. STDS com. 1969), Tech. Assn. Pulp Paper Industry, Comml. Devel. Assn., Assn. Corp. Growth (pres. So. Ohio Chpt, 1998). Avocations: golf, skiing, travel, gardening. Office: Adventa Global LLC 414 Walnut St Ste 607 Cincinnati OH 45202-3913 Office Phone: 513-579-8330 ext. 17. Personal E-mail: wiseowl726@aol.com. Business E-Mail: rlucke@agiglobal.net.

LUCKE, STEPHEN P., lawyer; b. 1957; AB in Econ. magna cum laude, Coll. Holy Cross, 1980; JD magna cum laude, Georgetown Univ., 1983. Bar: Minn. 1984, Wis. 1990. Law clerk, Hon. Myron H. Bright US Ct. Appeals (8th cir.), 1983—84; assoc. Dorsey & Whitney, Mpls., 1984—90, ptnr., trial group, co-head, ERISA litig., 1991. Mng. editor Georgetown Law Jour., 1982—83. Mem.: ABA, Hennepin County Bar Assn., Minn. State Bar Assn., Alpha Sigma Nu, Phi Beta Kappa. Office: Dorsey & Whitney LLP Ste 1500 50 S Sixth St Minneapolis MN 55402-1498 Office Phone: 612-343-7947. Office Fax: 612-340-8800. Business E-Mail: lucke.steve@dorsey.com.

LUCKER, JAY K., library consultant; b. NYC, Feb. 23, 1930; s. Joseph Jerome and Ella (Schwartz) L.; m. Marjorie Stern, Aug. 17, 1952 (dec. Aug. 1997); children— Amy Ellen, Nancy Judith. AB, Bklyn. Coll., City U. N.Y., 1951; MS, Columbia, 1952; postgrad., N.Y. U., 1955-57. Head procurement br., acquisition div. New York Pub. Library, 1954-57, first asst., acting chief, sci. and tech. div., 1957-59; asst. univ. librarian for sci. and tech., assoc. prof. Princeton U. Library, 1959-68, assoc. univ. librarian, prof., 1968-75; dir. librs. MIT, Cambridge, 1975-95; vis. prof. Grad. Sch. Libr. and Info. Sci. Simmons Coll., Boston, 1995-2001. Chmn. bd. dirs. Captain Libr. Svcs. Corp., 1972-75; vis. lectr. Drexel U. Grad. Sch. Libr. Svc., 1962-67; vice chmn. New Eng. Libr. Info. Network, 1978-79, chmn., 1980-82. Bd. dirs. Boston Libr. Consortium; mem. adv. coms. Brown U., Tufts U., Washington U., St. Louis, Libr. Congress, Engring. Info. Inc. Served with Signal Corps U.S. Army, 1952-54. Council on Library Resources fellow, 1970-71 Fellow AAAS; mem. ALA (council 1978-82), Am. Soc. Info. Sci., N.J. Library Assn. (Distinguished Service award coll. and univ. sect. 1975), Assn. Research Libraries (chmn. interlibrary loan com. 1976-80, dir. 1977-80, pres. 1980-81), Spl. Libraries Assn., Phi Beta Kappa, Alpha Phi Omega, Beta Phi Mu. E-mail: jklucker@mit.edu.

LUCKERT, MARLA JO, state supreme court justice; b. Goodland, Kans., July 20, 1955; d. William Gottleib and Gladys Iona (Rohr) L.; m. Steven. K. Morse, May 25, 1980; children: Sarah, Alisa. BA, Washburn U., 1977, JD, 1980. Bar: Kans. 1980, U.S. Dist. Ct. Kans. 1980, U.S. Ct. Appeals (10th cir.) 1980. Assoc. Goodell, Stratoon, Edmond & Palmer, Topeka, 1980—92; judge Third Jud. Dist., Kans. Supreme Ct., Kans., 1992—2000, chief judge, 2000—03; justice Kans. Supreme Ct., Kans., 2003—. Adj. prof. Washburn Univ. Sch. Law, Topeka, 1980-81, 1990—. Author: Kansas Consent Manual, 1988, Record Relations Guide, 1988, Kansas Law for Physicians, 1989. Pres. Mobile Meals of Topeka (Kans.), Inc., 1987-89, Mobile Meals of Topeka (Kans.) Found., 1989—; co-chair YWCA Nominating Com., Topeka, 1988-89. Recipient Woman of Excellence Award, YWCA, Topeka, Kans. Mem. ABA (co-chair young lawyers health law com. 1988-90), Am. Acad. Hosp. Attys., Kans. Assn. Hosp. Attys., Kans. Assn. Def. Counsel (bd. dirs. 1988—, disting. svc. award 1990), Kans. Bar Assn. (pres. young lawyers 1989-90, outstanding svc. award 1990), Topeka Bar Assn. (chair law day pubs. com.), Women Attys. Assn. Kans., Topeka (pres. 1988-89), Sam A. Crow Inn of Ct., Am. Judges Assn., Nat. Assn. Women Judges, Nat. Ctr. State Courts, Supreme Ct. Historical Soc., Am. Judicature Soc.; fellow Am. Bar Foundation, Kans. Bar Foundation. Office: Kansas Judicial Ctr 301 SW 10th Ave Topeka KS 66612-1507*

LUCKETT, BYRON EDWARD, JR., chaplain, retired military officer; b. Mineral Wells, Tex., Feb. 2, 1951; s. Byron Edward and Helen Alma (Hart) L.; m. Kathryn Louise Lambertson, Dec. 30, 1979; children: Florence Louise, Byron Edward III, Barbara Elizabeth, Stephanie Hart. BS, U.S. Mil. Acad., 1973; MDiv, Princeton Theol. Sem., 1982; MA, Claremont Grad. Sch., 1987. Commd. 2d lt. U.S. Army, 1973, advanced through grades to lt. col.; stationed at Camp Edwards E., Korea, 1974-75; bn. supply officer 563rd Engr. Bn., Kornwestheim, Germany, 1975-76; platoon leader, exec. officer 275th Engr. Co., Ludwigsburg, Germany, 1976-77; boy scout project officer Hdqrs., VII Corps, Stuttgart, Germany, 1977-78; student intern Moshannon Valley Larger Parish, Winburne, Penn., 1980-81; Protestant chaplain Philmont Scout Ranch, Cimarron, N.Mex., 1982; asst. pastor Immanuel Presbyn. Ch., Albuquerque, 1982-83, assoc. pastor, 1983-84; tchr. Claremont High Sch., 1985-86; Protestant chaplain 92nd Combat Support Group, Fairchild AFB, Wash., 1986-90; installation staff chaplain Pirinclik Air Station, Turkey, 1990-91; Protestant chaplain Davis-Monthan AFB, Ariz., 1991-95; dir. readiness ministries Offutt AFB, Nebr., 1995-96, sr. Protestant chaplain, 1996-98, Elmendorf AFB, AK, 1998-2000; wing chaplain Minot AFB, N.D., 2000—01; sr. career advisor Bernard Haldane Assocs., Las Vegas, Nev., 2001—02; on-call chaplain St. Rose Dominican Hosp., Henders, Nev., 2002—; sr. cons. IDC, 2003—04, account exec., 2004—. Mem. intern program coun. Claremont (Calif.) Grad. Sch.; affiliate faculty Regis U., Las Vegas, 2003—. Contbr. articles to profl. jours. Bd. dirs. Parentcraft, Inc., Albuquerque, 1984, United Campus Ministries, Albuquerque, 1984, Proclaim Liberty, Inc., Spokane, 1987-90, Amazing Grace Ministry, Las Vegas, 2005—; bd. dirs. western region Nat. Assn. Presbyn. Scouters, Irving, Tex., 1986-89, chaplain, 1991-93; mem. N.Mex. Employer Co, in Support of the Guard and Reserve, Albuquerque, 1984, Old Baldy coun. Boy Scouts Am., 1986; chmn. Fairchild Parent Coop., Fairchild AFB, 1986-87; pres. Co. Grade Officers Coun., Fairchild AFB, 1987-88. Capt. U.S. Army Reserve; chaplain USAF Res., 1983-86; lt. col. 1998. Recipient Dist. Award of Merit for Disting. Svc. Boy Scouts Am., 1977. Mem. Soc. Cin. Md., Mil. Order Fgn. Wars U.S., Civil Affairs Assn. Presbyterian. Office: IDC 2500 Paseo Verde Pkwy Henderson NV 89074 Personal E-mail: ekluckett@cox.net. Business E-Mail: eluckett@goidc.com.

LUCKEY, ALWYN HALL, lawyer; b. Biloxi, Miss., Oct. 3, 1960; s. Toxie Hall and Joy Evelyn (Smith) L.; m. Jeanne Elaine Carter, Aug. 4, 1984; children: Laurel McKay, Taylor Leah. BA in Zoology, U. Miss., 1982, JD, 1985. Bar: Miss. 1985, U.S. Dist. Ct. (so. and no. dist.) Miss. 1985, U.S. Ct. Appeals (5th cir.) 1985. Assoc. Richard F. Scruggs, Pascagoula, Miss., 1985-88, shareholder, 1988—, Asbestos Group PA, 1988-93; prin. Alwyn H. Luckey, Atty. at Law, Ocean Springs, Miss., 1993—. V.p., bd. dirs. Marine Mgmt., Inc., Ocean Springs, Miss., 1987—. Author: Mississippi Landlord Tenant Law, 1985. Deacon First Presbyn. Ch., Ocean Springs, 1989; chmn. Dole for Pres. com., Jackson County, 1988. Mem. Am. Trial Lawyers Assn., Miss. Bar Assn., Miss. Trial Lawyers Assn., Jackson County Bar Assn., Jackson County Young Lawyers Assn. (v.p.), Ocean Springs Yacht Club, Bienville Club, Treasure Oak Country Club. Avocations: tennis, boating, travel. Office: PO Box 724 Ocean Springs MS 39566-0724

LUCKEY, DORIS WARING, civic volunteer; b. Union City, NJ, Sept. 17, 1929; d. Jay Deloss and Edna May (Ware) Waring; m. George William Luckey, Mar. 29, 1958; children: G. Robert, Jana Elizabeth, John Andrew. AB, U. Rochester, 1950; CLU, Am. Coll., Bryn Mawr, Pa., 1957. With pers. dept., supr. life dept. Travelers Ins. Co., Rochester, NY, 1952-58; agt. asst. life underwriting Mass. Mut. Ins. Co., Rochester, NY, 1958. Chair, various past offices Bd. Coop. Ednl. Svc. and State Edn. Dept. Vocat. Tech. Adv. Com., Rochester and Albany, NY, 1975—2003, pres. Rochester, 1975—85, Monroe County Sch. Bd. Assn., Rochester, 1980—81; v.p. Penfield (N.Y.) Sch., 1978—81; mem., past pres. William Warfield Scholarship Fund Bd.; coord. Young Artist Competition Penfield Symphony Orch; former adv. to bd. St. John's Home for Aging Bd., former mem. fin., pension and pers. com., former bd. dir., former exec. com.; pres. Leslie Norwood Carter Music Scholarship Fund; vol. numerous other civic, cultural, ch. and artistic orgn.; former pres. new investments United Ch. Christ, Genesee Valley, trustee former ch. coun., former pres. ch. coun., former chair ch. and min. com., co-chair; property trustee Brighton United Ch. Christ, chair pastoral search com., 2001—02, co-chair investment com., co-chair long-range planning com; mem. program and mission com. Genesee Valley Assn. United Ch. Christ. Mem.: LWV (co-chmn. nominating com. Rochester Metro chpt., chair spkrs. bur. Rochester Metro chpt.), AAUW (past pres. Greater Rochester br., past bd. dirs., dist. 1 state rep.). Republican.

LUCKEY, ROBERT REUEL RAPHAEL, retired academic administrator; b. Houghton, N.Y., Nov. 19, 1917; s. James Seymour and Edith Bedell (Curtis) L.; m. Ruth Ida Brooks, Aug. 25, 1945; children: James, John, Linda, Peter, Daniel (dec.), Thomas. BS, BA, Houghton Coll., 1937; MA, N.Y. U., 1939; PhD, Cornell U., 1942; LittD, Houghton Coll., 1980; LLD, Marion Coll., 1987. Secondary tchr. Wilson (N.Y.) Cen. Sch., 1937-39; math. & physics instr. Houghton Coll., 1942, assoc. prof., prof. math. and physics, alumni dir., 1954, dir. devel., v.p. in devel.; pres. Ind. Wesleyan U. (formerly Marion (Ind.) Coll.), 1976-84, 1986-87. Pres. Seneca Council Boy Scouts Am., Olean, N.Y., 1964-65; assessor Township of Caneadea, N.Y., 1951-76. Recipient Silver Beaver award Boy Scouts Am., 1965; named Alumnus of Yr. Houghton Coll., 1976, Disting. Alumnus Houghton Coll., 1984, Sagamore of the Wabash by Gov. of Ind., 1980. Mem. Grant County C. of C. (bd. dirs. 1981-84). Republican. Wesleyan. Avocations: spectator sports, personal computers. Home: PO Box 24 Houghton NY 14744-8719 also: 22250 Melody Ln Brooksville FL 34601-6705 E-mail: rrrluckey@hotmail.com.

LUCKIE, ROBERT ERVIN, JR., advertising executive; b. Clanton, Ala., May 3, 1917; s. Robert Ervin and Eliza (Goodwyn) L.; m. Lois Katherine Drolet, May 15, 1942 (dec. May 1987); children: Katherine (Mrs. Andrew J. Shackelford), Robert Ervin III, Anne Claire Luckie Cobb, Thomas George. AB, Birmingham-So. Coll., 1940, LLD (hon.); HHD (hon.), U. Ala. Reporter-columnist Birmingham (Ala.) News, 1940-41, mem. advt. staff, 1945-48; chmn., ptnr. Tucker Wayne/Luckie & Co., Birmingham, 1958-99. Pres. Nat Advt. Agy. Network, 1960, chmn., Luckie/Birmingham, Inc., 1999—; bd. dirs. South Trust Bank. Chmn. for Ala. Radio Free Europe, 1964; co-chmn. Jefferson County United Appeal, 1968; pres. Met. Devel. Bd., 1976; bd. dirs. Blue Cross/Blue Shield, of Ala., Ala. Motorist's Assn.; trustee Birmingham-So. Coll., U. Ala. Birmingham Pres. Coun. Lt. comdr. USNR, 1942-45. Recipient Silver medal award Advt. Fedn. Am. and Printer's Ink, 1963, Disting. Alumni award Birmingham-So. Coll., 1967; named Advt. Man of Yr., Ad Club/Advt. Fedn. Am., 1963; inductee Birmingham Bus. Hall of Fame, U. Ala. Comm. Hall of Fame, 1999. Mem. Birmingham-So. Coll. Alumni Assn. (pres. 1966), Kiwanis (pres. 1964), Downtown Club, The Club (Birmingham) (pres. 1980-81), Birmingham Country Club (pres. 1975), Newcomen Soc., Omicron Delta Kappa, Kappa Alpha. Clubs: Kiwanis (pres. 1964), Birmingham Country (pres. 1975), Relay House (past pres.), Downtown, The Club (Birmingham) (pres. 1980-81). Methodist. Home: 3238 Country Club Rd Birmingham AL 35213-4115 Office: Luckie & Co 600 Luckie Dr Birmingham AL 35223-2429

LUCKING, PAUL, telecommunications executive; Various sr. mgmt. positions Fed. Express, SysteMed, CitiCorp.; founder, pres. Interface Solutions, Inc.; chief tech. officer, sr. v.p. ADT; COO, pres. subsidiaries Davel Comms., Inc., Tampa, Fla., 2000—. Office: Davel Communications 1001 Lakeside Ave E Fl 7 Cleveland OH 44114-1158

LUCKMAN, SHARON GERSTEN, arts administrator; b. Sioux City, Iowa, Oct. 10, 1945; d. Robert S. and Libbie (Izen) Gersten; m. Peter Luckman, Nov. 22, 1968 (div. 1979); children: Melissa, Gregory; m. Paul Shapiro, Dec. 13, 1981. BS, U. Wis., 1967; cert. Inst. Not-For-Profit Mgmt., Columbia U., 1982. Dir. 92d St YM/YHA Dance Ctr., N.Y.C., 1978-86; dir. devel. & new ventures Twyla Tharp Dance Found., N.Y.C., 1986-87, exec. dir., 1988; dir. Vol. Lawyers for Arts, N.Y.C., 1988-92; dir. devel. Alvin Ailey Dance Found., N.Y.C., 1992—95, exec. dir., 1995—. Dance tchr. 92nd St. Y, N.Y.C., 1963-78, Nassau C.C., Garden City, N.Y., 1963-78, Long Beach (N.Y.) Pub. Schs., 1963-78; dir. Brant Lake (N.Y.) Dance and Sports Ctr., 1980-86; bd. dirs. Dance USA. Chairperson Laban/Bartenieff Inst. Movement Studies, N.Y.C., 1984-87. Democrat. Jewish. Office: Alvin Ailey Dance Found Inc 211 W 61st St 3d Fl New York NY 10023-7832

LUCKNER, BRIAN WILLIAM, choir director, organist, composer; b. Massillon, OH, Apr. 22, 1959; s. William Joseph and Dorothy Margaret Luckner; m. Danielle Leanne Lang, Aug. 25, 2001; children: George William, Henry John. MusB, Oberlin Coll., 1981; MusM, U. Cin., 1983, MusD, 1992. Asst. organist Ch. of St. Joseph, Massillon, Ohio, 1971—77, St. John the Baptist Cath. Ch., Canton, Ohio, 1974—75; organist, choirmaster Christ Episcopal Ch., Oberlin, 1978—81, Holy Trinity Episcopal Ch., Cin., 1981—82; dir. music, organist Ch. Guardian Angels, Cin., 1983—87, Cathedral St. Joseph the Workman, La Crosse, Wis., 1988—; asst. liturgical music Basilica Nat. Shrine Immaculate Conception, Washington, 1987—88. Adj. faculty in organ, ch. music Viterbo U., La Crosse, Wis., 1995—97; dir. Diocese La Crosse Choir & Chorale, La Crosse, Wis., 1995—; instr. sacred music Holy Cross Sem. House of Formation, La Crosse, Wis., 1996—; chmn. of conf. Roman Cath. Cathedral Musicians, 1997—2002. Composer: choral music Welcome All Wonders, 1995, If I Have Washed your Feet, 1996, O Redeemen, 1997, Hosanna to the Son of David, 1998, The Spirit of the Lord Is upon Me, 2000, Easter Gospel Acclamation, 2000, Five Psalms for the Communion Procession, 2002, May We Abide in Union, 2003, Intercessions for the Elect and the Candidates, 2004, Dominus Dixit Ad Me, 2005. Mem.: Nat. Assn. Pastoral Musicians, Soc. Cath. Liturgy, Am. Choral Dirs. Assn., Am. Guild Organists. Avocations: carpentry, bicycling.

LUCKNER, HERMAN RICHARD, III, interior designer; b. Newark, Ohio, Mar. 14, 1933; s. Herman Richard and Helen (Friednour) L. BS, U. Cin., 1957. Cert. interior designer and appraiser. Interior designer Greiwe Inc., Cin., 1957-64; owner, internat. designer Designers Loft Interiors, Cin., 1964—; owner Designer Accents, Cin., 1991—. Mem. bd. adv. Ohio Valley Organ Procurement Ctr., Cin., 1987—, U. Cin. Fine Arts Collection and Hist. Southwest Ohio, 1987-97; bd. dirs. Cin. Club Travelers, 1997-2000. Mem.: Appraisers Assn. Am., Am. Soc. Interior Designers, Met. Club. Republican. Avocations: needlepoint, collecting 18th century chinese porcelain. Home and Office: 555 Compton Rd Cincinnati OH 45231-5005 Office Phone: 513-521-5434.

LUCKTENBERG, JERRIE CADEK, music educator; b. July 19, 1930; d. Ottokar Theodore and Sara (Hitchcock) Č; m. George Lucktenburg, 1953 (div. 1984); children: Judith, Kathryn, Ted. MusB, Curtis Inst., 1952; MusM, U. Ill., 1953; D of Mus. Arts, U. S.C., 1983. Concertizing as soloist and in chamber groups, Europe, Korea, Australia, U.S., 1954—96; assoc. prof. music Converse Coll., Spartanburg, SC, 1960—84; artist tchr., chmn. string dept. S.C. Gov.'s Sch. of Arts, Greenville, 1983—97; prof. music, chmn. string dept. U. So. Miss., Hattiesburg, 1984—96; concertmaster Pensacola (Fla.) Symphony, Meridian (Miss.) Symphony, 1986—96, Greater Spartanburg (S.C.) Philharm., 1996—2003. Author: The Joy of Shifting and Double Stops, a Violinist's Guide to Ease and Artistry, 1991; contbr. articles to profl. jours.; leader numerous workshops and clinics. Fulbright grantee State Acad. Music, Vienna, 1956-57; Ford Found. grantee, 1966-67; recipient Heart of Gold award The Arlington Assisted Living Facility, Hattiesburg, Miss., 1994, Tchr. Recognition award nat. winner Music Tchrs. Nat. Assn., 1974, Excellence in tchg. award, U. Southern Miss., 1990, Alumni Citation Outstanding Achievement as a performer and educator, U.S.C., 1991; citation for Exceptional Leadership and Merit award, 1992. Mem.: Suzuki Assn. of Ams., Music Educators Nat. Conf., Music Tchrs. Nat. Assn. (chmn. S.C. chpt. 1979—82, strings chmn. Miss. chpg. 1987—90), Am. String Tchrs. Assn. (life; founding pres. Miss. chpt. 1985, jour. reviewer 1987—97), Pi Kappa Lambda. Home: 311 Saranac Dr Spartanburg SC 29307-1141

LUCY, DENNIS DURWOOD, JR., neurologist, educator; b. Little Rock, July 3, 1934; s. Dennis Durwood and Ann Louise (Besiegel) L.; m. Patricia Wilch, Nov. 26, 1958; children: Stephen H., Vincent A., Denise D., David D. BS, MD, U. Ark., 1959. Diplomate: Am. Bd. Psychiatry and Neurology. Intern U. Ark. Med. Scis., 1959-60, resident in internal medicine, 1960-62, resident in psychiatry, 1962-63; resident in neurology U. Iowa Hosp., 1963-64, 65-66; from instr., acting head dept. neurology to prof. U. Ark., 1964—74, prof., 1974—; chmn. Coun. Departmental Chmn., 1980—81; chief of staff Univ. Hosp., 1973—76; chmn. acad. senate U. Ark. for Med. Scis., 2002—03. Bd. dirs. Ark. chpt. Multiple Sclerosis Soc., 1965-78; mem. Ark. Council Devel. Disabilities, 1971-74; bd. dirs. Ark. chpt. Epilepsy Soc., 1972-76; bd. dirs. Holy Souls Cath. Sch., 1974-77, pres. bd., 1976-77. Recipient Golden Apple award U. Ark., 1968-69 Mem. Am. Acad. Neurology, Alpha Omega Alpha. Roman Catholic. Home: 17 Robinwood Dr Little Rock AR 72227-2241 Office: 4301 W Markham St Little Rock AR 72205-7101 Office Phone: 501-686-5135.

LUCY, JANET ROSE, music educator; b. Hempstead, N.Y., June 10, 1960; d. James Joseph and Rita Rose Lucy. MusB in Viola Performance, Manhattan Sch. Music, 1983; student in Music, So. Meth. U., 1983—84, Stonybrook U., 1984—85; MA in Secondary Edn., Hofstra U., 1998. Cert. tchr. N.Y., 1999, N.Y.C., 2000. Tchr. music L.I. (N.Y.) Pub. Schs., 1987—94; freelance musician N.Y., 1993—; tchr. music N.Y.C. (N.Y.) Pub. Schs., 1995—2000, Bklyn. (N.Y.) Friends Sch., 2001—04, The Rudolf Steiner Sch., N.Y., 2004—. Tchr. music Manhattan Sch. Music, N.Y., 2001—02, Met. Youth Acad., Manhassett, NY, 2004—; coord. opera project Meet the Composer, N.Y., 1995—96; coord. project arts VH1 Save the Music, N.Y.C., 1998—2000; head Dept. Music Bklyn. (N.Y.) Friends Sch., 2001—04. Musician: (albums) Henry Cowel, 1994, David Soldier-War Prayer, 1994, Handel-Ezio, 1995, Alan Hoyhaness, 1995, William Grant Still-The American, 1995, An American Original, 1996, (performed with) Bar Harbor Chamber Music Festival, 1993, PiccoloSpoleto Festival, 1994, Alice Tully Hall Concert, 1995, Meml. Concert Raphael Bronstein, 1996, Brahms on Broadway, 1997, Golden Ctr, 1997. Recipient Meadows Artistic Achievement award, So. Meth. U., 1984; scholar, Manhattan Sch. Music, 1978—82. Mem.: Music Educators Nat. Conf. (educator 1991—94), Chamber Music Am. (violinist), Am. Fedn. Musicians (violinist). Democrat. Roman Catholic. Avocations: reading, movies, walking, travel. Home: 101 Cooper St 5J New York NY 10034 Office: The Rudolf Steiner Sch 15 East 79th St New York NY 10023 Office Phone: 212-535-2130.

LUCY, JOHN R., academic administrator, psychologist; b. Springfield, Va., Sept. 23, 1961; s. Robert M. and Mary White Lucy; m. Kathy Hull, June 25, 1988; children: Kyle, Landon. BBA, So. Meth. U., 1983; MA in Theology, Fuller Theol. Sem., 1990, PhD in Clin. Psychology, 1994. Lic. Psychologist Ga., 1995. Assoc. dean of students Agnes Scott Coll., Decatur, Ga., 2004—, dir. of personal counseling, 2000—04; dir. of counseling Oxford Coll. of Emory U., Oxford, Ga., 1995—2000; staff psychologist Jacksonville Naval Hosp., Fla., 1993—95; clin. psychology intern Nat. Naval Med. Ctr., Bethesda, Md., 1992—93. Adj. faculty Argosy U., Atlanta, 1997—2004. Lt. USN, 1992—95. Mem.: Nat. Assn. of Student Pers. Office: Agnes Scott Coll 141 E College Ave Decatur GA 30030 Office Phone: 404-471-6064.

LUCY, WILLIAM (BILL LUCY), labor union administrator; BS engring., Univ. Calif. Berkeley. Engr. Contra Costa Co.; pres. AFSCME Local 1675; exec asst. pres. AFSCME; founder, pres. Coalition Black Trade Unionists. Mem.: TransAfrica (mem. bd. dir.), NAACP (mem. bd. dir.). Office: Caolition Black Trade Unionists 628 Desoto Ave Clarksdale MS 38614 Office Phone: 662-627-6340.*

LUDDEN, JOHN FRANKLIN, retired economist; b. Michigan City, Ind., May 6, 1930; BS in Econs., U. Wis., 1952, MS in Econs., 1955; postgrad., U. Mich., 1955-59. Wage and hour investigator U.S. Dept. Labor, 1960, mgmt. intern, 1960-61, labor economist, 1963; economist, instr. U.S. Bur. of Labor Statis., 1961-63; economist Office of Internat. Ops. IRS, 1963-68, fin. economist Audit div., 1968-86, fin. economist Office of the Asst. Commr.

Internat., 1986-95; ret., 1995. With U.S. Army, 1952—54. Recipient spl. svc. award U.S. Dept. Treasury, 1967, 68, 87, spl. achievement award, 1984, Spl. Act award, 1990, Albert Gallatin award, 1995.

LUDDINGTON, BETTY WALLES, library director; b. Tampa, Fla., May 11, 1936; d. Edward Alvin and Ruby Mae (Hiott) L.; m. Robert Morris Schmidt, Sept. 20, 1957 (div. Dec. 1981); children: Irene Schmidt-Losat, Daniel Carl Schmidt. AA, U. South Fla., 1979, BA in Am. Studies and History, 1980, MA in Libr., Media and Info. Studies, 1982, EdS in Gifted Edn., 1986. Cert. tchr. media and gifted edn., Fla. Media intern Witter Elem. Sch., spring 1982; media specialist Twin Lakes Elem. Sch., 1982-84, Just Elem. Sch., 1984-87, Blake Jr. H.S., 1987-88, Dowdell Jr. H.S. (now Dowdell Mid. Sch.), 1988—. Educator Saturday enrichment program for gifted children U. South Fla., springs 1980, 84, 85; participant pilot summer program in reading and visual arts Just Elem. Sch., 1987; educator gifted edn. program in visual and performing arts Kingswood Elem. Sch., summers 1985, 86, gifted edn. program in video camera Apollo Beach Elem. Sch., summer 1989, Gifted Enrichment Prog. Imagi-lympics 2012, Maniscalco Elem. Sch., 1998, others. Author: (book of poetry) Aaron Tippin: A Hillbilly Knight, 1993; contbr. articles and poems to various books and periodical publs., 1986—. Parent vol. media ctr. Witter Elem. Sch., 1976-78; tchr. sponsor Storytelling Club, Dowdell Jr. H.S., 1994-95; news media liaison, tchr. vol. Dowdell Jr. H.S., 1993-96. Recipient Student Affairs Golden Signet award U. South Fla., 1980, Parent award for continuing support of Fla. chpt. # 39 Am. Indsl. Arts Student Assn., 1987-88, Editor's Choice awards for outstanding achievement in poetry Nat. Libr. of Poetry, 1996; nominee Tchr. of Month, Sta. WTSP-TV, 1994; recognized for contbn. of motivational activity for Sunshine State Young Reader's Award program Fla. Assn. for Media in Edn., Inc., 1985; named to Internat. Poetry Hall of Fame, 1996. Mem. Internat. Soc. Poets (Disting. mem. 1995), Hillsborough Classrm. Tchrs. Assn. (grantee 1988, 90), Hillsborough Assn. Sch. Libr. Media Specialists, Clan Wallace Soc. (life), Phi Kappa Phi, Kappa Delta Pi, Phi Alpha Theta (pres., v.p., rep. to honors coun. 1980, 81, Outstanding Student award), Omicron Delta Kappa (treas., chairperson, del., mem. selection com. 1981, Leslie Lynn Walbolt book award), Pi Gamma Mu. Episcopalian. Avocations: poetry, books, cats, country music. Home: 1032 E Robson St Tampa FL 33604-4344

LUDGUS, NANCY LUCKE, lawyer; b. Palo Alto, Calif., Oct. 28, 1953; d. Winston Slover and Betty Jean Lucke; m. Lawrence John Ludgus, Apr. 8, 1983. BA in Polit. Sci. with honors, U. Calif., Berkeley, 1975; JD, U. Calif., Davis, 1978. Bar: Calif. 1978, U.S. Dist. Ct. (no. dist.) Calif. 1978. Staff atty. Crown Zellerbach Corp., San Francisco, 1978-80, Clorox Co., Oakland, Calif., 1980-82, Nat. Semiconductor Corp., Santa Clara, Calif., 1982-85, corp. counsel, 1985-92, sr. corp. counsel, asst. sec., 1992-2000, assoc. gen. counsel, asst. sec., 2000—. Contbr. articles to profl. jours. Mem. ABA, Am. Corp. Counsel Assn., Calif. State Bar Assn., Santa Clara County Bar Assn., Phi Beta Kappa. Democrat. Avocations: travel, jogging, opera. Office: Nat Semiconductor Corp 2900 Semiconductor Dr # G3135 Santa Clara CA 95051 E-mail: nancy.lucke.ludgus@nsc.com.

LUDINGTON, TOWNSEND, English and American studies educator; b. Bryn Mawr, Pa., Jan. 31, 1936; s. Charles Townsend and Constance (Cameron) L.; m. Jane Ross, Feb. 22, 1958; children: David, Charles, James, Sarah. BA, Yale U., 1957; MA, Duke U., 1964; PhD, Duke U, 1967. Tchr. English Ransom Sch., Miami, Fla., 1960-62; from asst. prof. to prof. English U. N.C., Chapel Hill, 1967-78, Cary C. Boshamer prof. English and Am. Studies, 1982—, chair Am. studies curriculum, 1986—2001. Part-time instr. Duke U., 1963-66; resident scholar U.S. Internat. Communication Agy., 1980-81; vis. prof. U.S. Mil. Acad., West Point, N.Y., 1988-89 Author: John Dos Passos, 1980 (Mayflower award 1981), Marsden Hartley, 1992, Seeking the Spiritual: The Paintings of Marsden Hartley, 1998; Editor: The Fourteenth Chronicle, 1973, U.S.A., John Dos Passos, 1996, Three Soldiers, John Dos Passos, 1997, The Devil and Daniel Webster and Other Stories and Poems by Stephen Vincent Benet, 1999, A Modern Mosaic: Art and Modernism in the United States, 2000, Travel Books & Other Writings, John Dos Passos, 2003, Novels, 1920-1925, John Dos Passos, 2003. Mem. adv. com. Florence Griswold Mus.; elector Wadsworth Atheneum. Capt. USMC, 1957—60. Recipient Outstanding Svc. medal U.S. Army, 1988-89; Fulbright fellow, 1971-72, Nat. Humanities Ctr. fellow, 1985-86, Wurlitzer Found. fellow, 1996, Beinecke Libr. Yale U. fellow, 1998. Mem.: PEN, Am. Studies Assn. Democrat. Avocations: golf, reading. Office: U NC Curriculum in Am Studies Greenlaw Hall CB # 3520 Chapel Hill NC 27599-0001

LUDMERER, KENNETH MARC, medical educator; b. Long Beach, Calif., Jan. 13, 1947; s. Sol and Norma (Helfer) L.; m. Loren Rae Starobin, Aug. 9, 1987. AB, Harvard U., 1968; MA, Johns Hopkins U., 1971, MD, 1973. Med. resident, fellow Washington U., St. Louis, 1973-78; chief resident internal medicine Barnes Hosp., St. Louis, 1978-79; asst. prof. medicine, asst. prof. history Faculty Arts and Scis. Washington U., St. Louis, 1979-86, assoc. prof. medicine, assoc. prof. history, 1986-92, prof. medicine, prof. history, 1992—. Clin. scholars adv. com. mem. Robert Wood Johnson Found., Princeton, N.J., 1988-92; new pathway program evaluation com. mem. Assn. Am. Med. Colls., 1986-88; mem. nat. adv. com. Robert Wood Johnson Found. Clin. Scholars Program, Princeton, N.J., 1988-92; mem. adv. bd. Culpeper Found. Program in Med. Humanities, Stanford, Conn., 1992-93; mem. task force on med. edn. Acadia Inst.-Med. Coll. Pa., Phila., 1992-96; mem. vis. com. Harvard Med. Sch., Boston, 2000-2002, North Shore-L.I. Jewish Health Sys., Manhasset, N.Y., 2003—; med. edn. cons. numerous schs., hosps., profl. orgns., state govts., 2000—. Author: Genetics and American Society: A Historical Appraisal, 1972, Learning to Heal: The Development of American Medical Education, 1985, Time to Heal: American Medical Education from the Turn of the Century to the Era of Managed Care, 1999 (William Welch medal 2004); mem. editl. bd. Am. Jour. Medicine, 1981-96, Jour. History Medicine, 1981-83, 88-90, The Pharos, 1986—, History Edn. Quar., 1993-96, Annals Internal Medicine, 1993—. Mem. med. adv. com. St. Louis Sci. Ctr., 1985-87; trustee Mo. Hist. Soc., St. Louis, 1987-93, St. Louis History Mus., 1987-93, Jewish Fedn. St. Louis, 2002—, Sommers Children's Welfare Bur., St. Louis, 2000—; chair comty. rsch. peer rev. com. St. Louis Heart Assn., 1988-89. Faculty scholar gen. internal medicine Henry J. Kaiser Family Found., 1981-86; recipient Rsch. award Joseph Macy Jr. Found., 1989-96. Master ACP (com. on publ. policy 1988-93); fellow AAAS (tchg. and rsch. scholar 1980-83, pub. policy com. 1988-93), Am. Acad. Arts and Scis. (Midwest coun.); mem. Assn. Am. Physicians, Am. Clin. and Climatol. Assn., Am. Assn. History Medicine (coun. 1984-87), Am. Fedn. for Clin. Rsch., History Sci. Soc., Am. Osler Soc. (bd. govs. 1988—, v.p. 1991—), Phi Beta Kappa, Alpha Omega Alpha, Sigma Xi. Avocations: music, running, travel. Home: 42 Rio Vista Dr Saint Louis MO 63124-1745 Office: Washington U Sch Medicine Dept Medicine Box 8066 660 S Euclid Ave Saint Louis MO 63110 Business E-Mail: kludmere@im.wustl.edu.

LUDOLF, MARILYN MARIE KEATON, lay worker; b. Morganton, NC, July 19, 1932; d. Charles Jefferson and Dora Esther (Whitener) Keaton; m. Edwin Forrest Ludolf, Dec. 22, 1957; children: David Forrest, Jonathan Charles. BA, Lenoir Rhyne, 1954. Youth worker Cen. Bapt. Ch., Greenville, S.C., 1964-71, Park Bapt. Ch., Rock Hill, S.C., 1958-64; with coll. students Becks Bapt. Ch., Winston Salem, N.C., 1971-89; lay worker singles Calvary Bapt. Ch., Winston Salem, 1989—. Youth seminar leader youth activities Park Bapt., Rock Hill, S.C.; youth-Sunday sch. Tng. Union-All areas of Ch. Work, Greenville, S.C. and Winston Salem, N.C.; pub. spkr., sem. leader, Women's Conf. Keynoter. Author: Freed by Faith, 1995; contbr. articles to profl. jours. Chmn. Christian Women's Club Luncheon, Winston Salem, 2000-2002. Mem. Old Town Woman's Club (pres. 1975-77, Woman of Yr. 1977). Republican. Home: 3745 Whitehaven Rd Winston Salem NC 27106-2530 *Enjoy life. This is Not a Dress Rehearsal. It is a temporary assignment. We each choose our behavior daily. Choose life! The greatest decision I ever made was to let go and let God lead in my life!.*

LUDROF, JEFFREY A., insurance company executive; b. Allentown, Pa. BSBA, Bloomsburg U. From claims adjuster to dist. sales mgr. Erie Ins. Group, Allentown, 1981—89, asst. v.p., mgr. Erie, 1989—93, from regional v.p. to exec. v.p. ins. ops., 1993—2002, pres., CEO, 2002—. Bd. dirs. Ins. Inst. for Hwy. Safety. Bd. dirs. Erie Regional Chamber and Growth Partnership. Mem.: Nat. Assn. Ind. Insurers (bd. dirs., bd. govs.), Soc. Cert. Ins. Counselors, Soc. Chartered Property Casualty Underwriters. Office: Erie Ins Group 100 Erie Insurance Pl Erie PA 16530

LUDU, ANDREI, physicist, educator; b. Filipesti Targ, Prahova, Romania, Nov. 13, 1955; s. Andrei Stelian Ludu and Viorica Georgescu; m. Maria Missy Voinoiu, Aug. 22, 1980; 1 child, Delia Maria. BS, Bucharest U., 1979, MS, 1980, PhD, 1988. From lectr. theoretical physics to assoc. prof. Bucharest U., Romania, 1990—93, assoc. prof. Dept. of Theoretical Physics and Math, 1993—2001; asst. prof. physics Northwestern State U., Natchitoches, La., 2001—04, assoc. prof. physics, 2004—. Guest prof. Inst. Theoretical Physics Main U., Frankfurt, Germany, 1991—96, Justus Liebig U., Giessen, Germany; founder, co-dir. IDEAS Program Northwestern State U., Natchitoches, La., 2003—; sr. rschr. Dept. Physics and Astronomy La. State U., Baton Rouge, 1996—2001. Contbr. articles to profl. jours. (Mildred Hart Bailey Rsch. Award, 2003). Cpl. Romanian Army, 1975—76. Mem.: AAAS, Soc. Indsl. Application Focus Group, Soc. Indsl. & Applied Math., Soc. for Indsl. and Applied Math., N.Y. Acad. Sci., Am. Phys. Soc. Achievements include first to Nonlinear contour and surface dynamics, solitons on liquid drops, alpha and heavy fragments emission as new large amplitude collective motion of nuclear surface, q-groups applied to unified nuclear. Office: Northwestern State University Dept Chemistry and Physics Natchitoches LA 71497 Office Phone: 318-357-5225. Business E-Mail: ludua@nsula.edu.

LUDWIG, ALLAN IRA, photographer, educator, artist, writer; b. N.Y.C., June 9, 1933; s. Daniel and Honey (Fox) L.; m. Janine (Lowell), Aug. 1955 (div. 1991); children: Katherine Arabella, Pamela Vanessa, Adam Lowell; m. Gwendolyn (Akin), 1992; children: Allan B. Ludwig Jr., Alison Ludwig. *Grandparents on both sides of the family came from central Europe and settled in New York City. Both parents were born in New York. Daughter, Katherine, is a professor of medieval history at Catholic University in Washington, DC. Daughter, Pamela, is both an actress and screenwriter and lives in Los Angeles. Son, Adam, is a cabinetmaker and lives in New York City. Two youngest children, Allan Jr. and Alison, are still in school in New York City.* BFA, Yale U., New Haven, 1956, MA, 1962, PhD in Art History, 1964. Instr. R.I. Sch. of Design, 1956-58; asst. instr. Yale U., New Haven, 1958-64; asst. prof. Dickinson Coll., 1964-65, assoc. prof., 1965-68, Syracuse U., Syracuse, NY, 1968-69; pres. Automated Comm., Inc., 1969-75; dir. Ludwig Portfolios, N.Y.C., 1975-90; co-dir. Akin/Ludwig, N.Y.C., 1990—. Mem. exec. bd. Alternative Mus. N.Y.C., 1978-88, chmn. bd. dirs., 1982-83; cons. presses U. Mass., U. Ga., Boston Mus. Fine Arts, Smithsonian Instn. Author: Graven Images: New England Stonecarving and its Symbols, 1966, 3d edit., 1999; author exhbn. catalogues; one-person shows include: Silvermine (Conn.) Guild of Art, 1955, Davison Art Ctr., Wesleyan U., Middletown, Conn., 1961, Portland Mus. of Art, Portland, 1962, Miami Mus. and Arts Ctr., Miami, Fla., 1976, Jorgenson Art Gallery, U. Conn., Storrs, 1976, Alternative Mus., N.Y.C., 1977, Watson Art Gallery, Norton, Mass., 1978, Alonzo Gallery, N.Y.C., 1978, 79, Cayman Gallery, N.Y.C., 1980, IL.,Diaframma, Milan, Italy, 1981, Simon Gallery, Montclair, N.J., 1983, art gallery Farleigh Dickinson U., Madison, N.J., 1984, Ctr. for Creative Photography, Tucson, 1986, The Twining Gallery, N.Y.C., 1986, Cepa Gallery, Buffalo, 1986, The Shandai Gallery, Tokyo, Inst. of Tech., Tokyo, 1987, White Columns, N.Y.C., 1988, O'Kane Gallery, Houston, 1988, Farideh Cadot Gallery, N.Y.C., 1988, XYZ Gallery, Ghent, Belgium, 1989, Northlight Gallery, 1990, Ariz. State U., Tempe, 1990, Galerie Farideh Cadot, Paris, 1990, Pamela Auchincloss Gallery, N.Y.C., 1991, 92, 94, Gallery 954, Chgo., 1994, Gallery at 777, L.A., 1994, Houston Ctr. for Photography, 1995, Hudson River Mus. Westchester, Yonkers, N.Y., 1995, The Chrysler Mus., Norfolk, Va., 1995, 2002, CEPA Gallery, Buffalo, 1995, The Kemper Mus. Contemporary Art, Kansas City, Mo., 1997, Galerie Farideh Cadot, Paris, 1999, Ricco Maresca Gallery, N.Y.C., 1999; exhibited in group shows at Bannister Art Gallery, Providence, 1979, Westmoreland County (Pa.) Mus. Art, 1979, Ind. Am. Photography exhbn. Warsaw, Cracow, Katowice, Gdynia, Poland, 1980, Alonzo Gallery, N.Y.C., 1980, 81, 82, Alternative Mus., N.Y.C., 1981, Floating Found. for Photography, N.Y.C., 1981, World Photographic Archive, Parma, Italy, 1984, Diverse Works, Houston, 1985, The State Mus., Trenton, N.J., 1985, San Francisco Mus. Modern Art, 1986, Mus. Photog. Arts, San Diego, 1987, Public Image Gallery, N.Y.C. 1985, Houston Ctr. for Photog., 1988, Catherine Edelman Gall., Chgo., 1989, Univ. Gall., Clark U., Worcester, Mass., 1992, Long Beach (Calif.) Mus. Art, 1992, Preservation House, B.C., Can., 1992, Akin Gall., Boston, 1992, Internatl. Mus. Photography George Eastman House, Rochester, N.Y., 1993, The New Mus., N.Y.C., 1993, Akin Gall., Boston, 1993, Ctr. for Photography at Woodstock, 1993, Montage, Rochester, NY, 1993, Parko Gall., Tokyo, 1993, Addison Gall. Am. Art, Andover, Mass., 1994, Mus. Photographic Arts, San Diego, 1995, Mus, Contemporary Art, 1995, The Mercury Gall., Boston, 1995, Calif. Ctr. for the Arts Mus., 1996, Escondido, Calif., Univ. Art Mus., San Diego State U., 1997, Fullerton Mus. Ctr., 1997, The Mus. Modern Art, Oxford, England, 1997, The Julie Dermansky Gall., N.Y.C., 1995, 96,97, Moderna Museet, Stockholm, Sweden, 1998, Finish Mus. Photography, Helsinki, Finland, 1999, Ricco/Maresca Gall., NYC, 1999-2002, Marion Ctr. for Arts, Santa Fe, 2001, SF Camera-works, San Francisco, 2003. Regional chmn. Campaign for Yale Art Sch. Divsn., Met. N.Y.C. area, 1975-76; coun. mem., v.p. N.Y.C. Spl. Edn. of Dept. Edn., 2004-05. Bollingen Found. fellow, 1961-63, Jr. Sterling fellow Yale U., 1961-63, Am. Philos. Soc. fellow, 1964-66, Am. Coun. Learned Socs. fellow, 1967-68, NEH fellow, 1967; recipient USIS Merit award, 1966, Merit award Assn. State and Local History, 1967-68, Harriette Merrifield Forbes Award Assn., Gravestone Studies, U. Conn., 1981; Polaroid Found. grantee, 1987-88, Arts grantee N.J. State Coun., 1990, Agfa Corp. grantee, 1990, NEA grantee 1990-91. Democrat. E-mail: allani.ludwig@yahoo.com.

LUDWIG, ANTHONY L., music educator, minister; b. Knox, Ind., Dec. 5, 1955; s. Walter Duane and Amelia Sue Ludwig; m. Judith Sherril Oliver, Aug. 21, 1976; 1 child, Andrew David. BA in Music, Ctrl. Bible Coll., Springfield, Mo., 1977; MM in Choral Music, Ariz. State U., 1996. Lic. min. Bethany Cmty. Ch.; cert. secondary edn. tchr. Ariz. Dept. Edn. Worship pastor Assembly of God Denom., Springfield, Mo., 1977—88; music educator choral and piano Tempe (Ariz.) Union H.S. Dist., 1989—; worship pastor Bethany Cmty. Ch., Tempe, 1991—. Owner Note by Note Pub. Co., Chandler, Ariz., 1993—. Composer: (choral piece) Psalm 100. Mem.: Choral Dirs. Ariz. (treas. 1997—99), Music Educator's Nat. Conf. Avocations: scuba diving, hiking, board games, movies, woodworking. Home: 4876 W Tyson St Chandler AZ 85226 Office: Desert Vista HS 16400 S 32nd St Phoenix AZ 85048 Office Phone: 480-706-7600 1100.

LUDWIG, CHRISTA, retired mezzo soprano; b. Berlin; d. Anton and Eugenie (Besalla) L.; m. Walter Berry, Sept. 29, 1957 (div. 1970); 1 son, Wolfgang; m. Paul-Emile Deiber, Mar. 3, 1972. Ed. German schs. Prof. H.C. Senat, Berlin, 1995. Hon. mem. Vienna Philharm., 1995. Appeared at Staedtische Buehnenm, Frankfurt, W. Ger., 1946-52, Landestheatre, Darmstadt, W. Ger., 1952-54, Hannover, W. Ger., 1954-55, Vienna (Austria) State Opera, 1955—, Medaille, Ville de Paris, 1993, Shibuya-Price, Japan, 1993, others, U.S. appearances include Avery Fisher Hall, N.Y.C., 1978, Lyric Opera, Chgo., 1959-60, 70-71, 73-74, Philharmonic Hall, N.Y.C., 1968, 69, 72, 74, Goldene Ehrennadel Landtstadt, Vienna, 1997, others; guest artist London, Buenos Aires, Munich, Berlin, Tokyo, Salzburg Festival, Athens Festival, Saratoga Festival, Hunter Coll., Met. Mus., Scala Milano, Expo 67, Montreal, and others; rec. artist; author: (biography) In My Own Voice. Decorated Commdr. des Arts et des Lettres, France, 1988, Goldenes Ehren Zeichen Stadt, Salzburg, 1988, Goldene Ehrennadel Stadt und Land, Wien, Austria, 1988, Ordre Pour le Merit, France, 1997, France Officier Légion d'Honneur, 2004, Grosses Bundesverdienst Krewz, 2004; chevalier Legion d'Honneur, France, 1989; recipient Mozart medal, Mahler medal, Hugo Wolf medal, Fidelio medal Opera Wien, 1991, Shibuya prize Japan, 1993, Medaille ville Paris, 1993, Medaille Ville de Dijon, 1993, Echo Deutscher Preis, 1994, Karajan preis, Berliner Bär, 1994, Grosses Ehrenzeichen Osterreich, 1994, Ehrenmitglied der Wiener Philharm., Silver Rose, Vienna Philharm., Golden Ring, Vienna Staatsoper, Musician of Yr. award Musical Am., 1994, Cordandeur Pour le Merit France, 1997, Grosses Bundesverdienstivirez, Germany, 2004; named Kammersaengerin, Govt. of Austria, 1962. Mem. NARAS, Legion D'Honneur (officer 2003-).

LUDWIG, EDMUND VINCENT, federal judge; b. Phila., May 20, 1928; s. Henry and Ruth (Viner) L.; children: Edmund Jr., John, Sarah, David. AB, Harvard U., 1949, LLB, 1952. Assoc. Duane, Morris & Heckscher, Phila., 1956-59; ptnr. Barnes, Biester & Ludwig, Doylestown, Pa., 1959-68; judge Common Pleas Ct., Bucks County, Pa., 1968-85, U.S. Dist. Ct. (ea. dist.), Phila., 1985—. Faculty Pa. Coll. of the Judiciary, 1974-85; presenter Villanova (Pa.) U. Law Sch., 1975-80, lectr., 1984-97; vis. lectr. Temple Law Sch., 1977-80; clin. assoc. prof. Hahnemann U., Phila., 1977-85; mem. Pa. Juvenile Ct. Judge's Commn., 1978-85; chmn. Pa. Chief Justice's Ednl. Com., 1984-85; pres. Pa. Conf. State Trial Judges, 1981-82; co-chmn. 3d cir. task force on counsel for ind. litigants in civil cases, 1998. Contbr. articles to profl. jours. Chmn. Children and Youth Adv. Com., Bucks County, 1978-83; mem. Pa. Adv. Com. on Mental Health and Mental Retardation, 1980-85; founder, bd. dirs. Today, Inc., Newtown, Pa., 1971-85, Probation Vols., Bucks County, 1971-81; bd. dirs. New Directions for Women, Del. Valley, 1988—; mem. Pa. Joint Coun. Criminal Justice, Inc., 1979-80; mem. Joint Family Law Council Pa., 1979-85; vice chmn. Human Services Council Bucks County, 1979-81; mem. Com. to Study Unified Jud. System Pa., 1980-82, Pa. Legislative Task Force on Mental Health Laws, 1986-87; chmn. Juvenile Justice Alliance, Phila., 1992—; co-chmn. Doylestown (Pa.) Revitalization Bd., 1993-96; mem. 3d cir. task force on equal treatment in the cts., 1995-97; chmn. Doylestown (Pa.) Hist. Soc., 1995—. Recipient Disting. Svc. award Bucks County Corrections Assn., 1978, Spl. Svc. award Big. Bros., 1989, Humanitarian award United Way Bucks County, 1980, Founder's award Vol. Svcs., 1982, Spl. award Bucks County Juvenile Ct., 1985, Humanitarian award Ctrl. Bucks County C. of C., 1994, Disting. Jurist award John Peter Zenger Soc., 2000; Wasserstein Pub. Interest fellow Harvard Law Sch., 1996-97. Mem. ABA, Pa. Bar Assn. (chmn. com. legal svcs. to disabled 1990-92), Phila. Bar Assn. (pro bono pub. award 1998, Pub. Interest Disting. Svc. award 1998), Fed. Bar Assn. (hon.), Harvard Club (N.Y.C. and Phila., v.p. 1979-80), Harvard Law Sch. Assn. (exec. com. 1993—), Fed. Judges Assn. (bd. dirs. 1998—, v.p., mem. chmn. 1999—), U.S. Jud. Conf. (com. on ct. adminstrn. and case mgmt.), Am. Law Inst., Pa. Task Force on Medical Malpractice. Office: US Dist E Dist PA US Cthse 601 Market St # 12614 Philadelphia PA 19106-1775 Business E-Mail: Chambers_of_Judge__Edmund_V._Ludwig@paed.uscourts.gov.

LUDWIG, EDWARD J., medical technology executive; Grad., Holy Cross Coll., Columbia U. Bus. Sch. In mgmt. Becton, Dickinson and Co., Franklin Lakes, NJ, 1979—87, corp. planning & devel. mgr., 1987—89, pres. diagnostics divsn. Balt., 1989—94, sr. v.p. fin., CFO Franklin Lakes, NJ, 1995—99, exec. v.p., 1998—99, pres., 1999—, CEO, 2000—, chmn. bd., 2002—. Office: BD 1 Becton Dr Franklin Lakes NJ 07417-1815

LUDWIG, EUGENE ALLAN, financial consultant, former US Comptroller of the Currency, lawyer; b. Bklyn., Apr. 11, 1946; s. Jacob and Louise (Rabiner) L.; m. Carol Lynn Friedman, Mar. 11, 1978; children: Abigail Sarah, Elizabeth Madelaine Cathleen, David Maxwell. BA magna cum laude, Haverford Coll., 1968; BA, MA, Oxford U., Eng., 1970; LLB, Yale U., 1973. Bar: D.C. 1973. Assoc. Covington & Burling, Washington, 1973-81, ptnr., 1981-93; comptr. of the currency Dept. of the Treasury, Washington, 1993-98; vice chmn. Bankers Trust, New York, 1998-99; mng. ptnr. Promontory Fin. Group, Washington, 2000—. Pres. Yale Legis. Svcs., 1972-73; guest lectr. Harvard U., Georgetown U., 1974-77, 79, Yale U., 1989. Editor Yale Law Jour., 1972-73; mem. editorial bd., Jour. Internat. Banking Law, 1989; contbr. articles to profl. jours. Office: Promontory Fin Group 1201 Pennsylvania Ave NW Washington DC 20004 Business E-Mail: eludwig@promontory.com.

LUDWIG, GEORGE HARRY, retired physicist, electrical engineer; b. Johnson County, Iowa, Nov. 13, 1927; s. George McKinley and Alice (Helm) Ludwig; m. Rosalie F. Vickers, July 21, 1950; children: Barbara Rose, Sharon Lee Taylor, George Vickers, Kathy Ann Ramsay. BA in Physics cum laude, U. Iowa, 1956, MS, 1959, PhD in Elec. Engring., 1960. Head fields and particles instrumentation sect. Goddard Space Flight Center, NASA, 1960-65, chief info. processing div., 1965-71, assoc. dir. for data ops., 1971-72; dir. systems integration Nat. Environ. Satellite Service, NOAA, 1972-75, dir. ops., 1975-80, tech. dir., 1980; sr. scientist Environ. Rsch. Labs., NOAA, Boulder, Colo., 1980-81, dir. Environ. Rsch. Labs., 1981-83; asst. to chief scientist NASA Hdqrs., 1983-84; ind. cons. data mgmt. and space sta. design, 1983-92; sr. rsch. assoc. Lab. for Atmospheric and Space Physics, U. Colo., 1985-91; ret., 1992. Vis. sr. scientist NASA hdqrs. Calif. Inst. Tech., 1989—91; prin. designer radiation detection instrumentation for numerous sci. spacecraft including Explorer I, 1956—65; co-discoverer Van Allen radiation belts; expert on NASA sci. and applications rsch. data processing; overseer devel. and operation U.S. Nat. Environ. Satellite Sys. with its GOES and Tiros-N Spacecraft, 1972—80; dir. atmospheric and oceanic rsch. programs NOAA, 1981—83. Served from pvt to capt. USAF, 1946—52, pilot USAF, 1948—52. Named Van Allen scholar, 1958, rsch. fellow, U.S. Steel Found., 1958—60; recipient Exceptional Svc. medal, NASA, 1969, Program Adminstrn. and Mgmt. award, NOAA, 1977, Exceptional Sci. Achievement medal, NASA, 1984. Mem.: Am. Geophys. Union (life), IEEE (sr., life), Torch Club, Eta Kappa Nu, Phi Eta Sigma, Sigma Xi, Phi Beta Kappa. Home: 215 Aspen Trl Winchester VA 22602-1404 Personal E-mail: ludwiggh@visuallink.com.

LUDWIG, LAURA LONSHEIN, poet; b. Bklyn., July 26, 1955; d. Howard Lonshein, Gloria Lonshein; m. Ray Ludwig. Student, Franconia Coll., 1975—77. Writer Self-Employed, New York, NY, 1991—. Resident poet Joe Franklin Memory Lane Radio Show, WOR-AM, New York City, 1999—; screenwriter Joe Franklin Prodns., Inc., New York City, 1999—. Author (poetry, satires): Robo-Sapiens, 2001; author: (screenplays) Sounds Like a Plot, 2001, Reflections for the Renaissance, 2004; co-author (with Richard Ornstein): Of the Desk; prodr.(actress): classical concerts, ballet, opera, stage, short screenplays and T.V. programs,: (TV series) Earth is not on Tape;, co-author. Recipient Guardian Angel award, Hope for Children Found., 1999; grantee, N.Y. State Coun. for the Arts. Home: 71 Joel M Austin Rd N Cairo NY 12413 Office Phone: 518-622-9747.

LUDWIG, L(OWELL) MARK, social studies educator; b. Estevan, Can., Jan. 2, 1933; s. Daniel Robert and Minette Louise (Baue) L.; m. Elizabeth Ann Maimone, Nov. 25, 1968 (div. Oct. 1979); 1 child, Lara Elizabeth; m. Marlyn Ginsburg Josselson, Jan. 6, 1991. AB in Govt., Valparaiso U., 1959; BS in Edn., Kent State U., 1962, MA in History, 1967, PhD in Edn., 1976. Cert. tchr., Ohio. Tchr. social studies Nordonia H.S., Northfield, Ohio, 1959-69; prof. social scis. Cuyahoga Cmty. Coll., Cleve., 1970-86; adj. prof. Cleve. State U., 1987-89; program mgr. U.S. Dept. of Navy, Cleve., 1989-91; quality improvement advisor U.S. Dept. Def., Cleve., 1991-95; emeritus prof. Cuyahoga Cmty. Coll., 1989—, adj. prof., 1996—. Author: Introduction to Social Science, A Personalized course, Vols. I & II, 1977-78; contbr. articles to sci. and profl. jours. Fulbright fellow U.S. Dept. Edn., 1963, 72, 74. Democrat. Lutheran. Avocations: reading, highpointing, golf, hiking, travel. Home: 3675 Traynham Rd Shaker Heights OH 44122

LUDWIG, OLIVER GEORGE, chemistry educator; b. Nov. 15, 1935; s. Oliver George and Gertrude Ludwig. BS, Villanova (Pa.) U., 1957; MS, Carnegie Mellon U., 1960, PhD, 1962. NSF fellow math. lab. Cambridge (Eng.) U., 1962-63; asst. prof., faculty assoc. computing ctr. U. Notre Dame, Ind., 1963-68; assoc. prof. chemistry Villanova U., 1968—. Contbr. numerous articles to profl. jours. Mem. Am. Chem. Soc., Sigma Xi. Office: Villanova U Chemistry Dept Villanova PA 19085 Office Phone: 610-519-4873. E-mail: oliver.ludwig@villanova.edu.

LUDWIG, PATRICIA MARIE, pastor; b. Cleve., Feb. 3, 1945; d. Daniel Andrew and Nancy Jane (McGinley) Parulis; m. John G. Ellis, Jr., Dec. 26, 1977 (dec. Nov. 1990), Mark D. Hewitt, January 1, 2005; 1 child, Mark

Ludwig Ellis. BA, Elmhurst Coll., 1967; MDiv, Bethany Theol. Sem., Oak Brook, Ill., 1972. Ordained to ministry United Ch. of Christ, 1972. Dir. Christian edn. St. Peter's United Ch. of Christ, Chgo., 1967-68; assoc. pastor St. Paul Comty., Homewood, Ill., 1972-75, Salem United Ch. of Christ, Tonawanda, N.Y., 1975-80; pastor Cambria United Ch. of Christ, Lockport, N.Y., 1980-93; interim pastor various chs., N.Y., 1993-95; placement officer for Western N.Y., United Ch. of Christ, 1991—94; chaplain Wyndham Lawn Home for Children, Lockport, 1991-99; sr. pastor, adminstr. St. John's United Ch. of Christ, Buffalo, 1995-97; pastor 1st Bapt. Ch., Newfane, N.Y., 1997—. Bd. dirs. Niagara County Migrant and Rural Ministry; gen. synod del. United Ch. of Christ, 1993, 95; tchr. new mins. program Am. Bapt. Chs. N.Y. State, 2001—. Radio host Celebrate, 1978-91. Treas. Celebrants, 1981-2004; mem. Lockport Sr. Citizen Ctr. Bd., 1984-90, Planned Parenthood, Niagara Falls, N.Y., 1982-87, Lockport CROP Walk for Hunger, 1980—, treas., 1992—; mem. Joint Christian Edn. Com. Western N.Y., 1976-82, 85-88, chair, 1986-88; mem. Dept. Ch. and Ministry, 1991-98, chair, 1995-98; mem. com. on edn. and discipleship Niagara Area Bapt. Ch., 1999-2003; bd. dirs Habitat for Humanity, Lockport, 2000—, v.p., 2000-01, pres, 2001-03, sec., 2003—; chmn. dept. cmty. life Western Area United Ch. of Christ, 2001—, mem., advisor women's fellowship bd., 2004—; mem. So. Poverty Loan Ctr., 1999—. Recipient Woman of Yr. award Internat. Women's Decade, 1984, Golden Hammer award Habitat for Humanity, 1999; named one of Outstanding Young Women of Am., 1973. Mem. Assn. United Ch. Educators (editor newsletter 1985-91), Western Assn. United Ch. of Christ (vice moderator 1985-86, moderator 1986-87, sec. 1988-90), Lockport Clergy Assn. (convenor 1991-2003), Newfane Clergy Assn., Niagara Area Bapt. Assn., Bapt. Peace Fellowship of N.Am., Western N.Y. Peace Ctr. (bd. dirs. 1996-99, sec. 1997-99), Mental Health Assn. (compeer vol. 1998-2002, compeer adv. Niagara County 1999-2003), Amnesty Internat. Democrat. Avocations: jazz, collecting trivets, butterflies, classic movies, sacred dance. Home: 3985 Day Rd Lockport NY 14094-9451 Office Phone: 716-778-9216. Personal E-mail: butterflypreacher@juno.com.

LUDWIG, RICHARD JOSEPH, small business owner; b. Lakewood, Ohio, July 28, 1937; s. Mathew Joseph and Catherine Elizabeth (Sepich) L.; m. Erleen Catherine Halambeck Ramus, July 22, 1977; children: Charleen, Tracey, Charles, Cassandra. Student, Ohio State U., 1955-59; BBA Fenn Coll., Cleve. State U, 1963. C.P.A., Ohio. Sr. acct. Ernst & Whinney, Cleve., 1964-66; supervising acct. Ernst & Young, 1966-70; asst. treas. Midland Ross Corp., Cleve., 1970-71, treas., 1971-76; v.p. fin., treas. U.S. Realty Investments, 1976-78, v.p.-fin., chief fin. officer, 1978-79; owner Boston Mills Ski Resort, Inc., Peninsula, Ohio, 1979—2002; ptnr. White Oak Winery, Healdsburg, 1988—; owner Brandywine Ski Resort, Inc., Sagamore Hills, Ohio, 1990—2002; ptnr. Honor Mansion, Healdsburg, Calif., 2003—. Mem. Firestone Country Club (Akron, Ohio), Black Diamond Ranch Club (Lecanto, Fla.), Mediterra Country Club (Naples, Fla.), Mayacama Golf Club (Santa Rosa, Calif.), The Club at Mediterra (Naples), Stonewater Golf Club (Highland Heights, Ohio). Home: 15911 Roseto Way Naples FL 34110

LUDWIG, STEPHEN, pediatrics and emergency medicine educator; b. Phila., Nov. 12, 1945; m. Zella Wolgin, 1968; children: Susannah, Elisa, Aubrey. BA with honors, Pa. State U., 1966, BS, 1967; MD, Temple U., 1971. Diplomate Am. Bd. Pediat., Nat. Bd. Med. Examiners; cert. pediat. emergency medicine, CPR advanced life support, ATLS instr., PALS. Intern and resident pediat. Children's Hosp. Nat. Med. Ctr., Washington, 1971-74, chief resident, 1973-74; assoc. pediat. U. Pa. Sch. Medicine, Phila. Gen. Hosp., 1974-76; asst. prof. pediat. U. Pa. Sch. Medicine, Children's Hosp. Phila., 1976-83, assoc. prof. pediat., 1983-89; prof. pediat. U. Pa. Sch. Medicine, 1989—, prof. emergency medicine, 1994—. Asst. physician The Children's Hosp. Phila., 1974-76, sr. physician, 1979—, divsn. chief gen. pediat., 1988-95, assoc. physician-in-chief for med. edn. dept. pediat., 1995—, sec. med./dental staff, 1986-88, v.p. med./dental staff, 1988-90, exec. com. dept. pediat., 1993—,; attending physician, dir. in-patient svcs. Phila. Gen. Hosp., 1974-76, asst. chief svc. pediat. dept., 1989—; lectr. in field. Editor-in-chief Children's Doctors, 1995—; co-editor-in-chief Pediat. Emergency Care, 1985—; mem. editl. bd. Pediat. Emergency and Critical Care, 1987—, Jour. Ambulatory Pediat. Assn., 1998—; adv. editl. bd. Pediat. Emergency Trends, 1986—; contbg. editor Yearbook of Emergency Medicine, 1988-93; reviewer Clin. Pediat., 1979-93, Pediat., 1980—, Jour. AMA, 1986—, Yearbook Pediat., 1990—, Annals Emergency Medicine, 1990—, Archives Pediat. and Adolescent Medicine, 1992—; contbr. chpts. to books and articles to profl. jours. Grantee Robert Wood Johnson Found., 1982-83, 82-84, 85-87. Mem. Internat. Soc. Child Abuse and Neglect, Am. Acad. Pediat. (chmn. emergency medicine sect. 1984-86, chmn. com. on pediat. emergency medicine 1988-92, exec. bd. sect. on child abuse, membership chmn. 1988-90, Career Achievement award sect. pediat. emergency medicine 1992), Am. Pediat. Soc., Am. Pediat. Assn. (exec. bd. 1989-92, founding mem. pediat. emergency medicine interest group 1989—), Am. Bd. Pediat. (program dirs. com.), Am. Profl. Soc. Against Child Abuse, Am. Coll. Emergency Physician (co-chmn. edn. com. Pa. chpt. 1980-88, treas., co-chmn. edn. com. Pa. chpt. 1986-89), Ambulatory Pediat. Assn. (Nat. Tchg. award 1988), Phila. Emergency Physicians Soc. (steering com.), Phila. Pediat. Soc., Univ. Assn. for Emergency Medicine, Soc. Tchrs. Emergency Medicine, Phila. Trauma Consortium, Pediat. Emergency Medicine Fellowship Dirs. (chmn. 1984-87), Soc. for Pediat. Trauma (charter), Soc. for Pediat. Emergency Medicine (charter), Assn. Pediat. Program Dirs., Helfer Soc. (founder). Office Phone: 215-590-2162. E-mail: ludwig@email.chop.edu.

LUDZIK, STEVE, professional hockey coach; m. Mary Ann Ludzik; children: Stephen, Ryan. Hockey player Niagara Falls Flyers, Ont. Hockey League, 1981-82, Chgo. Blackhaws, NHL, 1982-88, Buffalo Sabres, NHL, 1988-89, Am. Hockey League's Rochester Americans, 1989-92; coach Muskegon Fury, Colonial Hockey League, 1993-94; head coach Detroit Vipers, Internat. Hockey League, 1994-99, Tampa Bay Lightning, NHL, 1999—2001, Mississauga Ice Dogs, Ontario Hockey League, 2002, San Antonio Rampage, 2003; asst coach Fl. Panthers, 2003—04; head coach San Antonio Rampage, 2004—. Office: San Antonio Rampage One SBC Center San Antonio TX 78219*

LUEBKE, NEIL ROBERT, philosophy educator; b. Pierce, Nebr., Sept. 15, 1936; s. Robert Carl and Cinderetta Amelia (Guthmann) L.; m. Phyllis Jean Madsen, June 15, 1957; children: Anne Elizabeth, Karen Marie. BA, Midland Coll., 1958; MA, Johns Hopkins U., 1962, PhD, 1968. Asst., assoc. then prof. philosophy Okla. State U., Stillwater, 1961-98, head philosophy dept., 1979-85, 89-96, Regents Svc. prof., 1997-98, prof. emeritus, 1998—. Dir. Exxon Critical Thinking Project, 1971-74 Contbr. articles to profl. jours. Woodrow Wilson nat. fellow, 1958-59 Mem. Am. Philos. Assn., Soc. Bus. Ethics, Mountain-Plains Philos. Conf. (chmn. 1971-72, 80-81), Southwestern Philos. Soc. (pres. 1981-82), Phi Kappa Phi (nat. pres. 1998-2001). Democrat. Lutheran. Home: 616 W Harned Ave Stillwater OK 74075-1303 Personal E-mail: nlueske@okstate.edu.

LUECHTEFELD, MONICA, retail executive; b. LA, Jan. 23, 1949; 1 child. BS, Mount St. Mary's Coll., LA, 1971. With recruiting office Mount St. Mary's Coll., LA; sales rep. Maloney's office supply, LA, 1979—93; from gen. mgr. So. Calif. Region to exec. v.p. E-Commerce Office Depot, Inc., Delray Beach, Fla., 1993—2000, exec. v.p. E-Commerce, 2000—. Office: Office Depot Inc 2200 Old Germantown Rd Delray Beach FL 33445*

LUECK, MARTIN R., lawyer; b. St. Paul, Sept. 25, 1956; BS, Winona State U., 1978; JD cum laude, William Mitchell Coll. Law, 1984. Bar: Minn. 1984, US Dist. Ct. Minn. 1984, US Dist. Ct. (no. dist.) Calif. 1987, US Dist. Ct. Ariz. 1998, US Ct. Appeals (fed. cir.) 1998, US Cir. Ct. Appeals (fed. cir.) 1998, US Supreme Ct. 1997, NY Supreme Ct. Appellate (3rd judicial dist.) 2003. Law clk. Sahr Kunert & Tamornino, Mpls., 1981—83; ptnr. Robins, Kaplan, Miller & Ciresi LLP, Mpls., 1983—, mem. exec. bd., 1996—, chmn. bus. litigation group, 1999—. Spkr, lectr. in field, 1992—; chair bus. litig. group, mem. exec. bd. Robins, Kaplan, Miller & Ciresi LLP, 1996—. Contbr. articles to profl. jour. Named one of Minn. Lawyer's 15 Attys. of Yr., 2003, Ten of Nations Top Litigators, The Nat. Law Jour., 2004. Mem.: ABA (mem. tng. the trial lawyer task force), Fed. Cir. Bar Assn., Hennepin County Bar Assn., Minn. Intellectual Property Law Assn., Am. Intellectual Property Law Assn. Office: Robins Kaplan Miller & Ciresi LLP 2800 LaSalle Pl 800 LaSalle Ave Minneapolis MN 55402-2015 Business E-Mail: mrluek@rkmc.com.

LUECKE, PAMELA, professor, former editor; BA in Philosophy, Carleton Coll., 1974; MA in Journalism, Northwestern U., 1975; MBA, U. Hartford, 1979. Features reporter Hartford Courant, Hartford, Conn., 1975—79; bus. editor The Louisville Times, Louisville, 1981—84; various positions The Courier-Journal, Louisville, 1981—89; asst. mng. editor/metro Hartford Courant, Hartford, Conn., 1989—95, deputy mng. editor, 1995; editorial page editor Lexington (Ky.) Herald-Leader, 1995—96, editor, v.p., 1996—2000, editor, sr. v.p., 2000—01; prof., Reynolds Chair Dept. Journalism and Mass Comm., Washington and Lee Univ., Va., 2001—. Office: Washington & Lee Univ Lexington VA 24450

LUECKENHOFF, MARK ALBERT, elementary school educator; b. Jefferson City, Mo., Sept. 24, 1955; s. Albert and Nancy (Hohenstreet) L.; m. Linda K. King, Jan. 8, 1977; children: Bethany, Phillip. BA, Ill. State U., 1977; MA, N.E. Mo. State U., 1982. Tchr. Lewis County C-1 Schs., Ewing, Mo., 1978—. Author: U.S. Neighbors, 1993; co-author: United States, 1993. Recipient Milken Family Found. award, 1996; named Mo. Elem. Social Studies Tchr. of the Yr., Mo. Coun. Social Studies, 1992. Mem. Mo. Geog. Alliance (newsletter editor 1993—). Home: 5 Lakeview Drive Ewing MO 63440-9445 Office: Highland Elem Sch PO Box 366 Ewing MO 63440-0366

LUEDEMAN, GERALD WARREN, radiologist; b. Kansas City, Mo., Jan. 17, 1941; s. Clarence Henry and Hazel McClure Luedeman; m. Brenda Jane Kvamme, Sept. 1, 1984; children: Robert Warren, Richard Brandt. AB, Harvard Coll., Cambridge, Mass., 1962; MD, George Washington U., Washington, 1966. Diplomate Am. Bd. Radiology, 1974, Am. Bd. Nuc. Medicine, 1976. Intern Grady Meml. Hosp., Atlanta, 1966—67; resident radiology Med. Coll. Va., Richmond, 1970—73; radiologist Ventura County Cmty. Hosp., Calif., 1973—75; pvt. practice Radiology Cons. PA, Winter Haven, Fla., 1975—. Capt. U.S. Army, 1967—69. Mem.: Radiol. Soc. N.Am., Am. Inst. of Ultrasound in Medicine, Soc. of Nuc. Medicine, Roentgen Ray Soc., Masons Lake Region Yacht and Country Club. Avocations: travel, reading, golf.

LUEDER, DIANNE CAROL, library director; b. Racine, Wis., Aug. 5, 1944; d. James Richard and Margaret Ann Helland; m. Roland Herman Lueder, Aug. 29, 1981 (dec. July 1993); children: Daniel Lee Bertelsen, Barbara Marie Lantz. BA, U. Wis.-Parkside, Kenosha, 1972; MLS, U. Wis., Milw., 1979. Ref./outreach libr. Elk Grove Village (Ill.) Libr., 1979-80; dir. Bartlett (Ill.) Pub. Libr., 1980-84; asst. exec. dir. DuPage Libr. Sys., Geneva, Ill., 1984-88; pres. Lueder Enterprises, Inc., Wauconda, Ill., 1988—2003; exec. dir. Roselle (Ill.) Pub. Libr., 1990—2001; libr. dir. Menomonie (Wis.) Pub. Libr., 2001—. Author: Administrator's Guide to Library Building Maintenance, 1992. V.p. Roselle Pub. Libr. Found., 1994-2001. Mem.: ALA, Wis. Libr. Assn., Menomonie Woman's Club, Rotary, Optimist Club (pres.). Lutheran. Avocations: flying, travel, learning Norwegian language. Home: 343 Red Cedar St Menomonie WI 54751 Office: Menomonie Pub Libr 600 Wolske Bay Rd Menomonie WI 54751 Office Phone: 715-232-2164. E-mail: dclueder@wwt.net.

LUEDERS, WAYNE RICHARD, lawyer; b. Milw., Sept. 23, 1947; s. Warren E. and Marjorie L. (Schramek) L.; m. Patricia L. Rasmus, Aug. 1, 1970 (div. Nov. 1990); children: Laurel, Daniel, Kristin; m. Kristine Harbrecht, May 22, 2004. BBA with honors, U. Wis., 1969; JD, Yale U., 1973, Yale Law Sch. Bar: Wis. 1973. Acct. Arthur Andersen & Co., Milw., 1969-70; atty. Foley & Lardner, Milw., 1973-80, ptnr., 1980—. Bd. dirs. numerous cos. Bd. dirs. Riveredge Nature Ctr., Milw., 1983-92, 96-99, Wis. Pro Soccer, 1986-2003, Milw. Art Mus., 1992-2001, Child Abuse Prevention Fund, Milw., 1989-2003, Michael Fields Agrl. Inst., 1991—, Florentine Opera Co., 1992—; class agt. Yale Law Sch., 1978—. With U.S. Army, 1969-75. Mem. ABA, AICPA (Wisc.), Wis. Bar Assn., Milw. Bar Assn., Estate Counselors Forum, Univ. Club (Milw.), Phi Kappa Phi. Avocations: theater, racquetball, violin. Office: Foley & Lardner LLP 777 E Wisconsin Ave Ste 3500 Milwaukee WI 53202-5306 Office Phone: 414-297-5786. Business E-Mail: wlueders@foley.com.

LUEDKE, FREDERICK LEE, manufacturing executive; b. Milw., Jan. 19, 1938; s. Frederick William and Martha Marie (Widiger) L.; m. Wilma Jeanne Seacat, July 3, 1960; children; Tracy Jeanne, Frederick William II. BSIE, Wichita State U., 1960; MBA, Harvard U., 1966. Mfg. tng. program GE, 1960-64; prodn. gen. supr. Polaroid Corp., Waltham, Mass., 1966-70; mgr. mfg. Millipore Corp., Bedford, Mass., 1970-76; dir. mfg. Berol Corp., Danbury, Conn., 1976-87; exec. v.p. Neoperl Inc., Waterbury, Conn., 1987-92; pres. Neoperl, Inc., Waterbury, Conn., 1992—. Bd. dirs. Naugatuck Valley Devel. Corp., 1994—, v.p., 1996—98; bd. dirs. Platt Bros. and Co., 1996—, Waterbury Partnership 2000, 1999—2001, Greater Waterbury Workforce Devel. Bd., 2001—; mem. Gov.'s coun. for Econ. Competitiveness and Tech., 1999—, Waterbury City Champion, Inner City Bus. Strategy Initiative, 1999. Founder Waterbury Neighborhood Coun., 1994; bd. dir. Waterbury Devel. Corp., 2004—; mem. Waterbury Planning and Fin. Assistance Bd., 2004—; pres. Luth. Ch. of Newtons, Mass., 1974—75, 1st Luth. Ch., Waterbury, 1988—89; bd. dirs. Danbury ARC, 1982—84, Easter Seals, 1993—2000, vice chmn., 1994—96, chmn., 1996—98; pres. bd. trustees East Hill Woods Retirement Ctr., Southbury, Conn., 1989—97; mem. Waterbury Found., 1991—; chmn. Incorporators of Waterbury Hosp., 1995—97; trustee Waterbury Hosp., 1997—, chmn., 2003—; bd. dirs. Greater Waterbury Health Network, 1999—, Waterbury Partnership for Growth, 2001—04. Mem. ASME, Am. Soc. Plumbing Engrs., Plumbing Mfrs. Inst. (pres. 1999-2000, bd. dirs. 1995-2000), Am. Soc. Sanitary Engring., Greater Waterbury C. of C. (bd. dirs. 2000—, Mfr. of Yr. 2003), Rotary (bd. dirs.), Waterbury Club (pres. 1996-98). Republican. Lutheran. Avocations: tennis, mountain hiking. Home: 98 Woodlawn Ter Waterbury CT 06710-1929 Office: Neoperl Inc 171 Mattatuck Heights Rd Waterbury CT 06705-3832

LUEDTKE, THOMAS, associate administrator procurement for NASA; BS in Polit. Sci. and History, U. Wis., Parkside; MS in Bus., JD, U. Wis. Contract specialist Naval Air Systems Command, Washington; dir. pricing policy divsn. Army Materiel Commnd Hdqtrs., Washington; chmn., army mem. Cost Principles Com. DAR Coun., Washington; dir. contract pricing and fin. divsn. NASA, Washington, dep. assoc. adminstr. for procurement, acting assoc. adminstr. for procurement, 1998—, assoc. adminstr. for procurement. Office: NASA Hdqtrs Code H Washington DC 20546-0001

LUEKEN, HAROLD W., retail executive; b. Bayshore, N.Y., Apr. 28, 1962; BA summa cum laude, Slippery Rock U., 1984; JD cum laude, Fordham U., 1988. Mng. dir., gen. counsel corp. investment Banc of Am. Securities, 2000—03; prin. Morgan Stanley Dean Witter & Co., NYC, 1994—2000; corp. assoc. Cravath, Swaine & Moore, NYC, 1989—94; fgn. assoc. Boden Oppenhoff & Schneider, Cologne, Germany, 1988—89; sr. v.p., gen. counsel, sec. Kmart Corp, Troy, Mich., 2003—. Office: Kmart Corp 3100 W Big Beaver Rd Troy MI 48084 Office Phone: 248-463-7408.

LUENING, ROBERT ADAMI, retired agricultural studies educator; b. Milw., Apr. 20, 1924; s. Edwin Garfield and Irma Barbara (Adami) L.; m. Dorothy Ellen Hodgskiss, Aug. 27, 1966. BS, U. Wis., 1961, MS, 1968. Dairy farmer, Hartland, Wis., 1942-58; fieldman Waukesha County Dairy Herd Improvement Assn., Waukesha, Wis., 1958; adult agr. instr. Blair Sch. Dist., Wis., 1961-63; extension farm mgmt. agt. U. Wis.-Racine, 1963-69; extension farm record specialist dept. agrl. and applied econs. U. Wis.-Madison, 1969-88; free-lance work, 1988—. Author: (with others) The Farm Management Handbook, 1972, 7th edit., 1991, Teacher's Manual, 1991, Managing Your Financial Future Farm Record Book Series, 1980, 4th edit., 1987, USDA Yearbook of Agriculture, 1989, Beef, Sheep and Forage Production in Northern Wisconsin, 1992, Dairy Farm Business Management, 1996, Poultry Farm Business Management, 1999, 2d edit., 2000, revised, 2004; writer mag. column: Agri-Vision, 1970-88. Founder, exec. pres. Lüning Family Orgns. U.S.A., Inc.; bd. dirs. Friends of the Max Kade Inst. for German-Am. Studies. Recipient John S. Donald Excellence in Teaching award U. Wis.-Madison, 1980; recipient Wis. State Farmer award Vocat. Agr. Inst. Wis., 1980, Second Mile award Wis. County Agts. Assn., 1980, Outstanding Svc. to Wis. Agr. award Farm and Industry Short Course, 1989. Mem. Wis. Soc. Farm Mgrs. and Rural Appraisers (hon., coll. v.p. 1976, chmn. editl. com. 1978-80, sec.-treas. 1968-80, pres. 1982, Silver Plow award 1988), Wis. State Geneal. Soc. (pres. S.C. chpt. 1995-96, pres. PAF Users group 1995), Epsilon Sigma Phi (Disting. Service award 1988), Alpha Gamma Rho, Kiwanis. Lodges: Masons. Presbyterian. Home: 5313 Fairway Dr Madison WI 53711-1038 Office: U Wis Dept Agrl and Applied Econs 427 Lorch St Madison WI 53706-1513 Business E-Mail: rluening@wisc.edu.

LUEPKER, RUSSELL VINCENT, epidemiology educator; b. Chgo., Oct. 1, 1942; s. Fred Joseph and Anita Louise (Thornton) L.; m. Ellen Louise Thompson, Dec. 22, 1966; children: Ian, Carl. BA, Grinnell Coll., 1964; MD with distinction, U. Rochester, 1969; MS, Harvard U., 1976; PhD (hon.), U. Lund, Sweden, 1996. Intern U. Calif., San Diego, 1969-70; resident Peter Bent Brigham Hosp., Boston, 1973-74; cardiology fellow Peter Bent Brigham Hosp./Med., Boston, 1974-76; asst. prof. divsn. epidemiology med. lab. physiol. hygiene U. Minn., Mpls., 1976-80, assoc. prof., 1980-87, prof. divsn. epidemiology and medicine, 1987—, dir. divsn. epidemiology, 1991—2004, Mayo prof. pub. health, 2000—. Cons. NIH, Bethesda, Md., 1980—, U. So. Calif., L.A., 1985—, Armed Forces Epidemiology Bd., 1993-97; vis. prof. U. Goteborg, Sweden, 1986, Ninewells Med. Sch., Dundee, Scotland, 1995. With USPHS, 1970—73. Harvard U. fellow, 1974-76, Bush Leadership fellow, 1990; recipient Prize for Med. Rsch. Am. Coll. Chest Physicians, 1970, Nat. Rsch. Svc. award Nat. Heart, Lung and Blood Inst., Bethesda, 1975-77, Disting. Alumni award Grinnell Coll., 1989. Fellow ACP, Am. Coll. Cardiology, Am. Heart Assn. (chmn. coun. on epidemiology 1992-94, chair program com. sci. sessions 1995-97, award of merit 1997), Am. Coll. Epidemiology; mem. Am. Epidemiol. Soc., Am. Soc. Preventive Cardiology (Joseph Stokes award 1999), Delta Omega Soc. (Nat. Merit award 1988). Office: Univ Minn Sch Pub Health Div Epidemiology 1300 S 2nd St Minneapolis MN 55454-1087 Office Phone: 612-624-6362. Business E-Mail: luepker@epi.umn.edu.

LUETKEHOELTER, GOTTLIEB WERNER (LEE LUETKEHOELTER), retired bishop, clergyman; b. Wheatwyn, Sask., Can., Nov. 16, 1929; s. Henry William and Marie Louise (Schlepper) L.; m. Betty Edwards, July 25, 1959; children— David Lee, Jonathan Richard. BA, U. Sask., 1952; B.D., Lutheran Coll. and Sem., Saskatoon, Sask., 1955; S.T.M., Vancouver Sch. Theology, 1975; DD, St. John's Coll., U. Manitoba, 1990, Luth. Theol. Sem., Saskatoon, 2000. Ordained to ministry United Luth. Ch. in Am., 1955. Pastor Markinch-Wheatwyn-Cupar Parish, 1955-57; pastor St. Mark's Luth. Ch., Regina, Sask., 1957-61, Erloeser Luth. Ch., Phila., 1961-63, Faith Luth. Ch., Burnaby, B.C., Can., 1963-69, Trinity Luth. Ch., Edmonton, Alta., Can., 1969-76; bishop Central Can. Synod, Luth. Ch. in Am., Winnipeg, Man., Can., 1976-85; bishop Man./Northwestern Ont. Synod, Evang. Luth. Ch. in Can., Winnipeg, Man., 1985-94; ret., 1994. Mem. exec. coun. Luth. Ch. in Am., N.Y.C., 1978-85, Anglican-Luth. Dialogue, Can., 1983-95; dir. Can. Luth. World Relief, 1989-98; lectr. Univ. Winnipeg, 1997-98. Bd. govs. Luth. Theol. Sem., Saskatoon, 1976-94, Schmieder resident, 1994-95, lectr. Luth. Theol. Sem., 1995-96. With Royal Can. Navy, 1952-54. Lutheran. Avocations: golf, swimming, writing. E-mail: lee7lue@shaw.ca.

LUETSCHWAGER, MARY SUSAN, transportation executive; b. Bloomingdale, Ind., Nov. 19, 1937; d. William Blaine Shade and Goldina VandaVeer (Newlin) Brown; children: Roger, Tisa, Julia, Angela, Robert, William; m. Bruce E. Luetschwager, Sept. 9, 2000. Grad. high sch., Rockville, Ind. Sec., treas. Tri-State Transport, Inc., 1968-73; road driver Roadway Express, Chicago Heights, Ill., 1977—, safety team capt., 1991-92, 94. Completed Passport Tour (Abate), 1990, 94, 2000; mem. Roadway Express Dist. Road Team Dist. 12, 1995-97. Past mem. newsletter com. focus group Roadway Express; mem. focus group Kenworth Driver's Bd., 1992—; active Motorcycle Safety Found., Basic Rider Course; Rider coach 1999-, ABATE of Ind., Ind. Dept. of Edn. Recipient truck driving competition awards and motorcycle rally trophies, 3d place 8/48 rally Motorcycle Endurance Rider's Assn., 1996; 1st woman to finish on a Harley-Davidson motorcycle World Famous Iron Butt Rally, 1995, finished 6th place out of 78 starts and 61 finishers in 8th Iron Butt Rally, 1997, placed 3d in twin-trailer truck driving championships in Ill., 2000; placed 2nd in competition at Delta Nu Alpha truck driving fraternity in Rockford Ill, 2001, 1st pl. award (grand champion overall) in twin-trailer divsn. of truck driving championships, Ill., 2001; named Ill. TDC Sportsman of the Yr., 1995. Mem. Am. Motorcycle Assn., Am. Bikers Aim Toward Edn., Am. Radio Relay League, Harley Owners Group (newsletter editor Calumet region chpt. 1994-96, 2005, Hammond, Ind., asst. dir. Calumet region chpt. 1996-99, 2002, historian, 2000—, sec. 2004), Ladies of Harley. Avocations: motorcycle endurance riding, amateur radio. Home and Office: PO Box 316 Griffith IN 46319-0316

LUFFSEY, WALTER STITH, air transportation executive, consultant; b. Richmond, Va., Mar. 15, 1934; s. Roland Emmit and Bernice Irene (Hall) L.; m. Louise Arlington Hicks, Dec. 19, 1956; children: Dennis Glenn, Melinda Denise. Student, U. Richmond, 1952—55, Agrl. Dept. Grad. Sch., 1963—65. With FAA, 1957—, supervisory air traffic control specialist Atlantic City, 1960-63, air traffic control specialist rsch., 1963-65, sr. air traffic control analyst systems rsch. and devel. svc., 1965-71, chief program analysis and reports br. Washington, 1971-72, asst. chief program mgmt. staff, 1972-73, spl. asst., assoc. adminstr. for engring. and devel., 1973-74, chief program mgmt. staff system rsch. and devel. svc., 1974-75, tech. asst., assoc. adminstr. policy devel. and rev., 1975-78, tech. asst., assoc. adminstr. policy and internat. aviation affairs, tech. asst. to the assoc. adminstr. for aviation stds., 1978-79, dep. assoc. adminstr. for aviation stds., 1979-80, assoc. adminstr. for aviation stds., 1980-85, assoc. adminstr. for air traffic, 1985-86, dir. advanced aviation sys. design team, 1986-89; sr. v.p. ops. and planning Tech. and Mgmt. Assistance, Washington, 1989-90, exec. v.p., 1990-97; pres. WSL Enterprises, Arlington, Va., 1989—. Author: Air Traffic Control: How to Become an FAA Air Traffic Controller, 1990; contbr. articles to profl. jours. Served with USAF/Va. Air N.G., 1955-58. Recipient Spl. Achievement award FAA, 1970, 78, 85, Disting. Svc. award Aviation Week and Space Tech.-Flight Safety Found., 1982, Laurel award, 2000, Sec.'s award, 1982, Meritorious Exec. award-Presdl. Rank, 1983, Adminstr.'s Superior Achievement award, 1985, others. Mem. AIAA (aero. policy com.), Soc. Sr. Aerospace Execs., Nat. Aero. Assn., Exptl. Aircraft Assn., Aircraft Owners and Pilots Assn., Profl. Women Contrs. Assn., Air Traffic Control Assn. (hon., past chair publs. com., Meritorious Achievement award 1965, Tech. Writing 1st pl. award), John Marshall Cadet Alumni Assn., Soc. Airway Pioneers, Va. Aero. Hist. Soc., Order of Quiet Birdmen, Silver Wings Fraternity, Aero Club, Nat. Aviation Club (past pres., gov. emeritus), Kiwanis (past pres. Crystal City). Home and Office: WSL Enterprises 9115 Alexandria Dr Weeki Wachee FL 34613 Personal E-mail: waltluffsey@prodigy.net.

LUFT, GARY ALAN, secondary school educator; b. Billings, Mont., Nov. 22, 1953; s. George Washington and Gladys Arlene Luft; m. Ella Sue Cowdrey, June 15, 1979; children: Garrett Paul, Chase Evan. BS, Wash. State U., 1976; postgrad., U. Ala., 1979-80; MS, Tex. Tech. U., 1986, PhD, 1989. Cert. tchr., Tex. Min. Univ. Ch. of Christ, Tuscaloosa, Ala., 1978-81, Sunset Ch. of Christ, Lubbock, Tex., 1981-84; tchg. asst. Tex. Tech. U., Lubbock, 1984-89; prof. Truman State U., Kirksville, Mo., 1989-90, U. Akron, Ohio, 1990-93; counselor Christian Counseling, Snyder, Tex., 1994-97; tchr. Roscoe (Tex.) H.S., 1996-97, Lee H.S., Midland, Tex., 1997—, asst. basketball coach, 1997—; adj. prof. Lubbock Christian U., 2003—. Adviser Parent Edn. Bd., Snyder, 1994-97. Mem. Nat. Coun. Tchrs. Math., Snyder C. of C. (dir. 1995-96). Home: 3411 Humble Ave Midland TX 79707-6608 E-mail: cubtech@grandecom.net.

LUFT, PAMELA, education educator, consultant; d. Marianne Gutteridge; m. Drew Tiene, June 12, 1998. MEd, Western Md. Coll./McDaniel Coll., Westminster, Md., 1976; MS, Johns Hopkins U., Balt., Md., 1987; PhD, U. Ill. Urbana Champaign, Urbana, Ill., 1995. Cert. tchg. Calif., 1991. Tchr./coord. Gallaudet U., PreCollege Programs, Washington, 1981—87; career ctr. coord. Calif. Sch. for the Deaf-Riverside, Riverside, Calif., 1991—92; asst. dir, deafmh dorms; behavior specialist Fla. Sch. for the Deaf and Blind, St. Augustine, Fla., 1987—89; rehab. counselor asst. Dept. of Vocat. Rehab., Champaign, Ill., 1995—95; assoc. prof. Kent State U., Ohio, 1995—. Bd. mem. Greater Akron Deaf Services (GADS), Akron, Ohio, 2003—; fund raising coord. History Through Deaf Eyes Task Force, Akron, Ohio, 2002—03; pres., conf. coord. Assoc. of Coll. Educators for the Deaf and Hard-of-Hearing, San Antonio, 2001—03; spl. edn. cons. Ohio Legal Rights Svcs., Columbus, Ohio, 1995—96; program and curriculum developer: educ interpreting, ASL fgn. lang. tchg. Kent State U., Kent, Ohio, 1998—2002, ASL coord., 2001—02. Author (editor): (textbook) Transition Planning for Secondary Students with Disabilities (2nd ed); author: Life Beyond the Classroom: Applications for Youth with Sensory Impairments. Grantee Grant Recipients of $500, 000 or more in One Yr., Kent State U., 2003, $498, 292 for RCD Tng., OSERS, 2003-2008, $1, 493, 187 for Transition Svcs. Tng. for Teachers of D/HH Students, 2001-2006, $340, 611 for Ednl. Interpreter and ASL Tng. Programs, Ohio Dept. of Edn., 1998-2004. Mem.: Conv. of Am. Instructors of the Deaf (CAID), Nat. Assn. of the Deaf (NAD), Assoc. of Coll. Educators for the Deaf and Hard-of-Hearing (pres., past pres., president-elect/conf. chair 2001—04), Ohio Assn. of the Deaf. Achievements include research in Transition preparation for tchrs., transition outcomes of D/HH students, technology survey for D/HH students, Instrnl. strategies in special edn. Office: Kent State Univ 405 White Hall Kent OH 44242-0001 Office Phone: 330-672-0593. Office Fax: 330-672-2512.

LUFT, RENE WILFRED, civil engineer; b. Santiago, Chile, Sept. 21, 1943; came to U.S., 1968; s. David and Malwina (Kelmy) L.; m. Monica Acevedo, Aug. 24, 1970; children: Deborah Elaine, Daniel Eduardo, Allegra Filomena; m. Laura J. Gigante, July 11, 1998. CE, U. Chile, 1967; MS, MIT, 1969, DSc, 1971. Registered profl. engr., Alaska, Calif., Wash., Mass., Nev., N.H., R.I., Republic of Chile; registered structural engr., Vt. Asst. prof. civil engring. U. Chile, 1967-68; research asst. MIT, Cambridge, Mass., 1969-71, vis. lectr., 1983-84; staff engr. Simpson, Gumpertz & Heger Inc., Arlington, Mass., 1971-74, sr. staff engr., 1975-78, assoc., 1978-83, sr. assoc., 1984-90, prin. San Francisco, 1990—, head design div., 1991-95. Sec. seismic adv. com. Mass. Bldg. Code Commn., 1978-80, chmn., 1981-82; mem. Boston seismic instrumentation com. U.S. Geol. Survey; mem. slabs on ground com. Post-Tensioning Inst., 1994—, also chmn. structural subcom., bd. dirs., 2001—. Contbr. articles to profl. jours. Mem. bldg. seismic safety coun. Earthquake Hazards Reduction Program, 1983-91. Mem. ASCE (outstanding award for paper 1995), Boston Soc. Civil Engrs. (chmn. seismic design adv. com. 1981-86, Clemens Herschel award for tech. paper 1980, pres.'s award for leadership in earthquake engring. 1984), Am. Concrete Inst., Earthquake Engring. Resch. Inst., Structural Engrs. Assn. Calif. (chmn. rsch. com. 2001—), NSPE (Young Engr. of Yr., 1979), Sigma Xi, Chi Epsilon. Home: 206 Windsor Dr Petaluma CA 94952-7516 Office: 222 Sutter St Ste 300 San Francisco CA 94108-4445 E-mail: rluft@sgh.com.

LUFT, ROBERT, energy executive; Mgmt. positions through sr. v.p. DuPont, 1978-96; pres. DuPont Europe; chmn. DuPont Internat., DuPont Dow Elastomers; dir. Entergy Corp., New Orleans, 1992—, acting CEO, 1998, bd. chmn. Bd. mem. U.S. Chemical Manufacturers Assn.; dir. Stonebridge Bank; mem. bd. vis. Univ. Pitts. Sch. Engring. Office: Entergy Corp 639 Loyola Ave New Orleans LA 70113 Mailing: Entergy Corp PO Box 61000 New Orleans LA 70161-1000

LUFTGLASS, MARIBETH, information technology manager; b. Clearwater, Fla., Sept. 15, 1961; d. Richard James and Elizabeth McGeachy Ernst; m. Robert Andrew Luftglass, Sept. 7, 1985; children: Jacob Daniel, David James, Adam Robert. B of Math. and Econs., Coll. of William and Mary, Va., 1983; MS, George Wash. U., Washington, DC, 1986. Sr. dir. info. tech. ARC, Washington, 1984—99; asst. supt. and chief info. officer Fairfax County Pub. Schs., Fairfax, Va., 1999—. Student mentor, Fairfax, Va., 1999—2005; deacon Providence Presbyn. Ch., Fairfax, Va., 2002—05. Recipient Heroine in Tech., Women in Tech., Inc., 2002. Home: 9004 Glenbrook Ct Fairfax VA 22031 Office: Fairfax County Pub Sch 4414 Holborn Ave Annandale VA 22003 Personal E-mail: luftglassm@aol.com. E-mail: maribeth.luftglass@fcps.edu.

LUFTGLASS, MURRAY ARNOLD, corporate financial executive; b. Bklyn., Jan. 2, 1931; s. Harry and Pauline (Yaged) L.; children by previous marriage: Paula Jean, Bryan Keith, Robert Andrew, Richard Eric; 1 child from 2d marriage: Andrew William. BS, Ill. Inst. Tech., 1952; MS, U. So. Calif., 1959; MBA, U. Conn., 1972. With Shell Chem. Co., Torrance, Calif., 1955-60, 64-66, N.Y.C., 1960-61, 66-69, Wallingford, Conn., 1961-64; asst. gen. mgr. Westchester Plastics div. Ametek, Inc., Mamaroneck, N.Y., 1969-75, dir. corp. devel. N.Y.C., 1975-76, v.p., 1976-83, sr. v.p. corp. devel., 1984-96; mng. dir. M&A London, LLC, 1996—. Contbr. articles to profl. jours., publs.; patentee in field. Lt. (j.g.) USN, 1952—55. Mem. NAM, Soc. Plastics Industry, Assn. Corp. Growth, Soc. Plastics Engrs., Tau Beta Pi, Beta Gamma Sigma, Phi Lambda Upsilon, Univ. Club (N.Y.C.). Office: M&A London LLC PO Box 150 Montclair NJ 07042-0150 Office Phone: 973-783-2266. Business E-Mail: murray@mandalondon.com.

LUGAR, DICK (RICHARD GREEN LUGAR), senator; b. Indpls., Apr. 4, 1932; s. Marvin L. and Bertha (Green) L.; m. Charlene Smeltzer, Sept. 8, 1956; children: Mark, Robert, John, David. BA, Denison U., 1954; BA, MA (Rhodes scholar), Oxford (Eng.) U., 1956. Mayor, Indpls., 1968-75; vis. prof. polit. sci. U. Indpls., 1976; mem. from Ind. US Senate, 1977—, chmn. com. fgn. rels., 1985-86, 2003—, chmn. com. on agr., nutrition and forestry, 1995-2001; chmn. Nat. Rep. Senatorial Com., 1983-84. Pres. Lugar Stock Farm, Inc.; mem. Indpls. Sch. Bd., 1964-67, v.p., 1965-66; vice chmn. Adv. Commn. on Intergovtl. Relations, 1969-75; pres. Nat. League of Cities, 1970-71; mem. Nat. Commn. Standards and Goals of Criminal Justice System, 1971-73; Del., mem. resolutions com. Republican Nat. Conv., 1968, del., mem. resolutions com., 1992, Keynote speaker, 1972, del., speaker, 1980., 88, 92, 96. Author: Letters to the Next President, 1988. Trustee Denison U., U. Indpls., 1970-2002; bd. dirs. Nat. Endowment for Democracy, 1992-2000, Nuclear Threat Initiative, 2000—. Served to lt. (j.g.) USNR, 1957-60. Pembroke Coll., Oxford U. hon. fellow Mem. Rotary, Blue Key, Phi Beta Kappa, Omicron Delta Kappa, Pi Delta Epsilon, Pi Sigma Alpha, Beta Theta Pi. Republican. Methodist. Office: US Senate 306 Hart Senate Bldg Washington DC 20510-0001*

LUGAR, THOMAS R., manufacturing executive; BS mech. engring., Purdue Univ. With Allison Div. Gen. Motors Co., Indpls., 1955-57; pres. Thomas L. Green & Co., Indpls., 1957—2001; chmn. Reading Bakery Systems. Served U.S. Army. Mem.: Cookie and Snack Bakers Assn., Biscuit & Cracker Manufacturers Assn. Office: Thomas L Green Co Inc 7802 Moller Rd Indianapolis IN 46268-2117

LUGENBEEL, EDWARD ELMER, publisher; b. Balt., June 6, 1932; s. Nimrod Augustus and Victoria Elizabeth (Shilling) L.; m. Alice Marie Smith, June 12, 1953; children: Craig Edward, Susan Elizabeth, Douglas Paul, Leslie Jean. BS, U. Md., 1954. With Prentice-Hall, Inc., N.J., 1957-76, exec. editor, asst. v.p., 1972-76; pres. D. Van Nostrand Co., div. Litton Ednl. Pub., Inc. (pubs. coll. textbooks), N.Y.C., 1976-81; v.p. Lynne Palmer Exec. Recruitment, Inc., N.Y.C., 1981-83; v.p., editl. dir. W.B. Saunders Med. Pubs., Phila., 1983-85; exec. editor Columbia U. Press, N.Y.C., 1985-98, ret., 1998-99. Cons. Columbia U. Earth Inst. Tchr. Tai Chi Chuan, Rockland County, N.Y., 1999—, SUNY-Rockland Cmty. Coll., 2000-01, Ramapo, Clarkstown and Nyack Sr. ctrs., Fountainview Sr. Residence, Pomona YM/YWHA. Served as 1st lt. USAF, 1954-57. Mem. AAAS, Am. Inst. Biol. Scis., Am. Geophys. Union, Soc. Vertebrate Paleontology, Internat. Assn. Landscape Ecology, Soc. Conservation Biology, Nyack Tai Chi Acad. (Black Sash Second degree 2005), Shukokai World Karate Union (Brown Belt), Delta Sigma Pi.

LUGER, DONALD R., engineering company executive; b. May 12, 1938; s. George A. and Elizabeth M. Luger; m. Pat Sanders, Feb. 17, 1968 (dec. 1982); m. Sharon L. Luger, May 14, 1983; children: Christopher Daniel, Morgan Kathleen. BCE, Auburn U., 1962, MSCE, 1964; exec. program, Stanford U., 1979. Registered profl. engr., N.C., Ga., Mich., Va., N.Y. Structural engr. NASA, Huntsville, Ala., summer 1962; area engr. E.I. DuPont Co., Nashville, 1964; structural engr. Hayes Internat. Corp., Huntsville, 1964-65; resident engr. Fibers Industries, Inc., Shelby, N.C. and, Greenville, S.C., 1965-66; project mgr. Lockwood Greene Engrs., Inc., Atlanta, 1967-71, 1971-74, v.p., corp. dir., 1974-78, sr. v.p., corp. dir., 1978-82, pres., 1982-99, CEO, 1983-99, chmn., 1989; pres. D.R. Luger Enterprises, Atlanta, 1999—. Mem. adv. bd. N.Am. br. AMEC, 2001-04. Mem. ASCE, NSPE, Ga. Soc. Profl. Engrs., Auburn U. Alumni Assn., Auburn Alumni Engring. Coun., Commerce Club. Office: CSP Inc Bldg 8 Ste 1000 3312 N Berkeley Lake Rd NW Duluth GA 30096

LUGG, CATHERINE ANNE, education educator; b. Elmira, NY, Mar. 15, 1963; d. Anna Elizabeth Pearson and Robert Sherer Lugg; life ptnr. Mary D. Aun, Sept. 22, 2001. MusB in Music Edn., Mansfield U., Pa., 1985; MusM in Flute Performance, Drake U., 1988, MusM in Edn., 1990; Ph.D. in Ednl. Theory and Policy, Pa. State U., 1995. Asst. prof. of edn. The Pa. State U., University Park, Pa., 1995—96; assoc. prof. of edn. Rutgers U., New Brunswick, NJ, 1996—. Assoc. dir. for publications U. Coun. for Eductational Adminstrn., New Brunswick, NJ, 2005—. Author: (book) Kitsch: From Education to Public Policy, For God and Country: Conservatism and American School Policy. Mem.: Am. Constn. Soc., Politics of Edn. Assn., History of Edn. Soc., Nat. Soc. for the Study of Edn., Am. Ednl. Rsch. Assn. (divsn. 1 program chair 2005—05). Avocations: reading, music. Office: Rutgers University 10 Seminary Place New Brunswick NJ 08901-1183 Office Phone: 732-932-7496 8220. E-mail: lugg@rci.rutgers.edu.

LUGIANO, MARYANN ELIZABETH, musician, educator; b. Wilkes-Barre, Pa., Sept. 7, 1971; d. Andrew Kasko, Jr. and Marion E. Kasko; m. Robert A. Lugiano, Jr., June 27, 1998; 1 child, Robert A. III. BMus, Wilkes U., Wilkes-Barre, Pa., 1989—93, MS in Edn., 1997—2001; MMus in Oboe Performance, Bklyn Conservatory at Bklyn Coll., 1993—95. Cert. tchr. State of Pa., 1998. Clk. Gateway Cinema Ctr., Edwardsville, Pa., 1989—96; counselor, faculty, adminstrn. Encore Music Camp Pa., Wilkes-Barre, 1990—98; faculty Performing Arts Inst., Kingston, Pa., 2000—01; tchr., k-8 gen. music Jim Thorpe Area Sch. Dist., Pa., 1996—. Oboist The Allentown Band, Pa., 1990—2001. Mem.: Jim Thorpe Edn. Assn. (assoc.), Pa. State Educators Assn. (assoc.), Nat. Educators Assn. (assoc.), Pa. Music Educators Assn. (assoc.), Music Educators Nat. Conf. (assoc.), Internat. Double Reed Soc. (assoc.). Avocations: reading, travel. Office: Jim Thorpe Area Sch Dist 2840 Route 903 Albrightsville PA 18210 Office Phone: 570-722-1150 3130. Office Fax: 570-722-0317. E-mail: mlugiano@jtasd.k12.pa.us.

LUGO, EMIL J., retired secondary school educator; b. N.Y.C., Sept. 7, 1946; s. Abraham and Margaret Lugo; m. Yvette Corsino-Lugo, July 19, 1980; children: Karl P., Cynthia M. BA, St. John's U., N.Y.C., 1968; MA, Fordham U., Bronx, 1976. Cert. tchr. secondary edn. N.Y. Tchr. social studies Automotive H.S., Bklyn., 1971—72, Washington Irving H.S., N.Y.C., 1973—76; tchr. social studies and Japanese lang. Stuyvesant H.S., N.Y.C., 1968—72, 1972—73, 1976—2000. Del. United Fedn. Tchrs., N.Y.C., 1973—75; N.C. English/Spanish interpreter, 2004—. Bd. dirs. Watauga, Avery, Mitchell, Yancey Counties Cmty. Action, Inc., 2005—. Recipient Tchr. Who Made a Difference award, N.Y. Times, 2001; grantee Summer Study grantee, N.Y. State, 1969; scholar Fulbright scholar, Fulbright/Japan Found., 1985. Mem.: High Country Amigos (English instr. 2000—). Republican. Roman Catholic. Avocation: home repair, remodeling, and japanese rock gardening. Home: 661 Hopewell Church Rd Boone NC 28607 E-mail: corsinolugo@aol.com.

LUGO-HERNANDEZ, EDUARDO A., research scientist; s. Antonio Lugo and Zaida Hernandez; m. Yadira Hernandez-Rodriguez, Aug. 8, 1998; children: Sergio E. Lugo-Hernandez, Fabian E. Lugo-Hernandez. PhD, DePaul U., 2003. Rsch. assoc. U. Mich., Ann Arbor, 2000—02; asst. rsch. scientist U. PR, Rio Piedras, 2003—, collaborator, 2004—. Consulting U. Mich., 2004—. Youth leader Assemblies of God Ch., Bayamon, PR, 1995—97. Grantee, NIMH, 2000—02. Mem.: APA (minority fellow 1997—2000). Achievements include development of project to evaluate Latino parents satisfaction with the special education system in Florida. Office: U PR Ave Universidad Num 55 Edificio Rivera Rio Piedras PR 00926 Office Phone: 787-764-0000 2956. Office Fax: 787-764-2615. Personal E-mail: ealugo@uprrp.edu.

LUH, HOWARD H., aerospace engineer; b. Tainan, Taiwan, Dec. 18, 1936; came to U.S., 1963; BS, Cheng-Kung U., Tainan, 1959; MS, Tex. A&M U., 1964; PhD, U. Calif., Berkeley, 1969. Prin. engr. Radiation Sys., Inc., McLean, Va., 1969-72; sr. tech. Space Sys./Loral, Palo Alto, Calif., 1972—. Contbr. over 37 articles to profl. jours.; patentee (18) in field. Mem. IEEE (chmn. antenna propagation Santa Clara Valley 1984-85). Office: Space Systems/Loral 3825 Fabian Way Palo Alto CA 94303 E-mail: luh.howard@ssd.loral.com.

LUHMAN, WILLIAM SIMON, community development administrator; b. Belvidere, Ill., May 15, 1934; s. Donald R. and H. Elizabeth (Rudberg) L. AB, Park Coll., 1956; MA, Fla. State U., 1957. City planner City of Moline, Ill., 1959-64; planning dir. Rock Island County, Ill., 1964-66; exec. dir. Bi-State Met. Planning Commn., Rock Island, 1966-71; dir. regional devel. Northeastern Ill. Planning Commn., Chgo., 1971-74, assoc. dir., 1975-76, dep. dir., 1977-79, acting exec. dir., 1979-80, asst. dir., 1980-81; v.p. Pub. Mgmt. Info. Svc., Chgo., 1981; asst. dir. No. Ill. U. Ctr. Govt. Studies, DeKalb, 1981-91, program coord., 1991; exec. dir. Growth Dimensions for Belvidere-Boone County, Ill., 1991—2001, pres., 1982-86, asst. dir., 2002—04. Vis. instr. Augustana Coll., Rock Island, 1967, 69. Bd. dirs. Rockford Area Coun. of 100, 1983-86; Boone County Regional Planning Commn., 1986—, chmn., 1986-90, 2002—; mem. Belvidere-Boone County Regional Planning Commn., 1986—, chmn., 1990-92; bd. dirs. Sch. Dist. 100 Found. for Excellence in Edn., 1992-99; mem. Sch. Dist. 100 Citizens Adv. Coun., 1999-2000, Sch. Dist. 100 Cmty. Strat. Planning, 1999; bd. dirs. Boone County United Way, 1999-2004; trustee Cmty. Found. of No. Ill., 2002-2004; active Boone County Arts Coun., Friends of Ida Pub. Libr., Belvidere Sister Cities Assn.; Ill. Regional Pub. Libr. Svc. Planning Panelist, 1996. Mem.: Am. Soc. Pub. Adminstrn., Am. Planning Assn. Home: 1538 Fremont St Belvidere IL 61008-5939 Office: 200 S State St Belvidere IL 61008-3687 E-mail: bluhman@growthdimensions.org, bluhman@aol.com.

LUHN, ROBERT KENT, writer, magazine editor; b. Oakland, Calif., Nov. 23, 1953; s. Joel Adrian and Norma Jeanne (Arnold) L.; 1 child, Pudge. Student, U. Calif., Davis, 1972-76. Freelance writer, 1968—. Broadcaster, 1979-82; sr. editor PC World mag., San Francisco, 1983-90, contbg. editor, 1990-94; contbg. editor Calif. Republic mag., San Francisco, 1990-94, editor in chief Computer Currents Mag., 1994-2000; exec. editor CNET, 2000—. Author: The Swedish Catfish & Other Tales, 1979, Collected Works, Vol. 3, 1985, Going West, 1988, The Wit is Out, 1993; contbr. fiction, features and poetry to numerous publs., including Harper's, Mother Jones, Omni, Am. Film, Hudson Rev., Nantucket Rev., Christian Sci. Monitor, San Francisco Chronicle, Chgo. Tribune, Phila. Inquirer, PC mag., Computerworld, The Oregonian, Exec. Update, Grapevine Weekly; columnist Computer Currents, 1993-95. Adv. bd. mem. Baykeeper, San Francisco, 1994-96. Mem. ACLU, Amnesty Internat., Greenpeace, Environ. Defense Fund. Avocations: tennis, quoits, writing.

LUHRS, CAROL, physician; b. N.Y.C., Dec. 29, 1951; d. Eugene Frederick and Jane Elsie Luhrs; m. David Robert Blumenthal, Apr. 12, 1981; children: Alex Michael, Kelly Anne. BA, Hunter Coll., 1973; MD, SUNY, Bklyn., 1977. Diplomate Am. Bd. Internal Medicine, Am. Bd. Hematology and Med. Oncology, Am. Bd. Palliative Medicine. Intern, resident in internal medicine Kings County Hosp.-Downstate Med. Ctr., Bklyn., 1977-80; fellow in hematology/oncology Bklyn. VA Med. Ctr., 1980-83, staff physician, 1983-84, NIH postdoctoral trainee in hematology, 1984-86, staff physician, 1986-94, chief hematology/oncology sect., 1995—; asst. prof. SUNY Hlth. Scis. Ctr., Bklyn., 1986-94, assoc prof. clin. medicine, 1996—. Contbr. articles to profl. jours. NIH grantee, 1986-91, VA grantee, 1992-95. Mem. Am. Soc. Hematology, Am. Fedn. Clin. Rsch., Am. Soc. Clin. Oncology. Office: Bklyn VA Med Ctr 800 Poly Pl Brooklyn NY 11209-7104

LUI, ANTHONY TAT YIN, physicist; b. Hong Kong, Dec. 29, 1945; s. Siu Wai and Choi Dai (Chow) L.; m. Theresa Susan Szabo, Nov. 10, 1973; children: Jennifer, Michael, Victoria. BS, Hong Kong U., 1969; MS, U. Calgary, 1971, PhD, 1974. Postdoctoral fellow U. Calgary, 1974-75, U. Alaska, Fairbanks, 1975-76; rsch. assoc. NRC of Can., Ottawa, Ont., 1977-79, The Johns Hopkins U./Applied Physics Lab., Laurel, Md., 1979-83, sr. staff, 1984-85, prin. profl. staff, 1986—. Mem. steering com. of CDAW, NASA, Greenbelt, Md., 1984-90; mem. Grand Tour Cluster SDT, NASA Hdqts., Washington, D.C., 1990-92, mem. Mercury Orbiter SDT, 1996-99; mem. inter-agy. cons. group, NASA, 1993—; cons. Los Alamos Nat. Lab., N.Mex., 1990-95; external examiner for PhD degree, U. Calgary, Can., 1992. Editor: Magnetotail Physics, 1987 (JHU/APL Outstanding Publ. 1987); assoc. editor Geophys. Rsch. Letters, 1997-2000; contbg. author: Amazing Mysteries of the World, 1983; contbr. articles to profl. jours. Linkage grantee, NATO, 1993—96. Mem.: Am. Geophys. Union (chair student awards com. 1996—98). Home: 10809 Beech Creek Way Columbia MD 21044-1031 Office: Johns Hopkins U/Applied Phy 11100 Johns Hopkins Rd Laurel MD 20723-6005 Business E-Mail: tony.lui@jhuapl.edu.

LUI, ELWOOD, lawyer; b. LA, Feb. 4, 1941; BS, UCLA, 1962, MBA, 1964, JD, 1969. Bar: Calif. 1970, D.C. 1990; CPA, Calif. Dep. atty. gen. State of Calif., 1969-71; judge mcpl. ct. LA Judicial Dist., 1975-79, LA County Superior Ct., 1980-81; assoc. justice 2nd appellate dist. Calif. Ct. Appeals, 1981-87; mem. Jones, Day, L.A.; ptnr.-in-charge San Francisco office Jones Day. Mem. Judicial Coun. Calif., 1983-87; adj. prof. law U. So. Calif., 1977-87, Loyola U., LA, 1984. Fellow: Am. Acad. Appellate Lawyers; mem.: Calif. Acad. Appellate Lawyers. Office: Jones Day Ste 4600 555 S Flower St Los Angeles CA 90050 also: Jones Day 26th Fl 555 California St San Francisco CA 94104 Office Phone: 213-489-3939, 415-626-3939. Office Fax: 415-875-5700. Business E-Mail: elui@jonesday.com.

LUI, ERIC MUN, civil engineering educator; came to U.S., 1977; BS in Civil and Environ. Engring., U. Wis., 1980; MS in Civil Engring., Purdue U., 1982, PhD, 1985. Teaching asst. Purdue U., W. Lafayette, Ind., 1981-82, rsch. asst., 1983-85, post-doctoral rsch. asst., 1985-86, lectr., 1985-86; asst. prof. Syracuse (N.Y.) U., 1986-91, assoc. prof., 1992, dept. chair, 2003. Engring. cons. in field; advisor ASCE Student Chpt., 1992—, Hong Kong Cultural Assn., 1997—. Co-author: Structural Stability-Theory and Implementation, 1987, Stability Design of Steel Frames, 1991; author: Handbands of Stuctual Engineering, 2005; editor (assoc.): ASCE Jour. Structural Engring., 1994—97; editor: (book), 1997—2000; author: monographs; contbr. more than 80 articles to profl. jours., papers to sci. procs., chapters to books. Recipient Bleyer scholarship U. Wis., 1979, Bates & Rogers Found. scholarship, 1980, David Ross fellowship Purdue U., 1982, 83; recipient Nellie Munsion award 1982, Crouse Hinds award for Excellence in Edn. Syracuse U., 1997. Mem. ASCE, AAUP, Am. Concrete Inst., Am. Acad. Mechanics, Am. Inst. Steel Constrn., Am. Soc. Engring. Edn., Coun. Tall Bldgs. and Urban Habitat, Structural Stability Rsch. Coun., Tau Beta Pi, Phi Kappa Phi, Sigma Xi. Avocations: painting, classical music, piano playing. Business E-Mail: emlui@syr.edu.

LUICK-THRAMS, MICHAEL, history educator, writer; b. Mason City, Iowa, Dec. 18, 1962; s. Lu Warren Luick and Phyllis Thrams. BS in History, Iowa State U., 1985; MA in History and English, Goddard Coll., 1991; PhD in Modern European History, Humboldt U., Germany, 1997. Social worker Omega House, Mpls., 1985—90; tchr. Friends Acad., Locust Valley, NY, 1991; instr. Ostravska U., Ostrava, Czech Republic, 1991—93, Berliner Volkshochschulen, Berlin, 1993—97; exec. dir. Traces, Des Moines, 1997—. Democrat. Avocations: travel, reading, swimming. Home: 110 S 9th St Clear Lake IA 50428 Office: Traces 4810 Ingersoll #1 Des Moines IA 50312 Office Phone: 515-255-4836. Personal E-mail: michaelluickthrams@yahoo.com.

LUIGS, CHARLES RUSSELL, retired gas and oil drilling industry executive; b. Evansville, Ind., Apr. 4, 1933; s. Charles Anthony and Agnes A. (Russell) L.; m. Mary M. McClaine, Sept. 7, 1957; children: Charles Edwin, James Russell, Carol Lynn, Susan Nadine, Michael Alan. BS in Petroleum Engring., U. Tex., 1957; student, St. Edwards U., 1951-52. With U.S., Industries, various locations, 1957-76, v.p., 1969-71, exec. v.p., 1971-74, pres., 1974-76; dir. U.S. Industries, 1971-76; pres., chief exec. officer, dir. Global Marine, Inc., 1977-98, chmn. bd., 1982-99; ret., 1999. Mem. NSPE. Home: PO Box 4577 Houston TX 77210-4577 Office: Global Santa Fe Corp 15375 Memorial Dr Houston TX 77079

LUING, GARY ALAN, financial management educator; b. Collins, Iowa, Apr. 24, 1937; s. Dwight Orn and Marjorie Mae (Clemons) L.; m. Sherry Lea Gates, Dec. 19, 1954; 1 child, Heather Sherry-Anne. BS cum laude, Stetson U., 1960; MA, U. Ill., 1961; Dr. Adminstrn. (hon.), Canadian Sch. Mgmt. Auditor Arthur Andersen & Co., Chgo., 1963; prof. Fla. Atlantic U., Boca Raton, 1965—, dean Sch. Bus., 1970-87. Cons. U.S. Treasury; expert witness on valuing closely held corps., 1972—; lectr., U.S., various fgn. countries; dir. Fla. Liquid Assets, Templeton Trust Co., Stewart Pvt. Found., 1999—; mem. faculty Internat. Assn. Fin. Planners. Editor Fla. C.P.A., 1974; assoc. editor Intellect, 1975-79; tax editor Quick Print, 1988—; contbr. articles to profl. jours. Chmn. Palm Beach County Transp. Com., 1972-75; treas. Ridge Audubon Soc., 1997-98. Served to 1st lt. U.S. Army, 1961-63. Recipient Disting. Svc., Fla. Accountants Assn., 1991, Alumni Assn. award for Outstanding Svcs., Fla. Atlantic Univ., 1997. Hon. fellow Internat. Soc. Preventive Medicine, Canadian Sch. Mgmt.; mem. AICPA, Am. Acctg. Assn., Acctg. Rsch. Assn., Beta Gamma Sigma, Beta Alpha Psi, Phi Beta Phi (pres. 1974), Phi Kappa Phi. Baptist. Home: 2612 Lake Front Dr Lake Wales FL 33898-7206 Office Phone: 863-696-4804. Personal E-mail: luing@msn.com. Business E-Mail: luing@fau.edu. *In the professions, as in life, so much is owed to those who have gone before.*

LUIPPOLD, PETER HENRY, lawyer; b. Oak Ridge, Tenn., June 29, 1960; s. Henry Edward and Amelia Helen (Johnston) L. BA, Vanderbilt U., 1982; JD, U. Tenn., 1985; LLM, Georgetown U., 1986. Bar: Tenn. 1986, D.C. 1988. Pvt. practice, Oak Ridge, 1986—. Legal cons. Found. for Am.-Chinese Cultural Exchs., N.Y.C., 1987-91, participant Trade and Law Symposium, Shanghai, People's Republic China, 1990; co-organizer Tenn.-Taiwan Trade Conf., Knoxville, 1989. Mem. ABA. Avocations: electronics, astronomy, photography. Home: 105 Stanton Ln Oak Ridge TN 37830-8408 E-mail: luippold@aol.com.

LUISI-POTTS, BILLIE, not-for-profit executive; b. NYC; d. Harold Meisller and Mollie Ulano Meisner; 1 child, Thecla Luisi. AB, Hunter Coll., 1962; AM, Fordham U., 1964. Author: Ergonomics: A Problem Solvers Handbook, 1990, Small Scaled Goatkeeping, 1984, A First Book of Clay, 1970. Dir., bd. mem. Seneca County, C. of C., 2002—; adv. bd. mem. Students in Free Enterprise, Kenka. Coll. Recipient Thanks Be to Grandmother Winifred Found. award, 1998. Mem.: Seneca Falls Rotary Club (pres.). Avocations: gardening, hiking, painting, clay arts. Office: Nat Women's Hall of Fame 76 Fall St Seneca Falls NY 13148 Personal E-mail: bluisipotts@yahoo.com.

LUJAN, ROSA EMMA, bilingual specialist, trainer, consultant, assistant principal; b. El Paso, Tex., May 17, 1949; d. Rosendo G. and Petra (Rubalcava) López; m. Daniel Lujan, Feb. 21, 1976; children: Lorena Janel, Daniel Omar, Carina Viani, Crystal Rose. BA in Elem. Edn., U. Tex. El Paso, 1972, MS in Edn., 1978, postgrad., 1988, N.Mex. State U. Tchr. Ysleta Ind. Sch. Dist., El Paso, 1972-74, bilingual tchr., 1974-90, immigrant tchr., 1990—, now bilingual program supr. project mariposa. Cons. Internat. Acad. Coop. Learning, 1994; mem. Tex. Task Force on Profl. Preparation and Profl. Devel.; nat. bd. dirs. profl. tchg. stds. com. English as a New Lang., 1994; cooperating tchr. U. Tex. El Paso, 1978—; tchr. tnr. Ysleta Ind. Sch. Dist., 1980—; rschr. tnr. Johns Hopkins, U. Tex. El Paso, Haifa U., Israel, 1988—; mentor tchr. U. Tex. El Paso, El Salvador C.A., Boise, Idaho, 1990—; bd. dirs. Nat. Bd. for Profl. Tchg. Stds. Editor: (bilingual newsletter) El Chisme Bilingüe, 1986—. Pres. Ysleta Assn. Bilingual Edn., 1975-76, SW Assn. Bilingual Edn., El Paso, 1990-91; mem. Mt. Carmel Sch. Bd., El Paso, 1991-94, Tex. Com. Student Learning, Austin, 1992—. Named Tex. Tchr. of Yr., Tex. Edn. Agy., 1991-92, Tex. Elem. Tchr. of Yr., 1991-92. Mem. Nat. Assn. Bilingual Edn., Tex. Assn. Bilingual Edn., Phi Kappa Phi, Delta Kappa Gamma, Kappa Delta Pi. Democrat. Roman Catholic. Avocations: reading, sewing, travel, dance. Office: Ysleta Ind Sch Dist 9600 Sims Dr El Paso TX 79925-7200

LUKABU KHABOUJI N'ZAJI, diplomat; m. Mme. Lukabu. Amb. from Zaire U.N., North Caldwell, N.J. Office: Perm Mission of Zaire to UN 2 Henry Ave Caldwell NJ 07006-4589

LUKACS, JOHN ADALBERT, historian, retired educator; b. Budapest, Hungary, Jan. 31, 1924; came to U.S., 1946, naturalized, 1953; s. Paul and Magdalena Maria L.; m. Helen Schofield, May 29, 1953 (dec. 1970); children: Paul, Annemarie; m. Stephanie Harvey, May 18, 1974 (dec. 2003); m. Pamela Grant Hall, Apr. 30, 2005. PhD, Palatine Joseph U., Budapest, 1946; fed. doctorate (hon.). Prof. history Chestnut Hill Coll., 1947-94, Chmn. dept. history, 1947-74, ret., 1994; vis. prof. history La Salle Coll., 1949-82, Columbia U., 1954-55, U. Toulouse, France, 1964-65, U. Pa., 1964, 67, 68, Johns Hopkins U., 1970-71, Fletcher Sch. Law, Diplomacy, 1971-72, Princeton U., 1988; vis. prof. U. Budapest, 1991, U. Pa., 1995-97. Author books, including: The Great Powers and Eastern Europe, 1953, A History of the Cold War, 1961, Decline and Rise of Europe, 1965, The Passing of the Modern Age, 1970, Historical Consciousness, 1968, 2d edit., 1985, The Last European War, 1939-41, 1976; 1945, Year Zero, 1978, Philadelphia: Patricians and Philistines, 1900-1950, 1981, Outgrowing Democracy: A historical interpretation of the U.S. in the 20th Century, 1984, Budapest 1900, 1988, Confessions of an Original Sinner, 1990, The Duel (Hitler vs. Churchill 10 May-31 August 1940), 1991, the End of the 20th Century (and the End of the Modern Age), 1993, Destinations Past, 1994, The Hitler of History, 1997, George F. Kennan and the Origins of Containment 1944-46, 1997, A Thread of Years, 1998, Five Days in London, 1999, At the End of an Age, 2002, Churchill, Visionary, Statesman, Historian, 2002, Democracy and Populism, 2005, A John Lukacs Reader: The Remembered Past, 2005; contbr. numerous articles, essays, revs. to hist. and lit. jours. Mem. Schuylkill Twp. (Pa.) Planning Commn. Recipient Ingersoll prize, 1991, Order of Merit, Republic Of Hungary, 1994, Matthias Corvinus chain, 2001. Fellow Soc. Am. Historians; mem. Am. Catholic Hist. Assn. (pres. 1977), Am. Philos. Soc. Home: Pickering Close 129 Valley Park Rd Phoenixville PA 19460

LUKACS, MICHAEL EDWARD, electro-optics researcher; b. N.Y.C., Mar. 25, 1946; s. William and Hannah (LeWitter-Wolf) L.; m. Diane Harriet Katz, Oct. 29, 1967. Student, CUNY, Queens, 1965-68; T-3, Radio Corp. Am. Inst. now Tech Careers Inst., N.Y.C., 1968-69. Tech. aide Bell Telephone Labs., Holmdel, NJ, 1969-72, sr. tech. aide, 1972-77, assoc. mem. tech. staff, 1977-81, mem. tech. staff, 1981-83, Bell Comm. Rsch., Red Bank, NJ, 1983-94, rsch. scientist, 1994-99, Telcordia Techs. (formerly Bell Comms. Rsch.), Red Bank, NJ, 1999—2002; prin. scientist Innovative Tech. Solutions-NovaSol, Honolulu, 2002—. Patentee cathode ray tube dynamic focus apparatus, cathode ray tube electro-optic linearization device, infinitely expandable video conferencing sys., video conf. sys. with multilayer keying of multi video images; (co-inventor) pel recursive motion compensated video coder; (inventor) "Lukacs" coding, disparity corrected predictive coding for 3-D video, "Personal Presence System" advanced multimedia video bridge, multilayer priority video keying, infinitely extensible video conferencing. Recipient Notable Achievement award Bell Labs Research Lab. 113, 1983; R&D 100 award, 1996. Mem. IEEE, Assn. Computing Machinery (Best Paper award 1994), Soc. Motion Picture TV Engrs., Lasers & Electro Optical Soc. (LEOS). Avocations: science fiction, autocross, antique belt buckles. Personal E-mail: whoswho@mikelukacs.com. E-mail: michael.lukacs@nova-sol.com.

LUKAS, EDWARD MICHAEL, retired secondary school educator; b. Pa., Sept. 9, 1944; s. Edward Alvin and Emily Marie (Serafin) Lukas; m. Carol Lukas; 1 stepchild, Cherié Johnson. BA, King's Coll., Wilkes-Barre, Pa., 1966; MS, Scranton U., Pa., 1973. Elem. sch. tchr. Crestwood Sch. Dist., 1967, secondary sch. tchr. Edwardsville, Pa., 1968—99; pers. trainer Edwardsville, 1980—. Defensive coord., asst. football coach Wilkes U., 1974—81; asst. football coach King's Coll., 1967; head football coach Crestwood Sch. Dist., 1968—69, disciplinarian, 1996—98; asst. football coach Bishop O'Reilly H.S., 1970—74, strength coach, 1970—74. Author: Weight Training - The Truth. Recipient Presdl. award for weight tng., 1977, Appreciation award, Crestwood Sch. Dist., 1990. Mem.: Pa. State Edn. Assn., Nat. Football Coachs Assn. Republican. Avocations: weightlifting, football coaching, collecting music. Home: 71 Williams St Edwardsville PA 18704-1770

LUKASIEWICZ, PAUL MANUS, music educator; b. Scranton, Pa., June 10, 1976; s. Paul and Marilyn Lukasiewicz. MusB in Music Edn., Marywood U., 1999. Cert. music edn. Pa., 1999. Ch. musician St. Catherine of Sienna's Ch., Moscow, Pa., 1990—; music tchr. Scranton (Pa.) Sch. Dist., 1999—; pvt. music tchr. Scranton, 1999—. Music camp tchr. Marywood Univ. Music Camp, Scranton, 1994—. Composer: (band composition) Latin In Scranton, (church hymn) Mass Parts, (music for anniversary mass) arrangement of Hymn to St. Ann, (band composition) Sergent Weber March. Mem.: Music Educators Nat. Conf., Pi Kappa Lambda. Achievements include 4th Degree Black Belt in Soo Bahk Do.

LUKASZEWSKI, JAMES EDMUND, communications executive; b. Kewaunee, Wis., Aug. 27, 1942; s. Edmund Ignatius and Virginia Francis Lukaszewski; m. Barbara Ann Bray, Dec. 18, 1964; children: Charles Todd, James Moir. BA, Metropolitan State U., 1974. Asst., press sec. State of Minn., Office of Governor Wendell R. Anderson, St. Paul, 1974-76; deputy commr. Dept. of Econ. Devel., State of Minn., St. Paul, 1976-78; pres. Media Info. Systems Corp., New Brighton, Minn., 1978-83, Brum & Anderson Exec. Tng., Inc., Mpls., 1984-86; ptnr. Chester Burger Co., N.Y.C., 1986-87; sr. v.p., dir. exec. communication programs Georgeson & Co., Inc., 1987-89; pres., chmn. bd. The Lukaszewski Group Inc., White Plains, N.Y., 1989—. Lectr. East Coast Comdr.'s media Tng. Symposium, USMC, 1986—, Nat. Media Conf., N.Y.C., 1986-89; adj. assoc. prof. mgmt. & comm. Div. Degree Studies, Mktg. & Mgmt., NYU Sch. Continuing and Profl. Studies, 1991—; civilian advisor to internat. disaster adv. com., US Dept. State, 1990-94, to USMC, 1986—; commencement spkr. NYU Summer Inst. in Pub. Rels., 1997-2000, 04—; lectr. Conf. Bd. of Can., 2000, 01, Chief EH&S Officers' Coun., The Conf. Bd., 2000, Canadian Investor Rels. Inst., 2001, AssoComunicazione, Milan, 2003, U.S. Army World Wide Pub. Affairs Symposium, 2004, Govt. Can. Communicators Conf., 2005; lectr., spkr. in field. Author: Executive Television Training Handbook, 1983, The Publicity Handbook, 1984, Having Effective Media Interviews, 1984, Having Effective Media Interviews, 1984, The Tactical Ingenuity Pyramid, 1989, Executive Action Crisis Management Anthology, 1992, Executive Action Crisis Management Workbook, 1992, 93, Executive Action Emergency Media Relations Guide, 1992, 93, Influencing Public Attitudes: Strategies that Reduce the Media's Power, 1992; War Stories and Crisis Communication Strategies, An Anthology, 2000, Crisis Communication Planning Strategies, A Workbook, 2000, Media Relations Strategies During Emergencies, A Guide, 2000, (chpts.) Executive Action Crisis Communication Plan Components and Models, 2005, Crisis Response: Inside Stories on Managing Image Under Siege, 1993, Disaster Recovery Testing: Exercising Your Contingency Plan, 1994, Environmental Health and Safety Auditing Handbook, 1994, Practical Public Affairs in an Era of Change: A Cutting Edge Guide for Government, Business and College, 1995; (video cassette) Executive Action Crisis Management System; contbg. editor Pub. Rels. Quar., 1997—; author Strategy quar. supplement to P.R. Reporter, 1998-2003; guest columnist, mem. editl. bd. PR News, 2000-01, 2003—; mem. editl. bd. Ragan's Pub. Rels. jour., 2000-2001; editor TRUST newsletter, 2001-02; mem. adv. bd. Media Rels. Insider, 2001—; contr. columnist O'Dwyer's PR Services Report, 2003-; contbr. articles to profl. jours Chmn. Bklyn. Park Tater Daze Celebration, Minn., 1972, Met. State U. Alumni Assn., St. Paul, 1974; chmn. venture fund drive Met. State U., 1990-91; trustee, v.p. Met. State U. Found., St. Paul, 1976-86. Recipient Silver Key award Bklyn. Park Jaycees, Minn., 1973, Drew Middleton award for Disting. Svc. in Support of USMC East Coast Comdrs. Media Tng. Symposium, 1992, Outstanding Svc. award Choice in Dying, 1996, Nat. Pub. Rels. Achievement award Ball State U., 2004; named Sound Citizen of Yr. Park Jaycees, 1972; named one of 28 Experts to Call When All Hell Breaks Loose, Corp. Legal Times, 2003, 22 Crunch-Time Counselors Who Should Be on the Speed Dial in a Crisis, PR Week, 2004. Fellow Pub. Rels. Soc. Am. (accredited; Pres.'s Citation award 1991, 2000, bd. ethics and profl. stds., 1990-, past mem. Counselors Acad., corp., employee rels. and pub. affairs/govt. sections, NYC and Westchester/Fairfield chpts., Patrick Jackson Disting. Svc. award 2004); mem. Internat. Assn. Bus. Communicators (accredited), Pub. Rels. Soc. NY, Ctr. for Study of Presidency, Internat. Churchill Soc., Issue Mgmt. Coun., Fairfield County Pub. Rels. Assn. Avocations: writing, lecturing. Home: 16 Sunset Dr Snug Harbor Danbury CT 06811-3132 Office: Ten Bank St Ste 530 White Plains NY 10606

LUKE, CLIFFORD JAMES, medical educator; b. Staines, Middlesex, Eng., Sept. 7, 1971; s. Ronald Clifford and Valerie Langstaff Luke; m. Juliet Elizabeth Dyer, Apr. 21, 2001; children: James Clifford, Elizabeth Dyer. BSc in Biochemistry with honors, U. Liverpool, Eng., 1994; PhD, U. of Surrey, Eng., 1998. Rsch. fellow Harvard Med. Sch., Boston, 1998—2001, instr., 2001—04; asst. prof. Magee Women's Rsch. Inst., Pitts., 2004—; rsch. assoc. Children's Hosp., Boston, 2001—04; asst. prof. U. Pitts., 2004—. Contbr. articles to profl. jours. Fellow Aaron Janoff Rsch. fellow, Alphaone Found., 2001—03. Mem.: Biochemistry Soc. (life). Office: Magee Womens Research Insititue 204 Craft Ave Pittsburgh PA 15213 Office Phone: 412-641-1938. Home Fax: 412-641-5425; Office Fax: 412-641-5425. Personal E-mail: cliffnjuli@msn.com. E-mail: rsicjl@mwri.magee.edu.

LUKE, DAVID LINCOLN, III, retired paper company executive; b. Tyrone, Pa., July 25, 1923; s. David Lincoln and Priscilla Warren Luke; m. Fanny R. Curtis, June 11, 1955. AB, Yale U., 1945; LLD (hon.), Juniata Coll., 1967, Lawrence U., 1976, Salem Coll., 1983, W. Va. U., 1984; DSc. (hon.), Cold Spring Harbor Lab., 2001. V.p., dir. Westvaco Corp., N.Y.C., 1953-57, exec. v.p., dir., 1957-62, pres., bd. dirs., 1962-80, chief exec. officer, 1963-88, chmn. bd. dirs., 1980-96. Trustee emeritus, past chmn. Cold Spring Harbor Lab.; hon. bd. dirs., former bd. dirs. Josiah Macy Jr. Found.; past chmn., trustee emeritus Hotchkiss Sch. Served from aviation cadet to capt. USMCR., 1942-45. Mem. St. Andrew's Soc., The River Club, Piping Rock Club, Megantic Fish and Game Corp., John's Island Club.

LUKE, DAVID RUSSELL, mathematician, educator; b. Clifton Forge, Va., Apr. 20, 1969; s. Anne (Nina) Roosevelt and Nicholas James Gibson (Stepfather), Douglas Siglar and Sarah Mullen Luke (Stepmother); m. Anja Karin Sturm, June 15, 2001. BA cum laude, U. Calif., Berkeley, Calif., 1991; MSc, U. Wash., 1997, PhD, 2001. Wissenchaftliche assistent U. Goettingen, Germany, 2001—03; postdoctoral fellow Pacific Inst. Math. Scis., Vancouver, Canada, 2003—04; asst. prof. U. Del., Newark, Del., 2004—. Assistant editor (films) The Ride to Wounded Knee, 1992; dir.(prodr., editor): (films) 29 and 7 Strong, 1995. Vol. VISTA Okanogan (Wash.) Cmty. Action Coun., 1994—95. Fellow, NASA, 1998—2001, Pacific Inst. Math. Scis., 2002—04. Mem.: IEEE, Soc. Indsl. and Applied Math., Am. Math. Soc. Independent. Office: University of Delaware Department of Mathematics Newark DE 19716-2553

LUKE, DOUGLAS SIGLER, investment company executive; b. Middletown, N.Y., Oct. 1, 1941; s. Douglas Sigler Luke and Joanne (Benton) Cowles; m. Anne Sturgis Roosevelt, June 20, 1964 (div. Sept. 1976); m. Sarah Chappell Mullen, Mar. 23, 1991; children: Haven Roosevelt, David Russell, Lindsay Hall. Student, Mexico City Coll., 1961; BA Fgn. Affairs, U. Va., 1964; MBA, The Darden Sch., Charlottesville, Va., 1966. Mem. staff chem. divsn. WestVaco Corp., Covington, Va., 1966-69; dir. corp. planning SCOA Industries, Columbus, Ohio, 1969-71; v.p. fin. Multicon Prop. divsn. Bethlehem Steel Corp., Columbus, 1971-72; gen. ptnr., CEO, Personal Investments, Columbus, 1972-79; v.p. Rothschild, Inc. (formerly New Court Securities), N.Y.C., 1979-83, sr. v.p., 1984-87, mng. dir., 1987-90; pres, CEO, WLD Enterprises, Inc., Ft. Lauderdale, Fla., 1991-98; pres., CEO HL Capital, Inc., N.Y.C., 1999—. Bd. dirs. MeadWestraco Corp., N.Y.C., Regency Ctrs. Corp., Jacksonville, Fla.; mem. adv. bd. Nat. Outdoor Leadership Sch., 1994-99, trustee, 2000—. Founding donor Adopt-a-Class, N.Y.C., 1988;mem. space adv. bd. U. Colo., 1985-89; bd. dirs. condrs. com. Columbus Symphony Orch., 1972-75; trustee The Columbus Acad., Gahanna, Ohio, 1973-77, Girl Scouts U.S., Piedmont Region, Roanoke, Va., 1967-69, Adirondack Coun., 2001—, Adirondack Nature Conservancy, Adirondack Land Trust, 2004—; high tech. com. working group N.Y.C. Partnership Inc., 1988-90. Mem. Ausable Club (St. Huberts, N.Y.), Adirondack Mountain Reserve (St. Huberts, trustee 1985-94, pres. 1988-91, chmn. 1991-94), Va. Club/Yale Club (N.Y.C.), Mashomack Fish and Game Preserve (Pine Plains, N.Y.). Avocations: skiing, fly fishing, horsepacking, fox hunting. Office: HL Capital Inc The Chrysler Bldg 48th Fl 405 Lexington Ave New York NY 10174 Office Phone: 212-983-3170. Business E-Mail: dluke@hlcapitol.com.

LUKE, GREGORIO, museum director; With Cultural Inst. Mex., LA; dir. Mus. Latin Am. Art, Long Beach, Calif., 1999—. Recipient Mayoral Citation, Washington, DC, 1992, Irving Leonard Award, Hispanic Soc. of Libr. of Congress, 1995, Edn. Award, March of Dimes, 2001. Office: Mus Latin Am Art 628 Alamitos Ave Long Beach CA 90802*

LUKE, JOHN ANDERSON, JR., paper, packaging and chemical company executive; b. Nov. 24, 1948; s. John Anderson Luke Sr. and Joy (Carter) Luke; m. Kathleen Allen, June 30, 1984; children: Lindsay Allen, Elizabeth Carter, John A. III. BA, Lawrence U., 1971; MBA, U. Pa., 1979. Unit sales mgr. Procter & Gamble, 1974—77; corp. assoc. Westvaco Corp., N.Y.C., 1979—81, sr. fin. analyst, 1981—82, asst. treas., 1982, treas., 1983—86, v.p., treas., 1986, sr. v.p. mktg., internat. and Brazilian subsidiary, 1987—90, exec. v.p., 1990—92, pres., CEO, 1992—, chmn., 1996—. Dir. FM Global, The Timken Co.; trustee Am. Enterprise Inst. for Pub. Policy Rsch.; chmn. Am. Forest Found., Nat. Assn. Mfr.; vice chmn. Sustainable Forestry Bd.; bd. dirs. Bank of N.Y., The Tinker Found., Ams. Soc., Bank of N.Y.; bd. trustees Lawrence U.; mem. President's Export Coun. Bd. govs. NCASI; dir. United Negro Coll. Fund. Officer USAF, 1971—74, S.E. Asia, Vietnam conflict. Mem.: Am. Forest and Paper Assn. (dir., exec. com.), The Commonwealth Club, The Links, Univ. Club. Office: Westvaco Corp 299 Park Ave Fl 12 New York NY 10171-0009*

LUKE, RANDALL DAN, retired manufacturing executive, lawyer; b. New Castle, Pa., June 4, 1935; s. Randall Beamer and Blanche Wilhelmina (Fisher) L.; m. Patricia Arlene Moody, Aug. 4, 1962 (div. Jan. 1977); children: Lisa Elin, Randall Sargent; m. Saralee Frances Krow, Mar. 1, 1979; 1 stepchild, Stephanie Sogg. BA in Econs. with honors, U. Pa., 1957, JD, 1960. Bar: Ohio 1960, Calif. 1962, Ill. 1989. Assoc., ptnr. Daus, Schwenger & Kottler, Cleve., 1965-70; ptnr. Kottler & Danzig, Cleve., 1970-75, Hahn, Loeser, Freedheim, Dean & Wellman, Cleve., 1975-81; assoc. gen. counsel The Firestone Tire & Rubber Co., Akron, Ohio, 1981-82, v.p., assoc. gen. counsel and sec., 1982-88, Bridgestone/Firestone, Inc., Akron, 1988-91, ret., 1991; of counsel Hahn Loeser & Parks, Cleve., 1991-2000; ret., 2000. Trustee, Akron Art Mus., 1982-87, Akron Symphony Orch., 1986-87, Cleve. Opera League, 1992-98. Served to Capt. USNR, 1960-81; ret. 1981. Mem.: Ill. Bar Assn., Calif. Bar Assn., Union Club, Mayfield Country Club, Cleve. Skating Club. Republican. Avocations: tennis, golf, skiing, swimming, physical fitness. Home: 13901 Shaker Blvd Cleveland OH 44120-1582 Personal E-mail: danluke945@msn.com.

LUKEHART, CHARLES MARTIN, chemistry professor; b. DuBois, Pa., Dec. 21, 1946; s. David Blair and Grace Dorothy L.; m. Marilyn Orleana McKinney, Aug. 4, 1973; children: Mark, Brian, Laura. BS in Chemistry, Pa. State U., 1968; PhD in Inorganic Chemistry, MIT, 1972. Postdoctoral assoc. Tex. A&M U., College Station, 1972-73; asst. prof. chemistry Vanderbilt U., Nashville, 1973-77, assoc. prof. chemistry, 1977-82, prof., 1982—. Author: Fundamental Transition Metal Organometallic Chemistry, 1985. Rsch. fellow Alfred P. Sloan Found., 1979-81. Mem. Am. Chem. Soc. (chmn. Nashville sect. 1979, 92), Materials Rsch. Soc. Office: Vanderbilt U Dept Chemistry VU Station B 351822 Nashville TN 37235 Office Phone: 615-322-2935. Business E-Mail: charles.m.lukehart@vanderbilt.edu.

LUKENBILL, GREGG, real estate developer, sports promoter; b. Sacramento, Aug. 15, 1954; s. Frank and Leona L.; children: Jake, Molly, Ben. BSBA, Calif. State U., 1995, MBA, 1997. Owner, developer, builder Lukenbill Enterprises, Sacramento Valley Region; mng. gen. ptnr. Sacramento Kings Profl. Basketball/NBA, 1983-92, ARCO Arena, 1985-93; pres. Hyatt Regency, Sacramento, 1986-92; owner Sky King Inc.; pilot, pres. Lunkenbill Engerprises. Office: UNITH 3600 Power Inn Rd Sacramento CA 95826-3826

LUKENS, ALAN WOOD, retired ambassador, retired federal official; b. Phila., Feb. 12, 1924; s. Edward Clark and Frances (Day) L.; m. Susan Atkinson, Dec. 29, 1962; children: Lewis Alan, Susan Lukens, Frances Lukens Bennett, Timothy Eric. AB, Princeton U., 1948; postgrad., U. Sorbonne, Paris, 1948, U. Madrid, 1948, Georgetown U., 1951; LLD (hon.), St. Lawrence U., 1987. Tchr. St. Albans Sch., Washington, 1950-51; joined U.S. Fgn. Svc., 1951; vice consul Ankara, Turkey, 1952, Istanbul, Turkey, 1953; pub. affairs officer Martinique, 1954-56; with news divsn. State Dept., 1956-57; U.S. del. 12th UN Gen. Assembly, 1957; mem. internat. staff NATO, Paris, 1958-60; consul Brazzaville, 1960; U.S. rep. to Independence of Congo, Brazzaville, Chad, Gabon, Central African Republic, 1961; charge d'affaires Am. Embassy, Bangui, Central African Republic, 1961, Paris, 1961-63, Rabat, Morocco, 1963-65; chief personnel Bur. African Affairs, State Dept., 1965-67; dep. chief mission, counselor embassy Dakar, 1967-70, Nairobi, 1970-72; chief jr. officer div. personnel State Dept., 1973-75; dir. Office Iberian Affairs, 1974-75; counselor, dep. chief mission Am. Embassy, Copenhagen, 1975-78; with Bur. African Affairs, Dept. State, Washington, 1978-79; consul gen. Cape Town, South Africa, 1979-82; dir. office analysis for Western Europe, Bur. Intelligence and Research, Dept. State, Washington, 1982-84; A.E.& P. People's Republic of Congo, 1984-87; cons. on internat. affairs and crisis mgmt. Dept. of State, 1987-93. Washington rep. for Alvensa Corp. and World Water Corp.; lectr. on Africa. Former mem. Peace Commn. Washington Nat. Cathedral; former trustee Episcopal Acad., Merion, Pa.; coun. mem. Woodrow Wilson House, Washington; v.p. Fgn. Policy Discussion Group, Washington. With AUS, 1943-46. Recipient Commendable Service award State Dept., 1961 Mem. Washington Inst. Fgn. Affairs (pres. DACOR, Diplomatic and Consular Officers Ret. 2001-03), Princeton Club N.Y.C., Washington Club, Nairobi (pres. Paris chpt. 1961-63), Fgn. Affairs Retirees Md. (pres.), 20th Armored Divsn. Assn. (pres.), Princeton U. Alumni Coun. (mem. exec. com., pres. Class of 1946), Explorers Club Washington (bd. dirs., chmn. Washington group 2003—), Chevy Chase Club (gov. 1995-2000), Am. Legion (comdr. Post 18 2005—). Episcopalian. Home: 18 Grafton St Chevy Chase MD 20815-3428 E-mail: alanwlukens@aol.com.

LUKENS, DAVID CLOUGH, mathematics professor; b. Helena, Mont., Dec. 11, 1934; s. Alexander Macons Lukens and Julia Parks Remington; m. Eleanor Reed Sutherland, Sept. 7, 0184; children: Caroline Wetherill, John Reed, Martha Elizabeth Gardina, Charles Edward. BS in Sci. Tech., MIT, 1957; MAT, Harvard U., 1957; MA in History of Sci., U. Toronto, 1976, PhD in History of Sci., 1979. Instr. MIT, Cambridge, Mass., 1957—58, Dean Jr. Coll., Franklin, 1961—67, Cuttigton Coll., Suacoco, Liberia, 1967—74; tchr. St. Procopine High Sch., Chgo., 1979—80, St. Scholastica High Sch., 1980—81; carpenter Wilmett Real Estate, Evanston, 1981—91; tchr. Shimer Coll., Waukegan, 1991—. Pres. Dean Jr. Coll. Faculty Assn., Franklin, 1964—67; sec. Skiner Coll. Faculty, Waukegan, 1992—97. 1st lt. USAF, 1958—61. Home: 727 Reba Pl Evanston IL 60202

LUKENS, JOHN PATRICK, lawyer; b. Washington, Aug. 10, 1944; s. John F. and Patricia A. Lukens; m. Donna Lukens, Sept. 24, 1987; 4 children. BS, U. Idaho, 1970, JD cum laude, 1973. Pub. defender Clark County Pub. Defender, Las Vegas, 1974—76; pvt. practice Las Vegas, 1976—87; chief dep. dist. atty. Clark County Dist. Atty., Las Vegas, 1987—97; pvt. practice Las Vegas, 1997—. Contbr. articles to profl. jours. Founder Sexual Abuse Investigation Team Clinic at Child Haven, Clark County Child Death Rev. com. With U.S. Army, 1967-69. Recipient award Com. on Victim's Rights, 1989. Office: 625 S 8th St Las Vegas NV 89101

LUKENS, MAX L., manufacturing company executive; b. Wash., May 6, 1948; m. Chris Lukens; children: K.C., Nick, Reid, Patrick, Steven. BS, Miami U., Oxford, Ohio, 1970, MBA, 1971. With Deloitte Haskins & Sells, Washington and Dayton, Ohio, 1970-81; v.p. fin. Reed Tubular Products, Baker Hughes Inc. (formerly Baker Internat.), Houston, 1982-84, v.p. fin. Milpark, 1984-89, v.p., CFO, 1984-89, pres. Hughes Tool Co., 1989-93, pres. Baker Hughes Prodn. Tools, 1989-93, pres., COO, 1995-96, pres., CEO, 1996-98; chmn., CEO Baker Hughes Inc., Houston, 1998-99; pres., CEO Stewart & Stevenson Svcs., Houston, 2002—. Bd. dir. NCI Building Systems, Inc., Stewart & Stevenson Svcs. Office: Stewart & Stevenson Svcs 2707 North Loop West Houston TX 77008

LUKER, KRISTIN, sociology educator; b. San Francisco, Aug. 15, 1946; d. James Wester and Bess (Littlefield) L. BA, U. Calif., Berkeley, 1968; PhD, Yale U., 1974. Postdoctoral fellow U. Calif., Berkeley, 1974-75, asst. prof. sociology San Diego, 1975-81, assoc. prof., 1981-85, prof., 1985-86, co-dir. women's studies program, 1984-85, prof. jurisprudence and social policy and sociology Berkeley, 1986—. Doris Stevens prof. women's studies, prof. sociology Princeton (N.J.) U., 1993-95. Author: Taking Chances: Abortion and the Decision Not To Contracept, 1976 (hon. mention Jessie Bernard award), Abortion and the Politics of Motherhood, 1984 (Charles Horton Dooley award, 1985). Bd. dirs. Ctr. for Women's Studies and Svcs., San Diego, Ctr. Population Options, Washington. Grantee Guggenheim Found., 1985. Mem. Am. Sociol. Assn., Sociologists for Women in Society. Office: U Calif Jurisprudence and Social Policy 2240 Piedmont Ave Berkeley CA 94720-2150

LUKIAN, ROBERT HERMANN, professional tennis player, educator; b. Murray, Utah, Mar. 27, 1933; s. Alexis N. Romanoff and Elsie Aichinger; m. Ruth Ann Mulder, Oct. 10, 1980; m. Virginia Hallock, 1959 (div. 1978); children: Paula Lorraine, Brian Robert. Student, Marquette U., 1952—54; BA in Geography and Speech, Ariz. State U., 1961, MA in Phys. Geography and Secondary Edn., 1966. Cert. elem., secondary and jr. coll. tchr., tennis profl. U.S. Profl. Tennis Assn. Tchr. 5th grade Scottsdale Sch. Dist., Ariz., 1961—66, tchr. H.S., 1967—92; tennis pro Ariz., 1970—. Coach golf, tennis, softball, cross-country Scottsdale Sch. Dist. With USMC, 1954—57, Korea. Avocations: harmonica, reading, crossword puzzles, horseback riding. Personal E-mail: lukian@aol.com.

LUKIN, LESLIE E., school system administrator; b. Bethpage, N.Y., Sept. 29, 1959; d. George Ashbee and Doris Bowles Eastman; m. Mark Edward Lukin, May 16, 1987; children: Caitlin Bowles, Erin Elizabeth. BA with distinction, U. Va., 1981; MA, U. Nebr., 1984, PhD, 1989. Asst. prof. U. Mo., Columbia, 1989—94; coord. assessment Kansas City Schs., Mo., 1994—96;

assessment specialist Lincoln Pub. Schs., Nebr., 1996—2004, dir. assessment and evaluation, 2004—. Mem. editl. bd. Applied Measurement Edn., Lawrence Erlbaun, 1996—; mem. Stars Adv. Bd., Lincoln, 1999—. Contbr. articles to profl. publs. Troop leader Girl Scouts U.S., Lincoln, 2000—04; mem. Leadership Lincoln, 2003—04. DuPont Merit scholar, U. Va., 1977—81. Mem.: ASCD, Nat. Assn. Test Dirs., Nat. Coun. Measurement Edn. (editl. bd. 2001—02, Excellence in Classroom Assessment Tng. in Tchr. Edn. 2002), Am. Ednl. Rsch. Assn. (chmn. awards com. classroom assessment spl. interest group), Phi Delta Kappa. Avocation: reading. Office: Lincoln Pub Schs 5901 O St Lincoln NE 68510 Office Phone: 402-436-1790. E-mail: llukin@lps.org.

LUKKEN, WALT(ER), commissioner; m. Dana Bostic Lukken; 1 child. BS with honors, Ind. U. Kelley Sch. Bus., 1989; JD, Lewis and Clark Law Sch., 1992. Bar: Ill. Leg. asst. in fin. and tax matters office of Senator Richard Lugar, Washington, 1992—97; profl. staff agr. com. US Senate, Washington, 1998—2002; commr. Commodity Futures Trading Commn., Washington, 2002—, chmn., designated fed. official Global Markets Adv. Comm., 2003—. Office: CFTC 1155 21st St NW Washington DC 20581 Office Phone: 202-418-5014. Office Fax: 202-418-5550.*

LUKS, ALLAN BARRY, executive director; b. N.Y.C., June 27, 1941; s. Joseph Moses and Evelyn (Gropper) L.; m. Karen Greenbaum, Feb. 22, 1969; children: Rachel, David. BA, U. N.C., 1963; JD, Georgetown Law Sch., 1966. Bar: N.Y. Vol. U.S. Peace Corps, Maracay, Venezuela, 1967-69; legal dir. Children's Aid Soc. East Harlem, N.Y.C., 1970-72; asst. dir. Life Ins. Industry Urban Investment Program, N.Y.C., 1972-75; sec.-treas. N.Y.C. Rand Inst., 1975-78; exec. dir. Alcoholism Coun. of Greater N.Y., N.Y.C., 1978-88, Inst. for the Advancement of Health, N.Y.C., 1988-90, Big Bros./Big Sisters of N.Y., N.Y.C., 1990—. Author N.Y.C. law, warning posters on drinking during pregnancy, 1983; adj. prof. Fordham U. Grad. Sch. Social Svc., N.Y.C., 1979-88; chmn. legal sect. Internat. Coun. on Alcohol and Addictions, Lausanne, Switzerland, 1980-88; mem. NGO-Crime Prevention and Criminal Justice, UN, N.Y.C., 1982-90. Author: Will America Sober Up?, 1983, The Healing Power of Doing Good, 1991; co-author: You Are What You Drink, 1989; editor Having Been There, 1979. Pres. Cadman Towers Housing, Bklyn., 1971-75; sch. bd. mem. N.Y.C. Sch. Bd. #13, Bklyn., 1975-80; v.p. Brooklyn Heights Assn., N.Y.C., 1982-86; adv. coun. mem. Jr. League N.Y., N.Y.C., 1984-88. Recipient Vol. Leadership award Mayor of N.Y., N.Y.C., 1987, Pub. Svc. award Crains N.Y. Bus. Mag., N.Y.C., 1994. Office: Big Bros/Big Sisters NYC 223 E 30th St New York NY 10016-8203 E-mail: aluks@bigsnyc.org.

LUKSA, JOSEPH EDWARD, music educator; b. Wilkes-Barre, Pa., Nov. 30, 1962; s. Edward E. Luksa; m. Jennifer V. Sluzele, Jan. 12, 1970; 1 child, Katherine Carmel. MusB, Moravian Coll., 1984. Cert. tchr. Pa., 1987. Automobile reconditioner Bonner Chevrolet, Kingston, Pa., 1984—95; guitarist Reflections Wedding and Dance Band, 1986—87, Forerunner Wedding and Dance Band, 1987—95, Grand Tour Wedding and Dance Band, 1995—97; music tchr. Wyo. Valley West Sch. Dist., Kingston, Pa., 1995—. Mem.: Am. Fedn. of Musicians (assoc.), Music Educator's Nat. Conf. (assoc.). Home: 417 Charles Street Luzerne PA 18709-1509 Office: Wyoming Valley West School District 201 Chester Street Kingston PA 18704 Personal E-mail: mrluksa@aol.com.

LULING-HAUGHTON, ROSEMARY ELENA KONRADIN, writer, lecturer, non-profit organization executive; b. London, Apr. 13, 1927; d. Peter T. and Sylvia E. (Thompson) Luling; m. Algernon E. Haughton, June 19, 1948; children: Susanna, Benet and Barnabas (twins), Dominic, Mark and Andrew (twins), Philip, Luke, Elizabeth, Emma. Student, Slade Sch. of Art, London, 1944-45, La Grande Chaumiere, Paris, 1944-45, Holburn Sch. Arts and Crafts, London, 1945-46; DD (hon.), U. Notre Dame, 1977; DLitt (hon.), St. Mary's Coll., Ind., 1983. Founder, assoc. dir. Wellspring House, Inc., Gloucester, Mass., 1980—. Author 35 books, including The Passionate God, The Catholic Thing, Song in a Strange Land, The Tower that Fell, Images for Change, Gifts in the Ruins; over 200 articles. Recipient Avila award, U. Dayton award. Roman Catholic. Avocations: woodcarving, gardening, english cottage, embroidery. Home and Office: 302 Essex Ave Gloucester MA 01930-2351 Office Phone: 978-281-3221. Business E-Mail: rosemary@wellspringhouse.org. E-mail: rhaughton@wellspringhouse.org.

LULL, WILLIAM PAUL, engineering consultant; b. Indpls., Nov. 5, 1954; s. William Roger and Florence Elizabeth (Morris) L.; m. Mary Ann Garrison, Dec. 22, 1989. Student, Ind. State U., 1973-75; BS in Arts & Design, MIT, 1978. Systems designer James Assocs., Architects, Engrs., Indpls., 1978-79; architect TVA, Knoxville, Tenn., 1980; mgr. energy mgmt. div. Dubin-Bloome, Engrs., N.Y.C., 1981; asst. chief of design Syska & Hennessy, Engrs., N.Y.C., 1982-83; prin. Garrison/Lull Inc., Princeton Junction, N.J., 1984—. Adj. assoc. prof. NYU, 1983—; lectr., presenter cons. environ. field. Author: Conservation Environment Guidelines for Libraries and Archives, 1990; co-author: Criteria for Storage of Paper-Based Archival Records, 1984, Humidity Control Design Guide, 2001; contbr. articles to profl. publs. Mem. ASHRAE (conf. presenter), Illuminating Engring. Soc. N.Am., Am. Inst. Conservation of Historic and Artistic Works (assoc.), Sigma Pi Sigma. Achievements include pioneering discipline of consulting on conservation environments for preservation of museum library and archival collections. Home: 7 High St Allentown NJ 08501-1914 Office: Garrison/Lull Inc PO Box 459 Princeton Junction NJ 08550-0459

LUM, DALE WHITNEY, lawyer; b. N.Y.C., Dec. 14, 1957; s. Dorey and Jean (Hom) L. AB, Columbia U., 1979, JD, 1982. Bar: Calif. 1983, U.S. Dist. Ct. (no. dist.) Calif. 1983, U.S. Ct. Appeals (9th cir.) 1983. Assoc. Parker, Milliken, Clark & O'Hara, LA, 1982, Brown & Wood LLP (now Sidley Austin Brown & Wood LLP), LA, 1983-90, ptnr., 1991—. Mem. ABA, Calif. Bar Assn. Presbyterian. Avocation: golf. Home: 1545 Bairn Dr Hillsborough CA 94010-7202 Business E-Mail: dlum@sidley.com.

LUM, JEAN LOUI JIN, nursing educator; b. Honolulu, Sept. 5, 1938; d. Yee Nung and Pui Ki (Young) L. BS, U. Hawaii, Manoa, 1960; MS in Nursing, U. Calif., San Francisco, 1961; MA, U. Wash., 1969, PhD in Sociology, 1972. Registered nurse, Hawaii. From instr. to prof. Sch. Nursing U. Hawaii Manoa, Honolulu, 1961-95, acting dean, 1982, dean, 1982-89, prof. emeritus, 1995—. Project coordinator Analysis and Planning Personnel Svcs., Western Interstate Commn. Higher Edn., 1977; extramural assoc. div. Rsch. Grants NIH, 1978-79; mem. mgmt. adv. com. Honolulu County Hosp., 1982-96; mem. exec. bd. Pacific Health Rsch. Inst., 1980-88; mem. health planning com. East Honolulu, 1978-81; mem. rsch. grants adv. coun. Hawaii Med. Svcs. Assn. Found., Nat. Adv. Coun. for Nursing Rsch., 1990-93. Contbr. articles to profl. jours. Trustee Straub Pacific Health Found., Honolulu; bd. dirs. Friends of the Nat. Inst. of Nursing Rsch., 1994-97. Recipient Nurse of Yr. award Hawaii Nurses Assn., 1982; named Disting. Practitioner in Nursing, Nat. Acads. of Practice, 1986; USPHS grantee, 1967-72. Fellow Am. Acad. Nursing; mem. Am. Nurses Assn., Am. Pacific Nursing Leaders Conf. (pres. 1983-87), Council Nurse Researchers, Nat. League for Nursing (bd. rev. 1981-87), Western Council Higher Edn. for Nurses (chmn. 1984-85), Western Soc. for Research in Nursing, Am. Sociol. Assn., Pacific Sociol. Assn., Assn. for Women in Sci., Hawaii Pub. Health Assn., Hawaii Med. Services Assn. (bd. dirs. 1985-92), Western Inst. Nursing, Mortar Bd., Phi Kappa Phi, Sigma Theta Tau (Kupuna award 2003), Alpha Kappa Delta, Delta Kappa Gamma. Episcopalian. Office: U Hawaii Manoa Sch Nursing Webster Hall 2528 The Mall Honolulu HI 96822

LUM, JOHNNY, physician assistant, consultant; b. Kowloon, Hong Kong, Oct. 3, 1954; arrived in US, 1955; s. So Hong Lum and Shok Hing Yuen; m. Nancy Virginia Caron, May 13, 1995. Cert. in Respiratory Therapy, Bay City Coll., 1978; BA in Physician Asst., Trevecca Nazarene U., 1986; cert. in Surg. Tech., Bridgeport (Conn.) Hosp. Sch. of Nursing, 2001. Physician asst. Bapt. Med. Ctr., Jacksonville, Fla., 1986—87, Correctional Med. Systems, Inc., Reidsville, Ga., 1987—92, Beth Israel Med. Ctr., N.Y.C., 1992—96, The Vein Treatment Ctr., N.Y.C., 1996—97, Arthritis Ctr. Conn., Waterbury, Conn., 1997—2003, Danbury (Conn.) Internal Medicine Assocs., 2003—, Waterbury Hosp., Conn., 2004—. Cons. Pfizer, Miami, 2003—; lead project designer world Trade Ctr. Site Meml. Competition Lower Manhattan (N.Y.) Devel. Corp., N.Y.C., 2003—. Mem.: Soc. Physician Asst. Rheumatology, Conn. Acad. Physician Assts., Am. Acad. Physician Asst. Home: 4-6 Union Avenue 20 Norwalk CT 06851 Office: Waterbury Hosp 64 Robbins St Waterbury CT 06708 Office Phone: 203-573-6548. Personal E-mail: jlum090@aol.com.

LUM, LARRY, lawyer; b. Hong Kong, Dec. 25, 1960; BA, SUNY, Stony Brook, 1983; JD, Albany Law Sch., Union U., 1986. Bar: NY 1987, US Dist. Ct. So., We. & Ea. Districts NY. Ptnr. Wilson, Elser, Moskowitz, Edelman & Dicker LLP, NYC. Mem.: ABA, Nat. Asian Am. Bar Assn., Assn. of the Bar of the City of NY. Office: Wilson Elser Moskowitz Edelman & Dicker LLP 23rd Fl 150 E 42nd St New York NY 10017-5639 Office Phone: 212-490-3000 ext. 2292. Office Fax: 212-490-3038. Business E-Mail: luml@wemed.com.

LUM, MARY, artist, art educator; BFA, U Mich.; MFA, Rochester Inst. Tech. Mem. faculty Sch. Art & Design, Albert U., NY, 1984—2004, prof. painting, co-chair MFA program in electronic integrated arts; mem. faculty painting and drawing Bennington Coll., Vt., 2005—. Work exhibited at, Hallwalls, Buffalo, NY, INTAR Gallery, NYC, Washington Project for the Arts, Washington, DC, So. Exposure, San Francisco, Art in General, NYC, Burchfield Art Ctr. and State Mus. of NY, Buffalo, Kean Coll., Union, NJ, Printed Matter, NYC, Ernest Rubenstein Gallery, U. Wis., Bernard Toale Gallery, Boston, Paris Project Room, 2002, Aldrich Contemporary Mus. Art, Ridgefield, CT, 2004. Grantee, Nat. Endowment for the Arts, NY Found. for the Arts, Constance Saltonstall Found. for the Arts, NY State Coun. on the Arts; Radcliffe Inst. Fellow, Harvard U., 2004—05, residency, Cite Internationale des Arts, Paris, Internat. Studio/Curatorial Program, NY, MacDowell Colony, Petersborough, NH, 2003. Office: Bennington Coll 1 Coll Dr Bennington VT 05201-6003*

LUM, RODGER G., city health department administrator; BS in Clin. Psychology, PhD in Clin. Psychology, U. Calif., Berkeley. Adj. faculty mem. Calif. Sch. Profl. Psychology, Alameda; exec. dir. Asian Cmty. Mental Health Svcs., Oakland, Calif., 1979—88; asst. dir. Alameda Co. Health Care Svcs. Agy., Oakland, Calif.; dir. Alameda Co. Social Svcs. Agy., Oakland, Calif., 1992—2001, Co. of San Diego Health and Human Svcs. Agy., San Diego, 2001—. Office: County of San Diego Health & Human Svcs Agency 1700 Pacific Hwy Rm 207 San Diego CA 92101

LUMAN, MITCHELL DEAN, museum administrator, director; b. Fostoria, Ohio, Sept. 14, 1959; s. Michael Dean Luman and Carol Johanna Pope; m. Loraine Marie Cook, June 18, 1982; children: Dean Michael, Jeremy Lee. BS in Edn., Ohio State U., Columbus, Ohio, 1981. Cert. Mgmt. U. So. Ind., 1996. Tchr. Cin. Pub. Schs., Cin., 1981—82; curator astronomy Hastings Mus., Hastings, 1982—85; george and dorothy eykamp dir. koch sci. ctr. and planetarium Evansville Mus. of Arts, History and Sci., Evansville, Ind., 1985—; fl. supr./planetarium operator Ctr. of Sci. and Industry, Columbus, Ohio, 1979—81. Peer reviewer Inst. of Mus. and Libr. Svcs., Washington, 1988—; site surveyor Am. Assn. of Mus., Washington, 1995—; co-chair alcon 98 Astron. League; developer Midwest Mus. Consortium, 1999—2002. Developer (exhibitions) Our Vanishing Sky. Pres. Wadesville-Blairsville Regional Sewer Dist., Wadesville, Ind., 2004; sch. bd. candidate North Posey Met. Sch. Dist., Poseyville, Ind., 2000. Fellow: Gt. Lakes Planetarium Assn. (hon. Svc. Award 2002); mem.: Am. Assn. of Musuems (assoc.), Internat. Dark Sky Assn. (assoc.). Achievements include design of Developer/Co-Developer of 30 original sci. and tech. exhbns. for museum display. Avocations: bicycling, astronomy. Office: Evansville Mus 411 SE Riverside Dr Evansville IN 47713 Office Phone: 812-425-2406. Home Fax: 812-421-7509; Office Fax: 812 425-2406. Personal E-mail: mluman@emuseum.org.

LUMB, WILLIAM VALJEAN, veterinarian; b. Sioux City, Iowa, Nov. 26, 1921; m. Lilly Carlson, 1949; 1 child, John W. DVM, Kans. State U., 1943; MS, Tex. A&M U., 1953; PhD in Vet. Medicine, U. Minn., 1957; DSc (hon.), Ohio State U., 1999. Intern, resident Angell Meml. Animal Hosp., Boston, 1946—48; from instr. to assoc. prof. medicine and surgery Tex. A&M U., 1949—52; asst. prof. clin. surgery Colo. State U., 1954—58; assoc. prof. surgery and medicine Mich. State U., 1958—60; assoc. prof. medicine Coll. Vet. Medicine, Colo. State U., Ft. Collins, 1960—63, dir. surg. lab., 1963—79, prof. surgery, 1963—81, emeritus prof., 1981—; prof. Ross U., St. Kitts, West Indies, 1986. Pres., CEO The Lubra Co., 1972—99. Author: Small Animal Anesthesia, 1963; author: (with E.W. Jones) Veterinary Anesthesia, 1973, 1984, Veterinary Anesthesia, Japanese and Spanish translations, 1979; editor: Vet Surgery, 1982; contbr. over 150 articles to profl. jours.; patentee in field. With Vet. Corps U.S. Army, 1943—46. Named Colo. Vet. of Yr., 1981; recipient Gaines medal, 1965, Ralston Purina Rsch. award, 1980, Disting. Svc. award, Kans. State U., 1982, Jacob Markowitz award, 1986, Glover Disting. Faculty award, Colo. State U., 2004. Mem.: NAS, AAAS, AVMA, Nat. Acads. of Practice, Am. Assn. Vet. Clinicians, N.Y. Acad. Sci., Am. Coll. Vet. Surgeons (founding diplomate, pres., chmn. bd. 1974—75), Am. Coll. Vet. Anesthesiologists (founding diplomate, Svc. award 1982). Address: 1905 Mohawk St Fort Collins CO 80525-1501

LUMBARD, ELIOT HOWLAND, lawyer, educator; b. Fairhaven, Mass., May 6, 1925; s. Ralph E. and Constance Y. L.; m. Jean Ashmore, June 21, 1947 (div.); m. Kirsten Dehner, June 28, 1981 (div.); children: Susan, John, Ann, Joshua Abel, Marah Abel. BS in Marine Transp., U.S. Mcht. Marine Acad., 1943—45; BS in Econs., U. Pa., 1949; JD, Columbia U., 1952; DSc (hon.), SUNY, 2005. Bar: N.Y. 1953, U.S. Supreme Ct. 1959, Pa. 1983. Assoc. Breed, Abbott and Morgan, N.Y.C., 1952-53; asst. U.S. atty. So. Dist. N.Y., 1953-56; assoc. Chadbourne, Parke, Whiteside & Wolff, N.Y.C., 1956-58; ptnr. Townsend & Lewis, N.Y.C., 1961-70, Spear and Hill, N.Y.C., 1970-75, Lumbard and Phelan, P.C., N.Y.C., 1977-82, Saul, Ewing, Remick & Saul, N.Y.C., 1982-84; pvt. practice law N.Y.C., 1984-86; ptnr. Haight, Gardner, Poor & Havens, N.Y.C., 1986-88; pvt. practice law N.Y.C., 1988-92; ret. Chief counsel N.Y. State Commn. Investigation, 1958-61; spl. asst. counsel for law enforcement to Gov. N.Y., 1961-67; organizer N.Y. State Identification and Intelligence Sys., 1963-67; chair Oyster Bay Conf. on Organized Crime, 1962-67; criminal justice cons. to Gov. Fla. and other states, 1967; chief criminal justice cons. to N.J. Legis., 1968-69; chmn. com. on organized crime N.Y.C. Criminal Justice Coordinating Coun., 1971-74; organizer schs. of criminal justice at SUNY Albany and Rutgers, Newark; mem. departmental disciplinary com. First Dept., N.Y. Supreme Ct., 1982-88; trustee bankruptcy Universal Money Order Co., Inc., 1977-82, Meritum Corp., 1983-89; spl. master in admiralty Hellenic Lines Ltd., 1984-86; chmn. Palisades Life Ins. Co. (former Equity Funding subs. 1974-75); bd. dir. RMC Industries Corp.; chair Am. Maritime History Project, Inc., Kings Point, N.Y., 1996—; lectr. trial practice NYU Law Sch., 1963-65; mem. vis. com. Sch. Criminal Justice, SUNY-Albany, 1968-75; adj. prof. law and criminal justice John Jay Coll. Criminal Justice, CUNY, 1975-86; arbitrator Am. Arbitration Assn. and N.Y. Civil Ct.-Small Claims Part, N.Y. County; mem. Vol. Master Program U.S. Dist. Ct. (so. dist.) N.Y. Contbr. articles to profl. jours. Bd. dirs. Citizens Crime Commn. N.Y.C., Inc., Big Bros. Movement, Citizens Union; trustee Trinity Sch., 1964-78, N.Y.C. Police Found., Inc., 1971-92, chmn., 1971-74, emeritus. Lt. j.g. USNR, 1943-52. Recipient Disting. Svc. award SUNY, Albany, 2000, US Merchant Marine Acad., 2005 Mem. Assn. Bar City N.Y., N.Y. County Lawyers Assn., ABA, N.Y. State Bar Assn., Maritime Law Assn., Down Town Assn. Club. Republican. Home: 10 Allds St #357 Nashua NH 03060

LUMBERG, JAMES JOSEPH, literature educator; b. Jacksonville, Fla., Feb. 23, 1942; s. Allen Bernard Lumberg and Margaret Mosher; children: James McGahn, Rachel. BA in English, St. Mary's Coll., 1964; MA in English, Calif. State U., L.A., 1992; MD, St. John's Sem., 1998. Tchr. high sch. L.A. Unified Sch. Dist., 1996—2003. Author of poems. Spl. advisor M.C. & S.B. Mesar Found., Santa Barbara; sponsor Homeless Shelter, Garden Grove. Home: 1030 Somberro Rd Pebble Beach CA 93953

LUMENG, LAWRENCE, physician, educator; b. Manila, Aug. 10, 1939; came to US, 1958; s. Ming and Lucia (Lim) Lu; m. Pauline Lumeng, Nov. 26, 1966; children: Carey, Emily. AB, Ind. U., 1960, MD, 1964, MS, 1969. Intern U. Chgo., 1964-65; resident Ind. U. Hosps., Indpls., 1965-67, fellow, 1967-69, asst. prof. Sch. of Medicine, 1971-73, assoc. prof. Sch. of Medicine, 1974-79, prof. Sch. of Medicine, 1979—2003, dir. div. gastroenterology and hepatology Sch. of Medieine, 1984—; chief gastroenterology sect. VA Med. Ctr., Indpls., 1979—2003. Merit rev. bd. VA. Cen. Office, Washington, 1981-84; alcohol biomed. res. rev. com. NIAAA, Washington, 1982-86; grant rev. panel USDA, Washington, 1985-2003. Contbr. over 290 articles to profl. jours. Maj. U.S. Army, 1969-71. Fellow ACP; mem. Am. Soc. Clin. Investigation, Am. Soc. Biol. Chemists, Rsch. Soc. on Alcoholism (treas. 1985-87, sec. 1987-89), Am. Gastroenterological Assn., Am. Assn. Study Liver Diseases, Am. Assn. Physicians, Cen. Soc. Clin. Rsch., Am. Liver Found. (vet. hepatitis C liver disease coun.), Am. Coll. Gastroenterology. Avocations: painting, music, gardening. Office: Ind U Med Ctr 975 W Walnut St Indianapolis IN 46202-5181 Office Phone: 317-274-3505. Business E-Mail: lluming@iupui.edu.

LUMET, SIDNEY, film director; b. Phila., June 25, 1924; s. Baruch and Eugenia (Wermus) L.; m. Rita Gam, 1949 (div. 1954); m. Gloria Vanderbilt, Aug. 27, 1956 (div. 1963); m. Gail Jones, Nov. 23, 1963 (div. 1978); m. Mary Gimbel, Oct. 1980; children: Amy, Jenny. Ed., Profl. Children's Sch.; student, Columbia. Tchr. acting High Sch. of Profl. Arts. Appeared as child actor in several plays including Dead End, 1935, George Washington Slept Here, 1940-41, My Heart's in the Highlands, 1939; dir. summer stock, 1947-49; assoc. dir., CBS, 1950, dir., 1951-57; Dir.(films) Twelve Angry Men, 1957, Stage Struck, 1958, That Kind of Woman, 1959, The Fugitive Kind, 1960, A View from the Bridge, 1961, Long Days Journey into Night, 1962, Fail Safe, 1964, The Pawnbroker, 1965, The Hill, 1965, The Group, 1966, The Appointment, 1969, (with Joseph L. Mankiewicz) King: A Filmed Record-...Montgomery to Memphis, 1969, The Anderson Tapes, 1971, Child's Play, 1972, The Offence, 1973, Serpico, 1974, Lovin' Molly, 1974, Murder on the Orient Express, 1974, Dog Day Afternoon, 1975, Network, 1976, Equus, 1977, The Wiz, 1978, Deathtrap, 1981, The Verdict, 1982, Garbo Talks, 1984, Power, 1985, The Morning After, 1986, Running on Empty, 1988, Family Business, 1989, A Stranger Among Us, 1992, Guilty As Sin, 1993, Gloria, 1998, Whistle, 2000, The Beautiful Mrs. Selderman, 2000, Rachel, quand du seigneur, 2004; dir., prodr. The Deadly Affair, 1966, Bye Bye Braverman, 1968, The Sea Gull, 1968, Last of the Mobile Hot Shots, 1970, Just Tell Me What You Want, 1980, Critical Care, 1997; dir., exec. prodr., Daniel, 1983, dir., screenwriter Prince of the City, 1981, Q & A, 1990, Night Falls on Manhattan, 1997; dir. (TV movies) All the King's Men, 1958, The Iceman Cometh, 1960, Rashomon, 1960, Strip Search, 2004; dir., prodr., Mr. Broadway, 1957; dir. (TV series) Studio One, 1948, Danger, 1950, Crime Photographer, 1951, CBS Television Workshop, 1952, You Are There, 1953, The United States Steel Hour, 1953, The Best of Broadway, 1954, The Elgin Hour, 1954, The Alcoa Hour, 1955, Playhouse 90, 1956; dir., writer, exec. prodr., 100 Centre Street, 2001; dir. (TV mini series) The Sacco-Vanzetti Story, 1960; over 200 plays for, TV Playhouse 90, Kraft TV Theatre, Studio One; staged: play Caligula, 1960; Author: (with Alfred A. Knopf) Making Movies, 1995. Recipient D.W. Griffith Lifetime Achievement award, 1993, Hon. Acad. award for Lifetime Achievement, 2005 Mem. Dirs. Guild Am. (hon. life). Address: ICM 8942 Wilshire Blvd Ste 219 Beverly Hills CA 90211-1934*

LUMLEY, JOHN LEASK, physicist, researcher; b. Detroit, Nov. 4, 1930; s. Charles S. and Jane Anderson Campbell (Leask) L.; m. Jane French, June 20, 1953; children: Katherine Leask, Jennifer French, John Christopher. BA, Harvard, 1952; MS in Engring., Johns Hopkins, 1954, PhD, 1957; Doctorate honoris causa, U. de Poitiers, France, 2004; Haute distinction honoris causa, Ecole Central de Lyon, France, 1987. Postdoctoral fellow Johns Hopkins, 1957-59; mem. faculty Pa. State U., 1959-77, prof. aerospace engring., 1963-74, Evan Pugh prof. aerospace engring., 1974-77; Willis H. Carrier prof. engring. Cornell U., 1977-2001, prof. emeritus, 2001—. Prof. d'echange U. d'Aix-Marseille, France, 1966-67; Fulbright sr. lectr. U. Liege; vis. prof. U. Louvain-La-Neuve, Belgium; Guggenheim fellow U. Provence and Ecole Centrale de Lyon, France, 1973-74. Author: (with H.A. Panofsky) Structure of Atmospheric Turbulence, 1964, Stochastic Tools for Turbulence, 1970, (with H. Tennekes) A First Course in Turbulence, 1971, (with P. Holmes and G. Berkooz) Turbulence, Coherent Structures, Dynamical Systems and Symmetry, 1996, Engines: An Introduction, 1999, Still Life with Cars: An Automotive Memoir, 2005; also articles; editor: (with A. Acrivos, L.G. Leal and S. Leibovich) Research Trends in Fluid Dynamics, 1996; tech. editor: Statistical Fluid Mechanics, 1971, 75, Variability of the Oceans, 1977; assoc. editor: Physics of Fluids, 1971-73; assoc. editor Ann. Rev. of Fluid Mechanics, 1976-85, co-editor, 1986-99, 03—, editor, 1999-03; chmn. tech. edit. bd. Izvestiya: Atmospheric and Oceanic Physics, 1971-96; editorial bd.: Fluid Mechanics: Soviet Research, 1972-94; editor Theoretical and Computational Fluid Dynamics, 1989-98; prin.: films Deformation of Continuous Media, 1963, Eulerian and Lagrangian Frames in Fluid Mechanics, 1968. Recipient medallion U. Liege, Belgium, 1971, Timoshenko medal ASME, 1993. Fellow Am. Acad. Arts and Scis., Am. Acad. Mechanics, Am. Phys. Soc. (exec. com. divsn. fluid dynamics 1972-75, 81-84, chmn. exec. com. divsn. fluid dynamics 1982, 87-89, Fluid Dynamics prize 1990), AIAA (fluid and plasma dynamics award 1982, Hugh L. Dryden rsch. lectureship 1996); mem. NAE, AAAS, N.Y. Acad. Sci., Soc. Natural Philosophy, Am. Geophys. Union, Johns Hopkins Soc. Scholars (charter), Sigma Xi. Home: 743 Snyder Hill Rd Ithaca NY 14850-8708 Office: Cornell U 256 Upson Hall Ithaca NY 14853-7501 Office Phone: 607-255-0992. Business E-Mail: jll4@cornell.edu.

LUMMIS, CYNTHIA MARIE, state official, lawyer; b. Cheyenne, Wyo., Sept. 10, 1954; d. Doran Arp and Enid (Bennett) L.; m. Alvin L. Wiederspahn, May 28, 1983; children: Annaliese Alex. BS, U. Wyo., 1976, BS, 1978, JD, 1985. Bar: Wyo. 1985, U.S. Dist Ct. of Wyo. 1985, U.S. Ct. of Appeals (10th cir.) 1986. Rancher Lummis Livestock Co., Cheyenne, 1972—; law clk. Wyo. Supreme Ct., Cheyenne, 1985-86; assoc. Wiederspahn, Lummis & Liepas, Cheyenne, 1986—; treas. State of Wyo., 1999—. Mem. Wyo. Ho. Judiciary Com., 1979-86, Ho. Agriculture, Pub. Lands & Water Resources Com., 1985-86, Wyo. State Senate, 1993-94, Senate Judiciary Com., 1993-94, Senate Mines, Minerals, Econ. Devel. Com., 1993-94, U. Wyo. Inst. for Environment and Natural Resource Policy and Rsch.; chmn. County Ct. Planning Com., Wyo., 1986-88, Ho. Rev. Com., 1987-92, Joint Revenue Interim Com., 1988-89, 91-92; mem. adv. bd. U. Mont. Ctr. for the Rocky Mountain West, 1998—. Sec. Meals on Wheels, Cheyenne, 1985-87; mem. Agrl. Crisis Support Group, Laramie County, Wyo., 1985-87; mem. adv. com. U. Wyo. Sch. Nursing, 1988-90; mem. steering com. Wyo. Heritage Soc., 1986-89. Mem.: Rep. Women's (Cheyenne) (legis. chmn. 1982). Republican. Lutheran. Office: State Treasurer 200 W 24th St Cheyenne WY 82002-0001

LUMPKIN, MURRAY M., federal agency administrator; m. Janet Lucille Rose, Dec. 22, 1978; 2 children. BA in German, Davidson Coll., 1975; MD, Wake Forest U., 1979; MSc in Med. Parasitology, U. London, 1984. Resident in pediats., fellow pediatric infectious disease Mayo Clinic, Rochester, Minn., 1979-83; chief pediatric infectious diseases E. Tenn. Children's Hosp., Knoxville, 1984-87; med. dir. Abbott Labs., Abbott Park, Ill., 1987-89; dir. divsn. anti-infective drug products FDA, Rockville, Md., 1989-93, dep. dir. Ctr. for Drug Evaluation and Rsch., 1993—2000, prin. assoc. commr., 2000—03, acting dep. commr. internat. and spl. programs, 2003—. Fulbright scholar. Mem. Am. Acad. Pediats. Avocations: history, geography, biking, organ, hiking. Office: FDA HF 3 5600 Fishers Ln Rockville MD 20852

LUMSDEN, IAN GORDON, art gallery director; b. Montreal, Que., Can., June 8, 1945; s. Andrew Mark and Isobel Dallas (Wilson) L.; m. Katherine Elizabeth Carson, July 28, 1979; 1 child, Craig Ian. BA, McGill U., 1968; postgrad., Mus. Mgmt. Inst., U. Calif., Berkeley, 1991. Curator art dept. N.B. Mus., Saint John, 1969; curator Beaverbrook Art Gallery, Fredericton, N.B., 1969-83, dir., 1983-2001; rsch. fellow Nat. Gallery, Canada, 2003—04. Mem. Cultural Property Export Rev. Bd., 1982-85; mem. program com. 49th Parallel Ctr. for Contemporary Can. Art, 1990-92, The Beaverbrook Art

Gallery Collection: Selected Works, 2000. Author exhbn. catalogues; contbr. articles to profl. jours. Mem. Can. Museums Assn. (sec.-treas. 1973-75), Can. Art Mus. Dirs. Orgn. (1st v.p. 1977-83, pres. 1983-85, treas. 1998-2001), Atlantic Provinces Art Gallery Assn. (chmn. 1970-72), Am. Assn. Museums, Union Club (St. John, N.B.), Can. Soc. for the Decorative Arts (dir. nat. coun. 1999). Mem. Anglican Ch. of Can. Home: 103 Bliss Carman Dr Fredericton NB Canada E3B 9P2 Office Phone: 506-455-7666. E-mail: lums@nb.sympatico.ca.

LUNA, MICHAEL DONOVAN, speech language pathologist; b. Panorama City, Calif., Dec. 10, 1968; s. Don Dickerson and Gloria Ruth Luna. BA in Comm. Sics. and Disorders, San Jose (Calif.) State U., 1993, MA in Speech Pathology and Audiology, 1995, MA in Edn. Adminstrn. and Supr., 2004. Lic. speech-lang. pathologist, Calif. Environ. chemist Animetrix, San Jose, 1989-90; warehouseman, dock worker W. W. Grainger, San Jose, 1990-95; speech-lang. pathologist San Jose Unified Sch. Dist., 1995-97, 99—; rsch. asst. Ariz. State U., Tempe, 1997-99, instr., 1998. Mem. leadership teams S. Valley Christian Ch., San Jose, 1993-96; sponsor Say No Drugs, San Jose, 1995; asst. scoutmaster Boy Scouts Am., San Jose, 1996. Specialist U.S. Army, 1990-91, Gulf War. Graduate scholar Ariz. State U., 1997. Mem. Am. Speech Lang. and Hearing Assn. Avocations: playing and writing music for piano, synthesizer, organ and guitar, cross-country running, kayaking, snow-boarding. Office: San Jose Unified Sch Dist Willow Glen Mid Sch 2105 Cottle Ave San Jose CA 95125-3502

LUNA, PATRICIA ADELE, marketing executive; b. Charleston, SC, July 22, 1956; d. Benjamin Curtis and Clara Elizabeth (McCrory) L. BS in History, Auburn U., 1978, MEd in History, 1980; MA in Adminstrn., U. Ala., 1981, EdS in Adminstrn., 1984, postgrad. in Adminstrn. Cert. tchr., Ga., Ala. History tchr. Harris County Mid. Sch., Ga., 1978-79, head dept., 1979-81; residence hall dir. univ. housing U. Ala., 1981-83, asst. dir. residence life, 1983-85; intern Cornell U., Ithaca, NY, 1983; dir. mktg. Golden Flake Snack Foods, Inc., Birmingham, Ala., 1985-89; sr. v.p. Quest U.S.A., Inc., Atlanta, 1989-90; pres. Promotion Mgmt. Group, Inc., Montgomery, Ala., 1990—. Cons. Capital Campaigns; lectr. in field. Author: Specialization: A Learning Module, 1979, Grantsmanship, 1981, Alcohol Awareness Programs, 1984, University Programming, 1984, Marketing Residential Life, 1985, The History of Golden Flake Snack Foods, 1986, Golden Flake Snack Foods, Inc., A Case Study, 1987, Cases in Strategic Marketing, 1989, Cases in Strategic Management, 1990, Frequency Marketing, 1992. Fundraiser U. Ala. Alumni Scholarship Fund, Tuscaloosa, 1983, Am. Diabetes Assn., Tuscaloosa, 1984, Urban Ministries, Birmingham, 1985-88; fundraiser, com. chmn. Spl. Olympics, Tuscaloosa, 1985; chmn. Greene County Relief Project, 1982-89; bd. dirs. Cerebral Palsy Found., Tuscaloosa, 1985-86; lay rector and com. chmn. Kairos Prison Ministry, Tutwiler State Prison, Ala., 1986-92; lobbyist, com. chmn. task force Justice Fellowship, 1988-91; bd. dirs. Internat. Found. Ewha U., Seoul, Korea, 1988-91; chmn. bd. dirs. Epiphany Ministries, 1991-98; bd. dirs. Hunting Coll. Fine Arts, chair Coll. Ministries, Whitfield Meml. United Meth. Ch., 1999-2000, chmn. capital fund campaign, 2000, chmn. stewardship bd. discipleship, 2000-02; chair Ala.-West. Fla. conf. United Meth. Ch., 2002; chair bd. discipleship Ala. UMC Conf., 2002—; retreat leader Upper Room, Acad. for Spiritual Formation, 2005—; com. chmn. Emmaus Ministry, 1985—; chmn. Chrysalis steering com., 1995-97; mem. bd. devel. Upper Rm. Ministries. Recipient Nat. award Joint Coun. Econ. Edn., 1979, Rsch. award NSF, 1979, Harry Denman Evangelism award, 2001; named to Hon. Order Ky. Cols. Commonwealth of Ky., 1985. Mem. Sales and Mktg. Execs. (chmn. com. 1985-86), Leadership Ala. (pres. 1982-83), Am. Mktg. Assn. (Disting. Leadership award 1987, Commemorative Medal of Honor 1988), Assn. Coll. and Univ. Housing Officers (com. chmn. 1983-85), Nat. Assn. Student Pers. Officers, Snack Food Assn. (mem. mktg. com. and conf. presenter), Internat. Coun. Shopping Ctrs. (Merit award 1991, program com.), Commerce Exec. Soc., Omega Rho Sigma (pres. 1983-84), Omicron Delta Kappa, Phi Delta Kappa, Kappa Delta Pi, Phi Alpha Theta. Mem. United Methodist Ch. Avocations: skiing, tennis, kayaking, community/church work, public speaking. Home and Office: 1327 Woodward AVE Montgomery AL 36106-2023 Office Phone: 334-262-9440. E-mail: patluna@charter.net.

LUNARDINI, CHRISTINE ANNE, writer, historian, school administrator; b. Holyoke, Mass., Jan. 27, 1941; d. Virgil Joseph and Christine Hildegarde (Cavanaugh) L. AA, Holyoke C.C., 1973; BA, Mt. Holyoke Coll., 1975; MA, Princeton U., 1979, PhD, 1981. Instr. history Princeton (N.J.) U., 1981-85; adminstrv. asst. Refco Inc., N.Y.C., 1985-87; assoc. prof. Pace U., N.Y.C., 1987-91; freelance writer, N.Y.C., 1991—; exec. asst. to pres. Lynn Chase Designs, Inc., N.Y.C., 1999-2000; dir. devel. St. Michael Acad., N.Y.C., 2000—. Vis. assoc. prof., Barnard Coll., Columbia U., N.Y.C., 1984-85; project mgr., sr. editor Carlson Pub., Bklyn., 1992-93. Author: From Equal Suffrage to Equal Rights: Alice Paul and the National Woman's Party 1910-1928, 1986, The American Peace Movement in the 20th Century, 1994, What Every American Should Know About Women's History, 1996, Women's Rights, 1996; editor, project mgr.: Black Women in America, An Historical Encyclopedia, 2 vols., 1993 (Dartmouth medal 1994), Columbia Guide to American Women: The Nineteenth Century, 1999; mem. editl. adv. bd. Am. Heritage Multi Media, Am. Heritage: Women in Am., 1994—. Princeton U. fellow, 1975—79, Woodrow Wilson nat. fellow, 1980, AAUW nat. fellow, 1980—81. Mem. NOW, Women's Bond Club N.Y., Phi Beta Kappa. Democrat. Episcopalian. Home: 26 Beaver St New York NY 10004-2311 Office: 425 W 33rd St New York NY 10001

LUND, BRUCE DONALD, small business executive; b. Niagara Falls, N.Y., May 4, 1951; s. Donald and Mary L.; m. Leverenz, May 20, 1984. BS in Botany and Zoology, Duke U., 1973; MS in Product Design, Ill. Inst. Tech., 1981. Apprentice The Leatherworks, Chapel Hill, NC, 1973—75; owner Earthwerk, San Antonio, 1975—78; toy designer Marvin Glass and Assocs., Chgo., 1979—84; founder Lund & Co. Invention Studio, Chgo., 1984—. Inventor: (games) Fireball Island, 1987, Slap Happy, Battle Masters, Man Overboard, Ballerhino, 1992, Quockshot, Dizzy Dryer, Travel Rockin Sockem Robots, Dragon Strike, Beware the Dragon, (toys) Stretch Rods, 1987, Live-In Limousine, 1988, Doodle Discs, Oozers, Monsters Rods Mud Runners, Baby Braids, Press to Dress, My Watch Dog, 1992, Love-A-Bye Babies, 1988, Twin Turbo Trains, Pop Watch, 1988, Domino Rally Spectacular Stunt Set, 1992, Vacman, MorphMan, Ice Man, Ramon the Robot, Electronic Talking Microscope, Scissor Critters, (puzzles) 3-D Puzzles, 1988, (dolls) Baby Sip'n Slurp, My Lickety Treats, Baby Go Boom, Somersault Sara, (plush) Norton Bear, First Steps Pooh, Get Up'n Bounce Tigger, Pounce and Bounce Tigger, Tumble Time Tigger, Happy Ears Eeyore, Hydrogen Powered Toy Rocket, Tsunami Waterguns. Recipient Oppenheim Platinum award, 2003, Create the Future award, NASA, 2003, 2004. Democrat. Lutheran. Achievements include patents in field of toys and game, hydrogen technology, martial arts, leather work. Avocations: motorcycling, weightlifting. Office: Lund & Co Invention Studio 4111 N Rockwell St Chicago IL 60618-2822

LUND, DANIEL PETER, lawyer; b. N.Y.C., Aug. 15, 1940; s. Adolph and Esther (Sinn) L.; m. Marilan Murdock, Feb. 20, 1967. AB cum laude, Princeton U., 1962; LLB, Columbia U., 1965. Bar: N.Y. 1965, U.S. Dist. Ct. D.C. 1974, U.S. Dist. Ct. (so. dist.) N.Y. 1974, U.S. Ct. Appeals (2d cir.) 1975. Counsel Blecher, Mendel & Fedele. Office: Ste 1609 1501 Broadway New York NY 10036-5601 E-mail: lunddp@earthlink.net.

LUND, DARYL BERT, food science educator; b. San Bernardino, Calif., Nov. 4, 1941; married June 15, 1963; children: Kristine, Eric. BS in Math., U. Wis., 1963, MS in food Sci., 1965, PhD in Food Sci., 1968. Rsch. asst. in food sci. U. Wis., Madison, 1963-67, instr., 1967-68, asst. prof., 1968-72, assoc. prof., 1972-77, prof. food sci., 1977-87, chmn. dept. food sci., 1984-87; chmn. dept. food sci., assoc. dir. agrl. experiment sta. Rutgers, the State U., New Brunswick, 1988-89, interim exec. dean agr. and natural resources, 1989-91, exec. dean agr./natural resources, 1991-95, exec. dir. N.J. Agrl. Experiment Sta., dean Cook Coll., 1991-95; Ronald P. Lynch dean of agr. and life scis. Cornell U., Ithaca, N.Y., 1995-2000; exec. dir. North Ctrl. Regional Assn., U. Wis., Madison, 2001—. Vis. engr. Western Regional Rsch. Lab., Berkeley, Calif., 1970-71; advisor for evaluation of food tech. dept. Inst. Agr., Bogor, Indonesia, 1973; mem. four-man evaluation team to review grad. edn. programs Brazilian univs., 1976; vis. prof. food process engring. Agrl. U., Wageningen, The Netherlands, 1979; invited vis. prof. food process engring. Univ. Coll., Dublin, 1982; invited advisor Inter-Univ. Ctr. on Food Sci. and Nutrition, Bogor, 1991; advisor Agrl. U., Bogor, 1992; Woodroof lectr. U. Ga., 2003; lectr. in field Contbr. over 200 articles to profl. jours.; editor 5 books; co-author text book. Fellow Inst. Food Sci. and Tech., UK, 2000; recipient Food Engring. award Dairy and Food Industries Supply Assn. and Am. Soc. Agrl. Engring., 1987, Internat. award, Inst. Food Technologists, 2001, Irving award for Svc., American Distance Education Consortium 2001, Carl Fellers award, IFT, 2003. Fellow Inst. Food Technologists (Wis. sect. 1968-87, N.Y. sect. 1988-95, ctrl. N.Y. 1995-2000), Internat. Union Food Sci. and Tech. (charter fellow); mem. AIChE, Am. Inst. Nutrition, Am. Soc. Agrl. Engrs., Am. Assn. Advancement Sci., Internat. Acad. Food Sci. and Tech., 1999 (charter mem.), Sigma Xi, Gamma Sigma Delta, Phi Tau Sigma. Avocations: golf, travel, wood working. Home: 151 E Reynolds St Cottage Grove WI 53527

LUND, DAVID NATHAN, artist; b. NYC, Oct. 16, 1925; s. Isidore and Mollie (Hirschfeld) Lifshitz; m. Sally Harriet Amster, June 17, 1961 (dec. Feb. 1988); children: Andrew Ethan, Giuliana Elizabeth; m. Judith Manelis (div. 2002). BA, Queens Coll., 1948; postgrad., NYU, 1948-50. Adj. asst. prof. painting, drawing, design Cooper Union Art Sch., 1955-57, 59-66, 67-74; instr. painting Cummington (Mass.) Sch. Arts, 1963; instr. in painting Haystack Sch., Deer Isle, Maine, 1963; instr. in drawing and painting Parsons Sch. Design, 1963-66, 67-69; lectr. in drawing Queens Coll., 1964-66; vis. prof. painting Washington U., St. Louis, 1966-67, 85; asst. prof. painting and drawing Columbia U., 1969-82; vis. prof. painting Boston U., 1975-76. Vis. critic; lectr. in field; juror Nat. Selection Com., Fulbright Grants In Art; cons. in painting Creative Artists Public Service, 1979-81; vis. artist Winston-Salem Arts Council and Associated Artists of Winston-Salem, 1975. One-man shows include Grand Central Moderns Gallery, N.Y.C., 1954, Galleria Trastevere, Rome, 1959, Grace Borgenicht Gallery, N.Y.C., 1960, 63, 66, 67, 69, 76, 78, 80, 83, 86, Martin Schweig Gallery, St. Louis, 1966, Kirkland Coll., 1971, Arts Council Winston-Salem, N.C., 1975, Creiger-Seson Gallery, Boston, 1981, Meredith Contemporary Art Gallery, Balt., 1982, U. Alaska, Fairbanks, 1983, Washington U., St. Louis, 1985, Allport Gallery, San Francisco, 1984, A.J. Laderman Fine Arts, Hoboken, N.J., 1990; group shows include Whitney Mus., N.Y.C., 1958, 60, 61, 62, 77, Galleria Schneider, Rome, 1959, Palazzo Venezia, Rome, 1959, Galleria San Marco, Rome, 1959, Washington Gallery Art, 1963, Am. embassy, Athens, Greece, 1966-67, White House, Washington, 1966-67, 67-68, 68-69, Nat. Collection Fine Arts, Washington, 1972-73; represented in permanent collections Whitney Mus., Balt. Mus., Art Gallery Ont., Toronto, Farnsworth Mus., Rockland, Me., Corcoran Gallery Art, Washington, Ft. Worth Art Center, U. Mass., Montclair (N.J.) Mus., Haas Gallery at Bloomsburg State Coll., Kranert Art Gallery, Champagne, Ill., also other public and pvt. collections. Fulbright grantee Rome, 1957-59 Mem. Nat. Acad. Design, Artists Equity. Jewish. Achievements include being subject of numerous profl. publs. Office Phone: 212-568-1472.

LUND, DENNIS PAUL, surgeon; b. Duluth, Minn., May 20, 1954; s. Paul Louis Lund and Yvonne Virginia (Morin) Ritchie; m. Cynthia Palmer Spencer, Sept. 4, 1982; children: Andrew Spencer, Paul Louis, Julia Haines. AB, Harvard Coll., 1976; MD, Harvard Med. Sch., Boston, 1980. Resident in surgery Mass. Gen. Hosp., Boston, 1980-83, 85-87, chief West surg. svc., 1987-88; resident in surgery Children's Hosp., Boston, 1988-90, asst. in surgery, 1990-93, assoc. in surgery, 1993—; instr. in surgery Harvard Med. Sch., Boston, 1990-93, asst. prof. in surgery, 1993—. Mem. pediatrics com. United Network for Organ Sharing, 1994—; trauma dir. Children's Hosp., Boston, 1990—. Contbr. articles to profl. jours., chpts. to books in field. Bd. dirs. Newton Hist. Soc., Newton, 1993—. Recipient Alworth Meml. scholarship, Duluth, Minn., 1976-80. Fellow ACS, Am. Acad. Pediats., Mass. Med. Soc., Ea. Assn. Surgery. Avocations: children, history, golf, music. Office: Childrens Hosp Dept Surgery 300 Longwood Ave Dept Surgery Boston MA 02115-5737

LUND, GEORGE EDWARD, retired electrical engineer; b. Phila., Feb. 17, 1925; s. Harold White and Hannah (Lawford) L.; m. Shirley Bolton Stevens, Sept. 24, 1960; 1 child, Gretchen Lund (Mrs. Kevin J. Collette); stepchildren: Marsha Stevens (Mrs. Donald Barnett), Roger Stevens, Sharon Stevens (Mrs. David Bailey). BEE, Drexel U., 1952; MEE, U. Pa., 1959; postgrad. in computer sci., Villanova U., 1981-83. Project engr. Burroughs Corp., Paoli, Pa., 1952-86, UNISYS Corp., Paoli, 1986-90, ret., 1990. Assoc. editor, contbr.: Digital Applications of Magnetic Devices, 1960; patentee in field. With USN, 1943-46, ETO. Mem. IEEE (sr.), Eta Kappa Nu. Republican. Methodist. Avocations: photography, amateur radio. Home: 323 Styer Rd Glenmoore PA 19343

LUND, JAMES LOUIS, lawyer; b. Long Beach, Calif., Oct. 4, 1926; s. G. Louis and Hazel Eunice (Cochran) L.; m. Jo Alvarez, Aug. 5, 1950; 1 son, Eric James. Student, Stanford U., 1943; BA in Math., U. So. Calif., 1946; postgrad., Grad. Sch. U.S. Naval Acad., Annapolis, MD, 1949; JD, Southwestern U., 1955; postgrad., U. So. Calif., 1956. Bar: Calif. 1955, U.S. Dist. Ct. (cen. dist.) Calif. 1955, U.S. Ct. Appeals (9th cir.) 1955, U.S. Tax Ct. 1955, U.S. Supreme Ct. Spl. agt. U.S. Govt., 1950-52; gen. mgr. Pacific ops., gen. counsel Holmes & Narver, Inc., LA, 1952-66; exec. v.p. Calif. Fabricators, Oakland and Honolulu, 1966-67; sr. ptnr. James Lund Law Firm, Beverly Hills, 1967-83; pres., founder Fortres Mgmt. Co.; sr. ptnr. James Lund Law Firm, Tehran, 1967—83, Tokyo, 1967—83, London, 1967—83; ptnr. Lund & Lund, 1983—. Chmn. bd. Envirotire, 1998—; dir. Superior Vision Svcs., Inc. Lt. comdr. USNR, 1943—46, lt. comdr. USNR, 1948—50. Mem. ABA, SAR, L.A. County Bar Assn., Internat. Bar Assn., Inter-Am. Bar Assn., Asia Pacific Lawyers Assn., Les Ambassadeurs Club (London). Office: Ste 1555 1901 Avenue Of The Stars Los Angeles CA 90067-6052 Office Phone: 310-286-2861. Business E-Mail: jlundesq@pacbell.net.

LUND, JOHN RICHARD, performing company executive; b. Phila., Mar. 30, 1960; s. Robert Lee and Catherine Mary (Walsh) L.; m. Yolande Simon, July 3, 1987; children: Eleonore, Eugenie. BA summa cum laude, St. Joseph's U., Phila., 1982; MA, Columbia U., 1984; PhD with gen. distinction, RAND Grad. Sch. Policy Studies, 1987. Def. analyst Maltese Mission to UN, N.Y.C., 1984; grad. fellow, policy analyst RAND Corp., Santa Monica, Calif., 1984-87, internat. policy analyst, 1988-92; mgr. transport devel. Euro Disney SCA, Marne-La-Vallee, 1992-93, mgr. telecom., transp., 1993-95, dir. telecom. and multimedia, 1995-96, dir. process re-engring., 1996—97, dir. exec. adminstrn., 1997-99, dir. operational labor mgmt., 1999—2000, v.p., chief of staff, 2001—03; v.p. process improvement Walt Disney Imagineering, Glendale, Calif., 2003—04; sr. v.p. strategic asset mgmt. Walt Disney Parks and Resorts, Glendale, Calif., 2004—. Dep. dir. RAND/Project AIR FORCE Office, Hdqrs. U.S. Air Forces in Europe, Ramstein AFB, Germany, 1988. Co-author: The New Calculus: Analyzing Airpower's Changing Role in Joint Theater Campaigns, 1993; contbr.: (with others) Transition and Turmoil in the Atlantic Alliance, 1991; author: Don't Rock the Boat: Reinforcing Norway in Crisis and War, 1989. Mem.: Internat. Inst. for Strategic Studies. Roman Catholic. Office: Walt Disney Parks and Resorts 1401 Flower St Glendale CA 91221 Home: 2887 Bottlebrush Dr Bel Air CA 90077-2011 Office Phone: 818-544-2700. Personal E-mail: john@john-lund.com. Business E-Mail: john.lund@disney.com.

LUND, RITA POLLARD, aerospace engineer, consultant; b. Vallscreek, W.Va., Aug. 28, 1950; d. Willard Garfield and Faye Ethel (Perry) Pollard. Student, Alexandria Hosp. Sch. Nursing, 1969-70, Columbia Pacific U., 1989-91. Notary pub. Va. Confidential asst. U.S. Ho. of Reps., Washington, 1975-76; exec. asst. White Ho. Domestic Policy Staff, Washington, 1977-82; exec. asst. to dep. sci. advisor to pres. White Ho. Sci. Office, Washington, 1982-83; asst. to pres. Telecom Futures Inc., Washington, 1983-84, v.p. for adminstrn., 1985-86; internat. accounts mgr. TFI Ltd., McLean, Va., 1987-89; ind. cons. telecom. Washington, 1989-90; aerospace cons., 1990—98; rep. Scott Sci. & Tech., Washington, 1992—2000; cons. Vanguard Space Corp., Washington, 1992—2000. Exec. dir. Puckett Bros. Corp., 1995—. Marriage commr. State of Va., 2000—; pres. Fairview Beach Residents Assn., 1997—2001. Mem.: AIAA, Competitive Alliance Space Enterprise, Am. Space Transp. Assn., Women in Aerospace, NAFE. Republican. Methodist. Avocations: travel, genealogy, reading.

LUND, VICTOR L., healthcare company executive; b. Salt Lake City, 1947; married BA, U. Utah, 1969, MBA, 1972. Audit mgr. Ernst and Whinney, Salt Lake City, 1972-77; sr. v.p. Skaggs Cos. Inc., from 1977; v.p., contr. Am. Stores Co., 1980-83, sr. v.p., contr., from 1983, exec. v.p., co-chief exec. officer, vice-chmn., chief fin. and adminstrv. officer, pres., CEO, dir., 1992-95, chmn., CEO, dir., 1995-99; vice chmn. bd. dirs. Albertsons Inc., Boise, 1999—2002; non-exec. chmn. bd. Mariner Health Care, Inc., Atlanta, 2002—. Bd. mem. Borders Group, Inc., Svc. Corp. Internat. NCR, State Bd. Regents, Utah. Office: Mariner Health Care Off of Non-Exec Chairman One Ravinia Drive Ste 1500 Atlanta GA 30346

LUNDAY, GERALDINE MARIE, elementary school educator, director; b. Memphis, May 23, 1943; d. Troy Cleo and Alice Mae Johnson; m. L. C. Lunday, Sept. 21, 1961; children: Cliff, Scott, Lisa, Stacy, Tracy. EdB, Blue Mountain (Miss.) Coll., 1980; MEd, U. Miss., 1984. Nat. bd. cert. tchr. Tchr. Ashland (Miss.) Elem. Sch., 1980—; dir. profl. devel. U. Miss., Oxford, 2001—. Cons. U. Miss., Oxford, 1998—2000. Mem.: NEA, Nat. Coun. Tchrs. English, Miss. Assn. Educators, Christian Writers Guild. Avocations: travel, poetry. Office: Ashland Elem Sch 768 Lamar Rd Ashland MS 38603

LUNDBACK, STAFFAN BENGT GUNNAR, lawyer; b. Stockholm, Mar. 23, 1947; arrived in U.S., 1965; s. B. Holger and Ingrid (Fjellstrom) L.; m. Lee Craig, June 14,1969; children: Hadley Elizabeth, Erik Burchfield. Student, U. Stockholm, 1966-67; BA, U. Rochester, 1970; JD, Boston U., 1974. Bar: N.Y. 1975, Fla. 1983. Assoc. Nixon Peabody, LLP, Rochester, NY, 1974—83, ptnr., 1983—. Bd. dirs. Scandinavian Seminar, Amherst, Mass., 1986-92; chmn. Scanamerican Properties, Inc., Atlanta, 1989-99. Mem. Swedish-Am. C. of C. (sec., bd. dirs. 1994—), Country Club of Rochester, Phi Beta Kappa. Avocations: music, literature, sports, current events, photography, golf. Office: Nixon Peabody LLP PO Box 31051 One Clinton First Sq Rochester NY 14603 Office Phone: 585-263-1212. Personal E-mail: slundback@aol.com. Business E-Mail: slundback@nixonpeabody.com.

LUNDBERG, GEORGE DAVID, II, medical editor in chief, pathologist; b. Pensacola, Fla., Mar. 21, 1933; s. George David and Esther Louise (Johnson) Lundberg; m. Nancy Ware Sharp, Aug. 18, 1956 (div.); children: George David III, Charles William, Jean Carol; m. Patricia Blacklidge Lorimer, Mar. 6, 1983; children: Christopher Leif, Melinda Suzanne. AA, North Park Coll., Chgo., 1950; BS, U. Ala., Tuscaloosa, 1952; MS, Baylor U., Waco, Tex., 1963; MD, Med. Coll. Ala., Birmingham, 1957; ScD (hon.), SUNY, Syracuse, 1988, Thomas Jefferson U., 1993, U. Ala., Birmingham, 1994, Med. Coll. Ohio, 1995. Intern Tripler Hosp., Hawaii; resident Brooke Hosp., San Antonio; assoc. prof. pathology U. So. Calif., L.A., 1967—72, prof., 1972—77; assoc. dir. labs. L.A. County-U. So. Calif. Med. Ctr., 1968—77; prof., chmn. dept. pathology U. Calif.-Davis, Sacramento, 1977—82; v.p. scientific info., editor Jour. AMA, Chgo., 1982—99, editor in chief scientific publ., 1991—95; editor-in-chief AMA Sci. Info. and Multimedia, Chgo., 1995—99, Medscape, 1999—2001, editor-in-chief emeritus, 2001—03; editor Medscape Gen. Medicine, 1999—; editor-in-chief and exec. v.p. Medicalogic/Medscape, 2000—02; spl. healthcare advisor to CEO WebMD, 2002—03; editor-in-chief Medscape Core, 2005—. Vis. prof. U. London, 1976, Lund U., Sweden, 1976; prof. clin. pathology Northwestern U., Chgo., 1982—; adj. prof. heatlh policy Harvard U., Boston, 1993—, vis. prof. pathology, 1994—96; sr. fellow Northwestern U., 1999—. Author, editor Managing the Patient Focused Laboratory, 1975, Using the Clinical Laboratory in Medical Decision Making, 1983, 1951, Landmark Articles in Medicine, 1984, AIDS From the Beginning, 1986, Caring for the Uninsured and Underinsured, 1991, Violence, 1992, 100 Years of JAMA Landmark Articles, 1997, Severed Trust: Why American Medicine Hasn't Been Fixed, 2001, paperback edit., 2002; contbr. articles to profl. jours. Lt. col. M.C. U.S. Army, 1956—67. Fellow: Am. Soc. Clin. Pathologists (past pres.); mem.: Inst. Med., N.Y. Acad. Scis., Am. Acad. Forensic Sci., Alpha Omega Alpha. Democrat. Episcopalian. Office: Medscape 76 9th Ave 10001 Office Phone: 408-876-5961. Personal E-mail: glundberg@webmd.net. Business E-Mail: glundberg@medscape.net.

LUNDBERG, SUSAN ONA, musical organization administrator; b. Mandan, N.D., Mar. 15, 1947; d. Robert Henry and Evelyn (Olson) L.; m. Paul R. Wick, July 2, 1972 (div. May 1976); 1 child, Melissa. BA, Stephens Coll., 1969; MLS, Western Mich. U., 1970; MPA, Calif. State U., Fullerton, 1980. Children's and reference libr. Bismarck (N.D.) Pub. Libr., 1970-71; reference libr. U. Tenn., Knoxville, 1971-72; coord. children's svcs. Orange County (Calif.) Pub. Libr., 1972-75; exec. dir. Bismarck-Manda Orch. Assn., 1992—. Exec. dir., founder Sleepy Hollow Summer Theatre, Bismarck, 1990—; trustee Gabriel J. Brown Trust, Bismarck, 1989—. Exhibitions include of paintings Scandinavian Threads of Inheritance, 2002. Chair Nat. Music Week N.D., 1990—, Friends of the Belle, 1997—; chair small budget orchs. Am. Symphony Orch. League, 2000-03; mem. civic chorus Bismarck-Mandary. Named Outstanding Leaders of Yr. Bismarck Tribune, 1995; recipient hon. portrait, Belle Mehus City Auditorium, Vol. award, DAR, 2004, Family Vol. award, Folk Fest, 2004. Mem. DAR (Vol. award 2004), Calif. Libr. Assn. (pres. children's svcs. 1971-72), Bismarck Art Assn. (pres. 1982-84), Bismarck Art and Galleries Assn. (bd. dirs. 1985-2000, pres. 1986-88, Honor Citation award 1992), Jr. Svc. League. Lutheran. Avocations: painting, singing. Home: 112 Ave E W Bismarck ND 58501 Office Phone: 701-258-8345.

LUNDBLAD, ROGER LAUREN, biotechnology consultant; b. San Francisco, Oct. 31, 1939; s. Lauren Alfred and Doris Ruth (Peterson) L.; m. Susan Hawly Taylor, Oct. 15, 1966 (div. 1985); children: Christina Susan, Cynthia Karin. BSc, Pacific Luth. U., 1961; PhD, U. Wash., 1965. Rsch. assoc. U. Wash., Seattle, 1965-66, Rockefeller U., NYC, 1966-68; asst. prof. U. NC, Chapel Hill, 1968-71, assoc. prof., 1971-77, prof. pathology and biochemistry, 1977-91, adj. prof., 1991—; dir. sci. tech. devel. Baxter-Hyland/Immuno, Duarte, Calif., 1991-99; biotech. cons., 2000—. Vis. scientist Hyland divsn. Baxter Healthcare, Glendale, Calif., 1988-89. Author: Chemical Reagents for Protein Modification, 1984, 2d edit., 1990, 3d edit., 2004; editor: Chemistry and Biology of Thrombin, 1977, Chemistry and Biology of Heparin, 1980, Techniques in Protein Modification, 1994; editor-in-chief: Biotechnology and Applied Biochemistry, 1996-2003; contbr. articles to profl. jours. Mem. Am. Soc. Biochem. Molecular Biology, Sigma Xi. Office: PO Box 16695 Chapel Hill NC 27516-6695 Office Phone: 919-929-5082. Personal E-mail: lundbladr@bellsouth.net.

LUNDE, ASBJORN RUDOLPH, lawyer; b. S.I., NY, July 17, 1927; s. Karl and Elisa (Andrews) L. AB, Columbia U., 1947, LLB, 1949. Bar: N.Y. 1949. Pvt. practice, N.Y.C., 1950-91; with Kramer, Marx, Greenlee & Backus and predecessors, 1950-68, mem., 1958-68; pvt. practice Columbia County, NY, 1991—. Bd. dirs., v.p. Orch. da Camera, Inc., 1964—, Sara Roby Found., 1971—; bd. dirs. Clarion Concerts in Columbia County, 1999—; mem. vis. com. dept. European paintings Met. Mus. Art. Fellow Met. Mus. Art (life); mem. ABA, N.Y. State Bar Assn., Assn. Bar City N.Y., Met. Opera Club, East India Club (London). Avocation: art collecting. Home and Office: 135 LaBranche Rd Hillsdale NY 12529-5713 Office Phone: 518-392-4430.

LUNDE, HAROLD IRVING, retired management educator; b. Austin, Minn., Apr. 18, 1929; s. Peter Oliver and Emma (Stoa) L.; m. Sarah Jeanette Lysne, June 25, 1955; children: Paul, James, John, Thomas. BA, St. Olaf Coll., 1952; MA, U. Minn., 1954, PhD, 1966. Assoc. prof. econs. Macalester Coll., St. Paul, 1957-64; fin. staff economist Gen. Motors Corp., N.Y.C., 1965-67; corp. sec. Dayton Hudson Corp., Mpls., 1967-70; mgr. planning and gen. research May Dept. Stores Co., St. Louis, 1970-72, v.p. planning and research, 1972-78; exec. v.p. adminstrn. Kobacker Stores, Inc., Columbus,

Ohio, 1979; prof. mgmt. Bowling Green (Ohio) State U., 1980-98, emeritus, 1998—. Bd. dir. and trustee AgCredit, Ohio, Goodwill Industries N.W. Ohio, U.S. Naval War Coll. Found., Newport, RI. Mem. Acad. Mgmt., Am. Econ. Assn., Nat. Assn. Bus. Economists, Decision Scis. Inst., Phi Beta Kappa, Phi Kappa Phi, Omicron Delta Kappa, Beta Gamma Sigma. Home: 880 Country Club Dr Bowling Green OH 43402-1602 Business E-Mail: hlunde@cba.bgsu.edu.

LUNDE, ØIVIND, cultural organization administrator, archaeologist, educator; b. Oslo, Aug. 21, 1943; s. Øivind and Ebba (Hansen) Lunde. PhD, U. Lund, Sweden, 1977. Inspector Riksantikvaren (Ctr. Office of Hist. Monuments and Sites), Oslo, 1968-78, prin. inspector, 1978-88, dir. archaeol. dept., 1989-91; dep. dir. gen. Directorate for Cultural Heritage, Oslo, 1991, dir. gen., 1991-96. Vis. prof. medieval archaeology, U. Lund, 1984; prof. II medieval archaeology, U. Oslo, 1985—; chmn. Norwegian Com. for Urban Historic Studies, 1978-88. Author: Trondheim's History in the Archaeological Deposits of the Town, 1977, others; contbr. articles to profl. jours. Mem. Nat. Coun. Museums, Norwegian Mus. Arch., European Assn. Archaeologists (exec. bd. 1993-96), Norwegian Acad. Sci. and Letters, Royal Norwegian Soc. Sci. and Letters. Office: Restoration Workshop PO Box 4447 NO 7418 7012 Trondheim Norway E-mail: oeivind.lunde@kirken.no.

LUNDE, RUTH NELSON, librarian; b. La Crosse, Wis., Jan. 29, 1914; d. O. Christian Nelson and Betsy Julie Munson; m. Olav Benjamin Lunde, June 12, 1937 (dec. Dec. 20, 1973); children: Stanley, Richard, Stephen(dec.), Betsy. Degree, La Crosse State Tchrs. Coll., 1934, U. Wis., 1936. Asst. libr. Employers Mutual Ins. Libr., Wausau, Wis., 1936—37; head social scis. Rockford (Ill.) Pub. Libr., 1962—84, ret., 1984. Tchr. genealogy Rock Valley Coll., Rockford, 1970—82. Active Boy Scouts Am., Peoria, Ill., 1949—52, Girl Scouts Am., Rockford, Ill., 1952—69. Mem.: Winnebago and Boone Counties Genealogy Soc., American Assn. State and Local History, Rockford (Ill.) Hist. Soc., Swedish Hist. Soc., Ill. State Geneal. Soc., Sons Norway. Home: 521 Vale Ave No Rockford IL 61107-4653

LUNDEBERG, PHILIP KARL BORAAS, curator, historian; b. Mpls., June 14, 1923; s. Olav Knutson and Vivian Juliet (Boraas) L.; m. Eleanore Lillian Berntson, July 18, 1953; 1 son, Karl Fredrik. BA summa cum laude, Duke U., 1944, MA, 1947; PhD, Harvard U., 1954. Asst. to historian U.S. Naval Ops. in World War II, Navy Dept., 1950-53; asst. prof. history St. Olaf Coll., 1953-55, U.S. Naval Acad., 1955-59; assoc. curator naval history Nat. Mus. History and Tech., Smithsonian Instn., 1959-61, curator of naval history, 1961-84, curator emeritus, 1984—. V.p. Am. Mil. Inst., 1968-71, pres., 1971-73; chmn. Internat. Congress Maritime Museums, 1972-75; v.p. U.S. Commn. on Mil. History, 1975-79, pres., 1980-83; sec. Internat. Com. Mus. Security, 1975-79; pres. Coun. Am. Maritime Museums, 1976-78. Author: The Continental Gunboat Philadelphia, 1966, 2d edit., 1995, Samuel Colt's Submarine Battery, 1974, American Anti-submarine Operations in the Atlantic, 1943-1945, 1997; co-author: Sea Power: A Naval History, 1960, 81; contbg. author: Guide to the Sources of U.S. Military History, 1975, 93, Seafaring and Society, 1987, To Die Gallantly, 1994, The Battle of the Atlantic (1939-1945), 1994; editor: Bibliographie de L'Histoire des Grandes Routes Maritimes: États-Unis d'Amèrique, 1970; exhibits: Armed Forces of U.S., 1961, By Sea and by Land, 1981. With USNR, 1943-83, 89, comdr. Res. ret., 1992. Decorated Bronze Star, Purple Heart; recipient Bronze medal Internat. Commn. Mil. History, 1975; Austin fellow Harvard U., 1949. Fellow Am. Mil. Inst. (Moncado prize 1964); mem. Coun. Am. Maritime Mus. (hon.), N.Am. Soc. for Oceanic History (K. Jack Bauer award 1998), Naval Hist. Found. (life), Internat. Congress Maritime Mus. (life), Soc. for Mil. History, Phi Beta Kappa. Home: 1107 Croton Dr Alexandria VA 22308-2009 Office Phone: 202-633-4011.

LUNDEEN, GEORGE WAYNE, sculptor; b. Holdrege, Nebr., Aug. 26, 1948; s. Warner Swan and Margurite (Hendrickson) L. B.A., Hastings Coll., 1971; M.F.A., U. Ill., 1973; hon. LHD, U. Neb., 1991. Artist-in-residence Tex. A&M U., College Station, 1978-79. One-man shows include: O'Brien's, Scottsdale, Ariz., Driscol's, Denver, Vail, Trails West, Laguna Beach; works include (bronze sculptures) Michelle (Nat. Acad. Art Watrous Gold medal 1982), Promise of the Prairie (Holdrege Nebr. award 1983). Fulbright-Hays grantee, Florence, Italy, 1973-74. Mem. Nat. Sculpture Soc. (Bronze medal 1981, 84, Silver medal 1982), Allied Artists Am. (Mont. award 1982); recipient, Pioneer award, Neb. legislature, 1995, Disting. Nebraskan, Gov. Neb., 1995; mem. NAD (academician). Studio: 338 E 4th St Loveland CO 80537 Office Phone: 970-669-7176 970) 669-7176. Business E-Mail: george@lundeensculpture.com.*

LUNDEEN, WILLIAM BRUCE, radiologist; b. Minn., 1928; s. Harry William and Alice Mary (Gessner) L.; m. Letitia Marguerite Hughey, June 6, 1981; 1 child, Letitia Marshall. BS, U. Richmond, 1951; MD, Med. Coll. Va., 1955. Diplomate Am. Bd. Radiology. Intern U. Minn. Hosps., 1955-56, resident, fellow, 1957-61; resident Med. Coll. VA Hosps., 1957-58; fellow radiation oncology U. Minn., 1960—61; assoc. clin. prof. radiation oncology Med. Coll. Va., 1961—; dir. radiation oncology Va. Hosp. Ctr., Arlington, 1975—. Gov.'s ad hoc com. self-referral med. practice Va. State Legis., Richmond, 1991-93; bd. health sys. H.S.A. No. Va., 1980-84. Staff sgt. USAAF, 1946—48, air weather svc. Fellow AMA, Am. Coll. Radiology; mem. Am. Soc. Therapeutic Radiology & Oncology, Med. Soc. Va., Arlington Med. Soc. (bd. dirs. 1979-83), Air Weather Assn., Annapolis Yacht Club, Alpha Omega Alpha. Republican. Episcopalian. Office: Virginia Hosp Ctr Arlington 1701 N George Mason Dr Arlington VA 22205-3698 Fax: (703) 558-5512.

LUNDEN, JOAN, television personality; b. Fair Oaks, CA, Sept. 19, 1950; d. Erle Murray and Gladyce Lorraine (Somervill) Blunden; m. Michael Krauss, 1978 (div. 1992); children: Jamie Beryl, Lindsay Leigh, Sarah Emily; m. Jeff Konigsberg, 2000; children: Kate Elizabeth, Max Aaron, Kimberly, Jack. Student, Universidad de Las Americas, Mexico City, U. Calif., Calif. State U., Am. River Coll., Sacramento, Calif. Began broadcasting career as co-anchor and prodr. at Sta. KCRA-TV and Radio, Sacramento, 1973-75; with Sta. WABC-TV, N.Y.C., 1975—97, co-anchor, 1976-80; co-host Good Morning America, ABC-TV, 1980-97; host spl. report TV for Whittle Comm.; host Everyday with Joan Lunden, 1989, Behind Closed Doors With Joan Lunden, 1994-2000 (ABC), 2000- (A&E); pres., host Women's Supermarket Network; film appearances include: Macho Callahan, 1970, What About Bob?, 1991, Free Willy 2, 1995, Conspiracy Theory, 1997; spl. appearances: (TV series) Murphy Brown, 1992, 93, LateLine, 1998; Author: Good Morning, I'm Joan Lunden, 1986, Joan Lunden's Mother's Minutes, 1986, Your Newborn Baby: Everything You Need to Know, 1988, Joan Lunden's Healthy Cooking, 1996, Joan Lunden's Healthy Living, 1997, Joan Lunden's A Bend in the Road Is Not the End of the Road, 1998, Wake-Up Calls: Making the Most Out of Every Day, 2000; syndicated columnist: Parent's Notes. Recipient Outstanding Mother of Yr. award, Nat. Mother's Day Com., 1982; Albert Einstein Coll. of Yeshiva U. Spirit of Achievement award; Nat. Women's Polit. Caucus award; NJ Divsn. of Civil Rights award; Baylor U. Outstanding Woman of the Year award; Decoration for Disting. Civilian Svc., US Army. Office: LMNO Prodns PO Box 4361 Los Angeles CA 90028 also: Creative Artists Agy c/o Debra Goldfarb 9830 Wilshire Blvd Beverly Hills CA 90212-1825 also: Rm 4332 1271 Avenue Of The Americas New York NY 10020-1401

LUNDERGAN, BARBARA KEOUGH, lawyer; b. Chgo., Nov. 6, 1938; d. Edward E. and Eleanor A. (Erickson) Keough; children: Matthew K., Mary Alice. BA, U. Ill., 1960; JD, Loyola U., Chgo., 1964. Bar: Ill. 1964, Ga. 1997, Minn. 2004, U.S. Dist. Ct. (no. dist.) Ill. 1964, U.S. Tax Ct. 1974. Of counsel with Hristendahl, Moersch & Dorsey P.A., Northfield, 1964—2004, ptnr., 1971-98, of counsel, 1998—2004. Fellow Am. Coll. Trust and Estate Counsel; mem. ABA (com. on fed. taxation), Ill. Bar Assn. (coun. sect. on fed. taxation 1983-91, chair 1989, coun. sect. on trusts and estates sect. coun. 1992-97, sec. 1996-97, editl. bd. Ill. Bar Jour. 1993-96), Chgo. Bar Assn. (chmn. trust law com. 1982-83, com. on fed. taxation). Office: Hristendahl Moersch and Dorsey PA 311 Water St Northfield MN 55057 Office Phone: 507-645-9358.

LUNDGREN, CARL WILLIAM, JR., physicist; b. Columbus, Sept. 17, 1933; s. Carl William and Anne Katherine (Kuntz) Lundgren; m. Virginia Anne Cullis, Dec. 7, 1963; children: David John, Janet Marie. BEE, U. Cin., 1957, MS, 1959, PhD, 1961. Coop undergrad. engr. govt. products divsn. Avco Corp., Cin., Evendale, Ohio, 1953-56; asst. supr., rsch. fellow U. Cin. Basic Sci. Rsch. Lab., 1959-61; tech. staff Bell Tel. Labs., Murray Hill, NJ, 1961-66, Holmdel and Middletown, NJ, 1966-84; dist. mgr. advanced fiber optics planning Bell Comm. Rsch., Inc., Red Bank, NJ, 1984-92; dir. transmission sys. engring. Bellcore, Morristown and Red Bank, 1992-95; dist. mgr., tech. cons. local access architecture AT&T, Holmdel, 1996-98, Middletown, 1998—. Contbr. articles to profl. jours. Capt. signal corps U.S. Army, 1961—63. Mem.: IEEE, AAAS, Nat. Spectrum Mgrs. Assn., Sierra Club, Gideons Internat., Omicron Delta Kappa, Phi Eta Sigma, Eta Kapa Nu, Tau Beta Pi, Delta Tau Delta. Republican. Episcopalian. Achievements include patents in field. Home: 60 Woodhollow Rd Colts Neck NJ 07722-1323 Office: AT&T R&D South 200 S Laurel Ave Middletown NJ 07748-1998 Office Phone: 732-420-2611. E-mail: cwlxxvcl@optonline.net.

LUNDGREN, CLARA ELOISE, public affairs administrator, journalist; b. Temple, Tex., Mar. 7, 1951; d. Claude Elton and Klara (Csirmaz) L. AA, Temple Jr. Coll., 1971; BJ, U. Tex., 1973; MA, Columbia Pacific U., 1986. Reporter Temple Daily Telegram, 1970-72; news editor Austin (Tex.) Am.-Statesman, 1972-75; mng. editor Stillhouse Hollow Pubs., Inc., Belton, 1975-77; pub. affairs officer Darnall Army Community Hosp., Ft. Hood, Tex., 1978-80; editor Ft. Hood Sentinel III Corps, 1980-85; command info. officer Pub. Affairs Office III Corps, Ft. Hood, 1985-87, community relations officer, 1987-88, dep. pub. affairs officer, 1988-94; pub. info. dir. Texas Dept. Transp., Austin, 1994—2000; cmty. rels. officer III Corps & Ft. Hood (Tex.) Pub. Affairs Office, 2003—. Pres. Episc. Ch. Women, Christ Ch.; bd. dirs. Belton Christian Youth Ctr. Recipient Nat. Observer Journalistic Achievement award Dow Jones & Co., 1971, Superior Civilian Svc. award Dept. Army, 1989, Meritorious Civilian Svc. award, 1992, Exceptional Civilian Svc. award, 1994, Comdr.'s award for pub. svc., 2005. Mem.: AUSA (Ctrl. Tex.-Ft. Hood chpt., v.p.), Rotary Club Killeen-Heights (dir. comty. svc.). Avocations: bicycling, volunteering. Office: Pub Affairs Office III Corps & Ft Hood Bldg 1001 Rm W105 Fort Hood TX 76544 Home: 314 W Upshaw Ave Temple TX 76501-1514 Office Phone: 254-287-0105. Business E-Mail: eloise.lundgren@hood.army.mil.

LUNDGREN, DENNIS D., communications educator; b. Benton Harbor, Mich., May 9, 1950; s. Walter O. and Helen F. Lundgren; m. Colleen K. Bowling, Dec. 18, 1971; 1 child, David S. MusB, Western Mich. U., 1975, EdS, 1982; MusM, Andrews U., 1979. Cert. adminstr. Mich., continuing tchr. cert. Mich. Tchr. and prin. Lakeshore Pub. Schs., Stevensville, Mich., 1975—94; dir. math. and sci. ctr. Berrien County (Mich.) Intermediate Sch. Dist., 1995—2004, dir. tech. and media svcs., 2004—. Assoc. The Cambridge Group, Montgomery, Ala., 1993—96. Congregation pres. Saron Luth. Ch., St. Joseph, Mich., 1998—2003. Finalist Tchr. of Yr., State of Mich., 1993. Mem.: ASCD, Mich. Assn. Computer Users in Learning, Nat. Assn. Secondary Sch. Principals, Nat. Assn. Specialized Secondary Schs. of Math., Sci. and Tech. (pres. 2003—04), Am. Choral Dirs. Assn. (life), Phi Delta Kappa. Office: Berrien County Intermediate Sch Dist 711 St Joseph Ave Berrien Springs MI 49103 Office Phone: 269-471-7725. Business E-Mail: dlundgre@remc11.k12.mi.us.

LUNDGREN, JOHN F., consumer products company executive, bank executive; b. Braintree, Mass., Sept. 3, 1951; BA cum laude, Dartmouth Coll., Hanover, N.H., 1973; MBA, Stanford U., Calif., 1975. Product mgr. Gillette, Boston, 1975—76; product mgr., group product mgr., mktg. dir. Am. Can, Greenwich, Conn., 1976—82; mktg. dir., strategic planning, mfg. planning James River Corp., Norwalk, Conn., 1982—88, v.p., corp. devel. Richmond, Va., 1988—90, v.p., strategic planning, mktg. & bus. devel. Brussels, 1990—95, pres., European consumer products, 1995—2001, Ga.-Pacific Corp., 2001—03; chmn., CEO The Stanley Works, New Britain, Conn., 2003—. Office: The Stanley Works 1000 Stanley Dr New Britain CT 06053

LUNDGREN, LEONARD, III, retired secondary education educator; b. San Francisco, June 22, 1933; s. Leonard II and Betty (Bosold) L.; m. Jane Gates, June 12, 1976. AA, City Coll. San Francisco, 1952; AB, San Francisco State U., 1954, MA, 1958, postgrad., 1958—71. Cert. tchr., Calif. Phys. edn. tchr., athletic coach Pelton Jr. High Sch., San Francisco, 1958-59; social studies tchr., dept. chair, phys. edn. tchr., athletic coach Luther Burbank Jr. High Sch., San Francisco, 1959-78; history, govt. econs., geography tchr. George Washington High Sch., San Francisco, 1978-93. Water safety instr. ARC, San Francisco, 1946-61; mem. Calif. Quality Teaching Ctr. Conf. Bd., 1965-67. Author: Guide for Films and Filmstrips, 1966, Teacher's Handbook for Social Studies, 1966, Guide for Minority Studies, 1968. V.p. Lakeside Property Owners Assn., San Francisco, 1986—88, legis. advocate, 1988—95; v.p. West of Twin Peaks Coun., San Francisco, 1986—87; pub. affairs polit. econ. cons. Calif. Fulbright scholar, Greece, 1963; recipient Svc. Pin, ARC, 1961. Mem.: AARP (cmty. coord. San Francisco 1996—97, rep. 2001—04), PTA (sch. v.p. 1980—81), NEA (life; del. 1970, 1972—76), San Francisco Classroom Tchrs. Assn. (pres. 1972—73, Gavel award 1973), Calif. Coun. Social Studies (v.p. San Francisco chpt. 1969—70), Nat. Coun. Social Studies, Calif. Tchrs. Assn. (state coun. rep. 1963—74), Calif. Assn. Health, Phys. Edn., Recreation and Dance (life; treas. San Francisco chpt. 1959—60), Calif. Ret. Tchrs. Assn. (life; legis. chmn. San Francisco divsn. 1995—99, 1st v.p. 1997—99, pres. 1999—2000, legis. co-chmn. 2001—04, Recognition award 2000), World Affairs Coun. No. Calif., San Francisco State U. Alumni Assn. (life; treas. 1959), Nat. Geog. Soc. (life), Fryers Club San Francisco, Commonwealth Club of Calif., Phi Delta Kappa (life; pres. chpt. 1965—66). Avocations: travel, swimming, gardening, research, service. *A career in education for me is my life from learning to teaching over and over again. History, government, geography and economics are my major subjects. World travel gives me the chance to see the places I studied and taught.*

LUNDGREN, RICHARD JOHN, real estate executive, preservationist, city planner; b. NYC, Dec. 13, 1940; s. John H. and Helen C. (Vetter) Lundgren; m. Nancy Whitin Truslow, Apr. 1, 1972 (dec. 2000); children: Andrew Auchincloss, Elizabeth Whitin. BS, Rensselaer Poly. Inst., 1964; MS, Pratt Inst., 1968; MPA, Harvard U., 1990. Sr. planner Herr Assocs., Boston, 1968-69; project dir. Boston Redevel. Authority, 1969-72; dir. planning Hilgenhurst & Assocs., Boston, 1972-77; v.p. Hunneman Comml. Co., Boston, 1977-82, sr. v.p., 1982—94, 2003—, pres., 1994—2003. Trustee The Trustees of Reservations, 1985—, Emerald Necklace Conservancy, 1997—, Mass. Farm and Conservation Lands Trust, 1985-92, Boston Local Devel. Corp., 1986-91; dir. Preservation Mass., 2002—, Initiative for a Competitive Inner City, Boston, 1999-2003, Vis. Nurse Assn. of Boston, 1972-82; mem. Met. Area Planning Coun., 1978-80, Boston Coord. Com., 1983, Mass. Gov.'s Com. on Pvt. Rental Housing Prodn., 1983-84, Boston Mayor's Com. on Linkage, 1983-84, Center City Task Force, 1983-87, Boston Mayor's Jobs Liaison Com., 1984-90, Park Plz. Civic Adv. Com., 1985-86; Boston Employment Com., 1986-88; chmn. Mass. Realtors Pub. Policy Com., 1989; adv. com. Boston U. Sch. for Real Estate Studies, 1986-91. With USCGR, 1968—72. Named Greater Boston Realtor of Yr., 1984. Fellow: Mass. Hist. Soc.; mem.: Inst. Real Estate Mgmt., Greater Boston Bldg. Owners and Mgrs. Assn. (bd. dirs. 1979—88, pres. 1982), Greater Boston Real Estate Bd. (bd. dirs. 1982—89, pres. 1983), Mass. Assn. Realtors, Nat. Assn. Realtors, New England Hist. Gen. Soc., Boston Athenaeum (propr.), The Country Club (gov.), Harvard Faculty Club, Somerset Club. Episcopalian. Home: Parker Hall 80 Parker Hill Ave Boston MA 02120 Office: Hunneman Comml Co 303 Congress St Boston MA 02111-2611

LUNDGREN, TERRY J., retail company executive; b. Long Beach, Calif., 1953; m. Nancy; two children. BA, U. Ariz., 1974. From. v.p. Bullock's to pres. Bullock's Wilshire Federated Dept. Stores, Inc., N.Y.C., 1975-88; chmn., CEO Neiman Marcus Stores Neiman Marcus Group Inc., 1990—94; chmn., CEO Federated Merchandising Group Federated Merchandising Group, 1994—98; pres., chief merchandising officer Federated Dept. Stores, Inc., N.Y.C., 1997—2002, COO, 2002—03, pres., CEO, 2003—, chmn., 2004—. Bd. dirs. Dallas Symphony Orch., Dallas Citizens Coun. Office: Federated Dept Stores Inc 151 W 34th St New York NY 10001-2101 also: Federated Dept Stores Inc 7 W 7th St Cincinnati OH 45202*

LUNDIN, BRUCE THEODORE, engineer, management consultant; b. Alameda, Calif., Dec. 28, 1919; s. Oscar Linus and Elizabeth Ellen (Erickson) L.; m. Barbara Ann Bliss, July 27, 1946 (wid. Feb. 1981); children: Dianne, Robert, Nancy; m. Jean Ann Oberlin, Mar. 22, 1982. BSME, U. Calif.-Berkeley, 1942; D of Engring. (hon.), U. Toledo, 1975. Chief engine research NASA Lewis Ctr., Cleve., 1952-58, asst. dir., 1958-61, assoc. dir., 1961-68, dir., 1969-77; dep. assoc. adminstrn. NASA, Washington, 1968-69. Adv. U.S. Air Force Sci. Adv. Bd., Washington, 1961-77; mem. Aerospace Safety Adv. Bd., Washington, 1961-72; staff dir. Pres.'s Commn. on the Accident at Three Mile Island, 1981; mem. TM1-2 Safety Adv. Bd., 1981-89; chmn. Rockwell Internat. Safety Oversight Panel, 1988-89. Pres. Westshore Unitarian Ch., Rocky River, Ohio, 1967-68; trustee Southwest Gen. Hosp., Berea, Ohio, 1970-75. Recipient Outstanding Leadership medal NASA, 1965, Pub. Service award NASA, 1971, 75, Disting. Service medal NASA, 1971, 77, Engineer of the Year award Nat. Space Club, 1975 Fellow AIAA; mem. Nat. Acad. Engring. Avocations: sailing, skiing, fishing. Home: 5859 Columbia Rd North Olmsted OH 44070-4611

LUNDIN, NORMAN KENT, artist, educator; b. Los Angeles, Dec. 1, 1938; s. John R. and Louise A. (Marland) L.; m. Sylvia Johnson; children: Kelly Jean, Christopher David. BA, Sch. Art Inst. Chgo., 1961; M.F.A., U. Cin., 1963. Asst. to dir. Cin. Art Mus., 1962-63; instr. art U. Wash., Seattle, 1964-66, asst. prof., 1966-68, assoc. prof., 1968-75, prof., 1976—. Vis. artist Hornsey Coll. Art, London, 1969-70; vis. prof. Ohio State U., Columbus, 1975; prof. San Diego State U., 1978; vis. prof. U. Tex.-San Antonio, 1982, Chelsea Coll. Art, London, 1996. Exhibited one-man shows, Francine Seders Gallery, Seattle, Space, L.A., Jack Rasmussen Gallery, Washington, Allen Stone, N.Y.C., Adams Middleton Gallery, Dallas, Allport Gallery, San Francisco, Stephen Haller Fine Art, N.Y.C., 1987-94, Schmidt-Bingham Gallery, N.Y.C., 1997, Koplin Gallery, L.A., 1997, Koplin DelRio Gallery, Los Angeles, 2005; group shows include Mus. Modern Art, N.Y.C., Whitney Mus. Am. Art, N.Y.C., Denver Art Mus., Seattle Art Mus., San Joes Mus. Art, Ca, 1982-1983, Fine Art Mus., Seattle, 2000, San Francisco Mus. Modern Art Nat. Endowment Arts grantee; Fulbright-Hays grantee Norway, 1963-64; Tiffany Found. grantee, 1968; Ford. Found. grantee Soviet Union, Eastern Europe, 1978-79 Office: U Wash Sch Art Seattle WA 98105

LUNDIN, SHIRLEY MATCOUFF, pre-school administrator, adult education educator, consultant; b. Chgo., Feb. 6, 1935; d. William and Emma Martha (Graf) Matcouff; m. Roy Charles Lundin, Sept. 1, 1956; children: Michael Roy, Laura Marie Lundin Simpkiss, Bethel Anne Lundin-Martinez. BA in Liberal Arts, Northwestern U., 1957; M in Adult Continuing Edn., Nat. Louis U., 1981; Myers Briggs Type Indicator Interpreter, Assn. for Psychol. Type, 1995. Cert. Vol. Adminstrn., 1991. Dir. HeadStart Ctr. Cmty. Action Program, Evansville, Ind., 1974-76; edn. coord. HeadStart Comty. Action Program in Evansville, 1976-78; asst. program coord. parent edn. program Triton Coll., River Grove, Ill., 1979-80; trainer/field advisor Comty. Econ. Devel. Agt. HeadStart for Child Devel. Assoc. Credential, Chgo., 1981-83; adult devel./program cons. Chgo. Field Ctr. Girl Scouts USA, N.Y.C., 1983-88; coord. vol. svcs. Frank Lloyd Wright Home and Studio Fedn., Oak Park, Ill., 1988-91; adj. faculty, vol. mgmt. curriculum coord. Wm. Rainey Harper Coll., Palatine, Ill., 1995—2001; cons., trainer, prin. Lundin & Assocs., Indian Head Park, Ill., 1991—. Trainer workshops and seminars in field of vol. program adminstrn.; trainer Heartland Internat. in U.S. and Belarus, 1998-; cons. in field. Co-author (manual) How to Start a Parent Cooperative Preschool, 1980; contbr. articles to profl. jours. Interim dir., bd. pres. Vol. Ctr., Oak Park, 1990—95; Am. vol. for internat. devel. Nat. Forum Fedn., Washington, 1996—97; mem. com. study of infrastructure Village of Oak Park, 1996; internat. trainer Heartland Internat., 1997—; regional chair Unitarian Universalist Svc. Com., Boston, 1977—80; bd. dirs. Sr. Citizens Ctr., Oak Park and River Forest, 1996—2001, pres., 1998—2001. Mem.: Assn. for Psychol. Type, Chgo. Assn. Psychol. Type, Chgo. Area Tech. Assistance Providers (newsletter editor 1992—94), Assn. Vol. Adminstrn. (bd. dirs., program chair, regional conf. chair Metro Chgo. 1995, profl. devel. com. Metro Chgo. 1993—97), Assn. Vol. Adminstrn. Internat. (mem. regional coun. 1992—95, profl. devel. com., tng. coord. bylaws chair 1995). Avocations: archaeology, choral singing, dream work, travel, family.

LUNDINE, LUCINDA R., artist, rancher, interior designer; b. Cedar Rapids, Iowa, Apr. 14, 1946; d. Luther Leroy and Lorraine Lundine. BA cum laude, Coe Coll., 1968; MA with honors, U. Iowa, Iowa City, 1977; grad., Sheffield Sch. Interior Design, 1988. CEO Cadillac Computer Creations, Cedar Rapids, 1973—83, Ridler, Bennet, Auten Investment Strategies, Cedar Rapids, 1983—90; owner/designer Adelle Schari Interiors, Cedar Rapids, 1988—94; CEO Dazzle Ranch, Alburnett, Iowa, 1993—, Bridlewreath Art Studio, Alburnett, 2002—. Author, children's column Cedar Rapids Gazette, 1971—79, author, book review column, 1971—82; v.p. Rock Island Arsenal Women's Club, Rock Island, Ill., 1999—; bd. mem. Seminole Valley Farm & Museum, Cedar Rapids, 2000—; editor/columnist Rock Island Arsenal Newsletter, 2002—03. Sec./webmaster Kenwood Sch. PTA, Cedar Rapids, 2001—; hist. Kenwood Pk. Neighborhood Assn., Cedar Rapids, 2001—. Named to Purple Arrow Hon. Soc., U. No. Iowa; recipient Founder's Day award, Nat. Sch. PTA Assn., 2002. Mem.: Nat. Edn. Assn. (life), Coe Coll. Martha Marquis Club, Cedar Rapids Creative Artists, Elmcrest Country Club (hist. 1991—). Meth. Avocations: golf, bridge, architecture, gardening, antique automobiles.

LUNDING, CHRISTOPHER HANNA, lawyer; b. Evanston, Ill., June 15, 1946; s. Franklin J. and Virginia (Hanna) L.; children: Elizabeth, Nelson, Alexander, Andrew, Kirsten; m. Barbara J. Fontana, Aug. 19, 1989. BA, Harvard U., 1968; JD, Yale U., 1971. Bar: NY 1972, Fla. 1972, U.S. Supreme Ct. 1975. Law clk. to judge 2d Cir. U.S. Ct. Appeals, NYC, 1971-72; assoc. Cleary, Gottlieb, Steen & Hamilton LLP, NYC, 1973-79, ptnr., 1980—2004, sr. counsel, 2005—. Chmn. Legal Svcs. NYC, 1987—94. Chmn. Belle Haven Tax Dist., Greenwich, Conn., 1986-96, 2001-05. Fellow Am. Bar Found. (life); mem. NY County Lawyers Assn. (bd. dirs. 1988-94). Office: Cleary Gottlieb Steen & Hamilton LLP One Liberty Plz Ste 3800 New York NY 10006 E-mail: CLunding@CGSH.com.

LUNDQUIST, CHARLES ARTHUR, academic administrator; b. Webster, SD, Mar. 26, 1928; s. Arthur Reynald and Olive Esther (Parks) L.; m. Patricia Jean Richardson, Nov. 28, 1951; children: Clara Lee, Dawn Elizabeth, Frances Johanna, Eric Arthur, Gary Lars. BS, S.D. State U., 1949, DSc, 1979; PhD, U. Kans., 1953. Asst. prof. engring. rsch. Pa. State U., 1953-54; sect. chief U.S. Army Ballistic Missile Agy., Huntsville, Ala., 1956-60; br. chief NASA-Marshall Space Flight Ctr., Huntsville, 1960-62; dir. Space Scis. Lab., 1973-81; asst. dir. sci. Smithsonian Astrophys. Obs., Cambridge, Mass., 1962-73; assoc. Harvard Coll. Obs., 1962-73; dir. rsch. U. Ala., Huntsville, 1982-90, assoc. v.p. for rsch., 1990-96, dir. consortium for materials devel. in space, 1985-98, dir. interactive projects office, 1999—. Editor: (with G. Veis) Smithsonian Institution Standard Earth, 1966, The Physics and Astronomy of Space Science, 1966, Skylab's Astronomy and Space Sciences, 1979. With U.S. Army, 1954—56. Recipient Exceptional Sci. Achievement medal NASA, 1971, Hermann Oberth award AIAA, 1978. Mem. AAAS, Am. Geophys. Union, Am. Astron. Soc., Am. Phys. Soc., Nat. Speleological Soc. Home: 214 Jones Valley Dr SW Huntsville AL 35802-1724 Office: U Ala Research Inst Rm E-37 Huntsville AL 35899-0001 Office Phone: 256-824-2684. Business E-Mail: lundquc@email.uah.edu. E-mail: lundquist5@comcast.net.

LUNDQUIST, DANA RICHARD, health facility administrator; b. Mpls., Sept. 12, 1941; s. R. Dana and Mary Jane (Norton) L.; children: Brenda A., Sheila R. BA, Valparaiso U., 1963; postgrad., U. Hawaii, 1963-64, U. Colo., 1963; MBA, U. Chgo., 1966. Adminstrv. asst. U. Chgo. Hosps. and Clinics, 1966—67, asst. supt., 1967—68, asst. dir., 1968—70; officer, bd. dirs. affiliates Hamot Health Systems, Inc., Erie, Pa., 1970—92, pres. parent co., 1981—92, cons., 1992—; sr. v.p. Highmark Blue Cross Blue Shield, 1993—97; exec. v.p. Hardware Hawaii, 1997—98. Lectr. grad. program in hosp. adminstrn. U. Chgo., 1967-70; mem. Erie County Hosp. Coun., 1978-92, pres., 1982; bd. dirs. Hosp. Coun. Western Pa., 1978-92, vice chmn.; exec. com. Pa. Coun. Tchg. Hosps., 1986-90; adv. coun. risk mgmt. Pa. Hosp. Ins. Co., 1982-90, bd. dirs. Vol. Hosps. Am. of Pa., 1985-92, chmn. bd.; bd. visitors The Behrend Coll., Pa. State U., 1990-92; bd. dirs. Pa. Med. Coll., 1991-92. Mem. Erie Conf. on Community Devel., 1981-92, bd. dirs., 1988-92; bd. dirs. N.W. Pa. Buy Right Coun., 1986-92, United Way Erie County, 1983-92; mem. pres.'s coun. Villa Maria Coll., Erie, 1981-90, bd. incorporators Gannon U., Erie, 1981-92; mem. governing bd. St. Paul's Luth. Ch., Erie, 1973-78, v.p., 1974-78; mem. Erie Down Town Coalition Steering Com., 1990-92, chmn., 1991-92, numerous other activities. Mem. Am. Coll. Healthcare Execs. (former regents adv. coun. Pa.); mem. Am. Hosp. Assn. (governing coun. sect. met. hosps. 1987, alt. ho. of dels. 1988), Hosp. Assn. Pa. (polit. action com. 1981-92), Pa. C. of C., U. Chgo. Hosp. Alumni Assn. (exec. com. 1967-70, 87-92, sec.-treas. 1988, pres. 1990-91), Rotary. Lutheran. Home and Office: PO Box 1227 Kailua HI 96734 Personal E-mail: danalundquist@yahoo.com.

LUNDQUIST, ERIC, editor-in-chief; Degree in journalism, Boston U. Computer journalist, 1978—; editor-in-chief Electronic Bus., Electronic Buyer's News; founding editor Electronic World News, Manhasset, NY; founding editor and pub. High Tech Mktg. News CMP Publications, 1990—92; editor PC Week, 1992—96; editor-in-chief eWEEK (formerly PC Week), 1996—, columnist; v.p. Ziff Davis Media Inc., 1997—. Recipient Best Computer Newspaper Award, Computer Press Assn., 2 Neal Awards for editl. excellence, Assn. Bus. Publishers. Office: eWEEK 500 Unicorn Dr Woburn MA 01801

LUNDQUIST, WEYMAN IVAN, lawyer; b. Worcester, Mass., July 27, 1930; s. Hilding Ivan and Florence Cecilia (Westerholm) L.; m. Joan Durrell, Sept. 15, 1956 (div. July 1977); children: Weyman, Erica, Jettora, Kirk; m. Kathryn E. Taylor, Dec. 28, 1978; 1 child, Derek. BA magna cum laude, Dartmouth Coll., 1952; LLB, Harvard U., 1955. Bar: Mass. 1955, Alaska 1961, Calif. 1963, Vt. 1994. Assoc. Thayer, Smith & Gaskill, Worcester, 1957-60; atty. U.S. Attys. Office, Mass. and Alaska, 1960-62; assoc. Heller, Ehrman, White & McAuliffe, San Francisco, 1963-65, ptnr., 1967—; counsel, v.p. State Mut. Life Ins. Co., Worcester, 1965-67. Vis. prof. environ. studies Dartmouth Coll., Hanover, NH, 1980, 84, adj. prof. Amos Tuck Bus. Sch., 1997—99, faculty advisor, 1998—; program chmn. 1990 Moscow Conf. on Law and Bilateral Econ. Rels.; mem. U.S. adv. com. Alaska/Can./Soviet No. Justice Conf., 1993—94, N.Y., San Francisco Cutting Edge Lawyer Liability Programs, 1989; assoc. dir. Inst. Arctic Studies, Dartmouth Coll., 1999—2003; bd. dirs. Univ. Press New Eng., 1996—2002, West Coast Magnetics, Stockton, Calif. Author: (fiction) The Promised Land, 1987, (nonfiction) The Art of Shaping the Case, 1999; contbr. articles to profl. jours. Trustee Natural Resources Def. Coun., 1982-91. Recipient CPR Significant Achievement award, 1987. Fellow ABA (founder and chmn. litig. sect. 1978-79, chmn. Soviet Bar Assn. liaison com. 1986, co-chmn. spl. com. for study discovery abuse 1976-83, spl. com. on tort liability sys. 1981-84, chmn. Soviet legal dialogue com. 1981-96, superfund 301e study group advisor to U.S. Congress 1983), Am. Coll. Trial Lawyers; fellow Dartmouth Coll. Dickey Ctr. for Internat. Understanding (sr.); mem. Worcester County Bar Assn., Dartmouth Lawyer's Assn. (founding mem.), Environ. Careers Orgn. (bd. dirs. 2001, chmn. 2002—), Am. Antiquarian Soc. (life, councillor), Assn. Life Ins. Coun., U.S. Supreme Ct. Hist. Soc., Swedish Am. C. of C. (pres., bd. dirs. west coast magnetics 1982-89) Avocations: squash, skiing, writing. Home: 16 Occum Rdg Hanover NH 03755-1410 Office: PO Box 5527 53 S Main St Ste 313 Hanover NH 03755-2022 Office Phone: 603-643-8610. Personal E-mail: wey@dartmouth.edu. Business E-Mail: wlundquist@hewm.com.

LUNDSTEDT, SVEN BERTIL, behavioral and social scientist, educator; b. N.Y.C., May 6, 1926; s. Sven David and Edith Maria L.; m. Jean Elizabeth Sanford, June 16, 1951; children: Margaret, Peter, Janet. AB, U. Chgo., 1952, PhD, 1955; SM, Harvard U., 1960. Lic. in psychology, N.Y., Ohio; cert. Council for Nat. Register of Health Services. Asst. dir. Found. for Research on Human Behavior, 1960-62; asst. prof. Case-Western Res. U., Cleve., 1962-64, assoc. prof., 1964-68; assoc. prof. adminstrv. sci. Ohio State U., Columbus, 1968-69, prof. pub. policy and mgmt., 1969—, Ameritech Research prof., 1987-89, prof. internat. bus. and pub. policy, 1988—, prof. mgmt. and human resources, 1990—2005, prof. emeritus, 2005—, mem. John Glenn Inst. for Pub. Svc. and Pub. Policy, 1999—. Affiliate scientist Battelle PNL, 1994—; chmn. Battelle endowment program for tech. and human affairs, 1976-80, mem. Univ. Senate, 2002—; dir. project on edn. of chief exec. officer Aspen Inst., 1978-80; advisor Task Force on Innovation, U.S. Ho. of Reps., 1983-84, Citizens Network for Fgn. Affairs, 1988—; mem. Am. Com. on U.S. Soviet Relations, 1985—, chair trade and negotiation project; cons. E.I. duPont de Nemours & Co., B.F. Goodrich Co., Bell Telephone Labs., Battelle Meml. Inst., Nat. Fulbright Award Com.; invited speaker Royal Swedish Acad. Scis., 1989. Author: Higher Education in Social Psychology, 1968; co-author: Managing Innovation, 1982, Managing Innovation and Change, 1989; author, editor: Telecommunications, Values and the Public Interest, 1990; contbr. articles to profl. jours. Pres., Cleve. Mental Health Assn., 1966-68; mem. Ohio Citizen's Task Force on Corrections, 1971-72. Served with U.S. Army, 1944-46 Harvard U. fellow, 1960; grantee Bell Telephone Labs., 1964-65, NSF, 1965-67, Kettering Found., 1978-80, Atlantic Richfield Found., 1980-82, German Marshall Fund of U.S. to conduct internat. ednl. joint ventures on econ. negotiations, Budapest, Hungary, 1990; recipient Ohio Ho. of Reps. award, 1986. Mem.: APA, Internat. Soc. Panetics (mem., sec. bd. govs., founding mem.), Am. Soc. for Pub. Adminstrn. (pres. Central Ohio chpt. 1975—77, founder, chmn. com. on bus. govt. relations 1977—79, editl. bd. Pub. Adminstrn. Rev. 1978—82), Am. Acad. Arts and Scis. (chmn. PIN com. on east/west trade negotiation), Internat. Inst. for Applied Systems Analysis (innovation task force, nat. adv. com. project. internat. negotiation with AAAS, founder, chmn. U.S. Midwest Assn. for IIASA 1986—, sr. social sci. advisor 1994—). Unitarian Universalist. E-mail: lundstedt.1@osu.edu.

LUNDSTROM, GILBERT GENE, bank executive, lawyer; b. Sept. 27, 1941; s. Vernon G. and Imogene (Jackett) L.; m. Joyce Elaine Ronin, June 26, 1965; children: Trevor A., Gregory G. BS, U. Nebr., 1964, JD, 1969; MBA, Wayne State U., 1966. Bar: U.S. Dist. Ct. (1st dist.) Nebr. 1969, Nebr. 1969, U.S. Ct. Appeals (5th cir.) 1970, U.S. Ct. Appeals (10th cir.) 1971, U.S. Ct. Appeals (8th cir.) 1974, U.S. Ct. Appeals (3d cir.) 1986. Ptnr. Woods & Aitken Law Firm, Lincoln, Nebr., 1969-93; CEO, chmn. bd. Tier One Bank, 1994—. Chmn., CEO Tier One Corp.; faculty law sch. U. Nebr., Lincoln, 1970-74; bd. dirs. Tier One Bank, TMS Corp. Ams., Sahara Enterprises, Inc., Sahara Coal Co., Chgo., SMCO, Inc.; vice-chmn. Fed. Home Loan Bank Topeka, 1996-2002. Bd. dirs. Folsom Children's Zoo, Lincoln, 1979-83, St. Elizabeth Hosp. Found., 1998-2002, Tier One Charitable Found, Jr. Achievement Found., Lincoln, U. Nebr. Found., U. Nebr. Found., Nebr. Art Assn Fellow Nebr. State Bar Assn.; mem. ABA, ATLA, Lincoln Bar Assn., Newcomer Soc. US, Nebr. Bankers Assn. (bd. dirs.), Country Club of Lincoln, Firethorn County Club, Masons, Scottish Rite (33 degree), Lincoln C. of C. (bd. dirs.) Republican. Methodist. Home: 9519 Firethorn Ln Lincoln NE 68520-1459 Office: Tier One Bank 1235 N St Lincoln NE 68508-2083

LUNDSTROM, MARJIE, editor, columnist; Grad., U. Nebr. Columnist, editor, nat. corr. The Denver Post, 1981-89; with The Sacramento Bee, 1989-90, 91—; nat. corr. Gannett News Svc., Washington, 1990-91. Recipient Pulitzer Prize for nat. reporting, 1991. Office: The Sacramento Bee PO Box 15779 Sacramento CA 95852-0779 E-mail: mlundstrom@sacbee.com.

LUNDSTROM, TAMMY SUE, health facility administrator; b. Virginia, Minn., Apr. 13, 1959; d. Richard Sanfred and Karen Warreth Lundstrom; m. Kamran Zakaria, Mar. 10, 1991; children: Benjamin Logan Zakaria, Nathaniel Logan Zakaria. BS in Biochemistry, U. Minn., 1983, MD, 1987; JD, Wayne State U., 2004. Diplomate American Board of Internal Medicine, American Board of Infectious Diseases. Resident in internal medicine Wayne State U., Detroit, 1990—92, fellow in infectious diseases, 1992; asst. prof. infectious diseases Wayne State U./Detroit Med. Ctr., 1992—97, med. dir. epidemiology, 1997—2000; v.p., chief quality and safety officer Detroit Med. Ctr., 2000—, sr. v.p., chief quality and safety officer, 2005—. Contbr. articles to profl. jours.; mem. editl. adv. bd. Briefings on Infection Control, 2003—, mem. Wayne State U. Law Rev., 2003. Mem.: Mich. Health and Hosp. Assn. (quality compliance and safety com. 2001—), Am. Coll. Physician Execs., Assn. Profls. in Infection Control and Epidemiology, Soc. Healthcare Epidemiology Am. Avocations: reading, rollerblading. Office: Detroit Med Ctr 4201 St Antoine UHC 2B Detroit MI 48209 E-mail: tlundstrom@dmc.org.

LUNDY, AUDIE LEE, JR., lawyer; b. Columbus, Ga., Mar. 10, 1943; s. Audie Lee and Mary Blanche (Snipes) L.; m. Ann Porter, June 11, 1966; children: Travis Stuart, Katherine Porter. BA, Yale U., 1965; LLB magna cum laude, Columbia U., 1968. Bar: N.Y. 1968, D.C. 1976, Pa., 1988, Md. 1990. Assoc. firm White & Case, N.Y.C., 1968-71, 74-75, London, 1971-74, Washington, 1975-78; asst. gen. counsel Campbell Soup Co., Camden, N.J., 1978, gen. counsel, 1979-88, v.p., gen. counsel, 1988-89; ptnr. Tydings & Rosenberg LLP, Balt., 1989—. Bd. mgrs. St. Christopher's Hosp. for Children, Phila., 1980-89, vice-chmn. 1986-89; trustee Food and Drug Law Inst., Washington, 1982-91, The Children's Guild, Inc., Balt., 1992-2005, chmn. 1997-99; chmn. Meritas Law Firms Worldwide, Mpls., 2005-. Mem. ABA, Am. Soc. Internat. Law, Assn. Gen. Counsel (emeritus). Republican. Presbyterian. Clus: Merion Cricket Home: 203 Goodwood Gdns Baltimore MD 21210-2531 Office: Tydings & Rosenberg LLP 100 E Pratt St Baltimore MD 21202-1009 Office Phone: 410-752-9705. Business E-Mail: llundy@tydingslaw.com.

LUNDY, BARBARA JEAN, training services executive; b. Chgo., Feb. 2, 1950; Tchr., facilitator Red Rocks C.C., Golden, Colo., 1986—90, AMI, St. Luke's Hosp., Denver, 1986—90; tchr. Arapaho C.C., Denver, 1991—95; tng. mgr. Denver Options, 1995. Mediator U. Denver; dir. Am. Poets and Fiction Writing, Denver. Author, poet, editor Market Mountain Writer's, 1978-81; co-author: You Can Collect Child Support, 1989; contbg. author Directory of Am. Poets and Fiction Writer's. Profl. vol. VIDA Vol., Pueblo, Colo., 1971-73; vol. dir. Legal Aid Soc., Denver, 1980-85; bd. mem., editl. bd. Colo. Women's Polit. Caucus, Denver, 1980-81; state commn. mem. Colo. Child Support Commn., Denver, 1984-85; co-founder Kids in Need Support (KINS), Denver, 1986-87; com. mem. Denver Dist. Ct., Bench, Bar, Cmty. Rels. Com., Denver, 1987-89. Mem. Assn. Persons Supported Employment (spkr. nat. conv. 1998), Hayna Writer's. Avocations: science, history and philosophy reading, piano, writing. Office: Denver Options 5250 Leetsdale Dr Ste 200 Denver CO 80246-1451 Office Phone: 303-636-5814. Personal E-mail: barbjlundy@earthlink.net. Business E-Mail: blundy@denveroptions.org.

LUNDY, DONNA S., speech pathology/audiology services professional; d. Carl and Edith D. Lundy. AA, Tulane U., New Orleans, 1973—75; BA, U. Fla., Gainesville, 1975—76; MA, U. Miami, 1976—78, PhD, 1992—2003. Certificate of Clinical Competence Am. Speech-Language-Hearing Assn., 1979. Speech pathologist Jackson Meml. Med. Ctr., Miami, Fla., 1979—89, U. Miami, Fla., 1989—. Chairperson, advocacy com. Am. Cancer Soc., Miami, Fla., 2003—; bd. mem. FLASHA Found., Orlando, Fla., 2004—, Am. Cancer Soc., Miami, Fla., 2004—. Fellow, Deafness Rsch. Soc., 2004. Mem.: Fla. Speech-Language-Hearing Assn. (v.p., publs. 1998—2000, v.p., continuing edn. 2000—02), Am. Acad. Otolaryngology (com. mem., neurolaryngology 2004—), Am. Speech-Language-Hearing Assn. (exec. bd. 1997—2004, assoc. coord., steering com. 2002—04). Office: Univ Miami 1474 NW 12th Ave Miami FL 33136 Office Phone: 305-243-5290. Office Fax: 305-243-5291. E-mail: dlundy@med.miami.edu.

LUNDY, HAROLD W., academic administrator; m. LaVerta May Lundy; children: Harold Jr., Baruch Barjona, Jamin Jay. BA, Dillard Univ; MS/Accounting, PhD, Univ of Wisconsin-Madison. Accounting Educator Univ of Wisconsin-Madison; Accounting Dept Head Savannah St College, Georgia; Accounting Educator Xavier Univ.; Auditor Federal Credit Union/Dillard Univ; Staff Accountant/Financial Analyst Mobil Oil Corp, Exxon Corporation, Arthur Young & Co., NY; Assistant to VP for Administration Grambling State Univ, Grambling, LA, 1980—, President, 1991—. Office: Grambling State U Office of President Grambling LA 71245

LUNDY, JOSEPH E., lawyer; b. Phila., Dec. 30, 1942; s. Martin L. and Adele E. (Zion) L.; m. Bonnie Verbit, Aug. 30, 1966; children: Seth Harris, Nancy Elizabeth. BS in Econs., U. Pa., 1965; JD, Temple U., 1968; LLM in Taxation, N.Y. U., 1969. Bar: Fla. 1968, Pa. 1969. Assoc. MacCoy, Evans & Lewis, Phila., 1969-73, ptnr., 1974-76, Montgomery, McCracken, Walker & Rhodes, Phila., 1976-88, Ballard, Spahr, Andrews & Ingersoll, Phila., 1988-97; prin. Price Waterhouse Coopers LLP, Phila., 1997—2004. Adj. prof. law Temple U., 1974—. Editor-in-Chief Jour. Taxation of Exempt Orgns. Assoc. trustee U. Pa., Phila.; bd. overseers U. Pa. Univ. Mus., Phila. Fellow Am. Coll. Tax Counsel; mem. ABA (exempt orgn. com., com. govt. subcoms.), Am. Acad. Hosp. Attys., Phila. Bar Assn. (vice chair tax sect. 1988-90, chair 1990-92). Office: Lundy Zateen, LLP Two Bala Plaza Ste 300 Bala Cynwyd PA 19004 Office Phone: 610-660-7788.

LUNDY, J(OSEPH) EDWARD, retired automobile company executive; b. Iowa, Jan. 6, 1915; s. Vern E. and Mary L. (Chambers) L. BA, U. Iowa, 1936. Fellow Princeton U., 1936-39, mem. econs. faculty, 1940-42, beginning as planning ofcl.; with Ford Motor Co., Dearborn, Mich., 1946-85, successively dir. fin. planning and analysis, gen. asst. contr., 1946-57, treas., 1957-61, v.p., contr., 1961-62, v.p. fin., 1962-67, exec. v.p., 1967-79, dir. and vice-chmn. fin. com., 1979-85. Dir. research and analysis Office Statis. Control, Hdqrs. USAAF, 1945 Served from pvt. to maj. USAAF, 1943-45. Decorated Legion of Merit. Mem. Dearborn Country Club, Phi Beta Kappa, Delta Upsilon. Clubs: Detroit Princeton. Roman Catholic. Home: 7 Brookwood Ln Dearborn MI 48120-1302

LUNDY, LARRY, food franchise company executive; b. New Orleans; married; 3 children. BS, Dillard U.; MBA, Pepperdine U. With Peat, Marc & Mitchell, Alexander Grant & Co.; contr. Pizza Hut, 1983-88, v.p., contr., v.p. restaurant devel., 1988; pres., CEO Lundy Enterprises, New Orleans. Named New Orleanian of Yr., Gambit newspaper, 1993. Office: Lundy Enterprises LLC 10555 Lake Forest Blvd Ste 1J New Orleans LA 70127-5215

LUNDY, SADIE ALLEN, small business owner; b. Milton, Fla., Mar. 29, 1918; d. Stephen Grover and Martha Ellen (Harter) Allen; m. Wilson Tate Lundy, May 17, 1939 (div. 1962); children: Wilson Tate Jr., Houston Allen, Micheal David, Robert Douglas, Martha Jo-Ellen. Degree in acctg., Graceland Coll., 1938. Acct. Powers Furniture Co., Milton, 1939-40; acct., v.p. Lundy Oil Co., Milton, 1941-52; controller First Fed. Savs. & Loan, Kansas City, Mo., 1953-55, Herald Pub. Co., Indepenence, Mo., 1956-58; mgr. Baird & Son Toy Co., Kansas City, 1959-62; regional mgr. Emmons Jewelers N.Y., Kansas City, 1963-65; owner, pres. Lundy Tax Svc., Independence, 1965-85; corp. sec. treas., purchasing mgr. Optimation, Inc., Independence, 1974-85, mgr., 1985—2001; COO Wasber Industries LLC, Independence, 2001—; dir. ops. ReEngineer Profit LLC, Independence, 2003—. Contbr. articles to profl. jours. Mem. com. Neighborhood Coun., Independence, 1985. Mem.: Am. Bus. Women's Assn., Independence C. of C. (mem. com. 1965—85), Independence Women's Club. Republican. Cmty. Of Christ Ch. Avocations: counseling, swimming, bicycling. Home: PO Box 520238 Independence MO 64052-0238 Office: ReEngineer Profit LLC PO 'Box 5200057 Independence MO 64053 E-mail: slundy@comcast.net.

LUNDY, VICTOR ALFRED, architect, educator; b. N.Y.C., Feb. 1, 1923; s. Alfred Henry and Rachel Lundy; m. Shirley Corwin, 1947 (div. 1959); children: Christopher Mark, Jennifer Alison; m. Anstis Manton Burwell, Sept. 19, 1960; 1 child, Nicholas Burwell. BArch, Harvard U., 1947, MArch, 1948. Registered architect, Tex., N.Y., Calif. Pvt. practice architecture, Sarasota, Fla., 1951-59, N.Y.C., 1960-75; prin. Victor A. Lundy & Assocs., Inc., Houston, 1976-84; design. prin., v.p. HKS Inc., Dallas, 1984-90. Vis. prof. Grad. Sch. Design, Harvard U., Sch. Architecture, Yale U., Columbia U., U. Calif., Berkeley, Calif. Poly. State U. San Luis Obispo, U. Houston, U. Rome, others; U.S. specialist-architect in U.S.I.A. exhibit, USSR, 1965. Responsible for design St. Paul's Luth. Ch., Sarasota, 1959, new sanctuary, 1970, 1st Unitarian Ch. of Fairfield County, Westport, Conn., 1961, 1st Unitarian Congl. Soc., Hartford, Conn., 1964, Ch. of Resurrection, East Harlem Protestant Parish, N.Y.C., 1966, exhbn. bldg. and exhibit for AEC in S.Am. (Buenos Aires, Rio de Janeiro, Bogota, Santiago), 1967 (Silver medal for exhbn. Archtl. League N.Y. 1965), recreation shelters for Nat. Mus. History and tech., Smithsonian Instn., Washington, 1967, U.S. States Tax Ct. bldg. and pla., Washington, 1976, U.S. Embassy, Colombo, Sri Lanka, for Office of Fgn. Bldgs., Dept. State, 1983 (U.S. Presdl. Design Awards Program 1988, Fed. Design Achievement award), Austin Centre-Omni Hotel, Austin, Tex., 1984, One Congress Pla., Austin, Tex., 1984, Walnut Glen Tower, Dallas, 1985, Mack Ctr. II, Tampa, Fla., 1990, Greyhound Corp. Ctr., Phoenix, 1991, GTE Telephone Ops. World Hdqrs., Irving, Tex., 1991, Tex. A&M Found Hdqs., 1999, others; archtl. work represented in Berlin Internat. Archtl. Exposition, 1957, Sao Paulo Internat. Biennial Exposition, 1957, 5th Congress Union Internat. Des Architectes, Moscow, 1958, Expo '70 Exhbn., Osaka, Japan, 1970, travelling exhbn. of architecture in S.Am. Sgt. inf. U.S. Army, 1943-46, ETO. Decorated Purple Heart; recipient Gold medal award Buenos Aires Sesquicentennial Internat. Exhbn., 1960, Gold medal award Buenos Aires Sesquicentennial Internt.Exhbn., 1960; Silver medal Archtl. League N.Y., 1965; Charles Hayden Meml. Scholastic scholar, 1939-43, Edward H. Kendall scholar Harvard U., 1947-48, Rotch travelling scholar Boston Soc. Architects, 1948-50; travelling fellow Harvard U., 1948-50; Dept. State grantee, 1965. Fellow AIA. Avocations: painting, sculpture. Home: 701 Mulberry Ln Bellaire TX 77401-3805

LUNDY-SLADE, BETTIE B., retired electronics executive; b. Marinette, Wis., Feb. 16, 1924; d. Adolph Gustav and Bertha Julian (Keller) Limberg; m. George Wesley Lundy II, Nov. 11, 1951 (div. 1956); children: George Wesley III, Genise Wynell, Charles Edward; m. Jim Donovan Slade, July 20, 1973. Lic. vocat. nurse, psychiat. technician, Calif. With Allis Chalmers, Milw., 1942-44, Gen. Dynamics, San Diego, 1959-65, Tetedyne Ryan, San Diego, 1966-76, Cubic, San Diego, 1976-86; ret., 1986. Author: (poetry) Do You Have a Minute, 1991, (biography) Growing Up on a Farm During the Depression, 1995, Book III Wistful Wanderings, 1992; artist over 100 paintings, 1986—. Den mother Boy Scouts Am., San Diego; Sunday sch. tchr. Luth. Ch., San Diego. With USN Waves, 1944-50. Recipient Sen. Cashman award Marinette, Wis., 1937, Letter of Appreciation Mother Teresa, 1992, Gen. Norman Schwarzkoph, 1993, Queen Elizabeth, 1993. Mem. Internat. Soc. Poets (life), Nat. Parks & Conservation, Smithsonian Assocs., Peal Ctr. Christian Living, Nat. Audubon Soc., Nat. Mus. Women in Arts. Republican. Avocations: soft sculpture, crocheting, short stories and poetry, oil, acrylic and water color painting. Home: 6315 Thorn St San Diego CA 92115-6908

LUNG, AURISTELA R., music educator; b. Barranquilla, Colombia, Jan. 14, 1955; arrived in U.S., 1958; d. Julio Rodríguez Buelvas and Estela Merlano Rodríguez. Grad., Watchtower Bible Sch. of Gilead, 1982; BA in Music Edn., U. Tex.-Pan Am. U., 1996; MA in Spanish Lit., U. Tex.-Pan. Am., 2000. Cert. bilingual educator, all-level music tchr. Missionary Jehovah's Witnesses, Colombia, 1982—85; piano tchr., owner Starr County Piano Studio, Rio Grande City, Tex., 1990—; 4th grade bilingual tchr. Rio Grande City Ctrl. Ind. Sch. Dist., 1997—99; instr. South Tex. Coll., Rio Grande City, 1999—. Vol. educator Jehovah's Witnesses, Roma, Tex., 1986—. Mem.: Magic Valley Music Tchrs. (sec. 1998—2005), Tex. Faculty Assocs., Tex. Music Tchrs. Assn., Phi Kappa Phi. Jehovah'S Witness. Avocations: reading, crocheting, travel, cat. Home: PO Box 804 Rio Grande City TX 78582 Office Phone: 956-488-5857. Business E-Mail: alung@southtexascollege.edu.

LUNG, CHANG See RIGNEY, JAMES JR.

LUNGREN, DANIEL EDWARD, congressman, former state attorney general; b. Long Beach, Calif., Sept. 22, 1946; s. John Charles and Lorain Kathleen (Youngberg) Lungren; m. Barbara Kolls, Aug. 2, 1969; children: Jeffrey Edward, Kelly Christine, Kathleen Marie. AB cum laude, Notre Dame U., 1968; postgrad., U. So. Calif., 1968—69; JD, Georgetown U., 1971. Bar: Calif. 1972. Staff asst. Sen. George Murphy, Sen. William Brock, 1969—71; spl. asst. to co-chmn. Rep. Nat. Com., dir. spl. programs, 1971—72; assoc., selected as ptnr. Ball, Hunt, Hart, Brown & Baerwitz, Long Beach, 1973—78; mem. U.S Congress from 42d Calif. dist., 1979—89, Rep. State Cen. Com. Calif., 1974—89; ptnr. Diepenbrock, Wulff, Plant & Hannegan, Sacramento, 1989—90; atty. gen. State of Calif., Sacramento, 1991—98; host, Dan Lungren Show Catholic Family Radio, San Diego; atty. private practice, 1999—2004; mem. U.S. Congress from 3d Calif. dist., 2005—; mem. judiciary com. Committeeman Rep. Nat. Com., 1988—96; bd. dirs. ARC Boy's Club, Long Beach, 1976—88. Recipient Good Samaritan award, L.A. Coun. Mormon Chs., 1976. Republican. Roman Catholic. Office: 2448 Rayburn House Office Bldg Washington DC 20515-0503 Office Phone: 202-225-5716.*

LUNGSTRUM, JOHN W., federal judge; b. Topeka, Nov. 2, 1945; s. Jack Edward and Helen Alice (Watson) L.; m. Linda Eileen Ewing, June 21, 1969; children: Justin Matthew, Jordan Elizabeth, Alison Paige. BA magna cum laude, Yale Coll., 1967; JD, U. Kans., 1970. Bar: Kans. 1970, Calif. 1970, admitted to practice: US Dist. Ct. (Ctrl. Dist.) Calif., US Ct. Appeals (10th Cir.). Assoc. Latham & Watkins, L.A., 1970-71; ptnr. Stevens, Brand, Lungstrum, Golden & Winter, Lawrence, Kans., 1972-91; U.S. Dist. judge Dist. of Kans., Kansas City, 1991—2001, chief judge, 2001—. Lectr. law U. Kans. Law Sch., 1973—; mem. faculty Kans. Bar Assn. Coll. Advocacy, Trial Tactics and Techniques Inst., 1983-86; chmn. Douglas County Rep. Ctrl. Com., 1975-81; mem. Rep. State Com.; del. State Rep. Conv., 1968, 76, 80; chair com. on ct. adminstrn. and case mgmt. Jud. Conf. US, 2000-05, mem. budget com., 2005-. Chmn. bd. dirs. Lawrence C. of C., 1990-91; pres. Lawrence United Fund, 1979; pres. Independence Days Lawrence, Inc., 1984, 85, Seem-to-be-Players, Inc., Lawrence Rotary Club, 1978-79; bd. dirs. Lawrence Soc. Chamber Music, Swarthout Soc. (corp. fund-raising chmn.); mem. Lawrence Art Commn., Williams Scholarship Fund, Lawrence League Women Voters, Douglas County Hist. Soc.; bd. trustees, stewardship chmn. Plymouth Congl. Ch.; pres. Lawrence Round Ball Club; coach Lawrence Summertime Basketball; vice chmn. U. Kans. Disciplinary Bd.; bd. govs. Kans Sch. Religion; bd. dirs. Kans. Day Club, 1980, 81. National Merit scholar, Yale Nat. scholar. Fellow Am. Bar Found.; mem. ABA (commn. Am. Jury 2004-05, past mem. litig. and ins. sect.), Douglas County Bar Assn., Johnson County Bar Assn., Wyandotte County Bar Assn., Kans. Bar Assn. (vice chair legis. com., subcom. litig., mem.CLE com.), U. Kans. Alumni Assn. (life), Judge Hugh Means Inn of Ct. (pres. 2005-), Phi Beta Kappa, Phi Gamma Delta, Phi Delta Phi. Avocations: basketball, hiking, skiing. Office: Robt J Dole US Courthouse Ste 517 500 State Ave Rm 517 Kansas City KS 66101-2400

LUNING, THOMAS P., lawyer; b. St. Louis, Oct. 11, 1942; AB magna cum laude, Xavier U., 1964; JD, Georgetown U., 1967. Bar: D.C. 1968, Ill. 1968. Law clk. to Hon. Spottswood W. Robinson III and to ct. U.S. Ct. Appeals (D.C. cir.), 1967-68; atty. Schiff Hardin & Waite, Chgo. Mng. editor Georgetown Law Jour., 1966-67. Mem. ABA, Ill. State Bar Assn., Chgo. Bar Assn., 7th Cir. Bar Assn., Chgo. Coun. Lawyers. Office: Schiff Hardin & Waite 6600 Sears Tower Chicago IL 60606 E-mail: tluning@schiffhardin.com.

LUNN, KITTY ELIZABETH, actress; b. New Orleans, Aug. 5, 1950; d. Hugh I. Morrison and Beatrice (McClung) Farrell; m. Andrew Macmillan, Dec. 21, 1989. Student, Washington Sch. Ballet, 1965-68, Neighborhood Playhouse Sch., 1968-70; degree summa cum laude, CUNY, 1995. Dancer Washington Ballet, 1965-68; radio producer WOR Radio, N.Y.C., 1983-85, WABC Talk Radio, N.Y.C., 1985-87; performer CBS TV, N.Y.C., 1990-93. Founder, artistic dir. Infinity Dance Theatre, 1995. Prin. works include Agnes of God, 1992-95, Edinburgh Festival, Fan's False Face Soc., 1990, The Waiting, 1990, Sand Dragons, 1990, As the World Turns, 1990-92, Awakenings, 1990, Eyes of a Stranger, 1979, Loving, 1995, Monograms, 1996-97, numerous TV appearances, 1978-86; dancer Cleve. Ballet, Dancing Wheels. Bd. dirs. Hosp. Audiences, Inc., N.Y.C., 1990—; dir. svcs. people with disabilities Actors' Work Program, N.Y.C., 1991—; mentor networking project YWCA, N.Y.C., 1991-95; mem. White House Conf. on Libr. and Info. Svcs., Washington, 1991; N.Y. State Libr. regent advisor; del. Dem. Nat. Conv., 1992. Named Belle Zeller scholar, CUNY, 1993, Woman of Excellence, 1994. Mem. SAG, AFTRA (nat. bd. dirs.), Nat. Alliance Broadcast Engrs. and Technicians, Actor's Equity Assn. (councillor Eastern Regional adv. bd. 1990—, chair performers with disabilities com. 1990—). Roman Catholic. Office: Actors' Equity Assn 165 W 46th St Fl 15 New York NY 10036-2500

LUNSFORD, CAROL A., special education educator; b. Farmville, Va., Aug. 2, 1947; d. Boyd Ray and Georgia Lee Pace; m. Charles T. Lunsford, Dec. 31, 1976; 1 child, Charles A. BA, Mars Hill (N.C.) Coll., 1969; Med, West Ga. U., 1976. Cert. tchr. spl. edn. Ga., 1997, ednl. leadership GA, 1997. Long distance operator Continental Telephone Va., Chase City, Va., 1970—70; tchr. 5th grade Rockingham County Schs., Reidsville, NC, 1970—71; tchr. 7th grade english lit., 1971—72; tchr. gen. math Fayette County Pub. Schs., Fayetteville, Ga., 1972—73, tchr. specific learning disabilities, 1973—2000. Drama coach, dir. play Bethany Sch., Reidsville, NC, 1970. Fireflies (Hon. Mention Acrylics award, 2004); author: Poems and Other Such Stuff (3rd Pl. Adult Divsn. Poetry Contest award, 2003), The Middle School Guide to Research Papers; co-author: Go With Us, Advent Devotional. Vol. storyteller various orgns. Mem.: AARP (newsletter editor 2004—), Fayette County Ret. Educators Assn. (pres. 2001—02), Fayette Soc. Fine Arts (newsletter editor 2004), Fayette Writers Guild (treas. publicity 2004—05), Fayette County C. of C. (mem. ptnrs. in edn. com. 2003), High Noon Toastmasters (sec. 2001—02, coord. youth leadership program 2003, v.p. publicity 2004—05, mentor, trainer).

LUNSFORD, W. BRUCE, health facility administrator, health and medical products executive; b. Nov. 11, 1947; m. Becky Lunsford, Aug. 29, 1970; children: Amy, Cindy, Brandy. BA, U. Ky., 1969; JD, Salmon P. Chase Coll. Law, 1974. CPA Ky., Ohio; bar: Ky. 1974, Ohio 1974. With Alexander Grant & Co., CPA, Cin., 1969—74, Keating, Muething and Klekamp Attys., Cin., 1974—79; dep. sec. Ky. Devel. Cabinet and Gov.'s Legis. Liaison, 1980—81; sec. Ky. Commerce Cabinet, 1981—83; of counsel, atty. Greenebaum Doll & McDonald, Louisville, 1984—91; chmn., pres., CEO Vencor Inc., Louisville, 1985—99; pres., CEO Ventas Inc., Louisville, 1998, chmn., 1998—. Bd. trustees U. Ky., 1983—87, Centre Coll., 1992—97, Shakertown at Pleasant Hill, Ky., Inc., 1992—; bd. trustees., sec. Bellarmine Coll., 1991—97; bd. govs. Salmon P. Chase Coll. Law, 1983—87; bd. dirs. Greater Louisville Fund for the Arts, 1990—97, Ky. Ctr. for the Arts Endowment Fund, Inc., 1992—97, Ky. Econs. Devel. Corp., 1989—, chmn., 1996—; bd. dirs., exec. com. Nat. City Bank, Ky., 1991—; bd. dirs. Res-Care, Inc., 1992—, Churchill Downs, Inc., 1995—, Nat. City Corp., 1995—; Fedn. Am. Health Sys., 1996—; bd. dirs. exec. com. Greater Louisville Econ. Devel. Partnership, 1992—. Named Entrepreneur of the Yr., Ky. and So. Ind., 1988, U. Ky. Bus. Leader of Yr., 1994; named to Kentuckiana Bus. Hall of Fame, 1993. Mem.: AICPA (Outstanding CPA in bus. and Ind. 1996), Omicron Delta Kappa. Office: Ventas Inc 10350 Ormsby Park Pl #300 Louisville KY 40223-6177

LUNT, ALAN NICHOLAS, rehabilitation services professional; b. Pitts., Dec. 11, 1955; s. Harry Edward and Carmela Lunt. BA, Rutgers U., 1979; AS, U. Medicine and Dentistry N.J., 1995, MS, 2001. Peer adv. Mental Health Assn. of Morris Co., Madison, NJ, 1995—96, Bridgeway, Elizabeth, NJ, 1995—2003. Contbr. articles to profl. jours. Mem. USPRA, Nat. Alliance for Mentally Ill, Mental Health Assn. of Morris County, N.J. Psychiat. Rehab. Assn. (bd. dir. 1997-2003). Avocation: piano. Home: 2 Deauville Dr Parsippany NJ 07054

LUNT, DAVID GARTH, music educator; b. Safford, Ariz., May 18, 1943; s. Garth Stowell Lunt and Olive Hardy; m. Judy Ann Merrell, July 15, 1966; children: Michael, Richard, Kristie, DeeAnn, Debra, Melanie, Kerrie, Steven. BS in Edn., No. Ariz. U., Flagstaff, 1968, MMusEd, 1969; DMA, U. Ariz., Tucson, 1988. Dir. choral activities Prescott H.S., Ariz., 1969—80, Ea. Ariz. Coll., Thatcher, 1980—2001, Thatcher H.S., 2001—. Piano technician Precision Piano Tuning, LLC, Thatcher, Ariz., 1970—; dist. music supr.; dept./divsn. music chair, 1975—85; choral arranger; studio musician; choral clinicician and adjudicator. Author: Development of Antiphonal Choral Works, 1987, composer songs. Bishop LDS Ch., Thatcher, Ariz., 1993—98, stake presidency counselor, 1998—. Named Most Admired Faculty Mem., Alumni Soc. Ea. Ariz. Coll., 1995; recipient Outstanding Tchr. Yr., Ariz. Music Educator Yr., Alumni award, Ea. Ariz. Coll., 1983, 1995. Mem.: Ariz. Choral Dirs. Assn. (pres. 1993—95), Music Educators Nat. Conf. (state pres. 1996—98). Republican. Avocations: mechanics, landscaping. Home: 2932 W Palo Verde St Thatcher AZ 85552-5336 Office: Thatcher HS PO Box 610 Thatcher AZ 85552 Business E-Mail: dave.lunt@eac.edu.

LUNT, HORACE GRAY, linguist, educator; b. Colorado Springs, Colo., Sept. 12, 1918; s. Horace Fletcher and Irene (Jewett) L.; m. Sally Herman, June 2, 1963; children: Elizabeth, Catherine. AB, Harvard U., 1941; MA, U. Calif., Berkeley, 1942; postgrad., Charles U., Prague, Czechoslovakia, 1946-47; PhD (Rockefeller fellow), Columbia U., 1950. Lectr. in Serbo-Croatian Columbia U., 1948-49; asst. prof. Slavic langs. and lit. Harvard U., 1949-54, asso. prof., 1954-60, prof., 1960—, Samuel H. Cross prof. Slavic langs. and lits., 1965-89, Samuel H. Cross prof. Slavic langs. and lits., emeritus, 1989—, chmn. dept. Slavic langs. and lits., 1959-73, 75-76, 82-83; chmn. Slavic and East European Lang. and Area Ctr., 1983-89; mem. exec. com. Russian Rsch. Ctr., 1970-91, fellow, 1991—; mem. exec. com. Harvard Ukrainian Research Inst., 1974-91, fellow, 1991—. Author: Grammar of the Macedonian Literary Language, 1952, Old Church Slavonic Grammar, 1955, 7th rev. edit., 2001, Fundamentals of Russian, 1958, 2d rev. ed., 1968, Progressive Palatalization of Common Slavic, 1981, (with M. Taube) The Slavonic Book of Esther: Text, Lexicon, Linguistic Analysis, Problems of Translation, 1998; editor: Harvard Slavic Studies, 1953-70. Served with U.S. Army, 1942-45. Guggenheim fellow, 1960-61 Mem. Macedonian Acad. Arts and Scis. (corr.). Home: Apt 11C 1105 Massachusetts Ave Cambridge MA 02138-5223 Office: Harvard U Barker Ctr Cambridge MA 02138

LUNT, LORA G., language educator, director; b. Princeton, N.J., Mar. 21, 1940; m. C. Richard K. Lunt; children: Emily Garland, Mary Jenney. BA in French Honors, Swarthmore Coll., 1962; MAT. in French, Johns Hopkins U., 1963; PhD in Arabic, Ind. U., 1978; PhD in French, McGill U., 2001. Instr. French U. Maine, Orono, 1963—64; ESL tchr. Peace Corps, Sfax, Tunisia, 1964—66; instr. French Canton Agrl. and Tech. Coll., NY, 1973; tchr. French Potsdam H.S., NY, 1973—80; adj. instr. French St. Lawrence U., Canton, NY, 1981; assoc. dean Arts and Scis. SUNY Potsdam, 1981—86, interim chair Modern Langs., 1987—88, instr. French, 1989—90, dir. Internat. Edn., 1990—. Editor: (book) The Potsdam Reader, 1982 (SUNY Potsdam President's Award Excellence Acad. Svc., 2000); contbr. articles newsletter N.E. Conf. Tchg. Fgn. Langs., 1988, articles including Institut des Belles Lettres Arabes, 1996; dir.: (grant project U.S. Dept. Edn.) Potsdam Coll. Fgn. Lang. Project, 1985, Potsdam Coll. Collaborative Project, 1989, (grant project U.S. Dept. State) Tunisia-SUNY Potsdam Bus. Edn. Partnership, 2002—06. Mem. World in Potsdam Diversity Festival, NY, 1998—; Clk. St. Lawrence Valley Friends Meeting, Potsdam, NY, 2000—01; Host Mother AFS, Potsdam, NY, 1977—78, 1983—84, 1987—88, Organizer of Bus Stop, 1987. Recipient Dictée Ameriques, Quebec, Can., 2002. Mem.: Northeast Modern Lang. Assn., Conseil Internat. des Etudes Francophones, NAFSA Orgn.Internat. Educators. Office: SUNY Potsdam 44 Pierrepont Ave Potsdam NY Office Phone: 315-267-2793. Office Fax: 315-267-2656. Business E-Mail: luntlg@potsdam.edu.

LUNT, OWEN RAYNAL, biologist, educator; b. El Paso, Tex., Apr. 8, 1921; s. Owen and Velma (Jackson) L.; m. Helen Hickman, Aug. 8, 1953; children: David, Carol, Janet. BA in Chemistry, 1947, PhD in Agronomy, 1951. Mem. faculty UCLA, 1951-93, prof. plant nutrition, 1964-72, prof. biology, 1972—, acting chmn. dept. biophysics, 1965-70, prof. emeritus, 1993; dir. Lab. Biomed. and Environ. Scis., 1968-93. Researcher in soil chemistry, fertility, plant physiology; tech. expert Internat. Atomic Energy Agy to Colombia, 1970, Kenya, 1983, Malaysia, 1985, Uruguay, 1987. Served with USN, 1944-46. Fellow Am. Soc. Agronomy, Soil Sci. Soc. Am.; Internat. Soc. Soil Sci., AAAS, Sigma Xi. Home and Office: 1200 Roberto Ln Los Angeles CA 90077-2334 Office Phone: 310-476-3597. *I was reared in a cheerful, harmonious family on a farm. During childhood, we were poor. We all had chores and the entire household was willing to work. The family was very generous with others who were less fortunate. Unwaivering allegiance to high ethical and moral standards was expected. The whole family was active in the Mormon church. Neither parent had finished high school, but they read extensively. From an early age, I understood the family would support me in securing any educational objectives. In retrospect, I believe I had one of the best of starts.*

LUO, JIANFENG, electrical engineer, electronics engineer, researcher; b. Xiangtan, Hunan, China, Feb. 12, 1975; s. Dewen Luo and Liqun Xu; m. Na Na Xu, Oct. 11, 2002. BS in Engring., Tsinghua U., Beijing, China, 1997; MS, U. Cin., 1998; PhD, U. Calif., Berkeley, Calif., 2003. Post doctoral fellow U. Calif., Berkeley, 2003; staff R&D engr. Synopsys Inc., Mountain View, Calif., 2004—. Cons. MEMGEN Inc., Burbank, Calif., 2003. Author: Integrated Modeling of Chemical Mechanical Planarization for Sub-Micron IC Fabrication: from particle scale to feature, die and wafer scales. Fellow, U. Calif., 1999—2000. Mem.: ASME, IEEE, Sigma Xi. Office: Synopsys Inc 700E Middlefield St Mountain View CA 94043 Office Phone: 650-584-1453. Personal E-mail: jianfeng.luo@gmail.com. Business E-Mail: jianfeng@synopsys.com.

LUO, JUNMING, medical researcher; b. Hanshou, China, July 10, 1962; s. Yongfu Luo and Fuyuan Rao; m. Shuhua Wang; 1 child, Cindy Xinjue. MS, Hunan Med. U., Changsha, China, 1989—92. Postdoctoral fellow Pa. State U., Hershey, 1998—2002; rsch. assoc. Brown Med. Sch., Providence, 2002—. Attending physician Ctrl. South U., Changsha, China, 1995—98. Achievements include research in autoimmunity and host defense molecule. Office: Dept Orthopaedics 1 Hoppin St Providence RI 02903 Office Phone: 401-793-8387. Office Fax: 401-444-5872. E-mail: junming_luo@brown.edu.

LUO, NIANZHU, mechanical engineer; b. Chengdu, China, Aug. 1, 1951; s. Qianhe and Jiqin (Feng) L.; m. Shufang Ye, Jan. 1, 1979; two children. BS, Southwest Jiaotong U., 1976; MS, U. Wis., 1986, PhD, 1989. Lectr. Southwest Jiaotong U., Sichuan, China, 1977-82; rsch. fellow U. Wis., Madison, 1983-85; from sr. engr. to tech. specialist Case Corp., Chgo., 1990-95; fluid power specialist Sauer-Sundstrand, Newtown, Pa., 1995-99; engring. mgr. Sauer-Danfoss Inc., 2000—. Mem. Soc. Automotive Engrs., Assn. Chinese Scientists & Engrs. Home: 261 Sassafras Dr Easley SC 29642-8264 Office Phone: 864-644-3007. Personal E-mail: nluo@yahoo.com.

LUO, SHAWN HAISHENG, retail company executive; b. Shantou, Guangdong, China, Apr. 4, 1961; came to U.S., 1990; s. Xu Luo and Shaofen Wu; m. Crystal Xiaoping Zheng, May 8, 1990. BS, Zhongshan U., Guangzhou, China, 1983; MS, Capital Normal U., Beijing, 1987; PhD, Claremont Grad. U., 1995. Mem. cons. team Info. Inst., U. So. Calif., Santa Monica, 1990-91, Chevron Oil Field Rsch. Co., La Habra, Calif., 1991-92; statis. analyst Pharmavite Corp., Mission Hills, Calif., 1996-98, mgr. prodn. planning San Fernando, Calif., 1998-2000; dir. supply chain cons. Quevera (formerly Millennia Vision Corp.), San Jose, Calif., 2000-01; dir. inventory productivity Circuit City Stores, Inc., Richmond, Va., 2001—03, dir. supply chain and inventory productivity, 2003—. Contbr. articles to sci. jours., including Jour. Math. and Computer Modeling, Math. Engring. in Industry, Jour. Math. Physics. Dissertation grantee Claremont Grad. U., 1993. Mem.: Am. Prodn. and Inventory Control Soc. Home: 2004 Kittiwake Ln Cedar Park TX 78613 Office: Circuit City Stores Inc 9950 Mayland Dr Richmond VA 23233

LUO, SHUHONG, microbiologist, researcher; s. Wenhua Luo and Wenyu Su; m. Min Cheng, Jan. 29, 1989; 1 child, Chengchao. BS, Hunan Med. Sch., 1980—83; MS, Ctrl. South China, 1988—91; PhD, Nanjing Med. U., 1992—95. Assoc. prof. Zhongshan U., Guangzhou, China, 1997—98; post-doctoral rsch. accociate U. of Ill. at Urbana-Champaign, 1998—2000, rsch. asst. prof., 2001—; postdoctoral rsch. assoc. Zhongshan U., Guangzhou, China. Vice sec.-gen. and mem. of coun. for the sixth coun. Soc. of Parasitology, Guangdong Province, China, 1997—2000. Recipient Outstanding Young Scientist award, Ministry of Pub. Health, China, 1998, Travel award for young scientists, XIV Int. Congress for Tropical and Med., 1996, IX Internat. Congress of Parasitology, 1998; fellow Post doctoral Rsch., Sci. Found., P.R. China, 1995—97; Malaria vaccine, China Med. Bd. (CMB), NY, 1998—2001, Studies On Malaria Vaccine, Nat. Natural Sci. Found., P.R.China, 1998—2001, Ministry of Pub. Health, P.R. China, 1998—99. Mem.: Soc. of Parasitology (assoc.), Am. Soc. of Parasitologists (assoc.), Am. Soc. for Tropical Medicine and Hygiene (assoc.), Am. Soc. for Microbiology (assoc.). Home: 300 Goldenrod Dr Savoy IL 61874-9332 Office: Univ of Ill at Urbana-Champai 2001 S Lincoln Ave Urbana IL 61802 Office Phone: 217-333-4598. Home Fax: 217-244-7421; Office Fax: 217-244-7421. Personal E-mail: sluo@uiuc.edu.

LUO, WENHONG, information scientist, educator; PhD, U. Ky., 1995. Asst. prof. Worcester (Mass.) Poly. Inst., 1996—2000; assoc. prof. Villanova (Pa.) U., 2000—05. Achievements include research in business computing, business intelligence, electronic commerce, management of information technology. Office: Villanova University 800 Lancaster Ave Villanova PA 19403 Office Phone: 610-519-5592.

LUONG, NAM THOAI, biochemist, researcher; b. Saigon, Vietnam, Nov. 20, 1977; s. Phat Minh Luong and Hue Thu Tran; m. Anh Boi Tran; 1 child, Sammy. BS, U. Hartford, 1999; postgrad., Harvard U. Rsch. chemist Cabot Corp., Billerica, Mass., 2000—. Mem.: Table Tennis Club. Avocations: table soccer, ping pong/table tennis, magic, piano, guitar. Office: 157 Concord Rd Billerica MA 01827

LUONGO, C. PAUL, public relations executive; b. Winchester, Mass., Dec. 31, 1930; s. Carmine and Carmela (Gilberti) L. Grad., Cambridge Sch. Radio-TV, 1955; diploma, Bentley Coll., 1951; BSBA, Suffolk U., 1955; MBA, Babson Coll., 1956; AAS (hon.), Grahm Jr. Coll., 1970. Jr. exec. Raytheon Co., Lexington, Mass., 1956-59; account exec. Young & Rubicam, Inc., 1959-62; v.p. Copley Advt. Agy., Boston, 1962-64; pres. C. Paul Luongo Co., Boston, 1964—. Guest appearances include: (TV programs) Today Show, NBC-TV, 1984-89, Tomorrow Show, NBC-TV; TV-radio programs, Can.; author: America's Best!, 1980; contbr. syndicated newspaper-mag. features to Pub. Rels. Today; contbg. editor Travel Smart, N.Y., mo. newsletter. Founder Anthony Spinazzola Meml. Scholarship Found., Boston U., 1986-88; vol. U.S.S. Constn. Mus., Boston, Sta. WGBH-TV, Boston, TV Auctions, 1991-2000; mem. WORLDBOSTON, Boston, Mus. Fine Arts, Black Ships Festival, Inc., Newport, R.I.; pub. rels. dir. centennial ba. Belcourt Castle, Newport, 1994. With AUS, 1952-54. Mem. Boston Stockbrokers Club, Boston Advt. Club, Newcomen Soc. N.Am., Am. Inst. Wine and Food, Japan-Am. Soc. R.I., Neighborhood Assn. of Back Bay, Inc., Back Bay Assn., Suffolk U. Gen. Alumni Assn. (bd. dirs. 1994-98), James Beard Found., Friends of the Boston Pops. Address: 545 Boylston St 9th Fl Boston MA 02116 Office Phone: 617-266-4210. *I believe in the work ethic, integrity and the maximum utilization of time for work and recreational activities. I loathe prejudice in any form, dishonesty and indolent people.*

LUONGO, ROBERTO, professional hockey player; b. Montreal, Quebec, Canada, Apr. 4, 1979; s. Pasqualina. Goaltender New York Islanders, 1999—2000, Florida Panthers, 2000—. Goaltender Team Can., World Championships, 2003, 04, Team Can., World Cup of Hockey, 2004. Named to NHL All-Star Game, 2004. Achievements include mem. Gold medal Canadian World Championships Team, 2003, 2004; set NHL record for saves in a single season (2,303), 2004; mem. World Cup Champion Team Can., 2004. Office: c/o Florida Panthers 1 Panther Pkwy Sunrise FL 33323

LUPERT, LESLIE ALLAN, lawyer; b. Syracuse, N.Y., May 24, 1946; s. Reuben and Miriam (Kaufman) L.; m. Roberta Gail Fellner, May 19, 1968; children: Jocelyn, Rachel, Susannah. BA, U. Buffalo, 1967; JD, Columbia U., 1971. Bar: N.Y. 1971. Ptnr. Orans Elsen & Lupert, N.Y.C., 1971—. Contbr. articles to profl. jours. Mem. ABA, N.Y. State Bar Assn. (trial lawyers sect.), Assn. of Bar of City of N.Y. (com. fed. legislation 1977-80, profl. and jud. ethics com. 1983-86, com. on fed. cts. 1986-89, 95-96), Phi Beta Kappa. Office: Orans Elsen & Lupert LLP 875 3d Ave 28th Fl New York NY 10021 Office Phone: 212-586-2211. Business E-Mail: llupert@oellaw.com.

LUPIANI, DONALD ANTHONY, psychologist; b. N.Y.C., June 7, 1946; s. Louis and Josephine (Boccia) L.; m. Linda Moyik, June 20, 1970; 1 child, Jennifer. BA, Iona Coll., 1968; MA, Columbia U., 1971, PhD, 1973; post-doctoral, Behavior Therapy Inst., White Plains, N.Y., 1976. Lic. psychologist, N.Y.; diplomat Am. Bd. Profl. Psychology, Am. Bd. Psychotherapy, Am. Acad. Behavioral Medicine, Intenat. Acad. Behavioral Medicine, Internat. Acad. Behavioral Medicine. Clin. assoc. Columbia U., N.Y.C., 1974-85, Fordham U., Bronx, N.Y., 1979-81; dir. psychology and spl. edn. svcs. Riverdale Country Sch., Bronx, 1973-87; chief psychologist Franciscan Order of Priests, N.Y.C., 1983—; pvt. practice Yonkers, N.Y., 1975—. Dir. spl. svcs. Riverdale Country Sch., Bronx., 1973-87; bd. dirs. St. Ursula Learning Ctr., Mt. Vernon, N.Y. Contbr. articles to profl. jours. Bd. dirs., mem. The St. Ursula Learning Ctr. Fellow Am. Orthopsychiat. Assn., Am. Coll. Psychology, Am. Acad. Sch. Psychology; mem. APA, N.Y. State Psychol. Assn., Westchester County Psychol. Assn. (chmn. ethics com. 1980-87). Roman Catholic. Avocations: woodworking, painting, drawing. Home and Office: 227 Mile Square Rd Yonkers NY 10701-5369

LUPICA, MICHAEL THOMAS, sports columnist; b. Oneida, N.Y., May 11, 1952; s. Benedict and Lee; married; 3 children. BA, Boston Coll., 1974. Corr. Boston Globe, 1970-74; columnist Boston Phoenix, 1971-75, Boston mag., 1974-75; feature writer Washington Star, 1974-75; basketball writer, columnist N.Y. Post, 1975-76; columnist N.Y. Daily News, 1980—; writer syndicated TV spls.; contbg. editor World Tennis, 1974-81. Contr.: (TV series) The Sports Reporters; host The Mike Lupica Show; co-author: (novels) Wait Till Next Year, 1988; author Reggie, 1984, Dead Air, 1986, Parcells, 1987, Extra Credits, 1988, Limited Partner, 1990, Mad as Hell, 1996, Jump, 1996, Summer of '98, 1999, Full Court Press, 2001, Red Zone, 2003, Wild Pitch, 2003, Too Far, 2004, Heat, 2005. Mem. Newspaper Guild Am. Achievements include youngest columnist (23 years old) to write for a major New York City newspaper. Office: NY Daily News 220 E 42nd St Fl 817 New York NY 10017-5806*

LUPIN, LOUIS MARTIN, lawyer; b. Mar. 1955; m. Margarita I. Lupin; children: Gabe, Daniel, Leanna. BA in Psychology, Swarthmore Coll., 1977; JD, Stanford U., 1985. Bar: 1985. Assoc. Cooley, Godward, Castro, Huddleson & Tatum, San Francisco, ptnr., 1992—95; sr. legal counsel QUALCOMM Inc., San Diego, 1995—96, v.p., proprietary rights counsel, 1996—98, sr. v.p., proprietary rights counsel, 1998—2000, sr. v.p., gen. counsel, 2000—. Exec. com. bd. visitors Stanford Law Sch. Mem.: San Francisco Bar Assn., Santa Clara County Bar Assn., ABA. Office: QUALCOMM Inc 5775 Morehouse Dr San Diego CA 92121-1714

LUPINO, JAMES SAMUEL, lawyer; b. Mpls., Oct. 23, 1952; s. Rocco and Marie (Furlong) L.; m. Diane Schaefer, May 14, 1983. BS, Augustana Coll., 1974; JD, Hamline U., 1977. Bar: Fla. 1977, Minn. 1977, U.S. Dist. Ct. (so. dist.) Fla. 1977, U.S. Dist. Ct. Minn. 1977, Colo. 1997. Assoc. Thomson, Nordby & Peterson, St. Paul, 1976-77; counsel Lone Star Industries, Greenwich, Conn., 1977-79; sole practice Coral Gables, Fla., 1980-86; ptnr. Storace & Lupino, Miami, Fla., 1986-87, 91-93, Storace, Lupino & Middelthon, Miami, 1987-91, Storace, Lupino, Gregg & Casey, Miami, 1993-95, Hershoff, Lupino, DeFoor & Gregg, Miami, 1995—. Mem. ABA, Fla. Bar Assn., Minn. Bar Assn., Assn. Trial Lawyer Am., Key Largo C. of C (bd. dirs.), Kiwanis, Upper Keys Rotary Club (bd. dirs.). Republican. Roman Catholic. Avocations: family, skiing, scuba, football. Office: Hershoff Lupino & Mulick LLP 90130 Old Hwy Tavernier FL 33070-2348

LUPIS, GIUSEPPE, musician; b. Bari, Italy, Feb. 13, 1968; s. Vito Lupis and Maria Serena; m. Sallie Bacon, May 18, 2002. Scientific diploma, Liceo Scientifico E. Fermi, Brindisi, Italy, 1986; piano diploma, Bari Conservatory of Music, 1989; postgrad. in DMA program, U. Ga., Athens, 2003—. Concert pianist U.S., Europe, S.Am., 1980—; prof. piano Music Conservatory, Monopoli, Italy, 1994—95, prof. chamber music Campobasso, Italy, 1996; prof. piano Vivaldi Inst., San Benedetto Del Tronto, Italy, 1994—96, Pergolesi Inst., Ancona, Italy, 1993—2001; artist in residence Wesleyan Coll., Macon, Ga., 2002; tchg. asst. U. Ga., Athens, 2003—. Artistic dir. Premio Nazionale M. Urbani, Urbisaglia, Italy, 2000—01, La Vittoria Theatre, Sarnano, Italy, 2000—01, UCSG Concert Season, San Ginesio, Italy, 1997—2000; jury mem. Premio Massimo Urbani competition, 1998, 2000—01, Citta' di Alcamo Internat. Singing Competition, 2000—01, Casamassima Nat. Competition, 2000. Performer (arranger): (CD) George Gershwin, 2000. Carabiniere Italian Army, 1990—91. Recipient Performance award, Macerata Feltria, 1996, Concerto Competition, U. GA, Athens, 2003, Dirs. Excellence List award, 2004, Franz Liszt award, 2005. Avocations: cooking, model trains. Home: 755 W Hancock Ave # 16 Athens GA 30601 Business E-Mail: lupodelu@uga.edu.

LUPO, RAPHAEL V., lawyer; b. Washington, Oct. 15, 1941; BSEE, George Washington U., 1963, JD, 1968. Bar: Va. 1968, D.C. 1968, U.S. Dist. Ct. D.C. 1968, U.S. Dist. Ct. (ea. dist.) Va. 1969, U.S. Patent and Trademark Office, U.S. Claims Ct. 1969, U.S. Ct. Appeals ((D.C. cir.) 1968, U.S. Ct. Appeals (4th cir.) 1969, U.S. Ct. Appeals (fed. cir.) 1982, U.S. Ct. Customs and Patent Appeals 1969, U.S. Supreme Ct. 1969, U.S. Ct. Appeals 1982. Assoc. solicitor U.S. Patent and Trademark Office, 1969-77; dep. asst. gen. counsel for patents Dept. Energy, 1977-80; atty. Spencer & Kaye, Washington, 1980-82, Lupo Lipman & Lever, Washington, 1982-89, Willian Brinks Olds Hofer Gilson & Lione, P.C., Washington; ptnr., mem. firm exec. mgmt. com., IP dept. chair McDermott Will & Emery LLP, Washington. Adj. prof. George Washington U. Law Sch., 1992; speaker 6th Annual Jud. Conf. U.S. Ct. Appeals (Fed. cir.), 1988, 10th Annual Jud. Conf. U.S. Ct. Appeals (Fed. cir.), 1992-1998; presenter in field. Co-author: Patent Litigation and Strategy, 1999. Mem. ABA (contbr. Patent Litigation Strategies Handbook section of Intellectual Property BNA 2000), D.C. Bar, Va. State Bar, Am. Intellectual Property Law Assn. Office: McDermott Will & Emery LLP 600 13th St NW Fl 12-8 Washington DC 20005-3005 Office Phone: 202-756-8366. Office Fax: 202-756-8087. Business E-Mail: rlupo@mwe.com.

LUPO, ROBERT EDWARD SMITH, real estate developer and investor; b. New Orleans, May 27, 1953; s. Thomas Joseph and Alvena Florence (Smith) L.; m. Mary Lynn Puissegur, June 16, 1980; children: Robert Thomas Smith, Francesca Marfise Smith. BArch, Tulane U., 1977. Owner Robert Edward Smith Lupo Properties, New Orleans, 1976—; cons. various firms, New Orleans, 1977—; COO Commodore Thomas J. Lupo Enterprises, Williams-Lupo, Smith-Lupo, New Orleans, 1981—; pres. Hedwig, Inc., Zephyr, Inc., Noroaltom Devel. Co., Inc., New Orleans, 1981—. Cons. Mrs. Thomas J. Lupo properties. Grad. Met. Area Leadership Forum, New Orleans, 1980; bd.

dirs., pres. New Orleans Mcpl. Yacht Harbor, 1989-93; life mem. Friends Audubon Zoo, 1983—; bd. dirs. New Orleans Met. Area Com., 1985-90; guardian mem. Boy Scouts Am., 1991—; mem. capital projects oversight com. Orleans Parish Sch. Bd., 1995—; mem. bd. commrs. Orleans Levee Dist., 1996—. Recipient Gov.'s award State of La., 1980, Tulane Assocs. award Tulane U., 1986; named One of 10 Best Dress Men, Men of Fashion, 1983, named to Hall of Fame, 1991. Mem. Aquarium Ams. (life), Assn. Naval Aviation (charter), Sigma Alpha Epsilon (founding). Clubs: Semreh. Republican. Roman Catholic. Office: 145 Robert E Lee Blvd New Orleans LA 70124-2552

LUPOLI, JOHN, JR., minister, photographer; b. Augsburg, Germany, Oct. 25, 1956; s. John Lupoli Sr. and Anna (Rufo) Lupoli; m. Patricia D. Cokos. BA in Theology, Carolina Christina U., 1988, MDiv, 1991, ThD, PhD, Carolina Christina U., 1993; DD, Corner Stone U., Israel, 1993. Commd. 2d lt. USAF, 1987, advanced through grades to lt. col., 1993; CEO, founder World Coun. Ind. Christian Ch., Harpers Ferry, W.Va., 1993—. Photographer Sun Chaser Studios, Calif. Humanitarian worker World Coun. Ind. Christian Chs., Namandzi, Malawi, 1994, New Delhi, 1996, Leper Colony, India, 1997; non-govtl. organizing rep. UN, 1994—. Republican. Jewish. Avocations: photography, camping. Office: World Coun Ind Christian Ch PO Box 406 Harpers Ferry WV 25425 Office Phone: 949-476-6903.

LUPTON, STEPHEN D., lawyer; b. 1944; LLB, Newcastle U., Eng., 1968. Barrister London Bar (Gray's Inn) 1970. Mgr. legal and secretarial services UK divsn. GM Corp., 1968—72; sec., group legal adviser for domestic appliance divsn. GEC Plc., 1972—75; European legal counsel NCH Corp., Irving, Tex., 1975—90; dir. legal services Massey Ferguson Group Ltd. (acquired by AGCO Corp. 1994), 1990—94; dir. legal services internat. AGCO Corp., Duluth, Minn., 1994—95, v.p., internat. counsel, 1995—99, sr. v.p., gen. counsel, 1999—2002, sr. v.p. corp. devel., gen. counsel, 2002—. Office: AGCO Corp 4205 River Green Pkwy Duluth GA 30096

LUPU, RADU, pianist; b. Galati, Romania, Nov. 30, 1945; s. Meyer and Ana (Gabor) L. Attended Conservatoire, Moscow, USSR, 1961-69. London debut, 1969, Berlin, 1972, U.S. debut with Cleve. Orch. in N.Y.C., appearances with worldwide maj. orchs., including Berlin Philharmonic, Vienna Philharmonic, Israel Philharmonic, Orch. de Paris, Concertgebouw, N.Y. Philharmonic, Phila. Symphony Orch., Chgo. Symphony Orch., Cleve. Symphony Orch.; recs. include Beethoven cycle with Israel Philharmonic and Zubin Mehta, Schubert Sonatas, Beethoven Sonatas, Mozart Sonatas for Violin and Piano with Szymon Goldberg, Schubert Lieder with Barbara Hendricks, Mozart and Schubert duets and Mozart Concerto for 2 pianos, both with Murray Perahia, Brahms Piano Concerto #1 Mozart and Beethoven Quintets in E Flat, Schubert Piano Duets with Daniel Barenboim. Recipient 1st prize Van Cliburn Internat. Piano Competition, 1966, Enescu Competition, 1967, Leeds Internat. Piano Competition, 1969, Abbiati prize Italian Critic's Assn., 1989, Edison award for Schumann Kinderszenen, Kreisleriana, 1995, Grammy award for Schubert D960 and D664 record, 1995. Office Phone: 01608 810330. Business E-Mail: artists@terryharrison.force9.co.uk.

LUPULESCU, AUREL PETER, medical educator, researcher, physician; b. Manastiur, Banat, Romania, Jan. 1, 1923; came to U.S., 1967, naturalized, 1973; s. Peter Vichentie and Maria Ann (Dragan) L. MD magna cum laude, Sch. Medicine, Bucharest, Romania, 1950; MS in Endocrinology, U. Bucharest, 1965; PhD in Biology, U. Windsor, Ont., Can., 1976. Diplomate Am. Bd. Internal Medicine. Chief lab. investigations Inst. Endocrinology, Bucharest, 1950-67; rsch. assoc. SUNY Downstate Med. Ctr., 1968-69; asst. prof. medicine Wayne State U., 1969-72, assoc. prof., 1973—. Vis. prof. Inst. Med. Pathology, U. Rome, 1967; cons. VA Hosp., Allen Park, Mich., 1971-73; sr. cancer rsch. scientist Wayne State U., 1991—. Author: Steroid Hormones, 1958, Advances in Endocrinology and Metabolism, 1962, Experimental Pathophysiology of Thyroid Gland, 1963, Ultrastructure of Thyroid Gland, 1968, Effect of Calcitonin on Epidermal Cells and Collagen Synthesis in Experimental Wounds As Revealed by Electron Microscopy Autoradiography and Scanning Electron Microscopy, 1976, Hormones and Carcinogenesis, 1983, Hormones and Vitamins in Cancer Treatment, 1990, Cancer Cell Metabolism and Cancer Treatment, 2001; reviewer various sci. jours.; contbr. chpts., numerous articles to profl. publs. Recipient Lifetime Sci. Achievement award, Internat. Biographical Ctr., 2003. Fellow Fedn. Am. Socs. for Exptl. Biology; mem. AMA, AAAS, Electron Microscopy Soc. Am., Soc. for Investigative Dermatology, N.Y. Acad. Scis., Am. Soc. Cell Biology, Soc. Exptl. Biology and Medicine. Republican. Achievements include research on hormones and tumor biology; studies regarding role of hormones and vitamins in cancer treatment and prevention. Home: 21480 Mahon Dr Southfield MI 48075-7525 Office: Wayne State U Sch Medicine 540 E Canfield St Detroit MI 48201-1928

LUQUE-ESCALONA, ROBERTO SABAS, writer; b. Holguin, Oriente, Cuba, Dec. 5, 1936; arrived in U.S., 1992; s. Ernesto Ramiro Luque and Dulce Maria Escalona; m. Miriam Ramos, Mar. 3, 1962 (div. Feb. 5, 1993); children: Veronica, Ernesto; m. Ana Casas, Dec. 18, 1996. BA in Polit. sci., U. Havana, Cuba, 1965. Columnist El Nuevo Herald, Miami, 1991—2001, Libre, Miami, 2000—03, Diario Las Americas, Miami, 2001—03; lectr. Sam Houston State U., Huntsville, Tex., 1993—94. Author: (historical book) The Tiger and the Children, 1990, (biography) Me, The Best of All, 1994, (novels) The Professor, 2002, 8 Ponpland St., 2003. Mem. Cuban Com. for Human Rights, Havana, 1987—92. Mem.: Cuban Exile PEN Club (v.p. 1999—2002). Republican. Avocations: reading, movies, baseball. Office: Diario Las Americas 2900 NW 39 St Miami FL 33142

LURAAS, SANDRA, elementary and secondary education educator; b. Seneca Falls, N.Y., Feb. 3, 1955; d. Antimo John and Helene (Arini) Scialdone; m. Robert Raymond Luraas, June 17, 1978; children: Suzanne Helene, Robert Ames. BA in Psychology, SUNY, Albany, 1981, MS in Edn., 1994. Cert. tchr., N.Y. Reading specialist Redemption Christian Acad., Troy, NY, 1979—, asst. dir. RCA Nature Camp, 1992-94. Sunday sch. tchr. Redemption Ch., Troy, 1977-91, 95—, instr. children's ministries, 1979-89, missions dir., 1989—; children's visitor St. Mary's Hosp., 1983. Recipient Tchr. of Yr. award Walmart, 1998. Apostolic Pentecostal. Avocations: gardening, fishing, swimming, hiking. Home: 1712 Highland Ave Troy NY 12180-3712 Office: Redemption Christian Acad 192 9th St Troy NY 12180-2304

LURAIN, JOHN ROBERT, III, gynecologist; b. Princeton, Ill., Oct. 27, 1946; s. John Robert Jr. and Elizabeth Helen (Grampp) L.; m. Nell Lee Snavely, June 14, 1969; children: Alice Elizabeth, Kathryn Anne. BA, Oberlin Coll., 1968; MD, U. N.C., 1972. Diplomate Am. Bd. Ob-Gyn., Am. Bd. Gynecologic Oncology. Resident in ob-gyn. U. Pitts./Magee-Womens Hosp., 1972-75; fellow in gynecologic oncology Roswell Park Cancer Inst., Buffalo, 1977-79; prof. gynecology and cancer rsch. Northwestern U., Feinberg Sch. Medicine, Chgo., 1979—; chief gyn. oncology svc. Northwestern Meml. Hosp., 1985—2004. Contbr. over 150 articles to profl. jours.; contbr. chapters to books. Lt. comdr. USN, 1975-77. Fellow: Am. Coll. Ob-Gyn.; mem.: Internat. Soc. Study Trophoblastic Diseases, Internat. Gynecol. Cancer Soc., Am Soc. Colposcopy and Cervical Pathology, Ctrl. Assn. Ob-Gyn., Am. Soc. Clin. Oncology, Soc. Gynecologic Oncologists. Avocations: golf, tennis. Office: Northwestern U Med Sch 333 E Superior St Chicago IL 60611-3015 Office Phone: 312-926-7365. Business E-Mail: jlurain@nmff.org.

LURASCHI, WILLIAM R., utilities executive, lawyer; BS finance, U. of Conn.; JD, Rutgers Sch. Law. Assoc. Chadbourne & Parke LLP; gen. counsel The AES Corp., Arlington, Va., 1994—, sec., 1996—2002, v.p., 1998—2002, sr. v.p., 2002—03, exec. v.p., 2003—. Office: The AES Corp 1001 N 19th St Arlington VA 22209

LURIA, MARTIN JAY, endocrinologist; b. Bklyn., Apr. 19, 1946; MD, NYU, 1971. Diplomate Am. Bd. Internal Medicine, Am. Bd. Endocrinology. Intern Kings County Hosp.-SUNY Downstate Med., 1971—72, resident in medicine, 1972—74; fellow in endocrinology Mt. Sinai Hosp., N.Y.C., 1974—76; chief sect. endocrinology Monmouth Med. Ctr., Long Branch, NJ, 1976—. Attending physician dept. medicine Riverview Med. Ctr., Red Bank, NJ, 1976—; mem. courtesy staff Bayshore Cmty. Hosp., Holmdel, NJ, 1976—; consulting physician in endocrinology Ctrl. State Hosp., Freehold, NJ, 1976—. Named one of Top Drs. 2003, Castle Connolly and N.J. Monthly Mag. Fellow: Am. Coll. Endocrinology. Office: 170 Morris Ave Ste F Long Branch NJ 07740-6660 Office Phone: 732-222-8874.

LURIA, MARY MERCER, lawyer; b. Boston, Dec. 29, 1942; d. Albert and Mabel (Jacomb) Mercer; m. Nelson J. Luria, June 19, 1967. AB, Radcliffe Coll., 1964; LLB, Yale U., 1967. Bar: N.Y. 1968. Assoc. Simpson, Thacher & Bartlett, N.Y.C., 1967-68, Hale & Dorr, Boston, 1968-69, Satterlee & Stephens, N.Y.C., 1969-74, ptnr., 1974-86, Patterson, Belknap, Webb & Tyler, N.Y.C., 1986-97, Davis & Gilbert, N.Y.C., 1997—. Mem. ABA, N.Y. State Bar Assn., Assn. Bar City N.Y. Avocations: gardening, photography. Office: Davis & Gilbert 1740 Broadway Fl 20 New York NY 10019-4379 Office Phone: 212-468-4813. E-mail: mluria@dglaw.com.

LURIE, ALISON, writer; b. Chgo., Sept. 3, 1926; children: John, Jeremy, Joshua. AB, Radcliffe Coll., 1947. Lectr. English Cornell U., 1968-73, adj. assoc. prof. English Ithaca, NY, 1973-76, assoc. prof., 1976-79, prof., 1979—. Author: V.R. Lang: A Memoir, 1959, Love and Friendship, 1962, The Nowhere City, 1965, Imaginary Friends, 1967, Real People, 1969, The War Between the Tates, 1974, Only Children, 1979, The Language of Clothes, 1981, Foreign Affairs, 1984, The Truth About Lorin Jones, 1988, Don't Tell the Grownups, 1990, Women and Ghosts, 1994, The Last Resort, 1998, Familiar Spirits, 2001, Boys and Girls Forever, 2003, Truth and Consequences, 2005. Recipient award in lit. Am. Acad. Arts and Letters, 1978, Pulitzer prize in fiction, 1985; fellow Yaddo Found., 1963-64, 66, Guggenheim Found., 1965, Rockefeller Found., 1967, Prix Femina Etranger, 1989. Business E-Mail: al28@cornell.edu.

LURIE, ALVIN DAVID, lawyer; b. N.Y.C., Apr. 16, 1923; s. Samuel and Rose L.; m. Marian Weinberg, Aug. 21, 1944; children: James, Jeanne, Margery, Jonathan. AB, Cornell U., 1943, LLB, 1944. Bar: N.Y. 1944, D.C. 1978. Ptnr. Lurie & Rubin, N.Y.C., 1961—68, Aranow, Brodsky, Bohlinger & Einhorn, N.Y.C., 1968—74; asst. commr. for employee plans and exempt orgns. IRS, Washington, 1974—78; ptnr. Chadbourne, Parke, Whiteside & Wolff, N.Y.C., 1978—84, Meyers, Tersigni, Lurie, Feldman & Gray, N.Y.C., 1984—94; atty. Alvin D. Lurie, N.Y.C., 1994—96; pres. Alvin D. Lurie, PC, New Rochelle, NY, 1996—; trustee N.Y. Ctr. Fin. Studies, 1980—. Mem. adv. bd. NYU Tax Inst., 1978-90; mem. adv. bd.Tax Mgmt., 1978—; mem. adv. bd. Tax Analysts and Advocates, 1995-2002; spl. counsel Small Bus. Coun. Am., 1978—; counsel N.Y. Soc. Fin. Svcs. Profls., 1978—. Author: Lurie's Commentaries on Pension Design, 1980, Lurie's Guide to VEBAs, 1983, Collected Commentaries on Pensions, 1984, ESOPs Made Easy, 1985; chair, editor NYU Rev. of Employee Benefits and Executive Compensation, 1998—; co-editor-in-chief Cornell Law Quar., 1943-44; pub. Pension & Benefit Power, 2002—; mem. editl. bd. LexisNexis Fed. Tax Libr., 2005; contbr. articles to profl. jours. Fellow Am. Coll. Tax Counsel; mem. ABA, N.Y. State Bar Assn. (chmn. spl. com. pension simplification 1986—2004), Assn. Bar City N.Y., Am. Coll. Employee Benefits Counsel (charter), N.Y. Bar Found. Office: 145 Huguenot St New Rochelle NY 10801-5200 Office Phone: 914-235-6575. E-mail: allurie@att.net. *Hard work, in intensive spurts, is my formula. The work must be varied, permitting application of different skills in constantly changing, creative ways. But one thing more is needed: carpe diem.*

LURIE, DAPHNE, clinical psychologist, lecturer, educator; b. Tel Aviv, May 31, 1965; came to U.S. 1966. d. Ranan and Tamar R.; m. Stephen Daniel Sprinkle, Aug. 17, 1999; 1 child: Samuel David. Grad. degree in psychology, Williams Coll., 1987; PhD, U. S.C., 1996. Psycholo. rschr. with Vietnam vets. Seattle Va. Med. Ctr., Nat. Ctr. Post-Traumatic Stress Disorder, 1988-89; predoctoral internship Seattle Va. Med. Ctr., 1994-96; counselor psychol. svcs., therapist, spvr. students Clemson U., 1997-01; pvt. practice, specializing in couples' counseling Clemson. Doctoral work and tchg., U. S.C., 1989-93. Mem. APA, S.C. Psychol. Assn. Mailing: Pmb 223 389 Hamilton St Geneva NY 14456-2920

LURIE, FEDOR, surgeon, researcher; s. Evgeniy Davidovich and Valentina Fedorovna Lurie; m. Galina Lurie, Nov. 12, 1976; children: Andrei, Evgenia. MD, Sverdlovskiy Med. Inst., Ekaterinburg, Russia, 1980; MSc, Inst. Math. and Mechanics, USSR Acad. Sci., Russia, 1984; PhD, Sverdlovskiy Med. Inst., Ekaterinburg, Russia, 1986. Med. diploma Sverdlovskiy Med. Inst., 1980. Asst. prof. surgery Sverdlovskiy Med. Inst., Ekaterinburg, Russia, 1980—84, assoc. prof. surgery, 1984—95; vis. prof. U. Calif. Davis, Sacramento, 1995—99, postgraduate rschr., 1999—2000; asst. clin. prof. surgery John A. Burns Sch. Medicine, U. Hawaii, Honolulu, 2000—. Dir. rsch. Straub Found., Honolulu, 2000—. Contbr. articles to profl. jours. Grantee, Hawaii Cmty. Found., 2001—03. Mem.: AMA, European Soc. for Vascular Surgery, Am. Venous Forum (outcomes com. 2004). Achievements include research in venous circulation. Office: Straub Foundation Ste 1045 1100 Ward Ave Honolulu HI 96814 Office Phone: 808-547-5936. Office Fax: 808-535-7545. Personal E-mail: tedlurie@yahoo.com. Business E-Mail: flurie@straub.net.

LURIE, JEFFREY, professional sports team executive; b. Sept. 8, 1951; married; 2 children. BA, Clark U.; MA in Psychology, Boston U.; PhD in Social Policy, Brandeis U. Pres., CEO Chestnut Hills Prodn., L.A.; dir. Harcourt Gen. Inc.; owner Phila. Eagles, 1994—. Mem. NFL expansion com., fin. com. Former trustee Clark U.; dir. Nat. Alliance for Autism Rsch., Boston; active local charitable cmty., Phila. Mem. Phila. C. of C. (exec. com.). Office: Nova Care Complex 1 Nova Care Way Philadelphia PA 19145-5996

LURIE, MAXINE NEUSTADT, historian; b. N.Y.C., Dec. 28, 1940; d. Harrison and Dora (Goldstein) Neustadt; m. Jonathan Lurie; children: David, Deborah, Daniel. BA, Alfred U., 1962; MA, U. Rochester, 1963; PhD, U. Wis., Madison, Wis., 1968. Asst. prof. Marquette U., Milw., 1967-69; coadjutant Rutgers U., Newark and New Brunswick, N.J., 1969-93, coord. undergrad. pub. history internships, 1992-94; asst. prof. Rutgers U. Libraries, New Brunswick, 1980-89, Seton Hall U., South Orange, N.J., 1993—, prof., dept. chair, 2000. Co-editor: Minutes East Jersey Proprietors, 1985, Encyclopedia N.J., 2004; compiler: N.J. Anthology, 1994; contbr. articles to profl. jours. Chair N.J. Studies Acad. Alliance, 1992—, bd. Advocates for N.J. History; adv. bd. N.J. State Historic Records, 1997. Recipient N.J. Hist. Commn. Rsch. Grant, 1985, Folger Inst. Fellowship, 1987, Bill of Rights Collaborative Grant, 1991, award N.J. Hist. Commn., 1995, Richard J. Hughes award 1997. Mem. Orgn. Am. Historians, Am. Hist. Assn., Mid-Atlantic Regional Archive Conf., N.J. Hist. Comm. Democrat. Jewish. Avocations: cooking, gardening, camping. Home: 6 Rye St Piscataway NJ 08854-4721 Office: Seton Hall U Dept History Fahy Hall South Orange NJ 07079 Office Phone: 973-275-2772. E-mail: luriemax@shu.edu.

LURIE, NICHOLAS H., marketing educator; PhD, U. Calif. Berkeley, 1999. Asst. prof. Kenan-Flagler Bus. Sch. U. NC, Chapel Hill, 1999—2005; asst. prof. Ga Inst. Tech. Coll. Mgmt., 2005—. Contbr. articles to profl. jours. (Ferber Award, 2004). Mem.: Assn. for Consumer Rsch. (assoc.). Office: Coll Mgmt U NC Chapel Hill Chapel Hill NC 27599-3490 also: Ga Inst Tech 800 W Peachtree St Atlanta GA 30332-0520

LURIE, RANAN RAYMOND, political organization worker, educator, cartoonist, artist; b. Port Said, Egypt, May 26, 1932; came to U.S., 1968, naturalized, 1974; s. Joseph and Rose (Sam) L. (parents Israeli citizens); m. Tamar Fletcher, Feb. 25, 1959; children: Rod, Barak, Daphne, Danielle. Student, Herzelia High Sch., Tel Aviv, Israel, 1949; student, Jerusalem Art Coll., 1951. Corr. Maariv Daily, 1950-52; features editor Hador Daily, 1953-54; editor-in-chief Tevel mag., 1954-55; staff polit. cartoonist Yedioth Aharonot Daily, 1955-66, Honolulu Advertiser, 1979; lectr. polit. cartooning U. Hawaii; univ. lectr. in fine arts, polit. cartoon and polit. analysis Am. Program Bur., Boston.; polit. cartoonist Time Internat. mag., 1994-97. Inventor 1st electronically syndicated bus.-news cartoon Lurie's Business World; 101 million readers of 1105 newspapers in 102 countries; 1999 Guiness Book of World Records; chief judge Internat. Cartoon Comp., Seoul, Korea, 1996, 97; sr. adj. fellow Ctr. Strategic and Internat. Studies, Washington. Author: Among the Suns, 1952, Lurie's Best Cartoons, 1961, Nixon Rated Cartoons, 1973, Pardon Me, Mr. President, 1974, Lurie's Worlds, 1980, So sieht es Lurie, 1981, Fed. Republic Germany, Lurie's Almanac (U.K.), 1982, (U.S.A.), 1983, Taro's International Politics, Japan, 1984, Lurie's Middle East, Israel, 1986; creator: The Expandable Painting, 1969; Cartoons used as guidelines in several encys., polit. sci. books.; 22 shows, Israel, Can., U.S., 1960-75, including, Expo 67, Can., Dominion Gallery, Montreal, Que., Can., Lim Gallery, Tel Aviv, 1965, Overseas Press Club, N.Y.C., 1962, 64, 75, U.S. Senate, Washington, Honolulu Acad. Fine Arts, 1979; represented by Circle Gallery, 1988-93; exhibited numerous group shows including, Smithsonian Instn., 1972, Circle Gallery, Washington, 1989; creator Japan's nat. cartoon symbol Taro-San, Taiwan's nat. cartoon symbol Cousin Lee; polit. cartoonist, Life Mag., N.Y.C., 1968-73, polit. cartoonist, interviewer, Die Welt, Bonn, W. Ger., 1980-81; contbr.: N.Y. Times, 1952—; contbg. editor, polit. cartoonist, Newsweek Internat., 1973-76, editor, polit. cartoonist, Vision Mag. of South Am., 1974-76, syndicated, United Features Syndicate, 1971-73; syndicated nationally by Los Angeles Times, also internationally by, N.Y. Times to over 260 newspapers, 1973-75, internationally by Editors Press Syndicate (345 newspapers), King Features Syndicate, 1975-83; syndicated in U.S. by Universal Press Syndicate, 1982-86, Cartoonews Internat. Syndicat, 1986—; polit. cartoonist, The Times of London, 1981-83, ABC's Nightline, 1991—, World News Show, 1993; sr. polit. analyst, editorial cartoonist Asahi Shimbun, Japan's largest daily newspaper, 1983-84; sr. analyst and polit. cartoonist U.S. News & World Report, 1984-85; chief editorial dir. Editors Press Service, 1985; joined staff MacNeil/Lehrer News Hour (PBS) as daily polit. cartoonist, analyst; editl. bd. Mid. East Quarterly, 1994—; creator, editor-in-chief Cartoon News Mag (now Cartoonews.com), 1996-2000, editor-in-chief Cartoonews.com, 2000-, The Current Events Ednl. Mag., 1996—; polit. cartoonist Fgn. Affairs Mag., 2000—. Chief judge Seoul (Republic of Korea) Internat. Cartoon Competition, 1996, 97. Served as maj. Combat Paratroop, Israeli Army Res., 1950-67. Recipient highest Israeli journalism award, 1954; U.S. Headliners award, 1972; named Outstanding Editorial Cartoonist of Nat. Cartoonist Soc., 1971-78; Salon award Montreal Cartoon, 1971; N.Y. Front Page award, 1972, 74, 77; cert. merit U.S. Publ. Designers, 1974; award Overseas Press Club, 1979; John Fischetti polit. cartoon award, 1982, 86; Ranan R. Lurie Internat. Polit. Cartoon ann. award created in his honor by Nat. Fedn. Hispanic Owned Newspapers, 1994, Ranan R. Lurie Internat. award for Polit. Cartooning created by U.N. Soc. of Writers, 1995, Annual Ranan Lurie Polit. Cartoon award created in his honor by U.N., 2000; recip. 1996 Hubert Humphrey 1st Amendment and Freedom of the Press Award, 1996; UN Corrs. Assn. ranan Lurie Polit. Cartoon award created in his honor, 1999; nominated for Nobel Peace Prize, 2002. Mem. Soc. Profl. Journalists, Nat. Cartoonists Soc. Am., Assn. Editorial Cartoonists, Mensa, Overseas Press Club, Friars Club. Inventor 1st electronically animated TV news cartoon; creator 1st syndicated bus.-news cartoon Lurie's Business World; 104 million readers of 1,105 newspapers in 104 countries; 1999 Guiness Book of World Records. Office: Cartoonews Internat 375 Park Ave Ste 1301 New York NY 10152-1399 E-mail: cartoonews@aol.com, luriehonor@aol.com. *The moment of truth will come when the cartoonist gauges the margin of time from the day he drew the cartoon. Then he can see how correctly he has evaluated the situation through his work. Eventually, the simple facts and reality always win. Then it becomes apparent that wishful thinking is meaningless and the capacity to evaluate the project and even predict the events that are happening will eventually cement the professional status and integrity of the political cartoonist.*

LURIE-WOLOK, CAROL P., librarian; b. Pietersburg, South Africa, Apr. 29, 1954; arrived in U.S., 1964; d. Aron Osher and Zifre (Palte) Lurie; m. Davin Levi Wolok, June 16, 1985; 1 child. AB, Radcliffe U., 1975; MS, Simmons U., 1982. Libr. Office of Energy Conservation, Boston, 1980-82, Hebrew Coll., Brookline, Mass., 1982-83, 87-90, Schechter, Newton, Mass., 1983-87. Translator: Esther, The Queen, 1983; contbr. book revs. to profl. jours.; author poetry. Recipient 1st prize Bur. Jewish Edn., 1986. Mem. Hadassah. Democrat. Jewish. Avocations: poetry, reading, writing, politics, peace.

LURIX, PAUL LESLIE, JR., chemist; b. Bridgeport, Conn., Apr. 6, 1949; s. Paul Leslie and Shirley Laurel (Ludwig) L.; m. Cynthia Ann Owens, May 30, 1970; children: Paul Christopher, Alexander Tristan, Einar Gabrielson. BA, Drew U., 1971; MS, postgrad., Purdue U., 1973. Tech. dir. Analysts, Inc., Linden, N.J., 1976-77; chief chemist Caleb Brett USA, Inc., Linden, 1977-80; v.p. Tex. Labs., Inc., Houston, 1980-82; pres. Lurix Corp., Fulshear, Tex., 1982—. Cons. LanData, Inc., Houston, 1980-88, Nat. Cellulose Corp., Houston, 1981-88, Met. Transit Authority, Houston, 1981—, Phillips 66, Houston, 1986—, Conoco, Inc., Houston, 1988—, Caronia Corp., Houston, 1988-98, WBC Holdings, Inc., 1989-96, M&H Engring., 1994-00, Compaq Computer, 1996—, Baylor Coll. Medicine, 2000—; dir. rsch. and devel. Stockbridge Software, Inc., Houston, 1986-88; v.p. Diesel King Corp., Houston, 1980-82. Contbr. articles to profl. jours. Fellow Am. Inst. Chemists; mem. AAAS, ASTM, Am. Chem. Soc., Soc. Applied Spectroscopy, N.Y. Acad. Sci., Kiwanis (pres. 1970-71), Phi Kappa Phi, Phi Lambda Upsilon, Sigma Pi Sigma. Republican. Methodist. Achievements include patents for distillate fuel additives and e-commerce; research on infrared spectroscopy, data base programming for science and industrial applications; subspecialities in infrared spectroscopy, information systems, storage, and retrieval (computer science).

LUSCH, CHARLES JACK, oncologist; b. Lehighton, Pa., Feb. 15, 1936; s. Charles Norman and Loretta (Gaumer) L.; m. Carole Faye Eckart, Aug. 17, 1957; children: Marjorie, Susan, Stephen, Robert. AB in Biology magna cum laude, Lafayette Coll., Easton, Pa., 1957; MD, Temple U., 1961. Diplomate in med. oncology, hematology, internal medicine, forensic medicine; diplomate Am. Bd. Forensic Medicine. Pres. Berks Hematology-Oncology Assocs., Reading, Pa., 1968—; chief sect. of med. oncology & hematology Reading Hosp. & Med. Ctr., Reading, 1970—; dir. Pa. State Hemophilia Ctr., Reading Hosp. & Med. Ctr., 1973—; v.p. Lusch Motor Parts, Lehighton, Pa., 1975—; chief sect. med. oncology & hematology Community Gen. Hosp., Reading, 1980—; asst. chief medicine Reading Hosp. and Med. Ctr., 1986—; med. dir. Pocono Internat. Raceway, 1980-85; chmn. institutional rev. bd. Reading Hosp. and Med. Ctr., 1986—, dir. continuing med. edn., 1987—; med. dir. Berks County Hospice, Berks County Vis. Nurse Assn., Reading, 1987—; dir. oncology svcs. Reading Hosp. and Med. Ctr., 1990—. Med. adv. com. Pa. Blue Shield, Camp Hill, Pa., 1987—; bd. dirs. Berks Home Health Car, Reading Cancer Ctr., Reading Hosp.; malpractice cons. Med. Protective Ins. Co., Ft. Wayne, Ind., 1985—; cons. in hematology and oncology Pottsville (Pa.) Hosp. and Good Samaritan Hosp., 1975—; clin. asst. prof. medicine Pa. Med. Sch., 1984—, Pa. State Med. Sch., 1981—, Pa. State Sch. Medicine, 2003—, Temple U. Med. Sch., clin. assoc. prof. 1990; clin. assoc. prof. medicine U. Pa., 2000—; sr. clin. instr. Mahnemann U. Med. Sch., 1968—; prin. investigator Ea. Coop Oncology Group, 1975-90, Nat. Surg. Adj. & Breast Project, 1986—. Contbr. articles to profl. jours.; editor The Med. Record (regional med. jour.), 1970-71. Advisor Future Physicians Am., Reading, 1965; bd. dirs. Berks County unit Am. Cancer Soc., Reading, 1968-78, Keystone Cmty. Blood Bank, Reading, 1970-80; adv. com. The Women's Ctr., Reading Hosp., 1987-88; mem. bd. divsn. ch. soc. Evang. Luth. Ch. Am., Chgo.; pres. ch. coun. Atonement Luth. Ch., Wyomissing, Pa.; pres. bd. dirs. Reading (Pa.) Symphony Orch., 2005—; pres. Reading Symohony Orch. Bd., 2005—. Lt. comdr. USPHS, 1965-67. Fellow ACP; mem. Pa. Soc. Hematology-Oncology (sec.-treas. 1986-87), Am. Soc. Clin. Oncology, Am. Soc. Hematology, Am. Fedn. Clin. Rsch., Acad. Hospice Physicians (publs. com. 1989—), U.S. Amateur Ballroom Dance Assn. (past pres. Reading chpt.), Sports Car Club Am., Phi Beta Kappa, Alpha Omega Alpha. Republican. Lutheran. Avocations: competition ballroom dancing, tennis, motor racing. Home: 1617 Meadowlark Rd Wyomissing PA 19610-2820 Office: Berks Hematology Oncology Assoc 301 S 7th Ave Reading PA 19611-1410 Office Phone: 610-374-4404. E-mail: bolero36@aol.com.

LÜSCHEN, GÜNTHER RUDOLF FRIEDO, social sciences educator; b. Oldenburg, Germany, Jan. 21, 1930; s. Gustav Hermann Anton and Elsa Pauline Elisabeth (Magnus) L.; m. Klara Maria Mertens, Dec. 22, 1958 (div. Aug. 1989); children: Birgit, Gerhard; m. Leila Antoun Sfeir, Nov. 18, 1989; 1 child, Gerlinde. PhD, U. Graz, Austria, 1959; MA, U. Bonn, Germany, 1960; D (hon.), U. Jyvaskyla, Finland, 1990. Rsch. assoc. U. Cologne, Germany, 1961-64; assoc. prof. U. Bremen, Germany, 1965-72; prof. U. Ill., 1966-90, prof. emeritus, 1990—; prof. Tech. U. Aachen, Germany, 1982-89, U. Düsseldorf, Germany, 1990-95, 2001—, U. Ala., Birmingham, 1995-2001. Pres. Internat. Com. Sociology of Sport/UNESCO, 1967-80, Rene-König-Gesellschaft, Cologne, Germany, 1993-96; mem. Rsch. Coun. Internat. Soc. Assn., 1966-74, 82. Author: Sociology of Sport, 1967, Health Systems in the European Union, 1995; co-author: Health Promotion Policy in Europe, 2000; editor: Deutsche Soziologie seit 1945, 1979, Das Moralische in der Soziologie, 1998; co-editor: Soziologie der Familie, 1970, Handbook of Social Science of Sport, 1981. Founder Polit. Action Group, Oldenburg, 1969. Recipient Fed. Merit Cross, German Pres., 1989, citation Internat. Com. Sociology of Sport, 1993, Nat. citation N.Am. Assn. Sociology Sport. Mem.: German Sociol. Assn., Am. Sociol. Assn., Midwest Sociol. Soc. (life), Internat. Sociol. Assn. (life). Avocations: tennis, guitar. Office: U Ill Dept Sociology 702 S Wright Urbana IL 61801 Home: 2103 Pond Urbana IL 61801 Office Phone: 217-244-2279. Business E-Mail: lueschen@uiuc.edu.

LUSCOMBE, GEORGE A. II, lawyer; b. Jefferson, Iowa, Oct. 22, 1944; BS, U. Ill., 1966, JD, 1969; LLM, George Washington U., 1972. Bar: Ill. 1969, U.S. Supreme Ct. 1972, U.S. Claims Ct. 1972, D.C. 1972. Asst. br. chief legislation and regulations divsn. IRS Office Chief Counsel, 1972-73; ptnr. Mayer, Brown, Rowe & Maw, LLP, Chgo. Adj. prof. law IIT, 1987-93; speaker in field. Mem. ABA (chmn. com. depreciation and investment tax credit, sect. taxation 1980-82), Ill. State Bar Assn. (chmn. fed. tax sect. coun. 1991-92), Chgo. Bar Assn. (chmn. gen. income tax divsn., fed. tax com. 1977-79), D.C. Bar. Office: Mayer Brown Rowe & Maw LLP 71 S Wacker Dr Chicago IL 60606-4637 Office Phone: 312-701-7099.

LUSE, KIMBERLY ANN, radiologist, educator; b. Fort Thomas, Ky., July 4, 1963; d. James Herbert and Ramona Jean Miller; m. Evan Ray Luse, Sr., Nov. 11, 1988; children: Jessica Lee, Sara Jean, Evan Ray Luse, Jr., Hannah Kimberly. AS, No. Ky. U., 1985, BS, 1994; MEd, Xavier U., 1998; EdD in Edn. Founds., U. of Cin., 2002. Cert. educator Nat. Profl. Orgn., 2000. Coop. edn. coord. Cin. (Ohio) State Tech. and C.C., 1996—99; asst. prof. of clin. The U. of Cin., 1999—2003; dir. clin. rsch. program imaging Proscan Imaging, 2003—; exec. asst. to pres., sec. to bd. regents No. Ky. U., 2004—. Presdl. mgmt. intern Fed. Govt., 2002—; nat. presentor Am. Healthcare Radiology Administrators, New Orleans, 2002—; faculty advisor Student Advanced Med. Imaging Tech. Orgn. U. of Cin., Cin., 2002—. Bd. dirs. Am. Heart Assn., 2004—; bd. mem. Brighton Ctr., Newport, Ky., 2001. Mem.: Am. Soc. of Radiology, Leadership No. Ky. Class of 2001 (Grad. of the cohort for 2001 current alumni 2001). Home: 71 Hanover Place Fort Thomas KY 41075 Office: Proscan Imaging 5400 Kennedy Ave Cincinnati OH 45213 E-mail: kimberly.luse@uc.edu.

LUSHER, JEANNE MARIE, pediatric hematologist, educator; b. Toledo, June 9, 1935; d. Arnold Christian and Violet Cecilia (French) L. BS summa cum laude, U. Cin., 1956, MD, 1960. Resident in pediat. Tulane divsn. Charity Hosp. La., New Orleans, 1961-64; fellow in pediat. hematology-oncology Child Rsch. Ctr. Mich., Detroit, 1964-65, St. Louis Children's Hosp./Washington U., 1965-66; instr. pediat. Washington U., St. Louis, 1965-66; from instr. to assoc. prof. Sch. Medicine Wayne State U., Detroit, 1966-74, prof., 1974-97, disting. prof., 1997—; dir. divsn. hematology-oncology Children's Hosp. Mich., Detroit, 1976—. Marion I. Barnhart prof. hemostasis rsch. Sch. Medicine Wayne State U., Detroit, 1989—; med. dir. Nat. Hemophilia Found., N.Y.C., 1987—94, chmn. med. and sci. adv. coun., 1994—2001, bd. dirs., 1997—2001, co-chmn. gene therapy working group, 2000—; pres. Wayne State U. Acad. of Scholars, 2004—05. Author, editor: Treatment of Bleeding Disorders with Blood Components, 1980, Sickle Cell, 1974, 76, 81, Hemophilia and von Willebrand Disease in the 1990's, 1991, Acquired Bleeding Disorders in Children, 1981, F VIII/von Willebrand Factor and Platelets in Health and Disease, 1987, Inhibitors to Factor VIII, 1994, Blood Coagulation Innhibitors, 1996. Mem. Citizens Info. Com., Pontiac Township, Mich., 1980-82; apptd. mem. Hazardous Waste Incinerator Commn., Oakland County, Mich., 1981. Recipient Disting. Alumnus award U. Cin. Alumni Assn., 1990, Lawrence Weiner award Wayne State U. Sch. Medicine Alumni Assn., 1991. Mem. Am. Bd. Pediat. (chmn. sub-bd. on hematology-oncology 1988-90), Am. Soc. Hematology (chmn. sci. com. pediat. 1991-92, sci. com. hemostasis 1998—), Am. Pediat. Soc., Soc. Pediat. Rsch., Internat. Soc. Thrombosis-Hemostasis (chmn. factor VIII/IX subcom. 1985-90, chmn. sci. and standardization com. 1996-98), Mich. Humane Soc., Wayne State U. Acad. Scholars (pres. 2004-05). Avocations: nature, wildlife. Office: Children's Hosp Mich 3901 Beaubien Blvd Detroit MI 48201-2119 E-mail: jlusher@med.wayne.edu.

LUSK, DEBORAH JAN HUTSON, business educator; d. Albert L. and Regina Hutson; m. Danny Lewis Lusk, Oct. 31, 1975; 1 child, Margaret Jean. MSE in Bus. Edn., Ark. State U., 1980. Cert. English Ark. State U., 1983. Instr. bus. edn. Evening Shade HS, Ark., 1977—88, Highland HS, Hardy, Ark., 1989—. Adv. com. Ozarka Coll., Melbourne, Ark., 2004—05. Recipient State Outstanding Jr. Mem., Ark. Soc. DAR, 1986, 1990, 2004 Class Nobel Educator Dist, Nat. Soc. of HS Scholars, 2004. Mem.: Delta Pi Epsilon. Business E-Mail: jlusk@hland.ncsc.k12.ar.us.

LUSK, HARLAN GILBERT, national park superintendent, business executive; b. Jersey City, June 22, 1943; s. Harlan H. and Mary M. (Kuhl) L.; m. Catherine L. Rutherford, Oct. 11, 1986. BA in History, Gettysburg Coll., 1965, D (hon.), 2001. Supervisory historian Cape Hatteras Nat. Seashore, Manteo, N.C., 1968; historian Nat. Pk. Svc., Washington, 1968-69; programs specialist So. Utah Group, Cedar City, 1968-70; pk. supt. Wolf Trap Farm Pk., Vienna, Va., 1970-72; supervisory pk. ranger Blue Ridge Pkwy., Roanoke, Va., 1972-74; pk. supt. Appomattox (Va.) Courthouse, Nat. Hist. Pk., 1974-76, Valley Forge (Pa.), Nat. Hist. Pk., 1976-81, Big Bend (Tex.) Nat. Pk., 1981-86, Glacier Nat. Pk., West Glacier, Mont., 1986-94; pk. supt. Albright Tng. Ctr. Grand Canyon Nat. Pk., Ariz., 1994-95; chief, Divsn. Tng. and Employee Nat. Park Svc., Washington, 1995-97; retired from park svc., 1997; chmn. Gil Lusk Assocs., 1997—; group mgr. The Cholla Group, 1997—. Organizer 1st regional conf. Rio Grande Border, States on Pks. and Wildlife, Laredo, Tex., 1985 Bd. dirs. Tech. Com. on Pks. and Recreation Cen. Va. Planning Dist., 1972-74, Fed. Exec. Assn. Roanoke Valley, 1972-74, Flathead Basin Commn., 1986-94, Flathead Conv. and Visitor Assn., 1986-94, Sonoran Inst., 1995-2001; prin. founder, 1st pres., Appomattox County Hist. Soc., 1974-76; trustee Sci. Mus. Assn. Roanoke Valley, 1972-74, Nature Conservancy Mont., 1994—; ex-officio Friends of Valley Forge, 1977-81; founder, ex-officio, bd. dirs. Valley Forge Pk. Interpretive Assn., 1977-81; founder Big Bend Area Travel Assn., chmn., 1984-86. Recipient Meritorious Svc. award. Dept. Interior, 1986, Disting. Svc. award, 1999. Mem. Glacier Natural History Assn. (ex officio 1986-94), Glacier Nat. Pk. Assocs. (founder, ex-officio 1989-94), George Wright Soc., Lions, Rotary. Avocations: golf, antiques, computers, collecting artwork, hiking. Home and Office: 1382 N Boyce Ave Green Valley AZ 85614-6259 E-mail: hglusk@msn.com.

LUSKIN, FREDERIC MICHAEL, psychologist, educator; b. NYC, May 5, 1954; BA, Binghamton U., 1976; MS, San Jose State, 1987; PhD, Stanford U., 1999. Cert. Lic. psychologist, marriage & family therapist, ednl. psychologist. Sch. psychologist, 1986—93; dir. Stanford Forgiveness Project Stanford U., 1996—2003; assoc. prof. Inst. Transpersonal Psychology, Palo Alto, Calif., 2002—03; rsch. assoc. Stanford U., 1999—2003. Author: Forgive for Good, 2002, Stress Free for Good, 2005.

LUSKIN, ROBERT DAVID, lawyer; b. Chgo., Jan. 21, 1950; s. Bert L. and S. Ruth (Katz) L.; m. Fairlea A. Sheehy, Aug. 23, 1975 (div. Mar. 2000); children: Peter Duncan, Charles Cassimer. BA magna cum laude, Harvard U., 1972, JD magna cum laude, 1979; postgrad., Oxford (Eng.) U., 1972-75. Bar: D.C. 1979, U.S. Ct. Appeals (1st, 2nd, 4th, 5th, 6th, 7th, 8th, 9th, 11th, D.C. and fed. cirs.) 1979, U.S. Supreme Ct., 1983. Law clk. to Hon. Louis F. Oberdorfer U.S. Dist. Ct. for D.C., Washington, 1979-80; spl. counsel organized crime racketeering sect. U.S. Dept. Justice, Washington, 1980-82; ptnr. Onek, Klein & Farr, Washington, 1982-89, Powell, Goldstein, Frazer & Murphy, Washington, 1989-93, Comey, Boyd & Luskin, Washington, 1993-99, Patton Boggs, LLP, 2000—. Lectr. in law U. Va. Sch. Law, 1992—. Rhodes scholar, 1972-75. Mem. ABA (chmn. RICO Forfeitures and Civil Remedies com. 1986-94, vice chmn. task force on forfeitures), Harvard Law Sch. Assn. Washignton (pres.). Home: 3415 Prospect St NW Washington DC 20007-3219 Office: Patton Boggs LLP 2550 M St NW Washington DC 20037 Office Phone: 202-457-6190. Business E-Mail: rluskin@msn.com.

LUSS, DAN, chemical engineering professor; b. Tel Aviv, May 5, 1938; came to U.S., 1963, naturalized, 1973; s. Manfred and Gertrude (Weinstein) L.; m. Amalia Rubin, Sept. 4, 1966; children: Noya, Limor. BS, Technion Inst. Tech., Haifa, Israel, 1960, MSc, 1963; PhD, U. Minn., 1966. Registered profl. engr., Tex. Asst. prof. chem. engring. U. Minn., Mpls., 1966-67, U. Houston, 1967-69, assoc. prof., 1969-72, prof., 1972—, chmn. dept., 1975-95, 99-00; assoc. dir. Tex. Ctr. for Superconductivity, 1988-92. Cons. to several chem. cos. Editor: Revs. in Chem. Engring.; mem. editorial bd. Sci. and Engring, Catalysis Rev. Fellow Am. Inst. Chem. Engrs. (Allan P. Colburn award 1973, Profl. Progress award 1979, Wilhelm award 1986, chmn. awards com., former mem. editorial bd. jour.,former dir.), Am. Chem. Soc. (Honor scroll award of Indsl. Engring. Chemistry div. 1967); mem. NAE, Am. Soc. Engring. Edn. (Curtis McGraw award 1977 3M-Chem. Engring. lectureship award 1985) Home: 115 Stablewood Ct Houston TX 77024 Office: U Houston Dept Chem Engring Houston TX 77204-4004 Office Phone: 713-743-4305. Business E-Mail: dluss@uh.edu.

LUSSIER, YVES A., biomedical researcher, medical educator, physician; b. Montreal, Quebec, Canada; s. André J. Lussier. BE, U. Sherboorke, Sherbrooke, QC, 1985; MD, U. Sherbrooke, Sherbrooke, QC, 1989; Post Doctoral Degree, Columbia U., N.Y.C., 2001. Lic. profl. enrging., Que., 1985; Med. Coun. of Can., 1989, full med. Coll. of Physicians of Que., 1991, Coll. of Physicians and Surgeons of Ont., 1998, Office of the Professions, N.Y., 2001. Sr. vp rsch. and devel., founder Purkinje.com, Montreal, Canada, 1990—94; adj. prof. U. Sherbrooke, Canada, 1995—2001; asst. prof. Columbia U., NY, 2001—; dir. of the biomedical informatics core NE Biodefense Ctr., NY, 2003—. Recipient Career Devel. Award, Nat. Libr. of Medicine, Nat. Inst. of Health, 2004, IBM Faculty award, 2003, 2004. Achievements include patents pending for Bioinformatics, Phenomics and Computational Terminologies. Office: Columbia Univ 639 W 168 St VC5 New York NY 10032 Office Phone: 212-305-0939. Business E-Mail: lussier@dbmi.columbia.edu.

LÜST, REIMAR, foundation president; b. Wuppertal, Germany, 1923; BS Physics, U. Frankfurt, Germany, 1949; Ph. D., Max-Planck Inst., Göttingen, Germany, 1955; Fulbright fellow, Enrico Fermi Inst. U. Chgo., Germany, 1955-56; Habilitation, U. Munich TH, Germany, 1959. Vis. prof. NYU, N.Y.C., 1959-60; mem. Max-Planck-Inst. f. Physik u. Astrophysik, Munich, Germany, 1960; vis. prof. MIT, Cambridge, 1961, Cal. Tech., Pasadena, 1962; dir. ESRO (European Space Research Organization), 1962-64, Inst. f. Extraterrestr. Physik, Max-Planck-Inst. f. Physik u. Astrophysik, Garching b. Munich, Germany, 1963; aus. ord. prof. U. Munich, Germany, 1963-72; hon. prof. U. Munich TH, Germany, 1963-72; v.p. ESRO, Germany, 1968-70; chmn. Wissenschaftsrat, Germany, 1969-72; pres. Max-Planck-Gesellschaft zur Förderung der Wissenschaften, 1972-84; gen. dir. Europäische Weltraumorganisation, Paris, France, 1984-90; pres. Alexander von Humboldt-Stiftung, Bonn, Germany, 1989-99, hon. pres., 1999—; prof. U. Hamburg, Germany, 1992. Max-Planck-Inst., Göttingen, Physics, 1951-55, Fulbright Fellow, Enrico Fermi Inst., U. Chgo., 1955-56, 99-2004; chmn. bd. Internat. U. Bremen, 1999-2004, hon. chmn. bd., 2005—. Hon. chmn. bd. govs. Internat. U. Bremen, 2005. Office: Humboldt Found Max Planck Inst Bundesstraße 53 D-20146 Hamburg Germany Office Phone: 0049-040-41173-301. E-mail: sengbusdi@dkrz.de.

LUSTBADER, ERIC VAN, writer; b. NYC, 1946; BS in Sociology, Columbia Coll. Worked for Elektra Records & CBS Records; writer Cash Box Magazine. Author: (short stories) In Darkness, Angels, 1983, The Devil on Myrtle Ave, 1995, Lassorio, 1995, The Singing Tree, 1995, 16 Mins., 1996, An Exaltation of Termagants, 1999, (novels) Sirens, 1981, Black Heart, 1983, Jian, 1985, Zero, 1987, Shan, 1988, French Kiss, 1989, Angel Eyes, 1991, Black Blade, 1992, Dark Homecoming, 1997, Pale Saint, 1999, (Sunset Warrior series) The Sunset Warrior, 1977, Shallows of Night, 1978, Dai-San, 1978, Beneath an Opal Moon, 1980, Dragons on the Sea of Night, 1997, (Nicholas Linnear series) The Ninja, 1980, The Miko, 1984, White Ninja, 1990, The Kaisho, 1993, Floating City, 1994, Second Skin, 1995, (Pearl Saga series) The Ring of Five Dragons, 2001, The Veil of One Thousand Tears, 2002, The Cage of Nine Banestones, 2003, (Bourne series) The Bourne Legacy, 2004. Office: c/o Henry Morrison Inc PO Box 235 Bedford Hills NY 10507

LUSTICA, KATHERINE GRACE, marketing executive, artist, consultant; b. Bristol, Pa., Nov. 20, 1958; d. Thomas Lustica and Elizabeth Delores (Moyer) De Groat. Student, Hussian Sch. Art, Phila., 1976-78, Rider Coll., 1980-82, U. Utah, 1993—. Comml. artist, illustrator Bucks County Courier Times Newspapers, Levittown, Pa., 1978-82; account exec. Trenton (N.J.) Times Newspapers, 1982-84; promotions and account exec. Diversified Suburban Newspapers, Murray (Utah) Printing, 1984-88; pub. Barclays Ltd. Salt Lake City, 1988-97; mktg. dir. Bora Bora Trading Co., Murray, Utah, 1997; mktg. mgmt. Clear Channel Entertainment, 1998—. Cover artist, illustrator Accent mag., Bristol, 1978-82; freelance artist, 1978-98; advt. and creative cons. Everett & Winthrop Products Group, Salt Lake City, 1988-90, Multi Techs. Internat., Salt Lake City, 1990-91. Newcombe scholar, 1981-82. Mem. Golden Key. Presbyterian. Avocation: black belt tae kwon do. Office: 419 E 100 S Salt Lake City UT 84111-1801

LUSTIG, GRAHAM, artistic director; b. London; Student, Royal Ballet. Joined Dutch Nat. Ballet, prin. dancer; co-founder Dance Advance; joined Sadler's Wells Royal Ballet (now Birmingham Royal Ballet), 1980, prin. dancer; artistic dir. Am. Repertory Ballet and Princeton Ballet Sch., 1999—. Choreographer-in-residence Washington Ballet; panelist Nat. Endowment Arts, 2003, Dance Grants and Policy panels, 2005. Choreographer Thanatos Instinct (Dutch Ministry on Culture award), (evening commd. works include) Peter Pan for Scottish Ballet, Uncertain Stages, George's Day Out and The Shrew for Introdans, D'Ensemble for No. Ballet Theatre, Appassionato for Singapore Dance Theatre, A Far Cry for Hartford Ballet, Borderlines for BalletMet. Bd. dirs. Choo-San Goh and H. Robert McGee; charter mem. Artists Coun. for Am. for Arts, 2003—. Recipient Dutch Ministry of Culture Award; grantee Winston Churchill Traveling Fellowship, 1987. Office: Am Repertory Ballet Co 301 N Harrison St Princeton NJ 08540-3512*

LUSTIG, MARGARET GALLAGHER, lawyer; b. Chgo., Aug. 5, 1956; d. Anthony Francis and Margaret Sarah (Sullivan) Gallagher; m. Patrick Foran Lustig, May 18, 1985; children: Margaret Sarah, Patrick Jr., Michael Gallagher. BA, Barat Coll., 1978; JD, Kent Coll., 1982. Bar: Ill 1982, U.S. Dist. Ct. (no. dist.) Ill. 1982. Law clk. Ill. Supreme Ct., Chgo., 1982-87; assoc. William M. Smith & Assocs., Orland Hills, Ill., 1987-97. Mem. Chgo. Bar Assn. Roman Catholic. Home and Office: 8240 W 93rd St Hickory Hills IL 60457-1936

LUSTIG, MICHAEL A., finance company executive; Sr. auditor, mgr. Arthur Young and Co.; various sr. positions including sr. v.p. corp. devel., COO Fuqua Industries, 1980-95; sr. v.p. ops. Profit Recovery Group Internats., Atlanta, 1996, pres., 1996—, also bd. dirs. Office: Profit Recovery Group Schultz Intl Inc 600 Galleria Pkwy SE #100 Atlanta GA 30339-5991

LUSTIG, SUSAN GARDNER, occupational therapist; b. Beloit, Wis., Apr. 27, 1942; d. James and Sally Howell; m. Karl Lustig, Aug. 16, 1969 (div. 1997); children: Kurt, Daniel, Benjamin, David, Amy, Richard, Lauren. BS with distinction, U. Minn., 1965. Lic. occupl. therapist. Occupl. therapist Minn. State Hosp., Hastings, 1965—66; occupl. therapy cons. Hawaii Divsn. Vocat. Rehab., Honolulu, 1966—67; occupl. therapist Kaneohe State Hosp., Kaneohe, Hawaii, 1967, Minn. VA Hosp., Mpls., 1967—68, unit supr., 1968—70; chief occupl. therapist, mgr. occupl. therapy dept. Avery Health Care Sys., Newland, NC, 1997—2000; established occupl. therapy depts. Autumn Care Marion.Autumn Care, Drexel, NC, 2000—01, occupl. therapist, 2001—. Mem Nat. Bd. Cert. Occupl. Therapy, 1997—; del. to Russia, People to People Amb. Program. Pres. LaSalle County Med. Aux., Ill., 1976—78; tutor, mentor Burke County Elem. Sch. Students; organist New Life Bapt. Ch., Newland, NC, 2003—, Crossmore 1st Bapt. Ch., NC, 1999—2001; organist, pianist, dir. of music Linville River Bapt. Ch., NC; organist, Sunday sch. tchr. Long Ridge Bapt. Ch., 2001—03; bd. dirs. Harrison County Sheltered Workshop, 1971—72, Ottawa Pub. Health Nursing, Ill., 1976—78, Cooking for Christ, 1998—2002, Heartland Christian Acad. Sch., 1986—88, Diversified Industries, Port Angeles, Wash., 1980—82. Mem.: N.C. Occupl. Therapy Assn., Nat. Bd. for Cert. of Occupl. Therapists, Am. Occupl. Therapy Assn. Republican. Baptist. Avocations: organ, antiques, woodcarving, ice skating, reading. Home: 15 Little Cow Camp Rd Newland NC 28657-8704

LUSZTIG, PETER ALFRED, university dean, educator; b. Budapest, Hungary, May 12, 1930; s. Alfred Peter and Susan (Szabo) L.; m. Penny Bicknell, Aug. 26, 1961; children: Michael, Cameron, Carrie. B in Com., U. B.C., Vancouver, Can., 1954; MBA, U. Western Ont., London, Can., 1955; PhD, Stanford U., 1964. Asst. to comptroller B.C. Electric, Vancouver, 1955-57; instr. fin. U. B.C., 1957-60, asst. prof. fin., 1962-64, assoc. prof., 1965—68, Killam sr. research fellow, 1968-69, prof., 1968—95, dean faculty commerce, 1977-91, dean emeritus, 1995—. Trustee BC Health Benefit Trust; bd. dirs. Canfor Corp.; fed. commr. BC Treaty Commn., 1995-2003; vis. prof. IMEDE, Switzerland, 1973-74, London Grad. Sch. Bur. Studies, 1968-69, Pacific Coast Banking Sch., 1977—1982; sr. advisor B.C. Ministry of Econ. Devel., Small Bus. and Trade, 1991. Author: Report of the Royal Commission on Automobile Insurance, 2 vols., 1968, Financial Management in a Canadian Setting, 6th rev. edit., 2001, Report of the Commission on the B.C. Tree Fruit Industry, 1990. Ford Found. faculty dissertation fellow, Stanford U., 1964.

LUTEN, KAREN A., English language educator; b. N.Y.C., Nov. 8, 1955; d. Colby John and Carol Ann (Green) L. BA, U. Pa., 1977; MA, Columbia U., 1984, PhD, 1992. From asst. to assoc. editor Metro. Opera Guild, N.Y.C., 1977-83; tchg. asst. Columbia U., N.Y.C., 1985-90; English tchr. Dalton Sch., N.Y.C., 1990—. Recipient Excellence in Tchg. award, Dalton Sch., 1996—97. Mem. Phi Beta Kappa. Avocations: theater, opera, ballet, guitar, reading. Home: 240 Cabrini Blvd Apt 1F New York NY 10033-1113

LUTER, JOSEPH WILLIAMSON, III, meat packing and processing company executive; b. Smithfield, Va., 1940; married. BBA, Wake Forest Coll., 1962. Pres. Smithfield Packing Co., Arlington, Va., 1964—69, Bryce Mountain Resort Inc., 1969—75; with Smithfield Foods Inc., Arlington, 1975—, pres., 1975—86, 1989—, CEO, 1975—, chmn., 1977—. Lectr. Harvard Bus. Sch., Darden Grad. Sch. Bus., Univ. Va.; mem. exec. com. Am. Meat Inst. Trustee Wake Forest Univ. Office: Smithfield Foods Inc 200 Commerce St Smithfield VA 23430-1204*

LUTES, DONALD HENRY, architect; b. San Diego, Mar. 7, 1926; s. Charles McKinley and Helen (Bjoraker) L.; m. Donnie Wageman, Aug. 14, 1949; children: Laura Jo, Gail Eileen, Dana Charles. BArch, U. Oreg., 2000. Pvt. archtl. practice, Springfield, Oreg., 1956-58; ptnr. John Amundson, Springfield, 1958-70; pres. Lutes & Amundson, Springfield, 1970-72; ptnr. Lutes/Sanetel, 1973-86. Adj. assoc. prof. architecture U. Oreg., 1964-66, 89-2000; chmn. Springfield Planning Commn., 1954-65, 93-99, Urban Design and Devel. Corp., 1968-70, Eugene Non-Profit Housing, Inc., 1970 Architect: Springfield Pub. Library, 1957, Mt. Hood Community Coll, 1965-79, Shoppers Paradise Expt. in Downtown Revitalization, 1957. Chmn. Springfield United Appeal, 1959. Served to 1st lt. AUS, 1943-46, 51-52. Decorate Bronze Star; named Jr. 1st Citizen, Springfield C. of C., 1957, 1st Citizen, 1968, Disting. Citizen, 1995. Fellow AIA (bd. dirs. 1987-90, v.p. 1991, doc. com. 1993-2000, Northwest & Pacific Region medal hon. 2003); mem. Rotary, Theta Chi. Home: 778 Crest Ln Springfield OR 97477-3601

LUTGEN, ROBERT RAYMOND, newspaper editor; b. Fairmont, Minn., Oct. 27, 1949; s. William J. and Barbara Estella (Sanger) L.; m. Teresa L. Palm, July 17, 1971; children: Mark, Kyle, Laura. BA, Ctrl. Wash. State Coll., 1971. Reporter, asst. city editor Yakima (Wash.) Herald Republic, 1970-77; city editor Bryan (Tex.) Eagle, 1977-81, Texarkana (Tex.) Gazette, 1981-83, mng. editor, 1983-87; asst. mng. editor Ark. Dem., 1987-91; mng. editor Ark. Dem.-Gazette, 1991-99, Chattanooga Times Free Press, 1999—. Recipient Best News Story award, Editorial Writing award, Headline Writing award AP Mng. Editors Assn., 1985. Mem. Ark. AP (pres. 1989-90), Mng. Editors Assn. (bd. dirs. 1986-91). Avocations: travel, golf, reading. Home: 141 S Brent Dr Ringgold GA 30736-8243 Office: Chattanooga Times Free Press 400 E 11th St Chattanooga TN 37403-4203 E-mail: lutgen1@aol.com.

LUTH, WILLIAM CLAIR, retired research manager; b. Winterset, Iowa, June 28, 1934; s. William Henry Luth and Ora Anna (Klingaman) Sorenson; m. Betty L. Heubrock, Aug. 23, 1953; children: Linda Diane, Robert William, Sharon Jean. BA in Geology, U. Iowa, 1958, MS in Geology, 1960; PhD in Geochemistry, Pa. State U., 1963. Rsch. assoc. in geochemistry Pa. State U., University Park, Pa., 1963-65; asst. prof. geochemistry MIT, Cambridge, Mass., 1965-68; assoc. prof. geology Stanford U., 1968-77, prof. geology, 1977-79; supr. geophysics div. Sandia Nat. Labs, Albuquerque, N. Mex., 1979-82, mgr. geoscis. dept., 1982-90; mgr. geoscis. rsch. program U.S. Dept. Energy, Washington, 1990-95, acting dir. divsn. engring. & geosci., 1994-95, dir. divsn. engring and geosci., 1996; ret., 1996. Geoscientist US ERDA/DOE Washington, 1976-78; faculty sabbatical Sandia Laboratories, Albuquerque, N. Mex., 1975, visiting staff mem. Los Alamos Nat. Lab, 1978. Contbr. articles to profl. jours. Served with U.S. Army, 1953-56. Grantee NSF, 1964-78. Avocations: photography, travel. Home: 653 N 63d Pl Mesa AZ 85205-6745 E-mail: wluth@cox.net.

LUTHER, DAVID BYRON, management consultant; b. Utica, N.Y., May 26, 1936; s. Everett David and Mary (Brown) Luther; m. Geraldine Frost; children: Leslie, Gregory, Valorie. BS, Syracuse U., 1958, MBA, 1961. Mfg. mgr. Corning Glass Works, 1962-74, dir. pers. resources, 1974-76, asst. corp. contr., 1976-78, dir. corp. planning, 1978-79, dir. info. svcs., 1979-80, v.p. pers., 1980-83, v.p. quality, 1983-85, sr. v.p., corp. dir. quality, 1985-94; founder, prin. Luther Quality Assocs., Corning, then Fairfield, Conn., 1994—. V.p. ops. Green Mountain Energy Resources, South Burlington, Vt., 1998—99; exec. in residence Syracuse U. Sch. Bus., 1994—96; mem. exec. session pub. sector mgmt. Harvard U. Kennedy Sch., 1998—2000; mem. conf. bd. steering com. Global Ctr. Performance Excellence; nat. chmn. Koalaty Kid Edn. Project; judge Malcolm Baldrige Nat. Quality Award, 1988—91. Fellow: Am. Soc. Quality (pres. 1994—95, chmn. 1995—96); mem.: Internat. Acad. Quality (v.p.). Office: Luther Quality Assoc PO Box 1008 Fairfield CT 06825 Home: 144 Stillson Rd PO 1008 Fairfield CT 06825 Office Phone: 203-333-5005. E-mail: davidbluther@cs.com.

LUTHER, ELISSA MEREDITH, art educator; b. Cin., Apr. 20, 1978; d. George Stears and Pamela Pascoe; m. Matthew Jacob Luther, June 21, 2003. BA and BFA, Coll. Mt. St. Joseph, 2001, postgrad., 2002—. Visual arts specialist Batavia Elem. Sch., Ohio, 2001—. Yearbook advisor Batavia Elem. Sch., 2001—. Silk paintings. Mem.: Ohio Edn. Assn., Ohio Art Edn. Assn., Nat. Art Edn. Assn. Office: Batavia Elem Sch 215 Broadway Batavia OH 45103

LUTHER, FLORENCE JOAN (MRS. CHARLES W. LUTHER), lawyer, educator; b. N.Y.C., June 28, 1928; d. John Phillip and Catherine Elizabeth (Duffy) Thomas; m. William J. Regan (dec.); children: Kevin P., Brian T.; m. Charles W. Luther, June 11, 1961. JD magna cum laude, U. Pacific, 1963. Bar: Calif. Mem. Luther, Luther, O'Connor & Johnson, Sacramento, 1964—; mem. faculty U. Pacific McGeorge Sch. Law, Sacramento, 1966-88, prof., 1968-88, prof. emeritus, 1988—. Judge Bank Am. Achievement awards, 1969-71. Bd. advisors Cmty. Property Jour., 1974—, state decision editor, 1974—. Bd. dirs. Sacramento Suicide Prevention League, 1969-70 Mem. ABA, AAUP, Am. Judicature Soc., Women's League Groups, Calif. Bar Assn., Sacramento County Bar Assn., Order of Coif, Iota Tau Tau. Office: PO Box 1030 Fair Oaks CA 95628-1030

LUTHER, NORMAN YEOMANS, mathematics professor; b. Palo Alto, Calif., June 3, 1936; s. Chester Francis and Helen Eva (Yeomans) L; m. Emily Rosalind Goforth, Sept. 4, 1958; children: Gregory Charles, Gordon Elliot, Melissa Alice, Marnie Ann. BA, BS in Math. and Psychology, Stanford U., 1958; PhD in Math., U. Iowa, 1963. NSF postdoctoral fellow U. Calif., Berkeley, 1963-64; mem. math. faculty Wash. State U., Pullman, 1964-87, Hawaii Pacific U., Honolulu, 1987-96; rsch. fellow Population Inst., East-West Ctr., Honolulu, 1981-83, 84, 1985-98. Vis. prof. Albany (Ga.) State Coll., 1971-72, U. Hawaii, Honolulu, 1982-84 Referee Am. Math. Monthly, 1976-78, Asian and Pacific Census Forum, 1981—; co-author: The Own-Children Method of Fertility Estimation, Chinese edit., 1991; contbr. articles, revs. to profl. publs. Danforth Found. assoc., 1972—. Mem. Am. Math. Soc., Math. Assn. Am., Population Assn. Am. Democrat. Achievements include research on mathematical demography.

LUTHER, SIGRID, music educator; b. Milw., July 27, 1948; d. Norman Cyrus and Marilyn Joyce (Carlson) Skogstad; m. David Alan Luther, Dec. 30, 1969; children: Kelly Lynn, Tara Joy. BA, Bob Jones U., 1970; MusM, La. State U., 1978, D in Musical Arts, 1986. Instr. music Pillsbury Bapt. Bible Coll., Owatonna, Tenn., 1970—73; staff accompanist New Orleans Bapt. Theol. Sem., 1974—76; tchg. asst. La. State U., Baton Rouge, 1976—78, 1983—84; prof. music, faculty chair Bryan Coll., Dayton, Tenn., 1978—, humanities chair, 1978—2002. Area chair Nat. Guild Piano Tchrs., Dayton, 1979—2001; founder, liaison Bryan Cmty. Music Sch., Dayton, 1985—. Named Hon. Alumna, Bryan Coll., 1995, Outstanding Tchr., Govs. Sch. for Arts, 1994; Boeppler scholar, Wis. Conservatory, 1966. Mem.: Chattanooga Music Tchrs. Assn. (pres. 1981—83, Tchr. of Yr. 1983), Rhea Arts Coun. (music festival founder and chair 2002—), Tenn. Music Tchrs. Assn. (pres. 1995—97, Tchr. of the Yr. 1995), Music Tchrs. Nat. Assn. (pres. so. divsn. 2000—02, bd. dirs. 2002—04, nat. cert. tchr. music, chair divsn. pres. adv. coun., founder, advisor student chpt., chair code of ethics revision 2004—), Pi Kappa Lambda, Phi Kappa Phi. Republican. Presbyterian. Avocation: interior decorating. Office: Bryan Coll PO Box 7818 Dayton TN 37321

LUTHER, THOMAS WILLIAM, retired dermatologist; b. Milw., Feb. 27, 1925; s. Elmer Charles and Ida Martha (Sohrweide) L.; m. Warrene E. Luther; children: Brian Thomas, Siri Karen Luther Witt. BS, U. Wis., 1947, MD, 1950. Diplomate Am. Bd. Dermatology. Intern West Suburban Hosp., Oak Park, Ill., 1950-51; resident VA Hosps., 1951-52, 55-56, U. Pa., 1954-55. Lt. USN, 1943-54. Fellow Am. Acad. Dermatology; mem. AMA, Wis. Med. Soc., Wis. Dermatologic Soc., Appleton Rotary. Avocations: archaeology, genealogy. Home: 1936 Palisades Dr Appleton WI 54915-1023 E-mail: tomandwarrene@aol.com.

LUTHER, WILLIAM LEE, secondary school educator; b. Philipsburg, Pa., Dec. 10, 1952; s. William Denis and Edna Patricia (Culp) L.; m. Carolyn Jane Shadburn, May 27, 1976 (div. June 1983). BS, Pa. State U., 1975. Tchr. Huntingdon (Pa.) Sch. Dist., 1977-79; carpenter Zimmerman Homes, Inc., State College, Pa., 1981-83, sales mgr., 1983-86, dir. sales, 1986—90; tchr. Bellefonte Area Sch., 2000—, jr. high girls softball coach, asst. boys golf coach. Bd. dirs. Zimmerman Homes, Inc., State College; owner, ptnr. Housewrights, Inc., State Coll., 1991-99; asst. coach jr. H.S. girls' softball team Bellefonte Area Sch. Dist. Mem. zoning hearing bd. Bellefonte Borough; chmn. Bellefonte Borough Zoning Hearing Bd. Mem.: U.S. Golf Assn. Republican. Roman Catholic. Avocations: golf, reading, weight training. Home: 1019 Tanney St Bellefonte PA 16823-2417 E-mail: wluther@basd.net.

LUTHER, WILLIAM P., former congressman; b. Fergus Falls, Minn., June 27, 1945; s. Leonard and Eleanor L.; m. Darlene Luther, Dec. 16, 1967; children: Alexander, Alicia. BS in Elec. Engring. with high distinction, U. Minn., 1967; JD cum laude, U. Minn. Law Sch., 1970. Judicial clerkship 8th cir. U.S. Ct. Appeals, 1970-71; atty. Dorsey & Whitney Law Firm, Mpls., 1971-74, William P. Luther Law Office, Mpls., 1974-83; founder, sr. ptnr. Luther, Ballenthin & Carruthers Law Firm, Mpls., 1983-92; state sen. 47th dist. State of Minn., 1977-94, asst. maj. leader, 1983-94; mem. U.S. Congress from 6th Minn. dist., 1995—2003; mem. commerce com., telecomm., trade & consumer protection, fin., hazardous materials subcoms. Democrat. also: 1811 Weir Dr Ste 150 Woodbury MN 55125-2291 Home: 6809 Shingle Creek Dr Minneapolis MN 55445-2647

LUTHEY, GRAYDON DEAN, JR., lawyer, educator; b. Topeka, Sept. 18, 1955; s. Graydon Dean Sr. and S. Anne (Murphy) L.; m. Deborah Denise McCullough, May 26, 1979; children: Sarah Elizabeth, Katherine Alexandra. BA in Letters with highest honors, U. Okla., 1976, JD, 1979; Fellow in Theology, Oxford (Eng.) U., 1976. Bar: Okla. 1979, U.S. Ct. Appeals (10th cir.) 1979, U.S. Dist. Ct. (no., we. and ea. dists.) Okla. 1980, U.S. Supreme Ct. 1982. Assoc. Jones, Givens, Gotcher, Bogan & Hilborne, Tulsa, 1979-84, ptnr., 1984-92, also bd. dirs.; ptnr. Hall, Estill, Hardwick, Gable, Golden & Nelson, Tulsa, 1992—, also bd. dirs. Adj. assoc. prof. U. Tulsa, 1985-87, adj. prof., 1987—; vis. fellow in theology Keble Coll., Oxford (Eng.) U., 1976; presiding judge Okla. Temporary Ct. Appeals, 1992-93; mem. Okla. Supreme Ct. Rules Com., 1992-94. Bd. dirs. Tulsa Ballet, 1987-2000; chmn. Tulsa Pub. facilties Authority, 1990-93; tustee Episcopal Theol. Sem. of S.W., 1991-99, exec. com., 1992-99; vice chmn. Univ. Hosps. Authority, 1993-94, chmn. 1994-98, sec., 1998-99; chancellor Episcopal Diocese Okla., 1986-99; mem. bd. visitors U. Okla. Coll. Arts and Scis., 1997—; mem. State of Okla. Futures Auth., 1998-2002, chmn., 1999-2002; mem. adv. bd. U. Okla. Tulsa, 2003-. Life Fellow Am. Bar Found. (chmn. Okla. chpt. 2003-); mem. ABA, Okla. Bar Assn. (chmn. continuing legal edn. com. 1989-91), Tulsa County Bar Assn. (bd. dirs. 1983-89, Disting. Svc. award 1988), Am. Law Inst., Am. Inns of Ct., Summit Club, So. Hills Country Club, Beta Theta Pi, Phi Beta Kappa, Omicron Delta Kappa. Office: Hall Estill Hardwick Gable Golden & Nelson 320 S Boston Ave Ste 400 Tulsa OK 74103-3704 Office Phone: 918-594-0431. Business E-Mail: dluthey@hallestill.com.

LUTHRINGSHAUSER, DANIEL RENE, manufacturing executive; b. Fontainebleau, France, July 23, 1935; came to U.S., 1937; s. Ernest Henri and Jeanne (Guerville) L.; m. Carol King; children: Mark Ernest, Heidi Elizabeth. BS, NYU, 1956, MBA, 1970. With exec. tng. program, internat. pub. relations Merck & Co. Inc., Rahway, N.J. and N.Y.C., 1962-65; dep. mktg. dir. Merck Sharp & Dohme Internat., Brussels, 1965-66; mktg. service dir. Paris, 1966-69; gen. mgr. Merck Sharp & Dohme/Chibret, Paris, 1970-74; v.p. mktg. Merrell (France), Paris, 1974-78; v.p. gen. mgr. Revlon Devel. Corp., Paris, 1978-82, Medtronic Europe, Paris, Africa, Middle East, 1982-86; v.p. internat. Medtronic Inc., Mpls., 1986-98; prin. DRL Internat. Cons., 1998—. Bd. dirs. Medtronic Found., Mpls., 1986—91, French-Am. C. of C., 2003—; chmn. Internat. Assn. of Prosthesis Mfrs., Paris, 1983—85; adj. prof. Grad. Sch. of Bus., Univ. St. Thomas. Bd. dirs. Am. Hosp. Paris, 1983-86, 94-95, Minn. Internat. Ctr., 1990—2003; mem. Am. Club Paris, 1970-80, Medtronic Found., Mpls., 1986-91. Served to capt. USAF, 1956-62. Recipient Gold medal Am. Mktg. Assn., 1956. Mem.: Mpls. Club, Ausable Club (Keene Valley, N.Y.). Avocations: gardening, golf, squash, skiing. Home: 480 Peavey Rd Wayzata MN 55391-1529 Office: PO Box 718 Wayzata MN 55391

LUTHY, JOHN FREDERICK, management consultant; b. Kansas City, Mo., Dec. 12, 1947; s. Walter Frederick Luthy and Loraine Florence Tramill; children: Roslyn, Bryan, John Paul. BA, Baker U., 1969; MS, U. Mo., 1973; MPA, Boise State U., 1978; EdD, U. Idaho, 1991. Mgr. State Com. Disease Edn., Topeka, 1973; dir. Divsn. Health Edn., Johnson County, Kans., 1973-75; state dir. Bur. Health Edn., Boise, Idaho, 1975-80; dir. Gen. Svcs. Adminstrn., Boise, 1980-84; dir. bus. devel. Morrison Knudsen Tech. Inc., Boise, 1984-86; pres. The Futures Corp., Boise, 1986—. Pres. Exec. Mgmt. Devel. Inst., Boise, 1991—; del. to China People to People, 1994. Author: (manual) Grantsmanship--A Time of Plenty, 1988; contbr. articles to profl. jours. Staff sgt. USAR, 1969-75. Recipient Nat. Early Career award APHA, 1978; named one of Outstanding Young Men of Am., U.S. Jaycees, 1977. Mem. ASTD, Am. Mgmt. Assn., U.S. Powerlifting Fedn. (exec. bd. dirs., regional chmn. 1981-86), Phi Delta Kappa. Avocations: mountain biking, power lifting, backpacking. Office: The Futures Corp 1109 Main St Ste 299A Boise ID 83702-5642 E-mail: futurescorp@aol.com.

LUTHY, RICHARD GODFREY, environmental engineering educator; b. June 11, 1945; s. Robert Godfrey Luthy and Marian Ruth (Ireland) Haines; m. Mary Frances Sullivan, Nov. 22, 1969; children: Matthew Robert, Mara Catherine, Jessica Bethlin. BSChemE, U. Calif., Berkeley, 1967; MS in Ocean Engring., U. Hawaii, 1969; MSCE, U. Calif., Berkeley, 1974, PhDCE, 1976. Registered profl. engr. Pa.; diplomate Am. Acad. Environ. Engrs. Rsch. asst. dept. civil engring. U. Hawaii, Honolulu, 1968-69; rsch. asst. div. san. and hydraulic engring. U. Calif., Berkeley, 1973-75; asst. prof. civil engring. Carnegie Mellon U., Pitts., 1975-80, assoc. prof., 1980-83, prof., 1983—, assoc. dean Carnegie Inst. Tech., 1986-89, head dept. civil and environ. engring., 1989-96, Lord prof. environ. engring., 1996-2000; Silas H. Palmer prof. dept. civil and environ. engring. Stanford (Calif.) U., 2000—, chmn. Dept. Civil and Environ. Engring., 2003—. Shimizu Corp. vis. prof. dept. civil engring. Stanford U., 1996-97; cons. sci. adv. bd. U.S. EPA, 1983—, Bioremediation Action com., 1990-92; cons. U.S. Dept. Energy, 1978—, various pvt. industries; del. water sci. and tech. bd. NAE, Washington and Beijing, 1988; mem. tech. adv. bd. Remediation Techs., Inc., Concord, Mass., 1989-94, Fostin Capital, Pitts., 1991-94, Balt. Gas & Elec., 1992-95, Pa. Dept. Environ. Protection, 1994-96; mem. sci. adv. com. Hazardous Substance Rsch. Ctr. Stanford U., 1994-99; chair Gordon Rsch. Conf. Environ. Scis., 1994; Nat. Rsch. Coun. Commn. on Innovative Remediation Tech., Com. on Intrinsic Remediation, Com. on Bioavailabilty, Water Sci. and Tech. Bd., 1997-2004, chair, 2000-04. Contbr. articles to tech. and sci. jours. Chmn. NSF/Assn. Environ. Engring. Prof. Conf. on Fundamental Rsch. Directions in Environ. Engring, Washington, 1988. Lt. C.E. Corps, USN, 1969-72. Recipient George Tallman Ladd award Carnegie Inst. Tech., 1977; AT&T Indsl. Ecology Faculty fellow, 2005. Mem. ASCE (Pitts. sect. Prof. of Yr. award 1987), Nat. Acad. Engring., Assn. Environ. Engring. Sci. Profs. (pres. 1987-88, Nalco award 1978, 82, Engring. Sci. award 1988, Svc. award 1999), Water Environ. Fedn. (rsch. com. 1982-86, awards com. 1981-84, 89-94, std. methods com. 1977—, groundwater com. 1989-90, editor jour. 1989-92, Eddy medal 1980, McKee medal 2000), Water Environ. Rsch. Found. (bd. 2003—), Internat. Assn. on Water Quality (Foudners award U.S. Nat. Com. 1986, 93, orgnl. com. 16th Biennial Conf. Washington 1992), Am. Chem. Soc. (divsn. environ. chemistry, mem. editl. adv. bd. Environ. Sci. Tech. 1992-95). Presbyterian.

LUTI, WILLIAM JOSEPH, federal agency administrator, retired military officer; b. Boston, Nov. 13, 1953; s. William Vincent and Marjorie Louise (Barnes) L.; m. Donna Margaret King, Dec. 13, 1990; children: Lauren Marie, Natalie Rose. BA in History, The Citadel, 1975; MA in Nat. Security Affairs, U.S. Naval War Coll., 1986; MA in Internat. Rels., Salve Regina Coll., 1986; MA in Law and Diplomacy, PhD in Internat. Rels., Tufts U., 1990. Commd. ensign USN, 1975, advanced through grades to capt., 1997; flight student Naval Air Station, Pensacola, Fla., 1975-76; div. officer VQ-1 (EA-3B aircraft), Agana, Guam, 1976-79; asst. dept. head VAQ-131 (EA-6B aircraft), Oak Harbor, Wash., 1979-82; dept. head VAQ-135 (EA-6B), Oak Harbor, 1986-88; commanding officer VAQ-130 (EA-6B squadron) USN, Oak Harbor, 1991-93; admiral's aide U.S. Naval Acad., Annapolis, Md., 1982-85; dep. dir. Chief of Navel Ops. Exec. Panel, Alexandria, Va., 1993-96; congl. fellow Office of Spkr. of the House Hon. Newt Gingrich, Washington, 1996—97; comdr. USS GUAM USN, 1997—98; spl. advisor to v.p., nat. security affairs The White House, 2001; dep. under sec. near ea. & south Asian affairs US Dept. Def., Washington, 2001—. Panelist Persian Gulf War Symposium, Naval Inst., Pensacola, 1992 Tchr.'s aide Hillcrest Elem. Sch., Oak Harbor, 1991-92. Decorated with Air medal U.S. Navy, Iraq, 1991. Mem. U.S. Naval Inst. (contbr. editor), Assn. of Naval Aviation, Phi Alpha Theta. Roman Catholic. Avocations: writing, golf, swimming. Office: US Dept Def 2400 Defense Pentagon Washington DC 20301*

LUTKENHOUSE, ANNE, non-profit executive; b. S.I., N.Y., Feb. 18, 1957; d. Emile Anthony and Jane Anne Lutkenhouse. BA magna cum laude, Wagner Coll., 1979; cert. Goethe Inst., N.Y.C., 1981, Emergency Med. Tech., State of N.Y., CPR Instr. Supr. Credit Suisse, N.Y.C., 1979-85; dist. office adminstr. N.Y. City Council, 1985-86; asst. dir., Appalachian Trail Field asst., N.Y.-N.J. Trail Conf., N.Y.C., 1986-01, asst. dir. Office of Grants and Rsch., Coll. S.I./CUNY, 2002—; mem. City U. of N.Y. Coun. of Grants Officers, 2002-; scholarship fundraising co-chmn., Wagner Coll.;dir. N.J. Appalachian Trail Ridge Runner Program; contbg. cons. Wagner Coll. Study Program, Bregenz, Austria, 1978-92. Photographer, producer photography show, 1984. instr. safety program ARC, S.I., 1977; campaign aide council member Fossella, N.Y. City Council, S.I., 1985; sec., bd. dirs. South Shore Swimming Club, Inc.; pres., bd. dirs. S.I. Chamber Music Players, 1984-86; co-chmn. Flag Day Parade, Tottenville Improvement Council, Inc., 1986; vol. Am.-Scandinavian Found.; producer Appalachian Trail 50th Anniversary Celebration, N.Y., 1987; alumni agt. telefund/ann. fund Wagner Coll., 1992. Recipient EMT Student Yr. award, St. Vincent's Cath. Med. Ctr./S.I. U. Hosp. Reg. Coun., 2003. Contbr. travel articles to mags; contbg. writer Appalachian Trailway News, 1987-2001, Appalachian Trail Guide to N.Y., N.J., 11th and 12th edits. Mem. NAFE, Am.-Scandinavian Found., Protectors of Pine Oak Woods, Norwegian-Am. C. of C. Democrat. Avocations: needlecrafts, ballet, skiing, travel. Home: 1100 Clove Rd Apt 9J Staten Island NY 10301-3633 Office: Coll of Staten Island/CUNY 1A-302 2800 Victory Blvd Staten Island NY 10314

LUTNICK, HOWARD W., brokerage house executive; b. New York; BA in Econ., Haverford Coll., 1983. With Cantor Fitzgerald, NYC, 1983—, pres. & CEO, 1991—, chmn., 1996—; founder, chmn., pres. & CEO eSpeed, NYC, 1999—. Spkr. in field. Bd. mgrs. Zachary & Elizabeth M. Fisher Ctr. Alzheimer's Disease Rsch., Rockefeller U.; trustee Solomon R. Guggenheim Mus.; bd. trustee, exec. com. Intrepid Mus. Found.; bd. dir. Tate Gallery Projects Ltd., Tate Mus.; bd. mgrs. Haverford Coll. Recipient Distinguished Pub. Svc. Award, Dept. Navy. Office: eSpeed Inc 135 East 57 th St New York NY 10022 Office Fax: 212-829-4866.*

LUTRINGER, RICHARD EMIL, lawyer; b. N.Y.C., Feb. 4, 1943; s. Emil Vincent Lutringer and Alice Hamilton Rich; m. Dagmar Bonitz, May 1, 1970 (div. 1980); m. Clarinda Higgins, Oct. 11, 1980 (div. 1999); m. Joanne Amelung LaVista, Nov. 27, 2004; children: Emily, Eric. AB, Coll. of William and Mary, 1964; JD in Internat. Affairs, Cornell U., 1967; MCL, U. Chgo., 1969. Bar: N.Y. 1972, U.S. Dist. Ct. (so. dist.) N.Y. 1972. Assoc. Whitman & Ransom, N.Y.C., 1971-80, ptnr., 1980-94, Morgan, Lewis & Bockius LLP, N.Y.C., 1994—2004, Schiff Hardin LLP, N.Y.C., 2004—. V.p. N.Y.-N.J. Trail Conf., N.Y.C., 1976-80; pres. German-Am. Roundtable, Inc., 2000—. Mem. ABA, Internat. Bar Assn., Assn. of Bar of City of N.Y. (chmn. com. fgn. and comparative law 1990-93), Am. Fgn. Law Assn. (pres. 1989-93, treas. 1986-89), European-Am. C. of C. (vice-chair trade com. 1992-98), German-Amer. C of C, Inc., Philadelphia (bd. dirs., 1999—, v.p., sec. 2001—), German Am. Law Assn. (bd. dirs. 2001—). Avocations: sailing, hiking, skiing. Home: 780 Mine Hill Rd Fairfield CT 06824 Office: Schiff Hardin LLP New York NY 10178-0060 Office Phone: 212-745-0820. Business E-Mail: rlutringer@schiffhardin.com.

LUTSYSHYN, OKSANA, concert pianist, organist; b. Sokal, Ukraine, July 22, 1964; d. Yaroslav and Lubov Lutsyshyn; m. Andrey Rafailovich Kasparov, Nov. 1, 1991. MusM, Moscow State Conservatory, 1987, MusD, 1991. Soloist and accompanist Chernovtsy State Philharmony, Chernovtsy, Ukraine, 1987—89; dir. ARK Mgmt., Bloomington, Ind., 1995—98; music dir., organist Prince Peace Luth. Ch., Virginia Beach, Va., 1999—; dir. Prince Peace Concert Series, 2000—. Pianist (concertizing) Concert Tours of Europe, Japan, Latin America, South Africa, South America and the United States, (recording) Andrey Kasparov's Toccata (Second prize Internat. Vienna Modern Masters Rec. Competition, 1997), (Grammy nomination, 1999), Recordings on VMM and CRS labels, (competition) William Kapell International Piano Competition (Prince George Coun. County Art prize, 1990), (recording) Appeared with violinist Joshua Bell and Josef Gingold in the BBC documentary, organist (organ recitals) Organ recitals throughout the United States and Ukraine. Bd. mem. Feldman Chamber Soc., Norfolk, Va., 2004—05; founding mem. Old Dominion U. Contemporary Musc. Ensemble, 1998—, Invencia Piano Duo, 2003—. Mem.: Coll. Music Soc. Home: 1460 Harmott Ave Norfolk VA 23509 Office: Prince Peace Luth Ch 424 Kings Grant Rd Virginia Beach VA 23452 Office Phone: 757-340-8420. Personal E-mail: oksana_lutsyshyn@yahoo.com.

LUTTER, PAUL ALLEN, lawyer; b. Chgo., Feb. 28, 1946; s. Herbert W. and Lois (Muller) L. BA, Carleton Coll., 1968; JD, Yale U., 1971. Bar: Ill. 1971, U.S. Tax Ct. 1986. Assoc. Ross & Hardies, Chgo., 1971-77, ptnr., 1978—2003, McGuire Woods, Chgo., 2003—04, Bryan Cave, Chgo., 2004—. Co-author: Illinois Estate Administration, 1993. Bd. dirs. Howard Brown Health Ctr., DIFFA Chgo. Mem. ABA, Chgo. Bar Assn. Home: 2214 N Magnolia Ave Chicago IL 60614-3104 Office: Bryan Cave 161 N Clark St Ste 4800 Chicago IL 60601

LUTTERODT, CLEMENT H., mathematician, educator; b. Nsawam, Ghana, Aug. 17, 1943; arrived in U.S., 1979; s. Samuel Augustus Christian Lutterodt and Olaonipekun Lutterodt (dec.); m. Sarah Anne French, Sept. 25, 1971; children: Tobias, Isabelle, Justine. BSc, U. Ghana, Legon, 1967, MSc, 1972; PhD, U. Birmingham, Eng., 1974. Lectr. U. Cape Coast, Ghana, 1973—78, sr. lectr., 1978—80; vis. asst. prof. U. South Fla., Tampa, 1980; asst. prof. Howard U., Washington, 1980—84, assoc. prof., 1984—90, prof., 1990—. Contbr. articles to profl. jours. Fellow, Internat. Ctr. for Theoretical Physics, Miramare, Italy, 1975, 1977, 1980, 1981, others. Mem.: Math Assn. Am., N.Y. Acad. Scis., Am. Math. Soc. Achievements include creation of the field of rational approximants in several complex variables. Avocations: ping pong/table tennis, walking, reading. Office: Howard Univ Dept Math 6th St NW Washington DC 20059

LUTTIG, J. MICHAEL, federal judge; b. Tyler, Tex., June 13, 1954; m. Elizabeth Luttig; 2 children. BA, Washington and Lee U., 1976; JD, U. Va., 1981. Asst. counsel The White House, 1981—82; law clk. to Judge Antonin Scalia US Ct. of Appeals DC Cir., 1982—83; law clerk to chief justice Warren Burger US Supreme Ct., 1983—84, spl. asst. to Chief justice Warren Burger, 1984—85; assoc. Davis Polk & Wardwell, 1985—89; prin. dep. asst. atty. gen., Office of Legal Counsel US Dept. Justice, 1989—90; asst. atty. gen., Office of Legal Counsel, counselor to atty. gen. US Dept. of Justice, 1990—91; judge US Ct. Appeals (4th cir.), McLean, Va., 1991—. Mem. Nat. Adv. Com. of Lawyers for Bush, 1988, Lawyers for Bush Com., 1988. Mem.: ABA, D.C. Bar Assn., Va. Bar Assn. Office: US Ct of Appeals 4th Cir US Courthouse 401 Courthouse Sq Fl 9 Alexandria VA 22314-5704 also: US Ct Appeals 11th Cir 56 Forsyth St NW Atlanta GA 30303*

LUTTRELL, HOWARD SPICER, music educator; b. Owensboro, Ky., Apr. 10, 1947; s. Howard S. and Jacqueline Smith Luttrell. MA, Western Ky. U., 1978; BME, Brescia U., 1971. Edn. Ky., 1978. Instrumental music instr. Brescia U., Owensboro, Ky., 1971—72; assoc. prof. of music Ky. Wesleyan Coll., Owensboro, 1973—75; band dir. Owensboro Cath. H.S., Owensboro, Ky., 1986—87, Albany H.S., Albany, Ga., 1987—88; dir. of instrumental music Avondale High Sch., DeKalb Ctr. for the Performing Arts, Avondale Estates, Ga., 1988—89; band dir. Franklin County H.S., Carnesville, Ga., 1989—92, Munford H.S., Munford, Tenn., 1992—94, Obion County H.S., Troy, Tenn., 1994—96, Hancock County H.S., Lewisport, Ky., 1969—85, Graves County H.S., Mayfield, Ky., 1996—97, Ripley H.S., Ripley, Tenn., 1997—2003; tchr. NW Miss. C.C., Senatobia, Miss., 2003—. Choir dir. Lewisport United Meth. Ch., Lewisport, Ky., 1969—72. Mem., chaplain Jaycees, Hawesville, Ky., 1969—73; county campaign chmn. for gov. Bert Combs Dem. Party of Ky., Lewisport, Ky., 1972—72; dir. Winds for Worship Hernando First Presbyn. Ch., Hernando, Miss., 2004—05. Recipient Ky. Col., Gov. Bert Combs, 1963, Gov. Julian Carroll, 1976, Outstanding Young Men of Am. award, 1981, Career Level III tchr., State of Tenn., 1994. Mem.: Miss. Assn. of C.C. Band Dirs. (mem.). Democrat. Presbyn. Avocations: travel, boating, music. Home: 660 W Commerce St Hernando MS 38632 Office: NW Miss Cmty Coll 4975 Hwy 51 N Senatobia MS 38668 Office Fax: 662-560-1118. Personal E-mail: hluttrel@midsouth.rr.com.

LUTTS, RALPH HERBERT, scholar, educator, museum administrator; b. Quincy, Mass., Jan. 7, 1944; s. Herbert Warren Lutts and Jean May (MacKenzie) Easton. BA in Biology, Trinity U., San Antonio, 1967; EdD, U. Mass., 1978. Curator, educator Mus. Sci., Boston, 1967-73; naturalist Hampshire Coll., Amherst, Mass., 1973-80, mem. natural sci. faculty, 1976-84; dir. Blue Hills Trailside Mus., Mass. Audubon Soc., Milton, 1980-90; dir. edn. Va. Mus. Natural History, Martinsville, 1990-92, dir. outreach divsn., 1992-94, rsch. assoc., 1994-97; mem. faculty Goddard Coll., Plainfield, Vt., 1995—, coord. MA concentration in environ. studies, 2002—; mem. adj. faculty U. Va., Charlottesville, 1995—; mem. adj. history faculty Va. Tech., 1998—. Pres. Alliance for Environ. Edn., 1988-89; founding pres. New Eng. Environ. Edn. Alliance, 1980-84; assoc. Ctr. for Animals and Pub. Policy, Tufts U. Sch. Vet. Medicine, North Grafton, Mass., 1989-90; dept. dir. mid-atlantic region Global Network of Environ. Edn. Ctrs., 1993-95; pres. Am. Nature Study Soc. (1995-97) Author: The Nature Fakers: Wildlife, Science and Sentiment, 1990; editor: The Wild Animal Story, 1998; founding editor New Eng. Jour. Environ. Edn., 1985-88; contbr. articles to profl. jours. Pres. Hitchcock Ctr. for Environ., Amherst, Mass., 1977-79; treas. Mass. Environ. Edn. Soc., 1982-84; mem. Blue Hills citizens' adv. com. Met. Dist. Commn., 1988-89, mgmt. adv. com., 1989-90; mem. sec.'s adv. group on environ. edn. Mass. Exec. Office for Environ. Affairs, 1989-90; mem. exec. com. Patrick Environ. Awareness Group, 1998-99; assoc. dir. Patrick Soil and Water Conservation Dist., 2001-2002. Recipient New Eng. award for achievement New Eng. Environ. Edn. Alliance, 1989; Paul Harris fellow Rotary Internat. Mem. Am. Soc. Environ. History, Assn. for Study of Lit. and Environ., Forest History Soc. (Ralph W. Hidy award 1993), N.Am. Assn. Environ. Edn., Am. Nature Study Soc. (bd. dirs. 1990-98, pres. 1995-97), Authors Guild, Popular Culture Assn. (area chair 1993-95), Nat. Writers Union, Appalachian Studies Assn., Soc. for Conservation Biology

LUTTWAK, EDWARD NICOLAE, academic administrator, policy and business consultant; b. Arad, Transylvania, Nov. 4, 1942; came to U.S., 1972, naturalized, 1981; s. Josif Menashe and Clara (Baruch) L.; m. Dalya Iaari, Dec. 14, 1970; children: Yael Rachel, Joseph Emmanuel. B.Sc. with honors, London Sch. Econs., 1964; PhD (Univ. fellow), Johns Hopkins U., 1975; D (hon.), U. Bath, Eng., 2004. Vis. prof. polit. sci. Johns Hopkins U., 1973-78; sr. fellow Georgetown U. Center Strategic and Internat. Studies, 1978-87, research prof. internat. security affairs, 1978-82, Burke chair in strategy, 1987—, dir. geo-econs., 1991-94, sr. fellow, 1994—; sr. fellow in preventive diplomacy Office of Sec. of Def., Nat. Security Coun. and Dept. State. Cons. Office of Sec. of Def., Nat. Security Coun., Dept. of Def. Army, Navy and U.S. Air Force, Fgn. (allied) Govs. and U.S., overseas bus. entities. Author: Coup d'Etat, 19 edits. including 12 for lang. translations, 1968-79, Dictionary of Modern War, 1971 (also Spanish edit.), The Political Uses of Sea Power,

1975 (also Japanese edit.), The Israeli Army, 1975, 85, (also Chinese edit.), The Grand Strategy of the Roman Empire, 1976 (also Hebrew, Italian and French edits.), Strategy and Politics: Collected Essays, 1980, The Grand Strategy of the Soviet Union, 1983 (also Italian and French edits.),The Pentagon and the Art of War: The Question of Military Reform, 1985 (also Italian, Japanese and Korean edits.), Strategy and History: Collected Essays, On the Meaning of Victory, 1986 (also Italian edit.), Strategy: The Logic of War and Peace, 1987 (also Chinese, French and Italian edits.), revised edit., 2001, 2d rev. edit., 2002, (with Stuart Koehl) Dictionary of Modern War, 1991 (also Italian edit.), The Endangered American Dream, 1993 (also French, Italian, German and Japanese edits.), (with G. Tremonti, Carlo Palanda) Il Fantasma della Poverta, 1995, (with Susanna Creperio) Cose e Davvero La Democrazia, 1996, Turbo Capitalism, U.K. edit., 1998, Turbo-Capitalism: Winners and Losers in the Global Economy, U.S. edit., 1999, French edit., 1999, Italian edit., 1999, Portuguese edit., 1999, Polish edit., 1999, German edit., 1999, Dutch edit., 1999, Japanese edit., 1999, Chinese edit., 1999, Taiwan edit., 1999, Spanish edit., 1999, La Renaissance De La Puissance Aerienne Strategique, 1999, Il Libro Della Liberta 2000 (with Susanna Creporop Verraiti), Strategy: The Logic of War and Peace, 2001, French edit., 2002, Italian edit., 2002, Hebrew edit., 2002; contbr. articles to Fgn. Affairs, London Rev. of Books, Times Lit. Supplement, Commentary National Interest Foreign Affairs Strategy: The Logic of War and Peace New, Revised and Enlarged Edit., 2001, translated edit. Independent. Jewish. Office: CSIS 1800 K St NW Washington DC 20006-2294

LUTVAK, MARK ALLEN, computer company executive; b. Chgo., Feb. 9, 1939; s. Joseph Issac and Jeanette Nettie (Pollock) L.; m. Gayle Helene Rotofsky, May 24, 1964; children: Jeffrey, Eric. BSEE, U. Mich., 1962; MBA, Wayne State U., Detroit, 1969. Sales rep. IBM Corp., 1962-64; from sales rep. to corp. product mgr. Burroughs Corp., Detroit, 1964-76; mgr. product mktg. Memorex Corp., Santa Clara, Calif., 1976-80, product program gen. mgr., 1980-81; dir. product mktg. Personal Computer divsn. Atari, Inc., Sunnyvale, Calif., 1981-83; dir. mktg., v.p. Durango Sys., San Jose, Calif., 1983-85; dir. mktg. ITTQUME Corp., San Jose, 1985-87; v.p. mktg. Optimem, Mountain View, Calif., 1987-88; dir. mktg. Priam Corp., San Jose, 1988-91; dir. Memorex, Santa Clara, 1991-94; owner Synergistic Mktg., 1994—. Prof. Applied Mgmt. Center, Wayne State U., 1967-72, Walsh U., Troy, Mich., 1974-76, West Valley Coll., Saratoga, Calif., 1977-78. Trustee, pres. brotherhood Temple Emanuel, San Jose, 1979-80. Mem. IEEE, Soc. Applied Math., Alpha Epsilon Pi. Home: 899 Balboa Ln Foster City CA 94404-2931 Office Phone: 650-349-5123. E-mail: mlutvak@sbcglobal.net.

LUTWAK, ERWIN, mathematician, educator; b. Chernovtsy, USSR, Feb. 9, 1946; came to U.S., 1956, naturalized, 1961; s. Herman and Anna (Halpern) L.; m. Nancy Ruth Selwyn, Mar. 7, 1968. BS, Poly. Inst. N.Y., Bklyn., 1968, MS, 1972; PhD, 1974. Instr. math. Poly. Inst. N.Y., Bklyn., 1975-77, asst. prof., 1977-81, assoc. prof., 1981-86, prof. 1986—, dept. head 1999—. Mem. editorial bd.: Advances in Math., Ency. of Math. and its Applications; co-editor: N.Y. Acad. Sci. publ., 1985; contbr. articles to sci. jours. Named Disting. Prof. of Yr., Student Govt., Poly. Univ., Bklyn., 1980. Mem. Am. Math. Soc., London Math. Soc., Math. Assn. Am., N.Y. Acad. Scis.(chmn. math. sect. 1988-91), Sigma Xi. Home: 1623 3rd Ave Apt 11C New York NY 10128-3639 Office: Poly U 333 Jay St Brooklyn NY 11201-2907

LUTZ, FRANCIS CHARLES, dean, civil engineering educator; b. Pottsville, Pa., Apr. 5, 1944; s. Charles Henry and Pauline Anna (Weislo) L.; m. Evelyn Florence Zommer, Apr. 29, 1972; 1 child, Stephanie Diane BSCE, N.J. Inst. Tech., 1966; MSCE, NYU, 1967, PhD, 1971. Assoc. M. Disko Assocs., West Orange, N.J., 1970-72; asst. prof. civil engring. Worcester Poly. Inst., Mass., 1972-76, prof., 1980-96, assoc. dean, 1980-90, dean undergrad. studies, 1990-95; dean sch. sci., tech. & engring. Monmouth U., West Long Branch, N.J., 1996—. Cons. Council on Environ. Quality, Washington, 1974-75; reviewer NSF Co-editor: Studies in Science, Technology and Culture, Worcester Poly. Inst.; contbr. articles to profl. jours. Trustee Worcester Ctr. for Crafts, 1992-96; mem. Boston Fed. Exec. Bd., 1972-74, Cen. Mass. Regional Planning Commn., Worcester, 1975-77. Am. Council on Edn. fellow, 1988-89; honors scholar NYU. Mem. ASCE, Am. Soc. Engring. Edn., Boynton Assn. (pres. 1982, 83), JETS (bd. dirs.), Sigma Xi, Chi Epsilon. Office: Monmouth U Office of Dean Sch Sci Tech & Engring West Long Branch NJ 07764-1898

LUTZ, FRANK WENZEL, education administration educator; b. St. Louis, Sept. 24, 1928; s. Vincent J. and Helen M. (Scrivens) L.; m. Susan Virginia Bleikamp, July 12, 1958; children: Paul E., Andrew C., Lynn S. AA, Harris Tchrs. Coll., 1948; BS, Washington U., 1950, MS, 1954, EdD, 1962. Instr. Washington U., St. Louis, 1961-62; from asst. to assoc. prof. NYU, N.Y.C., 1964-68; dir. divsn. policy studies Pa. State U., State College, 1968-73, prof. edn. adminstrn., 1974-80; dean Sch. Edn. Eastern Ill. U., 1980-82, asst. to v.p., 1982-83; prof., dir. Ctr. Policy Studies Tex. A&M-Commerce (formerly East State U.), Commerce, Tex., 1983-91, prof. edn. adminstrn., 1983-98, prof. emeritus, 1998; sr. nat. lectr. Nova S.E. U., Ft. Lauderdale, Fla., 1991-98; prof. edn. adminstrn. U. Tex.-Pan-Am., Edinburg, 1998—2002. Mem. adv. com. Opportunities Acad. Mgmt. Tng., Phila., 1975—90; mem., pres. Pattonville (Mo.) Sch. Bd., 1960—62; adv. bd. Nederland Columbine Clinic, 2001—03. Author seven books, numerous book chpts. in field; contbr. more than 200 articles to profl. jours. Chair Nederland Cmty. Ctr. Bd., 1998-2000; deacon 1st Presbyn. Ch., Commerce, Tex., 1989-91; clerk of session, Nederland Presbyn Ch., 2003-04. Doctoral fellow Washington U., 1960-61; grantee U.S. Office Edn., OEO. Mem. Am. Ednl. Rsch. Assn. (sec. Divsn. A 1970-72, dir. rsch. pre-session 1969, program com. 1970), Commerce Rotary (dist. 5810, pres. 1991-92, chair internat. svc. 1994-96, Found. award 1994, Paul Harris fellow), Peak-to-Peak Rotary (int. chair 2000—, Dist. 5450 world cmty. svc. and youth exch. com. 1999—, Rotarian of Yr. 1999-2001), Phi Delta Kappa (life, pres. Washington U. chpt. 1960, 1st v.p. East Tex. State U. chpt. 1985, Lafferty Faculty Senate Disting. scholarship award 1996). Avocations: appaloosa horses, opera, classical music. Home: PO Box 51 Nederland CO 80466-0051

LUTZ, JACOB A. (JAKE), III, lawyer; b. Radford, Va., 1956; BS in Fin. with distinction, Va. Polytechnic Inst. State Univ., 1978; JD, Coll. William and Mary, 1981. Bar: Va. 1982, Tenn. 1987. Atty. FDIC, Washington, 1981—84, sr. regional atty. Atlanta, 1984—87; assoc. Burid & Higgins, Memphis, 1987—90; ptnr., fin. institutions Troutman Sanders LLP, Richmond, 1990—, mng. ptnr., Richmond office, 1999—, and practice group leader, fin. institutions. Mem.: ABA, Am. Bar Found., Tenn. Bar Assn., Va. Bar Assn. Office: Troutman Sanders LLP Bank of Am Ctr 1111 E Main St Richmond VA 23219 Office Phone: 804-697-1490. Office Fax: 804-697-1339. Business E-Mail: jake.lutz@troutmansanders.com.

LUTZ, JOHN SHAFROTH, lawyer; b. San Francisco, Sept. 10, 1943; s. Frederick Henry and Helena Morrison (Shafroth) L.; m. Elizabeth Boschen, Dec. 14, 1968; children: John Shafroth, Victoria. BA, Brown U., 1965; JD, U. Denver, 1971. Bar: Colo. 1971, U.S. Dist. Ct. Colo. 1971, U.S. Ct. Appeals (2d cir.) 1975, D.C. 1976, U.S. Supreme Ct. 1976, U.S. Dist. Ct. (so. dist.) N.Y. 1977, U.S. Tax Ct. 1977, U.S. Ct. Appeals (10th cir.) 1979, N.Y. 1984, U.S. Ct. Appeals (9th cir.) 1990, U.S. Dist. Ct. (no. dist.) Calif. 1993. Trial atty. Denver regional office U.S. SEC, 1971-74; spl. atty. organized crime, racketeering sect. U.S. Dept. Justice (so. dist.) N.Y., 1974-77; atty. Kelly, Stansfield and O'Donnell, Denver, 1977-78; gen. counsel Boettcher & Co., Denver, 1987, spl. counsel, 1987-88, ptnr., 1988-93; of counsel LeBoeuf, Lamb, Greene and MacRae, LLP, Denver, 1993-94, ptnr., 1995—2001; dir. Fairfield and Woods, PC, Denver, 2002—. Spkr. on broker, dealer, securities law and arbitration issues. Contbr. articles to profl. jours. Bd. dirs. Cherry Creek Improvement Assn., 1980-84, Spalding Rehab. Hosp., 1986-89; chmn., vice-chmn. securities sub sect. Bus. Law Sect. of Colo. Bar, 1990, chmn., 1990-91. Lt. (j.g.) USNR, 1965-67. Mem. ABA, Colo. Bar Assn., Denver Bar Assn., Am. Law Inst., Securities Industry Assn. (state regulation com. 1982-86), Nat. Assn. Securities Dealers, Inc. (nat. arbitration com. 1987-91), St. Nicholas Soc. N.Y.C., Denver Law Club, Denver Country Club, Denver Athletic Club (dir. 1990-93), Univ. Club (Denver), Rocky Mountain Brown Club (founder, past pres.). Republican. Episcopalian. Office: Fairfield and Woods PC Wells Fargo Ctr 1700 Lincoln St #2400 Denver CO 80203 Office Phone: 303-894-4476. Business E-Mail: jlutz@fwlaw.com.

LUTZ, JOHN THOMAS, author; b. Dallas, Sept. 11, 1939; s. John Peter and Esther Jane (Gundelfinger) L.; m. Barbara Jean Bradley, Mar. 15, 1958; children: Steven, Jennifer, Wendy. Student, Meramec C.C., 1965. Author: The Truth of the Matter, 1971, Buyer Beware, 1976, Bonegrinder, 1977, Lazarus Man, 1979, Jericho Man, 1980, The Shadow Man, 1981; (with Steven Greene) Exiled, 1982; (with Bill Pronzini) The Eye, 1984, Nightlines, 1984, The Right to Sing the Blues, 1986, Tropical Heat, 1986, Ride the Lightning, 1987, Scorcher, 1987, Dancers Debt, 1988, Shadowtown, 1988, Kiss, 1988, Better Mousetraps (short story collection), 1988, Time Exposure, 1989, Flame, 1990, Diamond Eyes, 1990, SWF Seeks Same (Single White Female), 1990, Bloodfire, 1991, Hot, 1992, Dancing with the Dead, 1992, Spark, 1993, Thicker than Blood, 1993, (short story collection) Shadows Everywhere, 1994, Torch, 1994, Death by Jury, 1995, Burn, 1995, Lightning, 1996; (novel and screenplay) The Ex, 1996, Oops!, 1998; (with David August) Final Seconds, 1998; (short stories) Until You Are Dead, 1998, The Nudger Dilemmas, 2001, The Night Caller, 2001, The Night Watcher, 2002, The Night Spider, 2003, Endless Road, 2003; contbr. short stories and articles to mystery and private-eye mags, Darker Than Night, 2004, Fear the Night, 2005 Mem. Mystery Writers Am. (Scroll 1981, 2003, Edgar award 1986), Pvt.-Eye Writers Am. (Shamus award 1982, 88, Life Achievement award 1995), Short Mystery Fiction Soc. (Golden Derringer Life Achievement award 2001). Democrat. Home and Office: 880 Providence Ave Saint Louis MO 63119-2072

LUTZ, MATTHEW CHARLES, oil industry executive, geologist; b. Bunkie, La., Mar. 28, 1934; s. John Matthew and Maxie Mae (Andrus) L.; m. Patricia Dawnn Feazel, Apr. 11, 1953; children: Matt Jr., Cyndy, Tracey, Clay. BS, U. Southwestern La., 1956. Various geol. profl. positions Tidewater-Getty Oil Co., 1956-71; asst. dist. geologist Getty Oil Co., Houston, 1971-73, dist. geologist Midland, Tex., 1973-78, ctrl. divsn. geologist Tulsa, 1978-80, offshore dist. exploration mgr. Houston, 1980, so. divsn. exploration mgr., 1980-82, gen. mgr. offshore exploration and prodn., 1982-83, exploration mgr. so. divsn., 1983-84; sr. v.p. exploration Enserch Exploration, Inc., Dallas, 1984-92, also bd. dirs.; vice chmn. and bus. devel. mgr. Hunter Resources, Inc., Irving, Tex., 1993-95, also bd. dirs.; vice chmn. exploration and bus. devel. mgr. Magnum Hunter Resources, Inc., Irving, 1995-97, chmn., exec. v.p., 1997—2001, bd. dirs., 1993—2005; cons., 2005—. *During 28 years of service with Getty Oil Company, originated the exploration geological concepts that led to discovery of over 200 million barrels of oil at Pachuta Creek, East Nancy and West Nancy fields in Mississippi and Hatters Pond Field, Alabama. Moved the company into deep water Gulf of Mexico petroleum province and was recognized as one of its top oil finders. Upon joining Magnum Hunter Resources, provided strategic guidance and originated the petroleum exploration program and staff that led to the discovery and development of oil and gas in New Mexico, West Texas and the Gulf of Mexico.* Mem. Am. Assn. Petroleum Geologists, Houston Geol. Soc., Dallas Geol. Soc., Dallas Petroleum Club. Republican. Baptist. Avocations: golf, hunting, ranching.

LUTZ, RANDALL MATTHEW, lawyer; b. New Brunswick, N.J., June 1, 1945; s. Ralph P. and Gertrude (Goodman) L. BS with high honors, U. Md., 1967, JD, 1970. Bar: Md. 1970, U.S. Dist. Ct. Md. 1970, U.S. Ct. Appeals (4th cir.) 1970, U.S. Supreme Ct. 1975. Assoc. Burke, Gerber & Wilen, Balt., 1970-75; asst. atty. gen. State of Md., 1975-84; dir. criminal enforcement U.S. EPA, Washington, 1984-87; ptnr. Kaplan, Heyman, Greenberg, Engleman & Belgrade, Balt., 1987-90, Smith, Somerville & Case, LLC, Balt., 1990-98, Hodes, Ulman, Pessin & Katz, PA, Towson, Md., 1998—. Lectr. in field. Author: (column) Environmental Law jour.,1987-88. Mem. dist. cabinet Balt. area coun. Boy Scouts Am., 1974-75. Mem: ABA, Md. Bar Assn., Nat. Health Lawyers Assn. Office: Hodes Ulman Pessin & Katz PA 901 Dulaney Valley Rd Towson MD 21204-2600 E-mail: rlutz@hupk.com.

LUTZ, RAYMOND PRICE, retired industrial engineer, educator; b. Oak Park, Ill., Feb. 27, 1935; s. Raymond Price and Sibyl Elizabeth (Haralson) L.; m. Nancy Marie Cole, Aug. 23, 1958. BSME, U. N.Mex., 1958, MBA, 1962; PhD, Iowa State U., 1964. Registered profl. engr., N.Mex., Okla. With Sandia Corp., Albuquerque, summers 1958-63; instr. mech. engring. U. N.Mex., 1958-62; from asst. to assoc. prof. indsl. engring. N.Mex. State U., 1964-68; prof. head indsl. engring. U. Okla., 1968-73; prof., acting dean U. Tex. Sch. Mgmt., Dallas, 1973-76, dean, 1976-78, exec. dean grad. studies and rsch., 1979-92, prof. ops. mgmt., 1992-2001, ret., 2001. Cons. Bell Telephone Labs., Tex. Instruments, Kennecott Corp., Bath Iron Works, Sabre, Inc., City of Dallas, Oklahoma City; cons. U.S. Army, USAF, U.S. Dept. Transp., Los Angeles and Seattle public schs.; mem. shipbldg. productivity panel NRC Editor: The Engring. Economist, 1973-77, Indsl. Mgmt., 1983-87. Pres., bd. dirs. United Cerebral Palsy, Dallas, 1978, treas., 1984-88; bd. dirs., treas. Amigos Bibliographic Network, Dallas, 1984-90; chmn., bd. dirs. S.W. Police Inst., Dallas, 1980—; v.p., bd. dirs. Santa Fe Opera, 1988—, Dallas Opera, 1989-2001, Santa Fe Opera Found., 1993-2000, Santa Fe Women's Ensemble, 2005—; mem. dirs. coun. Desert Chorale, 2005— Fellow AAAS, Am. Inst. Indsl. Engrs. (v.p. industry and mgmt. divsns., trustee, dir. engring. economy divsn., systems engring. group); mem. Am. Soc. Engring. Edn. (chmn. engring. economy divsn., Eugene L. Grant award 1972), INFORMS, Dallas Classic Guitar Soc. (bd. dirs. 1993-96, v.p. 1994-96), Ops. Mgmt. Assn. (bd. dirs. 1994-98), Sigma Xi (bd. dirs. 1990-98, 99—, chmn. capital campaign 1992—, exec. com. 1992-95). Avocations: opera, hiking. Home: 1230 Turquoise Trl Cerrillos NM 87010-9716 E-mail: rplutz@att.net.

LUTZ, ROBERT ANTHONY, automotive company executive; b. Zurich, Switzerland, Feb. 12, 1932; came to U.S., 1939; s. Robert H. and Marguerite (Schmid) L.; m. Betty D. Lutz, Dec. 12, 1956 (div. 1979); children: Jacqueline, Carolyn, Catherine, Alexandra; m. Heide Marie Schmid, Mar. 3, 1980 (div. Dec. 1992); m. Denise Ford, Apr. 17, 1994; 2 stepchildren. BS in Prodn. Mgmt., U. Calif., Berkeley, 1961, MBA in Mktg. with highest honors, 1962; LLD (hon.), Boston U., 1988; DM (hon.), Kettering U., 2003. Research assoc., sr. analyst IMEDE, Lausanne, Switzerland, 1962-63; sr. analyst forward planning GM, N.Y.C., 1963-65, mgr. vehicle div. Paris, 1966-69; staff asst., mng. dir. Adam Opel, Russelsheim, Germany, 1965-66, asst. mgr. domestic sales, 1969, dir. sales Vorstand, 1969-70; v.p. Vorstand BMW, Munich, 1972-74; gen. mgr. Ford of Germany, Cologne, Germany, 1974-76; v.p. truck ops. Ford of Europe, Brentwood, Eng., 1976-77, pres., 1977-79, chmn., 1979-82, also bd. dirs.; exec. v.p. Ford Internat., Dearborn, Mich., 1982-84, Chrysler Motors Corp., Highland Park, Mich., 1986-88; pres. ops., pres., COO Chrysler Corp., Highland Park, Mich., 1988-96, vice chmn., 1996—98; chmn. Exide Corp., 1998—2002, pres., 1998—2000, CEO, 1998—2001; vice chmn., prod. devel. General Motors Corp., 2001—; chmn. General Motors N. Am., 2001—05; pres. GM Europe, 2004. Bd. dirs. Exide Technologies, 1998-, Kepner-Tregoe, Silicon Graphics, ASCOM, Switzerland; mem., former chmn. Hwy. Users Fedn. for Safety and Mobility. Author: Guts: The Seven Laws of Business That Made Chrysler the World's Hottest Car Company, 1998, Guts: 8 Laws of Business from One of the Most Innovative Business Leaders of our Time, 2003. Trustee: Mich. Cancer Found., USMC U. Found.; vice-chmn, bd. trustees, Marine Military Acad.; bd. dirs. United Way of Southeastern Mich.; mem. adv. bd. Walter A. Haas Sch. Bus., U. Calif., Berkeley, 1979—; chmn., The New Common School Found.; Capt. USMC, 1954-65. Named Alumnus of Yr., Sch. Bus., U. Calif., 1983; Kaiser Found. grantee, 1962. Mem. NAM (exec. com.), Phi Beta Kappa. Republican. Avocations: skiing, motorcycling, bicycling, helicopter flying, vintage cars, jet fighter flying. Office: GM Corp PO Box 300 Detroit MI 48265-3000 also: Exide Technologies 3000 Montrose Ave Reading PA 19605-2751*

LUTZER, ERWIN WESLEY, clergyman, author; b. Cofax, Sask., Can., Oct. 3, 1941; came to U.S., 1971; s. Gustav and Wanda (Lutke) L.; m. Rebecca Ann Hickman, Aug. 30, 1969; children: Lorisa, Lynette, Lisa. BTh, Winnipeg Bible Coll., 1963; ThM, Dallas Theol. Sem., 1967; MA, Loyola U., Chgo., 1974; LLD, Simon Greenleaf Sch. Law, 1984; DD, We. Conservative Bapt. Sem., 1987. Ordained to ministry Bapt. Ch., 1963, Christian and Missionary Alliance Ch., 1970. Pastor Edgewater Bapt. Ch., Chgo., 1971-76; prof. Bible and theology Moody Bible Ch., Chgo., 1976-80; sr. pastor The Moody Ch., Chgo., 1980—. Prof. Trinity, Deerfield, Ill., 1988, 97—. Author: Managing Your Emotions, 1983, When A Good Man Falls, 1986, Measuring Morality, 1989, Keep Your Dream Alive, 1991, Twelve Myths Americans Believe, 1993, Getting Closer to God, 1994, Hitler's Cross, 1995, The Serpent of Paradise, 1996, Putting Your Past Behind You, 1997, One Minute After You Die, 1997, Your Eternal Reward, 1998, others; host The Moody Church Hour, Songs in the Night, Running to Win; author 60-tape series. Avocation: tennis. Office: The Moody Ch 1609 N Lasalle St Chicago IL 60614-6004

LUTZKER, JOEL E., lawyer; b. Queens, NY, Dec. 30, 1951; BA in Physics, cum laude, NYU, 1972, JD, 1975. Bar: NY 1976, Conn. 1977, US Patent & Trademark Office. Atty. Bryan & Bollo, Stamford, Conn., 1976—80, Amster, Rothstein & Ebenstein, NYC, 1985—2001; ptnr., intellectual property dept. Schulte Roth & Zabel LLP. Contbr. articles to profl. jour.; spkr. in field. Mem.: Intellectual Property Owner's Assn., Licensing Exec. Soc., Internat. Trade Commn. Trial Lawyers Assn., Am. Intellectual Property Law Assn., NY Intellectual Property Law Assn., ABA, NY State Bar Assn., Sigma Pi Sigma. Office: Schulte Roth & Zabel LLP 919 Third Ave New York NY 10022 Office Phone: 212-756-2520. Office Fax: 212-593-5955. Business E-Mail: joel.lutzker@srz.com.

LUXEMBURG, WILHELMUS ANTHONIUS JOSEPHUS, mathematics professor; b. Delft, Netherlands, Apr. 11, 1929; s. Everardus H. and Digna L.; m. Geetruida Zappeij, Aug. 2, 1955; children— Ronald P., Jacqueline T. BA, U. Leiden, Netherlands, 1950, MA, 1953; PhD, Delft Inst. Tech., 1955. Postdoctoral fellow NRC, Can., 1955-56; mem. faculty U. Toronto, 1956-58; from mem. faculty to prof. emeritus Calif. Inst. Tech., Pasadena, 1958—2000, prof. emeritus, 2000—. Cons. Burroughs Corp., Pasadena, 1963-64 Mem. Am., Dutch math. socs., Math. Assn. Am., Canadian Math. Congress, Soc. for Indsl. and Applied Math., Royal Acad. Scis. Amsterdam (Humboldt award 1980) Research and publs. on theory of integration, spaces of measurable functions, ordinary differential equations, numerical analysis, topological linear spaces, Boolean algebras, axiomatic set theory, theory of Riesz spaces, non-standard analysis. Home: 817 S El Molino Ave Pasadena CA 91106-4411 Office Phone: 626-395-4344.

LUXENBERG, ARTHUR MARTIN, lawyer; b. N.Y.C., Apr. 14, 1959; s. Irwin Eugene and Joan Florence (Aronson) L.; m. Randi Joy Beeber Luxenberg, Aug. 14, 1984. Attended, Univ. Pa.; BA, Yeshiva Univ., N.Y.C., 1981; JD, Cardozo Sch. Law, Yeshiva Univ., N.Y.C., 1984. Bar: N.Y. 1985, U.S. Dist. Ct. (so. dist.) N.Y. 1988, U.S. Dist. Ct. (ea. dist.) N.Y. 1988, U.S. Ct. Appeals 2d cir. 1988. Assoc. law and appeals div. Morris J. Eisen P.C., N.Y.C., 1984-86, dir. law and appeals div., 1986—; founding mem. & mng. ptnr. Weitz & Luxenberg, N.Y.C., 1986—. Moot Ct. judge, Fordham U., N.Y.C., 1987-88. Co-author: Practicing Law Institute Course Book, 1988. Mem. N.Y. State Bar Assn., N.Y. State Trial Lawyers Assn. Office: Weitz & Luxenberg 180 Maiden Lane New York NY 10038-4925

LUXENBERG, MALCOLM NEUWAHL, ophthalmologist, educator; b. Philipsburg, Pa., July 29, 1935; s. Maurice and Henrietta (Neuwahl) L.; m. Sandra Diane Rosen, June 16, 1957; children: Steven Neuwahl, Cathy Ann. Student, Tulane U., 1953-56; MD, U. Miami, Fla., 1960. Diplomate: Am. Bd. Ophthalmology. Intern Cin. Gen. Hosp., 1960-61; resident in neurology U. Vt. Affiliated Hosps., Burlington, 1961-63; resident in ophthalmology Bascom Palmer Eye Inst., U. Miami-Jackson Meml. Hosp., Miami, Fla., 1963-66; asst. prof. ophthalmology Coll. Medicine, U. Iowa, Iowa City, 1968-70; chief ophthalmology service VA Hosp., Iowa City, 1968-70; practice medicine specializing in ophthalmology West Palm Beach, Fla., 1970-72; clin. asst. prof. ophthalmology Bascom Palmer Eye Inst., Sch. Medicine, U. Miami, 1971-72; prof., chmn. dept. ophthalmology Med. Coll. Ga., Augusta, 1972-2000, prof. emeritus, 2000—. Cons. ophthalmology VA Hosp., Augusta, 1972—; sr. surgeon USPHS, 1966-68. Mem. edtl. bd.: Archives of Ophthalmology, 1986-94. Recipient Outstanding Civilian Service Medal Dept. of Army, 1986. Mem. AMA, Am. Acad. Ophthalmology (hon. award 1986), Am. Ophthalmol. Soc., Assn. Univ. Profs. in Ophthalmology (pres. 1982-83), Ga. Soc. Ophthalmology, Med. Assn. Ga., Richmond County Med. Soc. Office: Med Coll Ga Dept Ophthalmology Augusta GA 30912 Office Phone: 706-721-1148.

LUYENDYK, BRUCE PETER, geophysicist, educator, institution administrator; b. Freeport, N.Y., Feb. 23, 1943; s. Pieter Johannes and Frances Marie (Blakeney) L.; 1 child, Loren Taylor Luyendyk. BS Geophysics, San Diego State Coll., 1965; PhD Marine Geophysics, Scripps Inst. Oceanography, 1969. Geophysicist Arctic Sci. and Tech. Lab. USN Electronics Lab. Ctr., 1965; lectr. San Diego State Coll., 1967-68; postgrad rsch. geologist Scripps Inst. Oceanography, 1969; postdoctoral fellow dept. geology and geophysics Woods Hole Oceanographic Instn., 1969-70, asst. scientist dept. geology and geophysics, 1970-73; asst. prof. U. Calif., Santa Barbara, 1973-75, assoc. prof., 1975-81, prof. dept. geol. scis., 1981—, acting dir. Inst. Crustal Studies, 1987-88, dir. Inst. Crustal Studies, 1988-97, chair dept. geol. scis., 1997—2003. Participant, chief sci. oceanographic cruises, geol. expdns.; coord. bd. So. Calif. Integrated GPS Network, 1997-2000. Editorial bd. Geology, 1975-79, Marine Geophysical Rschs., 1976-92, Jour. Geophysical Rsch., 1982-84, Tectonophysics, 1988-92, Pageoph, 1988-95; contbr. articles to profl. jours., chpts. to books, encys. Co-recipient Newcomb Cleveland prize AAAS, 1980; recipient Antarctic Svc. medal U.S. NSF, Dept. Navy, 1990, Disting. Alumni award San Diego State U., 1983, numerous rsch. grants, 1971—. Fellow Geol. Soc. Am., Am. Geophys. Union. Office: U Calif Santa Barbara Dept Geol Scis Santa Barbara CA 93106 Business E-Mail: luyendyk@geol.ucsb.edu.

LUZA, RADOMIR VACLAV, historian, educator; b. Prague, Czechoslovakia, Oct. 17, 1922; s. Vojtech V. and Milada (Vecera) L.; m. Libuse Ladislava Podhrazska, Feb. 5, 1949; children: Radomir V., Sabrina. JuDr, U. Brno, Czechoslovakia, 1948; MA, NYU, 1958, PhD, 1959. Assoc. prof. modern European history La. State U., New Orleans, 1966-67; prof. history Tulane U., New Orleans, 1967—. Scholar-in-residence Rockefeller Found., Bellagio Study Ctr., 1988; prof. gen. history Masaryk U., Brno, 1993—. Author: The Transfer of the Sudeten Germans, 1964, History of the International Socialist Youth Movement, 1970, (with V. Mamatey) A History of the Czechoslovak Republic, 1918-1948, 1973, Austro-German Relations in the Anschluss Era, 1975, Österreich und die Grossdeutsche Idee in der NS-Zeit, 1977, Geschichte der Tschechoslowakischen Republik 1918-1948, 1980, A History of the Resistance in Austria, 1938-1945, 1984, Der Widerstand in Österreich, 1938-1945, 1985, La Rèpublique Tchécoslovaque 1918-1948, 1987, The Czechoslovak Social Democracy Abroad, 1948-1989, 2001, The Hitler Kiss: A Memoir of the Czech Resistance, 2002; mem. editl. bd. East European Quar., Contemporary Austrian Studies. With Czech Resistance, 1939—45, WWII, col. Czech Army, 1995, ret. N, Czech Army. Recipient all Czechoslovak mil. decorations; prize Theodor Körner Found., Vienna, 1965, J. Hlavka Hon. medal Czechoslovak Acad. Arts and Scis., 1992, T.G. Masaryk medal Pres. of Czech Rep., 1996, Austrian Cross of Honor Sci. and Art I. Class, 1997, Meml. medal Czech Rep., 2000; grantee Social Rsch. Coun., Am. Philos. Soc., Coun. Learned Socs., Fulbright Com., NEH. Mem. Am. Hist. Assn., Czechoslovak History Conf., So. Conf. Slavic Studies, Am. Assn. Advancement Slavic Studies. Home: 2313 Twin Silo Dr Blue Bell PA 19422-3281 Office: Tulane U Dept History New Orleans LA 70118

LUZKY, LEONARD, protective services official, educator, non-commissioned officer; b. Nuremberg, Germany, Apr. 2, 1946; s. Igor Sergeavich and Feride Ablajkimova-Dorosh; m. Michele Pengitore, Nov. 26, 1998; 1 child, Dana Lyn Piscal;children from previous marriage: Alayna Dorso, Garrett Bayard. M in Human Resources, Pepperdine U., 1977. Cert. police tng. commn., 1967. Infantryman/rigger U.S. Army, 1963-66; sgt. Haledon (N.J.) Police Dept., 1967-73; officer, detective Dover Twp. Police, Toms River, N.J., 1973-95; col., dir. civilian pers. N.J. Army N.G., Ft. Dix,

1977—; safety officer Toms River Bd. Edn., 1999—. Adj. prof. Ocean County Coll., Toms River, 1990—; cons. 1st Response Protective Svcs., Bayville, N.J., 1995—. Mem. Mcpl. Alliance, Twp. of Dover, Toms River, 1993—. Named Policeman of Yr./Crime Prevention Practitioner, State of N.J., 1975, 89. Mem. N.J. Crime Prevention Officer's Assn. (life, pres. 1990-93, Practitioner of Yr. 1985, 90). Republican. Russian Orthodox. Avocation: singing. Home: 962 Riverbrook Ct Toms River NJ 08753-4490 Fax: (732) 573-1252. E-mail: lluzky@adelphia.net.

LY, ALLAN Q., medical technician; b. Feb. 7, 1973; arrived in U.S., 1978; s. Long Van Ly and Moni Giang. BS in Internat. Bus., Calif. State Poly. U., 1995; MBA, Woodbury U., 1997; AS in Marine Tech., Coll. Oceaneering, 2002. Cert. EMT-1 Calif.; comml. diver Coll. Oceaneering, Am. Welding Soc., helmet maintenance trng. Diving Sys. Internat., forklift safety trng., crane rigging safety. Customer svc. rep Bank of Am., Glendale, Calif., 1991—96; mktg. and rsch. KABC-TV, LA, 1999—2000; asst. mgr. Albertsons Inc., Monterey Pk, Calif., 1996—; hyperbaric oxygen technician The Brain Therapeutics Clin., Mission Viejo, Calif., 2002—. Mem. domestic alumni MBA Assn., Burbank, 1997—98, v.p. alumni rels., 1998—99. Avocations: basketball, diving, movies, dining out, camping. Home: 411 N Moore Ave Monterey Park CA 91754 Personal E-mail: med4sea@yahoo.com.

LYALL, KATHARINE CULBERT, former academic administrator, economist, educator; b. Lancaster, Pa., Apr. 26, 1941; d. John D. and Eleanor G. Lyall. BA in Econs., Cornell U., 1963, PhD in Econs., 1969; MBA, NYU, 1965. Economist Chase Manhattan Bank, N.Y.C., 1963-65; asst. prof. econs. Syracuse U., 1969-72; prof. econs. Johns Hopkins U., Balt., 1972-77, dir. grad. program in pub. policy, 1979-81; dep. asst. sec. for econs. Office Econ. Affairs, HUD, Washington, 1977-79; v.p. acad. affairs U. Wis. Sys., 1981-85; prof. of econ. U. Wis., Madison, 1982—; acting pres. U. Wis. Sys., Madison, 1985-86, 91-92, exec. v.p., 1986-91, pres., 1992—2004, pres. emeritus, 2005—. Bd. dirs. Marshall & Ilsley Bank, Alliant, Carnegie Found. for Advancement of Tchg. Author: Reforming Public Welfare, 1976, Microeconomic Issues of the 70s, 1978. Mem. Mcpl. Securities Rulemaking Bd., Washington, 1990-93. Mem. Am. Econ. Assn., Phi Beta Kappa. Office Phone: 608-262-2321. Business E-Mail: klyall@wisc.edu.

LYALL, LYNN, consumer products company executive; Sr. v.p. fin., info. svcs. & tech. Cadbury Schweppes, PLC; exec. v.p., CFO Blockbuster Entertainment, Inc.; exec. v.p. Alticor Inc., 1999—, CFO. Office: Alticor Inc 7575 Fulton St E Ada MI 49355

LYBECKER, MARTIN EARL, lawyer; b. Lincoln, Nebr., Feb. 11, 1945; s. Earl Edward and Jeanette Frances (Kiefer) L.; m. Andrea Kristine Tollefson, Dec. 27, 1969; children: Carl Martin, Neil Anders. BBA, U. Wash., 1967, JD, 1970; LLM in Taxation, NYU, 1971; LLM, U. Pa., 1973. Bar: Wash. 1970, D.C. 1972, Pa. 1982. Atty. investment mgmt. div. SEC, Washington, 1972-75, assoc. dir. div., 1978-81; assoc. prof. SUNY, Buffalo, 1975-78; ptnr. Drinker Biddle & Reath, Washington, 1981-87, Ropes & Gray, Washington, 1987—2002, Wilmer Cutler Pickering Hale and Dorr LLP, Washington, 2002—. Adj. prof. Georgetown U., Washington, 1974-75; vis. assoc. prof. Duke U., Durham, N.C., 1977-78, sr. lecturing fellow in law, 2000—. Contbr. articles to law revs. Fellow U. Pa. Ctr. for Study of Fin. Instns., 1971-72. Mem.: ABA (mem. subcom. on investment cos. and investment advisers, mem. com. on fed. regulation of securities bus. law sect., former chairperson com. on devels. in investment svcs. bus. law sect., chair com. on banking law), Am. Law Inst., Univ. Club. Washington. Home: 2806 Daniel Rd Bethesda MD 20815-3149 Office: Wilmer Cutler Pickering Hale and Dorr LLP 2445 M St NW Washington DC 20037-1420 Office Phone: 202-663-6240. Business E-Mail: martin.lybecker@wilmerhale.com.

LYCETT, SARA F. See FINNEGAN, SARA

LYDICK, NANCY M., psychologist; b. Belville, Tex., June 18, 1942; d. John Samuel Jr. and Dale (Crawford) McCelvey; m. Larry Stuart Lydick (div.); children: L. Drew, Todd W.; m. M'Baye Fara Gaye, Sept. 23, 1999. BA in Psychology, Antioch U., West L.A., 1980; MA in Marriage, Family and Child counseling, Asuza Pacific U., L.A., 1982; PhD in Gen. Psychology, U.S. Internat. U., San Diego, 1994. Lic. Marriage and Family Therapist Calif., Pa. Intern Calif. Family Study Ctr., 1982, L.A. Psychiat. Ctr., 1993—94; drug counselor, dual diagnosis Parkside Recovery/ Dept Human Svcs., Phila., 1999—, dir. family program, 2002—; pres., CEO For Love of the Family, Inc., 2004—. Presenter confs. and workshops Various Assns. and Groups, in U.S. and Can.; dir. workshops Dream, Sex Edn., Adolescents, Eating Disorders; interat. spkr. Women, Youth and Family (an Islamic perspective). Author (producer and dir.): (TV series) Women in Islam, 1996; author: (producer and host) Healing from the Heart, 1998; columnist (monthly mag. article) Ask Nasiha. Nat. Fellowship Ahmadu Bamba Internat. Sufi Sch.; presenter Development in Literacy; pres. Khidmatul Khadim Internat. Sufi Sch.; mem. Pa. Commn. for Healthy Families; Vol. thrift shop, Big Sisters program, fund raiser Fort Worth Jr. League, Tex., 1965—73; vol. book mobile Nat. Coun. Jewish Women, Fort Worth, 1964. Mem.: Pa. Commn. for Health and Families, Phila. Assn. Marriage and Family Therapy, Acad. Family Mediators, Assn. Family and Conciliation Cts., Assn. Play Therapy, Internat. Assn. Eating Disorders Specialists, Am. Psychol. Assn., Calif. Assn. Marriage and Family Therapy (clin. mem.), Am. Assn. Marriage and Family Therapy (clin. mem.), Kappa Kappa Gamma (Epsilon Alpha chpt.). Islam. Office: Parkside Recovery 5000 Parkside Ave Philadelphia PA 19131 E-mail: nm.lydick@verizon.net.

LYDON, AMANDA, chef; Undergrad Harvard Univ. Chef Truc, Radius, Chez Henri, Cambridge, Mass., Metro Brasserie, Boston, 2001—, UpStairs on the Square. Nominee James Beard award, 2000; named Best New Chef, Boston Mag., 2000; named one of Best Young Chefs in Am., Food & Wine Mag. Office: UpStairs on the Square 91 Winthrop St Cambridge MA 02138 Office Phone: 617-864-1933.

LYDON, NICHOLAS B. (NICK LYDON), pharmaceutical executive, researcher; b. Feb. 27, 1957; BSc, U. Leeds, Eng.; PhD, U. Dundee, Scotland, 1984. With Schering Plough, 1985; oncology rsch. team Ciba-Geigy AG (now Novartis Pharmaceuticals AG), 1985—87; founder, pres., CEO Kinetix Pharmaceutical Inc. (acquired by Amgen, Inc.), Medford, Mass., 1997—2000; v.p. small molecule drug discovery Amgen, Inc., Thousand Oaks, Calif., 2000—02; with Verizon Pharmaceutical Co., Calif., 2002. Past mem. Novartis Oncology Mgmt. Com. Recipient Sci. Prize, Warren Alpert Found., 2000, Bruce F. Cain Meml. award, Am. Assn. Cancer Rsch., 2002, Charles F. Kettering prize, GM Cancer Rsch. Found., 2002, Bruce F. Cain Meml. award, Am. Assn. Cancer Rsch., 2002. Achievements include (with Brian. J. Drucker) contribution to the development of a leukemia drug, Gleevac (STI571) that effectively treats chronic megelogenous leukemia and other forms of cancer.

LYERLA, BRADFORD PETER, lawyer; b. Savanna, Ill., Aug. 2, 1954; s. Ralph Herbert and Nancy Lee (Nelson) L.; m. Marilyn Wyse, Aug. 18, 1979; 3 children. BA, U. Ill., 1976, JD, 1980. Bar: Ill. 1980, U.S. Dist. Ct. (no. dist.) Ill. 1980, U.S. Dist. Ct. (no. dist.) Ind. 1982, U.S. Dist. Ct. (no. dist.) Calif. 1991, U.S. Dist. Ct. (ctrl. dist.) Ill. 1991, U.S. Dist. Ct. (no. dist.) Tex. 1999, U.S. Dist. Ct. (ea. dist.) Wis. 2000, U.S. Dist. Ct. Nebr. 1998, U.S. Dist. Ct. Colo. 2004, U.S. Ct. Appeals (7th cir.) 1983, U.S. Ct. Appeals (fed. cir.) 1991, U.S. Ct. Appeals (2d cir.) 2002, U.S. Supreme Ct. 1995. Trial lawyer, Chgo.; sr. ptnr. Marshall, Gerstein & Borun, Chgo. Lectr. on litigation and intellectual property law. Author publications in field; editor U. Ill. Law Rev., 1978-80. Bd. dirs. North Suburban Bd. of the Heartland Alliance, Wilmette, Ill., 1987-96, pres. 1993-94; bd. dirs. Traveler's and Immigrant's Aid, Chgo., 1991-95; bd. dirs., sec. Youth Svcs. Project, Inc., Chgo., 1987-91; mem. U. Ill. Pres.'s Coun.; founding mem. Cribbett Soc., U. Ill. Coll. Law; mem. Saints Faith Hope and Charity, Winnetka, Ill. Recipient John Powers Crowley Justice award People's Uptown Law Ctr., 1989. Fellow Am. Bar Found. (life); mem. ABA (editor litigation sect. intellectual properties litigation quar. 1990—, intellectual property sect. com. on unfair competition litigation), Ill. Bar Assn. (sect. coun. gen. practice sect. 1984-85, intellectual property sect. 1989—, co-editor intellectual property newsletter 1989-95, chair 1996-97), Chgo. Bar Assn. (legal ethics), Am. Intellectual Property Law Assn. (antitrust and fed. lit. com.), Intellectual Property Law Assn. Chgo. (patent litigation), Michigan Shores Club, Phi Beta Kappa, Phi Kappa Phi. Office: Marshall Gerstein & Borun 233 S Wacker Dr 6300 Sears Tower Chicago IL 60606 Office Phone: 312-474-6300. E-mail: blyerla@marshallip.com.

LYERLY, ELAINE MYRICK, advertising executive; b. Charlotte, NC, Nov. 26, 1951; d. J.M. and Annie Mary (Myrick) L.; m. Marc Rauch, Jan. 17, 1987. AA in Advt. and Comml. Design, Cen. Piedmont Community Coll., 1972. Freelance designer Sta. WBTV, Charlotte, N.C., 1972; fashion illustrator Matthews Belk, Gastonia, N.C., 1972-73; designer Monte Curry Mktg. and Communication Svcs., Charlotte, 1973-74, exec. v.p., 1974-77; pres. Repro/Graphics, Charlotte, 1975-77, Lyerly Agy. Inc., Charlotte, 1977—. Organizing dir. First Trust Bank. Illustrator: Mister Cookie Breakfast Cookbook, 1985. Former chmn. regional blood com. Greater Carolinas chpt. ARC, 1990-93, mem. nat. implementation com., 1991, chair nat. conv., 2001, mem. nat. bd. govs., 2002-, Red Cross, nat. exec. com. and chair pub. support, nat. co-chair task force non-episodic fundraising; bd. dirs. United Way, 1996, YMCA, Women's Impact Fund, 2003-, Levine Mus. of New South; bd. dirs., chair Child Care Resources, Inc., 2003-, Women's Impact Fund, 2002-; mem. bd. advisors Belmont Abbey Coll. Named Bus. Woman of Yr., Shearson Lehman Hutton/Queens Coll., 1989, N.C. Young Careerist Bus. and Profl. Women's Club, 1981; recipient ACE award Women in Comms., 1993, CPCC Hagemeyer award, 1996, Schley Lyons Leadership Charlotte award, 1999, Bus. Jour. Top 25 Women of Achievement award 2001. Mem. Women Execs., Women Bus. Owners (adv. coun., Leadership award 1990, Woman Bus. Owner of Yr. award 1994), Pub. Rels. Soc. Am. (Counselors Acad. 1985—), Charlotte C. of C. (bd. dirs., diversity coun., long-range planning com., Bus. Woman of Yr. award 1985), Hadassah. Republican. Jewish. Office: Lyerly Agy Inc 4819 Park Rd Charlotte NC 28209-3274 E-mail: elyerly@lyerly.com.

LYFORD, CABOT, sculptor; b. Sayre, Pa., May 22, 1925; s. Frederic Eugene and Eleanor (Cabot) L.; m. Joan Ardyth Richmond, June 22, 1953; children: Matthew, Julia, Thaddeus. BFA, Cornell U., 1950. Exec. trainee NBC, N.Y.C., 1952-54; producer and dir. J. Walter Thompson, N.Y.C., 1954-57, Sta. WGBH-TV, Boston, 1957-59; program mgr. Sta. WENH-TV, Durham, N.H., 1959-63; chmn. Dept. Art The Phillips Exeter (N.H.) Acad., 1963-86. Prin. sculptures include pub. monuments in Portland, Maine and Portsmouth, N.H., Berwick, Maine; represented in permanent collections at Portland Mus., Chattanooga Mus., Indpls. Mus., Wichita (Kans.) Mus., Ogunquit (Maine) Mus., Currier Gallery, Manchester, N.H., Addison Gallery, Andover, Mass., Theme sculpture New Bedford (Mass.) Whaling Mus.e With inf. U.S. Army, 1943-46, PTO. Recipient Sculpture prize Nat. Design Acad., 1990. Home: 4 Fish Point Rd New Harbor ME 04554-4606

LYJAK CHORAZY, ANNA JULIA, pediatrician, educator, retired health facility administrator; d. Walter and Cecilia (Swiatkowski) Lyjak; m. Chester John Chorazy, May 6, 1961; children: Paula Ann Chorazy Peters, Mary Ellen Chorazy-Cuccaro, Mark Edward Chorazy. BS, Waynesburg Coll., 1958; MD, Women's Med. Coll. Pa., 1960. Diplomate Am. Bd. Pediat. Intern St. Francis Gen. Hosp., Pitts., 1960-61; resident in pediat., tchg. fellow Children's Hosp. Pitts., 1961-63, pediatrician, devel. clinic, 1966-75; pediat. house physician Western Pa. Hosp., Pitts., 1963-66; med. dir. Rehab. Instn. Pitts., 1975-98, Children's Inst., Pitts., 1998—2001, interim med. dir., 2002—03. Clin. asst. prof. pediat. Children's Hosp. Pitts. and U. Pitts. Sch. Medicine, 1971—94, clin. assoc. prof. pediat., 1994—2001; pediat. cons. Children's Home Pitts., 1985—2001. Author chpts. to books. Co-chmn. EACH Joint Planning and Assessment, Pitts., 1980-85; mem. adv. com. 10th Nat. Conf. on Child Abuse, Pitts., 1993. Recipient Miracle Maker award, Children's Miracle Network, 1995, Disting. Alumni award, Waynesburg Coll., 2002. Fellow Am. Acad. Pediat.; mem. Pitts. Pediat. Soc. Avocations: reading, comedy, theater, music, opera. Home: 131 Washington Rd Pittsburgh PA 15221-4437 Office Phone: 412-420-2268.

LYLE, JAMES ARTHUR, real estate broker; b. Charlottesville, Va., Mar. 9, 1945; s. James Aaron and Sallie (Tuthill) Lyle; m. Martha Lee Gale, Jan. 28, 1978 (dec. June 2000); children: Cory Jackson, Martha Jessica; m. Yolanda Zarina Ramirez, Nov. 28, 2002. BS in Indsl. Mgmt., Ga. Inst. Tech., 1968. Cert. comml. investment mem. Mktg. rep. IBM, Atlanta, 1970-71; investment cons. La Salle Ptnrs., El Paso, Tex., 1971-76; owner James Arthur Lyle and Assocs., El Paso, 1976—. Bd. dirs. Hueco Mountain Estates, Inc., pres., 1983—; bd. dirs. Remington Oil and Gas Corp., 1997-2003. Vice chmn. El Paso City Plan Commn., 1978-82, chmn., 1997-2003; vice-chmn. Internat. Airport Bd., 1982; adv. bd. El Paso Bikeway, 1986-88; active El Paso County Planning Commn., 1986-98; bd. dirs. NCCJ, 1978-82, Southwestern Gen. Hosp., 1979-83, El Paso Econ. Devel. Bd., 1980-82; bd. dirs. Am. Heart Assn., 1989-93; mem. Leadership El Paso, 1981-82 1st lt. U.S. Army, 1968-70. Named Bus. Assoc. of Yr., Am. Bus. Womens Assn., 1984, S.W. Challenge Series Champion, 1991-2005, Ironman World Triathlon Championship, 1992, N.Mex. State Triathlon champion, 1999, Tuscon Triathlon Series Champion, 2001, Tex. Sr. Games Triathlon Champion, 2002; Border Grand Prix Series Champion, 2002; named to El Paso Sr. Games Hall of Fame, 2000, El Paso Athletic Hall of Fame, 2005. Mem. SAR (dist. v.p., Bronze Good Citizenship medal 1996, Cert. of Disting. Svc.), Nat. Assn. Realtors, Realtors Nat. Mktg. Inst., Nat. Assn. Indsl. and Office Parks, Tex. Property Exchangors (Best Exch. 1979), Tex. Assn. Realtors, Tex. Real Estate Polit. Action Com. (life), El Paso Bd. Realtors (bd. dirs. 1975-88, cert. comml. investment mem. 1975—, El Paso-West Tex. cert. comml. investment mem., pres., sec.-treas. 1975—, comml.-investment real estate coun. 1971—), El Paso Indsl. Devel. Bd., El Paso Investment Exch. Svc., Sons Confederate Vets, Sunturians (life), Half Fast Track Club (v.p. multisports), USA Triathlon (bd. dirs. 1995-2001), Team El Paso, Delta Sigma Pi (life), Sigma Alpha Epsilon (life). Republican. Episcopalian. Avocation: triathlons. Home: 811 Rim Rd El Paso TX 79902 Office: James Arthur Lyle & Assocs 720 Arizona Ave El Paso TX 79902-4402

LYLE, ROBERT EDWARD, chemist; b. Atlanta, Jan. 26, 1926; s. Robert Edward and Adaline (Cason) L.; m. Gloria Gilbert, Aug. 28, 1947 (dec. Dec. 1996); m. Anne Carroll Kohl, Aug. 1, 1997. BA, Emory U., 1945, MS, 1946; PhD, U. Wis., Madison, 1949. Asst. prof. Oberlin Coll., Ohio, 1949-51; asst. prof. U. N.H., Durham, 1951-53, assoc. prof., 1953-57, prof., 1957-76; prof., chmn. dept. chemistry U. North Tex., Denton, 1977-79; v.p. chemistry, chem. engr. S.W Rsch. Inst., San Antonio, 1979-91; v.p. GRL Cons., San Antonio, 1992—97, pres., 1997—. Vis. prof. U. Va., Charlottesville, 1973-74, U. Grenoble, France, 1976; adj. prof. Bowdoin Coll., Brunswick, Maine, 1975-79, U. Tex., San Antonio, 1985-2001. Mem. editl. bd. Index Chemicus, 1976—. USPHS fellow Oxford U., Eng., 1965; recipient honor scroll award Mass. chpt. Am. Inst. Chemistry, 1971; Harry and Carol Mosher co-awardee, 1986. Fellow AAAS; mem. Am. Chem. Soc. (councilor 1965-84, 86-92, medicinal chemistry divsn.), Royal Soc. Chemistry, Alpha Chi Sigma (editor Hexagon 1992-99, Kuebler award 1998). Methodist. Office: GRL Cons 12814 Kings Forest Dr San Antonio TX 78230-1511 Personal E-mail: geegeel@aol.com.

LYLE, VALARIE GAY, art educator, artist; d. James Franklin and Phyllis Eggers Lyle. BFA, Ringling Sch. Art Design, 1989; MFA, East Tenn. State U., 2001. Calendar editor Museums NY Mag., 1984—86, 1994—96; adj. art instr. East Tenn. State U., Johnson City, Tenn., 2001—03, N.E. State CC, Johnson City, 2002, Va. Highlands CC, Abingdon, 2003—04, Va. Intermont Coll., Bristol, 2005—. Art advisor, student art and lit. mag. The Mockingbird, East Tenn. State U., Johnson City, 2002—05. Exhibitions include Who We Are: The Figure in the 21st Century, A Difference of Opinion, Appalachian Corridors, Charleston, W.Va., The Figurative Gallery of Contemporary Art, From the Bar; New York City, 3.10 Exhibition by Peter Suschin, Nat. Conf. Edn. in Ceramic Arts, Bklyn. Waterfront Artists Coalition, Ise Foundation, NYC. Bd. mem. NC Folk Art Soc., 2004—05. Recipient Career Awards in Art, Nat. Soc. of Arts & Letters, Hono, HI, 1984, Gold Addy award of excellence, Tri-City Metro Advt. Fedn., 2004, 2005; grantee Exhbn. grant, Artist's Space, 1991; scholar Outstanding Fine Arts Student Scholarship, Binney & Smith Artist Materials Mfg. Co., Ethel and Stanley Glen Scholarship, Ringling Sch. of art and Design, 1987, Richard & Va. Crossley Scholarship, Ringling Sch. Art & Design, 1988. Mem.: NC Folk Art Soc., Tenn. Assn. Craft Artists, Nat. Coun. Edn. in Ceramic Arts, Coll. Art Assn., Peter Pugger Clay Pugmills (spokesperson 2003—), Knoxville Contra Dancers, Women's Mus. Art, Phi Kappa Phi Honor Soc. Achievements include writing and publishing one of the first fine art electronic thesis which is still considered exemplary by the international community of Graduate School Deans. Home: 2045 Carolina Ave Bristol TN 37620 Office: E Tenn State U PO Box 70708 Johnson City TN 37620 Office Phone: 423-439-5712. Personal E-mail: val@vallyle.com. Business E-Mail: lylev@etsu.edu.

LYLE, VIRGINIA REAVIS, retired archivist, genealogist; b. Nashville, Apr. 19, 1926; d. Damon Ashley and Nellie Alice (Vaughan) R.; m. John Reid Lyle, Sept. 25, 1943; 1 child, Judith L. Haggard. BA, Vanderbilt U., 1974, MLS, 1975. Cert. genealogist, archivist. Administrv. officer Commerce Union Bank, Nashville, 1961-70, 75-78; rsch. asst. R.C.H. Mathews, Jr., Nashville, 1970-75, 78-79; genealogist Nashville, 1980; archivist Metro Nashville-Davidson County Archives, Nashville, 1981-93; ret., 1993; organizing sec. Friends of Metro Archives, 1994-95. Sec. Homecoming '86 Metro Steering Com. for Tenn., 1986; mem. Pub. Libr. Bd., 1978-81; historian, archivist Dalewood United Meth. Ch., 1995—. Mem. Tenn. Archivists, Nat. Geneal. Soc., DAR, Ladies Hermitage Assn., Soc. Am. Archivists, Acad. Cert. Archivists, Woman's Club of Nashville (adv. bd.), Historical Soc. Hopkins Co., Nat. Trust Historical Preservation, Middle Tenn. Genealogical Soc., Century Soc. Geo. Peabody Coll., Vanderbilt Univ. Methodist. Home: 1421 Eastland Ave Nashville TN 37206-2626

LYLES, MARK BRADLEY, advanced technology company executive, dentist; b. Paducah, Ky., Dec. 3, 1957; s. Kendall Smith Lyles and Charlotte Dean (Ruley) Martell; m. Catherine Lynn Gregg, Mar. 17, 1984 (div. 1995); children: Austin Bradley, Dahlon Patrick. AS, BS, BA in Biology and Chemistry, Murray (Ky.) State U., 1978, MS, EdS, 1981; DMD, U. Louisville, 1986; PhD in Cellular and Structural Biology, U. Tex., San Antonio, 2001. Resident in oral and maxillofacial surgery U. Tex. Health Sci. Ctr., 1991-95; founder, chief exec. officer, pres. Talis Techs., Inc., San Antonio, 1992—; founder, pres., chief sci. officer Materials Evolution and Devel. U.S.A., Inc. (M.E.D. USA), San Antonio, 1993—. Presenter in field. Contbr. articles to profl. jours.; inventor use of ultra-low density fused fibrous ceramics for indsl. applications, use of fused fibrous ceramics in dental materials, implantable sys. for cell growth control, filters for polynuclear aromatic hydrocarbon containing smoke. Comdr. USNR, 1983—, recalled to active duty, 2003—. Recipient Dentist-Scientist award Nat. Inst. Dental Rsch., 1991-98; Dept. Chemistry and Bd. Regents scholar Murray State U., 1975-77, Imagineer of Yr. award Mind Sci. Found., 1997; Grad. Coop. Edn. fellow Nat. Ctr. Toxicol. Rsch., EPA, FDA, 1979-80, Grad. fellow U. Louisville, 1981-82. Mem. Am. Coll. Oral and Maxillofacial Surgeons (Walter Lorenz Residents Rsch. award 1994), Acad. Osseointegration, Acad. Gen. Dentistry, Navy Inst., Assn. Mil. Surgeons U.S., Naval Inst. Dental & Biomed. Rsch., Hon. Order Ky. Cols., Naval Res. Officers Assn., Phi Delta Kappa. Republican. Avocations: rifle and pistol marksmanship, weight training, sailing, travel, harley's. E-mail: jawbrkr@texas.net.

LYMAN, CHARLES EDSON, materials scientist, educator; b. Willimantic, Conn., Mar. 7, 1946; s. Edson Hunt and Sylvia (Hill) L.; m. Valerie Ann Livingston, Aug. 30, 1984. BS, Cornell U., 1968; PhD, MIT, 1974. Postdoctoral fellow dept. metallurgy Oxford (England) U., 1974-76; asst. prof. Rensselaer Poly. Inst., Troy, N.Y., 1976-80; staff scientist E.I. DuPont de Nemours, Wilmington, Del., 1980-84; assoc. prof. Lehigh U., Bethlehem, Pa., 1984-90, prof., 1990—. Electron microscopy steering com. Argonne (Ill.) Nat. Lab., 1984—. Author, editor: Scanning Electron Microscopy, X-Ray Microanalysis, and Analytical Electron Microscopy: A Laboratory Workbook, 1990; co-author: Scanning Electron Microscopy and X-ray Microanalysis, 2003; editor-in-chief: Microscopy and Microanalysis; contbr. articles to profl. jours. Mem. Microscopy Soc. Am. (pres. 1991), Microbeam Analysis Soc. (pres. 2000), Am. Soc. Materials Internat., Am. Chem. Soc., Burnside Plantation Inc. (pres. 1993), Historic Bethlehem, Inc. (pres. 1996-98). Home: 444 N New St Bethlehem PA 18018-5814 Office: Lehigh U Whitaker Lab 5 E Packer Ave Bethlehem PA 18015-3102 Office Phone: 610-758-4249. Business E-Mail: charles.lyman@lehigh.edu.

LYMAN, DOROTHY GRACE, artist, writer, arts and crafts shop executive; d. William Amasa and Dorothy Harriet (Marsh) Lyman; m. Fay Rosklin Sutton, Aug. 14, 1939 (div. 1958); children: Steven, Sierra, Daniel, Paul, Michael(dec.); m. LaMar Bushman, Jan. 15, 1965 (div. 1972); m. David Rex Gardner, Sept. 7, 1974 (div. 1989). Student, Art Instrn., Inc., 1954—56, U. Utah, 1969—72, Ririe Sch. Music, 1973—74. Cert. choral dir. Clk., Paris Co., 1941—42; welder Everett Pacific Shipyard, 1943—45; substitute tchr. Salt Lake City, 1954—57, 1969—72, Emery County, Utah, 1975—76, Carbon County (Utah) HS, 1977—87; pres., councillor drama and speech, music dir. Young Women's Mut. Improvement Assn., Salt Lake City, 1957—74, Lynndyl, Utah, 1974—78, Spring Glen, Utah, 1980—82. One-woman shows include Ricks Coll., Rexburg, Idaho, Springfield Mus. Art, Utah State Fair, 1967—68, others, exhibited in group shows at Utah State Capitol, Salt Lake City, 1969, also Salt Lake City pub. schs. and malls, others; newspaper corr.: Green Sheet, Sun Adv., Emery County Progress, Millard County Chronicle. Legis. reporter Utah State Women's Legis. Coun., 1974—76; counsellor ward status R.S. and YWMIA, 1957—74; GOP pres. legis. com. mem. at large; chmn. dist. Republican party, 1968—72; election judge, 1959—74; rep. Rep. Presdl. Task Force, 1984—88; pres. Ch. of Jesus Christ of Latter-day Saints Relief Soc., Eldredge Ward, 1964—68; tchr. Sunday Sch., 1957—83; temple worker Salt Lake LDS Temple, 1989—96, Jordan River Temple, 1989—96. Recipient Leadership awards, Ch. of Jesus Christ of Latter-day Saints, 1957—73, Golden Poet award, art awards, Utah State Fair, Salt Lake County Fair, Millard County Fair, Emery County Fair, Intermountain Soc. Artists, others, presdl. citation for outstanding commitment, Pres. Reagan, Pres. George H.W. Bush, Pres. George W. Bush. Mem.: Intermountain Soc. Artists, Sand and Sage Art Group (sec. 1972—74), U.S. Def. Com., Daus. Utah Pioneers, Eagles Aux. (chaplain 1977—81).

LYMAN, GARY HERBERT, epidemiologist, cancer researcher, educator; b. Buffalo, Feb. 24, 1946; s. Leonard Samuel and Beatrice Louise Lyman; children: Stephen Leonard, Christopher Henry. BA, SUNY, Buffalo, 1968, MD, 1972; MPH, Harvard U., 1982. Diplomate Am. Bd. Internal Medicine, Am. Bd. Oncology and Hematology. Resident in medicine U. NC, Chapel Hill, 1972-74; fellow in oncology Roswell Park Meml. Inst., Buffalo, 1974-77; rsch. instr. medicine SUNY Med. Sch., Buffalo, 1974-77; mem. faculty U. South Fla. Coll. Medicine, Tampa, 1977-2000, assoc. prof. medicine, 1980-86, prof. medicine, 1986-2000, dir. divsn. med. oncology, 1979-93, chief medicine H. Lee Moffitt Cancer and Rsch. Inst., 1985—93, prof. epidemiology and biostats., 1988-2000; Thomas Ordway prof. medicine divsn. hematology and oncology Albany (NY) Med. Coll., Union U., 2000—02, dir. Cancer Ctr., 2000—02; prof. biometry and stats. SUNY Sch. Pub. Health, 2000—02; prof. medicine, dept. medicine U. Rochester (NY) Sch. Medicine and Dentistry, 2002—; dir. health svcs. and outcomes rsch. James P. Wilmot Cancer Ctr., 2002—. Vis. prof. med. stats. London Sch. Hygiene and Tropical Medicine, 1997—98. Co-author: Geriatric Oncology, 1998, Comprehensive Geriatric Oncology, 1997, 2d edit., 2004; contbr. chpts. to books, over 250 articles to profl. jours. Spl. fellow Leukemia Soc. Am., 1976-77; postdoctoral fellow biostats. Harvard U., 1981-82; spl. clin. rellow Roswell Park Meml. Inst., 1975-76. Fellow ACP, Am. Coll. Preventive Medicine, Am. Coll. Clin. Pharmacology, Royal Coll. Physicians (Edinburgh); mem. Am. Soc. Clin. Oncology. Achievements include work in cancer clinical trials, biostatistics, epidemiology, clinical decision analysis. Office: U Rochester Med Ctr Box 704 601 Elmwood Ave Rochester NY 14642 Business E-Mail: gary_lyman@urmc.rochester.edu.

LYMAN, JOHN LESLIE, emergency physician; b. Berkeley, Calif., Dec. 3, 1946; BS in Psychology, U. Calif., Davis, 1969; MD, Wright State U., 1980. Diplomate Am. Bd. Emergency Medicine. Intern Miami Valley Hosp., Dayton, Ohio, 1980-81; resident in emergency medicine Wright State U., Dayton, 1981-83, asst. prof., 1983-86, assoc. prof., 1996—; pvt. practice Panama City, Fla., 1986-92; med. dir. emergency dept. U. Ala., 1992-94; regional med. dir. InPhyNet, Ft. Lauderdale, Fla., 1994-97, Premier Health Care, Dayton, 1997-2000, v.p. emergency medicine, 2000-01, chief med. officer, 2001—; CEO New Century Physicians, Dayton, 2001—. Assoc. prof. Wright State U. Sch. Medicine. Mem. Am. Coll. Emergency Physicians, Am. Coll. Physician Execs., Aerospace Med. Assn. Office: 332 Congress Park Dr Dayton OH 45459 Office Phone: 937-312-3608. E-mail: jlyman@phcsday.com.

LYMAN, PEGGY, artistic director, dancer, choreographer, educator; b. Cin., June 28, 1950; d. James Louis and Anne Earlene (Weeks) Morner; m. David Stanley Lyman, Aug. 29, 1970 (div. 1979); m. Timothy Scott Lynch, June 21, 1982 (div. 1997); 1 child, Kevin Lynch; m. Richard R. Hayes, Feb. 26, 2005. Grad. h.s., Cin. Solo dancer Cin. Ballet Co., 1964-68, Contemporary Dance Theater, 1970-71; chorus dancer N.Y.C. Opera, 1969-70; Radio City Music Hall Ballet Co., 1970; chorus singer, dancer Sugar, Broadway musical, N.Y.C., 1971-73; prin. dancer Martha Graham Dance Co., N.Y.C., 1973-88, rehearsal dir., 1989-90, assoc. rehearsal dir., 2005—; artistic dir. Martha Graham Ensemble, N.Y.C., 1990-91; faculty Martha Graham Sch., 1975—; co-artistic dir. Dance Conn., Hartford, 1998-2000. Head dance divns. No. Ky. U., 1977—78; artistic dir. Peggy Lyman Dance Co., N.Y.C., 1978—89; asst. prof. dance, guest choreographer Fla. State U., Tallahassee, 1982—89; guest choreographer So. Meth. U., Dallas, 1986; adjudicator Nat. Coll. Dance Festival Assn., 1983—; co-host To Make a Dance, QUBE cable TV, 1979; mem. guest faculty Am. Dance Festival, Durham, NC, 1984; site adjudicator NEA, 1982—84; tchr. Sch. Dance Conn., 1992—2004, East Conn. Concert Ballet, 1992—94; guest faculty Wesleyan U., Middletown, Conn., 1992; guest artist Conn. Coll., 1993; chair dance divsn. Hartt Sch., U. Hartford, Conn., 1994—2001, dir. dance divsn., Conn., 2002—04; freelance master tchr. internat. univs. Prin. dancer (TV spls.) Dance in America, 1976, 79, 84; guest with Rudolph Nureyev (CBS-TV) Invitation to the Dance, 1980; guest artist Theatre Choreographique Rennes, Paris, 1981, Rennes, France, 1983; Adelaide U., 1991; site dir. Martha Graham's Diversion of Angels for student concert U. Mich., 1992, Martha Graham's Panorama, U. Ill., Champaign-Urbana, 1993, Towson State U., 1997, Martha Graham's Diversion of Angels for Dutch Nat. Ballet, 1995, Diversion of Angels and Acts of Light for Dance Conn., 1998, Ballet Argentino, 1999, Lamentation For Ballet de Lorraine, 2004; choreographer: Conundrum (solo), 1982, Mantid (group), 1984, Roll, Spin, Draw, or Fold (group), 1984, Chope Dance (solo), 1985, Mirror's Edge (group), 1986, No Gavotte Bach (group), 1995, Interior Landscapes (group), 1997, Family Portrait (group), 1999, Yes, Is A World (group), 2002; co-creator (with John Feierabend) Move It (CD/DVD), 2003. Founding mem. Cin. Arts Coun., 1976-78. Mem. Am. Guild Mus. Artists. Office: care Martha Graham Sch Contemporary Dance 316 E 63d St New York NY 10021 Office Phone: 212-838-5886. Personal E-mail: lymanmhm@aol.com.

LYMAN, RICHARD WALL, foundation administrator, academic administrator, historian; b. Phila., Oct. 18, 1923; s. Charles M. and Aglae (Wall) Lyman; m. Elizabeth D. Schauffler, Aug. 20, 1947; children: Jennifer P., Holly Lyman Antolini, Christopher M., Timothy R. BA, Swarthmore Coll., 1947, LLD (hon.), 1974; MA, Harvard U., 1948, PhD, 1954, LLD (hon.), 1980, Washington U., St. Louis, 1971, Mills Coll., 1972, Yale U., 1975; LHD (hon.), U. Rochester, 1975, Coll. of Idaho, 1989. Teaching fellow, tutor, Harvard U., 1949-51; instr. Swarthmore Coll., 1952-53; instr., then asst. prof. Washington U., St. Louis, 1953-58; mem. faculty Stanford U., 1958-80, 88-91, prof. history, 1962-80, 88-91, Sterling prof., 1980-91, Sterling prof. emeritus, 1991—, assoc. dean Sch Humanities and Scis., 1964-66, v.p., provost, 1967-70, pres., 1970-80, pres. emeritus, 1980—, dir. Inst. Internat. Studies, 1988-91; pres. Rockefeller Found., 1980-88. Spl. corr. The Economist, London, 1953-66; bd. dirs. Coun. on Founds., 1982-88, Independent Sector, 1980-88, chair, 1983-86, Nat. Com. on U.S.-China Rels., 1986-92; dir. IBM, 1978-92, Chase Manhattan Corp., 1981-91. Author: The First Labour Government, 1957; editor: (with Lewis W. Spitz) Major Crises in Western Civilization, 1965, (with Virginia A. Hodgkinson) The Future of the Nonprofit Sector, 1989; editorial bd. Jour. Modern History, 1958-61. Mem. Nat. Coun. on Humanities, 1976-82, vice chmn., 1980-82; chmn. Commn. on Humanities, 1978-80; trustee Rockefeller Found., 1976-88, Carnegie Found. Advancement of Tchg., 1976-82, World Affairs Coun. of No. Calif., 1992-98; bd. dirs. Nat. Assn. Ind. Colls. and Univs., 1976-77, Assn. of Governing Bds. of Univs. and Colls., 1994-97, Am. Alliance for Rights and Responsiblities, 1993-2002; chmn. Assn. Am. Univs., 1978-79. With USAAF, 1943-46. Decorated officier Legion of Honor; recipient Clark Kerr award U. Calif., Berkeley, 1981; Fulbright fellow London Sch. Econs., 1951-52, hon. fellow, 1978—; Guggenheim fellow, 1959-60. Fellow Royal Hist. Soc.; mem. Am. Acad. Arts and Scis., Am. Hist. Assn., Council on Fgn. Relations, Am. Philos. Soc., Conf. Brit. Studies, Phi Beta Kappa. Office: Stanford U Sch Edn Stanford CA 94305-3096 Personal E-mail: rwlyman@hotmail.com.

LYMAN, WILLIAM WELLES, JR., retired architect; b. New London, Conn., Aug. 31, 1916; s. William Welles and Gladys Estelle (Latimer) L.; m. Margaret Helen Whittemore, July 12, 1941 (div. Sept. 1970); children: Cheryl, Steven, Philip, Susan, Donna, Patricia; m. Joan Evelyn Dalrymple, Sept. 26, 1970. BArch, U. Mich., 1939; MArch, Harvard U., 1940. Architect various orgns., Boston, 1941-42; pvt. practice Cambridge, Mass., 1947-53; chief designer Smith, Hinchman & Grylls, Detroit, 1953-56; architect Swanson Assocs., Bloomfield Hills, Mich., 1956-59, Smith & Smith Assocs., Royal Oak, Mich., 1959-62, Jickling Lyman & Powell Assocs., Inc., Birmingham, Mich., 1962-81, ret., 1981. Mem. faculty Harvard U., Cambridge, Mass., 1947-53; lectr. on early Am. furniture, 1975—. Pres. Cambridge Coun. PTAs, 1950-52, Harlan Sch. PTA, 1960-61; treas. Mass. Coun. for Better Schs., 1950-52; chmn. Citizens Elem. Curriculum Study Birmingham Pub. Schs., 1962-63; bd. dirs. South Oakland Symphony Soc., 1960-63, Birmingham Teen. Ctr., 1965-67, Birmingham Cmty. House, 1967-70, Profl. Skills Alliance, Detroit, 1973-75, Birmingham Hist. Bd., 1969-73, chmn., 1972-73; chmn. Birmingham Hist. Dist. Study Com., 1975-77, Cmty. Devel. Svcs., Portsmouth, N.H., 1993-96; pres. Birmingham Hist. Soc., 1980-81, bd. dirs. 1967-70; chmn. acquisitions com. John W. Hunter House, 1974-82; bd. govs. Warner House Assn., Portsmouth, N.H., 1983-91, chmn., 1986-88. U.S. Coast Guard, 1942-46. Fellow: AIA; mem.: York Pub. Libr. Assn. (trustee 1999—2002), Mich. Soc. Architects (pres. 1970). Unitarian Universalist. Home: 15 Victoria Ct York ME 03909-1454

LYN, JEAN, interior designer; b. Charlotte, N.C., Nov. 22, 1946; d. Frederic C. and Justine Keith Mayer; m. Nicolae Umberto Pollcappelli, July 15, 1976 (div. Apr. 1982). AA, Stephen's Coll., 1966; BA with honors in Interior Arch., U. Ky., 1968. Designer Loeffler Johnson, Ludnberg, Pitts., 1970—73, Morganell-Heumann & Assocs., L.A., 1973—76; design ptnr. Inventor Policappelli, 1976—81; prin., owner Jean Lyn & Assocs., 1981—. Achievements include design of copyright for eco homes; founder environmental endowments. Avocations: Bikram yoga, philosophy, hiking, bicycling, climbing. Office Phone: 480-585-9751.

LYNAM, GLORIA, elementary school educator; d. Abraham and Diana Beatrice Gerber; m. Roger Lynam. B Arts and Scis. with honors, U. Conn., 1973; MEd, Coll. St. Joseph Vt., 1991. Vt. profl. educator. Tchr. middle sch. lang. arts Rutland (Vt.) Town Sch., 1998—. Editor: student poetry anthologies, comic books. Grantee, Chapbooks for Learning, 1999, Excellence in Edn. grantee, SHOPA Found., 1999—2000, No strings art, Chaffee Art Gallery, 1999, Nat. writing project, Vt., 1999. Mem.: New Eng. League of Middle Schs. Assn., Vt. Assn. Middle Level Edn., Nat. Coun. Tchrs. Eng., Northern Vt. Artists Assoc., Vt. Watercolor Soc. Avocations: writing, reading, mountain biking, walking, watercolors.

LYNCH, BARBARA, chef, restaurant owner; m. Charles Petri. Chef Figs, Boston, Rocco's, Boston, 1993—95; exec. chef Galleria Italiana, Boston, 1995—98; chef, owner No. 9 Park, Boston, 1998—; owner B&G Oysters, Ltd., Boston, 2003—. Subject: (documentaries) Amuse Bouche - A Chef's Tale; Boston 24/7. Named Ten Best New Chefs, Food & Wine mag., Best Chef, Northeast, James Beard Found., 2003. Office: 9 Park St Boston MA 02108

LYNCH, BENJAMIN LEO, oral surgeon, educator; b. Omaha, Dec. 29, 1923; s. William Patrick and Mary (Rauber) L.; m. Colleen D. Cook, Nov. 10, 1956; children: Kathleen Ann, Mary Elizabeth, Patrick, George, Martha, Estelle. BSD, Creighton U., 1945, DDS, 1947, MA, 1953; fellow, U. Tex., 1947-48; MSD, Northwestern U., 1954. Diplomate Am. Bd. Oral and Maxillofacial Surgery. Asst. instr. oral surgery Creighton U., 1948-50, instr., 1950-52, asst. prof., 1952-53; dean Creighton U. (Sch. Dentistry), 1954-61, assoc. prof. oral surgery, 1954—57, prof. oral surgery, 1957-86, prof. emeritus, 1986—, dir. oral surgery dept., 1954-67; also coordinator grad. and postgrad. programs; chief oral surgeon Douglas County Hosp., Omaha, 1951-63; pres. dental staff Children's Meml. Hosp., Omaha, 1952, 59, co-founder cleft palate team, 1959; chmn. dept. dentistry Bergan-Mercy Hosp., Omaha, 1963-68; mem. exec. com., head dental staff Luth. Hosp., 1963-66; bd. dirs. Nebr. Dental Service Corp., 1972-78, pres., 1974-78; treas. Children's Meml. Hosp. Med.-dental staff, 1979-81. Guest lectr. Walter Reed Grad. Sch. Medicine, 1957-58. Mem. Omaha-Douglas County Health Bd., 1966-68, v.p., 1967, pres., 1968; exec. com. Nebr. divsn. Am. Cancer Soc., 1963-67; bd. dirs. Nebr. Blue Cross, 1968-89, Creighton U. Alumni Coun., Omaha chpt., 1989-91, Cath. Acad., Omaha, 2000—01; trustee United Cath. Social Svcs., 1989-95; adv. bd. to dean Creighton U. Dental Sch., 1984—, vice chmn., 1992-93, chmn., 1993-94; pres. Creighton U. Graybackers, 1991-94. Served at Walter Reed U.S. Army Med. Ctr., 1955-57. Recipient Alumni merit award Creighton U., 1978; named one of Ten Outstanding Young Omahans, 1952, 53, 58; inducted into Nebr. Dental Hall of Fame, 1981 Fellow Am. Coll. Dentists (pres. Nebr. chpt. 1973-74); mem. Am. Soc. Oral Surgeons, Midwest Soc. Oral Surgeons, Nebr. Soc. Oral Surgeons (founder 1957, pres. 1961), Nebr. Dental Soc. (trustee 1964-66), Omaha Dist. Dent Soc. (pres. 1963-64), Am. Coll. Oral-Maxillofacial Surgeons (founding mem.), Nebr. Soc. Dental Anesthesiology (founder, 1st pres.), Alpha Sigma Nu, Omicron Kappa Epsilon, Delta Sigma Delta. Home: 509 S Happy Hollow Blvd Omaha NE 68106-1224

LYNCH, BEVERLY LOVE, language educator; b. Newport News, Va., Dec. 15, 1950; d. Eugene Stone and Beverly (Pennell) Love; m. Kevin Timothy Lynch, Aug. 25, 1973; children: Robyn Michelle, Perry Kevin. *Father was the Director for Space and Senior Research Director at NASA. He was the author of archival works on space flight, a contributor to various periodicals, journals and textbooks, and the owner of 8 patents. He was the recipient of numerous awards, most notably: US National Rifle Champion, Hearst Trophy, Pershing Trophy, US Olympic Team, NASA's Exceptional Service Medal (twice), and the Clarenton Memorial Award. He was also a Fellow of the American Institute of Aeronautics and Astronautics and an Honorary Fellow of the Rhodes International Forum, International Jacks Club, and the Allied Special Forces Association.* BA, Furman U., 1972; MA in Spanish, Middlebury Coll., 1973. Instr. Spanish South Brunswick (NJ) HS, 1974—79; translator North Plainfield (NJ) Bd. Edn., 1979—81; instr. Spanish Watkinson Sch., West Hartford, Conn., 1980—82, Bancroft Sch., Worcester, Mass., 1983—84, Far Hills (NJ) Country Day Sch., 1988—90, West Morris Ctrl. HS, Chester, NJ, 1990—. Mem.: Fgn. Lang. Educators NJ, Am. Coun. on the Tchg. Fgn. Lang., Am. Assn. Tchrs. Spanish and Portuguese, Harmonium Choral Soc. Methodist. Avocations: jogging, cross stitch, needlepoint, travel, singing. Office: West Morris Ctrl High Sch Bartley Rd Chester NJ 07930

LYNCH, BEVERLY PFEIFER, education and information studies educator; b. Moorhead, Minn. d. Joseph B. and Nellie K. (Bailey) Pfeifer; m. John A. Lynch, Aug. 24, 1968. BS, N.D. State U., 1957, L.H.D. (hon.); MS, U. Ill., 1959; PhD, U. Wis., 1972. Librarian Marquette U., 1959-60, 62-63; exchange librarian Plymouth (Eng.) Pub. Library, 1960-61; asst. head serials div. Yale U. Library, 1963-65, head, 1965-68; vis. lectr. U. Wis., Madison, 1970-71, U. Chgo., 1975; exec. sec. Assn. Coll. and Research Libraries, 1972-76; univ. librarian U. Ill.-Chgo., 1977-89; dean, prof. Grad. Sch. Libr. and Info. Sci. UCLA, 1989-94, prof. Grad. Sch. Edn. and Info. Studies, 1977—89, dir. sr. fellows program, 1990—; interim pres. Ctr. for Rsch. Librs., Chgo., 2000-01; founding dir. Calif. Rare Book Sch., 2004—. Sr. fellow, vis. scholar UCLA, 1982. Author: (with Thomas J. Galvin) Priorities for Academic Libraries, 1982, Management Strategies for Libraries, 1985, Academic Library in Transition, 1989, Information Technology and the Remaking of the University Library, 1995. Recipient Cert. of Appreciation, Chinese Am. Librs. Assn., 2001; named Acad. Libr. of Yr., 1982, one of top sixteen libr. leaders in Am., 1990; fellow Indo-U.S. Subcommn. on Edn. and Culture, 1992-93. Mem. ALA (pres. 1985-86, coun. 1998-2004, com. on accreditation 1999-2002, chair 1999-2000, co-chair joint com. 2005—), Nat. Info. Stds. Orgn. (bd. dirs. 1996-2005, vice chair 1999-2001, chair 2001-03), Soc. Am. Archivists, Am. Assn. Mus., Acad. Mgmt., Am. Sociol. Assn., Assn. for the Study of Higher Edn., Bibliog. Soc. Am., Scottish Libr. Assn. (hon.), Caxton Club, Grolier Club, Book Club Calif., Phi Kappa Phi. Office: UCLA Grad Sch Edn Info Mailbox 951520 Los Angeles CA 90095-1520 Office Phone: 310-206-4294. Business E-Mail: bplynch@ucla.edu.

LYNCH, BILL, university football coach; b. Indpls., June 12, 1954; m. Linda Lux; children: Billy, Kelly, Joe, Kevin. BS, Butler U., 1972, MS, 1979. Offensive coord. football team Butler U., Indpls., 1977-83, No. Ill. U., DeKalb, 1984; head coach Butler, Indpls., 1985-89; quarterbacks coach Ind. U., Bloomington, 1993-94; asst. coach Orlando (Fla.) Renegades U.S. Football League, 1984; offensive coord. Ball State U., Muncie, Ind., 1990-92, head coach, 1995—. Office: Ball State Univ Athletic Dept 2000 W University Ave Muncie IN 47306-0002

LYNCH, CAROL, director special services, psychologist; d. Joseph Louis and Ellen (Birish) Dobkowski; 1 child, Eric Alexander. BA, William Paterson Coll., 1966; MA, NYU, 1970, PsyD, 1984. Lic. psychologist, N.J., N.Y. Tchr. Bloomfield (N.J.) Pub. Schs., 1966-68, psychologist, 1970-87; dir. spl. svcs. Waldwick (N.J.) Pub. Schs., 1987—, acting supt. schs., 1995-96, 98. Adj. clin. prof. NYU, N.Y.C., 1983-86 adj. prof. Montclair (N.J.) State Coll., 1984-85. Mem. prof. alumni coun. Sch. Edn., Health and Nursing, NYU, 1989—91; alumni coun. chair Sch. Edn., NYU, 1991—93, sec., 2002—03; sec., bd. trustees First Church of Religious Sci., New York, NY, 2001—. NYU fellow, 1981-82; recipient Best Practice award N.J. State Dept. Edn. for Fast Families Program, 1995, Disting. Grad. Brian E. Tomlinson Meml. award NYU, 1995, Exemplary Practice award N.J. Adminstrs. Assn./N.J. Sch. Bds. "Crisis Response Initiative," 2002. Mem. APA (sch. psychology task force 1989-90), N.J. Psychol. Assn. (treas. 1985-86, Sch. Psychologist of Yr. 2003), Nat. Assn. Sch. Psychologists (del. 1984-88), N.J. Assn. Sch. Psychologists (pres. 1982-83, Sch. Psychologist of Yr. 2003), Ea. Ednl. Rsch. Assn. (pres. 1993-95), Bergen County Assn. Lic. Psychologists (bd. dirs. 1991-93), NYU Sch. Psychology Alumni Assn. (founder 1988-92), Ramapo Valley Adminstrs. (v.p. 1996-98, pres. 1998—). Avocations: skiing, antiques collecting, tennis, gourmet cooking. Home: 124 Frank Ct Mahwah NJ 07430-2963 Office: Waldwick Pub Schs 155 Summit Ave Waldwick NJ 07463-2133 Office Phone: 201-652-5052. Personal E-mail: drcarollynch@msn.com. Business E-Mail: carol.lynch@waldwick.k12.nj.us.

LYNCH, CATHERINE GORES, social services administrator; b. Waynesboro, Pa., Nov. 23, 1943; d. Landis and Pamela (Whitmarsh) Gores; m. Joseph C. Keefe, Nov. 29, 1981; children: Shannon Maria, Lisa Alison, Gregory T. Keefe, Michael D. Keefe. BA magna cum laude with honors, Bryn Mawr Coll., 1965; postgrad., Cornell U., 1966-67. Cert. police instr. Mayor's intern Human Resources Adminstrn., N.Y.C., 1967; rsch. asst. Orgn. for Social and Tech. Innovation, Cambridge, Mass., 1967-69; cons. Ford Found., Bogota, Columbia, 1970; staff Nat. Housing Census, Nat. Bur. Statistics, Bogota, 1971; evaluator Foster Parent Plan, Bogota, 1972; rsch. staff FEDESARROLLO, Bogota, 1973-74; dir. Dade County Advocates for Victims, Miami, Fla., 1974-86; asst. to dep. dir. Dept. Human Resouces, Miami, 1986-87, computer liaison, 1987-88, asst. adminstr. placement svcs. program, 1988-89; exec. dir. Health Crisis Network, Miami, 1989-96; liaison HIV cmty. svc. State of Fla. Health and Rehab. Svcs., 1996-97; program ops. adminstr. adult protective svcs. Fla. Dept. Children and Families, 1997-2000; dir. grants mgmt. U. Miami Sch. Nursing, 2000—03; ann. giving and grants mgr. Audubon of Fla., 2003—05; dir. devel. svcs. Miami Children's Hosp. Found., 2005—. Guest lectr. local univs. Participant, co-chmn. various task forces rape, child abuse, incest, family violence, elderly victims of crime, nat. state, local levels, 1974-86, 1999-2000; developer workshops in field; participant, chair, co-chair task forces on HIV/AIDS impact; long term care, children and AIDS, AIDS orgnl. issues, 1991-96; mem. gov.'s task force on victims and witnesses, gov.'s task force on sex offenders and their victims, gov.'s Red Ribbon panel on AIDS, 1992-93, gov.'s interdepartmental work group, 1993-96; mem. ednl. rev. com. Am. Found AIDS Rsch., 1991-96; vice chair Metro-Dade HIV Svcs. Planning Coun., 1991-93; active Fla. HIV Svcs. Adv. Coun., 1991-96; rev. panel Fed. Spl. Projects of Nat. Significance, 1994, 96; adv. coun. Metro Dade Social Svcs., 1995-96; bd. dirs., v.p. Dade County Healthy Start Coalition, 2002—04; cert. expert witness on battered women syndrome in civil and criminal cts. Contbr. writings to field to publs. Recipient various pub. svcs. awards including WINZ Citizen of Day, 1979, Outstanding Achievement award Fla. Network Victim Witness Svcs., 1982, Pioneer award Metro-Dade Women's Assn., 1989; Fulbright scholar U. Central de Venezuela, Caracas, 1965-66; Lehman fellow Cornell U. Mem. Nat. Orgn. of Victim Assistance Programs (bd. dirs. 1977-83, Outstanding Program award 1984), Fla. Network of Victim/Witness Programs (bd. dirs., treas. 1980-81), Am. Soc. Pub. Adminstrs., Dade County Fedn. Health and Welfare Workers, Fla. Assn. Health and Social Svcs. (chpt. treas. 1979-80), LWV (bd. dirs. Dade County chpt. 1988-92, 2005—), Fla. Consortium Sch.-Based Health Ctrs. (sec. 2001-03). Office: Miami Children's Hosp Found 3000 SW 62d Ave Miami FL 33155 Office Phone: 786-268-1841. E-mail: clynch@mchf.org.

LYNCH, CHARLES ALLEN, investment company executive, director; b. Denver, Sept. 7, 1927; s. Laurence J. and Louanna (Robertson) L.; divorced; children: Charles A., Tara O'Hara, Casey Alexander; m. Justine Bailey, Dec. 27, 1992. BS, Yale U., 1950. With E.I. duPont de Nemours & Co., Inc., Wilmington, Del., 1950—69, dir. mktg., 1965—69; corp. v.p. SCOA Industries, Columbus, Ohio, 1969—72; corp. exec. v.p., also mem. rotating bd. W.R. Grace & Co., N.Y.C., 1972—78; chmn. bd., chief exec. officer Saga Corp., Menlo Park, Calif., 1978—86, also dir.; chmn., chief exec. officer DHL Airways, Inc., Redwood City, Calif., 1986—88; also dir.; pres., CEO Levolor Corp., 1988—89, also bd. dir., chmn. exec. com. of bd., 1989—90; chmn. Market Value Ptnrs. Co., Menlo Park, Calif., 1990—95; chmn., dir. Fresh Choice, Inc., Santa Clara, Calif., 1995—; also bd. dirs.; chmn. Market Value Ptnrs. Co., 1999—. Bd. dirs. Spectrum Organic Products, Inc., Sigaba Corp.; bd. dirs. Trade Point. Bd. dirs. United Way, 1990-92, past chmn. Bay Area campaign, 1987; vice chmn., dir. Bay Area Coun.; past chmn. Calif. Bus. Roundtable; past chmn. bd. trustees Palo Alto Med. Found. Mem. Yale Club (N.Y.C.), Internat. Lawn Tennis Club, Menlo Country Club (Calif.), Pacific Union Club (San Francisco), Coral Beach and Tennis Club (Bermuda), Vintage Club (Indian Wells, Calif.), Menlo Circus Club. Republican. Home: 96 Ridge View Dr Atherton CA 94027-6464 Office: 333 Ravenswood Ave Ste Ag320 Menlo Park CA 94025-3453 Office Phone: 650-859-5884. E-mail: clynch@mvp-co.com.

LYNCH, CHARLES ANDREW, chemicals executive; b. Bklyn., Jan. 6, 1935; s. Charles Andrew and Mary Martina (McEvoy) L.; m. Marilyn Anne Monaco, July 30, 1960; children: Nancy Callan, Cara Martina. BS, Manhattan Coll., 1956; PhD, U. Notre Dame, 1960. Rsch. chemist Esso Rsch. & Engrng. Co., Linden, N.J., 1960-65; rsch. supr. organic chemistry divsn. FMC Corp., Balt., 1965-72, rsch. mgr. indsl. chemistry divsn. Princeton, N.J., 1972-74; exec. v.p. Am. Oil & Supply Co., Newark, 1974-80; tech. dir., dir. sales & mktg., dir. rsch. & bus. devel., v.p. tech. Hatco Corp., Fords, N.J., 1981-95; with Calivera Cons., 1995—; account exec. N.J. Commerce, Econ. Growth and Tourism Commn., 1997—. Contbr. articles to profl. jours.; patentee in field (U.S. and foreign). Mem. Am. Chem. Soc., Soc. Tribologists and Lubrication Engrs. (chmn. N.Y. sect. 1980-81, 97-98), Ind. Lubricant Mfrs. Assn. (bd. dirs. 1985-88). Office Phone: 609-777-4277. Business E-Mail: charles.lynch@commerce.state.nj.us.

LYNCH, CHARLES THEODORE, SR., materials science engineering researcher, consultant, educator; b. Lima, Ohio, May 17, 1932; s. John Richard and Helen (Dunn) L.; m. Betty Ann Korkolis, Feb. 3, 1956; children: Karen Elaine Ostdiek, Charles Theodore Jr., Richard Anthony, Thomas Edward. BS, George Washington U., 1955; MS, U. Ill., 1957, PhD in Analytical Chemistry, 1960. Group leader ceramics div. Air Force Materials Lab., Wright-Patterson AFB, Ohio, 1962-66; lectr. in chemistry Wright State U., Dayton, Ohio, 1964-66; chief advanced metall. studies br. Air Force Materials Lab., Wright-Patterson AFB, Ohio, 1966-74, sr. scientist, 1974-81; head materials div. Office of Naval Rsch., Arlington, Va., 1981-85; pvt. practice cons. Washington, 1985-88; sr. engr. space ops. Vitro Corp., Washington, 1988-95, 96-98; cons. Burke, Va., 1996—; sr. cons. space ops. Marconi Systems Techs., Washington, 1998—99; v.p. RSC&L, Inc., Grayling, Mich., 1996—. USAF liaison mem. NMAB Panels on Solids Processing, Ion Implantation and Environ. Cracking, Washington, 1965-68, 78, 81; U.S. rep. AGARD structures and materials panel NATO, 1983-85. Co-author: Metal Matrix Composites, 1972; editor, author: Practical Handbook of Materials Science, 1989; editor: (series) Handbook of Materials Science, vol. I, 1974, vol. II, 1975, vol. III, 1975; vice chmn. editorial bd. Vitro Corp. Tech. Jour., 1989-92, chmn., 1993; contbr. articles to profl. jours. including Jour. Am. Ceramics Soc., Analytical Chemistry, Sci., Transactions AIME, Corr. Jour., Jour. Inorganic Chemistry, SAMPE, Jour. Less Common Metals. Mem., soloist George Washington U. Traveling Troubadours, Washington, 1950-55; choir dir. Trinity United Ch. of Christ, Fairborn, Ohio, 1966-81, Univ. Bapt. Ch., Champaign, Ill., 1957-60, Chapel II, Wright-Patterson AFB, Ohio, 1960-64; bd. dirs. Southport Home Owners' Assn., Burke, Va., 2002—; pres. Pub. Sch. PTO, 1967-69. 1st lt. USAF, 1960-62. Bailey scholar U. Ill., 1958-60; recipient Commendation medal USAF, 1962, Outstanding Achievement cert. NASA, 1992, award Soc. for Tech. Comm. Publ., 1993. Mem. Am. Chem. Soc. (treas. 1966-67, chmn. audit sect. 1967-68), ASM Internat. (sec. oxidation and corrosion com. 1980-81, chmn. 1981-82). Methodist. Achievements include patents for new corrosion inhibitors including encapsulated types, and for alkoxides and oxides; co-development of the refractory ceramic Zyttrite, the first high density translucent zirconia made from thermal or hydrolytic decomposition of mixed alkoxides followed by hot pressing; pioneered general approach of organometallic compounds as precursors of high purity, fine particulate, materials. Office: 5629 Kemp Ln Burke VA 22015-2041

LYNCH, CHARLOTTE ANDREWS, retired communications executive, consultant; b. Fall River, Mass., Mar. 25, 1928; d. Alan Hall and Florence (Worthen) Andrews; m. Francis Bradley Lynch, June 7, 1952; children: Sarah Faldetta, Richard, Stephen, William. AB in Philosophy, Radcliffe Coll., 1950; postgrad., U. Bridgeport, 1969-71. Adminstrv. asst. Mass. Congl. Confs. and Missionary Soc., Boston, 1951-52; journalist Town Crier newspaper, Westport, Conn., 1968; asst. dir. devel. Cape Cod Hosp., Hyannis, Mass., 1975-76; parish adminstr. S. Congl. Ch., Centerville, Mass., 1976-83; cons. to ethnic advt. agy. Loiminchay, Inc., N.Y.C., 1992-98; ret. Mem. Radcliffe Club Cape Cod (v.p. 1990-97, pres. 1997-2000, exec. com. 1990-2000), Harvard Club of Boston. Republican. Roman Catholic. Avocation: travel.

LYNCH, CONSTANCE, reading specialist; Guest spkr. WNYE, Bklyn., 1965, Bd. Edn., Bklyn., 1965, promotional policy adv. coun., 68; guest lectr., reading cons. Branch Coll., N.Y.C., NY, 1970. Author: Reflections, 1988, It Takes a Kitongoji, 1999, In Other Words, 2005, Reflections of the Day, 2005. Mem. MADD; vol. Charlotte County Retired Educator Assn., Port Charlotte, Fla., 1994—, v.p., 1995—99; vol. Unity Ch. of Peace, Port Charlotte, 1994—; mem. Christopher Reeves Found., Nat. Com. to Preserve Social Security and Medicare, Operation Smile. Recipient Life Mem. plaque, NAACP, 1994,

Voice of Civil Rights cert., 2005. Mem.: Peace River Ctr. for Writers, Nat. Women's Hist. Mus., Charlotte County Retired Educators Assn., Am. Assn. U. Women, Nat. Fed. for the Blind, Girls' HS Alumni Assn. Democrat. Avocations: sewing, music, poetry, dance. Home: 26287 Copiapo Cir Punta Gorda FL 33983

LYNCH, DAVID A., radiologist, educator; b. Cork, Ireland, May 15, 1956; s. Bill and Helen Lynch; m. Anne M. Keane, Aug. 27, 1981; children: Dermot W., Eimear M., Eileen E. MB, BCh, BAO, U. Coll. Dublin, 1979. Diplomate Am. Bd. Radiology, 1990. Asst. prof. radiology and medicine Health Sci. Ctr. U. Colo., Denver, assoc. prof. radiology and medicine Health Sci. Ctr., 1994—2000, prof. radiology and medicine Health Sci. Ctr., 2000—. Editor: (textbook) Imaging of Diffuse Lung Disease, Imaging of Diseases of the Chest. Fellow, Royal Coll. Surgeons, 1986, Royal Coll. Surgeons Ireland. Mem.: Soc. Thoracic Radiology, Radiologic Soc. N.Am., Fleischner Soc. Office: Univ Colorado Health Sci Ctr 4200 E Ninth Ave Denver CO 80220 Office Phone: 303-372-6129. E-mail: david.lynch@uchsc.edu.

LYNCH, DAVID WILLIAM, physicist, retired educator; b. Rochester, N.Y., July 14, 1932; s. William J. and Eleanor (Fouratt) L.; m. Joan N. Hill, Aug. 29, 1954 (dec. Nov. 1989); children: Jean Louise, Richard William, David Allan; m. Glenys R. Bittick, Nov. 14, 1992. BS, Rensselaer Poly. Inst., 1954; MS, U. Ill., 1955, PhD, 1958. Asst. prof. physics Iowa State U., 1959-63, assoc. prof., 1963-66, prof., 1966—2003, chmn. dept., 1985-90, disting. prof. liberal arts and scis., 1985—; on leave at U. Hamburg, Germany; and U. Rome, Italy, 1968-69; sr. physicist Ames Lab. of Dept. of Energy; acting assoc. dir. Synchrotron Radiation Ctr., Stoughton, Wis., 1984. Vis. prof. U. Hamburg, summer 1974; dir. Microelectronics Rsch. Ctr., Iowa State U., 1995-99. Fulbright scholar U. Pavia, Italy, 1958-59. Fellow: Am. Phys. Soc.; mem.: AAAS. Achievements include research on solid state physics. Home: 2020 Elm Cir West Des Moines IA 50265-4294 Office Phone: 515-294-3476. Business E-Mail: dwl@ameslab.gov.

LYNCH, DEBORAH ANN, college administrator; b. Cleve., June 12, 1947; d. Edward John and Dorothy Alice (Le Maitre) Dorony; m. Patrick Michael Lynch, Nov. 16, 1978 (dec. Dec. 11, 1989); 1 child, Ryan Woodward. BA, Kent (Ohio) State U., 1978; MS in Social Sci. Adminstrn., Case Western Res. U., 1980. Senate staff intern Com. on Labor and Human Resources, U.S. Senate, Washington, 1979-80; sr. planning assoc./evaluation assoc. United Way Svcs., Cleve., 1979-84; sr. planning assoc. Fedn. for Community Planning, 1984-85; cons. Mandel Ctr. for Non-Profit Orgn., Case Western Res. U., Cleve., 1986-90; dir. planning, mktg., pub. rels. Ursuline Coll., Pepper Pike, Ohio, 1990-92, dir. instl. planning, rsch. and assessment, 1990-95; exec. dir. Am. Kennel club Canine Health Found., 1995—. Cons. Inst. for Ednl. Renewal, 1991-94; chmn. strategic planning com. Cleve. Commn. Higher Edn., 1992-95. Contbr. articles to profl. jours. Trustee Women Infants and Children Program, Cleve., 1981-85, Ohio Conf. for Coll. and Univ. Planning, 1993-95. Recipient Ameritech Partnership Award for excellence in mktg. higher edn. Ohio Assn. Independent Colls. and Univs., 1992. Mem. Soc. for Coll. and Univ. Planning (planning com. 1993), Am. Kennel Club (columnist gazette 1985-93), Buckeye Keeshond Club (pres. 1981-83). Mem. Soc. Of Friends. Avocations: horseback riding, swimming, gardening, training and showing purebred dogs. Home: 340 Aspen Ct Aurora OH 44202-9153 Office: Ursuline Coll 2550 Lander Rd Cleveland OH 44124-4318

LYNCH, DENIS PATRICK, dentist, educator; b. Kansas City, Kans., Oct. 5, 1951; s. Patrick Edward and Helen Mary Lynch; m. Monica Colosimo, June 29, 1973; children: Sydney Alexis, Shannon Meredith. DDS, U. Calif., San Francisco, 1976; PhD, U. Ala., Birmingham, 1985. Asst. prof. U. Tex. Dental Br., Houston, 1981-88, assoc. dean acad. affairs, 1987-89, assoc. prof., 1989-93, exec. assoc. dean, 1988-92, U. Tenn., Memphis, 1993-97, prof. medicine, 1994—, prof. grad. health scis., 1998—, prof. biologic and diagnostic scis., 1993—. Cons. Commn. on Dental Accreditation, Chgo., 1990—. Author: The Mouth: Diagnosis and Treatment, 1998; author (chpt.): Development of a Houston Community-Based Dental Health Care Clinic for Indigent HIV-Positive Patients, 1994, Diseases of the Mouth, 1996, Stomatitis: Diagnosis and Treatment, 1998; reviewer Jour. Am. Dental Assn., 1988—. Instr. Confraternity of Christian Doctrine, Our Lady of Sorrow Ch., Birmingham, 1976-81; cons. Bering Dental Clinic, Houston, 1988-93; chair expert review panel for HIV/Hepatitis B Infected Dental Health Care Workers, Tex. State Bd. Dental Examiners, Houston, 1992-93; HIV/AIDS educator ARC, Houston, 1991-93. Fellow Am. Acad. Oral and Maxillofacial Pathology (chair parameters of care com. 1995-98); mem. ADA (spkr.'s bur. 1991-94), Internat. Assn. Dental Rsch. (pres. exptl. pathology group 1992-93), Am. Assn. Dental Schs. (del. exec. com. 1977-79). Roman Catholic. Avocations: golf, bridge, reading, travel. Home: 1924 Kilbirnie Dr Germantown TN 38139-3420 Office: Univ Tenn 875 Union Ave Memphis TN 38163-0001 Fax: 901-448-2671. E-mail: dlynch@utmem.edu.

LYNCH, DENNIS JAMES, plastic surgeon; b. Bayonne, N.J., Aug. 5, 1939; s. Dennis J. Lynch and Eileen Mallon; m. Mary; children: Dennis, David, Sarah. BS, Villanova U., 1961; MD, Georgetown U. Med. Ctr., 1965. Diplomate Am. Bd. Surgery, Am. Bd. Plastic Surgery. Resident U. Pa., Phila., 1965-74; plastic surgeon Scott & White Clinic, Temple, Tex., 1974—. Dir. divsn. plastic surgery Tex. A&M Med. Sch., Temple, 1974-87, chair dept. surgery, 1990-2004; bd. dirs. Scott & White Clinic, 1981-95. Mem. AMA, Am. Coll. Surgeons, Am. Cleft Palate Assn., Am. Assn. Plastic Surgeons, Tex. Soc. Plastic Surgeons, Am. Soc. Plastic & Reconstructive Surgeons (pres. elect 1996—, pres. 1997), Am. Bd. Plastic Surgery. Roman Catholic. Avocations: tennis, sailing. Office: Scott & White Meml Hosp 2401 S 31st St Temple TX 76508-0001 Office Phone: 254-724-2321. Business E-Mail: djlynch@swmail.sw.org.

LYNCH, DOUGLAS E., dean; b. Washington, D.C., May 7, 1964; s. William John Lynch and Gretchen Gail Holmes; m. Kuinera Jennifer De Kramer; 1 child, Cornelius. BA, Ariz. State U., 1987, postgrad., 1995; MBA, N.Y. U., N.Y.C., 1991; MPhil, PhD, Columbia U., 2005. Intern U.S. Embassy, Stockholm, 1984, Gov.'s Office, Phoenix, 1985; exec. asst. Coll. Bd., N.Y.C., 1989—95; asst. dir. Ariz. State U., Tempe, 1995—96; dir. mem. svcs. Coll. Bd., N.Y.C., 1996—99; asst. dean N.Y. U., N.Y.C., 1999—2004; vice dean U. Pa., Phila., 2004—. Author: Corporate-University Partnership, 2005; contbr. chapters to books. Mem. Goals 2000 Taskforce, Washington; with Congl. Nebr.-Based Commn., Washington. Recipient Pres. E-award, U.S. Dept. Commerce, 2002. Mem.: Am. Ednl. Rsch. Assn., Univ. Continuing Edn. Assn., Assn. Continuing Higher Edn. Democrat. Episcopalian. Office: Univ Pa 3700 Walnut St Philadelphia PA 19104 Office Phone: 215-573-5022. Business E-Mail: dougl@gse.upenn.edu.

LYNCH, FLORENCE, art gallery director; BS, MA in Art Adminstrn. With Salvatore Ala Gallery; independent curator Japan, Germany, France, Netherlands, Italy; founder, curator Florence Lynch Gallery, NYC. Named one of Seven Emerging Young Dealers in Chelsea, NY Arts Mag., 1999. Office: 531-539 W 25th St New York NY 10001 Office Phone: 212-924-3290. Office Fax: 212-924-2775. Business E-Mail: flynch@florencelynchgallery.com.*

LYNCH, FRANK THOMAS, aeronautical engineer, consultant; b. Binghamton, N.Y., Oct. 19, 1933; s. John Francis and Irene Elizabeth L.; m. Blanca Lynch, Dec. 10, 1966; children: Fernando, Maria, Monica, Manuel, Jose. BS in Aero. Engring., U. Notre Dame, 1955; postgrad., Cornell U., 1955-56. From propulsion airframe integration specialist to mgr. and sr. mgr. Douglas/McDonnell Douglas, Calif., 1956—93, program and technical mgr. integrated wing design, 1993-99; sr. mgr. subsonic aerodynamics tech. devel. Douglas/McDonnell Douglas (now The Boeing Co.), Long Beach, Calif., 1993-99; pvt. practice Yorba Linda, Calif., 1999—. Chmn. NASA Aerodynamics adv. group, 1995-97, Airframe Sys. adv. group, 1997-2000, Aerospace Tech. adv. group, 1998-2000, sr. adv. staff to Rand, 2003. Contbr. numerous articles to profl. publs., including Jour. of Aircraft, Aero. Jour., Prog. Aero. Sci., others; presenter in field. Recipient Disting. Pub. Svc. medal NASA, 1994; technical fellow McDonnell Douglas/Boeing Corp., 1992. Mem.: AIAA (aerodynamics award 1999). Roman Catholic. Avocations: writing, travel, grandkids. Home and Office: 5370 Via Maria Yorba Linda CA 92886-5014 Office Phone: 714-693-8797. Office Fax: 714-779-3541. Personal E-mail: aerofrank@sbcglobal.net.

LYNCH, GARY G., investment company executive, lawyer; b. Middletown, NY, July 25, 1950; BA, Syracuse U., 1972; JD, Duke U., 1975. Atty. SEC, 1976—89, dir., enforcement divsn., 1985—89; ptnr. Davis Polk & Wardwell, NYC, 1989—2001; gen. counsel Credit Suisse First Boston, NYC, 2001—, vice chmn. rsch. and legal, 2002—. Named Phi Beta Kappa. Mem.: DC Bar Assn., NY State Bar Assn. Office: Credit Suisse First Boston 11 Madison Ave New York NY 10010

LYNCH, GEORGE MICHAEL, auto parts manufacturing executive; b. Ft. Lauderdale, Fla., Apr. 7, 1943; s. Jack Traverse and Ruth Margarite (Koehler) L.; m. Carol Rollins, June 18, 1966; children: Kristin Ruth, Michael Scott. BSEE, Cornell U., 1965, MEE, 1966; MS in Indsl. Adminstrn., Carnegie-Mellon U., 1968. Fin. analyst, various supervisory positions Ford Motor Co., Dearborn, Mich., 1968-73, mgr. car product analysis, 1973-76, mgr. N.Am. ops. N.Am. contrs. analysis dept. office, 1976-77, mgr. programming and capacity dept., 1977-81, mgr. facilities and fin. staff mgmt. svcs., 1981-83, dir. fin. Ford of Australia, 1983-86, contr. Ford Tractor div. Troy, Mich., 1986-87; exec. v.p., chief fin. officer Ford New Holland, Inc., New Holland, Pa., 1987-97; v.p., contr. Dow Chem. Co., 1997-2000; exec. v.p., CFO Fed.-Mogul Corp., Southfield, Mich., 2000—. Mem. Orchard Lake Country Club, Birmingham Athletic Club (tennis chmn. 1977—), Phi Kappa Phi, Tau Beta Pi. Avocations: tennis, biking. Office: Fed Mogul Corp 26555 Northwestern Hwy Southfield MI 48034 Home: 2566 Kent Ridge Ct Bloomfield Hills MI 48301-2276 Office Phone: 248-354-9935.

LYNCH, GERARD E., federal judge; b. NYC, Sept. 4, 1951; s. Gerard Norman and Marjorie Ann (Werner) L.; m. Karen Marisak, June 10, 1972; 1 child, Christopher Marisak Lynch. BA, Columbia U., 1972, JD, 1975. Bar: N.Y. 1976, U.S. Supreme Ct., U.S. Ct. Appeals (2d, 4th and D.C. cirs.). Law clk. US Ct. Appeals, NYC, 1975-76, US Supreme Ct., Washington, 1976-77; asst. U.S. atty. So. Dist. NY, NYC, 1980-83; chief criminal div. U.S. Dist. Ct. (so. dist.) NY, NYC, 1990-92; assoc. independent counsel Iran/Contra, 1988-90; asst. prof. Columbia U., NYC, 1977-80, assoc. prof., 1980-87, prof. law, 1987—, vice dean, 1992—97, Paul J. Kellner prof. law; of counsel Howard, Darby & Levin, NYC, 1992—; judge U.S. Dist. Ct. (So. Dist.), NYC, 2000—. Office: US Courthouse 40 Centre St Room 803 New York NY 10007 Office Phone: 212-805-0427.*

LYNCH, HARRY JAMES, retired biologist; b. Glenfield, Pa., Jan. 18, 1929; s. Harry James and Rachel (McComb) L.; m. Pokum Lee Lynch. BS, Geneva Coll., Beaver Falls, Pa., 1957; PhD, U. Pitts., 1971; postgrad. Bio-Space Tech. Tng. Program, NASA and U. Va., 1970. Clin. chemist West Penn Hosp., Pitts., 1955-56; grad. teaching asst. U. Pitts., 1966-71, sr. teaching fellow, 1971; postdoctoral fellow MIT, Cambridge, 1973-75, rsch. assoc. dept. nutrition, lab. neuroendocrine regulation, 1973-75, lectr., 1976-81, rsch. scientist dept. brain and cognitive sci., 1982-92; ret., 1992. Contbr. more than 60 articles on the pineal gland to profl. jours. and books; patentee on implantable programmed microinfusion apparatus, 1981. With USN, 1950—54. NIH postdoctoral fellow 1971-73. Democrat. Avocation: study of animal behavior. Personal E-mail: harry_lynch@yahoo.com.

LYNCH, JAMES EDWARD, lawyer; b. Tampa, Fla., Aug. 5, 1951; s. John Thomas and Dorothy Bridget (Crosson) L.; m. Eileen Marie Baumgardner, Jan. 11, 1975; children: James Edward, Carolyn Marie. BA, LaSalle Coll., 1973; JD, Del. Law Sch., 1978. Bar: Pa. 1978, N.J. 1987, U.S. Dist. Ct. (ea. dist.) Pa. 1983, U.S. Dist. Ct. N.J. 1987, U.S. Dist. Ct. (ctrl. dist.) Pa. 1988, U.S. Ct. Appeals (3d cir.) 1984, U.S. Tax Ct. 1986, U.S. Supreme Ct. 1984. Terr. mgr. Clairol, Inc., N.Y.C., 1973-75; assoc. Ettinger, Silverman, Balka & Levy, Phila., 1978-80; ptnr. Lynch & Lynch, Bensalem, Pa., 1980-82, Kardos & Lynch, Newtown, Pa., 1982-87, Keane & Lynch, Newtown, 1987-88; prin. Law Offices of James E. Lynch, 1988—. Mem. ABA, Pa. Bar Assn., Bucks County Bar Assn., Philadelphia County Bar Assn., Upper Makefield Businessmen's Assn., Lower Bucks County C. of C., Men of LaSalle (bd. dirs.), Upper Makefield Soccer Assn. (bd. dirs.), Upper Makefield Baseball League (bd. dirs.) Gradu-Eights Club, Lions, Phi Alpha Delta. Republican. Roman Catholic. Office: Luxembourg Corp Ctr 503 Corporate Dr W Langhorne PA 19047-8011 also: 130 Durand Ave Trenton NJ 08611-3210 Home: 723 Falcon Dr Wyndmoor PA 19038-7101 E-mail: jel851951@hotmail.com.

LYNCH, JAYLEE JEAN, principal; b. Ft. Benning, Ga., Oct. 12, 1954; d. Donald and Janice Marie Dugas; m. Thomas Michael Lynch, Oct. 25, 1974; 1 child, Jason Thomas. BS in Elem. Edn., Ea. Mich. U., 1976, MA in Reading, 1983; MA in Adminstrn., Madonna U., 2001. Tchr. Our Lady Loretto Sch., Redford, Mich., 1976—77, St. Aloysius Sch., Romulus, 1977—90, St. Raphael Sch., Garden City, 1990—99; prin. Our Lady Victory, Northville, 1999—. Mem. city coun. City of Garden City, Mich., 1997—2001, mayor pro tem, 2001—03, mayor, 2003—. Mem.: Garden City Garden Club, Mich. Jaycees (life; regional v.p. 1985—86, state mgmt. v.p. 1986—87, sen.).

LYNCH, JESSICA, military officer; b. Palestine, W. Va., Apr. 26, 1983; d. Gregory O. and Deadra Lynch. Army Pvt. First Class, Hon. Med. Disability Discharge, 2003. Spokesperson Operation Purple. Decorated Purple Heart, Bronze Star, POW Medal; named West Virginian of Yr., 2003, Glamour Woman of Yr., 2003; recipient Heroes of Health award, 2003. Achievements include first POW/MIA recovered from Operation: Iraqi Freedom; subject of songs, poems, tributes, TV movies and reports; subject of Rick Bragg biography: I Am A Soldier Too: The Jessica Lynch Story, 2003; created the Jessica Lynch Found. to educate children of veterans.

LYNCH, JOHN BROWN, plastic surgeon, educator; b. Akron, Ohio, Feb. 5, 1929; s. John A. and Eloise L.; student Vanderbilt U., 1946-49; M.D., U. Tenn., 1952; children: John Brown, Margaret Frances Lynch Callihan; m. Mary Joyce Burrus, Dec. 1, 1994. Rotating intern John Gaston Hosp., Memphis, Tenn., 1953-54; resident in gen. surgery U. Tex. Med. Br., Galveston, 1956-59, resident in plastic surgery, 1959-62, instr., 1962, asst. prof. surgery, 1962-67, asso. prof., 1967-72, prof., 1972-73; prof., plastic surgery, chmn. dept. plastic surgery Vanderbilt U. Med. Center, 1973—. Served as capt. USAF, 1954-56. Diplomate Am. Bd. Plastic Surgery (chmn.). Fellow ACS; mem. Singleton Surg. Soc. (pres. 1982-83), AMA, Am. Soc. Plastic and Reconstructive Surgeons (pres. 1983-84), Am. Assn. Plastic Surgeons, Plastic Surgery Research Council, Am. Cleft Palate Assn., Am. Burn Assn., Soc. Head and Neck Surgeons, Internat. Burn Assn., Pan Am. Med. Assn., Am. Cancer Soc. (pres. Galveston County, Tex., Chpt. 1968), So. Med. Assn. (pres.-elect 1983-84), Tenn. med. Assn., Nashville Acad. Medicine, Tenn. Soc. Plastic Surgeons, Southeastern Soc. Plastic Surgeons, Southeastern Surg. Soc., H. William Scott, Jr. Soc., Nashville Surg. Soc., Am. Soc. Maxillofacial Surgeons, So. Surg. Assn., Am. Surg. Assn., Sigma Xi. Contbr. numerous articles to med. publs.; editor: (with S.R. Lewis) Symposium on the Treatment of Burns, 1973. Home: 5810 Hillsboro Pike Nashville TN 37215-4602 Office: Vanderbilt Hospital Nashville TN 37232-0001 E-mail: jblynchsr@aol.com.

LYNCH, JOHN EDWARD, JR., lawyer; b. Lansing, Mich., May 3, 1952; s. John Edward and Miriam Ann (Hyland) L.; m. Brenda Jayne Clark, Nov. 16, 1984; children: John E. III, Robert C., David B., Patrick D., Jacqueline E. AB, Hamilton Coll., 1974; JD, Case Western Res. U., 1977. Bar: Conn. 1978, Ohio 1980, U.S. Dist. Ct. (no. dist.) Ohio 1980, U.S. Ct. Appeals (6th cir.) 1980, Tex. 2000. Assoc. Thompson, Weir & Barclay, 1977-78; law clk. U.S. Dist. Judge, Cleve., 1978-80; assoc. Squire, Sanders and Dempsey, Cleve., 1980-86, ptnr., 1986-96; v.p., gen. counsel, sec. Caliber System, Inc., Akron, Ohio, 1996-98; sr. v.p. gen. couns. BP America, Inc., 1998-99; assoc. gen. counsel Upstream Western Hemisphere BP, 1999—2002; assoc. gen. counsel Upstream GP&R Global BP p.l.c., London, 2003—. Master bencher Am. Inns of Ct. Found., 1987-98; mem. civil justice reform act adv. group U.S. Dist. Ct. (no. dist.) Ohio. Del. Hamilton Coll. Alumni Coun., 1992-97, regional chair alumni admissions, 1993—97; trustee The Cath. Charities Corp., 1995-97; mem. Cuyahoga County Rep. Exec. Com., Cleve., 1984—98; mem. Seton Soc. St. Vincent Hosp. Fund. Roman Catholic. Avocations: golf, jogging. Home: Chilton House Ravenscroft Rd St Georges Hill Weybridge Surrey KT13 0NX England Office: BP Chertsey Rd Sunbury on Thames Middlesex TW16 7LN England Office Phone: 44 1932 771709. E-mail: lynchjl@bp.com.

LYNCH, JOHN F., lawyer; BSChemE, Rensselaer Poly. Inst., 1960; JD, Fordham U., 1964. Bar: DC Bar, Fla. State Bar, NY Bar, State Bar Tex., registered: US Ct. Appeals, Fed. Cir., US Patent & Trademark Office, US Supreme Ct. Engr. Hercules Power Co.; atty. Monsanto Company; atty. & patent agent Union Carbide Corp.; ptnr. & mem. exec. com. Howrey Simon Arnold & White LLP, Houston. Author: Patent Litig.: Procedure & Tactics, (articles) The Fraudulent Procurement Issue in Proposed Patent Legis.: Defining the Road to a Patent, 1973, Fraud in Patent Procurement: Genuine and Sham Charges, 1974, Privilege and Work Product in Patent Litig.: An Area of Contention, 1975, New Rule 56: The Second Time Around, 1992, An Argument for Eliminating the Defense of Patent Uninforceability Based on Inequitable Conduct, 1998. Named one of top 20 patent lawyers, Euromoney Legal Media Group's Best of the Best: 2000 Ed., 100 most influential lawyers in Am., Nat. Law Jour., 2000. Mem.: Tex. Bar Assn., Licensing Exec. Soc., Houston Intellectual Property Law Assn., Houston Bar Found., Houston Bar Assn., Fed. Cir. Bar Assn., Am. Intellectual Property Law Assn., ABA. Office: Howrey Simon Arnold & White LLP 750 Bering Dr Houston TX 77057 Office Phone: 713-787-1400. Office Fax: 713-787-1440. Business E-Mail: lynchj@howrey.com.

LYNCH, JOHN H., governor; b. Waltham, Mass., Nov. 25, 1952; s. William and Margaret Lynch; m. Susan Lynch; children: Jacqueline, Julia, Hayden. BA, U. NH, 1974; MBA, Harvard Bus. Sch., 1979; JD, Georgetown U. Law Ctr., 1984. Dir. admissions Harvard Bus. Sch.; pres., CEO Knoll, Inc., 1994—2001; pres. The Lynch Group, Manchester, 2001—04; gov. State of N.H., Concord, 2005—. Bd. dirs. Capitol Ctr. for Arts; past-pres. alumni assn. U. N.H.; bd. dirs. Catholic Med. Ctr., Manchester, Mass., 1997—2003; mem. bd. trustees Univ. Sys. NH, 2000—, chmn. bd. trustees, 2001—04; coach youth soccer, hockey and baseball teams. Democrat. Office: Office of the Gov 208-214 State House 107 N Main St Concord NH 03301*

LYNCH, JOHN JOSEPH, lawyer; b. Mt. Pleasant, Mich., Jan. 31, 1936; s. Edward N. Lynch and Dorothy K. Botsford; m. Sandra Claire Nunneley, Feb. 4, 1941; children: James, Michael, Patrick, Katherine. BS, John Carroll U., 1960; JD, U. Mich., 1963. Ptnr. Lynch Gallagher Lynch & Martineau, Mt. Pleasant, Mich., 1963—. Arbitrator Am. Arbitration Assn., U.S. Dist. Ct. (we. dist.) Mich., 1980; referee Cir. Ct., Mt. Pleasant, 1963-68. Bd. dir. C.M. Cmty. Hosp., Mt. Pleasant, 1965-80, Broomfield Fund., Mt. Pleasant, 1968-75. With USN, 1955-57. Recipient Plaque Am. Arbitration Assn., 1983, C.M. Cmty. Hosp., 1996. Mem. Mich. Oil and Gas Assn. (legal com.), Assn. Irish Am. Attys. Avocations: fly fishing, hunting, fishing, diving. Office: Lynch Gallagher Lynch & Martineau 555 N Main St Mount Pleasant MI 48858-1651

LYNCH, JOHN PETER, lawyer; b. Chgo., June 5, 1942; s. Charles Joseph and Anne Mae (Loughlin) Lynch; m. Judy Godvin, Sept. 21, 1968; children: Julie, Jennifer. AB, Marquette U., 1964; JD, Northwestern U., 1967. Bar: Ill. 1967, U.S. Ct. Appeals (7th cir.) 1979, U.S. Ct. Appeals (5th cir.) 1976, U.S. Supreme Ct. 1979. Atty. Kirkland & Ellis, Chgo., 1970—73, ptnr., 1973—76, Hedlund, Hunter & Lynch, Chgo., 1976—82, Latham, Watkins, Hedlund, Hunter & Lynch, Chgo., 1982—85, Latham & Watkins, Chgo., 1985—, and vice chair, global litig. dept., also resident ptnr. Paris, 2001—. Former mem. exec. com. Latham & Watkins. Notes and Comments editor: Northwestern U. Law Rev., 1967. Mem. vis. com. Northwestern U. Law Sch. Lt. USN, 1968—71. Mem.: ATLA, ABA, Ill. Bar Assn., Order of Coif, Met. Club, Exec. Club, City Club. Home: 439 Sheridan Rd Kenilworth IL 60043-1220 Office: Latham & Watkins Ste 5800 Sears Tower 233 S Wacker Dr Chicago IL 60606 also: Latham & Watkins 53 quai d'Orsay 75007 Paris France

LYNCH, JOHN ROBORG, neurologist; s. Sean Roborg and Alison Marah Lynch; m. Stacy Ross Racine, July 22, 1990; children: Hannah Racine, Henry Roborg. BA, Brown U., 1989; MD, Duke U., 1994, postgrad., 2004—. Diplomate Am. Bd. Psychiatry and Neurology, Am. Bd. Internal Medicine. Asst. prof. medicine and neurology Duke U. Med. Ctr., Durham, NC, 2004—. Dir. neurology Select Splty. Hosp., Durham, 2003—. Fellow: Am. Heart Assn. (stroke fellow 1999—2004). Avocations: mountain climbing, running. Office: Duke U Med Ctr 227E Bryan Research Bldg Durham NC 27710 Office Phone: 919-684-5128. Office Fax: 919-684-6514. Personal E-mail: lynch004@duke.edu.

LYNCH, JOHN TERRENCE, professional football player; b. Hinsdale, Ill., Sept. 25, 1971; m. Linda; 1 child, Jake. Student, Stanford U. Safety Tampa Bay Buccaneers, 1993—2003, Denver Broncos, 2004—. Active San Diguieto Boys Club; creator Lynch's Safety Zone; founder Lynch Family Legacy Scholarship. Named to 5 Pro-Bowls. Achievements include mem. of Super Bowl Championship Team, 2003. Office: c/o Denver Broncos 13655 Broncos Pkwy Englewood CO 80112

LYNCH, JOHN THOMAS, retired science administrator, physicist; b. Washington, Mar. 21, 1938; s. John Thomas and Mary Ellen (Kaye) L.; m. Leslie Gray, June 22, 1959 (div. June 1972); children: John Thomas III, Michael Gray; m. Carol Rollins, July 5, 1980. BS in Physics, Va. Poly. Inst., 1963; MS in Physics, U. Wis., 1965, PhD, 1972. Lab. technician Nat. Bur. Standards, Washington, 1957-60; rsch. scientist U. Wis., Madison, 1965-78; staff Los Alamos (N.Mex.) Nat. Labs., 1978-81; program scientist NASA Hdqs., Washington, 1981-85; program dir. aeronomy and astrophysics Polar programs NSF, Washington, 1985-2000; ret., 2000. Contbr. articles to sci. jours. Recipient Antarctic svc. medal USN, 1986; named Disting. Alumni fellow dept. physics U. Wis., Madison, 2003; a mountain in Antarctica is named in his honor. Avocations: music, sailing. Personal E-mail: JLynch137@comcast.net.

LYNCH, JOSEPH JAMES, philosophy educator; b. Decatur, Ala., Aug. 28, 1953; s. Joseph James Lynch and Edith Todd; life ptnr. Regina Dawn Hudachek; 1 child, Kane. BA, Va. Commonwealth U., 1982; MA, Claremont Grad. U., 1986, PhD, 1992. Lectr. philosophy Calif. State U., Fullerton, 1987—89, Calif. Poly. State U., San Luis Obispo, 1990—2001, asst. prof. philosophy, 2001—. Editor: (academic jour.) Between the Species, 1998; contbr. articles and revs. to profl. jours. Chair Coll. of Liberal Arts Caucus, Acad. Senate, San Luis Obispo, 2001—; lectr. rep. Calif. Faculty Assn., San Luis Obispo, 1995—2001. Recipient Oustanding Lectr. award, San Luis Obispo chpt. Calif. Faculty Assn., 2001, President's award, 2001. Mem.: Soc. for Study of Philosophy and Martial Arts (founder, chair 1997—2002), Soc. for Study of Ethics and Animals (Pacific coord. 1997—2002), Soc. for Study of Philosophy and Psychology, Am. Philos. Assn., Calif. Faculty Assn. (lectr. rep. 1995—2001), White Heron Sangha (bd. dirs. 2001—02). Green Party. Buddhist. Avocations: 2nd degree black belt in Hawaiian kempo, Taijiquan. Office: Calif Poly State U One Grand Ave San Luis Obispo CA 93407 Business E-Mail: jlynch@calpoly.edu.

LYNCH, JOSEPH MICHAEL, engineer, consultant; b. West New York, N.J., July 12, 1922; s. Peter Lawrence and Catherine Anne (Dritschel) L.; m. Anna Marie Lewandoski, June 8, 1943; children: Joan, Laurie, Peter, Joseph, Anna, Grace. ME in Engring., Stevens Inst. Tech., 1948; postgrad., Vanderbilt U., Pratt Grad. Sch. Planning, NYU. Registered profl. engr. and land surveyor, N.Y., N.J.; cert. profl. planner, N.J. Engr., supr. O'Kane Marine Repair Co., Hoboken, N.J., 1948-50; engr. Madison Contractors, Weehaken, N.J., 1950-53; engr., owner Mayo, Lynch & Assocs., Secaucus, N.J., 1953—. Chmn. bd. Plaza Nat. Bank, Secaucus, 1960-61; mcpl. engr. Towns of Weehawken, Secaucus, Hoboken, Bethel & Callicoon, N.Y. and N.J.; mem. adv. bd. New

Jersey Bank, Passaic, 1970-80. Chmn. Secaucus Planning Bd., 1960; adv. bd. mem. Passaic (N.J.) Planning Bd., 1970, N.J. Bank, Passaic; trustee Stevens Acad., Hoboken, N.J. Tech. sgt. U.S. Army, 1942-46. Fellow Soc. Civil Engrs. (various coms.); mem. NSPE (various coms.), Soc. Mcpl. Engrs. (various coms.), Profl. Land Surveyors. Roman Catholic. Achievements include U.S. patents for screening apparatus and treatment process; U.K. patent for apparatus. Home: 717 John St Secaucus NJ 07094-3207 Office: Mayo Lynch & Assocs Inc 333 Meadowlands Pkwy Secaucus NJ 07094-1814

LYNCH, KAREN RENZULLI, lawyer; b. Bridgeport, Conn., Feb. 4, 1946; d. Lidizio Amerigo and Cynthia Maria (Scott) Renzulli; m. Eugene Patrick Lynch Jr., Apr. 12, 1969; children: Tracy Regina, Kevin Anthony. BA, Manhattanville Coll., Purchase, N.Y., 1967; MPA, U. Hartford, West Hartford, Conn., 1975; JD, Western New Eng. Coll., Springfield, Mass., 1981. Bar: Conn. 1981, U.S. Dist. Ct. Conn. 1981. Mgmt. intern U.S. Army Chief of Staff, Washington, 1967-68; intelligence analyst U.S. Army for Sci. and Tech. Ctr., Washington, 1968-69; adminstr. N.Y. State Bd. Equalization, Albany, N.Y., 1969-70, U. Conn. Health Ctr., Farmington, 1971-76; pvt. practice West Hartford, 1981—. Law clk. U.S. Dist. Ct., Hartford, 1980; law intern Conn. Superior Ct., Hartford, 1981. Editor: Constabar News of Gen. Practice, 1985—88; mem. editl. bd. The Complete Lawyer, 1996—. Mem. Jewish Family Svc. Greater Hartford Task Force on Conservatorship, West Hartford, 1988; mem. legacy and planned giving com. Greater Hartford chpt. Am. Cancer Soc., 1992-98, bd. dirs., 1993-98, treas., 1993-97. Named to Best Lawyers in Am., Consumer Guide Trusts and Estates, 2001—. Mem. ABA (coun. sect. gen. practice div. 1987-91, bd. dirs. 1990-91, vice chmn. sole practitioners and small firms com. 1989-99, elder law com. 1991—, chmn. 2002-2003), Conn. Bar Assn. (exec. com. gen. practice sect. 1982—, vice chmn. 1990-91, Pro Bono Honor Roll 1996—), Hartford County Bar Assn. (chmn. legal svcs. com. Old Am. Day 1986), Hartford Assn. Women Attys. (bd. dirs. 1984-86), Consumer Guide for Trusts and Estates. Office: 45 S Main St PO Box 270715 West Hartford CT 06127-0715 Office Phone: 860-233-3786. E-mail: lynchlaw@juno.com.

LYNCH, LORETTA E., lawyer, former prosecutor; b. Durham, N.C., May 21, 1959; d. Lorenzo Lynch. Grad., Harvard Coll., 1981; JD, Harvard U., 1984. Bar: N.Y., U.S. Dist. Ct. (ea. dist. NY), U.S. Dist. Ct. (so. dist. NY), U.S. Ct. Appeals (2nd cir.). Litigation assoc. Cahill, Gordon & Reindel, 1984-90; with Office of U.S. Atty. for Ea. Dist. of N.Y., 1990—2001; chief L.I. offices, 1994-98; chief asst. U.S. States Atty., 1998—99; U.S. atty. ea. dist. N.Y. U.S. Dept. Justice, Bklyn., 2000—01; ptnr. Hogan & Hartson LLP, NYC, 2002—. Instr. Dept. Justice Criminal Trial Advocacy Prog.; adj. prof. St. John's Univ. Sch. Law; bd. dir. Fed. Reserve Bank N.Y., Office of the Appellate Defender; trustee Nat. Inst. Trial Advocacy; mem. Magistrate Judge Selection Panel Ea. Dist. N.Y., Judicial Screening Panel of Sen. Charles Schumer, NYC Charter Revision Commn., NY State Commn. on Jury, 2003—04; bd. advs. Brennan Ctr. for Justice, NYU Sch. Law. Author: White-Collar Crime: Counseling Corporate Clients Under Investigation, 2003. Bd. dirs. Nat. Inst. Law and Equity. Named one of Am.'s Top Black Lawyers, Black Enterprise Mag., 2003. Mem.: ABA (mem. sec. on litig.), Ea. Dist Com. on Civil Litigation, Fed. Bar. Coun., Assn. Bar N.Y.C. (chair Criminal Law Com.). Avocations: reading, tennis. Office: Hogan & Hartson 875 Third Ave New York NY 10022*

LYNCH, MARY JEAN, art educator, consultant; b. Hillsdale, Mich., Mar. 19, 1948; d. Paul A. and Marie C. (Larson) L.; m. Glenn A. Rowinski, Jan. 24, 1985. BA, Hillsdale Coll., 1970; BFA, Cleve. Inst. Art, 1981. Art tchr. Hillsdale (Mich.) Pub. Schs., 1970-72, Avon (Ohio) Pub. Schs., 1972-77; mus. vol. asst. Am. History Divsn. of Community Life Smithsonian Inst., Washington, 1982-83; art instr. after-sch. program Fairfax County Pub. Schs., Falls Church, Va., 1982-83; arts specialist key after sch.-program Six Schs. Complex, Washington, 1982-83; area coord., arts tchr. Fine Arts Summer program Chautauqua (N.Y.) Inst., 1981-85; art and art appreciation tchr. St. Mary's Acad., Alexandria, Va., 1983-85; art and art history instr. St. Stephen's Sch., Alexandria, Va., 1983-88; arts and crafts specialist, dir. Panzer Arts and Crafts Shop, Stuttgart, Germany, 1989-91; art tchr. St. Stephen's and St. Agnes Sch., Alexandria, 1997—. Workshop instr., summer camp instr. resident assocs. program, young assocs. and family activities Smithsonian Instn., Washington, 1983—85, 1991—; art cons., Alexandria, 1992—. Exhibited in group shows inlcuding Anton Gallery, Washington, 1987, Fredonia State Coll., 1983, 84, 85, Chautauqua Art Assn. Gallery, 1983-85 summers, Greater Reston Arts Ctr., 1983, Cleve. Inst. of Art, 1981. Recipient scholarship Cleve. Inst. Art, 1980-81. Mem. NEA, Nat. Arts Edn. Assn. Avocations: hiking, martial arts, woodworking, quilting, reading.

LYNCH, MATTHEW, artist, art educator; b. Ind., 1969; BFA, Ball State U., 1992; MFA, Syracuse U., 1995. Lectr. Concordia U., Montreal, Canada; co-founder & mem. SIMPARCH, 1996—; lectr. Weber State U., Ogden, Utah, 1997; resident Brandenburgischer Kunstverein, Potsdam, Germany, 1998, Ctr. Land Use Interpretation, LA, 1999, 2003; lectr. U. Utah, Salt Lake City, 1999, L'Ecole Nationale d'Art, France, Columbus Coll. Art & Design, Ohio, 2001, Documenta XI, Kassel, Germany, 2002; asst. prof.-fine arts Coll. Design, Architecture, Art & Planning- U. Cin., 2002—. Exhibitions include Highwayscape, Weber State U., Ogden, Utah, 1997, An Investigation of Trans-Architecture in Western Am., 1997, Rise Overrun, Plan B Evolving Arts, Santa Fe, 1997, L'Arche, Ecole Nationale d'Art, Cergy, France, 1998, SIMPARCH, Bemis Ctr. Contemporary Arts, Omaha, 1998, Ship from the Desert, Maschinenhalle, Potsdam, Germany, 1998, Moorings Project, 1998, Free Basin, Hyde Pk. Arts Ctr., Chgo., 2000, Spec, Renaissance Soc., U. Chgo., 2001, Mood River, Wexner Ctr. Arts, Columbus, Ohio, 2002, Documenta XI, Kassel, Germany, 2002, Session the Bowl, Deitch Projects, NY, 2002, Whitney Biennial, Whitney Mus. Am. Art, NY, 2004, InSITE, San Diego, 2005. Pollock-Krasner Grant, 1997, N. Mex. Arts Coun. Grant, 1997, Creative Capital Grant, 2002. Address: 1328 Pullan Ave Cincinnati OH 45223 Office Phone: 513-556-2083. E-mail: simparch@hotmail.com, matthew.lynch@uc.edu.*

LYNCH, MATTHEW J., retail executive; Grad., No. Ariz. U., Coll. Engring. Tech. Software engr. Sperry Aerospace; info. sys. mgmt. Air Wis. Airlines, Am. West Airlines, Honeywell, Aerospace Electronics Sys., 1985—93; v.p., info. tech. svcs. Runzheimer Internat., 1993—98; v.p., oper. tech. svcs. ShopKo, Green Bay, Wis., 1998—2003, sr. v.p., chief info. officer, 2003—. Office: ShopKo 700 Pilgrim Way Green Bay WI 54304

LYNCH, MICHAEL, lawyer, staffing company executive; BS in Bus. Adminstrn., JD, Marquette U. Tax mgr. Arthur Andersen & Co.; dir. corp. tax Manpower, Inc., Milw., 1990—93, v.p. corp. tax, 1993, v.p. internat. support services., internat. gen. counsel, 1999—. Office: Manpower Inc 5301 N Ironwood Rd Milwaukee WI 53217

LYNCH, NANCY ANN, computer scientist, educator; b. Bklyn., Jan. 19, 1948; d. Roland David and Marie Catherine (Adinolfi) Evraets; m. Dennis Christopher Lynch, June 14, 1969; children: Patrick, Kathleen (dec.), Mary. BS, Bklyn. Coll., 1968; PhD, MIT, 1972. Asst. prof. math. Tufts U., Medford, Mass., 1972-73, U. So. Calif., Los Angeles, 1973-76, Fla. Internat. U., Miami, 1976-77; assoc. prof. computer sci. Ga. Tech. U., Atlanta, 1977-82, MIT, Cambridge, 1982-86, prof. computer sci., 1986—, NEC prof. software sci. and engring., 1996—. Ellen Swallow Richards chair MIT, 1982-87, Cecil H. Green chair, 1994-96. Contbr. numerous articles to profl. jours. Fellow: Assn. Computing Machinery; mem.: NAE. Roman Catholic. Office: MIT 32-G668 Comp Sci & Artificial Intelligence Lab 32 Vassar St Cambridge MA 02139

LYNCH, PATRICK, lawyer; b. Pitts., Nov. 11, 1941; s. Thomas Patrick and Helen Mary (Grimes) Lynch; m. M. Linda Maturo, June 20, 1964; children: Megan, Kevin, Colin, Brendan, Erin, Brian, Liam, Eamonn, Kilian, Caitlin, Ryan, Declan, Cristin, Mairin, Sean. BA in philosophy, Loyola U., LA, 1964, LLB, 1966. Bar: Calif. 1967, US Dist. Ct. Ctrl., No., So., Ea. Districts Calif., US Ct. Appeals 9th Cir., US Supreme Ct. Ptnr. O'Melveny & Myers, Los Angeles, 1966—. Panelist PLI Annual Antritrust Law Inst., 1982—2000; exec. bd. Fed. Litig. Guide Reporter. Fellow: Am. Coll. Trial Lawyers; mem.: ABA, LA County Bar Assn. Office: OMelveny & Myers 400 S Hope St Los Angeles CA 90071-2899

LYNCH, PATRICK C., state attorney general; b. Providence, Feb. 4, 1965; s. Dennis and Irene Lynch; m. Christin Lynch; children: Kelsy, Graham. BA, Brown U., 1987; JD, Suffolk U., 1992. Bar: R.I. 1992, U.S. Dist. Ct. R.I. 1993. Clk. to Justice Joseph Rodgers Jr. R.I. Superior Ct., 1993—94; spl. asst. atty. gen. State of R.I., Providence, 1994—99, atty. gen., 2003—; assoc. Tillinghast Licht Perkins Smith and Cohen, LLP, Providence, 1999—2003. Sec., bd. dirs. Advent House; bd. mem. Camp St. Cmty. Ministries, Brown Club, RI; mem. Brown Hall of Fame Com.; former pres. bd. St. Raphael. Mem.: R.I. Bar Assn. Democrat. Office: 150 S Main St Providence RI 02903

LYNCH, PETER JOHN, retired dermatologist; b. Mpls., Oct. 22, 1936; s. Francis Watson and Viola Adeline (White) L.; m. Barbara Ann Lanzi, Jan. 18, 1964; children: Deborah, Timothy. Student, St. Thomas Coll., 1954-57; BS, U. Minn., 1958, MD, 1961. Intern U. Mich. Med. Ctr., 1961-62, resident in dermatology, 1962-65, asst. prof., then assoc. prof. dermatology, 1968-73; clin. instr. U. Minn., 1965; chief dermatology and venereal disease Martin Army Hosp., Columbus, Ga., 1966-68; asso. prof. to prof. dermatology U. Ariz., Tucson, 1973-86, chief sect. dermatology, 1973-86, asso. head dept. internal medicine, 1977-86; prof., head dermatology U. Minn. Med. Sch., Mpls., 1986-95; med. dir. ambulatory care U. Minn. Health Sys., 1993-95; prof., chmn. dept. dermatology U. Calif., Davis, 1995-2000, prof. emeritus, 2000—, tng. program dir., 2001—, Frederick G. Novy, Jr. prof., 2005—. Author: (with S. Epstein) Burckhardt's Atlas and Manual of Dermatology and Venereology, 1977, Dermatology for the House Officer, 1982, 3rd edit., 1994, (with W.M. Sams) Principles and Practice of Dermatology, 1992, 2nd edit., 1996, (with I.E. Edwards) Genital Dermatology, 1994. With AUS, 1966-68. Decorated Army Commendation Medal; recipient Disting. Service award for faculty U. Mich., 1970, Disting. Faculty award U. Ariz., 1981 Mem. Am. Acad. Dermatology (hon., bd. dirs. 1974-78, v.p. 1991-92), Assn. Profs. Dermatology (bd. dirs. 1976-80, pres. 1994-96), Internat. Soc. Study of Vulvar Disease (bd. dirs. 1976-79, pres. 1983), Soc. Investigative Dermatology, Am. Bd. Dermatology (bd. dirs. 1984-89), Gougerot Soc. (Bronze medal award), Alpha Omega Alpha. Democrat. Roman Catholic. Home: 802 Elmhurst Cir Sacramento CA 95825 Office: U Calif 4860 Y St # 3400 Sacramento CA 95817-2307

LYNCH, PETER L., retail executive; m. Maddy Lynch; 2 children. BS in Fin., Nichols Coll. V.p., gen. mgr. Star Markets, Boston; pres. Acme Markets subs. Am. Stores Co., Malvern, Pa.; exec. v.p. ops. Albertson's Inc., Boise, Idaho, 1999-2000, pres., COO, 2000—03; pres., CEO Winn-Dixie Stores, Inc., Jacksonville, Fla., 2004—. Mem. bd. dirs. Winn-Dixie Stores Inc, 2004—. Office: Winn-Dixie Stores Inc 5050 Edgewood Ct Jacksonville FL 32254*

LYNCH, ROBERT EMMETT, mathematics professor; b. Chgo., Feb. 5, 1932; s. Joseph Burke and Mildred Cecilia (Bildhauser) L.; m. Martha Bolling Hacker, Oct. 8, 1955; children: Barbara Ann, William Robert, Pamela Elizabeth. B Engring. Physics, Cornell U., 1954; MS, Harvard, 1959, PhD, 1963. Sr. rsch. mathematician Gen. Motors Rsch. Lab., Warren, Mich, 1961-64; assoc. prof. computer sci. and math. U. Tex., Austin, 1964-67, Purdue U., West Lafayette, Ind., 1967-85, prof., 1985—; prof. emeritus, 1998—. Author: (with Garrett Birkhoff) Numerical Solution of Elliptic Problems, 1984; (with John R. Rice) Computers, Their Impact and Use/with Basic, 1975, Computers, Their Impact and Use/With Fortran, 1977, Computers, Their Impact and Use/with PL/1, 1978. Lt. USAF, 1955-57. Address: 401 W Circle Dr North Muskegon MI 49445-2717

LYNCH, ROBERT MARTIN, lawyer, consultant; b. St. Louis, Mar. 28, 1950; s. Raymond Burns and Nancy Winn (Roeder) L.; m. Cynthia Kay Allmeyer, June 7, 1974; children: Christopher, Kelly, Stephanie. AB, St. Louis U., 1972, JD, 1975. Bar: Mo. 1975, D.C. 1985, Tex. 1992. Law clk. to presiding justice Mo. Ct. Appeals, St. Louis, 1975-76; atty. Southwestern Bell Telephone Corp., St. Louis, 1976-79, atty. network, 1979-83, gen. atty., 1983-88, v.p., asst. gen. counsel, 1988-91; v.p., gen. counsel Tex. office Southwestern Bell Telephone Co., Dallas, 1991-93, v.p., gen. counsel external affairs San Antonio, 1993-98; sr. v.p., gen. counsel external affairs SBC Comm., Inc., 1998—, sr. v.p., gen. counsel bus. and consumer markets, 1999-2000; sr. v.p. gen. counsel SBC Ops., Inc., 2000—02; sr. v.p. assoc. gen. counsel SBC Ameritech, 2002—03; pvt. cons., 2003—. Instr. paralegal studies St. Louis Community Coll., 1977—. Mem. ABA, Tex. Bar, Dallas Bar Assn., Mo. Bar Assn. (adminstrv. law com. coun.), St. Louis Bar Assn. (chmn. adminstrv. law com. 1981-82), Am. Corp. Counsel Assn. (chmn. communications com. St. Louis chpt., chmn. law dept. mgmt. com. 1997-98, bd. dirs. 1999—). Republican. Avocations: racquetball, writing. Home: 40 Brighton Way Apt 1N Saint Louis MO 63105-1658 E-mail: blynch@sbcglobal.net.

LYNCH, ROSEMARY G., secondary school educator; b. Fairmont, W.Va., Nov. 18, 1951; d. Okey James and Iva Marie (Seccuro) Moore; m. John Paul Lynch Sr., June 6, 1970; children: John Paul Jr., Scott, Ryan. AB, Shepherd Coll., 1985; MA, W.Va. U., 1990. Family and consumer svcs. tchr. Berkeley County Pub. Schs., Martinsburg, W.Va. Adj. faculty Shepherd Coll. Webmaster Martinsburg H.S. Band and South Middle Sch. Recipient ACE award Berkeley County Schs.; named. W.Va.'s Outstanding New Home Econs. Tchr., 1988, Outstanding Young Educator Martinsburg, 1988; named to Hall Fame, Martinsburg Band Boosters Mem. NEA, Am. Assn. Family Consumer Sci., Assn. Career Tech. Edn., W.Va. Edn. Assn., Berkeley County Edn. Assn., Shepherd Coll. Alumni Assn., W.Va. U. Alumni Assn., Kappa Omicron Nu. Home: 1606 W Race St Martinsburg WV 25401-2010 Office Phone: 304-267-3545.

LYNCH, SAMUEL CURLEE, JR., (SIR SAMI LYNCH), painter; b. Salisbury, NC, July 31, 1953; s. Samuel and Mae (Alexander) L. Student, Windsor (Ont., Can.) U., 1970-73, Acad. for Arts, N.Y.C., 1978, Raymond Duncan Acad., Paris, 1981, Writers Inst., Mamaroneck, N.Y., 1991-92. Registered Soc. N.Am. Artists, diamond banking account cons., DeBeers. Artist Windsor Sun, 1973-74; artist, editor asst. Akwesasne Notes, St. Regis, Que., Can., 1974; graphic artist Art Leadley, Windsor, 1974; counseling asst. S.W. Regional Centre, Cedar Springs, Ont., 1974-76; art dir., set. designer Video Variety, N.Y.C., 1977-79; instr. painting and sculpture Waterworks, Salisbury, 1980; artist, fashion designer DHR/555 Import-Export, N.Y.C. and Montreal, 1985-86; artist, writer, inventor, designer Fine Arts Restoration/Preservation Svc., Landis, N.C., 1986—; coml. product designer Landis, N.C., 1998—. Ptnr. Royal Whispers Note Card Co., prin. artist; v.p. Native Cultural Centre, Windsor, 1974; mem. Rowan Art Guild, Salisbury, 1980. Inventor art material Wings Easel; illustrator, editor The Oracle, 1985-87; works include Wedding Party/On a Summer's Night, Storm Shelter, Legends of the Firebird, 2002, Celestial Symphony, 2002; exhibited in group shows; represented in permenant collections Royal Family of Monaco/Consul de Monaco, Royal Collection of Hutt River Principality; cinematographer, creative dir.: (film) Sophistry, 2002; author: Anadolu Contemporary Royal Art, 2003; co-producer: (documentary) 90 Acre Ark of Safety, 2001. Artist, Landis Heritage Day Com., 1987-94; mem. Met. Soc. des Amis de la Fondation and Fondation Maeght. Decorated knight Royal Order (Hutt River Principality); recipient Bronze Medallion of Paris, Acad. Raymond Duncan, 1981, Prix du Centennaire, Musèo Duncan, 1981, Salon d'Aout award, 1981, certificate Vintner, Sursum Corda, Brussels, 2001, Archtl./Landscape Design Outstanding Artistic Ability award, 1966, Art award, 1970, Comte de Lyon-Satolas, 2000, Outstanding Achievement in arts medal, Princess Li Chieu-Hoang, Vietnam, 2001, Outstanding Artist citation Ordern Soverèin de Liechtenstein, 2001, Royal medal for Arts HM Volodar nad Volodarme of Ukraine, 2001, Duc de l'Iled' Oléron, 2001; Royal Patronage, Hutt River Province Principality, 1994, others; named His Royal Highness Prince of Trabzon, 2001, grand master Knights Order of St. John of Jerusalem. Mem. Societe des Amis de la Fondation Maeght. Avocations: horticulture, wine making, art and antiques collecting, music, architecture. Office: Sami Lynch PO Box 331 Landis NC 28088-0331 E-mail: royalwhispers@hotmail.com.

LYNCH, SANDRA LEA, federal judge; b. Oak Park, Ill., July 31, 1946; d. Bernard Francis and Eugenia Tyus Lynch; married; 1 child. AB in Philosophy, Wellesley Coll., 1968; JD cum laude, Boston U., 1971. Bar: Mass. 1971, U.S. Supreme Ct. 1974. Law clk. to Hon. Raymond J. Pettine U.S. Dist. Ct., Providence; asst. atty. gen. Commonwealth of Mass., Boston, 1974; gen. counsel Mass. Dept. Edn., Boston, 1974—78; ptnr. Foley, Hoag & Eliot, Boston, 1978—95; judge 1st cir. U.S. Ct. Appeals, Boston, 1995—. Contbr. articles to profl. jours. Past co-chair leading industries com. Greater Boston C. of C. Recipient Disting. Alumnae award, Boston U. Law Sch., 1993, Wellesley Coll., 1997, Disting. Svc. award, Planned Parenthood, 1991. Mem.: ABA, Boston Bar Assn. (pres. 1992—93, Jud. Excellence award 2001), Mass. Bar Assn., Nat. Assn. Women Judges, Women's Forum. Office: US Ct Appeals One Courthouse Way Ste 8710 Boston MA 02210-3010

LYNCH, STEPHEN F., congressman; b. Boston, Mar. 31, 1955; m. Margaret Lynch; 1 child, Victoria. BS, Wentworth Inst. of Tech., 1988; JD, Boston Coll., 1991; MPA, Harvard U., 1999. Ironworker US Steel Plant, General Motors, General Dynamics Shipyard, 1973—91; former atty. priv. practice; mem. Mass. Ho. of Reps., Boston, 1994—96, Mass. Senate, Boston, 1996—2001, U.S. Ho. Reps. from 9th Mass. dist., 2001—, mem. fin. svc. com., govt. reform com. Co-founder Congressional Labor and Working Families Caucus. Mem.: Boston Ironworkers Union (pres. Local 7). Democrat. Roman Catholic. Office: US Ho of Reps 319 Cannon Ho Office Bldg Washington DC 20515-2109*

LYNCH, THOMAS BERNARD, science educator; b. Winchester, Va., Aug. 20, 1953; s. Ashby Browning and Rosaline Phillips Lynch. BS, MS, Va. Poly. Inst. and State U., 1977; PhD, Purdue U., 1982. Asst. prof. dept. forestry Okla. State U., Stillwater, Okla., 1982—87, assoc. prof. dept. forestry, 1987—2001, prof. dept. forestry, 2001—. Assoc. editor: So. Jour. of Applied Forestry, 1996—2002 (SAF Cert. of Appreciation, 2002, USDA Cert. of Appreciation, 1993), Forest Sci., 2004—. Prison min. KAIROS, Hominy, Okla., 1997—2002. Grantee, USDA Forest Svc., 1985—2002, 1986—89, 1987—89, 1999—2006, Nekoosa Papers, Inc., 1989. Mem.: Am. Statis. Assn., Soc. of Am. Foresters (chair Okla. divsn. 1995, cert. forester 2002), Christian Leadership Ministries, Fellowship of Christian Faculty and Staff, Phi Sigma Soc., Gamma Sigma Delta, Xi Sigma Pi (ranger 1998—2000), Sigma Xi (treas. Okla. State U. chpt. 2002—04, v.p. 2004—). Achievements include development of Shortleaf Pine Stand Simulator (SLPSS) for growth of shortleaf pine forests; Equations for moment of inertia, center of gravity, and weight of loblolly pine tree stems; Monte Carlo integration for tree volume estimation by cylindrical shells; Prediction equations for loblolly pine veneer yield and grade; Sampling design for trees in a great plains riparian area; research in Estimators for forest growth and volume from permanently established points; Formulas for log center of gravity; Distance sampling for forest inventory. Avocations: Christian prison ministry, music (mandolin). Office: Okla State U Dept Forestry Agricultural Hall Rm 008C Stillwater OK 74078 Office Phone: 405-744-5447. Business E-Mail: tlynch@okstate.edu.

LYNCH, THOMAS J., telecommunications industry executive; married; 4 children. B, Rider U. Joined Gen. Instrument, 1982, controller cable set-top unit, CFO cable set-top unit, v.p. mktg. distbn. sys., v.p., gne. mgr. transmission network sys. strategic bus. unit Hatboro, Pa., 1994—97, sr. v.p., gne. mgr. satellite and broadcast network sys. strategic bus. unit San Diego, 1997—2000; corp. v.p., gen. mgr. satellite and broadcast network sys. broadband comms. sector (formerly Gen. Instrument Corp.) Comms. Enterprise Motorola, Inc., 2000, exec. v.p., 2000—, pres. integrated electronic sys. sector Schaumburg, Ill., 2000—02, pres., CEO Personal Communications Sector (PCS), 2002—. Office: Motorola 1303 Algonquin Schaumburg IL 60196

LYNCH, THOMAS JOSEPH, museum director; b. Omaha, Nebr., Feb. 15, 1960; s. James Humphery and Patricia Mae (Gaughan) L. BA in History, U. Nebr., 1984. Mus. asst. Father Flanagan's Boys' Home, Boys Town, Nebr., 1986-88, mus. assoc., 1988-93; CEO, mgr. Boys Town Hall of History and Fr. Flanagan's House, 1993—. Mem. adv. bd. RSVP; bd. dirs. Union Pacific R.R. Mus. Mem. Am. Assn. for State and Local History, Am. Mus. Assn., Nebr. Mus. Assn. (bd. dirs., former pres.), Nat. Hist. Landmark Stewards Assn. Office: Boys Town Hall of History 14057 Flanagan Blvd Boys Town NE 68010-7509 Business E-Mail: lyncht@boystown.org.

LYNCH, THOMAS PETER, retired investment company executive; b. N.Y.C., May 3, 1924; s. Michael Joseph and Margaret Mary (Fitzgerald) L.; m. Madeleine D'Eufemia, June 3, 1950; children: Francine, Richard. Student, Syracuse U., 1943-44; BBA, Baruch Coll., 1947. Acct. Deloitte, Haskins & Sells, N.Y.C., 1947-56; partner Bache & Co., N.Y.C., 1956-61; v.p. E.F. Hutton Co. Inc., N.Y.C., 1962-67; sr. v.p. E.F. Hutton Group Inc., 1967-72, exec. v.p., 1972-83, pres., dir., 1983-85; ret., 1985. Pres., dir. Cash Res. Mgmt. Inc., 1976-85 Served with U.S. Army, 1943-46. Decorated Bronze Star. Mem. AICPA, Fin. Execs. Inst., Canoe Brook Country Club, Baltusrol Golf Club, Johns Island Club, Morris County Golf Club.

LYNCH, THOMAS WIMP, lawyer; b. Monmouth, Ill., Mar. 5, 1930; s. William Brennan and Mildred Maurine (Wimp) L.; m. Elizabeth J. McDonald, July 30, 1952; children: Deborah, Michael, Maureen, Karen, Kathleen. BS in Geology, U. Ill., 1955, MS in Geology, 1958, JD, 1959. Bar: Ill. 1960, Okla. 1960, U.S. Supreme Ct. 1971, Tex. 1978. Staff atty. Amerada Hess Corp., Tulsa, 1959-72, asst. gen. counsel, 1972-75; mem. Hall, Estill, Hardwick, Gable, Collingsworth & Nelson, Tulsa, 1975; v.p., gen. counsel Tex. Pacific Oil Co., Inc., Dallas, 1975-80, Oryx Energy Co., Dallas, 1980-94; ret., 1994. Adj. prof. law U. Tulsa, 1974; trustee Ctr. Am. and Internat. Law, chmn., lectr. ann. Oil and Gas Short course, 1976-92; adv. bd. Oil and Gas Edn. Ctr.; chmn. Oil, Gas and Energy Resources Law sect. State Bar of Tex., 1995-96. Served with USN, 1948-49, U.S. Army, 1951-53. Mem. ABA, Okla. Bar Assn., Tex. Bar Assn., Dallas County Bar Assn. Roman Catholic.

LYNCH, TIMOTHY JEREMIAH-MAHONEY, lawyer, educator, theologian, realtor, writer; b. June 10, 1952; s. Joseph David and Margaret Mary (Mahoney) L. MS, JD in Taxation, Golden Gate U., 1981; MA, PhD in Modern European History, U. San Francisco, 1983; Licentiate, Inter-Am. Acad., Rio de Janeiro, 1988; PhD in Classics and Divinity/Theology, Harvard U., 1988; JSD in Constl. Law, Hastings Law Ctr., 1990. Bar: D.C. 1989, Calif., U.S. Ct. Appeals (2d cir.) 1989, U.S. Ct. Appeals (4th cir.) 1990; mem. Bar/Outer Temple/Comml. Bar of U.K.; European Econ. Ct. of 1st Instance. Legal bus., tax, counsel Lynch Real Estate, San Francisco, 1981-85; researcher, writer Kolb, Roche & Sullivan, San Francisco, 1986-88; chmn. internat. law dept. Timothy J.M. Lynch & Assocs., San Francisco, 1987-88, chmn., mng. dir. law dept., 1988—. Chmn., pres., CEO Lynch Real Estate Investment Corp., San Francisco, 1989—; ptnr. Lynch Investment Corp.; bd. lawyer/arbitrators Pacific Coast Stock Exch., NASD, 1994—; chmn. bd. Lynch Holdings Corp. Group; corp. counsel, sr. ptnr. L.A. Ctr. Internat. Comml. Arbitration, 1991—; vis. fellow classics, Inst. of Classical Studies, U. London; rsch. prof. Canon law and ecumenical ch. history grad. Theological Union U. Calif. Berkeley, 1992—; vis. scholar Patristic theology and classical philosophy of ecumenical doctrines, U. Laval, Quebec, Can., 1993—; vis. scholar Medieval ch. history U. Leeds, Eng., 1993-95; del. lectr. 24th Internat. Congress Arts Comms., Kreble Coll., Oxford U., 1997; arbitrator Iran-U.S. Claims Tribunal, The Hague, 1993; mem. internat. corp. adv. bd. J.P. Morgan and Co., N.Y.C.; bd. dirs. Morgan-Stanley Corp., N.Y.C.; chmn. Latin Am., African and Middle East Corp. Groups J.P. Morgan Internat., Corp.; adv. bd. Morgan Stanley Corp., N.Y.C.; mem. Orgn. Econ. Cooperation and Devel., mem. adv. com. Internat. Labor Orgn.; participant Forum/A Group of Internat. Leaders, Calif., 1995, mem. adv. bd. U.S.-Saudi Arabia Bus. Coun., OECD on Industry and Fin., Paris, 1995, others; apptd. U.S. amb. Spl. Del. to Commn. Security/Coop. in Europe on Econ. and Pub. Reforms in Russian Republics;

participant World Outlook Conf. on 21st Century, 1995; mem. Nat. Planning Assns., Washington, Brit.-North Am. Com. on Econ. and Pub. Policy Planning, Global Econ. Coun.; mem. adv. bd. Nat. Bus. Leadership Coun., Washington; mem. Arbitration Tribunal, Geneva; judge World Intellectual Property Orgns.; selected arbitrator, mem. tribunal; mem. arbitration bd., panel of arbitrators NAFTA Trade Policy; mem. adv. com. on private internat. law U.S. State Dept., Washington; mem. Dead Sea Scrolls Rsch. Project, 1998; mem. author and writers group on multi-vol. transl. series classical works from late Roman, medieval near eastern, patristic and early Christian ch. periods Princeton U., 1998, Cath. U. Am., 1998, U. Calif., Berkely, 1998; rsch. prof. Old and New Testament bibl. lit. commentary, 1998. Author: (10 vol. manuscript) History of Ecumenical Doctrines and Canon Law of Church; editorial bd. Internat. Tax Jour., 1993; author: Publishers National Endowment for Arts and Humanities Classical Translations: Latin, Greek, and Byzantine Literary Texts for Modern Theological-Philosophical Analysis of Social Issues; Essays on Issues of Religious Ethics and Social, Public Policy Issues, 1995, 96, others; editorial bd. Internat. Tax Jour., 1993, Melrose Press: Internat. Firm; contbr. articles to profl. jours. Dir., vice chmn. Downtown Assn. San Francisco; councillor, dir. Atlantic Coun. U.S., 1984—; corp. counsel, chmn. spl. arbitrator's tribunal on U.S.-Brazil trade, fin. and banking rels. Inter-Am. Comml. Arbitration Commn., Washington; chmn. nat. adv. com. U.S.-Mid. East rels. U.S. Mid. East Policy Coun., U.S. State Dept., Washington, 1989—; mem. Pres. Bush's Adv. Commn. on Econ. and Public Policy Priorities, Washington, 1989; mem. conf. bd. Mid. East Policy Coun., U.S. State Dept., Washington, 1994—; elected mem. Coun. of Scholars U.S. Libr. Congress, Washington; bd. dirs. Internat. Diplomacy Coun., San Francisco Opera, Ballet, Symphony Assns. Recipient Cmty. Svc. honors Mayor Dianne Feinstein, San Francisco, 1987, Leadership awards St. Ignatius Coll. Prep., 1984, Calif.'s Gold State award, 1990, AU-ABA Achievement award, 1990, Medal of Honor Order Internat. Ambs. Com. U.S. State Dept. and Foreign Svc. Inst., Washington D.C., World Lifetime Achievement award, Induction 20th Century Millenium Hall Fame and Dist. Leadership Hall Fame Am. Acad. Achievement, 1998, award Superior Talent in Bus. and Arts, Century Dist. Acheivement award, Am. Acad. Achievement, 1998, Internat. Cultural award, 1997, Presdl. Seal Honor, 1997, Decree Internat. Cultural Letters, 1997; named Civic Leader of Yr., Nat. Trust for Hist. Preservation, 1988, 89; named to Presdl. Order of Merit, 1991., Induction U.S. Lib. Congress 500 Leaders of Influence Hall Fame, 1998, Noble Installation Orders of Knighthood Royal British Legions by Queen Elizabeth II, 1998. Fellow World Jurist Assn., World Assn. Judges (Washington); mem. ATLA, Internat. Bar Assn. (various coms., internat. litigation, taxation, labor issue), Am. Arbitration Assn. (panelist, internat. decree), Am. Fgn. Law Assn. (various coms.), Am. Soc. Ch. History, Am. Inst. Archaeology (Boston), Pontifical Inst. Medieval Studies (Toronto, Can.), Am. Hist. Assn., Am. Philol. Assn., Inst. European Law, Medieval Acad. Am., U.S. Supreme Ct. Hist. Soc. (presdl. seal of honor, cultural diploma honor), J Canon Law Soc. U.S., Nat. Planning Assn., Nat. Assn. Scholars (Eminent Scholar of Yr. 1993), Netherlands Arbitration Inst. (mem. Gen. Panels of Arbitrators, mem. Permanent Ct. Arbitration), Calif. Coun. Internat. Trade (GATT com., tax com., legis. com.), Practicing Law Inst., Am. Fgn. Law Assn. (mem. editl. bd. Working Groups on Rsch. Jour. for Legal systems of Africa, Mid. East, Latin Am., EEC and Soviet Union), U.S.-China Bus. Coun. (export com., GATT com., banking and fin. com., import com.), Bay Area Coun. (corp. mem.), Nat. Acad. Conciliators (Spl. award), Internat. Bar (mem. U.S. Group on Model on Insolvency Corp. Acts), Ctr. Internat. Comml. Arbitration, Comml. Club (various positions), Am. Venture Capital Assn., Pacific Venture Capital Assn., Am. Soc. Internat. Law, Washington Fgn. Law Soc., Asia-Pacific Lawyers Assn., Soc. Profls. in Dispute Resolution, British Inst. Internat. and Comparative Law, Internat. Law Assn. (U.S. br.), Commercial Bar Assn. of United Kingdom (London), Inter-Pacific Bar Assn. (Tokyo; mem. arbitration intellectual property, consitutional taxation, labor, legal groups), Inst. European Law Faculty of Laws (United Kingdom), Urban Land Inst. Internat., Mid. East Inst. (Am.-Arab Affairs Coun.), Inter-Am. Bar Assn., 1987—, Calif. Trial Lawyers Assn., Ctr. Reformation Rsch. (co-chmn. Calif. State Com. on U.S-Mid. East Econ. and Polit. Rels.), Soc. Biblical Lit., Am. Acad. Arts and Letters, Am. Acad. Religion, World Lit. Acad., Coun. Scholars, Am. Com. on U.S.-Japan Rels., Japan Soc. No. Calif., Pan-Am. Assn. San Francisco, Soc. Indsl./Office Realtors, Assn. Entertainment Lawyers London, Royal Chartered Inst. Arbitrators (London), Soc. Indsl. and Office Realtors, Urban Land Inst., San Francisco Realtors Assn., Calif. Realtors Assn., Coun. Fgn. Rels., Chgo. Coun. Fgn. Rels., Conf. Bd., San Francisco Urban and Planning Assn., U.S. Trade Facilitation Coun., Asia Soc., Am. Petroleum Inst., Internat. Platform Assn., San Francisco C. of C. (bus. policy com., pub. policy com., co-chmn. congl. issues study group), Am. Inst. Diplomacy, Overseas Devel. Coun. (Mid. East, Russian Republics, Latin Am. studies group), Internat. Vis. Ctr. (adv. bd.), Fin. Execs. Inst., Nat. Assn. Corp. Dirs., Heritage Found. (bd. dirs.), Archaeological Inst. Am. (fellow coun. near east studies, Egyptology), Am. Literature Judicature Soc., Soc. of Biblical, Nat. Assn. Indsl. and Office Properties, World Literary Acad. (Cambridge, Eng.), Am. Acad. Arts & Letters, Am. Acad. Religion, Pres. Club, Nat. Assn. Bus. Economists, Villa Taverna Club, Palm Beach Yacht Club, Pebble Beach Tennis Club, Calif. Yacht Club, Commonwealth Club, City Club San Francisco, British Bankers Club, London, San Diego Track Club (registered athlete), Crow Canyon Country Club (bd. dirs.), Western Venture Capital Assn., Am. Venture Capital Assn., Authors Guild, Internat. Pen Soc., diplomate-delegate World Econ. Summit Conf., Paris, 1998, IOSECC Conf. Internat. Org. Securities Conf., Paris, 1998. Republican. Roman Catholic; Clubs: Crow Canyon Country Club, The Players. Avocations: theater, social entertainment events, opera, ballet, fine arts. Home: 501 Forest Ave Ste 108 Palo Alto CA 94301-2631

LYNCH, VICTOR K., lawyer; b. Latrobe, Pa., Sept. 9, 1929; s. Victor E. and Helen (Kamerer) L.; m. Jane Louise Sutherland, June 11, 1951 (div. 1970); children: G. Michael, Janet L. Mutschler, Steven J., David J., Thomas S., Victoria A. Dahmm. BS in Sanitary Engring., Pa. State U., 1951; LLD, Duquesne U., 1958. Bar: Pa. 1959. Design engr., constrn. insp. Chester Engrs., Pitts., 1953—54, project engr., 1954—58; assoc. Burgwin, Ruffin, Perry & Pohl, Pitts., 1958—62; ptnr. Ruffin, Perry, Springer, Hazlett & Lynch, Pitts., 1962—70; assoc. Litman, Litman, Harris & Specter, P.A., Pitts., 1971—74, Lynch, Lynch, Carr & Kabala, Pitts., 1974—78; ptnr. Lynch and Lynch, Pitts., 1978—. 1st lt. USAF, 1951-53. Recipient Bedell award Water Pollution Control Fedn., 1973. Mem. Water Pollution Control Assn. of Pa. (pres. 1972-73, Sludge Shoveler's award 1970, Johnny Clearwater award 1971), Pa. Soc. Profl. Engrs. Home: 1000 Grandview Ave Pittsburgh PA 15211-1362 Office: 403 Times Bldg 336 4th Ave Pittsburgh PA 15222-2004

LYNCH, WILLIAM J., career officer; b. Columbus, Ohio, Mar. 25, 1947; m. Marie E. Noser; three children. BS in Biology, John Carroll U., 1969; MD, Ohio State U., 1973. Commd. ensign USN; advanced through ranks to rear adm. USNR; family practice resident Naval Hosp., Jacksonville, Fla., 1973-79; pvt. practice Jacksonville Beach, Fla., 1979—; various assignments to chief of staff, asst. fleet support N931R, OPNAV. Decorated Meritorious Svc. medal with gold star, Nat. Def. medal with bronze star, Armed Forces Res. medal with silver hour glass, others. Mem. Naval Res. Assn. (life).

LYNCH, WILLIAM JOSEPH, lawyer; b. Providence, July 13, 1957; s. Dennis M. and Irene M. (MacIsaac) L.; m. Lynn M. Perna, Feb. 14, 1986; children: Jarred, Blair. BA, Brandeis U., 1979; JD, Suffolk U., 1982. Bar: R.I. 1982, U.S. Dist. Ct. R.I. 1984, U.S. Supreme Ct. 1988. Asst. atty. gen., dir. consumer protection Dept. Atty. Gen., Providence, 1983—85; lawyer Blais Cunningham Crowe & Chester, Pawtucket, RI, 1985—92, McIntyre, Tate, Lynch and Holt, Providence, 1992—. Mem. Pawtucket (R.I.) City Coun., 1986-92; vice chmn., dir. Sargent Rehab. Ctr., Providence, 1988—; dir. Boys & Girls Club, Pawtucket, 1988—, St. Raphael Acad., Pawtucket, 1989—; chmn. R.I. Dem. State Com., 1998—. Named R.I. Ethic Fellow R.I. Inst. for Internat. Sport, 1993. Office: McIntyre Tate Lynch and Holt 321 S Main St Providence RI 02903-7108 Office Phone: 401-351-7700.

LYNCH, WILLIAM REDINGTON, lawyer; b. N.Y.C., Nov. 17, 1928; s. Francis Russell Vincent and Helen Adams (Barrett) L.; m. Mary Pomeroy Grant, Aug. 22, 1958; children: Melissa L. Woolford, Elizabeth Barrett, Cynthia Pomeroy, Kimberly Townsend, Sarah Phillips. Student, Phillips Exeter Acad., 1944-47; BA, Yale U., 1951; JD, Columbia U., 1958. Bar: N.Y. 1959, Conn. 1963. Assoc. Milbank Tweed Hadley & McCloy, N.Y.C., 1958-62, Cummings & Lockwood, Stamford, Conn., 1962-66, ptnr., 1966—, ptnr. in charge Greenwich office, 1978-88. Bd. dirs. Greenwich Plaza Inc., 1970-74, Harrison & Ellis Inc., Cairo, Ga., 1985-87, Greenwich News Inc., 1986-90; chmn. ADM Mgmt. Corp., 1989-91. Chmn. Pub. Works Com., Greenwich, 1974-77, Greenwich United Way Campaign, 1975-76; vice chmn. Greenwich Bd. Edn., 1977-81, Rep. Town Meeting, 1967-77, dir., sec. Forum World Affairs, 1992-95. Lt. USNR, 1952-56. Mem. ABA, Conn. Bar Assn., Greenwich Bar Assn. (pres. 1979-80), Greenwich Field Club (pres. 1973-75), Round Hill Club (dir., sec. 1993-96). Congregationalist. Home: 100 Bedford Rd Greenwich CT 06831-2535 Office: Cummings & Lockwood 2 Greenwich Plz Ste 5 Greenwich CT 06830-6390 Office Phone: 203-863-6508.

LYNCH, WILLIAM THOMAS, JR., advertising agency executive; b. Evergreen Park, Ill., Dec. 3, 1942; s. William T. and Loretta J. L.; m. Kathleen; children: Kelly, Maureen, Kim, Meagan, Molly. BA, Loras Coll., 1964; MBA, U. Iowa, 1966. Media trainee Leo Burnett Co. Inc., Chgo., 1966-68, asst. account exec., 1968-76, v.p., 1976-79, sr. v.p., 1979-82, exec. v.p., 1981—86; vice chmn. Leo Burnett USA, Chgo., 1985-89, chmn., CEO, 1987—91; pres. Leo Burnett Worldwide, Chgo., 1993; CEO, pres. Leo Burnett Worldwide, Leo Burnett Co. Inc., Chgo., 1993-97; pres., CEO Liam Holdings, Prospect Heights, Ill., 1997—. Bd. dirs. Pella Corp., Krispy Kreme Doughnut Corp., SEI Info. Tech., Smurfit-Stone Container Corp. Bd. dir. U. Chgo. Grad. Sch. Bus., Northwestern Meml. Found.; bd. dirs., mem. exec. com. Big Shoulders Archdiocese of Chgo., Loras Coll. Mem. Econ. Club Chgo., Comml. Club Chgo. Roman Catholic. Avocations: running, skiing, gardening, golf. Office: Liam Holdings 206 N Pine St Prospect Heights IL 60070-1524

LYNCH, WILLIAM WALKER, banker; b. Washington, Sept. 18, 1926; s. Talbott and Gertrude (Farrell) L.; m. Barbara Van Sant, Apr. 21, 1951; children: John S., William Walker, Franklin P., Mark F. BA, George Washington U., 1950. Vice pres., treas., dir. Met. Mortgage Co., Washington, 1950-55; dir., mem. exec. com. Prog. Fed. Savs. & Loan Assn., Washington, 1953-58; v.p., treas., dir. Anderson & Co., Inc., Washington, 1953-59; with First Bank of Fla., West Palm Beach, Fla., 1959-98, exec. v.p., 1966-89, pres., chief exec. officer, 1989-94, chmn. bd., 1994-98. Chmn. 1st Palm Beach Bancorp., 1994-98; mem. tournament com. 53d PGA Championship, 1971; mem. tournament com. 19th World Cup, Internat. Golf Assn., 1971, 69th PGA Championship, 1987; dist. dir. Fla. League Fin. Instns., 1991; dir. Fed. Home Loan Bank of Atlanta, 1991-94; bd. dirs. Fla. Bankers Assn., 1994. Treas. Herbert Hoover Dike Dedication com., 1960; Asst. treas. Fla. Kennedy-Johnson campaign, 1960; bd. dirs. Am. Cancer Soc., 1967-69, 79—, hon. life dir. local United Way, 1962-64; trustee Media Rsch. Ctr.; hon. trustee Parent's T.V. Coun. With USNR, 1944-46. Recipient Free Enterprise Companion medal Palm Beach Atlantic Coll., 1989. Mem. West Palm Beach C. of C. (bd. dirs. 1970), Kiwanis (bd. dirs. West Palm Beach club 1961, v.p. 1970-71, pres. 1971-72), No. Palm Beach Country Club, Palm Beach Yacht Club, Pi Kappa Alpha. Republican. Roman Catholic. Home: 1032 Country Club Dr North Palm Beach FL 33408-3716

LYNCH, WILLIAM WRIGHT, JR., investment company executive, engineer; b. Dallas, Aug. 26, 1936; s. William Wright Sr. and Alma Martha (Hirsch) L.; m. June 11, 1960; children: Mary Margaret, Katherine. BSEE, U. Ariz., 1959; MBA, Stanford U., 1962. Pres. Ins. Bldg. Corp., Dallas, 1965-84; ptnr. Estacado Ptnrs., Dallas, 1985—, Encino Co., Dallas, 1970—, Cimarron Properties Co., Tucson, 1972-83. Pres., bd. dirs. Argus Realty Corp., Dallas, 1972—; bd. dirs. Lynch Properties Inc., Dallas, Lynch Investment Co., Dallas, Fleetwood Transp. Svcs., Inc., Dallas; adv. dir. Sun Valley Fruit Co., Albuquerque, LTD Enersyst Devel. Ctr., Inc., Dallas, 1995-98, TEWA Mouldings, Albuquerque, 1997-2004, Hacienda Packing, Albuquerque. Bd. dirs. Dallas Symphony Orch., 1966-74, Dallas Civic Music, 1970-77, Ednl. Opportunities Inc., Dallas, 1973-90, Dallas Coun. World Affairs, 1990-96; trustee W. W. Lynch Found., Dallas, 1968—. Capt. U.S. Army, 1959-60. Mem.: M.O. Club (Tucson), Verandah Club, Brook Hollow Club. Republican. Episcopalian. Office: Lynch Investment Co Ste 1600 LB-16 1845 Woodall Rodgers Fwy Dallas TX 75201-2295 Personal E-mail: w.w.lynch@sbcglobal.net.

LYNCHESKI, JOHN E., lawyer; b. Throop, Pa., Sept. 10, 1945; s. John W. and Laura B. (Oshetski) L.; m. Kathy D. Penhale, Aug. 26, 1967; children: John H., Marc E., Kristin E. BA in Econs., Cornell U., 1967; JD, U. Pitts., 1970. Bar: Pa. 1970, Fla. 1974, U.S. Supreme Ct. 1982, U.S. Ct. Appeals (3d cir.) 1970, U.S. Dist. Ct. (we. and mid. dists.) Pa. 1970. Assoc. Reed Smith Shaw & McClay, Pitts., 1970-71, 74-81; USN judge advocate Gen. Corps, Pensacola, Fla., 1971-74; dir. Manion Alder & Cohen, Pitts., 1981-84, Alder Cohen & Grigsby, Pitts., 1984-89. Mem. bd. visitors Robert Morris Coll. Sch. Mgmt., 1997-98; health adv. bd. U. Pitts. Sch. Law, 1996—; steering com. Law Fellows Sch. Law, 1992-98. Pres. Allegheny Beaver United Soccer, Pitts., 1986-94; bd. dirs., legal coun. Jaycees, Pa., 1977-78, pres., Upper St. Clair, 1976-77; mem. Chartiers Valley Adv. Bd. Lt. USNR. Mem. Am. Arbitration Assn. (nat. panel), Fed. Bar Assn., Pa. Bar Assn. (labor law com., health care law com., alternative dispute resolution com.), Fla. Bar Assn. (labor law sect.), Allegheny County Bar Assn. (labor and employment law sect., health law sect.) Am. Health Lawyers Assn. (chmn. labor and employment practice group. long term care practice group), Soc. for Human Resource Mgmt., Am. Soc. on Aging, Am. Hosp. Assn. Am. Soc. for Healthcare Risk Mgmt., Assisted Living Fedn. Am., Am. Coll. Healthcare Adminstrs. (pres. Pa. chpt.), Am. Soc. for Healthcare Human Resources Adminstrn. (nat. spkrs. bur.), W.Va. Healthcare Human Resources Assn., Federalist Soc., Am. Health Lawyers Assn., Alternative Dispute Resolution Svc., Bus. Dispute Resolution Alliance, Pa. Govs. Sportsmen's Adv. Coun., Chartiers Country Club (bd. dirs., pres.), Sewickley Heights Golf Club. Avocations: soccer, golf, hunting, fishing, outdoors. Office: Cohen & Grigsby PC 11 Stanwix St 15th Flr Pittsburgh PA 15222-1312 also: Ste 309 27200 Riverview Ctr Blvd Bonita Springs FL 34134

LYND, PHYLLIS, artist, educator; b. NYC, June 27, 1946; d. Louis and Frances (Orenbach) Leshaw; m. Edward Reed, Feb. 16, 1968 (div. 1969). B in French, Bklyn. Coll., 1966; MusM, Manhattan Sch. Music, 1972. Singer WGYN-FM, WQXR, BBC-TV, CBS, 1970—95; writer Boston Music, 1975—90; prodr. Longway Prodn., NYC, 1980—85; tchr. Ethical Culture, Hunter Coll., 2001—. Author: (instrn. book) Instant Folk Guitar, 1975, (musical revue) I've Come a Long Way, 1978; composer, lyricist: musical comedy I Love You Mme. President, 1985, composer, lyricist, librettist: Good God, 2001; performer: (CD) When I Fall in Love, 1998. Named Arthur Godfrey winner, NYC, 1965, CBS, NYC, 1968; scholar Scholarship, Nat. Music League, 1962; Philharm. scholar, NYC, 1959. Mem.: AFTRA, SAG, ASCAP (6 awards), Dramatist Guild. Achievements include reversing an antiquated cabaret law prohibiting instrumentalists from singing in restaurants; this new law (Cabaret Amendment of 1971) allowed singers to be hired in restaurants, launching many careers and giving singers exposure in N.Y.C. Office Phone: 212-873-5173.

LYNDALL, JANICE THOMPSON, vocational counselor; b. Mobile, Ala., Feb. 13, 1945; d. Sam M. and Julia H. Thompson; 1 child, Daniel T. Lyndall. BA in Psychology, U. South Ala., 1989, MS in Counseling, 1991. Cert. rehab. counselor, lic. profl. counselor, lic. bachelor social worker. Rehab. counselor Dept. Rehab. Svcs., Mobile, 1989-98; program mgr. Goodwill Easter Seals, Mobile, 1998—. Recipient Svc. award, Ind. Living Ctr., Mobile, 1994, 95. Mem. Nat. Rehab. Assn. (counselor divsn.), Ala. Rehab. Assn. (counselor divsn.), Mobile Lic. Profl. Counselor Assn., Friends of the Libr., Tillman's Corner Area C. of C. (bd. mem. 2000—), West Mobile Kiwanis. Baptist. Avocations: painting, writing poetry and fiction, arts and crafts, collectibles.

LYNDRUP, PEGGY B., lawyer; b. Winnipeg, Can., Mar. 27, 1949; BS in Edn. magna cum laude, U. N.D., 1969; MEd, Kent State U., 1971; JD summa cum laude, U. Louisville, 1979. Bar: Ky. 1979, U.S. Dist. Ct. (we. dist.) Ky. 1979, U.S. Dist. Ct. (ea. dist.) Ky. 1981. Atty. Greenebaum Doll & McDonald, PLLC, Louisville, 1979—. Recipient Disting. Alumnus award U. Louisville Sch. Law, 1989; Brandeis scholar. Mem. ABA, Louisville Bar Assn. (pres. 1989). Office: Greenbaum Doll & McDonald PLLC 3300 National City Tower Louisville KY 40202 E-mail: pbl@gdm.com.

LYNDS, GAYLE HALLENBECK, writer, editor; b. Omaha, June 23; d. Paul Duane and Marian Lucille (Tice) Hallenbeck; m. Thomas F. Stone, Aug. 14, 1966 (div. 1984); children: Paul F. Stone, Julia L. Stone; m. Dennis Lynds, Feb. 14, 1986. BA in Journalism, U. Iowa, 1967. Reporter Ariz. Rep., Phoenix, 1967; editor, rsch. asst. Iowa Ctr. for Edn. in Politics, Iowa City, 1968; editor GE-Tempo, Santa Barbara, Calif., 1968—71, Santa Barbara Mag., 1983—86, Prime Mag., Santa Barbara, 1986—89. Tchr. creative writing courses U. Calif., Santa Barbara, Pima Coll., Tucson, Asilomar Writing Conf., Monterey, Calif., So. Calif. Writers Conf., San Diego, others. Author: Masquerade, 1996, Mosaic, 1998, (with Robert Ludlum) The Hades Factor, 2000, Mesmerized, 2001, (with Robert Ludlum) The Paris Option, 2002, (with Robert Ludlum) The Altman Code, 2003, The Coil, 2004, I'd Kill For That (contbr. first chpt., edited by Mardla Talley), 2004 Mem. Authors Guild, Mystery Writers Am., Internat. Crime Writers, Internat. Thriller Writers, Inc. (co-founder)

LYNE, ADRIAN, film director; b. Peterborough, Cambridgeshire, Eng., Mar. 4, 1941; Dir. feature films: Foxes, 1980, Flashdance, 1983, 9 1/2 Weeks, 1986, Fatal Attraction, 1987 (Acad. award nomination), Jacob's Ladder, 1990, Indecent Proposal, 1993, Lolita, 1996, Unfaithful, 2002. Mem. Dirs. Guild Am.

LYNE, DOROTHY-ARDEN, secondary school educator; b. Orangeburg, N.Y., Mar. 9, 1928; d. William Henry and Janet More (Freston) Dean; m. Thomas Delmar Lyne, Aug. 16, 1952 (div. June 1982); children: James Delmar, Peter Freston, Jennifer Dean. BA, Ursinus Coll., 1949; MA, Fletcher Sch. Law and Diplomacy, 1950. Assoc. editor World Peace Found., Boston, 1950-51; editorial assoc. Carnegie Endowment Internat. Peace, N.Y.C., 1951-52; dir. Assoc. of Internat. Rels. Clubs, N.Y.C., 1952-53; editor The Town Crier, Westport, Conn., 1966-68; editorial assoc. Machinery Allied Products Inst., Wash., 1959-63; tchr. Helen Keller Mid. Sch., Easton, Conn., 1967-89. Vice chmn. Cooperative Ednl. Svcs., Fairfield, 1983-85. Editor: Documents in American Foreign Rels., 1950, Current Rsch. in Internat. Affairs, 1951. Chmn. Westport Zoning Bd. of Appeals, 1976-80, Westport Bd. of Edn., 1985-87; vice chmn. Westport Bd. of Edn., 1980-85; mem. Westport Charter Revision Commn., 1966-67. Democrat. Episcopalian.

LYNE, SUSAN MARKHAM, multi-media company executive, former broadcast executive; b. Boston, Apr. 30, 1950; d. Eugene and Ruth (Lally) L.; m. George Crile III; children: Susan Markham, Jane Halle; stepchildren: Katherine Murphy, Elizabeth McCook. Assoc. editor City Mag., San Francisco, 1975-76; west coast editor New Times, San Francisco, 1976-77, mng. editor NYC, 1978, The Village Voice, NYC, 1978-82; v.p. creative devel. IPC Films, NYC, 1982-85; ptnr. Lazar/Lyne Films, NYC, 1985-86; founder Premiere mag., NYC, 1987-96, editor-in-chief, publication dir., 1987—96; exec. v.p. acquisitions, development, and new bus. Walt Disney Motion Picture Group, 1996—98; exec. v.p. movies and miniseries ABC Entertainment, 1998—2002, pres., 2002—04; pres., CEO Martha Stewart Living Omnimedia, Inc., dir., 2004—. Bd. dirs. Lifetime Network, 1996—, Pub. Theater. Mem. Am. Soc. Mag. Editors (bd. dirs. 1993-96). Oversaw the development of recent hits including "Desperate Housewives", "Lost" and "Extreme Makeover, Home Edition". Also guided other programs, including "8 Simple Rules for Dating My Teenage Daughter", "The Bachelor" and "Hope and Faith".

LYNESS, JEFFREY MARC, psychiatrist, educator; b. Arlington, Va., June 18, 1960; married. BA, U. Rochester, 1983, MD, 1986. Diplomate Am. Bd. Psychiatry and Neurology, Am. Bd. Geriatric Psychiatry. Intern U. Rochester Med. Ctr., NY, 1986—87; resident Yale U., New Haven, 1987—90; fellow geriatric psychiatry U. Rochester Med. Ctr., Rochester, NY, 1990—91, sr. instr., fellow, 1990—93, asst. prof., 1993—99, assoc. prof., 1999—, chair third and fourth yr. instrn. com., 1996—2002, dir. program geriat. and neuropsychiatry, dir. med. student edn. psychiatry, 1999—, dir. geriatric psychiatry fellowship, 2000—. Author: Psychiatric Pearls, 1997. Recipient Young Investigator award, Nat. Alliance Rsch. Schizophrenia and Depression, 1999. Fellow: Gerontol. Soc. Am., Am. Psychiat. Assn. (Nancy C. A. Roeske, MD cert. Recognition 1997, Distinguished Fellow 2003); mem.: Internat. Psychogeriatrics Assn., Assn. Dirs. Med. Student Edn. Psychiatry, Internat. Coll. Geriatric Psychopharmacology, Am. Assn. Geriatric Psychiatry, Alpha Omega Alpha, Phi Beta Kappa. Office: U Rochester Med Ctr 300 Crittenden Blvd Rochester NY 14642

LYNETT, WILLIAM RUDDY, publishing, broadcasting company executive; b. Scranton, Pa., Jan. 18, 1947; s. Edward James and Jean O'Hara Lynett; m. Mary Jean Foley; children: Scott, Jennifer, Christopher P., Brigid P., Jean O. BS, U. Scranton, 1972. Pub. Scranton Times, 1966—; pres., chief exec. officer Shamrock Communications, Inc., 1971—; pres. Towanda Daily Rev., 1977-81, Owego Pennysaver Press, Inc., 1977-81. Owner, Pres. Mgmt. Program, Harvard U., 1990; vice-chmn. bd. dirs. WVIA TV. Bd. dirs. Cmty. Med. Ctr., Scranton, 1974—96; pres. Scranton Cultural Ctr.; chmn. Mayor's Libr. Fund Drive, 1974; chmn. spl. gifts divsn. Heart Fund, 1975; chmn. United Way of Lackawanna County, 1988; bd. govs. Scranton Area Found., chmn., 1996—97; trustee U. Scranton, 1990—96; chmn. Steamtown Nat. Pk. Grand Opening Com.; mem. exec. com. N.E. coun. Boy Scouts Am. Mem. Nat. Assn. Broadcasters, Pa. Assn. Broadcasters, Am. Newspaper Pubs. Assn., Pa. Newspaper Pubs. Assn., Greater Scranton C. of C. (chmn. membership drive 1980-81) Clubs: Scranton Country, Elks, K.C. Democrat. Roman Catholic. Office: 149 Penn Ave Scranton PA 18503-2022 Office Phone: 570-348-9107. E-mail: blynett@timeslamrock.com.

LYNGBYE, JØRGEN, hospital advisor, researcher; b. Andst, Denmark, July 23, 1929; arrived in Norway, 1988, permanent resident; s. Knud and Estrid Marie Schou (Nielsen) L.; m. Ulla von Holstein, July 15, 1967 (div. 1982); 1 child, Rie; m. Jintana Detwilaiphong, Jan. 3, 1994. MD, U. Copenhagen, 1956; PhD, U. Arhus, Denmark, 1969. Asst. U. Arhus, 1957-65; asst. prof. U. Copenhagen, 1966-72; sr. cons. Regional Hosp., Frederiksborg, Denmark, 1973-83, Førde, Norway, 1983; assoc. prof. molecular biology, 1984—89; prof. U. Thailand, 1990—91; dir. Regional Hosp., Molde, Norway, 1991—98; sci. advisor Copenhagen, 1999—. Author: Clinical Biochemistry, 1986, Twins--A Unique World Scenario, 1995, Norwegian Handbook of Laboratory Medicine, 1999, Danish Textbook of Laboratory Medicine, 2001, Niels Finsen, A Danish Nobel Prize Laureate, 2003, Ole Roemer, The Scientist, A Biography, 2004; contbr. articles to sci. jours. and newspapers. Sec. Danish Polit. Orgn., Copenhagen, 1977-81. Lt. Danish Army, 1951-66. Decorated WEO Order (Thailand); recipient prize Danish Sci. Soc., 1978, Prix Scientifique, France, 1980, prize Danish Soc. for Protection of Animals, 1987, Applied Physics award, 1993. Mem. Danish Med. Assn. (rep. 1978-83). Avocations: world ecology, philosophy, mathematics, nuclear physics, music. E-mail: jlyngbye.professor@mail.tele.dk.

LYNHAM, C(HARLES) RICHARD, manufacturing executive; b. Easton, Md., Feb. 24, 1942; s. John Cameron and Anna Louise (Lynch) L.; m. Elizabeth Joy Card, Sept. 19, 1964; children: Jennifer Beth, Thomas Richard. BME, Cornell U., 1965; MBA with distinction, Harvard U., 1969. Sales mgr. Nat. Carbide Die Co., McKeesport, Pa., 1969-71; v.p. sales Sinter-Met Corp., North Brunswick, N.J., 1971-72; sr. mgmt. analyst Am. Cyanamid Co., Wayne, N.J., 1972-74; gen. mgr. ceramics and additives div. Foseco Inc., Cleve., 1974-77, dir. mktg. steel mill products group, 1977-79; pres., chief exec. officer Exomet, Inc. subs. Foseco, Inc., Conneaut, Ohio, 1979-81, Fosbel Inc. subs. Foseco, Inc., Cleve., 1981-82; gen. mgr. splty. ceramics group Ferro Corp., Cleve., 1982-84, group v.p. splty. ceramics, 1984-92; owner, pres. Harbor Castings, Inc., North Canton, Ohio, 1992—, Island Castings, Inc., Muskegon, Mich., 2000—; owner, CEO Blue Ridge Castings, Inc., Piney Flats, Tenn., 2000—. Bd. dirs. Western Res. Bancorp., Inc. Patentee foundry casting ladle, desulphurization of metals. Past pres. bd. trustees Hospice of Medina County; treas., past pres. bd. trustees Bridge-sHome Health Care. Capt. C.E., U.S. Army, 1965-67. Decorated Bronze Star with one oak leaf cluster; recipient Frank H.T. Rhodes Exemplary Alumni Svc. award, Cornell U., 1999. Mem. Am. Foundrymen's Soc., Cornell U. Alumni Coun., Cornell U. Alumni Class 1963 (past v.p., past pres.), Cornell U. Alumni Fedn. (past pres., bd. dirs., past v.p.), Chippewa Yacht Club (commodore 1982), Cornell Club of N.E. Ohio (past pres., bd. dirs.), Harbor Bay Yacht Club. Republican. Congregationalist. Avocations: sailing, genealogy. Home: 970 Hickory Grove Ave Medina OH 44256-1616 Office: Harbor Castings Inc 4321 Strausser St NW North Canton OH 44720-7144

LYNKER, JOHN PAUL, newscaster; b. Bklyn., Aug. 30, 1927; s. Paul Warren and Evelyn Foland (Briggs) L.; m. Linda Ann Cairrao, Sept. 26, 1992; children: Roger John, Denise Suzanne Lynker Duclos, John Paul Jr., Whitney Ellen Lynker Trifiletti. Student, Steven's Inst. Tech., 1944, 46, Columbia U., 1946-49. News anchor WPAT Radio, Paterson, N.J., 1951-52, Sta. WVNJ, Newark, 1952-56, WWJ Radio, Detroit, 1960-65, KGO Radio (ABC), San Francisco, 1971-75, WEEI Radio (CBS), Boston, 1975-80, WTOP Radio, Washington, 1980—; pres., gen. mgr. WSKN (now WGHQ), Kingston, N.Y., 1956-60; freelance newscaster N.Y.C., 1965-71. Pres. The Programmers, N.Y.C., 1965-71. Bd. dirs. Arthritis Found., Washington; pres. Res. Officers' Assn., Boston, 1973, Washington, 1982; deacon Reformed Ch. of Am. Capt. USCGR, 1959-85. Recipient Legend award Washington Area Broadcasters Assn., 1992. Mem. VFW, Washington Automotive Press Assn. (pres. 1990-91), Internat. Motor Press Assn., Aircraft Owner and Pilots Assn., Radio and TV Corrs. Assn., Nat. Press Club, White House Corrs. Assn. Avocations: flying, boating, old cars. Office: WTOP Radio 3400 Idaho Ave NW Ste B Washington DC 20016-3046

LYNN, D. JOANNE, physician, researcher; b. Oakland, Md., July 2, 1951; d. John B. and Mary Dorcas (Clark) Harley; m. Barry W. Lynn; children: Christina, Nicholas. BS summa cum laude, Dickinson Coll., 1970; MD cum laude, Boston U., 1974; MA in Philosophy and Social Policy, George Washington U., 1981; MS Clin. Evaluative Scis., Dartmouth Coll., 1995. Diplomate Am. Bd. Internal Medicine. Resident internal Medicine The George Washington U. Med. Ctr., 1974-77; emergency rm. physician, triage physician Washington VA Hosp., 1977-78; faculty assoc. for medicine and humanities divsn. experimental programs George Washington U., Washington, 1978-81, dir. divsn. aging studies, 1988-92, prof. health care scis. and medicine, 1991-92, assoc. chairperson dept. health care scis., 1990-92, dir of the Ctr. to Improve the Care of the Dying, 1995-2000; prof. medicine, cmty. and family medicine, sr. assoc. Ctr. Evaluative Clin. Scis. Dartmouth-Hitchcock Med. Ctr., Hanover, N.H., 1992-95, assoc. dir. Ctr. for Aging, 1992-95; dir. RAND Ctr. to Improve Care of the Dying, Arlington, Va., 2000—02; pres. Ams. for Better Care of the Dying, 1995—2005; dir. The Washington Home Ctr. for Palliative Care Studies, 2002—05; sr. natural scientist RAND, 2005—. Robert Wood Johnson clin. scholar George Washington U., 1977-78, sr. fellow Ctr. Health Policy Rsch., 1991-92; asst. dir. med. studies The Pres. Commn. for Study of Ethical Problems in Medicine and Biomed. and Behavioral Rsch., 1981-83; med. dir. The Washington Home, 1983-89, Hospice of Washington, 1979-91, George Washington Cancer Home Care Program and Home Health Svcs. of The Washington Home, 1990-92, staff physician, 1979-92; fellow Hastings Ctr., 1984—; mem. working group on guidelines for care of terminally ill, 1985-87, rsch. project on ethical issues in care and treatment of chronically ill, 1985-87, working group on new physician-patient relationship, 1991-94, v.p., 1987, chair fellows nominating com., 1991; mem. coordinating coun. on life-sustaining med. treatment decision making by cts. Nat. Ctr. State Cts., 1989-93; fellow Kennedy Inst., 1991; mem. geriat. and gerontology adv. com. Dept. Vet. Affairs, 1991-97; mem. bioethics com. Vets. Health Adminstrn., 1991-93; active Washington Area Seminar on Sci., Tech., and Ethics, 1982-92, Nat. Clin. Panel on High-Cost Hospice Care, Washington, 1991; presenter in field. Author: (with J. Harrold) Handbook for Mortals: Guidance for People Facing Serious Illness, 1999, (with A. Kabenell and J. Lynch Schuster) Improving Care for the End of Life: A Sourcebook for Health Care Managers and Clinicians, 2000, Sick to Death and Not Going to Take It Any More, 2004; author chpts. to books; mem. editl. bd. The Ency. of Bioethics, 1994-95; mem. adv. editl. bd. Biolaw, 1983, The Hospice Jour., 1984—, Med. Ethics for the Physician, 1985-92, Med. Humanities Rev., 1986—, Cambridge Quar., 1991-95; contbr. articles, revs. to profl. jours. Peter Jeffries and Jeanne Arnold scholar, 1973; recipient Wellington Parlin Sci. Scholarship award, 1979, Dr. Bertha Curtis prize Boston U. Med. Sch., 1974, Nat. Bd. award Med. Coll. Pa., 1992. Master ACP (mem. subcom. on aging 1986-91), Am. Geriatrics Soc. (mem. com. public policy 1983-98, mem. ethics com. 1988, chair subcom. on ethics and policy 1986, chair ethics com. 1991-98, bd. dirs. 1991-97); mem. AAAS, APHA, Am. Fedn. Clin. Rsch., Am. Health Care Assn. (mem. task force on AIDS 1987-89), Am. Hosp. Assn. (mem. spl. com. on biomedical ethics 1983-85, 89-94), Am. Med. Dirs. Assn., Am. Soc. Law and Medicine, Am. Coll. Health Care Adminstrs. (mem. nat. adv. com. wandering patients 1987-88), Nat. Inst. on Aging (mem. senile dementia of Alzheimer's type, mem. rsch. ethics task force 1981-82, Am. Geriatrics Soc. rep. 1984-86), Soc. Health and Human Values (mem. gov. coun. 1981-84), Inst. Medicine (mem. com. on future issues in med. tech. devel. 1992-94), N.H. Med. Soc., Soc. Health and Human Values (mem. gov. coun. 1981-84), Internat. Hospice Inst. (mem. physician's adv. com. 1984-86), Med. Soc. D.C. (mem. legis. affairs com. 1985-92, vice chairperson 1991-92), Soc. Gen. Internal Medicine (mem. editl. adv. bd. Jour. 1988-91), Inst. of Medicine, Americans for Better Care of the Dying (pres. 1994-2005) Home: 2318 Ashboro Dr Chevy Chase MD 20815-3055 Business E-Mail: JLynn@medicaring.org.

LYNN, DAVID G., biology professor, chemistry professor; AB in Chem., Univ. NC, Chapel Hill; PhD in Organic/Biological Chem., Duke Univ. Prof., chem. Univ. Chgo.; Asa Griggs Candler prof. chem, biology Emory Univ., Atlanta. Adv. bds. in genetics to bioorganic and natural products NIH; rsch. prof. Howard Hughes Med. Inst., 2002—. Adv. bd. Amyloid: The Journal of Protein Folding Disorders, and Current Organic Synthesis. Adv. bd. Ga. Citizens for Integrity in Sci. Edn. Recipient Camille and Henry Dreyfus Teacher-Scholar award, Howard Hughes Med. Inst. grant, 2002; fellow Am. Chem. Soc., 1988—89; grantee NIH Fellowship, Columbia Univ., Sloan Rsch. Fellowship. Office: Dept Chem Emory Univ 1515 Pierce Dr Atlanta GA 30322 Office Phone: 404-727-9348. Office Fax: 404-727-6586. Business E-Mail: dlynn2@emory.edu.*

LYNN, DWIGHT EARL, insect cell culturist; b. Zanesville, Ohio, June 11, 1952; s. James Harding and Dorothy Myrtle (Kain) L. BSc in Agriculture, Ohio State U., 1974, MS, 1976, PhD, 1979. Rsch. assoc. Ohio State U., Columbus, 1974-79; postdoctoral rsch. assoc. U. Fla., Gainesville, 1979-81; rsch. entomologist USDA, Beltsville, Md., 1982—. Contbr. articles to Proceedings NAS, USA Sci., In Vitro, others. Mem. Soc. In-Vitro Biology Inc. (chmn. invertebrate divsn. 1986-88, program com. 1982-90, treas. 1996-98), Nat. Capital Area Tissue Culture Soc. Inc. (pres. 1990-92), Soc. for Invertebrate Pathology, Phi Sigma, Gamma Sigma Delta. Achievements include development of insect cell lines from many insect species; research in insect cell culture and insect pathology. Office: USDA ARS Insect Biocontrol Lab BARC-W Bldg 011A Rm 214 Beltsville MD 20705 E-mail: lynnd@ba.ars.usda.gov.

LYNN, EMERSON ELWOOD, JR., retired newspaper editor/publisher; b. Boulder, Colo., Aug. 18, 1924; s. Emerson Elwood and Ruth Merriman (Scott) L.; m. Mickey June Killough, Jan. 27, 1950; children: Emerson Killough, Michael Jay, Angelo Scott, Susan. BS, U. Chgo., 1947. Editor/pub. The Humboldt (Kans.) Union, 1951-58, The Bowie (Tex.) News, 1958-65, The Iola (Kans.) Register, 1965-2001. Chmn. Iola Industries, Inc.; mem. SEK, Inc.; chmn. bd. dirs. Huck Boyd Found., Manhattan, Kans., 2001-2002. Chmn. Allen County Hosp. Bd., Iola, 1970-77, adv. bd. Kans. Dept. Transp., Topeka, 1992-93; mem. panels on reform of probate code, Kans. Jud. Coun., others; mem. Pulitzer Prize Nominating Jury, 2000-20001. Sgt. USAF, 1942-46. Rotary Internat. fellow U. Melbourne, 1948-49. Mem. Rotary Internat. (pres.), Kans. Press Assn. (pres. 1979, Clyde Reed Master Editor award 1995), William Allen White Found. (pres. 1978). Republican. Presbyterian. Home: 821 S Buckeye St Iola KS 66749-3807 Office: The Iola Register 302 S Washington St Iola KS 66749-3255 Office Phone: 620-365-2111.

LYNN, EVADNA SAYWELL, investment analyst; b. Oakland, Calif., June 16, 1935; d. Lawrence G. Saywell; m. Richard Keppie Lynn, Dec. 28, 1962; children: Douglas, Melisa. BA, MA in Econs., U. Calif., Berkeley. CFA. With Dean Witter, San Francisco, 1958-61, 70-71, Dodge & Cox, San Francisco, 1961-69; fin. analyst, v.p. Clark, Dodge & Co., San Francisco, 1971-73, Wainwright Securities, N.Y.C., 1977-78; 1st v.p. Merrill Lynch Capital markets, N.Y.C., 1978-90; sr. v.p. Dean Witter Reynolds, N.Y.C., 1990-97; forest products cons., San Francisco, 1997—. Mem. Assn. for Investment Mgmt. and Rsch., San Francisco Security Analysts (treas. 1973-74), Fin. Women's Club San Francisco (pres. 1967). Office: Apt F 1824 Jackson St San Francisco CA 94109-2873

LYNN, EVELYN JOAN, state senator, consultant; b. NY, Feb. 2, 1930; d. Leo A. and Helen (Shep) Hoes. BA in Psychology, Queens Coll., N.Y., 1950; MA English and Edn., Stetson U., 1969; EdD, U. Fla., 1979. Cons. for bus., edn. and govt., 1979—; rep. Fla. House, 1994—2002, Fla. Senate Dist. 7, Fla., 2002—. Bd. dirs. Boys and Girls Clubs; mem. adv. bd. Annie E. Casey Found. Mem. Nat. Coun. State Legislators (com. vice chair). Home: PO Box 4236 Ormond Beach FL 32175-4236 Office Phone: 386-676-4000.

LYNN, GEORGE GAMBRILL, lawyer; b. Birmingham, Ala., Mar. 3, 1946; s. Henry Sharpe and Fariss (Gambrill) L.; m. Gabriella Hulsey, Aug. 30, 1969 (div. Aug. 1980); children: Gabriella Hansell, George Gambrill Jr. AB, Princeton U., 1968; JD, U. Va., Boehmes, 1974. Bar: Ala. 1974. Law clk. to Hon. Walter P. Gewin U.S. Ct. Appeals 5th Cir., Tuscaloosa, Ala., 1974-75; assoc., ptnr. Cabaniss, Johnston, Gardner, Dumas & O'Neal, Birmingham, 1975-84; ptnr. Maynard, Cooper & Gale, Birmingham, 1984—, mng. ptnr., 2000—. Mem. Ala. com. U.S. Civil Rights Commn., Birmingham, 1988-92; chmn. State of Ala. Ballet, Birmingham, 1989-95; bd. dirs. United Way of Ctrl. Ala., 2004—. Lt. (j.g.) USN, 1968-71, Vietnam. Mem. ABA, Ala. State Bar Assn. (chmn. sect. on antitrust and bus. torts 1988-89), Birmingham Bar Assn., Lex Mundi (bd. dirs. 2005—), Birmingham Rotary (trustee 1999-2002). Republican. Episcopalian. Avocations: tennis, travel. Home: 2712 Lockerbie Cir Birmingham AL 35223-2904 Office: Maynard Cooper & Gale 2400 Amsouth/Harbert Pla 1901 6th Ave N Birmingham AL 35203-2618 E-mail: glynn@maynardcooper.com.

LYNN, JEFFREY WHIDDEN, research physicist, educator; b. Hackensack, N.J., Mar. 2, 1947; s. Theodore John and Frances Whidden Lynn; m. Linda Mayo; children: Robert William, Heather Diane Hudspeth. BS, Ga. Inst. of Tech., 1969, MS, 1970, PhD, 1974. Rsch. fellow Oak Ridge (Tenn.) Nat. Lab., 1972—74; postdoctoral assoc. Brookhaven Nat. Lab., Upton, NY, 1974—76; prof. physics U. of Md., College Park, 1976—97; rsch. scientist NIST, Gaithersburg, Md., 1977—. Acting dir., founder Ctr. for Superconductivity Rsch., U. of Md., College Park, 1987—89; adj. prof. physics U. Md., College Park, 1997—. Author: (rsch. book) High Temperature Superconductivity; contbr. sci. revs. to profl. jours. Recipient Award for Sci. Achievement, Wash. Acad. of Scis., 1988, multiple grants, NSF, 1976—2003; fellow, Wash. Acad. of Scis., 1988. Fellow: Am. Phys. Soc. (exec. com. divsn. materials physics 1999—2002, chair topical group in magnetism 1999—2003, chair divsn. materials physics 2005—). Office: Nat Inst Stds and Tech NIST Ctr for Neutron Rsch Gaithersburg MD 20899-8562 Office Phone: 301-975-6246. E-mail: jeff.lynn@nist.gov.

LYNN, JOHN ERIC, nuclear physicist, researcher, consultant; arrived in U.S., 1985; s. William and Emily Lynn; m. Joyce Ward, Aug. 7, 1954; children: Shirley, David. BSc, U. Durham, 1953; DSc, U. Newcastle upon Tyne, 1970. Chartered physicist, fellow Inst. Physics, 1985. Group leader electron accelerator group U.K. Atomic Energy Authority, Harwell, England, 1971—78, head nuc. physics divsn., 1978—85, sr. individual merit scientist, 1977—89; fellow Argonne Nat. Lab., Ill., 1988—89; vis. staff mem. Los Alamos Nat. Lab., N.Mex., 1990—93; assoc. Sumner Assocs., Santa Fe, 1994—. Bd. mem. nuc. physics bd. Sci. Rsch. Coun., London, 1978—85. Author: (scientific monograph) Theory of Neutron Resonance Reactions. Fellow: Inst. Physics. Achievements include research in elucidation of the nature of different kinds of resonances in neutron reactions, especially in fission reactions and their relation to the shell structure effects in the fission barrier; application of neutron resonance; to measuring quantum vibrational properties of crystalline materials; theoretical evaluation of fission and capture cross sections for applications ranging from nuclear astrophysics to nuclear criticality safety. Avocations: travel, piano. Office: Sumner Assoc Office 100 Cienega St Santa Fe NM 87501

LYNN, KARYL CHARNA (KARYL LYNN KOPELMAN ZIETZ), writer, opera critic, television correspondent, producer, documentary filmmaker; b. N.Y.C., Oct. 11, 1943; d. Bernard and Vera Jean (Wantman) Kopelman; m. Neil J. Stone, Aug. 16, 1970 (div. 1975); m. Joachim Zietz, July 19, 1978 (div. 1994). BA in Chemistry, U. Pa., 1965; MA in Film and Broadcast Journalism, Am. U., 1980; spl. cert., Goettinger U., Germany, 1976. Rschr. Columbia Coll. Physicians and Surgeons, N.Y.C., 1967-70, NIH, Bethesda, Md., 1971-72; producer, writer Am. Chem. Soc., Washington, 1976-78; prodr., rschr. Zweites Deutsches Fernsehen, Mainz, Germany, 1978-89; prodr. ORF-Austrian TV, 1980-84; prodr., reporter European Television Svc., Cologne, Germany, 1985-88; prodr., dir., corr. KOPE Prodns., Washington, 1985—. Lectr. Smithsonian Inst., Arts Club, Chautauqua Instn., 1998, Italian Cultural Soc., 2004, Balt. Opera Guild, 2000, Italian Cultural Inst. (part of Italian Embassy), Washington, 2002, Italian Opera House Lectr. Series, Washington, 2003; site reporter NEA, 1994—95. Author: Opera! Guide to Western Europe's Great Houses, 1991, Eastern Europe's and USSR's Great Opera Houses, 1992, Opera-Going in South America, 1993, Opera Companies and Houses of the United States: A Comprehensive, Illustrated Reference, 1994, The National Trust Guide to Great Opera Houses in America, 1996, Italian Opera Directory, 1998, Opera Companies and Houses of Western Europe, Canada, Australia, New Zealand: A Comprehensive Illustrated Reference, 1999, Breve Storia dei Teatri d'Opera Italiani, 2001, The Guide to Italian Opera Houses and Festivals, 2005; prodr. (video) An Amish Portrait for USIA; prodr., dir., writer, interviewer documentary films; opera critic, contbr. articles to Opera Now, Orpheus Oper Internat., Toronto Globe and Mail, Opera News, Musica and Arte: Quaderno del Museo Teatrale alla Scala, Opera-Opera. Mem. Music Critics Assn., Coun. Internat. Nontheatrical Events, Internat. Platform Assn., Am. Women in Radio and TV, Author's Guild, Assn. Ind. Video and Filmakers, Washington Ind. Writers, Contemporary Authors, Cosmos Club. Avocations: sailing, jogging, bicycling, tennis, foreign languages. Office: KOPE Prodns Palisades Sta PO Box 40103 Washington DC 20016-0103 Personal E-mail: rifiuti4u@aol.com.

LYNN, LARRY (VERNE LAURISTON LYNN), engineering executive; b. Seattle, Sept. 5, 1930; s. Eldin Verne and Irma (Tuell) Lynn; m. Emily Jean Badger, Oct. 4, 1952 (div. 1988); m. Shirley Marie Pieczynski, Sept. 27, 1988. BS in Physics, Tufts U., 1951. Assoc. divsn. head, mem. steering com. Lincoln Lab. M.I.T., Lexington, Mass., 1953-79; dir. defensive systems Office of the Undersecretary of Defense, Washington, 1979-81; dep. dir. Adv. Rsch. Project Agy., Washington, 1981-85; v.p., COO Atlantic Aerospace Electronics, Greenbelt, Md., 1985-93; dep. under sec. defense Office Sec. Defense, Washington, 1993-95, dir. def. adv. rsch. project agy., 1995-98; pres., owner, cons. Larry Lynn Assocs., Naples, Fla., 1998—. Mem Def. Sci. Bd. Contbr. numerous articles to profl. jours. Lt. JG USNR, 1951-53. Fellow IEEE (life). Home and Office: 480 15th Ave S Naples FL 34102-7437 Office Phone: 239-261-7619. Personal E-mail: larry.lynn@attglobal.net.

LYNN, LAURENCE EDWIN, JR., academic administrator, educator; b. Long Beach, Calif., June 10, 1937; s. Laurence Edwin and Marjorie Louise (Hart) L.; m. Patricia Ramsey Lynn; 1 dau., Katherine Bell; children from previous marriage— Stephen Louis, Daniel Laurence, Diana Jane, Julia Suzanne. AB, U. Calif., 1959; PhD (Ford Found. fellow), Yale, 1966. Dir., dep. asst. sec. def. (OASD/SA) Dept. Def., Washington, 1965-69; asst. for program analysis NSC, Washington, 1969-70; assoc. prof. bus. Grad. Sch. Bus., Stanford (Calif.) U., 1970-71, vis. prof. pub. policy, 1982-83; asst. sec. planning and evaluation HEW, Washington, 1971-73; asst. sec. program devel. and budget U.S. Dept. Interior, Washington, 1973-74; sr. fellow Brookings Instn., 1974-75; prof. pub. policy John Fitzgerald Kennedy Sch. Govt. Harvard U., Cambridge, Mass., 1975-83; dean Sch. Social Service Adminstrn. U. Chgo., 1983-88, prof., sch. of social svc. adminstrn. and Harris grad. sch. pub. policy studies, 1983—2002, dir. Ctr. for Urban Rsch. and Policy Studies, 1986—2002; dir. Mgmt. Inst., 1992-99; Sydney Stein, Jr. prof., 1997—2002; George H.W. Bush chair and prof. Bush Sch. Govt. and Pub. Svc., Tex A&M U., 2002—. Author: Designing Public Policy, 1980, The State and Human Services, 1980, Managing the Public's Business, 1981, Managing Public Policy, 1987, Public Management as Art, Science and Profession, 1996, Teaching and Learning with Cases: A Guidebook, 1999; co-author: The President as Policymaker, 1981, Improving Governance: A New Logic for Empirical Research, 2001, Madison's Managers: Public Administration and the Constitution; contbr. articles to profl. jours. Bd. dirs. Chgo. Met. Planning Coun., 1984-89, Leadership Greater Chgo., 1989-92; mem. coun. of scholars Libr. of Congress, 1989-93. 1st lt. AUS, 1963-65. Recipient Sec. Def. Meritorious Civilian Svc. medal, Presdl. Cert. of Disting. Achievment, Vernon prize, best book award Acad. Mgmt., 1996. Fellow Nat. Acad. Public Adminstrn.; mem. ASPA, U. Calif. Alumni Assn., Coun. on Fgn. Rels., Assn. Pub. Policy Analysis and Mgmt. (past pres.), Pub. Mgmt. Rsch. Assn. (H. George Frederickson award 2005), Phi Beta Kappa. Office: 1081 Allen 4220 TAMU College Station TX 77843-4220 E-mail: llynn@bushschool.tamu.edu.

LYNN, LOIS ANN, lawyer; b. Butler, Mo., July 25, 1953; d. George William Lynn and Lois Isabel (Donalson) Davidson. BA in Polit. Sci., Wichita State U., 1979; JD, Washburn U., 1981. Bar: Kans. 1983. Staff atty. child support enforcement divsn. Kans. Social Rehab. Svcs., Wichita, 1984—87; pvt. practice, Wichita, 1987—. Campaign organizer Jack Williams for Congress, Wichita, 1976. Mem. Assn. Family and Conciliation Cts., Wichita Bar assn. Home: 7516 E 10th St N Wichita KS 67206-3855 Address: 300 N Main Ste 202 Wichita KS 67202 Office Phone: 316-262-6682.

LYNN, LORETTA WEBB (MRS. OLIVER LYNN JR.), singer; b. Butcher Hollow, Ky., Apr. 14, 1935; d. Ted and Clara (Butcher) Webb; m. Oliver V. Lynn, Jr., Jan. 10, 1948; children— Betty Sue Lynn Markworth, Jack Benny (dec.), Clara Lynn Lyell, Ernest Ray, Peggy, Patsy. Student pub. schs. Sec.-treas. Loretta Lynn Enterprises; v.p. United Talent, Inc.; hon. chmn. bd. Loretta Lynn Western Stores. Country vocalist with MCA records, 1961— (numerous gold albums); most recent album Just a Woman, 1985, (with Conway Twitty) Making Believe, 1988, Greatest Hits Live, 1992, The Country Music Hall of Fame, 1991, Country's Favorite Daughter (reissue), 1993. Author: Coal Miner's Daughter, 1976; appearance (TV movie) Loretta Lynn: The Seasons of My Life, 1992, Big Dreams and Broken Hears: The Dottie West Story, 1995; discs include (boxed set) Honky Tonk Girl: The Loretta Lynn Collection, 1994, (MCA special products) Hymns, 1995, Christmas Without Daddy, 1995, On Tour #1, 1996, On Tour #2, 1996, 20th Century Masters: The Millenium Collection, 1999, Still Woman Enough, 2000. Hon. rep. United Giver's Fund, 1971. Named Country Music Assn. Female Vocalist of Year 1967, 72, 73, Entertainer of Year, 1972, Top Duet of 1972, 73, 74, 75, Entertainer of Decade, Acad. Country Music 1980; recipient Grammy award 1971, Am. Music award 1978, Johnny Cash Visionary award, Country Music Television Music award, 2005; inducted into Country Music Hall of Fame, 1988; first country female vocalist to record certified Gold album.

LYNN, MICHAEL A., historic site director; BA with High Distinction, U. Va., 1974; MA in History Mus. Adminstrn., SUNY, Oneonta, 1980. Curatorial intern Fenimore House/N.Y. State Hist. Assn., Cooperstown, 1978-79; curator of collections Lynchburg Mus. System, Lynchburg, 1979-81; dir. Stonewall Jackson House, Lexington, 1981-94; exec. dir. Stonewall Jackson House/Found., 1994—, state hist. recs. bd., 2002—. Mem. Mus. and Hist. Sites Working Group Va. History Initiative, 1996—98; Va. state dir. Southeastern Mus. Conf., 1993—99; bd. dirs. Assn. for the Preservation of Civil War Sites, 1990—95, officer Va. Assn. of Mus.; others; mem. Rockbridge Area Tourism Devel. Bd., 2000—02, Lexington Archtl. Rev. Bd., 1999—; coun. mem.-at-large Southeastern Mus. Conf., 2000—03; spkr. in field. Vol. VISTA, Charlottesville, Va., 1975-77; mem. tourism adv. coun. Lexington, Rockbridge County, Buena Vista, 1996-99; founding bd. dirs. Lexington Downtown Devel. Assn., 1985-87, 89-95; elder Lexington Presbyn. Ch.; mem. task force Project Horizon: Alternatives for Abused Adults, 1983-84, founding bd. dirs., 1984-86, others. Office: Stonewall Jackson House 8 E Washington St Lexington VA 24450-2529

LYNN, MORTON DANIEL, orthopedist; b. Paterson, N.J., Apr. 4, 1939; s. Allan A. and Sophie (Schwartz) L.; m. Susan Z. Zeller, July 3, 1966; children: Allison, Elizabeth, Sarah, Geoffrey (dec.). AB, Dartmouth Coll., 1961; MD, Cornell U., 1965. Diplomate Nat. Bd. Med. Examiners, Am. Bd. Orthopedic Surgeons. Intern, resident in surgery U. Hosp., Cleve., 1965-67; resident in orthopedics Vanderbilt U. Hosp., Nashville, 1967-70; pvt. practice New Eng. Orthopedic Surgeons, Springfield, Mass., 1972—. Active staff Baystate Med. Ctr., Springfield, 1972—, Mercy Hosp., Springfield, 1982—, Shriners Hosp., Springfield, 1973—; asst. clin. instr. orthopedics N.Y. Med. Coll., N.Y.C., 1970-72, Boston U. Med. Sch., 1972-82, clin. asst. prof. orthopedics, 82—; v.p. med. staff Baystate Med. Ctr., 1989, 90, pres., 1991, 92. Contbr. articles to profl. jours. Lt. comdr. USPHS, 1970-72. Named Triplane Ankle Fracture, 1972. Fellow Am. Acad. Orthopedic Surgeons; mem. Mass. Med. Soc., AMA, New Eng. Orthopedic Soc., Eastern Orthopedic Soc., Am. Orthopedic Foot and Ankle Soc. Avocations: tennis, piano, fishing, skiing, golf. Office: New Eng Orthopedic Surgeons 300 Birnie Ave Springfield MA 01107-2316 Office Phone: 413-785-4666. Business E-mail: morton.lynn@neortho.com.

LYNN, NAOMI B., academic administrator; b. N.Y.C., Apr. 16, 1933; d. Carmelo Burgos and Maria (Lebron) Berly; m. Robert A. Lynn, Aug. 28, 1954; children: Mary Louise, Nancy Lynn Francis, Judy Lynn Chance, Jo-An Lynn Cooper. BA, Maryville (Tenn.) Coll., 1954; MA, U. Ill., 1958; PhD, U. Kans., 1970. Instr. polit. sci. Cen. Mo. State Coll., Warrensburg, Mo., 1966-68; asst. prof. Kans. State U., Manhattan, 1970-75, assoc. prof., 1975-80, acting dept. head, prof., 1980-81, head polit. sci. dept., prof., 1982-84; dean Coll. Pub. and Urban Affairs, prof. Ga. State U., Atlanta, 1984-91; chancellor U. Ill., Springfield, 1991-2001, chancellor emerita, 2001—. Cons. fed., state and local govts., Manhattan, Topeka, Atlanta, 1981-91; bd. dirs. Bank One Springfield; bd. trustees Maryville Coll., 1997—. Author: The Fulbright Premise, 1973; editor: Public Administration, The State of Discipline, 1990, Women, Politics and the Constitution, 1990; contbr. articles and textbook chpts. to profl. pubs. Bd. dirs. United Way of Sangamon County, 1991-98, Ill. Symphony Orch., 1992-95, Urban League, 1993-99, Ill. State Mus. Soc., 2002—. Recipient Disting. Alumni award Maryville Coll., 1986; fellow Nat. Acad. Pub. Adminstrn. Mem. Nat. Assn. Schs. Pub. Affairs and Adminstrn. (nat. pres.), Am. Soc. Pub. Adminstrn. (nat. pres. 1985-86), Am. Polit. Sci. Assn. (mem. exec. coun. 1981-83, trustee 1993—96, Am. Assn. State Colls. and Univs. (bd. dirs.), Midwest Polit. Sci. Assn. (mem. exec. coun. 1976-79), Women's Caucus Polit. Sci. (pres. 1975-76), Greater Springfield C. of C. (bd. dirs. 1991-99, mem. U.S. Senate jud. nominations commn. State Ill. 1999-2001), Pi Sigma Alpha (nat. pres.). Presbyterian.

LYNN, PATRICIA ANNE, student services representative; b. Newton, Iowa, Sept. 9, 1950; d. Harold Clifford (dec.) and Alice Marie (Uhlig) Johnson; divorced. AA in Psychology, Trinidad (Colo.) Jr. Coll., 1970; BS in Psychology, Ft. Lewis Coll., Durango, Colo., 1972; AA in Vet. Tech., Internat. Sch., Scranton, Pa., 1980. Customer svc. agt. Waco Scaffolding & Equipment,

Denver, 1980-83; leasing agt. Look Ltd. Realty, Federal Heights, Colo., 1983-84; sales assoc. Lynn & Assocs., Aurora, Colo., 1991—; customer svc. team leader EBSCO Industries, Golden, Colo., 1984-96; student svcs. rep. Coll. for Fin. Planning, Denver, 1997—. Political aide Dem. Party, Denver; docent Denver Zoo; vol. ARC, Aurora. Mem. Rocky Mountain Midget Racing Assn., Vintage Motor Racing Assn. Jehovah'S Witness. Avocations: auto racing, restoring antique cars. Home: 19013 E Carmel Cir Aurora CO 80011-3621 Office: Coll for Fin Planning 6161 S Syracuse Way Greenwood Village CO 80111 E-mail: trishia268@consultant.com.

LYNN, RICHARD JO, freelance/self-employed illustrator, journalist, cartoonist; s. Ralph H. and Mary Lucile Lynn. Student, Art Instrn. Schools, Inc., 1951—55. Freelance illustrator trade and juvenile periodicals, 1955—70; editl. cartoonist Twin Cir. Pubs., L.A., 1970—73; author, illustrator, cartoonist Richard Lynn Enterprises, Lagro, Ind., 1974—, FBN Publications, Wabash, Ind., 1978—80; pub., editor-in-chief Akron (Ind.)/Mentone News, 1980—81; CEO Parwell-Davis Features Syndicate, Lagro, 1989—. Guest spkr. convention San Diego Comics Con, 1977; web developer http://parwell.hypermart.net/, Lagro, Ind., 1998—; cons., spkr. in field. Author (illustrator): (syndicated newspaper cartoon strip) Sons of Liberty; book, anthology of newspaper cartoons, Comic Relief, comic books, The Space Giants and Cecil Kunkle, book, Wabash Canal Days, editorial cartoons during Watergate era, Published weekly in Twin Circle international Catholic weekly newspaper.; writer, photographer, reporter: Automotive Contact mag. Artist in edn. Ind. Arts Commn., Indpls. Recipient George Wash. Honor medal, Freedoms Found., Valley Forge, Pa., 1975, 1976. Mem.: So. Calif. Cartoonists Soc., Nat. Cartoonists Soc. (cartoonist Thanksgiving Day project 1986), Phi Theta Kappa. Achievements include first to published first comic book adaptation of TV series The Space Giants based on Japanese cartoon by Osamu Tesuka; development of Colonial Heroes E-book on 18th Century America; forthcoming online historical data to expand on cartoon series. Avocations: historical research, digital photography, multimedia. Office: Parwell-Davis Corp 3741 North 400 East Suite A Lagro IN 46941 Office Phone: 260-782-2345. E-mail: parwell@email.com.

LYNN, ROBERT WILLIAM, strategic planning consultant; b. Jan. 27, 1943; s. William Ernest and Jeannette (Reardon) Lynn; m. Sara E. Davis, Aug. 26, 1961 (dec. Nov. 1980); children: Robert, John, William, David, Michelle; m. Karen Gross, Mar. 3, 2001. AAS in Supervision, Purdue U., 1974, BS in Indsl. Engring., 1976; MBA, Ind.-Wesleyan U., 1991. Engr. No. Ind. Pub. Svc. Co., Crown Point, 1968-77, engring. supr. Gary, 1977-79, sr. cons. Hammond, 1979-82, mgr., 1982-89, asst. to sr. v.p. and gen. mgr. energy distbn., 1989-90, mgr. strategic planning, 1990-96, lectr., 1992-93; exec. dir. Nesi Integrated Energy Resources, Inc., 1997-2000; ind. strategic planning cons. Omaha, 2000—. Advisor Purdue U.-Hammond, 1979-2000. With USN, 1960-67. Mem. Inst. Indsl. Engrs. (sr. project award 1976). Avocations: woodcarving, sculpture. Home: 3020 NW 76th Ave Ankeny IA 50021 Office: Strategy Play Book 3020 NW 76th Ave Ankeny IA 50023-9479 Office Phone: 515-229-8547. E-mail: r.lynn@mchsi.com.

LYNN, THEODORE STANLEY, lawyer; s. Irving and Sydell Lynn; m. Linda Isabel Freeman, July 21, 1968; children: Jessica, Douglas. AB, Columbia U., 1958; LLB, Harvard U., 1961; LLM, NYU, 1962; SJD, George Washington U., 1972. Law clk. to Hon. Bruce M. Forrester U.S. Tax Ct., Washington, 1962-64; tchg. fellow in law George Washington U., Washington, 1963-64; ptnr. Webster & Sheffield, N.Y.C., 1964-90, Stroock & Stroock & Lavan LLP, N.Y.C., 1991—. Consult Adminstrn. Conf. U.S., Washington, 1974—75; founding counsel Pension Real Estate Assn., Washington, 1981—84. Author: Real Estate Limited Partnerships, 3d ed, 1991, Real Estate Investment Trusts, 1994, 11th edit., 2005; contbr. articles to profl jours. Sec. Manhattan Sch. Dance, 1974—93; trustee Birch Wathen Lenox Sch., N.Y.C., 1975—93; bd. dirs. Citizens Union, 1991—, vice-chair, 2001—04, treas., 2005—; dir. Sutton Area Cmty. Inc., 1995—; treas., trustee Citizens Union Found, 2000—; bd. dirs. Daniel K. Thorne Found.; spl. asst. Mayor John V Lindsay, N.Y.C., 1966—69; bd. dirs. Jewish Home and Hosp. Health Care Sys., 2003—, Manhattan Cmty. Bd. # 6, N.Y.C., 1977—; trustee John fellow Charitable Trust, 2003—. Mem.: Asn Bar City NY, Fed Bar Coun, Harvard Club, Univ Club. Office: Stroock & Stroock & Lavan 180 Maiden Ln Fl 17 New York NY 10038-4937 Office Phone: 212-806-6629. Business E-Mail: tlynn@stroock.com.

LYNN, THOMAS EDWARD, retired government agency administrator; b. St. Louis, Mo., May 19, 1930; s. Thomas Ulise and Mary Frances Lynn; m. Trudy Pearl White, June 17, 1966; children: Fran Christman, Kenneth Thomas, Tammy Hosea, Timothy Eugene, Sherry Sharp, Joseph Edward. Spl. agt. (investigator) U. S. Customs, Tampa, Fla., 1956—62; supervisory spl. agt. Insp. Gen. - USDA, Atlanta, 1962—89. Police crime analyst Gwinnett County Police Dept., Lawrenceville, Ga., 1989—95. Author: (poet, novelist, essayist, columnist) Writing (Numerous (poets of the yr.), (book) Over The Transom: Confessions Of A Wannabe Writer, 2002, (poetry - memorial) Old Comrades, 1995. Sgt. U.S. Army, 1952—53, Kanghwa, Korea. Mem.: Gulf Coast Writers Assn., Ga. Writers Assn. Home: 545 Birch Lane Lawrenceville GA 30044 Personal E-mail: lynn9493@bellsouth.net.

LYNN, WILLIAM STEPHEN, environmental services administrator; b. Ont., Canada; MA, U. Minn., 1992, PhD, 2000. Founder, sr. ethics advisor Practical Ethics, Beacon, 2004—. Contbr. articles to profl. jours. Bd. mem., ethics advisor Wolf Conservation Ctr. Found., South Salem, NY, 2002. Mem.: Internat. Union for Conservation of Nature, Soc. Conservation Biology, Internat. Soc. Anthrozoology, IUCN (chair 2002—03, mem. ethics specialist group), Assn. Am. Geographers. Independent. Unitarian-Universalist. Office: Practical Ethics 95 Liberty St Beacon NY 12508

LYNNE, MICHAEL, film company executive; b. 1941; m. Ninah Lynne; 2 children. BA in English Literature, Brooklyn Coll., 1961; JD, Columbia Law Sch., 1964. Atty. Barovick & Konecky; partner Blumenthal & Lynne, 1960—80; counsel New Line Cinema, 1980—90, COO, pres., 1990—2001, co-chmn., co-CEO, 2001—. Bd. dirs. New Line Cinema, 1983—; mem. NY Bar. Exec. prodr.: (films) Lord of the Rings: The Fellowship of the Ring, 2001, Lord of the Rings: The Two Towers, 2002, Lord of the Rings: The Return of the King, 2003. Bd. mem. Museum of Modern Art, Citymeals-on-Wheels, Am. Museum of the Moving Image, Drawing Ctr.; chair Museum Com. of Guild Hall East Hampton. Named one of Top 200 Collectors in the World, ARTnews Mag, 2004, 50 Most Powerful People in Hollywood, Premiere mag., 2002—05. Avocation: Collector of contemporary art. Office: New Line Cinema Corp 888 7th Ave Fl 20 New York NY 10106-0001*

LYNNE, SHELBY (SHELBY LYNN MOORER), country singer; b. Quantico, Va., Oct. 22, 1968; Singer: (albums) Sunrise, 1989, Tough All Over, 1990, Soft Talk, 1991, Temptation, 1993, Restless, 1995, I Am Shelby Lynne, 2000 (Grammy award best new artist, 2000), Love, Shelby, 2001, Identity Crisis, 2003, (singles) I'll Lie Myself to Sleep, 1990, Things Are Tough All Over, 1990, Feelin Kind of Lonely Tonight, 1993, (duet with George Jones) If I Could Bottle This Up, 1988; appearances (TV special) Willie Nelson and Friends, Outlaws and Angles, (TV series) Nashville Now. Named best new female artist, ACM, 1991; recipient Horizon award, CMA, 1991. Office: Capital Records 1750 N Vine St Hollywood CA 90028

LYNNE-O'BRIEN, VINCENT, theater director, actor; b. East Orange, N.J., Dec. 11, 1935; s. Patrick A. and Mary (Gallagher) O'B. BBA, Seton Hall U., 1957. Artistic dir. Shoreline Youth Theatre, Madison, Conn., 1978-85, Shubert Acad., Shubert Theatre, New Haven, 1990-95; dir. Alliance Theatre, New Haven, 1977-88, Stratford Cmty. Svcs., 1986-88, Jewish Cmty. Svcs., New Haven, 1986-87. Appearances include (on Broadway) The Boy Friend, No Time for Sargeants, Fiorello, Golden Boy, Best Laid Plans, Sweet Charity, Billy, (regional theaters) West Side Story, Mass Appeal, Tribute, Odd Couple, You Can't Take It with You, Diary of Ann Frank, The Sea Gull, Cape Cod-Wellfleet, 1999, You Can't Take It with You, Cape Cod-Orleans, 1999, On Golden Pond, (TV shows) Studio One, U.S. Steel, I Remember Mama, Voice of Firestone, Lucy Arnaz Show, I Bonino, Search for Tomorrow; (TV movies) Princess Daisey, Prisoner without a Name, Cell without a Number, Empire Falls; theatrical films include The Long Grey Line, Ragtime, Ghost Busters, Godfather III, Other Peoples Money, Amistad; dir. Life With Father, Broadway Bound. Dir. Daniel Hand Drama Soc., 1975-85; bd. dirs. ABC Program, 1984-86, Madison Arts and Sci. Council, 1985-86; commr. conservation com. Town of Eastham, Mass. Mem. Actors Equity Assn., Screen Actors Guild, Am. Fedn. TV and Radio Artists, Madison C. of C. (bd. dirs. 1979-85), Eastham Conservation Commn. Roman Catholic. Avocations: tennis, travel. Home: 11080 SE 173rd Pl Summerfield FL 34491 E-mail: vinmort@xpinternet.net.

LYNTON, MICHAEL, film company executive; b. London, Jan. 1, 1960; s. Mark and Marion Lynton; m. Jamie Alter, 1993. AB in History and Lit., Harvard Coll., 1982; MBA, Harvard Bus. Sch., 1987. Assoc. mergers and acquisitions The First Boston Corp./Credit Suisse First Boston, 1982-85; pres. Disney Pub. The Walt Disney Co., 1987—92, pres. Hollywood Pictures, 1992—96; chmn., CEO, penguin group Pearson plc, N.Y.C., 1996—2000; pres. AOL Internat., N.Y.C., 2000—03; CEO AOL Europe, 2000—03; pres. Time Warner Internat. (formerly AOL Time Warner Internat.), N.Y.C., 2002—03; chmn., CEO Sony Pictures Entertainment, Culver City, Calif., 2004—. Named one of 50 Most Powerful People in Hollywood, Premiere mag., 2004—05. Office: Sony Pictures Entertainment 10202 W Washington Blvd Culver City CA 90232*

LYNTON, SANDRA M., clinical psychologist; b. London, Eng., Nov. 17, 1957; came to U.S., 1983; d. Paul Stefan and Lya Lynton. BA with honors, U. Keele, Eng., 1982; MA, U. Colo., 1985; PsyD, Calif. Sch. Profl. Psychology, Berkeley, 1998. Women's counselor Women in Crisis Battered Women's Shelter, Jefferson County, Colo., 1985-87; social worker Ctr. for People with Disabilities, Boulder, Colo., 1988-93; program coord. OMI Children's Psychodiagnostic Assessments, San Francisco, 1993-95; pvt. practice Boulder, 1999—; clin. psychologist Childre's Specialized Svcs., Imperial County Behavial Svcs., El Centro, Calif., 2002—. Bd. dirs. Domestic Violence Initiative for Women with Disabilities, Denver, 1990-93; mem. Disability Task Force, City of Boulder, 1989-92, participant Task Force on Childhood Abuse, 1991-92; bd. dirs. Mental Health Ombuds Program Colo., Denver, 2004— Mem. APA. Avocations: art, music, outdoor wilderness. Personal E-mail: slynton@yahoo.com.

LYON, ANDREA D., law educator; b. Boston, Sept. 23, 1952; d. Harvey Tilden Lyon and Yolanda (Glockner) Miller; m. Arnold D. Glass; 1 child, Samantha Alliyah Lyon Glass; stepchildren: William Glass, Barbara Glass. BA, Rutgers U., 1973; JD, Antioch Sch. Law, 1976. Bar: Ill. 1976, D.C. 1978, U.S. Dist. Ct. (no. dist.) Ill. 1978, U.S. Supreme Ct. 1978, U.S. Ct. Appeals (7th cir.) 1986, Mich. 1995. Chief homicide task force atty. Cook County Pub. Defender, Chgo., 1976-90; dir. Ill. Capital Resource Ctr., Chgo., 1990-95; asst. clin. prof. law U. Mich. Law Sch., Ann Arbor, 1995-2000; assoc. prof., dir. Ctr. for Justice in Capital Cases, DePaul Coll. Law, Chgo., 2000—. Mem. faculty Nat. Criminal Def. Coll., Macon, Ga., 1983—. Author: Illinois Death Penalty Defense Motions Manual, 2001, Federal Mitigation Handbook, 2002. Bd. dirs. Black Ensemble Theater, Chgo., 1980-91. Recipient Stevens award Ill. Acad. Criminology 1991, Reginald Heber Smith award 1985, Justice for All award Northwestern Law Sch., 1998, Clarence Darrow award, 2003; tchg. awards 1998-2003. Avocations: swimming, dance. Office: Depaul U Coll Law 25 E Jackson Blvd Chicago IL 60604 E-mail: alyon1@depaul.edu.

LYON, BRUCE ARNOLD, lawyer, educator; b. Sacramento, Sept. 24, 1951; s. Arnold E. and Arlene R. (Cox) L.; m. Patricia J. Gibson, Dec. 14, 1974; children: Barrett, Andrew. AB with honors, U. Pacific, 1974; JD, U. Calif.-Hastings Coll. Law, 1977. Bar: Calif. 1977, U.S. Dist. Ct. (ea. and no. dists.) Calif. 1977. Ptnr. Ingoglia, Marskey, Kearney & Lyon, Sacramento, 1977-84; sole practice Auburn, Calif., 1984-91; ptnr. Robinson, Robinson & Lyon, Auburn, 1991-98, Robinson, Lyon & Springford LLP, Auburn, 1999—2004. Instr. in law Sierra Coll., Rocklin, Calif., 1983-98. Mng. editor Comment, A Jour. of Comm. and Entertainment Law, 1974; contbr. articles to trade publs. Bd. dirs. Auburn Cmty. Found., Gold Country Sci. and Tech. Found.; pres. Calif. Tule Elk Found. Mem.: ABA, Thurston Soc., Placer County Bar Assn., State Bar Calif., Native Sons of the Golden West, Mensa, Order of Coif. Office: Robinson & Lyon One California St Auburn CA 95603 Office Phone: 530-885-8900. Business E-Mail: brucelyon@rlsllp.com.

LYON, CARL FRANCIS, JR., lawyer; b. Sumter, S.C., May 9, 1943; s. Carl Francis and Sophie (Goldstrum) L.; m. Maryann Mercier; children— Barbara Ruth, Sarah Frances, Carl Francis, III. AB, Duke U., 1965, JD with honors, 1968. Bar: N.Y. 1969, D.C. 1977. Assoc., then ptnr. Mudge Rose Guthrie Alexander & Ferdon, N.Y.C., 1968-95, mem. exec. com., 1986-87, 94-95; ptnr. Orrick Herrington & Sutcliffe, N.Y.C., 1995—, mem. exec. com., 1998-2000. Contbr. articles to profl. publs. Mem. ABA (vice-chmn. spl. com. on energy fin. 1988-91), N.Y. State Bar Assn., D.C. Bar Assns., Am. Pub. Power Assn., Duke U. Law Alumni Coun., Order of Coif, Phi Alpha Delta. Office: Orrick Herrington Sutcliffe 666 5th Ave Rm 203 New York NY 10103-1798 Office Phone: 212-506-5180. Business E-Mail: cflyon@orrick.com.

LYON, DAVID WILLIAM, research and development company executive; b. Lansing, Mich., Mar. 26, 1941; s. Herbert Reid and Mary Kathleen (Slack) L.; m. Catherine McHugh Dillon, July 8, 1967. BS, Mich. State U., 1963; M in City and Regional Planning, U. Calif., Berkeley, 1966, PhD, 1972. Regional economist Fed. Res. Bank Phila., 1969-71; rsch. dir. human and econ. resources The N.Y.C.-Rand Inst., 1972-75, v.p., 1975; sr. economist The Rand Corp., Santa Monica, Calif., 1975-77, dep. v.p., 1977-79, v.p. domestic rsch. divsn., 1979-93, v.p. external affairs, 1993-94; pres., CEO Pub. Policy Inst. Calif., 1994—. Adj. prof. U. Pa., 1975; mem. adv. bd. Inst. for Civil Justice, 1987-93, Rand-Urban Inst. Program for Rsch. on Immigration Policy, 1988-91, Drug Policy Rsch. Ctr., 1989-93, So. Calif. Health Policy Rsch. Consortium, 1989-94, Rand Ctr. for U.S.-Japan Rels., 1989-93, Rand Ctr. for Asia-Pacific Policy, 1993-95; dir. Coll. Environ. Design Coun., U. Calif., Berkeley, 1979-90; Walker-Ames lectr., U. Wash. Mem. publs. com. Rand Jour. Econs., 1984-94; contbr. articles to profl. jours. Bd. dirs. Ctr. for Healthy Aging, Santa Monica, 1985-94, pres., 1989-91; mem. com. fgn. rels. San Francisco, Calif., 1996—, adv. coun. Coll. Environ. Design, U. Calif., Berkeley, 2000—. Mellon fellow in city planning, 1966-68; Econ. Devel. Adminstrn. grad. fellow, 1966. Mem. Coun. on Fgn. Rels., San Francisco Com. on Fgn. Rels., World Affairs Coun. No. Calif. (trustee 1999—), Japan Am. Soc. So. Calif. (bd. dirs. 1990-94), Japan Soc. No. Calif. (bd. dirs. 2000-), Asia Soc. (So. Calif. Ctr. adv. coun. 1988-2002, No. Calif. adv. bd. 2002—), Calif. Connected (cir. of advisors 2002-), Pacific Coun. on Internat. Policy, Delta Phi Epsilon, Lambda Alpha Internat. Office: Pub Policy Inst Calif 500 Washington St Ste 800 San Francisco CA 94111-2919 Business E-Mail: lyon@ppic.org.

LYON, JAMES BURROUGHS, lawyer; b. N.Y.C., May 11, 1930; s. Francis Murray and Edith May (Strong) L. BA, Amherst Coll., 1952; LLB, Yale U., 1955. Bar: Conn. 1955, U.S. Tax Ct. 1970. Asst. football coach Yale U., 1953-55; assoc. Murtha, Cullina LLP (and predecessor), Hartford, Conn., 1956-61, ptnr., 1961-96, counsel, 1996—. Adv. com., lectr. and session leader NYU Inst. on Fed. Taxation, 1973-86; mem. IRS Northeast Key Dist.'s Exempt Orgns. Liaison Group, Bklyn., 1993—. Mem. editl. bd. Conn. Law Tribune, 1988—. Chmn. 13th Conf. Charitable Orgn. N.Y.U. Inst. on Fed. Taxation, 1982; trustee Kingswood-Oxford Sch., West Hartford, Conn., 1961—91, hon. trustee, 1991—, chmn. bd. trustees, 1975—78; exec. com., chmn. Amherst Coll. Alumni Coun., 1963—69, alumni trustee candidate, 1970; chmn. bd. trustees Old Sturbridge Village, 1991—93, hon. trustee, 2002—; trustee Ellen Burr McManus Trust, Hartford, 1987—98, Ellen Battell Stoeckel Trust, Norfolk, Conn., 1994—, Hartford YMCA, 1985—99, St. Francis Hosp. Found., 1991—, Watkinson Libr., 1990—, pres., 2001—; trustee Wadsworth Atheneum, Hartford, 1968—93, pres., 1981—84, hon. trustee, 1993—; trustee Horace Bushnell Meml. Hall, Hartford, 1993—, sec., 1996—; corporator Inst. Living, 1981—, Hartford Hosp., 1975—, St. Francis Hosp., Hartford, 1976—, Hartford Pub. Libr., 1979—; bd. dirs. Conn. Policy and Econ. Com., Inc., 1991—98; mem. Conn. adv. com. New Eng. Legal Found., 1991—; mem. adv. com. Florence Griswold Mus., Old Lyme, Conn., 1991—; trustee Conn. Hist. Soc., 2000—, sec., 2002—; trustee Conn. Jr. Republic, Litchfield, 2000—; mem. N.E. regional coun. Nat. Club Assn., 1998—; trustee Conn. Pub. Radio and TV, 1979—86. Recipient Eminent Svc. medal Amherst Coll., 1967, Nathan Hale award Yale Club Hartford, 1982, Disting. Am. award No. Conn. chpt. Nat. Football Found. Hall of Fame, 1983, Community Svc. award United Way of the Capital Area, 1986, Disting. Alumnus award Kingswood Oxford Sch., 1998, Thomas Hooker award Ancient Burying Ground Assn., 2003; honored as a direct descendant of its founder Mary Lyon, Mt. Holyoke Coll., South Hadley, Mass. 1997. Fellow: ABA (co-chmn. subcom. on mus. and other cultural orgns. sect. of taxation 1988—, exempt orgn. com.), Am. Coll. Tax Counsel, Phi Beta Kappa; mem.: Am. Law Inst., Conn. State Srs. Golf Assn., Limestone Trout Club, Limestone Trout Club, Town and County Club, Univ. Club Hartford (pres. 1976—77), Mory's Assn. (New Haven), Wianno Club (Osterville, Mass.), Dauntless Club (Essex, Conn.), Union Club N.Y.C., Yale Club N.Y.C., Hartford Golf Club. Office: 185 Asylum St Hartford CT 06103-3408 Office Phone: 860-240-6007. Business E-Mail: jlyon@murthalaw.com.

LYON, JAMES KARL, German language educator; b. Rotterdam, Holland, Feb. 17, 1934; came to U.S., 1937; s. T. Edgar and Hermana (Forsberg) L.; m. Dorothy Ann Burton, Dec. 22, 1959; children: James, John, Elizabeth, Sarah, Christina, Rebecca, Matthew, Melissa. BA, U. Utah, 1958, MA, 1959; PhD, Harvard U., 1963. Instr. German Harvard U., Cambridge, Mass., 1962-63, asst. prof., 1966-71; assoc. prof. U. Fla., Gainesville, 1971-74; prof. U. Calif. San Diego, La Jolla, 1974-94, provost Eleanor Roosevelt Coll., 1987-94; prof. dept. Germanic and Slavic langs. Brigham Young U., Provo, Utah, 1994—. Vis. prof. U. Augsburg, Germany, 1993. Author: Konkordanz zur Lyrik Gottfried Benns, 1971, Bertolt Brecht and Rudyard Kipling, 1975, Brecht's American Cicerone, 1978, Bertolt Brecht in America, 1980, Brecht in den USA, 1994. Capt. M.I., U.S. Army, 1963-66. NEH fellow, 1970, Guggenheim Found. fellow, 1974; Ford Found. grantee, 1988, 91. Mem. MLA, Am. Assn. Tchrs. German, Internat. Brecht. Soc., Phi Beta Kappa. Democrat. Mem. Lds Ch. Avocations: back-packing, fishing. Office: Brigham Young U Dept Germanic & Slavic Lang 3106 JFSB Provo UT 84602-6120 E-mail: james_lyon@byu.edu.

LYON, JOSEPH LYNN, physician, medical educator; b. Salt Lake City, May 13, 1939; s. Thomas Edgar and Hermana (Forsberg) L.; m. June Fetzer, July 3, 1964; children: Natalee, Joseph, Stephen, Maryanne, Rachael, Janet. BS, U. Utah, 1964, MD, 1967; MPH, Harvard U., 1969. Diplomate Am. Bd. Preventive Medicine. Intern U. Calif., San Diego, 1967-68; resident Harvard U., 1968-70, Utah State Health Dept., 1971-72; asst. prof. U. Utah, Salt Lake City, 1974-80, assoc. prof., 1980-90, prof., 1990—. Contbr. articles to profl. jours. Mem.: Soc. for Epidemiologic Rsch. (sec.-treas. 1993). Mem. Lds Ch. Office: U Utah Dept Medicine Salt Lake City UT 84132-0001

LYON, MARINA, secondary school educator, translator; b. Chapaevsk, Russia, Mar. 15, 1967; arrived in U.S., 96; d. Nicholas Nuzhdin and Antonina Nuzhdina; m. Charles Lyon, July 20, 1963; 1 child, Anastasia. MA in Fgn. Langs., Kuibyshev State U., Samara, Russia, 1989. Cert. English/ESL tchr. English tchr. secondary sch., Chapaersk, Russia, 1989—90, vice prin., 1989—91; interpreter, translator U. Ky., Lexington, 1996—99; tchr. Russian, ESL Henry Clay H.S., Lexington, 1996—. Recipient Fame award for tchg., Fayette County Bd. Edn., 1999. Mem.: Ky. Fgn. Lang. Tchrs. Assn. Avocations: skiing, skating, gymnastics, dance. Home: 1004 Winding Cir Lexington KY 40517 Office: Henry Clay HS Fontain Rd 2100 Lexington KY 40502 E-mail: marina.lyon@usa.net.

LYON, MARTHA SUE, research engineer, retired military officer; b. Oct. 3, 1935; d. Harry Bowman and Erma Louise (Moreland) Lyon. BA in Chemistry, U. Louisville, 1959; MEd in Math., Northeastern Ill. U., 1974; postgrad., McGeorge Sch. Law, 1981-82, Northwestern Calif. U., 1999—, George Washington U., 1995—96. Cert. tchr. Ill., Ky. Rsch. assoc. U. Louisville Med. Sch., 1959-61, 62-63; commd. ensign USNR, 1965; advanced through grades to commr. USN, 1983; instr. instrumentation chemistry Northwestern U., Evanston, Ill., 1968-70; tchr. sci., chemistry, gifted math. Waukegan (Ill.) pub. schs., 1970-75; phys. scientist Libr. of Congress, Washington, 1975-76; rsch. engr. Lockheed Missiles & Space Co., Sunnyvale, Calif., 1976-77; instr., assoc. chmn. dept. physics U.S. Naval Acad., Annapolis, Md., 1977-80; analyst sys. analysis divsn. Office of Chief of Naval Ops. Staff, Washington, 1980-81; comdg. officer Naval Rsch. Ctr., Stockton, Calif., 1981-83; mem. faculty Def. Intelligence Coll., 1983-85; program mgr. Space and Naval Warfare Sys. Command, 1985-86; commdg. officer PERSUPPACT Memphis, 1986-88; program mgr. Space and Naval Warfare Sys. Command, 1988-91; sect. chief Def. Intelligence Agy., 1991-95. Chief marching divsn. Nat. Homecoming Parade and N.Y.C. Regional Parade Task Force Desert Storm, 1991; contractor mgr. supporting spl. asst. to Sec. of Def. for Gulf War Illnesses Investigations, 1997—98; pro bono work for Class Act Group; Fla. chpt. svc. officer, comdr. dist. 4 DAV. Mem. citizen rev. panel Fla. Foster Care Project Marion County, 1999; vet.'s advocate; mem. exec. com. Marion County Dem. Grantee, Am. Heart Assn., 1960—62, 1997—98, NSF, 1971, 1982. Mem.: Pvt. Investigators Assn. Va., Evidence Photographers' Internat. Coun., Internat. Soc. Bassists, Internat. Conf. Women in Sci. Engring. (protocol chair), Am. Soc. Photogrammetry, Am. Statis. Assn., Am. Fedn. Musicians, Soc. Women Engrs., Am. Chem. Soc., Mensa, Order Eastern Star, Delta Phi Alpha, Zeta Tau Alpha. Achievements include development of processes used in archival photography. E-mail: mslyon@att.net.

LYON, MARY LOU, retired secondary school educator; b. Wichita, Kans., Sept. 18, 1926; d. Theodore Joseph and Hazel Pearl (Johnson) Cochran; m. William Madison Lyon, Mar. 15, 1944 (div. July 1970); children: William Madison, Jr., Theodore Richard. AA, Coll. San Mateo, Calif., 1958; BA with distinction and honors, San Jose (Calif.) State U., 1960, lifetime secondary credential, 1961, MA, 1967. Cert. secondary edn. tchr., Calif. Tchr. Los Gatos (Calif.) HS, 1961, Blach Jr. HS Los Altos (Calif.) Elem. Dist., 1961-62, Homestead High, Fremont Union HS Dist., Cupertino, Calif., 1962—93, Metropoltitan Adult Edn. Program, San Jose, 1986—. Tchr. San Jose State U. Extension, Cupertino, 1974-76, Fremont Union High Sch. Adult Edn., 1977; various offices Calif. Coun. for Social Studies, Sacramento, 1962-80; historian, photographer Anza Trek Observance Bicentennial, Santa Clara County (Calif.) Bicentennial Commn., 1975-76; cons. Calif. map Hearne Bros. Map Co., 1981; speaker Genealogical Soc., San Jose Hist. Mus., Calif. Hist. Soc., others. Author, editor (pamphlet) Social Sci. Rev., 1975-76, San Francisco Westerners News from Telegraph Hill 1995-, Santa Clara County Trailblazers, 1997-2002, 04—; author, numerous books on Santa Clara County, photographer (one-woman show) Cupertino Hist. Soc., 1975; photographer: (textbook) Addison Wesley, 1980; author: Some Women in Santa Clara County, Some More Women in Santa Clara County, Elisha Stephens of the Stephens-Murphy Party of 1844, Some Men in Santa Clara History. Chair of site & times Conf. Calif. hist. soc., 1985—; commr. Santa Clara County Hist. Heritage, 1994—2003; delegate Calif. State Sesquicentennial commn. for CCHS, 1998—2000. Recipient history honor, Phi Alpha Theta, 1959—60, Award of excellence for tchng. Calif. history, Conf. of Calif. Hist. Soc., 1973, Honored as an Achiever, Santa Clara County Penwomen, 1976, Coke Wood award, Conf. of Calif. Hist. Soc., 1994, 1997, award of merit, Calif. Pioneers of Santa Clara County, 1999, Pres. award, Conf. of Calif. Hist. Soc., 1999, 2002. Mem. Conf. Calif. Hist. Soc. (various offices 1973—, pres. 1983-84, organizer confs., 2005, co-chair no. symposium 2005), Oreg.-Calif. Trail Assn. (publicity com. Calif.-Nev. Hawaii br. 1985—), Nat. Oreg.-Calif. Trail Assn., Westerners Internat. (bd. dirs.); mem. Cupertino Hist. Soc., San Jose Hist. Soc. (cons.), Santa Clara County Hist.Heritage Commn., Santa Clara County Pioneers, Golden Gate Park Assoc., Heritage Coun. of Santa Clara County, Lewis & Clark Hist. Assoc., Nat. Parks & Conservation Assoc., Menlo Park Hist. Soc., San Jose Hist. Mus. Assoc., San Francisco Corral of Westerners sheriff, 1995, others. Democrat. Congregational. Avocations: photography, travel, lecturing, western history. Home: 879 Lily Ave Cupertino CA 95014-4261 Personal E-mail: malyon_1999@yahoo.com.

LYON, PHILIP KIRKLAND, lawyer; b. Warren, Ark., Jan. 19, 1944; s. Leroy and Maxine (Campbell) L.; children by previous marriage: Bradford F., Lucinda H., Bruce P., Suzette P., John P., Martin K., Meredith J.; m. Jayne Carol Jack, Aug. 12, 1982. JD with honors, U. Ark., 1967. Bar: Ark. 1967, U.S. Supreme Ct. 1970, Tenn. 1989. Sr. ptnr., dir. ops. House, Wallace, Nelson & Jewell, P.A., Little Rock, 1967-86; pres. Jack, Lyon & Jones, P.A., Little Rock and Nashville, 1986—. Instr. bus. law, labor law, govt. bus. and collective bargaining U. Ark., Little Rock, 1969-72; lectr. practice skills and labor law U. Ark. Law Sch., 1979-80; bd. dirs. labor program Ctr. Am. and Internat. Law; editl. bd. dirs. Entertainment Law and Fin., 1993-2004. Author: Arkansas Employment Law Desk Book, 1997; co-author: Schlei and Grossman Employment Discrimination Law, 2d edit., 1982; editor-in-chief Ark. Law Rev., 1966—67, bd. dirs., 1978—93, v.p., 1990—92; editor: Arkansas Employment Law Letter, 1995—, Arkansas Employment Law Ctr., 1998—. Mem. Ark. State C. of C. (bd. dirs. 1984-88), Greater Little Rock C. of C. (chmn. cmty. affairs com. 1982-84, minority bus. affairs 1985-89). Inaugural fellow Coll. Labor and Employment Lawyers, 1996; recipient Golden Gavel award Ark. Bar. Assn., 1978, Writing Excellence award Ark. Bar Found., 1980. Mem.: ABA (select com. liaison office fed. contract compliance programs 1982—92, select com. liaison EEOC 1984—92, select com. immigration, co-chair ethics and profl. responsibility com. 2000—03, forum com. entertainment and sports industries), Nashville Bar Assn. (entertainment law com., lawyers concerned for lawyers com., employment law com.), Tenn. Bar Assn. (labor sect., lawyers helping lawyers com. 1989—), Ark. Bar Assn. (chmn. labor law com. 1977—78, chmn. labor law sect. 1978—79, chmn. lawyers helping lawyers com. 1988—94). Office: Jack Lyon & Jones PA 11 Music Cir S Ste 202 Nashville TN 37203-4335 also: Jack Lyon and Jones PA Ste 3400 425 W Capitol Little Rock AR 72201 also: Jack Lyon and Jones PA Shiloh Rd Jasper AR 72641-9744 Home: PO Box 121195 Nashville TN 37212 also: Owl Lyon Ranch HC 70 Box 478 Jasper AR 72641-9744 Office Phone: 615-259-4664. Business E-Mail: pklyon@jljnash.com. *One of the true secrets of success is to concentrate your efforts--for if you apply these efforts everywhere at once then you will accomplish very little anywhere.*

LYON, RICHARD, retired mayor, retired military officer; b. Pasadena, Calif., July 14, 1923; s. Norman Morais and Ruth (Hollis) L.; m. Cynthia Gisslin, Aug. 8, 1975; children: Patricia, Michael, Sean; children by previous marriage: Mary, Edward, Sally, Kathryn, Patrick (dec.), Susan. B.E., Yale U., 1944; MBA, Stanford U., 1953. Commd. ensign USN, 1944; advanced through grades to rear adm. SEAL, 1974; served as scout and raider in Pacific and China, World War II; with Underwater Demolition Team 5 in Korea; recalled to active duty as dep. chief Naval Res. New Orleans, 1978-81. Mem. Chief Naval Ops. Res. Affairs Adv. Bd., 1978-81; exec. v.p. Nat. Assn. Employee Benefits, Newport Beach, Calif., 1981-90; mem. Bd. Control, U.S. Naval Inst., 1978-81; pres. Civil Svc. Commn., San Diego County, 1990, Oceanside Unified Sch. Bd., 1991; mayor City of Oceanside, 1992-2000. Pres. bd. trustees Children's Hosp. Orange County, 1965, 72. Decorated Legion of Merit. Mem. Nat. Assn. Securities Dealers (registered prin.), Newport Harbor Yacht Club, Oceanside Yacht Club, Rotary (Anaheim, Calif. pres. 1966). Republican. Episcopalian. Home: 600 S The Strand Oceanside CA 92054-3902 Personal E-mail: lyonclan@cox.net.

LYON, RICHARD HAROLD, physicist, educator; b. Evansville, Ind., Aug. 24, 1929; s. Chester Clyde and Gertrude Lyon; m. Jean Wheaton; children: Katherine Lyon Davis, Geoffrey Cleveland, Suzanne Marie Riggle. AB, Evansville Coll., 1952; PhD in Physics (Owens-Corning fellow), MIT, 1955; DEng, U. Evansville, 1976. Asst. prof. elec. engring. U. Minn., Mpls., 1956-59; Mem. research staff Mass. Inst. Tech., 1955-56, lectr. mech. engring., 1963-69, prof. mech. engring., 1970-95, prof. emeritus, 1995—, head mechanics and materials div., 1981-86. NSF postdoctoral fellow U. Manchester, Eng., 1959-60; sr. scientist Bolt Beranek & Newman, Cambridge, 1960-66, v.p., 1966-70; chmn. Cambridge Collaborative, Inc., 1972-90; v.p. Grozier Pub., Inc., 1972; pres. Grozier Tech. Systems, 1976-82, RH Lyon Corp, 1976—; sr. scientist, Acentech, Inc., 2005. Author: Transportation Noise, 1974, Theory and Applications of Statistical Energy Analysis, 1975, 2d edit. (with R. DeJong), 1994, Machinery Noise and Diagnostics, 1987, Designing for Product Sound Quality, 2000; mem. editl. bd. Acoustical Soc. Japan, 1996—. Bd. dirs. Boston Light Opera, Ltd., 1975; mem. alumni bd. U. Evansville, 1988-94, trustee, 1995-98, chmn. ann. fund, 1996-97. Recipient Rayleigh medal Brit. Inst. Acoustics, 1995, Nat. Acad. Engring. award 1995, Disting. Alumni award U. Evansville, 1997, medal of Honor, U. Evansville, 2002, Gold medal Indian Acoustical Soc., 2003. Fellow: AAAS, Acoustical Soc. Am. (assoc. editor jour. 1967—74, exec. coun. 1976—79, v.p. 1989—90, pres. 1993—94, Silver medal in engring. acoustics 1998, Gold medal 2003), Internat. Inst. Acoustics and Vibrations (hon.); mem.: Brit. Inst. Acoustics (Rayleigh medal 1995), Nat. Acad. Engring., Sigma Xi, Sigma Pi Sigma. Achievements include research and publications in fields of nonlinear random oscillations, energy transfer in complex structures, sound transmission in marine and aerospace vehicles, building acoustics, product sound quality, environmental noise, machinery diagnostics, home theater audio systems. Home: 60 Prentiss Ln Belmont MA 02478-2021 Office: RH Lyon Corp 60 Prentiss Lane Belmont MA 02478 Office Phone: 617-489-2112. Business E-Mail: rhlyon@lyoncorp.com.

LYON, RONALD EDWARD, management consultant, computer consultant; b. Kansas City, Kans., Apr. 13, 1936; s. William Edward and Lillian (Gee) L.; m. Josette Paula Larré, July 24, 1959; children: Michael Alan, Mark Alexander, Matthew Adam, Collette Allison. Owner Hansler Outboard & Austin Aqua Sports, Austin, Tex., 1959-63; gen. mgr. Wayne Green Ent.-73 Mag., Peterboro, N.H., 1963-65; with Computer Control Corp., Peterboro, N.H., 1965-71; sales person Radio Shack (Tandy) & Sterling Elec. Co., Maine, N.H., Vt. areas, 1971-82; sales engr. Pall Corp./Russell Assocs., Inc., Watertown, Mass., 1982-87; mgr. eastern region Fansteel/Wellman Dynamics, 1984-87; CEO, COO Laryon Assocs., Inc., Keene, N.H., 1987—. With USAF, 1955—59. Mem. U.S. Power Squadron, Soc. for Preservation and Encouragement of Barber Shop Quartet Singing in Am. Avocations: sailing, amateur radio, computers, skiing, square dancing. Home: 12 Olde Towne Rd Munsonville NH 03457

LYON, WILFORD CHARLES, JR., insurance executive; b. Blackfoot, Idaho, June 1, 1935; s. Wilford Charles and Nellie Anna (Estenson) L.; m. Eleanor Perkins, Aug. 23, 1957; children: Katherine Ann, Wilford Charles III. BS, Ga. Inst. Tech., 1958; MA in Actuarial Sci., Ga. State Coll., 1962. Asst. v.p. Ind. Life and Accident Ins. Co., Jacksonville, Fla., 1963-69, asst. v.p., dir. methods and planning dept., 1969-70, v.p., home office coord., 1970-79, pres., chief adminstrv. officer, 1979-84, chmn. bd., CEO, 1984-96. Exec. compensation com., audit com. Fla. Bank, Inc., 1997-2004; trustee, exec. com. Edward Waters Coll., Jacksonville, 1983-96, chmn., bd. visitors, 1993-96, 2001-02. Pres. Jacksonville Jaycees, 1966; trustee Gator Bowl Assn., Jacksonville, 1981—, pres., 1981; pres. Jacksonville C. of C., 1984; trustee Cmty. TV, Inc., Jacksonville, 1980-93, chmn., 1991-92, exec. com., 2001-02; trustee Univ. Hosp., Jacksonville, Inc., 1985-86; bd. trustees Jacksonville Cmty. Found., 1999--; bd. dirs. YMCA Fla.'s First Coast, 1985—, sec., 1986, vice-chmn., 1987, chmn., 1988, chmn. devel. com. 2004—; chmn. 1991 Nat. Vol. Week, Vol. Jacksonville, Inc.; pres. bd. Cypress Village, Inc., 1998-99; bd. dirs. Bolles Sch., 2001—; deacon, elder, clk., trustee Presbyn. Ch. Recipient Disting Svc. award Jacksonville Jaycees, 1972, Jack Donnell award Outstanding Businessman of Yr., 1983, Dick Hutchinson award Sertoma Club South Jacksonville, 1972, Svc. to Mankind award, 1972, Boss of Yr. award Profl. Secs. Internat., 1972-73, Victory Crusade award Fla. Cancer Soc., 1969, Ins. Industry Cmty. Svc. award Jacksonville Assn. Life Underwriters, 1986, C.G. Snead Meml. award Jacksonville Assn. of Life Underwriters, 1991, Top Mgmt. award Sales and Mktg. Execs. of Jacksonville, 1990, Clanzel T. Brown award Jacksonville Urban League, 1991, Svc. to Youth award YMCA of Fla.'s First Coast, 1991, Humanitarian award NCCJ, 1994. Mem. Life Insurers Conf. (exec. com. 1981-91, chmn. membership com. 1981-86, sec. 1984-85, vice chmn. 1985-86, chmn. 1986-87), Am. Coun. Life Ins. (Fla. state v.p. 1981-96, bd. dirs. 1987-88, bd. dirs. Polit. Action Com. 1988-94), Southeastern Actuaries Club, Rotary Club Jacksonville (pres. Mandarin club 1977-78, Paul Harris fellow, dist. gov. 697 1985-86), Masons (33d degree), York Rite, Scottish Rite Bodies, Shriners (potentate Morocco Temple 1973, emeritus rep.). Republican. Home: 4035 Alhambra Dr W Jacksonville FL 32207

LYON, WILLIAM, SR., builder; b. 1923; Student, U. So. Calif. With Lyon & Son, Phoenix, 1945-50, William Lyon Devel. Co., Newport Beach, Calif., 1954-72, pres.; with William Lyon Co., Newport Beach, 1972—, now chmn. bd., CEO; and owner Martin Aviation, Orange County, Calif. Served to maj. gen. USAF, Pacific, European, Middle East theaters. WWII, pilot, 75 combat missions, Korean War. Decorated Disting. Svc. Medal, Disting. Flying Cross, Air Medal, Presdl. Unit Citation, others. Office: William Lyon Co 4490 Von Karman Ave Newport Beach CA 92660-2000*

LYON-HANSEN, EMILY FRANCES, language educator; b. Toledo, June 4, 1951; d. Gaylord Joe Lyon and Norma Duffield Stong; m. Lawrence Edward Testa (div.); children: Jeffrey Lawrence Testa, Abigail Marie Testa; m. George Arthur Hansen, Aug. 26, 2000. AA, Marshalltown C.C., 1971; BS, Iowa State U., 1973. Tchr. English, River Falls H.S., Wis., 1975—. Forensics coach, play dir. River Falls H.S., Wis. Actor: (plays) St. Croix Valley Theatre, 1982—2000. Lector trainer St. Bridget's Cath. Ch., River Falls, Wis., 1999—2005. Avocations: reading, listening to public radio, travel, gardening, home decorating.

LYONS, ANTHONY PATRICK, acoustician, acoustical engineer, researcher; b. Seoul, South Korea, Apr. 6, 1966; s. John Thomas and Mary Irene Lyons; m. Carrie Neuhard, July 30, 1968; 1 child, Natalie Rose; 1 child, Patrick Thomas. PhD, Tex.A&M U., 1995. Scientist SACLANT Undersea Rsch. Ctr., La Spezia, Italy, 1995—2000; sr. rsch. assoc. / assoc. prof. of acoustics Pa. State U. / Applied Rsch. Lab., State College, Pa., 2000—. Contbr. articles Jour. of Acoustical Soc.ric.EE Journal .Oceanic Engring., etc. Recipient A.B. Wood Medal, Inst. of Acoustics, 2003, Disting. Grad. Student Rsch. award, Tex. A&M U. Assn. of Former Students, 1991; fellow Bd. of Trustees fellowship, Henderson State U., Arkadelphia, AR, 1984—88. Mem.: Am. Geophys. Union, IEEE Oceanic Engring. Soc., Acoustical Soc. of Am. E-mail: apl2@psu.edu.

LYONS, BRIDGET GELLERT, language educator; b. Prague, Czechoslovakia, Aug. 28, 1932; came to U.S., 1940; d. Leopold and Marianne (Petschek) Gellert; m. Robert B. Lyons, Feb. 6, 1971. BA, Radcliffe Coll., 1954; MA, Oxford U., 1956; PhD, Columbia U., 1967. Instr. Rutgers U., New Brunswick, N.J., 1965-67, asst. prof., 1967-71, assoc. prof., 1971-78, prof., 1978—, chmn. dept. English, 1979-81, dir. grad. program in English, 1981-90. Author: Voices of Melancholy, 1971; co-editor: Renaissance Quar., 1978-92; editor: Reading in an Age of Theory, 1997. Mem. Renaissance Soc. Am. (exec. bd. 1978—) Home: 30 W 60th St New York NY 10023-7902 E-mail: robridge@rcn.com.

LYONS, BRUCE M., lawyer; b. New Rochelle, NY, Sept. 22, 1942; s. Mildred Goodavitch; m. Madeline Lyons, Nov. 29, 1971 (div. 1981); m. Marcia Mae Lyons, June 8, 1983; children: Scott, Marc. BA, U. Miami, 1964, JD, 1967. Bar: Fla. 1967, U.S. Dist. Ct. (so. dist.) Fla. 1967, U.S. Fed. Ct., 1969 U.S. Ct. Appeals (5th cir.) 1972, U.S. Supreme Ct. 1976, U.S. Ct. Appeals (11th cir.) 1981, D.C. 1993. Asst. county solicitor Broward County, 1967—71; mcpl. judge City of Coconut Creek, 1969—72; assoc. mcpl. judge City of Lauderdale Lakes, 1972—73; pres. Lyons & Sanders Chartered, Ft. Lauderdale, Fla. Advisor Nat. Criminal Justice Student Trial Advocacy Competition, 1990-91; trial practice instr. Nat. Coll. Criminal Def., Macon, Ga., 1991; mem. Broward County Narcotics Guidance Council, 1971; master of the bench, Stephen R. Booher Inn of Ct.; spkr. in field. Contbr. articles to profl. jours. Dir. The Starting Place, Hollywood, Fla.; mem. Youth Leadership of Broward County, Juvenile Delinquency and Gang Prevention Coun., Narcotics Guidance Coun. of Broward County. Mem. ABA (criminal justice coun. 1992-93, 95, vice-chmn. CLE 1996-97, chmn.-elect criminal justice sect. 1998, chmn. 1999-2000, chmn. def. function com. 1989-92), NACDL (pres. 1986-87, dir. 1976-81, sec. 1982-83, 2d v.p. 1984-85, pres. 1986-87, Robert C. Heeney award 1997), Broward County Criminal Def. Attys. Assn. (pres. 1988-89), Fla. Bar Assn. (mem. criminal rules com. 1988-89, exec. coun. criminal law sect. 1994), Broward County Bar Assn. (chmn. criminal law sect. 1976-77), Acad. Fla. Trial Lawyers (criminal law sect. chmn. 1974-76), Fed. Bar Assn., Fla. Assn. Criminal Def. Lawyers (dir. 1988-95), Am. Acad. Forensics Sci., Phi Delta Phi. Office: Lyons & Sanders 600 NE 3rd Ave Fort Lauderdale FL 33304-2618

LYONS, CHAMP, JR., state supreme court justice; b. Boston, Dec. 6, 1940; m. Emily Lee Oswalt, 1967; children— Emily Olive, Champ III. AB, Harvard U., 1962; LL.B., U. Ala., 1965. Bar: Ala. 1965, U.S. Supreme Ct. 1973. Law clk. U.S. Dist. Ct., Mobile, Ala., 1965-67; assoc. Capell, Howard, Knabe & Cobbs, Montgomery, Ala., 1967-70, ptnr., 1970-76, Helmsing, Lyons, Sims & Leach, Mobile, 1976-98; legal advisor Hon. Fob James, Jr. Gov. State Ala., 1998; assoc. justice Supreme Ct. of Ala., Montgomery, 1998—. Mem. adv. commn. on civil procedure Ala. Supreme Ct., 1971-98, chmn., 1985-98. Author: Alabama Practice, 1973, 3d edit., 1996; contbr. articles to law jours. Mem. ABA, Ala. Bar Assn., Mobile Bar Assn. (pres. 1991), Am. Law Inst., Ala. Law Inst., Farrah Law Soc., Harvard U. Alumni Assn. (S.E. regional dir. 1988-91, v.p.-at-large 1992-94, 1st v.p. 1994-95, pres. 1995-96).

LYONS, CHARLES HENRY, academic director; b. Boston, July 20, 1941; s. John Laurence and Adelaide (English) L.; m. Anne Warner Nason, Nov. 30, 1968; children: Mary Littlefield, Paul Laurence, Charles Philip. BA, Harvard U., 1963, MA in Tchg., 1964; PhD, Columbia U., 1970. Lectr. Syracuse (N.Y.) U., 1969-70; asst. to assoc. prof. Tchrs. Coll., Columbia U., N.Y.C., 1970-76; dir., overseas liaison Am. Coun. on Edn., Washington, 1976-82; exec. dir. Fulbright Found., Monrovia, Liberia, 1982-85; dir. internat. rsch. U. Ill., Chgo., 1985-87; dir. internat. affairs Conn. State U., New Britain, 1987-91; dir. internat. programs U. N.C., Greensboro, 1991—. Cons. U.S. AID, Washington, 1980-82. Author: To Wash An Aethiop White, 1975. Vol. U.S. Peace Corps, Nigeria, 1964-66; bd. dirs. Nat. Coun. Returned Peace Corps Vols., Washington, 1980-82; chmn. edn. com. Conn. World Trade Assn., Hartford, 1988-90. Recipient fellowship Fulbright Program, Germany, 1989. Avocation: amateur radio. Home: 313 N Tremont Dr Greensboro NC 27403-1546 E-mail: charleshlyons@yahoo.com.

LYONS, DAVID BARRY, philosophy and law educator; b. N.Y.C., Feb. 6, 1935; s. Joseph and Betty (Janower) L.; m. Sandra Yetta Nemiroff, Dec. 18, 1955; children— Matthew, Emily, Jeremy. Student, Cooper Union, 1952-54, 56-57; BA, Bklyn. Coll., 1960; MA (Gen. Electric Found. fellow), PhD (Woodrow Wilson dissertation fellow), Harvard U., 1963; postgrad., Oxford (Eng.) U., 1963-64. Asst. prof. philosophy Cornell U., Ithaca, NY, 1964-67, assoc. prof., 1967-71, prof., 1971-90, Susan Linn Sage prof. philosophy, 1990-95, chmn. dept. philosophy, 1978-84, prof. law, 1979-95, Boston U., 1995—, prof. philosophy, 1998—. Author: Forms and Limits of Utilitarianism, 1965, In the Interest of the Governed, 1973, Ethics and the Rule of Law, 1984, Moral Aspects of Legal Theory, 1993, Rights, Welfare, and Mill's Moral Theory, 1994; editor: Philos Rev., 1968-70, 73-75. Recipient Clark award Cornell U., 1976; Woodrow Wilson hon. fellow, 1960-61, Knox travelling fellow, 1963-64; Guggenheim fellow, 1970-71, Soc. for Humanities fellow, 1972-73, Nat. Endowment for Humanities fellow, 1977-78, 84-85, 93-94. Mem. Am. Philos. Assn., Am. Soc. Polit. and Legal Philosophy, Soc. Philosophy and Pub. Affairs. Office: Boston U Law Sch 765 Commonwealth Ave Boston MA 02215-1401 Office Phone: 617-353-3135. Business E-Mail: dbl@bu.edu.

LYONS, DENNIS GERALD, lawyer; b. Passaic, N.J., Nov. 20, 1931; s. Denis A.G. and Agnes C. (Dyt) L.; m. Anna Maria Nuñez, 1983; 1 child, Alexandra; children by previous marriage: Andrew, Sarah, Tessa. AB, Holy Cross Coll., 1952; JD, Harvard U., 1955. Bar: D.C. 1955, N.Y. 1956, U.S. Supreme Ct 1960. Law clk. U.S. Supreme Ct., Washington, 1958-60; assoc. firm Arnold & Porter, Washington, 1960-62, ptnr., 1963—; v.p., gen. counsel, dir. Gulf United Corp., Jacksonville, Fla., 1968-80; asst. sec. Braniff Airways, Dallas, 1966-77; trustee GMR Properties, Boston, 1971-81; dir. Gulf Broadcast Co., Dallas, 1983-86; vis. prof. law U. Va., Charlottesville, 1982-83. Pres. Harvard Law Rev., 1954-55 Served with USAF, 1955-58. Mem. ABA, Am. Law Inst. Office: Arnold & Porter 555 12th St NW Washington DC 20004-1206 Personal E-mail: lyonsden@erols.com. Business E-Mail: dennis_lyons@aporter.com.

LYONS, GENE MARTIN, political scientist, educator; b. Revere, Mass., Feb. 29, 1924; s. Abraham M. and Mary (Karger) L.; m. Micheline Pohl, Sept. 5, 1951; children: Catherine Anne, Daniel Eugene, Mark Lucien. BA, Tufts Coll., 1947; license en Scis. Politiques, Grad. Inst. Internat. Studies, Geneva, Switzerland, 1949; PhD, Columbia, 1958. Mgmt. officer Internat. Refugee Orgn., Geneva, 1948-52; budget and adminstrv. officer UN Korean Reconstrn. Agy., 1952-56; mem. faculty Dartmouth Coll., 1957-94, prof. govt., 1965-94, dir. Pub. Affairs Center, 1961-66, 73-75, assoc. dean faculty social scis., 1974-78; rsch. fellow Dickey Ctr. Dartmouth Coll., Hanover, N.H., 1994—. Vis. lectr. Sch. Mgmt. MIT, 1961-70; exec. sec. adv. com. govt. program behavioral scis. Nat. Acad. Scis., 1966-68; dir. dept. social scis. UNESCO, 1970-72; mem. U.S. Nat. Commn. for UNESCO, 1975-80, vice chmn., 1977-78; adv. U.S. del. UNESCO 19th Gen. Conf., 1976, 20th Gen. Conf., 1978; U.S. rep. to UNESCO European Conf., 1977; prof. associé U. Paris I, 1986; exec. dir. acad. council on the UN system, 1987-92. Author: Military Policy and Economic Aid: The Korean Case, 1961; co-author: (with J.W. Masland) Education and Military Leadership, 1959, (with L. Morton) Schools for Strategy, 1965, The Uneasy Partnership, 1969; editor, contbr. America: Purpose and Power, 1965, Social Science and the Federal Government, 1971; co-editor, contbr. Beyond Westphalia?, 1995, The United Nations System: The Policies of Member States, 1995, International Human Rights in the 21st Century, 2003—. Served with AUS, 1943—46. Mem. Acad. Coun. on UN System, Coun. on Fgn. Rels. Home: Main St Norwich VT 05055 Office: Dartmouth Coll Dickey Ctr Hanover NH 03755 E-mail: Gene.Lyons@Dartmouth.edu.

LYONS, GLORIA ROGERS, medical/surgical nurse, nursing educator; b. Durham, NC, Sept. 2, 1940; d. Roy Lee Rogers and Annie Bullock; m. James Lyons, Dec. 26, 1965; children: Jamesia, Anthony. BSN, Winston-Salem State U., 1962; MS, Tex. Woman's U., 1979. Cert. clin. nurse specialist. Charge nurse obstetrics Duke U. Med. Ctr., Durham, NC, 1962—65; charge nurse ob-gyn. John Hopkins Hosp., Balt., 1966; pub. health nurse Long Branch Pub. Health Agency, Long Branch, NJ, 1968; clin. rsch. nurse Clin. Rsch. Labs, Edgewood Arsenal, Md., 1966—68; charge nurse surgery Long Branch Med. Ctr., Long Branch, NJ, 1968—69; instr. LVN program Marlboro (N.J.) State Hosp., 1969—70; house supr. R.E. Thomason Gen. Hosp., El Paso, Tex., 1970—73; staff nurse emergency Darnall Army Cmty. Hosp., Fort Hood, Tex., 1974; coord. med.-surg. I Ctrl. Tex. Coll., Killeen, 1975—97, prof. emeritus, 2003—. Mem.: Tex. Retired Tchrs. Assn., Delta Sigma Theta.

LYONS, IRVING (BUD), III, corporate financial executive; BS in Indsl. Engring. and Ops. Rsch., U. Calif., Berkeley; MBA, Stanford U. V.p. Wells Fargo Mortgage Co.; founder, mng. ptnr. King & Lyons; joined Prologis, Fremont, Calif., 1993—, mng. dir., vice chmn., chief investment officer, 1997—. Office: Prologis Inc 47775 Fremont Blvd Fremont CA 94538

LYONS, JAMES EDWARD (JED), publishing executive; b. NYC, Feb. 7, 1952; s. James Vincent and Audrey Lucille (Garbers) L.; m. Blythe Mitchell Jones, June 6, 1981; children: James Edward Jr., Michael Davidson. BA cum laude, Bowdoin Coll., 1974. Advanceman and legis. asst. to Congressman William S. Cohen of Maine, Washington, 1972-75; pub. U. Press Am., Lanham, Md., 1975—, also bd. dirs.; pres. Madison Books, Inc., 1986—, U. Pub. Assocs. Inc., 1986—, Rowman and Littlefield Pubs., Inc., 1988—, Barnes and Noble Books, 1988—, Littlefield, Adams Quality Paperbacks, 1988—, Nat. Book Network, Inc. (divsn. Rowman and Littlefield Pubs.), 1986—, Scarecrow Press, Inc., 1995—, Vestal Press, 1997—, New Amsterdam Books, 1998—, Ivan R. Dee, 1998—, Lexington Books, Inc., 1998—. Nat. adv. com. to sec. HEW, 1974, The Derrydale Press, Inc., 1999—, Ardsley House, Pubs., 1999—, AltaMira Press, 1999—, Roberts Rinehart, 2000—, General Hall, 2000—, Madison House, 2000—, Sheed & Ward, 2002, Taylor Trade Pub., 2002, Gulf Pub., 2002, Republic of Tex. Press, 2003, Burnham Pubs., 2003, Collegiate Press, 2003, Jason Aronson, 2004, SR Books, 2004, Govt. Insts., 2004; panelist U.S. Dept. Edn., 1986-87; mem. USIA book and libr. adv. com., 1981-93; mem. bd. dir. Fidelity and Trust Bank, 2005-. Mem. Statue of Liberty-Ellis Island Centennial Commn., 1986-89; Presdl. appointee Nat. Commn. on Librs. and Info. Sci., 1991-93; trustee Georgetown U. Libr., 1981-92pres. St. Albans Sch. for Boys Parent's Club, 2002-03. Mem. Assn. Am. Pub. (exec. coun. profl. and scholarly pub. div. 1990-93, coll. div. faculty rels. com.), Soc. Scholarly Pub. (chmn. publ. com. 1979-80), Coun. on Fgn. Rels., Chief Execs. Orgn., Leaders Cir., Libr. of Congress (mem. exec. com. 2004-)Young Pres. Orgn. (bd. dir. 1994-99), Rolling Rock Club (Ligonier, Pa.), Chevy Chase Club, The Brook, Anglers Club of NY, Psi Upsilon. Presbyterian. Office: Rowman & Littlefield Pub Group National Book Network Ste 200 4501 Forbes Blvd Lanham MD 20706-4310 Office Phone: 301-459-3366. Office Fax: 301-429-5746. Business E-Mail: jlyons@rowman.com.

LYONS, JAMES ELLIOTT, lawyer; b. Lexington, Mo., Mar. 10, 1951; s. james Elliott and Elouise (Blackman) L.; m. Mary Jane McCarthy, June 30, 1979; children: Sean Austin, Caitlan Maureen. BA with honors, U. Mo., 1973; JD, NYU, 1976. Bar: Mo. 1976, N.Y. 1977, Calif. 1984. Assoc. Stinson Mag Thompson McEvers & Fizzell, Kansas City, Mo., 1976-77; assoc. Skadden, Arps, Slate et al., N.Y.C., L.A., 1977-84; law clk. to Hon. Robert W. Sweet U.S. Dist. Ct. (so. dist.) N.Y., 1978; ptnr. Skadden, Arps, Slate et al., L.A. and San Francisco, 1984—. Mem. ABA, Los Angeles County Bar Assn., Bar Assn. San Francisco, Mo. Bar Assn., Phi Beta Kappa Democrat. Office: Skadden Arps Slate et al 4 Embarcadero Ctr Ste 3800 San Francisco CA 94111-5974

LYONS, JAMES M., lawyer; b. Joliet, Ill., Jan. 6, 1947; AB, Coll. of Holy Cross, 1968; JD, DePaul U., 1971; LLD (hon.), Univ. Ulster, Belfast, No. Ireland, 2002. Bar: Colo. 1971, Ill. 1971, U.S. Dist. Ct. Colo. 1971, U.S. Dist. Ct. (no. dist.) Ill. 1971, U.S. Ct. Appeals (7th and 10th cirs.) 1971, U.S. Supreme Ct. 1971. Sr. trial ptnr., litigation & arbitration Rothgerber Johnson & Lyons LLP, Denver, 1971—. Mem. Colo. Supreme Ct. bd. law examiners, 1982-88; instr. Univ. Denver, Univ. Colo., Nat. Inst. Trial Advocacy; gen. counsel Clinton for Pres. Com., 1991-92, Office of Pres.-Elect, 1992-93; U.S. observer, Internat. Fund for Ireland, 1993-2001; spl. adv. to U.S. Pres. & Sec. State for econ. initiatives in Ireland & No. Ireland, 1997-2001; pres. Faculty of Fed. Advocates, US Dist. Ct. Colo. dist., 2003; vis. lectr. Univ. Ulster, No. Ireland, 2004; adj. prof. Univ. Denver, 2004. Assoc. editor DePaul Law Rev., 1970-71. Recipient St. Thomas More award, Catholic Lawyers Guild Colo., Learned Hand Nat. award, Am. Jewish Com., 1998. Fellow Am. Coll. Trial Lawyers, Internat. Acad. Trial Lawyers; master barrister Doyle's Inn chpt. Am. Inns of Ct.; mem. Ill. State Bar Assn., Colo. Bar Assn., Denver Bar Assn., Am. Bd. Trial Advocates. Office: Rothgerber Johnson & Lyons LLP Ste 3000 1 Tabor Ctr 1200 17th St Denver CO 80202 Office Phone: 303-623-9000. Office Fax: 303-623-9222. Business E-Mail: jlyons@rothgerber.com.

LYONS, JERRY LEE, mechanical engineer; b. St. Louis, Apr. 2, 1939; s. Ferd H. and Edna T. Lyons Diploma in Mech. Engring., Okla. Inst. Tech., 1964; MSME, S.W. U., 1983; PhD in Engring. Mgmt., Southwest U., 1984. Registered profl. engr., Calif.; diplomate Am. Bd. Forensic Engring. and Tech., Am. Coll. Forensic Examiners in forensic engring. and tech. (life). Project engr. Harris Mfg. Co., St. Louis, 1965-70, Essex Cryogenics Industries, St. Louis, 1963-65, 70-73; mgr. engring. rsch. Chemetron Corp., St. Louis, 1973-77; cons. fluid controls Wis. U., 1977—; pres., chief exec. Yankee Ingenuity, Inc., St. Louis, 1974—; v.p., gen. mgr. engring. R & D Essex Fluid Controls divsn. Essex Industries, Inc., St. Louis, 1977-90; pres. Lyons Pub. Co., St. Louis, 1983—; pres., CEO Innovative Controls subs. Yankee Ingenuity, Inc., Ft. Wayne, Ind., 1991—. Chmn. exec. bd. continuing engring. edn. in St. Louis for U. Mo., Columbia, 1980-81; bd. dirs. Intertech., Inc., Houston; cons. fluid power dept. Bradley U., Peoria, 1977-84. Author: Home Study Series Course on Actuators and Accessories, 1977, The Valve Designers Handbook, 1983, The Lyons' Encyclopedia of Valves, 1975, 93, The Designers Handbook of Pressure Sensing Devices, 1980, Special Process Applications, 1980; co-author: Handbook of Product Liability, 1991; contbr. articles to profl. jours.; patentee in field. With USAF, 1957-62. Recipient Winston Churchill medal, 1988, Dwight D. Eisenhower Achievement award of honor, 1990; named Businessman of Week (KEZK radio), Eminent Churchill fellow Winston Churchill Wisdom Soc., Business Man of Yr., Rep. Nat. Com., 2003. Fellow ASME; mem. N.Y. Acad. Scis., Soc. Mfg. Engrs. (life mem., cert. product design, chmn. Mo. registration com. 1975-90, chmn. St. Louis chpt. 1979-80, internat. dir. 1982-84, 85-87, engr. of yr. 1984, internat. award of merit 1985), Nat. Soc. Profl. Engrs., Mo. Soc. Profl. Engrs., St. Louis Soc. Mfg. Engrs. (chmn. profl. devel., registration and cert. com. 1975-79), Instrument Soc. Am. (sr. life mem., control valve stability com. 1978-84), Computer and Automated Sys. Assn. (1st chmn. St. Louis chpt. 1980-81), St. Louis Engrs. Club (award of merit 1977, Wisdom award of honor 1987, Wisdom Hall of Fame 1987), Am. Security Coun. (committeeman 1976—), Nat. Fluid Power Assn. (com. on pressure ratings 1975-77), Am. Legion. Lutheran. Achievements include patentee in field. Home: 1719 Wisteria Pl Fort Wayne IN 46818-8812 Office: Innovative Controls Inc 2705 Camino Court Fort Wayne IN 46808 Personal E-mail: a1yankee@aol.com.

LYONS, JOHN DAVID, literature and language professor; b. Springfield, Mass., Oct. 14, 1946; AB, Brown U., 1967; MA, Yale U., 1968, PhD, 1972. Asst. prof. French, Italian and comparative lit. Dartmouth Coll., Hanover, NH, 1972-78, assoc. prof., 1978-82, prof., 1982-87, chmn. comparative lit. program, 1981-84, chmn., prof. dept. French and Italian, 1987; dir. Am. Univ. Ctr. for Film and Critical Studies, Paris, 1984-85; prof. French U. Va., Charlottesville, 1987-92, Commonwealth prof. French, 1993—, chmn. dept., 1989-92, 98-99. Vis. prof. U. Paris III, 2005. Author: A Theatre of Disguise, 1978, The Listening Voice, 1982, Examplum, 1989, The Tragedy of Origins, 1996, Kingdom of Disorder, 1999, Before Imagination, 2005; co-editor: Mimesis: Mirror to Method, 1982, Dialectic of Discovery, 1983, Critical Tales, 1993; editor: Art, Architecture, Text: The Late Renaissance, 1985; assoc. editor Continuum, 1987—93, editor Academe, 1994—97, mem. editl. adv. bd. Philosophy and Literature, 1992—2002, French Forum. Recipient Robert Fish award for teaching Dartmouth Coll., 1978, Outstanding Tchr. award U. Va., 1996; Woodrow Wilson fellow, 1967, ACLS study fellow, 1978, NEH fellow, 1985-89, 92-93, ACLS contemplative practice fellow, 2002, J.S. Guggenheim fellow, 2002-03, Ctr. for Advanced Studies U. Va. fellow, 1987-89. Mem.: N.Am. Soc. for Seventeenth-Century French Lit. (pres. 2002).

LYONS, JOHN MATTHEW, telecommunications industry executive, broadcast executive; b. NYC, Nov. 5, 1948; s. Matthew Joseph and Anna (Coroneos) D.; m. Natalia Astakhova, Apr. 12, 1992; 1 child, Matthew. BSEE, Roosevelt U., Chgo., 1970, MSEE, 1976; PhD in Comm., Loyola U., Chgo., 1979; BSE, Century U., LA, 1981, MBA in Engring. Mgmt., 1982; PhD in Broadcasting (hon.), Sicluna U. Found., 1987. Registered profl. engr. Engr., prodr. Sta. WRFM, NYC, 1965-69; sr. facilities planning and project engr. Sta. WWRL-Radio, NYC, 1969-76; sr. facilities planning project engr. Sta. WWRL/WRVR, NYC, 1976-78; asst. chief engr. Sta. WOR, Inc., NYC, 1978-80; chief engr. Sta. WRKS-FM, NYC, 1980-90; sr. project mgr. DSI Comm. (now. DSI RF Sys. Inc. Somerset, NJ), Kenilworth, NJ, 1990-94, Vista Engring. Corp., NYC, 1994—; mgr. telecom. and broadcast ops. The Durst Orgn., 2002—. Pvt. cons. 1994—; dir. Raritan Ctr. Internat. Teleport, NJ, 1992-94; chief engr. WLTW/WAXQ, 1996-2002; ind. broadcasting cons., 1994—; mem. World Dance and Dancesport Coun., 1997—; pres. Lyon Records, NY, 1971—, Short Lines Co., NY, 1980—; chmn. master antenna com. Empire State Bldg., NY, 1980-88, exec. com., 1988-98, chmn. 1998-2002, Condé Nast Tower, 1999—, chmn. advt. industry com., 2000—; bd. dirs. The Document Ctr., NY; cons. broadcasting and telecom.; ofcl. photographer U.S. Imperial Soc. Tchrs. of Dance, 1991—, Blackpool Dance Festival, 1992—. Prodr.: (radio broadcast) The Cuban Missile Crisis, 1962 (Peabody award 1963); exec. prodr. (broadcast series) Radio: The First 50 Years, 1970, Sta. WOR 60th Anniversary Program, 1982 (Armstrong award 1983, Internat. Radio Festival award 1983), Sta. WOR 65th Anniversary Program, 1983; photography editor Amateur Dancers mag., Ability Mag.; contbg. photographer to Dance Scene mag., Dance News, Eng.; photographer Dance Beat, U.S.A., Australian Dance Rev., Dance Action, U.S.A., Japan Dance News, U.S. Imperial Soc. Tchrs. Dance, 1991—. Chmn. media curriculum com. Westchester Cmty. Coll., NY, 1987—. With USAF, 1967-70. Fellow Soc. Broadcast Engrs. (sr., life cert., bd. dirs. 1974-78), Internat. Biog. Assn.; mem. IEEE, ASCAP, Nat. Assn. Radio and Telecom. Engrs. (cert.), Broadcast Music, Inc., Audio Engring. Soc., Assn. Fed. Comms. Cons. Engrs., Internat. Radio and TV Soc., VA Hosp. Radio and TV Guild (v.p. 1976-82, 84—, pres. 1982-84, chmn. exec. com. 1984—, Bennie award 1981), Broadcast Pioneers, Broadcast Music, Am. Inst. Plant Engrs., U.S. Amateur Ballroom Dancers Assn. (regional v.p. 1987-89, dir. for internat. liaison 1989—), Knights of Malta, 1986. Avocations: competitive ballroom dancing, photography. Home: 305 E 86th St New York NY 10028-4702 Office: The Durst Orgn 4 Times Sq New York NY 10036 E-mail: dpintl@aol.com.

LYONS, JOHN W(INSHIP), retired civilian military employee, chemist, consultant; b. Reading, Mass., Nov. 5, 1930; m. Grace Hanley, Nov. 28, 1953; children: John, Louis, Margaret, Mary Ann. AB in Chemistry, Harvard U., 1952; AM in Phys. Chemistry, Washington U., St. Louis, 1963, PhD in Phys. Chemistry, 1964. With Monsanto Co., 1955-73, group leader, sect. mgr. research dept., inorganic chems. div., 1962-69, mgr. comml. devel., head fire safety center, 1969-73; mem. ad hoc panel on fire research Nat. Bur. Standards, Washington, 1971-73; dir. Ctr. for Fire Rsch., 1973-77, Nat. Engring. Lab., 1978-89, Nat. Inst. Standards and Tech., Gaithersburg, Md., 1990-93, Army Rsch. Lab., Adelphi, Md., 1993-98; ret., 1998. Co-chmn. U.S.-Japan Natural Resources Panel on Fire Rsch., 1975-78; mem. adv. com. on engring NSF, 1981-90; mem. bd. visitors Coll. Engring., U. Md., 1980-90, 99—, Biotech. Inst., 1999—; mem. adv. com. Naval Rsch. Lab., 1985; mem. com. on fed. labs. Office Sci. and Tech. Policy; mem. Nat. Rsch. Coun. Bd. on Army Sci. Tech.; chmn. standing com. on army tech. for Homeland Security; disting. rsch. prof. Ctr. Tech. and Nat. Security Policy, Nat. Def. U. Author: Viscosity and Flow Measurement, 1963, The Chemistry and Uses of Fire Retardants, 1970; Fire, 1985; contbr. numerous articles to profl. publs. Chmn. blue ribbon com. on rsch. and pub. svc. U. Md., 1993. Recipient gold medal Dept. Commerce, 1977, President's Mgmt. Improvement award White House, 1977, President's Disting. Exec. Rank award, 1981, E.U. Condon award, 1986; Disting. Svc. award U. Md. Coll. Engring., 1990, Centennial medal, 1994; 1st ann. Outstanding Achievement award Fire Retardant Chem. Assn., 1994. Fellow AAAS, Washington Acad. Sci.; mem. Am. Chem. Soc. (chmn. St. Louis sect. 1971-72), Nat. Fire Protection Assn. (bd. dirs. 1978-84), ASTM (bd. dirs. 1985-87), Nat. Acad. Engring., Sigma Xi. E-mail: jlyons@frederickmd.com.

LYONS, MARY E., academic administrator; b. Calif. BA, Sonoma St. Univ., 1971; MA, San Diego St. Univ., 1976; PhD, Sonoma St. Univ., 1983. Prof. Franciscan School of Theology, Berkeley, Calif., 1984—90; pres. Calif. Maritime Acad., Vallejo, 1990-96, Coll. of St. Benedict, St. Joseph, Minn., 1996—2003, Univ. San Diego, 2003—. Office: Office of the President Univ San Diego 5998 Alcala Pk San Diego CA 92110-2492

LYONS, MAXINE EVADNEY, small business owner, poet; b. Kingston, Jamaica, Nov. 7, 1962; arrived in U.S., 1995; d. Ezekiel West and Eunice May Hitnarinesingh; m. Norman W. Lyons, Dec. 31, 1989. AS, No. U. West Indies, Mandeville, Jamaica, 1985. Tchr. Continuation HS, Jamaica, 1980—81; sec. Precision Arts Ltd., Jamaica, 1986—88; sec., receptionist Speed-O-Graphic Printer, Jamaica, 1988—89; asst. mgr. Astra Hotel, Jamaica, 1990—91; sec. Jamaica Transformer Co., 1991—92. Owner Jamaica Pl., Bronx, 2000—; host poetry readings Magic Pot Restaurant, Bronx. TV appearance Good Day NY, 2002, Bronxnet TV, 2002 (named Small Bus. of Week, 2002); author: numerous poems. Recipient Shakespear trophy Excellence and medallion, 2003. Avocations: poetry, short stories, cooking, catering, music. Home: 3313 Eastchester Rd Bronx NY 10469 Office: Maroon Books PO Box 682 Bronx NY 10462 E-mail: poettothemax@verizon.net.

LYONS, MONA, lawyer; b. NYC, Jan. 10, 1950; BA, Coll. Potamac, 1972; JD, Catholic Univ. Am., 1975. Bar: DC 1975. Private practice, Washington. Named one of 75 Best Lawyers in Washington, Washingtonian Mag., 2002. Mem.: DC Bar. Office: Law Office of Mona Lyons 1666 Connecticut Ave NW Ste 500 Washington DC 20009 Office Phone: 202-387-7000. Office Fax: 202-387-7116.

LYONS, NICK, publishing executive; b. N.Y.C., June 5, 1932; s. Nathan and Rose (Bernstein) Ress; m. Mari Blumenau, Sept. 1, 1957; children: Paul, Charles, Jennifer, Anthony. BS in Econs., U. Pa., 1953; MA in Am. Lit., U. Mich., 1961, PhD in Am. Lit., 1963. Prof. English Hunter Coll., N.Y.C., 1961-88; exec. editor Crown Pubs., Inc., N.Y.C., 1963-78; pres. Nick Lyons Books, N.Y.C., 1979-84, Lyons & Burford, Pubs., N.Y.C., 1984-98; chmn. bd. dirs. The Lyons Press, N.Y.C., 1999—2001. Author: The Sony Vision, 1975, The Seasonable Angler, 1970, Bright Rivers, 1978, Confessions of a Fly Fishing Addict, 1988, Spring Creek, 1991, Full Creel, 2000. With U.S. Army, 1954-55. Avocation: fly fishing. Home: 342 W 84th St New York NY 10024-4202

LYONS, OREN, Native American chieftain, conservationist; BA, Syracuse U., 1958, LLD (hon.). Lic. profl. boxing second BN.Y. Mem. Onondaga Coun. of Chiefs of Six Nations of Iroquois Confederacy; Faithkeeper Turtle Clan of Onondaga Nation, 1970—; prof. Am. Studies State U. of N.Y., Buffalo, dir., Native Am. Studies Program. Native Am. rep. Corp. for Pub. Broadcasting, 1974—; Six Nations rep. to sub-commn. on prevention of discrimination and protection of minorities Commn. on Human Rights, UN Econ. and Social Coun., Washington, 1976; mem. Human Rights Divsn. of UN; bd. dirs. Harvard Project on Am. Econ. Devel.; chmn. bd. dirs. Honoring Contbns. in Governance of Am. Indian Nations; mem. exec. com. World Forum of Spiritual and Parliamentary Leaders on Human Survival, Oxford, England, 1998; hon. bd. dirs., co-founder Native Am. Ctr. for the Living Arts, Niagara Falls, NY; mem. adv. bd. Native Am. Family Nurse Practitioner Program; spkr., presenter in field. Author: Exiled in the Land of the Free, 1992, Voice of Indigenous Peoples, 1992, Native People Address the United Nations, 1994; pub.: Daybreak Mag.; co-editor: Exiled in the Land of the Free. Named to Lacrosse Nat. Hall of Fame, 1993; recipient Ellis Island Congl. Medal of Honor, 1990, Howard E. Johnson award, 1991, Audubon medal, Nat. Audubon Soc., 1993. Mem.: Am. Arbitration Assn., Salt City Amateur Boxing Club (bd. dirs.), Onandaga Athletic Club (founding mem.). Avocations: Native American history, international indigenous affairs, contemporary indigenous issues, international environmental issues. Office: The Onondaga Nation PO Box 200 Nedrow NY 13120-0200 also: Center for the Americas Univ of Buffalo 1010 Clemens Hall Buffalo NY 14260-4630

LYONS, PAUL VINCENT, lawyer; b. Boston, July 19, 1939; s. Joseph Vincent and Doris Irene (Griffin) L.; m. Elaine Marie Hurley, July 13, 1968; children: Judith Marie, Maureen Patricia, Paula Anne, Joseph Hurley BS cum laude, Boston Coll., 1960; MBA, NYU, 1962; JD, Suffolk U., Boston, 1968. Bar: Mass. 1968, U.S. Dist. Ct. Mass. 1969, U.S. Cir. Ct. (1st cir.) 1969, U.S. Supreme Ct. 1991. Div. adminstrn. mgr. Pepsi-Cola Co., N.Y.C., 1962-64; mem. bus. faculty Burdett Coll., Boston, 1964-68; atty. NLRB, Boston, 1968-73; assoc. Foley Hoag LLP, Boston, 1973-77, ptnr., 1978—. Mem. faculty Boston U., 1972-74. Mem. Town Meeting, Milton, Mass., 1986—2002, Pers. Bd., Milton, 1994—2004. Lt. U.S. Army, 1960—62. Mem. ABA, Mass. Bar Assn., Boston Bar Assn. Office: Foley Hoag LLP 155 Seaport Blvd Boston MA 02210-2175 Office Phone: 617-832-1000. Business E-Mail: plyons@foleyhoag.com.

LYONS, RICHARD KENT, economics professor; b. Palo Alto, Calif., Feb. 10, 1961; s. J. Richard and Ida (Primavera) L. BS in Bus. with highest honors, U. Calif., Berkeley, 1982; PhD in Econs., MIT, 1987. Rsch. analyst SRI Internat., Menlo Park, Calif., 1983-84; summer intern Orgn. for Econ. Cooperation & Devel., Paris, 1985, Bd. Govs., Fed. Res. System, Washington, 1986; asst. prof. Columbia U., NYC, 1987-91, assoc. prof., 1991-93; asst. prof. Haas Sch. Bus., U. Calif., Berkeley, Calif., 1993-96, assoc. prof., 1996—2000, prof., 2000—04, Sylvan Coleman Chair fin., 2004—, assoc. dean for academic affairs, 2004, acting dean, 2004—. Vis. prof. U. Toulouse, France, Stockholm U., Sweden, London Sch. Econs., Found. for Advanced Info. and Rsch., Japan, U. Aix-Marseille, France; rsch. assoc. Nat. Bur. Econ. Rsch., Cambridge, Mass., 1989—; chmn., dir. Matthews Asian Funds; dir. iShares Inc. (Barclays Global Investors); cons. IMF, World Bank, Fed. Res. Bank, European Commn.; adv. bd. Econ. Policy Review, NYC. Assoc. editor Calif. Mgmt. Rev., Jour. Fin. Markets; contbr. articles to profl. jours. NSF grad. fellow, 1984. Mem. Am. Econ. Assn., Coun. on Fgn. Rels., Phi Beta Kappa, Beta Gamma Sigma, Sigma Alpha Epsilon. Democrat. Avocations: squash, guitar, French. Office: U Calif Haas Sch Bus Berkeley CA 94720-1900 Office Phone: 510-643-2027.

LYONS, ROBERT WILLIAM, medical educator, epidemiologist, consultant; b. Westmont, N.J., June 23, 1937; s. William John and Anna Agnes (Sullivan) L.; m. Constance Cryer, June 18, 1966 (div. 1974); m. Virginia Palmer Riggs, Aug. 29, 1981. BS, Georgetown U., 1960; MD, Yale U., 1964. Diplomate Am. Bd. Internal Medicine, Am. Bd. Infectious Disease. From asst. prof. to asst. clin. prof. medicine Yale U., New Haven, Conn., 1970-79, assoc. clin. prof. medicine, 1979—; from asst. prof. to assoc. prof. medicine U. Conn. Med. Sch., Farmington, 1972-87, prof. medicine, 1988—. Acting chief infectious diseases U. Conn. Med. Sch., Farmington, 1975-81; chief infectious diseases St. Francis Hosp., Hartford, Conn., 1972—, Mt. Sinai Hosp., Hartford, 1990—. Contbr. articles to profl. jours. Pres. Conn. Infectious Disease Soc.; past pres. Hartford Med. Soc.; patron Yale Art Gallery, New Haven, 1991—, China Inst. N.Y., N.Y.C., 1992—. Lt. USNR, 1965-67. Fellow ACP, Infectious Disease Soc. Am., Jonathan Edwards Coll., Yale U.; mem. Internat. AIDS Soc., Asia Soc. (pres. cir. 1993—), Yale Club N.Y.C., Town and County Club, Hartford Club. Avocation: collecting asian art especially japanese prints. Office: St Francis Hosp 114 Woodland St Ste 1 Hartford CT 06105-1299

LYONS, TERRENCE ALLAN, mining executive; b. Grand Prairie, Alta., Can., Aug. 1, 1949; s. Allan Lynnwood and Mildred Helen (Smith) L. B in Applied Sci., U. B.C., 1972; MBA, U. Western Ont., 1974. Registered profl. engr., B.C. Gen. mgr. Southwestern Drug Co., Vancouver, B.C., Can., 1975-76; mgr. planning Versatile Corp., Vancouver, 1976-83, asst. v.p., 1983-86, v.p., dir., 1986-88; dir. B.C. Pacific Capital Corp., 1988—. Bd. dirs. Canaccord Capital Inc.; chmn. Northgate Minerals Corp. Author articles on mfg. tech. Office: Northgate Minerals Corp Ste 404-815 Hornby St Vancouver BC Canada V6Z 2E6 Office Phone: 604-681-4004. Business E-Mail: tlyons@northgateminerals.com.

LYONS, THOMAS PATRICK, economics professor; b. Groton, Conn., Sept. 8, 1953; BA in Asian Studies, Cornell U., 1979, MA in Econs., 1982, PhD in Econs., 1983. Asst. prof. econs. Dartmouth Coll., Hanover, N.H., 1983-87; vis. asst. prof. Cornell U., Ithaca, N.Y., 1986-88, asst. prof., 1988-91; assoc. prof., 1991-2000; dir. East Asia program Cornell U., Ithaca, N.Y., 1991-94, dir. undergrad. studies, econs., 1995—, prof., 2000—. Author: Economic Integration and Planning in Maoist China, 1987, China's War on Poverty, 1992, Economic Geography of Fujian: A Sourcebook, vols. 1 and 2, 1995, 97, China Maritime Customs and China's Trade Statistics 1859-1948, 2003; contbr. numerous articles to profl. jours. With USN, 1972-76. Rsch. grantee Ford Found., 1987. Mem. Am. Econ. Assn., Assn. for Asian Studies, Assn. Am. Geographers. Office: Cornell U Dept Econs Uris Hall Ithaca NY 14853-7601 Office Phone: 607-255-9534. Business E-Mail: tpl4@cornell.edu.

LYONS, WILLIAM BERRY, geologist, educator; b. Gainesville, Fla., Feb. 8, 1947; s. Robert William and Ruth Olive (Berry) L. BA, Brown U., 1969; MSc, U. Conn., 1972, PhD, 1979. Postdoctoral fellow, then rsch. scientist U. N.H., Durham, 1976-79, asst. prof., then assoc. prof., 1979-90; prof., dir. hydrology hydrogeology program U. Nev., Reno, 1990—. Mem. Am. Geophys. Union, Am. Soc. Limnology and Oceanography, Geochem. Soc. Avocations: running, reading. Office: Mackay Sch Mines Univ Nev Reno Reno NV 89557-0001

LYONS, WILLIAM HARRY, law educator; b. Fitchburg, Mass., Mar. 5, 1947; s. William Earl and Jeanette Underwood (Weed) L.; m. Karen Virginia Knapp, June 27, 1970; children: Virginia Lynne, Kevin Michael. BA, Colby Coll., Waterville, Maine, 1969; JD, Boston Coll., 1973. Bar: Maine 1973, Mass. 1973, Nebr. 1985, U.S. Dist. Ct. Maine 1974, U.S. Dist. Ct. Nebr. 1986, U.S. Tax Ct. 1986. Assoc. Vafiades, Brountas & Kominsky, Bangor, Maine, 1973-80, ptnr., 1980-81; prof. law U. Nebr., Lincoln, 1981—, Richard H. Larson prof. tax law, 1999—. Vis. prof. Boston Coll. Law Sch., 1997-98, Vt. Law Sch., spring 2001, U. Leiden, summer 2002, U. Limerick, summer 2003, Boston Coll. Law Sch., spring 2005; planning com. Gt. Plains Fed. Tax Inst., Lincoln, 1982—, program chmn., 1992, 2002, pres., 1993, 2003; adv. com. Gt. Plains Studies, Lincoln, 1983; prof. in residence IRS, 1987-88. Articles editor The Tax Lawyer, 1982-85; contbr. articles to profl. jours. Tax adviser Lincoln Nonprofit Devel. Corp., Lincoln, 1983—. Recipient Disting. Tchg. award Nebr. U. Found., Lincoln, 1984, Student Bar Assn. U. Nebr.-Lincoln Coll. Law, 1984-85, 97, 99, 2002, Chancellor's award for Exemplary Svc. to Students, 2003; Nebr. State Bar Found. Outstanding Legal Educator Award. Fellow Am. Coll. Tax Counsel (regent 8th Cir. 2003—); mem. ABA (group editor sect. of taxation newsletter 1986-88, chmn. individual investments and workouts com. 1995-97, chmn. important devel. subcom. 2001—), Maine State Bar Assn., Nebr. State Bar Assn., Am. Judicature Soc., Delta Theta Phi, Scribes. Democrat. Home: 5232 S Bristolwood Ln Lincoln NE 68516-1676 Office: U Nebr Coll Law PO Box 830902 Lincoln NE 68583-0902 Office Phone: 402-472-1246. E-mail: wlyons2@unl.edu.

LYSNE, ALLEN BRUCE, laboratory director; b. Owen, Wis. s. Almond P. and Helen A. (Childs) L.; children: Michael, Bruce, Brooke. BS, U. N.D., 1960. Lic. med. technologist, N.D. Bd. Clin. Lab. Practice; cert. clin. lab. scientist, Nat. Cert. Agy. Clin. lab. dir USPHS Indian Hosp., Fort Yates, N.D., 1961-62; asst. dir. biochemistry Dr. Salsbury's Lab., Charles City, Iowa, 1962-63; clin. lab. dir Lake Region Clinic, Devils Lake, N.D., 1963-69; CEO Meml. Hosp. Assn., Maddock, N.D., 1969-75; asst. exec. dir. ops. N.D. Health Care Rev., Minot, 1976-80; regional mgr. Colo. Found. Med. Care, Pueblo, Denver, Colo., 1980-87; dir. diagnositc svcs. Cmty. Hosp., Hillsboro, N.D., 1988-92; clin. lab. dir. Carroll County Meml. Hosp., Carrollton, Mo., 1992—. Chmn. Coun. on Aging, Pueblo, 1980-87. Mem. Am. Chem. Soc., Am. Assn. Clin. Lab. Sci., Am. Assn. Clin. Chemistry, Sci. Pub. Interest, Mo. Assn. Clin. Lab. Sci., N.Y. Acad. Scis. Achievements include research in effectiveness, toxicity and safety of 2 new drugs for coccidioidomycosis.

LYSTAD, MARY HANEMANN (MRS. ROBERT LYSTAD), sociologist, writer; b. New Orleans, Apr. 11, 1928; d. James and Mary (Douglass) Hanemann; m. Robert Lystad, June 20, 1953; children: Lisa Douglass, Anne Hanemann, Mary Lunde, Robert Douglass, James Hanemann. AB cum laude, Newcomb Coll., 1949; MA, Columbia U., 1951; PhD, Tulane U., 1955. Postdoctoral fellow social psychology S.E. La. Hosp., Mandeville, 1955-57; field rsch. social psychology Ghana, 1957-58, South Africa and Swaziland, 1968, China, 1986; chief sociologist Collaborative Child Devel. Project, Charity Hosp. La., New Orleans, 1958-61; feature writer African div. Voice Am., Washington, 1964-73; program analyst NIMH, Washington, 1968-78, asso. dir. for planning and coordination div. spl. mental health programs, 1978-80; chief Nat. Ctr. for Prevention and Control of Rape, 1980-83, Ctr. Mental Health Studies of Emergencies, 1983-89; pvt. cons. specializing on mental health implications social and econ. problems Bethesda, Md., 1990—. Cons. on youth Nat. Goals Research Staff, White House, Washington, 1969-70. Author: (nonfiction) Social Aspects of Alienation, 1969, As They See It: Changing Values of College Youth, 1972, Violence at Home, 1974, A Child's World As Seen in His Stories and Drawings, 1974, From Dr. Mather to Dr. Seuss: 200 Years of American Books for Chidlren, 1980, At Home in America, 1983; (fiction for children) Millicent the Monster, 1968, James the Jaguar, 1972, Jennifer Takes Over P.S. 94, 1972, Halloween Parade, 1973, That New Boy, 1973, Play Ball, 1997; editor: Innovations in Mental Health Services to Disaster Victims, 1985, Violence in the Home: Interdisciplinary Perspectives, 1986, Mental Health Response to Mass Emergencies: Theory and Practice, 1988. Recipient Spl. Recognition award USPHS, 1983, Alumna Centennial award Newcomb Coll., 1986. Home and Office: 4900 Scarsdale Rd Bethesda MD 20816-2440

LYTHCOTT, MARCIA A., newspaper editor; d. William and Florence; m. Stephen Lythcott (dec.). BA in journalism, U. Wisc., Madison. Assoc. food guide editor Chicago Tribune, Ill., editor, style section, editor, home section, 1993—94, op-ed editor, 1995—. Office: Chicago Tribune 435 N Michigan Ave Chicago IL 60611-4066

LYTLE, GARY R., communications executive; 4 children. BA in Bus. Adminstrn., MBA, Mich. State U. Various govt. rels. pos., including v.p. govt. affairs Mich. Bell, 1980—92; dir. fed. rels. Ameritech, 1992—94, v.p., fed. rels. Washington, 1994—99, corp. officer; cons. Lytle Consulting, 1999—2000; interim pres., CEO U.S. Telecom Assn., 2000—01; sr. v.p., fed. rels. Qwest Comm. Internat. Inc., Denver, 2001—.

LYTLE, JAMES DEVORE, retired dentist; b. Cin., Sept. 14, 1935; s. Floyd E. and Margaret G. (Gilfillen) L.; m. Alice Hague; children: Todd R., Ayn Lytle Holley, Holly Lytle Scherer, Loren Lytle Brunemann. DDS, Ohio State U., 1960, MS in Periodontics, 1961; Cert. in Prosthodontics, Boston U., 1970. Pvt. practice restorative dentistry James D. Lytle, Inc., Cin., 1961—98. Sec., vice chmn. Callahan Meml. Award Commn., Ohio; published in internat. jours.; lectr. internat. Elder Presbyn. Ch., Cin. Fellow Am. Coll. Dentists, Internat. Coll. Dentists; mem. ADA, Ohio Dental Assn., Cin. Dental Soc., Am. Acad. Restorative Dentistry (coun.), Am. Bd. Prosthodontics (diplomat), Am. Bd. Periodontology (diplomat), Am. Acad. Periodontology, Acad. Osseointegration, Acad. Implant Prosthodontics, Acad. Dentistry Internat., E.T. Carson Lodge, Univ. Club, Sigma Chi, Psi Omega. Republican. Avocations: travel, photography, archeology-anthropology, long distance running, evolution with scientific and biblical emphasis. Home: 8815 Indian Hill Rd Cincinnati OH 45243-3711

LYTLE, L(ARRY) BEN, insurance company executive, lawyer; b. Greenville, Tex., Sept. 30, 1946; children: Hugh, Larry. BS in Mgmt. Sci. and Indsl. Psychology, East Tex. State U., 1970; JD, Ind. U., 1980. Computer operator/programmer U.S. Govt., Ft. Smith, Ark., 1964-65; customer engr. Olivetti Corp., San Antonio, 1965-66; mgr. computer ops. and computer software LTV Electrosystems, Greenville, 1966-70; project mgr. electronic fin. system, dir. systems planning Assocs. Corp. N.Am., South Bend, Ind., 1970-75; asst. v.p. systems Am. Fletcher Nat. Bank, Indpls., 1975-76; with Anaheim Ins. Cos., Inc., Indpls., 1976-99; pres. Assoc. Ins. Cos., Inc., Indpls., 1987-99, COO, 1987-89, CEO, 1989-99. Chmn. bd. dirs. Anthem Cos., Inc., Acordia, Inc.; chmn. bd. dirs. AdminaStar, Inc., Health Networks Am., Inc., Novalis, Inc., Robinson-Conner Nev., Inc.; bd. dirs. The Shelby Ins. Group, Raffensperger, Hughes & Co., Inc., Indpls. Power and Light Co. Enterprises; mem. adv. bd. CID Venture Ptnrs., Ltd. Partnership; rschr., cons. state and fed. govt. orgns., including, Adv. Coun. on Social Security, Pepper Commn. of U.S. Congress, others. Chmn. health policy commn. State of Ind., Indpls., 1990-92; active various civic orgns., including United Negro Coll. Fund, Indpls. Mus. Art. Mem. ABA, Ind. Bar Assn., Indpls. Bar Assn., Ind. State C. of C. (bd. dirs.), Indpls. C. of C. (bd. dirs.). Home: PO Box 441830 Indianapolis IN 46244-1830 Office: Anthem Ins Cos Inc 120 Monument Cir Indianapolis IN 46204-4906

LYTLE, MICHAEL ALLEN, criminologist, consultant; b. Salina, Kans., Oct. 22, 1946; s. Milton Earl and Geraldine Faye (Young) L.; div.; 1 child, Eric Alexander. BA, Ind. U., 1973; grad. cert., Sam Houston State U., Huntsville, Tex., 1977; MEd, Tex. A&M U., 1978; postgrad., 1978-80; student, Nat. Def. U., 1988. Substitute high sch. tchr., Butler Cty., KS, 1969; instr. criminal justice Cleve. State C.C., Tenn., 1974-77; adj. instr. criminal justice U. Tenn., Chattanooga, 1975-76; tchg. asst. Tex. A&M U. Sys., 1977-80, intern adminstrv. asst. Office Vice Chancellor Legal Affairs and Gen. Counsel, 1980, staff assoc. Office Chancellor, 1980-81, asst. to chancellor, 1981-83, asst. dir. govt. rels., 1983-84, spl. asst. to chancellor for fed. rels., 1984-87; dir. rsch. devel. and spl. asst. to v.p. for rsch. and grad. studies Syracuse U., N.Y., 1987, exec. dir. govt. rels., 1987-89, sr. rsch. assoc. tech. and info. policy prog. Maxwell Sch. Citizenship and Pub. Affairs, 1987-92, dir. fed. rels., 1989-92, adj. prof. internatl. bus. studies, 1990-92; prin. and sr. couns. The Erik Alexander Group, 1992-93; exec. dir. instl. devel. U. Tex., Brownsville, 1993-95, sr. lectr. criminal justice, 1995-97; rsch. fellow Office Undersec. Def., 1997; sr. rsch. assoc. Sci. Applications Internat. Corp., 1997-99; adj. prof. criminal justice Marymount U. and Lutheran Colls., Wash. Consortiums, 1999—; dep. mgr. tech. svcs. divsn. Sci. Applications Internat. Corp., 2000—. Rep., Coun. on Fed. Rels., Assn. Am. Univs.; instl. rep. Rsch. Univs. Network; exec. dir. Tex. Com. for Employer Support of the Guard and Res., 1982-86; mem. US Mexico Com. Philanthropy and the Border, 1994-95, militarily critical techs. adv. com. US Internat. Bus. Studies, Tex. A&M Univ., 1986-87; res. asst. army attache to Rep. of Ireland, 1986-87; mem. exec. com. N.E. Parallel Architectures Ctr.; mem. Sec. of Army's adv. panel in ROTC affairs, 1988-92; cons. Nat. Inst. Justice, 2000--, Office of Victims of Crime, 2002--. Mem. editl. bd., Jour. Tech. Transfer, 1987-95, contbr. articles to profl. jours. Served with USAR, Vietnam and Bosnia. Trustee, Brownsville Hist. Mus. Assn., 1994-96. Decorated Legion of Merit, Bronze Star, Purple Heart, Meritorious Svc. medal with 2 oak leaf clusters, Joint Svc. Commendation medal, Army Commendation medal with 4 oak leaf clusters; recipient Disting. Alumni award Sam Houston State U., 2003. Fellow Inter-Univ. Seminar Armed Forces and Soc. Am. Coll. Forensic Examiners (life); mem. AAAS (bd. advs. nat. security and sci. comm. proj. mem. awd. sel. panel. sci. freedom and responsibilty), Nat. Assn. State Univs. and Land-Grant Colls. (vet. affairs and nat. svc. com.), Am. Soc. for Pub. Adminstrn. (exec. com. sect., past chair on Nat. Security and Def. Analysis), Atlantic Counc. U.S. (councilor), Forensic Sci. Soc., Acad. Criminal Justice Scis., Internat. Assn. for the Study of Organized Crime, Internat. Assn. Chief's Police, mem., US Attorney's Law Enforcement Coordinating Com., southern dist., Tex., 1995-97. Mem. Army and Navy Club, Capitol Hill Club, Sigma Xi, Phi Delta Kappa, Alpha Phi Sigma Republican. Episcopalian. Address: 260 S Reynolds St Apt 403 Alexandria VA 22304-4430

LYTTLE, DEBORAH JEAN, musician, educator; b. Portland, Oreg., Jan. 26, 1957; d. Clayton Frederick and Jean Carol Metzger; children: Andrew Jonathan, Anna Dawn. Student, Clackamas C.C., 1982; BA in Music, Marylhurst U., 1986; MA in Edn., Portland State U., Oreg., 1998—2001. Lic. Oreg. Tchg. Warner Pacific Coll, 1992. Music and spanish tchr. Linkup, Oregon City, Oreg., 1996—2001; music dir. Colegio Maya, Guatemala City, Guatemala, 2001—. Dir.: (concert) Messiah, 2004—05. Mem.: Internat. Soc. Music Edn., Music Educators Nat. Conf. Avocations: travel, music, reading, walking. Office: Colegio Maya Sectio 0280 PO Box 02-5289 Miami FL 33102-5289 Office Phone: 502-365-0037. Personal E-mail: whoswho@webwizardry.net. E-mail: dlyttle@cm.edu.gt.

LYTTON, BERNARD, urology educator; b. London, June 28, 1926; came to U.S., 1962; s. Morris and Pearl (Zuckerberg) L.; m. Norma M. Mendle, Oct. 28, 1963; children: Sharon, Simon, Timothy, Jennifer. MB, BS, U. London, 1948, FRCS, 1955. House officer, sr. registrar Royal London Hosp., 1948-50, 58-61; prof., chief urology Yale Univ. Sch. Medicine, New Haven, 1967-87, Donald Guthrie prof. surgery, 1987—96, prof. emeritus, 1996—, dir. Henry Koerner Ctr. Emeritus Faculty, 2001—; Master Jonathan Edwards Coll. Yale U., 1987-97. Squadron leader Royal Airforce Med. Br., Eng., 1950-52. Fellow ACS; mem. Am. Urol. Assn. (Hugh Hampton Young award 1985, pres. New Eng. sect. 1974), Am. Assn. Genito-Urinary Surgeons, Clin. Soc. Genito-Urinary Surgeons (pres. 2000-01), Soc. Pelvic Surgeons. Avocations: tennis, skiing, history, hiking. Home: 21 Autumn St New Haven CT 06511-2220 Office: Yale U Sch Medicine Sect Urology PO Box 208041 New Haven CT 06520-8041 Office Phone: 203-785-2815.

LYTTON, ROBERT LEONARD, civil engineer, educator; b. Port Arthur, Tex., Oct. 23, 1937; s. Robert Odell and Nora Mae (Verrett) Lytton; m. Eleanor Marilyn Anderson, Sept. 9, 1961; children: Lynn Elizabeth, Robert Douglas, John Kirby. BSCE, U. Tex., 1960, MSCE, 1961, PhD, 1967. Registered profl. engr., Tex., La., land surveyor, La. Cowhand Slaughter Ranch, Douglas, Ariz., 1963; assoc. Dannenbaum and Assocs., Cons. Engrs., Houston, 1963—65; U.S. NSF fellow U. Tex., Austin, 1965—67, asst. prof., 1967—68; NSF fellow Australian Commonwealth Sci. & Indsl. Rsch. Orgn., Melbourne, Australia, 1969—70; assoc. prof. Tex. A&M U., College Station, 1971—76, prof., 1976—90, Wiley chair prof., 1990—95, dir. ctr. for infrastructure engring., 1991—, Benson chair prof., 1995—; divsn. head Tex. Transp. Inst., 1982—91, head infrastructure and transp. divsn. civil engring. dept., 1993—95. Bd. dir. MLA Labs., Inc., Austin, Lyric Tech., LLC, Houston; v.p., bd. dir. Electronic Pavement and Infrastructure Charting, Inc., MLAW Cons., Inc., Austin, Geostructural Tool Kit, Inc.; prin. investigator strategic hwy. rsch. program A005 rsch. project, 1990—93; keynote spkr. 5th Internat. Conf. Rsch. Inst. Labs. Materials Testing, Limoges, France, 2004. Active St. Vincent de Paul Soc., Houston, 1963—65, Redemptorist Lay Mission Soc., Melbourne, Australia, 1969—70. Capt. U.S. Army, 1961—63. Named Soc. Am. Mil. Engrs. Outstanding Sr. Cadet, U. Tex., 1959; recipient SAR medal of Honor, St. Mary's U., 1957, Disting. Mil. Grad. award, 1960, Hamilton Watch award, Coll. Engring., 1960, Everite Bursary award, Coun. Sci. and Indsl. Rsch., South Africa, 1984, Disting. Achievement award, Tex. A&M U. Assn. Former Students, 1996, Zachary Sr. Rschr. award, Tex. Transp. Inst., 1996. Fellow: ASCE (John B. Hawley award Tex. sect. 1966), Post-Tensioning Inst. (adv. bd.); mem.: NSPE, Internat. Soc. Asphalt Pavements, Tex. Soc. Profl. Engrs., Assn. Asphalt Paving Technologists, Internat. Soc. Soil Mechanics and Geotechnical Engring. (U.S. rep. tech. com. TC-6 1987—, keynote adress 7th internat. conf. expansive soils 1992, keynote address 1st internat. conf. unsaturated soils 1995), Transp. Rsch. Bd. (chmn. com. A2LO6 1967—93, disting. lectr. 2000), Sigma Xi, Phi Kappa Phi, Tau Beta Pi, Chi Epsilon, Phi Kappa Delta. Roman Catholic. Achievements include patents for sys. identification; analysis of subsurface radar signals. Office: Tex A&M U 503A CE Tex Transp Inst Bldg College Station TX 77843-3136 E-mail: rllytton@mail.com.

LYTTON, WILLIAM BRYAN, lawyer; b. St. Louis, Mo., Aug. 22, 1948; s. William Bryan and Josephine (Lamy) L.; m. Christine Mary Miller; children— William Bryan IV, Laura Miller. AB, Georgetown U., 1970; JD, Am. U., Washington, 1973. Bar: D.C. 1973, U.S. Ct. Appeals (7th cir.) 1975, U.S. Supreme Ct. 1978, Pa. 1979, U.S. Dist. Ct. (ea. dist.) Pa. 1979, U.S. Ct. Appeals (3d cir.) 1979. Legal counsel, legis. asst. US Senator Charles H. Percy, 1973-75; asst. U.S. atty. US Dist. Ct., Chgo., 1975-78, US Dist. Ct. (ea. dist.), Pa., 1978-83, dep. chief spl. prosecutions div., 1980, dep. chief criminal div., 1980, chief criminal div., 1980-81, 1st asst. U.S. atty., 1981-83; ptnr. Kohn, Savett, Klein & Graf, P.C., Phila., 1983-87, 87-89; chief counsel, staff dir. Spl. Investigation Commn., Phila., 1985-86; dep. spl. counsellor to Pres. of U.S., Washington, 1987; v.p., gen. counsel GE Aerospace, King of Prussia, Pa., 1989-93; v.p., assoc. gen. counsel Martin Marietta & Lockheed Martin, 1993-95; v.p. and gen. coun. Internat. Paper, Purchase, NY, 1996—99, sr. v.p., gen. counsel, 1999—2002; exec. v.p., gen. counsel Tyco Internat. Ltd., Portsmouth, NH, 2002—. Contbr. articles to profl. jours. Committeeman Republican Party, Chester County, Pa.; mem. Easttown Twp. Bd. Suprs., 1990-95. Mem. ABA, Am. Corp. Counsel Assn. (bd. dirs. 1997—). Office: Tyco Internat Ltd 273 Corporate Dr 100 Portsmouth NH 03801-6807

LYU, SEUNG WON, metallurgical engineer, environmental scientist; b. Seoul, Korea, May 15, 1934; came to U.S., 1958; naturalized, 1968; s. Yohan and Kyun Shin (Kim) L.; m. Yun O. Chung; children: John A., Lori K. BS in Chem. Engring., Ind. Inst. Tech., Ft. Wayne, 1961; BS in Metall. Engring., Ill. Inst. Tech., Chgo., 1975; MAS in Environ. Sci., Governors State U., University Park, Ill., 1981. Registered profl. engr. Ill., Calif.; cert. ind. wastewater treatment operator, Ill. Metallurgist Verson Allsteel Press Co., Chgo., 1962-65; metall. engr. Am. Std.-ARI, Franklin Park, Ill., 1965-67; sr. rsch. metallurgist Continental Group, Oak Brook, Ill., 1967-70; sr. prin. engr. Am. Nat. Can Co., Chgo., 1970-83; asst. prof. Ill. Inst. Tech., Glen Ellyn, Ill., 1983-88; pres., chief engr. Prospect Testing Labs., Des Plaines, Ill., 1985—. Tech. cons. Korean Small and Medium Indsl. Promotion Corp., Seoul, 1983; metall. cons. Verson Allsteel Press Co., Chgo., 1985—. Bd. dirs. Korean-Am. Cmty. Svc., Chgo., 1989-95, Niles (Ill.) Korean Sch., 1990—. Mem. ASTM. Republican. Presbyterian. Achievements include 6 patents in metallurgy, tooling and container application; method of making tin-layered stock material; die and method of assembly and application; split punch design and wall/bottom profile for containers. Office: Prospect Testing Labs Inc 1245 E Forest Ave Des Plaines IL 60018-1564 Home: 1819 Krowka Dr Des Plaines IL 60018-2976

LYUBOMIRSKY, ILYA, engineering educator; b. Moscow, Feb. 7, 1968; arrived in U.S., 1976, permanent resident; BSEE, BS in Math., U. Md.-Coll. Park, 1991; MSEE Fannie and John Hertz Grad. fellow, Mass. Inst. Tech., 1994, PhD in Elec. Engring., 1999. Mem. tech. staff ONI Systems, Inc., San Jose, 2000—01; lead lightwave systems engr. CIENA Corp., Linthicum, Md., 2001—03; asst. prof. dept. elec. engring. U. Calif., Riverside, 2003—. Co-author: numerous articles on fiber-optic communications, infrared lasers, quantum optics, and plasma physics in various profl. publs. Office: Univ Calif Elec Engring A211 Bourns Hall Riverside CA 92521 Office Phone: 951-827-7701. Business E-Mail: ilyumbomi@ee.ucr.edu.